PREFACE

The Oxford Russian Dictionary is an amalgamation, harmonization and updating of *The Oxford Russian-English Dictionary* (1972, second edition 1984) and *The Oxford English-Russian Dictionary* (1984) — works which quickly established and have since maintained their reputations as the most comprehensive and authoritative in their class. The merits of these two major contributions to the field have been increased in the present combined work by the incorporation of a range of enhancements. The most important of these are the complete resetting of the text to afford greater ease of consultation, the addition of several thousand new words, meanings and phrases, and, for the convenience of users whose native language is not English, the provision of a transcription into the International Phonetic Alphabet of all English headwords. Such transcription has not been judged necessary in the Russian-English section since Russian pronunciation is generally phonetic.

The Dictionary, which is intended primarily, though by no means exclusively, for English-speaking users at college or university level, contains approximately 180,000 words and phrases. Since it is a general-purpose rather than a specialist work, technical, archaic, old-fashioned and slang terms are included sparingly, but attention has been given to the correct translation of colloquial and idiomatic language and to syntactical information. Vocabulary associated with the institutions of the former Soviet Union has been preserved in view of its historical importance and its continuing, if much reduced, currency in the post-Soviet Russian-speaking world.

My Russian collaborator in the task of updating has been Mr Aziz Ulugov, to whom I express my thanks. For unfailing linguistic assistance and moral support heartfelt thanks are also extended to my wife and fellow Russianist, Lis. Others who have contributed significantly to the work's successful completion are Bur Davis of Adobe Systems Inc., Tanya Kolker, Barry and Susan Kew, Maureen Jeffery, Robert Woodhouse, Peter Cox, Adrian Goodman, Roger Long, Arthur op den Brouw and, most especially, the late John Everest, whose wide-ranging skills played a key role until the very last months of compilation. Thanks are due, finally, to the editorial and technical staff of the Oxford University Press for the many services rendered in the course of the work's preparation.

Of the numerous reference works consulted in the process of revision the following were found to be of particular value: S. I. Ozhegov, *Slovar russkogo yazyka*, 21st edition, Moscow, 1990; Professor I. R. Galperin and others, *New English-Russian Dictionary*, 4th improved edition with a Supplement (Russkiy Yazyk Publishers, Moscow, 1987); V. V. Lopatin and others, *Orfografichesky slovar russkogo yazyka*, Moscow, 1991; D. I. Alekseyev and others, *Slovar sokrashcheny russkogo yazyka*, Moscow, 1983; Stephen Marder, *A Supplementary Russian-English Dictionary* (Slavica Publishers, Inc., Columbus, Ohio, 1992).

The principles of arrangement, provision of grammatical information etc., are given in the Guide to the Use of the Dictionary which follows.

COLIN HOWLETT

July 1993

GUIDE TO THE USE OF THE DICTIONARY

Russian-English Section

Presentation

1. A separate headword is given for each entry, and there is a separate entry for each word. The entries include a substantial quantity of idiomatic and illustrative phraseology.

2. The following devices are used to save space:

(i) The first letter of the headword, followed by a full point, represents the whole headword. Thus:

това́рный ... т. соста́в (= **това́рный соста́в**)

(ii) The swung dash, in conjunction with a vertical stroke, represents that part of the headword which is to the left of the vertical stroke. Thus:

роди́м|ый ... ~ое пятно́ (= **роди́мое пятно́**)

exceptions: the swung dash is not used in indicating the genitive singular of nouns or the 1st and 2nd persons singular of the present tense of verbs with unchanged stress (for examples, see below: *Grammatical Information*: *Nouns* and *Verbs*); and, in cross-references from the imperfective to the perfective verbal aspect, it may, when preceded by a prefix, represent the entire headword. Thus:

ста́|рить, ю, ишь *impf.* (*of* **со~**) ... (= *of* **соста́рить**)

Pronunciation

3. With the general exception of monosyllables, stress is indicated for every Russian word. A stress mark above the swung dash, where this sign represents two or more syllables, indicates shift of stress to the syllable immediately preceding the vertical stroke dividing the headword. Thus:

запи|са́ть, шу́, ~́шешь ... (= **запишу́, запи́шешь**)

4. Conversely, a stress mark above a syllable to the right of the swung dash indicates shift of stress away from the syllable(s) represented by the swung dash. Thus:

ва́хтер, а, *pl.* **~а́ ...** (= **вахтера́**)

5. Where a variant stress is permissible, both variants are shown. Thus:

скобл|и́ть, ю́, ~́ишь (= **ско́блишь** *or* **скобли́шь**)

Phraseology

6. Idiomatic phrases are frequently duplicated in entries for the component words. Phrases consisting of adjective and noun, however, are normally entered under the adjective component.

Meaning

7. Separate meanings of a word are indicated by means of Arabic numerals. Thus:

гада́тельный ... 1. pertaining to divination. **2.** based on conjecture, problematical.

8. Shades of meaning, represented by translations not considered strictly synonymous, are indicated by means of a semicolon: translations considered synonymous — by a comma. Thus:

га́дкий ... ugly, repulsive; vile, nasty.

9. Homonyms are indicated by repetition of the headword as a separate entry, followed by a superscript Arabic numeral. Thus:

газ¹, а *m.* gas.
газ², а *m.* gauze.

It should be noted that there is no accepted all-embracing criterion for differentiating homonymy from polysemy (plurality of meanings of a single word) or 'meaning' from 'shade of meaning'.

Explanation

10. Where necessary for the avoidance of ambiguity explanatory glosses are given in brackets in italic type. Thus:

интерпрета́тор, а *m.* interpreter (*expounder*). [i.e. *not* translator]

11. This device is used in particular in the case of words denoting specifically Russian or Soviet concepts (e.g. **да́ча, ка́ша; микрорайо́н, толка́ч**) and makes it possible to use one-word transliterations rather than clumsy paraphrases as a substitute for a translation.

12. Indications of style or usage are given, where appropriate, in brackets. Thus: (*coll.*), (*dial.*); (*fig.*), (*joc.*); (*agric.*), (*pol.*), etc.

Grammatical Information

13. The following grammatical information is given:

Nouns

The genitive singular ending and gender of all nouns are shown. Thus:

мо́лот, а *m.* hammer.
мо́лни|я, и *f.* lightning.
молок|о́, а́ *nt.* milk.
пья́ниц|а, ы *c.g.* drunkard.

Other case endings are shown where declensions or stress is, in relation to generally accepted systems of classification, irregular. Thus:

англича́н|ин, ина, *pl.* **~е, ~** *m.* Englishman.
бор|ода́, оды́, *a.* **∠оду,** *pl.* **∠оды, ~о́д,** *d.* **~ода́м** *f.* beard.

(But the inserted vowel in the genitive plural ending of numerous feminine nouns with nominative singular ending **-ка** is not regarded as irregular, e.g. **анлича́нка,** *g. pl.* **англича́нок.**)

Variant genitive case endings of certain *pluralia tantum* are indicated by a hyphen. Thus:

вы́молот|ки, ок-ков *no sg.* ... (= **вы́молоток** *or* **вы́молотков**)

Nouns ending **-ость** derived from adjectives have not been included where an appropriate English rendering can be obtained by adding *-ness* to the corresponding adjective (e.g., **зо́ркий ...** sharpsighted ... **зо́ркость ...** sharpsightedness ...).

Where an abbreviation is marked (*indecl.*) this indicates that, although not usually declined, it may be declined in order to avoid ambiguity. Thus:

переда́ча информа́ции ТАССом (*opp.* **ТАССа** *or* **ТАССу**)

Adjectives

Only the masculine nominative singular of the full form of the adjective is shown. Endings of the short forms, where these are found, are shown in brackets. Thus:

глу́п|ый (~, ~а́, ~о) ...

The neuter short form ending is omitted where stress is as for the feminine. Thus:

нау́ч|ный (~ен, ~на)

Verbs

Endings are shown of the 1st and 2nd persons singular of the present tense (or of the 1st person only of verbs with infinitive ending **-ать, -ова́ть, -ять, -еть** which retain stem and stress unchanged throughout the present tense). Thus:

говор|и́ть, ю, и́шь ...
чита́|ть, ю ...

Other endings of the present tense and endings of the past tense are shown where formation or stress are irregular. Thus:

ид|ти́, у́, ёшь, *past* **шёл, шла, шло** ...
стере́|чь, гу́, жёшь, гу́т, *past* **~г, ~гла́, ~гло́** ...

Participles and gerunds, and forms of the passive voice, are not shown unless having special semantic or syntactical features. Verbal aspects: the imperfective aspect is normally treated as the basic form of the simple verb, a cross-reference to the relevant perfective form being shown in brackets. Thus:

чита́|ть, ю *impf.* (*of* **про~**) ...

The corresponding entry is:

прочита́|ть, ю *pf. of* **чита́ть**

In the case, however, of compound verbs formed by means of a prefix, the perfective aspect is treated as the basic form. Thus:

зачит|а́ть, а́ю *pf.* (*of* **~ывать**) ...

Since, in a number of cases, a correspondence cannot, for semantic or other reasons, be firmly established (e.g. **иска́ть-сыска́ть**), the absence of a corresponding aspect is not necessarily noted.

Meanings and phraseology are shown under the basic form in each case unless peculiar to the other aspect.

Prefixes and Combining Forms

A number of prefixes and combining forms are shown as separate entries.Thus:

до...[1] *vbl. pref.*
гидро... *comb. form* hydro-
сов... *comb. form, abbr. of* **~е́тский**

Numerous compounded words, the meaning of which is judged sufficiently clear from a knowledge of the meaning of the prefix and the root-word, have, to save space, been excluded from the dictionary.

English-Russian Section

Orthography

1. The English spelling follows British usage; less usual American variations are noted, but not, e.g., such spellings as **honor**, or (as a rule) variants in which **e** replaces **ae** or **oe.** (See also paragraph 10 below.)

2. Russian cardinal numbers, given without 'tags' denoting inflection, are to be read in the nominative form. (This does not apply to year-dates).

3. Secondary stress is not indicated in Russian words unless they are hyphenated (or unless the syllable in question contains the letter ё). If stress is optional, as between two vowels, an accent is placed on both. When prepositions attract the accent from a noun, or не from a verb, the fact is shown by a stress mark; otherwise monosyllables are not generally shown as stressed. A form such as брази́л|ец (*fem.* -ья́нка) means that the feminine noun is stressed on the penultimate only (cf. paragraph 36(iii)).

Pronunciation

4. For the convenience of users whose native language is not English all headwords are transcribed into the International Phonetic Alphabet. An exception is made for those abbreviations, such as BBC, whose component letters are pronounced individually. Transcriptions are supplied, however, where an abbreviation is pronounced in the same way as its expansion, e.g. **c.** meaning 'century'. In compound words where the second element is listed elsewhere only the first element is generally transcribed.

A key to the phonetic symbols used is supplied below, immediately before the list of abbreviations used in the Dictionary.

Arrangement and presentation of entries: principal rules

5. These matters are explained in detail in paragraphs 10–39 below. Attention is drawn to the nesting principle (paragraph 21) and to the fact that compounds, whether hyphenated or written as one word, are listed under the first element and not the second: e.g. **pen-knife** under **pen**, not **knife.** As regards the placing of idioms see paragraph 22; and for the placing of labels such as (*coll.*) and (*sl.*), see paragraph 25. Paragraphs 35–39 deal with the presentation of Russian grammatical information, including verb aspects.

6. Attention is also drawn to paragraphs 24–25 on the subject of usage labels and their position; and to the fact that the oblique stroke / signifies an alternative affecting *one* word on either side of it (paragraphs 30–32).

7. For the use of the vertical stroke and swung dash (~) see paragraphs 16–17; for the approximate sign (≃), paragraph 25.

8. The gender of nouns in ь is only marked when they are *masculine* (paragraph 35(*a*)).

9. Many Russian nouns have an adjectival form (e.g. го́род — городско́й) corresponding to the attributive use of their English equivalent. Such adjectives are frequently given under the English noun-entry, preceded by the abbreviation *'attr.'*

Presentation: detailed rules

10. Headwords are printed in bold roman type except for non-naturalized foreign words and expressions, for which bold italic is used. Alternative spellings (including some of the less classifiable American variants) are presented alongside the preferred spelling in full or abbreviated form, or shown in brackets: these variants appear again in alphabetical sequence (unless adjacent to the main entry), as cross-references. Thus:

cosy (*US* **cozy**) **cozy** = **cosy**
hicc|up, -ough
curts(e)y

11. Similar treatment is applied to words in which an alternative termination can be used without affecting the sense. Thus:

cumb|ersome, -rous; submer|gence, -sion

Here as elsewhere (paragraphs 16–17), a vertical stroke (divider) is placed after those letters which are common to both forms and which, in the alternative form as shown, are replaced by a hyphen.

12. Also presented as headwords are a few two-word expressions of which the first element does not qualify for an individual entry, e.g. **Boxing Day; Parkinson's disease.**

13. Separate headword entries with superscript numerals are made for words which, though identical in spelling, differ in basic meaning and origin (**fine** as noun and verb; **fine** as adjective and adverb), or in pronunciation and/or stress (**house** and **supplement** as nouns and as verbs), or both (**tear** meaning 'teardrop' and **tear** meaning 'rip').

14. Separate entries for adverbs in '-ly' are made only when they have meanings or usage (idiom, compounds, etc.) which cannot conveniently be treated under the corresponding adjective. Examples are **hardly, really,** and **surely.** When there is no separate entry, and no instance of the adverb in the adjectival entry, it can be assumed that the corresponding Russian adverb is also formed regularly from the adjective. Thus **clumsy** неуклю́жий, нело́вкий implies that the Russian for 'clumsily' is неуклю́же or нело́вко; **critical** крити́ческий implies that 'critically' can be translated крити́чески, and so on.

15. Gerundive and participial forms of English verbs, used as nouns or adjectives, are often accommodated within the verb entry (transitive or intransitive as appropriate). Thus:

revolving doors is found under **revolve** *v.i.*
a retarded child is found under **retard** *v.t.*

but in certain cases, for the sake of clarity, such forms have been treated as independent headwords, e.g.

packing *n.*; **flying** *n.* and *adj.*; **barbed** *adj.*

16. Some headwords are divided by a vertical stroke in order that the unchanging letters preceding the stroke may subsequently be replaced, in inflected forms, by a swung dash. Where there is no divider, the swung dash represents the headword *in toto*, e.g.

house ... keep ~ ... ~hold ... a ~hold word ... ~-painter

17. The vertical divider is also used in both English and Russian to separate the main part of a word from its termination when it is necessary to show modifications or alternative forms of the latter: e.g. paragraphs 10, 35(*c*), and 36.

18. Within the headword entry each grammatical function has its own paragraph, introduced by a part-of-speech indicator (in this order): *n.*, *pron.*, *adj.*, *adv.*, *v.t.*, *v.i.*, *prep.*, *conj.*, *int.* A combined heading, e.g. **adagio** *n.*, *adj.*, *& adv.*, may sometimes be used for convenience; the most common instance is *v.t. & i.* when the two moods are not clearly distinguishable, or when the Russian intransitive is expressed by means of the suffix -ся.

19. Verb-adverb combinations forming 'phrasal verbs' normally appear in a separate paragraph headed '*with advs.*', immediately following simple verb usage; they are given in alphabetical order of the adverb, transitive and intransitive usage within each phrasal verb being separated. Only when the possible combinations are very few and uncomplicated are they contained within the *v.t.* or *v.i.* paragraph.

20. There are also a few verbs (e.g. **go**) where idiomatic usage with prepositions is extensive and complex enough to call for a separate paragraph headed '*with preps.*'.

21. Hyphenated or single-word compounds in which the headword forms the first element are brought together or 'nested' under the headword in a final paragraph headed '*cpds.*'. Here the headword is represented by a swung dash, and the second element, in bold type, determines the alphabetical sequence. An exception is made to the 'nesting' principle in some cases where compounds are particularly numerous, e.g. those beginning with such elements as **'back', 'by', 'out', 'over'** etc. Forms like **'bull's eye'** and **'Englishman'** (despite the reduced 'a') are treated as compounds. Phrases such as **'labour exchange'** will generally be found in the main paragraph of the entry for the first noun, in some cases preceded by '*attr.*' (for 'attributive').

22. Adjective-noun expressions generally appear under the adjective unless this has relatively little weight, as in **'good riddance'**; but some may also be repeated under the noun, e.g. **'French bean', 'French horn'** and **'French leave'.** Idioms of a more complex nature, and proverbs, are generally entered under the first noun, but here too the rule is not inflexible and some duplication may be found.

23. Within an entry differences of meaning or application are defined by synonym, context, or other means. Major differences may be distinguished by numerals in bold type. Thus:

> **gag** *n.* **1.** (*to prevent speech etc.*) … (*surgery*) … (*parl.*) … (*fig.*) … **2.** (*interpolation*) … **3.** (*joke*) …

24. A second type of label indicates status or level of usage: e.g. *arch*(aic), *liter*(ary), *coll*(oquial), *sl*(ang), *vulg*(ar). It may apply to the headword as a whole, to one of its functions or meanings, or to a single phrase or sentence, and is placed accordingly. Thus:

> **pep** (*coll.*) *n.* … *v.t.* (*usu.* ~ **up**)
> **tart** *n.* **1.** (*flat pie*) … **2.** (*sl.*, *prostitute*) … *v.t.* ~ **up** (*coll.*, *embellish*) …
> **bell** *n.* … **that rings a** ~ (*fig.*, *coll.*)

25. In cases where Russian has an expression corresponding closely in level of usage to a given colloquialism, vulgarism, or slang term in English, the status label (*coll.*), (*sl.*) etc. is placed *after* the Russian, and should be understood to apply equally to the preceding English equivalent. In other cases a 'literary' (non-colloquial) Russian translation is given, and the status label is placed immediately after the English. When both literary and colloquial Russian translations are given for the same English expression, the label appears *before* the second, colloquial one. Russian expressions, especially idioms or proverbs, which parallel rather than translate English ones are preceded by the symbol ≃.

26. The use of the comma or the semicolon to separate Russian words offered as translations of the same English word reflects a greater or lesser degree of equivalence; in the latter case an auxiliary English gloss is often used to express the nuance of difference. Thus:

> **inexhaustible** *adj.* (*unfailing*) неистощи́мый, неисчерпа́емый; … (*untiring*) неутоми́мый.

27. When shades of meaning of an adjective or verb have been defined in this way, and similar distinctions exist between derivative abstract nouns, the glosses are not usually repeated. Thus:

> **bookish** *adj.* (*literary*, *studious*) кни́жный; (*pedantic*) педанти́чный
> **bookishness** *n.* кни́жность; педанти́чность

28. To avoid ambiguity the semicolon is always used when the alternatives are complete phrases or sentences, and also in most cases between synonymous verbs. Thus:

what is he getting at? что он хо́чет сказа́ть?; куда́ он гнёт?
allow *v.t.* позв|оля́ть, -о́лить; разреш|а́ть, -и́ть

Idiom and illustration

29. The examples of characteristic and idiomatic usage in both languages, which illustrate and supplement the standard Russian equivalents, may consist of phrases or finite sentences. In the former case, where a verb is concerned, both aspects are generally given in Russian; in the latter, one or other aspect is chosen according to the context. For the method of giving aspectual information see paragraphs 36–39 below.

30. In both English and Russian there are many instances when one word in a phrase or sentence may be replaced by a synonymous alternative. This is shown by means of a comma in English, and an oblique stroke in Russian. Thus:

have, get one's hair cut стри́чься, по-
my better half моя́ дража́йшая/лу́чшая полови́на
lose one's hair (*lit.*) лысе́ть, об-/по- (either prefix may be used to form the perfective)

31. Non-synonymous alternatives are linked by the oblique stroke in *both* languages. Thus:

high/low tension высо́кое/ни́зкое напряже́ние

32. In all cases the oblique stroke expresses an alternative of only *one* word on either side of it. Other alternatives are shown in the form '(*or* ...)'. Thus:

the estate came (*or* **was brought) under the hammer**
I could do with a drink я охо́тно (*or* с удово́льствием) вы́пил бы

33. Optional extensions of words, phrases or sentences, which may be included at discretion, e.g. for greater clarity, are shown within brackets, and in ordinary roman or Cyrillic type.

34. Italics within brackets are used for such matters as labels of meaning and usage (paragraphs 24–25) and in connection with Russian grammatical information (paragraph 35). Russian italics (without stress marks) are used for brief definitions or explanations of English terms which have no counterpart in Russian: see e.g. at **commuter**; also to specify noun-objects of certain verbs in order to limit their application to that implicit in the English, e.g.

wall up *v.t.* заде́л|ывать, -ать (*дверь/окно*)

Grammatical Information

35. The following grammatical information is given in respect of words offered as translations of headwords:

(*a*) the gender of *masculine* nouns ending in -ь, except when this is made clear by an accompanying adjective (e.g. **polar bear** бе́лый медве́дь) or by the existence of a corresponding 'female' form (see (*e*) below).

(*b*) the gender of nouns (e.g. neuters in -мя, masculines in -а and -я, foreign borrowings in -и and -у) whose final letter does not serve as an indicator of gender. Nouns of common gender are designated (*c.g.*). Indeclinable nouns are designated (*indecl.*), preceded by a gender indicator if required. The many adjectives used as nouns (e.g. портно́й) are not specially marked.

(*c*) the gender (or, for *pluralia tantum*, the genitive plural termination) and number (*pl.*) of all plural nouns which translate a headword or compound. Thus:

timpani *n.* лита́вры (*f. pl.*).
pliers *n.* щипц|ы́ (*pl.*, *g.* -о́в); клёщ|и (*pl.*, *g.* -е́й).

This information, however is not given if the singular form has already appeared in the same entry, nor in the case of neuter plurals with an accompanying adjective, where the number and gender are self-evident from the terminations. Plurals of adjectives used substantivally are shown as (*pl.*).

(*d*) the nominative plural termination (-а́ or -я́) of certain masculine nouns when this form denotes a meaning different from that of the plural in -ы or -и, e.g.

icon ... о́браз (*nom. pl.* -а́).

(*e*) the forms of nouns used where Russian differs from English in making a verbal distinction between male and female. Thus:

teacher учи́тель (*fem.* -ница)

(*f*) aspectual information: see paragraphs 36–39 below.

(*g*) case usage with prepositions, e.g. **before** до+*g*.

(*h*) the case, with or without preposition, required to provide an equivalent to an English transitive verb. Thus:

attack *v.t.* нап|ада́ть, -а́сть на+*a*.

If no case is thus indicated, it is to be taken that the Russian verb is transitive.

(*i*) When English and Russian terms are equivalent as they stand, but both may be regularly extended e.g. by a prepositional phrase, the Russian idiom may be made explicit as in (*h*), but in brackets. Thus:

conduce *v.i.* спосо́бствовать (*impf.*) (+*d.*)

(*j*) Use is also made of oblique cases of the Russian pronouns кто and что (in brackets and italics) to indicate case/preposition usage after a verb. Thus:

suit (*adapt*) *v.t.* приспос|а́бливать, -о́бить (*что к чему*); согласо́в|ывать, -а́ть (*что с чем*)

Aspects

36. Aspectual information is given on all verbs (except быть, *impf.*) offered as renderings in infinitive form (except when they are subordinate to the finite verb in a sentence). If the verb is mono-aspectual, or used in a phrase to which only one aspect applies, it is designated either imperfective (*impf.*) or perfective (*pf.*) as the case may be. With verbs of motion a distinction is made between determinate (*det.*) and indeterminate (*indet.*) forms, the imperfective aspect being assumed unless otherwise stated. Bi-aspectual infinitives are shown as (*impf.*, *pf.*). In all other cases both aspects are indicated (the imperfective always preceding the perfective) as in the following examples:

(i) получ|а́ть, -и́ть; возра|жа́ть, -зи́ть; сн|оси́ть, -ести́.
(ii) позв|оля́ть, -о́лить; встр|еча́ть, -е́тить.
(iii) пока́з|ывать, -а́ть (i.e. *pf.* показа́ть); очаро́в|ывать, -а́ть.
(iv) гоня́ть, гнать; брать, взять; вынужда́ть, вы́нудить.
(v) смотре́ть, по-; греть, по- (i.e. *pf.* погре́ть); мости́ть, вы́- (i.e. *pf.* вы́мостить); лысе́ть, об-/по-.
(vi) и|мпровизи́ровать, сы-.

37. It will be seen from the above that

(i) when the first two or more letters of both aspects are identical, a vertical divider in the imperfective separates these letters from those which undergo change in the perfective. The perfective is then representated by the changed letters, preceded by a hyphen.

(ii) a 'change' includes change of stress only if the stress shifts *back* in the perfective to the previous vowel: the divider then precedes this vowel in the imperfective.

(iii) if it shifts forward, only the stressed syllable of the perfective is shown.

(iv) when the two aspects have only their first letter in common, or are in fact different verbs, or both begin with вы- (which is always accented in the perfective), both are given in full.

(v) perfectives of the type 'prefix+imperfective' are shown by giving the prefix only, followed by a hyphen. Prefixes are unstressed except for вы́-. Alternative prefixes are separated by an oblique stroke.

38. Where a verb has two possible imperfective or perfective forms, the alternative form is shown in brackets. Thus:

разв|ора́чивать (*or* -ёртывать), -ерну́ть.
возвра|ща́ться, -ти́ться (*or* верну́ться).
пали́ть (*or* опа́ливать), о-.

39. When two or three verbs separated by an oblique stroke are followed by the indication (*pf.*) or (*impf.*) this applies to both or all of them.

PHONETIC SYMBOLS USED IN THE DICTIONARY

Consonants

b	*b*ut	j	*y*es	p	*p*en	w	*w*e	ð	*th*is
d	*d*og	k	*c*at	r	*r*ed	z	*z*oo	ŋ	ri*ng*
f	*f*ew	l	*l*eg	s	*s*it	ʃ	*sh*e	x	lo*ch*
g	*g*et	m	*m*an	t	*t*op	ʒ	deci*s*ion	tʃ	*ch*ip
h	*h*e	n	*n*o	v	*v*oice	θ	*th*in	dʒ	*j*ar

Vowels

æ	c*a*t	iː	s*ee*	uː	t*oo*	əʊ	n*o*	aɪə	f*ire*
ɑː	*ar*m	ɒ	h*o*t	ə	*a*go	eə	h*air*	aʊə	s*our*
e	b*e*d	ɔː	s*aw*	aɪ	m*y*	ɪə	n*ear*		
ɜː	h*er*	ʌ	r*u*n	aʊ	h*ow*	ɔɪ	b*oy*		
ɪ	s*i*t	ʊ	p*u*t	eɪ	d*ay*	ʊə	p*oor*		

(ə) signifies the indeterminate sound as in gard*e*n, carn*a*l, and rhyth*m*.

(r) at the end of a word indicates an r that is sounded when a word beginning with a vowel follows, as in *clutter up* and *an acre of land*.

The mark ˜ indicates a nasalized sound, as in the following sounds that are not natural in English: æ̃ (t*im*bre) ɑ̃ (él*an*) ɔ̃ (garç*on*)

The main or primary stress of a word is shown by ˈ preceding the relevant syllable; any secondary stress in words of three or more syllables is shown by ˌ preceding the relevant syllable.

ABBREVIATIONS USED IN THE DICTIONARY

a.	accusative
abbr.	abbreviat|ion, -ed (to)
abs.	absolute
abstr.	abstract
acad.	academic
acc.	according
act.	active
adj., adjs.	adjectiv|e, -al; -es
admin.	administration
adv., advs.	adverb, -ial; -s
aeron.	aeronautics
agric.	agriculture
alg.	algebra
anat.	anatomy
anc.	ancient
anthrop.	anthropology
approx.	approximate(ly)
arch.	archaic
archaeol.	archaeology
archit.	architecture
astrol.	astrology
astron.	astronomy
attr.	attributive
Austral.	Austral(as)ian
aux.	auxiliary
bibl.	biblical
biol.	biology
bot.	botany
Br.	British; British usage
c.g.	common gender
chem.	chemistry
cin.	cinema(tography)
coll.	colloquial
collect.	collective
comb.	combin|ation, -ing
comm.	commerc|e, -ial
comp.	comparative
comput.	computing
concr.	concrete
conj., conjs.	conjunction; -s
cpd., cpds.	compound; -s
cul.	culinary
d.	dative
decl.	decl|ined, -ension
def. art.	definite article
det.	determinate
dial.	dialect(al)
dim.	diminutive
dipl.	diploma|cy, -tic
disp.	disputed
eccl.	ecclesiastical
econ.	economics
educ.	education, -al
elec.	electric|al, -ity
ellipt.	elliptical
emph.	empha|size(s), -sizing, -tic
eng.	engineering
Eng.	English
entom.	entomology
esp.	especially
ethnol.	ethnology
euph.	euphemis|m, -tic
exc.	except
excl.	exclamation
expr.	express|ed, -es, -ing, -ion
f.	feminine
fem.	female
fig.	figurative
fin.	financ|e, -ial
Fr.	French
freq.	frequentative
fut.	future (tense)
g.	genitive
geod.	geodesy
geog.	geography
geol.	geology
geom.	geometry
ger.	gerund
Ger.	German
Gk.	Greek
g. pl.	genitive plural
gram.	grammar
g. sg.	genitive singular
her.	heraldry
hist.	histor|y, -ical
hort.	horticulture
i.	instrumental; intransitive in '*v.i.*'
imper.	imperative
impers.	impersonal
impf.	imperfective
ind.	indirect
indecl.	indeclinable
indef.	indefinite
indet.	indeterminate
inf.	infinitive
inst.	instantaneous
int.	interjection
interrog.	interrogative
intrans.	intransitive
iron.	ironical
Ital.	Italian
joc.	jocular
journ.	journalism
Lat.	Latin
leg.	legal
ling.	linguistics
lit.	literal
liter.	literary
log.	logic
m.	masculine

math.	mathematics
mech.	mechanics
med.	medicin|e, -al
metall.	metallurgy
meteor.	meteorology
mil.	military
min.	mineralogy
mod.	modern
mus.	music(al)
myth.	mythology
n.	noun
naut.	nautical
nav.	naval
neg.	negative
nn.	nouns
nom.	nominative
nom.-a.	nominative-accusative
nt.	neuter
num., nums.	numer|al, -ical; -als
obj.	object
obs.	obsolete
oft.	often
onomat.	onomatopeia
opp.	opposite (to); as opposed to
opt.	optics
o.s.	oneself
p.	prepositional (case) *See also* p.p. *and* p.p.p.
palaeog.	palaeography
parl.	parliamentary
part.	participle
pass.	passive
path.	pathology
pej.	pejorative
pers.	person(s); personal
pert.	pertaining
pf.	perfective
pharm.	pharmaceutical
phil.	philosophy
philol.	philology
phon.	phonetic(s)
phot.	photography
phr., phrr.	phrase; -s
phys.	physic|s, -al
physiol.	physiology
pl.	plural
poet.	poet|ical, -ry
pol.	political
poss.	possessive
p.p.	past participle
p.p.p.	past participle passive
pr.	pronounce(d); pronunciation
pred.	predicate; predicative
pref.	prefix
prep., preps.	preposition; -s
pres.	present (tense)
pret.	preterite
pron., prons.	pronoun; -s
propr.	proprietary term
pros.	prosody
prov., provs.	proverb; -s
psych.	psychology
radiol.	radiology
rail.	railway
refl.	reflexive
rel.	relative
relig.	religion
rhet.	rhetorical
Rom.	Roman
Ru.	Russian
Sc.	Scottish
sc.	scilicet
sg.	singular
sl.	slang
s.o.	someone
soc.	social
stat.	statistics
sth.	something
subj.	subject
suff.	suffix
superl.	superlative
surv.	surveying
t.	transitive in 'v.t.'
tech.	technical
teleg.	telegraphy
teleph.	telephony
text.	textiles
theatr.	theatr|e, -ical
theol.	theology
thg.	thing
trans.	transitive
trig.	trigonometry
TV	television
typ.	typography
univ.	university
US	United States; United States usage
usu.	usually
v.	verb
var.	various
v. aux.	auxiliary verb
vbl.	verbal
vet.	veterinary
v.i.	intransitive verb
voc.	vocative
v.t.	transitive verb
vulg.	vulgar(ism)
vv.	verbs
zool.	zoology

The Russian -н. in illustrative phrases within entries stands for the enclitic -нибудь (in the words кто-нибудь, что-нибудь, etc.).

This dictionary includes some words which are, or are asserted to be, proprietary names or trade marks. These words are labelled (*propr.*). The presence or absence of this label should not be regarded as affecting the legal status of any proprietary name or trade mark.

RUSSIAN–ENGLISH

A

A (*abbr. of* **ампе́р**) amp, ampere.

а[1] *conj.* **1.** and; while, whereas; **вот ма́рки, а вот три рубля́ сда́чи** here are the stamps and here is three roubles change; **иди́те напра́во, пото́м нале́во, а пото́м ещё раз напра́во** turn right, then left, (and) then right again; **моя́ жена́ лю́бит о́перу, а я предпочита́ю кино́** my wife likes opera, while *or* whereas I prefer the cinema; **а и́менно** namely; to be exact. **2.** but; yet (*or not translated*); **пора́ идти́ — а мы то́лько что пришли́!** 'It's time to go.' 'But we've only just come!'; **хотя́ ты и не хо́чешь посове́товаться с врачо́м, а на́до** you may not want to see a doctor but you must; **я иду́ не в кино́, а в теа́тр** I am going to the theatre, not to the cinema. **3.: а то** or (else), otherwise; **спеши́, а то мы опозда́ем** hurry up or we'll be late.

а[2] *interrog. particle* (*coll.*) eh?; what('s that)?; huh?

а[3] *int.* (*expr. surprise, annoyance, pain, etc.*; *coll.*) ah, oh; **а ну его́!** oh, to hell with him!

а-а́ (*baby talk*): **сде́лать а.** to do a poo.

абажу́р, а *m.* lampshade.

аба́к|а, и *f.* (*and* **~**, **~а** *m.*) (*archit.*) abacus.

абба́т, а *m.* abbot; (Roman Catholic) priest.

аббати́с|а, ы *f.* abbess.

абба́тств|о, а *nt.* abbey.

аббревиату́р|а, ы *f.* abbreviation; acronym; **инициа́льная а.** initialism.

аберра́ци|я, и *f.* (*opt. and fig.*) aberration.

абза́ц, а *m.* **1.** (*typ.*) indention; **сде́лать а.** to indent; **нача́ть с но́вого ~а** to begin a new line, new paragraph. **2.** paragraph.

абисси́н|ец, ца *m.* Abyssinian.

Абисси́ни|я, и *f.* Abyssinia.

абисси́н|ка, ки *f. of* **~ец**

абисси́нский *adj.* Abyssinian.

абитурие́нт, а *m.* **1.** (*obs.*) (school-)leaver. **2.** university entrant.

абла́ут, а *m.* (*ling.*) ablaut.

аблати́в, а *m.* (*gram.*) ablative.

абля́ут = **абла́ут**

абонеме́нт, а *m.* subscription; season ticket; **сверх ~а** extra.

абонеме́нтн|ый *adj.*: **~ая ка́рточка** reader's *or* borrower's card; **~ая пла́та** (*TV, radio*) licence fee; **а. я́щик** P.O. (*abbr. of* Post Office) Box.

абоне́нт, а *m.* subscriber; (*library*) borrower, reader; (*theatre, etc.*) season-ticket holder; **а. ло́жи** box holder (*theatr.*).

абоне́нтск|ий *adj.* subscription; **~ое телеви́дение** subscription television, pay TV; **~ая пла́та** rental fee.

абони́р|овать, ую *impf. and pf.* to subscribe (to); to take out a booking (for), reserve a seat (for) (*a season at a theatre, a series of concerts, etc.*).

абони́р|оваться, уюсь *impf. and pf.* **1.** (**на**+*a.*) to subscribe (to); to take out a booking (for). **2.** *pass. of* **~овать**

аборда́ж, а *m.* (*naut.*) boarding; **взять на а.** to board.

аборда́ж|ный *adj. of* **~**; **а. крюк** (*naut.*) grapnel.

абориге́н, а *m.* aboriginal.

абориге́нный *adj.* aboriginal; native.

або́рт, а *m.* abortion; miscarriage; **внебольни́чный а.** backstreet abortion; **сде́лать а.** to have an abortion.

аборти́вн|ый *adj.* **1.** *adj. of* **або́рт**; **~ое сре́дство** abortifacient. **2.** (*biol.*) abortive.

аборти́ст, а *m.* abortionist.

абортма́хер, а *m.* (*coll.*) (backstreet) abortionist.

або́ртщик = **абортма́хер**

абракада́бр|а, ы *f.* gibberish, gobbledygook.

абра́ш|а, и *m.* (*coll., pej.*) Jew.

абрико́с, а *m.* **1.** apricot. **2.** apricot-tree.

абрико́с|овый *adj. of* **~**

абрикоти́н, а *m.* apricot liqueur.

а́брис, а *m.* contour(s); outline.

абсе́нт, а *m.* absinthe.

абсентеи́зм, а *m.* absenteeism.

абсентеи́ст, а *m.* absentee.

абсолю́т, а *m.* (*phil.*) the absolute.

абсолюти́зм, а *m.* (*pol.*) absolutism.

абсолюти́ст, а *m.* (*pol.*) absolutist.

абсолю́т|ный (~ен, ~на) *adj.* absolute; **а. слух** (*mus.*) perfect pitch.

абсорби́р|овать, ую *impf. and pf.* to absorb.

абсо́рбци|я, и *f.* absorption.

абстине́нт, а *m.* abstainer.

абстине́нтн|ый *adj.*: **а. синдро́м** (*med.*) withdrawal symptoms.

абстине́нци|я, и *f.* (*med.*) withdrawal symptoms; **наркоти́ческая а.** drug withdrawal symptoms.

абстраги́р|овать, ую *impf. and pf.* to abstract.

абстра́кт|ный (~ен, ~на) *adj.* abstract.

абстракциони́зм, а *m.* abstractionism.

абстракциони́ст, а *m.* abstractionist.

абстра́кци|я, и *f.* abstraction.

абсу́рд, а *m.* absurdity; **довести́ до ~а** to carry to the point of absurdity.

абсу́рдност|ь, и *f.* absurdity.

абсу́рд|ный (~ен, ~на) *adj.* absurd.

абсце́сс, а *m.* abscess.

абсци́сс|а, ы *f.* (*math.*) abscissa.

абха́з|ец, ца *m.* Abkhazian.

абха́з|ка, ки *f. of* **~ец**

абха́зский *adj.* Abkhazian.

а́бцуг, а *m.* (*obs.*) *only in phrr.* **с пе́рвого ~а; по пе́рвому ~у** right from the start.

ава́л|ь, я *m.* (*comm.*) banker's guarantee.

авангáрд, а *m.* **1.** advance-guard, van; vanguard (*also fig.*). **2.** (*fig.*) avant-garde.

авангарди́зм, а *m.* avant-gardism.

авангарди́ст, а *m.* avant-gardist.

авангард|и́стский *adj. of* **~ 2.**

аванга́рд|ный *adj. of* **~ 1.**

аванза́л, а *m.* ante-room.

аванпо́рт, а *m.* outer harbour.

аванпо́ст, а *m.* (*mil.*) outpost; forward position (*also fig.*).

ава́нс, а *m.* **1.** advance (*of money*); **получи́ть а.** to receive an advance. **2.** (*pl. only*; *fig.*) advances, overtures.

аванси́р|овать, ую *impf. and pf.* to advance (*money*).

ава́нсом *adv.* in advance, on account.

авансце́н|а, ы *f.* (*theatr.*) proscenium.

аванта́ж|ный (~ен, ~на) *adj.* (*obs., coll.*) fine, showing to advantage.

авантю́р|а, ы *f.* **1.** (*pej.*) adventure; venture, escapade; **пусти́ться в ~ы** to embark on adventures. **2.** (*coll.*) shady enterprise.

авантюри́зм, а *m.* adventurism.
авантюри́ст, а *m.* adventurist.
авантюр|исти́ческий *adj. of* **~и́зм**
авантюри́стк|а, и *f.* adventuress; gold-digger.
авантю́рно-плутовско́й *adj.* (*liter.*) picaresque.
авантю́р|ный (~ен, ~на) *adj.* adventurous; **а. рома́н** (*liter.*) adventure story.
ава́р, а *m.* (*hist.*) Avar.
ава́р|ец, ца *m.* Avar (*member of ethnic group inhabiting Caucasus*).
авари́йно-спаса́тельн|ый *adj.* (emergency-)rescue, life-saving; **~ые рабо́ты** rescue work *or* operation.
авари́йност|ь, и *f.* accidents, accident rate.
авари́йн|ый *adj.* **1.** *adj. of* **ава́рия; а. компле́кт** survival kit; **~ая маши́на** breakdown van; (*aeron.*): **~ая кома́нда** crash crew; **~ая поса́дка** crash landing; **а. сигна́л** distress signal. **2.** emergency, spare.
ава́ри|я, и *f.* **1.** damage; wreck, crash, accident; breakdown; **цепна́я а.** (*vehicle*) pile-up; (*fig.*, *iron.*) misfortune; **потерпе́ть ~ю** to crash, have an accident. **2.** (*leg.*) damages, average.
ава́р|ка, ки *f. of* **~** *and* **~ец**
ава́р|ский *adj. of* **~** *and* **~ец**
авгу́р, а *m.* augur; **язы́к ~ов** esoteric language.
а́вгуст, а *m.* August.
августе́йший *adj.* (*as title of emperors*) most august.
августи́н|ец, ца *m.* Augustinian, Austin friar.
а́вгуст|овский *adj. of* **~**
а́виа (*abbr. of* **авиапо́чтой**) '(by) airmail'.
авиа... *comb. form, abbr. of* **авиацио́нный**
авиаба́з|а, ы *f.* air base.
авиабиле́т, а *m.* airline ticket.
авиадеса́нт, а *m.* **1.** airborne assault landing. **2.** airborne assault force.
авиадеса́нтник, а *m.* paratrooper.
авиадеса́нтн|ый *adj.* airborne assault; **~ые войска́** airborne assault troops.
авиадиспе́тчер, а *m.* air-traffic controller.
авиадиспе́тчерск|ий *adj.*: **~ая слу́жба** (air) flight control.
авиакаскадёр, а *m.* stunt flyer.
авиакатастро́ф|а, ы *f.* air crash.
авиаколлекционе́р, а *m.* model aircraft collector.
авиакомпа́ни|я, и *f.* airline, air carrier.
авиаконстру́ктор, а *m.* aircraft designer.
авиакосми́ческий = авиацио́нно-косми́ческий
авиала́йнер, а *m.* airliner.
авиали́ни|я, и *f.* airway, air route.
авиама́тк|а, и *f.* aircraft-carrier.
авиамеха́ник, а *m.* aircraft mechanic; grease monkey.
авиамодели́зм, а *m.* aeromodelling.
авиамодели́ст, а *m.* aeromodeller.
авиамоде́л|ь, и *f.* model aircraft.
авиамоде́ль|ный *adj. of* **~**
авиано́с|ец, ца *m.* aircraft carrier.
авиапассажи́р, а *m.* airline passenger.
авиапербро́ск|а, и *f.* airlift.
авиаписьм|о́, а́, *pl.* **~а, авиапи́сем, ~ам** *nt.* air(mail) letter; aerogram(me).
авиапо́чт|а, ы *f.* air mail.
авиараке́т|а, ы *f.* air-launched missile.
авиасало́н, а *m.* air show.
авиасмо́тр = авиасало́н
авиаспо́рт, а *m.* aerial sports.
авиасъёмк|а, и *f.* air photography, aerial surveying.
авиа́тор, а *m.* aviator.
авиатра́нспортн|ый *adj.*: **~ая компа́ния** airline, air carrier.
авиатра́сс|а, ы *f.* air route, air lane, airway.
авиацио́нно-косми́ческ|ий *adj.* aerospace; **~ая промы́шленность** the aerospace industry.
авиацио́нн|ый *adj. of* **авиа́ция; ~ая промы́шленность** aircraft industry; **~ая шко́ла** flying school.
авиа́ци|я, и *f.* **1.** aviation. **2.** (*collect.*) aircraft; **бомбардиро́вочная а.** bomber force. **3.** aeronautics.
авиача́ст|ь, и *f.* air force unit.
авиашко́л|а, ы *f.* flying school.
ави́зо *nt. indecl.* **1.** (*comm.*) advice (note). **2.** (*naut.*) aviso, advice-boat.
авока́до *nt. indecl.* avocado (*tree*); **плод а.** avocado (*fruit*).
аво́сь *particle* (*coll.*) perhaps; **на а.** on the off-chance.
аво́ськ|а, и *f.* (*coll.*) string (shopping) bag.
авра́л, а *m.* **1.** (*naut.*) all-hands evolution; (*as int.*) all hands on deck! **2.** (*coll.*) rush job.
авра́л|ьный *adj.*: **~ьная рабо́та = авра́л**
авро́ра, ы *f.* (*poet.*) aurora, dawn.
австрали́|ец, йца *m.* Australian.
австрали́|йка, йки *f. of* **~ец**
австрали́йский *adj.* Australian.
Австра́ли|я, и *f.* Australia.
австри́|ец, йца *m.* Austrian.
австри́|йка, йки *f. of* **~ец**
австри́йский *adj.* Austrian.
А́встри|я, и *f.* Austria.
австрия́к, а *m.* (*coll.*, *obs.*) Austrian.
австрия́|чка, чки *f. of* **~к**
А́встро-Ве́нгри|я, и *f.* (*hist.*) Austria-Hungary.
а́встро-венге́рский *adj.* (*hist.*) Austro-Hungarian.
автарки́|я, и *f.* (*econ.*, *phil.*) self-sufficiency, autarky.
автенти́чный = аутенти́чный
авто́ *nt. indecl.* (*coll.*) (motor-)car.
авто... *comb. form* **1.** self-, auto-. **2.** *abbr. of* (*i*) **автомати́ческий** *and* (*ii*) **автомоби́льный**
автоава́ри|я, и *f.* road *or* traffic accident.
автоалкого́лик, а *m.* drunk driver.
автоантизапотева́тел|ь, я *m.* demister.
автоапте́чк|а, и *f.* (*car*) tyre repair kit.
автоа́тлас, а *m.* road atlas.
автобага́жник, а *m.* **1.** (*car*) roof *or* luggage rack. **2.** (*car*) boot.
автоба́з|а, ы *f.* motor-transport depot.
автобиографи́ческий *adj.* autobiographical.
автобиографи́чност|ь, и *f.* autobiographical nature, character.
автобиогра́фи|я, и *f.* autobiography; curriculum vitae, CV.
автоблокиро́вк|а, и *f.* (*rail.*) automatic block system.
авто́бус, а *m.* bus; (*inter-city vehicle*) coach; **а.-экспре́сс** express coach.
авто́бусник, а *m.* (*coll.*) bus driver; coach driver.
автобуфе́т, а *m.* mobile canteen.
автоваго́н, а *m.* rail car.
автоветера́н, а *m.* veteran car; vintage car.
автовладе́л|ец, ьца *m.* car owner.
автовокза́л, а *m.* bus terminal; coach station.
автово́р, а *m.* (*coll.*) car thief.
автоге́нный *adj.* (*tech.*) autogenous.
автоге́нщик, а *m.* oxyacetelene welder.
автого́нк|а, и *f.* car-race.
автого́нщик, а *m.* racing-driver.
авто́граф, а *m.* (*in var. senses*) autograph.
автогужево́й *adj.* vehicular.
автода́ч|а, и *f.* mobile home, caravan.
автоде́л|о, а *nt.* automobile engineering.
автодида́кт, а *m.* autodidact.
автодоро́г|а, и *f.* road; highway.
автодоро́жник, а *m.* highway engineer.
автодоро́жн|ый *adj.* road-transport; highway; **~ая катастро́фа** road *or* traffic accident.
автодрези́н|а, ы *f.* (*tech.*) motor trolley.
автодро́м, а *m.* **1.** vehicle testing point. **2.** motor-racing circuit.
автожи́р, а *m.* autogyro.
автозаво́д, а *m.* motor-car factory.
автозапра́вочн|ый *adj.* filling, refuelling; **~ая ста́нция** petrol- *or* filling-station.
автозапра́вщик, а *m.* petrol tanker.
автоинспе́ктор, а *m.* traffic inspector.
автоинспе́кци|я, и *f.* traffic inspectorate.
автоинформа́тор, а *m.* **1.** recorded (telephone) message. **2.** answerphone, (telephone) answering machine.
автока́р, а *m.* motor trolley.
автокаранда́ш, а́ *m.* propelling pencil.

автокаскадёр, а *m.* stunt driver.
автокатастро́ф|а, ы *f.* road *or* traffic accident.
автокефа́льный *adj.* (*eccl.*) autocephalous.
автокла́в, а *m.* (*tech.*) autoclave.
автоколо́нк|а, и *f.* petrol pump.
автоколо́нн|а, ы *f.* motorcade; convoy.
автокорри́д|а, ы *f.* stock-car race; stock-car racing.
автокосме́тик|а, и *f.* car care products.
автокра́н, а *m.* mobile crane, crane truck.
автокра́т, а *m.* autocrat.
автократи́ческий *adj.* autocratic.
автокра́ти|я, и *f.* autocracy.
автокро́сс, а *m.* autocross.
автоку́хн|я, и *f.* mobile kitchen.
авто́л, а *m.* motor oil.
автола́вк|а, и *f.* mobile shop.
автолебёдк|а, и *f.* winch truck.
автолиха́ч, а́ *m.* reckless driver, road-hog.
автолюби́тел|ь, я *m.* (private) motorist.
автомагази́н, а *m.* **1.** mobile shop. **2.** car dealer's, motorcar showroom.
автомагистра́л|ь, и *f.* motorway; **скоростна́я а.** expressway.
автомастерск|а́я, о́й *f.* car repair garage.
автома́т, а *m.* **1.** automatic machine, slot-machine; **биле́тный а.** ticket machine; **билья́рдный а.** pinball machine; **де́нежный а.** cash dispenser; **игрово́й а.** fruit machine; one-armed bandit; **парко́вочный а.** parking meter; **стира́льный а.** washing machine; **суши́льный а.** drier; **телефо́н-а.** pay phone; **торго́вый а.** vending machine; (*fig.*) automaton, robot. **2.** (*mil.*) (*coll.*) sub-machine-gun, tommy-gun.
автоматиза́ци|я, и *f.* automation.
автоматизи́рованн|ый *adj.* computer-aided; **~ое проекти́рование** CAD, computer-aided design.
автоматизи́р|овать, ую *impf. and pf.* **1.** to render automatic. **2.** to introduce automation (into); to automate.
автомати́зм, а *m.* automatism.
автома́тик|а, и *f.* **1.** automation. **2.** automatic equipment/devices.
автомати́ческ|ий *adj.* **1.** (*tech.*) automatic, self-acting; **~ая винто́вка** automatic (rifle); **~ая ру́чка** fountain-pen. **2.** (*fig.*) automatic, involuntary.
автомати́ч|ный (~ен, ~на) = ~еский 2.
автома́т|ный *adj. of* **~ 2.**
автома́тчик, а *m.* (*mil.*) sub-machine-gunner, tommy-gunner.
автомаши́н|а, ы *f.* motor vehicle.
автомеха́ник, а *m.* car mechanic.
автомобилево́з, а *m.* (*vehicle*) transporter.
автомобили́зм, а *m.* motoring.
автомобили́ст, а *m.* motorist.
автомоби́л|ь, я *m.* motor vehicle; (motor)car; **легково́й а.** (passenger) car; **грузово́й а.** lorry; **малолитра́жный а.** compact (car), mini; **микролитра́жный а.** subcompact (car); **сери́йный а.** stock car; **води́ть а.** to drive a car.
автомоби́л|ь-бо́мба, ~я-бо́мбы *m.* car bomb.
автомоби́л|ь-ветера́н, ~я-ветера́на *m.* = **автоветера́н**
автомоби́ль|ный *adj. of* **~**; **а. заво́д** motorcar factory; **~ая магнито́ла** (in-)car radio cassette; **а. спорт** motoring.
автомодели́зм, а *m.* car modelling.
автомодели́ст, а *m.* car modeller.
автомоде́л|ь, и *f.* model car.
автомотодро́м, а *m.* race-track.
автомотри́с|а, ы *f.* (*rail.*) diesel car.
автоно́ми|я, и *f.* autonomy.
автоно́м|ный (~ен, ~на) *adj.* autonomous.
автоотве́тчик = автоинформа́тор
автопавильо́н, а *m.* bus shelter.
автопансиона́т, а *m.* motel.
автопа́рк, а *m.* **1.** car fleet. **2.** car park.
автопаро́м, а *m.* car ferry.
автоперегру́зчик, а *m.* tip(per) truck.
автопогру́зчик, а *m.* lift truck.
автопо́езд, а, *pl.* **~а́** *m.* articulated lorry; juggernaut.
автопортре́т, а *m.* self-portrait.
автоприёмник, а *m.* car radio.
автоприце́п, а *m.* trailer, caravan; **жило́й а.** camper, mobile home; **тури́стский а.** travel trailer.
автопроисше́стви|е, я *nt.* road *or* traffic accident.
автопрока́тн|ый *adj.*: **~ая компа́ния** car hire company.
а́втор, а *m.* author; composer; (*fig.*) architect; **а. го́ла** (goal-)scorer; **а. предложе́ния, резолю́ции** mover of resolution.
авторазмора́живател|ь, я *m.* (*windscreen*) de-icer.
автора́лли *nt. indecl.* (car) rally.
авторалли́ст, а *m.* rallyist, rally driver.
автореферат, а *m.* abstract (*of dissertation, etc.*).
авториза́ци|я, и *f.* authorization.
авториз|о́ванный *p.p.p. of* **~ова́ть** *and adj.* authorized.
авториз|ова́ть, у́ю *impf. and pf.* to authorize.
авторитари́зм, а *m.* authoritarianism.
авторита́р|ный (~ен, ~на) *adj.* authoritarian.
авторите́т, а *m.* authority; **по́льзоваться ~ом** to enjoy authority, have prestige; **счита́ться ~ом** to be considered an authority.
авторите́тност|ь, и *f.* authoritativeness; trustworthiness.
авторите́т|ный (~ен, ~на) *adj.* authoritative; trustworthy; **а. исто́чник** an authoritative source (of information).
а́втор|ский *adj. of* **~**; **а. лист** (*typ.*) unit of 40,000 ens (*used in calculating author's royalties*); **~ское пра́во** copyright; *as n.* **~ские, ~ских** royalties.
а́вторско-правово́й *adj.* copyright.
а́вторств|о, а *nt.* authorship.
автору́чк|а, и *f.* fountain-pen.
автосало́н, а *m.* **1.** motorcar showroom. **2.** motor show.
автоса́н|и, е́й *no sg.* sledge car, motor sleigh.
автосекрета́р|ь, я́ *m.* answerphone, (telephone) answering machine.
автосе́рвис, а *m.* service station.
автосмо́тр = автосало́н 2.
автоспо́рт, а *m.* motor sports.
автоста́нци|я, и *f.* bus station; coach station.
автосто́п, а *m.* **1.** (*rail.*) automatic braking gear. **2.** hitch-hiking. **3.** hitch-hiking permit. **4.** (*tech.*) auto-stop.
автосто́пов|ец, ца *m.* hitchhiker, hitcher.
автосто́пщик = автосто́повец
автосто́рож, а *m.* anti-theft device (*for car*).
автостоя́нк|а, и *f.* car park.
автостра́д|а, ы *f.* motorway, motor highway; trunk-road; **скоростна́я а.** expressway; freeway.
автосуфлёр, а *m.* Autocue (*propr.*), teleprompter.
автосце́пк|а, и *f.* (*rail.*) automatic coupling.
автотелефо́н, а *m.* car phone.
автоти́пи|я, и *f.* (*typ.*) autotype.
автотра́нспорт, а *m.* motor transport.
автотра́сс|а, ы *f.* highway.
автотрюка́ч, а́ *m.* stunt driver.
автотури́зм, а *m.* motor touring.
автотури́ст, а *m.* motor tourer.
автоуго́нщик = автово́р
автофурго́н, а *m.* van.
автохто́н, а *m.* autochthon, aboriginal.
автохто́нный *adj.* autochthonous.
автоцисте́рн|а, ы *f.* tanker.
автошко́л|а, ы *f.* driving school; **преподава́тель** (*m.*) **~ы** driving instructor.
авуа́р|ы, ~ *no sg.* (*fin.*) holdings; foreign assets.
ага́ *int.* (*expr.* (*i*) *comprehension,* (*ii*) *malicious pleasure*) ah!; aha!
ага́в|а, ы *f.* (*bot.*) agave.
агаря́н|ин, ина, *pl.* **~е, ~** *m.* (*coll., obs.*) Hagarite.
ага́т, а *m.* (*min.*) agate.
ага́т|овый *adj. of* **~**
агглютинати́вный *adj.* (*ling.*) agglutinative.
агглютин|и́рующий = ~ати́вный
а́генс, а *m.* (*ling.*) agent.
аге́нт, а *m.* (*in var. senses*) agent; **рекла́мный а.** advertising agent; adman.
аге́нтств|о, а *nt.* agency; **а. печа́ти** news agency; **а. (для) по́мощи** aid *or* relief agency; **бракопосре́дническое а.**

marriage bureau; **информацио́нное а.** press agency.
агенту́р|а, ы *f.* **1.** secret service; **занима́ться ~ой** to be an agent. **2.** (*collect.*) agents.
агиогра́фи|я, и *f.* hagiography.
агит... *comb. form, abbr. of* **агитацио́нный**
агита́тор, а *m.* (*pol.*) agitator; canvasser; electioneer.
агитацио́н|ный (~ен, ~на) *adj.* (*pol.*) agitation; **~ная речь** campaign speech.
агита́ци|я, и *f.* (*pol.*) agitation; drive; **вести́ ~ю** to campaign; conduct a drive; **предвы́борная а.** electioneering; **вести́ предвы́борную ~ю** to electioneer.
агити́р|овать, ую *impf.* **1.** (*impf. only*) (*pol.*) to agitate, carry on agitation, campaign, electioneer. **2.** (*pf.* **с~**) (*coll.*) to canvass.
аги́тк|а, и *f.* (*pol.*) propaganda piece (*plays, posters, etc.*).
агитпро́п, а *m.* (*abbr. of* **отде́л агита́ции и пропага́нды**) agitation and propaganda section (*of central and local committees of the CPSU*).
агитпу́нкт, а *m.* agitation centre.
а́глицкий *adj.* (*coll., obs.*) English.
а́гн|ец, ца *m.* **1.** (*eccl.*) lamb (*Agnus Dei*). **2.** *fig. of a meek pers.*: **прики́нуться ~цем** to play the innocent.
агно́стик, а *m.* agnostic.
агностици́зм, а *m.* agnosticism.
агности́ческий *adj.* agnostic.
агонизи́р|овать, ую *impf. and pf.* to be in one's death-throes.
аго́ни|я, и *f.* (*med and fig.*) death-throes.
аго́рн, а *m.* (*cul.*) maple sugar.
аго́рновый *adj.*: **а. сиро́п** maple syrup.
агра́ри|й, я *m.* (*hist.*) landowner.
агра́рный *adj.* agrarian.
агрега́т, а *m.* **1.** (*tech.*) unit, assembly. **2.** aggregate.
агрега́тный *adj.* modular.
агресси́в|ный (~ен, ~на) *adj.* aggressive.
агре́сси|я, и *f.* (*pol.*) aggression.
агре́ссор, а *m.* aggressor.
агрикульту́р|а, ы *f.* agriculture.
агрикульту́рный *adj.* agricultural.
агро... *comb. form* agro-, agricultural, farm.
агроло́ги|я, и *f.* agrology, soil science.
агроно́м, а *m.* agronomist.
агроно́ми|я, и *f.* agronomics; agricultural science.
агроте́хник, а *m.* agricultural technician.
агроте́хник|а, и *f.* agricultural technology.
агрохимика́т|ы, ов *pl.* (*sg.* **~, ~а** *m.*) agrochemicals.
агрохими́ческий *adj.* agrochemical.
ад, а *m.* hell; (*fig.*) bedlam; **душе́вный а.** mental torment, anguish.
ада́жио (*mus.*) **1.** *adv.* **2.** *n.*; *nt. indecl.* adagio.
ада́мов *adj.*: **~о я́блоко** Adam's apple.
адапта́ци|я, и *f.* (*in var. senses*) adaptation.
ада́птер, а *m.* **1.** (*tech.*) adapter. **2.** (*mus.*) pick-up.
адвенти́ст, а *m.* (*relig.*) (Seventh-day) Adventist.
адвока́т, а *m.* barrister; (*fig.*) advocate.
адвокату́р|а, ы *f.* **1.** the profession of barrister. **2.** (*collect.*) the Bar, the legal profession.
Адди́с-Абе́б|а, ы *f.* Addis Ababa.
адеква́т|ный (~ен, ~на) *adj.* identical, coincident; adequate.
адено́ид, а *m.* (*med.*) adenoid.
аде́пт, а *m.* adherent, disciple.
аджа́р|ец, ца *m.* Adzharian.
аджа́р|ка, ки *f. of* **~ец**
аджа́рский *adj.* Adzharian.
адида́с|ки, ок *pl.* (*sg.* **~ка, ~ки** *f.*) (*coll.*) trainers.
администрати́вн|ый *adj.* administrative; **в ~ом поря́дке** administratively, by administrative means.
администра́тор, а *m.* administrator; manager (*of hotel, theatre, etc.*).
администра́торск|ая, ой *f.* (*hotel*) reception.
администра́ци|я, и *f.* administration; management.
администри́р|овать, ую *impf.* to administer; (*pej.*) to run (*an organization, etc.*) by means of orders and decrees.
адмира́л, а *m.* **1.** admiral. **2.** (*zool.*) Red Admiral.
адмиралте́й|ский *adj. of* **~ство**
адмиралте́йств|о, а *nt.* (*obs.*) **1.** naval dockyard. **2.** The Admiralty.
адмира́л|ьский *adj. of* **~**; **а. кора́бль** flagship; **а. чин, ~ьское зва́ние** flag rank; **а. час** (*joc., obs.*) midday drinking time.
адмира́льш|а, и *f.* admiral's wife.
а́дов *adj.* (*relig. and fig., coll.*) *of* **ад**
а́дрес, а, *pl.* **~а́, ~о́в** *m.* (*in var. senses*) address; **в а.** (+*g.*) (*fig.*) aimed at, directed at; **не по ~у** (*fig.*) mistakenly, at the wrong door, to the wrong quarter.
адреса́нт, а *m.* sender (*of mail*).
адреса́т, а *m.* addressee; **в слу́чае ненахожде́ния ~а** 'if undelivered'; **за ненахожде́нием ~а** 'not known' (*on letters*).
адрес-календа́р|ь, я́ *m.* (*obs.*) directory.
а́дрес|ный *adj. of* **~**; **~ная кни́га** directory; **а. стол** address bureau.
адрес|ова́ть, у́ю *impf. and pf.* to address, direct.
адрес|ова́ться, у́юсь *impf. and pf.* (**к**+*d.*) to address o.s. (to).
Адриати́ческ|ое мо́р|е, ~ого ~я *nt.* the Adriatic (Sea).
а́дски *adv.* (*coll.*) infernally, terribly, fearfully; **я а. за́нят** I am terribly busy.
а́дск|ий *adj.* infernal, diabolical; (*fig.*) hellish, intolerable; **~ая ску́ка** infernal bore; **~ая маши́на** infernal machine.
адсо́рбци|я, и *f.* (*chem.*) adsorption.
адъю́нкт, а *m.* **1.** (*obs.*) junior scientific assistant. **2.** advanced student in military academy.
адъюта́нт, а *m.* (*mil.*) aide-de-camp; **ста́рший а.** adjutant.
адюльте́р, а *m.* adultery.
адюльте́р|ный *adj. of* **~**
аж *adv. and conj.* (*coll.*) **1.** (*adv.*) **аж до** right up to; **аж на** (+*a.*) right on to. **2.** (*conj.*) so that, until; **она́ так закрича́ла, аж се́рдце похолоде́ло** she cried enough to break one's heart.
а́жио *nt. indecl.* (*comm.*) agio.
ажиота́ж, а *m.* **1.** (*comm.*) stockjobbing. **2.** (*fig.*) stir, hullabaloo.
ажита́ци|я, и *f.* (*obs.*) agitation, excitement; **быть в ~и** to be agitated, het up, in a state.
ажу́р[1]**, а** *m.* open-work.
ажу́р[2]**, а** *m.* (*comm.*): **учёт в ~е** the accounts are up to date; **всё в (по́лном) ~е** (*fig., coll.*) everything's fine *or* hunky-dory.
ажу́рн|ый *adj.* open-work; (*fig.*) delicate, fine; **~ые чулки́** open-work stockings; **~ая рабо́та** open-work; (*archit.*) tracery.
аз, а́ *m.* **1.** az (*Slavonic name of the letter A*). **2.** (*usu. pl.*; *coll.*) ABC; basics, elements, rudiments; **начина́ть с ~о́в** to begin at the beginning; **ни ~а́ не знать** (**о**+*p.*) not to know the first thing (about).
аза́ли|я, и *f.* (*bot.*) azalea.
аза́рт, а *m.* heat; excitement; fervour; **войти́ в а.** to grow heated, excited.
аза́рт|ный (~ен, ~на) *adj.* heated; venturesome; **~ная игра́** game of chance.
азбе́ст = асбе́ст
а́збук|а, и *f.* alphabet; the ABC (*also fig.*); **а. Мо́рзе** Morse code; **ручна́я/дакти́льная а.** sign language; **слогова́я а.** syllabary.
а́збучн|ый *adj.* alphabetical; **~ая и́стина** truism.
Азербайджа́н, а *m.* Azerbaijan.
азербайджа́н|ец, ца *m.* Azerbaijani(an).
азербайджа́н|ка, ки *f. of* **~ец**
азербайджа́нский *adj.* Azerbaijani.
азиа́т, а *m.* **1.** Asian; Asiatic. **2.** (*fig., obs.*) barbarian, savage.
азиа́т|ка, ки *f. of* **~**
азиа́тский *adj.* **1.** Asian; Asiatic. **2.** (*fig., obs.*) barbarous.
азиа́тчин|а, ы *f.* (*obs.*) barbarousness.
а́зимут, а *m.* (*astron.*) azimuth.
А́зи|я, и *f.* Asia; **Ма́лая А́.** Asia Minor.
Азо́вск|ое мо́р|е, ~ого ~я *nt.* the Sea of Azov.
Азо́рск|ие остров|а́, ~их ~о́в *no sg.* the Azores (*islands*).

азо́т, а *m.* (*chem.*) nitrogen; **о́кись ~а** nitric oxide.
азотистоки́слый *adj.* (*chem.*) nitrite.
азо́тистый *adj.* (*chem.*) nitrous.
азотноки́слый *adj.* (*chem.*) nitrate.
азо́тн|ый *adj.* (*chem.*) nitric; **~ая кислота́** nitric acid.
а́ир, а *m.* (*bot.*) sweet flag.
а́ист, а *m.* (*zool.*) stork.
ай *int.* (*expr.* (*i*) *fear*, (*ii*) *surprise and/or pleasure*) oh!; ow, ouch; **ай, бо́льно!** ow, that hurts!; **ай да** (*expr. approval*) what a ...!; **ай да молоде́ц!** well done!
айв|а́, ы́ *f.* **1.** quince. **2.** quince-tree.
айво́вый *adj.* quince.
айда́ *int.* (*coll.*) come along!; let's go!
а́йе-а́йе *m. indecl.* (*zool.*) aye-aye.
айкидо́ *nt. indecl.* aikido.
а́йсберг, а *m.* iceberg.
академи́зм, а *m.* academic manner.
акаде́мик, а *m.* **1.** academician (*member of an Academy*). **2.** (*coll., obs.*) student of an academy.
академи́ческий *adj.* academic(al); **а. мир** academia, academe; **а. о́тпуск** sabbatical (leave).
академи́ч|ный (~ен, ~на) *adj.* academic, theoretical.
акаде́ми|я, и *f.* academy.
акаде́мк|а, и *f.* (*sl.*) sabbatical (leave).
а́кань|е, я *nt.* 'akanie' (*pronunciation of unstressed Russian 'o' as 'a'*).
а́ка|ть, ю *impf.* to pronounce unstressed Russian 'o' as 'a'.
ака́фист, а *m.* (*eccl.*) acathistus (*series of doxological prayers*).
ака́ци|я, и *f.* (*bot.*) acacia.
аквала́нг, а *m.* aqualung.
акваланги́ст, а *m.* (skin *or* scuba) diver.
аквалaнги́ст|ка, ки *f. of* ~
аквамари́н, а *m.* (*min.*) aquamarine.
акваплáн, а *m.* aquaplane; **ката́ться на ~е** to aquaplane.
акварели́ст, а *m.* water-colourist.
аквaре́л|ь, и *f.* water-colours; **писа́ть ~ью** to paint in water-colours.
акваре́льный *adj.* water-colour.
аква́риум, а *m.* aquarium.
аквариуми́ст, а *m.* aquarist.
аквато́ри|я, и *f.* (*defined*) waters, water area.
акведу́к, а *m.* aqueduct.
акклиматиза́ци|я, и *f.* acclimatization.
акклиматизи́р|овать, ую *impf. and pf.* to acclimatize.
акклиматизи́р|оваться, уюсь *impf. and pf.* to become acclimatized.
аккомпанеме́нт, а *m.* (*mus.*) accompaniment (*also fig.*); **под а.** (*+g.*) to the accompaniment of.
аккомпаниа́тор, а *m.* (*mus.*) accompanist.
аккомпани́р|овать, ую *impf.* (*+d.*, **на**+*p.*; *mus.*) to accompany; **а. певцу́ на роя́ле** to accompany a singer on the piano.
акко́рд, а *m.* (*mus.*) chord; **заключи́тельный а.** (*fig.*) finale; **взять а.** to strike a chord (*on the piano*).
аккордео́н, а *m.* accordion.
аккордеони́ст, а *m.* accordionist.
акко́рдн|ый *adj.*: **~ая пла́та** payment by the job; **~ая рабо́та** piecework.
аккредити́в, а *m.* (*fin.*) letter of credit.
аккредит|ова́ть, у́ю *impf. and pf.* to accredit.
аккумули́р|овать, ую *impf. and pf.* to accumulate.
аккумуля́тор, а *m.* (*tech.*) accumulator; battery.
аккумуля́ци|я, и *f.* accumulation.
аккура́т *adv.* (*coll.*) *only in phrr.* **в а.** exactly, precisely; **в ~е** properly.
аккурати́ст, а *m.* (*coll.*) **1.** stickler for detail. **2.** tidiness fiend.
аккура́тност|ь, и *f.* **1.** exactness, thoroughness. **2.** tidiness, neatness.
аккура́т|ный (~ен, ~на) *adj.* **1.** exact, thorough. **2.** tidy, neat.
акмеи́зм, а *m.* (*liter.*) acmeism.
акмеи́ст, а *m.* (*liter.*) acmeist.
акри́д|ы, ~ *no sg., only in phr.* **пита́ться ~ами и ди́ким мёдом** to live on locusts and wild honey (*i.e. to live meagrely*).
акри́л, а *m.* acrylic.
акри́л|овый *adj. of* ~
акроба́т, а *m.* acrobat; **а.(-прыгу́н)** (*gymnast*) tumbler; **а. на велосипе́де** trick cyclist; **возду́шный а.** aerialist.
акроба́тик|а, и *f.* acrobatics.
акро́ним, а *m.* acronym.
акро́пол|ь, я *m.* (*hist.*) acropolis.
акрости́х, а *m.* acrostic.
акселера́т, а *m.* (*med.*) early developer, maturer.
акселера́тор, а *m.* accelerator.
акселера́ци|я, и *f.* (*med.*) early development, maturation; **а. ро́ста** accelerated growth.
аксельба́нт, а *m.* aiguillette.
аксессуа́р, а *m.* **1.** accessory. **2.** *pl.* (*theatr.*) props.
аксио́м|а, ы *f.* axiom.
акт, а *m.* **1.** act; **полово́й а.** sexual intercourse, intimacy. **2.** (*theatr.*) act. **3.** (*leg.*) deed, document; instrument; **обвини́тельный а.** indictment. **4.** (*obs.*) speech-day (*in schools*).
актёр, а *m.* actor (*also fig., pej.*); **а. на выходны́х роля́х** bit *or* walk-on player.
актёр|ский *adj. of* ~
актёрств|о, а *nt.* acting; (*fig.*) affectation, posing.
акти́в[1]**, а** *m.* (*fin.*) assets; (*fig.*) asset.
акти́в[2]**, а** *m.* (*pol.*) most active members; **парти́йный а.** party activists.
активиза́ци|я, и *f.* intensification.
активизи́р|овать, ую *impf. and pf.* to intensify; to stimulate, promote.
активи́ст, а *m.* (*pol.*) activist (*active member of political or social organization*).
акти́в|ный (~ен, ~на) *adj.* active, energetic.
акти́ни|я, и *f.* sea anemone.
а́ктов|ый *adj.*: **~ая бума́га** (*obs.*) official paper; **а. день** (official) non-working day (*due to bad weather*); **а. зал** assembly hall.
актри́с|а, ы *f.* actress.
актуа́льност|ь, и *f.* **1.** (*tech.*) actuality. **2.** topicality.
актуа́л|ьный (~ен, ~ьна) *adj.* **1.** (*tech.*) actual. **2.** topical, current; **а. вопро́с** pressing question, topical question.
аку́л|а, ы *f.* (*zool.*) shark (*also fig.*).
акупункту́р|а, ы *f.* acupuncture
аку́стик, а *m.* sound-man, sound technician.
аку́стик|а, и *f.* acoustics.
акусти́ческий *adj.* acoustic.
аку́т, а *m.* (*ling.*) acute accent.
акуше́р, а *m.* obstetrician; **подпо́льный а.** (backstreet) abortionist.
акуше́рк|а, и *f.* midwife.
акуше́рский *adj.* obstetric(al).
акуше́рств|о, а *nt.* obstetrics; midwifery.
акцелера́ция = акселера́ция
акце́нт, а *m.* accent.
акценти́р|овать, ую *impf. and pf.* to accent, accentuate.
акце́пт, а *m.* (*comm.*) acceptance.
акцепт|ова́ть, у́ю *impf. and pf.* (*comm.*) to accept.
акци́з, а *m.* (excise-)duty; **обложи́ть ~ом** to excise.
акционе́р, а *m.* shareholder, stockholder.
акционе́р|ный *adj. of* ~; **~ное о́бщество** joint-stock company.
а́кци|я[1]**, и** *f.* (*fin.*) share; **обыкнове́нная а.** ordinary share; **имення́я а.** nominal share; **привилегиро́ванная а.** preference share; (*fig., coll.*; *pl. only*) stock; **его́ ~и си́льно поднима́ются** his stock is rising rapidly.
а́кци|я[2]**, и** *f.* action.
алба́н|ец, ца *m.* Albanian.
Алба́ни|я, и *f.* Albania.
алба́н|ка, ки *f. of* **~ец**
алба́нский *adj.* Albanian.
а́лгебр|а, ы *f.* algebra.
алгебраи́ческий *adj.* algebraic(al).
алгори́тм, а *m.* algorithm.
алеба́рд|а, ы *f.* (*hist.*) halberd.
алеба́стр, а *m.* alabaster.
александри́йский *adj.* (*geog.*) Alexandrian; **а. лист** (*med.*)

senna; **а. стих** (*liter.*) Alexandrine (verse).
александри́т, а *m.* (*min.*) alexandrite.
Александри́|я, и *f.* Alexandria.
але́|ть, ю *impf.* (*of* **за~**) **1.** to redden, flush. **2.** to show red.
Алеу́тск|ие остров|а́, ~их ~о́в *no sg.* the Aleutians (*islands*).
Алжи́р, а *m.* **1.** Algeria. **2.** Algiers.
алжи́р|ец, ца *m.* Algerian.
алжи́р|ка, ки *f. of* **~ец**
алжи́рский *adj.* Algerian.
а́ли (*coll.*) = **и́ли**
а́либи *nt. indecl.* (*leg.*) alibi; **установи́ть а.** to establish an alibi.
алиме́нтщик, а *m.* (*coll.*) pers. paying alimony.
алиме́нтщиц|а, ы *f.* (*coll.*) woman in receipt of alimony.
алиме́нт|ы, ов *no sg.* (*leg.*) alimony, maintenance.
ал|ка́ть, ~́чу, ~́чешь *impf.* (*+g.*; *poet.*) to hunger (for), crave (for).
алка́ш, а́ *m.* (*coll., pej.*) boozer, dipso.
алкоголи́зм, а *m.* alcoholism.
алкого́лик, а *m.* alcoholic; (*coll.*) drunkard.
алкоголи́ческий *adj.* alcoholic.
алкого́л|ь, я *m.* alcohol; **прове́рить на а.** to breathalyze.
алкого́льный *adj.* alcoholic.
алкоме́тр, а *m.* breathalyzer.
алкоте́ст = **алкоме́тр**
Алла́х, а *m.* Allah; **А. его́ ве́дает** God knows; **одному́ ~у изве́стно** God alone knows.
аллегори́ч|еский *adj.* allegorical.
аллегори́ч|ный (~ен, ~на) = **~еский**
аллего́ри|я, и *f.* allegory.
алле́гро (*mus.*) **1.** *adv.* **2.** *n.*; *nt. indecl.* allegro.
аллерге́н, а *m.* allergen.
алле́ргик, а *m.* allergy sufferer.
аллерги́|я, и *f.* allergy.
алле́|я, и *f.* **1.** path, walk, ride. **2.** avenue.
аллига́тор, а *m.* alligator.
аллилу́йщик, а *m.* (*coll.*) toady, sycophant.
аллилу́йщин|а, ы *f.* (*coll.*) toadying, sycophancy.
аллилу́йя *nt. indecl. and as int.* alleluia, hallelujah.
аллитера́ци|я, и *f.* alliteration.
алло́ *int.* hello!
аллопа́т, а *m.* (*med.*) allopath(ist).
аллопа́ти|я, и *f.* (*med.*) allopathy.
аллопати́ческий *adj.* (*med.*) allopathic.
аллювиа́льный *adj.* (*geol.*) alluvial.
аллю́ви|й, я *m.* (*geol.*) alluvium.
аллю́р, а *m.* pace, gait (*of horses*).
алма́з, а *m.* (uncut) diamond.
ало́з|а, ы *f.* (*zool.*) shad.
ало́э *nt. indecl.* (*bot.*) aloe; (*med.*) aloes.
алта́р|ь, я́ *m.* **1.** (*eccl.*) altar; **возложи́ть, принести́ на а.** (*+g.*) to sacrifice (to). **2.** (*eccl.*) chancel; sanctuary.
алты́н, а *m.* (*obs.*) three-kopeck piece.
алты́нник, а *m.* (*obs., coll.*) skinflint.
алфави́т, а *m.* alphabet; (*comput., typ.*) character set.
алфави́тно-цифрово́й *adj.* alphanumeric.
алфави́тный *adj.* alphabetical; **а. указа́тель** index.
алхи́мик, а *m.* alchemist.
алхи́ми|я, и *f.* alchemy.
а́лчност|ь, и *f.* greed, avidity, cupidity.
а́лч|ный (~ен, ~на) *adj.* greedy, grasping.
а́лчущ|ий *pres. part. of* **алка́ть; ~ие и жа́ждущие** (*+g.*) those that hunger and thirst (after).
а́л|ый (~, ~а) *adj.* scarlet.
алыч|а́, и́ *f.* cherry-plum, myrobalan plum (*Prunus cerasifera*).
аль (*coll.*) = **и́ли**
альбатро́с, а *m.* albatross.
альбини́зм, а *m.* (*med.*) albinism.
альбино́с, а *m.* (*med.*) albino.
альбо́м, а *m.* album.
альвеоля́рный *adj.* (*ling.*) alveolar.
алько́в, а *m.* alcove.
алько́в|ный *adj.* **1.** *adj. of* **~. 2.** amorous, amatory; **~ные похожде́ния** amorous escapades; **а. фарс** bedroom comedy.
а́льма-ма́тер *f. indecl.* Alma Mater.
альмана́х, а *m.* **1.** literary miscellany. **2.** (*obs.*) almanac.
альпага́ = **альпака́**[1]
альпака́[1] *c.g. indecl. and nt. indecl.* **1.** *c.g.* alpaca (*animal*). **2.** *nt.* alpaca (*fabric*).
альпака́[2] *nt. indecl.* (*min.*) German silver.
альпа́ри *adv.* (*comm.*) at par.
альпи́йский *adj.* alpine.
альпина́ри|й, я *m.* rock garden.
альпиниа́да, ы *f.* mass ascent.
альпини́зм, а *m.* mountaineering.
альпини́ст, а *m.* mountain-climber.
А́льп|ы, ~ *no sg.* the Alps.
альт, а́, *pl.* **~ы́** *m.* (*mus.*) **1.** alto (*voice or singer*). **2.** viola.
альтера́ци|я, и *f.* (*mus.*) change in pitch of notes (*by a tone or semitone*); **зна́ки ~и** accidentals.
альтернати́в|а, ы *f.* alternative.
альтернати́в|ный (~ен, ~на) *adj.* alternative; **~ная техноло́гия** alternative technology.
альти́ст, а *m.* viola-player.
альт|о́вый *adj. of* **~; ~о́вая па́ртия** alto part.
альтруи́зм, а *m.* altruism.
альтруи́ст, а *m.* altruist.
альтруисти́ческий *adj.* altruistic.
а́льф|а, ы *f.* alpha; **от ~ы до оме́ги** from A to Z.
альфо́л|ь, и *f.* aluminium foil, tinfoil.
альфо́нс, а *m.* (*pej.*) gigolo.
алья́нс, а *m.* alliance.
алюми́ниевый *adj.* aluminium.
алюми́ни|й, я *m.* aluminium.
а-ля́ *prep.* à la.
аляпова́т|ый (~, ~а) *adj.* garish, cheap-looking; crude(ly fashioned).
Аля́ск|а, и *f.* Alaska.
аля́ск|а, и *f.* (*coll.*) **1.** anorak. **2.** *pl.* moon boots.
а-ля фурше́т, а *m.* buffet; fork lunch *or* supper.
Амазо́нк|а, и *f.* the Amazon (*river*).
амазо́нк|а, и *f.* **1.** (*myth.*) Amazon. **2.** horsewoman. **3.** riding-habit.
амальга́м|а, ы *f.* (*chem. and fig.*) amalgam.
амальгами́р|овать, ую *impf. and pf.* (*chem. and fig.*) to amalgamate.
амана́т, а *m.* (*dial.*) hostage.
а́мба *int.* (*sl.*) kaput!; it's all up!
амба́р, а *m.* barn, granary; warehouse, storehouse.
амба́рго = **эмба́рго**
амба́р|ный *adj. of* **~**
амбицио́з|ный (~ен, ~на) *adj.* arrogant, conceited.
амби́ци|я, и *f.* **1.** (*obs.*) pride; arrogance; **челове́к с ~ей** arrogant man; **вломи́ться в ~ю** to take offence. **2.** *pl.* claims (to) (**на**+*a.*).
а́мбр|а, ы *f.* amber; **се́рая а.** ambergris.
амбразу́р|а, ы *f.* (*mil., archit.*) embrasure.
амбре́ *nt. indecl.* scent, smell, fragrance (*now usu. iron.*).
амбро́зи|я, и *f.* ambrosia.
амбулато́ри|я, и *f.* (*med.*) out-patients department (*of hospital*); (*general practioner's*) surgery.
амбулато́р|ный *adj. of* **~ия; а. больно́й** out-patient; **а. приём** out-patient reception hours; surgery hours.
амбушю́р, а *m.* (*mus.*) mouthpiece.
амво́н, а *m.* (*eccl.*) ambo, pulpit.
амёб|а, ы *f.* (*zool.*) amoeba.
Аме́рик|а, и *f.* America.
америка́н|ец, ца *m.* American.
американи́зм, а *m.* (*ling.*) Americanism.
американи́стик|а, и *f.* American studies.
америка́н|ка, ки *f. of* **~ец**
америка́нск|ий *adj.* American; **~ие го́ры** Big Dipper, switchback (*fairground attraction*); **а. дя́дюшка** 'rich uncle' (*character, esp. in comedies, from whom a legacy is hoped for*); **а. замо́к** Yale (*propr.*) lock; **а. оре́х** Brazil nut.
америка́шк|а, и *c.g.* (*sl.*) yank.
амети́ст, а *m.* (*min.*) amethyst.

амети́ст|овый *adj. of* ~
амикошо́нств|о, а *nt.* (*coll.*) hail-fellow-well-met attitude.
аминокислот|а́, ы́ *f.* (*chem.*) aminoacid.
ами́нь *particle* (*eccl.*) amen.
аммиа́к, а *m.* (*chem.*) ammonia.
аммиа́чный *adj.* (*chem.*) ammoniac.
аммо́ни|й, я *m.* (*chem.*) ammonium.
амнисти́р|овать, ую *impf. and pf.* to amnesty.
амни́сти|я, и *f.* amnesty.
аморали́зм, а *m.* (*phil.*) amoralism.
амора́льност|ь, и *f.* amorality; immorality.
амора́л|ьный (~ен, ~ьна) *adj.* amoral; immoral.
амортиза́тор, а *m.* (*tech.*) shock-absorber.
амортиза́ци|я, и *f.* **1.** (*econ.*) amortization. **2.** (*tech.*) shock-absorption.
амортизи́р|овать, ую *impf. and pf.* to amortize.
амо́рф|ный (~ен, ~на) *adj.* amorphous.
ампе́р, а, *g. pl.* **а.** *m.* (*phys.*) ampere.
ампи́р, а *m.* Empire style (*of furniture, etc.*).
ампи́р|ный *adj. of* ~
амплиту́д|а, ы *f.* amplitude.
амплифика́ци|я, и *f.* (*liter.*) amplification, inflation.
амплуа́ *nt. indecl.* (*theatr.*) type; (*fig.*) role.
а́мпул|а, ы *f.* ampoule.
ампута́ци|я, и *f.* (*med.*) amputation.
ампути́р|овать, ую *impf. and pf.* (*med.*) to amputate.
Амстерда́м, а *m.* Amsterdam.
амуле́т, а *m.* amulet.
амуни́ци|я, и *f.* (*collect.*) (*mil., hist.*) accoutrements.
Аму́р, а *m.* **1.** (*myth.*) Cupid. **2.: аму́ры** (*pl. only*) (*coll.*) intrigues, love affairs.
аму́р|иться, юсь *impf.* (**с**+*i.*; *coll.*) to flirt (with), have an affair (with).
аму́рн|ый *adj.* (*coll.*) love; amorous; **~ые дела́** love affairs; **~ые пи́сьма** love letters.
амфетами́н, а *m.* (*pharm.*) amphetamine.
амфи́би|я, и *f.* (*zool., bot.*) amphibian.
амфибра́хи|й, я *m.* (*liter.*) amphibrach.
амфитеа́тр, а *m.* (*hist.*) amphitheatre; (*theatr.*) circle.
АН *f. indecl.* (*abbr. of* **Акаде́мия нау́к**) Academy of Sciences.
ан *conj.* (*dial.*) on the contrary; but in fact.
анабапти́зм, а *m.* Anabaptism.
анабапти́ст, а *m.* Anabaptist.
анабио́з, а *m.* (*biol.*) anabiosis.
анаболи́ческий *adj.*: **а. стеро́ид** anabolic steroid.
анагра́мм|а, ы *f.* anagram.
анаколу́ф, а *m.* (*liter.*) anacoluthon.
анакреонти́ческий *adj.* (*liter.*) anacreontic.
ана́лиз, а *m.* analysis; **а. кро́ви** blood test; **а. мочи́** (*med.*) urinalysis; **(радио)углеро́дный а.** carbon-dating.
анализи́р|овать, ую *impf.* to analyse.
анали́тик, а *m.* analyst.
анали́тик|а, и *f.* (*math.*) analytic geometry.
аналити́ческий *adj.* analytic(al).
ана́лог, а *m.* analogue.
аналоги́ческ|ий *adj.* analogical; **~ое рассужде́ние** reasoning by analogy.
аналоги́ч|ный (~ен, ~на) *adj.* analogous; **~ные слу́чаи** analogous cases.
анало́ги|я, и *f.* analogy; **по ~и (с**+*i.*) by analogy (with), on the analogy (of); **проводи́ть ~ю** to draw an analogy.
анало́|й, я *m.* (*eccl.*) lectern.
ана́льный *adj.* anal.
анана́с, а *m.* pineapple.
анана́с|ный *adj. of* ~
анана́с|овый *adj. of* ~; **а. сок** pineapple juice.
анапе́ст, а *m.* (*liter.*) anapaest.
анархи́зм, а *m.* (*pol.*) anarchism.
анархи́ст, а *m.* (*pol.*) anarchist.
анархи́ческий *adj.* anarchic(al).
ана́рхи|я, и *f.* anarchy.
ана́рхо-синдикали́зм, а *m.* (*pol.*) anarcho-syndicalism.
ана́рхо-синдикали́ст, а *m.* (*pol.*) anarcho-syndicalist.
ана́том, а *m.* anatomist.
анатоми́р|овать, ую *impf. and pf.* (*med.*) to dissect.
анатоми́ческий *adj.* anatomic(al); **а. теа́тр** dissecting room.
анатоми́чк|а, и *f.* (*coll.*) dissecting room.
анато́ми|я, и *f.* anatomy.
ана́фем|а, ы *f.* **1.** (*eccl.*) anathema; excommunication; (*fig.*): **преда́ть ~е** to anathematize. **2.** (*coll.*) accursed fellow.
анафема́тств|овать, ую *impf.* (*eccl.*) to excommunicate.
ана́фемский *adj.* (*coll.*) accursed.
анахоре́т, а *m.* hermit, anchorite; (*fig.*) recluse.
анахрони́зм, а *m.* anachronism.
анахрони́ческий *adj.* anachronistic.
анаш|а́, и́ *f.* (*sl.*) pot, hash; **закру́тка ~и́** joint (= *marijuana cigarette*).
анаши́ст, а *m.* (*sl.*) pot smoker; hash-head.
ангажеме́нт, а *m.* (*theatr.*) engagement.
ангажи́р|овать, ую *impf. and pf.* (*theatr.*) to engage.
анга́р, а *m.* (*aeron.*) hangar.
а́нгел, а *m.* angel; **а.-храни́тель** guardian angel; **а. во пло́ти** (*coll.*) (an absolute) angel; **день ~а** name-day; **морско́й а.** angelfish.
а́нгельск|ий *adj.* angelic (*also fig.*); **~ое терпе́ние** angelic patience; **а. о́браз** (*obs.*) monk's habit.
ангидри́д, а *m.* (*chem.*) anhydride.
ангидри́т, а *m.* (*chem.*) anhydrite.
анги́н|а, ы *f.* (*med.*) quinsy; tonsillitis.
англизи́ровать, ую *impf. and pf.* to anglicize.
англи́йск|ий *adj.* **1.** English; **~ая боле́знь** rickets; **~ая була́вка** safety-pin; **а. рожо́к** (*mus.*) cor anglais, alto oboe; **~ая соль** Epsom salts; *as n.* **а., ~ого** *m.* Baskerville (type). **2.** British.
англика́н|ец, ца *m.* Anglican.
англика́н|ка, ки *f. of* **~ец**
англика́нский *adj.* (*eccl.*) Anglican.
англи́ст, а *m.* Anglist.
англи́стик|а, и *f.* Anglistics.
англици́зм, а *m.* Anglicism.
англича́н|ин, ина, *pl.* **~е, ~** *m.* Englishman.
англича́нк|а, и *f.* Englishwoman.
А́нгли|я, и *f.* **1.** England. **2.** Britain.
а́нгло-бу́рск|ий *adj.*: **~ая война́** Boer War.
англоговоря́щий = англоязы́чный 1.
англома́н, а *m.* anglomane.
англоса́кс, а *m.* Anglo-Saxon.
англосаксо́нский *adj.* Anglo-Saxon.
англофи́л, а *m.* anglophile.
англофи́льств|о, а *nt.* anglophilia.
англофо́б, а *m.* anglophobe.
англофо́бств|о, а *nt.* anglophobia.
англоязы́чный *adj.* **1.** English-speaking, anglophone. **2.** English-language.
а́нгл|ы, ов *no sg.* (*hist.*) Angles.
Анго́л|а, ы *f.* Angola.
анго́л|ец, ца *m.* Angolan.
анго́л|ка, ки *f. of* **~ец**
анго́льский *adj.* Angolan.
анго́рск|ий *adj.* Angora; **~ая ко́шка** Angora cat, Persian cat; **~ая шерсть** Angora (wool).
андалу́з|ец, ца *m.* Andalucian.
андалу́з|ка, ки *f. of* **~ец**
андалу́зский *adj.* Andalucian.
Андалу́си|я, и *f.* Andalucia.
анда́нте *adv.* (*mus.*) andante.
андре́евский *adj.*: **а. крест** St. Andrew's cross; **а. флаг** ensign of Imperial Russ. Navy.
А́нд|ы, ~ *no sg.* the Andes.
анекдо́т, а *m.* **1.** anecdote, story. **2.** joke; **а. с бородо́й** old chestnut.
анекдоти́ческий *adj.* anecdotal.
анекдоти́ч|ный (~ен, ~на) *adj.* humorous.
анекдо́тчик, а *m.* raconteur.
анеми́ческий *adj.* anaemic.
анеми́ч|ный (~ен, ~на) *adj.* anaemic, pale.
анеми́|я, и *f.* anaemia.
анемо́н = анемо́на
анемо́н|а, ы *f.* (*bot.*) anemone.
анеро́ид, а *m.* aneroid (barometer).

анестези́р|овать, ую *impf. and pf.* (*med.*) to anaesthetize; **~ующее сре́дство** anaesthetic.
анестези́|я, и *f.* (*med.*) anaesthesia.
анимали́ст, а *m.* animal painter.
аними́зм, а *m.* animism.
аними́ст, а *m.* animist.
ани́с, а *m.* (*bot.*) **1.** anise. **2.** anise apples.
ани́совк|а, и *f.* (*coll.*) anisette.
ани́с|овый *adj. of* **~**; **~овое се́мя** aniseed; **~овая во́дка** anisette.
АНК *m. indecl.* (*abbr. of* **Африка́нский национа́льный конгре́сс**) ANC (*African National Congress*).
Анкар|а́, ы́ *m.* Ankara.
а́нкер, а *m.* **1.** (*tech.*) crutch (*in watch*). **2.** (*archit.*) anchor.
анке́т|а, ы *f.* questionnaire; poll, survey; **ви́зовая а.** visa application-form.
анкла́в, а *m.* enclave.
анна́л|ы, ов *no sg.* annals.
аннекси́р|овать, ую *impf. and pf.* (*pol.*) to annex.
анне́ксия|я, и *f.* (*pol.*) annexation.
аннота́ци|я *f.* annotation; blurb.
аннoти́р|овать, ую *impf. and pf.* to annotate.
аннули́р|овать, ую *impf. and pf.* to annul, nullify; to cancel; to abrogate.
аннуля́ци|я, и *f.* annulment; cancellation; abrogation.
ано́д, а *m.* (*phys.*) anode.
анома́ли|я, и *f.* anomaly.
анома́л|ьный (~ен, ~ьна) *adj.* anomalous.
анони́м, а *m.* anonymous author.
анони́мк|а, и *f.* (*coll.*) **1.** poison-pen letter. **2.** anonymous telephone call.
анони́м|ный (~ен, ~на) *adj.* anonymous.
анони́мщик, а *m.* (*coll.*) **1.** poison-pen writer. **2.** anonymous telephone caller.
ано́нс, а *m.* announcement, notice; (*cin.*) trailer.
анонси́р|овать, ую *impf. and pf.* (+*a. or* **o**+*p.*) to announce.
анора́к, а *m.* anorak.
аноре́кси|я, и *f.* anorexia; **больно́й** (*fem.* **больна́я**) **~ей** anorexic (*pers.*).
анорма́л|ьный (~ен, ~ьна) *adj.* abnormal.
анса́мбл|ь, я *m.* **1.** harmony. **2.** (*mus., theatr.*) ensemble, company.
антаблеме́нт, а *m.* (*archit.*) entablature.
антагони́зм, а *m.* antagonism.
антагони́ст, а *m.* antagonist.
Антаркти́д|а, ы *f.* Antarctica.
Анта́рктик|а, и *f.* the Antarctic.
антаркти́ческий *adj.* Antarctic.
Антве́рпен, а *f.* Antwerp.
анте́нн|а, ы *f.* **1.** (*zool.*) antenna. **2.** (*tech.*) aerial, antenna; **ко́мнатная а.** indoor aerial.
анте́нн|ый *adj. of* **~а**
анти... *pref.* anti-.
антиалкого́льн|ый *adj.*: **~ое движе́ние** temperance movement.
антиа́томный *adj.*: **а. марш** antinuclear march.
антибио́тик, а *m.* (*med.*) antibiotic.
антивеществ|о́, а *nt.* antimatter.
антигеро́|й, я *m.* anti-hero.
антигистами́н, а *m.* (*med.*) antihistimine.
антидепресса́нт, а *m.* (*med.*) antidepressant.
антидо́пинговый *adj.*: **а. контро́ль** dope testing.
антизапотева́тел|ь, я *m.* demister.
анти́к, а *m.* antique; veteran car, vintage car.
антиква́р, а *m.* antiquary.
антиквариа́т, а *m.* **1.** (*obs.*) antique-shop. **2.** (*collect.*) antiques.
антиква́рный *adj.* antiquarian; vintage.
антико́р, а *m.* anti-rust treatment, rustproofing.
антило́п|а, ы *f.* (*zool.*) antelope.
Анти́льск|ие о́стров|а́, ~их ~о́в *no sg.* the Antilles (*islands*).
антими́нс, а *m.* (*eccl.*) communion cloth.
антимо́ни|я[1], **и** *f.* (*min.*; *obs.*) antimony.
антимо́ни|я[2], **и** *f. only in phr.* **разводи́ть ~и** (*coll.*) to indulge in trivialities, idle chat.
антино́ми|я, и *f.* antinomy.
антиобледени́тел|ь, я *m.* (*aeron.*) anti-icer; de-icer.
антипати́ч|ный (~ен, ~на) *adj.* antipathetic.
антипа́ти|я, и *f.* antipathy.
антиперестро́ечный *adj.* (*pol.*) opposed to *perestroika*.
антипо́д, а *m.* antipode.
антиподи́ст, а *m.* foot juggler.
антиприга́рный *adj.* non-stick.
антираке́т|а, ы *f.* anti-missile missile, antimissile.
антираке́тчик, а *m.* ban-the-bomb campaigner.
антисанитари́|я, и *f.* insanitary conditions.
антисанита́р|ный *adj.* insanitary.
антисеми́т, а *m.* anti-Semite.
антисемити́зм, а *m.* anti-Semitism.
антисеми́тский *adj.* anti-Semitic.
антисе́птик, а *m.* **1.** antiseptic. **2.** preservative.
антисе́птик|а, и *f.* **1.** antisepsis. **2.** (*collect.*) antiseptics.
антисепти́ческий *adj.* antiseptic.
антисовети́зм, а *m.* anti-Sovietism.
антисове́тский *adj.* anti-Soviet.
антисове́тчик, а *m.* anti-Soviet (propagandist).
антисове́тчин|а, ы *f.* anti-Soviet propaganda.
антите́з|а, ы *f.* antithesis.
антите́зис, а *m.* (*phil.*) antithesis.
антите́л|о, а *nt.* antibody.
антитети́ческий *adj.* antithetical.
антифри́з, а *m.* antifreeze.
антицикло́н, а *m.* (*meteor.*) anti-cyclone.
античелове́ческий *adj.* inhuman.
анти́чност|ь, и *f.* antiquity; (*hist.*) classical antiquity.
анти́чный *adj.* ancient; classical; **а. мир** the ancient world; **а. про́филь** classical profile.
антологи́ческий *adj.* (*liter.*) anthological.
антоло́ги|я, и *f.* (*liter.*) anthology.
анто́нов *adj.* (*obs.*): **а. ого́нь** gangrene.
анто́новк|а, и *f.* Antonovka (*variety of winter apple*).
анто́новск|ий *adj.*: **~ие я́блоки = анто́новка**
антра́кт, а *m.* **1.** (*theatr.*) interval. **2.** (*mus.*) entr'acte.
антраци́т, а *m.* (*min.*) anthracite.
антраша́ *nt. indecl.* entrechat; **выде́лывать а.** (*coll.*) to cut capers.
антреко́т, а *m.* entrecôte, steak.
антрепренёр, а *m.* impresario.
антрепри́з|а, ы *f.* (*theatr.*) private theatrical concern.
антресо́л|ь, и *f.* (*usu. pl.*) **1.** mezzanine. **2.** shelf.
антропо́ид, а *m.* anthropoid.
антропо́лог, а *m.* anthropologist.
антропологи́ческий *adj.* anthropological.
антрополо́ги|я, и *f.* anthropology.
антропоме́три|я, и *f.* anthropometry.
антропоморфи́зм, а *m.* anthropomorphism.
антропоморфи́ческий *adj.* anthropomorphic.
антропомо́рфный *adj.* anthropoid.
антропофа́г, а *m.* cannibal.
антропофа́ги|я, и *f.* cannibalism.
антура́ж, а *m.* environment; (*collect.*) entourage, associates.
анфа́с *adv.* full face.
анфила́д|а, ы *f.* suite (of rooms).
анча́р, а *m.* (*bot.*) upas-tree (*Antiaris toxicaria*).
анчо́ус, а *m.* anchovy.
аншла́г, а *m.* notice; (*theatr.*) full house; **спекта́кль идёт с ~ом** the show is sold out, the house is full.
а́ншлюс(с), а *m.* anschluss.
аню́тины: а. гла́зки (*bot.*) pansy.
ао́рт|а, ы *f.* (*anat.*) aorta.
aпарта́ме́нт|ы, ов *pl.* (*sg.* **~, ~а** *m.*) apartment.
апартеи́д, а *m.* apartheid.
апати́т, а *m.* (*min.*) apatite.
апати́ч|ный (~ен, ~на) *adj.* apathetic.
апа́ти|я, и *f.* apathy.
апатри́д, а *m.* stateless person.
апа́ч, а *m.* Apache.
апа́ш *adj. indecl.* **руба́шка а.** (man's) open-necked shirt.
апелли́р|овать, ую *impf. and pf.* to appeal.

апелля́нт, а *m.* (*leg.*) appellant.
апелл|яцио́нный *adj. of* **~я́ция; а. суд** Court of Appeal.
апелля́ци|я, и *f.* (*leg.*) appeal.
апельси́н, а *m.* **1.** orange. **2.** orange-tree.
апельси́н|ный *adj. of* ~
апельси́нов|ый *adj.* orange; **~ое варе́нье** orange marmalade.
Апенни́н|ы, ~ *no sg.* the Apennines.
аперити́в, а *m.* apéritif.
аплоди́р|овать, ую *impf.* (+*d.*) to applaud.
аплодисме́нт|ы, ов *pl.* (*sg.* **а., ~а** *m.*) applause; **бу́рные а.** tumultuous applause.
апло́мб, а *m.* aplomb, assurance.
АПН *nt. indecl.* (*abbr. of* **Аге́нтство печа́ти «Но́вости»**) APN, Novosti Press Agency.
апоге́|й, я *m.* (*astron.*) apogee; (*fig.*) climax.
Апока́липсис, а *m.* (*bibl.*) (the Book of) Revelation, the Apocalypse.
апокалипти́ческий *adj.* apocalyptic.
апокриф|и́ческий *adj. of* **апо́криф**
апокрифи́ч|ный (~ен, ~на) *adj.* (*coll.*) apocryphal.
апо́криф|ы, ов *pl.* Apocrypha.
аполити́зм, а *m.* (*pol.*) political indifference; non-participation in politics.
аполити́чност|ь, и *f.* political indifference.
аполити́ч|ный (~ен, ~на) *adj.* apolitical; politically indifferent.
апологе́т, а *m.* apologist.
апологе́тик|а, и *f.* apologetics.
аполо́ги|я, и *f.* apologia.
апоплекси́ческий *adj.* (*med.*) apoplectic.
апопле́кси|я, и *f.* (*med.*) apoplexy.
апо́рт[1]**, а** *m.* **1.** Oporto apples (*tree*). **2.** Oporto apple(s) (*fruit*).
апо́рт[2] *int.* fetch! (*command to dog*)
апостерио́ри *adv.* (*phil.*) a posteriori.
апостерио́рный *adj.* (*phil.*) a posteriori.
апо́стол, а *m.* **1.** apostle (*also fig.*). **2.** (*eccl., liter.*) Books of the Apostles (*the Acts of the Apostles and the Epistles*).
апо́стольник, а *m.* wimple.
апо́стольский *adj.* apostolic.
апостро́ф, а *m.* apostrophe.
апофео́з, а *m.* apotheosis.
Аппала́ч|и, ей *no sg.* the Appalachians.
аппара́т, а *m.* **1.** apparatus; appliance; **ка́ссовый а.** cash register; **копирова́льный а.** photocopier; **косми́ческий лета́тельный аппара́т** spacecraft, space vehicle; **ку́хонный а.** food processor; **проекцио́нный а.** projector; **слуховóй а.** hearing aid; **спуска́емый а.** (*aeron.*) lander, landing vehicle, **телефо́нный а.** telephone set; **факси́мильный а.** fax (machine); **фотографи́ческий а.** camera; **а. «иску́сственная по́чка»** kidney machine; **а. на возду́шной поду́шке** hovercraft, ACV (*air-cushion vehicle*). **2.** (*physiol.*): **пищевари́тельный а.** digestive system. **3.** (*admin.*): **госуда́рственный а.** machinery of State; **суде́бный а.** judicial system. **4.** staff, personnel.
аппара́тно-програ́ммн|ый *adj.* (*comput.*) firmware; **~ые сре́дства** firmware.
аппара́тн|ый *adj.* (*comput.*) hardware; **~ые сре́дства** hardware.
аппарату́р|а, ы *f.* (*tech., collect.*) apparatus, equipment; (*comput.*) hardware.
аппара́тчик, а *m.* **1.** (machine) operative. **2.** (*pol.*) apparatchik (*in former USSR, member of Communist Party or governmental machine*).
аппе́ндикс, а *m.* (*anat.*) appendix.
аппендици́т, а *m.* (*med.*) appendicitis.
апперко́т, а *m.* uppercut.
аппети́т, а *m.* appetite; **прия́тного ~а!** bon appétit!
аппети́т|ный (~ен, ~на) *adj.* **1.** appetizing, mouth-watering. **2.** fetching, dishy (*of female*).
аппликату́р|а, ы *f.* (*mus.*) fingering.
апплика́ци|я, и *f.* (*tech.*) appliqué work.
апплике́ *adj. indecl.* plated.
аппрету́р|а, ы *f.* (*tech.*) dressing.
апре́л|ь, я *m.* April; **пе́рвое ~я** April Fool's Day; **с пе́рвым ~я!** April Fool!
апре́ль|ский *adj. of* ~
априо́ри *adv.* (*phil.*) a priori.
априо́р|ный (~ен, ~на) *adj.* (*phil.*) a priori.
апроба́ци|я, и *f.* approbation.
апроби́р|овать, ую *impf. and pf.* to approve.
апро́ш, а *m.* (*typ.*) space left between words.
апси́д|а, ы *f.* (*archit.*) apse.
апте́к|а, и *f.* chemist's (shop); **как в ~е** (*coll., joc.*) just so, exactly right.
апте́карский *adj.* chemist's; pharmaceutical; **а. магази́н** non-dispensing chemist's (shop).
апте́кар|ша, ши *f. of* **~ь**
апте́кар|ь, я *m.* chemist; pharmacist.
апте́чк|а, и *f.* first-aid set; medicine chest; **а. для ремо́нта шин** tyre repair kit.
апчхи́ *int.* atishoo.
ар, а *m.* are (*unit of land measurement*).
а́ра *m. indecl.* macaw.
ара́б, а *m.* Arab, Arabian.
арабе́ск, а *m.* arabesque.
арабе́ск|а, и *f.* = ~
араби́ст, а *m.* Arabic scholar, Arabist.
ара́б|ка, ки *f. of* ~
ара́бск|ий *adj.* Arab; Arabian; Arabic; **а. восто́к** the Arab countries (of the Near and Middle East); **~ая ло́шадь** Arab (horse); **~ие ци́фры** arabic numerals; **а. язы́к** Arabic.
арави́|ец, йца *m.* Arabian.
арави́|йка, йки *f. of* **~ец**
арави́йский *adj.* Arabian, of Arabia.
Ара́ви|я, и *f.* Arabia.
ара́к, а *m.* arrack (*rice or palm-sap spirit*).
аракче́евский *adj.* 'Arakcheyevan', despotic.
аракче́евщин|а, ы *f.* (*hist.*) the Arakcheyev regime; (*fig.*) despotism.
араме́йский *adj.* Aramaic.
аранжи́р|овать, ую *impf. and pf.* (*mus.*) to arrange.
аранжиро́вк|а, и *f.* (*mus.*) arrangement.
ара́п, а *m.* **1.** (*coll., obs.*) negro. **2.** (*sl.*) cheat, swindler; **на ~а** by bluffing.
ара́пник, а *m.* riding crop.
ара́п|ский *adj. of* ~; **~ские шту́чки** (*coll.*) tricks.
арауќари|я, и *f.* araucaria, monkey-puzzle tree.
ара́хис, а *m.* peanut, groundnut; **а. в са́харе** peanut brittle.
ара́хисов|ый *adj.*: **~ая па́ста** peanut butter; **~ое ма́сло** groundnut oil.
арб|а́, ы́, *pl.* **~ы** *f.* bullock-cart.
арбале́т, а *m.* arbalest, crossbow.
арби́тр, а *m.* arbiter, arbitrator; umpire, referee.
арбитра́ж, а *m.* arbitration.
арбу́з, а *m.* water-melon.
аргама́к, а *m.* argamak (*breed of race-horse*).
Аргенти́н|а, ы *f.* Argentina.
аргенти́н|ец, ца *m.* Argentinian.
аргенти́н|ка, ки *f. of* **~ец**
аргенти́нский *adj.* Argentine.
арго́ *nt. indecl.* argot, slang.
арго́н, а *m.* (*chem.*) argon.
арготи́зм, а *m.* slang expression.
арготи́ческий *adj. of* **арго́**
аргуме́нт, а *m.* argument.
аргумента́ци|я, и *f.* reasoning, argumentation.
аргументи́р|овать, ую *impf. and pf.* to argue; (*pf. only*) to prove.
А́ргус, а *m.* (*myth.*) Argus; (*fig.*) watchful guardian.
ареа́л, а *m.* (*bot. and zool.*) natural habitat; (*fig.*) region.
аре́н|а, ы *f.* arena, ring.
аре́нд|а, ы *f.* lease; **сдать в ~у** to rent, lease (*of owner, landlord*); **взять в ~у** to rent, lease (*of tenant*).
арендáтор, а *m.* tenant, lessee.
аре́нд|ный *adj. of* **~а; ~ная пла́та** rent; **а. подря́д** contract for lease (*of land*).
аренд|ова́ть, у́ю *impf. and pf.* to rent, lease (*of tenant*).

аре́ст, а *m.* arrest; **сиде́ть, находи́ться под ~ом** to be under arrest, in custody; **каза́рменный а.** confinement to barracks; **а. иму́щества** seizure, sequestration.
ареста́нт, а *m.* (*obs.*) prisoner.
аре́ста́нт|ский *adj. of* ~; **~ская ро́та** (*obs.*) penal battalion; *as n.* **~ская, ~ской** *f.* lock-up, cells.
арест|ова́ть, у́ю *pf.* (*of* **~о́вывать**) to arrest; to sequestrate.
аресто́вывa|ть, ю *impf. of* **арестова́ть**
ари́дный *adj.* arid.
ари́|ец, йца *m.* Aryan.
ари́йский *adj.* Aryan.
аристокра́т, а *m.* aristocrat.
аристократ|и́ческий *adj.* aristocratic.
аристокра́ти|я, и *f.* aristocracy.
аритми́ч|ный (~ен, ~на) *adj.* unrhythmical.
арифме́тик|а, и *f.* arithmetic.
арифмети́ческий *adj.* arithmetical.
арифмо́граф, а *m.* automatic calculating machine.
атифмо́метр, а *m.* calculating machine.
а́ри|я, и *f.* (*mus.*) aria.
а́рк|а, и *f.* arch.
арка́д|а, ы *f.* (*archit.*) arcade.
арка́дский *adj.* Arcadian.
арка́н, а *m.* lasso.
арка́н|ить, ю, ишь *impf.* (*pf.* **за~**) to lasso.
А́рктик|а, и *f.* the Arctic.
аркти́ческий *adj.* arctic.
арлеки́н, а *m.* harlequin.
арлекина́д|а, ы *f.* harlequinade.
армади́л, а *m.* armadillo.
армату́р|а, ы *f.* (*collect.*) fittings; (*tech.*) armature; steel *or* ferro-concrete reinforcement.
армату́р|ный *adj. of* **~а**
армату́рщик, а *m.* (*tech.*) fitter.
арме́|ец, йца *m.* **1.** soldier. **2.** (*obs.*) member of line regiment.
арме́йский *adj. of* **а́рмия**
Арме́ни|я, и *f.* Armenia.
а́рми|я, и *f.* **1.** army; **А. Спасе́ния** Salvation Army; **де́йствующая а.** front-line forces. **2.** (*obs.*) line regiments.
армя́к, а́ *m.* armyak (*peasant's coat of heavy cloth*).
армян|и́н, и́на, *pl.* **~́е, ~́** *m.* Armenian.
армя́н|ка, ки *f. of* **~и́н**
армя́нский *adj.* Armenian.
а́рник|а, и *f.* (*bot., med.*) arnica.
арома́т, а *m.* scent, odour, aroma, fragrance; (*of wine*) bouquet.
ароматиза́тор, а *m.* (*cul.*) flavouring.
аромати́ческий = **арома́тный**
аромати́ч|ный (~ен, ~на) = **арома́тный**
арома́т|ный (~ен, ~на) *adj.* aromatic, fragrant.
а́рочный *adj.* arched, vaulted.
арпе́дж|ио (*mus.*) **1.** *adv.* **2.** *n.*; *sg. nt. indecl., pl.* **~ии, ~ий** arpeggio.
арроро́ут, а *m.* arrowroot.
арсена́л, а *m.* arsenal.
арт. *abbr. of* **артилле́рия**
арт... *comb. form, abbr. of* **артиллери́йский**
арта́ч|иться, усь, ишься *impf.* (*coll.*) to jib, be restive.
артезиа́нский *adj.*: **а. коло́дец** artesian well.
арте́л|ь, и *f.* artel (*co-operative association of workmen or peasants*).
арте́ль|ный *adj. of* ~; (*coll.*) **1.** common, collective; **на ~ных нача́лах** on collective principles. **2.** chummy, sociable; **а. па́рень** a good mixer.
арте́льщик, а *m.* **1.** member of an artel. **2.** collector of money(s). **3.** (*obs.*) porter.
артериа́льный *adj.* (*anat.*) arterial.
артериосклеро́з, а *m.* (*med.*) arteriosclerosis.
арте́ри|я, и *f.* artery.
арти́кл|ь, я *m.* (*gram.*) article.
арти́кул, а *m.*: **во́инский а.** (*hist.*) Articles of War.
артику́л, а *m.* (*mil.*; *obs.*) firearms exercises; **выки́дывать а.** (*obs., coll.*) to play tricks.
артикули́р|овать, ую *impf.* (*ling.*) to articulate.
артикуля́ци|я, и *f.* (*ling.*) articulation.
артиллери́йск|ий *adj.* (*mil.*) artillery; **а. обо́з** artillery-train; **~ая подгото́вка** artillery preparation, preparatory bombardment; **а. склад** ordnance depot.
артилле́ри|я, и *f.* artillery.
арти́ст, а *m.* **1.** artist(e); **о́перный а.** opera singer; **а. бале́та** ballet dancer; **а. дра́мы** actor; **а. кино́** film actor. **2.** (*fig.*) artist, expert; **он — а. своего́ де́ла** he is a real artist (at his job).
артисти́зм, а *m.* artistry, virtuosity.
артисти́ческ|ий *adj.* artistic; *as n.* **~ая, ~ой** *f.* green-room, dressing-room.
артисти́чност|ь, и *f.* = **артисти́зм**
арти́ст|ка, ки *f. of* ~
артишо́к, а *m.* (*bot.*) artichoke.
артри́т, а *m.* (*med.*) arthritis; **больно́й** (*fem.* **больна́я**) **~ом** arthritic (*pers.*).
а́рф|а, ы *f.* harp.
арфи́ст, а *m.* harpist.
арфи́стк|а, и *f. of* ~
архаи́зм, а *m.* archaism.
архаи́ческий *adj.* archaic.
архаи́ч|ный (~ен, ~на) *adj.* archaic.
арха́нгел, а *m.* **1.** archangel. **2.** (*obs., iron.*) policeman.
арха́нгельский *adj.* archangelic.
арха́р, а *m.* (*zool.*) argali.
арха́ров|ец, ца *m.* (*coll.*) ruffian.
археографи́ческий *adj. of* **археогра́фия**
археогра́фи|я, и *f.* study (and publication) of early texts.
архео́лог, а *m.* archaeologist.
археологи́ческий *adj.* archaeological.
археоло́ги|я, и *f.* archaeology.
архи... *comb. form* arch-.
архи́в, а *m.* archives; **сдать в а.** (*coll.*) to shelve, throw out, leave out of account.
архива́риус, а *m.* keeper of archives.
архиви́ст, а *m.* archivist.
архи́в|ный *adj. of* ~; **~ная кры́са** (*coll.*) employee in the archives.
архидья́кон, а *m.* archdeacon.
архиепи́скоп, а *m.* archbishop.
архиере́|й, я *m.* member of higher orders of clergy (*bishop, archbishop or metropolitan*).
архимандри́т, а *m.* (*eccl.*) archimandrite.
архимиллионе́р, а *m.* multi-millionaire.
архипела́г, а *m.* archipelago.
архитекто́ник|а, и *f.* (*geol. and fig.*) architectonics.
архите́ктор, а *m.* architect.
архитекту́р|а, ы *f.* architecture.
архитекту́рный *adj.* architectural.
архитра́в, а *m.* (*archit.*) architrave.
арши́н, а *m.* **1.** arshin (*old Russ. measure, equivalent to 71 cm*). **2.** rule one arshin in length; **ме́рить на свой а.** to measure by one's own yardstick; **как бу́дто а. проглоти́л** (*coll.*) as stiff as a poker.
арши́нн|ый *adj.* (*coll.*) great big; whopping great; **~ая борода́** great long beard; **~ые заголо́вки** banner headlines.
ары́к, а *m.* irrigation canal (*in Central Asia*).
арьерга́рд, а *m.* (*mil.*) rearguard.
арьерга́рдный *adj.* (*mil.*) rearguard.
ас, а *m.* (*air*) ace.
асбе́ст, а *m.* asbestos.
асбе́стовый *adj.* asbestos.
асе́птик|а, и *f.* (*med.*) asepsis.
асепти́ческий *adj.* (*med.*) aseptic.
асе́ссор, а *m.* (*obs.*) assessor; **колле́жский а.** collegiate assessor (*8th grade in tsarist Russ. civil service, equivalent to rank of major in the army*).
асимметри́ческий *adj.* asymmetrical.
асимметри́ч|ный (~ен, ~на) *adj.* asymmetrical.
асимметри́|я, и *f.* asymmetry.
аске́т, а *m.* ascetic.
аскети́зм, а *m.* asceticism.
аскети́ческий *adj.* ascetic.

асоциа́льный *adj.* anti-social.
аспе́кт, а *m.* aspect, perspective.
а́спид[1], **а** *m.* (*zool.*) asp; (*fig.*) viper.
а́спид[2], **а** *m.* (*min.*) slate.
а́спид|ный *adj. of* ~[2]; **~ная доска́** slate.
аспира́нт, а *m.* post-graduate student.
аспиранту́р|а, ы *f.* **1.** post-graduate study. **2.** (*collect.*) post-graduate students.
аспири́н, а *m.* (*med.*) aspirin; **табле́тка ~а** an aspirin.
ассамбле́|я, и *f.* **1.** assembly. **2.** (*hist.*) ball.
ассенизацио́нный *adj.*: **а. обо́з** (*collect.*) sewage-disposal men.
ассениза́ци|я, и *f.* sewage disposal.
ассигна́ци|я, и *f.* (*hist.*) assignat (*a form of paper money in use 1769–c.1840*).
ассигнова́ни|е, я *nt.* (*fin.*) assignation, appropriation, allocation.
ассигн|ова́ть, у́ю *impf. and pf.* (*fin.*) to assign, appropriate, allocate.
ассигно́вк|а, и *f.* (*fin.*) assignment; grant (*of funds*).
ассимили́р|овать, ую *impf. and pf.* to assimilate.
ассимиля́ци|я, и *f.* assimilation.
ассири́|ец, йца *m.* **1.** Assyrian. **2.** Aysor.
ассири́|йка, йки *f. of* **~ец**
ассири́йский *adj.* Assyrian.
Асси́ри|я, и *f.* Assyria.
ассири́ян|ин, ина, *pl.* **~е, ~** *m.* (*obs.*) Assyrian.
ассири́ян|ка, ки *f. of* **~ин**
ассисте́нт, а *m.* **1.** assistant. **2.** (*in university, etc.*) junior member of teaching or research staff.
ассисти́р|овать, ую *impf.* (+*d.*) to assist.
ассона́нс, а *m.* assonance.
ассорти́ *nt. indecl.*: **шокола́дное а.** chocolate assortment.
ассортиме́нт, а *m.* assortment; range (*of goods*).
ассоциа́ци|я, и *f.* association.
ассоции́р|овать, ую *impf. and pf.* (**с**+*i.*; *phil.*) to associate (with).
АССР *f. indecl.* (*abbr. of* ***Автоно́мная Сове́тская Социалисти́ческая Респу́блика***) ASSR (*Autonomous Soviet Socialist Republic*).
астеро́ид, а *m.* (*astron.*) asteroid.
астигмати́зм, а *m.* (*med.*) astigmatism.
а́стм|а, ы *f.* (*med.*) asthma.
астма́тик, а *m.* (*med.*) asthmatic.
астмати́ческий *adj.* (*med.*) asthmatic.
а́стр|а, ы *f.* (*bot.*) aster.
астра́льный *adj.* astral.
астро́лог, а *m.* astrologer.
астрологи́ческий *adj.* astrological.
астроло́ги|я, и *f.* astrology.
астроля́би|я, и *f.* astrolabe; circumferentor.
астроно́м, а *m.* astronomer.
астрономи́ческий *adj.* astronomic(al).
астроно́ми|я, и *f.* astronomy.
астрофи́зик|а, и *f.* astrophysics.
асфа́льт, а *m.* asphalt.
асфальти́р|овать, ую *impf. and pf.* (*pf. also* **за~**) (*tech.*) to asphalt.
асфа́льтовый *adj.* asphalt.
асфи́кси|я, и *f.* (*med.*) asphyxia.
ась *int.* (*coll.*) what?; eh?; huh?
атави́зм, а *m.* atavism.
атависти́ческий *adj.* atavistic.
ата́к|а, и *f.* attack.
атак|ова́ть, у́ю *impf. and pf.* to attack, charge, assault; **а. с ты́ла** to take in rear; **а. с фла́нга** to take in flank.
атама́н, а *m.* **1.** (*hist.*) ataman (*Cossack chieftain*). **2.** (*coll.*) (gang-)leader, (robber) chief.
ата́с (*sl.*): **стоя́ть на ~е** to keep lookout; *int.* watch out!; beware!
атеи́зм, а *m.* atheism.
атеи́ст, а *m.* atheist.
атеисти́ческий *adj.* atheistic.
ателье́ *nt. indecl.* studio; **портно́вское а.** tailor's shop; **телевизио́нное а.** TV repair shop; **а. мод** fashion house.
атланти́зм, а *m.* (*pol.*) Atlanticism.
Атланти́ческ|ий океа́н, ~ого ~а *m.* the Atlantic Ocean; the Atlantic.
а́тлас, а *m.* atlas.
атла́с, а *m.* satin.
атла́систый *adj.* satiny.
атла́сный *adj.* satin.
Атла́сск|ие го́р|ы, ~их ~ *no sg.* the Atlas Mountains.
атле́т, а *m.* athlete; (*circus*) strongman.
атлети́зм, а *m.* **1.** athleticism. **2.** body-building.
атле́тик|а, и *f.* athletics; **лёгкая а.** (track-and-field) athletics; **тяжёлая а.** weightlifting; (*in athletics*) throwing events.
атлети́ческий *adj.* athletic.
атмосфе́р|а, ы *f.* atmosphere.
атмосфери́ческий *adj.* atmospheric.
атмосфе́рн|ый *adj.* atmospheric; **~ые оса́дки** atmospheric precipitation, rainfall.
ато́лл, а *m.* atoll.
а́том, а *m.* atom.
атомисти́ческий *adj.* atomistic.
а́томк|а, и *f.* (*coll.*) atomic power station.
а́томник, а *m.* (*coll.*) atomic scientist.
а́томност|ь, и *f.* (*chem.*) atomicity.
а́томн|ый *adj.* atomic; **~ая бо́мба** atomic bomb; **а. вес** (*chem.*) atomic weight.
атомохо́д, а *m.* nuclear-powered vessel.
а́томщик, а *m.* (*coll.*) **1.** nuclear scientist. **2.** (*pej.*) nuclearist
атрибу́т, а *m.* attribute.
атропи́н, а *m.* (*med.*) atropine.
атрофи́р|оваться, уюсь *impf. and pf.* to atrophy.
атрофи́|я, и *f.* atrophy.
АТС *f. indecl.* (*abbr. of* ***автомати́ческая телефо́нная ста́нция***) automatic telephone exchange.
атташе́ *m. indecl.* (*dipl.*) attaché.
аттеста́т, а *m.* testimonial; certificate; pedigree; **а. зре́лости** school-leaving certificate; **дать дурно́й а.** to give a bad character.
аттестацио́нн|ый *adj.*: **~ая коми́ссия** examination board.
аттеста́ци|я, и *f.* **1.** attestation. **2.** testimonial.
аттест|ова́ть, у́ю *impf. and pf.* to attest, recommend.
аттракцио́н, а *m.* (*theatr.*) attraction; (*fairground*) sideshow; **парк ~ов** amusement park.
ату́ *int.* (*hunting*) tally-ho!; halloo!
ать-два *int.* (*mil.*) hep, two!
ау́ *int.* **1.** halloo! **2.** (*coll.*) it's all up!; it's done for!
аудие́нци|я, и *f.* audience.
аудиовизуа́льный *adj.* audiovisual.
аудиоречево́й *adj.* audiolingual.
ауди́тор, а *m.* (*obs.*) auditor.
аудито́ри|я, и *f.* **1.** auditorium; lecture-hall. **2.** (*collect.*) audience; **зри́тельская а.** viewers; **слу́шательская а.** listeners.
ау́ка|ть, ю *impf.* to halloo.
ау́к|аться, аюсь *impf.* (*of* **~нуться**) to halloo to one another.
ау́к|нуть, ну, нешь *pf. of* **~ать**
ау́к|нуться, нусь *pf. of* **~аться; как ~нется, так и откли́кнется** serves you, *etc.*, right; do as you would be done by.
аукцио́н, а *m.* auction; **продава́ть с ~а** to auction.
аукционе́р, а *m.* = **аукциони́ст**
аукциони́ст, а *m.* auctioneer.
аукцио́н|ный *adj. of* ~; **а. зал** auction room.
ау́л, а *m.* aul (*mountain village in Caucasus or Central Asia*).
ауспи́ци|и, й *no sg.* auspices.
а́ут, а *m.* (*sport*) out (*also as int.*).
аутенти́ч|ный (~ен, ~на) *adj.* authentic.
аутодафе́ *nt. indecl.* auto-da-fé.
ауто́пси|я, и *f.* autopsy, post-mortem.
афа́зи|я, и *f.* (*med.*) aphasia.
афга́н|ец, ца *m.* Afghan; **«а.»** Afghan war vet(eran).
Афганиста́н, а *m.* Afghanistan.
афга́н|ка, ки *f. of* **~ец**

афга́нский *adj.* Afghan.
афе́р|а, ы *f.* (*coll.*) speculation; trickery.
афери́ст, а *m.* speculator; trickster.
афи́нск|ий *adj.* Athenian; **~ие вечера́, ~ие но́чи** orgies.
Афи́н|ы, ~ *no sg.* Athens.
афи́нян|ин, ина, *pl.* **~е, ~** *m.* Athenian.
афи́нян|ка, ки *f. of* **~ин**
афи́ш|а, и *f.* poster, placard; **театра́льная а.** playbill; **раскле́йщик ~** billsticker
афиши́р|овать, ую *impf.* to parade, advertise.
афори́зм, а *m.* aphorism.
афористи́ческий *adj.* aphoristic.
афористи́ч|ный (~ен, ~на) *adj.* aphoristic.
А́фрик|а, и *f.* Africa.
африка́анс, а *m.* Afrikaans.
африка́нер, а *m.* Afrikaner.
африка́н|ец, ца *m.* African.
африка́н|ка, ки *f. of* **~ец**
африка́нск|ий *adj.* African; **~ие стра́сти** (*coll.*) primitive passions.
афро́нт, а *m.* (*obs.*) insult.
аффе́кт, а *m.* (*psych., leg.*) fit of passion; temporary insanity.
аффекта́ци|я, и *f.* affectation.
аффекти́рованный *adj.* affected.
а́ффикс, а *m.* (*ling.*) affix.
ах *int.* ah! oh!; *as n.* **а́х|и, ~ов** *no sg.*, exclamations of 'ah!', 'oh!'
а́хань|е, я *nt.* (*coll.*) sighing.
а́ха|ть, ю *impf.* (*coll.*) to sigh, to exclaim 'ah!', 'oh!'.
ахилле́сов *adj.*: **~а пята́** Achilles heel; **~о сухожи́лие** (*anat.*) Achilles tendon.
ахине́|я *f.* (*coll.*) nonsense; **нести́ ~ю** to talk nonsense.
а́х|нуть, ну, нешь *pf.* **1.** *pf. of* **~ать; он и а. не успе́л** before he knew where he was. **2.** (*coll.*) to bang.
а́ховый *adj.* (*coll.*) **1.** breath-taking; **он па́рень а.** he is a great bloke. **2.** rotten.
ахромати́зм, а *m.* achromatism.
ахромати́ческий *adj.* achromatic.
ахтерште́в|ень, ня *m.* (*naut.*) stern-post.
ахти́ *int.* (*coll.*) alas!; **а. мне!** woe is me!; **не а. как, не а. како́й** not particularly, not particularly good; **он был студе́нтом не а. каки́м** he was not the brightest of students.
ацетиле́н, а *m.* (*chem.*) acetylene.
ацето́н, а *m.* (*chem.*) acetone.
ацте́к, а *m.* Aztec.
ашу́г, а *m.* ashug (*folk poet and singer in the Caucasus*).
аэра́ри|й, я *m.* sun terrace.
аэро... *comb. form* aero-; air-, aerial.
аэро́бик|а, и *f.* aerobics.
аэроби́ст, а *m.* aerobicist.
аэроби́ст|ка, ки *f. of* **~**
аэроби́ческий = аэро́бный
аэро́бн|ый *adj.* aerobic; **~ая гимна́стика** aerobics, aerobic exercises.
аэро́бус, а *m.* air bus.
аэровокза́л, а *m.* air terminal.
аэрогра́мм|а, ы *f.* aerogramme; air letter
аэро́граф, а *m.* air brush.
аэродина́мик|а, и *f.* aerodynamics.
аэродинами́ческ|ий *adj.* aerodynamic; **~ая труба́** wind tunnel.
аэродро́м, а *m.* aerodrome.
аэрозо́л|ь, я *m.* aerosol, spray; **а. для воло́с** hair spray.
аэрозо́льный *adj.*: **а. балло́н** spray can.
аэрокатастро́фа = авиакатастро́фа
аэрокосми́ческий *adj.* aerospace.
аэро́н, а *m.* travel sickness pill.
аэрона́вт, а *m.* aeronaut; balloonist.
аэрона́втик|а, и *f.* aeronautics.
аэропла́н, а *m.* (*obs.*) aeroplane.
аэропо́езд, а *m.* hovertrain, air train.
аэропо́рт, а *m.* airport.
аэропо́чт|а, ы *f.* (*obs.*) air mail.
аэросало́н = авиасало́н
аэроса́н|и, е́й *no sg.* aero-sleigh.
аэросе́в, а *m.* aerial sowing.
аэросни́м|ок, ка *m.* aerial photograph.
аэроста́т, а *m.* balloon; **а. загражде́ния** barrage balloon.
аэроста́тик|а, и *f.* aerostatics.
аэросъёмк|а, и *f.* aerial survey.
аэрохо́д, а *m.* hovercraft, air cushion vehicle (*abbr.* ACV).
АЭС *f. indecl.* (*abbr. of* **а́томная электроста́нция**) atomic power station.
аятолл|а́, ы́ *m.* ayatollah.
а/я *m. indecl.* (*abbr. of* **абонеме́нтный я́щик**) P.O. (*abbr. of* Post Office) Box.

Б

б *particle* = **бы** (*after words ending in vowel*).
б. (*abbr. of* **бы́вший**) former, ex-, one-time; **Санкт-Петербу́рг (б. Ленингра́д)** St Petersburg (formerly Leningrad).
ба *int.* (*coll.*) hullo!; well! (*expr. surprise*) **~! кого́ я ви́жу!** well I never, if it isn't ...
ба́б|а¹, ы *f.* **1.** married peasant woman. **2.** (*coll. or dial.*) wife, old woman; (*pl.*) womenfolk. **3.** (*coll.*) woman; **бой-б.** (*coll.*) virago; **ка́менная б.** stone image; **сне́жная б.** snowman. **4.** (*coll.*) 'old woman' (*said of a man*).
ба́б|а², ы *f.* (*tech.*) ram (*of pile-driver*).
ба́ба³, ы *f.* baba (*cylindrical cake*); **ро́мовая б.** rum-baba.
ба́ба-яга́, ба́бы-яги́ *f.* Baba-Yaga (*witch in Russ. folk-tales*).
баба́х *int.* (*expr. noise of heavily falling object*) bang!
баба́хн|уть, у, ешь *pf.* (*coll.*) to bang; (*impers.*): **~уло** there was a bang.
байби́т, а *m.* (*tech.*) babbit.
бабёнк|а и *f.* (*coll.*) bimbo, bit of skirt.
ба́б|ий *adj.* (*coll.*) women's; womanish; **~ье ле́то** Indian summer; **~ьи ска́зки** old wives' tales.
ба́бк|а¹, и *f.* **1.** (*coll., obs.*) grandmother. **2. (повива́льная) б.** midwife.
ба́бк|а², и *f.* **1.** (*anat.*) pastern. **2.** knuckle-bone; **~и** (*pl.*) babki (*Russ. children's game*). **3.** (*tech.*) mandrel.
ба́бк|а³, и *f.* (*dial.*) shock, stook (*of corn*).
ба́бник, а *m.* (*coll.*) ladies' man.
ба́бнича|ть, ю *impf.* **1.** (*dial.*) to be a midwife. **2.** (*coll.*) to be a ladies' man.
ба́бочк|а, и *f.* butterfly; **ночна́я б.** moth.
бабуи́н, а *m.* (*zool.*) baboon.
ба́бушк|а, и *f.* grandmother; (*coll.*) old woman; grandma, gran(nie) (*as mode of address to old woman*); **б.-ска́зочница** fairy-godmother; **б. на́двое сказа́ла** we shall see!
ба́бушкин *adj.* grandmother's; **~ы ска́зки** old wives' tales.
бабь|ё, я́ *nt.* (*collect.*) womenfolk.
бава́р|ец, ца *m.* Bavarian.
Бава́ри|я, и *f.* Bavaria.
бава́р|ка, ки *f. of* **~ец**
бава́рский *adj.* Bavarian.
бага́ж, а́ *m.* luggage; **сдать свои́ ве́щи в б.** to register one's luggage.
бага́жник, а *m.* luggage compartment; roof rack; boot (*of motor-car*).
бага́жнич|ек, ка *m.* glove compartment (*in car*).
бага́ж|ный *adj. of* **~; б. ваго́н** luggage van; **~ная квита́нция** luggage receipt.
Бага́мск|ие остров|а́, ~их ~о́в *no sg.* the Bahamas (*islands*).

ба́гги *m. indecl.* (*beach, dune etc.*) buggy.
багги́ст, а *m.* buggy-driver.
Багда́д, а *m.* Baghdad.
баг|о́р, ра́ *m.* boat-hook.
багре́ц, а́ *m.* crimson, purple.
ба́гр|ить, ю, ишь *impf.* **1.** to gaff. **2.** (*sl.*) to steal; pilfer.
багр|и́ть, ю́, и́шь *impf.* to paint purple, crimson; to incarnadine.
багрове́|ть, ю *impf.* (*of* **по~**) to turn crimson, purple.
багро́в|ый (~, ~а) *adj.* crimson, purple.
багря́н|ец, ца *m.* crimson, purple.
багряни́ц|а, ы *f.* (*hist.*) purple (mantle).
багря́нник, а *m.* (*bot.*) Judas-tree.
багря́н|ый (~, ~а) *adj.* (*poet.*) crimson, purple.
багу́льник, а *m.* (*bot.*) Labrador tea, wild rosemary (*Ledum*).
бадминто́н, а *m.* badminton.
бадминтони́ст, а *m.* badminton-player.
бад|ья́, ьи́, *g. pl.* **~е́й** *f.* tub.
ба́з|а, ы *f.* **1.** (*in var. senses*) base; depot; centre; **б. да́нных** database; **плаву́чая б.** factory ship. **2.** basis; **на ~е** (*+g.*) on the basis (of); **подвести́ ~у (под**+*a.*) to give good grounds (for).
база́льт, а *m.* basalt.
база́льтовый *adj.* basaltic.
база́р, а *m.* market; bazaar; **пти́чий б.** bird-colony on sea-shore; (*fig., coll.*) din, racket; **что за б.!** what a row!
база́р|ить, ю, ишь (*impf.*) (*coll.*) to wrangle, squabble.
база́рнича|ть, ю (*impf.*) to make a racket *or* din.
база́р|ный *adj. of* ~; (*coll.*) of the market-place, rough, crude; **~ная ба́ба** noisy woman, fishwife; **б. день** market-day; **~ная ру́гань** billingsgate.
базе́дов *adj.* (*med.*): **~а боле́знь** exophthalmic goitre (*Basedow's disease*).
Ба́зел|ь, я *m.* Basle.
базили́к, а *m.* (*bot.*) basil; **б. души́стый** sweet basil.
базили́к|а, и *f.* (*archit.*) basilica.
бази́ровани|е, я *nt.*: **ракéта назéмного/морско́го ~я** ground-based/sea-launched missile.
бази́р|овать, ую *impf.* (**на**+*p.*) to base (on).
бази́р|оваться, уюсь *impf.* (**на**+*p.*) **1.** to be based (on), to rest (on); **все его́ мне́ния ~уются на газе́тах** all his opinions are based on what he reads in the newspapers. **2.** (*mil.*) to base o.s. (on), be based (on).
ба́зис, а *m.* base; basis.
ба́зов|ый *adj.* **1.** basic; **б. курс** foundation course. **2.: б. ла́герь** base camp.
базу́к|а, и *f.* bazooka.
ба́иньки = бай-ба́й
ба|й, я *m.* bai (*rich landowner in Central Asia*).
бай-ба́й *int.* bye-byes; **пора́ б.!** time for bye-byes!
байба́к, а́ *m.* (*zool.*) steppe marmot; (*fig.*) lazybones.
байда́рк|а, и *f.* **1.** (Aleutian) canoe. **2.** (*sport*) kayak; **б.-дво́йка** kayak pair.
байда́рочник, а *m.* canoeist.
байда́р|очный *adj. of* **~ка; ~очная гре́бля** (canoe-) paddling.
ба́йк|а¹, и *f.* flannelette.
ба́йк|а², и *f.* (*coll.*) fairy story, cock-and-bull story.
ба́йковый *adj.* flannelette.
байрони́ческий *adj.* Byronic.
ба́йт, а *m.* (*comput.*) byte.
бак¹, и *m.* cistern; tank.
бак², и *m.* (*naut.*) forecastle.
бакала́вр, а *m.* bachelor (*holder of bachelor's degree*).
бакале́йн|ый *adj.* grocery; **~ая ла́вка** grocer's shop.
бакале́йщик, а *m.* grocer.
бакале́|я, и *f.* **1.** (*collect.*) groceries. **2.** grocer's shop.
ба́кан = ба́кен
бака́ут, а *m.* (*bot.*) lignum vitae, guaiacum.
ба́кен, а *m.* (*naut.*) buoy.
бакенба́рд|ы, ~ *pl.* (*sg.* **~а, ~ы** *f.*) side-whiskers.
ба́кенщик, а *m.* buoy-keeper.
ба́кен|ы, ов *pl.* (*sg.* **~, ~а** *m.*) (*obs.*) side-whiskers.
ба́к|и, ~ *no sg.* = **бакенба́рды**
баки́нский *adj.* (of) Baku.
баккара́¹ *nt. indecl.* (Baccarat) cut glass.
баккара́² *nt. indecl.* baccarat (card-game).
бакла́г|а, и *f.* flask, water-bottle.
баклажа́н, а *m.* (*bot.*) aubergine, egg-plant.
бакла́н, а *m.* (*zool.*) cormorant.
баклу́ши *now only in phr.* (*coll.*) **бить б.** to idle, fritter away one's time.
баклу́шнича|ть, ю *impf.* (*coll.*) to idle.
ба́к|овый *adj. of* ~²; bow; **б. гребе́ц** bow oarsman.
бактериа́льный *adj.* bacterial.
бактери́йный *adj.* bacterial.
бактерио́лог, а *m.* bacteriologist.
бактериологи́ческ|ий *adj.* bacteriological; **~ая война́** bacteriological, germ warfare.
бактериоло́ги|я, и *f.* bacteriology.
бактерици́дный *adj.* germicidal.
бакте́ри|я, и *f.* bacterium.
бакши́ш, а *m.* bakshish; tip; bribe; backhander.
бал, а, о ~е, на ~у́, *pl.* **~ы́** *m.* ball, dance; **ко́нчен б.!** it's all over; that's that.
балабо́л|ить, ю, ишь *impf.* (*coll.*) to chatter idly, gas.
балабо́лк|а, и *f. and c.g.* (*coll.*) **1.** *f.* pendant. **2.** *f.* (*child's*) rattle. **3.** *c.g.* chatterbox, gasbag.
балага́н, а *m.* **1.** booth (*at fairs*). **2.** low farce; (*fig.*) farce.
балага́н|ить, ю, ишь *impf.* (*coll.*) to play the fool.
балага́н|ный *adj. of* ~; farcical.
балага́нщик, а *m.* (*coll.*) **1.** showman. **2.** clown, joker.
балагу́р, а *m.* joker, clown.
балагу́р|ить, ю, ишь *impf.* to jest, joke.
балагу́рств|о, а *nt.* foolery, buffoonery.
бала́ка|ть, ю *impf.* (*dial.*) to chatter, natter.
балала́ечник, а *m.* balalaika-player.
балала́|ечный *adj. of* **~йка**
балала́йк|а, и *f.* balalaika.
баламу́т, а *m.* (*coll.*) trouble-maker.
баламу́|тить, чу, тишь *impf.* (*of* **вз~**) (*coll.*) to stir up, trouble (*water*); (*fig.*) to upset.
бала́нд|а, ы *f.* (*sl.*) skilly (*in prison or labour camp*).
бала́нс¹, а *m.* (*econ.*) balance; **платёжный б.** balance of payment; **торго́вый б.** balance of trade.
бала́нс², а *m.* pulpwood.
балансёр, а *m.* tightrope-walker.
баланси́р, а *m.* (*tech.*) **1.** bob, (balance) beam, equalizer; rocking beam, rocking shaft. **2.** balance-wheel (*in clock*).
баланси́р|овать, ую *impf.* **1.** (*impf. only*) to keep one's balance, balance. **2.** (*pf.* **с~**) (*bookkeeping*) to balance.
балахо́н, а *m.* loose overall; (*coll.*) shapeless garment.
балахо́нистый *adj.* baggy, shapeless.
балбе́с, а *m.* (*coll.*) booby.
балбе́снича|ть, ю *impf.* (*coll.*) to idle away one's time.
балд|а́, ы́ *f. and c.g.* **1.** *f.* (*tech.*) heavy hammer, sledge-hammer. **2.** *f.* (*dial.*) knob, knur. **3.** *c.g.* (*fig., coll.*) blockhead.
балдахи́н, а *m.* canopy.
балдёж, а́ *m.* (*sl.*) 'high', buzz (*state*); *int.* great!; brill!
балдёжный *adj.* (*sl.*) great, ace, brill.
балде́|ть, ю *impf.* (*sl.*) to be high, stoned; **б. от**+*g.* to 'dig', get a kick *or* buzz out of; **я от неё ~ю** she really turns me on.
балери́н|а, ы *f.* ballerina.
бале́т, а *m.* ballet; **б. на льду́** ice review *or* show.
балетме́йстер, а *m.* ballet-master.
бале́т|ный *adj. of* ~
балетома́н, а *m.* balletomane.
балетома́ни|я, и *f.* balletomania.
ба́лк|а¹, и *f.* beam, girder; **а́нкерная б.** tie-beam; **попере́чная б.** cross-beam; **решётчатая б.** lattice girder; **клёпаные ~и** riveted girders; **прока́тные ~и** rolled girders.
ба́лк|а², и *f.* gully; dried-up river-bed.
балка́нский *adj.* Balkan.
Балка́н|ы, ~ *no sg.* the Balkans.
балка́р|ец, ца *m.* Balkar(ian).
ба́лкер, а *m.* bulk carrier.
балко́н, а *m.* balcony; (*theatr.*) upper circle.
балл, а *m.* **1.** (*meteor.*) number; **ве́тер в пять ~ов** wind

force 5; **облачность в семь ~ов** 7/10ths cloud. **2.** mark (*in school*); **вы́сший б.** (*academic grade*) an 'A'; **он получи́л вы́сший б. по фи́зике** he got an 'A' for physics; **о́бщий б.** total mark(s); **проходно́й б.** pass mark; (*sport*) point; mark; score; **дополни́тельный/поощри́тельный б.** bonus point; **по́лный б.** perfect score.
балла́д|а, ы *f.* **1.** ballad. **2.** (*mus.*) ballade.
балла́ст, а *m.* ballast (*also fig.*).
балли́стик, а *m.* ballistics expert.
балли́стик|а, и *f.* ballistics.
баллисти́ческий *adj.* ballistic.
ба́лл|овый *adj. of* ~ **1.**
балло́н, а *m.* **1.** balloon (*vessel*); container (*of glass, metal, or rubber*); carboy; **аэрозо́льный б.** spray can; **б. с кислоро́дом** oxygen cylinder; **кати́ть б.** (**на**+*a.*) to run down, knock (*fig.*). **2.** (*motor-car, etc.*) balloon tyre.
баллоти́р|овать, ую *impf.* to ballot (for), vote (for).
баллоти́р|оваться, уюсь *impf.* **1.** (**в**+*a.*, **на**+*a.*) to stand (for), be a candidate (for); **б. на до́лжность секретаря́ па́ртии** to stand for secretary of the party. **2.** (*pass. of* **~овать**) to be put to the vote.
баллотиро́вк|а, и *f.* **1.** vote, ballot, poll. **2.** voting, balloting, polling.
баллотиро́в|очный *adj. of* **~ка**; **б. бюллете́нь** ballot paper.
ба́лл|ьный *adj. of* ~ **2.**
бало́в|анный *p.p.p. of* **~а́ть** *and adj.* (*coll.*) spoiled.
бал|ова́ть, у́ю *impf.* (*of* **из~**) **1.** to spoil, indulge; to pet, pamper. **2.** (*coll.*) to play about; to play up; **мото́р ~у́ет** the engine is playing up. **3.** (+*i.*; *coll.*) to play (with), amuse o.s. (with), toy (with). **4.** (*coll., obs., or dial.*) to get up to monkey business (*sc. to engage in brigandage, practise immorality, etc.*).
бал|ова́ться, у́юсь *impf.* **1.** to play about; to get up to monkey tricks. **2.** (+*i.*; *coll.*) to play (with), amuse o.s. (with), toy (with). **3.** (*coll.*) to indulge in. **4.** = **~ова́ть 4.**
ба́лов|ень, ня *m.* **1.** spoilt child; pet, favourite; **б. судьбы́** favourite of fortune. **2.** naughty child.
баловни́к, а́ *m.* (*coll.*) **1.** naughty child; mischievous pers. **2.** pet; favourite. **3.** (*obs.*) one who spoils s.o.
баловств|о́, а́ *nt.* (*coll.*) **1.** spoiling, over-indulgence; petting, pampering. **2.** mischievousness; monkey tricks.
ба́л|очный *adj.* (*tech.*) *of* **~ка 1.**
балти́|ец, йца *m.* sailor of the (Russian) Baltic Fleet.
балти́йский *adj.* Baltic.
балы́к, а́ *m.* balyk (*cured fillet of sturgeon, etc.*).
ба́льза, ы *f.* balsa(wood).
бальза́м, а *m.* balsam; (*fig.*) balm; **б. для воло́с** hair conditioner; **отте́ночный б.** (hair) rinse.
бальзами́н, а *m.* (*bot.*) balsam.
бальзами́р|овать, ую *impf.* (*of* **на~**) to embalm.
бальзамиро́вк|а, и *f.* embalming.
бальзамиро́вщик, а *m.* embalmer.
бальзами́ческ|ий *adj.* (*bot.*) balsam, balsamic; (*fig.*) balmy; **~ая пи́хта** fir; **б. во́здух** balmy air.
бальнео́лог, а *m.* (*med.*) balneologist.
бальнеологи́ческий *adj.* (*med.*) balneological.
бальнеоло́ги|я, и *f.* (*med.*) balneology.
бальнеотерапи́|я, и *f.* medicinal bathing.
ба́льник, а *m.* (*school sl.*; *obs.*) report.
ба́л|ьный *adj. of* ~; **~ьное пла́тье** ball-dress; **~ьные та́нцы** ballroom dancing.
балюстра́д|а, ы *f.* (*archit.*) balustrade.
баля́син|а, ы *f.* baluster.
баля́снича|ть, ю *impf.* (*coll.*) to jest.
баля́с|ы, ~ *no sg.* banister; **точи́ть б.** (*fig., coll.*) to jest.
БАМ *m.* (*indecl.*) (*abbr. of* **Байка́ло-Аму́рская (железнодоро́жная) магистра́ль**) Baikal-Amur railway.
бамбу́к, а *m.* bamboo.
бамбу́ков|ый *adj.* bamboo; **~ое положе́ние** (*coll.*) awkward position.
ба́мовский *adj.* (of the) BAM (*Baikal-Amur Railway*).
бана́льност|ь, и *f.* **1.** banality. **2.** banal remark; platitude.
бана́л|ьный (~ен, ~ьна) *adj.* banal, trite.
бана́н, а *m.* banana.
бананово́з, а *m.* banana boat.
бана́н|овый *adj. of* ~
Бангладе́ш, а *m.* Bangladesh.
бангладе́ш|ец, ца *m.* Bangladeshi.
бангладе́шк|а, и *f. of* **~ец**
бангладе́шский *adj.* Bangladeshi.
ба́нд|а, ы *f.* band, gang.
банда́ж, а́ *m.* **1.** bandage; **грыжево́й б.** truss. **2.** **спорти́вный б.** athletic supporter; jockstrap. **3.** (*tech.*) tyre, band (*of metal*).
бандеро́л|ь, и *f.* **1.** wrapper (*for dispatching newspapers, etc., by post*). **2.** 'printed matter', book post; **отправля́ть ~ью** to send as printed matter, by book post. **3.** label (*certifying payment of tax, etc.*).
банди́т, а *m.* bandit, brigand; gangster; thug; **вооружённый б.** armed robber.
бандити́зм, а *m.* brigandage; gangsterism; thuggery; **возду́шный б.** air piracy; **вооружённый б.** armed robbery.
банди́т|ский *adj. of* ~
банди́тств|овать, ую *impf.* to rampage.
банду́р|а, ы *f.* (*mus.*) bandura (*Ukrainian string instrument similar to large mandoline*).
бандури́ст, а *m.* (*mus.*) bandura-player.
банк, а *m.* **1.** (*fin.*) bank (*also in card-games*); **Всеми́рный б.** World Bank. **2.** faro (*card-game*).
ба́нк|а[1], **и** *f.* (*glass*) jar; tin, can; (*med.*) cupping-glass; **апте́чная б.** gallipot.
ба́нк|а[2], **и** *f.* (*naut.*) thwart; bank.
ба́нк|а[3], **и** *f.* bank, shoal.
банке́т[1], **а** *m.* banquet.
банке́т[2], **а** *m.* bank (*of earth or stones*), embankment.
банки́р, а *m.* banker.
банки́р|ский *adj. of* ~; **б. дом** banking-house.
банкно́т, а *m.* (*fin.*) bank-note.
банкно́т|а, ы *f.* = ~
ба́нк|овский *adj. of* ~; **б. биле́т** bank-note; **~овская кни́жка** passbook, bank-book.
ба́нк|овый *adj. of* ~; **б. аккредити́в** circular note; **б. биле́т** bank-note; **б. слу́жащий** bank clerk.
банкомёт, а *m.* banker (*at cards*); croupier.
банкро́т, а *m.* bankrupt; **объявля́ть ~ом** to declare bankrupt.
банкро́|титься, чусь, тишься *impf.* (*of* **о~**) to become bankrupt (*also fig.*).
банкро́тств|о, а *nt.* bankruptcy.
ба́нник, а *m.* (*mil.*) cleaning rod, rammer.
ба́н|ный *adj. of* **~я**; **б. ве́ник** besom used in Russ. baths, **(он) приста́л как б. лист** (*coll.*) (he) sticks like a leech.
бант, а *m.* bow; **завяза́ть ~ом** to tie in a bow.
ба́нтик, а *m. dim. of* **бант; гу́бки ~ом** Cupid's bow.
ба́нщик, а *m.* bath-house attendant.
ба́н|я, и *f.* (Russian) baths; bath-house; **крова́вая б.** blood-bath; **фи́нская б.** sauna; **зада́ть ~ю** (+*d.*; *coll.*) to give (s.o.) what for.
бапти́зм, а *m.* the doctrine of Baptists.
бапти́ст, а *m.* Baptist.
баптисте́ри|й, я *m.* baptist(e)ry.
бапти́стский *adj.* Baptist.
бар[1], **а** *m.* (snack-)bar; **пивно́й б.** pub.
бар[2], **а** *m.* (*naut.*) (sand-)bar.
бар[3], **а** *m.* (*phys.*) bar (*unit of atmospheric pressure*).
бараба́н, а *m.* drum (*also tech.*).
бараба́н|ить, ю, ишь *impf.* to drum, play the drum(s); (*fig., coll.*) to patter, gabble; **дождь ~ил в о́кна** the rain was drumming on the windows; **б. на роя́ле** to bang away on the piano.
бараба́н|ный *adj. of* ~; **~ная дробь** drum-roll; **~ная перепо́нка** (*anat.*) ear-drum, tympanum.
бараба́нщик, а *m.* drummer.
бара́к, а *m.* wooden barrack; hut (*mil.*; *also in hospitals, esp. as infectious diseases ward*).
бара́н, а *m.* ram; (wild) sheep; **смо́трит, как б. на но́вые воро́та** (*coll.*) he looks quite lost.
бара́н|ий *adj.* **1.** sheep's; **согну́ть в б. рог** (*coll.*) to make (s.o.) knuckle under. **2.** sheepskin; **б. полушу́бок** sheepskin

coat. **3.** mutton; **~ья котле́та** mutton chop.
бара́нин|а, ы *f.* mutton.
бара́нк|а, и *f.* **1.** baranka (*ring-shaped roll*). **2.** (*coll.*) steering-wheel.
бара́|ть, ю *impf.* (*vulg.*) to screw, hump.
барахл|и́ть, ю́, и́шь *impf.* (*coll.*) **1.** to pink (*of an engine*). **2.** to talk nonsense.
барахл|о́, а́ *nt.* (*collect.*; *coll.*) **1.** old clothes; jumble; goods and chattels, odds and ends; **торго́вец ~о́м** dealer in second-hand goods. **2.** trash, junk.
барахо́лк|а, и *f.* (*coll.*) flea market.
барах|о́льный *adj. of* **~ло́**
барах|о́льщик, а *m.* (*coll.*) dealer in second-hand goods.
бара́хта|ться, юсь *impf.* (*coll.*) to flounder; to wallow.
бара́|чный *adj. of* **~к**
бара́ш|ек, ка *m.* **1.** young ram; lamb; **б. в бума́жке** (*iron.*) bribe. **2.** lambskin. **3.** (*pl.*) 'white horses' (*on surface of sea, etc.*). **4.** (*pl.*) fleecy clouds. **5.** small curls; **зави́ться ~ком** to have one's hair done in small curls. **6.** (*tech.*) wing nut, thumbscrew. **7.** (*bot.*) catkin.
бара́шковый *adj.* lambskin.
Барба́дос, а *m.* Barbados.
барбадо́с|ец, ца *m.* Barbadian.
барбадо́с|ка, ки *f. of* **~ец**
барбадо́сский *adj.* Barbadian.
барбари́с, а *m.* barberry.
барбитура́т, а *m.* barbiturate.
барбо́с, а *m.* 'Barbos' (*name given to house-dogs*; *fig. of coarse, rude pers.*).
барви́н|ок, ка *m.* (*bot.*) periwinkle (*Vinca minor*).
бард, а *m.* bard.
бард|а́, ы́ *f.* distillery waste.
барда́к, а́ *m.* (*coll.*) brothel; **настоя́щий б.** (*fig.*) complete chaos.
бардач|о́к, ка́ *m.* (*coll.*) glove compartment (*in car*).
барелье́ф, а *m.* bas-relief.
Ба́ренцев|о мо́р|е, ~а ~я *nt.* the Barents Sea.
баре́тк|а, и *f.* (*coll., obs.*) (woman's) shoe, slipper.
ба́рж|а, и *f.* barge.
барж|а́, и́, *g. pl.* **~е́й = ба́ржа**
ба́ри|й, я *m.* (*chem.*) barium.
ба́р|ин, а, *pl.* **~е** *and* **~ы, ~** *m.* barin (*member of landowning gentry*); landowner; gentleman; master; (*as mode of address employed by peasants, servants, etc.*) sir; **оде́т ~ином** dressed like a gentleman; **жить ~ином** to live like a lord.
бари́т, а *m.* (*min.*) barytes.
барито́н, а *m.* baritone.
ба́рич, а *m.* barin's son; (*coll., pej.*) = **ба́рин**
ба́рк|а, и *f.* wooden barge.
баркаро́л|а, ы *f.* (*mus.*) barcarole.
барка́с, а *m.* launch; long boat.
бар-ко́д, а *m.* bar-code.
ба́рмен, а *m.* barman, bartender.
ба́рм|ы, ~ *no sg.* (*hist.*) small shoulder mantle (*worn by Moscow princes*).
баро́граф, а *m.* barograph, self-recording barometer.
баро́кко *nt. indecl.* baroque.
баро́метр, а *m.* barometer.
барометри́ческий *adj.* barometric.
баро́н, а *m.* baron.
бароне́сс|а, ы *f.* baroness.
баро́нский *adj.* baronial.
баро́нств|о, а *nt.* barony.
ба́рочник, а *m.* bargee.
ба́р|очный *adj. of* **~ка**
баро́чный *adj.* baroque.
баррика́д|а, ы *f.* barricade.
баррикади́р|овать, ую *impf.* (*of* **за~**) to barricade.
баррика́дник, а *m.* barricader.
баррика́д|ный *adj. of* **~а**
барс, а *m.* (*zool.*) ounce, snow leopard (*Uncia uncia*).
ба́рск|ий *adj. of* **ба́рин; б. дом** manor-house; **жить на ~ую но́гу** to live like a lord.
ба́рс|овый *adj. of* **~**
ба́рственный *adj.* lordly, grand.
ба́рств|о, а *nt.* **1.** lordliness. **2.** (*collect.*) gentry.
ба́рств|овать, ую *impf.* to live in idleness and plenty.
барсу́к, а́ *m.* badger.
барсу́чий *adj.* **1.** *adj. of* **барсу́к. 2.** badger-skin.
бару́ха, и *f.* (*sl.*) girlfriend.
барха́н, а *m.* (sand-)dune (*in steppe or desert*).
ба́рхат, а *m.* velvet.
бархати́ст|ый (~, ~а) *adj.* velvety.
ба́рхатк|а, и *f.* piece of velvet; velvet ribbon.
ба́рхатный *adj.* **1.** velvet; **б. сезо́н** autumn season, autumn months. **2.** (*fig.*) velvety.
ба́рхат|цы, цев *pl.* (*sg.* **~ец, ~ца** *m.*) (African) marigold (*Tagetes*).
бархо́тк|а, и *f.* velvet ribbon.
барч|о́нок, о́нка, *pl.* **~а́та, ~а́т** *m.* barin's son.
барчу́к, а́ *m.* (*coll.*) barin's son.
ба́рщин|а, ы *f.* (*hist.*) corvée.
бары́г|а, и *c.g.* (*sl.*) spiv.
ба́рын|я, и *f.* barin's wife; lady; mistress; (*as term of address employed by peasants, servants, etc.*) madam.
бары́ш, а́ *m.* profit.
бары́шник, а *m.* **1.** profiteer; speculator (*esp. in theatre tickets*); spiv. **2.** horse-dealer.
бары́шнича|ть, ю *impf.* to profiteer; (*+i.*) to speculate (in).
бары́шничеств|о, а *nt.* profiteering; speculation.
ба́рыш|ня, ни, *g. pl.* **~ень** *f.* **1.** girl of gentry family; (*as term of address employed by peasants, servants, etc.*) miss. **2.** (*coll.*) girl, young lady. **3.** (*coll., obs.*) female assistant; **телефо́нная б.** (*female*) telephone operator.
барье́р, а *m.* barrier (*also fig.*); **звуково́й б.** sound barrier; (*sport*) hurdle; **взять б.** to clear a hurdle; **поста́вить кого́-н. к ~у** to make s.o. fight a duel.
барьери́ст, а *m.* hurdler.
бас, а, *pl.* **~ы́** *m.* (*mus.*) bass.
ба́с|енный *adj. of* **~ня**
баси́ст|ый (~, ~а) *adj.* (*coll.*) bass.
ба|си́ть, шу́, си́шь *impf.* (*coll.*) to speak (*or* sing) in a deep voice.
баск, а *m.* Basque.
ба́ске́т, а *m.* (*coll.*) basketball (*sport*).
баскетбо́л, а *m.* basketball (*sport*).
баскетболи́ст, а *m.* basket-ball player.
баске́т|ки, ок *pl.* (*sg.* **~ка, ~ки** *f.*) basketball boots.
баск|о́нка, о́нки *f. of* **~**
ба́скский *adj.* Basque.
басма́ч, а́ *m.* (*hist.*) basmach (*member of anti-Soviet movement in Central Asia*).
басма́честв|о, а *nt.* (*hist.*) basmachestvo (*anti-Soviet movement in Central Asia*).
баснопи́с|ец, ца *m.* (*liter.*) fabulist.
баснoсло́ви|е, я *nt.* (*obs.*) **1.** mythology. **2.** (*collect.*) fabulous stories, fabrications.
басносло́в|ный (~ен, ~на) *adj.* **1.** mythical, legendary. **2.** (*fig., coll.*) fabulous.
ба́с|ня, ни, *g. pl.* **~ен** *f.* **1.** fable. **2.** (*fig., coll.*) fable, fabrication.
бас|о́вый *adj. of* **~; б. ключ** (*mus.*) bass clef.
бас|о́к, ка́ *m.* (*mus.*) **1.** low bass (voice). **2.** bass-string.
басо́н, а *m.* braid.
бассе́йн, а *m.* **1.** (*man-made*) pool; reservoir; **б. для пла́вания** swimming-pool; **плеска́тельный б.** paddling pool. **2.** (*geog.*) basin; **каменноу́го́льный б.** coalfield.
ба́ста *int.* (*coll.*) that's enough!; that'll do!
бастио́н, а *m.* (*mil. and fig.*) bastion.
баст|ова́ть, у́ю *impf.* to strike, go on strike; to be on strike.
бастр, а *m.* brown sugar.
баст|у́ющий *pres. part. of* **~ова́ть** *and adj.* striking; *as n.* **б., ~у́ющего** *m.* striker.
басурма́н, а *m.* (*obs.*) infidel (*esp. Mohammedan*).
баталёр, а *m.* (*naut.*) storeman; petty officer in charge of stores.
батали́ст, а *m.* painter of battle-pieces.
бата́ли|я, и *f.* **1.** (*obs.*) battle. **2.** (*coll.*) fight; row, squabble.
бата́л|ьный *adj. of* **~ия; ~ьная карти́на** battle-piece.

батальо́н, а *m.* (*mil.*) battalion; **стрелко́вый б.** rifle battalion; **б. свя́зи** signal battalion.
батальо́н|ный *adj. of* ~; **б. команди́р** battalion commander; *as n.* **б.**, **~ного** *m.* = **б. команди́р**
батаре́|ец, йца *m.* (*mil.*; *coll.*) gunner.
батаре́йк|а, и *f.* (*electric*) battery.
батаре́|йный *adj. of* **~я**; **~йная па́луба** (*naut.*) gun deck; **б. приёмник** (*radio*) battery set.
батаре́|я, и *f.* (*mil. and tech.*) battery; **б. парово́го отопле́ния** (central heating) radiator; **б. сухи́х элеме́нтов** dry battery; **аккумуля́торная б.** storage battery.
ба́теньк|а, и *m.* (*coll.*) (*familiar mode of address*) old chap!
бати́ст, а *m.* cambric, lawn.
бати́ст|овый *adj. of* ~
батисфе́р|а, ы *f.* bathysphere.
ба́тник, а *m.* shirt-waister (blouse).
бато́г, а́ *m.* (*obs. or dial.*) **1.** rod, cudgel; **не жале́ть ~о́в** not to spare the rod. **2.** walking-stick.
бато́н, а *m.* **1.** (*long*) loaf of bread. **2.** stick (*of confectionery*).
батра́к, а́ *m.* farm-labourer.
батра́|цкий *adj. of* **~к**
батра́честв|о, а *nt.* **1.** farm work. **2.** (*collect.*) farm-labourers.
батра́ч|ить, у, ишь *impf.* to work as a farm-labourer.
баттерфляи́ст, а *m.* butterfly swimmer.
баттерфля́|й, я *m.* butterfly (*swimming stroke*).
бату́д = **бату́т**
бату́н, а *m.* (*bot.*) Welsh onion.
бату́т, а *m.* (*sport*) trampoline.
батути́ст, а *m.* trampolinist.
батути́ст|ка, ки *f. of* ~
бату́т|ный *adj. of* ~; **б. спорт** trampolining.
ба́тьк|а, и *m.* (*coll. or dial.*) = **ба́тюшка 1.**
ба́тюшк|а, и *m.* **1.** (*coll.*) father; **как вас по ~е?** what is your patronymic? **2.** (*as mode of address to priest*) father. **3.** (*coll.*) old chap!; my dear fellow!
ба́тюшки *int.* **б. (мой)!** good gracious!
ба́т|я, и *m.* (*dial.*) = **~юшка**
ба́ул, а *m.* trunk.
бах *int.* bang!
бахаи́зм, а *m.* Bahaism.
бахаи́ст, а *m.* Bahai.
ба́ха|ть, ю *impf. of* **ба́хнуть**
ба́ха|ться, юсь *impf. of* **ба́хнуться**
бахва́л, а *m.* (*coll.*) braggart, boaster.
бахва́л|иться, юсь, ишься *impf.* (*coll.*; *+i.*) to brag (of).
бахва́льств|о, а *nt.* (*coll.*) bragging.
ба́хн|уть, у, ешь *pf.* (*coll.*) **1.** to bang; to bark (*of gunfire*). **2.** to bang, slap; **б. кого́-н. по спине́** to slap s.o. on the back.
ба́хн|уться, усь, ешься *pf.* (*coll.*) to bang, bump (o.s.); (*+i.*) **б. голово́й о стол** to bang one's head on the table.
Бахре́йн, а *m.* Bahrain
бахром|а́, ы́ *f.* fringe.
бахро́мчатый *adj.* fringed.
бахч|а́, и *f.* (water-)melon plantation; pumpkin (gourd) field.
бахче́вник, а *m.* melon-grower.
бахчево́дств|о, а *nt.* melon-growing.
бахч|ево́й *adj. of* **~а́**; **~евы́е культу́ры** melons and gourds.
бац *int.* = **бах**
ба́ца|ть, ю *impf.* **1.** *impf. of* **ба́цнуть. 2.** (*coll.*) to tap-dance.
баци́лл|а, ы *f.* bacillus.
бациллоноси́тел|ь, я *m.* (bacillus-)carrier.
ба́цн|уть, у, ешь *pf.* (*coll.*) = **ба́хнуть**
ба́шенк|а, и *f.* turret.
ба́ш|енный *adj. of* **~ня**; **~енные часы́** tower clock.
башибузу́к, а *m.* bashi-bazouk; Turkish irregular (soldier); (*fig.*) desperado.
башк|а́, и́ *no g. pl.*, *f.* (*coll.*) head; pate; **глу́пая б.** blockhead.
башки́р, а *m.* Bashkir.
башки́р|ец, ца *m.* (*obs.*) Bashkir.
башки́р|ка, ки *f. of* **~ец**
башки́рский *adj.* Bashkir.
башкови́т|ый (~, ~а) *adj.* (*coll.*) brainy.
ба́шл|и, ей *no sg.* (*sl.*) bread, dosh.
башлы́к, а *m.* hood.
башма́к, а́ *m.* shoe (*also tech.*); (*tech.*) chock; **быть под ~о́м у кого́-н.** to be under s.o.'s thumb.
башма́чник, а *m.* shoemaker, cobbler.
башма́|чный *adj. of* **~к**
башма|чо́к, чка́ *m. dim. of* **~к**; **вя́заный б.** bootee.
ба́ш|ня, ни, *g. pl.* **~ен** *f.* tower; turret; **пиза́нская кося́я б.** the Leaning Tower of Pisa.
башта́н, а *m.* = **бахча́**
ба|шу́, си́шь *see* **~си́ть**
баю́ка|ть, ю *impf.* to sing lullabies (to).
ба́юшки-баю́ *int.* lullaby.
баяде́р|а, ы *f.* = **~ка**
баяде́рк|а, и *f.* bayadère.
бая́н, а *m.* (*mus.*) bayan (*kind of accordion*); (*sl.*) hypo, 'spike' (= *hypodermic syringe*).
баяни́ст, а *m.* (*mus.*) bayan-player.
ба́|ять, ю, ешь *impf.* (*coll.*, *obs. or dial.*) to say, talk.
бде́ни|е, я *nt.* vigil; **всено́щное б.** (*eccl.*) all-night vigil.
бд|еть, *1st pers. sg. not used*, **~ишь** *impf.* (*obs.*), to keep watch, keep vigil; **б.** (**о**+*p.*) to watch (over).
бди́тельност|ь, и *f.* vigilance, watchfulness.
бди́тел|ьный (~ен, ~ьна) *adj.* vigilant, watchful.
бе: ни бе, ни ме (*coll.*) to not have a clue about sth.; **(ни кукаре́ку)** to not say a word.
бебе́ *nt. indecl.* (*coll.*) baby.
бебе́шк|а, и *c.g.* (*coll.*) baby; **наряжа́ться ~ой** to dress like a little girl.
бег, а, о ~́е, на ~у́, *pl.* **~а́, ~о́в** *m.* **1.** run, running; **~о́м, на ~у́** at the double; **на всём ~у́** at full speed; **б. на ме́сте** running on the spot; marking time (*also fig.*); **оздорови́тельный б.** jogging; **занима́ющийся оздорови́тельным ~ом** jogger; **б. трусцо́й** (*sport*) jogging. **2.** (*sport*) race; **б. на коро́ткие диста́нции** sprint; **б. на вре́мя** time trial. **3.** (*pl.*) the races (*for horses harnessed, not ridden*); trotting races; **быть на ~а́х** to be at the races. **4.: быть в ~а́х** to be on the run; **яви́ться из ~о́в** to come out of hiding.
бе́га|ть, ю *impf.* (*indet. of* **бежа́ть**) **1.** to run (about); (**за**+*i.*; *coll.*) to run (after), chase (after). **2.** (*of s.o.'s eyes*) to rove, roam.
бегемо́т, а *m.* hippopotamus.
бегле́ц, а *m.* fugitive.
бе́глост|ь, и *f.* fluency; dexterity.
бе́гл|ый *adj.* **1.** (*obs.*) fugitive. **2.** fluent, quick. **3.** superficial; cursory; **б. взгляд** fleeting glance; **~ое замеча́ние** passing remark; **б. звук** unstable sound, **б. осмо́тр** cursory inspection. **4.: б. гла́сный** (*gram.*) mobile vowel. **5.: б. ого́нь** (*mil.*) volley fire.
беговик|и́, о́в *no sg.* running shoes.
бег|ово́й *adj. of* ~; **~ова́я доро́жка** racetrack, running-track; **~ова́я ло́шадь** racehorse.
бего́м *adv.* running; at the double.
бего́ни|я, и *f.* (*bot.*) begonia.
беготн|я́, и́ *f.* (*coll.*) running about; bustle.
бе́гств|о, а *nt.* flight; escape; **обрати́ть в б.** to put to flight; **обрати́ться в б., спаса́ться ~ом** to take to flight.
бе|гу́, ~жи́шь *see* **~жа́ть**
бегу́н, а́ *m.* runner (*also tech.*); **(ме́льничные) ~ы́** runners, millstones.
бегун|о́к, ка́ *m.* **1.** (*tech.*) runner. **2.** (*pl.*) small front wheels (*of locomotive*). **3.** (*pl. only*) sulky. **4.** (*coll.*) clearance chit, loan slip.
бед|а́, ы́, *pl.* **~́ы** *f.* **1.** misfortune; calamity; **на ~у́** unfortunately; **на свою́ ~у́** to one's cost; **быть ~е́!** there's trouble brewing; **пришла́ б. — отворя́й ворота́** (*prov.*) it never rains but it pours; **семь ~ — оди́н отве́т** (*prov.*) in for a penny, in for a pound. **2.** (the) trouble, the matter; *as pred.* it is awful!; it is a trouble; **б. в том, что** the trouble is (that); **про́сто б.!** it's simply awful!; **б. мне с ним** (*coll.*) he's nothing but trouble; he's a handful; **не б.!** it doesn't matter; **что за б.!** what does it matter?; so what? **3.** (*coll.*) an awful lot. **4.: б. (как)** (*as adv.*; *coll.*) awfully, terribly.

бéдéкер, а *m.* (*arch.*) guide-book, Baedeker.
бедлáм, а *m.* bedlam.
беднé|ть, ю *impf.* (*of* **о~**) (*+i.*) to grow poor (in).
бéдност|ь, и *f.* poverty (*also fig.*); indigence; **ýровень/ порóг ~и** poverty line.
беднот|á, ы *f.* **1.** (*collect.*) the poor; **деревéнская б.** poor peasants. **2.** (*coll.*) poverty.
бéд|ный (~ен, ~нá) *adj.* poor; meagre; (*fig.*) barren, jejune.
бедня́г|а, и *m.* (*coll.*) poor fellow; poor devil.
бедня́жк|а, и *c.g. and f.* (*coll.*) **1.** *c.g. dim. of* **бедня́га. 2.** *f. of* **бедня́га**
бедня́к, á *m.* **1.** pauper. **2.** poor peasant.
бедня́|цкий *adj. of* **~к**
бедня́честв|о, а *nt.* (*collect.*) poor peasants.
бедня́чк|а, и *f.* poor peasant woman.
бедóв|ый (~, ~а) *adj.* (*coll.*) sharp, lively; mischievous; daredevil.
бедокýр, а *m.* (*coll.*) mischief-maker; joker.
бедокýр|ить, ю, ишь *impf.* (*of* **на~**) (*coll.*) to get up to mischief, play jokes.
бедолáг|а, и *c.g.* poor devil.
бéдренный *adj.* (*anat.*) femoral.
бед|рó, рá, *pl.* **~̈ра, ~̈ер, ~̈рам** *nt.* **1.** thigh; hip. **2.** (*joint of meat*) leg.
бéдствен|ный (~, ~на) *adj.* disastrous, calamitous.
бéдстви|е, я *nt.* calamity, disaster; **райóн ~я** disaster area; **сигнáл ~я** distress signal.
бéдств|овать, ую *impf.* to live in poverty.
бедуи́н, а *m.* bedouin.
бедуи́н|ский *adj. of* **~**
беж *adj. indecl.* beige.
бе|жáть, гý, жи́шь, гýт *impf.* (*det. of* **бéгать**) **1.** to run; (*fig.*) to run, fly; to boil over; **горя́чая водá ~жи́т из э́того крáна** hot water runs from this tap; **врéмя ~жи́т** time flies. **2.** (*impf. and pf.*) to escape.
бéжевый *adj.* beige.
бéжен|ец, ца *m.* refugee.
бéжен|ка, ки *f. of* **~ец**
бéженский *adj.* refugee.
бéженств|о, а *nt.* **1.** flight, exodus, refuge-seeking. **2.** (*collect.*) refugees.
без *prep.+g.* without; in the absence of; minus, less; **не б.** not without, not devoid (of); **б. вас** in your absence; **б. пяти́ (минýт) три** five (minutes) to three; **б. чéтверти час** a quarter to one; **б. мáлого** (*coll.*) almost, all but; **быть б. умá (от)** to be crazy (about); **не б. тогó** (*coll.*) that's about it, it can't altogether be denied.
без... *pref.* in-, un-, -less.
безавари́йный *adj.* accident-free.
безалáберност|ь, и *f.* disorder; lack of system.
безалáбер|ный (~ен, ~на) *adj.* disorderly; slovenly.
безалáберщин|а, ы *f.* (*coll.*) muddle; slovenliness.
безалкогóльный *adj.* non-alcoholic; **б. напи́ток** non-alcoholic drink, soft drink.
безапелляциóн|ный (~ен, ~на) *adj.* peremptory, categorical.
безáтомный = безъя́дерный
безбéд|ный (~ен, ~на) *adj.* well-to-do, comfortable.
безбилéтник, а *m.* fare dodger.
безбилéтный *adj.* ticketless; **б. пассажи́р** passenger travelling without ticket; (*on ship*) stowaway.
безбóжи|е, я *nt.* atheism.
безбóжник, а *m.* atheist.
безбóжно *adv.* (*coll.*) shamelessly, outrageously; **здесь б. дерýт** they fleece you shamelessly here.
безбóжн|ый *adj.* **1.** irreligious, anti-religious. **2.** (*coll.*) shameless, scandalous; **~ые цéны** outrageous prices.
безболéзнен|ный (~, ~на) *adj.* painless.
безборóдый *adj.* beardless (*also fig.*).
безбоя́знен|ный (~, ~на) *adj.* fearless.
безбрáчи|е, я *nt.* celibacy.
безбрáчный *adj.* celibate.
безбрéж|ный (~ен, ~на) *adj.* boundless.
безбрóвый *adj.* eyebrowless.
безбýр|ный (~ен, ~на) *adj.* calm, peaceful.
безвéри|е, я *nt.* unbelief.
безвéстност|ь, и *f.* obscurity.
безвéст|ный (~ен, ~на) *adj.* unknown; obscure; **~ное отсýтствие** absence in place unknown.
безвéтренный *adj.* calm.
безвéтри|е, я *nt.* calm.
безви́н|ный (~ен, ~на) *adj.* guiltless.
безвкýси|е, я *nt.* lack of taste.
безвкýсиц|а, ы *f.* lack of taste; **что за б.!** what bad taste!
безвкýс|ный (~ен, ~на) *adj.* tasteless.
безвлáсти|е, я *nt.* anarchy.
безвлáст|ный (~ен, ~на) *adj.* powerless.
безвóд|ный (~ен, ~на) *adj.* **1.** arid; waterless. **2.** (*chem.*) anhydrous.
безвóдь|е, я *nt.* aridity.
безвозврáт|ный (~ен, ~на) *adj.* irrevocable; **~ная ссýда** permanent loan.
безвоздýшный *adj.* airless.
безвозмéздный *adj.* gratuitous, free of charge; **б. труд** unpaid work.
безвóли|е, я *nt.* lack of will; weak will.
безволóсый *adj.* hairless, bald.
безвóл|ьный (~ен, ~ьна) *adj.* weak-willed.
безврéд|ный (~ен, ~на) *adj.* harmless; **экологи́чески б.** eco-friendly.
безвременéнник, а *m.* (*bot.*) Autumn crocus.
безврéменн|ый *adj.* untimely, premature; **~ая кончи́на** untimely decease.
безврéмень|е, я *nt.* (*obs.*) **1.** hard times. **2.** period of (social) stagnation.
безвы́ездно *adv.* uninterruptedly, without a break.
безвы́ездн|ый *adj.* uninterrupted; **~ое пребывáние** continuous residence.
безвы́ходно *adv.* uninterruptedly, without a break.
безвы́ход|ный (~ен, ~на) *adj.* **1.** hopeless, desperate; **быть в ~ном положéнии** to be in a desperate position. **2.** uninterrupted.
безглагóльный *adj.* **1.** (*gram.*) verbless. **2.** (*fig., poet.*) silent, dumb.
безглáзый *adj.* eyeless.
безглáс|ный (~ен, ~на) *adj.* (*fig.*) silent, dumb.
безголóв|ый (~, ~а) *adj.* **1.** headless; (*iron.*) brainless. **2.** (*fig., coll.*) forgetful, scatter-brained.
безголóсный *adj.* (*ling.*) unvoiced.
безголóс|ый *adj.* weak (*of voice*); voiceless; **он стал совсéм ~ым** his voice is quite ruined.
безгрáмотност|ь, и *f.* illiteracy.
безгрáмот|ный (~ен, ~на) *adj.* illiterate (*also fig.*); ignorant.
безграни́ч|ный (~ен, ~на) *adj.* infinite, limitless, boundless; (*fig.*) extreme, extraordinary.
безгрéшност|ь, и *f.* innocence.
безгрéш|ный (~ен, ~на) *adj.* innocent, sinless.
бездáрник, а *m.* mediocrity, third-rater.
бездáрност|ь, и *f.* **1.** lack of talent. **2.** pers. without talent; third-rater.
бездáр|ный (~ен, на) *adj.* talentless, undistinguished; third-rate; **б. актёр** ham; **б. певéц** third-rate singer.
бездáр|ь (*and* **бéздар|ь**), **и** *f.* (*coll.*) pers. without talent; third-rater.
бездéйствен|ный (~, ~на) *adj.* inactive.
бездéйстви|е, я *nt.* inaction, inertia, idleness; (*leg.*) (criminal) negligence.
бездéйств|овать, ую *impf.* to be inactive; to lie idle; not to work (*of a machine, etc.*).
бездéлиц|а, ы *f.* trifle, bagatelle; **такáя сýмма для негó б.** for him such a sum is a trifle.
бездéлк|а, и *f.* (*coll.*) **1.** trifle, bagatelle. **2.** knick-knack.
безделýшк|а, и *f.* knick-knack.
бездéль|е, я *nt.* idleness.
бездéльник, а *m.* **1.** idler, loafer. **2.** ne'er-do-well.
бездéльни|ца, цы *f. of* **~к**
бездéльнича|ть, ю *impf.* to idle, loaf.
бездéл|ьный (~ен, ~ьна) *adj.* (*coll.*) idle.
бездéнежный *adj.* **1.** impecunious. **2.** (*econ.*) non-monetary.
бездéнежь|е, я *nt.* lack of money, impecuniousness.

бездéтност|ь, и *f.* childlessness.
бездéт|ный (~ен, ~на) *adj.* childless.
бездефицúтный *adj.* (*econ.*) entailing no deficit; self-supporting.
бездéятельност|ь, и *f.* inactivity, inertia.
бездéятел|ьный (~ен, ~ьна) *adj.* inactive; sluggish.
бéздн|а, ы *f.* **1.** abyss, chasm. **2.** (*coll.*) a huge number; **б. хлопóт** a multitude, sea of troubles; **б. премýдрости** (*joc.*) a mine of information.
બездóждь|е, я *nt.* dry weather, drought.
бездоказáтел|ьный (~ен, ~ьна) *adj.* unsubstantiated.
бездóм|ный (~ен, ~на) *adj.* homeless; **~ная кóшка** stray cat.
бездóнный *adj.* bottomless; (*fig.*, *poet.*) fathomless.
бездорóж|ный (~ен, ~на) *adj.* without roads.
бездорóжь|е, я *nt.* **1.** absence of roads. **2.** bad condition of roads; season when roads are impassable.
бездохóд|ный (~ен, ~на) *adj.* (*econ.*) unprofitable.
бездýм|ный (~ен, ~на) *adj.* unthinking; feckless.
бездýши|е, я *nt.* heartlessness, callousness.
бездýш|ный (~ен, ~на) *adj.* **1.** heartless, callous. **2.** inanimate; (*fig.*) soulless.
безды́мный *adj.* smokeless; **б. пóрох** (*mil.*) smokeless powder.
бездыхáн|ный (~ен, ~на) *adj.* lifeless.
безé *nt. indecl.* meringue.
безжáлост|ный (~ен, ~на) *adj.* ruthless, pitiless.
безжúзнен|ный (~, ~на) *adj.* lifeless, inanimate; (*fig.*) spiritless.
беззабóт|ный (~ен, ~на) *adj.* carefree, light-hearted; careless.
беззавéт|ный (~ен, ~на) *adj.* selfless, wholehearted; **~ная хрáбость** selfless courage.
беззакóни|е, я *nt.* **1.** lawlessness. **2.** unlawful act.
беззакóннича|ть, ю *impf.* (*coll.*) to transgress, break the law.
беззакóн|ный (~ен, ~на) *adj.* **1.** illegal, unlawful. **2.** (*poet.*) lawless, wayward.
беззапрéтн|ый *adj.* **1.** permitted; **~ая сýмма инострáнной валю́ты** permitted amount of foreign currency. **2.** unrestrained.
беззастéнчив|ый (~, ~а) *adj.* shameless; **б. лгун** brazen, unblushing liar; **~ая ложь** barefaced lie.
беззащúт|ный (~ен, ~на) *adj.* defenceless, unprotected.
беззвёзд|ный (~ен, ~на) *adj.* starless.
беззвýч|ный (~ен, ~на) *adj.* soundless, noiseless.
беззéмéль|е, я *nt.* lack of land.
безземéльный *adj.* landless.
беззлóби|е, я *nt.* good nature, mildness.
беззлóб|ный (~ен, ~на) *adj.* mild, good-natured.
беззýб|ый *adj.* **1.** toothless; (*fig.*) impotent, harmless; **~ая злóба** impotent rage. **2.** (*zool.*) edentate.
безлáмповый *adj.* (*tech.*) valveless.
безлéс|ный (~ен, ~на) *adj.* woodless; treeless.
безлéсь|е, я *nt.* **1.** woodless tract. **2.** absence of forest.
безлúкий *adj.* featureless; faceless, impersonal.
безлúственный *adj.* leafless.
безлúч|ие, ия *nt.* = **~ность**
безлúчност|ь, и *f.* lack of personality; impersonality.
безлúч|ный (~ен, ~на) *adj.* **1.** without personality, characterless, impersonal. **2.** (*gram.*) impersonal.
безлошáдный *adj.* not possessing a horse.
безлýн|ный (~ен, ~на) *adj.* moonless.
безлю́д|ный (~ен, ~на) *adj.* uninhabited; sparsely populated; solitary, unfrequented.
безлю́дь|е, я *nt.* **1.** deficiency of population; absence of human life; **в дерéвне бы́ло пóлное б.** the village was completely deserted. **2.** lack of suitable company, lack of the right people; **на б. и Фомá дворянúн** (*prov.*) in the land of the blind the one-eyed is king.
безмéн, а *m.* steelyard.
безмéр|ный (~ен, ~на) *adj.* immense, excessive.
безмóзглый *adj.* (*coll.*) brainless.
безмóлви|е, я *nt.* silence; **царúт б.** silence reigns.
безмóлв|ный (~ен, ~на) *adj.* silent, mute, speechless; **~ное соглáсие** tacit consent.
безмóлвств|овать, ую *impf.* to keep silence.
безмолóчный *adj.* dairy-free.
безмотóрный *adj.* engineless.
безмятéжност|ь и *f.* serenity, placidity.
безмятéж|ный (~ен, ~на) *adj.* serene, placid.
безнадёж|ный (~ен, ~на) *adj.* hopeless; despairing; **большóй ~ен** the patient's case is hopeless.
безнадзóрност|ь, и *f.* neglect.
безнадзóрный *adj.* neglected.
безнакáзанно *adv.* with impunity; **э́то емý не пройдёт б.** he won't get away with this.
безнакáзанност|ь, и *f.* impunity.
безнакáзан|ный (~, ~на) *adj.* unpunished.
безналúчный *adj.* without cash transfer; **б. расчёт** (*fin.*) clearing.
безналóговый *adj.* tax-free.
безначáли|е, я *nt.* anarchy.
безначáльный *adj.* without beginning, from eternity.
безнóгий *adj.* **1.** legless; one-legged. **2.** deprived of the use of one's legs. **3.** (*zool.*) apod.
безнóсый *adj.* noseless; **б. чáйник** spoutless teapot.
безнрáвственност|ь, и *f.* immorality.
безнрáвствен|ный (~, ~на) *adj.* immoral.
безо *prep.* (*before g. of* **весь** *and* **вся́кий**) = **без**
безобúд|ный (~ен, ~на) *adj.* inoffensive.
безóблачност|ь и *f.* cloudlessness; (*fig.*) serenity.
безóблач|ный (~ен, ~на) *adj.* cloudless; (*fig.*) serene, unclouded.
безобрáзи|е, я *nt.* **1.** ugliness. **2.** outrage; (*pl.*) disgraceful things, shocking things. **3.** (*as pred*; *coll.*) it is disgraceful; **э́то прóсто б.!** it's simply disgraceful, scandalous.
безобрá|зить, жу, зишь *impf.* (*of* **о~**) **1.** to disfigure, mutilate. **2.** (*coll.*) to make a nuisance of o.s., make a disturbance.
безобрáзник, а *m.* (*coll.*) **1.** hooligan. **2.** naughty child.
безобрáзнича|ть, ю *impf.* (*coll.*) to carry on disgracefully, outrageously; to make a nuisance of o.s.; to get up to mischief.
безóбраз|ный (~ен, ~на) *adj.* **1.** unadorned; not employing images. **2.** vague.
безобрáз|ный (~ен, ~на) *adj.* **1.** ugly. **2.** disgraceful, scandalous, outrageous, shocking.
безогля́дный *adj.* reckless, impetuous.
безоговóрочн|ый (~а, ~о) *adj.* unconditional, unreserved.
безопáсност|ь, и *f.* safety, security; **пóяс/ремéнь ~и** seat belt; **Совéт Безопáсности** Security Council.
безопáс|ный (~ен, ~на) *adj.* safe, secure; **~ная брúтва** safety razor.
безорýж|ный (~ен, ~на) *adj.* unarmed.
безоскóлочн|ый *adj.*: **~ое стеклó** safety glass.
безосновáтел|ьный (~ен, ~ьна) *adj.* groundless.
безостанóвочный *adj.* unceasing; non-stop.
безотвéт|ный (~ен, ~на) *adj.* **1.** (*rare*) unanswered. **2.** meek, dumb.
безотвéтственност|ь, и *f.* irresponsibility.
безотвéтствен|ный (~, ~на) *adj.* irresponsible.
безотговóрочн|ый (~а, ~о) *adj.* unquestioning, implicit.
безоткáзный *adj.* **1.** dependable. **2.** trouble-free, faultless. **3.** certain, sure-fire.
безоткáтный *adj.* (*mil.*) non-recoil.
безотлагáтельный *adj.* urgent.
безотлýчно *adv.* continually; **онá нахóдится б. дóма** she is tied to the home, she never gets out.
безотлýч|ный (~ен, на) *adj.* ever-present; continuous.
безотносúтельно *adv.* **(к)** irrespective (of); **б. к егó плáнам я поéду зáвтра в Лóндон** irrespective of his plans I shall go to London tomorrow.
безотносúтел|ьный (~ен, ~ьна) *adj.* absolute, valid absolutely.
безотрáд|ный (~ен, ~на) *adj.* cheerless.
безотры́вн|ый *adj.*: **~ое обучéние** workers' education (*not involving taking time off from work*).
безотчётност|ь, и *f.* **1.** absence of control. **2.** unaccountableness; instinctiveness.

безотчёт|ный (~ен, ~на) *adj.* **1.** not liable to account, not subject to control. **2.** unaccountable, inexplicable; unreasoning, instinctive.
безоши́боч|ный (~ен, ~на) *adj.* correct; faultless, infallible; **~ное предсказа́ние** unerring prediction.
безрабо́тиц|а, ы *f.* unemployment.
безрабо́тн|ый *adj.* unemployed; *as n.* **~ые, ~ых** *pl.* the unemployed; **постоя́нно ~ые** the long-term unemployed.
безра́дост|ный (~ен, ~на) *adj.* joyless; dismal.
безразде́л|ьный (~ен, ~ьна) *adj.* undivided; **~ьная власть** complete sway; **~ьное иму́щество** indivisible property.
безразли́чи|е, я *nt.* indifference.
безразли́чно *adv.* indifferently; **относи́ться б. (к)** to be indifferent (to); **б. кто, где** no matter who, where.
безразли́ч|ный (~ен, ~на) *adj.* indifferent; **мне ~но** it's all the same to me.
безразме́р|ный (~ен, ~на) *adj.* one-size (*nylon, etc.*); **~ные носки́** stretch socks.
безрассве́т|ный (~ен, ~на) *adj.* continuous (*of night in polar regions*).
безрассу́д|ный (~ен, ~на) *adj.* reckless; foolhardy.
безрассу́дств|о, а *nt.* recklessness, foolhardiness.
безрасчёт|ный (~ен, ~на) *adj.* uneconomical.
безрезульта́тност|ь, и *f.* futility; failure.
безрезульта́т|ный (~ен, ~на) *adj.* futile; unsuccessful.
безре́льсов|ый *adj.* railless; **б. тра́нспорт** motor transport, **~ая доро́га** road.
безрессо́рный *adj.* unsprung.
безро́г|ий *adj.* hornless; **~ое живо́тное** pollard.
безро́д|ный (~ен, ~на) *adj.* **1.** without kith or kin. **2.** (*obs.*) of humble origin. **3.** (*fig.*) homeless, stateless.
безро́пот|ный (~ен, ~на) *adj.* uncomplaining, resigned; submissive.
безрука́вк|а, и *f.* sleeveless jacket *or* blouse.
безру́кий *adj.* **1.** armless. **2.** one-armed. **3.** (*fig.*) clumsy.
безры́бь|е, я *nt.* absence of fish; **на б. и рак ры́ба** (*prov.*) in the land of the blind the one-eyed is king.
безубы́точ|ный (~ен, ~на) *adj.* (*comm.*) not entailing loss; break-even.
безуда́р|ный (~ен, ~на) *adj.* (*ling.*) unaccented, unstressed.
безу́держ|ный (~ен, ~на) *adj.* unrestrained; impetuous.
безуе́здный *adj.*: **б. го́род** (*hist.*) town, not being principal town of uyezd, but possessing its own administration.
безукори́знен|ный (~, ~на) *adj.* irreproachable; impeccable.
безу́м|ец, ца *m.* **1.** (*obs.*) madman. **2.** crazy fellow.
безу́ми|е, я *nt.* **1.** madness, insanity. **2.** (*fig.*) madness; folly; **довести́ до ~я** to drive crazy; **люби́ть до ~я** to love to distraction.
безу́мно *adv.* madly, crazily, terribly, dreadfully; **я б. за́нят** I am terribly busy.
безу́м|ный (~ен, ~на) *adj.* **1.** mad, insane. **2.** (*fig.*) mad, crazy, senseless. **3.** (*coll.*) terrible; **~ные це́ны** absurd prices.
безумо́лч|ный (~ен, ~на) *adj.* incessant (*of noise*).
безу́мств|о, а *nt.* madness; foolhardiness.
безу́мств|овать, ую *impf.* to behave like a madman; to rave.
безупре́ч|ный (~ен, ~на) *adj.* irreproachable.
безуря́диц|а, ы *f.* disorder, confusion.
безуса́дочный *adj.* pre-shrunk, shrinkproof.
безусло́вно *adv.* **1.** unconditionally, absolutely. **2.** (*coll.*) of course, it goes without saying, undoubtedly.
безусло́вност|ь, и *f.* certainty.
безусло́в|ный (~ен, ~на) *adj.* **1.** unconditional, absolute. **2.** undoubted, indisputable.
безуспе́ш|ный (~ен, ~на) *adj.* unsuccessful.
безуста́нный *adj.* tireless, indefatigable.
безу́сый *adj.* having no moustache; (*fig.*) callow, immature, 'beardless'.
безуте́ш|ный (~ен, ~на) *adj.* inconsolable.
безу́хий *adj.* **1.** earless. **2.** one-eared.
безуча́сти|е, я *nt.* apathy, unconcern, neutrality.
безуча́стност|ь, и *f.* = **безуча́стие**
безуча́ст|ный (~ен, ~на) *adj.* apathetic, unconcerned, neutral.
безъя́дерный *adj.* nuclear-free.
безъязы́кий *adj.* dumb, without a tongue.
безъязы́ч|ный (~ен, ~на) *adj.* dumb, speechless.
безыде́йност|ь, и *f.* lack of principle(s); lack of ideals; lack of ideological content.
безыде́|йный (~ен, ~йна) *adj.* unprincipled; lacking ideals; lacking ideological content.
безызве́стност|ь, и *f.* **1.** uncertainty. **2.** obscurity.
безызве́ст|ный (~ен, ~на) *adj.* unknown, obscure.
безымя́нн|ый *adj.* nameless; anonymous; **б. па́лец** third finger, ring-finger; **~ая неде́ля** the third week in Lent.
безынициати́в|ный (~ен, ~на) *adj.* lacking initiative.
безынтере́с|ный (~ен, ~на) *adj.* **1.** uninteresting. **2.** (*obs.*) disinterested.
безыску́сствен|ный (~ен, ~на) *adj.* artless, ingenuous.
безысхо́д|ный (~ен, ~на) *adj.* irreparable; interminable; perpetual.
безэквивале́нтный *adj.* culture-specific, culturally bound.
бе|й, я *m.* bey (*Turkish title*).
бе́й(те) *imper. of* **бить**
бейдеви́нд *adv.* (*naut.*) close-hauled.
Бейру́т, а *m.* Beirut.
бейсбо́л, а *m.* baseball.
бейсболи́ст, а *m.* baseball player.
Бе́йсик *m.* (*comput.*) Basic.
бек, а *m.* (*sport; obs.*) back.
бека́р, а *m.* (*also as indecl. adj.*) (*mus.*) natural; **до б.** C natural.
бека́с, а *m.* (*zool.*) snipe.
бекаси́нник, а *m.* small shot.
бекаси́ный *adj. of* **бека́с**
беке́ш|а, и *f.* (*knee-length*) winter overcoat.
беко́н, а *m.* bacon.
беко́нный *adj.* bacon.
Белару́с|ь, и *f.* Belarus.
Белгра́д, а *m.* Belgrade.
белемни́т, а *m.* (*geol.*) belemnite.
белен|а́, ы́ *f.* (*bot.*) henbane; **что ты, ~ы́ объе́лся?** have you gone crazy?
беле́ни|е, я *nt.* bleaching.
белёный *adj.* bleached.
белесова́т|ый (~, ~а) *adj.* whitish.
белёсый *adj.* whitish.
беле́|ть, ю *impf.* (*of* **по~**) **1.** to grow white. **2.** (*no pf.*) to show up white.
беле́|ться, юсь *impf.* to show up white.
бел|е́ц, ьца́ *m.* (*eccl.*) novice.
бе́л|и, ей *no sg.* (*med.*) leucorrhoea.
белиберд|а́, ы́ *f.* (*coll.*) nonsense, rubbish.
белизн|а́, ы́ *f.* whiteness.
бели́л|а, ~ *no sg.* **1.** whitewash; correction fluid, Tippex (*propr.*); **закра́сить ~ами** to white/Tippex (*propr.*) out; **свинцо́вые б.** white lead; **ци́нковые б.** zinc white. **2.** ceruse.
бели́льный *adj.* bleaching.
бели́л|ьня, ьни, *g. pl.* **~ен** *f.* bleaching works, bleachery.
бел|и́ть, ю́, ~́ишь *impf.* **1.** (*pf.* **по~**) to whitewash. **2.** (*pf.* **на~**) to white(n) (*one's face, etc.*). **3.** (*pf.* **вы́~**) to bleach.
бел|и́ться, ю́сь, ~́ишься *impf.* **1.** *pass. of* **~и́ть**. **2.** (*pf.* **на~**) to whiten one's face.
бели́ц|а, ы *f.* (*eccl.*) female novice.
бе́л|ичий *adj. of* **~ка**[1]; **б. мех** squirrel (fur).
бе́лк|а[1], **и** *f.* squirrel; **верте́ться, кружи́ться как б. в колесе́** to put in much work without visible result; run round in circles.
бе́лк|а[2], **и** *f.* (*coll.*) bleaching.
белкови́н|а, ы *f.* (*chem.*) albumen.
белко́вый *adj.* (*chem.*) albuminous.
белладо́нн|а, ы *f.* (*bot.*) belladonna.
беллетриза́ци|я, и *f.* fictionalization.
беллетризи́р|овать, ую *impf. and pf.* to fictionalize.
беллетри́ст, а *m.* fiction writer.
беллетри́стик|а, и *f.* (*liter.*) fiction.
беллетристи́ческий *adj.* (*liter.*) fictional.
бело... *comb. form* white-.

белобро́вик, а *m.* (*orn.*) redwing.
белобры́с|ый (~, ~а) *adj.* (*coll.*) tow-haired.
белова́т|ый (~, а) *adj.* whitish.
белови́к, а́ *m.* fair copy (*of manuscript*).
белово́й *adj.* clean, fair; **б. экземпля́р** fair copy.
белогварде́|ец, йца *m.* (*pol.*) White Guard.
белогварде́|йский *adj.* *of* **~ец**
белоголо́вый *adj.* **1.** white-haired. **2.** fair(-haired).
белодере́в|ец, ца *m.* joiner.
бел|о́к[1], **ка́** *m.* (*biol., chem.*) albumen; protein.
бел|о́к[2], **ка́** *m.* white (of egg); glair.
бел|о́к[3], **ка́** *m.* white (of the eye).
белока́менный *adj.* (*folk poet.*) (built) of white stone (*esp. as epithet of Moscow*).
белокро́ви|е, я *nt.* (*med.*) leucaemia.
белоку́р|ый (~, ~а) *adj.* blond(e), fair(-haired).
белоли́ц|ый (~, ~а) *adj.* pale, white-faced.
белоподкла́дочник, а *m.* (*hist.*) student of aristocratic appearance and reactionary views.
белору́с, а *m.* Byelorussian (*formerly* White Russian).
белору́с|ка, ки *f.* *of* **~**
Белору́сси|я, и *f.* Byelorussia; (*obs.*) White Russia.
белору́сский *adj.* Byelorussian (*formerly* White Russian).
белору́чк|а, и *c.g.* (*coll., pej.*) pers. shirking rough *or* dirty (physical) work.
белоры́биц|а, ы *f.* white salmon.
Белосне́жк|а, и *f.* Snow-White.
белосне́ж|ный (~ен, ~на) *adj.* snow-white.
белоте́л|ый (~, ~а) *adj.* fair-skinned.
белошве́йк|а, и *f.* seamstress.
белошве́йн|ый *adj.* linen; **~ая мастерска́я** seamstress's workshop.
белоэмигра́нт, а *m.* (*pol.*) White Russian emigré.
белу́г|а, и *f.* **1.** beluga, white sturgeon (*Huso huso*). **2.** (*dial.*) white whale; **реве́ть ~ой** to bellow.
белу́|жий *adj.* *of* **~га**
белу́жин|а, ы *f.* (*meat of*) white sturgeon.
белу́х|а, и *f.* white whale (*Delphinapterus leucus*).
бе́л|ый (~, ~а́, ~о) *adj.* **1.** white; **~ая берёза** silver birch; **Б. дом** White House; (*Russian*) Parliament Building; **~ая кни́га** White Paper; **б. медве́дь** polar bear; **~ая сова́** snowy owl. **2.** (*opp. dark and in var. fig. senses*) white; fair; **б. биле́т** 'white chit' (*certificate of exemption from mil. service*); **~ое вино́** white wine; **~ое духове́нство** secular clergy; **~ое зо́лото** 'white gold' (= *cotton*); **~ое кале́ние** white heat, incandescence; **~ые кровяны́е ша́рики** white blood corpuscles, **~ое мя́со** white meat; **~ые но́чи** 'white nights', 'midnight sun'; **б. у́голь** 'white coal' (= *water power*); **б. хлеб** white bread, wheatmeal bread; **на ~ом све́те** in all the world; **средь ~а дня** in broad daylight; **э́то ши́то ~ыми ни́тками** it is all too obvious; it is quite transparent; *as n.* **~ые, ~ых** *pl.* white-skinned people, white men. **3.** clean; blank (= *unused*; *fig. unadorned*); **б. лист** clean sheet (*of paper*); **~ая страни́ца** blank page (*in book*); **~ые стихи́** blank verse. **4.** (= *of superior quality, of high class etc.*): **б. гриб** (edible) boletus (*mushroom*); **~ая кость** (*iron.*) blue blood; **~ая куха́рка** (*obs.*) head cook. **5.**: **~ая горя́чка** (*med.*) delirium tremens. **6.** (*pol.*) White (*also as n.*).
бельведе́р, а *m.* belvedere.
бельги́|ец, йца *m.* Belgian.
бельги́|йка, йки *f.* *of* **~ец**
бельги́йский *adj.* Belgian.
Бе́льги|я, и *f.* Belgium.
бель|ё, я́ *nt.* (*collect.*) linen; **да́мское б.** lingerie; **ни́жнее б.** underclothes; **посте́льное б.** bed-linen; **столо́вое б.** table-linen.
бель|ево́й *adj.* *of* **~ё**; **б. шкаф** linen cupboard; **~ева́я прище́пка** clothes-peg.
бельме́с, а *m.*: **ни ~а** (*coll.*) nothing; **он ни ~а не понима́ет** he hasn't a clue.
бельм|о́, а́, *pl.* **~а** *nt.* **1.** (*med.*) wall-eye; **как б. на глазу́** (*fig.*) a thorn in the flesh; bête noire. **2.** (*pl. only*; *also* **~ы**; *coll.*) eyes.
бельэта́ж, а *m.* **1.** first floor. **2.** (*theatr.*) dress circle.
беля́к, а́ *m.* white hare.
беля́н|а, ы *f.* (*obs.*) barge (*of unpainted wood, used on Volga and Kama rivers*).
беля́нк|а, и *f.* **1.** blonde woman, girl. **2.** cabbage butterfly. **3.** white mushroom.
бемо́л|ь, я *m.* (*also as indecl. adj.*) (*mus.*) flat; **ре б.** D flat.
бе́мск|ий *adj.*: **~ое стекло́** Bohemian glass.
Бенга́ли|я, и *f.* Bengal.
бенга́л|ец, ца *m.* Bengali.
бенга́л|ка, ки *f.* *of* **~ец**
бенга́льский *adj.* Bengali; Bengal; **б. ого́нь** Bengal light.
бенедикти́н, а *m.* benedictine (*liqueur*).
бенедикти́н|ец, ца *m.* (*eccl.*) Benedictine.
бенедикти́нский *adj.* (*eccl.*) Benedictine.
бенефи́с, а *m.* (*theatr.*) benefit performance; **устро́ить б.** (+*d.*; *sl.*) to give s.o. what for.
бенефи́с|ный *adj.* *of* **~**; **б. спекта́кль** benefit performance.
бенефициа́ри|й, я *m.* (*leg.*) beneficiary.
бенефициа́нт, а *m.* (*theatr.*) artist for whom benefit performance is given.
бенефи́ци|я, и *f.* (*eccl.*) living, benefice.
бензи́н, а *m.* benzine; petrol; **неэтили́рованный б.** unleaded petrol.
бензи́н|овый *adj.* *of* **~**; petrol; **~овая коло́нка** petrol pump.
бензино́ме́р, а *m.* petrol gauge.
бензинопрово́д, а *m.* petrol pipe.
бензо... *comb. form, abbr. of* **бензи́новый**
бензоба́к, а *m.* petrol tank.
бензово́з, а *m.* petrol tanker.
бензоколо́нк|а, и *f.* petrol pump.
бензо́л, а *m.* (*chem.*) benzol, benzene.
бензомото́рн|ый *adj.*: **~ая коси́лка** petrol-driven mower.
бензоспи́рт, а *m.* gasohol.
бензохрани́лищ|е, а *nt.* petrol tank.
Бенилю́кс, а *m.* Benelux.
бенуа́р, а *m.* (*theatr.*) boxes (*on level of the stalls*).
бербе́р, а *m.* Berber.
бербе́р|ка, ки *f.* *of* **~**
бербе́рский *adj.* Berber.
бергамо́т, а *m.* bergamot (*variety of pear*).
берда́нк|а, и *f.* (*obs.*) Berdan rifle.
бёрд|о, а *nt.* (*tech.*) reed (*of loom*).
берды́ш, а́ *m.* (*hist.*) pole-axe.
бе́рег, а, о ~е, на ~у́, *pl.* **~а́** *m.* bank; shore; land (*opp. sea*); **на ~у́ мо́ря** at the seaside; **вы́броситься на́ берег** to run aground; **вы́йти из ~о́в** to burst its banks; **сойти́ на б.** to go ashore.
бер|ёг, ~егла́ *see* **бере́чь**
берегов|о́й *adj.* coastal; waterside; **б. ве́тер** offshore wind, land-wind; **~а́я оборо́на** coastal defence; **~о́е пра́во** (*leg.*) right of salvage; **~о́е судохо́дство** coastal shipping; **~а́я ла́сточка** sand-martin.
бере|гу́, ~жёшь, ~гу́т *see* **бере́чь**
бере|ди́ть, жу́, ди́шь *impf.* (*of* **раз~**) (*coll.*) to irritate; **б. ста́рые ра́ны** (*fig.*) to re-open old wounds.
бережён|ый *adj.* (*coll.*) guarded, preserved; **~ая копе́йка рубль бережёт** (*prov.*) take care of the pennies and the pounds will take care of themselves; **~ого и Бог бережёт** God helps those who help themselves.
бережли́вост|ь, и *f.* thrift, economy.
бережли́в|ый (~, ~а) *adj.* thrifty, economical.
бе́режност|ь, и *f.* care; caution; solicitude.
бе́реж|ный (~ен, ~на) *adj.* careful; cautious; solicitous.
берёз|а, ы *f.* birch.
Берёзк|а, и *f.* Beryozka (*hard-currency shop*)
берёзник, а́ *no pl., m.* birch grove.
березня́к, а́ *no pl., m.* **1.** birch grove. **2.** birch-wood.
берёзовик, а *m.* brown mushroom (*Boletus scaber*).
берёз|овый *adj.* *of* **~а**; **~овая ка́ша** (*coll.*) the birch; a flogging.
бере́йтор, а *m.* riding-master.
бере́мене|ть, ю, ешь *impf.* (*of* **за~**) (*coll.*) to become pregnant.
бере́ме|нная (~нна) *adj.* (+*i.*) pregnant (with).

бере́менност|ь, и *f.* pregnancy; gestation; **быть на пя́том ме́сяце ~и** to be in the fifth month (of pregnancy).

бере́м|я, ени *nt.* (*dial.*) armful; bundle.

берёст|а, ы *no pl.*, *f.* birch-bark.

берёст|овый *adj.* *of* **~а**

берестяно́й = **берёстовый**

бере́т, а *m.* beret.

бер|е́чь, егу́, ежёшь, егу́т, *past* **~ёг, ~егла́** *impf.* **1.** to take care (of), look after; to keep, guard; **б. ка́ждую копе́йку** to count every penny; **б. своё вре́мя** not to waste one's time; **б. та́йну** to keep a secret. **2.** to spare; to spare the feelings (of).

бер|е́чься, егу́сь, ежёшься, егу́тся, *past* **~ёгся, ~егла́сь** *impf.* **1.** to be careful, take care. **2.** (*+g. or +inf.*) to beware (of), **~еги́тесь воро́в** beware of pickpockets!; **~еги́тесь перееда́ть!** mind you don't eat too much! **3.** *pass. of* **~е́чь**

бери́лл, а *m.* (*min.*) beryl.

бери́лли|й, я *m.* (*chem.*) beryllium, glucinium.

Бе́рингов|о мо́р|е, ~а ~я *f.* the Bering Sea.

бе́рков|ец, ца *m.* (*obs.*) berkovets (*old Russ. measure of weight, equivalent to 10 poods or 163.8 kg*).

бе́ркут, а *m.* golden eagle.

Берли́н, а *m.* Berlin.

берли́нск|ий *adj.* Berlin; **~ая лазу́рь** Prussian blue.

берло́г|а, и *f.* den, lair.

Берму́дск|ие остров|а́, ~их ~о́в *no sg.* the Bermudas (*islands*), Bermuda.

берму́д|ы, ов *no sg.* Bermuda shorts.

Берн, а *m.* Berne.

бертоле́тов *adj.*: **~а соль** potassium chlorate (*Berthollet's salt*).

бер|у́, ёшь *see* **брать**

берцо́в|ый *adj.* (*anat.*): **больша́я ~ая кость** shin-bone, tibia; **ма́лая ~ая кость** fibula.

бес, а *m.* demon, evil spirit; **рассыпа́ться ме́лким ~́ом** (**пе́ред**+*i.*; *coll.*) to fawn (on), ingratiate o.s. (with).

бесе́д|а, ы *f.* **1.** talk, conversation; **б. по душа́м** heart-to-heart (talk). **2.** discussion; **провести́ ~у** to give a talk; **б. по прочи́танному** discussion of what one has read (*in school, etc.*).

бесе́дк|а, и *f.* summer-house.

бесе́д|овать, ую *impf.* (**с**+*i.*) to talk, converse (with).

бесе́дчик, а *m.* (*coll.*) discussion-leader.

бесён|ок, ка, *pl.* **~я́та, ~я́т** *m.* imp, little devil (*also fig.*).

бе|си́ть, шу́, ~́сишь *impf.* (*of* **вз~**) (*coll.*) to enrage, madden, infuriate.

бе|си́ться, шу́сь, ~́сишься *impf.* (*of* **вз~**) **1.** to go mad (*of animals*). **2.** (*fig.*) to rage, be furious; **с жи́ру б.** (*coll.*) to grow fastidious, fussy; to be too well off.

беска́мерн|ый *adj.*: **~ая ши́на** tubeless tyre.

бескла́ссовый *adj.* classless.

бескозы́рк|а, и *f.* peakless cap; **матро́сская б.** sailor's cap.

бескозы́рный *adj.* (*cards*) without trumps.

бескомпроми́с|сный (~ен, на) *adj.* uncompromising.

бесконе́чно *adv.* infinitely, endlessly; (*coll.*) extremely; **я б. рад ва́шему успе́ху** I am extremely pleased about your success; **б. ма́лый** (*math.*) infinitesimal.

бесконе́чност|ь, и *f.* endlessness; infinity; **до ~и** endlessly.

бесконе́ч|ный (~ен, на) *adj.* endless; infinite; interminable; **~ная дробь** (*math.*) recurring decimal; **б. винт** (*tech.*) endless screw; **б. ряд** (*math.*) infinite series.

бесконтро́л|ьный (~ен, ~ьна) *adj.* uncontrolled; unchecked.

беско́рмиц|а, ы *f.* fodder shortage.

бескоро́вный *adj.* not possessing a cow.

бескоры́сти|е, я *nt.* disinterestedness.

бескоры́ст|ный (~ен, ~на) *adj.* disinterested; unselfish.

беско́стный *adj.* boneless.

бескофеи́нов|ый *adj.*: **б. ко́фе** decaffeinated coffee.

бескра́йний *adj.* boundless.

бескро́в|ный[1] **(~ен, ~на)** *adj.* **1.** anaemic, pale. **2.** bloodless; **~ная револю́ция** bloodless revolution.

бескро́вный[2] *adj.* (*obs.*) roofless; homeless.

бескры́лый *adj.* wingless; (*fig.*) uninspired, pedestrian, lacklustre.

бескульту́рь|е, я *nt.* lack of culture.

бесnова́ни|е, я *nt.* frenzy; raging.

бесnова́тый *adj.* possessed; raging, raving.

бесн|ова́ться, у́юсь *impf.* to be possessed; to rage, rave.

бесо́вский *adj.* devilish, diabolical.

беспа́лубный *adj.* without decks.

беспа́лый *adj.* lacking one *or* more fingers *or* toes.

беспа́мят|ный (~ен, ~на) *adj.* (*coll.*) forgetful.

беспа́мятств|о, а *nt.* **1.** unconsciousness; **впасть в б.** to lose consciousness. **2.** frenzy, delirium; **быть в ~е** to be beside o.s.; to be delirious.

беспардо́нный *adj.* shameless, brazen.

беспарти́йн|ый *adj.* non-party; *as n.* **б., ~ого** *m.*, *and* **~ая, ~ой** *f.* non-party man, woman.

беспа́спортный *adj.* not having a passport.

беспате́нтный *adj.* unlicensed.

беспербо́йный *adj.* uninterrupted; regular.

беспереса́дочный *adj.* direct; **б. по́езд** through train.

бесперспекти́в|ный (~ен, ~на) *adj.* having no prospects; hopeless.

беспеча́л|ьный (~ен, ~ьна) *adj.* carefree.

беспе́чност|ь, и *f.* carelessness, unconcern.

беспе́ч|ный (~ен, ~на) *adj.* careless, unconcerned; carefree.

беспило́тный *adj.* unmanned.

беспи́сьменный *adj.* having no written language.

беспла́новост|ь, и *f.* absence of plan.

беспла́новый *adj.* planless.

беспла́тно *adv.* free of charge, gratis.

беспла́т|ный (~ен, ~на) *adj.* free, gratuitous; **б. биле́т** free ticket, complimentary ticket.

бесплацка́ртный *adj.* without reserved seat(s); **б. по́езд** train with unreserved seats only; **б. пассажи́р** passenger travelling without reserving a seat.

беспло́ди|е, я *nt.* sterility, barrenness; infertility.

беспло́дност|ь, и *f.* fruitlessness, futility.

беспло́д|ный (~ен, ~на) *adj.* **1.** sterile, barren; infertile. **2.** (*fig.*) fruitless, futile.

беспло́тный *adj.* (*relig.*; *poet.*) incorporeal.

бесповоро́тност|ь, и *f.* irrevocability, finality.

бесповоро́тн|ый (~а, ~о) *adj.* irrevocable, final; **~ое реше́ние** final decision.

бесподо́б|ный (~ен, ~на) *adj.* matchless; incomparable; superlative; **~но!** *int.* superb!; splendid!

беспозвоно́чн|ый *adj.* (*zool.*) invertebrate; *as n.* **~ое, ~ого** *nt.* invertebrate.

беспоко́|ить, ю, ишь *impf.* **1.** (*pf.* **о~**) to disturb, bother. **2.** (*pf.* **по~**) to disturb, worry.

беспоко́|иться, юсь, ишься *impf.* **1.** (*pf.* **о~**) (**о**+*p.*) to worry, be worried *or* anxious (about). **2.** (*pf.* **по~**) (*coll.*) to worry, put o.s. out; **не ~йтесь!** don't trouble!; don't worry!

беспоко́|йный (~ен, ~йна) *adj.* **1.** agitated; anxious; uneasy; **~йное состря́ние** a state of agitation. **2.** disturbing; restless, fidgety; **б. ребёнок** fidgety child.

беспоко́йств|о, а *nt.* **1.** agitation; anxiety; unrest; **с ~ом** anxiously. **2.** disturbance; **причини́ть б.** (*+d.*) to disturb.

бесполе́з|ный (~ен, ~на) *adj.* useless.

беспо́л|ый *adj.* sexless; **~ое размноже́ние** asexual reproduction.

беспоме́стный *adj.* (*hist.*) not possessing an estate.

беспо́мощ|ный (~ен, ~на) *adj.* helpless, powerless; (*fig.*) feeble; **б. ум** feeble intellect.

беспоро́д|ный (~ен, ~на) *adj.* not thoroughbred, not pedigree; **~ная соба́ка** mongrel.

беспоро́ч|ный (~ен, ~на) *adj.* blameless, irreproachable, immaculate; **~ное зача́тие** (*relig.*) the Immaculate Conception; **~ная слу́жба** irreproachable service.

беспоря́д|ок, ка *m.* disorder, confusion (*pl. only*; *pol.*) disturbances, riots.

беспоря́доч|ный (~ен, ~на) *adj.* disorderly; untidy.

беспоса́дочный *adj.*: **б. перелёт** non-stop flight.

беспо́чвен|ный (~, ~на) *adj.* groundless; unsound.

беспо́шлинн|ый *adj.* (*econ.*) duty-free; **~ая торго́вля** free trade.

беспоща́д|ный (~ен, ~на) *adj.* merciless, relentless.

беспра́ви|е, я *nt.* **1.** lawlessness; arbitrariness. **2.** lack of rights.
беспра́вност|ь, и *f.* = **беспра́вие 2.**
беспра́в|ный (~ен, ~на) *adj.* without rights; deprived of rights.
беспредвзя́тый *adj.* unbiased, impartial.
беспреде́л, а *m.* (*coll.*) chaos, mayhem; **ценово́й б.** outrageous prices.
беспреде́л|ьный (~ен, ~ьна) *adj.* boundless, infinite.
беспредме́тник, а *m.* supporter of abstract art.
беспредме́тн|ый *adj.* **1.** aimless. **2.:** **~ая живопись** abstract painting.
беспрекосло́в|ный (~ен, ~на) *adj.* unquestioning, absolute; **он тре́бует ~ного повинове́ния** he demands unquestioning obedience.
беспрепя́тствен|ный (~, ~на) *adj.* free, clear, unimpeded.
беспреры́вно *adv.* continuously; uninterruptedly; **дождь шёл б. в тече́ние трёх дней** it rained for three days on end.
беспреры́в|ный (~ен, ~на) *adj.* continuous; uninterrupted.
беспреста́нно *adv.* continually, incessantly.
беспреста́н|ный (~ен, ~на) *adj.* continual; incessant.
беспрецеде́нт|ный (~ен,~на) *adj.* unprecedented.
беспри́был|ьный (~ен, ~ьна) *adj.* non-profit-making.
беспривє́т|ный (~ен, ~на) *adj.* unwelcoming.
бесприда́нниц|а, ы *f.* girl without dowry.
беспризо́рник, а *m.* waif, street urchin.
беспризо́рн|ый *adj.* **1.** neglected. **2.** stray, homeless; *as n.* **б., ~ого** *m.* waif, street urchin.
бесприме́р|ный (~ен, ~на) *adj.* unexampled, unparalleled; **~ная хра́брость** unexampled bravery.
беспри́месный *adj.* unalloyed.
беспринци́п|ный (~ен, ~на) *adj.* unscrupulous, unprincipled.
беспристра́сти|е, я *nt.* impartiality.
беспристра́стност|ь, и *f.* impartiality.
беспристра́ст|ный (~ен, ~на) *adj.* impartial, unbias(s)ed.
беспричи́нн|ый *adj.* causeless; pointless.
бесприю́т|ный (~ен, ~на) *adj.* homeless; not affording shelter; **~ная жизнь** life spent in roaming.
беспробу́д|ный (~ен, ~на) *adj.* **1.** deep, heavy (*of sleep*); **спать ~ным сном** to be in a deep sleep. **2.** unrestrained (*of drunkenness*).
беспроводно́й *adj.*: **б. телефо́н** cordless telephone.
беспро́волочный *adj.* wireless; **б. телегра́ф** wireless.
беспро́игрышн|ый *adj.* safe; without risk of loss; **~ая лотере́я** lottery in which no competitor loses.
беспросве́т|ный (~ен, ~на) *adj.* **1.** pitch-dark; **~ная тьма** thick darkness. **2.** (*fig.*) cheerless, hopeless; **~ное го́ре** unrelieved misery.
беспроце́нтный *adj.* (*fin.*) interest-free.
беспу́тиц|а, ы *f.* **1.** absence of roads. **2.** bad condition of roads. **3.** season when roads are impassable.
беспу́тник, а *m.* (*coll.*) debauchee.
беспу́тнича|ть, ю *impf.* (*coll.*) to lead a dissipated life, be a debauchee.
беспу́т|ный (~ен, ~на) *adj.* dissipated, dissolute.
беспу́тств|о, а *nt.* dissipation, debauchery.
Бессара́би|я, и *f.* Bessarabia.
бессвя́зност|ь, и *f.* incoherence.
бессвя́з|ный (~ен, ~на) *adj.* incoherent.
бессеме́йный *adj.* having no family.
бессе́менн|ый *adj.* **1.** (*obs.*) seedless. **2.** (*relig.*): **~ое зача́тие** the Virgin Birth (of Christ).
бессеменодо́льный *adj.* (*bot.*) acotyledonous.
бессемерова́ни|е, я *nt.* (*tech.*) Bessemer process.
бессеме́ровский *adj.* (*tech.*) Bessemer.
бессемя́нный *adj.* seedless.
бессерде́ч|ие, ия *nt.* = **~ность**
бессерде́чност|ь, и *f.* heartlessness; callousness.
бессерде́ч|ный (~ен, ~на) *adj.* heartless; callous.
бесси́ли|е, я *nt.* impotence; debility; (*fig.*) feebleness.
бесси́л|ьный (~ен, ~ьна) *adj.* impotent, powerless.
бессисте́мност|ь, и *f.* unsystematic character, lack of system.
бессисте́м|ный (~ен, ~на) *adj.* unsystematic.
бессла́ви|е, я *nt.* infamy.
бессла́в|ить, лю, ишь *impf.* (*of* **о~**) to defame.
бессла́в|ный (~ен, ~на) *adj.* infamous; inglorious.
бессле́дно *adv.* without leaving a trace; completely, utterly.
бессле́дн|ый *adj.* without leaving a trace; **~ое исчезнове́ние** complete disappearance.
бессслове́с|ный (~ен, ~на) *adj.* dumb, speechless; (*fig.*) silent; **~ные живо́тные** dumb animals; (*theatr.*) **~ная роль** non-speaking part.
бессме́н|ный (~ен, ~на) *adj.* permanent; continuous.
бессме́рти|е, я *nt.* immortality.
бессме́ртник, а *m.* (*bot.*) immortelle.
бессме́рт|ный (~ен, ~на) *adj.* immortal; undying.
бессмы́слен|ный (~, ~на) *adj.* senseless; foolish; meaningless, nonsensical; **б. посту́пок** senseless act; **~ная фра́за** meaningless sentence.
бессмы́слиц|а, ы *f.* nonsense.
бессне́жный *adj.* snowless.
бессо́вест|ный (~ен, ~на) *adj.* **1.** unscrupulous, dishonest. **2.** shameless, brazen.
бессодержа́тел|ьный (~ен, ~ьна) *adj.* empty; tame; dull.
бессозна́тел|ьный (~ен, ~ьна) *adj.* **1.** unconscious. **2.** involuntary.
бессо́нниц|а, ы *f.* insomnia, sleeplessness.
бессо́нный *adj.* sleepless.
бесспо́рно *adv.* indisputably; undoubtedly.
бесспо́р|ный (~ен, ~на) *adj.* indisputable, incontrovertible.
бессре́бреник, а *m.* disinterested pers.
бессро́чн|ый *adj.* without time-limit; **б. о́тпуск** indefinite leave; **~ое тюре́мное заключе́ние** imprisonment for life, life term.
бесстра́сти|е, я *nt.* **1.** impassiveness, impassivity. **2.** impartiality.
бесстра́ст|ный (~ен, ~на) *adj.* **1.** impassive. **2.** impartial.
бесстра́ши|е, я *nt.* fearlessness, intrepidity.
бесстра́ш|ный (~ен, ~на) *adj.* fearless, intrepid.
бессты́дник, а *m.* shameless pers.
бессты́дниц|а, ы *f.* shameless woman, hussy.
бессты́д|ный (~ен, ~на) *adj.* shameless.
бессты́дств|о, а *nt.* shamelessness.
бессты́жий *adj.* (*coll.*) shameless, brazen.
бессу́дный *adj.* arbitrary, summary.
бессчётный *adj.* innumerable.
беста́ктност|ь, и *f.* **1.** tactlessness. **2.** tactless action.
беста́кт|ный (~ен, ~на) *adj.* tactless.
бестала́н|ный (~ен, ~на) *adj.* **1.** untalented. **2.** (*folk poet.*) ill-starred, luckless; **~ная голо́вушка** poor devil.
бестеле́с|ный (~ен, ~на) *adj.* incorporeal.
бе́сти|я, и *f.* (*coll.*) rogue; **то́нкая б.** sly rogue.
бестова́рь|е, я *nt.* shortage of goods.
бестолко́вщин|а, ы *f.* (*coll.*) disorder, confusion.
бестолко́в|ый (~, ~а) *adj.* **1.** slow-witted, muddle-headed. **2.** disconnected, incoherent.
бе́столоч|ь, и *f.* (*coll.*) **1.** confusion. **2.** muddle-headed pers. (*also collect.*).
бестре́пет|ный (~ен, ~на) *adj.* (*poet.*) dauntless.
бестсе́ллер, а *m.* best-seller (*book*).
бесту́жевск|ий *adj.*: **~ие ку́рсы** (*hist.*) 'Bestuzhev courses' (*higher education courses for women established in St. Petersburg in 1879; named after the first director, K.N. Bestuzhev-Ryumin*).
бесту́жевк|а, и *f.* (*coll.*) member of 'Bestuzhev courses'.
бесфо́рмен|ный (~, ~на) *adj.* shapeless, formless.
бесхара́ктер|ный (~ен, ~на) *adj.* lacking in character; weak-willed.
бесхво́ст|ый *adj.* tailless; *as n.* **~ое, ~ого** *nt.* (*zool.*) ecaudate.
бесхи́трост|ный (~ен, ~на) *adj.* artless; unsophisticated; ingenuous.
бесхле́биц|а, ы *f.* (*coll.*) corn shortage; bread shortage.
бесхо́зн|ый *adj.* ownerless; **~ое иму́щество** property in abeyance.
бесхозя́йный *adj.* (*obs.*) ownerless.

бесхозя́йственност|ь, и *f.* thriftlessness; bad management.
бесхозя́йствен|ный (~, ~на) *adj.* thriftless; improvident.
бесхребе́т|ный (~ен, ~на) *adj.* (*fig.*) spineless, weak.
бесцве́т|ный (~ен, ~на) *adj.* colourless; (*fig.*) colourless, insipid.
бесце́л|ьный (~ен, ~ьна) *adj.* aimless; idle; **~ьная болтовня́** idle chat.
бесце́н|ный (~ен, ~на) *adj.* **1.** priceless, invaluable. **2.** (*obs.*) valueless.
бесце́н|ок, ка *m.* (*coll.*) *only in phr.* **за б.** very cheaply; **купи́ть за б.** to buy for a song.
бесцеремо́н|ный (~ен, ~на) *adj.* unceremonious; familiar; cavalier.
бесчелове́чност|ь, и *f.* inhumanity.
бесчелове́ч|ный (~ен, ~на) *adj.* inhuman.
бесче́|стить, щу, стишь *impf.* (*of* **о~**) to dishonour, disgrace.
бесче́ст|ный (~ен, ~на) *adj.* dishonourable; disgraceful.
бесче́сть|е, я *nt.* dishonour; disgrace.
бесчи́нный *adj.* (*obs.*) unseemly, scandalous.
бесчи́нств|о, а *nt.* excess; enormity.
бесчи́нств|овать, ую *impf.* to commit excesses.
бесчи́сленност|ь *f.* innumerable quantity.
бесчи́слен|ный (~, ~на) *adj.* innumerable.
бесчу́вственност|ь, и *f.* **1.** insensibility. **2.** insensitivity.
бесчу́вствен|ный (~, ~на) *adj.* **1.** insensible. **2.** insensitive, unfeeling.
бесчу́встви|е, я *nt.* **1.** loss of consciousness; **пья́ный до ~я** dead drunk; **бить до ~я** to knock insensible. **2.** insensitivity.
бесшаба́ш|ный (~ен, ~на) *adj.* (*coll.*) reckless.
бесшве́йный *adj.*: **б. переплёт** perfect binding.
бесшёрстный *adj.* hairless, woolless.
бесшёрст|ый = ~ный
бесшнурово́й = беспроводно́й
бесшо́вный *adj.* (*tech.*) seamless; jointless.
бесшоссе́йный *adj.* unsurfaced.
бесшу́м|ный (~ен, ~на) *adj.* noiseless.
бе́те́л|ь, я *m.* betel.
бето́н, а *m.* (*tech.*) concrete.
бетони́ровани|е, я *nt.* (*tech.*) concreting.
бетони́р|овать, ую *impf.* (*tech.*) to concrete.
бето́нный *adj.* (*tech.*) concrete.
бетоново́з, а *m.* concrete-delivery truck.
бетономеша́лк|а, и *f.* (*tech.*) concrete mixer.
бетоносмеси́тел|ь, я *m.* = **бетономеша́лка**
бето́нщик, а *m.* concrete worker.
бефстро́ганов *m. indecl.* (*cul.*) beef Stroganoff.
бехевиори́зм, а *m.* behaviourism.
бечев|а́, ы́ *no pl.*, *f.* tow-rope.
бечёвк|а, и *f.* string, twine.
бечевни́к, а́ *m.* tow-path.
бечев|о́й *adj. of* **~а́**; **~а́я тя́га** towing; *as n.* **~а́я, ~о́й** *f.* tow-path.
бешаме́л|ь, и *f.* (*cul.*) Bechamel sauce.
бе́шенств|о, а *nt.* **1.** (*med.*) hydrophobia; rabies. **2.** fury, rage; **довести́ до ~а** to enrage. **3.: б. ма́тки** (*med.*) nymphomania.
бе́шен|ый *adj.* **1.** rabid, mad; **~ая соба́ка** mad dog. **2.** furious; violent; **~ая ско́рость** furious pace; **~ые це́ны** (*coll.*) exorbitant prices. **3.: ~ые де́ньги** (*obs.*) easy money. **4.: б. огуре́ц** 'squirting' cucumber (*Ecballium elaterium*).
бешме́т, а *m.* beshmet (*kind of quilted coat*).
бз|деть, (д)жу, дишь *impf.* (*of* **набзде́ть**) (*vulg.*) **1.** to fart (*silently*). **2.** to bullshit. **3.** to be shit scared.
бздун, а́ *m.* (*vulg.*) **1.** farter, fart-arse. **2.** bullshitter. **3.** chicken (= *coward*).
бзик, а *m.* (*coll.*) quirk, oddity; **он с ~ом** he's loopy.
бзикану́тый *adj.* (*sl.*) loopy.
бзико́ванный = бзикану́тый
биатло́н, а *m.* biathlon.
биатлони́ст, а *m.* biathlete, biathlon competitor.
бибабо́ *nt. indecl.* glove puppet.
бибиси́шник, а *m.* (*coll.*) BBC announcer.
библеи́зм, а *m.* Biblical expression.
библе́йский *adj.* biblical.
библио́граф, а *m.* bibliographer.
библиографи́ческий *adj.* bibliographical.
библиогра́фи|я, и *f.* bibliography.
библиоте́к|а, и *f.* (*in var. senses*) library; **б. с вы́дачей книг на́ дом** lending-library; **б.-чита́льня** reading-room.
библиоте́кар|ша, ши *f. of* **~ь**
библиоте́кар|ь, я *m.* librarian.
библиотекове́дени|е, я *nt.* librarianship; library science.
библиоте́|чный *adj. of* **~ка**
библиофи́л, а *m.* bibliophile.
би́бли|я, и *f.* bible; the Bible.
би́бльдрук, а *m.* India paper.
бива́к, а *m.* (*mil.*) bivouac, camp; **стоя́ть ~ом, на ~ах** to bivouac, camp.
бива́|чный *adj. of* **~к**; **б. пункт** (*mil.*) bivouacking site, camping site.
би́в|ень, ня, *pl.* **~ни, ней** *m.* tusk.
бивуа́к = бива́к
бигл|ь, я *m.* beagle (*dog*).
бигуд|и́, е́й *no sg.* (*also indecl.*) (hair) curlers.
биде́ *nt. indecl.* bidet.
бидо́н, а *m.* can, churn; **б. для молока́** milk-can.
бие́ни|е, я *nt.* beating; throb; **б. се́рдца** heartbeat; **б. пу́льса** pulse.
бижуте́ри|я, и *f.* costume jewellery.
биза́н|ь, и *f.* (*naut.*) mizzen; **б.-ма́чта** mizzen-mast.
би́знес, а *m.* business; **рекла́мный б.** advertising.
бизнесме́н, а *m.* businessman.
бизнесме́нк|а, и *f.* (*coll.*) businesswoman.
бизо́н, а *m.* (*zool.*) bison.
бикарбона́т, а *m.* (*chem.*) bicarbonate.
бики́ни *nt. indecl.* bikini.
би́кс|а, ы *f.* (*sl.*) tart.
бикфо́рдов *adj.*: **б. шнур** (*tech.*) Bickford (safety) fuse.
билабиа́льный *adj.* (*ling.*) bilabial.
биле́т, а *m.* ticket; card; **входно́й б.** entrance ticket, permit; **еди́ный б.** rover ticket; **жёлтый б.** (*obs.*) prostitute's passport; **креди́тный б.** banknote; **обра́тный б.** return ticket; **отпускно́й б.** (*mil.*) leave-pass; **парти́йный б.** Party-membership card; **почётный б.** complimentary ticket; **пригласи́тельный б.** invitation card; **экзамена-цио́нный б.** examination question(-paper) (*at oral examination*).
билетёр, а *m.* ticket-collector.
билетёр|ша, ши *f. of* **~**; (*in cinema, etc.*) usherette.
били́нгв, а *m.* bilingual.
билингви́зм, а *m.* bilingualism.
биллио́н, а *m.* billion (= *a 1000 millions*).
билло́н, а *no pl.*, *m.* (*tech.*) billon (*debased silver*).
билл|ь, я *m.* (*pol.*) bill.
би́л|о, а *nt.* **1.** (*tech.*) beater. **2.** gong.
бильбоке́ *nt. indecl.* cup and ball (*toy*).
бильдаппара́т, а *m.* (*tech.*) telephote, photograph transmitter.
билья́рд, а *m.* **1.** billiard-table. **2.** billiards; **игра́ть в б.** to play billiards; **па́ртия в б., на ~е** game of billiards.
бильярди́ст, а *m.* billiards player.
билья́рд|ный *adj. of* **~**; **б. шар** billiard ball; *as n.* **~ная, ~ной** *f.* billiard-room.
биметалли́зм, а *m.* (*econ.*) bimetallism.
бимс, а *m.* (*naut.*) beam, transom.
бино́кл|ь, я *m.* binoculars; **полево́й б.** field glasses; **театра́льный б.** opera glasses.
бинокуля́рный *adj.* binocular.
бино́м, а *m.* (*math.*) binomial; **б. Ньюто́на** binomial theorem.
бинт, а́ *m.* bandage.
бинт|ова́ть, у́ю *impf.* to bandage.
бинто́вк|а, и *f.* bandaging.
био... *comb. form* bio-.
био́граф, а *m.* **1.** biographer. **2.** (*obs.*) cinematograph.
биографи́ческий *adj.* biographical.
биогра́фи|я, и *f.* biography; life story; curriculum vitae; CV.
биоинжене́р|ия, ии *f.* bioengineering.

биокре́м, а *m.* skin cream.
био́лог, а *m.* biologist.
биологи́ческий *adj.* biological.
биоло́ги|я, и *f.* biology.
биомедици́нский *adj.* biomedical.
биопротези́ровани|е, я *nt.* orthotics.
биоресу́рс|ы, ов *no sg.* bioresources.
биори́тм|ы, ов *no sg.* biorhythms.
биоста́нци|я, и *f.* biological research station.
биотехноло́ги|я, и *f.* biotechnology.
биосфе́р|а, ы *f.* biosphere.
биохими́ческий *adj.* biochemical.
биохи́ми|я, и *f.* biochemistry.
биоци́д, а *m.* biocide.
бипла́н, а *m.* biplane.
биполя́рност|ь, и *f.* (*phys.*) bipolarity.
биполя́рный *adj.* (*phys.*) bipolar.
би́рж|а, и *f.* **1.** exchange; **фо́ндовая б.** stock-exchange; **чёрная б.** black market (*in currency*); **б. труда́** labour exchange. **2.: изво́зчичья б.** (*obs.*) cabstand, cab-rank.
биржеви́к, а́ *m.* **1.** stockbroker. **2.** (*obs.*) cabby.
бирж|ево́й *adj. of* **∼а; б. ма́клер** stockbroker; **∼ева́я сде́лка** stock-exchange deal.
би́рк|а, и *f.* **1.** (*obs.*) tally (*notched stick*) **2.** name-plate; label-tag.
Би́рм|а, ы *f.* Burma.
бирма́н|ец, ца *m.* Burmese, Burman.
бирма́н|ка, ки *f. of* **∼ец**
бирма́нский *adj.* Burmese.
бирюз|а́, ы́ *no pl., f.* turquoise.
бирюзо́вый *adj.* turquoise.
бирю́к, а́ *m.* (*dial.*) lone wolf; (*fig.*) lone wolf, unsociable pers.; **смотре́ть ∼о́м** (*coll.*) to look gloomy, morose.
бирю́льк|а, и *f.* spillikin; **игра́ть в ∼и** to play at spillikins; (*fig.*) to occupy o.s. with trifles.
бирю́ч, а́ *m.* (*hist.*) crier, herald.
бис *int.* encore; **сыгра́ть, спеть на б.** to play, sing an encore.
бисексуа́льный *adj.* bisexual.
би́сер, а *no pl., m.* beads; **мета́ть б. пе́ред сви́ньями** (*fig.*) to cast pearls before swine.
би́серин|а, ы *f.* bead.
би́сер|ный *adj. of* **∼**; (*fig.*) minute; **б. по́черк** minute handwriting.
биси́р|овать, ую *impf. and pf.* to repeat, give an encore.
Биска́йск|ий зали́в, ∼ого ∼а *m.* the Bay of Biscay.
бискви́т, а *m.* **1.** sponge-cake. **2.** (*tech.*) biscuit (*unglazed pottery*).
бискви́т|ный *adj. of* **∼; б. руле́т** Swiss roll.
биссектри́с|а, ы *f.* (*math.*) bisector.
бисульфа́т, а *m.* (*chem.*) bisulphate.
бит, а *m.* (*comput.*) bit.
бит|а́, ы́ *f.* (*sport*) bat.
би́тв|а, ы *f.* battle; **б. за Атланти́ческий океа́н, на Ма́рне, под Полта́вой, при Трафа́льгаре** Battle of the Atlantic, of the Marne, of Poltava, of Trafalgar.
битко́м *adv. only in phr.* **б. наби́ть** (*coll.*) to pack, crowd; **авто́бус был б. наби́т** the bus was packed, crammed.
битло́вк|а, и *f.* polo-, roll- *or* turtle-neck (sweater).
битло́вый *adj.* Beatles.
битлома́ни|я, и *f.* Beatlemania.
би́тник, а *m.* beatnik.
би́тниковский *adj.* bohemian; hippie, hippie-like.
би́тничеств|о, а *nt.* bohemianism.
би́товый *adj.* (*comput.*) bit-mapped.
бит|о́к, ка́ *m.* (*round*) rissole.
биту́м, а *m.* (*min.*) bitumen.
битумино́зный *adj.* (*min.*) bituminous.
би́т|ый (∼, ∼а) *p.p.p. of* **∼ь** *and adj.*: **∼ая посу́да два живёт** (*prov.*) cracked pots last the longest; **б. час** (*coll.*) a full hour, a good hour; **∼ое стекло́** broken glass.
бить, бью, бьёшь *impf.* **1.** (*pf.* **по∼**) to beat (*a pers., an animal, etc.*). **2.** (*pf.* **по∼**) to beat, defeat (*in war, sports or games*); (*impf. only*) **б. ка́рту** (*cards*) to cover a card. **3.** (**уда́рить** *used in place of pf.*) to strike, hit; **б. кнуто́м** to whip, flog; **б. себя́ в грудь** to thump one's chest; **б. в лицо́** to strike, hit in the face (*also fig.*). **4.** (*impf. only*) to strike, hit; to beat, thump, bang; **б. в бараба́н** to beat a drum; **б. в ладо́ши** to clap one's hands; **б. по столу́** to bang on the table; **б. за́дом** to kick (*of a horse*); **б. чело́м** (*i*) (*hist.*) to present a petition, (*ii*) (*+d.*) to take off one's hat (to) (*fig.*). **5.** (*impf. only*) to kill, slaughter (*animals*); **б. гарпуно́м** to harpoon; **б. ры́бу острого́й** to spear fish. **6.** (*pf.* **с∼**) **б. ма́сло** to churn butter: **7.** (*impf. only*) to break, smash (*crockery, etc.*). **8.** (**уда́рить** *used in place of pf.*) to combat, fight (against), wage war (on); to damage, injure; **б. по хулига́нству** to combat hooliganism; **б. по чьему́-н. самолю́бию** to wound s.o.'s vanity; **б. по карма́ну** to cost one a pretty penny. **9.** (*pf.* **про∼**) to strike, sound; **б. (в) наба́т** to sound the alarm; **б. отбо́й** to beat a retreat (*also fig.*); **часы́ бьют пять** the clock is striking five; (*impers.*): **бьёт пять** it is striking five. **10.** (*impf. only*) to spurt, gush; **б. ключо́м** to gush out, well up; (*fig.*) to be in full swing. **11.** (*impf. only*) to shoot, fire; (*with fire-arms; also fig.*) to hit; to have a range (of); **б. из духово́го ружья́** to fire an air-gun; **б. в цель** to hit the target (*also fig.*); **б. наверняка́** (*fig.*) to take no chances; **б. на́ два киломе́тра** to have a range of two kilometres. **12.** (*impf. only*; **на**+*a.*) to strive (for, after); **б. на эффе́кт** to strive after effect.
бить|ё, я́ *nt.* (*coll.*) beating, flogging; smashing.
би́ться, бьюсь, бьёшься *impf.* **1.** (**с**+*i.*) to fight (with, against); **б. на поеди́нке** to fight a duel. **2.** (*of the heart*) to beat; **се́рдце его́ переста́ло б.** his heart stopped beating. **3.** (**о**+*a.*) to knock (against), hit (against), strike; **б. голово́й об стену** to bang one's head against a brick wall; **б., как ры́ба об лёд** to struggle desperately. **4.** to writhe, struggle; **б. в исте́рике** to writhe in hysterics. **5.** (**над**+*i.*; *fig.*) to struggle (with), exercise o.s. (over); **б. над зада́чей** to rack one's brains over a problem; **как бы он ни би́лся** however hard he tried. **6.** (*of crockery, etc.*) to break, smash; **легко́ б.** to be very fragile. **7.: б. об закла́д** to bet, wager.
битю́г, а́ *m.* bityug (*Russ. breed of cart-horse*); (*fig.*) strong man; **он настоя́щий б.** he is strong as a horse.
бифурка́ци|я, и *f.* bifurcation.
бифште́кс, а *m.* beefsteak.
бифште́ксн|ая, ой *f.* steakhouse.
би́цепс, а *m.* (*anat.*) biceps.
бич, а́ *m.* whip, lash; (*fig.*) scourge.
бичева́ = бечева́
бичева́ние, я *nt.* flogging; flagellation.
бич|ева́ть, у́ю *impf.* to flog; (*fig.*) to lash, castigate.
бичёвка = бечёвка
бичу́ющ|ий *adj.*: **∼ая сати́ра** scathing satire.
бишь *particle* (*expr. effort to recall name, etc.; coll.*) now (*or not translated*); **как б. его́ зову́т?** what is his name?; what was the name now?; **то б.** that is to say.
бла́г|о^1, а *nt.* good, the good; blessing; **о́бщее б.** the common weal; **жела́ю вам всех благ!** I wish you every happiness; **всех благ!** (*coll.*) all the best! **ни за каки́е ∼а** not for the world.
бла́го^2 *conj.* (*coll.*) since; seeing that; **скажи́те ему́ сейча́с, б. он здесь** tell him now since he is here.
благове́рн|ый *now used only facetiously as n.*; **б., ∼ого** *m.* husband; **∼ая, ∼ой** *f.* wife.
бла́говест, а *m.* ringing of church bell(s).
бла́гове|стить, щу, стишь *impf.* **1.** (*pf.* **от∼**) to ring for church. **2.** (*pf.* **раз∼**) (*coll., iron.*) to publish, spread news.
Благове́щени|е, я *nt.* (*eccl.*) the Annunciation.
благове́щен|ский *adj. of* **∼ие**
благови́д|ный (∼ен, ∼на) *adj.* **1.** (*obs.*) comely. **2.** specious, plausible; **б. предло́г** specious excuse.
благоволе́ни|е, я *nt.* goodwill, kindness; favour; **по́льзоваться чьим-н. ∼ем** to be in favour with s.o.
благовол|и́ть, ю́, и́шь *impf.* (**к**+*d.*) to be favourably disposed (toward), favour; **∼и́те** (*+inf.*) have the kindness (to); **∼и́те отве́тить на э́то письмо́** kindly answer this letter.
благово́ни|е, я *nt.* fragrance, aroma.
благово́нный *adj.* fragrant.
благовоспи́танност|ь, и *f.* good manners; good breeding.

благовоспи́тан|ный (~, ~на) *adj.* well-mannered; well brought up.

благовре́мени|е, я *nt. only in phr.* **во ~и** (*obs.*) opportunely.

благовре́менный *adj.* (*obs.*) timely.

благоглу́пост|ь, и *f.* pompous triviality.

благогове́|йный (~ен, ~йна) *adj.* reverential.

благогове́ни|е, я *nt.* reverence; veneration.

благогове́|ть, ю *impf.* (**пе́ред**+*i.*) to have a reverential attitude (towards).

благодар|и́ть, ю́, и́шь *impf.* (*of* **по~**) to thank; **~ю вас (за**+*a.*) thank you (for).

благода́рност|ь, и *f.* **1.** gratitude; **не сто́ит ~и** don't mention it. **2.** (*usu. pl.*) thanks, acknowledgement of thanks. **3.** (*coll.*) bribe. **4.** (*mil.*) citation, commendation.

благода́р|ный (~ен, ~на) *adj.* **1.** grateful. **2.** rewarding; worthwhile.

благода́рственн|ый *adj.* (*obs.*) expressing thanks; **б. моле́бен** thanksgiving service; **~ое письмо́** letter of thanks.

благода́рств|овать, ую *impf.* (*obs.*) only used in forms **~ую, ~уем, ~уй(те)** thank you.

благодаря́ *prep.*+*d.* thanks to, owing to, because of; **б. тому́, что** owing to the fact that; **б. хоро́шему кли́мату он ско́ро попра́вился** thanks to the good climate he soon recovered.

благода́т|ный (~ен, ~на) *adj.* beneficial; abundant; **б. край** land of plenty.

благода́т|ь, и *f.* **1.** plenty, abundance. **2.** (*relig.*) grace; **Сло́во о зако́не и ~и** (*hist.*) Sermon on Law and Grace.

благоде́нственный *adj.* (*obs.*) prosperous.

благоде́нстви|е, я *nt.* (*obs.*) prosperity.

благоде́нств|овать, ую *impf.* to prosper, flourish.

благоде́тел|ь, я *m.* benefactor.

благоде́тельниц|а, ы *f.* benefactress.

благоде́тел|ьный (~ен, ~ьна) *adj.* beneficial.

благоде́тельств|овать, ую *impf.* (+*d.*) to be a benefactor (to).

благодея́ни|е, я *nt.* good deed; blessing, boon.

благоду́шеств|овать, ую *impf.* (*coll.*) to take life easily.

благоду́ши|е, я *nt.* placidity, equability; good humour.

благоду́ш|ный (~ен, ~на) *adj.* placid, equable; good-humoured.

благожела́тел|ь, я *m.* well-wisher.

благожела́тел|ьный (~ен, ~ьна) *adj.* well-disposed; benevolent; **б. приём** a friendly, cordial reception; **~ьная реце́нзия** favourable review.

благожела́тельност|ь, и *f.* goodwill; benevolence.

благозву́чи|е, я *nt.* euphony.

благозву́чност|ь *f.* euphony.

благозву́ч|ный (~ен, ~на) *adj.* euphonious; melodious.

благ|о́й[1] *adj.* good; **~а́я мысль** a happy thought; **~и́е наме́рения** good intentions; **избра́ть ~у́ю часть** (*oft. iron.*) to choose the better part.

благ|о́й[2] *adj.* (*dial.*) crazy, cranky; **~и́м ма́том** (*coll.*) at the top of one's voice.

благоле́пи|е, я *nt.* (*obs.*) grandeur.

благомы́слящий *adj.* (*obs.*) right-thinking.

благонадёжност|ь, и *f.* reliability, trustworthiness; loyalty; **свиде́тельство о ~и** (*obs.*) certificate of loyalty.

благонадёж|ный (~ен, ~на) *adj.* reliable, trustworthy; loyal.

благонаме́ренност|ь, и *f.* (*obs.*) loyalty.

благонаме́рен|ный (~, ~на) *adj.* (*obs.*) loyal.

благонра́ви|е, я *nt.* good behaviour.

благонра́в|ный (~ен, ~на) *adj.* well-behaved.

благообра́зи|е, я *nt.* good looks; noble appearance.

благообра́з|ный (~ен, ~на) *adj.* good-looking; fine, fine-looking.

благополу́чи|е, я *nt.* well-being; prosperity.

благополу́чно *adv.* well, all right; happily; safely; **всё ко́нчилось б.** everything turned out happily.

благополу́ч|ный (~ен, ~на) *adj.* successful; safe; **б. коне́ц** happy ending.

благоприобре́тени|е, я *nt.* (*obs.*) acquisition.

благоприобре́тенн|ый *adj.* acquired; **всё иму́щество у него́ ~ое, не насле́дственное** his property is entirely acquired, not inherited.

благопристо́йност|ь, и *f.* decency, decorum.

благопристо́|йный (~ен, ~йна) *adj.* (*obs.*) decent, decorous.

благоприя́т|ный (~ен, ~на) *adj.* favourable; propitious; **~ные ве́сти** good news.

благоприя́тств|овать, ую *impf.* (+*d.*) to favour; **наибо́лее ~уемая держа́ва** (*econ.*) most favoured nation.

благоразу́ми|е, я *nt.* prudence; sense.

благоразу́м|ный (~ен, ~на) *adj.* prudent; sensible.

благорасположе́ни|е, я *nt.* (*obs.*) favour.

благорасполо́жен|ный (~, ~на) *adj.* (*obs.*) favourably disposed.

благорастворе́ни|е, я *nt.*: **б. возду́хов** (*eccl.*; *oft. joc.*) healthful climate.

благоро́ди|е, я *nt.* (*obs.*) **ва́ше б.** (*term of address to officers of rank up to and including that of captain*) your Honour.

благоро́д|ный (~ен, ~на) *adj.* noble; **б. газ** noble gas; **б. мета́лл** precious metal; **на ~ном расстоя́нии**at a decent distance.

благоро́дств|о, а *nt.* nobleness; nobility.

благоскло́нност|ь, и *f.* favour; **по́льзоваться чьей-н. ~ью** to be in s.o.'s good graces.

благоскло́н|ный (~ен, ~на) *adj.* favourable, gracious.

благослове́ни|е, я *nt.* (*eccl. and fig.*) blessing; benediction; **подойти́ под б.** (+*d.*) to ask a blessing (from); **с ~я** (+*g.*) with the blessing (of), with the consent (of).

благослове́н|ный (~, ~на) *adj.* (*eccl., poet.*) blessed, blest.

благослов|и́ть, лю́, и́шь *pf.* (*of* **~ля́ть**) **1.** to bless; to give one's blessing (to). **2.** to be grateful to; **б. свою́ судьбу́** to thank one's stars.

благослов|и́ться, лю́сь, и́шься *pf.* (*of* **~ля́ться**) (*coll.*) **1.** (**у**+*g.*) to receive the blessing (of). **2.** to cross o.s.

благослов|ля́ть(ся), ля́ю(сь) *impf. of* **~и́ть(ся)**

благососто́яни|е, я *nt.* well-being, welfare.

благотвори́тел|ь, я *m.* philanthropist.

благотвори́тельност|ь, и *f.* charity, philanthropy.

благотвори́тельный *adj.* charitable, philanthropic; **б. база́р** charity fête; **б. спекта́кль** charity performance.

благотво́р|ный (~ен, ~на) *adj.* beneficial; wholesome, salutary.

благоусмотре́ни|е, я *nt.* (*obs.*) consideration; **отда́ть на чьё-н. б.** to submit for s.o.'s consideration.

благоустра́ива|ть, ю *impf. of* **благоустро́ить**

благоустро́ен|ный (~, ~на) *p.p.p. of* **благоустро́ить** *and adj.* well-equipped, improved; comfortable; **б. дом** house with all modern conveniences.

благоустро́|ить, ю, ишь *pf.* (*of* **благоустра́ивать**) to equip with services and utilities, to improve.

благоустро́йств|о, а *nt.* equipping with services and utilities; improvement; **отде́л ~а** department of public services and utilities; **б. се́льских посёлков** improvement of rural settlements.

благоуха́ни|е, я *nt.* fragrance.

благоуха́нный *adj.* fragrant, sweet-smelling.

благоуха́|ть, ю *impf.* to be fragrant, to smell sweet.

благочести́в|ый (~, ~а) *adj.* pious, devout.

благоче́сти|е, я *nt.* piety.

благочи́ни|е, я *nt.* **1.** (*sg. only*) decency, decorum. **2.** (*eccl.*) deanery.

благочи́нн|ый *adj.* (*obs.*) decent, decorous; *as n.* (*eccl.*) **б., ~ого** *m.* rural dean.

блаже́н|ный (~, ~на) *adj.* blessed, blissful; (*eccl.*) the Blessed; **~ной па́мяти** of blessed memory; **~ное состоя́ние** (*state of*) bliss; *as n.* **б., ~ного** *m.* simple person.

блаже́нств|о, а *nt.* bliss, felicity; **на верху́ ~а** in perfect bliss.

блаже́нств|овать, ую *impf.* to be in a state of bliss.

блаж|и́ть, у́, и́шь *impf.* (*coll.*) to be capricious, to indulge whims, to be eccentric.

блажно́й *adj.* (*coll.*) capricious; eccentric.

блажь, и *f.* (*coll.*) whim, caprice.

бла́йзер = бле́йзер
бла́нжевый *adj.* (*obs.*) flesh-coloured.
бланк, а *m.* form; **анке́тный б.** questionnaire; **фи́рменный б.** letterhead; sheet of headed notepaper; **б. зака́за на кни́гу** order slip for book (*in library*); **запо́лнить б.** to fill in a form.
бла́нк|овый *adj. of* ~; **~овая на́дпись** endorsement.
бланманже́ *nt. indecl.* blancmange.
блат, а *m.* (*sl.*) **1.** crime. **2.** pull, protection, influence; string-pulling, wangling; **получи́ть по ~́у** to get on the quiet, come by through influence. **3.** thieves' cant, thieves' Latin.
блатме́йстер, а *m.* (*sl.*) racketeer.
блатни́к, а́ *m.* (*sl.*) wangler, fixer.
блатн|о́й *adj.* (*sl.*) criminal; **~а́я му́зыка** thieves' cant, thieves' Latin.
блатня́г|а, и *m.* (*sl.*) racketeer.
бл|ева́ть, юю́, юёшь *impf.* (*vulg.*) to puke.
блево́тин|а, ы *f.* (*vulg.*) **1.** vomit. **2.** (*fig.*) filth.
бледне́|ть, ю, ешь *impf.* (*of* **по~**) to grow pale; to pale.
бледноли́ц|ый *adj.* pale; *as n.* **б., ~ого** *m.* paleface.
бле́дност|ь, и *f.* paleness, pallor.
бле́д|ный (~ен, ~на́, ~но) *adj.* pale, pallid; **б. как полотно́** white as a sheet; (*fig.*) colourless, insipid; **~ная не́мочь** (*med.*) chlorosis.
бле́йзер, а *m.* blazer.
блёкл|ый *adj.* faded; wan; **~ая руда́** (*min.*) tetrahedrite.
блёк|нуть, ну, нушь, *past* ~, **~ла** *impf.* (*of* **по~**) to fade; to wither.
блеск, а *m.* **1.** brightness, brilliance, shine; splendour, magnificence, (*as int.*, *sl.*) **б.!** brilliant!; great!; super!; **б. наря́да** finery; **б. остроу́мия** brilliance of wit; **б. со́лнца** brightness of the sun; **во всём ~́е** in all (one's) glory; **прида́ть б.** to add lustre (to); **игра́ть с ~́ом на роя́ле** to play the piano brilliantly. **2.** (*min.*): **желе́зный б.** haematite; **свинцо́вый б.** galena.
блесн|а́, ы́, *pl.* **~́ы** *f.* spoon-bait.
блесн|у́ть, у́, ёшь *pf.* to flash; to shine; **у меня́ ~у́ла мысль** a thought flashed across my mind; **у нас ~у́ла наде́жда** we saw a ray of hope.
бле|сте́ть, щу́, сти́шь *and* **~́щешь** *impf.* to shine (*also fig.*); to glitter; to sparkle; **её глаза́ ~сте́ли ра́достью** her eyes shone with joy; **он не ~́щет умо́м** he is not overblessed with intelligence; he does not shine.
блёстк|а, и *f.* **1.** sparkle; **~и остроу́мия** flashes of wit. **2.** spangle, sequin; **усе́янный ~ами** spangled.
блестя́щ|ий (~, ~а, ~е) *pres. part. of* **блесте́ть** *and adj.* shining, bright; (*fig.*) brilliant; **б. ум** brilliant mind.
блеф, а *m.* bluff; **его́ угро́зы оказа́лись чи́стым ~́ом** his threats turned out to be pure bluff.
блеф|ова́ть, у́ю *impf.* (*coll.*) to bluff.
бле|щу́, ~́щешь *see* **~сте́ть**
бле́яни|е, я *nt.* bleat(ing).
бле́|ять, ю, ешь *impf.* to bleat.
ближа́йш|ий *superl. of* **бли́зкий**; nearest; next; immediate; **в ~ем бу́дущем** in the near future; **б. друг** closest friend; **б. нача́льник** immediate superior; **б. по́вод** (*leg.*, *phil.*) proximate cause, immediate cause; **б. ро́дственник** next of kin; **при ~ем рассмотре́нии** on closer examination; **~ее уча́стие** personal participation.
бли́|же *comp. of* **~зкий, ~зко** nearer; (*fig.*) closer.
ближневосто́чный *adj.* Middle East; Middle Eastern.
бли́жн|ий *adj.* **1.** near; neighbouring. **2.** (*mil.*) short range, close range, close; **б. ого́нь** close (range) fire. **3.** near, close (*of kinship*); *as n.* **б., ~его** *m.* (*fig.*) one's neighbour; **люби́ть ~его** to love one's neighbour.
близ *prep.+g.* near, close to, by.
бли́|зиться, жусь, зишься *impf.* to approach, draw near.
бли́з|кий (~ок, ~ка́, ~ко) *adj.* **1.** near, close; **на ~ком расстоя́нии** at a short distance, a short way off; at close range. **2.** (*of time*) near; imminent; **~кое бу́дущее** the near future. **3.** intimate, close, near; **б. ро́дственник** near relation; **быть ~ким с кем-н.** to be on intimate terms with s.o.; **быть ~ким** (*+d.*) to be dear (to); *as n.* **~кие, ~ких** one's nearest and dearest, one's people. **4.** (**к**) like; similar (to); close (to); **б. нам по ду́ху челове́к** kindred spirit; **~кая ко́пия** faithful copy; **~кая те́ма** congenial topic.
бли́зко *adv.* **1.** (**от**) near close (to); close by. **2.** (*fig.*, *coll.*) nearly, closely; **б. каса́ться** (*+g.*) to concern nearly; **б. познако́миться** (**с**+*i.*) to become closely acquainted (with). **3.** *as pred.* it is not far; **ему́ б. ходи́ть** he has not far to go.
близлежа́щий *adj.* neighbouring, near-by.
близне́ц, а́ *m.* twin (*also triplet, etc.*); **Б~ы́** (*astron.*) Gemini.
близору́к|ий (~, ~а) *adj.* short-sighted (*also fig.*).
близору́кост|ь, и *f.* short-sightedness; (*med.*) myopia (*also fig.*).
бли́зост|ь, и *f.* nearness, closeness, proximity; intimacy.
блик, а *m.* speck, patch of light; light, highlight; **со́лнечный б.** patch of sunlight; **~́и на карти́не** lights in a picture.
блин, а́ *m.* blin (*kind of pancake*); **пе́рвый б. ко́мом** (*prov.*) practice makes perfect; **пло́ский как б.** flat as a pancake.
блинда́ж, а́ *m.* (*mil.*) dug-out.
блиндир|ова́ть, у́ю *impf. and pf.* (*mil.*) to blind.
бли́нн|ая, ой *f.* pancake parlour
бли́н|чатый *adj. of* ~; **б. пиро́г** pancake pie (*made with pancakes, eggs and kasha*).
бли́нчик, а *m.* pancake; fritter.
блиста́тельност|ь, и *f.* brilliance, splendour.
блиста́тел|ьный (~ен, ~ьна) *adj.* brilliant, splendid.
блиста́|ть, ю *impf.* to shine; **б. отсу́тствием** (*iron.*) to be conspicuous by one's absence.
блиц, а *m.* flash (attachment).
блиц(-) *comb. form* lightning …; whirlwind …; **~визи́т** flying visit.
бли́цкриг, а *m.* blitzkrieg.
блок[1]**, а** *m.* (*tech.*) block, pulley, sheave.
блок[2]**, а** *m.* (*pol.*) bloc.
блок[3]**, а** *m.* module; carton; **б. пита́ния** power supply (unit); **па́мятный б.** (*philately*) commemorative sheet.
блока́д|а, ы *f.* blockade; **снять ~у** to raise the blockade; **прорва́ть ~у** to run the blockade.
блока́дник, а *m.* victim of siege of Leningrad (1941–44).
блок-аппара́т, а *m.* (*rail.*) signal-box.
блок-гара́ж, а́ *m.* carport.
блокга́уз, а *m.* (*mil.*) blockhouse.
блоки́р|овать, ую *impf. and pf.* **1.** to blockade. **2.** (*rail.*) to block.
блоки́р|оваться, уюсь *impf. and pf.* **1.** *pass. of* **~ова́ть.** **2.** (**с**+*i.*; *pol.*) to form a bloc with.
блокиро́вк|а, и *f.* (*rail.*) block system, signal system.
блокно́т, а *m.* notebook, notepad; **самостира́ющийся б.** magic slate.
блокпо́ст, а *m.* (*rail.*) blockhouse.
блок-схе́м|а, ы *f.* (*tech.*) flow chart.
блок-уча́ст|ок, ка *m.* (*rail.*) block section.
бло́нд|а, ы *f.* (*usu. pl.*) white silk lace.
блонди́н, а *m.* fair-haired man.
блонди́нист|ый (~, ~а) *adj.* (*coll.*) blonde, fair.
блонди́нк|а, и *f.* blonde, fair woman; **хими́ческая б.** peroxide blonde.
блонди́ночк|а, и *f.* (*coll.*) blonde piece.
блох|а́, и́, *pl.* **~́и, ~а́м** *f.* flea; **иска́ть ~** to nitpick (*fig.*).
бло́чный *adj.* modular.
блошело́вк|а, и *f.* flea collar.
бло|ши́ный *adj. of* **~ха́; б. уку́с** flea-bite.
бло́ш|ки, ек *f.* tiddly-winks; **игра́ть в б.** to play tiddly-winks.
блуд, а *m.* lechery, fornication.
блу|ди́ть[1]**, жу́, ди́шь** *impf.* to lecher, fornicate.
блу|ди́ть[2]**, жу́, ~́дишь** *impf.* (*coll.*) to wander, roam.
блудли́в|ый (~, ~а) *adj.* **1.** lascivious, lecherous. **2.** mischievous, roguish; thievish; **~ как кот, трусли́в как за́яц** thievish as a cat, timid as a hare.
блу́дн|и, ей *no sg.* (*coll.*) **1.** debauchery, lechery. **2.** getting up to mischief.
блудни́к, а́ *m.* (*obs.*) lecher, fornicator.
блудни́ц|а, ы *f.* (*obs.*) **1.** fornicatress, loose woman. **2.** whore.
блу́д|ный *adj. of* ~; **б. сын** (*eccl. and fig.*) prodigal son.
блужда́ни|е, я *nt.* wandering, roaming.
блужда́|ть, ю *impf.* to roam, wander; to rove; **б. по у́лицам**

to roam the streets.
блужда́|ющий *pres. part. of* **~ть; б. взгляд** vague, wandering expression; **~ющие звёзды** (*obs.*) the planets; **б. нерв** (*anat.*) vagus (nerve); **б. огонёк** will-o'-the-wisp; **~ющая по́чка** (*med.*) floating kidney.
блу́з|а, ы *f.* (working) blouse; smock.
блу́зк|а, и *f.* blouse.
блу́зник, а *m.* (*coll., obs.*) labourer.
блу́минг = блю́минг
блю́деч|ко, ка, *pl.* **~ки, ~ек, ~кам** *nt.* saucer; small dish; **б. для варе́нья** jam plate.
блю́д|о, а *nt.* dish (*concr. and abstr.*); **обе́д из трёх ~** three-course dinner; **вку́сное б.** a tasty dish; **как на ~е** (*of visibility of objects situated on even, open ground*) as on the palm of one's hand.
блюдоли́з, а *m.* (*coll.*) lickspittle.
блю|ду́, дёшь *see* **~сти́**
блю́д|це, ца, *g. pl.* **~ец** *nt.* saucer.
блю́минг, а *m.* (*tech.*) blooming (mill).
блю|сти́, ду́, дёшь, *past* **~л, ~ла́** *impf.* (*obs.*) to guard, watch over; to observe; **б. зако́ны** to abide by the law; **б. поря́док** to keep order.
блюсти́тел|ь, я *m.* keeper, guardian; **б. поря́дка** (*coll., iron.*) arm of the law.
блю|ю́, ёшь *see* **блева́ть**
бля́д|ский *adj.* (*vulg.*) *of* **~ь**; fucking.
бляду́н, а *m.* (*vulg.*) skirt chaser.
бляд|ь, и *f.* (*vulg.*) tart, whore (*esp. as term of abuse*); **трёхрублёвая б.** scrubber, cheap tart; *as int.* fuck!
блядю́г|а, и *f.* (*vulg.*) tart, scrubber.
бля́х|а, и *f.* **1.** name plate; number plate. **2.: ме́дная б.** (*as ornament on harness*) horse brass.
боа́ *m. indecl. and nt. indecl.* **1.** *m.* (*zool.*) boa, boa-constrictor. **2.** *nt.* boa; **мехово́е б.** fur boa.
боб, а́ *m.* bean; **ко́нский б.** field bean; **туре́цкий б.** kidney bean, haricot; **~ы́ разводи́ть** (*coll.*) to talk nonsense; **оста́ться, сиде́ть на ~а́х** (*coll.*) to get nothing for one's pains.
боб|ёр, ра́ *m.* **1.** (*sg. only*) beaver (fur). **2.** (*pl. only*) beaver collar.
боби́н|а, ы *f.* (*tech.*) bobbin.
бобк|и́, о́в *no sg.* (*bot.*) bayberries.
бобко́в|ый *adj.* bay; **~ое ма́сло** bay-oil.
боб|о́вый 1. *adj. of* **~; б. стручо́к** bean-pod. **2.** *as n.* **~о́вые, ~о́вых** leguminous plants.
бобр, а́ *m.* beaver; **уби́ть ~а́** to come off well, be in luck (*also iron.*).
бо́брик, а *m.* (*text.*) beaver, castor; **во́лосы ~ом** (*coll.*) French crop; crew cut; **постри́чься ~ом** to have a French crop, crew cut.
бобр|о́вый *adj. of* **~**; beaver; beaver-fur; **~о́вая струя́** (*med.*) castoreum.
бобсле́ист, а *m.* bobsleigher.
бо́бсле|й, я *m.* bobsleigh; bobsleighing.
бобы́л|ь, я́ *m.* **1.** (*obs.*) poor, landless peasant. **2.** solitary, lonely man; **жить ~ём** to lead a solitary, lonely existence.
Бог, а, *voc. sg.* **Бо́же** *m.* God; god; **Бо́же мой!** good God!, my God!; **Б. зна́ет!, Б. весть!** God knows!; **Б. его́ зна́ет!** who knows!; **не дай Б.!** God forbid!; **ра́ди ~а!** for God's sake!; **Б. с ним!** blow it; **с ~ом!** (*obs.*) good luck!; **сла́ва ~у** thank God!; **как Б. на́ душу поло́жит** anyhow, at random; **Б. с ним** let it pass; good luck to him (*iron.*); **обе́дать чем Б. посла́л** to take pot luck; **а он дава́й Б. но́ги** he took to his heels.
богаде́лк|а, и *f.* alms-woman.
богаде́л|ьня, ьни, *g. pl.* **~ен** *f.* almshouse, workhouse.
богар|а́, ы́ *f.* dry-farming (*in Central Asia*); dry-farming land.
бога́р|ный *adj. of* **~а́**
богате́|й, я *m.* (*coll.*) rich man.
богате́|ть, ю, ешь *impf.* (*of* **раз~**) to grow rich.
бога́тств|о, а *nt.* **1.** riches, wealth; **есте́ственные ~а** natural resources. **2.** (*fig.*) richness, wealth.
бога́т|ый (~, ~а) *adj.* (+*i.*) rich (in), wealthy; **страна́, ~ая го́рными проду́ктами** a country rich in mineral products; **~ая расти́тельность** luxuriant vegetation; **б. переплёт** a luxurious binding; **б. о́пыт** wide experience; **чем ~ы, тем и ра́ды** you are welcome to whatever we have; *as n.* **б., ~ого** *m.* rich man.
богаты́р|ский *adj. of* **~ь;** heroic; (*fig.*) powerful, mighty, Herculean; **б. э́пос** the Russ. folk-epic; **~ское сложе́ние** powerful physique; **б. сон** profound sleep.
богаты́рств|о, а *nt.* **1.** heroic qualities. **2.** (*collect.*) bogatyrs.
богаты́р|ь, я́ *m.* **1.** bogatyr (*hero in Russ. folklore*). **2.** (*fig.*) Hercules; hero.
бога́ч, а́ *m.* rich man; **~и́** (*collect.*) the rich.
богдыха́н, а *m.* (*hist.*) Chinese Emperor.
боге́м|а, ы *f.* (*fig.*) Bohemia; Bohemianism.
боге́м|ец, ца *m.* Bohemian.
боге́мистый *adj.* bohemian; arty-farty.
Боге́ми|я, и *f.* Bohemia.
боге́м|ка, ки *f. of* **~ец**
боге́м|ный *adj. of* **~а**
боге́мский *adj.* (*geog.*) Bohemian.
боги́н|я, и *f.* goddess (*also fig.*).
богобо́р|ец, ца *m.* theomachist.
богобо́р|ческий *adj. of* **~ец**
богобоя́знен|ный (~, ~на) *adj.* god-fearing.
богоду́л, а *m.* (*coll.*) boozer, dipso.
богоизбранный *adj.* (*rel.*): **б. наро́д** the Chosen people.
богоиска́тел|ь, я *m.* 'God-seeker'.
богома́з, а *m.* (*coll.*) icon-dauber.
Богома́тер|ь, и *f.* Mother of God; **лу́рдская ~** Our Lady of Lourdes; **Собо́р пари́жской ~и** (the cathedral of) Notre Dame.
богоме́рзкий *adj.* (*obs.*) **1.** impious. **2.** (*coll.*) hideous, repulsive.
богомо́л, а *m.* (*zool.*) praying mantis.
богомо́л|ец, ьца *m.* **1.** devout pers. **2.** pilgrim. **3.** one who prays (for s.o. else).
богомо́л|ка, ки *f.* **1.** (*zool.*) = **~**. **2.** *f. of* **~ец**
богомо́ль|е, я *nt.* pilgrimage.
богомо́л|ьный (~ен, ~ьна) *adj.* religious, devout.
богоно́с|ец, ца *m.* bearer of religious mission; **наро́д-б.** the Chosen People.
богоотсту́пник, а *m.* apostate.
богоотсту́пничеств|о, а *nt.* apostasy.
богоподо́б|ный (~ен, ~на) *adj.* god-like.
богопроти́в|ный (~ен, ~на) *adj.* **1.** (*obs.*) impious. **2.** (*coll.*) hideous, repulsive.
Богоро́диц|а, ы *f.* the Virgin, Our Lady; **сиде́ть ~ей** (*coll., iron.*) to sit with arms folded.
богоро́дич|ен, на *m.* (*eccl.*) hymn in praise of the Virgin.
богосло́в, а *m.* theologian.
богосло́ви|е, я *nt.* theology.
богосло́вский *adj.* theological.
богослуже́|бный *adj. of* **~ние;** liturgical; **~бная кни́га** prayer-book.
богослуже́ни|е, я *nt.* divine service, worship; liturgy.
богоспаса́емый *adj.* blessed (*usu. iron.*).
боготвор|и́ть, ю́, и́шь *impf.* **1.** to worship, idolize. **2.** to deify.
богоуго́д|ный (~ен, ~на) *adj.* (*obs.*) pleasing to God; **~ное заведе́ние** charitable institution.
богоху́льник, а *m.* blasphemer.
богоху́льный *adj.* blasphemous.
богоху́льств|о, а *nt.* blasphemy.
богоху́льств|овать, ую *impf.* to blaspheme.
богочелове́к, а *m.* (*theol.*) 'God-Man', God incarnate.
Богоявле́ни|е, я *nt.* (*eccl.*) Epiphany.
бод, а *m.* (*comput.*) baud.
бода́|ть, ю *impf.* (*of* **за~**) to butt.
бода́|ться, юсь *impf.* to butt (*intrans.*).
Бо́денское о́зеро = Конста́нцкое о́зеро
бодли́вост|ь, и *f.* disposition to butt.
бодли́в|ый (~, ~а) *adj.* given to butting; **~ая коро́ва** a cow that butts.
бодн|у́ть, у́, ёшь *pf.* to butt, give a butt.
бодр|и́ть, ю́, и́шь *impf.* to stimulate, invigorate; **зде́шний во́здух о́чень ~и́т** it is very bracing here.
бодр|и́ться, ю́сь, и́шься *impf.* to try to keep one's spirits

up, try to be cheerful.
бóдрост|ь, и *f.* cheerfulness; courage; good spirits.
бóдрствовани|е, я *nt.* keeping awake; vigilance.
бóдрств|овать, ую *impf.* to be awake, stay awake; to keep awake, keep vigil; **ей пришлóсь б. всю ночь при больнóм** she had to sit up all night with the sick man.
бóдр|ый (~, ~á, ~о) *adj.* cheerful, bright; hale and hearty.
бодр|я́щий *pres. part. of* **~и́ть** *and adj.* invigorating, bracing.
бодя́г|а, и *f.* fresh-water sponge; **разводи́ть ~у** to talk through one's hat.
боеви́к, á *m.* **1.** (*obs.*) member of revolutionary fighting group. **2.** (*coll.*) hit; **б. сезóна** the hit of the season.
боеви́тост|ь, и *f.* fighting spirit.
боев|óй *adj.* **1.** fighting, battle; **~ы́е дéйствия** operations; **б. дух** fighting spirit; **в б. готóвности** prepared for action, cleared for action; **~óе крещéние** baptism of fire; **б. патрóн** live cartridge; **б. поря́док** battle formation; **~ы́е припáсы** (live) ammunition; **~áя пружи́на** mainspring (*of gun*). **2.** urgent; **~áя задáча** urgent task. **3.** (*coll.*) militant; energetic; pushing; **~áя бáба** virago. **4.: б. механи́зм** striking mechanism (*of clock*).
боеголóвк|а, и *f.* (*mil.*) warhead.
боеготóвност|ь, и *f.* preparedness (for battle), combat readiness.
бо|ёк, йкá *m.* (*tech.*) firing-pin.
боеприпáс|ы, ов *no sg.* ammunition.
боеспосóбност|ь, и *f.* (*mil.*) fighting efficiency, fighting value.
боеспосóб|ный (~ен, ~на) *adj.* (*mil.*) efficient, battle-worthy.
бо|éц, йцá *m.* **1.** fighter; private soldier; **~йцы́ пéрвой áрмии** the men of the First Army; **петýх-б.** fighting-cock. **2.** butcher, slaughterman.
божб|á, ы́ *f.* swearing.
Бóже *see* **Бог**
бóжеск|ий *adj.* **1.** (*obs.*) divine. **2.** (*coll.*) fair, just; **~ая ценá** a fair price.
божéственност|ь, и *f.* divinity; divine nature.
божéствен|ный (~, ~на) *adj.* divine (*also fig.*); **б. гóлос** divine voice.
божеств|ó, á *nt.* deity, divine being.
бóж|ий, ья, ье *adj.* God's; **б. человéк** simple, otherworldly person; **я́сно, как б. день** it is as clear as could be; **~ья корóвка** (*zool.*) ladybird.
бож|и́ться, ýсь, ~ишься *impf.* (*of* **по~**) to swear.
божни́ц|а, ы *f.* **1.** icon-case. **2.** (*dial.*) chapel.
бож|óк, кá *m.* idol (*also fig.*).
бо|й[1], **я,** *pl.* **~и́, ~ёв** *m.* **1.** battle, fight, action, combat; **~и́** fighting; **в ~ю́** in action; **без ~я** without striking a blow; **взять с ~я** to take by force; **кулáчный б.** fisticuffs; **петуши́ный б.** cock-fight; **б. быкóв** bullfight. **2.** beating; **бить смéртным ~ем** to thrash within an inch of one's life. **3.** striking, strike (*of a clock*); **часы́ с ~ем** striking clock; **барабáнный б.** drum-beat. **4.** killing, slaughtering; **б. китóв** whaling; **б. тюлéней** sealing. **5.** breakage; broken objects; **стекля́нный б.** cullet; **в послéдней пáртии посýды бы́ло мнóго ~я** in the last consignment of crockery there were many breakages. **6.** accuracy (*of fire-arm*); **винтóвка с хорóшим ~ем** accurate rifle.
бо|й[2], **я,** *pl.* **~и, ~ев** *m.* message-boy; office-boy.
бой-бáб|а, ы *f.* (*coll.*) battleaxe.
бой-дéвк|а, и *f.* (*coll.*) tomboy.
бó|йкий (~ек, ~йкá, ~йко) *adj.* **1.** bold, spry, smart; **б. ум** ready wit; **б. язы́к** glib tongue. **2.** lively, animated; **~йкая торгóвля** brisk trade; **~йкая ýлица** busy street.
бóйкост|ь, и *f.* (*coll.*) **1.** smartness; glibness. **2.** liveliness, animation.
бойкóт, а *m.* boycott; **объяви́ть б.** (+*d.*) to declare a boycott (of).
бойкоти́р|овать, ую *impf.* to boycott.
бойни́ц|а, ы *f.* loop-hole, embrasure.
бóйн|я, и, *g. pl.* **бóен** *f.* slaughter-house, abattoir; (*fig.*) slaughter, butchery, carnage.
бойскáут, а *m.* Boy Scout.
бойскаути́зм, а *m.* scouting; the Boy Scout movement.
бойцóвый *adj.* fighting; **б. петýх** fighting-cock.
бóйче *comp. of* **бóйк|ий, ~о**
бок, а, о ~е, на ~ý, *pl.* **~á** *m.* side; flank; **в б.** sideways; **взять за ~á** to put the screw on; **схвати́ться за ~á (от смéха)** to split one's sides (with laughter); **нá б.** sideways, to the side; **на ~ý** on one side; **б. ó б.** side by side; **пó ~у** away with; **пó ~у учéние!** (we've done) enough studying!; **пóд ~ом** nearby, close at hand; **с ~у** from the side, from the flank; **с ~ нá б.** from side to side.
бокáл, а *m.* (wine)glass, goblet; **подня́ть б. (за**+*a.*) to drink the health (of), raise one's glass (to).
бокови́н|а, ы *f.* wall (*of tyre*).
боков|óй *adj.* side, flank, lateral, sidelong; **~áя кáчка** (*naut.*) rolling; **~áя ли́ния** collateral line; **~áя ýлица** side-street; **отпрáвиться на ~ýю** (*coll.*) to go to bed, turn in.
бóком *adv.* **1.** sideways; **ходи́ть б.** to sidle. **2.: вы́йти б.** (*coll.*) to turn out badly, give trouble.
бокс[1], **а** *m.* (*sport*) boxing.
бокс[2], **а** *m.* (*tech.*) boxcalf.
бокс[3], **а** *m.* short back and sides (*masculine hair-style*).
бокс[4], **а** *m.* box (*isolation compartment in hospital*).
боксёр, а *m.* (*sport*) boxer.
боксёр|ки, ок *no sg.* boxing boots.
бокси́р|овать, ую *impf.* (*sport*) to box.
бокси́т, а *m.* (*min.*) bauxite.
бóксовый *adj.* boxcalf.
болвáн, а *m.* (*coll.*) **1.** blockhead, dolt, twit. **2.** block (*esp. for shaping headgear*). **3.** (*in card-games*) dummy. **4.** (*obs.*) idol.
болвáнк|а, и *f.* **1.** (*tech.*) pig (*of iron, etc.*); **желéзо в ~ах** pig-iron. **2.** block (*for shaping headgear*).
Болгáри|я, и *f.* Bulgaria.
болгáр|ин, ина, *pl.* **~ы, ~** *m.* Bulgarian.
болгáр|ка, ки *f. of* **~ин**
болгáрский *adj.* Bulgarian.
бóле (*obs.*) = **бóлее**
болев|óй *adj. of* **боль; ~óе ощущéние** sensation of pain.
бóлее *adv.* more; **б. рóбкий** more timid; **б. тóлстый** thicker; **б. и б.** more and more; **он всё б. и б. слабéл** he was growing gradually weaker and weaker; **б. и́ли мéнее** more or less; **не б. и не мéнее, как** neither more nor less than; **б. всегó** most of all; **тем б., что** especially as.
болéзненност|ь, и *f.* **1.** sickliness; abnormality, morbidity. **2.** painfulness.
болéзнен|ный (~, ~на) *adj.* **1.** sickly; unhealthy; **б. румя́нец** unhealthy flush; (*fig.*) abnormal, morbid; **~ное любопы́тство** morbid curiosity. **2.** painful.
болезнетвóрный *adj.* (*med.*) morbific.
болéзный *adj.* (*dial.*) piteous; **мой б.!** poor thing!; my dear one!
болéзн|ь, и *f.* illness; disease; sickness; (*fig.*) abnormality; **б. Альцгéймера** Altzheimer's disease; **б. Дáуна** Down's syndrome; **б. движéния** travel sickness; **морскáя б.** sea-sickness; **б. рóста** growing pains.
болéльщик, а *m.* (*coll.*) fan, supporter.
болерó *nt. indecl.* (*dance or garment*) bolero.
болé|ть[1], **ю, ешь** *impf.* **1.** (+*i.*) to be ill, to be down (with), (*intrans.*) to ail; **онá с дéтства ~ет áстмой** she has suffered from asthma ever since she was a child; **б. душóй (за**+*a.*) to be worried (about). **2.** (**за**+*a.*; *coll.*) to be a fan (of), support.
бол|éть[2] *1st and 2nd pers. not used,* **~и́т** *impf.* to ache, hurt; **у меня́ зýбы ~я́т** I have toothache; **у негó ~и́т в ýхе** he has ear-ache; **у меня́ душá ~и́т (о**+*p.*) my heart bleeds (for, over).
болеутоля́ющ|ий *adj.* soothing, analgesic; **~ее срéдство** (*med.*) analgesic, anodyne.
боливи́|ец, йца *m.* Bolivian.
боливи́|йка, йки *f. of* **~ец**
боливи́йский *adj.* Bolivian.
Боли́ви|я, и *f.* Bolivia.
болиголóв, а *m.* (*bot.*) hemlock.
боли́д, а *m.* (*astron.*) fireball.
болóнк|а, и *f.* lap-dog.

боло́нь|я, и *f.* plastic mackintosh.
боло́тист|ый (~, ~а) *adj.* marshy, boggy, swampy.
боло́тн|ый *adj.* marsh; **~ая вода́** stagnant water; **б. газ** marsh gas; **~ая лихора́дка** marsh fever, malaria.
боло́т|о, а *nt.* marsh, bog, swamp; **торфяно́е б.** peatbog; (*fig.*) mire, slough.
болт, а́ *m.* (*tech.*) bolt; **нарезно́й б.** screw-bolt; **скрепля́ть ~а́ми** to bolt.
болта́нк|а, и *f.* (*aeron.*; *coll.*) bumps.
болта́|ть¹, ю *impf.* **1.** to stir; to shake; **б. ло́жкой в ча́шке ча́ю** to stir one's tea with a spoon. **2.** (*+i.*) to dangle (*arms or legs*).
болта́|ть², ю *impf.* (*coll.*) to chatter, jabber, natter; **б. глу́пости** to drivel; **б. по-неме́цки, по-францу́зски** *etc.*, to jabber German, French, *etc.*; **б. языко́м** to wag one's tongue.
болта́|ться¹, юсь *impf.* (*coll.*) **1.** to dangle, swing; to hang loosely; **он так похуде́л, вся оде́жда ~ется на нём** he has grown so thin that his clothes all hang on him. **2.** to hang about, loaf; **чего́ вы тут весь день ~етесь** why do you hang about here all day?
болта́|ться², ется *impf.* (*coll.*) *pass. of* **~ть²; здесь ~ется мно́го вздо́ру** a lot of nonsense is being talked here.
болтли́вост|ь, и *f.* garrulity, talkativeness.
болтли́в|ый (~, ~а) *adj.* garrulous, talkative; indiscreet.
болтн|у́ть¹, у́, ёшь *pf.* to give a stir, give a shake.
болтн|у́ть², у́, ёшь *pf.* to blurt out.
болтн|у́ться, ~ётся *pf.* to work loose; to come off.
болтовн|я́, и́ *f.* (*coll.*) talk; chatter; gossip; **пуста́я б.** idle talk.
болторе́зный *adj.* (*tech.*) **б. стано́к** bolt-screwing machine.
болту́н¹, а́ *m.* (*coll.*) **1.** chatterbox; gas-bag. **2.** gossip.
болту́н², а́ *m.* addled egg.
болту́шк|а, и *f.* (*coll.*) **1.** = **болту́нья. 2.** scrambled eggs. **3.** swill, mash. **4.** whisk.
бол|ь, и *f.* pain; ache; **б. в боку́** stitch; **зубна́я б.** toothache; **душе́вная б.** mental anguish.
больни́ц|а, ы *f.* hospital; **лечь в ~у** to go to hospital; **лежа́ть в ~е** to be in hospital; **вы́писаться из ~ы** to be discharged from hospital.
больни́|чный *adj. of* **~ца; ~чная ка́сса** hospital fund, club; **б. листо́к** medical certificate.
бо́льно¹ *adv.* **1.** painfully, badly; **б. ушиби́ться** to be badly bruised. **2.** *as pred.* it is painful (*also fig.*); **мне б. дыша́ть** it hurts me to breathe; **б., что мы должны́ расста́ться** I am sorry that we have to part.
бо́льно² *adv.* (*coll.*) very, exceedingly, badly; **он б. хитёр** he is exceedingly wily; **мне б. уж хо́чется пить** I badly want a drink.
бол|ьно́й (~́ен, ~ьна́) *adj.* ill, sick; diseased; sore (*also fig.*); **~ьны́е дёсны** sore gums; **б. зуб** bad tooth; **он тяжело́ ~́ен** he is seriously ill; **б. вопро́с** sore subject; **~ьно́е ме́сто** sore spot; **свали́ть с б. головы́ на здоро́вую** *see* **голова́**; *as n.* **б., ~ьно́го** *m.*, **~ьна́я, ~ьно́й** *f.* patient, invalid; **амбулато́рный б.** out-patient; **стациона́рный б.** in-patient; **б. анорекси́ей** anorexic (*pers.*); **б. артри́том** arthritic (*pers.*); **б. гемофили́ей** haemophiliac (*pers.*).
больша́к, а́ *m.* (*dial.*) **1.** head of the family. **2.** high road.
бо́льше 1. (*comp. of* **большо́й** *and* **вели́кий**) bigger, larger; greater; **Ло́ндон б. Пари́жа** London is larger than Paris. **2.** (*comp. of* **мно́го**) more; **чем б... тем б.** the more … the more; **б. того́** and what is more; **б. не** no more, no longer; **он б. не живёт на той у́лице** he does not live in that street any longer; **б. не бу́ду!** I won't do it again!; **б. нет вопро́сов?** any more questions?; **б. у** (*+g.*) (*tennis*) advantage. **3.** *adv.* (*coll.*) for the most part.
большевиза́ци|я, и *f.* bolshevization.
большевизи́р|овать, ую *impf. and pf.* to bolshevize.
большеви́зм, а *m.* Bolshevism.
большеви́к, а́ *m.* Bolshevik.
большеви́стский *adj.* Bolshevik, Bolshevist.
большеголо́вый *adj.* with a large head; macrocephalous.
бо́льш|ий *comp. of* **~о́й** *and* **вели́кий;** greater, larger; **~ей ча́стью, по ~ей ча́сти** for the most part; **са́мое ~ее** at most; **съезд бу́дет продолжа́ться са́мое ~ее три дня** the congress will last at most three days.
большинств|о́, а́ *nt.* majority; most (of); **в ~е́ слу́чаев** in most cases; **б. голосо́в** a majority vote.
больш|о́й *adj.* big, large; great; large-scale; (*coll.*) grown-up; **~а́я бу́ква** capital (letter); **~а́я доро́га** high road; **~ое знако́мство** wide range of acquaintance; **б. па́лец** thumb; **б. па́лец ноги́** big toe; **на б. па́лец** (*coll.*) in first-rate fashion, top-hole; **~о́й ско́ростью** (*rail.*) by fast goods (train); **б. свет** haut monde, society; **когда́ я бу́ду б.** when I grow up.
большу́х|а, и *f.* (*dial.*) mistress (of the house).
большу́щий *adj.* (*coll.*) huge.
боля́чк|а, и *f.* sore; scab; (*fig.*) defect.
бол|я́щий *pres. part. of* **~е́ть²**; *as n.* **б., ~я́щего** *m.* (*usu. joc.*) the patient.
бо́мб|а, ы *f.* bomb; **зажига́тельная б.** incendiary (device), petrol bomb, Molotov cocktail; **кассе́тная б.** cluster bomb; **б.-посы́лка** letter bomb; **самонаводя́щаяся б.** smart bomb.
бомбарди́р, а *m.* **1.** (*mil., hist.*) bombardier. **2.** (*aeron.*) bomb-aimer. **3.** (*zool.*) bombardier (*beetle*). **4.** (*sport*) striker.
бомбардир|ова́ть, у́ю *impf.* to bombard; to bomb; **б. про́сьбами** (*fig.*) to bombard with requests.
бомбардиро́вк|а, и *f.* bombardment; bombing; **ковро́вая б.** carpet bombing.
бомбардиро́вочный *adj.* bombing.
бомбардиро́вщик, а *m.* **1.** bomber; **пики́рующий б.** dive-bomber; **сре́дний б.** medium bomber. **2.** (*coll.*) bomber pilot.
бомбёжк|а, и *f.* (*coll.*) bombing.
бомб|и́ть, лю́, и́шь *impf.* to bomb.
бомбово́з, а *m.* bomber.
бо́мб|овый *adj. of* **~а; б. люк** bomb-bay door (*on aircraft*); **~овая нагру́зка** bomb-load; **б. уда́р** thud of exploding bomb.
бомбодержа́тел|ь, я *m.* bomb-rack.
бомбомёт, а *m.* (*mil.*) **1.** (*naut.*) depth-charge gun. **2.** (*obs.*) bomb-thrower.
бомбомета́ни|е, я *nt.* bomb-dropping, bomb-release.
бомбосбра́сывател|ь, я *m.* bomb-release gear.
бомбоубе́жищ|е, а *nt.* air-raid shelter, bomb-proof shelter.
бом-бра́мсел|ь, я *m.* (*naut.*) royal (sail).
бом-брам-сте́ньг|а, и *f.* (*naut.*) royal mast.
бомж, а *m.* (*abbr. of* **без определённого ме́ста жи́тельства**) homeless person, vagrant.
бомо́нд, а *m.* (*obs.*) beau monde, society.
бон, а *m.* (*naut.*) boom.
бонапарти́зм, а *m.* (*hist.*) Bonapartism.
бонаparти́ст, а *m.* (*hist.*) Bonapartist.
бонбонье́рк|а, и *f.* bonbonnière.
бонвива́н, а *m.* bon vivant.
бонда́р|ить, ю, ишь *impf.* (*dial.*) to cooper.
бонда́р|ный *adj. of* **~ство; ~ное ремесло́** the cooper's craft.
бонда́р|ня, ни, *g. pl.* **~ен** *f.* cooperage.
бо́нда́рств|о, а *nt.* coopering, cooperage.
бо́нда́р|ь, я/я́ *m.* cooper.
бо́нз|а, ы, *g. pl.* **~** *m.* bonze (*Buddhist priest*); (*fig.*) superior, distant pers.; bigwig; **парти́йный б.** Party boss.
бони́ст, а *m.* scripophile.
бони́стик|а, и *f.* scripophily.
бонмо́ *nt. indecl.* bon mot, witticism.
бонмоти́ст, а *m.* wit.
бо́нн|а, ы *f.* nursery-governess.
бонто́н, а *m.* (*coll., obs.*) bon ton.
бо́н|ы, ~ *pl.* (*sg.* **~а, ~ы** *f.*) **1.** cheques; vouchers, tokens. **2.** emergency paper money.
бор¹, а, о ~́е, на ~у́, *pl.* **~ы́, ~о́в** *m.* coniferous forest; **с ~́у да с со́сенки, с ~́у по со́сенке** chosen at random; **(я ви́жу), отку́да сыр б. загоре́лся** (I see) how it all started.
бор², а *m.* (*chem.*) boron.
бо́ргес, а *m.* (*typ.*) bourgeois.
борде́л|ь, я *m.* (*coll.*) brothel.

бордо́ 1. *nt. indecl.* claret. **2.** *as adj.* claret-coloured.
бордо́вый *adj.* claret-coloured.
бордю́р, а *m.* border (*of fabric, wallpaper, etc.*).
боре́ни|е, я *nt.* (*rhet.*) struggle, fight.
бор|е́ц, ца́ *m.* **1.** (**за**+*a.*) fighter (for); campaigner; activist; **б. за мир** peace campaigner; **б. за права́ же́нщин** women's liberationist; women's libber; **б. за эмансипа́цию живо́тных** animal liberationist. **2.** (*sport*) wrestler.
боржо́м, а *m.* (*and* **~и,** *nt. indecl.*) Borzhomi (*variety of mineral water*).
борз|а́я, о́й *f.*: **англи́йская б.** greyhound; **афга́нская б.** Afghan (hound); **ру́сская б.** borzoi, Russian wolfhound.
борз|о́й *adj. of* **~а́я**
борзопи́с|ец, ца *m.* (*iron.*) hack writer.
бо́рзый *adj.* (*obs. or poet.*) swift, fleet.
бормаши́н|а, ы *f.* (dentist's) drill.
бормота́ни|е, я *nt.* muttering.
бормо|та́ть, чу́, ~́чешь *impf.* to mutter.
бормоту́н, а́ *m.* (*coll.*) **1.** mutterer. **2.** (*breed of pigeons*) drummer.
бормоту́х|а, и *f.* (*coll.*) plonk (*cheap wine*).
борм|очу́, о́чешь *see* **~ота́ть**
Борне́о *nt. indecl.* Borneo.
бо́рн|ый *adj.* (*chem.*) boric, boracic, **~ая кислота́** boric, boracic acid.
бо́ров[1], а *m.* hog; (*fig.*) obese man.
бо́ров[2], а, *pl.* **~а́** *m.* (*tech.*) horizontal flue.
борови́к, а́ *m.* (*dial.*) (edible) boletus (*kind of mushroom*).
борови́нк|а, и *f.* borovinka (*variety of winter apple*).
бор|ово́й *adj. of* **~**[1]
бор|ода́, оды́, *a.* **~́оду,** *pl.* **~́оды, ~о́д, ~ода́м** *f.* **1.** beard; **отпусти́ть ~́оду** to grow a beard; **смея́ться в ~́оду** to laugh into one's beard. **2.** wattle (*of bird*).
борода́вк|а, и *f.* wart.
борода́вчатый *adj.* warty.
борода́ст|ый *adj.* (*coll.*) long-bearded, heavily bearded.
борода́т|ый (~, ~а) *adj.* bearded.
борода́ч, а́ *m.* **1.** (*coll.*) bearded man. **2.** (*bot.*) beard grass. **3.** (*zool.*) bearded vulture, lammergeyer.
боро́дк|а[1], и *f.* small beard, tuft.
боро́дк|а[2], и *f.* (*tech.*) key-bit; barb (*of hook*).
бор|озда́, озды́, *a.* **~́озду** *and* **~озду́,** *pl.* **~́озды, ~о́зд, ~озда́м** *f.* furrow; (*anat.*) fissure.
бороз|ди́ть, жу́, ди́шь *impf.* **1.** (*pf.* **вз~**) to furrow; to leave a furrow behind one; (*fig.*) to leave a wake. **2.** (*pf.* **из~**) to cover with furrows; **морщи́ны ~ди́ли его́ лоб** (*fig.*) wrinkles furrowed his brow; **б. океа́ны** (*poet.*) to plough, furrow the seas.
боро́здк|а, и *f.* furrow; groove.
боро́здчатый *adj.* furrowed; grooved.
бор|она́, оны́, *a.* **~́ону,** *pl.* **~́оны, ~о́н, ~она́м** *f.* (*agric.*) harrow.
борон|и́ть, ю́, и́шь *impf.* (*of* **вз~**) (*agric.*) to harrow.
борон|ова́ть, у́ю *impf.* (*of* **вз~**) = **~и́ть**
бороньб|а́, ы́ *f.* (*agric.*) harrowing.
бор|о́ться, ю́сь, ~́ешься *impf.* (**с**+*i.*; **за**+*a.*; **про́тив**+*g.*) to wrestle; (*fig.*) to struggle, fight (with; for; against); **б. с суеве́рием** to struggle against superstition; **б. со свое́й со́вестью** to wrestle with one's conscience.
борт, а, о ~́е, на ~у́, *pl.* **~а́, ~о́в** *m.* **1.** side (*of a ship*); **пра́вый б.** starboard side; **ле́вый б.** port side; **на ~у́** on board (*ship* or *aircraft*); **б.-о́-б.** broadside to broadside; **вы́бросить за́ б.** to throw overboard (*also fig.*); **челове́к за ~́ом!** man overboard! **2.** coat-breast. **3.** cushion (*billiards*).
борт|ево́й *adj. of* **~ь**
бортмеха́ник, а *m.* (*aeron.*) flight engineer.
бо́ртник, а *m.* wild-honey farmer.
бо́ртничеств|о, а *nt.* wild-honey farming.
борт|ово́й *adj. of* **~**; **б. журна́л** (ship's) log-book; **~ова́я ка́чка** (*naut.*) rolling.
бортпроводни́к, а́ *m.* air steward.
бортпроводни́ц|а, ы *f.* stewardess; air hostess.
бортради́ст, а *m.* radio operator (*aircraft*).
борт|ь, и *f.* hive of wild bees.
борщ, а́ *m.* (*cul.*) bor(t)sch.
борщ|о́к, ка́ *m.* (clear) beetroot soup.
борьб|а́, ы́ *f.* **1.** (*sport*) wrestling; **америка́нская б.** all-in wrestling; **класси́ческая/францу́зская б.** Greco-Roman wrestling; **спорти́вная б.** martial arts. **2.** (*fig.*) (**с**+*i.*; **за**+*a.*; **про́тив**+*g.*) struggle, fight (with; for; against); conflict; **душе́вная б.** mental strife; **кла́ссовая б.** the class struggle; **кампа́ния по ~е́ с престу́пностью** crime-prevention campaign; **б. за эмансипа́цию же́нщин** women's liberation struggle; women's lib.
босико́м *adv.* barefoot; **ходи́ть б.** to go barefoot.
боске́т, а *m.* spinney, copse.
Бо́сни|я и Герцегови́н|а, ~и и ~ы *f.* Bosnia and Herzegovina.
бос|о́й (~, ~а́, ~́о) *adj.* barefooted; **на ~́у но́гу** with bare feet, barefoot.
босоно́гий *adj.* barefooted.
босоно́жк|а, и *f.* **1.** barefoot dancer. **2.** (*pl.*) sandals; mules.
босто́н, а *m.* Boston (**1.** *card-game.* **2.** *kind of wool cloth.* **3.** *name of dance*).
Босфо́р, а *m.* the Bosp(h)orus.
boся́к, а́ *m.* tramp; down-and-out.
бося́|цкий *adj. of* **~к**
бот, а *m.* boat.
ботанизи́рк|а, и *f.* (*coll.*) plant-collecting box.
ботанизи́р|овать, ую *impf.* to collect plants (*for study*).
бота́ник, а *m.* botanist.
бота́ник|а, и *f.* botany.
ботани́ческий *adj.* botanical; **б. сад** botanical gardens.
ботв|а́, ы́ *f.* leafy tops of root vegetables (*esp. beet leaves*).
ботви́нь|я, и *f.* botvinia (*cold soup of fish, pot-herbs, and kvass*).
бо́тик, а *m.* (*obs.*) small boat.
бо́тик|и, ов *pl.* (*sg.* **~, ~а** *m.*) high (women's) over-shoes.
боти́н|ок, ка, *g. pl.* **б.** *m.* (*ankle-high*) boot.
боту́н = бату́н
ботфо́рт|ы, ов *pl.* (*sg.* **~, ~а** *m.*) (*obs.*) jackboots, Hessian boots.
бо́т|ы, ов *pl.* (*sg.* **~, ~а** *m.*) high overshoes.
бо́цман, а *m.* (*naut.*) boatswain.
боча́г, а́ *m.* (*dial.*) pool.
боча́р, а́, *pl.* **~ы́** *m.* cooper.
боча́р|ный *adj. of* **~**; coopering.
боча́р|ня, ни, *g. pl.* **~ен** *f.* (*dial.*) cooperage.
бо́чк|а, и *f.* **1.** barrel, cask; (*fig.*) **плати́ть де́ньги на ~у** to pay on the nail. **2.** barrel (*old Russ. liquid measure, equivalent to approx. 490 litres*). **3.** (*aeron.*) roll.
бочко́м *adv.* sideways; **пробира́ться б.** to sidle.
боч|о́к, ка́ *m.* (*coll.*) flank.
бочо́н|ок, ка *m.* small barrel, keg.
боязли́в|ец, ца *m.* wimp.
боязли́вост|ь, и *f.* timidity, timorousness.
боязли́в|ый (~, ~а) *adj.* timid, timorous.
бо́язно *adv. as pred.* (+*d.*; *coll.*) to be afraid, frightened, **ей б. остава́ться одно́й по вечера́м** she is frightened of being left alone in the evening.
боя́зн|ь, и *f.* (+*g. or* **пе́ред**+*i.*) fear (of), dread of; **б. темноты́** fear of the dark; **б. простра́нства** (*med.*) agoraphobia; **из ~и** for fear of, lest; **он промени́л фами́лию из ~и, что бу́дут смея́ться над ним** he changed his name for fear of being laughed at.
боя́р|ин, ина, *pl.* **~е, ~** *m.* (*hist.*) boyar.
боя́р|ский *adj. of* **~**; **~ские де́ти** (*hist.*) the lowest class of boyars.
боя́рств|о, а *nt.* (*collect.*; *hist.*) the boyars, the nobility.
боя́рын|я, и *f.* (*hist.*) boyar's wife.
боя́рышник, а *m.* (*bot.*) hawthorn.
боя́рышниц|а, ы *f.* pierid butterfly (*Aporia crataegi*).
боя́рыш|ня, ни, *g. pl.* **~ень** *f.* (*hist.*) (*unmarried*) daughter of a boyar.
бо|я́ться, ю́сь, и́шься *impf.* (+*g.*) **1.** to fear, be afraid (of); **она́ ~и́тся темноты́** she is afraid of the dark; **он ~и́тся пойти́ к врачу́** he is afraid to go to the doctor; **~ю́сь, что он (не) прие́дет** I am afraid that he will (not) come; **~ю́сь, как бы (что́бы) он не прие́хал** I am afraid

that he may come; ~**ю́сь сказа́ть** I would not like to say. **2.** to be afraid of, suffer from; **э́ти расте́ния ~я́тся хо́лода** these plants do not like the cold.
бра *nt. indecl.* sconce; lamp-bracket.
брава́д|а, ы *f.* bravado.
брави́р|овать, ую *impf.* (+*i.*) to brave, defy; **б. опа́сностью** to defy danger.
бра́во *int.* bravo!
браву́р|ный (~ен, ~на) *adj.* (*mus.*) bravura.
бра́вый *adj.* gallant; manly.
бра́г|а, и *f.* home-brewed beer.
брадобре́|й, я *m.* (*obs. or joc.*) barber.
бра́жник, а *m.* (*obs.*) reveller.
бра́жнича|ть, ю *impf.* (*obs.*) to revel, carouse.
бразд|а́, ы́ *f.* (*poet., obs.*) furrow.
бразд|ы́, ~ *now only in phr.* **б. правле́ния** the reins of government.
бразил|ец, ьца *m.* Brazilian.
Брази́ли|я, и *f.* **1.** Brazil. **2.** Brasilia.
брази́льский *adj.* Brazilian.
бразил|ья́нка, ья́нки *f. of* ~**ец**
бра́йлевский *adj.*: **б. шрифт** Braille.
Брайл|ь, я *m.*: **шрифт ~я** Braille.
брак[1]**, а** *m.* marriage; matrimony; **гражда́нский б.** civil marriage; (*obs.*) cohabitation; **свиде́тельство о ~е** certificate of marriage; **б. по расчёту** marriage of convenience; **рождённый вне ~а** born out of wedlock.
брак[2]**, а** *m.* waste; defective products, rejects.
бракёр, а *m.* (*tech.*) inspector.
бракера́ж, а *m.* (*tech.*) certification, inspection.
брако́ван|ный (~, ~а) *p.p.p. of* **бракова́ть** *and adj.* rejected; defective.
брак|ова́ть, у́ю *impf.* (*of* **за~**) to reject (*manufactured articles; also fig.*).
брако́вк|а, и *f.* rejection (*of defective articles*).
брако́вщик, а *m.* sorter (*of manufactured articles*).
брако́вщиц|а, ы *f. of* **брако́вщик**
бракоде́л, а *m.* (*coll.*) bad workman.
браконье́р, а *m.* poacher.
браконье́рств|о, а *nt.* poaching.
бракопосре́дническ|ий *adj.*: **~ое аге́нтство** marriage bureau.
бракоразво́дный *adj.* divorce; **б. проце́сс** divorce suit.
бракосочета́ни|е, я *nt.* wedding, nuptials.
брам-... *comb. form* (*naut.*) top-.
брами́н, а *m.* Brahmin.
брам-ре́|й, я *m.* (*naut.*) topgallant yard.
бра́мсел|ь, я *m.* (*naut.*) topsail.
брам-сте́ньг|а, и *f.* (*naut.*) topgallant (mast).
брандахлы́ст, а *m.* (*coll.*) **1.** slops; swipes. **2.** (*fig.*) worthless pers.
брандва́хт|а, ы *f.* guard-ship.
бра́ндер, а *m.* **1.** (*hist.*) fire-ship; **запусти́ть, подпусти́ть б.** (*fig.*) to put the cat among the pigeons. **2.** block-ship.
брандмайо́р, а *m.* (*obs.*) chief of the fire brigade.
брандма́уэр, а *m.* fire-proof wall.
брандме́йстер, а *m.* (*obs.*) chief fireman.
брандспо́йт, а *m.* **1.** fire-pump. **2.** nozzle. **3.** water-cannon.
бран|и́ть, ю́, и́шь *impf.* (*of* **вы́~**) to reprove; to scold; to abuse, curse (*coll.*).
бран|и́ться, ю́сь, и́шься *impf.* **1.** (*of* **по~**) (**с**+*i.*) to quarrel (with). **2.** to swear, curse (*intrans.*).
бра́нн|ый[1] *adj.* abusive; **~ое сло́во** swearword.
бра́нный[2] *adj.* (*obs., poet.*) martial.
бранч(л)и́в|ый (~, ~а) *adj.* (*coll.*) quarrelsome.
бра́ный *adj.* (*text.; obs.*) embroidered.
бран|ь[1]**, и** *f.* swearing; abuse; bad language.
бран|ь[2]**, и** *f.* (*obs., poet.*): **по́ле ~и** field of battle.
брас, а *m.* (*naut.*) brace.
брасле́т, а *m.* bracelet; (metal) watch-strap, watchband.
брас|ова́ть, у́ю *impf.* (*naut.*) to brace.
брасс, а *m.* (*sport*) breast stroke.
брат, а, *pl.* **~ья, ~ьев** *m.* **1.** brother; **моло́чный б.** foster-brother; **сво́дный б.** stepbrother; **единокро́вный б.** half-brother (*by father*); **единоутро́бный б.** half-brother (*by mother*); **двою́родный б.** cousin. **2.** (*fig.*) brother; comrade; **~ья-писа́тели** fellow-writers; **наш б.** (*coll.*) we, the likes of us; **ваш б.** (*coll.*) you, you and your sort. **3.** *as familiar or patronising term of address* old man; my lad; (*pl.*) friends, lads. **4.** (*eccl.*) lay brother; (*as style*) Brother, Friar; **б. милосе́рдия** male nurse. **5.: на ~а** (*coll.*) a head; **по два я́блока на ~а** two apples a head.
брата́ни|е, я *nt.* fraternization.
брата́|ться, юсь *impf.* (*of* **по~**) (**с**+*i.*) to fraternize (with).
братв|а́, ы́ *f.* (*collect.; coll.*) comrades; chaps, lads.
бра́т|ец, ца *m. affectionate or patronizing dim. of* ~; (*as term of address*) old man, old chap; boy.
бра́тин|а, ы *f.* (*hist.*) winebowl.
брати́ш|ка, ки, *g. pl.* **~ек** *m.* (*coll.*) **1.** little brother. **2.** = **брат 2.**
бра́ти|я, и, *g. pl.* **~й** *f.* (*collect.*) brotherhood, fraternity (*also fig.*); **доминика́нская б.** Dominican community; **актёрская б.** the acting fraternity.
бра́тнин *adj.* (*coll.*) brother's, belonging to one's brother.
брат|о́к, ка́ *m.* (*coll.*) = **брат 2.**
братоуби́йственный *adj.* fratricidal (*also fig.*).
братоуби́йств|о, а *nt.* fratricide (*act*).
братоуби́йц|а, ы *m.* fratricide (*agent*).
бра́тск|ий *adj.* brotherly, fraternal; **б. приве́т** fraternal greetings; **~ая моги́ла** communal grave (*esp. of war dead*).
бра́тств|о, а *nt.* (*abstr. and concr.*) brotherhood, fraternity.
брату́ш|ка, ки, *g. pl.* **~ек** *m. dim. of* **брат; ~ки** (*hist.; coll.*) 'the Little Brothers' (= *the Southern Slavs*).
бра|ть, беру́, берёшь, *past* **~л, ~ла́, ло** *impf.* (*of* **взять**). **1.** (*in var. senses*) to take; **б. наза́д, б. обра́тно** to take back; **б. курс (на**+*a.*) to make (for), head (for); **б. нача́ло (в**+*p.*) to originate (in); **б. но́ту** to sing, play a note; **б. поруче́ние** to undertake a commission; **б. приме́р (с**+*g.*) to follow the example (of); **б. сло́во** to take the floor; **б. в ско́бки** to place in brackets; **б. в плен** to take prisoner; **б. на букси́р** to take in tow; **б. на пору́ки** (*leg.*) to go bail (for); **б. на себя́** to take upon o.s.; **б. под аре́ст** to put under arrest; **б. кого́-н. по́д руку** to take s.o.'s arm. **2.** to take; to get, obtain; to book; to hire; **б. биле́ты** to take, book tickets; **б. верх** to get the upper hand; **б. такси́** to take a taxi; **б. своё** to get one's way; to make itself felt; **го́ды беру́т своё** age tells; **б. взаймы́** to borrow; **б. в аре́нду** to rent; **б. напрока́т** to hire. **3.** (**в**+*nom.-a.*) to take (as); **б. в жёны** to take to wife; **б. в свиде́тели** to call to witness. **4.** to seize; to grip; **б. власть** to seize power; **его́ берёт страх** he is in the grip of fear; **б. за се́рдце** to move deeply. **5.** to exact; to take (= *to demand, require*); **б. штраф** to exact a fine; **б. сло́во с кого́-н.** to get s.o.'s word; **б. вре́мя** to take time. **6.** to take; to surmount; **б. барье́р** to clear a hurdle. **7.** (+*i.*) to succeed (by means of, by dint of); **она́ берёт такти́чностью** the secret of her success is tact. **8.** (*usu.*+*neg.; coll.*) to work, operate; to be effective; (**на**+*a.; of a fire-arm*) to have a range (of); **э́ти но́жницы не беру́т** these scissors don't cut; **э́та винто́вка берёт на пятьсо́т ме́тров** this rifle has a range of, is effective at, five hundred metres. **9.** (+*adv. of place; coll.*) to bear; **б. вле́во** to bear left. **10.** (*dial.*) to gather, collect. **11.** (*impf. only*) (*coll.*) to take bribes.
бра́|ться, беру́сь, берёшься, *past* **~лся, ~ла́сь, ~ло́сь** *impf.* (*of* **взя́ться**). **1.** *pass. of* **~ть. 2. (за**+*a.*) to touch, lay hands (upon); **не бери́сь за то́рмоз!** don't touch the brake!; **б. за́ руки** to link arms. **3. (за**+*a.*) to take up; to get down (to); **б. за де́ло** to get down to business, get down to brass tacks; **б. за перо́** to take up the pen; **б. за чте́ние** to get down to reading. **4. (за**+*a. or* +*inf.*) to undertake; to take upon o.s.; **б. за поруче́ние** to undertake a commission; **б. вы́полнить рабо́ту** to undertake a job; **не беру́сь суди́ть** I do not presume to judge. **5.** (*3rd pers. only*) (*coll.*) to appear, arise; **не зна́ю, отку́да у них де́ньги беру́тся** I don't know where they get their money from. **6.: б. за ум** (*coll.*) to come to one's senses. **7.: б. нарасхва́т** to sell like hot cakes.
бра́т|ья[1] *see* ~
бра́ть|я[2]**, и** *f.* = **бра́тия**
бра́унинг, а *m.* Browning (*automatic pistol*).

брахицефа́л, а *m.* (*anthrop.*) brachycephalous pers.
брахицефа́ли|я *f.* (*anthrop.*) brachycephaly.
брахма́н, а *m.* = **брами́н**
бра́чн|ый *adj.* marriage; conjugal; **б. во́зраст** marriageable age; **~ая жизнь** married life; **~ая конто́ра** marriage bureau; **~ое свиде́тельство** marriage certificate; **б. наря́д** (*zool.*) breeding-dress; **~ое опере́ние** (*zool.*) breeding plumage.
бра́чущ|иеся, ихся *no sg.* the bride and groom; the happy couple; **дороги́е б.!** dearly beloved!
бра́шпиль, я *m.* (*naut.*) windlass, capstan.
бреве́нчатый *adj.* log, made of logs.
брев|но́, на́, *pl.* **~на, ~ен, ~нам** *nt.* log, beam; caber; **мета́ние ~а́** (*sport*) tossing the caber; (*fig.*) dullard, insensitive pers.
брег, а *pl.* **~а́** *m.* (*poet., arch.*) = **бе́рег**
брегéт, а *m.* (*obs.*) Bréguet (watch).
бред, а, о ~е, в ~у́ *m.* delirium; ravings; (*fig.*) gibberish; **соба́чий б.** twaddle, poppycock; **быть в ~у́** to be delirious.
бре́д|ень, ня *m.* drag-net.
бре́|дить, жу, дишь *impf.* to be delirious, rave; (*+i.*; *fig.*) to rave about, be mad about; **он ~дит джа́зом** he is crazy about jazz.
бре́|диться, дится *impf.* (*impers.+d.*; *coll.*) to dream (of); **ему́ всё ~дилось, что он па́дает в про́пасть** he was always dreaming that he was falling down a precipice.
бре́дн|и, ей *no sg.* ravings; fantasies.
бредово́й *adj.* **1.** delirious. **2.** (*fig.*) fantastic, nonsensical.
бредо́вый *adj.* crackpot, crazy.
бре|ду́, дёшь *see* **~сти́**
бре́|жу, дишь *see* **~дить**
бре́зг|ать, аю, аешь *impf.* (*of* **по~**) (*+i.*) to be squeamish, fastidious (about); **он ~ает есть немы́тые фру́кты** he is squeamish about eating unwashed fruit; **тако́й ниче́м бы не ~ал** he is the sort of pers. who would balk at nothing.
брезгли́в|ец, ца *m.* squeamish, fastidious pers.
брезгли́вост|ь, и *f.* squeamishness, fastidiousness; disgust.
брезгли́в|ый (~, ~а) *adj.* squeamish, fastidious; **~ое чу́вство** feeling of disgust.
брезе́нт, а *m.* tarpaulin.
брезе́нтовый *adj.* tarpaulin, canvas.
бре́зж|ить(ся), ~ит(ся) *impf.* to dawn; to glimmer; **~ила заря́** dawn was breaking.
брейд-вы́мпел, а *m.* (*naut.*) broad pennant.
брейк, а *m.* break-dancing; **му́зыка ~а** break music.
бре́йкер, а *m.* break-dancer.
брёл, а́ *see* **брести́**
брело́к, а *m.* (*bracelet*) charm; **б. для ключе́й** key ring.
бремен|и́ть, ю́, и́шь *impf.* (*obs.*) to burden.
бре́мсберг, а *m.* (*tech.*) gravity roadway.
бре́м|я, ~ени, ~енем, ~ени *nt.* burden; load; **разреши́ться от ~ени** to be delivered (of a child).
бре́нди *m. and nt. indecl.* brandy.
бре́нн|ый (~а, ~о) *adj.* transitory; perishable; **~ые оста́нки** mortal remains.
бренч|а́ть, у́, и́шь *impf.* **1.** (*+i.*) to jingle; **слы́шно бы́ло, как~а́ли шпо́ры** the jingling of spurs could be heard; **он всё ~а́л моне́тами в карма́не** he was always jingling coins in his pocket. **2.** (*coll.*) to strum; **б. на роя́ле** to strum on the piano.
бр|ести́, еду́, едёшь, *past* **~ёл, ~ела́** *impf.* **1.** to shuffle; to drag o.s. along. **2.** to amble, stroll pensively.
Брета́н|ь, и *f.* Brittany.
брете́льк|а, и *f.* shoulder-strap.
бретёр, а *m.* (*obs.*) duellist, swashbuckler, bully.
бретёр|ский *adj. of* **~**
брето́н|ец, ца *m.* Breton.
брето́н|ка, ки *f. of* **~ец**
брето́нский *adj.* Breton.
бре|ха́ть, шу́, ~шешь *impf.* (*coll.*) **1.** to yelp, bark. **2.** (*fig.*) to tell lies.
брехн|я́, и́ *no pl., f.* (*coll.*) lies; nonsense.
бреху́н, а́ *m.* (*coll.*) liar.
брехун|е́ц, ца́ *m.* (*coll.*) liar; (*fig., iron.*) lawyer.
бреш|у́, ~ешь *see* **бреха́ть**
бре́ш|ь, и *f.* breach; **проби́ть б.** (**в**+*p.*) to breach; (*fig.*) flaw, gap, deficit.
бре́|ю, ешь *see* **брить**
бре́ющий *pres. part. of* **брить; б. полёт** hedge-hopping flight.
бриг, а *m.* brig.
брига́д|а, ы *f.* **1.** (*mil.*) brigade; (*naut.*) subdivision. **2.** brigade, (work-) team; **поездна́я б.** train crew; **уда́рная б.** shock brigade.
бригади́р, а *m.* **1.** (*mil.*; *obs.*) brigadier. **2.** brigade-leader; team-leader; foreman.
бригади́рш|а, и *f.* (*obs.*) brigadier's wife.
брига́дник, а *m.* member of a brigade, team.
брига́д|ный *adj. of* **~а**
бриганти́н|а, ы *f.* brigantine.
бри́дер, а *m.* breeder reactor; **бы́стрый б.** fast-breeder (reactor).
бридж, а *m.* bridge (*card-game*).
бри́дж|и, ей *no sg.* breeches.
бриджи́ст, а *m.* bridge player.
бриз, а *m.* breeze.
briза́нтн|ый *adj.* high explosive; **~ые вещества́** high explosives; **б. снаря́д** high explosive shell.
брике́т, а *m.* briquette.
брил|лиа́нт, а *and* **~ья́нт, а** *m.* (cut) diamond, brilliant.
бриллиа́нт|овый *adj. of* **~**
брил|ья́нт = ~лиа́нт
брил|ья́нтовый = ~лиа́нтовый
брита́н|ец, ца *m.* Britisher, Briton.
брита́н|ка, ки *f. of* **~ец**
брита́нский *adj.* British; **б. мета́лл** Britannia metal.
Брита́ни|я, и *f.* Britain.
Брита́нск|ие остров|а́, ~их ~о́в *no sg.* the British Isles.
бри́тв|а, ы *f.* razor; **безопа́сная б.** safety razor.
бри́твенн|ый *adj.* shaving; **~ые принадле́жности** shaving things; **б. реме́нь** (razor-)strop.
бритоголо́вый *adj.* shaven-headed; **б. подро́сток** skinhead; *as n.* **бритоголо́в|ый, ого** *m.* skinhead.
бритт, а *m.* (ancient) Briton.
бри́т|ый (~, ~а) *p.p.p. of* **~ь** *and adj.* clean-shaven.
бр|ить, е́ю, е́ешь *impf.* (*pf.* **по~**) to shave.
бритьj|ё, я́ *nt.* shave; shaving.
бр|и́ться, е́юсь, е́ешься *impf.* to shave, have a shave.
бри́финг, а *m.* (press) briefing.
бри́чк|а, и *f.* (*obs.*) britzka (*light carriage*).
бро́вк|а, и *f.* **1.** *dim. of* **бровь. 2.** edge (*of running track*).
бров|ь, и, *pl.* **~и, ~е́й** *f.* eyebrow; brow; **~и дуго́й** arched eyebrows; **хму́рить ~и** to knit one's brows, frown; **он и ~ью не повёл** he did not turn a hair; **попа́сть не в б., а (пря́мо) в глаз** (*prov.*) to hit the nail on the head.
брод, а *m.* ford; **не зна́я ~у, не су́йся в во́ду** (*prov.*) look before you leap.
броди́льный *adj.* (*tech.*) fermentative; **б. чан** fermenting vat; **б. фериме́нт** fermenting-agent.
бро|ди́ть[1], жу́, ~дишь *impf.* to wander, roam; to amble, stroll; **б. по магази́ну** to browse round a shop; **б. по у́лицам** to roam the streets; **б. в потёмках** (*fig.*) to be in the dark, not to know one's way about; (*fig.*): **улы́бка ~ди́ла по её лицу́** a smile played about her face.
бро|ди́ть[2], ~дит *impf.* to ferment.
бродя́г|а, и *m.* tramp, vagrant; down-and-out.
бродя́жнича|ть, ю *impf.* to be a tramp, be on the road.
бродя́жничеств|о, а *nt.* vagrancy.
бродя́ч|ий *adj.* vagrant; wandering, roving; (*fig.*) restless; **~ие племена́** nomadic tribes; **~ая соба́ка** stray dog.
броже́ни|е, я *nt.* fermentation; **б. умо́в** (*fig.*) intellectual ferment.
бро|жу́, ~дишь *see* **~ди́ть**
бро́кер, а *m.* broker.
бро́кколи *f. indecl.* broccoli.
бром, а *m.* (*chem.*) bromine; (*med.*) bromide.
бро́мистый *adj.* (*chem.*) bromide; **б. на́трий** sodium bromide.
бро́м|овый *adj. of* **~**
броне... *comb. form* (*mil.*) armoured-.

бронеавтомоби́л|ь, я *m.* armoured car.
бронебо́йк|а, и *f.* (*coll.*) anti-tank rifle.
бронебо́йный *adj.* armour-piercing.
бронебо́йщик *m.* anti-tank rifleman.
броневи́к, á *m.* armoured car.
бронев|о́й *adj.* armoured; **~ы́е пли́ты** (*mil.*) armour plating.
бронежиле́т, а *m.* bulletproof vest.
броненóс|ец[1], **ца** *m.* (*naut.*) battleship; ironclad.
броненóс|ец[2], **ца** *m.* (*zool.*) armadillo.
броненóсный *adj.* armoured.
бронепóезд, а *m.* armoured train.
бронеси́л|ы, ~ *no sg.* armoured forces.
бронетáнков|ый *adj.* (*mil.*) armoured; **~ые чáсти** armoured units.
бронетранспортёр, а *m.* armoured troop carrier.
брóнз|а, ы *f.* **1.** bronze. **2.** (*collect.*) bronzes.
бронзир|овáть, у́ю *impf. and pf.* to bronze.
бронзирóвк|а, и *f.* bronzing.
бронзирóвщик, а *m.* bronzer.
бронзовщи́к, á *m.* worker in bronze.
брóнзов|ый *adj.* bronze; bronzed, tanned; **~ая болéзнь** (*med.*) Addison's disease; **б. век** (*archeol.*) the Bronze Age; **б. загáр** sunburn, sun-tan.
брони́рова|нный *p.p.p. of* **~ть** *and adj.* reserved.
бронирóв|анный *p.p.p. of* **~áть** *and adj.* armoured.
брони́р|овать, ую *impf.* (*of* **за~**) to reserve, book.
бронир|овáть, у́ю *impf. and pf.* to armour.
бронх, а *m.* (*anat.*) bronchial tube.
бронхиáльный *adj.* (*anat.*) bronchial.
бронхи́т, а *m.* (*med.*) bronchitis.
брóн|я *f.* reservation; commandeering; **получи́ть мéсто по ~е** to have a seat reserved.
брон|я́, и́ *f.* armour; armour-plating.
бросá|ть, ю *impf.* (*of* **брóсить**). **1.** to throw, cast, fling; **б. взгляд** to dart a glance; **б. обвинéния** to hurl accusations; **б. тень** to cast a shadow; (**на**+*a.*; *fig.*) to cast aspersions (on); **б. я́корь** to drop anchor; **б. на вéтер** to throw away, waste; **б. запасны́е войскá в бой** to fling reserves into the battle; (*impers.*): **егó ~ет то в жар, то в хóлод** he keeps going hot and cold. **2.** to leave, abandon, desert; **б. му́жа** to desert one's husband; **б. ору́жие** to lay down one's arms; **б. рабóту** to give up, throw up one's work. **3.** (+*inf.*) to give up, leave off; **он всё ~л кури́ть** he was forever trying to give up smoking.
брос|áться, áюсь *impf.* **1.** (*impf. only*) (+*i.*) to throw at one another, pelt one another (with); **по пути́ в шкóлу мы ~áлись снежкáми** we used to pelt one another with snowballs on the way to school. **2.** (*impf. only*) (+*i.*) to throw away; **б. деньгáми** to throw away, squander one's money. **3.** (*pf.* **∸иться**) (**на, в**+*a.*) to throw o.s. (on, upon), rush (to); **б. на еду́** to fall upon one's food; **б. на колéни** to fall on one's knees; **б. в объя́тия** (+*d.*) to fall into the arms (of); **б. на пóмощь** to rush to assistance; **б. на шéю** (+*d.*) to fall on the neck (of); **кровь ~áлась ей в лицó** the blood was rushing to her face. **4.** (*pf.* **∸иться**): **б. в глазá** to be striking, arrest attention. **5.** (*pf.* **∸иться**) (+*inf.*) to begin, start.
брó|сить, шу, сишь *pf. of* **~сáть; ~сь(те)!** stop it!; **хоть ~сь** (*coll.*) it is no good.
брó|ситься, шусь, сишься *pf. of* **~сáться**
брóс|кий (~ок, ~кá, ~ко) *adj.* (*coll.*) bright, loud, garish; **б. гáлстук** loud tie.
броскóм *adv.* (*coll.*) **1.** with one throw. **2.** with a spurt.
брóсовый *adj.* **1.** worthless; low-grade. **2.: б. э́кспорт** (*econ.*) dumping.
брос|óк, кá *m.* **1.** throw; **штрафнóй б.** (*sport*) free throw. **2.** bound; spurt; **он пришёл пéрвым в гóнке благодаря́ послéднему ~ку́** he came in first in the race by making a final spurt.
брóшк|а, и *f.* brooch.
брó|шу, сишь *see* **~сить**
брош|ь, и *f.* brooch.
брошир... (~овáть, *etc.*) = **брошюр...**
брошю́р|а, ы *f.* pamphlet, brochure.
брошюр|овáть, у́ю *impf.* (*of* **с~**) (*tech.*) to stitch.
брошюрóвк|а, и *f.* (*tech.*) stitching.
брошюрóвочн|ая, ой *f.* book-stitching shop.
брошюрóвщик, а *m.* (*tech.*) stitcher.
бру́дер, а *m.* brooder (*for poultry*).
брудершáфт, а *m. only in phr.* **вы́пить (на) б.** to drink 'Bruderschaft'.
брульóн, а *m.* (*obs.*) rough copy.
Бруне́|й, я *m.* Brunei.
брус, а, *pl.* **∸ья, ∸ьев** *m.* squared beam; **параллéльные ∸ья** (*sport*) parallel bars.
брускóв|ый *adj.* bar, bar-shaped; **~ое желéзо** bar-iron; **~ое мы́ло** bar soap.
брусни́к|а, и *f.* foxberry; red whortleberry (*Vaccinium vitis idaea*).
брусни́|чный *adj. of* **~ка**
брус|óк, кá *m.* bar; ingot; **б. мы́ла** bar of soap; **точи́льный б.** whetstone.
бру́ствер, а *m.* (*mil.*) breastwork, parapet.
бру́тто *adj. indecl.* gross; **вес б.** gross weight.
брыжéйк|а, и *f.* (*anat.*) mesentery.
бры́ж|и, ей *no sg.* ruff, frill.
бры́згалк|а, и *f.* **1.** sprinkler. **2.** water-pistol.
бры́з|гать, жу, жешь *impf.* (*of* **~нуть**) (+*i.*) **1.** to splash, spatter; to gush, spurt; **б. гря́зью (на**+*a.*) to splash mud (on to), spatter with mud. **2.** (*pres.* **~жу** *or* **~гаю**) to sprinkle.
бры́зга|ться, юсь *impf.* (*coll.*) to splash; to splash o.s., one another; **собáки лю́бят б. в лу́жах** the dogs enjoy splashing in the puddles; **б. духáми** to spray o.s. with scent.
бры́зг|и, ~ *no sg.* **1.** spray, splashes (*of liquids*). **2.** fragments (*of stone, glass, etc.*).
бры́з|жу, жешь *see* **~гать**
бры́з|нуть, ну, нешь *pf. of* **~гать; кровь ~нула из рáны** blood spurted from the wound.
брык|áть, áю *impf.* (*of* **~ну́ть**) to kick.
брыкá|ться, юсь *impf.* to kick; (*fig.*) to kick, rebel.
брыкли́в|ый (~, ~а) *adj.* (*coll.*) inclined to kick.
брык|ну́ть, ну́, нёшь *pf. of* **~áть**
брыку́н, á *m.* (*coll., dial.*) kicker.
брыл|ы́, ~ *pl.* (*sg.* **~á, ~ы́** *f.*) flews.
бры́нз|а, ы *f.* brynza (*sheep's milk cheese*).
брысь *int.* shoo! (*to a cat*).
Брю́гге *m. indecl.* Bruges.
брюзг|á, и́ *c.g.* grumbler.
брюзгли́в|ый (~, ~а) *adj.* grumbling, peevish.
брюзжáни|е, я *nt.* grumbling.
брюзж|áть, у́, и́шь *impf.* to grumble.
брю́кв|а, ы *f.* (*bot.*) swede.
брю́кв|енный *adj. of* **~а**
брю́к|и, ~ *no sg.* trousers; **б.-ю́бка** culottes.
брюнéт, а *m.* dark-haired man.
брюнéтк|а, и *f.* brunette.
Брюссéл|ь, я *m.* Brussels.
брю́ссельск|ий *adj.* Brussels; **~ая капу́ста** Brussels sprouts; **~ие кружевá** Brussels lace.
брюхáст|ый (~, ~а) *adj.* (*coll.*) big-bellied.
брюхá|тить, чу, тишь *impf.* (*of* **о~**) (*vulg.*) to put in the club; to knock up (*sc. impregnate*).
брюхáт|ый *adj.* (*coll.*) = **брюхáстый; ~ая** big with child.
брю́х|о, а, *pl.* **~и** *nt.* (*coll.*) belly; paunch; **ходи́ть с ~ом** (*vulg.*) to be big with child.
брюхонóг|ие, их (*zool.*) gasteropods.
брюши́н|а, ы *f.* (*anat.*) peritoneum; **воспалéние ~ы** (*med.*) peritonitis.
брюшк|ó, á, *pl.* **~и́, ~óв** *nt.* **1.** abdomen; (*coll.*) paunch. **2.** belly-pieces (*of fur-bearing animals or of fish as food*).
брюшнóй *adj.* abdominal; **б. тиф** typhoid (fever).
бряк *int.* bang!; crash!
бря́кань|е, я *nt.* (*coll.*) clatter.
бря́к|ать, аю *impf.* (*of* **~нуть**) (*coll.*) **1.** (+*i.*) to clatter; **б. посу́дой** to clatter crockery. **2.** to let fall with a bang; (*fig.*) to drop a clanger. **3.** to blurt out.
бря́к|аться, аюсь *impf.* (*of* **~нуться**) (*coll.*) to crash, fall heavily.
бря́к|нуть(ся), ну(сь), нешь(ся) *pf. of* **~ать(ся)**

бряца́ни|е, я *nt.* **1.** rattling. **2.** rattle; clang; clank, clanking; **б. шпор** the rattle of spurs; **б. ору́жием** sabre-rattling.
бряца́|ть, ю *impf.* (*+i. or* **на**+*p.*) to rattle; to clang; to clank; **б. цимба́лами** to clash cymbals; **б. ору́жием** (*fig.*) to rattle the sabre; **кимва́л ~ющий** (*iron.*) 'tinkling cymbal'.
БССР *f. indecl.* (*abbr. of* ***Белору́сская Сове́тская Социалисти́ческая Респу́блика***) Byelorussian Soviet Socialist Republic.
БТР *m. indecl.* (*abbr. of* **бронетранспортёр**) APC (*armoured personnel carrier*).
бу́б|ен, на, *g. pl.* **~ен** *m.* tambourine.
бубен|е́ц, ца́ *m.* little bell; **колпа́к с ~ца́ми** cap and bells.
бубе́нчик, а *m.* **1.** *dim. of* **бубене́ц. 2.** (*bot.*) harebell, campanula.
бу́блик, а *m.* boublik (*thick, ring-shaped bread roll*).
бу́б|на, ны, *g. pl.* **~ён** *f.* (*cards*) **1.** (*pl.*) diamonds; **ходи́ть с ~ён** to lead diamonds; **дво́йка ~ён** the two of diamonds. **2.** a diamond.
бубн|и́ть, ю́, и́шь *impf.* (*of* **про~**) (*coll.*) to grumble; to mutter; to drone on (*of a speaker*).
бубно́вый *adj.* (*cards*) diamond; **б. туз** ace of diamonds; (*hist.*; *fig.*) diamond-shaped patch on convict's coat.
бу́б|ны[1], **ен** *see* **~ен**
бу́б|ны[2], **ён** *see* **~на**
бубо́н, а *m.* (*med.*) bubo.
бубо́н|ный *adj. of* **~; ~ная чума́** (*med.*) bubonic plague.
буга́|й, я *m.* (*dial.*) bull (*also fig.*).
бу́гел|ь, я *m.* **1.** (*naut.*) hoop. **2.** (*elec.*) bow-collector.
буги-ву́ги *nt. indecl.* boogie-woogie.
буг|о́р, ра́ *m.* mound, knoll; bump, lump.
бугор|о́к, ка́ *m.* **1.** *dim. of* **~́** knob, protuberance. **2.** (*med.*) tubercle.
бугорча́тк|а, и *f.* (*med; obs.*) tuberculosis.
бугó́рчатый *adj.* **1.** covered with lumps. **2.** (*med.*) tuberculous. **3.** (*bot.*) tuberous.
бугри́ст|ый (~, ~а) *adj.* hilly; bumpy.
бугшпри́т = **бушпри́т**
Будапе́шт, а *m.* Budapest.
будди́зм, а *m.* Buddhism.
будди́йский *adj.* Buddhist.
будди́ст, а *m.* Buddhist.
бу́де *conj.* (*obs.*) if, provided that.
будёновк|а, и *f.* (*hist.*) budyonovka (*pointed helmet worn by Red Army men during period 1918–21*).
бу́дет 1. *3rd pers. sg. fut. of* **быть; б. ему́ за э́то!** he'll catch it. **2.** *as pred.* (*coll.*) that's enough; that'll do; **б. с вас э́того?** will that do?; **вы́пьем ещё одну́ буты́лку и б.** we'll drink one more bottle and call it a day; **уже́ за́ полночь, б. вам писа́ть** it's past midnight, it's time you stopped writing.
буди́льник, а *m.* alarm clock.
буди́р|овать, ую *impf.* (*obs.*) to sulk.
бу|ди́ть, жу́, ~́дишь *impf.* **1.** (*pf.* **раз~**) to wake, awaken, call. **2.** (*pf.* **про~**) (*fig.*) to rouse, arouse; to stir up; **б. мысль** to set (one) thinking, give food for thought.
бу́дк|а, и *f.* box, booth; stall; **железнодоро́жная б.** (*rail.*) trackman's hut, crossing-keeper's hut; **карау́льная б.** sentry-box; **соба́чья б.** dog kennel; **суфлёрская б.** prompt-box; **телефо́нная б.** telephone booth.
бу́д|ни, ней, *sg.* (*obs. or coll.*) **~ень, ~ня** *m.* **1.** weekdays; working days, workdays; **по ~ням** on weekdays. **2.** humdrum life; colourless existence.
бу́дний *adj.*: **б. день** weekday.
бу́днич|ный *adj.* **1.**: **б. день** weekday; **~ое расписа́ние** weekday timetable. **2.** everyday; dull, humdrum.
бу́днишний *adj.* = **бу́дничный**
будора́ж|ить, у, ишь *impf.* (*of* **вз~**) (*coll.*) to disturb; to excite.
бу́дочник, а *m.* **1.** (*obs.*) policeman on duty. **2.** (*rail.*) trackman; crossing-keeper.
бу́дто 1. *conj.* as if, as though; **он верну́лся с таки́м ви́дом, б. его́ изби́ли** he came back looking as if he had been beaten up. **2.** *conj.* that (*implying doubt as to the truth of a reported affirmation*); **он утвержда́ет, б. говори́т свобо́дно на десяти́ языка́х** he says that he speaks, he claims to speak ten languages fluently. **3.** (*also* **б. бы, как б.**) *particle* (*coll.*) apparently; allegedly, ostensibly; **она́ б. должна́ уха́живать за отцо́м** apparently she has to look after her father. **4.** *interrog. particle* (*coll.*) really?; **уж б. он так умён?** is he really all that clever?
бу́д|у, ешь *fut. of* **быть**
будуа́р, а *m.* boudoir.
будуа́р|ный *adj. of* **~**
бу́дучи *pres. ger. of* **быть** being.
бу́дущ|ий *adj.* future; next; ... to be; **~ее вре́мя** (*gram.*) future tense; **в ~ем году́** next year; **~ая мать** mother-to-be, expectant mother; **в б. раз** next time; *as n.* **~ее, ~его** *nt.* (*i*) the future; **в ближа́йшем ~ем** in the near future, (*ii*) (*gram.*) future tense.
бу́дущност|ь, и *f.* future; **ему́ предстои́т блестя́щая б.** a brilliant future lies before him.
бу́дь(те) *imper. of* **быть** (*sg. also used in place of* **е́сли**+*main v. to form protasis of conditional sentences*) **бу́дьте добры́, б. любе́зны** (*+inf. or imper.*) please; would you be good enough (to), kind enough (to); **будь, что бу́дет** come what may; **не будь вас, всё бы пропа́ло** but for you all would have been lost; **будь он бога́т, будь он бе́ден, мне всё равно́** be he rich or be he poor, it is all one to me.
бу|ёк, йка́ *m.* (*naut.*) anchor-buoy, lifebuoy.
бу́ер, а, *pl.* **~а́** *m.* **1.** ice-yacht, land-yacht. **2.** (*obs.*) small sailing-boat.
буера́к, а *m.* (*dial.*) gully; coomb.
буери́ст, а *m.* ice-yachtsman.
бу́ерный *adj.*: **б. спорт** ice-yachting.
буж, а́ *m.* (*med.*) probe.
буженй́н|а, ы *f.* boiled salted pork.
бу|жу́, ~́дишь *see* **~ди́ть**
буз|а́[1], **ы́** *f.* (*dial.*) bouza (*fermented beverage made from millet, buckwheat or barley*).
буз|а́[2], **ы́** *f.* (*coll.*) row; **подня́ть ~у́** to kick up a row.
бузи́л|а, ы *c.g.* (*coll.*) = **бузотёр**
бузин|а́, ы́ *f.* (*bot.*) elder.
бузи́нник, а *m.* (*bot.*) elder grove, elderbush.
бузи́н|ный *adj. of* **~а́**
бузи́|ть (*1st pers. not used*), **~шь** *impf.* (*coll.*) to kick up a row.
буз|ова́ть, у́ю *impf.* (*coll.*) to beat.
бузотёр, а *m.* (*coll.*) troublemaker, hell-raiser.
бузотёр|ка, ки *f. of* **~**
бузотёрств|о, а *nt.* (*coll.*) rowdyism.
бузу́н[1], **а́** *m.* salt-lumps (*precipitated in salt lakes*).
бузу́н[2], **а́** *m.* (*coll.*) rowdy.
бу|й, я, *pl.* **~и́, ~ёв** *m.* buoy.
бу́йвол, а *m.* (*zool.*) buffalo.
бу́йвол|овый *adj. of* **~; ~овая ко́жа** buff.
бу́|йный (~ен, ~йна́, ~́йно) *adj.* **1.** wild; violent, turbulent; tempestuous; ungovernable; **б. сумасше́дший** violent, dangerous lunatic; **б. хара́ктер** ungovernable character. **2.** luxuriant, lush; **б. рост** luxuriant growth.
бу́йств|о, а *nt.* unruly, riotous conduct.
бу́йств|овать, ую *impf.* (*coll.*) to create uproar; to behave violently.
бук, а *m.* beech.
бу́к|а, и *c.g.* (*coll.*) **1.** bogy(man), bugbear. **2.** (*fig.*) misanthrope, unsociable pers.; surly pers.; **смотре́ть ~ой** to look surly.
бука́шк|а, и *f.* small insect.
бу́кв|а, ы, *g. pl.* **~** *f.* letter (*of the alphabet*); **б. в ~у** literally; **б. зако́на** (*fig.*) the letter of the law.
буква́льно *adv.* literally; word for word.
буква́льн|ый *adj.* literal; **~ое значе́ние** literal meaning; **б. перево́д** word-for-word translation.
буква́р|ь, я́ *m.* ABC; primer.
бу́квенно-цифрово́й *adj.* alphanumeric.
бу́квенный *adj.* in letters.
бу́квиц|а, ы *f.* (*bot.*) wood betony.
буквое́д, а *m.* pedant.
буквое́дств|о, а *nt.* pedantry.
буке́т, а *m.* **1.** bouquet; bunch of flowers, posy. **2.** bouquet; aroma.

букини́ст, а *m.* second-hand bookseller.
букинисти́ческий *adj.*: **б. магазин** second-hand bookshop.
букле́т, а *m.* (fold-out) leaflet.
бу́кл|я, и *f.* curl; ringlet.
букме́кер, а *m.* bookmaker; bookie.
бу́ковый *adj.* beech(en); **б. жёлудь** beechnut.
буко́лик|а, и *f.* (*liter.*) bucolic literature.
буколи́ческий *adj.* bucolic, pastoral.
букс, а *m.* (*bot.*) box.
бу́кс|а, ы *f.* (*tech.*) axle-box.
букси́р, а *m.* **1.** tug, tugboat. **2.** tow-rope; **взять на б.** to take in tow; (*fig.*) to give a helping hand; **тяну́ть на ~е** to have in tow.
букси́р|ный *adj. of* **~; б. парохо́д** steam tug.
букси́р|овать, ую *impf.* to tow, have in tow.
буксиро́вк|а, и *f.* towing.
буксиро́вщик, а *m.* tug aircraft.
буксова́ни|е, я *nt.* skidding, wheel-spin.
букс|ова́ть, у́ю *impf.* to skid (*of wheels of locomotive, etc., to revolve on the spot without moving forward*).
бу́кс|овый *adj. of* **~**
булав|а́, ы́ *f.* mace.
була́вк|а, и *f.* pin; **англи́йская б.** safety-pin; **де́ньги на ~и** pin-money.
була́вочник, а *m.* **1.** pincushion, pin-box. **2.** pin-maker.
була́в|очный *adj. of* **~ка**
була́ный *adj.* Isabel(la), dun (*colour of horse*).
була́т, а *m.* (*hist.*) damask steel; (*fig.*) sword.
була́т|ный *adj. of* **~**; (*hist., poet.*; *conventional epithet of sword*).
булга́ч|ить, у, ишь *impf.* (*coll.*) to stir up, excite.
булими́|я, и *f.* bulimia.
бу́лин|ь, я *m.* (*naut.*) bowline.
бу́лк|а, и *f.* small loaf; white bread; **сдо́бная б.** bun.
бу́лл|а, ы *f.* (*Papal*) bull.
бу́лочн|ая, ой *f.* bakery; baker's shop.
бу́лочник, а *m.* baker.
булты́х *int.* plop!; splosh!; *as pred.*: **де́вочка б. в во́ду** the little girl fell splosh into the water.
бултых|а́ть, а́ю *impf.* (*of* **~ну́ть**) (*coll.*) **1.** to slop. **2.** to drop with a plopping noise (*into liquid*).
бултых|а́ться, а́юсь *impf.* (*coll.*) **1.** (*pf.* **~ну́ться**) to (fall) plop. **2.** (*impf. only*) to splash *or* thrash (about).
булты́х|нуть, ну-ну́, нешь-нёшь *pf. of* **~а́ть**
булты́х|нуться, нусь-ну́сь, нешься-нёшься *pf. of* **~а́ться**
булы́жник, а *m.* cobble-stone (*also collect.*).
бульва́р, а *m.* avenue; boulevard.
бульва́р|ный *adj. of* **~; ~ная пре́сса** the tabloids; gutter press; **б. рома́н** cheap novel.
бульдо́г, а *m.* bulldog.
бульдо́зер, а *m.* bulldozer.
бульдозери́ст, а *m.* bulldozer driver.
бу́лькань|е, я *nt.* gurgling.
бу́лька|ть, ю *impf.* to gurgle.
бульо́н, а *m.* broth; stock.
бульо́нный *adj.*: **б. ку́бик** stock cube.
бульва́рщин|а, ы *f.* (*pej.*) pulp literature.
бультерье́р, а *m.* bull terrier.
бум[1]**, а** *m.* (*coll.*) **1.** (*econ.*) boom. **2.** newspaper sensation.
бум[2]**, а** *m.* (*sport*) beam.
бум[3] *int.* boom! **ни ~-~** (*coll., joc.*) (*to know, understand, etc.*) bugger all; sweet FA (*Fanny Adams*).
бума́г|а[1]**, и** *f.* **1.** paper; **газе́тная б.** newsprint; **б. в клётку** squared paper; **почто́вая б.** notepaper; **2.** document; (*pl.*) (official) papers; **це́нные ~и** (*fin.*) securities.
бума́г|а[2]**, и** *f.* **(хлопча́тая) б.** cotton; **шерсть с ~ой** wool and cotton.
бумагодержа́тел|ь[1]**, я** *m.* (*fin.*) holder of securities, bondholder.
бумагодержа́тел|ь[2]**, я** *m.* paper-clip.
бумагомара́к|а, и *c.g.* = **бумагомара́тель**
бумагомара́ни|е, я *nt.* (*coll.*) scrawl.
бумагомара́тел|ь, я *m.* (*coll.*) scribbler; ink-slinger.
бумагопряде́ни|е, я *nt.* cotton-spinning.
бумагопряди́льн|ый *adj.* cotton-spinning; **~ая фа́брика** cotton mill.
бумагопряди́л|ьня, ьни, *g. pl.* **~ен** *f.* cotton mill.
бумагоре́зк|а, и *f.* shredder.
бума́жк|а, и *f.* **1.** *dim. of* **бума́га**; scrap of paper. **2.** note; (paper) money.
бума́жник[1]**, а** *m.* wallet.
бума́жник[2]**, а** *m.* paper-maker.
бума́|жный[1] *adj. of* **~га**[1]; (*fig.*) (existing only on) paper; **~жная волоки́та** red tape; **~жные де́ньги** paper money; **б. змей** kite; **~жная фа́брика** paper-mill.
бума́|жный[2] *adj. of* **~га**[2]; **~жная пря́жа** cotton yarn; **~жная ткань** cotton fabric.
бумажо́нк|а, и *f.* (*coll.*) scrap of paper.
бумазе́йный *adj.* fustian.
бумазе́|я, и *f.* fustian.
бумера́нг, а *m.* boomerang.
бу́нгало *nt. indecl.* bungalow.
бу́нкер, а *m.* (*tech.*) bunker.
бункер|ова́ть, у́ю *impf. and pf.* to bunker.
бункер|ова́ться, у́юсь *impf. and pf.* (*naut.*) to coal.
бункеро́вк|а, и *f.* coaling.
бунт[1]**, а,** *pl.* **~ы́** *m.* revolt; riot; mutiny.
бунт[2]**, а́** *m.* bale; packet; bundle.
бунта́рский *adj.* **1.** seditious; mutinous. **2.** (*fig.*) rebellious; turbulent; **б. дух** rebellious spirit.
бунта́рств|о, а *nt.* rebelliousness.
бунта́р|ь, я́ *m.* **1.** rebel (*also fig.*); insurgent; mutineer; rioter; **он б. в душе́** he is a rebel at heart. **2.** inciter to mutiny, rebellion.
бунт|ова́ть, у́ю *impf.* **1.** (*pf.* **взбунтова́ться**) to revolt, rebel; to mutiny; to riot; (*fig.*) to rage, go berserk. **2.** (*pf.* **вз~**) to incite to revolt, mutiny.
бунт|ова́ться, у́юсь *impf.* = **~ова́ть 1.**
бунт|ово́й *adj. of* **~**[2]
бунтовско́й *adj.* rebellious, mutinous.
бунтовщи́к, а́ *m.* rebel, insurgent; mutineer; rioter.
бунчу́к, а́ *m.* (*hist.*) staff of Cossack hetman.
бур[1]**, а** *m.* (*tech.*) auger.
бур[2]**, а** *m.* Boer.
бур|а́, ы́ *f.* (*chem.*) borax.
бура́в, а́, *pl.* **~а́** *m.* (*tech.*) auger; gimlet.
бура́в|ить лю, ишь *impf.* to bore, drill.
бура́вчик, а *m.* gimlet.
бура́к, а́ *m.* **1.** (*dial.*) beetroot. **2.** (*dial.*) cylindrical birch-bark box. **3.** cascade (*type of firework*).
бура́н, а *m.* snow-storm (*in steppes*).
бурбо́н, а *m.* (*coll., obs.*) coarse fellow; upstart.
бургоми́стр, а *m.* **1.** burgomaster. **2.** (*orn.*) glaucous gull.
бурго́нское = **бургу́ндское**
бургу́ндск|ий *adj.* Burgundian; *as n.* **~ое, ~ого** *nt.* burgundy (*wine*).
бурд|а́, ы́ *f.* slops.
бурдю́к, а́ *m.* wineskin, water-skin.
буреве́стник, а *m.* stormy petrel.
бур|ево́й *adj. of* **~я**; stormy.
бурело́м, а *m.* wind-fallen trees.
буре́ни|е, я *nt.* (*tech.*) boring, drilling; **о́пытное б.** test boring; **уда́рное б.** percussion drilling.
буре́|ть, ю, еш *impf.* (*of* **по~**) to grow brown.
буржуа́ *m. indecl.* bourgeois.
буржуази́|я, и *f.* bourgeoisie; **ме́лкая б.** petty bourgeoisie.
буржуа́з|ный (~ен, ~на) *adj.* bourgeois.
буржу́|й, я *m.* (*coll.*) bourgeois.
буржу́й|ка, ки *f.* **1.** *f. of* **~**. **2.** (*coll.*) small stove.
буржу́йский *adj.* (*coll.*) bourgeois.
бури́льный *adj.* (*tech.*) boring.
бури́льщик, а *m.* borer; driller, drill-operator.
бур|и́ть, ю́, и́шь *impf.* (*tech.*) to bore; to drill.
бу́рк|а[1]**, и** *f.* (*folk poet.*) chestnut horse.
бу́рк|а[2]**, и** *f.* felt cloak (*worn in Caucasus*).
бу́ркал|ы, ~ *no sg.* (*coll.*) eyes.
бу́рк|ать, аю *impf.* (*of* **~нуть**) (*coll.*) to mutter, growl out.
бу́рк|нуть, ну, нешь *pf. of* **~ать**
бурла́к, а́ *m.* barge hauler.

бурла́|цкий *adj. of* **~к**
бурла́честв|о, а *nt.* trade of barge hauler.
бурла́ч|ить, у, ишь *impf.* to be a barge hauler.
бурли́в|ый (~, ~а) *adj.* turbulent; seething.
бурл|и́ть, ю́, и́шь *impf.* to seethe, boil up (*also fig.*).
бурми́стр, а *m.* (*hist.*) bailiff.
бурну́с, а *m.* burnous.
бу́р|ный (~ен, ~на́) *adj.* **1.** stormy, rough; impetuous; **~ные аплодисме́нты** thunderous applause. **2.** rapid; energetic; **б. рост** rapid growth.
бурови́к, а́ *m.* (*tech.*) boring, drilling technician.
буров|о́й *adj.* boring; **~а́я вы́шка** derrick; **~а́я сква́жина** bore, bore-hole, well.
бу́рс|а, ы *f.* (*hist.*) seminary.
бурса́к, а́ *m.* (*hist.*) seminarist.
бурса́|цкий *adj. of* **~к**
бу́рский *adj.* Boer.
бу́ртик, а *m.* (*tech.*, *naut.*) fender.
буру́н, а́ *m.* breaker; bow-wave.
бурунду́к, а́ *m.* (*zool.*) chipmunk.
бурча́ни|е, я *nt.* (*coll.*) grumbling; (stomach-)rumbling.
бурч|а́ть, у́, и́шь *impf.* (*of* **про~**) (*coll.*) **1.** to mumble, mutter; to grumble. **2.** (*impf. only*) to rumble; to bubble; (*impers.*): **в котле́ ~и́т** the cauldron is bubbling; **у меня́ ~и́т в животе́** my stomach is rumbling.
бу́р|ый (~, ~а́, ~о) *adj.* brown; **б. медве́дь** brown bear; **~ая лиси́ца** red fox.
бурья́н, а *m.* tall weeds.
бу́р|я, и *f.* storm (*also fig.*); **б. в стака́не воды́** storm in a teacup; **б. и на́тиск** (*hist.*, *liter.*) 'Sturm und Drang'.
буря́т, а, *g. pl.* **б.** *m.* Buryat.
буря́т|ка, ки *f. of* **~**
буря́тский *adj.* Buryat.
бу́син|а, ы *f.* bead.
буссо́л|ь, и *f.* surveying compass.
бу́с|ы, ~ *no sg.* beads.
бут, а *m.* (*tech.*) rubble, quarry-stone.
бутафо́р, а *m.* (*theatr.*) property-man.
бутафо́ри|я, и *f.* (*theatr.*) properties; dummies (*in shop window*); (*fig.*) window-dressing, sham.
бутафо́р|ский *adj. of* **~ия;** (*fig.*) sham, mock-; illusory.
бутербро́д, а *m.* slice of bread and butter; sandwich; **зако́н ~а** Sod's Law, Murphy's Law.
бутербро́дн|ая, ой *f.* sandwich bar.
бути́л, а *m.* (*chem.*) butyl.
бутиле́н, а *m.* (*chem.*) butylene.
бу|ти́ть, чу́, ти́шь *impf.* (*of* **за~**) (*tech.*) to fill with rubble.
бу́товый *adj.* rubble.
буто́н, а *m.* **1.** bud. **2.** (*coll.*) pimple.
бутонье́рк|а, и *f.* buttonhole, posy.
бу́тс|ы, ~ *pl.* (*sg.* **~а, ~ы** *f.*) football boots.
буту́з, а *m.* (*coll.*) chubby lad.
буту́|зить, жу, зишь *impf.* (*coll.*) to punch.
буты́лк|а, и *f.* bottle.
буты́лочк|а, и *f.* small bottle; vial, phial.
буты́лочник, а *m.* glass-blower.
буты́л|очный *adj. of* **~ка; ~очного цве́та** bottle-green.
буты́л|ь, и *f.* large bottle; carboy, drum.
бу́фер, а, *pl.* **~а́** *m.* **1.** buffer. **2.** bumper. **3.** (*pl.*, *sl.*) boobs, knockers.
буфера́стый *adj.* (*coll.*) busty, bosomy.
бу́фер|ный *adj. of* **~; ~ное госуда́рство** (*pol.*) buffer state.
буфе́т, а *m.* **1.** sideboard. **2.** buffet, refreshment room; (refreshment) bar, counter.
буфе́тн|ая, ой *f.* pantry.
буфе́т|ный *adj. of* **~**
буфе́тчик, а *m.* barman, bartender.
буфе́тчиц|а, ы *f.* barmaid; counter assistant.
буфф *adj. indecl.* comic, buffo; **о́пера-б.** comic opera; **теа́тр-б.** comedy.
буффо́н, а *m.* (*theatr.*) buffoon; (*fig.*) buffoon, clown.
буффона́д|а, ы *f.* (*theatr.*) buffoonery, slapstick; (*fig.*) buffoonery.
бу́ф|ы, ~ *no sg.* gathers, puffs; **б. на рукава́х** puff sleeves.
бух *int.* bang!; plonk!; plop!; *as pred.* **он б. на зе́млю** he fell to the ground with a thud.
буха́нк|а, и *f.* loaf.
Бухаре́ст, а *m.* Bucharest.
буха́рский *adj.*: **б. ковёр** Bokhara carpet.
бу́х|ать, аю *impf.* (*of* **~нуть**) **1.** to thump, bang; **б. кулако́м в дверь** to bang on the door with one's fist. **2.** to let fall with a thud. **3.** to thud, thunder; **слы́шно бы́ло, как вдали́ ~али пу́шки** the thunder of cannon could be heard in the distance. **4.** (*fig.*, *coll.*) to blurt out.
бу́х|аться, аюсь *impf.* (*of* **~нуться**) (*coll.*) to fall heavily; to plonk o.s. down.
бухга́лтер, а, *pl.* **~ы** *m.* book-keeper, accountant.
бухгалте́ри|я, и *f.* **1.** book-keeping; **двойна́я б.** double-entry book-keeping. **2.** counting-house.
бухга́лтерский *adj.* book-keeping, account; **~ая кни́га** account book.
бу́х|нуть[1], ну, нешь, *past* **~нул** *pf. of* **~ать**
бу́х|нуть[2], ну, нешь, *past* **~, ~ла** *impf.* to swell, expand.
бу́х|нуться, нусь, нешься *pf. of* **~аться**
бухо́й *adj.* (*sl.*) sozzled (= *drunk*).
бу́хт|а[1], ы *f.* (*geog.*) bay, bight.
бу́хт|а[2], ы *f.* coil (*of rope*).
бу́хточк|а, и *f.* creek, cove, inlet.
бу́хты-бара́хты *only in phr.* (*coll.*) **с б.-б.** offhand; off the cuff; suddenly.
бу́цы = бу́тсы
бу́ч|а, и *f.* (*coll.*) row.
бу́чени|е, я *nt.* (*tech.*) washing in lye.
бу́ч|ить, у, ишь *impf.* (*tech.*) to wash in lye.
бу|чу́, ти́шь *see* **~ти́ть**
бу́ч|у, ишь *see* **~ить**
буш|ева́ть, у́ю *impf.* to rage; (*fig.*) to rage, storm.
бу́шел|ь, я *m.* bushel.
бушла́т, а *m.* (*naut.*) pea-jacket.
бу́шпри́т, а *m.* (*naut.*) bowsprit.
Буэ́нос-А́йрес, а *m.* Buenos Aires.
буя́н[1], а *m.* (*coll.*) rowdy, brawler.
буя́н[2], а *m.* (*obs.*) wharf.
буя́н|ить, ю, ишь, *impf.* (*coll.*) to make a row; to brawl.
буя́нств|о, а *nt.* (*coll.*) rowdyism, brawling.
бы (*abbr.* **б**) *particle* **1.** *indicates hypothetical sentence* (*see also* **е́сли**): **я мог бы об э́том догада́ться** I might have guessed it; **бы́ло бы о́чень прия́тно вас ви́деть** it would be very nice to see you. **2.** **(+ни)** *forms indef. prons.*: **кто бы ни** whoever; **что бы ни** whatever; **как бы ни** however; **кто бы ни пришёл** whoever comes; **что бы ни случи́лось** whatever happens; **как бы то ни́ бы́ло** however that may be, be that as it may. **3.** *expr. wish*: **я бы вы́пил пи́ва** I should like a drink of beer. **4.** *expr. polite suggestion or exhortation*: **вы бы отдохну́ли** you should take a rest.
быва́|ло 1. *see* **~ть. 2.** *particle indicating repetition of an action in past time*: **моя́ мать б. ча́сто пе́ла э́ту пе́сню** my mother would often sing this song.
быва́л|ый *adj.* **1.** experienced; worldly-wise. **2.** (*coll.*) habitual, familiar; **э́то де́ло ~ое** this is nothing new. **3.** (*obs.*) former.
быва́|ть, ю *impf.* **1.** to happen; to take place; **заседа́ния горсове́та ~ют раз в неде́лю** the town council meets once a week; **~ет, что поезда́ с се́вера опа́здывают** trains from the north are apt to be late, are sometimes late; **э́тому не б.!** this must not occur!, I forbid it! **2.** to be; to be present; to frequent; **он ~ет ка́ждый день в кабине́те с девяти́ часо́в утра́** he is in his office every day from nine a.m.; **они́ ре́дко ~ют в теа́тре** they seldom go to the theatre; **он ~ет у нас** he comes to see us. **3.** to be inclined to be, tend to be; **он ~ет раздражи́телен** he is inclined to be irritable. **4.: как ни в чём не ~ло** (*coll.*) as if nothing had happened; as if nothing were wrong; **как не ~ло** (*+g.*) to have completely disappeared; **головно́й бо́ли у меня́ как не ~ло** my headache has completely gone.
бы́вш|ий *p.p. of* **быть** *and adj.* former, ex-; one-time; ci-devant; **б. президе́нт** former president, ex-president; **~ие лю́ди** déclassés; **го́род Санкт-Петербу́рг, б. Ленингра́д**

St. Petersburg, formerly Leningrad.

бы́дл|о, а *nt.* (*collect.*; *dial.*; *also fig.*) cattle.

бык[1], **а́** *m.* **1.** bull; ox; **рабо́чий б.** draught ox; **бой ~о́в** bullfight; **взять ~а́ за рога́** (*fig.*) to take the bull by the horns; **здоро́в, как б.** as strong as a horse; **упере́ться, как б.** to be as stubborn as an ox. **2.** male (*of certain horned animals*); **оле́ний б.** stag. **3.** (*pl.*) the Bovidae.

бык[2], **а́** *m.* pier (*of a bridge*).

был|ево́й *adj. of* **~ина**

были́н|а, ы *f.* (*liter.*) bylina (*Russ. traditional heroic poem*).

были́нк|а, и *f.* blade of grass.

были́н|ный *adj. of* **~а**; epic.

бы́ло *particle* **1.** *indicates cancellation of projected or impending action*: nearly, on the point of; **он пое́хал б. с ни́ми, но заболе́л** he would have gone with them, but he fell ill; **чуть б.** very nearly; **я чуть б. не забы́л** I very nearly forgot; **они́ чуть б. не уби́ли его́** they all but killed him. **2.** *indicates cessation of action already, but only just, commenced*: **он отпра́вился б. с ни́ми, но верну́лся** he started out with them but turned back.

был|о́й *adj.* former, past, bygone; **в ~ы́е времена́** in days of old; *as n.* **~о́е, ~о́го** *nt.* (*poet.*) the past, olden time; **Было́е и ду́мы** 'My Past and Thoughts' (*title of work by A. I. Herzen*).

был|ь, и *f.* **1.** (*obs.*) fact. **2.** true story.

быль|ё, я́ *nt.* (*obs.*) grass; *now only in phr.* **~ём поросло́** long forgotten.

быстрин|а́, ы́, *pl.* **~́ы** *f.* (*geog.*) rapid(s).

быстрогла́з|ый (~, ~а) *adj.* saucy, sprightly, busybodyish.

быстроде́йстви|е, я *nt.* (*tech.*) speed, response time.

быстроде́йствующий *adj.* high-speed; quick-acting.

быстрозаморо́женный *adj.* (quick-)frozen.

быстролётный *adj.* high-speed; fleeting, transient.

быстроно́гий *adj.* (*poet.*) fleet of foot.

быстросбо́рный *adj.* quick-assembly.

быстросо́хнущий *adj.* quick-dry(ing).

быстросхва́тывающийся *adj.*: **б. бето́н** quick-setting concrete.

быстрот|а́, ы́ *f.* rapidity, quickness; speed.

быстроте́кущий *adj.* (*poet.*, *obs.*) swift-flowing.

быстроте́ч|ный (~ен, ~на) *adj.* fleeting, transient.

быстрохо́д|ный (~ен, ~на) *adj.* fast, high-speed; **б. танк** (*mil.*) cruiser tank.

бы́стр|ый (~, ~а́, ~о) *adj.* rapid, fast, quick; prompt.

быт, а, о ~́е, в ~у́ *no pl.*, *m.* way of life; life; **дома́шний б.** family life; **солда́тский б.** army life; **слу́жба ~́а** consumer services; **примене́ние персона́льных компью́теров в ~у́** the use of personal computers in the home.

быти|е́, я́ *nt.* (*phil.*) being, existence, objective reality; **б., по слова́м Ма́ркса, определя́ет созна́ние** existence, according to Marx, determines consciousness; **кни́га Б~я́** (*bibl.*) Genesis.

бы́тност|ь, и *f. only in phr.* **в б.** during a given period; **в б. мою́ студе́нтом** in my student days; **в б. его́ в Ри́ме** during his stay in Rome, in his Rome days.

быт|ова́ть, у́ет *impf.* to occur, be current; **были́ны ещё ~у́ют на се́вере** byliny still exist in the North.

бытови́зм, а *m.* excessive preoccupation with everyday themes; 'kitchen-sinkism'.

бытови́к, а́ *m.* (*coll.*) writer or artist of the kitchen-sink school.

быто́вк|а, и *f.* (*coll.*) site hut; rest-room.

быт|ово́й *adj. of* **~**; social; **~ова́я жи́вопись** genre painting; **~овы́е прибо́ры** domestic appliances; **~ова́я пье́са** domestic drama; **~ова́я револю́ция** social revolution; **~ова́я ЭВМ** home computer; **~ово́е явле́ние** everyday occurrence; **комбина́т ~ово́го обслу́живания** consumer service establishment (*multiple enterprise comprising hair-dressing, dry-cleaning, household appliance repair services, etc.*).

бытописа́ни|е, я *nt.* (*obs.*) annals, chronicles.

бытописа́тел|ь, я *m.* **1.** (*obs.*) historian, annalist. **2.** writer on social themes.

быть *pres. not used exc. 3rd pers. sg.* **есть** *and* (*obs.*) *3rd pers. pl.* **суть**, *fut.* **бу́ду, бу́дешь**, *past* **был, была́, бы́ло (не́ был, не была́, не́ было)** *imper.* **бу́дь(те)** (*see also* **бу́дет, бу́дь(те), бы́ло, есть**).

I. 1. to be (= *to exist*); **есть таки́е лю́ди** there are such people, such people do exist. **2.: б. у** (*see also* **есть**) to be in the possession (of); **у них была́ прекра́сная да́ча** they had a lovely dacha. **3.** to be (= *to be situated*, *be located*); **(к)** to come (to), be present (at); **здесь был тракти́р** there used to be an inn here; **где вы бы́ли вчера́?** where were you yesterday?; **он тут был не при чём** he had nothing to do with it; **они́ бу́дут к нам за́втра** they are coming (to see us) tomorrow; **на ней была́ ро́зовая ко́фточка** she had on a pink blouse. **4.** to be, happen, take place; **э́того не мо́жет б.!** it cannot be!; **что с ним бы́ло?** what happened to him?; **б. беде́** there's sure to be trouble; **как б.?** what is to be done?; **так и б.** so be it, all right, very well, have it your own way; **б. по сему́** (*obs.*) be it so enacted.

II. *as v. aux.* to be.

быть|ё, я́ *nt.* (*obs.*) mode of life.

быча́ч|ий *adj. of* **бык**[1]; **~ья ко́жа** oxhide; **~ья ше́я** bull neck.

бы́чий *adj.* = **быча́чий**

быч|о́к[1], **ка́** *m.* steer.

быч|о́к[2], **ка́** *m.* goby.

быч|о́к[3], **ка́** *m.* (*coll.*) cigarette butt.

бьеф, а *m.* reach; **ве́рхний б.** head water; **ни́жний б.** tail water.

бью, бьёшь *see* **бить**

бюва́р, а *m.* blotting-pad.

бюве́т, а *m.* pump-room.

бюдже́т, а *m.* budget.

бюдже́тный *adj.* budgetary; **б. год** fiscal year.

бюллете́н|ить, ю, ишь *impf.* (*coll.*) to be off sick.

бюллете́н|ь, я *m.* **1.** bulletin; **информацио́нный б.** newsletter. **2.** **(избира́тельный) б.** voting-paper. **3.** **(больни́чный) б.** medical certificate; **быть на ~е** (*coll.*) to be on sick-leave, be on the sick-list.

бю́ргер, а *m.* burgher; (*fig.*, *iron.*) philistine.

бюре́тк|а, и *f.* (*tech.*) burette.

бюро́ *nt. indecl.* **1.** bureau, office; **б. нахо́док** lost-property office; **спра́вочное б.** inquiry office; **туристи́ческое б.** travel agency. **2.** bureau, writing-desk.

бюрокра́т, а *m.* bureaucrat.

бюрократи́зм, а *m.* bureaucracy; red tape.

бюрократи́ческий *adj.* bureaucratic.

бюрокра́ти|я, и *f.* bureaucracy (*also collect.*).

бюст, а *m.* bust; bosom.

бюстга́льтер, а *m.* bra(ssière).

бя́з|евый *adj. of* **~ь**

бяз|ь, и *f.* coarse calico.

бя́к|а, и *f.* (*in children's speech*) nasty thing; nasty man.

бя́ша *int.* (*dial.*; *onomat.*) baa!

В

В (*abbr. of* **восто́к**) E, East.

в *prep.*

I. *+a. and p.* **1.** (*+a.*) into, to; (*+p.*) in, at; **пое́хать в Москву́** to go to Moscow; **роди́ться в Москве́** to be born in Moscow; **сесть в ваго́н** to get into the carriage; **сиде́ть в ваго́не** to be in the carriage; **оде́ться в смо́кинг** to put on a dinner-jacket; **быть в смо́кинге** to be in a dinner-jacket; **разби́ть на куски́** to smash to pieces; **са́хар в куска́х**

sugar in lumps; **привести́ в восто́рг** to delight, enrapture; **быть в восто́рге** to be delighted, be in raptures. **2.** *in reference to external attributes*: **руба́шка в клётку** check(ed) shirt; **лицо́ в весну́шках** freckled face. **3.** (*+nom.-a. pl. and p. pl.*) *in reference to occupation*: **пойти́ в стенографи́стки** to become a shorthand-typist; **служи́ть в куха́рках** to be a cook. **4.** *in reference to calendar units and periods of time*: **в понеде́льник** on Monday; **в январе́** in January; **в 1899-ом году́** in 1899; **в двадца́том ве́ке** in the twentieth century; **в четы́ре часа́** at four o'clock; **в четвёртом часу́** between three and four; **в на́ши дни** in our day; **в тече́ние** (*+g.*) during, in the course (of).

II. *+a.* **1.** *in reference to objects through which vision is directed*: **смотре́ть в окно́** to look out of the window; **смотре́ть в бино́кль** to look through binoculars. **2.** *in attribution of resemblance*: **быть в кого́-н.** to take after s.o.; **она́ вся в тётю** she is the image of her aunt. **3.** *indicating aim or purpose*: for, as; **сказа́ть в шу́тку** to say for a joke; **привести́ в доказа́тельство** to adduce as proof. **4.** *in specification of quantitative attributes*: **моро́з в де́сять гра́дусов** ten degrees of frost; **высото́й в три ме́тра** three metres high; **ве́сом в пять килогра́ммов** weighing five kilograms. **5.** (*+***раз** *and comp. adv.*) *indicates comparison in numerical terms*: **в два ра́за бо́льше** twice as big, twice the size; **в два ра́за ме́ньше** half as big, half the size. **6.** *of time*: in, within; **наде́юсь ко́нчить чернови́к в ме́сяц** I hope to finish the rough draft in a month. **7.** *indicates game or sport played*: **игра́ть в ка́рты, ша́хматы, те́ннис, футбо́л** to play cards, chess, tennis, football.

III. *+p.* **1.** at a distance of; **в трёх киломе́трах от го́рода** three kilometres from the town; **они́ живу́т в десяти́ мину́тах ходьбы́ отсю́да** they live ten minutes' walk from here. **2.** in; of (= *consisting of, amounting to*); **пье́са в трёх де́йствиях** play in three acts; **ра́зница в двух копе́йках** a difference of two kopecks.

в. (*abbr. of* **век**) C, century.

ва-ба́нк *adv.* (*cards*) **игра́ть, идти́ ва-б.** to stake everything; (*fig.*) to stake one's all.

ва́б|ить, лю, ишь *impf.* to lure, decoy.

Вавило́н, а *m.* Babylon.

вавило́нск|ий *adj.* Babylonian; **~ое столпотворе́ние** babel; **~ая ба́шня** the tower of Babel.

вавило́н|ы, ов *no sg.* (*coll.*) **1.** (*archit.*) scrolls. **2.** flourishes (*in handwriting*), scrawl; **выводи́ть, писа́ть в.** (*fig.*) to stagger, lurch (*of a drunken pers.*).

ва́г|а, и *f.* (*tech.*) **1.** weighing-machine. **2.** splinter-bar; swingle-tree. **3.** lever.

ваго́н, а *m.* **1.** carriage, coach; **мя́гкий, жёсткий в.** soft-seated, hard-seated carriage; **бага́жный в.** luggage van; **в.-рестора́н** dining-car, restaurant car; **служе́бный в.** guard's van; **спа́льный в.** sleeping-car; **това́рный в.** goods wagon, goods truck; **трамва́йный в.** tram-car; **в.-цисте́рна** tank truck. **2.** wagon-load; (*fig., coll.*) loads, lots; **игру́шек у него́ в.** he has loads of toys; **вре́мени у нас в.** we have masses of time.

ваготе́тк|а, и *f.* truck; trolley.

вагоне́тчик, а *m.* truck-, trolley-operator.

ваго́нник, а *m.* carriage-building worker.

ваго́н|ный *adj. of* **~**; **~ная ось** carriage axle; **в. парк** rolling-stock.

вагоновожа́т|ый, ого *m.* tram-driver.

вагонострое́ни|е, я *nt.* carriage-building.

вагонострои́тельный *adj.* carriage-building; **в. заво́д** carriage(-building) works.

ваго́нчик, а *m.* (*coll.*) site hut.

вагра́нк|а, и *f.* (*tech.*) cupola furnace.

ва́ди *nt. indecl.* wadi.

ва́женк|а, и *f.* (*dial.*) female reindeer.

важне́цк|ий *adj.* (*coll.*) good, good-quality; **вот у вас ~ие боти́нки** that's a good pair of boots you have on.

ва́жничани|е, я *nt.* airs and graces.

ва́жнича|ть, ю *impf.* (*coll.*) to give o.s. airs, get a swelled head; (*+i.*) to plume o.s. (on).

ва́жност|ь, и *f.* **1.** importance; significance; **де́ло большо́й ~и** a matter of great importance, of great moment; **не велика́ в.** (*coll.*) it's of no consequence; **э́ка в.** (*coll.*) what does it matter! **2.** pomposity, pretentiousness.

ва́ж|ный (~ен, ~на́, ~но) *adj.* **1.** important; weighty, consequential; **са́мое ~ное узна́ть, отку́да они́ прие́хали** the (important) thing is to discover where they have come from; **в свое́й стране́ он дово́льно в. челове́к** in his own country he is a man of some consequence; **~ная ши́шка** (*coll.*) bigwig, big knob. **2.** pompous, pretentious.

ва́з|а, ы *f.* vase, bowl; **в. для цвето́в** flower vase; **ночна́я в.** chamber-pot.

вазели́н, а *m.* Vaseline (*propr.*).

вазели́н|овый *adj. of* **~**; **~овое ма́сло** (*med.*) liquid paraffin.

вазомото́рный *adj.* (*med.*) vasomotor.

вазо́н, а *m.* (flower-)pot.

ва́и|я, и, *g. pl.* **~й** *f.* **1.** (*bot.*) fern-branch. **2.** palm(-branch); **неде́ля ~й** (*eccl.*) Palm Sunday.

ва́йя = **ва́ия**

вака́нси|я, и *f.* vacancy; **бу́дут две ~и в шта́те в бу́дущем году́** there will be two vacancies on the staff next year.

вака́нт|ный (~ен, ~на) *adj.* vacant (*of posts in an institution*).

вака́ци|я, и *f.* (*obs.*) vacation.

ва́кс|а, ы *f.* (shoe) polish; blacking.

ва́к|сить, шу, сишь *impf.* (*of* **на~**) to black, polish.

ва́куум, а *m.* (*tech.*) vacuum; **в.-маши́на, в.-насо́с** vacuum pump.

вакхана́ли|я, и *f.* **1.** (*usu. pl.*; *hist.*) bacchanalia. **2.** (*fig.*) orgy. **3.** (*fig.*) confusion, disorder.

вакха́нк|а, и *f.* **1.** Bacchante, maenad. **2.** (*fig.*) bawd, hussy.

вакхи́ческий *adj.* Bacchic.

вакци́н|а, ы *f.* vaccine.

вакцина́ци|я, и *f.* vaccination.

вакцини́р|овать, ую *impf. and pf.* to vaccinate.

ва́к|шу, сишь *see* **~сить**

вал[1], а, *pl.* **~ы́** *m.* billow, roller; **девя́тый в.** 'ninth wave' (*according to superstition, fatal to sailors*).

вал[2], а, *pl.* **~ы́** *m.* bank, earthen wall; (*mil.*) rampart; (*geol.*) swell.

вал[3], а, *pl.* **~ы́** *m.* (*tech.*) shaft.

вал[4], а *m.* (*econ.*) **1.** gross output (*as indicator of industrial efficiency, by contrast with profit*). **2.** = **план ~ово́й проду́кции** (*see* **~ово́й**).

валя́нда|ться, юсь *impf.* (*coll.*) **1.** to loiter, hang about. **2.** (**с***+i.*) to dawdle (over), mess about (with).

валансье́н *adj. indecl.* (*text.*) **кружева́ в.** Valanciennes lace.

Валга́лла = **Ва́льха́лла**

вале́жник, а *no pl., m.* (*collect.*) windfallen trees, branches.

вал|ёк, ька́ *m.* (*tech.*) **1.** battledore. **2.** swingle-tree. **3.** (*typ., etc.*) roller. **4.** (*agric.*) (threshing-)flail. **5.** (*naut.*) loom (*of an oar*).

ва́лен|ки, ок *pl.* (*sg.* **~ок, ~ка** *m.*) valenki (*felt boots*).

вале́нтност|ь, и *f.* (*chem.*) valency.

ва́леный = **ва́ляный**

валерья́н|а, ы *f.* (*bot.*) valerian.

валерья́нк|а, и *f.* (*coll.*) tincture of valerian.

валерья́нов|ый *adj.* (*med.*): **~ые ка́пли** tincture of valerian.

вале́т, а *m.* (*cards*) knave, jack; **спать ~ом** to sleep top to tail.

ва́лик, а *m.* **1.** (*tech.*) roller, cylinder; spindle, shaft. **2.** bolster.

вал|и́ть[1], ю, ~ишь *impf.* **1.** (*pf.* **по~** *and* **с~**) to throw down, bring down, send toppling; to overthrow; **в. кого́-н. с ног** to knock s.o. off his feet; **в. дере́вья** to fell trees; **нас всех ~и́л грипп** we were all being laid low by the 'flu. **2.** (*pf.* **с~**) to heap up, pile up; **в. всё в одну́ ку́чу** to lump everything together (*also fig.*); **в. вину́ (на***+a.***)** to lump the blame (on).

вал|и́ть[2], и́т *impf.* (*coll.*) **1.** to flock, throng, pour; **вало́м в.** to throng, go en masse; **лю́ди ~и́ли на стадио́н** people were flocking to the stadium; **снег ~и́т кру́пными хло́пьями** the snow is coming down in large flakes; **дым ~и́л из трубы́** smoke was belching from the chimney; **ему́ уж давно́ ~и́т сча́стье** he has had a long run of luck:

2.: ~и́(те)! go on!; have a go!; ~и́, беги́! be off with you!
вал|и́ться, ю́сь, ⁓ишься *impf.* (*of* **по~** *and* **с~**) to fall, collapse; to topple; **в. от уста́лости** to drop from tiredness; **у него́ всё из рук ⁓ится** (*coll.*) he is all fingers and thumbs; **де́ло у него́ ⁓ится из рук** his heart is not in the matter, he cannot put his mind to the matter; **на бе́дного Мака́ра все ши́шки ⁓ятся** (*prov.*) an unfortunate man would be drowned in a teacup.
ва́лк|а¹, и *f.* felling.
ва́лк|а², и *f.* (*text.*) fulling.
ва́л|кий (~ок, ~ка́, ~ко) *adj.* unsteady, shaky; (*naut.*) crank; **ни ша́тко, ни ~ко** middling; neither good nor bad.
валли́|ец, йца *m.* (*obs.*) Welshman.
валли́йк|а, и *f.* (*obs.*) Welshwoman.
валли́йский *adj.* (*obs.*) Welsh.
валло́н, а *m.* Walloon.
валло́н|ка, ки *f. of* ~
валло́нский *adj.* Walloon.
валова́н, а *m.* vol-au-vent.
валово́й *adj.* **1.** (*econ.*) gross; wholesale; **в. дохо́д** gross revenue; **в. сбор** gross yield; **план в. проду́кции** gross output plan. **2.** general, mass (*of migration of birds*).
вало́м *see* **вали́ть²**
вало́ш|ить, у, ишь *impf.* to castrate, geld.
валто́рн|а, ы *f.* (*mus.*) French horn.
валу́|й, я́ *m.* stinking russule (*mushroom*).
валу́н, а́ *m.* boulder.
Ва́льга́лла = Ва́льха́лла
ва́льдшнеп, а *m.* (*zool.*) woodcock.
вальс, а *m.* waltz.
вальси́р|овать, ую *impf.* to waltz.
Ва́льха́лл|а, ы *f.* Valhalla.
вальц|ева́ть, у́ю *impf.* (*tech.*) to roll.
вальцо́вк|а, и *f.* (*tech.*) **1.** rolling. **2.** rolling press.
вальцо́вщик, а *m.* (*tech.*) operative of rolling-mill, roller.
вальцо́в|ый *adj.* (*tech.*); **~ая ме́льница** rolling-mill.
вальц|ы́, о́в *no sg.* (*tech.*) rolling press.
ва́льщик, а *m.* (*dial.*) woodcutter.
вальяжный *adj.* (*coll.*) weighty, impressive; handsome; **вид у него́ в.** he has an impressive presence; **в. переплёт** handsome binding.
валю́т|а, ы *f.* (*fin., econ.*) **1.** currency; **курс ~ы** rate of exchange. **2.** (*collect.*) foreign exchange, hard currency.
валю́тка, и *f.* (*sl.*) = **Берёзка**
валю́тно-фина́нсов|ый *adj.*: **~ая би́ржа** foreign exchange market.
валю́т|ный *adj. of* **~а;** currency.
валю́тчик, а *m.* (*coll.*) speculator in foreign currency.
валя́льный *adj.* fulling.
валя́л|ьня, ьни, *g. pl.* **~ен** *f.* fulling-mill.
валя́льщик, а *m.* fuller.
валя́ни|е, я *nt.* (*tech.*) fulling, milling.
ва́ляный *adj.* felt.
валя́|ть, ю *impf.* **1.** (*impf. only*) to drag; **в. по́ полу** to drag along the floor. **2.** (*pf.* **вы́~**) to roll, drag; **в. в грязи́** to drag in the mire. **3.** (*pf.* **с~**) to knead. **4.** (*pf.* **с~**) to full; to felt. **5.** (*pf.* **на~**) (*coll.*) to botch, bungle; to muck about. **6.:** **в. дурака́** (*coll.*) to play the fool. **7.** **~й(те)!** (*coll.*) go ahead! carry on!
валя́|ться, юсь *impf.* **1.** to roll. **2.** (*coll.*) to lie about, loll; **весь день он ~ется в хала́те** he lies about in his dressing-gown all day; **её оде́жда ~лась везде́ по ко́мнате** her clothes lay scattered all over the room; **в. в нога́х у кого́-н.** (*fig.*) to fall down at s.o.'s feet.
вам *d. of* **вы**
ва́ми *i. of* **вы**
вамп *f. indecl.* vamp.
вампи́р, а *m.* **1.** vampire (*also fig.*). **2.** (*zool.*) vampire-bat.
вана́ди|й, я *m.* (*chem.*) vanadium.
ванда́л, а *m.* (*hist. and fig.*) Vandal; vandal.
вандали́зм, а *m.* vandalism.
ванили́н, а *m.* vanillin.
вани́л|ь, и *f.* vanilla.
вани́ль|ный *adj. of* ~
ва́нн|а, ы *f.* bath; **сидя́чая в.** hip-bath; **со́лнечная в.** sun-bath; **фотографи́ческая в.** photographic bath; **взять ~у, приня́ть ~у** to take a bath.
ва́нночк|а, и *f. dim. of* **ва́нна**; (*phot.*) developing tray; **глазна́я в.** eye-bath.
ва́нн|ый *adj. of* **~а**; *as n.* **~ая, ~ой** *f.* bathroom.
ва́нт|а, ы *f.* (*naut.*) shroud.
ва́ньк|а, и *m.* (*obs.*) cabby (*nickname of poor droshky-drivers*).
ва́нька-вста́нька, ва́ньки-вста́ньки *m.* tumbler (*toy*).
вапориза́тор, а *m.* (*tech.*) vaporizer.
вапориза́ци|я, и *f.* (*tech.*) vaporization.
вар, а *m.* **1.** pitch; cobbler's wax. **2.** (*dial.*) boiling water.
вара́кушк|а, и *f.* (*zool.*) bluethroat.
вара́н, а *m.* (*zool.*) giant lizard.
ва́рвар, а *m.* barbarian.
варвари́зм, а *m.* (*ling., liter.*) barbarism.
ва́рварский *adj.* barbarian; (*fig.*) barbaric.
ва́рварств|о, а *nt.* barbarity; vandalism.
варга́н|ить, ю, ишь *impf.* (*of* **с~**) (*coll.*) to botch, bungle.
ва́рев|о, а *nt.* (*coll., pej.*) broth; slop.
ва́режк|а, и *f.* mitten (*glove with thumb but no fingers*).
варен|е́ц, ца́ *m.* fermented boiled milk.
варе́ние = ва́рка
варе́ник, а *m.* varenik (*curd or fruit dumpling*).
варёнк|а, и *f.* (*coll.*) stone-washed *or* frosted denim garment; **ку́ртка/ю́бка-в.** stone-washed denim jacket/skirt.
варён|ки, ок *no sg.* (*coll.*) stone-washed *or* frosted denim jeans.
варёный *adj.* **1.** boiled. **2.** (*coll.*) limp.
варе́нь|е, я *nt.* preserve(s) (*containing whole fruit*), jam.
вариа́нт, а *m.* reading, variant; version; option; scenario; model; **нулево́й в.** (*pol.*) zero option; **расска́з был распространён во мно́гих ~ах** many versions of the story were circulated.
вариацио́нн|ый *adj.* variant; **~ое исчисле́ние** (*math.*) calculus of variations.
вариа́ци|я, и *f.* variation; **те́ма с ~ями** (*mus.*) theme and variations.
варико́зный *adj.* (*anat.*) varicose.
вар|и́ть, ю́, ⁓ишь *impf.* (*of* **с~**) **1.** to boil; to cook; **в. карто́фель** to boil potatoes; **в. обе́д** to cook dinner; **в. глинтве́йн** to mull wine; **в. пи́во** to brew beer. **2.** (*of the stomach*) to digest. **3.** to found (*steel*).
вар|и́ться, ю́сь, ⁓ишься *impf.* (*of* **с~**) **1.** to boil (*intrans.*); to cook (*intrans.*); **карто́фель уже́ полчаса́ ⁓ится** the potatoes have been on for half an hour already; **в. в со́бственном соку́** (*coll.*) to keep o.s. to o.s. **2.** *pass. of* **~и́ть**
ва́рк|а, и *f.* boiling; cooking; **в. варе́нья** preserve-making; **в. желе́за** iron-founding; **в. пи́ва** brewing.
ва́р|кий (~ок, ~ка́, ~ко) *adj.* **1.** heat-giving; **~кая печь** hot stove. **2.** tender (*of meat, etc.*).
варна́к, а́ *m.* (*dial.*) (escaped) convict.
ва́рниц|а, ы *f.* **1.** saltworks. **2.** saltpan.
варра́нт, а *m.* (*comm.*) custom-house license; warehouse warrant.
Варша́в|а, ы *f.* Warsaw.
варша́вский *adj.* (of) Warsaw.
варьете́ *nt. indecl.* variety (show); **теа́тр-в.** music-hall.
варьи́р|овать, ую *impf.* to vary, modify.
варя́г, а *m.* (*hist.*) Varangian.
варя́жский *adj.* (*hist.*) Varangian.
вас *g., a., and p. of* **вы**
васил|ёк, ька́ *m.* (*bot.*) cornflower.
васили́ск, а *m.* basilisk.
васил|ько́вый *adj. of* **~ёк**; cornflower blue.
васса́л, а *m.* vassal, liege(-man).
васса́льн|ый *adj.* vassal; **~ая зави́симость** vassalage.
ва́т|а, ы *f.* cotton wool; wadding; **са́харная в.** candyfloss; **пальто́ на ~е** wadded coat.
вата́г|а, и *f.* band, gang.
ватерклозе́т, а *m.* water-closet.
ватерли́ни|я, и *f.* (*naut.*) water-line; **грузова́я в.** load water-line.
Ватерло́о *nt. indecl.* Waterloo.

ва́тер-маши́н|а, ы *f.* (*text.*) water frame.
ватерпа́с, а *m.* (*tech.*) water-level, spirit-level.
ватерполи́ст, а *m.* water polo player.
ватерпо́ло *nt. indecl.* (*sport*) water polo.
Ватика́н, а *m.* the Vatican; **(госуда́рство-го́род) В.** the Vatican City.
ватика́нский *adj.* Vatican.
вати́н, а *m.* sheet wadding.
ва́тман, а *m.* Whatman paper.
ва́тник, а *m.* quilted jacket.
ва́тн|ый *adj.* wadded, quilted; **~ое одея́ло** quilt.
ватру́шк|а, и *f.* curd tart; cheese-cake.
ватт, а, *g. pl.* **в.** *m.* (*elec.*) watt.
ва́ттност|ь, и *f.* (*elec.*) wattage.
ва́учер, а *m.* voucher.
ва́учеризаци|я, и *f.* (*pol.*) voucherization.
ва́фельниц|а, ы *f.* waffle-iron.
ва́фельщик, а *m.* waffle-maker; waffle-vendor.
ва́ф|ля, ли, *g. pl.* **~ель** *f.* waffle; wafer.
вахла́к, а́ *m.* (*coll.*) lout; sloven.
ва́хмистр, а *m.* (*obs.*) cavalry sergeant-major.
ва́хт|а, ы *f.* **1.** (*naut.*) watch; **стоя́ть на ~е** to keep watch. **2.** (*fig.*) special (collective) effort, special stint (*in former USSR, of workers on anniversary of October revolution, etc.*).
ва́хт|енный *adj. of* **~а** (*naut.*); **в. журна́л** log(-book); **в. команди́р** officer of the watch; *as n.* **в., ~енного** *m.* watch.
ва́хтер, а, *pl.* **~а́** *m.* (*obs.*) senior watchman.
вахтёр, а *m.* janitor, porter.
вахтпара́д, а *m.* (*obs.*) changing of the guard.
ваш, ~́его; *f.* **~́а, ~́ей;** *nt.* **~́е, ~́его;** *pl.* **~́и, ~́их** *possessive pron.* your(s); **э́то в. каранда́ш** this is your pencil; **э́тот каранда́ш в.** this pencil is yours; **~́его мне не ну́жно** (*coll.*) I don't want anything of yours; **он зна́ет бо́льше ~́его** (*coll.*) he knows more than you; **не ~́е де́ло** it is none of your business; *as n.* **~́и, ~́их** your people, your folk.
ва́шгерд, а *m.* (*tech.*) buddle.
Вашингто́н, а *m.* Washington.
ваяни|е, я *nt.* (*obs.*) sculpture.
вая́тел|ь, я *m.* (*obs.*) sculptor.
ва́я|ть, ю *impf.* (*of* **из~**) to sculpt; to carve, chisel.
вбега́|ть, ю *impf.* (**в**+*a.*) to run (into).
вбе|жа́ть, гу́, жи́шь, гу́т *pf. of* **~га́ть**
вбер|у́, ёшь *see* **вобра́ть**
вбива́|ть, ю *impf. of* **вбить**
вби́вк|а, и *f.* knocking-in.
вбира́|ть, ы *impf. of* **вобра́ть**
вбить, вобью́, вобьёшь *pf.* (*of* **вбива́ть**) to drive in, hammer in; (*sport*) **в. мяч в воро́та** to score a goal; (*coll.*) **в. в го́лову** (+*d.*; *fig.*) to knock into s.o.'s head; **в. себе́ в го́лову** to get into one's head.
вблизи́ *adv.* **(от)** close by; not far (from); **они́ живу́т где́-то в.** they live somewhere near here; **в. был слы́шен водопа́д** the sound of a waterfall could be heard near by; **в. от библиоте́ки** not far from the library; **рассма́тривать в.** to examine closely.
вбок *adv.* sideways, to one side.
вбра́сывани|е, я *nt.* **в. (мяча́)** throw-in (*in football*).
вбра́сыва|ть, ю *impf. of* **вбро́сить**
вброд *adv.*: **переходи́ть в.** to wade; to ford.
вбро́|сить, шу, сишь *pf.* (*of* **вбра́сывать**) to throw in(to).
вв. (*abbr. of* **века́**) C, centuries.
вва́лива|ть, ю *impf. of* **ввали́ть**
вва́лива|ться, юсь *impf. of* **ввали́ться**
ввал|и́ть, ю́, ~́ишь *pf.* to hurl, heave into.
ввал|и́ться, ю́сь, ~́ишься *pf.* **1.** (*coll.*) to tumble into, sink into. **2.** (*fig.*, *coll.*) to burst into. **3.** to become hollow, sunken; **с ~и́вшимися щека́ми** hollow-cheeked.
введе́ни|е, я *nt.* **1.** leading in(to); **в. в заблужде́ние** leading into temptation; **В. (во Храм)** (*eccl.*) Feast of the Presentation of the Blessed Virgin. **2.** introduction; preamble; **в. в языкозна́ние** introduction to philology.
вве|ду́, дёшь *see* **~сти́**
ввез|ти́, у́, ёшь, *past* **~́,** **~ла́** *pf.* (*of* **ввози́ть**) to import.
ввек *adv.* (*now only used before neg.*) ever; **я э́того в. не забу́ду** I shall not forget it as long as I live.
вверг|а́ть, а́ю *impf. of* **~́нуть**
вве́рг|нуть, ну, нешь, *past* **~, ~ла** *pf.* (*of* **~а́ть**) (**в**+*a.*; *obs.*) to cause to fall (into); to reduce (to); **в. в тюрьму́** to cast into gaol; **в. в нищету́** to bring to ruin; **в. в отча́яние** to drive to despair.
вве́р|ить, ю, ишь *pf.* (*of* **~я́ть**) to entrust; **в. та́йну кому́-н.** to confide a secret in s.o.
вве́р|иться, юсь, ишься *pf.* (*of* **~я́ться**) (+*d.*) to trust (in), put one's faith (in), put o.s. in the hands of.
вверн|у́ть, у́, ёшь *pf.* (*of* **ввёртывать**) **1.** to screw in, insert. **2.** (*fig.*, *coll.*) to insert, put in; **в. замеча́ние** to insert a comment; **ему́ не удало́сь в. ни слове́чка** he could not get a word in.
вверста́|ть, ю *pf.* (*of* **ввёрстывать**) (*typ.*) to inset.
ввёрстыва|ть, ю *impf. of* **вверста́ть**
ввер|те́ть, чу́, ~́тишь *pf.* (*of* **~́тывать**) (*coll.*) to screw in.
ввёртыва|ть, ю *impf. of* **ввернуть** *and* **вверте́ть**
вверх *adv.* up, upward(s); **идти́ в. по ле́стнице** to go upstairs; **в. по тече́нию** upstream; **в. дном** upside down; topsy-turvy; **в. нога́ми** head over heels.
вверху́ *adv. and prep.*+*g.* above, overhead; **в. над кры́шами домо́в** above the roofs of the houses; **в. страни́цы** at the top of the page.
ввер|чу́, ~́тишь *see* **~те́ть**
вверя́|ть(ся), ю(сь) *impf. of* **вве́рить(ся)**
вве|сти́, ду́, дёшь, *past* **~́л, ~ла́** *pf.* (*of* **вводи́ть**) to introduce, bring in; **в. мо́ду** to introduce a fashion; **в. су́дно в га́вань** to bring a ship into harbour; **в. во владе́ние** (*leg.*) to put in possession; **в. в заблужде́ние** to mislead; **в. в искуше́ние** to lead into temptation; **в. в курс чего́-н.** to acquaint with the facts of sth.; **в. в расхо́д** to put to expense; (*math.*) to interpolate.
ввечеру́ *adv.* (*obs.*) in the evening.
ввива́|ть, ю *impf. of* **ввить**
ввиду́ *prep.*+*g.* in view (of); **в. тума́на полёт не состои́тся** in view of the fog the flight will not take place; **в. того́, что** as; **в. того́, что вы прие́хали** as you have come.
ввин|ти́ть, чу́, ти́шь *pf.* (*of* **~́чивать**) (**в**+*a.*) to screw (in); **в. што́пор в про́бку** to insert a corkscrew into a cork.
вви́нчива|ть, ю *impf. of* **ввинти́ть**
ввить, вовью́, вовьёшь *pf.* (*of* **ввива́ть**) to weave in.
ввод, а *m.* **1.** bringing in; **в. в бой** (*mil.*) throwing into battle; **в. во владе́ние** (*leg.*) putting in possession. **2.** (*elec.*) lead-in. **3.** (*comput.*) input; **в. да́нных** data input.
вво|ди́ть, жу́, ~́дишь *impf. of* **ввести́**
вво́дн|ый *adj.* introductory; (*gram.*) **~ое предложе́ние** parenthetic clause; **~ое сло́во** parenthetic word, parenthesis; **в. тон** (*mus.*) leading note.
вво|жу́[1], **~́дишь** *see* **вводи́ть**
вво|жу́[2], **~́зишь** *see* **ввози́ть**
ввоз, а *no pl.*, *m.* **1.** importation. **2.** import; (*collect.*) imports.
вво|зи́ть, жу́, ~́зишь *impf. of* **ввезти́**
вво́зн|ый *adj.* imported; import; **~ые континге́нты** quota of imports; **~ая по́шлина** import duty.
ввола́кива|ть, ю *impf. of* **вволо́чь**
вволо́|чь, ку́, чёшь, ку́т, *past* **~к, ~кла́** *pf.* (*coll.*) to drag in.
вво́лю *adv.* (*coll.*) to one's heart's content, ad lib.; **нае́сться в.** to eat one's fill.
вво́сьмеро *adv.* eight times; **в. бо́льше** eight times as much.
ввосьмеро́м *adv.* eight together; **они́ в. сде́лали рабо́ту** eight of them did the job together.
ВВС *no sg.*, *indecl.* (*abbr. of* ***вое́нно-возду́шные си́лы***) Air Force.
ввысь *adv.* up, upward(s).
ввя|за́ть, жу́, ~́жешь *pf.* (*of* **~́зывать**) to knit in; (*fig.*) to involve.
ввя|за́ться, жу́сь, ~́жешься *pf.* (**в**+*a.*; *coll.*) to meddle (in); to get involved (in); mixed up (in); **в. в неприя́тную исто́рию** to get mixed up in a nasty business; **в. в бой** (*mil.*) to become engaged.

ввя́зыва|ть(ся), ю(сь) *impf. of* **ввяза́ть(ся)**
вгиб, а *m.* bend inwards.
вгиба́|ть, ю *impf. of* **вогну́ть**
вглубь *adv. and prep.+g.* deep down; deep into, into the depths; **в. лесо́в** into the heart of the forest; **в. страны́** far inland.
вгля|де́ться, жу́сь, ди́шься *pf.* (*of* **~дываться**) (**в**+*a.*) to peer (at).
вгля́дыва|ться, юсь *impf. of* **вгляде́ться**
вгоня́|ть, ю *impf. of* **вогна́ть**
вгры́з|ться, у́сь, ёшься *pf.* (*coll.*) to get one's teeth into (*of animals*).
вда|ва́ться, ю́сь, ёшься *impf. of* **~ться**
вдав|и́ть, лю́, ~ишь *pf.* (*of* **~ливать**) to press in.
вда́влива|ть, ю *impf. of* **вдави́ть**
вда́лблива|ть, ю *impf. of* **вдолби́ть**
вдалеке́ *adv.* in the distance; **в. от** a long way from.
вдали́ *adv.* in the distance, far off; **в. от го́рода** a long way from the city; **держа́ться в.** to keep aloof, keep one's distance; **исчеза́ть в.** to vanish into thin air.
вдаль *adv.* afar, at a distance; **гляде́ть в.** to look into the distance.
вд|а́ться, а́мся, а́шься, а́стся, ади́мся, ади́тесь, аду́тся *pf.* (*of* **вдава́ться**) (**в**+*a.*) to jut out (into); **в. в подро́бности** to go into details; **в. в то́нкости** to split hairs.
вдвига́|ть(ся), ю(сь) *impf. of* **вдви́нуть(ся)**
вдвижно́й *adj.* insertable.
вдви́|нуть, ну, нешь *pf.* (*of* **~га́ть**) to push in(to).
вдви́|нуться, нусь, нешься *pf.* (*of* **~га́ться**) to push in, squeeze in.
вдво́е *adv.* twice; double; **в. бо́льше** twice as much, twice as big; **в. ста́рше** double the age; **сложи́ть в.** to fold double.
вдвоём *adv.* the two together; **они́ в. написа́ли статью** the two of them together wrote the article.
вдвойне́ *adv.* twice, double; doubly (*also fig.*); **плати́ть в.** to pay double; **он в. винова́т** he is doubly to blame.
вдева́|ть, ю *impf. of* **вдеть**
вде́вятеро *adv.* nine times.
вдевятеро́м *adv.* nine together.
вдёжк|а, и *f.* **1.** threading (*of a needle*). **2.** thread.
вде́л|ать, аю *pf.* (*of* **~ывать**) (**в**+*a.*) to fit (into), set (into); **в. ка́мень в кольцо́** to set a stone into a ring.
вде́лыва|ть, ю *impf. of* **вде́лать**
вде́н|у, ешь *see* **вдеть**
вдёргива|ть, ю *impf. of* **вдёрнуть**
вдёржк|а, и *f.* **1.** bodkin. **2.** threading.
вдёрн|уть, у, ешь *pf.* (*of* **вдёргивать**) to pull through; to thread; **в. ни́тку в иглу́** to thread a needle.
вде́сятеро *adv.* ten times; **в. бо́льше** ten times as much.
вдесятеро́м *adv.* ten together; **мы в.** ten of us.
вде|ть, ~ну, ~нешь *pf.* (*of* **~ва́ть**) (**в**+*a.*) to put in(to); **в. ни́тку в иглу́** to thread a needle.
ВДНХ *f. indecl.* (*abbr. of* ***Вы́ставка достиже́ний наро́дного хозя́йства СССР***) Exhibition of National Economic Achievements (*in Moscow*).
вдоба́вок *adv.* in addition; moreover; into the bargain.
вдов|а́, ы́, *pl.* **~ы** *f.* widow; **соло́менная в.** (*coll.*) grass widow.
вдове́|ть, ю *impf.* (*of* **о~**) to be a widow(er); to be widowed.
вдов|е́ц, ца́ *m.* widower; **соло́менный в.** grass widower.
вдо́в|ий *adj. of* **~а́**; **~ья часть насле́дства** (*leg.*) dower, jointure.
вдови́ц|а, ы *f.* (*obs.*) widow.
вдо́воль *adv.* (*coll.*) **1.** in abundance; **у нас вся́кого ро́да фру́ктов в.** we have abundance of every kind of fruit. **2.** enough; **он нае́лся в.** he ate his fill.
вдовств|о́, а́ *nt.* widowhood; widowerhood.
вдо́вств|овать, ую *impf.* (*obs.*) to be a widow, a widower; **~ующая императри́ца** the Dowager Empress.
вдо́в|ый (~) *adj.* widowed.
вдого́нку *adv.* after, in pursuit of; **бро́ситься вдого́нку** (**за**+*i.*) to rush (after).
вдолб|и́ть, лю́, и́шь *pf.* (*of* **вда́лбливать**) (*coll.*) **в. кому́-н. в го́лову** to drum, din into s.o.'s head.
вдоль 1. *prep.* (+*g. or* **по**+*d.*) along; **в. бе́рега** along the bank; **я поплы́л в. по реке́** I sailed down the river. **2.** *adv.* lengthwise, longways; **разре́зать мате́рию в.** to cut material lengthwise; **в. и поперёк** in all directions, far and wide; **он изъе́здил всю Росси́ю в. и поперёк** he has travelled the length and breadth of Russia; (*fig.*) minutely, in detail; **он зна́ет Шекспи́ра в. и поперёк** he knows Shakespeare inside out.
вдо́сталь *adv.* **1.** (*coll.*) in plenty. **2.** (*obs.*) completely.
вдох, а *m.* (*coll.*) breath; **сде́лать глубо́кий в.** to take a deep breath.
вдохнове́ни|е, я *nt.* inspiration.
вдохнове́нный *adj.* inspired.
вдохнови́тел|ь, я *m.* inspirer; inspiration (*of persons*); **он — наш в.** he is an inspiration to us.
вдохнови́тельн|ый *adj.* (*obs.*) inspiring; **~ая речь** an inspiring speech.
вдохнов|и́ть, лю́, и́шь *pf.* (*of* **~ля́ть**) (+*a. or* **на**+*a.*) to inspire (to); **его́ слова́ ~и́ли меня́** his words inspired me; **казнь бра́та ~и́ла его́ на борьбу́** his brother's execution inspired him to struggle.
вдохновля́|ть, ю *impf. of* **вдохнови́ть**
вдохн|у́ть, у́, ёшь *pf.* (*of* **вдыха́ть**) (**в**+*a.*) **1.** to breathe in, inhale; **в. све́жий во́здух в лёгкие** to breathe fresh air into one's lungs. **2.** to inspire (with), instil (into); **в. му́жество в кого́-н.** to inspire s.o. with courage, instil courage into s.o.
вдре́безги *adv.* to pieces, to smithereens; **разби́ть в.** to smash to smithereens; **в. пьян** (*coll.*) dead drunk.
вдруг *adv.* **1.** suddenly, all of a sudden; **все в.** all together; **не говори́те все в.** don't all speak at once. **2.** *as interrog. particle* (*coll.*) what if, suppose; **а в. они́ узна́ют?** but suppose they find out?
вдрызг, *adv.* (*coll.*) completely; **в. пьян** dead drunk.
вдува́ни|е, я *nt.* inflation, blowing up; (*med.*) pneumothorax.
вдува́|ть, ю *impf. of* **вдуть**
вду́м|аться, аюсь *pf.* (*of* **~ываться**) (**в**+*a.*) to think over, ponder, meditate (on).
вду́мчив|ый (~, ~а) *adj.* pensive, meditative; thoughtful.
вду́мыва|ться, юсь *impf. of* **вду́маться**
вду́н|уть, у, ешь *pf.* = **вдуть**
вду|ть, ~ю, ~ешь *pf.* (*of* **~ва́ть**) to blow into; **в. во́здух в ши́ну** to inflate, blow up a tyre.
вдыха́ни|е, я *nt.* inhalation.
вдыха́тельный *adj.* (*med.*) respiratory.
вдыха́|ть, ю *impf. of* **вдохну́ть**
вегетариа́н|ец, ца *m.* vegetarian.
вегетариа́нский *adj.* vegetarian.
вегетариа́нств|о, а *nt.* vegetarianism.
вегетати́вный *adj.* (*biol.*) vegetative.
вегетацио́нный *adj.* (*biol.*) vegetation; **в. пери́од** vegetation period.
вегета́ци|я, и *f.* vegetation.
ве́да|ть, ю *impf.* **1.** (*obs.*) to know. **2.** (+*i.*) to manage, be in charge of.
ве́дени|е, я *nt.* authority; **быть в ~и** (+*g.*) (*leg.*) to be under the jurisdiction (of); **э́то вне моего́ ~я** this is outside my province.
веде́ни|е, я *nt.* conducting, conduct; **в. де́ла** conduct of an affair, transaction.
ведёрный *adj.* **1.** of a bucket, pail. **2.** holding a bucketful, pailful. **3.** holding one vedro (*see* **ведро́ 2.**).
ведовств|о́, а́ *nt.* (*obs.*) sorcery.
ве́дома *only in phrr.*: **без в., с в.; без моего́ в.** unknown to me; **с моего́ в.** with my knowledge, with my consent.
ве́домост|ь, и, *pl.* **~и, ~е́й** *f.* **1.** list, register; **платёжная в.** pay-roll; **в. расхо́дов** expense-sheet. **2.** (*pl. only*) Gazette (*as name of newspaper*); **Моско́вские ~и** Moscow Gazette.
ве́домственный *adj.* departmental.
ве́домств|о, а *nt.* department; **Вое́нное в.** War Department.
ве́дом|ый (~, ~а) *adj.* (*obs.*) known; **вам э́то ~о?** did you know about it?

ведо́м|ый (~, ~а) *pres. part. pass. of* **вести́** (*obs.*) driven.
ве́дренный *adj. of* **вёдро** (*obs., coll.*); **в. день** a fine day.
вёдр|о, а *nt.* (*obs., coll.*) fine weather.
вед|ро́, ра́, *pl.* **~ра, ~ер** *nt.* **1.** bucket, pail; **по́лное в.** a pailful. **2.** vedro (*Old Russ. liquid measure, equivalent to approx. 12 litres*).
вед|у́, ёшь *see* **вести́**
веду́щ|ий *pres. part. act. of* **вести́** *and adj.* leading; (*tech.*) **~ее колесо́** driving-wheel; *as n.* **в., ~его** *m.* **1.** presenter; compère; anchorman. **2.** disk jockey, DJ. **3.** leader (*of flight*).
ведь *conj.* **1.** you see, you know (*but oft. requires no translation*); **она́ всё покупа́ет но́вые пла́тья — в. она́ о́чень бога́та** she is always buying new dresses — she is very rich, you know; **но в. э́то всем изве́стно** but everyone knows about this. **2.** is it not?; is it?; **в. э́то пра́вда?** it's the truth, isn't it?
ве́дьм|а, ы *f.* **1.** witch. **2.** (*coll.*) hag, harridan.
ведьм|овско́й *adj. of* **~а**
ве́ер, а, *pl.* **~а́** *m.* fan (*also fig.*); **обма́хиваться ~ом** to fan o.s.; **рассыпа́ться ~ом** (*mil., etc.*) to fan out.
веерообра́зный *adj.* fan-shaped; **в. свод** (*archit.*) fan tracery.
ве́жд|ы, ~ *pl.* (*sg.* **~а, ~ы** *f.*) (*obs., poet.*) eyelids.
ве́жливост|ь, и *f.* politeness, courtesy, civility.
ве́жлив|ый (~, ~а) *adj.* polite, courteous, civil.
везде́ *adv.* everywhere; **в. и всю́ду** here, there and everywhere.
вездесу́щ|ий (~, ~а) *adj.* ubiquitous, omnipresent (*initially as epithet of God*).
вездехо́д, а *m.* Landrover (*propr.*); (*mil.*) all-terrain vehicle (*abbr.* ATV); **песча́ный в.** beach *or* dune buggy.
везе́ни|е, я *nt.* luck.
вез|ти́, у́, ёшь, *past* **~, ~ла́** *impf.* (*of* **по~**) (*det. of* **вози́ть**) **1.** to cart, convey, carry (*of beasts of burden or mechanical transport*). **2.** (*coll.*) (*impers.+d.*) to have luck; **ему́ не ~ёт в ка́рты** he has no luck at cards.
Везу́ви|й, я *m.* (Mt.) Vesuvius.
везу́чий *adj.* (*coll.*) lucky.
вей[1] *imper. of* **вить**
вей[2] *imper. of* **ве́ять**
век, а, о ~е, на ~у́, *pl.* **~а́** (*obs.* **~и**) *m.* **1.** century. **2.** age; **ка́менный в.** Stone Age; **сре́дние ~а́** the Middle Ages; **испоко́н ~о́в** from time immemorial; **отжи́ть свой в.** to have had one's day, go out of fashion; **в ко́и-то ~и** once in a blue moon; **во ~и ~о́в** for all time; **на ~и ве́чные** for ever; **в. живи́ — в. учи́сь!** (*prov.*) live and learn! **3.** life, lifetime; **на моём ~у́** in my lifetime. **4.** *as adv.* for ages; **мы с ва́ми в. не вида́лись** we have not seen each other for ages.
ве́к|о, а, *pl.* **~и, ~** *nt.* eyelid.
век|ова́ть, у́ю, у́ешь *impf., usu. in phr.* **век в.** (*folk poet.*) to pass a lifetime.
векове́чный *adj.* eternal, everlasting.
вековóй *adj.* ancient, age-old.
векселеда́тел|ь, я *m.* (*comm.*) drawer (*of a bill*).
векселедержа́тел|ь, я *m.* (*comm.*) payee, holder (*of a bill*).
ве́ксел|ь, я, *pl.* **~я́** *m.* promissory note; bill of exchange; **в. на заграни́цу** foreign bill; **уплати́ть по ~ю** to meet a bill; **учи́тывать в.** to discount a bill.
ве́ксель|ный *adj. of* **~; в. курс** rate of exchange.
ве́кш|а, и *f.* (*dial.*) squirrel.
вёл, ~а́ *see* **вести́**
веле́невый *adj.* vellum.
веле́ни|е, я *nt.* (*obs.*) command, behest.
велеречи́в|ый (~, ~а) *adj.* (*obs. or iron.*) bombastic, magniloquent.
вел|е́ть, ю́, и́шь *impf. and pf.* (*+d. and inf. or* **что́бы**) **1.** to order; **я ~е́л ему́ сде́лать э́то** *or* **что́бы он сде́лал э́то** I ordered him to do this; **де́лайте, как вам ~ено** do as you are told. **2.: не в.** to forbid.
велика́н, а *m.* giant.
велика́нский *adj.* (*coll.*) gigantic.
велика́нш|а, и *f.* (*coll.*) giant(ess).
вели́к|ий (~, ~а, ~о) *adj.* **1.** (*short form* **~а, ~о**) great; **~ие держа́вы** the Great Powers; **Екатери́на Вели́кая** Catherine the Great; **В. князь** grand prince, grand duke; **~ая седми́ца** Passion Week; **В. четве́рг** Maundy Thursday. **2.** (*short form* **~а́, ~о́,** *pl.* **~и́**) big, large; **но́ги у неё о́чень ~и́** she has very big feet; **от ма́ла до ~а** (*coll.*) young and old. **3.** (*short form only*; **~а́, ~о́,** *pl.* **~и́**) (*+d. or* **для**) too big; **э́ти брю́ки мне ~и́** these trousers are too big for me.
Великобрита́ни|я, и *f.* Great Britain.
великова́т|ый (~, ~а) *adj.* (*coll.*) rather large, big; **э́ти боти́нки мне ~ы** these boots are rather big for me.
великовозра́ст|ный (~ен, ~на) *adj.* overgrown.
великодержа́вный *adj.* great-power.
великоду́ши|е, я *nt.* magnanimity, generosity.
великоду́шнича|ть, ю *impf.* to affect magnanimity, generosity.
великоду́ш|ный (~ен, ~на) *adj.* magnanimous, generous.
великокня́жеский *adj.* grand-ducal.
великоле́пи|е, я *nt.* splendour, magnificence.
великоле́п|ный (~ен, ~на) *adj.* **1.** splendid, magnificent; **в. дворе́ц** a magnificent palace. **2.** excellent; **э́то — ~ная иде́я** that's an excellent idea; **~но!** (*int.*) splendid!; excellent!
великому́ченик, а *m.* great martyr.
великопо́стный *adj.* (*eccl.*) Lenten.
великоро́дный *adj.* (*obs.*) of noble birth.
велико|ро́сс = ~ру́с
великору́с, а *m.* Great Russian.
великору́сский *adj.* Great Russian.
великосве́тск|ий *adj.* fashionable, society; **~ая жизнь** high life.
велича́вост|ь, и *f.* stateliness, majesty.
велича́в|ый (~, ~а) *adj.* stately, majestic.
велича́йш|ий *adj.* (*superl. of* **вели́кий**) greatest, extreme, supreme; **де́ло ~ей ва́жности** a matter of extreme importance; **с ~им удово́льствием** with the greatest pleasure.
велича́ни|е, я *nt.* **1.** glorification, extolling. **2.** songs of praise (*eccl.; also in honour of living persons*).
велича́|ть, ю *impf.* **1.** (*coll., dial.*) to call by patronymic; **как вас ~ют?** what is your patronymic? **2.** (*+a. and i.*; *obs. and iron.*) to call, dignify by the name of; **в. писа́ку ге́нием** to dignify a hack by the name of genius. **3.** (*folk poet.*) to honour with songs.
велича́|ться, юсь *impf.* **1.** *pass. of* **~ть. 2.** (*+i.*; *coll.*) to glory (in), plume o.s. (on).
вели́чественност|ь, и *f.* majesty, grandeur.
вели́чествен|ный (~, ~на) *adj.* majestic, grand.
вели́честв|о, а *nt.* majesty; **ва́ше в.** Your Majesty.
вели́чи|е, я *nt.* greatness; grandeur; **ма́ния ~я** megalomania.
величин|а́, ы́, *pl.* **~ы, ~а́м** *f.* **1.** size; **дом сре́дней ~ы́** a house of average size; **~о́ю с челове́ческую ру́ку** about the size of a man's hand. **2.** (*math.*) quantity, magnitude; value; **в. подъёма** up gradient; **в. укло́на** down gradient; **постоя́нная в.** constant. **3.** great figure; **литерату́рная в.** an eminent literary figure.
вело... *comb. form* bicycle-, cycle-.
велодро́м, а *m.* cycle track; velodrome.
велокро́сс, а *m.* cyclo-cross.
велори́кш|а, и *f.* pedicab.
велосипе́д, а *m.* bicycle; cycle; **во́дный в.** pedalo; **па́рный в.** tandem; **в.-пау́к** penny-farthing; **в.-такси́** pedicab.
велосипеди́ст, а *m.* bicyclist; cyclist.
велосипе́д|ный *adj. of* **~**
велотренажёр, а *m.* exercycle, exercise bicycle.
велофигури́ст, а *m.* trick cyclist.
вельбо́т, а *m.* whale-boat, whaler.
вельве́т, а *m.* velveteen; **в. в ру́бчик** corduroy.
вельве́товый *adj.* velveteen; corduroy.
вельми́ *adv.* (*obs. or iron.*) very.
вельмо́ж|а, и *m.* (*obs. or iron.*) grandee.
вельмо́ж|ный *adj. of* **~а**
веля́рный *adj.* (*ling.*) velar.
Ве́н|а, ы *f.* Vienna.
ве́н|а, ы *f.* (*anat.*) vein; **воспале́ние ~** phlebitis;

расширéние ~ varicose veins.
венгéр|ец, ца *m.* Hungarian.
венгéр|ка, ки *f.* **1.** *f. of* **~ец. 2.** Hungarian dance. **3.** dolman (*jacket*).
венгéрск|ий *adj.* Hungarian; *as n.* **~ое, ~ого** *nt.* Hungarian wine.
венгр, а *m.* = **венгéрец**
Вéнгри|я, и *f.* Hungary.
венéрик, а *m.* (*coll.*) venereal patient.
венéрин *adj. of* Venus; **в. волосóк** (*bot.*) maidenhair; **в. холм** (*palmistry*) mount of Venus.
венери́ческий *adj.* (*med.*) venereal.
венерóлог, а *m.* specialist in venereal diseases.
венерологи́|я, и *f.* science of venereal diseases.
Венесуэ́л|а, ы *f.* Venezuela.
венесуэ́л|ец, ца *m.* Venezuelan.
венесуэ́л|ка, ки *f. of* **~ец**
венесуэ́льский *adj.* Venezuelan.
вéн|ец, ца *m.* Viennese.
вен|éц, цá *m.* **1.** crown; (*fig.*) completion, consummation. **2.** (*fig.*) wedding; **вести́ под в.** to marry, lead to the altar; **под ~цóм** during the wedding. **3.** (*poet.*) wreath, garland. **4.** (*astron.*) corona. **5.** (*eccl.*) halo. **6.** row of beams (*in a house*).
венециáн|ец, ца *m.* Venetian.
венециáн|ка, ки *f. of* **~ец**
венециáнск|ий *adj.* Venetian; **~ая ярь** verdigris.
Венéци|я, и *f.* Venice.
венéчный *adj.* **1.** (*anat.*) coronal, coronary. **2.** *adj. of* **венéц**
вéнзел|ь, я, *pl.* **~я́, ~éй** *m.* monogram; **~я́ писáть** (*coll.*) to walk unsteadily (*of a drunken pers.*).
вéник, а *m.* **1.** besom. **2.** birch twigs (*used in Russ. baths*) **3.** (*cul.*) whisk.
вéнич|ек, ка *m.* (*cul.*) whisk.
вéн|ка, ки *f. of* **~ец**
вéн|о, а *nt.* (*anthrop.*) bride-price.
вен|óзный *adj. of* **~́а**; venous.
вен|óк, кá *m.* wreath, garland.
вéнск|ий *adj.* Viennese; **в. стул** bentwood chair; **~ая и́звесть** French chalk.
вентили́р|овать, ую *impf.* (*of* **про~**) to ventilate (*also fig.*).
вéнтил|ь, я *m.* (*tech.*) valve; (*mus.*) mute.
вентиля́тор, а *m.* ventilator; extractor (fan).
вентиля́ци|я, и *f.* ventilation.
венценóс|ец, ца *m.* (*epithet of monarch*; *rhet.*) wearer of crown, crowned head.
венчá|льный *adj. of* **~ние; ~льное кольцó** wedding ring; **в. наря́д** wedding dress.
венчáни|е, я *nt.* **1.: в. на цáрство** coronation. **2.** wedding ceremony.
венчá|ть, ю *impf.* **1.** (*pf.* **в.** *and* **у~**) to crown. **2.** (*pf.* **у~**) (*fig.*) to crown; **конéц ~ет дéло** all's well that ends well. **3.** (*pf.* **об~** *and* **по~**) to marry (*of officiating priest*).
венчá|ться, юсь *impf.* **1.** (*pf.* **об~** *and* **по~**) to be married, marry. **2.** *pass. of* **~ть**
вéнчик, а *m.* **1.** halo, nimbus. **2.** (*bot.*) corolla. **3.** edge, rim (*of vessel*). **4.** (*anat.*) crown (*of tooth*). **5.** (*tech.*) ring, bolt. **6.** (*eccl.*) paper band placed on forehead of dead pers.
вепр|ь, я *m.* wild boar.
вéр|а, ы *f.* (**в**+*a.*) faith, belief (in); trust, confidence; **приня́ть на ~у** to take on trust; **дать ~у** (+*d.*) to give credence (to); **си́мвол ~ы** (*eccl.*) the Creed.
верáнд|а, ы *f.* veranda.
вéрб|а, ы *f.* willow; willow branch.
вербáльн|ый *adj.* verbal; **~ая нóта** (*dipl.*) note verbale.
вербéн|а, ы *f.* (*bot.*) verbena.
верблю́д, а *m.* camel; **одногóрбый в.** Arabian camel, dromedary; **двугóрбый в.** Bactrian camel.
верблюжáтник, а *m.* camel driver.
верблю́|жий *adj. of* **~д; ~жья шерсть** camel's hair; **~жье сукнó** camel-hair cloth.
верблю́жин|а, ы *f.* camel-meat.
верблюж|óнок, óнка, *pl.* **~áта, ~áт** *m.* young camel, camel foal.
вéрб|ный *adj. of* **~а; ~ое воскресéнье** (*eccl.*) Palm Sunday; **в. базáр** Palm Sunday fair.
верб|овáть, у́ю *impf.* (*of* **за~** *and* **на~**) to recruit, enlist; (*fig.*) to win over.
вербóвк|а, и *f.* recruiting.
вербóвщик, а *m.* recruiter.
вéрбов|ый *adj.* willow; osier; **~ая корзи́на** wicker basket.
верди́кт, а *m.* verdict.
верёвк|а, и *f.* cord, rope; string; (*fig.*) noose; **в. для белья́** clothes-line; **свя́зывать ~ой** to rope, cord, tie up.
верёв|очный *adj. of* **~ка**
вéред, а *m.* (*dial.*) boil, abscess.
вере|ди́ть, жу́, ди́шь *impf.* (*of* **раз~**) (*coll.*) to knock, irritate (*a sore place; also fig.*).
верезж|áть, у́, и́шь *impf.* (*coll.*) to squeal.
верени́ц|а, ы *f.* row, file, line; **в. лошадéй** a string of horses; **в. идéй** a series of ideas.
вéреск, а *m.* (*bot.*) heather.
вéреск|овый *adj. of* **~**; *as pl. n.* **~овые, ~овых** (*bot.*) Ericaceae.
веретéниц|а, ы *f.* (*zool.*) slow-worm.
веретён|ный *adj. of* **~ó; ~ное мáсло** (*tech.*) axle grease; spindle oil.
веретен|ó, á, *pl.* **веретёна, веретён** *nt.* **1.** spindle; shank (*of an anchor*). **2.** (*tech.*) axle.
верéть|е, я *no pl., nt.* (*dial.*) sacking.
верещ|áть, у́, и́шь *impf.* (*coll.*) to squeal; to chirp (*of a cricket, etc.*).
вере|я́[1], **и́** *f.* (*dial.*) gate-post.
вере|я́[2], **и́** *f.* (*naut.*) wherry.
верзи́л|а, ы *c.g.* (*coll.*) lanky pers.
вери́г|и, ~ *pl.* (*sg.* **~а, ~и** *f.*) chains, fetters (*worn by ascetics; also fig.*).
вери́тельн|ый *adj.*: **~ая грáмота** (*dipl.*) letters of credence, credentials.
вéр|ить, ю, ишь *impf.* (*of* **по~**) (+*d.* *or* **в**+*a.*) to believe, have faith (in); to trust (in), rely (upon); **в. в Бóга** to believe in God; **в. в прогрéсс** to believe in progress; **в. в привидéния** to believe in ghosts; **э́тому человéку никтó не ~ит** no one believes that man; **он не ~ит своéй женé** he does not trust his wife; **в. нá слово** to take on trust; **я не ~ил свои́м ушáм, свои́м глазáм** I could not believe my ears, eyes.
вéр|иться, ится *impf.* (*impers.*+*d.*): **мне ~ится с трудóм** I find it hard to believe; **емý не ~ится, что лю́ди мóгут быть совершéнны** he cannot believe in the perfectibility of man.
вермишéл|ь, и *f.* vermicelli.
верн|ée *adv.* (*comp. of* **~́о**) rather; **писáтель и́ли, в., писáка** a writer or, rather, a hack.
вернисáж, а *m.* (*art*) **1.** private viewing. **2.** opening-day (*of an exhibition*).
вéрн|о *adv. of* **~ый**; *as particle* (*coll.*) probably, I suppose; **вы, в., ужé слыхáли нóвости** you have probably already heard the news.
верноподдáнический *adj.* (*obs. or iron.*) loyal, faithful.
верноподдáнств|о, а *nt.* (*obs. or iron.*) loyalty, allegiance.
верноподдáнн|ый *adj.* (*obs. or iron.*) loyal, faithful; *as n.* **в., ~ого** *m.* loyal subject.
вéрност|ь, и *f.* **1.** faithfulness, loyalty. **2.** truth, correctness.
верн|у́ть, у́, ёшь *pf.* (*of* **возвращáть**) **1.** to give back, return. **2.** to get back, recover, retrieve; **в. здорóвье** to recover one's health; **в. потéрянное врéмя** to make up for lost time. **3.** (*coll.*) to make come back.
верн|у́ться, у́сь, ёшься *pf.* (*of* **возвращáться**) to return, revert (*also fig.*); **в. домóй** to return home; **в. к прéжней рабóте** to return to one's old job.
вéр|ный (~ен, ~нá, ~но) *adj.* **1.** faithful, loyal, true; **в. свои́м убеждéниям** true to one's convictions. **2.** true, correct; **в. слух** a good ear; **~ны ли вáши часы́?** is your watch right?; **~но ли, что вы уезжáете?** is it true that you are going away? **3.** sure, reliable; **в. истóчник** reliable source; **~ная кóпия** faithful copy; **в. при́знак** sure sign. **4.** certain, sure; **~ная смерть** certain death.
вéровани|е, я *nt.* belief, creed; **~я дрéвних египтя́н** the beliefs of the ancient Egyptians.

вéр|овать, ую *impf.* (**в**+*a.*) to believe (in).
вероисповéдани|е, я *nt.* creed, denomination; **свобóда ~я** freedom of religion.
веролóм|ный (~ен, ~на) *adj.* treacherous, perfidious.
веролóмств|о, а *nt.* treachery, perfidy.
веронáл, а *m.* (*med.*) veronal.
верони́к|а, и *f.* (*bot.*) speedwell, veronica.
вероотстýпник, а *m.* apostate.
вероотстýпничеств|о, а *nt.* apostasy.
вероподóби|е, я *nt.* (*obs.*) likelihood.
вероподóб|ный (~ен, ~на) *adj.* (*obs.*) likely.
веротерпи́мост|ь, и *f.* (*relig.*) toleration.
веротерпи́м|ый (~, ~а) *adj.* (*relig.*) tolerant.
вероучéни|е, я *nt.* (*relig.*) dogma.
вероучи́тел|ь, я *m.* religious teacher, apologist.
верoя́ти|е, я *nt.* probability, likelihood; **по всемý ~ю, по всем ~ям** in all probability; **сверх вся́кого ~я** beyond all expectation.
верoя́тно *adv.* probably; **он, в., бóлен** probably he is ill; **он, в., приéдет ночны́м пóездом** he is likely to come, he will probably come by the night train.
верoя́тност|ь, и *f.* probability; **по всей ~и** in all probability; **теóрия ~и** (*math.*) theory of probability.
верoя́т|ный (~ен, ~на) *adj.* probable, likely; **э́то вполнé ~но** it is highly probable; **в. наслéдник** heir presumptive.
Версáл|ь, и *f.* Versailles.
версáльский *f.*: **в. договóр** Treaty of Versailles.
версификáтор, а *m.* versifier; (*also pej.*) **он не поэ́т, а в.** he is not a poet but a versifier.
версификáци|я, и *f.* versification.
вéрси|я, и *f.* version; **есть рáзные ~и э́того собы́тия** there are various versions of this story.
верст|á, ы́, *a.* **~ý** *and* **~́у**, *pl.* **~́ы**, **~́** *f.* verst (*old Russ. measurement, equivalent to approx. 1.06 kilometres*); verst-post; **зá ~у** (*coll.*) far off; **мéрить ~́ы** (*coll.*) to travel a long way; **колóменская в.** (*coll.*) beanpole, lanky person.
верстáк, á *m.* (*tech.*) joiner's *or* locksmith's bench.
верстáтк|а, и *f.* (*typ.*) composing-stick.
верстá|ть[1]**, ю** *impf.* (*of* **с~**) (*typ.*) to impose, make up into pages.
верстá|ть[2]**, ю** *impf.* (*of* **по~**) (*hist.*) **1.** to arrange in line; (**с**+*i.*; *fig.*) to rank (with), compare (with). **2.** (+*a.* *and i.*) to assign (to), **в. когó-н. помéстьем** to assign an estate to s.o. **3.** (**в**+*nom.-a.*) to recruit (for), conscript (for).
вёрстк|а, и *f.* (*typ.*) **1.** imposing, imposition. **2.** forme; made-up matter.
верст|овóй *adj. of* **~á; в. столб** milestone.
вéртел, а *m.* spit; skewer.
вертéп, а *m.* **1.** cave, den (*of thieves, etc.*). **2.** (*theatr.*) puppet-show of the Nativity; Nativity Play.
вер|тéть, чý, ~́тишь *impf.* (+*a. or i.*) to twirl, turn round and round; **в. трóстью** to twirl a cane; **онá ~́тит им, как хóчет** she can twist him round her little finger; **как ни ~ти́, нам придётся заплати́ть** there is nothing for it, we shall have to pay.
вер|тéться, чýсь, ~́тишься *impf.* **1.** to rotate, turn (round), revolve (*also fig.*); **разговóр у них всё ~́тится óколо войны** conversation with them always turns on the war; **егó фами́лия весь день ~тéлась у меня́ на кóнчике языкá** his name was on the tip of my tongue all day; **в. под ногáми, пéред глазáми** (*coll.*) to be under one's feet, in the way. **2.** (*coll.*) to move (among), mix (with); **он бóльшей чáстью ~́тится среди́ инострáнцев** he mixes mostly with foreigners. **3.** (*coll.*) to fidget. **4.** (*coll.*) to prevaricate; **отвéть на вопрóс пря́мо, не ~ти́сь** answer the question directly and don't prevaricate.
вертиголóвк|а, и *f.* = **вертишéйка**
вертикáл, а *m.* (*astron.*) vertical.
вертикáл|ь, и *f.* vertical line; file (*on chessboard*); down (*in crossword*).
вертикáльный *adj.* (*math.*) vertical.
вертихвóстк|а, и *f.* (*coll.*) flirt, coquette.
вертишéйк|а, и *f.* (*zool.*) wryneck.
вёрт|кий (~ок, ~кá, ~ко) *adj.* (*coll.*) nimble, agile.
вертлю́г, á *m.* **1.** (*anat.*) head of the femur. **2.** (*tech.*) swivel.
вертлю́|жный *adj. of* **~г**
вертля́в|ый (~, ~а) *adj.* (*coll.*) **1.** restless, fidgety. **2.** flighty, frivolous.
вертогрáд, а *m.* (*obs.*) garden.
вертодрóм, а *m.* heliport.
вертолёт, а *m.* helicopter; **боевóй в.** helicopter gunship, combat helicopter.
вертопрáх, а *m.* (*coll.*) frivolous pers.
вертопрáшнича|ть, ю *impf.* (*coll.*) to behave in a frivolous way.
вертýн, á *m.* (*coll.*) **1.** fidget; restless pers. **2.** tumbler-pigeon.
вертухá|й, я *m.* (*sl.*) screw (*prison warder*).
вертýшк|а, и *f.* (*coll.*) **1.** revolving object (*e.g. door, bookcase*). **2.** whirligig, teetotum (*toy*). **3.** flirt, coquette. **4.** turntable. **5.** 'hot line'.
вéр|ующий *pres. part. act. of* **~овать**; *as n.* **в., ~ующего** *m.* believer.
верф|ь, и *f.* dockyard; shipyard.
верх, а, *pl.* **~и́** *m.* **1.** top, summit (*also fig.*); **совещáние в ~áх** (*pol.*) summit conference; **в. глýпости** the height of folly. **2.** upper part, upper side; bonnet, hood (*of vehicle*); **«верх!»** (*sign*) 'this side up'; (*fig.*) **~и́** (*pl. only*) upper crust (*of society*); (*mus.*) high notes; **взять, одержáть в. (над)** to gain the upper hand (over). **3.** outside, top; right side (*of material*); **хватáть ~и́, нахватáться ~óв** (*fig., coll.*) to get a smattering (of), acquire a superficial knowledge (of); **скользи́ть по ~áм** to touch lightly on the surface.
Вéрхн|ее óзер|о, ~его ~а *nt.* Lake Superior.
вéрхн|ий *adj.* upper; **~яя одéжда** overcoat; outer clothing; **~яя палáта** (*pol.*) upper chamber; **в. реги́стр** (*mus.*) highest register; **~ее течéние (реки́)** upper reaches (of river); **в. я́щик** top drawer.
верховéнств|о, а *nt.* (*obs.*) leadership.
верхóвн|ый *adj.* supreme; **~ое комáндование** high command; **В. Совéт** Supreme Soviet.
верховóд, а *m.* (*coll.*) boss, leader.
верховó|дить, жу, дишь *impf.* (+*i.*; *coll.*) to lord it over, boss over; **он ~дит всéми в четвёртом клáссе** he rules the fourth form.
верх|овóй[1] *adj. of* **~óм; ~овáя ездá** riding; **~овáя лóшадь** saddle-horse; *as n.* **в., ~овóго** *m.* rider.
верховóй[2] *adj.* up-river.
верхóвь|е, я, *g. pl.* **~ев** *nt.* upper reaches.
верхогля́д, а *m.* (*coll.*) superficial pers.
верхогля́днича|ть, ю *impf.* (*coll.*) to be superficial.
верхогля́дств|о, а *nt.* (*coll.*) superficiality.
верхолáз, а *m.* steeplejack.
вéрхом *adv.* **1.** on high ground. **2.** quite full, brim-full; **нали́ть стакáн в.** to pour out a full glass.
верхóм *adv.* astride; on horseback; **éздить в.** to ride.
верхýшк|а, и *f.* **1.** top, summit; apex. **2.** (*fig., coll.*) bosses; **профсою́зная в.** trade-union bosses.
вéрченый *adj.* (*coll., pej.*) flighty, frivolous.
вер|чý, ~́тишь *see* **~тéть**
вéрш|а, и *f.* fish-trap (*made of osiers*).
верши́н|а, ы *f.* **1.** top, summit; peak; (*fig.*) peak, acme; **он дости́г ~ы слáвы** he had reached the summit of his fame. **2.** (*math.*) vertex; apex.
верш|и́ть ý, и́шь *impf.* **1.** (+*i.*) to manage, control; **в. всéми делáми** to run the whole show. **2.** (*dial.*) to top; **в. стог** to top a rick. **3.** (+*a.*) to decide.
вершкóвый *adj.* one vershok long.
верш|óк, кá *m.* vershok (*old Russ. measure of length, equivalent to 4.4 cm*); (*fig.*) smattering, superficial knowledge; **хватáть ~ки́** (+*g.*) to get a smattering (of).
вес, а, *pl.* **~á** *m.* **1.** weight; **ли́шний в.** excess baggage; (*fig.*) weight, authority; **на в.** by weight; **~́ом в сто фýнтов** weighing a hundred pounds; **на ~ý** balanced, hanging, suspended; **держáться на ~ý** to be balanced; **прибáвить, убáвить в ~́е** to put on, lose weight; **быть на в. зóлота** to be worth one's weight in gold; **имéть в ~́е** to carry weight. **2.** system of weights; **аптéкарский в.** apothecaries' weight. **3.: удéльный в.** specific gravity.
веселé|ть, ю *impf.* (*of* **по~**) to become gay, become bright.

весел|и́ть, ю́, и́шь *impf.* (*of* **по~**) to cheer, gladden; to amuse.

весел|и́ться, ю́сь, и́шься *impf.* (*of* **по~**) to enjoy o.s.; to amuse o.s.

весёлк|а, и *f.* (*bot.*) stinkhorn.

ве́село *adv.* gaily, merrily; *as pred.* (+*d.*) to enjoy o.s.; **нам тут о́чень в.** we very much enjoy being here; **мне в. бы́ло смотре́ть на вас** I enjoyed seeing you.

весёлост|ь, и *f.* **1.** gaiety; cheerfulness. **2.** (*pl. only*; *obs.*) merry-making.

весёл|ый (ве́сел, ~а́, ве́село) *adj.* gay, merry; cheerful; **у него́ ~ое настрое́ние сего́дня** he is in good spirits today.

весе́л|ье, ья, *g. pl.* **~ий** *nt.* **1.** gaiety, merriment. **2.** (*pl. only*; *obs.*) merry-making.

вес|е́льный *adj. of* **~ло́**; **~е́льная ло́дка** rowing-boat.

весельча́к, а́ *m.* (*coll.*) convivial fellow.

вес|е́нний *adj. of* **~на́**; **~е́ннее равноде́нствие** vernal equinox.

ве́|сить, шу, сишь *impf.* **1.** to weigh (*intrans.*); **~сит три то́нны** it weighs three tons. **2.** (*obs.*, *coll.*) to weigh (*trans.*).

ве́с|кий (~ок, ~ка) *adj.* weighty.

вес|ло́, ла́, *pl.* **~́ла, ~́ел, ~́лам** *nt.* oar; scull; paddle; **завязи́ть в.** to catch a crab; **подня́ть ~́ла** to rest on one's oars.

вес|на́, ны́, *pl.* **~́ны, ~́ен, ~́нам** *f.* spring (*season*).

весну́ш|ки, ек *pl.* (*sg.* **~ка, ~ки** *f.*) freckles.

весну́шчатый *adj.* freckled.

весня́нк|а, и *f.* **1.** (*zool.*) mayfly. **2.** (*ethnol.*) spring-song.

вес|ово́й 1. *adj. of* **~. 2.** sold by weight.

весовщи́к, а́ *m.* weigher; checkweighman.

весо́мост|ь, и *f.* (*phys.*) ponderability.

весо́м|ый (~, ~а) *adj.* (*phys.*) ponderable; (*fig.*) weighty; heavy.

вест, а *m.* (*naut.*) **1.** west. **2.** west wind.

веста́лк|а, и *f.* vestal (virgin).

вестго́т, а *m.* (*hist.*) Visigoth.

вестго́тский *adj.* (*hist.*) Visigothic.

ве́стерн, а *m.* western (*film*).

ве|сти́, ду́, дёшь, *past* **~́л, ~ла́** *impf.* (*det. of* **води́ть**) **1.** (*pf.* **по~**) to lead; to conduct; to take; **в. слепо́го** to lead a blind man. **2.** (*pf.* **про~**) (+*i.* **по**+*d.*) to run (over), pass (over, across); **в. смычко́м по стру́нам** to run one's bow over the strings. **3.** (*pf.* **про~**) to conduct; to carry on; **в. войну́** to wage war; **в. обще́ственную рабо́ту** to do social work; **в. ого́нь (по**+*d.*) to fire (on); **в. перегово́ры** to carry on negotiations; **в. перепи́ску (с**+*i.*) to correspond (with); **в. пра́вильный о́браз жи́зни** to lead a regular life; **в. проце́сс** to carry on a lawsuit. **4.** (*impf. only*) to drive; **в. кора́бль** to navigate a ship; **в. самолёт** to pilot an aircraft. **5.** (*impf. only*) to conduct, direct, run; **в. де́ло** to run a business; **в. собра́ние** to preside at a meeting; **в. хозя́йство** to keep house. **6.** (*impf. only*) to keep, conduct; **в. дневни́к** to keep a diary; **в. кни́ги** to keep books, keep accounts; **в. протоко́л** to keep minutes. **7.** (*impf. only*): **в. себя́** to behave, conduct o.s. **8.** (*impf. only*) **(к)** to lead (to) (*also fig.*); **куда́ ~дёт э́та доро́га?** where does this road lead (to)?; **э́то ни к чему́ не ~дёт** this is leading nowhere. **9.** (*impf. only*): **в. своё нача́ло (от)** to originate (in), take rise (in); **в. свой род (от)** to be descended (from). **10.: и у́хом не в.** (*coll.*) to pay no heed.

вестибю́л|ь, я *m.* hall, lobby.

вести́мо *adv.* (*dial.*) of course, certainly.

вест-и́нд|ец, ца *m.* West Indian.

Вест-И́нди|я, и *f.* the West Indies.

вест-и́нд|ка, ки *f. of* **~ец**

вест-и́ндский *adj.* West Indian.

ве|сти́сь, ду́сь, дёшься, *past* **вёлся, ~ла́сь** *impf.* (*of* **по~**) **1.** *pass. of* **~сти́. 2.** (*usu. impers.*; *coll.*) to be observed (*of customs, etc.*); **так ~дётся уже́ три́ста лет** this has been the custom for three hundred years. **3.** to multiply (*of domestic animals*).

ве́стник, а *m.* **1.** messenger, herald. **2.** (*in title of publications*) Bulletin.

ве́стни|ца, ицы *f. of* **~к 1.**

вестов|о́й *adj.* (*obs.*) signal; **~а́я раке́та** signal-rocket; *as n.* **в., ~о́го** *m.* orderly.

вестовщи́к, а́ *m.* (*coll.*, *obs.*) newsmonger, gossip.

ве́сточк|а, и *f.* (*coll.*) news; **да́йте о себе́ ~у, как то́лько прие́дете** let me hear from you as soon as you arrive.

вест|ь[1], и, *pl.* **~́и, ~е́й** *f.* news; piece of news; **пропа́сть бе́з ~и** (*mil.*) to be missing.

весть[2] *only in phrr.*: **Бог в.** God knows; **не в. что** goodness knows, heaven knows what; **не (Бог) в. како́й** trifling, insignificant.

вес|ы́, о́в *no sg.* **1.** scales, balance; **мостовы́е в.** weighbridge; **пружи́нные в.** spring balance; **бро́сить на в.** (*fig.*) to throw into the balance. **2. В.** the Scales, Libra (*sign of the Zodiac*).

весь[1], вся, всё, *g.* **всего́, всей, всего́,** *pl.* **все, всех** *pron.* all; **весь день** all day; **вся Фра́нция** the whole of France; **он весь в отца́** he is the (very) image of his father; **весь в лохмо́тьях** all in rags; **вы́йти весь** to be used up; **бума́га вся вы́шла** the paper is all used up, there is no paper left; **во в. го́лос** at the top of one's voice; **во всю мочь** with all one's might; **от всего́ се́рдца** from the bottom of one's heart, with all one's heart; **по всему́ го́роду** all over the town; **во-всю́** (*coll.*) like anything; **пре́жде всего́** before all, first and foremost; **при всём том** for all that, moreover; **вот и всё** that's all; **всего́ (хоро́шего)!** good-bye!, all the best!; **всё и вся** (*coll.*) all and everything; *as n.* **всё, всего́** *nt.* everything; **все, всех** *no sg.* all, everyone; **всем, всем, всем!** attention, everyone!

вес|ь[2], и *f.* (*obs.*) village.

весьма́ *adv.* very, highly; **в. успе́шный о́пыт** highly successful experiment.

ветви́ст|ый (~, ~а) *adj*: branchy, spreading.

ветвра́ч, а́ *m.* vet.

ветв|ь, и, *pl.* **~́и, ~е́й** *f.* branch, bough; (*fig.*) branch.

ве́т|ер, ра *m.* **1.** wind; **кре́пкий в.** (*naut.*) half a gale; **о́чень кре́пкий в.** fresh gale; **ти́хий в.** light air; **по ~ру** before the wind, down wind; **держа́ть нос по ~ру** (*fig.*) to trim one's sails to the wind; **под ~ром** leeward; **про́тив ~ра** close to the wind, in the teeth of the wind; **в. с бе́рега** off-shore wind; (*fig.*) **броса́ть слова́ на в.** to talk idly; **у него́ в. в голове́** he is a thoughtless fellow; **до ~ру пойти́** (*coll.*) to answer a call of nature; **мне до ~ру на́до** (*coll.*) I need to spend a penny; **подби́тый ~ром** (*coll.*) (*i*) empty-headed, (*ii*) light, flimsy. **2. ~ры** (*med.*) wind, flatulence.

ветера́н, а *m.* veteran.

ветерина́р, а *m.* veterinary surgeon.

ветерина́ри|я, и *f.* veterinary science; veterinary medicine.

ветерина́рный *adj.* veterinary.

ветер|о́к, ка́ *m.* breeze.

ве́тк|а, и *f.* branch; twig; **железнодоро́жная в.** branch-line.

вет|ла́, лы́, *pl.* **~́лы, ~́ел** *f.* (*bot.*) white willow.

ветлече́бниц|а, ы *f.* veterinary hospital.

ве́то *nt. indecl.* veto; **наложи́ть в. (на**+*a.*) to veto.

ве́точк|а, и *f.* twig, sprig, shoot.

вето́шник, а *m.* (*obs.*) old clothes dealer.

ве́тош|ь, и *f.* old clothes, rags.

ветр = ве́тер

ветрене́|ть, ет *impf.* (*impers.*; *coll.*) to become windy.

ве́треник, а *m.* (*coll.*) empty-headed, frivolous pers.

ве́трени|ца[1], цы *f. of* **~к**

ве́трениц|а[2], ы *f.* (*bot.*) anemone.

ве́тренност|ь, и *f.* empty-headedness, instability.

ве́трен|ый (~, ~а) *adj.* **1.** windy; **за́втра бу́дет ~о** it will be windy tomorrow. **2.** (*fig.*) empty-headed, unstable.

ветри́л|о, а *nt.* (*poet.*) sail.

ветробо́|й, я *no pl.*, *m.* (*dial.*, *collect.*) **1.** wind-fallen wood. **2.** windfalls (*fruit*).

ветрово́й *adj. of* **ве́тер**

ветрого́н, а *m.* **1.** (*tech.*) fan. **2. = ве́треник**

ветрого́нный *adj.* (*med.*) carminative.

ветроме́р, а *m.* (*phys.*) anemometer.

ветросилово́й *adj.* wind-powered.

ветроуказа́тел|ь, я *m.* (*aeron.*) drogue, wind cone, wind sock.

ветроулови́тел|ь, я *m.* (*aeron.*) rudder air scoop.

ветрочёт, а *m.* (*aeron.*) course and speed computer.
ветря́к, а́ *m.* **1.** (*tech.*) wind turbine. **2.** (*coll.*) windmill.
ветря́нк|а, и *f.* (*coll.*) **1.** windmill. **2.** chicken-pox.
ветрян|о́й *adj.* wind(-powered); **~а́я ме́льница** windmill.
ве́трян|ый *adj.*: **~ая о́спа** chicken-pox.
ве́тх|ий (~, ~а́, ~о) *adj.* old, ancient; dilapidated, tumbledown; decrepit; **В. заве́т** the Old Testament.
ветхозаве́тный *adj.* Old Testament; (*fig.*) antiquated.
ве́тхост|ь, и *f.* decrepitude; dilapidation.
ветчин|а́, ы́ *no pl.*, *f.* ham.
ветчи́н|ный *adj. of* **~а́**
ветша́|ть, ю *impf.* (*of* **об~**) to decay; to become dilapidated; to become decrepit.
ве́х|а, и *f.* landmark (*also fig.*); milestone; (*naut.*) spar-buoy; **сме́на ~** (*pol.*) volte-face; **смени́ть ~и** to execute a volte-face.
ве́ч|е, а *nt.* (*hist.*) veche (*popular assembly in medieval Russ. towns*).
вечево́й *adj. of* **ве́че**
ве́чер, а, *pl.* **~а́** *m.* **1.** evening; **по ~а́м** in the evenings; **под в., к ~у** towards evening. **2.** party; evening, soirée; **музыка́льный в.** musical evening; **вчера́ был в. у Ива́но́вых** the Ivanovs had a party last night; **в. па́мяти Че́хова** Chekhov commemoration meeting.
вечере́|ть, ет *impf.* (*impers.*) to grow dark; **~ет** night is falling.
вечери́нк|а, и *f.* (evening-)party.
вечерко́м *adv.* (*coll.*) in the evening.
вече́рн|ий *adj. of* **ве́чер; ~яя заря́** twilight, dusk; **в. звон** vesper chimes; **~ие ку́рсы** evening classes; **~ее пла́тье** evening dress; **~яя шко́ла** night-school.
вече́рник, а *m.* (*coll.*) night-school student.
вече́р|ня, ни, *g. pl.* **~ен** *f.* (*eccl.*) vespers.
ве́чером *adv.* in the evening.
ве́чер|я, и *f.* (*obs.*) supper; **Та́йная в.** (*bibl.*) the Last Supper.
ве́чник, а *m.* (*sl.*) lifer (*convict serving life sentence*).
ве́чно *adv.* for ever, eternally; always; **они́ в. ссо́рятся** they are always quarrelling.
вечнозелёный *adj.* (*bot.*) evergreen.
ве́чност|ь, и *f.* eternity; **ка́нуть в в.** to sink into oblivion; **це́лую в.** (*coll.*) for ages, for an age; **он не приходи́л сюда́ це́лую в.** he has not been here for ages.
ве́ч|ный (~ен, ~на) *adj.* **1.** eternal, everlasting; **~ная мерзлота́** permafrost; **засну́ть ~ным сном** to take one's last sleep. **2.** endless; perpetual; **~ное владе́ние** possession in perpetuity; **~ное перо́** fountain-pen.
вечо́р *adv.* (*coll.*, *obs.*) yesterday evening.
вечо́рк|а, и *f.* (*coll.*) evening paper.
ве́шалк|а, и *f.* **1.** peg, rack, stand. **2.** tab (*on clothes for hanging on pegs*). **3.** cloak-room.
ве́ша|ть[1]**, ю** *impf.* (*of* **пове́сить**) to hang; **в. бельё на верёвку** to hang washing on a line; **в. уби́йцу** to hang a murderer; **в. соба́к (на**+*a.* *or* **на ше́ю**+*d.*; *coll.*) to pin accusations (upon).
ве́ша|ть[2]**, ю** *impf.* (*of* **взве́сить**) to weigh, weigh out; **в. фунт ко́фе** to weigh out a pound of coffee.
ве́ша|ться[1]**, юсь** *impf.* (*of* **пове́ситься**) **1.** *pass. of* **~ть**[1]**;** to be hung; to be hanged. **2.** to hang o.s. **3.: в. на ше́ю кому́-н.** (*coll.*) to run after; **она́ всё ~ется молоды́м офице́рам на ше́ю** she is always running after young officers.
ве́ша|ться[2]**, юсь** *impf.* (*of* **с~**) to weigh o.s.
веш|и́ть, у́, и́шь *impf.* (*of* **про~**) (*geod.*) to mark out.
ве́шк|а, и *f.* landmark; surveying rod.
ве́шний *adj.* (*poet.*) vernal.
ве́|шу, сишь *see* **~сить**
веш|у́, и́шь *see* **~и́ть**
веща́ни|е, я *nt.* **1.** prophesying. **2.** (*radio*) broadcasting.
веща́|ть, ю *impf.* **1.** (*obs.*) to prophesy. **2.** (*coll.*) to pontificate, play the oracle, lay down the law. **3.** (*radio*) to broadcast.
вещ|ево́й *adj. of* **~ь; ~ево́е дово́льствие** payment in kind; (*mil.*) clothing, kit; **в. мешо́к** hold-all; kit-bag; **в. склад** storage warehouse, store; (*mil.*) stores.
веще́ственност|ь, и *f.* substantiality, materiality.
веще́ственн|ый *adj.* substantial, material; **~ые доказа́тельства** material evidence.
веществ|о́, а́ *nt.* substance; matter; **взры́вчатое в.** explosive; **канцероге́нное в.** carcinogen; **отравля́ющее в.** poison-gas; **пита́тельное в.** nutrient; **се́рое в.** grey matter.
вещи́зм, а *m.* materialism.
ве́щий *adj.* (*poet.*) prophetic.
вещ|и́ца, и́цы *f. dim. of* **~ь;** little thing; bagatelle.
вещмеш|о́к, ка́ *m.* kitbag, knapsack.
ве́щ|ный *adj. of* **~ь; ~ное пра́во** (*leg.*) law of estate.
вещу́н, а́ *m.* (*obs.*) soothsayer.
вещ|ь, и, *pl.* **~и, ~е́й** *f.* **1.** (*in var. senses*) thing; **пе́рвая любо́вь — чуде́сная в.** first love is a marvellous thing; **э́то в.!** (*expr. approval*; *coll.*) that's quite sth.!; **вот кака́я в.: президе́нт собира́ется посети́ть наш го́род** do you know what? the President is going to visit our town. **2.** (*pl.*) things (= (*i*) *belongings*; *baggage*; (*ii*) *clothes*); **ва́ши ли э́ти ~и?** are these things yours?; **тебе́ сле́дует носи́ть бо́лее тёплые ~и** you ought to be wearing warmer things; **со все́ми ~а́ми** bag and baggage. **3.** (*of artistic productions*) work; piece, thing; **его́ лу́чшие ~и ещё не переведены́** his best things have not yet been translated.
ве́ялк|а, и *f.* (*agric.*) winnowing-fan; winnowing-machine.
ве́яни|е, я *nt.* **1.** (*agric.*) winnowing. **2.** breathing, blowing (*of wind*). **3.** (*fig.*) current (*of opinion*), tendency, trend; **в. вре́мени** spirit of the times.
ве́|ять, ю, ешь *impf.* **1.** (*agric.*) to winnow. **2.** (*intrans.*) to blow (*of wind*); **~ял прохла́дный ветеро́к** a cool breeze was blowing; (*impers.*,+*i.*): **~ет весно́й** spring is in the air; **~ет но́выми иде́ями** new ideas are in the air. **3.** to wave, flutter; **знамёна ~яли по ве́тру** banners were fluttering in the wind.
вжива́|ться, юсь *impf. of* **вжи́ться**
вжи́|ться, ву́сь, вёшься *pf.* (**в**+*a.*; *coll.*) to get used (to), grow accustomed (to); **он с трудо́м ~вётся в вое́нную жизнь** he will find it hard to get used to army life.
взад *adv.* (*coll.*) back; **в. и вперёд** backwards and forwards, to and fro; **ни в. ни вперёд** neither backwards nor forwards; **он не мог дви́нуться ни в. ни вперёд** he could not budge an inch.
взаи́мност|ь, и *f.* reciprocity; return (*of affection*); **отвеча́ть кому́-н. ~ью** to reciprocate s.o.'s feelings, return s.o.'s love; **любо́вь без ~и** unrequited love.
взаи́м|ный (~ен, ~на) *adj.* mutual, reciprocal; **~ная по́мощь** mutual aid; **в. глаго́л** (*gram.*) reciprocal verb.
взаимоде́йстви|е, я *nt.* interaction; (*mil.*) co-operation, co-ordination.
взаимоде́йств|овать, ую *impf.* to interact; (*mil.*) to co-operate.
взаимоотноше́ни|е, я *nt.* interrelation.
взаимопо́мощ|ь, и *f.* mutual aid; **ка́сса ~и** mutual benefit; **догово́р о ~и** mutual assistance pact.
взаимосвя́з|ь, и *f.* interrelationship.
взаймы́ *adv.*: **взять в.** to borrow; **дать в.** to lend, loan.
взалка́|ть, ю *pf.* (*obs.*) to hunger (for) (+*g.* *or* +*inf.*; *fig.*, *now usu. iron.*).
взаме́н *prep.*+*g.* instead (of); in return (for), in exchange (for).
взаперти́ *adv.* **1.** under lock and key; **сиде́ть в.** to be locked up. **2.** in seclusion.
взапра́вду *adv.* (*coll.*) in truth, indeed.
вза́пуски *adv.*: **бе́гать в.** to chase one another.
взасо́с *adv.*: **целова́ться в.** (*coll.*) to exchange long-drawn-out kisses.
взатя́жку *adv.* **кури́ть в.** (*coll.*) to inhale (*in smoking*).
взаше́й *adv.* (*coll.*): **вы́гнать в.** to chuck out; to throw out (on one's neck).
взба́дрива|ть, ю *impf. of* **взбодри́ть**
взбаламу́|тить, чу, тишь *pf. of* **баламу́тить**
взба́лмошный *adj.* (*coll.*) unbalanced, eccentric.
взба́лтывани|е, я *nt.* shaking (up).
взба́лтыва|ть, ю *impf. of* **взболта́ть**
взбега́|ть, ю *impf.* (*of* **взбежа́ть**) to run up; **в. на́ гору** to

run up a hill; **в. по ле́стнице** to run upstairs.

взбе|жа́ть, гу́, жи́шь, гу́т *pf. of* **~га́ть**

взбелен|и́ться, ю́сь и́шься *pf.* (**на**+*a.*; *coll.*) to become enraged (with).

взбе|си́ть(ся), шу́(сь), ∸сишь(ся) *pf. of* **беси́ть(ся)**

взбива́|ть, ю *impf. of* **взбить**

взбира́|ться, юсь *impf. of* **взобра́ться**

взби́т|ый (~, ~а) *p.p.p. of* **~ь; ~ые сли́вки** whipped cream.

вз|бить, обью́, обьёшь *pf.* (*of* **~бива́ть**) **1.** to beat up; **в. сли́вки** to whip cream; **в. яи́чные белки́** to beat up white of egg. **2.** to shake up, fluff up.

взбодр|и́ть, ю *pf.* (*of* **взба́дривать**) to cheer up; to encourage.

взболта́|ть, ю *pf.* (*of* **взба́лтывать**) to shake (up) (*liquids*); **пе́ред приёмом в. миксту́ру** shake the bottle before taking.

взбороз|ди́ть, жу́, ди́шь *pf. of* **борозди́ть 1.**

взборон|и́ть, ю́, и́шь *pf. of* **борони́ть**

взбра́сыва|ть, ю *impf. of* **взбро́сить**

взбреда́|ть, ю *impf. of* **взбрести́**

взбре|сти́, ду́, дёшь, *past* **взбрёл, ~ла́** *pf.* (*of* **~да́ть**) (**на**+*a.*; *coll.*) to mount with difficulty; **в. в го́лову, на ум** to come into one's head; **ему́ ~ло́ на ум, что все его́ ненави́дят** he got it into his head that everyone hated him.

взбро́|сить, шу, сишь *pf.* (*of* **взбра́сывать**) (*coll.*) to throw up, toss up.

взбры́згива|ть, ю *impf. of* **взбры́знуть**

взбры́з|нуть, ну, нешь *pf.* (*of* **~гивать**) (*coll.*) to sprinkle, spatter.

взбудора́жива|ть, ю *impf. of* **взбудора́жить**

взбудора́ж|ить, у, ишь *pf.* (*coll.*) to agitate, work up.

взбунт|ова́ть(ся), у́ю(сь) *pf. of* **бунтова́ть(ся)**

взбух|а́ть, а́ю *impf. of* **∸нуть**

взбу́х|нуть, ну, нешь, *past* **~, ~ла** *pf.* (*of* **~а́ть**) to swell out.

взбу́ч|ить, у, ишь *pf.* (*coll.*) **1.** to thrash, beat. **2.** to reprimand.

взбу́чк|а, и *f.* (*coll.*) **1.** thrashing, beating. **2.** reprimand; **заката́ть кому́-н. ~у** to give s.o. a ticking-off; **получи́ть ~у** to be hauled over the coals.

взва́лива|ть, ю *impf. of* **взвали́ть**

взвал|и́ть, ю́ ∸ишь *pf.* (*of* **∸ивать**) to load, lift (onto); **в. мешо́к на́ спину** to hoist a pack onto one's back; **всю рабо́ту ~и́ли на но́вого учи́теля** (*coll.*) the new teacher was loaded with all the work; **всю вину́ ~и́ли на него́** he was made to shoulder all the blame.

взвар, а *m.* (*cul.*) stewed fruit and berries.

взве́|сить, шу, сишь *pf.* (*of* **~шивать** *and* **ве́шать**) to weigh; (*fig.*) to weigh, consider; **в. возмо́жные после́дствия посту́пка** to weigh the possible consequences of an action.

взве|сти́, ду́, дёшь, *past* **∸л, ~ла́** *pf.* (*of* **взводи́ть**) **1.** to lead up, take up; **в. куро́к (ружья́)** to cock (a gun). **2.** (**на**+*a.*) to impute (to); **на генера́ла ~ли́ обвине́ние в пораже́нии** blame for the defeat was laid at the general's door.

взвес|ь, и *f.* (*chem.*) suspension.

взве́шен|ный (~, ~а) 1. *p.p.p. of* **взве́сить. 2.** (*chem.*) suspended; **~ое состоя́ние** suspension.

взве́шивани|е, я *nt.* weighing.

взве́шива|ть, ю *impf. of* **взве́сить**

взвива́|ть(ся), ю(сь) *impf. of* **взви́ть(ся)**

взви́|деть, жу, дишь *pf. only in phr.* **све́та не в.** (*coll.*) to see stars.

взвизг, а *m.* (*coll.*) scream; yelp (*of a dog*).

взви́згива|ть, ю *impf. and freq. of* **взви́згнуть**

взви́згн|уть, у, ешь *pf.* to scream, cry out; to yelp (*of a dog*); **соба́ка жа́лобно ~ула** the dog let out a piteous yelp.

взвин|ти́ть, чу́, ти́шь *pf.* (*of* **взви́нчивать**) (*coll.*) to excite, work up; **в. це́ны** to inflate prices.

взви́нчен|ный (~, ~а) *p.p.p. of* **взвинти́ть** *and adj.* excited, worked up; highly-strung, nervy; **не́рвы у него́ всегда́ ~ы** he is always on edge; **~ные це́ны** inflated prices.

взви́нчива|ть, ю *impf. of* **взвинти́ть**

взвить, взовью́, взовьёшь *pf.* (*of* **взвива́ть**) to raise.

взви́ться, взовью́сь, взовьёшься *pf.* (*of* **взива́ться**) to rise; to fly up, soar (*of birds*); to be raised, go up (*of flags, etc.*); **за́навес взви́лся ро́вно в во́семь часо́в** the curtain went up at eight o'clock exactly.

взвод[1]**, а** *m.* (*mil.*) platoon.

взвод[2]**, а** *m.* (cocking) notch (*of guns*); **боево́й в., второ́й в.** full bent; **на боево́м ∸е** cocked; **на пе́рвом ∸е** at half-cock; **предохрани́тельный в.** safety notch; **на предохрани́тельном ∸е** at safety; **быть на ∸е** (*coll.*) to be in one's cups.

взво|ди́ть, жу́, ∸дишь *impf. of* **взвести́**

взвод|но́й *adj. of* **~**[2]**; ~на́я ру́чка** cocking handle.

взво́д|ный *adj. of* **~**[1]**;** *as n.* **в., ~ного** *m.* platoon commander.

взволно́ван|ный (~, ~а) *p.p.p. of* **взволнова́ть** *and adj.* agitated, disturbed; anxious, worried; **у неё в. вид** she has a worried look.

взволн|ова́ть, у́ю *pf. of* **волнова́ть**

взволн|ова́ться, у́юсь *pf. of* **волнова́ться**

взво́|ю, ешь *see* **взвыть**

взвыва́|ть, ю *impf. of* **взвыть**

взв|ыть, о́ю, о́ешь *pf.* (*of* **~ыва́ть**) to howl, set up a howl.

взгляд, а *m.* **1.** look; glance; gaze, stare; **бро́сить в.** (**на**+*a.*) to glance (at); **на в.** to judge from appearances; **на пе́рвый в., с пе́рвого ∸а** at first sight. **2.** view; opinion; **на мой в.** in my opinion, as I see it.

взгля́дыва|ть, ю *impf. of* **взгляну́ть**

взглян|у́ть, у́, ∸ешь *pf.* (**на**+*a.*) to look (at); to cast a glance (at); **в. на что-н. серьёзно** (*fig.*) to take a serious view of sth.

взговор|и́ть, ю́, и́шь *pf.* (*folk poet.*) to say.

взго́рь|е, я *nt.* (*dial.*) hillock.

взгре|ть, ю, ешь *pf.* (*coll.*) to thrash; (*fig.*) to give it hot.

взгроможда́|ть, ю *impf. of* **взгромозди́ть**

взгроможда́|ться, юсь *impf. of* **взгромозди́ться**

взгромоз|ди́ть, жу́, ди́шь *pf.* (*coll.*) to pile up.

взгромоз|ди́ться, жу́сь, ди́шься *pf.* (*coll.*) to clamber up.

взгрустн|у́ть, у́, ёшь *pf.* (*coll.*) to feel sad, depressed.

взгрустн|у́ться, ётся *pf.* (*impers.*, +*d.*; *coll.*) to feel sad, depressed; **ему́ ~у́лось** he feels depressed.

вздва́ива|ть, ю *impf. of* **вздво́ить**

вздв|о́ить, о́ю, о́ишь *pf.* (*of* **~а́ивать**) **в. ряды́** (*mil.*) to form fours.

вздёргива|ть, ю *impf. of* **вздёрнуть**

вздёрнут|ый (~, ~а) *p.p.p. of* **~ь; в. нос** snub nose.

вздёрн|уть, у, ешь *pf.* (*coll.*) **1.** to hitch up; to jerk up; **в. нос** to become proud. **2.** to hang.

вздор, а *no pl., m.* (*coll.*) nonsense; **городи́ть, моло́ть в.** to talk nonsense.

вздо́р|ить, ю, ишь *impf.* (*of* **по~**) (*coll.*) to squabble.

вздо́р|ный (~ен, ~на) *adj.* (*coll.*) **1.** foolish, stupid. **2.** cantankerous, quarrelsome.

вздорожа́ни|е, я *nt.* rise in price.

вздорожа́|ть, ю *pf. of* **дорожа́ть**

вздох, а *m.* sigh; deep breath; **испусти́ть после́дний в.** to breathe one's last.

вздохн|у́ть, у́, ёшь *pf.* (*of* **вздыха́ть**) **1.** to sigh. **2.** (*coll.*) to take breath, have a breathing-space; **дава́йте ~ём!** let's pause for breath!

вздра́гива|ть, ю *impf.* (*of* **вздро́гнуть**) to shudder, quiver.

вздремн|у́ть, у́, ёшь *pf.* (*coll.*) to have a nap, doze.

вздремн|у́ться, ётся *pf.* (*impers.*, +*d.*; *coll.*): **как раз по́сле еды́ ему́ ~у́лось** immediately after the meal he dozed off.

вздро́гн|уть, у, ешь *pf.* (*of* **вздра́гивать**) to start; to wince, flinch.

вздрю́ч|ить, у, ишь *pf.* (*coll.*) to thrash, beat, to reprimand.

вздува́|ть, ю *impf. of* **вздуть**[1]

взду́ма|ть, ю *pf.* (+*inf.*; *coll.*) to take it into one's head; **она́ ~ла носи́ть чёрные ве́щи** she took it into her head to wear black; **не ~й(те)** mind you don't; **не ~йте ныря́ть здесь!** mind you don't dive in here!; don't try to dive in here!

взду́ма|ться, ется *pf.* (*impers.*, +*d.*; *coll.*) to take it into one's head; **ему́ ~лось пое́хать в Аме́рику** he took it

into his head to go to America; **поступáть как ~ется** to follow one's fancy.
вздýти|е, я *nt.* (*med.*) swelling; **в. цен** (*fig.*) inflation of prices.
вздýт|ый[1] **(~, ~а)** *p.p.p. of* **~ь**[1] *and adj.* swollen.
вздýт|ый[2] **(~, ~а)** *p.p.p. of* **~ь**[2]
вздý|ть[1]**, ю, ешь** *pf.* (*of* **вздувáть**) **1.** to blow up, inflate. **2.** (*dial.*) to light (*a fire*).
вздý|ть[2]**, ю, ешь** *pf.* (*coll.*) to thrash, give a thrashing (to).
вздý|ться, юсь, ешься *pf.* to swell (*intrans.*).
вздымá|ть, ю *impf.* to raise.
вздымá|ться, юсь *impf.* to rise; **~лась мгла над óзером** mist was rising over the lake.
вздыхáни|е, я *nt.* (*obs.*) **1.** sighing. **2.** (*pl. only*) love-sickness.
вздыхáтел|ь, я *m.* (*coll., obs.*) admirer.
вздыхá|ть, ю *impf.* (*of* **вздохнýть**) **1.** to breathe; to sigh. **2.** (**о, по**+*p.*) to pine (for); to long, sigh (for).
взимáни|е, я *nt.* levy, collection.
взимá|ть, ю *impf.* to levy, collect, raise (*taxes*).
взирá|ть, ю *impf.* (**на**+*a.*) **1.** (*obs.*) to look (at), gaze (at). **2.: не ~я на** in spite of, notwithstanding; **не ~я на лúца** without respect of persons.
взлáмыва|ть, ю *impf. of* **взломáть**
взлезá|ть, ю *impf. of* **взлезть**
взлез|ть, у, ешь, *past* **~, ~ла** *pf.* (*of* **~áть**) to climb up.
взлелé|ять, ю, ешь *pf. of* **лелéять**
взлёт, а *m.* (upward) flight (*also fig.*); (*aeron.*) take-off; **в. фантáзии** flight of fancy.
взлетá|ть, ю *impf. of* **взлетéть**
взле|тéть, чý, тúшь *pf.* (*of* **~тáть**) to fly up; to take off; **в. по лéстнице** to fly upstairs; **в. на вóздух** to explode, blow up (*also fig.*); **в течéние едúного дня мечтý всей жúзни ~тéли на вóздух** the dreams of a lifetime exploded in a day.
взлёт|ный *adj. of* **~**; (*aeron.*): **~ная дорóжка** runway; **~но-посáдочная полосá** landing strip.
взлúз|а, ы (*coll.*) bald patch (*above the temples*).
взлом, а *m.* breaking open, breaking in; **крáжа со ~ом** house-breaking.
взломá|ть, ю *pf.* (*of* **взлáмывать**) to break open, force; to smash; **в. замóк** to force a lock; **в. неприятельскую оборóну** to force the enemy's defences.
взлóмщик, а *m.* burglar, house-breaker; **компьютерный в.** hacker.
взлохмá|тить, чу, тишь *pf. of* **лохмáтить** *and* **~чивать**
взлохмá|ченный (~чен, ~чена) *p.p.p. of* **~тить** *and adj.* tousled; dishevelled.
взлохмáчива|ть, ю *impf.* to tousle.
взлюб|úть, лю, ~ишь *pf., only with neg.*; **не в. с пéрвого взгля́да** to take an instant dislike (to).
взман|úть, ю́, úшь *pf. of* **манúть 2.**
взмах, а *m.* wave (*of hand*); flap, flapping (*of wings*); stroke (*of oars, etc.*); **одним ~ом** at one stroke.
взмáхива|ть, ю *impf. of* **взмахнýть**
взмахн|ýть, ý, ёшь *pf.* (+*i.*) to wave, flap; **в. платкóм** to wave a handkerchief.
взметн|ýть, ý, ёшь *pf.* (*of* **взмётывать**) (+*i.*) to throw up, fling up; **в. рукáми** to fling up one's hands.
взметн|ýться, ýсь ёшься *pf.* **1.** to leap up, fly up; **úскры ~ýлись из-под копы́т коня́** sparks flew up from the horse's hoofs. **2.** (**на**+*a.*) (*obs.*) to leap (upon), fly (at); **собáки ~ýлись на бродя́гу** the dogs flew at the tramp.
взмётыва|ть, ю *impf. of* **взметнýть**
взмётыва|ться, юсь *impf. of* **взметнýться**
взмол|úться, ю́сь, ~ишься *pf.* (**о**+*p.*) to beg (for); to beseech; **в. о пощáде** to beg for mercy.
взмóрь|е, я *nt.* sea-shore; seaside.
взмо|стúться, щýсь, стúшься *pf.* (*coll.*) (**на**+*a.*) to perch (on).
взму|тúть, чý, тúшь *pf. of* **мутúть**
взмывá|ть, ю *impf. of* **взмыть**
взмы́лива|ть(ся), ю(сь) *impf. of* **взмы́лить(ся)**
взмы́л|ить, ю, ишь *pf.* to cause to foam, lather.
взмы́л|иться, юсь, ишься *pf.* to foam (*intrans.*), froth.
взм|ыть, óю, óешь *pf.* (*of* **~ывáть**) to shoot upwards (*of a bird*).
взнос, а *m.* payment; fee, dues; subscription; **вступúтельный в.** entrance fee; **очереднóй в.** instalment; **профсою́зный в.** trade-union dues; **члéнский в.** membership fee.
взнуздá|ть, ю *pf.* to bridle.
взнýздыва|ть, ю *impf. of* **взнуздáть**
взобрá|ться, взберýсь, взберёшься, *past* **~лся, ~лáсь** *pf.* (*of* **взбирáться**) (**на**+*a.*) to climb (up), clamber (up); **им пришлóсь в. на склон холмá на четверéньках** they had to clamber up the slope on all fours.
взобь|ю́, ёшь *see* **взбить**
взовь|ю́, ёшь *see* **взвить**
взо|йтú, йдý, йдёшь, *past* **~шёл, ~шлá,** *p.p.* **~шéдший** *pf.* (*of* **всходúть** *and* **восходúть**) (**на**+*a.*) **1.** to mount, ascend; to rise; **в. на трибýну** to mount the platform; **сóлнце ~шлó в пять часóв сегóдня** the sun rose at five o'clock today; **посéвы ужé ~шлú** the crops are already standing; **тéсто не ~шлó** the dough would not rise. **2.** (*obs., coll.*) to enter.
взор, а *m.* look; glance; **обратúть на себя́ ~ы пýблики** to come into the public eye; **устремúть ~ы (на**+*a.*) to fasten one's eyes (on).
взорв|áть, ý, ёшь *pf.* (*of* **взрывáть**) **1.** to blow up; to detonate. **2.** (*fig.*) to exasperate, madden; (*impers.*): **егó ~áло, когдá онú сообщúли о своéй помóлвке** he exploded when they announced their engagement.
взорв|áться, ýсь, ёшься *pf.* (*of* **взрывáться**) to blow up, burst, explode (*also fig.*).
взо|шёл, шлá *see* **~йтú**
взра|стúть, щý, стúшь *pf.* to grow, cultivate; to bring up, nurture.
взрáщива|ть, ю *impf. of* **взрастúть**
взра|щý, стúшь *see* **~стúть**
взрев|éть, ý, ёшь *pf.* to let out a roar.
взрéж|у, ешь *see* **взрéзать**
взрé|зать, жу, жешь *pf.* to cut open.
взрезá|ть, ю *impf. of* **взрéзать**
взрéзыва|ть, ю *impf.* = **взрезáть**
взрóсл|ый *adj.* grown-up, adult; *as n.* **в., ~ого** *m.*; **~ая, ~ой** *f.*
взрыв, а *m.* explosion; (*fig.*) burst, outburst; **в. аплодисмéнтов** burst of applause; **в. негодовáния** outburst of indignation; **«Большóй в.»** (*astron.*) the Big Bang.
взрывá|ть[1]**, ю** *impf. of* **взорвáть**
взрывá|ть[2] *impf. of* **взрыть**
взрывá|ться, юсь *impf. of* **взорвáться**
взрывнúк, á *m.* explosives expert.
взрывн|óй *adj.* **1.** explosive; **~áя волнá** blast. **2.** (*ling.*) plosive.
взрывоопáсн|ый *adj.*: **~ая ситуáция** explosive situation.
взрывчáтк|а, и *f.* (*coll.*) explosive.
взры́вчат|ый *adj.* explosive; **~ое веществó** explosive.
взр|ыть, óю, óешь *pf.* (*of* **~ывáть**[2]) to plough up, turn up.
взрыхл|úть, ю́, úшь *pf.* to loosen, break up.
взрыхля́|ть, ю *impf. of* **взрыхлúть**
взъёбк|а, и *f.* (*vulg.*) bollocking.
взъедá|ться, юсь *impf. of* **взъéсться**
взъезжá|ть, ю *impf. of* **взъéхать**
взъерепéн|иться, юсь ишься *pf. of* **ерепéниться**
взъерóшен|ный (~, ~а) *p.p.p. of* **взъерóшить** *and adj.* tousled, dishevelled.
взъерóшива|ть(ся), ю(сь) *impf. of* **взъерóшить(ся)**
взъерóш|ить, у, ишь *pf.* (*of* **~ивать**) (*coll.*) to tousle, rumple.
взъерóш|иться, усь, ишься *pf.* (*of* **~иваться**) (*coll.*) to rumple one's hair; to become dishevelled.
взъ|éсться, éмся, éшься, éстся, едúмся, едúтесь, едя́тся, *past* **~éлся** *pf.* (*of* **~едáться**) (**на**+*a.*; *coll.*) to pitch into, go for (*fig.*).
взъé|хать, ду, дешь *pf.* (*of* **~зжáть**) to mount, ascend (*in a vehicle or on an animal*).
взывá|ть, ю *impf. of* **воззвáть**
взыгрá|ть, ю *pf.* **1.** to leap (for joy); **сéрдце во мне ~ло** my heart leapt. **2.** to become disturbed; **мóре ~ло** the sea grew rough.

взыска́ни|е, я *nt.* **1.** penalty; punishment; **подве́ргнуться ~ю** to incur a penalty. **2.** exaction, prosecution; **пода́ть на кого́-н. ко ~ю** (*leg.*) to proceed against s.o. (*for recovery of debt, etc.*).

взыска́тел|ьный (~ен, ~ьна) *adj.* exacting; demanding; severe.

взы|ска́ть[1], **щу́, ~щешь** *pf.* (*of* **~скивать**) **1.** to exact; to recover; **в. долг (с**+*g.*) to recover a debt (from). **2.** to call to account, make answer (for); **за неуда́чу в бою́ ~ска́ли с генера́лов** the generals were called to account for their failure in battle; **не ~щи́(те)!** (*coll.*) please forgive (me)!; don't be hard on (me)!

взы|ска́ть[2], **щу́, ~щешь** *pf.* (*of* **~скивать**) (+*i.*; *obs.*) to confer (on); to reward (with); **в. ми́лостями** to load with favours.

взы́скива|ть, ю *impf. of* **взыска́ть**

взыску́ющ|ий, его *m.* (*liter.*) 'seeker'.

взы|щу́, ~щешь *see* **~ска́ть**

взя́ти|е, я *nt.* taking; capture.

взя́тк|а, и *f.* **1.** bribe; backhander; **~и гла́дки,** *see* **гла́дкий. 2.** (*cards*) trick.

взя́т|ок, ка *m.* honey-gathering.

взя́точник, а *m.* bribe-taker.

взя́точничеств|о, а *nt.* bribery, bribe-taking, corruption.

взя|ть, возьму́, возьмёшь, *past* **~л, ~ла́, ~ло** *pf.* (*of* **брать**) **1.** *see* **брать. 2.** (*coll.*) to conclude, suppose; **с чего́ вы ~ли, что он не́мец?** what gave you the idea that he is a German? **3.: в. да, в. и, в. да и...** (*coll.*) to do sth. suddenly; **он ~л да убежа́л** he up and ran; **он возьми́ да скажи́** he up and spoke; **возьми́ да скажи́** speak up, speak your mind. **4.: чёрт возьми́!** (*coll.*) devil, deuce take it! **5.: ни дать ни в.** (*coll.*) exactly, neither more nor less.

взя́|ться, возьму́сь, возьмёшься, *past* **~лся, ~ла́сь, ~ло́сь** *pf.* (*of* **бра́ться**); **отку́да ни возьми́сь** (*coll.*) from nowhere, out of the blue; **отку́да ни возьми́сь налете́ла саранча́** out of the blue the locusts appeared.

виаду́к, а *m.* viaduct.

вибра́тор, а *m.* (*elec.*) vibrator; (*radio*) oscillator.

вибрафо́н, а *m.* (*mus.*) vibraphone, vibes.

вибра́ци|я, и *f.* vibration.

вибри́р|овать, ую *impf.* to vibrate; to oscillate.

вива́ри|й, я *m.* vivarium.

вивёр, а *m.* (*coll., obs.*) bon vivant.

вivéрр|а, ы *f.* (*zool.*) civet.

вивисе́кци|я, и *f.* vivisection.

виг, а *m.* (*hist.*) whig.

вигва́м, а *m.* wigwam.

виго́н|ь, и *f.* vicuña; vicuña wool.

вид[1], **а** *m.* **1.** air, look; appearance; aspect; **у вас хоро́ший в.** you look well; **име́ть мра́чный в.** to look gloomy, have a gloomy air; **приня́ть пра́здничный в.** to assume a festive air; **сде́лать в. бу́дто** to make it appear that, pretend that; **для ~у** for the sake of appearances; **на в., с ~у** in appearance; **знать по ~у** to know by sight; **под ~ом** (+*g.*) under the guise (of); **ни под каки́м ~ом** on no account. **2.** shape, form; condition; **в любо́м ~е** in any shape or form; **в тре́звом ~е** in a sober state; **в хоро́шем ~е** in good condition, in good shape. **3.** view; **ко́мната с ~ом на го́ры** room with a view of the mountains; **в. сбо́ку** side-view; **откры́тка с ~ом** picture postcard. **4.** (*pl.*) prospect; **~ы на бу́дущее** prospects for the future. **5.** sight; **потеря́ть и́з ~у** to lose sight (of); **упусти́ть и́з ~у** (*fig.*) to lose sight (of), fail to take into account; **поста́вить на в. кому́-н. что-н.** to reprimand s.o. for sth.; **быть на ~у́** to be in the public eye; **при ~е** (+*g.*) at the sight (of); **в ~у́** (+*g.*) in sight (of); **в ~у́ того́, что** as, since, seeing that; **име́ть в ~у́** (*i*) to plan, intend, (*ii*) to mean; **что вы име́ли в ~у́, говоря́ э́то?** what did you mean when you said that?, (*iii*) to bear in mind; **име́й(те) в ~у́** bear in mind, don't forget; **име́ться в ~у́** (*i*) to be intended, be envisaged, (*ii*) to be meant.

вид[2], **а** *m.* **1.** (*biol.*) species; **исчеза́ющий в.** endangered *or* threatened species. **2.** kind, sort. **3.** (*gram.*) aspect; **соверше́нный, несоверше́нный в.** perfective, imperfective aspect.

вид[3], **а** *m.*: **в. на жи́тельство** residence permit; identity card.

вида́к, а́ *m.* (*sl.*) = **ви́дик**

ви́дан|ный (~, ~а) *p.p.p. of* **вида́ть; ~ное ли э́то де́ло?** have you ever heard of such a thing?

вида́|ть, ю *impf.* (*of* **у~**) (*coll.*) to see; **его́ не в.** he is not to be seen; **ничего́ подо́бного я не ~л** I have never seen such a thing; **он ~л ви́ды** he has seen, knocked about, the world.

вида́|ться, юсь *impf.* (*of* **по~**) (**с**+*i.*; *coll.*) to meet; to see one another; **мы с жено́й три го́да не ~лись** my wife and I had not seen one another for three years.

ви́дени|е, я *nt.* sight, vision.

виде́ни|е, я *nt.* vision, apparition.

видео... *comb. form* video-.

видеоза́пис|ь, и *f.* video recording.

видеока́мер|а, ы *f.* video camera.

видеокассе́т|а, ы *f.* video cassette.

видеоле́нт|а, ы *f.* videotape.

видеомагнитофо́н, а *m.* video recorder.

видеоте́к|а, и *f.* video rental club.

видеотелефо́н, а *m.* videophone.

видеофо́н = **видеотелефо́н**

ви́|деть, жу, дишь *impf.* (*of* **у~**) to see; **в. кого́-н. насквозь** to see through s.o.; **в. во сне** to dream (of); **его́ то́лько и ~дели** (*coll.*) he was gone in a flash; **~дишь (ли)?; ~дите (ли)?** (*coll.*) (do) you see?

ви́|деться, жусь, дишься *impf.* **1.** to see one another; (**с**+*i.*) to see. **2.** (*pf.* **при~**) to appear; **ему́ ~делся стра́шный сон** he had a terrifying dream; **Га́млету ~делась тень отца́ на валу́** the ghost of his father appeared to Hamlet on the rampart.

ви́дик, а *m.* (*coll.*) video (recorder).

ви́димо *adv.* **1.** (*obs.*) visibly. **2.** evidently; **он, в., чу́вствовал себя́ оскорблённым** evidently he was offended.

ви́димо-неви́димо *adv.* (*coll.*) in immense quantity; **наро́ду бы́ло в.-н** there was an immense crowd.

ви́димост|ь, и *f.* **1.** visibility. **2.** outward appearance; **для ~и** for show, for appearances. **3.: по (всей) ~и** to all appearances.

ви́дим|ый (~, ~а) *p.p.p. of* **ви́деть** *and adj.* **1.** visible. **2.** apparent, evident; **без ~ой причи́ны** with no apparent cause. **3.** apparent, seeming.

видне́|ться, юсь, ешься *impf.* to be visible; **на горизо́нте ~лись огни́ корабля́** a ship's lights could be seen on the horizon.

ви́дно 1. *adv.* obviously, evidently; **она́, в., уста́ла** obviously she is tired; *as pred.* it is obvious, it is evident, it is apparent; **всем бы́ло в., что он лжёт** it was obvious to everyone, everyone could see that he was lying; **как в. из ска́занного** as is clear from the statement. **2.** *adv. as pred.* visible; in sight; **бе́рега ещё не́ было в.** the coast was not yet visible; **конца́ ещё не в.** the end is not yet in sight; **бы́ло хорошо́ в.** visibility was good.

ви́д|ный *adj.* **1.** (**~ен, ~на́, ~но**) visible; conspicuous. **2.** distinguished, prominent. **3.** (*coll.*) portly, stately; **в. мужчи́на** fine figure of a man.

видово́й[1] *adj. of* **вид**[1]; **в. объекти́в** (*phot.*) landscape lens; **в. фильм** travel film, travelogue.

видово́й[2] *adj.* (*of* **вид**[2]) **1.** (*biol.*) specific. **2.** (*gram.*) aspectual.

видоизмене́ни|е, я *nt.* **1.** modification, alteration. **2.** modification, variety.

видоизмен|и́ть, ю́, и́шь *pf.* (*of* **~я́ть**) to modify, alter.

видоизмен|и́ться, ю́сь, и́шься *pf.* (*of* **~я́ться**) **1.** to alter (*intrans.*). **2.** *pass. of* **~я́ть**

видоизмен|я́ть(ся), я́ю(сь) *impf. of* **~и́ть(ся)**

видообразова́ни|е, я *nt.* (*biol.*) formation of species.

ви́дыва|ть, ю *freq. of* **ви́деть** (*coll.*) to see.

ви́з|а, ы *f.* **1.** visa. **2.** official stamp.

визави́ 1. *adv.* opposite; **они́ сиде́ли в.** they sat opposite one another. **2.** *n.*; *c.g. indecl.* the pers. opposite, facing; **мы с мои́м в. завяза́ли разгово́р** I struck up a conversation with the pers. facing me.

византи́|ец, йца *m.* Byzantine.

Византи|й, я *m.* (*hist.*) Byzantium.
византи́|йка, йки *f. of* **~ец**
византи́йский *adj.* Byzantine.
византини́ст, а *m.* Byzantinist.
Византи́|я, и *f.* (*hist.*) Byzantine Empire.
визг, а *m.* scream, squeal, yelp.
визгли́в|ый (~, ~а) *adj.* **1.** shrill. **2.** given to screaming, squealing, yelping.
визготн|я́, и́ *f.* (*coll.*) screaming; squealing; yelping.
визж|а́ть, у́, и́шь *impf.* to scream; to squeal; to yelp.
визи́г|а, и *no pl., f.* viziga (*foodstuff prepared from gristle of fish of sturgeon family*).
визионе́р, а *m.* visionary, mystic.
визионе́рств|о, а *nt.* mystical propensities.
визи́р, а *m.* **1.** (*mil.*) sight; **навигацио́нный в.** (*aeron.*) drift sight. **2.** (*phot.*) view-finder.
визи́р|овать[1], **ую** *impf. and pf.* (*pf. also* **за~**) to visa, visé (*passport*).
визи́р|овать[2], **ую** *impf. and pf.* to sight; to take a sight (on).
визи́р|ь *m.* vizier.
визи́т, а *m.* visit; call; **нанести́ в.** to make an (*official*) visit; **отда́ть в.** to return a visit, call; **прийти́ с ~ом к кому́-н.** to visit s.o., pay s.o. a call.
визита́ци|я, и *f.* **1.** call; round (*of doctor*). **2.** search (*for contraband goods*).
визитёр, а *m.* visitor, caller.
визити́р|овать, ую *impf.* **1.** (*obs.*) to pay a visit. **2.** to make a round (*of doctor*).
визи́тк|а, и *f.* **1.** morning coat. **2.** business card.
визи́т|ный *adj. of* **~**; **~ная ка́рточка** visiting card; (business) card.
ви́к|а, и *no pl., f.* vetch, tares.
вика́ри|й, я *m.* (*eccl.*) vicar; suffragan.
вика́рный *adj.* (*eccl.*) suffragan.
ви́кинг, а *m.* Viking.
вико́нт, а *m.* viscount.
викториа́нский *adj.* Victorian.
виктори́н|а, ы *f.* quiz.
викто́ри|я, и *no pl., f.* pine strawberries.
ви́лк|а, и *f.* **1.** fork. **2.** (*elec.*): **ште́псельная в.** two-pin plug. **3.** (*mil*) bracket.
ви́лл|а, ы *f.* villa.
ви́ллис, а *m.* (*mil.*) jeep.
вил|о́к, ка́ *m.* (*dial.*) head of cabbage.
вилообра́з|ный (~ен, ~на) *adj.* forked.
ви́л|ы, ~ *no sg.* pitchfork; **э́то ещё ~ами на водé пи́сано** (*fig.*) it is still in the air.
вильн|у́ть, у́, ёшь *pf.* **1.** *pf. of* **виля́ть. 2.** to glide away; to turn off sharply, sidetrack.
Ви́льнюс, а *m.* Vilnius.
виля́ни|е, я *nt.* **1.** wagging. **2.** (*fig.*) prevarication; evasions.
виля́|ть, ю *impf.* (*of* **вильну́ть**) **1.** to wag; **в. хвосто́м** to wag one's tail; **хвост у соба́ки всё вре́мя ~л** the dog's tail was wagging the whole time. **2.** (*fig.*) to prevaricate; to be evasive.
вин|а́, ы́, *pl.* **~ы** *f.* fault, guilt; blame; **моя́ в.** it is my fault; **не по их ~é** through no fault of theirs; **поста́вить кому́-н. в ~у́** to accuse s.o. of, reproach s.o. with; **свали́ть ~у́ (на+***a.***)** to lay the blame (on).
виндсёрфинг, а *m.* **1.** windsurfing, sailboarding. **2.** sailboard.
виндсёрфинги́ст, а *m.* windsurfer, sailboarder.
винегре́т, а *m.* Russian salad; (*fig.*) medley, farrago.
ви́н|и, е́й *no sg.* (*coll.*) spades (*cards*).
вини́тельный *adj.* (*gram.*) **в. паде́ж** accusative case.
вин|и́ть, ю́ и́шь *impf.* **(в+***p.***)** to accuse (of); **(за+***a.***)** (*obs., call*) to reproach (for).
вин|и́ться, ю́сь, и́шься *impf.* (*of* **по~**) **(в+** *p.*; *coll.*) to confess (to).
вини́щ|е *nt.* (*coll.*) spirit *or* wine.
ви́нкел|ь, я, *pl.* **~я́** *m.* (*tech.*) set-square.
виннока́менн|ый *adj.* (*chem.*) **~ая кислота́** tartaric acid.
ви́нн|ый *adj.* wine; winy; vinous; **в. ка́мень** (*chem.*) tartar; **~ая кислота́** tartaric acid; **в. спирт** alcohol; **~ая я́года** dried figs.
вин|о́, а́, *pl.* **~а** *nt.* **1.** wine. **2.** (*sg. only*; *coll.*) vodka.
винова́т|ый (~, ~а) *adj.* guilty; to blame; **мы все ~ы в э́том** we are all to blame for this; **~!** sorry!; **без вины́ ~ый** innocent victim.
вино́вник, а *m.* author, initiator; culprit; **в. преступле́ния** perpetrator of a crime; **в. побе́ды** architect of victory.
вино́вность, и *f.* guilt.
вино́в|ный (~ен, ~на) *adj.* **(в+***p.***)** guilty (of); **объявля́ть ~ным** to bring in a verdict of guilty; **призна́ть себя́ ~ным** to plead guilty.
виногра́д, а (у) *m.* **1.** vine. **2.** (*collect*) grapes; **зе́лен в.!** sour grapes!
виногра́дарств|о, а *nt.* viticulture; wine-growing.
виногра́дар|ь, я *m.* wine-grower.
виногра́дин|а, ы *f.* (*coll.*) grape.
виногра́дник, а *m.* vineyard.
виногра́д|ный *adj. of* **~**; **~ная лоза́** vine; **в. сезо́н** vintage; **~ное су́сло** must.
виноде́л, а *m.* wine-grower.
виноде́ли|е, я *nt.* wine-making.
виноку́р, а *m.* distiller.
винокуре́ни|е, я *nt.* distillation.
виноку́р|енный *adj. of* **~е́ние; в. заво́д** distillery.
виноку́р|ня, ни, *g. pl.* **~ен** *f.* (*obs.*) distillery.
винотoрго́в|ец, ца *m.* wine-merchant.
винотoрго́вл|я, и *f.* **1.** wine-trade. **2.** wineshop.
виноче́рпи|й, я *m.* (*hist.*) cup-bearer.
винт[1], **а́** *m.* **1.** screw; **подъёмный в.** jack-screw; **упо́рный в.** stop screw; **устано́вочный в.** adjusting set screw. **2.** screw, propeller; **дать ~а́** (*sl.*) to take to one's heels, scarper. **3.** spiral; **ле́стница ~о́м** spiral staircase.
винт[2], **а́** *m.* vint (*card-game*).
винт[3], **а́** *m.* (*sl.*) rifle.
ви́нт|ик, а *m.* **1.** *dim. of* **~**[1]; **у него́ ~а не хвата́ет** (*coll.*) he has a screw loose somewhere. **2.** (*fig., coll., of a pers.*) cog.
вин|ти́ть[1], **чу́, ти́шь** *impf.* to screw up.
вин|ти́ть[2], **чу́, ти́шь** *impf.* (*coll.*) to play vint.
винто́вк|а, и *f.* rifle.
винт|ово́й *adj. of* **~**[1]; spiral; **~ова́я ле́стница** spiral staircase; **~ова́я наре́зка** thread (*of screw*); **в. парохо́д** steamer; **~ова́я переда́ча** (*tech.*) helical gear.
винтообра́з|ный (~ен, на) *adj.* spiral.
винторе́зный *adj.* (*tech.*) screw-cutting.
вин|чу́, ти́шь *see* **~ти́ть**
винье́тк|а, и *f.* vignette.
вио́л|а, ы *f.* viol; viola.
виолончели́ст, а *m.* (violon)cellist.
виолонче́л|ь, и *f.* (violon)cello.
ви́ппет, а *m.* whippet.
ви́ра[1] *int.* (*dockers' sl.*) lift!
ви́р|а[2], **ы** *f.* (*hist.*) wergeld.
вира́ж[1], **а** *m.* (*phot.*) intensifier; **в.-фикса́ж** tone-fixing bath.
вира́ж[2], **а́** *m.* **1.** turn; **круто́й в.** steep turn. **2.** bend, curve (*of road, racing-track, etc.*).
вирги́нский *adj.*: **в. таба́к** Virginia tobacco.
виpи́p|овать, ую *impf. and pf.* (*phot.*) to intensify.
виртуа́л|ьный (~ен, ~ьна) *adj.* virtual.
виртуо́з, а *m.* virtuoso.
виртуо́зност|ь, и *f.* virtuosity.
виртуо́з|ный (~ен, на) *adj.* masterly.
вируле́нт|ный (~ен, ~на) *adj.* (*med.*) virulent.
ви́рус, а *m.* (*med.*) virus; bug.
ви́рус|ный *adj. of* **~**
вирусоноси́тел|ь, я *m.* (*med.*) carrier.
ви́рш|и, ей *no sg.* **1.** (*liter.*) (syllabic) verses (*based on Polish form*). **2.** (*coll.*) doggerel.
вис, а *m.* (*sport*) hanging (on the pole).
ви́селиц|а, ы *f.* gallows, gibbet.
ви́сельник, а *m.* **1.** hanged man. **2.** (*coll.*) gallows-bird.
ви|се́ть, шу́, си́шь *impf.* to hang; to be hanging, be suspended; **в. на волоске́** to hang by a thread; **в. в во́здухе** (*i*) to be in the air, (*ii*) to be unfounded.
ви́ски *nt. indecl.* whisky; **шотла́ндское в.** Scotch (whisky).
виско́з|а, ы *f.* **1.** (*tech.*) viscose. **2.** (*coll.*) rayon.
Ви́сл|а, ы *f.* the Vistula (*river*).

вислоу́х|ий (~, ~а) *adj.* lop-eared.
ви́смут, а, *m.* (*chem.*) bismuth.
ви́сн|уть, у, ешь *impf.* (**на**+*p.*) to hang (*on*); to droop; **в. у кого́-н. на ше́е** (*fig., coll.*) to hang on s.o.'s neck.
вис|о́к, ка́ *m.* (*anat.*) temple.
високо́сный *adj.*: **в. год** leap-year.
висо́чный *adj.* (*anat.*) temporal.
вист, а *m.* whist (*card-game*).
висю́льк|а, и *f.* (*coll.*) pendant.
вися́чий *adj.* hanging, pendent; **в. замо́к** padlock; **в. мост** suspension bridge.
витали́зм, а *m.* (*phil.*) vitalism.
витали́ст, а *m.* (*phil.*) vitalist.
витами́н, а *m.* vitamin.
витаминизи́р|овать, ую *impf. and pf.* to fortify (*food*), enrich with vitamins.
витами́н|ный *adj.* **1.** *adj. of* ~; **~ная недоста́точность** vitamin deficiency. **2.** vitamin-rich *or* -packed.
витамин|о́зный = **~ный**
вита́|ть, ю *impf.* (*liter.*) to be; to wander (*of thoughts*); to hover; **он ~ет в ми́ре фанта́зий** he inhabits a world of fantasy; **он всё ещё говори́л, но мы́сли у него́ ~ли далеко́** he went on speaking but his thoughts were far away; **в. в облака́х** to be up in the clouds; **смерть ~ла над ней** death was hovering over her.
витиева́т|ый (~, ~а) *adj.* flowery, ornate, rhetorical.
вити́йств|о, а *nt.* (*obs.*) oratory, rhetoric.
вити́йств|овать, ую *impf.* (*obs.*) to orate.
вити́|я, и *m.* (*coll., iron*) orator.
вит|о́й *adj.* twisted; spiral; **~а́я ле́стница** spiral staircase.
вит|о́к, ка́ *m.* **1.** (*tech.*) spire. **2.** circuit (*of planet by space vehicle*); lap (*sport*). **3.** (*fig.*) round; **но́вый в. го́нки вооруже́ний** a new spiral in the arms race.
витра́ж, а *m.* stained-glass window.
витри́н|а, ы *f.* **1.** (shop-)window; **оформле́ние ~ы** window dressing. **2.** show-case.
ви|ть, вью, вьёшь, *past* **~л, ~ла́, ~ло** *impf.* (*of* **с~**) to twist, wind; **в. венки́** weave garlands; **в. гнездо́** to build a nest; **в. верёвки из кого́-н.** (*coll.*) to twist round one's little finger.
ви́|ться, вьюсь, вьёшься, *past* **~лся, ~ла́сь, ~ло́сь** *impf.* (*of* **с~**) **1.** to wind, twine. **2.** to curl, wave (*of hair*). **3.** to hover, circle (*of birds*). **4.** to writhe, twist (*of reptiles*).
витю́т|ень, ня *m.* wood-pigeon.
ви́тяз|ь, я *m.* (*poet., arch.*) knight; hero.
Вифлее́м, а *m.* Bethlehem.
вихля́|ть, ю *impf.* (*coll.*) to reel.
вихля́|ться, юсь *impf.* (*coll.*) to wobble.
вих|о́р, ра́ *m.* forelock.
вихра́ст|ый (~, ~а) *adj.* (*coll.*) shaggy; shock-headed.
вихрево́й *adj.* (*phys*) vortical.
вихр|ь, я *m.* **1.** whirlwind; **сне́жный в.** blizzard **2.** (*fig.*) vortex.
ви́це-... *comb. form* vice-.
вице-адмира́л, а *m.* vice-admiral.
вице-коро́л|ь я́ *m.* viceroy.
вицмунди́р, а *m.* uniform (*of civil-servants*).
ВИЧ *m. indecl.* (*abbr. of* **ви́рус иммунодефици́та челове́ка**) (*med.*) HIV (*human immunodeficiency virus*); **инфици́рованный В.** HIV-positive.
виши́ *nt. indecl.* Vichy (water).
вишнё|вк|а, и *f.* cherry brandy.
вишнёвый *adj.* **1.** cherry; **в. сад** cherry orchard. **2.** cherry-coloured.
ви́ш|ня, ни, *g. pl.* **~ен** *f.* **1.** cherry-tree. **2.** cherry; (*collect.*) cherries.
вишь (*contraction of* **ви́дишь**; *coll.*) look!; just look!; **в. что сде́лал!** look what he's done!
вка́лыва|ть, ю *impf.* **1.** *impf. of* **вколо́ть. 2.** *impf. only* (*sl.*) to work hard; to graft, slog *or* beaver away.
вка́п|ать, аю *pf.* (*of* **~ывать**[1]) (*coll.*) to pour in.
вка́пыва|ть[1]**, ю** *impf. of* **вка́пать**
вка́пыва|ть[2]**, ю** *impf. of* **вкопа́ть**
вка|ти́ть, чу́, ~тишь *pf.* (*of* **~тывать**) **1.** to roll into, onto; to wheel in, into; **в. бо́чку в подва́л** to roll a barrel into a cellar. **2.** (*fig., coll.*) to administer; to put in, on; **в. пощёчину** (+*d.*) to slap in the face; **в. в спи́сок** to place in a list.
вка|ти́ться, чу́сь, ~тишься *pf.* (*of* **~тываться**) to roll in (*intrans.*); (*coll.*) to run in.
вка́тыва|ть(ся), ю(сь) *impf. of* **вкати́ть(ся)**
вкл. (*abbr. of* **включи́тельно**) incl., including.
вклад, а *m.* **1.** (*fin.*) deposit; investment. **2.** endowment; (*fig.*) contribution; **внести́ ва́жный в. в нау́ку** to make an important contribution to learning.
вкла́дк|а, и *f.* supplementary sheet.
вклад|но́й 1. *adj. of* ~. **2.** supplementary, inserted; **в. лист** loose leaf.
вкла́дчик, а *m.* depositor; investor.
вкла́дыва|ть, ю *impf. of* **вложи́ть**
вкла́д|ыш, а *m.* **1.** = **~ка. 2.** (*tech.*) bush, bearing brass.
вкле́ива|ть, ю *impf. of* **вкле́ить**
вкле́|ить, ю, ~ишь *pf.* (*of* **~ивать**) to stick in; **в. сло́во в разгово́р** (*fig., coll.*) to put in a word.
вкле́йк|а, и *f.* **1.** sticking in. **2.** inset (*in a book*).
вклеп|а́ть, а́ю *pf.* (*of* **~ывать**) **1.** to rivet in. **2.** (*fig., coll.*) to mix up (in), involve (in).
вклеп|а́ться, а́юсь *pf.* (*of* **~ываться**) **1.** to be riveted in. **2.** (*fig., coll.*) to be mixed up in.
вклёпыв|ать(ся), аю(сь) *impf. of* **вклепа́ть(ся)**
вкли́нива|ть(ся), ю(сь) *impf. of* **вклини́ть(ся)**
вкли́н|ить, ю́, ~и́шь *pf.* to wedge in; **в. сло́во** (*fig., coll.*) to put a word in.
вкли́н|иться, ю́сь, ~и́шься *pf.* **1.** *pass. of* **~ить. 2.** (**в**+*a.*) to edge one's way into; (*mil.*) to drive a wedge (into).
включа́тел|ь, я, *m.* switch.
включ|а́ть(ся), а́ю(сь) *impf. of* **~и́ть(ся)**
включа́|я *pres. ger. of* **~ть**; *as prep.*+*a.* including, inclusive; **вы́ставка откры́та ка́ждый вень, в. воскресе́нье** the exhibition is open every day including Sundays.
включе́ни|е, я *nt.* **1.** inclusion, insertion; **со ~ем** (+*g.*) including. **2.** (*tech.*) switching on, turning on.
включи́тельно *adv.* inclusive; **с пя́того по девя́тое в.** from the 5th to the 9th inclusive.
включ|и́ть, у́, и́шь *pf.* (*of* **~а́ть**) **1.** (**в**+*a.*) to include (in); to insert (in); **в. в себя́** to include, comprise, take in; **в. в пове́стку дня** to enter on the agenda; **в. в спи́сок** to enter on a list. **2.** (*tech.*) to switch on, turn on; to plug in; **в. ра́дио** to put the wireless on; **в. ско́рость** to engage a gear; **в. сцепле́ние** to let in the clutch.
включ|и́ться, у́сь, и́шься *pf.* (*of* **~а́ться**) **1.** (**в**+*a.*) to join (in), enter (into); **в. в за́говор** to enter into a conspiracy. **2.** *pass. of* **~и́ть**
вкола́чива|ть, ю *impf. of* **вколоти́ть**
вкол|оти́ть, очу́, ~о́тишь *pf.* (*of* **~а́чивать**) to knock in, hammer in (*also fig.*); **в. в го́лову** (+*d.*; *coll.*) to knock into s.o.'s head; **в. себе́ в го́лову** to get it into one's head.
вкол|о́ть, ю́, ~ешь *pf.* (*of* **вка́лывать**) (**в**+*a.*) to stick (in, into).
вкол|очу́, ~о́тишь *see* **~оти́ть**
вконе́ц *adv.* (*coll.*) completely, absolutely.
вко́пан|ный (~, ~а) *p.p.p. of* **вкопа́ть; как в.** rooted to the ground.
вкопа́|ть, ю *pf.* to dig in.
вкорен|и́ть, ю́, и́шь *pf.* (*of* **~я́ть**) to inculcate.
вкорен|и́ться, ю́сь, и́шься *pf.* (*of* **~я́ться**) to be inculcated; to take root.
вкореня́|ть(ся), ю(сь) *impf. of* **вкорени́ть(ся)**
вкоротке́ *adv.* (*coll., obs*). **1.** shortly. **2.** in brief.
вкось *adv.* obliquely; slantwise; **вкривь и в.,** *see* **вкривь**
вкрад|у́сь, ёшься *see* **вкра́сться**
вкра́дчив|ый (~, ~а) *adj.* insinuating, ingratiating.
вкра́дыва|ться, юсь *impf. of* **вкра́сться**
вкра́п|ить, лю, ишь *pf.* (*of* **~ливать**) to sprinkle (with); (*fig.*) to intersperse (with); **он ~ил в речь цита́ты** he interspersed his speech with quotations.
вкра́пленник, а *m.* (*geol.*) phenocryst, porphyritic crystal.
вкра́плива|ть, ю *impf. of* **вкра́пить**
вкрапл|я́ть, я́ю *impf.* = **~ивать**
вкра́|сться, ду́сь, дёшься, *past* **~лся** *pf.* (*of* **~дываться**)

to steal in, creep in; **в. текст ~лось мно́го оши́бок** many mistakes have crept into the text; **в. в дове́рие к кому́-н.** to worm o.s., insinuate o.s. into s.o.'s confidence.

вкра́тце *adv.* briefly; succinctly.

вкривь *adv.* aslant; (*fig.*) wrongly, perversely; **всё, что говорю́, он понима́ет в.** he misinterprets everything I say; **в. и вкось** all over the place; (*fig., coll.*) indiscriminately.

вкруг = **вокру́г**

вкругову́ю *adv.* (*coll.*) round; **пусти́ть ча́шу в.** to send the cup round (*at banquets*).

вкру|ти́ть, чу́, ~́тишь *pf.* (*of* **~чивать**) to twist in.

вкруту́ю *adv.* (*coll.*): **яйцо́ в.** hard-boiled egg; **свари́ть яйцо́ в.** to hard-boil an egg.

вкру́чива|ть, ю *impf. of* **вкрути́ть**

вкру|чу́, ~́тишь *see* **~ти́ть**

вку́пе *adv.* (*obs.*) together.

вкус, а *m.* **1.** taste (*also fig.*); **про́бовать на в.** to taste; **войти́ во в.** (+*g.*) to begin to enjoy, develop a taste (for); **на в. и цвет това́рища нет** (*prov.*) tastes differ; **э́то де́ло ~́а** it is a matter of taste; **челове́к со ~́ом** a man of taste. **2.** manner, style; **во ~́е Ренесса́нса** in the Renaissance style.

вку|си́ть, шу́, ~́сишь *pf.* (*of* **~ша́ть**) **1.** (*obs.*) to taste, partake (of). **2.** (*fig., poet.*) to taste, savour, experience.

вку́с|ный (~ен, ~на́, ~но) *adj.* good, nice (*to taste*); appetizing, tasty.

вкусов|о́й *adj.* gustatory; **~ы́е вещества́** flavouring substances; **~ы́е о́рганы** organs of taste.

вкуша́|ть, ю *impf. of* **вкуси́ть**

вку|шу́, ~́сишь *see* **~си́ть**

вла́г|а, и *no pl., f.* moisture, liquid.

влага́лищ|е, а *nt.* (*anat., bot.*) vagina.

влага́|ть, ю *impf. of* **вложи́ть**

влагоме́р, а *m.* hygrometer.

владе́л|ец, ьца *m.* owner; proprietor.

владе́ни|е, я *nt.* **1.** ownership; possession; **вступи́ть во в. иму́ществом** to take possession of property. **2.** property, possession; domain, estate; **колониа́льные ~я** colonial possessions.

владе́тел|ь, я *m.* possessor; sovereign.

владе́тельный *adj.* sovereign.

владе́|ть, ю, ешь *impf.* (+*i.*) **1.** to own, possess. **2.** to control; to be in possession (of); **в. собо́й** to control o.s.; **им ~ют стра́сти** he is at the mercy of his passions. **3.** (*fig.*) to have (a) command (of); to have the use (of); **в. перо́м** to wield a skilful pen; **она́ ~ет шестью́ языка́ми** she has a command of six languages; **он не ~ет пра́вой руко́й** he has not the use of his right arm.

Влади́мирк|а, и *f.* (*coll.*) the Vladimir road (*the road to Siberia*); **идти́ по ~е** to be exiled, be going into exile.

влады́к|а, и *m.* **1.** master, sovereign. **2.** member of higher orders of clergy (*bishop, archbishop, or metropolitan*).

влады́честв|о, а *nt.* dominion, sway.

влады́честв|овать, ую *impf.* **(над**+*i.*) to hold sway, exercise dominion (over).

влады́чиц|а, ы *f.* **1.** mistress, sovereign. **2. В.** (*eccl.*) Our Lady.

влажне́|ть, ю, ешь *impf.* (*of* **по~**) to become damp, humid.

вла́жност|ь, и *f.* humidity, dampness.

вла́ж|ный (~ен, ~на́, ~но) *adj.* humid, damp; moist.

вла́мыва|ться, юсь *impf. of* **вломи́ться**

вла́ств|овать, ую *impf.* **(над**+*i.*) to rule, hold sway (over).

властели́н, а *m.* (*usu. fig.*) ruler; lord, master.

власти́тел|ь, я *m.* sovereign, potentate; **в. дум** dominant influence.

вла́ст|ный (~ен, ~на) *adj.* **1.** imperious, commanding; masterful. **2. (в**+*p.*; *leg.*) authoritative, competent; **я не ~ен в э́том де́ле** I have no competence to deal with this matter.

властолю́б|ец, ца *m.* power-seeker.

властолюби́в|ый (~, ~а) *adj.* power-loving; power-seeking.

властолю́би|е, я *nt.* love of power; lust for power.

власт|ь, и, *pl.* **~́и, ~е́й** *f.* **1.** power; **во ~́и** (+*g.*) at the mercy (of), in the power (of); **прийти́ к ~́и** to come to power; **у ~́и** in power. **2.** power, authority; (*pl.*) authorities; **ме́стная в., в. на места́х** local authority; **сове́тская в.** Soviet rule; **в. предержа́щая** (*arch.*) the powers that be. **3.: ва́ша в.** (*coll.*) as you like, please yourself.

власяни́ц|а, ы *f.* hair shirt.

влач|и́ть, у́, и́шь *impf.* (*obs., poet.*) to drag; **в. жа́лкое существова́ние** to drag out a miserable existence.

влач|и́ться, у́сь, и́шься *impf.* (*obs., poet.*) to drag o.s. along.

вле́во *adv.* to the left (*also fig., pol.*).

влеза́|ть, ю *impf. of* **влезть**

влез|ть, у, ешь, *past* **~, ~́ла** *pf.* (*of* **~а́ть**) **1.** to climb in, into, up; to get in, into; **в. на де́рево** to climb up a tree; **ей пришло́сь в. в окно́** she had to get in by the window; **в. в долги́** (*fig.*) to get into debt; **в. в ду́шу** (+*g.*) to worm o.s. into s.o.'s confidence; to worm confidences out of s.o. **2.** (*coll.*) to get on, board; **в. в авто́бус** to get on the bus. **3.** (*coll.*) to fit in, go in, go on; **все э́ти ве́щи не ~́ут в мою́ су́мку** these things will not all go into my bag; **сапоги́ мне не ~́ли** my boots would not go on; **ско́лько ~́ет** (*i*) as much as possible, (*ii*) as much as you like.

влеп|и́ть, лю́, ~́ишь *pf.* to stick in, fasten in; (*coll.*): **в. пощёчину кому́-н.** to slap s.o.'s face; **в. пу́лю в лоб кому́-н.** to put a bullet in s.o.'s brain.

влепля́|ть, ю *impf. of* **влепи́ть**

влет|а́ть, а́ю *impf. of* **~е́ть**

вле|те́ть, чу́, ти́шь *pf.* (*of* **~та́ть**) to fly in, into; (*fig., coll.*) to rush in, into; **в. в исто́рию** to get into trouble; (*impers.*): **ему́ опя́ть ~те́ло** he is in trouble again.

влече́ни|е, я *nt.* **(к)** attraction (to); bent (for); **он чу́вствует си́льное в. к Восто́ку** he is strongly drawn to the East; **сле́довать своему́ ~ю** to follow one's bent.

вле|чь, ку́, чёшь, ку́т, *past* **влёк, ~кла́** *impf.* to draw, drag; to attract; **в. за собо́й** to involve, entail.

вле́|чься, ку́сь, чёшься, ку́тся, *past* **~́кся, ~кла́сь** *impf.* **1. (к)** to be drawn (to); to be attracted (by). **2.** *pass. of* **~чь**

влива́ни|е, я *nt.* infusion; (*med.*) **внутриве́нное в.** intravenous administration.

влива́ть, ю *impf. of* **влить**

влипа́ть, ю *impf. of* **вли́пнуть**

вли́п|нуть, ну, нешь, *past* **~, ла** *pf.* (*coll.*) to get into a mess; to put one's foot in it; to get caught.

вли|ть, волью́, вольёшь, *past* **~л, ~ла́, ~́ло** *pf.* (*of* **~ва́ть**) **1.** to pour in; **в. по ка́пле** to instil, administer drops; (*med.*) to infuse; (*fig.*) to instil; **в. наде́жду в кого́-н.** to instil hope into s.o. **2.** (*mil.*) to bring in; **в. пополне́ния в часть** to reinforce a unit.

влия́ни|е, я *nt.* influence; **по́льзоваться ~ем** to have influence, be influential.

влия́тел|ьный (~ен, ~ьна) *adj.* influential.

влия́|ть, ю *impf.* (*of* **по~**) **(на**+*a.*) to influence, have an influence on, affect.

ВЛКСМ *m. indecl.* (*abbr. of* ***Всесою́зный Ле́нинский Коммунисти́ческий Сою́з Молодёжи***) All-Union Leninist Communist Youth League.

вложе́ни|е, я *nt.* **1.** enclosure; **со ~ем** 'enclosure' (*on letters*). **2.** (*fin.*) investment.

влож|и́ть, у́, ~́ишь *pf.* (*of* **вкла́дывать** *and* **влага́ть) 1.** to put in, insert; to enclose (*with a letter*); **он ~и́л всю свою́ ду́шу в рабо́ту** (*fig.*) he put his whole soul into his work; **в. в уста́ кому́-н.** to put into s.o.'s mouth. **2.** (*fin.*) to invest.

влом|и́ться, лю́сь, ~́ишься *pf.* (*of* **вла́мываться**) to break in, into; **в. в амби́цию** (*coll.*) to take offence.

вло́па|ться, юсь *pf.* (*coll.*) **1.** to get into an awkward situation. **2.** to fall in love.

влюб|и́ть, лю́, ишь *pf.* (*of* **~ля́ть**) **(в**+*a.*) to make fall in love (with).

влюб|и́ться, лю́сь, ~́ишься *pf.* (*of* **~ля́ться**) **(в**+*a.*) to fall in love (with).

влюблённост|ь, и *f.* love; being in love.

влюблён|ный (~, ~а́) *p.p.p. of* **влюби́ть** *and adj.* **1.** (*p.p.p.*) in love; **в. по́ уши** head over ears in love. **2.** (*adj.*) loving; tender.

влюбля́|ть, ю *impf. of* **влюби́ть**

влюбля́|ться, юсь *impf. of* **влюби́ться**
влю́бчив|ый (~, ~а) *adj.* (*coll.*) amorous, susceptible.
вля́па|ться, юсь *pf.* (*coll.*) to plunge into; (*fig.*) **в. в исто́рию** to get into a mess.
вм. (*abbr. of* **вме́сто**) instead of; in place of.
вма́|зать, жу, жешь *pf.* to cement, putty in.
вма́зыва|ть, ю *impf. of* **вма́зать**
вмен|и́ть, ю́, и́шь *pf.* (*of* **~я́ть**) (*d.*+**в**+*a.*) **1.** to regard (as); **в. в вину́** to lay to the charge of; **в. в заслу́гу** to regard as a merit; **в. в обя́занность** to impose as a duty; **он ~и́л себе́ в обя́занность чте́ние всех газе́т** he imposed on himself the duty of reading all the newspapers. **2.** to impute.
вменя́емост|ь, и *f.* (*leg.*) responsibility; liability.
вменя́ем|ый (~, ~а) *adj.* (*leg.*) responsible, liable; of sound mind.
вменя́|ть, ю *impf. of* **вмени́ть**
вме|си́ть, шу́, ~́сишь *pf.* (*of* **~́шивать**²) to knead in.
вме́сте *adv.* together; at the same time; **в. с тем** at the same time, also.
вмести́лищ|е, а *nt.* receptacle.
вмести́мост|ь, и *f.* capacity.
вмести́тел|ьный (~ен, ~ьна) *adj.* capacious; spacious, roomy.
вме|сти́ть, щу́, сти́шь *pf. of* **~ща́ть**
вме́сто *prep.*+*g.* instead of; in place of.
вмеша́тельств|о, а *nt.* interference; intervention; **поли́тика ~а** interventionism; **хирурги́ческое в.** surgical operation.
вмеша́|ть, ю *pf.* (*of* **вме́шивать**¹) (**в**+*a.*) **1.** to mix in. **2.** (*coll., fig.*) to mix up (in), implicate (in).
вмеш|а́ться, а́юсь *pf.* (*of* **~́иваться**) (**в**+*a.*) to interfere (in), meddle (with); to intervene (in); **в. в чужу́ю жизнь** to meddle with other people's lives; **полице́йский ~а́лся в дра́ку** a policeman intervened in the fight.
вме́шива|ть¹, ю *impf. of* **вмеша́ть**
вме́шива|ть², ю *impf. of* **вмеси́ть**
вме́шива|ться, юсь *impf. of* **вмеша́ться**
вмеща́|ть, ю *impf.* (*of* **вмести́ть**) **1.** to contain; to hold; to accommodate; **э́та бо́чка ~ет пятьдеся́т ли́тров** this barrel holds fifty litres; **зал ~ет пятьсо́т челове́к** the hall can seat five hundred. **2.** (**в**+*a.*) to put, place (in, into).
вмеща́|ться, юсь *impf.* (*of* **вмести́ться**) **1.** to go in; **ва́ши башмаки́ не ~ются в мой чемода́н** your shoes will not go in my case. **2.** *pass. of* **~ть 2.**
вмиг *adv.* in an instant; in a flash.
вмина́|ть, ю *impf. of* **вмять**
ВМК *m. indecl.* (*abbr. of* **внутрима́точный контрацепти́в**) IUD (*interuterine* (*contraceptive*) *device*).
ВМФ *m. indecl.* (*abbr. of* **вое́нно-морско́й флот**) Navy.
вмя́тин|а, ы *f.* dent.
вмять, вомну́, вомнёшь *pf.* (*of* **вмина́ть**) to press in.
внаём, внаймы́ *adv.*: **отда́ть в.** to let, hire out, rent; **взять в.** to hire, rent; **сдаётся в.** 'to let'.
внаки́дку *adv.* (*coll.*): **носи́ть в.** to wear thrown over the shoulders.
внакла́де *adv.* (*coll.*): **оста́ться в.** to be the loser, come off loser; **не оста́ться в.** (**от**+*g.*) to be none the worse off (for).
внакла́дку *adv.*: **пить чай в.** to drink tea with sugar in (*opp.* **вприку́ску**).
внача́ле *adv.* at first, in the beginning.
вне *prep.*+*g.* outside; out of; **в. зако́на** without the law; **объяви́ть в. зако́на** to outlaw; **в. ко́нкурса** hors concours; **в. о́череди** out of turn; **в. пла́на** over and above the plan; **в. себя́** beside o.s.; **в. вся́ких сомне́ний** beyond any doubt.
вне... *comb. form* extra-.
внебра́чный *adj.* extra-marital; **в. ребёнок** illegitimate child.
внебродве́йский *adj.* off-Broadway.
вневойскови́к, а́ *m.* civilian receiving military training.
вневойсков|о́й *adj.*: **~а́я подгото́вка** military training for civilians.
вневре́менный *adj.* timeless.
внедре́ни|е, я *nt.* **1.** introduction; inculcation; indoctrination. **2.** (*geol.*) intrusion.
внедр|и́ть, ю́, и́шь *pf.* (*of* **~я́ть**) **1.** to inculcate, instil; **в. в молоды́х привы́чку к чистоте́** to inculcate habits of cleanliness into the young. **2.** to introduce; **в. но́вые ме́тоды** to introduce new methods.
внедр|и́ться, ю́сь, и́шься *pf.* (*of* **~я́ться**) to take root.
внедря́|ть(ся), ю(сь) *impf. of* **внедри́ть(ся)**
внеза́пно *adv.* suddenly, all of a sudden.
внеза́пност|ь, и *f.* **1.** suddenness. **2.** (*obs.*) unexpected event.
внеза́пный *adj.* sudden.
внеземля́н|ин, ина, *pl.* **~е, ~** *m.* = **инопланетя́нин**
внеземно́й *adj.* alien, extra-terrestrial.
внекла́ссн|ый *adj.* out of school (hours); extra-curricular; **~ые заня́тия** out of school activities.
внекла́ссовый *adj.* (*pol.*) non-class.
внема́точный *adj.* (*med.*) extra-uterine.
вне́мл|ю, ешь *see* **внима́ть**
внеочередн|о́й *adj.* **1.** out of turn; **зада́ть в. вопро́с** to ask a question out of order. **2.** extraordinary; extra; **в. съезд** extraordinary congress; **~а́я сме́на** extra shift.
внепарти́йный *adj.* (*pol.*) non-party.
внепи́ковый *adj.* off-peak.
внепла́новый *adj.* (*econ.*) not provided for by the plan; extraordinary.
внерабо́ч|ий *adj.* leisure; leisure-time; **~ее вре́мя** leisure-time.
внесе́ни|е, я *nt.* **1.** bringing in, carrying in. **2.** paying in, deposit (*of money*). **3.** entry, insertion (*into an agreement, etc.*). **4.** moving, submission (*of a resolution*).
внеслужéбный *adj.* leisure-time.
внес|ти́, у́, ёшь, *past* **~́, ~ла́** *pf.* (*of* **вноси́ть**) **1.** to bring in, carry in; **в. ра́неных** to bring in the wounded. **2.** (*fig.*) to introduce, put in; **в. я́сность в де́ло** to clarify a matter; **в. свой вклад в де́ло** to do one's bit. **3.** to pay in, deposit. **4.** to bring in, move, table; **в. законопрое́кт** to bring in a bill; **в. предложе́ние** to move, table a resolution. **5.** to insert, enter; **в. попра́вки в текст ре́чи** to emend the text of a speech; **в. в спи́сок** to enter on a list. **6.** to bring about, cause; **в. раздо́ры** to cause bad feelings.
внестуди́йный *adj.* (*of radio or TV transmission*) outside.
внеуро́чный = **внеучéбный**
внеучéбн|ый *adj.* extracurricular, leisure-time.
внешко́льник, а *m.* adult education specialist.
внешко́льн|ый *adj.*: **~ое образова́ние** adult education.
вне́шне *adv.* outwardly.
вне́шн|ий *adj.* **1.** outer, exterior; outward, external; outside; **в. вид** outward appearance; **в. у́гол** (*math.*) external angle; **в. лоск** surface polish. **2.** foreign; **~яя поли́тика** foreign policy; **~яя торго́вля** foreign trade.
вне́шност|ь, и *f.* exterior; surface; appearance; **суди́ть по ~и** to judge by appearances.
внешта́тник, а *m.* (*coll.*) freelancer; casual; (*journ.*) stringer.
внешта́тный *adj.* not on permanent staff; not established; casual; untenured.
вниз *adv.* down, downwards; **в. голово́й** head first; **идти́ в. по ле́стнице** to go downstairs; **в. по тече́нию** downstream; **в. по Во́лге** down the Volga.
внизу́ *adv.* below; downstairs; *prep.*+*g.*: **в. страни́цы** at the foot of the page.
вник|а́ть, а́ю *impf. of* **~́нуть**
вни́к|нуть, ну, нешь, *past* **~, ~ла** *pf.* (*of* **~а́ть**) (**в**+*a.*) to go carefully (into), investigate thoroughly; **в. в обстоя́тельства уби́йства** to investigate the circumstances of a murder.
внима́ни|е, я *nt.* **1.** attention; heed; notice, note; **обраща́ть в.** (**на**+*a.*) (*i*) to pay attention, give heed (to), take note (of) (*ii*) to draw attention (to); **он весь в.** he is all ears; **принима́я во в.** taking into account. **2.** attention(s); kindness, consideration; **оказа́ть в.** to do a kindness; **по́льзоваться ~ем** to be the object of attentions. **3.** (*int.*): **в.!** look out! mind out!; **в. на старт!** (*sport*) get set!
внима́тельност|ь, и *f.* **1.** attentiveness. **2.** thoughtfulness, consideration.
внима́тел|ьный (~ен, ~ьна) *adj.* **1.** attentive. **2.** (**к**+*d.*) thoughtful, considerate (towards).
внима́|ть, ю *and* **вне́млю** *impf.* (*of* **внять**) (+*d.*; *poet.*,

obs.) to hear (*fig.*); to heed; **в. моли́тве** to hear prayer.

вничью́ *adv.* (*sport*) drawn; **па́ртия око́нчилась в.** the game ended in a draw; **на́ша хокке́йная кома́нда сыгра́ла сего́дня в.** our hockey team drew today.

вно́ве *adv. as pred.* new, strange; **всё во францу́зском быту́ ей бы́ло в.** everything about life in France was new to her.

вновь *adv.* **1.** afresh, anew; again. **2.** newly; **в. прибы́вший** newcomer; **в. избранный президе́нт** the president-elect.

вно|си́ть, шу́, ~́сишь *impf. of* **внести́**

ВНП *m. indecl.* (*abbr. of* **валово́й национа́льный проду́кт**) GNP (*Gross National Product*).

внук, а *m.* grandson; grandchild (*also fig.*).

вну́к|а, и *f.* (*obs.*) granddaughter.

вну́тренн|ий *adj.* **1.** inner, interior; internal; intrinsic; **~ие боле́зни** internal diseases; **в. мир** inner life, private world; **~ие причи́ны** intrinsic causes; **~ее сгора́ние** internal combustion; **в. смысл** inner meaning. **2.** home, inland; **~ие дохо́ды** inland revenue; **Министе́рство ~их дел** Ministry of Internal Affairs.

вну́тренност|ь, и *f.* **1.** interior. **2.** (*pl. only*) entrails, intestines; internal organs; (*anat.*) viscera.

внутри́ *adv. and prep.+g.* inside, within; **в. до́ма** inside the house.

внутри́... *comb. form* intra-.

внутриве́нный *adj.* (*med.*) intravenous.

внутрима́точный *adj.* intra-uterine.

внутрипарти́йный *adj.* within the Party, inner-Party.

внутрифи́рменный *adj.* in-house.

внутрь *adv. and prep.+g.* within, inside; inwards; **открыва́ться в.** to open inwards; **войти́ в. до́ма** to go inside the house.

внуча́т|а, ~ *no sg.* grandchildren.

внуча́тный *adj.*: **в. брат** second cousin; **в. племя́нник** great-nephew.

внуча́т|ый = ~ный

вну́чк|а, и *f.* granddaughter.

внуша́емост|ь, и *f.* suggestibility.

внуш|а́ть, а́ю *impf. of* **~и́ть**

внуше́ни|е, я *nt.* **1.** (*psych.*) suggestion. **2.** reproof, reprimand.

внуши́тел|ьный (~ен, ~ьна) *adj.* inspiring, impressive; (*coll.*) imposing, striking; **~ьное зда́ние** imposing edifice; **~ьное зре́лище** inspiring sight.

внуш|и́ть, у́, и́шь *pf.* (*of* **~а́ть**) (*+a.* and *d.*) to inspire (with); to instil; to suggest; **его́ вид ~и́л мне страх** the sight of him inspired me with fear; **в. уве́ренность в себе́** to instil self-confidence; **он уме́л в. слу́шателям, что он всегда́ прав** he had the power of suggesting to his audience that he was always right.

внюха|ться, юсь *pf.* (**в**+*a.*; *coll.*) to take a sniff (at) (*also fig.*).

внюхива|ться, юсь *impf. of* **внюхаться**

внят|ный (~ен, ~на) *adj.* **1.** distinct. **2.** (*obs.*) intelligible.

вня|ть *fut. not used, past* **~л, ~ла́, ~́ло,** *imper.* **вонми́(те),** *pf. of* **внима́ть**

во[1] *prep.* = **в**

во[2] *int.* (*coll.*) = **вот**

во́бл|а, ы *f.* vobla (*Caspian roach*).

вобр|а́ть, вберу́, вберёшь, *past* **~а́л, ~ала́, ~а́ло** *pf.* (*of* **вбира́ть**) to absorb, suck in; to inhale.

вове́к(и) *adv.* (*obs.*) for ever; **в. веко́в** for ever and ever.

вовлека́|ть, ю *impf. of* **вовле́чь**

вовл|е́чь, еку́, ечёшь, еку́т, *past* **~ёк, ~екла́** *pf.* to draw in, involve; to inveigle.

вовне́ *adv.* outside.

вовну́трь *adv. and prep.+g.* (*coll.*) inside.

во́время *adv.* at the proper time, at the normal time; in time; **говори́ть не в.** to speak out of turn.

во́все *adv.* (*+neg.*; *coll.*) at all; **он в. не бога́тый челове́к** he is not at all a rich man; **вы в. не по́няли, в чём де́ло** you have completely failed to grasp the point.

вовсю́ *adv.* to its (one's) utmost; with might and main; **бежа́ть в.** to run as fast as one's legs will carry one.

во-вторы́х *adv.* secondly, in the second place.

вогна́|ть, вгоню́, вго́нишь, *past* **~л, ~ла́, ~́ло** *pf.* (*of* **вгоня́ть**) to drive in; **в. гвоздь в сте́ну** to drive a nail into the wall; **в. в гроб** to be the death of; **в. в кра́ску** to put to the blush; **в. кого́-н. в пот** to make s.o. go hot and cold.

во́гнут|ый (~, ~а) *p.p.p. of* **~́ь** *and adj.* concave.

вогн|у́ть, у́, ёшь *pf.* (*of* **вгиба́ть**) to bend, curve inwards.

вод|а́, ы́, *a.* **~́у,** *pl.* **~́ы, ~́ам** (*obs.* **~а́м**) *f.* **1.** water; **е́хать ~о́й, по ~е́** to go by water; **жёлтая в.** (*med.*; *coll.*) glaucoma; **тёмная в.** (*med.*) amaurosis; **~о́й не разолье́шь** as thick as thieves; **выводи́ть на чи́стую ~́у** to show up, unmask; **и концы́ в ~́у** none will be the wiser; **как две ка́пли ~ы́ похо́жи** as like as two peas; **как с гу́ся в.** like water off a duck's back; **мно́го ~ы́ утекло́** much water has flowed under the bridge; **он ~ы́ не заму́тит** he could not hurt a fly; **как в ~́у опу́щенный** downcast, dejected; **чи́стой, чисте́йшей ~ы́** (*tech. and fig.*) of the first water. **2.** (*pl.*) the waters; watering-place, spa. **3.** (*coll.*) waffle; **~́у лить** to waffle (on).

водворе́ни|е, я *nt.* settlement; establishment.

водвор|и́ть, ю́, и́шь *pf.* **1.** to settle, install, house. **2.** to establish; **в. мир и споко́йствие** to introduce peace and quiet.

водворя́|ть, ю *impf. of* **водвори́ть**

водеви́л|ь, я *m.* (*theatr.*) **1.** vaudeville (*one-act comic piece with songs*). **2.** musical comedy.

води́тел|ь, я *m.* **1.** driver; **в. ри́тма** (*physiol.*) pacemaker. **2.** (*obs.*) leader.

води́тельств|о, а (*obs.*) leadership.

во|ди́ть, жу́, ~́дишь *impf.* (*indet. of* **вести́**) **1.** (*see also* **вести́**) to lead; to conduct; to drive. **2.** (*see also* **вести́**) **в. дру́жбу (с**+*i.*) to be friends with; **в. знако́мство (с**+*i.*) to keep up an acquaintance (with). **3.** (*+i.*, **по**+*d.*; *see also* **вести́**) to pass (over, across); **в. глаза́ми (по**+*d.*) to cast one's eye (over) (*only* **в.** *used in this phr.*). **4.** (*coll.*) to keep (*animals, birds, etc.*); **в. пчёл** to keep bees.

во|ди́ться, жу́сь, ~́дишься *impf.* **1.** (**с**+*i.*) to associate (with); to play (with); **он с на́ми бо́льше не ~́дится** he will not play with us anymore. **2.** to be, be found; **в э́той реке́ ~́дятся ло́соси** salmon abounds in this river; **львы́ не ~́дятся в Евро́пе** lions are not found in Europe; (*fig.*) **у него́ де́нег никогда́ не ~́дится** he never has any money. **3.** to be the custom; to happen; **так у нас ~́дится** it is the custom here; **э́то за ни́ми ~́дится** (*pej.*) they are always doing this.

води́ц|а, ы *f. dim. of* **вода́**

во́дк|а, и *f.* vodka; **дать на ~у** to tip; **кре́пкая в.** (*chem.*) aqua fortis; **ца́рская в.** (*chem.*) aqua regis.

во́дник, а *m.* water-transport worker.

воднолы́жник, а *m.* water-skier.

во́дн|ый *adj.* **1.** water; watery; **~ые лы́жи** (*i*) water-skiing, (*ii*) water-skis; **~ое по́ло** water polo; **в. пу́ть** waterways; **в. спорт** aquatic sports. **2.** (*chem.*) aqueous; **~ое соедине́ние** hydrate.

водобоя́зн|ь, и *f.* (*med.*) hydrophobia.

водовмести́лищ|е, а *nt.* reservoir.

водово́з, а *m.* water-carrier.

водоворо́т, а *m.* whirlpool; maelstrom (*also fig.*).

водогре́йк|а, и *f.* water-heater.

водоём, а *m.* reservoir (*natural or artificial*).

водоизмеще́ни|е, я *nt.* (*naut.*) displacement; **су́дно ~ем в шесть ты́сяч тонн** vessel of six thousand tons displacement.

водока́чк|а, и *f.* water-tower.

водола́з[1]**, а** *m.* diver; **в.-аквалангист** frogman.

водола́з[2]**, а** *m.* Newfoundland (dog).

водола́зк|а, и *f.* roll-, turtle- *or* polo-neck (sweater).

водола́з|ный *adj. of* **~**[1]; **в. костю́м** diving-suit.

водоле́|й, я *m.* **1.** (water-)bailer. **2.** (*coll., pej.*) waffler. **3. В.** (*astron.*) Aquarius.

водолече́бниц|а, ы *f.* hydropathic establishment.

водолече́бный *adj.* hydropathic.

водолече́ни|е, я *nt.* hydropathic treatment; water-cure.

водоли́в, а *m.* **1.** (water-)bailer, water-pumper. **2.** chief bargee.

водоме́р, а *m.* (*tech.*) water-gauge.

водоме́р|ный *adj. of* ~; **в. кран** gauge-cock; **~ное стекло́** gauge-glass; **~ная тру́бка** gauge-tube.
водомёт, а *m.* **1.** (*poet., obs.*) fountain. **2.** water cannon.
водомо́ин|а, ы *f.* gully, ravine (*formed by running water*).
водонапо́рн|ый *adj. only in phr.* **~ая ба́шня** water-tower.
водонепроница́ем|ый (~, ~а) *adj.* water-tight; waterproof; **~ая перебо́рка** (*naut.*) watertight bulkhead.
водоно́с, а *m.* **1.** water-carrier. **2.** (*dial.*) yoke (*for carrying water-buckets*).
водоотво́д, а *m.* drainage system.
водоотво́дн|ый *adj.* drainage; **~ая кана́ва** draining ditch; **~ая тру́бка** waste-pipe.
водоотли́вн|ый *adj.* discharge; **в. насо́с** hydrant; **~ая систе́ма** (*naut.*) bilge system.
водоочисти́тельный *adj.* water-purifying.
водопа́д, а *m.* waterfall.
водопла́вающ|ий *adj.*: **~ие пти́цы** waterfowl; **~ая маши́на** amphibious vehicle.
водопо́|й, я *m.* **1.** watering-place; water-trough; pond. **2.** watering (*of animals*).
водопрово́д, а *m.* **1.** water-pipe; (the) plumbing. **2.** water-supply; **дом с ~ом** house with running water.
водопрово́д|ный *adj. of* ~; **~ная магистра́ль** water-main; **~ная сеть** water-supply; **~ная ста́нция** waterworks.
водопрово́дчик, а *m.* plumber.
водопроница́ем|ый (~, ~а) *adj.* permeable to water.
водоразде́л, а *m.* (*geog.*; *fig.*) watershed.
водораспредели́тел|ь, я *m.* water-distributor.
водоре́з, а *m.* (*naut.*) cutwater.
водоро́д, а *m.* (*chem.*) hydrogen.
водоро́дистый *adj.* (*chem.*) hydrogen, hydride (of).
водоро́дн|ый *adj.* hydrogen; **~ая бо́мба** hydrogen bomb.
во́доросл|ь, и *f.* (*bot.*) alga; **морска́я в.** seaweed.
водосбо́р, а *m.* **1.** (*natural or artificial*) reservoir (*used for water-supply, irrigation, etc.*). **2.** (*tech.*) (*water-collecting*) header.
водосбо́рн|ый *adj.* **1.**: **~ая пло́щадь** (*geog.*) basin. **2.** (*tech.*) water-collecting.
водосли́в, а *m.* (*tech.*) waste-gate; sluice.
водоснабже́ни|е, я *nt.* water-supply.
водоспу́ск, а *m.* floodgate.
водосто́к, а *m.* drain; gutter.
водосто́|чный *adj. of* ~к; **~чная труба́** drain-pipe.
водотру́бный *adj.*: **в. котёл** (*tech.*) water-tube boiler.
водоупо́р|ный (~ен, ~на) *adj.* waterproof.
водоусто́йчивый *adj.* water-repellant.
водохо́дн|ый *adj.* amphibious; **~ая автомаши́на** (*mil.*) amphibious vehicle.
водохрани́лищ|е, а *nt.* reservoir; cistern, tank.
водоцисте́рн|а, ы *f.* water tender.
водочерпа́лк|а, и *f.* water-engine.
водочерпа́тельный *adj.* (*tech.*) water-lifting.
во́дочк|а, и *f.* (*coll.*) *dim. of* **во́дка**
во́д|очный *adj. of* ~**ка**
водружа́|ть, ю *impf. of* **водрузи́ть**
водру|зи́ть, жу́, зи́шь *pf.* (*of* **~жа́ть**) to hoist, erect.
водяне́|ть, ю *impf.* to grow watery.
водяни́к, а́ *m.* (*dial.*) water-sprite.
водяни́ст|ый (~, ~а) *adj.* watery; (*fig., coll.*) wishy-washy.
водя́нк|а, и *f.* (*med.*) dropsy.
водян|о́й[1] *adj.* **1.** *adj. of* **вода́**. **2.** water, aquatic; **~ы́е пти́цы** waterfowl; **~ы́е расте́ния** aquatic plants. **3.** water-driven, water-operated; **~а́я ме́льница** water-mill; **~о́е отопле́ние** hot-water heating. **4.**: **в. знак** watermark.
водян|о́й[2], **о́го** *m.* water-sprite.
водя́н|очный *adj. of* ~**ка**
во|ева́ть, ю́ю, ю́ешь *impf.* (**с**+*i.*) **1.** to wage war (with), make war (upon); to be at war. **2.** (*coll.*) to quarrel (with).
воево́д|а, ы *m.* **1.** (*hist.*) voivode (*commander of an army in medieval Russia*; *also, in Muscovite period, governor of a town or province*). **2.** governor of province (*in Poland*).
воево́дств|о, а *nt.* **1.** (*hist.*) office of voivode. **2.** province (*in Poland*).
воеди́но *adv.* together; **собра́ть в.** to bring together.
воен... *comb. form, abbr. of* **вое́нный**
военача́льник, а *m.* commander; leader in war.
воениза́ци|я, и *f.* militarization.
военизи́р|овать, ую *impf. and pf.* to militarize; to place on a war footing.
вое́нк|а, и *f.* (*coll.*) military training.
военко́м, а *m.* (*abbr. of* **вое́нный комисса́р**) military commissar.
военкома́т, а *m.* (*abbr. of* **вое́нный комиссариа́т**) military registration and enlistment office.
военко́р, а *m.* (*abbr. of* **вое́нный корреспонде́нт**) war correspondent.
вое́нно-... *comb. form, abbr. of* **вое́нный**
вое́нно-возду́шн|ый *adj.*: **~ые си́лы** Air Force(s).
вое́нно-морско́й *adj.* naval; **в. флот** the Navy.
военнообя́занн|ый, ого *m.* man liable for call-up (*including reservists*).
военнопле́нн|ый, ого *m.* prisoner of war.
вое́нно-полево́й *adj.* (*mil.*) field; **в. суд** court-martial.
военнослу́жащ|ий, его *m.* serviceman.
вое́нно-уче́бный *adj.* military training.
вое́нн|ый *adj.* military; war; army; **в. врач** (army) medical officer; **~ое вре́мя** wartime; **в. заво́д** munitions factory; **в. коммуни́зм** (*hist.*) War Communism; **в. мини́стр** Ministry of War; **В~ое министе́рство** War Ministry, War Office; **на ~ую но́гу** on a war footing; **в. о́круг** Command, military district; **~ое положе́ние** martial law; **~ое учи́лище** military college; *as n.* **в., ~ого** *m.* soldier, serviceman; **~ые** (*collect.*) the military.
военру́к, а *m.* (*abbr. of* **вое́нный руководи́тель**) military instructor.
вое́нщин|а, ы *f.* (*coll., pej.*) **1.** (*collect., obs.*) soldiery. **2.** militarists, military clique. **3.** military outlook.
вoери́зм, а *m.* voyeurism.
воери́ст, а *m.* voyeur; Peeping Tom.
вожа́к, а́ *m.* **1.** guide. **в. медве́дя, в. с медве́дем** bearleader; **в. слепо́го** blind man's guide. **2.** leader. **3.** leader (*of herd, flock*).
вожа́т|ый, ого *m.* **1.** guide. **2.** leader (*of youth organization*). **3.** (*coll.*) tram-driver. **4.** (*agric.*) leader (*of herd*).
вожделе́ни|е, я *nt.* desire, lust (*also fig.*).
вожделе́нн|ый *adj.* (*poet., obs.*) desired, longed-for; **~ое здра́вие** perfect health.
вожделе́|ть, ю, ешь *impf.* (**к**+*d.*) **1.** to long (for). **2.** (*obs.*) to lust (after).
вожде́ни|е, я *nt.* leading; driving; **в. корабля́** navigation; **в. самолёта** flying, piloting.
вожд|ь, я́ *m.* leader; chief.
вожжа́|ться, юсь *impf.* (**с**+*i.*; *coll.*) to bother o.s. (with), trouble o.s. (over).
во́жж|и, е́й *pl.* (*sg.* **~а́, ~и́** *f.*) reins; **отпусти́ть в.** to give a horse the reins; (*fig.*) to slacken the reins; **ему́ ~а́ под хвост попа́ла** (*coll.*) he has taken to acting capriciously.
во|жу́[1], **~ди́шь** *see* **~ди́ть**
во|жу́[2], **~зи́шь** *see* **~зи́ть**
ВОЗ *m.* (*indecl.*) (*abbr. of* ***Всеми́рная организа́ция здравоохране́ния***) WHO (*World Health Organization*).
воз, а, о ~е, на ~у́, *pl.* **~ы́** *m.* **1.** cart, wagon; **что с ~а упа́ло, то пропа́ло** (*prov.*) it is no use crying over spilt milk. **2.** cartload. **3.** (*fig., coll.*) load(s), heap(s); **в. вре́мени** loads of time.
возблагодар|и́ть, ю, и́шь *pf.* (*obs.*) to give thanks to.
возбран|и́ть, ю, и́шь *pf.* to prohibit, forbid; **в. вход подро́сткам не дости́гшим восемна́дцати лет** to prohibit entry to young people under the age of eighteen.
возбран|я́ть, я́ю *impf. of* **~и́ть**
возбраня́|ться, ется *impf.* to be prohibited, be forbidden; **купа́ться тут не ~ется** swimming is permitted here.
возбуди́мост|ь, и *f.* excitability.
возбуди́м|ый (~, ~а) *adj.* excitable.
возбуди́тел|ь, я *m.* **1.** agent; stimulus; (*fig.*) instigator; **дро́жжи — в. броже́ния** yeast is an agent for fermentation. **2.** (*med.*): **в. боле́зни** pathogenic organism. **3.** (*tech.*) exciter.
возбу|ди́ть, жу́, ди́шь *pf.* (*of* **~жда́ть**) **1.** to excite, rouse, arouse; **в. аппети́т** to whet the appetite; **в. любопы́тство**

to excite, stimulate curiosity. **2.** (**прóтив**+*g.*) to stir up (against), incite (against), instigate (against). **3.** (*leg.*) to institute; **в. дéло** (**прóтив**+*g.*) to institute proceedings (against), bring an acton (against); **в. иск** (**прóтив**+*g.*) to bring a suit (against); **в. ходáтайство** (**о**+*p.*) to submit a petition (for).

возбуждáемост|ь, и *f.* excitability.

возбуждá|ть, ю *impf. of* **возбудúть**

возбуждá|ющий *pres. part. act. of* **~ть; ~ющее срéдство** (*med.*) stimulant.

возбу|жý, дúшь *see* **~дúть**

возбуждéни|е, я *nt.* excitement; **в состоя́нии крáйнего ~я** in a state of extreme excitement.

возбу|ждённый *p.p.p. of* **~дúть** *and adj.* excited.

возведéни|е, я *nt.* **1.** raising; erection. **2.: в. во вторýю, в трéтью стéпень** (*math.*) raising to the second, third power. **3.: в. обвинéния** bringing of an accusation.

возвед|ý, ёшь *see* **возвестú**

возвелúчива|ть, ю *impf. of* **возвелúчить**

возвелúч|ить, у, ишь *pf.* (*of* **~ивать**) (*obs.*) to extol.

возве|стú, дý, дёшь, *past* **~́л, ~лá** *pf.* (*of* **возводúть**) **1.** to elevate; **в. в сан патриáрха** to elect to the patriarchate; **в. на престóл** to elevate to the throne. **2.** to raise, erect, put up; **в. высóтный дом** to erect a skyscraper **3.** (*math.*) to raise; **в. во вторýю стéпень** to raise to the second power; **в. в куб** to cube. **4.** to bring, advance, level (*a charge, an accusation. etc.*); **в. клеветý на когó-н.** to cast aspersions on s.o. **5.** (**к**+*d.*) to trace (to), derive (from); **в. происхождéние к нормáннам** to trace one's ancestry to the Northmen.

возве|стúть, щý, стúшь *pf.* (*of* **~щáть**) to proclaim, announce; **в. побéду** to proclaim a victory.

возвещá|ть, ю *impf. of* **возвестúть**

возве|щý, стúшь *see* **~стúть**

возво|дúть, жý, ~́дишь *impf. of* **возвестú**

возво|жý, ~́дишь *see* **~дúть**

возврáт, а *m.* return; repayment, reimbursement; **в. болéзни** relapse; **в. сóлнца** (*astron.*) solstice.

возвра|тúть, щý, тúшь *pf.* (*of* **~щáть**) **1.** to return, give back; to pay back; **в. имýщество** to restore property. **2.** to recover, retrieve; **в. дéньги, óтданные взаймы́** to recover a loan. **3.** to make return.

возвра|тúться, щýсь, тúшься *pf.* (*of* **~щáться**) to return; (*fig.*) to revert; **в. ко всем стáрым привы́чкам** to revert to all one's old habits.

возврáт|ный *adj.* **1.** *adj. of* **~; на ~ном путú** on the way back. **2.** (*med.*) recurring. **3.** (*gram.*) reflexive. **4.: ~ная пóшлина** drawback (duty).

возвращá|ть(ся), ю(сь) *impf. of* **возвратúть(ся)** *and* **вернýть(ся)**

возвращéн|ец, ца *m.* returnee, home-comer.

возвращéни|е, я *nt.* return; home-coming; **егó в. бы́ло отлóжено без срóка** his return was postponed indefinitely; **он настоя́л на немéдленном ~и кольцá** he insisted on immediate return of the ring.

возвра|щý, тúшь *see* **~тúть**

возвы́|сить, шу, сишь *pf.* (*of* **~шáть**) **1.** to raise, elevate; **в. в общéственном мнéнии** to raise in public opinion. **2.: в. гóлос** to raise one's voice.

возвы́|ситься, шусь, сишься *pf.* (*of* **~шáться**) (*in var. senses*) to rise, go up; **онú ~сились в нáшем мнéнии** they have risen in our estimation.

возвышá|ть, ю *impf.* **1.** *impf. of* **возвы́сить. 2.** (*impf. only*) to elevate, ennoble.

возвышá|ться, юсь *impf.* **1.** *impf. of* **возвы́ситься. 2.** (*impf. only*) (**над**+*i.*) to tower (above) (*also fig.*); **зáмок ~ется над гóродом** the castle towers above the city; **он ~ется умóм над товáрищами** he towers above his fellows in intellect.

возвышéни|е, я *nt.* **1.** rise; raising; **в. Москóвской Руси** the rise of Muscovite Russia. **2.** eminence; raised place.

возвы́шенност|ь, и *f.* **1.** (*geog.*) height; eminence. **2.** loftiness, sublimity.

возвы́шен|ный *p.p.p. of* **возвы́сить** *and adj.* **1.** high; elevated. **2.** lofty, sublime, elevated; **~ные идеáлы** lofty ideals; **в. стиль** elevated style.

возвы́|шу, сишь *see* **~сить**

возглáв|ить, лю, ишь *pf.* (*of* **~ля́ть**) to head, be at the head of.

возглавля́|ть, ю *impf. of* **возглáвить**

вóзглас, а *m.* **1.** cry, exclamation; **в. удивлéния** cry of astonishment; **в. с мéста** exclamation from the audience. **2.** (*eccl.*) concluding words of prayer (*pronounced in a loud voice*).

возгла|сúть, шý, сúшь *pf.* (*of* **~шáть**) to proclaim.

возглашá|ть, ю *impf. of* **возгласúть**

возглашéни|е, я *nt.* **1.** proclamation. **2.** exclamation. **3.** = **вóзглас 2.**

возгнá|ть, возгоню́, возгóнишь, *past* **~л, ~лá, ~ло** *pf. of* **возгоня́ть**

возгóнк|а, и *f.* (*chem.*) sublimation.

возгон|ю́, ~́ишь *see* **возгнáть**

возгоня́|ть, ю *impf.* (*chem.*) to sublimate.

возгорáемост|ь, и *f.* inflammability.

возгорáемый *adj.* inflammable.

возгорáни|е, я *nt.* (*tech.*) inflammation, ignition; **тóчка ~я** flash-point.

возгорá|ться, юсь *impf. of* **возгорéться**

возгор|дúться, жýсь, дúшься *pf.* to become proud; (+*i.*) to begin to pride o.s. (on).

возгор|éться, ю́сь úшься *pf.* **1.** to flare up (*also fig.*); **внезáпно ~éлась ссóра мéжду нúми** suddenly there flared up a quarrel between them. **2.** (+*i.*) to be inflamed (with); **онá ~éлась стрáстью к кинó** she was seized with a passion for the cinema.

возда|вáть, ю́, ёшь *impf. of* **воздáть**

воздá|м, шь, ст *see* **~ть**

воздá|ть, м, шь, ст, дúм, дúте, дýт, *past* **~л, ~лá, ~ло** *pf.* (*of* **~вáть**) to render; **в. комý-н. дóлжное** to give s.o. his due; **в. комý-н. по заслýгам** to reward s.o. according to his deserts.

воздая́ни|е, я *nt.* (*obs.*) recompense; retribution.

воздвигá|ть, ю *impf.* to raise, erect; **в. гонéние** (**на**+*a.*; *obs.*) to raise a hue-and-cry (after).

воздвигá|ться, юсь *impf.* **1.** *pass. of* **~ть. 2.** to rear (up) (*intrans.*).

воздвúг|нуть, ну, нешь, *past* **~, ~ла** *pf. of* **~áть**

воздвúг|нуться, нусь, нешься, *past* **~ся, ~лась** *pf. of* **~áться.**

Воздвижéни|е, я *nt.* (*eccl.*) Exaltation of the Cross (*Christian festival celebrated on 14 September*).

воздевá|ть, ю *impf. of* **воздéть**

воздéйстви|е, я *nt.* influence; **оказáть морáльное в.** (**на**+*a.*) to bring moral pressure to bear (upon); **он э́то сдéлал под физúческим ~ем** he did it under coercion.

воздéйств|овать, ую *impf. and pf.* (**на**+*a.*) to influence, affect; to exert influence, bring influence to bear (upon); to bring pressure to bear (upon); **в. на когó-н. сúлой примéра** to influence s.o. by one's example; **страсть к приключéниям ~овала на егó решéние сдéлаться моряком** love of adventure influenced his decision to become a sailor.

воздéл|ать, аю *pf.* (*of* **~ывать**) to cultivate, till.

воздéлыва|ть, ю *impf. of* **воздéлать**

воздержáвш|ийся *p.p. of* **воздержáться**; *as n.* **в., ~егося** *m.* abstainer; **предложéние бы́ло прúнято при трёх ~ихся** the motion was carried with three abstentions.

воздержáни|е, я *nt.* **1.** abstinence. **2.** abstention.

воздéржанност|ь, и *f.* abstemiousness; temperance.

воздéржан|ный (~, ~на) *adj.* abstemious; temperate.

воздерж|áться, ýсь *pf.* (*of* **~́иваться**) (**от**+*g.*) **1.** to restrain o.s., keep o.s. (from); to abstain (from); to refrain (from); **в. от мя́са** to abstain from meat; **я дóлее не мог в. от гнéва** I could no longer contain my rage. **2.** to abstain (from voting). **3.** to withhold acceptance (of).

воздéржива|ться, юсь *impf. of* **воздержáться**

воздéржност|ь, и *f.* = **воздéржанность**

воздéрж|ный (~ен, ~на) *adj.* = **~анный**

воздé|ть, ну, нешь *pf.* (*of* **~вáть**) *only in phr.* **в. рýки** (*obs.*) to lift up one's hands.

во́здух[1], **а** *no pl.*, *m.* air; **на (откры́том) ~е** out of doors; **вы́йти на в.** to go out of doors; **в ~е** (*fig.*) in the air; **в ~е носи́лось чу́вство предстоя́щей беды́** a sense of impending disaster was in the air; *as int.* **в.!** (enemy) aircraft approaching.
во́здух[2], **а**, *pl.* **~и** *m.* (*eccl.*) paten.
воздуходу́вк|а, и *f.* (*tech.*) blast-engine; blower.
воздуходу́вный *adj.* (*tech.*) blast.
воздухоме́р, а *m.* (*phys.*) aerometer.
воздухоохлажда́емый *adj.* air-cooled.
воздухопла́вани|е, я *nt.* aeronautics.
воздухопла́вател|ь, я *m.* **1.** aeronaut. **2.** balloonist.
воздухопла́вательный *adj.* **1.** aeronautic. **2.** (*mil.*) balloon.
возду́ш|ный *adj.* **1.** air, aerial; **~ная желе́зная доро́га** overhead railway; **~ные за́мки** castles in the air; **в. змей** kite; **~ная ли́ния** airline; **посла́ть ~ные поцелу́и** to blow kisses; **~ная прово́дка** overhead cable; **~ное сообще́ние** aerial communication; **~ная трево́га** air-raid warning; **в. шар** balloon; **~ная я́ма** air-pocket. **2.** air-driven, air-operated; **в. насо́с** air-pump. **3.** **(~ен, ~на)** airy, light; flimsy; **в. пиро́г** soufflé; **~ное пла́тье** flimsy dress.
воздыха́ни|е, я *nt.* (*obs.*) lamentation; complaint.
воздыха́|ть, ю *impf.* (*obs.*) = **вздыха́ть**
воз|жгу́, жжёшь, жгут *see* **~же́чь**
воз|же́чь, жгу́, жжёшь, жгу́т, *past* **~жёг, ~жгла́** *pf.* (*of* **~жига́ть**) (*obs.*) to light, kindle (*also fig.*).
возжига́|ть, ю *impf. of* **возже́чь**
воззва́ни|е, я *nt.* appeal; **в. к шахтёрам** appeal to miners.
возз|ва́ть, ову́, овёшь, *past* **~ва́л, ~вала́, ~ва́ло** *pf.* (*of* **взыва́ть**) (**к**+*d.*, **о**+*p.*) to appeal (to), call (for); **он ~ва́л к избира́телям о подде́ржке** he appealed to the electors for their support.
возз|ову́, овёшь *see* **~ва́ть**
воззре́ни|е, я *nt.* view, opinion, outlook.
воззр|е́ть, ю́, и́шь *pf. of* **взира́ть**
воззр|и́ться, ю́сь, и́шься *pf.* (**на**+*a.*; *coll.*) to stare (at).
во|зи́ть, жу́, ~́зишь *impf.* (*indet. of* **везти́**) **1.** to cart, convey; to carry; to draw (*of beasts of burden or mechanical transport*); **э́тот парово́з ~́зит до тридцати́ ваго́нов** this engine draws up to thirty coaches. **2.** (+*i.*, **по**+*d.*; *coll.*) to pass (over), run (over). **3.** (*coll.*) beat, flog.
во|зи́ться, жу́сь, ~́зишься *impf.* **1.** to play noisily, romp (*of children*). **2.** (**с**+*i.*, **над**+*i.*) to take trouble (over), spend time (on), busy o.s. (with); (*coll.*) to potter; to tinker (with), fiddle about (with); **он мно́го ~́зится над ле́кциями** he takes much trouble over the preparation of his lectures; **он лю́бит в. в саду́** he likes pottering about in the garden.
во́зк|а, и *f.* (*coll.*) carting, carriage.
возлага́|ть, ю *impf. of* **возложи́ть**
во́зле *adv. and prep.*+*g.* by, near; past; **он стоя́л в.** he was standing near-by; **ка́ждый день он хо́дит в. моего́ до́ма** he walks up and down past my house every day.
возлеж|а́ть, у́, и́шь *impf.* (*of* **возле́чь**) (*obs.*) to recline.
возл|е́чь, я́гу, я́жешь, я́гут, *imper.* **~я́г,** *past* **~ёг, ~егла́** *pf. of* **~ежа́ть**
возлик|ова́ть, у́ю *pf.* to rejoice.
возлия́ни|е, я *nt.* **1.** libation. **2.** (*coll.*) drinking-bout.
возлож|и́ть, у́, ~́ишь *pf.* (*of* **возлага́ть**) to lay on (*also fig.*); **в. вено́к на моги́лу** to lay a wreath on a grave; **наро́д ~и́л все наде́жды на но́вого президе́нта** the people had placed all their hopes on the new president.
возлюб|и́ть, лю́, ~́ишь *pf.* (*obs.*) to love.
возлю́бленн|ый *adj.* beloved; *as n.* (*i*) **в., ~ого** *m.* **1.** boy-friend. **2.** lover. (*ii*) **~ая, ~ой** *f.* **1.** girl-friend, sweetheart. **2.** mistress.
возля́|гу, жешь, гут *see* **возле́чь**
возме́зди|е, я *nt.* retribution; requital.
возме|сти́ть, щу́, сти́шь *pf.* (*of* **~ща́ть**) to compensate, make up (for); to replace; **в. поте́рянное вре́мя** to make up for lost time; **в. расхо́ды** to refund expenses.
возмечта́|ть, ю *pf.* **1.** to dream, start dreaming. **2.:** **в. о себе́** (*coll.*) to form a high opinion of o.s., become conceited.
возмеща́|ть, ю *impf. of* **возмести́ть**
возмеще́ни|е, я *nt.* **1.** compensation, indemnity; (*leg.*) damages; **получи́ть в. убы́тков по суду́** to be awarded damages. **2.** replacement; refund, reimbursement.
возме|щу́, сти́шь *see* **~сти́ть**
возмо́жно *adv.* **1.** possibly; (+*comp.*) as ... as possible; **в. лу́чше** as well as possible; **иди́те в. скоре́е** go as soon as possible. **2.** *as pred.* it is possible; **в., что мы за́втра уе́дем** we may possibly go away tomorrow.
возмо́жност|ь, и *f.* **1.** possibility; **по (ме́ре) ~и** as far as possible; **до после́дней ~и** to the uttermost. **2.** opportunity; **ему́ да́ли в. пое́хать в Росси́ю** he has been given an opportunity of going to Russia; **при пе́рвой ~и** at the first opportunity, at one's earliest convenience. **3.** (*pl.*) means, resources; **у него́ больши́е ~и** he has great potentialities.
возмо́ж|ный (~ен, ~на) *adj.* **1.** possible; **врач сде́лал для неё всё ~ное** the doctor did all in his power for her. **2.** the greatest possible; **с ~ной то́чностью** with the greatest possible accuracy, as accurately as possible.
возмо́|чь, гу́, жешь, гут, *past* **~г, ~гла́** *pf.* (*obs.*) to be able.
возмужа́лост|ь, и *f.* maturity; manhood.
возмужа́лый *adj.* mature; grown up.
возмужа́|ть, ю *pf.* **1.** to grow up. **2.** to gain in strength, become stronger.
возмути́тел|ьный (~ен, ~ьна) *adj.* **1.** disgraceful, scandalous. **2.** (*obs.*) seditious, subversive.
возму|ти́ть, щу́, ти́шь *pf.* **1.** (*obs.*) to disturb, trouble. **2.** (*fig., obs.*) to stir up, incite. **3.** to anger, rouse the indignation (of).
возму|ти́ться, щу́сь, ти́шься *pf.* **1.** to be indignant (at); to be exasperated (by); **все ~ти́лись его́ заявле́нием** all were filled with indignation by his announcement. **2.** (*obs.*) to rebel, rise in revolt.
возмуща́|ть, ю *impf. of* **возмути́ть**
возмуща́|ться, юсь *impf. of* **возмути́ться**
возмуще́ни|е, я *nt.* **1.** indignation. **2.** (*obs.*) revolt, rebellion. **3.** (*astron.*) perturbation. **4.:** **магни́тное в.** (*phys.*) magnetic disturbance.
возмущён|ный (~, ~а́) *p.p.p. of* **возмути́ть** *and adj.* (+*i.*) indignant (at).
возму|щу́, ти́шь *see* **~ти́ть**
вознагра|ди́ть, жу́, ди́шь *pf.* to reward; to recompense; to compensate, make up (for); **его́ ~ди́ли за заслу́ги золоты́ми часа́ми** he was rewarded for his services with a gold watch.
вознагражда́|ть, ю *impf. of* **вознагради́ть**
вознагражде́ни|е, я *nt.* **1.** reward, recompense; compensation. **2.** fee, remuneration.
вознаме́рива|ться, юсь *impf. of* **вознаме́риться**
вознаме́р|иться, юсь, ишься *pf.* (+*inf.*) to conceive a design, idea; **она́ ~илась сде́латься актри́сой** she conceived the idea of going on the stage.
вознегод|ова́ть, у́ю *pf.* to become indignant.
возненави́|деть, жу, дишь *pf.* to conceive hatred (for), come to hate.
вознесе́ни|е, я *nt.* ascent; **В.** (*eccl.*) Ascension (Day).
вознес|ти́, у́, ёшь, *past* **~́, ~ла́** *pf.* (*of* **возноси́ть**) (*poet.*) to raise, lift up; **в. моли́тву** to offer up a prayer.
вознес|ти́сь, у́сь, ёшься, *past* **~́ся, ~ла́сь** *pf.* (*of* **возноси́ться**) **1.** (*poet.*) to rise; to ascend. **2.** (*coll.*) to become conceited.
возник|а́ть, а́ю *impf.* (*of* **~́нуть**) to arise, spring up; **на на́ших глаза́х ~а́л но́вый го́род** a new town was springing up before our eyes; **у меня́ ~а́ет мысль** the thought occurs to me.
возникнове́ни|е, я *m.* rise, beginning, origin.
возни́к|нуть, ну, нешь, *past* **~, ~ла** *pf. of* **~а́ть**
возни́ц|а, ы *m.* coachman, driver.
возни́ч|ий, его *m.* **1.** (*obs.*) coachman, driver. **2.** **В.** (*astron.*) Auriga.
возно|си́ть, шу́, ~́сишь *impf. of* **вознести́**
возно|си́ться, шу́сь, ~́сишься *impf. of* **вознести́сь**
возноше́ни|е, я *nt.* (*obs.*) raising, elevation; **в. даро́в** (*eccl.*) elevation (*of the host*).
возно|шу́, ~́сишь *see* **~си́ть**

возн|я́, и́ *no pl., f.* (*coll.*) **1.** row, noise; **мыши́ная в.** (*fig.*) petty intrigues. **2.** bother, trouble; **у него́ мно́го ~и́ с автомоби́лем** he has a lot of trouble with his car.
возоблада́|ть, ю *pf.* (**над**+*i.*) to prevail (over).
возобнов|и́ть, лю́, и́шь *pf.* (*of* **~ля́ть**) **1.** to renew, resume. **2.** to restore.
возобновле́ни|е, я *nt.* renewal, resumption; revival (*of a play*).
возобновля́|ть, ю *impf. of* **возобнови́ть**
воз|о́к, ка́ *m.* closed sleigh.
возомн|и́ть, ю́, и́шь *pf.*: **в. о себе́** (*iron.*) to get a false idea of one's own importance; **в. себя́ авторите́том** to consider o.s. (*falsely*) an authority.
возоп|и́ть, лю́, и́шь *pf.* (*obs.*) to cry out.
возра́д|оваться, уюсь *pf.* (+*d.*; *obs.*) to be delighted (at).
возража́|ть, ю *impf. of* **возрази́ть; не ~ю** I have no objection; **вы не ~ете?** have you any objection(s)?; do you mind?
возраже́ни|е, я *nt.* **1.** objection; retort; **без ~й!** don't argue! **2.** (*leg.*) answer.
возра|зи́ть, жу́, зи́шь *pf.* (*of* **~жа́ть**) (**про́тив**+*g. or* **на**+*a.*) **1.** to object, raise an objection (to); to take exception (to); to retort; **про́тив э́того не́чего в.** nothing can be said against it. **2.** to say.
во́зраст, а *m.* age; **одного́ ~а** of the same age; **бра́чный в.** age of consent; **о́троческий в.** boyhood; **преде́льный в.** age-limit; **в. совершенноле́тия** age of majority; **быть на ~е** to be of age; **вы́йти из ~а** to pass the age, exceed the age-limit; **он вы́шел из ~а для вое́нной слу́жбы** he is over the age for military service; **преклóнный в.** declining years.
возраста́ни|е, я *nt.* growth, increase; increment.
возраст|а́ть, а́ю *impf. of* **~и́; ~а́ющая ско́рость** (*phys.*) accelerated velocity.
возраст|и́, у́, ёшь, *past* **возро́с, возросла́** *pf.* (*of* **~а́ть**) to grow, increase.
возраст|но́й *adj. of* **во́зраст; ~на́я гру́ппа** age group.
возро|ди́ть, жу́, ди́шь *pf.* (*of* **~жда́ть**) to regenerate; to revive; **его́ слова́ ~ди́ли в ней во́лю к жи́зни** his words revived in her the will to live.
возро|ди́ться, жу́сь, ди́шься *pf.* (*of* **~жда́ться**) to revive (*intrans.*).
возрожда́|ть, ю *impf. of* **возроди́ть**
возрожда́|ться, юсь *impf. of* **возроди́ться**
возрожде́н|ец, ца *m.* revivalist.
возрожде́ни|е, я *nt.* rebirth; revival; **эпо́ха Возрожде́ния** Renaissance.
возроп|та́ть, щу́, ∠щешь *pf.* (*obs.*) to cry out (*in protest*).
во́зчик, а *m.* carter, carrier.
возыме́|ть, ю, ешь *pf.* to conceive (*wish, intention, etc.*); **больно́й ~л жела́ние пое́сть фру́ктов** the invalid conceived a desire for fruit; **в. де́йствие** to take effect; **ва́ши предупрежде́ния наконе́ц ~ли де́йствие** your warnings have at last taken effect; **в. си́лу** to come into force.
возьм|у́(сь), ёшь(ся) *see* **взя́ть(ся)**
во́ин, а *m.* warrior; fighter.
во́инск|ий *adj.* **1.** military; **~ая пови́нность** liability for military service; **в. по́езд** troop-train. **2.** martial, warlike.
во́инствен|ный (~, ~на) *adj.* warlike; bellicose.
во́инств|о, а *nt.* (*collect.*; *obs.*) host, army.
во́инствующ|ий *adj.* militant; (*pol.*, *mil.*) hawkish; **~ая це́рковь** the church militant; **Сою́з ~их безбо́жников** (*hist.*) League of Militant Atheists.
вои́стину *adv.* (*obs.*) indeed; verily; **(Христо́с) в. воскре́с!** (*response at Orthodox Easter service*) He (Christ) is risen indeed!
во́ител|ь, я *m.* **1.** (*poet.*) warrior. **2.** (*coll.*) rowdy.
во́ительниц|а, ы *f.* **1.** (*poet.*) female warrior, Amazon. **2.** (*coll.*) shrew, termagant.
во|й, я *no pl., m.* howl, howling; wail, wailing.
вой|ду́, дёшь *see* **~ти́**
во́йлок, а *m.* felt; strip of felt.
во́йлочный *adj.* felt.
войн|а́, ы́, *pl.* **∠ы** *f.* war; warfare; **агресси́вная в.** war of aggression; **вести́ ~у́** to wage war; **объяви́ть ~у́** to declare war.
войск|а́, ~ *pl.* (*sg.* **∠о, ∠а** *nt.*) **1.** troops; forces; **наёмные в.** mercenaries. **2.** (*sg.*) army; (*hist.*) host (*of Cossacks*); **запоро́жское ∠о** the Zaporozhian host. **3.** (*sg.*; *fig.*) host, multitude.
войсков|о́й *adj.* **1.** military. **2.** (*hist.*) of the host; **в. круг** Cossack assembly; **в. старшина́** Lieutenant-Colonel (*of Cossack troops*).
во|йти́, йду́, йдёшь, *past* **~шёл, ~шла́** *pf.* (*of* **входи́ть**) (**в.**+*a.*) to enter; to go in(to); to come in(to); **в. в аза́рт** to grow heated; **в. в дове́рие к кому́-н.** to be taken into s.o.'s confidence; **в. в исто́рию** to go down to history; **в. в колею́** to carry on as normal; **в. в лета́** to get on (in years); **в. в мо́ду** to become fashionable; **в. в погово́рку** to pass into a proverb; **в. в роль** to (begin to) feel one's feet.
вока́бул|ы, ~ *no sg.* (*obs.*) foreign words (*as objects of study*).
вока́л, а *m.* vocalism, (the art of) singing.
вокали́з, а *m. and* **вокали́з|а, ы** (*obs.*) *f.* exercise in vocalization.
вокализа́ци|я, и *f.* (*ling.*, *mus*) vocalization.
вокали́зм, а *m.* (*ling.*) vowel-system.
вокали́ст, а *m.* (*mus.*) teacher of singing.
вока́льный *adj.* vocal; **в. ве́чер** sing-song.
вокза́л, а *m.* (large) station; station building; **железнодоро́жный в.** railway (*esp. main or terminus*) station; **морско́й в.** port arrival and departure building; **речно́й в.** river-boat station.
вокза́л|ьный *adj. of* **~**; station.
во́кмен, а *m.* Walkman (*propr.*), personal stereo.
вокру́г *adv. and prep.*+*g.* round, around, about; **путеше́ствие в. све́та** voyage round the world; **верте́ться в. да о́коло** (*coll.*) to beat about the bush.
ВОКС, а *m.* (*abbr. of* ***Всесою́зное о́бщество культу́рной свя́зи с заграни́цей***) (*hist.*) All-Union Society for Cultural Relations with Foreign Countries.
вол, а́ *m.* ox, bullock.
вола́н, а *m.* **1.** flounce (*on woman's skirt*). **2.** shuttlecock; **игра́ в в.** badminton, battledore and shuttlecock.
волапю́к, а *m.* Volapuk (*artificial international language*).
Во́лг|а, и *f.* the Volga (*river*).
волга́р|ь, я́ *m.* (*coll.*) native of Volga region.
волды́р|ь, я́ *m.* blister; bump.
волево́й *adj.* **1.** (*psych.*) volitional. **2.** strong-willed; tough.
волеизъявле́ни|е, я *nt.* will, pleasure; command; **по короле́вскому ~ю** at the king's pleasure, by royal command.
волейбо́л, а *m.* (*sport*) volley-ball.
волейболи́ст, а *m.* volley-ball player.
во́лей-нево́лей *adv.* (*coll.*) willy-nilly.
волжа́н|ин, ина, *pl.* **~е, ~** *m.* native of Volga region.
волжа́н|ка, ки *f. of* **~ин**
во́лжский *adj.* Volga, of the Volga.
волк, а, *pl.* **∠и, ~о́в** *m.* wolf; **морско́й в.** (*coll.*) old salt; **смотре́ть ∠ом** (*fig.*) to scowl; **в. в ове́чьей шку́ре** wolf in sheep's clothing; **хоть ∠ом вы́ть** (*coll.*) it's enough to make you despair; **с ~а́ми жить, по-во́лчьи выть** (*prov.*) when in Rome do as the Romans do; **сде́лать так, что́б и в. был сыт и о́вцы це́лы** (*prov.*) to run with the hare and hunt with the hounds.
волк-маши́н|а, ы *f.* (*text.*) willow, willy.
волкода́в, а *m.* wolf-hound.
волн|а́, ы́, *pl.* **∠ы, ∠а́м** *f.* (*in var. senses*) wave; breaker.
во́лн|а, ы *f.* (*dial.*) wool.
волне́ни|е, я *nt.* **1.** choppiness (*of water*). **2.** (*fig.*) agitation, disturbance; emotion; **прийти́ в в.** to become agitated, excited. **3.** (*usu. pl.*; *pol.*) disturbance(s); unrest.
волни́ст|ый (~, ~а) *adj.* wavy; watered (*of stuffs*); **~ое желе́зо** corrugated iron; **~ая ме́стность** undulating ground.
волн|ова́ть, у́ю, *impf.* (*of* **вз~**) to disturb, agitate (*also fig.*) to excite; to worry; **его́ всё ~ует** he is easily excited; **не ну́жно в. больно́го** the patient must not be disturbed.
волн|ова́ться, у́юсь *impf.* **1.** (*of water, etc.*) to be agitated,

choppy; to ripple, wave. **2.** to be disturbed, agitated; to worry, be nervous; to be excited; **она́ ~у́ется о де́тях** she worries about her children; **он всегда́ ~у́ется пе́ред экза́меном** he is always nervous before an examination. **3.** (*pol.*; *obs.*) to be in a state of ferment, of unrest; **наро́д всё бо́лее ~ова́лся** popular unrest was increasing.

волново́д, а *m.* (*elec.*) wave-guide.

волнов|о́й *adj.* wave, undulatory; **~а́я тео́рия** (*phys.*) wave theory.

волноло́м, а *m.* breakwater.

волноме́р, а *m.* (*tech.*) wave-meter.

волнообра́з|ный (~ен, ~на) *adj.* undulatory; wavy, undulating.

волнорé́з, а *m.* breakwater.

волноуказа́тел|ь, я *m.* (*radio*) wave detector.

волну́шк|а, и *f.* coral milky cap (*mushroom*).

волн|у́ющий *pres. part. act. of* **~ова́ть** *and adj.* disturbing, worrying; exciting, thrilling, stirring; **~у́ющие изве́стия** disturbing, exciting news; **~у́ющая по́весть** thrilling, exciting story.

вол|о́вий *adj. of* **~**; (*fig.*) very strong; **~о́вья шку́ра** oxhide; **у него́ ~о́вья си́ла** he is as strong as an ox.

во́лок, а *m.* portage; **перепра́вить ~ом** to portage.

воло́к(ся), ла́(сь) *see* **воло́чь(ся)**

волоки́т|а[1], **ы** *f.* (*coll.*) red tape; rigmarole, palaver.

волоки́т|а[2], **ы** *m.* (*coll.*) ladies' man; philanderer.

волоки́тств|о, а *nt.* (*coll.*) philandering.

волоки́тчик, а *m.* (*coll.*) red-tape merchant, red-tape monger.

волокни́ст|ый (~, ~а) *adj.* fibrous; stringy.

волок|но́, на́, *pl.* **~на, ~он, ~нам** *nt.* fibre, filament.

волонтёр, а *m.* (*obs.*) volunteer.

волоо́кий *adj.* (*poet.*) ox-eyed.

во́лос, а, *pl.* **~ы** (*and coll.* **~а́**), **воло́с, ~а́м** *m.* **1.** hair; (*pl.*) hair (*of the head*); **рвать на себе́ ~ы** to tear one's hair; **схвати́ть за́ ~ы** to take by the hair; **при ви́де тру́па ~ы у меня́ ста́ли ды́бом** the sight of the corpse made my hair stand on end; **э́то притя́нуто за́ волосы** it is far fetched; **ни на́ волос** not a bit; **у него́ ни на́ волос ума́** he has not a grain of sense. **2.** hair (*as material*); **подкла́дка из ко́нского ~а** horsehair lining.

волоса́тик[1], **а** *m.* (*zool.*) hair-worm.

волоса́тик[2], **а** *m.* (*coll.*) = **волоса́тый** *as n.*

волоса́т|ый (~, ~а) *adj.* hairy; hirsute; pilose; *as n.* **в., ~ого** *m.* (*coll.*) hippie, 'longhair'.

волоси́стый *adj.* (*min.*) fibrous.

волосн|о́й *adj.* (*phys.*) capillary; **~ы́е сосу́ды** (*anat.*) capillaries.

волос|о́к, ка́ *m.* **1.** *dim. of* **во́лос; на в. (от+*g.*)** within a hairbreadth (of); **висе́ть, держа́ться на ~ке́** to hang by a thread; **я не тро́нул ~ка́ у неё** I did not touch a hair of her head. **2.** hair-spring. **3.** (*elec.*) filament.

волосте́л|ь, я *m.* (*hist.*) volost head.

волостно́й *adj.* volost.

во́лост|ь, и, *pl.* **~и, ~е́й** *f.* (*hist.*) volost (*smallest administrative division of tsarist Russia*).

волосяно́й *adj.* hair, of hair; **в. покро́в** (*anat.*) scalp.

волоче́ни|е, я *nt.* dragging; (*tech.*) **в. про́волоки** wire-drawing.

волочи́льн|ый *adj.* (*tech.*) wire-drawing; **~ая доска́** draw-plate.

волочи́льщик, а *m.* (*tech.*) wire-drawer.

волоч|и́ть, у́, ~ишь *impf.* **1.** to drag; **в. но́гу** to drag one's foot; **в. но́ги** to shuffle one's feet; **е́ле но́ги в.** to be hardly able to drag one's legs along; **в. де́ло** to drag out an affair. **2.** (*tech.*) to draw.

волоч|и́ться, у́сь, ~ишься, *impf.* **1.** *pass. of* **~и́ть. 2.** to drag (*intrans.*), trail. **3.** (**за**+*i.*; *coll.*) to run after; **три ме́сяца он уже́ ~ится за ней** he has been running after her for three months.

вол|о́чь, оку́, очёшь, оку́т, *past* **~о́к, ~окла́** *impf.* (*coll.*) to drag.

вол|о́чься, оку́сь, очёшься, оку́тся, *past* **~о́кся, ~окла́сь** *impf.* (*coll.*) **1.** to drag (*intrans.*), trail. **2.** to drag (o.s.) along; to shuffle.

воло́шский *adj.* (*hist.*) Wallachian; **в. оре́х** (*obs.*) walnut.

волхв, а́ *m.* magician, sorcerer; soothsayer; **три ~а́** the Three Wise Men, the Magi.

волхв|ова́ть, у́ю *impf.* to practise magic, sorcery.

волча́нк|а, и *f.* (*med.*) lupus.

волч|е́ц, ца́ *m.* (*bot.*) thistle.

во́лч|ий *adj. of* **волк;** wolf, lupine; **в. аппети́т** (*coll.*) voracious appetite; **в. биле́т, в. па́спорт** (*hist.*, *coll.*) passport (*in tsarist Russia*) with note of political unreliability of holder; **у него́ в. па́спорт** he is a marked man; **~ья пасть** cleft palate; **~ья я́года** (*bot.*) spurge-flax; **~ья я́ма** (*mil.*) trou-de-loup.

волчи́х|а, и *f.* (*coll.*) she-wolf.

волчи́ц|а, ы *f.* she-wolf.

волч|о́к[1], **ка** *m.* **1.** top (*toy*); **верте́ться ~ко́м** to spin like a top. **2.** (*tech.*) gyroscope.

волч|о́к[2], **ка́** *m.* judas (*in door of prison cell*).

волч|о́нок, о́нка, *pl.* **~а́та, ~а́т** *m.* wolf-cub.

волше́бник, а *m.* magician; wizard.

волше́бниц|а, ы *f.* enchantress.

волше́б|ный (~ен, ~на) *adj.* **1.** magical; **в. жезл, ~ная па́лочка** magic wand; **~ное ца́рство** fairyland; **в. фона́рь** magic lantern. **2.** (*fig.*) bewitching; enchanting.

волшебств|о́, а́ *nt.* magic; (*fig.*) magic, enchantment.

волы́н|ить, ю, ишь *impf.* (*coll.*) to dawdle, delay, be dilatory, slack.

волы́нк|а[1], **и** *f.* bagpipes.

волы́нк|а[2], **и** *f.* dawdling, delay, dilatoriness, slacking; hold-up; **тяну́ть ~у** to dawdle, delay, be dilatory.

волы́нщик[1], **и** *m.* piper.

волы́нщик[2], **и** *m.* (*coll.*) dawdler, slacker.

вольго́тный *adj.* (*coll.*) free, free-and-easy.

волье́р, а *m.* cage; enclosure.

волье́р|а, и *f.* = **волье́р**

волье́рн|ый *adj.*: **~ое содержа́ние звере́й** the caging of wild animals.

во́льн|ая, ой *f.* (*hist.*) letter of enfranchisement (*given to freed serf*); **дать кому́-н. ~ую** to give s.o. his freedom.

во́льниц|а, ы *f. and c.g.* **1.** *f.* (*collect.*; *hist.*) freemen; outlaws (*runaway serfs, Cossacks, etc., in Muscovite Russia*). **2.** *c.g.* (*coll.*) self-willed pers., child.

во́льнича|ть, ю *impf.* (*pej.*) to take liberties, make free.

во́льн|о *adv. of* **~ый**; (*as mil. command*) **в.!** stand at ease!

во́льно́ *as pred.* (+*d. and inf.*) (*coll.*; *addressed to pers. complaining of misfortune*) **в. тебе́** it's of your own choosing; **ты простуди́лась? в. ж тебе́ бы́ло вы́йти без пальто́** have you caught cold? well, you *would* go out without a coat.

вольноду́м|ец, ца *m.* (*hist.*) free-thinker.

вольноду́м|ный (~ен, ~на) *adj.* (*hist.*) free-thinking.

вольноду́мств|о, а *nt.* (*hist.*) free-thinking.

вольнолюби́в|ый (~, ~а) *adj.* freedom-loving.

вольнонаёмн|ый *adj.* **1.** civilian (*employed in or for mil. establishment*); **в э́том ла́гере нет ~ого соста́ва** in this camp there are no civilian staff. **2.** (*obs.*) hired; free-lance.

вольноопределя́ющ|ийся, егося *m.* (*hist.*) 'volunteer' (*pers. with secondary education serving term in tsarist Russ. army on privileged conditions*).

вольноотпу́щенник, а *m.* (*hist.*) freedman; emancipated serf.

вольноотпу́щенн|ый *adj.* (*hist.*) freed, emancipated; *as n.* **в., ~ого** *m.* = **~ик**

вольнопрактику́ющий *adj.* conducting a private practice (*of doctors, etc.*).

вольнослу́шател|ь, я *m.* occasional student (*permitted to attend university, etc., lecture courses without having the formal status of student*).

во́льност|ь, и *f.* **1.** freedom; liberty; **поэти́ческая в.** poetic license; **позволя́ть себе́ ~и** to take liberties. **2.** (*usu. pl.*; *hist.*) liberties, rights.

во́л|ьный *adj.* **1.** free; **в. го́род** free city; **в. каза́к, ~ьная пти́ца** one's own master. **2.** (*econ.*) free, unrestricted; **в. ры́нок** free market; **~ьная прода́жа** unrestricted sale. **3.** (*obs.*) private; **жить на ~ьной кварти́ре** (*mil.*) to live out (*opp. in barracks*); **служи́ть по ~ьному на́йму** to work by private agreement; **перейти́ на ~ьные хлеба́** to turn free-lance. **4.** (*of clothing*) free, loose. **5.:** **в. перево́д** (*liter.*)

free translation; **~ьные стихи́** vers libre. **6.** (*sport*) free, free-style; **~ьная борьба́** free-style wrestling; **в. стиль** (*in swimming*) free-style; **в. уда́р** free-kick; **~ьные упражне́ния** free exercises. **7.: поста́вить на в. дух, на в. жар, на в. пар** (*cul.*) to leave to cook (*after source of heat has been removed or switched off*). **8.: в. ка́менщик** Freemason. **9. (~ен, ~ьна́)** free, familiar (*in behaviour*). **10. (~ен, ~ьна́,** *pl.* **~ьны́)** (*full form not used*) free, at liberty; **ты ~ен де́лать, что хо́чешь** you are a free agent; you are at liberty to do as you wish.

вольт[1]**, а,** *g. pl.* **в.** *m.* (*elec.*) volt.

вольт[2]**, а, о ~е, на ~у́** *m.* **1.** (*sport*) vault. **2.** volte (*in fencing*). **3.** (*sl.*) cheating (*at cards*); **вы́кинуть в.** (*fig., coll.*) to play a trick.

вольта́ж, а *m.* (*elec.*) voltage.

вольтерья́н|ец, ца *m.* (*hist.*) Voltairian, free-thinker.

вольтерья́нств|о, а *nt.* (*hist.*) Voltairianism, free-thinking.

вольтижёр, а *m.* (*sport*) trick-rider, equestrian acrobat.

вольтижи́р|овать, ую *impf.* (*sport*) to do acrobatics on horseback.

вольтижиро́вк|а, и *f.* (*sport*) acrobatics on horseback.

вольтме́тр, а *m.* (*elec.*) voltmetre.

во́льтов *adj.* (*elec.*) voltaic.

вольфра́м, а *m.* (*chem.*) tungsten.

вольфрами́т, а *m.* (*min.*) wolframite.

вольфра́м|овый *adj. of* **~; ~овая ла́мпочка** tungsten lamp; **~овая руда́** wolfram.

воль|ю́, ёшь *see* **влить**.

волюнтари́зм, а *m.* (*phil.*) libertarianism.

волюнтари́ст, а *m.* (*phil.*) libertarian.

волю́т|а, ы *f.* (*archit.*) volute, scroll.

во́л|я, и *no pl., f.* **1.** (*in var. senses*) will; volition; wish(es); **после́дняя в.** last will; **свобо́дная в.** free will; **в. к жи́зни** will to live; **си́ла ~и** will-power; **челове́к с си́льной ~ей** strong-willed pers.; **~ею суде́б** as the fates decree; **счита́ться с ~ей избира́телей** to take into account the wishes of the voters; **в. ва́ша** (*coll.*) (*i*) as you please, as you like, (*ii*) say what you like; **в свое́й ~е** in one's power; **по до́брой ~е** freely, of one's own free will; **не по свое́й ~е** against one's will. **2.** freedom, liberty; **вы́пустить, отпусти́ть на ~ю** to set at liberty; **на ~е** at liberty; at large; **с ~и** (*prison sl.*) from outside; **дать ~ю** (*+d.*) to give free play (to), give free rein (to). give vent (to); **дать ~ю рука́м** (*coll.*) to be free with one's hands, fists.

вон[1] *adv.* out; off, away; **вы́йти в.** to go away; **в. отсю́да!** get out!; **в. его́!** out with him!; **из рук в. пло́хо** wretchedly; **пье́са была́ сы́грана из рук в. пло́хо** the play was wretchedly played; **из ря́да в. выходя́щий** outstanding; **у меня́ э́то из ума́ в.** (*coll.*) it went right out of my mind.

вон[2] *particle* there, over there; **в. он идёт** there he goes; **куда́ вы положи́ли газе́ту? — на стол, в. та́м** where have you put the paper? — over there, on the table; **в. он кто!** so that's who he is!; **в. оно́ что** (*coll.*) so that's it!

во́на (*coll., dial.*) **1.** = **вон 2.. 2.** *as int.* **в.** so that's it!

вон|жу́, зи́шь *see* **~зи́ть**

вонза́|ть, ю *impf. of* **вонзи́ть**

вонза́|ться, юсь 1. *impf. of* **вонзи́ться. 2.** *pass. of* **~ть**

вон|зи́ть, жу́, жи́шь *pf.* (*of* **~за́ть**) **1.** (**в**+*a.*) to plunge, thrust (into). **2.** (*sl.*) to drink.

вон|зи́ться, жу́сь, зи́шься *pf.* (*of* **~за́ться**) **1.** to pierce, penetrate; **стрела́ ~зи́лась ему́ в се́рдце** the arrow pierced his heart. **2.** *pass. of* **~зи́ть**

вони́щ|а, и *f.* (*coll.*) stink, stench.

вонми́ *see* **внять**

вон|ь, и *no pl., f.* stink, stench.

воню́ч|ий (~, ~а) *adj.* stinking, fetid.

вонючк|а, и *f.* (*coll.*) stinker; (*zool.*) skunk.

воня́|ть, ю *impf.* **1.** (*+i.*) to stink, reek (of); **весь дом ~ет чесноко́м** the whole house reeks of garlic. **2.** (*pf.* **на~**) (*vulg.*) to fart.

вообража́|емый *pres. part. pass. of* **~ть** *and adj.* imaginary; fictitious.

вообража́л|а, ы *c.g.* (*coll.*) show-off.

воображá|ть, ю *impf.* (*of* **вообрази́ть**) **1.** to imagine, fancy; **в. жизнь в ка́менном ве́ке** to imagine life in the Stone Age; **он ~ет, что слы́шит го́лос своего́ у́мершего отца́** he imagines that the can hear the voice of his dead father; **~ю, как вы чу́вствуете себя́** I can imagine how you feel. **2.** (*coll.*): **в. о себе́** to fancy o.s.; **он сли́шком ~ет о себе́** he thinks too much of himself.

воображá|ться, юсь *impf.* **1.** (*+i.*; *obs.*) to imagine o.s.; (*impers.*): **ему́ ~ется, бу́дто он вели́кий учёный** he imagines that he is a great scholar. **2.** *pass. of* **~ть**

воображе́ни|е, я *nt.* imagination; fancy; **у неё живо́е в.** she has a lively imagination; **э́то одно́ твоё в.** it's just your imagination.

вообрази́м|ый (~, ~а) *pres. part. pass of* **вообрази́ть** *and adj.* imaginable.

вообра|зи́ть, жу́, зи́шь *pf. of* **~жа́ть; ~зи́(те)!** fancy!, (just) imagine!

вообра|зи́ться, жу́сь, зи́шься *pf. of* **~жа́ться**

вообще́ *adv.* **1.** in general; on the whole; **в. говоря́, я не люблю́ рабо́тать по ноча́м** generally speaking I do not like working at night; **он сейча́с за́нят, но в. он лени́вый челове́к** he is busy at the moment but on the whole he is a lazy man. **2.** always; altogether; **она́ вы́глядит бле́дной в., а не то́лько сего́дня** she always looks pale, not just today.

воодушев|и́ть, лю́, и́шь *pf.* (*of* **~ля́ть**) to inspire, rouse; to inspirit, hearten; **его́ ре́чь ~и́ла всю страну́** his speech was an inspiration to the whole nation.

воодушевле́ни|е, я *nt.* **1.** rousing; inspiriting. **2.** animation; enthusiasm, fervour; **говори́ть с больши́м ~ем** to speak with great fervour.

воодушевлён|ный (~, ~а́) *p.p.p. of* **воодушеви́ть** *and adj.* animated; enthusiastic, fervent.

воодушевля́|ть, ю *impf. of* **воодушеви́ть**

вооруж|а́ть(ся), а́ю(сь) *impf. of* **~и́ть(ся)**

вооруже́ни|е, я *nt.* **1.** arming. **2.** arms, armament; **в., состоя́щее из пу́шек и пулемётов** an armament consisting of cannon and machine-guns. **3.** equipment; **па́русное в.** (*naut.*) rig.

вооружён|ный (~, ~а́) *p.p.p. of* **вооружи́ть** *and adj.* armed; **в. до зубо́в** armed to the teeth; **в. но́выми све́дениями** armed with fresh information; **~ные си́лы** armed forces.

вооруж|и́ть, у́, и́шь *pf.* (*of* **~а́ть**) **1.** (*+i.*) to arm; to equip (with) (*also fig.*); **в. кора́бль** (*obs.*) to fit out a ship. **2.** (**про́тив**+*g.*) to set (against), instigate (against).

вооруж|и́ться, у́сь, и́шься *pf.* (*of* **~а́ться**) **1.** to arm o.s., take up arms; (*fig.*) to equip o.s., provide o.s.; **в. ули́ками** to provide oneself with evidence; **в. терпе́нием** to arm o.s. with patience. **2.** *pass. of* **~и́ть**

во́очию *adv.* **1.** with one's own eyes, for o.s.; **я в. убеди́лся в том, что он небре́жно пра́вил маши́ной** I could see for myself that he was driving carelessly. **2.** clearly, plainly; **показа́ть в.** to show clearly.

во-пе́рвых *adv.* first, first of all, in the first place.

воп|и́ть, лю́, и́шь *impf.* (*coll.*) to cry out; to howl; to wail.

вопи|ю́щий *pres. part. act. of* **~я́ть** *and adj.* scandalous; crying; **~ю́щее безобра́зие** crying shame; **~ю́щее противоре́чие** glaring contradiction; **глас ~ю́щего в пусты́не,** *see* **глас**

вопи|я́ть, ю́, ёшь *impf.* (*obs.*) to cry out, clamour; **в. об отмще́нии** to cry out for vengeance.

во́плениц|а, ы *f.* (*dial.*) (professional) mourner.

вопло|ти́ть, щу́, ти́шь *pf.* (*of* **~ща́ть**) to embody, incarnate; **в. в себе́** to be the embodiment (of), incarnation (of); **Ле́вин, в «А́нне Каре́нине» Толсто́го, ~ти́л в себе́ тип «ка́ющегося дворяни́на»** Levin, in Tolstoy's *Anna Karenina*, embodied the type of the 'repentant nobleman'.

воплоща́|ть, ю *impf. of* **воплоти́ть**

воплоще́ни|е, я *nt.* embodiment, incarnation; **он — в. здоро́вья** he is the picture of health; **в. Христа́** the Incarnation.

воплощён|ный (~, ~а́) *p.p.p. of* **воплоти́ть** *and adj.* incarnate; personified; **он — ~ная добросо́вестность** he is conscientiousness personified.

вопл|ь, я *m.* cry, wail; wailing, howling.

вопреки́ *prep.+d.* despite, in spite of; against, contrary to, in the teeth of; **он вы́шел в. предписа́нию врача́** he went out against doctor's orders; **в. предупрежде́ниям** regardless of warning; **в. сове́ту** contrary to advice.

вопро́с, а *m.* **1.** question; **зада́ть в.** to put, pose a question; **ко́свенный в.** (*gram.*) indirect question. **2.** question, problem; matter; **подня́ть, поста́вить в.** (**о**+*p.*) raise the question (of); **поста́вить под в.** to call in question; **возмо́жность сверхзвуково́го полёта бо́льше не под ~ом** the possibility of supersonic flight is no longer in question; **в. жи́зни и сме́рти** matter of life and death; **спо́рный в.** moot point; **что за в.!** what a question!, of course!; (*sometimes does not require translation*) **како́е ва́ше мне́ние по вопро́су приватиза́ции земли́?** what is your opinion about privatization of the land?

вопроси́тельный *adj.* interrogative; interrogatory; **в. знак** question-mark; **в. взгляд** inquiring look.

вопро|си́ть, шу́, си́шь *pf.* (*of* **~ша́ть**) (*obs.*) to question, inquire (of).

вопро́сник, а *m.* questionnaire.

вопро́сный *adj.* containing questions; **в. лист** question-paper; form.

вопроша́|ть, ю *impf. of* **вопроси́ть; ~ющий взгляд** inquiring look.

вопр|у́, ёшь *see* **впере́ть**

вопь|ю́, ёшь *see* **впить**

вор, а, *pl.* **~ы, ~о́в** *m.* **1.** thief; **карма́нный в.** pickpocket; **магази́нный в.** shoplifter. **2.** (*hist.*) criminal (*esp. one guilty of high treason*); **ту́шинский в.** (*hist.*) 'the impostor of Tushino' (*the second false Dmitri*).

во́рван|ь, и *f.* train-oil; blubber.

ворв|а́ться, у́сь, ёшься, *past* **~а́лся, ~ала́сь** *pf.* (*of* **врыва́ться²**) to burst (into); **он ~а́лся ко мне в ко́мнату** he burst into my room.

вори́шк|а, и *m* petty thief.

ворк|ова́ть, у́ю *impf.* (*of pigeons*) to coo; (*fig.*) to bill and coo.

воркотн|я́, и́ *f.* (*coll.*) grumbling.

вороб|е́й, ья́ *m.* sparrow; **ста́рый в., стре́ляный в.** (*fig.*) old hand; **ста́рого ~ья́ на мяки́не не проведёшь** (*prov.*) an old bird is not caught with chaff.

вороб|ьи́ный *adj. of* **~е́й; ~ьи́ная ночь 1.** short summer night. **2.** night of continuous thunder and/or summer-lighting.

воро́ванный *adj.* stolen.

ворова́т|ый (~, ~а) *adj.* thievish; furtive; **в. взгляд** furtive glance.

вор|ова́ть, у́ю *impf.* **1.** (*pf.* **с~**) to steal; **в. де́ньги у кого́-н.** to steal money from s.o. **2.** *impf.* only to be a thief; **с са́мых ра́нних лет он ~у́ет** he has been a thief from his earliest years.

воро́вк|а, и *f. of* **вор**

воровски́ *adv.* (*coll.*) furtively.

воровск|о́й *adj.* **1.** of thieves; **в. язы́к, ~о́е арго́** thieves' Latin, thieves' cant. **2.** (*hist.*) illegal; **~и́е де́ньги** counterfeit money.

воровств|о́, а́ *nt.* stealing; theft; **литерату́рное в.** plagiarism.

во́рог, а *m.* (*folk poet.*) **1.** foe. **2.** fiend.

ворожб|а́, ы́ *no pl., f.* sorcery; fortune-telling.

вороже|я́, и́ *f.* sorceress; fortune-teller.

ворож|и́ть, у́, и́шь *impf.* (*of* **по~**) to practise sorcery; to tell fortunes; **ему́ ба́бушка ~и́т** (*coll.*) (*i*) he holds good cards, (*ii*) he has a friend at court.

во́рон, а *m.* raven; **чёрный в.** (*obs.*) Black Maria, paddy wagon.

воро́н|а, ы *f.* **1.** crow; **бе́лая в.** rara avis (*of s.o. outstanding*); **в. в павли́ньих пе́рьях** daw in peacock's feathers; **ни па́ва, ни в.** neither one thing nor another; **пу́ганая в. куста́ бои́тся** (*prov.*) a burnt child dreads the fire. **2.** (*fig.*) gaper, loafer, Johnny-head-in-the-air; **~ счита́ть** (*coll.*) to be a gaper, loafer, Johnny-head-in-the-air.

воронён|ый *adj.* (*tech.*) blued; **~ая сталь** blue steel, burnished steel.

воро́н|ий *adj. of* **~а**

ворон|и́ть, ю́, и́шь *impf.* (*tech.*) to blue, burnish.

воро́нк|а, и *f.* **1.** funnel (*for pouring liquids*). **2.** (*mil.*) crater.

во́рон|ов *adj. of* **~;** *only in phr.* **цвет ~ова крыла́** raven (*of hair, etc.*).

ворон|о́й *adj.* black (*of horses*); **прокати́ть на ~ы́х** (*coll.*) to blackball.

воронь|ё, я́ *nt.* (*collect.*) carrion-crows (*also fig.*).

во́рот¹, а, *pl.* **~ы** *m.* collar (*of garment*); neckband; **схвати́ть за́ в.** to seize by the collar, collar.

во́рот², а *m.* (*tech.*) winch; windlass.

воро́т|а (*coll.* **~а́), ~** *no sg.* **1.** gate, gates; gateway; **шлю́зные в.** lock-gate; **въе́хать в в.** to enter the gates; **стоя́ть в ~ах** to stand in the gateway; **пришла́ беда́, отворя́й ~а́** (*prov.*) misfortunes never come singly. **2.** (*sport*) goal, goal-posts.

вороти́л|а, ы *m.* (*coll.*) bigwig, big noise.

воро|ти́ть¹, чу́, ~тишь *pf.* (*coll.*) **1.** to bring back; to get back; to call back; **сде́ланного не ~тишь** what's done can't be undone. **2.** to turn aside, back.

воро|ти́ть², чу́, ~тишь *impf.* (*coll.*) (+*i.*) to be in charge (of), run; **он тут всем ~тит** he runs the whole show here; **нос, ры́ло в. (от)** (*coll.*) to turn up one's nose (at); (*impers.*): **(с души́) меня́ ~тит от э́того де́ла** this business makes me sick.

воро|ти́ться, чу́сь, ~тишься *pf.* (*coll.*) to return.

воротни́к, а́ *m.* collar; **отложно́й в.** turn-down collar; **стоя́чий в.** stand-up collar.

воротнич|о́к, ка́ *m.* collar.

воро́т|ный *adj. of* **~а; в. створ** gate-post; (*med.*) **~ная ве́на** portal vein.

во́рох, а, *pl.* **~а́** *m.* heap, pile; (*fig., coll.*) heaps, masses, lots; **мне на́до в. пи́сем написа́ть** I have lots of letters to write; **в. новосте́й** lots of news.

воро́ча|ть, ю *impf.* (*coll.*) **1.** to turn, move; **в. глаза́ми** to roll one's eyes. **2.** (+*i.*; *fig.*) to have control (of); **в. ты́сячами, в. миллио́нами** to be rolling (*in money*).

воро́ча|ться, юсь *impf.* to turn, move (*intrans.*); **в. с бо́ку на́ бок** to toss and turn; **~йтесь!** (*coll.*) get a move on!

воро|чу́(сь), ~тишь(ся) *see* **~ти́ть(ся)**

ворош|и́ть, у́, и́шь *impf.* (*of* **раз~**) **1.: в. се́но** to turn, ted hay **2.** (*fig., coll.*) to stir up.

ворош|и́ться, у́сь и́шься *impf.* (*coll.*) to move about, stir.

ворс, а, *no pl., m.* pile; nap; **по ~у** with the pile, nap.

ворси́льн|ый *adj.* (*text.*): **~ая маши́на** teaser; **~ая ши́шка** teasel.

ворси́нк|а, и *f.* **1.** (*text.*) hair. **2.** (*physiol., bot.*) fibre.

ворси́ст|ый (~, ~а) *adj.* **1.** (*text.*) fleecy, with thick pile. **2.** (*bot.*) lanate.

ворсова́льн|ый *adj.*: **~ая маши́на** (*text.*) teaser.

ворс|ова́ть, у́ю *impf.* (*of* **на~**) (*text.*) to tease.

ворся́нк|а, и *f.* (*bot.*) teasel.

ворча́нь|е, я *nt.* grumbling; growling.

ворч|а́ть, у́, и́шь *impf.* (**на**+*a.*) to grumble (at); to growl (at); **в. себе́ по́д нос** to mutter (into one's beard); **э́ти соба́ки ~а́т на всех чужи́х люде́й** these dogs always growl at strangers.

ворчли́в|ый (~, ~а) *adj.* querulous.

ворчу́н, а́ *m.* (*coll.*) grumbler.

восвоя́си *adj.* (for) home; **он уже́ отпра́вился в.** he has already set out for home.

восемна́дцатый *adj.* eighteenth.

восемна́дцат|ь, и *num.* eighteen.

во́с|емь, ьми́, ьмью́, *and* **емью́** *num.* eight.

во́с|емьдесят, ьми́десяти *num.* eighty.

вос|емьсо́т, ьмисо́т, емьюста́ми (*coll.* **ьмиста́ми**) *num.* eight hundred.

во́семью *adv.* eight times (*in multiplication*).

воск, а *m.* wax, beeswax; **го́рный в.** (*min.*) ozocerite.

воскли́кн|уть, у, ешь *pf.* to exclaim.

восклица́ни|е, я *nt.* exclamation.

восклица́тельный *adj.* exclamatory; **в. знак** exclamation mark.

восклица́|ть, ю *impf.* (*of* **воскли́кнуть**) to exclaim.

воско́вк|а, и *f.* wax-paper; stencil (*for use in duplicating machine, etc.*).

восков|о́й *adj.* wax, waxen; **~а́я свеча́** wax candle; **~а́я бума́га** greaseproof paper; **~о́е лицо́** waxen complexion.

воскрес|а́ть, а́ю *impf.* (*of* **~нуть**) to rise again, rise from the dead; (*fig.*) to revive.
воскресе́ни|е, я *nt.* resurrection.
воскресе́нь|е, я *nt.* Sunday.
воскре|си́ть, шу́, си́шь, *pf.* (*of* **~ша́ть**) to raise from the dead, resurrect; (*fig.*) to resurrect, revive; **о́тдых ~си́л его́ си́лы** the rest revived his energies; **в. ста́рый обы́чай** to resurrect an old custom.
воскре́сник, а *m.* voluntary Sunday work.
воскре́с|нуть, ну, нешь, *past* **~, ~ла** *pf. of* **~а́ть**
воскре́сн|ый *adj.* Sunday.
воскреша́|ть, ю *impf. of* **воскреси́ть**
воскреше́ни|е, я *nt.* raising from the dead, resurrection; (*fig.*) revival.
воскур|и́ть, ю́, ~ишь *pf.* (*of* **~я́ть**) (*obs.*) to burn (*incense*); **в. фимиа́м кому́-н.** to sing one's praises.
воскур|я́ть, я́ю *impf. of* **~и́ть**
восле́д = вслед
воспале́ни|е, я *nt.* (*med.*) inflammation; **в. брюши́ны** peritonitis; **в. кишо́к** enteritis; **в. лёгких** pneumonia; **в. по́чек** nephritis; **ро́жистое в.** erysipelas.
воспалён|ный (~, ~а́) *p.p.p. of* **воспали́ть** *and adj.* sore; inflamed (*also fig.*); **~ное воображе́ние** fevered imagination.
воспали́тельный *adj.* (*med.*) inflammatory; **в. проце́сс** inflammation.
воспал|и́ть, ю́, и́шь *pf.* (*of* **~я́ть**) to inflame.
воспал|и́ться, ю́сь, и́шься *pf.* (*of* **~я́ться**) to become inflamed; (*+i.*; *obs.*) to become inflamed (with), be on fire (with); **в. гне́вом** to flare up with rage.
воспал|я́ть(ся), я́ю(сь) *impf. of* **~и́ть(ся)**
воспар|и́ть, ю́, и́шь *pf.* (*of* **~я́ть**) (*poet.*) to soar; **в. ду́хом** (*iron.*) to be carried away.
воспаря́|ть, ю *impf. of* **воспари́ть**
воспева́|ть, ю *impf. of* **воспе́ть**
восп|е́ть, ою́, оёшь *pf.* (*of* **~ева́ть**) (*poet.*) to sing (of), hymn; **в. по́двиги наро́дных геро́ев** to sing of the deeds of national heroes.
воспита́ни|е, я *nt.* **1.** education; upbringing. **2.** (good) breeding.
воспи́танник, а *m.* **1.** pupil; **в. сре́дней шко́лы** secondary schoolboy. **2.** ward (*a minor*).
воспи́танност|ь, и *f.* (good) breeding.
воспи́танный *p.p.p. of* **воспита́ть** *and adj.* well brought up.
воспита́тел|ь, я *m.* tutor, educator.
воспита́тельниц|а, ы *f.* governess.
воспита́тельный *adj.* educational; **в. дом** foundling hospital.
воспит|а́ть, а́ю *pf.* (*of* **~ывать**) **1.** to educate, bring up. **2.** to cultivate, foster; **в. са́мые хоро́шие накло́нности в ком-н.** to bring out the best in s.o. **3.** (**из**+*g.*) to make (of); **в. солда́т из сбро́да** to make an army of a rabble.
воспи́тыва|ть, ю *impf. of* **воспита́ть**
воспламене́ни|е, я *nt.* ignition.
воспламен|и́ть, ю, и́шь *pf.* (*of* **~я́ть**) to kindle, ignite; (*fig.*) to fire, inflame.
воспламен|и́ться, ю́сь, и́шься *pf.* (*of* **~я́ться**) to catch fire, ignite; (*fig.*) to take fire, flare up.
воспламеня́емост|ь, и *f.* inflammability.
воспламеня́емый *adj.* inflammable.
воспламеня́|ть(ся), ю(сь) *impf. of* **воспламени́ть(ся)**
воспо́лн|ить, ю, ишь *pf.* to fill in; **в. пробе́лы в свои́х зна́ниях** to fill in the gaps in one's knowledge.
восполня́|ть, ю *impf. of* **воспо́лнить**
воспо́льз|оваться, уюсь *pf. of* **по́льзоваться**
воспомина́ни|е, я *nt.* **1.** recollection, memory; **жить ~ями** to live on memories; **от его́ иму́щества оста́лось одно́ в.** of his possessions nothing is left. **2.** *pl.* (*liter.*) memoirs; reminiscences.
воспосле́д|овать, ую *pf.* (*obs.*) to follow, ensue; **~овал це́лый ряд несча́стных слу́чаев** a whole chapter of accidents ensued.
восп|ою́, оёшь *see* **~е́ть**
воспрепя́тств|овать, ую *pf. of* **препя́тствовать**
воспрети́тельный *adj.* prohibitive.
воспре|ти́ть, щу́, ти́шь *pf.* (*of* **~ща́ть**) (*+a. or inf.*) to forbid, prohibit; **в. вход** prohibit entry; **в. разгова́ривать за столо́м** to forbid talking at meals.
воспреща́|ть, ю *impf. of* **воспрети́ть**
воспреща́|ться, юсь *impf.* to be prohibited; **«кури́ть ~ется»** 'No Smoking'; **«посторо́нним вход ~ется»** 'Unauthorized persons not admitted'.
воспреще́ни|е, я *nt.* prohibition.
восприе́мник, а *m.* godfather.
восприе́мниц|а, ы *f.* godmother.
восприи́мчив|ый (~, ~а) *adj.* **1.** receptive; impressionable. **2.** susceptible; **он о́чень ~ к на́сморку** he is very susceptible to colds.
восприм|у́, ~ешь *see* **восприня́ть**
воспринима́ем|ый (~, ~а) *adj.* perceptible.
воспринима́|ть, ю *impf. of* **восприня́ть**
воспри|ня́ть, му́, ~мешь, *past* **~нял, ~няла́, ~няло** *pf.* (*of* **~нима́ть**) **1.** to perceive, apprehend; to grasp, take in. **2.** to take (for), interpret; **в. молча́ние как знак согла́сия** to take silence as a mark of consent. **3.: в. от купе́ли** (*eccl.*) to stand godfather, godmother (to).
восприя́ти|е, я *nt.* (*phil., psych.*) perception.
воспроизведе́ни|е, я *nt.* **1.** reproduction; **в. челове́ческого ро́да** reproduction of the human species; **ве́рное в. карти́ны Ру́бенса** faithful reproduction of a painting by Rubens. **2.** playback, replay; **заме́дленное/уско́ренное в.** slow-motion/high-speed replay.
воспроизве|сти́, ду́, дёшь, *past* **~л, ~ла́** *pf.* (*of* **воспроизводи́ть**) (*in var. senses*) to reproduce; **в. в па́мяти** to recall; **в. по́длинный докуме́нт** to reproduce an original document; **он то́лько ~л утвержде́ния профе́ссора** he merely echoed the professor's statements.
воспроизводи́тельный *adj.* reproductive.
воспроизво|ди́ть, жу́, ~дишь *impf. of* **воспроизвести́**
воспроизво́дств|о, а *nt.* (*econ.*) reproduction.
воспроти́в|иться, люсь, ишься *pf. of* **проти́виться**
воспря́н|уть, у, ешь *pf.* **1.** (*obs.*) to leap up. **2.** (*coll.*) to cheer up; **в. ду́хом** to take heart.
воспыла́|ть, ю *pf.* (*+i.*) to be inflamed (with); to blaze (with); **в. гне́вом** to blaze with anger; **в. любо́вью (к**+*d.*) to be smitten with love (for).
восседа́|ть, ю *impf. of* **воссе́сть**
восс|е́сть, я́ду, я́дешь, *past* **~е́л** *pf.* to sit (*in state, formally*); **в. на престо́л** to mount the throne.
восса́в|ить, лю, ишь *pf.* (*of* **~ля́ть**) (*obs.*) to hymn, praise.
восславля́|ть, ю *impf. of* **воссла́вить**
воссоедине́ни|е, я *nt.* reunion, reunification.
воссоедин|и́ть, ю́, и́шь *pf.* (*of* **~я́ть**) to reunite.
воссоединя́|ть, ю *impf. of* **воссоедини́ть**
воссозда|ва́ть, ю́, ёшь *impf. of* **~ть**
воссозда́ни|е, я *nt.* reconstruction.
воссоз|да́ть, да́м, да́шь да́ст, дади́м, дади́те, даду́т, *past* **~да́л, ~дала́, ~да́ло** *pf.* (*of* **~дава́ть**) to reconstruct, reconstitute; **он ~да́л в кни́ге собы́тия Троя́нской войны́** in his book he has reconstructed the events of the Trojan War.
восста|ва́ть, ю́, ёшь *impf. of* **~ть**
восста́в|ить, лю, ишь *pf.* (*obs.*) to set up, erect; **в. перпендикуля́р** (*math.*) to raise a perpendicular.
восставля́|ть, ю *impf. of* **восста́вить**
восстана́влива|ть, ю *impf. of* **восстанови́ть**
восста́ни|е, я *nt.* rising, insurrection.
восстанови́тел|ь, я *m.* **1.** renovator, restorer. **2.** restorative (*for hair*).
восстанови́тельн|ый *adj.* restorative; **в. перио́д** period of reconstruction; **~ые рабо́ты** restoration work.
восстанов|и́ть, лю́, ~ишь *pf.* (*of* **восстана́вливать**) **1.** to restore, renew; to rehabilitate; **в. мир** to restore peace; **в. хозя́йство страны́** to restore the economy of a country; **в. в па́мяти** to recall, recollect; **в. кого́-н. в права́х** to restore s.o.'s rights, rehabilitate; **его́ ~или в до́лжности заве́дующего** he has been reinstated as manager. **2.** (**про́тив**+*g.*) to set (against); **они́ ~или сосе́дей про́тив**

себя́ свое́й гру́бостью they have set their neighbours against them by their rudeness. **3.** (*chem.*) to reduce.
восстановле́ни|е, я *nt.* **1.** restoration, renewal; rehabilitation; **в. в права́х** restoration of rights, rehabilitation; **в. в до́лжности** reinstatement. **2.** (*chem.*) reduction.
восстановля́|ть, ю *impf.* **1.** *impf. of* **восстанови́ть. 2.** (*chem.*) to reduce.
восста́|ть, ну, нешь, *imper.* **~нь,** *pf.* (*of* **~ва́ть**) **1.** (*obs.*) to rise (up). **2.** (**на**+*a.*, **про́тив**+*g.*) to rise (against); (*fig.*) to be up in arms (against), fly in the face (of); **всё дереве́нское населе́ние ~ло на врага́** the whole countryside rose against the enemy; **вы ~ли про́тив здра́вого смы́сла** you are flying in the face of the dictates of common sense.
воссыла́|ть, ю *impf.* (*obs.*) to offer up, send up.
восто́к, а *m.* **1.** east; **на в., с ~а** to, from the east. **2. В.** the East; the Orient; **Бли́жний В.** the Middle East; **Да́льний В.** the Far East.
востокове́д, а *m.* orientalist.
востокове́дени|е, я *nt.* oriental studies.
востокове́дный *adj.* of oriental studies.
востокове́д|ческий *adj.* = **~ный**
восто́рг, а *m.* delight; rapture; **быть в ~е (от**+*g.*) to be delighted (with); **приходи́ть в в. (от**+*g.*) to go into raptures (over).
восторга́|ть, ю *impf.* to delight, enrapture.
восторга́|ться, юсь *impf.* (+*i.*) to be delighted (with); to go into, be in raptures (over); **она́ ~ется бале́том** she goes into raptures over the ballet.
восто́рженност|ь, и *f.* **1.** enthusiasm. **2.** proneness to enthusiasm.
восто́ржен|ный (~, ~на) *adj.* enthusiastic, rapturous; **~ная голова́** exalté; **в. приём** enthusiastic reception; **его́ нове́йшая пье́са получи́ла ~ные о́тзывы** his latest play has had rave reviews.
восторжеств|ова́ть, у́ю *pf. of* **торжествова́ть**
восто́чник, а *m.* (*coll.*) orientalist.
восто́чн|ый *adj.* east, eastern; oriental; **~ая це́рковь** the Eastern Church.
востре́бовани|е, я *nt.* claiming, demand; **до ~я** to be called for, on demand; **посла́ть паке́т до ~я** to send a parcel to be called for, send a parcel poste restante.
востре́б|овать, ую *pf.* to claim, call for (*from post-office, etc.*).
вострепе|та́ть, щу́, ~щешь *pf.* (*obs.*) to begin to tremble.
востро́ *adv.* (*coll.*): **держа́ть у́хо в.** to keep a sharp lookout.
вострогла́зый *adj.* (*coll.*) sharp-eyed; bright-eyed.
вострonóсый *adj.* (*coll.*) sharp-nosed.
во́ст|рый (~ёр, ~ра́, ~ро) *adj.* (*dial.*) sharp.
восхвале́ни|е, я *nt.* eulogy.
восхвал|и́ть, ю́, ~ишь *pf.* (*of* **~я́ть**) to laud, extol, eulogize.
восхваля́|ть, ю *impf. of* **восхвали́ть**
восхити́тел|ьный (~ен, ~ьна) *adj.* entrancing, ravishing; delightful; delicious; **~ьная пе́сня** an entrancing song; **из рестора́на нёсся в. за́пах** a delicious smell came from the restaurant.
восхи́|тить, щу, тишь *pf.* (*poet.*, *obs.*) to carry away.
восхи|ти́ть, щу́, ти́шь *pf.* (*fig.*) to carry away, delight, enrapture; **красота́ италья́нских озёр его́ ~ти́ла** he was carried away by the beauty of the Italian lakes.
восхи|ти́ться, щу́сь, ти́шься *pf.* (+*i.*) to be carried away (by); to admire; **все ~ти́лись его́ хра́бростью** his courage was the admiration of all.
восхища́|ть(ся), ю(сь) *impf. of* **восхити́ть(ся)**
восхище́ни|е, я *nt.* delight, rapture; admiration.
восхищён|ный (~, ~а́) *p.p.p. of* **восхити́ть** *and adj.* rapt; admiring; **в. взгляд** rapt gaze.
восхи́|щу, тишь *see* **~тить**
восхи|щу́(сь), ти́шь(ся) *see* **~ти́ть(ся)**
восхо́д, а *m.* **1.** rising; **в. со́лнца** sunrise. **2.** (*obs.*) the east.
восхо|ди́ть, жу́, ~дишь *impf.* **1.** *impf. of* **взойти́. 2.** (*impf. only*) **(к)** to go back (to), date (from); **в. к дре́вности** to go back to antiquity.
восход|я́щий *pres. part. of* **~и́ть** *and adj.* **~я́щая звезда́, ~я́щее свети́ло** (*fig.*) rising star; **~я́щее поколе́ние** rising generation; **~я́щая интона́ция** (*ling.*), **~я́щее ударе́ние** (*mus.*) rising intonation.
восхожде́ни|е, я *nt.* ascent; **в. на Монбла́н** the ascent of Mont Blanc.
восчу́вств|овать, ую *pf.* (*obs. or iron.*) to feel.
восше́стви|е, я *nt.* **(на престо́л)** accession (to the throne).
восьм|а́я *see* **~о́й**
восьмери́чн|ый *adj.* eightfold; **и ~ое** name of letter **'и'** in old Russ. orthography.
восьмёрк|а, и *f.* **1.** (*coll.*) eight; number eight (*of buses, etc.*). **2.** (*cards*) eight; **в. черве́й** eight of hearts. **3.** eight (*boat*). **4.** figure of eight.
во́сьмер|о, ы́х *num.* **1.** eight; **нас бы́ло в.** there were eight of us; **в. сане́й** eight sledges. **2.** eight pairs; **в. перча́ток** eight pairs of gloves.
восьми́... *comb. form* eight-, octo-.
восьмивесе́льный *adj.* eight-oared.
восьмигра́нник, а *m.* (*math.*) octahedron.
восьмидесятиле́тний *adj.* **1.** of eighty years; **в. юбиле́й** eightieth anniversary. **2.** eighty-year-old.
восьмидеся́тник, а *m.* 'man of the eighties' (*of 19th century*).
восьмидеся́тый *adj.* eightieth.
восьмикла́ссник, а *m.* eighth-former (*pupil*).
восьмикла́ссни|ц|а, ы *f. of* **~к**
восьмикра́тный *adj.* eightfold; octuple.
восьмиле́тний *adj.* **1.** eight-year. **2.** eight-year-old.
восьмино́г = осьмино́г
восьмисо́тый *adj.* eight-hundredth.
восьмисти́ши|е, я *nt.* (*liter.*) octave, octet.
восьмисто́пный *adj.* (*liter.*) eight-foot, octonarian.
восьмиуго́льник, а *m.* (*math.*) octagon.
восмиуго́льный *adj.* octagonal.
восьмичасово́й *adj.* eight-hour; **в. рабо́чий день** eight-hour (working-)day.
восьм|о́й *adj.* eighth; *as n.* **~а́я, ~о́й** *f.* (*in var. senses*) an eighth.
восьму́шк|а, и *f.* **1.** (*coll.*) eighth of a pound (*in weight*). **2.** octavo; **писа́ть на ~е** to write on octavo.
вот *particle* **1.** here (is), there (is); this is; **в. мой дом** here is my house, this is my house; **в. авто́бус** here's, there's the bus; **в. авто́бус идёт** here comes the bus; **в. и я** here I am; **в. мы пришли́** here we are; **в. где я живу́** this is where I live. **2.** (*emph. prons.*; *unstressed*): **в. э́ти ту́фли ей нра́вились** *these* are the shoes she liked; **в. ему́ я бы э́того не поруча́л** I would not trust *him* with this. **3.** (*in excl.*; *always stressed*) here's a ..., there's a ... (for you); **во́т тип!** there's a character (for you)!; **во́т так исто́рия!** here's a pretty kettle of fish!; (*expr. surprise*) **во́т как!, во́т что!** really? you don't mean to say so!; **слы́шали ли вы но́вость? коро́ль у́мер. В. как!** have you heard the news? the king is dead. No! (not) really?; **в. так та́к! в. тебе на́!** well!; well, I never!; **говоря́т, что Пётр обручи́лся с Ли́зой. В. так та́к!** they day Peter and Elizabeth are engaged. Well!; (*surprise and disapproval*) **в. ещё!** indeed!; what(ever) next!; good heavens!; **не дашь ли мне пять фу́нтов взаймы́? ну, во́т ещё!** will you lend me five pounds? well, what next!; (*approval and/or encouragement*) **в. та́к!, в.-в.!** that's right!; that's it!; (*accompanying blows*) **во́т тебе!** take that!; **во́т тебе, во́т тебе!** take that, and that!; (*expr. disagreeable surprise at unwelcome turn of events or at non-occurrence of expected event*) **вот тебе́ и...** so much for ...; **вот тебе́ и пое́здка в Пари́ж!** so much for the trip to Paris!; we've (you've, *etc.*) had the trip to Paris!
вот-во́т *adv.* just, on the point of; **вода́ в.-в. закипи́т** the water is just boiling, is on the boil; **по́езд в.-в. придёт** the train is just coming.
воти́р|овать, ую *impf. and pf.* to vote (for); **в. увеличе́ние дота́ций студе́нтам** to vote an increase of students' grants.
votиро́вк|а, и *f.* voting.
votк|а́ть, у́, ёшь, *past* **~а́л, ~ала́, ~а́ло** *pf.* to interweave.
воткн|у́ть, у́, ёшь *pf.* (*of* **втыка́ть**) (**в**+*a.*) to stick (into),

drive (into); **в. кол в зе́млю** to drive a stake into the ground; **она́ ~у́ла ему́ гвозди́ку в петли́цу** she stuck a carnation in his buttonhole.

вотр|у́, ёшь *see* **втере́ть**

во́тский *adj.* Votyak.

во́тум, а *no pl., m.* vote; **в. (не)дове́рия** (+*d.*) vote of (no) confidence (in).

во́тчин|а, ы *f.* (*hist.*) inherited estate, lands; allodium, patrimony (*in Muscovite Russia as opposed to* **поме́стье**).

во́тчинник, а *m.* (*hist.*) great landowner (*in Muscovite Russia*).

во́тчинный *adj.* (*hist.*) allodial, patrimonial.

вотще́ *adv.* (*obs.*) in vain, to no purpose.

вотя́к, а́ *m.* Votyak (*former name of Udmurt*).

вотя́цкий *adj.* = **во́тский**

вотя́|чка, чки *f. of* **~к**

воцаре́ни|е, я *nt.* accession (to the throne).

воцар|и́ться, ю́сь, и́шься *pf.* (*of* **~я́ться**) **1.** to come to the throne. **2.** (*fig.*) to set in; **в лесу́ ~лась тишина́** in the forest silence fell.

воцаря́|ться, юсь *impf. of* **воцари́ться**

вочелове́чени|е, я *nt.* (*theol.*) incarnation.

вочелове́ч|иться, усь, ишься *pf.* (*theol.*) to become man, be incarnate.

вош|ёл, ла́ *see* **войти**

во́шк|а, и *f.* (*coll.*) louse.

вошь, вши, *i.* **~ю,** *pl.* **вши, вшей** *f.* louse.

воща́нк|а, и *f.* **1.** wax-paper; waxed cloth. **2.** cobbler's wax. **3.** stencil.

вощано́й *adj.* wax.

вощёный *adj.* waxed.

вощи́н|а, ы *f.* **1.** (*collect.*) empty honeycomb. **2.** unrefined beeswax.

вощ|и́ть, у́, и́шь *impf.* (*of* **на~**) to wax; to polish with wax.

во́|ю, ешь *see* **выть**

вою́|ю, ешь *see* **воева́ть**

воя́ж, а *m.* (*obs.or iron.*) journey, travels.

вояжёр, а *m.* **1.** (*obs. or iron.*) traveller. **2.** commercial traveller.

воя́к|а, и *m.* (*coll., iron.*) warrior; fire-eater.

впада́|ть, ю *impf.* **1.** *impf. of* **впасть. 2.** *impf. only* (*of rivers*) to fall (into), flow (into); **Ока́ ~ет в Во́лгу** the Oka flows into the Volga. **3.** *impf. only* (**в**+*a.*) to verge (on), approximate (to).

впаде́ни|е, я *nt.* confluence; mouth (*of rivers*).

впа́дин|а, ы *f.* cavity, hollow; **глазна́я в.** eye-socket.

впад|у́, ёшь *see* **впасть**

впа́ива|ть, ю *impf. of* **впая́ть**

впа́йк|а, и *f.* **1.** soldering-in. **2.** soldered-in piece.

впа́л|ый *adj.* hollow, sunken; **~ые щёки** hollow cheeks.

впа|сть, ду́, дёшь *pf.* (*of* **~да́ть**) **1.** (**в**+*a.*) to fall (into), lapse (into), sink (into); **в. в бе́дность** to fall into penury; **в. в грех** to lapse into sin; **в. в де́тство** to sink into dotage; **в. в неми́лость** to fall into disgrace. **2.** (*of eyes, cheeks*) to fall in, sink.

впа|я́ть, я́ю *pf.* (*of* **~ивать**) to solder in.

вперви́нку *adv.* (*coll.*) for the first time; **ему́ не в. е́хать в Росси́ю** it is not the first time he has been to Russia.

вперв|о́й *adv.* (*coll.*) = **~ы́е**

впервы́е *adv.* for the first time, first; **семи́десяти лет он в. полете́л на самолёте** at the age of seventy he went in an aeroplane for the first time; **когда́ в. я прие́хал в Ло́ндон** when I first came to London.

вперева́лку *adv.* (*coll.*): **ходи́ть в.** to waddle.

вперего́нки *adv.* (*coll.*): **бе́гать в.** to run races.

вперёд *adv.* **1.** forward(s), ahead; (*of clocks and watches*) fast; **взад и в.** back and forth; **большо́й шаг в.** (*fig.*) a big step forward; **ра́зве ва́ши часы́ не иду́т в.?** surely your watch is fast?; **в.!** (*mil, command*) forward! **2.** in future, henceforward; **в. будь осторо́жнее** be more careful in future. **3.** in advance; **заплати́ть в.** to pay in advance; **дать очки́ в.** (*sport*) to give points; **дав мне пять очко́в в., он всё-таки вы́играл** he gave me five points and still won.

впереди́ 1. *adv.* in front, ahead. **2.** *adv.* in (the) future; ahead. **3.** *prep.*+*g.* in front of, before; **лейтена́нт марширова́л в. взво́да** the lieutenant marched at the head of the platoon.

впереме́жку *adv.* (*coll.*) alternately; **на пара́де солда́ты и моряки́ шли в.** soldiers and sailors alternated in the parade.

впереме́шку *adv.* (*coll.*) pell-mell, higgledy-piggledy; in confusion; **все его́ ве́щи лежа́ли в. на полу́ ко́мнаты** all his things lay in confusion on the floor of the room.

впер|е́ть, вопру́, вопрёшь, *past* **≁, ≁ла** *pf.* (*of* **впира́ть**) (*coll.*) **1.** to barge in; **он про́сто ≁ в дом, не дожда́вшись приглаше́ния** he simply barged into the house without waiting to be invited. **2.** to shove in, thrust in.

впер|е́ться, вопру́сь, вопрёшься, *past* **≁ся, ≁лась** *pf.* (*of* **впира́ться**) (*coll.*) to barge in.

впер|и́ть, ю́, и́шь *pf.* (*of* **~я́ть**) (**в**+*a.*) to direct (upon); **в. взор** to fasten one's gaze (upon).

впер|и́ться, ю́сь, и́шься *pf.* (*of* **~я́тся**) (*coll.*) to stare (at), fasten one's eyes (upon).

вперя́|ть(ся), ю(сь) *impf. of* **впери́ть(ся)**

впечатле́ни|е, я *nt.* impression; **~я де́тства** childhood impressions; **произвести́ в.** (**на**+*a.*) to make an impression (upon); **его́ речь произвела́ в. на всех** his speech made an impression on all; **у меня́ создало́сь в., что она́ недово́льна** I formed the impression that she was dissatisfied.

впечатли́тельност|ь, и *f.* impressionability.

впечатли́тел|ьный (~ен, ~ьна) *adj.* impressionable.

впечатля́ющий *adj.* impressive.

впива́|ть, ю *impf.* **1.** *impf. of* **впить. 2.** *impf. only* to drink in, enjoy (*esp. olfactory sensations*).

впива́|ться[1], юсь *impf. of* **впи́ться[1]**

впива́|тся[2], юсь *impf. of* **впи́ться[2]**

впира́|ть(ся), ю(сь) *impf. of* **впере́ть(ся)**

впи́санный *p.p.p. of* **вписа́ть** *and adj.* (*math.*) inscribed.

впи|са́ть, шу́, ≁шешь *pf.* (*of* **≁сывать**) **1.** to enter; to insert; **в. своё и́мя в спи́сок** to enter one's name on a list; **в. фра́зу в ру́копись статьи́** to insert a sentence into the manuscript of an article. **2.** (*math.*) to inscribe.

впи|са́ться, шу́сь, ≁шешься *pf.* (*of* **≁сываться**) (*coll.*) to be enrolled, join.

впи́ск|а, и *f.* (*coll.*) **1.** entry. **2.** insertion; **страни́ца была́ полна́ впи́сок** the page was full of insertions.

впи́сыва|ть(ся), ю(сь) *impf. of* **вписа́ть(ся)**

впит|а́ть, а́ю *pf.* (*of* **≁ывать**) to absorb; (*fig.*) to absorb, take in; **за удиви́тельно коро́ткий срок он ~а́л в себя́ всю филосо́фию Ка́нта** in an amazingly short time he had absorbed the whole of Kant's philosophy.

впит|а́ться, а́юсь *pf.* (*of* **≁ываться**) (**в**+*a.*) to soak (into).

впи́тыва|ть(ся), ю(сь) *impf. of* **впита́ть(ся)**

впи|ть, вопью́, вопьёшь, *past* **~л, ~ла́, ≁ло** *pf.* (*of* **~ва́ть**) to imbibe, absorb.

впи́|ться[1], вопью́сь, вопьёшься, *past* **~лся, ~ла́сь** *pf.* (*of* **~ва́ться**) (**в**+*a.*) **1.** to stick (into); to bite; to sting; **ко́шка ~ла́сь в неё когтя́ми** the cat stuck its claws into her; **ва́ша соба́ка ~ла́сь мне в но́гу** your dog has bitten me in the leg; **гвоздь ~лся мне в но́гу** a nail stuck into my foot. **2.: в. взо́ром, глаза́ми** to fix, fasten one's eyes (upon).

впи́|ться[2], вопью́сь, вопьёшься, *past* **~лся, ~ла́сь** *pf.* (*coll.*) to become hardened to drink.

впих|а́ть, а́ю *pf.* (*coll.*) = **~ну́ть**

впи́хива|ть, ю *impf. of* **впиха́ть** *and* **впихну́ть**

впих|ну́ть, ну́, нёшь *pf.* (*of* **≁ивать**) to stuff in, cram in; to shove; **в. кого́-н. в ко́мнату** to shove s.o. into a room.

вплавь *adv.* swimming; **каки́м о́бразом перепра́вился он че́рез ре́ку? в.** how did he get across the river? he swam it.

впле|сти́, ту́, тёшь, *past* **≁л, ~ла́** *pf.* (*of* **~та́ть**) (**в**+*a.*) to plait (into), intertwine; (*fig., coll.*) to involve (in); **вы ~ли́ меня́ в хоро́шенькое де́ло** you have got me into a fine mess.

вплета́|ть, ю *impf. of* **вплести́**

впле|ту́, тёшь *see* **~сти́**

вплотну́ю *adv.* close; (*fig.*) in (real) earnest; **поста́вить стол в. к стене́** to put the table right against the wall;

приня́ться за де́ло в. to get to grips with the matter, tackle the matter in real earnest.
вплоть *adv.* **1.**: **в. до** (right) up to; **он шути́л в. до моме́нта ка́зни** he was joking right up to the moment of his execution; **мы танцева́ли в. до утра́** we danced till morning; **всё живо́е исче́зло, в. до крыс** every living thing had vanished, even the rats. **2. в.** (**к**+*d.*) right against, right up to; **толпа́ подошла́ в. к воро́там** the crowd came right up to the gates.
вплыва́|ть, ю *impf. of* **вплыть**
вплы|ть, ву́, вёшь, *past* **~л, ~ла́, ~́ло** *pf.* (*of* **~ва́ть**) to swim in; to sail in, steam in.
вперва́лку *adv.* (*coll.*) side by side (*in prone position; only of human beings*).
вполгла́за *adv.* (*coll.*): **спать в.** to sleep with one eye open.
вполго́лоса *adv.* in an undertone, under one's breath.
вполз|а́ть, а́ю *impf. of* **~ти́**
вполз|ти́, у́, ёшь, *past* **~, ~ла́** *pf.* (*of* **~а́ть**) to creep in, crawl in; to creep up, crawl up.
вполне́ *adv.* fully, entirely; quite; **э́то в. доста́точно** that is quite enough; **он в. знако́м с пра́вилами игры́** he is perfectly familiar with the rules of the game; **он в. понима́ет, в како́й он опа́сности** he is quite aware of his danger.
вполоборо́та *adv.* half-turned; (*of a portrait, etc.*) half-face.
вполови́ну *adv.* (*coll.*) by half; **за две неде́ли коли́чество прису́тствующих уменьши́лось в.** after two weeks the attendance had dropped by half.
вполпьяна́ *adv.* (*coll.*) half seas over.
впопа́д *adv.* (*coll.*) to the point; opportunely; **вы спроси́ли о́чень в.** your question was very much to the point.
впопыха́х *adv.* (*coll.*) **1.** in a hurry, hastily. **2.** in one's haste; **в. я оста́вил мой зо́нтик в по́езде** in my haste I left my umbrella on the train.
впо́ру *adv.* (*coll.*) **1.** at the right time, opportunely; **его́ прие́зд был о́чень в.** his arrival was very opportune. **2.** just right, exactly; **быть, прийти́сь в.** to fit; **э́тот костю́м мне соверше́нно в.** this suit fits me perfectly; **бе́дному да во́ру вся́кое пла́тье в.** (*prov.*) beggars cannot be choosers. **3.** *as pred.* it is possible; **так поступа́ть в. лишь дураку́** only a fool would behave like that; **тут в. двои́м спра́виться** there is enough work here for two.
впорхн|у́ть, у́, ёшь *pf.* (*of birds or butterflies*) to flit in(to), flutter in(to); (*fig.*) to fly (into).
впосле́дствии *adv.* subsequently; afterwards.
впотьма́х *adv.* (*coll.*) in the dark; (*fig.*) **броди́ть в.** to be in the dark.
впра́вду *adv.* (*coll.*) really, in reality.
впра́ве *as pred.*: **быть в.** (+*inf.*) to have a right (to); **он был в. серди́ться на вас** he had a right to be angry with you.
впра́в|ить, лю, ишь *pf.* (*of* **~ля́ть**) **1.** (*med.*) to set, reduce (*fractured or dislocated bone*). **2.** to tuck in (*shirt, trousers*).
впра́вк|а, и *f.* (*med.*) setting, reduction.
вправля́|ть, ю *impf. of* **впра́вить**
впра́во *adv.* (**от**+*g.*) to the right (of).
впредь *adv.* in future, henceforward; **в. до** until; **в. до конца́ ме́сяца** until the end of the month; **в. до распоряже́ния** until further notice.
впригля́дку *adv.* (*coll., joc.*) *only in phr.* **пить чай в.** to have tea without sugar.
вприку́ску *adv.* (*coll.*) *only in phr.* **пить чай в.** to drink unsweetened tea while holding a lump of sugar in the mouth (*opp.* **внакла́дку**).
вприпры́жку *adv.* (*coll.*) skipping; hopping.
вприся́дку *adv.*: **пляса́ть в.** to dance squatting.
впро́голодь *adv.* half-starving.
впрок *adv.* **1.** for future use; **загото́вить в.** to lay in, store; to preserve, put by; **загото́вить я́йца в.** to put down eggs. **2.** to advantage; **э́то не пойдёт ему́ в.** it will not profit him, he will do no good by it; **ху́до на́житое в. не идёт** (*prov.*) ill-gotten wealth never thrives.
впроса́к *adv.* (*coll.*): **попа́сть в.** to put one's foot into it.
впросо́нках *adv.* (*coll.*) half asleep.
впро́чем *adv. and conj.* **1.** however, but; **он у́мный челове́к, в. он ча́сто ошиба́ется** he is a clever man, but he often makes mistakes. **2.** (*expr. indecisiveness, revision of opinion*) or rather; **приезжа́йте за́втра, в. лу́чше бы́ло бы послеза́втра** come tomorrow, or rather, the day after would be better.
впры́гива|ть, ю *impf. of* **впры́гнуть**
впры́г|нуть, ну, нешь *pf.* (*of* **~ивать**) (**в, на**+*a.*) to jump (into, on).
впры́скивани|е, я *nt.* injection.
впры́скива|ть, ю *impf. of* **впры́снуть**
впры́сн|уть, у, ешь *pf.* (*of* **впры́скивать**) to inject.
впряга́|ть(ся), ю(сь) *impf. of* **впря́чь(ся)**
впрямь *adv.* (*coll.*) really, indeed.
впря|чь, гу́, жёшь, гу́т, *past* **впряг, ~гла́, ~гло́** *pf.* (*of* **~га́ть**) (**в**+*a.*) to harness (to), put (to).
впря́|чься, гу́сь, жёшься, гу́тся, *past* **впря́гся, ~гла́сь** *pf.* (*of* **~га́ться**) **1.** (**в**+*a.*) to harness o.s. (to). **2.** *pass. of* **~чь**
впуск, а *m.* admission, admittance.
впуска́|ть, ю *impf. of* **впусти́ть**
впускн|о́й *adj.* admittance; inlet; **~а́я труба́** inlet pipe.
впу́сте *adv.* (*obs.*) fallow; **лежа́ть в.** to lie fallow.
впу|сти́ть, щу́, ~́стишь *pf.* (*of* **~ска́ть**) to admit, let in.
впусту́ю *adv.* (*coll.*) for nothing, to no purpose.
впу́т|ать, аю *pf.* (*of* **~ывать**) to twist in; (*fig.*) to entangle, involve, implicate.
впу́т|аться, аюсь *pf.* (*of* **~ываться**) *pass. of* **~ать;** (*fig.*) to get mixed up (in).
впу́тыва|ть(ся), ю(сь) *impf. of* **впу́тать(ся)**
впу|щу́, ~́стишь *see* **~сти́ть**
впя́теро *adv.* five times; **в. бо́льше** five times as much.
впятеро́м *adv.* five (together); **в э́ту игру́ мо́жно игра́ть в.** five can play this game.
враг, а́ *m.* **1.** enemy; (*collect*) the enemy. **2.** (*obs.*) the Fiend, the Devil.
вражд|а́, ы́ *f.* enmity, hostility.
вражде́б|ный (~ен, ~на) *adj.* hostile.
вражд|ова́ть, у́ю *impf.* (**с**+*i. and* **ме́жду собо́ю**) to be at enmity, at odds (with).
вра́жеский *adj.* (*mil.*) enemy.
вра́ж|ий *adj.* (*folk poet.*) enemy; hostile; **~ья си́ла** (*obs.*) Satan, the Devil.
враз *adv.* (*coll.*) all together, simultaneously.
вразби́вку *adv.* (*coll.*) at random.
вразбро́д *adv.* (*coll.*) separately; in disunity.
вразбро́с *adv.* (*coll.*) separately; **се́ять в.** (*agric.*) to sow broadcast.
вразва́лку *adv.* (*coll.*): **ходи́ть в.** to waddle.
вразно́с *adv.* (*coll.*): **торгова́ть в.** to peddle.
вразре́з *adv., only in phr.* **идти́ в.** (**с**+ *i.*) to go against; **э́то идёт в. с мои́ми интере́сами** it goes against my own interests.
вразря́дку *adv.* (*typ.*): **набра́ть в.** to (letter-)space.
вразуми́тел|ьный (~ен, ~ьна) *adj.* **1.** intelligible; perspicuous. **2.** instructive.
вразум|и́ть, лю́, и́шь *pf.* (*of* **~ля́ть**) to teach, make understand; **ниче́м их не ~и́шь** they will never learn.
вразумля́|ть, ю *impf. of* **вразуми́ть**
вра́к|и, ~ *no sg.* (*coll.*) nonsense, rubbish.
врал|ь, я́ *m.* (*coll.*) liar; chatterbox.
вран|ьё, я́ *nt.* (*coll.*) lies; nonsense.
врасплох *adv.* unexpectedly, unaware; **заста́ть, захвати́ть, засти́гнуть в.** to take unawares.
врассыпну́ю *adv.* in all directions; helter-skelter.
враста́ни|е, я *nt.* growing in.
враст|а́ть, а́ю *impf.* (*of* **~и́**) to grow in(to); **~а́ющий но́готь** ingrowing nail.
враст|и́, у́, ёшь, *past* **врос, вросла́** *pf. of* **~а́ть**
врастя́жку *adv.* (*coll.*) **1.** at full length; **упа́сть в.** to fall flat. **2. говори́ть в.** to drawl.
врат|а́, ~ *no sg.* (*poet., obs.*) = **воро́та**
врата́р|ь, я́ *m.* **1.** (*sport*) goalkeeper. **2.** (*obs.*) gate-keeper.
вр|ать, у, ёшь, *past* **~ал, ~ала́, ~а́ло** *impf.* (*of* **на~** *and* **со~**) (*coll.*) **1.** to lie, tell lies. **2.** to talk nonsense.
врач, а́ *m.* doctor, physician; **де́тский в.** paediatrician; **зубно́й в.** dentist.

врачебный *adj.* medical.
врач|евать, ую *impf.* (*of* **у~**) (*obs.*) to doctor, treat; (*fig.*) to heal.
вращательный *adj.* rotary.
враща|ть, ю *impf.* to revolve, rotate; **в. глазами** to roll one's eyes.
враща|ться, юсь *impf.* to revolve, rotate (*intrans.*); **он ~ется в художественных кругах** he moves in artistic circles.
вращени|е, я *nt.* rotation; revolution.
вред, а *no pl.*, *m.* harm, hurt, injury; damage; **без ~а (для+g.)** without detriment (to).
вредител|ь, я *m.* **1.** (*agric.*) pest; vermin. **2.** (*pol.*) wrecker, saboteur.
вредитель|ский *adj. of* **~ 2.**
вредительств|о, а *nt.* **1.** wrecking, sabotage. **2.** act of sabotage.
вре|дить, жу, дишь *impf.* (*of* **по~**) (*+d.*) to injure, harm, hurt; **в. здоровью** to be injurious to health.
вредно *adv. as pred.* it is harmful, it is injurious; **в. для торговли** it is bad for trade.
вред|ный (~ен, ~на, ~но) *adj.* harmful, injurious; unhealthy.
вре|жу(сь), жешь(ся) *see* **~зать(ся)**
вре|жу, дишь *see* **~дить**
вре|зать, жу, жешь *pf.* (*of* **~зать**) to cut in; to set in, socket.
врез|ать, аю *impf. of* **~ать**
вре|заться, жусь, жешься *pf.* (*of* **~заться**) **(в+a.) 1.** to cut (into); to force one's way (into); **в. в землю** to dig into the ground; **в. в толпу** to run into a crowd. **2.** to be engraved (on); **черты её лица ~зались в его память** her features were engraved on his memory. **3.** (*pf. only*) (*coll.*) to fall in love (with).
врез|аться, аюсь *impf. of* **~аться**
врезыва|ть(ся), ю(сь) *impf.* = **врезать(ся)**
временами *adv.* at times, now and then, now and again.
временник, а *m.* chronicle, annals.
временной *adj.* **1.** (*phil.*) temporal. **2.** (*gram.*) tense. **3.** (*tech.*) time.
временн|ый *adj.* temporary; provisional; **В~ое правительство** (*hist.*) the Provisional Government (*of Russia, March–November 1917*); **~ое правительство** caretaker government; **~ое соглашение** interim agreement.
временщик, а *m.* (*coll.*) casual (worker); seasonal worker.
временщик, а *m.* (*hist.*) favourite (*enjoying position of trust or power*).
врем|я, ени, енем, ени, *pl.* **~ена, ~ён, ~енам** *nt.* **1.** time; times; **во в. оно** (*arch. or joc.*) in the old days; **в данное в.** at present, at the present moment; **в мирное в.** in peace-time **(в) первое в.** at first; **(в) последнее в.** lately, of late; **в своё в.** (*i*) (*in ref. to past*) in one's time, once, at one time, (*ii*) (*in ref. to future*) in due course; in one's own time; **в скором ~ени** in the near future, shortly, before long; **в то же (самое) в.** at the same time, on the other hand; **до поры до ~ени** for the time being; **за последнее в.** lately, of late; **на в.** for a while; **на первое в.** for the initial period, initially; **по среднеевропейскому ~ени** by Central European time; **с незапамятных ~ён** from time immemorial, time out of mind; **с течением ~ени** in the course of time; **всё в.** all the time, continually; **раньше ~ени** prematurely; **самое в.** (*+inf. or +d.*; *coll.*) just the time (to, for); the (right) time (to, for); **апрель — самое в. побывать в Париже** April is the (right) time to be in Paris; **сколько ~ени?** what is the time?; **тем ~енем** meanwhile. **2.: в. года** season. **3.** (*gram.*) tense. **4.: в то в. как** while, whereas. **5.: во в.** (*+g.*) during, in.
времяисчислени|е, я *nt.* calendar (*system of reckoning time*).
времянк|а, и *f.* **1.** small stove. **2.** step-ladder. **3.** temporary structure or fitting.
времяпрепровождени|е, я *nt.* way of spending one's time.
вретищ|е, а *nt.* (*obs.*) sackcloth.
врид, а *m.* (*abbr. of* **временно исполняющий должность**) acting (*director, manager, etc.*).
врио *m. indecl.* (*abbr. of* **временно исполняющий обязанности**) = **врид**
вровень *adv.* **(c+i.)** level (with); **в. с краями** to the brim.
вроде 1. *prep.+g.* like; **у него есть галстук в. моего** he has a tie like mine; **нечто в.** (*coll.*) a sort of, a kind of; **оркестр начал играть нечто в. фокстрота** the band began to play some sort of foxtrot. **2.** *particle* such as, like; **весь его разговор состоит из односложных слов в. «да» и «нет»** his entire conversation consists of monosyllables such as 'yes' and 'no'.
врождён|ный (~, ~а) *adj.* innate; congenital.
врознь *adv.* (*obs.*) = **врозь**
врозь *adv.* separately, apart.
вро|ю(сь), ~ешь(ся) *see* **врыть(ся)**
вруб, а *m.* (*mining*) cut.
вруб|ать(ся), аю(сь) *impf. of* **~ить(ся)**
вруб|ить, лю, ~ишь *pf.* (*of* **~ать**) to cut in(to).
вруб|иться, люсь, ~ишься *pf.* (*of* **~аться**) **(в+a.) 1.** to cut one's way (into), hack one's way (through). **2.** (*coll.*) to twig, cotton on.
врубов|ый *adj.*: **~ая машина** coal-cutter.
врукопашную *adv.* hand to hand; **схватиться в.** to come to grips.
врун, а *m.* (*coll.*) liar.
врун|ья, ьи *f. of* **~**
вруч|ать, аю *impf. of* **~ить**
вручени|е, я *nt.* handing, delivery; **в. солдату медали** investiture of a soldier with a medal; (*leg.*) service (*of summons, etc.*).
вруч|ить, у, ишь *pf.* (*of* **~ать**) to hand, deliver; to entrust; **в. судебную повестку** to serve a subpoena.
вручител|ь я *m.* bearer (*of message, writ, etc.*).
вручную *adv.* by hand.
врыва|ть, ю *impf. of* **врыть**
врыва|ться[1], юсь *impf. of* **врыться**
врыва|ться[2], юсь *impf. of* **ворваться**
вр|ыть, ою, оешь *pf.* (*of* **~ывать**) to dig in(to), bury (in).
вр|ыться, оюсь, оешься *pf.* (*of* **~ываться[1]**) to dig o.s. (into), bury o.s. (in).
вряд (ли) *adv. coll.* hardly, scarcely (*expr. doubt*); **в. ли стоит** it is hardly worth it; **в. ли они уже придут** they will scarcely come now.
вса|дить, жу, ~дишь, *pf.* (*of* **~живать**) **1.** to thrust, plunge (into); **в. нож в спину** (*+d.*) to stab in the back (*also fig.*); **в. пулю в лоб кому-н.** to put a bullet in s.o.'s brains. **2.** (*coll.*) to put, sink (into); **он ~дил весь свой капитал в одно рискованное предприятие** he has sunk all his capital in one doubtful venture.
всадник, а *m.* **1.** rider, horseman; **конкурный в.** showjumper. **2.** (*hist.*) knight.
всадниц|а, ы *f.* horsewoman.
всажива|ть, ю *impf. of* **всадить**
вса|жу, ~дишь *see* **~дить**
всамделишный *adj.* (*coll.*) real(-live), honest-to-goodness.
всасывани|е, я *nt.* suction; absorption.
всасыва|ть(ся), ю(сь), *impf. of* **всосать(ся)**
все... *comb. form* all-, omni-, pan-; most (*gracious etc.*).
всё 1. *pron. see* **весь. 2.** *adv.* always; all the time; **он в. отвечает одно и то же** he always gives the same answer; **он в. ругается** he swears all the time. **3. в. (ещё)** still; **дождь в. (ещё) идёт** it is still raining; **дождь в. (ещё) шёл** it kept on raining. **4.** (*coll.*) only, all; **он провалился на экзамене, — в. из-за тебя!** he has failed his examination — all because of you! **5.** *as conj.* however, nevertheless; **как ни стараюсь, в. не разбираю, что он говорит** however hard I try, I cannot make out what he says. **6.** *as particle* (*strengthening comp.*): **в. более и более** more and more; **он в. толстеет** he is getting fatter and fatter.
всеведени|е, я *nt.* omniscience.
всеведущий *adj.* omniscient.
всевидящий *adj.* all-seeing.
всевласти|е, я *nt.* absolute power.
всевластный *adj.* all-powerful.
всевобуч, а *m.* (*abbr. of* **всеобщее военное обучение**) universal military training.

всевозмо́жный *adj.* various; all kinds of; every possible; **в. това́р** goods of all kinds.
всево́лновый *adj.* (*radio*) all-wave.
Всевы́шний *adj.* (*relig.*) the Most High, the Almighty (*also as n.*).
всегда́ *adv.* always; **как в.** as ever.
всегда́шний *adj.* usual, customary, wonted.
всего́ *adv.* **1.** in all, all told; **в. упла́чено две ты́сячи рубле́й** in all two thousand roubles has been paid. **2.** only; **в.-на́всего** all in all; **нас бы́ло в. пя́теро** there were only five of us; **в. ничего́** (*coll.*) practically nothing; **то́лько и в.** (*coll.*) that's all. **3.** (*good*)bye!
вседержи́тел|ь, я *m.* (*relig.*) the Almighty.
вседне́вный *adj.* (*obs.*) daily, everyday.
вседозво́ленност|ь, и *f.* permissiveness; **о́бщество ~и** the permissive society.
всезна́йк|а, и *c.g.* (*coll., iron.*) know-all; smart Alec, clever Dick.
всезна́йств|о, а *nt.* (*coll., iron.*) knowingness; behaviour of a know-all.
вселе́ни|е, я *nt.* installation, quartering; moving in.
вселе́нн|ая, ой *no pl., f.* universe.
вселе́нский *adj.* universal; (*eccl.*) ecumenical; **в. собо́р** ecumenical council.
всел|и́ть, ю́, и́шь *pf.* (*of* **~я́ть**) **1.** to install, quarter (in) **2.** (*fig., rhet.*) to inspire (in); **в. страх** (**в**+*a.*) to strike fear (into).
всел|и́ться, ю́сь, и́шься *pf.* (*of* **~я́ться**) (**в**+*a.*) **1.** to move in(to). **2.** (*fig.*) to be implanted (in); to seize.
вселя́|ть(ся), ю(сь) *impf. of* **всели́ть(ся)**
всеме́рный *adj.* utmost, with all the means at one's disposal.
все́меро *adv.* seven times.
всеме́ро́м *adv.* seven (together).
всеми́лостивейший *adj.* (*hist.*) most gracious.
всеми́рный *adj.* world; world-wide.
всемогу́честв|о, а *nt.* omnipotence.
всемогу́щ|ий (~, ~а) *adj.* omnipotent, all-powerful; (*of God*) Almighty.
всенаро́дн|ый *adj.* national; nation-wide; **~ая пе́репись** general census.
всенаро́дно *adv.* **1.** throughout the nation. **2.** publicly.
всенижа́йший *adj.* most humble
все́нощн|ая, ой *f.* (*eccl.*) night service (vespers and matins).
всео́буч, а *m.* (*abbr. of* ***всео́бщее обуче́ние***) universal education.
всео́бщ|ий *adj.* general; universal; across-the-board; **~ая во́инская пови́нность** universal military service; **~ая забасто́вка** general strike.
всеобъе́млющ|ий (~, ~а) *adj.* all-embracing, comprehensive.
всеору́жи|е, я *nt. only in phr.* **во ~и** fully armed; **во ~и сведе́ний** in full possession of the facts.
всеохва́тный = **всеобъе́млющий**
всеплане́тный *adj.* global, worldwide.
всепоглоща́ющий *adj.* all-consuming (*also fig.*).
всепого́дный *adj.* all-weather.
всепо́дданейш|ий *adj.* (*obs.*) loyal, humble; **~ее проше́ние** humble petition.
всепожира́ющий *adj.* all-consuming.
всеросси́йский *adj.* All-Russian.
всерьёз *adv.* seriously, in earnest.
всесезо́нный *adj.* year-round.
всеси́л|ьный (~ен, ~ьна) *adj.* all-powerful.
всеславя́нский *adj.* pan-Slav(ic).
всесожже́ни|е, я *nt.* holocaust.
всесосло́вный *adj.* of all classes.
всесою́зный *adj.* All-Union (*with reference to former USSR, esp. in designations of institutions, associations, etc., as opposed to those of individual republics*).
всесторо́нний *adj.* all-round; thorough, detailed.
всё-таки *conj. and particle* for all that, still, all the same.
всеуслы́шани|е, я *nt. only in phr.* **во в.** publicly, for all to hear; **объяви́ть во в.** to announce publicly.
всеце́ло *adv.* completely; exclusively.
всеча́сный *adj.* (*obs.*) hourly.
всея́дный *adj.* omnivorous.
вска́кива|ть, ю *impf. of* **вскочи́ть**
вска́пыва|ть, ю *impf. of* **вскопа́ть**
вскара́бк|аться, аюсь *pf.* (*of* **кара́бкаться** *and* **~иваться**) (**на**+*a.*; *coll.*) to scramble (up, on to) clamber (up, on to).
вскара́бкива|ться, юсь *impf. of* **вскара́бкаться**
вска́рмлива|ть, ю *impf. of* **вскорми́ть**
вскачь *adv.* at a gallop.
вски́дыва|ть(ся), ю(сь) *impf. of* **вски́нуть(ся)**
вски́|нуть, ну, нешь *pf.* (*of* **~дывать**) to throw up; **в. на пле́чи** to shoulder; **в. глаза́** to look up suddenly.
вски́|нуться, нусь, нешься *pf.* (*of* **~дываться**) (**на**+*a.*; *coll.*) **1.** to leap up (on to). **2.** (*fig.*) to turn (on), go (for).
вскипа́|ть, ю *impf. of* **вскипе́ть**
вскип|е́ть, лю́, и́шь *pf.* (*of* **~а́ть**) **1.** to boil up. **2.** (*fig.*) to flare up, fly into a rage; **в. негодова́нием** to flare with indignation.
вскипя|ти́ть, чу́, ти́шь *pf. of* **кипяти́ть**
вскипя|ти́ться, чу́сь, ти́шься *pf.* **1.** *pass. of* **вскипяти́ть** **2.** (*coll.*) to flare up, fly into a rage.
всклоко́чен|ный (~, ~а) *p.p.p. of* **всклоко́чить** *and adj.* (*coll.*) dishevelled, tousled
всклоко́чива|ть, ю *impf. of* **всклоко́чить**
всклоко́ч|ить, у, ишь *pf.* (*of* **~ивать**) (*coll.*) to dishevel, tousle.
вскло́чива|ть, ю *impf. of* **вскло́чить**
вскло́ч|ить, у, ишь *pf.* (*of* **~ивать**) (*coll.*) to dishevel, tousle.
всколыхн|у́ть, у́, ёшь *pf.* to stir; to rock; (*fig.*) to stir up.
всколыхн|у́ться, у́сь, ёшься *pf.* to rock (*intrans.*); (*fig.*) to be roused.
вскользь *adv.* slightly; in passing; **упомяну́ть в.** to mention in passing.
вскопа́|ть, ю *pf.* (*of* **вска́пывать**) to dig up.
вско́ре *adv.* soon, shortly after.
вскорм|и́ть, лю́, ~ишь *pf.* (*of* **вска́рмливать**) to rear.
вскоч|и́ть, у́, ~ишь *pf.* (*of* **вска́кивать**) **1.** (**в, на**+*a.*, **с**+*g.*) to leap up (into, on to; from). **2.** (*coll.*) to come up (*of bumps, boils, etc.*). **3. в.** (**в копе́ечку**) (+*d.*; *coll.*) to cost dear.
вскри́кива|ть, ю *impf. of* **вскри́кнуть**
вскри́к|нуть, ну, нешь *pf.* (*of* **~ивать**) to cry out.
вскрич|а́ть, у́, и́шь *pf.* to exclaim.
вскро́|ю, ешь *see* **вскрыть**
вскруж|и́ть, у́, ~и́шь *pf. only in phr.* **в. го́лову кому́-н.** to turn s.o.'s head.
вскрыва́|ть(ся), ю(сь) *impf. of* **вскры́ть(ся)**
вскры́ти|е, я *nt.* **1.** opening, unsealing. **2.** (*fig.*) revelation, disclosure. **3.** (*geog.*) opening (*of rivers after break-up of ice*). **4.** (*med.*) lancing. **5.** autopsy; (*med.*) dissection; post-mortem (*examination*).
вскр|ыть, о́ю, о́ешь *pf.* (*of* **~ыва́ть**) **1.** to open, unseal. **2.** (*fig.*) to reveal, disclose; **в. ко́зыря** (*cards*) to turn up a trump. **3.** (*med.*) to lance, open. **4.** (*med.*) to dissect.
вскр|ы́ться, о́юсь, о́ешься *pf.* (*of* **~ыва́ться**) **1.** to come to light, be revealed. **2.** (*geog.*) to become clear (of ice; *of rivers*); become open. **3.** (*med.*) to break, burst.
всласть *adv.* (*coll.*) to one's heart's content.
вслед 1. *adv.* (**за**+*i.*) after; **посла́ть письмо́ в.** to forward a letter. **2.** *prep.*+*d.* after; **смотре́ть в.** to follow with one's eyes.
всле́дствие *prep.*+*g.* in consequence of, owing to; **в. дождя́ па́ртия в те́ннис не состоя́лась** owing to the rain the game of tennis did not take place.
вслепу́ю *adv.* **1.** blindly. **2.** blindfold; **печа́тать в.** to touch-type.
вслух *adv.* aloud.
вслу́ш|аться, аюсь *pf.* (*of* **~иваться**) (**в**+*a*) to listen attentively (to).
вслу́шива|ться, юсь *impf. of* **вслу́шаться**
всма́трива|ться, юсь *impf. of* **всмотре́ться**
всмотр|е́ться, ю́сь, ~ишься *pf.* (*of* **всма́триваться**) (**в**+*a*) to peer (at); to scrutinize.
всмя́тку *adv.*: **яйцо́ в.** soft-boiled, lightly-boiled egg; **сапоги́**

в. (*coll.*) nonsense; **все его́ мы́сли — про́сто сапоги́ в.** all his ideas are quite half-baked.
вс|ова́ть, ую́, уёшь *pf.* (*of* **~о́вывать**) (*coll.*) to put in, stick in; to slip in.
всо́выва|ть, ю *impf. of* **всова́ть** *and* **всу́нуть**
всос|а́ть, у́, ёшь *pf.* (*of* **вса́сывать**) to suck in; (*fig.*) to absorb, imbibe; **в. с молоко́м ма́тери** to imbibe with one's mother's milk.
всос|а́ться, у́сь, ёшься *pf.* (*of* **вса́сываться**) (**в**+*a.*) **1.** to fasten upon (*with mouth, lips, etc.*) **2.** to soak through (into).
вспа́ива|ть, ю *impf. of* **вспои́ть**
вспа́рива|ть, ю *impf. of* **вспа́рить**
вспа́р|ить, ю, ишь *pf.* (*of* **~ивать**) **1.** (*dial.*) to steam. **2.** (*coll.*) to put into a sweat. **3.** (*coll.*) to thrash.
вспа́рхива|ть, ю *impf. of* **вспорхну́ть**
вспа́рыва|ть, ю *impf. of* **вспоро́ть**
вспа|сть, ду́, дёшь, *past* **~л** *pf.* (*obs.*) *only in phrr.* **в. на ум, на мысль** (+*d.*) to occur to one.
вспа|ха́ть, шу́, ~́шешь *pf.* (*of* **~́хивать**) to plough up
вспа́хива|ть, ю *impf. of* **вспаха́ть**
вспа́шк|а, и *f.* ploughing.
вспаш|у́, ~́ешь *see* **вспаха́ть**
вспе́нива|ть(ся), ю(сь) *impf. of* **вспе́нить(ся)**
вспе́н|ить, ю, ишь *pf.* (*of* **~ивать**) to make foam, make froth, make lather; **в. коня́** get one's horse into a lather.
вспе́н|иться, юсь, ишься *pf.* (*of* **~иваться**) to froth; to lather (*intrans.*).
вспетуш|и́ться, у́сь, и́шься *pf. of* **петуши́ться**
всплакн|у́ть, у́, ёшь *pf.* to shed a few tears, have a little cry.
всплеск, а *m.* splash.
всплёскива|ть, ю *impf. of* **всплесну́ть**
всплес|ну́ть, ну́, нёшь *pf.* (*of* **~́кивать**) to splash; **в. рука́ми** to clasp one's hands (*under stress of emotion*).
всплыва́|ть, ю *impf. of* **всплыть**
всплы|ть, ву́, вёшь, *past* **~л, ~ла́, ~́ло** *pf.* (*of* **~ва́ть**) to rise to the surface, surface; (*fig.*) to come to light, be revealed; **~́ли но́вые све́дения об обстоя́тельствах уби́йства** new evidence has come to light about the circumstances of the murder; **э́тот вопро́с ~вёт вероя́тно на сле́дующем собра́нии** this question will probably come up at the next meeting.
вспо|и́ть, ю́, и́шь *pf.* (*of* **вспа́ивать**) to nurse; to rear; **в.-вскорми́ть** (*fig., coll.*) to bring up.
вспола́скива|ть, ю *impf. of* **всполосну́ть**
всполосн|у́ть, у́, ёшь *pf.* (*of* **вспола́скивать**) to rinse.
всполо́х, а *m.* (*obs.*) alarm.
всполо́х|и, ов *no sg.* **1.** (flashes of) summer lightning; (*collect.*) flashes, glow (*from fire, explosion, etc.*) **2.** (*dial.*) Northern lights.
всполош|и́ть, у́, и́шь *pf.* (*of* **полоши́ть**) (*coll.*) to rouse; to alarm.
всполош|и́ться, у́сь, и́шься *pf.* (*of* **полоши́ться**) (*coll.*) to take alarm.
вспомина́|ть(ся), ю(сь) *impf. of* **вспо́мнить(ся)**
вспо́м|нить, ню, нишь *pf.* (*of* **~ина́ть**) to remember, recall, recollect.
вспо́м|ниться[1], **нюсь, нишься** *pf.* (*of* **~ина́ться**) (*impers.,* +*d.*): **мне,** *etc.,* **~нилось** I, *etc.,* remembered.
вспо́мн|иться[2], **юсь, ишься** *pf.* (*obs.*) to collect o.s.
вспомога́тельн|ый *adj.* auxiliary; subsidiary, branch; **в. глаго́л** (*gram.*) auxiliary verb; **~ое обору́дование** (*comput.*) peripherals.
вспомоществова́ни|е, я *nt.* (*obs.*) relief, assistance.
вспомян|у́ть, у́, ~́ешь *pf.* (+*a. or* **о**+*p.*; *coll.*) to remember.
вспор|о́ть, ю́, ~́ешь *pf.* (*of* **вспа́рывать**) (*coll.*) to rip open.
вспорхн|у́ть, у́, ёшь *pf.* to take wing.
вспоте́|ть, ю *pf.* (*of* **поте́ть**) to come out in a sweat; to mist over (*of spectacles, etc.*).
вспры́гива|ть, ю *impf. of* **вспры́гнуть**
вспры́г|нуть, ну, нешь *pf.* (*of* **~ивать**) (**на**+*a.*) to jump up (on to), spring up (on to).
вспры́скивани|е, я *nt.* (*med.*) injection.
вспры́скива|ть, ю *impf. of* **вспры́снуть**
вспры́с|нуть, ну, нешь *pf.* (*of* **~кивать**) **1.** to sprinkle; (*fig., coll.*) to celebrate; **в. сде́лку** to wet a bargain. **2.** (*med.*) to inject.
вспу́гива|ть, ю *impf. of* **вспугну́ть**
вспуг|ну́ть, ну́, нёшь *pf.* (*of* **~́ивать**) to scare away; to put up (*birds*).
вспух|а́ть, а́ю *impf. of* **~́нуть**
вспу́х|нуть, ну, нешь *pf.* (*of* **~а́ть**) to swell up.
вспу́чива|ть, ю *impf. of* **вспу́чить**
вспу́ч|ить, у, ишь *pf.* (*of* **~ивать**) (*usu. impers.*) to distend; **у него́ живо́т ~ило** his abdomen is distended.
вспыл|и́ть, ю́, и́шь *pf.* to flare up; **в.** (**на**+*a.*) to fly into a rage (with).
вспы́льчив|ый (~, ~а) *adj.* hot-tempered; irascible.
вспы́хива|ть, ю *impf. of* **вспы́хнуть**
вспы́х|нуть, ну, нешь *pf.* (*of* **~ивать**) **1.** to burst into flames, blaze up; to flash out; (*fig.*) to flare up; to break out; **на грани́це ~нули бой** fighting flared up on the frontier. **2.** to blush.
вспы́шк|а, и *f.* flash; (*phot.*) flash (attachment); **электро́нная в.** flashgun; (*astron.*) flare; (*fig.*) outburst, burst; outbreak (*of epidemic, etc.*).
вспять *adv.* (*obs.*) back(wards).
встава́ни|е, я *nt.* rising; **почти́ть ~ем** to stand in honour (of).
вста|ва́ть, ю́, ёшь *impf. of* **~ть**
вста́в|ить, лю, ишь *pf.* (*of* **~ля́ть**) to put in, insert; **в. в ра́му** to frame; **в. себе́ зу́бы** to have a set of (false) teeth made; **в. шпо́ны** (*typ.*) to interline; **в. перо́** (+*d.*; *obs., vulg.*) to give the sack, give the boot.
вста́вк|а, и *f.* **1.** fixing, insertion; framing, mounting. **2.** inset. **3.** interpolation.
вставля́|ть, ю *impf. of* **вста́вить**
вставн|о́й *adj.* inserted; **~ы́е зу́бы** false teeth; **~ы́е ра́мы** double window-frames.
встарь *adv.* of old, in olden time(s).
встаскива|ть, ю *impf. of* **встащи́ть**
вста|ть, ну, нешь *pf.* (*of* **~ва́ть**) **1.** to get up, rise; to stand up; **он ра́но ~л сего́дня у́тром** he got up early this morning; **он вчера́ ~л впервы́е со дня несча́стного слу́чая** he got up yesterday for the first time since his accident; **в. с ле́вой ноги́** to get out of bed on the wrong side; **в. из-за стола́** to rise from table; (*fig.*) **в. на свои́ но́ги** to stand on one's own feet; **в. гру́дью за** (+*a.*) to stand up for. **2.** to stand; **в. на рабо́ту** to start work. **3.** (**в**+*a.*) to go (into), fit (into); **большо́й шкаф не ~нет в э́ту ко́мнату** the large cupboard will not go into this room. **4.** (*fig.*) to arise, come up; **тот же са́мый вопро́с ~л на про́шлом собра́нии** the same question arose at the last meeting. **5.** (*coll.*) to get out, get off (*means of conveyance*).
встащ|и́ть, у́, ~́ишь *pf.* (*of* **вста́скивать**) (*coll.*) to pull up.
встрева́|ть, ю *impf. of* **встрять**
встрево́жен|ный (~, ~на) *p.p.p. of* **встрево́жить** *and adj.* anxious.
встрево́ж|ить, у, ишь *pf. of* **трево́жить**
встрёпанный *p.p.p. and adj.* (*coll.*) dishevelled; **как в.** full of beans.
встреп|а́ть, лю́, ~́лешь *pf.* (*of* **~́ывать**) (*coll.*) to dishevel.
встрепен|у́ться, у́сь, ёшься *pf.* **1.** to rouse o.s., start (up). **2.** to begin to beat faster (*of heart*).
встрёпк|а, и *f.* (*coll.*) **1.** scolding. **2.** shock.
встрёпыва|ть, ю *impf. of* **встрепа́ть**
встре́|тить, чу, тишь *pf.* (*of* **~ча́ть**) **1.** to meet (with), encounter; **в. сопротивле́ние** to encounter resistance. **2.** to greet, receive; **в. аплодисме́нтами** to greet with cheers; **в. Но́вый год** to see the New Year in.
встре́|титься, чусь, тишься *pf.* (*of* **~ча́ться**) (**с**+*i.*) **1.** to meet (with), encounter, come across; **в. с затрудне́ниями** to encounter difficulties. **2.** to be found, occur.
встре́ч|а, и *f.* **1.** meeting, encounter; reception; **в. в верха́х** (*pol.*) summit; **в. выпускнико́в** old boys' *or* old girls' reunion; **в. Но́вого го́да** New Year's Eve party. **2.** (*sport*) match, meeting.
встреча́|ть, ю *impf. of* **встре́тить**
встреча́|ться, юсь *impf.* **1.** *impf. of* **встре́титься. 2.** *impf.*

only to be found, be met with; **в Шотла́ндии ещё ~ются ди́кие ко́шки** wild cats are still to be found in Scotland.
встре́чный *adj.* **1.** proceeding from opposite direction; oncoming; **в. ве́тер** head wind; **в. по́езд** oncoming train; *as n.* **пе́рвый в.** the first pers. you meet, anyone; **(ка́ждый) в. и попере́чный** every Tom, Dick, and Harry. **2.** counter; **в. иск** (*leg.*) counter-claim; **в. план** counter-plan; **в. бой** (*mil.*) encounter battle; (*naut.*) action on opposite courses.
встро́енн|ый *adj.* built-in; **~ые програ́ммы** (*comput.*) firmware.
вструхн|у́ть, у́, ёшь *pf.* (*coll.*) to be alarmed.
встря́ск|а, и *f.* (*coll.*) **1.** shaking; **он получи́л си́льную ~у** he has been badly shaken up, he has received a severe shock. **2.** real telling off.
встря|ть, ну, нешь *pf.* (*of* **встрева́ть**) (**в**+*a.*; *coll.*) to get mixed up (in); **в. в разгово́р** to butt in(to a conversation).
встря́хива|ть(ся), юсь *impf. of* **встряхну́ть(ся)**
встрях|ну́ть, ну́, нёшь *pf.* (*of* **∸ивать**) to shake; (*fig.*) to shake up, rouse.
встрях|ну́ться, ну́сь, нёшься *pf.* (*of* **∸иваться**) **1.** to shake o.s. **2.** (*fig.*) to rouse o.s.; to cheer up; **~ни́тесь!** pull yourself together. **3.** (*coll.*) to have a fling.
вступа́|ть(ся), ю(сь) *impf. of* **вступи́ть(ся)**
вступи́тельн|ый *adj.* introductory; **в. взнос** entrance fee; **~ая ле́кция** inaugural lecture.
вступ|и́ть, лю́, ∸ишь *pf.* (*of* **~а́ть**) **1.** (**в**+*a.*) to enter (into), join (in); **в. в бой** to join battle; **в. в де́йствие** to come into force; **в. в брак** to marry; **в. в свои́ права́** to come into one's own. **2.** (**на**+*a.*) to mount, go up; **в. на престо́л** to ascend the throne.
вступ|и́ться, лю́сь, ∸ишься *pf.* (*of* **~а́ться**) **1.** (**за**+*a.*) to stand up (for), take (s.o.'s) part. **2.** (*coll.*) to intervene.
вступле́ни|е, я *nt.* **1.** entry, joining. **2.** prelude, opening, introduction, preamble.
всу́е *adv.* (*obs.*) in vain; **призва́ть в. и́мя Бо́жье** to take the name of God in vain.
всу́н|уть, у, ешь *pf.* (*of* **всо́вывать**) to stick in; to slip in.
всухомя́тку *adv.* (*coll.*): **есть в.** to live on, eat cold food without liquids.
всу́чива|ть, ю *impf. of* **всучи́ть**
всуч|и́ть, у́, ∸ишь *pf.* (*of* **∸ивать**) **1.** to entwine. **2.** (+*d.*; *fig.*, *coll.*, *pej.*) to foist (on), palm off (on).
всхли́п|нуть, ну, нешь *pf.* (*of* **∸ывать**) to sob.
всхли́пывань|е, я *nt.* sobbing; sobs.
всхли́пыва|ть, ю *impf. of* **всхли́пнуть**
всхо|ди́ть, жу́, ∸дишь *impf. of* **взойти́**
всхо́д|ы, ов *no sg.* (cereal-)shoots.
всхо́жест|ь, и *f.* (*agric.*) germinating capacity.
всхо́жий *adj.* (*agric.*) capable of germinating.
всхрап|ну́ть, ну́, нёшь *pf.* **1.** *pf. of* **∸ывать. 2.** (*coll.*) to have a nap.
всхра́пыва|ть, ю *impf.* (*of* **всхрапну́ть**) to snore; to snort (*of a horse*).
всып|ать, лю, лешь *pf.* (*of* **~а́ть**) **1.** (**в**+*a.*) to pour (into). **2.** (+*d.*; *coll.*) to swear at; to beat; thrash, give what for; **в. по пе́рвое число́** to knock into the middle of next week.
всыпа́|ть, ю *impf. of* **всы́пать**
всы́пк|а, и *f.* rating; beating, drubbing.
всю́ду *adv.* everywhere.
вся *see* **весь**[1]
вся́к *short form* (*obs.*) *of* **∸ий;** *as pron.* (*obs.*) everyone.
вся́к|ий *adj.* **1.** any; **без ~ого сомне́ния** beyond any doubt; **во ~ом слу́чае** in any case, at any rate; *as pron.* anyone. **2.** all sorts of; every; **на в. слу́чай** against every eventuality; to be on the safe side; **тут мно́го ~их моше́нников** here are all sorts of rogues.
вся́чески *adv.* (*coll.*) in every way possible; **в. стара́ться** to try one's hardest, try all ways.
вся́ческ|ий *adj.* (*coll.*) all kinds of; **все и ~ие уло́вки** every sort and kind of trick.
вся́чин|а, ы *f.* (*coll.*): **вся́кая в.** all kinds of things; odds and ends.
вся́чинк|а, и *f.* (*coll.*): **жить со ~ой** to have one's up and downs.
Вт (*abbr. of* **ватт**) W, watt.

вта́йне *adv.* secretly, in secret.
вта́лкива|ть, ю *impf. of* **втолкну́ть**
вта́птыва|ть, ю *impf. of* **втопта́ть**
вта́скива|ть(ся), ю(сь) *impf. of* **втащи́ть(ся)**
втач|а́ть, а́ю *pf.* (*of* **∸ивать**) (**в**+*a.*) to stitch in(to).
вта́чива|ть, ю *impf. of* **втача́ть**
вта́чк|а, и *f.* **1.** stitching in. **2.** patch.
втащ|и́ть, у́, ∸ишь *pf.* (*of* **вта́скивать**) (**в**+*a.* **на**+*a.*) to drag (into, on to).
втащ|и́ться, у́сь ∸ишься *pf.* (*of* **вта́скиваться**) (*coll.*) to drag o.s.
втека́|ть, ю *impf. of* **втечь**
втёмную *adv.* without seeing one's cards; (*fig.*) blindly, in the dark; **де́йствовать в.** to take a leap in the dark.
втемя́ш|ить, у, ишь *pf.* (+*d.*; *coll.*) to impress (upon); **в. что-н. кому́-н. в башку́** to get sth. into s.o.'s skull.
втемя́ш|иться, усь, ишься *pf.* (+*d.*; *coll.*) to get into one's head.
втер|е́ть, вотру́, вотрёшь, *past* **∸,** **∸ла** *pf.* (*of* **втира́ть**) (**в**+*a.*) to rub in(to); **в. очки́ кому́-н.** (*fig.*, *coll.*) to bluff, pull the wool over s.o.'s eyes.
втер|е́ться, вотру́сь, вотрёшься, *past* **∸ся, ∸лась** *pf.* (*of* **втира́ться**) **1.** (**в**+*a.*; *coll.*) to insinuate *or* worm o.s. into; **ему́ удало́сь в. в дове́рие к премье́р-мини́стру** he succeeded in worming his way into the confidence of the Prime Minister. **2.** to sink in(to), soak in(to).
вте|са́ться, шу́сь, ∸шешься *pf.* (*of* **∸сываться**) (**в**+*a.*; *coll.*) to insinuate o.s. in(to), brazen one's way in(to).
втёсыва|ться, юсь *impf. of* **втеса́ться**
вте|чь, ку́, чёшь, ку́т, *past* **∸к, ~кла́** *pf.* (*of* **~ка́ть**) to flow in(to).
втира́ни|е, я *nt.* **1.** rubbing in. **2.** embrocation, liniment.
втира́|ть(ся), ю(сь) *impf. of* **втере́ть(ся)**
вти́скива|ть(ся), ю(сь) *impf. of* **вти́снуть(ся)**
вти́с|нуть, ну, нешь *pf.* (*of* **~кивать**) (**в**+*a.*) to squeeze in(to).
вти́с|нуться, нусь, нешься *pf.* (*of* **~киваться**) (*coll.*) to squeeze (o.s.) in(to).
втихомо́лку *adv.* (*coll.*) surreptitiously; on the quiet, on the sly.
втих|у́ю *adv.* (*coll.*) = **~омо́лку**
втолкн|у́ть, у́, ёшь *pf.* (*of* **вта́лкивать**) (**в**+*a.*; *coll.*) to push in(to), shove in(to).
втолк|ова́ть, у́ю *pf.* (*of* **~о́вывать**) (+*d.*; *coll.*) to din (into), ram (into).
втолко́выва|ть, ю *impf. of* **втолкова́ть**
втоп|та́ть, чу́, ∸чешь *pf.* (*of* **вта́птывать**) to trample in; **в. в грязь** (*fig.*) to drag in the mire.
вто́р|а, ы *f.* (*mus.*) second voice; second violin.
втора́чива|ть, ю *impf. of* **второчи́ть**
вторг|а́ться, а́юсь *impf. of* **∸нуться**
вто́рг|нуться, нусь, нешься, *past* **~ся, ~лась** *pf.* (*of* **~а́ться**) (**в**+*a.*) to invade; to encroach (upon), trespass (on), intrude (in) (*also fig.*).
вторже́ни|е, я *nt.* invasion; intrusion.
вто́р|ить, ю, ишь *impf.* (+*d.*) **1.** (*mus.*) to play, sing second part (to). **2.** (*fig.*, *pej.*) to echo, repeat; **он про́сто ~ит отцо́вским мне́ниям** he simply echoes his father's opinions.
втори́чн|ый *adj.* **1.** second; **~ое предупрежде́ние** second warning. **2.** secondary; **~ые половы́е при́знаки** secondary sexual characteristics.
вто́рник, а *m.* Tuesday.
вто́рни|чный *adj. of* **~к**
второбра́чный *adj.* (*obs.*) (born) of second marriage.
второго́дник, а *m.* pupil remaining in same form for second year.
Второзако́ни|е, я *nt.* (*bibl.*) Deuteronomy.
втор|о́й *adj.* **1.** second; **~а́я мо́лодость** second youth; **~а́я скри́пка** second violin; (*fig.*) second fiddle; **в. час** (it is) past one; **из ~ы́х рук** (at) second hand. **2.** *as n.* **~о́е, ~о́го** *nt.* main course (*of meal*). **3.** *as particle* **~о́е** (*coll.*) in the second place.
второкла́ссник, а *m.* second-form boy.
второкла́ссниц|а, ы *f.* second-form girl.

второкла́ссный *adj.* second-class; (*pejor*) second-rate.
второку́рсник, а *m.* second-year student.
второочередно́й *adj.* secondary.
второпя́х *adv.* **1.** hurriedly, in haste. **2.** in one's hurry.
второразря́дный *adj.* second-rate.
второсо́ртный *adj.* second-quality; inferior.
второстепе́нный *adj.* secondary; minor.
второч|и́ть, у́, и́шь *pf.* (*of* **втора́чивать**) to strap to one's saddle.
трав|и́ть, лю́, ⁓ишь *pf.* (*of* **⁓ливать**) (**в**+*a.*) to inveigle (into).
втра́влива|ть, ю *impf. of* **втрави́ть**
втре́ска|ться, юсь *pf.* (**в**+*a.*; *coll.*) to fall (for), fall in love (with).
в-тре́тьих *adv.* thirdly, in the third place.
втри́дешева *adv.* (*coll.*) three times as cheap; excessively cheaply; **прода́ть в.** to sell for a song.
втри́дорога *adv.* (*coll.*) triple the price; extremely dear(ly); **плати́ть в.** to pay through the nose.
втро́е *adv.* three times; treble.
втроём *adv.* three (together); **мы пое́хали в Ло́ндон в.** the three of us went to London.
втройне́ *adv.* three times as much, treble.
втуз, а *m.* (*abbr. of* ***вы́сшее техни́ческое уче́бное заведе́ние***) technical college.
вту́лк|а, и *f.* **1.** (*tech.*) bush. **2.** plug; bung.
вту́не *adv.* (*obs.*) in vain.
втык, а *m.* (*coll.*) dressing-down, rocket; **сде́лать в.** (+*d.*) to tear s.o. off a strip.
втыка́|ть, ю *impf. of* **воткну́ть**
вты́чк|а, и *f.* (*coll.*) **1.** sticking in. **2.** plug, bung.
втю́р|иться, юсь ишься *pf.* (**в**+*a.*; *coll.*) to fall in love (with).
втя́гива|ть(ся), ю(сь) *impf. of* **втяну́ть(ся)**
втяжно́й *adj.* (*tech.*) suction.
втя|ну́ть, ну́, ⁓нешь *pf.* (*of* **⁓гивать**) **1.** to draw (in, into, up), pull (in, into, up); to absorb, take in; **в. живо́т** to pull in one's stomach; **в. жи́дкость** to take in a liquid. **2.** (*fig.*) to draw (into), involve (in); **в. в спор** to draw into an argument.
втя|ну́ться, ну́сь, ⁓нешься *pf.* (*of* **⁓гиваться**) (**в**+*a.*) **1.** to draw (into), enter; **коло́нна ⁓ну́лась в уще́лье** the column entered the defile. **2.** (*of cheeks*) to sag, fall in. **3.** (*coll.*) to get accustomed (to), used (to); **вы ско́ро ⁓нетесь в рабо́ту** you will soon get used to the work. **4.** to become keen (on); **он о́чень ⁓ну́лся в игру́ в те́ннис** he has become very keen on tennis.
втя́па|ться, юсь *pf.* (**в**+*a.*; *coll.*) to get involved (in); to get into a mess.
вуале́тк|а, и *f.* veil.
вуали́р|овать, ую *impf.* (*of* **за⁓**) to veil, draw a veil (over).
вуа́л|ь, и *f.* veil.
вуз, а *m.* (*abbr. of* ***вы́сшее уче́бное заведе́ние***) institution of higher education.
ву́зов|ец, ца *m.* student (*at any institution of higher education*).
ву́зов|ка, ки *f. of* **⁓ец**
ву́з|овский *adj. of* **⁓**
вулка́н, а *m.* volcano; **де́йствующий, потýхший в.** active, extinct volcano; **жить (как) на ⁓е** (*fig.*) to be living on the edge of a volcano.
вулканиза́ци|я, и *f.* (*tech.*) vulcanization.
вулканизи́р|овать, ую *impf. and pf.* (*tech.*) to vulcanize.
вулкани́зм, а *m.* (*geol.*) vulcanism.
вулканиз|ова́ть, у́ю = ⁓и́ровать
вулкани́ческий *adj.* volcanic (*also fig.*).
вульгариза́тор, а *m.* vulgarizer.
вульгариза́ци|я, и *f.* vulgarization.
вульгаризи́р|овать, ую *impf. and pf.* to vulgarize.
вульгари́зм, а *m.* (*ling.*) vulgarism.
вульга́рност|ь, и *f.* vulgarity.
вульга́р|ный (⁓ен, ⁓на) *adj.* (*in var. senses*) vulgar; **в. маркси́зм** vulgar Marxism.
вундерки́нд, а *m.* infant prodigy.
вурдала́к, а *m.* werewolf; vampire.

вход, а *m.* **1.** entry. **2.** entrance.
вхо|ди́ть, жу́, ⁓дишь *impf. of* **войти́**
вход|но́й *adj. of* **⁓**; **⁓на́я пла́та** entrance fee.
вход|я́щий *pres. part. of* **⁓и́ть** *and adj.* incoming; **в. журна́л** book of entries; **в. у́гол** (*math.*) re-entrant angle; *as n.* **⁓я́щая, ⁓я́щей** *f.* incoming paper.
вхожде́ни|е, я *nt.* entry.
вхо́ж|ий (⁓, ⁓а) *adj.* (*coll.*): **быть ⁓им (в**+*a.*, **к)** to be (well) received (at); to be well in (with).
вхолосту́ю *adv.* (*tech.*): **рабо́тать в.** to run idle.
вцеп|и́ться, лю́сь, ⁓ишься *impf.* (*of* **⁓ля́ться**) (**в**+*a.*) to seize hold of (by).
вцепля́|ться, юсь *impf. of* **вцепи́ться**
вчера́ *adv.* yesterday; (*in past-tense narration*) the day before.
вчера́|шний *adj. of* **⁓**; **есть у вас ⁓шняя «Пра́вда»** have you yesterday's 'Pravda'?; **иска́ть ⁓шнего дня** to waste time on a hopeless quest.
вчерне́ *adv.* in rough; **я написа́л свою́ ле́кцию в.** I have made a rough draft of my lecture.
вчер|ти́ть, чу́, ⁓тишь *pf.* (*of* **⁓чивать**) (*math.*) to inscribe.
вче́рчива|ть, ю *impf. of* **вчерти́ть**
вче́тверо *adv.* four times; four times as much; **сложи́ть в.** to fold in four.
вчетверо́м *adv.* four (*together*).
в-четвёртых *adv.* fourthly, in the fourth place.
вчин|и́ть, ю́, и́шь *pf.* (*of* **⁓я́ть**) (*leg.*; *obs.*): **в. иск** to bring an action.
вчиня́|ть, ю *impf. of* **вчини́ть**
вчи́стую *adv.* (*coll.*, *obs.*) **1.** finally, definitively; **он был уво́лен в.** he was pensioned off. **2.** completely.
вчит|а́ться, а́юсь *pf.* (*of* **⁓ываться**) (**в**+*a.*) to get a grasp (of) (*a text*).
вчи́тыва|ться, юсь *impf.* **1.** *impf. of* **вчита́ться. 2.** *impf. only* to try to grasp the meaning (of).
вчу́же *adv.* disinterestedly, vicariously; **я в. любова́лся его́ успе́хом** his success gave me vicarious pleasure.
вше́стеро *adv.* six times; six times as much.
вшестеро́м *adv.* six (together).
вшива́|ть, ю *impf. of* **вшить**
вши́ве|ть, ю *impf.* (*of* **за⁓** *and* **обо⁓**) to become lice-ridden.
вши́вк|а, и *f.* (*coll.*) **1.** sewing in. **2.** patch.
вшивно́й *adj.* sewn-in.
вши́в|ый (⁓, ⁓а) *adj.* lousy, lice-ridden.
вширь *adv.* in breadth.
вшить, вошью́, вошьёшь *pf.* (*of* **вшива́ть**) (**в**+*a.*) to sew in(to).
въеда́|ться, юсь *impf. of* **въе́сться**
въе́длив|ый (⁓, ⁓а) *adj.* (*coll.*) corrosive; (*fig.*) acid; **⁓ое замеча́ние** acid remark; **в. челове́к** caustic pers.
въе́дчив|ый (⁓, ⁓а) *adj.* = **въе́дливый**
въезд, а *m.* **1.** entry; **«В. запрещён»** 'No entry'. **2.** entrance.
въезд|но́й *adj. of* **⁓**; **⁓на́я ви́за** entry visa.
въезжа́|ть, ю *impf. of* **въе́хать**
въе́|сться, мся, шься, стся, ди́мся, ди́тесь дя́тся, *past* **⁓лся** *pf.* (*of* **⁓да́ться**) (**в**+*a.*) to eat (into).
въе́|хать, ду, дешь *pf.* (*of* **⁓зжа́ть**) (**в**+*a.*) to enter, ride in(to), drive in(to); to ride, drive up; **в. в мо́рду, в ры́ло** (+*d.*; *vulg.*) to slap in the face.
въя́в|е *adv.* = **⁓ь**
въявь *adv.* (*obs.*) **1.** openly; **ви́деть в.** to see with one's own eyes. **2.** in reality; **и в. случи́лось так, как я сказа́л** it really did happen as I said.
вы, вас, вам, ва́ми, вас *pron.* (*pl. and formal mode of address to one pers.*) you; **быть на в.** (**с**+*i.*) to be on formal terms (with).
вы... *pref. indicating* **1.** motion outwards. **2.** action directed outwards. **3.** acquisition (*as outcome of a series of actions*). **4.** completion of a process.
выба́лтыва|ть, ю *impf. of* **вы́болтать**
выбега́|ть, ю *impf. of* **вы́бежать**
вы́бега|ться, юсь *pf.* **1.** (*coll.*) to wear o.s. out with running. **2.** to become sterile (*of livestock*).
вы́бе|жать, гу, жишь, гут *pf.* (*of* **⁓га́ть**) to run out.
вы́бел|ить, ю, ишь *pf. of* **бели́ть 3.**
вы́белк|а, и *f.* bleaching; whitening.

вы́бер|у, ешь *see* **вы́брать**
выбива́|ть(ся), ю(сь) *impf. of* **вы́бить(ся)**
выбира́|ть(ся), ю(сь) *impf. of* **вы́брать(ся)**
вы́б|ить, ью, ьешь *pf.* (*of* **~ива́ть**) **1.** to knock out; to dislodge; **в. из седла́** to unseat, unhorse; **в. из колей** (*fig.*) to unsettle, upset; **в. дурь из кого́-н.** to knock the nonsense out of s.o. **2.** to beat (clean); **в. ковёр** to beat a carpet. **3.** to beat; to stamp; to print (*fabrics*); **в. медь** to beat copper; **в. меда́ль** to strike a medal. **4.** to beat down; **град ~ил посе́вы** the hail had beaten down the crops. **5.** to beat out; to drum; **в. бараба́нную дробь** to beat a tattoo.
вы́б|иться, ьюсь, ьешься *pf.* (*of* **~ива́ться**) **1.** to get out; to break loose (from); **в. из колей** to go off the rails; **в. в лю́ди** to make one's way in the world; **в. из сил** to strain o.s. to breaking point; to wear o.s. out. **2.** to come out, show (*intrans.*; *usu. of hair, from under hat*).
вы́боин|а, ы *f.* **1.** rut, pot-hole. **2.** dent; groove.
вы́бойк|а, и *f.* **1.** beating (*of metals*). **2.** (*text.*) print.
вы́бойчатый *adj.* (*text.*) printed.
вы́болта|ть, ю *pf.* (*of* **выба́лтывать**) (*coll.*) to let out, blurt out.
вы́болта|ться, юсь *pf.* (*coll.*) **1.** to talk o.s. to a standstill. **2.** to talk (*to let out secrets*).
вы́бор, а *m.* **1.** choice; option. **2.** selection; assortment; **в э́том магази́не име́ется большо́й в. конфе́т** this shop has a large selection of sweets. **3.** (*pl. only*) election(s); **дополни́тельные ~ы** by-election.
вы́борк|а, и *f.* **1.** selection; sample. **2.** (*coll.*) excerpt.
вы́борност|ь, и *f.* appointment by election.
вы́борн|ый *adj.* **1.** elective. **2.** electoral; **в. бюллете́нь** ballot-paper. **3.** elected; *as n.* **в., ~ого** *m.* delegate.
вы́борочный *adj.* selective.
вы́борщик, а *m.* **1.** elector (*in indirect elections*); **колле́гия ~ов** electoral college. **2.** selector.
вы́бор|ы, ов *see* **~**
вы́бран|ить, ю, ишь *pf. of* **брани́ть**
выбра́сывател|ь, я *m.* ejector (*in firearms*).
выбра́сыва|ть(ся), ю(сь) *impf. of* **вы́бросить(ся)**
вы́б|рать, еру, ерешь *pf.* (*of* **~ира́ть**) **1.** to choose, select, pick out. **2.** to elect. **3.: в. пате́нт** (*leg.*) to take out a patent. **4.** to take (everything) out. **5.** (*naut.*) to haul in.
вы́б|раться, ерусь, ерешься *pf.* (*of* **~ира́ться**) **1.** to get out; **в. из затрудне́ний** to get out of a difficulty. **2.** to move (house). **3.** (*coll.*) to (manage to) get to; **несмотря́ на боле́знь мать всё-таки ~ралась в це́рковь** in spite of being ill mother managed to get to church.
выбрива́|ть(ся), ю(сь) *impf. of* **вы́брить(ся)**
вы́бр|ить, ею, еешь *pf.* (*of* **~ива́ть**) to shave.
вы́бр|иться, еюсь, еешься *pf.* (*of* **~ива́ться**) to shave, have a shave.
вы́бро|сить, шу, сишь *pf.* (*of* **выбра́сывать**) **1.** to throw out; **в. за́ борт** to throw overboard (*also fig.*); **в. на у́лицу** to throw on to the street. **2.** to reject, discard, throw away; **в. зря** to waste; **в. из головы́** to put out of one's head, dismiss. **3.** (*in var. senses*) to put out; **в. флаг** to hoist a flag; **в. ло́зунг** to put out, launch a slogan.
вы́бро|ситься, шусь, сишься *pf.* (*of* **выбра́сываться**) to throw o.s. out, leap out; (*naut.*) **в. на мель, на́ берег** to run aground; **в. с парашю́том из самолёта** to bale out of an aircraft.
вы́броск|а, и *f.* (*mil.*) (air)drop.
выбыва́ни|е, я *nt.* knock-out (*sports competition*).
выбыва́|ть, ю *impf. of* **вы́быть**
вы́быти|е, я *nt.* departure; **за ва́шим ~ем письмо́ бы́ло возвращено́ отправи́телю** in view of your having gone away the letter was returned to the sender.
вы́б|ыть, уду, удешь *pf.* (*of* **~ыва́ть**) (**из**) to leave, quit; **в. из стро́я** (*mil.*) (*i*) to leave the ranks (*ii*) to become a casualty.
выва́лива|ть(ся), ю(сь) *impf. of* **вы́валить(ся)**
вы́вал|ить, ю, ишь *pf.* (*of* **~ивать**) **1.** to throw out. **2.** (*coll.*) to pour out (*intrans.*; *of a crowd*).
вы́вал|иться, юсь, ишься *pf.* (*of* **~иваться**) to fall out, tumble out.
вы́валя|ть, ю *pf.* (*of* **валя́ть 2.**) to drag (in, through) (*mud, snow, etc.*).
вы́валя|ться, юсь *pf.* (**в**+*p.*) to get covered (*in mud, snow, etc.*).
выва́рива|ть, ю *impf. of* **вы́варить**
вы́вар|ить, ю, ишь *pf.* (*of* **~ивать**) **1.** to boil down; to extract by boiling; **в. соль из морско́й воды́** to extract salt from sea water. **2.** to boil thoroughly. **3.** to remove (*stains, etc.*) by boiling.
вы́варк|а, и *f.* decoction, extraction.
вы́вед|ать, аю *pf.* (*of* **~ывать**) to find out; **в. секре́т у кого́-н.** to worm a secret out of s.o.
выведе́ни|е, я *nt.* **1.** leading out, bringing out. **2.** deduction, conclusion. **3.** hatching (out); growing (*of plants*); breeding, raising. **4.** putting up, erection. **5.** getting out, removal (*of stains*); extermination (*of pests*).
вы́ведр|ить, ит *pf.* (*impers.*; *dial.*) to become fine, clear up (*of weather*).
выве́дыва|ть, ю *impf.* **1.** *impf. of* **вы́ведать**. **2.** *impf. only* to investigate, try to find out; **в. чьи-н. наме́рения** to sound out s.o.'s intentions.
вы́вез|ти, у, ешь, *past* **~, ~ла** *pf.* (*of* **вывози́ть**) **1.** to take out, remove; to bring out. **2.** (*econ.*) to export. **3.** (*coll.*) to save, rescue; **счастли́вый слу́чай ~ меня́** a lucky chance saved me. **4.: в. в свет** to bring out (into society).
вы́вер|ить, ю, ишь *pf.* (*of* **~я́ть**) to adjust; to regulate (*clocks and watches*).
вы́верк|а, и *f.* adjustment; regulation (*of clocks and watches*).
вы́вер|нуть, ну, нешь *pf.* (*of* **~тывать**) **1.** to unscrew; to pull out. **2.** (*coll.*) to twist, wrench. **3.** (*coll.*) to dislocate. **4.** to turn (inside) out.
вы́вер|нуться, нусь, нешься *pf.* (*of* **~тываться**) **1.** to come unscrewed. **2.** (*coll.*) to slip out. **3.** (*coll.*) to get out (of), extricate o.s. (from). **4.** (*coll.*) to appear, emerge (*from behind sth., from round a corner*). **5.** (*coll.*) to be dislocated.
вы́верт, а *m.* (*coll.*) **1.** caper; **танцева́ть с ~ами** to caper. **2.** mannerism; affectation; **челове́к с ~ом** eccentric.
вы́вер|теть, чу, тишь *pf.* (*coll.*) to unscrew.
вывёртыва|ть(ся), ю(сь) *impf. of* **вы́вернуть(ся)**
вывёрчива|ть, ю *impf. of* **вы́вертеть**
выверя́|ть, ю *impf. of* **вы́верить**
вы́ве|сить[1], шу, сишь *pf.* (*of* **~шивать**) **1.** to put up; to post up. **2.** to hang out (*linen, flags, etc.*).
вы́ве|сить[2], шу, сишь *pf.* (*of* **~шивать**) to weigh.
вы́веск|а, и *f.* **1.** sign, signboard. **2.** (*fig.*) screen, pretext; **он обману́л её под ~ой любе́зности** he deceived her under the mask of kindness. **3.** (*sl.*) mug (= *face*).
вы́ве|сти, ду, дешь, *past* **~л, ~ла** *pf.* (*of* **выводи́ть**) **1.** to lead out, bring out; **в. самолёт из што́пора** to pull an aeroplane out of a spin; **в. кого́-н. в лю́ди** to help s.o. on in life; **в. из заблужде́ния** to undeceive; **в. кого́-н. из себя́** to drive s.o. out of his wits; **в. из стро́я** to disable, put out of action (*also fig.*); **в. из терпе́ния** to exasperate; **в. кого́-н. на доро́гу** (*fig.*) to set s.o. on the right path; **в. на чи́стую во́ду** show up. **2.** to turn out, force out; **в. из соста́ва прези́диума** to remove from the presidium. **3.** to remove (*stains*); to exterminate (*pests*). **4.** to deduce, conclude. **5.** to hatch (out); to grow (*plants*); to breed, raise. **6.** to put up, erect. **7.** to depict, portray (*in a liter. work*). **8.** to write, draw, trace out painstakingly. **9.: в. балл, в. отме́тку** to give a mark.
вы́ве|стись, дусь, дешься *pf.* (*of* **выводи́ться**) **1.** to go out of use; to lapse. **2.** to disappear; to come out (*of stains*); to become extinct. **3.** to hatch out (*intrans.*).
выве́тривани|е, я *nt.* **1.** airing. **2.** (*geol.*) weathering.
выве́трива|ть(ся), ю(сь) *impf. of* **вы́ветрить(ся)**
вы́ветр|ить, ю, ишь *pf.* (*of* **~ивать**) **1.** to air; to ventilate; to remove (by ventilation); **в. дурно́й за́пах** to remove a bad smell. **2.** (*fig.*) to remove. **3.** (*impers.*; *geol.*) to weather.
вы́ветр|иться, юсь, ишься *pf.* (*of* **~иваться**) **1.** (*geol.*) to weather. **2.** to disappear (*by action of wind or fresh air*; *also fig.*); **в. из па́мяти** to be effaced from memory.
выве́шива|ть, ю *impf. of* **вы́весить**
вы́вин|тить, чу, тишь *pf.* (*of* **~чивать**) to unscrew.

вы́вин|титься, чусь, тишься *pf.* (*of* **~чиваться**) to come unscrewed.
выви́нчива|ть(ся), ю(сь) *impf. of* **вы́винтить(ся)**
вы́вих, а *m.* **1.** dislocation; dislocated part. **2.** (*fig.*, *coll.*) kink; oddity, quirk.
вывихива|ть, ю *impf. of* **вы́вихнуть**
вы́вих|нуть, ну, нешь *pf.* (*of* **~ивать**) to dislocate, put out (of joint); **он ~нул себе́ но́гу** he has dislocated his foot.
вы́вод, а *m.* **1.** deduction, conclusion. **2.** (*elec.*) outlet; leading-out wire. **3.** leading out, bringing out; **в. войск** withdrawal *or* pull-out of troops; **в. да́нных** (*comput.*) output. **4.** hatching (out); growing (*of plants*); breeding, raising.
выво|ди́ть(ся), жу́(сь), ~дишь(ся) *impf. of* **вы́вести(сь)**
вы́водк|а, и *f.* **1.** removal (*of stains.*) **2.** exercising (*of horses*).
выводно́й *adj.* **1.** (*tech.*) discharge. **2.** (*anat.*) excretory.
вы́вод|ок, ка *m.* brood (*also fig.*); hatch; litter.
выво|жу́[1], **~дишь** *see* **~ди́ть**
выво|жу́[2], **~зишь** *see* **~зи́ть**
вы́воз, а *m.* **1.** export. **2.** removal.
вы́во|зить, жу, зишь *pf.* (**в**+*p.*; *coll.*) to cover (*in mud, snow, etc.*).
выво|зи́ть, жу́, ~зишь *impf. of* **вы́везти**
вы́возк|а, и *f.* (*coll.*) carting out.
вывозно́й *adj.* export.
выволакива|ть, ю *impf. of* **вы́волочь**
вы́волочк|а, и *f.* (*coll.*) **1.** dragging out. **2.** beating. **3.** dressing-down.
вы́воло|чь, ку, чешь, кут, *past* **~к, ~кла** *pf.* (*of* **волакивать**) (*coll.*) to drag out.
вывора́чива|ть, ю *impf. of* **вы́воротить**
вы́воро|тить, чу, тишь *pf.* (*of* **вывора́чивать**) (*coll.*) **1.** to pull out, shake loose. **2.** to twist, wrench. **3.** to turn (inside) out. **4.** to overturn.
вы́гад|ать, аю *pf.* (*of* **~ывать**) to gain; to save, economize; **что вы ~али на э́том?** what did you gain by it?
выга́дыва|ть, ю *impf. of* **вы́гадать**
вы́гарк|и, ов *no sg.* slag.
вы́гиб, а *m.* curve; curvature.
выгиба́|ть(ся), ю(сь) *impf. of* **вы́гнуть(ся)**
вы́гла|дить, жу, дишь *pf. of* **гла́дить 1.**
вы́гля|деть[1], **жу, дишь** *pf.* (*coll.*) to discover; to spy out.
вы́гля|деть[2], **жу, дишь** *impf.* to look (like); **он ~дит о́чень молоды́м** he looks very young; **он ~дит грузи́ном** he looks like a Georgian; **она́ пло́хо ~дит** she does not look well.
выгля́дыва|ть, ю *impf. of* **вы́глянуть**
вы́гля|нуть, ну, нешь *pf.* (*of* **~дывать**) **1.** to look out. **2.** to peep out, emerge, become visible; **из-за туч ~нуло со́лнце** the sun peeped out from behind the clouds.
вы́г|нать, оню, онишь *pf.* (*of* **~оня́ть**) **1.** to drive out; to expel; **в. со слу́жбы** (*coll.*) to sack. **2.** to distil. **3.** (*coll.*) to make (*a sum of money, etc.*).
выгнива́|ть, ю *impf. of* **вы́гнить**
вы́гни|ть, ю, ешь *pf.* (*of* **~ва́ть**) to rot away; to rot at the core.
вы́гнут|ый (~, ~а) *p.p.p. of* **~ь** *and adj.* curved; convex.
вы́гн|уть, у, ешь *pf.* (*of* **выгиба́ть**) to bend; **в. спи́ну** to arch the back.
вы́гн|уться, усь, ешься *pf.* (*of* **выгиба́ться**) to bend (*intrans.*).
выгова́рива|ть, ю *impf.* **1.** *impf. of* **вы́говорить. 2.** *impf. only* (+*d.*; *coll.*) to reprimand, tell off.
вы́говор, а *m.* **1.** accent; pronunciation. **2.** reprimand; rebuke; dressing-down, ticking-off.
вы́говор|ить, ю, ишь *pf.* (*of* **выгова́ривать**) **1.** to articulate, speak. **2.** (*leg.*) to reserve; to stipulate; **в. себе́ пра́во расторже́ния контра́кта** to reserve the right of annulment of contract.
вы́говор|иться, юсь, ишься *pf.* (*coll.*) to speak out.
вы́год|а, ы *f.* advantage, benefit; profit, gain; interest.
вы́годно *adv.* **1.** advantageously. **2.** *as pred.* it is profitable, it pays.
вы́год|ный (~ен, ~на) *adj.* advantageous, beneficial; profitable.
вы́гон, а *m.* pasture; common.
вы́гонк|а, и *f.* distillation.
выгоня́|ть, ю *impf. of* **вы́гнать**
выгора́жива|ть, ю *impf. of* **вы́городить**
выгора́|ть, ет *impf. of* **вы́гореть**
вы́гор|еть[1], **ит** *pf.* (*of* **~а́ть**) **1.** to burn down, burn out (*intrans.*). **2.** to fade.
вы́гор|еть[2], **ит** *pf.* (*of* **~а́ть**) (*3rd pers. only or impers.*; *coll.*) to succeed, come off.
вы́горо|дить, жу, дишь *pf.* (*of* **выгора́живать**) **1.** to fence off. **2.** (*fig.*, *coll.*) to shield, screen.
вы́гравир|овать, ую *pf. of* **гравирова́ть**
выгра́нива|ть, ю *impf. of* **вы́гранить**
вы́гран|ить, ю, ишь *pf.* (*of* **~ивать**) (*tech.*) to cut (*crystal, glass*).
вы́греб[1], **а** *m.* **1.** raking out; clearing away. **2.** cesspool.
вы́гре|б[2] *see* **~сти**
выгреба́|ть, ю *impf. of* **вы́грести**
выгребн|о́й *adj.* refuse; **~а́я я́ма** cesspool.
вы́гре|сти[1], **бу, бешь,** *past* **~б, ~бла** *pf.* (*of* **~ба́ть**) to rake out; to clear away.
вы́гре|сти[2], **бу, бешь,** *past* **~б, ~бла** *pf.* (*of* **~ба́ть**) to row (out), pull (out).
выгружа́|ть(ся), ю(сь) *impf. of* **вы́грузить(ся)**
вы́гру|зить, жу, зишь *pf.* (*of* **~жа́ть**) to unload, unlade; to disembark.
вы́гру|зиться, жусь, зишься *pf.* (*of* **~жа́ться**) to disembark; (*mil.*) to detrain, debus.
вы́грузк|а, и *f.* unloading; disembarkation.
вы́грузчик, а *m.* unloader; stevedore.
выгрыза́|ть, ю *impf. of* **вы́грызть**
вы́грыз|ть, у, ешь, *past* **~, ~ла** *pf.* (*of* **~а́ть**) to gnaw out.
вы́гул, а *m.* **1.** range, pasture. **2.: в. соба́к** dog walking; **«Вы́гул соба́к запрещён»** 'Dogs must be kept on a leash'.
выгу́лива|ть, аю *impf. of* **вы́гулять**
вы́гуля|ть, ю *pf.* (*of* **выгу́ливать**) to walk (*a dog, etc.*).
выда|ва́ть(ся), ю́(сь), ёшь(ся) *impf. of* **вы́дать(ся)**
вы́дав|ить, лю, ишь *pf.* (*of* **~ливать**) **1.** to press out, squeeze out (*also fig.*); **в. улы́бку** to force a smile. **2.** to break, knock out.
выда́влива|ть, ю *impf. of* **вы́давить**
выда́ива|ть, ю *impf. of* **вы́доить**
выда́лблива|ть, ю *impf. of* **вы́долбить**
вы́дань|е, я *nt. only in phr.* (*coll.*, *obs.*) **на в.** marriageable.
вы́да|ть, м, шь, ст, дим, дите, дут *pf.* (*of* **~ва́ть**) **1.** to give (out), issue, produce; **в. ве́ксель** to draw a bill; **в. зарпла́ту** to pay out wages; **в. про́пуск** to issue a pass; **в. кого́-н. за́муж (за**+*a.*) to give s.o. in marriage (to); **в. на-гора́** (*tech.*) to hoist, wind (to the surface); **в. у́голь на-гора́** to produce coal. **2.** to give away, betray; to deliver up, extradite; **в. голово́й** to betray. **3. (за**+*a.*) to pass off (as), give out to be; **(себя́)** to pose (as); **в. себя́ за свяще́нника** to pose as a clergyman.
вы́да|ться, мся, шься, стся, димся, дитесь, дутся *pf.* (*of* **~ва́ться**) **1.** to protrude, project, jut out; (*fig.*) to stand out, be conspicuous. **2.** (*coll.*) to happen; **как то́лько ~лся хоро́ший денёк, мы пое́хали в дере́вню** on the first fine day that came along we went into the country.
вы́дач|а, и *f.* **1.** issuing. **2.** issue; payment. **3.** extradition.
выдаю́щийся *pres. part. of* **выдава́ться** *and adj.* prominent, salient; (*fig.*) eminent, outstanding; prominent.
выдвига́|ть(ся), ю(сь) *impf. of* **вы́двинуть(ся)**
выдвиже́н|ец, ца *m.* worker promoted to an administrative post.
выдвиже́ни|е, я *nt.* **1.** nomination. **2.** promotion, advancement.
выдвиже́н|ка, ки *f. of* **~ец**
выдвиже́нчеств|о, а *nt.* system of promotion of workers to positions of responsibility and authority.
выдвижно́й *adj.* sliding; (*tech.*) telescopic.
вы́дви|нуть, ну, нешь *pf.* (*of* **~га́ть**) **1.** to move out, pull out. **2.** (*fig.*) to bring forward, advance; **в. обвине́ние** to bring an accusation. **3.** to promote; **в. на до́лжность**

секретаря́ to promote to the post of secretary. **4.** to nominate, propose; **в. чью-н. кандидату́ру, кого́-н. в кандида́ты** to propose s.o. as candidate.
вы́дви|нуться, нусь, нешься *pf.* (*of* **~га́ться**) **1.** to move forward, move out; to slide in and out (*of a drawer, etc.*). **2.** to rise, get on (in the world). **3.** *pass. of* **~нуть**
вы́двор|ить, ю, ишь *pf.* (*of* **~я́ть**) (*coll. and leg.*; *obs.*) to evict; (*fig.*) to throw out.
выдворя́|ть, ю *impf. of* **вы́дворить**
вы́дел, а *m.* apportionment.
вы́дел|ать, аю *pf.* (*of* **~ывать**) **1.** to manufacture; to process. **2.** to dress, curry (*leather*).
выделе́ни|е, я *nt.* **1.** (*physiol.*) secretion; excretion. **2.** (*chem.*) isolation. **3.** apportionment.
выдели́тельный *adj.* (*physiol.*) secretory; excretory.
вы́дел|ить, ю, ишь *pf.* (*of* **~я́ть**) **1.** to pick out, single out; (*mil.*) to detach, detail; (*typ.*) **в. курси́вом** to italicize. **2.** to assign, earmark; to allot. **3.** (*physiol.*) to secrete; to excrete. **4.** (*chem.*) to isolate. **5.** to emit.
вы́дел|иться, юсь, ишься *pf.* (*of* **~я́ться**) **1.** to take one's share (*of a legacy*). **2.** (+*i.*) to stand out (for); to make a mark (by); **он ~ился остроу́мием** he was noted for his wit. **3.** to ooze out, exude. **4.** *pass. of* **~ить**
вы́делк|а, и *f.* **1.** manufacture. **2.** workmanship. **3.** dressing, currying.
выде́лыва|ть, ю *impf. of* **вы́делать; что ты тепе́рь ~ешь?** (*coll.*) what are you up to now?
выделя́|ть(ся), ю(сь) *impf. of* **вы́делить(ся)**
выдёргива|ть, ю *impf. of* **вы́дернуть**
вы́держанност|ь, и *f.* **1.** consistency. **2.** self-possession; firmness.
вы́держа|нный (~н, ~на) *p.p.p. of* **~ть** *and adj.* **1.** consistent; **~нная поли́тика** consistent policy. **2.** self-possessed; firm. **3.** mature; seasoned (*of wine, cheese, wood, etc.*)
вы́держ|ать, у, ишь *pf.* (*of* **~ивать**) **1.** to bear, hold; **лёд вас не ~ит** the ice will not hold you. **2.** (*fig.*) to bear, stand (up to), endure; to contain o.s.; **не в.** to give in, break down; **я не мог э́того бо́льше в.** I could stand it no longer; **ва́ши мне́ния не ~ат кри́тики** your opinions will not stand up to criticism; **выраже́ние лица́ у него́ бы́ло тако́е коми́чное, что я не ~ал** his expression was so funny that I could not contain myself. **3.: в. экза́мен** to pass an examination. **4.: в. не́сколько изда́ний** to run into several editions. **5.** to keep, lay up; to mature; to season. **6.: в. под аре́стом** to keep in custody. **7.** to maintain, sustain; **в. роль** to keep up a part, sustain an act; **в. хара́ктер** to stand firm; **в. па́узу** to pause.
выде́ржива|ть, ю *impf. of* **вы́держать**
вы́держк|а[1], **и** *f.* **1.** endurance; self-possession. **2.** (*phot.*) exposure.
вы́держк|а[2], **и** *f.* excerpt, quotation.
вы́дер|нуть, ну, нешь *pf.* (*of* **~гивать**) to pull out.
выдира́|ть, ю *impf. of* **вы́драть**[1]
выдира́|ться, юсь *impf. of* **вы́драться**
вы́до|ить, ю, ишь *pf.* (*of* **выда́ивать**) **1.** to milk (dry). **2.** to obtain (by milking).
вы́долб|ить, лю, ишь *pf.* (*of* **выда́лбливать**) **1.** to hollow out, gouge out. **2.** (*coll.*) to learn by rote.
вы́дох, а *m.* exhalation.
вы́дохн|уть, у, ешь *pf.* (*of* **выдыха́ть**) to breathe out.
вы́дохн|уться, усь, ешься *pf.* (*of* **выдыха́ться**) to have lost fragrance, smell; (*of wines, etc.*) to be flat; (*fig.*) to be past one's best, be played out.
вы́др|а, ы *f.* otter (*also fig., coll., of a thin, unattractive woman*).
вы́д|рать[1], **еру, ерешь** *pf.* (*of* **~ира́ть**) to tear out.
вы́д|рать[2], **еру, ерешь** *pf.* (*of* **драть 4.**) (*coll.*) to thrash, flog.
вы́д|раться, ерусь, ерешься *pf.* (*of* **~ира́ться**) (*coll.*) to extricate o.s.
вы́дрессир|овать, ую *pf. of* **дрессирова́ть**
вы́дуб|ить, лю, ишь *pf. of* **дуби́ть**
выдува́лк|а, и *f.* (soap) bubble blower.
выдува́льщик, а *m.* glass-blower.
выдува́|ть, ю *impf. of* **вы́дуть**
вы́дувк|а, и *f.* (*tech.*) (glass-)blowing.
выдувно́й *adj.* blown (*of glass*).
вы́думан|ный (~, ~а) *p.p.p. of* **вы́думать** *and adj.* made-up, fabricated; **~ная исто́рия** fabrication, fiction.
вы́дум|ать, аю *pf.* (*of* **~ывать**) to invent; to make up, fabricate; **он по́роха не ~ает** he will not set the Thames on fire; **не вы́думай напи́ться!** mind you don't get drunk!
вы́думк|а, и *f.* **1.** invention; idea (*discovery, device*); **голь на ~и хитра́** (*prov.*) necessity is the mother of invention. **2.** (*coll.*) inventiveness. **3.** (*coll.*) invention, fabrication (*lie*).
вы́думщик, а *m.* (*coll.*) **1.** inventor. **2.** fabricator (*liar*).
выду́мыва|ть, ю *impf. of* **вы́думать; не ~й** (*coll.*) don't argue; **де́лай то, что тебе́ ве́лено, а не ~й** do what you are told and don't argue.
вы́ду|ть, ю, ешь *pf.* (*of* **~ва́ть**) **1.** to blow out. **2.** (*impf.* **дуть**) (*tech.*) to blow. **3.: в. ого́нь** (*coll.*) to blow up a fire. **4.** (*impf.* **дуть**) (*coll.*) to drain, toss off (*drink*).
выдыха́ни|е, я *nt.* exhalation.
выдыха́|ть(ся), ю(сь) *impf. of* **вы́дохнуть(ся)**
выеда́|ть, ю *impf. of* **вы́есть**
вы́еденн|ый *p.p.p. of* **вы́есть; не сто́ит ~ого яйца́** it is not worth a brass farthing.
вы́езд, а *m.* **1.** departure. **2.** exit (*concr.*). **3.** (*obs.*) turn-out, equipage. **4.** (*obs.*) going out (*to balls, theatres, etc.*).
вы́ез|дить, жу, дишь *pf.* (*of* **~жа́ть**) to break(-in); to train (*horses*).
вы́ездк|а, и *f.* **1.** breaking-in; training (*of horses*). **2.** (*equestrian event*) dressage.
выезд|но́й *adj. of* **вы́езд; ~на́я се́ссия суда́** assizes; **в. матч** (*sport*) away match; **в. лаке́й** (*obs.*) footman; **~но́е пла́тье** (*obs.*) evening dress; party dress.
выезжа́|ть, ю *impf. of* **вы́ездить** *and* **вы́ехать**
вы́емк|а, и *f* **1.** taking out, collection (*of letters from letter-box*); **в. докуме́нтов** seizure of documents. **2.** excavation. **3.** hollow; groove; (*archit.*) fluting. **4.** (*rail.*) cutting. **5.** (*tailoring*) cut, cutting.
вы́е|сть, м, шь, ст, дим, дите, дят *pf.* (*of* **~да́ть**) to eat away; (*coll.*) to corrode.
вы́е|хать, ду, дешь *pf.* (*of* **~зжа́ть**) **1.** to go out, depart (*in or on a vehicle or on an animal*); to drive out; to ride out. **2.** to leave, move (*from dwelling-place*). **3.** (**на**+*p.*) (*fig., coll.*) to make use (of), exploit, take advantage (of).
выжа́рива|ть, ю *impf. of* **вы́жарить**
вы́жар|ить, ю, ишь *pf.* (*of* **~ивать**) (*coll.*) **1.** to heat up. **2.** to roast to a turn; to fry up.
вы́ж|ать[1], **му, мешь** *pf.* (*of* **~има́ть**) **1.** to press out, wring (out); to squeeze out; **в. после́дние си́лы из кого́-н.** to squeeze the last ounce of effort out of s.o.; **~атый лимо́н** (*fig.*) a has-been. **2.** (*sport*) to lift (*weights*).
вы́ж|ать[2], **ну, нешь** *pf.* (*of* **~ина́ть**) to reap clean.
вы́жд|ать, у, ешь *pf.* (*of* **выжида́ть**) (+*g.*) to wait (for); to bide one's time.
вы́ж|ечь, гу, жешь *pf.* (*of* **~ига́ть**) **1.** to burn down; to burn out; to scorch. **2.** (*med.*) to cauterize. **3.** to make a mark, etc., by burning; **в. клеймо́** (**на**+*p.*) to brand.
вы́жжен|ный *p.p.p. of* **вы́жечь** *and adj.* **~ная земля́** scorched earth.
выжива́ни|е, я *nt.* survival; **в. наибо́лее приспосо́бленных** (*biol.*) survival of the fittest.
выжива́|ть, ю *impf. of* **вы́жить**
вы́жиг|а, и *c.g.* (*coll.*) cunning rogue; skinflint.
выжига́ни|е, я *nt.* **1.** scorching; **в. по де́реву** poker-work. **2.** (*med.*) cauterization.
выжига́|ть, ю *impf. of* **вы́жечь; в. по де́реву** to do poker-work.
выжида́ни|е, я *nt.* waiting; temporizing.
выжида́тельн|ый *adj.* waiting; temporizing; **занима́ть ~ую пози́цию** to temporize, play a waiting game.
выжида́|ть, ю *impf. of* **вы́ждать**
вы́жим, а *m.* (*sport*) press-up.
выжима́л|а, ы *c.g.* (*sl.*) exploiter.
выжима́ни|е, я *nt.* **1.** squeezing; wringing. **2.** (*sport*) (weight-)lifting.
выжима́|ть, ю *impf. of* **вы́жать**[1]

вы́жимк|и, ов *no sg.* husks, marc; **льняны́е в.** linseed-cake.
выжина́|ть, ю *impf. of* **вы́жать**[2]
вы́жи|ть, ву, вешь *pf.* (*of* **~ва́ть**) **1.** to survive; to live through. **2.** (*coll.*) to live on in spite of sth., hold out, stick it out; **они́ три ме́сяца ~ли на плаву́чей льди́не** they stuck it out for three months on an ice-floe. **3.: в. из ума́** to lose possession of one's faculties. **4.** (*coll.*) to drive out, hound out; to get rid of.
вы́жлец, а *m.* (*hunting*) hound.
выжля́тник, а *m.* (*hunting*) whipper-in.
вызва́нива|ть, ю *impf. of* **вы́звонить**
вы́з|вать, ову, овешь *pf.* (*of* **~ыва́ть**) **1.** to call (out); to send for; **в. актёра** to call for an actor; **в. врача́** to call a doctor, send for a doctor; **в. ученика́** to call out a pupil; **в. по телефо́ну** to ring up; **в. в суд** (*leg.*) to summon(s), subpoena. **2.** to challenge; **в. на дуэ́ль** to challenge to a duel, call out; **в. на открове́нность** to draw out. **3.** to call forth, provoke; to cause; to stimulate, rouse; **в. любопы́тство** to provoke curiosity; **в. пожа́р** to cause a fire.
вы́з|ваться, овусь, овешься *pf.* (*of* **~ыва́ться**) (*+inf. or* **в**+*a.*) to volunteer; to offer; **в. помо́чь** to offer to help; **в. в экспеди́цию** to volunteer for an expedition.
вы́звезд|ить, ит *pf.* (*impers.*): **~ит, ~ило** the stars are (were) out; it is (was) a starlit night.
вы́звол|ить, ю, ишь *pf.* (*of* **~я́ть**) (*coll.*) to help out; **в. из беды́** to get out of trouble.
вызволя́|ть, ю *impf. of* **вы́зволить**
вы́звон|ить, ю, ишь *pf.* (*of* **вызва́нивать**) **1.** to ring (out) (*of bells*). **2.** (*fig.*) to ring, jingle.
выздора́влива|ть, ю *impf. of* **вы́здороветь**
вы́здорове|ть, ю, ешь *pf.* (*of* **выздора́вливать**) to recover, get better.
выздоровле́ни|е, я *nt.* recovery; convalescence.
вы́зов, а *m.* **1.** call; **в. по телефо́ну** telephone call. **2.** summons. **3.** challenge; **бро́сить в.** to throw down a challenge.
вы́золо|тить, чу, тишь *pf. of* **золоти́ть**
вы́золочен|ный (~, ~а) *p.p.p. of* **вы́золотить** *and adj.* gilt.
вызрева́|ть, ю *impf. of* **вы́зреть**
вы́зре|ть, ю, ешь *pf.* (*of* **~ва́ть**) to ripen.
вы́зубр|ить, ю, ишь *pf.* (*of* **зубри́ть**[2]) (*coll.*) to learn by heart.
вызыва́|ть(ся), ю(сь) *impf. of* **вы́звать(ся)**
вызыва́|ющий *pres. part. act. of* **~ть** *and adj.* defiant; provocative.
вы́игр|ать, аю *pf.* (*of* **~ывать**) to win; to gain; **в. вре́мя** to gain time; **он ~ал в моём мне́нии** he has gone up in my estimation.
выи́грыва|ть, ю *impf. of* **вы́играть**
вы́игрыш, а *m.* **1.** win; winning. **2.** gain, winnings; prize; **быть в ~е** to be winner; (*fig.*) to be the gainer; stand to gain.
вы́игрышн|ый *adj.* **1.** winning; **в. ход** winning move; **в. заём** premium bonds (issue); **в. биле́т** lottery ticket. **2.** advantageous; effective; **~ое положе́ние** advantageous position; **~ая нару́жность** winsome appearance.
вы́и|скать, щу, щешь *pf.* to light upon, track down, run to earth.
вы́и|скаться, щусь, щешься *pf.* (*coll., iron.*) to turn up, put in an appearance.
выи́скива|ть, ю *impf.* to seek out, try to trace.
вы́|йти, йду, йдешь, *past* **~шел, ~шла** *pf.* (*of* **~ходи́ть**) **1.** to go out; to come out; **она́ вчера́ ~шла в пе́рвый раз по́сле боле́зни** she went out yesterday for the first time since her illness; **в. в лю́ди** to get on in the world; **в. в отста́вку** to retire; **в. в офице́ры** to be commissioned, get a commission; **в. в тира́ж** (*of a bond, etc.; fin.*) to be drawn; (*fig.*) to take a back seat; **в. в фина́л** (*sport*) to reach the final; **в. из берего́в** to overflow its banks; **в. из бо́я** (*mil.*) to disengage; **в. из ваго́на** to alight from a carriage; **в. из во́зраста** to pass the age limit; **в. из головы́, из па́мяти, из ума́** (*coll.*) to go out of one's head; **в. из грани́ц** (*+g.*), **из преде́лов** (*+g.*) (*fig.*) to exceed the bounds (of); **в. из долго́в** to get out of debt; **в. из игры́** to go out of a game; **в. из положе́ния** to get out of a (tight) spot; **в. из себя́** to lose one's temper; **в. из терпе́ния** to lose patience; **в. на вы́зовы** (*theatr.*) to take a call; **в. на прогу́лку** to go out for a walk; **в. на сце́ну** to come on to the stage. **2. (в свет)** (*of publications*) to come out, appear. **3.** (*of photographs or persons photographed*) to come out; **вы хорошо́ ~шли на э́том сни́мке** you have come out well in this photo. **4.: в., в. за́муж (за**+*a.*) (*of a woman*) to marry. **5.** to come (out); to turn out (*also impers.*); to ensue; **не в.** (*+i. of n.; coll.*) to be lacking (in); **в. победи́телем** to come out victor; **из него́ ~шел бы хоро́ший лётчик** he would have made a good pilot; **из э́того куска́ мате́рии ~шла хоро́шенькая блу́зка** that piece of material has made a pretty blouse; **из э́того ничего́ не ~йдет** nothing will come of it; **~шло, (что) он ни одного́ сло́ва не по́нял** it turned out that he did not understand a single word; **как бы чего́ не ~шло** (*coll.*) it will come to no good; **ро́стом не ~шел** (*coll.*) he has not grown much; **умо́м не ~шел** (*coll.*) he is not too bright. **6.** to be by origin; **она́ ~шла из крестья́н** she is of peasant origin, comes of peasant stock. **7.** to be used up; (*of a period of time*) to have expired; **горчи́ца вся ~шла** the mustard is used up; **срок уже́ ~шел** time is up. **8.: года́ ~шли** (*+d. or g.; coll.*) (*i*) to be of age, (*ii*) to be over the age (for).
вы́ка|зать, жу, жешь *pf.* (*of* **~зывать**) (*coll.*) to manifest, display (*abstract qualities*).
выка́зыва|ть, ю *impf. of* **вы́казать**
выка́лива|ть, ю *impf. of* **вы́калить**
вы́кал|ить, ю, ишь *pf.* (*of* **~ивать**) (*tech.*) to fire.
выка́лыва|ть, ю *impf. of* **вы́колоть**
выка́пчива|ть, ю *impf. of* **вы́коптить**
выка́пыва|ть(ся), ю(сь) *impf. of* **вы́копать(ся)**
вы́карабк|аться, аюсь *pf.* (*of* **~иваться**) to scramble out; (*fig., coll.*) to get (o.s.) out; **в. из боле́зни** to get over an illness.
выкара́бкива|ться, юсь *impf. of* **вы́карабкаться**
выка́рмлива|ть, ю *impf. of* **вы́кормить**
вы́кат|ать, аю *pf.* (*of* **~ывать**[1]) **1.** to roll out. **2.** (*impf.* **ката́ть**) to smooth out; to mangle (*linen*). **3.** (*coll.*) to roll (in).
вы́кат|аться, аюсь *pf.* (*of* **~ываться**[1]) (*coll.*) **1.** *pass. of* **~ать. 2.** to roll (*intrans.*)
вы́ка|тить, чу, тишь *pf.* (*of* **~тывать**[2]) **1.** to roll out; to wheel out. **2.** (*coll.*) to come rolling out, come bowling out; (*fig.*) to hare out. **3.: в. глаза́** (*coll.*) to open one's eyes wide, stare.
вы́ка|титься, чусь, тишься *pf.* (*of* **~тываться**[2]) to roll out (*intrans.*).
вы́катк|а[1], **и** *f.* mangling.
вы́катк|а[2], **и** *f.* rolling out.
выка́тыва|ть(ся)[1], **ю(сь)** *impf. of* **вы́катать(ся)**
выка́тыва|ть(ся)[2], **ю(сь)** *impf. of* **вы́катить(ся); ~йся** (*coll.*) be off!; get out!
вы́ка|ть, ю *impf.* (*coll.*) to address formally, address as **'вы'**.
вы́кач|ать, аю *pf.* (*of* **~ивать**) to pump out; (*fig., coll.*) to extort.
выка́чива|ть, ю *impf. of* **вы́качать**
вы́качк|а, и *f.* pumping out; (*fig., coll.*) extortion.
выка́шива|ть, ю *impf. of* **вы́косить**
выка́шлива|ть(ся), ю(сь) *impf. of* **вы́кашлять(ся)**
вы́кашл|ять, яю *pf.* (*of* **~ивать**) to cough up.
вы́кашл|яться, яюсь *pf.* (*of* **~иваться**) to clear one's throat.
выки́дыва|ть, ю *impf. of* **вы́кинуть**
вы́кидыш, а *m.* (*med.*) **1.** miscarriage; abortion. **2.** foetus (*after miscarriage or abortion*).
вы́ки|нуть, ну, нешь *pf.* (*of* **~дывать**) **1.** to throw out, reject. **2.** to put out; **в. флаг** to hoist a flag. **3.** (*med.*) to have a miscarriage; to have an abortion. **4.** (*coll.*): **в. но́мер, штýку, фо́кус** to play a trick.
выкипа́|ть, ет *impf. of* **вы́кипеть**
вы́кип|еть, ит *pf.* (*of* **~а́ть**) to boil away.
вы́кипя|тить, чу, тишь *pf.* to boil out, boil through.

вы́кладк|а, и *f.* **1.** laying-out; lay-out. **2.** (*tech.*) facing; **в. кирпичо́м** bricking. **3.** (*mil.*) kit; **в по́лной ~е** in full marching order. **4.** (*math.*) computation.

выкла́дыва|ть, ю *impf. of* **вы́ложить**

вы́кл|евать, юю, юешь *pf.* (*of* **~ёвывать**) **1.** to peck out. **2.** to peck up.

вы́кл|еваться, ююсь, юешься *pf.* (*of* **~ёвываться**) to hatch out (*of birds*).

выклёвыва|ть(ся), ю(сь) *impf. of* **вы́клевать(ся); пока́ что ничего́ не ~ется** (*coll.*) at the moment nothing is happening, there are no bites.

выкле́ива|ть, ю *impf. of* **вы́клеить**

вы́кле|ить, ю, ишь *pf.* (*of* **∸ивать**) (*coll.*) to paste up; **в. обо́ями** to paper.

выклика́|ть, ю *impf. of* **вы́кликнуть**

вы́клик|нуть, ну, нешь *pf.* (*of* **~а́ть**) to call out; **в. по спи́ску** to call over the roll.

выключа́тел|ь, я *m.* switch; **шнуро́вой в.** pull-switch.

выключа́|ть, ю *impf. of* **вы́ключить**

вы́ключ|ить, у, ишь *pf.* (*of* **~а́ть**) **1.** to turn off, switch off. **2.** to remove, exclude; **в. кого́-н. из спи́ска** to take s.o.'s name off a list. **3.** (*typ.*) to justify.

выкля́нчива|ть, ю *impf.* **1.** *impf. of* **вы́клянчить. 2.** *impf. only* **в. что-н. у кого́-н.** to try to get sth. out of s.o.

вы́клянч|ить, у, ишь *pf.* (*of* **∸ ивать**) (**у**+*g.*; *coll.*) to cadge (from, off), get (out of).

вы́к|овать, ую, уешь *pf.* (*of* **~о́вывать**) to forge (*also fig.*).

выко́выва|ть, ю *impf. of* **вы́ковать**

выковы́рива|ть, ю *impf. of* **вы́ковырять**

вы́ковыр|ять, яю *pf.* (*of* **∸ивать**) to pluck out, pick out; (*coll.*) to hunt out.

выкола́чива|ть, ю *impf. of* **вы́колотить**

вы́коло|тить, чу, тишь *pf.* (*of* **выкола́чивать**) **1.** to knock out, beat out. **2.** to beat (*a carpet, etc.*). **3.** (*coll.*) to extort, wring out. **4.** (*coll.*) to make (money).

вы́кол|оть, ю, ешь *pf.* (*of* **выка́лывать**) **1.** to thrust out; **в. глаза́ кому́-н.** to put out s.o.'s eyes; **хоть глаз ~и,** *see* **глаз. 2.** to tattoo.

вы́колуп|ать, аю *pf.* (*of* **∸ывать**) (*coll.*) to pick out.

выколу́пыва|ть, ю *impf. of* **вы́колупать**

вы́копа|ть, ю *pf.* (*of* **выка́пывать**) **1.** to dig; **в. я́му** to dig a hole. **2.** (*impf. also* **копа́ть**) to dig up, dig out; to exhume; (*fig., coll.*) to unearth.

вы́копа|ться, юсь *pf.* (*of* **выка́пываться**) (*coll.*) to dig o.s. out.

вы́коп|тить, чу, тишь *pf.* (*of* **выка́пчивать**) to smoke (*trans.*).

вы́корм|ить, лю, ишь *pf.* (*of* **выка́рмливать**) to rear, bring up.

вы́корм|ок, ка *m.* (*coll.*) fosterling; (*fig.*) protégé; (*pejor*) creature.

вы́кормышь, а *m.* = **вы́кормок**

вы́корч|евать, ую *pf.* (*of* **~ёвывать**) to uproot; (*fig.*) to root out, extirpate.

выкорчёвыва|ть, ю *impf. of* **вы́корчевать**

вы́ко|сить, шу, сишь *pf.* (*of* **выка́шивать**) to mow clean.

выкра́дыва|ть(ся), ю(сь), *impf. of* **вы́красть(ся)**

выкра́ива|ть, ю *impf. of* **вы́кроить**

вы́кра|сить, шу, сишь *pf.* (*of* **∸шивать**) to paint; to dye.

вы́кра|сть, ду, дешь, *past* **~л** *pf.* (*of* **∸дывать**) to steal; (*fig.*) to plagiarize.

вы́кра|сться, дусь, дешься, *past* **~лся** *pf.* (*of* **∸дываться**) (*coll.*) to steal away, steal out.

выкра́шива|ть, ю *impf. of* **вы́красить**

вы́крест, а *m.* (*coll.*) convert (*to Christianity, esp. of Jews*).

вы́кре|стить, щу, стишь *pf.* (*coll.*) to convert (*to Christianity*).

вы́крик, а *m.* cry, shout; yell.

выкри́кива|ть, ю *impf. of* **вы́крикнуть**

вы́крик|нуть, ну, нешь *pf.* (*of* **∸ивать**) to cry out; to yell.

вы́кристаллиз|оваться, уюсь *pf.* (*of* **~о́вываться**) to crystallize (*also fig.*).

выкристаллизо́выва|ться, юсь *impf. of* **вы́кристаллизоваться**

вы́кро|ить, ю, ишь *pf.* (*of* **выкра́ивать**) **1.** (*tailoring*) to cut out. **2.** (*fig.*) to find; **в. вре́мя** to make, find time.

вы́кройк|а, и *f.* pattern; **снять ~у** to cut out a pattern.

выкрута́с|ы, ов *no sg.* (*coll.*) intricate movements, figures; flourishes (*in handwriting*); (*fig.*) peculiarities, idiosyncrasies; **говори́ть с ~ами** to speak affectedly; **челове́к с ~ами** eccentric.

вы́кру|тить, чу, тишь *pf.* (*of* **∸чивать**) **1.** to unscrew. **2.** (*tech.*) to twist; **в. верёвку** to twist a rope; (*coll.*) **ему́ ~тили ру́ку** they twisted his arm.

вы́кру|титься, чусь, тишься *pf.* (*of* **∸чиваться**) **1.** to come unscrewed. **2.** (*fig., coll.*) to extricate o.s., get o.s. out (of); **ему́ удало́сь в. из беды́** he has managed to get himself out of the mess.

выкру́чива|ть(ся), ю(сь) *impf. of* **вы́крутить(ся)**

выкувы́рива|ть, ю *impf. of* **вы́кувырнуть**

вы́кувыр|нуть, ну, нешь *pf.* (*of* **∸кивать**) (*coll.*) to overturn.

вы́куп, а *m.* **1.** (*leg.*) redemption. **2.** ransom; redemption-fee, redemption-dues.

вы́купа|ть(ся), ю(сь) *pf. of* **купа́ть(ся)**

выкуп|а́ть, а́ю *impf. of* **вы́купить**

вы́куп|ить, лю, ишь *pf.* (*of* **~а́ть**) **1.** to ransom. **2.** to redeem; **в. из-под зало́га** to get out of pawn.

выкупно́й *adj.* redemption.

выку́рива|ть, ю *impf. of* **вы́курить**

вы́кур|ить, ю, ишь *pf.* (*of* **∸ивать**) **1.** to smoke; to finish smoking; **пойдёмте, — но, пре́жде всего́, ~ите ва́шу папиро́су!** let's go, but first of all finish your cigarette. **2.** to smoke out; (*fig., coll.*) to drive out. **3.** to distil.

вы́ку|сить, шу, сишь *pf.* (*of* **∸сывать**) to bite through; **на́кось, ~си!** (*coll.*) you'll get nothing out of me!; you shan't have it!

выку́сыва|ть, ю *impf. of* **вы́кусить**

вы́куша|ть, ю *pf.* (*obs.*) to drink.

вы́ку|шу, сишь *see* **~сить**

вы́ку|ю, ешь *see* **вы́ковать**

выла́влива|ть, ю *impf. of* **вы́ловить**

вы́лаз, а *m.* (*coll.*) opening (*in animal's burrow, etc.*).

вы́ла|зить, жу, зишь *pf.* (*coll.*) to climb all over.

выла́|зить, жу, зишь *impf.* (*dial.*) to fall out, come out.

вы́лазк|а, и *f.* **1.** (*mil.*) sally, sortie (*also fig.*). **2.** ramble, excursion, outing.

вы́лака|ть, ю *pf.* (*of* **лака́ть**) to lap up.

выла́мыва|ть, ю *impf. of* **вы́ломать** *and* **вы́ломить**

выла́щива|ть, ю *impf. of* **вы́лощить**

вы́леж|ать, у, ишь *pf.* (*of* **∸ивать**) (*coll.*) to remain lying down; to stay in bed, keep one's bed.

вы́леж|аться, усь, ишься *pf.* (*of* **∸иваться**) (*coll.*) **1.** to have a thorough rest. **2.** to ripen; to mature (*of tobacco, etc.*).

вылёжива|ть(ся), ю(сь) *impf. of* **вы́лежать(ся)**

вылеза́|ть, ю *impf. of* **вы́лезть**

вы́лезт|и = ~ь

вы́лез|ть, у, ешь, *past* **~, ~ла** *pf.* (*of* **~а́ть**) **1.** to crawl out; to climb out; (*coll.*) to get out, alight. **2.** to fall out, come out; **по́сле боле́зни у него́ ~ли почти́ все во́лосы** almost all his hair fell out after his illness. **3.** (**с**+*i.*; *coll., pej.*) to come out with; **он, должно́ быть, ~ет с каки́м-н. глу́пым замеча́нием** he is sure to come out with some fatuous remark.

вы́леп|ить, лю, ишь *pf. of* **лепи́ть**

вы́лет, а *m.* flight (*of birds*); (*aeron.*) take-off; commencement of flight; sortie; **зал ~а** departure lounge.

вылета́|ть, ю *impf. of* **вы́лететь**

вы́ле|теть, чу, тишь *pf.* (*of* **~та́ть**) **1.** to fly out; (*aeron.*) to take off; (*fig., coll.*) to rush out, dash out; **в. пу́лей** to go like a shot from a gun; **не дожда́вшись отве́та, он ~тел из ко́мнаты** without waiting for an answer he rushed from the room; **в. из головы́** to escape one; **его́ сообще́ние ~тело у меня́ из головы́** I clean forgot his message; **в. в трубу́** (*coll.*) to become bankrupt, go broke. **2.: в. со слу́жбы** (*fig., coll.*) to be given the sack.

выле́чива|ть(ся), ю(сь) *impf. of* **вы́лечить(ся)**

вы́леч|ить, у, ишь *pf.* (*of* **∸ивать**) (**от**) to cure (of) (*also fig.*)

вы́леч|иться, усь, ишься *pf.* (*of* **∸иваться**) (**от**) to

recover (from), be cured (of); to get over (*also fig.*); **он ~ился от нарко́мании** he has been cured of his drug-addiction.
вы́леч|у[1], **ишь** *see* **~ить**
вы́ле|чу[2], **тишь** *see* **~теть**
вылива́|ть(ся), ю(сь) *impf. of* **вы́лить(ся)**
вы́ли|зать, жу, жешь *pf.* (*of* **~зывать**) to lick clean, lick up.
выли́зыва|ть, ю *impf. of* **вы́лизать**
вы́линя|ть, ю *pf. of* **линя́ть**
вы́лит|ый (~, ~а) *p.p.p. of* **~ь**; (*fig., coll.; long form only*) **он — в. оте́ц** he is the spitting image of his father.
вы́л|ить, ью, ьешь *pf.* (*of* **~ива́ть**) **1.** to pour out; to empty (out). **2.** (*tech.*) to cast, found; to mould.
вы́л|иться, ьюсь, ьешься *pf.* (*of* **~ива́ться**) **1.** to run out, flow out; (*fig.*) to flow (from), spring (from); **её жа́лобы ~ились пря́мо из се́рдца** her complaints came straight from the heart. **2.** (**в**+*a. or* **в фо́рму** +*g.*) to take the form (of); to be expressed, express itself (in); **никто́ не знал, во что ~ьется его́ восто́рг** no one knows how his feeling of delight would express itself.
вы́лов|ить, лю, ишь *pf.* (*of* **выла́вливать**) **1.** to fish out; **уто́пленника наконе́ц ~или из реки́** the drowned man has at last been fished out of the river. **2.** to draw out (*catch all the fish in a stream, etc.*) **в. всю ры́бу в пруду́** to draw out a pond.
вы́лож|ить, у, ишь *pf.* (*of* **выкла́дывать**) **1.** to lay out, spread out; (*fig., coll.*) to tell; to reveal, make an exposé (of). **2.** (+*i.*) to cover, lay (with); **в. дёрном** to turf; **в. ка́мнем** to face with masonry, revet; (*tailoring*) to decorate, embellish (with). **3.** (*dial.*) to geld.
вы́лом, а *m.* **1.** breaking open; breaking off. **2.** breach.
вы́лома|ть, ю *pf.* (*of* **выла́мывать**) to break open; to break off.
вы́лом|ить, лю, ишь *pf.* (*coll.*) = **вы́ломать**
вы́ломк|а, и *f.* breaking off.
вы́лощен|ный (~, ~а) *p.p.p. of* **вы́лощить** *and adj.* **1.** glossy. **2.** (*coll., fig.*) polished, smooth.
вы́лощ|ить, у, ишь *pf.* (*of* **выла́щивать**) to polish; (*fig., coll.*) to make polished, sophisticated.
вы́лу|дить, жу, дишь *pf.* (*of* **~живать**) to tin(-plate).
выл́ужива|ть, ю *impf. of* **вы́лудить**
вы́лу|жу, дишь *see* **~дить**
вы́луп|ить, лю, ишь *pf.* (*of* **~ля́ть**) (*coll.*) to peel; to shell; **в. глаза́** to goggle.
вы́луп|иться, люсь, ишься *pf.* (*of* **~ля́ться**) to hatch (out); **не счита́й утя́т, пока́ не ~ились** (*prov.*) don't count your chickens before they are hatched.
вылупля́|ть(ся), ю(сь) *impf. of* **вы́лупить(ся)**
вылу́щива|ть, ю *impf. of* **вы́лущить**
вы́лущ|ить, у, ишь *pf.* (*of* **~ивать**) **1.** to shell (peas). **2.** (*med.*) to remove (*by surgical operation*).
вы́л|ью, ьешь *see* **~ить**
вы́ма|зать, жу, жешь *pf.* (*of* **ма́зать 2.** *and* **~зывать**) (+*i.*) to smear (with), daub (with); (*coll.*) to dirty; **в. свои па́льцы в черни́лах** to make one's fingers inky.
вы́ма|заться, жусь, жешься *pf.* (*of* **ма́заться 1.** *and* **~зываться**) (*coll.*) to get dirty, make o.s. dirty.
выма́зыва|ть(ся), ю(сь) *impf. of* **вы́мазать(ся)**
выма́лива|ть, ю *impf.* **1.** *impf. of* **вы́молить. 2.** *impf. only* to beg for.
выма́лыва|ть, ю *impf. of* **вы́молоть**
выма́нива|ть, ю *impf. of* **вы́манить**
вы́ман|ить, ю, ишь *pf.* (*of* **~ивать**) **1.** (**у**+*g.*) to cheat, swindle (out of); to wheedle (out of); **у него́ ~или поже́ртвование** they wheedled a contribution out of him. **2.** (**из**+*g.*) to entice (from), lure (out of, from).
вы́мар|ать, аю *pf.* (*of* **~ывать**) (*coll.*) **1.** to soil, dirty. **2.** to strike out, cross out.
выма́рива|ть, ю *impf. of* **вы́морить**
вы́марк|а, и *f.* striking out, crossing out, deletion.
выма́рыва|ть, ю *impf. of* **вы́марать**
выма́тыва|ть(ся), ю(сь) *impf. of* **вы́мотать(ся)**
вы́махн|уть, у, ешь *pf.* (*coll.*) to fly out; to leap out.
выма́чива|ть, ю *impf. of* **вы́мочить**
выма́щива|ть, ю *impf. of* **вы́мостить**
вы́межева|ть, ю *pf.* (*of* **вымежёвывать**) (*agric.*) to measure out (*strips of land*).
вымежёвыва|ть, ю *impf. of* **вы́межевать**
вы́м|ени, енем *see* **~я**
выме́нива|ть, ю *impf. of* **вы́менять**
вы́мен|ять, яю *pf.* (*of* **~ивать**) (**на**+*a.*) to receive in exchange, barter (for); **в. проду́кты на оде́жду** to barter produce for clothing.
вы́м|ереть, ру, решь, *past* **~ер, ~ерла** *pf.* (*of* **~ира́ть**) **1.** to die out, become extinct. **2.** to become desolate, deserted.
вымерз|а́ть, а́ю *impf. of* **вы́мерзнуть**
вы́мерз|нуть, ну, нешь, *past* **~, ~ла** *pf.* (*of* **~а́ть**) **1.** to be killed by frost. **2.** to freeze (right through).
выме́рива|ть, ю *impf. of* **вы́мерить**
вы́мер|ить, ю, ишь *pf.* (*of* **~ивать**) to measure.
вы́мер|ший *p.p. of* **~еть** *and adj.* extinct.
вы́меря|ть, ю = **вы́мерить**
вымеря́|ть, ю = **выме́ривать**
вы́ме|сти, ту, тешь, *past* **~л** *pf.* (*of* **~та́ть**) **1.** to sweep out; to sweep clean; **в. сор** to sweep out refuse; **в. ко́мнату** to sweep a room clean. **2.** (*coll.*) to throw out, chuck out.
вы́ме|стить, щу, стишь *pf.* (*of* **~ща́ть**) **1.** (+*d.*; *obs.*) to retaliate, take reprisals (against). **2.** (**на**+*p.*) to vent; **в. зло́бу на ком-н.** to vent one's anger on s.o.
вы́мет|ать[1], **аю** *pf.* (*of* **~ывать**) **1.** to put out, cast out (*a net, etc.*). **2.**: **в. икру́** to spawn.
вы́мет|ать[2], **аю** *pf.* (*of* **~ывать**) **в. пе́тли** to make buttonholes.
вымета́|ть, ю *impf. of* **вы́мести**
вымета́|ться, юсь *impf.* (*coll.*) to clear out, clear off (*intrans.*).
вымётыва|ть, ю *impf. of* **вы́метать**
вымеща́|ть, ю *impf. of* **вы́местить**
вы́ме|щу, стишь *see* **~стить**
вымина́|ть, ю *impf. of* **вы́мять**
вымира́|ть, ю *impf. of* **вы́мереть**
вы́м|ну, нешь *see* **~ять**
вымога́тел|ь, я *m.* extortioner.
вымога́тельский *adj.* extortionate.
вымога́тельств|о, а *nt.* extortion.
вымога́|ть, ю *impf.* to extort; to wring (out); **угро́зами он нере́дко ~л у неё обеща́ния** he frequently wrung promises out of her by means of threats.
вы́моин|а, ы *f.* (*dial.*) gully.
вымока́|ть, ю *impf. of* **вы́мокнуть**
вы́мок|нуть, ну, нешь, *past* **~, ~ла** *pf.* (*of* **~а́ть**) **1.** (*of crops, foodstuffs, etc.*) to rot, ret; to become soggy. **2.** to be drenched, be soaked; **мы ~ли до ни́тки** we are soaked to the skin.
вымола́чива|ть, ю *impf. of* **вы́молотить**
вы́молв|ить, лю, ишь *pf.* to say, utter (*usu. with neg.*); **за весь ве́чер он сло́ва не ~ил** he did not say a word all evening.
вы́мол|ить, ю, ишь *pf.* (*of* **выма́ливать**) to obtain by asking, by entreaties; to beg (for) and obtain; **(у Бо́га)** to obtain by prayer.
вы́молот, а *m.* **1.** threshing. **2.** grain (obtained by threshing).
вы́моло|тить, чу, тишь *pf.* (*of* **вымола́чивать**) to thresh (out).
вы́молот|ки, ок-ков *no sg.* (*dial.*) chaff.
вы́м|олоть, елю, елешь *pf.* (*of* **выма́лывать**) (*coll.*) to obtain by grinding.
вымора́жива|ть, ю *impf. of* **вы́морозить**
вы́мор|ить, ю, ишь *pf.* (*of* **мори́ть**[1] *and* **выма́ривать**) to exterminate; **го́лодом в.** to starve out.
вы́моро|зить, жу, зишь *pf.* (*of* **вымора́живать**) **1.** to cool; to air, give an airing (to). **2.** to freeze out; to freeze to death (*trans.*).
вы́морочн|ый *adj.* (*leg.*) escheated; **~ое иму́щество** escheat.
вы́мо|стить, щу, стишь *pf.* (*of* **мости́ть** *and* **выма́щивать**) to pave.

вы́мота|ть, ю *pf.* (*of* **выма́тывать**) (*coll.*) **1.** to wind (*wool*). **2.** to wind off, use up (*wool*); (*fig.*) to use up; to exhaust; **в. ду́шу** to annoy, wear out; **они́ ~ли не́рвы друг дру́гу** they got on one another's nerves.
вы́мота|ться, юсь *pf.* (*of* **выма́тываться**) (*coll.*) **1.** *pass. of* **~ть. 2.** to be worn out.
вы́моч|ить, у, ишь *pf.* (*of* **выма́чивать**) **1.** to soak, drench. **2.** to ret (*flax, hemp*); to steep, macerate.
вы́мо|щу, стишь *see* **~стить**
вы́м|ою, оешь *see* **~ыть**
вы́мпел, а *m.* **1.** pendant, pennant. **2.** (*naut.*) unit; **эска́дра в соста́ве двадцати́ ~ов** a squadron consisting of twenty units. **3.** message bag (*used for messages dropped by air*).
вы́мр|у, ешь *see* **вы́мереть**
вы́мучен|ный (~, ~а) *p.p.p. of* **вы́мучить** *and adj.* forced; (*liter.*) laboured.
выму́чива|ть, ю *impf. of* **вы́мучить**
вы́муч|ить, у, ишь *pf.* (*of* **~́ивать**) **(из+g.)** to extort (from), force (out of); **он наконе́ц ~ил согла́сие у отца́** at last he extorted his father's consent.
вы́муштр|овать, ую *pf. of* **муштрова́ть**
вымыва́|ть(ся), ю(сь) *impf. of* **вы́мыть(ся)**
вы́мыс|ел, ла *m.* **1.** invention, fabrication. **2.** fantasy, flight of imagination.
вы́мы|слить, слю, слишь *pf.* (*of* **~шля́ть**) (*obs.*) to think up, invent; to imagine.
вы́м|ыть, ою, оешь *pf.* (*of* **мыть** *and* **~ыва́ть**) **1.** to wash; to wash out, off; **в. го́лову кому́-н.** to give s.o. a dressing-down. **2.** to wash away.
вы́м|ыться, оюсь, оешься *pf.* (*of* **мы́ться** *and* **~ыва́ться**) to wash o.s.
вы́мышлен|ный (~, ~а) *p.p.p. of* **вы́мыслить** *and adj.* fictitious, imaginary.
вымышля́|ть, ю *impf. of* **вы́мыслить**
вы́м|я, ени, ени, енем, ени, *pl.* **~ена́, ~ён, ~ена́м** *nt.* udder
вы́м|ять, ну, нешь *pf.* (*of* **~ина́ть**) **1.** to knead, work (*clay*). **2.** (*dial.*) to trample down.
вына́шива|ть, ю *impf. of* **выноси́ть**
вынесе́ни|е, я *nt.*: **в. пригово́ра** (*leg.*) pronouncement of sentence.
вы́нес|ти, у, ешь *pf.* (*of* **выноси́ть**) **1.** to carry out, take out; to take way; (*of sea or river current, etc.*) to carry away; **в. поко́йника** to carry out a body for burial; **в. на бе́рег** to wash ashore; **в. ле́вую но́гу** to step off with the left foot; **в. на поля́** to enter in the margin (*of a book*); **в. под строку́** to make a footnote; **в. сор из избы́** to wash one's dirty linen in public. **2.** (*fig.*) to take away, carry away, derive; **в. прия́тное впечатле́ние** to be favourably impressed. **3.: в. вопро́с (на собра́ние, на обсужде́ние)** to put, submit a question (to a meeting, for discussion). **4.: в. на свои́х плеча́х** (*fig.*) to shoulder, take the full weight (of), bear the full brunt (of). **5.** to bear, stand, endure; **не в.** to be unable to stand, be unable to take, be allergic (to) (*diet, treatment, etc.*). **6.: в. благода́рность** to express gratitude, return thanks; **в. пригово́р** (+*d.*) to pass sentence (on), pronounce sentence (on); **в. реше́ние** to decide; (*leg.*) to pronounce judgement.
вы́нес|тись, усь, ешься, *past* **~ся, ~лась** *pf.* (*of* **выноси́ться**) (*coll.*) to fly out, rush out.
вы́ни|зать, жу, жешь *pf.* (*of* **~́зывать**) (*obs.*) to decorate, adorn (*with string of beads, pearls, etc.*)
выни́зыва|ть, ю *impf. of* **вы́низать**
вынима́|ть, ю *impf. of* **вы́нуть**
вынима́|ться, ется *impf.* (*of* **вы́нуться**) (*coll.*) to come out; **э́тот я́щик не ~ется** this drawer does not come out.
вы́нос, а *m.* **1. (из це́ркви)** bearing-out, carrying-out (*of bier, at funerals*). **2.** trace; **ло́шадь под ~ом** trace-horse.
вы́но|сить, шу, сишь *pf.* (*of* **вына́шивать**) to bear, bring forth (*a child at full term*); **в. мысль** (*fig.*) to give birth to an idea.
выно|си́ть, шу́, ~́сишь *impf.* **1.** *impf. of* **вы́нести. 2.** *impf. only* (+*neg.*) to be unable to bear, be unable to stand; **я его́ не ~шу́** I can't stand him. **3.: хоть святы́х ~си́** (*coll.*) it is intolerable.
вы́носк|а, и *f.* **1.** taking out, carrying out. **2.** marginal note; footnote.
выно́сливост|ь, и *f.* (power of) endurance; staying-power.
выно́слив|ый (~, ~а) *adj.* hardy (*also hort.*); robust, sturdy (*equipment*).
выносн|о́й *adj.* **1.** detachable, removable; portable. **2.** inserted in footnote. **3.: ~а́я ло́шадь** trace-horse.
вы́ношен|ный (~, ~а) *p.p.p. of* **вы́носить** *and adj.* **в. ребёнок** child born at full term; **в. прое́кт** (*fig.*) mature project.
вы́но|шу, сишь *see* **~сить**
выно|шу́, ~́сишь *see* **~си́ть**
вы́ну|дить, жу, дишь *pf.* (*of* **~жда́ть**) **1.** (+*inf.*) to force, compel; **его́ ~дили уе́хать из страны́** he was forced to leave the country. **2. (у+g.)** to extort, force (from, out of); **они́ ~дили у него́ призна́ние в свое́й вине́** they have extorted an admission of guilt from him.
вынужда́|ть, ю *impf. of* **вы́нудить**
вы́нужден|ный (~, ~а) *p.p.p. of* **вы́нудить** *and adj.* forced, compulsory; **~ная поса́дка** (*aeron.*) forced landing.
вы́н|уть, у, ешь *pf.* (*of* **~има́ть**) **1.** to take out; to pull out, extract; to draw out (*money from bank, etc.*). **2.: ~ь да поло́жь** (*coll.*) (right) here and now, on the spot; there and then; **он тре́бует шампа́нского — ~ь да поло́жь** he demands champagne (right) here and now.
выны́рива|ть, ю *impf. of* **вы́нырнуть**
вы́ныр|нуть, ну, нешь *pf.* (*of* **~́ивать**) to come up, come to the surface (*of diver*); (*fig., coll.*) to turn up; **как для него́ характе́рно — он опя́ть ~нул без гроша́** how like him to turn up without a farthing again!
вы́нюх|ать, аю *pf.* (*of* **~́ивать**) (*coll.*) to sniff up; (*fig.*) to nose out, sniff out; **в формулиро́вке предложе́ния он ~ал что́-то недо́брое** he smelled a rat in the wording of the offer.
вынюхива|ть, ю *impf. of* **вы́нюхать**
выня́нчива|ть, ю *impf. of* **вы́нянчить**
вы́нянч|ить, у, ишь *pf.* (*of* **~́ивать**) (*coll.*) to bring up, nurse.
вы́пад, а *m.* **1.** (*fig.*) attack. **2.** (*sport*) lunge, thrust.
выпада́|ть, ю *impf. of* **вы́пасть**
выпаде́ни|е, я *nt.* **1.** falling out. **2.** (*med.*) prolapse.
выпа́ива|ть, ю *impf. of* **вы́поить**
выпа́лива|ть, ю *impf. of* **вы́палить**
вы́пал|ить, ю, ишь *pf.* (*of* **~́ивать**) (*coll.*) **1. (в+a.)** to shoot, fire (at). **2.** (*fig.*) to blurt out. **3.** (*dial.*) to fire (*trans.*), burn up.
выпа́лыва|ть, ю *impf. of* **вы́полоть**
выпа́рива|ть, ю *impf. of* **вы́парить**
вы́пар|ить, ю, ишь *pf.* (*of* **~́ивать**) **1.** to steam; to clean, disinfect (by steaming). **2.** (*chem.*) to evaporate. **3.** to clean (*in a steam-bath*).
вы́парк|а, и *f.* (*coll.*) **1.** steaming. **2.** evaporation.
выпарно́й *adj.* (*tech.*) evaporation.
выпа́рхива|ть, ю *impf. of* **вы́порхнуть**
выпа́рыва|ть, ю *impf. of* **вы́пороть 1.**
вы́пас, а *m.* pasture.
вы́па|сть, ду, дешь, *past* **~л** *pf.* (*of* **~да́ть**) **1.** to fall out. **2.** to fall (*of rain, snow, etc.*); **но́чью ~ло мно́го сне́гу** there was a heavy fall of snow in the night. **3.** to befall, fall (to); **им ~ло тяжёлое испыта́ние** a severe test has befallen them; **ему́ ~л жре́бий стоя́ть на карау́ле в день Рождества́** it fell to his lot to be on guard on Christmas Day. **4.** to occur, turn out; **ночь ~ла звёздная** it turned out a starry night. **5.** (*sport*) to lunge, thrust.
вы́па|хать, шу, шешь *pf.* (*of* **~́хивать**) **1.** to exhaust (*soil*). **2.** to turn up with the plough.
выпа́хива|ть, ю *impf. of* **вы́пахать**
вы́пачка|ть, ю *pf.* to soil, dirty; to stain.
вы́пачка|ться, юсь *pf.* to make o.s. dirty.
вы́па|шу, шешь *see* **~хать**
вы́пе|к *see* **~чь**
выпека́|ть, ю *impf. of* **вы́печь**
выпе́ндрива|ться, аюсь *impf.* (*coll.*) to show off.
вы́п|ереть, ру, решь, *past* **~ер, ~ерла** *pf.* (*of* **~ира́ть**) **1.** to push out, shove out. **2.** to stick out, bulge out, protrude. **3.** (*sl.*) to throw out, kick out, sling out.

вы́пест|овать, ую *pf. of* **пе́стовать**
вы́печк|а, и *f.* **1.** baking. **2.** batch (*of loaves, etc.*).
вы́пе|чь, ку, чешь, кут, *past* **~к, ~кла** *pf.* (*of* **~ка́ть**) to bake.
выпива́л|а, ы *c.g.* (*coll.*) tippler.
выпива́|ть, ю *impf.* **1.** *impf. of* **вы́пить. 2.** (*impf. only; coll.*) to be fond of the bottle.
вы́пивк|а, и *f.* (*coll.*) **1.** drinking-bout. **2.** (*collect.*) drinks.
выпиво́н, а *m.* (*coll.*) booze-up, drinking session.
выпиво́х|а, и *c.g.* (*sl.*) tippler; boozer.
вы́пи|вши *past ger. of* **~ть;** (*coll.*) drunk (*also used as predicative adj.*).
выпи́лива|ть, ю *impf. of* **вы́пилить**
вы́пил|ить, ю, ишь *pf.* (*of* **~ивать**) to saw, saw up, saw off; **в. ра́мку ло́бзиком** to make a fretwork frame.
вы́пилк|а, и *f.* **1.** sawing. **2.** sawn-up, sawn-off object.
выпира́|ть, ю *impf. of* **вы́переть**
вы́пи|сать, шу, шешь *pf.* (*of* **~сывать**) **1.** to copy out; to excerpt. **2.** to delineate scrupulously; to trace out. **3.** to write out; **в. квита́нцию** to write out a receipt. **4.** to order; to subscribe (to); to send for (*in writing*); **в. кни́гу** to order a book; **е́сли ей ста́нет ху́же, вам придётся в. её сы́на** if she gets worse you will have to send for her son. **5.** to strike off the list; **в. из больни́цы** to discharge from hospital.
вы́пи|саться, шусь, шешься *pf.* (*of* **~сываться**) **1.** to leave (*on discharge*); to be discharged; **он уже́ ~сался из больни́цы** he is already out of hospital. **2.** (*obs.*) to write o.s. out.
вы́писк|а, и *f.* **1.** copying, excerpting. **2.** writing out. **3.** extract, excerpt; **~и из газе́т** newspaper extracts. **4.** ordering; subscription. **5.** discharge.
выпи́сыва|ть(ся), ю(сь) *impf. of* **вы́писать(ся)**
вы́пис|ь, и *f.* extract, copy; **метри́ческая в.** birth certificate.
вы́п|ить, ью, ьешь *pf.* (*of* **выпива́ть** *and* **пить**) to drink; to drink up, off; **~ьем!** cheers!; bottoms up!
выпи́хива|ть, ю *impf. of* **вы́пихнуть**
вы́пих|нуть, ну, нешь *pf.* (*of* **~ивать**) (*coll.*) to shove out, bundle out.
вы́пи|шу, шешь *see* **~сать**
вы́плав|ить, лю, ишь *pf.* (*of* **~ля́ть**) to smelt.
вы́плавк|а, и *f.* **1.** smelting. **2.** smelted metal.
выплавля́|ть, ю *impf. of* **вы́плавить**
вы́пла|кать, чу, чешь *pf.* **1.** (*coll., folk poet.*) to sob out. **2.** (*coll.*) to obtain by weeping, by tearful entreaties. **3.** (*coll., folk poet.*): **в. (все) глаза́** to cry one's eyes out.
вы́пла|каться, чусь, чешься *pf.* (*coll.*) to have a good cry, have one's cry out.
вы́плат|а, ы *f.* **1.** payment. **2.** (*coll.*) payment by instalments; **купи́ть на ~у** to purchase by instalments.
вы́пла|тить, чу, тишь *pf.* (*of* **~чивать**) **1.** to pay (out). **2.** to pay off (*debts*).
выпла́чива|ть, ю *impf. of* **вы́платить**
вы́пла|чу[1], **тишь** *see* **~тить**
вы́пла|чу[2], **чешь** *see* **~кать**
выплёвыва|ть, ю *impf. of* **вы́плюнуть**
вы́пле|скать, щу, щешь *pf.* (*of* **~скивать**) to splash out.
выплёскива|ть, ю *impf. of* **вы́плескать** *and* **вы́плеснуть**
вы́плес|нуть, ну, нешь *pf.* (*of* **~кивать**) to splash out; **в. с водо́й и ребёнка** (*fig.*) to throw out the baby with the (bath-)water.
вы́пле|сти, ту, тешь *pf.* (*of* **~та́ть**) **1.** to undo, untie. **2.** to weave.
выплета́|ть, ю *impf. of* **вы́плести**
выплыва́|ть, ю *impf. of* **вы́плыть**
вы́плы|ть, ву, вешь *pf.* (*of* **~ва́ть**) **1.** to swim out; (*fig.*) **она́ ~ла из ко́мнаты** she sailed out of the room. **2.** to come to the surface, come up; (*fig., coll.*) to emerge; to appear; to crop up; **пре́жнее недоразуме́ние сно́ва ~ло** the old misunderstanding has cropped up again.
вы́плюн|уть, у, ешь *pf.* (*of* **выплёвывать**) to spit out
вы́по|ить, ю, ишь *pf.* (*of* **выпа́ивать**) to feed (*livestock*).
выпола́скива|ть, ю *impf. of* **вы́полоскать**
выполза́|ть, ю *impf. of* **вы́ползти**
вы́полз|ок, ка *m.* (*dial.*) **1.** slough. **2.** worm.
вы́полз|ти, у, ешь, *past* **~, ~ла** *pf.* (*of* **~а́ть**) (**из**+*g.*) to crawl out, creep out (from).
вы́полир|овать, ую *pf.* (*coll.*) to polish (up).
выполне́ни|е, я *nt.* execution, carrying-out; fulfilment.
выполни́м|ый (~, ~а) *pres. part. pass. of* **вы́полнить** *and adj.* practicable, feasible.
вы́полн|ить, ю, ишь *pf.* (*of* **~я́ть**) to execute, carry out; to fulfil; **в. свои́ обя́занности** to discharge one's obligations, do one's duty; **в. приказа́ние** to carry out an order.
выполня́|ть, ю *impf. of* **вы́полнить**
вы́поло|скать, щу, щешь *pf.* (*of* **выпола́скивать**) to rinse out.
вы́пол|оть, ю, ешь *pf.* (*of* **выпа́лывать**) to weed out.
вы́порот|ок, ка *m.* unborn animal (*removed from female for fur*).
вы́пор|оть[1], **ю, ешь** *pf.* (*of* **выпа́рывать**) (*coll.*) to rip out, rip up.
вы́пор|оть[2], **ю ешь** *pf. of* **поро́ть**[2]
вы́порхн|уть, у, ешь *pf.* (*of* **выпа́рхивать**) to flit out (*of birds*); (*fig., coll.*) to dart out.
вы́поте|ть, ю, ешь *pf.* (*coll.*) to sweat out.
вы́потрош|ить, у, ишь *pf. of* **потроши́ть**
вы́прав|ить, лю, ишь *pf.* (*of* **~ля́ть**) **1.** to straighten (out). **2.** to correct; to improve. **3.** (*coll.*) to get, obtain (documents); **в. па́спорт** to get a passport.
вы́прав|иться, люсь, ишься *pf.* (*of* **~ля́ться**) **1.** to become straight. **2.** to improve (*intrans.*).
вы́правк|а, и *f.* **1.** bearing. **2.** (*typ.*) correction.
выправля́|ть(ся), ю(сь) *impf. of* **вы́править(ся)**
выпра́стыва|ть(ся), ю(сь) *impf. of* **вы́простать(ся)**
выпра́шива|ть, ю *impf.* **1.** *impf. of* **вы́просить. 2.** *impf. only* to solicit, try to get; **он всё ~ет разреше́ние на вы́езд** he is always trying to get permission to go abroad.
выпрева́|ть, ю *impf. of* **вы́преть**
вы́пре|ть, ю, ешь *pf.* (*of* **~ва́ть**) (*coll., dial.*) to rot (*of crops*).
выпрова́жива|ть, ю *impf. of* **вы́проводить**
вы́прово|дить, жу, дишь *pf.* (*of* **выпрова́живать**) (*coll.*) to send packing; to show the door (to).
вы́про|сить, шу, сишь *pf.* (*of* **выпра́шивать**) (**у**+*g.*) to get (out of), obtain, elicit (by begging); **наконе́ц он ~сил разреше́ние на вы́езд** at last he elicited permission to go abroad.
вы́проста|ть, ю *pf.* (*of* **выпра́стывать**) (*coll.*) **1.** to free, work loose. **2.** to empty.
вы́проста|ться, юсь *pf.* (*of* **выпра́стываться**) (*coll.*) **1.** to free o.s., work (o.s.) free. **2.** to defecate.
вы́про|шу, сишь *see* **~сить**
вы́п|ру, решь *see* **~ереть**
выпры́гива|ть, ю *impf. of* **вы́прыгнуть**
вы́прыг|нуть, ну, нешь *pf.* (*of* **~ивать**) to jump out, spring out.
выпряга́|ть, ю *impf. of* **вы́прячь**
выпрями́тел|ь, я *m.* (*elec.*) rectifier.
вы́прям|ить, лю, ишь *pf.* (*of* **~ля́ть**) **1.** to straighten (out). **2.** (*elec.*) to rectify.
вы́прям|иться, люсь, ишься *pf.* (*of* **~ля́ться**) to become straight; **в. во весь рост** to draw o.s. up to one's full height.
выпрямля́|ть(ся), ю(сь) *impf. of* **вы́прямить(ся)**
вы́пря|чь, гу, жешь, гут, *past* **~г, ~гла** *pf.* (*of* **~га́ть**) to unharness.
выпу́гива|ть, ю *impf. of* **вы́пугнуть**
вы́пуг|нуть, ну, нешь *pf.* (*of* **~ивать**) to scare off; to start (*game*).
вы́пукло-во́гнутый *adj.* (*phys.*) convexo-concave.
вы́пуклост|ь, и *f.* **1.** protuberance; prominence, bulge. **2.** (*phys.*) convexity. **3.** relief (*in sculpture, etc.*). **4.** (*sg. only; fig.*) clarity, distinctness.
вы́пуклый *adj.* **1.** protuberant; prominent, bulging. **2.** (*phys.*) convex. **3.** in relief. **4.** (*fig.*) clear, distinct.
вы́пуск, а *m.* **1.** output; issue; discharge (*of steam, gases, etc.*); **в. из печа́ти** publication; **в. новосте́й** newscast; **сро́чный в. новосте́й** newsflash. **2.** part, number, instalment (*of serial publication*); **дебю́тный в.** launch *or*

premier issue; **сери́йный в.** mass production. **3.** leavers; graduates (*those who complete studies at the same time*); **он — са́мый блестя́щий из прошлого́днего ~а по хи́мии** he is the most brilliant of those who graduated in chemistry last year. **4.** cut, omission. **5.** (*obs.*) edging, piping. **6.: брю́ки на в.**, *see* **навы́пуск**

выпуска́|ть, ю *impf. of* **вы́пустить**

выпуска́|ющий *pres. part. act. of* **~ть;** *as n.* **в., ~ющего** *m.* pers. responsible for seeing newspaper *or* journal through press.

выпускни́к, а́ *m.* **1.** graduate; **бы́вший в.** old boy. **2.** final-year student.

выпускни́|ца, цы *f. of* **~к**

выпуск|но́й *adj. of* **вы́пуск; в. кла́пан** (*tech.*) exhaust valve; **в. кран** (*tech.*) discharge cock; **~на́я труба́** (*tech.*) exhaust pipe; **~на́я цена́** (*econ.*) market price; **в. экза́мен** final examination, finals; *as n.* **в., ~но́го** *m.*, **~на́я, ~но́й** *f.* final-year student.

вы́пу|стить, щу, стишь *pf.* (*of* **~ска́ть**) **1.** to let out; to release; **в. во́ду из ва́нны** to let the water out of a bath; **в. из тюрьмы́** to release from prison; **в. (пулемётную) о́чередь** (*mil.*) to fire a burst. **2.** to put out, issue; to turn out, produce; **в. в прода́жу** to put on the market; **в. заём** to float a loan; **в. офице́ров** to turn out officers; **в. кинокарти́ну** to release a film. **3.** to cut (out), omit. **4.** (*tailoring*) to let out, let down. **5.** to show; **в. свои́ ко́гти** to show one's claws. **6.** (*typ.*) to see through the press.

вы́пут|ать, аю *pf.* (*of* **~ывать**) to disentangle.

вы́пут|аться, аюсь *pf.* (*of* **~ываться**) to disentangle o.s., extricate o.s. (*also fig.*).

выпу́тыва|ть(ся), ю(сь) *impf. of* **вы́путать(ся)**

вы́пуч|енный *p.p.p. of* **~ить** *and adj.* (*coll.*): **с ~енными глаза́ми** wide-eyed, goggle-eyed.

выпу́чива|ть, ю *impf. of* **вы́пучить**

вы́пуч|ить, у, ишь *pf.* (*of* **~ивать**) **в. глаза́** (*coll.*) to open one's eyes wide.

вы́пушк|а, и *f.* edging, braid, piping.

вы́пыт|ать, аю *pf.* (*of* **~ывать**) (**у**+*g.*) to elicit, extort (*information, secrets, etc., from*).

выпы́тыва|ть, ю *impf.* **1.** *impf. of* **вы́пытать. 2.** *impf. only* to try to discover (*by interrogation*); **в. секре́т у кого́-н.** to try to get a secret out of s.o.

вып|ь, и *f.* (*zool.*) bittern.

выпя́лива|ть, ю *impf. of* **вы́пялить**

вы́пял|ить, ю, ишь *pf.* (*of* **~ивать**) (*coll.*) to stick out; **в. глаза́** to open one's eyes wide, stare.

вы́пя|тить, чу, тишь *pf.* (*of* **~чивать**) (*coll.*) **1.** to stick out; **в. грудь** to stick out one's chest. **2.** (*fig.*) to over-emphasize.

вы́пя|титься, чусь, тишься *pf.* (*of* **~чиваться**) (*coll.*) to stick out (*intrans.*), protrude.

выпя́чива|ть(ся), ю(сь) *impf. of* **вы́пятить(ся)**

вырабо́тыва|ть, ю *impf. of* **вы́работать**

вы́работа|ть, ю *pf.* (*of* **вырабо́тывать**) **1.** to manufacture; to produce, make. **2.** to work out, draw up; **в. пове́стку дня для заседа́ния** to draw up an agenda for a meeting; **в. хоро́ший стиль** to work up a good style; **в. си́лу хара́ктера** to develop, acquire strength of character. **3.** (*coll.*) to earn, make. **4.** (*tech.*) to work out (*a mine*).

вы́работк|а, и *f.* **1.** manufacture; production, making. **2.** working-out, drawing-up. **3.** output, yield. **4.** (*coll.*) make; **хоро́шей ~и** well-made. **5.** (*tech.*) (mine-)working.

выра́внивани|е, я *nt.* smoothing-out, levelling; equalization; alignment; (*typ.*) justification.

выра́внива|ть(ся), ю(сь) *impf. of* **вы́ровнять(ся)**

выража́|ть, ю *impf. of* **вы́разить**

выража́|ться, юсь *impf.* **1.** *impf. of* **вы́разиться; мя́гко ~ясь** to put it mildly. **2.** (*coll.*) to swear, use swear-words.

выраже́ни|е, я *nt.* (*in var. senses*) expression.

вы́ражен|ный (~, ~а) *p.p.p. of* **вы́разить** *and adj.* pronounced, marked; **он говори́т по-англи́йски, но с ре́зко ~ным неме́цким акце́нтом** he speaks English, but with a very pronounced German accent.

вырази́тел|ь, я *m.* mouthpiece, spokesperson; exponent; **он был еди́нственным в исто́рии страны́ ~ем стремле́ний всего́ наро́да** he was the only pers. in the country's history to have articulated the aspirations of the entire people.

вырази́тел|ьный (~ен, ~ьна) *adj.* expressive; significant; **~ьное чте́ние** elocution.

вы́ра|зить, жу, зишь *pf.* (*of* **~жа́ть**) to express; to convey; to voice; **его́ докла́д ~зил взгля́ды прису́тствующих на ми́тинге** his report conveyed the views of the meeting.

вы́ра|зиться, жусь, зишься *pf.* (*of* **~жа́ться**) **1.** to express o.s. **2.** (**в**+*p.*) to manifest itself (in.). **3.** (**в**+*p.*) to amount to, come to; **изде́ржки ~зились в шести́ рубля́х** the costs came to six roubles.

вы́разуме|ть, ю *pf.* (*obs.*) to understand.

выраста́|ть, ю *impf. of* **вы́расти**

вы́р|асти, асту, астешь, *past* **~ос, ~осла** *pf.* (*of* **~аста́ть**) **1.** to grow (up). **2.** (**в**+*a.*) to grow (into), develop (into), become; **их дру́жба ~осла в любо́вь** their friendship grew into love. **3.** (**из**+*g.*) to grow (out of) (*clothing*). **4.** to increase; **населе́ние за пять лет ~осло на два́дцать проце́нтов** in five years the population had increased by twenty per cent. **5.** to appear, rise up; **пе́ред на́шими глаза́ми ~ос Арара́т** Mount Ararat rose up before our eyes. **6.: в. в чьих-н. глаза́х** to rise in s.o.'s estimation.

вы́ра|стить, щу, стишь *pf.* (*of* **~щивать**) to bring up (*children*); to rear, breed (*livestock*); to grow, cultivate (*plants*).

выра́щива|ть, ю *impf. of* **вы́растить**

вы́рв|ать[1], у, ешь *pf.* (*of* **вырыва́ть[1]**) **1.** to pull out, tear out; **в. зуб** to pull out a tooth; **в. себе́ зуб (у врача́)** to have a tooth out; **он ~ал кни́гу у меня́ из рук** he snatched the book out of my hands. **2.** (*fig.*) to extort, wring; **в. призна́ние у кого́-н.** to wring a confession out of s.o.

вы́рв|ать[2], у, ешь *pf. of* **рвать[2]**

вы́рв|аться, усь, ешься *pf.* (*of* **вырыва́ться**) **1.** (**из**+*g.*) to tear o.s. away (from); to break out (from), break loose (from), break free (from); to get away (from); **в. из чьих-н. объя́тий** to tear o.s. away from s.o.'s embrace; **в. из чьих-н. рук** to break loose from s.o.'s grip; **едва́ ли мне уда́стся до ле́та в. из Москвы́** I shall hardly manage to get away from Moscow before the summer. **2.** to come loose, come out; **не́сколько страни́ц ~алось из э́той кни́ги** several pages have come out of this book. **3.** (*of a sound, a remark, etc.*) (**из, у**+*g.*) to break (from), burst (from), escape; **из груди́ старика́ ~ался стон** a groan broke from the old man. **4.** to shoot up, shoot out; **пла́мя ~алось из трубы́** a flame shot up from the chimney; **четвёртая маши́на вдруг ~алась вперёд на пе́рвое ме́сто** the fourth car suddenly shot ahead into first place.

вы́рез, а *m.* cut; notch; **пла́тье с больши́м ~ом** low-necked dress; **покупа́ть (арбу́з) на в.** (*coll.*) to buy (a water-melon) on trial.

вы́ре|зать, жу, жешь *pf.* (*of* **~за́ть**) **1.** to cut out; to excise. **2.** to cut, carve; to engrave. **3.** (*fig.*) to slaughter, butcher.

выреза́|ть, ю *impf. of* **вы́резать**

вы́резк|а, и *f.* **1.** cutting-out, excision; carving; engraving. **2. газе́тная в.** press-cutting. **3.** fillet steak.

вырезн|о́й *adj.* **1.** cut; carved. **2.** low-necked, décolleté. **3.: ~а́я откры́тка** (cut-out) reply coupon.

выре́зывани|е, я *nt.* cutting-out; excision; carving; engraving.

выре́зыва|ть, ю *impf.* = **выреза́ть**

вы́реш|ить, у, ишь *pf.* (*coll.*) to decide finally.

вы́рис|овать, ую *pf.* (*of* **~о́вывать**) to draw carefully, draw in detail.

вы́рис|оваться, уется *pf.* (*of* **~о́вываться**) to appear (in outline); to stand out; **на горизо́нте ~овалась го́рная цепь** a mountain chain stood out against the horizon.

вырисо́выва|ть(ся), ю(сь) *impf. of* **вы́рисовать(ся)**

вы́ровня|ть, ю *pf.* (*of* **выра́внивать**) **1.** to smooth (out), level; **в. доро́гу** to level a road; **в. шаг** to regulate one's pace. **2.** to equalize; to align; (*typ.*) to justify. **3.** (*mil.*) to draw up in line; **в. ряды́** to dress ranks. **4.: в. самолёт** to straighten out an aeroplane.

вы́ровня|ться, юсь, *pf.* (*of* **выра́вниваться**) **1.** to become level; to become even; (*mil.*) to form up; to dress, take up dressing; (*sport*) to equalize. **2.** (*fig.*) to catch up, draw level; **несмотря́ на боле́знь, ему́ удало́сь в. с други́ми ученика́ми кла́сса** despite his illness he has managed to catch up with the rest of the class. **3.** (*fig.*) to improve, get better; (*coll.*) to become more equable.
вы́род|иться, ится *pf.* (*of* **вырожда́ться**) to degenerate.
вы́род|ок, ка *m.* (*coll.*) degenerate; **он — в. в на́шей семье́** he is the black sheep of our family.
вырожда́|ться, юсь *impf. of* **вы́родиться**
вырожде́н|ец, ца *m.* degenerate.
вырожде́ни|е, я *nt.* degeneration.
вы́рон|ить, ю, ишь *pf.* to drop.
вы́рост, а *no pl., m.* **1.** growth, excrescence; offshoot. **2.: шить на в.** to make (*clothes*) with room for growth.
вы́ростковый *adj.* calf(-leather).
вы́рост|ок, ка *m.* year-old calf; calf-leather.
вы́р|ою, оешь *see* **~ыть**
выруба́|ть(ся), ю(сь) *impf. of* **вы́рубить(ся)**
вы́руб|ить, лю, ишь *pf.* (*of* **~а́ть**) **1.** to cut down, fell; to hew out. **2.** to cut out; **в. ды́ру** to make a hole. **3.** to carve (out).
вы́руб|иться, люсь, ишься *pf.* (*of* **~а́ться**) to cut one's way out.
вы́рубк|а, и *f.* **1.** cutting down, felling; hewing out; **в. ле́са** *or* **лесо́в** deforestation. **2.** (*dial.*) clearing (*in forest*).
вы́руга|ть(ся), ю(сь) *pf. of* **руга́ть(ся)**
выру́лива|ть, ю *impf. of* **вы́рулить**
вы́рул|ить, ю, ишь *pf.* (*of* **~́ивать**) (*aeron.*) to taxi.
выруча́|ть, ю *impf. of* **вы́ручить**
вы́руч|ить, у, ишь *pf.* (*of* **~а́ть**) **1.** to rescue; to come to the help, aid (of). **2.** to gain; to make (*coll.*); **он ~ил мно́го де́нег от прода́жи свои́х карти́н** he has made a lot of money from the sale of his pictures; **в. затра́ченное** to recover one's expenses.
вы́ручк|а, и *f.* **1.** rescue, assistance; **прийти́ на ~у** to come to the rescue. **2.** gain; proceeds, receipts; earnings.
вырыва́ни|е[1], я *nt.* **1.** pulling out; extraction (*of teeth, etc.*). **2.** uprooting.
вырыва́ни|е[2], я *nt.* digging (up).
вырыва́|ть[1], ю *impf. of* **вы́рвать[1]**
вырыва́|ть[2], ю *impf. of* **вы́рыть**
вырыва́|ться, юсь *impf. of* **вы́рваться**
вы́р|ыть, ою, оешь *pf.* (*of* **~ыва́ть[2]**) to dig up, dig out, unearth; **в. труп** to exhume a corpse; **где вы ~ыли э́ту ру́копись?** (*fig., coll.*) where did you dig up this manuscript?
вы́ря|дить, жу, дишь *pf.* (*coll.*) to dress up (*trans.*).
вы́ря|диться, жусь, дишься *pf.* (*coll.*) to dress up (*intrans.*).
выряжа́|ть(ся), ю(сь) *impf. of* **вы́рядить(ся)**
вы́са|дить, жу, дишь *pf.* (*of* **~́живать**) **1.** to set down; to help down; to make alight; **в. на бе́рег** to put ashore; **в. деса́нт** (*mil.*) to make a landing; **пья́ницу ~дили из авто́буса** the drunken man was made to get off the bus. **2.** (*hort.*) to transplant. **3.** (*coll.*) to smash; to break in.
вы́са|диться, жусь, дишься *pf.* (*of* **~́живаться**) (**из, c**+*g.*) to alight (from), get off; **в. (с су́дна)** to land, disembark; **в. (с самолёта)** to land.
вы́садк|а, и *f.* **1.** debarkation, disembarkation; landing. **2.** (*hort.*) transplanting.
выса́жива|ть(ся), ю(сь) *impf. of* **вы́садить(ся)**
вы́са|жу, дишь *see* **~дить**
выса́сыва|ть, ю *impf. of* **вы́сосать**
вы́свата|ть, ю *pf.* (*coll., obs.*) to make a match, arrange a marriage (with).
высва́тыва|ть, ю *impf.* **1.** *impf. of* **вы́сватать. 2.** *impf. only* to try to make a match, arrange a marriage (with); to seek in marriage.
высве́рлива|ть, ю *impf. of* **вы́сверлить**
вы́сверл|ить, ю, ишь *pf.* to drill, bore.
вы́све|тить, чу, тишь *pf.* (*of* **высве́чивать**) **1.** to light up, illuminate. **2.** (*fig.*) to highlight.
высве́чива|ть, ю *impf. of* **вы́светить**
вы́сви|стать, щу, щешь *pf.* (*of* **~́стывать**) (*coll.*) **1.** to whistle; **в. мело́дию** to whistle a tune. **2.** to whistle for, whistle up.
вы́сви|стеть, щу, стишь *pf.* = **~стать**
высви́стыва|ть, ю *impf. of* **вы́свистать**
вы́свобо|дить, жу, дишь *pf.* **1.** to free, liberate; to disentangle, disengage. **2.** (*coll.*) to help (to) escape; **не́которые ме́стные жи́тели ~дили заключённых** some of the locals helped the prisoners escape.
высвобожда́|ть, ю *impf. of* **вы́свободить**
вы́сев|ки, ок *no sg.* bran, siftings.
высе́ива|ть, ю *impf. of* **вы́сеять**
высека́|ть, ю *impf. of* **вы́сечь[2]**
вы́се|ку, чешь *see* **~чь**
выселе́н|ец, ца *m.* evacuee.
выселе́ни|е, я *nt.* eviction.
вы́сел|ить, ю, ишь *pf.* (*of* **~я́ть**) **1.** to evict. **2.** to evacuate, move.
вы́сел|иться, юсь, ишься *pf.* (*of* **~я́ться**) to move (*from one dwelling-place to another*).
вы́сел|ок, ка *m.* settlement.
выселя́|ть(ся), ю(сь) *impf. of* **вы́селить(ся)**
вы́семен|иться, ится *pf.* (*agric.*) to go to seed.
вы́сечк|а, и *f.* carving; hewing.
вы́се|чь[1], ку, чешь, кут, *past* **~к, ~кла** *pf.* (*of* **сечь[1]**) to beat, flog.
вы́се|чь[2], ку, чешь, кут, *past* **~к, ~кла** *pf.* (*of* **~ка́ть**) to cut (out); to carve, sculpture; to hew; **в. ого́нь** to strike fire (*from a flint*).
вы́се|ять, ю *pf.* (*of* **~́ивать**) (*agric.*) to sow.
вы́си|деть, жу, дишь *pf.* (*of* **~́живать**) **1.** to hatch (out) (*of birds; also fig.*). **2.** to stay; to sit out (*trans.*); **мы ~дели до конца́ ле́кции** we sat the lecture out.
вы́сидк|а, и *f.* (*coll.*) **1.** incubation. **2.** imprisonment.
выси́жива|ть, ю *impf. of* **вы́сидеть**
вы́|ситься, шусь, сишься *impf.* to tower (up), rise.
выска́блива|ть, ю *impf. of* **вы́скоблить**
вы́ска|зать, жу, жешь *pf.* (*of* **~́зывать**) to express; to state; **в. мне́ние** to advance an opinion; **в. предположе́ние** to suggest, come out with a suggestion.
вы́ска|заться, жусь, жешься *pf.* (*of* **~́зываться**) **1.** to speak out; to speak one's mind; to have one's say. **2.** to speak (for *or* against); **никто́ не ~зался про́тив законопрое́кта** no one spoke against the bill.
выска́зывани|е, я *nt.* **1.** utterance. **2.** pronouncement; opinion.
выска́зыва|ть(ся), ю(сь) *impf. of* **вы́сказать(ся)**
выска́кива|ть, ю *impf. of* **вы́скочить**
выска́льзыва|ть, ю *impf. of* **вы́скользнуть**
вы́скобл|ить, ю, ишь *pf.* (*of* **выска́бливать**) to scrape out; to erase; (*med.*) to remove.
вы́скользн|уть, у, ешь *pf.* (*of* **выска́льзывать**) to slip out (*also fig.*); **аре́стант ~ул из рук охра́ны** (*coll.*) the prisoner slipped through his escort's fingers.
вы́скоч|ить, у, ишь *pf.* (*of* **выска́кивать**) **1.** to jump out; to leap out, spring out; (*fig., coll.*) to butt in, come out (with); **он ~ил с кра́йне неуме́стным замеча́нием** he came out with an extremely uncalled-for remark. **2.** (*of a boil, etc.*) (*coll.*) to come up. **3.** (*coll.*) to drop out, fall out. **4.: в. в лю́ди** (*fig., coll.*) to fall on one's feet.
вы́скочк|а, и *c.g.* (*coll.*) upstart, parvenu.
выскреба́|ть, ю *impf. of* **вы́скрести**
вы́скре|сти, бу, бешь, *past* **~б, ~бла** *pf.* **1.** to scrape out, scrape off. **2.** to rake out.
вы́слан|ный (~, ~а) *p.p.p. of* **вы́слать;** *as n.* **в., ~ного** *m.*, **~ная, ~ной** *f.* exile, deportee
вы́|слать, шлю, шлешь *pf.* (*of* **~сыла́ть**) **1.** to send, send out, dispatch. **2.** (*pol.*) to exile; to deport.
вы́сле|дить, жу, дишь *pf.* to trace; to track down.
высле́жива|ть, ю *impf.* **1.** *impf. of* **вы́следить. 2.** *impf. only* to be on the track of; to shadow.
вы́сле|жу, дишь *see* **~дить**
вы́слуг|а, и *f.* period of service; **за ~у лет** for long service, for meritorious service; **за ~ой двадцати́ лет** on the expiry of twenty year's service.

высл́ужива|ть(ся), ю(сь) *impf. of* **вы́служить(ся)**
вы́служ|ить, у, ишь *pf.* **1.** to qualify for, obtain (*as result of service*); **он ~ил повыше́ние** he has qualified for promotion. **2.** to serve (out); **он ~ил два́дцать пять лет на Да́льнем Восто́ке** he has completed twenty-five years' service in the Far East.
вы́служ|иться, усь, ишься *pf.* **1.** to gain promotion, be promoted. **2.** (*coll.*, *pej.*) to gain favour (with), get in (with); **он ~ился пе́ред бригади́ром** he is well in with the foreman.
вы́слуша|ть, ю *pf.* (*of* **выслу́шивать**) **1.** to hear out. **2.** (*med.*) to sound; to listen to.
выслу́шивани|е, я *nt.* (*med.*) auscultation.
выслу́шива|ть, ю *impf. of* **вы́слушать**
высма́трива|ть, *impf. of* **вы́смотреть**
высме́ива|ть, ю *impf. of* **вы́смеять**
вы́сме|ять, ю, ешь *pf.* (*of* **~́ивать**) to deride, ridicule.
вы́смол|ить, ю, ишь *pf. of* **смоли́ть**
вы́сморка|ть(ся), ю(сь) *pf. of* **сморка́ть(ся)**
вы́смотр|еть, ю, ишь *pf.* (*of* **высма́тривать**) **1.** to scrutinize, look through. **2.** to spy out; to locate (*by eye*). **3.** (*coll.*) **в. глаза́** to tire one's eyes out.
высо́выва|ть(ся), ю(сь) *impf. of* **вы́сунуть(ся)**
высо́к|ий (~, ~а́, ~́о) *adj.* (*in var. senses*) high; tall; lofty; elevated, sublime; (*mus.*) high, high-pitched; **~ая вода́** high water, high tide; **в. стиль** elevated style; **в. гость** distinguished visitor; **я о нём ~ого мне́ния** I have a high opinion of him; **в ~ой сте́пени** highly; **~ие догова́ривающиеся сто́роны,** *see* **догова́риваться**
высо́ко́ *adv.* **1.** high (up); **лежа́ть в. над у́ровнем мо́ря** to be high above sea level. **2.** *as pred.* it is high (up); it is a long way up; **окно́ бы́ло в. от земли́** the window was high up off the ground.
высоко... *comb. form* high-, highly-; (*meteor.*) alto-.
высокоблагоро́ди|е, я *nt.* **(ва́ше) в.** (your) Honour, (your) Worship (*title, in tsarist Russia, of civil servants of the eighth to the sixth classes and of officers from the rank of major to that of colonel*).
высокого́рный *adj.* Alpine, mountain.
высокока́чественный *adj.* high-quality.
высококвалифици́рованный *adj.* highly qualified; **в. рабо́тник** (highly-)skilled workman.
высокоме́ри|е, я *nt.* haughtiness, arrogance.
высокоме́рнича|ть, ю *impf.* (*coll.*) to behave haughtily, arrogantly.
высокоме́р|ный (~ен, ~на) *adj.* haughty, arrogant.
высокомолекуля́рный *adj.* (*phys.*) high-molecular.
высокопа́р|ный (~ен, ~на) *adj.* (*liter.*) high-flown, stilted; bombastic, turgid.
высокопоста́вленный *adj.* high-ranking.
высокопревосходи́тельств|о, а *nt.* **(ва́ше) в.** (your) Excellency (*title, in tsarist Russia, of officers and civil servants of the first and second class*).
высокопреосвяще́нств|о, а *nt.* **(ва́ше) в.** (your) Eminence, (your) Grace (*title of archbishops and metropolitans of the Orthodox Church*).
высокопреподо́би|е, я *nt.* **(ва́ше) в.** (your) Reverence (*title of archimandrites, abbots and archpriests of the Orthodox Church*).
высокопро́б|ный (~ен, ~на) *adj.* sterling, standard; (*fig.*) sterling, of high quality.
высокоро́ди|е, я *nt.* **(ва́ше) в.** (your) Honour, (your) Worship (*title, in tsarist Russia, of civil servants of the fifth class*).
высокосо́ртный *adj.* high-grade.
высокоторже́ственный *adj.* solemn.
высокоуважа́емый *adj.* (*obs.*; *mode of address in letters*) honoured (Sir), respected (Sir).
высокоу́м|ный (~ен, ~на) *adj.* (*iron.*) clever, brainy.
высокочасто́тный *adj.* (*elec.*) high-frequency.
высокочти́мый *adj.* (*obs.*) highly esteemed.
высокоэффекти́в|ный (~ен, на) *adj.* high-efficiency.
вы́сол|ить, ю, ишь *pf.* (*coll.*) to salt well.
вы́сос|ать, у, ешь *pf.* (*of* **выса́сывать**) **1.** to suck out, suck dry. **2.** (*fig., coll.*) to get out (of), extort (from); **в. все со́ки из** to exhaust, wear out; **в. из па́льца** to invent, fabricate; **всё э́то из па́льца ~ано** it is a complete fabrication.
высот|а́, ы́, *pl.* **~́ы, ~́** *f.* **1.** height, altitude; (*mus.*) pitch; **го́род нахо́дится на ~е́ ты́сячи фу́тов над у́ровнем мо́ря** the town is a thousand feet above sea level; **набра́ть ~у́** (*aeron.*) to gain altitude. **2.** height, eminence (*concr.*); **кома́ндные ~́ы** commanding heights (*also fig.*). **3.** high level; high quality. **4.** (*fig.*): **на до́лжной ~е́** up to the mark; **быть, оказа́ться на ~е́ положе́ния** to rise to the occasion; **быть на ~е́ зада́чи** to be equal to a task. **5.** (*math.*): **в. треуго́льника** altitude of a triangle.
высо́тник, а *m.* **1.** workman employed on construction of skyscrapers. **2.** high-altitude flier. **3.** (*coll.*) high-jumper.
высо́тн|ый *adj.* **1.** high-altitude. **2.: ~ое зда́ние** high-rise building, tower block.
высотоме́р, а *m.* **1.** (*aeron.*) altimeter. **2.** (*mil.*) height-finder.
вы́сох|нуть, ну, нешь, *past* **~, ~ла** *pf.* (*of* **высыха́ть**) **1.** to dry (out); to dry up (*of rivers, etc.*). **2.** to wither, fade; (*fig.*) to waste away, fade away.
вы́сох|ший *p.p. act. of* **~нуть** *and adj.* dried-up; shrivelled; wizened.
высоча́йш|ий *adj.* **1.** *superl. of* **высо́кий. 2.** (*epithet of tsar or emperor*) imperial, royal; **проше́ние на ~ее и́мя** petition to His Imperial Majesty.
высоче́нный *adj.* (*coll.*) very high, very tall.
высо́честв|о, а *nt.* **(ва́ше) в.** (your) Highness.
вы́сп|аться, люсь, ишься *pf.* (*of* **высыпа́ться**[2]) (*coll.*) to have a good sleep; to have one's sleep out.
выспева́|ть, ю *impf. of* **вы́спеть**
вы́спе|ть, ю *pf.* (*coll.*) to ripen.
выспра́шива|ть, ю *impf. of* **вы́спросить**
вы́спренний *adj.* high-flown; bombastic.
вы́спро|сить, шу, сишь *pf.* (*of* **выспра́шивать**) (*coll.*) **1.** to inquire. **2.** to inquire of, interrogate; to pump **посла́ ~сили о поли́тике прави́тельства его́ страны́** the ambassador was pumped about his government's policy; **~сили у посла́ наме́рения его́ прави́тельства** the ambassador was pumped about his government's intentions.
вы́став|ить, лю, ишь *pf.* (*of* **~ля́ть**) **1.** to bring out, bring forward; to display, exhibit; **в. на прода́жу** to display for sale; **в. на свет** to expose to the light; **в. напока́з** to show off, parade. **2.** (*mil.*) to post (*guard, etc.*). **3.** (*+i.*) to represent (as), make out (as); **в. в плохо́м све́те** to represent in an unfavourable light; **в. в смешно́м ви́де** to make a laughing-stock (of); **его́ ~или тру́сом** he was made out to be a coward. **4.** to put forward; to adduce; **в. свою́ кандидату́ру** to come forward as a candidate; **в. до́воды** to adduce arguments. **5.** to put down, set down (*in writing*); **в. отме́тки** to put down marks; **в. число́ на письме́** to date a letter. **6.** to take out, remove; **в. око́нную ра́му** to take out a window frame. **7.** (*coll.*) to send out, turn out, throw out; to give the brush-off (to); **в. из ко́мнаты** to send out of the room; **в. со слу́жбы** to sack.
вы́став|иться, люсь, ишься *pf.* (*of* **~ля́ться**) **1.** (*coll.*) to lean out; to thrust o.s. forward; (*fig., pej.*) to show off. **2.** to exhibit (*intrans.*; *of an artist*).
вы́ставк|а, и *f.* **1.** exhibition, show; display. **2.** (show-)window, (shop-)window.
выставля́|ть, ю *impf. of* **вы́ставить**
выставля́|ться, юсь *impf. of* **вы́ставиться**
выставно́й *adj.* removable.
вы́став|очный *adj. of* **~ка; в. комите́т** exhibition committee.
выста́ива|ть(ся), ю(сь) *impf. of* **вы́стоять(ся)**
вы́стега|ть[1]**, ю** *pf. of* **стега́ть**[2]
вы́стега|ть[2]**, ю** *pf.* (*coll.*) to thrash, flog.
выстёгива|ть, ю *impf. of* **вы́стегнуть**
вы́стегн|уть, у, ешь *pf.* (*coll.*) to flick out.
вы́стел|ить, ю, ешь *pf.* = **вы́стлать**
вы́ст|елю, елешь *see* **~лать**
выстила́|ть, ю *impf. of* **вы́стлать** *and* **вы́стелить**
вы́стира|ть, ю *pf. of* **стира́ть**[2]
вы́ст|лать, елю, елешь *pf.* to cover; to pave; **они́ ~лали лино́леумом пол во всех ко́мнатах** they have covered all their floors with linoleum.

вы́сто|ять, ю, ишь *pf.* (*of* **выста́ивать**) **1.** to stand; **нам пришло́сь в. весь путь** we had to stand the whole way. **2.** to stand one's ground.
вы́сто|яться, юсь, ишься *pf.* (*of* **выста́иваться**) **1.** to mature, ripen. **2.** to become stale, flat. **3.** to rest (*of horses*).
выстра́гива|ть, ю *impf. of* **вы́строгать**
вы́страда|ть, ю *pf.* **1.** to suffer; to go through. **2.** to gain, achieve through suffering.
выстра́ива|ть(ся), ю(сь) *impf. of* **вы́строить(ся)**
выстра́чива|ть, ю *impf. of* **вы́строчить**
вы́стрел, а *m.* shot; report; **произвести́ в.** to fire a shot; **разда́лся в.** a shot rang out; **на в.** (**от**+ *g.*) (*coll.*) within gunshot (of).
выстре́лива|ть, ю *impf. of* **вы́стрелять**
вы́стрел|ить, ю, ишь *pf.* to shoot, fire; **я ~ил в него́ три ра́за** I fired three shots at him.
вы́стреля|ть, ю *pf.* (*of* **выстре́ливать**) (*coll.*) **1.** to use up in shooting; **мы ~ли все патро́ны** we had used up all our cartridges. **2.** to kill off (*by shooting*).
вы́стри|г, гу, жешь *see* **~чь**
выстрига́|ть, ю *impf. of* **вы́стричь**
вы́стри|чь, гу, жешь, гут, *past* **~г, ~гла** *pf.* to cut, clip out; to shear.
вы́строга|ть, ю *pf.* (*of* **строга́ть** *and* **выстра́гивать**) (*tech.*) to plane, shave.
вы́стро|ить, ю, ишь *pf.* (*of* **выстра́ивать**) **1.** to build. **2.** to draw up, order, arrange; (*mil.*) to form up.
вы́стро|иться, юсь, ишься *pf.* (*of* **выстра́иваться**) **1.** (*mil.*) to form up (*intrans.*). **2.** *pass. of* **~ить**
вы́строч|ить, у, ишь *pf.* (*of* **выстра́чивать**) to hemstitch.
вы́струга|ть, ю *pf.* = **вы́строгать**
вы́сту|дить, жу, дишь *pf.* (*coll.*) to cool; (*impers.*): **дом ~дило** the house had grown cold.
высту́жива|ть, ю *impf. of* **вы́студить**
вы́сту|жу, дишь *see* **~дить**
вы́стука|ть, ю *pf.* (*of* **высту́кивать**) (*coll.*) **1.** (*med.*) to tap. **2.** to tap out; **в. мело́дию** to tap out a tune; **в. сообще́ние** to tap out a message (*prison sl.*); to type out.
высту́кивани|е, я *nt.* percussion; tapping.
высту́кива|ть, ю *impf. of* **вы́стукать**
вы́ступ, а *m.* **1.** protuberance, projection, ledge; **в. фро́нта** (*mil.*) salient. **2.** (*tech.*) lug.
выступа́|ть, ю *impf.* **1.** *impf. of* **вы́ступить. 2.** (*impf. only*) to project, jut out, stick out. **3.** (*impf. only*) to strut, pace.
вы́ступ|ить, лю, ишь *pf.* **1.** to come forward; to come out; **герои́ня ~ила из-за кули́с** the heroine came forward from the wings; **в. в похо́д** (*mil.*) to take the field; **сыпь ~ила у неё на рука́х** a rash has come out on her arms. **2.** (**из**+*g.*) to go beyond; **в. из берего́в** to overflow its banks. **3.** to appear (*publicly*); to come out (with, as); **в. в печа́ти** to appear in print; **в. за предложе́ние** to come out in favour of a proposal; **в. защи́тником** (*leg.*) to appear for the defence; **в. с ре́чью** to make a speech; **в. по ра́дио с докла́дом** to give a broadcast talk, give a talk on the radio.
выступле́ни|е, я *nt.* **1.** appearance (*in public*); speech. **2.** setting out.
выстыва́|ть, ю *impf. of* **вы́стыть**
вы́сты|ть, ну, нешь *pf.* (*coll.*) to cool off, become cold.
вы́су|дить, жу, дишь *pf.* (*coll.*) to obtain by court decision.
высу́жива|ть, ю *impf. of* **вы́судить**
вы́су|жу, дишь *see* **~дить**
вы́сун|уть, у, ешь *pf.* (*of* **высо́вывать**) to put out, thrust out; **в. язы́к** to put one's tongue out; **бежа́ть ~ув язы́к** (*coll.*) to run without pausing for breath; **нельзя́ но́су в. (из дому)** (*coll.*) one can't show one's face (outside).
вы́сун|уться, усь, ешься *pf.* (*of* **высо́вываться**) to show o.s., thrust o.s. forward; **в. в окно́** to lean out of the window.
высу́шива|ть, ю *impf. of* **вы́сушить**
вы́суш|ить, у, ишь *pf.* **1.** to dry (out). **2.** (*coll.*) to emaciate. **3.** (*coll., fig.*) to make callous, make hard.
вы́считa|ть, ю *pf.* **1.** to calculate, compute; to reckon out. **2.** (*coll.*) to deduct.
высчи́тыва|ть, ю *impf. of* **вы́считать**
вы́с|ший *adj.* (*comp. and superl. of* **высо́кий**) highest; supreme; high; higher; **~шего ка́чества** of the highest quality; **~шая ме́ра наказа́ния** supreme penalty; (*leg.*) capital punishment; **суд ~шей инста́нции** High Court; **~шее образова́ние** higher education; **~шее о́бщество** (high) society; **~шее уче́бное заведе́ние** higher education establishment; **~шая шко́ла** university; **в ~шей сте́пени** in the highest degree.
высыла́|ть, ю *impf. of* **вы́слать**
вы́сылк|а, и *f.* **1.** sending, dispatching. **2.** expulsion; exile.
вы́сып|ать, лю, лешь *pf.* **1.** to pour out; to empty (out); to spill; (*fig., coll.*) to pour out, tell; **в. все свои́ забо́ты** to pour out all one's troubles; **ну, ~айте всё!** come on, spill the beans! **2.** (*coll.*) to pour out (*intrans.*). **3.** to break out (*of a rash, etc.*); (*impers.*): **у него́ ~ало на всем те́ле** he has come out in a rash all over.
высыпа́|ть, ю *impf. of* **вы́сыпать**
вы́сып|аться, люсь, лешься (*coll.* **~ешься)** *pf.* **1.** *pass. of* **~ать. 2.** to pour out; to spill (*intrans.*).
высыпа́|ться[1], юсь *impf. of* **вы́сыпаться**
высыпа́|ться[2], юсь, *impf. of* **вы́спаться**
вы́сыпк|а, и *f.* **1.** (*coll.*) pouring out, spilling. **2.** (*hunting*) descent (*of birds, etc.*).
высыха́|ть, ю *impf. of* **вы́сохнуть**
выс|ь, и *f.* height; (*usu. pl.*) summit; (*fig.*) the world of fantasy; **он всё вита́ет в забо́лачной ~и** he lives in the clouds.
выта́лкива|ть, ю *impf. of* **вы́толкать** *and* **вы́толкнуть**
вы́танц|евать(ся), ует(ся) *pf. of* **вытанцо́вывать(ся)**
вытанцо́выва|ть, ю *impf.* (*coll.*) to execute assiduously (*steps of a dance*).
вытанцо́выва|ться, ется *impf.* (*coll.*) to succeed, come off; **де́ло не ~ется** it is not coming off.
вытáплива|ть, ю *impf. of* **вы́топить**
вытáптыва|ть, ю *impf. of* **вы́топтать**
вытара́щива|ть, ю *impf. of* **вы́таращить**
вы́таращ|ить, у, ишь *pf.* (*coll.*): **в. глаза́** to open one's eyes wide.
вы́таска|ть, ю *pf.* (*coll.*) to drag out, fish out.
выта́скива|ть, ю *impf. of* **вы́таскать** *and* **вы́тащить**
вы́тача|ть, ю *pf. of* **тача́ть**
выта́чива|ть, ю *impf. of* **вы́точить**
вы́тачк|а, и *f.* tuck, dart.
вы́тащ|ить, у, ишь *pf.* (*of* **выта́скивать**) **1.** to drag out; to pull out, extract; (*coll.*) **в. кого́-н.** to drag s.o. out, drag s.o. off; **они́ ~или его́ в. кино́** they have dragged him off to the cinema; **в. кого́-н. из беды́** to help s.o. out of trouble. **2.** (*coll.*) to steal, pinch; **у меня́ ~или бума́жник** I have had my wallet stolen.
вы́твер|дить, жу, дишь *pf.* (*coll.*) to get by heart.
вытве́ржива|ть, ю *impf. of* **вы́твердить**
вытворя́|ть, ю *impf.* (*coll.*) to get up to, be up to; **что ты тепе́рь ~ешь?** what are you up to now?
вытека́|ть, ю *impf.* **1.** *impf. of* **вы́течь. 2.** (*impf. only*) to flow (from, out of) (*of a river*). **3.** (*impf. only*) (*fig.*) to result, follow (from); **отсю́да ~ет, что вы оши́блись** from this it follows that you are mistaken.
вы́те|ку, чешь, кут *see* **~чь**
вы́т|ереть, ру, решь, *past* **~ер, ~ерла** *pf.* (*of* **~ира́ть**) **1.** to wipe (up); to dry, rub dry; **в. но́ги** to wipe one's feet; **в. посу́ду** dry the crockery; **в. пыль со стола́** to dust the table. **2.** (*coll.*) to wear out, wear threadbare.
вы́терп|еть, лю, ишь *pf.* to bear, endure; to suffer; **я е́ле ~ел, когда́ он сказа́л э́то** I could hardly stand it when he said that.
вы́терт|ый (~, ~а) *p.p.p. of* **вы́тереть** *and adj.* threadbare.
вы́те|сать, шу, шешь *pf.* to square off.
вытесне́ни|е, я *nt.* **1.** ousting; supplanting. **2.** (*phys.*) displacement.
вы́тесн|ить, ю, ишь *pf.* **1.** to crowd out; to force out; (*fig.*) to oust; to supplant. **2.** (*phys.*) to displace.
вытесня́|ть, ю *impf. of* **вы́теснить**
вытёсыва|ть, ю *impf. of* **вы́тесать**
вы́те|чь, ку, чешь, кут, *past* **~к, ~кла** *pf.* (*of* **~ка́ть**) to flow out, run out; **у него́ глаз ~к** he has lost an eye.

вы́те|шу, шешь *see* **~сать**
вытира́|ть, ю *impf. of* **вы́тереть**
вы́тисн|ить, ю, ишь *pf.* to stamp, imprint, impress.
вы́тисн|уть, у, ешь *pf.* = **~ить**
вытисня́|ть, ю *impf. of* **вы́тиснить**
вы́тк|ать, у, ешь *pf.* to weave, finish weaving; **в. ковёр** to weave a carpet; **в. цветы́ на ковре́** to weave a flower pattern on a carpet.
вы́толка|ть, ю *pf.* (*of* **выта́лкивать**) (*coll.*) to throw out; **его́ ~ли в ше́ю** (*sl.*) he was thrown out on his neck.
вы́толкн|уть, у, ешь *pf.* (*of* **выта́лкивать**) **1.** to throw out. **2.** (*coll.*) to push out, force out.
вы́топ|ить, лю, ишь *pf.* (*of* **выта́пливать**) **1.** (*coll.*) to heat. **2.** to melt (down).
вы́топ|тать, чу, чешь *pf.* (*of* **выта́птывать**) to trample down.
вытора́чива|ть, ю *impf. of* **вы́торочить**
вы́торг|овать, ую *pf.* **1.** to gain, obtain (*by bargaining, haggling*); to get a reduction (of); **он ~овал де́сять рубле́й из цены́ э́тих сапо́г** he got a reduction of ten roubles on the price of these boots, he got these boots reduced by ten roubles; (*fig., coll.*) to manage to get; **он ~овал отсро́чку для оконча́ния диссерта́ции** he has managed to get an extension of time to finish his dissertation. **2.** (*coll.*) to make (a profit of), to net, clear.
выторго́выва|ть, ю *impf.* **1.** *impf. of* **вы́торговать. 2.** to try to get (*by bargaining*); to haggle over.
вы́тороч|ить, у, ишь *pf.* (*of* **вытора́чивать**) to unstrap from the saddle.
вы́точен|ный (~, ~а) *p.p.p. of* **вы́точить** *and adj.* **сло́вно в.** chiselled (*of facial features*); perfect, perfectly-formed (*of bodies*).
вы́точ|ить, у, ишь *pf.* (*of* **выта́чивать**) **1.** to turn (*tech.*). **2.** (*coll.*) to sharpen. **3.** (*coll.*) to gnaw through.
вы́трав|ить, лю, ишь *pf.* (*of* **трави́ть**[1] *and* **~ля́ть**) **1.** to exterminate, destroy. **2.** to remove, get out (*by chemical action*); **в. пятно́** to remove a stain. **3.** to etch. **4.** (*of cattle, etc.*) to trample down (*crops etc.*).
вытра́влива|ть, ю *impf.* (*coll.*) = **вытравля́ть**
вытравля́|ть, ю *impf. of* **вы́травить**
вытравно́й *adj.* corrosive, erosive.
вытра́ива|ть, ю *impf. of* **вы́троить**
вытра́лива|ть, ю *impf. of* **вы́тралить**
вы́трал|ить, ю, ишь *pf.* (*mil.*) to sweep (*mines*).
вы́треб|овать, ую *pf.* **1.** to obtain on demand. **2.** to send for, summon(s); **в. кого́-н. в суд пове́сткой** to summons s.o.
вытрезви́ловк|а, и *f.* (*coll.*) = **вытрезви́тель**
вытрезви́тел|ь, я *m.* detoxification centre.
вы́трезв|ить, лю, ишь *pf.* to sober.
вы́трезв|иться, люсь, ишься *pf.* (*coll.*) to sober up (*intrans.*).
вытрезвля́|ть(ся), ю(сь) *impf. of* **вы́трезвить(ся)**
вы́тро|ить, ю, ишь *pf.* (*of* **вытра́ивать**) (*dial., tech.*) **1.** to distil three times. **2.** to plough up three times.
вы́т|ру, решь *see* **~ереть**
вы́тру|сить, шу, сишь *pf.* (*coll.*) to drop, let fall; to spill.
вытряса́|ть, ю *impf. of* **вы́трясти**
вы́тряс|ти, у, ешь, *past* **~, ~ла** *pf.* **1.** to shake out. **2.** to clean by shaking out; **в. ковёр** to shake out a carpet.
вытряха́|ть, ю *impf.* (*dial., coll.*) = **вытря́хивать**
вытря́хива|ть, ю *impf. of* **вы́тряхнуть**
вы́тряхн|уть, у, ешь *pf.* to drop, let fall; to shake out.
выту́рива|ть, ю *impf. of* **вы́турить**
вы́тур|ить, ю, ишь *pf.* (*coll.*) to throw out, chuck out.
выть, во́ю, во́ешь *impf.* to howl (*of animals, the wind, etc.*); (*fig., coll.*) to howl, wail.
вы́ть|ё, я́ *no pl., nt.* (*coll.*) howling; wailing.
вы́тяга|ть, ю *pf.* (*obs.*) to win (by a lawsuit)
вытя́гива|ть(ся), ю(сь) *impf. of* **вы́тянуть(ся)**
вытяже́ни|е, *nt.* stretching.
вы́тяжк|а, и *f.* **1.** drawing out, extraction. **2.** (*chem., med.*) extract. **3.** stretching, extension; **на ~у,** *see* **навы́тяжку**
вытяжн|о́й *adj.* for extracting, for drawing out; **в. пла́стырь** drawing plaster; **в. трос** rip cord (*of parachute*); **~а́я труба́** ventilating pipe; **в. шкаф** fume cupboard.
вы́тянут|ый (~, ~а) *p.p.p. of* **~ь** *and adj.* stretched; **~ое лицо́** (*fig.*) a long face.
вы́тян|уть, у, ешь *pf.* (*of* **вытя́гивать**) **1.** to stretch (out); to extend. **2.** to draw out, extract (*also fig.*); (*impers.*): **газ ~уло в окно́** the gas had escaped through the window; (*fig., coll.*) **в. всю ду́шу** (+*d. or* **у**+*g.*) to wear (s.o.) out; **в. все жи́лы** (**у, из**+*g.*) to exhaust. **3.** (*coll.*) to endure, stand, stick; **он до́лго не ~ет при тако́м кли́мате** he won't stick it for long in a climate like that. **4.** (*coll.*) to weigh. **5.** (*coll.*) to flog.
вы́тян|уться, усь, ешься *pf.* (*of* **вытя́гиваться**) **1.** to stretch (*intrans.*); to stretch o.s. (out); **он засну́л ~увшись на полу́** he fell asleep stretched out on the floor; **лицо́ у неё ~улось** (*coll.*) her face lengthened, her face fell. **2.** (*coll.*) to grow, shoot up. **3.** to stand erect; **в. в стру́нку, в. во фронт** (*mil.*) to stand at attention.
вы́у|дить, жу, дишь *pf.* **1.** to catch. **2.** (*fig., pej.*) to extract, dig up.
выу́жива|ть, ю *impf. of* **вы́удить**
вы́утюж|ить, у, ишь *pf. of* **утю́жить**
вы́ученик, а *m.* pupil (*of a craftsman*); disciple, follower.
выу́чива|ть, ю *impf. of* **вы́учить**
вы́уч|ить, у, ишь *pf.* (*of* **учи́ть** *and* **~́ивать**) **1.** to learn. **2.** (+*a. and d. or* +*inf.*) to teach; **он ~ил нас испа́нскому языку́** he taught us Spanish; **он ~ил её пра́вить маши́ной** he has taught her to drive (a car).
вы́уч|иться, усь ишься *pf.* (*of* **учи́ться**) (+*d. or inf.*) to learn.
вы́учк|а, и *f.* teaching, training; **отда́ть на ~у** (+*d.*) to apprentice (to); **он прошёл хоро́шую ~у** he has had a sound schooling; **боева́я в.** (*mil.*) battle training.
выха́жива|ть, ю *impf. of* **вы́ходить**
вы́харка|ть, ю *pf.* (*coll.*) to hawk (up).
выха́ркива|ть, ю *impf. of* **вы́харкать**
вы́харк|нуть, ну, нешь *pf.* = **~ать**
выхва́лива|ть, ю *impf. of* **вы́хвалить**
вы́хвал|ить, ю, ишь *pf.* to praise.
выхваля́|ть, ю *impf.* = **выхва́ливать**
выхваля́|ться, юсь *impf.* **1.** (*coll.*) to sing one's own praises, blow one's own trumpet. **2.** *pass. of* **~ть**
вы́хва|тить, чу, тишь *pf.* **1.** to snatch out, snatch away from; **он про́сто ~тил газе́ту из-под моего́ но́са** he simply snatched up the newspaper from under my nose. **2.** to pull out, draw; **в. нож** to draw a knife. **3.** to pull out, take out, pick up (*at random*); **он ~тил кни́гу из ку́чи и на́чал чита́ть** he picked up a book from the pile and began to read; **в. цита́ту** (*fig.*) to quote at random.
выхва́тыва|ть, ю *impf. of* **вы́хватить**
вы́хвачен|ный (~, ~а) *p.p.p. of* **вы́хватить; ~ из жи́зни** true to life, taken from the life.
вы́хва|чу, тишь *see* **~тить**
вы́хлеба|ть, ю *pf.* (*coll.*) to eat up.
вы́хлеб|нуть, ну, нешь *pf.* = **~ать**
выхлёбыва|ть, ю *impf. of* **вы́хлебать**
вы́хлеста|ть, ю *pf.* (*coll.*) **1.** to flog, lash. **2.** to flick out. **3.** (*sl.*) to drink off, drain.
вы́хлестн|уть, у, ешь *pf.* (*coll.*) **1.** to flick out. **2.** to splash out.
выхлёстыва|ть, ю *impf. of* **вы́хлестнуть**
выхлоп, а *m.* (*tech.*) exhaust.
выхлопа́тыва|ть, ю *impf. of* **вы́хлопотать**
выхлопно́й *adj.* (*tech.*) exhaust.
вы́хлопо|тать, чу, чешь *pf.* (*of* **выхлопа́тывать**) to obtain (*after much trouble*).
вы́ход, а *m.* **1.** going out; leaving, departure; **в. за́муж** marriage (*of woman*); **в. в отста́вку** retirement. **2.** way out, exit; outlet; **из э́того положе́ния ~а не́ было** (*fig.*) there was no way out of this situation; **дать в.** (+*d.*) to give vent (to); **знать все хо́ды и ~ы** (*coll.*) to know all the ins and outs. **3.** appearance (*of a publication*); (*theatr.*) entrance. **4.** (*econ.*) output; yield. **5.** (*geol.*) outcrop. **6.** (*eccl.*): **вели́кий, ма́лый в.** great, little entrance. **7.: быть на ~ах** (*theatr.*) to play a supernumerary part.
вы́ход|ец, ца *m.* **1.** emigrant; immigrant; **он роди́лся в США, а роди́тели бы́ли ~цами из Гре́ции** he was born

in the United States but his parents were emigrants from Greece; **в. с того́ све́та** apparition, ghost. **2.** pers. springing from different social group; **он — в. из крестья́н** he is of peasant origin.

вы́хо|дить[1], **жу, дишь** *pf.* (*of* **выха́живать**) (*coll.*) **1.** to tend, nurse. **2.** to rear, bring up; to grow (*plants*).

вы́хо|дить[2], **жу, дишь** *pf.* (*of* **выха́живать**) (*coll.*) to pass (through); go all over.

выхо|ди́ть, жу́, ~дишь *impf.* **1.** *impf. of* **вы́йти. 2.** (*impf. only*) to look out (on), give (on), face; **его́ ко́мната ~дит о́кнами на у́лицу** his room looks onto the street. **3.: не в. из головы́, из ума́** to be unforgettable, stick in one's mind. **4.** *as pred.* **~дит** (*coll.*) it turns out.

вы́ходк|а, и *f.* **1.** (*pej.*) trick; escapade. **2.** outburst. **3.** (*coll.*) initial step of a dance.

выходни́к, а́ *m.* (*coll.*) pers. working on day off.

выходн|о́й *adj.* **1.** exit; **~а́я дверь** street door. **2.: в. день** day off, free day, rest-day; **~а́я оде́жда** 'best' clothes, walking-out clothes; **~о́е пла́тье** party dress; *as n.* (*i*) **в., ~о́го** *m.* = **в. день**, (*ii*) **в., ~о́го** *m.*, **~а́я, ~о́й** *f.* pers. having day off; **он сего́дня в.** it is his day off today. **3.: ~о́е посо́бие** (*also as n.* **~ы́е, ~ы́х**) gratuity on discharge; severance pay. **4.** (*theatr.*): **~а́я роль** supernumerary part. **5.** (*typ.*): **в. лист** title-page; **~ы́е све́дения** imprint.

выход|я́щий *pres. part. of* **~и́ть; из ря́да вон ~я́щий** outstanding; *as n.* **в., ~я́щего** *m.* (*chess, cards*) extra player, bye; **в. пе́рвом ту́ре он был ~я́щим** he had a bye in the first round.

вы́хо|жу, дишь *see* **~дить**

выхо|жу́, ~дишь *see* **~ди́ть**

выхола́жива|ть, ю *impf. of* **вы́холодить**

выхола́щива|ть, ю *impf. of* **вы́холостить**

вы́хол|енный *p.p.p. of* **~ить** *and adj.* well-cared-for; well-groomed.

вы́хол|ить, ю, ишь *pf.* to care for, tend.

вы́холо|дить, жу, дишь *pf.* (*of* **выхола́живать**) to cool.

вы́холо|стить, щу, стишь *pf.* (*of* **выхола́щивать**) to castrate, geld; (*fig.*) to emasculate.

вы́холо|щенный *p.p.p. of* **~стить** *and adj.* castrated, gelded; (*fig.*) emasculated; **~щенная ло́шадь** gelding.

вы́хухолевый *adj.* musquash.

вы́хухол|ь, я *m.* **1.** desman, musk-rat. **2.** (*fur*) musquash.

вы́цапа|ть, ю *pf.* (**у**+*g.*; *coll.*) to seize, grasp.

вы́царапа|ть, ю *pf.* (*coll.*) **1.** to scratch; (+*a. and d.*) to scratch out; **они́ почти́ ~ли друг дру́гу глаза́** they almost scratched each other's eyes out. **2.** (*fig.*) to extract, get (out of); **он ~л у отца́ ещё де́сять рубле́й** he has got another ten roubles out of his father.

выцара́пыва|ть, ю *impf. of* **вы́царапать**

вы́цве|сти (*coll.* **~сть**), **ту, тешь,** *past* **~л** *pf.* to fade.

выцвета́|ть, ю *impf. of* **вы́цвести**

вы́цве|тший *p.p. of* **~сти** *and adj.* faded.

вы́це|дить, жу, дишь *pf.* **1.** to filter, rack (off); to decant. **2.** (*fig., coll.*) to drink off, drain.

выце́жива|ть, ю *impf. of* **вы́цедить**

выча́лива|ть, ю *impf. of* **вы́чалить**

вы́чал|ить, ю, ишь *pf.* to haul up, beach (*a boat*).

вычека́нива|ть, ю *impf. of* **вы́чеканить**

вы́чекан|ить, ю, ишь *pf.* to mint; to strike; **в. меда́ль** to strike a medal.

вы́ч|ел, ла *see* **~есть**

вычёркива|ть, ю *impf. of* **вы́черкнуть**

вы́черкн|уть, у, ешь *pf.* to cross out, strike out; to expunge, erase; **в. кого́-н. из спи́ска живы́х** to give up as dead.

вы́черпа|ть, ю *pf.* (**из**+*g.*) to take out (*fluids*); to bail (out); **в. во́ду из ло́дки** bail out a boat.

выче́рпыва|ть, ю *impf. of* **вы́черпать**

вы́чер|тить, чу, тишь *pf.* to draw; to trace.

вы́черчен|ный (~, ~а) *p.p.p. of* **вы́чертить** *and adj.* finely-drawn; **~ные бро́ви** pencilled eyebrows.

выче́рчива|ть, ю *impf. of* **вы́чертить**

вы́чер|чу, тишь *see* **~тить**

вы́че|сать, шу, шешь *pf.* (*of* **~́сывать**) to comb out.

вы́ческ|а, и *no pl., f.* combing out.

вы́чес|ки, ок *no sg.* (*text*) combing.

вы́ч|есть, ту, тешь, *past* **~ел, ~ла,** *pres. ger.* **~тя** *pf.* (*of* **~ита́ть**) **1.** (*math.*) to subtract. **2.** to deduct, keep back; **пять проце́нтов из ва́шего жа́лованья ~ли на страхова́ние** five per cent of your salary has been kept back for insurance.

вычёсыва|ть, ю *impf. of* **вы́чесать**

вы́чет, а *m.* deduction; **за ~ом** (+*g.*) except; less, minus, allowing for; **он зараба́тывает две́сти рубле́й в ме́сяц за ~ом нало́гов** he earns two hundred roubles a month less taxes.

вы́че|шу, шешь *see* **~сать**

вычисле́ни|е, я *nt.* calculation.

вычисли́тел|ь, я *m.* **1.** calculator. **2.** (*mil.*) plotter. **3.** calculating-machine.

вычисли́тельн|ый *adj.* calculating, computing; **~ая маши́на** computer.

вы́числ|ить, ю, ишь *pf.* to calculate, compute.

вычисля́|ть, ю *impf. of* **вы́числить**

вы́чи|стить, щу, стишь *pf.* (*of* **чи́стить** *and* **~ща́ть**) **1.** to clean (up, out). **2.** (*fig.*) to purge; to expel; **его́ ~стили из па́ртии** he has been expelled from the party.

вычита́ем|ое, ого *nt.* (*math.*) subtrahend.

вычита́ни|е, я, *nt.* (*math.*) subtraction.

вы́чита|ть, ю *pf.* (*of* **вычи́тывать**) **1.** (*coll.*) to find (*by reading, perusing*); **я ~л сообще́ние о его́ сме́рти в одно́й из вчера́шних газе́т** I found a report of his death in one of yesterday's newspapers. **2.** (*typ.*) to read (*manuscripts, proofs*).

вычита́|ть, ю *impf. of* **вы́честь**

вы́читк|а, и *f.* (*typ.*) reading.

вычи́тыва|ть[1], **ю** *impf.* = **вычита́ть**

вычи́тыва|ть[2], **ю** *impf.* **1.** *impf. of* **вы́читать. 2.** *impf. only* to reprimand, tell off.

вычища́|ть, ю *impf. of* **вы́чистить**

вы́чи|щу, стишь *see* **~стить**

вы́ч|ту, тешь *see* **~есть**

вы́чур|ы, ~, *sg.* **~а, ~ы** *f.* **1.** fancy; mannerism; (*liter.; obs.*) conceit. **2.** (*obs.*) intricate pattern (*on fabrics*).

вы́чур|ный (~ен, ~на) *adj.* fanciful; mannered; precious.

вы́шага|ть, ю *pf.* (*coll.*) to pace out.

выша́рива|ть, ю *impf. of* **вы́шарить**

вы́шар|ить, ю, ишь *pf.* (*coll.*) to rummage out, ferret out.

вышвы́рива|ть, ю *impf. of* **вы́швырнуть** *and* **вы́швырять**

вы́швырн|уть, у, ешь *pf.* to throw out, hurl out (*fig., coll.*) to chuck out.

вы́швыря|ть, ю *pf.* (*coll.*) to throw out.

вы́ше 1. *comp. of* **высо́кий** *and* **высо́ко́**; higher, taller. **2.** *prep.*+*g.* above, beyond; over; **э́то в. моего́ понима́ния** it is beyond my comprehension, it passes my understanding; **в. свои́х сил** beyond one's powers, beyond one; **зада́ча оказа́лась в. его́ сил** the task proved to be beyond him; **быть в.** (+*g.*) to rise superior (to); **в по́лдень температу́ра подняла́сь в. восьми́десяти гра́дусов** by midday the temperature had risen to over eighty degrees; **дере́вня на Во́лге, в. Сара́това** a village on the Volga, above Saratov. **3.** *adv.* (*liter.*) above; **смотри́ в.** *vide supra.*

выше... *comb. form* above-, afore-.

вышеизло́женный *adj.* foregoing.

вы́|шел, шла *see* **~йти**

вышелу́шива|ть, ю *impf. of* **вы́шелушить**

вы́шелуш|ить, у, ишь *pf.* to peel; to shell.

вышена́званный *adj.* aforenamed.

вышеозна́ченный *adj.* aforesaid, above-mentioned.

вышеприведённый *adj.* above-cited; **в. приме́р** the above-cited example, the example above.

вышере́ченный *adj.* (*obs., now iron.*) aforementioned.

вышеска́занный *adj.* aforesaid.

вышестоя́щ|ий *adj.* higher; (*pol.*) **~ие о́рганы вла́сти** the higher organs of power.

вышеука́занный *adj.* foregoing.

вышеупомя́нутый *adj.* afore-mentioned.

вышиба́л|а, ы *m.* **1.** (*sl.*) chucker-out; bouncer. **2.** (*coll.*) rude fellow.

вышиба́|ть, ю *impf. of* **вы́шибить**

вы́шиб|ить, у, ешь, *past* **~, ~ла** *pf.* (*coll.*) **1.** to knock

out; **в. ду́шу, в. дух (из**+*g.*) to bump off, beat to death. **2.** to chuck out.
вышива́льный *adj.* embroidery.
вышива́льщиц|а, ы *f.* needle-woman.
вышива́ни|е, я *nt.* embroidery, needle-work.
вышива́|ть, ю *impf. of* **вы́шить**
вы́шивк|а, и *f.* embroidery, needle-work.
вышивно́й *adj.* embroidered.
вышин|а́, ы́, *pl.* **∠ы** *f.* height; **в ~е́** aloft, high up; **~о́й в ты́сячу ме́тров** a thousand metres high, up.
вы́ш|ить, ью, ьешь, *imper.* **~ей** *pf.* (*of* **~ива́ть**) to embroider (on; with); **в. узо́р на пла́тье** to embroider a pattern on a dress; **в. узо́р гла́дью** to embroider a pattern in satin-stitch.
вы́шк|а, и *f.* **1.** turret. **2.** (watch-)tower; **диспе́тчерская в.** (*aeron.*) control tower; **сторожева́я в.** watch-tower; **бурова́я в.** derrick. **3.** high board. **4.** (*coll.*) capital punishment, the death penalty; **ему́ да́ли ~у** he was given a death sentence.
вы́школ|ить, ю, ишь *pf. of* **шко́лить**
вы́шлиф|овать, ую *pf.* **1.** (*tech.*) to polish. **2.** (*fig., coll.*) to polish, give a polish to; to smarten up.
вышлифо́выва|ть, ю *impf. of* **вы́шлифовать**
вы́|шлю, шлешь *see* **~слать**
вышмы́гива|ть, ю *impf. of* **вы́шмыгнуть**
вы́шмыгн|уть, у, ешь *pf.* (*coll.*) to slip out.
вы́шн|ий *adj.* heavenly, divine; **~яя си́ла** the power of the Most High.
вышны́рива|ть, ю *impf. of* **вы́шнырнуть** *and* **вы́шнырять**
вы́шнырн|уть, у, ешь *pf.* (*coll.*) to jump out.
вы́шныря|ть, ю *pf.* (*coll.*) **1.** to rush all round. **2.** to smell out, scent out (*information*).
вышпа́рива|ть, ю *impf. of* **вы́шпарить**
вы́шпар|ить, ю, ишь *pf.* (*coll.*) to smoke out; to scald out (*insects, etc.*).
выштукату́рива|ть, ю *impf. of* **вы́штукатурить**
вы́штукатур|ить, ю, ишь *pf.* to stucco.
вы́шу|тить, чу, тишь *pf.* to laugh at, make fun of; to poke fun at.
вышу́чива|ть, ю *impf. of* **вы́шутить**
выщела́чива|ть, *impf. of* **вы́щелочить**
выщёлкива|ть, ю *impf.* (*coll.*) (*of nightingales, etc.*) to warble forth; (*fig.; of horses' hoofs*) to clatter.
вы́щелоч|ить, у, ишь *pf.* (*of* **выщела́чивать**) **1.** (*chem.*) to leach, lixiviate. **2.** to steep, soak (*linen*) to lye.
вы́щерб|ить, лю, ишь *pf.* (*of* **~ля́ть**) (*coll.*) to dent; to jag.
выщербля́|ть, ю *impf. of* **вы́щербить**
вы́щип|ать, лю, лешь *pf.* to pull out, pull up; **в. пе́рья у ку́рицы** to pluck a hen.
вы́щипн|уть, у, ешь *pf.* to pull out; to pluck out.
выщи́пыва|ть, ю *impf. of* **вы́щипать** *and* **вы́щипнуть**
вы́щупа|ть, ю *pf.* **1.** (*med.*) to find (*by probing*). **2.** (*coll.*) to run one's hands over; to ransack.
выщу́пыва|ть, ю *impf. of* **вы́щупать**
вы́|я, и *f.* **1.** (*obs. or rhet.*) neck. **2.** nape (of the neck).
вы́яв|ить, лю, ишь *pf.* (*of* **~ля́ть**) **1.** to display, reveal. **2.** to bring out; to make known. **3.** (*pej.*) to show up, expose.
вы́яв|иться, люсь, ишься *pf.* (*of* **~ля́ться**) to appear, come to light, be revealed.
выявле́ни|е, я *nt.* revelation; showing up, exposure.
выявля́|ть(ся), ю(сь) *impf. of* **вы́явить(ся)**
выясне́ни|е, я *nt.* elucidation; explanation.
вы́ясн|ить[1], ю, ишь *pf.* to elucidate; to clear up, explain.
вы́ясн|ить[2], ит *pf.* (*impers.; dial.*) to clear up (*of weather*).
вы́ясн|иться, ится *pf.* to become clear; to turn out, prove (*intrans.*); **как ~илось, он лгал всё вре́мя** he was lying all the time as it turned out.
выясн|я́ть(ся), я́ю(сь) *impf. of* **вы́яснить(ся)**
Вьетна́м, а *m.* Vietnam.
вьетна́м|ец, ца *m.* Vietnamese.
вьетна́м|ка, ки *f. of* **~ец**
вьетна́м|ки, ок *no sg.* (*coll.*) flip-flops.
вьетна́мский *adj.* Vietnamese.
вью, вьёшь *see* **вить**
вью́г|а, и *f.* snow-storm, blizzard.
вью́|жный *adj. of* **~га**
вьюк, а *m.* pack; load.
вьюн, а́ *m.* **1.** loach (*fish*). **2.** (*fig., coll.*) restless, mobile pers.; **верте́ться ~о́м, ви́ться ~о́м о́коло кого́-н.** to be all over s.o., try to get round s.o.
вьюн|о́к, ка́ *m.* (*bot.*) bindweed, convolvulus.
вьюр|о́к, ка́ *m.* (*zool.*) mountain finch, brambling.
вью́ч|ить, у, ишь *impf.* (*of* **на~**) to load (up).
вью́чн|ый *adj.* pack; **~ое живо́тное** beast of burden; **~ое седло́** pack-saddle.
вью́шк|а, и *f.* damper.
вью́щ|ийся *pres. part. of* **ви́ться** *and adj.*: **~иеся во́лосы** curly hair; **~ееся расте́ние** (*bot.*) creeper, climber; **в. плющ** tree ivy.
вя|жу́, ∠жешь *see* **~за́ть**
вя́жущий *pres. part. act. of* **вяза́ть** *and adj.* **1.** astringent. **2.** (*tech.*) binding, cementing.
вяз, а *m.* elm(-tree).
вяза́льн|ый *adj.* knitting; **в. крючо́к** crochet hook; **~ая спи́ца** knitting-needle.
вяза́льщик, а *m.* **1.** knitter. **2.** binder.
вяза́ни|е, я *nt.* **1.** knitting. **2.** binding, tying.
вя́занк|а, и *f.* (*coll.*) knitted garment (*jumper, jacket, etc.*).
вяза́нк|а, и *f.* bundle; truss.
вя́заный *adj.* knitted.
вяза́нь|е, я *nt.* knitting (*object in process of being knitted*).
вя|за́ть, жу́, ∠жешь *impf.* **1.** (*pf.* **с~**) to tie, bind; (*tech.*) to tie, clamp; **в. кому́-н. ру́ки** to tie s.o.'s hands. **2.** (*pf.* **с~**) to knit. **3.** (*impf. only*) to be astringent; (*impers.*): **у меня́ ∠жет во рту** my mouth feels constricted.
вя|за́ться, жу́сь, ∠жешься *impf.* (**с**+*i.*) to accord, agree (with); to fit in, be in keeping (with), tally; **ва́ше предположе́ние о причи́не ава́рии не ∠жется с э́тими све́дениями** your theory as to the cause of the crash does not fit in with this evidence; **его́ вычисле́ния никогда́ не ~за́лись с мои́ми** his calculations never tallied with mine; **де́ло не ~за́лось, пока́ вы не прие́хали** the business was making no progress until you came.
вязи́га = **визи́га**
вя́зк|а, и *f.* **1.** tying, binding. **2.** knitting. **3.** bunch, string; **в. ключе́й** bunch of keys.
вя́з|кий (~ок, ~ка́, ~ко) *adj.* **1.** viscous, sticky; boggy. **2.** (*tech.*) ductile, malleable; tough. **3.** (*coll.*) astringent.
вя́зкост|ь, и *f.* **1.** viscosity, stickiness; bogginess. **2.** (*tech.*) ductility, malleability; toughness.
вя́зн|уть, у, ешь *impf.* (**в**+*p.*) to stick, get stuck (in); to sink (into); **в. в грязи́** to stick in the mud.
вя́зовый *adj.* elm.
вя́з|че *comp. of* **~кий** *and* **~ко**
вя́зчик, а *m.* binder.
вяз|ь, и *no pl., f.* **1.** (*palaeog.*) ornamental, ligatured script. **2.** interwoven ornament (*in pattern*).
вя́ка|ть, ю *impf.* (*coll., dial.*) to speak indistinctly; to talk nonsense, blather.
вя́лени|е, я *nt.* (*of meat, fish, etc.*) drying; dry-curing; jerking.
вя́леный *adj.* dried.
вя́л|ить, ю, ишь *impf.* (*of* **про~**) to dry (*in the sun*); to dry-cure, jerk (*meat, fish, etc.*).
вя́лост|ь, и *f.* flabbiness; limpness; (*fig.*) sluggishness; inertia; slackness.
вя́л|ый *adj.* **1.** faded. **2.** (**~, ~а́, ~о**) flabby, flaccid; limp; (*fig.*) sluggish, inert; slack; **~ое настрое́ние** sluggish disposition; **в. ры́нок** (*econ.*) slack market.
вя́н|уть, у, ешь, *past* **~ул, ~ула** *and* **вял, вя́ла** *impf.* (*of* **за~**) to fade, wither; (*fig.*) to droop, flag; **у́ши ~ут от тако́го разгово́ра** it makes one sick to listen to such talk.
вя́хир|ь, я *m.* wood-pigeon.
вя́щ|ий *adj.* (*obs. or joc.*) greater; **к ~ему несча́стью** to crown the misfortune; **для ~ей предосторо́жности** to make assurance doubly sure.

Г

г (*abbr. of* **грамм**) g, gr, gram(me)(s).
г. *abbr. of* **1. год** year. **2. гора́** mountain; Mount, Mt. **3. го́род** city, town. **4. господи́н** Mr.
га (*abbr. of* **гекта́р**) ha, hectare(s).
Гаа́г|а, и *f.* The Hague.
габарди́н, а *m.* gaberdine.
габари́т, а *m.* (*tech.*) **1.** (*rail.*) clearance. **2.** size, dimension (*of a machine*).
габари́т|ный *adj. of* ~; **~ные воро́та** (*rail.*) clearance gauge; **~ная высота́** overall height; overhead clearance; **г. свет** sidelight, parking light.
Габо́н, а *m.* Gabon.
гава́|ец, йца *m.* Hawaiian.
Гава́йи *m. indecl.* Hawaii.
гава́|йка, йки *f. of* **~ец**
гава́йский *adj.* Hawaiian.
Гава́н|а, ы *f.* Havana.
гава́нн|а, ы *f.* (*coll.*) Havana (*tobacco or cigar*).
га́ван|ский *adj. of* **~ь**
га́ван|ь, и *f.* harbour.
га́вка|ть, ю *impf.* (*coll.*) to bark.
Гавр, а *m.* Le Havre.
га́врик, а *m.* (*sl.*) **1.** petty crook. **2.** mate.
га́г|а, и *f.* eider-duck.
гага́ка|ть, ет *impf.* (*dial. or coll.*; *onomat.*, *of geese*) to cackle.
гага́р|а, ы *f.* (*zool.*) loon, diver.
гага́рк|а, и *f.* (*zool.*) razorbill.
гага́т, а *m.* (*min.*) jet.
гага́чий *adj. of* **га́га; г. пух** eider-down.
гад, а *m.* **1.** (*obs.*) amphibian, reptile. **2.** (*fig.*, *coll.*) repulsive pers.; (*pl.*) vermin.
гада́лк|а, и *f.* fortune-teller.
гада́ни|е, я *nt.* **1.** divination, fortune-telling; **г. на ка́ртах** card-reading, cartomancy; **г. по руке́** palmistry. **2.** guess-work.
гада́тел|ьный (~ен, ~ьна) *adj.* problematic, conjectural, hypothetical; **~ьная кни́га** fortune-telling book.
гада́|ть, ю *impf.* **1.** (*pf.* **по~**) (**на**+*p. or* **по**+*d.*) to tell fortunes (by); **г. на кофе́йной гу́ще** to make wild guesses. **2.** *impf. only* (**о**+*p.*) to guess, conjecture, surmise.
Гаде́с, а *m.* Hades.
га́дин|а, ы *f.* (*fig.*) reptile; (*coll.*) repulsive pers.; (*pl.*) vermin.
га́|дить, жу, дишь *impf.* (*of* **на~**) **1.** (*of animals*) to defecate. **2.** (**на**+*a. or p.*, **в**+*p.*) to foul, defile. **3.** (+*d.*; *coll.*) to play dirty tricks (on).
га́д|кий (~ок, ~ка́, ~ко) *adj.* nasty, vile, repulsive; **г. утёнок** ugly duckling.
га́дк|о[1] *adv. of* **~ий**
га́дко[2] *as pred.* **мне,** *etc.*, **г.** I, *etc.*, loathe (it); I, *etc.*, am repelled.
гадли́вост|ь, и *f.* aversion, disgust.
гадли́в|ый (~, ~а) *adj.*: **~ое чу́вство** (feeling of) disgust.
га́дост|ный (~ен, ~на) *adj.* disgusting; (*coll.*) poor, bad.
га́дост|ь, и *f.* **1.** (*coll.*) filth, muck. **2.** dirty trick; **он спосо́бен на вся́кую г.** he is capable of the lowest trick; **говори́ть ~и** to say foul things.
гадю́к|а, и *f.* **1.** adder, viper. **2.** (*coll.*) repulsive pers.
га́ер, а *m.* (*obs.*) buffoon, clown.
га́ерств|о, а *nt.* (*obs.*) buffoonery, tomfoolery.
га́ерств|овать, ую *impf.* (*obs.*, *pej.*) to play the buffoon; to clown.
га́ечный *adj. of* **га́йка; г. ключ** spanner, wrench.
га́же *comp. of* **га́дкий**
газ[1], **а** *m.* **1.** gas; **г. (не́рвно)паралити́ческого де́йствия** nerve gas. **2.** (*coll.*): **на по́лном ~́е (~у́)** at top speed; **дать г.** to step on the gas, step on it; **peда́ль** (*f.*) **га́за** accelerator, gas pedal; **сба́вить г.** to reduce speed; **быть под ~́ом** to be tipsy. **3.** (*pl.*; *med.*) wind; **скопле́ние ~́ов** flatulence, wind.
газ[2], **а** *no pl.*, *m.* gauze.
газан|у́ть, у́, ёшь *pf.* (*sl.*) **1.** to step on it (*in a car*). **2.** to scram.
газа́ци|я, и *f.* aeration.
газго́льдер, а *m.* gasholder.
газе́л|ь[1], **и** *f.* (*zool.*) gazelle.
газе́л|ь[2], **и** *f.* (*liter.*) ghazal (*Arabic verse form*).
газе́т|а, ы *f.* newspaper; **г. табло́идного форма́та** tabloid.
газе́тниц|а, ы *f.* newspaper stand *or* holder.
газе́т|ный *adj. of* **~а; ~ная бума́га** news-print; **г. коро́ль** *or* **магна́т** press baron; **г. стиль** journalese.
газе́тчик, а *m.* **1.** newspaper-seller; newspaper-boy. **2.** (*coll.*) journalist.
га́зик, а *m.* 'Gazik' (*small lorry produced by Gorky motor-vehicle works*).
газиро́ванный *adj.* aerated.
газир|овать, ую (*and* **газир|ова́ть, у́ю)** *impf.* to aerate.
газиро́вк|а, и *f.* **1.** aeration. **2.** (*coll.*) aerated water.
газифика́ци|я, и *f.* **1.** supplying with gas. **2.** gasification.
газифици́р|овать, ую *impf. and pf.* **1.** to supply with gas; to install gas (in). **2.** (*tech.*) to extract gas (from).
газобалло́н, а *m.* gas cylinder.
газ|ова́ть, у́ю *impf.* (*coll.*) to step on the gas, put one's foot down.
газови́к, а́ *m.* gas industry worker.
газовщи́к, а́ *m.* gas-works employee; gas-man.
га́зов|ый[1] *adj. of* **газ**[1]; **~ая коло́нка** geyser; **~ая плита́** gas-cooker, gas-stove; **г. рожо́к** gas-burner; gas bracket; **~ая сва́рка** oxy-acetylene welding; **г. счётчик** gas-meter; **~ая ата́ка** (*mil.*) gas attack; **~ая ка́мера** gas chamber.
га́зовый[2] *adj. of* **газ**[2]
газогенера́тор, а *m.* (*tech.*) gas generator, gas producer.
газокали́льн|ый *adj.* **г. колпачо́к** gas mantle; **~ая ла́мпа** incandescent gas-lamp.
газоли́н, а *m.* gasoline.
газоме́р, а *m.* gas-meter.
газомёт, а *m.* (*mil.*) gas projector.
газомото́р, а *m.* (*tech.*) gas-engine.
газо́н, а *m.* grass-plot, lawn; **«по ~ам ходи́ть воспреща́ется»** 'Keep off the grass'.
газонепроница́емый *adj.* gas-proof, gas-tight.
газонокоси́лка, и *f.* lawn-mower.
газообра́з|ный (~ен, ~на) *adj.* (*phys.*) gaseous, gasiform.
газопрово́д, а *m.* gas pipeline; gas-main.
газопровод|ный *adj. of* ~
газоубе́жищ|е, а *nt.* gas-proof shelter.
газохрани́лищ|е, а *nt.* gas-holder; gasometer.
ГАИ *f. indecl.* (*abbr. of* **госуда́рственная автомоби́льная инспе́кция**) State Motor-Vehicle Inspectorate.
Гаи́ти *m. indecl.* Haiti.
гаитя́н|ец, ца *m.* = **гаитя́нин**
гаитя́н|ин, ина, *pl.* **~е, ~** *m.* Haitian.
гаитя́н|ка, ки *f. of* **~ин**
гаитя́нский *adj.* Haitian.
га́ишник, а *m.* (*coll.*) traffic-cop.
Гайа́н|а, ы *f.* Guyana.
гайа́н|ец, ца *m.* Guyanese.
гайа́н|ка, ки *f. of* **~ец**
гайа́нский *adj.* Guyanese.
гайдама́к, а *m.* (*hist.*) haydamak (*Ukrainian Cossack*; *also member of anti-Bolshevik Ukrainian cavalry detachment in 1918*).
гайдама́|цкий *adj. of* **~к**
гайду́к, а́ *m.* (*hist.*) heyduck (**1.** *rebel against Turkish domination in Balkans.* **2.** *footman in house of wealthy landowner*).
га́йк|а, и *f.* nut, female screw; **бара́шковая г.** wing-nut;

закрутить ~и (*fig.*) put the screws on; **у него в голове не хватает ~и** (*coll.*) he's got a screw loose.
гайморит, а *m.* (*med.*) antritis.
гайморов *adj.*: **~а полость** (*anat.*) antrum of Highmore.
гак[1], **а** *m.* (*naut.*) hook.
гак[2], **а** *m.* (*coll.*) superfluity; **часа три с ~ом** about three hours or more.
гакаборт, а *m.* (*naut.*) taffrail.
гала *adj. indecl.* gala; **г.-представление** gala performance.
галактик|а, и *f.* (*astron.*) galaxy.
галантерейност|ь, и *f.* (*obs., coll.*) urbanity, gallantry.
галантере|йный *adj.* **1.** *adj. of* **~я**; **~йная кожа** fancy leather; **г. магазин** haberdashery, fancy-goods shop. **2.** (*obs., coll.*) urbane, gallant.
галантере|я, и *f.* haberdashery, fancy goods.
галантир, а *m.* galantine.
галантност|ь, и *f.* gallantry (= *courtliness*).
галант|ный (~ен, ~на, ~но) *adj.* gallant (= *courtly*).
гал|дёж, а *m.* (*coll.*) din, racket.
галд|еть, *1st pers. not used,* **ишь** *impf.* (*coll.*) to make a din, racket.
галеон, а *m.* galleon.
галер|а, ы *f.* galley.
галере|я, и *f.* (*in var. senses*) gallery.
галёрк|а, и *f.* (*theatr.*; *coll.*) **1.** gallery, 'the gods'. **2.** 'the gods' (= *those occupying gallery seats.*)
галер|ный *adj. of* **~а**
галет|а, ы *f.* (ship's) biscuit.
галечник, а *m.* (*collect.*) pebbles, shingle.
галечный *adj.* pebble, shingle; pebbly, shingly.
Галилейск|ое мор|е, ого ~я *f.* the Sea of Galilee.
Галиле|я, и *f.* Galilee.
галиматья|я, и *f.* (*coll.*) rubbish, nonsense.
галиси|ец, йца *m.* Galician (*in Spain*).
галиси|йка, йки *f. of* **~ец**
галисийский *adj.* Galician (*in Spain*).
Галиси|я, и *f.* Galicia (*Spain*).
галифе *nt. pl. indecl.* riding-breeches, jodhpurs.
галицийский *adj.* Galician (*Eastern Europe*).
Галици|я, и *f.* Galicia (*Eastern Europe*).
галичан|ин, ина, *pl.* **~е, ~** *m.* Galician (*Eastern Europe*).
галичан|ка, ки *f. of* **~ин**
галк|а, и *f.* daw, jackdaw; **считать галок** (*i*) to stand gaping, gawp (*ii*) to loaf.
галл, а *m.* Gaul.
галли|й, я *m.* (*chem.*) gallium.
галлицизм, а *m.* Gallicism.
галломани|я, и *f.* Gallomania.
галлон, а *m.* gallon.
галлофоби|я, и *f.* Gallophobia.
галльский *adj.* Gallic.
галлюцинаци|я, и *f.* hallucination.
галлюциниро|вать, ую *impf.* to have hallucinations.
галлюциноген, а *m.* hallucinogen.
галлюциногенный *adj.* hallucinogenic.
галоген, а *m.* (*chem.*) halogen.
галоид, а *m.* (*chem.*) haloid.
галоп, а *m.* **1.** gallop; **~ом** at a gallop; **лёгкий г.** canter; **скакать ~ом** to gallop; **поднять в г.** to put into a gallop. **2.** galop (*dance*).
галопир|овать, ую *impf.* to gallop.
гал|очий *adj. of* **~ка**
галош|а, и *f.* **1.** galosh; **сесть в ~у** (*coll.*) to get into a fix, into a spot. **2.** (*sl.*) French letter, johnny.
галс, а *m.* (*naut.*) tack; **правым (левым) ~ом** on the starboard (port) tack.
галстук, а *m.* (neck)tie, cravat; **заложить, залить за г.** (*coll.*) to booze; **г.-бабочка** bow-tie, dicky bow.
галун, а *m.* lace, galloon.
галушк|а, и *f.* (*cul.*) dumpling.
гальванизаци|я, и *f.* (*phys.*) galvanization.
гальванизир|овать, ую *impf. and pf.* (*phys.*) to galvanize.
гальванический *adj.* (*phys.*) galvanic.
гальвано *nt. indecl.* (*typ.*) electrotype.
гальванометр, а *m.* (*phys.*) galvanometer.
гальванопластик|а, и *f.* electroplating.
гал|ька, ьки *f.* **1.** (*g. pl.* **~ек**) pebble. **2.** (*collect.*) pebble, shingle.
гальюн, а *m.* (*naut.*) (the) heads.
гам, а *m.* (*coll.*) din, uproar.
гамадрил, а *m.* (*zool.*) hamadryad (*baboon*).
гамак, а *m.* hammock.
гамаш|а, и *f.* gaiter, legging.
гамбургер, а *m.* (ham)burger.
гамбургерн|ая, ой *f.* burger bar.
гамм|а[1], **ы** *f.* (*mus.*) scale; gamut (*also fig.*); **г. красок** colour range.
гамм|а[2], **ы** *f.* gamma (*letter of Greek alphabet*); **г.-лучи** (*phys.*) gamma-rays.
Ган|а, ы *f.* Ghana.
Ганг, а *m.* the Ganges (*river*).
гангли|й, я *m.* (*anat.*) ganglion.
гангрен|а, ы *f.* gangrene.
гангренозный *adj.* gangrenous.
гангстер, а *m.* gangster.
гандбол, а *m.* handball.
гандболист, а *m.* handball-player.
гандикап, а *m.* (*sport*) handicap.
ган|ец, ца *m.* Ghanaian.
ганзейский *adj.* (*hist.*) Hanseatic.
Ганновер, а *f.* Hanover.
ганноверский *adj.* Hanoverian.
ганский *adj.* Ghanaian.
гантел|ь, и *f.* (*sport*) dumb-bell.
гараж, а *m.* garage.
гарант, а *m.* (*leg.*) guarantor.
гарантийный *adj.* guarantee.
гарантир|овать, ую *impf. and pf.* **1.** to guarantee, vouch for. **2.** (**от**+*g.*) to guarantee (against).
гаранти|я, и *f.* guarantee; safeguard.
гардемарин, а *m.* (*hist.*) **1.** naval cadet. **2.** **(корабельный) г.** midshipman.
гардероб, а *m.* **1.** wardrobe (*article of furniture*). **2.** cloakroom. **3.** (*collect.*) wardrobe (*clothes belonging to one pers.*).
гардеробн|ая, ой *f.* cloakroom.
гардеробщик, а *m.* cloakroom attendant.
гардеробщи|ца, цы *f. of* **~к**
гардин|а, ы *f.* curtain.
гар|евой *adj. of* **~ь; ~евая дорожка** cinder path.
гарем, а *m.* harem.
гарк|ать, аю *impf. of* **~нуть**
гарк|нуть, ну, нешь *pf.* (*of* **~ать**) (*coll.*) to bark (out), bawl (out); **г. на кого-н.** to bark at s.o.
гармонизаци|я, и *f.* (*mus.*) harmonization.
гармонизир|овать, ую *impf. and pf.* (*mus.*) to harmonize (*trans.*).
гармоник|а, и *f.* **1.** accordion, concertina; **губная г.** mouth organ. **2.**: **~ой, в ~у** *as adv.* pleated; concertina'ed.
гармонир|овать, ую *impf.* (**с**+*i.*) to harmonize (*intrans.*) (with); to tone (with).
гармонист[1], **а** *m.* accordion player, concertina player.
гармонист[2], **а** *m.* (*mus.*) specialist in harmony.
гармонический *adj.* **1.** (*mus.*) harmonic. **2.** harmonious. **3.** (*tech.*) rhythmic.
гармонич|ный (~ен, ~на, ~но) *adj.* harmonious.
гармони|я[1], **и** *f.* **1.** (*mus.*) harmony. **2.** (*fig.*) harmony, concord.
гармони|я[2], **и** *f.* (*coll.*) accordion, concertina.
гармон|ь, и *f.* (*coll.*) accordion, concertina.
гармошк|а, и *f.* = **гармонь**
гарн|ец, ца *m.* (*obs.*) garnets (*old Russ. dry measure, equivalent to* 3.28 *litres*).
гарнизон, а *m.* garrison.
гарнизон|ный *adj. of* **~; ~ная служба** garrison duty.
гарнир, а *m.* (*cul.*) trimmings, garnish.
гарнитур, а *m.* set; suite.
гарнитур|а, ы *f.* (*typ., comput.*): **шрифтовая г.** fo(u)nt; **г. русского/латинского шрифта** Cyrillic/Latin fo(u)nt.
гарн|ый *adj.* (*obs.*): **~ое масло** lamp oil.
гарпи|я, и *f.* harpy.

гарпу́н, а́ *m.* harpoon.
гарпу́н|ный *adj. of* ~; **~ная пу́шка** harpoon-gun.
гарт, а *m.* type-metal; printer's pie.
га́рус, а *m.* worsted (yarn); **вышивка ~ом** worsted work.
гарц|ева́ть, у́ю *impf.* to caracole, prance.
гар|ь, и *f.* **1.** burning; **па́хнет ~ью** there's a smell of burning. **2.** cinders, ashes.
гаси́льник, а *m.* (*obs.*) extinguisher.
гаси́тел|ь, я *m.* extinguisher; (*fig.*) suppressor; **г. просвеще́ния** obscurantist.
га|си́ть, шу́, ~сишь *impf.* (*of* **по~**) **1.** (*pf. also* **за~**) to put out, extinguish; **г. свет** to put out the light. **2.: г. и́звесть** to slake lime. **3.** (*fig.*) to suppress, stifle. **4.** to cancel; **г. долг** to liquidate a debt; **г. почто́вую ма́рку** to frank a postage stamp.
га́с|нуть, ну, нешь, *past* ~, **~ла** *impf.* (*of* **по~**) to be extinguished, go out; to grow feeble; **он ~нет не по дням, а по часа́м** he is sinking hourly.
гастри́т, а *m.* gastritis.
гастри́ческий *adj.* gastric.
гастролёр, а *m.* **1.** artiste on tour. **2.** (*coll.*) casual worker.
гастроли́р|овать, ую *impf.* to tour, be on tour (*of an artiste*).
гастро́л|ь, и *f.* tour; temporary engagement (*of artiste*).
гастро́льный *adj.* touring (*of artistes*).
гастроно́м[1]**, а** *m.* gastronome, gourmet.
гастроно́м[2]**, а** *m.* grocer's (shop).
гастрономи́ческий *adj.* **1.** gastronomical. **2.: г. магази́н** grocer's (shop).
гастроно́ми|я, и *f.* **1.** connoisseur's taste in food. **2.** provisions, delicatessen.
га|ти́ть, чу́, ти́шь *impf.* to make a road (of brushwood) across (*marshy ground*).
ГАТТ *nt. indecl.* GATT (*abbr. of* General Agreement on Tariffs and Trade — *Генера́льное соглаше́ние о тари́фах и торго́вле*).
гат|ь, и *f.* road of brushwood; **бреве́нчатая г.** corduroy road.
га́убиц|а, ы *f.* (*mil.*) howitzer.
га́уб|ичный *adj. of* **~ица**
гауптва́хт|а, ы *f.* (*mil.*) **1.** (*obs.*) guardhouse, guardroom. **2.** detention cell.
га́ч|и, ей *pl.* (*sg.* **~а, ~и** *f.*) (*dial.*) **1.** trousers. **2.** haunches (*of an animal*).
гаше́ни|е, я *nt.* extinguishing; slaking.
гашён|ый *p.p.p. of* **гаси́ть** *and adj.*: **~ая и́звесть** slaked lime.
гаше́тк|а, и *f.* trigger.
гаши́ш, а *m.* hashish.
гвалт, а *m.* (*coll.*) row, uproar, rumpus.
гварде́|ец, йца *m.* (*mil.*) guardsman.
гварде́йский *adj.* (*mil.*) Guards'; **г. миномёт** multi-rail rocket launcher.
гва́рди|я, и *f.* (*mil.*) Guards; **~и** (*preceding* **капита́н** *etc.*, *in titles of rank*) Guards.
Гватема́л|а, ы *f.* Guatemala.
гватема́л|ец, ца *m.* Guatemalan.
гватема́л|ка, ки *f. of* **~ец**
гватема́льский *adj.* Guatemalan.
гвине́|ец, йца *m.* Guinean.
гвине́|йка, йки *f. of* **~ец**
гвине́йский *adj.* Guinean.
Гвине́|я, и *f.* Guinea.
гвоздево́й *adj.* feature, main; (*journ.*): **г. материа́л** feature item; **г. но́мер** main attraction, star turn; **г. матч сезо́на** the highlight of the season.
гво́здик, а *m.* tack (*small nail*).
гвозди́к|а[1]**, и** *f.* (*bot.*) pink(s); **пе́ристая г.** carnation(s); **туре́цкая г., борода́тая г.** sweet william.
гвозди́к|а[2]**, и** *f.* (*collect.*) cloves.
гво́здик|и, ов *no sg.* stilettos, stiletto heels (= *stiletto-heeled shoes*).
гвозди́льный *adj.* nail, nail-making.
гвоз|ди́ть, жу́, ди́шь *impf.* (*coll.*) **1.** to bang, bash; to bang away; **2.** to repeat, keep on.
гвозди́|чный[1] *adj. of* **~ка**[1]
гвозди́|чный[2] *adj. of* **~ка**[2]; **~чное ма́сло** oil of cloves.
гвозд|ь, я́, *pl.* **~и, ~е́й** *m.* **1.** nail; tack; peg; **пове́сить шля́пу на г.** to hang one's hat on a peg; **~ём засе́сть** (*fig.*) to become firmly fixed. **2.** (*+g.*; *fig.*, *coll.*) the crux (of); the pièce de résistance (of); highlight (of); **г. вопро́са** the crux of the matter; **г. ве́чера** the highlight of the evening; **г. сезо́на** the hit of the season. **3.: (и) никаки́х ~е́й!** (*coll.*) and that's that!; and that's the end of it!
гг. *abbr. of* **1.** *го́ды* years. **2.** *города́* cities, towns. **3.** *господа́* Messrs.; Mr and Mrs.
где *adv.* **1.** (*interrog. and rel. adv.*) where; **г. бы ни** wherever; **г. бы то ни́ было** no matter where. **2.** (*coll.*) somewhere; anywhere. **3.: г...., г....** (*coll.*) in one place ..., in another .... **4. г. (уж)** (*+d. and inf.*) (*coll.*) how should one, how is one to; **г. мне знать?** how should I know?
где́-либо *adv.* anywhere.
где́-нибудь *adv.* somewhere; anywhere.
где́-то *adv.* somewhere.
ГДР *f. indecl.* (*abbr. of* ***Герма́нская Демократи́ческая Респу́блика***) GDR (*German Democratic Republic*).
гебист, а *m.* (*coll.*) KGB man *or* agent.
гебраист, а *m.* Hebraist.
Гебри́дск|ие о́стров|а́, ~их ~о́в *no sg.* the Hebrides.
гебри́дский *adj.* Hebridean.
гегельян|ец, ца *m.* Hegelian.
гегелья́нств|о, а *nt.* Hegelianism.
гегемо́н, а *m.* leader.
гегемони́зм, а *m.* (*pol.*) 'hegemonism'.
гегемо́ни|я, и *f.* hegemony, supremacy.
гедони́зм, а *m.* hedonism.
гедони́ст, а *m.* hedonist.
гедонисти́ческий *adj.* hedonistic.
гей *int.* hi!
ге́йзер, а *m.* geyser.
гейм, а *m.* game.
гекато́мб|а, ы *f.* hecatomb.
гекза́метр, а *m.* hexameter.
гекко́н, а *m.* gecko.
гекса́эдр, а *m.* (*math.*) hexahedron.
гекта́р, а *m.* hectare.
гекто... *comb. form* hecto-.
ге́ли|й, я *m.* (*chem.*) helium.
геликопте́р, *m.* (*obs.*) = **вертолёт**
гелио́граф, а *m.* heliograph.
гелиотро́п, а *m.* (*bot. and min.*) heliotrope.
гелиоцентри́ческий *adj.* heliocentric.
гельминтоло́ги|я, и *f.* helminthology.
ге́мм|а, ы *f.* stone with engraved design.
гемоглоби́н, а *m.* (*physiol.*) haemoglobin.
геморроида́льн|ый *adj.* (*med.*) haemorrhoidal; **~ая ши́шка** pile.
геморро́|й, я *m.* (*med.*) haemorrhoids, piles.
гемофи́лик, а *m.* haemophiliac.
гемофили́|я, и *f.* (*med.*) haemophilia.
ген, а *m.* (*physiol.*) gene.
ген... *comb. form, abbr. of* **генера́льный**
генеалоги́ческий *adj.* genealogical.
генеало́ги|я, и *f.* genealogy.
ге́незис, а *m.* origin, source, genesis.
генера́л, а *m.* general (*mil.*; *also*, *hist.*, *denotes status of member of first four grades of tsarist Russ. civil service*); **г.-майо́р** major-general; **г.-лейтена́нт** lieutenant-general; **г.-полко́вник** colonel-general; **г.-губерна́тор** governor-general.
генера́л-ба́с, а *m.* (*mus.*) figured bass.
генерали́ссимус, а *m.* generalissimo.
генералите́т, а *m.* (*collect.*) the generals; the top brass.
генера́лк|а, и *f.* (*coll.*) dress rehearsal.
генера́льн|ый *adv.* (*in var. senses*) general; **г. констру́ктор** chief designer; **~ая ли́ния па́ртии** (*pol.*) Party general line; **~ая репети́ция** dress rehearsal; **~ое сраже́ние** decisive battle; **г. штаб** general staff.
генера́льский *adj.* general's; **г. чин** rank of general.
генера́льш|а, и *f.* (*coll.*) general's wife.

генера́тор, а *m.* (*tech.*) generator; **г. колеба́ний** oscillator; **г. то́ка** current generator.
генера́тор|ный *adj. of* ~; **г. газ** producer gas.
гене́тик|а, и *f.* genetics.
генети́ческий *adj.* genetic.
гениа́льност|ь, и *f.* genius; greatness.
гениа́л|ьный (~ен, ьна) *adj.* of genius, great; brilliant; **~ьная иде́я** a stroke of genius.
ге́ни|й, я *m.* genius; a genius; **злой г.** evil genius.
генита́ли|и, й *no sg.* (*med.*) genitalia, genitals.
ге́н|ный *adj. of* ~; **~ная инжене́рия** genetic engineering; **~ная дактилоско́пия** genetic fingerprinting.
генсе́к, а *m.* (*abbr. of* ***генера́льный секрета́рь***) General-Secretary; Secretary-General.
генсове́т, а *m.* General Council.
Ге́ну|я, и *f.* Genoa.
геншта́б, а *m.* general staff.
генштаби́ст *m.* (*coll.*) general staff officer.
гео... *comb. form, abbr. of* **географи́ческий**
гео́граф, а *m.* geographer.
географи́ческий *adj.* geographical.
геогра́фи|я, и *f.* geography.
геодези́ст, а *m.* land-surveyor.
геодези́ческий *adj.* geodesic, geodetic.
геоде́зи|я, и *f.* geodesy, (land-)surveying.
гео́лог, а *m.* geologist.
геологи́ческий *adj.* geological.
геоло́ги|я, и *f.* geology.
гео́метр, а *m.* geometrician.
геометри́ческий *adj.* geometric(al).
геоме́три|я, и *f.* geometry.
георги́н, а *m.* (*bot.*) dahlia.
георги́н|а, ы *f.* = ~
геофи́зик|а, и *f.* geophysics.
геофизи́ческий *adj.* geophysical.
гепа́рд, а *m.* cheetah.
гепати́т, а *m.* hepatitis.
гепе́ушник, а *m.* OGPU agent.
гера́льдик|а, и *f.* heraldry.
геральди́ческий *adj.* heraldic.
гера́н|ь, и *f.* geranium.
герб, а́ *m.* arms, coat of arms.
герба́ри|й, я *m.* herbarium.
гербици́д, а *m.* herbicide, weed-killer.
гербо́вник, а *m.* armorial.
ге́рбов|ый *adj.* **1.** heraldic. **2.** bearing a coat of arms; **~ая бума́га** stamped paper; **~ая ма́рка** duty stamp. **3.: г. сбор** stamp-duty.
геркуле́с, а *m.* **1.** (a) Hercules (*strong man*). **2.** (*sg. only*) rolled oats; porridge.
геркуле́совский *adj.* Herculean.
герма́н|ец, ца *m.* **1.** Teuton; ancient German; **~цы** the Germanic, Nordic peoples. **2.** (*coll.*) German.
германиза́ци|я, и *f.* Germanization.
германизи́р|овать, ую *impf. and pf.* to Germanize.
германи́зм, а *m.* Germanism.
герма́ни|й, я *m.* (*chem.*) germanium.
германи́ст, а *m.* specialist in Germanic studies.
германи́стик|а, и *f.* Germanic studies.
Герма́ни|я, и *f.* Germany.
герма́нск|ий *adj.* **1.** Germanic; Teutonic; **~ие языки́** Germanic languages. **2.** (*coll.*) German.
гермафроди́т, а *m.* hermaphrodite.
гермети́чески *adv.*: **г. закры́тый** hermetically sealed.
гермети́ческ|ий *adj.* **1.** hermetic, sealed; air-tight; water-tight; **~ая каби́на** (*aeron.*) pressurized cabin. **2.** hermetic, secret.
гернсе́йский *adj.* Guernsey.
Ге́рнси *m. indecl.* Guernsey.
герои́зм, а *m.* heroism.
геро́ик|а, и *f.* heroics; heroic spirit; heroic style.
геро́инщик, а *m.* (*coll.*) heroin addict.
герои́н|я, и *f.* heroine.
герои́ческ|ий *adj.* heroic; **~ие ме́ры** heroic measures.
геро́|й, я *m.* hero; (*liter.*) character.
геро́йский *adj.* heroic.
геро́йств|о, а *nt.* heroism.
геро́льд, а *m.* (*hist.*) herald.
ге́рпес, а *m.* herpes.
герунди́в, а *m.* (*gram.*) gerundive.
геру́нди|й, я *m.* (*gram.*) gerund.
герц, а, *g. pl.* **г.** *m.* (*phys.*) hertz, cycle per second.
ге́рцог, а *m.* duke; **г. Эдинбу́ргский** the Duke of Edinburgh.
герцоги́н|я, и *f.* duchess.
ге́рцогский *adj.* ducal.
ге́рцогств|о, а *nt.* duchy.
геста́по *nt. indecl.* Gestapo.
геста́пов|ец, ца *m.* Gestapo agent.
гетероге́нный *adj.* heterogeneous.
гетеросексуали́ст, а *m.* heterosexual.
гетеросексуа́льный *adj.* heterosexual.
ге́тман, а *m.* (*hist.*) hetman.
ге́тр|ы, гетр *pl.* (*sg.* **~а, ~ы** *f.*) **1.** gaiters. **2.** (*sport, coll.*) football socks. **3.** leg-warmers.
ге́тто *nt. indecl.* ghetto.
гешефт, а *m.* (*coll.*) deal, speculation.
г-жа (*abbr. of* **госпожа́**) Mrs; Miss; Ms.
гиаци́нт, а *m.* **1.** (*bot.*) hyacinth. **2.** (*min.*) jacinth.
ги́бел|ь, и *f.* **1.** death; destruction, ruin; loss; wreck; downfall. **2.** (+*g.*; *coll.*) masses (of), swarms (of), hosts (of).
ги́бел|ьный (~ен, ~ьна) *adj.* disastrous, fatal.
ги́б|кий (~ок, ~ка́, ~ко) *adj.* **1.** flexible, pliant; lithe, lissom; floppy; **г. диск** (*comput.*) floppy (disk); **~кая пласти́нка** flexidisc; **г. стан** slender build. **2.** adaptable, versatile. **3.** tractable.
ги́бкост|ь, и *f.* **1.** flexibility, pliancy. **2.** versatility, resourcefulness.
ги́бл|ый *adj.* (*coll.*) bad, rotten, good-for-nothing; **~ое де́ло** we've had it.
ги́б|нуть, ну, нешь, *past* ~, **~ла** *impf.* (*of* **по~**) to perish.
Гибралта́р, а *f.* Gibraltar.
Гибралта́рск|ий зали́в, ~ого ~а *m.* the Strait of Gibraltar.
гибри́д, а *m.* hybrid, mongrel.
гибридиза́ци|я, и *f.* hybridization.
гига... *comb. form* giga-
гигаба́йт, а *m.* (*comput.*) gigabyte.
гига́нт, а *m.* giant; **(пласти́нка-)г.** LP, long-player.
гига́нтский *adj.* gigantic.
гигие́н|а, ы *f.* hygiene, hygienics.
гигиени́ческ|ий *adj.* hygienic, sanitary; **~ая повя́зка** sanitary towel; **~ая бума́га** toilet paper.
гигро́метр, а *m.* hygrometer.
гигроско́п, а *m.* hygroscope.
гигроскопи́ческий *adj.* hygroscopic.
гид, а *m.* guide.
гида́льго *m. indecl.* hidalgo.
ги́др|а, ы *f.* (*myth., zool.; fig.*) hydra.
гидра́влик|а, и *f.* hydraulics.
гидравли́ческий *adj.* hydraulic.
гидра́нт, а *m.* hydrant.
гидра́т, а *m.* (*chem.*) hydrate.
гидро... *comb. form* hydro-.
гидро́граф, а *m.* **1.** hydrograph. **2.** hydrographer.
гидрографи́ческий *adj.* hydrographic.
гидрогра́фи|я, и *f.* hydrography.
гидродина́мик|а, и *f.* hydrodynamics.
гидрокостю́м, а *m.* wet suit.
гидро́лиз, а *m.* (*chem.*) hydrolysis.
гидроло́ги|я, и *f.* hydrology.
гидролока́тор, а *m.* sonar.
гидроме́три|я, и *f.* hydrometry.
гидро́окис|ь, и *f.* hydroxide.
гидропа́ти|я, и *f.* hydropathy.
гидропу́льт, а *m.* **1.** stirrup pump. **2.** water-cannon. **3.** spray gun.
гидросамолёт, а *m.* hydroplane.
гидроста́нци|я, и *f.* hydro-electric (power-)station.
гидроста́тик|а, и *f.* hydrostatics.

гидросульфи́т, а *m.* (*chem.*) hydrosulphite.
гидротерапи́|я, и *f.* hydrotherapy.
гидроте́хник, а *m.* hydraulic engineer.
гидроте́хник|а, и *f.* hydraulic engineering.
гидроустано́вк|а, и *f.* (*tech.*) hydro-electric power-plant.
гидрофо́н, а *m.* (*naut.*) hydrophone.
гидроэлектри́ческий *adj.* hydro-electric.
гидроэлектроста́нци|я, и *f.* hydro-electric power-station.
гие́н|а, ы *f.* hyena.
гик, а *m.* (*coll.*) whoop.
ги́к|ать, аю *impf.* (*of* **~нуть**) (*coll.*) to whoop.
ги́к|нуть, ну, нешь *pf.* (*of* **~ать**) to whoop.
гил|ь, и *f.* (*obs., coll.*) nonsense.
гильде́йский *adj. of* **ги́льдия**
ги́льди|я, и *f.* (*hist.*) guild; class, order (*of merchants in tsarist Russia*).
ги́льз|а, ы *f.* case, empty; **патро́нная г.** cartridge-case; **папиро́сная г.** cigarette-paper; **г. цили́ндра** (*tech.*) cylinder sleeve.
гильоти́н|а, ы *f.* guillotine.
гильотини́р|овать, ую *impf. and pf.* to guillotine.
Гимала́|и, ев *no sg.* the Himalayas.
гимала́йский *adj.* Himalayan.
гимн, а *m.* hymn; **госуда́рственный г.** national anthem.
гимнази́ст, а *m.* grammar-school boy.
гимнази́стк|а, и *f.* grammar-school girl.
гимна́зи|я, и *f.* grammar school, high school.
гимна́ст, а *m.* gymnast; **возду́шный г.** aerialist; **г. на трапе́ции** trapeze artist.
гимнастёрк|а, и *f.* soldier's blouse.
гимна́стик|а, и *f.* gymnastics; **атлети́ческая г.** (sports) gymnastics; **аэро́бная г.** aerobic exercises; **худо́жественная г.** eurhythmics, rhythmic gymnastics.
гимнасти́ческ|ий *adj.* gymnastic; **г. зал** gymnasium; **~ие снаря́ды** gymnastic apparatus.
гинеко́лог, а *m.* gynaecologist.
гинекологи́ческий *adj.* gynaecological.
гинеколо́ги|я, и *f.* gynaecology.
гине́|я, и *f.* guinea.
гипе́рбол|а, ы *f.* **1.** hyperbole. **2.** (*math.*) hyperbola.
гиперболи́ческий *adj.* **1.** hyperbolical. **2.** (*math.*) hyperbolic.
гиперболи́ч|ный (~ен, ~на) *adj.* exaggerated.
гипергликеми́|я, и *f.* hyperglycaemia.
гиперто́ник, а *m.* hypertensive.
гипертони́|я, и *f.* (*med.*) hypertonia, high blood-pressure.
гипертрофи́рованный *adj.* (*biol.*) hypertrophied.
гипертрофи́|я, *f.* (*biol.*) hypertrophy.
гипно́з, а *m.* hypnosis.
гипнотизёр, а *m.* hypnotist.
гипнотизи́р|овать, ую *impf.* (*of* **за~**) to hypnotize.
гипноти́зм, а *m.* hypnotism.
гипно́тик, а *m.* hypnotic, (hypnotic) subject.
гипноти́ческий *adj.* hypnotic.
гипосульфи́т, а *m.* (*chem*) hyposulphite.
гипо́тез|а, ы *f.* hypothesis.
гипотену́з|а, ы *f.* (*math.*) hypotenuse.
гипотети́ческий *adj.* hypothetical.
гиппопота́м, а *m.* hippopotamus.
гипс, а *m.* **1.** (*min.*) gypsum, plaster of Paris. **2.** plaster cast. **3.** (*med.*) plaster.
гипс|ова́ть, у́ю *impf.* (*of* **за~**) to plaster; to gypsum.
ги́псовый *adj.* **1.** gypseous. **2.** plaster; **г. сле́пок** plaster-cast.
гиреви́к, а́ *m.* (*sport*) weight-lifter.
гир|ево́й *adj. of* **~́я**
гирля́нд|а, ы *f.* garland, wreath.
гироко́мпас, а *m.* gyrocompass.
гироско́п, а *m.* gyroscope.
гироскопи́ческий *adj.* gyroscopic.
ги́р|я, и *f.* weight; **г. для гимна́стики** dumb-bells.
гистерэктоми́|я, и *f.* hysterectomy.
гистогра́мм|а, ы *f.* histogram.
гисто́лог, а *m.* histologist.
гистологи́ческий *adj.* histological.
гистоло́ги|я, и. *f.* histology.
гит, а *m.* (*sport*) heat.

гита́р|а, ы *f.* guitar; **г.-ритм** rhythm guitar.
гитари́ст, а *m.* guitarist.
гитлери́зм, а *m.* Hitlerism; Naz(i)ism.
ги́тлеров|ец, ца *m.* Hitlerite, Nazi; German soldier (*in Second World War*).
ги́тлеровский *adj.* Hitlerite, Nazi.
ги́чк|а, и *f.* (*naut.*) gig.
Глав... *and* **...глав...** *comb. forms, abbr. of* **гла́вное управле́ние**, *as* **Главга́з (*Гла́вное управле́ние га́зового хозя́йства*)**, **Росглавко́ж (*Гла́вное управле́ние коже́венной промы́шленности Министе́рства лёгкой промы́шленности РСФСР*)**
глав... *comb. form, abbr. of* **гла́вный**
глав|а́^{1}**, ы́,** *pl.* **~́ы** *f. and c.g.* **1.** *f.* (*obs. or rhet.*) head. **2.** *c.g.* head, chief; **г. делега́ции** head of a delegation; **быть во ~е́** (+*g.*) to be at the head (of), lead; **во ~е́** (**с**+*i.*) under the leadership (of), led (by). **3.: поста́вить во ~у́ угла́** to regard as of paramount importance. **4.** *f.* (*archit.*) cupola (*of a church*).
глав|а́^{2}**, ы́,** *pl.* **~́ы** *f.* chapter (*of a book*).
глава́р|ь, я́ *m.* leader; ringleader.
главе́нств|о, а *nt.* supremacy.
главе́нств|овать, ую *impf.* (**в**+*p.*, **над**+*i.*) to have command (over), hold sway (over).
главк, а *m.* (*abbr. of* **гла́вный комите́т**) central directorate (*department of Ministry controlling either branch of industry falling within competence of Ministry or establishments in a particular area*).
главко́м, а *m.* (*abbr.*) = **главнокома́ндующий**
главнокома́ндующ|ий, его *m.* Commander-in-Chief (*abbr.* C.-in-C.); **верхо́вный г.** Supreme Commander.
гла́вн|ый *adj.* chief, main principal; head, senior; **г. врач** head physician; **г. инжене́р** chief engineer; **~ая кварти́ра** (*mil., obs.*) headquarters; **~ая кни́га** ledger; **~ое предложе́ние** main clause; **~ое управле́ние** main directorate, central directorate; **~ым о́бразом** chiefly, mainly, for the most part; *as n.* **~ое, ~ого** *nt.* the chief thing, the main thing; the essentials.
глаго́л, а *m.* **1.** (*gram.*) verb. **2.** (*arch.*) word.
глаго́лиц|а, ы *f.* (*ling.*) the Glagolitic alphabet.
глаголи́ческий *adj.* (*ling.*) Glagolitic.
глаго́льный *adj.* verbal.
гладиа́тор, а *m.* gladiator.
гладиа́торский *adj.* gladiatorial.
глади́льн|ый *adj.* ironing; **~ая доска́** ironing-board.
гла́|дить, жу, дишь *impf.* (*of* **по~**^{1}) **1.** (*pf. also* **вы́~**) to iron, press. **2.** to stroke; **г. по голо́вке** (*coll.*) to pat on the back; **г. про́тив ше́рсти** to rub the wrong way.
гла́д|кий (~ок, ~ка́, ~ко) *adj.* **1.** smooth; (*of hair*) straight; (*of fabrics*) plain, self-coloured, unfigured; **с него́ взя́тки ~ки** (*coll.*) you'll get nothing out of him. **2.** fluent, facile. **3.** (*coll.*) sleek, well-nourished.
гла́д|ко *adv. of* **~кий;** smoothly, swimmingly; **де́ло сошло́ г.** the affair went off smoothly; **г. вы́бритый** clean-shaven.
гладкокра́шеный *adj.* self-coloured.
гладкоство́льный *adj.* (*of firearms*) smooth-bore.
глад|ь^1**, и** *f.* smooth surface (*of water*); **тишь да г.** (*coll.*) peace and quiet.
глад|ь^2**, и** *f.* satin-stitch; **вышива́ть ~́ью** to satin-stitch.
гла́же, *comp. of* **гла́дкий, гла́дко**
гла́жень|е, я *nt.* ironing.
глаз, а, о ~́е, в ~у́, *pl.* **~а́, ~, ~а́м** *m.* eye; eyesight; **дурно́й г.** evil eye; **невооружённый г.** naked eye; **не в бровь, а в г.** (*coll.*) to hit the mark, strike home; **в ~а́** to one's face; **я его́ в ~а́ не вида́л** I have never seen him; **в ~а́х** (+*g.*) in the eyes (of); **он был геро́ем в ~а́х ма́тери** he was a hero in his mother's eyes; **ни в одно́м ~у́** (*coll.*) not at all drunk; **за ~а́** (*i*) in absence; **руга́ть кого́-н. за ~а́** to abuse s.o. behind his back, (*ii*) (*coll.*) enough, more than enough; **на ~а́, на ~а́х** before one's eyes; **не попада́йся мне на ~а́!** keep out of my sight!; **дитя́ вы́росло на роди́тельских ~а́х** the child grew before its parents' eyes; **на г.** approximately, by eye; **с ~у на́ г.** tête-à-tête, cheek-by -jowl; **с г. доло́й** out of sight; **убира́йся с г. доло́й!** get out of my sight; **с г. доло́й — из се́рдца**

вон out of sight, out of mind; **не спуска́ть с г., г. с**+*g.* not to let out of one's sight; **с пья́ных г.** in a drunken condition, drunk; **смотре́ть во все ~а́** to be all eyes; **хоть г. вы́коли** it's pitch dark; **закрыва́ть ~а́ (на**+*a.*) to close one's eyes (to), connive (at); **открыва́ть кому́-н. ~а́ (на**+*a.*) to open s.o.'s eyes (to); **премье́р-мини́стр откры́л нам ~а́ на неизбе́жность войны́** the Prime Minister opened our eyes to the fact that war was inevitable; **идти́ куда́ ~а́ глядя́т** to follow one's nose.

глаза́ст|ый (~, ~а) *adj.* (*coll.*) big-eyed; quick-sighted.

глазена́п|ы, ов *no sg.* (*coll., joc.*) eyes.

глазе́т, а *m.* brocade.

глазе́|ть, ю *impf.* (*of* **по~**) (**на**+*a.*; *coll.*) to stare (at), gawk (at).

глазир|о́ванный *p.p.p. of* **~ова́ть** *and adj.* glazed; glossy; (*cul.*) iced, glacé.

глазир|ова́ть, у́ю *impf. and pf.* to glaze; (*cul.*) to ice.

глазиро́вк|а, и *f.* glazing; icing; **торт с ~ой** iced cake.

глазни́к, а́ *m.* (*coll.*) oculist.

глазни́ц|а, ы *f.* eye-socket.

глазн|о́й *adj. of* **глаз; г. врач** oculist; **г. нерв** optic nerve; **~о́е я́блоко** eyeball.

глаз|о́к, ка́, *pl.* **~ки, ~ок** *and* **~ки́, ~ко́в** *m.* **1.** (*pl.* **~ки**) *dim. of* **~; одни́м ~ко́м** with half an eye; **де́лать, стро́ить ~ки кому́-н.** to make eyes at s.o.; **аню́тины ~ки** (*bot.*) pansy. **2.** (*pl.* **~ки́**) pigmented spot (*on some birds and insects*). **3.** (*pl.* **~ки́**) (*coll.*) peephole; inspection hole; glory hole (*of furnace*); head (*of periscope*). **4.** (*pl.* **~ки́**) bud; eye (*of potato*). **5.** (*pl.* **~ки́**) (*tech.*) eye, eyelet.

глазоме́р, а *m.* **1.** measurement by eye. **2.** ability to judge by eye; **хоро́ший г.** good eye.

глазоме́р|ный *adj. of* **~; ~ное определе́ние** estimation by eye.

глазу́н|ья, ьи, *g. pl.* **~ий** *f.* fried eggs.

глазу́р|ь, и *f.* **1.** glaze (*on pottery*). **2.** (*cul.*) icing.

гла́нд|а, ы *f.* (*anat.*) tonsil; **удали́ть ~ы** to take out tonsils.

глас, а *m.* **1.** (*obs.*) voice; **г. вопию́щего в пусты́не** the voice of one crying in the wilderness. **2.** (*eccl.*) tune.

гла|си́ть, шу́, си́шь *impf.* **1.** (*obs.*) to announce. **2.** to say, run; **докуме́нт ~си́т сле́дующее** the paper runs as follows; **как ~си́т погово́рка** as the saying goes.

гла́сно[1] *adv.* openly, publicly.

гла́сно[2] *as pred.* (*obs.*) it is well known.

гла́сност|ь, и *f.* **1.** publicity; **преда́ть ~и** to give publicity (to), make known, publish. **2.** *glasnost*, openness.

гла́сный[1] *adj.* open, public; **г. суд** public trial.

гла́сн|ый[2] *adj.* vowel, vocalic; *as n.* **г., ~ого** *m.* vowel.

гла́сн|ый[3]**, ого** *m.* (*hist.*) (*town, province, etc.*) councillor.

глаша́та|й, я *m.* **1.** (*hist.*) town crier, public crier. **2.** (*fig., rhet.*) herald.

гле́тчер, а *m.* glacier.

гли́н|а, ы *f.* clay; **валя́льная г.** fuller's earth; **жи́рная г.** loam; **огнеупо́рная г.** fire-clay; **фарфо́ровая г.** china clay, porcelain clay; **ма́зать ~ой** to clay.

гли́нист|ый *adj.* clayey, argillaceous; **~ая по́чва** loam.

глинobи́тный *adj.* pisé (*of clay, mixed with straw, gravel, etc.*).

глинозём, а *m.* (*chem.*) alumina.

глинтве́йн, а *m.* mulled wine; **де́лать г.** to mull wine.

гли́нян|ый *adj.* **1.** clay; earthenware; **~ая посу́да** earthenware crockery. **2.** clayey.

гли́ссер, а *m.* (*naut.*) speed-boat.

глист, а́ *m.* (intestinal) worm.

глистого́нный *ad.* (*med.*) vermifuge.

глицери́н, а *m.* glycerine.

гл. об. (*abbr. of* **гла́вным о́бразом**) mostly, chiefly.

глоба́льный *adj.* global; (*fig.*) extensive, in-depth.

гло́бус, а *m.* globe.

гло|да́ть, жу́, ~жешь *impf.* to gnaw (*also fig.*).

гло́кеншпил|ь, я *m.* glockenspiel.

глота́|ть, ю *impf.* to swallow.

гло́тк|а, и *f.* **1.** (*anat.*) gullet. **2.** (*coll.*) throat.

глот|о́к, ка́ *m.* gulp, mouthful; drink.

гло́х|нуть, ну, нешь, *past* **~, ~ла** *impf.* **1.** (*pf.* **о~**) to become deaf. **2.** (*pf.* **за~**) to die away, subside (*of noise*). **3.** (*pf.* **за~**) to become wild, go to seed.

глу́б|же *comp. of* **~о́кий** *and* **~око́**

глубин|а́, ы́, *pl.* **~ы** *f.* **1.** depth. **2.** (*pl.*) (the) depths, deep places. **3.** heart, interior (*also fig.*); **в ~е́ ле́са** in the heart of the forest; **в ~е́ веко́в** in ancient times; **в ~е́ души́** at heart, in one's heart of hearts; **от ~ы́ души́** with all one's heart. **4.** (*fig.*) depth, profundity; intensity.

глуби́нк|а, и *f.* (*coll.*) the sticks, the back of beyond; **жить в ~е** to live (way) out in the sticks.

глуби́нн|ый *adj.* **1.** deep; deep-laid; deep-sea; **~ая бо́мба** depth charge; **г. лов ры́бы** deep-sea fishing. **2.** remote, out-of-the-way.

глубо́к|ий (~, ~а́, ~о́) *adj.* **1.** (*in var. senses*) deep; **~ая вспа́шка** deep ploughing; **г. сон** deep sleep; **~ая таре́лка** soup-plate; **~ая оборо́на** defence in depth; **в ~ом тылу́** (*mil.*) deep in the rear; **г. вира́ж** (*aeron.*) steep turn. **2.** profound; thorough, thoroughgoing; considerable, serious; **~ие зна́ния** thorough knowledge; **~ая оши́бка** serious error. **3.** (*of time, age, seasons*) late; advanced; extreme; **до ~ой но́чи** (until) far into the night; **~ая дре́вность** extreme antiquity; **~ая ста́рость** extreme old age; **~ая стару́ха** a very old woman; **наступи́ла ~ая зима́** it was mid-winter. **4.** (*fig.*; *of feelings, etc.*) deep, profound, intense; **с ~им приско́рбием** (*in obituary formula*) with deep regret.

глубоко́[1] *adv.* deep; (*fig.*) deeply, profoundly; **г. сиде́ть в воде́** (*of a vessel*) to draw much water.

глубо́ко́[2] *as pred.* it is deep.

глубоково́д|ный (~ен, ~на) *adj.* **1.** deep-water. **2.** deep-sea.

глубокомы́сленный *adj.* thoughtful; serious.

глубокомы́сли|е, я *nt.* profundity; perspicacity.

глубокоуважа́емый *adj.* much-esteemed; (*in formal letters*) dear.

глубоме́р, а *m.* depth gauge.

глубоча́йший *superl. of* **глубо́кий**

глуб|ь, и *f.* depth; **г. реки́** the river-bottom.

глум|и́ться, лю́сь, и́шься *impf.* (**над**+*i.*) to mock (at); to desecrate.

глумле́ни|е, я *nt.* mockery; gibe; desecration.

глумли́вый *adj.* (*coll.*) mocking; gibing.

глупе́|ть, ю *impf.* (*of* **по~**) to grow stupid.

глуп|е́ц, ца́ *m.* fool, blockhead.

глуп|и́ть, лю́, и́шь *impf.* (*of* **с~**) to make a fool of o.s.; to do sth. foolish.

глупова́т|ый (~, ~а) *adj.* silly; rather stupid.

глу́пост|ь, и *f.* **1.** foolishness, stupidity. **2.** foolish, stupid action; foolish, stupid thing. **3.** (*usu. pl.*) nonsense; **~и!** (stuff and) nonsense!

глу́п|ый (~, ~а́, ~о) *adj.* foolish, stupid; silly; (*coll.*) **она́ ещё ~а́** she is still young and innocent.

глупы́ш[1]**, а́** *m.* (*coll.*) silly; silly little thing.

глупы́ш[2]**, а́** *m.* (*zool.*) fulmar.

глуха́р|ь, я́ *m.* **1.** (*zool.*) capercailzie, woodgrouse. **2.** (*coll.*) deaf pers. **3.** (*tech.*) propeller (*with hexahedral or square head*).

глу́хо[1] *adj. of* **глухо́й;** (*coll.*) = **на́глухо**

глу́хо[2] *as pred.* **1.** it is lonely, deserted. **2.** (*coll.*) it is no good.

глухова́т|ый (~, ~а) *adj.* somewhat deaf, hard of hearing.

глух|о́й (~, ~а́, ~о) *adj.* **1.** deaf (*also fig.*); **он был ~ к на́шим мольба́м** he was deaf to our entreaties; *as n.* **г., ~о́го** *m.* deaf man; **~а́я, ~о́й** *f.* deaf woman. **2.** (*of sound*) muffled, confused, indistinct. **3.** indistinct, obscure; **~а́я молва́** rumours. **4.** (*ling.*) voiceless; **5.** thick, dense; wild; **г. лес** dense forest. **6.** remote, out-of-the-way; god-forsaken; **в ~о́й прови́нции** in the depths of the country; **~а́я у́лица** lonely street. **7.** sealed; blank, blind; **~а́я стена́** blind wall. **8.** (*of clothing*) buttoned-up, done up; not open. **9.: г. ряд** (*mil.*) blank file. **10.** (*of times or seasons*) dead; late; **~а́я ночь** dead of night; **~а́я пора́** slack period; **г. сезо́н** dead season.

глухома́н|ь, и *f.* (*coll.*) out-of-the-way place, backwoods.

глухонем|о́й *adj.* deaf and dumb; *as n.* **г., ~о́го** *m.* deaf mute; **язы́к (для) ~ы́х** sign language.

глухот|а́, ы́ *f.* deafness.

глу́|ше *comp. of* **~хо́й** *and* **~хо**
глуши́тел|ь, я *m.* **1.** (*tech.*) silencer, muffler. **2.** (*fig.*) suppressor.
глуш|и́ть, у́, ~и́шь *impf.* **1.** (*pf.* **о~**) to stun, stupefy; **г. ры́бу** to stun fish (*by means of explosives*). **2.** (*pf.* **за~**) to muffle (*sounds*); **г. боль** to dull pain; **г. мото́р** to stop the engine; **г. радиопереда́чи** to jam broadcasts. **3.** (*pf.* **за~**) (*coll.*) to put out (*a fire, etc.*). **4.** (*pf.* **за~**) to choke, stifle (*growth*). **5.** (*pf.* **за~**) (*fig.*) to suppress, stifle; **г. кри́тику** to suppress criticism. **6.** (*impf. only*) (*sl.*) to soak up (= *to drink in large quantities*).
глуш|ь, и́ *f.* overgrown part (*of forest or garden*); backwoods (*also fig.*); **жить в ~и́** to live in the back of beyond.
глы́б|а, ы *f.* clod; lump, block.
глюко́з|а, ы *f.* glucose, grape sugar, dextrose.
гля|де́ть, жу́, ди́шь *impf.* (*of* **по~**) **1.** (**на**+*a.*) to look (at); to peer (at); to gaze (upon); **г. ко́со (на**+*a.*) to take a poor view (of); **г. в о́ба** to be on one's guard; **г. в гроб** to have one foot in the grave; **г. сквозь па́льцы (на**+*a.*) to wink (at), shut one's eyes (to), turn a blind eye (to); **идти́ куда́ глаза́ ~дя́т** to follow one's nose. **2.** (**на**+*a.*; *coll.*) to look to (= *to take as an example*). **3.** (**на**+*a.*) to heed, mark; **не́чего на них г.** don't take any notice of them. **4.** (*coll.*) to look for, seek (*with ones eyes*). **5.** (*impf. only*) to show, appear. **6.** (*impf. only*) (**на**+*a.*) to look (on to), face, give (on to). **7.** (*impf. only*) (+*i. or adv.*; *coll.*) to look after, look like, appear; **она́ ~ди́т пла́ксой** she looks a cry-baby. **8.** (**за**+*i.*; *coll.*) to look after, see to. **9.: ~ди́(те)** (*expr. warning or threat*) mind (out); **~ди́ не** (+*imper.*) mind you don't .... **10.: того́ и ~ди́** (*coll.*) it looks as if; I'm afraid; **того́ и ~ди́ бу́дет бу́ря** I'm afraid there's going to be a storm. **11.: ~́дя (по**+*d.*, *coll.*) depending (on).
гля|де́ться, жу́сь, ди́шься *impf.* (*of* **по~**) (**в**+*a.*) to look at o.s. (in).
глядь *int.* lo and behold!; hey presto!
гля́н|ец, ца *m.* gloss, lustre.
гля́|нуть, ну, нешь *pf.* (**на**+*a.*) glance (at).
глянцеви́т|ый (~, ~а) *adj.* glossy, lustrous.
гля́нцев|ый *adj.* glossy, lustrous; **~ая кра́ска** gloss paint.
гм *int.* hm!
г-н (*abbr. of* **господи́н**) Mr; Master; (*on envelope*) **~у** (+*d.*) Mr ...; ... Esq.; **~у В. Джо́нсу** W. Jones, Esq.
гна|ть, гоню́, го́нишь, *past* **~л, ~ла́, ~́ло** *impf.* **1.** (*det. of* **гоня́ть**) to drive. **2.** to urge (on); to whip up (*an animal*); (*coll.*) to drive (*a vehicle*) hard. **3.** (*coll.*) to dash, tear. **4.** to hunt, chase; (*fig.*) to persecute. **5.** to turn out, turf out. **6.** to distil. **7.** (*usu. imper.*; *coll.*) to give. **8.** (*dial.*) to raft (*timber*).
гна́|ться, гоню́сь, го́нишься, *past* **~лся, ~ла́сь, ~́ло́сь** *impf.* (*indet. of* **гоня́ться**) (**за**+*i.*) to pursue; to strive (for, after); (*fig.*) to keep up with.
гнев, а *m.* anger, rage, wrath; **не во гнев будь ска́зано** if you don't mind me saying so.
гне́ва|ться, юсь *impf.* (*of* **раз~**) (**на**+*a.*; *obs.*) to be angry (with).
гнев|и́ть, лю́, и́шь *impf.* (*of* **про~**) (*obs.*) to anger, enrage.
гневли́в|ый (~, ~а) *adj.* (*obs.*) irascible.
гне́в|ный (~ен, ~на́, ~но) *adj.* angry, irate.
гнедо́й *adj.* bay (*colour of horse*).
гнез|ди́ться, жу́сь, ди́шься *impf.* **1.** to nest, build one's nest; to roost. **2.** (*fig.*) to have its seat; to be lodged.
гнезд|о́, а́, *pl.* **гнёзда** *nt.* **1.** nest; eyrie. **2.** den, lair (*also fig.*); **г. сопротивле́ния** (*mil.*) pocket of resistance. **3.** brood (*also fig.*). **4.** (*bot., med.*) nidus; cluster. **5.** (*tech.*) socket; seat; housing. **6.** (*ling.*) 'nest' (*group of words of same root*).
гнездова́ни|е, я *nt.* nesting; **пора́ ~я** nesting season.
гнездово́й *adj. of* **гнездо́**
гнездо́вь|е, я *nt.* nesting-site.
гнейс, а *m.* (*min.*) gneiss.
гне|сти́, ту́, тёшь *impf.* to oppress, weigh down; to press; **его́ ~ту́т забо́ты** he is weighed down by cares.
гнёт, а *m.* **1.** (*obs.*) press; weight. **2.** oppression, yoke (*fig.*).
гнету́щий *pres. part. act. of* **гнести́** *and adj.* oppressive.
гни́д|а, ы *f.* nit; (*fig.*) scumbag, worm.
гние́ни|е, я *nt.* decay, putrefaction, rot.
гнил|о́й (~, ~а́, ~о) *adj.* **1.** rotten (*also fig.*); decayed; putrid; corrupt. **2.** (*of weather*) damp, muggy.
гнилокро́ви|е, я *nt.* (*med.*) septicaemia.
гни́лостный *adj.* **1.** putrefactive. **2.** putrid.
гни́лост|ь, и *f.* rottenness (*also fig.*); putridity.
гнилу́шк|а, и *f.* piece of rotten wood; (*coll.*) rotten stump (*of tooth*).
гнил|ь, и *f.* **1.** rotten stuff. **2.** mould.
гниль|ё, я́ *nt.* (*collect.*) rotten stuff.
гнильц|а́, ы́ *f.* (*coll.*) rottenness; **с ~о́й** slightly rotten.
гни|ть, ю́, ёшь *impf.* (*of* **с~**) to rot, decay; to decompose.
гноекро́ви|е, я *nt.* (*med.*) pyaemia.
гное́ни|е, я *nt.* suppuration.
гноетече́ни|е, я *nt.* suppuration.
гно|и́ть, ю́, и́шь *impf.* (*of* **с~**) to let rot, allow to decay; **г. наво́з** to ferment manure; **г. в тюрьме́** to leave to rot in prison.
гно|и́ться, ю́сь, и́шься *impf.* to suppurate, discharge matter.
гно́ищ|е, а *nt.* (*obs.*) garbage dump
гно|й, я, в ~́е *or* **в ~ю́** *m.* pus, matter.
гнойни́к, а́, *m.* abscess; ulcer.
гно́йный *adj.* purulent.
гном, а *m.* gnome.
гно́м|а, ы *f.* maxim, aphorism.
гноми́ческий *adj.* gnomic.
гно́мон, а *m.* gnomon, sun-dial.
гносеоло́ги|я, *f.* (*phil.*) gnosiology; theory of knowledge.
гно́стик, а *m.* gnostic.
гностици́зм, а *m.* gnosticism.
гнус, а *m.* (*collect.*) midges.
гнуса́в|ить, лю, ишь *impf.* to speak through one's nose.
гнуса́вост|ь, и *f.* twang; nasal intonation.
гнуса́в|ый (~, ~а) *adj.* nasal.
гну́сност|ь, и *f.* **1.** vileness, foulness. **2.** vile, foul action.
гну́с|ный (~ен, ~на́, ~но) *adj.* vile, foul.
гну́т|ый *p.p.p. of* **гнуть** *and adj.* bent; **~ая ме́бель** bent-wood furniture.
гнуть, гну, гнёшь *impf.* (*of* **со~**) **1.** to bend, bow (*trans.*); **г. спи́ну, ше́ю (пе́ред**+*i.*) (*coll.*) to cringe (before), kowtow (to); **г. свою́ ли́нию** to have it one's own way. **2.** (*coll.*) to drive at; aim at; **я не понима́ю, куда́ ты гнёшь** I don't know what you are driving at.
гнуть|ё, я́ *nt.* bending.
гну́ться, гнусь, гнёшься *impf.* (*of* **со~**) **1.** to bend (*intrans.*), be bowed; to stoop. **2.** (*impf. only*) to bend (*intrans.*), be flexible.
гнуш|а́ться, а́юсь *impf.* (*of* **по~**) **1.** (+*g. or i.*) to abhor, have an aversion (to). **2.** (+*inf.*) to disdain (to).
гобеле́н, а *m.* Gobelin, tapestry.
гобои́ст, а *m.* (*mus.*) oboist.
гобо́|й, я *m.* oboe.
гова́рива|ть, (*pres. tense not used*), *impf.* (*freq. of* **говори́ть** *coll.*); **он ~л** he often used to say, he would often say.
гове́нь|е, я *nt.* fasting (*as preparation for Communion*).
гов|е́ть, е́ю, е́ешь *impf.* (*eccl.*) to prepare for Communion (*by fasting*); (*coll.*) to fast, go without food.
говн|о́, а́ *nt.* (*vulg.*) shit.
говное́д, а *m.* (*vulg.*) turd, shit(bag) (*pers.*).
говню́к = говное́д
го́вор, а *m.* **1.** sound of voices (*usu. human, but also fig.*); **г. волн** the murmur of the waves. **2.** (*coll.*) talk, rumour. **3.** mode of speech, accent. **4.** dialect.
говори́л|ьня, ьни, *g. pl.* **~ен** *f.* (*coll., pej.*) talking-shop.
говор|и́ть, ю, и́шь *impf.* **1.** (*impf. only*) to (be able to) speak, talk; **он ещё не ~и́т** he can't speak yet; **г. по-францу́зски** to speak French. **2.** (*pf.* **сказа́ть**) to say; to tell; to speak, talk; **г. пра́вду** to tell the truth; **г. де́ло** to talk sense; **~я́т** they say, it is said; **~я́т тебе́!** (*emph. command*) do you hear?; **что вы ~и́те?** (*expr. incredulity*) you don't mean to say so!; **~и́т Москва́!** (*introducing radio programme*) this is Radio Moscow!; **не́чего (и) г.** it goes without saying, needless to say; **что и г.** (*coll.*) it cannot be denied; **что ни ~и́** say what you like; **и не ~и́!** certainly!,

of course!; **ина́че ~я́** in other words; **со́бственно ~я́** strictly speaking; **не ~я́ уже́** (**о**+*p.*) not to mention. **3.** (*pf.* **по~**) (**о**+*p.*) to talk (about), discuss. **4.** (*impf. only*) to mean, convey, signify; **э́ти карти́ны мне ничего́ не ~я́т** these pictures convey nothing to me. **5.** (*impf. only*) (**о**+*p.*) to point (to), indicate, betoken, testify (to); **всё ~и́т о том, что он ко́нчил самоуби́йством** everything points to his having committed suicide. **6.** (*impf. only*) **г. в по́льзу** (+*g.*) to tell in favour (of); to support, back.

говор|и́ться, и́тся *impf. pass. of* **~и́ть; как ~и́тся** as they say, as the saying goes.

говорли́вост|ь, и *f.* garrulity, talkativeness.

говорли́в|ый (~, ~а) *adj.* garrulous, talkative.

говор|о́к, ка́ *m.* (*coll.*) **1.** sound of voices; hum of conversation. **2.** accent, speech.

говору́н, а́ *m.* (*coll.*) talker, chatterer.

говору́н|ья, ьи, *g. pl.* **~ий** *f. of* **~**

говя́дин|а, ы *f.* beef.

говя́жий *adj.* beef.

го́гол|ь, я *m.* (*zool.*) golden-eye (*Clangula bucephala*); **ходи́ть ~ем** to strut.

го́голь-мо́гол|ь *and* **го́гель-мо́гел|ь, я** *m.* egg-flip.

го́гот, а *m.* cackle (*of geese*); (*coll.*) loud laughter.

гогота́нь|е, я *nt.* cackling.

гого|та́ть, чу́, ~́чешь *impf.* **1.** to cackle (*of geese*). **2.** (*coll.*) to cackle, roar with laughter.

год, а, в ~у́, о ~́е, *pl.* **~́ы** *and* **~а́,** *g.* **~о́в** *and* **лет** *m.* **1.** (*g. pl.* **лет**) year; **високо́сный г.** leap year; **кру́глый г.** (*as adv.*) the whole year round; **в бу́дущем, про́шлом ~у́** next, last year; **в теку́щем ~у́** during the current year; **в г.** a year, per annum; **из ~́а в г.** year in, year out; **г. о́т ~у** every year; **спустя́ три ~́а** three years later; **через три ~́а** in three years' time; **бе́з ~у неде́ля** (*coll.*) only a few days; **мы ~́ы не вида́лись** we have not met for years; **встреча́ть Но́вый г.** to see the New Year in; **ей пошёл пятна́дцатый г.** she is in her fifteenth year. **2. двадца́тые, тридца́тые,** *etc.*, **~́ы** (*g.* **~о́в**) the twenties, the thirties etc. **3. ~а́** *and* **~́ы, ~о́в** (*pl. only*) years, age, time; **шко́льные ~а́** schooldays; **в ~́ы** (+*g.*) in the days (of); during; **в те ~́ы** in those days; **в ~а́х** advanced in years; **не по ~а́м** beyond one's years, precocious(ly).

года́ми *adv.* for years (*on end*).

годи́н|а, ы *f.* **1.** (*rhet.*) time, period; **г. войны́** war-time; **тяжёлая г.** hard times. **2.** (*arch.*) year.

го|ди́ть, жу́, ди́шь *impf.* (*coll.*) to wait, loiter.

го|ди́ться, жу́сь, ди́шься *impf.* **1.** (**на**+*a.*, **для**+*g.*, *or* +*d.*) to be fit (for), be suited (for), do (for), serve (for); **э́та мате́рия ни на что, никуда́ не ~ди́тся** this material is no good (for anything); **не ~ди́тся** it's no good, it won't do. **2.** (**в**+*nom.-a.*) to serve (as), be suited to be; **он не ~ди́тся в офице́ры** he is not cut out to be an officer. **3.** (**в**+*nom.-a.*) to be old enough to be; **она́ ~ди́тся тебе́ в ма́тери** she is old enough to be your mother. **4.: не ~ди́тся** (+*inf.*) it does not do (to), one should not.

годи́чн|ый *adj.* **1.** lasting a year; **~ое путеше́ствие** a year's journey. **2.** annual, yearly; **г. съезд** annual conference; **~ые ко́льца** (*bot.*) annual rings.

го́дност|ь, и *f.* fitness, suitability; validity.

го́д|ный (~ен, ~на́, ~но) *adj.* fit, suitable, valid; **г. к вое́нной слу́жбе** fit for military service; **г. к пла́ванию** seaworthy; **биле́т го́ден три ме́сяца** the ticket is valid for three months.

годова́лый *adj.* one year old, yearling.

годови́к, а́ *m.* (*dial.*) yearling (*animal*).

годово́й *adj.* annual, yearly; **г. дохо́д** annual revenue.

годовщи́н|а, ы *f.* anniversary.

гой[1] *int.* (*folk poet.*) hail!

го|й[2], **я** *m.* goy, gentile.

гол, а *m.* (*sport*) goal; **заби́ть г.** to score a goal.

гола́вл|ь, я *m.* chub (*fish*).

го́лб|ец, ца *m.* (*dial.*) store-room, cellar.

Голго́ф|а, ы *f.* Calvary (*also fig.*).

голена́стый *adj.* **1.** (*coll.*) long-legged. **2.** *as pl. n.* (*zool.*) waders, Grallatores.

голени́щ|е, а *nt.* top (*of a boot*).

го́лен|ь, и *f.* shin.

гол|е́ц, ьца́ *m.* loach (*fish*).

голизн|а́, ы́ *f.* nakedness.

голи́к, а́ *m.* **1.** (*dial.*) besom. **2.** (*naut.*) seamark.

голки́пер, а *m.* (*sport*) goalkeeper.

голла́нд|ец, ца *m.* Dutchman; **лету́чий г.** Flying Dutchman.

Голла́нди|я, и *f.* Holland.

голла́ндк|а[1], **и** *f.* Dutchwoman; Dutch girl.

голла́ндк|а[2], **и** *f.* **1.** tiled stove. **2.** animal (*cow, hen, etc.*) of Dutch breed. **3.** (*naut.*) jumper.

голла́ндск|ий *adj.* Dutch; **~ая печь** tiled stove; **~ое полотно́** holland (*cloth*); **г. сыр** Dutch cheese.

голли́зм, а *m.* (*pol.*) Gaullism.

голли́стский *adj.* (*pol.*) Gaullist.

голов|а́, ы́, *a.* **го́лову,** *pl.* **го́ловы, голо́в, ~а́м** *f. and c.g.* **1.** *f.* head (*also fig.*); **г. в го́лову** (*mil.*) shoulder to shoulder; **на све́жую го́лову** while one is fresh; **быть ~о́й, на́ голову вы́ше кого́-н.** (*fig.*) to be head and shoulders above s.o.; **с ~ы́ до ног** from head to foot; **с ~о́й погрузи́ться, окуну́ться, уйти́ (во что-н.)** (*fig.*) to throw o.s. (into sth.), plunge (into sth.), get up to one's neck (in sth.); **свали́ть с больно́й ~ы́ на здоро́вую** to lay the blame on s.o. else; **че́рез чью-н. го́лову** (*fig.*) behind s.o.'s back; **у неё г. шла кру́гом** her head was going round and round; **у меня́ г. кру́жится** I feel giddy; **у них г. кру́жится от успе́хов** they are giddy with success; **вы́дать ~о́й** (*obs.*) to give away, betray; **вы́мыть, намы́лить кому́-н. го́лову** to give s.o. a dressing-down; **го́лову пове́сить** to hang one's head. **2.** *f.* head (*of cattle*). **3.** *f.* (*fig.*) head (*as unit of calculation*); **с ~ы́** per head. **4.** *f.* (*fig.*) head; brain, mind; wits; **он па́рень с ~о́й** he's a bright lad; **лома́ть го́лову** to rack one's brains; **не теря́ть ~ы́** to keep one's head; **ей пришла́ в го́лову мысль** it occurred to her, it struck her, the thought crossed her mind. **5.** *f.* (*fig.*) head (= *person*); **горя́чая г.** hothead; **сме́лая г.** bold spirit. **6.** *f.* (*fig.*) head, life; **на свою́ го́лову** to one's cost, to one's misfortune; **заплати́ть, поплати́ться за что-н. ~о́й** to pay for sth. with one's life; **отвеча́ть, руча́ться ~о́й за что-н.** to stake one's life on sth. **7.** *c.g.* (*fig.*) head; pers. in charge; **городско́й г.** (*obs.*) mayor; **сам себе́ г.** one's own master. **8.** *f.* **г. са́хару** sugar-loaf; **г. сы́ру** a cheese; **г. капу́сты** head of cabbage. **9.** *idiomatic phrr.*: **в пе́рвую го́лову** in the first place; first and foremost; **в ~а́х** at the head of the bed.

голова́стик, а *m.* tadpole.

голове́шк|а, и *f.* brand, smouldering piece of wood.

голови́зн|а, ы *f.* jowl (*of sturgeon*).

голо́вк|а, и *f.* **1.** *dim. of* **голова́. 2.** head, cap, nose; tip; **г. по́ршня** piston head; **г. лу́ка** an onion, onion bulb; **спи́чечная г.** match-head. **3.** (*collect.*; *coll.*) heads, big shots. **4.** (*pl.*) vamp (*of boot*). **5.** (*obs.*) head-scarf (*worn by married peasant or merchant-class women*).

головн|о́й *adj.* **1.** *adj. of* **голова́; ~а́я боль** headache; **г. плато́к** head-scarf; **г. убо́р** headgear, head-dress. **2.** (*anat.*) encephalic; **г. мозг** brain, cerebrum. **3.** (*obs.*) brain, cerebral; **~а́я рабо́та** brain work. **4.: г. го́лос** (*mus.*) head-voice, falsetto. **5.** (*fig.*) head, leading; **~а́я железнодоро́жная ста́нция** railhead; **г. отря́д** (*mil.*) vanguard, leading detachment; **~а́я похо́дная заста́ва** (*mil.*) advance party.

головн|я́[1], **и́,** *g. pl.* **~е́й** *f.* charred log.

головн|я́[2], **и́,** *g. pl.* **~е́й** *f.* blight, smut, rust (*disease of crops*).

головокруже́ни|е, я *nt.* giddiness, dizziness (*also fig.*); vertigo.

головокружи́тельн|ый *adj.* dizzy, giddy; vertiginous (*also fig.*); **~ая высота́** dizzy height; **~ые перспекти́вы** breath-taking prospects.

головоло́мк|а, и *f.* puzzle, conundrum.

головоло́мный *adj.* puzzling; baffling; **г. вопро́с** puzzler.

головомо́йк|а, и *f.* (*coll.*) reprimand, dressing-down.

головоно́г|ие, их *pl.* (*sg.* **~ое, ~ого** *nt.*) (*zool.*) cephalopoda.

головоре́з, а *m.* (*coll.*) **1.** cutthroat; bandit; desperado. **2.** blackguard, rascal.

головотя́п, а *m.* (*coll.*) bungler, muddler.
головотя́пств|о, а *nt.* (*coll.*) bungling.
голо́вушк|а, и *f.* **1.** *affectionate dim. of* **голова́; пропа́ла моя́ г.** it's all up with me; I've had it. **2.** (*folk poet.*; *coll.*) fellow, chap; **бе́дная г.** poor wretch.
голограмм|а, ы *f.* hologram.
го́лод, а (у) *m.* **1.** hunger; starvation; **во́лчий г.** ravenous appetite; **умира́ть с ~у** to die of starvation; **мори́ть ~ом** to starve (*trans.*). **2.** famine. **3.** dearth, acute shortage; **шерстяно́й г.** wool shortage.
голода́ни|е, я *nt.* **1.** starvation. **2.** fasting.
голод|а́ть, а́ю *impf.* **1.** to hunger, starve. **2.** to fast, go without food.
голода́|ющий *pres. part. act. of* **~ть** *and adj.* starving, hungry, famished; *as n.* **г., ~ющего** *m.*, **~ющая, ~ющей** *f.* starving pers.
голо́д|ный (го́лоден, ~на́, ~но) *adj.* **1.** hungry; **г. как соба́ка, как волк** hungry as a hunter; **сексуа́льно г.** sex-starved. **2.** (*caused by*) hunger, starvation; **~ные бо́ли** hunger-pangs; **г. похо́д** hunger-march; **~ная смерть** starvation. **3.** (*of food, food supplies*) meagre, scanty, poor; **г. год** lean year; **г. край** barren country; **г. паёк** starvation rations.
голодо́вк|а, и *f.* **1.** starvation. **2.** hunger-strike; **объяви́ть ~у** to go on hunger-strike.
голодра́|нец, нца *m.* (*coll.*) beggar.
голоду́х|а, и *f.* (*coll.*) hunger.
гололёд, а *m.* = **гололе́дица**
гололе́диц|а, ы *f.* black ice.
голоно́гий *adj.* bare-legged; bare-foot.
го́лос, а, *pl.* **~а́** *m.* **1.** voice; **во весь г.** at the top of one's voice; **быть в ~е** to be in good voice; **с ~а** by ear; **г. за ка́дром** voice-over. **2.** (*mus.*) voice, part; **фу́га на четы́ре ~а** four-part fugue. **3.** (*fig.*) voice, word, opinion; **в оди́н г.** with one accord, unanimously; **име́ть свой г.** to have one's say. **4.** vote; **пра́во ~а** the vote, suffrage, franchise; **пода́ть г.** (**за**+*a.*) to vote (for), cast one's vote (for); **победи́ть большинство́м ~о́в** to outvote.
голосемя́нный *adj.* (*bot.*) gymnospermous.
голоси́ст|ый (~, ~а) *adj.* loud-voiced; vociferous; loud.
голо|си́ть, шу́, си́шь *impf.* **1.** (*coll.*) to sing loudly; to cry. **2.** (*obs.*) to wail; to keen; **г. по поко́йнику** to keen a dead pers.
голосло́вно *adv.* without adducing any proof.
голосло́в|ный (~ен, ~на) *adj.* unsubstantiated, unfounded; unsupported by evidence.
голосова́ни|е, я *nt.* voting; poll; **всео́бщее г.** universal suffrage; **поста́вить на г.** to put to the vote.
голос|ова́ть, у́ю *impf.* (*of* **про~**) **1.** (**за**+*a.*, **про́тив**+*g.*) to vote (for; against); **г. нога́ми** to vote with one's feet. **2.** to put to the vote, vote on. **3.** (*sl.*) to thumb a lift.
голосоведе́ни|е, я *nt.* (*mus.*) harmonisation of themes.
голосов|о́й *adj.* vocal; (*anat.*) **~ы́е свя́зки** vocal chords; **~а́я щель** glottis.
голоу́сый *adj.* (*coll.*) clean-shaven; (*fig.*) young, immature.
голошта́нник, а *m.* (*coll.*) ragamuffin.
голубево́дств|о, а *nt.* pigeon breeding.
голубегра́мм|а, ы *f.* (*mil.*) pigeon(-carried) message.
голу́беньк|ий, ого *m.* = **голубо́й** *as n.*
голубеста́нци|я, и *f.* (postal-)pigeon loft.
голубе́|ть, ю *impf.* (*of* **по~**) to show blue; to turn blue.
голуб|е́ц[1], ца́ *m.* (*min.*) mountain-blue, azurite.
голуб|е́ц[2], ца́ *m.* (*usu. pl.*) golubets (*rissole rolled in cabbage-leaves*).
голубизн|а́, ы *f.* blueness.
голуби́к|а, и *f.* great bilberry, bog whortleberry (*Vaccinium uliginosum*).
голуби́н|ый *adj.* **1.** *adj. of* **го́лубь; ~ая по́чта** pigeon post. **2.** (*fig.*) dove-like.
голу́|бить, блю, бишь *impf.* (*of* **при~**) (*folk poet.*) to caress, fondle.
голуби́ц|а[1], ы *f.* = **голуби́ка**
голуби́ц|а[2], ы *f.* **1.** female pigeon, dove. **2.** (*fig.*; *of a girl*) innocent creature.
голу́бк|а, и *f.* **1.** female pigeon, dove **2.** (*fig.*; *as term of endearment*) (my) dear, (my) darling.
голубогла́з|ый (~, ~а) *adj.* blue-eyed.
голуб|о́й *adj.* pale blue, sky-blue; **~а́я кровь** (*fig.*) blue blood; **г. песе́ц** blue fox; **~о́е то́пливо** 'blue fuel' (= *natural gas*); **г. экра́н** the small screen (*i.e. TV*); *as n.* **голуб|о́й, о́го** *m.* gay (= *homosexual*).
голуб|о́к, ка́ *m.* **1.** *dim. of* **го́лубь;** *fig.* = **голу́бчик. 2.** (*bot.*) columbine, aquilegia.
голу́бушк|а, и *f.* **1.** (*coll.*; *as mode of address*) (my) dear. **2.** *affectionate dim. of* **голу́бка 1.**
голу́бчик, а *m.* (*coll.*; *as mode of address*) **1.** my dear; dear friend; dear (so and so). **2.** (*iron.*) my friend.
го́луб|ь, я, *g. pl.* **~е́й** *m.* **1.** pigeon, dove; **г. свя́зи** (*mil.*) carrier-pigeon. **2.** (*fig.*; *as mode of address to man*) = **голу́бчик**
голубя́тник, а *m.* **1.** pigeon-fancier. **2.** pigeon-hawk.
голубя́т|ня, ни, *g. pl.* **~ен** *f.* dovecot(e), pigeon loft.
го́л|ый (~, ~а́, ~о) *adj.* **1.** naked, bare (*also fig.*); **~ая голова́** (*i*) bare head, (*ii*) bald head; **г. про́вод** naked wire; **~ыми рука́ми** with one's bare hands; (*fig.*) without a hand's turn. **2.** (*coll.*) poor; **~ как со́кол** poor as a church mouse. **3.** (*coll.*) unmixed, pure, neat; **г. спирт** pure spirit. **4.** (*fig., coll.*) bare, pure, unadorned; **~ые ци́фры** bare figures.
голытьб|а́, ы́ *f.* (*collect.*; *coll.*) the poor.
голы́ш, а́ *m.* **1.** (*coll.*) naked child; naked pers. **2.** (*obs.*) pauper. **3.** round flat stone.
гол|ь, и *no pl.*, *f.* **1.** (*collect.*) the poor; **г. перека́тная** the down-and-outs, the utterly destitute; **г. на вы́думки хитра́** necessity is the mother of invention. **2.** (*obs.*) bare place, barren place.
голь|ё, я́ *nt.* **1.** (*cul.*) tripe. **2.** raw hide.
гольём *adv.* (*coll.*) **1.** bare, clean. **2.** neat, unmixed.
гольф, а *m.* **1.** golf; **игро́к в г.** golfer. **2. ~ы** (*coll.*) plus-fours; knee-length stockings.
голя́к, а́ *m.* (*coll.*) beggar, tramp.
гомеопа́т, а *m.* homoeopath(ist).
гомеопати́ческий *adj.* **1.** homoeopathic. **2.** (*fig.*) minute, very small.
гомеопа́ти|я, и *f.* homoeopathy.
гомери́ческий *adj.* Homeric (= *on heroic scale*); **г. смех** Homeric laughter.
гоме́ровский *adj.* Homeric (= *pertaining to Homer*); **г. вопро́с** the Homeric question.
го́мик, а *m.* (*coll., pej.*) fairy, queer, poof(ter).
гоминьда́н, а *m.* (*pol.*) Kuomintang
гоминьда́нов|ец, ца *m.* member, supporter of Kuomintang.
гоминьда́новский *adj.* Kuomintang.
гомоге́нный *adj.* homogeneous.
го́мон, а *m.* (*coll.*) hubbub.
гомон|и́ть, ю́, и́шь *impf.* (*coll.*) to talk noisily, shout (*of large number of people*).
гомосе́к = **го́мик**
гомосексуали́зм, а *m.* homosexuality.
гомосексуали́ст, а *m.* homosexual; gay.
гомосексуа́льный *adj.* homosexual; gay.
гон, а *m.* **1.** dash, rush. **2.** hunt, chase, pursuit. **3.** (*area of*) hunt. **4.** (*of animals*) heat; **во вре́мя ~а** (when) on heat. **5.** (*agric.*) row.
гондо́л|а, ы *f.* **1.** gondola. **2.** (*aeron.*) car (*of balloon*); (*tech.*) nacelle. **3.** (*rail.*) gondola.
гондолье́р, а *m.* gondolier.
гондо́н, а *m.* (*vulg.*) condom; French letter, johnny.
Гондура́с, а *m.* Honduras.
гондура́с|ец, ца *m.* Honduran.
гондура́с|ка, ки *f. of* **~ец**
гондура́сский *adj.* Honduran.
гоне́ни|е, я *nt.* persecution.
гон|е́ц, ца́ *m.* courier; (*fig.*) herald, harbinger.
гонио́метр, а *m.* (*phys.*) goniometer.
гони́тел|ь, я *m.* persecutor.
го́нк|а, и *f.* **1.** dashing, rushing. **2.** (*coll.*) haste, hurry. **3.** (*sport*) race; **гребны́е ~и** boat race; **г. вооруже́ний** arms race. **4.** (*coll., obs.*) scolding, dressing-down. **5.** (*dial.*) floatage, raftage.

го́н|кий (~ок, ~ка́, ~ко) *adj.* **1.** fast; **~кая соба́ка** hound. **2.** (*of trees*) fast-growing.
Гонко́нг, а *m.* Hong Kong.
гоноко́кк, а *m.* (*med.*) gonococcus.
Гонолу́лу *m. indecl.* Honolulu.
го́нор, а *m.* (*coll.*) arrogance, conceit.
гонора́р, а *m.* fee, honorarium; **а́вторский г.** royalties.
гонорé|я, и *f.* gonorrhoea.
го́ночный *adj. of* **го́нка; г. автомоби́ль** racing car.
гонт, а *m.* (*collect.*; *tech.*) shingles.
гонтов|о́й *adj. of* **гонт; ~а́я кры́ша** shingle roof.
гонча́р, а́ *m.* potter.
гонча́рн|ый *adj.* potter's; **~ые изде́лия** pottery; **г. круг** potter's wheel.
го́нч|ая, ей *f.* hound.
го́нщик, а *m.* **1.** racer; **велосипеди́ст-г.** racing cyclist. **2.** drover. **3.** rafter.
гоню́(сь), го́нишь(ся) *see* **гна́ть(ся)**
гоня́|ть, ю *impf.* **1.** (*indet. of* **гнать**) to drive. **2.** (*coll.*) to make run errands. **3.** (**по**+*d.*; *coll.*) to make run over, grill (on) (*sth. learnt, read, etc.*). **4.: г. голубе́й** to race pigeons. **5.: г. ло́дыря, соба́к** (*coll.*) to idle, kick one's heels.
гоня́|ться, юсь *impf.* **1.** (*indet. of* **гна́ться**) (**за**+*i.*) to chase, pursue, hunt. **2.** (**с**+*i.*; *obs.*) to race.
гоп *int.* hup!; jump!
гопа́к, а́ *m.* gopak (*Ukrainian dance*).
гопля́ *int.* hup!; jump!
го́пник, а *m.* (*sl.*) yob(bo).
гопкомпа́ни|я, и *f.* (*sl.*) bunch of yobs.
гор... *comb. form, abbr. of* **1. городско́й. 2. го́рный**
гор|а́, ы́, *a.* **~́у,** *pl.* **~́ы,** *a.* **~а́м** *f.* **1.** mountain; hill; **г. Эвере́ст** Mount Everest; **г. с плеч** a load off one's mind; **ката́ться с ~ы́** to toboggan; **в ~́у** uphill; **идти́ в ~́у** to go uphill; (*fig.*) to go up in the world; **не за ~а́ми** (*fig.*) not far off; **по́д ~у** downhill (*also fig.*); **пир ~о́й** lavish, riotous feast; **наде́яться на кого́-н. как на ка́менную ~́у** to place implicit faith in s.o.; **стоя́ть за кого́-н. ~о́й** to be solidly behind s.o. **2.** (*fig.*) heap, pile, mass.
гора́зд (~а, ~о) *pred. adj.* (+*inf. or* **на**+*a.*; *coll.*) good (at), clever (at); **он на всё г.** he's a Jack of all trades; **кто во что г.** each in his own way; **он г. вы́пить** he is no mean drinker.
гора́здо *adv.* (+*comp. adjs. and advs.*) much, far, by far; **г. лу́чше** far better.
горб, а́, о ~е́, на ~у́ *m.* **1.** hump; (*dial.*) back; **свои́м ~о́м** by the sweat of one's brow; **испыта́ть на своём ~у́** to learn by bitter experience. **2.** protuberance, bulge; **~о́м** (*as adv.*) sticking out.
горба́т|ый (~, ~а) *adj.* humpbacked, hunchbacked; gibbous; **г. мост** humpback bridge; **г. нос** hooked nose; **~ого моги́ла испра́вит** (*prov.*) can the leopard change his spots?
горбачёв|ец, ца *m.* (*coll.*) 'Gorbyite', (M. S.) Gorbachev supporter.
горби́нк|а, и *f.* small protuberance; **нос с ~ой** aquiline nose.
го́рб|ить, лю, ишь *impf.* (*of* **с~**) to arch, hunch; **г. спи́ну** to arch one's back.
го́рб|иться, люсь, ишься *impf.* (*of* **с~**) to stoop, become bent.
горбоно́с|ый (~, ~а) *adj.* hook-nosed.
горбу́н, а́ *m.* hunchback.
горбу́ш|а¹, и *f.* humpback salmon.
горбу́ш|а², и *f.* sickle.
горбу́шк|а, и *f.* crust (*of loaf*).
горбы́л|ь, я́ *m.* (*tech.*) slab.
горделиво́ст|ь, и *f.* haughtiness, pride.
горде́ли́в|ый (~, ~а) *adj.* haughty, proud.
горде́ц, а *m.* arrogant man.
го́рдиев *adj.*: **г. у́зел** Gordian knot.
гор|ди́ться, жу́сь, ди́шься *impf.* **1.** (+*i.*) to be proud (of), pride o.s. (on). **2.** to put on airs, be haughty.
го́рдост|ь, и *f.* (*in var. senses*) pride.
го́рд|ый (~, ~а́, ~о, ~ы́) *adj.* (*in var. senses*) proud.
горды́н|я, и *f.* arrogance; aloofness.
горде́чк|а, и *f.* arrogant woman.
го́р|е, я *nt.* **1.** grief, sorrow, woe; **на своё г.** to one's sorrow. **2.** misfortune, trouble; **г. в том, что...** the trouble is that .... **3.** *as pred.* (+*d.*; *coll.*) woe (unto), woe betide.
горе́ *adv.* (*arch.*) on high; upwards; **г. сердца́** (*eccl.*) sursum corda.
го́ре... *comb. form* sorry, woeful; apology for a ...; **г.-поэ́т** poetaster; **г.-войска́** a Fred Karno's army.
гор|ева́ть, ю́ю, ю́ешь *impf.* **1.** (**о**+*p.*) to grieve (for). **2.** (*coll. or dial.*) to be in need, be penurious.
горево́й *adj.* (*coll. or dial.*) piteous, unhappy.
горе́лк|а¹, а *f.* burner; **г. Бу́нзена** Bunsen burner; **приму́сная г.** Primus (*propr.*) stove.
горе́лк|а², и *f.* (*dial.*) vodka.
горе́л|ки, ок *no sg.* (*game of*) catch.
горе́л|ый *adj.* **1.** burnt; **па́хло ~ым** there was a smell of burning. **2.** rotten, decomposed (*of skins*).
горелье́ф, а *m.* (*art*) high relief.
горемы́к|а, и *c.g.* (*coll.*) unlucky individual, victim of misfortune.
горемы́ч|ный (~ен, ~на) *adj.* hapless, ill-starred; down on one's luck.
горе́ни|е, я *nt.* burning, combustion; (*fig.*) enthusiasm.
го́рест|ный (~ен, ~на) *adj.* sad, sorrowful; pitiful, mournful.
го́рест|ь, и *f.* **1.** sorrow, grief. **2.** (*pl.*) afflictions, misfortunes, troubles.
гор|е́ть, ю́, и́шь *impf.* **1.** to burn, be on fire. **2.** to burn, be alight; **в ку́хне у них ~е́л свет** the lights were burning in their kitchen; **~и́т ли пе́чка?** is the stove alight?; **де́ло ~и́т** things are going like a house on fire; **земля́ ~е́ла у него́ под нога́ми** (*i*) he went like greased lightning, (*ii*) the place was getting too hot for him, (*iii*) he was impatient to be off. **3.** (+*i.*; *fig.*) to burn (with); **г. жела́нием** (+*inf.*) to burn with the desire (to), be impatient (to). **4.** to glitter, shine. **5.** to rot, ferment.
го́р|ец, ца *m.* mountain-dweller, highlander.
го́реч|ь, и *f.* **1.** bitter taste. **2.** bitter stuff. **3.** bitterness.
го́рж|а, и *f.* (*mil.*) gorge.
горже́тк|а, и *f.* boa, throat-wrap.
горздра́в(отде́л), а *m.* (*abbr. of* ***городско́й отде́л здравохране́ния***) city health department.
горизо́нт, а *m.* **1.** horizon (*also fig.*), skyline. **2.: г. воды́** (*tech.*) water-level.
горизонта́л|ь, и *f.* **1.** horizontal; **по ~и** (*in crossword*) across. **2.** (*geog.*) contour line.
горизонта́л|ьный (~ен, ~ьна) *adj.* horizontal; **г. полёт** (*aeron.*) horizontal flight, level flight.
гори́лк|а, и *f.* = **горе́лка²**
гори́лл|а, ы *f.* gorilla.
гори́ст|ый (~, ~а) *adj.* mountainous, hilly.
горихво́стк|а, и *f.* redstart (*bird*).
горицве́т, а *m.* (*bot.*) lychnis; ragged robin.
го́рк|а, и *f.* **1.** hillock. **2.** cabinet, stand. **3.** (*aeron.*) steep climb. **4.: кра́сная г.** (*coll.*) the week following Easter week.
го́ркн|уть, у, ешь *impf.* (*of* **про~**) to turn rancid.
горко́м, а *m.* (*abbr. of* ***городской комите́т***) town, city committee.
горла́н, а *m.* (*coll.*) bawler; rowdy.
горла́н|ить, ю, ишь *impf.* (*coll.*) to bawl.
горла́ст|ый (~, ~а) *adj.* (*coll.*) noisy, loudmouthed.
го́рлинк|а, и *f.* = **го́рлица**
го́рлиц|а, ы *f.* **1.** turtle-dove. **2.** (*obs.*) = **голу́бка**
го́рл|о, а *nt.* **1.** throat; **дыха́тельное г.** windpipe; **драть г.** to bawl; **во всё г.** at the top of one's voice; **по г.** up to the neck (*also fig.*); **сыт по г.** full up; (*fig.*) fed up; **приста́ть с ножо́м к ~у** (+*d.*) to press, importune; **приста́вить нож к чьему́-н. ~у** to hold a knife to one's throat; **промочи́ть г.** (*coll.*) to wet one's whistle; **слова́ застря́ли у меня́ в ~е** the words stuck in my throat; **схвати́ть за г.** to catch, take by the throat. **2.** neck (*of a vessel*). **3.** narrow entrance to a gulf, bay.
горлови́н|а, ы *f.* mouth, orifice; manhole hatch; **г. вулка́на** crater.

горловóй *adj.* **1.** *adj. of* **гóрло**; throat; guttural. **2.** raucous.
горлодёр, а *m.* (*coll.*) **1.** bawler. **2.: табак-г.** rough shag.
гóрлыш|ко, ка, *g. pl.* **~ек** *nt.* **1.** *dim. of* **гóрло. 2.** neck (*of a bottle*).
гормóн, а *m.* (*physiol.*) hormone.
гормонáльный *adj.* hormone(-containing).
горн[1], **а** *m.* furnace, forge.
горн[2], **а** *m.* bugle.
гóрн|ий *adj.* **1.** (*arch., poet.*) heavenly, celestial; lofty. **2.: ~ее мéсто** (*eccl.*) east end (*of church, area behind altar*).
горнúл|о, а *nt.* **1.** (*obs.*) hearth, furnace. **2.** (*fig.*) crucible.
горнúст, а *m.* bugler.
гóрниц|а, ы *f.* **1.** (*obs.*) chamber. **2.** (*dial.*) clean part of peasant's hut.
гóрничн|ая, ой *f.* (house)maid; stewardess (*on ship*).
горнов|óй *adj. of* **горн**[1]; *as n.* **г., ~óго** *m.* furnace-worker.
горнозавóдский *adj.* mining and metallurgical.
горнозавóдчик, а *m.* owner of a mine *or* foundry.
горнолы́жник, а *m.* alpine skier.
горнолы́жный *adj.*: **г. спорт** alpine skiing.
горнопромы́шленност|ь, и *f.* mining industry.
горнопромы́шленный *adj.* mining.
горнорабóч|ий, его *m.* miner.
горностáевый *adj.* ermine.
горностá|й, я *m.* **1.** (*zool.*) ermine; stoat. **2.** ermine (*fur*).
гóрн|ый *adj.* **1.** *adj. of* **горá**; mountain; mountainous; **~ая болéзнь** altitude *or* mountain sickness; **~ые лы́жи** alpine skis; **~ая цепь** mountain range; **~ая артиллéрия** (*mil.*) mountain artillery. **2.** mineral; **г. лён** asbestos; **~ая порóда** rock; **г. хрустáль** rock crystal. **3.** mining; **~ое дéло** mining; **г. инститýт** College of Mines. **4.: ~ое сóлнце** artificial sunlight.
горня́к, á *m.* (*coll.*) **1.** miner. **2.** mining engineer; mining student.
горня́|цкий *adj. of* **~к 1.**
горовосходúтел|ь, я *m.* mountaineer.
гóрод, а, *pl.* **~á** *m.* **1.** town; city; **г.-побратúм** twin city; **вы́ехать зá г.** to go out of town; **жить зá ~ом** to live out of town, in the suburbs; **ни к селý, ни к ~у** (*coll.*) for no reason at all, inappropriate(ly). **2.** (*sports and games*) base; home.
гор|одúть, ожý, óдишь *impf.* to enclose, fence; **огорóд г.** to make unnecessary fuss; **г. чепухý, чушь** to talk nonsense.
городúш|ко, ка, *g. pl.* **~ек** *m.* small town.
городúщ|е, а *nt.* **1.** very large town. **2.** (*archaeol.*) site of ancient settlement.
город|кú, кóв *pl.* (*sg.* **~óк, ~кá** *m.*) gorodki (*game similar to skittles*).
городнúч|ий, его. *m.* (*hist.*) governor of a town.
городов|óй[1] *adj.* (*obs.*) *of* **гóрод; ~óе положéние** municipal statutes.
городов|óй[2], **óго** *m.* (*hist.*) policeman.
город|óк, кá *m.* **1.** small town; **воéнный г.** cantonment; **г. мúра** peace camp; **университéтский г.** campus. **2.** block of wood (*in game* **городкú**).
городóшник, а *m.* gorodki player.
городóшни|ца, цы *f. of* **~к**
городск|óй *adj.* urban; city; municipal; (*coll.*) *as n.* **г., ~óго** *m.* city-dweller, town-dweller.
городьб|á, ы́ *f.* **1.** fencing, enclosure. **2.** fence, hedge.
горожáн|ин, ина, *pl.* **~е, ~** *m.* city-dweller, town-dweller; townsman.
горожáн|ка, ки *f. of* **~ин**; townswoman.
горoскóп, а *m.* horoscope.
горóх, а (у) *no pl., m.* **1.** pea. **2.** (*collect.*) peas; **как óб стену, в стéну, от стены́ г.** (*coll.*) like being up against a brick wall; **при царé Горóхе** in days of yore.
горóхов|ый *adj.* **1.** pea. **2.** greenish-khaki; pea-green; **~ое пальтó** (*hist.; coll.*) agent of secret police; **чýчело ~ое** scarecrow; **шут г.** buffoon, laughing-stock.
горóш|ек, ка *m.* **1.** *dim. of* **горóх; душúстый г.** (*bot.*) sweet peas; **мéлким ~ком рассыпáться (пéред**+*i.*) to cringe (before). **2.** (*collect.*) spots, polka dots, spotted design (*on material*).
горóшин|а, ы *f.* a pea.
гóрский *adj. of* **гóрец**; mountain, highland.
горсовéт, а *m.* town, city soviet.
гóрсточк|а, и *f.* handful.
горст|ь, и, *g. pl.* **~éй** *f.* **1.** cupped hand; **держáть рýку ~ью** to cup one's hand. **2.** handful (*also fig.*).
гортáнный *adj.* **1.** (*anat.*) laryngeal. **2.** (*ling.*) guttural.
гортáн|ь, и *f.* larynx; **у негó язы́к прилúп к ~и** he was struck dumb; he was tongue-tied.
гортéнзи|я, и *f.* hydrangea.
гóрче *comp. of* **гóрький**
горч|úть, úт *impf.* (*impers.*) to have a bitter taste.
горчúц|а, ы *f.* mustard.
горчúчник, а *m.* mustard-poultice.
горчúчниц|а, ы *f.* mustard-pot.
горчúчн|ый *adj. of* **горчúца; г. газ** mustard gas; **~ое сéмя** mustard seed.
гóрше *comp. of* **гóрький**
горшéчник, а *m.* potter.
горшéчный *adj.* pottery; **г. товáр** pottery, earthenware.
гóрший (*obs.*) *comp. of* **гóрький**; more bitter (*fig.*).
горш|óк, кá *m.* pot; jug; vase; **ночнóй г.** chamber pot; (*infant's*) potty.
горшóчн|ый *adj.*: **~ое растéние** pot plant.
гóрьк|ая, ой *f.* vodka; **пить ~ую** (*coll.*) to hit the bottle.
гóр|ький (~ек, ~ькá, ~ько) *adj.* **1.** (*comp.* **~че**) bitter; **~ькое мáсло** rancid butter. **2.** (*comp.* **~ше, ~ший**) (*fig.*) bitter; hard; **~ькие слёзы** bitter tears; **~ьким óпытом узнáть** to learn by bitter experience. **3.** (*coll.*) hapless, wretched. **4.: г. пья́ница** (*coll.*) inveterate drunkard.
гóрько[1] *adv.* bitterly.
гóрько[2] *as pred.* **1.: у меня́ г. во рту** I have a bitter taste in my mouth. **2.** it is bitter; **мне г.** I am sorry, I am grieved.
горю́н, á *m.* (*coll.*) unfortunate.
горю́н|ья, ьи, *g. pl.* **~ий** *f. of* **~**
горю́ч|ее, его *nt.* fuel.
горю́чест|ь, и *f.* combustibility; inflammability.
горю́ч|ий *adj.* **1.** combustible, inflammable. **2.** (*folk poet.*) burning; **~ие слёзы** bitter tears.
гóрюшк|о, а *nt.* (*coll.*) grief, affliction; **а емý и ~а мáло** he does not care a jot.
горячелóмкий *adj.* (*tech.*) hot-shot.
горя́ч|ечный *adj. of* **~ка**; feverous; **г. бред** delirium; **~ечная рубáшка** strait-jacket.
горя́ч|ий (~, ~á, ~ó) *adj.* **1.** hot (*also fig.*); **по ~им следáм** (*i*) (+*g.*) hot on the heels (of), (*ii*) (*fig.*) forthwith; **под ~ую рýку** in the heat of the moment. **2.** passionate; ardent, fervent. **3.** hot-tempered; mettlesome; **~ая головá** hothead. **4.** heated; impassioned; **г. спор** heated argument. **5.** busy; **~ее врéмя** busy season. **6.** (*tech.*) high-temperature; **~ая обрабóтка** heat treatment.
горячúтельн|ый *adj.* (*obs.*) hot, warming; **~ые напúтки** strong drink.
горяч|úть, ý, úшь *impf.* (*of* **раз~**) to excite, irritate.
горяч|úться, ýсь, úшься *impf.* (*of* **раз~**) to get excited, become impassioned.
горя́чк|а, и *f. and c.g.* **1.** *f.* fever (*also fig.*). **2.** *f.* feverish activity; feverish haste; **порóть ~у** (*coll.*) to act impetuously, in the heat of the moment. **3.** *c.g.* (*coll.*) hothead; firebrand.
горя́чност|ь, и *f.* zeal, fervour, enthusiasm; impulsiveness.
горячó[1] *adv.* hot.
горячó[2] *as pred.* it is hot.
гос... *comb. form, abbr. of* **госудáрственный**
госбезопáсник, а *m.* (*coll.*) KGB officer.
госдéп, а *m.* (*abbr.*) = **госдепартáмент**
госдепартáмент, а *m.* (*US*) State Department.
Госиздáт, а *m.* (*abbr. of* ***Госудáрственное издáтельство***) State Publishing House.
госнóмер, а *m.* (*automobile*) licence plate.
гóспелз *m. indecl.* gospel music.
госпитализáци|я, и *f.* hospitalization.
гóспитал|ь, я *m.* hospital (*esp. mil.*).
госпитáльный *adj. of* **гóспиталь**
Госплáн, а *m.* (*abbr. of* ***Госудáрственная плáновая комúссия***) State Planning Commission (*in former USSR*).

госпо́д|ень, ня, не *adj.* (*eccl.*) the Lord's; **моли́тва ~ня** the Lord's Prayer.

го́споди *int.* good heavens!; good Lord!; good gracious!

господ|и́н, и́на, *pl.* **~а́, ~́, ~а́м** *m.* **1.** master; **сам себе́ г.** one's own master; **г. своего́ сло́ва** a man of one's word. **2.** gentleman; **э́ти ~а́** (*oft. iron.*) these gentlemen. **3.** (*as style*) (*i*) Mr, (*ii*) Master; **~а́** (*as form of address*) (*i*) gentlemen, (*ii*) ladies and gentlemen; (*as style*) (*i*) Messrs, (*ii*) Mr and Mrs.

господ́ский *adj.* seigniorial, manorial; **г. дом** manor-house.

госпо́дств|о, а *nt.* **1.** supremacy, dominion, mastery. **2.** predominance.

госпо́дств|овать, ую *impf.* **1.** to hold sway, exercise dominion. **2.** to predominate, prevail. **3.** (**над**+*i.*) to command, dominate; to tower (above).

госпо́дств|ующий *pres. part. act. of* **~овать** *and adj.* **1.** ruling; **г. класс** ruling class. **2.** predominant, prevailing. **3.** (*of physical features*) commanding.

Госпо́дь, Го́спода, *voc.* **Го́споди** *m.* God, the Lord; **Г. его́ зна́ет** (the) Lord knows!

госпож|а́, и́ *f.* **1.** mistress. **2.** lady. **3.** (*as style*) Mrs.; Miss.

госпожи́н|ки, ок *no sg.* (*dial.*) fast before the feast of the Assumption.

госсекрета́р|ь, я́ *m.* Secretary of State.

ГОСТ, а *or* **гост, а** *m.* (*abbr. of* ***госуда́рственный общесою́зный станда́рт***) State All-Union Standard (*in former USSR*).

гостево́й *adj.* guest, guests'.

гостеприи́м|ный (~ен, ~на) *adj.* hospitable.

гостеприи́мств|о, а *nt.* hospitality.

гости́н|ая, ой *f.* **1.** drawing-room, sitting-room. **2.** drawing-room suite.

гости́н|ец, ца *m.* (*coll.*) present.

гости́ниц|а, ы *f.* hotel, inn.

гости́н|ичный *adj. of* **~ица**

гостинодво́|рец, рца *m.* (*obs.*) shopkeeper (*in a bazaar*).

гости́ный *adj.*: **г. двор** arcade, bazaar.

гости́ть, гощу́, гости́шь *impf.* (**у**) to stay (with), be on a visit (to).

гост|ь, я, *g. pl.* **~е́й** *m.* guest, visitor; **кома́нда ~е́й** (*sport*) visiting team; **пойти́ в ~́и** (**к**+*d.*) to visit; **быть в гостя́х (у)** to be a guest (at, of), be visiting; **в гостя́х хорошо́, а до́ма лу́чше** there's no place like home.

го́ст|ья, ьи, *g. pl.* **~ий** *f. of* **~ь**

госуда́рственност|ь, и *f.* State system; statehood.

госуда́рственн|ый *adj.* State, public; **г. переворо́т** coup d'état; **~ая изме́на** high treason; **~ое пра́во** public law; **~ая слу́жба** public service; **г. слу́жащий** civil servant; **Г. сове́т** (*hist.*) State Council; **~ые экза́мены** final examinations (*in higher education institutions*).

госуда́рств|о, а *nt.* State.

госуда́рын|я, и *f.* **1.** sovereign; **Г.** (*as form of address*) Your Majesty. **2.** (*obs.*) mistress; **ми́лостивая г.** (*as form of address*) madam.

госуда́р|ь, я *m.* **1.** sovereign; **Г.** (*as form of address*) Your Majesty, Sire. **2.** (*obs.*) master; **ми́лостивый г.** (*as form of address*) sir.

гот, а *m.* (*hist.*) Goth.

го́тик|а, и *f.* (*archit.*) Gothic style.

готи́ческий *adj.* (*art*) Gothic; **г. шрифт** Gothic script, black-letter.

готова́л|ьня, ьни, *g. pl.* **~ен** *f.* case of drawing instruments.

гото́в|ить, лю, ишь *impf.* **1.** to prepare, make ready; to train. **2.** to cook. **3.** to lay in, store. **4.** (+*d.*; *fig.*) to have in store (for).

гото́в|иться, люсь, ишься *impf.* **1.** (**к**+*d. or* +*inf.*) to get ready (for, to); to prepare o.s. (for), make preparations (for). **2.** to be at hand, in the offing, impending, imminent; **~ятся кру́пные собы́тия** great events are in the offing.

гото́вност|ь, и *f.* **1.** readiness, preparedness; **в боево́й ~и** ready for action; (*naut.*) cleared for action. **2.** readiness, willingness.

гото́во *as pred.*: **и г.** (*coll.*) and that's that.

гото́в|ый (~, ~а) *adj.* **1.** (**к**+*d.*) ready (for), prepared (for); **г. к де́йствию** ready for action; **я не ~** I'm not ready; **г. к услу́гам** (*epistolary formula*) yours faithfully. **2.** (**на**+*a. or* +*inf.*) ready (for, to), prepared (for, to); willing (to); **мы ~ы на всё** we are prepared for anything; **она́ не ~а идти́** she is not willing to go. **3.** (+*inf.*) on the point (of), on the verge (of), ready (to); **он ~ был ка́ждую мину́ту расхохота́ться** he was on the verge of bursting out laughing. **4.** ready-made, finished; ready-to-wear; **~ое пла́тье** ready-made clothes; **~ые изде́лия** finished articles. **5.**: **на всём ~ом** with all found; **на ~ых харча́х** with full board and lodging. **6.** (*short form only*; *coll.*) (*i*) finished (= *dead*), (*ii*) tight, plastered (= *drunk*).

го́тский *adj.* Gothic (*of the Goths and Gothic language*).

гофма́ршал, а *m.* (*hist.*) Marshal of the (Imperial) Court.

гофме́йстер, а *m.* (*hist.*) steward of the household.

гофриро́ванн|ый *p.p.p. of* **гофрирова́ть** *and adj.* **~ое желе́зо** corrugated iron; **~ые во́лосы** waved hair; **~ая ю́бка** pleated skirt; **~ый воротни́к** goffered collar.

гофрир|ова́ть, у́ю *impf. and pf.* **1.** to corrugate; to wave; to crimp. **2.** to goffer.

гофриро́вк|а, и *no pl., f.* **1.** corrugation; goffering; waving. **2.** waves (*of hair*).

гр. (*abbr. of* **граждани́н** *or* **гражда́нка**) citizen.

граб, а *m.* (*bot.*) hornbeam.

гра́бар|ь, я *m.* (*dial.*) navvy.

грабёж, а́ *m.* robbery (*also fig., coll.*).

граби́ловк|а, и *f.* (*coll.*) **1.** rip-off establishment, clip-joint. **2.** extortion, rip-off.

граби́тел|ь, я *m.* robber; **у́личный г.** mugger.

граби́тельский *adj.* **1.** predatory. **2.** extortionate, exorbitant (*of prices*).

граби́тельств|о, а *nt.* (*obs.*) robbery.

гра́б|ить[1], лю, ишь *impf.* (*of* **о~**) to rob, pillage; (*fig.*) to rob.

гра́б|ить[2], лю, ишь *impf.* to rake.

гра́блени|е, я *nt.* raking.

гра́бленый *adj.* stolen.

гра́б|ли, лей *or* **~ель** *no sg.* rake.

гра́б|овый *adj. of* **~**

гравёр, а *m.* engraver.

гравёр|ный *adj. of* **~; ное иску́сство** engraving.

гра́ви|й, я *m.* gravel.

грави́йн|ый *adj. of* **гра́вий; ~ые карье́ры** gravel pits.

гравирова́льн|ый *adj.* engraving; **~ая доска́** steel plate, copper plate; **~ая игла́** etching needle.

гравир|ова́ть, у́ю, у́ешь *impf.* (*of* **вы́~**) to engrave.

гравиро́вк|а, и *f.* engraving.

гравиро́вщик, а *m.* engraver.

гравитацио́нный *adj.* gravitation(al).

гравита́ци|я, и *f.* (*phys.*) gravitation.

гравю́р|а, ы *f.* engraving, print; etching; **г. на де́реве** woodcut; **г. на лино́леуме** linocut; **г. на ме́ди** copper-plate engraving.

град[1], а *m.* **1.** hail. **2.** (*fig.*) hail, shower, torrent; volley.

град[2], а *m.* (*arch. or poet.*) city, town.

града́ци|я, и *f.* gradation, scale.

градие́нт, а *m.* gradient.

гра́дин|а, ы *f.* (*coll.*) hailstone.

гради́р|ня, ни, *g. pl.* **~ен** *f.* **1.** salt-pan. **2.** (water-)cooling tower.

гради́р|овать, ую *impf. and pf.* to evaporate, graduate (*salt*).

градоби́ти|е, я *nt.* damage done by hail.

градово́й *adj. of* **град 1.**

гра́дом *adv.* thick and fast; **уда́ры посы́пались г.** blows showered down, rained down.

градонача́льник, а *m.* (*hist.*) town governor (*of a town independent administratively of its province*).

градонача́льств|о, а *nt.* (*hist.*) **1.** town, borough (*independent administratively of province*). **2.** town governor's office.

градострои́тел|ь, я *m.* town-planner.

градострои́тельный *adj.* town-planning.

градострои́тельств|о, а *nt.* town-planning.

градуи́р|овать, ую *impf. and pf.* **1.** to graduate (*to mark with lines to indicate degrees, etc.*) **2.** to grade.

гра́дус, а *m.* **1.** degree (*unit of measurement*); **у́гол в 40**

~ов angle of 40 degrees; **сего́дня 20 ~ов тепла́, моро́за** it is twenty degrees above, below zero today. **2.** (*fig.*) degree, pitch; stage; **в после́днем ~е** in the final; stage (*of an illness*). **3.: под ~ом** (*coll.*) under the weather, one over the eight.

гра́дусник, а *m.* thermometer.

гра́дус|ный *adj. of* ~; **~ная се́тка** (*geog.*) grid.

граждани́н, а, *pl.* **гра́ждане, гра́ждан** *m.* **1.** citizen; **пото́мственный почётный г.** (*hist.*) hereditary honorary citizen (*title conferred in tsarist Russia on pers. not of gentle birth for service.*) **2.** person.

гражда́н|ка[1], ки *f. of* ~**и́н**; citizeness.

гражда́нк|а[2], и *f.* (*coll.*) **1.** = **гражда́нская а́збука. 2.** the Civil War (*in Russia 1917–1921*).

гражда́нк|а[3], и *f.* (*coll.*) **1.** civilian life; civvy street; **на ~е** in civvy street. **2.** civvies, civilian clothing.

гражда́нск|ий *adj.* **1.** (*leg., etc.*) civil; citizen's; civic; **г. иск** civil suit; **предъяви́ть г. иск** (**к**+*d.*) to bring a civil suit (against); **г. ко́декс** civil code; **~ое пра́во** civil law; **~ая смерть** deprivation of civil rights. **2.** civil, secular (*opp. ecclesiastical*); **г. брак** (*i*) civil marriage, (*ii*) (*coll., obs.*) cohabitation, free union; **~ая панихи́да** civil funeral rite. **3.** civilian (*opp. military*); **~ое пла́тье** civilian clothes, civvies, mufti. **4.** civic, befitting a citizen; **~ие доброде́тели** civic virtues. **5.** (*of poetry, etc.*) civic, having social content. **6.: ~ая война́** civil war. **7.: ~ая а́збука, ~ая печа́ть** Russian type (*introduced by Peter the Great in place of Church Slavonic*).

гражда́нственност|ь, и *f.* **1.** civilization; civil society. **2.** civic spirit.

гражда́нств|о, а *nt.* **1.** citizenship, nationality; **права́ ~а** civic rights; **получи́ть права́ ~а** to be granted civic rights; (*fig.*) to achieve general recognition. **2.** (*collect.; obs.*) citizenry.

грамза́пис|ь, и *f.* gramophone recording.

грамм, а *m.* gramme, gram.

грамма́тик, а *m.* grammarian.

грамма́тик|а, и *f.* **1.** grammar. **2.** grammar(-book).

граммати́ческий *adj.* grammatical.

граммофо́н, а *m.* gramophone (*with loudspeaker horn*).

граммофо́н|ный *adj. of* ~; **~ная пласти́нка** gramophone record.

гра́мот|а, ы *f.* **1.** reading and writing, ability to read and write. **2.** official document; deed.

грамоте́|й, я *m.* (*coll.*) **1.** one who can read and write. **2.** scholar.

гра́мотк|а, и *f.* (*coll.*) letter, note.

гра́мотност|ь, и *f.* **1.** literacy (*also fig.*). **2.** grammatical correctness. **3.** competence.

гра́мот|ный (~ен, ~на) *adj.* **1.** literate; able to read and write. **2.** grammatically correct. **3.** competent. **4.: полити́чески г.** politically aware.

грампласти́нк|а, и *f.* gramophone record.

гран, а *m.* grain (*unit of weight*); **в э́том нет ни ~а и́стины** there is not a grain of truth in it.

грана́т[1], а *m.* **1.** pomegranate. **2.** pomegranate tree.

грана́т[2], а *m.* (*min.*) garnet.

грана́т|а, ы *f.* (*mil.*) shell, grenade; **ручна́я г.** hand-grenade.

грана́тник, а *m.* pomegranate tree.

грана́т|ный *adj. of* ~**а**; **г. ого́нь** shell-fire.

грана́товый[1] *adj.* pomegranate.

грана́т|овый[2] **1.** *adj. of* ~[2]. **2.** rich red.

гранатомёт, а *m.* (*mil.*) grenade cup discharger, grenade thrower.

гранатомётчик, а *m.* grenade-thrower, grenadier.

гранд, а *m.* grandee (*Spanish nobleman*).

грандио́зност|ь, и *f.* grandeur; immensity.

грандио́з|ный (~ен, ~на) *adj.* grandiose; mighty; vast.

гране́ни|е, я *nt.* cutting (*of precious stones, glass*).

гранён|ый *adj.* **1.** cut, faceted; **~ое стекло́** cut glass. **2.** cut-glass.

грани́льный *adj.* lapidary; diamond-cutting.

грани́л|ьня, ьни, *g. pl.* **~ен** *f.* lapidary workshop; **г. алма́зов** diamond-cutting shop.

грани́льщик, а *m.* lapidary; **г. алма́зов** diamond-cutter.

грани́т, а *m.* granite.

грани́тный *adj.* granite.

гран|и́ть, ю́, и́шь *impf.*, to cut, facet; (*coll.*) **г. мостову́ю** to loaf, saunter, promenade.

грани́ц|а, ы *f.* **1.** frontier, border; **за ~ей** abroad; **е́хать за ~у** to go abroad. **2.** (*fig.*) boundary, limit; **вы́йти из ~** to overstep the limits, overstep the mark; **перейти́ все ~ы** to pass all bounds; **в ~ах прили́чия** within the bounds of decency.

грани́ч|ить, у, ишь *impf.* (**с**+*i.*) **1.** to border (upon), be contiguous (with). **2.** (*fig.*) to border (on), verge (on); **э́то ~ит с изме́ной** it borders on treason.

гра́нк|а, и *f.* (*typ.*) slip, galley-proof.

гранули́р|овать, ую *impf. and pf.* to granulate.

грануля́ци|я, и *f.* (*tech., astron., med.*) granulation.

гран|ь, и *f.* **1.** border, verge; **на ~и сумасше́ствия** on the verge of insanity; **«поли́тика на ~и войны́»** brinkmanship. **2.** side, facet; edge. **3.** (*math.*) period.

грасси́р|овать, ую *impf.* to pronounce one's *r*'s in the French manner.

грат, а *m.* (*tech.*) barb, burr.

граф, а *m.* count.

граф|а́, ы́ *f.* (*book-keeping, etc.*) column (*of a table or page*); section.

гра́фик[1], а *m.* **1.** graph, chart. **2.** schedule; **пло́тный г.** packed *or* heavy schedule; **скользя́щий г. рабо́ты** flexible working hours; flexitime; **то́чно по ~у** according to schedule.

гра́фик[2], а *m.* draughtsman.

гра́фик|а, и *f.* **1.** (*art*) drawing; (*comput.*) graphics; **экра́нная г.** on-screen graphics. **2.** script.

графи́н, а *m.* carafe; decanter.

графи́н|я, и *f.* countess.

графи́т, а *m.* **1.** (*min.*) graphite, black-lead. **2.** pencil-lead.

графи́т|ный *adj.* = **~овый**

графи́товый *adj.* graphite.

граф|и́ть, лю́, и́шь *impf.* (*of* **раз~**) to rule (*paper*).

графи́ческий *adj.* graphic.

графлёный *adj.* (vertically) ruled.

графо́лог, а *m.* graphologist.

графоло́ги|я, и *f.* graphology.

графома́н, а *m.* graphomaniac; (*fig.*) pulp-writer, hack.

графома́ни|я, и *f.* graphomania.

графопострои́тел|ь, я *m.* plotter (*instrument*).

графопрое́ктор, а *m.* overhead projector.

гра́фский *adj. of* **граф**

гра́фств|о, а *nt.* **1.** title of count. **2.** county.

грацио́з|ный (~ен, ~на) *adj.* graceful.

гра́ци|я, и *f.* **1.** gracefulness. **2. Г.** (*myth.*) Grace; (*fig.*) beauty. **3.** corselette.

грач, а́ *m.* (*zool.*) rook.

грач|и́ный *adj. of* ~

грач|о́нок, о́нка, *pl.* **~а́та, ~а́т** *m.* (*zool.*) rooklet, rookling.

гребёнк|а, и *f.* **1.** comb; **стричь под ~у** to crop close; **стричь всех под одну́ ~у** to treat all alike, reduce all to the same level. **2.** (*tech.*) rack; (*text.*) hackle.

гребе́нчатый *adj.* **1.** (*zool.*) cristate; pectinate. **2.** comb-shaped; **г. подши́пник** (*tech.*) collar thrust bearing.

гре́б|ень, ня *m.* **1.** comb. **2.** (*tech.*) comb; (*text.*) hackle. **3.** (*of bird*) comb, crest; **петуши́ный г.** cock's comb. **4.** crest (*of hill or wave*). **5.** (*archit.*) ridge-piece, roof-tree. **6.** (*agric.*) ridge.

греб|е́ц, ца́ *m.* rower, oarsman.

гребеш|о́к[1], ка́ *m.* = **гре́бень**

гребеш|о́к[2], ка́ *m.* (*zool.*) scallop.

гре́бл|я[1], и *f.* **1.** rowing. **2.** (*dial.*) raking.

гре́бл|я[2], и *f.* (*dial.*) dyke.

гребневи́д|ный (~ен, ~на) *adj.* comb-shaped, pectinate.

гребнечеса́льн|ый *adj.*: **~ая маши́на** (*text.*) hackling machine, comber.

гребни́ст|ый (~, ~а) *adj.* (high-)crested.

гребн|о́й *adj.* **1.** rowing; **г. спорт** rowing. **2.: г. вал** propeller shaft; **г. винт** propeller screw; **~о́е колесо́** paddle wheel.

греб|о́к, ка́ *m.* **1.** stroke (*in rowing*). **2.** blade (*of a mill-wheel or paddle-wheel*).

грегориа́нский *adj.* = **григориа́нский**
грёз|а, ы *f.* day-dream, reverie.
гре́|жу *see* **~зить**
гре́|зить, жу, зишь *impf.* to dream; **г. наяву́** to day-dream.
гре́|зиться, жусь, зишься *impf.* (*of* **при~**) (*impers.*, *+d.*) to dream; **мне ~зилось, что...** I used to dream that ....
гре́йгаунд, а *m.* greyhound.
гре́йдер, а *m.* (*tech.*) **1.** grader. **2.** (*coll.*) earth road (*levelled but unmetalled*).
гре́йдер|ный *adj. of* **~**; **~ная доро́га** grader road.
гре́йпфрут, а *m.* grapefruit.
гре́йхаунд = **гре́йгаунд**
грек, а *m.* Greek.
гре́ко-ки́прский *adj.* Greek-Cypriot.
гре́лк|а, и *f.* hot-water bottle; **электри́ческая г.** electric blanket.
грем|е́ть, лю́, и́шь *impf.* to thunder, roar; peal; rattle; (*fig.*) to resound, ring out; **и́мя его́ ~е́ло по всей Евро́пе** his name resounded throughout Europe.
грему́ч|ий *adj.* roaring; **г. газ** detonating-gas; **~ая змея́** rattlesnake; **~ая ртуть** (*chem.*) fulminate of mercury; **г. сту́день** nitrogelatine, blasting gelatine.
грему́шк|а, и *f.* **1.** rattle (*child's toy*). **2.** sleigh-bell.
гре́н|а, ы *f.* (*collect.*) silkworm eggs.
гренаде́р, а *m.* grenadier.
гренаде́р|ский *adj. of* **~**; **г. полк** Grenadiers.
гре́нк|а, и *f.* (*coll.*) piece of toast.
Гренла́нди|я, и *f.* Greenland.
гренла́ндский *adj.* Greenland.
грен|о́к, ка́ *m.* (finger of) toast; (*cul.*) croûton.
гре|сти́, бу́, бёшь, *past* **~б, ~бла́** *impf.* **1.** to row. **2.** to rake; **г. лопа́той де́ньги** (*coll.*) to rake in the shekels.
греть, гре́ю, гре́ешь *impf.* **1.** (*intrans.*) to give out warmth. **2.** (*trans.*) to warm, heat; **г. (себе́) ру́ки** to warm one's hands; (*fig.*, *coll.*, *pej.*) to be on to a good thing.
гре́|ться, юсь, ешься *impf.* **1.** to warm o.s. **2.** *pass. of* **греть**
грех, а́ *m.* **1.** (*relig. or fig.*) sin; **первоpо́дный г.** original sin; **г. попола́м** (*coll.*) they're (just) as bad as each other; **приня́ть на себя́ г.** to take the blame upon o.s.; **не́чего ~а́ таи́ть** it must be owned; **есть тако́й г.** I own it; **пода́льше от ~а́** get out of harm's way; **как на г.** as ill-luck would have it. **2.** *as pred.* (*+inf.*; *coll.*) it is a sin, it is sinful; **не г.** (*+inf.*) it does not, would not hurt (to); there is no harm (in); **не г. вы́пить рю́мочку-две** there is no harm in (drinking) a glass or two. **3.: с ~о́м попола́м** (only) just; **мы с ~о́м попола́м расшифрова́ли твой по́черк** we just managed to decipher your handwriting.
грехо́в|ный (~ен, ~на) *adj.* sinful.
греховó́дник, а *m.* (*coll.*, *obs.*) sinner; (*of a child*) naughty boy.
грехово́дни|ца, цы *f. of* **~к**
грехово́днича|ть, ю *impf.* (*coll.*, *obs.*) to be a sinner.
грехопаде́ни|е, я *nt.* (*bibl.*) the Fall; (*fig.*) fall.
Гре́ци|я, и *f.* Greece.
гре́цкий *adj.*: **г. оре́х** walnut.
гре́ч|а, и *f.* (*coll.*) buckwheat.
греча́нк|а, и *f. of* **грек**
гре́ческий *adj.* Greek; Grecian.
гречи́х|а, и *f.* buckwheat.
гре́чнев|ый *adj.* buckwheat; **~ая ка́ша** buckwheat porridge.
греш|и́ть, у́, и́шь *impf.* **1.** (*pf.* **со~**) to sin. **2.** (*pf.* **по~**) (**про́тив**+*g.*; *fig.*) to sin (against).
гре́шник, а *m.* sinner.
гре́шни|ца, цы *f. of* **~к**
гре́ш|ный (~ен, ~на́) *adj.* sinful; culpable; **г. челове́к** (*parenth.*) I am ashamed to say; **~ным де́лом** (*parenth.*) much as I regret it, I am ashamed to say.
греш|о́к, ка́ *m.* peccadillo.
гриб, а́ *m.* fungus; mushroom; **съедо́бный г.** mushroom, edible fungus; **несъедо́бный г.** toadstool; **уче́ние о ~а́х** (*bot.*) mycology; **г. съесть** (*obs.*) to be unsuccessful, meet with failure; **расти́ как ~ы́** to spring up like mushrooms.
грибко́вый *adj.* fungoid.
грибни́ц|а, ы *f.* **1.** mushroom spawn. **2.** (*coll.*) mushroom soup.
грибн|о́й *adj. of* **гриб**; fungoid; mushroom; **г. дождь** sun shower; **~а́я похлёбка** mushroom soup.
гриб|о́к, ка́ *m.* **1.** *dim. of* **гриб.** **2.** (*biol.*) fungus, microorganism. **3.** mushroom (*for darning stockings*).
гри́в|а, ы *f.* **1.** mane. **2.** wooded ridge. **3.** (*dial.*) shoal.
грива́ст|ый (~, ~а) *adj.* with a long mane.
гри́венник, а *m.* (*coll.*) ten-kopeck piece.
гри́вн|а, ы *f.* **1.** (*hist.*) grivna (*unit of currency in medieval Russia*). **2.** (*obs.*) ten kopecks. **3.** (*hist.*) pendant.
гривуа́з|ный (~ен, ~на) *adj.* obscene, indecent.
григориа́нск|ий *adj.* Gregorian; **г. календа́рь, ~ое летосчисле́ние** Gregorian Calendar.
гри́дниц|а, ы *f.* (*hist.*) quarters of body-guard.
грид|ь, и *f.* (*collect.*; *hist.*) (*prince's*) body-guard.
гри́зли *m. indecl.* grizzly (bear)
гриль-ба́р, а *m.* grillroom.
грим, а *m.* make-up (*theatr. only*); grease-paint.
грима́с|а, ы *f.* grimace; **де́лать ~ы** to make *or* pull faces.
грима́сник, а *m.* grimacer.
грима́снича|ть, ю *impf.* to grimace; to make *or* pull faces.
гримёр, а *m.* (*theatr.*, *etc.*) make-up artist.
гримёрн|ая, ой *f.* (*theatr.*, *etc.*) make-up (room).
гримёр|ша, ши (*coll.*) *f. of* **~**
гримир|ова́ть, у́ю, *impf.* **1.** (*theatr.*) (*pf.* **на~**) to make up. **2.** (*pf.* **за~**) (*+i.*) to make up (as); (*+i. or* **под**+*a.*; *fig.*) to make to appear, make out (as); **г. Наполео́на геро́ем, под геро́я** to paint Napoleon as a hero.
гримир|ова́ться, у́юсь *impf.* (*of* **за~**) (*theatr.*) to make up (*intrans.*); (*+i. or* **под**+*a.*; *fig.*) to make o.s. out, seek to appear; **г. патрио́том, под патрио́та** to make o.s. out a patriot.
гримиро́вк|а, и *f.* (*theatr.*) making-up.
грим-убо́рн|ая, ой *f.* (*theatr.*, *etc.*) dressing-room.
Гри́нвич, а *m.* Greenwich; **вре́мя по ~у** Greenwich (Mean) Time (*abbr. GMT*).
грипп, а *m.* influenza.
гриппо́зный *adj.* influenzal; **г. больно́й** flu victim *or* sufferer.
гриф[1], а *m.* **1.** (*myth.*) gryphon. **2.** (*zool.*) vulture.
гриф[2], а *m.* (*mus.*) finger-board (*of stringed instruments*).
гриф[3], а *m.* seal, stamp.
гриф[4], а *m.* (*sport*) grip (*in wrestling*).
гри́фел|ь, я *m.* slate-pencil; (*pencil*) lead.
гри́фельн|ый *adj.* slate; **~ая доска́** slate; **г. сла́нец** (*geol.*) grapholite.
грифо́н, а *m.* **1.** (*myth.*, *archit.*) gryphon. **2.** griffon (*dog*).
гроб, а, о ~е, в ~у́, *pl.* **~ы́** *and* **~а́** *m.* **1.** coffin; **идти́ за ~ом** to follow the coffin. **2.** (*obs.*) grave, burial-place. **3.** (*fig.*) the grave (= *death*); **вогна́ть в г.** to drive to the grave; **до ~а, по г. жи́зни** (*coll.*) until death, as long as one shall live; **стоя́ть одно́й ного́й в ~у́** to have one foot in the grave.
гро́б|ить, лю, ишь *impf.* (*sl.*) to destroy; to ruin.
гробни́ц|а, ы *f.* tomb, sepulchre.
гробов|о́й *adj.* **1.** *adj. of* **гроб; ~а́я доска́** (*fig.*) the grave; **ве́рный до ~о́й доски́** faithful unto death. **2.** sepulchral, deathly; **г. го́лос** sepulchral voice; **~о́е молча́ние** deathly silence.
гробовщи́к, а́ *m.* coffin-maker; undertaker.
гробокопа́тел|ь, я *m.* (*obs.*) gravedigger (*iron.* = *dry-as-dust historian*, *etc.*).
грог, а *m.* grog.
гроз|а́, ы́, *pl.* **~ы** *f.* **1.** (thunder)storm. **2.** calamity, disaster. **3.** (*fig.*; *of a pers. or thing*) terror. **4.** (*obs.*) threats.
гроздь, и, *pl.* **~и, ~е́й** *and* **~ья, ~ьев** *f.* cluster, bunch (*of fruit or flowers*)
гро|зи́ть, жу́, зи́шь *impf.* **1.** (*pf.* **при~**) (*+d. and i. or +inf.*) to threaten; **он ~зи́л мне револьве́ром** he was threatening me with a revolver; **г. уби́ть кого́-н.** to threaten to kill s.o. **2.** (*pf.* **по~**) (*+i.*) to make threatening gestures; **г. кулако́м кому́-н.** to shake one's fist at s.o. **3.** (*no pf.*) to threaten; **ему́ ~зи́т банкро́тство** he is threatened with bankruptcy; **дом ~зи́т паде́нием** the house threatens to collapse.
гро|зи́ться, жу́сь, зи́шься *impf.* (*of* **по~**) (*coll.*) **1.** (*+inf.*)

to threaten. **2.** to make threatening gestures.

гро́з|ный (~ен, ~на́, ~но) *adj.* **1.** menacing, threatening. **2.** dread, terrible; formidable; **~ная опа́сность** terrible danger. **3.** (*coll.*) stern, severe.

гроз|ово́й *adj. of* **~а́; ~ова́я ту́ча** storm-cloud, thunder-cloud.

гром, а, *pl.* **⁓ы, ~о́в** *m.* thunder (*also fig.*); **уда́р ⁓а** thunderclap; **г. среди́ я́сного не́ба** a bolt from the blue; **мета́ть ⁓ы и мо́лнии** (*fig.*) to fulminate.

грома́д|а[1]**, ы** *f.* mass, bulk, pile (+*g.*); a mass (of), heaps (of).

грома́д|а[2]**, ы** *f.* (*hist.*) gromada (*rural commune or assembly in Ukraine and Byelorussia*).

грома́дин|а, ы *f.* (*coll.*) vast object.

грома́д|ный (~ен, ~на) *adj.* huge, vast, enormous, colossal.

громи́л|а, ы *m.* (*coll.*) **1.** burglar. **2.** thug.

гром|и́ть, лю́, и́шь *impf.* (*of* **раз~**) **1.** to destroy; (*mil.*) to smash, rout. **2.** (*fig.*) to lambaste; to fulminate against.

гро́м|кий (~ок, ~ка́, ~ко) *adj.* **1.** loud. **2.** famous; notorious; **~кое поведе́ние** infamous conduct. **3.** fine-sounding, specious; **~кие слова́** (*iron.*) big words.

гро́мко *adv.* loud(ly); aloud.

громкоговори́тел|ь, я *m.* loud-speaker.

громкоголо́сый *adj.* loud-voiced.

громове́рж|ец, ца *m.* the thunderer (*epithet of Zeus; myth, and fig.*).

громов|о́й *adj.* **1.** *adj. of* **гром; ~ы́е раска́ты** peals of thunder. **2.** thunderous, deafening; **~ы́е рукоплеска́ния** thunderous applause. **3.** crushing, smashing.

громогла́сно *adv.* **1.** loudly. **2.** out loud, publicly.

громогла́с|ный (~ен, ~на) *adj.* **1.** loud; loud-voiced. **2.** public, open.

громозву́ч|ный (~ен, ~на) *adj.* (*obs.*) **1.** loud. **2.** (*fig.*) triumphal; highflown.

громоз|ди́ть, жу́, ди́шь *impf.* (*of* **на~**) to pile up, heap up.

громоз|ди́ться, жу́сь, ди́шься *impf.* **1.** to tower. **2.** (*coll.*) to clamber up.

громо́зд|кий (~ок, ~ка) *adj.* cumbersome, unwieldy.

громоотво́д, а *m.* lightning-conductor (*also fig.*).

громоподо́б|ный (~ен, ~на) *adj.* thunderous.

гро́м|че *comp. of* **~кий** *and* **~ко**

громыха́|ть, ю *impf.* (*coll.*) to rumble.

гросс, а *m.* gross.

гро́ссбу́х, а *m.* ledger.

гроссме́йстер, а *m.* **1.** grand master (*at chess*). **2.** (*hist.*) Grand Master (*of order of knights in Middle Ages*).

грот[1]**, а** *m.* grotto.

грот[2]**, а** *m.* mainsail.

грот-... *comb. form* (*naut.*) main-.

гроте́ск, а *m.* (*art*) grotesque.

гроте́скный *adj.* grotesque.

гроте́сковый *adj.*: **г. шрифт** (*typ.*) sanserif.

гро́х|ать(ся), аю(сь) *impf. of* **~нуть(ся)**

гро́хн|уть, у, ешь *pf.* (*coll.*) **1.** to crash, bang. **2.** (*trans.*) to drop with a crash, bang down.

гро́хн|уться, усь, ешься *pf.* (*coll.*) to fall with a crash.

гро́хот[1]**, а** *m.* crash, din; thunder.

гро́хот[2]**, а** *m.* (*tech., agric.*) riddle, screen, sifter.

грохота́нь|е, я *nt.* crashing; rumbling.

грох|ота́ть, очу́, о́чешь *impf.* **1.** to crash; roll, rumble; roar. **2.** (*coll.*) to roar (*with laughter*).

грохо|ти́ть, чу́, ти́шь *impf.* (*of* **про~**) (*tech., agric.*) to riddle, sift, screen.

грош, а́ *m.* **1.** half-kopeck piece. **2.** grosz (*Polish unit of currency*). **3.** *pl.* **~и́, ~е́й** (*fig., coll.*) penny, farthing; **э́тому г. ме́дный, ло́маный цена́; э́то ~а́ ме́дного, ло́маного не сто́ит** it's not worth a brass farthing; **ни в г. не ста́вить** not to give a brass farthing (for); **купи́ть за ~и́** to buy for a song; **рабо́тать за ~и́** work for peanuts. **4.** *pl.* **⁓и, ⁓ей** (*sl.*) lolly, brass (= *money*).

гроше́вый *adj.* (*coll.*) **1.** dirt-cheap; (*fig.*) cheap, shoddy. **2.** insignificant, trifling.

грубе́|ть, ю, ешь *impf.* (*of* **о~**) to grow coarse, rude.

груб|и́ть, лю́, и́шь *impf.* (*of* **на~**) (+*d.*) to be rude (to).

грубия́н, а *m.* (*coll.*) boor.

грубия́н|ить, ю, ишь *impf.* (*of* **на~**) (+*d.*; *coll.*) to be rude (to); to behave boorishly.

гру́бо *adv.* **1.** coarsely, roughly. **2.** crudely. **3.** rudely. **4.** roughly (= *approximately*); **г. говоря́** roughly speaking.

грубова́т|ый (~, ~а) *adj.* rather coarse, rude.

гру́бост|ь, и *f.* **1.** rudeness; coarseness; grossness. **2.** rude remark; coarse action; **говори́ть ~и** to be rude.

грубошёрстный *adj.* (*of cloth, etc.*) coarse.

гру́б|ый (~, ~а́, ~о) *adj.* **1.** coarse, rough; **~ое сукно́** coarse fabric; **г. го́лос** gruff voice. **2.** (*of workmanship, etc.*) crude, rude. **3.** gross, flagrant; **г. обма́н** gross deception. **4.** rude; coarse, crude; **~ое сло́во** rude, coarse word. **5.** rough (= *approximate*); **в ~ых черта́х** in rough outline.

гру́д|а, ы *f.* heap, pile.

груда́ст|ый (~, ~а) *adj.* broad-chested; big-breasted, big-bosomed.

груди́н|а, ы *f.* (*anat.*) breastbone.

груди́нк|а, и *f.* brisket; breast (*of lamb, etc.*).

грудни́ц|а, ы *f.* (*med.*) mastitis.

грудн|о́й *adj.* **1.** breast; chest; **г. го́лос** chest-voice; **~а́я жа́ба** (*med.*) angina pectoris; **~а́я железа́** (*anat.*) mammary gland; **~а́я кле́тка** (*anat.*) thorax. **2.** at the breast; **г. ребёнок** infant in arms. **3.: г. мох** (*bot.*) Iceland moss.

грудобрю́шн|ый *adj.*: **~ая прегра́да** (*anat.*) diaphragm.

груд|ь, и́, о ⁓и, в (на) ~и́, *pl.* **⁓и ~е́й** *f.* **1.** breast, chest; **стоя́ть ⁓ью (за**+*a.*) to stand up (for), champion; **г. с ⁓ью, г. на́ г. би́ться** to fight hand to hand **2.** (*female*) breast; bosom, bust; **корми́ть ⁓ью** to breast-feed; **отня́ть от ~и́** to wean. **3.** (shirt)-front.

гружёный *adj.* loaded, laden.

груз, а *m.* **1.** weight; load, cargo, freight; **поле́зный г.** payload. **2.** (*fig.*) weight, burden. **3.** (*pendulum*) bob.

груздь, я́, *pl.* **⁓и, ~е́й** *m.* milk-agaric (*mushroom*).

грузи́л|о, а *nt.* sinker.

грузи́н, а, *g. pl.* **г.** *m.* Georgian.

грузи́н|ка, ки *f. of* **~**

грузи́нский *adj.* Georgian.

гру|зи́ть, жу́, ⁓зи́шь *impf.* **1.** (*pf.* **за~** *and* **на~**) to load; to lade, freight; **г. су́дно** to lade a ship. **2.** (*pf.* **по~**) **(в, на**+*a.*) to load; **г. това́р на су́дно** to put a cargo aboard a ship.

гру|зи́ться, жу́сь, ⁓зи́шься *impf.* (*of* **по~**) to load (*intrans.*), take on cargo.

Гру́зи|я, и *f.* Georgia (*Transcaucasia*).

гру́зк|а, и *f.* lading.

грузне́|ть, ю, ешь *impf.* (*of* **по~**) to grow heavy, corpulent.

гру́зност|ь, и *f.* weightiness, bulkiness; unwieldiness; corpulence.

гру́зн|уть, у, ешь *impf.* to go down, sink.

гру́з|ный (~ен, ~на́, ~но) *adj.* weighty, bulky; unwieldy; corpulent.

грузови́к, а́ *m.* lorry.

грузовладе́л|ец, ьца *m.* owner of freight.

грузов|о́й *adj.* goods, cargo, freight; **~о́е движе́ние** goods traffic; **~о́е су́дно** cargo boat, freighter.

грузооборо́т, а *m.* turnover of goods.

грузоотправи́тел|ь, я *m.* consignor of goods.

грузо(-)пассажи́рский *adj.*: **г. автомоби́ль** utility vehicle.

грузоподъёмност|ь, и *f.* payload capacity; freight-carrying capacity.

грузоподъёмный *adj.*: **г. кран** (*loading*) crane.

грузополуча́тел|ь я *m.* consignee.

грузопото́к, а *m.* goods traffic.

грузотакси́ *nt. indecl.* 'taxi-lorry' (*lorry operated for hire from taxi-station*).

гру́зчик, а *m.* docker, stevedore.

грум, а *m.* groom.

грунт, а *m.* **1.** soil, earth; bottom; **пересади́ть в г.** to plant out. **2.** priming, prime coating (*of a picture*).

грунт|ова́ть, у́ю *impf.* (*of* **за~**) (*art*) to prime.

грунто́вк|а, и *f.* priming, first coat (*of paint*).

грунтов|о́й *adj. of* **грунт; ~ы́е во́ды** subsoil waters; **~а́я доро́га** dirt road, earth road.

гру́пп|а, ы *f.* (*in var. senses*) group; club; **г. кро́ви** (*med.*)

blood group; **г. любúтелей бéга** jogging club; **дошкóльная г.** playgroup; **оператúвная г.** task force.

группир|овáть, ýю *impf.* (*of* **с~**) to group; to classify.

группир|овáться, ýется *impf.* (*of* **с~**) to group, form groups.

группирóвк|а, и *f.* **1.** grouping, classification; **г. сил** (*mil.*) distribution of forces. **2.** group, grouping.

группово́д, а *m.* group leader.

группов|óй *adj.* group; **~ы́е заня́тия** group study, group work; **~ы́е úгры** team games; **г. полёт** formation flying; **г. снúмок** group photograph.

групповщúн|а, ы *f.* clique-formation, cliquishness.

гру|стúть, щý, стúшь *impf.* to grieve, mourn; (**по**+*d.*) to pine (for).

грýстно[1] *adv.* sadly, sorrowfully.

грýстно[2] *as pred.* it is sad; **ей г.** she feels sad; **нам г. узнáть, что...** we are sorry to hear that....

грýст|ный (~ен, ~нá, ~но) *adj.* **1.** sad, melancholy. **2.** sad(-making); (*coll.*) grievous, distressing.

груст|ь, и *f.* sadness, melancholy.

грýш|а, и *f.* **1.** pear. **2.** pear-tree. **3.: землянáя г.** Jerusalem artichoke. **4.** pear-shaped object; **боксёрская г.** punchball.

грушевúд|ный (~ен, ~на) *adj.* pear-shaped.

грýшевый *adj.* pear; **г. компóт** stewed pears.

грушóвк|а, и *f.* **1.** pear liqueur. **2.** grushovka (*variety of apple tree*).

гры́ж|а, и *f.* (*med.*) hernia, rupture.

грыжевóй *and* **гры́жевый** *adj.* hernial; **г. бандáж** truss.

гры́зл|о, а *nt.* bit (*of bridle*).

грызн|я́, ú *f.* (*coll.*) **1.** fight (*of animals*). **2.** squabble.

гры́з|ть, ý, ёшь, *past* **~, ~ла** *impf.* **1.** to gnaw; to nibble; **г. нóгти** to bite one's nails. **2.** (*coll.*) to nag (at). **3.** (*fig.*) to devour, consume; **нас ~ло любопы́тство** we were consumed with curiosity.

гры́з|ться, ýсь, ёшься, *past* **~ся, ~лась** *impf.* **1.** to fight (*of animals*). **2.** (*coll.*) to squabble, bicker.

грызýн, á *m.* rodent.

гры́мз|а, ы *c.g.* (*coll.*) grumbler.

грю́ндер, а *m.* company promoter.

грю́ндерств|о, а *nt.* company promotion.

гряд|á, ы́, *pl.* **~ы, ~, ~áм** *f.* **1.** ridge. **2.** bed (*in garden*). **3.** row, series.

гря́дил|ь, я *m.* plough-beam.

гря́дк|а[1], **и** *f. dim. of* **грядá**

гря́дк|а[2], **и** *f.* edge (*of cart or sledge*).

гря́дков|ый *adj.* *of* **гря́дка**[1]; **~ая культýра** (*hort.*) growing in beds.

грядовóй *adj.* (*hort.*) growing, grown in beds.

грядýщ|ий *pres. part. act. of* **грястú** (*obs.*) *and adj.* (*rhet.*): coming, future; **~ие дни** days to come; **на сон г.** (*coll.*) at bedtime, before going to bed; *as n.* **~ее, ~его** *nt.* the future.

грязев|óй *adj.* mud; **~áя вáнна** mud-bath.

грязелечéбниц|а, ы *f.* institution for mud-cures, therapeutic mud-baths.

грязелечéни|е, я *nt.* mud-cure.

грязнé|ть, ю *impf.* to get covered in mud, become dirty.

грязн|úть, ю́, úшь *impf.* (*of* **на~**) **1.** to make dirty, soil; (*fig.*) to sully, besmirch. **2.** to litter.

грязн|úться, ю́сь, úшься *impf.* to become dirty.

гря́зн|о[1] *adv. of* **~ый**

гря́зно[2] *as pred.* it is dirty.

грязнýл|я, и *c.g.* (*coll.*) guttersnipe; slut.

гря́зн|уть, у, ешь *impf.* to sink in the mire (*also fig.*).

гря́з|ный (~ен, ~нá, ~но) *adj.* **1.** muddy, mud-stained. **2.** dirty; **~ное бельё** dirty washing (*also fig.*). **3.** untidy; slovenly; **~ная тетрáдь** untidy copy-book. **4.** (*fig.*) dirty, filthy; **~ное дéло** dirty business. **5.** mud-grey. **6.** refuse, garbage; **~ное ведрó** refuse-pail, garbage-pail, slop-pail.

гряз|ь, и, о ~и, в ~ú *f.* **1.** mud (*also fig.*); **месúть г.** (*coll.*) to wade through mud; **забросáть ~ью, смешáть с ~ью; втоптáть, затоптáть в г.** (*fig.*) to sling mud (at). **2.** (*pl.*) (*therapeutic*) mud; mud-baths; mud-cure. **3.** dirt, filth (*also fig.*).

гря́н|уть, у, ешь *pf.* **1.** (*of sounds and fig.*) to burst out, crash out; **~ул гром** there was a clap of thunder; **~ул вы́стрел** a shot rang out. **2.** to strike up (*a song, etc.*).

гря́н|уться, усь, ешься *pf.* to crash.

гря|стú, дý, дёшь (*impf.*) (*obs.*) to approach.

гуáно *nt. indecl.* guano.

Гуанчжóу = Кантóн

гуáшь, и *f.* (*art*) gouache; gouache painting.

губ|á[1], **ы́,** *pl.* **~ы, ~áм** *f.* **1.** lip; **надýть ~ы** to pout; **по ~áм комý-н. помáзать** (*coll.*) to raise false hopes in s.o.; **у негó гýба не дýра** (*coll.*) he knows which side his bread is buttered; **молокó на ~áх не обсóхло** he is still green. **2.** (*pl.*) pincers.

губ|á[2], **ы́,** *pl.* **~ы, ~áм** *f.* bay, inlet, firth (*in northern Russia*).

губ|á[3], **ы́,** *pl.* **~ы, ~áм** *f.* tree-fungus.

губ|á[4], **ы́,** *pl.* **~ы, ~áм** *f.* (*hist.*) guba (*judicial division of Muscovite Russia*).

губáст|ый (~, ~а) *adj.* (*coll.*) thick-lipped.

губернáтор, а *m.* governor.

губернáторск|ий *adj.* of a governor; (*joc.*) **положéние хýже ~ого** a critical situation, a tight spot.

губернáторств|о, а *nt.* governorship.

губернáторш|а, и *f.* (*coll.*) governor's wife.

губéрни|я, и *f.* (*hist.*) guberniya, province; **пошлá писáть г.** (*joc.*) everything is in commotion.

губéрн|ский *adj.* *of* **~ия; г. гóрод** principal town of province.

губúтел|ь, я *m.* destroyer.

губúтел|ьный (~ен, ~ьна) *adj.* destructive, ruinous; baneful, pernicious.

губ|úть, лю́, ~ишь *impf.* (*of* **по~**) to destroy; to be the undoing (of); to ruin, spoil.

губ|úться ~ится *impf.* (*of* **по~**) to be destroyed; to be wasted.

гýб|ка[1], **ки** *f. dim. of* **губá**[1]

гýбк|а[2], **и** *f.* sponge; **мыть ~ой** to sponge.

губн|óй[1] *adj.* **1.** lip; **~áя помáда** lipstick. **2.** (*ling.*) labial.

губ|нóй[2] *adj. of* **~á**[4]

губошлёп, а *m.* (*coll.*) **1.** mumbler. **2.** lout.

гýбчат|ый *adj.* porous, spongy; **~ое желéзо** sponge iron, porous iron; **г. каучýк** foam rubber.

гувернáнтк|а, и *f.* governess.

гувернёр, а *m.* tutor.

гугенóт, а *m.* (*hist.*) Huguenot.

гугнúв|ый (~, ~а) *adj.* (*coll.*) speaking through the nose.

гугý *only in phr.* **ни г.!** not a word!; **об э́том ни г.!** don't let it go any further!; don't breathe a word (about this)!

гуд, а *m.* (*coll.*) buzzing; drone; hum.

гудéни|е, я *nt.* buzzing; drone; hum; honk (*of a motor-car horn, etc.*).

гу|дéть, жý, дúшь *impf.* **1.** to buzz; to drone; to hum; (*impers.*): **у меня́ ~дéло в ушáх** there was a buzzing in my ears. **2.** (*of a factory whistle, steamer's siren, etc.*) to hoot; to honk. **3.** (*coll.*) to ache.

гуд|óк, кá *m.* **1.** hooter, siren, horn, whistle. **2.** hoot(ing); honk; toot; **по ~кý** when the whistle blows. **3.** (*hist.*) rebeck (*three-stringed viol*).

гудрóн, а *m.* tar.

гудронúр|овать, ую *impf. and pf.* to tar.

гудрóн|ный *adj. of* **~; ное шоссé** tarred highroad.

гуж, á *m.* **1.** tug (*part of harness*); **взя́лся за г., не говорú, что не дюж** (*prov.*) in for a penny in for a pound. **2.** cartage.

гужев|óй *adj.* **1.** *adj. of* **гуж. 2.** cart; **~áя дорóга** cart-track; **г. трáнспорт** cartage, animal-drawn transport.

гужóм *adv.* **1.** by cartage; **возúть г.** to cart. **2.** (*dial.*) in file.

гýзк|а, и *f.* rump (*of a bird*).

гýзн|о, а *nt.* (*vulg.*) arse, bum.

гул, а *m.* rumble; hum; boom.

ГУЛАГ *m.* (*indecl.*) (*abbr. of* ***Глáвное управлéние исправúтельно-трудовы́х лагерéй***) GULAG, Main Administration for Corrective Labour Camps.

гýл|кий (~ок, ~кá, ~ко) *adj.* **1.** resonant; echoing. **2.** booming, rumbling.

гуллúв|ый (~, ~а) *adj.* (*coll.*) gadabout.

гульб|а́, ы́ *f.* (*coll.*) idling; revelry.
гу́льбищ|е, а *nt.* **1.** (*obs.*) promenade. **2.** (*coll.*) revels, carousal.
гу́льден, а *m.* **1.** (*hist.*) gulden (*coin*). **2.** guilder (*Dutch unit of currency*).
гульн|у́ть, у́, ёшь *pf.* (*coll.*) to make merry.
гу́л|я, и *c.g.* (*coll.*) dove, pigeon.
гуля́к|а, и *c.g.* (*coll.*) idler; flâneur; playboy.
гуля́нк|а, и *f.* (*coll.*) **1.** fête; outdoor party. **2.** feast.
гуля́н|ье, ья, *g. pl.* **~ий** *nt.* **1.** walking; (going for a) walk. **2.** fête; outdoor party. **3.** (*obs. or dial.*) pleasure-ground.
гуля́|ть, ю *impf.* (*of* **по~**) **1.** to walk, stroll; to take a walk, go for a walk; **г. по рука́м** to pass from hand to hand. **2.** (*impf. only*) (*coll.*) not to be working; (*of land*) to be untilled; **мы сего́дня ~ем** we have got the day off today. **3.** (*coll.*) to make merry, have a good time; to carouse, go on the spree. **4.** (**с+***i.*; *coll.*) to go (with) (= *have a sexual relationship with*). **5.** (*of a baby*; *coll.*) to lie awake.
гуля́ш, а *m.* (*cul.*) goulash.
гуля́щ|ий *adj.* (*coll.*) idle; *as n.* **~ая, ~ей** *f.* streetwalker.
ГУМ, а *or* **гум, а** *m.* (*abbr. of* **госуда́рственный универса́льный магази́н**) GUM, State Department Store.
гумани́зм, а *m.* **1.** humanism. **2.** (*hist.*) the revival of learning.
гумани́ст, а *m.* humanist.
гуманисти́ческий *adj.* humanist.
гуманита́рн|ый *adj.* **1.** pertaining to the humanities; **~ые нау́ки** the humanities, the Arts (*opp. natural sciences*). **2.** humane.
гума́нност|ь, и *f.* humanity, humaneness.
гума́н|ный (~ен, ~на) *adj.* humane.
гумённый *adj. of* **гумно́**
гуме́нц|е, а *nt.* **1.** *dim. of* **гумно́**. **2.** (*eccl.*) tonsure.
гу́мка|ть, ю *impf.* (*coll.*) to repeat frequently 'hm!'.
гу́мм|а, ы *f.* (*med.*) gumma (*kind of tumour*).
гу́мми *nt. indecl.* gum.
гуммиара́бик, а *m.* gum arabic.
гуммигу́т, а *m.* gamboge.
гуммила́стик, а *m.* india-rubber.
гумми́р|овать, ую *impf. and pf.* to (stick with) gum.
гуммо́зный *adj.* (*med.*) gummatous.
гум|но́, на́, *pl.* **~́на, ~́ен** *and* **~ён, ~́нам** *nt.* **1.** threshing-floor. **2.** barn.
гу́мус, а *m.* (*agric.*) humus.
гундо́|сить, шу, сишь *impf.* (*coll.*) to speak through one's nose.
гунн, а *m.* (*hist.*) Hun.
гу́нтер, а *m.* hunter (*horse*).
гу́н|я, и *f.* (*obs or dial.*) old rags.
гури́|ец, йца *m.* Gurian (*inhabitant of western districts of Caucasian Georgia*).
гури́|йка, йки *f. of* **~ец**
гури́йский *adj.* Gurian.
гу́ри|я, и *f.* houri.
гу́рк(х)а *m. indecl.* Gurkha.
гу́рк(х)ский *adj.* Gurkha.
гурма́н, а *m.* gourmet, epicure.
гурма́нств|о, а *nt.* connoisseurship (*of food and drink*).
гурт[1]**, а** *m.* herd, drove; flock.
гурт[2]**, а** *m.* **1.** milling (*of a coin*). **2.** frieze.
гуртовщи́к, а́ *m.* **1.** herdsman; drover. **2.** (*obs.*) cattle-dealer.
гурто́м *adv.* (*coll.*) **1.** wholesale; in bulk. **2.** together; in a body, en masse.
гу́ру *m. indecl.* guru.
гурьб|а́, ы́ *f.* crowd, gang.
гуса́к, а́ *m.* gander.
гуса́р, а *m.* hussar.
гуса́рский *adj.* hussar.
гус|ёк, ька́ *m.* goose.
гу́с|ельный *adj. of* **~ли**
гу́сениц|а, ы *f.* **1.** (*zool.*) caterpillar. **2.** (caterpillar) track.
гу́сеничн|ый *adj.* (*zool., tech.*) caterpillar; **~ая ле́нта** (*tech.*) caterpillar track; **г. тра́ктор** caterpillar tractor; **г. ход** caterpillar drive.
гус|ёнок, ёнка, *pl.* **~я́та** *m.* gosling.
гуси́н|ый *adj.* goose; **~ая ко́жа** goose-flesh; **~ые ла́пки** crow's feet; **~ое перо́** goose-quill.
гуси́т, а *m.* (*hist.*) Hussite.
гу́сл|и, ей *no sg.* (*mus.*) psaltery, gusli.
гусля́р, а́-а *m.* psaltery player.
густе́|ть, ет *impf.* (*of* **по~**) to thicken, get thicker, get denser.
гу|сти́ть, щу́, сти́шь *impf.* to thicken (*trans.*).
гу́сто[1] *adv.* thickly, densely.
гу́сто[2] *as pred.* (*coll.*) there is much, there is plenty; **у меня́ де́нег не г.** I'm a bit hard up, a bit pushed.
густоволо́сый *adj.* thick-haired, shaggy.
густ|о́й (~́, ~а́, ~́о) *adj.* **1.** (*in var. senses*) thick, dense; **~а́я листва́** thick foliage; **г. тума́н** dense fog; **~ое населе́ние** dense population; **~ы́е бро́ви** bushy eyebrows. **2.** (*of sound or colour*) deep, rich.
густоли́ственный *adj.* with thick foliage, leafy.
густонаселённый *adj.* densely populated.
густопсо́вый *adj.* **1.** a breed of borzoi. **2.** (*fig.*) out-and-out.
густот|а́, ы́ *f.* **1.** thickness, density. **2.** (*of sound or colour*) deepness, richness.
гусы́н|я, и *f.* goose.
гус|ь, я, *pl.* **~́и, ~е́й** *m.* goose; **как с ~́я вода́** like water off a duck's back; **хоро́ш гусь!** (*iron.*) a fine fellow indeed!
гусько́м *adv.* in (single) file, in crocodile.
гуся́тин|а, ы *f.* goose(-meat).
гуся́тник, а *m.* **1.** goose-pen, goose-run. **2.** goshawk.
гу́т|а, ы *f.* (*obs.*) glass-foundry.
гутали́н, а *m.* shoe-polish.
гути́р|овать, ую *impf.* (*obs.*) to savour.
гуто́р|ить, ю, ишь *impf.* (*dial.*) to natter.
гуттапе́рч|а, и *f.* gutta percha.
гуттапе́рч|евый *adj. of* **~а**
гуцу́л, а *m.* Huzul (*Ukrainian inhabitant of Carpathian region*).
гуцу́л|ка, ки *f. of* **~**
гуцу́льский *adj.* Huzul.
гу́щ|а, и *f.* **1.** dregs, lees, grounds, sediment; **кофе́йная г.** coffee grounds. **2.** thicket; (*fig.*) thick, centre, heart; **в са́мой ~е собы́тий** in the thick of things.
гу́ще *comp. of* **густо́й, гу́сто**
гущин|а́, ы́ *f.* (*coll.*) **1.** thickness. **2.** thicket.
гэ́льский *adj.* Gaelic.
ГЭС *f. indecl.* (*abbr. of* **гидроэлектроста́нция**) hydro-electric power-station.
гюйс, а *m.* (*naut.*) jack.
гяу́р, а *m.* giaour.

Д

д. (*abbr. of* **дом**) house.
да[1] *particle* **1.** yes. **2.** (*interrog*) yes?, is that so?, really?, indeed?; **он мно́го лет прожива́л в Пари́же. — Да? а я и не знал** he lived in Paris for many years. Really? I didn't know. **3.** (*emph.*) why; well; **да не мо́жет быть!** why, that's impossible!; **д. нет!** of course not!; not likely!; **да в чём де́ло?** well, what's it all about? **4.** *emph. pred.*: **когда́-н. да ко́нчится** it must end some time; **э́то что́-н. да зна́чит** there's sth. behind this. **5. (вот) э́то да!** (*coll.*) splendid!; super!
да[2] *particle* (*+3rd pers. pres. or fut. of v.*) may, let; **да здра́вствует..!** long live …!
да[3] *conj.* **1.** (*mainly in conventional phrr.*) and; **день да ночь** day and night; **ко́жа да ко́сти** skin and bone. **2.: да (и *or* ещё)** and (besides); and what is more; **бы́ло за́ полночь, да и снег шёл** it was past midnight and (what is

more) it was snowing; **принеси́те мне во́дки, да поскоре́е!** bring me some vodka, and (be) quick about it!; **он занима́лся, занима́лся, да и провали́лся на экза́мене** he studied and studied and then he (went and) failed his exam. **3.: да и то́лько** and that's all, and no more; **она́ ворчи́т, да и то́лько** she does nothing but grouse. **4.** but; **я охо́тно проводи́л бы тебя́, да вре́мени не́ту** I would gladly come with you but I haven't the time.

дабы́ *conj.* (*obs.*) in order (to, that).

дава́й(те) *as particle* **1.** (*+inf. or 1st pers. pl. of fut.*) let's; **дава́йте приостано́вимся мину́точку-две** let's pause for a minute or two; **дава́йте заку́рим** let's light up. **2.** (*+imper.*; *coll.*) come on; **дава́й, расскажи́ что-н.** come on, tell us a story. **3.** (*+inf.*; *coll.*) *expr. inception of action*: **а он дава́й бежа́ть** he just took to his heels.

да|ва́ть, ю, ёшь *impf. of* **дать**

да|ва́ться, ю́сь, ёшься *impf.* (*of* **~́ться**) **1.** *pass. of* **дава́ть. 2.** to let o.s. be caught; **не д.** (*+d.*) to dodge, evade. **3.: легко́ д.** to come easily, naturally; **ру́сский язы́к ему́ легко́ даётся** Russian comes easily to him.

да́веча *adv.* (*coll.*) lately, recently.

да́вешний *adj.* (*coll.*) recent; late.

дави́л|о, а *nt.* press.

дави́льный *adj.*: **д. пресс** winepress.

дави́л|ьня, ьни, *g. pl.* **~ен** *f.* winepress.

дави́льщик, а *m.* presser, treader.

дав|и́ть, лю́, ~́ишь *impf.* **1.** (*also* **на**+*a.*) to press (upon); (*fig.*) to oppress, weigh (upon), lie heavy (on); (*impers.*): **се́рдце ~ит** (my) heart is heavy. **2.** to crush; to trample. **3.** to squeeze (*juice out of fruit, etc*).

дав|и́ться, лю́сь ~́ишься *impf.* (*of* **по~**) **1.** (*+i. or* **от**) to choke (with); **д. от ка́шля** to choke with coughing. **2.** (*pf.* **у~**) (*coll.*) to hang o.s. **3.** *pass. of* **~и́ть**

да́вка, и *f.* (*coll.*) **1.** crushing, squeezing. **2.** throng, crush.

давле́ни|е, я *nt.* pressure (*also fig.*); **под ~ем** (*+g.*) under pressure (of); through stress (of).

да́вленый *adj.* pressed, crushed.

давне́нько *adv.* (*coll.*) for quite a long time.

да́вн|ий *adj.* **1.** ancient. **2.** of long standing; **с ~их пор, времён** of old, for a long time.

давни́шний *adj.* (*coll.*) = **да́вний**

давно́ *adv.* **1.** long ago; **он д. у́мер** he died long ago; **д. бы так** (*expr. approval of s.o.'s action*) not before (it was) time. **2.** for a long time (*up to and including the present moment*); long since; **мы д. живём в дере́вне** we have been living in the country for a long time.

давнопроше́дш|ий *adj.* remote (*in time*); **~ее вре́мя** (*gram.*) pluperfect tense.

да́вност|ь, и *f.* **1.** antiquity; remoteness. **2.** long standing. **3.** (*leg.*) prescription.

давны́м-давно́ *adv.* (*coll.*) very long ago, ages (and ages) ago.

дагерроти́п, а *m.* daguerrotype.

дагерроти́пный *adj.* daguerrotype.

дагеста́н|ец, ца *m.* Dagestani.

дагеста́н|ка, ки *f. of* **~ец**

дагеста́нский *adj.* Dagestani.

да́же *particle* even; **е́сли д.** even if; **о́чень д. пло́хо** extremely bad.

да́к|ать, аю *impf.* (*coll.*) to keep saying 'yes'.

дактили́ческий *adj.* (*liter.*) dactylic.

дактилоло́ги|я, и *f.* finger-speech.

дактилоскопи́|я, и *f.* dactyloscopy, identification by means of fingerprints; **ге́нная д.** genetic fingerprinting.

да́ктил|ь, я *m.* (*liter.*) dactyl.

дакти́льн|ый *adj.*: **~ая а́збука** sign language.

дала́й-ла́м|а, ы *m.* Dalai Lama.

да́лее *adv.* further; **не д., как вчера́, он был здесь** he was here only yesterday; **и так д.** (*abbr.* **и т. д.**) and so on, etcetera.

далёк|ий (~, ~а́, ~о́ *and* ~о) *adj.* **1.** (*in var. senses*) distant, remote; far(away); **д. путь** long journey; **~ое про́шлое** distant past; **д. от и́стины** wide of the mark; **я ~ от того́, что́бы жела́ть** I am far from wishing. **2.** (*only with neg.*; *coll.*) clever, bright; **она́ не о́чень ~а́** she is not awfully bright.

далеко́ *and* **далёко**[1] *adv.* **1.** far, far off; **(от)** far (from); **д. зайти́** (*fig.*) to go too far, burn one's boats; **д. пойти́** (*fig.*) to go far (= *to be a success*). **2.** far, by a long way, by much; **д. за** (*of time*) long after; **д. не** far from; **она́ д. не краса́вица** she is far from beautiful.

далеко́ *and* **далёко**[2] *as pred.* it is far, it is a long way; (*+d.* **до** *fig.*) to be far (from), be much inferior (to); **ему́ д. до соверше́нства** he is far from perfect.

дале́че *adv.* (*obs. or dial.*) = **далеко́**

дал|ь, и, о ~́и, в ~и́ *f.* **1.** distance; distant prospect. **2.** (*coll.*) distant spot. **3.: така́я д.!** (*coll.*) it is so far, such a long way!

дальневосто́чный *adj.* Far Eastern.

дальне́йш|ий *adj.* further, furthest; **в ~ем** (*i*) in future, henceforth, (*ii*) below, hereinafter.

да́льн|ий *adj.* **1.** distant, remote; **Д. Восто́к** the Far East (*of former USSR*); **~ее пла́вание** long voyage; **~его де́йствия** long-range; **~его сле́дования** (*of a train*) long-distance. **2.** (*of kinship*) distant. **3.: без ~их слов** without more ado.

дальнобо́йност|ь, и *f.* (*mil.*) long range.

дальнобо́йный *adj.* (*mil.*) long-range.

дальнови́дени|е, я *nt.* (*obs.*) television.

дальнови́дност|ь, и *f.* foresight.

дальнови́д|ный (~ен, ~на) *adj.* far-sighted.

дальнозо́р|кий (~ок, ~ка) *adj.* long-sighted.

дальнозо́ркост|ь, и *f.* long sight.

дальноме́р, а *m.* range-finder.

дальноме́рщик, а *m.* range-finder operator.

да́льност|ь, и *f.* distance; range; **д. полёта снаря́да** range of a missile.

дальтони́зм, а *m.* colour-blindness, Daltonism.

дальто́ник, а *m.* colour-blind pers.

да́льше *adj. and adv.* **1.** *comp. of* **далёкий. 2.** (*adv.*) farther; **ти́ше е́дешь, д. бу́дешь** (*prov.*) more haste, less speed; **д. не́куда** (*coll.*) that's the limit. **3.** (*adv.*) further; **расска́зывать д.** to go on (telling a story); **д.!** go on! **4.** (*adv.*) then, next; **они́ не зна́ли, что д. де́лать** they did not know what to do next. **5.** (*adv.*) longer; **ждать д. нельзя́ бы́ло** it was impossible to wait any longer.

да́м|а, ы *f.* **1.** lady. **2.** partner (*in dancing*). **3.** (*cards*) queen.

Дама́ск, а *m.* Damascus

дама́ск, а *m.* damask.

дама́сск|ий *adj.*: **~ая сталь** Damascus steel.

да́мб|а, ы *f.* dike.

да́мк|а, и *f.* king (*at draughts*).

да́м|ский *adj. of* **~а; ~ская су́мка** ladies' handbag; **д. кавале́р, д. уго́дник** ladies' man.

дан, а *m.* (*judo*) dan.

Да́ни|я, и *f.* Denmark.

да́нник, а *m.* (*hist.*) tributary.

да́нн|ые, ых *no sg.* **1.** data; facts, information; **необрабо́танные д.** raw data. **2.** qualities, gifts, potentialities. **3.** grounds.

да́нн|ый *p.p.p. of* **дать** *and adj.* given; present; in question; **в д. моме́нт** at the present moment, at present; **в ~ом слу́чае** in this case, in the case in question; **~ая (величина́)** (*math.*) datum.

данти́ст, а *m.* dentist.

дан|ь, и *f.* **1.** (*hist.*) tribute; **обложи́ть ~́ью** to lay under tribute. **2.** (*fig.*) tribute; debt; **отда́ть д.** (*+d.*) to appreciate, recognize.

дар, а, *pl.* **~ы́** *m.* **1.** gift, donation; grant; **посме́ртный д.** bequest. **2.** (*+g.*) gift (of); **д. сло́ва** (*i*) the gift of the gab, (*ii*) speech, ability to speak. **3.** (*pl.*) (*eccl.*) the sacraments (*of bread and wine*).

дарвини́зм, а *m.* Darwinism.

дарвини́ст, а *m.* Darwinist.

Дардане́лл|ы, ~ *no sg.* the Dardanelles.

даре́ни|е, я *nt.* donation.

дарён|ый *adj.* received as a present; **~ому коню́ в зу́бы не смо́трят** (*prov.*) one should not look a gift horse in the mouth.

дари́тел|ь, я *m.* donor.

дар|и́ть, ю́, ~́ишь *impf.* (*of* **по~**) **1.** (*+d. of pers.*) to give, make a present. **2.** (*+a. of pers. and i.*) to favour (with), bestow (upon); **д. кого́-н. улы́бкой** to bestow a smile upon s.o.

дармовщи́на = **даровщи́нка**
дармовщи́нка = **даровщи́нка**
дармое́д, а *m.* (*coll.*) parasite, sponger, scrounger.
дармое́днича|ть, ю *impf.* (*coll.*) to sponge, scrounge.
дармое́дств|о, а *nt.* (*coll.*) parasitism, sponging, scrounging.
дарова́ни|е, я *nt.* **1.** (*obs.*) donation, giving. **2.** gift, talent
дар|ова́ть, у́ю *impf. and pf.* to grant, confer.
дарови́тост|ь, и *f.* giftedness.
дарови́т|ый (~, ~а) *adj.* gifted, talented.
дарово́й *adj.* free (of charge), gratuitous.
даровщи́на = **даровщи́нка**
даровщи́нк|а, и *f.*: **на ~у** (*coll.*) for nothing, for free, buckshee.
да́ром *adv.* **1.** free (of charge), gratis; **э́то вам д. не пройдёт** you'll pay for this. **2.** in vain, to no purpose; **пропа́сть д.** to be wasted. **3.** *as conj.*: **д. что** (*coll.*) although.
даро́носиц|а, ы *f.* (*eccl.*) pyx.
дарохрани́тельниц|а, ы *f.* (*eccl.*) tabernacle.
да́рственн|ый *adj.* **1.** (*obs.*) received as a present. **2.** confirming a gift; **~ая на́дпись** dedicatory inscription; **~ая за́пись** (*leg.*) settlement, deed.
да́т|а, ы *f.* date.
да́тельный *adj.* (*gram.*) dative.
дати́р|овать, ую *impf. and pf.* to date (= (*i*) *affix a date to*, (*ii*) *establish the date of*).
да́тский *adj.* Danish.
датча́н|ин, ина, *pl.* **~е, ~** *m.* Dane.
датча́н|ка, ки *f. of* **~ин**
дать, дам, дашь, даст, дади́м, дади́те, даду́т, *past* **дал, дала́, да́ло, да́ли** *pf.* (*of* **дава́ть**) **1.** to give; **д. взаймы́** to lend (*money*); **д. на во́дку, на чай** to tip; **д. обе́д** to give a dinner; **д. уро́ки** to give lessons; **д. показа́ния** to testify, depose. **2.** to give, administer; **д. лека́рство** to give medicine; **д. кому́-н. пощёчину** (*coll.*) to box s.o.'s ears. **3.** (**по**+*d.*, **в**+*a.*; *coll.*) to give (it); to hit; **д. кому́-н. по́ уху** to clip s.o. round the ear; **я те дам!** (*coll.*; *expr. vague threat*) I'll give you what-for!; I'll teach you! **4.** (*fig.*) to give; **д. кля́тву** to take an oath; **д. нача́ло** (+*d.*) to give rise (to); **д. сло́во** to pledge one's word; **д. себе́ труд** (+*inf.*) to put o.s. to the trouble (of). **5.** (*fig.*) to give, grant; **д. во́лю** (+*d.*) to give (free) rein (to), give vent (to); **д. газ** (*coll.*) to open the throttle; **д. доро́гу** (+*d.*) to make way (for); **д. но́гу** (*aeron.*) to give (it) rudder; **не д. поко́я** (+*d.*) to give no peace; **д. кому́-н. сло́во** to give s.o. the floor (*at a meeting*); **д. ход** (+*d.*) to set in motion, get going; **д. ход кому́-н.** (*coll.*) to help s.o. on, give s.o. a leg-up. **6.** + *certain nn. expr. action related to meaning of n.*; **д. залп** to fire a volley; **д. звоно́к** to ring (*a bell*); **д. отбо́й** to ring off (*on telephone*); **д. отпо́р** (+*d.*) to repulse; **д. течь** to spring a leak; **д. тре́щину** to crack. **7.** (+*inf.*) to let; **д. поня́ть** to give to understand; **д. себя знать, д. себя́ почу́вствовать** to make o.s. (itself) felt; **да́йте ему́ говори́ть** let him speak. **8.: дай**+*1st pers. of fut. expr. decision to take some action*: **дай вы́купаюсь** I think I'll take a bath. **9.: ни д. ни взять** (*i*) exactly the same, neither more nor less, (*ii*) as like as two peas.
да́ться, да́мся, да́шься *etc.*, *past* **да́лся, дала́сь** *pf.* **1.** *pf. of* **дава́ться. 2.** (+*d.*) to have become an obsession (with).
дацзыбао́ *nt. indecl.* wall posters (*in China*).
да́ч|а[1], **и** *f.* **1.** giving. **2.** helping, portion.
да́ч|а[2], **и** *f.* **1.** dacha (*holiday cottage in the country in environs of city or large town*); **д.-(авто)прице́п** mobile home. **2.: быть на ~е** to be in the country; **пое́хать на ~у** to go to the country.
да́ч|а[3], **и** *f.* (*forestry*) (piece of) woodland.
дачевладе́л|ец, ьца *m.* owner of a dacha.
дачевладе́л|ица, ицы *f. of* **~ец**
да́чник, а *m.* (holiday) visitor (*in the country*).
да́ч|ный *adj. of* **~а**[2]; **д. о́тдых** country holiday; **д. по́езд** suburban train.
дашна́к, а *m.* (*hist.*) Dashnak (*member of Armenian nationalist movement*).
дая́ни|е, я *nt.* (*rhet.*; *obs. or iron*) donation, contribution.
два (*f.* **две), двух, двум, двумя́, о двух** *num.* two; **два-три, две-три** two or three, a couple; **ни д. ни полтора́** (*coll.*) neither one thing nor another; **в двух слова́х** briefly, in short; **в д. счёта** in no time, in two ticks; **в двух шага́х** a short step away; **ка́ждые д. дня** every other day, on alternate days.
двадцати... *comb. form* twenty-.
двадцатигра́нник, а *m.* (*math.*) icosahedron.
двадцатиле́ти|е, я *nt.* **1.** period of twenty years. **2.** twentieth anniversary.
двадцатиле́тний *adj.* **1.** twenty-year, of twenty years. **2.** twenty-year-old.
двадцатипятиле́ти|е, я *nt.* **1.** period of twenty-five years. **2.** twenty-fifth anniversary.
двадца́т|ый *adj.* twentieth; **одна́ ~ая** a twentieth; **~ое января́** the twentieth of January; **~ые го́ды** the twenties.
два́дцат|ь, и́, *i.* **ью** *num.* twenty; **д. оди́н**, etc., twenty-one, etc.; **д. одно́** (*card-game*) vingt-et-un.
два́дцатью *adv.* twenty times.
два́жды *adv.* twice; **я́сно как д. два четы́ре** as plain as a pikestaff.
дванадеся́тый *and* **двунадеся́тый** *adj.*: **д. пра́здник** (*eccl.*) major festival (*each of the twelve major festivals of the Russ. Orthodox Church*).
двенадцатипе́рстн|ый *adj.*: **~ая кишка́** (*anat.*) duodenum.
двенадцатисло́жный *adj.* dodecasyllabic.
двена́дцатый *adj.* twelfth.
двена́дцат|ь, и *num.* twelve.
двер|но́й *adj. of* **~ь; д. проём** doorway; **~на́я ру́чка** door-handle.
две́р|ца, ы, *g. pl.* **~ец** *f.* door (*of car, cupboard, etc.*).
двер|ь, и, о ~́и, в ~и́, *pl.* **~́и, ~е́й,** *i.* **~я́ми** *and* **~ьми́** *f.* door; **в ~я́х** in the doorway; **у ~е́й** close at hand; **при закры́тых ~я́х** behind closed doors, in camera.
две́сти, двухсо́т, двумста́м, двумяста́ми, о двухста́х *num.* two hundred.
дви́гател|ь, я *m.* motor, engine; (*fig.*) mover, motive force.
дви́гательн|ый *adj.* **1.** motive; **~ая си́ла** moving force, impetus. **2.** (*anat.*) motor.
дви́га|ть, ю *and* **дви́жу** *impf.* (*of* **дви́нуть**) **1.** **(~ю)** to move. **2.** **(~ю)** (+*i.*) to move (*part of the body*); to make a movement (of). **3.** **(дви́жу)** to set in motion, get going (*also fig.*); **д. вперёд** (*fig.*) to advance, further.
дви́га|ться, юсь *and* **дви́жусь** *impf.* (*of* **дви́нуться**) **1.** to move (*intrans.*); **д. вперёд** to advance (*also fig.*). **2.** to start, get going. **3.** *pass. of* **~ть**
движе́ни|е, я *nt.* **1.** (*in var. senses*) movement; motion; **д. вперёд** forward movement, advance; **привести́ в д.** to set in motion; **д. сторо́нников ми́ра** peace movement; **д. «зелёных»** the green movement. **2.** (*physical*) movement, exercise. **3.** traffic; **д. в одно́м направле́нии** one-way traffic; **пра́вила у́личного ~я** traffic regulations. **4.: д. по слу́жбе** promotion, advancement. **5.** impulse.
дви́жимост|ь, и *f.* movables, chattels; personal property.
дви́жим|ый *pres. part. pass. of* **дви́гать** *and adj.* **1.** (*part.*) moved, prompted, actuated. **2.** (*adj.*) movable; **~ое иму́щество** movable, personal property.
движко́в|ый *adj.* slide; **~ые регуля́торы** slide controls.
движ|о́к, ка́ *m.* **1.** (*tech.*) slide, runner. **2.** (wooden) shovel. **3.** (*coll.*) (small) engine, motor.
дви́жущ|ий *pres. part. act. of* **дви́гать** *and adj.*: **~ие си́лы** driving force.
дви́|нуть, ну, нешь *pf.* **1.** *pf. of* **~гать. 2.** (*coll.*) to hit, cosh.
дви́|нуться, нусь, нешься *pf. of* **~гаться**
дво́е, двои́х *num.* **1.** (+*m. nn. denoting persons, pers. prons. in pl. or nn. used only in pl.*) two; **д. сынове́й** two sons; **нас бы́ло д.** there were two of us; **д. сане́й** two sledges; **д. су́ток** forty-eight hours. **2.** (+*nn. denoting objects usu. found in pairs*) two pairs; **д. глаз** two pairs of eyes; **д. чуло́к** two pairs of stockings; **на свои́х (на) двои́х** on Shanks's pony.
двоебо́рь|е, я *nt.* (*sport*) biathlon.
двоебра́чи|е, я *nt.* bigamy.
двоевла́сти|е, я *nt.* diarchy.
двоеду́ши|е, я *nt.* duplicity.

двоеду́ш|ный (~ен, ~на) *adj.* two-faced.
двоеже́н|ец, ца *m.* bigamist (*of a man*).
двоежёнств|о, а *nt.* bigamy (*of man*).
двоему́жи|е, я *nt.* bigamy (*of woman*).
двоему́жниц|а, ы *f.* bigamist (*of a woman*).
двоемы́сли|е, я *nt.* doublethink.
двоето́чи|е, я *nt.* (*gram.*) colon.
дво́ечник, а *m.* (*coll.*) low-achiever (*pupil receiving an 'unsatisfactory' mark*).
дво|и́ть, ю́, и́шь *impf.* **1.** to double. **2.** to divide in two. **3.** (*chem.*) to rectify, distil. **4.** to plough a second time.
дво|и́ться, ю́сь, и́шься *impf.* **1.** to divide in two (*intrans.*). **2.** to appear double; **у него́ ~и́лось в глаза́х** he saw (objects) double.
двои́чн|ый *adj.* (*math.*) binary; **~ая автомати́ческая вычисли́тельная маши́на** binary computer; **~ая ци́фра** binary digit, bit.
дво́йк|а, и *f.* **1.** (*figure*) two. **2.** (*coll.*) No. 2 (*bus, tram, etc.*). **3.** 'two' (*out of five, acc. to marking system used in Russ. educational establishments*). **4.** (*cards*) two; **д. треф** two of clubs. **5.** pair-out (*boat*).
двойни́к, а́ *m.* **1.** (*a person's*) double. **2.** (*coll.*) twin.
двойн|о́й *adj.* double, twofold, binary; **д. подборо́док** double chin; **~а́я бухгалте́рия** double-entry book-keping; **~ая фами́лия** double-barrelled surname; **вести́ ~у́ю игру́** to play a double game.
дво́|йня, йни, *g. pl.* **~ен** *f.* twins.
двойня́шк|а, и *f.* **1.** (*coll.*) twin. **2.** twin, double (*e.g. two trees growing together*).
дво́йственност|ь, и *f.* **1.** duality. **2.** duplicity.
дво́йствен|ный (~, ~на) *adj.* **1.** dual; **~ное число́** (*gram.*) dual number. **2.** two-faced. **3.** bipartite.
двойча́тк|а, и *f.* twin kernel, philippine.
двор, а́ *m.* **1.** yard, court, courtyard. **2.** (*peasant*) homestead. **3.: ско́тный д.** farmyard; **пти́чий д.** poultry-yard. **4.: на ~е́** out of doors, outside; **по ~а́м, ко ~а́м** (*obs*) to one's home, home(wards); **со ~а́** (*obs.*) from home. **5.** (royal) court; **при ~е́** at court. **6.: быть ко ~у́** to be (found) suitable; **быть не ко ~у́** not to be wanted.
двор|е́ц, ца́ *m.* palace; **Д. бракосочета́ния** Wedding Palace.
дворе́цк|ий, ого *m.* butler, major-domo.
дво́рник, а *m.* **1.** dvornik; caretaker, janitor. **2.** (*coll.*) windscreen-wiper.
дво́рницк|ий *adj.* *of* **дво́рник 1.**; *as n.* **~ая, ~ой** *f.* dvornik's lodge.
дво́рничих|а, и *f.* (*coll.*) **1.** wife of dvornik. **2.** yardwoman.
дво́рн|я, и *f.* (*collect.*) servants, menials (*before 1861*).
дворня́г|а, и *f.* (*coll.*) mongrel (dog).
дворня́жк|а, и *f.* = **дворня́га**
дворо́в|ый *adj.* **1.** *adj. of* **двор 1., 2.**; **~ые постро́йки** outbuildings, farm buildings; **~ая соба́ка** watch-dog. **2.: ~ые лю́ди** house-serfs; *as n.* **д., ~ого** *m.*, **~ая, ~ой** *f.* house-serf.
дворцо́вый *adj. of* **дворе́ц; д. переворо́т** palace revolution.
дворян|и́н, и́на, *pl.* **~е, ~** *m.* nobleman, member of the gentry.
дворя́н|ка, ки *f. of* **дворяни́н**
дворя́нск|ий *adj.* of the nobility; of the gentry; **~ое зва́ние** the rank of gentleman.
дворя́нств|о, а *nt.* (*collect.*) nobility, gentry.
двою́родный *adj.* related through grandparent; **д. брат** (first) cousin (*male*); **д. дя́дя** (first) cousin once removed.
двоя́кий *adj.* double, two-fold.
двоя́ко *adv.* in two ways.
двояково́гнутый *adj.* (*phys.*) concavo-concave
двояковы́пуклый *adj.* (*phys.*) convexo-convex.
дву..., двух... *comb. form* bi-, di-, two-, double-.
двубо́ртный *adj.* double-breasted.
двувидово́й *adj.* (*gram.*) biaspectual.
двугла́в|ый *adj.* two-headed; **~ая мы́шца** (*anat.*) biceps; **д. орёл** double-headed eagle.
двугла́сн|ый, ого *m.* (*gram.*) diphthong.
двуго́рбый *adj.* two-humped; **д. верблю́д** Bactrian camel.
двугра́нный *adj.* two-sided; dihedral.
двугри́венн|ый, ого *m.* (*coll.*) twenty-kopeck piece.
двудо́льный *adj.* **1.** two-part. **2.** (*bot.*) dicotyledonous.
двудо́мный *adj.* (*bot.*) diclinous.
двужи́льный *adj.* **1.** (*coll.*) strong; hardy, tough. **2.** (*tech.*) twin-core.
двузна́чный *adj.* two-digit.
двузу́бый *adj.* two-prong, two-tine.
двуко́лк|а, и *f.* two-wheeled cart.
двуко́нный *adj.* two-horse.
двукопы́тный *adj.* cloven-footed.
двукра́тный *adj.* twofold, double; reiterated.
двукры́л|ый *adj.* dipterous; *as n.* **~ые, ~ых** (*zool.*) Diptera.
двули́к|ий (~, ~а) *adj.* two-faced (*also fig.*).
двули́чи|е, я *nt.* double-dealing, duplicity.
двули́чност|ь, и *f.* duplicity.
двули́ч|ный (~ен, ~на) *adj.* (*fig.*) two-faced; hypocritical.
двунадеся́тый = дванадеся́тый
двуно́гий *adj.* two-legged, biped.
двуо́кис|ь, и *f.* (*chem.*) dioxide.
двупе́рсти|е, я *nt.* (*eccl.*) making the sign of the cross with two fingers (*as done by the Old Believers*).
двупе́рст(н)ый *adj.* (*eccl.*) two-fingered; with two fingers (*of making the sign of the cross*).
двупла́нный *adj.* two-dimensional.
двупо́лый *adj.* bisexual.
двупо́ль|е, я *nt.* (*agric.*) two-field rotation of crops.
двуправору́кост|ь, и *f.* ambidexterity, ambidextrousness.
двуро́г|ий *adj.* two-horned; **~ая луна́** crescent moon.
двуру́чный *adj.* two-handed; two-handled.
двуру́шник, а *m.* double-dealer.
двуру́шнича|ть, ю *impf.* to play a double game.
двуру́шничеств|о, а *nt.* double dealing.
двусве́тный *adj.* with two tiers of windows.
двуска́тн|ый *adj.* with two sloping surfaces; **~ая кры́ша** gable roof.
двусло́жный *adj.* disyllabic.
двусме́нный *adj.* in two shifts, two-shift.
двусмы́сленност|ь, и *f.* **1.** ambiguity. **2.** ambiguous expression, double entendre.
двусмы́слен|ный (~, ~на) *adj.* ambiguous.
двуспа́льный *adj.* double (*of beds*).
двуство́лк|а, и *f.* double-barrelled gun.
двуство́льный *adj.* double-barrelled.
двуство́рчат|ый *adj.* bivalve; **~ые две́ри** folding doors.
двусти́ши|е, я *nt.* (*liter.*) distich, couplet.
двусто́пный *adj.* (*liter.*) of two feet (*verse*).
двусторо́нн|ий *adj.* **1.** double-sided; **~ее воспале́ние лёгких** double pneumonia; **ку́ртка ~ей но́ски** reversible jacket. **2.** two-way. **3.** bilateral; **~ее соглаше́ние** bilateral agreement.
двутавро́в|ый *adj.*: **~ая ба́лка** I-beam.
двууглеки́сл|ый *adj.* (*chem.*) bicarbonate; **д. натр, ~ая со́да** sodium bicarbonate.
двуутро́бк|а, и *f.* (*zool.*) marsupial.
двуха́томный *adj.* diatomic.
двухвёрстк|а, и *f.* (*coll.*) map on scale of two versts to the inch.
двухвёрстный *adj.* **1.** two versts in length. **2.** in proportion of two versts to the inch.
двухвесе́льный *adj.* pair-oar.
двухгоди́чный *adj.* of two years' duration.
двухгодова́лый *adj.* two-year-old.
двухдне́вный *adj.* two-day.
двухдюймо́вый *adj.* two-inch.
двухкварти́рный *adj.* containing two flats.
двухколе́йный *adj.* (*rail.*) double-track.
двухколёсный *adj.* two-wheeled.
двухкра́сочный *adj.* two-tone.
двухлеме́шный *adj.*: **д. плуг** two-share plough.
двухле́тний *adj.* **1.** of two year's duration. **2.** two-year-old. **3.** (*bot.*) biennial.
двухле́тник, а *m.* (*bot.*) biennial.
двухма́чтовый *adj.* two-masted.

двухме́стн|ый *adj.* two-seater; **~ая каю́та** two-berth cabin; **д. но́мер** double room.
двухме́сячник, а *m.* bimonthly.
двухме́сячный *adj.* **1.** of two months' duration. **2.** two-month-old. **3.** (*of periodicals, etc.*) appearing every two months.
двухмото́рный *adj.* twin-engined.
двухнеде́льник, а *m.* (*coll.*) fortnightly (*magazine, etc.*).
двухнеде́льный *adj.* **1.** of two weeks' duration. **2.** two-week-old. **3.** (*of publications*) fortnightly.
двухпала́тный *adj.* (*pol.*) bicameral, two-chamber.
двухпа́лубный *adj.* (*naut.*) having two decks.
двухпарти́йный *adj.* (*pol.*) two party; bipartisan.
двухпласти́ночный *adj.*: **д. альбо́м** double (*record*) album.
двухря́дный *adj.* double-row.
двухсо́тенный *adj.* (*coll.*) costing two hundred roubles.
двухсотле́ти|е, я *nt.* bicentenary.
двухсотле́тний *adj.* **1.** of two hundred year's duration. **2.** bicentenary.
двухсо́тый *adj.* two-hundredth.
двухстепе́нн|ый *adj.*: **~ые вы́боры** indirect elections.
двухсу́точный *adj.* forty-eight-hour.
двухта́ктный *adj.* (*tech.*) two-stroke.
двухто́мник, а *m.* (*coll.*) two-volume book, work.
двухты́сячный *adj.* **1.** two-thousandth. **2.** costing two thousand roubles.
двухцве́тный *adj.* two-coloured.
двухчасово́й *adj.* **1.** two-hour. **2.** (*coll.*) two o'clock.
двухъя́русный *adj.* two-tier(ed).
двухэта́жный *adj.* two-storeyed; double-deck.
двучле́н, а *m.* (*math.*) binomial.
двучле́нный *adj.* (*math.*) binomial.
дву́шк|а, и *f.* (*coll.*) two-kopeck piece.
двуязы́чи|е, я *nt.* bilingualism.
двуязы́ч|ный (~ен, ~на) *adj.* bilingual.
-де (*coll.*) *enclitic particle indicating attribution of utterance to another speaker*; **они́-де не мо́гут прийти́** (they say) they can't come.
дебаркаде́р, а *m.* **1.** landing-stage. **2.** (*obs.*) platform (*in rail. station*).
дебати́р|овать, ую *impf.* to debate.
деба́т|ы, ов *no sg.* debate.
дебе́л|ый (~, ~а) *adj.* (*coll.*) plump, corpulent.
де́бет, а *m.* debit.
дебет|ова́ть, у́ю *impf. and pf.* to debit.
деби́л, а *m.* moron.
деби́т, а *m.* (*tech.*) yield, output (*of oil, etc.*).
дебито́р, а *m.* debtor.
деблоки́р|овать, ую *impf. and pf.* (*mil.*) to relieve, raise the blockade (of).
дебо́ш, а *m.* (*coll.*) riot; uproar, shindy.
дебоши́р, а *m.* (*coll.*) rowdy, brawler, hell-raiser.
дебоши́р|ить, ю, ишь *impf.* (*coll.*) to kick up a row, create a shindy.
дебоши́рств|о, а *nt.* (*coll.*) rowdyism, hell-raising.
де́бр|и, ей *no sg.* **1.** jungle; thickets. **2.** the wilds. **3.** (*fig.*) maze, labyrinth; **запу́таться в ~ях** (+*g.*) to get bogged down in.
дебюрократиза́ци|я, и *f.* debureaucratization.
дебю́т, а *m.* **1.** début. **2.** (*chess*) opening.
дебюта́нт, а *m.* débutant.
дебюта́нтк|а, и *f.* débutante.
дебюти́р|овать, ую *impf. and pf.* to make one's debut.
дебю́т|ный *adj. of* **~**; **д. спекта́кль** (*theatr.*) début, first performance; **д. ход** (*chess*) opening move.
де́в|а, ы *f.* **1.** (*obs.*) girl, maiden; unmarried girl; **ста́рая д.** (*coll.*) old maid. **2. Д.** (*relig.*) the Virgin. **3. Д.** (*astron.*) Virgo.
девалориза́ци|я, и *f.* debunking.
девальва́ци|я, и *f.* (*econ.*) devaluation.
дева́|ть, ю 1. *impf. of* **деть. 2.** (*in past tense* = **деть**) to put, do (with); **куда́ ты ~л письмо́ ?** what have you done with the letter?
дева́|ться, юсь 1. *impf. of* **де́ться; она́ не зна́ла, куда́ д. от смуще́ния** she did not know where to put herself for embarrassment. **2.** (*in past tense* = **де́ться**) to get to, disappear; **куда́ ~лись мои́ часы́?** where has my watch got to?
де́вер|ь, я, *pl.* **~ья́, ~е́й** *and* **~ьёв** (*coll.*) brother-in-law (*husband's brother*).
девиа́ци|я, и *f.* (*tech.*) deviation.
деви́з, а *m.* motto; device (*in heraldry*).
деви́з|а, ы *f.* bill of exchange (*cheque, etc.*) payable in foreign currency.
деви́ц|а, ы *f.* (*obs.*) unmarried woman, spinster; girl; **в ~ах** unmarried, before marriage.
деви́ческий = де́вичий
деви́честв|о, а *nt.* girlhood; spinsterhood.
де́вич|ий *adj.* girlish; maidenly; **~ья фами́лия** maiden name; **~ья па́мять** (*joc.*) a memory like a sieve; **~ья ко́жа** (*pharm.*) althea paste.
деви́чник, а *m.* (*ethnol.*) party for girls given by a bride on the eve of her wedding; (*fig.*) hen party.
де́вичь|я, ей *f.* (*obs.*) maid's room.
де́вк|а, и *f.* **1.** (*coll. and dial.*) girl, wench, lass; **засиде́ться в ~ах** to remain a long time unmarried; **оста́ться в ~ах** to become an old maid. **2.** (*coll.*) tart, whore.
Девома́тер|ь, и *f.* (*relig.*) the Virgin Mother.
дево́н, а *m.* (*geol.*) Devonian period.
дево́нский *adj.* (*geol.*) Devonian.
де́вочк|а, и *f.* (little) girl.
де́вственник, а *m.* virgin.
де́вственниц|а, ы *f.* virgin.
де́вственност|ь, и *f.* virginity; chastity; **обе́т ~и** vow of chastity.
де́вствен|ный (~, ~на) *adj.* **1.** virgin; **~ная плева́** (*anat.*) hymen. **2.** virginal; innocent. **3.** (*fig.*) virgin; **д. лес** virgin forest.
де́вств|о, а *nt.* spinsterhood.
де́вушк|а, и *f.* **1.** (unmarried) girl. **2.** (*obs.*) maid. **3.** (*coll.*; *as mode of address to shop assistant, etc.*) miss.
девча́т|а, ~ *no sg.* (*coll.*) girls.
девчо́нк|а, и *f.* (*coll.*) **1.** slut. **2.** kid; slip of a girl.
девчу́рк|а, и *f.* (*coll.*) little girl.
девчу́шк|а, и *f.* (*coll.*) little girl.
девяно́ст|о *g., d., i. and p.* **а** *num.* ninety.
девяно́стый *adj.* ninetieth.
девятерно́й *adj.* ninefold.
де́вятер|о, ы́х *num.* **1.** (+*m. nn. denoting persons, pers. prons. in pl. or nn. used only in pl.*) nine. **2.** (+*nn. denoting objects usu. found in pairs*) nine pairs.
девятидеся́тый (*obs.*) = **девяно́стый**
девятикра́тный *adj.* ninefold.
девятиле́тний *adj.* **1.** nine-year; of nine years' duration. **2.** nine-year-old.
девятисо́тый *adj.* nine-hundredth.
девя́тк|а, и *f.* **1.** (*figure*) nine. **2.** (*coll.*) No. 9 (*bus, tram, etc.*). **3.** (*coll.*) group of nine objects. **4.** (*cards*) nine.
девятна́дцатый *adj.* nineteenth.
девятна́дцат|ь, и *num.* nineteen.
девя́тый *adj.* ninth; **д. вал** 'the ninth wave' (*symbol of impending danger*).
де́вят|ь, и́, *i.* **ью́** *num.* nine.
девятьсо́т, девятисо́т, девятиста́м, девятьюста́ми, о девятиста́х *num.* nine hundred.
де́вятью *adv.* nine times.
дегаза́тор, а *m.* decontaminator.
дегазацио́нн|ый *adj. of* **дегаза́ция; ~ая часть** decontamination unit.
дегаза́ци|я, и *f.* decontamination.
дегази́р|овать, ую *impf. and pf.* to decontaminate.
дегенера́т, а *m.* degenerate.
дегенерати́вност|ь, и *f.* degeneracy.
дегенерати́в|ный (~ен, ~на) *adj.* degenerate.
дегенера́ци|я, и *f.* degeneration.
дегенери́р|овать, ую *impf. and pf.* to degenerate.
дёг|оть, тя *no pl., m.* tar; **ло́жка ~тя в бо́чке мёда** a fly in the ointment.
деграда́ци|я, и *f.* degradation.

деградир|овать, ую *impf. and pf.* to become degraded.
дёгтемаз, а *m.* mud-slinger.
дегтярн|ый *adj.* tar; **~ая вода** (*pharm.*) tar water; **~ое мыло** coal-tar soap.
дегустатор, а *m.* taster.
дегустаци|я, и *f.* tasting; **д. вин** wine-tasting.
дегустир|овать, ую *impf. and pf.* to carry out a tasting (of).
дед, а *m.* **1.** grandfather; (*pl.*; *fig.*) grandfathers, forefathers. **2.** (*coll.*; *as mode of address to an old man*) grand-dad, grandpa. **3.: д.-мороз** Father Christmas, Santa Claus.
дедовский *adj.* **1.** grandfather's. **2.** old-world; old-fashioned.
дедовщин|а, ы *f.* (*mil. sl.*) bullying, harassment (*of subordinates*).
дедуктивный *adj.* deductive.
дедукци|я, и *f.* deduction.
дедуцир|овать, ую *impf. and pf.* to deduce.
дедушк|а, и *m.* grandfather.
деепричасти|е, я *nt.* (*gram.*) gerund (*e.g.* **читая, читавши**).
деепричаст|ный *adj. of* **~ие**
дееспособност|ь, и *f.* **1.** energy, activity. **2.** (*leg.*) capability.
дееспособ|ный (~ен, ~на) *adj.* **1.** energetic, active. **2.** (*leg.*) capable.
деж|а, и, *pl.* **~и, ~ей** *f.* (*dial.*) vat.
дежур|ить, ю, ишь *impf.* **1.** to be on duty. **2.** to be in constant attendance, not to leave one's post.
дежурк|а, и *f.* **1.** duty room. **2.** pilot flame.
дежурн|ый *adj.* **1.** duty; on duty; **д. офицер** (*mil.*) orderly officer; **д. пункт** (*mil.*) guard-room; **~ая аптека** chemist's shop open after normal closing hour *or* on holiday. **2.: ~ое блюдо** plat du jour. **3.** *as n.* **д., ~ого** *m.*, **~ая, ~ой** *f.* man, woman on duty; **кто д.?** who is on duty? **д. по школе** teacher on duty; **д. по полётам** (*aeron.*) duty pilot. **4.** *as n.* **~ая, ~ой** *f.* duty room.
дежурств|о, а *nt.* (being on) duty; **расписание ~а** rota, (*mil.*) roster; **смениться с ~а** to come off duty, be relieved.
дезабилье *nt. indecl.* déshabillé.
дезавуир|овать, ую *impf. and pf.* to repudiate, disavow.
дезактизатор, а *m.* decontaminant.
дезертир, а *m.* deserter.
дезертир|овать, ую *impf. and pf.* to desert.
дезертирств|о, а *nt.* desertion.
дезинсекционн|ый *adj. of* **дезинсекция; ~ые средства** insecticides
дезинсекци|я, и *f.* insecticide.
дезинфектант, а *m.* disinfectant.
дезинфекционный *adj. of* **дезинфекция**
дезинфекци|я, и *f.* disinfection; (*coll.*) disinfectant.
дезинфицир|овать, ую *impf. and pf.* to disinfect.
дезинформаци|я, и *f.* misinformation.
дезинформир|овать, ую *impf. and pf.* to misinform.
дезодорант, а *m.* **1.** deodorant. **2.** air freshener.
дезодоратор, а *m.* deodorant, deodorizer.
дезодораци|я, и *f.* deodorization.
дезорганизаци|я, и *f.* disorganization.
дезорганиз|овать, ую *impf. and pf.* to disorganize.
дезориентаци|я, и *f.* disorientation.
дезориентир|овать, ую *impf. and pf.* to disorient; to cause to lose one's bearings, confuse.
дезориентир|оваться, уюсь *impf. and pf.* to lose one's bearings.
деизм, а *m.* deism.
деист, а *m.* deist.
действенност|ь, и *f.* efficacy; effectiveness.
действен|ный (~, ~на) *adj.* efficacious; effective.
действи|е, я *nt.* **1.** action, operation; activity; **ввести в д.** to bring into operation, bring into force. **2.** functioning (*of a machine etc.*). **3.** effect; action; **под ~ем** (*+g.*) under the influence (of); **не оказывать никакого ~я** to have no effect. **4.** action (*of a story, etc.*); **д. происходит во время Первой мировой войны** the action takes place during the First World War. **5.** act (*of a play*). **6.** (*math.*) operation.
действительно *adv.* really; indeed.
действительност|ь, и *f.* **1.** reality. **2.** realities; conditions, life; **современная китайская д.** present-day conditions in China; **в ~и** in reality, in fact. **3.** validity (*of a document*). **4.** efficacy (*of a medicine, etc.*).
действител|ьный (~ен, ~ьна) *adj.* **1.** real, actual; true, authentic; **~ьное положение вещей** the true state of affairs; **это были его ~ьные слова** these were his actual words; **~ьная служба** (*mil.*) active service; **~ьное число** (*math.*) real number; **д. член Академии наук** (full) member of the Academy of Sciences. **2.** valid; **удостоверение ~ьно на шесть месяцев** the licence is valid for six months. **3.** efficacious (*of a medicine, etc.*). **4.** (*tech.*) effective. **5.: д. залог** (*gram.*) active voice.
действ|овать, ую *impf.* **1.** (*impf. only*) to act; to work, function; to operate; **телефон не ~ует** the telephone is not working, is out of order; **~ует ли у больного кишечник?** are the patient's bowels open? **2.** (*pf.* **по~**) (**на**+*a.*) to affect, have an effect (upon), act (upon); **лекарство ~ует** the medicine is taking effect; **д. кому-н. на нервы** to get on s.o.'s nerves. **3.** (*impf. only*) (*+i.*; *coll.*) to work, operate; to use; **д. локтями** to use one's elbows.
действующ|ий *pres. part. act. of* **действовать** *and adj.*: **~ая армия** army in the field; **д. вулкан** active volcano; **~ее лицо** (*i*) (*theatr., liter.*) character, (*ii*) active participant; **~ие лица** (*theatr.*) dramatis personae.
дека... *comb. form* deca-.
дек|а, и *f.* (*mus.*) **1.** sounding-board. **2.** deck; **магнитофонная д.** tape deck.
декабрист, а *m.* (*hist.*) Decembrist.
декабрист|ский *adj. of* **~**
декабр|ь, я *m.* December.
декабрь|ский *adj. of* **~**
декад|а, ы *f.* **1.** ten-day period. **2.** (ten-day) festival.
декаданс, а *m.* decadence.
декадент, а *m.* decadent.
декадентский *adj.* decadent.
декадентств|о, а *nt.* decadence.
декадник, а *m.* (*pol.*) ten-day campaign.
декад|ный *adj. of* **~а**
декалитр, а *m.* decalitre.
декалькир|овать, ую *impf. and pf.* (*art*) to transfer.
декалькомани|я, и *f.* transfer-making; transfer (*of a design on to glass, pottery, etc.*).
декаметр, а *m.* decametre.
декан, а *m.* dean (*of university*).
деканат, а *m.* **1.** office of dean (*of university*). **2.** dean's office (*building*).
деканств|о, а *nt.* (*of university*) duties of dean, deanship.
декатир|овать, ую *impf. and pf.* (*text.*) to sponge (*woollen cloth, to prevent shrinking*).
декаэдр, а *m.* (*math.*) decahedron.
деквалификаци|я, и *f.* loss of professional skill.
декел|ь, я *m.* (*typ.*) tympan.
декламатор, а *m.* reciter, declaimer.
декламаци|я, и *f.* recitation, declamation.
декламир|овать, ую *impf.* (*of* **про~**) **1.** to recite, declaim. **2.** (*pej.*) to rant.
декларативност|ь, и *f.* (*pej.*) tendency to make pronouncements for effect; pretentiousness.
декларатив|ный (~ен, ~на) *adj.* **1.** declaratory; solemn. **2.** (*pej.*) made for effect, pretentious.
деклараци|я, и *f.* declaration; **налоговая д.** tax return.
деклариp|овать, ую *impf. and pf.* to declare, proclaim.
деклассированный *adj.* déclassé.
дековильк|а, и *f.* (*tech.*) tub (*on colliery rail., etc.*).
декокт, а *m.* (*med.*; *obs.*) decoction.
декольте *nt. indecl.* décolleté (*also as adj.*); décolletage.
декольтированный *adj.* **1.** décolleté. **2.** bare(d).
декоратив|ный (~ен, ~на) *adj.* decorative, ornamental.
декоратор, а *m.* decorator; scene-painter.
декораци|я, и *f.* **1.** scenery, décor. **2.** (*fig.*) window-dressing.
декорир|овать, ую *impf. and pf.* to decorate.
декорум, а *m.* decorum.
декрет, а *m.* **1.** decree. **2.** (*coll.*) maternity leave; **уйти в д.** to take maternity leave.
декретир|овать, ую *impf. and pf.* to decree.

декре́тниц|а, ы *f.* (*coll.*) woman on maternity leave.
декре́т|ный *adj. of* ~; **д. о́тпуск** maternity leave.
декстри́н, а *m.* (*chem.*) dextrine.
де́ланност|ь, и *f.* artificiality; affectation.
де́ланный *p.p.p. of* **де́лать** *and adj.* artificial, forced, affected.
де́ла|ть, ю *impf.* (*of* **с**~) **1.** to make (= *to construct, produce*). **2.** to make (= *to cause to become*); **д. кого́-н. несча́стным** to make s.o. unhappy; **д. из кого́-н. посме́шище** to make a laughing-stock of s.o. **3.** to do; **д. не́чего** there is nothing for it; it can't be helped; **от не́чего д.** for want of anything better to do; **д. под себя́** to foul *or* wet one's bed. **4.** (*+var. nn.*) to make, do, give; **д. вид** to pretend, feign; **д. вы́воды** to draw conclusions; **д. вы́говор** (*+d.*) to reprimand; **д. гла́зки** (*+d.*; *coll.*) to make eyes (at); **д. докла́д** to give a report; **д. комплиме́нт** (*+d.*) to pay a compliment; **д. предложе́ние** (*+d.*) to propose (*marriage*) (to); **д. уси́лия** to make an effort; **д. честь** (*+d.*) (*i*) to honour, (*ii*) to do credit. **5.** (*of distance covered*) to do, make; **д. два́дцать узло́в** (*naut.*) to make twenty knots.
де́ла|ться, юсь *impf.* (*of* **с**~) **1.** to become, get, grow. **2.** to happen; **что там ~ется?** what is going on? **что с ней ~ется?** what is the matter with her? **3.** (*coll.*) to break out, appear.
делега́т, а *m.* delegate.
делега́т|ский *adj. of* ~
делега́ци|я, и *f.* delegation; group.
делеги́р|овать, ую *impf. and pf.* to delegate.
делёж, а́ *m.* sharing, division; partition.
делёж|ка, ки *f.* (*coll.*) = ~
деле́ни|е, я *nt.* **1.** (*in var. senses*) division; **д. кле́ток** (*biol.*) cell-fission; **знак ~я** (*math.*) division sign. **2.** (*on graduated scale*) point, degree, unit.
дел|е́ц, ьца́ *m.* (*pej.*) smart operator, pers. on the make.
Де́ли *m. indecl.* Delhi.
деликате́с, а *m.* dainty; delicacy; **магази́н ~ов** delicatessen.
делика́тнича|ть, ю *impf.* (*coll.*) to be overnice; (**с**+*i.*) to treat unnecessarily softly, be too soft with s.o.
делика́тност|ь, и *f.* (*in var. senses*) delicacy.
делика́т|ный (~ен, ~на) *adj.* (*in var. senses*) delicate.
дели́м|ое, ого *nt.* (*math.*) dividend.
дели́мост|ь, и *f.* divisibility.
дели́тел|ь, я *m.* divisor.
дел|и́ть, ю́, ∠ишь *impf.* **1.** (*pf.* **раз**~) to divide; **д. по́ровну** to divide into equal parts; **д. шесть на́ три** to divide six by three. **2.** (*pf.* **по**~) (**с**+*i.*) to share (with); **д. с кем-н. го́ре и ра́дость** to share s.o.'s sorrows and joys.
дел|и́ться, ю́сь ∠ишься *impf.* **1.** (*pf.* **раз**~) (**на**+*a.*) to divide (into). **2.** (*impf. only*) (**на**+*a.*) to be divisible (by). **3.** (*pf.* **по**~) (+*i.*, **с**+*i.*) to share (with); to communicate (to), impart (to); **д. куско́м хле́ба с кем-н.** to share a crust of bread with s.o.; **д. ве́стью с кем-н.** to impart news to s.o.; **д. впечатле́ниями с кем-н.** to compare notes with s.o.
де́л|о, а, *pl.* **~а́, ~, ~а́м** *nt.* **1.** business, affair(s); **ме́жду ~ом** (*coll.*) at odd moments, between times; **по ~у, по ~а́м** on business; **э́то моё д.** that is my affair; **име́ть д.** (**с**+*i.*) to have to do (with), deal (with); **не вме́шивайтесь не в своё д.** mind your own business; **как (ва́ши) ~а́?** how are things going (with you)?, how are you getting on?; **за чем д. ста́ло?** what's holding things up?; **привести́ свой ~а́ в поря́док** to put one's affairs in order; **без ~а не входи́ть** no entry except on business; **таки́е-то ~а́** (*coll.*) so that's how it is!; **д. в шля́пе** (*coll.*) it's in the bag; **говори́ть д.** to talk sense; **вот э́то д.!** (*coll.*) now you're talking; **д. за ва́ми** it's up to you; **како́е мне до э́того д.?** what has this to do with me?; **что тебе́ за д.?** what does it matter to you?; **пе́рвым ~ом** in the first instance, first of all. **2.** cause; **д. ми́ра** the cause of peace; **э́то д. его́ жи́зни** it's his life's work. **3.** (+*adj.*) occupation; (*obs.*) business, concern; **вое́нное д.** soldiering; military science; **го́рное д.** mining. **4.** matter point; **д. вку́са** matter of taste; **д. привы́чки** matter of habit; **д. че́сти** point of honour; **д. в том, что...** the point is that ...; **в то́м-то и д.** that's (just) the point; **не в э́том д.** that's not the point; **совсе́м друго́е д.** quite another matter; **д. идёт о** (+*p.*) it is a matter of .... **5.** fact, deed; thing; **на са́мом ~е** in actual fact, as a matter of fact; **и на слова́х и на ~е** in word and deed; **на слова́х..., на ~е же** in theory, nominally ... but actually; **в са́мом ~е** really, indeed. **6.** (*leg.*) case; cause; **вести́ д.** to plead a cause; **возбуди́ть д. (про́тив)** to bring an action (against), institute proceedings (against). **7.** file, dossier; **ли́чное д.** personal file; **приложи́ть к ~у** to file. **8.** battle, fighting. **9.** *idiomatic phrr.*: **то и д.** continually, time and again; **то ли д.** (*coll.*) what a difference (*how much better*).
делови́тост|ь, и *f.* business-like character, efficiency.
делови́т|ый (~, ~а) *adj.* business-like, efficient.
делов|о́й *adj.* **1.** business; work; **~о́е письмо́** business letter; **~а́я пое́здка** business trip; **~о́е вре́мя** working time. **2.** business-like.
делопроизводи́тел|ь, я *m.* chief clerk; **д. шко́лы** school secretary.
делопроизво́дств|о, а *nt.* office work, clerical work; record keeping.
де́льн|ый *adj.* **1.** business-like, efficient. **2.** sensible, practical; **~ое предложе́ние** sensible suggestion.
де́льт|а, ы *f.* delta.
дельтаклу́б, а *m.* hang-gliding club.
дельтапла́н, а *m.* hang-glider (*craft*).
дельтапланери́ст, а *m.* hang-glider (*pers.*).
дельтапланери́ст|ка, ки *f. of* ~
дельтапла́нер|ный *adj. of* **~и́зм; д. спорт** hang-gliding.
дельтапланери́зм, а *m.* hang-gliding.
дельтови́дн|ый *adj.* delta-shaped; **д. самолёт** delta-wing aircraft; **~ая мы́шца** (*anat.*) deltoid muscle.
дельфи́н, а *m.* dolphin.
дельфина́ри|й, я *m.* dolphinarium.
деля́г|а, и *m.* **1.** (*coll.*) pers. pursuing his own interests. **2.** (*obs.*) good worker.
деля́нк|а, и *f.* plot (of land); piece (of woodland).
деля́ческий *adj.* narrow-minded, narrowly pragmatic (*not related to moral or philosophical principle*).
деля́честв|о, а *nt.* narrow-mindedness, narrowly pragmatic attitude.
демаго́г, а *m.* demagogue.
демагоги́ческий *adj.* demagogic.
демаго́ги|я, и *f.* demagogy.
демаркацио́нн|ый *adj.*: **~ая ли́ния** line of demarcation.
демарка́ци|я, и *f.* demarcation.
демаски́р|овать ую *impf. and pf.* (*mil.*) to unmask.
демикото́н, а *m.* (*text.*) jean.
демилитариза́ци|я, и *f.* demilitarization.
демилитаризи́р|овать ую *impf. and pf.* to demilitarize.
демисезо́нн|ый *adj.*: **~ое пальто́** light overcoat (*for spring and autumn wear*).
демиу́рг, а *m.* demiurge, creator.
демобилизацио́нный *adj.* demobilization.
демобилиза́ци|я, и *f.* demobilization.
демобилиз|ова́ть у́ю *impf. and pf.* to demobilize.
демограф|и́ческий *adj. of* **∠ия; д. взрыв** population explosion.
демогра́фи|я, и *f.* demography.
демокра́т, а *m.* **1.** democrat. **2.** plebeian.
демократиза́ци|я, и *f.* democratization.
демократизи́р|овать, ую *impf. and pf.* to democratize
демократи́ческий *adj.* **1.** democratic. **2.** plebeian.
демокра́ти|я, и *f.* **1.** democracy; **стра́ны наро́дной ~и** the People's Democracies. **2.** the common people, lower classes.
де́мон, а *m.* demon.
демони́ческий *adj.* demonic, demoniacal.
демонстра́нт, а *m* (*pol.*) demonstrator.
демонстрати́в|ный (~ен, ~на) *adj.* **1.** demonstrative, done for effect. **2.** demonstration; **~ная ле́кция** demonstration lecture. **3.** (*mil.*) feint, decoy.
демонстра́тор, а *m.* demonstrator.
демонстра́ци|я, и *f.* **1.** (*in var. senses*) demonstration; **д. му́скулов** (*pol.*) muscle-flexing. **2.** (*public*) showing (*of a film, etc.*); **повто́рная д.** repeat, rerun. **3.** (*mil.*) feint, manœuvre.

демонстри́р|овать, ую *impf. and pf.* 1. to demonstrate, make a demonstration. 2. (*pf. also* про~) to show, display; to give a demonstration (of); д. но́вый кинофи́льм to show a new film.
демонта́ж, а *m.* (*tech.*) dismantling.
демонти́р|овать, ую *impf. and pf.* (*tech.*) to dismantle.
демореализа́ци|я, и *f.* demoralization.
деморализ|ова́ть, у́ю *impf. and pf.* to demoralize.
де́мос, а *m.* (*hist.*) the people, plebs.
де́мпинг, а *m.* (*econ.*) dumping.
де́мпфер, а *m.* (*tech.*) damper; shock absorber.
денатурализа́ци|я, и *f.* (*leg.*) denaturalization.
денатурализ|ова́ть у́ю *impf. and pf.* (*leg.*) to denaturalize.
денатура́т, а *m.* methylated spirits.
денатури́р|овать, ую *impf. and pf.* (*chem.*) to denature.
денационализа́ци|я, и *f.* 1. (*pol.*) denationalization. 2. loss or suppression of natural characteristics.
денационализи́р|овать, ую *impf. and pf.* (*pol.*) to denationalize.
денацифика́ци|я, и *f.* denazification.
денацифици́р|овать, ую *impf. and pf.* to denazify.
де́нди *m. indecl.* dandy.
дендри́т, а *m.* (*anat.*, *min.*) dendrite.
дендроло́ги|я, и *f.* dendrology.
де́нежк|а, и *f.* 1. (*obs.*) half-kopeck coin. 2. *usu. pl.* (*coll.*) money; пла́кали на́ши ~и that's our money down the drain.
де́нежный *adj.* 1. monetary; money; д. автома́т cash dispenser; д. знак bank-note; д. перево́д money order; д. ры́нок money-market; д. штраф fine; д. я́щик strong-box. 2. (*coll.*) moneyed; д. челове́к a man of means.
ден|ёк, ька́ *m.*, *dim. of* день
денни́к, а́ *m.* (*dial.*) loose box.
денни́ц|а, ы *f.* (*poet.*) 1. dawn. 2. morning star.
де́нно *adv.*: д. и но́щно day and night.
денно́й *adj.* (*obs.*) day, daylight.
деномина́ци|я, и *f.* (*econ.*) denomination.
денонса́ци|я, и *f.* (*dipl.*) denouncement.
денонси́р|овать, ую *impf. and pf.* (*dipl.*) to denounce.
денщи́к, а́ *m.* (*mil.*, *obs.*) batman.
де́нь, дня *m.* 1. day; afternoon; в 4 ч. дня at 4 p.m.; днём in the afternoon; д.-деньско́й all day long; д. рожде́ния birthday; д. откры́тых двере́й open day; д. в д. to the day; д. ото дня with every passing day, day by day; в оди́н прекра́сный д. one fine day; во дни о́ны in those days; изо дня в д. day after day; на друго́й, сле́дующий д. next day; на дню (*obs.*) in the course of the day; на днях (*i*) the other day, (*ii*) one of these days, any day now; не по дням, а по часа́м hourly, fast, rapidly; со дня на́ д. daily, from day to day; че́рез д. every other day, on alternate days; Д. сме́ха April Fool's Day; кану́н Дня всех святы́х Halloween; Д. поминове́ния Remembrance Day; второ́й д. Рождества́ Boxing Day. 2. (*pl.*) days (= (*i*) *time*, *period*, (*ii*) *life*); его́ дни сочтены́ his days are numbered.
де́н|ьги, ег, ьгам *or* **ьга́м** *pl.* (*sg.* (*coll.*) ~ьга́, ~ьги́ *f.*) money; кро́вные д. hard-earned money; ме́лкие д. small change; нали́чные д. cash, ready money; при ~ьга́х in funds; не при ~ьга́х hard up; не за каки́е д. not for all the tea in China.
деньжа́т|а, ~ *no sg.* (*coll.*) money, cash.
деньжо́н|ки, ок *no sg.* (*coll.*) money, cash.
деонтоло́ги|я, и *f.* medical ethics.
департа́мент, а *m.* department.
департиза́ци|я, и *f.* (*pol.*) dismantling of (Communist) party control; 'departyization'.
депе́ш|а, и *f.* 1. dispatch. 2. (*obs.*) telegram.
депо́ *nt. indecl.* (*rail.*) depot; shed, roundhouse; пожа́рное д. fire-station.
депо́в|ец, ца *m.* engine-shed worker.
депо́|вский *adj. of* ~
депози́т, а *m.* (*fin.*) deposit.
депозита́ри|й, я *m.* depository.
депози́тор, а *m.* (*fin.*) depositor.
депоне́нт, а *m* (*fin.*) depositor.
депони́р|овать, ую *impf. and pf.* (*fin.*, *leg.*) to deposit.
депорта́нт, а *m.* deportee.
депорта́ци|я, и *f.* deportation.
депорти́р|овать, ую *impf. and pf.* to deport.
депресси́вн|ый *adj. of* депре́ссия; д. пери́од (*econ.*) depression, slump; ~ое состоя́ние (*econ. and psych.*) depression.
депре́сси|я, и *f.* 1. (*econ.*) depression, slump. 2. (*psych.*) depression.
депута́т, а *m.* deputy; delegate; пала́та ~ов Chamber of Deputies.
депута́ци|я, и *f.* deputation.
дёр, у *m.*: (за)да́ть ~у (*coll.*) to take to one's heels.
дератиза́ци|я, и *f.* rodent control.
де́рвиш, а *m.* dervish.
дёрга|ть, ю *impf.* (*of* дёрнуть) 1. to pull, tug; д. кого́-н. за рука́в to tug at s.o.'s sleeve, pluck by the sleeve. 2. to pull out; д. зу́бы (*i*) to pull out teeth, (*ii*) to have teeth out (*at the dentist's*); д. лён to pull flax. 3. (*impf. only*) to harass, pester. 4. (*impf. only*) (*coll.*) to cause to twitch; (*impers.*) to twitch; его́ всего́ ~ло he was twitching all over. 5. (*impf. only*) (+*i.*; *coll.*) to move sharply, jerk; д. плеча́ми to shrug one's shoulders.
дёрга|ться, юсь *impf.* (*of* дёрнуться) 1. *pass. of* ~ть. 2. to twitch; рот у него́ непреста́нно ~ется his mouth twitches incessantly.
дерга́ч[1], а́ *m.* (*zool.*) landrail, corncrake.
дерга́ч[2], а́ *m.* (*tech.*) nail extractor.
деревене́|ть, ю *impf.* (*of* о~) to grow stiff, numb.
деревéнский *adj.* 1. village. 2. rural, country.
деревéнщик, а *m.* (*liter.*) member of 'village prose' school.
деревéнщин|а, ы *c.g.* (*coll.*) (country) bumpkin.
дере́в|ня, ни, *g. pl.* **~е́нь** *f.* 1. village. 2. (the) country (*opp. the town*).
де́рев|о, а, *pl.* **~́ья, ~́ьев** *nt.* 1. tree; за ~́ьями ле́са не ви́деть not to see the wood for the trees. 2. (*sg. only*) wood (*as material*).
дерево-землянóй *adj.* (*mil.*) earth-and-timber.
деревообдéлочник, а *m.* woodworker.
деревообдéлочный *adj.* wood-working.
деревообрабо́тк|а, и *f.* woodworking.
деревýшк|а, и *f.* hamlet.
де́ревц|е, а *and* **деревц|о́, а́** *nt.* sapling.
деревяни́ст|ый (~, ~а) *adj.* 1. ligneous. 2. hard (*of fruit*, *etc.*).
деревя́нн|ый *adj.* 1. wood; wooden. 2. (*fig.*) wooden; expressionless, dead; dull; ~ое выраже́ние лица́ wooden expression; д. го́лос expressionless voice. 3.: ~ое ма́сло lamp-oil (*low-grade olive oil*).
деревя́шк|а, и *f.* 1. piece of wood. 2. (*coll.*) wooden leg.
держа́в|а, ы *f.* 1. (*pol.*) power; вели́кие ~ы the Great Powers. 2. (*hist.*) orb (*as emblem of monarchy*).
держа́вный *adj.* 1. holding supreme power, sovereign. 2. powerful.
держа́лк|а, и *f.* 1. (*coll.*) handle. 2. umbrella stand. 3. base (*of standard lamp*).
де́ржаный *adj.* (*coll.*) used, worn, second-hand.
держа́тел|ь, я *m.* 1. (*fin.*) holder. 2. bracket; socket; holder.
держ|а́ть, у́, ~́ишь *impf.* 1. to hold; to hold on to; ~и́те во́ра! stop thief! 2. to hold up, support. 3. (*in var. senses*) to keep, hold; д. в посте́ли to keep in bed; д. банк (*card-games*) to be banker; д. курс (на+*a.*) to hold course (for), head (for); (*fig.*) to be working (for); д. путь (к, на+*a.*) to head (for), make (for); д. пари́ to bet; д. чью-н. сто́рону to take s.o.'s side; д. язы́к за зуба́ми to hold one's tongue; д. в ку́рсе to keep posted; д. в неве́дении to keep in the dark; д. в плену́ to hold prisoner. 4. to keep (= *to own*, *possess*); д. лошаде́й to keep horses. 5. д. себя́ to behave. 6. + *certain nn.* = *to carry out*; д. корректу́ру to read proofs; д. ре́чь to make a speech; д. экза́мен to sit, take an examination.
держ|а́ться, у́сь, ~́ишься *impf.* 1. (за+*a.*) to hold (on to); ~и́тесь за пери́ла hold on to the banister. 2. (на+*p.*) to be held up (by), be supported (by); д. на ни́точке to hang by a thread (*also fig.*). 3. to keep, stay, be; д. вме́сте

to stick together; **д. в стороне́** to hold aloof. **4.** to hold o.s.; (*fig.*) to behave. **5.** to last; to hold together; **у неё всё ещё ~ится америка́нский акце́нт** she still retains her American accent; **э́тот стол у вас е́ле ~ится** this table of yours is on its last legs. **6.** to hold out, stand firm; to hold one's ground. **7.** (+*g.*) to keep (to); **д. ле́вой стороны́** to keep to the left; **д. бе́рега** to hug the shore. **8.** (+*g.*) to adhere (to), stick (to); **д. те́мы** to stick to the subject; **д. убежде́ний** to have the courage of one's convictions. **9.: то́лько ~и́сь!** (*int.*) and how!

дерза́ни|е, я *nt.* daring.

дерз|а́ть, а́ю *impf.* (*of* **~ну́ть**) to dare.

дерз|и́ть, (у́), и́шь *impf.* (*of* **на~**) (+*d.*; *coll.*) to be impertinent (to), cheek.

де́рз|кий (~ок, ~ка́, ~ко) *adj.* **1.** impertinent, cheeky. **2.** daring, audacious.

дерзнове́ни|е, я *nt.* (*obs.*) audacity.

дерзнове́н|ный (~ен, ~на) *adj.* **1.** (*obs.*) impertinent, insolent. **2.** daring, audacious.

дерзн|у́ть, у́, ёшь *pf. of* **дерза́ть**

де́рзост|ный (~ен, ~на) *adj.* (*obs.*) = **де́рзкий**

де́рзост|ь, и *f.* **1.** impertinence; cheek; rudeness; **говори́ть ~и** to be impertinent, cheeky, rude. **2.** daring, audacity.

дерива́т, а *m.* (*tech.*) derivative.

дерива́ци|я, и *f.* **1.** (*mil.*) drift. **2.** (*math.*) derivation. **3.** canalization.

дермати́н, а *m.* leatherette.

дермати́т, а *m.* dermatitis.

дермато́лог, а *m.* dermatologist.

дерматоло́ги|я, и *f.* dermatology.

дёрн, а *m.* turf.

дерни́н|а, ы *f.* (a) turf, sod.

дерни́ст|ый (~, ~а) *adj.* turfy.

дерн|ова́ть, у́ю *impf.* to cover with turf; to make a turf edging round.

дерно́вый *adj. of* **дёрн**

дёрн|уть, у, ешь *pf.* **1.** *pf. of* **дёргать; чёрт ~ет (~ул), нелёгкая ~ет (~ула)** *or* (*impers.*) **~ет (~уло) кого́-н.** (+*inf.*; *coll.*) to be possessed (to do sth.); **чёрт меня́ ~ул дать сло́во** I don't know what possessed me to promise. **2.** to get going, get cracking. **3.** (*coll.*) to go off. **4.** (*coll.*) to drink up; to take a swig. **5.** (*coll.*) to start vigorously to do sth.; **д. плясову́ю** to strike up a (dance) tune.

дёрн|уться, усь, ешься *pf.* (*of* **дёргаться**) to start up (with a jerk), to dart.

дер|у́, ёшь *see* **драть**

дерьм|о́, а́ *nt.* (*vulg.*) dung, muck (*also fig.*).

дерьмо́вый *adj.* (*coll.*) crappy (= *inferior*).

дерю́г|а, и *f.* sackcloth, sacking.

дерю́жный *adj.* sackcloth.

деря́бн|уть, у, ешь *pf.* (*sl.*) **1.** to make (= *to acquire by sharp practice*). **2.** to drink up.

деса́нт, а *m.* (*mil.*) **1.** (*airborne or amphibious*) landing; **д. с бо́ем** opposed landing. **2.** landing force.

деса́нтник, а *m.* paratrooper.

деса́нтный *adj.* (*mil.*) landing.

дёсенный *adj.* (*anat.*) gingival.

десе́рт, а *m.* dessert.

десе́рт|ный *adj. of* **~; ~ная ло́жка** dessert spoon; **~ное вино́** sweet wine.

де́скать *particle indicating reported speech* (*coll.*): **она́, д., ничего́ подо́бного не хоте́ла сказа́ть** she said she had not meant anything of the kind.

десн|а́, ы́, *pl.* **~̀ы, дёсен** *f.* (*anat.*) gum.

десни́ц|а, ы *f.* (*obs. or poet.*) right hand.

де́спот, а *m.* despot.

деспоти́зм, а *m.* despotism.

деспоти́ческий *adj.* despotic.

деспоти́ч|ный (~ен, ~на) *adj.* despotic.

деспоти́|я, и *f.* despotism.

дестабилизи́р|овать, ую *impf. and pf.* (*pol.*) to destabilize.

дест|ь, и, *g. pl.* **~е́й** *f.* quire (*of paper*) (**ру́сская д.** = 24 sheets; **метри́ческая д.** = 50 sheets).

десятери́к, а́ *m.* measure or object containing ten units.

десятери́чн|ый *adj.* (*obs.*) tenfold; **и ~ое** name of letter 'i' in old Russ. orthography.

десятерно́й *adj.* tenfold.

де́сятер|о, ы́х *num.* **1.** (+*m. nn. denoting persons*, *pers. prons. in pl. or nn. used only in pl.*) ten. **2.** (+*nn. denoting objects usu. found in pairs*) ten pairs.

десятибо́р|ец, ца *m.* decathlete.

десятибо́рь|е, я *nt.* (*sport*) decathlon.

десятигра́нник, а *m.* decahedron.

десятизу́б|ый *adj.*: **~ые ко́шки** (*mountaineering*) crampons.

десятикра́тный *adj.* tenfold.

десятиле́ти|е, я *nt.* **1.** decade. **2.** tenth anniversary.

десятиле́тк|а, и *f.* ten-year (secondary) school.

десятиле́тний *adj.* **1.** ten-year, decennial. **2.** ten-year-old.

десяти́н|а, ы *f.* **1.** dessiatine, desyatin (*old Russ. land measure, equivalent to 2.7 acres or 1.09 hectares*). **2.** tithe.

десятирублёвк|а, и *f.* (*coll.*) ten-rouble note.

десятисло́жный *adj.* (*liter.*) decasyllabic.

десятиуго́льник, а *m.* (*math.*) decagon.

десяти́чн|ый *adj.* decimal; **~ая дробь** decimal fraction.

деся́тка, и *f.* **1.** (*figure*) ten. **2.** (*coll.*) No. 10 (*bus, tram, etc.*). **3.** (*coll.*) group of ten objects. **4.** (*cards*) ten. **5.** (*coll.*) ten-rouble note. **6.** ten-oared boat.

деся́тник, а *m.* (*obs.*) foreman.

деся́т|ок, ка *m.* **1.** ten. **2.** ten years, decade (*of life*). **3.** (*pl.*) (*math.*) tens. **4.** (*pl.*) tens. **5.: не ро́бкого ~ка** plucky.

деся́тск|ий, ого *m.* (*hist.*) peasant policeman.

деся́т|ый *num.* tenth; **расска́зывать из пя́того в ~ое, с пя́того на ~ое** to relate inconsequentially; **э́то де́ло ~ое** (*coll.*) it is of no consequence.

де́сят|ь, и́, ью *num.* ten.

де́сятью *adv.* ten times (*in multiplication*).

дет... *comb. form, abbr. of* **де́тский**

детализа́ци|я, и *f.* working out in detail.

детализи́р|овать, ую *and* **детализ|ова́ть, у́ю** *impf. and pf.* to work out in detail.

дета́л|ь, и *f.* **1.** detail. **2.** part, component (*of a machine, etc.*).

дета́л|ьный (~ен, ~ьна) *adj.* detailed; minute.

детвор|а́, ы́ *no pl.*, *f.* (*collect.*; *coll.*) children.

детдо́м, а *m.* children's home.

детдо́мов|ец, ца *m.* (*coll.*) resident of a children's home.

детекти́в, а *m.* **1.** detective. **2.** detective story; whodunit.

детекти́вный *adj.*: **д. рома́н** detective story.

детекти́вщик, а *m.* (*coll.*) writer of detective stories *or* whodunits.

дете́ктор, а *m.* (*tech.*) detector; spark indicator.

детёныш, а *m.* young (*of animals*; *whelp, cub, calf, etc.*).

детерге́нт, а *m.* detergent.

детермини́зм, а *m.* determination.

детермини́ст, а *m.* determinist.

де́т|и, ~е́й, ~ям, ~ьми́, о ~ях *pl.* (*sg.* **дитя́** *nt.*) children; **д. боя́рские,** *see* **боя́рский**

дети́н|а, ы *m.* (*coll.*) big fellow, hefty chap.

дети́н|ец, ца *m.* (*hist.*) citadel.

де́тищ|е, а, *g. pl.* **~** *nt.* child, offspring; (*fig.*) child, creation; brainchild.

деткомбина́т, а *m.* (*coll.*) day nursery.

де́тный *adj.* (*coll.*) having children.

детона́тор, а *m.* (*tech.*) detonator.

детона́ци|я, и *f.* (*tech.*) detonation.

детони́р|овать¹, ую *impf.* (*tech.*) to detonate.

детони́р|овать², ую *impf.* to sing, play out of tune.

деторо́дный *adj.* genital.

деторожде́ни|е, я *nt.* procreation.

детоуби́йств|о, а *nt.* infanticide (*action*).

детоуби́йц|а, ы *c.g.* infanticide (*agent*).

детплоща́дк|а, и *f.* playground.

детри́т, а *m.* **1.** (*physiol.*) detritus. **2.** vaccine.

детса́д, а *m.* kindergarten, nursery school; **д.-я́сли** day nursery.

детса́дов|ец, ца *m.* (*coll.*) child attending kindergarten.

де́тск|ая, ой *f.* nursery.

де́тск|ий *adj.* **1.** child's, children's; **д. дом** children's home; **д. сад** kindergarten, nursery school; **~ая сме́ртность** infantile mortality; **~ая ко́мната** (*i*) = **~ая,** (*ii*) room for mothers and children (*at rail. station, etc.*), (*iii*) juvenile

delinquents' room (*at police station*); **~ая коло́ния** reformatory (school); **д. труд** child labour. **2.** childish; **д. язы́к** baby-talk. **3.: ~ое ме́сто** (*anat.*) placenta.
де́тскост|ь, и *f.* childishness.
де́тств|о, а *nt.* childhood; **с ~а** from childhood, from a child; **впада́ть в д.** to lapse into dotage.
деть, де́ну, де́нешь *pf.* (*of* **дева́ть**) to put, do (with); **куда́ ты дел моё перо́?** what have you done with my pen?; **не знать, куда́ глаза́ д.** not to know where to look; **э́того никуда́ не де́нешь** there's no getting away from it; there's no disputing it.
де́|ться, нусь, нешься *pf.* (*of* **дева́ться**) to get to, disappear.
де-фа́кто *adv.* de facto.
дефе́кт, а *m.* defect.
дефекти́в|ный (~ен, ~на) *adj.* defective; handicapped; **д. ребёнок** (mentally) defective *or* (physically) handicapped child.
дефе́ктный *adj.* imperfect, faulty.
дефекто́лог, а *m.* specialist on mental defects and physical handicaps (*in children*).
дефектол|оги́ческий *adj. of* **~о́гия**
дефектоло́ги|я, и *f.* study of mental defects and physical handicaps (*in connection with education of blind, spastic, etc., children*).
дефектоско́п, а *m.* (*tech.*) fault detector.
дефектоскопи́|я, и *f.* (*tech.*) fault detection.
дефиле́ *nt. indecl.* (*mil.*) defile.
дефили́р|овать, ую *impf.* (*of* **про~**) to march past, go in procession.
дефини́ци|я, и *f.* definition.
дефи́с, а *m.* hyphen.
дефици́т, а *m.* **1.** (*econ.*) deficit; **д. торго́вого бала́нса** trade gap. **2.** shortage, deficiency; **д. в то́пливе** fuel shortage.
дефици́т|ный (~ен, ~на) *adj.* **1.** (*econ.*) showing a loss. **2.** in short supply; scarce.
дефля́ция, и *f.* **1.** (*econ.*) deflation. **2.** (*geol.*) deflation, wind erosion.
деформа́ци|я, и *f.* deformation.
деформи́р|овать, ую *impf. and pf.* to deform; to transform.
деформи́р|оваться, уюсь *impf. and pf.* to change one's shape; to become deformed.
дехка́н|ин, ина, *pl.* **~е, ~** *m.* peasant (*in Uzbekistan and Tadzhikistan*).
дехка́н|ский *adj. of* **~ин**
децентрализа́ци|я, и *f.* decentralization.
децентрализ|ова́ть, у́ю *impf. and pf.* to decentralize.
деци... *comb. form* deci-.
децили́тр, а *m.* decilitre.
децима́льный *adj.* decimal.
децимéтр, а *m.* decimetre.
дешеве́|ть, ю *impf.* (*of* **по~**) to fall in price, become cheaper.
дешеви́зн|а, ы *f.* cheapness; low price.
дешев|и́ть, лю́, и́шь *impf.* (*coll.*) to underprice.
дешёвк|а, и *f.* **1.** low price; **купи́ть по ~е** to buy cheap. **2.** sale at reduced prices; **купи́ть на ~е** (*coll.*) to buy at a sale. **3.** (*fig.*) cheap stuff; worthless object.
дешéвле *comp. of* **дешёвый** *or* **дёшево; д. па́реной ре́пы** dirt-cheap.
дёшево *adv.* cheap, cheaply; (*fig.*) cheaply, lightly; **д. да гни́ло** cheap and nasty; **д. и серди́то** cheap but good; **д. отде́латься** to get off lightly; **э́то вам д. не пройдёт** this will cost you dear; **д. остри́ть** to make cheap jokes; **д. сто́ить** to be of no account.
дешёв|ый (дёшев, дешева́, дёшево) *adj.* **1.** cheap. **2.** (*fig.*) cheap; empty, worthless; **~ая острота́** cheap crack.
дешифри́р|овать, ую *impf. and pf.* to decipher, decode.
дешифро́вк|а, и *f.* decipherment, deciphering, decoding.
деэскала́ци|я, и *f.* (*mil., pol.*) de-escalation.
де-ю́ре *adv.* de jure.
дея́ни|е, я *nt.* (*obs. or rhet.*) act; action; **Дея́ния апо́столов** the Acts of the Apostles.
де́ятел|ь, я *m.* agent; **госуда́рственный д.** statesman; **обще́ственный д.** public figure; **заслу́женный д. иску́сства, нау́ки** Honoured Artist, Scientist (*honorific title in former USSR*).
де́ятельност|ь, и *f.* **1.** activity, activities; work; **обще́ственная д.** public work; **педагоги́ческая д.** educational work, teaching. **2.** (*physiol, psych., etc.*) activity, operation; **д. се́рдца** operation of the heart.
де́ятел|ьный (~ен, ~ьна) *adj.* active, energetic.
де́|яться, ется *impf.* (*coll.*) to happen; **что там ~ется?** what's going on?
джаз, а *m.* **1.** jazz band. **2.** jazz music.
джаз-анса́мбл|ь, я *m.* jazz-combo.
джаз-ба́нд, а *m.* jazz band.
джази́ст, а *m.* jazzman, jazz musician.
джазме́н, а *m.* = **джази́ст**
джаз-му́зык|а, и *f.* jazz.
джа́зовый *adj.* jazz.
джем, а *m.* jam.
дже́мпер, а *m.* jumper.
джентльме́н, а *m.* gentleman.
джентльме́нск|ий *adj.* gentlemanly; **~ое соглаше́ние** gentlemen's agreement.
джентльме́нств|о, а *nt.* gentlemanliness.
джерсе́ *nt. indecl.* = **дже́рси**
Дже́рси *m. indecl.* Jersey.
дже́рси́ *nt. indecl.* jersey (*material*).
джерсо́вый *adj. of* **дже́рси́**
джерсе́йск|ий *adj.*: **~ая коро́ва** Jersey (cow).
джи́г|а, и *f.* jig.
джиги́т, а *m.* Dzhigit (*Caucasian horseman*).
джигит|ова́ть, у́ю *impf.* to engage in trick riding.
джигито́вк|а, и *f.* trick riding (*originally by Caucasian horsemen*).
джин[1]**, а** *m.* gin (*liquor*); **д. с то́ником** gin and tonic.
джин[2]**, а** *m.* (*tech.*) (cotton-)gin.
джинн, а *m.* genie.
джинсо́вый *adj.* denim.
джи́нс|ы, ов *no sg.* jeans.
джип, а *m.* jeep.
джи́у-джи́тсу *nt. indecl.* ju-jitsu.
джо́ггинг, а *m.* jogging, fun-running; jog, fun-run.
джо́йстик, а *m.* (*comput.*) joystick.
джо́нк|а, и *f.* junk (*Chinese sailing vessel*).
Джо́рджи|я, и *f.* Georgia (*USA*).
джо́ул|ь, я, *g. pl.* **~ей** *m.* (*phys.*) joule.
джу́нгл|и, ей *no sg.*, jungle; **«шко́льные д.»** 'blackboard jungle'.
джут, а *m.* jute.
джу́т|овый *adj. of* **~**
дзот, а *m.* (*abbr. of* ***де́рево-земляна́я огнева́я то́чка***) (*mil.*) earth-and-timber emplacement.
ДЗУ *nt. indecl.* (*abbr. of* ***долговре́менное запомина́ющее устро́йство***) (*comput.*) ROM (*read-only memory*).
дзэн-будди́зм, а *m.* Zen-Buddhism.
дзю(-)до́ *nt. indecl.* judo.
дзюдои́ст, а *m.* judoist, judoka.
диабе́т, а *m.* diabetes.
диабе́тик, а *nt.* diabetic.
диа́гноз, а *nt.* diagnosis.
диагно́ст, а *m.* diagnostician.
диагно́стик|а, и *f.* diagnostics.
диагности́р|овать, ую *impf. and pf.* to diagnose.
диагона́л|ь, и *f.* diagonal; **по ~и** diagonally.
диагона́л|ьный (~ен, ~ьна) *adj.* diagonal.
диагра́мм|а, ы *f.* diagram; chart; **кругова́я** *or* **се́кторная д.** pie chart.
диаде́м|а, ы *f.* diadem.
диа́кон, а *m.* = **дья́кон**
диакони́сс|а, ы *f.* deaconess.
диакрити́ческий *adj.*: **д. знак** (*ling.*) diacritical mark.
диале́кт, а *m.* dialect.
диалекта́льный *adj.* dialectal.
диалекти́зм, а *m.* (*ling.*) dialecticism.
диале́ктик, а, *m.* (*phil.*) dialectician.
диале́ктик|а, и *f.* (*phil.*) dialectics.

диалекти́ческий[1] *adj.* (*phil.*) dialectical.
диалекти́ческий[2] *adj.* (*ling.*) dialectal.
диале́ктный *adj.* (*ling.*) dialectal.
диалектологи́ческий *adj.* (*ling.*) dialectological.
диалектоло́ги|я, и *f.* (*ling.*) dialectology.
диало́г, а *m.* dialogue.
диалоги́ческий *adj.* having dialogue form.
диало́говый *adj.* (*comput.*) interactive.
диама́нт, а *m.* (*obs.*) diamond.
диама́т, а *m.* (*abbr. of* ***диалекти́ческий материали́зм***) dialectical materialism.
диа́метр, а *m.* diameter.
диаметра́льно *adv.*: **д. противополо́жный** diametrically opposite.
диаметра́льный *adj.* **1.** diametral. **2.** diametrical.
диапазо́н, а *m.* **1.** (*mus.*) diapason, range. **2.** (*fig.*) range, compass; **у него́ о́чень большо́й д. интере́сов** he has a very wide range of interests. **3.** (*tech.*; *fig.*) range; **д. волн** (*radio*) wave band; **д. скоросте́й** (*aeron.*) air speed bracket.
диапозити́в, а *m.* (*phot.*) slide, transparency.
диатри́б|а, ы *f.* diatribe.
диафи́льм, а *m.* slide film.
диафра́гм|а, ы *f.* **1.** diaphragm. **2.** (*phys.*) stop; (*phot.*) aperture.
ди́в|а, ы *f.* (*obs.*) diva, prima donna.
дива́н[1]**, а** *m.* divan (*couch*); sofa; **д.-крова́ть** sofa bed.
дива́н[2]**, а** *m.* **1.** (*hist.*) divan (*Turkish Council of State*). **2.** (*liter.*) divan (*Persian name for collection of lyric poetry*).
дива́н|ный *adj. of* ~[1]; (*obs.*) *as n.* **~ная, ~ной** *f.* divan-room.
диверса́нт, а *m.* saboteur.
диве́рси|я, и *f.* **1.** (*mil.*) diversion. **2.** sabotage.
дивертисме́нт, а *m.* (*theatr.*) variety show, music-hall entertainment; divertissement (*ballet programme*).
дивиде́нд, а *m.* dividend.
дивизио́н, а *m.* (*mil.*) **1.** battalion (*of artillery or cavalry*). **2.** division (*of small warships*).
дивизио́н|ный *adj.* **1.** *adj. of* **диви́зия; д. кома́ндный пункт** division command post. **2.** *adj. of* ~
диви́зи|я, и *f.* (*mil.*) division.
див|и́ть, лю́, и́шь *impf.* (*coll.*) to amaze.
див|и́ться, лю́сь, и́шься *impf.* (*of* **по~**) (*+d.*) to be surprised, wonder, marvel (at); (**на***+a.*) to look upon with wonder.
ди́в|ный (~ен, ~на) *adj.* **1.** amazing; **что тут ~ного?** what's extraordinary about that? **2.** marvellous, wonderful.
ди́в|о, а *nt.* wonder, marvel; **~у да́ться** to wonder, marvel; **что за д.!** how extraordinary!; **на д.** marvellously; *as pred.* it is amazing; **не д.** it is no wonder.
дидакти́ческий *adj.* didactic.
дие́з, а *m.* (*and as indecl. adj.*) (*mus.*) sharp; **ре-д.** D sharp.
дие́т|а, ы *f.* diet; **посади́ть на ~у** to place on a diet; **соблюда́ть ~у** to keep to a diet.
диете́тик|а, и *f.* dietetics.
диетети́ческий *adj.* dietetic; **д. магази́н** health food shop; **в. проду́кт** dietetic foodstuff.
дието́лог, а *m.* nutritionist.
диза́йн, а *m.* design.
диза́йнер, а *m.* designer.
ди́зел|ь, я *m.* diesel engine.
ди́зельный *adj.* diesel
дизентери́|я, и *f.* dysentery.
дика́р|ский *adj. of* **~ь**
дика́рств|о, а *nt.* shyness.
дика́р|ь, я́ *m.* **1.** savage; (*fig.*) barbarian. **2.** (*fig.*, *coll.*) shy, unsociable pers. **3.** (*coll.*) non-official holiday-maker.
ди́к|ий (~, ~а́, ~о) *adj.* **1.** wild (*opp. tame, cultivated*); **~ая ко́шка** wild cat; **~ое по́ле** (*hist.*) steppe frontier region; **~ое я́блоко** crab-apple. **2.** savage (= *pertaining to primitive society*; *also as n.* **д., ~ого** *m.*). **3.** wild (= *unrestrained*); **~ие кри́ки** wild cries; **д. восто́рг** wild delight. **4.** queer, absurd; fantastic, preposterous, ridiculous; **~ое предложе́ние** fantastic suggestion. **5.** shy; unsociable. **6.** (*obs.*) dark-grey. **7.**: **~ое мя́со** (*med.*) proud flesh. **8.** not officially organized.
ди́к|о[1] *adv.* **1.** *adv. of* **~ий; д. расти́** to grow wild. **2.** in fright; startled; **д. озира́ться** to look around wildly.
ди́ко[2] *as pred.* it is absurd, it is ridiculous; **д. задава́ть таки́е вопро́сы** it is ridiculous to ask such a question.
дикобра́з, а *m.* porcupine.
дико́вин|а, ы *and* **~ка, ~ки** *f.* (*coll.*) marvel, wonder; **э́то мне не в ~(к)у** I see nothing remarkable about it.
дико́винный *adj.* strange, unusual, remarkable.
дикорасту́щий *adj.* wild.
ди́кост|ь, и *f.* **1.** wildness; savagery. **2.** shyness; unsociableness. **3.** absurdity, queerness; **э́то соверше́нная д.** it is quite absurd.
дикта́нт, а *m.* dictation.
дикта́т, а *m.* (*pol.*) diktat.
дикта́тор, а *m.* dictator.
дикта́торский *adj.* dictatorial.
дикта́торств|о, а *nt.* **1.** dictatorship. **2.** (*coll.*) dictatorial attitude.
диктату́р|а, ы *f.* dictatorship; **в. пролетариа́та** dictatorship of the proletariat.
дикт|ова́ть, у́ю, у́ешь *impf.* (*of* **про~**) to dictate.
дикто́вк|а, и *f.* dictation; **под чью-н. ~у** to s.o.'s dictation; (*fig.*) at s.o.'s bidding.
ди́ктор, а *m.* (radio-)announcer.
диктофо́н, а *m.* Dictaphone (*propr.*).
ди́кци|я, и *f.* diction; enunciation.
диле́мм|а, ы *f.* dilemma.
ди́лер, а *m.* dealer.
дилета́нт, а *m.* dilettante, dabbler.
дилета́нтств|о, а *nt.* dilettantism.
дилижа́нс, а *m.* stage-coach.
динами́зм, а *m.* dynamism.
дина́мик, а *m.* loudspeaker; (*audio equipment*) **ба́совый д.** woofer; **высокочасто́тный д.** tweeter.
дина́мик|а, и *f.* **1.** dynamics. **2.** (*fig.*) dynamics; movement, action; **в пье́се ма́ло ~и** there is little action in this play.
динами́т, а *m.* dynamite.
динами́тчик, а *m.* **1.** dynamiter. **2.** (*coll.*) terrorist.
динами́ческий *adj.* dynamic.
дина́мо *nt. indecl.* = **дина́мо-маши́на**
дина́мов|ец, ца *m.* member of the 'Dynamo' football team.
дина́мо-маши́н|а, ы *f.* dynamo.
дина́р, а *m.* dinar.
династи́ческий *adj.* dynastic.
дина́сти|я, и *f.* dynasty; **д. Тюдо́ров** the House of Tudor.
ди́нго *m. indecl.* (*zool.*) dingo.
диноза́вр, а *m.* dinosaur.
дио́д, а *m.*: **светоизлуча́ющий д.** light-emitting diode, LED.
диора́м|а, ы *f.* diorama.
дип... *comb. form, abbr. of* **дипломати́ческий**
дипкурье́р, а *m.* diplomatic courier.
дипло́м, а *m.* **1.** diploma; degree (*certificate*). **2.** (*coll.*) degree work, research. **3.** pedigree.
диплома́нт, а *m.* diploma-winner.
диплома́т, а *m.* **1.** diplomat, diplomatist (*lit. and fig.*). **2.** attaché case, (rigid) briefcase.
диплома́тик|а, и *f.* (*palaeog.*) diplomatic(s).
дипломати́ческий *adj.* diplomatic; **д. ко́рпус** corps diplomatique; **д. курье́р** diplomatic courier; Queen's Messenger.
дипломати́ч|ный (~ен, ~на) *adj.* (*fig.*) diplomatic.
диплома́ти|я, и *f.* diplomacy; **д. каноне́рок** gunboat diplomacy.
дипломи́рованный *adj.* graduate; professionally qualified, certificated.
дипло́мник, а *m.* student engaged on degree thesis.
дипло́м|ный *adj. of* **~; ~ная рабо́та** degree work, degree thesis.
директи́в|а, ы *f.* directive; instruction.
дире́ктор, а, *pl.* **~а́** *m.* director, manager; **д. шко́лы** head (master, mistress); principal.
директри́с|а[1]**, ы** *f.* (*obs.*) head mistress.
директри́с|а[2]**, ы** *f.* **1.** (*math.*) directrix. **2.** (*mil.*): **д. стрельбы́** base line.

дире́кци|я, и *f.* management; board (of directors).
дирижа́бл|ь, я *m.* airship, dirigible.
дирижёр, а *m.* conductor (*of band or orchestra*).
дирижёр|ский *adj. of* ~; **~ская па́лочка** conductor's baton.
дирижи́р|овать, ую *impf.* (+*i.*; *mus.*) to conduct.
дисгармони́р|овать, ую *impf.* **1.** (*mus.*) to be out of tune. **2.** (*fig.*) to clash, jar; to be out of keeping.
дисгармо́ни|я, и *g.* (*mus. and fig.*) disharmony; discord.
диск, а *m.* **1.** disk; **д. номеронабира́теля** telephone dial. **2.** (*sport*) discus. **3.** (cartridge-)drum (*of automatic weapon*). **4.** disc, record; **д.-гига́нт** long-playing record, LP.
ди́скант, а *m.* (*mus.*) treble.
дисквалифика́ци|я, и *f.* disqualification.
дисквалифици́р|овать, ую *impf. and pf.* to disqualify.
диске́т, а *m.* (*comput.*) diskette; **пусто́й д.** blank diskette.
диске́т|а, ы *f.* = **диске́т**
диск-жоке́|й, я *m.* disc-jockey.
дискобо́л, а *m.* discus-thrower.
диск|ова́ть, у́ю *impf.* (*agric.*) to disc-harrow.
дискове́чер, а *m.* disco(thèque) (*event*).
дисково́д, а *m.* (*comput.*) disk drive.
ди́сков|ый *adj.* disc-shaped; **~ая борона́** disc-harrow.
диско́нт, а *m.* (*fin.*) discount.
дисконти́р|овать, ую *impf. and pf.* (*fin.*) to discount.
ди́скос, а *m.* (*eccl.*) paten.
дискоте́к|а, и *f.* disco(thèque) (*place*).
дискоте́|чный *adj. of* **~ка**
дискредити́р|овать, ую *impf. and pf.* to discredit.
дискриминацио́нный *adj.* discriminatory.
дискримина́ци|я, и *f.* discrimination; **д. же́нщин** sexism; **д. по во́зрасту** ageism.
дискримини́р|овать, ую *impf. and pf.* to discriminate against; to deprive of equality of rights, **д. национа́льные меньшинства́** to discriminate against national minorities.
дискуссио́нн|ый *adj.* **1.** *adj. of* **диску́ссия; д. клуб** debating club; **в ~ом поря́дке** as a basis for discussion. **2.** debatable, open to question.
диску́сси|я, и *f.* discussion.
дискути́р|овать, ую *impf. and pf.* (+*a. or* **о**+*p.*) to discuss.
дислока́ци|я, и *f.* **1.** (*mil.*) stationing, distribution (*of troops*). **2.** (*geol.*) displacement. **3.** (*med.*) dislocation.
дислоци́р|овать, ую *impf. and pf.* (*mil.*) to station (*troops*).
диспансе́р, а *m.* (*med.*) clinic, (health) centre (*for treatment and prevention of disease*).
диспансериза́ци|я, и *f.* clinic system, health centre system.
диспепси́|я, и *f.* dyspepsia.
диспе́тчер, а *m.* controller (*of movement of transport, etc.*); (*aeron.*) flying control officer.
диспе́тчер|ский *adj. of* ~; (*aeron.*): **~ская вы́шка** control tower; **~ская слу́жба** flying control organization; *as n.* **~ская, ~ской** *f.* controller's office; (*aeron.*) control tower.
диспле́|й, я *m.* (*comput.*) display, VDU (*visual display unit*).
ди́спут, а *m.* disputation, debate; public defence of dissertation.
диссерта́нт, а *m.* author of dissertation.
диссерта́ци|я, и *f.* dissertation, thesis.
диссиде́нт, а *m.* (*relig.*) nonconformist.
диссимиля́ци|я, и *f.* dissimilation.
диссона́нс, а *m.* (*mus. and fig.*) dissonance, discord.
диссони́р|овать, ую *impf.* to strike a discordant note, be discordant.
дистанцио́нн|ый *adj.*: **д. взрыва́тель, ~ая тру́бка** time fuse; **~ое управле́ние** remote control.
дistáнци|я, и *f.* **1.** distance; **на большо́й, ма́лой ~и** at a great, short distance. **2.** (*sport*) distance; **сойти́ с ~и** to withdraw, scratch. **3.** (*mil.*) range. **4.** (*rail.*) division, region.
дистилли́р|овать, ую *impf. and pf.* to distil.
дистилля́ци|я, и *f.* distillation.
дистрофи́|я, и *f.* (*med.*) dystrophy.
дисципли́н|а, ы *f.* (*in var. senses*) discipline.
дисциплина́рный *adj.* disciplinary; **д. батальо́н** penal battalion.
дисциплини́рова|нный *p.p.p. of* **~ть** *and adj.* disciplined.
дисциплини́р|овать, ую *impf. and pf.* to discipline.
дитя́, *g. and d.* **~ти,** *i.* **~тею,** *p.* **о ~ти;** *pl.* **де́ти** *nt.* child; baby.
дифира́мб, а *m.* **1.** dithyramb. **2.** (*fig.*) eulogy; **петь ~ы** (+*d.*) to sing the praises (of), extol, eulogize.
дифтер|ийный *adj. of* **~и́я**; diphtheritic.
дифтер|и́т, а *m.* = **~и́я**
дифтер|и́тный = **~и́йный**
дифтери́|я, и *f.* diphtheria.
дифто́нг, а *m.* diphthong.
диффама́ци|я, и *f.* (*leg.*) defamation, libel.
дифференциа́л, а *m.* **1.** (*math.*) differential. **2.** (*tech.*) differential gear.
дифференциа́льн|ый *adj.* differential; **~ое исчисле́ние** (*math.*) differential calculus.
дифференци́р|овать, ую *impf. and pf.* to differentiate.
дича́|ть, ю *impf.* (*of* **о~**) to run wild, become wild; (*fig.*) to become unsociable.
дичи́н|а, ы *f.* (*coll.*) game.
дич|и́ться, у́сь, и́шься *impf.* (+*g.*; *coll.*) to be shy (of); to avoid.
дич|о́к, ка́ *m.* **1.** wilding (*wild fruit-bearing plant*). **2.** (*fig.*) shy pers.
дич|ь, и *f.* **1.** (*collect.*) game; wildfowl. **2.** wilderness, wilds. **3.** (*coll.*) nonsense; **поро́ть д.** to talk nonsense.
диэле́ктрик, а *m.* (*phys.*) dielectric, non-conductor.
длан|ь, и *f.* (*arch. or poet.*) palm (*of hand*).
длин|а́, ы́ *f.* length; **в ~у́** longwise, lengthwise; **во всю ~у́** at full length; **ме́ры ~ы́** long measures; **~о́й в шесть ме́тров** six metres long.
длинно... *comb. form* long-.
длинново́лновый *adj.* (*radio*) long-wave.
длиннот|а́, ы́, *pl.* **~́ы** *f.* **1.** (*obs or coll.*) length. **2.** (*pl.*) longueurs, prolixities.
длиннофо́кусный *adj.*: **д. объекти́в** telephoto lens.
длинню́щий *adj.* (*coll.*) (terribly) long.
дли́н|ный (~ен, ~на́, ~но) *adj.* long; lengthy; **д. рубль** (*coll.*) easy money, quick money; **у него́ д. язы́к** he has a long tongue.
дли́тельност|ь, и *f.* duration.
дли́тел|ьный (~ен, ~ьна) *adj.* long, protracted, long-drawn-out; **~ьная боле́знь** lingering illness.
дл|и́ться, и́тся *impf.* (*of* **про~**) to last.
для *prep.*+*g.* **1.** for (the sake of); **э́то д. тебя́** this is for you. **2.** (*expr. purpose*) for; **маши́на д. выка́чивания воды́** machine for pumping out water; **я э́то сде́лал то́лько д. ви́ду** I only did for appearances' sake; **д. того́, что́бы...** in order to .... **3.** for, to (= *in relation to, in respect of*); **д. нас не сто́ит** for us it is not worth while; **вре́дно д. дете́й** bad for children; **непроница́емый д. воды́** waterproof. **4.** for, of (= *in relation to a stated norm*); **он о́чень высо́к д. свои́х лет** he is very tall for his age; **э́то поведе́ние типи́чно д. них** such behaviour is typical of them.
днева́л|ить, ю, ишь *impf.* (*coll.*) to be on duty.
днева́льн|ый, ого *m.* (*mil.*) orderly, fatigue man.
днева́ть, дню́ю, дню́ешь *impf.* to spend the day; **д. и ночева́ть** to spend all one's time.
днёвк|а, и *f.* day's rest.
дневни́к, а́ *m.* diary, journal; **вести́ д.** to keep a diary.
дневн|о́й *adj.* **1.** day; **в ~о́е вре́мя** during daylight hours; **д. свет** daylight; **~а́я сме́на** day shift; **д. спекта́кль** matinée. **2.** day's, daily; **~а́я зарпла́та** day's pay.
днём *adv.* **1.** in the day-time, by day. **2.** in the afternoon; **сего́дня д.** this afternoon.
дни́щ|е, а *nt.* bottom (*of vessel or barrel*).
ДНК *f. indecl.* (*abbr. of* **дезоксирибонуклеи́новая кислота́**) (*chem.*) DNA (*deoxyribonucleic acid*).
дно, дна, *pl.* **до́нья, до́ньев** *nt.* **1.** bottom (*of sea, river, etc.*); **идти́ ко дну** to go to the bottom, sink; **золото́е д.** (*fig.*) gold-mine. **2.** bottom (*of vessel*); **вверх дном** upside down; **пить до дна** to drink to the dregs; **(пей) до дна!** bottoms up!; **ни дна ему́ ни покры́шки!** (*coll.*) bad luck to him!
дноуглуби́тел|ь, я *m.* dredger.
до *prep.*+ *g.* **1.** (*of place or indicating length, etc.*) to, up to; as far as; **от Ло́ндона до Москвы́** from London to

Moscow; **доехать до Парижа** to go as far as Paris; **юбка до колен** knee-length skirt. **2.** (*of time*) to, up to; until, till; **до шести часов** till six o'clock; **работать от девяти (часов) до шести** to work from nine (o'clock) to six; **до сих пор** up to now, till now, hitherto; **до тех пор** till then, before; **до тех пор, пока** until; **до свидания!** good-bye!; au revoir! **3.** before; **до войны** before the war; **до нашей эры (до н. э.)** before Christ (*abbr.* BC); **до того, как** before. **4.** (*expr. degree or limiting point*) to, up to, to the point of; **до боли** until it hurt(s); **до того..., что** to the point where; **мы до того устали, что и заснуть не удалось** we were too tired even to be able to sleep. **5.** under, up to (= *not over, not more than*); **дети до пяти лет** children under five; under-fives; **зарабатывать до тысячи рублей** to earn up to a thousand roubles. **6.** about, approximately; **у нас в больнице до двух тысяч коек** in our hospital there are about two thousand beds. **7.** with regard to, concerning; **что до меня** as far as I am concerned; **у меня до тебя дело** (*coll.*) I want (to see) you, I want a word with you; **не быть охотник до** not to be keen on, not to like; **мне,** *etc.*, **не до** (*coll.*) I, *etc.*, don't feel like, am not in the mood for; **мне не до разговора** I am not in a mood for talk.

до...[1] *vbl. pref.* **1.** *expr. completion of action*: **дочитать книгу** to finish (reading) a book. **2.** *indicates that action is carried to a certain point*: **дочитать до страницы 270** to read as far as page 270. **3.** *expr. supplementary action*: **докупить** to buy in addition. **4.** (*+refl. vv.*) *expr. eventual attainment of object*: **дозвониться** to ring until one gets an answer. **5.** (*+refl. vv.*) *expr. continuation of action with injurious consequences*: **доиграться до беды** (*coll.*) to carry on until one gets into a mess.

до...[2] *pref. of nn. and adjs., used to indicate priority in chronological sequence* (pre-).

добав|ить, лю, ишь *pf.* (*of* **~лять**) (*+a. or g.*) to add.

добавк|а, и *f.* **1.** addition. **2.** second helping.

добавлени|е, я *nt.* addition; appendix, addendum; extra.

добавля|ть, ю *impf. of* **добавить**

добавочн|ый *adj.* additional, supplementary; accessory; **~ое время** (*sport*) extra time; **д. налог** surtax; **~ая труба** (*tech.*) extension pipe.

добега|ть, ю *impf. of* **добежать**

добега|ться, юсь *pf.* (**до**+*g.*) to run o.s. (to the point of); **д. до усталости** to tire o.s. out running.

добе|жать, гу, жишь, гут *pf.* (*of* **~гать**) (**до**+*g.*) to run (to, as far as); to reach (*also fig.*).

добела *adv.* **1.** to white heat; **раскалённый д.** white-hot. **2.** clean, white; **чёрного кобеля не отмоешь д.** (*prov.*) the leopard can't change his spots.

добива|ть, ю *impf. of* **добить**

добива|ться, юсь *impf.* **1.** *impf. of* **добиться. 2.** (*+g.*) to try to get, strive (for), aim (at).

добира|ть, ю *impf. of* **добрать**

добира|ться, юсь *impf. of* **добраться**

до|бить, бью, бьёшь *pf.* (*of* **~бивать**) to finish off, do for, deal the final blow (*also in var. senses corresponding to meanings of pref. and simple v.*).

до|биться, бьюсь, бьёшься *pf.* (*of* **добиваться**) (*+g.*) to get, obtain, secure; **д. своего** to get one's way; **не д. толку от кого-н.** to be unable to get any sense out of s.o.

доблест|ный (~ен, ~на) *adj.* valiant, valorous.

доблест|ь, и *f.* valour, gallantry; **трудовая д.** devoted work *or* service.

до|брать, беру, берёшь, *past* **~брал, ~брала, ~брало** *pf.* (*of* **~бирать**) **1.** to finish gathering. **2.** (*typ.*) to finish setting up.

до|браться, берусь, берёшься, *past* **~брался, ~бралась, ~бралось** *pf.* (*of* **~бираться**) **1.** (**до**+*g.*) to get (to), reach. **2.** (*coll.*) to get, deal with; **я до тебя ~берусь!** I'll get you!

добрачн|ый *adj.* pre-marital; **~ая фамилия** maiden name.

добре|сти, ду, дёшь, *past* **~л, ~ла** *pf.* (**до**+*g.*) to get (to), reach (*slowly or with difficulty*).

добре|ть[1]**, ю, ешь** *impf.* (*of* **по~**) to become kinder.

добре|ть[2]**, ю, ешь** *impf.* (*of* **раз~**) (*coll.*) to become corpulent, put on weight.

добр|о[1]**, а** *nt.* **1.** good; good deed; **желаю вам ~а** I wish you well; **от ~а ~а не ищут** let well alone; **нет худа без ~а** every cloud has a silver lining; **это не к ~у** it is a bad omen, it bodes ill; **поминать ~ом** to speak well (of), remember kindly. **2.** (*collect.*; *coll.*) goods, property. **3.: дать/получить добро** to give/get the go-ahead.

добро[2] *particle* (*coll.*) good; all right.

добро[3]**: д. пожаловать!** welcome!

добро[4] *as conj.* (**+бы**) it would be a different matter if; there would be some excuse if.

доброво́л|ец, ьца *m.* volunteer.

добровольно *adv.* voluntarily, of one's own free will.

доброволь|ный (~ен, ~ьна) *adj.* voluntary.

добровольческий *adj.* volunteer.

добродетел|ь, и *f.* virtue.

добродетель|ный (~ен, ~ьна) *adj.* virtuous.

добродуши|е, я *nt.* good-nature.

добродуш|ный (~ен, ~на) *adj.* good-natured; genial.

доброжелател|ь, я *m.* well-wisher.

доброжелатель|ный (~ен, ~ьна) *adj.* benevolent.

доброкачествен|ный (~, ~на) *adj.* **1.** of good quality. **2.** (*med.*) benign.

добром *adv.* (*coll.*) of one's own free will, voluntarily.

добронрав|ный (~ен, ~на) *adj.* (*obs.*) well-behaved.

добропорядоч|ный (~ен, ~на) *adj.* respectable.

добросердеч|ный (~ен, ~на) *adj.* good-hearted.

добросовест|ный (~ен, ~на) *adj.* conscientious.

добрососедский *adj.* (good-)neighbourly; friendly.

добрососедств|о, а *nt.* (good-)neighbourliness.

доброт|а, ы *f.* goodness, kindness.

добротност|ь, и *f.* (good) quality; **д. сукна** quality of cloth.

доброт|ный (~ен, ~на) *adj.* of good, high quality; durable.

доброхот, а *m.* (*obs.*) well-wisher.

доброхот|ный (~ен, ~на) *adj.* (*obs.*) **1.** benevolent. **2.** voluntary.

добрый (~, ~а, ~о, ~ы) *adj.* **1.** (*in var. senses*) good; **~ое имя** good name; **д. конь** good horse; **д. знакомый** good friend; **д. малый** decent chap; **~ое утро!** good morning!; **всего ~ого!** good-bye!, all the best!; **в д. час!** good luck!; **по ~у по здорову** while the going is (was) good. **2.** kind, good; **будьте ~ы** (*+imper.*) please, would you be so kind as to. **3.** (*coll.*) a good (= *fully, not less than*); **осталось нам идти ~ых пять км** we had still a good five kilometres to go. **4.: по ~ой воле** of one's own free will. **5.: чего ~ого** (*introducing expr. of anticipation of unpleasant eventuality*) who knows; it may be.

добряк, а *m.* (*coll.*) good-natured pers.

добу|диться, жусь, ~дишься *pf.* (*coll.*) to wake, succeed in waking.

добыва|ть, ю *impf. of* **добыть**

добытчик, а *m.* (*coll.*) **1.** getter (*of minerals, etc.*). **2.** bread-winner.

до|быть, буду, будешь, *past* **~был, ~была, ~было** *pf.* (*of* **~бывать**) **1.** to get, obtain, procure. **2.** to extract, mine, quarry.

добыч|а, и *f.* **1.** extraction (*of minerals*), mining, quarrying. **2.** booty, spoils, loot. **3.** (*hunting*) bag; catch (*of fish*). **4.** mineral products; output.

довարив|ать, аю *impf. of* **доварить**

довар|ить, ю, ~ишь *pf.* (*of* **~ивать**) **1.** to finish cooking; to do to a turn. **2.** to cook a little longer.

доведа|ться, юсь *pf.* (*obs. or coll.*) to find out by inquiry.

довез|ти, у, ёшь, *past* **~, ~ла** *pf.* (*of* **довозить**[1]) to take (to).

доверенност|ь, и *f.* **1.** warrant, power of attorney; **получить деньги по ~и** to obtain money by proxy. **2.** (*obs.*) trust.

довер|енный *p.p.p. of* **~ить** *and adj.* trusted; **~енное лицо**; *as n.* **д., ~енного** *m.* agent, proxy; pers. empowered to act for s.o.

довери|е, я *nt.* trust, confidence; **меры ~я** confidence-building measures; **пользоваться чьим-н. ~ем** to enjoy s.o.'s confidence; **поставить вопрос о ~и** to call for a vote of confidence.

доверител|ь, я *m.* principal (*pers. empowering another to act for him*).
доверительный *adj.* **1.** confiding. **2.** (*obs.*) confidential (= *classified*; *of documents*). **3.** (*obs.*) empowering to act for one.
дове́р|ить, ю, ишь *pf.* (*of* **~я́ть**) (+*d.*) to entrust (to).
дове́р|иться, юсь, ишься *pf.* (*of* **~я́ться**) (+*d.*) to trust (in), confide (in).
до́верху *adv.* to the top; to the brim.
дове́рчивост|ь, и *f.* trustfulness, credulity.
дове́рчив|ый (~, ~а) *adj.* trustful, credulous; gullible.
доверш|а́ть, а́ю *impf. of* **~и́ть**
доверше́ни|е, я *nt.* completion, consummation; **в д. всего́** to crown all; on top of it all.
доверш|и́ть, у́, и́шь *pf.* (*of* **~а́ть**) to complete.
довер|я́ть, я́ю *impf.* **1.** *impf. of* **~ить. 2.** (*impf. only*) (+*d.*) to trust, confide (in).
довер|я́ться, я́юсь *impf. of* **~иться**
дове́с|ок, ка *m.* makeweight.
дове|сти́, ду́, дёшь, *past* **~л, ~ла́** *pf.* (*of* **доводи́ть**) **1.** (**до**+*g.*) to lead (to), take (to), accompany (to). **2.** (**во**+*g.*) to bring (to); to drive (to), reduce (to); **д. до соверше́нства** to perfect; **д. до сумасше́ствия** to drive mad; **д. до слёз** to reduce to tears; **д. до све́дения** (+*g.*) to inform, let know, bring to the notice (of).
дове|сти́сь, дётся, *past* **~ло́сь** *pf.* (*of* **доводи́ться**) (*impers.*, +*d.*; *coll.*) to have occasion (to); to manage (to); to happen (to); **нам ~ло́сь заста́ть его́ до́ма** we happened to catch him in.
довин|ти́ть, чу́, ти́шь *pf.* (*of* **~чивать**) to screw up.
дови́нчива|ть, ю *impf. of* **довинти́ть**
довле́|ть, ет *impf.* **1.** (*obs*) to suffice; **д. себе́** to be self-sufficient; **~ет дне́ви зло́ба его́** sufficient unto the day is the evil thereof. **2.** (**над**+*i.*; *vulg.*) to dominate, prevail over.
до́вод, а *m.* argument.
дово|ди́ть, жу́, ~дишь *impf. of* **довести́**
дово|ди́ться, жу́сь, ~дишься *impf.* **1.** *impf. of* **довести́сь. 2.** (+*d. and i.*) to be related (to as); **он ~дится ей племя́нником** he is her nephew.
дово́дк|а, и *f.* (*tech.*) finishing; lapping.
довое́нный *adj.* pre-war; ante-bellum.
дово|зи́ть[1]**, жу́, ~зишь** *impf. of* **довезти́**
дово|зи́ть[2]**, жу́, ~зишь** *pf.* (*coll.*) to finish carrying.
дово́льно[1] *adv.* **1.** enough; *as pred.* it is enough; **с нас э́того д.** we've had enough of this; **д. спо́рить!** stop arguing! **2.** quite, fairly; rather, pretty **д. хоро́ший фильм** quite a good film; **д. глу́пый челове́к** rather a stupid pers.
дово́льно[2] *adv.* contentedly.
дово́л|ьный (~ен, ~ьна) *adj.* **1.** contented, satisfied; **д. вид** contented expression. **2.** (+*i.*) contented (with), satisfied (with), pleased (with); **д. собо́й** pleased with o.s., self-satisfied; **он не осо́бенно ~ен но́вой рабо́той** he does not like his new job very much. **3.** (*obs.*) considerable.
дово́льстви|е, я *nt.* (*mil.*) allowance (*of money*, *food or clothing*).
дово́льств|о, а *nt.* **1.** content, contentment. **2.** (*coll.*) ease, prosperity.
дово́льств|овать, ую *impf.* **1.** (*obs.*) to satisfy, make content. **2.** (*mil.*) to supply, maintain.
дово́льств|оваться, уюсь *impf.* (*of* **у~**) **1.** (+*i.*) to be content (with), be satisfied (with). **2.** *pass. of* **~овать**
довооруж|а́ться, аюсь *impf. of* **~и́ться**
довооруже́ни|е, я *nt.* (*mil.*, *pol.*) strengthening of one's defences; **д. НАТО** modernization of NATO.
довооруж|и́ться, у́сь, и́шься *pf.* (*of* **~а́ться**) (*mil.*, *pol.*) to strengthen one's defences.
довре́менный *adj.* (*obs.*) premature.
довы́бор|ы, ов *no sg.* by-election.
дог, а *m.* mastiff; **да́тский д.** Great Dane; **далма́тский д.** Dalmatian.
догад|а́ться, а́юсь *pf.* (*of* **~ываться**) to guess; to have the sense to.
дога́дк|а, и *f.* **1.** surmise, conjecture; **теря́ться в ~ах** to be lost in conjecture. **2.** (*coll.*) imagination; **прояви́ть ~у** to be on the spot.
дога́длив|ый (~, ~а) *adj.* quick-witted, shrewd.
дога́дыва|ться, юсь *impf.* **1.** *impf. of* **догада́ться. 2.** (*impf. only*) to suspect.
догля|де́ть, жу́, ди́шь *pf.* (*coll.*) **1.** to watch to the end, see through. **2.** to keep an eye out; (**за**+*i.*) to keep an eye (on).
до́гм|а, ы *f.* **1.** dogma, dogmatic assertion. **2.** (*pl.*) foundations, bases (*of a theory*, *intellectual discipline*, *etc.*).
до́гмат, а *m.* **1.** (*relig.*) doctrine, dogma; **д. непогреши́мости Па́пы** the doctrine of the infallibility of the Pope. **2.** tenet, foundation; **одни́м из ~ов ло́гики явля́ется зако́н тожде́ственности** the law of identity is one of the foundations of logic.
догмати́зм, а *m.* dogmatism (*in general*, *also in Marxist pol. jargon*, *as a deviation opposed to revisionism*).
догма́тик, а *m.* **1.** dogmatic pers. **2.** 'dogmatist' (*in Marxist pol. jargon*, *as opposed to revisionist*).
догмати́ческий *adj.* dogmatic.
до|гна́ть, гоню́, го́нишь, *past* **~гна́л, ~гнала́, ~гна́ло** *pf.* (*of* **~гоня́ть**) **1.** to catch up (with) (*also fig.*); **д. и перегна́ть За́пад** (*pol. slogan*) to catch up with and pass the West. **2.** (**до**+*g.*) to drive (to); (*fig.*, *coll.*) to raise (to).
догова́рива|ть, ю *impf. of* **договори́ть**
догова́рива|ться, юсь *impf.* **1.** *impf. of* **договори́ться. 2.** (*impf. only*) (**о**+*p.*) to negotiate (about), treat (for); **Высо́кие ~ющиеся сто́роны** (*dipl.*) the High Contracting Parties.
догово́р, а *and* (*coll.*) **до́говор,** *pl.* **~а́** *m.* agreement; (*pol.*) treaty, pact; **Варша́вский д.** Warsaw Pact; **заключи́ть ми́рный д.** to conclude a peace treaty.
договорённост|ь, и *f.* agreement, understanding; (*pol.*) accord.
договор|и́ть, ю́, и́шь *pf.* (*of* **догова́ривать**) to finish saying; to finish telling.
договор|и́ться, ю́сь, и́шься *pf.* (*of* **догова́риваться**) **1.** (**о**+*p.*) to come to an agreement, understanding (about); to arrange; **~и́лись!** agreed!; it's a deal! **2.** (**до**+*g.*) to come (to); to talk (to the point of).
догово́рник, а *m.* (*coll.*) worker under contract for a particular job.
догово́рн|ый *adj.* **1.** agreed; contractual; **~ая цена́** agreed price. **2.** fixed by treaty.
догола́ *adv.* stark naked; **разде́ться д.** to strip to the skin.
догоня́л|ки, ок *no sg.* (*children's game*) 'it', tag.
догоня́|ть, ю *impf. of* **догна́ть**
догор|а́ть, а́ю *impf. of* **~е́ть**
догор|е́ть, ю́, и́шь *pf.* (*of* **~а́ть**) to burn down, burn out.
догружа́|ть, ю *impf. of* **догрузи́ть**
догру|зи́ть, жу́, ~зи́шь *pf.* (*of* **~жа́ть**) **1.** to finish loading. **2.** to load in addition.
догу́лива|ть, ю *impf. of* **догуля́ть**
догуля́|ть, ю *pf.* (*of* **догу́ливать**) (*coll.*) to spend in pleasure (the remainder of); **дава́йте ~ем о́тпуск** let's make the most of what's left of the holidays.
дода|ва́ть, ю́, ёшь *impf. of* **~ть**
дода́|ть, м, шь, ст, ди́м, ди́те, ду́т, *past* **до́дал, ~ла́, до́дало** *pf.* (*of* **~ва́ть**) to make up (the rest of); to pay up.
доде́л|ать, аю *pf.* (*of* **~ывать**) to finish.
доде́лыва|ть, ю *impf. of* **доде́лать**
доду́м|аться, аюсь *pf.* (*of* **~ываться**) (**до**+*g.*) to hit (upon) (*afterthought*).
доду́мыва|ться, юсь *impf. of* **доду́маться**
доеда́|ть, ю *impf. of* **дое́сть**
доезжа́|ть, ю *impf. of* **дое́хать**
доезжа́ч|ий, его *m.* whipper-in.
дое́ни|е, я *nt.* milking.
до|е́сть, е́м, е́шь, е́ст, еди́м, еди́те, едя́т *pf.* (*of* **~еда́ть**) to eat up, finish eating.
до|е́хать, е́ду, е́дешь *pf.* (*of* **~езжа́ть**) **1.** (**до**+*g.*) to reach, arrive (at). **2.** (*fig.*, *coll.*) to wear out.
дож, а *m.* (*hist.*) doge.
дожа́рива|ть, ю *impf. of* **дожа́рить**
дожа́р|ить, ю, ишь *pf.* (*of* **~ивать**) to finish roasting, frying; to roast, fry to a turn.
дожд|а́ться, у́сь, ёшься, *past* **~а́лся ~ала́сь, ~ало́сь** *pf.* **1.** (+*g.*) to wait (for); **д. конца́ спекта́кля** to wait until

the end of the show. **2.**: **д. того́, что** to end up (by); **он ~а́лся того́, что ему́ показа́ли дверь** he ended up by being shown the door.
дождева́льный *adj.*: **д. аппара́т** (*agric.*) water-sprinkler.
дождева́ни|е, я *nt.* (*agric.*) irrigation by sprinkling.
дождеви́к, а́ *m.* **1.** (*coll.*) raincoat. **2.** puff-ball (*Lycoperdon giganteum*).
дождев|о́й *adj. of* **дождь; ~а́я ка́пля** rain-drop; **~о́е о́блако** rain-cloud, nimbus; **~о́е пла́тье** oilskins.
дождеме́р, а *m.* rain-gauge.
до́ждик, а *m.* shower.
дожди́нк|а, и *f.* (*coll.*) rain-drop.
дожд|и́ть, и́т *impf.* (*impers.*; *coll.*) to rain, be raining.
дождли́в|ый (~, ~а) *adj.* rainy.
дожд|ь, я́ *m.* **1.** rain (*also fig.*); **под ~ём** in the rain; **кратковре́менный д.** (light) shower; **ме́лкий д.** drizzle; **проливно́й д.** downpour; **кисло́тные ~и́** acid rain; **д. идёт** it is raining; **д. льёт как из ведра́** it's raining cats and dogs; it's bucketing down. **2.** (*fig.*) rain, hail, cascade; **д. искр** cascade of sparks; **д. руга́тельств** torrent of abuse; **сы́паться ~ём** to rain down, cascade.
дожива́|ть, ю *impf.* **1.** *impf. of* **дожи́ть. 2.** (*impf. only*) to live out; **д. свой век** to live out one's days.
дожига́тел|ь, я *m.* (*tech.*) afterburner.
дожида́|ться, юсь *impf.* (*of* **дожда́ться**) (+*g.*) to wait (for).
дожи́н|ки, ок *no sg.* (*dial.*) harvest festival.
до|жи́ть, живу́, живёшь, *past* **~́жил, ~лила́, ~́жило** *pf.* (*of* **~жива́ть**) **1.** (**до**+*g.*) to live (till); to attain the age (of); **она́ ~жила́ до конца́ войны́** she lived to see the end of the war. **2.** (**до**+*g.*) to come (to), be reduced (to); **до чего́ мы ~́жили!** what have we come to! **3.** (*coll.*) to stay, spend (the rest of); **я доживу́ ле́то в Пари́же** I shall spend the rest of the summer in Paris.
до́з|а, ы *f.* dose.
дозапра́вк|а, и *f.* refuelling.
дозасто́йный *adj.* pre-stagnation (*euph., i.e. pre-Brezhnev*).
доза́тор, а *m.* measure, measuring hopper.
до|зва́ться, зову́сь, зовёшься, *past* **~зва́лся, ~звала́сь, ~звало́сь** *pf.* (*coll.*) to call until one gets an answer; **его́ не ~зовёшься** he never comes when he is called.
дозволе́ни|е, я *nt.* (*obs.*) permission.
дозво́л|енный *p.p.p. of* **~ить** *and adj.* permitted.
дозво́л|ить, ю, ишь *pf.* (*of* **~я́ть**) (*obs. or coll.*) to permit, allow.
дозвол|я́ть, я́ю, *impf. of* **~́ить**
дозвон|и́ться, ю́сь и́шься *pf.* (*coll.*) (**до**+*g.*, **к**+*d.*) to ring (*at doorbell, on telephone*) until one gets an answer; to get through (*on telephone*); **я не мог к тебе́ д.** I rang you but could get no reply, could not get through.
дозвуково́й *adj.* subsonic.
дози́р|овать, ую *impf. and pf.* to measure out (in doses).
дозиро́вк|а, и *f.* dosage.
дозна|ва́ться, ю́сь, ёшься *impf.* **1.** *impf. of* **~́ться. 2.** (*only impf.*) (**о**+*p.*) to inquire (about).
дозна́ни|е, я *nt.* (*leg.*) inquiry; inquest.
дозн|а́ться, а́юсь *pf.* (*of* **~ава́ться**) to find out, ascertain.
дозо́р, а *m.* patrol.
дозо́р|ный *adj. of* **~; ~ная шлю́пка** patrol boat; *as n.* **д., ~ного** *m.* (*mil.*) scout.
дозрева́|ть, ю *impf. of* **дозре́ть**
дозре́лый *adj.* fully ripe.
дозр|е́ть, е́ю *pf.* (*of* **~ева́ть**) to ripen.
доигр|а́ть, а́ю *pf.* (*of* **~́ывать**) to finish (playing).
доигр|а́ться, а́юсь *pf.* (*of* **~́ываться**) (**до**+*g.*) to play (until); (*fig.*) to get o.s. (into), land o.s. (in); **вот и ~а́лся!** now you've (he's, *etc.*) done it!
доигрыва|ть(ся), ю(сь) *impf. of* **доигра́ть(ся)**
дои́льн|ый *adj.*: **~ая маши́на** milking machine.
до́ильщица, ы *f.* = **доя́рка**
до|иска́ться, ищу́сь, и́щешься *pf.* (*of* **~и́скиваться**) (*coll.*) **1.** (+*g.*) to find, discover. **2.** to find out, ascertain.
дои́скива|ться, юсь *impf.* **1.** *impf. of* **доиска́ться. 2.** (*impf. only*) to try to find out.
доистори́ческий *adj.* prehistoric.
доисто́ри|я, и *f.* prehistory.
до|и́ть, ю́, ~́ишь *impf.* (*of* **по~**) to milk; (*fig.*) to milk (*of money*).
до|и́ться, ~́ится *impf.* **1.** to give milk; **хорошо́ д.** to be a good milker. **2.** *pass. of* **~и́ть**
до́йк|а, и *f.* milking.
до́йн|ый *adj.* milch; **~ая коро́ва** milch cow (*also fig.*).
до|йти́, йду́, йдёшь, *past* **~шёл, ~шла́** *pf.* (*of* **~ходи́ть**) **1.** (**до**+*g.*) (*in var. senses*) to reach; **письмо́ ~шло́ до меня́ то́лько сего́дня** the letter only reached me today; **слух ~шёл до нас** a rumour reached us; **д. до све́дения** (+*g.*) to come to the notice (of), come to the ears (of); **д. до того́, что...** to reach a point where ...; **ру́ки не ~шли́** (**до**+*g.*) I, *etc.*, had no time (for). **2.** (*coll.*) (**до**+*g.*) to make an impression (upon), get through (to), penetrate (to), touch; **его́ про́поведь про́сто не ~шла́ до слу́шателей** his homily left his audience quite unmoved. **3.** (*impers.*; *also* **де́ло ~йдёт, ~шло́ до**+*g.*) to come (to), be a matter (of); **де́ло ~шло́ до проце́сса** it came to a court case. **4.** (*coll.*) to be done (= *to be cooked*); to be ripe.
док, а *m.* dock.
до́к|а, и *c.g.* (*coll.*) expert, authority.
доказа́тел|ьный (~ен, ~ьна) *adj.* demonstrative, conclusive.
доказа́тельств|о, а *nt.* **1.** proof, evidence. **2.** (*maths.*) demonstration.
док|аза́ть, ажу́, а́жешь *pf.* (*of* **~а́зывать**) **1.** to demonstrate, prove; **счита́ть ~а́занным** to take for granted; **что и тре́бовалось д.** (*maths.*) quod erat demonstrandum (*abbr.* Q.E.D.). **2.** (*coll.*): **д. на кого́-н.** to inform on s.o.
доказу́ем|ый (~, ~а) *adj.* demonstrable.
дока́зыва|ть, ю *impf.* **1.** *impf. of* **доказа́ть. 2.** (*impf. only*) to argue, try to prove.
дока́нчива|ть, ю *impf. of* **доко́нчить**
дока́пыва|ться, юсь *impf. of* **докопа́ться**
док|ати́ться, ачу́сь, а́тишься *pf.* (*of* **~а́тываться**) **1.** (**до**+*g.*) to roll (to). **2.** (*of sounds*) to roll, thunder, boom. **3.** (*fig., coll.*) (**до**+*g.*) to sink (into), come (to); **д. до преступле́ния** to sink into crime.
дока́тыва|ться, юсь *impf. of* **докати́ться**
до́кер, а *m.* docker.
докла́д, а *m.* **1.** report; lecture; paper; talk, address; **чита́ть д.** to give a report, read a paper. **2.** announcement (*of arrival of guest, etc.*); **войти́ без ~а** to enter unannounced.
докладн|о́й *adj.*: **~а́я запи́ска** report, memorandum; *as n.* **~а́я, ~о́й** *f.* = **~а́я запи́ска.**
докла́дчик, а *m.* speaker, lecturer; reader of a report.
докла́дыва|ть(ся), ю(сь) *impf. of* **доложи́ть(ся)**
доко́ле (and доко́ль) *adv.* (*obs.*) **1.** (*interrog.*) how long. **2.** (*rel.*) as long as; until.
доколу́мбов *adj.* pre-Columbian; **~о иску́сство** pre-Columbian art.
докона́|ть, ю *pf.* (*coll.*) to finish off, be the end (of).
доко́нч|ить, у, ишь *pf.* (*of* **дока́нчивать**) to finish, complete.
докопа́|ться, юсь *pf.* (*of* **дока́пываться**) (**до**+*g.*) **1.** to dig down (to). **2.** (*fig.*) to get to the bottom (of); to find out, discover.
до́красна́ *adv.* to redness; to red heat; **раскалённый д.** red-hot.
докрич|а́ться, у́сь, и́шься *pf.* **1.** to shout until one is heard. **2.**: **д. до хрипоты́** to shout o.s. hoarse.
до́ктор, а, *pl.* **~а́** *m.* doctor.
доктора́льный *adj.* didactic.
доктора́нт, а *m.* pers. working for degree of doctor.
до́ктор|ский *adj. of* **~; ~ская диссерта́ция** thesis for degree of doctor.
до́кторш|а, и *f.* (*coll.*) **1.** doctor's wife. **2.** woman-doctor.
доктри́н|а, ы *f.* doctrine.
доктринёр, а *m.* doctrinaire.
доктринёрский *adj.* doctrinaire
доктринёрств|о, а. *nt.* doctrinaire attitude.
доку́да *adv.* (*coll.*) **1.** (*interrog.*) how far. **2.** (*rel.*) as far as.
доку́к|а, и *f.* (*obs. or coll.*) tiresome request.
докуме́нт, а *m.* **1.** document, paper; **предъяви́ть ~ы** to produce one's papers. **2.** (*leg.*) deed; instrument.

документали́ст, а *m.* documentary film-maker.
документа́льный *adj.* documentary; **д. фильм** documentary (film).
документа́ци|я, и *f.* **1.** documentation. **2.** (*collect.*) documents, papers.
документи́р|овать, ую *impf. and pf.* to document.
докуп|а́ть[1], **а́ю** *impf. of* **~и́ть**
докупа́|ть[2], **ю** *pf.* to finish bathing (*trans.*).
докуп|и́ть, лю́, ~́ишь *pf.* (*of* **~а́ть**[1]) to buy in addition.
докуча́|ть, ю *impf.* (+*d. and i.*; *coll.*) to bother (with), pester (with), plague (with).
доку́члив|ый (~, ~а) *adj.* (*coll.*) tiresome, importunate.
доку́ч|ный (~ен, ~на) *adj.* (*coll.*) tiresome, boring.
дол, а *m.* (*poet.*) dale, vale; **за гора́ми, за ~а́ми** far and wide; **по гора́м, по ~а́м** up hill and down dale.
долбёжк|а, и *f.* (*sl.*) swotting; **учи́ться в ~у** to learn by rote.
долб|и́ть, лю́, и́шь *impf.* **1.** to hollow; to chisel, gouge. **2.** (*coll.*) to repeat, say over and over. **3.** (*sl.*) to swot (up); to learn by rote.
долбоёб, а *m.* (*vulg.*) wanker, dickhead.
долг, а, о ~́е, в ~у́, *pl.* **~и́** *m.* **1.** duty; **по ~́у слу́жбы** in the performance of one's duty. **2.** debt; **в д.** on credit; **войти́, влезть в ~и́** to get into debt; **быть у кого́-н. в ~у́** to be indebted to s.o.; **отда́ть после́дний д.** to pay the last honours; **д. платежо́м кра́сен** one good turn deserves another.
до́л|гий (~ог, ~га́, ~го) *adj.* long, of long duration; **~гая пе́сня** (*fig.*) a long story; **отложи́ть в д. я́щик** to shelve, put off.
до́лго *adv.* **1.** long, a long time. **2.: д. ли** (+*inf. or* **до**+*g.*) one may easily, it can easily happen that; **д. ли до беды́** accidents will happen.
долгове́ч|ный (~ен, ~на) *adj.* lasting; long-lived.
долгов|о́й *adj. of* **долг 2.**; **~о́е обяза́тельство** promissory note; **~о́е отделе́ние** (*hist.*) debtor's prison.
долговре́менн|ый *adj.* of long duration; **~ая огнева́я то́чка, ~ое огнево́е сооруже́ние** (*mil.*) pillbox (*of reinforced concrete*).
долговя́з|ый (~, ~а) *adj.* (*coll.*) lanky.
долгогри́вый *adj.* shaggy-maned.
долгоде́нстви|е, я *nt.* (*obs.*) long life.
долгожи́тел|ь, я *m.* old-timer, senior citizen.
долгоигра́ющ|ий *adj.*: **~ая пласти́нка** long-playing (gramophone) record.
долголе́ти|е, я *nt.* longevity.
долголе́тний *adj.* of many years; of many years' standing, long-standing.
долгоно́сик, а *m.* weevil.
долгосро́чный *adj.* long-term; of long duration.
долгот|а́, ы́, *pl.* **~́ы** *f.* **1.** (*sg. only*) duration. **2.** longitude.
долготерпели́в|ый (~, ~а) *adj.* long-suffering.
долготерпе́ни|е, я *nt.* long-suffering.
долгун|е́ц, ца́ *m.* **(лён-)д.** long-stalked flax (*commercial brand*).
долево́й[1] *adj.* lengthwise.
долев|о́й[2] *adj. of* **до́ля; ~о́е отчисле́ние** royalty.
до́лее *comp. of* **до́лго**
долет|а́ть, а́ю *impf. of* **~е́ть**
доле|те́ть, чу́, ти́шь, *pf.* (*of* **~та́ть**) (**до**+*g.*) **1.** to fly (to, as far as). **2.** to reach (*also fig.*); to be wafted (to).
должа́|ть, ю *impf.* (*of* **за~**) (*obs.*) **1.** (**у**+*g.*) to borrow (from). **2.** (+*d.*) to owe.
до́лж|ен (~на́, ~но́) *pred. adj.* **1.** owing; **он д. мне три рубля́** he owes me three roubles. **2.** (+*inf.*) *expr. obligation*; **я д. идти́** I must go, I have to go; **он д. был отказа́ться** he had to refuse. **3.** (+*inf.*) *expr. probability or expectation*; **она́ ~на́ ско́ро прийти́** she should be here soon; **~но́ быть** probably; **вы с ним, ~но́ быть, уже́ знако́мы** you must have met him; you probably met him.
долженств|ова́ть, у́ю *impf.* (+*inf.*; *obs.*) to be obliged (to); to be intended (to).
должни́к, а́ *m.* debtor.
до́лжно *as pred.* (+*inf.*) one should, ought (to).
должностн|о́й *adj.* official; **~о́е лицо́** official, functionary, public servant; **~о́е преступле́ние** malfeasance in office.
до́лжност|ь, и, *g. pl.* **~е́й** *f.* post, appointment, office; duties.
до́лжн|ый *adj.* due, fitting, proper; **~ым о́бразом** properly; *as n.* **~ое, ~ого** due; **воздава́ть д.** (+*d.*) to do justice.
долива́|ть, ю *impf. of* **доли́ть**
доли́вк|а, и *f.* refilling, replenishment; refuelling.
доли́н|а, ы *f.* valley.
доли́н|ный *adj. of* **~а**
дол|и́ть, ью́, ьёшь, *past* **~́ил, ~ила́, ~́ило** *pf.* (*of* **~ива́ть**) **1.** to add; to pour in addition. **2.** to fill (up); to refill.
до́ллар, а *m.* dollar.
долож|и́ть[1], **у́, ~́ишь** *pf.* (*of* **докла́дывать**) **1.** (+*a. or* **о**+*p.*) to report; to give a report (on). **2.** (**о**+*p.*) to announce (*a guest, etc.*).
долож|и́ть[2], **у́, ~́ишь** *pf.* (*of* **докла́дывать**) to add.
долож|и́ться, у́сь, ~́ишься *pf.* (*of* **докла́дываться**) to announce one's arrival.
доло́й *adv.* (+*a.*; *coll.*) down (with), away (with); **д. изме́нников!** down with the traitors!; **уйди́ с глаз д.!** out of my sight! **2.** off (with); **ша́пки д.!** hats off!
долот|о́, а́, *pl.* **~́а, ~́** *nt.* chisel.
до́лу *adv.* (*poet.*) down, downwards.
до́льк|а, и *f.* segment, clove.
до́льний *adj.* (*poet.*) **1.** *adj. of* **дол. 2.** earthly, terrestrial.
до́льше *adv.* longer.
до́л|я, и, *g. pl.* **~е́й** *f.* **1.** part, portion; share; quota, allotment; **войти́ в ~ю** (**с**+*i.*) to go shares (with); **в его́ слова́х не́ было и ~и и́стины** there was not a grain of truth in his words; **кни́га в четвёртую, восьму́ю ~ю листа́** quarto, octavo. **2.** (*anat., bot.*) lobe. **3.** lot, fate; **вы́пасть на чью-н. ~ю** to fall to s.o.'s lot. **4.** (*obs.*) dolia (*measure of weight, equivalent to 44 milligrams*).
дом, а (у), *pl.* **~а́** *m.* **1.** (*in var. senses*) building, house; block (of flats); **д. культу́ры** palace of culture; ≃ arts (and leisure) centre; **д. о́тдыха** rest home, holiday home; **Д. учёных** Scientists' Club; **д. терпи́мости** brothel; **д.-музе́й…** … House; **д.-музе́й Пу́шкина** Pushkin House. **2.** home; house, household; **вести́ д.** to keep house, run the house; **хлопота́ть по ~́у** to busy o.s. with housework, with domestic chores; **на ~у́** at home; **брать рабо́ту на́ д.** to take work home; **тоска́ по ~́у** homesickness. **3.** house (= *dynasty*), lineage; **д. Рома́новых** the House of Romanov.
дом… *comb. form, abbr. of* **1. домо́вый. 2. дома́шний**
до́ма *adv.* at home, in; **быть как д.** to feel at home; **бу́дьте как д.** make yourself at home; **у него́ не все д.** he's not all there.
домаркси́стский *adj.* pre-Marxist.
домаха́|ть, ю *pf.* (*coll.*) (**до**+*g.*) to get (to).
дома́шн|ий *adj.* **1.** house; home; domestic; **д. а́дрес** home address; **~ие забо́ты** household chores; **~ее пла́тье** house dress; **~яя рабо́тница** domestic servant; **~яя хозя́йка** housewife; **под ~им аре́стом** under house arrest. **2.** home-made; homespun; home-brewed. **3.** tame (*opp. wild*); domestic; **~ие живо́тные** domestic animals; **~ие пти́цы** poultry. **4.** *as n.* **~ие, ~их** one's people, one's family.
дома́шност|ь, и *f.* (*coll. or dial.*) **1.** housekeeping. **2.** household equipment.
доме́н, а *m.* (*hist.*) domain, state lands.
до́менн|ый *adj. of* **до́мна; ~ая печь** blast furnace.
до́менщик, а *m.* blast-furnace operator.
до́мик, а *m. dim. of* **дом**
домина́нт|а, ы *f.* **1.** (*mus.*) dominant. **2.** (*fig.*) leitmotif.
доминика́н|ец, ца *m.* Dominican (monk).
Доминика́нск|ая Респу́блик|а, ~ой ~и *f.* the Dominican Republic.
доминио́н, а *m.* dominion (*member of British Commonwealth*).
домини́р|овать, ую *impf.* **1.** to dominate, prevail (*fig.*). **2.** (*geog.*) (**над**+*i.*) to dominate, command.
домино́ *indecl.*, **1.** dominoes (*game*). **2.** domino (*costume*).
доми́ш|ко, ~ка, *pl.* **~ки, ~ек, ~кам** *m.* (*coll.*) small, wretched house; hovel.

домко́м, а *m.* (*abbr. of* **домо́вый комите́т**) house management committee.
домкра́т, а *m.* (*tech.*) jack.
до́мн|а, ы *f.* blast furnace.
домо... *comb. form* **1.** home-. **2.** *abbr. of* (*i*) **домо́вый** *and* (*ii*) **дома́шний**
домови́н|а, ы *f.* (*dial.*) coffin.
домови́т|ый (~, ~а) *adj.* thrifty, economical; **~ая хозя́йка** good housewife.
домовладе́л|ец, ьца *m.* house-owner; land-lord.
домовни́ц|а, ы *f.* (*coll. or dial.*) housekeeper.
домовни́ча|ть, ю *impf.* (*coll. or dial.*) to keep house.
домово́дств|о, а *nt.* (art of) housekeeping; household management; home economics.
домов|о́й, о́го *m.* (*folklore*) brownie, house-sprite.
домо́в|ый *adj.* **1.** house; household; **~ая кни́га** house register, register of tenants; **~ая конто́ра** house-manager's office; **д. пау́к** house-spider. **2.** housing; **д. трест** housing trust.
домога́тельств|о, а *nt.* **1.** solicitation, importunity. **2.** demand, bid; **д. госпо́дства** bid for power.
домога́|ться, юсь *impf.* (+*g.*) to seek (after), solicit, covet.
домоде́льный *adj.* home-made.
домо́й *adv.* home, homewards; **нам пора́ д.** it's time for us to go home.
домоправи́тел|ь, я *m.* (*obs.*) steward.
домоправле́ни|е, я *nt.* (*obs.*) household management.
доморо́щенный *adj.* **1.** home-bred. **2.** (*fig.*) crude; primitive; homespun.
домосе́д, а *m.* stay-at-home.
домостро́евский *adj.* authoritarian, harsh.
домострое́ни|е, я *nt.* house-building.
домострои́тельный *adj.* house-building.
домотка́ный *adj.* home-spun.
домоуправле́ни|е, я *nt.* house management (committee).
домохозя́|ин, ина, *pl.* **~ева, ~ев** *m.* **1.** householder. **2.** (*obs.*) head of peasant household.
домохозя́йк|а, и *f.* housewife.
домоча́д|ец, ца *m.* (*obs.*) member of household.
до́мр|а, ы *f.* (*mus.*) domra (*Russ. stringed instrument similar to mandolin*).
домрабо́тниц|а, ы *f.* domestic (servant), maid; **приходя́щая д.** home help; daily.
домраче́|й, я *m.* (*obs.*) = **домри́ст**
домри́ст, а *m.* domra-player.
дому́шник, а *m.* (*sl.*) burglar, housebreaker.
домч|а́ть, у́, и́шь *pf.* (*coll.*) to bring quickly (*in a vehicle, etc.*).
домч|а́ться, у́сь, и́шься *pf.* (*coll.*) to reach quickly (*at a run or gallop*).
до́мыс|ел, ла *m.* conjecture.
дон *int.* (*onomat.*) ding-dong.
донага́ *adv.* stark naked.
дона́шива|ть, ю *impf. of* **доноси́ть**[1]
доне́льзя *adv.* to the utmost; in the extreme; **он д. упря́м** he is obstinate in the extreme.
донесе́ни|е, я *nt.* dispatch, report, message; **д. о боевы́х поте́рях** casualty report.
донес|ти́[1]**, у́, ёшь,** *past* **~́, ~ла́** *pf.* (*of* **доноси́ть**[2]) (**до**+*g.*) to carry (to, as far as); to carry, bear (*a sound or smell*).
донес|ти́[2]**, у́, ёшь,** *past* **~́, ~ла́** *pf.* (*of* **доноси́ть**[3]) **1.** to report, announce; (+*d.*) to inform. **2.** (**на**+*a.*) to inform (on, against), denounce.
донес|ти́сь, у́сь, ёшься, *past* **~́ся, ~ла́сь** *pf.* (*of* **доноси́ться**[2]) **1.** (*of sounds or smells, also of news, etc.*) to reach; **до нас уже́ ~́ся слух** a rumour had already reached us. **2.** (*coll.*) to reach quickly.
дон|е́ц, ца́ *m.* Don Cossack.
донжуа́н, а *m.* Don Juan, philanderer.
донжуа́нств|о, а *nt.* philandering.
до́низу *adv.* to the bottom.
донима́|ть, ю *impf. of* **доня́ть**
донкихо́тский *adj.* quixotic.
донкихо́тств|о, а *adj.* quixotry.
до́нник, а *m.* (*bot.*) melilot, sweet clover.
до́нный *adj. of* **дно**; **д. лёд** ground ice; **д. заря́д** (*mil.*) base charge.
до́нор, а *m.* (blood-)donor.
до́нор|ский *adj. of* **~**; **д. пункт** blood donation centre.
доно́с, а *m.* denunciation, information, delation.
дон|оси́ть[1]**, ошу́, ~о́сишь** *pf.* (*of* **дона́шивать**) **1.** to finish carrying. **2.** to wear out. **3.: д. ребёнка** to bear at full term.
дон|оси́ть[2,3]**, ошу́, ~о́сишь** *impf. of* **донести́**[1,2]
дон|оси́ться[1]**, ~о́сится** *pf.* to wear out, be worn out.
дон|оси́ться[2]**, ~о́сится** *impf. of* **донести́сь**
доно́счик, а *m.* informer.
донско́й *adj.* (of the river) Don; **д. каза́к** Don Cossack.
до́нц|е, а *nt. dim. of* **дно**
доны́не *adv.* (*rhet.*) hitherto.
до|ня́ть, йму́, йме́шь, *past* **~́нял, ~няла́, ~́няло** *pf.* (*of* **~нима́ть**) (*coll.*) to weary, tire out, exasperate.
дообе́денный *adj.* pre-prandial.
дооктя́брьский *adj.* pre-October (*before the Russ. Revolution of October 1917*).
допека́|ть, ю *impf. of* **допе́чь**
допетро́вский *adj.* pre-Petrine (*before time of tsar Peter the Great*).
допе́|чь, ку́, чёшь, ку́т, *past* **~́к, ~кла́** *pf.* (*of* **~ка́ть**) **1.** to bake until done; to finish baking. **2.** (*fig., coll.*) to wear out, plague, pester.
допива́|ть, ю *impf. of* **допи́ть**
до́пинг, а *m.* **1.** stimulant. **2.** (*fig.*) **(психологи́ческий) д.** boost, shot in the arm.
до́пинговый *adj.*: **д. контро́ль** dope test; dope testing.
допи|са́ть, шу́, ~́шешь *pf.* (*of* **~́сывать**) **1.** to finish writing. **2.** to add.
допи́сыва|ть, ю *impf. of* **дописа́ть**
доп|и́ть, ью́, ьёшь, *past* **~́йл, ~ила́, ~́йло** *pf.* (*of* **~ива́ть**) to drink (up).
допла́т|а, ы *f.* additional payment; excess fare.
допл|ати́ть, ачу́, ~а́тишь *pf.* (*of* **~а́чивать**) to pay in addition, in excess.
допла́чива|ть, ю *impf. of* **доплати́ть**
доплыва́|ть, ю *impf. of* **доплы́ть**
доплы́|ть, ву́, вёшь, *past* **~л, ~ла́, ~ло** *pf.* (*of* **~ва́ть**) (**до**+*g.*) to swim (to, as far as); to sail (to, as far as); (*fig.*) to reach.
допо́длинно *adv.* (*coll.*) for certain.
допо́длинный *adj.* (*coll.*) authentic, genuine.
дополне́ни|е, я *nt.* **1.** supplement, addition; addendum. **2.** (*gram.*) object; **прямо́е д.** direct object; **ко́свенное д.** indirect object.
дополни́тельно *adv.* in addition.
дополни́тельн|ый *adj.* supplementary, additional, extra; **~ое вре́мя** (*sport*) extra time; **д. окла́д** extra pay; **д. у́гол** (*math.*) supplement; **~ые цвета́** complementary colours.
допо́лн|ить, ю, ишь *pf.* (*of* **~я́ть**) to supplement, add to; (*fig.*) to embellish (*a story, etc.*); **д. друг дру́га** to complement one another.
дополн|я́ть, я́ю, *impf. of* **~́ить**
допото́пный *adj.* antediluvian.
допра́шива|ть, ю *impf. of* **допроси́ть**
допризы́вник, а *m.* youth undergoing pre-conscription military training.
допризы́вный *adj.* pre-conscription.
допро́с, а *m.* (*leg.*) interrogation, examination; **перекрёстный д.** cross-examination.
допр|оси́ть, ошу́, о́сишь *pf.* (*of* **~а́шивать**) (*leg.*) to interrogate, question, examine.
допр|оси́ться, ошу́сь, ~о́сишься *pf.* (*coll.*) **1.** to obtain, find out by asking; **у него́ ничего́ не ~о́сишься** one cannot get anything out of him. **2.** (+*g. or inf.*) to make, get (*to do sth.*).
до́пуск, а *m.* **1.** right of entry, admittance. **2.** (*tech.*) tolerance.
допуска́|ть, ю *impf. of* **допусти́ть**
допусти́м|ый (~, ~а) *adj.* permissible, admissible; **~ая нагру́зка** permissible load.
допу|сти́ть, щу́, ~́стишь *pf.* (*of* **~ска́ть**) **1.** (**до**+*g.* **к**+*d.*) to admit (to); **д. к ко́нкурсу** to allow to compete. **2.** to

allow, permit; to tolerate. **3.** to grant, assume; **∼стим** let us suppose, let us assume. **4.** to commit.

допуще́ни|е, я *nt.* assumption.

допыт|а́ться, а́юсь *pf.* (*of* **∼ываться**) to find out.

допы́тыва|ться, юсь *impf. of* **допыта́ться;** (*impf. only*) to try to find out, try to elicit.

до́пьяна́ *adv.* (*coll.*) dead drunk; **напои́ть д.** to make dead drunk.

дораст|а́ть, а́ю *impf. of* **∼и́**

дораст|и́, у́, ёшь, *past* **доро́с, доросла́** *pf.* (*of* **дорасти́ть**) **1.** (**до**+*g.*) to grow (to); (fig.) to attain (to), come up (to). **2. не д. что́бы** (+*inf.*) not to be old enough (to); **она́ ещё не доросла́, что́бы е́здить на велосипе́де** she is not old enough yet to ride a bicycle.

дорв|а́ться, у́сь, ёшься, *past* **∼а́лся, ∼а́ло́сь** *pf.* (**до;** *coll.*) to fall upon, seize upon.

дореволюцио́нный *adj.* pre-revolutionary.

дорефо́рменный *adj.* pre-reform (*esp. with reference to the emancipation of serfs and other reforms in Russia in the 1860s*).

дори́ческий *adj.* (*ling., archit.*) Doric, Dorian.

доро́г|а, и *f.* **1.** road, way (*also fig.*); **желе́зная д.** railway(s); **д. пе́рвого кла́сса** first-class road; **д. госуда́рственного значе́ния** national highway; **вы́йти на ∼у** to get on, succeed; **дать, уступи́ть кому́-н. ∼у** to let s.o. pass, make way for s.o. (*also fig.*); **идти́ свое́й ∼ой** to go one's own way; **перебежа́ть, переби́ть кому́-н. ∼у** to steal a march on s.o.; **пойти́ по плохо́й ∼е** to be on the downward path; **стать кому́-н. попере́к ∼и** to stand in s.o.'s way; **туда́ ему́ и д.** (*coll.*) it serves him right; **ска́тертью д.!** good riddance! **2.** journey; **отпра́виться в ∼у** to set out; **запасти́ прови́зии на ∼у** to lay in supplies for the journey; **в ∼е** on the journey, en route; **с ∼и** after the journey, from the road. **3.** (the) way, route; **показа́ть ∼у** to show the way, direct; **сби́ться с ∼и** to lose one's way; **нам с ни́ми бы́ло по ∼е** we went the same way; **нам с ни́м да́льше не́ было по ∼е** our ways parted (*also fig.*).

до́рого *adv.* dear, dearly; **д. обойти́сь** (+*d.*) to cost one dear; **д. бы я дал, что́бы...** (*coll.*) I would give anything to ....

дорогови́зн|а, ы *f.* dearness, expensiveness.

доро́гой *adv.* on the way, en route.

дорог|о́й (до́рог, дорога́, до́рого) *adj.* **1.** dear, expensive; costly; **по ∼о́й цене́** at a high price; **∼а́я побе́да** dearly-bought victory. **2.** dear; precious; *as n.* **д., ∼о́го** *m.*, **∼а́я, ∼о́й** *f.* (my) dear.

доро́д|ный (∼ен, ∼на) *adj.* portly, burly.

дородово́й *adj.* antenatal.

доро́дств|о, а *nt.* **1.** portliness, burliness. **2.** (*obs.*) courage, prowess.

дорожа́|ть, ет *impf.* (*of* **вз∼** *and* **по∼**) to rise (in price), go up.

доро́же *comp. of* **дорого́й** *and* **до́рого**

дорож|и́ть, у́, и́шь *impf.* (+*i.*) to value; to prize, set store (by).

дорож|и́ться, у́сь, и́шься *impf.* (*coll.*) to ask too high a price, overcharge.

доро́жк|а, и *f.* **1.** path, walk; **велосипе́дная д.** cycle-path *or* way. **2.** (*sport*) track; lane. **3.** (*aeron.*) runway. **4.** strip (*of carpet, linoleum or fabric*); runner. **5.** (*of tape recorder*) track.

доро́жник, а *m.* road-worker.

доро́жно-тра́нспортн|ый *adj.*: **∼ое происше́ствие** road *or* traffic accident.

доро́жн|ый *adj.* **1.** *adj. of* **доро́га; д. знак** road sign; **д. отде́л** highways department; **∼ая поли́ция** traffic police; **∼ое строи́тельство** road-building. **2.** travel, travelling; **д. буди́льник** travel alarm; **∼ые расхо́ды** travelling expenses. **3.** *as n.* **д., ∼ого** *m.* (*obs.*) traveller.

дорса́льный *adj.* dorsal.

дортуа́р, а *m.* (*obs.*) dormitory.

ДОСААФ *m.* (*indecl.*) (*abbr. of* ***Доброво́льное о́бщество соде́йствия а́рмии, авиа́ции и флоту́***) Voluntary Society for Cooperation with the Army, Air Force and Navy.

доса́д|а, ы *f.* vexation, disappointment, spite; **кака́я д.!** what a nuisance!

доса|ди́ть[1]**, жу́, ди́шь** *pf.* (*of* **∼жда́ть**) (+*d.*) to annoy, vex.

доса|ди́ть[2]**, жу́, ∼дишь** *pf.* to finish planting.

доса́длив|ый (∼, ∼а) *adj.* expressing vexation, irritation, disappointment; **д. жест** gesture of vexation.

доса́дно *as pred.* it is vexing, annoying; disappointing.

доса́д|ный (∼ен, ∼на) *adj.* vexing, annoying; disappointing.

доса́д|овать, ую *impf.* (**на**+*a.*) to be annoyed (with), be vexed (with).

досажда́|ть, ю *impf. of* **досади́ть**[1]

досе́ле *adv.* (*obs.*) up to now.

доси|де́ть, жу́, ди́шь *pf.* (*of* **∼живать**) (**до**+*g.*) to sit (until), stay (until).

доси́жива|ть, ю *impf. of* **досиде́ть**

доск|а́, и́, *a.* **∼у,** *pl.* **∼и,** *g.* **досо́к,** *d.* **∼а́м** *f.* **1.** board, plank; **д. для объявле́ний** notice-board; **д. почёта** board of honour (*with photographs and names of outstanding workers*); **ро́ликовая** *or* **ро́ллинговая д.** skateboard; **как д. (худо́й)** thin as a rake; **проче́сть от ∼и́ до ∼и́** to read from cover to cover; **ста́вить на одну́ ∼у** (**с**+*i.*) to put on a level (with); **пьян в ∼у** (*sl.*) dead drunk. **2.** slab; plaque, plate.

доско́к, а *m.* (*gymnastics*) landing.

доскона́л|ьный (∼ен, ∼ьна) *adj.* thorough.

до|сла́ть, шлю́, шлёшь *pf.* (*of* **∼сыла́ть**) **1.** to send in addition; to send the remainder. **2.** (*mil.*) to seat, chamber (*a cartridge, etc.*).

рассле́довани|е, я

досле́довани|е, я *nt.* (*leg.*) supplementary examination, further inquiry; **напра́вить де́ло на д.** to remit a case for further inquiry.

досле́д|овать, ую *impf. and pf.* (*leg.*) to submit to supplementary examination, further inquiry.

досло́вно *adv.* verbatim, word for word.

досло́вный *adj.* literal, verbatim; **д. перево́д** literal translation.

дослу́жива|ть(ся), ю(сь) *impf. of* **дослужи́ть(ся)**

дослуж|и́ть, у́, ∼ишь *pf.* (*of* **∼ивать**) (**до**+*g.*) to serve (until); to finish a period of service.

дослуж|и́ться, у́сь, ∼ишься *pf.* (*of* **∼иваться**) to obtain as a result of service; **д. до чи́на майо́ра** to rise to the rank of major; **д. до пе́нсии** to qualify for a pension.

досма́трива|ть, ю, *impf. of* **досмотре́ть**

досмо́тр, а *m.* examination (*at Customs, etc.*).

досмотр|е́ть, ю́, ∼ишь *pf.* (*of* **досма́тривать**) **1.** (**до**+*g.*) to watch, look at (to, as far as); **мы ∼е́ли пье́су до тре́тьего а́кта** we saw the play as far as the third act. **2. не д.** to overlook, to allow to escape one's notice.

досмо́трщик, а *m.* inspector, examiner.

досове́тский *adj.* pre-Soviet.

доспева́|ть, ю *impf. of* **доспе́ть**

доспе́|ть, ю, ешь *pf.* (*of* **∼ва́ть**) to ripen, mature; **вре́мя ∼ло** (*obs.*) the time has come.

доспе́х|и, ов *pl.* (*sg.* **∼, ∼а** *m.*) armour.

досро́чный *adj.* ahead of schedule, early.

доста|ва́ть(ся), ю́(сь), ёшь(ся) *impf. of* **∼ть(ся)**

доста́в|ить, лю, ишь *pf.* (*of* **∼ля́ть**) **1.** to deliver, convey; to supply, furnish. **2.** to give, cause; **д. слу́чай** to afford an opportunity; **д. удово́льствие** to give pleasure.

доста́вк|а, и *f.* delivery, conveyance (*of goods, etc.*).

доставля́|ть, ю *impf. of* **доста́вить**

доста́вщик, а *m.* delivery man, roundsman.

доста́ива|ть, ю *impf. of* **достоя́ть**

доста́т|ок, ка *m.* **1.** sufficiency. **2.** prosperity; **жить в ∼ке** to be comfortably off; **сре́днего ∼ка** middle-income. **3.** (*pl. only*) income.

доста́точно[1] *adv.* sufficiently, enough.

доста́точно[2] *as pred.* it is enough; **д. сказа́ть** suffice it to say; **д. бы́ло одного́ взгля́да** one glance was enough.

доста́точност|ь, и *f.* **1.** sufficiency. **2.** (*obs.*) easy circumstances.

доста́точ|ный (∼ен, ∼на) *adj.* **1.** sufficient. **2.** (*coll.*) prosperous, well-to-do.

доста́|ть, ну, нешь *pf.* (*of* **∼ва́ть**) (+*d.*) **1.** to fetch; to take out; **д. плато́к из карма́на** to take a handkerchief out of one's pocket. **2.** (+*g. or* **до**+*g.*) to touch; to reach; **д.**

руко́й до потолка́ to touch the ceiling. **3.** to get, obtain. **4.** (*impers.*, +*g.*; *coll.*) to suffice.

доста́|ться, нусь, нешься *pf.* (*of* **~ва́ться**) (+*d.*) **1.** to pass (to) (by inheritance); **ему́ ~лось большо́е име́ние** he came into a large estate. **2.** to fall to one's lot. **3.** (*impers.*; *coll.*): **ему́** *etc.*, **~нется** he, *etc.*, will catch it.

достига́|ть, ю *impf. of* **дости́гнуть** *and* **дости́чь**

дости́г|нуть, ну, нешь, *past* **~, ~ла** *pf.* (*of* **~а́ть**) **1.** (+*g. or* **до**+*g.*) to reach; **д. га́вани** to reach harbour; **д. ста́рости** to reach old age; **слух ~ до на́ших уше́й** a rumour had come to our ears. **2.** (+*g.*) to attain, achieve.

достиже́ни|е, я *nt.* achievement, attainment.

достижи́м|ый (~, ~а) *adj.* accessible; attainable.

дости́чь = дости́гнуть

достове́рност|ь, и *f.* authenticity; trustworthiness.

достове́р|ный (~ен, ~на) *adj.* authentic; trustworthy; reliable.

достодо́лжный *adj.* (*obs.*) due, just.

достое́вщин|а, ы *f.* **1.** mental imbalance (*as exemplified esp. by characters in the novels of Dostoevsky*). **2.** analysis of character in the manner of Dostoevsky.

досто́инств|о, а *nt.* **1.** merit, virtue. **2.** (*sg. only*) dignity; **чу́вство со́бственного ~а** self-respect. **3.** (*econ.*) value; **моне́ты ма́лого ~а** coins of small denomination. **4.** (*obs.*) rank, title.

досто́йно *adv.* **1.** suitably, fittingly, adequately, properly. **2.** (*obs.*) with dignity.

досто́|йный (~ин, ~йна) *adj.* **1.** (+*g.*) worthy (of), deserving; **д. внима́ния** worthy of note; **д. похвалы́** praiseworthy. **2.** deserved; fitting, adequate; **~йная награ́да** deserved reward. **3.** suitable, fit. **4.** worthy.

достопа́мят|ный (~ен, ~на) *adj.* memorable.

достопочте́нный *adj.* (*obs.*) venerable; (*iron.*) worthy.

достопримеча́тельност|ь, и *f.* sight; place, object of note; **осма́тривать ~и** to go sight-seeing, see the sights.

достопримеча́тел|ьный (~ен, ~ьна) *adj.* remarkable, notable.

достоя́ни|е, я *nt.* property.

досто|я́ть, ю́, и́шь *pf.* (*of* **доста́ивать**) to wait standing (until).

досту́ка|ться, юсь *pf.* (*coll.*) to get what one had been asking for, get the punishment one deserves.

до́ступ, а *m.* **1.** entrance. **2.** access, admission, admittance.

досту́п|ный (~ен, ~на) *adj.* **1.** accessible; easy of access. **2.** (**для**+*g*) open (to); available (to). **3.** simple; easily understood; intelligible. **4.** (*of prices*) moderate, reasonable; **~ные це́ны** affordable prices. **5.** affable, approachable. **6.**: **~ная же́нщина** (*obs.*) loose woman, woman of easy virtue.

достуч|а́ться, у́сь, и́шься *pf.* (*coll.*) to knock until one is heard.

досу́г, а *m.* **1.** leisure, leisure-time; **на ~е** at leisure, in one's spare time. **2.** *as pred.* (+*d. and inf.*; *coll.*) to have time (to, for); **где мне д. чита́ть?** what time have I for reading?

досу́ж|ий *adj.* (*coll.*) **1.** leisure; **~ее вре́мя** leisure-time, spare time. **2.** idle; **~ие разгово́ры** idle talk.

до́суха *adv.* (until) dry; **вы́тереть д.** to rub dry.

досчита́|ть, ю *pf.* (*of* **досчи́тывать**) **1.** to finish counting. **2.** (**до**+*g.*) to count (up to); **д. до ста** to count up to a hundred.

досчи́тыва|ть, ю *impf. of* **досчита́ть**

досыла́|ть, ю *impf. of* **досла́ть**

досы́п|ать, лю, лешь *pf.* (*of* **~а́ть**) to pour in, fill up.

досып|а́ть, а́ю *impf. of* **~ать**

до́сыта *adv.* (*coll.*) to satiety.

досье́ *nt. indecl.* dossier, file.

досю́да *adv.* (*coll.*) as far as here, up to here.

досяга́емост|ь, и *f.* reach; (*mil.*) range; **вне преде́лов ~и** beyond reach.

досяга́ем|ый (~, ~а) *adj.* attainable, accessible.

дот, а *m.* (*abbr. of* **долговре́менная огнева́я то́чка**) (*mil.*) (*reinforced concrete*) pill-box.

дота́скива|ть(ся), ю(сь) *impf. of* **дотащи́ть(ся)**

дота́ци|я, и *f.* (State) grant, subsidy.

дотащ|и́ть, у́, ~ишь *pf.* (*of* **дота́скивать**) (*coll.*) (**до**+*g.*) to carry, drag (to).

дотащ|и́ться, у́сь, ~ишься *pf.* (*of* **дота́скиваться**) (*coll.*) to drag o.s.; **ра́неный едва́ ~и́лся до свои́х пози́ций** the wounded man hardly managed to drag himself to his lines.

дотемна́ *adv.* until it gets (got) dark.

дотла́ *adv.* utterly, completely; **разорён д.** razed to the ground; **сгоре́ть д.** to burn to the ground.

дото́ле *adv.* (*obs.*) until then, hitherto.

дото́шный *adj.* (*coll.*) meticulous.

дотра́гива|ться, юсь *impf. of* **дотро́нуться**

дотро́н|уться, усь, ешься *pf.* (*of* **дотра́гиваться**) (**до**+*g.*) to touch.

дотя́гива|ть(ся), ю(сь), ешь(ся) *impf. of* **дотяну́ть(ся)**

дотян|у́ть, у́, ~ешь *pf.* (*of* **дотя́гивать**) (**до**+*g.*) **1.** to draw, drag, haul (to, as far as). **2.** (*coll.*) to reach, make. **3.** to stretch out (to, as far as). **4.** (*coll.*) to hold out (till); to live (till); **он до утра́ не ~ет** he won't last till morning. **5.** (*coll.*) to put off (till).

дотян|у́ться, у́сь, ~ешься *pf.* (*of* **дотя́гиваться**) (**до**+*g.*) **1.** to reach; to touch. **2.** (*coll.*) to stretch (to), reach; **о́чередь ~у́лась до конца́ у́лицы** the queue stretched to the end of the street. **3.** (*coll.*; *of time*) to drag by (until).

доу́чива|ть(ся), ю(сь) *impf. of* **доучи́ть(ся)**

доуч|и́ть, у́, ~ишь *pf.* (*of* **~ивать**) **1.** to finish teaching; (**до**+*g.*) to teach (up to). **2.** to finish learning; (**до**+*g.*) to learn (up to, as far as).

доуч|и́ться, у́сь, ~ишься *pf.* (*of* **~иваться**) **1.** to complete one's studies, finish one's education. **2.** (**до**+*g.*) to study (up to, till).

дох|а́, и́, *pl.* **~и** *f.* fur-coat (*with fur on both sides*).

до́хлый *adj.* **1.** dead (*of animals*). **2.** (*coll.*) sickly; weakly (*of human beings*).

дохля́тин|а, ы *f. and c.g.* (*coll.*) **1.** *f.* carcass; (*collect.*) carrion. **2.** *c.g.* feeble, sickly pers.

до́х|нуть, ну, нешь, *past* **~, ~ла** *impf.* (*of* **по~**) to die (*of animals*).

дохн|у́ть, у́, ёшь *pf.* **1.** to breathe (*of a single breath*) **тут д. не́где** there is no room to breathe here. **2.** to blow.

дохо́д, а *m.* income; receipts; revenue.

доходи́ть, жу́, ~дишь *impf. of* **дойти́**

дохо́дност|ь, и *f.* profitableness; income.

дохо́д|ный (~ен, ~на) *adj.* **1.** profitable, lucrative, paying. **2.** *adj. of* **~**

дохо́дчив|ый (~, ~а) *adj.* intelligible, easy to understand.

доходя́г|а, и *m.* (*sl.*) goner.

дохристиа́нский *adj.* pre-Christian.

доце́нт, а *m.* senior lecturer, (university) reader.

доценту́р|а, ы *f.* **1.** post of senior lecturer; readership. **2.** (*collect.*) = **доце́нты.**

до́чери, до́черью *see* **дочь**

до́черин = доче́рнин

доче́рн|ий *adj.* **1.** daughter's. **2.** daughter; branch; **~ее предприя́тие** (*comm.*) branch (*establishment*).

доче́рнин *adj.* (*coll.*) daughter's.

до́чиста *adv.* **1.** clean; **вы́мыть д.** to wash clean. **2.** (*fig.*, *coll.*) clean, completely; **его́ обыгра́ли д.** they cleaned him out (*at cards*).

дочит|а́ть, а́ю *pf.* (*of* **~ывать**) **1.** to finish reading. **2.** (**до**+*g*) to read (to, as far as).

дочит|а́ться, а́юсь *pf.* (*of* **~ываться**) (*coll.*) (**до**+*g.*) to read (to the point of).

дочи́тыва|ть(ся), ю(сь) *impf. of* **дочита́ть(ся)**

до́чк|а, и *f.* (*coll.*) = **дочь**

дочу́рк|а, и *f.* (*coll.*) *dim. of* **дочь**

доч|ь, ~ери, *i.* **~ерью,** *pl.* **~ери, ~ере́й, ~еря́м, ~ерьми́, о ~еря́х** *f.* daughter.

дошко́льник, а *m.* **1.** preschooler. **2.** specialist on training of preschool-age children.

дошко́льни|ца, ы *f. of* **~к**

дошко́льный *adj.* preschool.

до́шлый *adj.* (*coll.*) cunning, shrewd.

доща́ник, а *m.* flat-bottomed boat.

доща́тый *adj.* made of planks, boards; **д. насти́л** duckboards.

доще́чк|а, и *f.* **1.** *dim. of* **доска́. 2.** door-plate, name-plate.
доя́рк|а, и *f.* milkmaid.
д-р *abbr. of* **1. до́ктор** Dr, Doctor. **2. дире́ктор** Director.
др.: и ~ (*abbr. of* **и други́е**) & co.; *et al.*
дра́г|а, и *f.* (*tech.*) drag, dredge.
драги́р|овать *impf. and pf.* (*tech.*) to drag, dredge.
драго́й *adj.* (*obs. or poet.*) dear, precious.
драгома́н, а *m.* dragoman.
драгоце́нност|ь, и *f.* **1.** jewel; gem; precious stone; (*pl.*) jewellery. **2.** object of great value; (*pl.*) valuables.
драгоце́н|ный (~ен, ~на) *adj.* precious (*also fig.*); **~ные ка́мни** precious stones.
драгу́н, а, *g. pl.* **~** *m.* dragoon.
дража́йш|ий *superl. of* **дорого́й; ~ая полови́на** 'better half'.
драже́ *nt. indecl.* dragée; **шокола́дное д.** chocolate drop.
дразн|и́ть, ю́, ~ишь *impf.* **1.** to tease; **его́ ~и́ли тру́сом** they used to mock him by calling him a coward. **2.** to excite; to tantalize.
дра́|ить, ю, ишь *impf.* (*naut.*) to polish; to swab.
драйв, а *m.* drive (*in tennis*).
дра́к|а, и *f.* fight; **у них дошло́ до ~и** they came to blows.
драко́н, а *m.* **1.** dragon. **2.** (*heraldry*) wyvern.
драко́новский *adj.* Draconian.
дра́ла *as pred.* (*coll.*) (he) ran off, made off; **встал да и д.** he got up and made off; **дать д.** to take to one's heels.
дра́м|а, ы *f.* **1.** drama. **2.** (*fig.*) tragedy, calamity.
драматиза́ци|я, и *f.* dramatization.
драматизи́р|овать, ую *impf. and pf.* to dramatize.
драмати́зм, а *m.* **1.** (*theatr.*) dramatic effect. **2.** (*fig.*) dramatic character, quality; tension.
драмати́ческ|ий *adj.* **1.** dramatic; drama, theatre; **~ое иску́сство** dramatic art, art of the theatre; **д. теа́тр** theatre (*opp. cinema, ballet, opera*). **2.** dramatic, theatrical; **~им то́ном** in a dramatic tone. **3.** (*fig.*) dramatic; tense. **4.** (*mus.*) strong (*of a voice*).
драмати́ч|ный (~ен, ~на) *adj.* (*fig.*) dramatic.
драмату́рг, а *m.* playwright, dramatist.
драматурги́|я, и *f.* **1.** dramatic art. **2.** (*collect.*) plays, drama; **д. Че́хова** the plays of Chekhov. **3.** dramatic theory, drama.
драмкруж|о́к, ка́ *m.* dramatic circle.
драндуле́т, а *m.* (*coll., joc.*) jalopy, old banger.
драни́ц|а, ы *f.* (*dial.*) = **дра́нка**
дра́нк|а, и *f.* (*tech.*) **1.** lathing, shingle. **2.** lath.
дра́ночный *adj. of* **дра́нка**
дра́ный *adj.* (*coll.*) tattered, ragged.
дран|ь, и *f.* (*collect.; tech.*) lathing, shingle.
драп, а *m.* thick woollen cloth.
драпан|у́ть, у́, ёшь *pf. of* **дра́пать**
дра́па|ть, ю *impf.* (*of* **~ну́ть**) (*sl.*) to clear out, scarper.
драпир|ова́ть, у́ю *impf.* to drape.
драпир|ова́ться, у́юсь *impf.* **1.** (**в**+*a. or i.*) to drape o.s. (in); (*fig.*) to affect, make a parade (of). **2.** *pass. of* **~ова́ть**
драпиро́вк|а, и *f.* **1.** draping. **2.** curtain; hangings.
драпиро́вщик, а *m.* upholsterer.
дра́п|овый *adj. of* **~**
драпри́ *nt. indecl.* **1.** draperies. **2.** hangings, curtains.
дра́тв|а, ы *f.* waxed thread.
дра|ть, деру́, дерёшь, *past* **~л, ~ла́, ~ло** *impf.* **1.** (*impf. only*) to tear (up, to pieces); **д. го́рло** (*coll.*) to bawl; **д. нос** (*coll.*) to turn up one's nose, put on airs; **д. на себе́ во́лосы** (*fig.*) to tear one's hair. **2.** (*pf.* **со~**) to tear off; **д. лы́ко (с лип)** to bark (lime-trees); **д. шку́ру** to flay. **3.** (*pf.* **за~**) to kill (*of wild animals*). **4.** (*pf.* **вы́~**) (*coll.*) to beat, flog, thrash; to tear out; **д. зу́бы** to pull out teeth. **5.** (*pf.* **со~**) (**с**+*g.*; *fig., coll.*) to fleece; to sting; **д. с живо́го и мёртвого** to fleece unmercifully. **6.** (*pf.* **по~**): **чёрт его́ (по)дери́!** damn him! **7.** (*impf. only*) (*coll.*) to sting, irritate; **д. у́ши** (+*d.*) to jar (on); (*impers.*): **у меня́ в го́рле дерёт** I have a sore throat. **8.** (*impf. only*) (*coll.*) to run away, make off; **д. во все лопа́тки, со всех ног** to run as fast as one's legs can carry one.
дра́|ться, деру́сь, дерёшься, *past* **~лся, ~ла́сь, ~ло́сь** *impf.* **1.** (**с**+*i.*) to fight (with); **д. на дуэ́ли** to fight a duel. **2.** (*fig.*) (**за**+*a.*) to fight, struggle (for). **3.** (*pf.* **по~**) to hit, to give a hiding.
дра́хм|а, ы *f.* **1.** drachma (*Greek unit of currency*). **2.** dram (*apothecaries' weight*).
драце́н|а, ы *f.* (*bot.*) club palm, cabbage-tree (*Cordyline australis*).
драч[1], а́ *m.* (*tech.*) plane.
драч[2], а́ *m.* (*coll.*) flayer, knacker.
драчли́вост|ь, и *f.* pugnacity.
драчли́в|ый (~, ~а) *adj.* pugnacious.
драчу́н, а́ *m.* (*coll.*) pugnacious, quarrelsome fellow.
драчу́н|ья, и, *g. pl.* **~ий** (*coll.*) *f. of* **~**
ДРВ *f. indecl.* (*abbr. of* **Демократи́ческая Респу́блика Вьетна́м**) Democratic Republic of Vietnam.
дребеде́н|ь, и *f.* (*coll.*) nonsense; **сплошна́я д.** absolute rubbish.
дре́безг, а *m.* (*coll.*) **1.** tinkling sound (*as of breaking glass, etc.*). **2.** (*pl. only*) **разби́ть(ся) в (ме́лкие) ~и** to smash to smithereens.
дребезж|а́ть, и́т *impf.* to jingle, tinkle.
древеси́н|а, ы *f.* **1.** wood (*substance*); wood-pulp. **2.** timber.
древе́сниц|а, ы *f.* (*zool.*) **1.** tree-frog. **2.** leopard moth.
древесноволокни́ст|ый *adj.*: **~ая плита́** fibreboard.
древесностру́жечн|ый *adj.*: **~ая плита́** chipboard.
древе́сн|ый *adj. of* **де́рево; ~ая ма́сса** wood-pulp; **д. са́хар** wood sugar, xylose; **д. спирт** wood alcohol; **д. у́голь** charcoal; **д. у́ксус** (*chem.*) wood vinegar, pyroligneous acid.
дре́вк|о, а, *pl.* **~и, ~ов** *nt.* pole, staff; shaft (*of spear, etc.*); **д. зна́мени** flagstaff.
древлехрани́лищ|е, а *nt.* (*obs.*) archive.
древнегре́ческий *adj.* ancient, classical Greek.
древнеевре́йский *adj.* ancient, classical Hebrew.
древнеру́сский *adj.* Old Russian.
древнецерко́внославя́нский *adj.* (*ling.*) Old Church Slavonic.
дре́в|ний (~ен, ~ня) *adj.* **1.** ancient; **~няя исто́рия** ancient history; **~ние языки́** classical languages; *as n.* **~ние, ~них** the ancients. **2.** very old, aged.
дре́вност|ь, и *f.* **1.** (*sg. only*) antiquity. **2.** (*pl.*; *archaeol.*) antiquities.
дре́в|о, а, *pl.* **~еса́, ~е́с, ~еса́м** *nt.* (*poet.*) tree; **д. позна́ния добра́ и зла** the tree of the knowledge of good and evil.
древови́д|ный (~ен, ~на) tree-like; **д. па́поротник** tree-fern.
древонасажде́ни|е, я *nt.* **1.** tree-plantation. **2.** planting of trees.
дрези́н|а, ы *f.* (*rail.*) trolley, hand car.
дрейф, а *m.* (*naut.*) drift, leeway; **лечь в д.** to heave to; **лежа́ть в ~е** to lie to.
дре́йф|ить, лю, ишь *impf.* (*of* **с~**) (*coll.*) to be a coward, funk.
дрейф|ова́ть, у́ю *impf.* (*naut.*) to drift; **~у́ющий лёд** drift ice; **нау́чная ~у́ющая ста́нция** drift-ice research unit.
дрек, а *m.* (*naut.*) grapnel.
дреко́ль|е, я *nt.* (*collect.*) staves (*as weapon*).
дрел|ь, и *f.* (*tech.*) (hand-)drill.
дрем|а́, ы́ (*and* **дрём|а, ы**) *f.* (*poet.*) drowsiness, sleepiness.
дрем|а́ть, лю́, ~лешь *impf.* to doze; to slumber; **не д.** (*also fig.*) to be watchful; to be wide awake.
дрем|а́ться, ~лется *impf.* (*impers.,* +*d.*) to feel sleepy, drowsy.
дремо́т|а, ы *f.* drowsiness, sleepiness, somnolence.
дремо́тный *adj.* drowsy, sleepy, somnolent.
дрему́ч|ий (~, ~а) *adj.* (*poet.*) thick, dense (*of a forest*); (*fig.*) utter, complete.
дрена́ж, а *m.* **1.** (*tech. and med.*) drainage. **2.** (*med.*) drainage-tube.
дренажи́р|овать, ую *impf. and pf.* (*med.*) to drain.
дрена́ж|ный *adj. of* **~; ~ная труба́** drain-pipe.
дрени́р|овать, ую *impf. and pf.* to drain.
дресв|а́, ы́ *f.* gravel.
дрессиро́ванн|ый *p.p.p. of* **дрессирова́ть** *and adj.*: **~ые живо́тные** performing animals.
дрессир|ова́ть, у́ю *impf.* (*of* **вы́~**) to train (*animals*); (*fig.*) to school.
дрессиро́вк|а, и *f.* training.

дрессиро́вщик, а *m.* trainer.
дриа́д|а, ы *f.* (*myth.*) dryad.
дри́блинг, а *m.* (*sport*) dribbling.
дроби́лк|а, и *f.* (*tech.*) crusher.
дроби́льн|ый *adj.* (*tech.*) crushing; **~ая маши́на** crusher.
дроби́н|а, ы *f.* pellet.
дроб|и́ть, лю́, и́шь *impf.* (*of* **раз~**) **1.** to break up, crush, smash (to pieces). **2.** (*fig.*) to subdivide, split up.
дроб|и́ться, и́тся *impf.* (*of* **раз~**) **1.** to break to pieces, smash, smash to pieces. **2.** to divide, split up.
дробле́ни|е, я *nt.* **1.** crushing, breaking up. **2.** (*fig.*) subdivision, splitting up. **3.** (*biol.*) cell-division.
дроблёный *adj.* splintered, crushed, ground.
дробни́ц|а, ы *f.* ammunition-pouch.
дро́б|ный (~ен, ~на) *adj.* **1.** separate; subdivided, split up; minute. **2.** staccato, abrupt; **д. стук** staccato knocking; **д. дождь** fine rain. **3.** (*math.*) fractional.
дробови́к, а́ *m.* shot-gun.
дроб|ь, и, *pl.* **~и, ~е́й** *f.* **1.** (*collect.*) small shot. **2.** drumming; tapping; trilling. **3.** (*math.*) fraction. **4.** oblique stroke.
дров|а́, ~, ~а́м *no sg.* firewood; **наколо́ть д.** to chop firewood; **кто в лес, кто по дрова́** (*fig.*) at sixes and sevens, inharmoniously.
дро́вн|и, ~е́й *no sg.* (*peasant*) wood-sledge.
дровоко́л, а *m.* (*obs.*) woodcutter.
дровосе́к, а *m.* **1.** woodcutter. **2.** (*pl.*) (*zool.*) Cerambycidae.
дровяни́к, а́ *m.* **1.** (*obs.*) firewood merchant. **2.** (*coll.*) woodshed.
дров|яно́й *adj. of* **~а́; д. сара́й** woodshed; **д. склад** wood pile, wood store.
дрог|а́, и́, *a.* **~у,** *pl.* **~и** *f.* centre pole (*of cart*).
дро́г|и, ~ *no sg.* **1.** dray cart. **2.** hearse.
дро́г|нуть[1]**, ну, нешь,** *past* **~, ~ла** *impf.* to be chilled, freeze.
дро́гн|уть[2]**, у, ешь,** *past* **~ул, ~ула** *pf.* **1.** to shake, move; to quaver; to flicker. **2.** to waver, falter; **у меня́ рука́ не ~ет** (*+inf.*) I shall not hesitate to ....
дрожа́ни|е, я *nt.* trembling, vibration.
дрожа́тельный *adj.* tremulous, shivery; **д. парали́ч** (*med.*) shaking palsy, Parkinson's disease.
дрож|а́ть, у́, и́шь *impf.* **1.** to tremble; to shiver, shake; to quiver; to vibrate; to quaver; to flicker; **д. от хо́лода, испу́га** to shiver with cold, with fright. **2.** (**за**+*a. or* **пе́ред** *i.*; *fig.*) to tremble (for; before). **3.** (**над**+*i.*) to grudge; **д. над ка́ждой копе́йкой** to count every penny.
дрожж|ево́й *adj. of* **~и; ~евы́е грибки́** (*bot.*) Ascomycetes.
дро́жж|и, е́й *no sg.* yeast, leaven; **ста́вить на ~а́х** to leaven; **пивны́е д.** barm, brewer's yeast.
дро́ж|ки, ~ек, ~кам *no sg.* droshky.
дрож|ь, и *f.* **1.** shivering, trembling; tremor, quaver. **2.** (*varied*) tints.
дрозд, а́ *m.* thrush; **пе́вчий д.** song-thrush; **чёрный д.** blackbird; **дать ~а́** (*+d.*) to tear s.o. off a strip.
дрок, а *m.* (*bot.*) gorse.
дромаде́р, а *m.* (*zool.*) dromedary.
дро́ссел|ь, я *m.* (*tech.*) throttle, choke.
дро́тик, а *m.* javelin.
дрочён|а, ы *f.* (*cul.*) batter.
дрочи́л|а, ы *c.g.* (*vulg.*) wanker (= *masturbator*).
дрочи́ть, дро́чу́, дро́чишь *impf.* (*vulg.*) wank, toss off.
дрочи́ться = **дрочи́ть**
друг[1]**, а,** *pl.* **друзья́, друзе́й** *m.* friend; **д. до́ма** friend of the family; **д. по перепи́ске** pen friend *or* pal.
друг[2] (*short form of* **~о́й**) **д. ~а** each other, one another; **д. за ~ом** one after another; **д. с ~ом** with each other.
друг|о́й *adj.* **1.** other, another; different; **и тот и д.** both; **ни тот ни д.** neither; **никто́ д.** none other; **э́то ~о́е де́ло** that is another matter; **~и́ми слова́ми** in other words; **с ~о́й стороны́** on the other hand; **на д. день** the next day; *as n.* **~и́е, ~и́х** others. **2.** second. **3.** (*coll.*) the odd.
дру́жб|а, ы *f.* friendship; **не в слу́жбу, а в ~у** out of friendship.
дружелю́би|е, я *nt.* friendliness.
дружелю́б|ный (~ен, ~на) *adj.* friendly, amicable.
дру́жеск|ий *adj.* friendly; **быть на ~ой ноге́ (с**+*i.*) to be on friendly terms (with).
дру́жественн|ый *adj.* friendly, amicable; **~ая держа́ва** friendly power; (*comput.*) user-friendly.
дру́жеств|о, а *nt.* (*obs.*) friendship.
дружи́н|а, ы *f.* **1.** (*hist.*) (prince's) armed force. **2.** militia unit, detachment (*in tsarist Russia*); **боева́я д.** (*hist.*) armed workers' detachment. **3.** squad, team; **доброво́льная наро́дная д.** voluntary people's (militia) patrol (*in former USSR, organized to assist police in maintaining public order, combating hooliganism, etc.*).
дружи́нник, а *m.* **1.** (*hist.*) member of (prince's) armed force. **2.** (*hist.*) member of militia detachment; member of armed band. **3.** member of voluntary people's (militia) patrol, vigilante; **д. противовозду́шной оборо́ны** air-raid warden.
друж|и́ть, у́, ~ишь *impf.* **1.** (**с**+*i.*) to be friends (with), on friendly terms (with). **2.** (*obs.*) to make friends, unite.
друж|и́ться, у́сь, ~ишься *impf.* (*of* **по~**) (**с**+*i.*) to make friends (with).
дружи́щ|е, а *m.* (*coll.*) old chap (*as mode of address*).
дру́жк|а[1]**, и** *m.* (*ethnol.*) best man (*at wedding*).
дру́жк|а[2]**: друг ~у,** *etc.* (*coll.*) = **друг дру́га,** *etc.*
дру́жно *adv.* **1.** harmoniously, in concord. **2.** simultaneously, in concert; **раз, два, ~!** heave-ho!; all together! **3.** rapidly, smoothly (*of coming of spring, thawing of snow, etc.*).
дру́ж|ный (~ен, ~на́, ~но) *adj.* **1.** amicable; harmonious. **2.** simultaneous, concerted; **~ные уси́лия** concerted efforts. **3.: ~ная весна́** spring with rapid, uninterrupted thawing of snow.
друж|о́к, ка́ *m.* (*coll.*) pal; (*as mode of address*) my dear.
друзья́ *see* **друг**
друммо́ндов *adj.*: **д. свет** (*theatr.*) limelight.
дры́г|ать, аю *impf.* (*of* **~нуть**) (+*i.*; *coll.*) to jerk, twitch.
дры́г|нуть, ну, нешь *pf. of* **~ать**
дры́х|нуть, ну, нешь, *past* **~** *and* **~нул, ~ла** *impf.* (*coll.*) to sleep.
дря́бл|ый (~, ~а́, ~о) *adj.* flabby (*also fig.*); flaccid; sluggish.
дря́бн|уть, у, ешь *impf.* (*coll.*) to become flabby.
дря́гил|ь, я, *m.* (*obs.*) carrier, porter.
дрязг, а (у) *m.* (*collect.*; *obs. or dial.*) refuse, rubbish.
дря́зг|и, ~ *no sg.* (*coll.*) squabbles; annoyances, unpleasantnesses.
дрян|но́й (~ен, ~на́, ~но) *adj.* (*coll.*) worthless, rotten; good-for-nothing.
дрян|ь, и *f.* (*coll.*) **1.** trash, rubbish. **2.** *as pred.* it is rotten, it is no good; **пого́да — д.** the weather is awful. **3.** (*of a pers.*) a bad lot, a good-for-nothing.
дряхле́|ть, ю *impf.* (*of* **о~**) to grow decrepit.
дря́хлост|ь, и *f.* decrepitude, senile infirmity.
дря́хл|ый (~, ~а́, ~о) *adj.* decrepit, senile.
дуайе́н, а *m.* (*dipl.*) doyen.
дуали́зм, а *m.* (*phil.*) dualism.
дуб, а, *pl.* **~ы́** *m.* **1.** oak; **дать ~а** to snuff it; to kick the bucket. **2.** (*coll.*) blockhead, numskull.
дуба́|сить, шу, сишь *impf.* (*of* **от~**) (*coll.*) **1.** to cudgel. **2.** (**по**+*d.* **в**+*a.*) to bang (on).
дуби́льн|ый *adj.* tanning, tannic; **~ое ве́щество** tannin; **~ая кислота́** tannic acid.
дуби́л|ьня, ьни, *g. pl.* **~ен** *f.* tannery.
дуби́льщик, а *m.* tanner.
дуби́н|а, ы *f.* **1.** club, cudgel. **2.** (*coll.*) blockhead, numskull.
дуби́нк|а, и *f.* truncheon, baton.
дуб|и́ть, лю́, и́шь *impf.* (*of* **вы́~**) to tan.
дублёнк|а, и *f.* (*coll.*) sheepskin coat.
дублёный *adj.* tanned; (*fig.*) leathery, weather-beaten.
дублёр, а *m.* (*theatr.*) understudy; (*cin.*) stand-in.
дубле́т, а *m.* duplicate.
дублика́т, а *m.* duplicate.
Ду́блин, а *m.* Dublin.
дубли́р|овать, ую *impf.* **1.** to duplicate; **д. роль** (*theatr.*) to understudy a part. **2.** (*cinema*) to dub. **3.: д. че́рез**

копи́рку to make a carbon copy (of).
дубня́к, á *nt.* wood of oak-trees.
дубова́т|ый (~, ~а) *adj.* (*coll.*) coarse; stupid, thick.
дубо́в|ый *adj.* **1.** oak; **д. лист** oak-leaf; **д. гроб** oak coffin. **2.** (*fig.*, *coll.*) coarse; thick; **~ая голова́** blockhead, numskull. **3.** (*fig.*, *coll.*) rock hard, bullet-like (= *inedible*).
дуб|о́к, ка́ *m.* oakling.
дубра́в|а, ы *f.* **1.** oak forest. **2.** (*poet.*) leafy grove.
дубь|ё, я́ *no pl.*, *nt.* (*collect.*; *coll.*) **1.** cudgels. **2.** fools, blockheads.
Дувр, а *m.* Dover.
Ду́врск|ий проли́в, ~ого ~а *m.* the Strait of Dover.
дуг|а́, и́, *pl.* **~и** *f.* **1.** shaft-bow (*part of harness*). **2.** arc, arch; **бро́ви ~о́й** arched brows; **согну́ть в ~у́, в три ~и́** (*coll.*) to bring under, compel to submit.
дуг|ово́й *adj.* of **~а́; ~ова́я ла́мпа** arc-lamp; **~ова́я сва́рка** arc welding.
дугообра́з|ный (~ен, ~на) *adj.* arched, bow-shaped.
дуд|е́ть, *1st pers. not used*, **и́шь** *impf.* (*coll.*) to play the pipes, fife.
ду́дк|а, и *f.* pipe, fife; **пляса́ть под чью-н. ~у** (*fig.*) to dance to s.o.'s tune.
ду́дки *int.* (*coll.*) not if I know it!; not on your life!
ду́жк|а, и *f.* **1.** *dim. of* **дуга́. 2.** hoop (*at croquet*). **3.** handle.
дука́т, а *m.* ducat.
ду́л|о *nt.* muzzle, barrel (*of firearms*); **д. без наре́зки** smooth bore.
ду́л|ьный *adj. of* **~о; ~ьная ско́рость** muzzle velocity.
ду́л|ьце, ьца, *g. pl.* **~ец** *nt.* **1.** *dim. of* **~о. 2.** (*mus.*) mouthpiece (*of wind instruments*).
ду́м|а, ы *f.* **1.** thought, meditation; (*folk poet.*): **ду́мать ~у** to meditate, brood. **2.** duma (*Ukrainian folk ballad*). **3.** (*hist.*) duma, council, representative assembly; **Госуда́рственная Д.** the State Duma.
ду́ма|ть, ю *impf.* (*of* **по~**) **1.** (**о**+*p. or* **над**+*i.*) to think (about); to be concerned (about); **мно́го о себе́ д.** to have a high opinion of o.s. **2.** (*impf. only*) **д. что...** to think, suppose that ...; **я ~ю!** of course!; I should think so! **3.** (+*inf.*) to think of, intend; **он ~ет пое́хать в Ло́ндон** he is thinking of going to London; **и не ~ю** (+*inf.*) I would not dream (of); **и д. не смей** (+*inf.*) don't dare (to). **4.** (+*ind. question*) to wonder.
ду́ма|ться, ется *impf.* (*impers.*, +*d.*) to seem; **мне ~ется** I think, I fancy; **~ется** it seems.
ду́м|ец, ца *m.* (*hist.*) member of duma; councillor.
ду́мк|а, и *f.* **1.** *dim. of* **ду́ма 1.. 2.** (*coll.*) small pillow. **3.** dumka (*Ukrainian folk-lyric*).
ду́мный *adj.* (*hist.*) of the Boyars' Council.
ду́м|ский *adj. of* **~а 3.; ~ские де́ньги** credit notes (*issued by the Provisional Government in 1917*).
Дуна́|й, я *m.* the Danube (*river*).
дунове́ни|е, я *nt.* puff, breath (*of wind*).
ду́н|уть, у, ешь *pf.* to blow.
ду́пел|ь, я *pl.* **~я́** *m.* (*zool.*) great snipe.
дупле́т, а *m.* doublet (*at billiards*).
дупли́ст|ый (~, ~а) *adj.* hollow.
дупл|о́, а́, *pl.* **~а, ду́пел** *nt.* **1.** hollow (*in tree-trunk*). **2.** cavity (*in a tooth*).
-дур *adj. indecl.* (*mus.*) major.
ду́р|а, ы *f. of* **дура́к**
дура́к, а́ *m.* **1.** (*hist.*) jester, fool. **2.** fool, ass; **д. ~о́м** an utter fool; **не д.** (+*inf.*) (to be) expert (at); **оста́вить в ~а́х** to make a fool of; **оста́ться в ~а́х** to be fooled, make a fool of o.s.; **валя́ть, лома́ть ~а́** the play the fool; to make a fool of o.s.; **на ~а** for fun, for a joke; **~а́м зако́н не пи́сан** (*prov.*) fools rush in where angels fear to tread; **нашёл ~а́!** not likely!; no thanks!
дурале́|й, я *m.* = **дура́к 2.**
дура́цкий *adj.* (*coll.*) stupid, foolish, idiotic; **д. колпа́к** dunce's cap.
дура́честв|о, а *nt.* folly, absurdity; foolish trick.
дура́ч|ить, у, ишь *impf.* (*of* **о~**) to fool, dupe.
дура́ч|иться, усь, ишься *impf.* to play the fool.
дурач|о́к, ка́ *m.* **1.** *affectionate dim. of* **дура́к. 2.** (*coll.*) idiot, imbecile.
дура́шлив|ый (~, ~а) *adj.* (*coll.*) stupid.
ду́р|ень, ня *m.* (*coll.*) fool, simpleton.
дуре́|ть, ю *impf.* (*of* **о~**) to become stupid.
дур|и́ть, ю́, и́шь *impf.* (*coll.*) **1.** to be naughty (*of children*); to play tricks. **2.** to be obstinate (*esp. of horses*).
дурма́н, а *m.* **1.** (*bot.*) thorn-apple (*Datura stramonium*). **2.** (*coll.*) drug, narcotic; intoxicant.
дурма́н|ить, ю, ишь *impf.* (*of* **о~**) to stupefy.
дурне́|ть, ю *impf.* (*of* **по~**) to grow ugly.
ду́рно *adv. of* **дурно́й**
ду́рно *as pred.* (*impers.*, +*d.*): **мне,** *etc.*, **д.** I, *etc.*, feel faint, bad, queer.
дур|но́й (~ен, ~на́, ~но) *adj.* **1.** (*in var. senses*) bad, evil; nasty; **д. вкус** nasty taste; **д. глаз** the evil eye; **~ные мы́сли** evil thoughts; **~ные привы́чки** bad habits; **д. сон** bad dream. **2. (собо́ю)** ugly. **3.** (*coll.*) foolish, stupid; soft(-headed). **4.: ~на́я боле́знь** (*coll.*) venereal disease.
дурнот|а́, ы́ *f.* (*coll.*) faintness; nausea; **у́тренняя д.** morning sickness; **чу́вствовать ~у́** to feel faint, sick.
дурну́шк|а, и *f.* (*coll.*) plain girl, plain Jane.
ду́рост|ь, и *f.* (*coll.*) folly, stupidity.
дуршла́г, а *m.* (*cul.*) colander.
дур|ь, и *f.* (*coll.*) **1.** foolishness, stupidity; **вы́бить, вы́колотить д. (из)** to knock the nonsense (out of). **2.** (*sl.*) dope.
ду́с|я, и *f.* (*coll.*, *affectionate mode of address*) darling.
ду́тик|и, ов *no sg.* (*coll.*) après-ski boots.
ду́т|ый *p.p.p. of* **~ь** *and adj.* **1.** hollow. **2.** inflated; **~ые ши́ны** pneumatic tyres. **3.** (*fig.*) inflated, exaggerated; **~ые ци́фры** exaggerated figures.
дуть, ду́ю, ду́ешь *impf.* **1.** (*pf.* **по~**) to blow; **сего́дня ду́ет ве́тер с за́пада** there is a west wind today; **от окна́ ду́ет** there is a draught from the window; **в ус не ду́ет** (*coll.*) he does not give a damn. **2.** (*pf.* **вы~**) to blow (*glassware*). **3.** (*pf.* **от~**) (*coll.*) to thrash; **д. и в хвост и в гри́ву** to urge on, drive relentlessly. **4.** (*pf.* **вы~**) (*coll.*) to drink deep. **5.** (*coll.*) to rush. **6.** (*coll.*) to do sth. (*e.g.*, *to play a musical instrument*) with abandon, energetically.
дуть|ё, я́ *nt.* **1.** (*tech.*) blowing, blast; **про́ба че́рез д.** bubble test. **2.** (glass-)blowing.
ду́|ться, юсь, ешься *impf.* (*coll.*) **1. (на**+*a.*) to grumble (at), pout (at). **2. (в**+*a.*) to play with abandon.
дух, а *m.* **1.** (*relig.*, *phil.*, *and fig.*) spirit; **свято́й д.** the Holy Spirit, the Holy Ghost; **д. ве́ка** Zeitgeist (*spirit of the age*). **2.** spirit(s); heart; mind; **настрое́ние ~а, расположе́ние ~а** mood, temper, humour; **быть в ~е** to be in good (high) spirits; **не в ~е** in low spirits; **па́дать ~ом** to lose heart, become despondent; **собра́ться с ~ом** to take heart, pluck up one's courage; **прису́тствие ~а** presence of mind; **хва́тит ~у (на**+*a.*) to have the strength (for); **у меня́ ~у не хвата́ет** (+*inf.*) I have not the heart (to); **э́то не в моём ~е** it is not to my taste; **что́-то в э́том ~е** sth. of the sort. **3.** breath; (*coll.*) air; **перевести́ д.** to take breath; **испусти́ть д.** (*fig.*) to give up the ghost; **во весь д.** (*coll.*) at full speed, flat out; **одни́м ~ом** in one breath; (*fig.*) at one go, at a stretch; **о нём ни слу́ху ни ~у** nothing is heard of him. **4.** spectre, ghost. **5.** (*coll.*) smell.
духа́н, а *m.* dukhan (*inn in Caucasus*).
дух|и́, о́в *no sg.* perfume, scent.
духобо́р, а *m.* (*relig.*) Dukhobor.
духобо́рств|о, а *nt.* the Dukhobor religious sect.
ду́хов *adj.*: **Д. день** (*eccl.*) Whit Monday.
духове́нств|о, а *nt.* (*collect.*) clergy, priesthood.
духови́д|ец, ца *m.* clairvoyant; medium.
духови́т|ый (~, ~а) *adj.* (*coll.*, *dial.*) aromatic.
духо́вк|а, и *f.* oven.
духо́вн|ая, ой *f.* testament, will.
духовни́к, а́ *m.* (*eccl.*) confessor.
духо́вност|ь, и *f.* spirituality.
духо́вн|ый *adj.* **1.** spiritual; inner, inward; **~ые запро́сы** spiritual demands; **д. мир** inner world; **д. о́блик** spiritual make-up. **2.** ecclesiastical, church; religious; **~ое лицо́** ecclesiastic; **~ая му́зыка** church music, sacred music; **д. оте́ц** confessor, spiritual director; **д. сан** holy orders. **3.:**

~ое завеща́ние (last) will, testament. **4.: ~ое о́ко** (the) mind's eye.

духов|о́й *adj.* **1.** (*mus.*) wind; **д. инструме́нт** wind instrument; **д. орке́стр** brass band. **2.** (hot-)air; **~о́е отопле́ние** hot-air heating; **~а́я печь** oven; **~о́е ружьё** air-gun; **д. утю́г** iron. **3.** (*cul.*) steamed.

духот|а́, ы́ *f.* stuffiness, closeness; stuffy heat.

душ, а *m.* shower-bath; **приня́ть д.** to take a shower(-bath).

душ|а́, и́, *a.* **~́у,** *pl.* **~́и** *f.* **1.** soul; (*fig.*) heart; **без ~и́ (от** *obs.*) beside o.s. (with); **д. в ~́у** at one, in harmony; **в ~е́** (*i*) inwardly, secretly, (*ii*) at heart; **для ~и́** for one's private satisfaction; **за ~о́й** to one's name; **у него́ за ~о́й ни гроша́** he hasn't a penny to his name; **от ~и́** from the heart; **от всей ~и́** with all one's heart; **по ~е́** (*+d.*) to one's liking; **по ~а́м говори́ть (с**+*i.*) to have a heart-to-heart talk (with); **вложи́ть ~́у (в**+*a.*) to put one's heart (into); **изли́ть, отвести́ ~́у** to pour out one's heart; **~и́ не ча́ять (в**+*p.*) to think the world of; to dote on; **ско́лько ~е́ уго́дно** to one's heart content; **~о́й и те́лом** heart and soul; **ни ~о́й, ни те́лом** in no wise, in no respect. **2.** feeling, spirit; **говори́ть с ~о́й** to speak with feeling. **3.** (*fig.*) (the) soul; moving spirit; inspiration; **д. о́бщества** the life and soul of the party. **4.** (*fig.*) spirit (= *person*); **сме́лая д.** a bold spirit. **5.** (*fig.*) soul (= *person*); **на ~́у** per head; **потребле́ние на ~́у населе́ния** per-capita consumption; **ни (живо́й) ~и́** not a (living) soul. **6.: душа́ моя́!** (*coll.*; *affectionate mode of address*) my dear, darling.

душев|а́я, о́й *f.* shower-room.

душевнобольн|о́й *adj.* insane; suffering from mental illness; *as n.* **д., ~о́го** *m.*, **~а́я, ~о́й** *f.* insane pers.; mental patient.

душе́вн|ый *adj.* **1.** mental, psychical; **~ая боле́знь** mental illness; **~ое потрясе́ние** nervous shock. **2.** sincere, cordial, heartfelt; **~ая бесе́да** friendly chat; **д. челове́к** understanding pers.

душев|о́й[1] *adj.* per head; **~о́е потребле́ние** consumption per head.

душево́й[2] *adj. of* **душ**

душегре́йк|а, и *f.* (*woman's*) sleeveless jacket (*usu. wadded or fur-lined*).

душегу́б, а *m.* (*coll.*) murderer.

душегуби́тельный *adj.* soul-destroying.

душегу́б|ка, ки *f.* **1.** *f. of* **~. 2.** dugout (canoe). **3.** (*hist.*) mobile gas-chamber.

душегу́бств|о, а *nt.* (*coll.*) murder.

ду́шеньк|а, и *c.g.* (*obs., coll.*) darling (*affectionate mode of address*).

душеполе́з|ный (~ен, ~на) *adj.* (*obs.*) edifying.

душеприка́зчик, а *m.* (*leg.*; *obs.*) executor.

душеприка́зчиц|а, ы *f.* (*leg.*; *obs.*) executrix.

душераздира́ющий *adj.* heart-rending.

душеспаси́тел|ьный (~ен, ~ьна) *adj.* (*eccl. or iron.*) salutary, edifying.

ду́шечк|а, и *c.g.* = **ду́шенька**

душещипа́тельный *adj.*: **д. фильм** tear-jerker, weepie.

души́ст|ый (~, ~а) *adj.* fragrant, sweet-scented.

души́тел|ь, я *m.* strangler, suffocator; (*fig.*) suppressor.

душ|и́ть[1], **у́, ~́ишь** *impf.* (*of* **за~**) **1.** to strangle; to stifle, smother, suffocate; (*fig.*) to stifle, suppress; **д. поцелу́ями** to smother with kisses. **2.** (*impf. only*) to choke; **его́ ~и́л ка́шель, гне́в** he choked with coughing, with rage.

душ|и́ть[2], **у́, ~́ишь** *impf.* (*of* **на~**) to scent, perfume.

душ|и́ться[1], **у́сь, ~́ишься** *impf., pass. of* **~и́ть**[1]

душ|и́ться[2], **у́сь, ~́ишься** *impf.* (*of* **на~**) (+*i.*) to perfume o.s. (with); **она́ всегда́ ~́ится францу́зскими духа́ми** she always uses French perfume.

ду́шк|а, и *c.g.* (*coll.*) dear (person); **он тако́й д., она́ така́я д.** he, she is such a dear.

душма́н, а *m.* Dushman (= *Afghan revolutionary*).

душма́н|ский *adj. of* **~**

душни́к, а́ *m.* vent (*in stove*).

ду́шно *as pred.* it is stuffy; it is stifling, suffocating; **мне ста́ло д.** I felt suffocated.

ду́ш|ный (~ен, ~на́, ~но) *adj.* stuffy, close, sultry; stifling.

душ|о́к, ка́ *m.* (*coll.*) **1.** smell (*esp. of decaying matter*); **с ~ко́м** high, tainted. **2.** (*fig.*) smack, taint; tinge; **газе́та с либера́льным ~ко́м** (*pej.*) newspaper with a liberal tinge.

дуэли́ст, а *m.* duellist.

дуэ́л|ь, и *f.* duel; **вы́звать на д.** to challenge; **дра́тся на ~и** to fight a duel.

дуэля́нт, а *m.* = **дуэли́ст**

дуэ́н|ья, ьи, *g. pl.* **~ий** *f.* duenna.

дуэ́т, а *m.* duet.

ды́б|а, ы *f.* (*hist.*) rack (*instrument of torture*).

ды́б|иться, ится *impf.* **1.** to stand on end. **2.** (*of a horse*) to rear, prance.

ды́бом *adv.* on end; **во́лосы у него́ вста́ли д.** his hair stood on end.

дыбы́: на д. on to the hind legs; **станови́ться на д.** to rear, prance; (*fig.*) to kick, resist.

ды́лд|а, ы *c.g.* (*coll.*) lanky fellow, girl.

дым, а (у), о ~́е, в ~у́, *pl.* **~ы́** *m.* **1.** smoke; **в д.** (*coll.*) completely; **там д. коромы́слом** (*coll.*) it's a bedlam there. **2.** (*hist.*) household, hearth (*as unit for taxation*).

дым|и́ть, лю́, и́шь *impf.* (*of* **на~**) to smoke (*intrans.*), emit smoke.

дым|и́ться, и́тся *impf.* to smoke (*intrans.*); (*of fog*) to billow.

ды́мк|а, и *f.* **1.** haze (*also fig.*). **2.** (*obs.*) gauze.

ды́мный *adj.* smoky; **д. по́рох** black powder, gunpowder.

дымов|о́й *adj. of* **дым; ~а́я заве́са** (*mil.*) smoke-screen; **~а́я ма́ска** (anti-)smoke mask; **д. снаря́д** (*mil.*) smoke-shell; **~а́я труба́** flue, chimney; funnel, smoke-stack.

дымога́рн|ый *adj.*: **д. котёл** fire-tube boiler; **~ая труба́** flue, fire tube.

дым|о́к, ка́ *m.* puff of smoke.

дымомёт, а *m.* (*mil.*) smoke projector.

дымохо́д, а *m.* flue.

ды́мчат|ый (~, ~а) *adj.* smoke-coloured.

ды́нный *adj. of* **ды́ня**

ды́н|я, и *f.* melon.

дыр|а́, ы́, *pl.* **~́ы** *f.* **1.** hole; **заткну́ть ~у́** (*fig.*) to stop a gap. **2.** (*fig., coll.*) hole (= *remote place*). **3.** (*pl. only*) gaps, shortcomings.

дыроко́л, а *m.* hole-puncher, punch.

дыря́в|ить, лю, ишь *impf.* (*coll.*) to make a hole (in).

дыря́в|ый (~, ~а) *adj.* full of holes, holey.

ды́хал|о, а *nt.* blowhole.

дыха́ни|е, я *nt.* breathing; breath; **второ́е д.** (*fig.*) second wind; **иску́сственное д.** artificial respiration.

дыха́тельн|ый *adj.* respiratory; **~ое го́рло** (*anat.*) windpipe; **~ые пути́** respiratory tract.

дыш|а́ть, у́, ~́ишь *impf.* (+*i.*) to breathe; **д. ме́стью** to breathe vengeance; **е́ле д.** to be at one's last gasp; (*fig.*) to be on one's last legs.

ды́шл|о, а *nt.* shaft, pole, beam (*attached to front axle of cart, etc., drawn by two horses*).

дья́вол, а *m.* devil; **како́го ~а?; за каки́м ~ом?; на кой ~?** (*coll.*) why the devil?; why the deuce?

дьявол|ёнок, ёнка, *pl.* **~я́та, ~я́т** *m.* (*coll.*) imp.

дья́вольский *adj.* devilish, diabolical; (*coll.*) damnable.

дья́вольщина, ы *f.* (*coll.*) devilment; **что за д.!** what the hell's going on?

дьяк, а́ *m.* (*hist.*) **1.** (prince's) scribe. **2.** clerk, secretary.

дья́кон, а, *pl.* **~а́, ~о́в** *m.* (*eccl.*) deacon.

дья́кониц|а, ы *f.* (*coll.*) deacon's wife.

дья́конств|о, а *nt.* (*eccl.*) diaconate.

дьяч|о́к, ка́ *m.* (*eccl.*) sacristan, sexton; reader.

дю́же *adv.* (*coll. or dial.*) terribly, awfully.

дю́ж|ий (~, ~а́, ~е) *adj.* (*coll.*) sturdy, hefty, robust.

дю́жин|а, ы *f.* dozen; **чёртова д.** baker's dozen.

дю́жинный *adj.* ordinary, commonplace.

дюйм, а *m.* inch.

дюймо́вк|а, и *f.* (*coll.*) **1.** inch(-thick) plank. **2.** one-inch nail.

дюймо́вый *adj.* one-inch.

дю́н|а, ы *f.* dune.

дюра́л|ь, я *m.* = **~юми́ний**

дюралюми́ни|й, я *m.* (*tech.*) duralumin.

дюше́с, а *m.* Duchess pear.

дя́гил|ь, я *m.* (*bot.*) angelica.

дя́деньк|а, и *m. affectionate form of* **дя́дя**
дя́дин *adj.* uncle's.
дя́дьк|а, и *m.* **1.** *pej. form of* **дя́дя. 2.** (*coll.*) = **дя́дя 2.. 3.** (*obs.*) tutor (*in noble families*); usher (*in boys' private school*).
дя́дюшк|а, и *m.* (*coll.*) *affectionate form of* **дя́дя**; (*fig.*): **д. Сэм** Uncle Sam.
дя́д|я, и, *pl.* **~и, ~ей** *and* **~ья́, ~ьёв** *m.* **1.** uncle. **2.** (*coll.*) mister (*as term of address by child to any mature male*).
дя́т|ел, ла *m.* woodpecker.

Е

ЕАСТ *f. indecl.* (*abbr. of* **Европе́йская ассоциа́ция свобо́дной торго́вли**) EFTA (*European Free Trade Association*).
ёбаный *adj.* (*vulg.*) fucking.
еб|а́ть, у́, ёшь *impf.* (*of* **уе́ть**) (*vulg.*) to fuck; **ёб твою мать! 1.** fuck you! **2.** *int.* fuck!; fucking hell!
ёбл|я, и *f.* (*vulg.*) fucking.
ев... *comb. form* (*in words derived from Greek*) eu-.
Ева́нгели|е, я *nt.* (*collect.*) the Gospels; **е.** gospel (*also fig.*).
еванге́лик, а *m.* (an) evangelical.
евангели́ст, а *m.* **1.** Evangelist. **2.** (an) evangelical.
евангели́ческ|ий *adj.* evangelical; **~ая це́рковь** Evangelical Church.
ева́нгельский *adj.* gospel
евге́ник|а, и *f.* eugenics.
евкали́пт(овый) = эвкали́пт(овый)
е́внух, а *m.* eunuch.
еврази́|ец, йца *m.* Eurasian.
еврази́|йка, йки *f. of* **~ец**
еврази́йский *adj.* Eurasian.
еврази́йств|о, а *nt.* Eurasianism (*theory asserting special character of Russ. and related Eastern cultures*).
Евра́зи|я, и *f.* Eurasia.
евре́|й, я *m.* Jew; Hebrew; **ве́рующий е.** Orthodox Jew.
евре́йк|а, и *f.* Jewess.
евре́йский *adj.* Jewish.
евре́йств|о, и *nt.* **1.** (*collect.*) Jewry, the Jews. **2.** Jewishness.
евро... *comb. form* Euro-.
Евро́п|а, ы *f.* Europe.
Европарла́мент, а *m.* Europarliament.
европе́|ец, йца *m.* European.
европеиза́ци|я, и *f.* Europeanization.
европеизи́р|овать, ую *impf. and pf.* to Europeanize.
европе́|йка, йки *f. of* **~ец**
европе́йск|ий *adj.* European; Western.
ЕВС *f. indecl.* (*abbr. of* **Европе́йская валю́тная систе́ма**) EMS (*European Monetary System*).
евста́хиев *adj.*: **~а труба́** (*anat.*) Eustachian tube.
Евфра́т, а *m.* the Euphrates (*river*).
евхаристи́ческий *adj.* (*eccl.*) eucharistal.
евхари́сти|я, и *f.* (*eccl.*) Eucharist.
егерме́йстер, а *m.* (*obs.*) master of the hunt.
е́гер|ский *adj. of* **~ь; е. полк** regiment of chasseurs.
е́гер|ь, я, *pl.* **~и, ~ей** *and* **~я́, ~е́й** *m.* **1.** huntsman. **2.** (*mil.*) chasseur.
Еги́пет, а *m.* Egypt.
еги́петск|ий *adj.* Egyptian; (*fig.*) severe, hard; **~ая тьма** pitch darkness; **~ая синь** Egyptian blue (*a copper pigment*).
египто́лог, а *m.* Egyptologist.
египтоло́ги|я, и *f.* Egyptology.
египтя́н|ин, ина, *pl.* **~е, ~** *m.* Egyptian.
египтя́н|ка, ки *f. of* **~ин**
его́ 1. *g. and a. sg. of* **он**; *g. sg. of* **оно́. 2.** (*possessive adj.*) his; its.
егоз|а́, ы́ *m.and f.* (*coll.*) fidget.
его|зи́ть, жу́, зи́шь *impf.* (*coll.*) **1.** to fidget. **2.** (**пе́ред+*i.***) to fawn (upon).
егозли́в|ый (~, ~а) *adj.* (*coll.*) fidgety.
ед|а́, ы́ *f.* **1.** food. **2.** meal; **во вре́мя ~ы́** at meal-times, during a meal, while eating.
еда́|ть *no pres., past* **~л, ~ла** (*coll.*) *freq. of* **есть**[1]
едва́ *adv. and conj.* **1.** (*adv.*) hardly, barely, only just (= *with difficulty*); **мы е. попа́ли на по́езд** we only just caught the train. **2.** (*adv.*) hardly, scarcely, barely, only just (= *only slightly*); **печь е. гори́т** the fire is barely alight. **3. едва́-едва́** *emph. variant of* **е. 1., 2.. 4.: е. ли** (*adv.*) hardly, scarcely (*in judgements of probability*); **е. ли он отка́жется от тако́го соблазни́тельного предложе́ния** he will hardly refuse such a tempting offer. **5.: е. (ли) не** (*adv.*) nearly, almost, all but; **я е. не по́мер со́ смеху** I nearly died laughing; **э́та оши́бка е. ли не грубе́йшая из заме́ченных мно́ю** that is perhaps (= *I am inclined to think*) the worst howler I have ever seen. **6.** (*conj.*) hardly, scarcely, barely; **е...., как** scarcely ... when; no sooner ... than; **е. самолёт взлете́л, как оди́н из мото́ров зае́ло** no sooner had the plane taken off than one of the engines seized up.
еди́м *see* **есть**[1]
едине́ни|е, я *nt.* unity.
един|и́ть, ю́, и́шь *impf.* (*obs.*) to unite.
едини́ц|а, ы *f.* **1.** one; figure 1; (*math.*) unity. **2.** (*in var. senses*) unit; **е. мо́щности** unit of power; **~ы вое́нно-морско́го фло́та** naval units. **3.** 'one' (*lowest mark in Russ. university and school marking system*). **4.** individual; **(то́лько) ~ы** only a few, only a handful.
едини́чност|ь, и *f.* singleness; single occurrence.
едини́чн|ый *adj.* **1.** single, unitary; **е. слу́чай** solitary instance; **~ые слу́чаи** isolated cases. **2.** individual; **~ое се́льское хозя́йство** farming on an individual basis.
единобо́жи|е, я *nt.* monotheism.
единобо́рств|о, а *nt.* (*rhet.*) single combat.
единобра́чи|е, я *nt.* monogamy.
единобра́чный *adj.* monogamous; (*bot.*) monogamian, monogynous.
единове́р|ец, ца *m.* **1.** co-religionist. **2.** member of Edinoverie (*see* **~ие**).
единове́ри|е, я *nt.* **1.** community of religion. **2.** Edinoverie (*an Old Believer sect which reached an organizational compromise with the official Orthodox Church*).
единове́р|ный (~ен, ~на) *adj.* (*+d. or* **c**+*i.*) of the same faith (as).
единове́р|ческий *adj. of* **~ие 2.**
единовла́сти|е, я *nt.* autocracy, absolute rule.
единовла́ст|ный (~ен, ~на) *adj.* autocractic; dictatorial; **е. прави́тель** absolute ruler.
единовре́менно *adv.* **1.** but once, once only. **2.** simultaneously.
единовре́менн|ый *adj.* **1.** extraordinary, unique; **~ое посо́бие** extraordinary grant. **2.** (*+d. or* **c**+*i.*) simultaneous (with).
единогла́си|е, я *nt.* unanimity.
единогла́сно *adv.* unanimously; **при́нято е.** carried unanimously.
единогла́сный *adj.* unanimous.
единодержа́ви|е, я *nt.* (*obs.*) monarchy, autocracy.
единодержа́в|ный (~ен, ~на) *adj.* (*obs.*) having autocratic powers, unlimited powers.
единоду́ши|е, я *nt.* unanimity.
единоду́ш|ный (~ен, ~на) *adj.* unanimous.
еди́ножды *adv.* (*obs.*) once; **е. три — три** three ones are three.
единокро́в|ный (~ен, ~на) *adj.* **1.** (*obs.*) consanguineous; **е. брат** half-brother. **2.** of the same stock.
единоли́чник, а *m.* individual peasant-farmer (*working his own holding*).

единоли́чн|ый *adj.* individual; personal; **~ое реше́ние** individual decision; **~ое хозя́йство** individual peasant holding.
единомы́сли|е, я *nt.* agreement of opinion; like-mindedness.
единомы́шленник, а *m.* **1.** pers. who holds the same views; like-minded pers.; **мы с ним ~и по вопро́сам вне́шней поли́тики** we agree, we think the same way on matters of foreign policy. **2.** confederate, accomplice.
единонасле́ди|е, я *nt.* (*leg.*) primogeniture.
единонача́ли|е, я *nt.* one-man management; unified management; combined (*military and political*) command.
единонача́льник, а *m.* **1.** combined (military and political) commander. **2.** sole director.
единообра́зи|е, я *nt.* uniformity.
единообра́з|ный (~ен, ~на) *adj.* uniform.
единоплеме́нник, а *m.* member of the same tribe; fellow-countryman.
единоплеме́нный *adj.* of the same tribe; of the same nationality.
единоро́г, а *m.* **1.** (*myth.*) unicorn. **2.** (*hist.*) 'unicorn' (*name of kind of cannon*). **3.** (*zool.*) narwhal.
единоро́дный *adj.* (*obs.*) only-begotten; **е. сын** only son.
единосу́щный *adj.* (*theol.*) (+*d.*) consubstantial (with).
единоутро́б|ный (~ен, ~на) *adj.* (*obs.*) uterine; **е. брат** half-brother, uterine brother.
еди́нственно *adv.* only, solely; **е. возмо́жный ход** the only possible move; **она́ прису́тствовала е. из любопы́тства** she came solely out of curiosity.
еди́нственн|ый *adj.* **1.** only, sole; one and only; **е. сын** only son; **он е. пережи́л кораблекруше́ние** he was the sole survivor of the shipwreck; **е. в своём ро́де** the only one of its kind, unique specimen; **~ое число́** (*gram.*) singular (number). **2.** (*obs.*) unique, unequalled.
еди́нств|о, а *nt.* (*in var. senses*) unity.
еди́н|ый (~, ~а) *adj.* **1.** one; single, sole; **не́ было там ни ~ой души́** there was not a soul there; **всё ~о** (*coll.*) it's all one; **все до ~ого** to a man. **2.** united, unified; **е. и недели́мый** one and indivisible; **~ая сре́дняя шко́ла** comprehensive school. **3.** common, single; **~ая во́ля** single will, purpose.
еди́те *see* **есть**[1]
е́д|кий (~ок, ~ка́, ~ко) *adj.* **1.** caustic; acrid, pungent; **е. натр** (*chem.*) caustic soda; **е. за́пах** pungent smell. **2.** caustic, sarcastic.
е́дкост|ь, и *f.* **1.** causticity; pungency; (*fig.*) sarcasm. **2.** sarcasm, sarcastic remark.
едо́к, а́ *m.* **1.** mouth; head; **у него́ в семье́ де́сять ~о́в** he has ten mouths to feed; **на ~а́** per head. **2.** (*coll.*) (big) eater; **плохо́й е.** a poor eater.
е́д|у, ешь *see* **е́хать**
еду́н, а́ *m.* (*coll.*) mouth (= **едо́к 2.**).
е́дучи *pres. ger.* (*coll.*) *of* **е́хать**
е́д|че *comp. of* **~кий**
едя́т *see* **есть**[1]
её 1. *g. and a. of* **она́**. **2.** (*possessive adj.*) her.
ёж, ежа́ *m.* hedgehog (*also mil. = obstruction of barbed wire entangled with stakes or iron bars*); **~у поня́тно** (*coll.*) it's as plain as can be.
е́ж|а, и *f.* (*agric.*) orchard grass (*Dactylis*).
ежеви́к|а, и *f.* **1.** (*collect.*) blackberries. **2.** bramble, blackberry bush.
ежеви́|чный *adj.* *of* **~ка; ~чное варе́нье** bramble preserve.
ежего́дник, а *m.* annual, year-book.
ежего́дный *adj.* annual, yearly.
ежедне́вн|ый *adj.* daily; everyday; **~ая лихора́дка** quotidian fever.
ежекварта́льник, а *m.* quarterly.
ежекварта́льный *adj.* quarterly.
е́жели *conj.* (*obs. or coll.*) if.
ежеме́сячник, а *m.* monthly (magazine).
ежеме́сячный *adj.* monthly.
ежемину́тный *adj.* **1.** occurring every minute, at intervals of a minute; **у нас есть е. авто́бусный рейс в го́род** we have a one-minute bus service to town. **2.** incessant, continual.
еженеде́льник, а *m.* weekly (*newspaper, magazine*).
еженеде́льный *adj.* weekly.
ежено́щный *adj.* nightly.
ежесеку́ндный *adj.* **1.** occurring every second. **2.** (*coll.*) incessant, continual.
ежесу́точный *adj.* daily (= *occurring every 24 hours*).
ежеча́сный *adj.* hourly.
ёжик, а *m.* **1.** *dim. of* **ёж. 2.: стри́чься ~ом** to have a crew cut. **3.** brush (*for cleaning Primus stove, etc.*); steel wool.
ёж|иться, усь, ишься *impf.* (*of* **съ~**) **1.** to shiver, huddle o.s. up (*from cold, fever, etc.*). **2.** (*fig., coll.*) to shrink (*from fear, shyness, etc.*).
ежи́х|а, и *f.* female hedgehog.
ежо́в|ый *adj. of* **ёж; держа́ть в ~ых рукави́цах** (*coll.*) to rule with a rod of iron.
езд|а́, ы́ *f.* **1.** ride, riding; drive, driving; going; **е. на велосипе́де** bicycling. **2.** *in phrr. indicating distance from one point to another*; journey; **отсю́да до о́зера — до́брых три часа́ ~ы́** from here to the lake is a good three hours' journey.
е́з|дить, жу, дишь *impf.* **1.** (*indet. of* **е́хать**) to go (*in or on a vehicle or on an animal*); to ride, drive; **е. верхо́м** to ride (on horseback). **2.** to (be able to) ride, drive. **3. (к)** to visit (*habitually*). **4.** (*coll.*) to slip.
езд|ово́й *adj. of* **~а́; ~овы́е соба́ки** draught-dogs; *as n.* **е., ~ово́го** *m.* (*mil.*) driver.
ездо́к, а́ *m.* **1.** rider; horseman. **2.: туда́ я бо́льше не е.** I am not going there again.
езжа́|ть *no pres., past* **~л, ~ла** (*coll.*), *freq. of* **е́здить; ~й(те)** (*as imper. of* **е́хать**) go!; get going!
е́зжен|ый *adj.*: **~ая доро́га** beaten track; (*coll.*): **~ая ло́шадь** broken-in horse.
ей *d. and i. of* **она́**
ей-Бо́гу *int.* (*coll.*) truly!; really and truly!
ей-е́й *int.* (*coll.*) truly!; in very truth!
ёк|ать, аю *impf.* (*of* **~нуть**) (+**се́рдце**) (*coll.*) to miss a beat; to go pit-a-pat.
ёкн|уть, у, ешь *pf. of* **ёкать**
ектен|ья́, ьи́, *g. pl.* **~и́й** *f.* (*eccl.*) ektenia (*part of Orthodox liturgy consisting of versicles and responses*).
ел, е́ла *see* **есть**[1]
е́ле *adv.* **1.** hardly, barely, only just (= *with difficulty*); **его́ речь была́ е. слышна́** his speech was hardly audible. **2.** hardly, scarcely, barely, only just (= *only slightly*); **по́езд е. дви́гался** the train was scarcely moving. **3.: е́ле-е́ле** *emph. variant of* **е.; он е.-е. спа́сся** he had a very narrow escape.
е́левый *adj.* (*bot.*) fir, spruce.
еле́|й, я *m.* (*eccl.*) anointing oil; unction; (*fig.*) unction; balm.
еле́й|ный *adj.* **1.** (*eccl.*) *adj. of* **~. 2.** unctuous.
елеосвяще́ни|е, я *nt.* (*eccl.*) extreme unction.
ел|е́ц, ьца́ *m.* dace (*fish*).
елизаве́ти́нский *adj.* Elizabethan.
ели́ко *adv.* (*obs.*) as far as, as much as; **е. возмо́жно** as far as possible.
елисе́йский *adj.* Elysian.
ёлк|а, и *f.* fir(-tree), spruce; **рожде́ственская е.** Christmas-tree; **заже́чь ~у** to light up the Christmas-tree; **быть на ~е** (*coll.*) to be at a Christmas, New Year's party; *int.* **~и-па́лки!** (*coll.*) sugar!; flip(ping hell)!; hell's bells!
ел|о́вый *adj. of* **~ь; ~о́вые ши́шки** fir-cones; **голова́ ~о́вая** (*coll.*) blockhead, numskull.
ело́|зить, жу, зишь *impf.* (*coll.*) to crawl.
ёлочк|а, и *f.* **1.** *dim. of* **ёлка. 2.** herring-bone (pattern); **он но́сит зелёный пиджа́к ~ой, в ~у** he wears a green herring-bone jacket. **3.** *pl.* (*typ.*) guillemets.
ёлочн|ый *adj. of* **ёлка; ~ые украше́ния** Christmas-tree decorations.
ел|ь, и *f.* spruce (*Picea*); fir(-tree); (*comm.*) white wood; **обыкнове́нная е.** Norway spruce, common spruce (*Picea abies*).
е́льник, а *m.* **1.** fir-grove, fir-plantation. **2.** (*collect.*) fir-wood; fir-twigs.
ем *see* **есть**[1]

ём|кий (~ок, ~ка) *adj.* capacious.

ёмкост|ь, и *f.* capacity, cubic content; **ё. цисте́рны** tankage; **ме́ры ~и** measures of capacity; **ё. ры́нка** (*econ.*) market capacity.

е́мл|ю, ешь *see* **има́ть**

ему́ *d. of* **он, оно́**

ендов|а́, ы́ *f.* (*hist.*) flagon (*large copper or earthenware vessel with spout formerly used in Russia for pouring out wine, beer, mead, etc.*).

ено́т, а *m.* **1.** (*zool.*) raccoon. **2.** raccoon (fur).

ено́т|овый *adj. of* **~; ~овая шу́ба** raccoon coat, coonskin coat.

епанч|а́, и́, *g. pl.* **~е́й** *f.* (*hist.*) cloak, mantle.

епархиа́лк|а, и *f.* (*hist.*; *coll.*) church secondary schoolgirl.

епархиа́льн|ый *adj.* (*eccl.*) diocesan; **~ое учи́лище** (*obs.*) church secondary school for girls (*mainly for children of the Orthodox clergy*).

епа́рхи|я, и *f.* (*eccl.*) diocese, see; bishopric; eparchy (*in Orthodox Church*).

епи́скоп, а *m.* bishop.

епископа́льный *adj.* (*eccl.*) episcopalian.

епи́скопский *adj.* episcopal.

епи́скопств|о, а *nt.* episcopate.

епитим|ья́, ьи́, *g. pl.* **~и́й** *f.* (*eccl.*) penance.

епитрахи́л|ь, и *f.* (*eccl.*) stole.

ер, а *m.* (hard) yer (*name of Russ. letter* **'ъ'**).

ерала́ш, а *m.* **1.** (*coll.*) jumble, confusion; **у него́ в голове́ по́лный е.** his thoughts are in complete confusion. **2.** mixture of preserved fruits. **3.** eralash (*card-game*).

ерепе́н|иться, юсь, ишься *impf.* (*of* **взъ~**) (*coll.*) to bristle (*fig.*).

е́рес|ь, и, *pl.* **~и, ~ей** *f.* **1.** heresy. **2.** (*coll.*): **городи́ть е.** to talk nonsense.

ерети́к, а́ *m.* heretic.

ерети́ческий *adj.* heretical.

ёрза|ть, ю *impf.* (*coll.*) to fidget.

ермо́лк|а, и *f.* skull-cap.

еро́ш|ить, у, ишь *impf.* (*coll.*) to rumple, ruffle; to dishevel.

еро́ш|иться, ится *impf.* (*coll.*) to bristle, stick up.

ерунд|а́, ы́ *f.* (*coll.*) **1.** nonsense, rubbish; **говори́ть ~у́** to talk nonsense; **е. на по́стном ма́сле** twaddle, poppycock. **2.** trifle, trifling matter; child's play.

ерунди́стик|а, и *f.* (*coll.*) nonsense.

ерунд|и́ть, *1st pers. sg. not used,* **~и́шь** *impf.* (*coll.*) to talk nonsense; to play the fool.

ерундо́в|ский *adj.* = **~ый**

ерундо́вый *adj.* (*coll.*) **1.** foolish. **2.** trifling.

ёрш[1], **ерша́** *m.* **1.** (*fish*) ruff. **2.** (lamp-chimney) brush. **3.** notched nail *or* spike. **4.** hair sticking up; **~о́м** (*as adv.*) sticking up, on end.

ёрш[2], **ерша́** *m.* (*coll.*) mixture of beer and vodka.

ерши́ст|ый (~, ~а) *adj.* (*coll.*) **1.** bristling; sticking up. **2.** (*fig.*) obstinate; unyielding.

ерш|и́ться, у́сь, и́шься *impf.* (*coll.*) **1.** to stick up. **2.** to grow heated, fly into a rage.

ершо́вый *adj. of* **ёрш**[1] **1.**

еры́ *nt. indecl.* yery (*name of Russ. letter* **'ы'**).

ер|ь, я *m.* (soft) yer (*name of Russ. letter* **'ь'**).

есау́л, а *m.* (*hist.*) esaul (*Cossack captain*).

е́сли *conj.* if; **е. не** unless; **е. то́лько** provided; **е. бы не** but for, if it were not for; **е. бы не ты, он мог бы ко́нчить самоуби́йством** but for you he might have committed suicide; **е. бы** (*in exclamations*) if only; **что е...?** what if ...?; **что, е. бы** (*introducing suggestion of course of action*) what about, how about; **е. бы да кабы́** if ifs and ans were pots and pans.

ессе́|й, я *m.* (*relig.*) Essene.

ессентук|и́, о́в *no sg.* Essentuki (*kind of mineral water*).

ест *see* **есть**[1]

есте́ственник, а *m.* **1.** scientist. **2.** science student.

есте́ственно[1] *adv.* **1.** naturally. **2.** *as particle* naturally, of course.

есте́ственно[2] *as pred.* it is natural.

есте́ствен|ный (~, ~на) *adj.* (*in var. senses*) natural; **~ные бога́тства** natural resources; **~ное прикры́тие** (*mil.*) natural cover; **~ная на́добность, ~ная потре́бность** (*euph.*) needs of nature; **~ные нау́ки** natural sciences; **е. отбо́р** (*biol.*) natural selection.

естеств|о́, а́ *nt.* **1.** nature; essence; **е. вопро́са** the nature of the question. **2.** (*obs.*) Nature.

естествове́д, а *m.* (*obs.*) (natural) scientist.

естествове́дени|е, я *nt.* (*obs.*) natural history; (natural) science.

естествозна́ни|е, я *nt.* (natural) science.

естествоиспыта́тел|ь, я *m.* (natural) scientist.

есть[1], **ем, ешь, ест, еди́м, еди́те, едя́т,** *past* **ел, е́ла,** *imper.* **ешь,** *impf.* (*of* **съ~**) **1.** to eat; **е. глаза́ми** to devour with one's eyes. **2.** (*impf. only*) to corrode, eat away. **3.** (*impf. only*) to sting, cause to smart. **4.** (*impf. only*) (*coll.*) to torment; to nag.

есть[2] **1.** *3rd pers. sg.* (*also, rarely, substituted for all persons*) *pres. of* **быть; и е.** (*coll.*) yes, indeed; **как е.** (*coll.*) entirely, completely. **2.** there is; there are; **у меня́, него́** *etc.*, **е.** I have, he has, *etc.*; **е. тако́е де́ло** (*coll.*) all right; O.K.

есть[3] *int.* (*mil.*; *in acknowledgement of a superior's order*) yes, sir; (*naut.*) aye-aye; very good.

еть (*and* **ети́), ебу́, ебёшь,** *past* **ёб, ебли́** *impf.* = **еба́ть**

ефре́йтор, а *m.* (*mil.*) lance-corporal.

е́хать, е́ду, е́дешь *impf.* (*of* **по~**) (*det. of* **е́здить**) to go (*in or on a vehicle or on an animal*); to ride, drive; **е. верхо́м** to ride (*on horseback*); **е. по́ездом, на по́езде** to go by train; **е. на парохо́де** to go by boat; **е. в Ригу** (*vulg.*) to puke, spew; **да́льше е. не́куда** (*coll.*) that's the end, last straw.

ехи́дн|а, ы *f.* **1.** (*zool.*) echidna. **2.** Australian viper. **3.** (*fig., coll.*) viper, snake.

ехи́днича|ть, ю *impf.* (*of* **съ~**) (*coll.*) to employ malicious innuendo; to be malicious.

ехи́д|ный (~ен, ~на) *adj.* (*coll.*) malicious, spiteful, snide; venomous (*fig.*).

ехи́дств|о, а *nt.* (*coll.*) malice, spite; innuendo.

ехи́дств|овать, ую *impf.* (*coll.*) = **ехи́дничать**

ешь *see* **есть**[1]

ещё *adv.* **1.** still; yet; **е. не, нет е.** not yet; **всё е.** still; **пока́ е.** for the present, for the time being; **э́то е. ничего́!** that's nothing! **2.** some more; any more; yet, further; again; **мо́жно нали́ть е. (вина́** *etc.***)?** may I pour you some more (wine, *etc.*)?; **есть ли е. хлеб?** is there any more bread?; **е. оди́н** one more, yet another; **е. раз** (*i*) once more, again, (*ii*) *as int.* encore!; **наде́юсь, е. приду́** I hope I shall come again. **3.** already; as long ago as, as far back as; **е. в 1900-ом году́** in 1900 already; as long ago as 1900; **что тут но́вого? е. Маркс э́то дока́зывал** what is new in this? (Why,) Marx argued thus. **4.** (*+comp.*) still, yet, even; **е. гро́мче** even louder; **е. и е.** more and more. **5.** (*+prons. and advs.*) *as emph. particle*; **кого́ е. мы не спра́шивали?** whomever did we not ask? **ты ви́дел инду́са? — како́го е. инду́са?** have you seen the Indian? — What Indian, for heaven's sake? **6.: е. бы** (*i*) yes, rather!; and how!; I'll say!, (*ii*) it would be surprising if ...; **е. бы вы с ни́ми не сошли́сь** it would be surprising if you and they didn't get on. **7.: а е.** *expr. reproach or sarcastic criticism*: **тепе́рь ворчи́шь, а е. сам предложи́л** you grumble now, but it was you who suggested it.

ЕЭС *nt. indecl.* (*abbr. of* **Европе́йское экономи́ческое соо́бщество**) EEC (*European Economic Community*).

е́ю *i. of* **она́**

ея́ *g. of* **она́** *in pre-1918 orthography.*

Ж

Ж (*abbr. of* **Же́нская (убо́рная)**) Ladies (*lavatory*).

ж = же

жа́б|а[1], **ы** *f.* (*zool.*) toad.

жа́б|а[2], **ы** *f.* (*med.*) quinsy; **грудна́я ж.** angina pectoris.

жа́берный *adj.* (*zool.*) branchiate.

жа́б|ий *adj. of* **~а**[1]

жабо́ *nt. indecl.* jabot.

жа́бр|ы, ~ *pl.* (*sg.* **~а, ~ы** *f.*) (*zool.*) gills; branchia; **взять за ж.** (*fig., coll.*) to bring pressure to bear upon.

жаве́лев *adj.*: **~а вода́** liquid bleach.

жаве́л|ь, я́ *m.* = **~ева вода́**.

жа́ворон|ок, ка *m.* (*zool.*) lark; **лесно́й ж.** wood lark; **хохла́тый ж.** crested lark.

жа́дин|а, ы *c.g.* (*coll.*) greedy pers.

жадне́|ть, ы *impf.* (*coll.*) to become greedy.

жа́днича|ть, ю *impf.* (*coll.*) to be greedy; to be mean.

жа́дност|ь, и *f.* **1.** greed; greediness; avidity. **2.** avarice, meanness.

жа́д|ный (~ен, ~на́, ~но) *adj.* **1.** (**к**+*d.*) greedy (for); avid (for); **он всегда́ был ~ным к но́вым ощуще́ниям** he was always greedy for new sensations. **2.** avaricious, mean.

жадю́г|а, и *c.g.* (*coll.*) cheapskate, penny-pincher.

жа́жд|а, ы *no pl., f.* thirst; (+*g.*; *fig.*) thirst, craving (for); **ж. зна́ний** thirst for knowledge.

жа́жд|ать, у *impf.* (*obs.*) to be thirsty; (+*g. or inf.*; *fig.*) to thirst (for, after); **а́лчущие и ~ущие,** *see* **а́лчущий**

жаке́т, а *m.* **1.** (*obs.*) morning coat. **2.** (*ladies'*) jacket.

жаке́тк|а, и *f.* (*coll.*) jacket.

жакт, а *m.* (*abbr. of* ***жили́щно-аре́ндное кооперати́вное това́рищество***) (*hist.*) housing lease co-operative society.

жа́кт|овский *adj. of* **~**

жале́йк|а, и *f.* (*mus.*; *dial.*) zhaleyka (*kind of pipe played by peasants, made from cow's horn or birchbark*).

жале́|ть, ю *impf.* (*of* **по~**) **1.** to pity, feel sorry (for). **2.** (**о**+*p. or* +*g.*; **что**) to regret, be sorry (for, about); **~ю об утра́ченном вре́мени** I regret the waste of time; **~ю, что не оста́лся до конца́ ма́тча** I am sorry I did not stay till the end of the match. **3.** (+*a. or g.*) to spare; to grudge; **не ~я сил** not sparing o.s., unsparingly.

жа́л|ить, ю, ишь *impf.* (*of* **у~**) to sting; to bite.

жа́л|иться[1], **юсь, ишься** *impf.* (*coll.*) to sting; to bite.

жа́л|иться[2], **юсь, ишься** *impf.* (*dial.*) to complain.

жа́л|кий (~ок, ~ка́, ~ко) *adj.* pitiful, pitiable, pathetic, wretched (= (*i*) *arousing pity*, (*ii*) *arousing contempt*); **име́ть ж. вид** to be a sorry sight.

жа́лк|о[1] *adv. of* **~ий**

жа́лко[2] *as pred.* (*impers.*) **1.** (+*d. and g.*) to pity, feel sorry (for); **ей ж. бы́ло себя́** she felt sorry for herself. **2.** (it is) a pity, a shame; (+*d. and g. or a.*) it grieves (me, *etc.*); to regret, feel sorry; **мне ста́ло ж. да́нного обеща́ния** I began to regret giving a promise. **3.** (+*g. or* +*inf.*) to grudge.

жа́л|о, а *nt.* **1.** sting (*also fig.*). **2.** point (*of pin, needle, etc.*).

жа́лоб|а, ы *f.* complaint; **пода́ть ~у** (**на**+*a.*) to make, lodge a complaint (about).

жа́лоб|ный (~ен, ~на) *adj.* **1.** plaintive; doleful, mournful. **2.** *adj. of* **~а**; **~ная кни́га** complaints book.

жа́лобщик, а *m.* **1.** pers. lodging complaint. **2.** (*leg.*) plaintiff.

жа́лова|нный *p.p.p. of* **~ть** *and adj.* (*hist.*) granted, received as grant; **~нная гра́мота** letters patent, charter.

жа́ловань|е, я *nt.* **1.** salary. **2.** (*obs.*) reward; donation.

жа́л|овать, ую *impf.* (*of* **по~**) **1.** (+*a. and i. or* +*d. and a.*) to grant (to); to bestow, confer (on); to reward (with); **ж. сторо́нников землёй, ж. сторо́нникам зе́млю** to grant land to one's supporters, reward one's supporters with (grants of) land. **2.** (*coll.*) to favour, regard with favour. **3.** (**к**; *obs.*) to visit, come to see.

жа́л|оваться, уюсь *impf.* (*of* **по~**) (**на**+*a.*) to complain (of, about); **он всё ~уется офице́рам на харчи́** he is always complaining to officers about the food; **ж. в суд** to go to law.

жалоно́сный *adj.* (*zool.*) stinging, possessing a sting.

жа́лостлив|ый (~, ~а) *adj.* (*coll.*) **1.** compassionate, sympathetic. **2.** pitiful.

жа́лост|ный (~ен, ~на) *adj.* (*coll.*) **1.** piteous; doleful, mournful. **2.** compassionate, sympathetic.

жа́лост|ь, и *f.* pity, compassion; **из ~и (к)** out of pity (for); **кака́я ж.!** what a pity!; **ж. к себе́** self-pity.

жаль *as pred.* (*impers.*) **1.** (+*d. and a. or g.*) to pity, feel sorry (for); **мне ж. тебя́** I pity you. **2.** (it is) a pity; (+*d.*) it grieves (me, *etc.*); to regret, feel sorry; **ж., что вас там не бу́дет** it is a pity you will not be there; **нам ж. бы́ло расстава́ться** it grieved us to part. **3.** (+*g. or* +*inf.*) to grudge. **4.** *as adv.* unfortunately.

жа́л|ьче (*coll.*) *comp. of* **~ко**

жалюзи́ *nt. indecl.* Venetian blind, jalousie.

жанда́рм, а *m.* gendarme.

жандарме́ри|я, и *f.* (*collect.*) gendarmerie.

жанда́рм|ский *adj. of* **~**

жанр, а *m.* **1.** genre. **2.** genre-painting.

жанри́ст, а *m.* genre-painter.

жа́нр|овый *adj. of* **~**

жанти́льнича|ть, ю *impf.* (*coll.*) to behave in an affected way, put on airs.

жанти́л|ьный (~ен, ~ьна) *adj.* (*coll.*) affected.

жар, а (у), о ~е, в ~у́ *no pl., m.* **1.** heat; heat of the day; hot place; **в ~у́** (+*g.*) in the heat (of). **2.** (*coll.*) embers; **как ж. горе́ть** to gleam, glitter; **чужи́ми рука́ми ж. загреба́ть** to use others to pull one's chestnuts out of the fire. **3.** fever; (high) temperature. **4.** (*fig.*) heat, ardour; **с ~ом приня́ться за что-н.** to set about sth. with a will.

жар|а́, ы́ *f.* heat; hot weather.

жарго́н, а *m.* **1.** jargon; slang, cant (*of a particular social or occupational group*). **2.** (*obs.*) Yiddish (language).

жарго́н|ный *adj. of* **~**

жардинье́рк|а, и *f.* flower-stand, jardinière.

жа́рев|о, а *nt.* (*collect.*; *coll.*) roast *or* fried food.

жа́рен|ое, ого *nt.* (*coll.*) roast meat.

жа́реный *adj.* roast, broiled; fried; grilled.

жа́р|ить, ю, ишь *impf.* **1.** (*pf.* **за~** *or* **из~**) **(на огне́)** to roast, broil; **(на сковороде́)** to fry; **(на решётке)** to grill. **2.** (*of the sun*) to burn, scorch. **3.** (*coll.*) *used as substitute for other vv. to emph. speed of action or vigour of performance*: **~ь за по́мощью!** run for help as fast as you can!; **ж. на гармо́шке** to bash out a tune on the accordion.

жа́р|иться, юсь ишься *impf.* **1.** (*pf.* **за~** *or* **из~**) to roast, fry (*intrans.*). **2.: ж. на со́лнце** (*coll.*) to roast, grill (o.s.), bask in the sun. **3.** *pass. of* **~ить**

жа́р|кий (~ок, ~ка́, ~ко) *adj.* **1.** hot; torrid; tropical; **ж. по́яс** (*geog.*) torrid zone. **2.** (*fig.*) hot, heated; ardent; passionate; **ж. спор** heated argument.

жа́р|ко[1] *adv. of* **~кий**

жа́рко[2] *as pred.* it is hot; **мне,** *etc.*, **ж.** I am, *etc.*, hot.

жарк|о́е, о́го *nt.* roast (meat).

жаро́в|ня, ни, *g. pl.* **~ен** *f.* brazier.

жарово́й *adj.* **1.** *adj. of* **жар 1.**. **2.** caused by heat; **ж. уда́р** heat-stroke.

жар|о́к, ка́ *m.* (*coll.*) fever; (slight) temperature.

жаропонижа́ющ|ий *adj.* (*med.*) febrifugal; *as n.* **~ее, ~его** *nt.* febrifuge.

жаропро́чн|ый *adj.* ovenproof; **~ая кастрю́ля** casserole (dish).

жаросто́йкий *adj.* (*tech.*) heat-resisting, heatproof.

жаротру́бный *adj.*: **ж. котёл** (*tech.*) fire-tube boiler, flue boiler.

жароупо́рный = жаросто́йкий

жар-пти́ц|а, ы *f.* (*folklore*) the Fire-bird.
жа́р|че *comp. of* **~кий** *and* **~ко**
жары́н|ь, и *f.* (*coll.*) intense heat (*of atmosphere*); very hot weather.
жасми́н, а *m.* jasmin(e), jessamin(e).
жа́тв|а, ы *no pl., f.* reaping, harvesting; harvest (*also fig.*).
жа́тв|енный *adj. of* **~а; ~енная маши́на** binder, harvester, reaping-machine.
жа́тк|а, и *f.* binder, harvester, reaping-machine.
жать[1], **жму, жмёшь** *impf.* (*no pf.*) **1.** to press, squeeze; **ж. ру́ку** to shake (s.o.) by the hand. **2.** to press out, squeeze out. **3.** to pinch, be tight (*of shoes or clothing*); (*impers.*): **в плеча́х жмёт** it is tight on the shoulders. **4.** (*fig., coll.*) to oppress.
жать[2], **жну, жнёшь** *impf.* (*of* **с~**) to reap, cut, mow.
жа́ться, жму́сь, жмёшься *impf.* **1.** to huddle up; **ж. в у́гол** to skulk in a corner. **2.** (**к**) to press close (to), draw closer (to). **3.** (*coll.*) to hesitate, vacillate. **4.** (*coll.*) to stint o.s.; to be stingy.
жбан, а *m.* (wooden) jug.
жва́чк|а, и *f.* **1.** chewing, rumination. **2.** cud; **жева́ть ~у** to chew the cud, ruminate; (*fig.*) to repeat sth. monotonously. **3.** (*coll.*) chewing-gum
жва́чн|ый *adj.* (*zool.*) ruminant; *as n.* **~ое, ~ого** *nt.* ruminant.
жгу, жжёшь, жгут *see* **жечь**
жгут, а́ *m.* **1.** plait; braid; wisp. **2.** (*med.*) tourniquet.
жгу́тик, а *m.* (*zool.*) flagellum.
жгу́чест|ь, и *f.* burning heat.
жгу́ч|ий (~, ~а, ~е) *adj.* burning hot (*also fig.*); **~ая боль** smart, smarting pain; **ж. брюне́т** pers. with jet-black hair and eyes; **ж. вопро́с** burning question.
ж. д. (*abbr. of* ***желе́зная доро́га***) railway.
ждать, жду, ждёшь, *past* **ждал, ждала́, жда́ло** *impf.* **1.** (*+g.*) to wait (for); to await; **заста́вить ж.** to keep waiting; **не заста́вить себя́ ж.** to come quickly; **ж. не дожда́ться** (*coll.*) to wait impatiently, be on tenterhooks; **что нас ждёт?** what is in store for us?; **того́ и жди** (*coll.*) any time now, any minute. **2.** (*+g.*) to expect (= *to hope for*). **3.** (**+что**) to expect; **мы жда́ли, что вы поя́витесь на ми́тинге** we expected you to come to the meeting.
же[1] *conj.* **1.** but; **иди́, е́сли тебе́ охо́та, я же оста́нусь здесь** you go, if you feel like it, but I shall stay here. **2.** (*introducing clause elucidating or modifying preceding clause*) and; **с тех пор как я его́ зна́ю, зна́ю же я его́ два́дцать лет, я всегда́ ве́рил ему́** ever since I have known him, and I have known him for twenty years, I have always trusted him; **Ока́ впада́ет в Во́лгу, Во́лга же в Каспи́йское мо́ре** the Oka flows into the Volga, and the Volga flows into the Caspian Sea. **3.** after all; **расскажи́ ей — она́ же твоя́ мать** tell her — she's your mother, after all.
же[2] *emph. particle*: **когда́ же они́ прие́дут?** whenever will they come?; **что же ты де́лаешь?** whatever are you doing, what *are* you doing?; **сего́дня же он собира́лся прие́хать** it was today that he intended to come.
же[3] *particle expr. identity*: **тот же, тако́й же** the same, idem; **тогда́ же** at the same time; **там же** in the same place, ibidem; **Петрося́н, он же Петро́в** Petrosyan, alias Petrov.
жева́ни|е, я *nt.* mastication; rumination.
жёваный *adj.* (*coll.*) chewed up; crumpled.
жева́тельн|ый *adj.* masticatory, manducatory; **~ая рези́нка** chewing gum.
жева́ть, жую́, жуёшь *impf.* to chew, masticate; to ruminate; **ж. губа́ми** to munch; (*fig.*) **ж. жва́чку,** *see* **жва́чка; ж. вопро́с** to chew over a question.
жёг, жгла *see* **жечь**
жезл, а́ *m.* **1.** rod; staff (of office); baton; (*eccl.*) crozier; (*hist.*) warder. **2.** staff (*token of authority to proceed on single-line railways*). **3.** Jacob's staff (*used by surveyors*).
жезлов|о́й *adj.*: **~а́я систе́ма** staff system (*on single-line railways*).
жела́ни|е, я *nt.* **1.** (*+g.*) wish (for), desire (for); **бу́дет по ва́шему ~ю** it shall be as you wish; **я всегда́ стара́юсь счита́ться с ва́шими ~ями** I always try to consult your wishes; **при всём ~и** with the best will in the world. **2.** desire, lust.
жела́|нный *p.p.p. of* **~ть** *and adj.* wished for, longed for, desired, beloved; **ж. гость** welcome visitor.
жела́тельно[1] *adv.* preferably.
жела́тельно[2] *as pred.* it is desirable; it is advisable, preferable; **ж., что́бы вы прису́тствовали** it is desirable that you should be present, your presence is desirable.
жела́тел|ьный (~ен, ~ьна) *adj.* **1.** desirable; advisable, preferable; **2.: ~ьное наклоне́ние** (*gram.*) optative mood.
желати́н, а *no pl., m.* gelatin(e).
желати́новый *adj.* gelatinous.
жела́|ть, ю *impf.* (*of* **по~**) **1.** (*+g.*) to wish (for), desire. **2.** (**что́бы** *or +inf.*) to wish, want; **я ~ю, что́бы вы при́няли уча́стие в игре́** I want you to join in the game; **~ете ли вы познако́миться с ним?** do you wish to meet him? **3.** (*+d. and g. or inf.*) to wish (*s.o. sth.*); **~ю вам вся́ких благ** (*coll.*) I wish you every happiness; **~ю вам успе́ха** good luck!; **э́то оставля́ет ж. лу́чшего, мно́гого** it leaves much to be desired.
жела́|ющий *pres. part. act. of* **~ть; ~ющие** persons interested, those who so desire.
желва́к, а́ *m.* (*med.*) tumour; (*fig.*) moving knot of muscle.
желе́ *nt. indecl.* jelly.
желез|а́, ы́, *pl.* **же́лезы, ~́, ~а́м** *f.* (*anat.*) gland *pl.*; (*coll.*) tonsils; **же́лезы вну́тренней секре́ции** endocrine glands.
желе́зистый[1] *adj.* (*anat.*) glandular.
желе́зист|ый[2] **(~, ~а)** *adj.* ferriferous; (*chem.*) ferrocyanide (of); ferruginous; chalybeate (*of water*); **ж. препара́т** iron preparation.
желе́зк|а, и *f.* (*coll.*) **1.** piece of iron. **2.** (*obs.*) railway. **3.** chemin-de-fer (*card-game*).
желёзк|а, и *f.* (*anat.*) glandule.
железне́ни|е, я *nt.* (*tech.*) iron plating.
железнодоро́жник, а *m.* railwayman.
железнодоро́жн|ый *adj.* rail, railway; **~ая ве́тка** branch line; **~ая перево́зка** rail transport; **~ое полотно́** permanent way; **ж. путь** (railway) track; **ж. у́зел** (railway) junction.
желе́зн|ый *adj.* **1.** iron (*also fig.*); (*chem.*) ferric, ferrous; **ж. блеск** (*min.*) haematite; **ж. век** the Iron Age; **~ое де́рево** (*bot.*) lignum vitae (*Guaiacum officinale*); **ж. за́навес** the 'Iron Curtain'; **~ая кислота́** ferric acid; **ж. колчеда́н** (*min.*) iron pyrites; **~ая ко́мната** strong-room; **ж. купоро́с** (*min.*) green vitriol; **ж. лом** scrap iron; **~ые опи́лки** iron filings; **за ~ой решёткой** (*coll.*) behind bars; **~ая руда́** iron-stone, iron-ore; **~ые това́ры** ironmongery, hardware; **~ая трава́** (*bot.*) vervain. **2.: ~ая доро́га** railway(s); **по ~ой доро́ге** by rail; **~ая доро́га ме́стного значе́ния** local line. **3.** (*sl.*) reliable, dependable.
железня́к, а́ *m.* (*min.*) iron-stone, iron clay.
желе́з|о, а, *pl.* (*obs. or poet.*) **~ы** *nt.* **1.** iron; **ж. в болва́нках** pig-iron; **о́кись ~а** (*chem.*) ferric oxide. **2.** (*collect.*) iron; hardware. **3.** (*pl.*) (*obs.*) fetters, irons.
желе́зо... *comb. form* iron-, ferro-.
железобето́н, а *m.* (*tech.*) reinforced concrete, ferro-concrete.
железобето́н|ный *adj. of* **~**
железоплави́льный *adj.*: **ж. заво́д** (*tech.*) iron foundry.
железопрока́тный *adj.*: **ж. заво́д** (*tech.*) rolling mill.
жёлоб, а, *pl.* **~а́, ~о́в** *m.* gutter; trough; chute.
желоб|о́к, ка́ *m.* (*tech.*) groove, channel, flute.
жело́бчатый *adj.* (*tech.*) channelled, fluted.
жело́нк|а, и *f.* (*tech.*) sludge pump, sand pump.
желте́|ть, ю *impf.* **1.** (*pf.* **по~**) to turn yellow. **2.** (*impf. only*) to be yellow, show up yellow.
желте́|ться, ется *impf.* to be yellow, show up yellow.
желтизн|а́, ы́ *f.* yellowness; yellow spot; sallow complexion.
желти́нк|а, и *f.* (*coll.*) yellow spots; yellow shade.
жел|ти́ть, чу́, ти́шь *impf.* to colour yellow.
желтова́т|ый (~, ~а) *adj.* yellowish; sallow.
желт|о́к, ка́ *m.* yolk.
желтоко́жий *adj.* yellow-skinned.
желтоли́ц|ый (~, ~а) *adj.* sallow.
желторо́т|ый (~, ~а) *adj.* **1.** yellow-beaked. **2.** (*fig.*) inexperienced, green.

желтофио́л|ь, и *f.* (*bot.*) wallflower.
желтоцве́т, а *m.* (*bot.*) golden rod.
желт|о́чный *adj. of* **~о́к**
желту́х||а, и *f.* (*med.*) jaundice.
желту́|шный *adj. of* **~ха**; jaundiced.
жёлт|ый (~, ~а́, ~о *and* **~о́)** *adj.* yellow; **ж. биле́т** (*hist., coll.*) 'yellow ticket' (*prostitute's passport in tsarist Russia*); **~ая вода́** (*med.*) glaucoma; **ж. дом** (*coll., obs.*) lunatic asylum; **~ая лихора́дка** yellow fever; **~ая пре́сса** the yellow press.
желт|ь, и *f.* yellow (paint).
желудёвый *adj. of* **жёлудь; ж. ко́фе** acorn coffee.
желу́д|ок, ка *m.* stomach; **несваре́ние ~ка** indigestion.
желу́доч|ек, ка *m.* (*anat.*) ventricle.
желу́дочно-кише́чный *adj.* gastro-intestinal.
желу́дочный *adj.* stomach; stomachic, gastric; **ж. зонд** stomach pump; **ж. сок** gastric juice.
жёлуд|ь, я, *g. pl.* **~е́й** *m.* acorn.
жёлч|ный (~ен, ~на) *adj.* **1.** bilious; **ж. ка́мень** gall-stone; **ж. пузы́рь** gall-bladder. **2.** (*fig.*) peevish, irritable; atrabilious.
жёлч|ь (*coll.* **желчь**), **и** *no pl., f.* bile, gall (*also fig.*); **разли́тие ~и** (*med.*) jaundice.
жема́н|иться, юсь, ишься *impf.* (*coll.*) to attitudinize, behave with false modesty.
жема́нниц|а, ы *f.* (*coll.*) affected creature.
жема́ннича|ть, ю *impf.* (*coll.*) to behave affectedly.
жема́н|ный (~ен, ~на) *adj.* affected.
жема́нств|о, а *nt.* affectedness.
же́мчуг, а, *pl.* **~а́** *m.* pearl(s); **ме́лкий ж.** seed-pearls.
жемчу́жин|а, ы *f.* pearl (*also fig.*).
жемчу́жниц|а, ы *f.* **1.** pearl-oyster. **2.** pearl disease.
жемчу́жн|ый *adj. of* **же́мчуг**; (*fig.*) pearly(-white); **~ая боле́знь** pearl disease; **~ое ожере́лье** pearl necklace.
жен... *comb. form, abbr. of* **же́нский**
жен|а́, ы́, *pl.* **~́ы, ~́, ~́ам** *f.* **1.** wife; **быть у ~ы́ под башмако́м** to be henpecked. **2.** (*poet., obs.*) woman.
жена́т|ый (~) *adj.* married; **ж. (на+p.)** married (to; *of man*).
Жене́в|а, ы *f.* Geneva.
жене́вский *adj.* Genevan.
же́нин *adj.* (*obs.*) wife's.
жен|и́ть, ю́, ~́ишь *impf. and pf.* (*pf. also* **по~**) to marry (off); **без меня́ меня́ ~и́ли** (*fig., coll.*) I was roped in without being consulted.
жени́тьб|а, ы *no pl., f.* marriage.
жен|и́ться, юсь, ~́ишься *impf. and pf.* **(на+p.)** (*of man*) to marry, get married (to).
жени́х, а́ *m.* **1.** fiancé; **смотре́ть ~о́м** (*coll.*) to look happy. **2.** bridegroom. **3.** suitor. **4.** eligible bachelor.
жениха́|ться, юсь *impf.* (*coll. or dial.*) to be engaged; to be courting.
жениxо́вский *adj.* (*coll.*) *of* **жени́х**
жениxо́вств|о, а *nt.* (*coll.*) engagement; courting(-days).
жёнк|а, и *f.* (*coll.*) **1.** *affectionate form of* **жена́**. **2.** (*obs. or dial.*) woman.
женолю́б, а *nt.* ladies' man.
женолюби́в|ый (~) *adj.*: **ж. челове́к** ladies' man.
женолю́би|е, я *nt.* fondness for women.
женоненави́стник, а *m.* misogynist.
женоненави́стнический *adj.* misogynous.
женоненави́стничеств|о, а *nt.* misogyny.
женоподо́б|ный (~ен, ~на) *adj.* effeminate; poofy.
женотде́л, а *m.* (*hist.*) women's section (*section of Communist party committees dealing with political work among women*).
жен-премье́р, а *m.* (*theatr.*) jeune premier.
же́нск|ий *adj.* **1.** woman's; female; feminine; **~ое зва́ние, ~ая на́ция, ~ое сосло́вие** (*obs.*) the female sex; **ж. вопро́с** the question of women's rights; **~ое ца́рство** petticoat government. **2.** (*gram.*) feminine. **3.** *as n.* **~ое, ~ого** (*coll.*) menstruation.
же́нственност|ь, и *f.* femininity; (*pej.*) effeminacy.
же́нствен|ный (~, ~на) *adj.* feminine, womanly; (*pej.*) womanish, effeminate.
же́нщин|а, ы *f.* woman; **ж.-полице́йский** policewoman.
женьше́н|ь, я *m.* (*bot., med.*) ginseng.

жёрдочк|а, а, *f.* (*coll.*) pole; perch (*in bird-cage*).
жерд|ь, и, *pl.* **~́и, ~е́й** *f.* pole; stake; **худо́й, как ж.** (*coll.*) thin as a lath.
жерёб|ая (~а) *adj.* in foal.
жереб|ёнок, ёнка, *pl.* **~я́та, ~я́т** *m.* foal, colt.
жереб|е́ц, ца́ *m.* stallion.
жереб|и́ться, и́тся *impf.* (*of* **о~**) to foal.
жере́бчик, а *m. dim. of* **жеребе́ц; мыши́ный ж.** (*obs.*) old lecher.
жеребьёвк|а, и *f.* casting of lots, sortition; (*sport*) draw (*for play-off*).
жереб|я́чий *adj. of* **~ёнок; ж. смех** (*coll.*) horse-laugh.
же́рех, а *m.* chub (*fish*).
жерли́ц|а, ы *f.* kind of fishing tackle (*for catching pike, etc.*).
жерл|о́, а́, *pl.* **~́а, ~** *nt.* mouth, orifice; muzzle (*of gun*); **ж. вулка́на** crater.
жёрнов, а, *pl.* **~а́, ~о́в** *m.* millstone.
же́ртв|а, ы *f.* **1.** sacrifice (*also fig.*); **принести́ ~у** (*+d.*) to make a sacrifice (to); **принести́ в ~у** to sacrifice. **2.** victim; **пасть ~ой** (*+g.*) to fall victim (to.).
же́ртвенник, а *m.* **1.** sacrificial altar. **2.** (*eccl.*) credence table.
же́ртвенный *adj.* sacrificial.
же́ртвовател|ь, я *m.* donor.
же́ртв|овать, ую, *impf.* (*of* **по~**) **1.** to make a donation (of), present. **2.** (*+i.*) to sacrifice, give up.
жертвоприноше́ни|е, я *nt.* sacrifice; oblation.
жест, а *m.* gesture (*also fig.*).
жестикули́р|овать, ую *impf.* to gesticulate.
жестикуля́ци|я, и *f.* gesticulation.
жёст|кий (~ок, ~ка́, ~ло) *adj.* hard; tough; (*fig.*) rigid, strict; **ж. ваго́н** hard-seated carriage, 'hard' carriage; **~кая вода́** hard water; **~кие во́лосы** wiry hair.
жёст|ко[1] *adj. of* **~кий**
жёстко[2] *as pred.* it is hard.
жесткокры́л|ые, ых *pl.* (*sg.* **~ое, ~ого** *nt.*) (*zool.*) Coleoptera.
жесто́к|ий (~, ~а́, ~о) *adj.* cruel; brutal; (*fig.*) severe, sharp.
жестокосе́рд|ный (~ен, ~на) *adj.* hard-hearted.
жестокосе́рд|ый = ~ный
жесто́кост|ь, и *f.* cruelty, brutality.
жесто|ча́йший *superl. of* **~́кий**
жёст|че *comp. of* **~кий** *and* **~ко**
жест|ь, и *f.* tin-plate.
жестя́ник, а *m.* tinman, tin-smith.
жестя́нк|а, и *f.* **1.** tin, can; **ж. из-под сарди́нок** sardine tin. **2.** (*coll.*) piece of tin.
жест|яно́й *adj. of* **~ь; ~яна́я посу́да** tinware.
жестя́нщик, а *m.* tinman, tin-smith.
жето́н, а *m.* **1.** medal. **2.** counter. **3.** token; **проездно́й ж.** travel token.
жечь, жгу, жжёшь, жгут, *past* **жёг, жгла** *impf.* **1.** (*pf.* **с~**) to burn (up, down); **ж. му́сор** to burn up refuse. **2.** (*impf. only*) to burn, sting; (*impers.*): **от э́того ликёра жжёт го́рло** this liqueur burns one's throat.
же́чься, жгусь, жжёшься, жгу́тся, *past* **жёгся, жглась** *impf.* **1.** to burn, sting (*intrans.*) **2.** (*coll.*) to burn o.s.
жже́ни|е, я *nt.* **1.** burning. **2.** burning pain; heartburn.
жжёнк|а, и *f.* hot punch.
жжёный *adj.* burnt, scorched; **ж. ко́фе** roasted coffee.
жжёшь *see* **жечь**
жива́ть *no pres.* (*coll.*) *freq. of* **жить**
жив|е́й, *see* **~́о 5.**
живе́те *nt. indecl.* old name of letter **ж.**
жив|е́ц[1], **ца́** *m.* live bait, sprat.
жив|е́ц[2], **ца́** *m.* (*obs., coll.*) member of Living Church.
живи́тел|ьный (~ен, ~ьна) *adj.* life-giving; bracing; **~ьная вла́га** (*coll.*) intoxicating liquor.
жив|и́ть, лю́, и́шь *impf.* to give life to, animate; to brace.
жив|и́ться, лю́сь, и́шься *impf.* (*+i.; obs.*) to live (on), make a living (by).
живи́ц|а, ы *f.* soft resin.
жи́вност|ь, и *no pl., f.* (*collect.; coll.*) poultry, fowl.
жи́в|о *adj.* **1.** vividly. **2.** with animation. **3.** keenly; extremely, exceedingly; **он ж. чу́вствовал оскорбле́ние** he felt deeply insulted. **4.** (*coll.*) quickly, promptly. **5. ж.!; ~е́й!**

(*coll.*) get a move on!; look lively!
живодёр, а *m.* knacker; (*fig.*) fleecer, flay-flint; profiteer.
живодёр|ня, ни, *g. pl.* **~ен** *f.* (*coll.*) knacker's yard.
живодёрств|о, а *nt.* (*coll.*) cruelty.
жив|о́й (~, ~á, ~о) ** *adj.* **1. living, live, alive; **он ещё в ~ы́х** he is still alive; **остáться в ~ы́х** to survive, escape with one's life; **~ (и) здорóв** (*coll.*) safe and sound; **ни ~ ни мёртв** (*coll.*) petrified (*with fright, astonishment*); **ж. вес** live weight; **~áя водá** (*folklore*) water of life; **~áя и́згородь** (quickset) hedge; **ж. инвентáрь** livestock; **~ы́е карти́ны** tableaux (vivants); **шить на ~ýю ни́тку** to tack; **на ~ýю ни́тку** (*coll.*) hastily, anyhow; **стоя́ть в ~óй óчереди** to queue in person; **ж. портрéт** (+*g.*) the living image (of); **~áя рáна** open wound; **~áя си́ла** (*mil.*) men and beasts (*opp. matériel*); **~ы́м слóвом рассказáть** to tell by word of mouth; **ж. уголóк** nature corner (*in a school*); **~ы́е цветы́** natural flowers; **нé было ви́дно ни (однóй) ~óй души́** there was not a living soul to be seen; **на нём нé было ~óго мéста** he was all battered and bruised; **забрáть, задéть за ~óе** to touch, sting to the quick. **2.** lively; keen; brisk; animated; **ж. ум** lively mind; **проявля́ть ж. интерéс (к)** to take a keen interest (in); **принимáть ~óе учáстие (в**+*p.*) to take an active part (in); to feel keen sympathy with. **3.** lively, vivacious; bright; **~ы́е глазá** bright eyes. **4.** keen, poignant. **5.** (*short form only*; +*i.*) *expr. raison d'être*: **он ~ одни́ми шáхматами** he lives for chess alone; **чем онá ~á?** what makes her tick?
жи́вокост|ь, и *f.* (*bot.*) larkspur.
живопи́с|ать, ую *impf. and pf.* (*obs.*) to describe vividly, paint a vivid picture.
живопи́с|ец, ца *m.* painter; **ж. вы́весок** sign-painter.
живопи́с|ный (~ен, ~на) *adj.* **1.** pictorial. **2.** picturesque (*also fig.*); **~ное мéсто** beauty spot.
жи́вопис|ь, и *f.* **1.** painting. **2.** (*collect.*) paintings; **италья́нская ж.** paintings of the Italian school; **стенна́я ж.** murals.
живородя́щий *adj.* (*zool.*) viviparous.
живорождéни|е, я *nt.* (*zool.*) viviparity.
живоры́бный *adj.*: **ж. садóк** fishpond.
жи́вост|ь, и *f.* liveliness, vivacity; animation.
живóт, а *m.* **1.** abdomen, belly; stomach; (*coll.*) **у негó ж. подвóдит** he feels hungry; **жéнщина с ~óм** (*coll.*) pregnant woman. **2.** (*arch.*) life; **не на ж., а на смерть** to the death; **не щадя́ ~á своегó** not counting the cost. **3.** (*obs. or dial.*) animals, beasts; (*pl.*) goods and chattels.
животвор|и́ть, ю́, и́шь *impf.* (*of* **о~**) to revive.
животвóр|ный (~ен, ~на) *adj.* life-giving.
животвор|я́щий *pres. part. act. of* **~и́ть** *and adj.* (*obs. or poet.*) life-giving; **ж. крест** (*theol.*) the life-giving cross.
живóтик, а *m.* (*coll.*) tummy.
животи́н|а, ы *f.* (*coll.*) domestic animal; (*fig.*) beast.
животновóд, а *m.* cattle-breeder.
животновóдств|о, а *nt.* stock-raising, animal husbandry.
животновóдческий *adj.* cattle-breeding, stock-raising.
живóтно|е, го *nt.* animal; **кóмнатное ж.** pet; (*fig., pej.*) beast, brute.
живóтный *adj.* **1.** animal; **ж. жир** animal fat; **ж. ýголь** animal charcoal; **ж. э́пос** (*liter.*) bestiary. **2.** bestial, brute.
животрепéщущий *adj.* **1.** topical; stirring, exciting. **2.** lively, full of life. **3.** (*joc.*) unsound, unstable.
живýчест|ь, и *f.* **1.** vitality, tenacity of life. **2.** (*fig.*) firmness, stability.
живýч|ий (~, ~а) *adj.* **1.** tenacious of life; (*bot.*) hardy; **он ~ как кóшка** he has nine lives like a cat. **2.** (*fig.*) firm, stable.
жи́вчик, а *m.* **1.** (*coll.*) lively pers. **2.** (*biol.*) spermatozoon. **3.** (*coll.*) perceptible pulsing of artery on temple *or* twitching of eyelid.
живь|ё, я́ *nt.* (*collect.*; *dial.*) live things.
живьём *adv.* **1.** (*coll.*) alive; **петь ж.** to sing live; **постарáйтесь схвати́ть егó ж.** try to catch him alive. **2.** (*dial.*) anyhow; in rough and ready fashion.
жиган|ýть, ý, ёшь *pf.* (*coll.*) to lash.
жи́голо *m. indecl.* gigolo.
жид, á *m.* (*obs. or pej.*) **1.** (*obs.*) Jew. **2.** (*pej. and vulg.*) Yid.
жи́дкий (~ок, ~кá, ~ко) *adj.* **1.** liquid; fluid; **~кое тóпливо** liquid fuel, fuel oil. **2.** watery; (*of liquids*) weak, thin; **ж. чай** weak tea. **3.** sparse, scanty; **~кая бородá** straggly beard. **4.** (*coll.*; *of voice or sound*) weak, thin. **5.** (*fig.*) weak, feeble.
жидкокристалли́ческий *adj.*: **ж. индикáтор** liquid-crystal display, LCD.
жи́дкостный *adj.* (*tech.*) liquid; fluid.
жи́дкост|ь, и *f.* **1.** liquid; fluid; **мóющая ж.** washing-up liquid; **корректи́рующая ж.** correction fluid. **2.** wateriness; weakness, thinness (*also fig.*).
жидóвк|а, и *f.* (*obs. or pej.*) Jewess.
жидóвск|ий *adj.* (*obs. or pej.*) Jewish; **~ая смолá** (*min.*) Jew's pitch.
жи́ж|а, и *no pl., f.* liquid; swill; slush.
жи́|же *comp. of* **~дкий**
жи́жиц|а, ы *f.* (*coll.*) *dim. of* **жи́жа**
жизнедéятельност|ь, и *f.* **1.** (*biol.*) vital activity. **2.** (*obs.*) life's work
жизнедéятел|ьный (~ен, ~ьна) *adj.* **1.** (*biol.*) active. **2.** lively; energetic.
жи́зненност|ь, и *f.* **1.** vitality. **2.** closeness to life; (art) lifelikeness.
жи́знен|ный (~, ~на) *adj.* **1.** life; (*biol.*) vital; **~ные отправлéния** vital functions; **ж. путь** life; **~ные си́лы** vitality, sap; **ж. ýровень** standard of living. **2.** close to life; lifelike. **3.** (*fig.*) vital, vitally important; **ж. вопрóс** question of vital importance; **~ные цéнтры страны́** nerve-centres of a country.
жизнеобеспéчени|е, я *nt.*: **систéма ~я** life-support system.
жизнеописáни|е, я *nt.* biography.
жизнерáдостност|ь, и *f.* joie de vivre; cheerfulness.
жизнерáдост|ный (~ен, ~на) *adj.* full of joie de vivre; cheerful.
жизнеспосóбност|ь, и *f.* (*biol.*) viability; (*fig.*) vitality.
жизнеспосóб|ный (~ен, ~на) *adj.* capable of living; (*biol.*) viable; (*fig.*) vigorous, flourishing.
жизнестó|йкий (~ек, ~йка) *adj.* tenacious of life; tough, durable.
жизн|ь, и *f.* life; existence; **ж. моя́!** my dear!; **заробóтать на ж.** to earn one's living; **как ж.?** (*coll.*) how are you?; **лиши́ть себя́ ~и** to take one's life; **не на ж., а на смерть** to the death; **ни в ж.** never, not for anything; **óбраз ~и** way of life; **вести́ ширóкий óбраз ~и** to live in style; **по ж.** for life; **провести́ что-н. в ж.** to put sth. into practice; **прожéчь ж.** to dissipate one's life, fritter away one's life; **~и не рад** (*coll.*) upset, distressed, miserable; **из-за э́того он и ~и не рад** he is very vexed about it.
жиклёр, а *m.* (*tech.*) (carburettor) jet.
жил... *comb. form, abbr. of* **1. жили́щный. 2. жилóй 1.**
жи́л|а[1], ы *f.* **1.** vein; tendon, sinew; **тянýть ~ы (из**+*g.*; *coll.*) to torment, rack. **2.** (*min.*) vein, lode. **3.** filament, strand (*of cable*).
жи́л|а[2], ы *c.g.* (*coll., pej.*) skinflint.
жилéт, а *m.* waistcoat; **пуленепробивáемый ж.** bulletproof vest; **спасáтельный ж.** life-jacket.
жилéтк|а, и *f.* (*coll.*) waistcoat; **плáкать в ~у** (+*d.*) to cry on s.o.'s shoulders.
жилéт|ный *adj. of* **~; ж. кармáн** waistcoat pocket, vest-pocket.
жил|éц, ьцá *m.* **1.** lodger; tenant. **2.** (*obs.*) inhabitant; **он не ж. (на бéлом свéте)** (*coll.*) he is not long for this world.
жи́лист|ый (~, ~а) *adj.* **1.** having prominent veins. **2.** sinewy; (*fig.*) wiry; **~ое мя́со** stringy meat.
жи́л|ить, ю, ишь *impf.* (**у**; *coll.*) to swindle.
жи́л|иться[1], юсь, ишься *impf.* (*coll.*) to heave, strain.
жи́л|иться[2], юсь, ишься *impf.* (*pej., coll.*) to stint; to be miserly.
жил|и́ца, и́цы *f. of* **~éц**
жили́чк|а, и *f.* (*coll.*) = **жили́ца**
жили́щ|е, а *nt.* **1.** dwelling, abode; habitation. **2.** lodging; (living) quarters.
жили́щно-строи́тельн|ый *adj.*: **~ое óбщество** building society.
жили́щ|ный *adj. of* **~е; ~ные услóвия** housing conditions; **~но-бытовы́е услóвия** living conditions.

жи́лк|а, и *f.* 1. (*anat., geol.*) vein; (*zool., bot.*) fibre, rib (*of insect's wing or of leaf*). 2. (*fig.*) vein, streak; bent; **артисти́ческая ж.** artistic streak; **попа́сть в ~у** (*obs.*) to do sth. opportunely.

жилкова́ни|е, я *nt.* (*zool., bot.*) nervation.

жилмасси́в, а *m.* housing estate.

жи́л|о, а *nt.* (*obs. or dial.*) habitation.

жилова́т|ый (~, ~а) *adj.* (*coll.*) with prominent veins.

жил|о́й *adj.* 1. dwelling; residential; inhabited; **ж. дом** dwelling house, block of flats (*opp. office block, etc.*); **ж. кварта́л** residential area; **~ы́е ко́мнаты** rooms lived in; **~а́я пло́щадь = жилпло́щадь.** 2. habitable, fit to live in.

жилотде́л, а *m.* housing department (*of local council*).

жилпло́щад|ь, и *f.* 1. floor space. 2. housing, accommodation (= *available dwelling space*).

жилстрои́тельств|о, а *nt.* house building.

жилфо́нд, а *m.* housing, accommodation.

жиль|ё, я́ *nt.* 1. habitation; dwelling; **мы не нашли́ никако́го при́знака ~я́** we could find no sign of life. 2. lodging; (living) accommodation. 3. (*obs.*) storey, floor.

жи́льн|ый *adj.* venous; **~ая поро́да** (*geol.*) veinstone, matrix, gangue.

жим, а *m.* (*sport*) press (*in weight-lifting*).

жи́молост|ь, и *f.* (*bot.*) honeysuckle.

жи́нк|а, и *f.* (*dial.*) = **жёнка**

жир, а (у), о ~́е, в ~у́, *pl.* **~ы́** *m.* fat; grease.

жира́ф, а *m.* giraffe.

жира́ф|а, ы *f.* = **~**

жире́|ть, ю *impf.* (*of* **о~** *and* **раз~**) to grow fat, stout, plump.

жирномоло́чный *adj.* (*agric.*) giving milk with high fat content.

жи́р|ный (~ен, ~на́, ~го) *adj.* 1. fatty; (*chem.*) aliphatic; rich (*of food*); greasy; **~ная кислота́** fatty acid, aliphatic acid; **~ное пятно́** grease stain. 2. fat, plump. 3. rich (*of soil*); lush (*of vegetation*); **~ная земля́** loam. 4. (*typ.*) bold, heavy; **ж. шрифт** bold(-face) type. 5. (*coll.*): **ж. кусо́к** fat sum (*of money*); **~но бу́дет!** that's too much!

жи́ро *nt. indecl.* (*fin.*) endorsement.

жир|ова́ть[1], **у́ю** *impf.* to lubricate, oil, grease.

жир|ова́ть[2], **у́ет** *impf.* to fatten (*intrans.*).

жирови́к, а́ *m.* 1. (*med.*) fatty tumour, lipoma. 2. (*min.*) steatite, soapstone.

жиров|о́й *adj.* 1. fatty, aliphatic; (*anat.*) adipose; **~а́я ткань** adipose tissue; **~о́е перерожде́ние** (*med.*) fatty degeneration. 2.: **~а́я промы́шленность** fat-products industry. 3.: **~о́е яйцо́** wind-egg.

жирово́ск, а *m.* (*physiol.*) adipocere.

жиропо́т, а *m.* (*tech.*) suint, yolk (*of wool*).

жиропри́ка́з, а *m.* (*fin.*) (banking) order.

жироско́п, а *m.* (*phys.*) gyroscope.

жите́йск|ий *adj.* 1. worldly; of life, of the world; **~ая му́дрость** worldly wisdom; **~ое мо́ре** the ups and downs of life. 2. everyday; **де́ло ~ое** (*coll.*) there's nothing extraordinary in that.

жи́тел|ь, я *m.* inhabitant; dweller; **ми́рные ~и** civilians; civilian population.

жи́тельство, а *nt.* residence; **вид на ж.** residence permit; **ме́сто ~а** residence, domicile; **ме́сто постоя́нного ~а** permanent address.

жи́тельств|овать, ую *impf.* (*obs.*) to reside, dwell.

жити|е́, я́ *nt.* 1. life, biography; **~я́ святы́х** Lives of the Saints. 2. (*obs.*) life, existence.

жити́йн|ый *adj. of* **житие́**; **~ая литерату́ра** hagiology, hagiography.

жи́тниц|а, ы *f.* granary (*also fig.*).

жи́тный *adj.* cereal; **ж. двор** (*obs.*) life, granary.

жи́т|о, а *no pl., nt.* (*unground*) corn (*denotes rye in Ukraine, barley in northern Russia, spring-sown cereals in general in eastern Russia.*).

жить, живу́, живёшь, *past* **жил, жила́, жи́ло (не́ жил, не жила́, не́ жило)** *impf.* 1. to live; **ж. в Москве́** to live in Moscow; **ж. ве́село** to have a good time; **ж. припева́ючи** to be in clover; **ж. на широ́кую но́гу** to live in style; **ж. со дня на́ день** to live from hand to mouth; **ж. да ж. бы ему́** (*of a pers. untimely dead*) he should have lived to see another day; **жил-бы́л** once upon a time there lived … (*formula for opening of fairy-tale*). 2. (*+i. or* **на**+*a.*) to live (on); (*+i.; fig.*) to live (in, for); **нам не́чем ж.** we have nothing to live on; **ж. на свои́ сре́дства** to support o.s., live on one's own means; **ж. наде́ждами** to live in hopes; **ж. иску́сством** to live for art. 3. (**в**+*p.*; *of domestic servants*) to work (as); **ж. в прислу́гах (у)** to be a maid (at), work as a maid (for).

жить|ё, я́ *nt.* (*coll.*) 1. life; existence; **~я́ тут нет от мух** the flies make life here impossible. 2. habitation, residence; **кварти́ра гото́ва для ~я́** the flat is ready for habitation.

житьё-бытьё, житья́-бытья́ *nt.* (*coll.*) life; existence.

жи́ться, живётся, *past* **жило́сь** *impf.* (*impers., +d.; coll.*) to live, get on; **ей ве́село живётся** she leads a gay life; **как вам жило́сь в Аме́рике?** how did you get on in America?

ЖКИ *m. indecl.* (*abbr. of* **жидкокристалли́ческий индика́тор**) LCD (*liquid-crystal display*).

жлоб, а *m.* (*coll.*) 1. slob. 2. prat, nerd.

жмот, а *m.* (*coll.*) miser.

жму, жмёшь *see* **жать**[1]

жму́рик, а *m.* (*sl.*) goner, stiff.

жму́р|ить, ю, ишь *impf.* (*of* **за~**): **ж. глаза́** to screw up one's eyes, narrow one's eyes.

жму́р|иться, юсь, ишься *impf.* (*of* **за~**) to screw up one's eyes, narrow one's eyes.

жму́р|ки, ок *no sg.* blind man's buff.

жмых|и́, о́в *pl.* (*sg.* **~, ~а́** *m.*) (*agric.*) oil-cake.

жне́йк|а, и *f.* (*agric.*) binder, harvester, reaping-machine.

жнец, а́ *m.* reaper.

жне|я́, и́ *f.* (*obs. or dial.*) 1. *f. of* **~ц.** 2. reaping-machine.

жни́в|о, а *nt.* (*dial.*) = **~ьё**

жнивь|ё, я́, *pl.* **~́я** *nt.* 1. stubble-field. 2. (*sg. only*) stubble. 3. (*sg. only*) (*dial.*) harvest, harvest-time.

жнитв|о́, а́ *nt.* (*dial.*) 1. stubble. 2. harvest, harvest-time.

жни́ц|а, ы *f. of* **жнец**

жну, жнёшь *see* **жать 2.**

жоке́|й, я *m.* jockey.

жоке́йк|а, и *f.* (*coll.*) jockey cap.

жоке́й|ский *adj. of* **~**

жо́лоб = жёлоб

жо́лудь = жёлудь

жом, а *m.* 1. (*tech.*) press. 2. (*sg., collect.*) husks, marc.

жонглёр, а *m.* juggler.

жонглёрств|о, а *nt.* sleight-of-hand; juggling (*also fig.*).

жонгли́р|овать, ую *impf.* (*+i.*) to juggle (with) (*also fig.*); **он лю́бит ж. ци́фрами** he likes juggling with figures.

жо́п|а, ы *f.* (*vulg.*) arse; arsehole; **ну ты и ж.!** you arsehole!; **иди́** *or* **пошёл в ~у!** fuck off!; **лени́вая ж.** lazy bugger; **пьян(ый) в ~у** pissed as a fart *or* newt.

жо́пник = жо́почник

жополи́з, а *m.* (*vulg.*) arse-licker.

жо́почник, а *m.* (*vulg.*) 1. arse-licker. 2. queer, poof(ter).

жо́рнов = жёрнов

жох, а *m.* (*coll.*) rogue.

жрань|ё, я́ *nt.* (*vulg.*) guzzling, hogging.

жратв|а́, ы *f.* (*vulg.*) 1. guzzling, hogging. 2. (*sl.*) grub.

жр|ать, у́, ёшь, *past* **~а́л, ~ала́, ~а́ло** *impf.* (*of* **со~**) 1. (*of animals*) to eat. 2. (*vulg.*) to guzzle, gobble.

жре́би|й, я *m.* 1. lot; **броса́ть, мета́ть ж.** to cast lots; **вы́нуть, тяну́ть ж.** to draw lots. 2. (*fig.*) lot, fate, destiny; **ж. бро́шен** the die is cast.

жрец, а́ *m.* priest (*of heathen religious cult*); (*fig.*) devotee.

жре́ческий *adj.* priestly.

жре́честв|о, а *nt.* priesthood.

жри́ц|а, ы *f.* priestess; **ж. любви́** woman of easy virtue.

жу́желиц|а, ы *f.* (*zool.*) ground beetle.

жужжа́ни|е, я *nt.* hum, buzz, drone; humming, buzzing, droning.

жужж|а́ть, у́, и́шь *impf.* to hum, buzz, drone; to whiz (*of projectiles*).

жуи́р, а *m.* playboy.

жуи́р|овать, ую *impf.* to lead a gay life, life of pleasure.

жук, а́ *m.* 1. beetle; **ма́йский ж.** may-bug, cockchafer. 2. (*coll.*) rogue, twister.

жу́лик, а *m*. petty thief; cheat, swindler; (card-)sharper.
жуликова́т|ый (~, ~а) *adj.* (*coll.*) roguish.
жуль|ё, я́ *nt.* (*collect.*; *coll.*) rogues.
жу́льнича|ть, ю *impf.* (*of* **с~**) (*coll.*) to cheat; to swindle.
жу́льнический *adj.* (*coll.*) roguish; underhand, dishonest.
жу́льничеств|о, а *nt.* (*coll.*) **1.** cheating (*at games*). **2.** underhand, dishonest action; sharp practice.
жупа́н, а *m.* (*hist.*) zhupan (*kind of jerkin worn by Poles and Ukrainians*).
жу́пел, а *m.* **1.** bugbear, bogy. **2.** (*relig.*) brimstone.
журавл|и́ный *adj. of* **∠ь; ~и́ные но́ги** spindle shanks.
жура́вл|ь, я́ *m.* **1.** (*zool.*) crane; **не сули́ ~я́ в не́бе, а дай сини́цу в ру́ки** (*prov.*) a bird in the hand is worth two in the bush. **2.** (*well*) sweep, shadoof.
жур|и́ть, ю́, и́шь *impf.* (*coll.*) to reprove, take to task.
журна́л, а *m.* **1.** magazine; periodical; journal. **2.** journal, diary; register; **ж. заседа́ний** minutes, minute-book.
журнали́ст, а *m.* **1.** journalist. **2.** ledger-clerk.
журнали́стик|а, и *f.* **1.** journalism; **ж. с че́ковой кни́жкой** chequebook journalism. **2.** (*collect.*) periodical press.
журнали́стский *adj.* journalistic.
журна́л|ьный *adj. of* **~; ~ьная статья́** magazine article.
журфи́кс, а *m.* (*obs.*) at-home.
журча́ни|е, я *nt.* purling, babbling, murmur.
журч|а́ть, у́, и́шь *impf.* to purl, babble, murmur (*of water*; *also fig.*, *poet.*).
жу́т|кий (~ок, ~ка́, ~ко) *adj.* terrible, terrifying; awe-inspiring, eerie.
жу́тко[1] *adv.* terrifyingly; (*coll.*) terribly, awfully.
жу́тко[2] *as pred.* (*impers.*, *+d.*): **мне,** *etc.*, **ж.** I, *etc.*, am terrified, feel awestruck.
жут|ь, и *f.* **1.** terror; awe; **воспомина́ния о де́тстве для него́ — пря́мо ж.** memories of childhood simply terrify him. **2.** *as pred.* = **∠ко**[2]
жу́хл|ый (~, ~а) *adj.* withered, dried-up; hardened; tarnished.
жу́х|нуть, нет, *past* **~, ~ла** *impf.* to dry up; to become hard; to become tarnished.
жу́ч|ить, у, ишь *impf.* (*coll.*) to scold.
жу́чк|а, и *f.* (*coll.*) house-dog.
жуч|о́к, ка́ *m.* **1.** *dim. of* **жук. 2.** (*coll.*) wood-engraver (*insect*).
жу|ю́, ёшь *see* **жева́ть**
ЖЭК, а *or* **жэк, а** *m.* (*abbr. of* ***жили́щно-эксплуатацио́нная конто́ра***) housing office.
жюри́ *indecl.* **1.** *nt.* (*collect.*) judges (*of competition, etc.*). **2.** *m.* (*obs.*) umpire, referee.

З

З (*abbr. of* **за́пад**) W, West.
за *prep.* **I.** *+a. and i.* (*+a.*: *indicates motion or action*; *+i.*: *indicates rest or state*). **1.** behind; **за крова́ть, за крова́тью** behind the bed. **2.** beyond; across, the other side of; **за боло́то, за боло́том** beyond the marsh; **за́ борт, за бо́ртом** overboard; **за́ угол, за угло́м** round the corner; **за́ городом** out of town; **за рубежо́м** abroad. **3.** at; **сесть за роя́ль** to sit down at the piano; **сиде́ть за роя́лем** to be at the piano. **4.** (*denoting occupation*) at, to (*or translated by part.*); **приня́ться за рабо́ту** to set to work, get down to work; **заста́ть кого́-н. за рабо́той** to find s.o. at work, working; **сесть за кни́гу** to sit down with a book, get down to reading; **проводи́ть всё своё вре́мя за чте́нием** to spend all one's time reading. **5.: вы́йти за́муж за** (*+a.*) (*of a woman*) to marry; **(быть) за́мужем за** (*+i.*) (to be) married (to).

II. *+a.* **1.** after (*of time*); over (*of age*); **далеко́ за́ полночь** long after midnight; **ему́ уже́ за со́рок** he is already over forty. **2.** *expr. distance in space or time*: **самолёт разби́лся за ми́лю от дере́вни** the aeroplane crashed a mile from the village; **за два дня до его́ сме́рти** two days before his death; **за час** an hour before, an hour early. **3.** during, in the space of; **за́ ночь** during the night, overnight; **за су́тки** in the space of twenty-four hours; **за после́днее вре́мя** recently, lately, of late. **4.** (*+vv. having sense of to take hold of, etc.*) by; **вести́ за́ руку** to lead by the hand. **5.** (*in var. senses*) for; **плати́ть за биле́т** to pay for a ticket; **подписа́ть за дире́ктора** to sign for the director; **боя́ться, ра́доваться за кого́-н.** to fear, be glad for s.o.; **слыть за знатока́** to pass for an expert; **есть за трои́х** to eat (enough) for three; **за ва́ше здоро́вье!** your health!; cheers!

III. *+i.* **1.** after; **друг за дру́гом** one after another; **год за го́дом** year after year; **сле́довать за кем-н.** to follow s.o. **2.** (*fig.*) after; **следи́ть за детьми́** to look after children; **уха́живать за больны́м** to look after a sick pers.; **волочи́ться за же́нщиной** (*coll.*) to run after a woman. **3.** for (= *in order to fetch*, *obtain*); **идти́ за молоко́м** to go for milk; **посла́ть за до́ктором** to send for a doctor; **зайти́ за кем-н.** to call for s.o. **4.** at, during; **за за́втраком** at breakfast. **5.** for, on account of, because of; **за неиме́нием, недоста́тком** (*+g.*) for want of; **за темното́й** for the darkness, on account of the darkness; **за чем де́ло ста́ло?** what's up? **6.** (*+prons.*) (*i*) *ascribes habits, qualities*, (*ii*) *imputes responsibility*: **за ним во́дятся стра́нности** he has his peculiarities; **за тобо́й пять рубле́й** you are owing five roubles; **о́чередь за ва́ми** it is your turn. **7.** *indicates provenance of a document, etc.*: **письмо́ за по́дписью гла́вного реда́ктора** a letter signed by the editor-in-chief.
за... *pref.* **I.** (*of vv.*) **1.** *indicates commencement of action*: **зала́ять** to start barking. **2.** *indicates direction of action beyond given point*: **заверну́ть за́ угол** to turn a corner. **3.** *indicates continuation of action to excess*: **закорми́ть** to overfeed. **4.** *forms pf. aspect of some vv.*

II. (*of nn. and adjs.*) trans-; **Закавка́зье** Transcaucasia; **заатланти́ческий** transatlantic.
заадрес|ова́ть, у́ю *pf.* (*coll.*) to address, write the address (on).
заале́|ть, ет *pf. of* **але́ть**
заале́|ться, ется = **~ть**
зааплоди́р|овать, ую *pf.* to break out into applause, start clapping.
зааренд|ова́ть у́ю *pf.* (*of* **~о́вывать**) to rent, lease.
зааренд́овыва|ть, ю *impf. of* **заарендова́ть**
заарка́н|ить, ю, ишь *pf. of* **арка́нить**
заарта́ч|иться, усь, ишься *pf.* (*coll.*) to become restive, stubborn.
заасфальти́р|овать ую *pf. of* **асфальти́ровать**
заатланти́ческий *adj.* transatlantic.
зааха|ть, ю *pf.* (*coll.*) to begin to sigh, begin to groan.
заба́в|а, ы *f.* **1.** game; pastime. **2.** amusement, fun; **он э́то сде́лал для ~ы** he did it for fun.
забавля́|ть, ю *impf.* to amuse, entertain, divert.
забавля́|ться, юсь *impf.* to amuse o.s.
заба́вник, а *m.* (*coll.*) amusing *or* entertaining pers.; humorist.
заба́вн|о[1] *adv. of* **~ый**
заба́вно[2] *as pred.* it is amusing, funny; **мне з.** I find it amusing, funny; **з.!** how funny!
заба́в|ный (~ен, ~на) *adj.* amusing; funny.
забаллоти́р|овать, ую *pf.* to blackball, reject, fail to elect.
заба́лтыва|ть, ю *impf. of* **заболта́ть**[1] **2.**
забараба́н|ить, ю, ишь *pf.* to begin to drum.
забаррикади́р|овать, ую *pf. of* **баррикади́ровать**
забаст|ова́ть, у́ю *pf.* to go, come out on strike.
забасто́вк|а, и *f.* strike; **всео́бщая з.** general strike; **голо́дная з.** hunger strike; **италья́нская з.** sit down strike, go-slow; **неофициа́льная з.** wildcat strike.
забасто́в|очный *adj. of* **~ка**
забасто́вщик, а *m.* striker.
забве́ни|е, я *nt.* **1.** oblivion; **преда́ть ~ю** to consign to oblivion. **2.** (*obs.*) unconsciousness; drowsiness.

забве́нный *adj.* (*obs.*) forgotten.
забе́г, а *m.* (*sport*) heat, race.
забега́ловк|а, и *f.* (*coll.*) snack bar.
забе́га|ть, ю *pf.* **1.** to start running. **2.** to assume a shifty expression.
забега́|ть, ю *impf. of* **забежа́ть**
забе́га|ться, юсь *pf.* (*coll.*) to run o.s. to a standstill.
забе|жа́ть, гу́, жи́шь, гу́т *pf.* (*of* **~га́ть**) **1.** to run up. **2.** (**к**; *coll.*) to drop in (to see). **3.** to run off; to stray. **4.: з. вперёд** to run ahead; (*fig.*, *coll.*) to anticipate.
забеле́|ть, ет *pf.* to begin to turn white.
забел|и́ть, ю́, ~и́шь *pf.* **1.** to whiten, paint white. **2.** (*coll.*) to add milk, cream (to); **з. чай молоко́м** to put milk in tea.
забе́лк|а, и *f.* (*coll.*) **1.** whitening. **2.** milk or cream added to tea, etc.
забере́мене|ть, ю *pf.* (*of* **бере́менеть**) to become pregnant.
забеспоко́|иться, юсь, ишься *pf.* to begin to worry.
забива́ни|е, я *nt.* (*coll.*) jamming (*of radio transmissions*).
забива́|ть(ся), ю(сь) *impf. of* **заби́ть(ся)**[1]
заби́вк|а, и *f.* (*coll.*) driving in; blocking up, stopping up.
забинт|ова́ть, у́ю *pf.* (*of* **~о́вывать**) to bandage.
забинт|ова́ться, у́юсь *pf.* (*of* **~о́вываться**) to bandage o.s.
забинто́выва|ть(ся), аю(сь) *impf. of* **забинтова́ть(ся)**
забирать(ся), ю(сь) *impf. of* **забра́ть(ся)**
заби́т|ый (~, ~а) *p.p.p. of* **~ь** *and adj.* cowed, downtrodden.
заб|и́ть[1]**, ью́, ьёшь** *pf.* (*of* **~ива́ть**) **1.** to drive in, hammer in, ram in; **з. себе́ в го́лову** to get (it) firmly fixed in one's head. **2.** (*sport*) to score; **з. мяч** to kick the ball into the goal; **з. гол** to score a goal. **3.** to seal, stop up, block up; **з. ще́ли па́клей** to caulk up cracks with oakum. **4.** to obstruct; (*of plants*) to choke; (*coll.*) to jam (*radio transmissions*). **5.** (*+i.*; *coll.*) to cram, stuff (with). **6.** to beat up, knock senseless; (*fig.*) to render defenceless. **7.** (*coll.*) to beat (*at sth.*); to outdo, surpass. **8.** to slaughter (*cattle*).
заб|и́ть[2]**, ью́, ьёшь** *pf.* (*in var. senses*; *trans. and intrans.*) to begin to beat (*in some cases forms pf. aspect of* **бить**); **з. трево́гу** to sound the alarm; **у нас из сква́жины ~и́ла нефть** we have struck oil.
заб|и́ться[1]**, ью́сь, ьёшься** *pf.* (*of* **~ива́ться**) **1.** (**в**+*a.*) to hide (in), take refuge (in). **2.** (**в**+*a.*) to get (into), penetrate. **3.** (*+i.*) to become cluttered (with), clogged (with).
заб|и́ться[2]**, ью́сь, ьёшься** *pf.* to begin to beat (*intrans.*).
забия́к|а, и *c.g.* (*coll.*) squabbler; trouble-maker; bully.
заблаговре́менно *adv.* in good time; well in advance; **з. предупреди́ть** to warn in advance.
заблаговре́менный *adj.* timely, done in good time.
заблагорассу́|дить, жу, дишь *pf.* (*obs.*) to think fit.
заблагорассу́д|иться, ится *pf.* (*impers.*) to like, think fit; to come into one's head; **он придёт, когда́ ему́ ~ится** he will come when he thinks fit, when he feels so disposed.
забле|сте́ть, щу́, сти́шь *and* **~щешь** *pf.* to begin to shine, glitter, glow.
забле́|ять, ю, ешь *pf.* to begin to bleat.
заблу|ди́ться, жу́сь ~дишься *pf.* to lose one's way, get lost; **з. в трёх со́снах** to lose one's way in broad daylight.
заблу́дш|ий *adj.* (*obs.*) lost, stray; **~ая овца́** a lost sheep.
заблужда́|ться, юсь *impf.* to be mistaken.
заблужде́ни|е, я *nt.* error; delusion; **ввести́ в з.** to delude, mislead; **впасть в з.** to be deluded.
забода́|ть, ю *pf. of* **бода́ть**
забо́|й[1]**, я** *m.* (*mining*) (pit-)face.
забо́|й[2]**, я** *m.* slaughtering.
забо́йник, а *m.* (*tech.*) beetle, rammer.
забо́йщик, а *m.* face-worker, (coal-)hewer, getter (*in mine*).
забола́чива|ть(ся), ет(ся) *impf. of* **заболо́тить(ся)**
заболева́емост|ь, и *f.* sickness rate; number of cases; **з. полиомиели́том утро́илась за про́шлую неде́лю** the number of cases of infantile paralysis has tripled during the last week.
заболева́ни|е, я *nt.* **1.** sickness, illness. **2.** falling sick, falling ill.
заболева́|ть[1]**, ю** *impf. of* **заболе́ть**[1]
заболева́|ть[2]**, ет** *impf. of* **заболе́ть**[2]
заболе́|ть[1]**, ю, ешь** *pf.* (*of* **~ва́ть**[1]) to fall ill, fall sick; (*+i.*) to be taken ill (with), go down (with).
забол|е́ть[2]**, ит** *pf.* (*of* **~ева́ть**[2]) to (begin to) ache, hurt; **у меня́ ~е́л зуб** I have toothache.
за́болон|ь, и *f.* (*bot.*) alburnum, sap-wood.
заболо́|тить, чу, тишь *pf.* (*of* **забола́чивать**) to swamp, turn into swamp (*intrans.*).
заболо́|титься, тится *pf.* (*of* **забола́чиваться**) to turn into swamp (*intrans.*).
заболта́|ть[1]**, ю** *pf.* **1.** (*+i.*) to begin to swing. **2.** (*impf.* **заба́лтывать**) to mix (in).
заболта́|ть[2]**, ю** *pf.* (*coll.*) to start chattering, nattering.
заболта́|ться[1]**, юсь** *pf.* (*coll.*) to begin to swing.
заболта́|ться[2]**, юсь** *pf.* (*coll.*) to become engrossed in conversation.
забо́р[1]**, а** *m.* fence.
забо́р[2]**, а** *m.* **1.** taking away. **2.** obtaining on credit.
забо́рист|ый (~, ~а) *adj.* (*coll.*) **1.** strong (*of liquor*, *tobacco*, *etc.*). **2.** (*fig.*) **з. анекдо́т** risqué story; **з. моти́в** racy tune.
забо́р|ный[1] *adj.* **1.** *adj. of* **~**[1]. **2.** coarse, indecent; risqué; **~ная литерату́ра** pornography.
забо́р|ный[2] *adj. of* **~**[2]; **~ная кни́жка** (*i*) ration book, (*ii*) account (*book in which purchases obtained on credit are entered*).
забо́ртный *adj.* (*naut.*) outboard; **з. дви́гатель** outboard engine; **з. кла́пан** (*tech.*) seacock; **з. трап** companion ladder.
забо́т|а, ы *f.* **1.** cares, trouble(s); **без ~** carefree; (*coll.*) **вот не́ было ~ы!** there was trouble enough already; **ему́ ма́ло ~ы** what does he care? **2.** care, attention(s); concern; **з. о челове́ке** concern for people's welfare.
забо́|тить, чу, тишь *impf.* to trouble, worry, cause anxiety.
забо́|титься, чусь, тишься *impf.* (*of* **по~**) (**о**+*p.*) **1.** to worry, be troubled (about). **2.** to take care (of); to take trouble (about); to care (about); **она́ всё ~тится о де́тях** she is always thinking of the children; **он ни о чём не ~тится** he does not care about anything.
забо́тливост|ь, и *f.* solicitude, care, thoughtfulness.
забо́тлив|ый (~, ~а) *adj.* solicitous, thoughtful; caring.
забрако́в|анный *p.p.p. of* **~а́ть**; **з. това́р** rejects.
забрак|ова́ть, у́ю *pf. of* **бракова́ть**
забра́л|о, а *nt.* visor; **с откры́тым ~ом** openly, frankly.
забра́сыва|ть, ю *impf. of* **заброса́ть** *and* **забро́сить**
забра́|ть[1]**, заберу́, заберёшь,** *past* **~л, ~ла́, ~ло** *pf.* (*of* **забира́ть**) **1.** to take (*in one's hands*); to take (with one); **з. во́жжи** to take the reins; **з. с собо́й ве́щи** to take one's things with one; **з. себе́ в го́лову** to take it onto one's head; **з. за живо́е** to touch to the quick. **2.** to take away; to seize, appropriate. **3.** (*of emotions*; *coll.*) to come over, seize; **его́ ~ла́ охо́та пое́хать в Аме́рику** he was seized with a desire to go to America. **4.** to take in (*part of a garment*, *etc.*). **5.** to turn off, aside. **6.** (*tech.*) to catch; (*of an anchor*) to bite.
забра́|ть[2]**, заберу́, заберёшь,** *past* **~л, ~ла́, ~ло** *pf.* (*of* **забира́ть**) to stop up, block up.
забра́|ться, заберу́сь, заберёшься, *past* **~лся, ~ла́сь, ~ло́сь** *pf.* (*of* **забира́ться**) **1.** (**в**+*a.*) to get (into); (**в, на**+*a.*) to climb (into, on to); **з. в чужо́й дом** to get into s.o. else's house. **2.** to get to; to hide out, go into hiding; **куда́ они́ ~лись?** where have they got to?
забре́|дить, жу, дишь *pf.* to become delirious.
забре́зж|ить, ит *pf.* to begin to dawn; to begin to appear; **чуть ~ил свет** it was barely light; (*impers.*): **~ило** it is just beginning to get light.
забре|сти́, ду́, дёшь, *past* **~л, ~ла́** *pf.* (*coll.*) **1.** to drop in. **2.** to go astray, wander off.
забр|и́ть, е́ю, е́ешь *pf.* (*obs.*) to call up (into the army); **з. лоб** (*+d.*) = **з.**
заброни́р|овать, ую *pf.* (*of* **брони́ровать**) to reserve.
забронир|ова́ть, у́ю *pf.* (*of* **бронирова́ть**) to armour.
забро́с, а *m.*: **в ~е** (*coll.*) in a state of neglect.
заброса́|ть, ю *pf.* (*of* **забра́сывать**) (*+i.*) **1.** to fill (up) (with); **з. я́му золо́й** to fill up a hole with ashes. **2.** to shower (with), bespatter (with); **з. кого́-н. гря́зью** to sling

mud at s.o. (*also fig.*); **з. кого́-н. бла́нками** to deluge s.o. with forms.

забро́|сить, шу, сишь *pf.* (*of* **забра́сывать**) **1.** to throw (*with force or to a distance*); to cast (*also fig.*); **кто ~сил мя́чик в окно́?** who threw a ball through the window?; **вое́нная слу́жба ~сила его́ на Да́льний Восто́к** military service took him to the Far East. **2.** to throw (*a part of the body, etc.*); **з. го́лову наза́д** to throw one's head back. **3.** (*pf. only*) to mislay. **4.** to throw up, give up, abandon; to neglect, let go; **з. иссле́дования** to throw up one's research; **з. дете́й** to neglect children. **5.** to take, bring (*to a certain place*). **6.** to leave behind (*somewhere*).

забро́шенност|ь, и *f.* **1.** neglect. **2.** desertion.

забро́|шенный *p.p.p. of* **~сить** *and adj.* **1.** neglected. **2.** deserted, desolate.

забры́зг|ать[1], **аю** *pf.* (*of* **~ивать**) (+*i.*) to splash; to bespatter (with).

забры́з|гать[2], **жет** *pf.* to begin to play (*of a fountain*).

забры́згива|ть, ю *impf. of* **забры́згать**[1]

забубённ|ый *adj.* (*coll.*) reckless; wild; **~ая голо́вушка** desperate fellow, reprobate.

заб|у́ду, у́дешь *see* **~ы́ть**

забукси́р|овать, ую *pf.* to take in tow.

забулды́г|а, и *m.* (*coll.*) debauchee, profligate.

забу|ти́ть, чу́, ти́шь *pf.* (*of* **бути́ть**) to fill with rubble; (+*i.*) to fill in (with).

забуха́|ть, ет *impf. of* **забу́хнуть**

забу́х|нуть, нет, *past* **~,** **~ла** *pf.* to swell; to become stuck.

забуя́н|ить, ю, ишь *pf.* to become unruly, get out of hand.

забыва́|ть(ся), ю(сь) *impf. of* **забы́ть(ся)**

забы́вчив|ый (~, ~а) *adj.* forgetful; absent-minded.

заб|ы́ть, у́ду, у́дешь *pf.* (*of* **~ыва́ть**) **1.** (+*a.*, *o*+*p. or inf.*) to forget; **и ду́мать ~у́дь!** (*coll.*) get it out of your head!; **себя́ не з.** to take care of o.s. **2.** to leave behind, forget (to bring); **вы опя́ть ~ы́ли биле́ты** you have forgotten the tickets again.

забыть|ё, я́, в ~и́ *nt.* **1.** drowsy state. **2.** half-conscious state, oblivion. **3.** (state of) distraction; **в ~и́** distractedly.

заб|ы́ться, у́дусь, у́дешься *pf.* (*of* **~ыва́ться**) **1.** to doze off, drop off. **2.** to become unconscious, lose consciousness. **3.** to sink into a reverie. **4.** to forget o.s. **5.** *pass. of* **~ы́ть**

зав, а *m.* (*coll.*) *abbr. of* **~е́дующий**

зав. (*abbr. of* **заве́дующий**) manager.

зав... *comb. form, abbr. of* **1. заве́дующий. 2. заводско́й, заво́дский**

зава́л, а *m.* obstruction, blockage.

зава́лива|ть(ся), ю(сь) *impf. of* **завали́ть(ся)**

зава́линк|а, и *f.* zavalinka (*mound of earth round a Russ. peasant hut serving as protection from the weather and oft. used for sitting out*).

завал|и́ть, ю́, ~́ишь *pf.* (*of* **~́ивать**) **1.** to block up, obstruct; to fill (*so as to block up*); **з. вход мешка́ми с песко́м** to block up the entrance with sandbags. **2.** (+*i.*; *coll.*) to pile (with); to fill cram-full (with); (*fig.*) to overload with; **прила́вок ~́ен коро́бками** the stall is piled high with boxes; **реда́кция ~́ена рабо́той** the editors are snowed under with work. **3.** (*coll.*) to throw back; to tip up, cant. **4.** (*coll.*) to knock down, demolish. **5.** (*fig.*, *coll.*) to make a mess (of), muck up. **6.** (*impers.*; *coll.*) to block up, stuff up; **у меня́ у́хо ~и́ло** my ear feels blocked up.

завал|и́ться, ю́сь, ~́ишься *pf.* (*of* **~́иваться**) **1.** to fall; to collapse; **нож ~и́лся за шкаф** the knife has fallen behind the cupboard. **2.** (*coll.*) to lie down; **з. спать** to fall into bed. **3.** (*coll.*) to overturn, tip up. **4.** (*fig.*, *coll.*) to miscarry, come to grief; (*of a pers.*) to slip up.

зава́лк|а, и *f.* **1.** filling up. **2.** (*tech.*) (furnace) charge.

за́вал|ь, и *f.* (*collect.*; *coll.*) shop-soiled goods; trash.

заваля́|ться, ется *pf.* (*coll.*) **1.** to be still on hand; **э́тот това́р ~ется** these goods will not sell. **2.** to remain without attention; to be shelved.

заваля́щий *adj.* (*coll.*) long unsold, shop-soiled; worthless, useless.

зава́рива|ть(ся), ет(ся) *impf. of* **завари́ть(ся)**

завар|и́ть, ю́, ~́ишь *pf.* (*of* **~́ивать**) **1.** to make (*drinks, etc., by pouring on boiling water*); **з. чай** to brew tea; **з. ка́шу** (*fig.*) to start trouble; **ну и ~и́л ка́шу!** now the fat's in the fire. **2.** to scald. **3.** (*tech.*) to weld. **4.** (*coll.*) to start, initiate.

завар|и́ться, ~́ится *pf.* (*of* **~́иваться**) **1.** (*of drinks*) to have brewed. **2.** (*coll.*) to start; **~и́лось бо́льшое де́ло** there's big trouble brewing.

зава́рк|а, и *f.* **1.** brewing (*of tea, etc.*). **2.** scalding. **3.** (*tech.*) welding. **4.** (*coll.*) enough tea for one brew.

заварно́й *adj.* (*cul.*) boiled.

завару́х|а, и *f.* (*coll.*) commotion, stir.

заведе́ни|е, я *nt.* **1.** establishment, institution. **2.** (*obs.*) custom, habit; **здесь уж тако́е з.** it is the custom here.

заве́д|овать, ую *impf.* (+*i.*) to manage, superintend; to be in charge (of).

заве́домо *adv.* wittingly; (+*adj.*) known to be; **з. зна́я** being fully aware; **переда́ть з. необосно́ванный слух** to pass on a rumour known to be unfounded.

заве́домый *adj.* notorious; undoubted.

заве|ду́, дёшь *see* **~сти́**

заве́дующ|ий, его *m.* (+*i.*) manager; head; pers. in charge (of); **з. уче́бной ча́стью** director of studies; **з. отде́лом** head of a department.

завез|ти́, у́, ёшь, *past* **~́,** **~ла́** *pf.* (*of* **завози́ть**) **1.** to convey, deliver; **з. запи́ску по доро́ге домо́й** to deliver a note on the way home. **2.** to take (to a distance *or* out of one's way).

заверб|ова́ть, у́ю *pf. of* **вербова́ть**

завере́ни|е, я *nt.* assurance; protestation.

завери́тел|ь, я *m.* witness (*to a signature, etc.*).

заве́р|ить, ю, ишь *pf.* (*of* **~я́ть**) **1.** (**в**+*p.*) to assure (of). **2.** to certify; **з. по́дпись** to witness a signature.

заве́рк|а, и *f.* certification.

заверн|у́ть, у́, ёшь *pf.* (*of* **завёртывать**) **1.** (**в**+*a.*) to wrap (in); **~и́те его́ в одея́ло** wrap in a blanket. **2.** to tuck up, roll up (*sleeve, etc.*). **3.** to turn (*intrans.*); **з. напра́во** to turn to the right. **4.** (*coll.*) to drop in, call in. **5.** to screw tight; to turn off (*by screwing*); **з. га́йку** to screw a nut tight; **з. кран** to turn off a tap; **з. во́ду** to turn the water off. **6.** (*of weather conditions*; *coll.*) to come on, come down.

заверн|у́ться, у́сь, ёшься *pf.* (*of* **завёртываться**) **1.** (**в**+*a.*) to wrap o.s. up (in), muffle o.s. (in). **2.** *pass. of* **~у́ть**

завер|те́ть, чу́, ~́тишь *pf.* **1.** to begin to twirl. **2.: з. кого́-н.** (*fig.*, *coll.*) to turn s.o.'s head.

завер|те́ться, чу́сь, ~́тишься *pf.* **1.** to begin to turn, begin to spin. **2.** (*coll.*) to become flustered; to lose one's head.

завёртк|а, и *f.* **1.** wrapping up. **2.** (*coll.*) package.

завёртыва|ть(ся), ю(сь) *impf. of* **заверну́ть(ся)**

заверш|а́ть, а́ю *impf. of* **~и́ть**

заверше́ни|е, я *nt.* completion; end; **в з.** in conclusion.

заверш|и́ть, у́, и́шь *pf.* (*of* **~а́ть**) to complete, conclude, crown.

завер|я́ть, я́ю *impf. of* **~́ить**

заве́с|а, ы *f.* (*obs.*) curtain; **дымова́я з.** (*mil.*) smoke-screen; (*fig.*) veil, screen; **приподня́ть ~у** to lift the veil.

заве́|сить, шу, сишь *pf.* (*of* **~шивать**) to curtain (off.).

заве|сти́, ду́, дёшь, *past* **~́л,** **~ла́** *pf.* (*of* **заводи́ть**[1]) **1.** to take, bring (*to a place*); to leave, drop of (*at a place*). **2.** to take (to a distance *or* out of one's way). **3.** to set up; to start; **з. де́ло** (*coll.*) to set up in business; **з. птицефе́рму** to start a poultry farm; **з. перепи́ску с кем-н.** to start up a correspondence with s.o. **4.** to acquire. **5.** to institute, introduce (*as a custom*); **з. привы́чку** (+*inf.*) to get into the habit (of); **у нас так ~дено́** this is our custom. **6.** to wind (up), start (*a mechanism*); **з. часы́** to wind up a clock; **з. мото́р** to crank an engine; **как ~дённый** (*coll.*) like a machine.

заве|сти́сь, ду́сь, дёшься, *past* **~́лся,** **~ла́сь** *pf.* (*of* **заводи́ться**) **1.** to be; to appear; **в по́гребе ~ли́сь кры́сы** there are rats in the cellar. **2.** to be established, be set up; **~ло́сь обыкнове́ние** it has become a habit. **3.** (+*i.*; *coll.*) to acquire; **з. свои́м до́мом** to acquire a home of one's own. **4.** (*of a mechanism*) to start (*intrans.*).

заве́т, а *m.* **1.** (*rhet.*) behest, bidding, ordinance. **2.: Ве́тхий, Но́вый з.** the Old, the New Testament.

заве́тн|ый *adj.* cherished; intimate; secret, hidden; **стать кинозвездо́й — её ~ая мечта́** her secret ambition is to become a film-star.
заве́тренный *adj.* leeward.
заве́ш|ать, аю *pf.* (*of* **~ивать**) (*+a. and i.*) to hang (all over); **он ~ал сте́ны своего́ кабине́та фотогра́фиями** he has hung the walls of his study with photographs.
заве́шива|ть, ю *impf. of* **заве́сить** *and* **заве́шать**
завеща́ни|е, я *nt.* will, testament.
завеща́тел|ь, я *m.* (*leg.*) testator.
завеща́тельниц|а, ы *f.* (*leg.*) testatrix.
завеща́|ть, ю *impf. and pf.* (*+a. and d.*) to leave (to), bequeath (to); (*leg.*) to devise (to).
заве́|ять, ет *pf.* **1.** to begin to blow (*of the wind*). **2.** (*of blizzard, etc.*) to cover.
завзя́тый *adj.* (*coll.*) inveterate, out-and-out, downright; incorrigible.
завива́|ть(ся), ю(сь) *impf. of* **зави́ть(ся)**
зави́вк|а, и *f.* **1.** waving; curling; **сде́лать себе́ ~у** to have one's hair waved. **2.** (hair-)wave.
зави́|деть, жу, дишь *pf.* (*coll.*) to catch sight of.
зави́д|ки, ок *no sg.* (*coll.*): **меня́**, *etc.*, **беру́т з.** I, *etc.*, feel envious.
зави́дно *as pred.* (*impers.*, *+d.*) to feel envious.
зави́д|ный (~ен, ~на) *adj.* enviable.
зави́д|овать, ую *impf.* (*of* **по~**) (*+d.*) to envy.
завиду́щий *adj.* (*coll.*) envious, covetous.
завизж|а́ть, у́, и́шь *pf.* to begin to scream, squeal.
визи́р|овать, ую *pf. of* **визи́ровать**[1]
завин|ти́ть, чу́, ти́шь *pf.* (*of* **~́чивать**) to screw up.
завин|ти́ться, чу́сь, ти́шься *pf.* (*of* **~́чиваться**) to screw up (*intrans.*).
зави́нчива|ть(ся), ю(сь) *impf. of* **завинти́ть(ся)**
завира́льный *adj.* (*coll.*) false; nonsensical.
завира́|ться, юсь *impf. of* **завра́ться**
завиру́х|а, и *f.* (*dial.*) **1.** snow-storm. **2.** (*coll.*) bother, fuss.
зависа́|ть, ю *impf.* (*aeron.*) to hover.
зави́|сеть, шу, сишь *impf.* **(от) 1.** to depend (on). **2.** to lie in the power (of); **я помогу́ тебе́, наско́лько от меня́ ~сит** I will help you as far as in me lies.
зави́симость *f.* dependence; **в ~и (от)** depending (on), subject (to).
зави́сим|ый (~, ~а) *adj.* **(от)** dependent (on).
зави́стлив|ый (~, ~а) *adj.* envious.
зави́стник, а *m.* envious pers.
за́вист|ь, и *f.* envy.
завит|о́й *and* **~́ый (зави́т, ~а́, зави́то)** *adj.* curled; waved.
завит|о́к, ка́ *m.* **1.** curl, lock. **2.** flourish (*in handwriting*). **3.** (*archit.*) volute, scroll. **4.** (*bot.*) tendril. **5.** (*anat.*) helix.
зав|и́ть, ью́, ьёшь, *past* **~и́л, ~ила́, ~и́ло** *pf.* (*of* **~ива́ть**) to curl, to wave, to twist, wind; **з. го́ре верёвочкой** (*coll.*) to pack up one's troubles.
зав|и́ться, ью́сь, ьёшься, *past* **~и́лся, ~ила́сь** *pf.* (*of* **~ива́ться**) **1.** to curl, wave, twine (*intrans.*). **2.** to curl, wave one's hair; to have one's hair curled, waved.
завко́м, а *m.* (*abbr. of* ***заводско́й комите́т***) factory committee.
завладева́|ть, ю *impf. of* **завладе́ть**
завладе́|ть, ю *pf.* (*of* **~ва́ть**) (*+i.*) to take possession (of); to seize, capture (*also fig.*); **свои́м красноре́чием он ~л внима́нием слу́шателей** he gripped the audience with his eloquence.
завлека́тел|ьный (~ен, ~ьна) *adj.* (*coll.*) alluring; fascinating, captivating.
завлека́|ть, ю *impf. of* **завле́чь**
завле́|чь, ку́, чёшь, ку́т, *past* **~́к, ~кла́** *pf.* (*of* **~ка́ть**) **1.** to lure, entice. **2.** to fascinate, captivate.
заво́д[1], **а** *m.* **1.** factory, mill; works; **нефтеочисти́тельный з.** oil refinery. **2.** **(ко́нский) з.** stud(-farm).
заво́д[2], **а** *m.* **1.** winding up. **2.** winding mechanism; **игру́шка с ~ом** clockwork toy. **3.** period of running (*of clock, etc.*); **часы́ с су́точным ~ом** twenty-four-hour clock.
заво́д[3], **а** *m. only in phr.* **э́того (и) в ~е нет** (*coll.*) it has never been the custom.
заводи́л|а, ы *c.g.* (*coll.*) instigator; live-wire.
заво|ди́ть[1], **жу́, ~́дишь** *impf. of* **завести́**
заво|ди́ть[2], **жу́, ~́дишь** *pf.* (*coll.*) to walk off one's feet.
завод|и́ться, ~́ится *impf. of* **завести́сь**
заво́дк|а, и *f.* winding up; starting.
заводн|о́й *adj.* **1.** clockwork. **2.** (*tech.*) winding. starting; **~а́я рукоя́тка, ру́чка** starting crank.
заводоуправле́ни|е, я *nt.* works management.
заво́д|ский *adj. of* **~**[1]; **~ская ло́шадь** stud-horse; *as n.* **з., ~ского** *m.* factory worker.
завод|ско́й = **~́ский; з. треуго́льник** (*coll.*) 'factory triangle' (= *leadership comprising factory manager, Party secretary, and trade union secretary*).
заво́дчик[1], **а** *m.* **1.** factory-owner, mill-owner.
заво́дчик[2], **а** *m.* (*coll., obs.*) instigator, author.
за́вод|ь, и *f.* creek, backwater.
завоева́ни|е, я *nt.* **1.** winning. **2.** conquest; (*fig.*) achievement, gain, attainment; **нове́йшие ~я те́хники** the latest achievements of technology.
завоева́тел|ь, я *m.* conqueror.
завоева́тельн|ый *adj.* aggressive; **~ая война́** war of conquest.
заво|ева́ть, ю́ю, ю́ешь *pf.* (*of* **~ёвывать**) to conquer; (*fig.*) to win, gain; **з. о́бщие симпа́тии** to gain general sympathy.
завоёвыва|ть, ю *impf. of* **завоева́ть**; to try to get.
заво́з, а *m.* delivery; carriage.
заво|зи́ть[1], **жу́, ~́зишь** *impf. of* **завезти́**
заво|зи́ть[2], **жу́, ~́зишь** *pf.* (*coll.*) to dirty, soil.
заво|зи́ться[1], **жу́сь, ~́зишься** *impf., pass. of* **~зи́ть**[1]
заво|зи́ться[2], **жу́сь, ~́зишься** *pf.* (*coll.*) to begin to play about.
заво́зный *adj.* brought in; imported.
завола́кива|ть(ся), ю(сь) *impf. of* **заволо́чь(ся)**
заво́лжск|ий *adj.* (situated, living) on the left bank of the Volga; **~ие ста́рцы** (*hist.*) trans-Volga monks (*adherents of 'non-possessor' doctrine of Nil Sorsky*).
заволн|ова́ться, у́юсь *pf.* to become agitated.
заволо́|чь, ку́, чёшь, ку́т, *past* **~к, ~кла́** *pf.* (*of* **завола́кивать**) to cloud; to obscure; **тума́н ~к со́лнце** the sun was obscured by fog; **её глаза́ ~кло́ слеза́ми** her eyes were clouded with tears.
заволо́|чься, чётся, ку́тся, *past* **~кся, ~кла́сь** *pf.* (*of* **завола́киваться**) to cloud over, become clouded.
завоп|и́ть, лю́, и́шь *pf.* (*coll.*) to cry out, yell; to give a cry.
завора́жива|ть, ю *impf. of* **заворожи́ть**
завора́чива|ть[1], **ю** *impf.* = **завёртывать**
завора́чива|ть[2], **ю** *impf.* **1.** *impf. of* **заворoти́ть. 2.** (*impf. only*) (*+i.*; *coll.*) to be boss (of).
заворож|и́ть, у́, и́шь *pf.* (*of* **завора́живать**) to cast a spell (over), bewitch; (*fig.*) to fascinate.
заворо́т, а *m.* (*coll.*) **1.** turn, turning. **2.** bend (*in road, river, etc.*).
завор|оти́ть, очу́, о́тишь *pf.* (*of* **завора́чивать**[2]) **1.** to turn. **2.** to turn in; to drop in. **3.** to roll up; to tuck up.
заворо́шк|а, и *f.* (*coll.*) complication(s).
завр|а́ться, у́сь, ёшься, *past* **~а́лся, ~ала́сь** *pf.* (*of* **завира́ться**) (*coll.*) to become entangled in lies; to become an inveterate liar.
завсегда́ *adv.* (*coll.*) always.
завсегда́та|й, я *m.* habitué, frequenter, regular; **театра́льный з.** regular theatre-goer; **з. ба́ров** barfly.
за́втра *adv.* tomorrow; (*in past-tense narration*) the next day; **до з.!** see you tomorrow!; **не ны́нче-з.** (*coll.*) any day now.
за́втрак, а *m.* breakfast; lunch(eon); **второ́й з.** elevenses, mid-morning snack; **корми́ть ~ами** (*coll.*) to feed with empty hopes.
за́втрака|ть, ю *impf.* (*of* **по~**) to (have) breakfast; to (have) lunch.
за́втрашн|ий *adj.* tomorrow's; **з. день** tomorrow; **забо́титься о ~ем дне** to take thought for the morrow.
завуали́ров|анный *p.p.p. of* **~ать** *and adj.* (*phot.*) fogged.
завуали́р|овать, ую *pf. of* **вуали́ровать**
за́вуч, а *m.* (*abbr. of* ***заве́дующий уче́бной ча́стью***) director of studies.

завхо́з, а *m.* (*abbr. of* **заве́дующий хозя́йством**) bursar, steward.
завши́ве|ть, ю *pf. of* **вши́веть**
завши́вленный *adj.* (*coll.*) lice-ridden.
завыва́|ть, ю *impf.* to howl; to sough.
завы́|сить, шу, сишь *pf.* (*of* **~ша́ть**) to raise too high; **з. отме́тку на экза́мене** to give too high a mark in an examination.
зав|ы́ть, о́ю, о́ешь *pf.* to begin to howl.
завыша́|ть, ю *impf. of* **завы́сить**
завя|за́ть[1], **жу́, ~́шешь** *pf.* (*of* **~́зывать**) **1.** to tie (up); to knot; **з. шнýрки боти́нок** to tie up one's shoe-laces. **2.** to bind (up). **3.** (*fig.*) to start; **з. бой** to join battle; **з. перепи́ску** to start a correspondence; **з. разгово́р** to strike up a conversation.
завяза́|ть[2], **ю** *impf. of* **завя́знуть**
завя|за́ться, ~́жется *pf.* (*of* **~́зываться**) **1.** *pass. of* **~за́ть. 2.** to start; to arise. **3.** (*bot.*) to set.
завязи́|ть, ть, *1st pers. not used,* **шь** *pf.* (*coll.*) to get stuck (*trans.*).
завя́зк|а, и *f.* **1.** string, lace, band. **2.** beginning, start; opening (*of novel, etc.*).
завя́з|нуть, ну, нешь, *past* **~, ~ла** *pf.* (*of* **~а́ть**[2]) to stick, get stuck; **з. в долга́х** to be over head and ears in debt.
завя́зыва|ть(ся), ет(ся) *impf. of* **завяза́ть(ся)**
за́вяз|ь, и *f.* (*bot.*) ovary.
завя́лый *adj.* (*obs.*) withered, faded.
завя́|нуть, ну, нешь, *past* **~л** *pf. of* **вя́нуть**
загад|а́ть, а́ю *pf.* (*of* **~́ывать**) **1.: з. зага́дки** to ask riddles. **2.** to guess one's fortune; to decide, settle (*by tossing a coin, etc.*). **3.** to think of (*= to select arbitrarily, at random*); **~а́йте число́** think of a number. **4.** to plan ahead, look ahead. **5.** (*coll.*) to give orders.
зага́|дить, жу, дишь *pf.* (*of* **~живать**) (*coll.*) to soil, dirty, befoul.
зага́дк|а, и *f.* riddle; enigma; mystery.
зага́доч|ный (~ен, ~на) *adj.* enigmatic; mysterious.
зага́дыва|ть, ю *impf. of* **загада́ть**
зага́жива|ть, ю *impf. of* **зага́дить**
зага́р, а *m.* sunburn, (sun-)tan.
загаса́|ть, ет *impf. of* **зага́снуть**
зага|си́ть, шу́, ~́сишь *pf. of* **гаси́ть 1.**
зага́с|нуть, нет, *past* **~, ~ла** *pf.* (*of* **~а́ть**) (*coll.*) to go out.
загвоз|ди́ть, жу́, ди́шь *pf.* **1.** (*obs.*) to spike (a gun). **2.** (*coll.*) to pose, set (*a problem, etc.*).
загво́здк|а, и *f.* (*coll.*) snag, obstacle; **вот в чём з.!** there's the rub!
заги́б, а *m.* **1.** fold; bend. **2.** (*coll.*) exaggeration; (*pol.*) deviation.
загиба́|ть(ся), ю(сь) *impf. of* **загну́ть(ся)**
заги́бщик, а *m.* (*pol.*; *coll.*) deviationist.
загипнотизи́р|овать, ую *pf. of* **гипнотизи́ровать**
загипс|ова́ть, у́ю *pf. of* **гипсова́ть**
загла́ви|е, я *nt.* title; heading; **под ~ем** entitled, headed.
загла́в|ный *adj. of* **~ие; з. лист** title-page; **~ная бу́ква** capital letter; **~ные бу́квы** initials; **~ная роль** (*theatr.*) title-role, name-part; **~ное сло́во** headword.
загла́|дить, жу, дишь *pf.* (*of* **~живать**) **1.** to iron (out), press. **2.** (*fig.*) to make up (for), make amends (for); **з. грехи́** to expiate one's sins.
загла́|диться, дится *pf.* (*of* **~живаться**) **1.** to iron out (*intrans.*); to become smooth. **2.** (*fig.*) to fade.
загла́жива|ть, ю *impf. of* **загла́дить**
загла́жива|ться, ется *impf. of* **загла́диться**
загла́зно *adv.* (*coll.*) behind s.o.'s back.
загла́зн|ый *adj.* (*coll.*) done, said in s.o.'s absence, behind s.o.'s back; **~ое реше́ние** (*leg.*) judgment by default; **~ая клевета́** scandal uttered about s.o. behind his back; backbiting.
загла́тыва|ть, ю *impf. of* **заглота́ть**
заглота́|ть, ю *pf.* (*of* **загла́тывать**) to swallow.
загло́тный *adj.* (*coll.*): **з. коммуни́ст** die-hard Communist.
загло́хн|уть, у, ешь *pf. of* **гло́хнуть 2., 3.**
заглуш|а́ть, а́ю *impf. of* **~и́ть**
заглуш|и́ть, у́, и́шь *pf.* (*of* **глуши́ть** *and* **~а́ть**) **1.** to drown, deaden, muffle (*sound*). **2.** to jam (*radio transmissions*). **3.** (*of plants*) to choke. **4.** (*fig.*) to suppress, stifle. **5.** to alleviate, soothe.
заглу́шк|а, и *f.* **1.** (*tech.*) choke, plug, stopper. **2.** lid (*for central tube of samovar*).
загляде́нь|е, я *nt.* (*coll.*) lovely sight; **э́то про́сто з.!** isn't that lovely?; what a beautiful sight!
загля|де́ться, жу́сь, ди́шься *pf.* (*of* **~́дываться**) (**на**+*a.*; *coll.*) to stare (at); to be unable to take one's eyes off; to be lost in admiration (of).
загля́дыва|ть, ю *impf. of* **загляну́ть**
загля́дыва|ться, юсь *impf. of* **загляде́ться**
заглян|у́ть, у́, ~́ешь *pf.* (*of* **загля́дывать**) **1.** to peep; to glance; **она́ ~у́ла в окно́ и уви́дела, что де́ти засну́ли** she peeped in at the window and saw that the children had gone to sleep; **з. в газе́ты** to glance at the newspapers. **2.** (*coll.*) to look in, drop in; **~и́те к нам, пожа́луйста!** please look in (on us)!
загна́ива|ть(ся), ю(сь) *impf. of* **загнои́ть(ся)**
за́гнанный *p.p.p.* of **загна́ть** *and adj.* **1.** tired out, exhausted; (*of a horse*) winded; **как з. зверь** at the end of one's tether. **2.** down-trodden, cowed.
загна́|ть, загоню́, заго́нишь, *past* **~л, ~ла́, ~ло** *pf.* (*of* **загоня́ть**[1]) **1.** to drive in; **з. коро́в в хлев** to drive the cows into the shed, get the cows in; **з. мяч в воро́та** (*sport*) to score, shoot a goal. **2.** to drive (off). **3.** to tire out, exhaust; to override (*a horse*). **4.** (*coll.*) to drive home; **з. сва́и в зе́млю** to drive piles into the ground. **5.** (*sl.*) to flog (*= to sell*). **6.: з. копе́йку** (*sl.*) to make (some) money.
загнива́ни|е, я *nt.* rotting, putrescence; (*fig.*) decay; (*med.*) suppuration.
загнива́|ть, ю *impf. of* **загни́ть**
загни́|ть, ю́, ёшь, *past* **~л, ~ла́, ~ло** *pf.* (*of* **~ва́ть**) to begin to rot; to rot, decay (*also fig.*); (*med.*) to fester.
загно|и́ть, ю́, и́шь *pf.* (*of* **загна́ивать**) (*coll.*) **1.** to allow to fester. **2.** to allow to rot, allow to decay.
загно|и́ться, и́тся *pf.* (*of* **загна́иваться**) to fester.
загн|у́ть, у́, ёшь *pf.* (*of* **загиба́ть**) **1.** to turn up, turn down; to bend, fold; to crease; **з. страни́цу** to dog-ear a page. **2.** to turn (*intrans.*); **з. за́ угол** to turn a corner. **3.** (*coll.*) to utter (*a swear-word or vulgarism*); **ну и слове́чко ~у́л!** (*iron.*) what language! **4.** (*coll.*) to ask (*an exorbitant price*).
загн|у́ться, у́сь, ёшься *pf.* (*of* **загиба́ться**) **1.** to turn up, stick up; to turn down. **2.** (*sl.*) to turn up one's toes (*= to die*).
загова́рива|ть, ю *impf. of* **заговори́ть**[1]
загова́рива|ться, юсь *impf.* (*of* **заговори́ться**) **1.** to be carried away by a conversation. **2.** (*impf. only*) to rave; to ramble (*in speech*); **говори́, да не ~йся!** talk sense!
за́говень|е, я *nt.* (*eccl.*) last day before fast.
загове́|ться, юсь *pf.* (*eccl.*) to eat meat for the last time (*before a fast*).
за́говор, а *m.* **1.** plot, conspiracy. **2.** charm, spell.
заговор|и́ть[1], **ю́, и́шь** *pf.* (*of* **загова́ривать**) **1.** (*coll.*) to talk s.o.'s head off; to tire out with much talk. **2.** to cast a spell (over); (**от**) to put on a spell (against); to exorcize; **з. зу́бы кому́-н.** (*coll.*) to distract s.o. with smooth talk.
заговор|и́ть[2], **ю́, и́шь** *pf.* **1.** to begin to speak. **2.** to (be able to) speak; to learn to speak.
заговор|и́ться, ю́сь, и́шься *pf. of* **загова́риваться**
загово́рщик, а *m.* conspirator, plotter.
загово́рщицкий *adj.* (*coll.*) conspiratorial.
загог|ота́ть, очу́, о́чешь *pf.* to begin to cackle; (*coll.*) to begin to guffaw.
загогу́лин|а, ы *f.* (*coll.*) flourish.
за́годя *adv.* (*coll.*) in good time.
загол|и́ть, ю́, и́шь *pf.* (*of* **~я́ть**) to bare.
заголо́в|ок, ка *m.* **1.** title; heading. **2.** headline.
заголя́|ть, ю *impf. of* **заголи́ть**
заго́н, а *m.* **1.** driving in; rounding-up. **2.** enclosure (*for cattle*); pen. **3.** strip (of ploughed land). **4.: быть в ~е** (*fig.*) to be kept down; **у кого́-н. в ~е** under s.o.'s thumb. **5.: в ~е** (*sl.*) to one's credit, 'chalked up'; **у него́ в ~е три дня** he had three days' (work) to his credit.

загóнщик, а *m.* (*hunting*) beater.
за|гоню́, гóнишь *see* **~гнáть**
загоня́|ть[1], **ю** *impf. of* **загнáть**
загоня́|ть[2], **ю** *pf.* (*coll.*) **1.** to tire out; to work to death. **2.** (*sl.*) to grill (*with questions*).
загорáжива|ть(ся), ю(сь) *impf. of* **загороди́ть(ся)**
загорá|ть(ся), ю(сь) *impf. of* **загорéть(ся)**
загóрб|ок, ка *m.* (*coll.*) upper part of the back (*between shoulder-blades*).
загор|ди́ться, жу́сь, ди́шься *pf.* (*coll.*) to become proud, become stuck-up.
загорéлый *adj.* sunburnt; brown, bronzed.
загор|éть, ю́, и́шь *pf.* (*of* **~áть**) to become sunburnt, become brown; to acquire a tan.
загор|éться, ю́сь, и́шься *pf.* (*of* **~áться**) **1.** to catch fire; to begin to burn; (*impers.*): **в библиотéке ~éлось** a fire broke out in the library. **2.** (*+i.*; **от**) to blaze (with), burn (with) (*fig.*); **егó глазá ~éлись от гнéва** his eyes blazed with anger; **онá ~éлась от смущéния** she went red with embarrassment. **3.** (*impers., +d.*; *coll.*) to want very much; to have a burning desire; **ей ~éлось уви́деть Рим** she had a burning desire to see Rome. **4.** (*fig.*) to break out, start; **~éлась дрáка** a fight broke out.
загоро|ди́ть, жу́, ~ди́шь *pf.* (*of* **загорáживать**) **1.** to enclose, fence in. **2.** to barricade; to obstruct; **з. комý-н. свет** to stand in s.o.'s light.
загоро|ди́ться, жу́сь, ~ди́шься *pf.* (*of* **загорáживаться**) **1.** to barricade o.s.; **з. ши́рмой** to screen o.s. off. **2.** *pass. of* **~ди́ть**
загорóдк|а, и *f.* (*coll.*) **1.** fence. **2.** enclosure.
зáгородн|ый *adj.* out-of-town; country; **~ая экскýрсия** excursion into the country.
заго|сти́ться, щу́сь, сти́шься *pf.* (*coll.*) to outstay one's welcome.
заготови́тел|ь, я *m.* official in charge of (State) procurements.
заготов|и́тельный *adj. of* **~ка; з. аппарáт** official organization in charge of (State) procurements; **з. пункт** storage place; **~и́тельная ценá** (*econ.*) fixed price (*for purchases by State*).
заготóв|ить, лю, ишь *pf.* (*of* **~ля́ть**) **1.** to lay in; to make a stock (of), stockpile, store. **2.** to prepare.
заготóвк|а, и *f.* **1.** (State) procurement (*of agricultural products, timber, etc.*). **2.** laying in; stocking up, stockpiling. **3.** half-finished product; (*tech.*) blank, billet.
заготовля́|ть, ю *impf. of* **заготóвить**
заготóвщик, а *m.* = **заготови́тель**
заграбáст|ать, аю *pf.* (*of* **~ывать**) (*coll., pej.*) to seize; to make off with.
заграбáстыва|ть, ю *impf. of* **заграбáстать**
загрáб|ить, лю, ишь *pf.* (*coll.*) to seize; to plunder.
заградúтел|ь я *m.* (*naut.*) minelayer.
заградúтельный *adj.* (*mil.*) barrage; (*naut.*) mine-laying; **з. аэростáт** barrage balloon; **з. огóнь** defensive fire.
загра|ди́ть, жу́, ди́шь *pf.* (*of* **~ждáть**) to block, obstruct; **з. путь** to bar the way.
заграждá|ть, ю *impf. of* **загради́ть**
заграждéни|е, я *nt.* **1.** blocking, obstruction. **2.** obstacle, barrier, obstruction.
заграни́ц|а, ы *f.* (*coll.*) foreign countries (*see also* **грани́ца**).
заграни́чный *adj.* foreign (**1.** = *of foreign make, etc.* **2.** = *for foreign travel, etc.*; **з. пáспорт** foreign passport).
загребá|ть, ю *impf. of* **загрести́**[1]; **чужи́ми рукáми жар з.**, *see* **жар**
загрёбистый *adj.* (*coll.*) greedy.
загребн|óй *adj.*: **~óе веслó** stroke oar; *as n.* **з., ~óго** *m.* stroke (*rower*).
загребу́щий *adj.* (*coll.*) greedy.
загрем|éть[1], **лю́, и́шь** *pf.* (*coll.*) to crash down.
загрем|éть[2], **лю́, и́шь** *pf.* to begin to thunder.
загре|сти́[1], **бу́, бёшь,** *past* **~̈б, ~блá** *pf.* (*of* **~бáть**) (*coll.*) to rake up, gather; (*fig.*) to rake in; **з. жар** to bank up the fire; **з. дéньги** to rake in the shekels.
загре|сти́[2], **бу́, бёшь,** *past* **~̈б, ~блá** *pf.* to begin to row.
загри́в|ок, ка *m.* **1.** withers (*of horse*). **2.** (*coll.*) nape (of the neck).
загримир|овáть(ся), у́ю(сь) *pf. of* **гримировáть(ся)**
загрипп|овáть, у́ю *pf.* (*coll.*) to catch flu, go down with the flu.
загрóбн|ый *adj.* **1.** beyond the grave; **~ая жизнь** life after death. **2.** sepulchral (*of voice*).
загромождá|ть, ю *impf. of* **загромозди́ть**
загромоз|ди́ть, жу́, ди́шь *pf.* (*of* **загромождáть**) to block up, encumber; (*fig.*) to pack, cram; **з. расскáз подрóбностями** to cram a story with detail.
загрох|отáть, очу́, óчешь *pf.* to begin to rumble, begin to rattle.
загрубéлый *adj.* coarsened, callous.
загрубé|ть, ю *pf.* to become coarsened; to become callous (*also fig.*).
загружá|ть, ю *impf. of* **загрузи́ть 2., 3.**
загру́женност|ь (*and* **загружённост|ь**), **и** *f.* **1.** utilised capacity (*of transport services, etc.*). **2.** programme (*of work*), commitment.
загр|узи́ть, ужу́, у́зи́шь *pf.* **1.** (*impf.* **грузи́ть**) to load. **2.** (*impf.* **~ужáть**) (*tech.*) to feed, charge, prime; **з. тóпливо в печь** to stoke a furnace. **3.** (*impf.* **~ужáть**) (*coll.*) to keep fully occupied, provide with a full-time job; to fill out (*a period of time*) with occupations.
загру|зи́ться, жу́сь, зи́шься *pf.* (*of* **~жáться**) **1.** (*+i.*) to load up (with), take on. **2.** (*coll.*) to take on a job, a commitment.
загру́зк|а, и *f.* **1.** loading. **2.** (*tech.*) feeding, charging, priming. **3.** capacity (*of work*), load; **завóд рабóтает при пóлной ~е** the factory is working at full capacity.
загру́з|очный *adj. of* **~ка; з. ковш, я́щик** hopper; **з. лотóк** feed chute, loading chute.
загрунт|овáть, у́ю *pf. of* **грунтовáть**
загру|сти́ть, щу́, сти́шь *pf.* to grow sad.
загрызá|ть, ю *impf. of* **загры́зть**
загры́з|ть, у́, ёшь *past* **~, ~ла** *pf.* (*of* **~áть**) **1.** to bite to death; (*fig.*) to worry the life out of, worry to death. **2.** to tear to pieces.
загрязнéни|е, я *nt.* soiling; pollution; contamination.
загрязни́тел|ь, я *m.* polluter; pollutant.
загрязн|и́ть, ю́, и́шь *pf.* (*of* **~я́ть**) to soil, make dirty; to pollute.
загрязн|и́ться, ю́сь, и́шься *pf.* (*of* **~я́ться**) to make o.s. dirty, become dirty.
загрязня́|ть(ся), ю(сь) *impf. of* **загрязни́ть(ся)**
ЗАГС, а *or* **загс, а** *m.* (*abbr. of* **(отдéл) зáписи áктов граждáнского состоя́ния**) registry office.
загси́р|оваться, уюсь *impf. and pf.* (*coll.*) to get married (in a registry office).
загуб|и́ть, лю́, ~ишь *pf.* **1.** to ruin; **з. чей-н. век, з. чью-н. жизнь** to make s.o.'s life a misery. **2.** (*coll.*) to squander.
загу́бник, а *m.* mouthpiece.
загу́л, а *m.* (*coll.*) drinking(-bout).
загуля́|ть, ю *pf.* (*coll.*) to take to drink, start drinking.
зад, а, о ~е, на ~у́, *pl.* **~ы́** *m.* **1.** back; **~ом наперёд** back to front. **2.** hind quarters; buttocks; croup, rump; **бить ~ом** to kick (*of animal*). **3.** (*pl.*) = **задвóрки 1.. 4.: повтори́ть ~ы́** (*coll.*) to repeat what one had learned before; to pass on stale news.
задáбрива|ть, ю *impf. of* **задóбрить**
задавáк|а, и *c.g.* (*coll.*) snob, big-head.
задавáла = **задавáка**
зада|вáть, ю́, ёшь *impf. of* **~ть**
зада|вáться[1], **ю́сь, ёшься** *impf. of* **~ться**
зада|вáться[2], **ю́сь, ёшься** *impf.* (*coll.*) to give o.s. airs, put on airs.
задав|и́ть, лю́, ~ишь *pf.* to crush; to run over, knock down.
задáни|е, я *nt.* task, job.
задáрива|ть, ю *impf. of* **задари́ть**
задар|и́ть, ю́, ~ишь *pf.* (*of* **~ивать**) **1.** to load with presents. **2.** to bribe.
задáром *adv.* (*coll.*) **1.** for nothing; very cheaply; **купи́ть з.** to buy for a song. **2.** in vain, to no purpose.
задáстый *adj.* (*coll.*) fat-arsed.
задáтк|и, ов *no sg.* instincts, inclinations.
задáт|ок, ка *m.* deposit, advance.

за|да́ть, да́м, да́шь, *past* **∠дал, ~дала́, ∠дало** *pf.* (*of* **~дава́ть**) to set; to give; **з. уро́к** to set a lesson; **з. вопро́с** to put a question; **з. бал** to give a dance; **з. корм коро́вам** to feed the cows; **з. тон** to set the tone; **з. тя́гу** to take to one's heels; **з. стра́ху** (*+d.*) to strike terror (into); **я ему́ ~да́м!** (*coll.*) I'll give him what-for!

за|да́ться, да́мся, да́шься, *past* **~да́лся, ~дала́сь** *pf.* (*of* **~дава́ться**[1]) **1.: з. це́лью, мы́слью** (*+inf.*) to set o.s. (to), make up one's mind (to); **з. вопро́сом** to ask o.s. the question. **2.** (*coll.*) to turn out (well); to work out, succeed; **пое́здка не ~дала́сь** the trip was not a success.

зада́ч|а, и *f.* **1.** (*math., etc.*) problem. **2.** task; mission.

зада́чник, а *m.* book of (mathematical) problems.

задви́га|ть, ю *pf.* to begin to move.

задвига́|ть, ю *impf. of* **задви́нуть**

задвига́|ться, юсь *impf.* **1.** *impf. of* **задви́нуться. 2.** (*impf. only*) to be drawable, be slidable.

задви́жк|а, и *f.* bolt; catch, fastening; (*tech.*) slide-valve.

задвижно́й *adj.* sliding.

задви́н|уть, у, ешь *pf.* (*of* **задвига́ть**) **1.** to push; **з. задви́жку** to shoot a bolt. **2.** to bolt; to bar; to close; **з. за́навес** to draw a curtain (across).

задви́н|уться, усь, ешься *pf.* (*of* **задвига́ться**) to shut; to slide (*intrans.*)

задво́р|ки, ок *no sg.* **1.** backyard; (*fig.*) out-of-the-way place, backwoods. **2.: быть на ~ках** (*fig.*) to take a back seat.

задева́|ть[1]**, ю** *impf. of* **заде́ть**

задева́|ть[2]**, ю** *pf.* (*coll.*) to mislay; **куда́ ~л мой очки́?** where did I put my spectacles?

задева́|ться[1]**, юсь** *impf., pass. of* **~ть**[1]

задева́|ться[2]**, юсь** *pf.* (*coll.*) to disappear; **куда́ ты ~лся?** where did you get to?

заде́л, а *m.* (*coll.*) **1.** undertaking (*begun but not completed*). **2.** (*tech.*) surplus (*of goods or products*). **3.** amount (*of work done, etc.*) in hand.

заде́л|ать, аю *pf.* (*of* **~ывать**) to do up; to block up, close up; **з. посы́лку** to do up a parcel; (*naut.*) **з. течь** to stop up a leak.

заде́ла|ться[1]**, юсь** *pf., pass. of* **~ть**

заде́л|аться[2]**, аюсь** *pf.* (*of* **~ываться**) (*coll.*) to become; to turn; **он ~лся литературове́дом** he has turned literary critic.

заде́лк|а, и *f.* doing up; blocking up, stopping up.

заде́лыва|ть(ся), ю(сь) *impf. of* **заде́лать(ся)**

задёрга|ть[1]**, ю** *pf.* (*+a. or i.*) to begin to tug.

задёрга|ть[2]**, ю** *pf.* to wear out (*by tugging on the reins*); (*fig., coll.*) to break the spirit of (*by nagging, etc.*).

задёргива|ть, ю *impf. of* **задёрнуть**

задеревене́лый *adj.* numb(ed), stiff.

задеревене́|ть, ю *pf.* (*coll.*) to become numb, become stiff.

задержа́ни|е, я *nt.* **1.** detention; arrest. **2.** (*med.*): **з. мочи́** retention of urine. **3.** (*mus.*) suspension.

заде́ржанн|ый, ого *m.* detainee.

задерж|а́ть, у́ ∠ишь *pf.* (*of* **∠ивать**) **1.** to detain; to delay; **до́ждик ~а́л нача́ло ма́тча** the start of the match was delayed by a shower. **2.** to withhold, keep back; to retard; **з. зарпла́ту** to stop wages; **з. дыха́ние** to hold one's breath. **3.** to detain, arrest.

задерж|а́ться, у́сь ∠ишься *pf.* (*of* **∠иваться**) **1.** to stay too long; to linger. **2.** *pass. of* **~а́ть**

заде́ржива|ть(ся), ю(сь) *impf. of* **задержа́ть(ся)**

заде́ржк|а, и *f.* delay; hold-up.

задёрн|уть, у, ешь *pf.* (*of* **задёргивать**) **1.** to pull; to draw; **з. за́навески** to draw the curtains. **2.** to cover; to curtain off.

заде́т|ый (~, ~а) *p.p.p. of* **~ь**; **1.: з. насме́шками** stung by taunts. **2.** (*med.; coll.*) affected; **пра́вое лёгкое у него́ ~о** he has a spot on his right lung.

заде́|ть, ну, нешь *pf.* (*of* **~ва́ть**[1]) **1.** to touch, brush (against), graze; (*fig.*) to offend, wound; **его́ ~ло за живо́е** he was stung to the quick. **2.** to catch (on, against).

за́дешево *adv.* (*coll.*) very cheaply.

зади́р|а, ы *c.g.* (*coll.*) bully; trouble-maker.

задира́|ть(ся)[1]**, ю(сь)** *impf. of* **задра́ть(ся)**

задира́|ться[2]**, юсь** *impf.* (*coll.*) to pick a quarrel.

задненёбный *adj.* (*ling.*) velar.

заднепрохо́дный *adj.* (*anat.*) anal.

заднеязы́чный *adj.* (*ling.*) velar, back.

за́дн|ий *adj.* back, rear; hind; **~яя мысль** ulterior motive; **з. план** background; **з. прохо́д** (*anat.*) anus; **~им умо́м кре́пок** (*coll.*) wise after the event; **з. фона́рь** tail-light; **з. ход** (*tech.*) backward movement; (*naut.*) stern-board; **дать з. ход** to back; **~им число́м** later, with hindsight; **поме́тить ~им число́м** to antedate; **быть без ~их ног** (*coll.*) to be falling off one's feet; **ходи́ть на ~их ла́пках (пе́ред)** (*coll.*) to dance attendance (on).

за́дник, а *m.* **1.** back, counter (*of shoe*). **2.** (*theatr.*) backdrop.

за́дниц|а, ы *f.* (*vulg.*) arse, buttocks.

задо́бр|ить, ю, ишь *pf.* (*of* **зада́бривать**) to cajole; to coax; to win over (*by bribes, etc.*).

зад|о́к, ка́ *m.* back (*of conveyance or furniture*).

задолб|и́ть, лю́, и́шь *pf.* **1.** to begin to peck. **2.** (*coll.*) to learn off by rote.

задо́лго *adv.* long before; **он ко́нчил рабо́ту з. до ве́чера** he finished the work long before evening.

задолжа́|ть, ю *pf. of* **должа́ть**

задолжа́|ться, юсь *pf.* (*coll.*) to run into debt.

задо́лженност|ь, и *f.* debts; **погаси́ть з.** to pay off one's debts.

за́дом *adv.* backwards; **е́хать з.** to reverse, back up.

задо́р, а *m.* fervour, ardour; passion.

задо́ринк|а, и *f.* unevenness, roughness; (*fig., coll.*) **без сучка́, без ~и** *or* **ни сучка́, ни ~и** without a hitch.

задо́р|иться, юсь ишься *impf.* (*coll.*) to become provocative.

задо́р|ный (~ен, ~на) *adj.* **1.** fervent, ardent; impassioned. **2.** provocative; quick-tempered.

задох|ну́ться, ну́сь, нёшься, *past* **∠ся, ∠лась** *and* **~ну́лся, ~ну́лась** *pf.* (*of* **задыха́ться**) **1.** to suffocate; to choke; (*fig.*): **з. от гне́ва** to choke with anger. **2.** to pant; to gasp for breath.

задра́знива|ть, ю *impf. of* **задразни́ть**

задразн|и́ть, ю́, ∠ишь *pf.* (*coll.*) to tease unmercifully.

задра́ива|ть, ю *impf. of* **задра́ить**

задра́|ить, ю, ишь *pf.* (*naut.*) to batten down.

задрапир|ова́ть, у́ю *pf.* (*+a. and i.*) to drape (with).

задрапир|ова́ться, у́юсь *pf.* (*+a. or* **в***+a.*) to drape o.s. (with), wrap o.s. up (in).

задрапиро́выва|ть(ся), ю(сь) *impf. of* **задрапирова́ть(ся)**

зад|ра́ть, еру́, ерёшь, *past* **~ра́л, ~рала́, ~ра́ло** *pf.* (*of* **~ира́ть**) **1.** to tear to pieces; to kill (*of wolves, etc.*). **2.** (*coll.*) to lift up; to pull up; **з. го́лову** to crane one's neck; **з. нос** (*fig.*) to cock one's nose. **3.** to break (*finger-nail, etc.*); **з. ко́жу на па́льце** to split a finger. **4.** (*coll.*) to insult; to provoke.

зад|ра́ться, ерётся, *past* **~ра́лся, ~рала́сь, ~ра́ло́сь** *pf.* (*of* **~ира́ться**) **1.** to break (*intrans.; finger-nail, etc.*); to split (*intrans.*). **2.** (*coll.*) to ride up (*of clothing*). **3.** *pass. of* **~ра́ть**

задрем|а́ть, лю́, ∠лешь *pf.* to doze off, begin to nod.

задри́пан|ный (~, ~а) *adj.* (*coll.*) bedraggled.

задрож|а́ть, у́, и́шь *pf.* to begin to tremble; to begin to shiver.

за́друг|а, и *f.* (*ethnol.*) zadruga (*patriarchal commune among the southern Slav peoples*).

задры́га|ть, ю *pf.* (*coll.*) to begin to jerk, begin to twitch.

задува́|ть, ю *impf. of* **заду́ть**

заду́ма|ть, ю *pf.* (*of* **заду́мывать**) **1.** (*+a. or inf.*) to plan; to intend; to conceive the idea (of). **2.: з. число́** to think of a number.

заду́ма|ться, юсь *pf.* to become thoughtful, pensive; to fall to thinking; **о чём вы ~лись?** what are you thinking about?

заду́мчивост|ь, и *f.* thoughtfulness, pensiveness; reverie.

заду́мчив|ый (~, ~а) *adj.* thoughtful, pensive.

заду́мыва|ть, ю *impf. of* **заду́мать**

заду́мыва|ться, юсь *impf.* to be thoughtful, be pensive; to meditate; to ponder; **не ~ясь, он согласи́лся** he agreed without a moment's thought.

задур|úть, ю́, úшь *pf.* (*coll.*) to start playing the fool; **он мне едвá не ~úл гóлову** he nearly drove me crazy.

задý|ть, ю, ешь *pf.* (*of* **~вáть**) **1.** to blow out. **2.** (*tech.*): **з. дóмну** to blow in a blast-furnace. **3.** to begin to blow.

задушéв|ный (~ен, ~на) *adj.* sincere; cordial; intimate.

задуш|úть, ý, ~ишь *pf. of* **душúть**[1]

зад|ы́[1] *see* ~

зад|ы́[2] = **~вóрки**

задым|úть, лю́, úшь *pf.* **1.** to begin to (emit) smoke. **2.** to blacken with smoke. **3.** (*mil.*) to lay a smoke-screen.

задымúться, úтся *pf.* **1.** to begin to (emit) smoke. **2.** to be blackened with smoke.

задымля́|ть, ю *impf. of* **задымúть 2., 3.**

задыхá|ться, юсь *impf. of* **задохнýться**

задыш|áть, ý, ~ишь *pf.* to begin to breathe.

заёб|а, ы *c.g.* (*vulg.*) **1.** pain in the arse (*pers.*). **2.** (silly) prick, wanker.

заедáни|е, я *nt.* (*tech.*) jamming.

заедá|ть(ся), ю(сь) *impf. of* **заéсть(ся)**

заéзд, а *m.* **1.** calling in (*en route*). **2.** (*sport*) lap, round, heat.

заéз|дить, жу, дишь *pf.* to override (*a horse*); (*fig.*) to wear out; to work too hard.

заезжá|ть, ю *impf. of* **заéхать**

заéзженный *adj.* (*coll.*) **1.** hackneyed, trite. **2.** worn out.

заéзж|ий *adj.* visiting; **~ая трýппа** touring company; **он здесь з. человéк** he is a stranger, he is passing through; **з. двор** (*obs.*) wayside inn.

заём, зáйма *m.* loan.

заёмн|ый *adj.* loan; **~ое письмó** (*leg.*) acknowledgement of debt.

заёмщик, а *m.* borrower, debtor.

заёрза|ть, ю *pf.* (*coll.*) **1.** to begin to fidget. **2.** to dirty, wear out as a result of fidgeting.

заé|сть[1]**, м, шь, ст, дúм, дúте, дя́т,** *past* **~л** *pf.* (*of* **~дáть**) **1.** to bite to death; (*fig.*) to torment, oppress; **егó ~ла тоскá** he fell a prey to melancholy. **2.** (*impers.*; *tech.*) to jam; (*naut.*) to foul; **канáт ~ло** the cable has fouled. **3.** (*dial.*) to seize, appropriate.

заé|сть[2]**, м, шь, ст, дúм, дúте, дя́т,** *past* **~л** *pf.* (*of* **~дáть**) (*+a. and i.*) to take (with); **он ~л пилю́лю сáхаром** he took the pill with sugar.

заé|сться, мся, шься, стся, дúмся, дúтесь, дя́тся, *past* **~лся** *pf.* (*of* **~дáться**) (*coll.*) to become fastidious, become fussy.

заé|хать, ду, дешь *pf.* (*of* **~зжáть**) **1.** **(к)** to call in (at); **(в**+*a.*) to enter, ride into, drive into; **(за**+*a.*) to go beyond, past; **(за**+*i.*) to call for; to fetch. **2.** to go too far (*also fig.*); **он ~хал в канáву** he landed in the ditch; **ведь кудá он ~хал со своим хвастовствóм!** look where he got himself with his boasting! **3.** (*+d.* **в**+*a.*; *coll.*) to strike; **я ~хал емý в мóрду** I gave him a sock on the jaw.

зажáр|ить(ся), ю(сь), ишь(ся) *pf. of* **жáрить(ся)**

заж|áть, мý, мёшь *pf.* (*of* **~имáть**) to squeeze; to press; to clutch; **з. в рукé** to grip; **з. рот комý-н.** (*fig.*) to stop s.o.'s mouth; **з. крúтику** to suppress criticism.

заж|гý, жёшь, гýт *see* **~éчь**

зажд|áться, ýсь, ёшься, *past* **~áлся, ~алáсь, ~алóсь** *pf.* (*coll.*) to be tired of waiting (for).

зажелтé|ть, ю, ешь *pf.* **1.** to turn yellow. **2.** to begin to appear, begin to show up yellow.

зажел|тúть, чý, тúшь *pf.* (*coll.*) to paint yellow; to stain yellow.

заж|éчь, гý, жёшь, гýт, *past* **~ёг, ~глá** *pf.* (*of* **~игáть**) to set fire to; to kindle, light; to ignite; **з. спúчку** to strike a match; (*fig.*, *rhet.*) to kindle; to inflame.

заж|éчься, гýсь, жёшься, гýтся, *past* **зажёгся, зажглáсь** *pf.* (*of* **~игáться**) to catch fire; to light up; (*fig.*) to flame up.

заживá|ть(ся), ю(сь) *impf. of* **зажúть(ся)**

зажив|úть, лю́, úшь *pf.* to heal.

заживля́ть, ю *impf. of* **заживúть**

зáживо *adv.* alive; **з. погребённый** buried alive.

зажигáлк|а, и *f.* **1.** (cigarette) lighter. **2.** (*coll.*) incendiary (bomb).

зажигáни|е, я *nt.* ignition; **ключ (от) зажигáния** ignition key.

зажигáтел|ьный (~ен, ~ьна) *adj.* **1.** incendiary; **~ьная бóмба** fire bomb, incendiary (device); **буты́лка с ~ьной смéсью** petrol bomb, Molotov cocktail. **2.** stirring, rousing; **~ьная речь** rousing speech.

зажигá|ть(ся), ю(сь) *impf. of* **зажéчь(ся)**

зажúл|ить, ю, ишь *pf.* (*coll.*) to fail to return (*sth. borrowed*).

зажúлива|ть, ю *impf. of* **зажúлить**

зажúм, а *m.* **1.** (*tech.*) clamp; clutch; clip. **2.** (*elec.*) terminal. **3.** (*fig.*) suppression; clamping down.

зажимá|ть, ю *impf. of* **зажáть**

зажúмист|ый (~, ~а) *adj.* (*coll.*) **1.** strong, powerful; **у негó ~ая рукá** he has a strong grip. **2.** tight-fisted, stingy.

зажимнóй *adj.* (*coll.*) tight-fisted.

зажúмный *adj.* (*tech.*) clamping; **з. винт** clamping screw.

зажúмщик, а *m.* (*coll.*) suppressor.

зажирéлый *adj.* (*dial.*) excessively stout, overweight.

зажирé|ть, ю *pf.* (*coll.*) to put on weight to excess.

зажит|óй *p.p.p. of* **~ь** *and adj.* earned; *as n.* **~óе, ~óго** (*coll.*) earned income.

зажúточност|ь, и *f.* prosperity; easy circumstances.

зажúточ|ный (~ен, ~на) *adj.* well-to-do; prosperous.

зáжит|ый = **~óй**

зажú|ть, вý, вёшь, *past* **зáжил, ~лá, зáжило** *pf.* (*of* **~вáть**) **1.** to heal (*intrans.*); to close up (*of wound*). **2.** to begin to live; **з. по-нóвому** to begin a new life; **з. семéйной жúзнью** to settle down; **з. трудовóй жúзнью** to begin to earn one's own living.

зажú|ться, вýсь, вёшься, *past* **~лся, ~лáсь** *pf.* (*of* **~вáться**) (*coll.*) to live to a great age; to exceed one's allotted span.

зажмýр|ить(ся), ю(сь), ишь(ся) *pf. of* **жмýрить(ся)**

зажужж|áть, ý, úшь *pf.* to begin to buzz; to begin to drone.

зажýлива|ть, ю *impf. of* **зажýлить**

зажýл|ить, ю, ишь *pf.* (*coll.*) to obtain by fraud.

зажýхлый *adj.* (*coll.*) tarnished, dull; dry, stiff (*of leather, etc.*).

заз|вáть, овý, овёшь, *past* **~вáл, ~валá, ~вáло** *pf.* (*of* **~ывáть**) (*coll.*) to press (to come); to press an invitation on.

зазвен|éть, úт *pf.* to begin to ring.

зазвóнист|ый (~, ~а) *adj.* (*coll.*) loud.

зазвон|úть, ю́, úшь *pf.* to begin to ring.

зазвуч|áть, ý, úшь *pf.* to begin to sound; to begin to resound.

заздрáвный *adj.* to the health (of), in honour (of); **онú вы́пили з. тост за послá** they drank the ambassador's health.

зазевá|ться, юсь *pf.* **(на**+*a.*; *coll.*) to stand gaping (at); to gape (at).

зазеленé|ть, ю *pf.* to turn green.

зазелен|úть, ю́, úшь *pf.* (*coll.*) to paint green; to colour green.

заземлéни|е, я *nt.* (*elec.*) **1.** earthing. **2.** earth.

заземл|úть, ю́, úшь *pf.* (*elec.*) to earth.

заземл|я́ть, я́ю *impf. of* **~úть**

зазим|овáть, ýю *pf.* to winter; to pass the winter.

зазúм|ок, ка *m.* (*dial.*) **1.** first snow. **2.** first frost(s). **3.** fresh sledge track.

зазна|вáться, ю́сь, ёшься *impf. of* **~ться**

зазнáвшийся *adj.* (*coll.*) stuck-up, hoity-toity.

зазнáйка = **задавáка**

зазнáйств|о, а *nt.* (*coll.*) conceit.

зазнá|ться, юсь *pf.* (*of* **~вáться**) (*coll.*) to give o.s. airs, become conceited.

зазнóб|а, ы *f.* **1.** (*folk poet.*) passion. **2.** (*coll.*) sweetheart.

зазноб|úть, лю́, úшь *pf.* (*coll.*) **1.** to be frozen; to get shivery. **2.** (*impers.*): **егó ~úло** he is beginning to be feverish.

зазнóбушк|а, и *f.* (*folk poet.*) sweetheart.

заз|овý, овёшь *see* **~вáть**

зазóр[1]**, а** *m.* (*coll.*) shame, disgrace.

зазóр[2]**, а** *m.* gap; (*tech.*) clearance; (*mil.*) windage.

зазóр|ный (~ен, ~на) *adj.* (*coll.*) shameful, disgraceful.

зазрéни|е, я *nt.*: **без ~я (сóвести)** (*coll.*) without a twinge of conscience.

за́зр|ить, ит *pf., only in phr.* **со́весть ~ит, ~ила** (*coll.*) conscience forbids, forbade (it).
зазу́брен|ный (~, ~а) *p.p.p. of* **зазубри́ть**[1] *and adj.* notched, jagged, serrated.
зазу́брива|ть, ю *impf. of* **зазубри́ть**
зазу́брин|а, ы *f.* notch, jag.
зазубр|и́ть[1], **ю́, и́шь** *pf.* (*of* **зубри́ть** *and* **~ивать**) to notch, serrate.
зазубр|и́ть[2], **ю́, ~ишь** *pf.* (*of* **зубри́ть** *and* **~ивать**) (*sl.*) **1.** to learn by rote. **2.** to start cramming.
зазы́в, а *m.* (*coll.*) pressing invitation.
зазыва́л|а, ы *c.g.* (*fairground*) barker.
зазыва́|ть, ю *impf. of* **зазва́ть**
зазя́б|нуть, ну, нешь, *past* **~, ~ла** *pf.* (*coll.*) **1.** to become frozen. **2.** (*hort.*) to die of frost.
заигра́|ть, ю *pf.* **1.** to begin to play; **з. весёлый моти́в** to strike up a lively tune. **2.** to begin to sparkle. **3.** to wear out (*cards, etc.*); **з. пье́су** to stage a play so often that it becomes stale.
заи́грыва|ть[1], **ю** *impf. of* **заигра́ть**
заи́грыва|ть[2], **ю** *impf.* (**с**+*i.*; *coll.*) to flirt (with); to make advances (to) (*also fig.*).
заи́к|а, и *c.g.* stammerer, stutterer.
заика́ни|е, я *nt.* stammer(ing), stutter(ing).
заика́|ться, юсь *impf.* **1.** to stammer, stutter; to falter (*in speech*). **2.** (**о**+*p.*; *coll.*) to hint (at), to mention in passing; **он никогда́ не ~ется о свое́й про́шлой жи́зни** he never breathes a word about his past life.
заикн|у́ться, у́сь, ёшься *pf. of* **заика́ться 2.**
заи́мк|а, и *f.* (*hist.*) **1.** squatting (*on land*). **2.** squatter's holding. **3.** isolated arable field.
заимода́в|ец, ца *m.* creditor, lender.
заимообра́зно *adv.* on credit, on loan.
заимообра́з|ный (~ен, ~на) *adj.* **1.** borrowed, taken on credit. **2.** lent, loaned.
заи́мствовани|е, я *nt.* borrowing.
заи́мствован|ный (~, ~а) *p.p.p. of* **заи́мствовать; ~ное сло́во** (*ling.*) loan-word.
заи́мств|овать, ую *impf.* (*of* **по~**) to borrow.
заи́ндеве|ть, ет *pf.* (*of* **и́ндеветь**) (*coll.*) to be covered with hoar-frost.
заинтересо́ван|ный (~, ~а) *p.p.p. of* **заинтересова́ть** *and adj.* (**в**+*p.*) interested (in); **он ~ в возмо́жности торго́вых сноше́ний с Да́льним Восто́ком** he is interested in the possibility of trade relations with the Far East; **~ная сторона́** interested party.
заинтерес|ова́ть, у́ю *pf.* to interest; to excite the curiosity (of).
заинтерес|ова́ться, у́юсь *pf.* (+*i.*) to become interested; to take an interest (in).
заинтриг|ова́ть, у́ю *pf. of* **интригова́ть 2.**
Заи́р, а *m.* Zaire.
заи́р|ец, ца *m.* Zairean.
заи́р|ка, ки *f. of* **~ец**
заи́рский *adj.* Zairean.
заи́скива|ть, ю *impf.* (**у** *or* **пе́ред**) to try to ingratiate o.s. (with).
заи́скива|ющий *pres. part. act. of* **~ть** *and adj.* ingratiating.
заискр|и́ться, ю́сь, и́шься *pf.* to begin to sparkle.
зай|ду́, дёшь *see* **~ти́**
за́ймищ|е, а *nt.* (*dial.*) water-meadow.
займодержа́тел|ь, я *m.* loan-holder.
займ|у́, ёшь *see* **заня́ть**
за|йти́, йду́, йдёшь, *past* **~шёл, ~шла́** *pf.* (*of* **~ходи́ть**[1]) **1.** (**к, в**+*a.*) to call (on); to look in (at); **по пути́ домо́й я ~шёл к Ивано́вым** I dropped in at the Ivanovs on the way home; **не забу́дьте з. в апте́ку** don't forget to look in at the chemist's. **2.** (**за**+*i.*) to call for, fetch. **3.** (**в**+*a.*) to get (*to a place*); to find o.s. (*in a place*); **мы ~шли в во́ду по го́рло** we got up to our necks in water; **разгово́р ~шёл о выступле́нии президе́нта по ра́дио** the conversation turned on the President's broadcast; **з. на цель** (*aeron.*) to be over the target; **з. в тыл врага́** (*mil.*) to take the enemy in the rear. **4.** (**за**+*a.*) to go behind; to turn; to go on, continue (after); to set (*of sun, etc.*); (*fig., obs.*) to wane; **з. за́ угол** to turn a corner; **з. плечо́м** (*mil.*) to wheel; **заседа́ние ~шло́ далеко́ за́ полночь** the meeting went on until long after midnight; **з. сли́шком далеко́** (*fig.*) to go too far.
за́йчик, а *m.* (*coll.*) **1.** *affectionate dim. of* **за́яц. 2.** reflection of a sunray. **3.** catkin.
зайчи́х|а, *f.* doe-hare.
зайч|о́нок, о́нка, *pl.* **~а́та, ~а́т** *m.* leveret.
закабал|и́ть, ю́, и́шь *pf.* to enslave.
закабал|и́ться, ю́сь, и́шься *pf.* **1.** (+*d.*) to tie o.s. in slavery (to). **2.** *pass. of* **~и́ть**
закабал|я́ть(ся), я́ю(сь) *impf. of* **~и́ть(ся)**
закавка́зский *adj.* Transcaucasian.
Закавка́зь|е, я *nt.* Transcaucasia.
закавы́ч|ить, у, ишь *pf.* (*coll.*) to place in inverted commas.
закавы́чк|а, и *f.* (*coll.*) **1.** obstacle, hitch. **2.** innuendo.
закадро́вый *adj.*: **з. го́лос** (*TV, cin.*) voice-over.
закады́чный *adj.*: **з. друг** (*coll.*) bosom friend.
зака́з[1], **а** *m.* order; **ваш з. ещё не гото́в** your order is not ready yet; **на з.** to order; **мне де́лают костю́м на з.** I am having a suit made to measure; **социа́льный з.** (*pol.*) demand formulated by a social class.
зака́з[2], **а** *m.* (*obs.*) prohibition.
зака|за́ть[1], **жу́, ~жешь** *pf.* (*of* **~зывать**) to order; to reserve.
зака|за́ть[2], **жу́, ~жешь** *pf.* (+*inf. or a.*; *obs. or coll.*) to forbid.
зака́зник, а *m.* (*game*) reserve.
заказн|о́й *adj.* **1.** made to order; made to measure. **2.: ~о́е письмо́** registered letter; **посла́ть письмо́ ~ы́м** to send a letter registered; *as n.* **~о́е, ~о́го** *nt.* registered postal packet.
зака́зчик, а *m.* customer, client.
зака́зыва|ть, ю *impf. of* **заказа́ть**[1]
зака́ива|ться, юсь *impf. of* **зака́яться**
зака́л, а *m.* **1.** (*tech.*) temper; (*fig.*) stamp, cast; **он челове́к ста́рого ~а** he is one of the old school. **2.** (*fig.*) strength of character; guts, backbone.
закалён|ный (~, ~а́) *p.p.p. of* **закали́ть** *and adj.* hardened, hard; **з. в боя́х** battle-hardened.
зака́лива|ть, ю *impf. of* **закали́ть**
закал|и́ть, ю́, и́шь *pf.* (*of* **~ивать** *and* **~я́ть**) (*tech.*) to temper; to case-harden; (*fig.*) to temper, harden; to make hard, hardy.
зака́лк|а, и *f.* tempering; hardening; (*sport*) conditioning.
зака́лыва|ть, ю *impf. of* **заколо́ть**
закаля́|ть, ю *impf. of* **закали́ть**
закамене́лый *adj.* (*coll.*) hard as stone.
закамене́|ть, ю *pf.* (*coll.*) to turn to stone, become petrified.
зака́нчива|ть, ю *impf. of* **зако́нчить**
зака́п|ать, аю (*obs.* **~лю, ~лешь**) *pf.* **1.** to begin to drip; **дождь ~ал** it began to spot with rain. **2.** (*impf.* **~ывать**) to spot; **вот ты ~ала себе́ пла́тье черни́лами** look, you have spotted your dress with ink.
зака́пыва|ть(ся), ю(сь) *impf. of* **закопа́ть(ся)** *and* **зака́пать 2.**
зака́рмлива|ть, ю *impf. of* **закорми́ть**
закаспи́йский *adj.* Trans-Caspian.
зака́т, а *m.* setting; **з. (со́лнца)** sunset; **он пришёл на ~е** he came at sunset; (*fig.*) decline; **на ~е дней** in one's declining years.
заката́|ть, ю *pf.* (*of* **зака́тывать**) **1.** to begin to roll. **2.** (**в**+*a.*) to roll up (in). **3.** to roll out. **4.: з. в тюрьму́** (*sl.*) to throw into prison.
зака́тист|ый (~, ~а) *adj.* (*coll.*) rolling; **з. смех** peals of laughter.
зака|ти́ть, чу́, ~тишь *pf.* (*of* **~тывать**) (*coll.*) to roll; **з. глаза́** to screw up one's eyes (*in pain*); **она́ ~ти́ла ему́ пощёчину** she slapped his face; **з. исте́рику** to go off into hysterics; **з. сце́ну** to make a scene.
зака|ти́ться, чу́сь, ~тишься *pf.* (*of* **~тываться**) **1.** to roll (*intrans.*); **ма́льчик пла́кал, потому́ что мяч ~ти́лся под стол** the little boy was crying because the ball had rolled under the table. **2.** to set (*of heavenly bodies*); (*fig.*) to wane; to vanish, disappear; **его́ сла́ва давно́ ~ти́лась**

his fame had long since waned; **моя́ звездá ~ти́лась** my luck is out. **3.** (*coll.*) to go off; **он ~ти́лся на недéлю в Лóндон** he went off to London for a week; **з. смéхом** to go off into peals of laughter

закáтный *adj.* sunset.

закáтыва|ть, ю *impf. of* **закатáть** *and* **закати́ть**

закáтыва|ться, юсь *impf. of* **закати́ться**

закачá|ть, ю *pf.* **1.** to begin to shake, begin to swing; **он ~л головóй** he began shaking his head. **2.** to rock (to sleep). **3.** (*impers.*) to make feel sick by rocking; **я собирáюсь в каю́ту: меня́ ~ло** I am going to my cabin; I feel sick.

закачá|ться, юсь *pf.* to begin to rock (*intrans.*), begin to sway.

закáшива|ть, ю *impf. of* **закоси́ть**

закáшля|ться, юсь *pf.* to have a fit of coughing.

закá|яться, юсь, ешься *pf.* (*of* **~иваться**) (*+inf.*; *coll.*) to forswear; to swear to give up; **он ~ялся кури́ть** he has sworn that he will give up smoking.

заквá|сить, шу, сишь *pf.* (*of* **~шивать**) to ferment; to leaven.

заквáск|а, и *f.* ferment; leaven; (*fig.*, *coll.*) **у негó хорóшая з.** he promises well, he has received a good start in life.

заквáшива|ть, ю *impf. of* **заквáсить**

закидá|ть, ю *pf.* (*coll.*) **1.** (*+a. and i.*) to bespatter (with); to shower (with); **з. камня́ми** to stone; **кандидáтов ~ли вопрóсами** the candidates were plied with questions; **з. гря́зью** (*fig.*) to sling mud (at). **2.** to fill up (with); to cover (with).

заки́дк|а, и *f.* refusal (*in equestrian event*).

заки́дыва|ть, ю *impf. of* **закидáть** *and* **заки́нуть**

заки́дыва|ться, юсь *impf. of* **заки́нуться**

заки́н|уть, у, ешь *pf.* to throw (out, away); to cast, toss; **з. нóгу нá ногу** to cross one's legs; **з. винтóвку зá спину** to sling a rifle on one's back; **з. у́дочку** (*fig.*, *coll.*) to put out a feeler; **з. словéчко (о+*p.*)** (*coll.*) to throw out a hint (about); **~ьте словéчко за меня́** put in a word for me.

заки́н|уться, усь, ешься *pf.* **1.** to fall back. **2.** to jib, shy (*of a horse*).

закипá|ть, ю *impf. of* **закипéть**

закип|éть, лю́, и́шь *pf.* to begin to boil; to be on the boil; (*fig.*) to be in full swing.

закисá|ть, ю *impf. of* **заки́снуть**

заки́с|нуть, ну, нешь, *past* **~, ~ла** *pf.* **1.** to turn sour. **2.** (*fig.*, *coll.*) to become apathetic.

зáкис|ь, и *f.* (*chem.*) protoxide; **з. азóта** nitrous oxide; **з. желéза** ferrous oxide.

заклáд, а *m.* (*obs.*) **1.** pawning; mortgaging; **мои́ часы́ в ~е** my watch is in pawn. **2.** bet, wager; **би́ться об з.** to bet, wager.

заклáдк|а[1], **и** *f.* laying (*of bricks, etc.*).

заклáдк|а[2], **и** *f.* bookmark.

закладн|áя, óй *f.* (*leg.*, *obs.*) mortgage(-deed).

заклад|нóй[1] *adj. of* **~ка**[1]; **~нáя рáма** fixed frame.

заклад|нóй[2] *adj. of* **~**; **~нáя квитáнция** pawn-ticket.

заклáдчик, а *m.* (*obs.*) pawner; mortgagor.

заклáдыва|ть, ю *impf. of* **заклáсть** *and* **заложи́ть**

заклáни|е, я *nt.* immolation, sacrifice; **идти́ (как) на з.** to go to the slaughter.

заклá|сть, ду́, дёшь, *past* **~л, ~лá, ~лo** *pf.* (*coll.*) to fill up; to block up; to pile.

зак|лáть, олю́, óлешь, *past* **~лáл** *pf.* (*obs.*) to sacrifice, immolate.

закл|евáть, юю́, юёшь *pf.* **1.** to begin to peck; to begin to bite (*of fish*). **2.** to peck to death; (*fig.*, *coll.*) to go for.

заклёвыва|ть, ю *impf. of* **заклевáть**

заклéива|ть(ся), ю(сь) *impf. of* **заклéить(ся)**

заклé|ить, ю, ишь *pf.* to glue up; to stick up; **з. конвéрт** to seal an envelope.

заклé|иться, ится *pf.* to stick (*intrans.*).

заклейм|и́ть, лю́, и́шь *pf. of* **клейми́ть**

заклепá|ть, ю *pf.* (*of* **заклёпывать**) (*tech.*) to rivet.

заклёпк|а, и *f.* (*tech.*) **1.** riveting. **2.** rivet.

заклёпник, а *m.* (*tech.*) riveting hammer.

заклёпыва|ть, ю *impf. of* **заклепáть**

заклинáни|е, я *nt.* **1.** incantation; spell. **2.** exorcism.

заклинáтел|ь, я *m.* exorcist; **з. змей** snake-charmer.

заклинá|ть, ю *impf.* (*of* **закля́сть**) **1.** to conjure; to invoke. **2.** to exorcize (*by means of incantation*). **3.** to enchant, endow with magical powers. **4.** to conjure, adjure; to entreat.

закли́нива|ть, ю *impf. of* **заклини́ть**

заклин|и́ть, ю́, и́шь *pf.* **1.** to wedge, fasten with a wedge. **2.** to jam.

заключá|ть, ю *impf. of* **заключи́ть**

заключ|áться, аюсь *impf.* (*of* **~и́ться**) **1.** *pass. of* **~áть.** **2.** (*impf. only*) (**в**+*p.*) to consist (of); to lie (in); **глáвное затруднéние ~áется в недостáтке дéнежных средств** the principal difficulty consists in the lack of funds. **3.: з. в монасты́рь** to enter a monastery.

заключéни|е, я *nt.* **1.** conclusion, end; **в з.** in conclusion. **2.** conclusion, inference. **3.: з. договóра** conclusion of a treaty. **4.** (*leg.*) resolution, decision; **передáть на з.** to submit for a decision. **5.** confinement, detention; **тюрéмное з.** imprisonment.

заключён|ный (~, ~á, ~о) *p.p.p. of* **заключи́ть;** *as n.* **з., ~ного** *m.*, *and* **~ная, ~ной** *f.* (*leg.*) prisoner, convict.

заключи́тельн|ый *adj.* final, concluding; **з. аккóрд** (*mus.*) finale; **~ое словó** concluding remarks.

заключ|и́ть, у́, и́шь *pf.* (*of* **~áть**) **1.** (*+i.*) to conclude, end (with). **2.** to conclude, infer. **3.** to conclude, enter into; **з. брак** to contract marriage; **з. договóр** to conclude a treaty; **з. сдéлку** to strike a bargain. **4.: з. в себé** to contain, enclose; to comprise; **з. в скóбки** to enclose in brackets. **5.** to confine; **з. в тюрьму́** to imprison; **з. под стрáжу** to take into custody.

заключ|и́ться, у́сь, и́шься *pf. of* **~áться**

закля́|сть, ну́, нёшь, *past* **~л, ~лá, ~ло** *pf. of* **заклинáть**

закля́|сться, ну́сь, нёшься, *past* **~лся, ~лáсь, ~лось** *pf.* (*obs.*) to swear to give up.

закля́ти|е, я *nt.* (*obs.*) **1.** incantation. **2.** oath, pledge.

закля́тый *adj.* **1.** (*coll.*) passionate; inveterate; **з. враг** sworn enemy. **2.** enchanted, bewitched; **з. дом** haunted house.

зак|овáть, ую́, уёшь *pf.* **1.** to chain; **з. в кандалы́** to shackle, put in irons; (*fig.*, *obs.*) to chain, bind, hold down; (*poet.*) **морóз ~овáл зéмлю** the land was in the grip of frost. **2.** to begin to forge. **3.** to injure in shoeing (*a horse*).

закóвыва|ть, ю *impf. of* **заковáть**

заковыля́|ть, ю *pf.* (*coll.*) to begin to hobble.

заковы́рист|ый (~, ~а) *adj.* (*coll.*) subtle, complicated; odd.

заковы́чк|а, и *f.* = **закавы́чка**

закóл, а *m.* weir.

заколáчива|ть, ю *impf. of* **заколоти́ть**

заколдóван|ный (~, ~а) *p.p.p. of* **заколдовáть** *and adj.* bewitched, enchanted; spellbound; (*fig.*) **з. круг** vicious circle.

заколд|овáть, у́ю *pf.* to bewitch, enchant; to lay a spell (on).

заколдóвыва|ть, ю *impf. of* **заколдовáть**

заколеб|áться, ∠люсь, ∠лешься *pf.* to begin to shake; (*fig.*) to begin to waver, begin to vacillate.

закóлк|а, и *f.* **1.** stabbing. **2.** pinning. **3.** hairpin.

заколóд|ить, ит *pf.* (*impers.*, *+d.*; *dial.*) to stand in the way (of), impede; **почему́ он не приéхал? ~ило ему́, что ли?** why hasn't he come? has he been held up?

заколо|ти́ть, чу́, ∠тишь *pf.* (*of* **заколáчивать**) (*coll.*) **1.** to board up; to nail up. **2.** to knock in, drive in. **3.** to beat the life out of; to knock insensible. **4.** to begin to knock; **в дверь ~ти́ли** there was a knocking on the door.

заколо|ти́ться, чу́сь, ∠тишься *pf.* (*coll.*) **1.** *pass. of* **~ти́ть.** **2.** to begin to beat; **сéрдце у неё ~ти́лось** her heart began to thump.

закол|óть, ю́, ∠ешь *pf.* (*of* **закáлывать** *and* **колóть**[2]) **1.** to stab (to death), spear, stick. **2.** to pin (up). **3.** to begin to chop. **4.** (*impers.*): **у меня́,** *etc.*, **~óло в бокý** I, *etc.*, have a stitch in my side.

закол|óться, ю́сь, ∠ешься *pf.* to stab o.s.

заколы|хáться, ∠шется *pf.* to begin to sway; to begin to wave, begin to flutter.

закольц|евáть, у́ю, у́ешь *pf. of* **кольцевáть**

закóн, а *m.* law; **свод ~ов** code, statute book; **объяви́ть вне ~а** to outlaw; **з. Бóжий** (*as school subject, etc.*) scripture, divinity; **з. пóдлости** Sod's Law, Murphy's Law.

зако́нник, а *m.* (*coll.*) **1.** one versed in law, lawyer. **2.** one who keeps to letter of the law.
законнорождённый *adj.* legitimate (*child*).
зако́нност|ь, и *f.* lawfulness, legality.
зако́н|ный (~ен, ~на, ~но) *adj.* lawful, legal; legitimate, rightful; **з. брак** lawful wedlock; **з. владе́лец** rightful owner.
законове́д, а *m.* **1.** jurist. **2.** tutor in law.
законове́дени|е, я *nt.* jurisprudence, law.
законода́тел|ь, я *m.* legislator; lawgiver; **з. мо́ды** trendsetter.
законода́тельный *adj.* legislative.
законода́тельств|о, а *nt.* legislation.
закономе́рност|ь, и *f.* regularity; conformity with a law; normality.
закономе́р|ный (~ен, ~на) *adj.* **1.** regular, natural. **2.** *as pred.* **~но** it is in order.
законопа́|тить, чу, тишь *pf.* **1.** to caulk up; **з. у́ши** (*fig., coll.*) to block up one's ears. **2.** (*fig., coll.*) to coop up; pack off (to).
законопа́|титься, чусь, тишься *pf.* (*coll.*) to box o.s. up, shut o.s. up.
законопа́чива|ть(ся), ю(сь) *impf. of* **законопа́тить(ся)**
законоположе́ни|е, я *nt.* (*leg.*) statute.
законопослу́шный *adj.* (*obs.*) law-abiding.
законопрое́кт, а *m.* (*pol., leg.*) bill.
законосовеща́тельн|ый *adj.* (*pol., leg*) concerned with discussion and/or preparation of bills; **~ая коми́ссия** consultative commission.
законоуче́ни|е, я *nt.* (*obs.*) religious instruction.
законоучи́тел|ь, я *m.* (*obs.*) religious teacher.
законсерви́р|овать, ую *pf. of* **консерви́ровать**
законспири́р|овать, ую *pf.* (*of* **конспири́ровать**) to keep secret, keep dark.
закронтракт|ова́ть, у́ю *pf.* (*of* **контрактова́ть**) to contract (for), enter into a contract (for).
законтракт|ова́ться, у́юсь *pf.* (*of* **контрактова́ться**) to contract to work (for); to hire o.s. out (to).
законфу́|зиться, жусь, зишься *pf.* to show embarrassment.
зако́нченност|ь, и *f.* finish; completeness.
зако́нчен|ный (~, ~а) *p.p.p. of* **зако́нчить** *and adj.* finished; complete; (*coll.*) consummate; **он явля́ется ~ным проза́иком** he is a finished prose-writer; **з. лгун** consummate liar.
зако́нч|ить, у, ишь *pf.* (*of* **зака́нчивать**) to end, finish.
зако́нч|иться, усь, ишься *pf.* (*of* **зака́нчиваться**) to end, finish (*intrans.*).
закопа́|ть, ю *pf.* (*of* **зака́пывать**) **1.** to begin to dig. **2.** to bury.
закопа́|ться, юсь *pf.* (*of* **зака́пываться**) (*coll.*) **1.** to begin to rummage. **2.** to bury o.s. **3.** (*mil.*) to dig in.
закопёрщик, а *m.* **1.** foreman pile-driver. **2.** (*fig., coll.*) ringleader.
закопте́лый *adj.* (*coll.*) sooty; smutty.
закопт|е́ть, и́т *pf.* (*of* **копте́ть**[1]) to become covered with soot.
закоп|ти́ть, чу́, ти́шь *pf.* (*of* **копти́ть**) **1.** to smoke. **2.** to blacken with smoke.
закоп|ти́ться, чу́сь, ти́шься *pf.* **1.** to be smoked. **2.** to become covered with soot.
закорене́лый *adj.* deep-rooted; ingrained; inveterate.
закорене́|ть, ю, ешь *pf.* **1.** (*fig.*) to take root. **2.** (**в**+*p.*) to become steeped (in); **он ~л в греха́х** he became an inveterate sinner.
зако́р|ки, ок *no sg.* (*coll.*) back, shoulders; **он перенёс де́вочку че́рез ре́ку́ на ~ках** he carried the little girl across the river on his shoulders.
закорм|и́ть, лю́, ~ишь *pf.* (*of* **зака́рмливать**) to overfeed; to stuff.
закорю́чк|а, и *f.* (*coll.*) **1.** hook; flourish (*in handwriting*). **2.** (*fig., dial.*) hitch, snag.
зако|си́ть, шу́, ~сишь *pf.* (*of* **зака́шивать**) (*agric.*) **1.** to begin to mow, begin to scythe. **2.** to mow up, scythe up.
закосне́лый *adj.* incorrigible, inveterate.
закосне́|ть, ю *pf. of* **косне́ть**
закостене́лый *adj.* ossified; stiff.
закостене́|ть, ю *pf.* to ossify; (*fig.*): **он ~л от хо́лода** he became stiff with cold.
закостыля́|ть, ю *pf.* (*coll.*) to hobble, limp.
закоу́л|ок, ка *m.* **1.** back street, (dark) alley. **2.** (*coll.*) secluded corner; **обыска́ть все углы́ и ~ки** to search in every nook and cranny; **знать все ~ки** (*fig.*) to know all the ins and outs.
закочене́лый *adj.* numb with cold.
закочене́|ть, ю, ешь *pf. of* **кочене́ть**
закра́дыва|ться, юсь *impf. of* **закра́сться**
закра́ива|ть, ю *impf. of* **закрои́ть**
закра́ин|а, ы *f.* **1.** (*geog.*) zakraina (*water at edge of frozen river, lake, etc.*). **2.** (*tech.*) flange.
закра́па|ть, ю *pf.* **1.** to begin to fall (*of raindrops*). **2.** to spot.
закра́пыва|ть, ю *impf. of* **закра́пать 2.**
закра́|сить, шу, сишь *pf.* (*of* **~шивать**) **1.** to paint over, paint out. **2.** to begin to paint.
закрасне́|ть, ю, ешь *pf.* to begin to show red.
закрасне́|ться, юсь, ешься *pf.* **1.** to begin to show red. **2.** to blush.
закра́|сться, ду́сь, дёшься, *past* **~лся** *pf.* (*of* **~дываться**) to steel in, creep in; (*fig.*): **у меня́ ~лось подозре́ние** a suspicion crept into my mind.
закра́шива|ть, ю *impf. of* **закра́сить**
закре́п|а, ы *f.* catch; fastener.
закрепи́тел|ь, я *m.* (*chem., phot.*) fixing agent, fixer.
закрепи́тельный *adj.*: **з. тало́н** voucher.
закреп|и́ть, лю́, и́шь *pf.* **1.** to fasten, secure; (*naut.*) to make fast; (*phot.*) to fix. **2.** (*fig.*) to consolidate; **мы ~и́ли прошлого́дние успе́хи** we have consolidated last year's successes. **3.** (+*a.* **за**+*i.*) to allot, assign (to); to appoint, attach (to); **з. за собо́й** to secure; **за на́ми ~и́ли одну́ из но́вых кварти́р** we have been assigned one of the new flats; **он ~и́л за собо́й места́ на за́втрашнее представле́ние в Большо́м теа́тре** he has secured seats for tomorrow's performance at the Bolshoi Theatre. **4.** (*impers.; coll.*): **его́,** *etc.*, **~и́ло** he, *etc.*, has got over his diarrhoea.
закреп|и́ться, лю́сь, и́шься *pf.* **1.** *pass. of* **~и́ть. 2.** (**на**+*a.*) to consolidate one's hold (on).
закрепля́|ть(ся), ю(сь) *impf. of* **закрепи́ть(ся)**
закрепо|сти́ть, щу́, сти́шь *pf.* to enserf.
закрепоща́|ть, ю *impf. of* **закрепости́ть**
закрепоще́ни|е, я *nt.* **1.** enserfment. **2.** slavery; serfdom.
закрив|и́ть, лю́, и́шь *pf.* **1.** to bend; to fold. **2.** (*coll.*) to begin to bend.
закрив|и́ться, лю́сь, и́шься *pf.* **1.** to become crooked. **2.** (*coll.*) to begin to bend (*intrans.*).
закривля́|ть(ся), ю(сь) *impf. of* **закриви́ть(ся)**
закристаллиз|ова́ться, у́юсь *pf. of* **кристаллизова́ться**
закрич|а́ть, у́, и́шь *pf.* **1.** to cry out. **2.** to begin to shout; to give a shout.
закро|и́ть, ю́, и́шь *pf.* (*of* **закра́ивать**) **1.** to cut out. **2.** (*tech.*) to groove.
закро́|й, я *m.* **1.** cutting out. **2.** cut; style (*of dress*). **3.** (*tech.*) groove.
закро́йны|й *adj.* for cutting clothes; **~е но́жницы** cutting-out scissors.
закро́йщик, а *m.* cutter.
за́кром, а, *pl.* **~а́** *m.* corn-bin; (*fig., rhet.*) granary.
закругле́ни|е, я *nt.* **1.** rounding, curving. **2.** curve; curvature. **3.** (*liter.*) well-rounded period.
закруглён|ный (~, ~а́) *p.p.p. of* **закругли́ть** *and adj.* rounded; (*liter.*) well-rounded.
закругл|и́ть, ю, и́шь *pf.* to make round; **з. фра́зу** to round off a sentence.
закругл|и́ться, ю́сь, и́шься *pf.* to become round.
закругля́|ть(ся), ю(сь) *impf. of* **закругли́ть(ся)**
закруж|и́ть, у́, ~и́шь *pf.* **1.** to begin to whirl (*trans. and intrans.*); **з. кому́-н. го́лову** (*fig., coll.*) to turn s.o.'s head. **2.** to make giddy, make dizzy; **она́ его́ совсе́м ~и́ла** (*fig., coll.*) she has swept him off his feet. **3.** (*dial.*) to lead astray.
закруж|и́ться, у́сь, ~и́шься *pf.* **1.** to begin to whirl, begin

to go round; **у меня́ голова́ ~и́лась** my head began to swim. **2.** *pf. of* **кружи́ться**

закрута́с|ы, ов *no sg.* (*coll., obs.*) flourishes.

закру|ти́ть, чу́, ~́тишь *pf.* **1.** to twist; to twirl; to wind round; **они́ ~ти́ли ему́ ру́ки за́ спину** they twisted his arms behind his back. **2.** to turn; to screw in; (*fig.*) **з. слове́чко** to make a caustic remark. **3.** (*fig., coll.*) to turn s.o.'s head. **4.** (*coll., dial.*) to go drinking.

закру|ти́ться, чу́сь, ~́тишься *pf.* **1.** to twist; to twirl; to wind round (*intrans.*). **2.** to begin to whirl.

закру́тка = самокру́тка

закру́чива|ть(ся), ю(сь) *impf. of* **закрути́ть(ся)**

закрыва́|ть(ся), ю(сь) *impf. of* **закры́ть(ся)**

закры́ти|е, я *nt.* **1.** closing; shutting. **2.** (*mil.*) cover.

закры́т|ый (~, ~а) *p.p.p. of* **~ь** *and adj.* closed, shut; private; **с ~ыми глаза́ми** (*fig.*) blindly; **~ое голосова́ние** secret ballot; **при ~ых дверя́х** behind closed doors, in private; **~ое заседа́ние** private meeting; **з. ко́нкурс** closed competition; **~ое мо́ре** inland sea; **~ое пла́тье** high-necked dress; **в ~ом помеще́нии** indoors; **з. просмо́тр** private view; **з. распредели́тель** store closed to non-members; **~ое уче́бное заведе́ние** (private) boarding-school.

закр|ы́ть, о́ю, о́ешь *pf.* (*of* **~ыва́ть**) **1.** to close, shut; **з. глаза́** to pass away; **я ему́ ~ы́л глаза́** I attended him on his deathbed; **з. глаза́ (на+***a.*) to shut one's eyes (to); **з. ско́бки** to close brackets; **з. счёт** to close an account. **2.** to shut off, turn off. **3.** to close down, shut down. **4.** to cover.

закр|ы́ться, о́юсь, о́ешься *pf.* (*of* **~ыва́ться**) **1.** to close, shut; to end; to close down; (*intrans.*). **2.** to cover o.s.; to take cover; **они́ ~́лись от дождя́ зонто́м** they took cover from the rain beneath the awning. **3.** *pass. of* **~ы́ть**

закули́сный *adj.* (occurring) behind the scenes; (*fig.*) secret; underhand, undercover.

за́куп, а *m.* (*hist.*) zakup (*peasant in Kievan Russia repaying loan by means of labour*).

закупа́|ть, ю *impf. of* **закупи́ть**

закупа́|ться[1]**, юсь** *impf., pass. of* **~ть**

закупа́|ться[2]**, юсь** *pf.* (*coll.*) to bathe excessively.

закуп|и́ть, лю́, ~́ишь *pf.* (*of* **~а́ть**) **1.** to buy up (wholesale). **2.** to lay in; to stock up with. **3.** (*obs.*) to bribe.

заку́пк|а, и *f.* purchase.

закупно́й *adj.* bought, purchased.

заку́порива|ть, ю *impf. of* **заку́порить**

заку́пор|ить, ю, ишь *pf.* **1.** to cork; to stop up. **2.** (*fig., coll.*) to shut up; coop up.

заку́порк|а, и *f.* **1.** corking. **2.** (*med.*) embolism, thrombosis.

заку́п|очный *adj. of* **~ка**; **~очная цена́** purchase price.

заку́пщик, а *m.* purchaser; buyer.

заку́рива|ть(ся), ю(сь) *impf. of* **закури́ть(ся)**

закур|и́ть, ю́, ~́ишь *pf.* **1.** to light up (*cigarette, pipe, etc.*). **2.** to begin to smoke; **ещё не ко́нчив шко́лу он ~и́л** he began to smoke before he had left school. **3.** (*dial.*) to begin to distil.

закур|и́ться, ю́сь, ~́ишься *pf.* **1.** to begin to smoke (*intrans.*). **2.** (*coll.*) to smoke excessively; to make o.s. ill by excessive smoking.

заку|си́ть[1]**, шу́, ~́сишь** *pf.* (*of* **~́сывать**) to bite; (*fig.*): **з. удила́** to take the bit between the teeth; **з. язы́к** to hold one's tongue, to shut up.

заку|си́ть[2]**, шу́, ~́сишь** *pf.* (*of* **~́сывать**) **1.** to have a snack, have a bite; **з. на́скоро** to snatch a hasty bite. **2.** (*+a. and i.*) to take (with); **з. во́дку ры́бкой** to drink vodka with fish hors-d'œuvres.

заку́ск|а, и *f.* (*usu. pl.*) hors-d'œuvre; snack; **на ~у** for a titbit; (*fig., coll.*) as a special treat.

заку́с|очный *adj. of* **~ка**; *as n.* **~очная, ~очной** *f.* snack bar.

заку́сыва|ть, ю *impf. of* **закуси́ть**

заку́т, а *m.* (*dial.*) **1.** storeroom. **2.** kennel; (pig-)sty.

заку́та|ть, ю *pf.* (*of* **заку́тывать**) to wrap up, muffle; **з. в одея́ло** to tuck up (in bed).

заку́та|ться, юсь *pf.* (*of* **заку́тываться**) to wrap o.s. up, muffle o.s.

заку|ти́ть, чу́, ~́тишь *pf.* to begin to drink; to go drinking.

заку|ти́ться, чу́сь, ~́тишься *pf.* (*coll.*) to spend (all) one's time drinking.

заку́тк|а, и *f.* (*dial.*) **1.** *dim. of* **заку́т. 2.** chimney-corner (*in peasant's hut*).

заку́тыва|ть(ся), ю(сь) *impf. of* **заку́тать(ся)**

зал, а *m.* hall; **з. ожида́ния** waiting room; **демонстрацио́нный з.** showroom; **з. вы́лета** (*airport*) departure lounge; **з. игровы́х автома́тов** amusement *or* video game arcade.

за́л|а, ы *f.* (*obs. or coll.*) = **~**

зала́в|ок, ка *m.* (*dial.*) chest, locker.

зала́|дить, жу, дишь *pf.* (*coll.*) **1.** (*+inf.*) to take to; **он ~дил заходи́ть к нам по вечера́м** he has taken to calling in on us in the evening. **2.: з. одно́ и то́ же** to harp on the same string.

залакир|ова́ть, у́ю *pf.* to varnish over; (*fig.*) to make shiny.

зала́мыва|ть, ю *impf. of* **заломи́ть**

залата́|ть, ю *pf. of* **лата́ть**

зал|га́ться, гу́сь, жёшься, гу́тся, *past* **~га́лся, ~гала́сь, ~гало́сь** *pf.* (*coll.*) to become an inveterate liar.

залега́ни|е, я *nt.* (*geol.*) **1.** bedding. **2.** bed, seam.

залега́|ть, ю *impf. of* **зале́чь**

заледене́лый *adj.* **1.** covered with ice; ice-bound. **2.** ice-cold, icy.

заледене́|ть, ю *pf.* (*of* **ледене́ть**) (*coll.*) **1.** to be covered with ice; to freeze up, ice up. **2.** to become cold as ice; to become numb.

залежа́лый *adj.* (*coll.*) **1.** stale. **2.** long unused.

залеж|а́ться, у́сь, и́шься *pf.* **1.** to lie too long; to lie idle a long time. **2.** (*econ.*) to find no market. **3.** become stale.

залёжива|ться, юсь *impf. of* **залежа́ться**

за́леж|ь, и *f.* **1.** (*geol.*) deposit, bed, seam. **2.** (*agric.*) fallow land. **3.** (*sg. only; collect.; coll.*) stale goods.

залеза́|ть, ю *impf. of* **зале́зть**

зале́з|ть, у, ешь, *past* **~, ~ла** *pf.* **1.** (**на+***a.*) to climb (up, on to). **2.** (**в+***a.; coll.*) to get (into); to creep (into); **з. кому́-н. в карма́н** to pick s.o.'s pocket; **з. в во́ду по го́рло** to get up to one's neck in water; **он ~ в отцо́вские сапоги́** he got into his father's boots; **з. в долги́** to run into debt.

зален|и́ться, ю́сь, ~́ишься *pf.* (*coll.*) to grow lazy.

залепе|та́ть, чу́, ~́чешь *pf.* (*coll.*) to begin to babble.

залеп|и́ть, лю́, ~́ишь *pf.* (*+a. and i.*) to paste up, paste over; to glue up; **всю стéну ~и́ли афи́шами** the whole wall had been pasted over with bills; **глаза́ у него́ ~и́ло сне́гом** his eyes were stuck up with snow; **з. кому́-н. пощёчину** (*vulg.*) to slap s.o.'s face.

залепля́|ть, ю *impf. of* **залепи́ть**

залета́|ть[1]**, ю** *pf.* (*coll.*) to begin to fly.

залета́|ть[2]**, ю** *impf. of* **залете́ть**

зале|те́ть, чу́, ти́шь *pf.* **1.** (**в+***a.*) to fly (into); (**за+***a.*) to fly (over, beyond); **пти́ца ~те́ла в ко́мнату** a bird flew into the room; **мы ~те́ли за Се́верный по́люс** we flew over the North Pole. **2.** (**в+***a.*) to fly (into), land (*on the way*); **нам пришло́сь з. в Стокго́льм за горю́чим** we had to land at Stockholm to refuel. **3.** (*fig., coll.*): **з. высоко́, з. далеко́** to go up in the world.

залётн|ый *adj.* (*coll.*): **~ая пти́ца** bird of passage (*also fig.*); **з. гость** unexpected visitor.

зале́чива|ть, ю *impf. of* **залечи́ть**

залеч|и́ть, у́, ~́ишь *pf.* **1.** to heal; to remedy **2.** (*coll.*): **з. до́ сме́рти** to doctor to death; to murder (*by unskilful treatment*).

залеч|и́ться, ~́ится *pf.* (*coll.*) to heal (up).

зал|е́чь, я́гу, я́жешь, я́гут, *past* **~ёг, ~егла́** *pf.* (*of* **~ега́ть**) **1.** to lie down; to lie low; to lie in wait. **2.** (*geol.*) to lie, be deposited; **здесь руда́ ~егла́ на глубине́ ста ме́тров** there is a deposit of ore here at a depth of a hundred metres. **3.** (*fig.*) to take root; to become ingrained. **4.** (*med.*) to become blocked; **нос у него́ ~ёг, у него́ в носу́ ~егло́** his nose is blocked.

зали́в, а *m.* bay; gulf; creek, cove.

залива́|ть[1]**, ю** *impf.* (*coll.*) to lie, tell lies.

залива́|ть[2]**(ся), ю(сь)** *impf. of* **зали́ть(ся)**

зали́вист|ый (~, ~а) *adj.* (of sound) modulating.

зали́вк|а, и *f.* mending; stopping up, filling in (*with liquid substance*).

заливн|о́е, о́го *nt.* fish or meat in aspic.

заливн|о́й *adj.* **1.: з. луг** water-meadow. **2.** for pouring; **~а́я труба́** funnel. **3.** (*folk poet.*) trilling. **4.** jellied; **~а́я ры́ба** fish in aspic.

зали|за́ть, жу́, ~́жешь *pf.* **1.** to lick clean. **2.: з. себе́ во́лосы** to sleek down one's hair.

зали́зыва|ть, ю *impf. of* **зализа́ть**

зал|и́ть, ью́, ьёшь, *past* **~́ил, ~ила́, ~́ило** *pf.* (*of* **~ива́ть**) **1.** to flood, inundate; (*fig.*): **ко́мнату ~́ило све́том** the room was flooded with light; **толпа́ ~ила́ у́лицы** the crowd filled the streets to overflowing. **2.** (*+a. and i.*) to pour (over); to spill (on); **кто ~и́л но́вую ска́терть черни́лами?** who has spilled ink on the new table-cloth?; **з. кра́ской** to give a wash of paint; **з. ту́шью** to ink in. **3.** to quench, extinguish (*with water*); **з. пожа́р** to put out a fire; **з. го́ре (вино́м)** to drown one's sorrows. **4.** to stop up (*with liquid substance, as putty, rubber solution, etc.*); **з. гало́ши** to mend galoshes. **5.** to begin to pour (*intrans.*).

зал|и́ться, ью́сь, ьёшься, *past* **~и́лся́, ~ила́сь** *pf.* (*of* **ива́ться**) **1.** to be flooded, inundated. **2.** to pour; to spill (*intrans.*); **вода́ ~ила́сь мне за воротни́к** water has gone down my neck. **3.** to spill on o.s.; **ты весь ~илс́я су́пом** you have spilled soup all over yourself. **4.** (*+i.*) to break into, burst into; **соба́ка ~ила́сь ла́ем** the dog began to bark furiously; **з. пе́сней** to break into a song; **з. слеза́ми** to burst into tears, dissolve in tears. **5.** to set (*of jellies*).

залихва́тск|ий *adj.* (*coll.*) devil-may-care; **~ая пе́сня** rollicking song.

зало́г[1]**, а** *m.* **1.** deposit; pledge; security; (*leg.*) bail; **под з.** (*+g.*) on the security of; **отда́ть в з.** to pawn; to mortgage; **вы́купить из ~а** to redeem; to pay off mortgage (on); **усе́рдие — з. успе́ха** hard work is the key to success. **2.** (*fig.*) pledge, token.

зало́г[2]**, а** *m.* (*gram.*) voice.

зало́г|овый *adj. of* **~; ~овое свиде́тельство** mortgage-deed.

залогода́тел|ь, я *m.* depositor; mortgagor.

залогодержа́тел|ь, я *m.* pawnee.

залож|и́ть, у́, ~́ишь *pf.* (*of* **закла́дывать**) **1.** to put (behind); **он ~и́л ру́ки за́ спину** he put his hands behind his back. **2.** to lay (the foundation of). **3.** (*coll.*) to mislay. **4.** (*+i.*) to pile up, heap up (with); to block up (with); (*impers., +d.*): **мне нос ~и́ло** my nose is blocked, is stuffed up. **5.** to mark, put a marker in; **я ~и́л страни́цу девяно́сто** I have put a marker in at page ninety. **6.** to pawn; to mortgage. **7.** to harness. **8.** to lay in, store, put by.

зало́жник, а *m.* hostage.

залом|и́ть, лю́, ~́ишь *pf.* (*of* **зала́мывать**) **1.** to break off. **2.** (*coll.*): **з. це́ну** to ask an exorbitant price; **з. ша́пку** to cock one's hat.

залосн|и́ться, и́тся *pf.* (*coll.*) to become shiny.

залп, а *m.* volley; salvo; **вы́стрелить ~́ом** to fire a volley, salvo; **~́ом** (*fig., coll.*) without pausing for breath; **вы́пить ~́ом** to drain at one draught.

залуп|и́ть, лю́, ~́ишь *pf.* (*coll.*) **1.** to peel off; to tear off. **2.** to ask an exorbitant price for. **3.** to begin to beat. **4.** to beat up.

залуп|и́ться, ~́ится *pf.* (*coll.*) to peel off, flake off.

залупя́|ть(ся), ет(ся) *impf. of* **залупи́ть(ся)**

залуча́|ть, ю *impf. of* **залучи́ть**

залуч|и́ть, у́, и́шь *pf.* (*coll.*) to entice, lure.

заль|сти́ть, щу́, сти́шь *pf.* (*coll.*) **1.** (*+d.*) to begin to flatter. **2.** (*dial.*) to win over by flattery.

залюб|ова́ться, у́юсь *pf.* (*+i.*) to be lost in admiration (of).

заля́па|ть, ю *pf.* (*coll.*) to make dirty.

зам, а *m.*(*coll.*) *abbr. of* **~ести́тель**

зам. (*abbr. of* **замести́тель**) deputy.

зам... *comb. form, abbr. of* **замести́тель**

зама́|зать, жу, жешь *pf.* (*of* **ма́зать** *and* **~зывать**) **1.** to paint over; to efface; (*fig.*) to slur over. **2.** to putty; to lute. **3.** to daub, smear, to soil.

зама́|заться, жусь, жешься *pf.* (*of* **ма́заться** *and* **~зываться**) to smear o.s.; to get dirty.

зама́зк|а, и *f.* **1.** putty; **(бе́лая) з.** correction fluid. **2.** closing up with putty, luting.

зама́зыва|ть(ся), ю(сь) *impf. of* **зама́зать(ся)**

зама́й *only in phr.* **не з.** (*dial.*) don't touch, leave alone.

зама́лива|ть, ю *impf. of* **замоли́ть**

зама́лчива|ть, ю *impf. of* **замолча́ть**

зама́нива|ть, ю *impf. of* **замани́ть**

заман|и́ть, ю́, ~́ишь *pf.* to entice, lure; to decoy.

зама́нчив|ый (~, ~а) *adj.* tempting, alluring.

замара́|ть, ю *pf.* (*of* **мара́ть 1.**) **1.** to soil, dirty; (*fig.*) to disgrace; **з. свою́ репута́цию** to sully one's reputation. **2.** to blot out, efface.

замара́|ться, юсь *pf. of* **мара́ться 1.**

замара́шк|а, и *c.g.* (*coll.*) slut, sloven; grubby child.

зама́рива|ть, ю *impf. of* **замори́ть**

замарин|ова́ть, у́ю *pf. of* **маринова́ть**

замаскир|ова́ть, у́ю *pf.* to mask; to disguise; to camouflage; **з. свои́ чу́вства** (*fig.*) to conceal one's feelings.

замаскир|ова́ться, у́юсь *pf.* to disguise o.s.

замаскиро́выва|ть(ся), ю(сь) *impf. of* **замаскирова́ть(ся)**

зама́слива|ть(ся), ю(сь) *impf. of* **зама́слить(ся)**

зама́сл|ить, ю, ишь *pf.* **1.** to oil, grease. **2.** to make oily, make greasy. **3.** (*fig., sl.*) to butter up.

зама́сл|иться, юсь, ишься *pf.* to become oily, become greasy.

заматере́лый *adj.* hardened, inveterate.

заматере́|ть, ю *pf.* to become hardened.

замат|оре́лый = ~ере́лый

зама́тыва|ть(ся), ю(сь) *impf. of* **замота́ть(ся)**

зама́х, а *nt.* threatening gesture.

зама|ха́ть, шу́, ~́шешь *pf.* to begin to wave.

зама́хива|ться, юсь *impf. of* **замахну́ться**

замахн|у́ться, у́сь, ёшься *pf.* (*+i.*) to raise threateningly; **он да́же ~у́лся руко́й на беззащи́тную стару́ху** he even lifted up his hand against a defenceless old woman.

зама́чива|ть, ю *impf. of* **замочи́ть**

зама́шк|а, и *f.* (*coll., pej.*) way, manner.

зама́щива|ть, ю *impf. of* **замости́ть**

зама́|ять, ю, ешь *pf.* (*coll.*) to tire out, wear out.

зама́|яться, юсь, ешься *pf.* (*coll.*) to be tired out, exhausted.

замая́ч|ить, у, ишь *pf.* to loom; **вдали́ ~или огни́ га́вани** the lights of the harbour loomed up in the distance.

замби́|ец, йца *m.* Zambian.

замби́йк|а, и *f.* Zambian.

замби́йский *adj.* Zambian.

За́мби|я, и *f.* Zambia.

замедле́ни|е, я *nt.* **1.** slowing down, deceleration; (*mus.*) ritardando. **2.** delay; **без ~я** without delay, at once.

заме́дленн|ый *p.p.p. of* **заме́длить** *and adj.* retarded; delayed; **бо́мба ~ого де́йствия** delayed-action bomb; **~ое воспроизведе́ние** slow-motion replay.

заме́дл|ить, ю, ишь *pf.* **1.** to slow down, retard; **з. шаг** to slacken one's pace; **з. ход** to reduce speed. **2.** (*+inf. or +i. or* **с***+i.*) to delay (in); to be long (in); **отве́т не ~ил прийти́** the answer was not long in coming; **з. (с) отве́том** to delay in answering.

заме́дл|иться, ится *pf.* **1.** to slow down; to slacken, become slower. **2.** *pass. of* **~ить**

замедля́|ть(ся), ет(ся) *impf. of* **заме́длить(ся)**

замел|и́ть, ю́, и́шь *pf.* (*coll.*) to chalk over.

заме́н|а, ы *f.* **1.** substitution; replacement; **з. сме́ртной ка́зни тюре́мным заключе́нием** commutation of death sentence to imprisonment. **2.** substitute.

замени́|мый *pres. part. pass. of* **~ть** *and adj.* replaceable.

замени́тел|ь, я *m.* (*+g.*) substitute; **з. ко́жи** leather substitute; **з. са́хара** sweetener.

замен|и́ть, ю́, ~́ишь *pf.* **1.** (*+a. and i.*) to replace (by), substitute (for); **мы ~и́ли кероси́н электри́чеством** we have replaced oil by electricity; **з. ма́сло маргари́ном** to use margarine instead of butter. **2.** to take the place of; **она́ ~и́ла ребёнку мать** she was (like) a mother to the child; **тру́дно бу́дет з. его́** it will be hard to replace him.

замен|я́ть, я́ю *impf. of* **~и́ть**

зам|ере́ть, ру́, рёшь, *past* **~́ер, ~ерла́, ~́ерло** *pf.* (*of* **~ира́ть**) **1.** to stand still; to freeze, be rooted to the spot;

to die (*fig.*); **се́рдце моё ∼́ерло, когда́ дверь откры́лась** my heart stopped beating when the door opened. **2.** to die down, die away; **к полу́ночи стрельба́ ∼ерла́** towards midnight firing died down.

замерза́ни|е, я *nt.* freezing; **то́чка ∼я** freezing point; **на то́чке ∼я** (*fig.*) at a standstill.

замерза́|ть, ю *impf. of* **замёрзнуть**

замёрз|нуть, ну, нешь, *past* **∼, ∼ла** *pf.* (*of* **∼а́ть**) to freeze (up); to freeze to death; to be killed by frost.

за́мертво *adv.* **1.** like one dead; **она́ упа́ла з.** she collapsed in a dead faint. **2.** (*coll.*) dead drunk.

заме|си́ть, шу́, ∼́сишь *pf.* (*of* **∼́шивать**) to mix; **з. те́сто** to knead dough.

заме|сти́, ту́, тёшь, *past* **∼̈л, ∼ла́** *pf.* (*of* **∼та́ть**) **1.** to sweep up. **2.** to cover (up); (*impers.*): **доро́гу ∼ло́ сне́гом** the road is covered with snow; (*fig.*): **з. следы́** to cover up one's traces.

замести́тел|ь, я *m.* substitute; deputy; **з. дире́ктора** deputy director; **з. председа́теля** (*comm.*) vice-chairman (of the board); **быть ∼ем** (+*g.*) to stand proxy (for), substitute (for).

замести́тельств|о, а *nt.* position of deputy; acting tenure of office; **по ∼у** by proxy.

заме|сти́ть, щу́, сти́шь *pf.* (*of* **∼ща́ть**) **1.** (+*a. and i.*) to replace (by); to substitute (for). **2.** (+*a. and i.*) to appoint (to); **они́ ∼сти́ли ка́федру психоло́гии не́мцем** they have appointed a German to the chair of psychology. **3.** to deputize for, act for; to serve in place of.

замета́|ть[1]**, ю** *impf. of* **замести́**

замета́|ть[2]**, ю** *pf.* (*of* **замётывать**) to tack, baste; *p.p.p. as pred.* (*coll.*): **замётано!** all right!; agreed!

заме|та́ться, чу́сь, ∼́чешься *pf.* to begin to rush about; to begin to toss.

заме́|тить, чу, тишь *pf.* (*of* **∼ча́ть**) **1.** to notice, remark; **∼тили ли вы, что он ча́сто повторя́ется?** have you noticed that he often repeats himself?; **я ∼тил за ним скло́нность повторя́ться** I have noticed that he has a tendency to repeat himself. **2.** to take notice (of); to make a note (of). **3.** to remark, observe; **«соверше́нно ве́рно» — ∼тил он** 'perfectly true', he remarked.

заме́тк|а, и *f.* **1.** mark. **2.** note; **∼и на поля́х** marginal notes; **взять на ∼у** (*coll.*) to make a note (of). **3.** notice; paragraph; **ни одна́ газе́та не удосто́ила вы́ставки ∼ой** not a single newspaper gave the exhibition a notice.

заме́т|ный (∼ен, ∼на) *adj.* **1.** noticeable; appreciable; **ме́жду ни́ми есть ∼ная ра́зница в во́зрасте** there is an appreciable difference in age between them; **∼но** (*as pred.*) it is noticeable; **∼но, как он не лю́бит говори́ть о де́тстве** it is noticeable that he does not like talking about his childhood. **2.** outstanding.

замётыва|ть, ю *impf. of* **замета́ть**[2]

замеча́ни|е, я *nt.* **1.** remark, observation. **2.** reprimand; reproof; **он у меня́ на ∼и** (*obs.*) he is in my bad books.

замеча́тел|ьный (∼ен, ∼ьна) *adj.* remarkable; splendid, wonderful.

замеча́|ть, ю *impf. of* **заме́тить**

заме́чен|ный (∼, ∼а) *p.p.p. of* **заме́тить; з.** (**в**+*p.*) discovered, noticed, detected (in); **он был неоднокра́тно ∼ во взя́точничестве** he was several times discovered taking bribes.

замечта́|ться, юсь *pf.* to give o.s. up to day-dreaming; to fall into a reverie; **он опя́ть ∼лся** he is day-dreaming again.

замеша́тельств|о, а *nt.* confusion; embarrassment; **привести́ в з.** to throw into confusion; **прийти́ в з.** to be confused, be embarrassed.

замеша́|ть, ю *pf.* (**в**+*a.*) to mix up, entangle (in).

замеша́|ться, юсь *pf.* (**в**+*a.*) **1.** to become mixed up, entangled (in). **2.** to mix (with), mingle (in, with); **з. в толпу́** to mingle with the crowd.

заме́шива|ть(ся), ю(сь) *impf. of* **замеси́ть** *and* **замеша́ть(ся)**

заме́шк|а, и *f.* (*coll.*) delay.

заме́шка|ться, юсь *pf.* (*coll.*) to linger, tarry.

замеща́|ть, ю *impf. of* **замести́ть**

замеще́ни|е, я *nt.* **1.** substitution. **2.** appointment; **бу́дет ко́нкурс на з. вака́нтной до́лжности** there will be a competition to fill the vacancy.

замза́в, а *m.* (*abbr. of* **замести́тель заве́дующего**) assistant manager.

замина́|ть, ю *impf. of* **замя́ть**

зами́нк|а, и *f.* (*coll.*) **1.** hitch. **2.** hesitation (*in speech*).

замира́ни|е, я *nt.* dying out, dying down; **он ждал с ∼ем се́рдца** he waited with a sinking heart.

замира́|ть, ю *impf. of* **замере́ть**

замире́ни|е, я *nt.* peace-making.

замир|и́ть, ю́, и́шь *pf.* (*obs.*) to pacify; to reconcile.

замир|и́ться, ю́сь, и́шься *pf.* (**с**+*i.*; *obs*) to make peace (with).

замиря́|ть(ся), ю(сь) *impf. of* **замири́ть(ся)**

за́мкнут|ый (∼, ∼а) *adj.* **1.** exclusive. **2.** reserved; **адмира́л — о́чень з. челове́к** the admiral is a very reserved pers.; **вести́ ∼ую жизнь** to lead an unsociable life.

замкн|у́ть, у́, ёшь *pf.* (*of* **замыка́ть**) to lock; to close; **з. ше́ствие, з. коло́нну** to bring up the rear; **з. цепь** (*elec.*) to close the circuit.

замкн|у́ться, у́сь, ёшься *pf.* (*of* **замыка́ться**) **1.** *pass. of* **∼у́ть. 2.** to shut o.s. up; **з. в круг** to form a circle; (*fig.*) **з. в себе́** to become reserved, retire into o.s.

замле́|ть, ю *pf.* (*coll.*) to become numb; to go to sleep (*of a limb*).

зам|ну́, нёшь *see* **∼я́ть**

замоги́льный *adj.* sepulchral (*of voice*).

за́м|ок, ка *m.* castle; **возду́шные ∼ки** castles in the air.

зам|о́к, ка́ *m.* **1.** lock; **америка́нский з.** Yale lock; **вися́чий з.** padlock; **секре́тный з.** combination lock; **под ∼ко́м** under lock and key; **за семью́ ∼ка́ми** well and truly hidden. **2.** (*archit.*) keystone. **3.** bolt (*of fire-arm*). **4.** clasp (*of necklace, etc.*); clip (*of ear-ring*).

замока́|ть, ет *impf. of* **замо́кнуть**

замо́кн|уть, ет *pf.* to become drenched, become soaked.

замо́лв|ить, лю, ишь *pf.* (*coll.*): **з. слове́чко за** (+*a.*) to put in a word (for); **прошу́ вас з. слове́чко за меня́ у нача́льства** will you, please, put in a word for me with the authorities.

замол|и́ть, ю́, ∼́ишь *pf.* (*of* **зама́ливать**); **з. грехи́** to atone for one's sins by prayer.

замолка́|ть, ю *impf. of* **замо́лкнуть**

замо́лк|нуть, ну, нешь, *past* **∼, ∼ла** *pf.* to fall silent; to stop, cease (*speaking, etc.*); **внеза́пно пе́ние ∼ло** suddenly the singing ceased.

замолч|а́ть[1]**, у́, и́шь** *pf.* to fall silent; (*fig.*), to cease corresponding.

замолч|а́ть[2]**, у́, и́шь** *pf.* (*of* **зама́лчивать**) (*coll.*) to keep silent about; to hush up.

замора́живани|е, я *nt.* freezing; **з. зарпла́ты** wage-freezing.

замора́жива|ть, ю *impf. of* **заморо́зить**

заморд|ова́ть, у́ю *pf.* (*coll.*) to torment.

замор|и́ть, ю́, и́шь *pf.* (*of* **зама́ривать**) (*coll.*) **1.** to overwork; **з. ло́шадь** to founder a horse. **2.** to underfeed; **з. червячка́** to have a bite, have a snack.

заморо́|женный *p.p.p. of* **∼зить** *and adj.* frozen; iced; **∼женное мя́со** frozen meat; **∼женное шампа́нское** iced champagne.

заморо́|зить, жу, зишь *pf.* (*of* **замора́живать**) to freeze; to ice.

за́морозк|и, ов *no sg.* (light) frosts.

замо́рский *adj.* oversea(s).

замо́рыш, а *m.* (*coll.*) weakling; runt.

замо|сти́ть, щу́, сти́шь *pf.* (*of* **мости́ть** *and* **зама́щивать**) to pave.

замо́тан|ный (∼, ∼а) *adj.* (*coll.*) fagged- *or* worn-out, shattered.

замота́|ть, ю *pf.* (*of* **зама́тывать**) **1.** to wind, twist; to roll up. **2.** (*fig.*) to tire out. **3.** (*sl.*) to pinch, whip. **4.** (+*i.*) to begin to shake; **з. голово́й** to begin to shake one's head; **з. хвосто́м** to begin to wag its tail.

замота́|ться, юсь *pf.* (*of* **зама́тываться**) (*coll.*) **1.** to wind round. **2.** to be tired out, be fagged out. **3.** to begin to shake; to begin to swing (*intrans.*).

замоч|и́ть, у́, ≁ишь *pf.* (*of* **зама́чивать**) **1.** to wet; to soak; **з. лён** to ret (rate, rait) flax. **2.** (*fig., coll.*) to celebrate.
замо́чник, а *m.* locksmith.
замо́чн|ый *adj. of* **замо́к; ~ая сква́жина** keyhole.
зампре́д, а *m.* (*abbr. of* **замести́тель председа́теля**) vice-chairman; deputy chairman.
за́муж *adv.*: **вы́йти з. за кого́-н.** to marry s.o. (*of woman*); **вы́дать кого́-н. з.** (**за**+*a.*) to give s.o. in marriage (to); **она́ вы́шла з. за моряка́, несмотря́ на то́, что её оте́ц всё мечта́л вы́дать её за врача́** she has married a sailor despite the fact that her father always dreamed of marrying her to a doctor.
за́мужем *adv.*: **быть з.** (**за**+*i.*) to be married (to) (*of woman*).
заму́жеств|о, а *nt.* marriage (*of woman*); **у неё о́чень счастли́вое з.** she is very happily married.
заму́жняя *adj.* married (*of woman*).
замундшту́чива|ть, ю *impf. of* **замундшту́чить**
замундшту́ч|ить, у, ишь *pf.* to bit.
замур|ова́ть, у́ю *pf.* to brick up; to immure.
замуро́выва|ть, ю *impf. of* **замурова́ть**
заму́сл|ить, ю, ишь = замусо́лить
замусо́лива|ть, ю *impf. of* **замусо́лить**
замусо́л|ить, ю, ишь *pf.* to beslobber.
заму|ти́ть, чу́, ~ти́шь *pf. of* **мути́ть; он воды́ не ~ти́т** he won't cause any trouble.
замухры́шк|а, и *c.g.* (*coll., pej.*) poor specimen.
заму́чива|ть, ю *impf. of* **заму́чить**
заму́ч|ить, у, ишь *pf.* (*of* **му́чить** *and* **~ивать**) to torment; to wear out; to plague the life out of; to bore to tears.
заму́ч|иться, усь, ишься *pf.* (*of* **му́читься**) to be worn out, worried to death.
за́мш|а, и *f.* chamois (leather); suede.
замшеви́дный *adj.* suedette, suede-cloth.
за́мш|евый *adj. of* **~а**
замше́лый *adj.* mossy, moss-covered.
замше́|ть, ет *pf.* to be overgrown with moss.
замыва́|ть, ю *impf. of* **замы́ть**
замыка́ни|е, я *nt.* locking; **коро́ткое з.** (*elec.*) short circuit.
замы́ка|ться, юсь *pf.* (*coll.*) to be tired out.
замыка́|ть(ся), ю(сь) *impf. of* **замкну́ть(ся)**
за́мыс|ел, ла *m.* project, plan; design, scheme; idea; **его́ но́вая пье́са осно́вана на о́чень оригина́льном ~ле** his new play is based on a very original idea; **злы́е ~лы** evil designs.
замы́сл|ить, ю, ишь *pf.* (*of* **замышля́ть**) (+*a. or inf.*) to plan; to contemplate, meditate; **он ~ил самоуби́йство** he contemplated suicide; **они́ ~или убежа́ть под покро́вом темноты́** they had planned to escape under cover of darkness.
замыслова́т|ый (~, ~а) *adj.* intricate, complicated.
зам|ы́ть, о́ю, о́ешь *pf.* (*of* **~ыва́ть**) to wash off, wash out.
замышля́|ть, ю *impf. of* **замы́слить**
зам|я́ть, ну́, нёшь *pf.* (*of* **~ина́ть**) (*coll.*) to put a stop to; **з. разгово́р** to change the subject.
зам|я́ться, ну́сь, нёшься *pf.* (*coll.*) to stumble; to stop short (*in speech*).
за́навес, а *m.* curtain; **под з.** (*theatr.*) near the end of an act.
занаве́|сить, шу, сишь *pf.* (*of* **~шивать**) to curtain; to cover.
занаве́с|ка, ки *f.* curtain (*of light material*).
занаве́шива|ть, ю *impf. of* **занаве́сить**
занаво́|зить, жу, зишь *pf.* **1.** (*dial.*) to manure. **2.** (*coll.*) to befoul.
зана́шива|ть, ю *impf. of* **заноси́ть**[2]
зане́ *conj.* (*arch.*) since, because.
занеме́|ть, ю *pf.* (*coll.*) to grow numb.
занемога́|ть, ю *impf. of* **занемо́чь**
занемо́|чь, гу́, жешь, гут, *past* **~г, ~гла́** *pf.* to fall ill, be taken ill.
занес|ти́, у́, ёшь, *past* **≁, ~ла́** *pf.* (*of* **заноси́ть**[1]) **1.** to bring, import. **2.** to raise, lift; **з. но́гу в стре́мя** to raise one's foot into the stirrup. **3.** to note down; **з. в протоко́л** to enter in the minutes. **4.** (*coll.*) to carry (away); **куда́ его́ нелёгкая ~ла́?** where the devil has he got to?; (*impers.*): **каки́м ве́тром вас сюда́ ~ло́?** what wind blows you here? **5.** (*impers.*): **з. сне́гом** to cover with snow; **доро́гу ~ло́ сне́гом** the road is snowed up.
занес|ти́сь, у́сь, ёшься, *past* **≁ся, ~ла́сь** *pf.* (*of* **заноси́ться**[1]) (*coll., pej.*) to be carried away (*fig.*).
Занзиба́р, а *m.* Zanzibar.
занима́тел|ьный (~ен, ~ьна) *adj.* entertaining, diverting; absorbing.
занима́|ть[1]**, ю** *impf.* (*of* **заня́ть**) **1.** to occupy; **з. го́род** to occupy a city; **з. кварти́ру** to occupy a flat; **крова́ть ~ет мно́го ме́ста** the bed takes up a lot of room; **он ~ет высо́кое положе́ние** (*fig.*) he occupies a high post. **2.** to occupy; to interest; **она́ ника́к не могла́ з. дете́й** she simply could not keep the children occupied; **его́ ~ют бо́льше всего́ вопро́сы филосо́фии** his chief interest is in philosophy. **3.** to take (*of time*); **э́то ~ет мно́го вре́мени** this takes a lot of time. **4.** (*impers.; coll.*): **дух ~ет** it takes your breath away!
занима́|ть[2]**, ю** *impf.* (*of* **заня́ть**) to borrow.
занима́|ться[1]**, юсь** *impf.* (*of* **заня́ться**) (+*i.*) **1.** to be occupied (with), be engaged (in); to work (at, on); to study; **чем вы ~лись вчера́?** what were you doing yesterday?; **он ~ется подгото́вкой но́вой экспеди́ции** he is engaged in preparations for a new expedition; **до заму́жества она́ ~лась му́зыкой** before her marriage she was studying music. **2.** to busy o.s. (with); to devote o.s. (to); **з. собо́й** to devote attention to one's appearance. **3.** (**с**+*i.*) to assist; to attend to.
занима́|ться[2] *impf.* (*of* **заня́ться**) to catch fire; **~лась заря́** day was breaking.
за́ново *adv.* anew.
зано́з|а, ы *f. and c.g.* **1.** *f.* splinter. **2.** *c.g.* (*fig., coll.*) thorn in the flesh; nagger.
зано́зист|ый (~, ~а) *adj.* (*coll.*) splintery; (*fig.*) nagging.
зано|зи́ть, жу́, зи́шь *pf.* to get a splinter into.
зано́с[1]**, а** *m.* snow-drift.
зано́с[2]**, а** *m.* **1.** bringing, importing, import. **2.** raising, lifting.
зано|си́ть[1]**, шу́, ≁сишь** *impf. of* **занести́**
зано|си́ть[2]**, шу́, ≁сишь** *pf.* (*of* **зана́шивать**) to wear out.
зано|си́ться[1]**, шу́сь, ≁сишься** *impf. of* **занести́сь**
зано|си́ться[2]**, ≁сится** *pf.* to be worn out; to wear out (*intrans.*).
зано́сный *adj.* alien, imported.
зано́счив|ый (~, ~а) *adj.* arrogant, haughty.
заноч|ева́ть, у́ю *pf.* (*coll.*) to stay for the night.
зану́д|а, ы *c.g.* (*coll.*) tiresome pers., pain in the neck.
зану́дливый = зану́дный
зану́д|ный (~ен, ~на) *adj.* (*coll.*) tiresome.
занумер|ова́ть, у́ю *pf.* (*of* **нумерова́ть**) to number.
заня́ти|е, я *nt.* **1.** occupation; pursuit. **2.** (*pl.*) studies; work; **часы́ ~й** working hours.
заня́т|ный (~ен, ~на) *adj.* (*coll.*) entertaining, amusing.
занято́й *adj.* busy.
за́нятост|ь, и *f.* being busy; **у нас в э́ту неде́лю больша́я з.** we are very busy this week; (*econ.*): **по́лная з.** full employment.
за́нят|ый (~, ~а́, ~о) *p.p.p. of* **≁ь** *and adj.* **1.** occupied; **здесь ~о** this place is taken; **~о** engaged (*of telephone number*); **на э́том заво́де ~о свы́ше ты́сячи рабо́чих** over a thousand people are employed in this factory; **быть ~ым собо́й** to be self-centred. **2.** busy.
зан|я́ть(ся), займу́(сь), займёшь(ся), *past* **≁ял(ся), ~яла́(сь), ≁яло(сь)** *pf. of* **занима́ть(ся)**; (*impers.; coll.*): **у кого́-н. дух ≁яло** to be out of breath; (*fig.*) to be (left) breathless; **от э́того у меня́ дух ≁яло** it took my breath away.
зао́блачн|ый *adj.* (*poet., fig.*) beyond the clouds; **~ая высь,** *see* **высь**
заодно́ *adv.* **1.** in concert, at one; **де́йствовать з.** to act in concert; **насчёт э́того мужчи́ны — з. с же́нщинами** on this the men are in agreement with the women. **2.** (*coll.*) at the same time; **купи́те з. и апельси́нов** buy some oranges at the same time.
заозёрный *adj.* situated on the other side of the lake.
заокеа́нский *adj.* transoceanic.

заор|а́ть, у́, ёшь *pf.* (*coll.*) to begin to bawl, begin to yell.
заострённост|ь, и *f.* pointedness, sharpness.
заострённый *p.p.p. of* **заостри́ть** *and adj.* pointed, sharp.
заостр|и́ть, ю́, и́шь *pf.* to sharpen; (*fig.*) to stress, emphasize; **з. внима́ние (на+***a.***)** to stimulate an interest (in).
заостр|и́ться, и́тся *pf.* to become sharp; to become pointed.
заостр|я́ть(ся), я́ет(ся) *impf. of* **~и́ть(ся)**
зао́чник, а *m.* student taking correspondence course; external student.
зао́чно *adv.* **1.** in one's absence. **2.** by correspondence course, externally.
зао́чн|ый *adj.* **1.** (*leg.*): **з. пригово́р** judgment by default. **2.: з. курс** correspondence course; **~ое обуче́ние** postal tuition.
за́пад, а *m.* **1.** west. **2.** the West; the Occident.
запада́|ть, ю *impf. of* **запа́сть**
за́падник, а *m.* Westernizer, Westernist.
за́падничеств|о, а *nt.* Westernism.
за́падный *adj.* west, western; westerly.
западн|я́, и́, *g. pl.* **~е́й** *f.* trap, snare; **попа́сть в ~ю́** to fall into a trap (*also fig.*).
запа́здывани|е, я *nt.* **1.** lateness, being late. **2.** (*tech.*) lag.
запа́здыва|ть, ю *impf. of* **запозда́ть** (*impf. only*; *tech.*) to lag.
запа́ива|ть, ю *impf. of* **запая́ть**
запа́йк|а, и *f.* soldering.
запак|ова́ть, у́ю *pf.* to pack (up); to wrap up, do up.
запако́выва|ть, ю *impf. of* **запакова́ть**
запа́ко|стить, щу, стишь *pf. of* **па́костить 1.**
запа́л[1]**, а** *m.* fuse; touchhole.
запа́л[2]**, а** *m.* heaves; broken wind.
запа́лива|ть, ю *impf. of* **запали́ть**[1]
запал|и́ть[1]**, ю́, и́шь** *pf.* (*coll.*) to set fire to, kindle; to light.
запал|и́ть[2]**, ю́, и́шь** *pf.* (*dial.*) **1.** to water (*a horse*) when overheated. **2.** to override (*a horse*).
запал|и́ть[3]**, ю́, и́шь** *pf.* (*coll.*) **1.** to open fire. **2.** (+*i.*) to hurl.
запа́л|ьный *adj. of* **~**[1]; **~ьная свеча́** sparking plug.
запа́льчивост|ь, и *f.* (quick) temper.
запа́льчив|ый (~а) *adj.* quick-tempered.
запа́мят|овать, ую *pf.* (*obs.*, *coll.*) to forget.
запанибра́та *adv.* (*coll.*): **быть з. с кем-н.** to be hail-fellow-well-met with s.o.
запанибра́тский *adj.* (*coll.*) hail-fellow-well-met.
запанибра́тств|о, а *nt.* (*coll.*, *obs.*) hail-fellow-well-met terms.
запа́рива|ть(ся), ю(сь) *impf. of* **запа́рить(ся)**
запа́р|ить, ю, ишь *pf.* **1.** (*coll.*) to put into a sweat. **2.** to stew; to bake.
запа́р|иться, юсь, ишься *pf.* **1.** (*coll.*) to get into a sweat. **2.** to be worn out.
запарк|ова́ть, у́ю *pf. of* **паркова́ть**
запарк|ова́ться, у́юсь *pf. of* **паркова́ться**
запарши́ве|ть, ю *pf. of* **парши́веть**
запа́рыва|ть, ю *impf. of* **запоро́ть**
запа́с, а *m.* **1.** supply, stock; reserve; **з. това́ров** stock-in-trade; **прове́рить з.** to take stock; **про з.** for emergency; **отложи́ть про з.** to put by; **истощи́ть з. терпе́ния** (*fig.*) to exhaust one's reserves of patience; **приобрести́ большо́й з. слов** to acquire a large vocabulary. **2.** (*mil.*) reserve; **его́ уво́лили в з.** he has been transferred to the reserve. **3.** hem; **вы́пустить з.** to let out.
запаса́|ть(ся), ю(сь) *impf. of* **запасти́(сь)**
запа́слив|ый (~, ~а) *adj.* thrifty; provident.
запа́сни́к[1]**, а** *m.* (*coll.*) reservist.
запа́сник[2]**, а** *m.* repository, depository; storeroom.
запасн|о́й *adj.* **1.** spare; reserve; **з. вы́ход** emergency exit; **з. путь** siding; **з. батальо́н** (*mil.*) depot battalion; **з. сте́ржень** re-fill (*for pen*); **~а́я часть** spare part; **з. я́корь** (*naut.*) sheet anchor, spare bower anchor. **2.** *as n.* **з., ~о́го** *m.* reservist.
запа́сн|ый *adj.* = **~о́й**
запас|ти́, у́, ёшь, *past* **~̈, ~ла́** *pf.* (*of* **~а́ть**) (+*a. or g.*) to stock, store; to lay in a stock of.
запас|ти́сь, у́сь, ёшься, *past* **~̈ся, ~ла́сь** *pf.* (*of* **~а́ться**) (+*i.*) to provide o.s. (with); to stock up (with); **з. терпе́нием** (*fig.*) to arm o.s. with patience.
запа́|сть, ду́, дёшь, *past* **~л** *pf.* (*of* **~да́ть**) to fall (behind); to sink down; **слова́ его́ ~ли мне в ду́шу** (*fig.*) his words are imprinted in my mind.
запат|ова́ть, у́ю *pf. of* **патова́ть**
за́пах, а *m.* smell.
запа|ха́ть, шу́, ~̈шешь *pf.* (*agric.*) **1.** to plough in. **2.** to begin to plough.
запа́хива|ть[1]**(ся), ю(сь)** *impf. of* **запахну́ть(ся)**
запа́хива|ть[2]**, ю** *impf. of* **запаха́ть**
запа́хн|уть, у, ешь *pf.* to begin to emit a smell.
запахн|у́ть, у́, ёшь *pf.* (*of* **запа́хивать**[1]) **1.** to wrap over (*folds of a garment*). **2.** (*coll.*) **з. за́навеску** to draw the curtain.
запахн|у́ться, у́сь, ёшься *pf.* **(в+***a.***)** to wrap o.s. tighter (into).
запа́чка|ть, ю *pf. of* **па́чкать 1.**
запа́шк|а, и *f.* **1.** ploughing up. **2.** plough-land, arable land.
запаш|о́к, ка́ *m.* (*coll.*) faint smell.
запая́|ть, ю *pf.* (*of* **запа́ивать**) **1.** to solder. **2.** (*coll.*): **з. кому́-н. в у́хо** to box s.o.'s ears.
запе́в, а *m.* introduction (*to song*); solo part.
запева́л|а, ы *m.* leader (of choir); precentor; (*fig.*, *coll.*) leader, instigator.
запева́|ть, ю *impf.* (*of* **запе́ть**) to lead the singing, set the tune.
запека́нк|а, и *f.* **1.** baked pudding; casserole; **ри́совая з.** rice pudding; **карто́фельная з.** shepherd's pie. **2.** spiced brandy.
запека́|ть(ся), ю(сь) *impf. of* **запе́чь(ся)**
запелена́|ть, ю *pf. of* **пелена́ть**
запе́н|ить, ю, ишь *pf.* to froth up.
запе́н|иться, юсь, ишься *pf.* to begin to froth up, begin to foam (*intrans.*).
зап|ере́ть, ру́, рёшь, *past* **~̈ер, ерла́, ~̈ерло** *pf.* (*of* **~ира́ть**) **1.** to lock; **з. на засо́в** to bolt. **2.** to lock in; to shut up. **3.** to bar; to block up.
зап|ере́ться, ру́сь, рёшься, *past* **~̈ерся́, ~ерла́сь, ~̈ерлось** *pf.* (*of* **~ира́ться**) **1.** to lock o.s. in. **2. (в+***p.*; *coll.*) to refuse to admit; to refuse to speak (about); to shut up (*intrans.*).
зап|е́ть, ою́, оёшь *pf.* **1.** *pf. of* **~ева́ть. 2.** to begin to sing; **з. пе́сню** to break into a song; **з. друго́е** (*fig.*) to change one's tune. **3.** (*coll.*): **з. пе́сню** to plug a song.
запеча́т|ать, аю *pf.* (*of* **~ывать**) to seal.
запечатлева́|ть(ся) *impf. of* **запечатле́ть(ся)**
запечатле́ни|е, я *nt.* (*biol.*) imprinting.
запечатле́|ть, ю *pf.* to imprint, impress, engrave; **з. что-н. в па́мяти** (*fig.*) to imprint sth. on one's memory.
запечатле́|ться, юсь *pf.* (*fig.*) to imprint itself, stamp itself, impress itself; **черты́ его́ лица́ ~лись у де́вочки в па́мяти** his features stamped themselves in the little girl's memory.
запеча́тыва|ть, ю *impf. of* **запеча́тать**
запе́|чь, ку́, чёшь, ку́т, *past* **~̈к, ~кла́** *pf.* (*of* **~ка́ть**) to bake.
запе́|чься, чётся, ку́тся, *past* **~̈кся, ~кла́сь** *pf.* (*of* **~ка́ться**) **1.** to bake (*intrans.*). **2.** to clot, coagulate. **3.** to become parched.
запива́|ть, ю *impf. of* **запи́ть**
запина́|ться, юсь *impf.* (*of* **запну́ться**) to hesitate; to stumble, halt (*in speech*); to stammer; **з. ного́й** to trip up; **з. о ка́мень** to strike against a stone.
запи́нк|а, и *f.* hesitation (*in speech*).
запира́тельств|о, а *nt.* (*pej.*) denial, disavowal.
запира́|ть(ся), ю(сь) *impf. of* **запере́ть(ся)**
запи|са́ть, шу́, ~̈шешь *pf.* (*of* **~̈сывать**) **1.** to note, make a note (of); to take down (in writing); to record (*with apparatus*); **(на плёнку)** to tape; **(на ви́део)** to video; **з. ле́кцию** to take notes of a lecture. **2.** to enter, register, enrol; **~ши́те меня́ пожа́луйста на приём к врачу́** please, make an appointment with the doctor for me. **3.** (+*a.* **на+***a.*; *leg.*) to make over (to); **он ~са́л всю со́бственность на свою́ племя́нницу** he made over all his property to his

niece. **4.** (*coll.*) to begin to write, begin to correspond.
запи|са́ться, шу́сь, ~́шешься *pf.* (*of* **~́сываться**) **1.** to register, enter one's name, enrol; **з. в клуб** to join a club; **з. к врачу́** to make an appointment with the doctor. **2.** to forget the time in writing. **3.** *pass. of* **~са́ть**
запи́ск|а, и *f.* **1.** note; **делова́я з.** memorandum, minute. **2. ~и** (*pl.*) notes; memoirs; (*as title of learned journals*) transactions.
записн|о́й[1] *adj.*: **~а́я кни́жка** notebook.
записно́й[2] *adj.* (*coll.*) inveterate; regular.
запи́сыва|ть(ся), ю(сь) *impf. of* **записа́ть(ся)**
за́пис|ь, и *f.* **1.** writing down; recording. **2.** entry; record; (*leg.*) deed; **метри́ческая з.** registration of vital statistics.
зап|и́ть, ью́, ьёшь, *past* **~́ил, ~ила́, ~́ило** *pf.* (*of* **~ива́ть**) **1.** (*coll.*; *past* **~́ил**) to take to drink; to go on a blind. **2.** (*past* **~и́л**; *+a. and i.*) to wash down (with); to take (with, after); **з. пилю́лю водо́й** to take a pill with water.
запиха́|ть, ю *pf.* (*coll.*) to cram into.
запи́хива|ть, ю *impf. of* **запиха́ть**
запих|ну́ть, ну́, нёшь *pf.* (*coll.*) = **~а́ть**
запи́чка|ть, ю *pf.* (*coll.*) to stuff, cram.
запи|шу́, ~́шешь *see* **~са́ть**
запла́кан|ный (~, ~а) *adj.* tear-stained; in tears.
запла́|кать, чу, чешь *pf.* to begin to cry.
запланир|овать, ую *pf. of* **плани́ровать**[1]
запла́т|а, ы *f.* patch (*in garments*); **наложи́ть ~у (на**+*a.*) to patch.
заплата́|ть, ю *pf.* (*of* **плата́ть**) (*coll.*) to patch.
запла|ти́ть, чу́, ~́тишь *pf. of* **плати́ть**
запла́чк|а, и *f.* (*anthrop.*; *dial.*) lamentation (*of a bride, in course of wedding rite*; *at funerals*).
запла́|чу, чешь *see* **~кать**
запла|чу́, ~́тишь *see* **~ти́ть**
заплёван|ный (~, ~а) *p.p.p. of* **заплева́ть** *and adj.* bespattered (with spittle); dirty.
запл|ева́ть, юю́, юёшь *pf.* (*coll.*) to spit on; to spit at; (*fig.*) to rain curses on.
заплёвыва|ть, ю *impf. of* **заплева́ть**
запле|ска́ть, ска́ю, *and* **~щу́, ~́щешь** *pf.* **1.** to splash. **2.** to begin to splash.
заплёскива|ть, ю *impf. of* **заплеска́ть** *and* **заплесну́ть**
запле́сневелый *adj.* mouldy, mildewed.
запле́сневе|ть, ю *pf. of* **пле́сневеть**
заплесн|у́ть, у́, ёшь *pf.* (*of* **заплёскивать**) (*coll.*) to splash into; to swamp.
запле|сти́, ту́, тёшь, *past* **~̈л, ~ла́** *pf.* to braid, plait.
запле|сти́сь, ту́сь, тёшься, *past* **~̈лся, ~ла́сь** *pf.* **1.** (*coll.*) to stumble, be unsteady on one's legs; to falter (*in speech*). **2.** (*dial.*) to wind (*intrans.*). **3.** *pass. of* **~сти́**
заплета́|ть(ся), ю(сь) *impf. of* **заплести́(сь)**
запле́чный *adj.* over the shoulder; **з. мешо́к** rucksack; **з. ма́стер** (*obs.*) executioner.
заплéч|ье, ья, *g. pl.* **~ий** *nt.* shoulder-blade.
запломбир|ова́ть, у́ю *pf.* (*of* **пломбирова́ть** *and* **~о́вывать**) **1.: з. зуб** to stop, fill a tooth. **2.** to seal.
запломбиро́выва|ть, ю *impf. of* **запломбирова́ть**
заплута́|ться, юсь *pf.* (*coll.*) to lose one's way, stray.
заплы́в, а *m.* round, heat (*of water sports*).
заплыва́|ть, ю *impf. of* **заплы́ть**
заплы́|ть[1], **ву́, вёшь,** *past* **~л, ~ла́, ~ло** *pf.* to swim far out; to sail away.
заплы́|ть[2], **ву́, вёшь,** *past* **~л, ~ла́, ~ло** *pf.* to be swollen; to be bloated; **~вшие жи́ром глаза́** bloated eyes.
запн|у́ться, у́сь, ёшься *pf. of* **запина́ться**
запове́да|ть, ю *pf.* (*of* **запове́дывать**) (*rhet.*) to command.
запове́дник, а *m.* reserve; preserve; sanctuary; **госуда́рственный з.** national park.
запове́дн|ый *adj.* **1.** prohibited; **з. лес** forest reserve; **~ое име́ние** entailed estate. **2.** (*poet.*) precious.
запове́дыва|ть, ю *impf. of* **запове́дать**
за́повед|ь, и *f.* precept; (*relig. and fig.*) commandment; **де́сять ~ей** the Ten Commandments.
запода́зрива|ть, ю *impf. of* **заподо́зрить**
заподо́зр|ить, ю, ишь *pf.* **1.** (*+a.* **в**+*p.*) to suspect (of); **его́ ~или в прича́стности к за́говору** he was suspected of complicity in the plot. **2.** (*obs.*) to suspect, be suspicious of; **з. чьи́-н. наме́рения** to suspect s.o.'s intentions.
запо́ем *adv.*: **пить з.** to be a heavy drinker; (*fig.*, *coll.*) heavily, unrestrainedly; **чита́ть з.** to read avidly; **кури́ть з.** to smoke like a chimney.
запозда́лый *adj.* belated.
запозда́|ть, ю *pf.* (*of* **запа́здывать**) (**с**+*i.*) to be late (with); **он ~л с упла́той аре́нды** he is late in paying his rent.
запо|и́ть, ю́, и́шь *pf.* (*coll.*, *dial.*) to give too much to drink (to).
запо́|й, я *m.* (addiction to periodical) hard drinking; **пить ~ем,** *see* **~ем; страда́ть ~ем** to be addicted to the bottle.
запо́й|ный *adj. of* **~; з. пери́од** drunken bout; **з. пья́ница** chronic drunkard.
запола́скива|ть, ю *impf. of* **заполоска́ть** *and* **заполосну́ть**
запо́лза|ть, ю *pf.* to begin to crawl.
заполза́|ть, ю *impf. of* **заползти́**
заполз|ти́, у́, ёшь, *past* **~́, ~ла́** *pf.* (**в, под**+*a.*) to creep, crawl (into, under).
запо́лн|ить, ю, ишь *pf.* (*of* **~я́ть**) to fill in, fill up; **чем вы ~или вре́мя?** how did you fill in the time? **з. бланк** to fill in a form; **з. пробе́л** to fill a gap.
заполня́|ть, ю *impf. of* **запо́лнить**
заполон|и́ть, ю́, и́шь *pf.* (*of* **~я́ть**) (*folk poet. and arch.*) to take captive; (*fig.*) to captivate, enthral.
заполон|я́ть, я́ю *impf. of* **~и́ть**
заполо|ска́ть, щу́, ~́щешь *pf.* (*of* **запола́скивать**) (*coll.*) **1.** to begin to rinse. **2.** to rinse out.
заполо|ска́ться, щу́сь, ~́щешься *pf.* (*coll.*) **1.** to begin to paddle. **2.** to enjoy paddling.
заполосн|у́ть, у́, ёшь *pf.* (*of* **запола́скивать**) (*coll.*) to rinse out.
заполуч|а́ть, а́ю *impf. of* **~и́ть**
заполуч|и́ть, у́, ~́ишь *pf.* (*of* **~а́ть**) (*coll.*) to get hold of, pick up; **я мог бы з. биле́ты на представле́ние в суббо́ту** I could get tickets for Saturday's performance; **з. на́сморк** to pick up a cold.
заполя́рный *adj.* (*geog.*) **1.** polar (*situated within one or other of the polar circles*). **2.** trans-polar; **з. возду́шный путь** trans-polar air route.
заполя́рь|е, я *nt.* (*geog.*) polar regions.
запомина́|ть(ся), ю(сь) *impf. of* **запо́мнить(ся); ~ющее устро́йство** computer memory.
запо́мн|ить, ю, ишь *pf.* (*of* **запомина́ть**) **1.** to memorize. **2.** (*pf. only*) (*+neg.*; *coll.*) to remember; **никто́ не ~ит тако́й жары́** no one remembers such heat.
запо́мн|иться, юсь, ишься *pf.* (*of* **запомина́ться**) to be retained, stick in one's memory; **ему́ ~ился день землетрясе́ния** the day of the earthquake is stuck in his memory.
за́понк|а, и *f.* cuff-link; stud.
запо́р[1], **а** *m.* **1.** bolt; lock; **на ~(е)** locked; bolted (and barred). **2.** (*coll.*) closing; locking; bolting.
запо́р[2], **а** *m.* constipation.
запора́шива|ть, ет *impf. of* **запороши́ть**
запоро́ж|ец, ца *m.* (*hist.*) Zaporozhian Cossack.
запоро́жский *adj.* (*hist.*) Zaporozhian.
запор|о́ть, ю́, ~́ешь *pf.* (*of* **запа́рывать**) (*coll.*) **1.** to flog to death. **2.** to begin to talk (nonsense).
запорош|и́ть, и́т *pf.* (*of* **запора́шивать**) **1.** (*+i.*) to powder (with); (*impers.*): **доро́гу ~и́ло сне́гом** the road was powdered with snow; **глаза́ мои́ ~и́ло пы́лью** there is dust in my eyes. **2.** to begin to powder.
запорхн|у́ть, у́, ёшь *pf.* (*coll.*) to flutter (away, in).
запо|сти́ться, щу́сь, сти́шься *pf.* (*coll.*) **1.** to begin to fast. **2.** to make o.s. weak by fasting.
запотева́|ть, ю *impf. of* **запоте́ть**
запоте́лый *adj.* misted; dim (*from perspiration*).
запоте́|ть, ю *pf.* (*of* **поте́ть** *and* **~ва́ть**) to mist over.
започива́|ть, ю *pf.* (*obs.*) to retire (*for the night*).
зап|ою́, оёшь *see* **~е́ть**
запра́вдашный (*coll.*, *dial.*) true, authentic.

заправи́л|а, ы *m.* (*coll.*) boss.
запра́в|ить, лю, ишь *pf.* (*of* **~ля́ть**) **1.** to insert; **з. брю́ки в сапоги́** to tuck one's trousers into one's boots. **2.** to prepare; to adjust; **з. ла́мпу** to trim a lamp; **з. автомоби́ль бензи́ном** to fill a car up with petrol. **3.** (*+i.*) to mix in; to season (with); **з. со́ус муко́й** to thicken a sauce with flour.
запра́в|иться, люсь, ишься *pf.* (*of* **~ля́ться**) **1.** (*coll.*) to satisfy hunger; to eat one's fill. **2. з. (горю́чим)** to refuel (*intrans.*).
запра́вк|а, и *f.* **1.** seasoning; **з. для сала́та** salad dressing. **2.** refuelling. **3.** petrol *or* service station.
заправля́|ть(ся), ю(сь) *impf. of* **запра́вить(ся)**
запра́вочн|ый *adj.*: **з. пункт, ~ая ста́нция** (petrol) filling station.
запра́вский *adj.* (*coll.*) real, true; thorough; **он — з. моря́к** he is a real sailor.
запра́вщик, а *m.* petrol station attendant.
запра́шива|ть, ю *impf. of* **запроси́ть**
запреде́льный *adj.* (*obs.*) **1.** lying beyond the bounds (of). **2.** fantastic; other-worldly.
запресто́льн|ый *adj.* (*eccl.*) situated behind the altar; **з. о́браз** altar-piece; **~ое украше́ние** reredos.
запре́т, а *m.* prohibition, ban; **наложи́ть з. (на**+*a.*) to place a ban (on).
запрети́тельн|ый *adj.* prohibitive; prohibitory; (*econ.*): **~ая по́шлина** prohibitive duty.
запре|ти́ть, щу́, ти́шь *pf.* (*of* **~ща́ть**) to prohibit, forbid, ban; **врач ~ти́л мне кури́ть, врач ~ти́л мне куре́ние** the doctor has forbidden me to smoke; **з. пье́су** to ban a play.
запре́тн|ый *adj.* forbidden; **~ая зо́на** (*mil.*) restricted area; **~ая те́ма** taboo subject.
запреща́|ть, ю *impf. of* **запрети́ть**
запреща́|ться, ется *impf.* to be forbidden, to be prohibited; (*in official notices, etc.*): **«вход ~ется»** 'No Entry'; **«кури́ть ~ется»** 'No Smoking'.
запреще́ни|е, я *nt.* prohibition; (*leg.*): **з. на иму́щество** distraint, arrest on property; **суде́бное з.** injunction.
запримé|тить, чу, тишь *pf.* (*coll.*) **1.** to notice, perceive. **2.** to recognize, spot; **я ~тил его́ в толпе́ по кра́сной руба́шке** I spotted him in the crowd by his red shirt.
заприхо́д|овать, ую *pf. of* **прихо́довать**
запрограмми́р|овать, ую *pf. of* **программи́ровать**
запрода|ва́ть, ю́, ёшь, *impf. of* **~́ть**
запрода́ж|а, и *f.* (*comm.*) forward contract, provisional sale.
запрода́ж|ный *adj. of* **~а; ная за́пись** document concerning sale.
запрод|а́ть, а́м, а́шь, а́ст, адди́м, ади́те, аду́т, *past* **~́ал, ~ала́, ~́ало** *pf.* (*of* **~ава́ть**) (*comm.*) to conclude a forward contract (on), sell on part-payment; to agree to sell.
запроекти́р|овать, ую *pf. of* **проекти́ровать**[1] **1.**
запроки́дыва|ть, ю *impf. of* **запроки́нуть**
запроки́н|уть, у, ешь *pf.* (*coll.*) to throw back; **он захохота́л, ~ув го́лову** he threw back his head and guffawed.
запроки́н|уться, усь, ешься *pf.* (*coll.*) to lean back, slump back.
запропада́|ть, ю *impf. of* **запропа́сть**
запропа|сти́ть, щу́, сти́шь *pf.* (*coll.*) to mislay.
запропа|сти́ться, щу́сь, сти́шься *pf.* (*coll.*) to get lost, disappear; **куда́ ты ~сти́лся?** where on earth did you get to?
запропа́|сть, ду́, дёшь, *past* **~л** *pf.* (*of* **~да́ть**) (*coll.*) to get lost, disappear.
запро́с, а *m.* **1.** inquiry; (*pol.*) question. **2.** overcharging; **це́ны без ~а** fixed prices. **3.** (*pl. only*) spiritual needs.
запро|си́ть, шу́, ~́сишь *pf.* (*of* **запра́шивать**) **1.** (**о**+*p.*) to inquire (about); (*+a.*) to inquire (of), question; **мини́стра ~си́ли о его́ расхо́дах** the Minister was questioned about his expenditure. **2.: з. сли́шком высо́кую це́ну** to ask an exorbitant price.
за́просто *adv.* (*coll.*) without ceremony, without formality.
запротоколи́р|овать, ую *pf.* to enter in the minutes.
запротоко́л|ить, ю, ишь *pf.* (*coll.*) = **~и́ровать**
запро|шу́, ~́сишь *see* **~си́ть**
зап|ру́, рёшь *see* **~ере́ть**
запру́д|а, ы *f.* **1.** dam, weir. **2.** mill-pond.
запру|ди́ть, жу́, ~́дишь *pf.* **1.** (**~́дишь**) to dam. **2.** (**~ди́шь**) (*fig., coll.*) to block (up); to fill to overflowing.
запружа́|ть, ю *impf. of* **запруди́ть**
запру́жива|ть, ю *impf.* = **запружа́ть**
запры́га|ть, ю *pf.* to begin to jump; (*coll.*): **се́рдце у неё ~ло** her heart began to thump.
запры́гива|ть, ю *impf. of* **запры́гнуть**
запры́гн|уть, у, ешь *pf.* (**за**+*a.*; *coll.*) to leap (over).
запры́ска|ть, ю *pf.* (*coll.*) **1.** to begin to sprinkle. **2.** to besprinkle.
запры́скива|ть, ю *impf. of* **запры́скать**
запряга́|ть, ю *impf. of* **запря́чь**
запря́жк|а, и *f.* **1.** harnessing. **2.** equipage.
запря́|тать, чу, чешь *pf.* (*coll.*) to hide.
запря́|таться, чусь, чешься *pf.* (*coll.*) to hide o.s.
запря́тыва|ть(ся), ю(сь) *impf. of* **запря́тать(ся)**
запря|чь, гу́, жёшь, гу́т, *past* **~г, ~гла́** *pf.* (*of* **~га́ть**) to harness (*also fig.*); **з. воло́в** to yoke oxen.
запря|чься, гу́сь, жёшься, гу́тся, *past* **~гся, ~гла́сь** *pf.* **1.** *pass. of* **~чь. 2.** (*fig., coll.*) to harness o.s.; to buckle to, get down to.
запу́ганный *p.p.p. of* **запуга́ть** *and adj.* broken-spirited.
запуга́|ть, ю *pf.* to intimidate, cow.
запу́гива|ть, ю *impf. of* **запуга́ть**
запу́дрива|ть, ю *impf. of* **запу́дрить**
запу́др|ить, ю, ишь *pf.* to powder.
запузы́рива|ть, ю *impf.* (*sl.*) to do sth. vigorously; **з. на фортепья́но** to knock out a tune on the piano.
запул|и́ть, ю́, и́шь *pf.* (*+a. or i.*; *coll., dial.*) to sling, chuck; **з. ка́мнем в окно́** to sling a stone at a window.
запус|ка́ть, ка́ю *impf. of* **~ти́ть**
запусте́лый *adj.* neglected; desolate.
запусте́ни|е, я *nt.* neglect; desolation.
запусте́|ть, ет *pf.* to fall into neglect; to become desolate.
запу|сти́ть[1]**, щу́, ~́стишь** *pf.* (*of* **~ска́ть**) **1.** (*+i.* **в**+*a.*; *coll.*) to throw (at), fling (at); **он ~сти́л кирпичо́м в окно́** he flung a brick at the window. **2.** (**в**+*a.*) to thrust (*hands, etc.*, into); **ко́шка ~сти́ла ко́гти в мышь** the cat dug its claws into the mouse; **з. ко́гти, ла́пы, ру́ки** (**в**+*a.*; *fig.*) to get one's hands on; **з. глаза́** (*pej.*) to let one's eyes roam. **3.** to start (up) (*mechanism*); **з. мото́р** to start up the engine; **з. раке́ту** to launch a rocket. **4.** (**в**+*a.*) (*coll.*) to put (into), let loose (in); **з. коро́в на луг** to let cows loose in a meadow.
запу|сти́ть[2]**, щу́, ~́стишь** *pf.* (*of* **~ска́ть**) **1.** to neglect, allow to fall into neglect; **з. дела́** to neglect one's affairs; **з. сад** to neglect a garden. **2.** to allow to develop unchecked; **он ~сти́л на́сморк и тепе́рь заболе́л бронхи́том** he neglected his cold and now he is ill with bronchitis.
запу́тан|ный *p.p.p. of* **запу́тать** *and adj.* tangled; (*fig.*) intricate, involved; **з. вопро́с** knotty question.
запу́та|ть, ю *pf.* **1.** to tangle (up). **2.** (*fig.*) to confuse; to complicate; to muddle; **его́ сообще́ние ~ло де́ло** his statement has complicated matters; **тако́го ро́да вопро́сы то́лько ~ют кандида́тов** questions of this kind will only confuse the candidates. **3.** (**в**+*a.*; *fig.*) to involve (in).
запу́та|ться, юсь *pf.* **1.** to become entangled; to foul (*intrans.*); (**в**+*p.*; *fig.*) to entangle o.s. (in), be caught (in). **2.** (**в**+*p.*; *fig.*) to become entangled (in), become involved (in); to become complicated; **з. в долга́х** to become involved in debts; **докла́дчик ~лся в слова́х** the lecturer became tied up in knots.
запу́тыва|ть(ся), ю(сь) *impf. of* **запу́тать(ся)**
запуш|и́ть, и́т *pf.* to cover lightly (*of snow or frost*).
запу́щен|ный *p.p.p. of* **запусти́ть**[2] *and adj.* neglected.
запча́ст|и, е́й *pl.* (*sg.* **~ь, ~и** *f.*; *abbr. of* **запасны́е ча́сти**) spare parts; spares.
запыла́|ть, ю *pf.* to blaze up, flare up.
запыл|и́ть, ю́, и́шь *pf.* (*of* **пыли́ть**) to cover with dust, make dusty.
запыл|и́ться, ю́сь, и́шься *pf.* (*of* **пыли́ться**) to become dusty.

запыхá|ться, юсь *impf.* (*coll.*) to puff, pant.
запы́ха|ться, юсь *pf.* (*coll.*) to be out of breath.
запьяне́|ть, ю *pf.* (*coll.*) to get drunk.
запья́нств|овать, ую *pf.* to take to drink.
запя́стье|е, я *nt.* **1.** wrist; (*anat.*) carpus. **2.** (*poet.*) bracelet.
запят|áя, óй *f.* **1.** comma. **2.** (*coll.*) difficulty, snag.
запя́т|ки, ок *no sg.* footboard (*at back of carriage*).
запятнá|ть, ю *pf. of* **пятнáть**
зарабáтыва|ть(ся), ю(сь) *impf. of* **заработать(ся)**
зарабóта|ть, ю *pf.* **1.** to earn. **2.** to begin to work; to start (up).
зарабóта|ться, юсь *pf.* (*coll.*) **1.** to overwork, tire o.s. out with work. **2.** to work late; **он вчерá ~лся далекó зá пóлночь** he went on working long after midnight last night.
зáработн|ый *adj.*: **~ая плáта** wages, pay, salary.
зáработ|ок, ка *m.* **1.** earnings; **лёгкий з.** easy money. **2.** (*pl. only*) (seasonal) labour, work.
зарáвнива|ть, ю *impf. of* **заровня́ть**
заражáемост|ь, и *f.* susceptibility to infection.
заражá|ть(ся), ю(сь) *impf. of* **заразúть(ся)**
заражéни|е, я *nt.* infection.
зара|жу́, зи́шь *see* **~зи́ть**
зарáз *adv.* (*coll.*) at once; at a sitting; at one fell swoop.
зарáз|а, ы *f.* **1.** infection, contagion. **2.** (*fig.*, *coll.*) pest, plague (*of pers.*).
заразúтел|ьный (~ен, ~ьна) *adj.* infectious; catching; **з. смех** infectious laughter.
зара|зúть, жу́, зи́шь *pf.* (*of* **~жáть**) (+*i.*) to infect (with); (*also fig.*) **з. своúм примéром** to infect with one's example.
зара|зúться, жу́сь, зи́шься *pf.* (*of* **~жáться**) (+*i.*) to be infected (with); catch (*also fig.*).
зарáз|ный (~ен, ~на) *adj.* **1.** infectious; contagious. **2.** of *or* for infectious diseases; **з. барáк** infectious diseases ward; **з. больнóй** patient suffering from infectious disease, infectious case; *as n.* **з.**, **~ного** *m.*, **~ная**, **~ной** *f.* infectious case.
зарáне *adv.* (*obs.*) = **~е**
зарáнее *adv.* beforehand; in good time; **заплатúть з.** to pay in advance; **преступлéние с з. обду́манным намéрением** premeditated crime; **рáдоваться з.** (+*d.*) to look forward (to).
зарапорт|овáться, у́юсь *pf.* (*coll.*) to let one's tongue run away with one.
зарастá|ть, ю *impf. of* **зарасти́**
зараст|и́, у́, ёшь, *past* **зарóс, зарослá** *pf.* **1.** (+*i.*) to be overgrown (with). **2.** (*of a wound*) to heal, skin over.
зарв|áться, у́сь, ёшься, *past* **~áлся, ~алáсь, ~áлóсь** *pf.* (*of* **зарывáться**) (*coll.*) to go too far; to overstep the mark.
зардé|ть, ю *pf.* (*poet.*) = **~ться 1.**
зардé|ться, юсь *pf.* **1.** (*poet.*) to redden, grow red. **2.** to blush.
зáрев|о, а *nt.* glow; **з. (от) пожáра** the glow of a fire.
зар|евóй *adj. of* **~éво**
зарегистрúр|овать, ую *pf.* (*of* **регистрúровать**) to register.
зарегистрúр|оваться, уюсь *pf.* (*of* **регистрúроваться**) **1.** to register o.s. **2.** (*coll.*) to register one's marriage. **3.** *pass. of* **~овать**
зарегистр|овáть(ся), у́ю(сь) *pf.* = **~úровать(ся)**
зарéз, а *m.* **1.** (*coll.*) disaster; **до ~у** extremely, badly, urgently; **мне до ~у нужны́ пять рублéй** I badly need five roubles. **2.** (*dial.*) killing, slaughtering.
зарé|зать, жу, жешь *pf.* **1.** to murder; to knife; **з. свинью́** to stick a pig; (*of a wolf*) to devour, kill; **хоть зарéжь** (*coll.*) extremely, urgently; come what may. **2.** (*fig.*) to undo, be the undoing of; to do for; **без ножá з.** to do for; to make mincemeat of.
зарезá|ть(ся), ю(сь) *impf. of* **зарéзать(ся)**
зарé|заться, жусь, жешься *pf.* (*coll.*) to cut one's throat.
зарéзыва|ть(ся), ю(сь) *impf.* = **зарезáть(ся)**
зарекá|ться, юсь *impf. of* **зарéчься**
зарекоменд|овáть, у́ю *pf. only in phr.* **з. себя́** (+*i.*) to prove o.s., show o.s. (to be); **хорошó з. себя́** to show to advantage.
зарекомендóвыва|ть, ю *impf. of* **зарекомендовáть**
заре|ку́сь, чёшься, ку́тся *see* **~чься**
зарéчный *adj.* situated on the other side of the river.
зарéчь|е, я *nt.* part of town, etc., on the other side of a river.
зарé|чься, ку́сь, чёшься, ку́тся, *past* **~кся, ~клáсь** *pf.* (*of* **~кáться**) (+*inf.*; *coll.*) to renounce; to promise to give up, vow to give up; **он ~кся курúть** he has promised to give up smoking.
заржáве|ть, ет *pf.* (*of* **ржáветь**) to rust; to have got rusty.
заржáвлен|ный (~, ~а) *adj.* rusty.
зарис|овáть, у́ю *pf.* (*of* **~óвывать**) to sketch.
зарис|овáться, у́юсь *pf.* (*of* **~óвываться**) (*coll.*) to spend too much time drawing.
зарисóвк|а, и *f.* **1.** sketching. **2.** sketch.
зарисóвыва|ть(ся), ю(сь) *impf. of* **зарисовáть(ся)**
зáр|иться, юсь, ишься *impf.* (*of* **по~**) (**на**+*a.*; *coll.*) to hanker (after).
зарни́ц|а, ы *f.* summer lightning.
заровня́|ть, ю *pf.* (*of* **зарáвнивать**) to level, even up; **з. я́му** to fill up a hole.
заро|дúть, жу́, дúшь *pf.* (*of* **~ждáть**) to generate, engender (*also fig.*).
заро|дúться, жу́сь, дúшься *pf. pass. of* **~дúть;** (*fig.*) to arise; **у негó ~дúлось сомнéние** a doubt arose in his mind.
зарóдыш, а *m.* (*biol.*) foetus; (*bot.*) bud; (*fig.*) embryo, germ; **подавúть в ~е** to nip in the bud.
зарóдышевый *adj.* embryonic.
зарождá|ть(ся), ю(сь) *impf. of* **зародúть(ся)**
зарождéни|е, я *nt.* conception; (*fig.*) origin.
заро|жу́, дúшь *see* **~дúть**
зарóк, а *m.* **1.** (solemn) promise, vow, pledge, undertaking; **дать з.** to pledge o.s., give an undertaking. **2.** (*dial.*) charm, incantation.
зарон|úть, ю́, ~ишь *pf.* **1.** (*coll.*) to drop (behind); to let fall. **2.** (*fig.*) to excite, arouse; **з. сомнéния** to give rise to doubts.
зарон|úться, ю́сь, ~ишься *pf.* (**в**+*a.*; *obs.*) to sink in, make an impression (on).
заронЯ́|ть, ю *impf. of* **заронúть**
зáросл|ь, и *f.* brake; thicket.
зар|óю, óешь *see* **~ы́ть**
зарплáт|а, ы *f.* (*abbr. of* ***зáработная плáта***) wages, pay, salary.
зарубá|ть, ю *impf. of* **зарубúть**
зарубéжный *adj.* foreign.
заруб|úть, лю́, ~ишь *pf.* (*of* **~áть**) **1.** to kill (*with sabre, axe, etc.*). **2.** to notch, make an incision (on); **~ú э́то себé на носу́, на лбу, на стенé** (*coll.*) put that in your pipe and smoke it. **3.** (*tech.*) to hew.
зару́бк|а, и *f.* **1.** notch; incision. **2.** (*tech.*) hewing.
зарубц|евáться, у́ется *pf.* (*of* **рубцевáться** *and* **~óвываться**) to cicatrize.
зарубцóвыва|ться, ется *impf. of* **зарубцевáться**
зару́бщик, а *m.* (coal-)hewer.
заругá|ть, ю *pf.* (*coll.*) to abuse, scold.
зарумя́нива|ть(ся), ю(сь) *impf. of* **зарумя́нить(ся)**
зарумя́н|ить, ю, ишь *pf.* to redden.
зарумя́н|иться, юсь, ишься *pf.* **1.** to redden (*intrans.*); to blush, colour. **2.** (*coll.*) to brown, bake brown.
заруч|áться, áюсь *impf. of* **~úться**
заруч|úться, у́сь, úшься *pf.* **1.** (+*i.*) to secure; **з. поддéржкой** to enlist support; **з. соглáсием** to obtain consent. **2.** (*sl.*) to secure o.s. (*in a suit at cards*).
зару́чк|а, и *f.* (*coll.*) pull, protection.
зарывá|ть, ю *impf. of* **зары́ть**
зарывá|ться[1], юсь *impf. of* **зары́ться**
зарывá|ться[2], юсь *impf. of* **зарвáться**
зарыдá|ть, ю *pf.* to begin to sob.
зар|ы́ть, óю, óешь *pf.* (*of* **~ывáть**) to bury; **з. талáнт в зéмлю** (*fig.*) to bury one's talent, hide one's light under a bushel.
зар|ы́ться, óюсь, óешься *pf.* (*of* **~ывáться**) **1.** to bury o.s.; **з. лицóм в поду́шку** to bury one's head in the pillow; **з. в дерéвне** (*fig.*, *coll.*) to bury o.s. in the country; **з. в**

книги to bury o.s. in one's books. **2.** (*mil.*) to dig in. **3.** (*dial.*) to become fussy.

зар|я́, и́, *a.* **~ю́** *and* (*rare*) **зо́рю,** *pl.* **зо́ри, зорь, ~я́м** *and* **зо́рям** *f.* **1.** (*a.* **~ю́**) dawn, daybreak; **на ~е́** at dawn, at daybreak; **встать с ~ёй** to rise at crack of dawn; **что ты встал ни свет ни з.?** what made you get up at this unearthly hour? **2.** (*a.* **~ю́**) (**вече́рняя**) **з.** sunset, evening glow; **от ~и́ до ~и́** from night to morning, all night long. **3.** (*a.* **~ю́**) (*fig.*) start, outset; dawn, threshold. **4.** (*a.* **зо́рю,** *d. pl.* **зо́рям**) (*mil.*) reveille; retreat; **бить зо́рю** to beat retreat.

заря́д, а *m.* **1.** charge (*also elec.*), cartridge; **холосто́й з.** blank cartridge; (*fig., coll.*) round (*of drinks*). **2.** (*fig.*) fund, supply.

заря|ди́ть[1], **жу́, ~́ди́шь** *pf.* (*of* **~жа́ть**) **1.** to load (*fire-arm*). **2.** (*elec.*) to charge.

заря|ди́ть[2], **жу́, ди́шь** *pf.* (*coll.*) to keep on, persist in; **с утра́ ~ди́л дождь** it has kept on raining since the morning; **он ~ди́л одно́ и то же** he keeps saying the same thing over and over again.

заря|ди́ться, жу́сь, ~́ди́шься *pf.* (*of* **~жа́ться**) **1.** to be loaded; (*elec.*) to be charged. **2.** (*fig., coll.*) to cheer o.s. up, revive o.s.

заря́дк|а, и *f.* **1.** loading (*of fire-arms*); (*elec.*) charging. **2.** exercises; drill.

заря́д|ный *adj. of* **~; з. я́щик** ammunition wagon.

заряжа́|ть(ся), ю(сь) *impf. of* **заряди́ть(ся)**

заряжа́|ющий *pres. part. act. of* **~ть;** *as n.* **з., ~ющего** *m.* (*mil.*) loader.

заря|жу́, ~́ди́шь *see* **~ди́ть**

заса́д|а, ы *f.* ambush.

заса|ди́ть, жу́, ~́дишь *pf.* (*of* **~́живать**) **1.** (+*a. and i.*) to plant (with); **з. сад плодо́выми дере́вьями** to plant a garden with fruit-trees. **2.** (+*a.* **в**+*a.*; *coll.*) to plant (into), plunge (into), drive (into). **3.** (*coll.*) to shut in, confine; to keep in; **з.** (**в тюрьму́**) to put in prison, lock up; **боле́знь на це́лый ме́сяц ~ди́ла меня́ в го́спиталь** illness kept me in hospital for a whole month. **4.** (+*a.* **за**+*a.*; *coll.*) to set (to); **его́ ~ди́ли за изуче́ние ру́сского языка́** he was set to learn Russian. **5.** (**в**+*a.*) get (*a knife, axe, etc.*) stuck (in).

заса́дк|а, и *f.* planting.

заса́жива|ть, ю *impf. of* **засади́ть**

заса́жива|ться, юсь *impf.* **1.** *impf. of* **засе́сть. 2.** *pass. of* **~ть**

заса|жу́, ~́дишь *see* **~ди́ть**

заса́лива|ть[1], **ю** *impf. of* **заса́лить**

заса́лива|ть[2], **ю** *impf. of* **засоли́ть**

заса́л|ить, ю, ишь *pf.* (*of* **~ивать**[1]) to soil, make greasy.

заса́рива|ть, ю *impf. of* **засори́ть**

заса́сыва|ть, ю *impf. of* **засоса́ть**

заса́харен|ный *p.p.p. of* **заса́харить** *and adj.* candied; **~ные фру́кты** crystallized fruits, candied fruits.

заса́харива|ть, ю *impf. of* **заса́харить**

заса́хар|ить, ю, ишь *pf.* (*of* **~ивать**) to candy.

засверка́|ть, ю *pf.* to begin to sparkle, begin to twinkle.

засве|ти́ть, чу́, ~́ти́шь *pf.* **1.** to light. **2.** (+*d.* **в**+*a.*; *coll.*) to strike, hit; **з. кому́-н. в физионо́мию кулако́м** to stick one's fist in s.o.'s face.

засве|ти́ться, ~́тится *pf.* to light up (*also fig.*).

засветле́|ть, ю *pf.* to show up.

за́светло *adv.* (*coll.*) before nightfall, before dark.

засве|чу́, ~́тишь *see* **~ти́ть**

засвиде́тельств|овать, ую *pf. of* **свиде́тельствовать 2.**

засви|ста́ть, щу́, ~́щешь *pf.* = **~сте́ть**

засви|сте́ть, щу́, сти́шь *pf.* to begin to whistle.

засда|ва́ться, ю́сь, ёшься *impf. of* **~́ться**

засда́|ться, мся, шься, стся, ди́мся, ди́тесь, ду́тся, *past* **~лся, ~ла́сь** *pf.* (*sl.*) to misdeal.

засе́в, а *m.* **1.** sowing. **2.** seed, seed-corn. **3.** sown area.

засева́|ть, ю *impf. of* **засе́ять**

заседа́ни|е, я *nt.* meeting; conference; session, sitting.

заседа́тел|ь, я *m.* assessor; **присяжный з.** juryman.

заседа́|ть, ю *impf.* to sit; to meet.

засе́ива|ть, ю *impf. of* **засе́ять**

засе́|к, кла *see* **~чь**

засе́к|а, и *f.* abat(t)is.

засека́|ть(ся), ет(ся) *impf. of* **засе́чь(ся)**

засекре́|тить, чу, тишь *pf.* **1.** to place on secret list; to classify as secret, restrict. **2.** to give access to secret documents; to admit to secret work.

засекре́ченный *p.p.p. of* **засекре́тить** *and adj.* hush-hush, secret.

засекре́чива|ть, ю *impf. of* **засекре́тить**

засе|ку́, чёшь, ку́т *see* **~́чь**

засе́|л, ла *see* **~сть**

заселе́ни|е, я *nt.* settlement; colonization.

заселённый *p.p.p. of* **засели́ть** *and adj.* populated; inhabited; **ре́дко з.** sparsely populated.

засел|и́ть, ю́, и́шь *pf.* (*of* **~я́ть**) to settle; to colonize; to populate; **з. но́вый дом** to occupy a new house.

засел|я́ть, я́ю *impf. of* **~и́ть**

засемен|и́ть, ю́, и́шь *pf.* to begin to mince (*of gait*).

зас|е́сть, я́ду, я́дешь, *past* **~е́л** *pf.* (*of* **~а́живаться**) (*coll.*) **1.** (**за**+*a. or* +*inf.*) to sit down (to). **2.** to sit firm, sit tight; to ensconce o.s.; **з. в тюрьму́** to go to prison. **3.** (**в**+*p.*) to lodge (in), stick (in); **пу́ля ~е́ла у него́ в боку́** a bullet had lodged in his side; **моти́в ~е́л у меня́ в голове́** (*fig.*) the tune has stuck in my head.

засе́чк|а, и *f.* **1.** notch, mark. **2.** (*geog.*) intersection. **3.** (*med.*) canker. **4.** (*typ.*) serif.

засе́|чь, ку́, чёшь, ку́т, *past* **~к, ~кла** *pf.* (*of* **~ка́ть**) **1.** to flog to death. **2.** to notch. **3.** (*geog.*) to determine by intersection.

засе́|чься, чётся, ку́тся, *past* **~кся, ~кла́сь** *pf.* (*of* **~ка́ться**) to overreach itself, cut, hitch (*of horse*).

засе́|ять, ю, ешь *pf.* (*of* **~ва́ть** *and* **~ивать**) to sow.

заси|де́ть, ди́т *pf.* (*of* **~́живать**) (*coll.*) to fly-spot.

заси|де́ться, жу́сь, ди́шься *pf.* (*of* **~́живаться**) (*coll.*) to sit too long, stay too long; to sit up late; to stay late; **з. за рабо́той** to sit up late working; **з. в де́вках,** *see* **де́вка**

заси́женный *p.p.p. of* **засиде́ть** *and adj.* (*coll.*): **з.** (**му́хами**) fly-blown.

заси́жива|ть(ся), ю(сь) *impf. of* **засиде́ть(ся)**

заси́ль|е, я *no pl.,* (*pej.*) domination, sway.

заси́м *adv.* (*obs.*) hereafter, after this.

засине́|ть(ся), ю(сь) *pf.* to become blue; to appear blue (in the distance).

заси́нива|ть, ю *impf. of* **засини́ть**

засин|и́ть, ю́, и́шь *pf.* (*of* **~́ивать**) **1.** to over-blue (*in laundering*). **2.** to cover with blue paint.

засин|я́ть, я́ю *impf.* = **~́ивать**

засия́|ть, ю *pf.* **1.** to begin to shine, begin to beam. **2.** to appear, come out; **ме́сяц ~л из-за туч** the moon appeared from behind the clouds.

заска|ка́ть, чу́, ~́чешь *pf.* **1.** to begin to jump, to break into a gallop. **2.** (*impf.* **~́кивать**) (**в**+*a.*) to gallop (away to, up to).

заска|ка́ться, чу́сь, ~́чешься *pf.* (*coll.*) to gallop until exhausted.

заска́кива|ть, ю *impf. of* **заскака́ть 2.** *and* **заскочи́ть**

засквo|зи́ть, зи́т *pf.* to begin to show light through.

заскирд|ова́ть, у́ю *pf. of* **скирдова́ть**

заскоб|и́ть, лю́, и́шь *pf.* (*coll.*) to place in brackets.

заско́к, а *m.* (*coll.*) **1.** leap, jump. **2.** crazy idea; **э́то у тебя́ з.?** have you gone crazy?; are you out of your mind?

заскору́злый *adj.* **1.** hardened, calloused. **2.** (*fig.*) coarsened, callous. **3.** (*fig.*) backward, retarded.

заскору́з|нуть, ну, нешь, *past* **~, ~ла** *pf.* **1.** to harden, coarsen, become callous; (*also fig.*). **2.** (*fig.*) to stagnate; to become retarded.

заскоч|и́ть, у́, ~́ишь *pf.* (*of* **заска́кивать**) **1.** (**за**+*a.,* **на**+*a.*) to jump, spring (behind, onto). **2.** (**в**+*a.*; *fig.*) to drop in (to, at).

засла|сти́ть, щу́, сти́шь *pf.* (*of* **~́щивать**) **1.** to take (*medicine, etc.*) with sth. sweet. **2.** to sweeten, put sugar into.

за|сла́ть, шлю́, шлёшь *pf.* (*of* **~сыла́ть**) to send, dispatch; **з. не по а́дресу** to send to the wrong address; **з. шпио́на** to send out a spy.

засла́щива|ть, ю *impf. of* **засласти́ть**
засле|ди́ть, жу́, ди́шь *pf.* (*of* **∼живать**) (*coll.*) to leave dirty foot-marks on.
засле́жива|ть, ю *impf. of* **заследи́ть**
засле|зи́ться, зи́тся *pf.* to begin to water.
заслеп|и́ть, лю́, и́шь *pf.* (*of* **∼ля́ть**) (*coll.*) to blind.
заслепля́|ть, ю *impf. of* **заслепи́ть**
засло́н, а *m.* **1.** screen, barrier. **2.** (*mil.*) covering force.
заслон|и́ть, ю́, и́шь *and* (*coll.*) **∼ишь** *pf. and* (*of* **∼я́ть**) **1.** to hide, cover; to shield, screen. **2.** (*fig.*) to push into the background.
заслон|и́ться, ю́сь, и́шся *and* (*coll.*) **∼ишься** *pf.* (*of* **∼я́ться**) **1. (от)** to shield o.s., screen o.s. (from). **2.** *pass. of* **∼и́ть**
засло́нк|а, и *f.* oven-door; stove-door.
заслон|я́ть(ся)[1], **я́ю(сь)** *impf. of* **∼и́ть(ся)**
заслоня́|ться[2], **юсь** *pf.* (*coll.*) to begin to pace up and down.
заслу́г|а, и *f.* merit, desert; service; contribution; **их наказа́ли по ∼ам** they have been punished according to their deserts; **у него́ больши́е ∼и пе́ред родны́м го́родом** he has rendered great services to his home town.
заслу́женно *adv.* deservedly; according to (one's) deserts.
заслу́жен|ный (*and* **∼ный**) *p.p.p. of* **заслужи́ть** *and adj.* **1.** deserved, merited. **2.** meritorious, of merit; (*as honorific in former USSR*) Honoured. **3.: ∼ный профе́ссор** professor emeritus. **4.** (*fig., joc.*) time-honoured; good old.
заслу́жива|ть, ю *impf.* (*of* **заслужи́ть**) (+*g.*) to deserve, merit.
заслу́жива|ться, юсь *impf.* **1.** *impf. of* **заслужи́ться. 2.** *pass. of* **∼ть**
заслуж|и́ть, у́, ∼ишь *pf.* (*of* **∼ивать**) (+*a.*) **1.** to deserve, merit; win, earn. **2.** (*coll., obs.*) to repay, pay back. **3.** (*dial.*) to atone for, make up for.
заслуж|и́ться, у́сь, ∼ишься *pf.* (*of* **∼иваться**) (*coll.*) to serve for too long.
заслу́ш|ать, аю *pf.* (*of* **∼ивать**) to hear, listen to (*a public or official pronouncement*).
заслу́ш|аться, аюсь *pf.* (*of* **∼иваться**) (+*g.*) to listen spellbound (to).
заслу́шива|ть(ся), ю(сь) *impf. of* **заслу́шать(ся)**
заслы́ш|ать, у, ишь *pf.* **1.** to hear, catch. **2.** (*coll.*) to smell; **з. за́пах** to detect a smell.
заслы́ш|аться, ится, *pf.* (*coll.*) to begin to be audible; to be able to be heard.
заслю́нива|ть, ю *impf. of* **заслюни́ть**
заслюн|и́ть, ю́, и́шь *pf.* (*of* **слюни́ть** *and* **∼ивать**) (*coll.*) to slobber over.
засма́лива|ть, ю *impf. of* **засмоли́ть**
засма́ркива|ть, ю *impf. of* **засморка́ть**
засма́трива|ть, ю *impf.* (**в**+*a.*; *coll.*) to look (into); to peep (into); **з. в окно́ к кому́-н.** to look in at s.o.'s window.
засма́трива|ться, юсь *impf. of* **засмотре́ться**
засме́ива|ть, ю *impf. of* **засмея́ть**
засме|я́ть, ю́, ёшь *pf.* (*coll.*) to ridicule.
засме|я́ться, ю́сь, ёшься *pf.* to begin to laugh.
засмол|и́ть, ю́, и́шь *pf.* to tar; to caulk.
засмо́рканный *p.p.p. of* **засморка́ть** *and adj.* (*coll.*) snotty.
засморка́|ть, ю *pf.* (*coll.*) to make snotty.
засмотр|е́ться, ю́сь, ∼ишься *pf.* (*of* **засма́триваться**) (**на**+*a.*) to be lost in contemplation (of), be carried away (by the sight of).
засне́женный *adj.* snow-covered.
заснима́|ть, ю *impf. of* **засня́ть**
засн|иму́, и́мешь *see* **∼я́ть**
засн|у́ть, у́, ёшь *pf.* (*of* **засыпа́ть**[1]) to go to sleep. fall asleep; (*fig.*) to die down; (*rhet.*): **з. ве́чным сном** to go to one's eternal rest.
засн|я́ть, иму́, и́мешь, *past* **∼я́л, ∼яла́, ∼я́ло** *pf.* (*of* **∼има́ть**) to photograph, snap (*coll.*); (*cinema sl.*) to shoot.
засо́в, а *m.* bolt, bar.
засо́ве|ститься, щусь, стишься *pf.* (+*inf.*; *coll.*) to feel ashamed (to).
засо́выва|ть, ю *impf. of* **засу́нуть**
засо́л, а *m.* salting; pickling.
засол|и́ть, ю́, ∼ишь *pf.* (*of* **заса́ливать**[2]) to salt; to pickle.
засо́льщик, а *m.* salter, pickler.
засоре́ни|е, я *nt.* littering, obstruction, clogging up.
засор|и́ть, ю́, и́шь *pf.* (*of* **заса́ривать** *and* **∼я́ть**) **1.** to clog, block up, stop. **2.** to litter; to get dirt into; (*fig.*): **з. чью-н. ду́шу** to poison s.o.'s mind.
засор|и́ться, ю́сь, и́шься *pf.* (*of* **заса́риваться** *and* **∼я́ться**) to become obstructed, blocked up.
засоря́|ть(ся), ю(сь) *impf. of* **засори́ть(ся)**
засо́с, а *m.* sucking in.
засос|а́ть, у́, ёшь *pf.* (*of* **заса́сывать**) **1.** to suck in, engulf, swallow up (*also fig.*). **2.** (*coll.*) to exhaust by sucking. **3.** to begin to suck.
засо́х|нуть, ну, нешь, *past* **∼, ∼ла** *pf.* (*of* **засыха́ть**) **1.** to dry (up). **2.** to wither.
за́спанный *p.p.p. of* **заспа́ть** *and adj.* (*coll.*) sleepy.
засп|а́ть, лю́, и́шь, *past* **∼а́л, ∼ала́, ∼а́ло** *pf.* (*of* **засыпа́ть**[2]) (*dial.*) to smother (*a baby*) in one's sleep, overlie.
засп|а́ться, лю́сь, и́шься, *past* **∼а́лся, ∼ала́сь, ∼а́лось** *pf.* (*of* **засыпа́ться**[1]) (*coll.*) to oversleep.
заспирт|ова́ть, у́ю *pf.* (*of* **∼о́вывать**) to preserve in alcohol.
заспирто́выва|ть, ю *impf. of* **заспиртова́ть**
засп|лю́, и́шь *see* **∼а́ть**
заспо́р|ить, ю, ишь *pf.* to begin to argue.
заспо́р|иться, юсь, ишься *pf.* (*coll.*) to get carried away by argument.
заспор|и́ться, ю́сь, и́шься *pf.* (*coll.*) to go well; to be a success.
засрам|и́ть, лю́, и́шь *pf.* (*coll.*) to put to shame.
засра́н|ец, ца *m.* (*vulg.*) shit, turd (*pers.*).
засра́н|ка, ки *f. of* **∼**
заста́в|а, ы *f.* **1.** gate (*of town*). **2.** (*hist., mil.*) barrier. **3.** (*mil.*) picket; outpost.
заста|ва́ть, ю́, ёшь *impf. of* **∼ть**
заста́в|ить[1], **лю, ишь** *pf.* (*of* **∼ля́ть**[1]) **1.** to cram, fill; **з. ко́мнату ме́белью** to cram a room with furniture. **2.** to block up, obstruct. **3.** (*library sl.*): **з. кни́гу** to put a book in the wrong place.
заста́в|ить[2], **лю, ишь** *pf.* (*of* **∼ля́ть**[2]) (+*a. and inf.*) to compel, force, make; **он ∼ил нас ждать себя́ два часа́** he kept us waiting for two hours; **они́ не ∼или до́лго проси́ть себя́** they agreed with alacrity.
заста́вк|а, и *f.* (*typ.*) headpiece.
заставля́|ть[1,2], **ю** *impf. of* **заста́вить**[1,2]
заста́в|очный *adj. of* **∼ка**
заста́ива|ться, юсь *impf. of* **застоя́ться**
заста́|ну, нешь *see* **∼ть**
застарева́|ть, ю *impf. of* **застаре́ть**
застаре́лый *adj.* inveterate; chronic.
застаре́|ть, ю *pf.* (*of* **∼ва́ть**) (*coll.*) to become inveterate; to become chronic.
заста́|ть, ну, нешь *pf.* (*of* **∼ва́ть**) to find; **∼ли ли вы его́ до́ма?** did you find him in?; **я ∼л его́ ещё спя́щим** I found him still asleep; **з. врасплo̍х** to catch napping; **з. на ме́сте преступле́ния** to catch red-handed.
заста|ю́, ёшь *see* **∼ва́ть**
застега́|ть, ю *pf.* (*coll.*) **1.** to begin to flog. **2.: з. до́ сме́рти** to flog to death.
застёгива|ть, ю *impf. of* **застегну́ть**
застёгива|ться, юсь *impf.* **1.** *impf. of* **застегну́ться. 2.** *pass. of* **∼ть. 3.** to fasten, do up (*intrans.*); **во́рот ∼ется на пу́говицу** the collar does up with a button.
застег|ну́ть, ну́, нёшь *pf.* (*of* **∼ивать**) to fasten, do up; **з. (на пу́говицы)** to button up.
застег|ну́ться, ну́сь, нёшься *pf.* (*of* **∼иваться**) to button o.s. up; **з. на все пу́говицы** to do up all one's buttons.
застёжк|а, и *f.* fastening; clasp, buckle, hasp; **з. «ве́лкро»** Velcro fastener; **з.-мо́лния** zip fastener.
застекл|и́ть, ю́, и́шь *pf.* (*of* **∼я́ть**) to glaze, fit with glass; **з. портре́т** to frame a portrait.
застекл|я́ть, я́ю *impf. of* **∼и́ть**
застел|и́ть, ю́, ∼ешь *pf.* = **застла́ть 1.**
засте́н|ок, ка *m.* torture-chamber.

застéнчив|ый (~, ~а) *adj.* shy; bashful.
засти́|г, гла *see* **~чь**
засти|гáть, гáю *impf. of* **~́гнуть** *and* **~́чь**
засти́|гнуть = **~чь**
застилá|ть, ю *impf. of* **застлáть**
засти́лк|а, и *f.* **1.** covering. **2.** floor-covering.
застир|áть, áю *pf.* (*of* **~́ывать**) (*coll.*) **1.** to wash off. **2.** to ruin by washing. **3.** (*rare*) to begin to wash.
засти́рыва|ть, ю *impf. of* **застирáть**
зá|стить, щу, стишь *impf.* (*coll.*): **з. свет** to stand in the light.
засти́|чь, гну, гнешь, *past* **~г, ~гла** *pf.* (*of* **~гáть**) to catch; to take unawares; **нас ~гла грозá** we were caught by the storm.
заст|лáть, елю́, éлешь *pf.* (*of* **~илáть**) **1.** (*+i*) to cover (with); **з. ковро́м** to carpet, lay a carpet (over). **2.** (*fig.*) to hide from view; to cloud; **облакá ~лáли солнце** clouds obscured the sun; **слёзы ~лали её глазá** tears dimmed her eyes.
застó|й, я *m.* stagnation (*fig.*); **в ~е** at a standstill; (*pol.*, *pej.*) **пери́од ~я** the years of stagnation (*i.e. period in office of L. Brezhnev*); (*econ.*) depression; **з. крóви** (*med.*) haemostasia.
застóй|ный *adj.* stagnant (*fig.*); **~ные гóды** (*pol.*, *pej.*) = **~**; (*econ.*) unwanted, idle as a result of depression.
застóльн|ый *adj.* table-, occurring at table; **~ая бесéда** table-talk; **~ая пéсня** drinking-song; **~ая речь** after-dinner speech.
застóпорива|ть(ся), ю(сь) *impf. of* **застóпорить(ся)**
застóпор|ить, ю, ишь, *pf.* (*of* **~ивать**) (*tech.*) to stop; (*fig.*, *coll.*) to bring to a standstill.
застóпор|иться, юсь, ишься *pf.* (*of* **~иваться**) (*tech.*) to stop (*of a machine*); (*fig.*, *coll.*) to come to a standstill.
засто|я́ться, ю́сь, и́шься *pf.* (*of* **застáиваться**) **1.** to stand too long. **2.** to stagnate. **3.** (*coll.*) to linger.
застрáгива|ть, ю *impf. of* **застрогáть 2.**
застрáива|ть, ю *impf. of* **застрóить**
застрахóван|ный *p.p.p. of* **застраховáть** *and adj.* insured; *as n.* **з., ~ного** *m.* insured pers.
застрах|овáть, у́ю *pf.* (*of* **страховáть** *and* **~óвывать**) (**от**) to insure (against).
застрах|овáться, у́юсь *pf.* (*of* **страховáться** *and* **~óвываться**) to insure o.s.
застрахóвыва|ть(ся), ю(сь) *impf. of* **застраховáть(ся)**
застрáчива|ть, ю *impf. of* **застрочи́ть**
застращá|ть, ю *pf.* (*coll.*) to frighten, intimidate.
застрáщива|ть, ю *impf. of* **застращáть**
застревá|ть, ю *impf. of* **застря́ть**
застрéлива|ть(ся), ю(сь) *impf. of* **застрели́ть(ся)**
застрел|и́ть, ю́, ~́ишь *pf.* (*of* **~́ивать**) to shoot (dead).
застрел|и́ться, ю́сь, ~́ишься *pf.* (*of* **~́иваться**) to shoot o.s.; to blow one's brains out.
застрéльщик, а *m.* **1.** (*mil.*) skirmisher, tirailleur. **2.** (*fig.*) pioneer, leader; **з. нóвых мод** trendsetter.
застреля́|ть, ю *pf.* (*coll.*) to begin to shoot, begin to fire.
застрéх|а, и *f.* (*dial.*) eaves.
застригá|ть, ю *impf. of* **застри́чь 2.**
застри́|чь, гу́, жёшь, гу́т, *past* **~г, ~гла** *pf.* (*coll.*) **1.** to begin to cut. **2.** (*impf.* **~гáть**) to cut (nails) too short.
застрогá|ть, ю *pf.* **1.** to begin to plane. **2.** (*pf. of* **застрáгивать**) to plane (down).
застрó|ить, ю, ишь *pf.* (*of* **застрáивать**) **1.** to build (over, on, up). **2.** to begin to build.
застрóйк|а, и *f.* building; **прáво ~и** building permit.
застрóйщик, а *m.* pers. building (or having built for him) his own house.
застроч|и́ть, у́, ~́ишь *pf.* **1.** (*impf.* **застрáчивать**) to sew up, stitch up. **2.** (*coll.*) to begin to scribble, dash off (*a letter, etc.*). **3.** (*coll.*) to rattle away (*of or with automatic weapons*).
застругá|ть, ю, *pf.* = **застрогáть**
застру́гива|ть, ю *impf. of* **застругáть**
застря́|ну, нешь *see* **~ть**
застря́па|ться, юсь *pf.* (*coll.*) to devote too much time to cooking.
застря́|ть, ну, нешь *pf.* (*of* **застревáть**) **1.** to stick; **з. в грязи́** to get stuck in the mud; **словá ~ли у негó в гóрле** the words stuck in his throat. **2.** (*fig.*, *coll.*) to be held up; to become bogged down.
засту|ди́ть, жу́, ~́дишь, *pf.* (*of* **~́живать**) (*coll.*) to expose to cold; to aggravate by exposure to cold.
засту|ди́ться, жу́сь, ~́дишься *pf.* (*of* **~́живаться**) (*coll.*) to catch cold, catch a chill.
засту́жива|ть(ся), ю(сь) *impf. of* **застуди́ть(ся)**
засту|жу́, ~́дишь *see* **~ди́ть**
зáступ, а *m.* spade.
заступá|ть(ся), ю(сь) *impf. of* **заступи́ть(ся)**
заступ|и́ть, лю́, ~́ишь *pf.* (*of* **~áть**) **1.** to take the place of; **з. отцá сиротé** to become a father to an orphan. **2. (на пост)** to take up (a post).
заступ|и́ться, лю́сь, ~́ишься *pf.* (**за**+*a.*) to stand up for; to take s.o.'s part; to plead (for).
засту́пник, а *m.* defender, protector.
засту́пничеств|о, а *nt.* intercession.
застывá|ть, ю *impf. of* **засты́ть**
засты|ди́ть, жу́, ди́шь *pf.* (*coll.*) to shame, cause to feel shame.
засты|ди́ться, жу́сь, ди́шься *pf.* (*coll.*) to feel shame; to become confused.
засты|жу́, ди́шь *see* **~ди́ть**
засты́лый *adj.* (*coll.*) congealed; stiff.
засты́|ну, нешь *see* **~ть**
засты́|нуть = **~ть**
засты́|ть *and* **~нуть, ну, нешь** *pf.* (*of* **~вáть**) **1.** to thicken, set; to harden; to congeal, coagulate. **2.** (*coll.*) to become stiff; (*fig.*): **з. от у́жаса** to be paralysed with fright. **3.** (*coll.*) to freeze (*also fig.*).
засу|ди́ть, жу́, ~́дишь *pf.* (*of* **~́живать**) (*coll.*) to condemn.
засуе|ти́ться, чу́сь, ти́тся *pf.* **1.** to begin to bustle about, begin to fuss. **2.** to wear o.s. out with fussing.
засу́жива|ть, ю *impf. of* **засуди́ть**
засу|жу́, ~́дишь *see* **~ди́ть**
засу́н|уть, у, ешь *pf.* (*of* **засóвывать**) to shove *or* thrust in; to tuck in; **з. ру́ки в кармáн** to thrust one's hands into one's pockets.
засу́сл|ить, ю, ишь *pf. of* **су́слить**
засусóл|ить, ю, ишь *pf. of* **сусóлить**
зáсух|а, и *f.* drought.
засухоустóйчив|ый (~, ~а) *adj.* (*agric.*) drought-resisting.
засу́чива|ть, ю *impf. of* **засучи́ть**
засуч|и́ть, у́, ~́ишь *pf.* (*of* **~́ивать**) (**рукавá**, *etc.*) to roll up (*sleeves, etc.*).
засу́шива|ть(ся), ю(сь) *impf. of* **засуши́ть(ся)**
засуш|и́ть, у́, ~́ишь *pf.* (*of* **~́ивать**) to dry up (*plants*; *also fig.*).
засуш|и́ться, у́сь, ~́ишься *pf.* (*of* **~́иваться**) to dry up (*intrans.*), shrivel.
засу́шлив|ый (~, ~а) *adj.* droughty, dry.
засчит|áть, áю *pf.* (*of* **~́ывать**) to take into consideration; **з. в уплáту дóлга** to reckon towards payment of a debt.
засчи́тыва|ть, ю *impf. of* **засчитáть**
засылá|ть, ю *impf. of* **заслáть**
засы́лк|а, и *f.* sending, dispatching.
засы́п|ать[1]**, лю, лешь** *pf.* (*of* **~áть**[3]) **1.** to fill up. **2.** (*+i.*) to cover (with), strew (with); **за одну́ ночь дорóжка былá ~ана опáвшими ли́стьями** in a single night the path was strewn with fallen leaves. **3.** (*+i.*; *fig.*, *coll.*) **з. вопрóсами** to bombard with questions; **з. поздравлéниями** to shower congratulations (on). **4.** (*+a. or g.* **в**+*a.*; *coll.*) to put (into), add (to); **з. овсá в я́сли** to pour oats into the manger.
засы́п|ать[2]**, лю, лешь** *pf.* (*of* **~áть**[4]) (*sl.*) to give away, betray.
засыпá|ть[1]**, ю** *impf. of* **засну́ть**
засыпá|ть[2]**, ю** *impf. of* **заспáть**
засыпá|ть[3,4]**, ю** *impf. of* **засы́пать**[1,2]
засы́п|аться[1]**, люсь, лешься** *pf.* (*of* **~áться**[2]) **1.** to get into; **песóк ~ался мне в башмаки́** I have got sand into my shoes. **2.** (*+i.*) *pass. of* **~ать**[1]
засы́п|аться[2]**, люсь, лешься** *pf.* (*of* **~áться**[3]) (*coll.*) **1.**

to be caught; (*sl.*) to be nabbed. **2.** to come to grief, slip up.
засыпа́|ться[1], **юсь** *impf. of* **заспа́ться**
засыпа́|ться[2,3], **юсь** *impf. of* **засы́паться**[1,2]
засы́пк|а, и *f.* **1.** filling up; covering, strewing. **2.** pouring in, putting in.
засыха́|ть, ю *impf. of* **засо́хнуть**
зас|я́ду, я́дешь *see* **~есть**
затавр|и́ть, ю́, и́шь *pf.* (*of* **таври́ть**) to brand (*cattle, etc.*).
затаён|ный *p.p.p. of* **затаи́ть** *and adj.* secret; suppressed; **~ная мечта́** secret dream.
зата́ива|ть(ся), ю(сь) *impf. of* **затаи́ть(ся)**
зата|и́ть, ю́, и́шь *pf.* (*of* **~́ивать**) **1.** to conceal; to suppress; **з. дыха́ние** to hold one's breath. **2.** to harbour, cherish; **з. оби́ду (на+*a.*)** to nurse a grievance (against).
зата|и́ться, ю́сь, и́шься *pf.* (*of* **~́иваться**) (*coll.*) to hide (*intrans.*); **з. в себе́** (*fig.*) to become reserved, retire into o.s.
зата́лкива|ть, ю *impf. of* **затолка́ть** *and* **затолкну́ть**
затанц|ева́ться, у́юсь *pf.* (*coll.*) to dance until exhausted.
зата́плива|ть[1,2], **ю** *impf. of* **затопи́ть**[1,2]
зата́птыва|ть, ю *impf. of* **затопта́ть**
зата́сканный *p.p.p. of* **затаска́ть** *and adj.* worn; threadbare; (*fig.*) hackneyed, trite.
затаск|а́ть, а́ю *pf.* (*of* **~́ивать**[1]) (*coll.*) **1.** to wear out; to make dirty (with wear); (*fig.*) to make hackneyed, make trite. **2.** to drag about; **з. по суда́м** to drag through the courts. **3.** to begin to drag.
затаск|а́ться, а́юсь *pf.* (*of* **~́иваться**) (*coll.*) to wear out, become worn out; to become dirty (with wear).
зата́скива|ть[1], **ю** *impf. of* **затаска́ть**
зата́скива|ть[2], **ю** *impf. of* **затащи́ть**
зата́скива|ться, юсь *impf. of* **затаска́ться**
зата́чива|ть, ю *impf. of* **заточи́ть**[1]
затащ|и́ть, у́, ~́ишь *pf.* (*of* **зата́скивать**[2]) (*coll.*) to drag off, drag away; (*fig.*): **они́ ~и́ли его́ в теа́тр** they have dragged him off to the theatre.
затвердева́|ть, ю *impf. of* **затверде́ть**
затверде́лост|ь, и *f.* = **затверде́ние**
затверде́лый *adj.* hardened.
затверде́ни|е, я *nt.* **1.** hardening. **2.** (*med.*) induration, callosity. **3.** (*med.*) callus.
затверде́|ть, ю *pf.* (*of* **~ва́ть**) to harden, become hard; to set.
затвер|ди́ть, жу́, ди́шь *pf.* (*of* **~́живать**) (*coll.*) **1.** to learn by rote. **2.: з. одно́ и то же** to harp on one string.
затве́ржива|ть, ю *impf. of* **затверди́ть**
затво́р, а *m.* **1.** shutting; bolting. **2.** bolt, bar; breech-block (*of fire-arm*); water-gate, flood-gate; (*phot.*) shutter. **3.** (*eccl.*) cell; seclusion, solitude.
затвор|и́ть, ю́, ~́ишь *pf.* (*of* **~я́ть**) to shut, close.
затвор|и́ться, ю́сь ~́ишься *pf.* (*of* **~я́ться**) **1.** to shut, close (*intrans.*). **2.** to shut o.s. in, lock o.s. in. **3.** (*eccl.*) to become a recluse; **з. в монасты́рь, в монастыре́** to go into a monastery, become a monk.
затво́рник, а *m.* hermit, anchorite, recluse; **он живёт соверше́нным ~ом** (*fig.*) he is a complete recluse.
затво́рни|ческий *adj. of* **~к**; solitary; **~ческая жизнь** the life of a recluse.
затво́рничеств|о, а *nt.* (*eccl.*) seclusion, solitary life.
затвор|я́ть(ся), я́ю(сь) *impf. of* **~и́ть(ся)**
затева́|ть, ю *impf. of* **зате́ять**
зате́йлив|ый (~, ~а) *adj.* **1.** intricate, involved; **~ая речь** involved discourse; **~ое украше́ние** intricate ornament. **2.** ingenious, original; inventive; **~ая игру́шка** ingenious toy.
зате́йник, а *m.* **1.** practical joker; humorist. **2.** entertainer; organizer (*of entertainments*).
зате́|йный (~ен, ~йна) *adj.* (*coll.*) = **~йливый**
зате́йщик, а *m.* (*coll.*) instigator.
затёк, ла́ *see* **зате́чь**
затека́|ть, ю́ *impf. of* **зате́чь**
зате|ку́, чёшь, ку́т *see* **~́чь**
зате́м *adv.* **1.** after that, thereupon, then, next. **2.** for that reason; **з. что** because, since, as; **заче́м ты прие́хала? з., что слыха́ла, что ты заболе́л** why have you come? because I heard that you had been taken ill; **з. что́бы** in order that; **она́ прие́хала з., что́бы уха́живать за тобо́й** she has come (in order) to look after you.
затемне́ни|е, я *nt.* **1.** darkening; obscuring (*also fig.*). **2.** (*med.*) dark patch. **3.** (*mil.*) black-out. **4.** (*psych.*) black-out.
затемн|и́ть, ю́, и́шь *pf.* (*of* **~я́ть**) **1.** to darken; to obscure (*also fig.*). **2.** (*mil.*) to black-out.
затемн|и́ться, ю́сь, и́шься *pf.* (*of* **~я́ться**) to become dark; to become obscure; (*fig.*) to become obscured, become clouded.
за́темно *adv.* (*coll.*) before daybreak.
затемн|я́ть(ся), я́ю(сь) *impf. of* **~и́ть(ся)**
затен|и́ть, ю́, и́шь *pf.* (*of* **~я́ть**) to shade.
затен|я́ть, я́ю *impf. of* **~и́ть**
зате́плива|ть(ся), ю(сь) *impf. of* **зате́плить(ся)**
зате́пл|ить, ю, ишь *pf.* (*of* **~ивать**) (*obs.*, *folk poet.*) to light (*candle, etc.*).
зате́пл|иться, юсь, ишься *pf.* (*of* **~иваться**) (*obs.*, *folk poet.*) to begin to gleam.
зат|ере́ть, ру́, рёшь, *past* **~ёр, ~ёрла** *pf.* (*of* **~ира́ть**) **1.** to rub out. **2.** to block, jam; (*impers.*): **су́дно ~ёрло льда́ми** the ship was ice-bound; (*fig.*, *coll.*): **з. кого́-н.** to keep s.o. down, impede s.o.'s career. **3.** (*coll.*) to make dirty, soil.
зат|ере́ться, ру́сь, рёшься, *past* **~ёрся, ~ёрлась** *pf.* (*of* **~ира́ться**) (*coll.*) **1.** (**в**+*a.*) to get (into), worm one's way (into). **2.** to begin to rub o.s.
зате́рива|ть(ся), ю(сь) *impf. of* **затеря́ть(ся)**
зате́рпн|уть, ет *pf. of* **те́рпнуть**
зате́рянный *p.p.p. of* **затеря́ть** *and adj.* forgotten, forsaken.
затер|я́ть, я́ю *pf.* (*of* **~́ивать**) (*coll.*) to lose, mislay.
затер|я́ться, я́юсь *pf.* (*of* **~́иваться**) to be lost, be mislaid; (*fig.*) to become forgotten; **моё перо́ ~я́лось** (*coll.*) my pen has vanished; **з. в толпе́** to be lost in a crowd.
зате|са́ть, шу́, ~́шешь *pf.* (*of* **~́сывать**) to rough-hew; to sharpen (*stake, etc.*).
зате|са́ться, шу́сь, ~́шешься *pf.* (*of* **~́сываться**) (*coll.*) to worm one's way in, intrude.
затесн|и́ть, ю́, и́шь *pf.* (*of* **~я́ть**) (*coll.*) **1.** to jostle, press. **2.** (*fig.*) to oppress, persecute.
затесн|и́ться, ю́сь, и́шься *pf.* (*of* **~я́ться**) (*coll.*) to begin to crowd.
затесн|я́ть(ся), я́ю(сь) *impf. of* **~и́ть(ся)**
затёсыва|ть(ся), ю(сь) *impf. of* **затеса́ть(ся)**
зате́|чь, ку́, чёшь, ку́т, *past* **~́к, ~кла́** *pf.* (*of* **~ка́ть**) **1.** (**в**+*a.*; **за**+*a.*) to pour, flow, leak (into; behind). **2.** to swell up. **3.** to become numb; **у меня́ нога́ ~кла́** I have pins and needles in my foot.
зате́|я, и *f.* **1.** undertaking, enterprise, venture. **2.** (*usu. pl.*) piece of fun; escapade; practical joke. **3.** (*pl.*, *obs*) embellishment, ornament; (*liter.*) conceit; **жить без ~й** to live simply, unpretentiously.
зате́|ять, ю *pf.* (*of* **~ва́ть**) (*coll.*) to undertake, venture; to organize; **з. дра́ку** to start a fight.
затира́|ть(ся), ю(сь) *impf. of* **затере́ть(ся)**
зати́ск|ать, аю *pf.* (*of* **~ивать**) (*coll.*) to smother with caresses.
зати́скива|ть(ся), ю(сь) *impf. of* **зати́скать** *and* **зати́снуть(ся)**
зати́с|нуть, ну, нешь *pf.* (*of* **~кивать**) (*coll.*) to squeeze in.
зати́с|нуться, нусь, нешься *pf.* (*of* **~киваться**) (*coll.*) to squeeze (o.s.) in.
затих|а́ть, а́ю *impf. of* **~́нуть**
зати́х|нуть, ну, нешь, *past* **~, ~ла** *pf.* (*of* **~а́ть**) to die down, abate; to die away, fade (*of noise*).
зати́ш|е, я *nt.* calm; lull.
затк|а́ть, у́, ёшь, *past* **~а́л, ~ала́, ~а́ло** *pf.* (*+a. and i.*) to cover all over with a woven pattern.
заткн|у́ть, у́, ёшь *pf.* (*of* **затыка́ть**) **1.** (*+a. and i.*) to stop up; to plug; **з. буты́лку про́бкой** to cork a bottle; **з. рот, гло́тку кому́-н.** (*coll.*) to shut s.o. up; **~и́ гло́тку!** shut your mouth! **2.** to stick, thrust; **з. кого́-н. за по́яс** (*fig.*, *coll.*) to outdo s.o.
заткн|у́ться, у́сь, ёшься *pf.* (*coll.*) to shut up; **~и́сь!** shut up!
затмева́|ть, ю *impf. of* **затми́ть**

затмéни|е, я *nt.* **1.** (*astron.*) eclipse. **2.** (*fig., coll.*) black-out, mental derangement.
затм|и́ть, и́шь *pf.* (*of* **~ева́ть**) **1.** to darken. **2.** (*fig.*) to eclipse; to overshadow.
затó *conj.* (*coll.*) but then, but on the other hand; but to make up for it; **дóрого, з. хорóшая вещь** it is expensive, but then it is good.
затовáренност|ь, и *f.* (*econ.*) glut.
затовáренный *p.p.p. of* **затовáрить** *and adj.* (*econ.*) surplus.
затовáривани|е, я *nt.* glutting; overstocking.
затовáрива|ть(ся), ю(сь) *impf. of* **затовáрить(ся)**
затовáр|ить, ю, ишь *pf.* (*of* **~ивать**) (*econ.*) to accumulate (excess stock of), overstock.
затовáр|иться, юсь, ишься *pf.* (*of* **~иваться**) (*econ.*) **1.** to be over-stocked. **2.** (*coll.*) to have a surplus.
затолкá|ть, ю *pf.* (*of* **затáлкивать**) to jostle (*to the point of discomfort*).
затолкн|ýть, ý, ёшь *pf.* (*of* **затáлкивать**) (*coll.*) to shove in.
затóн, а *m.* **1.** backwater. **2.** (river-)boat yard. **3.** dam, weir.
затон|ýть, ý, ⁓ешь *pf.* to sink (*intrans.*).
затоп|и́ть[1], **лю́, ⁓ишь** *pf.* (*of* **затáпливать**) to light (*a stove*); to turn on the heating.
затоп|и́ть[2], **лю́, ⁓ишь** *pf.* (*of* **~ля́ть**) **1.** to flood; to submerge. **2.** to sink; **з. корáбль** to scuttle a ship.
затóпк|а, и *f.* **1.** fire-lighting. **2.** kindling(-wood).
затопля́ть, ю *impf. of* **затопи́ть**[2]
затоп|тáть, чý, ⁓чешь *pf.* (*of* **затáптывать**) to trample (down, in); to trample underfoot.
затоп|чý, ⁓чешь *see* **~тáть**
затóр[1], **а** *m.* blocking, obstruction; **з. ýличного движéния** traffic-jam, congestion.
затóр[2], **а** *m.* mash (*in brewing and distilling*).
затормо|зи́ть, жý, зи́шь *pf. of* **тормози́ть**
затормош|и́ть, ý, и́шь *pf.* (*coll.*) to pester.
затóр|ный *adj. of* **~**[2]
заточ|áть, áю *impf. of* **~и́ть**[2]
заточéни|е, я *nt.* confinement; incarceration, captivity.
заточ|и́ть[1], **ý, ⁓ишь** *pf.* (*of* **затáчивать**) to sharpen.
заточ|и́ть[2], **ý, ~и́шь** *pf.* (*of* **~áть**) to confine, shut up; to incarcerate.
затравенé|ть, ет *pf. of* **травенéть**
затрав|и́ть, лю́, ⁓ишь *pf.* (*of* **трави́ть**[1] *and* **⁓ливать**) to hunt down, bring to bay; (*fig., coll.*) to persecute; to badger; to worry the life out of.
затрáвк|а, и *f.* **1.** (*tech.*) priming-tube. **2.** touchhole.
затрáвлива|ть, ю *impf. of* **затрави́ть**
затрáвник, а *m.* (*tech.*) priming-tube.
затрáгива|ть, ю *impf. of* **затрóнуть**
затрапéз|ный[1] *adj.* taking place in the refectory, at the table; **~ная бесéда** table-talk.
затрапéзный[2] *adj.* (*obs.*) working-, every-day (*of clothing*).
затрáт|а, ы *f.* expense; outlay.
затрá|тить, чу, тишь *pf.* (*of* **~чивать**) to expend, spend.
затрáчива|ть, ю *impf. of* **затрáтить**
затрéб|овать, ую *pf.* to request, require; to ask for.
затреп|áть, лю́, ⁓лешь *pf.* (*of* **⁓̈ывать**) **1.** to wear out; to make dirty (with wear). **2.** (*fig.*) to wear out; **з. чьё-н. и́мя** to give s.o. a bad name. **3.** to begin to scutch.
затреп|áться, лю́сь, ⁓лешься *pf.* (*of* **⁓̈ываться**) **1.** to wear out (*intrans.*), be worn out. **2.** (*fig.*): **я совсéм ~áлся** (*coll.*) I have stayed gossiping too long. **3.** to begin to flutter.
затрёпыва|ть(ся), ю(сь) *impf. of* **затрепáть(ся)**
затрéщин|а, ы *f.* (*coll.*) box on the ears.
затрóн|уть, у, ешь *pf.* (*of* **затрáгивать**) **1.** to affect; to touch, graze. **2.** (*fig.*) to touch (on); **з. вопрóс** to broach a question; **з. чьё-н. самолю́бие** to wound s.o.'s self-esteem.
затруднéни|е, я *nt.* difficulty.
затруднённый *p.p.p. of* **затрудни́ть** *and adj.* laboured.
затрудни́тельност|ь, и *f.* difficulty; straits.
затрудни́тел|ьный (~ен, ~ьна) *adj.* difficult; embarrassing.
затрудн|и́ть, ю́, и́шь *pf.* (*of* **~я́ть**) **1.** to trouble; to cause trouble (to); to embarrass. **2.** to make difficult; to hamper.
затрудн|и́ться, ю́сь, и́шся *pf.* (*of* **~я́ться**) (*+inf. or i.*) to find difficulty (in); **з. отвéтом** to find difficulty in replying; **он ~и́лся испóлнить мою́ прóсьбу** he found difficulty in complying with my request.
затрудн|я́ть(ся), я́ю(сь) *impf. of* **~и́ть(ся)**
затумáн|ивать(ся), иваю(сь), иваешь(ся) *impf. of* **~ить(ся)**
затумáн|ить, ю, ишь *pf.* (*of* **~ивать**) **1.** to befog; to cloud, dim; (*impers.*): **~ило горизóнт** the horizon was obscured by fog; **слёзы ~или её глазá** tears dimmed her eyes. **2.** (*fig.*) to obscure.
затумáн|иться, юсь, ишься *pf.* (*of* **~иваться**) **1.** to grow foggy, become clouded (with). **2.** (*fig.*) to grow sad. **3.** (*fig.*) to become obscure.
затуп|и́ть, лю́, ⁓ишь *pf.* (*of* **~ля́ть**) to blunt; to dull.
затуп|и́ться, лю́сь, ⁓ишься *pf.* (*of* **~ля́ться**) to become blunt(ed).
затупля́|ть(ся), ю(сь) *impf. of* **затупи́ть(ся)**
затýрка|ть, ю *pf.* (*coll.*) to nag.
затухáни|е, я *nt.* extinction; (*tech.*) damping; fading.
затух|áть, áет *impf. of* **⁓нуть**
затýх|нуть, нет, *past* **~, ~ла** *pf.* (*of* **~áть**) **1.** to go out, be extinguished. **2.** (*fig., coll.*) to die away (*of sounds*); (*tech.*) to damp, to fade.
затуш|евáть, ýю *pf.* (*of* **~ёвывать**) **1.** to shade. **2.** (*fig., coll.*) to conceal; to draw a veil over.
затушёвыва|ть, ю *impf. of* **затушевáть**
затуш|и́ть, ý, ⁓ишь *pf.* to put out, extinguish; (*fig.*) to suppress.
зáтхлый *adj.* mouldy, musty; stuffy; (*fig.*) stagnant.
затыкá|ть, ю *impf. of* **заткнýть**
заты́л|ок, ка *m.* **1.** back of the head; (*anat.*) occiput; scrag (*cut of meat*). **2.: станови́ться в з.** to form up in file.
заты́лочный *adj.* (*anat.*) occipital.
заты́чк|а, и *f.* (*coll.*) **1.** stopping up; plugging. **2.** stopper; plug; spigot; (*fig.*) stopgap.
затя́гива|ть(ся), ю(сь) *impf. of* **затянýть(ся)**
затяжелé|ть, ю *pf.* (*coll., dial.*) to become pregnant.
затя́жк|а, и *f.* **1.** inhaling (*in smoking*). **2.** prolongation; (*coll.*) dragging out. **3.** delaying, putting off. **4.** (*tech.*) tie-beam.
затяжн|óй, *adj.* long drawn-out, protracted; **~áя болéзнь** lingering illness.
затя́нут|ый *p.p.p. of* **⁓ь** *and adj.* tightly buttoned, corseted.
затя|нýть, нý, ⁓нешь *pf.* (*of* **⁓гивать**) **1.** to tighten; (*naut.*) to haul taut. **2.** to cover; to close; (*impers.*): **нéбо ~нýло тýчами** it has clouded over; **рáну ~нýло** the wound has closed. **3.** (*coll.*) to drag down, drag in; (*fig.*) to inveigle. **4.** (*coll.*) to drag out, spin out. **5.: з. пéсню** (*coll.*) to strike up a song.
затя|нýться, нýсь, ⁓нешься *pf.* (*of* **⁓гиваться**) **1.** to lace o.s. up; **з. пóясом** to tighten one's belt. **2.** to be covered; to close (*intrans.*), skin over (of a wound). **3.** (*coll.*) to be delayed; to linger; to be dragged out, drag on (*intrans.*); **вечери́нка ~нýлась до пóлночи** the party dragged on till midnight. **4.** to inhale (*in smoking*).
заýл|ок, ка *m.* (*coll.*) back street.
заýмн|ый *adj.* abstruse, unintelligible; nonsensical.
зáум|ь, и *no pl., f.* nonsense.
зауны́в|ный (~ен, ~на) *adj.* doleful.
заупокóйн|ый *adj.* for the repose of the soul (*of the dead*); **~ая слýжба** requiem.
заупря́м|иться, люсь, ишься *pf.* to begin to be obstinate, turn obstinate.
заýря́д, а *m.* (*obs.*) **1.** acting rank, brevet rank. **2.** (*fig., coll.*) mediocrity.
заýря́д|ный (~ен, ~на) *adj.* ordinary, commonplace; mediocre.
заусéниц|а, ы *f.* **1.** agnail, hangnail. **2.** (*tech.*) wire-edge.
заýтра *adv.* (*poet., obs.*) on the morrow.
заýтрен|я, и *f.* (*eccl.*) prime.
заутю́жива|ть, ю *impf. of* **заутю́жить**
заутю́ж|ить, у, ишь *pf.* to iron (out).
заýченный *p.p.p. of* **заучи́ть** *and adj.* studied.
заýчива|ть(ся), ю(сь) *impf. of* **заучи́ть(ся)**

зау|чи́ть, чу́, ∼чишь *pf.* (*of* **∼чивать**) **1.** to learn by heart. **2.** (*coll.*) to din learning into.
зауч|и́ться, у́сь, ∼ишься *pf.* (*of* **∼иваться**) (*coll.*) to overstudy.
зауша́тельский *adj.* disparaging, abusive.
зауша́тельств|о, а *nt.* disparagement, abuse.
зауш|а́ть, а́ю *impf. of* **∼и́ть**
зауше́ни|е, я *nt.* box on the ears; (*fig.*) slap in the face, insult.
зауш|и́ть, у́, и́шь *pf.* (*of* **∼а́ть**) (*obs.*) to box on the ears; (*fig.*) to insult.
зау́шниц|а, ы *f.* (*med.*) mumps.
зау́шный *adj.* behind the ears; (*med.*) parotid.
зафаршир|ова́ть, у́ю *pf. of* **фарширова́ть**
зафикси́р|овать, ую *pf. of* **фикси́ровать**
зафрахт|ова́ть, у́ю *pf.* (*of* **фрахтова́ть** *and* **∼о́вывать**) to charter, freight.
зафрахто́выва|ть, ю *impf. of* **зафрахтова́ть**
заха́жива|ть, ю *freq. of* **заходи́ть**[1]; **он часте́нько к нам ∼л** he often used to drop in (to see us).
заха́п|ать, аю *pf.* (*of* **∼ывать**) (*coll.*) to grab, lay hold of.
заха́пыва|ть, ю *impf. of* **заха́пать**
захва́лива|ть, ю *impf. of* **захвали́ть**
захвал|и́ть, ю́, ∼ишь *pf.* (*coll.*) to praise to excess; to spoil by flattery.
захва́т, а *m.* **1.** seizure, capture; usurpation. **2.** (*tech.*) claw.
захва́танный *p.p.p. of* **захвата́ть** *and adj.* soiled by handling, thumbed; (*fig., coll.*) trite, hackneyed.
захват|а́ть, а́ю *pf.* (*of* **∼ывать**[2]) (*coll.*) to make dirty by handling; to thumb.
захва|ти́ть, чу́, ∼тишь *pf.* (*of* **∼тывать**[1]) **1.** to take; **з. горсть ви́шен** to take a handful of cherries; **они́ ∼ти́ли с собо́й дете́й** they have taken the children with them. **2.** to seize; to capture; **з. власть** to seize power; **мы ∼ти́ли три́ста пле́нных** we took three hundred prisoners. **3.** (*fig.*) to carry away; to thrill, excite; **кни́га меня́ ∼ти́ла** I was thrilled by the book. **4.** (*coll.*) to catch; **з. после́дний по́езд** to catch the last train; **я успе́л з. его́ в кабине́те** I managed to catch him in his office; **∼ти́ла ли тебя́ гроза́?** were you caught by the storm? **5.** to stop (*an illness, etc.*) in time. **6.** (*impers.*): **от э́того у меня́ дух ∼ти́ло** it took my breath away.
захва́тнический *adj.* (*pej.*) aggressive.
захва́тчик, а *m.* invader; aggressor.
захва́тыва|ть[1]**, ю** *impf. of* **захвати́ть**
захва́тыва|ть[2]**, ю** *impf. of* **захвата́ть**
захва́тыва|ющий *pres. part. act. of* **∼ть**[1] *and adj.* (*fig.*) gripping; **слу́шать но́вости с ∼ющим интере́сом** to listen to news with keen interest.
захвора́|ть, ю *pf.* (*coll.*) to be taken ill.
захиле́|ть, ю *pf. of* **хиле́ть**
захире́лый *adj.* faded; ailing.
захире́|ть, ю *pf. of* **хире́ть**
захлеб|ну́ть, ну́, нёшь *pf.* (*of* **∼ывать**) (*coll.*) **1.** to swallow, take a mouthful of. **2.** (+ *a. and i.*) to take (with), wash down (with).
захлеб|ну́ться, ну́сь, нёшься *pf.* (*of* **∼ываться**) **1.** to choke (*intrans.*); to swallow the wrong way. **2.** (*fig., coll.*): **з. от восто́рга** to be transported with delight; **ата́ка ∼ну́лась** (*mil.*) the attack misfired.
захлёбыва|ть, ю *impf. of* **захлебну́ть**
захлёбыва|ться, юсь *impf.* (*of* **захлебну́ться**) to choke (*intrans.*); (*fig.*): **з. от сме́ха** to choke with laughter; **говори́ть ∼ющимся го́лосом** to speak in a voice choked with emotion.
захлест|а́ть, а́ю *pf.* (*of* **∼ывать**[1]) (*coll.*) **1.** to flog to death **2.** to begin to pour (*of rain*).
захлест|ну́ть, ну́, нёшь *pf.* (*of* **∼ывать**[2]) **1.** to fasten, secure. **2.** to flow over, swamp, overwhelm; (*fig.*): **её ∼ну́ла волна́ сча́стья** a wave of happiness flowed over her.
захлёстыва|ть[1]**, ю** *impf. of* **захлеста́ть**
захлёстыва|ть[2]**, ю** *impf. of* **захлестну́ть**
захло́п|нуть, ну, нешь *pf.* (*of* **∼ывать**) **1.** to slam. **2.** to shut in.
захло́п|нуться, нусь, нешься *pf.* (*of* **∼ываться**) to slam to; to close with a bang.
захлопо|та́ться, чу́сь ∼чешься *pf.* (*coll.*) to be worn out (with bustling about).
захло́пыва|ть(ся), ю(сь) *impf. of* **захло́пнуть(ся)**
захлороформи́р|овать, ую *pf. of* **хлороформи́ровать**
захмеле́|ть, ю *pf. of* **хмеле́ть**
захо́д, а *m.* **1. (со́лнца)** sunset. **2.** stopping (at), putting in (at); **э́тот парохо́д пришёл из Аме́рики без ∼а в Шербу́р** this ship has arrived from America without calling at Cherbourg.
захо|ди́ть[1]**, жу́, ∼дишь** *impf. of* **зайти́**
захо|ди́ть[2]**, жу́, ∼дишь** *pf.* to begin to walk; **он ∼ди́л по ко́мнате** he began to pace up and down the room.
захо|ди́ться, жу́сь, ∼дишься *pf.* (*coll.*) to tire o.s. out with walking, walk o.s. off one's feet.
захо́жий *adj.* (*coll.*) newly-arrived; **он — з. челове́к** he is a stranger.
захо|жу́, ∼дишь *see* **∼ди́ть**
захолоде́|ть, ю *pf.* (*coll.*) to become cold; (*impers.*) to turn cold.
захолу́стный *adj.* remote; **з. быт** (*fig.*) provincial life.
захолу́ст|ье, ья, *g. pl.* **∼ий** (*coll.* **∼ьев**) *nt.* out-of-the-way place.
захороне́ни|е, я *nt.* burial.
захорон|и́ть, ю́, ∼ишь *pf.* (*of* **хорони́ть**) **1.** to bury **2.** (*dial.*) to hide.
захо|те́ть(ся), чу́(сь) ∼чешь(ся), ти́м(ся), ти́те(сь), тя́т(ся) *pf. of* **хоте́ть(ся)**
захребе́тник, а *m.* (*dial.*) parasite.
захуда́лый *adj.* impoverished, decayed.
заца́п|ать, аю *pf.* (*of* **∼ывать**) (*coll.*) to grab; to lay hold of.
заца́пыва|ть, ю *impf. of* **заца́пать**
зацве|сти́, ту́, тёшь, *past* **∼л, ∼ла́** *pf.* (*of* **∼та́ть**) to break into blossom.
зацвета́|ть, ю *impf. of* **зацвести́**
зацве|ту́, тёшь *see* **∼сти́**
зацел|ова́ть, у́ю *pf.* (*coll.*) to smother with kisses, rain kisses on.
зацеп|и́ть, лю́, ∼ишь *pf.* (*of* **∼ля́ть**) **1.** to hook. **2.** (**за**+ *a.*) to catch (on); **з. ного́й за ка́мень** to catch one's foot on a stone; (*tech.*) to engage (*gears*); (*fig.*) to sting.
зацеп|и́ться, лю́сь, ∼ишься *pf.* (*of* **∼ля́ться**) (**за**+*a.*) **1.** to catch (on); **чуло́к у неё ∼и́лся за гвоздь** her stocking caught on a nail. **2.** to catch hold (of).
заце́пк|а, и *f.* (*coll.*) **1.** peg, hook. **2.** hooking. **3.** (*fig.*) pull, protection. **4.** hitch, catch (*fig.*).
зацепля́|ть(ся), ю(сь) *impf. of* **зацепи́ть(ся)**
зачаро́ванный *p.p.p. of* **зачарова́ть** *and adj.* spell-bound.
зачар|ова́ть, у́ю *pf.* (*of* **∼о́вывать**) to bewitch, enchant, captivate.
зачаро́выва|ть, ю *impf. of* **зачарова́ть**
зача|сти́ть, щу́, сти́шь *pf.* (*coll.*) **1.** (+ *inf.*) to take (to); **он ∼сти́л игра́ть в те́ннис по вечера́м** he has taken to playing tennis in the evening; **они́ ∼сти́ли к нам в го́сти** they have taken to visiting us, they have become regular visitors at our house. **2.** to begin to go fast; **докла́дчик ∼сти́л так, что переводи́ть его́ слова́ ста́ло невозмо́жно** the lecturer began to go so fast that it was impossible to translate; **дождь ∼сти́л** it began to rain cats and dogs.
зачасту́ю *adv.* (*coll.*) often, frequently.
зача́ти|е, я *nt.* (*physiol.*) conception.
зача́т|ок, ка *m.* **1.** embryo. **2.** rudiment (*biol.*). **3.** (*usu. pl.*; *fig.*) beginning, germ.
зача́точн|ый *adj.* rudimentary; **в ∼ом состоя́нии** in embryo.
зач|а́ть, ну́, нёшь, *past.* **∼а́л, ∼ала́, ∼а́ло** *pf.* (*of* **∼ина́ть**) **1.** to conceive (*trans. and intrans.*). **2.** (+ *a. or inf.*) (*coll.*) to begin.
зача́х|нуть, ну, нешь, *past* **∼нул** *and* **∼, ∼ла** *pf. of* **ча́хнуть**
зача|щу́, сти́шь *see* **∼сти́ть**
зач|ёл, ла́ *see* **∼е́сть**
заче́м *interrog. and rel. adv.* why; what for; **з. ты пришла́?** why did you come? **вот з. пришла́** that's why I came.
заче́м-то *adv.* for some reason or other.

зачёркива|ть, ю *impf. of* **зачеркну́ть**
зачерк|ну́ть, ну́, нёшь *pf.* (*of* **~ивать**) to cross out, strike out.
зачерне́|ть, ю *pf.* to show black.
зачерне́|ться, юсь *pf.* to turn black.
зачерн|и́ть, ю́, и́шь *pf.* (*of* **черни́ть 1.** *and* **~я́ть**) to blacken, paint black.
зачерн|я́ть, я́ю *impf. of* **~и́ть**
заче́рп|ать, аю *pf.* to begin to ladle.
зачерп|ну́ть, ну́, нёшь *pf.* (*of* **~ывать**) to draw up, scoop; to ladle.
заче́рпыва|ть, ю *impf. of* **зачерпну́ть**
зачерстве́лый *adj.* stale; (*fig.*) hard-hearted.
зачерстве́|ть, ю *pf. of* **черстве́ть 1.**
зачер|ти́ть, чу́, ~тишь *pf.* (*of* **~чивать**) **1.** to cover with pencil-strokes. **2.** to sketch.
заче́рчива|ть, ю *impf. of* **зачерти́ть**
зачер|чу́, ~тишь *see* **~ти́ть**
заче|са́ть, шу́, ~шешь *pf.* **1.** to begin to scratch. **2.** (*impf.* **~сывать**) to comb back.
заче|са́ться, шу́сь, ~шешься *pf.* (*coll.*) **1.** to begin to scratch o.s. **2.** to begin to itch.
зач|е́сть, ту́, тёшь, *past* **~ёл, ~ла́** *pf.* (*of* **~и́тывать**[1]) **1.** to take into account, reckon as, credit; **з. де́сять рубле́й в упла́ту до́лга** to account ten roubles towards payment of a debt; **з. проведённый на вое́нной слу́жбе год за два го́да** to reckon a year spent on war service as two years. **2.** (+*d. and a.*) to pass (*trans.*); **мы ~ли́ ему́ перево́д с францу́зского** we passed him in French translation.
зачёсыва|ть, ю *impf. of* **зачеса́ть**
зачёт, а *m.* **1.** reckoning; **в з. пла́ты** in payment. **2.** test (*in school, etc.*); **получи́ть з., сдать з.** (**по+** *d.*) to pass a test (in); **поста́вить** (+ *d.*) **з.** (**по+** *d.*) to pass (in); **поста́вили мне з. по исто́рии** they have passed me in history.
зачётк|а, и *f.* (*coll.*) (student's) record book.
зачёт|ный *adj. of* **~. 1.: ~ная квита́нция** receipt. **2.: ~ная кни́жка** (student's) record book; **~ная се́ссия** test period; **~ная стрельба́** classification shoot.
зачехл|и́ть, ю́, и́шь *pf. of* **чехли́ть**
зач|ешу́, ~е́шешь *see* **~еса́ть**
зачи́н, а *m.* (*liter.*) beginning; introduction (*of folk-tale, etc.*).
зачина́тел|ь, я *m.* (*rhet.*) author, founder.
зачина́|ть, ю *impf. of* **зача́ть**
зачи́нива|ть, ю *impf. of* **зачини́ть**
зачин|и́ть, ю́, ~ишь *pf.* (*of* **~ивать**) (*coll.*) to mend; to patch; to sharpen (*a pencil*).
зачи́нщик, а *m.* (*pej.*) instigator, ring-leader.
зачисле́ни|е, я *nt.* enrolment.
зачи́сл|ить, ю, ишь *pf.* (*of* **~я́ть**) **1.** to include; **з. в счёт** to enter in an account. **2.** to enrol, enlist; **з. в штат** to take on the staff, on the strength.
зачи́сл|иться, юсь, ишься *pf.* (*of* **~я́ться**) (**в+** *a.*) **1.** to join, enter. **2.** *pass. of* **~ить**
зачисл|я́ть(ся), я́ю(сь) *impf. of* **~ить(ся)**
зачи́|стить, щу, стишь *pf.* (*of* **~ща́ть**) **1.** to smooth out. **2.** to clean up, clean out.
зачит|а́ть, а́ю *pf.* (*of* **~ывать**[2]) (*coll.*) **1.** to read out. **2.** to borrow and fail to return to its owner, take and keep (*a book*). **3.** to exhaust (*by continual reading aloud*). **4.** (*university sl.*) to exceed one's allotted time (*in lecturing*). **5.** (*no impf.*) to begin to read.
зачит|а́ться, а́юсь *pf.* (*of* **~ываться**) **1.** to become engrossed in reading; to go on reading; **вчера́ я ~а́лся далеко́ за́ полночь** last night I went on reading until long after midnight. **2.** (*coll.*) to make o.s. stale by excessive reading.
зачи́тыва|ть[1]**, ю** *impf. of* **зачéсть**
зачи́тыва|ть[2]**, ю** *impf. of* **зачита́ть**
зачи́тыва|ться, юсь *impf.* **1.** *impf. of* **зачита́ться. 2.** *pass. of* **~ть**[2]
зачища́|ть, ю *impf. of* **зачи́стить**
зачи́|щу, стишь *see* **~стить**
зач|ну́, нёшь *see* **~а́ть**
зачтён|ный (~, ~а́) *p.p.p. of* **зачéсть**
зач|ту́, тёшь *see* **~е́сть**

зачумлённый *adj.* infected with plague.
зачу́|ять, ю, ешь *pf.* (*coll.*) to scent, smell.
заша́рка|ть, ю *pf.* (*coll.*) **1.** (*impf.* **заша́ркивать**) to scratch (*with one's feet*). **2.** to begin to scrape (one's feet).
заша́ркива|ть, ю *impf. of* **заша́ркать 1.**
зашварт|ова́ть, у́ю *pf.* (*of* **~о́вывать**) (*naut.*) to moor, tie up.
зашварт|ова́ться, у́юсь *pf.* (*of* **~о́вываться**) (*naut.*) to moor, tie up (*intrans.*).
зашварто́выва|ть(ся), ю(сь) *impf. of* **зашвартова́ть(ся)**
зашвы́рива|ть, ю *impf. of* **зашвырну́ть** *and* **зашвыря́ть**
зашвыр|ну́ть, ну́, нёшь *pf.* (*of* **~ивать**) (*coll.*) to throw, fling (away).
зашвыр|я́ть, я́ю *pf.* (*of* **~ивать**) (+*a. and i.*; *coll.*) to shower (with); **з. кого́-н. ка́мнями** to stone s.o., throw stones at s.o.
зашелохн|у́ть, у́, ёшь *pf.* (*obs.*) to ripple.
зашиб|а́ть, а́ю *impf.* (*coll.*) **1.** *impf. of* **~и́ть. 2.** to drink (*intrans.*).
зашиб|а́ться, а́юсь *impf. of* **~и́ться**
зашиб|и́ть, у́, ёшь, *past* **~, ~ла** *pf.* (*of* **~а́ть**) (*coll.*) **1.** to bruise, knock, hurt; **он ~ себе́ коле́но** he has bruised his knee. **2.: з. деньгу́** (*sl.*) to coin money.
зашиб|и́ться, у́сь, ёшься, *past* **~ся, ~лась** *pf.* (*of* **~а́ться**) (*coll.*) to bruise o.s., knock o.s.
зашива́ть, ю *impf. of* **заши́ть**
заш|и́ть, ью́, ьёшь *pf.* (*of* **~ива́ть**) **1.** to mend. **2.** to sew up; **з. посы́лку в холст** to sew up a parcel in sacking. **3.** (*med.*) to put (a) stitch(es) in.
зашифр|ова́ть, у́ю *pf.* (*of* **шифрова́ть** *and* **~о́вывать**) to encipher, put into code.
зашифро́выва|ть, ю *impf. of* **зашифрова́ть**
за|шлю́, шлёшь *see* **~сла́ть**
зашнур|ова́ть, у́ю *pf.* (*of* **шнурова́ть** *and* **~о́вывать**) to lace up.
зашнуро́выва|ть, ю *impf. of* **зашнурова́ть**
зашпакл|ева́ть, ю́ю *pf.* (*of* **шпаклева́ть** *and* **~ёвывать**) to putty (*woodwork, etc., before painting*).
зашпаклёвыва|ть, ю *impf. of* **зашпаклева́ть**
зашпи́л|ить, ю, ишь *pf.* (*of* **~ивать**) to pin up, fasten with a pin.
зашпи́лива|ть, ю *impf. of* **зашпи́лить**
зашта́тный *adj.* (*obs.*) supernumerary, extra; **з. чино́вник** official not on permanent staff; **з. го́род** unimportant town (*not being, or having ceased to be, the administrative centre of an* uyezd).
заштемпелева́|ть, ю *pf.* (*of* **штемплева́ть**) to stamp, postmark.
заштóпа|ть, ю *pf.* (*of* **што́пать**) to darn.
заштрих|ова́ть, у́ю *pf. of* **штрихова́ть**
заштукату́рива|ть, ю *impf. of* **заштукату́рить**
заштукату́р|ить, ю, ишь *pf.* (*of* **~ивать**) to plaster.
защеко|та́ть, чу́, ~чешь *pf.* (*coll.*) **1.** to torment by tickling. **2.** to begin to tickle.
защёлк|а, и *f.* click, latch (*of lock*); catch, pawl.
защёлкива|ть, ю *impf. of* **защёлкнуть**
защёлк|нуть, ну, нешь *pf.* (*of* **~ивать**) (*coll.*) to latch.
защем|и́ть, лю́, и́шь *pf.* (*of* **~ля́ть**) **1.** to pinch, jam, nip; **з. па́лец** to pinch one's finger. **2.** (*impers.*; *coll.*): **у неё ~и́ло се́рдце** her heart aches.
защемля́|ть, ю *impf. of* **защеми́ть**
защип|ну́ть, ну́, нёшь *pf.* (*of* **~ывать**) to take (*with pincers, tongs, etc.*); to nip, tweak; to curl (*hair*); to punch (*tickets*).
защи́пыва|ть, ю *impf. of* **защипну́ть**
защи́т|а, ы *no pl., f.* defence; protection; (*collect.*) the defence (*leg. and sport*); **в ~у** (+*g.*) in defence (of); **под ~ой** (+*g.*) under the protection (of); **свиде́тели ~ы** witnesses for the defence; **з. окружа́ющей среды́** *or* **приро́ды** environmentalism, conservation.
защи|ти́ть(ся), щу́(сь), ти́шь(ся) *pf. of* **~ща́ть(ся)**
защи́тник, а *m.* **1.** defender, protector; (*leg.*) counsel for the defence; **колле́гия ~ов** the Bar; **з. окружа́ющей среды́** *or* **приро́ды** environmentalist, conservationist. **2.** (*sport*) (full-)back; **ле́вый, пра́вый з.** left, right back.

защи́тн|ый *adj.* protective; **~ая окра́ска** (*zool.*) protective coloration; **~ые очки́** goggles; **з. цвет** khaki.

защища́|ть, ю *impf.* **1.** (*impf. of* **защити́ть**) to defend, protect. **2.** (*no pf.*) to defend (*leg.*); to stand up for; **з. диссерта́цию** to defend a thesis (*before examiners*).

защища́|ться, юсь *impf.* (*of* **защити́ться**) **1.** to defend o.s., protect o.s. **2.** *pass. of* **~ть**

за́|щу, стишь *see* **~стить**

заяви́тел|ь, я *m.* (*leg.*) declarant, deponent.

заяв|и́ть, лю́, ~́ишь *pf.* (*of* **~ля́ть**) **1.** (*+a.*, **о**+*p. or* **что**) to announce, declare; **з. свои́ права́** (**на**+*a.*) to claim one's rights (to); **з. об ухо́де со слу́жбы** to announce one's retirement. **2.** (*obs.*) to certify, attest.

заяв|и́ться, лю́сь, ~́ишься *pf.* (*coll.*) to appear, turn up.

зая́вк|а, и *f.* (**на**+*a.*) claim (for); demand (for).

заявле́ни|е, я *nt.* **1.** statement, declaration. **2.** application; **пода́ть з.** to put in an application.

заявля́|ть, ю *impf. of* **заяви́ть**

зая́длый *adj.* (*coll.*) inveterate.

за́|яц, йца *m.* **1.** hare; (*prov.*) **одни́м уда́ром уби́ть двух ~йцев** to kill two birds with one stone. **2.** (*coll.*) stowaway; gate-crasher; fare-dodger; **е́хать ~йцем** to travel without paying for a ticket.

за́я|чий *adj. of* **~ц; ~чья губа́** (*med.*) harelip; (*bot.*) **~чья ла́пка** hare's foot; **з. щаве́ль** wood sorrel.

збру́|я, и = **сбру́я**

зва́ни|е, я *nt.* **1.** (*obs.*) profession, calling. **2.** rank; title; **ры́царское з.** knighthood.

зва́ный *adj.* **1.** invited. **2.** with invited guests; **з. ве́чер** guest-night; **з. обе́д** dinner-party.

зва́тельный *adj.* (*gram.*): **з. паде́ж** vocative case.

зва|ть, зову́, зовёшь, *past* **~л, ~ла́, ~́ло** *impf.* (*of* **по~́**) **1.** to call; **з. на по́мощь** to call for help. **2.** to ask, invite. **3.** (*impf. only*) to call; **как вас зову́т?** what is your name? **меня́ зову́т Влади́мир** my name is Vladimir; I am called Vladimir.

зва́|ться, зову́сь, зовёшься, *past* **~́лся́, ~ла́сь, ~́ло́сь** *impf.* (*+i.*; *coll.*) to be called; **её сестра́ ~ла́сь Татья́ной** her sister was called Tatyana.

звезд|а́, ы́, *pl.* **~̈ы, ~̈, ~̈ам** *f.* **1.** star; **но́вая з.** (*astron.*) nova; (*fig.*): **з. экра́на** film star; **ве́рить в свою́ ~у́** to believe in one's lucky star; **роди́ться под счастли́вой ~о́й** to be born under a lucky star; **он ~̈ с не́ба не хвата́ет** (*coll.*, *iron.*) he won't set the Thames on fire. **2.** (*zool.*): **морска́я з.** starfish.

звёздно-полоса́тый *adj.*: **з. флаг** the Stars and Stripes, the Star-Spangled Banner, Old Glory (= *national flag of USA*).

звёзд|ный *adj. of* **~а́; ~ная ка́рта** celestial map; **~ная ночь** starlit night; **з. час** finest hour.

звездообра́з|ный (~ен, ~на) *adj.* star-shaped; **з. дви́гатель** (*tech.*) radial engine.

звездопа́д, а *m.* meteor shower.

звездочёт, а *m.* (*obs.*) astrologer.

звёздочк|а, и *f.* **1.** *dim. of* **звезда́**. **2.** asterisk.

звен|е́ть, ю́, и́шь *impf.* **1.** to ring; **у неё ~е́ло в уша́х** there was a ringing in her ears. **2.** (*+i.*) **з. моне́тами** to jingle coins; **з. стака́нами** to clink glasses.

звен|о́, а́, *pl.* **~́ья, ~́ьев** *nt.* **1.** link (*of a chain*; *also fig.*). **2.** (*fig.*) team, section (*in agriculture, etc.*); (*aeron.*) flight. **3.** row (*of logs*).

звен|ьево́й *adj. of* **~о́;** *as n.* **з., ~ьево́го** *m.* teamleader; section leader (*of Pioneers*).

звер|ёк[1], **ька́** *m. dim. of* **~ь**

звер|ёк[2], **ька́** *m.* (*sl.*) pusher, (drug-)dealer.

зверёныш, а *m.* (*coll.*) young of wild animal.

звере́|ть, ю, ешь *impf.* (*of* **о~**) to become brutalized.

звери́н|ец, ца *m.* menagerie.

звер|и́ный *adj. of* **~ь;** of wild animals; **~и́ное число́** (*bibl.*) number of the Beast.

зверобо́|й[1], **я** *m.* hunter, trapper.

зверобо́|й[2], **я** *m.* (*bot.*) St John's wort.

зверово́д, а *m.* fur farmer.

зверово́дств|о, а *nt.* fur farming.

зверово́д|ческий *adj. of* **~ство**

зверoло́в, а *m.* hunter, trapper.

зверoло́в|ный *adj. of* **~; з. про́мысел** hunting, trapping.

зверoподо́б|ный (~ен, ~на) *adj.* beast-like; bestial.

зверофе́рм|а, ы *f.* fur farm.

звéрски *adv.* **1.** brutally, bestially. **2.** (*coll.*) terribly, awfully; **я з. уста́л** I am terribly tired.

звéрский *adj.* **1.** brutal, bestial. **2.** (*coll.*) terrific, tremendous; **у него́ з. аппети́т** he has a tremendous appetite.

звéрств|о, а *nt.* brutality; atrocity; **~а** atrocities (*in war, etc.*).

звéрств|овать, ую *impf.* to behave with brutality; to commit atrocities.

звер|ь, я, *pl.* **~́и, ~е́й** *m.* **1.** wild animal, wild beast; **пушно́й з.** fur-bearing animal. **2.** (*fig.*) brute, beast; **смотре́ть ~́ем** to look (very) savage, look (very) fierce.

звер|ьё, я́ *no pl.*, *nt.* (*collect.*) wild animals, wild beasts; (*fig.*) brutes, beasts.

звон, а *m.* **1.** (ringing) sound, peal; **з. моне́т** chinking of coins; **з. стака́нов** clinking of glasses; **слы́шал з., да не зна́ет, где он** he does not know what he is talking about. **2.** (*fig.*, *coll.*) rumour; gossip.

звона́р|ь, я́ *m.* **1.** bell-ringer. **2.** (*fig.*, *coll.*) rumour-monger; gossip.

звон|и́ть, ю́, и́шь *impf.* **1.** (*pf. of* **по~**) (**в**+*a.*) to ring; **з. кому́-н. (по телефо́ну)** to telephone s.o., ring s.o. up; **вы не туда́ ~и́те** you've got the wrong number; **~я́т** s.o. is ringing; **з. во все колокола́** (*fig.*) to set all the bells a-ringing. **2.** (**о**+*p.*) to gossip (about).

звон|и́ться, ю́сь, и́шься *impf.* (*of* **по~**) to ring (*a doorbell*).

зво́н|кий (~ок, ~ка́, ~ко) *adj.* **1.** ringing, clear; **~кая моне́та** hard cash, coin. **2.** (*ling.*) voiced.

звон|ко́вый *adj. of* **~о́к**

зво́нниц|а, ы *f.* belfry (*of old Russ. churches*).

звон|о́к, ка́ *m.* bell; **дать з.** to ring; **з. по телефо́ну** telephone call; **встава́ть по ~ку́** to get up when the bell goes.

зво́н|че *and* (*coll.*) **~че́е** *comp. of* **~кий** *and* **~ко**

звук, а *m.* sound; **пусто́й звук** (*fig.*) (mere) name, empty phrase; **я звал её, а она́ ни ~́а** I kept calling her but she never uttered a sound; (*ling.*) **гла́сный з.** vowel; **согла́сный з.** consonant.

звукови́к, а́ *m.* (*mil.*, *coll.*) member of sound-locating or sound-ranging unit.

звук|ово́й *adj. of* **~; з. барье́р** sound barrier; **~ова́я волна́** sound wave; **~ово́е измене́ние** (*ling.*) sound change; **~ово́е кино́, з. фильм** sound-film(s), talkie(s).

звукоза́пис|ь, и *f.* sound recording.

звуконепроница́емый *adj.* sound-proof.

звукоопера́тор, а *m.* (*cin.*) sound recordist, sound man.

звукоподража́ни|е, я *nt.* onomatopoeia.

звукоподража́тельный *adj.* onomatopoeic.

звукопрово́дный *adj.* (*phys.*) sound-conducting.

звукоря́д, а *m.* (*mus.*) scale.

звукоснима́тел|ь, я *m.* (*radio*) pickup.

звукоула́вливател|ь, я *m.* (*mil.*) sound-locator.

звукоуловите́л|ь, я *m.* = **звукоула́вливатель**

звуча́ни|е, я *nt.* **1.** (*ling.*) phonation. **2.** sound(s).

звуч|а́ть, у́, и́шь *impf.* (*of* **про~**) **1.** to be heard; to sound; **вдали́ ~а́ли голоса́** voices could be heard in the distance; **э́тот пасса́ж ~и́т прекра́сно** (*mus.*) this passage sounds splendid. **2.** (*+adv. or i.*; *fig.*) to sound; to express, convey; **з. трево́гой** to sound a note of alarm; **з. и́скренно** to ring true.

зву́ч|ный (~ен, ~на́, ~но) *adj.* sonorous.

звя́кань|е, я *nt.* jingling; tinkling.

звя́к|ать, аю *impf. of* **~нуть**

звя́к|нуть, ну, нешь *pf.* (*of* **~ать**) **1.** (*+i.*) to jingle; to tinkle. **2.** (*+d.*) **з. (по телефо́ну)** (*coll.*) to ring up.

зга *only in phr.* **ни зги не ви́дно** it is pitch dark.

зда́ни|е, я *nt.* building, edifice; premises.

здесь *adv.* **1.** (*of place*) here; (*on letters*) local. **2.** (*coll.*) here, at this point (*of time*); in this; **з. мы засмея́лись** here we burst out laughing; **з. нет ничего́ смешно́го** there is nothing funny in this.

зде́шний *adj.* local; of this place; **вы з. жи́тель? нет, я не з.** are you a local? no, I am a stranger here.

здоро́ва|ться, юсь *impf.* (*of* **по~**) (**с**+*i.*) to greet; to pass

the time of day (with); **з. зá руку** to shake hands (*in greeting*).
здоровéнн|ый *adj.* (*coll.*) burly, strapping, beefy; **~ая бáба** strapping woman; **з. гóлос** powerful voice.
здоровé|ть, ю, ешь *impf.* (*of* **по~**) (*coll.*) to become stronger.
здóрово (*coll.*) **1.** (*adv.*) splendidly, magnificently; **ты з. порабóтал** you have worked splendidly. **2.** (*adv.*) very, very much; **вчерá они́ з. вы́пили** they had a great deal to drink yesterday. **3.** (*int.*) well done!
здорóво[1] *int.* (*coll.*) hullo.
здорóв|о[2] *adv. of* **~ый**[1]; healthily, soundly; **(за) з. живёшь** for nothing, without rhyme or reason.
здорóв|ый[1] **(~, ~а)** *adj.* **1.** healthy; **бýдь(те) ~(ы)!** (*on parting*) good luck!; (*to s.o. sneezing*) (God) bless you! **2.** health-giving, wholesome; (*fig.*) sound, healthy; **з. кли́мат** healthy climate; **~ая идéя** sound idea.
здорóв|ый[2] **(~, ~á, ~ó)** *adj.* (*coll.*) **1.** robust, sturdy. **2.** strong, powerful; sound; **з. морóз** sharp frost; **~ая трёпка** sound thrashing. **3.** (*short form +inf.*) clever (at), good (at), expert; **он ~ льсти́ть жéнщинам** he is expert at flattering women.
здорóвь|е, я *no pl., nt.* health; **пить за чьё-н. з.** to drink s.o.'s health; **за вáше з.!** your health!; **как вáше з.?** how are you?; **на з.** to your heart's content, as you please; **грýппа ~я** keep-fit group.
здоровя́к, á *m.* (*coll.*) pers. in the pink of health.
здрав... *comb. form, abbr. of* **здравоохрани́тельный**
здрáви|е, я *nt.* (*obs.*) health; **~я желáю!** *soldiers' reply to senior officer's greeting.*
здрáвиц|а, ы *f.* toast; **провозгласи́ть ~у за** (*+a.*) to propose a toast to.
здрáвниц|а, ы *f.* sanatorium.
здравомы́слящий *adj.* sensible, judicious.
здравоохранéни|е, я *nt.* (*care of*) public health; **Министéрство ~я** Ministry of Health; **óрганы ~я** (public) health services.
здравоохрани́тельный *adj.* public health.
здравотдéл, а *m.* health department (*of local authority*).
здравпýнкт, а *m.* first-aid station.
здрáвств|овать, ую *impf.* to be healthy; to thrive, prosper; **~уй(те)!** how do you do; how are you; **да ~ует!** long live!
здрáв|ый (~, ~а) *adj.* **1.** sensible; **з. смысл** common sense. **2.** (*obs.*) healthy; **~ и невреди́м** safe and sound; **быть в ~ом умé** to be in one's right mind.
зéбр|а, ы *f.* **1.** (*zool.*) zebra. **2.** zebra crossing.
зéбр|овый *adj. of* **~а**
зев, а *m.* **1.** (*anat.*) pharynx; **воспалéние ~́а** (*med.*) pharyngitis. **2.** (*obs.*) jaws.
ревáк|а, и *c.g.* idler, gaper.
зев|áть, áю *impf.* **1.** (*pf.* **~нýть**) to yawn. **2.** (*no pf.*) (*coll.*) to gape, stand gaping; **не ~áй!** keep your wits about you! **3.** (*pf.* **про~**) (*coll.*) to miss opportunities, let chances slip through one's fingers. **4.** (*no pf.*) (*dial.*) to shout, bawl.
зевá|ться, ется *impf.* (*impers.*, *+d.*) (*coll.*) to have an urge to yawn; **мне сегóдня ~ется** I can't stop yawning today.
зев|нýть, нý, нёшь *pf. of* **~áть 1.**
зев|óк, кá *m.* yawn.
зевóт|а, ы *f.* (fit of) yawning.
зелёненьк|ая, ой *f.* (*coll.*, *obs.*) three-rouble note.
зеленé|ть, ю *impf.* **1.** (*pf.* **по~**) to turn green, come out green. **2.** to show green.
зелен|и́ть, ю́, и́шь *impf.* (*of* **по~**) to make green, paint green.
зелёнк|а, и *f.* (*coll.*) 'brilliant green' (*an antiseptic embrocation*).
зеленн|óй *adj.*: **~áя лáвка** greengrocer's (shop).
зелёноберéтчик, а *m.* (*mil.*) Green Beret.
зеленовáт|ый (~, ~а) *adj.* greenish.
зеленоглáз|ый (~, ~а) *adj.* green-eyed.
зеленщи́к, á *m.* greengrocer.
зелён|ый (зéлен, ~á, зéлено) *adj.* green (*of colour*; *of vegetation*; *unripe*; *also fig.*); **~ое винó** (*folk poet. or coll.*) vodka; **з. горóшек** green peas; **~ые насаждéния** (plantations of) trees and shrubs; **~ая скýка** intolerable boredom; **~ое я́блоко** green apple; **з. юнéц** greenhorn; **~ая ýлица** 'go' (*of traffic signals*); **дать ~ую ýлицу** (*fig.*) to give the go-ahead, green-light (to); **прогнáть по ~ой ýлице** (*hist.*) to make to run the gauntlet.
зéлен|ь, и *no pl.*, *f.* **1.** green colour. **2.** (*collect.*) verdure. **3.** (*collect.*) greens (*green vegetables*).
зелен|я́, éй *no sg.* shoots, seedlings (*of cereal crops*).
зелó *adv.* (*arch.*) very.
зéл|ье, ья, *g. pl.* **~ий** *nt.* **1.** potion; **приворóтное з.** philtre. **2.** (*fig.*) poison; **з. замóрское** (*obs.*) tobacco. **3.** (*fig.*, *coll.*) venomous pers.; pest (*sl.*).
зельц, а *m.* (*cul.*) brawn.
зéмельн|ый *adj.* land; **з. банк** (*hist.*) Land Bank; **з. надéл** allotment; **~ая рéнта** ground-rent; **~ая сóбственность** (property in) land.
зéм|ец, ца *m.* member of zemstvo.
землевéдени|е, я *nt.* physical geography.
землевладéл|ец, ьца *m.* landowner.
землевладéл|ьческий *adj. of* **~ец**
землевладéни|е, я *nt.* land-ownership.
земледéл|ец, ьца *m.* (peasant) farmer.
землеедéли|е, я *nt.* agriculture, farming.
землеедéльческий *adj.* agricultural.
землекóп, а *m.* navvy.
землемéр, а *m.* land-surveyor.
землемéри|е, я *nt.* land-surveying, geodesy.
землемéрный *adj.* geodetic; **з. шест** Jacob's staff.
землепáшеств|о, а *nt.* (*obs.*) tillage.
землепáш|ец, ца *m.* (*obs.*) tiller.
землепóльзовани|е, я *nt.* land-tenure.
землепрохóд|ец, ца *m.* (*obs.*) explorer.
землерóйк|а, и *f.* (*zool.*) shrew.
землетрясéни|е, я *nt.* earthquake.
землеустрóйств|о, а *nt.* land-tenure regulations.
землечерпáлк|а, и *f.* (*tech.*) dredger, excavator.
землечерпáни|е, я *nt.* (*tech.*) dredging.
земли́ст|ый (~, ~а) *adj.* earthy; sallow (*of complexion*).
зем|ля́, ли́, *a.* **~́лю**, *pl.* **~́ли, ~éль, ~́лям** *f.* **1.** earth; (dry) land; **уви́деть ~́лю** to sight land; **упáсть на ~́лю** to fall to the ground. **2.** land; soil (*fig.*); **помéщичья з.** (*collect.*) landed estates; **на чужóй ~лé** on foreign soil. **3.** earth, soil. **4.** (*in Germany*) Land, state; (*in Austria*) province; **Óгненная З~** Tierra del Fuego.
земля́к, á *m.* fellow-countryman, pers. from same district.
земляни́к|а, и *no pl.*, *f.* (*collect.*) wild strawberries.
земля́н|ин, ина, *pl.* **~е, ~** *m.* **1.** (*hist.*) landholder. **2.** earth-dweller, earthling, terrestrial.
земляни́|чный *adj. of* **~ка**
земля́нк|а, и *f.* dug-out; adobe cottage.
землян|óй *adj.* **1.** earthen, of earth; **~ые рабóты** excavations. **2.** earth-; **~áя грýша** Jerusalem artichoke; **з. орéх** peanut; **з. червь** earth-worm.
земля́честв|о, а *nt.* **1.** friendly society of persons coming from same district. **2.** national group (*of foreign students at Russian universities*).
земля́чк|а, и *f. of* **земля́к**
зéмно *adv.*, *only in phr.* **з. кля́няться** (*obs.*) to bow to the ground.
земновóдн|ый *adj.* amphibious; *as n.* (*zool.*) **~ые, ~ых** amphibia; *sg.* **~ое, ~ого** *nt.* amphibian.
земн|óй *adj.* **1.** earthly; terrestrial; **~áя корá** (earth-)crust; **з. шар** the globe; **з. поклóн** bow to the ground. **2.** (*fig.*) mundane.
земнорóдный *adj.* (*poet.*, *rhet.*) earth-born, mortal.
зéм|ский *adj.* **1.** *of* **~ля́ 2.**; (*hist.*): **з. начáльник** land captain (*holder of office established in 1889*); **~ское ополчéние** militia; **3. собóр** Assembly of the Land (*in Muscovite Russia*). **2.** *of* **~ство**
зéмств|о, а *nt.* **1.** zemstvo (*elective district council in Russia, 1864–1917*). **2.** zemstvo system (*of local administration*).
зéмщин|а, ы *f.* (*hist.*) **1.** populace. **2.** zemshchina (*boyar domains, as opposed to oprichnina, under Tsar Ivan IV*).
зени́т, а *m.* zenith (*also fig.*)
зени́тк|а, и *f.* (*mil*; *coll.*) anti-aircraft gun.
зени́тн|ый *adj.* **1.** (*astron.*) zenithal; **~ое расстоя́ние** zenith-distance. **2.** (*mil.*) anti-aircraft.
зени́тчик, а *m.* (*mil.*) anti-aircraft gunner.
зени́ц|а, ы *f.* (*arch.*) pupil (*of the eye*); **берéчь как ~у óка** to keep as the apple of one's eye.

зерка́лк|а, и *f.* (*coll.*) reflex camera.
зе́ркал|о, а, *pl.* **~а́, зерка́л, ~а́м** *nt.* looking-glass, mirror (*also fig.*); **криво́е з.** distorting mirror.
зерка́льн|ый *adj. of* **зе́ркало**; (*fig.*) smooth; **~ое стекло́** plate glass; **~ое окно́** plate-glass window; **з. фотоаппара́т** reflex camera; **~ое изображе́ние** looking-glass reflection; **~ая пове́рхность** smooth surface; **з. карп** (*zool.*) mirror carp.
зерни́ст|ый (~, ~а) *adj.* granular; **~ая икра́** unpressed caviar(e).
зер|но́, на́, *pl.* **~на, ~ен, ~нам** *nt.* **1.** grain; seed; (*fig.*) grain; kernel, core; **горчи́чное з.** mustard seed; **жемчу́жное з.** pearl; **ко́фе в ~нах** coffee beans; **з. и́стины** grain of truth. **2.** (*collect., sg. only*) grain, cereal.
зернобобо́в|ые, ых *no sg.* (*agric.*) grain legumes.
зернови́д|ный (~ен, ~на) *adj.* granular.
зерново́з, а *m.* grain carrier (*ship*).
зернов|о́й *adj.* grain, cereal; **~ы́е зла́ки** cereals; **~а́я торго́вля** grain trade.
зернодроби́лк|а, и *f.* (*agric.*) corn-crusher.
зерносовхо́з, а *m.* State grain farm.
зерносуши́лк|а, и *f.* (*agric.*) grain dryer.
зернохрани́лищ|е, а *nt.* granary.
зерца́л|о, а *nt.* **1.** (*arch.*) looking-glass. **2.** (*pl. only*; *hist.*) breastplate.
ЗЕС *m. indecl.* (*abbr. of* ***Западноевропе́йский сою́з***) WEU (*Western European Union*).
зефи́р, а *m.* **1. 3.** (*poet.*) Zephyr. **2.** zephyr (*material*).
зигза́г, а *m.* zigzag.
зижди́тел|ь, я *m.* (*obs. or rhet.*) founder, author; (*relig.*) the Creator.
зижди́тельный *adj.* (*obs.*) creative.
зи́жд|иться, ется *impf.* (**на**+*p.*; *obs. or rhet.*) to be founded (on), based (on).
зил, а *m.* Zil (*motor-vehicle produced by Likhachev factory*).
зим, а *m.* Zim (*motor-vehicle produced by former Molotov factory*).
зим|а́, ы́, *a.* **~у,** *pl.* **~ы,** *d.* **~ам** *f.* winter; **на́ ~у** for the winter; **всю ~у** all winter; **ско́лько лет, ско́лько ~,** *see* **ле́то**
Зимба́бве *nt. indecl.* Zimbabwe.
зимбабви́|ец, йца *m.* Zimbabwean.
зимбабви́|йка, йки *f. of* **~ец**
зимбабви́йский *adj.* Zimbabwean.
зи́м|ний *adj. of* **~а́**; winter; wintry.
зим|ова́ть, у́ю *impf.* (*of* **пере~** *and* **про~**) to winter, pass the winter; to hibernate; **знать, где ра́ки ~у́ют,** *see* **рак**
зимо́вк|а, и *f.* **1.** wintering, hibernation; **оста́ться на ~у** to stay for the winter. **2.** polar station.
зимо́вщик, а *m.* winterer.
зимо́вь|е, я *nt.* winter quarters, winter hut.
зимо́й *adv.* in winter.
зиморо́д|ок, ка *m.* (*zool.*) kingfisher.
зипу́н, а́ *m.* homespun coat.
зис, а *m.* Zis (*motor-vehicle produced by former Stalin factory*).
зия́ни|е, я *nt.* **1.** gaping, yawning. **2.** (*ling.*) hiatus.
зия́|ть, ю *impf.* to gape, yawn; **~ющая бе́здна** yawning abyss.
злак, а *m.* (*bot.*) grass; **хле́бные ~и** cereals.
зла́т|о, а *nt.* (*arch.*; *poet.*) gold.
златове́рхий *adj.* (*folk poet.*) with roof(s) of gold.
Златовла́ск|а, и *f.* Goldilocks.
златогла́вый *adj.* gold-domed; with gold cupolas.
златоку́дрый *adj.* (*poet.*) golden-haired.
зла́чн|ый *adj.* (*obs*) lush; (*coll.*): **~ое ме́сто** den of vice.
зле́йший *superl. of* **злой**
зл|ить, ю, ишь *impf.* (*of* **обо~** *and* **разо~**) to anger; to vex; to irritate.
зл|и́ться, юсь, и́ься *impf.* (*of* **обо~** *and* **разо~**) **1.** (**на**+*a.*) to be in a bad temper; to be angry (with). **2.** (*fig., poet.*) to rage (*of a storm*).
зло[1], **зла,** *no pl. except g.* **зол** *nt.* **1.** evil; harm; **отплати́ть ~м за добро́** to repay good with evil. **2.** evil, misfortune, disaster; **из двух зол вы́брать ме́ньшее** to choose the lesser of two evils; **жела́ть кому́-н. зла** to bear s.o. malice. **3.** (*sg. only*) malice, spite; vexation; **он э́то сде́лал то́лько со зла** he did it purely from malice, out of spite; **меня́ з. берёт** it vexes me, it annoys me, I feel vexed, annoyed.
зло[2] *adv. of* **~й**
зло́б|а, ы *f.* malice; spite; anger; **по ~е** out of spite; **со ~ой** maliciously; **з. дня** topic of the day, latest news; **довле́ет дне́ви з. его́** (*arch.*) sufficient unto the day is the evil thereof.
зло́б|иться, люсь, ишься *impf.* (**на**+*a.*; *coll.*) to feel malice (towards); to be in a bad temper (with).
зло́б|ный (~ен, ~на) *adj.* malicious, spiteful; bad-tempered.
злободне́вност|ь, и *f.* topical interest, topical character.
злободне́вн|ый *adj.* topical; **~ые вопро́сы** burning topics of the day.
зло́бств|овать, ую *impf.* to bear malice; (**на**+*a.*) to have it in (for).
злове́щ|ий (~, ~а) *adj.* ominous, ill-omened; sinister.
злово́ни|е, я *nt.* stink, stench.
злово́н|ный (~ен, ~на) *adj.* fetid, stinking.
зловре́д|ный (~ен, ~на) *adj.* pernicious; noxious.
злоде́|й, я *m.* **1.** villain, scoundrel (*also joc.*). **2.** (*theatr.*; *obs.*) villain.
злоде́йский *adj.* villainous.
злоде́йств|о, а *nt.* **1.** villainy. **2.** crime, evil deed.
злоде́йств|овать, ую *impf.* to act villainously.
злодея́ни|е, я *nt.* crime, evil deed.
зложела́тельный *adj.* (*obs.*) malevolent.
злой (зол, зла, зло) *adj.* **1.** evil; bad; **з. ге́ний** evil genius. **2.** wicked; malicious; malevolent; vicious; **зла́я улы́бка** malevolent smile; **со злым у́мыслом** with malicious intent; (*leg.*) of malice prepense. **3.** (*short form only*) angry; **быть злым (на**+*a.*) to be angry (with). **4.** (*of animals*) fierce, savage; **«зла́я соба́ка»** 'beware of the dog!' **5.** dangerous; severe; **з. моро́з** severe frost. **6.** (*coll.*) bad, nasty; **з. ка́шель** bad cough. **7.** (*sl.*) terrible (= *keen, enthusiastic*).
злока́чественн|ый *adj.* (*med.*) malignant; **~ая о́пухоль** malignant tumour; **~ое малокро́вие** pernicious anaemia.
злоключе́ни|е, я *nt.* mishap, misadventure.
злоко́зненный *adj.* (*obs.*) crafty, wily; perfidious.
злонаме́рен|ный (~, ~на) *adj.* ill-intentioned.
злонра́ви|е, я *nt.* (*obs.*) bad character; depravity.
злонра́в|ный (~ен, ~на) *adj.* (*obs.*) having a bad character; depraved.
злопа́мятност|ь, и *f.* = **злопа́мятство**
злопа́мят|ный (~ен, ~на) *adj.* rancorous.
злопа́мятств|о, а *nt.* rancour.
злополу́ч|ный (~ен, ~на) *adj.* unlucky, ill-starred.
злопыха́тел|ь, я *m.* (*coll.*) disingenuous, spiteful critic.
злопыха́тельский *adj.* (*coll.*) disingenuously spiteful, malevolent; ranting.
злопыха́тельств|о, а *nt.* (*coll.*) malevolence; ranting.
злора́дный *adj.* gloating, maliciously rejoicing at others' misfortune.
злора́дств|о, а *nt.* Schadenfreude (*malicious delight in others' misfortunes*).
злора́дств|овать, ую *impf.* to rejoice at, gloat over, others' misfortunes.
злосло́ви|е, я *nt.* scandal, backbiting.
злосло́в|ить, лю, ишь *impf.* to say spiteful things.
зло́ст|ный (~ен, ~на) *adj.* **1.** malicious. **2.** conscious, intentional; **~ное банкро́тство** fraudulent bankruptcy; **з. неплате́льщик** persistent defaulter (*in payment of debt*). **3.** inveterate, hardened.
злост|ь, и *f.* malicious anger, fury; **их з. берёт на него́** they are furious with him.
злосча́ст|ный (~ен, ~на) *adj.* ill-fated, ill-starred.
зло́т|ый, ого *m.* zloty (*Polish currency*).
злоумы́шленник, а *m.* (*obs.*); plotter; criminal.
злоумы́шленный *adj.* (*obs.*) with criminal intent.
злоумышля́|ть, ю *impf.* (*obs.*) to plot.
злоупотреб|и́ть, лю́, и́шь *pf.* (*of* **~ля́ть**) (+*i.*) to abuse; to indulge in to excess; to overdo; **з. вла́стью** to abuse power; **з. чьим-н. внима́нием** to take up too much of s.o.'s time.
злоупотребле́ни|е, я *nt.* (+*i.*) abuse (of); **з. дове́рием** breach of confidence.

злоупотреб|ля́ть, ля́ю *impf. of* **~и́ть**
злоязы́чи|е, я *nt.* (*obs.*) slander, back-biting.
злоязы́ч|ный (~ен, ~на) *adj.* (*obs.*) slanderous.
злы́д|ень, ня *m.* (*dial.*) **1.** (*obs.*) rogue, rascal. **2.** wicked pers.; wicked creature.
злю́к|а, и *c.g.* (*coll.*) curmudgeon, crosspatch; (*used of woman only*) shrew.
злю́чк|а, и *c.g.* = **злю́ка**
злю́щий *adj.* (*coll.*) furious.
змееви́д|ный (~ен, ~на) *adj.* serpentine; sinuous, snaky.
змееви́к, а́ *m.* **1.** (*tech.*) coil(-pipe). **2.** (*min.*) serpentine, ophite.
змеёныш, а *m.* young snake.
зме|и́ный *adj.* **1.** *adj. of* **~я́; ~и́ная ко́жа** snake-skin. **2.** cunning, crafty; wicked.
змеист|ый (~, ~а) *adj.* serpentine, sinuous.
зме|и́ться, и́ся *impf.* to wind, coil; (*fig., poet. pej.*) to glide; **по её лицу́ ~и́лась улы́бка** a smile stole across her face.
змей, змея́ *m.* **1.** (*obs. or coll.*) = **змея́**. **2.** dragon. **3.** **(бума́жный) з.** kite; **запусти́ть змея́** to fly a kite.
зме́йк|а, и *f.* **1.** *dim. of* **змея́; бежа́ть ~ой** to glide. **2.** (*typ.*) swung dash. **3.** (*mil.*) broken file.
зме́йковый *adj.*: **з. аэроста́т** kite balloon.
зме|я́, и́, *pl.* **≁и, ~й** *f.* snake (*also fig.*); **отогре́ть, пригре́ть ~ю́ на свое́й груди́** to cherish a snake in one's bosom.
зми́|й, я *m.* (*arch.*) serpent, dragon; the Serpent (*Old Testament representation of the Devil*); **напи́ться до зелёного ~я** (*coll.*) to get blind drunk.
знава́ть *pres. not used, impf.* (*coll.*) *freq. of* **знать**
знак, а *m.* **1.** (*in var. senses*) sign; mark; token, symbol; (*comput.*) character; **з. вста́вки** caret; **номерно́й з.** licence plate; **па́мятный з.** plaque; **≁и препина́ния** stops, punctuation marks; **≁и отли́чия** decorations (and medals); **≁и разли́чия** (*mil.*) badges of rank, insignia; **в з.** (*+g.*) as a mark (of), as a token (of), to show. **2.** omen. **3.** signal; **пода́ть з.** to give a signal.
знако́м|ить, лю, ишь *impf.* (*of* **по~**) (*+a.* **с***+i.*) to acquaint (with); to introduce (to).
знако́м|иться, люсь, ишься *impf.* (*of* **по~**) (**с***+i.*) **1.** to meet, make the acquaintance (*of a pers.*). **2.** to introduce o.s.; **~ьтесь!** (*informal mode of introduction*) may I introduce you? **3.** to become acquainted (with), familiarize o.s. (with); to study, investigate; **з. с ме́стностью** to get to know a locality; **з. с тео́рией относи́тельности** to go into the theory of relativity.
знако́мств|о, а *nt.* **1.** (**с***+i.*) acquaintance (with); **слу́жба ~** dating service. **2.** acquaintances; (*collect.*) acquaintance; **у него́ большо́е з.** he has a wide circle of acquaintances; **по ~у** by exploiting one's personal connections, by pulling strings. **3.** (**с***+i.*) knowledge (of).
знако́м|ый (~, ~а) *adj.* **1.** familiar; **его́ лицо́ мне ~о** his face is familiar. **2.** (**с***+i.*) familiar (with); **быть ~ым (с***+i.*) to be acquainted (with), know; **я с ней ~ с де́тства** I have known her since childhood. **3.** *as n.* **з., ~ого** *m.*, **~ая, ~ой** *f.* acquaintance, friend.
знамена́тел|ь, я *m.* (*math.*) denominator; **о́бщий з.** common denominator; **привести́ к одному́ ~ю** (*fig.*) to reduce to the common denominator.
знамена́тел|ьный (~ен, ~ьна) *adj.* **1.** significant, important. **2.** (*gram.*) principal (*opp. subordinate*).
зна́м|ени, енем, *etc.*, *see* **~я**
зна́мени|е, я *nt.* sign; **~я вре́мени** signs of the times.
знамени́тост|ь, и *f.* celebrity.
знамени́т|ый (~, ~а) *adj.* **1.** celebrated, famous, renowned; **печа́льно з.** infamous, notorious. **2.** (*coll.*) outstanding, superlative.
знамен|ова́ть, у́ю *impf.* to signify, mark.
знамено́с|ец, ца *m.* standard-bearer (*also fig.*).
знамёнщик, а *m.* (*mil.*) colour bearer.
зна́мо *as pred.* (*coll. or dial.*) it is well known.
зна́м|я, *g., d., and p.* **~ени,** *i.* **~енем,** *pl.* **~ёна, ~ён** *nt.* banner; standard; **под ~енем** (*+g.*; *fig.*, *rhet.*) in the name of; **высо́ко держа́ть з. свобо́ды** to keep the flag of freedom flying.
зна́ни|е, я *nt.* **1.** knowledge; **тео́рия ~я** (*phil.*) theory of knowledge; **у него́ хоро́шее з. сце́ны** he has a good knowledge of the stage; **со ~ем де́ла** capably, competently. **2.** (*pl. only*) learning; accomplishments.
зна́т|ный (~ен, ~на́, ~но) *adj.* **1.** (*adj. of* **~ь**[2]) in an exalted station. **2.** outstanding, distinguished; **~ные лю́ди** celebrities, leading figures. **3.** (*coll.*) splendid; **~ные бли́нчики** splendid pancakes; **~ная су́мма** splendid sum (*of money*).
знато́к, а́ *m.* expert; connoisseur.
зна|ть[1]**, ю** *impf.* to know, have a knowledge of; **≁ете ли вы Алекса́ндрова?** do you know Alexandrov?; **з. в лицо́** to know by sight; **з. своё де́ло** to know one's job; **з. своё ме́сто** to know one's place; **з. ме́ру** to know when to stop; **не з. поко́я** to know no peace; **з. толк (в***+p.*) to be knowledgeable (about); **з. уро́к** to know a lesson; **он хорошо́ ≁ет Пу́шкина** he has a good knowledge of Pushkin; **з. себе́ це́ну** to know one's own value; **они́ не ≁ли о на́ших наме́рениях** they were unaware of our intentions; **дать кому́-н. з.** to let s.o. know; **да́йте мне з. о вас** let me hear from you; **дать себя́ з.** to make itself felt; **он з. не хо́чет** he won't listen; **~й (себе́)** unconcerned; **она́ ~й себе́ пе́ла** she was singing away quite unconcerned; **то и ~й** (*coll.*) continually; **как з., почём з.?** who can tell?, how should I know?; **кто его́ ≁ет, Бог его́ ≁ет, чёрт его́ ≁ет** (*coll.*) goodness knows!; God knows!; the devil (only) knows!; **≁ешь (ли), ≁ете (ли)** (*coll.*) you know, do you know what.
знат|ь[2]**, и** *no pl., f.* (*collect.*) the nobility, the aristocracy.
знать[3] *as pred.* (*coll.*) evidently, it seems.
зна́|ться, юсь *impf.* (**с***+i.*; *coll.*) to associate (with).
зна́хар|ка, ки *f. of* **~ь**
зна́хар|ь, я *m.* sorcerer, witch-doctor; quack(-doctor).
зна́ч|ащий *pres. part. act. of* **~ить** *and adj.* significant, meaningful.
значе́ни|е, я *nt.* **1.** meaning, significance. **2.** importance, significance; **придава́ть большо́е з.** (*+d.*) to attach great importance (to); **э́то не име́ет ~я** it is of no importance. **3.** (*math.*) value.
зна́чимост|ь, и *f.* significance.
зна́чимый *adj.* significant.
зна́чит (*coll.*) so, then; well then; **он у́мер до войны́? з., вы не́ были с ним знако́мы** he died before the war? then you didn't know him.
значи́тел|ьный (~ен, ~ьна) *adj.* **1.** considerable, sizeable; **в ~ьной сте́пени** to a considerable extent. **2.** important; **игра́ть ~ьную роль** to play an important part. **3.** significant, meaningful.
зна́ч|ить, у, ишь *impf.* **1.** to mean, signify. **2.** to mean, have significance, be of importance; **ничего́ не ~ит** it is of no importance; **получи́ть приглаше́ние на бал о́чень мно́го ~ит для неё** to be invited to a dance means a great deal to her.
зна́ч|иться, усь, ишься *impf.* to be; to be mentioned, appear; **з. в о́тпуску** to be on leave; **з. в спи́ске** to appear on a list.
знач|о́к, ка́ *m.* **1.** badge. **2.** mark (*in margin of book, etc.*).
зна́|ющий *pres. part. act. of* **~ть** *and adj.* expert; learned, erudite.
зноб|и́ть, и́т *impf.* **1.** (*coll.*) to chill. **2.** (*impers.*): **меня́,** *etc.*, **~и́т** I, *etc.*, feel shivery, feverish.
зно́б|кий (~ок, ~ка́, ~ко) *adj.* (*dial.*) **1.** sensitive to cold. **2.** chilly.
зно|й, я *m.* intense heat; sultriness.
зно́|йный (~ен, ~йна) *adj.* hot, sultry; torrid; burning (*also fig.*).
зоб, а, *pl.* **~ы́, ~о́в** *m.* **1.** crop, craw (*of birds*). **2.** (*med.*) goitre.
зоба́ст|ый (~, ~а) *adj.* (*coll.*) **1.** with a large crop (*of birds*). **2.** goitrous.
зов, а *m.* **1.** call, summons. **2.** (*coll.*) invitation.
зов|у́, ёшь *see* **звать**
зодиа́к, а *m.* (*astron.*) zodiac; **зна́ки ~а** signs of the zodiac.
зодиака́льный *adj.* (*astron.*) zodiacal, of the zodiac.
зо́дчес|кий *adj. of* **~тво**
зо́дчеств|о, а *nt.* architecture.

зо́дч|ий, его *m.* (*obs.*) architect.
зол[1] *see* **злой**
зол[2] *g. pl. of* **зло**[1]
зол|а́, ы *no pl., f.* ashes, cinders.
золо́вк|а, и *f.* sister-in-law (*husband's sister*).
золота́рник, а *m.* (*bot.*) golden rod.
золоти́льщик, а *m.* gilder.
золоти́ст|ый (~, ~а) *adj.* golden (*of colour*).
золо|ти́ть, чу́, ти́шь *impf.* (*of* **вы́~** *and* **по~**) to gild.
золо|ти́ться, ти́тся *impf.* **1.** to become golden. **2.** to shine (*of sth. golden*).
зо́лотк|о, а *nt.* (*coll.*) sweetheart, sweetie(-pie).
золотни́к[1], **а́** *m.* zolotnik (*old Russ. measure of weight, equivalent to 4.26 grams*); **мал з., да до́рог** (*coll.*) small but precious.
золотни́к[2], **а́** *m.* (*tech.*) slide valve; **цилиндри́ческий з.** piston valve.
золотнико́вый *adj. of* **золотни́к**[2]; **з. дви́гатель** pusher-type engine; **з. приво́д** eccentric drive.
зо́лот|о, а *no pl., nt.* gold; (*collect.*) gold (*coins, ware*); **«бе́лое з.»** 'white gold' (= *cotton*); **«голубо́е з.»** 'blue gold' (= *natural gas*); **«чёрное з.»** 'black gold' (= *oil*); **плати́ть ~ом** to pay in gold; **есть на ~е** to eat off gold plate; (*fig.*) **она́ настоя́щее з.** she is pure gold, a treasure; **не всё то з., что блести́т** (*prov.*) all is not gold that glitters; **на вес ~а** worth its weight in gold.
золотоволо́сый *adj.* golden-haired.
золотоиска́тел|ь, я *m.* gold-prospector; gold-digger.
золот|о́й *adj.* **1.** gold; golden (*also fig.*); **~ы́х дел ма́стер** goldsmith; **з. песо́к** gold-dust; **з. запа́с** (*econ.*) gold reserves; **~а́я ры́бка** goldfish; **~о́е руно́** (*myth.*) golden fleece; **з. век** the Golden Age; **~о́е дно** (*fig.*) gold-mine; **~а́я молодёжь** jeunesse dorée, gilded youth; **~ы́е ру́ки** skilful fingers; **~а́я середи́на** golden mean; **~о́е сече́ние** (*math.*) golden section. **2.** (*coll.*) invaluable, precious; **мой з.!** my precious!; my darling! **3.** *as n.* **з., ~о́го** *m.* gold coin; ten-rouble piece.
золотоно́сный *adj.* gold-bearing; **з. райо́н** gold-field.
золотопромы́шленник, а *m.* owner of gold-mines.
золотопромы́шленност|ь, и *f.* gold-mining.
золоторо́т|ец, ца *m.* (*obs., coll.*) tramp, down-and-out.
золототы́сячник, а *m.* (*bot.*) centaury.
золотошве́йный *adj.* of gold embroidery.
золоту́х|а, и *f.* (*med.*) scrofula.
золоту́шный *adj.* (*med.*) scrofulous.
золоче́ни|е, я *nt.* gilding.
золочёный *adj.* gilded, gilt.
Зо́лушк|а, и *f.* Cinderella.
зо́льник, а *m.* (*tech.*) ashpit.
зо́н|а, ы *f.* **1.** zone; area, belt; **з. де́йствий** (*mil.*) zone of operations; **з. досяга́емости** (*mil.*) field of fire; **з. пораже́ния** (*mil.*) area under fire. **2.** (*geol.*) stratum, layer.
зона́льный *adj.* zone; regional.
зонд, а *m.* **1.** (*med.*) probe. **2.** (*geol.*) bore. **3.** weather-balloon, sonde.
зонди́р|овать, ую *impf.* (*med. and fig.*) to sound, probe; **з. по́чву** (*fig.*) to explore the ground.
зо́н|ный *adj. of* **~а**; (*rail.*) regional.
зонт, а́ *m.* **1.** umbrella. **2.** awning. **3.** (chimney) cowl.
зо́нтик, а *m.* **1.** umbrella; sunshade, parasol. **2.** (*bot.*) umbel.
зо́нти|чный *adj. of* **~к**; (*bot.*) umbellate, umbelliferous.
зоо... *comb. form, abbr. of* **зоологи́ческий**
зоо́лог, а *m.* zoologist.
зоологи́ческий *adj.* **1.** zoological; **з. парк, з. сад** zoological garden(s). **2.** (*fig.*) brutish, bestial.
зооло́ги|я, и *f.* zoology.
зоомагази́н, а *m.* pet-shop.
зоопа́рк, а *m.* zoo; **«сафа́ри» з.** safari park.
зооте́хник, а *m.* livestock specialist.
зооте́хник|а, и *f.* zootechny, animal science.
зоотехни́ческий *adj.* (farm) animal-research; livestock-research; **з. институ́т** animal-research institute.
зоофе́рм|а, ы *f.* fur farm.
зо́ри *see* **заря́**
зо́р|кий (~ок, ~ка́, ~ко) *adj.* **1.** sharp-sighted. **2.** (*fig.*) perspicacious, penetrating; vigilant.
зо́рьк|а, и *f.* (*folk poet.*) *affectionate form of* **заря́**
зо́рю *see* **заря́**
зра́з|ы, ~ *pl.* (*sg.* (*rare*) **~а, ~ы** *f.*) (*cul.*) zrazy (*meat cutlets stuffed with rice, buckwheat kasha, etc.*).
зрач|о́к, ка́ *m.* pupil (*of the eye*).
зре́лищ|е, а *nt.* **1.** sight. **2.** spectacle; show; pageant.
зре́лищ|ный *adj. of* **~е**; **~ные предприя́тия** places of entertainment.
зре́лост|ь, и *f.* ripeness; maturity (*also fig.*); **полова́я з.** puberty; **аттеста́т ~и** school-leaving certificate.
зре́л|ый (~, ~а́, ~о) *adj.* ripe; mature (*also fig.*); **дости́гнуть ~ого во́зраста** to reach maturity; **з. ум** mature mind; **по ~ом размышле́нии** on reflection, on second thoughts.
зре́ни|е, я *nt.* (eye)sight; **по́ле ~я** (*phys.*) field of vision; **обма́н ~я** optical illusion; **то́чка ~я** point of view; **под э́тим угло́м ~я** from this standpoint.
зре|ть[1], **ю, ешь** *impf.* (*of* **со~́**) to ripen; to mature (*also fig.*); **у нас ~́ет план** our plans are maturing.
зреть[2], **зрю, зришь** *impf.* (*of* **у~́**) (*obs.*) **1.** to behold. **2.** (**на**+*a.*) to gaze (upon).
зри́м|ый (~, ~а) *p.p.p. of* **зреть**[2] *and adj.* visible.
зри́тел|ь, я *m.* spectator, observer; **быть ~ем** to look on.
зри́тельн|ый *adj.* **1.** visual; optic; **з. нерв** optic nerve; **~ая па́мять** visual memory; **~ая труба́** telescope. **2.:** **з. зал** hall, auditorium.
зря *adv.* (*coll.*) to no purpose, for nothing; **болта́ть з.** to chatter idly; **рабо́тать з.** to plough the sand.
зря́чий *adj.* sighted (*opp. blind*).
зуа́в, а *m.* zouave.
зуб, а *m.* **1.** (*pl.* **~́ы, ~о́в**) tooth; **з. му́дрости** wisdom tooth; **вооружённый до ~о́в** armed to the teeth; **име́ть з. (про́тив), точи́ть ~́ы (на**+*a.*; *coll.*) to have it in for s.o.; **положи́ть ~́ы на по́лку** (*coll.*) to tighten one's belt; **он по-неме́цки ни в з. толкну́ть** (*coll.*) he does not know a word of German; **не по ~а́м** beyond one's capacity; **э́то пробле́ма мне не по ~а́м** (*coll.*) I cannot get my teeth into this problem; **э́то у меня́ в ~а́х навя́зло** (*coll.*) it sticks in my gullet, I am sick and tired of it; **у тебя́ з. на́ з. не попада́ет** your teeth are chattering; **хоть ви́дит о́ко, да з. неймёт** (*coll.*) there's many a slip 'twixt the cup and lip; **~́ы заговори́ть** *see* **заговори́ть**[1]; **держа́ть язы́к за ~а́ми** to hold one's tongue. **2.** (*pl.* **~́ья, ~́ьев**) tooth, cog.
зуба́ст|ый (~, ~а) *adj.* (*coll.*) sharp-toothed; (*fig.*) sharp-tongued.
зуб|е́ц, ца́ *m.* **1.** tooth, cog; **з. ви́лки** prong. **2.** merlon (*of wall*). **3.** (*radar*) blip.
зуби́л|о, а *nt.* (*tech.*) point-tool, chisel.
зу́бно-губно́й *adj.* (*ling.*) labio-dental.
зубн|о́й *adj.* **1.** dental; **~а́я боль** tooth-ache; **з. врач** dentist; **~а́я па́ста** tooth-paste; **з. порошо́к** tooth-powder; **~а́я щётка** tooth-brush. **2.** (*ling.*) dental.
зубо́вн|ый *adj. only in phrr.* **скре́жет з.** gnashing of teeth; **де́лать что-н. со скре́жетом ~ым** to do sth. with extreme unwillingness.
зубоврачё́бн|ый *adj. of* **зубно́й врач; з. кабине́т** dental surgery; **~ая шко́ла** dental school.
зубоврачева́ни|е, я *nt.* dentistry.
зуб|о́к, ка́, *pl.* **~́ки́** *m.* **1.** (*g. pl.* **~́ок**) *dim. of* **~; подари́ть на з.** (*coll.*) to bring a present for a (new-born) baby; **вы́учить на з.** (*coll.*) to learn by rote; **попа́сть на з. кому́-н.** (*coll., fig.*) to be torn to pieces by s.o. **2.** (*g. pl.* **~ко́в**) bit (*of coal-cutting machine*).
зуболече́бниц|а, ы *f.* dental surgery.
зубоска́л|ить, ю, ишь *impf.* (*coll.*) to scoff, mock.
зубоска́льств|о, а *nt.* (*coll.*) scoffing, mocking.
зуботы́чин|а, ы *f.* (*vulg.*) sock on the jaw.
зубочи́стк|а, и *f.* toothpick.
зубр, а *m.* **1.** (*zool.*) (European) bison. **2.** (*fig.*) die-hard.
зубрёжк|а, и *f.* (*coll.*) cramming.
зубри́л|а, ы *c.g.* (*coll.*) crammer.
зубр|и́ть[1], **ю́, ~́ишь** *impf.* (*of* **за~**) to notch, serrate.
зубр|и́ть[2], **ю́, ~́ишь** *impf.* (*of* **вы́~** *and* **за~**) (*coll.*) to cram.
зубро́вк|а, и *f.* **1.** sweet grass, holy grass. **2.** zubrovka (*sweet-grass vodka*).

зубча́тк|а, и *f.* (*tech.*) rack-wheel.
зубча́т|ый *adj.* **1.** (*tech.*) toothed, cogged; **~ая желе́зная доро́га** rack-railway; **~ое колесо́** rack-wheel, cogwheel, pinion; **з. насо́с** gear pump; **~ая ре́йка** rack. **2.** jagged, indented.
зуд, а *m.* itch; (*fig.*) itch, urge; **писа́тельский з.** the urge to write, to be a writer.
зуд|а́, ы *c.g.* (*coll.*) bore (*pers.*).
зуд|е́ть, и́т *impf.* **1.** (*coll.*) to itch (*intrans.*). **2.** (*fig.*) to itch, feel an itch (*to do sth.*).
зу|ди́ть, жу́, ди́шь *impf.* (*coll.*) **1.** to nag at. **2.** to cram.
зу|ёк, йка́ *m.* (*zool.*) plover.
зулу́с, а *m.* Zulu.
зулу́с|ка, ки *f. of* **~**
зулу́сский *adj.* Zulu.
зу́ммер, а *m.* (*tech.*) buzzer; tone; **з. за́нятости** engaged tone.
ЗУПВ *nt. indecl.* (*abbr. of* ***запомина́ющее устро́йство с произво́льной вы́боркой***) (*comput.*) RAM (*random-access memory*).
зурн|а́, ы́ *f.* (*mus.*) zurna (*type of clarinet*).
зы́б|иться, лется (*past and 1st and 2nd pers. of pres. not used*) *impf.* (*obs.*) to be ruffled (*of the sea*); to toss (*intrans.*).
зы́бк|а, и *f.* (*dial.*) cradle.
зы́б|кий (~ок, ~ка́, ~ко) *adj.* unsteady, shaky; (*fig.*) vacillating.
зыбу́н, а́ *m.* marshy ground; bog.
зыбу́ч|ий *adj.* unsteady, unstable; **~ие пески́** quicksands.
зыб|ь, и, *pl.* **~и, ~е́й** *f.* (*on water*) ripple; **мёртвая з.** swell; (*poet.*) lop.
зык, а *m.* (*coll.*) loud voice; loud cry.
зы́к|ать, аю *impf. of* **~нуть**
зы́к|нуть, ну, нешь *pf.* (*of* **~ать**) **1.** to shout, cry out. **2.** to whistle, whiz(z).
зы́ч|ный (~ен, ~на) *adj.* (*coll.*) loud, shrill.
зюйд, а *m.* (*naut.*) **1.** south. **2.** southerly wind.
зюйдве́стк|а, и *f.* sou'wester (hat).
зэк, а *m.* (*sl.*) prisoner, convict.
зя́б|кий (~ок, ~ка́, ~ко) *adj.* chilly, sensitive to cold.
зя́б|левый *adj. of* **~ь; ~левая вспа́шка** autumn ploughing.
зя́блик, а *m.* chaffinch.
зя́б|нуть, ну, нешь, *past* **~, ~ла** *impf.* to suffer from cold, feel the cold.
зяб|ь, и *f.* (*agric.*) land ploughed in autumn for spring sowing.
зят|ь, я, *pl.* **~ья́, ~ьёв** *m.* **1.** son-in-law. **2.** brother-in-law (*sister's husband or husband's sister's husband*).

И

и[1] *conj.* **1.** and; **добро́ и зло** good and evil; *indicating temporal sequence*: **я встал и вы́мылся и побри́лся** I got up and washed and shaved; *introducing narrative*: **и наста́ло у́тро** and then came the morning; *emph. questions*: **и ра́зве э́то не пра́вда?** and is it not the truth?; *adversative*: **мужчи́на, и пла́чет!** a man, and crying!; **и так да́лее, и про́чее** (*abbr.* **и т. д., и пр.**) etcetera, and so on, and so forth. **2.: и... и** both ... and; **и тот и друго́й** both. **3.** too; (*with negation*) either; **она́ сказа́ла, что и муж придёт** she said that her husband would come too; **и он не знал** he did not know either. **4.** even; **и знато́к ошиба́ется** even an expert may be mistaken; **я не мог бы и поду́мать об э́том** I would not (even) think of it. **5.** (*emph.*): **в то́м-то и де́ло** that is the whole point. **6. и... да** (*concessive*): **я и пое́хал бы, да не́когда** (*coll.*) I should like to go, but I have not time; **и рад э́то сде́лать, но не могу́** much as I should like to, I can't.
и[2] *int.* (*expr. disagreement*; *coll.*) oh!; **и, по́лно!** that's quite enough!; (*iron.*) you don't say (so)!
ибе́р, а *m.* Iberian.
ибери́йский *adj.* Iberian.
Ибе́ри|я, и *f.* Iberia.
ибе́р|ка, ки *f. of* **~**
и́бис, а *m.* (*zool.*) ibis.
и́бо *conj.* for.
и́в|а, ы *f.* willow; **корзи́ночная и.** osier; **плаку́чая и.** weeping willow.
Ива́н, а *m.* John; **И. Купа́л|а, ы** (*and* **~о, ~а**) *no pl.*, St John Baptist's Day (*24 June, Old Style*); **ночь на Ива́на Купа́лу** Midsummer's Night.
ива́н-да-ма́рья, ива́н-да-ма́рьи *no pl., f.* (*bot.*) **1.** cow-wheat (*Melampyrum nemorosum*). **2.** heart's ease (*Viola tricolor*).
Ива́нов *adj.*: **И. день** St John's Day, Midsummer's Day (*24 June, Old Style*).
ива́новск|ий[1] *adj. only in phr.* **во всю ~ую** (*coll.*) with all one's might; extremely loudly; **крича́ть во всю ~ую** to shout at the top of one's voice; **скака́ть во всю ~ую** to go hell-for-leather.
ива́новский[2] *adj.*: **и. червя́к** (*dial.*) glow-worm.
ива́н-чай, ива́н-чая́ *no pl., m.* (*bot.*) rose-bay, willow-herb.
иваси́ *f. indecl.* west Pacific sardine.
ивня́к, а́ *no pl., m.* **1.** osier-bed. **2.** (*collect.*) osier(s).
и́в|овый *adj. of* **~а**
и́волг|а, и *f.* (*zool.*) oriole.
иври́т, а *m.* (modern) Hebrew.
игл|а́, ы́, *pl.* **~ы, ~** *f.* **1.** needle. **2.** (*bot.*) needle; thorn, prickle; **ело́вая и.** fir-needle. **3.** quill, spine (*of porcupine, etc.*).
игли́ст|ый (~, ~а) *adj.* prickly; covered with quills; **и. скат** thornback (fish).
иглова́т|ый (~, ~а) *adj.* (*coll.*) prickly.
игълови́д|ный (~ен, ~на) *adj.* needle-shaped.
иглодержа́тел|ь, я *m.* needle-holder.
иглоко́ж|ие, их *pl.* (*sg.* **~ее, ~его** *nt.*) (*zool.*) Echinodermata; echinoderms.
иглообра́з|ный (~ен, ~на) *adj.* needle-shaped.
иглотерапе́вт, а *m.* acupuncturist.
иглотерапи́|я, и *f.* acupuncture.
иглоука́лывани|е, я *nt.* = **иглотерапи́я**
игнори́р|овать, ую *impf. and pf.* to ignore; to disregard.
и́г|о, а *nt.* yoke (*fig.*); **тата́рское и.** (*hist.*) the Tatar yoke.
иго́лк|а, и *f.* needle; **сиде́ть как на ~ах** to be on thorns, on tenterhooks; **каблуки́ на ~ах** stiletto heels.
иго́лочк|а, и *f. dim. of* **иго́лка**; (*coll.*) **оде́тый с ~и** spick and span; **костю́м с ~и** brand-new suit.
иго́льник, а *m.* needle-case; pin-cushion.
иго́льниц|а, ы *f.* = **иго́льник**
иго́льн|ый *adj. of* **игла́; ~ое у́шко** eye of a needle.
иго́льчат|ый *adj.* **1.** needle-shaped; **~ые каблуки́** stiletto heels. **2.** (*min.*) needle(-shaped), acicular; **~ые криста́ллы** acicular crystals; **~ая руда́** needle ore. **3.** (*tech.*) needle; **и. кла́пан** needle valve; **и. при́нтер** dot-matrix printer.
иго́рный *adj.* playing, gaming; **и. дом** gaming-house; **и. прито́н** gambling-den; **и. стол** gaming table.
игр|а́, ы́, *pl.* **~ы** *f.* **1.** play (*action*), playing; **гря́зная и.** foul play; **у скрипа́чки была́ блестя́щая и.** the violinist's performance was brilliant; **и. све́та на стене́** the play of light on the wall; **и. слов** play upon words; **биржева́я и.** stock exchange speculation; **и. приро́ды** freak, sport of nature. **2.** game; **аза́ртная и.** game of chance; **ко́мнатные ~ы** indoor games, party games; **одино́чные ~ы** (*tennis*) singles; **па́рные ~ы** (*tennis*) doubles; **олимпи́йские ~ы** Olympic games; (*fig.*) **опа́сная и.** dangerous game; **и. не сто́ит свеч** the game is not worth the candle; **игра́ть, вести́ большу́ю, кру́пную ~у́** to play for high stakes; **раскры́ть чью-н. ~у́** to uncover s.o.'s game. **3.** (*sport, cards*) game (*part of set, match, etc.*); **взять ~у́ при свое́й пода́че** to win one's service. **4.** (*cards*) hand; **сдать хоро́шую ~у́** to deal a good hand. **5.** turn (*to play*); **сейча́с твоя́ и.** it is your turn now.

игрáлищ|е, а *nt.* (*obs., rhet.*) plaything.
игрáльн|ый *adj.* playing; **~ые кáрты** playing cards; **~ые кóсти** dice.
и́граный *adj.* (*coll.*) (already) used.
игрá|ть, ю *impf.* (*of* **сыгрáть**) **1.** to play; **и. пьéсу** to put on a play; **и. роль** to play a part; **и. Лéди Макбéт** to play, take the part of, Lady Macbeth; **э́то не ~ет рóли** it is of no importance, it does not signify; **и. комéдию** to act (*fig.*); **и. симфóнию** to play a symphony; **и. пéрвую, вторýю скри́пку** (*fig.*) to play first, second fiddle; **и. комý-н. в рýку** (*fig.*) to play into s.o.'s hand; **и. глазáми** to flash one's eyes; **и. словáми** to play upon words; **и. ферзём** to move the queen (*at chess*); **и. в кáрты, тéннис, футбóл, шáхматы** *etc.*, to play cards, tennis, football, chess, *etc.*; **и. в загáдки** to talk in riddles; **и. в прятки** to play hide-and-seek; (*fig.*) to be secretive; **и. в скрóмность** to feign modesty; **и. на роя́ле, скри́пке** *etc.*, to play the piano, the violin, etc.; **и. на бильярде** to play billiards; **и. на би́рже** to speculate on the Stock Exchange; **и. на** (+*p.*) to play on (*fig.*); **и. на чýвствах толпы́** to play on the emotions of a crowd. **2.** (*impf. only*) (+*i. or* **с**+*i.*) to play with, toy with, trifle with (*also fig.*); **и. чьи́ми-н. чýвствами** to trifle with s.o.; **и. с огнём** (*fig.*) to play with fire. **3.** (*impf. only*) to play; to sparkle (*of wine, jewellery, etc.*); **улы́бка ~ла на её лицé** a smile played on her face.
игрá|ющий *pres. part. act. of* **~ть;** *as n.* **и., ~ющего** *m.* player.
и́грек, а *m.* (the letter) **y**; (*math.*) **y** (*second unknown quantity*).
игрéневый *adj.* skewbald.
игрéц, á *m.* **1.** (*obs.*) musician, strolling player. **2.** (*coll.*) player; **швец и жнец, и в дýду и.** jack-of-all-trades.
игри́в|ый (~, ~а) *adj.* playful; skittish (*of a woman*); (*coll.*) naughty, ribald.
игри́ст|ый (~, ~а) *adj.* sparkling (*of wine*).
игр|овóй *adj. of* **~á; и. автомáт** fruit machine; one-armed bandit.
игрóк, á *m.* **1.** (**в**+*a.*, **на**+*p.*) player (of); **и. в футбóл** football-player; **хорóший и. на балалáйке** a good balalaika player. **2.** gambler.
игротéк|а, и *f.* compendium of children's games; games store.
игрýшечный *adj.* **1.** toy; **и. паровóз** toy-engine. **2.** (*coll.*) tiny.
игрýшк|а, и *f.* toy; (*fig.*) plaything.
и́гр|ывать *pres. not used*; *freq. of* **~áть** (*coll.*).
игуáн|а, ы *f.* (*zool.*) iguana.
игýмен, а *m.* (*eccl.*) Father Superior (*of monastery*).
игýмен|ья, ьи, *g. pl.* **~ий** *f.* (*eccl.*) Mother Superior (*of a convent*).
идеáл, а *m.* ideal.
идеализи́р|овать, ую *impf. and pf.* to idealize.
идеали́зм, а *m.* (*in var. senses*) idealism.
идеали́ст, а *m.* (*in var. senses*) idealist.
идеалисти́ческий *adj.* (*phil.*) idealist(ic).
идеалисти́ч|ный (~ен, ~на) *adj.* idealistic.
идеáл|ьный (~ен, ~ьна) *adj.* **1.** (*phil.*) ideal. **2.** (*coll.*) ideal, perfect; **~ьное состоя́ние** perfect *or* mint condition.
идéйк|а, *f.* (*pej.*) *dim. of* **идéя**
идéйност|ь, и *f.* **1.** ideological content. **2.** 'progressive' character (*of work of art, etc. — from Marxist point of view*). **3.** principle, integrity (*from Marxist point of view*).
идé|йный (~ен, ~йна) *adj.* **1.** ideological. **2.** expressing an idea *or* ideas; committed, engagé; **~йная пьéса** play of ideas. **3.** 'progressive' (*from Marxist point of view*); **~йное искýсство** 'progressive' art. **4.** high-principled, acting on principle (*from Marxist point of view*).
идентификáци|я, и *f.* identification.
идентифици́р|овать, ую *impf. and pf.* to identify.
идент́ич|ный (~ен, ~на) *adj.* identical.
идеогрáмм|а, ы *f.* (*ling.*) ideogram.
идеогрáфи|я, и *f.* (*ling.*) ideography.
идеóлог, а *m.* ideologist; (*coll.*) idea-monger.
идеологи́ческий *adj.* ideological.
идеолóги|я, и *f.* ideology.
идёт (*3rd pers. sg. pres. of* **идти́**) *as int.* (*coll.*) (all) right!
идé|я, и *f.* **1.** idea (*also coll.*); notion, concept; (*phil.*) Idea; **борóться за ~ю** to fight for an idea; **подáть ~ю** to suggest, make a suggestion; **навя́зчивая и.** obsession, idée fixe; **счастли́вая и.** happy thought. **2.** point, purport (*of a work of art, of fiction, etc.*).
идилли́ческий *adj.* idyllic.
иди́лли|я, и *f.* idyll (*liter. and fig.*).
идиóм|а, ы *f.* (*and* **~, ~а** *m.*) idiom.
идиомати́зм, а *m.* idiom.
идиомáтик|а, и *f.* (*ling.*) **1.** study of idiom(s). **2.** (*collect.*) idiom, idiomatic expressions.
идиомати́ческий *adj.* idiomatic.
идиосинкрази́|я, и *f.* **1.** idiosyncrasy. **2.** (*med.*) allergy.
идиóт, а *m.* idiot, imbecile (*med. and coll.*).
идиоти́зм[1]**, а** *m.* idiocy, imbecility (*med. and coll.*).
идиоти́зм[2]**, а** *m.* (*ling.*) idiom.
идиоти́ческий *adj.* idiotic, imbecile.
идиóтский *adj.* idiotic, imbecile.
и́диш *m. indecl.* Yiddish (*language*).
и́дол, а *m.* **1.** idol (*also fig.*); **стоя́ть, сидéть ~ом** to stand, sit like a stuffed dummy. **2.** (*coll., pej.*) callous or obtuse pers.
идолопоклóнник, а *m.* idolater.
идолопоклóннический *nt.* idolatrous.
идолопоклóнств|о, а *nt.* idolatry.
ид|ти́ (итти́), ý, ёшь, *past* **шёл, шла** *impf.* (*of* **пойти́**; *det. of* **ходи́ть**) **1.** to go; (*impf. only*) to come; **и. в гóру** to go uphill; **автóбус ~ёт** the bus is coming; **кто ~ёт?** who goes there?; **и. гуля́ть** to go for a walk; **и. в продáжу** to go for sale, be up for sale; **и. в нóгу** to keep in step (*also fig.*); **и. на охóту** to go hunting; **и. на смéну** (+*d.*) to take the place (of), succeed. **2.** (**на**+*a.*) to enter; (**в**+*nom.-a.*) to become; **и. на госудáрственную слýжбу** to enter Government service; **и. в лётчики** to become an airman. **3.** (**в**+*a.*) to be used (for); (**на**+*a.*) to go to make; **и. в корм** to be used for fodder; **и. в лом** to go for scrap; **и. на юбку** to go to make a skirt **4.** (**из, от**) to come (from), proceed (from); **из трубы́ шёл чёрный дым** black smoke was coming from the chimney. **5.** (*of news, etc.*) to go round; **шла мóлва, что...** word went round that ..., rumour had it that .... **6.** (*coll.*) to sell, be sold; **хорошó и.** to be selling well; **и. за бесцéнок** to go for a song. **7.** (*of machines, machinery, etc.*) to go, run, work. **8.** (*of rain, etc.*) to fall; **дождь, снег ~ёт** it is raining, snowing. **9.** (*of time*) to pass; **шли гóды** years passed; **ей ~ёт тридцáтый год** she is in her thirtieth year. **10.** to go on, be in progress; (*of entertainments*) to be on, be showing; **перегово́ры ~ýт** are in progress; **сегóдня ~ёт «Ревизóр»** 'The Government Inspector' is on tonight. **11.** (+*d. or* **к**) to suit, become; **э́та шля́па ей не ~ёт** this hat does not become her. **12.** (**в, на**+*a.*; *coll.*) to go (in, on). **13.** (+*i*, or **с**+*g.*) to play, lead, move (*at chess, cards, etc.*); **и. ферзём** to move one's queen; **и. с червéй** to lead a heart. **14.** (**о**+*p.*; *of a discussion, etc.*) to be (about); **дéло ~ёт, речь ~ёт о том, что...** the point is that ..., it is a matter of ....
и́д|ы, ~ *no sg.* (*hist.*) Ides.
иегови́ст, а *m.* (*relig.*) Jehovah's witness.
иезуи́т, а *m.* (*eccl.*) Jesuit.
иезуи́тский *adj.* (*eccl.*) Jesuit; (*fig.*) Jesuitical.
иéн|а, ы *f.* yen (*Japanese currency*).
иерархи́ческий *adj.* hierarchic(al).
иерáрхи|я, и *f.* hierarchy.
иерати́ческ|ий *adj.* hieratic; **~ое письмó** (*ling.*) hieratic script.
иерé|й, я *m.* priest.
иерéйский *adj.* priestly.
иеремиáд|а, ы *f.* jeremiad.
Иерихóн, а *m.* Jericho.
иерóглиф, а *m.* hieroglyph; ideogram, ideograph.
иероглифи́ческий *adj.* hieroglyphic.
иеромонáх *m* (*eccl.*) father (*priest in monastic order, as opposed to lay brother*).
Иерусали́м, а *m.* Jerusalem.
иждивéн|ец, ца *m.* dependant.
иждивéни|е, я *nt.* **1.** maintenance; **на чьём-н. ~и** at s.o.'s expense; **жить на своём ~и** to maintain o.s., keep o.s. **2.** (*obs.*) means, funds.
иждивéнчеств|о, а *nt.* dependence.
и́же *rel. pron.* (*arch.*) who, which; *now only in phr.* **и и́же с ним(и)** (and others) of that ilk, and company.

и́жиц|а, ы *f.* 'izhitsa' (*last letter of Church Slavonic and pre-1918 Russ. alphabet*); **от аза́ до ~ы** (*fig.*) from A to Z; **прописа́ть ~у** (+*d.*) (*obs. or joc.*) to lecture, bring to book; to give a lesson (to); **с нога́ми ~ей** (*coll.*) knock-kneed.

из (изо) *prep.*+*g.* from, out of; of. **1.** *indicates place of origin of action, source, etc.*: **прие́хать из Ло́ндона** to come from London; **пить из ча́шки** to drink out of a cup; **узна́ть из газе́т** to learn from the newspapers; **из достове́рных исто́чников** from reliable sources, on good authority; **вы́йти из себя́** to be beside o.s.; **вы́йти из употребле́ния** to pass out of use, become obsolete; **он из крестья́н** he is of peasant origin. **2.** *with numeral or in partitive sense*: **оди́н из её покло́нников** one of her admirers; **ни оди́н из ста** not one in a hundred; **мла́дший из всех** the youngest of all; **главне́йшие собы́тия из исто́рии Росси́и** the principal events in the history of Russia; **трус из тру́сов** a craven. **3.** *indicates material*: **из чего́ э́то сде́лано?** what is it made of?; **варе́нье из абрико́сов** apricot jam; **обе́д из трёх блюд** a three-course dinner; **ло́жки из серебра́** silver spoons; **буке́т из кра́сных гвозди́к** bouquet of carnations; (*fig.*; *of human potential*) **из него́ вы́йдет хоро́ший труба́ч** he will make a good trumpet-player. **4.** *indicates agency*: **изо всех сил** with all one's might; **из после́дних средств** with one's last penny. **5.** *indicates cause, motive*: **из благода́рности** in gratitude; **из ли́чных вы́год** for private gain; **из ре́вности** from jealousy; **мно́го шу́му из ничего́** a lot of fuss about nothing.

из... (*also* **изо...**, **изъ...** *and* **ис...**) *vbl. pref. indicating*: **1.** motion outwards. **2.** action over entire surface of object, in all directions. **3.** expenditure of instrument *or* object in course of action; continuation *or* repetition of action to extreme point; exhaustiveness of action.

изб|а́, ы́, *a.* **~́у**, *pl.* **~́ы** *f.* **1.** izba (*peasant's hut or cottage*); **и.-чита́льня, ~ы́-чита́льни** *f.* village reading-room. **2.** (*hist.*) government office (*in Muscovite Russia*).

изба́б|иться, люсь, ишься *pf.* (*coll.*) to become womanish, effeminate.

избави́тел|ь, я *m.* deliverer.

изба́в|ить, лю, ишь *pf.* (*of* **~ля́ть**) (**от**) to save, deliver (from); **~ьте меня́ от ва́ших замеча́ний** spare me your remarks; **~ьте меня́!** leave me alone!; **~и Бог!** God forbid!

изба́в|иться, люсь, ишься *pf.* (*of* **~ля́ться**) (**от**) to be saved (from), escape; to get out (of); to get rid (of); **и. от привы́чки** to get out of a habit.

избавле́ни|е, я *nt.* deliverance.

избавля́|ть(ся), ю(сь) *impf. of* **изба́вить(ся)**

избало́ванный *p.p.p. of* **избалова́ть** *and adj.* spoilt.

избал|ова́ть, у́ю *pf.* (*of* **балова́ть** *and* **~о́вывать**) to spoil (*a child, etc.*).

избал|ова́ться, у́юсь *pf.* (*of* **~о́вываться**) to become spoilt.

избало́выва|ть(ся), ю(сь) *impf. of* **избалова́ть(ся)**

изба́ч, а́ *m.* village librarian.

избе́га|ть, ю *pf.* (*coll.*) to run about, run all over.

избег|а́ть, а́ю *impf.* (*of* **~́нуть** *and* **избежа́ть**) (+*g. or inf.*) to avoid; (*impf. only*) to shun; to escape, evade; **и. встреча́ться с кем-н.** to avoid meeting s.o.; **и. штра́фа** to evade a penalty.

избе́га|ться, юсь *pf.* (*coll.*) **1.** to exhaust o.s. by running (about). **2.** to get out of hand (*of an undisciplined child*).

избе́г|нуть, ну, нешь, *past* **~нул** *and* **~, ~ла** *pf. of* **~а́ть**

избежа́ни|е, я *nt.*: **во и.** (+*g.*) in order to avoid.

избе|жа́ть, гу́, жи́шь, гу́т *pf. of* **~га́ть**

избива́|ть(ся), ю(сь) *impf. of* **изби́ть(ся)**

избие́ни|е, я *nt.* **1.** slaughter, massacre; **и. младе́нцев** (*bibl.*; *also fig. of persecutions*) Massacre of the Innocents. **2.** (*leg.*) assault and battery; **и. гомосексуали́стов** gay-bashing.

избира́тел|ь, я *m.* elector, voter; **колe´блющийся и.** floating voter.

избира́тельност|ь, и *f.* (*radio*) selectivity.

избира́тельн|ый *adj.* **1.** electoral; **и. бюллете́нь** voting-paper; **~ая кампа́ния** election campaign; **и. о́круг** electoral district; **~ое пра́во** suffrage; franchise; **и. спи́сок** electoral; roll, register of voters; **~ая у́рна** ballot-box; **и. уча́сток** polling station; **и. ценз** voting qualification. **2.** (*tech.*) selective.

избира́|ть, ю *impf. of* **избра́ть**

изби́т|ый *p.p.p. of* **~ь** *and adj.*; (*fig.*) hackneyed, trite.

из|би́ть, обью́, обьёшь *pf.* (*of* **~бива́ть**) **1.** to beat unmercifully, beat up. **2.** to slaughter, massacre. **3.** (*coll.*) to wear down, ruin.

из|би́ться, обью́сь, обьёшься *pf.* (*of* **~бива́ться**) (*coll.*) **1.** to bruise o.s. **2.** to be worn out, be ruined.

избл|ева́ть, юю́, юёшь *pf.* (*of* **~ёвывать**) **1.** (*obs.*) to bring up, throw up; (*fig.*) to bring out (*coarse or vituperative language*). **2.** (*coll.*) to vomit over.

изблёвыва|ть, ю *impf. of* **изблева́ть**

изб|но́й *adj. of* **~а́**

избо́ин|а, ы *no pl.*, *f.* (*agric.*) oilcake.

изболе́|ть(ся), ю(сь) *pf.* (*coll.*) to be in torment.

избо́рник, а *m.* (*hist.*, *liter.*) miscellany, anthology.

изборо|зди́ть, жу́, зди́шь *pf. of* **борозди́ть**

избоче́н|иваться, иваюсь *impf. of* **~иться**

избоче́н|иться, юсь, ишься *pf.* (*of* **~иваться**) (*coll.*) to stand in a challenging pose (with one hip forward and one hand on it).

избра́ни|е, я *nt.* election.

избра́нник, а *m.* (*rhet.*) elect, chosen one; favoured one, darling.

избра́нн|ица, ицы *f. of* **~ик**

и́збран|ный *p.p.p. of* **избра́ть** *and adj.* **1.** selected; **~ные сочине́ния Пу́шкина** selected works of Pushkin; **вновь и.** ... elect; **вновь и. президе́нт** president elect. **2.** select; *as n.* **~ные, ~ных** *no sg.*, élite.

из|бра́ть, беру́, берёшь, *past* **~бра́л, ~брала́, ~бра́ло** *pf.* (*of* **~бира́ть**) (+*a. and i.*) to elect (as, for); to choose; **его́ ~бра́ли чле́ном парла́мента** he has been elected a Member of Parliament.

и́збура- *comb. form* brownish-; **и.-жёлтый** brownish-yellow.

избу́шк|а, и *f. dim. of* **изба́**

избыва́|ть, ю *impf. of* **избы́ть**

избы́т|ок, ка *m.* surplus, excess; abundance, plenty; **в ~ке** in plenty; **от ~ка се́рдца, от ~ка чувств** out of the fullness of the heart.

избы́точ|ный (~ен, ~на) *adj.* **1.** surplus. **2.** abundant, plentiful.

из|бы́ть, бу́ду, бу́дешь, *past* **~бы́л, ~была́, ~бы́ло** *pf.* (*of* **~быва́ть**) (*obs.*) to rid o.s. of.

изб|яно́й *adj. of* **~а́**

изваяни|е, я *nt.* statue, sculpture; graven image.

изваяя́|ть, ю *pf. of* **вая́ть**

изве́д|ать, аю *pf.* (*of* **~ывать**) to come to know, learn the meaning of; **и. го́ре** to taste, have the taste of, grief.

изве́дыва|ть, ю *impf. of* **изве́дать**

изве́ка *adv.* (*obs.*) of old.

и́зверг, а *m.* monster, cruel pers., fiend; **и. ро́да челове́ческого** scum of the earth.

изверг|а́ть, а́ю *impf.* (*of* **~́нуть**) to throw out, disgorge; (*physiol.*) to excrete; (*fig.*) to eject, expel.

изверг|а́ться, а́юсь *impf.* (*of* **~́нуться**) **1.** to erupt (*of volcanoes*). **2.** *pass. of* **~а́ть**

изве́рг|нуть(ся), ну(сь), нешь(ся), *past* **~(ся)** *and* **~нул(ся), ~ла(сь)** *pf. of* **~а́ть(ся)**

изверже́ни|е, я *nt.* **1.** eruption (*of volcano*). **2.** ejection, expulsion; (*physiol.*) excretion. **3.** (*pl. only*; *obs.*) excreta, ordure.

изве́рженный *p.p.p. of* **изве́ргнуть** *and adj.* (*geol.*) igneous, eruptive, volcanic.

изве́рива|ться, юсь *impf. of* **изве́риться**

изве́р|иться, юсь, ишься *pf.* (*of* **~иваться**) (**в**+*a. or p.*) to lose faith (in), lose confidence (in); **и. в люде́й, и. в лю́дях** to lose faith in people.

извер|ну́ться, ну́сь, нёшься *pf.* (*of* **~́тываться**[1] *and* **извора́чиваться**) (*coll.*) to dodge, take evasive action (*also fig.*); **и. при отве́те** to give an evasive answer.

извер|те́ться, чу́сь, ~́тишься *pf.* (*of* **~́тываться**[2]) (*coll.*) **1.** to wear out (*intrans.*) as a result of turning (*of propeller, etc.*). **2.** (*no impf.*; *fig.*) to become flighty; to go to the bad.

извёртыва|ться[1]**, юсь** *impf. of* **изверну́ться**

извёртыва|ться², **юсь** *impf. of* **изверте́ться**
изве|сти́, ду́, дёшь, *past* **~́л, ~ла́** *pf.* (*of* **изводи́ть**) (*coll.*) **1.** to spend, use up; to waste. **2.** to destroy, exterminate. **3.** to vex, exasperate; to torment.
изве́сти|е, я *nt.* **1.** (**о**+*p.*) news (of); intelligence; information; **после́дние ~я** the latest news. **2.** (*pl. only*; *as title of periodicals*) proceedings, transactions; **~я Акаде́мии нау́к** Proceedings of the Academy of Sciences.
изве|сти́сь, ду́сь, дёшься, *past* **~́лся, ~ла́сь** *pf.* (*of* **изводи́ться**) (*coll.*) **1.** to consume o.s., eat one's heart out; to exhaust o.s., wear o.s. out; **и. от за́висти** to consume o.s. with envy. **2.** to perish, disappear. **3.** *pass. of* **~сти́**
изве|сти́ть, щу́, сти́шь *pf.* (*of* **~ща́ть**) to inform, notify.
извёстк|а, и *f.* (slaked) lime.
известк|ова́ть, у́ю *impf. and pf.* (*agric.*) to lime.
известко́вый *adj. of* **и́звесть**
изве́стно 1. *as pred.* it is (well) know; **как и.** as is well known; **наско́лько мне и.** as far as I know. **2.** (*as particle*; *coll.*) of course, certainly.
изве́стност|ь, и *f.* **1.** fame, reputation; repute; notoriety; **приноси́ть и.** (+*d.*) to bring fame (to); **по́льзоваться гро́мкой ~ью** to be far-famed. **2.** publicity; **привести́ в и.** to make known, make public; **поста́вить кого́-н. в и.** to inform, notify. **3.** (*coll.*) notability, prominent figure.
изве́ст|ный (~ен, ~на) *adj.* **1.** (+*d.*) well-known (to); (+*i.*) (well-)known (for); (**за**+*a.*) (well-)known (as); **он ~ен свое́й бо́дростью** he is well known for his cheerfulness; **челове́к, и. как пья́ница.** a well-known drunkard. **2.**: **печа́льно и.** infamous, notorious. **3.** (a) certain; **~ным о́бразом** in a certain way; **в ~ных слу́чаях** in certain cases; **до ~ной сте́пени, в ~ной ме́ре** to a certain extent. **4.** *as n.* **~ное, ~ного** *nt.* (*math.*) the known.
известня́к, а́ *m.* limestone.
известняко́вый *adj.* limestone.
и́звест|ь, и *f.* lime; **гашёная и.** slaked lime; **негашёная и.** quicklime; **хло́рная и.** chloride of lime; **раство́р ~и** mortar, grout; whitewash; **преврати́ть в и.** to calcify.
изве́т, а *m.* (*obs.*) denunciation, delation.
изве́тчик, а *m.* (*obs.*) informer, delator.
изветша́лый *adj.* (*obs.*) dilapidated.
изветша́|ть, ет *pf.* (*obs.*) to become completely dilapidated.
извеща́|ть, ю *impf. of* **извести́ть**
извеще́ни|е, я *nt.* notification, notice; (*comm.*) advice; **~я морепла́вателям** Instructions to Mariners.
изви́в, а *m.* winding, bend.
извива́|ть, ю *impf. of* **изви́ть**
извива́|ться, юсь *impf.* (*of* **изви́ться**) **1.** to coil (*intrans.*); to wriggle. **2.** (*impf. only*) to twist, wind (*intrans.*); to meander.
изви́лин|а, ы *f.* bend, twist; **~ы мо́зга** (*anat.*) convolutions of the brain.
изви́лист|ый (~, ~а) *adj.* winding; tortuous; sinuous; (*of river*) meandering.
извине́ни|е, я *nt.* **1.** excuse. **2.** apology; **приня́ть ~я** to accept an apology. **3.** pardon; **прошу́ ~я** I beg your pardon, I apologize.
извини́тел|ьный (~ен, ~ьна) *adj.* **1.** excusable, pardonable. **2.** apologetic.
извин|и́ть, ю́, и́шь *pf.* (*of* **~я́ть**) **1.** to excuse (= *to pardon*); **~и́те (меня́)!** I beg your pardon; excuse me!; (I'm) sorry!; **~и́те, что я опозда́л** sorry I'm late; **прошу́ и. меня́ за беста́ктное замеча́ние** I apologize for my tactless remark; **~и́те за выраже́ние** (*coll.*) if you will excuse the expression; **уж ~и́(те)!** (*coll.*; *expr. disagreement*) excuse me! **2.** to excuse (= *to justify*); **э́то ниче́м нельзя́ и.** this is inexcusable.
извин|и́ться, ю́сь, и́шься *pf.* (*of* **~я́ться**) **1.** (**пе́ред**) to apologize (to); **~и́тесь за меня́** present my apologies, make my excuses. **2.** (+*i.*) to excuse o.s. (on account of, on the ground of); to make excuses.
извин|я́ть, я́ю *impf. of* **~и́ть**
извин|я́ться, я́юсь *impf. of* **~и́ться; ~я́юсь** (*coll.*) I apologize; (I'm) sorry!.
извиня́|ющийся *pres. part. of* **~ться** *and adj.* apologetic.
из|ви́ть, овью́, овьёшь, *past* **~ви́л, ~вила́, ~ви́ло** *pf.* (*of* **~вива́ть**) to coil, twist, wind (*trans.*).
из|ви́ться, овью́сь, овьёшься, *past* **~ви́лся, ~вила́сь** *pf. of* **~вива́ться**
извлека́|ть(ся), ю(сь) *impf. of* **извле́чь(ся)**
извлече́ни|е, я *nt.* **1.** extraction; (*math.*) **и. ко́рня** extraction of root, evolution. **2.** extract, excerpt.
извле́|чь, ку́, чёшь, ку́т, *past* **~́к, ~кла́** *pf.* (*of* **~ка́ть**) to extract; (*fig.*) to extricate; to derive, elicit; **и. уро́к (из)** to learn a lesson (from); **и. дохо́д, по́льзу, удово́льствие (из)** to derive profit, benefit, pleasure (from); **и. ко́рень** (*math.*) to find the root.
извле́|чься, ку́сь, чёшься, ку́тся, *past* **~́кся, ~кла́сь** *pf.* (*of* **~ка́ться**) to come out (*to be extracted*).
извне́ *adv.* from without.
изво́д¹, а *m.* (*coll.*) **1.** waste. **2.** vexation.
изво́д², а *m.* (*liter.*) recension, text (*of a manuscript document*).
изво|ди́ть(ся), жу́(сь), ~́дишь(ся) *impf. of* **извести́(сь)**
изво́з, а *m.* (*hist.*) carrying (*on horse-drawn carts*); **промышля́ть ~ом** to be a carrier (*by trade*).
изво|зи́ть, жу́, ~́зишь *pf.*; **и. в грязи́** (*coll.*) to drag through the mud.
изво́знича|ть, ю *impf.* to be a carrier.
изво́з|ный *adj. of* **~**; **и. про́мысел** carrier's trade.
изво́зчик, а *m.* **1.** carrier; **(легково́й) и.** cabman, cabby; **(ломово́й) и.** carter, drayman. **2.** (*coll.*) cab; **е́хать на ~е** to go in a cab.
изво́зчи|чий *adj. of* **~к**; **~чья би́ржа** cab-stand, cab-rank.
изволе́ни|е, я *nt.* (*obs.*) will, pleasure; **по ~ю Бо́жию** Deo volente.
изво́л|ить, ю, ишь *impf.* **1.** (+*inf. or g.*; *obs or iron. except in imper.*) to wish, desire; **чего́ ~ите?** what can I do for you?; **~ь(те)** (*coll.*) if you wish, all right; with pleasure; **~ь, я оста́нусь** all right, I will stay; **да́йте мне папиро́су. — ~ьте** give me a cigarette. — with pleasure! **2.** (+*inf.*; *expr. respectful attention* (*obs.*) *or ironical disapproval*) to deign, be pleased (*oft. equivalent to polite form of indicative of following v.*); **ба́рин ~ит спать** the master is asleep; **а как вы ~ите пожива́ть?** and, pray, how are you?; **~ь(те)** kindly, please be good enough; **~ьте молча́ть!** kindly be quiet!
изво́льнича|ться, юсь *pf.* (*coll.*) to become wayward, get out of hand.
извора́чива|ться, юсь *impf. of* **изверну́ться**
изворо́т, а *m.* **1.** bend, twist. **2.** (*pl.*; *fig.*) tricks, wiles.
изворо́тист|ый (~, ~а) *adj.* (*coll.*) = **изворо́тливый**
изворо́тлив|ый (~, ~а) *adj.* versatile, resourceful; wily, shrewd.
изврa|ти́ть, щу́, ти́шь *pf.* (*of* **~ща́ть**) **1.** to pervert. **2.** to misinterpret, misconstrue; **и. и́стину** to distort the truth; **и. чью-н. мысль** to misinterpret s.o.
извраща́|ть, ю *impf. of* **изврати́ть**
извраще́ни|е, я *nt.* **1.** perversion. **2.** misinterpretation, distortion (*fig.*).
извращённый *p.p.p. of* **изврати́ть** *and adj.* perverted; unnatural.
изга́|дить, жу, дишь *pf.* (*of* **~жи́вать**) (*coll.*) **1.** to befoul, soil. **2.** (*fig.*) to make a mess of.
изга́|диться, жусь, дишься *pf.* (*of* **~живаться**) (*coll.*) to turn nasty (*of weather*); to go to the bad.
изга́жива|ть(ся), ю(сь) *impf. of* **изга́дить(ся)**
изги́б, а *m.* **1.** bend, twist; winding. **2.** inflection (of voice); nuance.
изгиба́|ть(ся), ю(сь) *impf. of* **изогну́ть(ся)**
изгла́|дить, жу, дишь *pf.* (*of* **~живать**) to efface, wipe out (*also fig.*); **и. из па́мяти** to blot out of one's memory.
изгла́жива|ть, ю *impf. of* **изгла́дить**
изгна́ни|е, я *nt.* **1.** banishment; expulsion. **2.** exile.
изгна́нник, а *m.* exile (*pers.*).
из|гна́ть, гоню́, го́нишь, *past* **~гна́л, ~гнала́, ~гна́ло** *pf.* (*of* **~гоня́ть**) to banish, expel; to exile; **и. из употребле́ния** to prohibit the use of, ban; **и. плод** (*med.*) to procure an abortion.
изго́|й, я *m.* (*hist.*) izgoy (*pers. in Kievan Russ. society with changed status*; *e.g. illiterate son of priest, ruined merchant, freed slave*); (*fig.*) outcast.

изголо́вь|е, я *nt.* head of the bed; **сиде́ть у ~я** to sit at the bedside; **служи́ть ~ем** to serve as a pillow.
изголода́|ться, юсь *pf.* **1.** to be famished, starve. **2.** (**по**+*d.*) to yearn for.
из|гоню́, го́нишь *see* **~гна́ть**
изгоня́|ть, ю *impf. of* **изгна́ть**
изго́рб|иться, люсь, ишься *pf.* (*coll.*) **1.** to arch the back (*of a cat, etc.*). **2.** to warp (*intrans.*).
и́згород|ь, и *f.* fence; **жива́я и.** hedge.
изгота́влива|ть, ю *impf.* = **изготовля́ть**
изготови́тел|ь, я *m.* manufacturer, producer.
изгото́в|ить, лю, ишь *pf.* (*of* **~ля́ть**) **1.** to manufacture. **2.** (*obs.*) to prepare; **и. ружьё** (*mil.*) to come to the ready. **3.** (*obs.*) to cook.
изгото́в|иться, люсь, ишься *pf.* (*of* **~ля́ться**) **1.** to get ready, place o.s. in readiness. **2.** *pass. of* **~ить**
изгото́в|ка, ки *f.* = **~ле́ние; взять ружьё на ~ку** (*mil.*) to come to the ready.
изготовле́ни|е, я *nt.* **1.** manufacture. **2.** (*mil.*) preparation; 'ready' position.
изготовля́|ть(ся), ю(сь) *impf. of* **изгото́вить(ся)**
изгрыз|а́ть, а́ю *impf. of* **~́ть**
изгры́з|ть, у́, ёшь *past* **~, ~ла** *pf.* (*of* **~а́ть**) to gnaw to shreds.
изда|ва́ть, ю́, ёшь, *impf. of* **~́ть**
изда|ва́ться, ётся *impf. of* **~́ться**
и́здавна *adv.* for a long time; from time immemorial.
издал|ека́ (*more rarely* **~ёка**) *adv.* from afar; from a distance; **го́род ви́ден и.** the town is visible from afar; **прие́хать и.** to come from a distance; **говори́ть и.** (*coll.*) to speak in a roundabout way.
и́здал|и *adv.* = **~ека́**
изда́ни|е, я *nt.* **1.** publication; promulgation (*of law*). **2.** edition; **пе́рвое и.** first edition; **испра́вленное и.** revised edition; **репри́нтное и.** reprint.
изда́тел|ь, я *m.* publisher.
изда́тель|ский *adj. of* **~** *and* **~ство; ~ское де́ло** publishing; **~ская фи́рма** publishing house.
изда́тельств|о, а *nt.* publishing house.
изда́|ть, м, шь, ст, ди́м, ди́те, ду́т, *past* **~л, ~ла́, ~ло** *pf.* (*of* **~ва́ть**) **1.** to publish; **и. зако́н** to promulgate a law; **и. ука́з** to issue an edict. **2.** to produce, emit (*a smell*); to let out (*a sound*); **и. крик** to let out a cry.
изда́|ться, стся, *past* **~лся, ~ла́сь, ~лось** *pf.* to be published.
изд-во (*abbr. of* **изда́тельство**) publishing house.
издева́тельский *adj.* mocking.
издева́тельств|о, а *nt.* **1.** mocking, scoffing. **2.** mockery; taunt, insult.
издева́|ться, юсь *impf.* (**над**) to mock (at), scoff (at).
издёвк|а, и *f.* (*coll.*) taunt, insult.
изде́ли|е, я *nt.* **1.** (*sg. only*) make; **куста́рного ~я** hand-made; **фа́бричного ~я** factory-made. **2.** (manufactured) article; (*pl.*) wares.
издёрган|ный *p.p.p. of* **издёргать** *and adj.* harassed; overstrained; **~ные не́рвы** shattered nerves.
издёрг|ать, аю *pf.* (*of* **~ивать**) (*coll.*) **1.** to pull to pieces. **2.** to harass; to overstrain.
издёрг|аться, аюсь *pf.* (*of* **~иваться**) (*coll.*) **1.** *pass. of* **~ать. 2.** to become overwrought, become unhinged.
издёргива|ть(ся), ю(сь) *impf. of* **издёргать(ся)**
издерж|а́ть, у́, ~́ишь *pf.* (*of* **~́ивать**) to spend; to expend.
издерж|а́ться, у́сь, ~́ишься *pf.* (*of* **~́иваться**) (*coll.*) **1.** to have spent all one has, be spent up. **2.** *pass. of* **~а́ть**
изде́ржива|ть(ся), ю(сь) *impf. of* **издержа́ть(ся)**
изде́рж|ки, ек *pl.* (*sg.* **~ка, ~ки** *f.*) expenses; **суде́бные и.** (*leg.*) costs; **и. произво́дства** production costs.
издира́|ть, ю *impf. of* **изодра́ть**
издо́льщин|а, ы *f.* (*hist., econ.*) share-cropping.
издо́х|нуть, ну, нешь *past* **~, ~ла** *pf.* (*of* **издыха́ть**) to die (*of animals*); (*sl.*; *of human beings*) to peg out, kick the bucket.
издре́вле *adv.* (*obs.*) from the earliest times.
издроб|и́ть, лю́, и́шь *pf.* to pulverize, granulate.
издыха́ни|е, я *nt.* (one's) last breath; **до после́днего ~я** to one's last breath; **при после́днем ~и** at one's last gasp.
издыха́|ть, ю *impf. of* **издо́хнуть**
изжа́р|ить(ся), ю(сь) ишь(ся) *pf. of* **жа́рить(ся) 1., 2.**
изжёванный *p.p.p. of* **изжева́ть** *and adj.* (*coll.*) **1.** crumpled. **2.** (*fig.*) hackneyed.
изж|ева́ть, ую́, уёшь *pf.* (*of* **~ёвывать**) (*coll.*) to chew up.
изжёвыва|ть, ю *impf. of* **изжева́ть**
и́зжелта- *comb. form* yellowish-.
из|же́чь, ожгу́, ожжёшь, ожгу́т, *past* **~жёг, ~ожгла́** *pf.* (*of* **~жига́ть**) (*coll.*) **1.** to burn all over; to burn holes in; **она́ ~ожгла́ ру́ки утюго́м** she has burned her hands all over on the iron. **2.** to use up (*fuel, by burning*).
из|же́чься, ожгу́сь, ожжёшься, ожгу́тся, *past* **~жёгся, ~ожгла́сь** *pf.* (*of* **~жига́ться**) (*coll.*) **1.** to burn o.s. all over; to be covered with burns; **но́ги у неё ~ожгли́сь от кислоты́** her legs were all covered with burns from the acid. **2.** to be burned up, be used up (*of fuel*).
изжива́|ть, ю *impf. of* **изжи́ть**
изжига́|ть(ся), ю(сь) *impf. of* **изже́чь(ся)**
изжи́ти|е, я *nt.* elimination.
изжи́|ть, ву́, вёшь, *past* **~л, ~ла́, ~ло** *pf.* (*of* **~ва́ть**) **1.** to eliminate. **2.** (*obs.*) to overcome (gradually); **и. разочарова́ние** to get over a disappointment. **3.: и. себя́** to become obsolete.
изжо́г|а, и *f.* heartburn.
из-за *prep.*+*g.* **1.** from behind; **из-за две́ри** from behind the door; **встать из-за стола́** to rise from the table; **прие́хать из-за мо́ря** to come from oversea(s); (*fig.*): **сплéтничать о ком-н. из-за угла́** to gossip about s.o. behind his back. **2.** because of, through; **не засыпа́ть из-за шу́ма** to be unable to get to sleep because of the noise; **ссо́риться из-за пустяко́в** to fall out over trifles; **то́лько из-за тебя́ мы опозда́ли** it was all because of you that we were late. **3.** for; **жени́ться из-за де́нег** to marry for money.
и́зззелена- *comb. form* greenish-.
иззя́б|нуть, ну, нешь, *past* **~, ~ла** *pf.* (*coll.*) to feel frozen, feel chilled to the marrow.
излага́|ть, ю *impf. of* **изложи́ть**
изла́мыва|ть(ся), ю(сь) *impf. of* **излома́ть(ся)**
изле́нива|ться, юсь *impf. of* **излени́ться**
излен|и́ться, ю́сь, ~́ишься *pf.* (*of* **~́иваться**) (*coll.*) to grow incorrigibly lazy, become a lazybones.
излёт, а *m.* (*tech.*) end of trajectory; **пу́ля на ~е** spent bullet.
излече́ни|е, я *nt.* **1.** medical treatment; **он был на ~и в Москве́** he was undergoing medical treatment in Moscow; **отпра́вить в го́спиталь на и.** to send to hospital for treatment. **2.** recovery.
изле́чива|ть(ся), ю(сь) *impf. of* **излечи́ть(ся)**
излечи́м|ый (~, ~а) *adj.* curable.
излеч|и́ть, у́, ~́ишь *pf.* (*of* **~́ивать**) to cure.
излеч|и́ться, у́сь, ~́ишься *pf.* (*of* **~́иваться**) (**от**) to make a complete recovery (from); (*fig.*) to rid o.s. (of), shake off.
излива́|ть(ся), ю(сь) *impf. of* **изли́ть(ся)**
из|ли́ть, олью́, ольёшь, *past* **~ли́л, ~лила́, ~ли́ло** *pf.* (*of* **~лива́ть**) **1.** (*obs.*) to pour out, shed. **2.** (*fig.*) to pour out, give vent to; **и. свой гнев на** (+*a.*) to vent one's anger (on); **и. ду́шу** to unbosom o.s.
из|ли́ться, олью́сь, ольёшься, *past* **~ли́лся, ~лила́сь, ~ли́ло́сь** *pf.* (*of* **~лива́ться**) **1.** (*obs. or poet.*) to stream, pour out (*intrans.*); **~лили́сь слёзы** tears welled up. **2.** (**в**+*p.*) to find expression (in). **3.** (**в**+*p.*) to give vent to one's feelings (in); (**на**+*a.*) to vent itself (on); **его́ гнев ~ли́лся на всех окружа́ющих** his anger vented itself on all about him.
изли́ш|ек, ка *m.* **1.** surplus; remainder. **2.** excess; **нам э́того хва́тит с ~ком** we have more than enough, enough and to spare; **и. осторо́жности** excessive caution.
изли́шеств|о, а *nt.* excess; over-indulgence.
изли́шеств|овать, ую *impf.* to go to excess, over-indulge o.s.
изли́шне *adv.* excessively; unnecessarily, superfluously.

изли́ш|ний (~ен, ~ня, ~не) *adj.* excessive; unnecessary, superfluous.
излия́ни|е, я *nt.* outpouring, effusion (*fig.*).
излов|и́ть, лю́, ~́ишь *pf.* (*coll.*) to catch.
изловч|и́ться, у́сь, и́шься *pf.* (*coll.*) to contrive, manage; **он ~и́лся и вы́бил ору́жие из руки́ проти́вника** he contrived to knock his opponent's weapon out of his hand; **он ~и́лся попа́сть в цель** he managed to hit the target.
изложе́ни|е, я *nt.* exposition, account; **кра́ткое и.** synopsis, outline.
излож|и́ть, у́, ~́ишь *pf.* (*of* **излага́ть**) to expound, state; to set forth; to word, draft; **и. на бума́ге** to commit to paper.
изло́жниц|а, ы *f.* (*tech.*) mould.
изло́м, а *m.* **1.** break, fracture; sharp bend. **2.: душе́вный и.** mental unbalance.
изло́ман|ный *p.p.p. of* **излома́ть** *and adj.* **1.** broken. **2.** winding, tortuous. **3.** (*fig.*) unbalanced, unhinged; warped.
излома́|ть, ю *pf.* (*of* **изла́мывать**) **1.** to break, smash. **2.** (*coll.*) to break (*in health*); (*impers.*) to have (crippling) rheumatism; **всю спи́ну у неё ~ло** she is crippled with rheumatism in her back. **3.** (*fig.*, *coll.*) to warp, corrupt.
излома́|ться, юсь *pf.* (*of* **изла́мываться**) **1.** to be broken, be smashed. **2.** (*fig.*, *coll.*) to be affected; to resort to hypocrisy.
излуч|а́ть, а́ю *impf.* (*of* **~и́ть**) to radiate (*also fig.*); **её глаза́ ~а́ли не́жность** her face radiated tenderness.
излуч|а́ться, а́ется *impf.* (*of* **~и́ться**) **1.** (**из**) to emanate (from). **2.** *pass. of* **~а́ть**
излуче́ни|е, я *nt.* radiation; emanation.
излу́чин|а, ы *f.* bend, wind.
излу́чист|ый (~, ~а) *adj.* winding, meandering.
излуч|и́ть(ся), у́(сь), шь(ся) *pf. of* **~а́ть(ся)**
излю́бленный *adj.* favourite.
изма́|зать, жу, жешь, *pf.* (*of* **ма́зать 3.** *and* **~зывать**) (*coll.*) **1.** to make dirty, smear; **и. пальто́ кра́ской** to get paint all over one's coat. **2.** to use up (*paint, grease, etc.*).
изма́|заться, жусь, жешься *pf.* (*of* **ма́заться 1.** *and* **~зываться**) (*coll.*) **1.** to get dirty; **он ~зался в кра́ске** he has got paint all over himself. **2.** *pass. of* **~зать**
изма́зыва|ть(ся), ю(сь) *impf. of* **изма́зать(ся)**
измар|а́ть, а́ю *pf.* (*of* **~́ывать**) to make dirty, soil.
изма́рыва|ть, ю *impf. of* **измара́ть**
изма́тыва|ть(ся), ю(сь) *impf. of* **измота́ть(ся)**
изма́чива|ть(ся), ю(сь) *impf. of* **измочи́ть(ся)**
изма́|ять, ю *pf.* (*coll.*) to exhaust, tire out.
изма́|яться, юсь *pf.* (*coll.*) to be exhausted, tired out.
измельча́ни|е, я *nt.* growing small; growing shallow; (*fig.*) becoming shallow, becoming superficial.
измельча́|ть, ю *pf. of* **мельча́ть**
измельч|и́ть, у́, и́шь *pf. of* **мельчи́ть**
изме́н|а, ы *f.* betrayal; treachery; **госуда́рственная и.** high treason; **супру́жеская и.** unfaithfulness, (conjugal) infidelity.
измене́ни|е, я *nt.* change, alteration; (*gram.*) inflexion.
измен|и́ть[1], ю́, ~́ишь *pf.* (*of* **~я́ть**) to change, alter; (*pol.*) **и. законопрое́кт** to amend a bill.
измен|и́ть[2], ю́, ~́ишь *pf.* (*of* **~я́ть**) (+*d.*) to betray; to be unfaithful (to); (*fig.*) **зре́ние ~и́ло ему́** his eyesight had failed him; **сча́стье нам ~и́ло** our luck is out.
измен|и́ться, ю́сь, ~́ишься *pf.* (*of* **~я́ться**) **1.** to change, alter (*intrans.*); to vary (*intrans.*); **и. к лу́чшему, к ху́дшему** to change for the better, for the worse; **и. в лице́** to change countenance.
изме́нник, а *m.* traitor.
изме́ннический *adj.* treacherous, traitorous.
изме́нчивост|ь, и *f.* **1.** changeableness; mutability; inconstancy, fickleness. **2.** (*biol.*) variability.
изме́нчив|ый (~, ~а) *adj.* changeable; inconstant, fickle; **~ая пого́да** changeable weather.
изменя́ем|ый *pres. part. pass. of* **изменя́ть** *and adj.* variable; **~ые величи́ны** (*math.*) variables.
измен|я́ть(ся), я́ю(сь) *impf. of* **~и́ть(ся)**
измере́ни|е, я *nt.* **1.** measurement, measuring; sounding, fathoming (*of sea bottom*); taking (*of temperature*). **2.** (*math.*) dimension; **двух, трёх ~й** two-, three-dimensional.
измери́м|ый (~, ~а) *adj.* measurable.
измери́тел|ь, я *m.* **1.** measuring instrument, gauge. **2.** (*econ.*) index.
измери́тельный *adj.* (for) measuring.
изме́р|ить, ю, ишь *pf.* (*of* **~я́ть**) to measure; **и. кому́-н. температу́ру** to take s.o.'s temperature.
измер|я́ть, я́ю *impf. of* **~́ить**
изможд|ённый (~, ~а́) *adj.* emaciated; worn out.
измок|а́ть, а́ю *impf. of* **~́нуть**
измо́к|нуть, ну, нешь *past* **~, ~ла** *pf.* (*of* **~а́ть**) (*coll.*) to get soaked, get drenched.
измо́р, а *no pl., m.*: **взять ~ом** to reduce by starvation, starve out; (*fig.*, *coll.*): **взять кого́-н. ~ом** to nag, worry s.o. into doing sth.
измор|и́ть, ю́, и́шь *pf.* (*coll.*) to wear out, exhaust.
и́змороз|ь, и *f.* hoar-frost; rime.
и́зморос|ь, и *f.* drizzle.
измота́|ть, ю *pf.* (*of* **изма́тывать**) (*coll.*) to exhaust, wear out.
измота́|ться, юсь *pf.* (*of* **изма́тываться**) (*coll.*) to be exhausted, worn out.
измоча́лива|ть(ся), ю(сь) *impf. of* **измоча́лить(ся)**
измоча́л|ить, ю, ишь *pf.* (*of* **~ивать**) to shred; to reduce to shreds (*also fig., coll.*).
измоча́л|иться, юсь, ишься *pf.* (*of* **~иваться**) to become frayed, be in shreds; (*fig., coll.*) to be worn to a shred, go to pieces.
измоч|и́ть, у́, ~́ишь *pf.* (*of* **изма́чивать**) (*coll.*) to soak through.
измоч|и́ться, у́сь, ~́ишься *pf.* (*of* **изма́чиваться**) (*coll.*) to be soaked through.
изму́ч|ать, аю *pf.* = **~ить**
изму́ч|аться, аюсь *pf.* = **~иться**
изму́ченный *p.p.p. of* **изму́чить** *and adj.* worn out, tired out; **у вас и. вид** you look worn out.
изму́чива|ть(ся), ю(сь) *impf. of* **изму́чить(ся)**
изму́ч|ить, у, ишь *pf.* **1.** (*pf. of* **~ивать**) to torment; to tire out, exhaust. **2.** *pf. of* **му́чить**
изму́ч|иться, усь, ишься *pf.* **1.** *pf.* (*of* **~иваться**) to be tired out, be exhausted. **2.** *pf. of* **му́читься**
измыва́тельств|о, а *nt.* (*coll.*) mocking, scoffing.
измыва́|ться, юсь *impf.* (**над**; *coll.*) to mock (at), scoff (at).
измы́зг|ать, аю *pf.* (*of* **~ивать**) (*coll.*) **1.** to make dirty all over. **2.** to wear threadbare.
измы́зг|аться, аюсь *pf.* (*of* **~иваться**) (*coll.*) **1.** to get dirty all over. **2.** to become threadbare.
измы́згива|ть(ся), ю(сь) *impf. of* **измы́згать(ся)**
измы́лива|ть, ю *impf. of* **измы́лить**
измы́л|ить, ю, ишь *pf.* (*of* **~ивать**) to use up (*soap*).
измы́сл|ить, ю, ишь *pf.* (*of* **измышля́ть**) **1.** to fabricate, invent. **2.** to contrive.
измыта́р|ить, ю, ишь *pf.* (*coll.*) to wear out; to try.
измыта́р|иться, юсь, ишься *pf.* (*coll.*) to be worn out; to be sorely tried.
измышле́ни|е, я *nt.* fabrication, invention (*action and product*).
измышля́|ть, ю *impf. of* **измы́слить**
измя́т|ый *p.p.p. of* **~ь** *and adj.* **1.** crumpled, creased. **2.** (*fig.*) haggard, jaded.
из|мя́ть(ся), омну́, омнёт(ся) *pf. of* **мя́ть(ся)[1]**
изна́нк|а, и *f.* the wrong side (*of material, clothing*); **с ~и** on the inner side; **вы́вернуть на ~у** to turn inside out; **и. жи́зни** the seamy side of life.
изнаси́ловани|е, я *nt.* rape, assault, violation.
изнаси́л|овать, ую *pf.* (*of* **наси́ловать 2.**) to rape, assault, violate.
изнача́льный *adj.* primordial.
изна́шивани|е, я *nt.* wear; wear and tear.
изна́шива|ть(ся), ю(сь) *impf. of* **износи́ть(ся)**
изне́женност|ь, и *f.* delicacy; softness; effeminacy.
изне́женный *p.p.p. of* **изне́жить** *and adj.* **1.** pampered; delicate. **2.** soft, effete; effeminate.
изне́жива|ть(ся), ю(сь) *impf. of* **изне́жить(ся)**
изне́ж|ить, у, ишь *pf.* (*of* **~ивать**) to pamper, coddle; to render effeminate.

изнéж|иться, усь, ишься *pf.* (*of* **~иваться**) to go soft, become effete; to become effeminate.
изнемогá|ть, ю *impf. of* **изнемóчь**
изнеможéни|е, я *nt.* exhaustion; **быть в ~и** to be utterly exhausted; **рабóтать до ~я** to work to the point of exhaustion.
изнеможён|ный (~, ~á) *adj.* exhausted.
изнемó|чь, гý, ~жешь, ~гут, *past* **~г, ~глá** *pf.* (*of* **~гáть**) (**от**) to be exhausted (from), grow faint (from).
изнéрвнича|ться, юсь *pf.* (*coll.*) to get into a state of nerves.
изничтож|áть, áю *impf. of* **~ить**
изничтóж|ить, у, ишь *pf.* (*of* **~áть**) (*coll.*) to destroy, wipe out.
изнóс, а (у) *m.* (*coll.*) wear; wear and tear, deterioration; **не знать ~у (а)** to wear well; **носи́ть что-н. до ~у** (a) to wear sth. until quite worn out; (*+d.*) **э́тим боти́нкам нет ~у (а)** these boots will stand any amount of hard wear.
изно|си́ть, шý, ~сишь *pf.* (*of* **изнáшивать**) to wear out.
изно|си́ться, шýсь, ~сишься *pf.* (*of* **изнáшиваться**) to wear out (*intrans.*); (*fig., coll.*) to be used up, be played out; to age (prematurely).
износостóйкий *adj.* hard-wearing, wear-resistant.
изнóшенный *p.p.p. of* **износи́ть** *and adj.* worn out; **и. костю́м** threadbare suit; (*fig., coll.*) worn (prematurely) aged.
изнурéни|е, я *nt.* (*physical*) exhaustion.
изнурённый *p.p.p. of* **изнури́ть** *and adj.* (*physically*) exhausted, worn out; jaded; **у негó был и. вид** he looked worn out; **и. гóлодом** faint with hunger.
изнури́тел|ьный (~ен, ~ьна) *adj.* exhausting; gruelling; **~ьная болéзнь** wasting disease.
изнур|и́ть ю́, и́шь *pf.* (*of* **~я́ть**) to exhaust, wear out.
изнур|я́ть, я́ю *impf. of* **~и́ть**
изнутри́ *adv.* from within; **дверь запирáется и.** the door fastens on the inside.
изнывá|ть, ю *impf. of* **изны́ть**
изн|ы́ть, óю, óешь *pf.* (*of* **~ывáть**) to languish, be exhausted; **и. от жáжды** to be tormented by thirst; **и. от тоски́** (**по**+*d.*; *poet.*) to pine (for).
изо *prep.* = **из**
изо...[1] *pref.* = **из...**
изо...[2] *comb. form* **1.** = iso-. **2.** = *abbr. of* **изобрази́тельный**
изобáр|а, ы *f.* (*meteor.*) isobar.
изобáт|а, ы *f.* (*geog.*) isobath, depth contour.
изоби́|деть, жу, дишь *pf.* (*coll.*) to hurt, insult.
изоби́ли|е, я *nt.* abundance, plenty, profusion; **рог ~я** cornucopia.
изоби́л|овать, ую *impf.* (*+i.*) to abound (in), be rich (in).
изоби́л|ьный (~ен, ~ьна) *adj.* **1.** abundant. **2.** (*+i.*) abounding in.
изоблич|áть, áю *impf.* **1.** *impf. of* **~и́ть. 2.** (*no pf.*) (*+a.* **в**+*p.*) to show (to be), point to (as being); **все егó постýпки ~áли в нём мошéнника** his every action pointed to his being a swindler; **егó похóдка ~áет в нём морякá** one can tell by his gait that he is a sailor.
изобличéни|е, я *nt.* exposure; conviction.
изобличи́тельный *adj.* damning.
изоблич|и́ть, ý, и́шь *pf.* (*of* **~áть**) (*+a.* **в**+*p.*) to expose (as), convict (of); to unmask; **егó ~и́ли во лжи** he stands convicted as a liar.
изображá|ть(ся), ю(сь) *impf. of* **изобрази́ть(ся)**
изображéни|е, я *nt.* **1.** (*artistic*) representation. **2.** representation, portrayal; image; imprint; effigy; **и. в зéркале** reflection.
изобрази́тельн|ый *adj.* graphic; decorative; **~ые искýсства** fine arts.
изобра|зи́ть, жý, зи́шь *pf.* (*of* **~жáть**) **1.** (*+i.*) to depict, portray, represent (as); **и. из себя́** (*+a.*; *coll.*) to make o.s. out (to be), represent o.s. (as); **и. Гáмлета слáбым человéком** to portray Hamlet as a weak character (*of actor or producer*); **и. из себя́ хорóшего певцá** to make o.s. out a good singer. **2.** to imitate, take off.
изобра|зи́ться, зи́тся *pf.* (*of* **~жáться**) **1.** to appear, show itself. **2.** *pass. of* **~жáться**

изобре|сти́, тý, тёшь *past* **~л, ~лá** *pf.* (*of* **~тáть**) to invent; to devise, contrive.
изобретáтел|ь, я *m.* inventor.
изобретáтельност|ь, и *f.* inventiveness.
изобретáтел|ьный (~ен, ~ьна) *adj.* inventive; resourceful.
изобретáтель|ский *adj. of* **~**
изобретáтель|ство, ства *nt.* = **~ность**
изобретá|ть, ю *impf. of* **изобрести́**
изобретéни|е, я *nt.* invention (*process and product*).
изóгнут|ый *p.p.p. of* **~ь** *and adj.* bent, curved, winding.
изогн|ýть, ý, ёшь *pf.* (*of* **изгибáть**) to bend, curve.
изогн|ýться, ýсь, ёшься *pf.* (*of* **изгибáться**) to bend, curve (*intrans.*).
изогрáф, а *m.* (*obs.*) icon-painter.
изогрáфи|я, и *f.* (*obs.*) icon-painting.
изóдранный *p.p.p. of* **изодрáть** *and adj.* tattered.
из|одрáть, дерý, дерёшь, *past* **~одрáл, ~одралá, ~одрáло** *pf.* (*of* **~дирáть**) (*coll.*) **1.** to tear to pieces; to tear in several places. **2.** to scratch all over.
изо|йти́, йдý, йдёшь, *past* **~шёл, ~шлá** *pf. of* **исходи́ть**[2]
изол|гáться, гýсь, жёшься, гýтся, *past* **~гáлся, ~галáсь, ~гáлось** *pf.* to become an inveterate, hardened liar.
изоли́рованный *p.p.p. of* **изоли́ровать** *and adj.* **1.** isolated; separate. **2.** (*tech.*) insulated.
изоли́р|овать, ую *impf. and pf.* **1.** to isolate; to quarantine. **2.** (*tech.*) to insulate.
изолирóвк|а, и *f.* (*tech.*) **1.** insulation. **2.** (*coll.*) insulating tape.
изолирóвочный *adj.* (*tech.*) insulating.
изоля́тор[1]**, а** *m.* (*tech.*) insulator.
изоля́тор[2]**, а** *m.* **1.** (*med.*) isolation ward. **2.** solitary confinement cell. **3.** (*pol.*) 'isolator' (*in former USSR, special prison for political detainees and espionage suspects*).
изоляциони́зм, а *m.* (*pol.*) isolationism.
изоляциони́ст, а *m.* (*pol.*) isolationist.
изоля|циóнный *adj. of* **~ция; ~циóнная лéнта** (*tech.*) insulating tape.
изоля́ци|я, и *f.* **1.** isolation; (*med.*) quarantine. **2.** (*tech.*) insulation.
изомáслян|ый *adj.*: **~ая кислотá** (*chem.*) isolbutyric acid.
изомéрный *adj.* (*chem.*) isomeric.
изомóрфный *adj.* (*min.*) isomorphous.
изóрванный *p.p.p. of* **изорвáть** *and adj.* tattered, torn.
изорв|áть, ý, ёшь, *past* **~áл, ~алá, ~áло** *pf.* (*of* **изрывáть**[1]) to tear (to pieces).
изорв|áться, ётся, *past* **~áлся, ~алáсь, ~áлось** *pf.* (*coll.*) to be in tatters.
изотéрм|а, ы *f.* (*geog.*) isotherm.
изотерми́ческий *adj.* **1.** (*phys.*) isothermal. **2.** having regulated temperature.
изотóп, а *m.* (*chem.*) isotope.
изохрóнный *adj.* isochronous.
изошýтк|а, и *f.* (*coll.*) cartoon, humorous drawing.
изощрéни|е, я *nt.* sharpening (*fig.*); refinement.
изощрённый *p.p.p. of* **изощри́ть** *and adj.* refined; keen.
изощр|и́ть, ю́, и́шь *pf.* (*of* **~я́ть**) to sharpen (*fig.*); to cultivate, refine; **и. слух** to train one's ear; **и. ум** to cultivate one's mind.
изощр|и́ться, ю́сь, и́шься *pf.* (*of* **~я́ться**) **1.** to acquire refinement. **2.** (**в**+*p.*) to excel (in); **и. в придýмывании каламбýров** to excel in punning.
изощр|я́ть(ся), я́ю(сь) *impf. of* **~и́ть(ся)**
из-под *prep.+g.* **1.** from under; **сдéлать что-н. из под пáлки** to do sth. under the lash; **у негó укрáли бумáжник из-под нóсу** he had his wallet stolen from under his nose; **из-под полы́** on the sly; under the counter. **2.** from near; **мы приéхали из-под Москвы́** we have come from near Moscow. **3.** (for) (*indicates purpose of object*); **бáнка из-под варéнья** jam-jar.
изразé|ц, цá *m.* tile.
израз|цóвый *adj. of* **~éц**
Израи́л|ь, я *m.* Israel.
изрáильский *adj.* **1.** (*hist.*) Israelitish. **2.** Israeli.
израильтя́н|ин, ина, *pl.* **~е, ~** *m.* **1.** (*hist.*) Israelite. **2.** Israeli.

израильтя́н|ка, ки *f. of* **~ин**
изра́н|ить, ю, ишь *pf.* to cover with wounds.
израсхо́д|овать(ся), ую(сь) *pf. of* **расхо́довать(ся)**
и́зредка *adv.* now and then; from time to time.
изре́занный *p.p.p. of* **изре́зать** *and adj.*: **и. бе́рег** indented coastline.
изре́|зать, жу, жешь *pf.* (*of* **~зывать** *and* **~за́ть**) **1.** to cut to pieces; to cut up. **2.** (*geog.*) to indent.
изрез|а́ть, а́ю *impf.* (*coll.*) *of* **~́ать**
изре́зыва|ть, ю *impf. of* **изре́зать**
изрека́|ть, ю *impf. of* **изре́чь**
изрече́ни|е, я *nt.* apophthegm, dictum, saying.
изре́|чь, ку́, чёшь, ку́т, *past* **~̈к, ~кла́** *pf.* (*of* **~ка́ть**) (*obs. or iron.*) to speak (solemnly); to utter; **так ~̈к** thus he spake; **и. му́дрое сло́во** to utter a word of wisdom.
изреше|ти́ть, чу́, ти́шь *pf.* (*of* **~́чивать**) to pierce with holes; **и. пу́лями** to riddle with bullets.
изреше́чива|ть, ю *impf. of* **изрешети́ть**
изрис|ова́ть, у́ю *pf.* (*of* **~о́вывать**) **1.** to cover with drawings. **2.** (*coll.*) to use up (*pencil, paper, etc.*).
изрисо́выва|ть, ю *impf. of* **изрисова́ть**
изруб|а́ть, а́ю *impf. of* **~и́ть**
изруб|и́ть, лю́, ~́ишь *pf.* (*of* **~а́ть**) to chop up; to hack to pieces; to mince (*meat*).
изруга́|ть, ю *pf.* to abuse, curse violently.
изрыва́|ть¹, ю *impf. of* **изорва́ть**
изрыва́|ть², ю *impf. of* **изры́ть**
изрыг|а́ть, а́ю *impf.* (*of* **~ну́ть**) to vomit, throw up; **пу́шки ~а́ли дым и пла́мень** the cannon were belching forth smoke and flames; (*fig.*): **и. руга́тельства** to let forth a stream of oaths.
изрыг|ну́ть, ну́, нёшь *pf. of* **~а́ть**
изры́т|ый *p.p.p. of* **~ь** pitted; **и. о́спой** pock-marked.
изр|ы́ть, о́ю, о́ешь *pf.* (*of* **~ыва́ть²**) to dig up; to dig through.
изря́дно *adv.* (*coll.*) fairly, pretty; tolerably; **я и. уста́л** I am pretty tired; **они́ вчера́ ве́чером и. вы́пили** they had a fair amount to drink last night.
изря́д|ный (~ен, ~на) *adj.* (*coll.*) fair, handsome; fairly large, tolerable; **~ое коли́чество** a fair amount; **и. пья́ница** a pretty heavy drinker.
изуве́р, а *m.* **1.** bigot, fanatic, zealot. **2.** fiend, monster.
изуве́рский *adj.* **1.** bigoted, fanatical. **2.** fiendish.
изуве́рств|о, а *nt.* **1.** bigotry, fanaticism; (fanatical) cruelty; zealotry. **2.** fiendishness.
изуве́чива|ть, ю *impf. of* **изуве́чить**
изуве́ч|ить, у, ишь *pf.* (*of* **~ивать**) to maim, mutilate.
изуве́ч|иться, усь, ишься *pf.* (*coll.*) **1.** to maim o.s., mutilate o.s. **2.** *pass. of* **~ить**
изукра́|сить, шу, сишь *pf.* (*of* **~шивать**) to decorate (lavishly); **и. дом фла́гами** to bedeck a house with flags; (*coll., iron.*) **и. синяка́ми** to 'adorn' with bruises.
изукра́шива|ть, ю *impf. of* **изукра́сить**
изуми́тел|ьный (~ен, ~ьна) *adj.* amazing, astounding.
изум|и́ть, лю́, и́шь *pf.* (*of* **~ля́ть**) to amaze, astound.
изум|и́ться, лю́сь, и́шься *pf.* (*of* **~ля́ться**) to be amazed, astounded.
изумле́ни|е, я *nt.* amazement.
изумлённый *p.p.p. of* **изуми́ть** *and adj.* amazed, astounded; dumbfounded.
изумля́|ть(ся), ю(сь) *impf. of* **изуми́ть(ся)**
изумру́д, а *m.* emerald.
изумру́дный *adj.* **1.** emerald. **2.** emerald(-green).
изуро́дованный *p.p.p. of* **изуро́довать** *and adj.* maimed, mutilated; disfigured.
изуро́д|овать, ую *pf. of* **уро́довать**
изу́стно *adv.* (*obs.*) orally, by word of mouth.
изуч|а́ть, а́ю *impf.* (*of* **~и́ть**) to learn; (*impf. only*) to study; **он два го́да ~а́ет гре́ческий язы́к** he has been studying Greek for two years.
изуче́ни|е, я *nt.* study, studying.
изуч|и́ть, у́, ~́ишь *pf.* (*of* **~а́ть**) **1.** to learn; **за шесть ме́сяцев она ~и́ла и испа́нский и италья́нский языки́** in six months she had learned both Spanish and Italian. **2.** to come to know (very well), come to understand; **он кра́йне за́мкнут, но я всё-таки ~и́л его́** he is extremely reserved, but I came to understand him in the end.
изъ... *pref.* = **из...**
изъеда́|ть, ю *impf. of* **изъе́сть**
изъе́денный *p.p.p. of* **изъе́сть** *and adj.*: **и. мо́лью** moth-eaten.
изъе́з|дить, жу, дишь *pf.* (*of* **~живать**) **1.** to travel all over, traverse; **мы ~дили весь свет** we have been all round the world. **2.** (*coll.*) to wear out (*vehicle or road surface*).
изъе́зженный *p.p.p. of* **изъе́здить** *and adj.*, well-worn, rutted.
изъе́зжива|ть, ю *impf. of* **изъе́здить**
изъе́|сть, ст, дя́т, *past* **~л, ~ла** *pf.* (*of* **~да́ть**) **1.** to eat away. **2.** to corrode.
изъяви́тельн|ый *adj., only in phr.* **~ое наклоне́ние** (*gram.*) indicative mood.
изъяв|и́ть, лю́, ~́ишь *pf.* (*of* **~ля́ть**) to indicate, express; **и. своё согла́сие** to give one's consent.
изъявле́ни|е, я *nt.* expression.
изъявля́|ть, ю *impf. of* **изъяви́ть**
изъязв|и́ть, лю́, и́шь *pf.* (*of* **~ля́ть**) (*med.*) to ulcerate.
изъязвле́ни|е, я *nt.* (*med.*) ulceration.
изъязвлённый *p.p.p. of* **изъязви́ть** *and adj.* ulcered, ulcerous.
изъязвля́|ть, ю *impf. of* **изъязви́ть**
изъя́н, а *m.* **1.** defect, flaw; **това́р с ~ом** defective goods; **у него́ мно́го ~ов** he has many defects. **2.** damage, loss.
изъясне́ни|е, я *nt.* (*obs.*) explanation; declaration.
изъясни́тельный *adj.* (*obs.*) explanatory.
изъясн|и́ть, ю́, и́шь *pf.* (*of* **~я́ть**) (*obs.*) to explain, expound.
изъясн|и́ться, ю́сь, и́шься *pf.* (*of* **~я́ться**) (*obs.*) to express o.s.; **и. в любви́** to declare one's love.
изъясн|я́ть(ся), я́ю(сь) *impf. of* **~и́ть(ся)**
изъя́ти|е, я *nt.* **1.** withdrawal; removal; **и. из обраще́ния (моне́ты)** (*fin.*) immobilization (of currency). **2.** exception; **без вся́кого ~я** without exception; **в и. из пра́вил** as an exception to the rule.
из|ъя́ть, ыму́, ы́мешь *pf.* (*of* **~ыма́ть**) to withdraw; to remove; **и. из обраще́ния** to withdraw from circulation; to immobilize (*currency*); **и. в по́льзу госуда́рства** to confiscate.
изыма́|ть, ю *impf. of* **изъя́ть**
из|ыму́, ы́мешь *see* **~ъя́ть**
изыска́ни|е, я *nt.* (*usu. pl.*) investigation, research; prospecting; survey.
изы́сканност|ь, и *f.* refinement.
изы́скан|ный 1. (~, ~а) *p.p.p. of* **изыска́ть. 2. (~, ~на)** *adj.* refined; recherché.
изыска́тел|ь, я *m.* prospector.
изыска́тельский *adj.* prospecting.
изы|ска́ть, щу́, ~́щешь *pf.* (*of* **~́скивать**) to find (*after search or investigation*); to search out; **и. сре́дства на постро́йку домо́в** to find funds for house-building.
изы́скива|ть, ю *impf.* (*of* **изыска́ть**) to search out; to try to find.
изю́бр, а *m.* (*zool.*) Manchurian deer.
изю́м, а (у) *no pl., m.* raisins; sultanas; **э́то не фунт ~у!** (*joc.*) it is no light matter, it is no joke.
изю́мин|а, ы *f.* raisin.
изю́мин|ка, ки *f., dim. of* **~а**; (*fig.*) pep, go, spirit; **с ~кой** spirited; **в ней нет ~ки** she has no go in her.
изя́честв|о, а *nt.* elegance, grace.
изя́щ|ный (~ен, ~на) *adj.* elegant, graceful; (*obs.*) **~ные иску́сства** fine arts; **~ная литерату́ра** belles-lettres.
ика́ни|е, я *nt.* hiccupping.
ик|а́ть, а́ю *impf.* (*of* **~ну́ть**) to hiccup.
ик|ну́ть, ну́, нёшь *pf. of* **~а́ть**
ико́н|а, ы *f.* icon.
ико́н|ный *adj. of* **~а**
иконобо́р|ец, ца *m.* (*hist.*) iconoclast.
иконобо́рческий *adj.* (*hist.*) iconoclastic.
иконобо́рчеств|о, а *nt.* (*hist.*) iconoclasm.
иконогра́фи|я, и *f.* **1.** iconography. **2.** (*collect.*) portraits.
иконопи́с|ец, ца *m.* icon-painter.

иконопи́сный *adj.* **1.** *adj. of* **и́конопись. 2.** (*fig.*) icon-like (*severe, severely beautiful*).
и́конопис|ь, и *f.* icon-painting.
иконоста́с, а *m.* (*eccl.*) iconostasis.
ико́рный *adj. of* **икра́**[1]
ико́т|а, ы *f.* hiccups.
икр|а́[1], **ы́** *no pl. f.* **1.** (hard) roe; spawn; **мета́ть ~у́** to spawn; (*fig., coll.*) to rage. **2.** caviar(e); pâté; **зерни́стая и.** soft caviar(e); **па́юсная и.** pressed caviar(e); **баклажа́нная и.** aubergine pâté.
икр|а́[2], **ы́**, *pl.* **~ы** *f.* (*anat.*) calf.
икри́нк|а, и *f.* (*coll.*) grain of roe.
икри́ст|ый (~, ~а) *adj.* containing much roe.
икр|и́ться, ю́сь, и́шься *impf.* to spawn.
икромета́ни|е, я *nt.* spawning.
икряно́й *adj.* **1.** hard-roed. **2.** (made from) roe.
икс, а *m.* (*the letter*) x; (*math*) x (*unknown quantity*).
икс-луч|и́, е́й *no sg.* (*obs.*) X-rays.
ил, а *m.* silt.
и́ли *conj. or*; **и.... и.** either ... or; **и. вы меня́ не понима́ете?** don't you understand me?
и́лист|ый (~, ~а) *adj.* covered in silt; containing silt.
иллю́зи|я, и *f.* illusion.
иллюзо́р|ный (~ен, ~на) *adj.* illusory.
иллюмина́тор, а *m.* (*naut.*) porthole.
иллюмина́ци|я, и *f.* illumination.
иллюмини́р|овать, ую *impf. and pf.* to illuminate (*in var. senses*).
иллюстрати́в|ный (~ен, ~на) *adj.* illustrative; **и. материа́л** illustration(s).
иллюстра́тор, а *m.* illustrator.
иллюстра́ци|я, и *f.* illustration (*in various senses*).
иллюстри́р|ованный *p.p.p. of* **~овать** *and adj.* illustrated.
иллюстри́р|овать, ую *impf. and pf.* (*pf. also* **про~**) to illustrate (*also fig.*).
ило́т, а *m.* (*hist. or fig.*) helot.
и́л|овый *adj.* = **~истый**
иль = и́ли
и́льк|а, и *f.* (*zool.*) **1.** (North American) mink. **2.** mink (*fur*).
и́льк|овый *adj. of* **~а**
ильм, а *m.* (*bot.*) elm (*Ulmus scabra*).
и́льм|овый *adj. of* **~**
им 1. *i. of prons.* **он, оно́. 2.** *d. of pron.* **они́**
им. (*abbr. of* **и́мени**) named after; **стадио́н им. Ле́нина** Lenin Stadium.
имажини́зм, а *m.* (*liter.*) imagism.
имажини́ст, а *m.* (*liter.*) imagist.
има́м, а *nt.* imam (*Mohammedan priest or leader*).
има́ть (*inf. and past not used*), **е́млю, е́млешь** *impf.* (*arch., now only iron.*) to take.
имби́р|ный *adj. of* **~ь**
имби́р|ь, я́ *m.* ginger.
и́м|ени, енем *see* **~я**
име́ни|е, я *nt.* **1.** estate, landed property. **2.** (*sg. only*; *obs.*) property, possessions.
имени́нник, а *m.* one whose name-day it is; **сиде́ть, смотре́ть ~ом** (*joc.*) to look cheery, look on top of the world.
имени́н|ный *adj. of* **~ы; и. пиро́г** name-day cake.
имени́н|ы, ~ *no sg.* **1.** name-day (*day of saint after whom pers. is named*); **спра́вить и.** to celebrate one's name-day. **2.** name-day celebration; **пойти́ на и. к кому́-н.** to go to s.o.'s name-day party.
имени́тельный *adj.* (*gram.*) nominative.
имени́т|ый (~, ~а) *adj.* (*obs.*) distinguished.
и́менно *adv.* **1. (а) и.** namely; to wit, videlicet (viz); **нас там бы́ло тро́е, а и.: Петро́в, Ивано́в и я** there were three of us there, namely Petrov, Ivanov, and myself. **2.** just, exactly; to be exact; **где и. она́ живёт?** where exactly does she live?; **в то вре́мя я был в Росси́и, а и. в Оде́ссе** I was in Russia then, in Odessa to be exact; **вот и. э́то я и говори́л** that's just what I was saying; **вот и.!** exactly!; precisely!
имен|о́й *adj.* **1.** nominal; **~ы́е а́кции** (*fin.*) inscribed stock; **~о́е кольцо́** ring engraved with owner's name; **и. спи́сок** nominal roll; **и. ука́з** edict signed by tsar; **и. чек** cheque payable to pers. named; **и. экземпля́р** autographed copy. **2.** *adj. of* **и́мя 3.**
имено́ван|ный *p.p.p. of* **именова́ть** *and adj.*; (*math.*): **~ное число́** concrete number.
имен|ова́ть, у́ю *impf.* (*of* **на~**) to name.
имен|ова́ться, у́юсь *impf.* **1.** (*+i.*) to be called; to be termed. **2.** *pass. of* **~ова́ть**
именосло́в, а *m.* **1.** (*arch.*) list of names, roll. **2.** (*eccl.*) litany (*of saints*).
имену́емый *pres. part. pass. of* **именова́ть; царь Ива́н, и. Гро́зным** Tsar Ivan, called the Terrible.
име́|ть, ю, ешь *impf.* **1.** to have (*of abstract possession*); **и. возмо́жность** (*+inf.*) to have an opportunity (to), be in a position (to); **и. де́ло (с+i.)** to have dealings (with), have to do (with); **и. значе́ние (для)** to matter (to), be important (to); **и. ме́сто** to take place; **и. на́глость, несча́стье** etc. (*+inf.*) to have the effrontery, the misfortune, *etc.* (to); **и. стыд** to be ashamed; **и. в виду́** to bear in mind, think of, mean; **ничего́ не и. про́тив** (*+g.*) to have no objection(s) (to); **и. сто ме́тров в высоту́** to be 100 metres high. **2.** (*+inf. forms fut. tense in formal utterance*; *obs.*) **за́втра ~ет быть банке́т** there is to be a banquet tomorrow.
име́|ться, ется *impf.* to be; to be present, be available (**~ется у, ~ются у** *are equivalent to* **есть у); в на́шем го́роде ~ется два кино́** there are two cinemas in our town, we have two cinemas in our town; **бана́нов у нас не ~ется** we have no bananas, bananas are not to be had here; **и. налицо́** to be available, be on hand.
име́|ющийся *pres. part. of* **~ться** *and adj.* available; present.
и́ми *i. of pron.* **они́**
имита́тор, а *m.* **1.** mimic; impressionist. **2.** simulator; **и. полёта** flight simulator.
имита́ци|я, и *f.* **1.** mimicry; mimicking. **2.** imitation (*artefact*); **и. же́мчуга** imitation pearl. **3.** (*mus.*) imitation.
имити́р|овать, ую *impf.* **1.** to mimic. **2.** to make imitation goods. **3.** (*mus.*) imitate.
имманéнт|ный (~ен, ~на) *adj.* (*phil., theol.*) immanent.
иммигра́нт, а *m.* immigrant.
иммигра|цио́нный *adj. of* **~ция; ~цио́нные зако́ны** immigration laws.
иммигра́ци|я, и *f.* **1.** immigration. **2.** (*collect.*) immigrants.
иммигри́р|овать, ую *impf. and pf.* to immigrate.
иммора́л|ьный (~ен, ~ьна) *adj.* immoral.
иммуниза́ци|я, и *f.* (*med.*) immunization.
иммунизи́р|овать, ую *impf. and pf.* (*med.*) to immunize.
иммуните́т, а *m.* (*med., leg.*) immunity.
иммун|ный (~ен, ~на) *adj.* **(к)** immune (to).
императи́в, а *m.* (*phil., gram.*) imperative.
императи́в|ный (~ен, ~на) *adj.* imperative.
импера́тор, а *m.* emperor.
импера́торский *adj.* imperial.
императри́ц|а, ы *f.* empress.
империа́л[1], **а** *m.* (*obs.*) imperial (*Russ. gold coin of 10 or, after 1897, 15 roubles*).
империа́л[2], **а** *m.* (*obs.*) imperial, outside (*of omnibus or tram*).
империали́зм, а *m.* imperialism.
империали́ст, а *m.* imperialist.
империалисти́ческий *adj.* imperialist(ic).
импе́ри|я, и *f.* empire.
импе́рский *adj.* imperial.
импи́чмент, а *m.* impeachment.
импоза́нт|ный (~ен, ~на) *adj.* imposing, striking.
импони́р|овать, ую *impf.* (*+d.*) to impress, strike (*fig.*); **его́ зна́ния ~овали всем знако́мым** everyone he knew was impressed by his learning.
и́мпорт, а *m.* **1.** import. **2.** (*coll.*) Western *or* foreign goods.
импортёр, а *m.* importer.
импорти́р|овать, ую *impf. and pf.* (*econ.*) to import.
и́мпорт|ный *adj. of* **~; ~ные по́шлины** import duties; **~ные това́ры** foreign imports, (imported) foreign goods.
импоте́нт, а *m.* impotent man.
импоте́нт|ный (~ен, ~на) *adj.* (*med.*) impotent.

импоте́нци|я, и *f.* (*med.*) impotence.
импреса́рио *m. indecl.* impresario.
импрессиони́зм, а *m.* (*art*) impressionism.
импрессиони́ст, а *m.* (*art*) impressionist.
импрессионисти́ческий *adj.* (*art*) impressionistic.
импрессиони́ст|ский *adj.* = **~и́ческий**
импровиза́тор, а *m.* improviser.
импровиза́торский *adj.* improvisational.
импровиза́ци|я, и *f.* improvisation.
импровизи́рова|нный *p.p.p. of* **~ть** *and adj.* improvised; impromptu, extempore.
импровизи́р|овать, ую *impf.* (*of* **сымпровизи́ровать**) to improvize; to extemporize.
и́мпульс, а *m.* impulse, impetus.
импульси́в|ный (~ен, ~на) *adj.* impulsive.
и́мут *3rd pers. pl. of arch. v.* **я́ти; мёртвые сра́му не и.** (*rhet.*) 'de mortuis nil nisi bonum'.
иму́ществ|енный *adj. of* **~о; и. ценз** property qualification; **и. иск** (*leg.*) real action.
иму́ществ|о, а *nt.* property, belongings; stock; **дви́жимое и.** (*leg.*) personalty, personal estate; **недви́жимое и.** realty, real estate.
иму́щий *adj.* propertied; well-off; **власть иму́щие** the powers that be.
и́м|я, *g., d., and p.* **~ени,** *i.* **~енем,** *pl.* **~ена́, ~ён, ~ена́м** *nt.* **1.** first, Christian name; name; **вы́мышленное и.** alias, false name; **по ~ени О́льга** Olga by name; **во и.** (*+g.*) in the name of; **посла́ть на и.** (*+g.*) to address to; **запиши́те счёт на моё и.** put it down to my account; **от ~ени** (*+g.*) on behalf of; **то́лько по ~ени** only in name, only nominally; **он тепе́рь изве́стен под други́м ~енем** he now goes by, under another name; **~енем зако́на** in the name of the law; **~ени** (*+g.*) named in honour of (*usu. not translated*); **Вое́нная акаде́мия ~ени Фру́нзе** the Frunze Military Academy; **называ́ть ве́щи свои́ми ~ена́ми** to call a spade a spade. **2.** (*fig.*) name, reputation; **челове́к с больши́м ~енем** a man with a big name; **у него́ европе́йское и.** he has a European reputation; **приобрести́ и.** to acquire, make a name; **замара́ть своё и.** to ruin one's good name; **кру́пные ~ена́ в о́бласти фи́зики** great names in the field of physics. **3.** (*gram.*) noun, nomen (*any part of speech declined, as opposed to conjugated*); **и. прилага́тельное** adjective; **и. существи́тельное** noun, substantive; **и. числи́тельное** numeral.
имяре́к, а *m.* **1.** (*obs. or joc.*) so-and-so. **2.** (*in official forms, etc.*) *indicates space for signatory's name.*
ин... *comb. form, abbr. of* **иностра́нный**
инакомы́сли|е, я *nt.* nonconformism, heterodoxy.
инакомы́сящ|ий *adj.* differently minded; heterodox; nonconformist; *as n.* **и., ~его** *m.* dissident.
и́наче 1. (*adv.*) differently, otherwise; **так и́ли и.** in either event, at all events; **не ина́че (как)** (*coll.*) precisely, of course; **не ина́че как полко́вник** none other than the colonel. **2.** (*conj.*) otherwise, or (else); **спеши́те, и. вы опозда́ете** hurry up, or you will be late.
инвали́д, а *m.* invalid; **и. войны́** disabled serviceman; **и. труда́** industrial invalid.
инвали́дност|ь, и *f.* disablement; **посо́бие по ~и** disablement relief; **перейти́ на и.** to be registered as a disabled pers.; **по ~и перейти́ на пе́нсию** (*mil.*) to be invalided out on pension; **уво́литься по ~и** (*mil.*) to be invalided out.
инвали́д|ный *adj. of* **~; и. дом** home for invalids.
инвалю́т|а, ы *f.* foreign currency.
инвекти́в|а, ы *f.* invective.
инвентариза́ци|я, и *f.* inventory making, inventorying, stock-taking.
инвентариз|ова́ть, у́ю *impf. and pf.* to inventory.
инвента́р|ный *adj. of* **~ь; ~ная о́пись** inventory.
инвента́р|ь, я́ *m.* **1.** stock; equipment, appliances; **живо́й и.** livestock; **сельскохозя́йственный и.** agricultural implements; **торго́вый и.** stock-in-trade. **2.** inventory.
инве́рси|я, и *f.* (*liter.*) inversion.
инвести́р|овать, ую *impf. and pf.* to invest.
инвести́тор = инве́стор
инвеститу́р|а, ы *f.* investiture.
инвести́ци|я, и *f.* investment.
инве́стор, а *m.* (*fin.*) investor.
инволю́ци|я, и *f.* (*physiol.*) involution.
ингаля́тор, а *m.* (*med.*) inhaler.
ингаля|цио́нный *adj. of* **~́ция**
ингаля́ци|я, и *f.* (*med.*) inhaling.
ингредие́нт, а *m.* ingredient.
ингу́ш, а́, *g. pl.* **~е́й** *m.* Ingush.
ингу́ш|ка, ки *f. of* **~**
ингу́шский *adj.* Ingush.
Инд, а *m.* the Indus (*river*).
и́ндеве|ть, ет *impf.* (*of* **за~**) to become covered with hoar-frost.
инде́|ец, йца, *pl.* **~йцы, ~йцев** *m.* (American) Indian.
инде́йк|а, и *f.* turkey(-hen).
инде́|йский *adj. of* **~ец; и. пету́х** turkey-cock.
и́ндекс, а *m.* index; **и. цен** (*econ.*) price index; **почто́вый и.** post-code.
инд|иа́нка, иа́нки *f. of* **~е́ец** *and* **~и́ец**
индиви́д, а *m.* individual.
индивидуализа́ци|я, и *f.* individualization.
индивидуализи́р|овать, ую *impf. and pf.* to individualize.
индивидуали́зм, а *m.* individualism.
индивидуали́ст, а *m.* individualist.
индивидуалисти́ческий *adj.* individualistic.
индивидуалисти́ч|ный (~ен, ~на) *adj.* individualistic
индивидуа́льност|ь, и *f.* individuality.
индивидуа́л|ьный (~ен, ~ьна) *adj.* individual; **~ьные осо́бенности** individual peculiarities; **~ьное хозя́йство** individual holding; **в ~ьном поря́дке** individually; **и. слу́чай** individual case, single case.
индиви́дуум, а *m.* individual.
инди́го *nt. indecl.* **1.** indigo (*colour*). **2.** (*bot.*) indigo plant.
инди́|ец, йца, *pl.* **~йцы, ~йцев** *m.* Indian.
и́нди|й, я *m.* (*chem.*) indium.
инди́йский *adj.* Indian.
Инди́йск|ий океа́н, ~ого ~а *m.* the Indian Ocean.
индикати́в, а *m.* (*gram.*) indicative.
индика́тор, а *m.* **1.** (*tech.*) indicator; (*comput.*) display; **жидко-кристалли́ческий и.** liquid-crystal display, LCD; **светово́й и.** indicator light. **2.** (*chem.*) reagent.
индика́тор|ный *adj. of* **~; ~ная диагра́мма** indicator diagram; **~ная мо́щность** indicated horse-power (*abbr.* i.h.p.).
инди́кт, а *m.* (*hist.*) indiction (*period of 15 years*).
индифере́нтност|ь, и *f.* indifference.
индифферо́нт|ный (~ен, ~на) *adj.* **(к)** indifferent (to).
И́нди|я, и *f.* India.
индогерма́нский *adj.* Indo-Germanic.
индоевропе́|ец, йца *m.* Indo-European.
индоевропе́|йка, йки *f. of* **~ец**
индоевропе́йский *adj.* Indo-European.
Индокита́|й, я *m.* Indo-China.
индокита́йский *adj.* Indo-Chinese.
индонези́|ец, йца, *pl.* **~йцы, ~йцев** *m.* Indonesian.
индонези́|йка, йки *f. of* **~ец**
индонези́йский *adj.* Indonesian.
Индоне́зи|я, и *f.* Indonesia.
индоссаме́нт, а *m.* (*fin.*) endorsement, indorsation.
индосса́нт, а *m.* (*fin.*) endorser.
индосса́т, а *m.* (*fin.*) endorsee.
индосси́р|овать, ую *impf. and pf.* (*fin.*) to endorse.
индуи́зм, а *m.* Hinduism.
индуи́стский *adj.* Hindu.
индукти́вный *adj.* (*phil., phys.*) inductive.
инду́ктор, а *m.* (*elec.*) inductor, field magnet.
инду́ктор|ный *adj. of* **~; и. вы́зов** induction call; **и. телефо́нный аппара́т** magneto telephone, sound power telephone.
индукци|о́нный *adj. of* **~я; ~о́нная кату́шка** induction coil.
инду́кци|я, и *f.* (*phil., phys.*) induction.
индульге́нци|я, и *f.* (*eccl.*) indulgence.

инду́с, а *m.* Hindu; (*obs.*) Indian.
инду́с|ка, ки *f. of* ~
инду́сский *adj.* Hindu; (*obs.*) Indian.
индустриализа́ци|я, и *f.* industrialization.
индустриализи́р|овать, ую *impf. and pf.* to industrialize.
индустриа́льный *adj.* industrial.
инду́стри|я, и *f.* industry.
индю́к, а́ *m.* turkey(-cock); **наду́лся как и.** (*coll.*) he got on his high horse.
индюш|а́чий *adj.* = ~**ечий**
индю́ш|ечий *adj. of* ~**ка**
индю́шк|а, и *f.* turkey(-hen).
индюш|о́нок, о́нка, *pl.* ~**а́та,** ~**а́т** *m.* turkey-poult.
и́не|й, я *no pl., m.* hoar-frost, rime.
ине́ртност|ь, и *f.* inertness, sluggishness, inaction.
ине́рт|ный (~ен, ~на) *adj.* inert (*phys. and fig.*); sluggish, inactive.
ине́рци|я, и *f.* (*phys. and fig.*) inertia; momentum; **двигаться по ~и** to move under its own momentum; (*fig.*): **де́лать что-н. по ~и** to do sth. from force of inertia, mechanically.
инжене́р, а *m.* pers. with higher technical education; engineer; **гражда́нский и. путе́й сообще́ния, и.-строи́тель** civil engineer.
инжене́ри|я, и *f.* engineering; **ге́нная и.** genetic engineering.
инжене́рн|ый *adj.* engineering; ~**ые войска́** (*mil.*) Engineers; ~**ое де́ло** engineering.
инженю́ *f. indecl.* (*theatr.*) ingénue.
инжи́р, а *m.* fig.
инжи́рный *adj.* fig.
и́нист|ый (~, ~а) *adj.* rimy, covered with hoar-frost.
инициа́л|ы, ов *pl.* (*sg.* ~, ~**а** *m.*) initials.
инициати́в|а, ы *f.* initiative; **по со́бственной ~е** on one's own initiative; **стратеги́ческая оборо́нная и.** Strategic Defense Initiative, SDI.
инициати́в|ный *adj.* **1.** initiating, originating; ~**ная гру́ппа** organizing body, action committee. **2.** (~**ен,** ~**на**) full of initiative, enterprising; dynamic, go-getting.
инкасса́тор, а *m.* (*fin.*) collector, receiver (*of bill, cheque, etc.*).
инкасса́ци|я, и *f.* encashment, collection, receipt (*of money or bills*).
инкасси́р|овать, ую *impf. and pf.* (*fin.*) to encash, collect, receive (*money, bill*).
инка́ссо *nt. indecl.* (*fin.*) encashment.
ин-ква́рто *adv.* (*also as indecl. adj. and m.n.*) (*typ.*) quarto.
инквизи́тор, а *m.* inquisitor.
инквизи́торский *adj.* inquisitorial.
инквизи́ци|я, и *f.* inquisition.
и́нк|и, ов *no sg.* the Incas.
инко́гнито 1. *adv.* incognito. **2.** *n.*; *nt. indecl.* incognito (*concealed identity*). **3.** *n.*; *c.g. indecl.* incognito (*pers.*).
инкорпора́ци|я, и *f.* incorporation.
инкорпори́р|овать, ую *impf. and pf.* to incorporate.
инкримини́р|овать ую *impf. and pf.* (+*a. and d.*) to charge (with); **ему́ ~уют поджо́г** he is being charged with arson.
инкруста́ци|я, и *f.* inlaid work, inlay.
инкрусти́р|овать ую *impf. and pf.* to inlay.
и́нкский *adj.* Incan.
инкуба́тор, а *m.* incubator.
инкубацио́нный *adj.* incubative, incubatory; **и. пери́од** (*med.*) incubation.
инкуба́ци|я, и *f.* incubation (*of chickens and med.*).
инкуна́бул|ы, ~ *pl.* (*sg.* ~**а,** ~**ы** *f.*) (*liter.*) incunabula.
инове́р|ец, ца *m.* (*relig.*) adherent of different faith, creed.
инове́ри|е, я *nt.* (*relig.*) adherence to different faith, creed.
инове́рный *adj.* (*relig.*) belonging to different faith, creed.
иногда́, *adv.* sometimes.
иногоро́дн|ий *adj.* **1.** of, from another town; ~**яя по́чта** mail for, from other towns. **2.** *as n.* **и.,** ~**его** *m.* (*hist.*) non-Cossack peasant living in Cossack community.
инозе́м|ец, ца *m.* (*obs.*) foreigner.
инозе́мный *adj.* (*obs.*) foreign.
ин|о́й *adj.* **1.** different; other; ~**ы́ми слова́ми** in other words; **не кто и., как; не что ~о́е, как** none other than; **тот и́ли и.** one or other, this or that. **2.** some; **и. раз** sometimes; **и. (челове́к) мог и согласи́ться** some might agree.
и́нок, а *m.* monk.
и́нокин|я, и *f.* nun.
ин-окта́во *adv.* (*also as indecl. adj. and m. n.*) (*typ.*) octavo.
инокули́р|овать, ую *impf. and pf.* to inoculate.
инокуля́ци|я, и *f.* inoculation.
иномы́сли|е, я *nt.* (*obs.*) dissent, difference of opinion.
инопланета́рный *adj.* alien, extraterrestrial.
инопланетя́н|ин, а, *pl.* ~**е,** ~ *m.* alien, extraterrestrial.
иноплеме́нник, а *m.* (*obs.*) member of different tribe, nationality.
иноплеме́нный *adj.* (*obs.*) of another tribe, nationality; foreign.
иноро́д|ец, ца *m.* (*hist.*) non-Russian (*member of national minority in tsarist Russia*).
иноро́дн|ый *adj.* heterogeneous; ~**ое те́ло** (*med. or fig.*) foreign body.
иноро́д|ческий *adj. of* ~**ец**
иносказа́ни|е, я *nt.* allegory.
иносказа́тел|ьный (~ен, ~ьна) *adj.* allegorical.
иносла́вный *adj.* (*relig.*) non-Orthodox.
иностра́н|ец, ца *m.* foreigner.
иностра́нный *adj.* foreign.
инотде́л, а *m.* foreign department (*of Russian institutions*).
инофи́рм|а, ы *f.* foreign company.
инохо́д|ец, ца *m.* ambler (*horse*).
и́ноход|ь, и *f.* amble.
и́ноческий *adj.* monastic.
и́ночеств|о, а *nt.* monasticism; monastic life.
иноязы́чн|ый *adj.* **1.** speaking another language. **2.** belonging to another language; ~**ое сло́во** loan-word.
инсинуа́ци|я, и *f.* insinuation.
инсинуи́р|овать, ую *impf. and pf.* to insinuate.
инсоля́ци|я, и *f.* (*phys., med*) isolation.
инспекти́р|овать, ую *impf.* to inspect.
инспе́ктор, а, *pl.* ~**а́,** ~**о́в** *m.* inspector; (*mil.*) inspecting officer; **и. мане́жа** ringmaster; **порто́вый и.** harbourmaster.
инспе́ктор|ский *adj. of* ~
инспе́кци|я, и *f.* **1.** inspection; **и. на ме́сте** (*mil.*) on-site inspection. **2.** inspectorate.
инспира́тор, а *m.* inciter.
инспири́р|овать, ую *impf. and pf.* to incite; to inspire; **кто ~овал э́ту статью́?** who inspired this article?; **и. слу́хи** to start rumours.
инста́нци|я, и *f.* (*leg.*) instance; (*pol.*) level of authority; **суд пе́рвой ~и** court of first instance; **по ~ям** from instance to instance, through all stages; (*mil.*) **кома́ндная и.** chain of command.
инсти́нкт, а *m.* instinct.
инстинкти́в|ный (~ен, ~на) *adj.* instinctive.
институ́т, а *m.* **1.** institution; **и. бра́ка, и. ча́стной со́бственности** the institution of marriage, of private property. **2.** (*educational or scientific*) institute, institution; school; **медици́нский и.** medical school; **педагоги́ческий и.** teacher training college. **3.** girls' private boarding school (*in tsarist Russia*).
институ́тк|а, и *f.* boarding schoolgirl (*in tsarist Russia*); (*fig., coll.*) innocent, unsophisticated girl.
институ́т|ский *adj. of* ~ **2., 3.**
инструкта́ж, а *m.* instructing; (*mil., aeron.*) briefing.
инструкти́в|ный (~ен, ~на) *adj.* instructional.
инструкти́р|овать, ую *impf. and pf.* (*pf. also* **про~**) to instruct, give instructions to.
инстру́ктор, а *m.* instructor.
инстру́ктор|ский *adj. of* ~
инстру́кци|я, и *f.* instructions, directions.
инструме́нт, а *m.* instrument; tool, implement; (*sg.*; *collect.*) tools.
инструментали́ст, а *m.* (*mus.*) instrumentalist.
инструмента́льн|ая, ой *f.* tool-shop.
инструмента́льн|ый *adj.* **1.** (*mus.*) instrumental. **2.** (*tech.*) tool-making; ~**ая сталь** tool steel.

инструментáльщик, а *m.* tool-maker, instrument-maker.
инструментáри|й, я *m.* (*collect.*) instruments, tools.
инструмент|овáть, ýю *impf. and pf.* (*mus.*) to arrange for instruments.
инструментóвк|а, и *f.* (*mus.*) instrumentation.
инсулúн, а *m.* (*med.*) insulin.
инсýльт, а *m.* (*med.*) cerebral thrombosis; (apoplectic) stroke.
инсургéнт, а *m.* (*obs.*) insurgent.
инсуррéкци|я, и *f.* (*obs.*) insurrection.
инсценúр|овать, ую *impf. and pf.* **1.** to dramatize, adapt for stage *or* screen (*a novel, etc.*). **2.** (*fig.*) to feign, stage; **и. óбморок** to stage a faint.
инсценирóвк|а, и *f.* **1.** dramatization, adaptation for stage *or* screen. **2.** (*fig.*) pretence; act.
интегрáл, а *m.* (*math.*) integral.
интегрáльн|ый *adj.* (*math.*) integral; **~ое исчислéние** integral calculus.
интегрáци|я, и *f.* (*math.*) integration.
интегрúр|овать, ую *impf. and pf.* (*math.*) to integrate.
интеллéкт, а *m.* intellect; **искýсственный и.** (*comput.*) artificial intelligence.
интеллектуáл|ьный (~ен, ~на) *adj.* intellectual.
интеллигéнт, а *m.* member of the intelligentsia, intellectual.
интеллигéнт|ный (~ен, ~на) *adj.* cultured, educated.
интеллигéнт|ский *adj.* (*pej.*) *of* **~**; dilettante.
интеллигéнци|я, и *f.* **1.** (*hist.*) intelligentsia. **2.** (*collect.*) professional class(es).
интендáнт, а *m.* (*mil.*) quartermaster.
интендáнтств|о, а *nt.* (*mil.*) quartermaster service, commissariat.
интенсúв|ный (~ен, ~на) *adj.* intensive.
интенсифицúр|овать, ую *impf. and pf.* to intensify.
интервáл, а *m.* (*in var. senses*) interval; **и. строк** (*typ.*) line spacing.
интервéнт, а *m.* (*pol.*) interventionist.
интервéнци|я, и *f.* (*pol.*) intervention.
интервью́ *nt. indecl.* (*press*) interview; **и. в прямóм эфúре** live (*TV or radio*) interview.
интервьюéр, а *m.* (*press*) interviewer.
интервьюúр|овать, ую *impf. and pf.* to interview.
интерéс, а *m.* **1.** interest (= *attention*); **представля́ть и.** to be of interest; **проявúть и. (к)** to show interest (in). **2.** interest (= *advantage*); (*pl.*) interests; **какóй мне и.?** how do I stand to gain?; **в вáших ~ах поéхать** it is in your interest to go; **игрáть на и.** (*coll., obs.*) to play for money.
интерéснича|ть, ю *impf.* (*coll.*) to show off.
интерéсно *as pred.* it is, would be interesting; **и. знать, кто э́тот высóкий инострáнец** it would be interesting to know who the tall foreigner is; **и., что из негó вы́йдет** I wonder how he will turn out.
интерéс|ный (~ен, ~на) *adj.* **1.** interesting; **в ~ном положéнии** (*euph.*) in an interesting condition. **2.** striking, attractive.
интерес|овáть, ýю *impf.* to interest.
интерес|овáться, ýюсь *impf.* (*+i.*) to be interested (in).
интерлю́ди|я, и *f.* (*mus.*) interlude.
интермéди|я, и *f.* (*theatr.*) interlude.
интермéццо *nt. indecl.* (*mus.*) intermezzo.
интернáт, а *m.* **1.** boarding school. **2.** boarding house (*at private school*).
интернационáл, а *m.* **1.** international (*organization*); **Пéрвый И.** (*hist.*) the First International. **2. И.** the 'Internationale'.
интернационализáци|я, и *f.* internationalization.
интернационализúр|овать, ую *impf. and pf.* to internationalize.
интернационалúзм, а *m.* internationalism.
итнернационалúст, а *m.* internationalist.
интернационáльный *adj.* international.
интернúрова|нный *p.p.p. of* **~ть;** *as n.* **и., ~нного** *m.* internee.
интернúр|овать, ую *impf. and pf.* to intern.
интерпеллúр|овать *impf. and pf.* (*pol.*) to interpellate.
интерпелля́ци|я, и *f.* (*pol.*) interpellation; question in Parliament.
интерполúр|овать, ую *impf. and pf.* to interpolate.
интерполя́ци|я, и *f.* interpolation.
интерпретáтор, а *m.* interpreter (*expounder*).
интерпретáци|я, и *f.* interpretation; **нóвая и. рóли Гáмлета** a new interpretation of the part of Hamlet.
интерпретúр|овать, ую *impf. and pf.* to interpret (*expound*).
интерфéйс, а *m.* (*comput.*) interface.
интерферéнци|я, и *f.* (*phys.*) interference.
интерьéр, а *m.* (*art*) interior.
интúмност|ь, и *f.* intimacy.
интúм|ный (~ен, ~на) *adj.* intimate.
интоксикáци|я, и *f.* (*med.*) intoxication; **алкогóльная и.** alcoholic poisoning.
интонáци|я, и *f.* intonation.
интонúр|овать, ую *impf.* to intone.
интрúг|а, и *f.* **1.** intrigue. **2.** (*obs.*) (love-)affair. **3.** plot of story *or* play.
интригáн, а *m.* intriguer, schemer.
интригáн|ка, ки *f. of* **~**
интриг|овáть, ýю *impf.* **1.** (*no pf.*) to intrigue, carry on an intrigue. **2.** (*pf.* **за~**) to intrigue (*excite curiosity of*).
интродýкци|я, и *f.* (*mus.*) introduction.
интроспéкци|я, и *f.* introspection.
интуитивúзм, а *m.* (*phil.*) intuitionism.
интуитúв|ный (~ен, ~на) *adj.* intuitive.
интуúци|я, и *f.* intuition.
интурúст, а *m.* foreign tourist.
инфантéри|я, и *f.* (*obs.*) infantry.
инфантилúзм, а *m.* infantilism.
инфантúльный *adj.* infantile.
инфáркт, а *m.* (*med.*) infarct; infarction; coronary thrombosis; heart attack.
инфекциóнн|ый *adj.* infectious; **~ая больнúца** isolation hospital.
инфéкци|я, и *f.* infection.
инфернáльный *adj.* infernal, of hell.
инфильтрáци|я, и *f.* infiltration.
инфинитúв, а *m.* (*gram.*) infinitive.
инфицúр|овать, ую *impf. and pf.* to infect.
инфлюэ́нц|а, ы *f.* influenza.
инфля́ци|я, и *f.* (*econ.*) inflation.
ин-фóлио *adv.* (*also as indecl. adj. and m. n.*) (*typ.*) folio.
информáтик, а *m.* information scientist.
информáтик|а, и *f.* information science, informatics.
информáтор, а *m.* **1.** informant; **политúческий и.** political information officer. **2. автоматúческий и.** answering machine.
информ|ациóнный *adj. of* **~áция**
информáци|я, и *f.* information; news item.
Информбюрó *nt. indecl.* (*abbr. of* ***Информациóнное бюрó коммунистúческих и рабóчих пáртий***) (*hist.*) Cominform (*Communist Information Bureau*).
информúр|овать, ую *impf. and pf.* to inform.
инфракрáсный *adj.* infrared.
инфузóри|я, и *f.* (*zool.*) infusoria.
инцидéнт, а *m.* incident (*quarrel, clash*); **пограничный и.** frontier incident.
инъектúр|овать, ую, уешь *impf. and pf.* to inject.
инъéкци|я, и *f.* injection.
и. о. (*abbr. of* ***исполня́ющий обя́занности***) *+g.* acting ....
иóд, ~истый, ~ный, ~офóрм *see* **йод,** *etc.*
иóн, а *m.* (*phys.*) ion.
ионизáци|я, и *f.* (*phys., med.*) ionization.
ионúческ|ий *adj.* Ionian, Ionic; **~ая колóнна** Ionic column.
иóнный *adj.* (*phys., med.*) ionic.
Иордáн, а *f.* the Jordan (*river*).
иордáн|ец, ца *m.* Jordanian.
Иордáни|я, и *f.* Jordan.
иордáн|ка, ки *f. of* **~ец**
иордáнский *adj.* Jordanian.
иóта = **йóта**
иподья́кон, а *m.* (*eccl.*) subdeacon.
ипомé|я, и *f.* (*bot.*) morning glory.
ипостáс|ь, и *f.* (*theol.*) hypostasis.

ипоте́к|а, *f.* mortgage.
ипоте́|чный *adj. of* **~ка**
ипохо́ндрик, а *m.* hypochondriac.
ипохо́ндри|я, и *f.* hypochondria.
ипподро́м, а *m.* hippodrome; racecourse.
ипри́т, а *m.* mustard gas, yperite.
ИРА *f. indecl.* (*abbr. of* **Ирла́ндская республика́нская а́рмия**) IRA (*Irish Republican Army*).
Ира́к, а *m.* Iraq.
ира́к|ец, ца *m.* Iraqi.
ира́кский *adj.* Iraqi.
Ира́н, а *m.* Iran.
ира́н|ец, ца *m.* Iranian.
ира́н|ка, ки *f. of* **~ец**
ира́нский *adj.* Iranian.
ира́|чка, чки *f. of* **~кец**
и́рбис, а *m.* (*zool.*) ounce.
ири́ди|й, я *m.* (*chem.*) iridium.
иридодиагно́стик|а, и *f.* iridology.
иридо́лог, а *m.* iridologist.
и́рис, а *m.* (*bot.*) iris.
ири́с, а *m.* toffee.
ири́ск|а, и (*coll.*) *f.* (a) toffee.
ирла́нд|ец, ца *m.* Irishman.
Ирла́нди|я, и *f.* Ireland.
ирла́нд|ка, ки *f. of* **~ец**
ирла́ндский *adj.* Irish.
ирмо́с, а *m.* (*eccl. mus.*) introduction (*to hymn or canon*).
и́род, а *m.* (*coll.*) tyrant, monster.
ироке́з, а *m.* **1.** Iroquois. **2.** (*coll.*) Mohican (*hairstyle*).
иронизи́р|овать, ую *impf.* **(над)** to speak ironically (about).
ирони́ческий *adj.* ironic(al).
ирони́ч|ный (~ен, ~ьна) *adj.* = **~еский**
иро́ни|я, и *f.* irony.
иррациона́л|ьный (~ен, ~ьна) *adj.* irrational; **~ьное число́** (*math.*) irrational number, surd.
иррегуля́рн|ый *adj.* irregular; **~ые войска́** (*mil.*) irregulars.
ирригаци|я, и *f.* (*agric. and med.*) irrigation.
ис... *pref.* = **из...**
иск, а *m.* (*leg.*) suit, action; **предъяви́ть и. (к) кому́-н.** to sue, prosecute s.o., bring an action against s.o.; **отказа́ть в ~е** to reject a suit; **и. за клевету́** libel action; **и. за оскорбле́ние де́йствием** action for assault and battery.
искажа́|ть, ю *impf. of* **искази́ть**
искаже́ни|е, я *nt.* distortion, perversion; **~я в те́ксте** corruptions of a text.
искажённый *p.p.p. of* **искази́ть** *and adj.* distorted, perverted.
иска|зи́ть, жу́, зи́шь *pf.* (*of* **~жа́ть**) to distort, pervert, twist; to misrepresent; **боль ~зи́ла черты́ её лица́** pain has distorted her features; **и. чьи-н. слова́** to twist s.o.'s words; **и. фа́кты** to misrepresent the facts.
искале́ч|енный *p.p.p. of* **~ить** *and adj.* crippled, maimed.
искале́чива|ть, ю *impf. of* **искале́чить**
искале́ч|ить, у, ишь *pf.* (*of* **~ивать** *and* **кале́чить**) **1.** to cripple, maim. **2.** (*coll.*) to break.
иска́лыва|ть, ю *impf. of* **исколо́ть**
иска́ни|е, я *nt.* **1.** (*+g.*) search (for), quest (of). **2.** (*pl.*) strivings.
иска́п|ать, аю *pf.* (*of* **~ывать**[1]) (*coll.*) to sprinkle all over, spill all over; **и. свои́ брю́ки черни́лами** to spill ink all over one's trousers.
иска́пыва|ть[1]**, ю** *impf. of* **иска́пать**
иска́пыва|ть[2]**, ю** *impf. of* **ископа́ть**
иска́тел|ь, я *m.* **1.** seeker, searcher; **и. же́мчуга** pearl-diver. **2.** (*tech.*) (view-)finder.
иска́тел|ьный (~ен, ~ьна) *adj.* ingratiating.
иска́тельств|о, а *nt.* (*arch.*) obsequiousness.
иска́ть, ищу́, и́щешь *impf.* **1.** (*+a.*) to look for, search for; to seek (*sth. concr.*); **и. иго́лку, кварти́ру** to be looking for a needle, for a flat. **2.** (*+g.*) to seek, look for (*sth. abstr.*); **и. ме́ста** to look for a job; **и. слу́чая, сове́та** to seek an opportunity, seek advice. **3.** (**с**+*g. or* **на**+*p.*; *leg.*) to claim (from). **4.** (*+inf.*; *obs.*) to seek (to).

исключ|а́ть, а́ю *impf. of* **~и́ть**
исключа́|я *pres. ger. of* **~ть** *and prep.+g.* excepting, with the exception of; **и. прису́тствующих** the present company excepted.
исключе́ни|е, я *nt.* **1.** exception; **за ~ем** (*+g.*) with the exception (of). **2.** exclusion; expulsion; **по ме́тоду ~я** by process of elimination.
исключи́тельно *adv.* **1.** exceptionally. **2.** exclusively, solely. **3.** exclusive; **до страни́цы семь и.** to page seven exclusive.
исключи́тел|ьный (~ен, ~ьна) *adj.* **1.** exceptional; **и. слу́чай** exceptional case; **~ьной ва́жности** of exceptional importance. **2.** exclusive; **~ьное пра́во** exclusive right, sole right. **3.** (*coll.*) excellent.
исключ|и́ть, у́, и́шь *pf.* (*of* **~а́ть**) **1.** to exclude; to eliminate; **и. из спи́ска** to strike off a list. **2.** to expel; to dismiss. **3.** to rule out; **не ~ено́, что́ на́ши проигра́ют** our side could conceivably lose.
искове́рка|нный *p.p.p. of* **~ть** *and adj.* (*coll.*) corrupt(ed); **~нное сло́во** corrupted word, corruption.
искове́рка|ть, ю *pf. of* **кове́ркать**
иск|ово́й *adj. of* **~**; **~ово́е заявле́ние** (*leg.*) statement of claim.
иско́ж|а, и *f.* leatherette, leatherine.
искола́чива|ть, ю *impf. of* **исколоти́ть**
исколе|си́ть, шу́, си́шь *pf.* (*coll.*) to travel all over.
исколо|ти́ть, чу́, ~тишь *pf.* (*of* **искола́чивать**) (*coll.*) **1.** to beat; **и. кого́-н. до полусме́рти** to beat s.o. within an inch of his life. **2.** to spoil, damage by knocking in nails, etc.
искол|о́ть, ю́, ~ешь *pf.* (*of* **иска́лывать**) to prick all over, cover with pricks.
иско́мка|ть, ю *pf. of* **ко́мкать**
иско́м|ый *adj.* sought for; *as n.* **~ое, ~ого** *nt.* (*math.*) unknown quantity.
искони́, *adv.* (*rhet.*) from time immemorial.
иско́нный *adj.* primordial; immemorial.
ископа́ем|ое, ого *nt.* **1.** mineral. **2.** fossil (*also fig., iron.*).
ископа́емый *adj.* fossilized.
ископа́|ть, ю *pf.* (*of* **иска́пывать**[2]) to dig up.
искорёж|ить(ся), у(сь), ишь(ся) *pf. of* **корёжить(ся)**
искорене́ни|е, я *nt.* eradication.
искорен|и́ть, ю́, и́шь *pf.* (*of* **~я́ть**) to eradicate.
искорен|я́ть, я́ю *impf. of* **~и́ть**
и́скорк|а, и *f. dim. of* **и́скра**
и́скоса *adv.* (*coll.*) aslant, sideways; **взгляд и.** sidelong glance.
и́скр|а, ы *f.* spark; (*fig.*) flash; **промелькну́ть, как и.** to flash by; **и. наде́жды** glimmer of hope; **у меня́ ~ы из глаз посы́пались** (*coll.*) I saw stars.
искре́ни|е, я *nt.* (*tech.*) sparking.
и́скренн|е = **~о**
и́скрен|ний (~ен, ~на) *adj.* sincere, candid.
и́скренно *adv.* sincerely, candidly; **и. ваш, и. пре́данный вам** (*epistolary formula*) Yours sincerely; Yours faithfully.
и́скренност|ь, и *f.* sincerity, candour.
искрив|и́ть, лю́, и́шь *pf.* (*of* **~ля́ть**) to bend; (*fig.*) to distort.
искривле́ни|е, я *nt.* bend; (*fig.*) distortion; **и. позвоно́чника** curvature of the spine.
искривля́|ть, ю *impf. of* **искриви́ть**
искри́ст|ый (~, ~а) *adj.* sparkling.
искр|и́ть, и́т *impf.* (*tech.*) to spark.
и́скр|иться, ~и́тся *impf.* to sparkle; to scintillate (*also fig.*).
искровен|ённый *p.p.p. of* **~и́ть** *and adj.* blood-stained.
искровен|и́ть, ю́, и́шь *pf.* (*coll.*) **1.** to wound so as to draw blood. **2.** to stain with blood.
искр|ово́й *adj. of* **~а**; **и. зазо́р, и. промежу́ток** (*elec.*) spark-gap; **и. разря́дник** (*radio*) spark discharger; **и. телегра́ф** (*obs.*) wireless telegraph.
искрогаси́тел|ь, я *m.* (*tech.*) spark-extinguisher.
искромётный *adj.* sparkling; (*fig.*) **и. взгляд** flashing glance.
искромса́|ть, ю *pf. of* **кромса́ть**
искроудержа́тел|ь, я *m.* (*tech.*) spark-arrester.

искрош|и́ть, у́, ~́ишь *pf.* (*of* **кроши́ть**) to crumble; to mince; (*fig.*) to cut to pieces (*with sabres*).

искрош|и́ться, ~́ится *pf.* (*of* **кроши́ться**) to crumble (*intrans.*).

искупа́|ть[1], ю *pf.* (*coll.*) to bath.

искуп|а́ть[2], а́ю *impf. of* **~и́ть**

искупа́|ться[1], юсь *pf.* (*coll.*) to bathe; to take a bath.

искупа́|ться[2], юсь *impf., pass. of* **~ть[2]**

искупи́тел|ь, я *m.* (*theol.*) redeemer.

искупи́тел|ьный (~ен, ~ьна) *adj.* expiatory, redemptive; **~ьная же́ртва** sin offering.

искуп|и́ть, лю́, ~́ишь *pf.* (*of* **~а́ть[2]**) **1.** (*theol. and fig.*) to redeem; to expiate, atone for. **2.** to make up for, compensate for.

искупле́ни|е, я *nt.* redemption, expiation, atonement.

иску́с, а *m.* novitiate, probation (*in religious orders*); test, ordeal.

искус|а́ть, а́ю *pf.* (*of* **~́ывать**) to bite badly, all over; to sting badly, all over.

искуси́тел|ь, я *m.* tempter.

иску|си́ть, шу́, си́шь *pf. of* **~ша́ть**

иску|си́ться, шу́сь, си́шься *pf.* **1.** (**в**+*p.*) to become expert (at), become a past master (in, of). **2.** *pass. of* **~си́ть**

иску́сник, а *m.* (*coll.*) expert, past master.

иску́с|ный (~ен, ~на) *adj.* skilful; expert.

иску́сственник, а *m.* (*coll.*) bottle-fed baby.

иску́сственност|ь, и *f.* artificiality.

иску́сствен|ный *adj.* **1.** artificial, synthetic; man-made; **~ное пита́ние (младе́нца)** bottle feeding; **~ная цепь** (*tech.*) phantom circuit. **2.** (**~, ~на**) (*fig.*) artificial, feigned.

иску́сств|о, а *nt.* **1.** art; **изобрази́тельные, изя́щные ~а** fine arts. **2.** craftsmanship, skill; **и. верхово́й езды́** horsemanship; **де́лать что-н. из любви́ к ~у** to do sth. for its own sake.

искусствове́д, а *m.* art historian.

искусствове́дени|е, я *nt.* history of art, art history.

иску́сыва|ть, ю *impf. of* **искуса́ть**

искуша́|ть, ю *impf.* (*of* **искуси́ть**) to tempt; to seduce; **и. судьбу́** to tempt fate; tempt Providence.

искуше́ни|е, я *nt.* temptation; seduction; **ввести́ в и.** to lead into temptation; **подда́ться ~ю, впасть в и.** to yield to temptation.

искушённый *p.p.p. of* **искуси́ть** *and adj.* experienced; tested.

исла́м, а *m.* Islam.

исла́нд|ец, ца *m.* Icelander.

Исла́нди|я, и *f.* Iceland.

исла́нд|ка, ки *f. of* **~ец**

исла́ндский *adj.* Icelandic.

испа́ко|стить, щу, стишь *pf. of* **па́костить**

испа́н|ец, ца *m.* Spaniard.

Испа́ни|я, и *f.* Spain.

испа́нк|а[1], и *f.* Spanish woman.

испа́нк|а[2], и *f.* (*coll.*) Spanish 'flu.

испа́нский *adj.* Spanish.

испаре́ни|е, я *nt.* **1.** evaporation. **2.** exhalation; fumes.

испа́рин|а, ы *f.* perspiration.

испар|и́ть, ю́, и́шь *pf.* (*of* **~я́ть**) to evaporate (*trans.*); to exhale.

испар|и́ться, ю́сь, и́шься *pf.* (*of* **~я́ться**) to evaporate; (*fig., joc.*) to vanish into thin air.

испар|я́ть(ся), я́ю(сь) *impf. of* **~и́ть(ся)**

испа|ха́ть, шу́, ~́шешь *pf.* (*of* **~́хивать**) (*coll.*) to plough all over.

испа́хива|ть, ю *impf. of* **испаха́ть**

испа́чка|ть, ю *pf. of* **па́чкать**

испепел|и́ть, ю́, и́шь *pf.* (*of* **~я́ть**) to reduce to ashes, incinerate.

испепел|я́ть, я́ю *impf. of* **~и́ть**

испестр|ённый *p.p.p. of* **~и́ть** *and adj.* speckled, mottled; variegated.

испестр|и́ть, ю́, и́шь *pf.* (*of* **~я́ть**) to speckle; to mottle; to make variegated.

испестр|я́ть, я́ю *impf. of* **~и́ть**

испечённый *p.p.p. of* **испе́чь; вновь и.** (*coll.*) new-fledged.

испе́|чь, ку́, чёшь, ку́т, *past* **~̈к, ~кла́** *pf. of* **печь**

испещр|и́ть, ю́, и́шь *pf.* (*of* **~я́ть**) (+*a. and i.*) to spot (with); to mark all over (with); **и. сте́ну на́дписями** to cover a wall with inscriptions.

испещр|я́ть, я́ю *impf. of* **~и́ть**

испи|са́ть, шу́, ~́шешь *pf.* (*of* **~́сывать**) **1.** to cover with writing; **он уже́ ~са́л два́дцать тетра́дей** he has already filled up twenty exercise books. **2.** to use up (in writing) (*pencil, paper, etc.*).

испи|са́ться, шу́сь, ~́шешься *pf.* (*of* **~́сываться**) (*coll.*) **1.** to be used up (*of writing instrument*). **2.** to write o.s. out; to be used up (*of a writer*).

испи́сыва|ть(ся), ю(сь) *impf. of* **исписа́ть(ся)**

испито́й *adj.* (*coll.*) haggard, gaunt; hollow-cheeked.

испи́|ть, изопью́, изопьёшь, *past* **~л, ~ла́ ~ло** *pf.* **1.** (*dial.*) to have a drink of, sup. **2.** (*fig., rhet.*) to drain.

исповеда́л|ьня, ьни, *g. pl.* **~ен** *f.* (*eccl.*) confessional.

испове́дани|е, я *nt.* creed, confession (*of faith*).

испове́д|ать, аю *pf.* (*coll.*) = **~овать[1]**

испове́д|аться, аюсь *pf.* (*coll.*) = **~оваться[1]**

испове́д|овать[1], ую *impf. and pf.* **1.** (*eccl.*) to confess (*trans.*), hear confession (of). **2.** (*coll.*) to draw out. **3.** to confess.

испове́д|овать[2], ую *impf.* to profess (*a faith*).

испове́д|оваться[1], уюсь *impf. and pf.* **1.** (+*d. or* **у**; *eccl.*) to confess, make one's confession (to). **2.** (+*d. or* **пе́ред**; *fig., coll.*) to confess; to unburden o.s. of, acknowledge; **он мне ~овался в свои́х сомне́ниях** he confessed his doubts to me.

испове́д|оваться[2], уюсь *impf. and pf., pass. of* **~овать[2]**

исопове́дыва|ть(ся), ю(сь) *impf.* (*obs.*) = **испове́довать(ся)**

и́споведь, и *f.* (*eccl.*) confession; **быть на ~и** to be at confession.

испога́нива|ть, ю *impf. of* **испога́нить**

испога́н|ить, ю, ишь *pf.* (*of* **~ивать**) (*coll.*) to foul, defile.

испо́д, а *m.* (*dial.*) underside, bottom; wrong side (*of garment*).

и́сподволь *adv.* (*coll.*) in leisurely fashion; by degrees.

исподло́бья *adv.* from under the brows (*distrustfully, sullenly*).

исподни́зу *adv.* (*coll.*) from underneath.

испо́дн|ий *adj.* (*obs.*) under; *as n.* **~ее, ~его** *nt.* undergarment.

исподтишка́ *adv.* (*coll., pej.*) in an underhand way; on the quiet, on the sly; **смея́ться и.** to laugh in one's sleeve.

испоко́н *adv.*; *only in phrr.* **и. ве́ку, и. веко́в** from time immemorial.

испола́ть *int.* (*rhet.*) hail!

испо́лза|ть, ю *pf.* (*coll.*) to crawl all over.

исполи́н, а *m.* giant.

исполи́нский *adj.* gigantic.

исполко́м, а *m.* (*abbr. of* **исполни́тельный комите́т**) executive committee.

исполне́ни|е, я *nt.* **1.** fulfilment (*of wish*); execution (*of order*); discharge (*of duties*); **привести́ в и.** to carry out, execute. **2.** performance (*of play, etc.*); execution (*of music*); (*theatr., mus.*) **в ~и** (+*g.*) (as) played (by), (as) performed (by).

испо́лненный *p.p.p. of* **испо́лнить** *and adj.* (+*g.*) full (of).

исполни́м|ый (~, ~а) *adj.* feasible, practicable, realizable.

исполни́тел|ь, я *m.* **1.** executor; **суде́бный и.** bailiff. **2.** (*theatr., mus., etc.*) performer; **и. поп-му́зыки** pop musician; **соста́в ~ей** cast.

исполни́тельност|ь, и *f.* assiduity; expedition.

исполни́тел|ьный *adj.* **1.** executive; **и. лист** (*leg.*) writ, court order. **2.** (**~ен, ~ьна**) efficient and dependable.

испо́лн|ить[1], ю, ишь *pf.* (*of* **~я́ть**) **1.** to carry out, execute (*orders, etc.*); to fulfil (*a wish*); **и. обеща́ние** to keep a promise; **и. про́сьбу** to grant a request. **2.** to perform; **и. роль** (+*g.*) to take the part (of).

испо́лн|ить[2], ю, ишь *pf.* (*of* **~я́ть**) (+*a. and i. or g.*; *obs.*) to fill (with); **сообще́ние о побе́де ~ило всех ра́достью (ра́дости)** the report of the victory delighted everyone.

испо́лн|иться, юсь, ишься *pf.* (*of* **~я́ться**) **1.** to be fulfilled. **2.** (+*i. or g.*; *obs.*) to become filled (with). **3.** (*impers.*, +*d.*; *expr. passage of time*): **ему́ ~илось семь лет** he is seven, he was seven last birthday; **~илось пять**

лет с тех пор, как он уе́хал в Аме́рику five years have passed (it is five years) since he went to America.
исполн|я́ть(ся), я́ю(сь) *impf. of* **~и́ть(ся); ~я́ющий обя́занности** (+*g.*) acting.
исполос|ова́ть, у́ю *pf. of* **полосова́ть**
и́сполу *adv.* half and half; **де́лать что-н. и.** to go halves; **обрабо́тать зе́млю и.** to farm land on the métayage system.
испо́льзовани|е, я *nt.* utilization; **повто́рное и.** recycling.
испо́льз|овать, ую *impf. and pf.* to make (good) use of, utilize; to turn to account.
испо́льщик, а *m.* métayer; sharecropper (*under half-and-half system*).
испо́льщин|а, ы *f.* métayage, sharecropping.
испо́р|тить(ся), чу(сь), тишь(ся) *pf. of* **по́ртить(ся)**
испо́рченност|ь, и *f.* depravity.
испо́рчен|ный *p.p.p. of* **испо́ртить** *and adj.* **1.** depraved; corrupted. **2.** (*of perishable goods, etc.*) spoiled; bad, rotten; **~ные зу́бы** rotten teeth; **~ное мя́со** tainted meat. **3.** (*coll.*) spoiled (*child*).
испоха́б|ить, лю, ишь *pf.* (*coll.*) to corrupt.
испо́шл|ить, ю, ишь *pf.* (*coll.*) to vulgarize.
исправи́лк|а, и *f.* (*coll.*) reformatory.
исправи́м|ый (~, ~а) *adj.* corrigible.
исправи́тельно-трудово́й *adj.* corrective labour; **и.-т. ко́декс** corrective labour code.
исправи́тельный *adj.* correctional; corrective; **и. дом** reformatory.
испра́в|ить, лю, ишь *pf.* (*of* **~ля́ть**) **1.** to rectify, correct, emend. **2.** to repair, mend. **3.** to reform, improve, amend.
испра́в|иться, люсь, ишься *pf.* (*of* **~ля́ться**) **1.** to improve (*intrans.*); to reform (*intrans.*), turn over a new leaf. **2.** *pass. of* **~ить**
исправле́ни|е, я *nt.* **1.** correcting; repairing. **2.** improvement; correction; **и. текста** emendation of a text.
испра́влен|ный *p.p.p. of* **испра́вить** *and adj.* improved, corrected; **~ное изда́ние** revised edition; **и. хара́ктер** reformed character.
исправля́|ть, ю *impf.* **1.** *impf. of* **испра́вить. 2.** (*obs.*): **и. обя́занности** (+*g.*) to carry out the duties (of), act as.
исправля́|ться, юсь *impf. of* **испра́виться**
испра́вник, а *m.* (*hist.*) police chief (*head of uyezd constabulary in tsarist Russia*).
испра́вност|ь, и *f.* **1.** good condition; **в (по́лной) ~и** in good working order, in good repair. **2.** punctuality; preciseness; meticulousness.
испра́в|ный (~ен, ~на) *adj.* **1.** in good order. **2.** punctual; precise; meticulous.
испражне́ни|е, я *nt.* **1.** defecation. **2.** faeces.
испражн|и́ться, ю́сь, и́шься *pf. of* **~я́ться**
испражн|я́ться, я́юсь *impf.* (*of* **~и́ться**) to defecate.
испра́шива|ть, ю *impf.* (*of* **испроси́ть**) to beg, solicit; **и. ми́лость** to ask a favour.
испро́б|овать, ую *pf.* **1.** to test. **2.** to make trial of, try out; **и. все возмо́жности** to try everything, leave no stone unturned.
испро|си́ть, шу́, ~́сишь *pf.* (*of* **испра́шивать**) to obtain (by asking).
испрям|и́ть, лю́, и́шь *pf.* (*of* **~ля́ть**) (*coll.*) to straighten (out).
испрямля́|ть, ю *impf. of* **испрями́ть**
испу́г, а (у) *m.* fright; alarm; **с ~у** from fright.
испу́ганный *p.p.p. of* **испуга́ть** *and adj.* frightened, scared, startled.
испуга́|ть(ся), ю(сь) *pf. of* **пуга́ть(ся)**
испуска́|ть, ю *impf. of* **испусти́ть**
испу|сти́ть, щу́, ~́стишь *pf.* (*of* **~ска́ть**) to emit, let out; **и. вздох** to heave a sigh; **и. дух** to breathe one's last; **и. крик** to utter a cry.
испыта́ни|е, я *nt.* **1.** test, trial; (*fig.*) ordeal; **быть на ~и** to be on trial, be on probation. **2.** examination; **вступи́тельные ~я, приёмные ~я** entrance examination.
испы́т|анный *p.p.p. of* **~а́ть** *and adj.* tried, well-tried.
испыта́тел|ь, я *m.* tester; **лётчик-и.** test pilot.
испыта́тельн|ый *adj.* test, trial; probationary; **~ая коми́ссия** examining board; **и. полёт** test-flight; **и. полиго́н** (*mil.*) testing ground; **и. пробе́г** trial run; **и. срок, и. стаж** period of probation; **~ая ста́нция** experimental station.
испыт|а́ть, а́ю *pf.* (*of* **~́ывать**) **1.** to test, put to the test; **и. чьё-н. терпе́ние** to try s.o.'s patience. **2.** to feel, experience.
испыту́ющий *adj.*: **и. взгляд** searching look.
испы́тыва|ть, ю *impf. of* **испыта́ть**
иссека́|ть, ю *impf. of* **иссе́чь**
и́ссера- *comb. form* grey-; **и.-голубо́й** grey-blue.
иссече́ни|е, я *nt.* (*med.*) excision, removal (*by means of operation*).
иссе́|чь[1], ку́, чёшь, ку́т, *past* **~к, ~кла́** *pf.* (*of* **~ка́ть**) **1.** (*obs.*) to carve (*in stone, etc.*). **2.** (*med.*) to excise, remove (*by means of operation*).
иссе́|чь[2], ку́, чёшь, ку́т, *past* **~к, ~кла** *pf.* (*of* **~ка́ть**) **1.** to cut up, cleave. **2.** (*obs.*) to cut (*with a whip, etc.*), lash, cover with lashes.
и́ссиня- *comb. form* bluish-.
иссле|ди́ть, жу́, ди́шь *pf.* (*of* **~́живать**) (*coll.*) to cover with dirty footprints.
иссле́довани|е, я *nt.* **1.** investigation; research; exploration; **и. больно́го** examination of a patient; **и. кро́ви** blood analysis, test; **он занима́ется ~ями по ру́сской исто́рии** he is engaged in research on Russian history. **2.** (*scientific*) paper; study.
иссле́довател|ь, я *m.* researcher; investigator; explorer.
иссле́довательский *adj.* research.
иссле́д|овать уюю *impf. and pf.* to investigate, examine; to research into; to explore; to analyse.
иссле́жива|ть, ю *impf. of* **исследи́ть**
иссо́х|нуть, ну, нешь, *past* **~, ~ла** *pf.* (*of* **иссыха́ть**) **1.** to dry up. **2.** to wither; (*fig., coll.*) to decline, fade away.
и́сстари *adv.* from of old, of yore; **так и. ведётся** it is an old custom.
исстрада́|ться, юсь *pf.* to become worn out, wretched (with suffering).
исстре́лива|ть ю *impf. of* **исстреля́ть**
исстрел|я́ть, я́ю *pf.* (*of* **~́ивать**) **1.** to use up (*ammunition*). **2.** (*coll.*) to riddle (*with shot*).
исступле́ни|е, и *nt.* frenzy; **и. восто́рга** ecstasy, transport; **гне́вное и.** rage.
исступлённост|ь, и *f.* state of frenzy.
исступлённый *adj.* frenzied; ecstatic.
иссуш|а́ть, а́ю *impf. of* **~и́ть**
иссуш|и́ть, у́, ~́ишь *pf.* (*of* **~а́ть**) to dry up; (*fig.*) to consume, waste.
иссыха́|ть, ю *impf. of* **иссо́хнуть**
иссяк|а́ть, а́ю *impf. of* **~́нуть**
иссяќ|нуть, ну, нешь, *past* **~, ~ла** *pf.* (*of* **~а́ть**) to run dry, dry up; (*fig.*) to run low, fail.
istáплива|ть, ю *impf. of* **истопи́ть**
istáск|анный *p.p.p. of* **~а́ть** *and adj.* **1.** worn out; threadbare. **2.** (*fig., coll.*) worn; haggard.
истаск|а́ть, а́ю *pf.* (*of* **~́ивать**) to wear out.
истаск|а́ться, -а́юсь *pf.* (*of* **~́иваться**) to wear out (*intrans.*); (*fig., coll.*) to be worn out.
istáскива|ть(ся), ю(сь) *impf. of* **истаска́ть(ся)**
istáчива|ть, ю *impf. of* **источи́ть[1]**
istá|ять, ю, ешь *pf.* to melt (completely); **и. от тоски́** to pine, languish.
истека́|ть, ю *impf. of* **исте́чь**
исте́|кший *p.p. of* **~чь** *and adj.* past, preceding; **в тече́ние ~кшего го́да** during the past year; **15-го числа́ ~кшего ме́сяца** on the 15th ult(imo).
истер|е́ть, изотру́, изотрёшь, *past* **~́, ~́ла** *pf.* (*of* **истира́ть**) **1.** to grate. **2.** to wear out, use up (*by rubbing*); **и. в порошо́к** to reduce to powder.
истер|е́ться, изотрётся, *past* **~́ся, ~́лась** *pf.* (*of* **истира́ться**) to wear out (*intrans.*), be worn out (*by rubbing*).
исте́рз|анный *p.p.p. of* **~а́ть** *and adj.* tattered, lacerated; (*fig.*) tormented.
истерза́|ть, ю *pf.* **1.** to tear in pieces; to mutilate. **2.** to torment, worry the life out of.

исте́рик, а *m.* hysterical man.
исте́рик|а, и *f.* hysterics.
истери́ческий *adj.* hysterical; **и. припа́док** fit of hysterics.
истери́чк|а, и *f.* hysterical woman.
истери́ч|ный (~ен, ~на) *adj.* hysterical.
истери́|я, и *f.* (*med.*) hysteria; (*fig.*): **вое́нная и.** war hysteria.
истёртый *p.p.p. of* **истере́ть** *and adj.* worn, old.
ист|е́ц, ца́ *m.* (*leg.*) plaintiff; petitioner (*in divorce case*).
истече́ни|е, я *nt.* **1.** outflow; **и. кро́ви** haemorrhage. **2.** expiry, expiration; **по ~и сро́ка каранти́на** on the expiry of the quarantine period.
исте́|чь, ку́, чёшь, ку́т, *past* **~́к, ~кла́** *pf.* (*of* **~ка́ть**) **1.** (*obs.*) to flow out. **2.: и. кро́вью** to bleed profusely; (*fig., rhet.*) to pour out one's life-blood. **3.** to expire, elapse; **вре́мя ~кло́** time is up.
и́стин|а, ы *f.* truth; **изби́тая и.** truism; **свята́я и.** God's truth; gospel truth; **во ~у** (*obs.*) in truth, verily.
и́стин|ный (~ен, ~на) *adj.* true, veritable; **~ная высота́** true altitude; **~ное со́лнечное вре́мя** apparent solar time.
истира́ни|е, я *nt.* abrasion.
истира́|ть(ся), ю(сь) *impf. of* **истере́ть(ся)**
истле|ва́ть, ва́ю *impf. of* **~́ть**
истле́|ть, ю *pf.* (*of* **~ва́ть**) **1.** to rot, decay. **2.** to smoulder to ashes.
истма́т, а *m.* (*abbr. of* **истори́ческий материали́зм**) historical materialism.
и́стово *adv.* (*obs.*) properly, religiously, devoutly; assiduously, punctiliously; **и. крести́ться** to cross o.s. religiously.
и́стов|ый (~, ~а) *adj.* (*obs.*) proper; devout; assiduous, punctilious.
исто́к, а *m.* source.
истолкова́ни|е, я *nt.* interpretation, commentary.
истолкова́тел|ь, я *m.* interpreter, commentator, expounder.
истолк|ова́ть, у́ю *pf.* (*of* **~о́вывать**) to interpret, expound; to comment upon; **и. замеча́ние в дурну́ю сто́рону** to put a nasty construction on a remark.
истолко́выва|ть, ю *impf. of* **истолкова́ть**
истол|о́чь, ку́, чёшь, ку́т, *past* **~о́к, ~кла́** *pf.* to pound, crush.
исто́м|а, ы *f.* lassitude; (*pleasurable*) languor.
истом|и́ть, лю́, и́шь *pf.* (*of* **томи́ть** *and* **~ля́ть**) to exhaust, weary.
истом|и́ться, лю́сь, и́шься *pf.* (*of* **~ля́ться**) **(от)** to be exhausted, worn out (with, from); to be weary (of); **и. от жа́жды** to be faint with thirst.
истом|лённый *p.p.p. of* **~и́ть** *and adj.* exhausted, worn out.
истомля́|ть(ся), ю(сь) *impf. of* **истоми́ть(ся)**
истоп|и́ть, лю́, ~́ишь *pf.* (*of* **иста́пливать**) **1.** to heat up. **2.** (*coll.*) to spend, use up (*fuel*). **3.** to melt down.
истопни́к, а́ *m.* stoker, boiler-man.
истоп|та́ть, чу́, ~́чешь *pf.* **1.** to trample (down, over). **2.** (*coll.*) to wear out (*footwear*).
исторг|а́ть, а́ю *impf. of* **~́нуть**
исто́рг|нуть, ну, нешь, *past* **~, ~ла** *pf.* (*of* **~а́ть**) **1.** (*rhet.*) to throw out, expel; **и. из свое́й среды́** to ostracize. **2.** (**у** *or* **из**; *obs.*) to rest, wrench (from); (*fig.*) to force (from), extort; **и. обеща́ние** to extort a promise.
истори́зм, а *m.* historical method.
исто́рийк|а, и *f.* (*coll.*) **1.** anecdote, story. **2.** episode, incident.
исто́рик, а *m.* historian.
историо́граф, а *m.* historiographer.
историогра́фи|я, и *f.* historiography.
истори́ческий *adj.* **1.** historical. **2.** historic.
истори́чност|ь, и *f.* historicity.
истори́ч|ный (~ен, ~на) *adj.* historical.
исто́ри|я, и *f.* **1.** history; **войти́ в ~ю** to go down in history. **2.** (*coll.*) story. **3.** (*coll.*) incident, event; scene, row; **вчера́ случи́лась со мно́й заба́вная и.** a funny thing happened to me yesterday; **вот так и.!** here's a pretty kettle of fish!; **ве́чная** (*or* **обы́чная**) **и.!** the (same) old story!

истоск|ова́ться, у́юсь *pf.* (**по**+*d.*) to yearn (for); to be wearied with longing (for).
источ|а́ть, а́ю *impf.* (*of* **~и́ть**[2]) (*obs.*) to shed; to give off, impart.
источ|и́ть[1]**, у́, ~́ишь** *pf.* (*of* **иста́чивать**) **1.** to grind down. **2.** to eat away, gnaw through.
источ|и́ть[2]**, у́, ~́ишь** *pf. of* **~а́ть**
исто́чник, а *m.* **1.** spring. **2.** (*fig.*) source; **и. информа́ции** source of information; **ве́рный и.** reliable source; **и. све́та** source of light; **и. боле́зни** (*med.*) nidus; **служи́ть ~ом** (+*g.*) to be a source (of).
источникове́дени|е, я *nt.* source study.
исто́шный *adj.* (*coll.*) heart-rending.
истощ|а́ть(ся), а́ю(сь) *impf. of* **~и́ть(ся)**
истоще́ни|е, я *nt.* emaciation; exhaustion; depletion; **война́ на и.** war of attrition.
истощ|ённый *p.p.p. of* **~и́ть** *and adj.* emaciated; exhausted.
истощ|и́ть, у́, и́шь *pf.* (*of* **~а́ть**) to emaciate; to exhaust; to drain, sap; **и. ко́пи** to work out mines.
истощ|и́ться, у́сь, и́шься *pf.* (*of* **~а́ться**) to become emaciated; to become exhausted (*also fig.*); **все на́ши запа́сы ~и́лись** all our supplies had run out.
истра́|тить, чу, тишь *pf. of* **тра́тить**
истра́|титься, чусь, тишься *pf.* **1.** *pass. of* **~тить. 2.** (*coll.*) to overspend.
истреби́тел|ь, я *m.* **1.** destroyer. **2.** fighter (*aircraft*); **и.-бомбардиро́вщик** fighter bomber; **и.-перехва́тчик** interceptor fighter.
истреби́тель|ный *adj.* **1.** destructive. **2.** *adj. of* **~ 2.; ~ная авиа́ция** fighters (*collect.*), Fighter Command.
истреб|и́ть, лю́, и́шь *pf.* (*of* **~ля́ть**) to destroy; to exterminate, extirpate.
истребле́ни|е, я *nt.* destruction; extermination, extirpation.
истребля́|ть, ю *impf. of* **истреби́ть**
истре́бовани|е, я *nt.* demand, order.
истре́б|овать, ую *pf.* to obtain on demand.
истрёп|анный *p.p.p. of* **~а́ть** *and adj.* torn, frayed; worn.
истреп|а́ть, лю́, ~́лешь *pf.* (*of* **~́ывать**) to tear, fray; to wear to rags; **и. не́рвы** (*coll.*) to fray one's nerves.
истрёпыва|ть, ю *impf. of* **истрепа́ть**
истре́ска|ться, ется *pf.* (*coll.*) to crack, become cracked.
истука́н, а *m.* idol, statue (*fig., coll.; of a pers. devoid of feeling or understanding*).
и́стый *adj.* true, genuine; keen; **и. учёный** a true scholar; **и. люби́тель живо́тных** a genuine animal-lover.
исты́к|ать, аю *pf.* (*of* **~ивать**) (*coll.*) to riddle, pierce all over.
исты́кива|ть, ю *impf. of* **исты́кать**
истяза́ни|е, я *nt.* torture.
истяза́тел|ь, я *m.* torturer.
истяза́|ть, ю *impf.* to torture.
исхле|ста́ть, щу́, ~́щешь *pf.* (*of* **~́стывать**) (*coll.*) **1.** to lash, flog. **2.** to wear out (*a whip*).
исхлёстыва|ть, ю *impf. of* **исхлеста́ть**
исхлопа́тыва|ть, ю *impf. of* **исхлопота́ть**
исхлопо|та́ть, чу́, ~́чешь *pf.* (*of* **исхлопа́тывать**) (*coll.*) to obtain (*by dint of application in the right quarters*).
исхо́д, а *m.* **1.** outcome, issue; end; **быть на ~е** to be nearing the end, be coming to an end; **на ~е дня** towards evening; **день был на ~е** the day was drawing to a close. **2.** (*bibl.*) **И.** (*the Book of*) Exodus.
исхода́тайств|овать, ую *pf.* to obtain (*by petition, after official application*).
исхо|ди́ть[1]**, жу́, ~́дишь** *pf.* (*coll.*) to go, walk all over.
исхо|ди́ть[2]**, жу́, ~́дишь** *impf.* (*of* **изойти́**) **1.** (*impf. only*) (**из**) to issue (from), come (from); to emanate (from); **отку́да ~ди́л э́тот слух?** where did this rumour come from? **2.** (*impf. only*) (**из**) to proceed (from), base o.s. (on); **и. из необосно́ванных предположе́ний** to proceed from unfounded assumptions. **3.: и. кро́вью** to become weak through loss of blood; **и. слеза́ми** to cry one's heart out.
исхо́дн|ый *adj.* initial; **~ая то́чка, ~ое положе́ние** point of departure; **и. пункт маршру́та** (*aeron.*) flight departure point; **~ая ста́дия** initial phase.

исходя́щ|ая, ей *f.* outgoing paper.
исхуда́лый *adj.* emaciated, wasted.
исхуда́ни|е, я *nt.* emaciation.
исхуда́|ть, ю *pf.* to become emaciated, become wasted.
исцара́п|ать, аю *pf.* (*of* **~ывать**) to scratch badly; to scratch all over.
исцара́пыва|ть, ю *impf. of* **исцара́пать**
исцеле́ни|е, я *nt.* **1.** healing, cure. **2.** recovery.
исцел|и́мый *pres. part. pass. of* **~и́ть** *and adj.* curable.
исцели́тел|ь, я *m.* healer.
исцел|и́ть, ю́, и́шь *pf.* (*of* **~я́ть**) to heal, cure.
исцел|я́ть, я́ю *impf. of* **~и́ть**
исча́ди|е, я *nt.* (*rhet.*) offspring, progeny; *esp. in phr.* **и. а́да** fiend, devil incarnate.
исча́х|нуть, ну, нешь, *past* **~, ~ла** *pf.* to waste away.
исчез|а́ть, а́ю *impf.* (*of* **~́нуть**) to disappear, vanish.
исчезнове́ни|е, я *nt.* disappearance.
исче́з|нуть, ну, нешь, *past* **~, ~ла** *pf. of* **~а́ть**
исчёрк|ать, аю (*and* **~а́ть, ~а́ю**) *pf.* **1.** to cover with crossings-out. **2.** to scribble all over.
и́счерна- *comb. form* blackish-.
исче́рп|ать, аю *pf.* (*of* **~ывать**) **1.** to exhaust, drain; **и. все свои́ сре́дства** to exhaust all one's resources; (*fig.*): **и. терпе́ние** to exhaust s.o.'s patience. **2.** to settle, conclude; **и. вопро́с** to settle a question; **и. пове́стку дня** to conclude the agenda.
исче́рпыва|ть, ю *impf. of* **исче́рпать**
исче́рпыва|ющий *pres. part. act. of* **~ть** *and adj.* exhaustive.
исчер|ти́ть, чу́, ~́тишь *pf.* (*of* **~́чивать**) **1.** to cover with lines. **2.** to use up (*pencil, chalk, etc.*).
исче́рчив|ать, ю *impf. of* **исчерти́ть**
исчи́рка|ть, ю *pf.* (*coll.*) to use up (*matches*).
исчисле́ни|е, я *nt.* calculation; (*math.*) calculus.
исчи́сл|ить, ю, ишь *pf.* (*of* **~я́ть**) to calculate, compute; to estimate.
исчисл|я́ть, я́ю *impf. of* **~́ить**
исчисля́|ться, ется *impf.* (*+i. or* **в**+*a.*) to amount to, come to; to be estimated (at); **убы́тки ~лись в сто рубле́й** the damages came to one hundred roubles; **поте́ри ~ются ты́сячами** the casualties are estimated at thousands.
ита́к *conj.* thus; so then.
Ита́ли|я, и *f.* Italy.
италья́н|ец, ца *nt.* Italian.
италья́н|ка, ки *f. of* **~ец**
италья́нск|ий *adj.* Italian; **~ая забасто́вка** sit-down strike; work-to-rule.
и т. д. (*abbr. of* ***и так да́лее***) etc., etcetera, and so on.
итерати́вный *adj.* (*ling.*) iterative.
ито́г, а *m.* **1.** sum, total; **о́бщий и.** grand total. **2.** (*fig.*) result; **подвести́ и.** to sum up; **в ~е** as a result, in the upshot; **в коне́чном ~е** in the end.
итого́ *adv.* in all, altogether.
ито́говый *adj.* total, final.
ито́ж|ить, у, ишь *impf.* to sum up, add up.
и т. п. (*abbr. of* ***и тому́ подо́бное***) etc., etcetera, and so on.
итте́рби|й, я *m.* (*chem.*) ytterbium.
итти́ = идти́
и́ттри|й, я *m.* (*chem.*) yttrium.
иудаи́зм, а *m.* Judaism.
иуде́|й, я *m.* Jew (*by religion*).
иуде́й|ка, ки *f. of* **~**
иуде́йский *adj.* (*hist. and relig.*) Judaic.
их[1] *a. and g. of* **они́**
их[2] *possessive adj.* **1.** their(s); **их маши́на ме́ньше, чем на́ша** their car is smaller than ours. **2.** (*obs.*; *in formal speech*) his; her; **э́то их пальто́** this is her coat.
ихневмо́н, а *m.* (*zool.*) ichneumon.
и́хний *possessive adj.* (*coll.*) their(s).
ихтиоза́вр, а *m.* ichthyosaurus.
ихтио́л, а *m.* (*med.*) ichthyol
ихтио́лог, а *m.* ichthyologist.
ихтиологи́ческий *adj.* ichthyological.
ихтиоло́ги|я, и *f.* ichthyology.
иша́к, а́ *m.* **1.** donkey, ass (*also fig.*). **2.** hinny.
иша́|чий *adj. of* **~к**
и́шиас, а *m.* (*med.*) sciatica.
ишь *int.* (*coll.*) *expr. surprise or disgust*: look!; **и. ты! = и.!** *or expr. disagreement or objection.*
ище́йк|а, и *f.* bloodhound, tracker dog, sleuth-hound (*also fig., pej.*).
и́щущий *pres. part. act. of* **иска́ть** *and adj.*: **и. взгляд** searching, wistful look.
ию́л|ь, я *m.* July.
ию́ль|ский *adj. of* **~**
ию́н|ь, я *m.* June.
ию́нь|ский *adj. of* **~**

Й

Йе́мен, а *m.* Yemen.
йе́мен|ец, ца *m.* Yemeni.
йе́мен|ка, ки *f. of* **~ец**
йе́менский *adj.* Yemeni.
йе́ти *m. indecl.* yeti, abominable snowman.
йог, а *m.* yogi.
йо́г|а, и *f.* yoga.
йогу́рт, а *m.* yog(h)urt.
йод, а *m.* iodine.
йо́дист|ый *adj.* (*chem.*) containing iodine; **й. ка́лий** potassium iodide; **~ая соль** iodized salt.
йо́д|ный *adj. of* **~**; **и. раство́р** tincture of iodine.
йодофо́рм, а *m.* iodoform.
йот, а *m.* (*ling.*) *letter* J; yod (*name of sound* [j]).
йо́т|а, ы *f.* iota; **ни на ~у** not a jot, not an iota.
йота́ци|я, я *f.* (*ling.*) appearance of yod before vowel; vowel softening.
йоти́р|овать, ую *impf. and pf.* (*ling.*) to pronounce (*vowels*) with yod; to give soft pronunciation.
Йоха́ннесбург, а *m.* Johannesburg.

К

°К (*abbr. of* **гра́дусов по Ке́львину**) K., degrees Kelvin; **273°К** 273K.
к (*abbr. of* **кило́**) k, kg, kilo(s), kilogram(s).
к, ко *prep.+d.* **1.** (*of space and fig.*) to, towards; **мы приближа́лись к Берли́ну** we were nearing Berlin; **прислони́те его́ к стене́** place it against the wall; **лицо́м к лицу́** face to face; **к лу́чшему** for the better; **моли́тва к Бо́гу** prayer to God; **любо́вь к де́тям** love of children; **к о́бщему удивле́нию** to everyone's surprise; **к (не)сча́стью** (un)fortunately; **к чёрту его́!** to hell with him!; **шля́па ей к лицу́** her hat becomes her; **к ва́шим услу́гам** at your service; (*in addition to*) **приба́вить три к пяти́** to add three and five; **к тому́ же** besides, moreover. **2.** (*of time*) to, towards; by; **зима́ подходи́ла к концу́** winter was drawing to a close; **к утру́** towards morning, by morning; **к пе́рвому января́** by the first of January; **я приду́ к восьми́ (часа́м)** I will be there by eight (o'clock); **к тому́ вре́мени**

by then, by that time; **к сро́ку** on time. **3.** for; **к чему́?** what for?; **э́то ни к чему́** it is no good, no use; **к обе́ду, к у́жину** *etc.*, for dinner, for supper, *etc.* **4.** (*in titles of pamphlets, articles in newspapers and periodicals, etc.*) on; on the occasion of; **к столе́тию со дня рожде́ния Льва Толсто́го** on (the occasion of) the centenary of the birth of Lev Tolstoy; **к вопро́су о...** *oft. requires no translation.*

-ка *particle* (*coll.*) **1.** *modifying force of imper.*: **скажи́-ка мне** come on now, tell me; **да́й-ка мне посмотре́ть** come on, let me take a look; **ну́-ка** well; **ну́-ка спо́йте что-н.!** come on, give us a song! **2.** *with 1st pers. sg. of fut., expr. tentative decision*: **напишу́-ка ей письмо́** I think I'll write to her; **куплю́-ка тот га́лстук** maybe I'll buy that tie.

каба́к, а́ *m.* (*obs.*) tavern, low bar; (*coll., fig.*) pigsty.

кабал|а́, ы́ *f.* **1.** (*hist.*) kabala (*agreement exacting obligation of labour for creditor in case of non-payment of debt*). **2.** (*hist.*) debt-slavery, kabala slavery. **3.** (*fig.*) servitude, bondage.

к. (*abbr. of* **копе́йка**) k, kopeck(s).

кабал|и́ть, ю́, и́шь *impf.* to enslave.

каба́л|ьный (~ен, ~ьна) *adj.* **1.** relating to, bound by kabala; **к. холо́п** kabala serf. **2.** (*fig.*) imposing bondage, enslaving; **~ьные усло́вия** crushing terms. **3.** (*fig.*) in bondage.

каба́н[1]**, а́** *m.* **1.** wild boar. **2.** boar (*male domestic pig*).

каба́н[2]**, а́** *m.* block (*of unprocessed mineral ore, etc.*).

каба́н|ий *adj. of* ~[1]

кабар|га́, ги́, *g. pl.* **~о́г** *f.* (*zool.*) musk-deer.

кабарди́н|ец, ца *m.* Kabardinian.

кабаре́ *nt. indecl.* cabaret.

каба́тчик, а *m.* (*obs.*) publican, tavern-keeper.

каба́|цкий *adj.* **1.** *adj. of* **~к. 2.** (*fig., coll.*) coarse, vulgar; **~цкие нра́вы** public bar manners; **голь ~цкая** (*folk poet.*) tavern riff-raff.

кабач|о́к[1]**, ка́** *m.* **1.** *dim. of* **каба́к. 2.** (*coll.*) small restaurant.

кабач|о́к[2]**, ка́** *m.* vegetable marrow.

каббал|а́, ы́ *f.* (*relig. and fig.*) cab(b)ala.

каббали́стик|а, и *f.* (*relig. and fig.*) cab(b)alism.

каббалисти́ческий *adj.* (*relig. and fig.*) cab(b)alistic.

ка́бел|ь, я *m.* (*elec. and naut.*) cable; **возду́шный к.** overhead cable; **к. абоне́нта** service cable.

ка́бель|ный *adj. of* ~; **к. кана́т** cable-laid rope; **~ное телеви́дение** cable television.

ка́бельтов, а, *pl.* **~ы, ~ых, ~ым, ~ыми** *m.* (*naut.*) **1.** cable('s length) (*measure = 185.2 metres*). **2.** cable, hawser.

ка́бельтовый *adj.* (*naut.*) of one cable's length.

кабеста́н, а *m.* (*tech.*) capstan.

каби́н|а, ы *f.* cabin; cockpit; cab (*of a lorry*); cubicle; booth; **(для купа́льщиков)** bathing-hut.

кабине́т[1]**, а** *m.* **1.** study; consulting-room, surgery; **физи́ческий к.** physics laboratory; **лингафо́нный к.** language laboratory; **отде́льный к.** private room (*in restaurant*); **к. заду́мчивости** (*euph., joc.*) lavatory; **к. красоты́** beauty parlour. **2.** suite (*of furniture*).

кабине́т[2]**, а** *m.* (*pol.*) cabinet.

кабине́т|ный *adj.* **1.** *adj. of* ~[1]. **2.: к. портре́т** cabinet photograph. **3.** (*fig.*) theoretical; **к. учёный, страте́г** armchair scientist, strategist.

каби́н|ка, ки *f. dim. of* **~а**

каблогра́мм|а, ы *f.* cable(gram).

каблу́к, а́ *m.* heel (*of footwear*); **ту́фли на рези́новых ~а́х** rubber-heeled shoes; **быть под ~о́м у кого́-н.** (*fig., coll.*) to be under s.o.'s thumb.

каблуч|о́к, ка́ *m.* **1.** *dim. of* **каблу́к. 2.** (*archit.*) ogee.

кабота́ж, а *m.* **1.** cabotage; coasting-trade. **2.** coastal shipping.

кабота́жник, а *m.* coaster, coasting vessel.

кабота́жнича|ть, ю *impf.* to coast; to ply coastwise.

кабота́ж|ный *adj. of* ~; **~ное пла́вание** coastwise navigation.

кабриоле́т, а *m.* cabriolet.

Кабу́л, а *m.* Kabul.

кабы *conj.* (*coll. and folk poet.*) if; **е́сли бы да к.,** *see* **е́сли**

кавале́р[1]**, а** *m.* **1.** partner (*at dance*); (*in mixed company on social occasions*) (gentle-)man; **была́ весёлая вечери́нка, но ~ов не хвата́ло** it was a good party but there were not enough men. **2.** (*coll.*) admirer, cavalier; **да́мский к.** carpet-knight.

кавале́р[2]**, а** *m.* **(о́рдена)** knight, holder (of an order); **гео́ргиевский к.** holder of the St George Cross.

кавалерга́рд, а *m.* horse-guardsman.

кавалерга́рд|ский *adj. of* ~

кавалер|и́йский *adj.* **1.** *adj. of* **~́ия. 2.** of a cavalryman, of a horseman.

кавалери́ст, а *m.* **1.** cavalryman. **2.** (*coll.*) horseman.

кавале́ри|я, и *f.* cavalry; **лёгкая к.** light horse.

кавале́рственн|ый *adj. only in phr.* **~ая да́ма** Dame of the Order of St Catherine.

кавалька́д|а, ы *f.* cavalcade.

кавarда́к, а́ *m.* (*coll.*) mess, muddle.

ка́верз|а, ы *f.* (*coll.*) **1.** chicanery. **2.** mean trick, dirty trick; **устро́ить ~у кому́-н.** to play s.o. a mean trick.

ка́вер|зить, жу, зишь *impf.* (*of* **на~**) (*coll., pej.*) to play mean, dirty tricks.

ка́верзник, а *m.* (*coll.*) one who plays (enjoys playing) mean, dirty tricks.

ка́верзный *adj.* (*coll.*) **1.** (*pej.*) given to playing mean, dirty tricks. **2.** tricky, ticklish.

каве́рн|а, ы *f.* (*med. and geol.*) cavity.

Кавка́з, а *m.* Caucasus.

кавка́з|ец, ца *m.* Caucasian.

кавка́з|ка, ки *f. of* **~ец**

кавка́зский *adj.* Caucasian.

каву́н, а *m.* (*dial.*) water-melon.

кавы́ч|ки, ек *no sg.* inverted commas, quotation marks; **откры́ть к.** to quote; **закры́ть к.** to unquote; **в ~ках** in inverted commas, in quotes; (*fig., coll.*) so-called, would-be; **демокра́тия в ~ках** so-called 'democracy'; **знато́к в ~ках** would-be expert.

кага́л, а *m.* **1.** (*hist.*) kahal (*assembly of elders of Jewish communes*). **2.** (*fig., coll.*) bedlam, uproar.

кагебе́шник, а *m.* (*coll.*) KGB agent.

кагеби́ст = кагебе́шник

кагэбэ́шник = кагебе́шник

када́стр, а *m.* (*leg.*) land-survey.

када́стровый *adj.* (*leg.*) cadastral.

каде́нци|я, и *f.* **1.** (*mus. and liter.*) cadence. **2.** (*mus.*) cadenza.

каде́т[1]**, а** *m.* cadet.

каде́т[2]**, а** *m.* (*abbr. of* **конституцио́нный демокра́т**) (*pol., hist.*) Constitutional Democrat (*abbr.* Cadet).

каде́т|ский[1] *adj. of* ~[1]; **к. ко́рпус** (*hist.*) military school.

каде́т|ский[2] *adj. of* ~[2]

кади́л|о, а *nt.* (*eccl.*) thurible, censer.

кади́л|ьный *adj.* **1.** *adj. of* **~о. 2.** of incense; **к. за́пах** smell of incense.

Ка́дис, а *m.* Cadiz.

ка|ди́ть, жу́, ди́шь *impf.* (*eccl.*) to burn incense; (*+d.; fig., coll.*) to burn incense to, flatter.

ка́дк|а, и *f.* tub, vat.

ка́дми|й, я *m.* (*chem.*) cadmium.

ка́дочник, а *m.* cooper.

ка́д|очный *adj. of* **~ка**

кадр[1]**, а** *m.* **1.** (*mil.*) cadre; (*pl.; collect.*) (regular, peace-time) establishment; **он слу́жит в ~́ах** he is a regular (soldier). **2.** (*pl. only*) personnel; **отде́л ~́ов** personnel department (*of institution, factory, etc.*). **3.** (*pl. only*) specialists; skilled workers (*esp. of trained functionaries of a political party*); **руководя́щие ~́ы парти́йной организа́ции Моско́вской о́бласти** the leadership of the Party organization in Moscow oblast.

кадр[2]**, а** *m.* (*cinema*) **1.** frame, still. **2.** close-up.

кадри́л|ь, и *f.* quadrille (dance).

кадрови́к, а́ *m.* **1.** (*mil.*) regular (soldier). **2.** member of permanent staff; experienced, skilled man.

ка́дровый *adj.* **1.** (*mil.*) regular. **2.** experienced, skilled; trained.

кады́к, а́ *m.* (*coll.*) Adam's apple.

каёмк|а, и *f.* (*coll.*) *dim. of* **кайма́**

каёмчатый *adj.* with edge(s), with border(s).
каждéни|е, я *nt.* (*eccl.*) censing.
каждогóдный *adj.* (*obs.*) annual.
каждоднéвный *adj.* daily; diurnal.
кáжд|ый *adj.* **1.** every, each; **к. день** every day; **~ые два дня** every two days; **~ую веснý** every spring; **к. из них получи́л по пять фýнтов** they received five pounds each; **на ~ом шагý** at every step. **2.** *as n.* everyone; **всех и ~ого** (*coll.*) all and everyone, all and sundry.
кажи́сь (*coll.*, *dial.*) it seems, it would seem.
ка|жý[1], **ди́шь** *see* **~ди́ть**
ка|жý[2], **~́жешь** *see* **~зáть**
казáк, á, *pl.* **~́и́** *m.* Cossack; **игрáть в ~и́-разбóйники** to play cowboys and Indians *or* cops and robbers.
казаки́н, а *m.* kazakin (*man's knee-length coat with pleated skirt*).
казáн, á *m.* (*dial.*) copper (*vessel*).
Казáн|ь, и *f.* Kazan.
казáрм|а, ы *f.* barracks (*also fig.*; *coll. of ugly, clumsy buildings*).
казáрм|енный *adj. of* **~а;** (*fig.*, *pej.*): **к. вид** barrack-like appearance; **~енная острóта** barrack-room humour.
ка|зáть, жý, ~́шешь *impf.* (*coll.*) to show; **не к. глаз, нóсу** not to show up.
ка|зáться, жýсь, ~́жешься *impf.* (*of* **показáться**) **1.** to seem, appear; **он ~́жется ýмным** he appears clever; **онá ~́жется стáрше свои́х лет** she looks older than she is. **2.** (*impers.*): **(мне,** *etc.*) **~́жется, ~зáлось** it seems, seemed (to me, *etc.*); apparently; **мне ~́жется, что он был прав** I think he was right; **всё, ~зáлось, шло хорошó** everything seemed to be going well; **зáвтра, ~́жется, начинáются егó кани́кулы** apparently his holidays begin tomorrow; **вы, ~́жется, из Москвы́?** you are from Moscow, I believe?; **~зáлось бы** it would seem, one would think.
казáх, а *m.* Kazakh.
казáхский *adj.* Kazakh.
Казахстáн, а *m.* Kazakhstan.
казáцкий *adj.* Cossack.
казáчеств|о, а *nt.* (*collect.*) the Cossacks.
казáчий *adj.* Cossack.
казá|чка, чки *f. of* **~к**
казач|óк[1], **кá** *m.* **1.** (*coll.*) *affectionate dim. of* **казáк. 2.** (*hist.*) page, boy-servant.
казач|óк[2], **кá** *m.* kazachok (*Ukrainian dance*).
казá|шка, шки *f. of* **~х**
казеи́н, а *m.* (*chem.*) casein.
казеи́н|овый *adj. of* **~**
каземáт, а *m.* casemate.
казёнк|а, и *f.* (*coll.*, *obs.*) **1.** state liquor store, wine-shop. **2.** (state-retailed) vodka.
казённик, а *m.* breech ring (*of firearm*).
казённокóштный *adj.* (*obs.*): **к. студéнт** state-aided student, student receiving education and maintenance at state expense.
казённ|ый *adj.* **1.** (*hist.*) fiscal; of State, of Treasury; **~ое имýщество** State property; **на к. счёт** at public cost; (*joc.*, *coll.*) free, gratis; **~ое винó** (*obs.*) vodka (*sold under State monopoly*); **~ая палáта** (provincial) revenue department. **2.** (*fig.*) bureaucratic, formal; **к. язы́к** language of officialdom, official jargon. **3.** (*fig.*) banal, undistinguished, conventional. **4.: ~ая часть = казнá 4.**
казёнщин|а, ы *f.* (*coll.*) **1.** conventionalism. **2.** red tape.
казими́р, а *m.* (*text.*) kerseymere.
казими́р|овый *adj. of* **~**
казинó *nt. indecl.* casino.
казн|á, ы́ *no pl.*, *f.* **1.** (*hist.*) Exchequer, Treasury; public purse, public coffers. **2.** the State (*as a legal pers.*); **перейти́ из чáстных рук в ~ý** to pass from private ownership to the State. **3.** (*folk poet.*) money; property. **4.** (*mil.*) breech, breech end.
казначé|й, я *m.* **1.** treasurer, bursar. **2.** (*mil.*) paymaster; (*naut.*) purser.
казначéй|ский *adj.* **1.** *of* **~. 2.** *of* **~ство; к. билéт** treasury note.
казначéйств|о, а *nt.* Treasury, Exchequer.
казначéйш|а, и *f.* (*obs.*, *coll.*) wife of treasurer.
казначé|я, и *f.* (*eccl.*) treasurer.
казн|и́ть, ю́, и́шь *impf. and pf.* **1.** to execute, put to death. **2.** (*impf. only*; *fig.*) to punish, chastise; to castigate.
казн|и́ться, ю́сь, и́шься *impf.* **1.** *pass. of* **~и́ть. 2.** (*coll.*) to blame o.s.; to torment o.s. (*with remorse*).
казнокрáд, а *m.* embezzler of public funds.
казнокрáдств|о, а *nt.* embezzlement of public funds.
казн|ь, и *f.* execution, capital punishment; **смéртная к.** death penalty; (*fig.*) torture, punishment.
кáзов|ый *adj.* (*obs.*) for show; **к. товáр** shop-window goods; **~ая сторонá дéла** the bright side of the affair.
казуáльный *adj.* random; accidental.
казуáр, а *m.* (*zool.*) cassowary.
казуи́ст, а *m.* casuist (*also fig.*).
казуи́стик|а, и *f.* casuistry (*also fig.*).
казуисти́ческий *adj.* casuistic(al).
кáзус, а *m.* **1.** (*leg.*) exceptional case, special case; (*med.*) isolated case. **2.** (*coll.*) extraordinary occurrence; **вот так к.!** here's an amazing thing; here's a rum start! **3.: к. бéлли** casus belli.
кáзусный *adj.* (*obs.*) involved.
Кáин, а *m.* (*coll.*) Cain (*fratricide, murderer*).
кáин|ов *adj. of* **~; ~ова печáть** the mark of Cain.
Каи́р, а *m.* Cairo.
кайл|á, ы́ *f.* (miner's) hack.
кайл|ó, á *nt.* = **~á**
ка|ймá, ймы́, *pl.* **~ймы, ~ём, ~ймáм** *f.* edging, border; hem, selvedge.
каймáн, а *m.* (*zool.*) cayman.
кайнозóйский *adj.* (*geol.*) Cenozoic.
кáйр|а, ы *f.* (*zool.*) guillemot.
кайф, а *m.* (*sl.*) kicks, 'high'; turn-on; buzz; **быть под ~ом** (*sl.*) to be spaced out; **лови́ть к.** (*sl.*) to get stoned.
кайф|овáть, ýю *impf.* (*sl.*) **1.** to get stoned *or* smashed (*on drugs* or *alcohol*). **2.** to enjoy o.s.
кайфóвый *adj.* (*sl.*) cool, far-out, mind-blowing.
кайфолóм, а *m.* (*sl.*) killjoy, party-pooper.
как[1] *adv. and particle* **1.** how; **к. вам нрáвится Москвá?** how do you like Moscow?; **к. чýдно!** how wonderful! **к. вы поживáете?** how do you do?; **к. (вáши) делá?** how are you getting on?; **забы́л, к. э́то дéлается** I have forgotten how to do this; **к. вам не сты́дно!** you ought to be ashamed!; **к. егó фами́лия, к. егó зовýт?** what is his name?, what is he called?; **к. называ́ется э́тот цветóк?** what is this flower called?; **к. вы дýмаете?** what do you think?; **к. егó женá отнóсится к э́тому вопрóсу?** what does his wife think about the question?; *expr. surprise and/or displeasure*; **к.! ты опя́ть здесь** what! are you here again?; **к. же так?** how is that?; (*coll.*): **к. знать?** who knows?; (*coll.*) **к. сказáть** it all depends; **кýпишь ли э́то для меня́? ну, э́то ещё к. сказáть** will you buy it for me? well, that all depends; (*coll.*): **к. есть** completely, utterly; **он к. есть дурáк** he is a complete fool; (*coll.*): **расскажи́ нам, к. и что** tell us all about it, tell us how it's going; (*coll.*): **к.-никáк** nevertheless, for all that; **к.-никáк, но мы попáли вó время** nevertheless, we managed to arrive in time; **к. же** (*coll. or iron.*) naturally, of course. **2.** *with fut. tense of pf. vv. expr. suddenness of action*: (*coll.*): **мы спокóйно слýшали рáдио, а — он к. вскóчит!** we were listening quietly to the wireless when all of a sudden he jumped up; **онá к. закричи́т!** she suddenly cried out. **3.: к. ни, к.... ни** however; **к. ни пóздно** however late it is; **к. он ни умён** clever as he is; **к. ни старáйтесь** however hard you may try, try as you may. **4.** (*following* **бедá, прéлесть, страх, ужáсно,** *etc.*, *in elliptical construction*; *coll.*) terribly, awfully, wonderfully, etc.; **мне страх к. хóчется пить!** I have a terrible thirst!; **онá прéлесть к. одéта** she is beautifully dressed.
как[2] *conj.* **1.** as; like; **бéлый, к. снег** white as snow; **совéтую тебé э́то к. друг** I give this advice as a friend; **он говори́т по-рýсски к. настоя́щий рýсский** he speaks Russian like a native; **бýдьте к. дóма** make yourself at home; **к. напримéр** as, for instance; **к. нарóчно** as luck would have it; **к. попáло** anyhow, at sixes and sevens; (*with comp.*) **к.**

мо́жно, к. нельзя́ as … as possible; **к. мо́жно, скоре́е** as soon as possible; **к. нельзя́ лу́чше** as well as possible. **2.: к...., так и** both … and; **к. ма́льчики, так и де́вочки** both the boys and the girls. **3.** *following vv. of perceiving not translated*: **я ви́дел, к. она́ ушла́** I saw her go out; **ты слы́шал, к. часы́ би́ли по́лночь?** did you hear the clock strike midnight? **4.** (*coll.*) when; since; **к. пойдёшь, зайди́ за мной** when you go, call for me; **прошло́ два го́да, к. мы встре́тились** it is two years since we met; **к. ско́ро** (*obs.*), **к. то́лько** as soon as, when; **к. вдруг** when suddenly. **5.** (+*neg.*) but, except, than; **что ему́ остава́лось де́лать, к. не созна́ться?** what could he do but confess? **6.: в то вре́мя к.; до того́ к.; ме́жду тем к.; тогда́ к.,** *see* **вре́мя, до, ме́жду, тогда́. 7.: к. бу́дто, к. бы, к.-либо, к.-нибудь, к. ра́з, к.-то** *see separate entries.*

кака́: (*baby-talk*) **сде́лать к.** to (do a) poo.

какаду́ *m. indecl.* (*zool.*) cockatoo.

кака́о *nt. indecl.* **1.** cocoa. **2.** cacao(-tree).

кака́о|вый *adj. of* ~; **~вые бобы́** cocoa-beans.

ка́к|ать, аю *impf.* (*baby-talk*) to (do a) poo.

кака́шк|а, и *f.* (*vulg.*) turd.

как бу́дто 1. *conj.* as if, as though; **она́ побледне́ла, к. б. уви́дела при́зрак** she turned pale as if she had seen a ghost; **к. б. вы не зна́ете!** as if you didn't know! **2.** *particle* (*coll.*) apparently, it would seem; **они́ к. б. за́втра прие́дут** apparently they are coming tomorrow.

как бы 1. (+*inf.*) how; **к. б. э́то сде́лать?** how is it to be done, I wonder. **2.: к. б. ни** however; **к. б. то ни́ было** however that may be, be that as it may. **3.** as if, as though; **к. б. в шу́тку** as if in jest. **4.: к. б. не** (*expr. anxious expectation*) what if, supposing; (*following v.*) (that, lest); **к. б. он не был в дурно́м настрое́нии!** what if he is in a bad temper!; **бою́сь, к. б. он не был в дурно́м настрое́нии!** I am afraid (that) he may be in a bad temper. **5.** (*coll.*): **к. б. не так!** not likely, certainly not.

ка́к-либо *adv.* somehow.

ка́к-нибудь *adv.* **1.** somehow (or other). **2.** (*coll.*) anyhow; **он всё де́лает к.-н.** he does things all anyhow. **3.** (*coll.*) some time; **загляни́те к.-н.** look in some time.

как-ника́к *adv.* (*coll.*) nevertheless, for all that.

како́в (~а́, ~о́, ~ы́) *pron.* (*interrog., and in exclamations expr. strong feeling*) what; of what sort; **к. результа́т?** what is the result?; **к. он?** what is he like?; **к. он собо́й?** what does he look like?; **а пого́да-то ~а́!** what (*splendid, filthy*) weather!; **вот он к.!** (*coll.*) what a chap!

каково́ *adv.* (*coll.*) how; **к. ему́ живётся?** how is he getting on?; **к. мне э́то слы́шать!** I am extremely sorry to hear it.

каково́й *rel. pron.* (*obs.*) which.

как|о́й *pron.* **1.** (*interrog. and rel.; and in exclamations*) what; **~и́е у вас впечатле́ния о Ло́ндоне?** what are your impressions of London?; **~о́е сего́дня число́?** what is today's date?; **~и́м о́бразом?** how?; **не зна́ю, ~у́ю кни́гу ему́ дать** I don't know what book to give him; **~а́я беда́!** what a misfortune, how unfortunate!; **~а́я на́глость!** what impudence!; **~а́я хоро́шенькая де́вушка!** what a pretty girl! **2. (тако́й) к.** such as; **он (тако́й) плут, ~и́х никогда́ не быва́ло** he is a rogue such as never was, there has never been such a rogue; **гнев, ~о́го он никогда́ не испы́тывал** anger such as he had never felt. **3.: к. ни** whatever, whichever; **к. есть, к. ни на есть** (*coll.*): whatever you please, any you please; **дай мне ~у́ю ни на есть кни́гу** give me any book you please. **4.** *expr. negation*: (*in rhet., questions*) **к. он учёный?** what kind of scholar is that?, how can you call him a scholar?; (*coll.*) **понра́вился ли тебе́ э́тот фильм? ~о́е! я не вы́терпел и получа́са!** did you like the film? what! I stuck it less than half an hour; **~о́е там** nothing of the kind, quite the contrary; **ты хорошо́ спал? ~о́е там!** did you sleep well? I most certainly did not! **5.: к. тако́й?** which (exactly)?; **пришёл Ивано́в. — К. тако́й Ивано́в?** Ivanov is here. Which Ivanov? **6.** (*coll.*) any; **нет ли у вас ~о́го вопро́са?** have you any questions?; **ни в ~у́ю** in no circumstances, not for anything.

како́й-либо *pron.* = **како́й-нибудь 1.**

как|о́й-нибудь *pron.* **1.** some; any; **мы э́то сде́лаем ~и́м-н. спо́собом** we shall do it somehow; **да́йте мне кни́гу хоть ~у́ю-н.** give me a book, any one at all. **2.** (*with numerals*) some (*and not more*), only; **за́мок нахо́дится в ~и́х-н. трёх киломе́трах отсю́да** the castle is some three kilometres from here; **~и́е-н. пять рубле́й** some five roubles.

как|о́й-то *pron.* **1.** some, a. **2.** a kind of; **э́то ~а́я-то боле́знь** it is a kind of disease.

какофони́ческий *adj.* cacophonous.

какофо́ни|я, и *f.* cacophony.

как ра́з *adv.* just, exactly; **к. р. то, что мне ну́жно** just what I need; **к. р. вас я иска́л** you are the very pers. I was looking for; *as pred.*: **э́ти ту́фли мне к. р.** these shoes are just right.

ка́к-то *adv.* **1.** somehow; **он к.-то ухитри́лся сде́лать э́то** he managed to do it somehow; **в э́том до́ме к.-то всегда́ хо́лодно** somehow it is always cold in this house. **2.** how; **посмотрю́, к.-то он вы́вернется из э́того положе́ния** I wonder how he will get himself out of this situation. **3.** (*coll.*): **к.-то (раз)** once. **4.** namely, as for example.

ка́ктус, а *m.* (*bot.*) cactus.

кал, а *m.* faeces, excrement.

каламбу́р, а *m.* pun.

каламбури́ст, а *m.* punster.

каламбу́р|ить, ю, ишь *impf.* (*of* **с~**) to pun.

каламбу́рный *adj.* punning.

каламя́нк|а, и *f.* (*text.*) stout linen cloth; calamanco.

каланч|а́, и́, *g. pl.* **~е́й** *f.* watch-tower; **пожа́рная к.** fire observation tower; (*fig., coll.*) bean-pole.

кала́ч, а́ *m.* kalach (*kind of white, wheatmeal loaf*); **меня́ ~о́м туда́ не зама́нишь** (*coll.*) nothing will induce me to go there; (*fig., coll.*) **тёртый к.** pers. who has knocked about the world.

кала́чиком *adv.* (*coll.*) in the shape of a kalach; **лежа́ть к.** to lie curled up.

кала́ч|ный *adj. of* ~

калейдоско́п, а *m.* kaleidoscope.

калейдоскопи́ческий *adj.* kaleidoscopic.

кале́к|а, и *c.g.* cripple.

календа́р|ный *adj. of* **~ь; к. ме́сяц** calender month; **~ное и́мя** name derived from that of a saint.

календа́р|ь, я́ *m.* calender; (*sport*) fixture list.

кале́нд|ы, ~ *no sg.* (*hist.*) calends.

кале́ни|е, я *nt.* incandescence; **бе́лое к.** white heat; **довести́ до бе́лого ~я** (*fig., coll.*) to rouse to fury.

калён|ый *adj.* **1.** red-hot. **2.: ~ые оре́хи** roasted nuts.

кале́ч|ить, у, ишь *impf.* (*of* **искале́чить**) to cripple, maim, mutilate; (*fig.*) to twist, pervert.

кале́ч|иться, усь, ишься *impf.* (*of* **искале́читься**) **1.** to become a cripple. **2.** *pass. of* **~ить**

ка́ли *nt. indecl.* (*chem.; obs.*) potash; *now only in phr.* **е́дкое к.** caustic potash.

кали́бр, а *m.* **1.** calibre. **2.** (*tech.*) gauge.

калибр|ова́ть, у́ю *impf.* (*tech.*) to calibrate.

калибро́вк|а, и *f.* (*tech.*) calibration.

ка́лиевый *adj.* (*chem.*) potassic, potassium.

ка́ли|й, я *m.* (*chem.*) potassium.

кали́йн|ый *adj.* (*chem.*) potassium; **~ое удобре́ние** potash fertilizer.

кали́к|а, и *m.* **1.** (*hist.*) pilgrim. **2.** (*folk poet.*): **~и перехо́жие** wandering minstrels.

кали́льн|ый *adj.* (*tech.*): **к. жар** temperature of incandescence; **~ая печь** temper furnace; **~ая се́тка** (incandescent) mantle.

кали́н|а, ы *no pl., f.* (*bot.*) guelder rose, snowball-tree.

кали́н|овый *adj. of* **~а**

кали́тк|а, и *f.* (wicket-)gate.

кал|и́ть, ю́, и́шь *impf.* **1.** (*tech.*) to heat. **2.** to roast (*chestnuts, etc.*).

кали́ф, а *m.* caliph; **к. на час** (*iron.*) king for a day.

калифорни́|ец, йца *m.* Californian.

калифорни́|йка, йки *f. of* **~ец**

калифорни́йский *adj.* Californian.

Калифо́рни|я, и *f.* California.

каллиграфи́ческий *adj.* calligraphic.

каллигра́фи|я, и *f.* calligraphy.
калмы́к, а́ *m.* Kalmuck, Kalmyk.
калмы́цкий *adj.* Kalmuck, Kalmyk.
калмы́|чка, чки *f. of* **~к**
ка́л|овый *adj. of* **~**
ка́ломел|ь, и *f.* calomel.
калори́йност|ь, и *f.* calorie content.
калори́йный *adj.* high-calorie; fattening.
калори́метр, а *m.* (*phys.*) calorimeter.
калориме́три|я, и *m.* (*phys.*) calorimetry.
калори́фер, а *m.* (*tech.*) heater, radiator.
кало́ри|я, и *f.* calorie; **больша́я к.** large (kilogram-)calorie; **ма́лая к.** small (gram-)calorie.
кало́ш|а, и *f.* = **гало́ша**
калу́жниц|а, ы *f.* (*bot.*) king-cup, marsh marigold.
калы́м, а *no pl., m.* **1.** (*ethnol.*) bride-money. **2.** (*coll.*) earnings on the side.
калы́м|ить, лю, ишь *impf.* (*coll.*) to moonlight, do work on the side.
калы́мщик, а *m.* (*coll.*) moonlighter.
кальвини́зм, а *m.* Calvinism.
кальвини́ст, а *m.* Calvinist.
кальвинисти́ческий *adj.* Calvinistic(al).
ка́л|ька, ьки, *g. pl.* **~ек** *f.* **1.** tracing-paper. **2.** (tracing-paper) copy. **3.** (*ling.*) loan translation, calque.
кальки́р|овать, ую *impf.* (*of* **с~**) **1.** to trace. **2.** (*ling.*) to make a loan translation of.
калькули́р|овать, ую *impf.* (*of* **с~**) (*comm.*) to calculate.
калькуля́тор, а *m.* (*comm.*) calculator.
калькуля|цио́нный *adj. of* **~́ция; ~цио́нная ве́домость** cost sheet; cost record.
калькуля́ци|я, и *f.* (*comm.*) calculation.
Кальку́тт|а, ы *f.* Calcutta.
кальма́р, а *m.* (*zool.*) squid.
кальсо́н|ы, ~ *no sg.* pants, drawers.
ка́льциевый *adj.* (*chem.*) calcium, calcic.
ка́льци|й, я *m.* (*chem.*) calcium.
кальцина́ци|я, и *f.* (*chem.*) calcination.
кальци́т, а *m.* (*min.*) calcite.
кальја́н, а *m.* hookah.
каля́ка|ть, ю *impf.* (*of* **по~**) (*coll.*) to chat.
кама́зский *adj.* KamAZ (*of the Kama motor-vehicle factory*).
камари́ль|я, и *f.* camarilla, clique.
кама́ринск|ая, ой *f.* kamarinskaya (*Russ. folk-dance*).
ка́мбал|а, ы *f.* **1.** flat-fish (*generic term*). **2.** plaice; flounder.
ка́мби|й, я *m.* (*bot.*) cambium.
Камбо́дж|а, и *f.* Cambodia.
камбоджи́|ец, йца *m.* Cambodian.
камбоджи́|йка, йки *f. of* **~ец**
камбоджи́йский *adj.* Cambodian.
ка́мбуз, а *m.* (*naut.*) galley, caboose.
камво́льный *adj.* (*text.*) worsted.
каме́дистый *adj.* gummy.
каме́д|ь, и *f.* gum.
камел|ёк, ька́ *m.* fire-place.
каме́ли|я, и *f.* (*bot.*) camellia.
камене́|ть, ю *impf.* (*of* **о~**) to become petrified, turn to stone; (*fig.*) to harden (*intrans.*).
камени́ст|ый (~, ~а) *adj.* stony.
ка́менк|а[1], и *f.* stove (*in bath-house in rural Russia*).
ка́менк|а[2], и *f.* (*zool.*) wheat-ear.
каменноуго́льн|ый *adj.* coal; **к. бассе́йн** coal-field; **~ые ко́пи** coal-mine.
ка́менн|ый *adj.* **1.** stone-; stony; **к. век** the Stone Age; **~ая кла́дка** stone-work; **~ая соль** rock-salt; **к. у́голь** coal; **~ая боле́знь** (*med.*) gravel; **к. мешо́к** (*hist.*; *rhet.*) prison cell; **к. о́кунь** bass (*fish*). **2.** (*fig.*) stony; hard, immovable; **~ое се́рдце** stony heart.
каменоло́м|ня, ни, *g. pl.* **~ен** *f.* quarry.
каменотёс, а *m.* (stone)mason.
ка́менщик, а *m.* (stone)mason, bricklayer; (*hist.*): **во́льные ~и** Freemasons.
ка́м|ень, ня, *pl.* **~ни, ~не́й** *and* (*coll.*) **~е́нья, ~е́ньев** *m.* stone; tartar; **зубно́й к.** dental tartar; **па́дать ~нем** to fall like a stone; **~ня на ~не не оста́вить** to raze to the ground; (*fig.*): **боса́ть ~нем (в+*a.*)** to cast stones (at); **у него́ к. на се́рдце лежи́т** a weight sits heavy on his heart; **держа́ть к. за па́зухой (на+*a.*, про́тив)** to harbour a grudge (against); **к. с души́ мое́й свали́лся** a load has been taken off my mind.
ка́мер|а, ы *f.* **1.** chamber (*in var. senses*); **морози́льная к.** freezer compartment (*of refrigerator*); **тюре́мная к.** prison cell; **к. хране́ния (багажа́)** cloak-room. **2.** **(фотографи́ческая) к.** camera. **3.** inner tube (*of tyre*); bladder (*of football*).
камерге́р, а *m.* chamberlain.
камерди́нер, а *m.* valet.
камери́стк|а, и *f.* lady's maid.
ка́мер|ный[1] *adj. of* **~а**
ка́мерн|ый[2] *adj.* (*mus.*): **к. конце́рт** chamber concert; **~ая му́зыка** chamber music.
камерто́н, а *m.* tuning-fork.
ка́мер-ю́нкер, а *m.* gentleman of the bedchamber.
ка́меш|ек, ка *m. dim. of* **ка́мень**; pebble; (*fig., coll.*): **бро́сить к. в чей-н. огоро́д** to make digs at s.o.
каме́|я, и *f.* cameo.
камзо́л, а *m.* camisole.
камика́дзе *m. indecl.* kamikaze pilot.
камила́вк|а, и *f.* (*eccl.*) kamelaukion (*Orthodox priest's headgear*).
ками́н, а *m.* fire-place; (open) fire.
ками́н|ный *adj. of* **~; ~ная по́лка** mantelpiece; **~ная решётка** fender, fireguard.
камк|а́, и́ *f.* (*text.*) damask.
камко́рдер, а *m.* camcorder.
камло́т, а *m.* (*text.*) camlet.
камло́т|овый *adj. of* **~**
камнедроби́лк|а, и *f.* stone-breaker, stone-crusher.
камнело́мк|а, и *f.* (*bot.*) saxifrage.
камнепа́д, а *m.* rockfall.
камо́рк|а, и *f.* (*coll.*) closet, very small room; box room.
кампане́йск|ий *adj.* (*pej.*): **~ая рабо́та** work done in spurts.
кампане́йщин|а, ы *f.* (*pej.*) system of working in spurts (*opp. working according to plan, methodically*).
кампа́ни|я, и *f.* **1.** (*mil. and fig.*) campaign. **2.** (*naut.*) cruise.
кампе́шев|ый *adj.* (*bot.*): **~ое де́рево** peachy wood, logwood.
кампучи́|ец, йца *m.* Kampuchean.
кампучи́|йка, йки *f. of* **~ец**
кампучи́йский *adj.* Kampuchean.
Кампучи́|я, и *f.* Kampuchea.
камуфле́т, а *m.* (*mil.*) camouflet; (*fig., coll., joc.*) dirty trick.
камуфля́ж, а *no pl., m.* camouflage.
камфар|а́, ы́ *f.* camphor.
камфа́р|ный *adj. of* **~а́**
камф|ора́ = ~ара́
камфо́рк|а, и *f.* = **конфо́рка**
камча́тк|а[1], и *f.* (*text.*) damask linen.
камча́тк|а[2], и *f.* (*joc.*) the back row(s) of the classroom; **сиде́ть на ~е** to sit at the back (of the classroom).
камча́т(н)ый *adj.* **1.** (*folk poet.*) damask. **2.** damasked, figured (*of linen*).
камы́ш, а́ *m.* reed, rush (*also collect.*).
камы́ш|евый *adj. of* **~**
камыш|о́вый *adj. of* **~́; ~о́вое кре́сло** cane chair; **~о́вая жа́ба** natterjack.
кана́в|а, ы *f.* ditch; **сто́чная к.** gutter.
канавокопа́тел|ь, я *m.* (*tech.*) trench digger, trench excavator.
Кана́д|а, ы *f.* Canada.
кана́д|ец, ца, *g. pl.* **~цев** *m.* Canadian.
кана́д|ка, ки *f. of* **~ец**
кана́дск|ий *adj.* Canadian; **~ая пи́хта** balsam fir.
кана́л, а *m.* **1.** canal. **2.** (*in var. senses*) channel; **дипломати́ческие ~ы** diplomatic channels. **3.** (*anat.*) duct, canal; **мочеиспуска́тельный к.** urethra. **4.** bore (*of barrel of gun*).
канализа|цио́нный *adj. of* **~́ция; ~цио́нная труба́** sewer(-pipe).
канализа́ци|я, и *f.* **1.** sewerage. **2.** sewer (system).

канализи́р|овать, ую *impf. and pf.* to provide with sewerage-system.
кана́льский *adj.* (*coll., obs.*) rascally, roguish.
кана́льств|о, а *nt.* (*coll., obs.*) trickery, knavery.
кана́л|ья, ьи, *g. pl.* **~ий** *c.g.* (*coll.*) rascal, scoundrel.
канапе́ *nt. indecl.* canapé.
канаре́|ечный *adj.* **1.** *adj. of* **~йка. 2.** canary(-coloured).
канаре́йк|а, и *f.* **1.** canary. **2.** (*coll., fig.*) police car.
кана́т, а *m.* rope; cable, hawser.
кана́т|ный *adj. of* **~; к. заво́д** rope-yard; **~ная желе́зная доро́га** funicular railway; **к. пля́сун** rope-dancer.
канатохо́д|ец, ца *m.* rope-walker.
Ка́нберр|а, ы *f.* Canberra.
канв|а́, ы́ *no pl., f.* canvas; (*fig.*) groundwork; outline, design; **к. рома́на** the outline of a novel.
канв|о́вый *adj. of* **~а́**
кандал|ы́, о́в *no sg.* shackles, fetters; **ручны́е к.** manacles, handcuffs; **закова́ть в к.** to put into irons.
канда́л|ьный *adj. of* **~ы́**
канделя́бр, а *m.* candelabrum.
кандида́т, а *m.* **1.** candidate; **к. в чле́ны коммунисти́ческой па́ртии** candidate-member of the Communist Party. **2.** kandidat (*in former USSR, holder of first higher degree, awarded on dissertation*).
кандида́тск|ая, ой *f.* (*coll.*) doctoral thesis.
кандида́т|ский *adj. of* **~; к. ми́нимум** qualifying examinations for admission to the course leading to the degree of kandidat; **к. стаж** (*pol.*) probation period (*period as candidate-member of the CPSU*).
кандидату́р|а, ы *f.* candidature; **вы́ставить чью-н. ~у** to nominate s.o. for election.
кани́кул|ы, ~ *no sg.* (*school*) holidays; (*university, etc.*) vacation.
кани|куля́рный *adj. of* **~́кулы**
кани́стр|а, ы *f.* jerrycan.
кани́те́л|ить, ю, ишь *impf.* (*of* **про~**) (*coll., pej.*) to drag out; **к. кого́-н.** to waste s.o.'s time.
кани́те́л|иться, юсь, ишься *impf.* (*of* **про~**) (*coll., pej.*) to waste time; to mess about; to maunder.
кани́те́л|ь, и *f.* **1.** gold thread, silver thread; wire-ribbon. **2.** (*fig., coll.*) long-drawn-out proceedings; **тяну́ть, разводи́ть к.** to spin out, drag out, proceedings, procrastinate; **дово́льно ~и!** this has gone on, dragged on long enough!
кани́те́л|ьный (~ен, ~ьна) *adj.* (*coll.*) **1.** long-drawn out; tedious. **2.: к. челове́к** procrastinator. **3.** *adj. of* **~ь 1.**
кани́те́льщик, а *m.* **1.** wire-ribbon spinner. **2.** (*fig., coll.*) time-waster.
канифа́с, а *m.* (*obs.*) **1.** sail-cloth. **2.** dimity.
канифо́л|ить, ю, ишь *impf.* (*of* **на~**) to rosin.
канифо́л|ь, и *f.* rosin, colophony.
канка́н, а *m.* cancan.
канкани́р|овать, ую *impf.* (*coll.*) to dance the cancan.
каннелю́р|а, ы *f.* (*archit.*) flute.
каннииба́л, а *m.* cannibal.
каннибали́зм, а *m.* cannibalism.
канои́ст, а *m.* canoeist.
кано́н, а *m.* (*in var. senses*) canon.
канона́д|а, ы *f.* cannonade.
канонe̋рк|а, и *f.* gunboat.
канонe̋рск|ий *adj.*: **~ая ло́дка** gunboat.
канониза́ци|я, и *f.* (*eccl.*) canonization.
канонизи́р|овать, ую *impf. and pf.* (*eccl. and fig.*) to canonize.
канониз|ова́ть, у́ю *impf. and pf.* = **~и́ровать**
кано́ник, а *m.* (*eccl.*) canon.
канони́р, а *m.* gunner.
канони́ческ|ий *adj.* **1.** (*eccl.*) canonical; (*liter.*) definitive. **2.** (*eccl.*): **~ое пра́во** canon law.
канони́чност|ь, и *f.* (*eccl. and liter.*) canonicity.
канотье́ *nt. indecl.* boater (*hat*).
кано́э *nt. indecl.* canoe.
кант, а *m.* **1.** edging, piping. **2.** mount (*for pictures, etc.*).
канта́т|а, ы *f.* (*mus.*) cantata.
кантиа́н|ец, ца *m.* (*phil.*) Kantian.
кантиа́нский *adj.* (*phil.*) Kantian.
кантиле́н|а, ы *f.* (*mus.*) cantilena.
кант|ова́ть[1], у́ю *impf.* (*of* **о~**) to border; to mount (*picture, etc.*).
кант|ова́ть[2], у́ю *impf.* (*tech.*) to cant.
Канто́н, а *m.* Canton; Guangzhou.
канто́н, а *m.* (*administrative unit*) canton.
кантона́льный *adj.* cantonal.
канто́н|ец, ца *m.* Cantonese.
кантони́ст, а *m.* (*hist.*) soldier's son.
канто́н|ка, ки *f. of* **~ец**
канто́нский *m.* Cantonese.
ка́нтор, а *m.* cantor.
кану́н, а *m.* eve; (*eccl.*) vigil; **к. Но́вого го́да** New Year's eve.
ка́н|уть, у, ешь *pf.* (*obs.*) to drop, sink; **к. в ве́чность, к. в Ле́ту** (*fig.*) to sink into oblivion; **как в во́ду к.** to disappear without a trace, vanish into thin air.
канцеляри́ст, а *m.* clerk.
канцеля́ри|я, и *f.* office.
канцеля́р|ский *adj. of* **~; ~ские принадле́жности** stationery; **~ская рабо́та** clerical work; **к. стол** office desk; **~ская кры́са** (*fig., pej.*) office drudge; **к. по́черк** clerkly hand; **к. слог** officialese.
канцеля́рщин|а, ы *f.* (*coll.*) red tape.
канцероге́н, а *m.* carcinogen.
канцероге́нн|ый *adj.* carcinogenic; **~ое вещество́** carcinogen.
ка́нцлер, а *m.* chancellor.
канцо́н|а, ы *f.* (*mus.*) canzonet.
канцтова́р|ы, ов *no sg.* (*abbr. of* **канцеля́рские това́ры**) office supplies.
кань́он, а *m.* (*geog.*) canyon.
каню́к, а́ *m.* **1.** (*zool.*) buzzard. **2.** (*fig., dial.*) moaner, grumbler.
каню́ч|ить, у, ишь *impf.* (*coll., pej.*) to moan, grumble; to pester.
каоли́н, а m. china clay, kaolin.
кап... *comb. form, abbr. of* **капиталисти́ческий**
ка́п|а, ы *f.* gumshield.
ка́п|ать, аю (*obs.* **~лю, ~лешь**) *impf.* (*of* **~нуть**) **1.** (*3rd pers. only*) to drip, drop; to trickle; to dribble; to fall (in drops); **из глаз у неё ~али слёзы** tear-drops were falling from her eyes; **дождь ~ает** it is spotting with rain; **с потолка́ ~ало** there was a drip from the ceiling; **над на́ми не ~лет** (*fig., coll.*) we can take our time; there is no hurry. **2.** to pour out (*in drops*); **к. лека́рство в рю́мку** to pour medicine into a glass. **3.** (*+i.; coll.*) to spill; **ты ~аешь водо́й на ска́терть** you are spilling water on the cloth.
капе́лл|а, ы *f.* **1.** choir. **2.** chapel; **к. Богома́тери** Lady chapel.
капелла́н, а *m.* chaplain.
капе́л|ь, и *f.* **1.** drip (*of thawing snow*). **2.** thaw.
капельди́нер, а *m.* (*obs.*) usher, box-keeper (*in theatre*).
ка́пельк|а, и *f.* **1.** small drop; **к. росы́** dew-drop; **вы́пить всё до ~и** to drink to the last drop. **2.** (*sg. only; fig.*) grain, minute quantity; **в нём нет ни ~и здра́вого смы́сла** he has not a grain of common sense; **она́ ни ~и не смути́лась** she was not a whit put out; *as adv.* **~у** (*coll.*) a little; **подожди́ ~у!** wait a moment.
капельме́йстер, а *m.* (*mus.*) conductor, bandmaster.
капельме́йстер|ский *adj. of* **~; ~ская па́лочка** conductor's baton.
ка́пельниц|а, ы *f.* (*medicine*) dropper.
ка́пельный *adj.* (*coll.*) tiny.
ка́пер, а *m.* (*naut.*) privateer.
ка́перс, а *m.* **1.** (*bot.*) caper. **2.** (*pl. only; cul.*) capers.
ка́перств|о, а *nt.* (*naut.*) privateering.
капилля́р, а *m.* (*phys., anat.*) capillary.
капилля́рный *adj.* (*phys., anat.*) capillary.
капита́л, а *m.* (*fin.*) capital; **к. и проце́нты, к. с проце́нтами** principal and interest.
капита́л|ец, ьца *m. dim. of* **~**; *coll.* a tidy sum.
капитализа́ци|я, и *f.* (*fin.*) capitalization.
капитализи́р|овать, ую *impf. and pf.* (*fin.*) to capitalize.

капитали́зм, а *m.* capitalism.
капитали́ст, а *m.* capitalist.
капиталисти́ческий *adj.* capitalist(ic).
капиталовложе́ни|е, я *nt.* capital investment.
капита́льн|ый *adj.* capital; main, fundamental; most important; **к. вопро́с** fundamental question; **к. ремо́нт** major repairs; **~ая стена́** main wall.
капита́н, а *m.* captain.
капита́н|ский *adj. of* ~; **к. мо́стик** captain's bridge.
капите́л|ь, и *f.* **1.** (*archit.*) capital. **2.** (*typ.*) small capitals.
Капитоли́йск|ий холм, ~ого ~а́ *m.* Capitol Hill.
капи́тул, а *m.* (*eccl., hist.*) chapter (*of canons or of members of an order*).
капитули́р|овать, ую *impf. and pf.* **(пе́ред)** to capitulate (to).
капитуля́нт, а *m.* (*pej.*) faint-heart; truckler.
капитуля́нтств|о, а *nt.* truckling.
капитуля́ци|я, и *f.* capitulation.
ка́пищ|е, а *nt.* (*heathen*) temple.
капка́н, а *m.* trap; **попа́сться в к.** to fall into a trap (*also fig.*).
капка́н|ный *adj. of* ~; **к. про́мысел** trapping.
капли́ц|а, ы *f.* (*Roman Catholic*) chapel.
каплу́н, а́ *m.* capon.
ка́п|ля, ли, *g. pl.* **~ель** *f.* **1.** drop; **по ~ле, к. за ~лей** drop by drop; **до ~ли** to the last drop; **похо́жи как две ~ли воды́** as like as two peas; **~ли в рот не беру́** (*euph.*) I never touch a drop (*sc. of alcoholic liquor*); (*fig.*): **к. в мо́ре** a drop in the ocean; **после́дняя к.** the last straw; **би́ться до после́дней ~ли кро́ви** to fight to the last. **2.** (*pl.*; *med.*) drops. **3.** (*fig., coll.*) drop, bit; **у него́ (нет) ни ~ли благоразу́мия** he hasn't a drop of sense; **ни ~ли** (*as adv.*) not a bit, not a whit.
ка́п|нуть, ну, нешь *pf.* (*of* **~ать**) to drop, let fall a drop.
кап|о́к, ка́ *no pl., m.* (*text.*) kapok.
ка́пор, а *m.* hood; bonnet.
капо́т, а *m.* **1.** house-coat (*woman's informal indoor attire*). **2.** capote (*French soldier's greatcoat*). **3.** (*tech.*) hood, bonnet, cowl; **к. мото́ра** (*aeron.*) engine cowling.
капра́л, а *m.* (*mil.*) corporal.
капра́л|ьский *adj. of* ~
капра́льств|о, а *nt.* (*mil.*) rank of corporal.
каприз, а *m.* caprice, whim; vagary; **к. судьбы́** twist of fate.
капри́зник, а *m.* capricious pers., capricious child.
капри́знича|ть, ю *impf.* to behave capriciously; (*of a child*) to play up.
капри́з|ный (~ен, ~на) *adj.* **1.** capricious; (*of a child*) wilful. **2.** freakish.
капризу́л|я, и *c.g.* (*coll.*) capricious, self-willed child.
каприфо́л|ь, и *f.* (*bot.*) honeysuckle.
капри́ччио *nt.* (*mus.*) capriccio.
капро́н, а *nt.* kapron (*synthetic fibre, similar to nylon*).
капро́н|овый *adj. of* ~
ка́псул|а, ы *f.* capsule.
ка́псюл|ь, я *m.* (percussion) cap (*in explosives*).
ка́псюль|ный *adj. of* ~; **~ное ружьё** percussion musket.
каптена́рмус, а *m.* (*mil.*) quartermaster-sergeant.
капу́ст|а, ы *f.* cabbage; **спа́ржевая к.** broccoli, calabrese; **кормова́я к.** kale.
капу́стник, а *m.* **1.** cabbage field. **2.** cabbage worm. **3.** actors', artists', *or* students' party.
капу́стниц|а, ы *f.* cabbage butterfly.
капу́ст|ный *adj. of* **~а**
капу́т *m. indecl.* (*coll.*) end, destruction; *used as adj. or adv.* done for, kaput; **тут ему́ и к.** he's done for; it's all up with him.
капуци́н, а *m.* **1.** Capuchin (friar). **2.** (*zool.*) capuchin monkey. **3.** (*bot.*) nasturtium.
капюшо́н, а *m.* hood, cowl.
ка́р|а, ы *f.* (*rhet.*) punishment, retribution.
караби́н, а *m.* carbine.
карабине́р, а *m.* car(a)bineer.
кара́бка|ться, юсь *impf.* (*of* **вс~**) (*coll.*) to clamber.
карава́|й, я *m.* cottage loaf.
карава́н, а *m.* **1.** caravan. **2.** convoy (*of ships, etc.*)
карава́н-сара́|й, я *m.* caravanserai.
караґа́ч, а *m.* (*bot.*) elm.
кара́емый *adj.* (*leg.*) punishable.
Кар(а)и́бск|ое мо́р|е, ~ого ~я *m.* the Caribbean Sea; the Caribbean.
карайм, а *m.* Karaite (*member of Jewish sect who reject the Talmud*).
каракалпа́к, а *m.* (*ethnol.*) Karakalpak.
Кара́кас, а *m.* Caracas.
карака́тиц|а, ы *f.* **1.** (*zool.*) cuttlefish. **2.** (*fig., joc.*) short-legged, clumsy pers.
кара́ковый *adj.* dark-bay.
кара́кул|евый *adj. of* **~ь**
кара́кул|ь, я *no pl., m.* astrakhan (fur).
каракульч|а́, и́ *f.* astrakhan (fur).
кара́кул|я, и *f.* scrawl, scribble.
карамбо́л|ь, я *m.* (*in billiards*) cannon.
караме́л|ь, и *no pl., f.* **1.** (*collect.*) caramels. **2.** caramel
караме́льк|а, и *f.* (*coll.*) caramel.
караме́ль|ный *adj. of* ~
каранда́ш, а́ *m.* pencil.
каранда́ш|ный *adj. of* ~; **к. рису́нок** pencil drawing.
каранти́н, а *m.* **1.** quarantine; **сня́тие ~а** (*naut.*) pratique; **подве́ргнуть ~у** to place in quarantine. **2.** quarantine station.
каранти́н|ный *adj. of* ~; **~ное свиде́тельство** (*naut.*) bill of health.
карапу́з, а *m.* (*coll.*) chubby lad.
кара́с|ь, я́ *m.* (*fish*) crucian; **серебряный к.** Prussian carp.
кара́т, а *m.* carat.
карате́ *nt. indecl.* karate.
каратеист *m.* = **карати́ст**
кара́тел|ь, я *m.* **1.** (*obs.*) punisher, chastiser. **2.** member of punitive expedition.
кара́тельный *adj.* punitive.
карати́ст, а *m.* karate enthusiast, karateka.
кара́|ть, ю *impf.* (*of* **по~**) to punish, chastise.
карау́л, а *m.* **1.** guard; watch; **вступи́ть в к.** to mount guard; **нести́ к., стоя́ть в ~е** to be on guard; **смени́ть к.** to relieve the guard. **2.** *word of command*: **на к.!** present arms!; **взять на к.** to present arms. **3.** *as int.* help!; **крича́ть к.** to shout for help.
карау́л|ить, ю, ишь *impf.* **1.** to guard. **2.** (*coll.*) to lie in wait for, watch out for.
карау́лк|а, и *f.* (*coll.*) guardroom.
карау́л|ьный *adj. of* ~; **~ьная бу́дка** sentry-box; *as n.* **к., ~ьного** *m.* sentry, sentinel, guard.
карау́л|ьня, ьни, *g. pl.* **~ен** *f.* guardroom.
карау́льщик, а *m.* (*coll.*) sentry, guard.
Кара́чи *m. indecl.* Karachi.
кара́ч|ки, ек *no sg.* (*coll.*): **на к., на ~ках** on all fours; **стать на к.** to get on all fours.
карби́д, а *m.* (*chem.*) carbide.
карбо́ван|ец, ца *m.* **1.** karbovanets (*Ukrainian unit of currency*). **2.** (*pl.*) money.
карбо́лк|а, и *f.* (*coll.*) carbolic acid.
карбо́ловый *adj.* (*chem.*) carbolic.
карбона́т, а *m.* (*chem.*) carbonate.
карбору́нд, а *m.* carborundum.
карбу́нкул, а *m.* (*min., med.*) carbuncle.
карбюра́тор, а *m.* (*tech., chem*) carburettor.
карбюри́р|овать, ую *impf. and pf.* (*chem.*) to carburet.
карг|а́, и́, *pl.* **~и́, ~, ~а́м** *f.* **1.** (*dial.*) crow. **2.** (*coll.*): **ста́рая к.** hag, harridan, crone.
ка́рд|а, ы *f.* (*tech.*) card.
кардамо́н, а *m.* (*bot.*) cardamom.
кардина́л, а *m.* (*eccl.*) cardinal.
кардина́льный *adj.* cardinal.
кардина́л|ьский *adj. of* ~
кардиогра́мм|а, ы *f.* cardiogram.
кардио́лог, а *m.* cardiologist.
кардиостимуля́тор, а *m.* (*med.*) pacemaker (*artificial*).
каре́ *nt. indecl.* (*mil.*) square.
каре́л, а *m.* Karelian.
Каре́ли|я, и *f.* Karelia.
каре́л|ка, ки *f. of* ~

каре́льск|ий *adj.* Karelian; **~ая берёза** Karelian birch.
каре́т|а, ы *f.* carriage, coach; **к. запряжённая па́рой, четвёркой** carriage and pair, coach and four; **почто́вая к.** stage-coach; **к. ско́рой по́мощи** (*obs.*) ambulance.
каре́тк|а, и *f.* (*tech.*) carriage, frame.
каре́тник, а *m.* **1.** coach-house. **2.** coach-builder.
кариати́д|а, ы *f.* (*archit.*) caryatid.
ка́рий *adj.* (*of colour of eyes*) brown, hazel; (*of colour of horses*) chestnut, dark-chestnut.
карикату́р|а, ы *f.* **1.** caricature. **2.** cartoon.
карикатури́ст, а *m.* **1.** caricaturist. **2.** cartoonist.
карикату́р|ить, ю, ишь *impf.* (*coll., obs.*) to caricature.
карикату́р|ный *adj. of* **~а**; **~ная фигу́ра** ludicrous figure.
карио́з, а *m.* (*med.*) caries, decay.
карио́зный *adj.* (*med.*) carious.
карка́с, а *m.* (*tech.*) frame; (*fig.*) framework.
карка́с|ный *adj. of* **~**; **к. дом** framehouse.
ка́рк|ать, аю *impf.* (*of* **~нуть**) **1.** to caw, croak. **2.** (*fig.*) to croak, prophesy ill.
ка́рк|нуть, ну, нешь *pf. of* **~ать 1.**
ка́рлик, а *m.* dwarf; pygmy.
ка́рликов|ый *adj.* (*anthrop., bot., and fig.*) dwarf; pygmean; **~ые племена́** the Pygmies.
ка́рли|ца, цы *f. of* **~к**
кармази́н, а *m.* (*obs.*) cramoisy, crimson (*cloth*).
кармази́н|ный *adj. of* **~**; **к. цвет** crimson.
карма́н, а *m.* pocket; (*fig., coll.*): **э́то мне не по ~у** I can't afford it; **бить по ~у** to cost a pretty penny; **наби́ть себе́ к.** to fill one's pockets; **то́щий к.** empty pocket; **держи́ к. ши́ре!** you've got a hope!; **не лезть за сло́вом в к.** to have a ready tongue.
карма́нник, а *m.* pickpocket.
карма́н|ный *adj. of* **~**; **к. вор** pickpocket; **~ные де́ньги** pocket money.
карма́нщик = **карма́нник**
карми́н, а *m.* carmine.
карми́нный *adj.* carmine.
карнава́л, а *m.* carnival.
карни́з, а *m.* (*archit.*) **1.** cornice. **2.** ledge.
кароте́л|ь, и *f.* carrot (*variety having short roots*).
карп, а *m.* (*fish*) carp.
Карпа́т|ы, ~ *no sg.* the Carpathians.
карт, а *m.* (*sport*) go-cart.
ка́рт|а, ы *f.* **1.** (*geog.*) map. **2.** (playing-)card; **игра́ть в ~ы** to play cards; **име́ть хоро́шие ~ы** to have a good hand; **его́ ка́рта би́та** (*fig.*) his game is up; **поста́вить на ~у** to stake, risk; **на ~е** at stake; **раскры́ть свои́ ~ы** to show one's hand.
карта́в|ить, лю, ишь *impf.* to burr.
карта́вост|ь, и *f.* (*ling.*) burr.
карта́вый *adj.* **1.** pronounced gutturally. **2.** having a burr.
картве́л, а *m.* (*ethnol.*) Georgian.
картёж, а́ *no pl., m.* (*coll.*) card-playing; gambling school.
картёжник, а *m.* (*coll.*) card-player; gambler (at cards).
картёжный *adj.* (*coll.*) card-playing; gambling.
картезиа́нский *adj.* (*phil.*) Cartesian.
карте́л|ь, я *m.* (*fin.*) cartel.
ка́ртер, а *m.* (*tech.*) crank case.
карте́ч|ный *adj. of* **~ь**
карте́ч|ь, и *f.* **1.** (*mil.*) case-shot; grape-shot. **2.** buck-shot.
карти́н|а, ы *f.* **1.** (*in var. senses*) picture. **2.** (*theatr.*) scene; **жива́я к.** tableau (vivant).
ка́ртинг, а *m.* go-carting.
карти́нк|а, и *f.* picture; illustration; **к.-зага́дка** jig-saw puzzle; **лубо́чные ~и** crude, coloured woodcuts; (*pej.*) crude pictures; **мо́дная к.** fashion-plate; **переводны́е ~и** transfers.
карти́н|ный (~ен, ~на) *adj.* **1.** *adj. of* **~а**; **~ная галере́я** art gallery, picture-gallery. **2.** picturesque.
карто́граф, а *m.* cartographer.
картографи́р|овать, ую *impf.* to map, draw a map of.
картографи́ческий *adj.* cartographic.
картогра́фи|я, и *f.* cartography.
карто́н, а *m.* **1.** cardboard, pasteboard. **2.** (*artists' sl.*) sketch, cartoon.
картона́ж, а *m.* cardboard article; cardboard box.
картона́ж|ный *adj of* **~**; **~ная фа́брика** cardboard box factory.
карто́нк|а, и *f.* cardboard box; **к. для шля́пы** hat-box, bandbox.
карто́н|ный *adj. of* **~**; (*fig.*): **к. до́мик** house of cards.
картоте́к|а, и *f.* card-index.
картофелекопа́лк|а, и *f.* (*agric.*) potato-digger.
картофелечи́стк|а, и *f.* potato peeler.
карто́фелин|а, ы *f.* (*coll.*) potato.
карто́фел|ь, я *no pl., m.* **1.** (*collect.*) potatoes; **к. в мунди́ре** jacket potatoes; **жа́реный к.** fried potatoes; **молодо́й к.** new potatoes. **2.** potato plant.
карто́фель|ный *adj. of* **~**; **~ное пюре́** mashed potatoes.
ка́рточк|а, и *f.* **1.** card; **визи́тная к.** visiting card, business card; **к. вин** wine-list; **катало́жная к.** index card; **к. ку́шаний** bill of fare; **продово́льственная к.** food-card, ration card. **2.** season ticket. **3.** (*coll.*) photo.
ка́рточ|ный *adj.* **1.** *adj. of* **ка́рта; к. долг** gambling-debt; **к. стол** card-table; (*coll.*): **к. до́мик** house of cards (*also fig.*); **к. фо́кус** card trick. **2.** *adj. of* **~ка; к. катало́г** card index; **~ная систе́ма** rationing system.
карто́шк|а, и *f.* (*coll.*) **1.** (*collect.*) potatoes. **2.** potato; **нос ~ой** bulbous nose.
карту́з, а́ *m.* **1.** (peaked) cap. **2.** (*mil.*) powder bag. **3.** (*obs.*) paper-bag.
карусе́л|ь, и *f.* roundabout, merry-go-round.
карусе́ль|ный *adj. of* **~**; (*tech.*): **к. стано́к** vertical lathe.
Карфаге́н, а *m.* Carthage.
карфаге́нский *adj.* Carthaginian.
карфаге́нян|ин, ина, *pl.* **~е, ~** *m.* Carthaginian.
карфаге́нян|ка, ки *f. of* **~ин**
ка́рцер, а *m.* cell, lock-up.
карье́р[1]**, а** *m.* career, full gallop; **во весь к.** at full speed, in full career; **пусти́ть ло́шадь в к., ~ом** to put a horse into full gallop; (*fig., coll.*) **с ме́ста в к.** straight away, without more ado.
карье́р[2]**, а** *m.* quarry; sand-pit.
карье́р|а, ы *f.* career; **сде́лать ~у** to make good, get on.
карьери́зм, а *m.* careerism.
карьери́ст, а *m.* careerist.
карье́р|ный *adj. of* **1. ~**[1,2]. **2. ~а**
каса́ни|е, я *nt.* contact; (*math.*): **то́чка ~я** point of contact.
каса́тельн|ая, ой *f.* (*math.*) tangent.
каса́тельно *prep.+g.* touching, concerning.
каса́тельств|о, а *nt.* **(к)** connection (with); **я не име́л никако́го ~а к э́тому заявле́нию** I had nothing to do with this statement.
каса́тик, а *m.* (*folk poet.*) darling.
каса́т|ка, ки *f.* **1.** (*zool.*) swallow. **2.** (*zool.*) killer whale. **3.** (*folk poet.*) *f. of* **~ик**
каса́|ться, юсь *impf.* (*of* **косну́ться**) **1.** (*+g.*) to touch. **2.** (*+g.; fig.*) to touch (on, upon); **к. больно́го вопро́са** to touch on a sore subject. **3.** (*+g. or* **до;** *fig*) to concern, relate (to); **э́то тебя́ не ~ется** it is no concern of yours; **что ~ется** as to, as regards, with regard to.
ка́ск|а, и *f.* helmet.
каска́д, а *m.* **1.** cascade; **к. красноре́чия** (*fig.*) flood of eloquence. **2.** leaping from horseback (*as circus turn*).
каскадёр, а *m.* stunt man.
каска́д|ный *adj.* **1.** *adj. of* **~**. **2.** (*theatr.*) music-hall.
Каспи́йск|ое мо́р|е, ~ого ~я *nt.* the Caspian Sea.
ка́сс|а, ы *f.* **1.** cash-box; till, cash register; cash-desk; **уплати́ть в ~у** to pay at the cash-desk; **несгора́емая к.** safe. **2.** cash. **3.** booking-office; box-office; **к. взаимопо́мощи** benefit fund, mutual aid fund; **сберега́тельная к.** savings bank. **4.** (*typ.*) case.
касса|цио́нный *adj. of* **~ция**; **~цио́нная жа́лоба** appeal; **к. суд** Court of Appeal, Court of Cassation.
касса́ци|я, и *f.* (*leg.*) **1.** cassation. **2.** (*coll.*) **пода́ть ~ю** to appeal.
кассе́т|а, ы *f.* cassette; (*phot.*) plate-holder.
кассе́т|ный *adj. of* **~а**; **к. магнитофо́н** cassette recorder.
касси́р, а *m.* cashier.
касси́р|овать, ую *impf. and pf.* (*leg.*) to annul, quash.

касси́р|ша, ши *f. of* ~
ка́сс|овый *adj. of* **~а; ~овая кни́га** cash-book; **к. счёт** cash-account.
ка́ст|а, ы *f.* caste.
кастанье́т|ы, ~ *pl.* (*sg.* **~а, ~ы** *f.*) castanets.
кастеля́нш|а, и *f.* linen-keeper (*in institution*).
касте́т, а *m.* knuckleduster.
касти́льский *adj.* Castilian.
касто́р, а *m.* (*text.*) beaver, castor (cloth).
касто́рк|а, и *f.* (*coll.*) castor oil.
касто́ров|ый[1] *adj.*: **~ое ма́сло** castor oil.
касто́р|овый[2] *adj. of* **~; ~овая шля́па** beaver (hat).
кастра́т, а *m.* eunuch.
кастра́ци|я, и *f.* castration.
кастри́р|овать, ую *impf. and pf.* to castrate; to geld.
кастрю́л|я, и *f.* saucepan.
кат[1], **а** *m.* (*dial. or obs*) executioner.
кат[2], **а** *m.* (*naut.*) cat; **к.-ба́лка** cathead.
катава́си|я, и *f.* (*coll.*) confusion, muddle.
катаклизм, а *m.* cataclysm.
катако́мб|а, ы *f.* catacomb.
катала́жк|а, и *f.* (*coll.*) lock-up.
катала́нский *adj.* Catalan (*of language*).
ката́лиз, а *m.* (*chem.*) catalysis.
катализа́тор, а *m.* (*chem.*) catalyst.
ката́лк|а, и *f.*: **де́тская к.** baby buggy, pushchair.
катало́г, а *m.* catalogue.
каталогиза́тор, а *m.* cataloguer.
каталогизи́р|овать, ую *impf. and pf.* to catalogue.
катало́жн|ая, ой *f.* catalogue room.
катало́|жный *adj. of* **~г**
катало́н|ец, ца *m* Catalan, Catalonian.
Катало́ни|я, и *f.* Catalonia.
катало́н|ка, ки *f. of* **~ец**
катало́нский *adj.* Catalan; Catalonian.
ка́тал|ь, я *m.* porter, barrow man.
катамара́н, а *m.* catamaran.
ката́ни|е, я *nt.* **1.** rolling. **2.**: **к. в экипа́же** driving; **к. верхо́м** riding; **к. на ло́дке** boating; **к. на конька́х** skating; **к. на ро́ликах** roller skating; **фигу́рное к.** figure skating; **к. с гор** tobogganing.
ка́тань|е, я *nt., only in phr.* **не мытьём, так ~ем** (*coll.*) by hook or by crook.
катапу́льт|а, ы *f.* (*hist. and aeron.*) catapult.
Ка́тар, а *m.* Qatar.
ката́р, а *m.* catarrh.
катара́кт, а *m.* (*geog.*) cataract.
катара́кт|а, ы *f.* (*med.*) cataract.
катара́льный *adj.* catarrhal.
ка́тарсис, а *m.* catharsis.
катастро́ф|а, ы *f.* catastrophe, disaster; accident.
катастрофи́ческий *adj.* catastrophic.
катастрофи́ч|ный (~ен, ~на) *adj.* catastrophic.
кат|а́ть, а́ю *impf.* **1.** (*indet. of* **~и́ть**) to roll; to wheel, trundle. **2.** to drive, take for a drive. **3.** to roll (*from clay, dough, etc.*). **4.** (*pf.* **вы́~**) **к. бельё** to mangle linen.
кат|а́ться, а́юсь *impf.* **1.** (*indet. of* **~и́ться**) to roll (*intrans.*); (*coll.*) **к. от бо́ли** to roll in pain; **к. со́ смеху** to split one's sides with laughter. **2.** to go for a drive; **к. верхо́м** to ride, go riding; **к. на велосипе́де** to cycle, go cycling; **к. на конька́х** to skate, go skating; **к. на ло́дке** to go boating.
катафа́лк, а *m.* **1.** catafalque. **2.** hearse.
катафо́т, а *m.* cat's eye (*on road*); reflector.
категори́чески *adv.* categorically; **к. отказа́ться** to refuse flatly.
категори́ческий *adj.* categorical.
катагори́ч|ный (~ен, ~на) *adj.* categorical.
катего́ри|я, и *f.* category.
ка́тер, а, *pl.* **~а́** *m.* (*naut.*) cutter; **мото́рный к.** motor-launch; **сторожево́й к.** patrol boat; **торпе́дный к.** motor torpedo-boat.
ка́тер|ный *adj. of* ~
кате́тер, а *m.* (*med.*) catheter.
катехи́зис, а *m.* catechism.
ка|ти́ть, чу́, ∠тишь *impf.* (*of* **по~**) **1.** *det. of* **~та́ть. 2.** (*coll.*) to bowl along, rip, tear.
ка|ти́ться, чу́сь, ∠тишься *impf.* (*of* **по~**) **1.** *det. of* **~та́ться; к. с горы́** to slide downhill; **к. по́д гору** (*fig.*) to go downhill. **2.** (*coll.*) to rush, tear. **3.** to flow, stream; (*fig.*) to roll; **слёзы ~ти́лись по её щека́м** tears were rolling down her cheeks; **день ∠тится за днём** day after day rolls by. **4.** (*coll.*): **~ти́сь; ~ти́тесь отсю́да!** get out!; clear off!
ка́т|кий (~ок, ~ка́) *adj.* (*coll.*) **1.** that can be rolled easily. **2.** slippery.
като́д, а *m.* (*phys.*) cathode.
като́дн|ый *adj.* (*phys.*) cathodic; **~ые лучи́** cathode rays; **~ая тру́бка** cathode-ray tube.
кат|о́к[1], **ка́** *m.* skating-rink.
кат|о́к[2], **ка́** *m.* **1.** (*in var. senses*) roller. **2.** **(для белья́)** mangle.
като́лик, а *m.* (Roman) Catholic.
католико́с, а *m.* Catholicos (*head of the Armenian Church*).
католици́зм, а *m.* (Roman) Catholicism.
католи́ческий *adj.* (Roman) Catholic.
католи́честв|о, а *nt.* (Roman) Catholicism.
католи́чк|а, и *f. of* **като́лик**
ка́торг|а, и *no pl., f.* penal servitude, hard labour (*in a place of exile*).
каторжа́н|ин, ина, *pl.* **~е, ~** *m.* convict; ex-convict.
ка́торжник, а *m.* convict.
ка́тор|жный *adj. of* **~га; ~жные рабо́ты** hard labour; (*fig.*) drudgery; **~жная тюрьма́** convict prison.
кату́шк|а, и *f.* **1.** reel, bobbin; (*text.*) spool. **2.** (*elec.*) coil, bobbin.
ка́тыш, а *m.* **1.** pellet, ball. **2.** block of wood.
ка́тыш|ек, ка *m.* (*coll.*) pellet.
катю́ш|а, и *f.* (*mil.; coll.*) Katyusha (*lorry-mounted multiple rocket launcher*).
кауза́льный *adj.* (*phil.*) causal.
ка́урый *adj.* (*of colour of horses*) light-chestnut.
каусти́ческий *adj.* (*chem.*) caustic.
каучу́к, а *m.* (india-)rubber, caoutchouc.
каучу́к|овый *adj. of* **~**; rubber.
каучуконо́с, а *m.* (*bot.*) rubber-bearing plant.
кафе́ *nt. indecl.* café; **к.-моро́женое** ice-cream parlour.
ка́федр|а, ы *f.* **1.** pulpit; rostrum, platform; **говори́ть с ~ы** to speak from the platform. **2.** (*fig.; at a university*) chair; **получи́ть ~у** to obtain a chair. **3.** (*fig.; at a university*) department, sub-faculty; **заседа́ние ~ы** sub-faculty meeting.
кафедра́льный *adj.*: **к. собо́р** cathedral.
ка́фел|ь, я *m.* Dutch tile.
ка́фель|ный *adj. of* **~; ~ная печь** tiled stove.
кафете́ри|й, я *m.* cafeteria.
кафешанта́н, а *m.* café chantant.
кафоли́ческий *adj.* (*epithet of the Orthodox Church*) ecumenical, universal.
ка́фр, а *m.* Kaffir.
ка́фрский *adj.* Kaffir.
кафта́н, а *m.* caftan.
каца́п, а *m.* 'butcher' (*term of abuse used by Ukrainians of Russians*).
кача́лк|а, и *f.* rocking-chair; **конь-к.** rocking-horse.
кача́ни|е, я *nt.* **1.** rocking, swinging; **к. ма́ятника** swing of pendulum. **2.** pumping.
кач|а́ть, а́ю *impf.* (*of* **~ну́ть**) **1.** (*+a. or i.*) to rock, swing; to shake; **к. колыбе́ль** to rock a cradle; **к. голово́й** to nod, shake one's head; (*impers.*): **его́ ~а́ло из стороны́ в сто́рону** he was reeling; **ло́дку ~а́ет** the boat is rolling. **2.** to lift up, chair (*as mark of esteem or congratulation*). **3.** to pump.
кач|а́ться, а́юсь *impf.* (*of* **~ну́ться**) **1.** to rock, swing (*intrans.*); (*of vessel*) to roll, pitch. **2.** to reel, stagger.
каче́л|и, ей *no sg.* (*child's*) swing; see-saw.
ка́чественный *adj.* **1.** qualitative. **2.** high-quality.
ка́честв|о, а *nt.* **1.** quality; **ни́зкого ~а** poor quality; low-grade; **в ~е** (*+g.*) in the character (of), in the capacity (of); **в ~е преподава́тельницы она́ отли́чна** (in her capacity) as a teacher she is excellent. **2.** (*chess*): **вы́играть,**

проигра́ть к. to gain, lose an exchange.
ка́чк|а, и *f.* rocking; tossing; (*naut.*): **бортова́я к.** rolling; **килева́я к.** pitching.
ка́чкий *adj.* (*coll.*) unstable, wobbly.
кач|ну́ть(ся), ну́(сь), нёшь(ся) *pf. of* **~а́ть(ся)**
ка|чу́, ~́тишь *see* **~ти́ть**
качу́рк|а, и *f.* (*zool.*) petrel.
ка́ш|а, и *f.* **1.** kasha (*dish of cooked grain or groats*); **ма́нная к.** semolina; **ри́совая к.** boiled rice. **2.** (*fig., coll.*): **берёзовая к.** the birch; **с ним ~и не сва́ришь** one can't get on with him; **у него́ к. во рту** he mumbles; **ма́ло ~и ел** (*of s.o. young and/or inexperienced*); **сапоги́ у тебя́ ~и про́сят** your boots are agape; **завари́ть ~у** to start sth., stir up trouble; **расхлёбывать ~у** to put things right.
кашало́т, а *m.* (*zool.*) cachalot, sperm-whale.
кашева́р, а *m.* (*obs.*) cook (*in mil. unit or workmen's canteen*).
ка́ш|ель, ля *m.* cough.
кашеми́р, а *m.* (*text.*) cashmere.
каши́ц|а, ы *f.* (*coll.*) thin gruel; **бума́жная к.** paper pulp.
ка́ш|ка[1], ки *f. dim. of* **~а**; pap.
ка́шк|а[2], и *f.* (*bot.*; *coll.*) clover.
ка́шлян|уть, у, ешь *pf.* to give a cough.
ка́шля|ть, ю *impf.* **1.** to cough. **2.** to have a cough.
Кашми́р, а *m.* Kashmir.
кашми́р|ец, ца *m.* Kashmiri.
кашми́р|ка, ки *f. of* **~ец**
кашми́рский *adj.* Kashmiri.
кашне́ *nt. indecl.* scarf, muffler.
кашта́н, а *m.* **1.** chestnut; **таска́ть ~ы из огня́** (*fig.*) to pull the chestnuts out of the fire. **2.** chestnut-tree; **ко́нский к.** horse-chestnut.
кашта́н|овый *adj.* **1.** *adj. of* **~**. **2.** chestnut(-coloured).
каю́к[1], а *m.* caique.
каю́к[2] (*coll.*) *only in phr.* **к. (пришёл)** (*+d.*) it's the end (of); **тут ему́ и к.** his number's up; he's done for.
каю́р, а *m.* dog-team (*or* reindeer-team) driver.
каю́т|а, ы *f.* cabin, stateroom.
каю́т-компа́ни|я, и *f.* **1.** (*on warships*) wardroom. **2.** (*on passenger vessels*) passengers' lounge.
ка́|ющийся *pres. part. of* **~яться** *and adj.* repentant, contrite, penitent.
ка́|яться, юсь, ешься *impf.* **1.** (*pf.* **рас~**) (**в**+*p.*) to repent (of); **он сам тепе́рь ~ется** he is sorry himself now. **2.** (*pf.* **по~**) (**в**+*p.*) to confess. **3.** (*coll.*): **~юсь** I am sorry to say; I (must) confess; **я, ~юсь, совсе́м об э́том забы́л** I am sorry to say I had forgotten all about it.
кв. (*abbr. of* **кварти́ра**) flat, apartment.
квадра́нт, а *m.* **1.** (*math.*) quadrant. **2.** (*mil.*) quadrant, gunner's clinometer.
квадра́т, а *m.* (*math.*) square; **возвести́ в к.** to square; **в ~е** squared; (*fig., joc.*): **дура́к в ~е** doubly a fool.
квадра́тн|ый *adj.* square; (*anat.*): **~ая мы́шца** quadrate muscle; (*math.*): **к. ко́рень** square root; **~ое уравне́ние** quadratic equation.
квадрату́р|а, ы *f.* (*math.*) quadrature; (*fig.*): **к. кру́га** squaring the circle.
квадрилльо́н, а *m.* (*math.*) quadrillion.
ква́зи... *comb. form* quasi-.
квазизвезд|а́, ы́ *f.* (*astron.*) quasar.
ква́кань|е, я *nt.* croaking.
ква́ка|ть, ю *impf.* to croak.
ква́кн|уть, у, ешь *pf.* to give a croak.
ква́кушк|а, и *f.* (*coll.*) frog.
квалификац|ио́нный *adj. of* **~́ия**; **~ио́нная коми́ссия** board of experts.
квалифика́ци|я, и *f.* qualification.
квалифици́рова|нный (~н, ~на) *p.p.p. of* **~ть** *and adj.* **1.** qualified, skilled. **2.: к. труд** skilled work, specialist work.
квалифици́р|овать, ую *impf. and pf.* **1.** to check, test. **2.** to qualify (as); **как к. тако́е поведе́ние?** how should one qualify such conduct?
квант, а *m. and* **~́а, ~́ы** *f.* (*phys.*) quantum.
ква́нт|овый *adj. of* **~**; **~овая тео́рия** quantum theory.
ква́рт|а, ы *f.* **1.** (*liquid measure*) quart. **2.** (*mus.*) fourth. **3.** (*fencing and cards*) quart.
кварта́л, а *m.* **1.** block (*of buildings*); **к. кра́сных фонаре́й** red-light district; **кита́йский к.** Chinatown; (*obs.*) quarter, ward. **2.** quarter (*of year*).
кварта́льн|ый *adj.* **1.** quarterly; **к. отчёт** quarterly account. **2.** of quarter of city; *as n.* **к., ~ого** *m.* (*hist.*; *coll.*) non-commissioned police officer.
кварте́т, а *m.* (*mus.*) quartet(te).
кварти́р|а, ы *f.* **1.** flat; lodging; apartment(s); **к. и стол** board and lodging; **сдаётся к.** flat, apartment(s) to let; **гла́вная к.** (*mil.*) general headquarters. **2.** *pl.* (*mil.*) quarters, billets; **зи́мние ~ы** winter quarters.
квартира́нт, а *m.* lodger, tenant.
квартира́нт|ка, ки *f. of* **~**
квартирме́йстер, а *m.* (*mil. and naut.*) quartermaster.
кварти́рник, а *m.* (*obs.*) craftsman working at home.
кварти́р|ный *adj. of* **~а**; **~ная пла́та** rent; **~ное расположе́ние** (*mil.*) billeting.
квартир|ова́ть, у́ю *impf.* **1.** (*coll.*) to lodge. **2.** (*mil.*) to be billeted, be quartered.
квартиронанима́тел|ь, я *m.* tenant.
квартирохозя́ин, а *m.* landlord.
квартирохозя́йк|а, и *f.* landlady.
квартпла́т|а, ы *f.* (*abbr. of* ***кварти́рная пла́та***) rent.
кварц, а *m.* (*min.*) quartz.
ква́рц|евый *adj. of* **~**
кварци́т, а *m.* (*min.*) quartzite.
квас, а, *pl.* **~ы́** *m.* kvass.
ква́|сить, шу, сишь *impf.* to pickle; to make sour.
квас|но́й *adj. of* **~**; **к. патриоти́зм** (*fig.*) jingoism.
квас|о́к, ка́ *m.* **1.** *dim. of* **~**. **2.** (*coll.*) sour tang.
квасцо́вый *adj.* (*chem.*) aluminous.
квасц|ы́, о́в *no sg.* (*chem.*) alum.
квашени́н|а, ы *f.* **1.** (*coll.*) sauerkraut. **2.** (*agric.*) fermented vegetable leaves.
ква́шен|ый *adj.* sour, fermented; **~ая капу́ста** sauerkraut.
квашн|я́, и́, *g. pl.* **~е́й** *f.* **1.** kneading trough. **2.** (*dial.*) leavened dough.
Квебе́к, а *m.* Quebec.
квебе́кский *adj.* Quebec.
квёл|ый (~, ~а́, ~л) *adj.* (*dial. or fig.*) weakly, poorly.
квёрху *adv.* up, upwards.
кви́нт|а, ы *f.* (*mus.*) fifth; (*coll.*): **пове́сить нос на ~у** to look dejected.
квинта́л, а *m.* = **це́нтнер**
квинте́т, а *m.* (*mus.*) quintet(te).
квинтэссе́нци|я, и *f.* quintessence.
квит, ~́ы *as pred.* (*coll.*) quits; **мы с тобо́й ~́ы** we are quits.
квитанц|ио́нный *adj. of* **~́ия**
квита́нци|я, и *f.* receipt; **бага́жная к.** luggage-ticket.
квит|о́к, ка́ *m.* (*coll.*) ticket, check.
кво́рум, а *m.* quorum.
кво́т|а, ы *f.* quota.
кг (*abbr. of* **кило́**) k, kg, kilo(s), kilogram(me)(s).
КГБ *m. indecl.* (*abbr. of* ***Комите́т госуда́рственной безопа́сности***) KGB, State Security Committee.
кеба́б, а *m.* kebab.
кеба́бн|ая, ой *f.* kebab house.
ке́гель = кегль
кегельба́н, а *m.* bowling alley; skittle alley.
ке́гл|и, ей *pl.* (*sg.* **~я, ~и** *f.*) **1.** skittles, ninepins; **спорти́вные к.** bowls. **2.** (*sg.*) skittle; pin.
кегл|ь, я *m.* (*typ.*) point; **к. 8** 8 point.
кедр, а *m.* cedar; **гимала́йский к.** deodar; **лива́нский к.** cedar of Lebanon; **сиби́рский к.** Siberian pine; **европе́йский к.** Cembran (Arolla) pine.
кедро́вк|а, и *f.* (*zool.*) nutcracker.
кедр|о́вый *adj. of* **~**; **к. стла́ник** dwarf Siberian pine (*Pinus pumila*).
ке́д|ы, ов *or* **~** *pl.* (*sg.* **кед, а** *m. or* **ке́д|а, ы** *f.*) baseball boots, tennis shoes.
кейнсиа́нский *adj.* Keynesian.
кейнсиа́нств|о, а *nt.* Keynesianism.
кейф, а *m.* (*coll., obs.*) (taking one's) ease, putting one's feet up.
кекс, а *m.* fruit-cake.

ке́лар|ь, я *m.* (*eccl.*) cellarer.
келе́йник, а *m.* (*eccl.*) lay brother.
келе́йно *adv.* in secret, privately; **они́ к. реши́ли де́ло** they decided the matter in camera.
келе́йный *adj.* **1.** *adj. of* **ке́лья. 2.** (*fig., pej.*) secret, private.
Кёльн, а *m.* Cologne.
кельт, а *m.* Celt.
ке́льтский *adj.* Celtic.
ке́л|ья, ьи, *g. pl.* **~ий** *f.* (*eccl.*) cell.
кем *i. of* **кто**
кема́р|ить, ю, ишь *impf.* (*sl.*) to kip, grab some shut-eye.
Ке́мбридж, а *m.* Cambridge.
ке́мбриджский *adj.* Cambridge; Cantabrigian.
ке́мпинг, а *m.* camping-site.
кенгуру́ *m. indecl.* kangaroo.
ке́ндо *nt. indecl.* kendo.
Ке́ни|я, и *f.* Kenya.
кенота́ф, а *m.* cenotaph.
кента́вр, а *m.* (*myth.*) centaur.
Ке́нтербери *m. indecl.* Canterbury.
кентербери́йский *adj.* Canterbury.
ке́пк|а, и *f.* (*coll.*) cloth cap.
кера́мик|а, и *f.* ceramics.
керами́ческий *adj.* ceramic.
ке́рвел|ь, я *m.* (*bot.*) chervil; **ди́кий к.** cow-parsley.
keрогáз, а *m.* paraffin stove.
кероси́н, а *m.* paraffin, kerosene.
кероси́нк|а, и *f.* (*coll.*) paraffin stove.
кероси́н|овый *adj. of* **~; ~овая ла́мпа** oil lamp.
ке́сарев *adj.* (*med.*): **~о сече́ние** Caesarean section.
ке́сар|ь, я *m.* monarch, lord.
кессо́н, а *m.* (*tech.*) caisson, coffer-dam.
кессо́н|ный *adj. of* **~; ~ная боле́знь** caisson disease; the bends.
ке́т|а, ы *f.* Siberian salmon.
кетме́н|ь, я́ *m.* (*agric.*) ketmen (*kind of hoe used in Central Asia*).
ке́т|овый *adj. of* **~а**
ке́тч, а *m.* (*coll.*) all-in wrestling.
кетчи́ст, а *m.* (*coll.*) all-in wrestler.
кефа́л|ь, и *f.* grey mullet.
кефи́р, а *m.* kefir.
кибернéтик|а, и *f.* cybernetics.
кибернети́ческий *adj.* cybernetic.
киби́тк|а, и *f.* **1.** kibitka, covered wagon. **2.** nomad tent.
кибу́ц, а *m.* kibbutz.
кив|а́ть, а́ю *impf.* (*of* **~ну́ть**) **1.** **(голово́й)** to nod (one's head); to nod assent. **2.** (**на**+*a.*) to motion (to); (*fig.*) refer (to), put the blame (on to).
ки́вер, а, *pl.* **~а́** *m.* shako.
ки́ви *f.* & *nt. indecl.* **1.** (*f.*) (*zool.*) kiwi. **2.** (*nt.*) kiwi fruit.
кив|ну́ть, ну́, нёшь *pf. of* **~а́ть**
кив|о́к, ка́ *m.* nod.
ки|да́ть, да́ю *impf.* (*of* **~нуть**) to throw, fling, cast (*usage as for* **броса́ть**).
ки|да́ться, да́юсь *impf.* (*of* **~нуться**) **1.** to throw o.s., fling o.s.; to rush. **2.** (+*i.*) to throw, fling, shy. **3.** *pass. of* **~да́ть**
Ки́ев, а *m.* Kiev.
киевля́н|ин, ина, *pl.* **~е, ~** *m.* Kievan.
киевля́н|ка, ки *f. of* **~ин**
ки́евский *adj.* Kiev; Kievan.
кизи́л, а *m.* (*bot.*) cornel.
кизя́к, а́ *m.* pressed dung (*used as fuel*).
ки|й, я́, *pl.* **~и́, ~ёв** *m.* (*billiard*) cue.
кики́мор|а, ы *f.* **1.** (*folklore*) kikimora (*hobgoblin in female form*). **2.** (*fig., coll.*): **вы́глядеть ~ой** to look a fright.
кикс, а *m.* (*sl.*) miss (*at billiards*).
кил|а́, ы́ *f.* (*dial.*) rupture, hernia.
килева́ни|е, я *nt.* (*naut.*) careening, careenage.
кил|ева́ть, у́ю *impf.* (*naut.*) to careen.
кил|ево́й *adj. of* **~ь; ~ева́я ка́чка** pitching.
кило́ *nt. indecl.* kilogram(me).
килоба́йт, а *m.* (*comput.*) kilobyte.
килова́тт, а *m.* (*elec.*) kilowatt.
килогра́мм, а *m.* kilogram(me).
килокало́ри|я, и *f.* large calorie.
киломе́тр, а *m.* kilometre.
километра́ж, а *m.* kilometres (*travelled, flown etc.*), distance.
кил|ь, я *m.* **1.** (*naut.*) keel. **2.** (*aeron.*) fin.
кильва́тер, а *m.* (*naut.*) wake; **идти́ в к.** (+*d.*) to follow in the wake (of).
кильва́тер|ный *adj. of* **~; ~ная коло́нна** line ahead.
ки́льк|а, и *f.* sprat.
кима́рить = кема́рить
кимва́л, а *m.* cymbal.
кимоно́ *nt. indecl.* kimono.
кингсто́н, а *m.* (*naut.*) Kingston valve; **откры́ть ~ы** to scuttle (a ship).
кинда́л|ь, я *m.* macadamia (nut).
кинемато́граф, а *m.* **1.** (*obs.*) cinematograph. **2.** cinema, cinematography. **3.** (*obs.*) cinema, picture-house.
кинематографи́ст, а *m.* cinematographer, film-maker.
кинематографи́ческий *adj.* cinematographic.
кинематогра́фи|я, и *f.* cinematography.
кинеско́п, а *m.* television tube.
кине́тик|а, и *f.* (*phys.*) kinetics.
кинети́ческий *adj.* (*phys.*) kinetic.
кинжа́л, а *m.* dagger.
кинжа́л|ьный *adj.* **1.** *adj. of* **~. 2.** (*mil.*) close-range, hand-to-hand.
кинз|а́, ы *f.* (*cul.*) fresh coriander (leaves).
кино́ *nt. indecl.* (*abstr. and concr.*) cinema.
кино... *comb. form, abbr. of* **кинематографи́ческий**
киноаппара́т, а *m.* cine-camera.
киноаппарату́р|а, ы *f.* cinematographic equipment.
киноарти́ст, а *m.* film actor.
киноарти́стк|а, и *f.* film actress.
киноателье́ *nt. indecl.* film studio.
кинобоеви́к, а́ *m.* hit film.
ки́новар|ь, и *f.* cinnabar, vermilion.
кинове́д, а *m.* student of film, film historian.
кинове́дени|е, я *nt.* film studies.
кинове́дческий *adj.*: **к. факульте́т** department of film studies.
кинодел|е́ц, ьца́ *m.* movie mogul.
кинодрамату́рг, а *m.* screenwriter.
кинонжурна́л, а *m.* newsreel.
кинoза́л, а *m.* **1.** cinema. **2.** auditorium.
кинозвезд|а́, ы́, *pl.* **~ы, ~, ~ам** *f.* film star.
кинозри́тел|ь, я *m.* cinema-goer.
кинока́мер|а, ы *f.* cine-camera.
кинокарти́н|а, ы *f.* (*non-documentary*) film; motion picture; movie.
кинокоме́ди|я, и *f.* comedy.
киноле́нт|а, ы *f.* reel (of film).
кино́лог, а *m.* cynologist.
кинолюби́тел|ь, я *m.* amateur film-maker, cineast(e).
киноман́, а *m.* cinephile, film freak.
киномеха́ник, а *m.* projectionist.
кинообозрева́тел|ь, я *m.* film critic.
кинoопера́тор, а *m.* camera-man.
кинопередви́жк|а, и *f.* portable (motion picture) projector.
киноплёнк|а, и *f.* (ciné) film.
кинопро́б|а, ы *f.* screen test.
кинопрока́тчик, а *m.* film distributor.
кинопросмо́тр, а *m.* film screening.
кинорежиссёр, а *m.* film director.
кинорепорта́ж, а *m.* news film.
киносеа́нс, а *m.* (cinema) performance, showing.
киносту́ди|я, и *f.* film studio.
киносцена́ри|й, я *m.* screenplay.
киносценари́ст, а *m.* scriptwriter; scripter.
киносъёмк|а, и *f.* filming, shooting.
киносъём|очный *adj. of* **~ка; ~очная кома́нда** film crew; **к. аппара́т** film *or* movie camera.
кинотеа́тр, а *m.* cinema.
киноустано́вк|а, и *f.* projecting machine.
кинофика́ци|я, и *f.* **1.** inclusion in cinema circuit. **2.** adaptation for the cinema, for the screen.
кинофи́льм, а *m.* film; **комеди́йный к.** comedy (*film*).

кинофици́р|овать, ую *impf. and pf.* **1.** to include in cinema circuit, bring cinema to. **2.** to adapt for the cinema, for the screen.
кинохро́ник|а, и *f.* newsreel.
кино́шк|а, и *f.* (*coll.*) **1.** cinema; the flicks. **2.** film, movie.
кино́шник, а *m.* (*coll.*) **1.** film-maker. **2.** film-goer, movie buff.
ки́|нуть(ся), ну(сь), нешь(ся) *pf. of* **~да́ть(ся)**
кио́ск, а *m.* kiosk, stall; **газе́тный к.** news-stand.
киоскёр, а *m.* stall-holder.
кио́т, а *m.* icon-case.
ки́п|а, ы *f.* **1.** pile, stack. **2.** (*measure*) pack, bale; **к. хло́пка** bale of cotton.
кипари́с, а *m.* (*bot.*) cypress.
кипе́ни|е, я *nt.* boiling; **то́чка ~я** boiling point.
кип|е́ть, лю́, ишь *impf.* (*of* **вс~**) to boil, seethe; **к. ключо́м** to gush up; **к. негодова́нием** (*fig.*) to seethe with indignation; **рабо́та ~е́ла** work was in full swing; **как в котле́ к.** to be hard pressed.
Кипр, а *m.* Cyprus.
кипре́|й, я *m.* (*bot.*) willow-herb.
киприо́т, а *m.* Cypriot.
киприо́т|ка, ки *f. of* **~**
ки́прский *adj.* Cypriot.
кипу́честь, и *f.* ebullience, turbulence.
кипу́ч|ий (~, ~а) *adj.* **1.** boiling, seething. **2.** (*fig.*) ebullient, turbulent; **~ая де́ятельность** feverish activity.
кипяти́льник, а *m.* kettle, boiler, boiling-tank.
кипяти́льный *adj.* boiling; **к. бак** copper.
кипя|ти́ть, чу́, ти́шь *impf.* (*of* **вс~**) to boil.
кипя|ти́ться, чу́сь, ти́шься *impf.* **1.** to boil (*intrans.*). **2.** (*fig., coll.*) to get excited. **3.** *pass. of* **~ти́ть**
кипят|о́к, ка́ *m.* **1.** boiling water. **2.** (*fig., coll.*) testy pers., irritable pers.
кипячёный *adj.* boiled.
кира́с|а, ы *f.* (*mil., hist.*) cuirass.
кираси́р, а *m.* (*mil., hist.*) cuirassier.
кирги́з, а *m.* Kirghiz.
Кирги́зи|я, и *f.* Kirghizia.
кирги́з|ка, ки *f. of* **~**
кирги́зский *adj.* Kirghiz.
ки́рз|а́, ы *and* **ы́** *f.* kersey.
ки́рз|овый *adj. of* **~а́**
кири́ллиц|а, ы *f.* Cyrillic alphabet.
ки́рк|а, и *f.* (Protestant) church.
кирк|а́, и́ *f.* pick(axe).
кирк|о́вый *adj. of* **~а́**
киркомоты́г|а, и *f.* pickaxe.
кирпи́ч, а́ *m.* **1.** brick. **2.** (*collect.*) bricks; **необожжённый, сама́нный к.** adobe. **3.** (*coll.*) no-entry sign.
кирпи́ч|ик, а *m.* **1.** *dim. of* **~**. **2.** (*pl.*) bricks (*as child's plaything*).
кирпи́ч|ный *adj. of* **~**; **к. заво́д** brickworks; **к. чай** brick-tea.
киря́|ть, ю *impf.* (*sl.*) to booze.
ки́с|а, ы *f.* = **~ка**
кисе́|йный *adj. of* **~я́**; (*coll., obs.*): **~йная ба́рышня** prim young lady.
кисе́л|ь, я́ *m.* kissel (*kind of blancmange*); (*fig., coll.*): **деся́тая (***or* **седьма́я) вода́ на ~е́** distant connexion, distant relative; **за семь вёрст ~я́ хлеба́ть** to go a long way for nothing; to go on a fool's errand.
кисе́ль|ный *adj. of* **~**; **моло́чные ре́ки, ~ные берега́** land flowing with milk and honey.
кисе́т, а *m.* tobacco pouch.
кисе|я́, и́ *f.* muslin.
ки́ск|а, и *f.* (*coll.*) puss, pussy-cat.
кис-ки́с *int.* puss-puss! (*when calling cat*).
ки́сленький *adj.* (*coll.*) slightly sour.
кисле́|ть, ю *impf.* (*coll.*) to become sour.
кисли́нк|а, *f., only in phr.* **с ~ой** (*coll.*) slightly sour, sourish.
кислова́т|ый (~, ~а) *adj.* sourish; acidulous.
кисло́ро́д, а *m.* oxygen.
кислоро́дно-ацетиле́новый *adj.* oxy-acetylene.
кислоро́дный *adj.* (*chem.*) oxygen.
ки́сло-сла́дкий *adj.* sour-sweet.
кислот|а́, ы́, *pl.* **~́ы** *f.* **1.** sourness; acidity. **2.** (*chem.*) acid.
кисло́тност|ь, и *f.* (*chem.*) acidity.
кисло́тный *adj.* (*chem.*) acid.
кислотоупо́рный *adj.* (*tech.*) acid-proof; acid resistant.
ки́с|лый (~ел, ~ла́, ~ло) *adj.* **1.** sour; (*fig.*): **~лое настрое́ние** sour mood; **~лая улы́бка** sour smile. **2.** fermented; **~лая капу́ста** sauerkraut; **~лые щи** sauerkraut soup. **3.** (*chem.*) acid.
кисля́тин|а, ы *f.* (*coll.*) **1.** sour(-tasting) stuff. **2.** (*fig., pej.*) sour puss, misery.
ки́с|нуть, ну, нешь, *past* **~, ~ла** *impf.* **1.** to turn sour. **2.** (*fig., coll.*) to mope; to look sour.
кист|а́, ы́ *f.* (*med.*) cyst.
кистеви́дный *adj.* (*bot.*) racemose.
кисте́н|ь, я́ *m.* bludgeon, flail.
ки́сточк|а, и *f.* **1.** brush; **к. для бритья́** shaving-brush. **2.** tassel.
кист|ь[1]**, и,** *pl.* **~́и, ~е́й** *f.* **1.** (*bot.*) cluster, bunch; **к. виногра́да** bunch of grapes. **2.** brush; **маля́рная к.** paintbrush. **3.** tassel.
кист|ь[2]**, и,** *pl.* **~́и, ~е́й** *f.* hand.
кит, а́ *m.* whale.
китаеве́д, а *m.* sinologist, sinologue.
китаеве́дени|е, я *nt.* sinology.
кита́|ец, йца, *pl.* **~йцы, ~йцев** *m.* Chinese, Chinaman.
китаизи́р|овать, ую *impf.* to Sinicize, Sinify.
китаи́ст, а *m.* sinologist, sinologue.
Кита́|й, я *m.* China.
кита́йк|а, и *f.* (*text.*) nankeen.
кита́йск|ий *adj.* Chinese; **~ая гра́мота** double Dutch; **к. и́дол** joss; **к. храм** josshouse; **~ая тушь** India(n) ink.
кита́йско-... *comb. form* Sino-.
китайч|о́нок, о́нка, *pl.* **~а́та, ~а́т** *m.* Chinese child.
китая́нк|а, и *f. of* **кита́ец**
ки́тел|ь, я, *pl.* **~я́, ~е́й** *m.* (*single-breasted, military or naval*) tunic, jacket (*with high collar*).
китобо́|ец, йца *m.* whaler (*ship*).
китобо́|й, я *m.* **1.** whaler (*pers.*). **2.** whaler (*ship*).
китобо́йн|ый *adj.* whaling; **к. про́мысел** whaling; **~ое су́дно** whaler.
кит|о́вый *adj. of* **~**; **к. жир** blubber; **к. ус** whalebone, baleen.
китоло́в = **китобо́й 1.**
кито|ло́вный *adj.* = **~бо́йный**
китообра́зный *adj.* (*zool.*) cetacean.
кич|и́ться, у́сь, и́шься *impf.* (+*i.*) to plume o.s. (on); to strut.
ки́чк|а, и *f.* (*dial.*) **1.** kichka (*married woman's head-dress*). **2.** (*fig.*) front (*of boat*).
кичли́вост|ь, и *f.* conceit; arrogance.
кичли́в|ый (~, ~а) *adj.* conceited, arrogant, haughty, strutting.
киш|е́ть, у́, и́шь *impf.* (+*i.*) to swarm (with), teem (with).
кише́чник, а *m.* (*anat.*) bowels, intestines; **очи́стить к.** to open the bowels.
киш|е́чный *adj. of* **~е́чник** *and* **~ка́**; intestinal.
киш|ка́, ки́, *g. pl.* **~о́к** *f.* **1.** (*anat.*) gut, intestine; **двенадцатипе́рстная к.** duodenum; **пряма́я к.** rectum; **слепа́я к.** caecum; **то́нкая, то́лстая к.** small, large intestine; (*fig., coll.*): **к. тонка́!** he, *etc.*, isn't up to that!; **вы́пустить ~ки́** to disembowel; **лезть из ~о́к** to put one's guts into; **надорва́ть ~ки́ (со́ смеху)** to laugh o.s. sick; **тяну́ться ~ко́й** to go in file. **2.** hose; **поли́ть ~ко́й** to hose.
кишла́к, а́ *m.* kishlak (*village in Central Asia*).
кишла́|чный *adj. of* **~к**
кишми́ш, а́ *no pl., m.* raisins, sultanas.
кишмя́ *adv., only in phr.* **к. кише́ть** to swarm.
КЛА *m. indecl.* (*abbr. of* ***косми́ческий лета́тельный аппара́т***) spacecraft, space vehicle.
клавеси́н, а *m.* (*mus.*) harpsichord.
клавиату́р|а, ы *f.* keyboard.
клавико́рд|ы, ов *no sg.* (*mus.*) clavichord.

кла́виш, а *m.* key (*of piano, typewriter, etc.*); **к. пробе́ла** space-bar.
кла́виш|а, и *f.* = ~
кла́виш|ный *adj. of* ~; **~ные инструме́нты** keyboard instruments.
клад, а *m.* treasure; (*fig., coll.*) treasure(-house); **моя́ секрета́рша — настоя́щий к.** my secretary is a real treasure.
кла́дбищ|е, а *nt.* cemetery, graveyard; churchyard.
кладби́щенский *adj. of* **кла́дбище; к. сто́рож** sexton.
кла́дез|ь, я *m., arch., now only in phr.* **к. прему́дрости** mine of information.
кла́дк|а, и *f.* laying; **ка́менная к.** masonry; **кирпи́чная к.** brickwork.
кладов|а́я, о́й *f.* pantry, larder; storeroom.
кладо́вк|а, и *f.* (*coll.*) pantry, larder.
кладовщи́к, а́ *m.* storeman.
кла|ду́, дёшь *see* **~сть**
кла́дчик, а *m.* bricklayer.
клад|ь, и *f.* **1.** (*sg. only*) load; **ручна́я к.** hand luggage. **2.** haycock.
кла́к|а, и *no pl., f.* (*collect.*) claque.
клакёр, а *m.* (*theatr.*) claqueur.
клан, а *m.* clan.
кла́ня|ться, юсь *impf.* (*of* **поклони́ться**) **1.** (*+d. or* **с***+i.*) to bow (to); to greet; **к. в по́яс** to bow from the waist; (*fig.*): **мы с ним не ~емся** I am not on speaking terms with him; **честь име́ю к.** *obs. leave-taking formula.* **2.** to send, convey greetings; **~йтесь ему́ от меня́** give him my regards. **3.** (*+d. or* **пе́ред**; *coll.*) to cringe (before); to humiliate o.s. (before). **4.** (*+d. and i.*; *obs.*) lay before, offer; **к. кому́-н. хле́бом-со́лью** to offer s.o. hospitality.
кла́пан, а *m.* **1.** (*tech.*) valve; **предохрани́тельный к.** safety valve. **2.** (*mus.*) vent. **3.** (*anat.*): **серде́чный к.** mitral valve. **4.** (*on clothing, etc.*) flap.
кларне́т, а *m.* clarinet.
кларнети́ст, а *m.* clarinettist.
класс, а *m.* **1.** (*in various senses*) class; **госпо́дствующий, пра́вящий к.** ruling class; **к. млекопита́ющих** (class of) mammalia; **игра́ высо́кого ~а** high class play. **2.** class-room.
кла́ссик, а *m.* **1.** (*in various senses*) classic; classic(al) author. **2.** classical scholar.
кла́ссик|а, и *f.* the classics.
классифика́тор, а *m.* classifier.
классифика́ци|я, и *f.* classification.
классифици́р|овать, ую *impf. and pf.* to classify.
классици́зм, а *m.* **1.** (*liter., art*) classicism. **2.** classical education.
класси́ческий *adj.* (*in var. senses*) classic(al).
кла́сс|ный *adj.* (*of* ~) **1.: ~ная доска́** blackboard; **~ная ко́мната** classroom; **~ная рабо́та** class work. **2.: к. ваго́н** passenger coach. **3.** (*sport*) first-class. **4.** (*sl.*) classy.
кла́ссовост|ь, и *f.* class character.
кла́ссов|ый *adj.* (*pol.*) class; **~ая борьба́** class struggle; **к. враг** class enemy; **~ые разли́чия** class distinctions; **~ое созна́ние** class-consciousness.
кла́сс|ы, ов (*children's game*) hopscotch.
кла|сть, ду́, дёшь, *past* **~л, ~ла** *impf.* (*of* **положи́ть**) **1.** to lay; to put (*into prone position or fig.*); to place; **к. больно́го на носи́лки** to lay a patient on a stretcher; **к. са́хар в чай** to put sugar in one's tea; **к. на ме́сто** to replace; **к. не на ме́сто** to mislay; **к. на му́зыку** to set to music; **к. в лу́зу, к. шара́** (*billiards*) to pocket a ball; **к. я́йца** to lay eggs (*of birds and insects*); **к. руль** (*naut.*) to put the wheel over; **к. нача́ло, к. коне́ц чему́-н.** to start sth., put an end to sth.; (*fig.*): **к. под сукно́** to shelve. **2.** (*pf.* **сложи́ть**) to build. **3.** to assign, set aside (*time, money*); **мы ~дём пятьдеся́т рубле́й на э́ту пое́здку** we are setting aside fifty roubles for this trip.
кла́узул|а, ы *f.* (*leg.*) clause, proviso, stipulation.
клаустрофо́би|я, и *f.* claustrophobia.
клёв, а *m.* biting, bite; **сего́дня хоро́ший к.** the fish are biting well today.
кл|ева́ть, юю́, юёшь *impf.* (*of* **~ю́нуть**) **1.** to peck. **2.** (*of fish*) to bite; **вчера́ ры́ба не ~ева́ла** the fish were not biting yesterday. **3.** (*coll.*): **к. но́сом** to nod (*from drowsiness*). **4.** (*fig., impers., coll.*): **~юёт** things are going well, better.
кл|ева́ться, ~юётся *impf.* (*of birds*) to peck (one another).
кле́вер, а *m.* (*bot.*) clover.
кле́вер|ный *adj. of* ~
клевет|а́, ы́ *f.* slander; calumny, aspersion; libel; **возвести́ на кого́-н. ~у́** to slander s.o., cast aspersions on s.o.
клеве|та́ть, щу́, ~щешь *impf.* (*of* **на~**) (**на**+*a.*) to slander, calumniate; to libel.
клеветни́к, а́ *m.* slanderer.
клеветн|и́ца, и́цы *f. of* **~и́к**
клеветни́ческ|ий *adj.* slanderous; libellous, defamatory; **~ая кампа́ния** smear campaign.
клеве|щу́, ~щешь *see* **~та́ть**
клев|о́к, ка́ *m.* (*coll.*) **1.** peck. **2.** (*mil.*) burst (of shrapnel) on impact.
клевре́т, а *m.* (*obs.*) minion, creature.
клёвый *adj.* (*sl.*) brill, knockout, fantastic.
кле|ево́й *adj. of* **~й; ~ева́я кра́ска** size paint.
клеёнк|а, и *f.* oil-cloth.
клеёнчатый *adj.* oilskin.
клеёный *adj.* gummed, glued.
кле́|ить, ю, ишь *impf.* **1.** (*pf.* **с~**) to glue; to gum; to paste. **2.** (*pf.* **под~**): **к. де́вушку** (*sl.*) to pick up a girl.
кле́|иться, ится *impf.* (*coll.*) **1.** to become sticky. **2.** (*fig.*; *usu. with neg.*) to get on, go well; **моя́ рабо́та что́-то пло́хо ~ится** my work is not going too well somehow; **разгово́р не ~ился** the conversation was sticky. **3.** *pass. of* **~ить**
кле|й, я, о ~е, на ~ю́ *m.* glue; **мучно́й к.** paste; **пти́чий к.** bird-lime; **пчели́ный к.** propolis; **ры́бий к.** isinglass; fish-glue; **к. и но́жницы** (*iron.*) scissors and paste.
кле́йк|а, и *f.* glueing.
кле́йк|ий *adj.* sticky; **~ая бума́га (для мух)** fly-paper; **~ая ле́нта** adhesive tape.
клейкови́н|а, ы *f.* gluten.
кле́йкост|ь, и *f.* stickiness.
клеймёный *adj.* branded.
клейм|и́ть, лю́, и́шь *impf.* (*of* **за~**) to brand, stamp; (*fig.*) to brand, stigmatize; **к. позо́ром** to hold up to shame.
клейме́ни|е, я *nt.* branding, stamping.
клейм|о́, а́, *pl.* **~а** *nt.* **1.** brand, stamp; **проби́рное к.** hall-mark, mark of assay; **фабри́чное к.** trade-mark; **к. позо́ра** (*fig.*) stigma. **2.** border panel (*of icon*).
кле́йстер, а *m.* paste.
клёкот, а *m.* (*of birds*) scream.
клеко|та́ть, чу́, ~чешь *impf.* (*of birds*) to scream.
клема́тис, а *m.* clematis.
кле́мм|а, ы *f.* (*elec.*) terminal.
клён, а *m.* maple.
клено́вый *adj. of* **клён**
клепа́л|о, а *nt.* (*tech.*; *obs.*) riveting hammer.
клепа́льн|ый *adj.* riveting; **~ая маши́на** riveter, riveting machine.
клепа́льщик, а *m.* riveter (*operator*).
клёпаный *adj.* (*tech.*) riveted.
клепа́|ть[1]**, ю** *impf.* (*tech.*) to rivet.
клеп|а́ть[2]**, лю́, ~лешь** *impf.* (*of* **наклепа́ть**) (**на**+*a.*; *coll.*) to slander, cast aspersions (on).
клёпк|а[1]**, и** *f.* riveting.
клёпк|а[2]**, и** *f.* stave, lag; (*fig., coll.*): **у него́ како́й-то ~и не хвата́ет** he has got a screw loose.
клептома́н, а *m.* kleptomaniac.
клептома́ни|я, и *f.* kleptomania.
клерикали́зм, а *m.* (*pol.*) clericalism.
клер|ова́ть, у́ю *impf.* (*tech.*) to refine, clarify.
клёст, а́ *m.* (*zool.*) crossbill.
кле́тк|а, и *f.* **1.** cage; coop; hutch. **2.** (*on paper*) square; (*on material*) check. **3.** (*anat.*): **грудна́я к.** thorax. **4.** (*biol.*) cell.
клетн|ева́ть, ю́ю, ю́ешь *impf.* (*naut.*) to serve (*a rope*).
клету́шк|а, и *f.* (*coll.*) closet, tiny room.
клетча́тк|а, и *f.* **1.** (*bot., tech.*) cellulose. **2.** (*anat.*) cellular tissue.

клéтчатый *adj.* **1.** checked; **к. платóк** checked head-scarf. **2.** (*biol.*) cellular.
клет|ь, и, *pl.* **∸и, ~éй** *f.* **1.** (*dial.*) store-room; shed. **2.** (*in mines*) cage.
клёцк|а, и *f.* (*cul.*) dumpling.
клёш, а *m.* (*and indecl. adj.*) flare; **~и, брюки-к.** flared trousers, bell-bottomed trousers; **юбка-к.** flared skirt.
клешн|я́, и́, *g. pl.* **~éй** *f.* claw (*of a crustacean*).
клещ, á *m.* (*zool.*) tick.
клещевúн|а, ы *f.* (*bot.*) Palma Christi (*castor-oil plant*).
клéщ|и, éй *no sg.* **1.** pincers, tongs; (*fig., coll.*): **э́того из меня́ ~áми не вы́тянешь** wild horses shall not drag it from me. **2.** (*mil.; fig.*) pincers, pincer-movement.
клúвер, а *m.* (*naut.*) jib.
клиéнт, а *m.* client.
клиентýр|а, ы *f.* (*collect.*) clientèle.
клúзм|а, ы *f.* (*med.*) enema, clyster; **стáвить ~у** (+*d.*) to give an enema.
клик, а *m.* (*poet.*) cry, call.
клúк|а, и *f.* clique.
клú|кать, чу, чешь *impf.* (*of* **~кнуть**) **1.** (*coll.*) to call, hail. **2.** (+*a. and i.; dial.*) to call (*name*); **егó ~чут Ивáном** he is called Ivan. **3.** (*of geese and swans*) to honk.
клúк|нуть, ну, нешь *pf. of* **~ать**
кликýш|а, и *f.* hysterical woman.
кликýшеский *adj.* hysterical.
кликýшеств|о, а *nt.* hysterics.
клúмакс, а *m.* = **климактéрий**
климактéри|й, я *m.* (*physiol.*) climacteric, menopause.
климактерúческий *adj.* (*physiol.*) climacteric, menopausal; **к. перúод** menopause.
клúмат, а *m.* climate.
климатúческий *adj.* climatic.
клин, а, *pl.* **∸ья, ∸ьев** *m.* **1.** wedge; **загнáть к. (в**+*a.*) to drive a wedge (into); **бородá ∸ом** wedge-shaped beard; (*fig.*) **вбить к. (мéжду)** to drive a wedge (between); **к. ∸ом вышибáется** (*prov.*) like cures like; **свет не ∸ом сошёлся** there are plenty more fish in the sea. **2.** (*archit.*) quoin. **3.** gore (*in skirt*); gusset (*in underwear*). **4.** (*agric.*) field; **озúмый к.** winter field; **посевнóй к.** sown area.
клúник|а, и *f.* clinic.
клиницúст, а *m.* clinician.
клинúческий *adj.* clinical.
клиновúдный *adj.* wedge-shaped; V-shaped.
клин|овóй *adj. of* **~; к. затвóр** (*mil.*) breech mechanism.
клин|óк, кá *m.* blade.
клинообрáз|ный (~ен, ~на) *adj.* wedge-shaped; **~ные письменá** cuneiform characters.
клинопúсный *adj.* cuneiform.
клúнопис|ь, и *f.* cuneiform (characters, text).
клúныш|ек, ка *m.*: **борóдка ~ком** goatee.
клúпер, а *m.* (*naut.*) clipper.
клúпс|ы, ~ *or* **ов** *pl.* (*sg.* **~, ~а** *m. or* **~а, ~ы** *f.*) clip-on earrings; clip-ons.
клир, а *m.* (*collect.; eccl.*) the clergy (*of a parish*).
клúринг, а *m.* (*fin.*) clearing, clearance.
клúринг|овый *adj. of* **~**
клúрос, а *m.* choir (*part of church*).
клистúр, а *m.* (*med.; obs.*) enema, clyster.
клúтор, а *m.* (*anat.*) clitoris.
клич, а *m.* (*rhet.*) call; **боевóй к.** war-cry; **клúкнуть к.** to issue a call.
клúчк|а, и *f.* **1.** name (*of domestic animal, pet*). **2.** nickname. **3.** alias.
клишé *nt. indecl.* (*typ. and fig.*) cliché.
клоáк|а, и *f.* **1.** cesspit, sink, sewer (*also fig., concr., and abstr.*). **2.** (*zool.*) cloaca.
клобýк, á *m.* (*eccl.*) klobuk (*headgear of Orthodox monk*).
клозéт, а *m.* (*coll., obs.*) water closet, W.C.
клозéт|ный *adj. of* **~; ~ная бумáга** toilet paper.
клок, á *pl.* **клóчья, клóчьев** *and* **~и́, ~óв** *m.* **1.** rag, shred; **разорвáть в клóчья** to tear to shreds, tatters. **2.** tuft; **к. сéна** wisp of hay; **к. шéрсти** flock.
клóкот, а *no pl., m.* bubbling; gurgling.
клоко|тáть, чý, ∸чешь *impf.* to bubble; to gurgle; to boil up (*also fig.*); **в нём всё ~тáло от гнéва** he was seething with rage.
клон, а *m.* (*biol.*) clone.
клонúр|овать, ую *impf. and pf.* to clone.
клон|úть, ю́, ∸ишь *impf.* **1.** to bend; to incline; (*impers.*): **лóдку ~úло нá бок** the boat was heeling; **старикá ужé ~úло ко снý** the old man was already nodding off. **2.** (*fig., coll.*) to lead (*conversation*); **кудá ты ∸ишь?** what are you driving at?
клон|úться, ю́сь, ∸ишься *impf.* **1.** to bow, bend (*intrans.*). **2.** (**к**+*d., fig.*): to be nearing; to be leading up (to), be heading (for); **день ~úлся к вéчеру** the day was declining; **дéло ∸ится к развя́зке** the affair is coming to a head; **к чемý э́то ∸ится?** what is it leading up to?
клоп, á *m.* **1.** bedbug. **2.** (*fig., coll.; in addressing a child*) kid.
клопóвник, а *m.* (*coll.*) bug-infested place.
клоп|óвый *adj. of* **~**
клопомóр, а *m.* insecticide.
клóун, а *m.* clown.
клоунáд|а, ы *f.* clownery, clowning; clown acts.
клóун|ский *adj. of* **~; к. колпáк** fool's cap.
клох|тáть, чý, ∸чешь *impf.* (*coll.*) to cluck.
клочковáт|ый (~, ~а) *adj.* **1.** tufted, shaggy. **2.** patchy, scrappy.
клоч|óк, кá *m. dim. of* **клок; разорвáть в ~кú** to tear to shreds, tatters; **к. бумáги** scrap of paper; **к. земли́** plot of land; **к. лазýри средú облакóв** a patch of blue sky between the clouds.
клуб[1]**, а** *m.* **1.** club; **к. любúтелей бéга** jogging club; **к. здорóвья** keep-fit club; **к. одинóких сердéц** Lonely Hearts Club. **2.** club-house; **офицéрский к.** officers' mess.
клуб[2]**, а,** *pl.* **~ы́, ~óв** *m.* puff; **~ы́ пы́ли** clouds of dust.
клýб|ень, ня *m.* (*bot.*) tuber.
клуб|úть, úт *impf.* to blow up, puff out; **к. пыль** to raise clouds of dust.
клуб|úться, úтся *impf.* to swirl; to curl, wreathe.
клубневóй *adj.* (*bot.*) tuberose.
клубнеплóд|ы, ов *pl.* (*sg.* **~, ~а** *m.*) (*bot., agric.*) root crops, tuber crops.
клубнúк|а, и *f.* **1.** (cultivated) strawberry. **2.** (*collect.*) (cultivated) strawberries.
клубнú|чный *adj. of* **~ка; ~чное варéнье** strawberry preserve.
клýб|ный *adj. of* **~**[1]
клуб|óк, кá *m.* **1.** ball; **свернýться ~кóм, в к.** to roll o.s. up into a ball. **2.** (*fig.*) tangle, mass; **к. интрúг** network of intrigue; **к. противорéчий** mass of contradictions. **3.** (*fig.*) lump (in the throat); **слёзы у неё подступúли ~кóм к гóрлу** a lump rose in her throat.
клýмб|а, ы *f.* (flower-)bed.
клупп, а *m.* (*tech.*) die-stock, screw-stock.
клýш|а, и *f.* **1.** (*dial.*) broody hen. **2.** lesser black-backed gull.
клык, á *m.* **1.** canine (tooth). **2.** fang; tusk.
клюв, а *m.* beak; bill.
клюз, а *m.* (*naut.*) hawse-hole.
клюк|á, и́ *f.* walking-stick.
клю́к|ать, аю *impf. of* **~нуть**
клю́кв|а, ы *f.* cranberry (*Oxycoccus palustris*); (*coll.*): **вот так к.!** here's a pretty kettle of fish!; **развéсистая к.** myth, fable (*of credulous travellers' fabrications*).
клю́кв|енный *adj. of* **~а; к. кисéль** cranberry jelly; **к. морс** cranberry drink.
клю́к|нуть, ну, нешь *pf.* (*of* **~ать**) (*coll.*) to take a drop.
клю́н|уть, у, ешь *pf. of* **клевáть**
ключ[1]**, á** *m.* **1.** (*in var. senses*) key; clue; **заперéть на к.** to lock; **гáечный к.** spanner, wrench; **францýзский к.** monkey-wrench; **к.-шестигрáнник** Allen key; **к. к шúфру** key to a cipher; (*mil.*): **к. мéстности** key-point. **2.** (*archit.*) keystone. **3.** (*mus.*) key, clef; **басóвый к.** bass clef; **скрипúчный к.** treble clef.
ключ[2]**, á** *m.* spring; source; **кипéть ~óм** to bubble over; **бить ~óм** to spout, jet; (*fig.*) to be in full swing.
ключáр|ь, я́ *m.* (*eccl.*) sacristan.
ключ|евóй[1] *adj. of* **~**[1]**; ~евы́е óтрасли промы́шленности** key industries; (*mil.*): **~евы́е позúции** key positions;

(*mus.*): **к. знак** clef.
ключ|евóй² *adj. of* ~²; **~евáя водá** spring water.
ключи́ц|а, ы *f.* (*anat.*) clavicle, collar-bone.
клю́чник, а *m.* (*obs.*) steward.
клю́чниц|а, ы *f.* (*obs.*) housekeeper.
клю́шк|а, и *f.* (*sport*) (golf-)club; (hockey) stick; (*coll.*) walking-stick.
клюшконóс, а *m.* caddie.
кл|ю́ю, юёшь *see* **~евáть**
кля́кс|а, ы *f.* blot, smudge.
кля|нý, нёшь *see* **~сть**
кля́нч|ить, у, ишь *impf.* **(у)** (*coll.*) to beg (of).
кляп, а *m.* gag; **засýнуть к. в рот** (*+d.*) to gag.
кля|сть, нý, нёшь, *past* **~л, ~лá, ~ло** *impf.* to curse.
кля́|сться, нýсь, нёшься, *past* **~лся, ~лáсь** *impf.* (*of* **по~**) **(в**+*p.*, *+inf. or* **+что)** to swear, vow; **к. в вéрности** to vow fidelity; **к. отомсти́ть** to vow vengeance; **к. чéстью** to swear on one's honour.
кля́тв|а, ы *f.* oath, vow; **гиппокрáтова к.** Hippocratic oath; **лóжная к.** perjury; **дать ~у** to take an oath.
кля́тв|енный *adj. of* **~а; дать ~енное обещáние** to promise on oath.
клятвопреступлéни|е, я *nt.* perjury.
клятвопрестýпник, а *m.* perjurer.
кля́уз|а, ы *f.* **1.** (*coll.*) slander, scandal; tale-bearing. **2.** (*leg., obs.*) barratry; **затевáть ~у** to institute vexatious litigation.
кля́узник, а *m.* (*coll.*) scandalmonger; tale-bearer.
кля́узнича|ть, ю *impf.* (*of* **на~**) (*coll.*) to spread slander; to bear tales.
кля́узн|ый *adj.* (*coll.*) captious, pettifogging; **случи́лось ~ое дéло** a tiresome thing happened.
кля́ч|а, и *f.* (*pej.*; *of horse*) jade.
км (*abbr. of* **киломéтр**) km, kilometre(s).
КНДР *f. indecl.* (*abbr. of* ***Корéйская Нарóдно-Демократи́ческая Респýблика***) Korean People's Democratic Republic.
кнел|ь, и *f.* (*collect.*; *cul.*) quenelles.
кнехт, а *m.* (*naut.*) bollard, bitts.
кни́г|а, и *f.* **1.** book; **Бéлая к.** White Paper (= *official government report*); **тебé и ~и в рýки** (*coll.*) you know best. **2.** number (*of a journal, magazine*).
книговéдени|е, я *nt.* bibliography.
книговедéни|е, я *nt.* book-keeping.
книгоéд, а *m.* (*zool. and fig.*) bookworm.
книгоиздáтел|ь, я *m.* publisher.
книгоиздáтельский *adj.* publishing.
книгоиздáтельств|о, а *nt.* **1.** publishing-house. **2.** publishing.
книголю́б, а *m.* bibliophile.
книгонóш|а, и *c.g.* book-pedlar, colporteur.
книгопечáтани|е, я *nt.* (book-)printing.
книгопечáт|ный *adj. of* **~ание; к. станóк** printing-press.
книготоргóв|ец, ца *m.* bookseller.
книготоргóвл|я, и *f.* **1.** book trade. **2.** bookshop.
книгохрани́лищ|е, а *nt.* **1.** library. **2.** book-stack.
кни́жечк|а, и *f.* booklet.
кни́жк|а¹, **и** *f.* **1.** *dim. of* **кни́га; записнáя к.** notebook; **к.-календáрь** pocket diary; **к.-ши́рмочка** pop-up book. **2.** (*document*) book, card; **забóрная к.** ration book; **расчётная к.** pay-book; **чéковая к.** cheque-book. **3.** **(сберегáтельная) к.** savings-bank book; **положи́ть дéньги на ~у** to deposit money at a savings bank; **на кни́жку** on credit.
кни́жк|а², **и** *f.* (*zool.*) third stomach (*of ruminants*).
кни́жник, а *m.* **1.** (*bibl.*) scribe. **2.** bibliophile. **3.** bookseller.
кни́жн|ый *adj.* **1.** *adj. of* **кни́га; к. знак** book-plate; **~ая пóлка** bookshelf; **к. шкаф** bookcase. **2.** bookish, abstract; pedantic; **к. стиль** pedantic style; **~ая учёность** book-learning; **к. червь** bookworm.
кни́зу *adv.* downwards.
кни́ксен, а *m.* curts(e)y.
кни́ц|а, ы *f.* (*tech., naut.*) knee, gusset.
кнóпк|а, и *f.* **1.** drawing-pin; **прикрепи́ть ~ой** to pin. **2.** press-button (*fastener*). **3.** (*elec.*) button; knob; **нажáть все ~и** (*fig., coll.*) to pull wires, do all in one's power.
кнóп|очный *adj. of* **~ка; к. телефóн** push-button telephone.
КНР *f. indecl.* (*abbr. of* ***Китáйская Нарóдная Респýблика***) People's Republic of China.
кнут, á *m.* whip; (*hist.*) knout; **щёлкать ~óм** to crack a whip; **поли́тика ~а и пря́ника** (*pol.*) carrot and stick policy.
кнутови́щ|е, а *nt.* whip-handle.
княги́н|я, и *f.* princess (*wife of prince*).
княжéни|е, я *nt.* (*hist.*) reign.
кня́жеств|о, а *nt.* principality.
кня́ж|ить, у, ишь *impf.* (*hist.*) to reign.
кня́жич, а *m.* prince (*prince's unmarried son*).
княж|нá, ны́, *g. pl.* **~óн** *f.* princess (*prince's unmarried daughter*).
княз|ёк, ькá *m.* **1.** (*coll.*) princeling. **2.** (*tech.*) roof-ridge.
княз|ь, я, *pl.* **~ья́, ~éй** *m.* prince; **вели́кий к.** (*in medieval Russia*) grand prince; (*in tsarist Russia*) grand duke.
К° (*abbr. of* **компáния**) Co., Company.
ко *see* **к**
коагуля́ци|я, и *f.* coagulation.
коалиц|иóнный *adj. of* **~ия**
коали́ци|я, и *f.* (*pol.*) coalition.
кóбальт, а *m.* (*chem.*) cobalt.
кóбальт|овый *adj. of* **~; ~овая крáска** cobalt; **~овое стеклó** smalt.
кобéл|ь, я́ *m.* **1.** (*male*) dog. **2.** (*coll.*) lech(er).
кобéн|иться, юсь, ишься *impf.* (*coll.*) to be capricious; to make faces.
кóбз|á, ~ы *f.* kobza (*Ukrainian mus. instrument similar to guitar*).
кобзáр|ь, я́ *m.* kobza-player.
КÓБОЛ, а *m.* (*comput.*) COBOL.
кóбр|а, ы *f.* cobra.
кобур|á, ы́ *f.* holster.
кóбчик, а *m.* (*zool.*) merlin.
кобы́л|а¹, **ы** *f.* mare.
кобы́л|а², **ы** *f.* **1.** (*hist.*) punishment-bench. **2.** vaulting-horse.
кобы́л|ий *adj. of* **~а**¹
кобы́лк|а¹, **и** *f.* filly.
кобы́лк|а², **и** *f.* bridge (*of stringed instruments*).
кóваный *adj.* **1.** forged; hammered. **2.** (*fig.*) terse.
ковáр|ный (~ен, ~на) *adj.* insidious, crafty; perfidious.
ковáрств|о, а *nt.* insidiousness, craftiness; perfidy.
ковáть, кую́, куёшь *impf.* **1.** (*pf.* **вы́~**) to forge (*also fig.*); to hammer (*iron*); **к. побéду** to forge victory; **куй желéзо, покá горячó** (*prov.*) strike while the iron is hot. **2.** (*pf.* **под~**) to shoe (*horses*).
ковбó|й, я *m.* cowboy.
ковбóй|ский *adj. of* **~; к. фильм** western (*film*).
ковбóйк|а, и *f.* (*coll.*) **1.** cowboy hat. **2.** cowboy shirt.
ков|ёр, рá *m.* carpet; rug; mat; **к.-самолёт** magic carpet.
ковéрка|ть, ю *impf.* (*of* **ис~**) **1.** to spoil, ruin (*concr. and abstr*). **2.** (*fig.*) to distort; to mangle, mispronounce; **к. чужýю мысль** to distort s.o. else's ideas **к. словá** to mangle words; **он ~ет францýзский язы́к** he murders the French language.
коверкóт, а *m.* covert coat.
ковéрн|ый, ого *m.* clown.
кóвк|а, и *f.* **1.** forging. **2.** shoeing.
кóв|кий (~ок, ~кá, ~ко) *adj.* malleable, ductile.
кóвкост|ь, и *f.* malleability, ductility.
коври́г|а, и *f.* loaf.
коври́жк|а, и *f.* gingerbread; **ни за каки́е ~и** (*coll.*) not for love nor money.
кóврик, а *m.* rug; **к. для вáнной** bath mat.
ковроочисти́тел|ь, я *m.* carpet cleaner.
коврочи́стк|а, и *f.* carpet sweeper.
ковчéг, а *m.* **1.** ark; **Нóев к.** Noah's ark. **2.** (*eccl.*) shrine.
ковш, á *m.* **1.** scoop, ladle, dipper. **2.** (*tech.*) bucket.
кóв|ы, ~ *no sg.* (*obs.*) snare, trap; toils; **стрóить к. кому-н.** to lay a trap for s.o.
ковы́л|ь, я́ *m.* (*bot.*) feather-grass.
ковыля́|ть, ю *impf.* (*coll.*) to hobble; to stump; (*of child*) to toddle.

ковыр|ну́ть, ну́, нёшь *pf. of* **~я́ть**
ковыр|я́ть, я́ю *impf.* (*of* **~ну́ть**) (*coll.*) **1.** to dig into; (**в**+*p.*) to pick (at); **к. в зуба́х** to pick one's teeth. **2.** to tinker (up), potter.
ковыря́|ться, юсь *impf.* (*coll.*) **1.** (**в**+*p.*) to rummage (in). **2.** to tinker.
когда́[1] *adv.* **1.** (*interrog. and rel.*) when; (*coll.*): **есть к.!** there's no time for it!; **есть к. мне болта́ть!** I've no time for talk! **2.**: **к. (бы) ни** whenever; **к. бы вы ни пришли́, к. (вы) ни придёте** whenever you come. **3.** (*coll.*): **к...., к.** sometimes ... sometimes; **я занима́юсь к. у́тром, к. ве́чером** sometimes I work in the morning, sometimes in the evening. **4.** (*coll.*): **к. как** it depends. **5.** (*coll.*) = **когда́-нибудь**
когда́[2] *conj.* **1.** when; while, as; **я её встре́тил, к. шёл домо́й** I met her as I was going home. **2.** (*coll.*) if; **к. так, согла́сен с тобо́й** if that is the case, I agree.
когда́-либо *adv.* = **когда́-нибудь**
когда́-нибудь *adv.* **1.** (*in future*) some time, some day. **2.** ever; **вы бы́ли к.-н. в Кита́е?** have you ever been to China?
когда́-то *adv.* **1.** (*in past*) once; some time; formerly. **2.** (*in future*) some day (*indefinitely distant*); **к.-то ещё бу́дет тако́й прия́тный ве́чер** it will be a long time before we have such a pleasant evening again.
кого́ *a. and g. of* **кто**
когóрт|а, ы *f.* cohort.
ко́г|оть, тя, *pl.* **~ти, ~те́й** *m.* claw; talon; **показа́ть свои́ ~ти** (*fig.*) to show one's teeth; **попа́сть в ~ти (к кому́-н.)** to fall into the clutches (of s.o.).
когти́ст|ый (~, ~а) *adj.* sharp-clawed.
когти́т|ь, ~ *impf.* (*dial.*) to claw to pieces, tear with claws.
код, а *m.* code; **персона́льный к.** personal identification number, PIN; **телегра́фный к.** cable code; **по ~у** in code.
ко́д|а, ы *f.* (*mus.*) coda.
коде́ин, а *m.* (*pharm.*) codeine.
ко́декс, а *m.* **1.** (*leg. and fig.*) code; **мора́льный к.** moral code; **уголо́вный к.** criminal code. **2.** (*liter.*) codex.
коди́рующий *adj.*: **к. преобразова́тель** (*comput.*) digitizer; **к. планше́т** digitizing tablet.
кодифика́ци|я, и *f.* codification.
кодифици́р|овать, ую *impf. and pf.* (*leg.*) to codify.
ко́дов|ый *adj. of* **код**; **~ое назва́ние** code-name.
кодоско́п, а *m.* overhead projector.
ко́е-где́ (*and* **кой-где́**) *adv.* here and there, in places.
ко́е-ка́к (*and* **кой-ка́к**) *adv.* (*coll.*) **1.** anyhow (*badly, carelessly*). **2.** somehow (or other), just (*with great difficulty*); **к.-к. мы доплы́ли до того́ бе́рега** somehow we managed to swim to the other side.
ко́е-како́й (*and* **кой-како́й**) *pron.* some.
ко́е-кто́ (*and* **кой-кто́**), **ко́е-кого́** *pron.* somebody; some people.
ко́ечный *adj. of* **ко́йка; к. больно́й** in-patient.
ко́е-что́ (*and* **кой-что́**), **ко́е-чего́** *pron.* something; a little.
ко́ж|а, и *f.* **1.** skin; hide; (*anat.*) cutis; **гуси́ная к.** goose-flesh; (*fig., coll.*) **из ~и (вон) лезть** to go all out, do one's utmost; **к. да ко́сти** skin and bone. **2.** leather; **свина́я к.** pig-skin; **теля́чья к.** calf. **3.** peel, rind; (*bot.*) epidermis.
кожа́н[1], **а́** *m.* (*obs.*) leather coat.
кожа́н[2], **а́** *m.* large bat.
ко́жанк|а, и *f.* (*coll.*) leather jacket, jerkin.
ко́жаный *adj.* leather(n).
кожгалантере́|я, и *f.* leather goods.
коже́венный *adj.* leather; leather-dressing, tanning; **к. заво́д** tannery; **к. това́р** leather goods.
коже́вник, а *m.* currier, leather-dresser, tanner.
кожзамени́тел|ь, я *m.* imitation leather, leatherette.
кожими́т, а *m.* imitation leather, leatherette.
ко́жиц|а, ы *f.* **1.** thin skin, film. pellicle; **к. колбасы́** sausage-skin. **2.** peel, skin (*of fruit*).
ко́жник, а *m.* (*coll.*) dermatologist.
ко́жный *adj.* skin; (*med.*) cutaneous.
кожур|а́, ы́ *f.* rind, peel, skin (*of fruit*).
кожу́х, а́ *m.* **1.** leather jacket, sheepskin jacket. **2.** (*tech.*) housing, casing, jacket; **к. гребно́го колеса́** paddle-box.
коз|а́, ы́, *pl.* **~ы** *f.* **1.** goat. **2.** she-goat. **3.** (*coll.*) tomboy.
коз|ёл, ла́ *m.* he-goat; **к. отпуще́ния** scapegoat; **от него́ как от ~ла́ молока́** he is good for nothing.
козеро́г, а *m.* **1.** (*zool.*) wild (mountain) goat, ibex. **2. К.** (*astrol., astron.*) Capricorn; **тро́пик К~а** (*geog.*) Tropic of Capricorn.
козе́тк|а, и *f.* (*coll.*) settee.
ко́з|ий *adj. of* **~а́; к. пасту́х** goatherd; **~ья но́жка** (*med.*) molar forceps; (*coll.*) roll-up, roll-your-own (*home-made cigarette*).
козл|ёнок, ёнка, *pl.* **~я́та, ~я́т** *m.* kid.
коз|ли́ный *adj. of* **~ёл; ~ли́ная боро́дка** goatee; **к. го́лос** reedy voice.
козло́вый *adj.* goatskin.
ко́з|лы, ел, лам *no sg.* **1.** (coach-)box. **2.** trestle(s); saw-horse. **3.** (*mil.*): **соста́вить винто́вки в к.** to pile arms.
козл|я́та, я́т *see* **~ёнок**
козля́т|ки, ок *no sg., affectionate dim. of* **~а**
ко́зн|и, ей *pl.* (*sg.* (*rare*) **~ь, ~и** *f.*) (*obs.*) machinations, intrigues; snare.
козово́д, а *m.* goat breeder.
козово́дств|о, а *nt.* goat-breeding.
козодо́|й, я *m.* (*zool.*) nightjar, goatsucker.
козу́л|я, и *f.* roe(buck).
козыр|ёк, ька́ *m.* **1.** (cap) peak; **взять под к.** (*+d.*) to salute. **2.** (*mil.*) head cover (*in trenches*).
козыр|но́й *adj. of* **ко́зырь**
козыр|ну́ть, ну́, нёшь *pf. of* **~я́ть**
ко́зыр|ь, я, *pl.* **~и, ~е́й** *m.* **1.** (*cards and fig.*) trump; **объяви́ть ~я** to call one's hand; **откры́ть свои́ ~и** (*fig.*) to lay one's cards on the table; **покры́ть ~ем** to trump; **ходи́ть с ~я** to lead trumps; (*fig.*) to play a trump card; **гла́вный к.** (one's) trump card. **2.** (*coll.*) card, swell; **ходи́ть ~ем** to swagger.
козыр|я́ть[1], **я́ю** *impf.* (*of* **~ну́ть**) (*coll.*) **1.** (*cards*) to lead trumps, play a trump; (*fig.*) to play one's trump card. **2.** (*+i.*) to show off.
козыр|я́ть[2], **я́ю** *impf.* (*of* **~ну́ть**) (*+d.*; *coll.*) to salute.
козя́вк|а, и *f.* (*coll.*) small insect.
ко́итус, а *m.* coition, coitus; **к. прерыва́емый** coitus interruptus.
кой *interrog. and rel. pron.* (*obs.*) which; **до ко́их пор?** how long?; **ни в ко́ем слу́чае** on no account; (*coll.*): **на к. чёрт?** why in the world; what the devil for?
ко́йк|а, и *f.* **1.** berth, bunk (*on board ship*). **2.** bed (*in hospital*).
койо́т, а *m.* coyote.
кок, а *m.* **1.** (ship's) cook. **2.** quiff.
ко́к|а, и *f.* (*bot.*) coca.
кокаи́н, а *m.* cocaine.
кокаини́зм, а *m.* cocainism.
кокаини́ст, а *m.* cocaine addict.
кока́рд|а, ы *f.* cockade.
ко́к|ать, аю *impf.* (*of* **~нуть**) (*coll.*) to crack, break,
коке́тк|а, и *f.* coquette.
коке́тлив|ый (~, ~а) *adj.* coquettish.
коке́тнича|ть, ю *impf.* **1.** (**с**+*i.*) to coquet(te), flirt (with). **2.** (*+i.*) to show off, flaunt.
коке́тств|о, а *nt.* coquetry.
коки́л|ь, я *m.* (*tech.*) chill mould.
коки́льн|ый *adj.*: **~ое литьё** (*tech.*) chill casting.
кокк, а *m.* (*med.*) coccus.
коклю́ш, а *m.* whooping-cough.
коклю́шк|а, и *f.* bobbin.
ко́к|нуть, ну, нешь *pf. of* **~ать**
ко́кон, а *m.* cocoon.
коко́с, а *m.* **1.** coco(-tree). **2.** coconut.
коко́с|овый *adj. of* **~; ~овое волокно́** coir; **~овое ма́сло** coconut oil; **к. оре́х** coconut; **~овая па́льма** coco(-tree), coconut tree.
коко́тк|а, и *f.* courtesan, cocotte.
коко́шник, а *m.* kokoshnik (*Russ. peasant woman's head-dress*).
кокс, а *m.* coke; **вы́жиг ~а** (*tech.*) coke firing.
коксова́льн|ый *adj.* (*tech.*) coking; **~ая печь** coke oven.

кокс|ова́ть, у́ю *impf.* (*tech.*) to coke.
кокс|ова́ться, у́юс *impf.* (*tech.*) to coke (*intrans.*).
ко́кс|овый *adj. of* ~; **~овая печь** coke oven; **~овое число́** coking value.
кокс|у́ющийся *pres. part. act. of* **~ова́ться** *and adj.*; **к. у́голь** coking coal.
кокте́йл|ь, я *m.* cocktail; cocktail party; **моло́чный к.** milk shake.
кол, а́ *m.* **1.** (*pl.* **~ья, ~ьев**) stake, picket; **сажа́льный к.** dibber; **посади́ть на́ к.** to impale; (*coll.*): **стоя́ть ~о́м в го́рле** to stick in one's throat; **ему́ хоть к. на голове́ теши́** he is very pig-headed; **у него́ нет ни ~а́ ни двора́** he has neither house nor home. **2.** (*pl.* **~ы́, ~о́в**) (*coll.*) a 'very poor' (*lowest possible school mark*). **3.** (*sl.*) rouble; smacker.
кол... *comb. form, abbr. of* **коллекти́вный**
ко́лб|а, ы *f.* (*chem.*) retort.
колбас|а́, ы́, *pl.* **~ы** *f.* sausage; **кровяна́я к.** black pudding.
колба́сник, а *m.* sausage-maker; pork butcher.
колба́с|ный *adj. of* **~а́**; **к. яд** ptomaine.
колго́т|ки, ок *no sg.* tights.
колдо́бин|а, ы *f.* (*dial.*) **1.** rut, pothole (*in road*). **2.** deep place (*in lake, river, etc.*).
колд|ова́ть, у́ю *impf.* to practise witchcraft.
колдовско́й *adj.* magical; (*fig.*) magical, bewitching.
колдовств|о́, а́ *nt.* witchcraft, sorcery, magic.
колдо́говор, а *m.* collective agreement.
колду́н, а́ *m.* sorcerer, magician, wizard.
колду́н|ья, ьи, *g. pl.* **~ий** *f.* witch, sorceress.
колеба́ни|е, я *nt.* **1.** (*phys.*) oscillation, vibration; **к. ма́ятника** swing of the pendulum. **2.** fluctuation, variation; **к. ку́рса** (*fin.*) stock exchange fluctuations, fluctuations in the rate of exchange. **3.** (*fig.*) hesitation, wavering, vacillation.
колеба́тельный *adj.* (*tech.*) oscillatory, vibratory.
колеб|а́ть, ~лю, ~лешь *impf.* (*of* **по~**) to shake; (*fig.*): **к. обще́ственные усто́и** to shake the foundations of society.
колеб|а́ться, ~люсь, ~лешься *impf.* (*of* **по~**) **1.** to shake to and fro, sway; (*phys.*) to oscillate. **2.** to fluctuate, vary. **3.** (*fig.*) to hesitate; to waver, vacillate.
коле́нк|а, и *f.* (*coll.*) knee.
коленко́р, а *m.* (*text.*) calico; (*coll.*): **э́то совсе́м друго́й к.** that's quite another matter.
коленко́р|овый *adj. of* ~
коле́н|ный *adj. of* **~о**; (*anat.*): **к. суста́в** knee-joint; **~ная ча́шка** patella, knee-cap.
коле́н|о, а *nt.* **1.** (*pl.* **~и, ~ей, ~ям**) knee; **преклони́ть ~и** to genuflect; **стать на ~и (пе́ред)** to kneel (to); **стоя́ть на ~ях** to be kneeling, be on one's knees; **по к., по ~и** knee-deep, up to one's knees; (*coll.*): **ему́ мо́ре по к.** he doesn't care a damn for anything; **поста́вить кого́-н. на ~и** to bring s.o. to his knees. **2.** (*pl. only*; **~и, ~ей, ~ям**) lap; **сиде́ть у кого́-н. на ~ях** to sit on s.o.'s lap. **3.** (*pl.* **~ья, ~ьев**) (*tech.*) knee, joint; (*bot.*) joint, node; **к. трубы́** knee pipe, elbow pipe. **4.** (*pl.* **~а, ~, ~ам**) bend (*of river, etc.*). **5.** (*pl.* **~а, ~, ~ам**) (*obs.*) generation; **ро́дственники до пя́того ~а** cousins five times removed; **двена́дцать ~ изра́илевых** the twelve tribes of Israel. **6.** (*pl.* **~а, ~, ~ам**) (*coll.*) figure (*in dance, song, etc.*); **выде́лывать к.** to execute a figure; (*pej.*): **вы́кинуть к.** to play a trick.
коленопреклоне́ни|е, я *nt.* genuflection.
коле́н|це, ца, *g. pl.* **~ец** *nt.* (*coll.*): **вы́кинуть к.** to play a trick.
коле́нчат|ый *adj.* (*tech.*) elbow-shaped, cranked; **к. вал** crankshaft; **к. рыча́г** toggle lever, bell crank; **~ая труба́** knee pipe.
ко́лер[1], **а** *m.* (*art*) colour, shade.
ко́лер[2], **а** *m.* (*vet.*) staggers.
колёсик|о, а *nt.* **1.** *dim. of* **колесо́**. **2.** castor.
коле|си́ть, шу́, си́шь *impf.* (*coll.*) **1.** to go in a roundabout way. **2.** to go all over, travel about.
коле́сник, а *m.* wheelwright.
колесни́ц|а, ы *f.* chariot; **погреба́льная к.** hearse; **триумфа́льная к.** triumphal car.
колёс|ный *adj.* **1.** *adj. of* **~о́**. **2.** wheeled, on wheels.
колес|о́, а́, *pl.* **~а** *nt.* **1.** wheel; **гребно́е к.** paddle-wheel; **запасно́е к.** spare wheel; **зубча́тое к.** cog-wheel; **махово́е к.** fly-wheel; **к. обозре́ния** Big Wheel (*fairground attraction*); **рулево́е к.** driving wheel; **цепно́е к.** sprocket; **грудь ~о́м** (*fig.*) well-developed chest; *as adv.* with chest well out; **вста́вить кому́-н. па́лки в ~а** to put a spoke in s.o.'s wheel; **кружи́ться, как бе́лка в ~е́** to run round in circles; **но́ги ~о́м** bandy legs; **кувырка́нье «~о́м»** cartwheel (*acrobatics*); **ходи́ть ~о́м** to cartwheel. **2.** *pl.* (*coll.*) transport, a motor; **быть на ~ах** to have (one's own) transport.
колесова́ни|е, я *nt.* breaking on the wheel.
колес|ова́ть, у́ю *impf. and pf.* to break on the wheel.
коле́ч|ко, ка, *pl.* **~ки, ~ек, ~кам** *nt.* (*coll.*) ringlet.
коле|я́, и́ *f.* **1.** rut; (*fig.*): **войти́ в ~ю́** to settle down (again); **вы́битый из ~и́** unsettled. **2.** (*rail.*) track; gauge.
ко́ли (*and* **коль**) (*obs. or dial.*) if; (*coll.*): **к. на то пошло́** while we are about it; **коль ско́ро** if, as soon as.
коли́бри *c.g. indecl.* (*zool.*) humming-bird.
ко́лик|и, ~ *no sg.* (*med.*) colic; **смея́ться до ~** (*coll.*) to make o.s. ill with laughing.
колир|ова́ть, у́ю *impf.* (*hort.*) to graft.
колиро́вк|а, и *f.* (*hort.*) grafting.
коли́т, а *m.* (*med.*) colitis.
коли́чественный *adj.* quantitative; **~ое числи́тельное** cardinal number.
коли́честв|о, а *nt.* quantity, amount; number.
ко́лк|а, и *f.* chopping.
ко́л|кий[1] **(~ок, ~ка́ ~ко)** *adj.* easily split.
ко́л|кий[2] **(~ок, ~ка́ ~ко)** *adj.* prickly; (*fig.*) sharp, biting, caustic.
ко́лкост|ь, и *f.* **1.** (*fig.*) sharpness. **2.** sharp, caustic remark; **говори́ть ~и** to make sharp remarks.
коллаборациони́ст, а *m.* (*pol.*; *pej.*) collaborator.
коллаборациони́ст|ский *adj. of* ~
colláж
колла́ж, а *m.* collage.
колле́г|а, и *c.g.* colleague.
коллегиа́л|ьный (~ен, ~ьна) *adj.* joint, collective; corporate; **~ьное реше́ние** collective decision.
колле́ги|я, и *f.* **1.** board, collegium. **2.** college; **к. адвока́тов, к. правозасту́пников** the Bar; **к. вы́борщиков** electoral college.
колле́дж, а *m.* college.
колле́жский *adj.* (*in titles of officials in tsarist Russia*) collegiate; **а. сове́тник** collegiate counsellor.
коллекти́в, а *m.* group, body; (*in many phrr. does not require separate translation*) **к. машини́стов** engine-drivers; **нау́чный к.** (the) scientists; **парти́йный к.** Party members.
коллективиза́ци|я, и *f.* collectivization.
коллективизи́р|овать, ую *impf. and pf.* to collectivize.
коллективи́зм, а *m.* collectivism.
коллективи́ст, а *m.* collectivist.
коллекти́вн|ый *adj.* collective; joint; **~ое владе́ние** joint ownership; **~ое хозя́йство** collective farm; **~ое руково́дство** (*pol.*) collective leadership (*opp. one-man rule*).
колле́ктор, а *m.* **1.** (*elec.*) commutator. **2.** (*in sewage system*) manifold. **3.: библиоте́чный к.** central library.
коллекционе́р, а *m.* collector.
коллекциони́р|овать, ую *impf.* to collect.
колле́кци|я, и *f.* collection.
ко́лли *c.g. indecl.* collie (*dog*).
колли́зи|я, и *f.* clash, conflict.
колло́ди|й, я *m.* (*chem.*) collodion.
колло́ид, а *m.* (*chem.*) colloid.
коллоида́льный *adj.* (*chem.*) colloidal.
колло́идный *adj.* (*chem.*) colloidal.
колло́квиум, а *m.* oral examination.
колоб|о́к, ка́ *m.* small round loaf.
колобро́|дить, жу, дишь *impf.* (*coll.*) **1.** to roam, wander; to loaf. **2.** to make a noise; to get up to mischief.
коловоро́т, а *m.* (*tech.*) brace.
коловра́тност|ь, и *f.* (*obs.*) mutability, inconstancy.
коловра́т|ный (~ен, ~на) *adj.* **1.** rotary. **2.** (*fig.*, *obs.*) inconstant, changeable.

коловраще́ни|е, я *nt.* (*obs.*) rotation.
коло́д|а[1], **ы** *f.* **1.** block, log. **2.** (water-)trough.
коло́д|а[2], **ы** *f.* pack (*of cards*).
коло́де|зный *adj. of* **~ц**
коло́де|зь, зя *m.* (*obs.*) = **~ц**
коло́д|ец, ца *m.* **1.** well. **2.** (*tech.*) shaft.
коло́дк|а, и *f.* **1.** boot-tree; last. **2.** (*tech.*) shoe. **3.** (*pl.*; *hist.*) stocks; **наби́ть ~и на́ ноги кому́-н.** to put s.o. in stocks.
коло́дник, а *m.* convict (*in stocks*).
кол|о́к, ка́ *m.* (*mus.*) peg.
ко́локол, а, *pl.* **~а́, ~о́в** *m.* bell.
колоко́льный *adj. of* **ко́локол; к. звон** peal, chime.
колоко́л|ьня, ьни, *g. pl.* **~ен** *f.* steeple, bell-tower, church-tower; (*coll.*): **смотре́ть со свое́й ~ьни на что-н.** to take a narrow, parochial view of sth.
колоко́льчик, а *m.* **1.** small bell; handbell. **2.** (*bot.*) bluebell.
ко́ломаз|ь, и *f.* wheel grease.
Коло́мбо *m. indecl.* Colombo.
колониа́льный *adj.* colonial; **к. магази́н** (*obs.*) grocer's shop.
колониза́тор, а *m.* colonizer.
колониза́ци|я, и *f.* colonization.
колониз|ова́ть, у́ю *impf. and pf.* to colonize.
колони́ст, а *m.* colonist.
коло́ни|я, и *f.* (*in various senses*) colony; settlement.
коло́нк|а, и *f.* **1.** geyser. **2.** (*street*) water fountain. **3.: бензи́новая к.** petrol pump. **4.** (*typ.*) column; **газе́тная полоса́ в шесть коло́нок** newspaper page with six columns; **к. цифр** column of figures. **5.** (*coll.*) (loud)speaker.
коло́нн|а, ы *f.* column; (*mil.*) **та́нковая к.** tank column; **похо́дная к.** column of route; **со́мкнутая к.** close column; **к. по три** column of threes.
колонна́д|а, ы *f.* colonnade.
коло́нный *adj.* columned.
колон|о́к, ка́ *m.* (*zool.*) Siberian weasel, kolinsky.
колонти́тул, а *m.* (*typ.*) running title.
колонци́фр|а, ы *f.* (*typ.*) folio, page number.
колора́дский *adj.*: **к. жук** Colorado beetle.
колорату́р|а, ы *f.* (*mus.*) coloratura.
колорату́р|ный *adj. of* **~а**
колори́ст, а *m.* (*art*) colourist.
колори́т, а *m.* colouring, colour; (*fig.*): **ме́стный к.** local colour; **он прида́л расска́зу о встре́че я́ркий к.** he painted a glowing picture of the encounter.
колори́т|ный (~ен, ~на) *adj.* colourful, picturesque, graphic (*also fig.*); **язы́к у него́ о́чень к.** his language is highly coloured.
ко́лос, а, *pl.* **~ья, ~ьев** *m.* (*agric.*) ear, spike.
колоси́ст|ый (~, ~а) *adj.* (*agric.*) full of ears.
коло|си́ться, си́тся *impf.* (*agric.*) to form ears.
колосни́к, а́ *m.* **1.** furnace-bar, grate-bar; (*pl.*) fire-bars. **2.** (*pl.*; *theatr.*) flies; grid-iron.
коло́сс, а *m.* colossus.
колосса́льный *adj.* colossal; (*coll.*) terrific, great.
коло|ти́ть, чу́, ~тишь *impf.* (*of* **поколоти́ть**) **1.** (**по**+*d.*, **в**+*a.*) to strike (on); to batter (on), pound (on); **к. в дверь** to bang on the door. **2.** (*coll.*) to thrash, drub. **3.** (*impf. only*): **к. лён** to scutch flax. **4.** (*impf. only*) (*coll.*) to break, smash. **5.** (*impf. only*) (*coll.*) to shake; (*impers.*): **его́ ~ти́ла лихора́дка** he was shaking with fever.
коло|ти́ться, чу́сь, ~тишься *impf.* (*of* **поколоти́ться**) **1.** (**о**+*a.*) to beat (against); to strike (against); **к. голово́й об сте́ну** to beat one's head against a wall. **2.** (*impf. only*) (*coll.*) to pound; to shake; **се́рдце у неё ~ти́лось** her heart was pounding. **3.** *pass. of* **~ти́ть**
колоту́шк|а, и *f.* **1.** (*coll.*) punch. **2.** beetle (*tech.*). **3.** (*wooden*) rattle (*used by night watchman*).
ко́лот|ый[1] **(~, ~а)** *p.p.p. of* **~ь**[1] *and adj.*; **к. са́хар** chipped sugar.
ко́лот|ый[2] **(~, ~а)** *p.p.p. of* **~ь**[2] *and adj.*; **~ая ра́на** stab.
кол|о́ть[1], **ю́, ~ешь** *impf.* (*of* **расколо́ть**) to break, chop, split; **к. дрова́** to chop wood; **к. оре́хи** to crack nuts.
кол|о́ть[2], **ю́, ~ешь** *impf.* (*of* **заколо́ть**) **1.** to prick; (*impers.*): **у меня́ ~ет в боку́** I have a stitch in my side. **2.** to stab. **3.** to slaughter (*cattle*). **4.** (*fig.*) to sting, taunt; **к. глаза́ кому́-н.** (+*i.*) to cast a thing in s.o.'s teeth; **пра́вда глаза́ ~ет** (*prov.*) home truths are unpalatable.
ко́лоть|е, я (*and* **колоть|ё, я́**) *nt.* (*coll.*) stitch.
кол|о́ться[1], **ю́сь, ~ешься** *impf.*, *pass. of* **~о́ть**[1]
кол|о́ться[2], **ю́сь, ~ешься** *impf.* to prick (*intrans.*).
коло́ш|а, и *f.* (*tech.*) blast furnace charge.
колошма́|тить, чу, тишь *impf.* (*of* **отколошма́тить**) (*coll.*) to beat, thrash.
колошни́к, а́ *m.* (*tech.*) furnace throat.
колошник|о́вый *adj. of* **~; к. газ** blast furnace gas.
колпа́к, а́ *m.* **1.** cap; **ночно́й к.** nightcap; **шутовско́й к.** fool's cap; **к. колеса́** hubcap. **2.** lamp-shade; (*tech.*) cowl; **бронево́й к.** armoured hood; **стекля́нный к.** bell-glass; (*fig.*, *coll.*): **жить под стекля́нным ~о́м** to live in the public view, have no privacy; **держа́ть под стекля́нным ~о́м** to keep in cotton-wool (= *to treat as a child*). **3.** (*fig.*, *coll.*) simpleton.
колпач|о́к, ка́ *m.* **1.** *dim. of* **колпа́к. 2.** (gas) mantle.
колту́н, а́ *m.* (*med.*) plica (polonica).
колумба́ри|й, я *m.* columbarium.
колумби́|ец, йца *m.* Colombian.
колумби́|йка, йки *f. of* **~ец**
колумби́йский *adj.* Colombian.
Колу́мби|я, и *f.* Colombia.
колу́н, а́ *m.* (wood-)chopper, hatchet.
колупа́|ть, ю *impf.* (*coll.*) to pick, scratch.
колхо́з, а *m.* (*abbr. of* **коллекти́вное хозя́йство**) collective farm.
колхо́зник, а *m.* member of collective farm.
колхо́зн|ица, ицы *f. of* **~ик**
колхо́з|ный *adj. of* **~; ~ное строи́тельство** organization of collective farms; **к. строй** collective farm system.
колча́н, а *m.* quiver.
колчеда́н, а *m.* (*min.*) pyrites.
колчено́гий *adj.* (*coll.*) **1.** lame. **2.** rickety, wobbly (*of furniture*).
колыбе́л|ь, и *f.* cradle; (*fig.*): **к. нау́ки** the cradle of learning; **с ~и** from the cradle; **от ~и до моги́лы** from the cradle to the grave.
колыбе́ль|ный *adj. of* **~; ~ная пе́сня** lullaby; **~ная смерть** cot death.
колыма́г|а, и *f.* (*obs.*) heavy, unwieldy carriage; (*iron.*) wagon, bus.
колы|ха́ть, ~шу, ~шешь *impf.* (*of* **~хну́ть**) to sway, rock.
колы|ха́ться, ~шется *impf.* (*of* **~хну́ться**) to sway, heave; to flutter; to flicker.
колых|ну́ть(ся), ну́(сь), нёшь(ся) *pf. of* **~а́ть(ся)**
ко́лыш|ек, ка *m.* peg.
коль *see* **ко́ли**
колье́ *m. indecl.* necklace.
кол|ьну́ть, ьну́, ьнёшь *inst. pf. of* **~о́ть**[2]
кольра́би *f. indecl.* (*bot.*) kohlrabi.
кольт, а *m.* colt (*pistol*).
кольц|ева́ть, у́ю *impf.* **1.** (*of* **закольцева́ть**) to girdle, ring-bark (*a tree*). **2.** (*of* **окольцева́ть**) to ring (*bird's leg.*, *etc.*).
кольцев|о́й *adj.* annular; circular; **~а́я доро́га** ring road; **~а́я развя́зка** roundabout.
кольцеобра́з|ный (~ен, ~на) *adj.* ring-shaped.
кол|ьцо́ ~ьца́, *pl.* **~ьца, ~ец, ~ьцам** *nt.* **1.** ring; **сверну́ться ~ьцо́м** to coil up; **годи́чное к.** (*bot.*) ring; **обруча́льное к.** wedding ring; **трамва́йное к.** circle, terminus (on tram-route). **2.** (*tech.*) ring; collar; hoop.
ко́льчат|ый *adj.* annulate(d); **~ые че́рви** (*zool.*) Annelida.
кольчу́г|а, и *f.* shirt of mail, hauberk.
колю́ч|ий (~, ~а) *adj.* prickly; thorny; (*fig.*) sharp, biting; **~ая и́згородь** prickly hedge; **~ая про́волока** barbed wire; **к. язы́к** sharp tongue.
колю́чк|а, и *f.* (*coll.*) **1.** prickle; thorn; quill (*of porcupine*). **2.** burr.
ко́люшк|а, и *f.* (*fish*) stickleback.
ко́л|ющий *pres. part. act. of* **~о́ть**[2] *and adj.*; **~ющая боль** shooting pain.
коляд|а́, ы *f.* kolyada (*custom of house-to-house Christmas carol-singing*).

коляд|ова́ть, у́ю *impf.* to go round carol-singing.

коля́ск|а, и *f.* **1.** carriage, barouche. **2.** **(де́тская** *or* **прогу́лочная) к.** pram; pushchair; **инвали́дная к.** wheelchair; **к.-су́мка** shopping trolley, shopper. **3.** (*motor-cycle*) side-car.

ком[1], **а,** *pl.* **~́ья, ~́ьев** *m.* lump; ball; clod; **сне́жный к.** snow-ball; (*fig.*): **к. в го́рле** lump in the throat; **пе́рвый блин ~́ом** (*prov.*) practice make perfect.

ком[2] *p. of* **кто**

ком... *comb. form, abbr. of* **1. коммунисти́ческий. 2. кома́ндный. 3. команди́р**

...ком *comb. form, abbr. of* **1. комите́т. 2. комисса́р. 3. комиссариа́т**

ко́м|а, ы *f.* (*med.*) coma.

кома́нд|а, ы *f.* **1.** (word of) command, order; **пода́ть ~у** to give a command. **2.** command; **приня́ть ~у (над)** to take command (of). **3.** (*mil.*) party, detachment, crew; (*naut.*) crew, ship's company; **пожа́рная к.** fire-brigade. **4.** (*sport*) team.

команди́р, а *m.* (*mil.*) commander, commanding officer; (*naut.*) captain.

командир|ова́ть, у́ю *impf. and pf.* to post; to dispatch, send on a mission.

командиро́вк|а, и *f.* **1.** posting, dispatching (*on official business*). **2.** mission; (official business) trip; **е́хать в ~у** to go on a mission; **он в ~е** he is away on business, on a commission; **я получи́л ~у в Казахста́н** I have been given a commission to execute in Kazakhstan; **нау́чная к.** scientific mission. **3.** (*coll.*) warrant, authority (*for travelling on official business, on commission*).

командиро́в|очный *adj. of* **~ка; ~очные де́ньги** travelling allowance; **~очное удостовере́ние** warrant, authority (*for travelling on official business, on commission*); *as n.* **~очные, ~очных** travelling allowance, travelling expenses.

команди́тн|ый *adj.* (*comm.*): **~ое това́рищество** sleeping partnership.

кома́нд|ный *adj.* **1.** *adj. of* **~а; ~ная до́лжность** duties of a commander; **к. пункт** command post; **к. соста́в** the officers (*of a military unit*). **2.** (*fig.*) commanding; **~ные высо́ты** commanding heights, key points.

кома́ндовани|е, я *nt.* **1.** commanding, command; **приня́ть к. (над)** to take command (of, over). **2.** (*collect.*) command.

кома́нд|овать ую *impf.* (*of* **c~**) **1.** to give orders. **2.** (*+i.*) to command, be in command (of). **3.** (*fig., coll.*) (*+i. or* **над**) to order about. **4.** (*fig.*) **(над)** to command (*terrain*).

командо́р, а *m.* **1.** (*hist.*) knight commander. **2.** commodore (*of yacht club*).

кома́ндующ|ий, его *m.* commander.

кома́р, а́ *m.* gnat, mosquito; (*coll.*): **к. но́са не подто́чит** not a thing can be said against it.

комар|и́ный *adj. of* **~́; к. уку́с** mosquito bite; (*fig., coll.*) minute, midget.

комато́зный *adj.* (*med.*) comatose.

комба́йн, а *m.* (*tech.*) combine, multi-purpose machine; **зерново́й к.** combine harvester; **ку́хонный к.** food processor.

комба́йнер, а *m.* (*agric.*) combine operator.

комба́т, а *m.* (*abbr. of* ***команди́р батальо́на***) battalion commander.

комбико́рм, а, *pl.* **~а́** *m.* (*agric.*) mixed fodder.

комбико́рм|овый *adj. of* **~**

комбина́т, а *m.* **1.** industrial complex; combine; **де́тский к.** day nursery; **к. бытово́го обслу́живания,** *see* **бытово́й. 2.** comprehensive school.

комбина́тор, а *m.* (*pej.*) schemer, contriver; wheeler-dealer.

комбинато́рный *adj.* (*math.*) combinative.

комбинац|ио́нный *adj. of* **~́ия**

комбина́ци|я[1], **и** *f.* **1.** combination; (*econ.*) merger. **2.** (*fig.*) scheme, system; (*pol., sport*) manœuvre.

комбина́ци|я[2], **и** *f.* (*underwear*) **1.** slip. **2.** combinations.

комбинезо́н, а *m.* **1.** overalls; dungarees. **2.** jump-suit.

комбини́рованный *adj.* combined.

комбини́р|овать, ую *impf.* (*of* **c~**) **1.** to combine, arrange. **2.** (*coll., pej.*) to scheme, contrive; to devise a scheme, a system.

комбри́г, а *m.* (*abbr. of* ***команди́р брига́ды***) brigade commander.

комди́в, а *m.* (*abbr. of* ***команди́р диви́зии***) division(al) commander.

комедиа́нт, а *m.* **1.** (*obs.*) actor. **2.** (*pej.*) play-actor; hypocrite.

комеди́йный *adj.* (*liter., theatr.*) comic; comedy; **к. актёр** comedy actor.

коме́ди|я, *f.* **1.** comedy. **2.** (*fig., pej.*) play-acting; farce; **лома́ть ~ю, разы́грывать ~ю** to put on an act, enact a farce.

ко́м|ель, ля *m.* butt, butt-end (*of tree, etc.*).

коменда́нт, а *m.* **1.** (*mil.*) commandant; **к. го́рода** town major; **к. (ста́нции)** R.T.O. (*Railway Transportation Officer*). **2.** manager; warden; **к. теа́тра** theatre manager; **к. общежи́тия** warden of a hostel.

коменда́нт|ский *adj. of* **~; к. час** (*mil.*) curfew.

комендату́р|а, ы *f.* commandant's office.

комендо́р, а *m.* (*naut.*) seaman gunner.

коме́т|а, ы *f.* comet.

коми́зм, а *m.* **1.** comedy, the comic element; **к. положе́ния** the funny side of a situation. **2.** comicality; **с ~ом передразни́ть кого́-н.** to give a comical imitation of s.o.

ко́мик, а *m.* **1.** comic actor. **2.** (*fig.*) comedian, comical fellow.

ко́микс, а *m.* comic(-book); comic strip.

Коминте́рн, а *m.* (*hist.*) (*abbr. of* ***Коммунисти́ческий Интернациона́л***) Comintern.

коминте́рн|овский *adj. of* **~**

Коминфо́рм *m.* = **Информбюро́**

комисса́р, а *m.* commissar, commissioner; **верхо́вный к.** high commissioner.

комиссариа́т, а *m.* commissariat.

комисса́р|ский *adj. of* **~**

комиссионе́р, а *m.* (commission-)agent, factor, broker.

комиссио́нк|а, и *f.* (*coll.*) commission shop.

комисс|ио́нный *adj. of* **~́ия 2.; к. магази́н** commission shop (*where second-hand goods are sold on commission*); *as n.* **~ио́нные, ~ио́нных** (*comm.*) commission; **получи́ть ~ио́нные** to receive a commission.

коми́сси|я, и *f.* **1.** commission, committee; **к. по разоруже́нию** disarmament commission; **сле́дственная к.** committee of investigation. **2.** (*comm.*) commission; **брать на ~ю** to take on commission.

комите́т, а *m.* committee; **специа́льный к.** select committee; ad hoc committee.

коми́ческ|ий *adj.* **1.** comic; **~ая о́пера** comic opera. **2.** comical, funny.

коми́ч|ный (~ен, ~на) *adj.* comical, funny.

ко́мка|ть, ю *impf.* (*of* **c~**) **1.** (*pf. also* **иско́мкать**) to crumple. **2.** (*fig., coll.*) to make a hash of, muff.

коммента́ри|й, я *m.* **1.** commentary. **2.** (*pl.*) comment; **~и изли́шни** comment is superfluous.

коммента́тор, а *m.* commentator.

комменти́р|овать, ую *impf. and pf.* to comment (upon).

коммерса́нт, а *m.* merchant; business man.

комме́рци|я, и *f.* commerce, trade.

комме́рческ|ий *adj.* **1.** commercial; mercantile; **к. флот** mercantile marine. **2.** of trade off the ration, on free market; **к. магази́н** shop retailing goods officially controlled at prices above those fixed; **~ие це́ны** free market prices.

коммивояжёр, а *m.* commercial traveller.

комму́н|а, ы *f.* (*in var. senses*) commune.

комму́налк|а, и *f.* (*coll.*) communal flat.

комму́нальник, а *m.* municipal employee.

комму́нальн|ый *adj.* **1.** communal; municipal; **~ая кварти́ра** 'communal' flat (*in which kitchen and toilet facilities are shared by a number of tenants*); **~ые услу́ги** public utilities; **~ое хозя́йство** municipal economy. **2.** *adj. of* **комму́на**

коммуни́зм, а *m.* communism.

коммуникацио́нн|ый *adj.*: **~ая ли́ния** line of communication.

коммуника́ци|я, и *f.* (*in var. senses*) communication; (*mil.*)

line of communication.
коммуни́ст, а *m.* communist.
коммунисти́ческ|ий *adj.* communist; **~ое строи́тельство** the building of communism.
коммута́тор, а *m.* (*elec.*) **1.** commutator. **2.** switchboard.
коммюнике́ *nt. indecl.* communiqué.
ко́мнат|а, ы *f.* room; **тёмная к.** (*phot.*) darkroom.
ко́мнатн|ый *adj.* **1.** of a room. **2.** indoor; pet; **~ые и́гры** indoor games; **~ые расте́ния** indoor plants; **~ая соба́чка** lap-dog; **~ая температу́ра** room temperature.
комо́д, а *m.* chest of drawers.
ком|о́к, ка́ *m. dim. of* **~; сверну́ться в к.** to roll o.s. up into a ball; (*fig.*) **к. в го́рле** lump in the throat; **к. не́рвов** bundle of nerves.
комо́лый *adj.* (*dial.*) polled.
компа́кт-ди́ск, а *m.* compact disk, CD; **пройгрыватель** (*m.*) **~ов** compact disk *or* CD player.
компа́кт|ный (~ен, ~на) *adj.* compact, solid.
компане́йск|ий *adj.* (*coll.*) **1.** sociable, companionable. **2.** equally shared; **расхо́ды на ~их нача́лах** expenses qually shared; **устро́ить ве́чер на к. счёт** to go shares in giving a party.
компа́ни|я, и *f.* (*in var. senses*) company; **доче́рняя к.** subsidiary; **к.-производи́тель** manufacturer, producer; **води́ть ~ю с кем-н.** (*coll.*) to associate with s.o.; **расстро́ить ~ю** to break up a party; **соста́вить кому́-н. ~ю** to keep s.o. company; **я провёл ве́чер в ~и с Воло́дей** I spent the evening in Volodya's company; **он тебе́ не к.** he is no company for you; **пойти́ це́лой ~ей** to go all together; **гуля́ть ~ей** to go about in a group; (*coll.*): **за ~ю** for company; **ну, ещё стака́нчик с тобо́й за ~ю!** well, just one more to keep you company!
компаньо́н, а *m.* **1.** (*comm.*) partner. **2.** companion.
компаньо́н|ка, ки *f.* **1.** *f. of* **~. 2.** (lady's) companion; chaperon(e).
компа́рти|я, и *f.* Communist Party.
ко́мпас, а *m.* compass; **гла́вный к.** standard compass; **морско́й к.** mariner's compass.
ко́мпас|ный *adj. of* **~; ~ная стре́лка** compass needle; **к. я́щик** binnacle.
компатрио́т, а *m.* compatriot.
компа́унд, а *m.* (*tech.*) compound.
компе́ндиум, а *m.* compendium, digest.
компенсацио́нный *adj.* compensatory, compensating; (*tech.*) **к. ма́ятник** compensation-pendulum.
компенса́ци|я, и *f.* compensation.
компенси́р|овать, ую *impf. and pf.* **1.** to compensate, indemnify (for). **2.** (*tech.*) to compensate, equilibrate.
компете́нт|ный (~ен, ~на) *adj.* competent.
компете́нци|я, и *f.* competence; **э́то не в мое́й ~и** it is outside my competence; it is beyond my scope.
компили́ровать, ую *impf.* (*of* **с~**) (*pej.*) to compile.
компиляти́в|ный (~ен, ~на) *adj. of* **компиля́ция; к. труд** compilation.
компиля́тор, а *m.* (*pej.*) compiler.
компиля́ци|я, и *f.* (*pej.*) compilation.
ко́мплекс, а *m.* (*in var. senses*) complex; set; **к. неполноце́нности** inferiority complex; **к. мероприя́тий** package of measures.
ко́мплексн|ый *adj.* **1.** (*math.*) complex; **~ое число́** complex number. **2.** over-all, all-embracing, all-in; **к. обе́д** table d'hôte dinner.
компле́кт, а *m.* **1.** complete set; kit; outfit; **к. белья́** bedding, bed-clothes; **к. спорти́вного сти́ля** casual outfit; **шрифтово́й к.** (*typ.*) fo(u)nt. **2.** complement; specified number; **сверх ~а** above the specified number; **у нас ещё не хвата́ет двух челове́к до по́лного ~а** we are still two short of the full complement.
компле́ктный *adj.* complete.
комплект|ова́ть, у́ю *impf.* (*of* **у~**) **1.** to complete; to replenish; **к. журна́л** to acquire a complete set of a periodical. **2.** (*mil.*) to bring up to strength; to (re)man.
компле́кци|я, и *f.* build; (bodily) constitution.
комплеме́нт, а *m.* complement.
комплиме́нт, а *m.* compliment; **сде́лать к.** (*+d.*) to pay a compliment (to).
компло́т, а *m.* (*obs.*) plot, conspiracy.
компози́тор, а *m.* (*mus.*) composer.
компози́ци|я, и *f.* (*in various senses*) composition; **класс ~и** (*mus.*) composition class.
компоне́нт, а *m.* component.
компон|ова́ть, у́ю *impf.* (*of* **скомпонова́ть**) to put together, arrange; to group; **к. статью́** to put together an article.
компоно́вк|а, и *f.* putting together, arrangement; grouping.
компо́ст, а *m.* (*hort.*) compost.
компо́стер, а *m.* punch (*for bus tickets etc.*).
компости́р|овать, ую *impf.* (*of* **про~**) to punch (*bus tickets, etc.*).
компо́ст|ный *adj. of* **~; ~ная я́ма** compost pit.
компо́т, а *m.* compote, stewed fruit.
компре́сс, а *m.* (*med.*) compress; **согрева́ющий к.** hot compress; **поста́вить к.** to apply a compress.
компре́ссор, а *m.* (*tech., med.*) compressor.
компромети́р|овать, ую *impf.* (*of* **с~**) to compromise.
компроми́сс, а *m.* compromise; **идти́ на к.** to make a compromise, meet half-way.
компроми́сс|ный *adj. of* **~; ~ное реше́ние** compromise settlement.
компью́тер, а *m.* computer; **ИБМ-совмести́мый к.** IBM-compatible computer; **к.-блокно́т** notebook computer; **к.-калькуля́тор** scientific calculator; **наколе́нный к.** laptop (computer).
компью́тер|ный *adj. of* **~**; computerized.
комсомо́л, а *m.* (*abbr. of* ***коммунисти́ческий сою́з молодёжи***) Komsomol (*Young Communist League*).
комсомо́л|ец, ьца *m.* Komsomol (member).
комсомо́л|ка, ки *f. of* **~ец**
комсомо́л|ьский *adj. of* **~**
комсо́рг, а *m.* (*abbr. of* ***комсомо́льский организа́тор***) Komsomol organizer.
кому́ *d. of* **кто**
комфо́рт, а *m.* comfort.
комфорта́бельный *adj.* comfortable.
кон, а, о ~е, на ~у́ *m.* **1.** (*in games of chance*) kitty; **поста́вить де́ньги на́ к.** to place one's stake, put one's money in (the kitty); **быть, стоя́ть на ~у́** (*fig.*) to be at stake. **2.** (*games*) game; round.
кона́|ться, юсь *impf.* (*dial.*) to draw lots (*for first turn at a game*).
конве́йер, а *m.* (*tech.*) conveyor (*belt*); **сбо́рочный к., к. сбо́рки** assembly line.
конве́йер|ный *adj. of* **~; ~ная систе́ма** conveyor (belt) system.
конве́кци|я, и *f.* (*phys.*) convection.
конве́нт, а *m.* (*pol.*) convention.
конвенциона́льный *adj.* conventional.
конвенц|ио́нный *adj. of* **~ия; к. тари́ф** agreed tariff.
конве́нци|я, и *f.* (*leg.*) convention, agreement.
конверге́нци|я, и *f.* convergence.
конве́рси|я, и *f.* (*econ.*) conversion.
конве́рт, а *m.* **1.** envelope. **2.** (*gramophone record*) sleeve. **3.** sleeping bag (*for infants*).
конверти́р|овать, ую *impf. and pf.* (*econ.*) to convert.
конве́ртор, а *m.* (*tech.*) converter.
конвои́р, а *m.* escort.
конвои́р|овать, ую *impf.* to escort, convoy.
конво́|й, я *m.* escort, convoy; **вести́ под ~ем** to convoy, conduct under escort.
конво́й|ный *adj. of* **~; ~ное су́дно** escort vessel; *as n.* **к., ~ного** *m.* escort.
конвульси́в|ный (~ен, ~на) *adj.* (*med.*) convulsive.
конву́льси|я, и *f.* (*med.*) convulsion.
конгениа́л|ьный (~ен, ~ьна) *adj.* congenial; (*+d.*) well suited (to), in harmony (with); **перево́д, к. оригина́лу** translation in the spirit of the original
конгломера́т, а *m.* **1.** conglomeration. **2.** (*geol.*) conglomerate.
Ко́нго *nt. indecl.* the Congo (*river and state*).
конголе́з|ец, ца *m.* Congolese.

конголе́з|ка, ки *f. of* **~ец**
конголе́зский *adj.* Congolese.
конгре́сс, а *m.* congress.
кондач|о́к *only in phr.* (*coll.*): **с ~ка́** off-hand, perfunctorily.
конденса́тор, а *m.* condenser.
конденсацио́нн|ый *adj.* condensing, obtained by condensation; **~ая вода́** condensation water; **к. горшо́к** condensing vessel.
конденса́ци|я, и *f.* condensation.
конденси́р|овать, ую *impf. and pf.* to condense.
конди́тер, а *m.* confectioner, pastry-cook.
конди́терск|ая, ой *f.* confectioner's, sweet-shop; pastry-cook's.
конди́терск|ий *adj.*: **~ие изде́лия** confectionery; **к. магази́н = ~ая**
кондиционе́р, а *m.* air-conditioner.
кондициони́ровани|е, я *nt.* conditioning; **к. во́здуха** air conditioning.
кондициони́р|овать, ую *impf.* to condition.
конди́ци|я, и *f.* **1.** (*comm.*) standard. **2.** (*hist.*): **жить на ~ях** to be a resident tutor.
ко́ндо́вый *adj.* **1.** having solid, close-grained timber (*also fig. as epithet of old Russia*). **2.** (*fig.*) of the good old-fashioned sort.
ко́ндор, а *m.* (*zool.*) condor.
кондотье́р, а *m.* (*hist.*) condottiere; soldier of fortune.
кондуи́т, а *m.* conduct-book.
конду́ктор[1]**, а,** *pl.* **~а́, ~о́в** *m.* (*bus, tram*) conductor; (*rail.*) guard.
конду́ктор[2]**, а,** *pl.* **~ы, ~ов** *m.* (*elec.*) conductor.
конду́кторш|а, и *f.* (*coll.*) conductress.
конево́д, а *m.* horse-breeder.
конево́дств|о, а *nt.* horse-breeding.
конево́д|ческий *adj. of* **~ство**
кон|ёк, ька́ *m.* **1.** *dim. of* **~ь; морско́й к.** (*zool.*) hippocampus, sea-horse. **2.** ornament on peak of gable. **3.** (*fig., coll.*) hobby-horse; hobby; **сесть на своего́ ~ька́** to mount one's hobby-horse. **4.** (*zool.*) pipit. **5.** *see* **~ьки́**
кон|е́ц, ца́ *m.* **1.** (*in var. senses*) end; **о́стрый к.** point; **то́лстый к.** butt(-end); **то́нкий к.** tip; **в к.** (*coll.*) completely; **в ~це́ ~цо́в** in the end, after all; **и де́ло с ~цо́м** and there's an end to it; **из ~ца́ в к.** from end to end, all over; **~цы́ с ~ца́ми своди́ть** (*coll.*) to make both ends meet; **на э́тот (тот) к.** to this (that) end; **на худо́й к.** (*coll.*) at the worst, if the worst comes to the worst; **оди́н к.** (*coll.*) it comes to the same thing in the end; **со всех ~цо́в** from all quarters; **хорони́ть ~цы́** (*coll.*) to bury, remove traces; **и ~цы́ в во́ду** and none will be the wiser; **пришёл ему́ к.** that's the end of him; **отда́ть ~цы́** (*coll.*) to kick the bucket, to snuff it. **2.** (*coll.*) distance, way (*from one place to another*); **в оди́н к.** one way; **в о́ба ~ца́** there and back. **3.** (*naut.*) rope's end.
коне́чно *adv.* of course, certainly; no doubt; **он, к., прав** no doubt he is right; **к. да!** rather!; **к. нет!** certainly not!
коне́чност|ь[1]**, и** *f.* finiteness.
коне́чност|ь[2]**, и** *f.* (*anat.*) extremity.
коне́ч|ный (~ен, ~на) *adj.* **1.** final, last; ultimate; **~ная ста́нция** terminus; **~ная цель** ultimate aim; **в ~ном ито́ге, счёте** ultimately, in the last analysis. **2.** finite.
кони́н|а, ы *no pl., f.* horse-flesh.
кони́ческ|ий *adj.* conic(al); **~ое сече́ние** conic section.
ко́нк|а, и *f.* horse-tramway; horse-drawn tram.
конкистадо́р, а *m.* (*hist.*) conquistador.
конкла́в, а *m.* conclave.
конкорда́т, а *m.* concordat.
конкретизи́р|овать, ую *impf. and pf.* to render concrete, give concrete expression to.
конкре́т|ный (~ен, ~на) *adj.* concrete; specific.
конкубина́т, а *m.* concubinage.
конку́р, а *m.* showjumping.
конкуре́нт, а *m.* competitor; rival.
конкуре́нци|я, и *f.* competition; **вне ~и** hors-concours.
конкури́р|овать, ую *impf.* (**с**+*i.*) to compete (with).
конку́рн|ый *adj.*: **к. вса́дник** showjumper (*pers.*); **~ая ло́шадь** showjumper (*horse*).
ко́нкурс, а *m.* competition; contest; **к. красоты́** beauty contest; **уча́стник ~а** contestant; **объяви́ть к. (на**+*a.*) to announce a vacancy (for); **вне ~а** hors-concours; (*fig.*) in a class by itself.
конкурса́нт, а *m.* competitor; contestant.
ко́нкурс|ный *adj. of* **~; к. экза́мен** competitive examination.
ко́нник, а *m.* cavalryman; rider, equestrian.
ко́нниц|а, ы *f.* cavalry; horse (*collect.; mil.*).
конногварде́|ец, йца *m.* (*mil.*) **1.** horse-guardsman. **2.** (*in tsarist Russ. army*) life-guard.
коннозаво́дств|о, а *nt.* **1.** horse-breeding. **2.** stud(-farm).
коннозаво́дчик, а *m.* owner of stud(-farm).
коннокаскадёр, а *m.* trick (*horseback*) rider.
конноспорти́вн|ый *adj.* equestrian; **~ая шко́ла** riding school.
ко́н|ный *adj. of* **~ь;** horse; mounted; equestrian; **~ная а́рмия** cavalry army; **~ная артилле́рия** horse artillery; **к. двор** stables; **к. приво́д** horse-drive; **к. спорт** equestrianism; **~ная ста́туя** equestrian statue; **на ~ной тя́ге** horse-drawn; **~ная я́рмарка** horse-market.
конова́л, а *m.* **1.** horse-doctor, farrier. **2.** (*coll.*) quack(-doctor).
коново́д[1]**, а** *m.* (*mil.*) horse-holder.
коново́д[2]**, а** *m.* (*coll.*) ringleader.
коново́|дить, жу, дишь *impf.* (+*i.*; *coll.*) to be ringleader (of).
ко́новяз|ь, и *f.* tether; tethering-post.
конокра́д, а *m.* horse-thief.
конокра́дств|о, а *nt.* horse-stealing.
конопа́|тить, чу, тишь *impf.* (*of* **законопа́тить**) to caulk.
конопа́тк|а, и *f.* **1.** caulking. **2.** caulking-iron.
конопа́тчик, а *m.* caulker.
конопа́тый *adj.* (*dial.*) freckled; pock-marked.
конопа́|чу, тишь *see* **~тить**
конопл|я́, и́ *f.* (*bot.*) hemp.
конопля́ник, а *m.* hemp-field.
конопля́нк|а, и *f.* (*zool.*) linnet.
конопля́|ный *adj. of* **~; ~ное ма́сло** hempseed oil.
коносаме́нт, а *m.* (*comm.*) bill of lading.
консе́нсус, а *m.* consensus.
консерва́нт, а *m.* preservative.
консервати́в|ный (~ен, ~на) *adj.* conservative.
консервати́зм, а *m.* conservatism.
консерва́тор, а *m.* (*esp. pol.*) conservative.
консервато́ри|я, и *f.* conservatoire, academy of music.
консерва́торский *adj.* conservative.
консервато́р|ский *adj. of* **~ия**
консерва́ци|я, и *f.* **1.** conservation. **2.** temporary closing-down.
консерви́рован|ный (~, ~а) *p.p.p. of* **консерви́ровать** *and adj.*; **~ные фру́кты** bottled fruit, tinned fruit.
консерви́р|овать, ую *impf. and pf.* (*pf. also* **за~**) **1.** to preserve (*to tin, bottle, etc.*). **2.: к. предприя́тие** to close down an enterprise temporarily.
консе́рв|ный *adj. of* **~ы; ~ная ба́нка** tin; **к. нож** tin-opener; **~ная фа́брика** cannery.
консервооткрыва́тел|ь, я *m.* tin *or* can opener.
консе́рв|ы, ов *no sg.* **1.** tinned goods. **2.** goggles.
консигна́нт, а *m.* consignor.
консигна́тор, а *m.* consignee.
консигна́ци|я, и *f.* consignment.
конси́лиум, а *m.* (*med.*) consultation.
консисте́нци|я, и *f.* (*phys., med.*) consistence.
консисто́ри|я, и *f.* (*eccl.*) consistory.
ко́н|ский *adj. of* **~ь; ~ские бобы́** broad beans; **к. во́лос** horse-hair; **к. заво́д** stud(-farm); **~ские состяза́ния** horse-races; **к. хвост** 'pony-tail' (*hairstyle*).
консолида́ци|я, и *f.* consolidation.
консолиди́р|овать, ую *impf. and pf.* **1.** to consolidate. **2.** (*fin.*) to fund.
консо́л|ь, и *f.* (*archit.*) **1.** console, cantilever. **2.** pedestal.
консоме́ *nt. indecl.* (*cul.*) consommé.
консона́нс, а *m.* (*mus.*) consonance.

консонанти́зм, а *m.* (*ling.*) system of consonants.
консо́рциум, а *m.* (*fin.*) consortium.
конспе́кт, а *m.* **1.** synopsis, summary, abstract. **2.** notes (*for a lecture*).
конспекти́в|ный (~ен, ~на) *adj.* concise, summary.
конспекти́р|овать, ую *impf.* (*of* **за~** *and* **проконспекти́ровать**) to make an abstract of.
конспирати́в|ный (~ен, ~на) *adj.* secret, clandestine.
конспира́тор, а *m.* conspirator.
конспира́ци|я, и *f.* security, secrecy (*of an illegal organization*).
конспири́р|овать, ую *impf.* (*of* **за~**) to observe the rules of security (*in an illegal organization*).
конста́нт|а, ы *f.* (*math.*, *phys.*) constant.
Константино́пол|ь, я *m.* (*hist.*) Constantinople.
Конста́нцк|ое о́зер|о, ~ого ~а *nt.* Lake Constance.
констата́ци|я, и *f.* ascertaining; verification, establishment.
констати́р|овать, ую *impf. and pf.* to ascertain; to verify, establish; **к. смерть** to certify death; **к. факт** to establish a fact.
констелля́ци|я, и *f.* (*astron.*) constellation.
конституи́р|овать, ую *impf. and pf.* to constitute, set up.
конституционали́зм, а *m.* (*pol.*) constitutionalism.
конституциона́льный *adj.* (*med.*, *physiol.*) constitutional.
конституцио́нный *adj.* (*pol.*) constitutional.
конститу́ци|я, и *f.* (*pol.*, *med.*) constitution.
конструи́р|овать, ую *impf. and pf.* (*pf. also* **с~**) **1.** to construct; to design. **2.** to form (*a government*, *etc.*).
конструктиви́зм, а *m.* (*art*) constructivism.
конструкти́вный *adj.* **1.** structural; constructional; **к. фа́ктор** (*tech.*) efficiency factor, construction factor. **2.** constructive.
констру́ктор, а *m.* designer, constructor.
констру́ктор|ский *adj. of* **~**; **~ское бюро́** design office.
констру́кци|я, и *f.* **1.** construction, structure; design. **2.** (*gram.*) construction.
ко́нсул, а *m.* consul.
ко́нсульский *adj.* consular.
ко́нсульств|о, а *nt.* consulate.
консульта́нт, а *m.* consultant, adviser; tutor (*in higher education institution*).
консультати́вный *adj.* consultative, advisory.
консультац|ио́нный *adj. of* **~ия**; **~ио́нное бюро́** advice bureau; **~ио́нная пла́та** consultation fee.
консульта́ци|я, и *f.* **1.** consultation; specialist advice. **2.** advice bureau; **де́тская к.** children's clinic; **же́нская к.** ante-natal clinic; **юриди́ческиая к.** legal advice office. **3.** tutorial; supervision (*in higher education institution*).
консульти́р|овать, ую *impf.* **1.** (**с**+*i.*) to consult. **2.** (*pf.* **про~**) to advise; to act as tutor (to).
консульти́р|оваться, уюсь *impf.* (*of* **про~**) **1.** (**с**+*i.*) to consult. **2.** to have a consultation; to obtain advice; to be a pupil of.
конта́кт, а *m.* **1.** contact; **вступи́ть в к. с кем-н.** to come into contact, get in touch with s.o.; **быть в ~е (с**+*i.*) to be in touch (with). **2.** (*elec.*) **к. приёмный** socket; **к. штыково́й** plug.
конта́ктн|ый *adj.* (*tech.*) **1.** contact; **к. рельс** contact rail, live rail; **~ая сва́рка** point welding; **~ные ли́нзы** (*med.*) contact lenses. **2.** (*coll.*) sociable.
контамина́ци|я, и *f.* (*ling.*) contamination.
конте́йнер, а *m.* container.
контейнерово́з, а *m.* container ship *or* carrier.
конте́кст, а *m.* context.
континге́нт, а *m.* **1.** (*econ.*) quota. **2.** contingent; batch; **к. войск** a military force; **к. новобра́нцев** batch, squad of recruits.
контине́нт, а *m.* continent.
континента́льный *adj.* continental.
контокорре́нт, а *m.* account current (a/c).
конто́р|а, ы *f.* office, bureau; **почто́вая к.** post office.
конто́рк|а, и *f.* (writing-)desk, bureau.
конто́р|ский *adj. of* **~а**; **~ская кни́га** (account-)book; ledger.
конто́рщик, а *m.* clerk.
ко́нтр|а[1], **ы** *f.* (*coll.*) (*pl.*) disagreement, dispute; **быть в ~ах (с**+*i.*) to be at odds (with); **у них вы́шли ~ы** they have fallen out.
ко́нтр|а[2], **ы** *c.g.* (*sl.*) counter-revolutionary.
контраба́нд|а, ы *f.* **1.** contraband, smuggling; **занима́ться ~ой** to smuggle. **2.** contraband (*goods*).
контрабанди́ст, а *m.* smuggler, contrabandist.
контраба́ндный *adj.* contraband; bootleg.
контраба́с, а *m.* (*mus.*) double-bass.
контраге́нт, а *m.* contractor.
контр-адмира́л, а *m.* rear-admiral.
контра́кт, а *m.* contract.
контракта́ци|я, и *f.* contracting (for).
контракт|ова́ть, у́ю *impf.* (*of* **за~**) to contract for (*supply of*, *performance of work by*); **к. рабо́тников** to engage workmen.
контракт|ова́ться, у́юсь *impf.* (*of* **за~**) **1.** to contract, undertake (*to supply goods*, *perform work*). **2.** *pass. of* **~ова́ть**
контра́кт|овый *adj. of* **~**; **~овая я́рмарка** trade fair, industrial fair.
контра́льто *nt. indecl.* (*mus.*) contralto.
контра́льто|вый *adj. of* **~**
контрама́рк|а, и *f.* complimentary ticket; free pass; pass-out.
контрапу́нкт, а *m.* (*mus.*) counterpoint.
контрапункти́ческий *adj.* (*mus.*) contrapuntal.
контрапу́нкт|ный *adj.* = **~и́ческий**
ко́нтрас *no sg. indecl.* (*pol.*) (*Nicaraguan*) Contras.
контрассигна́ци|я, и *f.* countersign.
контрассигни́р|овать, ую *impf. and pf.* to countersign.
контрассигно́вк|а, и *f.* countersign.
контра́ст, а *m.* contrast; **по ~у (с**+*i.*) by contrast (with).
контрасти́р|овать, ую *impf.* (**с**+*i.*) to contrast (with).
котнра́стный *adj.* contrasting.
контрата́к|а, и *f.* (*mil.*) counter-attack.
контратак|ова́ть, у́ю *impf. and pf.* to counter-attack.
контрацепти́в, а *m.* contraceptive; **внутрима́точный к.** intrauterine (contraceptive) device, IUD.
контрга́йк|а, и *f.* (*tech.*) lock-nut, check-nut.
контрибу́ци|я, и *f.* (war) indemnity; contribution; **наложи́ть ~ю (на**+*a.*) to impose an indemnity (on); to lay under contribution.
ко́нтрик, а *m.* (*sl.*) = **ко́нтра**[2]
контркульту́р|а, ы *f.* counterculture.
контр-манёвр, а *m.* (*mil.*) counter-manœuvre.
контрма́рш, а *m.* (*mil.*) countermarch.
контрнаступле́ни|е, я *nt.* counter-offensive.
контрове́рз|а, ы *f.* controversy.
контролёр, а *m.* inspector; ticket-collector.
контроли́р|овать, ую *impf.* (*of* **про~**) to check; **к. биле́ты** to inspect tickets; (*mil.*) to monitor, verify.
контро́ллер, а *m.* (*elec.*) controller.
контро́л|ь, я *m.* **1.** control. **2.** check(ing); inspection; **предста́вить ци́фры ~ю** to check one's figures; (*tech.*, *mil.*) monitoring; (*mil.*) verification; **ме́ры по ~ю** verification measures. **3.** (*collect.*) inspectors.
контро́льно-прове́рочный *adj.*: **к. пу́нкт** checkpoint.
контро́льно-пропускно́й = **контро́льно-прове́рочный**
контро́ль|ный *adj. of* **~**; **~ная вы́шка** (*naut.*) conning tower; **~ная коми́ссия** control commission; **~ная рабо́та** test (*in school*, *etc.*); **~ная систе́ма** (*radio*) monitoring system; **~ные ци́фры** (*econ.*) scheduled figures; **к. пле́нный** (*mil.*) prisoner for identification.
контрпа́р, а *m.* (*tech.*) counter-steam, back-steam.
контрпрете́нзи|я, и *f.* counter-claim.
контрприка́з, а *m.* countermand.
контрразве́дк|а, и *f.* counter-espionage; counter-intelligence.
контрразве́дчик, а *m.* member of counter-espionage; counter-intelligence agent.
контрреволюционе́р, а *m.* counter-revolutionary.
контрреволюцио́нный *adj.* counter-revolutionary.
контрреволю́ци|я, и *f.* counter-revolution.
контруда́р, а *m.* (*mil.*) counter-blow.

контрфо́рс, а *m.* (*archit.*) buttress, counterfort.
контршпиона́ж, а *m.* counterespionage.
контрэска́рп, а *m.* (*mil.*) counterscarp.
конту́жен|ный (~, ~а) *p.p.p. of* **конту́зить** *and adj.*; **~ные** (*mil.*) shell-shock cases.
конту́|зить, жу, зишь *pf.* to contuse; to shell-shock.
конту́зи|я, и *f.* contusion, bruising; shell-shock.
ко́нтур, а *m.* **1.** contour. **2.** (*elec.*) circuit.
ко́нтурный *adj. of* **~**; **~ная карта** contour map.
конур|а́, ы́ *f.* kennel (*also fig., coll.*)
ко́нус, а *m.* cone.
конусообра́з|ный (~ен, ~на) *adj.* conical.
конфедера́т, а *m.* (*hist.*) confederate.
конфедерати́вный *adj.* confederative.
конфедера́тк|а, и *f.* (*hist.*) konfederatka (*Polish national or mil. headgear*).
конфедера́ци|я, и *f.* confederation.
конфекцио́н, а *m.* ready-made clothes shop.
конфера́нс, а *m.* (*theatr.*) compèring.
конферансье́ *m. indecl.* (*theatr.*) compère, master of ceremonies (*abbr.* MC).
конфере́нц-за́л, а *m.* conference chamber.
конфере́нци|я, и *f.* conference.
конфе́т|а, ы *f.* sweet; **шокола́дная к.** chocolate; **коро́бка шокола́дных ~** box of chocolates; **~ы-соса́лки** fruit drops.
конфе́т|ка, ки *f.* **1.** = **~а. 2.** (*fig.*) cracker, pip, lulu; **его́ но́вая маши́на — к.** his new car is a honey; **ух, к.!** what a dish! (*i.e. attractive female*).
конфе́тниц|а, ы *f.* sweet dish *or* bowl.
конфе́т|ный *adj.* **1.** *adj. of* **~а**; **~ная бума́жка** sweet wrapper. **2.** (*coll., pej.*) sugary, treacly.
конфетти́ *nt. indecl.* confetti.
конфигура́ци|я, и *f.* configuration, conformation.
конфиденциа́л|ьный (~ен, ~ьна) *adj.* confidential.
конфирма́нт, а *m.* (*eccl.*) confirmation candidate.
конфирма́ци|я, и *f.* **1.** (*eccl.*) confirmation. **2.** (*obs.*) ratification.
конфирм|ова́ть, у́ю *impf. and pf.* **1.** (*eccl.*) to confirm. **2.** (*obs.*) to ratify.
конфиска́ци|я, и *f.* confiscation, seizure.
конфиск|ова́ть, у́ю *impf. and pf.* to confiscate.
конфли́кт, а *m.* **1.** clash, conflict. **2.** (*pol.*) dispute.
конфли́кт|ный *adj. of* **~**; **~ная коми́ссия** arbitration tribunal.
конфликт|ова́ть, у́ю *impf.* (**с**+*i.*) (*coll.*) to clash (with), come up (against).
конфо́рк|а, и *f.* ring (*on cooking stove*); crown, top ring (*in samovar*).
конфронта́ци|я, и *f.* (*pol.*) confrontation, showdown.
конфу́з, а *m.* discomfiture, embarrassment; **како́й к. (получи́лся)!** how awkward!; how embarrassing!; **привести́ в к.** to place in an embarrassing position.
конфу́|зить, жу, зишь *impf.* (*of* **с~**) to confuse, embarrass; to place in an embarrassing position.
конфу́|зиться, жусь, зишься *impf.* (*of* **с~**) **1.** to feel embarrassed; to be shy. **2.** (+*g.*) to feel ashamed (of); to be shy (in front of).
конфу́злив|ый (~, ~а) *adj.* bashful; shy.
конфу́зный *adj.* (*coll.*) awkward, embarrassing.
концев|о́й *adj.* final; **~а́я строка́** end-line.
концентра́т, а *m.* **1.** concentrated product. **2.** (*geol.*) concentrate.
концентрацио́нный *adj.*: **к. ла́герь** concentration camp.
концентра́ци|я, и *f.* (*in var. senses*) concentration.
концентри́рова|нный *p.p.p. of* **~ть** *and adj.* concentrated.
концентри́р|овать, ую *impf.* (*of* **с~**) (*in var. senses*) to concentrate; (*mil.*) to mass; (*fig.*): **к. внима́ние на вопро́се** to concentrate one's attention on a question.
концентри́р|оваться, уюсь *impf.* (*of* **с~**) **1.** to mass, collect (*intrans.*). **2.** (*fig.*; **на**+*p.*) to concentrate.
концентри́ческий *adj.* concentric.
концентри́чност|ь, и *f.* concentricity.
конце́нтр|ы, ов *pl.* (*sg.* **~, ~а** *m.*) concentric circles.
конце́пт, а *m.* (*phil.*) concept.
концептуали́зм, а *m.* (*phil.*) conceptualism.
конце́пци|я, и *f.* conception, idea.
конце́рн, а *m.* (*econ.*) concern.
конце́рт, а *m.* (*mus.*) **1.** concert; recital; **симфони́ческий к.** symphony concert; **быть на ~е** to be at a concert; (*coll.*): **коша́чий к.** (*fig.*) hooting, barracking. **2.** concerto.
концерта́нт, а *m.* performer (*in a concert*).
концерти́н|а, ы *f.* concertina.
концерти́но *nt. indecl.* **1.** concertino. **2.** = **концерти́на**
концерти́р|овать, ую *impf.* to give concerts.
концертме́йстер, а *m.* (*mus.*) **1.** leader (*of orchestra*). **2.** solo performer.
конце́рт|ный *adj. of* **~**; **к. роя́ль** concert grand (piano).
концессионе́р, а *m.* concessionaire.
конце́сси|я, и *f.* (*econ.*) concession.
концла́гер|ь, я *m.* (*abbr. of* **концентрацио́нный ла́герь**) concentration camp.
концо́вк|а, и *f.* **1.** (*typ.*) tail-piece; colophon. **2.** (*fig.*) ending (*of liter. work*).
конч|а́ть(ся), а́ю(сь) *impf. of* **~́ить(ся)**
ко́нч|енный *p.p.p. of* **~ить;** *as int.* **~ено!** enough!; **всё ~ено!** it's all over!; **с ним всё ~ено** it's all up with him.
ко́нчен|ый *adj.* (*coll.*) decided, settled; **э́то де́ло ~ое** the matter is settled; **к. челове́к** (*coll.*) goner.
ко́нчик, а *m.* tip; point; **на ~е языка́** on the tip of one's tongue.
конч́ин|а, ы *f.* (*rhet.*) decease, demise; end.
ко́нч|ить, у, ишь *pf.* (*of* **~а́ть**) **1.** to finish, end; **к. речь выраже́нием благода́рности** to end a speech with thanks; **на э́том он ~ил** here he stopped; **я ~ил** that is all (I have to say); **к. шко́лу** to finish school course; **к. университе́т** to graduate, go down (*from university*); **к. самоуби́йством** to commit suicide; **к. пло́хо, ду́рно, скве́рно** to come to a bad end. **2.** (**с**+*i.*) to be finished (with), give up. **3.** (+*inf.*) to stop. **4.** (*coll.*) to come (= *have an orgasm*).
ко́нч|иться, усь, ишься *pf.* (*of* **~а́ться**) **1.** (+*i.*) to end (in), finish (by); to come to an end; **э́тим де́ло не ~илось** that was not the end of it; **де́ло ~илось ниче́м** it came to nothing. **2.** (*obs.*) to die, expire.
конъекту́р|а, ы *f.* (*philol.*) conjecture.
конъекту́рный *adj.* (*philol.*) conjectural.
конъюнктиви́т, а *m.* (*med.*) conjunctivitis.
конъюнкту́р|а, ы *f.* **1.** state of affairs, juncture; **междунаро́дная к.** international situation. **2.** (*econ.*) state of the market.
конъюнкту́р|ный *adj. of* **~а 2.**; **~ные це́ны** (free) market prices.
конъюнкту́рщик, а *m.* (*coll., pej.*) opportunist, time-server.
кон|ь, я́, *pl.* **~́и, ~е́й** *m.* **1.** horse; **боево́й к.** war-horse, charger; **на́ к., по ~́ям!** (*mil. command*) mount!; (*prov.*) **дарёному ~ю в зу́бы не смо́трят** never look a gift horse in the mouth; **не в ~я корм** pearls before swine. **2.** (vaulting-)horse; **к. с ру́чками** pommel-horse. **3.** (*chess*) knight.
кон|ьки́,ько́в *pl.* (*sg.* **~ёк, ~ька́** *m.*) skates; **к. на ро́ликах** roller skates; **ката́ться на ~ька́х** to skate.
конькобе́ж|ец, ца *m.* skater.
конькобе́жный *adj.* skating.
конья́к, а́ (у́) *m.* brandy.
конья́|чный *adj. of* **~к**
ко́нюх, а *m.* groom, stable-man.
коню́ш|ня, ни, *g. pl.* **~ен** *f.* stable; **А́вгиевы ~ни** (*myth. or fig.*) Augean stables.
кооперати́в, а *m.* **1.** cooperative society. **2.** (*coll.*) cooperative store.
кооперати́вн|ый *adj.* cooperative; **~ое движе́ние** (*econ., pol.*) the cooperative movement; **~ое това́рищество** cooperative society.
коопера́тор, а *m.* cooperator, member of the cooperative society.
коопера́ци|я, и *f.* **1.** cooperation. **2.** (*collect.*) cooperative societies; **потреби́тельская, сельскохозя́йственная к.** consumers', agricultural cooperative societies.
коопери́р|овать, ую *impf. and pf.* (*econ.*) **1.** to organize on cooperative lines. **2.** to recruit to a cooperative organization.

кооперúр|оваться, уюсь *impf.* (*of* **с~**) (*econ.*) **1.** to cooperate. **2.** *pass. of* **~овать**
кооптáци|я, и *f.* co-optation.
кооптúр|овать, ую *impf. and pf.* to co-opt.
координáт|а, ы *f.* (*math.*) coordinate; *pl.* (*coll.*) contact details (*address, telephone number, etc.*).
координáтный *adj.* (*math.*) coordinate.
координáтор, а *m.* coordinator.
координáци|я, и *f.* coordination.
координúр|овать, ую *impf. and pf.* to coordinate.
копáл, а *m.* copal.
копáни|е, я *nt.* digging.
коп|áть, áю *impf.* **1.** (*pf.* **~нýть**) to dig. **2.** (*pf.* **вы́~**) to dig up, dig out.
копá|ться, юсь *impf.* **1.** (**в**+*p.*) to rummage (in); to root (in); (*fig.*): **к. в душé** to be given to soul-searching. **2.** (*coll.*; **с**+*i.*) to dawdle (over). **3.** *pass. of* **~ть**
копéечк|а, и *f. dim. of* **копéйка**; (*coll.*): **э́то влетúт тебé в ~у** it will cost you a pretty penny.
копéечн|ый *adj.* **1.** one-kopeck; worth one kopeck. **2.** (*in price*) minute, insignificant; **~ые расхóды** trifling expenses. **3.** (*fig., coll.*) petty; twopenny-halfpenny.
копéйк|а, и, *g. pl.* **копéек** *f.* kopeck; **к. в ~у** exactly; **до послéдней ~и** to the last farthing; **зашибúть, сколотúть ~у** to turn an honest penny; **к. рубль бережёт** (*prov.*) take care of the pence, the pounds will take care of themselves.
Копенгáген, а *m.* Copenhagen.
коп|ёр, рá *m.* (*tech.*) **1.** pile-driver. **2.** mine headframe.
кóп|и, ей *pl.* (*sg.* **~ь, ~́и** *f.*) mines.
копúлк|а, и *f.* money-box.
копúрк|а, и *f.* (*coll.*) carbon paper, copying paper; **писáть под ~у** to make a carbon copy.
копировáльн|ый *adj.* copying; **~ая бумáга** carbon paper.
копúр|овать, ую *impf.* (*of* **с~**) to copy; to imitate, mimic.
копирóвк|а, и *f.* copying.
копирóвщик, а *m.* copyist.
коп|úть, лю́, ~́ишь *impf.* (*of* **на~**) to accumulate, amass; to store up; **к. дéньги** to save up; (*fig.*): **к. сúлы** to save one's strength.
коп|úться, лю́сь, ~́ишься, *impf.* (*of* **на~**) to accumulate (*intrans.*).
кóпи|я, и *f.* copy; duplicate; replica; **печáтная к.** (*comput.*) hard copy; **резéрвная к.** (*comput.*) backup; **заве́ренная к.** (*leg.*) attested copy; **снять ~ю** (**с**+*g.*) to copy, make a copy (of); (*fig.*): **он тóчная к. своегó отцá** he is the very image of his father.
коп|нá, ны́, *pl.* **~́ны, ~ён, ~нáм** *f.* shock, stook (*of corn*); **к. сéна** haycock; (*fig., coll.*) heap, pile; **к. волóс** shock of hair.
копн|úть, ю́, úшь, *impf.* (*of* **с~**) (*agric.*) to shock, stook; to cock (*hay*).
коп|нýть, нý, нёшь *pf. of* **~áть**
копотлúв|ый (~, ~а) *adj.* (*coll.*) slow, sluggish; **~ое дéло** slow, sticky job.
копотн|я́, ú *f.* (*coll.*) dawdling.
копотýн, á *m.* (*coll.*) dawdler.
кóпот|ь, и *f.* soot; lamp-black.
копош|úться, ýсь, úшься *impf.* **1.** to swarm. **2.** (*fig., coll.*) to stir, creep in; **у меня́ в головé ~úлось сомнéние** a doubt was beginning to stir in my head. **3.** (*coll.*) to potter about.
кóпр|а, ы *f.* copra.
коп|рóвый *adj. of* **~ёр**
копт|éть[1], úт *impf.* (*of* **за~**) (*coll.*) to be blackened (*from smoke, with soot*).
коп|тéть[2], чý, тúшь *impf.* (**над**) (*coll.*) **1.** to swot (at), plug away (at). **2.** to vegetate, rot away (*fig.*).
коптúлк|а, и *f.* (*coll.*) oil-lamp (*of primitive design*).
коптúльный *adj.* for smoking.
коптúл|ьня, ьни, *g. pl.* **~ен** *f.* smoking-shed.
коп|тúть, чý, тúшь *impf.* **1.** (*pf.* **за~**) to smoke, cure in smoke. **2.** (*pf.* **за~**) to blacken (*with smoke*); **к. стеклó** to smoke glass; **к. нéбо** (*coll.*) to idle one's life away. **3.** (*pf.* **на~**) to smoke (*intrans.*).
копýн, á *m.* (*coll.*) dawdler.
копчéни|е, я *nt.* **1.** smoking, curing in smoke. **2.** (*collect.*) smoked products.
копчён|ый *adj.* smoked, smoke-dried; **~ая селёдка** bloater.
кóпчик, а *m.* (*anat.*) coccyx.
коп|чý[1], тúшь *see* **~тéть[2]**
коп|чý[2], тúшь *see* **~тúть**
копы́тн|ый *adj.* **1.** hoof. **2.** (*zool.*) hoofed, ungulate; *as n.* **~ые, ~ых** ungulates.
копы́т|о, а *nt.* hoof.
коп|ь *see* **~́и**
коп|ьё[1], ья́, *pl.* **~́ья, ~́ий, ~́ьям** *nt.* spear, lance; **метáние ~ья́** (*sport*) javelin throwing; **бúться на ~́ьях** to tilt, joust; (*fig., iron.*): **~́ья ломáть (из-за)** to break a lance (over).
коп|ьё[2], ья́ *nt.*: **у меня́ ни ~я́** (*coll.*) I haven't a penny.
копьевúд|ный (~ен, ~на) *adj.* (*bot.*) lanceolate.
копьеметáтел|ь, я *m.* javelin-thrower.
...кор *comb. form, abbr. of* **корреспондéнт**
кор|á, ы́ *f.* **1.** (*bot.*) cortex; bark, rind. **2.** (*anat.*): **к. головнóго мóзга** cerebral cortex. **3.** crust; **земнáя к.** (earth-)crust; (*fig.*): **под ~óй егó сурóвости бы́ло дóброе сéрдце** he had a kind heart beneath his hard exterior.
кораб|éльный *adj. of* **~́ль; ~éльная авиáция** shipborne aircraft; **к. лес** ship timber; **к. инженéр** naval architect; **к. мáстер** shipwright.
корабéльщик, а *m.* **1.** (*obs.*) sea-captain. **2.** (*coll.*) shipwright.
кораблевождéни|е, я *nt.* navigation.
кораблекрушéни|е, я *nt.* ship-wreck; **потерпéть к.** to be ship-wrecked.
кораблестроéни|е, я *nt.* ship-building.
кораблестрóител|ь, я *m.* ship-builder, naval architect.
корáбл|ик, а *m.* **1.** *dim. of* **~ь. 2.** toy boat. **3.** (*zool.*) nautilus; argonaut.
корáбл|ь, я́ *m.* **1.** ship, vessel; **линéйный к.** battleship; **флáгманский к.** flagship; **космúческий к.** spaceship; **челнóчный (космúческий) к.** space shuttle; **садúться на к.** to go on board (ship); **сжечь свои́ ~и́** (*fig.*) to burn one's boats; **большóму ~ю́ большóе плáванье** (*prov.*) a great ship asks deep waters. **2.** (*archit.*) nave.
корáлл, а *m.* coral.
корáллов|ый *adj.* **1.** coral. **2.** coralline; coral-red; **~ые устá** coral lips.
Корáн, а *m.* the Koran.
корвéт, а *m.* (*naut.*) corvette.
кóрд|а, ы *f.* lunge (longe); **гоня́ть лóшадь на ~е** to lunge a horse.
кордебалéт, а *m.* corps de ballet.
кордúт, а *m.* cordite.
кордóн, а *m.* cordon.
кор|евóй *adj. of* **~ь**
корé|ец, йца *m.* Korean.
корёж|ить, у, ишь *impf.* (*of* **ис~**) (*coll.*) **1.** to bend, warp; (*impers.*): **егó ~ило от бóли** he was writhing with pain. **2.** (*fig.*) to make indignant.
корёж|иться, усь, ишься *impf.* (*of* **ис~**) (*coll.*) **1.** to bend, warp (*intrans.*). **2.**: **к. от бóли** to writhe with pain.
корéйк|а, и *f.* brisket (*of pork or veal*).
корéйский *adj.* Korean.
коренáст|ый (~, ~а) *adj.* **1.** thickset, stocky. **2.** with strong roots.
коренизáци|я, и *f.* (*pol.*) indigenization.
коренизúр|овать, ую *impf. and pf.* (*pol.*) to place under local (indigenous) authority.
коренúт|ься, ся *impf.* (**в**+*p.*) to be rooted (in).
коренни́к, á *m.* shaft-horse, thill-horse, wheeler.
коренн|óй *adj.* radical, fundamental; **к. зуб** molar (tooth); **к. жúтель** native; **~óе населéние** indigenous population; **~áя лóшадь = ~úк**
кóр|ень, ня, *pl.* **~ни, ~нéй** *m.* **1.** (*in var. senses*) root; **в ~не** radically; **в ~ню́** between the shafts; **вы́рвать с ~нем** to uproot, tear up by the roots (*also fig.*); **краснéть до ~нéй волóс** to blush to the roots of one's hair; **пустúть ~ни** to take root (*also fig.*); **смотрéть в к. чегó-н.** to get

at the root of sth.; **хлеб на ∼ню́** standing crop. **2.** (*math.*) root; radical; **знак ∼ня** radical sign; **куби́ческий к.** cube root; **показа́тель ∼ня** root index.

коре́нь|я, ев *no sg.* roots (*of vegetables, herbs, etc., for culinary and medicinal purposes*).

ко́реш, а *m.* (*sl.*) pal, mate.

кореш|о́к, ка́ *m.* **1.** spine (*of book*). **2.** counterfoil. **3.** *dim. of* **ко́рень. 4.** (*sl.*) pal, mate.

Коре́|я, и *f.* Korea.

коре|я́нка, я́нки *f. of* **∼́ец**

корзи́н|а, ы *f.* basket.

корзи́нк|а, и *f.* small basket, punnet; **рабо́чая к.** work-basket; (*bot.*) calathide.

корзи́н|ный *adj. of* **∼а; ∼ное произво́дство** basket-making.

корзи́нщик, а *m.* basket-maker.

коридо́р, а *m.* corridor, passage.

коридо́р|ный *adj. of* **∼**; *as n.* **к., ∼ного** *m.* boots (*in hotel*).

кори́нк|а, и *no pl., f.* currants.

кори́нфский *adj.* (*archit.*) Corinthian.

кор|и́ть, ю́, и́шь *impf.* (*+a.* **за**) to upbraid (for); (*+a. and i.*) to reproach (with), cast in s.o.'s teeth.

корифе́|й, я *m.* (*rhet.*) coryphaeus (*fig.*), leading light.

кори́ц|а, ы *f.* cinnamon.

коричневоруба́шечник, а *m.* (*hist.*) Brown-shirt.

кори́чневый *adj.* brown.

ко́рк|а, и *f.* **1.** crust. **2.** peel, rind. **3.** scab. **4.** (*fig.*): **прочита́ть от ∼и до ∼и** to read from cover to cover; **руга́ть, брани́ть кого́-н. на все ∼и** (*coll.*) to give it s.o. hot; tear s.o. off a strip.

корм, а, о ∼́е, на ∼́е *and* **на ∼у́,** *pl.* **∼а́, ∼о́в** *m.* **1.** fodder; forage; **пти́чий к.** birdseed; **на подно́жном ∼у́** at grass. **2.** feeding.

корм|а́, ы́ *f.* (*naut.*) stern, poop.

кормёжк|а, и *f.* (*coll.*) feeding.

корми́л|ец, ьца *m.* **1.** bread-winner. **2.** (*obs.*) benefactor. **3.** (*dial. mode of address to man*) old man.

корми́лиц|а, ы *f.* **1.** wet-nurse. **2.** (*obs.*) benefactress.

корми́л|о, а *nt.* (*naut. and fig.*) helm; (*fig., rhet.*): **быть у ∼а правле́ния** to be at the helm.

корм|и́ть, лю́, ∼́ишь *impf.* **1.** (*pf.* **на∼** *and* **по∼**) to feed; **к. с ло́жки** to spoon-feed; **к. гру́дью** to nurse, (breast-)feed; **не ∼я́ (е́хать)** (*obs.*) (to ride) non-stop; (*coll.*): **его́ хле́бом не ∼и́, то́лько дай смотре́ть футбо́л** he is mad about watching football. **2.** (*pf.* **про∼**) keep, maintain.

корм|и́ться, лю́сь, ∼́ишься *impf.* **1.** (*pf.* **по∼**) to eat, feed (*intrans.*). **2.** (*pf.* **про∼**) (*+i.*) to live (on); **к. уро́ками** to make a living by giving tuition.

кормле́ни|е, я *nt.* **1.** feeding. **2.** (*hist.*) 'feeding' (*in Muscovite Russia, system by which boyars responsible for local administration retained revenues for their own use*).

корм|ово́й[1] *adj. of* **∼а́; ∼ово́е весло́** scull; **к. флаг** ensign; **∼ова́я часть** after-part, stern-part; **∼ова́я ру́бка** roundhouse.

корм|ово́й[2] *adj. of* **∼**; fodder, forage; **∼овы́е культу́ры, расте́ния** fodder crops; **∼ова́я свёкла** mangel-wurzel.

корму́шк|а, и *f.* (*agric.*) (feeding-)trough, (feeding-)rack, manger.

ко́рмч|ий, его *m.* (*arch. or fig., rhet.*) helmsman, pilot; **∼ая кни́га** (*hist., liter.*) Nomocanon.

корна́|ть, ю *impf.* (*of* **о∼** *and* **об∼**) (*coll.*) to crop, cut short.

корневи́щ|е, а *nt.* (*bot.*) rhizome.

кор|нево́й *adj. of* **∼́ень; ∼невы́е языки́** (*ling.*) isolating languages.

корнепло́д, а *m.* root plant.

ко́рнер, а, *pl.* **∼ы** *or* **∼а́** *m.* (*sport*) corner; **заби́ть гол с ∼а** to score a goal from, off a corner.

корнере́зк|а, и *f.* (*agric.*) root-cutting machine.

корне́т, а *m.* (*mil. and mus.*) cornet.

корне́т-а-писто́н, а *m.* (*mus.*) cornet-à-piston(s).

корнети́ст, а *m.* (*mus.*) cornet-player, cornetist.

корни́йский *adj.* = **корну́эльский**

корнишо́н, а *m.* (*cul.*) gherkin.

корноу́х|ий (∼, ∼а) *adj.* (*coll.*) crop-eared.

ко́рнский *adj.* = **корну́эльский**

ко́рнуо́ллский *adj.* Cornish.

корну́эльский *adj.* Cornish (*of language*).

ко́роб, а, *pl.* **∼а́** *m.* **1.** box, basket (*of bast*). **2.** (*tech.*) box, chest. **3.** (*mil.*) body (*of machine-gun*). **4.** body (*of a carriage*). **5.** (*fig., coll.*): **це́лый к. новосте́й** heaps of news; **наговори́ть с три ∼а** to spin a long yarn.

коробе́йник, а *m.* (*obs.*) pedlar.

коро́б|ить, лю, ишь *impf.* (*of* **по∼**) **1.** to warp. **2.** (*fig.*) to jar upon, grate upon; (*impers.*): **меня́ ∼ит от его́ акце́нта** his accent jars upon me.

коро́б|иться, люсь, ишься *impf.* (*of* **по∼** *and* **с∼**) to warp, buckle.

коро́бк|а, и *f.* box, case, canister; **дверна́я к.** door-frame; **к. скоросте́й** (*tech.*) gear-box; **черепна́я к.** (*anat.*) cranium.

короб|о́к, ка́ *m.* small box.

коро́бочк|а, и *f.* **1.** *dim. of* **коро́бка. 2.** (*bot.*) boll.

коро́бчат|ый *adj.* box shaped; (*tech.*): **∼ое желе́зо** channel iron.

коро́в|а, ы *f.* cow; **морска́я к.** sea-cow, manatee.

корова́|й, я *m.* = **карава́й**

коро́в|ий *adj. of* **∼а; ∼ье ма́сло** butter.

коро́в|ка, ки *f. affectionate dim. of* **∼а; бо́жья к.** lady-bird.

коро́вник[1]**, а** *m.* cow-shed.

коро́вник[2]**, а** *m.* cow-man.

коро́вниц|а, ы *f.* dairy-maid.

короле́в|а, ы *f.* queen.

короле́вич, а *m.* king's son.

короле́в|на, ны, *g. pl.* **∼ен** *f.* king's daughter.

короле́вск|ий *adj.* royal; king's; regal, kingly; **∼ая ко́бра** king cobra; (*chess*): **к. слон** king's bishop.

короле́вств|о, а *nt.* kingdom.

корол|ёк, ька́ *m.* **1.** (*zool.*): **желтоголо́вый к.** goldcrest; **красноголо́вый к.** firecrest. **2.** blood-orange. **3.** (*min.*) regulus.

коро́л|ь, я́ *m.* king; (*fig.*) baron; **газе́тный к.** press baron; **нефтяно́й к.** oil king.

коромы́сл|о, а *nt.* **1.** yoke (*for carrying buckets*); beam (*of scales*). **2.** (*tech.*) rocking shaft, rocker arm. **3.** (*coll.*): **там шёл дым ∼ом** all hell was let loose.

коро́н|а, ы *f.* **1.** crown (*also fig.*); coronet. **2.** (*astron.*) corona.

коронаротромбо́з, а *m.* coronary thrombosis; coronary.

корона́рный *adj.* coronary.

корона|цио́нный *adj. of* **∼́ция**

корона́ци|я, и *f.* coronation.

коро́нк|а, и *f.* crown (*of tooth*).

коро́нн|ый *adj.* crown, of state; (*theatr.*): **∼ая роль** best part.

корон|ова́ть, у́ю *impf. and pf.* to crown.

коро́ст|а, ы *f.* scab.

коросте́л|ь, я́ *m.* (*zool.*) corncrake, landrail.

корота́|ть, ю *impf.* (*of* **с∼**) (*coll.*) to pass, while away (time).

коро́т|кий (ко́роток, ∼ка́, ко́ротко́, *pl.* **∼́ки́)** *adj.* **1.** short; brief; **э́то пальто́ тебе́ ∼ко́** this coat is too short for you; **рассказа́ть в ∼ких слова́х** to tell in a few words; **∼кая распра́ва** short shrift; **к. уда́р** short and sharp blow; (*coll.*): **ру́ки ко́ротки!** just try!; you couldn't if you tried!; **у́м ∼ок** limited intelligence. **2.** (*fig.*) close, intimate; (*coll.*): **быть на ∼кой ноге́ с кем-н.** to be on intimate terms with s.o.

ко́ротк|о́[1] *see* **∼ий**

ко́ротко[2] *adv.* **1.** briefly; **к. говоря́** in short. **2.** intimately.

коротковолнови́к, а́ *m.* radio ham.

коротково́лновый *adj.* (*radio*) short-wave.

короткометра́жк|а, и *f.* (*coll.*) short (film); **рекла́мная к.** commercial, ad(vert).

короткометра́жный *adj.*: **к. фильм** short (film).

коро́ткост|ь, и *f.* (*coll.*) intimacy, familiarity.

коротышк|а, и *c.g.* (*coll.*) dumpy, tubby pers.; squab.

кор|о́че *comp. of* **∼о́ткий** *and* **∼́отко** shorter; **к. говоря́** in short, to cut a long story short.

ко́рочк|а, и *f. dim. of* **ко́рка**

корп|éть, лю́, и́шь *impf.* (**над, за**+ *i.*) (*coll.*) to pore (over), sweat (over).
кóрпи|я, и *f.* (*obs.*) lint.
корпорати́вный *adj.* corporative.
корпорáци|я, и *f.* corporation.
кóрпус[1], **а,** *pl.* **~ы** *m.* **1.** body; trunk, torso. **2.** length (*of animal, as unit of measurement*); **нáша лóшадь опереди́ла други́х на три ~а** our horse won by three lengths. **3.** hull; (*tech.*) frame, body, case. **4.** (*typ.*) long primer.
кóрпус[2], **а,** *pl.* **~á, ~óв** *m.* **1.** (*mil.*) corps; **кадéтский, морскóй к.** military school, naval college; **дипломати́ческий к.** diplomatic corps. **2.** building; block.
корректи́в, а *m.* amendment, correction.
корректи́р|овать, ую *impf.* (*of* **про~**) to correct.
корректирóвщик, а *m.* (*mil.*) **1.** spotter. **2.** spotter (aircraft).
коррéкт|ный (~ен, ~на) *adj.* correct, proper.
коррéктор, а *m.* proof-reader, corrector.
корректу́р|а, ы *f.* **1.** proof-reading, correction. **2.** proof(-sheet); **держáть ~у** to read, correct proofs; **к. в грáнках** galley proof(s); **к. в листáх** page proof(s). **3.** (*mil.*) correction, adjustment (*of fire*).
корректу́р|ный *adj. of* **~а; ~ные знáки** proof symbols; **к. óттиск** proof(-sheet).
коррéкци|я, и *f.* (*med.*) correction.
корреля́т, а *m.* correlate.
корреляти́вный *adj.* correlative.
корреля́ци|я, и *f.* correlation.
корреспондéнт, а *m.* correspondent.
корреспондéнци|я, и *f.* **1.** correspondence; **заказнáя, простáя к.** registered, non-registered mail. **2.** newspaper contribution from a correspondent.
корреспонди́р|овать, ую *impf.* (*in var. senses*) to correspond.
коррóзи|я, и *f.* (*chem.*) corrosion.
коррумпи́ров|анный (~ан, ~ана) *adj.* corrupt, venal.
коррýпци|я, и *f.* (*pol.*) corruption.
корсáж, а *m.* bodice, corsage.
корсáр, а *m.* corsair.
корсéт, а *m.* corset.
корсéтниц|а, ы *f.* corsetière.
Кóрсик|а, и *f.* Corsica.
корсикáн|ец, ца *m.* Corsican.
корсикáн|ка, ки *f. of* **~ец**
корсикáнский *adj.* Corsican.
корт, а *m.* (tennis-)court.
кортéж, а *m.* cortège; motorcade.
кортизóн, а *m.* cortisone.
кóртик, а *m.* dagger, dirk.
кóрточ|ки, ек *no sg.*: **сидéть на ~ках, сесть на к.** to squat.
корýнд, а *m.* (*min.*) corundum.
Кóрфу *m. indecl.* Corfu.
корчáг|а, и *f.* (*dial.*) earthenware pot, ewer.
корч|евáть, ýю *impf.* to stub, grub up, root out.
корчёвк|а, и *f.* stubbing, grubbing up, rooting out.
корчéмств|о, а (*obs.*) bootlegging.
кóрч|и, ей *pl.* (*sg.* **~а, ~и** *f.*) (*coll.*) convulsions, spasm; **мýчиться в ~ах** to writhe with pain; **злáя ~а** (*med.*) ergotism.
кóрч|ить, у, ишь *impf.* (*of* **с~**) **1.** to contort; (*coll.*): **к. гримáсы, рóжи** to make, pull faces. **2.** (*impf. only*) (*coll.*): **к. из себя́** to pose (as); **к. дуракá** to play the fool.
корч|мá, мы́, *g. pl.* **~éм** *f.* (*obs.*) inn, tavern (*in Ukraine and Byelorussia*).
корчмáр|ь, я́ *m.* (*obs.*) innkeeper.
кóршун, а *m.* (*zool.*) kite; (*fig.*): **налетéть, набрóситься ~ом (на**+*a.*) to pounce (on), swoop (onto).
коры́ст|ный (~ен, ~на) *adj.* mercenary, mercenary-minded.
корыстолю́б|ец, ца *m.* profit-seeker, mercenary-minded pers.
корыстолюби́в|ый (~, ~а) *adj.* self-interested, mercenary-minded.
корыстолю́би|е, я *nt.* self-interest, cupidity.
коры́ст|ь, и *f.* (*coll.*) **1.** profit, gain; **какáя тебé в э́том к.?** what are you getting out of it? **2.** cupidity.
коры́т|о, а *nt.* wash-tub; trough; **остáться у разби́того ~а** to be no better off than before, be back where one started.
кор|ь, и *f.* measles.
коры|ё, я́ *nt.* (*collect., dial.*) bark (*stripped from the tree*).
кóрюшк|а, и *f.* smelt (*fish*).
коря́в|ый (~, ~а) *adj.* (*coll.*) **1.** rough, uneven; gnarled. **2.** (*fig.*) clumsy, uncouth. **3.** (*dial.*) pock-marked.
коря́г|а, и *f.* snag (*tree or boughs impeding navigation*).
кос|á[1], **ы́,** *a.* **~ý,** *pl.* **~ы** *f.* plait, pigtail, braid.
кос|á[2], **ы́,** *a.* **~ý,** *pl.* **~ы** *f.* scythe; **нашлá к. на кáмень** he (has) met his match; he ran (has run) into a brick wall.
кос|á[3], **ы́,** *a.* **~ý,** *pl.* **~ы** *f.* (*geog.*) **1.** spit. **2.** (*dial.*) belt (*of trees*).
косáр|ь[1], **я́** *m.* mower (*agent*).
косáр|ь[2], **я́** *m.* chopper (*tool*).
косáтк|а, и *f.* killer whale.
кос|áя, óй *f.* (*sl.*) grand, thou, ...K; **он зарабáтывает 35 ~ы́х в год** he makes 35K a year.
кóсвенн|ый *adj.* indirect, oblique; **~ые ули́ки** circumstantial evidence; (*gram.*): **к. падéж** oblique case; **~ая речь** indirect speech.
косéканс, а *m.* (*math.*) cosecant.
коси́лк|а, и *f.* mowing-machine, mower; **газóнная к.** lawn mower.
кóсинус, а *m.* (*math.*) cosine.
ко|си́ть[1], **шý, ~сишь** *impf.* (*of* **с~**) to mow; to cut; (*fig.*) to mow down; **~си́ ~сá покá росá** (*prov.*) make hay while the sun shines.
ко|си́ть[2], **шý, си́шь** *impf.* (*of* **с~**) **1.** to squint; **к. на óба глазá** to have a squint in both eyes. **2.** (+*a. or i.*) to twist, slant (*mouth, eyes*). **3.** to be crooked.
ко|си́ться, шýсь, си́шься *impf.* (*of* **по~**) **1.** to slant. **2.** (*coll.*) (**на**+ *a.*) to cast a sidelong look (at); (*fig.*) to look askance (at).
коси́ц|а, ы *f.* **1.** lock (*of hair*) **2.** (*dim. of* **косá**[1]) pigtail.
космá|тить, чу, тишь *impf.* (*coll.*) to tousle.
космáт|ый (~, ~а) *adj.* shaggy.
космéтик|а, и *f.* cosmetics, make-up.
космети́ческ|ий *adj.* cosmetic; **к. кабинéт** beauty parlour; **~ая мáска** face-pack; **~ая сýмочка** vanity bag *or* case; **к. ремóнт** redecoration (*papering, painting of interior of house*); refurbishment.
космети́чк|а, и *f.* (*coll.*) **1.** beautician. **2.** vanity bag *or* case.
кóсмик, а *m.* (*coll.*) **1.** cosmic ray specialist. **2.** being from outer space.
косми́ческ|ий *adj.* cosmic, outer space; **к. корáбль** spaceship, spacecraft; **~ое телеви́дение** satellite television broadcasting.
космогóни|я, и *f.* cosmogony.
космогрáфи|я, и *f.* cosmography.
космодрóм, а *m.* space-vehicle launching site.
космолёт, а *m.* (space) shuttle.
космонáвт, а *m.* astronaut, cosmonaut, spaceman.
космонáвтик|а, и *f.* astronautics, (*outer*) space exploration.
космополи́т, а *m.* cosmopolite.
космополити́зм, а *m.* cosmopolitanism.
космополити́ческий *adj.* cosmopolitan.
кóсмос, а *m.* cosmos; outer space.
космотéхник|а, и *f.* space technology.
кóсм|ы, ~ *no sg.* (*coll.*) locks, mane.
коснé|ть, ю *impf.* (*of* **за~**) **1.** (**в**+ *p.*) to stagnate (in). **2.** to stick.
косноязы́чи|е, я *nt.* confused articulation.
косноязы́ч|ный (~ен, ~на) *adj.* speaking thickly.
косн|ýться, ýсь, ёшься *pf. of* **касáться**
кóс|ный (~ен, ~на) *adj.* inert, sluggish; stagnant.
кóсо *adv.* slantwise, askew; obliquely; **смотрéть к.** to look askance, scowl.
кособóк|ий (~, ~а) *adj.* (*coll.*) crooked, lop-sided.
косоворóтк|а, и *f.* (*Russ.*) shirt, blouse (*with collar fastening at side*).
косоглáзи|е, я *nt.* squint, cast in the eye.
косоглáз|ый (~, ~а) *adj.* cross-eyed, squint-eyed.

косого́р, а *m.* slope, hill-side.
кос|о́й[1] **(~, ~а́. ~́о)** *adj.* **1.** slanting; oblique; **к. по́черк** sloping handwriting; **к. у́гол** (*math.*) oblique angle; **~а́я черта́** oblique stroke; **~а́я са́жень в плеча́х** (*coll.*) broad shoulders. **2.** squinting; cross-eyed. **3.: к. взгляд** (*fig.*) sidelong glance.
кос|о́й[2], **о́го** *m.* (*folk poet.*) hare.
косола́п|ый (~, ~а) *adj.* pigeon-toed; (*fig.*) clumsy.
косоуго́льный *adj.* (*math.*) oblique-angled.
Ко́ста-Ри́к|а, и *f.* Costa Rica.
костарика́н|ец, ца *m.* Costa Rican.
костарика́н|ка, ки *f. of* **~ец**
костарика́нский *adj.* Costa Rican.
костёл, а *m.* (Roman Catholic) church.
костене́|ть, ю *impf.* (*of* **о~**) to grow stiff; to grow numb.
кост|ёр, ра́ *m.* bonfire; camp-fire; **сжечь на ~ре́** to burn at the stake.
кости́ст|ый (~, ~а) *adj.* bony.
ко|сти́ть, щу́, сти́шь *impf.* (*coll.*) to abuse.
костля́в|ый (~, ~а) *adj.* bony.
ко́стный *adj.* osseous; (*anat.*): **к. мозг** marrow.
костое́д|а, ы *f.* (*med.*) caries.
костопра́в, а *m.* bone-setter.
ко́сточк|а, и *f.* **1.** *dim. of* **кость**; (*coll.*): **вое́нная к.** old soldier, military man; **перемыва́ть ~и** (+ *d.*) to gossip about, pull to pieces; **разбира́ть по ~ам** to go through (a thing, matter) with a fine comb. **2.** stone, pit (*of fruit*). **3.** ball (*of abacus*). **4.** bone (*of corset, etc.*).
косточковыта́лкивател|ь, я *m.* pitter.
костре́ц, а́ *m.* leg of meat.
косты́л|ь, я́ *m.* **1.** crutch; **ходи́ть на ~я́х** to walk on crutches. **2.** (*tech.*) spike, drive. **3.** (*aeron.*) tail skid.
костыля́|ть, ю *impf.* (*coll.*) **1.** to cudgel. **2.** to hobble.
кост|ь, и, *pl.* **~́и, ~е́й** *f.* **1.** bone; **слоно́вая к.** ivory; (*fig., coll.*) **бе́лая к.** blue blood; **язы́к без ~е́й** loose tongue; **лечь ~ьми́** (*rhet.*) to fall in battle; **пересчита́ть кому́-н. ~́и** to give s.o. a drubbing. **2.** die; **игра́ть в ~́и** to dice.
костю́м, а *m.* **1.** dress, clothes; **в ~е Ада́ма, Е́вы** (*joc.*) in one's birthday suit; **маскара́дный к.** fancy-dress. **2.** suit; costume; **англи́йский к.** tailor-made coat and skirt; **вече́рний к.** dress suit; **пара́дный к.** full dress; **купа́льный к.** swimsuit.
костюме́р, а *m.* (*theatr.*) wardrobe master.
костюме́р|ный *adj. of* **~**; *as n.* **~ная, ~ной** *f.* (*theatr.*) wardrobe (room).
костюме́рш|а, и *f.* (*coll., theatr.*) wardrobe mistress.
костюмиро́ва|нный *p.p.p. of* **~́ть** *and adj.* **1.** in costume; in fancy-dress. **2.: к. бал, ве́чер** fancy-dress ball.
костюмир|ова́ть, у́ю *impf. and pf.* (*theatr.*) to dress.
костюмир|ова́ться, у́юсь *impf. and pf.* to put on costume; to put on fancy-dress.
костю́м|ный *adj. of* **~**; **~ная пье́са** period play.
костя́к, а́ *m.* skeleton; (*fig.*) backbone.
костян|о́й *adj.* (*made of*) bone; **~а́я мука́** bone-meal; **к. но́жик** ivory knife.
костя́шк|а, и *f.* **1.** *dim. of* **кость. 2.** knuckle. **3.** ball (*of abacus*).
косу́л|я, и *f.* roe deer.
косу́шк|а, и *f.* (*obs.*) half-bottle of vodka.
косы́нк|а, и *f.* (triangular) kerchief, scarf.
косьб|а́, ы́ *f.* mowing.
костя́к[1], **а́** *m.* **1.** (door-)post; jamb; cheek. **2.** slope; sloping object.
кося́к[2], **а́** *m.* **1.** herd (*of mares with only one stallion*). **2.** shoal, school; flock.
кося́к[3], **а́** *m.* (*sl.*) joint (= *marijuana cigarette*).
кот, а́ *m.* **1.** tom-cat; **морско́й к.** (*zool.*) sea-bear; (*coll.*): **к. напла́кал** nothing to speak of; practically nothing; **купи́ть ~а́ в мешке́** to buy a pig in a poke; (*prov.*) **не всё ~у́ ма́сленица, придёт и вели́кий пост** after dinner comes the reckoning. **2.** (*sl.*) pimp.
кота́нгенс, а *m.* (*math.*) cotangent.
кот|ёл, ла́ *m.* **1.** copper, cauldron; (*fig.*): **о́бщий к.** common stock. **2.** (*tech.*) boiler. **3.** (*pl.*) hopscotch.
котел|о́к, ка́ *m.* **1.** pot. **2.** mess-tin. **3.** bowler (hat).
коте́льн|ая, ой *f.* boiler-house.
коте́л|ьный *adj. of* **~̈ 2.**; **~ьное желе́зо** boiler plate.
коте́льщик, а *m.* boiler-maker.
кот|ёнок, ёнка, *pl.* **~я́та, ~я́т** *m.* kitten.
ко́тик, а *m.* **1.** fur-seal. **2.** sealskin. **3.** *affectionate dim. of* **кот. 4.** (*affectionate mode of address*) darling. **5.** (*pl.*) *dim. of* **коты**
ко́тик|овый *adj. of* **~ 1., 2.**; **к. про́мысел** sealing; sealskin trade; **~овая ша́пка** sealskin cap.
котилльо́н, а *m.* cotillion.
коти́р|овать, ую *impf. and pf.* (*fin.*) to quote.
коти́р|оваться, уюсь *impf. and pf.* **1.** (*fin.*) **(в+***a.***)** to be quoted (at). **2.** (*fig.*) to be rated.
котиро́вк|а, и *f.* (*fin.*) quotation.
ко|ти́ться, чу́сь, ти́шься *impf.* (*of* **о~**) to kitten, have kittens; to have young.
котле́т|а, ы *f.* cutlet; burger; rissole, patty; **отбивна́я к.** chop.
котле́тн|ая, ой *f.* burger bar.
котлова́н, а *m.* (*tech.*) foundation ditch, trench.
котлови́н|а, ы *f.* (*geog.*) hollow, basin.
кот|ова́ть, у́ю *impf.* (*sl.*) to be courting.
кото́мк|а, и *f.* wallet; knapsack.
кото́р|ый *pron.* **1.** *interrog. and rel.* which; **к. час?** what time is it?; **в ~ом часу́ он зашёл?** what time did he call?; **к. раз?** how many times?; (*coll.*): **к. раз я тебе́ э́то говорю́?** how many times have I told you! **2.** *rel.* who. **3.** (*coll.*): **к.... к.** some … some (others); **~ые бы́ли в чулка́х, ~ые с го́лыми нога́ми** some were wearing stockings and some were bare-legged.
кото́рый-либо *pron.* = **кото́рый-нибудь**
кото́рый-нибудь *pron.* some; one or other.
котте́дж, а *m.* small (detached) house.
коту́рн, а *m.* (*theatr., hist.*) buskin; **станови́ться на ~ы** (*fig.*) to assume a tragic tone.
кот|ы́, о́в *no sg.* (*dial.*) (*woman's*) fur slippers.
кот|я́та, я́т *see* **~ёнок**
ко́уш, а *m.* (*naut.*) thimble.
ко́фе *m. indecl.* coffee; **к. гля́се́** iced coffee; **раствори́мый к.** instant coffee; **к. в зёрнах** coffee beans.
кофева́рк|а, и *f.* coffee-maker.
кофеи́н, а *m.* caffeine.
ко́фе|й, я *m.* (*coll., obs.*) coffee.
кофе́йник, а *m.* coffee-pot.
кофе́йниц|а, ы *f.* **1.** coffee-grinder. **2.** coffee tin.
коф|е́йный *adj. of* **~́е**
кофе́|йня, йни, *g. pl.* **~ен** *f.* (*obs.*) coffee-house.
ко́фт|а, ы *f.* **1.** (*woman's*) jacket, cardigan. **2.** (*coll.*) (*woman's*) short, warm overcoat.
ко́фточк|а, и *f.* blouse.
коча́н, а́ (*and dial.* **кочна́)** *m.*: **к. капу́сты** head of cabbage.
коч|ева́ть, у́ю *impf.* **1.** to be a nomad, to roam from place to place, wander. **2.** (*of birds and animals*) to migrate.
кочёвк|а, и *f.* (*coll.*) **1.** nomad camp. **2.** wandering; nomadic existence.
коче́вник, а *m.* nomad.
кочево́й *adj.* **1.** nomadic. **2.** (*of birds and animals*) migratory.
кочевря́ж|иться, усь *impf.* (*coll.*) **1.** to be obstinate. **2.** to pose, put on airs.
коче́в|ье, ья, *g. pl.* **~ий** *nt.* **1.** nomad encampment. **2.** nomad territory.
кочега́р, а *m.* stoker, fireman.
кочега́рк|а, и *f.* stoke-hole, stoke-hold.
кочене́|ть, ю *impf.* (*of* **за~** *and* **о~**) to become numb; to stiffen.
кочер|га́, ги́, *g. pl.* **~ёг** *f.* poker.
кочеры́жк|а, и *f.* cabbage-stalk, cabbage-stump.
ко́чет, а *m.* (*dial.*) cock.
ко́чк|а, и *f.* hummock; tussock.
кочкова́т|ый (~, ~а) *adj.* hummocky, tussocky.
ко|чу́сь, ти́шься *see* **~ти́ться**
кош, а *m.* **1.** (nomad's) tent. **2.** (*hist.*) camp (*of Zaporozhian Cossacks*).
коша́тник, а *m.* **1.** dealer in (stolen) cats. **2.** (*coll.*) cat-lover.

кош|а́чий *adj. of* **∼́ка**; feline; **к. глаз** (*min.*) cat's eye; **к. конце́рт** caterwauling; (*fig.*) hooting, barracking; **∼а́чьи ухва́тки** catlike (cattish) ways; *as n.* (*zool.*) **∼а́чьи, ∼а́чьих** Felidae.
кош|ево́й *adj. of* **∼́**; **к. атама́н** commander of Cossack camp.
кошел|ёк, ька́ *m.* purse; (*fig.*): **туго́й к.** tight-filled purse.
коше́л|ь, я́ *m.* **1.** (*obs.*) purse. **2.** (*dial.*) bag.
кошени́л|евый *adj. of* **∼ь**
кошени́л|ь, и *f.* cochineal.
коше́рный *adj.* kosher.
ко́шк|а, и *f.* **1.** cat; **(к.-)манкс, бесхво́стая к.** Manx cat; (*fig., coll.*) **игра́ть в ∼и-мы́шки** to play cat-and-mouse; **жить как к. с соба́кой** to lead a cat-and-dog life; **чёрная к. пробежа́ла ме́жду ни́ми** they have fallen out; **но́чью все ∼и се́ры** when candles are out all cats are grey; **у него́ ∼и скребу́т на се́рдце** he is heavy-hearted. **2.** (*tech., naut.*) grapnel, drag. **3.** (*pl.*) crampons; climbing-irons. **4.** (*pl.*) cat-o'-nine tails.
кошм|а́, ы́, *pl.* **∼́ы, ∼** *f.* large piece of felt.
кошма́р, а *m.* nightmare (*also fig.*).
кошма́р|ный (∼ен, ∼на) *adj.* nightmarish; (*fig.*) horrible, awful.
кошт, а *m.* (*obs.*) expense; **на казённом ∼́е** at Government expense.
ко|шу́, си́шь *see* **∼си́ть**
коще́|й, я *m.* **1.** Koshchey (*an evil being in Russ. folk-lore*) *fig. of a tall, thin old man.* **2.** (*fig., coll.*) miser.
кощу́нствен|ный (∼, ∼на) *adj.* blasphemous.
кощу́нств|о, а *nt.* blasphemy.
кощу́нств|овать, ую *impf.* to blaspheme.
коэффицие́нт, а *m.* (*math.*) coefficient, factor; (*tech.*): **к. мо́щности** power factor; **к. поле́зного де́йствия** efficiency; **к. поте́рь** loss factor; **к. у́мственных спосо́бностей** intelligence quotient, IQ.
КП *f. indecl.* (*abbr. of* ***Коммунисти́ческая па́ртия***) Communist Party.
КПСС *f. indecl.* (*abbr. of* ***Коммунисти́ческая па́ртия Сове́тского Сою́за***) CPSU (*Communist Party of the Soviet Union*).
кр. (*abbr. of* **край**) kray, krai.
краб, а *m.* (*zool.*) crab.
кра́вч|ий, его *m.* royal carver (*in Muscovite Russia*).
кра́г|и, ∼ *pl.* (*sg.* **∼а, ∼и** *f.*) **1.** leggings. **2.** cuffs (of gloves).
кра́ден|ый *adj.* stolen; **∼ое** (*collect.*) stolen goods.
кра|ду́, дёшь *see* **∼́сть**
кра́дучись *adv.* stealthily; **идти́ к.** to creep, slink.
краеве́д, а *m.* student of local lore; history and economy.
краеве́дени|е, я *nt.* study of local lore, history and economy.
краеве́д|ческий *adj. of* **∼ение; к. музе́й** museum of local lore, history, and economy; folk museum.
краево́й *adj. of* **край 4.**
краеуго́льный *adj.* (*rhet.*) basic; **к. ка́мень** corner-stone.
кра́ж|а, и *f.* theft; larceny; **к. со взло́мом** burglary; **магази́нная к.** shoplifting; **квалифици́рованная к.** (*leg.*) aggravated theft.
кра|й, я, о ∼́е, в ∼ю́, *pl.* **∼я́, ∼ёв** *m.* **1.** edge; brim; brink (*also fig.*); **пере́дний к.** (*mil.*) first line, forward positions; **быть на ∼ю́ моги́лы** to have one foot in the grave; **конца́-∼́ю нет** there is no end to it; **∼́ем у́ха слу́шать** to overhear; **на ∼ю́ све́та** at the world's end; **че́рез к.** overmuch, beyond measure; **хлебну́ть че́рез к.** (*coll.*) to have a drop too much. **2.** side (*of meat*); **то́лстый к.** rib-steak; **то́нкий к.** chine (of beef), upper cut. **3.** land, country; **в на́ших ∼я́х** in our part of the world; **в чужи́х ∼я́х** in foreign parts. **4.** (*administrative division of former USSR*) kray, krai.
край... *comb. form, abbr. of* **краево́й**
крайко́м, а *m.* (*abbr. of* ***краево́й комите́т***) kray *or* krai committee.
кра́йне *adv.* extremely.
кра́йн|ий *adj.* **1.** (*in var. senses*) extreme; last; uttermost; **К. Се́вер** the Far North; **в ∼ем слу́чае** in the last resort; **по ∼ей ме́ре** at least; **∼яя плоть** (*anat.*) foreskin, prepuce. **2.** (*sport*) outside, wing; **к. напада́ющий** outside forward, wing forward.
кра́йност|ь, и *f.* **1.** extreme; **в ∼и** in the last resort; **до ∼и** in the extreme, extremely. **2.** extremity; **быть в ∼и** to be reduced to extremity.
Кра́ков, а *f.* Cracow.
краковя́к, а *m.* (*dance*) Cracovienne.
крал, а *see* **красть**
кра́л|я, и *f.* (*coll.*) beauty; (*cards*) queen.
крамо́л|а, ы *f.* (*obs.*) sedition.
крамо́льник, а *m.* (*obs.*) maker of, participant in sedition; plotter.
крамо́льный *adj.* (*obs.*) seditious.
кран[1]**, а** *m.* tap; (*tech.*) cock; **запо́рный к.** stopcock; **к.-смеси́тель** mixer tap.
кран[2]**, а** *m.* crane; **к.-двуно́га** (*naut.*) sheerlegs.
кра́н|ец, ца *m.* (*naut.*) fender.
краниоло́ги|я, и *f.* craniology.
крановщи́к, а́ *m.* crane operator.
кра́н|овый *adj. of* **∼**[1,2]
крап, а *no pl., m.* **1.** specks. **2.** pattern on the backs of playing cards.
кра́п|ать, ает *and* **лет** *impf.* to spatter; **дождь ∼лет** it is spitting with rain.
крапи́в|а, ы *f.* (stinging-)nettle; (*collect.*) nettles; **глуха́я к.** dead nettle.
крапи́вник, а *m.* (*zool.*) wren.
крапи́вниц|а, ы *f.* nettle-rash.
крапи́в|ный *adj. of* **∼а; ∼ная лихора́дка** nettle-rash; **∼ное се́мя** (*obs., joc., of civil servants*) tribe of quill-drivers, pen-pushers.
кра́пин|а, ы *f.* speck; spot.
кра́пин|ка, ки *f.* = **∼а**
краплёный *adj.* (*of cards*) marked.
крас|а́, ы́ *f.* **1.** (*obs.*) beauty; (*iron.*): **во всей свое́й ∼е́** in all one's glory. **2.** (*rhet.*) ornament.
краса́в|ец, ца *m.* handsome man; Adonis; good-looker (*male*).
краса́виц|а, ы *f.* beauty (*beautiful woman*); good-looker (*female*).
краса́вк|а, и *f.* belladonna.
краса́вчик, а *m.* (*coll.*) **1.** = **краса́вец. 2.** (*iron.*) dandy.
краси́вост|ь, и *f.* (*mere*) prettiness.
краси́в|ый (∼, ∼а) *adj.* beautiful; handsome; fine.
краси́льный *adj.* appertaining to dyes.
краси́л|ьня, ьни, *g. pl.* **∼ен** *f.* dye-house, dye-works.
краси́льщик, а *m.* dyer.
краси́тел|ь, я *m.* dye(-stuff); **пищево́й к.** food colouring.
кра́|сить, шу, сишь *impf.* (*of* **по∼**) **1.** to paint; to colour; **он кра́сит ло́дку в бе́лое с голубы́м** he is painting the boat white and blue. **2.** to dye; to stain (*wood, glass*). **3.** (*impf. only*) to adorn.
кра́|ситься, шусь, сишься *impf.* **1.** (*pf.* **на∼**) to make up. **2.** (*of newly dyed or newly-painted objects*) to stain. **3.** *pass. of* **∼сить**
кра́ск|а, и *f.* **1.** painting; colouring; dyeing. **2.** paint; dye; **акваре́льная к.** water-colour; **(водо-)эмульсио́нная к.** emulsion (*paint*); **ма́сляная к.** oil-colour; **типогра́фская к.** printer's ink; **писа́ть ∼ами** to paint; **к. для ресни́ц** mascara. **3.** (*pl., fig.*) colours; **сгуща́ть ∼и** (*coll.*) to lay it on thick. **4.** blush; **вогна́ть кого́-н. в ∼у** (*coll.*) to make s.o. blush.
краскопу́льт, а *m.* = **краскораспыли́тель**
краскораспыли́тел|ь, я *m.* paint sprayer, spray-gun.
красне́|ть, ю *impf.* (*of* **по∼**) **1.** to redden, become red. **2.** to blush, colour; (*fig.*): **к. за**+*a.* to blush for. **3.** (*impf. only*) to show red.
красне́|ться, юсь *impf.* to show red.
красноарме́|ец, йца *m.* Red Army man.
красноарме́|йский *adj. of* **∼ец** *and* **Кра́сная А́рмия.**
краснобá|й, я *m.* (*coll.*) phrase-monger, rhetorician.
краснобá́йств|о, а *nt.* (*coll.*) eloquence, fair-sounding speech.
краснобрига́дов|ец, ца *m.* Red Brigader, member of the Red Brigade.
красно́бу́рый *adj.* reddish-brown.
красновáт|ый (∼, ∼а) *adj.* reddish.

красногвардé|ец, йца *m.* (*hist.*) Red Guard.
красногвардé|йский *adj. of* **~ец**
краснодерéв|ец, ца *m.* cabinet-maker.
краснодерéв|щик, щика *m.* = **~ец**
краснозвёздный *adj.* bearing the Red Star (*emblem of the former USSR and Soviet Army*).
краснознамённый *adj.* holding the order of the Red Banner (*decoration in former USSR*); **к. полк** Red Banner regiment.
краснокóж|ий (~, ~а) *adj.* red-skinned; *as n.* **к., ~его** *m.* redskin.
краснокрéстный *adj.* Red Cross.
краснолéсь|е, я *nt.* pine forest.
краснолúцый *adj.* red-faced, rubicund.
красноречúв|ый (~, ~а) *adj.* eloquent; expressive; (*fig.*) telltale, significant.
краснорéчи|е, я *nt.* eloquence; oratory.
краснот|á, ы́ *f.* **1.** redness. **2.** red spot.
краснофлóт|ец, ца *m.* Red Navy man.
краснофлóт|ский *adj. of* **~ец** *and* **Крáсный Флот.**
краснощёкий *adj.* rosy-cheeked.
краснýх|а, и *f.* (*med.*) German measles.
крáс|ный (~ен, ~нá, ~но) *adj.* **1.** red (*also fig., pol.*); **~ное дéрево** mahogany; **~ная шáпочка** Little Red Riding Hood; **к. уголóк** 'Red Corner' (*room in factories, etc., providing recreational and educational facilities*); (*fig.*): **~ная строкá** (first line of) new paragraph; **сказáть для ~ного словцá** to say as a joke, for effect; **~ная ценá** (*coll.*) outside figure, the most which one is willing to pay; **проходúть ~ной нúтью** to stand out, run through (*of theme, motif*); **пустúть ~ного петухá** (*coll.*) to set fire, commit act of arson; **попáсть под ~ную шáпку** (*coll., obs.*) to become a soldier. **2.** (*obs., folk poet. or coll.*) beautiful; (*fig.*) fine; **~ная дéвица** bonny lass; **лéто ~ное** glorious summer; (*prov.*) **долг платежóм ~ен** one good turn deserves another; **к. угол** place of honour (*in peasant hut*). **3.** *signifies that object qualified is of high quality or value*; **~ная ры́ба** cartilaginous fish; (*obs.*): **к. товáр** textiles; **к. зверь** superior types of game (*such as bear, elk*); **к. лес** conifer forest.
крас|овáться, ýюсь *impf.* **1.** to impress by one's beauty, stand out vividly. **2.** (+*i.*) (*coll.*) to flaunt, show off.
красот|á, ы, *pl.* ~́ы *f.* beauty; *as int.* (*coll.*) **к.!** splendid!
красóтк|а, и *f.* (*coll.*) **1.** good-looking girl; (*coll.*) good-looker (*female*). **2.** (*obs.*) sweetheart.
крáс|очный *adj.* **1.** *adj. of* **~ка. 2. (~очен, ~очна)** colourful, highly coloured.
кра|сть, дý, дёшь, *past* **~л, ~́ла** *impf.* (*of* **у~**) to steal.
крá|сться, дýсь, дёшься, *past* **~лся, ~лась** *impf.* to steal, creep, sneak.
крат *only in phr.* **вó сто к.** hundredfold.
крáтер, а *m.* crater.
крáт|кий (~ок, ~кá, ~ко) *adj.* short; brief; concise; **в ~ких словáх** in short, briefly; *as n.* **~кая, ~кой** *f. only in* **и с ~кой** *old name of Russ. letter* **й** (*now* **и ~кое**).
крáтко *adv.* briefly.
кратковрéменный *adj.* of short duration, brief; transitory.
краткосрóч|ный (~ен, ~на) *adj.* short-term.
крáтн|ое, ого *nt.* (*math.*) multiple; **óбщее наимéньшее к.** least common multiple.
крáт|ный (~ен, ~на) *adj.* (+*d.*) divisible without remainder (by); **дéвять — числó ~ное трём** nine is a multiple of three.
крат|чáйший *superl. of* **~́кий**
крáт|че *comp. of* **~кий** *and* **~ко**
крах, а *m.* (*fin. and fig.*) crash; failure.
крахмáл, а *m.* starch.
крахмáлист|ый (~, ~а) *adj.* containing starch.
крахмáл|ить, ю, ишь *impf.* (*of* **на~**) to starch.
крахмáл|ьный *adj. of* **~**; starched; **к. воротничóк** stiff collar.
крáше (*coll.*) *comp. of* **красúв|ый** *and* **~о; к. в гроб кладýт** pale as a ghost.
крáшени|е, я *nt.* dyeing.
крашенúн|а, ы *f.* (*obs.*) coarse, thick linen.
крáшен|ый *adj.* **1.** painted; coloured; **~ое яйцó** pace egg, (decorated) Easter egg. **2.** dyed. **3.** made-up, wearing make-up; (*pej.*) painted.
краю́х|а, и *f.* (*coll.*) thick slice of bread.
креатýр|а, ы *f.* creature, minion.
кревéтк|а, и *f.* (*zool.*) shrimp; prawn.
креветколóвн|ый *adj.*: **~ое сýдно** shrimper, shrimp boat.
крéдит, а *m.* (*book-keeping*) credit.
кредúт, а *m.* credit; **откры́ть, предостáвить к.** to give credit; **отпустúть в к.** to supply on credit; (*fig.*): **пóльзоваться ~ом (у+*g.*)** to have credit (with).
кредúтк|а, и *f.* (*coll.*) credit card; (*obs.*) bank-note.
кредúт|ный *adj. of* **~; к. билéт** (*obs.*) bank-note.
кредит|овáть, ýю *impf. and pf.* (*fin.*) to credit, give credit (to).
кредит|овáться, ýюсь *impf. and pf.* (*fin.*) **1.** to obtain funds on credit. **2.** *pass. of* **~овáть**
кредитóр, а *m.* creditor; **к. по закладнóй** mortgagee.
кредитоспосóбность, и *f.* creditworthiness, credit rating.
кредитоспосóб|ный (~ен, ~на) *adj.* creditworthy.
крéдо *nt. indecl.* credo.
крез, а *m.* Crœsus.
крéйсер, а, *pl.* ~ы *and* **~á** (*naut.*) cruiser; **линéйный к.** battle cruiser.
крéйсер|ский *adj. of* **~; ~ская скóрость** cruising speed.
крéйсерств|о, а *nt.* (*naut.*) cruise, cruising.
крейсúр|овать, ую *impf.* (*naut.*) to cruise.
крéкер, а *m.* cracker.
крéкинг, а *m.* (*tech.*) **1.** cracking (*oil refining*). **2.** oil refinery.
крéкинг-процéсс, а *m.* (*tech.*) cracking (*oil refining*).
крекúр|овать, ую *impf. and pf.* (*tech.*) to crack.
крем, а *m.* (*in var. senses*) cream; **(сапóжный) к.** shoe-polish; **увлажня́ющий к.** moisturizer; **защúтный к.** sunblock; **к.-мáска** face-pack.
кремальéр|а, ы *f.* (*tech.*) rack and pinion gear.
крематóри|й, я *m.* crematorium.
кремац|иóнный *adj. of* **~́ия; ~иóнная печь** incinerator.
кремáци|я, и *f.* cremation.
крем|éнь, ня́ *m.* flint; (*fig.*) hard-hearted pers.; skinflint.
кремеш|óк, кá *m.* piece of flint.
кремлевéд, а *m.* Kremlinologist; Kremlin-watcher.
кремлевéдени|е, я *nt.* Kremlinology; Kremlin-watching.
кремл|ёвский *adj. of* **~ь**
кремленóлог = кремлевéд
кремленолóги|я, и *f.* Kremlinology, Kremlin-watching.
кремл|ь, я́ *m.* citadel; **(москóвский) К.** the Kremlin.
кремнёв|ый *adj.* made of flint; **~ое ружьё** flint-lock.
кремнезём, а *m.* (*min., chem.*) silica.
кремнекúслый *adj.* (*chem.*) silicic; **к. нáтрий** sodium silicate.
крéмниевый *adj.* (*chem.*) silicic.
крéмни|й, я *m.* (*chem.*) silicon.
кремнúстый *adj.* **1.** (*min.*) siliceous. **2.** (*obs.*) stony.
крéм|овый *adj.* **1.** *adj. of* **~. 2.** cream(-coloured).
крен, а *m.* (*naut.*) list, heel; (*aeron.*) bank; **дать к.** (*naut.*) to list, heel (over); (*aeron.*) to bank.
крéндел|ь, я, *pl.* ~и *and* **~я́, ~éй** *m.* (*cul.*) pretzel; **ни за какúе ~я́** (*coll.*) not for anything; **выпúсывать ~я́** to stagger, lurch; **свернýться ~ем** to curl up.
крен|úть, ю́, úшь *impf.* (*of* **на~**) to cause to heel, list.
крен|úться, ю́сь, úшься *impf.* (*of* **на~**) (*naut.*) to list, heel (over); (*aeron.*) to bank.
креóл, а *m.* creole.
креóл|ьский *adj. of* **~**
креп, а *m.* crêpe; **трáурный к.** mourning crape.
крепдешúн, а *m.* crêpe de chine.
крепёжный *adj.*: **к. лес** pit-props.
крепúльщик, а *m.* (*tech.*) timberer (*in mines*).
крепúтельный *adj.* **1.** (*tech.*) strengthening. **2.** (*med.*) astringent.
креп|úть, лю́, úшь *impf.* **1.** (*tech. and fig.*) to strengthen; (*mining*) to timber. **2.** (*naut.*) to make fast, hitch, lash; **к. парусá** to furl sails. **3.** (*med.*) to constipate, render costive.
креп|úться, лю́сь, úшся *impf.* **1.** to hold out. **2.** *pass. of* **~úть**
крéп|кий (~ок, ~кá, ~ко) *adj.* **1.** strong; sound; sturdy,

robust; (*fig.*) firm; **к. моро́з** hard frost; **~кие напи́тки** spirits. **~кое словцо́** (*coll.*) swear-word, strong language; **к. сон** sound sleep; **к. чай** strong tea; **~ок на́ ухо** hard of hearing. **2.** (*coll.*) well-off.

кре́пко *adv.* strongly; firmly; soundly; (*coll.*): **к.-на́крепко** very firmly; **к.-на́крепко завяза́ть** to tie really tight.

крепкоголо́в|ый (~, ~а) *adj.* (*coll.*) pig-headed.

крепколо́б|ый (~, ~а) *adj.* (*coll.*) pig-headed.

крепле́ни|е, я *nt.* **1.** strengthening; fastening. **2.** (*mining*) timbering. **3.** (*naut.*) lashing; furling. **4.** (*ski*) binding.

креплёный *adj.* (*of wines*) fortified.

кре́пн|уть, у, ешь *impf.* (*of* **о~**) to get stronger.

крепостни́к, а́ *m.* advocate of serfdom.

крепостни́|ческий *adj. of* **~к** *and* **~чество**

крепостни́честв|о, а *nt.* serfdom.

крепостн|о́й[1], **и** *adj.* serf; **к. крестья́нин** (*peasant*) serf; **~о́е пра́во** serfdom; *as n.* **к., ~о́го** *m.* serf.

крепостно́й[2] *adj. of* **кре́пость**[2]

кре́пост|ь[1], **и** *f.* (*in var. senses*) strength.

кре́пост|ь[2], **и** *f.* fortress.

кре́пост|ь[3], **и** *f.* (*hist., leg.*): **ку́пчая к.** deed of purchase.

крепча́|ть, ет *impf.* to grow stronger, get up (*of wind*); to get harder (*of frost*).

кре́п|че *comp. of* **~кий** *and* **~ко**

крепы́ш, а́ *m.* (*coll.*) brawny fellow; sturdy child.

креп|ь, и *f.* (*mining*) timbering.

кре́с|ло, ла, *g. pl.* **~ел** *nt.* arm-chair, easy-chair; **высо́кое к.** (*child's*) high chair; **инвали́дное к.** wheelchair; **к.-кача́лка** rocking chair, rocker; (*theatr.*) stall.

кресс-сала́т, а *m.* cress.

крест, а́ *m.* **1.** cross; **поста́вить к.** (**на**+*p.*) to give up for lost; **целова́ть к.** (+*d.*) (*obs.*) to take an oath (to). **2.** the sign of the cross; **осени́ть себя́ ~о́м** to cross o.s., make the sign of the cross.

крест|е́ц, ца́ *m.* (*anat.*) sacrum.

крести́льный *adj.* baptismal.

крести́н|ы, ~ *no sg.* **1.** christening. **2.** christening-party.

крести́тел|ь, я *m.*: **Иоа́нн К.** (*relig.*) John the Baptist.

кре|сти́ть, щу́, ~́стишь *impf.* **1.** (*pf.* **к.** *or* **о~**) to baptize, christen. **2.** (*no pf.*) (+*a.* **у**) to be godfather, godmother (*to the child of*); (*obs., coll.*): **мне с ни́ми дете́й не к.** I have no connection with them. **3.** (*pf.* **пере~**) to make the sign of the cross over.

кре|сти́ться, щу́сь, ~́стишься *impf.* **1.** (*pf.* **к.** *or* **о~**) to be baptized, be christened. **2.** (*pf.* **пере~**) to cross o.s.

крест-на́крест, *adv.* crosswise.

кре́стник, а *m.* god-son, god-child.

кре́стниц|а, ы *f.* god-daughter, god-child.

кре́ст|ный *adj. of* **~**; **~ное зна́мение** sign of the cross; **к. ход** (religious) procession; **~ное целова́ние** oath-taking; (*coll.*): **с на́ми ~ная си́ла!** good heavens!

крёстн|ый *adj.*: **к. оте́ц** (*also as n.* **к., ~ого** *m.*) god-father; **~ая мать** (*also as n.* **~ая ~ой** *f.*) god-mother; **~ые де́ти** god-children.

крестови́к, а́ *m.* garden-spider.

крестови́н|а, ы *f.* (*rail.*) frog.

кресто́вник, а *m.* (*bot.*) ragwort, groundsel.

крест|о́вый *adj. of* **~**; **к. похо́д** crusade.

крестоно́с|ец, ца *m.* crusader.

крестообра́з|ный (~ен, ~на) *adj.* cruciform; (*bot., zool.*) cruciate.

крестоцве́тн|ые, ых (*bot.*) cruciferae.

крестцо́вый *adj.* (*anat.*) sacral.

крестья́н|ин, ина, *pl.* **~е, ~** *m.* peasant.

крестья́нк|а, и *f.* peasant woman.

крестья́нский *adj.* peasant.

крестья́нств|о, а *nt.* **1.** (*collect.*) the peasants, peasantry. **2.** (*obs.*) the life of a peasant, farm-labouring.

крестья́нств|овать, ую *impf.* (*obs.*) to till the soil.

крети́н, а *m.* cretin; (*fig., coll.*) idiot, imbecile.

кретини́зм, а *m.* cretinism; (*fig., coll.*) idiocy, imbecility.

крето́н, а *m.* (*text.*) cretonne.

кре́чет, а *m.* (*zool.*) gerfalcon.

креще́ндо *nt. indecl.* & *adv.* (*mus.*) crescendo.

креще́ни|е, я *nt.* **1.** baptism, christening; **боево́е к.** baptism of fire. **2.** Epiphany.

креще́н|ский *adj. of* **~ие 2.**; **к. моро́з, хо́лод** *of severe frost, cold*; (*fig., coll.*) coldness, severity.

крещён|ый *adj.* baptized; *as n.* **к., ~ого** *m.* (*coll.*) Christian.

кре|щу́, ~́стишь *see* **~сти́ть**

крив|а́я, о́й *f.* (*math., econ., etc.*) curve; (*coll.*): **к. вывезет** sth. will turn up; **его́ на ~о́й не объе́дешь** you won't catch him napping.

кри́вд|а, ы *f.* (*arch. and folk poet.*) falsehood; injustice.

криве́|ть, ю *impf.* (*of* **о~**) to lose an eye.

кривизн|а́, ы́ *f.* crookedness; curvature.

крив|и́ть, лю́, и́шь *impf.* (*of* **с~**) to bend, distort; (*coll.*): **к. гу́бы, рот** to twist one's mouth, curl one's lip; **к.** (*pf.* **по~**) **душо́й** to act against one's conscience.

крив|и́ться, лю́сь, и́шься *impf.* **1.** (*pf.* **по~**) to become crooked, bent. **2.** (*pf.* **с~**) (*coll.*) to make a wry face.

кривля́к|а, и *c.g.* (*coll.*) poseur, pseud.

кривля́нь|е я *nt.* affectation.

кривля́|ться, юсь *impf.* (*coll.*) to be affected, behave in an affected manner.

кривобо́к|ий (~, ~а) *adj.* lop-sided.

кривогла́з|ый (~, ~а) *adj.* blind in one eye.

криводу́ши|е, я *nt.* (*obs.*) duplicity, crookedness.

криводу́ш|ный (~ен, ~на) *adj.* (*obs.*) dishonest, crooked.

крив|о́й (~, ~а́, ~́о) *adj.* **1.** crooked; **~о́е зе́ркало** distorting mirror; **~а́я улы́бка** wry smile; (*fig.*): **~ы́е пути́** crooked ways. **2.** (*coll.*) one-eyed.

криволине́йный *adj.* (*math.*) curvilinear; (*tech.*): **к. паз** cam slot, cam groove.

кривоно́г|ий (~, ~а) *adj.* bandy-legged, bow-legged.

кривото́лк|и, ов *no sg.* false interpretations.

кривоши́п, а *m.* (*tech.*) crank; crankshaft.

кри́зис, а *m.* crisis.

крик, а *m.* cry, shout; *pl.* clamour, outcry; **после́дний к. мо́ды** the last word in fashion.

крикли́в|ый (~, ~а) *adj.* **1.** clamorous, bawling. **2.** loud, penetrating. **3.** (*fig., coll.*) loud; blatant.

кри́кн|уть, у, ешь *inst. pf. of* **крича́ть**

краку́н, а́ *m.* (*coll.*) **1.** shouter, bawler. **2.** babbler.

крил|ь, я *m.* krill.

кримина́л, а *m.* (*coll.*) **1.** foul play. **2.** crime.

криминали́ст, а *m.* (*leg.*) specialist in crime detection.

криминали́стик|а, и *f.* (*science of*) crime detection.

кримина́льный *adj.* criminal.

кримино́лог, а *m.* criminologist.

криминоло́ги|я, и *f.* criminology.

кри́нка = крынка

кринол́ин, а *m.* crinoline.

криптогра́мм|а, ы *f.* cryptogram.

криптогра́фи|я, и *f.* cryptography.

криста́лл, а *m.* **1.** crystal; **маги́ческий к.** crystal ball. **2.** (*comput.*) (silicon) chip.

кристаллиза́ци|я, и *f.* crystallization.

кристаллиз|ова́ть, у́ю *impf. and pf.* (*pf. also* **за~**) to crystallize (*trans.*).

кристаллиз|ова́ться, у́юсь *impf.* (*of* **вы~** *and* **за~**) to crystallize (*intrans.*; *also fig.*).

кристаллографи́ческий *adj.* crystallographic.

кристаллогра́фи|я, и *f.* crystallography.

криста́л|ьный *adj.* **1.** crystalline. **2. (~ен, ~ьна)** (*fig.*) crystal-clear.

Крит, а *m.* Crete.

кри́тский *adj.* Cretan.

крите́ри|й, я *m.* criterion.

кри́тик, а *m.* critic.

кри́тик|а, и *f.* **1.** criticism. **2.** critique.

критика́н, а *m.* (*coll., pej.*) fault-finder, carper.

критика́нств|овать, ую *impf.* (*coll., pej.*) to engage in fault-finding; to carp.

критик|ова́ть, у́ю *impf.* to criticize.

критици́зм, а *m.* **1.** critical attitude. **2.** (*phil.*) criticism.

крити́ческий *adj.* (*in var. senses*) critical; **к. моме́нт** (*fig.*) crucial moment.

кри́ц|а, ы *f.* (*tech.*) bloom.

кри|ча́ть, чу́, чи́шь *impf.* (*of* **~́кнуть**) **1.** to cry, shout; to

yell, scream; **к. (на**+*a.*) to shout (at); **к. о по́мощи** to call for help. **2. (о**+*p.*) (*coll.*, *pej.*) to make a song (about), cry out (against).
крича́|щий *pres. part. act. of* **~ть** *and adj.* (*fig.*, *coll.*) loud; blatant.
кри́|чный *adj. of* **~ца** (*tech.*); **к. горн** finery, bloomery; **~чное произво́дство** finery process.
кришнайт, а *m.* Hare Krishna (follower).
кришнаи́тский *adj.* Hare Krishna; Krishna-Consciousness.
кроа́т, а *m.* = **хорва́т**
кроа́тский *adj.* = **хорва́тский**
кров, а *m.* roof; shelter; **оста́ться без ⁓а** to be left without a roof over one's head.
крова́в|ый *adj.* **1.** bloody; (*fig.*): **~ая ба́ня** blood-bath. **2.** blood-stained.
крова́тк|а, и *f.*: **перено́сная де́тская к.** carry-cot.
крова́т|ь, и *f.* bed; bedstead; **двухъя́русная к.** bunk bed.
кро́в|ельный *adj. of* **~ля**
кро́вельщик, а *m.* roof-maker.
кровено́сн|ый *adj.* appertaining to the circulation of the blood; **~ая систе́ма** circulatory system; **к. сосу́д** blood-vessel.
крови́нк|а, и *f.* (*coll.*) drop of blood; **у него́ ни ~и в лице́** he is deathly pale.
кро́в|ля, ли, *g. pl.* **~ель** *f.* roof.
кро́вн|ый *adj.* **1.** blood; **~ое родство́** blood relationship, consanguinity; **~ая месть** blood feud. **2.** (*of animals*) thorough-bred. **3.** (*fig.*) vital, deep, intimate; **моё ~ое де́ло** an affair which concerns me closely; **~ые интере́сы** vital interests; **~ые де́ньги** money earned by the sweat of one's brow. **4.** (*fig.*) deadly; **~ая оби́да** deadly insult.
кровожа́д|ный (~ен, ~на) *adj.* blood-thirsty.
кровоизлия́ни|е, я *nt.* (*med.*) haemorrhage.
кровообраще́ни|е, я *nt.* circulation of the blood.
кровоостана́вливающ|ий *adj.*: **~ее сре́дство** styptic.
кровопи́йц|а, ы, *g. pl.* **~** *c.g.* (*fig.*, *rhet.*) blood-sucker.
кровоподтёк, а *m.* bruise.
кровопроли́ти|е, я *nt.* bloodshed.
кровопроли́тный *adj.* bloody; sanguinary.
кровопуска́ни|е, я *nt.* (*med.*) blood-letting, phlebotomy.
кровосмеси́тельный *adj.* incestuous.
кровосмеше́ни|е, я *nt.* incest.
кровосо́с, а *m.* **1.** vampire bat. **2.** (*dial.*) vampire. **3.** (*coll.*) blood-sucker; (*sl.*) (drug) pusher.
кровосо́сн|ый *adj.*: **~ая ба́нка** cupping-glass.
кровотече́ни|е, я *nt.* haemorrhage; bleeding.
кровоточи́вост|ь, и *f.* (*med.*) haemophilia.
кровоточи́в|ый (~, ~а) *adj.* **1.** bleeding. **2.** (*med.*; *obs.*) haemophiliac.
кровоточи́т|ь, ~, *impf.* to bleed.
кровоха́ркани|е, я *nt.* blood-spitting; (*med.*) haemoptysis.
кров|ь, и, о ⁓и, в ~и́, *g. pl.* **~е́й** *f.* blood (*also fig.*); **в к., до ⁓и** till it bleeds, till blood flows; **изби́ть, разби́ть в к.** to draw blood; **пусти́ть к.** (+*d.*) to bleed (*trans.*); (*fig.*): **по ⁓и** by birth; **к. с молоко́м** (*coll.*) the very picture of health, blooming; **у него́ к. кипи́т** his blood is up; **страсть к игре́ у него́ в ~и́** gambling is in his blood; **войти́ в плоть и к.** to become ingrained; **по́ртить кому́-н. к.** to put s.o. out, annoy s.o.; **се́рдце у меня́ облива́ется ⁓ью** my heart bleeds; **пить чью-н. к.** (*rhet.*) to suck s.o.'s blood, batten on s.o.
кровяни́ст|ый (~, ~а) *adj.* containing some blood.
кров|яно́й *adj. of* **~ь**
кро|и́ть, ю́, и́шь *impf.* (*of* **с~**) to cut (out).
кро́йк|а, и *f.* cutting (out).
кроке́т, а *m.* **1.** croquet. **2.** (*cul.*) croquette.
кроке́т|ный *adj. of* **~**
кроки́ *nt. indecl.* sketch-map; rough sketch.
кроки́р|овать, ую *impf.* to sketch.
крокир|ова́ть, у́ю *impf. and pf.* (*at croquet*) to roquet.
крокоди́л, а *m.* crocodile.
крокоди́л|ов *and* **~овый** *adj. of* **~**
крокодиловодство|о, а *nt.* crocodile farming.
кро́кус, а *m.* **1.** (*bot.*) crocus. **2.** jeweller's rouge, colcothar.
кро́лик, а *m.* rabbit.
кроликово́д, а *m.* rabbit-breeder.
кроликово́дств|о, а *nt.* rabbit-breeding.
кро́ли|ковый *and* **~чий** *adj. of* **~к; ~чий мех** rabbit-skin.
крол|ь, я *m.* (*sport*) crawl (stroke).
крольча́тник, а *m.* rabbit-hutch.
крольчи́х|а, и *f.* doe-rabbit.
кромань́о́н|ец, ца *m.* Cro-Magnon man.
кроманьо́нский *adj.* Cro-Magnon.
кро́ме *prep.*+*g.* **1.** except. **2.** besides, in addition to; **к. того́** besides, moreover, furthermore; (*coll.*): **к. шу́ток** joking apart.
кроме́шн|ый *adj.*: **ад к.** inferno; **тьма ~ая** (*New Testament*) outer darkness; (*fig.*) pitch darkness.
кро́мк|а, и *f.* edge; (*of material*) selvage; **пере́дняя, за́дняя к.** leading (*aeron.*) edge, trailing edge; **к. на ~у** with edges overlapping, (*naut.*) clinker-built; **к. тротуа́ра** kerb.
кромса́|ть, ю *impf.* (*of* **ис~**) (*coll.*) to cut up carelessly.
крон, а *m.* chrome yellow.
кро́н|а[1]**, ы** *f.* crown (*of a tree*).
кро́н|а[2]**, ы** *f.* (*unit of currency*) crown.
кронпри́нц, а *m.* crown prince.
кронци́ркул|ь, я *m.* (*tech.*) calipers.
кро́OOншнеп, а *m.* (*zool.*) curlew.
кронште́йн, а *m.* (*tech.*) bracket; corbel.
кропа́|ть, ю *impf.* (*coll.*) **1.** (*obs.*) to mend, patch. **2.** to potter away at. **3.** to scribble.
кропи́л|о, а *nt.* (*eccl.*) aspergillum.
кроп|и́ть, лю́, и́шь *impf.* (*of* **о~**) **1.** to besprinkle; to asperse. **2.** (*intrans.*; *of rain*) to trickle, spot.
кропотли́в|ый (~, ~а) *adj.* **1.** laborious; **~ая рабо́та** minute, laborious work. **2.** painstaking, precise; minute.
кросс, а *m.* (*sport*) cross-country (race).
кроссво́рд, а *m.* crossword.
кроссме́н, а *m.* cross-country runner.
кроссови́к, а́ *m.* = **кроссме́н**
кроссо́в|ки, ок *pl.* (*sg.* **~ка, ~ки** *f.*) running shoes, trainers; **соревнова́тельные к.** racing shoes.
крот, а́ *m.* **1.** mole. **2.** moleskin.
кро́т|кий (~ок, ~ка́, ~ко) *adj.* gentle; mild, meek.
кротови́н|а, ы *f.* mole-hill.
крот|о́вый *adj.* **1.** *of* **~**; **~о́вая нора́** mole-hill. **2.** moleskin.
кро́тост|ь, и *f.* gentleness; mildness, meekness.
крох|а́, и́, *pl.* **⁓и, ~а́м** *f.* crumb (*pl. also fig.*).
крохобо́р, а *m.* **1.** penny-pincher, skinflint. **2.** hair-splitter.
крохобо́рств|о, а *nt.* **1.** penny-pinching. **2.** hair-splitting.
крохобо́рств|овать, ую *impf.* **1.** to penny-pinch. **2.** to split hairs.
кро́хотный *adj.* (*coll.*) tiny, minute.
кро́шев|о, а *nt.* (*coll.*) **1.** (*cul.*) hash. **2.** medley.
кро́шечк|а, и *f. dim. of* **кро́шка**
кро́шечный *adj.* (*coll.*) tiny, minute.
крош|и́ть, у́, ⁓ишь *impf.* **1.** (*pf.* **ис~, на~** *or* **рас~**) to crumb, crumble; to chop, hack; (*fig.*) to hack to pieces. **2.** (*pf.* **на~**) (+*i.*) to drop, spill crumbs (of); **к. хле́бом на́ пол** to drop crumbs on to the floor.
крош|и́ться, ⁓ится *impf.* (*of* **ис~** *and* **рас~**) to crumble, break into small pieces.
кро́шк|а, и *f.* **1.** crumb. **2.** (*fig.*) a tiny bit; **ни ~и** not a bit. **3.** (*coll.*, *affectionate of a child*) little one.
круасса́н, а *m.* (*cul.*) croissant.
круг, а, *pl.* **~и́** *m.* **1.** (*p. sg.* **в, на ~у́** = *circular area*; **в, на ~е** = *circumference*) circle; **движе́ние по ⁓у** movement in a circle; **на к.** on average, taking it all round; **к. сы́ра** a cheese; **~и́ (на воде́)** ripples (on water); **стать в к.** to form a circle. **2.** (*sport*; *p. sg.* **на ~у́) беговóй к.** race-course, ring; **к. почёта** lap of honour. **3.** (*fig.*; *p. sg.* **в ~у́**) sphere, range; compass; **вне ⁓а свои́х обя́занностей** outside one's province. **4.** (*fig.*; *p. sg.* **в ~у́**) circle (*of persons*); **официа́льные ~и́** official quarters; **в семе́йном ~у́** in the family circle.
кру́гленьк|ий *adj.* (*coll.*) **1.** *dim. of* **кру́глый; ~ая су́мма** a round sum. **2.** rotund, portly.
кругле́|ть, ю *impf.* (*of* **по~**) to become round.
круглова́т|ый (~, ~а) *adj.* roundish.
круглогодово́й *adj.* year-round.

круглогу́бц|ы, ев *no sg.* (*tech.*) round pliers.
круглоли́ц|ый (~, ~а) *adj.* moon-faced, chubby-faced.
круглоро́т|ые, ых (*zool.*) Cyclostomata.
круглосу́точный *adj.* round-the-clock, twenty-four-hour.
кру́гл|ый (~, ~а́, ~о) *adj.* **1.** (*in var. senses*) round; **к. год** all the year round; **~ые су́тки** day and night; **к. по́черк** round hand; **~ая су́мма** round sum; **в ~ых ци́фрах, для ~ого счёта** in round figures. **2.** (*coll.*) complete, utter, perfect; **к. дура́к** perfect fool; **~ое неве́жество** crass ignorance; **к., ~ая сирота́** orphan (*having neither father nor mother*)
круглы́ш, а́ *m.* (*dial.*) rounded stone.
кругов|о́й *adj.* circular; **~а́я пору́ка** mutual responsibility, guarantee; **~а́я ча́ша** loving-cup; **~а́я доро́га** roundabout route; **~а́я оборо́на** all-round defence.
круговоро́т, а *m.* rotation, circulation.
кругозо́р, а *m.* **1.** prospect. **2.** (*fig.*) horizon, range of interests.
круго́м[1] *adv.* **1.** round, around; **он обошёл маши́ну к.** he walked around the car. **2.** (all) round, round about; **к. всё бы́ло ти́хо** all around was still. **3.** (*coll.*) completely, entirely; **он был к. в долга́х** he was head over heels in debt; **вы к. винова́ты** you are entirely to blame, you haven't a leg to stand on.
круго́м[2] *prep.+g.* round, around.
кругооборо́т, а *m.* circuit, circulation.
кругообра́з|ный (~ен, ~на) *adj.* circular.
кругосве́тный *adj.* round-the-world.
кружа́л|о[1]**, а** *nt.* (*archit.*) bow member, curve piece.
кружа́л|о[2]**, а** *nt.* (*hist.*) tavern, pothouse.
круж|ева́, ~́ев, ~ева́м = ~́ево
кружевни́ц|а, ы *f.* lace-maker.
кружев|но́й *adj. of* **~а́** *and* **кру́жево**
кру́жев|о, а *nt.* lace
круж|и́ть, у́, ~́ишь *impf.* **1.** to whirl, spin round; (*fig.*): **к. кому́-н. го́лову** to turn s.o.'s head. **2.** to circle. **3.** (*coll.*) to wander.
круж|и́ться, у́сь, ~́ишься *impf.* (*of* **за~**) to whirl, spin round; to circle; **у меня́ ~́ится голова́** my head is going round, I feel giddy.
кру́жк|а, и *f.* **1.** mug; tankard; (*measure*): **к. пи́ва** glass of beer; **ме́рная к.** (*cul.*) measuring cup. **2.** collecting-box. **3.** (*med.*) douche.
кружковщи́н|а, ы *f.* clannishness, cliquishness.
круж|ко́вый *adj. of* **~о́к 2.**
кру́жный *adj.* roundabout, circuitous.
круж|о́к, ка́ *m.* **1.** *dim. of* **круг; стри́чься в к.** to have one's hair bobbed. **2.** (*liter., pol., etc.*) circle, study group.
круи́з, а *m.* cruise.
круп[1]**, а** *m.* (*med.*) croup.
круп[2]**, а** *m.* croup, crupper (*of horse*).
круп|а́, ы́, *pl.* **~́ы** *f.* **1.** (*collect.*) groats; **гре́чневая к.** buckwheat; **ма́нная к.** semolina; **овся́ная к.** oatmeal; **перло́вая к.** pearl-barley. **2.** (*fig.*) sleet.
крупени́к, а́ *m.* buckwheat pudding with curd.
крупи́нк|а, ы *f.* grain.
крупи́ц|а, ы *f.* grain, fragment, atom; **у него́ нет ни ~ы́ здра́вого смы́сла** he hasn't a grain of common sense.
крупне́|ть, ю *impf.* (*of* **по~**) to grow larger.
кру́пн|о *adv. of* **~ый; к. наре́зать** to cut into large pieces; **к. писа́ть** to write large; **к. поспо́рить (с+*i.*)** to have high words (with), have a slanging-match (with).
крупногабари́т|ный (~ен, ~на) *adj.* large.
крупнозерни́стый *adj.* coarse-grained, large-grained.
крупнокали́берный *adj.* large-calibre.
крупномасшта́б|ный (~ен, ~на) *adj.* large-scale; (*fig.*) ambitious.
кру́п|ный (~ен, ~на́, ~но) *adj.* **1.** large, big; large-scale; (*fig.*) prominent, outstanding; **~ные де́ньги** money in large denominations; **~ные поме́щики** big landowners; **~ная промы́шленность** large-scale industry; **к. рога́тый скот** (horned) cattle; **~ным ша́гом** at a round pace; **засня́ть ~ным пла́ном** (*cinema*) to take a close-up (of). **2.** coarse; **к. песо́к** coarse sand; **к. шаг** (*tech., aeron.*) coarse pitch. **3.** important; serious; **~ная неприя́тность** serious trouble; **к. разгово́р** (*fig.*) high words.
круп|о́зный *adj. of* **~**[1]**; ~о́зное воспале́ние лёгких** lobar pneumonia.
крупору́шк|а, и *f.* (*agric.*) hulling mill, peeling mill.
крупча́тк|а, и *f.* finest wheaten flour.
крупча́тый *adj.* granular.
крупье́ *m. indecl.* croupier.
крутизн|а́, ы́ *f.* **1.** steepness. **2.** steep slope.
крути́льн|ый *adj.* (*tech.*) torsion(al); (text.) doubling; **~ая маши́на** twisting machine, (*text.*) twiner.
кру|ти́ть, чу́, ~́тишь *impf.* (*of* **за~** *and* **с~**) **1.** to twist; to twirl; **к. верёвку** to twist a rope; **к. папиро́су** to roll a cigarette; **к. усы́** to twirl one's moustache; **к. шёлк** to twist, throw silk; (*coll.*; *+i.*) **она́ ~́тит им, как хо́чет** she twists him round her little finger. **2.** to turn, wind (*tap, handle, etc.*). **3.** to whirl (*trans.*). **4.** (*coll.*; **с+*i.***) to go out (with), have an affair (with).
кру|ти́ться, чу́сь, ~́тишься *impf.* **1.** to turn, spin, revolve. **2.** to whirl. **3.** (*fig., coll.*) to be in a whirl.
кру́то *adv.* **1.** steeply. **2.** suddenly; abruptly, sharply; **к. поверну́ть** to turn round sharply. **3.** (*coll.*) sternly, severely; drastically; **к. распра́виться с кем-н.** to give s.o. short shrift. **4.** thoroughly; **к. замеси́ть те́сто** to make a thick dough; **к. отжа́ть** to squeeze dry, wring out thoroughly; **к. посоли́ть** to put (too) much salt (into).
крут|о́й (~, ~а́, ~́о) *adj.* **1.** steep; **к. вира́ж** (*aeron.*) steep turn. **2.** sudden; abrupt, sharp. **3.** (*coll.*) stern, severe; drastic; **к. нрав** stern temper; **~ы́е ме́ры** drastic measures. **4.** (*cul.*) thick; well-done; **к. кипято́к** fiercely boiling water; **~о́е яйцо́** hard-boiled egg.
кру́ч|а, и *f.* steep slope, cliff.
кру́|че *comp. of* **~то́й** *and* **~то**
круче́ни|е, я *nt.* **1.** (*text.*) twisting, spinning. **2.** (*tech.*) torsion.
кручён|ый *adj.* **1.** twisted; **~ые ни́тки** lisle thread. **2.** (*sport*) spinning, turning; with spin on.
кручи́н|а, ы *f.* (*folk poet.*) sorrow, woe.
кручи́н|иться, юсь, ишься *impf.* (*folk poet.*) to sorrow, grieve.
кру|чу́, ~́тишь *see* **~ти́ть**
круше́ни|е, я *nt.* **1.** wreck; ruin; **к. по́езда** derailment. **2.** (*fig.*) ruin; collapse; downfall.
круши́н|а, ы *f.* (*bot.*) buckthorn.
круш|и́ть, у́, и́шь *impf.* to shatter, destroy (*also fig.*).
круш|и́ться, у́сь, и́шься *impf.* (*obs. or poet.*) to sorrow, be afflicted.
крыжо́венный *adj.* gooseberry.
крыжо́вник, а *m.* **1.** gooseberry bush(es). **2.** (*collect.*) gooseberries.
крыла́тк|а[1]**, и** *f.* **1.** (*obs.*) (man's) loose cloak with cape. **2.** (*bot.*) ash-key.
крыла́тк|а[2]**, и** *f.* (*tech.*) wing nut; vane.
крыла́т|ый *adj.* winged (*also fig.*): **~ые слова́** pithy saying(s); (*tech.*): **к. болт** butterfly bolt; **~ая га́йка** wing nut.
крыл|е́чко, е́чка *nt. dim. of* **~ьцо́**
крыл|о́, а́, *pl.* **~́ья, ~́ьев** *nt.* (*in var. senses*) wing; sail, vane (*of windmill*); splash-board, mud-guard, wing (*of car, carriage*).
крылоно́г|ие, их (*zool.*) Pteropoda.
кры́лыш|ко, ка, *pl.* **~ки, ~ек, ~кам** *nt. dim. of* **крыло́;** (*fig.*): **под ~ком** under the wing (*of*).
крыл|ьцо́, ьца́, *pl.* **~́ьца, ~ец, ~ьца́м** *nt.* porch; perron; front (*or* back) steps.
Крым, а *m.* the Crimea.
кры́мский *adj.* Crimean.
крымча́к, а́ *m.* inhabitant of the Crimea.
кры́нк|а, и *f.* earthenware pot, pitcher.
кры́с|а, ы *f.* rat; **су́мчатая к.** opossum; **канцеля́рская к.** (*fig., coll.*) quill-driver.
крыс|ёнок, ёнка, *pl.* **~я́та, ~я́т** *m.* young rat.
крыс|и́ный *adj. of* **~́а; к. яд** rat poison.
крысоло́в, а *m.* rat-catcher.
крысоло́вк|а, и *f.* **1.** rat-trap. **2.** (*dog*) rat-catcher, ratter.
кры́т|ый *p.p.p. of* **~ь** *and adj.* covered; sheltered, with an awning; **к. ры́нок** covered market.
крыть, кро́ю, кро́ешь *impf.* (*of* **по~**) **1.** to cover; to roof;

to coat (*with paint*); (*cards*) to cover, trump. **2.** (*coll.*) to swear (at); **емý нéчем к.** he hasn't a leg to stand on.
крыться, крóюсь, крóешься *impf.* **1.** (**в**+*p.*) to be, lie (in). **2.** to be concealed.
крыш|а, и *f.* roof.
крышк|а, и *f.* **1.** lid; cover. **2.** (*sl.*) death, end; **емý к.** he's done for; he's finished.
крэк, а *m.* crack (*drug*).
крю|к, кá *m.* **1.** (*pl.* **~кú, ~кóв**) hook; **(альпинúстский) к.** piton; (*pl.* **~чья, ~чьев**) hook (*for supporting load*). **2.** detour; (*coll.*): **дать ~ку, сдéлать к.** to make a detour. **3.** (*mus.*) (*pl.* **~кú, ~кóв**) kryuk (*old Russ. neum*).
крючúть, ит *impf.* (*of* **с~**) (*impers., coll.*): **егó ~ит (от бóли)** he is writhing (in pain).
крючковáт|ый (~, ~а) *adj.* hooked.
крючкотвóр, а *m.* (*obs., coll.*) pettifogger.
крючкотвóрств|о, а *nt.* (*obs., coll.*) chicanery.
крючник, а *m.* carrier, stevedore.
крюч|óк, кá *m.* **1.** hook; **спусковóй к.** trigger. **2.** (*fig.*; *obs., pej.*) hitch, catch. **3.** (*fig., obs*) pettifogger.
крюшóн, а *m.* cup (*beverage*).
крядý *adv.* (*coll.*) running; **три дня к. онá опáздывала на слýжбу** three days running she was late for work.
кряж, а *m.* **1.** (mountain-)ridge. **2.** block, log.
кряжист|ый (~, ~а) *adj.* thick; (*fig.*) thick-set.
крякать, аю *impf.* (*of* **~нуть**) **1.** to quack. **2.** (*coll.*) to wheeze.
крякв|а, ы *f.* wild duck, mallard.
кряк|нуть, ну, нешь *inst. pf. of* **~ать**
крях|тéть, чý, тúшь *impf.* to groan; to wheeze, grunt.
ксёндз, á *m.* Roman Catholic (*esp. Polish*) priest.
ксéр|ить, ю, ишь *impf.* (*of* **откcéрить**) (*coll.*) to xerox.
ксерогрáфи|я, и *f.* xerography.
ксерокопúр|овать, ую *impf. and pf.* to xerox, photocopy.
ксерокóпи|я, и *f.* Xerox (*propr.*), xerograph.
ксéрокс, а *m.* **1.** xerography. **2.** Xerox(-machine) (*propr.*). **3.** xerox.
ксилогрáфи|я, и *f.* **1.** wood-engraving. **2.** woodcut.
ксилофóн, а *m.* (*mus.*) xylophone.
кстáти *adv.* **1.** to the point, apropos **2.** opportunely; **вы пришлú как раз к.** you came just at the right moment; **э́тот подáрок оказáлся óчень к.** the present has proved most welcome. **3.** (*coll.*) at the same time, incidentally; **к. зайдúте пожáлуйста в аптéку** will you please call at the chemist's at the same time. **4.: к. (сказáть)** by the way; **к., где вы купúли э́тот гáлстук?** by the way, where did you buy that tie?
ктúтор, а *m.* churchwarden.
кто, когó, комý, кем, ком *pron.* **1.** (*interrog.*) who; **к. э́то такóй?** who is that?; **к. из вас э́то сдéлал?** which of you did it? **к. идёт?** (*mil.*) who goes there?; **к. когó** (*sc.* **побьёт)?** who will win? **2.** (*rel.*) who (*normally after pron. antecedent*); **тот, к.** he who; **те, к.** those who; **блажéн, к....** blessed is he who ...; **спасáйся к. мóжет!** every man for himself! **3.** (*indef.*): **к. (бы) ни** who(so)-ever; **к. ни придёт** whoever comes; **к. бы то нú был** whoever it may be. **4.** (*indef.*) some ... others; **к. что лю́бит, комý что нрáвится** tastes differ; **разбежáлись к. кудá** they scattered in all directions; **к. в лес, к. по дровá** (*coll.*) to be (*etc.*) at sixes and sevens. **5.** (*coll., indef.*) anyone; **éсли к. позвонúт, дай мне знать** if anyone rings, let me know. **6.: к.-к., а... (когó-когó, а..., комý-комý, а...)** *contrasts action, attitude, etc., of one or more members of a group with that of remainder* (*coll.*): **когó-когó, а меня́ э́то вполнé устрáивает** I don't know about anyone else, but it suits me fine.
ктó-либо, когó-либо *pron.* = **ктó-нибудь**
ктó-нибудь, когó-нибудь *pron.* anyone, anybody; someone, somebody.
ктó-то, когó-то *pron.* someone, somebody.
куафёр, а *m.* (*obs.*) coiffeur.
куафю́р|а, ы *f.* (*obs.*) coiffure.
куб¹, а, *pl.* **~ы́** *m.* **1.** (*math.*) cube; **два в ~е** two cubed. **2.** (*coll.*) cubic metre.
куб², а, *pl.* **~ы́** *m.* boiler, water-heater, (tea)-urn; still.
Кýб|а, ы *f.* Cuba.
кубáн|ец, ца *m.* Kuban Cossack.
кубáнк|а, и *f.* flat, round fur hat.
кубáнский *adj.* (*geog.*) (of the) Kuban.
кýбарем *adv.* (*coll.*) head over heels, headlong; **скатúться к.** to roll head over heels.
кубáр|ь, я́ *m.* peg-top.
кубатýр|а, ы *f.* cubic content.
кубúзм, а *m.* (*art*) cubism.
кýбик, а *m.* **1.** *dim. of* **куб. 2.** (*pl.*) blocks, bricks (*as children's toy*). **3.** (*coll.*) cubic centimetre.
кубúн|ец, ца *m.* Cuban.
кубúн|ка, ки *f. of* **~ец**
кубúнский *adj.* Cuban.
кубúческий *adj.* cubic; **к. кóрень** (*math.*) cube root.
кубовúд|ный (~ен, ~на) *adj.* cube-shaped, cuboid.
куб|овóй *adj. of* **~²**
кýбовый *adj.* indigo.
кýб|ок, ка *m.* goblet, bowl, beaker; **переходя́щий к.** (*sport etc.*) (challenge) cup; **встрéча на к.** cup-tie.
кубомéтр, а *m.* cubic metre.
кýбрик, а *m.* (*naut.*) crew's quarters; orlop(-deck).
кубы́шк|а, и *f.* (*coll.*) **1.** (*obs.*) money-box. **2.** (*joc.*) dumpy woman. **3.** yellow water-lily. **4.** holothurian, sea cucumber. **5.** locust pod.
кувáлд|а, ы *f.* sledge-hammer (*also fig., coll., of a clumsy woman*).
кувéз, а *m.* (*med.*) incubator.
Кувéйт, а *m.* Kuwait.
кувéйт|ец, ца *m.* Kuwaiti.
кувéйт|ка, ки *f. of* **~ец**
кувéйтский *adj.* Kuwaiti.
кувéрт, а *m.* (*obs.*) place (*at table*); **стол на двáдцать ~ов** table laid for twenty persons.
кувшúн, а *m.* jug; pitcher.
кувшúнк|а, и *f.* (*bot.*) water-lily.
кувырк|áться, áюсь *impf.* (*of* **~нýться**) to turn somersaults, go head over heels.
кувырк|нýться, нýсь, нёшься *inst. pf. of* **~áться**
кувыркóм *adv.* (*coll.*) head over heels; topsy-turvy; **полетéть к.** to go head over heels; **всё пошлó к.** everything went haywire.
кугуáр, а *m.* (*zool.*) puma, cougar; mountain-lion.
кудá *adv.* **1.** (*interrog. and rel.*) where (*expr. motion*), whither; **к. ты идёшь?** where are you going?; **к. он положúл мою́ кнúгу?** where did he put my book? **2.: к. (бы) ни** wherever; **к. бы то нú было** anywhere; (*coll.*): **к. ни кинь** wherever one looks, on all sides; **к. ни шло** come what may. **3.** (*coll.*) what for; **к. вам стóлько багажá?** what do you want so much luggage for? **4.** (*+comp.; coll.*) much, far; **сегóдня мне к. лýчше** I am much better today. **5.** (*coll.*): **хоть к.** fine, excellent. **6.** (*expr. doubt, incredulity; coll.*) how (could that be; could you, he, etc.); **к часý я намéрен дочитáть до странúцы 200 — к. тебé!** I intend to reach page 200 by one o'clock — you'll never do it!; **узнáли ли тебя́ онú? к. им** did they recognize you? how could they? **7.** (*coll., iron.*): **к. как** very; **к. как прия́тно слýшать егó гóлос** it is *so* nice to listen to his voice.
кудá-либо *adv.* = **кудá-нибудь**
кудá-нибудь *adv.* anywhere; somewhere.
кудá-то *adv.* somewhere.
кудáхтань|е, я *nt.* cackling, clucking.
кудáх|тать, чу, чешь *impf.* to cackle, cluck.
кудéл|ь, и *f.* (*text.*) tow.
кудéсник, а *m.* magician, sorcerer.
кудáтлый *adj.* (*coll.*) shaggy.
кудреват|ый (~, ~а) *adj.* rather curly; (*fig.*) florid, ornate.
кýдр|и, éй *no sg.* curls.
кудря́в|иться, люсь, ишься *impf.* to curl.
кудря́в|ый (~, ~а) *adj.* **1.** curly; curly-headed. **2.** leafy, bushy; **~ая капýста** curly kale. **3.** (*fig.*) florid, ornate.
кудря́ш|ки, ек *no sg.* (*coll.*) ringlets.
кузéн, а *m.* cousin.
кузúн|а, ы *f.* cousin.
кузнéц, á *m.* (black)smith; farrier.

кузне́чик, а *m.* grasshopper.

кузне́чный *adj.* blacksmith's; **к. мех** bellows.

ку́зниц|а, ы *f.* forge, smithy.

ку́зов, а, *pl.* **~ы** *and* **~а́** *m.* **1.** basket. **2.** body (*of carriage, etc.*).

кукаре́ка|ть, ю *impf.* to crow.

кукареку́ cock-a-doodle-doo.

ку́киш, а *m.* (*coll.*) fig (*gesture of derision or contempt, generally accompanying refusal to comply with a request, and consisting of extending clenched fist with thumb placed between index and middle fingers*); **показа́ть кому́-н. к.** *to make this gesture* (*cf.* to cock a snook, give the V-sign); **к. в карма́не** *of defiance expr. in the absence of the pers. defied*; **получи́ть к. с ма́слом** to come away empty-handed, receive a snub.

ку́к|ла, лы, *g. pl.* **~ол** *f.* doll; puppet; **ручна́я к.** glove puppet; **тростева́я к.** string puppet; **теа́тр ~ол** puppet-theatre.

ку-клукс-кла́н, а *m.* Ku Klux Klan.

куклуксклáнов|ец, ца *m.* Ku Klux Klaner.

кук|ова́ть, у́ю *impf.* to (cry) cuckoo.

ку́колк|а, и *f.* **1.** (*affectionate dim. of* **ку́кла**) dolly. **2.** (*zool.*) chrysalis, pupa.

ку́кол|ь[1]**, я** *m.* (*bot.*) cockle.

ку́кол|ь[2]**, я** *m.* (*eccl.*) cowl.

ку́кольник, а *m.* (*coll.*) puppeteer.

ку́кольн|ый *adj.* **1.** doll's; **к. теа́тр** puppet-theatre.; **~ая коме́дия** (*fig., coll.*) farce; play-acting. **2.** doll-like.

ку́к|ситься, шусь, сишься *impf.* (*coll.*) to sulk; to be in the dumps.

кукуру́з|а, ы *f.* maize, Indian corn; **возду́шная к.** popcorn.

кукуру́з|ный *adj. of* **~а**

куку́шк|а[1]**, и** *f.* cuckoo, **часы́ с ~ой** cuckoo clock.

куку́шк|а[2]**, и** *f.* small steam locomotive.

кула́к[1]**, а́** *m.* **1.** fist; **брониро́ванный к.** the mailed fist; **дойти́ до ~о́в** to come to blows; **смея́ться в ~** to laugh in one's sleeve. **2.** (*mil.*) striking force.

кула́к[2]**, а́** *m.* kulak.

кула́к[3]**, а́** *m.* (*tech.*) cam.

кула́|цкий *adj. of* **~к**[2]

кула́честв|о, а *nt.* (*collect.*) the kulaks.

кула́чк|а, и *f. of* **кула́к**[2]

кула́чк|и *only in phrr.* **идти́ на к.** to come to blows; **би́ться на ~ах** to engage in fisticuffs.

кулач|ко́вый *adj. of* **~о́к**[2]; **к. вал** camshaft.

кула́|чный *adj. of* **~к**[1,3]; **к. бой** fisticuffs; **~чное пра́во** fist-law.

кула|чо́к[1]**, чка́** *m. dim. of* **~к**[1]

кулач|о́к[2]**, ка́** *m.* (*tech.*) cam.

кулебя́к|а, и *f.* kulebyaka (*pie containing meat, fish, or vegetables, etc.*).

кул|ёк, ька́ *m.* bag (*made from bast or paper*); **из ~ька́ в рого́жку** (*coll.*) out of the frying-pan into the fire.

куле́ш, а́ *m.* (*coll.*) thin gruel.

ку́ли *m. indecl.* coolie.

кули́к, а́ *m.* (*zool.*) stint; sandpiper (*Calidris*).

кулина́р, а *m.* cookery specialist.

кулина́ри|я, и *f.* cookery.

кулина́рный *adj.* culinary.

кули́с|а, ы *f.* (*tech.*) link.

кули́с|ный *adj. of* **~а; к. ка́мень** sliding block, link block, guiding shoe; **~ное распределе́ние** link gear, link motion, slide block mechanism.

кули́с|ы, ~ *pl.* (*sg.* **~а, ~ы** *f.*) (*theatr.*) wings, side-scenes, slips; **за ~ами** behind the scenes (*also fig.*).

кули́ч, а́ *m.* Easter cake.

кули́чк|и *only in phrr.* (*coll.*): **у чёрта на ~ах, к чёрту на к.** at (to) the world's end.

куло́н[1]**, а** *m.* pendant.

куло́н[2]**, а** *m.* (*elec.*) coulomb.

кулуа́р|ный *adj. of* **~ы**

кулуа́р|ы, ов *sg. not used* lobby (*in Parliament; also fig.*).

кул|ь, я́ *m.* sack (*formerly also variable dry measure, equivalent to approx. 82–147 kilograms*).

ку́льман, а *m.* drawing-board.

кульминацио́нный *adj.*: **к. пункт** culmination point.

кульмина́ци|я, и *f.* culmination.

кульмини́р|овать, ую *impf. and pf.* to culminate.

культ, а *m.* (*in var. senses*) cult; **служи́тели ~а** ministers of religion; **к. ли́чности** (*hist.*) cult of personality (*esp. of J. V. Stalin*).

культ... *comb. form, abbr. of* **культу́рный**

культба́з|а, ы *f.* recreation centre.

культива́тор, а *m.* (*agric.*) cultivator (*machine*).

культива́ци|я, и *f.* (*agric.*) treatment of the ground with a cultivator (*machine*).

культиви́ровани|е, я *nt.* cultivation (*also fig.*).

культиви́р|овать, ую *impf.* to cultivate (*also fig.*).

культма́ссов|ый *adj.*: **~ая рабо́та** education of the masses.

ку́льт|овый *adj. of* **~; ~овая му́зыка** religious music.

культпохо́д, а *m.* **1.** cultural crusade. **2.** educational (field) trip (*visit by group to museum, theatre, etc.*).

культрабо́тник, а *m.* recreation officer.

культтова́р|ы, ов *no sg.* recreational supplies.

культу́р|а, ы *f.* **1.** (*in var. senses*) culture. **2.** standard, level; **к. ре́чи** standard of speech; **повы́сить ~у земледе́лия** to raise the standard of farming. **3.** (*agric.*): **зерновы́е ~ы** cereals; **кормовы́е ~ы** forage crops. **4.** (*agric.*) cultivation, growing; **к. карто́феля** potato-growing.

культури́зм, а *m.* body-building.

культури́ст, а *m.* body-builder.

культу́рничеств|о, а *nt.* (*pej.*) culture-mongering (*promotion of cultural and/or educational activities to exclusion of political questions*).

культу́рно *adv.* in a civilized manner.

культу́рно-бытов|о́й *adj.*: **~о́е обслу́живание** culture and welfare service.

культу́рно-просвети́тельный *adj.* cultural and educational.

культу́рност|ь, и *f.* (level of) culture; cultivation; (*fig.*): **он отлича́лся ~ью** he was exceptionally cultivated.

культу́р|ный (~ен, ~на) *adj.* **1.** cultured, cultivated. **2.** (*in var. senses*) cultural. **3.** (*agric., hort.*) cultured; cultivated.

культуртре́гер, а *m.* (*iron.*) 'Kulturträger', pers. with civilizing mission.

культ|я́, и́ *f.* stump (*of maimed or amputated limb*).

культя́|пка, пки *f.* (*coll.*) = **~**

кум, а, *pl.* **~овья́, ~овьёв** *m.* god-father of one's child; fellow-sponsor; father of one's god-child; gossip (*in arch. sense*).

кум|а́, ы́ *f.* **1.** god-mother of one's child; fellow-sponsor; mother of one's god-child; gossip (*in arch. sense*), cummer (*dial.*). **2.** *in folklore, conventional epithet of fox.*

куман|ёк, ька́ *m.* (*coll.*) *affectionate of* **кум**; *as form of address* my friend.

кума́ч, а́ *m.* red calico.

куми́р, а *m.* idol (*also fig.*)

куми́р|ня, ни, *g. pl.* **~ен** *f.* pagan temple.

кум|и́ться, лю́сь, и́шься *impf.* (*of* **по~**) (**с**+*i.*; *coll.*) to become god-parent to s.o.'s child; (*fig.*) to become acquainted (with).

кумовств|о́, а́ *nt.* **1.** relationship of god-parent to parent, *or* of god-parents. **2.** (*fig.*) favouritism, nepotism.

кумуляти́вн|ый *adj.* cumulative; (*mil.*): **к. заря́д** hollow charge; **снаря́д ~ого де́йствия** hollow-charge of projectile.

ку́мушк|а, и *f.* **1.** *affectionate of* **кума́**; *as form of address* my good woman. **2.** (*coll.*) gossip, scandal-monger.

кумы́с, а *m.* koumiss (*fermented mare's milk*).

кумысолече́бниц|а, ы *f.* koumiss-cure institution.

кумысолече́ни|е, я *nt.* koumiss cure, treatment.

куна́к, а́ *m.* friend (*among the mountain-dwellers of the Caucasus*).

кунжу́т, а *m.* (*bot.*) sesame.

кунжу́т|ный *adj. of* **~**

ку́н|ий *adj. of* **~и́ца**

куни́ц|а, ы *f.* (*zool.*) marten.

кунстка́мер|а, ы *f.* cabinet of curiosities.

кунту́ш, а́ *m.* (*hist.*) kuntush (*kind of coat worn by Polish noblemen*).

кун-фу́ *nt. indecl.* kung fu.

кунштю́к, а *m.* (*coll.*) trick, dodge.

кýп|а, ы *f.* group, clump (*of trees*).
купáла *see* **Ивáн**
купáльник, а *m.* bathing costume.
купáльный *adj.* bathing, swimming; **к. костю́м** swimming costume.
купáл|ьня, ьни, *g. pl.* **~ен** *f.* (*enclosed*) bathing-place; dressing-shed.
купáльщик, а *m.* bather.
купá|ть, ю *impf.* (*of* **вы́~**) to bathe; to bath.
купá|ться, юсь *impf.* (*of* **вы́~**) to bathe; to have, take a bath; (*coll.*): **к. в зóлоте** to roll in money.
купé *nt. indecl.* compartment (*of rail. carriage*).
купéл|ь, и *f.* (*eccl.*) font.
куп|éц, цá *m.* merchant.
купéческ|ий *adj.* merchant, mercantile; **~ое сослóвие** the merchant class.
купéчеств|о, а *nt.* (*collect.*) the merchants.
купин|á, ы *f.* (*arch.*) bush; **неопали́мая к.** (*bibl.*) the burning bush.
куп|и́ть, лю́, ~́ишь *pf.* (*of* **покупáть**) to buy, purchase.
куплéт, а *m.* **1.** stanza, strophe. **2.** (*pl.*) satirical ballad(s), song(s) (*containing topical allusions*).
куплети́ст, а *m.* singer of satirical songs, ballads.
кýпл|я, и *f.* buying, purchase.
кýпол, а, *pl.* **~á** *m.* cupola, dome.
куполообрáз|ный (~ен, ~на) *adj.* dome-shaped.
кýпол|ьный *adj. of* **~**
купóн, а *m.* **1.** coupon; (*theatr.*) ticket. **2.** suit-length.
купорóс, а *m.* (*chem.*) vitriol.
кýпч|ая, ей *f.* (*also* **к. крéпость**) (*hist., leg.*) deed of purchase.
купчи́х|а, и *f.* **1.** *f. of* **купéц. 2.** merchant's wife.
купю́р|а, ы *f.* **1.** cut (*in liter., music., etc., work*). **2.** (*fin.*) denomination (*of paper money, bonds, etc.*).
кур, а *m.* (*arch.*) cock; *now only in phr.* (*coll.*): **как к. вó щи (попáсть)** (to get o.s.) into the soup.
кýр|а, ы *f.* (*obs.*) = **~ица**
кураг|á, и́ *f.* (*collect.*) dried apricots.
курáж, á *m.* (*obs.*) boldness, spirit; **вы́пить для ~á** to summon up Dutch courage; **быть в ~é** to be lit up.
курáж|иться, усь, ишься *impf.* (*coll.*) to swagger, boast; **(над)** to bully.
курáнт|ы, ов *no sg.* **1.** chiming clock.; chimes. **2.** (*hist.*) gazette.
курáтор, а *m.* **1.** (*obs.*) curator. **2.** (academic) supervisor, tutor.
курбéт, а *m.* (*sport and fig.*) curvet; handstand.
кýрв|а, ы *f.* (*vulg.*) whore, tart.
кургáн, а *m.* barrow, burial mound; tumulus.
кургýз|ый (~, ~а) *adj.* (*coll.*) **1.** too short and/or tight. **2.** bob-tailed. **3.** short, stumpy.
курд, а *m.* Kurd.
Курдистáн, а *m.* Kurdistan.
кýрдский *adj.* Kurdish.
курдю́к, á *m.* fat(ty) tail (*of certain breeds of sheep*).
курдя́нк|а, и *f.* Kurdish woman.
кýрев|о, а *nt.* (*coll.*) tobacco, baccy; sth. to smoke; **у меня́ нет ~а** I haven't got a smoke.
курéни|е, я *nt.* **1.** smoking. **2.** incense.
кур|ёнок, ёнка, *pl.* **~я́та, ~я́т** *m.* (*dial.*) chicken.
курéн|ь, я́ *m.* **1.** (*dial.*) hut, shanty. **2.** (*hist.*) kuren (*unit of Zaporozhian Cossack troop*).
курзáл, а *m.* kursaal.
куриáльный *adj.* (*leg., eccl.*) curial.
кури́лк|а[1], и *f.* (*coll.*) smoking-room.
кури́лка[2] *only in phr.* **жив к.!** there's life in the old dog yet.
кури́льниц|а, ы *f.* (*obs.*) censer; incense-burner.
кури́л|ьня, ни, *g. pl.* **~ен** *f.*: **к. óпиума** opium-den.
кури́льщик, а *m.* smoker.
кури́н|ые, ых (*zool.*) Gallinaceae.
кури́н|ый *adj.* hen's; chicken's; **~ая грудь** pigeon-chest; **~ая слепотá** (*med.*) night-blindness; (*bot.*) buttercup.
кури́р|овать, ую *impf.* to supervise.
кури́тельн|ый *adj.* smoking; **~ая бумáга** cigarette paper; **~ая (кóмната)** smoking-room.
кур|и́ть, ю́, ~́ишь *impf.* (*of* **по~**) **1.** to smoke; **к. трýбку** to smoke a pipe. **2.** (+*a. or i.*) to burn; to fumigate (with); **к. лáданом** to burn incense; **к. фимиáм комý-н.** (*fig.*) to burn incense to s.o. **3.** to distil.
кур|и́ться, ~́ится *impf.* **1.** to smoke (*intrans.*). **2.** (+*i.*) to emit (smoke, steam). **3.** *pass. of* **~и́ть**
кýр|ица, ицы, *pl.* **~ы, ~** *f.* hen; (*fig., coll.*): **мóкрая к.** milksop, wet hen; **~ам нá смех** it would make a cat laugh; **дéнег у негó ~ы не клюю́т** he is rolling in money.
куркýм|а, ы *f.* curry.
курн|óй *adj.*: **~áя избá** hut having stove but without chimney.
курнóс|ый (~, ~а) (*coll.*) snub-nosed.
куровóдств|о, а *nt.* poultry-breeding.
кур|óк, кá *m.* cocking-piece; **взвести́ к.** to cock; **спусти́ть к.** to pull the trigger.
куролé|сить, шу, сишь *impf.* (*of* **на~**) (*coll.*) to play tricks, get up to mischief.
куропáтк|а, и *f.* (*zool.*) **(сéрая)** partridge; **бéлая к.** willow grouse; **тундрянáя к.** ptarmigan.
курóрт, а *m.* health resort.
курóртник, а *m.* health resort visitor.
курóрт|ный *adj. of* **~**; **~ное лечéние** spa treatment.
курослéп, а *m.* (*bot.*) buttercup.
кýрочк|а, и *f.* **1.** pullet. **2.** moor-hen.
курс, а *m.* **1.** (*in var. senses*) course; **нóвый к.** (*pol.*) new policy; **«нóвый к.»** (*hist.*) New Deal; **бáзовый к.** foundation course; **ускóренный к.** crash *or* intensive course; **быть на трéтьем ~́е** to be in the third year (*of a course of studies*); **держáть к. (на**+*a.*) to head (for); **быть в ~́е дéла** to be au courant, be in the know. **2.** (*fin.*) rate (of exchange).
курсáнт, а *m.* **1.** member of a course. **2.** student (*of mil. school or academy*).
курси́в, а *m.* italic type, italics; **~ом** in italics.
курси́вный *adj.* (*typ.*) italic.
курси́р|овать, ую *impf.* **(мéжду)** to ply, run (between).
курси́стк|а, и *f.* (*obs.*) girl-student.
курсóвк|а, и *f.* board and treatment authorization (*at health resort*).
кýрсор, а *m.* (*comput.*) cursor.
куртáж, а *m.* (*comm.*) brokerage.
куртизáнк|а, и *f.* courtesan.
курти́н|а, ы *f.* **1.** (*mil., obs.*) curtain. **2.** flower-bed.
кýртк|а, и *f.* (*man's*) jacket; **штормовáя к.** anorak; parka.
курфю́рст, а *m.* (*hist.*) elector.
курчáв|иться, ится *impf.* to curl.
курчáв|ый (~, ~а) *adj.* (*coll.*) curly; curly-headed.
курч|óнок, óнка, *pl.* **~áта, ~áт** *m.* (*coll.*) chicken.
кýр|ы[1] *see* **~ица**
кýры[2] *only in phr.* **стрóить к.** (+*d.*) (*joc.*) to flirt (with), pay court (to).
курьёз, а *m.* curious, amusing incident; **для, рáди ~а** for fun.
курьёз|ный (~ен, ~на) *adj.* curious; funny.
курьéр, а *m.* messenger; courier.
курьéр|ский *adj.* **1.** *adj. of* **~. 2.** fast; **к. пóезд** express; **на ~ских** (*coll.*) post-haste.
кур|я́та *see* **~ёнок**
куря́тин|а, ы *f.* chicken, fowl (*as meat*).
куря́тник, а *m.* hen-house, hen-coop.
кус, а, *pl.* **~ы́** *m.* (*coll.*) morsel.
кусá|ть, ю *impf.* to bite; to sting; **к. себé лóкти** (*fig.*) to be whipping the cat.
кусá|ться, юсь *impf.* **1.** to bite (= *to be given to biting*). **2.** to bite one another. **3.** (*coll.*) to be exorbitant; **э́то — хорóшая вещь, но ~ется** it's good, but they sting you for it.
кусáч|ки, ек *no sg.* pliers; wire-cutters.
кусковóй *adj.* broken in lumps; **к. сáхар** lump sugar.
кус|óк, кá *m.* lump; piece, bit; slice; cake (*of soap*); **заробóтать к. хлéба** to earn one's bread and butter.
куст[1], á *m.* bush, shrub; **спря́татся в ~ы́** (*fig.*) to scarper, make o.s. scarce.

куст^{2}, **а́** *m.* (*econ.*) group.
куста́рник, а *m.* (*collect.*) bush(es), shrub(s); shrubbery.
куста́рник|овый *adj. of* ~; **~овое расте́ние** shrub.
куста́рнича|ть, ю *impf.* **1.** to be a handicraftsman; to exercise a craft at home. **2.** (*coll., pej.*) to use primitive methods; to work in an amateurish manner.
куста́рничеств|о, а *nt.* (*pej.*) work done by primitive methods; amateurish, inefficient work.
куста́рн|ый *adj.* **1.** handicraft; **~ые изде́лия** hand-made goods; **~ая промы́шленность** cottage industry. **2.** (*fig., pej.*) amateurish, primitive.
куста́рщин|а, ы *f.* = **куста́рничество**
куста́р|ь, я́ *m.* handicraftsman.
кусти́ст|ый (~, ~а) *adj.* bushy.
куст|и́ться, и́тся *impf.* (*agric.*) to tiller.
кустова́ни|е, я *nt.* (*elec.*) interconnection.
кустов|о́й *adj. of* **куст**^{2}; **~о́е совеща́ние** group conference.
кусторе́з, а *m.* hedge trimmer.
ку́та|ть, ю *impf.* (*of* **за~**) (**в**+*a.*) to muffle up (in).
ку́та|ться, юсь *impf.* (*of* **за~**) (**в**+*a.*) to muffle o.s. up (in).
кутёж, а́ *m.* drinking-bout; riot, binge.
кутерьм|а́, ы́ *f.* (*coll.*) commotion, stir, bustle, hubbub.
кути́л|а, ы *m.* fast liver; hard drinker.
ку|ти́ть, чу́, ~́тишь *impf.* (*of* **~тну́ть**) to booze; to go on the booze.
кут|ну́ть, ну́, нёшь *inst. pf.* (*of* **~и́ть**) to go on the booze, to go on a binge.
куту́зк|а, и *f.* (*coll.*) jail, lock-up.
куха́рк|а, и *f.* cook.
кухми́стерск|ая, ой *f.* (*obs.*) eating-house, cook-shop.
ку́х|ня, ни, *g. pl.* **~онь** *f.* **1.** kitchen; cook-house. **2.** cooking, cuisine. **3.** (*fig., coll.; sg. only*) intrigues, machinations.
ку́хонн|ый *adj.* kitchen; **~ая плита́** kitchen-range; **к. шкаф** dresser; (*joc.*): **~ая латы́нь** low Latin.
ку́ц|ый (~, ~а) *adj.* **1.** tailless; bob-tailed. **2.** (*of clothing*) short; (*fig.*) limited, abbreviated.
ку́ч|а, и *f.* **1.** heap, pile; (*coll.*): **вали́ть всё в одну́ ~у** to lump everything together. **2.** (*coll.; +g.*) heaps (of), piles (of); **у него́ к. де́нег** he has heaps of money; **ку́ча мала́** sacks on the mill (*children's game*).
кучево́й *adj.* (*meteor.*) cumulous.
ку́чер, а, *pl.* **~а́, ~о́в** *m.* coachman, driver.
кучерско́й *adj.* coachman's.
кучеря́в|ый (~, ~а) *adj.* (*dial.*) curly; curly-haired.
ку́ч|ка, ки *f. dim. of* **~а; к. люде́й** small group of people.
ку́чный *adj.* (*of shots*) closely-grouped.
ку|чу́, ~́тишь *see* **~ти́ть**
куш^{1}, **а** *m.* (*coll.*) large sum (*of money*).
куш^{2} *int.* (*coll.; to a dog*) (lie) down!
куша́к, а́ *m.* sash, girdle.
ку́шань|е, я *nt.* food; dish.
ку́ша|ть, ю *impf.* (*of* **по~** *and* **с~**) (*in polite invitation to eat*) to eat, have, take.
куше́тк|а, и *f.* couch.
ку́щ|а, и, *g. pl.* **~** *and* **~ей** *f.* **1.** (*obs., poet.*) tent, hut; **пра́здник ~ей** (Jewish) Feast of Tabernacles. **2.** foliage; crest (*of tree*).
кущéни|е, я *nt.* (*bot.*) tillering, stooling.
ку|ю, ёшь *see* **кова́ть**
кхме́р|ы, ов *pl.* (*sg.* **~, а** *m.*) the Khmers; **кра́сные к.** the Khmer Rouge.
Кыргызста́н, а *m.* Kyrgyzstan.
кэб, а *m.* cab.
кюве́т, а *m.* **1.** (*mil.*) cuvette, cunette. **2.** ditch (*at side of road*).
кюве́тк|а, и *f.* (*phot.*) cuvette, bath.
кюрасо́ *nt. indecl.* curaçao (*liqueur*).
кюре́ *m. indecl.* (*eccl.*) curé.

Л

Л. (*abbr. of* **Ленингра́д**) Leningrad.
л (*abbr. of* **литр**) l, litre(s).
лаба́з, а *m.* (*obs.*) corn-chandler's shop, ware-house; grain merchant's shop, ware-house.
лаба́зник, а *m.* (*obs.*) corn-chandler, grain merchant.
лабиализа́ци|я, и *f.* (*ling.*) labialization.
лабиализ|ова́ть, у́ю *impf. and pf.* (*ling.*) to labialize.
лабиа́льный *adj.* (*ling.*) labial.
лабио-дента́льный *adj.* (*ling.*) labio-dental.
лабири́нт, а *m.* (*in var. senses*) labyrinth, maze.
лабора́нт, а *m.* laboratory assistant.
лаборато́ри|я, и *f.* laboratory.
лаборато́р|ный *adj. of* **~ия**
Лабрадо́р, а *m.* Labrador.
лабрадо́р, а *m.* (*min.*) labradorite.
ла́бух, а *m.* (*sl.*) musician, 'muso'.
ла́в|а^{1}, **ы** *f.* lava.
ла́в|а^{2}, **ы** *f.* (*mining*) drift.
ла́в|а^{3}, **ы** *f.* (Cossack) cavalry charge.
лава́нд|а, ы *f.* (*bot.*) lavender.
лава́ш, а *m.* lavash (*flat white loaf*).
лави́н|а, ы *f.* avalanche (*also fig.*).
лави́р|овать, ую *impf.* **1.** (*naut.*) to tack; **л. про́тив ве́тра** to beat up against the wind. **2.** (*fig.*) to manœuvre, avoid taking sides.
ла́вк|а^{1}, **и** *f.* bench.
ла́вк|а^{2}, **и** *f.* shop; store.
ла́вочк|а^{1}, **и** *f. dim. of* **ла́вка**^{1}
ла́вочк|а^{2}, **и** *f. dim. of* **лавка**^{2}; (*fig., coll.*) shady concern; gang; **на́до закры́ть э́ту ла́вочку** a stop must be put to this business.
ла́вочник, а *m.* shop-keeper, retailer.
лавр, а *m.* **1.** (*bot.*) laurel; bay(-tree). **2.** (*pl., fig.*) laurels; **пожина́ть ~́ы** to win laurels; **почи́ть на ~́ах** to rest on one's laurels.
ла́вр|а, ы *f.* monastery (*of highest rank*).
лаврови́шн|евый *adj. of* **~я; ~евые ка́пли** laurel water.
лаврови́шн|я, и *f.* (*bot.*) cherry-laurel.
ла́вр|о́вый *adj. of* ~; **~о́вый вено́к** laurel wreath, (*fig.*) laurels; **~о́вый лист** bay leaf; **~овая ро́ща** laurel grove; *as n.* **~овые, ~овых** (*bot.*) Lauraceae.
ла́вр|ский *adj. of* **~а**
лавса́н, а *m.* lavsan (*Terylene(propr.)-like synthetic fibre*).
лаг, а *m.* (*naut.*) **1.** log. **2.** broadside; **пали́ть всем ~ом** to fire a broadside.
ла́герник, а *m.* (*coll.*) inmate of camp.
ла́гер|ный *adj. of* **~ь; ~ная жизнь** nomadic existence; **л. сбор** (*mil.*) annual camp; **~ная те́ма** (*liter.*) 'the (concentration) camp theme' (*in former USSR, genre of anti-Stalinist literature*).
ла́гер|ь, я *m.* **1.** (*pl.* **~я́, ~е́й**) camp; **жить в ~я́х** to camp out; (*mil.*): **располага́ться, стоя́ть ~ем** to camp, be encamped; **снять л.** to break up, strike camp. **2.** (*pl.* **~и, ~ей**) (*fig.*) camp; **де́йствовать на два ~я** to have a foot in both camps.
лагли́н|ь, я *m.* (*naut.*) log-line.
лагу́н|а, ы *f.* lagoon.
лад, а, о ~́е, в ~у́, *pl.* **~ы́, ~о́в** *m.* **1.** (*mus. and fig.*) harmony, concord; **петь в л., не в л.** to sing in, out of tune; **запе́ть на друго́й л.** (*fig.*) to sing a different tune; **жить в ~у́ (с**+*i.*) to live in harmony (with); **быть не в**

~**а́х (с**+*i.*) to be at odds (with), at variance (with); (*coll.*) **идти́, пойти́ на л.** to go well, be successful; **де́ло не идёт на л.** things are not going well. **2.** manner, way; **на ра́зные** ~**ы** in various ways; **на свой л.** in one's own way; after one's own fashion; **на ста́рый л.** in the old style. **3.** (*mus.*) stop; fret (*of stringed instrument*).

ла́д|а, ы *c.g.* (*folk poet.*) beloved.

ла́дан, а *m.* incense, frankincense; **л. ро́сный** (*pharm.*) benzoin; **дыша́ть на л.** (*fig., coll.*) to have one foot in the grave.

ла́данк|а, и *f.* amulet.

ла́|дить, жу, дишь *impf.* **1.** (**с**+*i.*) to get on (with), be on good terms (with); **они́ не** ~**дят** they don't get on. **2.** (*coll.*) to prepare, make ready; to tune (*mus. instrument*). **3.** (*coll.*): **л. одно́ и то же** to harp on the same string.

ла́д|иться, ится *impf.* (*coll.*) to go well, succeed.

ла́дно *adv.* (*coll.*) **1.** harmoniously. **2.** well; all right; **всё ко́нчилось л.** everything ended happily. **3.** *particle* **л.!** all right!; very well!

ла́д|ный (~**ен,** ~**на́,** ~**но)** *adj.* (*coll.*) **1.** fine, excellent. **2.** harmonious.

ладо́нный *adj.* (*anat.*) palmar.

ладо́н|ь, и *f.* palm (*of hand*); **быть (ви́дным) как на** ~**и** to be clearly visible.

ладо́ши *only in phrr.* **бить, ударя́ть, хло́пать в л.** to clap one's hands.

лад|ья́, ьи́, *g. pl.* ~**е́й** *f.* **1.** (*poet.*) boat. **2.** (*chess*) castle, rook.

лаж, а *m.* (*comm.*) agio.

ла́ж|а, и *f.* (*sl.*) crap, garbage; **поро́ть** ~**у** to talk crap.

лажо́вый *adj.* (*sl.*) crap(py), bum, lousy.

ла́|жу[1]**, дишь** *see* ~**дить**

ла́|жу[2]**, зишь** *see* ~**зить**

лаз, а *m.* **1.** (*tech.*) manhole. **2.** (*hunting*) track; **стать на л.** (+*g.*) to get on the track (of).

ла́зан|ки, ок *no sg.* (*cul.*) lasagne.

лазаре́т, а *m.* **1.** (*mil.*) field hospital; sick quarters; (*naut.*) sick-bay. **2.** (*obs.*) infirmary.

ла́з|ать, аю *impf.* (*coll.*) = ~**ить**

лазе́йк|а, и *f.* hole, gap; (*fig., coll.*) loophole; **оста́вить себе́** ~**у** to leave o.s. a loophole.

ла́зер, а *m.* (*phys., tech.*) laser.

ла́зер|ный *adj. of* ~; **л. при́нтер** laser printer.

ла́|зить, жу, зишь *impf.* (*indet. of* **лезть**) **1.** (**на**+*a.*, **по**+*d.*) to climb, clamber (on to, up); **л. на стéну** to climb a wall; **л. по дере́вьям** to climb trees; **л. по кана́ту** to swarm up a rope. **2.** (**в**+*a.*) to climb (into), get (into); **л. в окно́** to get in through the window.

лазо́ревк|а, и *f.* (*zool.*) blue tit.

лазо́ревый *adj.* (*poet.*) sky-blue, azure; **л. ка́мень** (*min.*) lapis lazuli.

лазу́ревый *adj.* = **лазо́ревый, лазу́рный**

лазу́р|ный (~**ен,** ~**на)** *adj.* sky-blue, azure.

лазу́р|ь, и *f.* azure; **берли́нская л.** Prussian blue.

лазу́тчик, а *m.* (*mil., obs.*) spy, scout.

ла|й, я *m.* bark(ing).

ла́йб|а, ы *f.* (*one- or two-masted*) sailing boat (*used formerly in Baltic Sea and on rivers Dnieper and Dniester*).

ла́йк|а[1]**, и** *f.* Eskimo dog.

ла́йк|а[2]**, и** *f.* kid-skin.

ла́йк|овый *adj. of* ~**а**[2]; ~**овые перча́тки** kid gloves.

ла́йнер, а *m.* (*naut., aeron.*) liner.

лак, а *m.* varnish, lacquer; **япо́нский л.** black japan; **л. для воло́с** hair spray.

лака́|ть, ю *impf.* (*of* **вы́**~) to lap (up).

лаке́|й, я *m.* footman, man-servant; lackey, flunkey (*also fig., pej.*).

лаке́й|ский *adj. of* ~; (*fig.*) servile.

лаке́йств|о, а *nt.* servility; dancing attendance.

лаке́йств|овать, ую *impf.* **(пе́ред)** to dance attendance (on), kow-tow (to).

лакиро́в|анный *p.p.p. of* ~**а́ть** *and adj.* varnished, lacquered; ~**анная ко́жа** patent leather; ~**анные ту́фли** patent-leather shoes.

лакир|ова́ть, у́ю *impf.* (*of* **от**~) to varnish, lacquer; (*fig., pej.*) to varnish.

лакиро́вк|а, и *f.* **1.** varnishing, lacquering (*also fig., pej.*). **2.** varnish. **3.** (*fig.*) gloss, polish.

лакиро́вщик, а *m.* varnisher (*also fig., pej.*).

ла́кмус, а *m.* (*chem.*) litmus.

ла́кмус|овый *adj. of* ~; ~**овая бума́га** litmus paper.

ла́ков|ый *adj.* varnished, lacquered; ~**ые ту́фли** patent-leather shoes; (*bot.*): ~**ое де́рево** varnish-tree.

ла́ком|ить, лю, ишь *impf.* (*of* **по**~) (*coll.*) to regale (with), treat (to).

ла́ком|иться, люсь, ишься *impf.* (*of* **по**~) (+*i.*) to treat o.s. (to).

ла́комк|а, и *c.g.* gourmand; **быть** ~**ой** to have a sweet tooth.

ла́комств|о, а *nt.* dainty, delicacy.

ла́ком|ый (~**,** ~**а)** *adj.* **1.** dainty, tasty; **л. кусо́к** titbit, tasty morsel (*also fig.*). **2.** (*coll.*) **(до)** fond (of), partial (to).

лакони́зм, а *m.* laconic brevity.

лакони́ческий *adj.* laconic.

лакони́ч|ный (~**ен,** ~**на)** *adj.* = ~**еский**

лакрима́тор, а *m.* tear gas.

лакри́ц|а, ы *f.* (*bot.*) liquorice.

лакро́сс, а *m.* lacrosse.

лакта́ци|я, и *f.* lactation.

лактобацилли́н, а *m.* yoghurt.

лакто́з|а, ы *f.* (*chem.*) lactose.

ла́м|а[1]**, ы** *f.* (*zool.*) llama.

ла́м|а[2]**, ы** *m.* (*relig.*) lama.

ламаи́зм, а *m.* (*relig.*) Lamaism.

Ла-Ма́нш, а *m.* the (English) Channel.

ламбреке́н, а *m.* pelmet.

ла́мп|а, ы *f.* **1.** lamp; **предохрани́тельная л.** safety-lamp; **рудни́чная л.** Davy lamp; **л. дневно́го све́та** fluorescent lamp. **2.** (*radio*) valve; tube; **односе́точная л.** one-grid valve; **двухсе́точная л.** space charge electrode; **смеси́тельная л.** frequency changer valve.

лампа́д|а, ы *f.* icon-lamp.

лампа́дн|ый *adj.*: ~**ое ма́сло** lamp-oil.

лампа́с, а *m.* stripe (*on side of trousers*).

ла́мп|овый *adj. of* ~**а**; ~**овое стекло́** lamp-chimney; (*tech.*) **л. выпрями́тель** tube rectifier; **л. генера́тор** valve oscillator, vacuum tube generator.

ла́мпочк|а, и *f.* **1.** *dim. of* **ла́мпа. 2.** (electric light) bulb; (*tech.*) **л. нака́ливания** incandescent lamp; **стосвечо́вая л.** 100-watt bulb. **3.: до** ~**и** (*sl.*) to hell (with it).

ланге́т, а *m.* breaded cutlet.

лангу́ст, а *m.* (*also* **лангу́ст|а,** ~**ы** *f.*) spiny lobster; rock lobster.

ландо́ *nt. indecl.* landau.

ландскне́хт, а *m.* **1.** (*hist.*) lansquenet, landsknecht. **2.** (*card game*) lansquenet.

ландша́фт, а *m.* landscape.

ла́ндыш, а *m.* lily of the valley.

лани́т|а, ы *f.* (*arch.*) cheek.

ланоли́н, а *m.* (*pharm.*) lanolin.

ланце́т, а *m.* (*med.*) lancet; **вскрыть** ~**ом** to lance.

ланце́т|ный *adj.* **1.** *adj. of* ~. **2.** (*bot.*) lanceolate.

ланцетови́д|ный (~**ен,** ~**на)** *adj.* (*bot.*) lanceolate.

лан|ь, и *f.* fallow deer; doe (*of fallow deer*).

Лао́с, а *m.* Laos.

лао́с|ец, ца *m.* Laotian.

лао́с|ка, ки *f. of* ~**ец**

лао́сский *adj.* Laotian.

лаотя́н|ин, ина, *pl.* ~**е,** ~ *m.* = **лао́сец**

лаотя́нк|а, и *f.* = **лао́ска**

лаотя́нский *adj.* = **лао́сский**

ла́п|а, ы *f.* **1.** paw; pad (*joc. of human hand*); (*fig., coll.*): **попа́сть в** ~**ы к кому́-н.** to fall into s.o.'s clutches; **в** ~**ах у кого́-н.** in s.o.'s clutches. **2.** (*tech.*) tenon, dovetail. **3.** (*naut.*) fluke (*of anchor*). **4.** (*fig.*) bough (*of coniferous tree*).

лапида́р|ный (~**ен,** ~**на)** *adj.* lapidary, terse.

ла́п|ка, ки *f. dim. of* ~**а**; **лягуша́чьи** *or* **лягу́шечьи** ~**ки** (*cul.*) frog's legs; (*fig., coll.*): **стоя́ть ходи́ть на за́дних** ~**ках (пе́ред)** to dance attendance (upon).

лапла́нд|ец, ца *m.* Lapp, Laplander.

Лапла́нди|я, и *f.* Lapland.

лаплáнд|ка, ки *f. of* **~ец**
лаплáндский *adj.* Lappish.
лáпотник, а *m.* **1.** bast-shoe maker. **2.** (*obs., coll.*) peasant.
лáпот|ный *adj. of* **~ь; ~ная Россúя** (*rhet.*) the old (*opp. post-1917*) Russia.
лáп|оть тя, *pl.* **~ти, ~тéй** *m.* bast shoe, bast sandal; **ходúть в ~тях** to wear bast shoes, sandals.
лáпочк|а, и *f.* (*coll.*) **1.** (my) pet, darling, sweetheart (*form of direct address*). **2.** sweetie (*pers.*); **онá такáя л.!** she's such a sweetie!
лапсердáк, а *m.* lapserdak (*long overcoat worn by Jews*).
лапт|á, ы́ *f.* **1.** (*Russ. ball game*) lapta. **2.** lapta bat.
лáпчатый *adj.* **1.** (*bot.*) palmate. **2.** web-footed; **гусь л.** (*fig., coll.*) cunning fellow, sly one.
лапш|á, ú *f.* **1.** noodles. **2.** noodle soup.
лар|ёк, ькá *m.* stall.
лар|éц, цá *m.* casket, small chest.
ларёчник, а *m.* (*coll.*) stall-holder.
ларингúт, а *m.* laryngitis
ларингоскóп, а *m.* laryngoscope.
ларинготомú|я, и *f.* laryngotomy.
лáрчик, а *m.* small box; (*coll.*): **а л. прóсто открывáлся** the explanation was quite simple.
лáр|ы, ов *pl.* (*sg.* **~, ~а** *m.*): **л. и пенáты** lares and penates.
лар|ь, я́ *m.* **1.** chest, coffer; bin; **л. с мукóй** bin containing flour. **2.** stall.
лáск|а[1], **и** *f.* **1.** caress, endearment; (*pl.*) petting; **предварúтельные ~и** foreplay. **2.** kindness.
лáс|ка[2], **и,** *g. pl.* **~ок** *f.* (*zool.*) weasel.
ласкáтельн|ый *adj.* **1.** caressing; **~ое úмя** pet name. **2.** (*obs.*) cajoling, unctuous. **3.** (*gram.*) affectionate, expressing endearment.
ласкá|ть, ю *impf.* **1.** to caress, fondle, pet. **2.** (*obs.*) to comfort, console.
ласкá|ться, юсь *impf.* **1.** (**к**) to make up to; to snuggle up to; to coax; (*of a dog*) to fawn (upon). **2.** (*coll.*) to exchange caresses.
лáсковый *adj.* affectionate, tender; (*fig.*) gentle; **л. вéтер** soft wind.
лассó *nt. indecl.* lasso.
ласт, а *m.* flipper.
лáстик[1], **а** *m.* (*material*) lasting.
лáстик[2], **а** *m.* (*coll.*) india-rubber.
лá|ститься, щусь, стишься *impf.* (**к, óколо**) (*coll.*) to make up (to), fawn (upon).
лáстовиц|а, ы *f.* gusset (*in shirt*).
ластоногó|ое, ого *nt.* (*zool.*) Pinniped.
лáсточк|а, и *f.* **1.** swallow; **береговáя л.** sand-martin; **городскáя л.** (house) martin; **прыжóк в вóду ~ой** swallow-dive; **пéрвая л.** (*fig.*) the first signs; **однá л. весны́ не дéлает** (*prov.*) one swallow does not make a summer. **2.** sweetheart (*form of direct address*).
лáт|анный *p.p.p. of* **~áть** *and adj.* worn, patched.
лататы́ *only in phr.* (*coll.*): **задáть л.** to take to one's heels.
латá|ть, ю *impf.* (*of* **за~**) (*coll.*) to patch.
латвú|ец, йца *m.* Latvian.
латвú|йка, йки *f. of* **~ец**
латвúйский *adj.* Latvian.
Лáтви|я, и *f.* Latvia.
лáтекс, а *m.* latex.
латинизáци|я, и *f.* Latinization.
латинизúр|овать, ую *impf. and pf.* to Latinize.
латинúзм, а *m.* **1.** Latin construction (*borrowed by another language*). **2.** Latin loan-word.
латинúст, а *m.* Latin scholar.
латúниц|а, ы *f.* Roman alphabet, Roman letters.
латúнский *adj.* Latin.
латúнств|о, а *nt.* (*obs.*) **1.** the Roman Catholic faith. **2.** (*collect.*) Roman Catholics.
латúнщин|а, ы *f.* Latin culture; Latinity.
латúнян|ин, ина, *pl.* **~е, ~** *m.* **1.** (*hist.*) inhabitant of Latium. **2.** (*obs.*) Roman Catholic.
латифу́нди|и, й *pl.* (*sg.* **~я, ~и** *f.*) latifundia.
латифундúст, а *m.* **1.** latifundist (*large land-owner in South America*). **2.** (*pej.*) land baron (*exploitative land-owner*).
лáтк|а, и *f.* (*coll.*) patch.
лáтник, а *m.* armour-clad warrior.
лату́к, а *m.* (*bot.*) lettuce.
лату́нный *adj.* brass.
лату́н|ь, и *f.* brass.
лáт|ы, ~ *no sg.* (*hist.*) armour.
латы́н|ь, и *f.* (*coll.*) Latin.
латы́ш, á, *pl.* **~ú, ~éй** *m.* Lett.
латы́ш|ка, ки *f. of* **~**
латы́шский *adj.* Lettish, Latvian.
лауреáт, а *m.* prize-winner; laureate; **л. Нóбелевской прéмии** Nobel prize-winner *or* laureate; (*cin.*) **л. прéмии Óскара** Oscar-winner.
лафá *as pred.*; (*impers.; coll.*): **тебé, емý,** *etc.* **л.** you are, he is *etc.*, in clover, having a wonderful time.
лафéт, а *m.* (*mil.*) gun-carriage.
лáцкан, а, *pl.* **~ы, ~ов** *m.* lapel.
лачу́г|а, и *f.* hovel, shack.
лá|ять, ю, ешь *impf.* to bark; to bay.
лá|яться, юсь, ешься *impf.* (*coll.*) (**на**+*a.*) to rail, snarl (at).
лба, лбу *etc., see* **лоб**
лгать, лгу, лжёшь, лгут, *past* **лгал, лгалá, лгáло** *impf.* **1.** (*pf.* **со~**) to lie; to tell lies. **2.** (*pf.* **на~**) (**на**+*a.*) to slander.
ЛГУ *m. indecl.* (*abbr. of* ***Ленингрáдский госудáрственный университéт***) Leningrad State University.
лгун, á *m.* liar.
лгунúшк|а, и *m.* (*coll.*) paltry liar.
лебед|á, ы́ *f.* (*bot.*) goose-foot, orach.
лебед|ёнок, ёнка, *pl.* **~я́та, ~я́т** *m.* cygnet.
лебедúн|ый *adj. of* **лéбедь; ~ая пóступь** graceful gait; (*fig.*) **~ая пéсня** swan-song; **~ая шéя** swan-neck; (*tech.*) S-bend pipe.
лебёдк|а[1], **и** *f.* (female) swan, pen(-swan).
лебёдк|а[2], **и** *f.* (*tech.*) winch, windlass.
лéбед|ь, я, *pl.* **~и, ~éй** *m.* swan, cob(-swan).
лебе|зúть, жу́, зúшь *impf.* (*coll.*) (**пéред**) to fawn (upon), cringe (to).
леб|я́жий *adj. of* **∠едь; л. пух** swansdown.
лев[1], **льва** *m.* lion; **морскóй л.** sea-lion; **муравьúный л.** ant lion.
лев[2], **а** *m.* (*Bulgarian monetary unit*) lev.
левáд|а, ы *f.* (*dial.*) **1.** meadow. **2.** riparian woodlands (*flooded at season of thaw; in Southern Russia*).
левáк, á *m.* **1.** (*pol.*) leftist. **2.** (*coll.*) moonlighter; black marketeer.
Левáнт, а *m.* the Levant.
левантúйский *adj.* Levantine.
левантúн|ец, ца *m.* Levantine.
левантúн|ка, ки *f. of* **~ец**
левáцкий *adj.* (*pol., pej.*) ultra-left.
левáчеств|о, а *nt.* **1.** (*pol.*) leftism. **2.** (*coll.*) moonlighting; black marketeering.
левé|ть, ю *impf.* (*of* **по~**) (*pol.*) to become more left, move to the left.
левиафáн, а *m.* leviathan.
левизн|á, ы́ *f.* (*pol.*) leftishness.
левкó|й, я *m.* (*bot.*) stock, gilly-flower.
лéво *adv.* (*naut.*) to port; **л. руля́!** port helm! **л. на борт!** hard-a-port!
левобережный *adj.* left-bank.
левоэкстремúст, а *m.* radical leftist.
леврéтк|а, и *f.* Italian greyhound.
левш|á, ú, *i.* **~óй,** *g. pl.* **~éй** *c.g.* left-hander; **боксёр-л.** southpaw.
лéв|ый *adj.* **1.** left; left-hand; (*naut.*) port; **л. борт** port side, port hand; **~ая сторонá** left-hand side, (*of horse, carriage, etc.*) near side; (*of material*) wrong side; (*fig.*): **встать с ~ой ногú** to get out of bed on the wrong side. **2.** illegal, unofficial; **~ая рабóта** work on the side. **3.** (*pl.*) left-wing; *as n.* **л., ~ого** *m.* left-winger; (*pl.; collect.*) the left.
легáв|ая, ой *f.* (**длинношёрстая**) setter; (**короткошёрстая**) pointer.
легáв|ый, ого *m.* (*coll.*) police spy, informer.
легализáци|я, и *f.* legalization.

легализ|и́ровать(ся), и́рую(сь) = **~ова́ть(ся)**
легализ|ова́ть, у́ю *impf. and pf.* to legalize.
легализ|ова́ться, у́юсь *impf. and pf.* to become legalized.
лега́л|ьный (~ен, ~ьна) *adj.* legal.
лега́т, а *m.* legate.
лега́то *mus.* **1.** *adv.* legato. **2.** *n.*; *nt. indecl.* slur.
леге́нд|а, ы *f.* legend.
легенда́р|ный (~ен, ~на) *adj.* legendary (*also fig.*).
легио́н, а *m.* (*in var. senses*) legion; **Иностра́нный л.** the Foreign Legion; **о́рден почётного ~а** Legion of Honour; **и́мя им л.** their name is legion.
легионе́р, а *m.* legionary.
леги́рова|нный *p.p.p. of* **~ть** *and adj.* alloy(ed).
леги́р|овать, ую *impf.* to alloy.
легислату́р|а, ы *f.* term of office.
лёг|кий (~ок, ~ка́, ~ко́, *pl.* **~ки́** *or* **~ки)** *adj.* **1.** light (*in weight*). **2.** easy; **л. слог** simple style; **у него́ л. хара́ктер** he is easy to get on with; **~ко́ сказа́ть!** easier said than done! **3.** (*in var. senses*) light; slight; **~кая атле́тика** (*sport*) field and track athletics; **~кая просту́да** slight cold; **л. слу́чай (заболева́ния)** mild case; **~кие фигу́ры** (*chess*) minor pieces; **~кое чте́ние** light reading(-matter); (*coll.*): **~ок на поми́не, вы ~ки́ на поми́не!** talk of the devil!; (*coll.*): **у него́ ~кая рука́** he is lucky; he has luck; **с ва́шей ~ой руки́** once you start(ed) the ball rolling; **же́нщина лёгкого поведе́ния** woman of easy virtue.
легко́ *adv.* easily, lightly, slightly; **э́то ему́ л. даётся** it comes easily to him; **л. косну́ться** to touch lightly.
легкоатле́т, а *m.* (track-and-field) athlete.
легкове́ри|е, я *nt.* credulity, gullibility.
легкове́р|ный (~ен, ~на) *adj.* credulous, gullible.
легкове́с, а *m.* (*sport*) light-weight.
легкове́с|ный (~ен, ~на) *adj.* **1.** light-weight; light. **2.** (*fig.*, *pej.*) superficial.
легководола́з, а *m.* frogman.
легково́й *adj.* passenger (*conveyance*); **л. автомоби́ль** (motor) car; **л. изво́зчик** cab, cabman.
легкову́шк|а, и *f.* (*coll.*) car, motor.
лёгк|ое, ого *nt.* **1.** (*anat.*) lung; **воспале́ние одного́ ~ого, обо́их ~их** single, double pneumonia. **2.** (*sg. only*; *cul.*) lights.
легкомы́слен|ный (~, ~на) *adj.* light(-minded), thoughtless; flippant, frivolous, superficial; **л. посту́пок** thoughtless action.
легкомы́сли|е, я *nt.* light-mindedness, thoughtlessness; flippancy, levity.
легкопла́в|кий (~ок, ~ка) *adj.* fusible, easily melted.
лёгкост|ь, и *f.* **1.** lightness. **2.** easiness.
легóнько *adv.* (*coll.*) **1.** slightly. **2.** gently.
лёгочный *adj.* (*med.*) pulmonary.
легча́|ть, ет *impf.* (*of* **по~**) **1.** to lessen, abate. **2.** (*impers.*, *+d.*) to get better; to feel better.
ле́г|че *comp. of* **≃кий** *and* **~ко́; больно́му л.** the invalid is feeling better; **мне от э́того не л.** I am none the better for it; (*coll.*): **час о́т часу не л.** worse and worse; **л. на поворо́тах!** mind what you say!
лёд, льда, о льде́, на льду́ *m.* ice; **л. разби́т, л. сло́ман** (*fig.*) the ice is broken.
леда́щий *adj.* (*coll.*) puny; feeble.
ледене́|ть, ю *impf.* (*of* **за~** *and* **о~**) (*intrans.*) **1.** to freeze. **2.** to become numb with cold; (*fig.*): **кровь ~ет** (one's) blood runs cold.
леден|е́ц, ца́ *m.* fruit-drop; **ки́слый л.** acid-drop.
ледени́ст|ый (~, ~а) *adj.* frozen; icy.
леден|и́ть, и́т *impf.* (*of* **о~**) (*trans.*) to freeze; (*fig.*) to chill.
леден|я́щий *pres. part. of* **~и́ть** *and adj.* chilling, icy.
ледери́н, а *m.* leathercloth, leatherine.
ле́ди *f. indecl.* lady.
ле́дник, а *m.* **1.** ice-house. **2.** ice-box; **ваго́н-л.** refrigerator van.
ледни́к, а́ *m.* glacier.
ледни́ковый *adj.* glacial; **л. пери́од** ice age.
ледови́тый *adj.*: **Се́верный Л. океа́н** the Arctic Ocean.
ледо́в|ый *adj.* ice; **~ые пла́вания** Arctic voyages; **~ое побо́ище** the Battle on the Ice (*fought on 5 April 1242 between the army of Alexander Nevsky and the Teutonic Knights*).
ледоко́л, а *m.* ice-breaker.
ледоко́л|ьный *adj. of* **~**
ледоре́з, а *m.* **1.** (*naut.*) ice-cutter. **2.** (*tech.*) starling.
ледору́б, а *m.* ice-axe.
ледоста́в, а *m.* freezing-over (*of river*).
ледохо́д, а *m.* drifting of ice, floating of ice (*at time of freeze-up and thaw*).
леды́шк|а, и *f.* (*coll.*) **1.** piece of ice. **2.** (*fig.*, *joc.*) iceberg.
лед|яно́й *adj.* **1.** *adj. of* **≃**; **~яна́я гора́** ice slope (*for tobogganing*); iceberg. **2.** icy (*also fig.*); ice-cold. **3.**: **~яно́е стекло́** frosted glass.
ле́ер, а *m.* (*naut.*) taut rope, yard.
лёжа *adv.* lying down, in lying position.
лежа́к, а́ *m.* chaise longue, deck chair.
лежа́лый *adj.* stale, old.
лежа́нк|а, и *f.* stove-bench (*a shelf on which it is possible to sleep, running along the side of a Russ. stove*).
леж|а́ть, у́, и́шь *impf.* (*in var. senses*) to lie; to be (situated); **л. в больни́це** to be in hospital; **л. больны́м** to be laid up; **врач веле́л мне л.** the doctor told me to stay in bed; **л. на боку́, на печи́** (*fig.*, *coll.*) to idle away one's time; **л. у кого́-н. на душе́** to be on one's mind; **э́то ~и́т у меня́ на со́вести** it lies heavy on my conscience; **э́то ~и́т на ва́шей отве́тственности** this is your responsibility; **у меня́ душа́ не ~и́т (к)** I have a distaste (for), an aversion (to, from, for).
леж|а́ться, и́шься *impf.* (*+d.*): **ему́ не ~а́лось в посте́ли** he would, could not stay in bed.
лежа́ч|ий *adj.* lying, recumbent; **л. больно́й** bed-patient; **~его не бьют** never hit a man when he is down.
ле́жбищ|е, а *nt.* breeding ground (*of certain aquatic mammals*); **л. тюле́ней** seal-rookery.
лежебо́к|а, и *c.g.* (*coll.*) lazy-bones, lie-abed.
ле́ж|ень, ня *m.* (*tech.*) **1.** ledger; foundation beam; mud sill. **2.** (*rail.*) sleeper.
лёжк|а, и *f.* **1.** (*coll.*) lying. **2.** (*coll.*) lying position; **лежа́ть в ~у** to be on one's back (*of sick pers.*); **напи́ться в ~у** to become dead drunk. **3.** lair (*of wild animal*).
лежмя́ *adv.* (*coll.*): **лежа́ть л.** to lie without getting up; to lie helpless.
ле́зви|е, я *nt.* **1.** edge (*of cutting instrument*). **2.** safety-razor blade.
лезги́нк|а, и *f.* lezginka (*Caucasian dance*).
лез|ть, у, ешь, *past* **~, ≃ла** *impf.* (*of* **по~**) **1.** (**на**+*a.*, **по**+*d.*) to climb (up, on to). **2.** (**в**+*a.*, **под**+*a.*) to clamber, crawl (through, into, under). **3.** to make one's way stealthily; **куда́ ≃ешь?** (*coll.*) where do you think you're going? **4.** (**в**+*a.*) to thrust the hand (into). **5.** (**в**+*a.*) to fit (into). **6.** to stick out (*intrans.*). **7.** to slip out of position. **8.** to come on (*in spite of obstacles*). **9.** (**в**+*a.*) to try to climb (*into a higher station in life*). **10.** to fall out (*of hair, fur*). **11.** to come to pieces (*of fabrics, leather, etc.*); **л. на́ стену** (*fig.*, *coll.*) to climb up the wall; **не л. в карма́н за сло́вом** not to be at a loss for a word; **л. в пе́тлю** (*coll.*) to stick one's neck out.
ле|й, я *m.* leu (*Romanian monetary unit*).
лейб-гва́рди|я, и *f.* (*hist.*) Life-Guards.
лейб-ме́дик, а *m.* (*hist.*) physician in ordinary.
лейбори́ст, а *m.* (*pol.*) Labourite.
лейбори́стск|ий *adj.* (*pol.*) Labour; **~ая па́ртия** Labour Party.
ле́йденск|ий *adj.*: **~ая ба́нка** (*phys.*) Leyden jar.
ле́йк|а[1], **и** *f.* **1.** watering-can. **2.** (*naut.*) bail. **3.** funnel (*for pouring liquids*).
ле́йк|а[2], **и** *f.* Leica (*propr.*) (camera).
лейкеми́|я, и *f.* (*med.*) leukaemia.
лейко́м|а, ы *f.* (*med.*) leucoma.
лейкопла́стыр|ь, я *m.* sticking plaster.
лейкоци́т, а *m.* (*physiol.*) leucocyte.
Ле́йпциг, а *m.* Leipzig
лейтена́нт, а *m.* lieutenant; **мла́дший л.** 'junior lieutenant'; **ста́рший л.** 'senior lieutenant'; (*corresponding to the three*

Russ. Army ranks of **мла́дший л., л.** *and* **ста́рший л.** *are the two Br. Army ranks of* second lieutenant *and* lieutenant).
лейтмоти́в, а *m.* (*mus. and fig.*) leitmotif.
лека́л|о, а *nt.* **1.** (*tech.*) template, gauge, pattern. **2.** instrument for drawing curves.
лека́рственный *adj.* medicinal; officinal.
лека́рств|о, а *nt.* medicine; drug.
ле́кар|ь, я, *pl.* **~и, ~е́й** *m.* (*obs. or pej.*) physician.
ле́ксик|а, и *f.* vocabulary; lexis.
лексико́граф, а *m.* lexicographer.
лексикографи́ческий *adj.* lexicographical.
лексикогра́фи|я, и *f.* lexicography.
лексико́лог, а *m.* lexicologist.
лексиколо́ги|я, и *f.* lexicology.
лекси́ческий *adj.* lexical.
ле́ктор, а *m.* lecturer.
лекто́ри|й, я *m.* **1.** centre organizing public lectures. **2.** lecture-hall.
лекто́ри|я, и *f.* (*obs.*) reading-room (*in university library*).
ле́ктор|ский *adj. of* **~**; *as n.* **~ская, ~ской** *f.* lecturers' common room.
ле́кторств|о, а *nt.* lecturing; lectureship.
лектри́с|а, ы *f.* lecturer, lectrice.
лекцио́нный *adj. of* **ле́кция; л. зал** lecture-room; **л. ме́тод преподава́ния** teaching method based on lectures.
ле́кци|я, и *f.* lecture; **чита́ть ~ю** to lecture, deliver a lecture; (*fig., coll.*) to read a lecture.
леле́|ять, ю *impf.* **1.** to coddle, pamper. **2.** (*fig.*) to cherish, foster; **л. мечту́** to cherish a hope.
ле́мех, а (*and* **леме́х, а́**) *m.* ploughshare.
лем|е́шный *adj. of* **≗е́х**
ле́мм|а, ы *f.* (*math.; liter.*) lemma.
ле́мминг, а *m.* (*zool.*) lemming.
лему́р, а *m.* (*zool.*) lemur.
лен, а *m.* (*hist.*) fief, fee; **отда́ть в л.** to give in fee.
лён, льна *m.* (*bot.*) flax; **л.-долгуне́ц** long-fibred flax; **го́рный л.** (*min.*) asbestos.
лендло́рд, а *m.* landlord, land-owner (*in Great Britain and Ireland*).
лени́в|ец, ца *m.* **1.** lazy-bones; sluggard. **2.** (*zool.*) sloth. **3.** (*tech.*) idler, idling sprocket.
лени́в|ый (~, ~а) *adj.* **1.** lazy, idle; sluggish. **2.** (*cul.*) prepared in accordance with a hasty recipe.
Ленингра́д, а *m.* Leningrad.
ле́нин|ец, ца *m.* Leninist.
лениниа́н|а, ы *f.* (*collect.*) Leniniana (*works of literature and art devoted to V.I. Lenin.*)
ленини́зм, а *m.* Leninism.
ле́нинский *adj.* of Lenin; Leninist.
лен|и́ться, ю́сь, ≗ишься *impf.* **1.** to be lazy, idle. **2.** (*+inf.*) to be too lazy (to); **он призна́лся, что он ~и́лся им писа́ть** he admitted that he had been too lazy to write to them.
ле́нник, а *m.* (*hist.*) vassal, feudatory.
ле́нный *adj.* (*hist.*) feudatory; feudal.
ле́ност|ь, и *f.* laziness, idleness; sloth.
ле́нт|а, ы *f.* ribbon, band; tape; **а́ннинская л.** ribbon of Order of St Anne; **гу́сеничная л.** caterpillar track; **изоляцио́нная л.** insulating tape; **кинематографи́ческая л.** (reel of) film; **патро́нная л.** cartridge belt; **ви́ться ~ой** to twist, meander.
ле́нт|очный *adj. of* **~а; л. глист, л. червь** tape-worm; **~очная пила́** band-saw; **л. то́рмоз** band brake; **л. транспортёр** conveyor belt; **~очная застро́йка** (*fig.*) ribbon development.
лентя́|й, я *m.* lazy-bones; sluggard.
лентя́йнича|ть, ю *impf.* (*coll.*) to be lazy, idle; to loaf.
ленц|а́, ы́ *f.* (*coll.*) disposition to laziness; **он с ~о́й** he is inclined to be lazy.
ле́нчик, а *m.* saddle-tree.
лен|ь, и *f.* **1.** laziness, idleness; indolence. **2.** *as pred.* (*+d. and inf.; coll.*) to feel too lazy (to), not to feel like; **ему́ бы́ло л. вы́ключить ра́дио** he was too lazy to turn the wireless off; **на́до бы пойти́, да л.** I ought to go, but I don't feel like it; **все, кому́ не л.** anyone who feels like it.
леопа́рд, а *m.* leopard.
леота́рд, а *m.* leotard.
лепестко́вый *adj.* (*bot.*) petalled.
лепест|о́к, ка́ *m.* petal.
ле́пет, а *m.* babble (*also fig.*); prattle.
лепе|та́ть, чу́, ≗чешь *impf.* to babble; to prattle.
лепёшк|а, и *f.* **1.** flat cake; (*fig., coll.*): **разби́ться, расшиби́ться в ~у** to strain every nerve, go through fire and water. **2.** (*medicinal*) tablet, pastille.
леп|и́ть, лю́, ≗ишь *impf.* **1.** (*pf.* **вы́~** *and* **с~**) to model, fashion; to mould; **л. гнездо́** to build a nest. **2.** (*pf.* **на~**) (*coll.*) to stick (on). **3.** (*sl.*) to lie, tell lies.
леп|и́ться, лю́сь, ≗ишься *impf.* **1.** (**по**+*d.*) to cling (to) (*of things adhering to a steep or precipitous surface*). **2.** (*coll.*) to crawl.
ле́пк|а, и *f.* modelling.
лепн|о́й *adj.* modelled, moulded; **~о́е украше́ние** stucco moulding.
лепрозо́ри|й, я *m.* leper hospital.
ле́пт|а, ы *f.* mite; **внести́ свою́ ~у** to contribute one's mite.
ле́пщик, а *m.* modeller, sculptor.
лес, а (у), *pl.* **~а́** *m.* **1.** (**в ~у́**) forest, wood(s); **вы́йти из ≗а (и́з ~у)** to come out of the wood; **купи́ть л.** to buy woodland; **кра́сный, чёрный л.** coniferous, deciduous forest; **тропи́ческий л.** rainforest; **быть как в ~у́** (*fig., coll.*) to be all at sea; **л. ру́бят — ще́пки летя́т** (*prov.*) you can't make omelettes without breaking eggs; **кто в л., к. по дрова́** (to be, *etc.*) at sixes and sevens. **2.** (**в ≗е**) (*sg. only; collect.*) timber; **л. на корню́** standing timber.
лес|а́[1] *pl. of* **~**
лес|а́[2]**, о́в** *pl.* scaffolding.
леса́[3]**, ле́сы,** *pl.* **ле́сы** *or* **лёсы, лес** *or* **лёс** *f.* fishing-line.
лесби́йск|ий *adj.* of Lesbos; **~ая любо́вь** lesbianism.
лесбия́нк|а, и *f.* lesbian.
ле́сенк|а, и *f.* (*coll.*) *dim. of* **ле́стница**; short flight of stairs; short ladder.
леси́н|а, ы *f.* (*dial.*) trunk (*of a timber tree*).
леси́ст|ый (~, ~а) *adj.* wooded, woody.
лесни́к, а́ *m.* forester.
лесни́честв|о, а *nt.* forest area.
лесни́ч|ий, его *m.* forestry officer; forest warden.
лес|но́й *adj. of* **~; л. двор, склад** timber-yard; **~но́е де́ло** timber industry; **л. институ́т** forestry institute, school of forestry; **~ны́е насажде́ния** afforestation; **л. пито́мник** nursery forest.
лесово́д, а *m.* forestry specialist; graduate of forestry institute.
лесово́дств|о, а *nt.* forestry.
лесово́з, а *m.* timber ship; timber lorry.
лесозаво́д, а *m.* timber mill.
лесозаготі́вк|а, *f.* **1.** timber cutting. **2.** logging; wooding. **3.** (*pl.*) (State) timber purchasing.
лесозащи́тный *adj.* appertaining to the protection of the forests.
лес|о́к, ка́ *m.* small wood, copse, grove.
лесоматериа́л, а *m.* timber.
лесонасажде́ни|е, я *nt.* **1.** afforestation. **2.** (forest) plantation.
лесоохране́ни|е, я *nt.* forest preservation.
лесопа́рк, а *m.* forest park.
лесопи́лк|а, и *f.* saw-mill.
лесопи́льн|ый *adj.* sawing; **л. заво́д** saw-mill; **~ая ра́ма** log frame; gang saw.
лесопи́л|ьня, ьни, *g. pl.* **~ен** *f.* = **~ка**
лесополос|а́, ы́ *f.* woodland belt, forest belt.
лесопоса́д|ки, ок forest plantations.
лесопромы́шленник, а *m.* timber merchant.
лесопромы́шленност|ь, и *f.* timber industry.
лесору́б, а *m.* lumber-man.
лесосе́к|а, и *f.* (wood-)cutting area.
лесоспла́в, а *m.* timber rafting.
лесосте́п|ь, и *f.* (*geog.*) forest-steppe.
лесота́ск|а, и *f.* (*tech.*) log conveyer.
лесоту́ндр|а, ы *f.* (*geog.*) forest-tundra.

леспромхо́з, а *m.* (*abbr. of* **лесно́е промы́шленное хозя́йство**) (State) timber industry enterprise.
лёсс, а *m.* (*geol.*) loess.
ле́стниц|а, ы *f.* stairs, staircase; ladder; **верёвочная л.** rope-ladder; **пара́дная л.** front staircase; **пожа́рная л.** fire-escape; **складна́я л.** steps, step-ladder; **чёрная л.** backstairs.
ле́стни|чный *adj. of* ~**ца; ~чная кле́тка** well (*of stairs*).
ле́ст|ный (~ен, ~на) *adj.* **1.** complimentary. **2.** flattering; **ему́ бы́ло ~но, что...** he felt flattered that ....
лест|ь, и *f.* flattery; adulation.
лёт, а, на ~у́, о ~е *m.* flight, flying; **стреля́ть в пти́цу в л.** to shoot at a bird in flight; **на ~у́** in the air, on the wing; (*fig., coll.*) hurriedly, in passing; **хвата́ть на ~у́** to be quick to grasp (*an idea, etc.*); to be quick on the uptake.
Ле́т|а, ы *f.* (*myth.*) Lethe; **ка́нуть в ~у** to sink into oblivion.
лет|а́, ~ *pl.* **1.** years; age; **ско́лько вам ~?** how old are you?; **ему́ бо́льше, ме́ньше сорока́ ~** he is over, under forty; **с де́тских лет** from childhood; **мы одни́х лет** we are (of) the same age; **сре́дних лет** middle-aged; **быть в ~а́х** to be elderly, getting on (in years); **на ста́рости ~** in one's old age. **2.** *g. pl.* (*as g. pl. of* **год**) years; **прошло́ мно́го ~** many years (have) passed, elapsed. **3.** *pl. of* **ле́то**
лета́льный *adj.* lethal, fatal.
летарги́ческий *adj.* lethargic.
летарги́|я, и *f.* lethargy.
лета́тельн|ый *adj.* flying; **л. аппара́т** aircraft; (*zool.*): **~ая перепо́нка** wing membrane (*in bats*).
лет|а́ть, а́ю *indet. of* **~е́ть**
лета́|ющий *pres. part. of* **~ть** *and adj.*; **~ющая лягу́шка** (*zool.*) tree-frog.
ле|те́ть, чу́, ти́шь *impf.* (*of* **по~**) **1.** to fly. **2.** (*fig.*) (*in var. senses*) to fly; to rush, tear; **л. на всех пара́х** to run at full tilt; **л. стрело́й** to go like an arrow. **3.** (*fig., coll.*) to fall, drop (*intrans.*); **ли́стья ~тя́т** the leaves are falling; **а́кции ~тя́т вниз** shares are plummeting.
лётк|а, и *f.* (*tech.*) tap hole; slag notch.
ле́тний *adj.* summer; **л. сад** pleasure garden(s).
ле́тник, а *m.* (*bot.*) annual.
лётн|ый *adj.* (*suitable for, appertaining to*) flying; **~ое де́ло** flying; **~ое по́ле** airfield; **л. соста́в** aircrew.
ле́т|о, а, *pl.* **~а́** *nt.* summer; **ба́бье л.** Indian summer; (*coll.*): **ско́лько ~, ско́лько зим** it's ages since we met!
лет|о́к, ка́ *m.* (*bee-keeping*) entrance (*in hive*).
ле́том *adv.* in summer.
летопи́с|ец, ца *m.* chronicler, annalist.
летопи́сный *adj.* annalistic.
ле́топис|ь, и *f.* chronicle, annals.
летосчисле́ни|е, я *nt.* chronology.
лету́н, а́ *m.* **1.** flyer, flier. **2.** (*fig., coll.*) rolling-stone, drifter; jobhopper.
лету́чест|ь, и *f.* (*chem.*) volatility.
лету́ч|ий *adj.* **1.** flying; **~ая мышь** bat; **~ая ры́ба** flying-fish. **2.** (*fig.*) passing, ephemeral; brief; **л. листо́к** leaflet; **л. ми́тинг** emergency, extraordinary meeting. **3.** (*med.*) shifting. **4.** (*chem.*) volatile.
лету́чк|а, и *f.* (*coll.*) **1.** leaflet. **2.** emergency meeting, extraordinary meeting. **3.** mobile detachment; (*med.*) mobile dressing station; **ремо́нтная л.** emergency repairs team; **хирурги́ческая л.** mobile surgical unit.
лётчик, а *m.* pilot; aviator, flyer; **л.-испыта́тель** test-pilot; **л.-истреби́тель** fighter pilot.
лецити́н, а *m.* lecithin.
лече́бник, а *m.* book of home cures.
лече́бниц|а, ы *f.* clinic.
лече́бн|ый *adj.* **1.** medical. **2.** medicinal; **~ая гимна́стика** remedial gymnastics.
лече́ни|е, я *nt.* (medical) treatment; **амбулато́рное л.** out-patient treatment.
леч|и́ть, у́, ~ишь *impf.* to treat (*medically*); **его́ ~ат от шо́ка** he is being treated for shock.
леч|и́ться, у́сь, ~ишься *impf.* **1.** **(от)** to receive, undergo (medical) treatment (for); **л. впры́скиваниями** to take a course of injections. **2.** *pass. of* **~и́ть**
ле|чу́¹, ти́шь *see* **~те́ть**
леч|у́², ~ишь *see* **~и́ть**
лечь, ля́гу, ля́жешь, ля́гут, *past* **лёг, легла́,** *imper.* **ляг, ля́гте** *pf.* (*of* **ложи́ться**) **1.** to lie (down); **л. в больни́цу** to go (in) to hospital; **л. в посте́ль, л. спать** to go to bed; (*coll.*): **неуже́ли де́ти ещё не легли́?** aren't the children in bed yet?; **л. в осно́ву** (+*g.*) to underlie; (*naut.*): **л. в дрейф** to lie to, heave to. **2.** **(на+*a.*)** to fall (on); (*rhet.*): **л. костьми́** to fall in battle; (*fig.*): **отве́тственность ля́жет на вас** it will be your duty, it will be incumbent upon you; **подозре́ние легло́ на иностра́нцев** suspicion fell upon the foreigners; **л. на со́весть** to weigh on one's conscience.
ле́ш|ий, его *m.* (*in Russ. myth.*) wood-goblin; **к ~ему!** (*coll. expletive*) go to the devil!; **како́го ~его...** what the devil, why the devil ....
лещ, а́ *m.* (*fish*) bream.
лещи́н|а, ы *f.* (*bot.*) hazel.
лже... *comb. form* pseudo-, false-, mock-.
лжеприся́г|а, и *f.* (*leg.*) perjury.
лжесвиде́тел|ь, я *m.* false witness.
лжесвиде́тельств|о, а *nt.* false evidence.
лжесвиде́тельств|овать, ую *impf.* to give false evidence.
лжеуче́ни|е, я *nt.* false doctrine.
лжец, а́ *m.* liar.
лжёшь *see* **лгать**
лжи́вост|ь, и *f.* falsity, mendacity.
лжи́в|ый (~, ~а) *adj.* **1.** lying; mendacious. **2.** false, deceitful.
ли (ль) 1. *interrog. particle* **возмо́жно ли?** is it possible?; **придёт ли он?** is he coming? **2.** *conj.* whether, if; **не зна́ю, придёт ли** I don't know whether he is coming; **посмотри́, идёт ли по́езд** go and see if the train is coming. **3.: ли... ли** whether ... or; **сего́дня ли, за́втра ли** whether today or tomorrow; **ра́но ли, по́здно ли, но приду́** I shall come sooner or later.
лиа́н|а, ы *f.* (*bot.*) liana.
либера́л, а *m.* liberal.
либерали́зм, а *m.* **1.** liberalism. **2.** (*pej.*) tolerance.
либера́льнича|ть, ю *impf.* (*of* **с~**) (**с**+*i.*; *coll., pej.*) to act the liberal; to show (excessive) tolerance (towards).
либера́л|ьный (~ен, ~ьна) *adj.* **1.** liberal. **2.** (excessively) tolerant.
либери́|ец, йца *m.* Liberian.
либери́|йка, йки *f. of* **~ец**
либери́йский *adj.* Liberian.
Либе́ри|я, и *f.* Liberia.
ли́бо *conj.* or; **л.... л.** (either) ... or; **л. пан, л. пропа́л** all or nothing.
либретти́ст, а *m.* librettist.
либре́тто *nt. indecl.* libretto.
Лива́н, а *m.* (the) Lebanon.
лива́н|ец, ца *m.* Lebanese.
лива́н|ка, ки *f. of* **~ец**
лива́нский *adj.* Lebanese.
ли́в|ень, ня *m.* heavy shower, downpour; cloud-burst; (*fig.*) **л. свинца́** hail of bullets.
ли́вер¹, а *m.* (*cul.*) pluck.
ли́вер², а *m.* (*tech.*) pipette.
ли́вер|ный *adj. of* **~¹; ~ная колбаса́** liver sausage.
ливи́|ец, йца *m.* Libyan.
ливи́|йка, йки *f. of* **~ец**
ливи́йский *adj.* Libyan.
Ли́ви|я, и *f.* Libya.
ливмя́ *adv.* (*coll.*): **л. лить** (*of rain*) to pour, come down in torrents.
ли́в|невый *adj. of* **~ень;** (*meteor.*) cumulo-nimbus.
ливре́|йный *adj. of* **~я; л. слуга́** livery servant.
ливре́|я, и *f.* livery.
ли́г|а, и *f.* league; **Л. на́ций** (*hist.*) League of Nations.
лигату́р|а¹, ы *f.* (*chem.*) base metal (*added to precious metals to harden them*).
лигату́р|а², ы *f.* (*ling. and med.*) ligature.
лигни́н, а *m.* (*chem.*) lignin(e).
лигни́т, а *m.* (*min.*) lignite.
ли́дер, а *m.* **1.** leader (*of political party or organization*). **2.** (*sport*) leader (*in tournament, etc.*). **3.** (*naut.*) flotilla leader.

ли́дерств|о, а *nt.* **1.** leadership (*of pol. party or public organization*). **2.** (*sport*) first place, lead; **занима́ть л.** to be in the lead.
лиди́р|овать, ую *impf.* (*sport*) to take first place, be in the lead.
ли|за́ть, жу́, ~́жешь *impf.* (*of* **~зну́ть**) to lick; (*fig., coll.*): **л. ру́ки (но́ги, пя́тки) кому́-н.** to lick s.o.'s boots.
ли|за́ться, жу́сь, ~́жешься *impf.* (*coll.*) to neck, smooch.
ли́зис, а *m.* (*med.*) lysis.
лиз|ну́ть, ну́, нёшь *inst. pf. of* **~а́ть**
лизоблю́д, а *m.* (*coll., pej.*) lickspittle.
лизо́л, а *m.* (*chem.*) lysol.
лик[1], **а** *m.* **1.** (*obs.*) face. **2.** representation of face (*on icon*). **3.: л. луны́** face of the moon.
лик[2], **а** *m.* (*eccl., arch.*) assembly; **причи́слить к ~́у святы́х** to canonize.
ликбе́з, а *m.* (*abbr. of* **ликвида́ция безгра́мотности**) campaign against illiteracy.
ликвида́тор, а *m.* (*comm., etc.*) liquidator.
ликвида́ци|я, и *f.* **1.** (*comm.*) liquidation; **л. долго́в** settlement of debts. **2.** (*pol., etc.*) liquidation; elimination, abolition.
ликвиди́р|овать, ую *impf. and pf.* **1.** (*comm.*) to liquidate, wind up. **2.** to liquidate; to eliminate, abolish.
ликвиди́р|оваться, уюсь *impf. and pf.* **1.** to wind up (one's activities). **2.** *pass. of* **~овать**
ликви́дн|ый *adj.* (*fin.*) liquid; **~ые сре́дства** ready money.
ликёр, а *m.* liqueur.
ликова́ни|е, я *nt.* rejoicing, exultation.
лик|ова́ть, у́ю *impf.* to rejoice, exult.
лик-тро́с, а *m.* (*naut.*) bolt-rope.
лик|у́ющий *pres. part. of* **~ова́ть** *and adj.* exultant, triumphant.
лиле́йный *adj.* **1.** (*poet.*) lily-white. **2.** (*bot.*) liliaceous.
лилипу́т, а *m.* Lilliputian.
ли́ли|я, и *f.* lily.
лилове́|ть, ю *impf.* (*of* **по~**) to turn violet.
лило́вый *adj.* lilac, violet.
лима́н, а *m.* **1.** estuary. **2.** flood plain.
лима́н|ный *adj. of* **~**
лими́т, а *m.* quota; limit.
лимити́р|овать, ую *impf. and pf.* to establish a quota (*or* maximum) in respect of.
лимитро́ф, а *m.* border state (*esp. of the Baltic states in relation to the former USSR*).
лимитро́ф|ный *adj. of* **~**
лимо́н, а *m.* lemon; **вы́жатый л.** (*fig., coll.*) has-been.
лимона́д, а *m.* **1.** lemonade; lemon squash. **2.** squash (*of fruit or berries, not necessarily lemon, as beverage*).
лимо́н|ить, ю, ишь *impf.* (*of* **с~**) (*thieves' sl.*) to knock off, pinch.
лимонноќислый *adj.* (*chem.*) citric acid.
лимо́нн|ый *adj.* lemon; **~ая кислота́** (*chem.*) citric acid.
лимузи́н, а *m.* limousine.
ли́мф|а, ы *f.* (*physiol.*) lymph.
лимфати́ческий *adj.* (*physiol.*) lymphatic (*also fig., obs.*).
лингафо́нный *adj.*: **л. кабине́т** language laboratory.
лингви́ст, а *m.* linguist.
лингви́стик|а, и *f.* linguistics.
лингвисти́ческий *adj.* linguistic.
лингвострановéдени|е, я *nt.* linguistic and regional studies.
лингвострановéд|ческий *adj. of* **~ение; л. слова́рь** dictionary of linguistic and regional studies.
лине́йк|а[1], **и** *f.* **1.** line (*on paper, blackboard, etc.*); **писа́ть по ~ам** to write on the lines; **но́тные ~и** (*mus.*) staves. **2.** ruler; **логарифми́ческая л.** slide-rule. **3.** (*typ.*): **набо́рная л.** setting-rule. **4. ла́герная л.** camp line(s).
лине́йк|а[2], **и** *f.* (*obs.*) break, wagonette.
лине́йн|ый *adj.* **1.** (*math.*) linear; **~ые ме́ры** long measures. **2.** (*mil., naut.*) of the line; **л. кора́бль** battleship.
лин|ёк, ька́ *m.* (*naut.*) rope's end, colt.
ли́нз|а, ы *f.* lens.
ли́ни|я, и *f.* (*in var. senses*) line; (*fig.*): **л. поведе́ния** line of conduct, policy; **провести́ ~ю в поли́тике** to pursue a policy; **вести́** (*coll. also* **гнуть**) **свою́ ~ю** to have one's own way; **вести́ ~ю на что-н.** to direct one's efforts towards sth.; **по ~и наиме́ньшего сопротивле́ния** on the line of least resistance.
линко́р, а *m.* (*abbr. of* **лине́йный кора́бль**) battleship.
лино-бати́ст, а *m.* lawn, cambric.
лино́ваный *adj.* lined, ruled.
лин|ова́ть, у́ю *impf.* (*of* **на~**) to rule.
линогравю́р|а, ы *f.* linocut.
лино́леум, а *m.* linoleum.
Линч, а *m.*: **зако́н ~́а, суд ~́а** lynch law.
линч|ева́ть, у́ю *impf. and pf.* to lynch.
лин|ь[1], **я́** *m.* (*zool.*) tench.
лин|ь[2], **я́** *m.* (*naut*) line.
ли́ньк|а, и *f.* moult(ing).
линю́ч|ий (~, ~а) *adj.* (*coll.*) liable to fade.
линя́лый *adj.* (*coll.*) **1.** faded, discoloured. **2.** having moulted.
линя́|ть, ет *impf.* **1.** (*pf.* **по~**) to fade, lose colour; (*of paint*) to run. **2.** (*pf.* **вы́~**) (*of animals*) to shed hair; to cast the coat; (*of birds*) to moult, shed feathers; (*of snakes*) to slough.
ли́п|а[1], **ы** *f.* lime(-tree).
ли́п|а[2], **ы** *f.* (*sl.*) forgery.
ли́п|ка, ки *f. dim. of* **~а**[1]; (*coll.*): **ободра́ть как ~ку** to fleece.
ли́п|кий (~ок, ~ка́, ~ко) *adj.* sticky, adhesive; **л. пла́стырь** sticking plaster.
ли́п|нуть, ну, нешь, *past* **~, ~ла** *impf.* **(к)** to stick (to), adhere (to).
липня́к, а́ *m.* (*coll.*) lime-grove.
ли́п|овый[1] *adj. of* **~а**[1]; **л. мёд** white honey; **л. цвет** lime-blossom; **л. чай** limeleaf tea.
ли́повый[2] *adj.* (*sl.*) sham, fake, forged.
липу́чк|а, и *f.* (*coll.*) **1.** adhesive tape, Sellotape (*propr.*). **2.** Velcro (*propr.*) (fastener).
ли́р|а[1], **ы** *f.* lyre.
ли́р|а[2], **ы** *f.* (*monetary unit*) lira.
лири́зм, а *m.* lyricism.
ли́рик, а *m.* lyric poet.
ли́рик|а, и *f.* **1.** lyric poetry; lyrics. **2.** (*fig., pej.*) lyricism.
лири́ческ|ий *adj.* **1.** lyric; (*liter.*): **л. беспоря́док** poetic disorder; **~ое отступле́ние** lyrical digression. **2.** (*of disposition, etc.*) lyrical.
лири́ч|ный (~ен, ~на) *adj.* lyrical.
ли́р|ный *adj.* (*obs. or poet.*) of **~а**[1]
лирохво́ст, а *m.* lyre-bird.
лис, а *m.* (*obs.*) (dog-)fox.
лис|а́, ы́, *pl.* **~́ы** *f.* fox; **чернобу́рая л.** silver fox; **Л. Патрике́евна** (*in Russ. folk-tales*) Reynard; **прики́дываться ~о́й** (*fig., coll.*) to fawn, toady.
ли́сел|ь, я, *pl.* **~я́** *m.* (*naut.*) studding-sail.
лис|ёнок, ёнка, *pl.* **~я́та, ~я́т** *m.* fox-cub.
ли́с|ий *adj. of* **~а́; л. мех** fox fur; **л. хвост** (fox-)brush.
лис|и́ть, и́шь *impf.* (*coll.*) to fawn, flatter.
лиси́ц|а, ы *f.* fox; vixen.
лиси́чк|а, и *f.* **1.** *dim. of* **лиси́ца. 2.** (*mushroom*) chanterelle. **3.** paper-chase.
Лиссабо́н, а *m.* Lisbon
лист[1], **а́,** *pl.* **~́ья, ~́ьев** *m.* leaf (*of plant*); blade (*of cereal*).
лист[2], **а́,** *pl.* **~ы́, ~о́в** *m.* **1.** leaf, sheet (*of paper, etc.*); (*metal*) plate; **в л.** in folio; **корректу́ра в ~а́х** page-proofs; **печа́тный л.** printer's sheet, quire; **игра́ть с ~а́** (*mus.*) to play at sight. **2.: исполни́тельный л.** (*leg.*) writ of execution; **опро́сный л.** questionnaire; **охра́нный л.** safe-conduct; **похва́льный л.** (*obs.*) certificate of progress and good conduct (*in schools*).
листа́ж, а́ *m.* number of sheets (*in a book*).
листа́|ть, ю *impf.* (*coll.*) to turn over the pages of.
листв|а́, ы́ *f.* (*collect.*) leaves, foliage.
ли́ственниц|а, ы *f.* (*bot.*) larch.
ли́ственный *adj.* (*bot.*) deciduous.
листо́вк|а, и *f.* leaflet.
лист|ово́й *adj. of* **~; ~ово́е желе́зо** sheet iron; **~ова́я рессо́ра** laminated spring.

лист|о́к, ка́ *m.* **1.** *dim. of* ~[1]. **2.** leaflet. **3.** form, pro-forma. **4.** (*sl.*) rag (*newspaper*).
листопа́д, а *m.* (*autumn*) fall of the leaves.
листоре́з, а *m.* paper-knife.
лит... *comb. form, abbr. of* **литерату́рный**
лита́врщик, а *m.* kettle(drummer).
лита́вр|ы, ~ *pl.* (*sg.* ~**а,** ~**ы** *f.*) kettledrum.
Литв|а́, ы́ *f.* Lithuania.
литви́н, а *m.* (*obs.*) Lithuanian.
литви́н|ка, ки *f. of* ~
лите́йн|ая, ой *f.* foundry, smelting-house.
лите́йный *adj.* founding, casting.
лите́йщик, а *m.* founder, caster, smelter.
ли́тер, а *m.* (*coll.*) travel warrant.
ли́тер|а, ы *f.* **1.** (*typ.*) type. **2.** (*obs.*) letter (*of the alphabet*).
литера́тор, а *m.* literary man, man of letters.
литерату́р|а, ы *f.* literature; **худо́жественная л.** belles-lettres, literature.
литерату́р|ный (~**ен,** ~**на)** *adj.* literary; ~**ная со́бственность** copyright.
литературове́д, а *m.* specialist in study of literature; literary critic.
литературове́дени|е, я *nt.* study of literature; literary criticism.
литерату́рщин|а, ы *f.* (*coll.*) striving after literary effect; self-conscious writing.
ли́терный *adj.* **1.** marked with a letter. **2.** (*sl.*) hush-hush (*of factories, etc., designated only by a letter of the alphabet for security reasons*).
литер|ова́ть, у́ю *impf. and pf.* to rate by system of letters.
ли́ти|й, я *m.* (*chem.*) lithium.
ли́тник, а *m.* (*tech.*) pouring gate, pouring channel, flow gate.
литобрабо́тник, а *m.* ghost-writer.
лито́в|ец, ца *m.* Lithuanian.
лито́в|ка, ки *f. of* ~**ец**
лито́вский *adj.* Lithuanian.
лито́граф, а *m.* lithographer.
литографи́р|овать, ую *impf. and pf.* to lithograph.
литогра́фи|я, и *f.* **1.** lithograph. **2.** lithography.
литогра́фск|ий *adj.* lithographic; ~**ая печа́ть** lithograph.
лит|о́й *adj.* cast; ~**а́я сталь** cast steel, ingot steel.
литр, а *m.* litre.
литра́ж, а́ *m.* capacity (*in litres*).
литро́вый *adj.* litre (*of one litre capacity*).
литурги́ческий *adj.* liturgical.
литурги́|я, и *f.* liturgy.
литфа́к, а *m.* (*abbr. of* **литерату́рный факульте́т**) literature department.
Литфо́нд, а *m.* Writers' Foundation.
лить, лью, льёшь, *past* **лил, лила́, ли́ло,** *imper.* **лей** *impf.* **1.** to pour (*trans. and intrans.*); to shed, spill; **л. слёзы** to shed tears; **дождь льёт как из ведра́** it is raining cats and dogs; **л. во́ду на чью-н. ме́льницу** to play into s.o.'s hands. **2.** (*tech.*) to found, cast, mould.
лит|ьё, я́ *no pl., nt.* (*tech.*) **1.** founding, casting, moulding. **2.** (*collect.*) castings, mouldings.
ли́|ться, льётся, *past* ~́**лся,** ~**ла́сь,** ~́**ло́сь** *impf.* **1.** to flow; to stream, pour. **2.** *pass. of* ~**ть**
лиф, а *m.* bodice.
лифт, а *m.* lift, elevator.
лифтёр, а *m.* lift operator, lift-boy.
ли́фчик, а *m.* **1.** brassière. **2.** (*child's*) bodice.
лиха́ч, а́ *m.* **1.** (*obs.*) driver of smart cab. **2.** reckless driver; road-hog. **3.** daredevil.
лиха́честв|о, а *nt.* **1.** reckless driving. **2.** recklessness, daredevilry.
лихв|а́, ы́ *f.* interest; **отплати́ть с** ~**о́й** to repay with interest.
ли́х|о[1]**, а** *nt.* (*poet.*) evil, ill; **не помина́йте** ~**ом** (*coll.*) remember me (us) kindly; **узна́ть, почём фунт** ~**а** (*coll.*) to fall on hard times, plumb the depths of misfortune.
ли́х|о[2]**, а** *adv. of* ~**о́й**[2]; **л. заломи́ть ша́пку** to cock one's hat at a jaunty angle.
лиходе́|й, я *m.* (*obs.*) evil-doer.
лиходе́йств|о, а *nt.* (*obs.*) evil-doing.
лихои́м|ец, ца *m.* (*obs.*) usurer; extortioner.
лихои́мств|о, а *nt.* (*obs.*) extortion; bribe-taking; bribery and corruption.
лих|о́й[1] **(**~**,** ~**а́,** ~́**о)** *adj.* (*dial. and folk poet.*) evil; ~**а́ беда́ нача́ло** (*or* **нача́ть**) (*coll.*) the first step is the hardest.
лих|о́й[2] **(**~**,** ~**а́,** ~́**о)** *adj.* (*coll.*) dashing, spirited; jaunty.
лихора́|дить, жу, дишь *impf.* **1.** to be in a fever. **2.** (*impers.*): **меня́** ~**дит** I feel feverish.
лихора́дк|а, и *f.* **1.** fever (*also fig.*); **сенна́я л.** hay fever; **перемежа́ющаяся (боло́тная) л.** malaria. **2.** rash; coldsore.
лихора́доч|ный (~**ен,** ~**на)** *adj.* feverish (*also fig.*).
ли́хост|ь, и *f.* (*coll.*) spirit, mettle; swagger.
ли́хтер, а *m.* (*naut.*) lighter.
лиц|ева́ть, у́ю *impf.* (*of* **пере**~) to turn (*clothing*).
лицев|о́й *adj.* **1.** (*anat.*) facial. **2.** exterior; ~**а́я сторона́** (*of building*) façade, front; (*of material*) right side; (*of coin, etc.*) obverse. **3.:** ~**а́я ру́копись** illuminated manuscript. **4.** (*book-keeping*): **л. счёт** personal account.
лицеде́|й, я *m.* (*obs.*) **1.** actor. **2.** (*fig.*) hypocrite, dissembler.
лицеде́йств|о, а *nt.* (*obs.*) **1.** acting. **2.** theatrical performance. **3.** (*fig.*) play-acting, dissembler.
лицезр|е́ть, ю́, и́шь *impf.* (*obs. and iron.*) to behold with one's own eyes.
лицеи́ст, а *m.* pupil of Lyceum, lycée.
лице́|й, я *m.* **1.** Lyceum (*high school or law school in pre-revolutionary Russia*). **2.** lycée (*in France*).
лице́й|ский *adj. of* ~
лицеме́р, а *m.* hypocrite, dissembler.
лицеме́ри|е, я *nt.* hypocrisy, dissimulation.
лицеме́р|ить, ю, ишь *impf.* to play the hypocrite, dissemble.
лицеме́р|ный (~**ен,** ~**на)** *adj.* hypocritical.
лице́нзи|я, и *f.* (*econ.*) licence.
лицеприя́ти|е, я *nt.* (*obs.*) partiality.
лицеприя́т|ный (~**ен,** ~**на)** *adj.* (*obs.*) partial, based on partiality.
лицеприя́тств|овать, ую *impf.* (*obs.*) to be partial; to show bias.
лиц|о́, а́, *pl.* ~́**а** *nt.* **1.** face; **черты́** ~**а́** features; **измени́ться, перемени́ться** ~**о́м, в** ~**е́** to change countenance; **сказа́ть в л. кому́-н.** to say to s.o.'s face; **знать кого́-н. в л.** to know s.o. by sight; **на нём** ~**а́ нет** he looks awful; ~**о́м в грязь не уда́рить** not to disgrace o.s.; **быть к** ~**у́** (*+d.*) to suit, become; (*fig.*) to become, befit; **нам не к** ~**у́ таки́е посту́пки** such actions do not become us; ~**о́м к** ~**у́** face to face; **поста́вить** ~**о́м к** ~**у́** to confront; **они́ на одно́ л.** (*coll.*) they are as like as two peas; **ра́дость была́ напи́сана у неё на** ~**е́** joy was written all over her face; **показа́ть своё (настоя́щее) л.** to show one's true worth; **пе́ред (пред)** ~**о́м** (*+g.*) in the face (of); **с** ~**а́ некраси́в** (*coll.*) ugly; **(исче́знуть) с** ~**а́ земли́** (to vanish) from the face of the earth. **2.** exterior; (*of material*) right side; (*fig.*): **показа́ть това́р** ~**о́м** to show sth. to advantage; to make the best of sth. **3.** person; **гражда́нское л.** civilian; **де́йствующее л.** (*theatr., liter.*) character; **де́йствующие** ~́**а** dramatis personae; **должностно́е л.** official, functionary; **духо́вное л.** clergyman; **перемещённые** ~́**а** displaced persons; **подставно́е л.** dummy, man of straw; **физи́ческое л.** (*leg.*) natural person; **юриди́ческое л.** (*leg.*) juridical person; **в** ~**е́** (*+g.*) in the person (of); **невзира́я на** ~́**а** without respect of persons; **от** ~**а́** (*+g.*) in the name (of), on behalf (of). **4.** identity.
личи́н|а[1]**, ы** *f.* mask; (*fig.*) guise; **под** ~**ой** (*+g.*) in the guise (of), under cover (of); **сорва́ть** ~**у с кого́-н.** to unmask s.o.
личи́н|а[2]**, и** *f.* (*tech.*) scutcheon, key-plate.
личи́нк|а[1]**, и** *f.* larva, grub; maggot.
личи́нк|а[2]**, и** *f.* (*mil.*): **боева́я л.** bolt head (*of rifle*); elevator (*in machine-gun*).
ли́чно *adv.* personally, in person.
личн|о́й *adj.* **1.** face; **л. крем** face cream. **2.** (*anat.*) facial.
ли́чност|ь, и *f.* **1.** personality. **2.** person, individual; **тёмная л.** shady character; **удостовере́ние** ~**и** identity card; **установи́ть чью-н. л.** to establish s.o.'s identity. **3.** (*pl.*)

personal remarks, personalities; **переходи́ть на ~и** to become personal.

ли́чн|ый *adj.* personal, individual; private; **~ое местоиме́ние** (*gram.*) personal pronoun; **~ая охра́на** body-guard; **л. секрета́рь** private secretary; **~ая со́бственность** personal property; **л. соста́в** staff.

лиша́|й, я́ *m.* **1.** (*bot.*) lichen. **2.** (*med.*) herpes; **опоя́сывающий л.** shingles; **стригу́щий л.** ringworm; **чешу́йчатый л.** psoriasis.

лиша́йник, а *m.* (*bot.*) lichen.

лиш|а́ть(ся), а́ю(сь) *impf. of* **~и́ть(ся)**

ли́ш|ек, ка *m.* (*coll.*) surplus; **с ~ком** odd, and more, just over; **де́сять миль с ~ком** ten odd miles, ten miles and a bit; **хвати́ть ~ку** (*coll.*) to have one too many.

лише́н|ец, ца *m.* disfranchised person (*in USSR up to 1936*).

лише́ни|е, я *nt.* **1.** deprivation; **л. гражда́нских прав** (*leg.*) disfranchisement. **2.** privation, hardship.

лишён|ный (~, ~а́, ~о́) *p.p.p. of* **лиши́ть** *and adj.* (+*g.*) lacking (in), devoid (of); **он не лишён остроу́мия** he is not without wit.

лиш|и́ть, у́, и́шь *pf.* (*of* **~а́ть**) (+*g.*) to deprive (of); **л. кого́-н. насле́дства** to disinherit s.o.; **л. себя́ жи́зни** to take one's life.

лиш|и́ться, у́сь, и́шься *pf.* (*of* **~а́ться**) (+*g.*) to lose, be deprived (of); **л. зре́ния** to lose one's sight; **л. чувств** to faint away.

ли́шн|ий *adj.* **1.** superfluous; unnecessary; unwanted; **бы́ло бы не ~е** (+*inf.*) it would not be out of place; **он здесь л.** he is one too many here. **2.** left over; spare, odd; **л. раз** once more; **с ~им** (*coll.*) and more, odd; **со́рок фу́нтов с ~им** forty pounds odd.

лишь *adj. and conj.* only; **не хвата́ет л. одного́** one thing only is lacking; **л. вошёл, соба́ка зала́яла** no sooner had he entered than the dog began to bark; **л. то́лько** as soon as; **л. бы** if only, provided that; **л. бы он мог прие́хать** provided that he can come.

лоб, лба, о лбе́, во (на) лбу́, *pl.* **лбы, лбов** *m.* forehead, brow; **пока́тый л.** receding forehead; **стреля́ть в л.** to fire point-blank; **ата́ка в л.** frontal attack; **пусти́ть себе́ пу́лю в л.** to blow out one's brains; (*coll.*): **на лбу́ напи́сано** writ large on one's face; **что в л., что по́ лбу** it is all one; it comes to the same thing; **будь он семи́ пяде́й во лбу** be he a Solomon.

лоба́ст|ый (~, ~а) *adj.* having a large forehead.

ло́бби *nt. indecl.* (*pol.*) lobby.

лобби́зм, а *m.* (*pol.*) lobbyism.

лобби́ст, а *m.* (*pol.*) lobbyist.

лобза́ни|е, я *nt.* (*obs.*) kiss.

лобза́|ть, ю *impf.* (*obs.*) to kiss.

ло́бзик, а *m.* fret-saw.

лобко́в|ый *adj.*: **~ая кость** (*anat.*) pubis.

ло́бн|ый *adj.* (*anat.*) frontal; **~ое ме́сто** (*hist.*) place of execution.

лобов|о́й *adj.* frontal, front; **~а́я ата́ка** (*mil.*) frontal attack; **л. фона́рь** headlight; **~о́е сопротивле́ние** (*aeron.*) drag.

лобогре́йк|а, и *f.* (*agric.*) harvester, reaping machine (*of simple design*).

лоб|о́к, ка́ *m.* (*anat.*) pubis.

лоботря́с, а *m.* (*coll.*) lazy-bones, idler.

лобыза́|ть, ю *impf.* (*obs.*) to kiss.

лов, а *m.* **1.** = **~ля. 2.** = **уло́в**

ловела́с, а *m.* (*coll.*) Lovelace, lady-killer.

лов|е́ц, ца́ *m.* fisherman; hunter; **л. же́мчуга** pearl-diver, pearler.

лов|и́ть, лю́, ~́ишь *impf.* (*of* **пойма́ть**) to (try to) catch; (*fig.*) **л. ры́бу в му́тной воде́** to fish in troubled waters; **л. чей-н. взгляд** to try to catch s.o.'s eye; **л. (удо́бный) моме́нт, слу́чай** to seize an opportunity; **л. ка́ждое сло́во** to devour every word; **л. себя́ на чём-н.** to catch o.s. at sth.; **л. кого́-н. на сло́ве** to take s.o. at his word; **л. ста́нцию** (*radio*) to try to pick up a station.

ловка́ч, а́ *m.* (*coll.*) dodger.

ло́в|кий (~ок, ~ка́, ~́ко) *adj.* **1.** adroit, dexterous, deft; **л. ход** master stroke. **2.** cunning, smart. **3.** (*coll.*) comfortable.

ло́вк|о *adv. of* **~ий; л. ли вам здесь сиде́ть?** (*coll.*) are you comfortable sitting here?

ло́вкост|ь, и *f.* **1.** adroitness, dexterity, deftness; **л. рук** sleight of hand. **2.** cunning, smartness.

ло́в|ля, ли, *g. pl.* **~ель** *f.* **1.** catching, hunting; **ры́бная л.** fishing; **л. силка́ми** snaring. **2.** fishing-ground.

лову́шк|а, и *f.* snare, trap (*also fig.*); **пойма́ть в ~у** to ensnare, entrap.

ло́в|че (*and* **~че́е**) *comp. of* **~кий** *and* **~ко**

ло́вчий[1] *adj.* **1.** hunting. **2.** serving as snare, trap.

ло́вч|ий[2], его *m.* (*hist.*) huntsman, master of hounds.

лог, а, в ~́е *or* **в ~у́,** *pl.* **~а́, ~о́в** *m.* broad gully.

логари́фм, а *m.* (*math.*) logarithm.

логарифми́р|овать, ую *impf. and pf.* (*math.*) to find the logarithm of.

логарифми́ческ|ий *adj.* (*math.*) logarithmic; **~ая лине́йка** slide-rule.

ло́гик|а, и *f.* logic.

логи́ческий *adj.* logical.

логи́чност|ь, и *f.* logicality.

логи́ч|ный (~ен, ~на) *adj.* = **~еский**

ло́говищ|е, а *nt.* den, lair.

ло́гов|о, а *nt.* = **~ище**

логопа́ти|я, и *f.* speech defect.

логопе́д, а *m.* speech therapist.

логопед|и́ческий *adj. of* **~́ия**

логопе́ди|я, и *f.* speech therapy.

ло́дк|а, и *f.* boat; **двухвесе́льная л.** pair-oar; **го́ночная л.** gig, yawl; **подво́дная л.** submarine; **спаса́тельная л.** life-boat; **лета́ющая л.** flying-boat; **ката́ться на ~е** to go boating.

ло́дочк|а, и *f. dim. of* **ло́дка**

ло́дочник, а *m.* boatman.

ло́д|очный *adj. of* **~ка**

лоды́жк|а, и *f.* **1.** (*anat.*) ankle-bone. **2.** (*mil.*) tumbler (*part of the lock of a machine-gun*).

ло́дырнича|ть, ю *impf.* (*coll.*) to loaf, idle.

ло́дыр|ь, я *m.* (*coll.*) loafer, idler; **гоня́ть ~я** to loaf, idle.

ло́ж|а[1], и *f.* **1.** (*theatr.*) box. **2.** (*Masonic*) lodge.

ло́ж|а[2], и *f.* (gun-)stock.

ложби́н|а, ы *f.* (*geog.*) narrow, shallow gully; **л. бю́ста** (*fig., coll.*) cleavage.

ло́ж|е, а *nt.* **1.** (*obs.*) bed, couch. **2.** bed, channel (*of river*). **3.** gun-stock.

ло́жечк|а[1], и *f. dim. of* **ло́жка**

ло́жечк|а[2], и *f.*: **под ~ой** in the pit of the stomach.

лож|и́ться, у́сь, и́шься *impf. of* **лечь**

ло́жк|а, и *f.* **1.** spoon; **десе́ртная л.** dessert-spoon; **столо́вая л.** table-spoon; **ча́йная л.** tea-spoon; **че́рез час по ча́йной ~е** (*fig., coll.*) in minute doses. **2.** spoonful; **л. дёгтя в бо́чке мёда** a fly in the ointment.

ложно... *comb. form* pseudo-.

ло́жност|ь, и *f.* falsity, error.

ло́ж|ный (~ен, ~на) *adj.* false, erroneous; sham, dummy; **~ная скро́мность** false modesty; **~ная трево́га** false alarm.

ложь, лжи *f.* lie, falsehood.

лоз|а́, ы́, *pl.* **~́ы** *f.* **1.** rod; **«волше́бная л.»** dowsing rod. **2.** withe. **3.** vine.

лозня́к, а́ *m.* willow-bush.

лозоиска́тел|ь, я *m.* dowser, water diviner.

лозоиска́тельств|о, а *nt.* dowsing, water divining.

ло́зунг, а *m.* **1.** slogan, catchword; watch-word. **2.** (*mil., obs.*) pass-word.

лойя́льн|ость, ~ый = **лоя́льн|ость, ~ый**

локализа́ци|я, и *f.* localization.

локализ|ова́ть, у́ю *impf. and pf.* to localize.

лока́льный *adj.* local.

лока́ут, а *m.* (*pol.*) lock-out.

локаути́р|овать, ую *impf. and pf.* (*pol.*) to lock-out.

локомоби́л|ь, я *m.* traction-engine, portable engine.

локомоти́в, а *m.* locomotive.

ло́кон, а *m.* lock, curl, ringlet.

локотни́к, а́ *m.* arm (*of a chair*); elbow-rest.

ло́к|оть, тя, *pl.* **~ти, ~те́й** *m.* **1.** elbow; **с про́дранными ~тя́ми** out at elbow(s); **рабо́тать ~тя́ми** (*coll.*) to elbow one's way; **чу́вство ~тя** (*fig.*) feeling of comradeship; **бли́зок л., да не уку́сишь** (*prov.*) so near and yet so far. **2.** (*measure*) (*obs.*) cubit, ell.

локтев|о́й *adj.* (*anat.*): **~а́я кость** ulna; funny-bone.

лом, а, *pl.* **~́ы, ~о́в** *m.* **1.** crow-bar. **2.** (*sg. only*; *collect.*) scrap, waste; **желе́зный л.** scrap-iron.

лома́к|а, и *c.g.* (*coll.*) poseur, pseud.

ло́ман|ый *adj.* broken; **л. англи́йский язы́к** broken English; **~ого гроша́ не сто́ит** (*coll.*) it is not worth a brass farthing.

лома́нь|е, я *nt.* (*coll.*) affectation; mincing, simpering.

лома́|ть, ю *impf.* (*of* **с~**) **1.** to break; to fracture. **2.** (*no pf.*) (*fig.*): **л. себе́ го́лову (над)** to rack one's brains (over); **л. дурака́** to play the fool; **л. ру́ки** to wring one's hands; **л. ша́пку (пе́ред)** to bow obsequiously (to). **3.** (*no pf.*): **л. ка́мень** to quarry stone. **4.** (*no pf.*; *of pain, sickness*) (*coll.*) to rack; to cause to ache; (*impers.*): **меня́ всего́ ~ло** I was aching all over.

лома́|ться, юсь *impf.* **1.** (*pf.* **с~**) to break (*intrans*). **2.** (*no pf.*) (*of voice*) to crack, break. **3.** (*pf.* **по~**) (*coll.*) to pose, put on airs. **4.** (*pf.* **по~**) (*coll.*) to make difficulties, be obstinate.

ломба́рд, а *m.* pawn-shop; **заложи́ть в л.** to pawn.

ломба́рд|ец, ца *m.* Lombard.

Ломба́рди|я, и *f.* Lombardy.

ломба́рдский *adj.* Lombard.

ломба́рд|ный *adj. of* **~**; **~ная квита́нция** pawn ticket.

ло́мберный *adj.*: **л. стол** card-table.

лом|и́ть, лю́, ~́ишь *impf.* (*coll.*) **1.** to break. **2.** to break through, rush. **3.** (*impers.*) to cause to ache; **у меня́ ~́ит спи́ну** my back aches. **4.** (*coll.*): **л. це́ну** to demand an extortionate price.

лом|и́ться, лю́сь, ~́ишься *impf.* **1.** to be (near to) breaking; **(от)** to burst (with), be crammed (with); **ве́тви ~ятся от плодо́в** the boughs are groaning with fruit. **2.** (*coll.*) to force one's way; **л. в откры́тую дверь** (*fig.*) to force an open door.

ло́мк|а, и *f.* **1.** breaking (*also fig.*). **2.** (*usu. pl., obs.*) quarry.

ло́м|кий (~ок, ~ка́, ~ко) *adj.* fragile, brittle.

ломови́к, а́ *m.* drayman, carter.

ломов|о́й *adj.* dray, draught; **л. изво́зчик = ломови́к; ~а́я ло́шадь** cart-horse, draught-horse; **~а́я подво́да** dray; *as n.* **л., ~о́го** *m.* **= ломови́к**

ломоно́с, а *m.* (*bot.*) clematis.

ломо́т|а, ы *f.* (*coll.*) rheumatic pain, ache.

ломо́т|ный *adj. of* **~а**

лом|о́ть, тя́, *pl.* **~ти́, ~те́й** *m.* large flat slice; round (*of bread*); **отре́занный л.** *fig., of pers. no longer dependent, standing on his own feet.*

ло́мтик, а *m.* slice; **ре́зать ~ами** to slice.

Ло́ндон, а *m.* London.

ло́ндон|ец, ца *m.* Londoner.

ло́ндон|ка, ки *f. of* **~ец**

ло́ндонский *adj.* London.

лонжеро́н, а *m.* (*tech.*) longeron; (*aeron.*) (wing) spar.

ло́н|о, а *no pl., nt.* (*obs.*) bosom, lap; **л. семьи́** the bosom of the family; **на ~е приро́ды** in the open air.

лопар|ка, ки *f. of* **~ь**[1]

лопа́рский *adj.* Lapp(ish).

лопа́р|ь[1]**, я́** *m.* Lapp, Laplander.

лопа́р|ь[2]**, я́** *m.* (*naut.*) fall.

ло́паст|ный *adj. of* **~ь**; (*bot.*) laciniate.

ло́паст|ь, и, *pl.* **~и, ~е́й** *f.* **1.** blade; fan, vane (*of propeller, etc.*); (wheel) paddle; **л. о́си** axle tree. **2.** (*bot.*) lamina.

лопа́т|а, ы *f.* spade, shovel; **грести́ де́ньги ~ой** (*fig., coll.*) to rake it (*sc.* money) in.

лопа́тк|а, и *f.* **1.** shovel; trowel, scoop; (*cul.*) spatula; blade (*of turbine*). **2.** (*anat.*) shoulder-blade, scapula; (*part of joint of meat*) shoulder; **положи́ть на о́бе лопа́тки** to throw (*in wrestling*); **бежа́ть во все ~и** (*coll.*) to run as fast as one's legs can carry one.

ло́па|ть, ю *impf.* (*of* **с~**) (*coll.*) to gobble up.

ло́п|аться, аюсь *impf. of* **~нуть**

ло́п|нуть, ну, нешь *pf.* (*of* **~аться**) **1.** to break, burst; to split, crack; **чуть не л. от сме́ха** to split one's sides with laughter, burst with laughter; (*fig.*): **у меня́ терпе́ние ~нуло** my patience is exhausted. **2.** (*fig., coll.*) to fail, be a failure; (*fin.*) to go bankrupt, crash.

лопо|та́ть, чу́, ~́чешь *impf.* (*coll.*) to mutter, mumble.

лопоу́х|ий (~, ~а) *adj.* lop-eared.

лопу́х, а́ *m.* **1.** (*bot.*) burdock. **2.** (*sl.*) fool.

лорд, а *m.* lord; **пала́та ~́ов** House of Lords.

лорд-ка́нцлер, а *m.* Lord Chancellor.

лорд-мэ́р, а *m.* Lord Mayor.

лоре́тк|а, и *f.* (*obs.*) courtesan, cocotte.

лорне́т, а *m.* lorgnette.

лорни́р|овать, ую *impf. and pf.* to quiz(z).

Лос-А́нджелес, а *m.* Los Angeles.

лоси́н|а, ы *f.* **1.** elk-skin, chamois leather. **2.** (*pl.*; *hist.*) buckskin breeches. **3.** (*meat*) elk.

лос|и́ный *adj. of* **~ь**

лоск, а *m.* lustre, gloss, shine (*also fig.*); **в л.** (*coll.*) completely, entirely; **пья́ный в л.** blind drunk.

ло́скут, а *no pl., m.* (*collect.*) rags, pieces.

лоску́т, а́, *pl.* **~ы́, ~о́в** *and* **~ья, ~ьев** *m.* rag, shred, scrap.

лоску́тник, а *m.* rag merchant, rag dealer.

лоску́тн|ый *adj.* **1.** scrappy. **2.** made of scraps; **~ое одея́ло** patchwork quilt; **~ая мона́рхия** *iron. of Austro-Hungarian Empire.*

лосн|и́ться, ю́сь, и́шься *impf.* to be glossy, shine.

лососи́н|а, ы *f.* salmon (flesh).

лосо́с|ь, я, *pl.* **ло́соси, ло́сосей** *m.* salmon; **каспи́йский л.** Caspian sea-trout.

лос|ь, я, *pl.* **~́и, ~е́й** *m.* elk.

лосьо́н, а *m.* lotion; aftershave; make-up remover.

лот[1]**, а** *m.* (*naut.*) (sounding-)lead, plummet.

лот[2]**, а** *m.* (*obs.*) lot (*unit of measurement equivalent to 12.8 grams*).

Лотари́нги|я, и *f.* (*hist.*) Lorraine.

лотере́|йный *adj. of* **~я; л. биле́т** lottery-ticket.

лотере́|я, и *f.* lottery, raffle; **разы́грывать в ~ю** to raffle, dispose of by lottery.

ло́тлин|ь, я *m.* (*naut.*) leadline.

лото́ *nt. indecl.* lotto; bingo.

лот|о́к, ка́ *m.* **1.** hawker's stand; hawker's tray. **2.** chute; gutter; (*tech.*) trough; **ме́льничный л.** mill-race.

ло́тос, а *m.* (*bot.*) lotus.

лото́чник, а *m.* hawker.

лото́шник, а *m.* (*coll.*) lotto player, bingo player.

лоха́нк|а, и *f.* (wash-)tub; **по́чечная л.** (*anat.*) calix (of the kidney).

лоха́н|ь, и *f.* (wash-)tub.

лохма́|тить, чу, тишь *impf.* (*of* **вз~**) (*coll.*) to tousle.

лохма́|титься, чусь, тишься *impf.* (*coll.*) to become tousled, dishevelled.

лохма́т|ый (~, ~а) *adj.* **1.** shaggy(-haired). **2.** dishevelled, tousled.

лохмо́ть|я, ев *no sg.* rags; **в ~ях** in rags, ragged.

ло́ци|я, и *f.* (*naut.*) sailing directions.

ло́цман, а *m.* **1.** (*naut.*) pilot. **2.** pilot-fish.

лошадёнк|а, и *f.* (*pej.*) jade.

лошади́н|ый *adj.* of horses; equine; **~ая до́за** (*joc.*) very large dose; **~ая си́ла** horse-power.

лоша́дк|а, и *f.* **1.** *dim. of* **ло́шадь**; (*in child's speech*) gee-gee. **2.** hobby-horse; rocking-horse.

лоша́дник, а *m.* (*coll.*) horse-lover.

ло́шад|ь, и, *pl.* **~и, ~е́й, ~я́м, ~ьми́, ~я́х** *f.* horse; **бегова́я, скакова́я л.** race-horse; **верхова́я л.** saddle-horse; **выю́чная л.** pack-horse; **заводна́я л.** (*mil.*) led horse; **заво́дская л.** stud-horse; **кавалери́йская л.** troop-horse, cavalry horse; **коренна́я л.** shaft-horse; **ломова́я л.** dray-horse; **пристяжна́я л.** outrunner; **упряжна́я л.** draught horse; **чистокро́вная л.** thoroughbred; **сади́ться на л.** to mount; **ходи́ть за ~ью** to groom a horse.

лоша́к, а́ *m.* hinny.

лощён|ый *adj.* glossy, polished; **~ая пря́жа** glazed yarn; (*fig.*): **~ые мане́ры** polished manners; **л. молодо́й челове́к** (*coll.*) swell, masher.

лощи́н|а, ы *f.* (*geog.*) hollow, depression.

лощ|и́ть, у́, и́шь *impf.* (*of* **на~**) **1.** to polish. **2.** to gloss, glaze.
лоя́льност|ь, и *f.* fairness; honesty; loyalty.
лоя́л|ьный (~ен, ~ьна) *adj.* fair; honest; loyal (*to the State authorities*).
луб, а, *pl.* **∠ья, ∠ьев** *m.* (*bot.*) (lime) bast.
луб|о́к[1], **ка́** *m.* **1.** (*med.*) splint. **2.** strip of bast.
луб|о́к[2], **ка́** *m.* **1.** cheap popular print. **2.** (*fig.*) popular literature.
луб|о́чный[1] *adj. of* **~о́к**[1]
луб|о́чный[2] *adj. of* **~о́к**[2]; **~о́чная карти́нка** cheap popular print.
луб|яно́й *adj. of* **~**
луг, а, о ∠е, на ~у́, *pl.* **~а́, ~о́в** *m.* meadow; **заливно́й л.** water-meadow.
лугово́дств|о, а *nt.* grass farming, meadow cultivation.
луг|ово́й *adj. of* **~**; **л. бе́рег** lower bank (= *right bank of most rivers in European Russia*); **~ова́я соба́чка** (*zool.*) prairie-dog.
луди́льщик, а *m.* tinsmith, tinman.
лу|ди́ть, жу́, ∠дишь *impf.* (*of* **вы~** *and* **по~**) (*tech.*) to tin.
лу́ж|а, и *f.* puddle, pool; **сесть в ~у** (*fig., coll.*) to get into a mess; to slip up.
лужа́йк|а, и *f.* grass-plot, (forest) glade; **л. для игры́ в шары́** bowling green.
луже́ни|е, я *nt.* (*tech.*) tinning.
лужён|ый *adj.* tinned, tin-plate; **~ая гло́тка** (*fig., coll.*) throat of cast iron, iron palate.
луж|о́к, ка́ *m. dim. of* **луг**
лу́з|а, ы *f.* (billiard-)pocket.
лук[1], **а** *m.* (*collect.*) onions; **зелёный л.** spring onions; **л.-поре́й** leek; **голо́вка ∠а** onion; **л.-шнитт** chives.
лук[2], **а** *m.* bow; **натяну́ть л.** to bend, draw a bow.
лук|а́, и́, *pl.* **∠и** *f.* **1.** bend (*of river, road, etc.*). **2.** pommel (*of saddle*); **за́дняя л.** rear arch; **пере́дняя л.** front arch.
лука́в|ец, ца *m.* (*coll.*) crafty, sly pers.; (*joc.*) slyboots.
лука́в|ить, лю, ишь *impf.* (*of* **с~**) to be cunning.
лука́вств|о, а *nt.* craftiness, slyness.
лука́в|ый (~, ~а) *adj.* **1.** crafty, sly, cunning; *as n.* **л., ~ого** *m.* the Evil One. **2.** arch.
лу́ковиц|а, ы *f.* **1.** an onion. **2.** (*bot., anat.*) bulb. **3.** 'onion' cupola (*of Russ. churches*). **4.** (*coll.*) 'turnip' watch.
лу́кови|чный *adj. of* **~ца**; bulbous.
лукодро́м, а *m.* archery range.
лукомо́рь|е, я *nt.* (*poet.*) cove, creek.
луко́ш|ко, ка, *pl.* **~ки, ~ек** *nt.* bast basket; punnet.
лун|а́, ы́, *pl.* **∠ы** *f.* moon; the Moon.
лу́на-па́рк, а *m.* funfair.
лунати́зм, а *m.* sleep-walking, somnambulism.
луна́тик, а *m.* sleep-walker, somnambulist.
лунати́ческий *adj.* somnambulistic.
лу́нк|а, и *f.* hole; (*anat.*) alveolus, socket.
лу́нник[1], **а** *m.* (*bot.*) honesty.
лу́нник[2], **а** *m.* lunar probe, lunik.
лу́н|ный *adj. of* **~а́**; (*astron.*) lunar; **л. год** lunar year; **~ное затме́ние** lunar eclipse; **~ная ночь** moonlit night; **л. свет** moonlight; **л. ка́мень** (*min.*) moonstone.
лунохо́д, а *m.* **1.** lunar rover, Moon buggy. **2.** (*pl., coll.*) moon boots.
лун|ь, я́ *m.* (*zool.*) harrier; **полево́й л.** henharrier; **седо́й, бе́лый, как л.** white as snow (*of hair*).
лу́п|а, ы *f.* magnifying glass.
лупи́н, а *m.* (*bot.*) lupin(e).
луп|и́ть[1], **лю́, ∠ишь** *impf.* **1.** (*pf.* **об~**) to peel; to bark. **2.** (*pf.* **с~**) (*coll.*) to fleece; **л. с кого́-н. втри́дорога** to make s.o. pay through the nose.
луп|и́ть[2], **лю́, ∠ишь** *impf.* (*of* **от~**) (*coll.*) to thrash, flog.
луп|и́ться, ∠ится *impf.* (*of* **об~**) to peel (off), scale; (*coll.*) to come off, chip (*of paint, plaster, etc*).
лупогла́зый *adj.* (*coll.*) pop-eyed, goggle-eyed.
лупц|ева́ть, у́ю *impf.* (*of* **от~**) (*coll.*) to beat, flog.
луч, а́ *m.* ray; beam; **рентге́новские, рентге́новы ~и́** X-rays; **л. наде́жды** (*fig.*) ray, gleam of hope.
луч|ево́й *adj.* **1.** *adj. of* **~**. **2.** radial. **3.** (*anat.*): **~ева́я кость** radius. **4.** (*med.*): **~ева́я боле́знь** radiation sickness.
лучеза́р|ный (~ен, ~на) *adj.* (*poet.*) radiant, resplendent.
лучи́н|а, ы *f.* **1.** splinter, chip (*of kindling wood; also collect.*). **2.** torch (*for lighting peasant hut*).
лучи́ст|ый (~, ~а) *adj.* **1.** radiant (*also fig. and phys.*); **л. грибо́к** (*med.*) Actinomyces. **2.** radial.
луч|и́ть, у́, и́шь *impf.*: **л. ры́бу** to spear fish (*at night, by torchlight*).
луч|и́ться, и́тся *impf.* (*poet.*) to shine brightly, sparkle.
лучко́в|ый *adj.* bow-shaped; **~ая пила́** frame-saw.
лу́чник, а *m.* (*hist.*) archer.
лу́чше *adj. and adj.* **1.** (*comp. of* **хоро́ший** *and* **хорошо́**) better; **тем л.** so much the better; **л. всего́, л. всех** best of all; **как мо́жно л.** as well as possible, to the best of one's abilities; *as pred.* it is better; **л. ли вам сего́дня?** are you better today?; **л. не спра́шивай** better not ask; **нам л. верну́ться** we had better go back. **2.** *as particle* rather, instead; **ты им говори́ или, л., я позвоню́** you talk to them, or, rather, I'll give them a ring; **дава́йте л. поговори́м об э́том** let's talk it over instead.
лу́чш|ий *adj.* (*comp. and superl. of* **хоро́ший**) better; best; **к ~ему** for the better; **в ~ем слу́чае** at best; **всего́ ~его!** all the best!
лущ|и́ть, у́, и́шь *impf.* **1.** (*pf.* **об~**) to shell, hull, pod (*peas, etc.*); to crack (*nuts*). **2.** (*pf.* **вз~**) to remove stubble (from).
Лха́с|а, ы *f.* Lhasa.
лы́ж|а, и *f.* ski; snow-shoe; **го́рные ∠и** alpine skis; **бе́гать, ходи́ть на ~ах** to ski; **навостри́ть ~и** (*fig.*) to take to one's heels, show a clean pair of heels; **напра́вить ~и** (*fig.*) to head (for).
лы́жник, а *m.* skier.
лы́ж|ный *adj. of* **~а**; **л. спуск** ski-run.
лыжн|я́, и́ *f.* ski-track.
лы́к|о, а, *pl.* **~и** *nt.* bast; **драть л.** to bark lime-trees; **не вся́кое л. в стро́ку** one must make allowances; **я не ~ом шит** I was not born yesterday; **~а не вя́жет** (*of the incoherent speech of a drunk pers.*).
лысе́|ть, ю *impf.* (*of* **об~** *and* **по~**) to grow bald.
лы́син|а, ы *f.* bald spot, bald patch; star (*on horse's forehead*).
лысу́х|а, и *f.* (*zool.*) coot.
лы́с|ый (~, ~а́, ~о) *adj.* bald.
ль = ли
льв|ёнок, ёнка, *pl.* **~я́та, ~я́т** *m.* young lion, lion cub.
льви́н|ый *adj. of* **лев**[1]; **~ая до́ля** (*fig.*) the lion's share; (*bot.*): **л. зев, ~ая пасть** snap-dragon; **л. зуб** dandelion.
льви́ц|а, ы *f.* lioness.
льв|я́та *see* **~ёнок**
льго́т|а, ы *f.* privilege; advantage.
льго́тник, а *m.* (*coll.*) privileged pers.
льго́тн|ый *adj.* privileged; favourable; **л. биле́т** privilege ticket, free ticket; **~ые дни** (*comm.*) days of grace; **на ~ых усло́виях** on preferential terms.
льда *g. sg. of* **лёд**
льди́н|а, ы *f.* block of ice, ice-floe.
льди́нк|а, и *f.* piece of ice.
льди́стый *adj.* icy; ice-covered.
льна, льну *see* **лён**
льново́д, а *m.* flax grower.
льново́дств|о, а *nt.* flax growing.
льнопряде́ни|е, я *nt.* flax spinning.
льнопряди́льн|ый *adj.* flax-spinning; **~ая фа́брика** flax-mill.
льнопряди́л|ьня, ьни, *g. pl.* **~ен** *f.* flax-mill.
льнотреби́лк|а, и *f.* (*agric.*) flax puller.
льнотрепа́лк|а, и *f.* (*agric.*) scutching-sword; swingling machine.
льнуть, льну, льнёшь *impf.* (*of* **при~**) (**к**) **1.** to cling (to), stick (to). **2.** (*fig., coll.*) to have a weakness (for). **3.** (*fig., coll.*) to make up (to), (*sl.*) try to get in (with).
льнян|о́й *adj.* **1.** of flax; **~о́е ма́сло** linseed-oil; **~о́е се́мя** linseed, flax-seed; **~о́го цве́та** flaxen. **2.** linen; **~а́я промы́шленность** linen industry.
льстец, а́ *m.* flatterer.

льсти́в|ый (~, ~а) *adj.* flattering; (*of a pers.*) smooth-tongued.

льстить, льщу, льстишь *impf.* (*of* **по~**) **1.** (*+d.*) to flatter; to gratify; **э́то льстит его́ самолю́бию** it flatters his self-esteem. **2.** (*+a., with refl. pron. only*) to delude; **л. себя́ наде́ждой** to flatter o.s. with the hope.

льсти́ться, льщусь, льсти́шься *impf.* (*of* **по~**) (**на**+*a., obs., +i.*) to be tempted (by).

лью, льёшь *see* **лить**

люб, ~а́, ~́о *adj. as pred.* (*coll.*) dear; pleasant; **она́ мне ~а́** she is dear to me; **~́о** (*+inf.*) it is pleasant (to); **~́о-до́рого** it is a real pleasure.

любвеоби́л|ьный (~ен, ~ьна) *adj.* loving; full of love.

любе́знича|ть, ю *impf.* (**с**+*i.*) (*coll.*) **1.** to pay compliments (to); to pay court (to). **2.** to stand on ceremony (with).

любе́зност|ь, и *f.* **1.** courtesy; politeness, civility. **2.** kindness; **оказа́ть, сде́лать кому́-н. л.** to do s.o. a kindness. **3.** compliment; **говори́ть ~и кому́-н.** to pay s.o. compliments.

любе́з|ный (~ен, ~на) *adj.* **1.** courteous; polite; obliging. **2.** kind, amiable; **л. чита́тель** gentle reader; **бу́дьте ~ны...** (*polite form of request*) be so kind as .... **3.** (*obs.*) dear; (*as mode of address to inferior*) my (good) man. **4.** *as n.* **л., ~ного** *m.*, **~ная, ~ной** *f.* (*coll. and folk poet.*) beloved.

люби́м|ец, ца *m.* favourite, darling.

люби́мчик, а *m.* (*pej.*) pet, blue-eyed boy.

люби́м|ый (~, ~а) *adj.* **1.** beloved, loved. **2.** favourite.

люби́тел|ь, я *m.* **1.** (*+g. or +inf.*) lover; **л. му́зыки** music-lover; **л. оздорови́тельного бе́га** jogger; **л. мастери́ть** do-it-yourselfer, (home) handyman; **л. саморекла́мы** publicity-seeker; **л. соба́к** dog-fancier; **он л. сплетни́чать** he loves gossiping. **2.** amateur.

люби́тельский *adj.* **1.** amateur; **л. спекта́кль** amateur performance. **2.** amateurish. **3.** choice.

люби́тельств|о, а *nt.* amateurishness.

люб|и́ть, лю́, ~́ишь *impf.* **1.** to love. **2.** to like, be fond (of). **3.** (*of plants, etc.*) (*coll.*) to need, require, like; **фиа́лки ~́ят тень** violets like shade.

люб|ова́ться, у́юсь *impf.* (*of* **по~**) (*+i.*, **на**+*a.*) to admire; to feast one's eyes (upon); **л. на себя́ в зе́ркало** to admire o.s. in the looking glass.

любо́вник, а *m.* **1.** lover. **2.** (*theatr.*) jeune premier.

любо́вниц|а, ы *f.* mistress.

любо́вн|ый *adj.* **1.** love-; **~ая исто́рия** love-affair; **л. напи́ток** love-potion; **~ое письмо́** love-letter. **2.** loving.

люб|о́вь, ви́, *i.* **~о́вью** *f.* (**к**) love (for, of); **де́лать что-н. с ~о́вью** to do sth. with enthusiasm, con amore.

любозна́тел|ьный (~ен, ~ьна) *adj.* inquisitive.

любо́й 1. *adj.* any; either (*of two*); **л. цено́й** at any price. **2.** *as n.* anyone.

любопы́т|ный (~ен, ~на) *adj.* (*in var. senses*) curious; interesting; *as n.* **л., ~ного** *m.* curious, inquisitive pers.; (*impers.*; *+d. and inf.*): **~но знать, что с ним ста́ло** it would be interesting to know what happened to him; **мне ~но слу́шать, о чём они́ спо́рят** I am curious to hear what they are arguing about; **~но, придёт ли она́** I wonder if she will come.

любопы́тств|о, а *nt.* curiosity; **пра́здное л.** idle curiosity.

любопы́тств|овать, ую *impf.* (*of* **по~**) to be curious.

любостяжа́ни|е, я *nt.* (*obs.*) cupidity.

лю́б|ящий *pres. part. act. of* **~и́ть** *and adj.* loving, affectionate; **л. Вас** (*in letters*) yours affectionately.

лю́гер, а *m.* (*naut.*) lugger.

люд, а *m.* (*collect.*; *coll.*) people; **рабо́чий л.** working-people.

лю́д|и, е́й, ~́ям, ~ьми́, о ~́ях *no sg.* **1.** (*pl. of* **челове́к**) people; **вы́биться, вы́йти в л.** to rise in the world, get on in life; **вы́вести кого́-н. в л.** to put s.o. on his feet, set s.o. up; **уйти́ в л.** to go away from home (*to work*); **на ~ях** in the presence of others, in company; **на ~я́х и смерть красна́** (*prov.*) two in distress make sorrow less. **2.** (*mil.*) men. **3.** (*obs.*) servants.

лю́д|ный (~ен, ~на) *adj.* **1.** populous, thickly-populated. **2.** crowded.

людое́д, а *m.* **1.** cannibal; man-eater; **тигр-л.** man-eating tiger. **2.** ogre.

людое́дств|о, а *nt.* cannibalism.

людск|а́я, ой *f.* (*obs.*) servants' hall.

людск|о́й *adj.* **1.** human; **~и́е пересу́ды** talk of the town. **2.** (*mil.*): **л. соста́в** personnel, effectives. **3.** (*obs.*) servants'.

люизи́т, а *m.* (*chem.*) lewisite.

люк, а *m.* **1.** (*naut.*) hatch, hatchway; manhole. **2.** (*theatr.*) trap. **3.: светово́й л.** sky-light.

люкс[1]**, а** *m.* (*phys.*) lux (*unit of light*).

люкс[2] *adj. indecl.* de luxe, luxury.

Лю́ксембу́рг, а *m.* Luxemburg.

люксембу́ргский *m.* Luxemburg.

люксембу́рж|ец, ца *m.* Luxemburger.

лю́ксовский = лю́ксовый

лю́ксовый *adj.* (*coll.*) plush, luxury.

лю́льк|а[1]**, и** *f.* cradle.

лю́льк|а[2]**, и** *f.* (*dial.*) pipe.

люмба́го *nt. indecl.* lumbago.

люмина́л, а *m.* (*pharm.*) luminal.

люминесце́нтн|ый *adj.* luminescent; **~ые ла́мпы** fluorescent lighting.

люминесце́нци|я, и *f.* (*phys.*) luminescence.

лю́мпен-пролетариа́т, а *m.* Lumpenproletariat.

люне́т, а *m.* **1.** (*mil.*) lunette. **2.** (*tech.*) rest, support, collar plate.

лю́рик, а *m.* (*zool.*) little auk.

лю́стр|а, ы *f.* chandelier.

люстри́н, а *m.* lustrine, lutestring.

люстри́н|овый *adj. of* **~**

лютера́н|ин, ина, *pl.* **~е, ~** *m.* (*relig.*) Lutheran.

лютера́нский *adj.* (*relig.*) Lutheran.

лютера́нств|о, а *nt.* (*relig.*) Lutheranism.

лю́тик, а *m.* (*bot.*) buttercup.

лю́тиков|ые, ых (*bot.*) ranunculi.

лю́тн|евый *adj. of* **~я**

лю́т|ня, ни, *g. pl.* **~ен** *f.* (*mus.*) lute.

лю́т|ый (~, ~а́, ~́о) *adj.* ferocious, fierce, cruel (*also fig.*).

люф|а́, ы́ *f.* (*bot.*) loofah.

люце́рн|а, ы *f.* (*bot.*) lucerne.

лю́эс, а *m.* (*med*) syphilis.

люэти́ческий *m.* (*med.*) syphilitic.

ля *nt. indecl.* (*mus.*) A; **ля дие́з** A sharp; **ля бемо́ль** A flat.

ляг(те) *imper: of* **лечь**

лягáвая = лега́вая

ляг|а́ть, а́ю *impf.* (*of* **~ну́ть**) to kick.

ляга́|ться, юсь *impf.* to kick (*intrans*); to kick one another.

ляг|ну́ть, ну́, нёшь *inst. pf. of* **~а́ть**

ля́|гу, жешь, гут *see* **лечь**

лягуша́тник, а *m.* paddling pool.

лягуш|а́чий (*and* **~́ечий**) *adj. of* **~́ка**

лягу́шк|а, и *f.* frog.

лягуш|о́нок, о́нка, *pl.* **~а́та, ~а́т** *m.* young frog.

ляд, а *m.* (*coll.*): **на кой л.?** what the devil, why the devil?; **ну его́ к ~́у!** to hell with him!

ляду́нк|а, и *f.* cartridge-pouch.

ля́жк|а, и *f.* thigh, haunch.

лязг, а *no pl., m.* clank, clang; clack (*of teeth*).

ля́зга|ть, ю *impf.* (*+i.*) to clank, clang; **он ~л зуба́ми** his teeth were chattering; **л. це́пью** to rattle a chain.

ля́мз|ить, ю, ишь *impf.* (*of* **с~**) (*sl.*) to pinch (*= to steal*).

ля́мк|а, и *f.* strap; **тяну́ть ~ами, на ~ах** to tow, take in tow; **тяну́ть ~у** (*fig., coll.*) to toil, sweat, be engaged in drudgery.

ляп, а *m.* (*coll.*) blunder, gaffe.

ля́п|ать, аю *impf.* (*coll.*) **1.** (*pf.* **на~**) to make hastily *or* any old how. **2.** *impf. of* **~нуть**

ля́пис, а *m.* (*chem.*) lunar caustic, silver nitrate.

ля́пис-лазу́р|ь, и *f.* lapis lazuli.

ля́п|нуть, ну, нешь *pf.* (*of* **~ать**) (*coll.*) **1.** to blurt out, blunder out. **2.** to strike, slap; **л. кого́-н. по́ уху** to box s.o.'s ears.

ля́псус, а *m.* blunder, lapsus; slip (*of tongue, pen*).

ля́сы *only in phr.* (*coll.*) **точи́ть л.** to chatter, talk idly.

лях, а *m.* (*hist.*) Pole.

М

М *abbr. of* **1. метро́** Metro, Underground. **2. *Мужска́я (убо́рная)*** Gents, Gentlemen (*lavatory*).
М. (*abbr. of* **Москва́**) Moscow.
м (*abbr. of* **метр**) m, metre(s).
м. *abbr. of* **1. мину́та** min., minute(s). **2. мыс** (*geog.*) C., Cape.
мавзоле́|й, я *m.* mausoleum.
мавр, а *m.* Moor.
Маври́к|ий, ого *m.* Mauritius.
маврита́н|ец, ца *m.* Mauritanian.
Маврита́ни|я, и *f.* Mauritania.
маврита́н|ка, ки *f. of* **~ец**
маврита́нский *adj.* Moorish; (*archit., etc.*) **1.** Moresque. **2.** Mauritanian.
ма́врский *adj.* (*obs.*) Moorish.
маг[1]**, а** *m.* **1.** (*hist.*) magus; Magian. **2.** magician, wizard.
маг[2]**, а** *m.* (*abbr. of* **магнитофо́н**) (*coll.*) tape recorder.
магази́н, а *m.* **1.** shop; **винно-во́дочный м.** off-licence; **гастрономи́ческий м.** grocer's (shop); **м. деликате́сов** delicatessen; **м. канцпринадле́жностей** stationer's; **многофилиа́льный м.** chain store; **мо́дный м.** boutique; **м. натура́льных проду́ктов** health-food shop; **универса́льный м.** department store. **2.** (*obs.*) store, depot; (*mil.*) magazine. **3.** (*in fire-arm*) magazine.
магази́н|ный *adj. of* **~**; **~ная коро́бка** magazine (*of fire-arm*).
магази́нщик, а *m.* **1.** (*coll., obs.*) shop-keeper. **2.** (*sl.*) shop-lifter.
магара́дж|а, и *m.* Maharaja(h).
магары́ч, а́ *m.* (*coll.*) entertainment (*provided by pers. on making a good bargain*); wetting a bargain; **поста́вить м.** to stand a round (of drinks); **с вас м.!** you owe us a drink!
маги́ст|ерский *adj. of* **~р 3.**
магист|е́рский *adj. of* **~р 1., 2.**
маги́стр, а *m.* **1.** holder of a master's degree. **2.** master's degree. **3.** head of a knightly *or* monastic order.
магистра́л|ь, и *f.* main; main line; **га́зовая м.** gas main; **доро́жная м.** arterial road; **железнодоро́жная м.** main (railway) line.
магистра́ль|ный *adj. of* **~**; **м. локомоти́в** long-haul locomotive.
магистра́т, а *m.* city, town council.
магистрату́р|а, ы *f.* magistracy.
маги́ческий *adj.* magic(al).
ма́ги|я, и *f.* magic.
магна́т, а *m.* **1.** (*hist.*) member of Upper House of Diet in Poland *or* Hungary. **2.** magnate.
магнези́т, а *m.* (*min.*) magnesite.
магне́зи|я, и *f.* (*chem.*) magnesia.
магнетизёр, а *m.* (*obs.*) mesmerist.
магнетизи́р|овать, ую *impf.* (*obs.*) to mesmerize.
магнети́зм, а *m.* **1.** magnetism. **2.** (*phys.*) magnetics. **3.** (*obs.*) hypnotism.
магнети́т, а *m.* (*min.*) magnetite.
магнети́ческий *adj.* magnetic.
магне́то *nt. indecl.* (*tech.*) magneto.
магнетро́н, а *m.* (*radio*) magnetron.
ма́гниевый *adj.* magnesium.
ма́гни|й, я *m.* (*chem.*) magnesium.
магни́т, а *m.* magnet.
магни́тный *adj.* magnetic; **м. железня́к** magnetite, lodestone.
магнито́л|а, ы *f.* radio cassette (recorder); **крупногабари́тная м.** large radio cassette (recorder); 'ghetto blaster'.
магнитоле́нт|а, ы *f.* magnetic tape.
магнитоте́к|а, и *f.* tape library.
магнитофо́н, а *m.* tape-recorder, tape-recording machine; **видеокассе́тный м.** video (cassette) recorder, VCR; **кату́шечный м.** reel-to-reel tape-recorder; **м.-пле́йер** personal stereo, Walkman (*propr.*).
магнитофо́н|ный *adj. of* **~**; **~ная за́пись** tape-recording.
магнито-электри́ческий *adj.* electromagnetic.
магно́ли|я, и *f.* (*bot.*) magnolia.
магомета́н|ин, ина, *pl.* **~е, ~** *m.* Mohammedan.
магомета́нств|о, а *nt.* Mohammedanism.
маго́т, а *m.* Barbary ape.
Мадагаска́р, а *m.* Madagascar.
мада́м *f. indecl.* **1.** madam(e). **2.** (*obs., coll.*) governess. **3.** (*obs.*) dressmaker.
Маде́йр|а, ы *f.* Madeira.
мадемуазе́л|ь, и *f.* **1.** mademoiselle. **2.** (*obs., coll.*) governess.
маде́р|а, ы *f.* Madeira (wine).
маджо́нг, а *m.* mah-jong.
мадо́нн|а, ы *f.* madonna.
мадрига́л, а *m.* madrigal.
Мадри́д, а *m.* Madrid.
мадья́р, а, *pl.* **~ы, ~** *m.* Magyar.
мадья́рский *adj.* Magyar.
маёвк|а, и *f.* **1.** May Day meeting (*workers' gathering on 1 May, illegal before the 1917 Russ. revolution*). **2.** springtime outing, picnic.
мает|а́, ы́ *f.* (*coll.*) trouble, bother.
мажо́р, а *m.* **1.** (*mus.*) major key. **2.** (*fig.*) a cheerful mood; **быть в ~е** to be in high spirits.
мажордо́м, а *m.* major-domo.
мажо́рный *adj.* **1.** (*mus.*) major. **2.** (*fig.*) cheerful.
ма́занк|а, и *f.* (*dial.*) cottage of daubed brick or wood (*esp. in southern Russia*).
ма́заный *adj.* **1.** (*coll.*) dirty, stained, soiled. **2.** adobe.
ма́|зать, жу, жешь *impf.* **1.** (*pf.* **на~, по~**) to oil, grease, lubricate. **2.** (*pf.* **вы́~, на~, по~**) to smear (with), anoint (with); **м. хлеб ма́слом** to spread butter on bread, butter bread; **м. по губа́м** (*fig., coll.*) to excite false expectations. **3.** (*pf.* **за~, из~**; *coll.*) to soil, stain. **4.** (*pf.* **на~**; *coll.*) to daub. **5.** (*pf.* **про~**[2]; *coll.*) to miss (*in shooting, football, etc.*)
ма́|заться, жусь, жешься *impf.* **1.** (*pf.* **вы́~, за~, из~**) to soil o.s., stain o.s. **2.** (*coll.*) to soil, stain (*of objects; intrans.*). **3.** (*pf.* **на~, по~**) to make up; **она́ си́льно ~жется** (*coll.*) she makes up heavily.
мази́лк|а[1]**, и** *f.* paint-brush.
мази́лк|а[2]**, и** *c.g.* (*coll., pej.*) dauber.
ма́з|кий (~ок, ~ка́, ~ко) *adj.* (*coll.*) liable to stain, soil (*of newly-painted wall, etc.*).
мазн|у́ть, у́, ёшь *pf.* **1.** to dab. **2.** (*coll.*) to hit.
мазн|я́, и́ *f.* (*coll.*) **1.** daub. **2.** poor play.
маз|о́к, ка́ *m.* **1.** dab; stroke (*of paint-brush*); **класть после́дние ~ки́** (*fig.*) to put the finishing touches. **2.** (*med.*) smear (*for microscopic examination*). **3.** (*coll.*) miss (*in shooting, football, etc.*).
мазохи́зм, а *m.* (*med.*) masochism.
мазохи́ст, а *m.* masochist.
мазу́рик, а *m.* (*sl.*) rogue, swindler.
мазу́рк|а, и *f.* mazurka.
мазу́т, а *m.* (*tech.*) fuel oil
маз|ь, и *f.* **1.** ointment. **2.** grease; **де́ло на ~и́** (*fig., coll.*) things are going swimmingly.
маи́с, а *m.* maize.
маи́с|овый *adj. of* **~**; **~овая ка́ша** polenta.
ма|й, я *m.* May.
майда́н, а *m.* **1.** public square. **2.** (*sl.*) gambling-den (*in bazaar or prison*).
ма́йк|а, и *f.* **м.(-безрука́вка)** singlet; **м. (-полурука́вка)** T-shirt; **се́тчатая м.** string vest.
ма́йна *int.* (*naut.*) heave-ho!
майо́лик|а, и *f.* majolica.

майоне́з, а *m.* (*cul.*) mayonnaise.
майо́р, а *m.* major (*mil. rank*).
майора́н, а *m.* (*bot.*) marjoram.
майора́т, а *m.* (*leg.*) **1.** (right of) primogeniture. **2.** entailed estate.
Майо́рка = Мальо́рка
майо́р|ский *adj. of* ~
ма́й|ский *adj. of* ~; **м. жук** may-bug, cockchafer.
ма́йя *c.g. indecl. and adj. indecl.* Maya.
мак, а *m.* **1.** poppy. **2.** (*collect.*) poppy-seed.
мака́к|а, и *f.* (*zool.*) macaque.
мака́о *m. indecl. and nt. indecl.* **1.** *m.* (*zool.*) macaw. **2.** *nt.* macao (*gambling game*).
Мака́р: куда́ М. теля́т не гоня́л to the back of beyond.
макарони́зм, а *m.* (*liter.*) macaronism.
макарони́ческий *adj.* (*liter.*) macaronic.
макаро́нник, а *m.* baked macaroni pudding.
макаро́н|ный *adj. of* **~ы**
макаро́н|ы, ~ *pl.* (*sg.* **~а, ~ы** *f.*) macaroni.
мак|а́ть, а́ю *impf.* (*of* **~ну́ть**) to dip.
македо́н|ец, ца *m.* Macedonian.
Македо́ни|я, и *f.* Macedonia.
македо́н|ка, ки *f. of* **~ец**
македо́нский *adj.* Macedonian; **Александр ~** Alexander the Great.
маке́т, а *m.* **1.** model. **2.** (*mil.*) dummy.
макиавелли́зм, а *m.* Machiavellianism.
макиавеллисти́ческий *adj.* Machiavellian.
макинто́ш, а *m.* mackintosh.
маккарти́зм, а *m.* (*pol.*) McCarthyism.
маккарти́ст, а *m.* (*pol.*) McCarthyite.
макла́к, а́ *m.* (*obs.*) **1.** second-hand dealer. **2.** jobber, middleman.
макла́честв|о, а *nt.* (*obs.*) **1.** second-hand dealing. **2.** jobbing.
ма́клер, а *m.* (*comm.*) broker.
ма́клерств|о, а *nt.* (*comm.*) brokerage.
мак|ну́ть, ну́, нёшь *pf. of* **~а́ть**
ма́ковк|а, и *f.* **1.** poppy-head. **2.** (*coll.*) crown (*of head*). **3.** (*coll.*) cupola.
ма́к|овый *adj. of* ~; *as n.* **~овые, ~овых** (*bot.*) Papaveraceae; (*fig., coll.*): **как ~ов цвет** blooming, ruddy (*of complexion*).
макраме́ *nt. indecl.* macramé.
макрамэ́ = макраме́
макре́л|ь, и *f.* mackerel.
макроко́см, а *m.* macrocosm.
макроскопи́ческий *adj.* macroscopic.
макроцефа́ли|я, и *f.* (*anthrop.*) macrocephalism.
ма́кси *nt. indecl.* maxi (*garment*); **ма́кси-ю́бка** maxi-skirt.
макси́м, а *m.* Maxim gun.
ма́ксим|а, ы *f.* maxim.
максимали́зм, а *m.* (*hist.*) maximalism.
максимали́ст, а *m.* (*hist.*) maximalist.
максима́льный *adj.* maximum.
макси́мк|а, и *f.* (*coll.*) slow train.
ма́ксимум, а *m.* **1.** maximum. **2.** *as adv.* at most; **м. сто рубле́й** a hundred roubles at most.
макулату́р|а, ы *f.* **1.** (*typ.*) spoiled sheet(s), spoilage. **2.** (*fig.*) pulp literature. **3.** paper for recycling.
маку́шк|а, и *f.* **1.** top, summit. **2.** crown (*of head*); **у нас у́шки на ~е** (*fig.*) we are on the qui vive, on our guard.
Мала́ви *nt. indecl.* Malawi.
Ма́лаг|а, и *f.* Malaga.
мала́г|а, и *f.* Malaga (wine).
малагаси́|ец, йца *m.* Malagasy.
малагаси́|йка, йки *f. of* **~ец**
Малагаси́йск|ая Респу́блик|а, ~ой ~и *f.* the Malagasy Republic.
малагаси́йский *adj.* Malagasy.
мала́|ец, йца *m.* Malay.
Мала́йзи|я, и *f.* Malaysia.
мала́|йка, йки *f. of* **~ец**
мала́йский *adj.* Malay, Malayan.
Мала́й|я, и *f.* Malaya.
малаха́|й, я *m.* (*dial.*) malakhai (= **1.** *fur cap with large ear-flaps.* **2.** *beltless caftan*).
малахи́т, а *m.* (*min.*) malachite.
мал|ева́ть, ю́ю, ю́ешь *impf.* (*of* **на~**) **1.** (*coll.*) to paint; **не так стра́шен чёрт, как его́ ~ю́ют** (*prov.*) the devil is not so black as he is painted.
мале́йший *adj.* (*superl. of* **ма́лый**) least, slightest.
мал|ёк, ька́ *m.* young fish; (*collect.*) fry.
ма́леньк|ий *adj.* **1.** little, small; **~ие лю́ди** humble folk; **игра́ть по ~ой** to play for small stakes; **идти́ по ~ому** (*baby talk*) to do a wee-wee. **2.** slight; diminutive **3.** young; *as n.* **м., ~ого** *m.*, **~ая, ~ой** *f.* the baby, the child; **~ие** the young.
мале́нько *adv.* (*coll.*) a little, a bit.
ма́л|е́ц, ьца-ьца́ *m.* (*coll.*) lad, boy.
Мали́ *nt. indecl.* Mali.
мали́|ец, йца *m.* Malian.
мали́|йка, йки *f. of* **~ец**
мали́йский *adj.* Malian.
мали́н|а, ы *no pl., f.* **1.** (*collect.*) raspberries. **2.** raspberry-bush; raspberry-cane. **3.** raspberry juice. **4.** *fig., coll. of sth. pleasurable* (*cf.* '*a piece of cake*'); **у нас житьё — м.** we are in clover.
мали́нник, а *no pl. m.* raspberry-canes.
мали́н|ный *adj. of* **~а**
мали́новк|а[1]**, и** *f.* (*zool.*) robin (redbreast).
мали́новк|а[2]**, и** *f.* (*coll.*) raspberry-flavoured vodka.
мали́новый[1] *adj.* **1.** raspberry. **2.** crimson.
мали́новый[2] *adj. only in phr.* **м. звон** mellow chime.
ма́лк|а, и *f.* (*tech.*) bevel.
ма́ло *adv.* little few; not enough; **у нас м. вре́мени** we have little time; **э́того ма́ло** this is not enough; **об э́том м. кто зна́ет** few (people) know about it; **я м. где быва́л** I have been in few places; **м. ли что!** what does it matter!; **м. ли что мо́жет случи́ться** who knows what may happen, anything may happen; **м. того́** moreover; **м. того́, что...** not only ..., it is not enough that ...; **м. того́, что он сам прие́хал, он привёз всех това́рищей** it was not enough that he came himself, but he had to bring all his friends.
малоазиа́тский *adj.* of Asia minor.
малоблагоприя́т|ный (~ен. ~на) *adj.* unfavourable.
малова́ж|ный (~ен, ~на) *adj.* of little importance, insignificant.
малова́т (~а, ~о) *adj.* (*coll.*) on the small side; **м. ро́стом** undersized.
малова́то *adv.* (*coll.*) not quite enough; not very much.
малове́р, а *m.* sceptic.
малове́ри|е, я *nt.* lack of faith, scepticism.
малове́р|ный (~ен, ~на) *adj.* lacking faith, lacking conviction, sceptical.
маловероя́т|ный (~ен, ~на) *adj.* unlikely, improbable.
малове́с|ный (~ен, ~на) *adj.* light-weight; (*comm.*) light, short-weight.
маловóдный *adj.* containing little water; shallow; dry (*of land*).
малово́дь|е, я *nt.* **1.** shortage of water. **2.** low water-level, shallowness.
малвы́год|ный (~ен, ~на) *adj.* unprofitable, unrewarding.
малоговоря́щий *adj.* not enlightening, not illuminating.
малогра́мот|ный (~ен, ~на) *adj.* **1.** semiliterate. **2.** crude, ignorant.
малодействи́тел|ьный (~ен, ~ьна) *adj.* ineffective.
малодоказа́тел|ьный (~ен, ~ьна) *adj.* not persuasive, unconvincing.
малодостове́р|ный (~ен, ~на) *adj.* improbable; not well-founded.
малодохо́д|ный (~ен, ~на) *adj.* unprofitable.
малоду́шеств|овать, ую *impf.* to lose heart; to be faint-hearted.
малоду́ши|е, я *nt.* faint-heartedness, pusillanimity.
малоду́ш|ный (~ен, ~на) *adj.* faint-hearted, pusillanimous.
малое́зжен(н)ый *adj.* **1.** (*of horse, etc.*) little ridden; (*of carriage*) little used. **2.** (*of road*) little used, unfrequented.

малоéзж|ий *adj.* = ~**ен(н)ый 2.**
маложи́р|ный (~**ен,** ~**нá,** ~**но**) *adj.* low-fat.
малозамéт|ный (~**ен,** ~**на**) *adj.* **1.** barely visible, barely noticeable. **2.** ordinary, undistinguished.
малоземéль|е, я *nt.* shortage of (arable) land
малоземéльный *adj.* having insufficient (arable) land.
малознакóм|ый (~, ~**а**) *adj.* little-known, unfamiliar.
малознaчи́тел|ьный (~**ен,** ~**ьна**) *adj.* of little significance, of little importance.
малоизвéданный *adj.* little-known.
малоимýщ|ий (~, ~**а**) *adj.* needy, indigent.
малокали́берный *adj.* small-calibre; (*of fire-arm*) small-bore.
малокалори́йный *adj.* low-calorie.
малокрóви|е, я *nt.* anaemia.
малокрóв|ный (~**ен,** ~**на**) *adj.* anaemic.
малолéтн|ий *adj.* **1.** young; juvenile. **2.** *as n.* **м.,** ~**его** *m.* infant; juvenile, minor.
малолéтств|о, а *nt.* infancy; nonage, minority.
малолитрáжк|а, и *f.* (*coll.*) compact (car); mini.
малолитрáжный *adj.* of small (*cylinder*) capacity; **м. автомоби́ль** compact (car); mini.
малолю́дност|ь, и *f.* scarcity of people; poor attendance (*at meeting, etc.*).
малолю́д|ный (~**ен,** ~**на**) *adj.* **1.** not crowded, unfrequented; ~**ное собрáние** poorly attended meeting. **2.** thinly populated.
малолю́д|ье, ья *nt.* = ~**ность**
мало-мáльски *adv.* (*coll.*) in the slightest degree, at all.
маломáльский *adj.* (*coll.*) slightest, most insignificant.
малометрáжн|ый *adj.*: ~**ая кварти́ра** small flat.
маломóч|ный (~**ен,** ~**на**) *adj.* (*econ.*) having small resources; ~**ные крестья́не** poor peasants.
маломóщ|ный *adj.* lacking power; ~**ное предприя́тие** small concern.
малонадёжный *adj.* unreliable, undependable.
малонаселённый *adj.* thinly, sparsely populated.
малообеспéченный *adj.* needy, poverty-stricken.
малообщи́тел|ьный (~**ен,** ~**на**) *adj.* unsociable, uncommunicative.
малооплáчиваемый *adj.* low-paid, badly-paid (*of work*).
малосновáтел|ьный (~**ен,** ~**ьна**) *adj.* **1.** unfounded. **2.** (*of pers.*) undependable.
малоподви́ж|ный (~**ен,** ~**на**) *adj.* not mobile, slow-moving.
малоподéржанный *adj.* little used, almost unused.
мало-помáлу *adv.* (*coll.*) little by little, bit by bit.
малопоня́тлив|ый (~, ~**а**) *adj.* (*coll.*) not very bright, slow in the uptake.
малопоня́т|ный (~**ен,** ~**на**) *adj.* hard to understand; obscure.
малопри́был|ьный (~**ен,** ~**ьна**) *adj.* bringing little profit, of little profit.
малопригóд|ный (~**ен,** ~**на**) *adj.* of little use.
малорáзвит|ый (~, ~**а**) *adj.* **1.** undeveloped. **2.** underdeveloped. **3.** uneducated.
малоразговóрчив|ый (~, ~**а**) *adj.* taciturn.
малорóсл|ый (~, ~**а**) *adj.* undersized, stunted.
малорóсс, а *m.* (*obs.*) Little Russian (*Ukrainian*).
малоросси́йский *adj.* (*obs.*) Little Russian (*Ukrainian*).
Малорóсси|я, и *f.* (*obs.*) Little Russia, Ruthenia.
малороссия́н|ин, ина, *pl.* ~**е** *m.* = **малорóсс**
мало|рýсский *adj.* = ~**росси́йский**
малосвéдущ|ий (~, ~**а**) *adj.* ill-informed.
малосемéйный *adj.* having a small family.
малоси́л|ьный (~**ен,** ~**ьна**) *adj.* **1.** weak, feeble. **2.** (*tech.*) low-powered.
малосодержáтел|ьный (~**ен,** ~**ьна**) *adj.* uninteresting; (*fig.*) empty, shallow.
малосóл|ьный (~**ен,** ~**ьна**) *adj.* slightly, inadequately salted.
малосостоя́тел|ьный[1] (~**ен,** ~**ьна**) *adj.* poor, poorer.
малосостоя́тел|ьный[2] (~**ен,** ~**ьна**) *adj.* unconvincing.
мáлост|ь, и *f.* (*coll.*) **1.** a bit; trifle, bagatelle. **2.** *as adv.* a little, a bit; **м. поспáть** to take a nap.
малосущéствен|ный (~, ~**на**) *adj.* of small importance, immaterial.
малотирáжн|ый *adj.* small-circulation; ~**ое издáние** limited edition.
малоубеди́тел|ьный (~**ен,** ~**ьна**) *adj.* unconvincing.
малоупотреби́тел|ьный (~**ен,** ~**ьна**) *adj.* infrequent, rarely used.
малоуспéш|ный (~**ен,** ~**на**) *adj.* unsuccessful.
малоформáтный *adj.* miniature.
малоцéн|ный (~**ен,** ~**на**) *adj.* of little value.
малочи́сленност|ь, и *f.* small number; paucity.
малочи́слен|ный (~, ~**на**) *adj.* small (in numbers); scanty.
мáл|ый[1] (~, ~**á,** ~**ó**) *adj.* little, (too) small; **м. рóстом** short, of small stature; **м. ход!** (*naut.*) slow speed (ahead)!; **э́ти сапоги́ мне** ~**ы** these boots are too small for me; ~ ~**á мéньше** (*coll.*) *of children of one family, viewed in descending order of size*; **от** ~**а до вели́ка** young and old (*i.e. all, regardless of age*); **по** ~**ой мéре** at least; **с** ~**ых лет** from childhood; *as n.* ~**ое,** ~**ого** *nt.* little; **сáмое** ~**ое** (*coll.*) at the least; **без** ~**ого** almost, all but; **за** ~**ым дéло стáло** (*frequently iron.*) one small thing is lacking.
мáл|ый[2], **ого** *m.* (*coll.*) fellow, chap; lad, boy.
малы́ш, á *m.* (*coll.*) child, kid; little boy.
мáльв|а, ы *f.* (*bot.*) mallow, hollyhock.
мальв|á, ы́ *f.* (*collect., coll.*) children, kids.
мальвáзи|я, и *f.* malmsey (*wine*).
Мальóрк|а, и *f.* Majorca.
Мáльт|а, ы *f.* Malta.
мальти́|ец, йца *m.* Maltese.
мальти́|йка, йки *f. of* ~**ец**
мальти́йский *adj.* Maltese.
мальтузиáнский *adj.* Malthusian.
мальтузиáнств|о, а *nt.* Malthusianism.
мáльчик, а *m.* **1.** boy, lad; (male) child; **м. с пáльчик** Tom Thumb. **2.** (*obs.*) apprentice.
мальчикóвый *adj.* boy's, boys'.
мальчи́шеский *adj.* **1.** boyish. **2.** (*pej.*) childish, puerile.
мальчи́шеств|о, а *nt.* boyishness; (*pej.*) childishness.
мальчи́шк|а, и *m.* (*coll.*) urchin, boy; **в сравнéнии с одноклáссниками он м.** in comparison with his classmates he is a child.
мальчи́шник, а *m.* stag-party.
мальчугáн, а *m.* (*coll., affectionate*) little boy.
малю́сенький *adj.* (*coll.*) tiny, wee.
малю́тк|а, и *c.g.* baby, tot.
маля́р, á *m.* (house-)painter, decorator.
маляри́йный *adj.* malarial.
маляри́|я, и *f.* (*med.*) malaria.
маля́р|ный *adj. of* ~
мáм|а, ы *f.* mummy, mamma.
мамалы́г|а, и *f.* (*dial.*) polenta.
мамáш|а, и *f.* (*coll.*) mummy, mamma.
мамелю́к, а *m.* (*hist.*) Mameluke.
мáменькин *adj.* mother's; **м. сынóк** (*coll., iron.*) mother's darling.
мáмин *adj.* mother's.
мáмк|а, и *f.* (*obs.*) (wet-)nurse.
мамóн|а, ы *f.* Mammon.
мáмонт, а *m.* mammoth.
мáмонт|овый *adj. of* ~; ~**овое дéрево** (*bot.*) sequoia, Wellingtonia.
мáмочк|а, и *f.* (*coll.*) mummy.
манáт|ки, ок *no sg.* (*sl.*) possessions, goods and chattels.
манат|ья́, ьи́, *g. pl.* ~**éй** *f.* monk's habit.
мангани́т, а *m.* (*min.*) manganite.
мáнго *nt. indecl.* (*bot.*) mango.
мáнго|вый *adj. of* ~
мáнгровый *adj.* (*bot.*) mangrove.
мангýст|а, ы *f.* (*zool.*) mongoose.
мандари́н[1], **а** *m.* mandarin (*Chinese official*).
мандари́н[2], **а** *m.* mandarin(e), tangerine.
мандари́н|ный *adj. of* ~[2]
мандари́н|овый *adj.* = ~**ный**
мандари́н|ский *adj. of* ~[1]
мандáт, а *m.* **1.** warrant. **2.** (*pol.*) mandate; credentials.

мандáт|ный *adj.* *of* **~**; **~ная комиссия** credentials committee; **~ная систéма голосовáния** card vote system; **~ная террито́рия** mandated territory.
мандоли́н|а, ы *f.* (*mus.*) mandolin(e).
мандолини́ст, а *m.* mandolin(e)-player.
мандрагóр|а, ы *f.* (*bot.*) mandrake.
мандрáж, á *m.* (*coll.*) butterflies, the jitters.
мандри́л, а *m.* (*zool.*) mandrill.
манёвр, а *m.* **1.** (*in var. senses*) manœuvre; (*pl.*; *mil.*) manœuvres. **2.** (*pl.*) shunting.
манёвренност|ь, и *f.* manœuvrability.
манёвр|енный *adj.* *of* **~**; **~енная войнá** war of movement; **~енный самолёт** manœuvrable aircraft; **м. паровóз** shunting engine.
маневри́р|овать, ую *impf.* (*of* **с~**) **1.** to manœuvre. **2.** (*+i.*) to make good use (of), use to advantage. **3.** (*rail.*) to shunt.
маневрóвый *adj.* (*rail.*) shunting.
манéж, а *m.* **1.** riding-school, manège. **2.** (*circus*) ring; **инспéктор ~а** ringmaster. **3. спорти́вный м.** sports hall. **4. (дéтский) м.** play-pen.
манéжик, а *m.* play-pen.
манéж|ить, у, ишь *impf.* **1.** to break in (*a horse*). **2.** (*fig.*, *coll.*) to tire out (*with waiting*).
манекéн, а *m.* lay figure, dummy.
манекéнщик, а *m.* male model.
манекéнщиц|а, ы *f.* mannequin.
манéр, а *m.* (*coll.*) manner; **таки́м ~ом** in this manner, in this way; **на англи́йский м.** in the English manner.
манéр|а, ы *f.* **1.** manner, style; **м. вести́ себя́** way of behaving; **м. держáть себя́** bearing, carriage; **у негó неприя́тная м. опáздывать на свидáния** he has an unpleasant way of being late for appointments; **петь в ~е Карýзо** to sing in the style of Caruso. **2.** (*pl.*) manners; **у негó плохи́е ~ы** he has no manners.
манéрк|а, и *f.* (*mil.*) mess tin.
манéрнича|ть, ю *impf.* (*coll.*) to behave affectedly.
манéрност|ь, и *f.* affectation; preciosity.
манéр|ный (~ен, ~на) *adj.* affected; precious.
манжéт|а, ы *f.* cuff.
маниакáльный *adj.* maniacal.
мáни|е, я *nt.* (*arch.*) *now only in phrr.* **~ем, по ~ю (руки́, жезлá** *etc.***)** with a motion (*of the hand*, *the baton*, *etc.*); (*fig.*): **по ~ю (богóв, царя́** *etc.***)** by the will (of the gods, the Tsar, *etc.*).
маникю́р, а *m.* manicure.
маникю́рш|а, и *f.* manicurist.
Мани́л|а, ы *f.* Manila.
мани́льск|ий *adj.*: **~ая бумáга** Manil(l)a paper.
манипули́р|овать, ую *impf.* to manipulate.
манипуля́ци|я, и *f.* **1.** manipulation. **2.** (*fig.*) machination, intrigue.
ман|и́ть, ю́, ~́ишь *impf.* **1.** (*pf.* **по~**) to beckon. **2.** (*pf.* **вз~**) (*fig.*) to attract; to lure, allure.
манифéст, а *m.* manifesto; proclamation.
манифестáнт, а *m.* (*pol.*, *etc.*) demonstrator.
манифестáци|я, и *f.* (street) demonstration.
манифести́р|овать, ую *impf. and pf.* to demonstrate, take part in a demonstration.
мани́шк|а, и *f.* (false) shirt-front, dicky.
мáни|я, и *f.* **1.** mania; **м. вели́чия** megalomania. **2.** (*fig.*) passion, craze; **у неё м. противорéчить** she has a passion for contradicting.
манки́р|овать, ую *impf. and pf.* **1.** (*+i.*) to neglect. **2.** to be absent; (*+a.*; *obs.*) to miss, be absent from. **3.** (*+d.*; *obs.*) to be impolite to.
мáнн|а, ы *f.* manna; **ждать (***+g.***) как ~ы небéсной** to await with impatience; **питáться ~ой небéсной** (*joc.*) to be half-starved.
мáнн|ый *adj.*: **~ая крупá** semolina.
мановéни|е, я *nt.* (*obs.*) beck, nod; **~ем руки́** with a wave of one's hand.
манóметр, а *m.* (*tech.*) pressure-gauge, manometer.
манометри́ческий *adj.* (*tech.*) manometric.
мансáрд|а, ы *f.* attic, garret.
манти́ль|я, и *f.* mantilla.
манти́сс|а, ы *f.* (*math.*) mantissa.
мáнти|я, и *f.* cloak, mantle; robe, gown.
мантó *nt. indecl.* (*lady's*) coat.
манускри́пт, а *m.* manuscript.
мануфактýр|а, ы *f.* **1.** manufactory. **2.** (*obs.*) textile mill. **3.** (*sg. only*; *collect.*) cotton textiles.
мануфактýр|ный *adj.* *of* **~а**
манчéстер, а *m.* (*text.*) velveteen.
маньчжýр, а *m.* Manchu; Manchurian.
Маньчжýри|я, и *f.* Manchuria.
маньчжýр|ский *adj.* *of* **~**
маньяк, а *m.* maniac, pers. in the grip of an obsession.
маои́зм, а *m.* Maoism.
маои́стский *adj.* Maoist.
мáори *c.g. indecl.* Maori.
маори́йский *adj.* Maori.
марабý *nt. indecl.* (*zool.*) marabou.
марáзм, а *m.* (*med.*) marasmus; **стáрческий м.** senility, dotage; (*fig.*) decay.
марак|овáть, ýю *impf.* (*coll.*) to have some notion (about), be not completely at sea.
марáл, а *m.* (*zool.*) Siberian deer.
маraски́н, а *m.* maraschino (*liqueur*).
марáтел|ь, я *m.* (*coll.*) dauber; scribbler.
марá|ть, ю *impf.* (*coll.*) **1.** (*pf.* **за~**) to soil, dirty; (*fig.*) to sully, stain; **м. рýки (о***+a.***)** to soil one's hands (on). **2.** (*pf.* **на~**) to daub; to scribble. **3.** (*pf.* **вы~**) to cross out, strike out.
марá|ться, юсь *impf.* (*coll.*) **1.** (*pf.* **за~**) to soil o.s., get dirty. **2.** (*no pf.*) to be dirty; to stain (*intrans.*). **3.** (*no pf.*; *fig.*) to soil one's hands. **4.** (*of infants*; *euph.*) to soil o.s., make a mess. **5.** *pass. of* **~ть**
марафéт, а *m.* **1.** (*sl.*) coke (= *cocaine*). **2.: навести́ м.** to spruce *or* tidy up.
марафóн|ец, ца *m.* marathon runner.
марафóнский *adj.*: **м. бег** (*sport*) Marathon race.
марáшк|а, и *f.* (*typ.*) turn.
мáрган|ец, ца *m.* (*chem.*) manganese.
мáрган|цевый *adj.* *of* **~ец**
марганцóвистый *adj.* (*chem.*) manganous, manganic.
марганцóвый *adj.* = **мáрганцевый**
маргари́н, а *m.* margarine.
маргари́н|овый *adj.* *of* **~**; (*fig.*) bogus, ersatz.
маргари́тк|а, и *f.* (*bot.*) daisy.
маргинáли|и, ев *and* **ий** *no sg.* marginalia.
мáрев|о, а *nt.* **1.** mirage. **2.** heat haze.
марéн|а, ы *f.* (*bot.*) madder.
марéнго *adj. indecl.* black flecked with grey.
мáри *indecl.* (*collect.*) the Mari (*inhabitants of Mari Autonomous Republic in former USSR, formerly the Cheremis*).
мари́|ец, йца *m.* Mari.
мари́йский *adj.* Mari.
мари́н|а, ы *f.* (*art*) seascape.
мари́нáд, а *m.* marinade; pickles.
марини́ст, а *m.* painter of seascapes.
маринóв|анный *p.p.p. of* **~áть** *and adj.* (*cul.*) pickled.
марин|овáть, ýю *impf.* **1.** (*pf.* **за~**) to pickle. **2.** (*pf.* **про~**) (*fig.*, *coll.*) to put off, shelve.
марионéт|ка, ки *f.* marionette; puppet (*also fig.*); **теáтр ~ок** puppet-theatre.
марионéт|очный *adj.* *of* **~ка**; **~очное госудáрство** puppet state.
марихуáн|ец, ца *m.* (*coll.*) pot smoker; hash-head.
мáрк|а[1], и *f.* **1.** (postage-)stamp. **2.** (*monetary unit in Germany and Finland*) mark. **3.** mark; brand; **фабри́чная м.** trade-mark; **какóй мáрки?** what make? **4.** counter. **5.** grade, sort, brand; **товáр вы́сшей ~и** goods of the highest grade. **6.** (*fig.*) name, reputation; **держáть ~у** to maintain one's reputation.
мáрк|а[2], и *f.* (*hist.*) mark (*medieval German territorial unit or rural commune*).
маркгрáф, а *m.* (*hist.*) margrave.
маркёр, а *m.* (*in var. senses*) marker.

ма́рке́тинг, а *m.* marketing.
маркетри́ *indecl. adj. and nt. n.* marquetry.
марки́з, а *m.* marquis, marquess.
марки́з|а[1], **ы** *f.* marchioness.
марки́з|а[2], **ы** *f.* sun-blind; awning; marquee.
маркизе́т, а *m.* (*text.*) voile.
маркизе́т|овый *adj. of* ~
ма́р|кий (~ок, ~ка) *adj.* easily soiled.
маркир|ова́ть, у́ю *impf. and pf.* (*in var. senses*) to mark; to brand.
маркита́нт, а *m.* (*hist.*) sutler.
маркси́зм, а *m.* Marxism.
маркси́зм-ленини́зм, а-а *m.* Marxism-Leninism.
маркси́ст, а *m.* Marxist.
маркси́стский *adj.* Marxist, Marxian.
маркси́стско-ле́нинский *adj.* Marxist-Leninist.
маркше́йдер, а *m.* mine-surveyor.
маркше́йдер|ский *adj. of* ~; **~ская съёмка** mine surveying.
ма́рл|евый *adj. of* **~я**; **м. бинт** gauze bandage.
ма́рл|я, и *f.* gauze; cheesecloth.
мармела́д, а *m.* fruit jelly (*sweets*).
мармори́р|овать, ую *impf. and pf.* (*tech.*) to marble.
мародёр, а *m.* marauder, pillager.
мародёрск|ий *adj.* marauding; **~ие це́ны** (*fig., coll.*) exorbitant prices.
мародёрств|о, а *nt.* pillage, looting.
мародёрств|овать, ую *impf.* to maraud, pillage, loot.
мароке́н, а *m.* **1.** morocco(-leather). **2.** (*text.*) marocain.
мароке́н|овый *adj. of* ~
марокка́н|ец, ца *m.* Moroccan.
марокка́н|ка, ки *f. of* **~ец**
марокка́нский *adj.* Moroccan.
Маро́кко *nt. indecl.* Morocco.
ма́р|очный *adj. of* **~ка**[1]; **~очное вино́** fine wine.
марс[1], **а** *m.* (*naut.*) top.
Марс[2], **а** *m.* (*astron., myth.*) Mars (*in myth. sense, a.* **~а**).
марсал|а́, ы́ *f.* Marsala (*wine*).
Марсе́л|ь, я *m.* Marseilles.
ма́рсел|ь, я *m.* (*naut.*) topsail.
Марселье́з|а, ы *f.* Marseillaise.
марсиа́н|ин, ина, *pl.* **~е, ~** *m.* Martian.
ма́рс|овый *adj. of* **~**[1]
март, а *m.* March.
марте́н, а *m.* (*tech.*) **1.** open-hearth furnace. **2.** open-hearth steel.
марте́новский *adj.* (*tech.*) open-hearth.
мартенси́т, а *m.* (*tech.*) martensite.
мартинга́л, а *m.* martingale.
мартироло́г, а *m.* martyrology.
ма́рт|овский *adj. of* ~
марты́шк|а, и *f.* marmoset; (*fig., coll.*) monkey.
марципа́н, а *m.* marzipan.
марш[1], **а** *m.* (*in var. senses*) march; **м. проте́ста** protest march; **м. голо́дных** hunger march.
марш[2] *int.* (*as word of command*) forward!; **ша́гом м.!** quick march!; (*coll.*) off you go!
марш[3], **а** *m.* flight of stairs.
ма́ршал, а *m.* marshal.
ма́ршал|ьский *adj. of* ~
ма́ршальств|о, а *nt.* rank of marshal.
ма́рш|евый *adj. of* **~**[1]; **м. поря́док** marching order; **~евые ча́сти** drafts, reinforcements.
маршир|ова́ть, у́ю *impf.* to march; **м. на ме́сте** to mark time.
марширо́вк|а, и *f.* marching.
марш-марш, а *m.* quick march.
маршру́т, а *m.* **1.** route, itinerary. **2.** through goods-train.
маршрутиза́ци|я, и *f.* conveyance by through goods-train.
маршру́тк|а, и *f.* (*coll.*) fixed-route taxi.
маршру́т|ный *adj. of* ~; **м. по́езд** through goods-train; **~ное такси́** fixed-route taxi.
маседуа́н, а *m.* (*cul.*) macedoine.
ма́ск|а, и *f.* mask; **противога́зовая м.** gas-mask; (*fig.*): **сбро́сить с себя́ ~у** to throw off the mask.
маскара́д, а *m.* masked ball, masquerade.
маскара́д|ный *adj. of* **~**; **м. костю́м** fancy dress.
Маска́т, а *m.* Muscat; **Ома́н и Маска́т** Muscat and Oman.
маскир|ова́ть, у́ю *impf.* (*of* **за~**) to mask, disguise; (*mil.*) to camouflage; **м. свои́ наме́рения** (*fig.*) to disguise one's intentions.
маскиро́вк|а, и *f.* masking, disguise; (*mil.*) camouflage.
ма́слениц|а, ы *f.* Shrove-tide; carnival; **не всё ко́ту м.,** *see* **кот**
ма́слени|чный *adj. of* **~ца**
маслёнк|а, и *f.* **1.** butter-dish. **2.** oil-can.
масл|ёнок, ёнка, *pl.* **~я́та, ~я́т** *m. Boletus lutens* (*edible mushroom*).
ма́слен|ый *adj.* **1.** buttered; oiled, oily, **~ая неде́ля** = **~ица**; **~ые кра́ски** = **ма́сло 3.**. **2.** (*fig., coll.*) oily, unctuous. **3.** (*fig., coll.*) voluptuous, sensual.
масли́н|а, ы *f.* **1.** olive-tree. **2.** olive.
ма́сл|ить, ю, ишь *impf.* (*of* **на~** *and* **по~**) **1.** to butter. **2.** to oil; to grease.
ма́сл|иться, ится *impf.* **1.** to leave greasy marks. **2.** (*coll.*) to shine; to glisten. **3.** *pass. of* **~ить**
ма́сличный *adj.* (*of plants*) oil-yielding.
масли́|чный *adj. of* **~на**; **М~чная гора́** Mount of Olives.
ма́с|ло, ла, *pl.* **~ла́, ~ел, ~ла́м** *nt.* **1. (сли́вочное)** butter; **топлёное м.** clarified butter. **2.** oil; **как по ~лу** (*fig., coll.*) swimmingly. **3.** oil (paints); **писа́ть ~лом** to paint in oils.
маслобо́йк|а, и *f.* **1.** churn. **2.** oil-press.
маслобо́йн|ый *adj.*: **м. заво́д** = **~я**
маслобо́|йня, йни, *g. pl.* **~ен** *f.* **1.** creamery. **2.** oil-mill.
маслоде́л, а *m.* **1.** butter manufacturer. **2.** oil manufacturer.
маслоде́ли|е, я *nt.* **1.** butter manufacturing. **2.** oil manufacturing.
маслозаво́д, а *m.* **1.** creamery, butter-dairy. **2.** oil-mill.
масломе́р, а *m.* oil gauge; dipstick.
маслопрово́д, а *m.* oil pipe, oil pipe-line.
маслоро́дный *adj.*: **м. газ** (*chem.*) ethylene.
маслосисте́м|а, ы *f.* lubrication system.
масляни́ст|ый (~, ~а) *adj.* fatty; **м. сыр** full-fat cheese.
ма́сл|яный *adj. of* **~о**; **~яная кислота́** (*chem.*) butyric acid; **~яные кра́ски** oil paints.
масо́н, а *f.* Freemason, Mason.
масо́нский *adj.* Masonic.
масо́нств|о, а *nt.* Freemasonry.
ма́сс|а, ы *f.* **1.** (*in var. senses*) mass; *pl.* (*pol.*) the masses; **в ~е** on the whole, in the mass. **2.** (*ceramics*) paste. **3.: древе́сная м.** wood-pulp. **4.** (*coll.*) a lot, lots.
масса́ж, а *m.* massage; **то́чечный м.** shiatsu, acupressure.
массажи́ст, а *m.* masseur.
массажи́стк|а, и *f.* masseuse.
масси́в, а *m.* (*geog.*) massif, mountain-mass; (*fig.*) expanse; **жили́щный м.** housing unit; **лесно́й м.** forest tract.
масси́в|ный (~ен, ~на) *adj.* massive.
масси́ровани|е, я *nt.* massing, concentration.
масси́рова|нный *p.p.p. of* **~ть**[1] *and adj.* (*mil.*) massed, concentrated.
масси́р|овать[1], **ую** *impf. and pf.* (*mil.*) to mass, concentrate.
масси́р|овать[2], **ую** *impf. and pf.* to massage.
массови́к, а́ *m.* organizer of popular cultural and recreational activities.
массо́вк|а, и *f.* (*coll.*) **1.** mass meeting. **2.** group excursion. **3.** crowd scene (*in play, film*).
ма́ссов|ый *adj.* (*in var. senses*) mass; popular; **~ые аре́сты** mass arrests; **~ое произво́дство** mass production.
маста́к, а́ *m.* (*coll.*) expert, past master.
ма́стер, а, *pl.* **~а́** *m.* **1.** foreman. **2.** master craftsman, skilled workman; **золоты́х дел м.** goldsmith. **3.** **(на+***a.*, *or* +*inf.***)** expert, master (at, of); (*sport*) vet(eran); **м. (по ремо́нту)** repairman; **телевизио́нный м.** TV repairman; **м. на все ру́ки** all-round expert; **быть ~ом своего́ де́ла** to be an expert at one's job; **он м. танцева́ть вальс** he is an expert at the waltz.
мастер|и́ть, ю́, и́шь *impf.* (*of* **с~**) (*coll.*) to make, build; **мы ~и́м себе́ са́ни** we are making ourselves a sledge.
мастеров|о́й, о́го *m.* (*obs.*) workman, (factory-)hand.

мастерск|а́я, о́й *f.* workshop; studio; (*in factory*) shop; **авторемо́нтная м.** car repair garage.
мастерски́ *adv.* skilfully; in masterly fashion.
мастерско́й *adj.* masterly.
мастерств|о́, а́ *nt.* **1.** trade, craft. **2.** skill, craftsmanship.
масти́к|а, и *f.* **1.** mastic. **2.** putty. **3.** floor-polish.
масти́к|овый *adj. of* **~а; ~овое де́рево** mastic (tree).
масти́т, а *m.* (*med.*) mastitis.
масти́т|ый (~, ~а) *adj.* venerable; **м. учёный** old and eminent scholar.
мастодо́нт, а *m.* mastodon.
мастурби́р|овать, ую *impf.* to masturbate.
масты́рк|а, и *f.* (*drug sl.*) joint (= *marijuana cigarette*).
маст|ь, и, *pl.* **~и, ~е́й** *f.* **1.** colour (*of animal's hair or coat*). **2.** (*cards*) suit; **ходи́ть в м.** to follow suit.
масшта́б, а *m.* scale; **м. — две ми́ли в дю́йме** the scale is two miles to the inch; (*fig.*): **в большо́м, ма́леньком ~е** on a large, small scale; **конфли́кт большо́го ~а** large-scale conflict.
масшта́бност|ь, и *f.* (*fig.*) (large) scale, range, dimensions.
масшта́б|ный (~ен, ~на) *adj.* **1.** scale; **~ная моде́ль** scale model. **2.** large-scale.
мат[1], **а** *m.* (*chess*) checkmate, mate; **объяви́ть м.** (*+d.*) to mate.
мат[2], **а** *m.* (floor-, door-)mat.
мат[3], **а** *m.* mat (*roughened or frosted groundwork*); **нанести́ м.** (**на**+*a.*) to mat, frost.
мат[4], **а** *m.* (*coll.*) *only in phr.* **благи́м ~ом** at the top of one's voice.
мат[5], **а** *m.* foul language, abuse; **руга́ться ~ом** to use foul language.
матема́тик, а *m.* mathematician.
матема́тик|а, и *f.* mathematics.
математи́ческ|ий *adj.* mathematical; **~ое обеспе́чение** (*computer*) software.
матере́|ть, ю *impf.* (*coll.*) **1.** to grow to full size. **2.** (*fig.*) to become hardened.
матереуби́йств|о, а *nt.* matricide (*act*).
матереуби́йц|а, ы *c.g.* matricide (*agent*).
материа́л, а *m.* (*in var. senses*) material; stuff; **м. (для печа́тания)** copy; **гвоздево́й м.** feature (item).
материали́зм, а *m.* materialism.
материализ|ова́ть(ся), у́ю(сь) *impf. and pf.* to materialize (*trans. and intrans.*).
материали́ст, а *m.* materialist.
материалисти́ческий *adj.* (*phil.*) materialist.
материалисти́ч|ный (~ен, ~на) *adj.* (*pej.*) materialistic.
материа́льност|ь, и *f.* materiality.
материа́льно-техни́ческий *adj.* (*mil.*) logistical.
материа́л|ьный (~ен, ~ьна) *adj.* (*in var. senses*) material; **~ьная заинтересо́ванность** material incentive(s); **~ьные затрудне́ния** financial difficulties; **~ьное положе́ние** economic conditions; **~ьная часть** (*tech., mil.*) equipment, matériel.
матери́к, а́ *m.* **1.** continent, mainland. **2.** subsoil.
материко́вый *adj.* continental.
матери́нский *adj.* maternal, motherly.
матери́нств|о, а *nt.* maternity, motherhood.
матер|и́ться, ю́сь и́шься *impf.* (*coll.*) to use foul language.
мате́ри|я[1], **и** *f.* **1.** (*phil.*) matter. **2.** (*med.*) matter, pus. **3.** (*fig., coll.*) subject, topic (of conversation).
мате́ри|я[2], **и** *f.* (*text.*) material, cloth.
ма́терный *adj.* (*coll.*) obscene, abusive.
матеро́й *adj.* (*coll.*) full-grown, grown-up; **м. волк** (*fig.*) an old hand.
мате́рчатый *adj.* (*coll.*) made of cloth.
матерщи́н|а, ы *f.* (*coll.*) foul language.
матёрый *adj.* (*coll.*) **1.** experienced, practised. **2.** inveterate, out-and-out.
матине́ *nt. indecl.* **1.** matinée coat. **2.** (*obs.*) matinée.
ма́тиц|а, ы *f.* (*tech.*) tie-beam, joist.
ма́тк|а, и *f.* **1.** (*anat.*) uterus, womb. **2.** female (*of animals*); queen (bee). **3.** (*coll.*) mother. **4.** (*naut.*) (submarine) tender.
ма́тов|ый *adj.* mat(t); dull; suffused (*of light*); **~ое стекло́** frosted glass.
ма́точник, а *m.* **1.** queen bee's cell. **2.** (*bot.*) style, ovary.
ма́точн|ый *adj.* **1.** (*anat.*) uterine. **2.** (*min.*): **~ая поро́да** matrix.
матра́с, а *m.* mattress; **надувно́й м.** air bed, inflatable mattress.
матра́|ц = ~с
матрёшк|а, и *f.* matrioshka, (set of) nested Russian dolls.
матриарха́льный *adj.* matriarchal.
матриарха́т, а *m.* matriarchy.
матри́кул, а *m.* student's record card.
ма́триц|а, ы *f.* **1.** (*typ.*) matrix. **2.** (*tech.*) die, mould.
матрици́р|овать, ую *impf. and pf.* (*typ.*) to make matrix-moulds (of).
матро́с, а *m.* sailor, seaman.
матро́ск|а[1], **и** *f.* sailor's jacket.
матро́ск|а[2], **и** *f.* (*coll.*) sailor's wife.
ма́тушк|а, и *f.* (*coll.*) **1.** mother; **~и (мои́)!** *excl. of surprise or fright.* **2.** priest's wife. **3.** (*as familiar form of address to an elderly woman*) gran(ny), ma.
матч, а *m.* (*sport*) match; **междунаро́дный м.** (*cricket, rugby*) test (match); **повто́рный м.** rematch, return match.
мат|ь, *g., d., p.* **~ери, ~ерью,** *pl.* **~ери, ~ере́й** *f.* **1.** mother; **бу́дущая м.** expectant mother; **м.-одино́чка** single mother. **2.** (*coll.*) *familiar term of address to a woman.*
ма́ть-и-ма́чех|а, и *f.* (*bot.*) coltsfoot.
ма́узер, а *m.* Mauser (*automatic pistol or rifle*).
мафио́зи *m. indecl.* Mafioso.
мафио́зник, а *m.* (*coll.*) = **мафио́зи**
мафио́зо = мафио́зи
ма́фи|я, и *f.* Mafia.
мах, а (у) *m.* swing, stroke; (*coll.*): **дать ~у** to let a chance slip; to make a blunder; **одни́м ~ом, с одного́ ~у** at one stroke, in a trice; **с ~у** rashly, without thinking.
маха́льн|ый, ого *m.* (*mil., sport*) signaller.
ма|ха́ть, шу́, ~шешь *impf.* (*of* **~хну́ть**) (*+i.*) to wave; to brandish; to wag; to flap.
махи́н|а, ы *f.* (*coll.*) bulky and cumbersome object.
махина́тор, а *m.* (*coll.*) schemer, wangler.
махина́ци|я, и *f.* machination, intrigue.
мах|ну́ть, ну́, нёшь *pf.* **1.** *pf. of* **~а́ть; м. руко́й (на**+*a.*) (*fig., coll.*) to give up as a bad job. **2.** (*coll.*) to go, travel. **3.** (*coll.*) to rush; to leap.
махови́к, а́ *m.* fly-wheel.
махов|о́й *adj.* **1.** (*tech.*): **~о́е колесо́** fly-wheel. **2.** (*zool.*): **~ы́е пе́рья** wing-feathers.
ма́хонький *adj.* (*coll.*) titchy.
махо́рк|а, и *f.* makhorka (*inferior kind of tobacco*).
махро́в|ый *adj.* **1.** (*bot.*) double. **2.** dyed-in-the-wool, out-and-out; **~ая порногра́фия** hard-core pornography. **3.** (*text.*) terry.
мац|а́, ы́ *no pl., f.* matzos, matzoth (*Jewish biscuits of unleavened wheatmeal*).
маче́те *nt. indecl.* machete.
ма́чех|а, и *f.* stepmother.
ма́чт|а, ы *f.* mast.
ма́чт|овый *adj. of* **~а**
маши́н|а, ы *f.* **1.** machine, mechanism (*also fig.*); **бумагоре́зальная м.** guillotine; **бумагоре́зательная м.** shredder; **ку́хонная м.** food processor; **фотонабо́рная м.** typesetter; **(посудо)мо́ечная м.** dishwasher. **2.** car; **м. «ско́рой по́мощи»** ambulance; **пятидве́рная м.** hatchback; **служе́бная м.** company car. **3.** (*obs., coll.*) train.
машина́л|ьный (~ен, ~ьна) *adj.* mechanical (*fig.*); **м. отве́т** an automatic response.
машиниза́ци|я, и *f.* mechanization.
машинизи́р|овать, ую *impf. and pf.* to mechanize.
машини́ст, а *m.* **1.** machinist, engineer (*workman in charge of machinery*). **2.** (*rail.*) engine-driver. **3.** (*theatr.*) scene-shifter.
машини́стк|а, и *f.* (girl-)typist; **м.-стенографи́стка** shorthand-typist.
маши́н|ка, ки *f. dim. of* **~а; (пи́шущая) м.** typewriter.
маши́нно-тра́кторн|ый *adj.*: **~ая ста́нция** (*hist.*) machine and tractor station.
маши́н|ный *adj. of* **~а; ~ая гра́фика** computer graphics;

~ное обуче́ние computer-aided learning.
машинопи́сный *adj.* typewritten; **м. текст** typescript.
маши́нопис|ь, и *f.* **1.** typewriting. **2.** typescript.
машинострое́ни|е, я *nt.* mechanical engineering, machinery construction.
машиностро|и́тельный *adj. of* **~е́ние**
машиночита́емый *adj.* (*comput.*) machine-readable.
маэ́стро *m. indecl.* maestro; master.
мая́к, а́ *m.* **1.** lighthouse; beacon (*also fig.*). **2.** (*fig.*) leading light.
ма́ятник, а *m.* pendulum.
ма́|яться, юсь, ешься *impf.* (*coll.*) **1.** (**c**+*i.*) to toil (with, over). **2.** to pine, suffer.
мая́ч|ить, у, ишь *impf.* (*coll.*) **1.** to loom (up), appear indistinctly. **2.** to lead a wretched life.
мая́чник, а *m.* lighthouse-keeper.
м. б. (*abbr. of* ***мо́жет быть***) maybe, perhaps.
МБР *f. indecl.* (*abbr. of* ***межконтинента́льная баллисти́ческая раке́та***) ICBM (*intercontinental ballistic missile*).
МВД *nt. indecl.* (*abbr. of* ***Министе́рство вну́тренних дел***) Ministry of Internal Affairs.
МВТ *nt. indecl.* (*abbr. of* ***Министе́рство вне́шней торго́вли***) Ministry of Foreign Trade.
МВФ *m. indecl.* (*abbr. of* ***Междунаро́дный валю́тный фонд***) IMF (*International Monetary Fund*).
мг (*abbr. of* ***миллигра́мм***) mg, milligram(s).
м. г. (*abbr. of* ***мину́вшего го́да***) last year.
мгл|а, ы *f.* **1.** haze; mist. **2.** gloom, darkness.
мгли́ст|ый (~, ~а) *adj.* hazy.
мгнове́ни|е, я *nt.* instant, moment; **в м. о́ка** in the twinkling of an eye.
мгнове́н|ный (~ен, ~на) *adj.* instantaneous.
МГУ *m. indecl.* (*abbr. of* ***Моско́вский госуда́рственный университе́т***) Moscow State University.
ме́бел|ь, и *f.* furniture; (*fig.*): **для ~и** figurehead, fifth wheel (*said of a useless pers.*).
ме́бельщик, а *m.* upholsterer; furniture-dealer.
меблиро́|ванный *p.p.p. of* **~ва́ть** *and adj.* furnished.
меблир|ова́ть, у́ю *impf. and pf.* to furnish.
меблиро́вк|а, и *f.* **1.** furnishing. **2.** furniture, furnishings.
мегаба́йт, а *m.* (*comput.*) megabyte.
мегаге́рц, а *m.* (*radio*) megahertz.
мегалома́ни|я, и *f.* megalomania.
мегало́полис, а *m.* megalopolis.
мегафо́н, а *m.* megaphone.
мегéр|а, ы *f.* (*coll.*) shrew, termagant.
мего́м, а *m.* (*elec.*) megohm.
мёд, а, о ~е, в ~у́, *pl.* **~ы́, ~о́в** *m.* **1.** honey. **2.** mead.
мед... *comb. form, abbr. of* **медици́нский**
медали́ст, а *m.* medallist; medal winner.
меда́л|ь, и *f.* medal.
медальо́н, а *m.* medallion, locket.
медбра́т, а *m.* male nurse.
медве́диц|а, ы *f.* she-bear; (*astron.*): **Больша́я М.** the Great Bear (Ursa Major); **Ма́лая М.** the Little Bear (Ursa Minor).
медве́дк|а, и *f.* **1.** (*zool.*) mole-cricket. **2.** handcart. **3.** (*tech.*) punch press.
медве́д|ь, я *m.* **1.** bear (*also fig.*); **бамбу́ковый м.** giant panda; **бе́лый м.** polar bear. **2.** (*obs., coll.*) bearskin.
медвеж|а́та *pl. of* **~о́нок**
медвежа́тин|а, ы *f.* bear's flesh.
медвежа́тник, а *m.* **1.** bear-leader. **2.** bear-hunter. **3.** bear-pit, bear-garden. **4.** (*sl.*) safe-cracker, cracksman.
медве́|жий *adj. of* **~дь; м. у́гол** (*coll.*) god-forsaken place; **~жья услу́га** well-meant action having opposite effect; **~жья боле́знь** (*euph.*) diarrhoea induced by fear.
медвеж|о́нок, о́нка, *pl.* **~а́та, ~а́т** *m.* bear-cub; **плю́шевый м.** teddy (bear).
медвя́н|ый *adj.* **1.** (*poet.*) honeyed. **2.** smelling of honey. **3.: ~ая роса́** honey-dew.
медели́янск|ий *adj.*: **~ая соба́ка** mastiff.
медеплави́льный *adj.* copper-smelting.
меджли́с, а *m.* Majlis (*Iranian parliament*).
медиа́н|а, ы *f.* (*math.*) median.
медиа́тор, а *m.* plectrum, pick.
ме́дик, а *m.* **1.** physician, doctor. **2.** medical student.
медикаме́нт, а *m.* medicine.
мединститу́т, а *m.* medical school.
медита́ци|я, и *f.* meditation; **трансцендента́льная м.** transcendental meditation, TM.
медити́р|овать, ую *impf.* to meditate.
медици́н|а, ы *f.* medicine.
медици́нский *adj.* medical.
мед|и́чка, и́чки *f.* (*coll.*) *of* **~ик 2.**
ме́дленно *adv.* slowly.
ме́длен|ный (~, ~на) *adj.* slow.
медли́тел|ьный (~ен, ~ьна) *adj.* sluggish; slow, tardy.
ме́дл|ить, ю, ишь *impf.* to linger; to tarry; (**c**+*i.*) to be slow (in); **он ~ит с отве́том** he is a long time replying.
ме́дник, а *m.* copper-smith; tinker.
ме́дно-кра́сный *adj.* copper-coloured.
меднолите́йный *adj.* copper-smelting.
ме́дн|ый *adj.* **1.** copper; brazen (*also fig.*); **м. лоб** (*fig., coll.*) blockhead; **учи́ться на ~ые гроши́, на ~ые де́ньги** to receive a poor boy's schooling. **2.** (*chem.*) cupric, cuprous; **м. колчеда́н** copper pyrites; **м. купоро́с** copper sulphate, bluestone.
медо́вый *adj. of* **мёд; м. ме́сяц** honeymoon.
мед|о́к[1], ка́ *m. dim. of* **мёд**
медо́к[2], а *m.* Médoc (*wine*).
медоно́сн|ый *adj.* melliferous, nectariferous; **пчела́ ~ая** honey-bee.
медосмо́тр, а *m.* medical (examination), checkup; **пройти́ м.** to have a checkup.
медоточи́в|ый (~, ~а) *adj.* (*obs.*) mellifluous, honeyed.
медпу́нкт, а *m.* first-aid station.
медсестр|а́, ы́ *f.* (*medical*) nurse.
меду́з|а, ы *f.* **1.** (*zool.*) jellyfish, medusa. **2. М.** (*myth.*) Medusa.
медуни́ц|а, ы *f.* (*bot.*) lungwort.
мед|ь, и *f.* copper; **жёлтая м.** brass.
медя́к, а́ *m.* (*coll.*) copper (coin).
медяни́ц|а, ы *f.* slow-worm, blind-worm.
медя́нк|а[1], и *f.* grass-snake.
медя́нк|а[2], и *f.* (*chem.*) verdigris.
меж = ме́жду
меж... *comb. form* inter-.
меж|а́, и́, *pl.* **~и, ~, ~а́м** *f.* boundary; boundary-strip.
межгородско́й *adj.* inter-city.
междоме́ти|е, я *nt.* (*gram.*) interjection.
междоусо́би|е, я *nt.* civil strife; internecine strife (*esp. in medieval Russia*).
междоусо́б|ица, ицы *f.* (*obs.*) = **~ие**
междоусо́бный *adj.* internecine; intestine.
ме́жду *prep.*+*i.* (+*g. pl., obs.*) **1.** between; **м. де́лом** at odd moments; **м. на́ми (говоря́)** between ourselves; between you and me; **м. про́чим** incidentally; **м. тем** meanwhile; **м. тем, как** while, whereas; **м. двух огне́й** between two fires. **2.** among, amongst.
междуве́домственный *adj.* inter-departmental.
междугоро́дный *adj.* inter-town, inter-urban; long-distance; **м. телефо́нный разгово́р** long-distance *or* trunk call.
междунаро́дник, а *m.* specialist on international law *or* affairs.
междунаро́дный *adj.* international.
междупу́ть|е, я *nt.* (*rail.*) track spacing.
междуря́дь|е, я *nt.* (*agric.*) space between rows.
междусобо́йчик, а *m.* (*coll.*) get-together, do.
междустро́чный *adj.* (*typ.*) interlinear; **м. пробе́л** (*typ.*) leading.
междуца́рстви|е, я *nt.* interregnum.
межева́ни|е, я *nt.* land surveying, survey.
меж|ева́ть, у́ю *impf.* to survey; to establish the boundaries (of).
межеви́к, а́ *m.* surveyor.
меж|ево́й *adj. of* **~а́; м. знак** landmark, boundary-mark.
меже́н|ь, и *f.* **1.** lowest water-level (*in river or lake*). **2.** (*dial.*) midsummer.
межеу́м|ок, ка *m.* (*coll.*) **1.** pers. of limited intelligence; a mediocrity. **2.** pers. *or* thing lacking definite qualities.

межеу́мочный *adj.* (*coll.*) mediocre; ill-defined; neither one thing nor another.
межзу́бный *adj.* (*ling.*) interdental.
межкле́точный *adj.* (*biol.*) intercellular.
межконтинента́льный *adj.* inter-continental; **м. баллисти́ческий снаря́д** intercontinental ballistic missile.
межли́чностный *adj.* interpersonal.
межнациона́льный *adj.* interethnic.
межплане́тн|ый *adj.* interplanetary; **~ая автомати́ческая ста́нция** 'interplanetary automatic station' (*unmanned space research vehicle*).
межра́совый *adj.* interracial.
межрёберный *adj.* (*anat.*) intercostal.
межсезо́нь|е, я *nt.* (*sport*) off-season.
мездр|а́, ы́ *f.* inner side (*of hide*).
мезозо́йский *adj.* (*geol.*) Mesozoic.
мезолити́ческий *adj.* (*archaeol.*) mesolithic.
мезони́н, а *m.* **1.** attic story. **2.** mezzanine (floor).
Ме́кк|а, и *f.* Mecca.
Ме́ксик|а, и *f.* Mexico.
мексика́н|ец, ца *m.* Mexican.
мексика́н|ка, ки *f.* *of* **~ец**
мексика́нский *adj.* Mexican.
мел, а, о ~е, в ~у́ *m.* chalk; whiting; white-wash.
меланези́|ец, йца *m.* Melanesian.
меланези́|йка, йки *f.* *of* **~ец**
меланези́йский *adj.* Melanesian.
Мелане́зи|я, и *f.* Melanesia.
мела́нжев|ый *adj.* (*text.*): **~ая ни́тка** blended yarn; **~ое произво́дство** blended yarn fabric production.
меланхо́лик, а *m.* melancholic (*pers.*).
меланхоли́ческий *adj.* melancholy.
меланхоли́ч|ный (~ен, ~на) *adj.* = **~еский**
меланхо́ли|я, и *f.* melancholy; (*med.*) melancholia.
мела́сс|а, ы *f.* molasses.
меле́|ть, ет *impf.* (*of* **об~**) to grow shallow.
мелиор|ати́вный *adj.* *of* **~а́ция**
мелиора́тор, а *m.* (*agric.*) specialist in melioration, land improvement.
мелиора́ци|я, и *f.* (*agric.*) melioration, land improvement (*either by drainage or by irrigation*).
мелиори́р|овать, ую *impf.* *and pf.* (*agric.*) to reclaim.
мел|и́ть, ю́, и́шь *impf.* (*of* **на~**) to chalk; to polish with whiting.
ме́л|кий (~ок, ~ка́, ~ко) *adj.* **1.** small, petty. **2.** shallow; shallow-draught. **3.** (*of rain, sand, etc.*) fine; **м. шаг** (*tech.*) fine pitch. **4.** (*fig.*) petty, small-minded; **~кая душо́нка** petty pers.; **~кая со́шка** small fry.
ме́лко *adv.* **1.** fine, into small particles. **2.** not deep; **м. пла́вать** (*fig., coll.*) to lack depth.
мелкобуржуа́з|ный (~ен, ~на) *adj.* petty-bourgeois.
мелково́д|ный (~ен, ~на) *adj.* shallow.
мелково́дь|е, я *nt.* shallow water.
мелкозерни́ст|ый (~, ~а) *adj.* fine-grained, small-grained.
мелколе́сь|е, я *nt.* young forest.
мелкопоме́стный *adj.* (*hist.*) small (*of landowners*).
мелкосо́бственнический *adj.* relating to small property holders.
мелкот|а́, ы́ *f.* **1.** smallness; (*fig.*) pettiness, meanness. **2.** (*collect.; coll.*) small fry.
мелкотова́рный *adj.* (*econ.*) small-scale.
мелкошту́чник, а *m.* (*coll.*) pilferer.
мелово́й *adj.* **1.** consisting of chalk. **2.** white as chalk. **3.** cretaceous.
мелодекламаци|я, и *f.* recitation of poetry to musical accompaniment.
мело́дик|а, и *f.* melodics.
мелоди́ческий *adj.* melodious, tuneful.
мелоди́ч|ный (~ен, ~на) *adj.* = **~еский**
мело́ди|я, и *f.* melody, tune.
мелодра́м|а, ы *f.* melodrama.
мелодрамати́ческий *adj.* melodramatic.
мел|о́к, ка́ *m.* piece of chalk; **игра́ть на м.** (*cards, billiards, etc.*) to play on credit.
мелома́н, а *m.* music-lover.
мелочно́й[1] *adj.* (*obs.*) retail.
мелочно́й[2] = **ме́лочный**
ме́лочност|ь, и *f.* pettiness, small-mindedness, meanness.
ме́лоч|ный (~ен, ~на) *adj.* **1.** petty, trifling. **2.** (*pej.*) petty, paltry, small-minded.
ме́лоч|ь, и, *pl.* **~и, ~е́й** *f.* **1.** (*collect.*) small items; small fry; **кру́пные я́блоки мы съе́ли, оста́лась м.** we had eaten the big apples, only the small ones were left. **2.** (*collect.*) small coin; (small) change. **3.** (*pl.*) trifles, trivialities; **разме́ниваться на ~и, по ~а́м** to fritter away one's energies.
мел|ь, и, о ~и, на ~и́ *f.* shoal; bank; **песча́ная м.** sandbank; **на ~и́** aground; (*fig.*) on the rocks, in low water; **сесть на м.** to run aground; **сиде́ть (как рак) на ~и́** (*fig., coll.*) to be on the rocks, be in low water.
мельк|а́ть, а́ю *impf.* (*of* **~ну́ть**) to be glimpsed fleetingly.
мельк|ну́ть, ну́, нёшь, *inst. pf. of* **~а́ть; у меня́ ~ну́ла мысль** I had a sudden idea.
ме́льком *adv.* in passing, cursorily.
ме́льник, а *m.* miller.
ме́льниц|а, ы *f.* mill; **э́то вода́ на на́шу ~у** (*fig., coll.*) it affords support to our cause.
ме́льничих|а, и *f.* (*coll.*) miller's wife.
ме́льни|чный *adj.* *of* **~ца**
мельхио́р, а *m.* cupro-nickel, German silver.
мельхио́р|овый *adj.* *of* **~**
мельча́йший *superl. of* **ме́лкий**
мельча́|ть, ю *impf.* (*of* **из~**) **1.** to grow shallow. **2.** to become small; to grow smaller. **3.** (*fig.*) to become petty.
ме́л|ьче *comp. of* **~кий** *and* **~ко**
мельч|и́ть, у́, и́шь *impf.* (*of* **из~** *and* **раз~**) **1.** to crush, crumble. **2.** to reduce in size. **3.** to reduce the significance of.
мелю́, ме́лешь *see* **моло́ть**
мелюзг|а́, и́ *f.* (*collect.; coll.*) small fry.
мембра́н|а, ы *f.* (*phys.*) membrane; (*tech.*) diaphragm.
мемора́ндум, а *m.* (*dipl.*) memorandum.
мемориа́л, а *m.* **1.** (*comm.*) day-book. **2.** (*obs.*) note-book.
мемориа́льный *adj.* memorial.
мемуари́ст, а *m.* author of memoirs.
мемуа́р|ы, ов *no sg.* memoirs.
ме́н|а, ы *f.* exchange, barter.
менажёр, а *m.* (*sport*) manager.
менажи́р|овать, ую *impf.* (*sport*) to manage, be manager (of).
мена́рхе *nt. indecl.* (*med.*) menarche.
ме́неджер, а *m.* manager; **м. по сбы́ту** sales manager.
ме́нее *adv.* (*comp. of* **ма́ло**) less; **тем не м.** none the less.
менестре́л|ь, я *m.* (*hist.*) minstrel.
ме́нзул|а, ы *f.* (*tech.*) plane-table.
мензу́рк|а, и *f.* (*pharm.*) measuring-glass.
менинги́т, а *m.* (*med.*) meningitis.
мени́ск, а *m.* (*math., phys.*) meniscus.
менов|о́й *adj.* (*econ.*) exchange; **~а́я торго́вля** barter.
мено́р|а, ы *f.* (*relig.*) menorah.
менструа́льный *adj.* (*physiol.*) menstrual.
менструа́ци|я, и *f.* (*physiol.*) menstruation.
менструи́р|овать, ую *impf.* (*physiol.*) to menstruate.
мент, а *m.* (*sl.*) copper, bogey.
ме́нтик, а *m.* (*obs.*) hussar's pelisse.
менто́вк|а, и *f.* (*sl.*) paddy wagon.
менто́вск|ая, ой *f.* (*sl.*) cop-shop.
ментол, а *m.* (*chem.*) menthol.
ме́нтор, а *m.* (*obs.*) mentor.
менту́р|а, ы *f.* (*sl.*) the fuzz, the Old Bill.
менуэ́т, а *m.* minuet.
ме́ньше *comp. of* **ма́ленький** *and* **ма́ло** smaller, less.
меньшеви́зм, а *m.* (*pol.*) Menshevism.
меньшеви́к, а́ *m.* (*pol.*) Menshevik.
меньшеви́стский *adj.* (*pol.*) Menshevist.
ме́ньш|ий *adj.* (*comp. of* **ма́ленький, ма́лый**) lesser, smaller; younger; **по ~ей ме́ре** at least; **са́мое ~ее** at the least.
меньшинств|о́, а́ *nt.* minority.
меньшо́й *adj.* (*coll.*) youngest.
меню́ *nt. indecl.* menu, bill of fare.

меня́ *a. and g. of* **я**
меня́л|а, ы *m.* (*coll.*) money-changer.
меня́льный *adj.* (*comm.*) money-changing.
меня́|ть, ю *impf.* **1.** (*no pf.*) to change. **2.** (+*a.* **на**+*a.*; *pf.* **об~, по~**) to exchange (for).
меня́|ться, юсь *impf.* **1.** (*no pf.*) to change; **м. в лице́** to change countenance. **2.** (+*i.*; *pf.* **об~, по~**) to exchange; **м. с кем-н. ко́мнатами** to exchange rooms with s.o.
ме́р|а, ы *f.* (*in var. senses*) measure; **вы́сшая м. наказа́ния** capital punishment; **~ы по укрепле́нию дове́рия** (*pol.*) confidence-building measures; **в ~у** (+*g.*) to the extent (of); **по ~е возмо́жности, по ~е сил** as far as possible; **по ~е того́, как** as, (in proportion) as; **по кра́йней, ма́лой, ме́ньшей ~е** at least; **в ~у** fairly; **сверх ~ы, чрез ~у, не в ~у** excessively, immoderately; **знать ~у,** *see* **знать**[1]
ме́ргел|ь, я *m.* (*geol.*) marl.
мере́жк|а, и *f.* hem-stitch, open work.
мере́нг|а, и *f.* meringue.
мере́ть, мру, мрёшь, *past* **мёр, мёрла** *impf.* (*coll.*) **1.** to die (*in large numbers*); **мрут, как му́хи** they are dying like flies. **2.** (*of the heart*) to stop beating.
мере́щ|иться, усь, ишься *impf.* (*of* **по~**) (*coll.*; +*d.*) **1.** to seem (to), appear (to); **она́ мне ~ится** her image haunts me; **э́то тебе́ ~ится** you only imagine you see it. **2.** (*obs.*) to appear dimly.
мерза́в|ец, ца *m.* (*coll.*) swine, bastard.
ме́рз|кий (~ок, ~ка́, ~ко) *adj.* disgusting, loathsome; abominable, foul.
мерзлот|а́, ы́ *f.* frozen condition of ground; **ве́чная м.** permafrost.
мерзлотове́дени|е, я *nt.* study of frozen soil conditions.
мёрзлый *adj.* frozen, congealed.
мёрз|нуть, ну, нешь, *past* **~, ~ла** *impf.* (*of* **за~**) to freeze.
ме́рзост|ь, и *f.* **1.** vileness, loathsomeness. **2.** loathsome thing, nasty thing; abomination; **м. запусте́ния** (*bibl. or iron.*) abomination of desolation.
меридиа́н, а *m.* meridian.
мери́л|о, а *nt.* standard, criterion.
мери́льный *adj.* measuring.
ме́рин, а *m.* gelding; **врёт как си́вый м.** (*coll.*) he's a barefaced liar; **он глуп как си́вый м.** (*coll.*) he's as thick as they come.
мерино́с, а *m.* **1.** merino (sheep). **2.** merino (wool).
мерино́совый *adj.* merino.
ме́р|ить, ю, ишь *impf.* **1.** (*pf.* **с~**) to measure; **м. взгля́дом** to look up and down. **2.** (*pf.* **по~, при~**) to try on (*clothing, footwear*).
ме́р|иться, юсь, ишься *impf.* (*of* **по~**) (+*i.*) to measure (against); **м. ро́стом с кем-н.** to compare heights with s.o.
ме́рк|а, и *f.* measure; **подходи́ть ко всему́ с одно́й ~ой** (*fig.*) to apply the same standard to all alike.
меркантили́зм, а *m.* **1.** (*econ.*) mercantilism. **2.** (*fig.*) mercenary spirit.
меркант́ил|ьный *adj.* **1.** mercantile. **2. (~ен, ~ьна)** (*fig., pej.*) mercenary.
ме́рк|нуть, нет, *past* **~нул** *and* **~, ~ла** *impf.* (*of* **по~**) to grow dark, grow dim; (*fig.*) to fade.
Мерку́ри|й, я *m.* (*myth., astron*) Mercury.
мерла́н, а *m.* (*fish*) whiting.
мерлу́шк|а, и *f.* lambskin.
ме́рный *adj.* **1.** measured; rhythmical. **2.** (*tech.*) measuring.
мероприя́ти|е, я *nt.* measure; event.
мерсериза́ци|я, и *f.* (*tech.*) mercerization.
мерсеризо́в|анный *p.p.p. of* **~а́ть** *and adj.* (*tech.*) mercerized.
мерсериз|ова́ть, у́ю *impf. and pf.* (*tech.*) to mercerize.
мерси́ *particle* (*joc.*) ta.
ме́ртвенный *adj.* deathly, ghastly.
мертве́|ть, ю *impf.* **1.** (*pf.* **о~**) to grow numb; (*med.*) to mortify. **2.** (*pf.* **по~**) to be benumbed (*with fright, grief, etc.*).
мертве́ц, а́ *m.* corpse, dead man.
мертве́цк|ая, ой *f.* (*coll.*) mortuary, morgue.
мертве́цки *adv.* (*coll.*) *only in phrr.* **м. пьян** dead drunk; **напи́ться м.** to become dead drunk.
мертвечи́н|а, ы *f.* **1.** (*collect.*) carrion. **2.** (*fig., coll.*) deadness, (a) dead thing.
мертв|и́ть, лю́, и́шь *impf.* to deaden.
мертворождённый *adj.* still-born.
мёртв|ый (~, ~а́, ~о, *pl.* **~ы;** *in fig. senses* **~о́, ~ы́)** *adj.* dead; **ни жив ни ~** more dead than alive; **~ая зыбь** (*naut.*) swell; **м. инвента́рь** (*agric.*) dead stock; **м. капита́л** (*fin.*) dead stock, unemployed capital; **~ая пе́тля** (*aeron.*) loop; **пить ~ую** (*coll.*) to drink hard; **~ое простра́нство** (*geog., mil.*) dead ground; **спать ~ым сном** (*coll.*) to sleep like the dead; **быть на ~ой то́чке** to be at a standstill; **~ая хва́тка** mortal grip; **м. час** quiet time (*in sanatoria, etc.*).
мертвя́к, а́ *m.* (*sl.*) stiff (= *corpse*).
мерца́|ть, ю *impf.* to twinkle, glimmer, flicker.
ме́сив|о, а *nt.* **1.** mash. **2.** (*fig., coll.*) medley; jumble.
ме|си́ть, шу́, ~сишь *impf.* (*of* **с~**) to knead; **м. грязь** (*coll., joc.*) to wade through mud.
месмери́зм, а *m.* mesmerism.
ме́сс|а, ы *f.* (*relig., mus.*) mass.
мессиа́нский *adj.* Messianic.
мессиа́нств|о, а *nt.* Messianism.
месси́|я, и *m.* Messiah.
места́ми *adj.* (*coll.*) here and there, in places.
месте́ч|ко[1]**, ка,** *pl.* **~ки, ~ек, ~кам** *nt.* small town (*in Ukraine and Byelorussia*).
месте́ч|ко[2]**, ка,** *pl.* **~ки, ~ек, ~кам** *nt. dim. of* **ме́сто; тёплое м.** (*coll.*) cushy job.
ме|сти́, ту́, тёшь, *past* **мёл, ~ла́** *impf.* **1.** to sweep. **2.** to whirl; (*impers.*): **~тёт** there is a snow-storm.
местко́м, а *m.* (*abbr. of* ***ме́стный комите́т***) local (trade union) committee.
ме́стничес|кий *adj. of* **~тво**
ме́стничеств|о, а *nt.* **1.** (*hist.*) order of precedence (*based on birth and service*). **2.** (*pej.*) regionalism, giving priority to local interests.
ме́стност|ь, и *f.* **1.** locality, district; area. **2.** (*mil.*) ground, country, terrain.
ме́стный *adj.* **1.** (*in var. senses*) local; **м. колори́т** local colour. **2.** (*gram.*) locative.
-ме́стный *comb. form* -seated, -seater.
ме́ст|о, а, *pl.* **~а́, ~, ~а́м** *nt.* **1.** place; site; **больно́е м.** (*fig.*) tender spot, sensitive point; **де́тское м.** (*anat.*) afterbirth, placenta; **о́бщее м.** platitude; **отхо́жее м.** latrine; **пусто́е м.** blank (space); (*fig.*) a nobody, a nonentity; **сла́бое м.** (*fig.*) weakness, weak spot; **у́зкое м.** bottleneck; **м. де́йствия, м. происше́ствия** scene (of action); **на ~е преступле́ния** in the act, red-handed; **знать своё м.** (*fig.*) to know one's place; **име́ть м.** to take place; **поста́вить на своё м., указа́ть кому́-н. его́ м.** (*fig.*) to put s.o. in his place; **не находи́ть себе́ ~а** (*fig.*) to fret, worry; **не к ~у** (*fig.*) out of place; **по ~а́м!** to your places!; **ни с ~а!** don't move!; stay put!; **честь и м.!** (*obs., now joc.*) kindly be seated! **2.** (*in theatre, etc.*) seat; (*on ship or train*) berth, seat. **3.** space; room; **нет ~а** there is no room. **4.** post, situation; job; **быть без ~а** to be out of work. **5.** passage (*of book or mus. work*). **6.** piece (*of luggage*). **7.** (*pl.*) the provinces, the country; **на ~а́х** in the provinces; **делега́ты с ~** provincial delegates.
местоблюсти́тел|ь, я *m.* (*eccl.*) locum tenens.
местожи́тельств|о, а *nt.* (place of) residence; **без определённого ~а** of no fixed abode.
местоиме́ни|е, я *nt.* (*gram.*) pronoun.
местоиме́нный *adj.* (*gram.*) pronominal.
местонахожде́ни|е, я *nt.* location, the whereabouts.
местоположе́ни|е, я *nt.* site, situation, position.
местопребыва́ни|е, я *nt.* abode, residence.
месторожде́ни|е, я *nt.* **1.** (*geol.*) deposit; layer. **2.** (*obs.*) birth-place.
мест|ь, и *f.* vengeance, revenge.
ме́сяц, а *m.* **1.** month; **медо́вый м.** honeymoon. **2.** moon; **молодо́й м.** new moon.
месяцесло́в, а *m.* (*obs.*) calender.
ме́сячник, а *m.* month (*marked by special observances or devoted to some special cause*).
ме́сячн|ый *adj.* monthly; *as n.* **~ые, ~ых** *no sg.* (*coll.*) (menstrual) period.

метаболи́зм, а *m.* metabolism.
мета́лл, а *m.* metal; **презре́нный м.** filthy lucre.
металлиза́ци|я, и *f.* (*tech.*) metallization.
металлизи́р|овать, ую *impf. and pf.* to metallize.
металли́ст, а *m.* **1.** metal-worker. **2.** (*coll.*, *mus.*) heavy metallist.
металли́ческий *adj.* metal; metallic (*also fig.*); **~ая болва́нка** pig-metal; **~ая отли́вка** cast metal; **м. рок** heavy metal (rock).
металлоиска́тел|ь, я *m.* metal-detector.
металлоно́с|ный (~ен, ~на) *adj.* metalliferous.
металлообраба́тывающий *adj.* metal-working.
металлоплави́льный *adj.* smelting.
металлопрока́тный *adj.* (*tech.*) rolling.
металлопромы́шленност|ь, и *f.* metal industry.
металлоре́жущий *adj.* metal-cutting.
металлу́рг, а *m.* metallurgist.
металлурги́ческий *adj.* metallurgical; **м. заво́д** metal works, iron and steel works.
металлу́рги|я, и *f.* **1.** metallurgy. **2.** metallurgical science.
метаморфо́з, а *m.* = **~а**
метаморфо́з|а, ы *f.* metamorphosis.
мета́н, а *m.* (*chem.*) methane, marsh gas.
мета́ни|е, я *nt.* **1.** throwing, casting, flinging. **2.:** **м. икры́** spawning.
метано́л, а *m.* (*chem.*) methanol, methyl alcohol.
метате́з|а, ы *f.* (*ling.*) metathesis.
мета́тел|ь, я *m.* (*sport*) thrower; **м. ди́ска** discus thrower.
мета́тельный *adj.* missile; **м. снаря́д** projectile.
ме|та́ть[1], **чу́, ~́чешь** *impf.* (*of* **~тну́ть**) **1.** to throw, cast, fling; **м. гро́мы и мо́лнии** (*fig.*, *coll.*) to rage, fulminate; **рвать и м.** (*coll.*) to be in a rage; **м. жре́бий** to cast lots; **м. се́но** to stack hay. **2.:** **м. икру́** to spawn. **3.** (*cards*): **м. банк** to keep the bank.
мета́|ть[2], **ю** *impf.* (*of* **на~, с~**) to baste, tack; **м. пе́тли** to edge buttonholes.
ме|та́ться, чу́сь, ~́чешься *impf.* to rush about; to toss (*in bed*).
метафи́зик, а *m.* metaphysician.
метафи́зик|а, и *f.* metaphysics.
метафизи́ческий *adj.* metaphysical.
мета́фор|а, ы *f.* metaphor.
метафори́ческий *adj.* metaphorical.
мете́л|ица, ицы *f.* (*poet.*) = **~ь**
метёлк|а, и *f.* **1.** *dim. of* **метла́; под ~у** (*fig.*, *coll.*) entirely, to the last particle. **2.** (*bot.*) panicle.
мете́л|ь, и *f.* snow-storm; blizzard.
мете́льчатый *adj.* (*bot.*) panicular, paniculate.
мете́льщик, а *m.* sweeper.
метео... *comb. form, abbr. of* **метеорологи́ческий**
метеопрогнози́ровани|е, я *nt.* weather forecasting.
метео́р, а *m.* **1.** meteor. **2.** hydrofoil (*vessel*).
метеори́зм, а *m.* (*med.*) flatulence.
метеори́т, а *m.* (*astron.*) meteorite.
метеори́ческий *adj.* meteoric.
метео́р|ный *adj. of* **~**
метеоро́лог, а *m.* meteorologist; weather forecaster; (*coll.*) weatherman.
метеорологи́ческ|ий *adj.* meteorological; **~ая ста́нция** weather station.
метеороло́ги|я, и *f.* meteorology.
метеосво́дк|а, и *f.* weather report.
метеоста́нци|я, и *f.* meteorological station.
метиза́ци|я, и *f.* (*biol.*) cross-breeding.
мети́зный *adj.* metal-ware, hardware.
мети́з|ы, ов *no sg.* (*abbr. of* **металли́ческие изде́лия**) metal wares, hardware.
мети́л, а *m.* (*chem.*) methyl.
мети́с, а *m.* **1.** (*biol.*) mongrel, half-breed. **2.** (*anthrop.*) metis, mestizo.
ме́|тить[1], **чу, тишь** *impf.* (*of* **на~** *and* **по~**) to mark.
ме́|тить[2], **чу, тишь** *impf.* (*of* **на~**) **1.** (**в**+*a*) to aim at; (*fig.*, *coll.*; **в**+*nom.-a. pl.*) to aim (at), aspire (to); **он всегда́ ~тил в профессора́** it had always been his aim (ambition) to become a professor. **2.** (*fig.*; **в**+*a.*, **на**+*a.*) to drive (at), mean.
ме́тк|а, и *f.* **1.** marking. **2.** mark.
ме́т|кий (~ок, ~ка́, ~ко) *adj.* well-aimed, accurate; **м. стрело́к** a good shot; (*fig.*): **~кое замеча́ние** apt remark; **~ко вы́разиться** to be very much to the point.
ме́ткост|ь, и *f.* marksmanship; accuracy; (*fig.*) neatness, pointedness.
мет|ла́, лы́, *pl.* **~́лы, ~́ел, ~́лам** *f.* broom.
метлови́щ|е, а *nt.* broomstick.
мет|ну́ть, ну́, нёшь *inst. pf. of* **~а́ть**[1]
ме́тод, а *m.* method; **печа́тать слепы́м ~ом** to touch-type.
мето́д|а, ы *f.* (*obs.*) method.
методи́зм, а *m.* (*relig.*) Methodism.
мето́дик|а, и *f.* **1.** method(s), system; principles; **м. препода-ва́ния ру́сского языка́** methods of teaching Russian; **м. пожа́рного де́ла** principles of fire-fighting. **2.** methodology.
методи́ст[1], **а** *m.* methodologist; specialist (*on principles of, methods of teaching, etc.*).
методи́ст[2], **а** *m.* (*relig.*) Methodist.
методи́ст|ский *adj. of* **~**[2]
метод|и́ческий *adj.* **1.** methodical, systematic. **2.** *adj. of* **~́ика; м. приём** procedure; **~и́ческое совеща́ние** conference on (*teaching, etc.*) methods.
методи́ч|ный (~ен, ~на) *adj.* methodical, orderly.
методо́лог, а *m.* methodologist.
методологи́ческий *adj.* methodological.
методоло́ги|я, и *f.* methodology.
метони́ми|я, и *f.* (*liter.*) metonymy.
мето́п, а *m.* (*archit.*) metope.
метр[1], **а** *m.* (*unit of measurement and liter.*) metre.
метр[2], **а** *m.* (*obs. or joc.*) master.
метра́ж, а *m.* **1.** metric area. **2.** length in metres.
метранпа́ж, а *m.* (*typ.*) maker-up.
метрдоте́л|ь, я *m.* head waiter.
ме́трик|а[1], **и** *f.* (*liter.*) metrics.
ме́трик|а[2], **и** *f.* birth-certificate.
метри́ческий[1] *adj.* metric.
метри́ческ|ий[2] *adj.* (*liter.*) metrical; **~ое ударе́ние** ictus, metrical stress.
метри́ческ|ий[3] *adj.*: **~ая кни́га** register of births; **~ое свиде́тельство** birth-certificate.
метро́ *nt. indecl.* (*abbr. of* **~полите́н**) **1.** underground (railway system); the tube. **2.** (*coll.*) metro station; tube station.
метро... *comb. form, abbr. of* **метрополите́нный**
метрологи́ческий *adj.* metrological.
метроло́ги|я, и *f.* metrology.
метроно́м, а *m.* (*phys.*, *mus.*) metronome.
метрополите́н, а *m.* underground (railway); metro(politan railway).
метрополите́н|ный *adj. of* **~**
метропо́ли|я, и *f.* mother country, centre (*of empire*).
ме|ту́, тёшь *see* **~сти́**
ме́т|че *comp. of* **~кий** *and* **~ко**
ме́тчик, а *m.* (*tech.*) **1.** punch, stamp. **2.** marker.
метчи́к, а́ *m.* (*tech.*) tap-borer, screw-tap.
мех[1], **а о ~́е, в ~у́ (~́е), на ~у́,** *pl.* **~а́, ~о́в** *m.* fur; **на ~у́** fur-lined.
мех[2], **а,** *pl.* **~и́, ~о́в** *m.* **1.** (*pl.*) bellows. **2.** wine-skin, water-skin.
механиза́тор, а *m.* **1.** specialist on mechanization. **2.** (*agric.*) machine operator, machine servicer.
механиза́ци|я, и *f.* mechanization.
механизи́рова|нный *p.p.p. of* **~ть** *and adj.* mechanized.
механизи́р|овать, ую *impf. and pf.* to mechanize.
механи́зм, а *m.* mechanism, gear(ing); (*pl.*; *collect.*) machinery (*also fig.*).
меха́ник, а *m.* **1.** mechanic. **2.** student of, specialist in mechanics.
меха́ник|а, и *f.* **1.** mechanics. **2.** (*fig.*, *coll.*) trick; knack; **подвести́ (подстро́ить) ~у кому́-н.** to play a trick on s.o.
механи́ст, а *m.* (*phil.*) mechanist.
механисти́ческий *adj.* (*phil.*) mechanistic.
механи́ческий *adj.* **1.** (*in var. senses*) mechanical; power-driven; **м. моме́нт** momentum; **м. пресс** power press; **м. тка́цкий стано́к** power loom; **м. цех** machine shop. **2.** of

mechanics. **3.** (*phil.*) mechanistic.
механи́ч|ный (~ен, ~на) *adj.* (*fig.*) mechanical, automatic.
Ме́хико *m. indecl.* Mexico City.
мехово́й *adj. of* **мех**[1]
меховщи́к, а́ *m.* furrier.
мецена́т, а *m.* Maecenas, patron.
мецена́тств|о, а *nt.* patronage of literature, of arts.
ме́ццо-сопра́но *indecl.* (*mus.*) **1.** *nt.* mezzo-soprano (*voice*). **2.** *f.* mezzo-soprano (*singer*).
ме́ццо-ти́нто *nt. indecl.* (*art*) mezzotint.
меч, а́ *m.* sword; **дамо́клов м.** sword of Damocles; **преда́ть огню́ и ~у́** to put to the sword; **скрести́ть ~и́** (*fig., rhet.*) to cross swords.
мечено́с, а *m.* = **меч-ры́ба**
мечено́с|ец, ца *m.* **1.** sword-bearer. **2.** (*hist.*) member of German Order of Knights of the Sword. **3.** *pl.* (*zool.*) swordtails.
ме́чен|ый *adj.* marked; **~ые а́томы** (*phys.*) labelled, tagged atoms.
мече́т|ь, и *f.* mosque.
мечехво́ст, а *m.* horseshoe crab.
меч-ры́б|а, ы *f.* sword-fish.
мечт|а́, ы́ (*g. pl. not used*) *f.* dream, day-dream.
мечта́ни|е, я *nt.* day-dreaming, reverie.
мечта́тел|ь, я *m.* dreamer; day-dreamer.
мечта́тел|ьный (~ен, ~ьна) *adj.* dreamy.
мечта́|ть, ю *impf.* (**о**+*p.*) to dream (of, about); **м. мно́го, высоко́** *etc.*, **о себе́** (*coll.*) to think much of o.s.
ме́|чу, тишь *see* **~тить**
ме|чу́, ~чешь *see* **~та́ть**[1]
меша́лк|а, и *f.* (*coll.*) mixer, stirrer; agitator (*in washing machine*).
мешани́н|а, ы *f.* (*coll.*) medley, jumble.
меша́|ть[1], **ю** *impf.* (*of* **по~**) **1.** (+*d.* +*inf.*) to prevent (from); to hinder, impede, hamper; **что ~ет вам прие́хать в Москву́?** what prevents you from coming to Moscow? **2.** (+*d.*) to disturb; **вам не ~ет, что я игра́ю на пиани́но?** does it disturb you when I play the piano?; **не ~ло бы** (+*inf.*) (*coll.*) it would not be a bad thing (to).
меша́|ть[2], **ю** *impf.* **1.** (*pf.* **по~**) to stir, agitate; **м. у́голь в пе́чке** to poke the fire; **м. в котле́** to stir the cauldron. **2.** (*pf.* **с~**) (**с**+*i.*) to mix (with), blend (with). **3.** (*pf.* **с~**) to confuse, mix up.
меша́|ться, юсь *impf.* **1.** (*coll.*; **в**+*a.*) to interfere (in), meddle (with); **не ~йтесь не в своё де́ло!** mind your own business! **2.** (*pf.* **с~**) *pass. of* **~ть**[2]
ме́шка|ть, ю *impf.* (*coll.*; **с**+*i.*) to linger, tarry (over); to loiter.
мешкова́т|ый (~, ~а) *adj.* **1.** (*of clothing*) baggy. **2.** awkward, clumsy.
мешкови́н|а, ы *f.* sacking, hessian.
ме́шкот|ный (~ен, ~на) *adj.* (*coll.*) **1.** sluggish, slow. **2.** long (*of a job*).
меш|о́к, ка́ *m.* **1.** bag; sack; **вещево́й м.** haversack, knapsack; kit-bag; **ка́менный м.** (*hist.*; *rhet.*) prison cell; **огнево́й м.** (*mil.*) fire pocket; **~ки́ под глаза́ми** bags under the eyes. **2.** bag (*old Russ. dry measure, equivalent to 3–5 poods or approx. 49–82 kilograms*). **3.** (*fig., coll.*) oaf, clumsy clot.
мешо́ч|ек, ка *m. dim. of* **мешо́к**; sac, follicle, utricle; **м. с ча́ем** tea bag.
мещан|и́н, и́на, *pl.* **~е, ~** *m.* **1.** (*hist.*) petty bourgeois (*member of urban lower middle class comprising small traders, craftsmen, junior officials, etc.*). **2.** (*fig.*) Philistine.
меща́н|ский *adj. of* **~и́н; (*fig.*)** Philistine; bourgeois, vulgar, narrow-minded.
меща́нств|о, а *nt.* **1.** (*collect.*) petty bourgeoisie, lower middle class. **2.** (*fig.*) philistinism, vulgarity, narrow-mindedness.
мзд|а, ы *no pl., f.* (*arch., now joc.*) recompense, payment (*iron.* = *bribe*).
мздоим|ец, ца *m.* (*obs.*) bribe-taker.
мздоимств|о, а *nt.* (*obs.*) bribery.
ми *nt. indecl.* (*mus.*) me (mi); E.
МИГ, а *or* **«миг», а** *m.* (*abbr. of* **Микоя́н и Гуре́вич**) 'Mig' (*aircraft*).
миг, а *m.* moment, instant.
мига́лк|а, и *f.* (*coll.*) **1.** flashing light. **2.** blinker.
мига́ни|е, я *nt.* **1.** winking; twinkling. **2.** blinking.
мига́тельн|ый *adj.*: **~ая перепо́нка** nict(it)ating membrane.
миг|а́ть, а́ю *impf.* (*of* **~ну́ть**) **1.** to blink. **2.** (+*d.*) to wink (at); (*fig.*) to wink, twinkle.
миг|ну́ть, ну́, нёшь *inst. pf. of* **~а́ть**
ми́гом *adv.* (*coll.*) in a flash; in a jiffy.
миграцио́нный *adj. of* **мигра́ция**
мигра́ци|я, и *f.* migration.
мигре́н|ь, и *f.* migraine.
мигри́р|овать, ую *impf.* to migrate.
МИД, а *m.* (*abbr. of* **Министе́рство иностра́нных дел**) Ministry of Foreign Affairs; (*Br.*) Foreign Office.
ми́дел|ь, я *m.* (*naut.*) midship section.
ми́ди *nt. indecl.* midi (*garment*); **ми́ди-ю́бка** midi-skirt.
ми́ди|я, и *f.* mussel.
мизансце́н|а, ы *f.* (*theatr.*) mise en scène.
мизантро́п, а *m.* misanthrope.
мизантропи́ческий *adj.* misanthropic.
мизантро́пи|я, и *f.* misanthropy.
мизги́р|ь, я́ *m.* (*dial.*) spider.
мизере́ре *nt. indecl.* (*eccl.*) miserere.
ми́зе́р|ный (~ен, ~на) *adj.* scanty, wretched.
мизи́н|ец, ца *m.* little finger; little toe; **он не сто́ит ва́шего ~ца** (*fig.*) he is not a patch on you.
мизи́н|цевый *adj. of* **~ец**
мике́нский *adj.* Mycenean.
Мике́н|ы, ~ *no sg.* (*hist.*) Mycenae.
миколо́ги|я, и *f.* mycology.
микро... *comb. form* micro-
микроавто́бус, а *m.* minibus.
микроампе́р, а *m.* (*elec.*) microampere.
микро́б, а *m.* microbe.
микробио́лог, а *m.* microbiologist.
микробиоло́ги|я, и *f.* microbiology.
микрово́лнов|ый *adj.*: **~ая пе́чка** microwave (oven).
микроди́ск, а *m.* (*comput.*) floppy (disk), diskette.
микрока́рт|а, ы *f.* microfiche.
микроко́кк, а *m.* (*biol., med.*) micrococcus.
микрокомпью́тер, а *m.* microcomputer.
микроко́см, а *m.* microcosm.
микролитра́жк|а, и *f.* (*coll.*) subcompact (car).
микрометри́ческий *adj.* micrometrical.
микроме́три|я, и *f.* micrometry.
микро́н, а *m.* (*phys.*) micron.
микрооргани́зм, а *m.* (*biol.*) micro-organism; **разлага́емый ~ами** biodegradable.
микроплёнк|а, и *f.* microfilm.
микропроце́ссор, а *m.* microprocessor.
микрорайо́н, а *m.* **1.** mikrorayon *or* mikroraion (*administrative subdivision of urban rayon in former USSR*). **2.** (*town planning*) neighbourhood unit; **м. шко́лы** school catchment area.
микроско́п, а *m.* microscope.
микроскопи́ческий *adj.* microscopic.
микроскопи́ч|ный (~ен, ~на) *adj.* = **~еский**
микроскопи́|я, и *f.* microscopy.
микрострукту́р|а, ы *f.* microstructure.
микросхе́м|а, ы *f.* microcircuit.
микрофи́ш|а, и *f.* (micro)fiche.
микрофо́н, а *m.* microphone; mouthpiece (*of telephone*).
микроцефа́л, а *m.* (*med.*) microcephalic.
микроцефа́ли|я, и *f.* (*med.*) microcephaly.
микроэлектро́ник|а, и *f.* microelectronics.
микроэлеме́нт, а *m.* **1.** (*tech.*) microelement, micro-component. **2.** trace element.
ми́ксер, а *m.* (*cul.*) blender, liquidizer.
миксту́р|а, ы *f.* (liquid) medicine, mixture.
мила́ш|а, и *f.* (*coll.*) darling.
мила́шк|а, и *f.* **1.** (*coll.*) pretty girl; nice girl. **2.** (*vulg.*) sweetheart, tart.
ми́ленький *adj.* **1.** pretty; nice; sweet; dear. **2.** (*as form of address*) darling.

милитаризáци|я, и *f.* militarization.
милитари́зм, а *m.* militarism.
милитариз|овáть, ýю *impf. and pf.* to militarize.
милитари́ст, а *m.* militarist.
милитаристи́ческий *adj.* militaristic.
милиц|éйский *adj. of* **~ия**
милиционéр, а *m.* **1.** policeman (*in former USSR*). **2.** militiaman.
мили́ци|я, и *f.* militia (*in former USSR, civil police force*); **м. нрáвов** vice squad.
миллиáрд, а *m.* milliard; (*US*) billion.
миллиардéр, а *m.* multimillionaire; billionaire.
миллиáрдный *adj.* **1.** milliardth; (*US*) billionth. **2.** worth a milliard.
миллибáр, а *m.* (*meteor.*) millibar.
милливóльт, а *m.* (*elec.*) millivolt.
миллигрáмм, а *m.* milligram(me).
миллили́тр, а *m.* millilitre.
миллимéтр, а *m.* millimetre.
миллиметрóвк|а, и *f.* (*coll.*) graph paper.
миллиóн, а *m.* million.
миллионéр, а *m.* **1.** millionaire. **2.** (*fig.*) one who has accomplished sth. which can be estimated in millions of units; **лётчик-м.** pilot who has flown more than a million kilometres.
миллиóнный *adj.* **1.** millionth. **2.** worth millions. **3.** million-strong.
ми́л|овать, ую *impf.* (*of* **по~**) to pardon, spare.
мил|овáть, ýю *impf.* (*folk poet.*) to caress, fondle.
мил|овáться, ýюсь *impf.* (*folk poet.*) to exchange caresses.
милови́д|ный (~ен, ~на) *adj.* pretty, nice-looking.
милóрд, а *m.* (mi)lord.
милосéрди|е, я *nt.* mercy, charity; **сестрá ~я** (*obs.*) nurse.
милосéрд|ный (~ен, ~на) *adj.* merciful, charitable.
ми́лостив|ый (~, ~а) *adj.* (*obs.*) gracious, kind; **м. госудáрь** (*form of address*) sir; (*in letters*) (Dear) Sir; **~ая госудáрыня** madam; (*in letters*) (Dear) Madam.
ми́лостын|я, и *no pl., f.* alms.
ми́лост|ь, и *f.* **1.** favour, grace; *pl.* favours; **~и прóсим!** (*coll.*) welcome!; you are always welcome!; **сдéлай(те) м.** (*obs.*) be so kind, be so good; **скажи́(те) на м.!** (*coll., iron.*) you don't say (so)! **2.** mercy; charity; **сдáться на м. победи́теля** to surrender at discretion; **из ~и** out of charity. **3.** (*form of address to superior*): **вáша м.** your worship.
ми́лочк|а, и *f.* (*coll.*) dear, darling.
ми́л|ый (~, ~á, ~л) *adj.* **1.** nice, sweet; lovable; **э́то óчень ~о с вáшей стороны́** it is very nice of you. **2.** dear; *as n.* **м., ~ого** *m.*, **~ая, ~ой** *f.* dear, darling.
мильтóн, а *m.* (*sl.*) copper, bogey.
ми́л|я, и *f.* mile.
мим, а *m.* (*theatr.*) mime.
мимеóграф, а *m.* duplicating machine.
ми́мик|а, и *f.* mimicry.
мимикри́|я, и *f.* (*biol.*) mimicry, mimesis.
мими́ст, а *m.* mimic.
мими́ческий *adj.* mimic.
ми́мо *adv. and prep.+g.* by, past; **пройти́, проéхать м.** to pass by, to pass; **м.!** miss(ed)!
мимоéздом *adv.* (*coll.*) in passing.
мимóз|а, ы *f.* (*bot.*) mimosa.
мимолёт|ный (~ен, ~на) *adj.* fleeting, transient.
мимохóдом *adv.* in passing; **м. упомянýть** (*fig., coll.*) to mention in passing.
мин. (*abbr. of* **минýта**) min., minute(s).
ми́н|а[1]**, ы** *f.* **1.** (*mil., naut.*) mine; booby trap. **2.** (*mil.*) mortar shell, bomb.
ми́н|а[2]**, ы** *f.* mien, expression; **сдéлать весёлую (хорóшую) ~у при плохóй игрé** to put a brave face on a sorry business.
минарéт, а *m.* minaret.
миндалеви́дн|ый *adj.* almond-shaped; **~ая железá** (*anat.*) tonsil.
миндáлин|а, ы *f.* **1.** almond. **2.** (*anat.*) tonsil.
миндáл|ь, я́ *m.* **1.** almond-tree. **2.** (*collect.*) almonds.
миндáльнича|ть, ю *impf.* (**с**+*i.*; *coll.*) to sentimentalize (over), be excessively soft (towards).
миндáль|ный *adj. of* **~**
минёр, а *m.* (*mil.*) mine-layer.
минерáл, а *m.* mineral.
минерáлк|а, и *f.* (*coll.*) mineral water.
минералоги́ческий *adj.* mineralogical.
минералóги|я, и *f.* mineralogy.
минерáльный *adj.* mineral.
минéт, а *m.* (*vulg.*) blow-job.
Минздрáв, а *m.* (*abbr. of* **Министéрство здравоохранéния**) Ministry of Health.
миниатю́р|а, ы *f.* (*art*) miniature.
миниатюриз|овáть, ýю *impf. and pf.* to miniaturize.
миниатюри́ст, а *m.* miniature-painter, miniaturist.
миниатю́р|ный (~ен, ~на) *adj.* **1.** *adj. of* **~а. 2.** (*fig.*) diminutive, tiny, dainty.
мини(-)компью́тер, а *m.* minicomputer.
минимáл|ьный (~ен, ~ьна) *adj.* minimum.
мини(-)маши́н|а, ы *f.* = **мини(-)компьютер**
ми́нимум, а *m.* **1.** minimum; **м. зáработной плáты** minimum wage; **прожи́точный м.** living wage; **техни́ческий м.** essential technical qualifications. **2.** (*as adv.*) at the least, at the minimum.
мини́р|овать, ую *impf. and pf.* (*mil., naut.*) to mine.
министéрский *adj.* ministerial.
министéрств|о, а *nt.* (*pol.*) ministry.
мини́стр, а *m.* (*pol.*) minister; **м.-президéнт, премьéр-м.** Prime Minister, premier.
мини-трус|ы́, óв *no sg.* (*woman's*) briefs, panties.
мини-футбóл, а *m.* ≃ five-a-side.
миниЭВМ *f. indecl.* = **мини(-)компьютер**
ми́ни-ю́бк|а (*and* **миниюбк|а**)**, и** *f.* miniskirt.
ми́нн|ый *adj.* (*mil.*) mine; **~ое загражде́ние** minefield.
мин|овáть, ýю *impf. and pf.* **1.** to pass (by); **~ýя подрóбности** omitting details. **2.** (*pf. only*) to be over, be past; **опáсность ~овáла** the danger is past. **3.** (*only with* **не**+*g.*) to escape; **не м. тебé тюрьмы́** you cannot escape being sent to prison.
минóг|а, и *f.* (*zool.*) lamprey.
миноискáтел|ь[1]**, я** *m.* (*mil.*) mine-detector (*apparatus*).
миноискáтель[2]**, я** *m.* (*mil.*) sapper.
миномёт, а *m.* (*mil.*) mortar; **гвардéйский м.** multi-rail rocket launcher.
миномёт|ный *adj. of* **~**
миномётчик, а *m.* (*mil.*) mortar man.
миноно́с|ец, ца *m.* (*naut.*) torpedo-boat; **эскáдренный м.** destroyer.
минóр, а *m.* **1.** (*mus.*) minor key. **2.** (*fig.*) gloomy, depressed; **быть в ~е** to have the blues, be in the dumps.
минóрн|ый *adj.* **1.** (*mus.*) minor. **2.** (*fig.*) gloomy, depressed; **быть в ~ом настроéнии** to have the blues, be in the dumps.
минýвш|ий *adj.* past; *as n.* **~ее, ~его** *nt.* the past.
ми́нус, а *m.* **1.** (*math.*) minus. **2.** (*fig., coll.*) defect, shortcoming.
ми́нусовый *adj.* (*elec.*) negative.
минýт|а, ы *f.* (*in var. senses*) minute.
минýт|ный *adj.* **1.** *adj. of* **~а**; **~ная стрéлка** minute-hand. **2.** momentary; transient, ephemeral; **~ная встрéча** brief encounter.
мин|ýть, ~ешь *pf.* **1.** (*past* **~ýл, ~ýла**) = **миновáть. 2.** (*past* **~ул, ~ула**) (+*d.*) to pass (*only in expressions of age*); **емý ~уло двáдцать лет** he has turned twenty.
миньóн, а *m.* (*typ.*) minion (*7-point type*).
миокарди́т, а *m.* (*med.*) myocarditis.
миóлог, а *m.* myologist.
миолóги|я, и *f.* myology.
миопи́|я, и *f.* (*med.*) myopia.
миоцéн, а *m.* Miocene.
мир[1]**, а** *m.* peace; **почётный м.** peace with honour; **прóчный м.** lasting peace; **заключи́ть м.** to make peace; **м. вам!** peace be with you!; **иди́те с ~ом** go in peace.
мир[2]**, а,** *pl.* **~ы́** *m.* world (*also fig.*); universe; **академи́ческий м.** academia; **живóтный м.** fauna; **расти́тельный м.** flora;

престу́пный м. the underworld; **не от ~а сего́** (*coll.*) other-worldly, not of this world; **в ~у́** in the world (*opp. in a monastery*); **ходи́ть по́ ~у** to beg, live by begging; **пусти́ть по́ ~у** to ruin utterly; **на ~у́ и смерть красна́** (*prov.*) company in distress makes trouble less.

мир³, а *m.* (*hist.*) mir (*Russ. village community*); **всем ~ом** all together; **с ~у по ни́тке го́лому руба́шка** (*prov.*) every little helps.

мирабе́л|ь, и *f.* mirabelle plum.

мира́ж, а *m.* mirage (*also fig.*); optical illusion.

мира́кл|ь, я *m.* (*liter.*, *theatr.*) miracle-play.

мирво́л|ить, ю, ишь *impf.* (+*d.*; *coll.*) to connive (at); to be over-indulgent (towards).

мир|и́ть, ю́, и́шь *impf.* **1.** (*pf.* **по~**) to reconcile. **2.** (*pf.* **при~**) (**с**+*i.*) to reconcile (to); **больша́я зарпла́та ~и́ла его́ с неприя́тными усло́виями рабо́ты** high wages reconciled him to unpleasant working conditions.

мир|и́ться, ю́сь, и́шься *impf.* (**с**+*i.*) **1.** (*pf.* **по~**) to be reconciled (with), make it up (with). **2.** (*pf.* **при~**) to reconcile o.s. (to); **м. со свои́м положе́нием** to accept the situation.

ми́р|ный (~ен, ~на) *adj.* **1.** *adj. of* **~¹**; **2.** peaceful; peaceable; **~ное сосуществова́ние** (*pol.*) peaceful co-existence.

ми́р|о, а *nt.* (*eccl.*) chrism; **одни́м ~ом ма́заны** (*fig.*, *joc.*) tarred with the same brush.

миров|а́я, о́й *f.* peaceful settlement; amicable agreement.

мировоззре́ни|е, я *nt.* (world-)outlook, Weltanschauung; (one's) philosophy.

мир|ово́й¹ *adj. of* **~²**; **~ова́я война́** world war; **~ова́я скорбь** Weltschmerz; (*coll.*, *joc.*) first-rate, first-class.

мирово́й² *adj.* (*obs.*) conciliatory; (*hist.*): **м. посре́дник** arbitrator **м. судья́** Justice of the Peace.

мироврия́ти|е, я *nt.* perception of the world.

мирое́д, а *m.* (*obs.*, *coll.*) extortioner, bloodsucker (*among peasants*).

мирозда́ни|е, я *nt.* the universe.

миролюби́вост|ь, и *f.* peaceable disposition.

миролюби́в|ый (~, ~а) *adj.* peaceable, pacific.

миролю́би|е, я *nt.* peaceableness.

мироощуще́ни|е, я *nt.* attitude, disposition.

миропома́зани|е, я *nt.* (*eccl.*) anointing.

миропонима́ни|е, я *nt.* = **мировосприя́тие**

миросозерца́ни|е, я *nt.* = **мировоззре́ние**

миротво́р|ец, ца *m.* peace-maker.

ми́рр|а, ы *f.* (*bot.*) myrrh.

мирско́й¹ *adj.* secular, lay; mundane, worldly.

мир|ско́й² *adj. of* **~³**; **~ска́я схо́дка** peasants' meeting.

мирт, а *m.* (*bot.*) myrtle.

ми́рт|овый *adj. of* **~**

миря́н|ин, ина, *pl.* **~е, ~** *m.* (*obs.*) layman (*opp. clergy*).

ми́ск|а, и *f.* basin, bowl.

ми́сс *f. indecl.* Miss.

миссионе́р, а *m.* missionary.

миссионе́р|ский *adj. of* **~**

миссионе́рств|о, а *nt.* missionary work.

ми́ссис *nt. indecl.* missis, Mrs.

ми́сси|я, и *f.* **1.** (*in var. senses*) mission. **2.** legation.

ми́стер, а *m.* mister, Mr.

мисте́ри|я, и *f.* **1.** (*relig.*) mystery; **элевси́нские ~и** the Eleusinian mysteries. **2.** (*hist.*, *theatr.*) mystery, miracle-play.

ми́стик, а *m.* mystic.

ми́стик|а, и *f.* mysticism.

мистифика́тор, а *m.* hoaxer.

мистифика́ци|я, и *f.* hoax, leg-pull.

мистифици́р|овать, ую *impf. and pf.* to hoax, mystify.

мистици́зм, а *m.* mysticism.

мисти́ческий *adj.* mystic(al).

мистра́л|ь, я *m.* mistral (wind).

мите́н|ки, ок *pl.* (*sg.* **~ка, ~ки** *f.*) mittens.

ми́тинг, а *m.* (political) mass-meeting; rally; **м. проте́ста** protest rally.

митинг|ова́ть, у́ю *impf.* (*coll.*) **1.** to hold a mass-meeting (about). **2.** (*pej.*) to discuss endlessly.

митинго́вый *adj. of* **ми́тинг**

миткал|евый *adj. of* **~ь**

миткал|ь, я́ *m.* (*text.*) calico.

ми́тр|а, ы *f.* (*eccl.*) mitre.

митрополи́т, а *m.* (*eccl.*) metropolitan.

митрополи́|чий *adj. of* **~т**

митропо́ли|я, и *f.* (*eccl.*) metropolitan see.

ми́ттел|ь, я *m.* (*typ.*) English (*14-point type*).

миф, а *m.* myth (*also fig.*).

мифи́ческий *adj.* mythic(al).

мифологи́ческий *adj.* mythological.

мифоло́ги|я, и *f.* mythology.

мифотво́рчеств|о, а *nt.* myth-making.

мице́ли|й, я *m.* (*bot.*) mycelium.

ми́чман, а, *pl.* (*in naval usage*) **~а́, ~о́в** *m.* (*naut.*) **1.** (*in Russian Navy*) warrant officer. **2.** (*in Imperial Russ. Navy*) midshipman.

ми́чман|ский *adj. of* **~**

мише́н|ь, и *f.* target (*also fig.*).

ми́шк|а, и *m.* (*dim. of* **Михаи́л**) **1.** (*pet-name for*) bear. **2.** teddy bear.

мишур|а́, ы́ *f.* **1.** tinsel. **2.** (*fig.*) trumpery.

мишу́рный *adj.* tinsel, trumpery, tawdry (*also fig.*).

миэли́т, а *m.* (*med.*) myelitis.

мл (*abbr. of* **миллили́тр**) ml, millilitre(s).

младе́н|ец, ца *m.* baby, infant.

младе́нческий *adj.* infantile.

младе́нчеств|о, а *nt.* infancy, babyhood.

младовегетариа́н|ец, ца *m.* lactovegetarian.

млад|о́й (~, ~а́, ~о) *adj.* (*arch. or poet.*) young; **стар и ~** one and all (*without respect of age*).

младопи́сьменный *adj.*: **м. язы́к** language having newly acquired a written form.

мла́дост|ь, и *f.* (*arch. or poet.*) youth.

мла́дший *adj.* (*comp. and superl. of* **молодо́й**) **1.** younger. **2.** the youngest. **3.** junior; **м. кома́ндный соста́в** non-commissioned officers; **м. офице́рский соста́в** junior officers, subaltern officers; **м. лейтена́нт** second lieutenant (*see also* **лейтена́нт**).

млекопита́ющ|ее, его *nt.* (*zool.*) mammal.

мле|ть, ю *impf.* **1.** (*obs.*) to grow numb. **2.** (**от**) to be overcome (*with delight, with fright, etc.*).

мле́чный *adj.* milk; lactic; **м. сок** (*bot.*) latex; (*physiol.*) chyle; **М. Путь** (*astron.*) the Milky Way, the Galaxy.

млн. (*abbr. of* **миллио́н**) m, million(s).

млрд. (*abbr. of* **миллиа́рд**) b., billion(s) (= *thousand million*).

мм (*abbr. of* **миллиме́тр**) mm, millimetre(s).

мне *d. and p. of* **я**

мнемони́ческий *adj.* mnemonic.

мне́ни|е, я *nt.* opinion.

мнимоуме́рший *adj.* apparently dead.

мни́м|ый *adj.* **1.** imaginary (*also math.*); **~ая величина́** imaginary quantity. **2.** sham, pretended; **м. больно́й** hypochondriac.

мни́тельност|ь, и *f.* **1.** hypochondria. **2.** mistrustfulness, suspiciousness.

мни́тел|ьный (~ен, ~ьна) *adj.* **1.** hypochondriac; valetudinarian. **2.** mistrustful, suspicious.

мн|ить, ю, ишь *impf.* **1.** (*obs.*) to think, imagine. **2.:** **м. мно́го о себе́** to think a lot of o.s.

мни́т|ься, ~ся *impf.* (*impers.*; *obs. or poet.*): **~ся** it seems, methinks.

мно́г|ие, их *adj. and n.* many; **во ~их отноше́ниях** in many respects.

мно́го *adv.* (+*g.*) much; many; a lot (of); **м. вре́мени** much time; **м. лет** many years; **о́чень м. знать** to know a great deal; **м. лу́чше** much better; **ни м., ни ма́ло** (*coll.*) neither more nor less.

много... *comb. form* many-, poly-, multi-.

многоа́томный *adj.* (*phys.*) polyatomic.

многобо́жи|е, я *nt.* polytheism.

многобо́р|ец, ца *m.* all-round athlete, multi-eventer.

многобо́рь|е, я *nt.* multi-discipline event *or* competition.

многобра́чи|е, я *nt.* polygamy.

многобра́ч|ный (~ен, ~на) *adj.* polygamous.
многова́то *adv.* (*coll.*) a bit too much, rather much (many).
многовеково́й *adj.* centuries-old.
многовла́сти|е, я *nt.* = **многонача́лие**
многово́д|ный (~ен, ~на) *adj.* (*of rivers, etc.*) full, having high water-level.
многово́дь|е, я *nt.* **1.** fullness, high water-level **2.** time of high water-levels.
многоговоря́щий *adj.* revealing, suggestive.
многогра́нник, а *m.* (*math.*) polyhedron.
многогра́нный *adj.* (*math.*) polyhedral; (*fig.*) many-sided; multi-faceted.
многоде́тност|ь, и *f.* possession of many children.
многоде́т|ный (~ен, ~на) *adj.* having many children.
многодне́вн|ый *adj.*: **м. путь** a journey lasting several days; **~ое автомоби́льное ра́лли** multi-stage motor rally.
мно́г|ое, ого *nt.* much, a great deal; **во ~ом** in many respects.
многоже́н|ец, ца *m.* polygamist.
многожёнств|о, а *nt.* polygamy.
многожи́льный *adj.* (*tech.*) multiple.
многозада́чный *adj.*: **м. режи́м (рабо́ты)** (*comput.*) multitasking.
многозаря́дн|ый *adj.*: **~ая боеголо́вка** multiple warhead.
многоземе́л|ьный (~ен, ~ьна) *adj.* possessing, owning much land; **~ьное хозя́йство** large-scale cultivation.
многозначи́тельност|ь, и *f.* significance.
многозначи́тел|ьный (~ен, ~ьна) *adj.* significant.
многозна́ч|ный (~ен, ~на) *adj.* **1.** (*math.*) expressed by several figures. **2.** (*ling.*) polysemantic; **~ное сло́во** polyseme.
многокаска́дный *adj.* (*radio*) multistage.
многоклё́точный *adj.* (*biol.*) multi-cellular.
многокра́сочный *adj.* polychromatic, many-coloured.
многокра́тный *adj.* **1.** repeated, re-iterated; multiple. **2.** (*gram.*) frequentative, iterative.
многола́мповый *adj.* multi-valve.
многоле́ти|е, я *nt.* expression of wishes for long life.
многоле́тний *adj.* **1.** lasting *or* living many years; of many years' standing. **2.** (*bot.*) perennial.
многоле́тник, а *m.* (*bot.*) perennial.
многоли́кий *adj.* many-sided.
многолю́дност|ь, и *f.* populousness; size (*of meeting, etc.*).
многолю́д|ный (~ен, ~на) *adj.* populous; crowded.
многолю́дств|о, а *nt.* throng.
многомиллио́нный *adj.* of many millions.
многому́жи|е, я *nt.* polyandry.
многонациона́л|ьный (~ен, ~ьна) *adj.* multi-national.
многонача́ли|е, я *nt.* multiple authority (*absence of clearly-defined spheres of authority*).
многоно́жк|а, и *f.* (*zool.*) myriapod.
многообеща́ющий *adj.* **1.** promising, hopeful. **2.** significant.
многообра́зи|е, я *nt.* variety, diversity.
многообра́з|ный (~ен, ~на) *adj.* varied, diverse.
многопо́ль|е, я *nt.* (*agric.*) crop-rotation system involving seven or eight fields.
многопо́ль|ный *adj. of* **~е**
многора́совый *adj.* multiracial.
многоречи́в|ый (~, ~а) *adj.* loquacious, verbose, prolix.
многосеме́|йный (~ен, ~йна) *adj.* having a large family.
многосло́в|ный (~ен, ~на) *adj.* verbose, prolix.
многосло́жный *adj.* **1.** complex, complicated. **2.** polysyllabic.
многосло́йн|ый *adj.* multi-layer; multi-ply; **~ая фане́ра** plywood.
многостано́чник, а *m.* workman operating a number of machines simultaneously.
многостепе́нн|ый *adj.* many-stage; **~ые вы́боры** election by several stages.
многосторо́н|ний (~ен, ~ня) *adj.* **1.** (*math.*) polygonal; multilateral (*also fig.*). **2.** (*fig.*) many-sided, versatile.
многострада́л|ьный (~ен, ~ьна) *adj.* suffering, unfortunate.
многоступе́нчатый *adj.* (*tech.*) multi-stage.
многотира́жк|а, и *f.* (*coll.*) factory newspaper; house organ.
многотира́жный *adj.* published in large editions; large-circulation.
многото́мный *adj.* multivolume.
многото́чи|е, я *nt.* (*typ.*) ellipsis *or* suspension points.
многотру́д|ный (~ен, ~на) *adj.* arduous.
многоуважа́емый *adj.* respected; (*in letters*) dear.
многоуго́льник, а *m.* (*math.*) polygon.
многоуго́льный *adj.* (*math.*) polygonal.
многофа́зный *adj.* (*elec.*) polyphase.
многоцве́тный *adj.* **1.** many-coloured, multi-coloured. **2.** (*typ.*) polychromatic. **3.** (*bot.*) multiflorous.
многоцелево́й *adj.* multipurpose.
многочи́слен|ный (~, ~на) *adj.* numerous.
многочле́н, а *m.* (*math.*) multinomial.
многоэта́жный *adj.* multi-storey, high-rise.
мно́жественност|ь, и *f.* plurality.
мно́жественн|ый *adj.* plural; **~ое число́** (*gram.*) plural (number).
мно́жеств|о, а *nt.* a great number, a quantity; multitude; (*math.*) set.
мно́жим|ое, ого *nt.* (*math.*) multiplicand.
мно́жител|ь, я *m.* multiplier, factor.
мно́ж|ить, у, ишь *impf.* **1.** (*pf.* **по~, у~**) (*math.*) to multiply. **2.** (*pf.* **у~**) to increase, augment.
мно́ж|иться, усь, ишься *impf.* (*of* **у~**) **1.** to multiply, increase (*intrans.*). **2.** *pass. of* **~ить**
мной, мно́ю *i. of* **я**
МНР *f. indecl.* (*abbr. of* ***Монго́льская Наро́дная Респу́блика***) Mongolian People's Republic.
мобилиза|цио́нный *adj. of* **~ция**
мобилиза́ци|я, и *f.* mobilization.
мобилизо́ванност|ь, и *f.* complete readiness for action.
мобилизо́в|анный *p.p.p. of* **~а́ть**; *as n.* mobilized soldier.
мобилиз|ова́ть, у́ю *impf. and pf.* (**на**+*a.*) to mobilize (for).
моби́льный *adj.* mobile.
могика́н|е, ~ *pl.* (*sg.* **могика́нин, а** *m.*, **могика́нк|а, и** *f.*) the Mohicans; **после́дний из ~** the last of the Mohicans.
моги́л|а, ы *f.* grave; **свести́ в ~у** to bring to one's grave.
моги́льник, а *m.* (*archaeol.*) burial ground.
моги́льный *adj.* **1.** *adj. of* **моги́ла. 2.** sepulchral.
моги́льщик, а *m.* grave-digger.
мо|гу́, ~гут *see* **мочь**
могу́ч|ий (~, ~а) *adj.* mighty, powerful.
могу́ществен|ный (~, ~на) *adj.* powerful; potent.
могу́честв|о, а *nt.* power, might.
мо́д|а, ы *f.* fashion, vogue; **выходи́ть из ~ы** to go out of fashion; **по после́дней ~е** in the latest fashion.
мода́льност|ь, и *f.* (*phil.*) modality.
мода́льный *adj.* modal.
модели́зм, а *m.* modelling.
модели́р|овать, ую *impf. and pf.* (*pf. also* **с~**) to model, fashion.
моде́л|ь, и *f.* (*in var. senses*) model, pattern.
моделье́р, а *m.* fashion designer, couturier.
моде́ль|ный *adj.* **1.** *adj. of* **~. 2.** fashionable.
моде́льщик, а *m.* (*tech.*) modeller, pattern maker.
моде́м, а *m.* (*comput.*) modem.
модера́тор, а *m.* (*tech.*) governor.
моде́рн, а *m.* modernist style (*in art, furnishing, etc.*); *as indecl. adj.* modern; **м.-бале́т** modern dance.
модерниза́ци|я, и *f.* modernization; updating.
модернизи́р|овать, ую *impf. and pf.* to modernize; to update.
модерни́зм, а *m.* (*art*) modernism.
модерниз|ова́ть, у́ю *impf. and pf.* = **~и́ровать**
модерни́ст, а *m.* (*art*) modernist.
моде́рновый = **моде́рный**
моде́рный *adj.* (*coll.*) modern; trendy, with-it.
моди́стк|а, и *f.* milliner, modiste.
модифика́ци|я, и *f.* modification.
модифици́р|овать, ую *impf. and pf.* to modify.
мо́дник, а *m.* (*coll.*) dandy.
мо́днича|ть, ю *impf.* (*coll.*) **1.** to dress in the latest fashion. **2.** (*coll.*) to behave affectedly.
мо́д|ный (~ен, ~на́, ~но) *adj.* **1.** fashionable, stylish. **2.** *adj. of* **~а**; **м. журна́л** fashion magazine.

модули́р|овать, ую *impf.* (*mus. and tech.*) to modulate.
мо́дул|ь, я *m.* (*math.*) modulus.
модуля́ци|я, и *f.* (*mus. and tech.*) modulation.
мо́дус, а *m.* modus.
моёвк|а, и *f.* (*orn.*) kittiwake.
мо́жет *see* **мочь**
можжевёловый *adj.* juniper.
можжеве́льник, а *m.* (*bot.*) juniper.
мо́жно *pred.* (*impers.+ inf.*) **1.** it is possible; **м. бы́ло э́то предви́деть** it was possible to foresee it, it could have been foreseen; **как м.**+*comp.* as ... as possible; **как м. скоре́е** as soon as possible. **2.** it is permissible, one may; **м. идти́?** may I (we) go?; **м.! (***sc.* **войти́)** come in!
моза́ик|а, и *f.* mosaic; inlay.
моза́ичный *adj.* inlaid, mosaic, tesselated.
Мозамби́к, а *m.* Mozambique.
мозамби́кский *adj.* Mozambican.
мозг, а, в ~у́, *pl.* **~и́, ~о́в** *m.* **1.** brain (*also fig.*), nerve tissue; **головно́й м.** brain, cerebrum; **спинно́й м.** spinal cord; **шевели́ть ~а́ми** (*coll.*) to use one's head. **2.** (*anat.*) marrow; **до ~а косте́й** (*fig., coll.*) to the core.
мо́зглый *adj.* dank.
мозгля́вый *adj.* (*coll.*) weakly, puny.
мозгови́т|ый (~, ~а) *adj.* (*coll.*) brainy.
мозгово́й *adj.* (*anat.*) cerebral; (*fig.*) brain.
Мо́зел|ь, я *m.* the Moselle (*river*).
мозельве́йн, а *m.* Moselle (*wine*).
мозжеч|о́к, ка́ *m.* (*anat.*) cerebellum.
мозж|и́ть, и́т *impf.* (*coll.*) to ache; **мозжи́т нога́** my leg is aching; (*impers.*): **мозжи́т но́гу** my leg is aching; **мозжи́т в ноге́** I've an ache in my leg.
мозо́лист|ый (~, ~а) *adj.* callous(ed); (*fig.*) toil-hardened; **~ые ру́ки** horny hands.
мозо́л|ить, ю, ишь *impf.* (*of* **на~**) to make callous; **м. глаза́** (*+d.*; *fig., coll.*) to plague (with one's presence).
мозо́л|ь, и *f.* corn; callus, callosity; **ру́ки в ~ях** callus(ed) hands; **наступи́ть кому́-н. на люби́мую м.** (*fig., coll.*) to tread on s.o.'s pet corn.
мозо́ль|ный *adj. of* **~; м. пла́стырь** corn-plaster.
мой *possessive adj.* my; mine; **ты зна́ешь лу́чше моего́** (*coll.*) you know better than I; *as n.* **мои́, мои́х** my people; **по-мо́ему** in my opinion; as I think right.
мо́йк|а, и *f.* **1.** washing. **2.** (*tech.*) washer.
мо́йщик, а *m.* washer; cleaner; **м. о́кон** window-cleaner; **м. посу́ды** dishwasher (*pers.*), washer-up.
мо́кко *m. indecl.* mocha (coffee).
мо́к|нуть, ну, нешь, *past* **~, ~ла** *impf.* **1.** (*pf.* **вы~**) to become wet, become soaked. **2.** to soak (*intrans.*).
мокри́ц|а, ы *f.* wood-louse.
мокрова́тый *adj.* moist, damp.
мокро́т|а, ы *f.* (*med.*) phlegm.
мокрот|а́, ы́ *f.* humidity, moistness.
мокру́шник, а *m.* (*sl.*) hit man (= *paid assassin*).
мо́кр|ый (~, ~а́, ~о) *adj.* wet, damp; soggy; (*impers., pred.*) **~о** it is wet; **~ая ку́рица** (*coll.*) milksop; **у неё глаза́ на ~ом ме́сте** (*coll.*) she is easily moved to tears.
мол[1], **а** *m.* mole, pier.
мол[2] (*contraction of* **мо́лвил**) he says (said), they say (said), *etc.* (*indicating reported speech*); **он, м., никогда́ там не́ был** he said he had never been there.
молв|а́, ы́ *f.* (*obs.*) rumour, talk; **идёт м.** it is rumoured, rumour has it; **дурна́я м.** ill repute.
мо́лв|ить, лю, ишь *pf.* (*obs.*) to say.
молдава́н|ин, ина, *pl.* **~е, ~** *m.* Moldovan; Moldavian.
молдава́н|ка, ки *f. of* **~ин**
молдав|а́нский = **~ский**
Молда́ви|я, и *f.* (*hist.*) Moldavia.
молда́вский *adj.* Moldovan; Moldavian.
Молдо́в|а, ы *f.* Moldova.
моле́б|ен, на *m.* (*eccl.*) service; public prayer.
моле́бстви|е, я *nt.* = **моле́бен**
моле́кул|а, ы *f.* (*phys.*) molecule.
молекуля́рный *adj.* molecular.
моле́л|ьня, ьни, *g. pl.* **~ен** *f.* chapel, meeting-house (*of relig. sects*).
моле́ни|е, я *nt.* **1.** praying. **2.** entreaty, supplication.
молески́н, а *m.* (*text.*) moleskin.
молибде́н, а *m.* (*chem.*) molybdenum.
молибде́н|овый *adj. of* **~**
моли́тв|а, ы *f.* prayer.
моли́твенник, а *m.* prayer-book.
моли́тв|енный *adj. of* **~а**
мол|и́ть, ю́, ~ишь *impf.* (*a. and* **о**+*p.*) to pray (for), entreat (for), supplicate (for), beseech; **~ю́ вас о по́мощи** I beg you to help me.
мол|и́ться, ю́сь, ~ишься *impf.* **1.** (*pf.* **по~; о**+*p.*) to pray (for), offer prayers (for); **он ~ится Бо́гу** he is saying his prayers. **2.** (*fig.*; **на**+*a.*) to idolize.
мо́лкн|уть, у, ешь *impf.* (*poet.*) to fall silent.
моллю́ск, а *m.* mollusc; shell-fish.
молниено́сно *adv.* with lightning speed, like lightning.
молниено́с|ный (~ен, ~на) *adj.* (quick as) lightning; **~ная война́** blitzkrieg.
молниеотво́д, а *m.* lightning-conductor.
молни́р|овать, ую *impf. and pf.* to inform by express telegram.
мо́лни|я, и *f.* **1.** lightning. **2. (телегра́мма-)м.** express telegram. **3. (застёжка-)м.** zip-fastener.
молодёж|ный *adj. of* **~ь**
молодёж|ь, и *f.* (*collect.*) youth; young people.
молоде́|ть, ю, ешь *impf.* (*of* **по~**) to grow young again.
молод|е́ц, ца́ *m.* fine fellow; **вести́ себя́ ~цо́м** (*coll.*) to put up a good show; *as int.* **м.!** well done!
молоде́цкий *adj.* (*coll.*) dashing, spirited.
молоде́честв|о, а *nt.* spirit, mettle, dash.
моло|ди́ть, жу́, ди́шь *impf.* to make look younger.
моло|ди́ться, жу́сь, ди́шься *impf.* to try to look younger than one's age.
молоди́ц|а, ы *f.* (*dial.*) young married (peasant) woman.
моло́д|ка, ки *f.* **1.** = **~и́ца. 2.** pullet.
молодня́к, а́ *m.* (*collect.*) **1.** saplings. **2.** young animals; cubs. **3.** (*coll.*) the younger generation.
молодожён|ы, ов *pl.* (*sg.* **~, ~а** *m.*) **1.** newly-married couple, newly-weds. **2.** (*sg.*) newly-married man.
молод|о́й (мо́лод, ~а́, мо́лодо) *adj.* **1.** young; youthful (*also of inanimate objects*); **м. задо́р** youthful hotheadedness; **м. карто́фель** new potatoes; **м. ме́сяц** new moon; **мо́лодо-зе́лено!** (*iron., of young or inexperienced pers.*) he has a lot to learn! **2.** *as n.* (*coll.*) **м., ~о́го** *m.* bridegroom; **~а́я, ~о́й** *f.* bride; **~ы́е, ~ы́х** newly-married couple, newly-weds.
мо́лодост|ь, и *f.* youth; youthfulness.
молоду́х|а, и *f.* (*dial.*) = **молоди́ца**
молодцева́т|ый (~, ~а) *adj.* dashing, sprightly.
моло́дчик, а *m.* (*coll.*) **1.** rogue, rascal. **2.** (*pej.*) lackey, myrmidon.
молодчи́н|а, ы *m.* (*coll.*) fine fellow; *as int.* **м.!** well done!
мо́лод|ь, и *f.* young; fry.
моложа́вост|ь, и *f.* youthful appearance (*for one's years*).
моложа́в|ый (~, ~а) *adj.* young-looking; **име́ть м. вид** to look young for one's age.
моло́|же *comp. of* **~до́й**
моло́зив|о, а *no pl., nt.* colostrum; (*of cow*) beestings.
моло́к|и, ~ *no sg.* soft roe, milt.
молок|о́, а́ *no pl., nt.* milk.
молокови́з, а *m.* milk tanker.
молокосо́с, а *m.* (*coll.*) greenhorn, raw youth.
мо́лот, а *m.* hammer; **кузне́чный м.** sledge-hammer.
молоти́лк|а, и *f.* threshing-machine.
молоти́л|о, а *nt.* (*agric.*) swingle.
молоти́льщик, а *m.* thresher.
моло|ти́ть, чу́, ~тишь *impf.* (*of* **с~**) to thresh.
молотобо́|ец, йца *m.* (*tech.*) hammerer; blacksmith's striker.
молот|о́к[1], **ка́** *m.* hammer; gavel; **отбо́йный м.** pneumatic drill; **прода́ть с ~ка́** to sell by auction.
молото́к[2] *int.* (*sl.*) attaboy!; good lad!
молото́ч|ек, ка *m.* **1.** *dim. of* **молото́к. 2.** (*anat.*) malleus.
мо́лот-ры́б|а, ы *f.* (*zool.*) hammer-head shark.
мо́лот|ый (~, ~а) *p.p.p. of* **моло́ть** *and adj.* ground.
моло́ть, мелю́, ме́лешь *impf.* (*of* **с~**) to grind, mill; **м.**

вздор (*fig.*, *coll.*) to talk nonsense *or* rot.
молотьб|а́, ы́ *f.* threshing.
молоча́|й, я *m.* (*bot.*) spurge, euphorbia.
моло́чн|ая, ой *f.* dairy; creamery.
моло́чник[1], **а** *m.* milk-jug; milk-can.
моло́чник[2], **а** *m.* milkman.
моло́чниц|а[1], **ы** *f.* milk-seller; dairy-maid.
моло́чниц|а[2], **ы** *f.* (*med.*) thrush.
моло́чност|ь, и *f.* (*agric.*) yield (*of cow*).
моло́чн|ый *adj.* **1.** *adj. of* **молоко́; м. брат** foster-brother; **~ое стекло́** frosted glass; opal glass; **~ое хозя́йство** dairy-farm(ing). **2.** milky; lactic; **~ая кислота́** (*chem.*) lactic acid.
мо́лча *adv.* silently, in silence.
молчали́в|ый (~, ~а) *adj.* **1.** taciturn, silent. **2.** tacit, unspoken.
молча́льник, а *m.* (*relig.*) silentiary.
молча́ни|е, я *nt.* silence.
молч|а́ть, у́, и́шь *impf.* to be silent, keep silence.
молч|ко́м *adv.* (*coll.*) = **~а́**
молчо́к *m. indecl.* (*coll.*) silence; **об э́том — м.!** not a word of (about) this!
мол|ь[1], **и** *f.* (clothes-)moth.
мол|ь[2], **и** *f.* (*chem.*) mole (*gram molecule*).
мольб|а́, ы́ *f.* entreaty, supplication.
мольбе́рт, а *m.* easel.
моля́щ|ийся, егося *m.* worshipper.
моме́нт, а *m.* **1.** moment; instant; **голево́й м.** scoring opportunity; **лови́ м.!** now's your chance!; go for it! **2.** feature, element, factor (*of process*, *situation*, *etc.*). **3.** (*phys.*) moment; **м. ине́рции** moment of inertia.
момента́льно *adv.* in a moment, instantly.
момента́льный *adj.* instantaneous; **м. сни́мок** snapshot.
моме́нтами *adv.* (*coll.*) now and then.
мона́д|а, ы *f.* (*phil.*) monad.
Мона́ко *nt. indecl.* Monaco.
мона́кский *adj.* Monegasque.
мона́рх, а *m.* monarch.
монархи́зм, а *m.* monarchism.
монархи́ст, а *m.* monarchist.
монархи́ческ|ий *adj.* monarchic(al).
мона́рхи|я, и *f.* monarchy.
мона́рший *adj. of* **мона́рх**
монасты́рский *adj.* monastic, conventual.
монасты́р|ь, я́ *m.* monastery; **(же́нский)** convent; **в чужо́й м. со свои́м уста́вом не су́йся** (*prov.*) when in Rome do as the Romans do.
мона́х, а *m.* monk; friar; **постри́чься в ~и** to take the monastic vows; **жить ~ом** (*fig.*, *iron.*) to have a monkish existence.
мона́хин|я, и *f.* nun; **постри́чся в ~и** to take the veil.
мона́шенк|а, и *f.* **1.** (*coll.*) nun. **2.** (*zool.*) praying mantis.
мона́шеский *adj.* monastic; (*fig.*, *joc.*) monkish.
мона́шеств|о, а *nt.* **1.** monasticism. **2.** (*collect.*) monks, regular clergy.
Монбла́н, а *m.* Mont Blanc.
монго́л, а *m.* Mongol, Mongolian.
Монго́ли|я, и *f.* Mongolia.
монго́л|ка, ки *f. of* **~**
монголове́дени|е, я *nt.* Mongolian studies.
монго́льский *adj.* Mongolian.
моне́т|а, ы *f.* coin; **зво́нкая м.** specie, hard cash; **разме́нная м.** change; **ходя́чая м.** currency; **плати́ть кому́-н. той же ~ой** (*fig.*) to give s.o. a dose of his own medicine; **приня́ть за чи́стую ~у** (*fig.*, *coll.*) to take at face value, take in good faith.
монетари́ст, а *m.* (*econ.*) monetarist.
монетари́ст|ский *adj. of* **~**
моне́тный *adj.* monetary; **м. двор** mint.
монетоприёмник, а *m.* coin-box (*of automatic machine*).
моне́тчик, а *m.* coiner.
мони́зм, а *m.* (*phil.*) monism.
мони́ст|о, а *nt.* necklace.
монито́р, а *m.* (*tech.*) monitor.
монито́ринг, а *m.* monitoring.
монога́ми|я, и *f.* monogamy; (*zool.*) pair-bonding.
монога́мный *adj.* monogamous.
моногра́мм|а, ы *f.* monogram.
моногра́фи|я, и *f.* monograph.
моно́кл|ь, я *m.* (*single*) eye-glass, monocle.
моноко́к, а *m.* (*aeron.*) monocoque.
монокульту́р|а, ы *f.* (*agric.*) one-crop system, monoculture.
моноли́т, а *m.* monolith.
моноли́тност|ь, и *f.* monolithic character, solidity.
моноли́т|ный (~ен, ~на) *adj.* monolithic (*also fig.*; *pol.*); (*fig.*) solid.
моноло́г, а *m.* monologue, soliloquy.
моно́м, а *m.* (*math.*) monomial.
монома́н, а *m.* (*med.*) monomaniac.
монома́ни|я, и *f.* (*med.*) monomania.
монометалли́зм, а *m.* (*econ.*) monometallism.
монопла́н, а *m.* monoplane.
монополиза́ци|я, и *f.* monopolization.
монополизи́р|овать, ую *impf. and pf.* to monopolize.
монополи́ст, а *m.* monopolist.
монополисти́ческий *adj.* monopolistic.
монопо́ли|я, и *f.* (*econ. and fig.*) monopoly.
монопо́л|ьный *adj. of* **~ия; ~ьное пра́во** exclusive rights.
моноре́льсовый *adj.* monorail.
моноспекта́кл|ь, я *m.* one-man show.
монотеи́зм, а *m.* monotheism.
монотеисти́ческий *adj.* monotheistic.
моноти́п, а *m.* (*typ.*) monotype.
моното́нный *adj.* monotonous.
монофто́нг, а *m.* (*ling.*) monophthong.
монохо́рд, а *m.* (*mus.*) monochord.
монохро́мный *adj.* monochrome.
моноци́кл, а *m.* unicycle.
монпансье́ *nt. indecl.* fruit drops.
Монреа́л|ь, я *m.* Montreal.
монстр, а *m.* monster.
монта́ж, а *m.* **1.** (*tech.*) assembling, mounting, installation. **2.** (*cin.*) montage; (*art*, *mus.*, *liter.*) arrangement; **м. о́перы по ра́дио** arrangement of an opera for radio.
монтажёр, а *m.* (*cin.*, *phot.*) montage specialist.
монта́жник, а *m.* rigger, erector, fitter.
монта́ж|ный *adj. of* **~**; *as n.* **~ная, ~ной** *f.* (*tech.*) assembly shop; (*cin.*) clipping room.
Мо́нте-Ка́рло *m. indecl.* Monte-Carlo.
монтёр, а *m.* **1.** fitter. **2.** electrician.
монти́р|овать, ую *impf.* (*of* **с~**) **1.** (*tech.*) to assemble, mount, fit. **2.** (*art*, *cin.*, *etc.*) to mount; to arrange.
монуме́нт, а *m.* monument.
монумента́льный *adj.* monumental (*also fig.*).
мопс, а *m.* pug(-dog).
мор, а *m.* (*obs. and coll.*) wholesale deaths, high mortality.
морализи́р|овать, ую *impf.* to moralize.
морали́ст, а *m.* moralist.
мора́л|ь, и *f.* **1.** (code of) morals, ethics. **2.** (*coll.*) moralizing; **чита́ть м.** to moralize. **3.** moral (*of a story*, *etc.*).
мора́льный *adj.* (*in var. senses*) moral; ethical.
морато́ри|й, я *m.* (*leg.*, *comm.*) moratorium.
морг[1], **а** *m.* morgue, mortuary.
морг[2], **а** *m.* (*obs.*) *land measure, equivalent to approx. 1.25 acres/0.5 hectares* (*in Poland and Lithuania*).
морганати́ческий *adj.* morganatic.
морг|а́ть, а́ю *impf.* (*of* **~ну́ть**) to blink; to wink.
морг|ну́ть, ну́, нёшь *pf. of* **~а́ть; гла́зом не ~ну́в** (*coll.*) without batting an eyelid.
мо́рд|а, ы *f.* **1.** snout, muzzle. **2.** (*coll.*; *of human face*) mug.
морда́ст|ый (~, ~а) *adj.* (*coll.*) **1.** with a large muzzle. **2.** (*of people*) with a big, fat face.
мордв|а́, ы́ *f.* (*collect.*) the Mordva, the Mordvinians.
мордви́н, а *m.* Mordvinian.
мордви́н|ка, ки *f. of* **~**
мордо́вский *adj.* Mordvinian.
мо́р|е, я, *pl.* **~я́, ~е́й** *nt.*: **за́ ~ем** oversea(s); **из-за ~я** from overseas; **на́ м.** at sea; **у ~я** by the sea; **ему́ м. по коле́но** (*coll.*) he doesn't care a damn.
море́н|а, ы *f.* (*geol.*) moraine.
море́н|ный *adj. of* **~а**

морёный *adj.* (*of wood*) water-seasoned.
мореплáвани|е, я *nt.* navigation, seafaring.
мореплáвател|ь, я *m.* navigator, seafarer.
мореплáвательный *adj.* nautical, navigational.
морехóд, а *m.* seafarer.
морехóдност|ь, и *f.* seaworthiness.
морехóдный *adj.* nautical.
морехóдств|о, а *nt.* (*obs.*) navigation.
морж, á *m.* walrus; (*coll.*) (*open-air*) winter bather.
моржевáни|е, я *nt.* (*open-air*) winter bathing.
моржи́х|а, и *f. of* **морж**
морж|óвый *adj. of* ~
Мóрзе *indecl.* Morse; **áзбука М.** Morse code.
морзи́ст, а *m.* Morse code signaller.
морзя́нк|а, и *f.* (*coll.*) Morse code.
мори́лк|а, и *f.* (*tech.*) mordant.
мор|и́ть[1], ю́, и́шь *impf.* **1.** (*pf.* **вы́~** *and* **по~**) to exterminate. **2.** (*pf.* **у~**) to exhaust, wear out; **м. гóлодом** to starve. **3.** (*dial.*) to quench.
мор|и́ть[2], ю́, и́шь *impf.* to stain (*wood*); **м. дуб** to fume oak.
моркóвк|а, и *f.* (*coll.*) a carrot.
моркóв|ный *adj. of* **~ь**
моркóв|ь, и *f.* carrots.
мормóн, а *m.* (*relig.*) Mormon.
морóв|óй *adj.*: **~óе повéтрие, ~áя я́зва** plague, pestilence.
морóжениц|а, ы *f.* ice cream maker (*appliance*).
морóжен|ое, ого *nt.* ice(-cream); **м. в шоколáде** choc-ice.
морóженщик, а *m.* ice-cream vendor.
морóженщи|ца, ы *f. of* **~к**
морóжен|ый *adj.* frozen, chilled; **~ое мя́со** chilled meat.
морóз, а *m.* **1.** frost; **у меня́ м. по кóже подирáет (пошёл)** it makes (made) my flesh creep. **2.** (*usu. in pl.*) intensely cold weather.
морози́лк|а, и *f.* (*coll.*) freezer compartment; freezer.
морози́льник, а *m.* deep-freezer.
морози́льщик, а *m.* (*coll.*) refrigerator ship.
морó|зить, жу, зишь *impf.* (*of* **по~**) **1.** to freeze, congeal. **2.** (*impers.*): **~зит** it is freezing.
морóзн|ый *adj.* frosty; (*impers., pred.*) **~о** it is freezing.
морозостóйкий *adj.* (*bot.*) frost-resisting.
морозоустóйчив|ый (~, ~а) *adj.* = **морозостóйкий**
морóк|а, и *f.* (*coll., fig.*) darkness, confusion; **с ним однá м.** you can get no sense out of him.
морос|и́ть, и́т *impf.* to drizzle.
мóрось = **и́зморось**
морóч|ить, у, ишь *impf.* (*of* **об~**) (*coll.*) to fool, pull the wool over the eyes of; **м. гóлову комý-н.** to take s.o. in.
морóшк|а, и *f.* cloudberry (*Rubus chamaimorus*).
морс, а *m.* fruit drink.
морск|óй *adj.* **1.** sea; maritime; marine, nautical; **м. волк** (*coll.*) old salt, sea-dog; **~áя звездá** starfish; **м. ёж** (*zool.*) sea-urchin, echinus; **~áя иглá** needle-fish, pipe-fish; **~áя капýста** (*bot.*) sea-kale; **м. конёк** (*zool.*) sea-horse, hippocamp; **~áя пéнка** (*min.*) meerschaum; **м. разбóйник** pirate; **~áя сви́нка** guinea-pig; **~áя свинья́** porpoise. **2.** naval; **~áя пехóта** marines; **м. флот** navy, fleet.
морти́р|а, ы *f.* (*mil.*) mortar.
морти́р|ный *adj. of* **~а**
морфéм|а, ы *f.* (*ling.*) morpheme.
мóрфи|й, я *m.* (*pharm.*) morphia, morphine.
морфини́зм, а *m.* addiction to morphine.
морфини́ст, а *m.* morphine addict.
морфологи́ческий *adj.* morphological.
морфолóги|я, и *f.* morphology.
морщи́н|а, ы *f.* wrinkle; crease.
морщи́нист|ый (~, ~а) *adj.* wrinkled, lined; creased.
мóрщ|ить, у, ишь *impf.* **1.** (*pf.* **на~**) **м. лоб** to knit one's brow. **2.** (*pf.* **с~**) to wrinkle, pucker; **м. гýбы** to purse one's lips.
морщ|и́ть, и́т *impf.* to crease, ruck up (*intrans.*).
мóрщ|иться, усь, ишься *impf.* **1.** (*pf.* **на~**) to knit one's brow. **2.** (*pf.* **по~** *and* **с~**) to make a wry face, wince. **3.** (*pf.* **с~**) to crease, wrinkle.
моря́к, á *m.* sailor.
москáл|ь, я́ *m.* (*obs., pej.*) Muscovite.
москатéл|ь, и *f.* (*collect.*) dry-salter's wares (*paints, oil, gum, etc.*).
москатéль|ный *adj. of* ~; **~ная торгóвля** dry-saltery.
москатéльщик, а *m.* dry-salter.
Москв|á, ы́ *f.* **1.** Moscow; **М. не срáзу строи́лась** (*prov.*) Rome wasn't built in a day; **М. слезáм не вéрит** (*prov.*) tears will get you nowhere. **2.** the Moskva (*river*).
москвитя́н|ин, ина, *pl.* **~е** *m.* (*obs.*) Muscovite.
москви́ч, á *m.* **1.** Muscovite. **2.** Moskvich (*trade name of Russian-made motor car*).
москви́ч|ка, ки *f. of* ~ **1.**
моски́т, а *m.* mosquito.
моски́т|ный *adj. of* ~; **~ная сéтка** mosquito net.
Москóви|я, и *f.* (*hist.*) Muscovy.
москóвк|а, и *f.* (*zool.*) coal tit.
москóвск|ий *adj.* (of) Moscow; **~ая Русь** (*hist.*) Muscovy.
мост, ~á, о ~́е, на ~ý, *pl.* **~ы́** *m.* **1.** bridge. **2.** (*tech.*) shaft.
мóстик, а *m.* **1.** *dim. of* **мост. 2.: капитáнский м.** (*naut.*) (*captain's*) bridge.
мости́льщик, а *m.* paver.
мо|сти́ть, щý, сти́шь *impf.* **1.** (*pf.* **вы́~, за~**) to pave. **2.** (*pf.* **на~**) to lay (*a floor*).
мостк|и́, óв *no sg.* **1.** planked walkway. **2.** wooden platform (*at edge of stream, on scaffolding*).
мостов|áя, óй *f.* road(way), carriage way.
мост|овóй *adj. of* ~
мóськ|а, и *f.* (*coll.*) pug-dog.
мот, а *m.* prodigal, spendthrift.
мотáльный *adj.* (*tech.*) winding.
мот|áть[1], áю *impf.* **1.** (*pf.* **за~, на~**) to wind, reel; **м. себé что-н. на ус** (*fig., coll.*) to make a mental note of sth. **2.** (*pf.* **~нýть**) (*+i.; coll.*) to shake (*head, etc.*).
мотá|ть[2], ю *impf.* (*of* **про~**) (*coll.*) to squander.
мотá|ться[1], ется *impf.* (*coll.*) to dangle.
мотá|ться[2], юсь *impf.* (*coll.*) to rush about; **м. пó свету** to knock about the world.
мотéл|ь, я *m.* motel.
моти́в[1], а *m.* **1.** motive. **2.** reason; **привести́ ~ы в пóльзу предложéния** to adduce reasons in support of an assertion.
моти́в[2], а *m.* **1.** (*mus.*) tune. **2.** (*mus. and fig.*) motif.
мотиви́р|овать, ую *impf. and pf.* to give reasons (for), justify.
мотивирóвк|а, и *f.* reason(s), justification.
мот|нýть, нý, нёшь *pf. of* **~áть[1]**
мото... *comb. form, abbr. of* **1. мотóрный[1]. 2. моторизóванный. 3. мотоциклéтный**
мотобóт, а *m.* motor-boat.
мотови́л|о, а *nt.* (*tech.*) reel.
мотóвк|а, и *f.* (*coll.*) *of* **мот**
мотовóз, а *m.* petrol engine (*on rail. for shunting, etc.*).
мотовскóй *adj.* wasteful, extravagant.
мотовств|ó, á *nt.* wastefulness, extravagance, prodigality.
мотогóн|ки, ок *no sg.* motor-cycle races.
мотогóнщик, а *m.* motor cycle racer.
мотодрези́н|а, ы *f.* motor trolley (*on rails*).
мотодрóм, а *m.* motor-cycle racing track.
мотозавóд, а *m.* motorcycle factory.
мот|óк, кá *m.* skein, hank.
мотоклýб, а *m.* motorcycle club.
мотоколя́ск|а, и *f.* motorized wheel-chair.
мотокрóсс, а *m.* moto-cross, scramble.
мотокроссмéн, а *m.* moto-cross competitor.
мотомеханизи́рованный *adj.* (*mil.*) mechanized.
мотопéд, а *m.* moped.
мотопехóт|а, ы *f.* motorized infantry.
мотопил|á, ы́ *f.* power saw.
мотопланёр, а *m.* powered glider.
мотóр, а *m.* motor, engine; **подвеснóй м.** outboard engine.
моторесýрс, а *m.* (*tech.*) life (*of an engine, etc.*)
моторизáци|я, и *f.* motorization.
моторизóв|анный *p.p.p. of* **~áть** *and adj.* (*mil.*) motorized.
моториз|овáть, ýю *impf. and pf.* to motorize.
моторист, а *m.* motor-mechanic.
мотóрк|а, и *f.* (*coll.*) motor-boat.

мото́р|ный[1] *adj. of* ~; **м. ваго́н** front car (*of set, on electric railway or tramway, and containing power unit*); **~ная устано́вка** power plant, power unit.
мото́рный[2] *adj.* (*physiol., psych.*) motor.
моторо́ллер, а *m.* (motor-)scooter.
мотоспо́рт, а *m.* motorcycle racing.
мототра́сс|а, ы *f.* trail bike track.
мототрюка́ч, а́ *m.* motorcycle stunt rider.
мотоци́кл, а *m.* motor-cycle; **кро́ссовый м.** trail bike.
мотоцикле́т, а *m.* = **мотоци́кл**
мотоцикле́т|ный *adj. of* ~
мотоцикли́ст, а *m.* motor-cyclist; biker; **м. свя́зи** (*mil.*) dispatch-rider.
мотошле́м, а *m.* crash helmet.
моты́г|а, и *f.* hoe, mattock.
моты́ж|ить, у, ишь *impf.* to hoe.
мотыл|ёк, ька́ *m.* butterfly, moth.
моты́л|ь[1], **я́** *m.* mosquito grub (*used to feed fish in aquaria*).
моты́л|ь[2], **я́** *m.* (*tech.*) crank.
мотылько́в|ые, ых (*bot.*) Papilionaceae.
мох, мха *and* **мо́ха, о мхе** *and* **о мо́хе, во (на) мху́,** *pl.* **мхи, мхов** *m.* moss.
мохна́т|ый (~, ~а) *adj.* hairy, shaggy; **~ое полоте́нце** Turkish towel.
моцио́н, а *m.* exercise; constitutional; **де́лать, соверша́ть м.** to take exercise.
моч|а́, и́ *f.* urine, water.
моча́л|ить, ю, ишь *impf.* **1.** to strip into fibres. **2.** (*coll.*) to torment, vex.
моча́лк|а, и *f.* loofah; washing-up mop.
моча́л|о, а *nt.* bast.
мочеви́н|а, ы *f.* (*chem.*) urea.
мочево́й *adj.* urinary, uric; **м. пузы́рь** (*anat.*) bladder.
мочего́нный *adj.* (*med.*) diuretic.
мочеиспуска́ни|е, я *nt.* urination.
мочеиспуска́тельный *adj.*: **м. кана́л** (*anat.*) urethra.
мочёный *adj.* soaked.
мочеотделе́ни|е, я *nt.* urination.
мочеполово́й *adj.* (*anat.*) urino-genital.
мочето́чник, а *m.* (*anat.*) ureter.
моч|и́ть, у́, ~ишь *impf.* (*of* **на~**) **1.** to wet, moisten. **2.** to soak; to steep, macerate; **м. селёдку** to souse herring.
моч|и́ться, у́сь, ~ишься *impf.* (*of* **по~**) (*coll.*) to urinate, make water.
мо́чк|а[1], **и** *f.* soaking, macerating; retting.
мо́чк|а[2], **и** *f.* **1.** (*anat.*) lobe of the ear. **2.** (*bot.*) fibril.
мочь[1], **могу́, мо́жешь, мо́гут,** *past* **мог, могла́** *impf.* (*of* **с~**) to be able; **мо́жет быть, быть мо́жет** perhaps, maybe; **мо́жет** (*coll.*) = **мо́жет быть; не мо́жет быть!** impossible!; **как живёте-мо́жете?** (*coll.*) how are you?; how are things with you?; **не могу́ знать** (*obs.*) I don't know.
моч|ь[2], **и** *f.* (*coll.*) power, might; **во всю м., изо всей ~и, что есть ~и** with all one's might, with might and main; **~и нет (как)** it is unendurable, unbearable; **~и нет, как хо́лодно** it's so cold, I can stand it no longer.
моше́нник, а *m.* rogue, scoundrel; swindler.
моше́ннича|ть, ю *impf.* (*of* **с~**) to play the swindler.
моше́ннический *adj.* rascally, swindling.
моше́нничеств|о, а *nt.* swindling; cheating (*at games*).
мо́шк|а, и *f.* midge.
мошкар|а́, ы́ *f.* (*collect.*) (swarm of) midges.
мош|на́, ны́, *pl.* **~ны́, ~о́н** *f.* purse, pouch; **больша́я, туга́я м.** (*fig., coll.*) well-filled purse; **наби́ть ~ну́** (*fig., coll.*) to fill one's purse.
мошо́нк|а, и *f.* (*anat.*) scrotum.
мошо́ночный *adj.* scrotal.
мощéни|е, я *nt.* paving.
мощённый *p.p.p. of* **мости́ть**
мощёный *adj.* paved.
мо́щ|и, е́й *no sg.* (*relig.*) relics; **живы́е м.** (*coll., joc., of a very thin pers.*) walking skeleton.
мо́щност|ь, и *f.* power; (*tech.*) capacity, rating; output; **номина́льная м.** rated power, rated capacity; **дви́гатель ~ью в сто лошади́ных сил** hundred horsepower engine.
мо́щ|ный (~ен, ~на́, ~но) *adj.* powerful, mighty; vigorous.
мо|щу́, сти́шь *see* **~сти́ть**
мощ|ь, и *f.* power, might.
мо́|ю, ешь *see* **мыть**
мо́ющ|ий *pres. part. act. of* **мыть** *and adj.* detergent; **~ие сре́дства** detergents.
мо́ющ|ийся *adj.* washable; **~иеся обо́и** washable wallpaper.
мраз|ь, и *no pl., f.* (*coll.*) rubbish; (*pej. of human beings*) dregs, scum.
мрак, а *m.* darkness, gloom (*also fig., rhet.*); **покры́то ~ом неизве́стности** shrouded in mystery; **у него́ м. на душе́** he is in the dumps, in a black mood.
мракобе́с, а *m.* obscurantist.
мракобе́си|е, я *nt.* obscurantism.
мра́мор, а *m.* marble.
мра́морный *adj.* marble; (*fig.*) (white as) marble; marmoreal.
мра́морщик, а *m.* marble-cutter.
мрачне́|ть, ю *impf.* (*of* **по~**) to grow dark; to grow gloomy.
мра́ч|ный (~ен, ~на́, ~но) *adj.* **1.** dark, sombre. **2.** (*fig.*) gloomy, dismal.
мре́|ть, ешь *impf.* (*coll.*) to be dimly visible.
мсти́тел|ь, я *m.* avenger.
мсти́тел|ьный (~ен, ~ьна) *adj.* vindictive.
мсти́ть, мщу, мстишь *impf.* (*of* **ото~**) (+*d.* **за**+*a.*) to take vengeance (on for), revenge o.s. (upon for); (**за**+*a.*) to avenge; **м. врагу́** to take vengeance on one's enemy; **м. за дру́га** to avenge one's friend.
МТС *f. indecl.* (*abbr. of* ***маши́нно-тра́кторная ста́нция***) (*hist.*) machinery and tractor station.
муа́р, а *m.* moire, watered silk.
муа́ровый *adj.* moiré.
муда́к, а́ *m.* (*vulg.*) prick, arsehole (*pers.*).
му|де́ть, жу́, ди́шь *impf.* (*of* **промуде́ть**) (*vulg.*) to talk balls *or* bollocks.
муджахи́д|ы, ов *no sg.* mujahidin, mujahedin, mujahedeen.
му́ди́, муде́й *pl.* (*sg.* **муде́** *nt. indecl.*) (*vulg.*) bollocks, balls, nuts (= *testicles*).
муди́ла *c.g.* = **муда́к**
муди́стик|а, и *f.* (*vulg.*) bollocks, balls (= *nonsense*).
мудн|я́, и́ *f.* (*vulg.*) (a load of) bollocks, balls (= *nonsense*); **поро́ть ~ю́** to talk balls *or* bollocks.
мудоёб = **долбоёб**
мудрен|е́е *comp. of* **~ый** *only in phr.* (*coll.*): **у́тро ве́чера м.** sleep on it.
мудрён|ый (~, ~а́) *adj.* (*coll.*) **1.** strange, queer, odd; **не ~о́, что...** it is no wonder that .... **2.** difficult, abstruse, complicated.
мудре́ц, а́ *m.* (*rhet.*) sage, wise man; **на вся́кого ~а́ дово́льно простоты́** (*prov.*) Homer sometimes nods.
мудр|и́ть, ю́, и́шь *impf.* (*of* **на~**) (*coll.*) to subtilize; to complicate matters unnecessarily; **не ~и́те!** don't try to be clever!
му́дрост|ь, и *f.* wisdom; **в э́том нет никако́й ~и** (*coll.*) there is nothing mysterious about it.
му́дрств|овать, ую *impf.* (*obs. coll.*) to philosophize; to bandy sophistries.
му́др|ый (~, ~а́, ~о) *adj.* wise, sage.
муж, а *m.* **1.** (*pl.* **~ья́, ~е́й, ~ья́м**) husband. **2.** (*pl.* **~и́, ~е́й, ~а́м**) (*obs. or rhet.*) man; **госуда́рственный м.** statesman; **м. нау́ки** man of science; **учёный м.** scholar.
мужа́|ть, ю *impf.* (*obs.*) to grow up, reach manhood.
мужа́|ться, юсь *impf.* to take heart, take courage; **~йтесь!** courage!
мужело́ж|ец, ца *m.* bugger, sodomite.
мужело́жств|о, а *nt.* buggery, sodomy.
мужен|ёк, ька́ *m.* (*coll.*) hubby.
мужененави́стниц|а, ы *f.* misandrist.
мужененави́стнический *adj.* misandrist, misandrous.
мужененави́стничеств|о, а *nt.* misandry.
мужеподо́б|ный (~ен, ~на) *adj.* mannish; masculine.
му́ж|еский *adj.* (*obs.*) = **~ско́й; м. род** (*gram.*) masculine gender.
му́жествен|ный (~, ~на) *adj.* manly, steadfast.
му́жеств|о, а *nt.* courage, fortitude.
мужи́к, а́ *m.* **1.** muzhik, moujik (*Russ. peasant*). **2.** (*fig.*) lout, clod, bumpkin. **3.** (*coll.*) bloke, guy. **4.** (*dial.*) husband.

мужиковáт|ый (~, ~а) *adj.* (*coll.*) loutish, boorish.
мужи́цкий *adj. of* **мужи́к 1.**
мýжний *adj.* (*coll.*) husband's.
мýжн|ин *adj.* = **~ий**
мужск|óй *adj.* masculine; male; **м. портнóй** gentlemen's tailor; **м. род** (*gram.*) masculine gender; **~áя шкóла** boys' school.
мужчи́н|а, ы *m.* man.
мýз|а, ы *f.* muse.
музееве́дени|е, я *nt.* museum management studies.
музе́|й, я *m.* museum; **м. восковы́х фигýр** waxworks.
музе́й|ный *adj. of* ~
мýзык|а, и *f.* **1.** music; **м. лёгкого жáнра** light music. **2.** instrumental music. **3.** (*coll.*) band; **воéнная м.** military band. **4.** (*fig.*, *coll.*) (*complicated*, *protracted*) business, affair; **блатнáя м.** thieves' cant; **он испóртил всю ~у** he upset the apple-cart.
музыкáльност|ь, и *f.* **1.** melodiousness. **2.** musical talent.
музыкáл|ьный (~ен, ~ьна) *adj.* (*in var. senses*) musical; **м. комбáйн** music centre.
музыкáнт, а *m.* musician; **ýличный м.** busker.
музыкове́д, а *m.* musicologist.
музыкове́дени|е, я *nt.* musicology.
мýк|а, и *f.* torment; torture; (*pl.*) pangs, throes; **родовы́е ~и** birth-pangs; **хождéние по ~ам** (*relig.*) Purgatory; (*fig.*) (*series of*) trials and tribulations, purgatory.
мук|á, и́ *f.* meal; flour; **перемéлется — м. бýдет** (*coll.*) it will all come right in the end.
мукомóл, а *m.* miller.
мукомóльный *adj.* flour-grinding.
мул, а *m.* mule.
мулáт, а *m.* mulatto.
мулл|á, ы́ *m.* mullah.
мýльд|а, ы *f.* **1.** (*geol.*) flexure. **2.** (*tech.*) charging box, charging trough.
мýльтик, а *m.* (*coll.*) = **мультипликáция**
мультипликáтор, а *m.* **1.** (*in var. tech. senses*) multiplier. **2.** (*film*) animator, cartoonist.
мультипликáци|я, и *f.* (animated) cartoon (*film*).
мультфи́льм, а *m.* = **мультипликáция**
мультя́шк|а, и *f.* (*coll.*) = **мультипликáция**
муля́ж, á *m.* (*art*) cast, (*life-size*) model.
мумификáци|я, и *f.* mummification.
мумифици́р|оваться, уется *impf. and pf.* to be (become) mummified.
мýми|я[1]**, и** *f.* mummy (*embalmed corpse*).
мýми|я[2]**, и** *f.* mummy (*brown pigment*).
мунди́р, а *m.* full-dress uniform; **полковóй м.** regimentals; **картóфель в ~е** potatoes cooked in their jackets.
мундштýк, á *m.* **1.** mouth-piece (*of Russ. cigarette*); cigarette-holder. **2.** mouth-piece (*of musical instrument*, *pipe*). **3.** curb, curb-bit.
муниципализи́р|овать, ую *impf. and pf.* to municipalize
муниципалитéт, а *m.* municipality; town council; **здáние ~а** town hall.
муниципáльн|ый *adj.* municipal; **~ая квартúра** council flat.
мур|á, ы́ *f.* (*coll.*) mess; nonsense.
мурав|á[1]**, ы́** *f.* (*poet.*) grass, sward.
мурав|á[2]**, ы́** *f.* (*tech.*) glaze.
мурав|éй, ья́ *m.* ant.
муравéйник, а *m.* **1.** ant-hill. **2.** ant-bear.
мурáв|ить, лю, ишь *impf.* to glaze (*pottery*).
мурáвленый *adj.* (*tech.*) glazed.
муравьéд, а *m.* (*zool.*) ant-eater.
мурав|ьи́ный *adj.* **1.** *adj. of* **~éй. 2.** (*chem.*) formic.
мурáш, á *m.* = **~ка**
мурáшк|а, и *f.* **1.** (*dial.*) small ant. **2.** (*coll.*) small insect; **~и по спинé бéгают** it gives one the creeps.
мурл|ó, á *nt.* (*coll.*) (ugly) mug.
мурлы|кать, чу, чешь *impf.* **1.** to purr. **2.** (*coll.*) to hum.
мускáт, а *m.* **1.** nutmeg. **2.** (*kind of grape*) muscadine, muscat. **3.** muscatel, muscat (*wine*).
мускáт|ный *adj. of* **~; м. орéх** nutmeg; **м. цвет** mace.
мýскул, а *m.* muscle; **у негó ни оди́н м. не дрóгнул** (*fig.*) he didn't move a muscle.
мускулатýр|а, ы *f.* (*collect.*) muscular system.
мýскулист|ый (~, ~а) *adj.* muscular, sinewy, brawny.
мýскульный *adj.* muscular.
мýскус, а *m.* musk.
мýскусн|ый *adj.* musky; **м. бык** musk-ox; **~ая кры́са** musk-rat, musquash; **~ая ýтка** musk-duck, Muscovy duck.
мусли́н, а *m.* muslin.
мусли́н|овый *adj. of* ~
мýсл|ить, ю, ишь *impf.* (*of* **на~**) (*coll.*) **1.** to wet moisten (*with saliva*); **м. ни́тку** to moisten a thread (*when threading a needle*). **2.** to beslobber; to soil (*with wet or sticky hands*); **м. кни́гу** to dog-ear, soil a book.
мýсл|иться, юсь, ишься *impf.* (*of* **на~**) to slobber over o.s.; to dirty o.s.
мусóл|ить, ю, ишь *impf.* (*of* **за~, на~**) **1.** = **мýслить. 2.** (*fig.*) to spend much time (over); **м. вопрóс** to drag out a question.
мýсор, а *m.* **1.** sweepings, dust; rubbish, refuse, garbage. **2.** débris. **3.** (*pl.* **~á, ~óв**) (*sl.*) copper, bogey.
мýсор|ить, ю, ишь *impf.* (*of* **на~**) (*coll.*) to litter, leave litter about.
мýсор|ный *adj. of* **~; ~ная повóзка** dust cart; **м. я́щик** dustbin.
мусородроби́лк|а, и *f.* waste-disposal unit.
мусоропровóд, а *m.* refuse chute.
мусоросжигáтел|ь, я *m.* incinerator.
мусоросжигáтельн|ый *adj.*: **~ая печь** incinerator.
мусороубóрочный *adj.* refuse collection.
мýсорщик, а *m.* **1.** dustman. **2.** scavenger.
мусс, а *m.* (*cul.*) mousse.
мусси́р|овать, ую *impf.* **1.** to whip up, make to foam. **2.** (*fig.*) to puff up (*reports*), inflate (*significance of sth.*).
муссóн, а *m.* (*geog.*) monsoon.
муст, а *nt.* must.
мустáнг, а *m.* (*zool.*) mustang.
мусульмáн|ин, ина, *pl.* **~е, ~** *m.* Muslim, Moslem.
мусульмáнский *adj.* Muslim, Moslem.
мусульмáнств|о, а *nt.* Islam, Mohammedanism.
мутáнт, а *m.* (*biol.*) mutant.
мутáци|я, и *f.* (*biol.*) mutation.
му|ти́ть, чý, ти́шь *impf.* **1.** (*pf.* **вз~, за~**) (*pres. also* **~́тишь** *etc.*) to trouble, make muddy (*liquids*). **2.** (*pf.* **по~**) (*fig.*) to stir up, upset. **3.** (*pf.* **по~**) (*fig.*) to dull, make dull. **4.** (*impers.*): **меня́,** *etc.*, **~ти́т** I *etc.* feel sick.
му|ти́ться, чýсь, ти́шься *impf.* **1.** (*pf.* **за~**) (*pres. also* **~́тишься** *etc.*) to grow turbid (*of liquids*). **2.** (*pf.* **по~**) (*fig.*) to grow dull, dim. **3.** (*impers.*; *coll.*): **у меня́ ~ти́тся в головé** my head is going round.
мутнé|ть, ет *impf.* (*of* **по~**) to grow turbid, grow muddy; (*fig.*) to grow dull.
мýтност|ь, и. *f.* **1.** turbidity. **2.** dullness.
мýт|ный (~ен, ~нá, ~но) *adj.* **1.** turbid; **в ~ной водé ры́бу лови́ть** (*fig.*) to fish in troubled waters. **2.** (*fig.*) dull(ed); confused; **~ные глазá** lacklustre eyes; **~ное сознáние** dulled consciousness.
мутóвк|а[1]**, и** *f.* whisk.
мутóвк|а[2]**, и** *f.* (*bot.*) whorl.
мýтор|ный (~ен, ~на) *adj.* (*coll.*) disagreeable; dreary, sombre; **у негó бы́ло ~но на душé** he was in a sombre mood.
мут|ь, и *f.* **1.** lees, sediment. **2.** murk.
мýфел|ь, я *m.* (*tech.*) muffle.
муфлóн, а *m.* (*zool.*) moufflon.
мýфт|а, ы *f.* **1.** muff. **2.** (*tech.*) sleeve joint, coupling; **соедини́тельная м.** coupling sleeve, clutch sleeve; (*etec.*) connecting box; **м. сцеплéния** clutch.
мýфти|й, я *m.* (*relig.*) mufti.
мýх|а, и *f.* fly; **какáя м. егó укуси́ла** (*fig.*, *coll.*) what's bitten him?; **дéлать из ~и слонá** (*fig.*) to make a mountain out of a mole-hill; **быть под ~ой, с ~ой** (*coll.*) to be three sheets in the wind; **зашиби́ть ~у** to hit the bottle.
мухобóйк|а, и *f.* (*coll.*) fly swatter.
мухолóвк|а, и *f.* **1.** fly-paper. **2.** (*bot.*) Venus's fly-trap, sundew. **3.** (*zool.*) fly-catcher.

мухомо́р, а *m.* **1.** fly agaric (*mushroom*). **2.** (*coll.*) decrepit old pers.
мухо́ртый *adj.* (*colour of horse*) bay with yellowish markings.
муче́ни|е, я *nt.* torment, torture.
му́ченик, а *m.* martyr.
му́чени|ца, цы *f. of* **~к**
му́чени|ческий *adj. of* **~к; му́ка ~ческая** (*coll.*) excruciating torment.
му́ченичеств|о, а *nt.* martyrdom.
му́ченск|ий *adj. only in phr.* **му́ка ~ая** (*coll.*) excruciating torment.
мучи́тел|ь, я *m.* torturer; tormenter.
мучи́тел|ьный (~ен, ~ьна) *adj.* excruciating; agonizing.
му́ч|ить, у, ишь *impf.* (*of* **за~, из~**) to torment; to worry, harass.
му́ч|иться, усь, ишься *impf.* (*of* **за~, из~**) **1.** (+*i.*, **от**) *pass. of* **~ить; м. от бо́ли** to be racked with pain. **2.** (**из-за**) to worry (about), feel unhappy. **3.** (**над**) to torment o.s. (over, about).
мучни́к, а́ *m.* dealer in flour and meal.
мучни́ст|ый (~, ~а) *adj.* farinaceous.
мучн|о́е, о́го *nt.* farinaceous foods.
мучно́й *adj. of* **мука́**
му́шк|а[1]**, и** *f.* **1.** *dim. of* **му́ха; шпа́нская м.** (*med.*) Spanish fly, cantharides. **2.** (*artificial*) beauty-spot (*on face*).
му́шк|а[2]**, и** *f.* foresight (*of fire-arm*); **взять на ~у** to take aim (at).
мушке́т, а *m.* musket.
мушкетёр, а *m.* musketeer.
мушта́бел|ь, я *m.* maulstick.
муштр|а́, ы *f.* **1.** drill. **2.** regimentation.
муштр|ова́ть, у́ю *impf.* (*of* **вы́~**) to drill.
муэдзи́н, а *m.* muezzin.
МФА *m. indecl.* (*abbr. of* **междунаро́дный фонети́ческий алфави́т**) IPA (*International Phonetic Alphabet*).
мха, мху *see* **мох**
МХАТ, а *m.* (*abbr. of* **Моско́вский худо́жественный академи́ческий теа́тр**) Moscow Arts Theatre.
мчать, мчу, мчишь *impf.* to rush, whirl along (*trans.*; *coll. also intrans.*).
мч|а́ться, усь, и́шься *impf.* to rush, race, tear along; **м. во весь опо́р** to go at full speed; **вре́мя ~и́тся** time flies.
мши́ст|ый (~, ~а) *adj.* mossy.
мще́ни|е, я *nt.* vengeance, revenge.
мы, *a., g., p.* **нас,** *d.* **нам,** *i.* **на́ми** *pron.* we; **мы с ва́ми** you and I.
мы́з|а, ы *f.* farmstead, country house (*in Estonia and other regions bordering on Gulf of Finland*).
мы́зга|ть, ю *impf.* (*coll.*) to soil, crumple.
мы́ка|ть, ю *impf.* (*tech.*) to ripple, hackle (*flax*); **го́ре м.** (*fig., coll.*) to lead a dog's life.
мы́ка|ться, юсь *impf.* (*coll.*) to roam, wander.
мы́л|ить, ю, ишь *impf.* (*of* **на~**) to soap; to lather; **м. кому́-н. го́лову** (*fig., coll.*) to give s.o. a dressing-down.
мы́л|иться, юсь, ишься *impf.* (*of* **на~**) **1.** to soap o.s. **2.** to lather, form a lather.
мы́л|кий (~ок, ~ка́, ~ко) *adj.* freely lathering.
мы́л|о, а, *pl.* **~а́, ~, ~а́м** *nt.* **1.** soap. **2.** (*of horse*) foam, lather.
мылова́р, а *m.* soap-boiler.
мыловаре́ни|е, я *nt.* soap-boiling.
мылова́р|енный *adj. of* **~е́ние; м. заво́д** soap works, soap factory.
мы́льниц|а, ы *f.* soap-dish; soap-box.
мы́л|ьный *adj. of* **~о; м. ка́мень** soapstone, steatite; **~ьные хло́пья** soap-flakes.
мыс, а *m.* (*geog.*) cape, promontory.
мы́сик, а *m.* **1.** (*coll.*) protuberance; jutting out part. **2.** widow's peak.
мы́сленн|ый *adj.* mental; **м. о́браз** mental image; **~ое пожела́ние** unspoken wish.
мысли́м|ый (~, ~а) *adj.* conceivable, thinkable.
мысли́тел|ь, я *m.* thinker.
мысли́тельный *adj.* intellectual, of thought; **м. проце́сс** thought process.
мы́сл|ить, ю, ишь *impf.* **1.** to think; to reason. **2.** to conceive.
мысл|ь, и *f.* (**о**+*p.*) thought (of, about); idea; **за́дняя м.** ulterior motive, arrière pensée; **о́браз ~́ей** way of thinking, views; **у него́ э́того и в ~́ях не́ было** it never even crossed his mind; **быть с кем-н. одни́х ~́ей** to be of the same opinion as s.o.; **пода́ть м.** to suggest an idea; **собира́ться с ~́ями** to collect one's thoughts.
мыт, а *m.* (*vet.*) strangles.
мыта́р|ить, ю, ишь *impf.* (*of* **за~**) (*coll.*) to harass, torment, try.
мыта́р|иться, юсь, ишься *impf.* (*of* **за~**) (*coll.*) to be harassed; to suffer afflictions, undergo trials.
мыта́рств|о, а *nt.* ordeal, affliction, hardship.
мы́тар|ь, я *m.* **1.** (*in Bible*) publican. **2.** (*hist.*) collector of transit dues.
мыть, мо́ю, мо́ешь *impf.* (*of* **вы́~, по~́**) to wash.
мыть|ё, я́ *nt.* wash, washing; **не ~ём, так ка́таньем** by hook or by crook.
мы́ть|ся, мо́юсь, мо́ешься *impf.* (*of* **вы́~, по~**) **1.** to wash (o.s.). **2.** *pass. of* **~**
мыч|а́ть, у́, и́шь *impf.* **1.** to low, moo; to bellow. **2.** (*fig., coll.*) to mumble.
мыша́ст|ый (~, ~а) *adj.* mouse-coloured, mousey.
мышело́вк|а, и *f.* mouse-trap.
мы́шечный *adj.* muscular.
мыш|и́ный *adj. of* **~ь; ~и́ная возня́ (суета́)** pointless fussing over trifles; **м. жере́бчик** (*obs.*) old lecher.
мы́шк|а[1]**, и** *f. dim. of* **мышь**
мы́шк|а[2]**, и** *f.* oxter; **под ~у, под ~и, под ~ой, под ~ами** under one's arm; in one's armpit(s); **взять под ~у** to put under one's arm; **нести́ под ~ой** to carry under one's arm.
мышле́ни|е, я *nt.* thinking, thought.
мыш|о́нок, о́нка, *pl.* **~а́та, ~а́т** young mouse.
мы́шц|а, ы *f.* muscle.
мыш|ь, и, *pl.* **~́и, ~е́й** *f.* **1.** mouse. **2.: летý́чая м.** bat.
мышья́к, а́ *m.* (*chem., pharm.*) arsenic.
мышьяко́вистый *adj.* (*chem.*) arsenious.
мышьяко́вый *adj.* (*chem.*) arsenic.
Мья́нм|а, ы *f.* Myanmar (*formerly Burma*).
Мэн: о́-в М., ~а М. *m.* the Isle of Man.
мэ́нский *adj.*: **м. язы́к** Manx (*language*).
мэр, а *m.* mayor.
мэ́ри|я, и *f.* **1.** town council. **2.** town hall.
мю́зикл, а *m.* musical.
мю́зик-хо́лл, а *m.* music-hall.
Мю́нхен, а *m.* Munich.
мя́г|кий (~ок, ~ка́, ~ко) *adj.* soft; (*fig.*) mild, gentle; **м. ваго́н** (*rail.*) soft-(seated) carriage, sleeping car; **м. знак** (*ling.*) soft sign (*name of Russ. letter* **'ь'**); **~кое кре́сло** easy chair; **~кая поса́дка** soft landing (*of space vehicle*); **м. хлеб** new bread.
мя́гко *adv.* softly; (*fig.*) mildly, gently; **м. выража́ясь** (*iron.*) to put it mildly, to say the least.
мягконабивн|о́й *adj.*: **~а́я игру́шка** soft *or* cuddly toy.
мягкосерде́чи|е, я *nt.* soft-heartedness.
мягкосерде́ч|ный (~ен, ~на) *adj.* soft-hearted.
мягкоте́лый *adj.* soft; (*fig.*) spineless.
мягкошёрстный *adj.* soft-haired.
мя́г|че *comp. of* **~кий** *and* **~ко**
мягчи́тельный *adj.* (*med.*) emollient.
мягч|и́ть, у́, и́шь *impf.* (*of* **с~**) to soften.
мяки́н|а, ы *f.* chaff; **ста́рого воробья́ на ~е не проведёшь** (*prov.*) an old bird is not caught with chaff.
мя́киш, а *m.* inside, soft part (*of loaf*).
мя́к|нуть, ну, нешь, *past* **~, ~ла** *impf.* (*of* **раз~**) to soften; to become soft (*also fig.*).
мя́кот|ь, и *f.* **1.** fleshy part of body. **2.** pulp (*of fruit*).
мя́лк|а, и *f.* (*tech.*) brake (*for flax or hemp*).
мя́мл|ить, ю, ишь *impf.* (*coll.*) **1.** (*pf.* **про~**) to mumble. **2.** (*no pf.*) to vacillate; to procrastinate.
мя́мл|я, и, *g. pl.* **~ей** *c.g.* (*coll.*) **1.** mumbler. **2.** irresolute pers.
мяси́ст|ый (~, ~а) *adj.* fleshy; meaty; pulpy.
мясн|а́я, о́й *f.* butcher's (shop).

мясни́к, á *m.* butcher.
мяс|но́й *adj. of* ∼**о; ∼ные консе́рвы** tinned meat.
мя́с|о, а *nt.* **1.** flesh; **сла́дкое м.** (*anat.*) sweetbread; **вы́рвать пу́говицу с ∼ом** to rip out a button with a bit of cloth. **2.** meat; **пу́шечное м.** (*fig.*) cannon fodder. **3.** (*coll.*) beef.
мясое́д, а *m.* **1.** meat-eater. **2.** (*eccl.*) season during which the eating of meat is permitted (*esp. from Christmas to Shrovetide*).
мясокомбина́т, а *m.* meat processing and packing factory.
мясоотбива́лк|а, и *f.* meat tenderizer.
мясопу́ст, а *m.* (*eccl.*) **1.** season during which it is forbidden to eat meat. **2.** Shrovetide.
мясору́бк|а, и *f.* mincing-machine.
мясохладобо́|йня, йни, *g. pl.* **∼ен** *f.* combined slaughter-house and meat store.
мя|сти́сь, ту́сь, тёшься *impf.* (*obs.*) to be disturbed.
мя́т|а, ы *f.* (*bot.*) mint; **пе́речная м.** peppermint.
мяте́ж, á *m.* mutiny, revolt.
мяте́жник, а *m.* mutineer, rebel.
мяте́жный *adj.* **1.** rebellious, mutinous. **2.** (*fig.*) restless; stormy.
мя́тн|ый *adj.* mint; **∼ые леденцы́** peppermints.
мя́т|ый *p.p.p. of* **∼ь** *and adj.*; **м. пар** (*tech.*) waste steam, exhaust steam.
мять, мну, мнёшь *impf.* **1.** (*pf.* **раз∼**) to work up, knead; **м. гли́ну** to pug clay; **м. лён** to brake flax. **2.** (*pf.* **из∼, с∼**) to crumple; to rumple (*a dress, etc.*); **м. траву́** to trample grass.
мя́ться[1], **мнётся** *impf.* (*of* **из∼, по∼** *and* **с∼**) to become crumpled; to rumple up easily.
мя́ться[2], **мну́сь, мнёшься** *impf.* (*coll.*) to vacillate, hum and ha.
мяу́ка|ть, ю, *impf.* to mew, miaow.
мяч, á *m.* ball.
мя́чик, а *m. dim. of* **мяч**

Н

на́[1] *int.* (*coll.*) here; here you are; here, take it; **на́ кни́гу!** here, take the book!; **вот тебе́ на́!** well, I never!; well, how d'you like that?
на[2] *prep.* **I.** +*a.* **1.** on (to); to; into; over, through; **положи́те кни́гу на стол** put the book on the table; **сесть на авто́бус, по́езд** to board a bus, a train; **сесть на парохо́д** to go on board; **на Украи́ну** to (the) Ukraine; **на се́вер** to the North; **на се́вер от** (to the) north of; **на заво́д** to the factory; **на конце́рт** to a concert; **слепо́й на оди́н глаз** blind in one eye; **перевести́ на англи́йский** to translate into English; **положи́ть на му́зыку** to set to music; **сла́ва его́ греме́ла на весь мир** his fame resounded throughout the world. **2.** (*of time*) at; on; until, to (*or untranslated*); **на друго́й день, на сле́дующий день** (the) next day; **на Но́вый год** on New Year's day; **на Рождество́** at Christmas; **на Па́сху** at Easter; **отложи́ть на бу́дущую неде́лю** to put off until the following week. **3.** for; **на два дня** for two days; **на́ зиму** for the winter; **на э́тот раз** this time, for this once; **на чёрный день** (*fig.*) for a rainy day; **собра́ние назна́чено на понеде́льник** the meeting is fixed for Monday; **на что э́то тебе́ ну́жно?** what do you want it for?; **ко́мната на двои́х** a room for two; **уро́к на за́втра** the lesson for tomorrow; **лес на постро́йку** building timber; **учи́ться на инжене́ра** (*coll.*) to study engineering; **на беду́** unfortunately. **4.** by (*or untranslated*); **коро́че на дюйм** shorter by an inch; **купи́ть на вес** to buy by weight; **опозда́ть на час** to be an hour late; **четы́ре ме́тра (в длину́) на два (в ширину́)** four metres (long) by two (broad); **помно́жить пять на три** to multiply five by three; **дели́ть на два** to divide into two. **5.** worth (*of sth.*); **на рубль ма́рок** a rouble's worth of stamps.
II. +*p.* **1.** on, upon; in; at; **на столе́** on the table; **на бума́ге** on paper (*also fig.*); **на Украи́не** in (the) Ukraine; **на се́вере** in the North; **на заво́де** at the factory; **на конце́рте** at a concert; **на со́лнце** in the sun; **на чи́стом, во́льном во́здухе** in the open air; **на дворе́, на у́лице** out of doors; **на рабо́те** at work; **на излече́нии** undergoing medical treatment; **на вёслах** under oars; **на мо́ре** at sea; **идти́ на паруса́х** to go sailing; **игра́ть на роя́ле** to play the piano; **висе́ть на потолке́** to hang from the ceiling; **жа́рить на ма́сле** to fry; **на свои́х глаза́х** before one's eyes; **на его́ па́мяти** within his recollection; **писа́ть на неме́цком языке́** to write in German; **оши́бка на оши́бке** blunder upon blunder. **2.** (*of time*) in (*or untranslated*); during; **на э́той неде́ле** this week; **на лету́** in flight, during (the) flight; **на кани́кулах** during the holidays. **3.** (*made, prepared with, of*); on (= *operated by means of*); **на ва́те** padded; **матра́ц на рессо́рах** sprung mattress; **э́тот дви́гатель рабо́тает на не́фти** this engine runs on oil.
на... *as vbl. pref.* **I.** *forms pf. aspect.*
II. *indicates* **1.** action continued to sufficiency, to point of satisfaction or exhaustion. **2.** action relating to determinate quantity or number of objects.
наб. (*abbr. of* **на́бережная**) Embankment.
наба́в|ить, лю, ишь *pf.* (*of* **∼ля́ть**) to add (to), increase; **н. ша́гу** to quicken one's pace.
наба́вк|а, и *f.* addition, increase; extra charge; **н. к зарпла́те** rise (in wages).
набавля́|ть, ю, *impf. of* **наба́вить**
наба́вочный *adj.* (*coll.*) extra, additional.
набаламу́|тить, чу, тишь *pf.* (*coll.*) to make trouble; to upset.
набалда́шник, а *m.* knob; walking-stick handle.
набало́в|анный *p.p.p. of* **∼а́ть** *and adj.* spoiled.
набал|ова́ть, у́ю *pf.* (*coll.*) **1.** to spoil. **2.** to get up to mischief.
набальзами́р|овать, ую *pf. of* **бальзами́ровать**
наба́т, а *m.* alarm bell, tocsin; **бить (ударя́ть) (в) н.** to sound the alarm (*also fig.*).
наба́т|ный *adj. of* ∼
набе́г, а *m.* raid; foray, inroad, incursion.
набе́га|ть, ю, *pf.* (*coll.*) to cause o.s. (*heart trouble, etc.*) by running.
набега́|ть, ю, *impf.* **1.** *impf. of* **набежа́ть. 2.** (*impers., coll.*) to ruck up.
набе́га|ться, юсь *pf.* to be tired out with running about; to have one's fill of running.
набе|гу́, жи́шь, гу́т *see* **∼жа́ть**
набедоку́р|ить, ю, ишь *pf. of* **бедоку́рить**
набе|жа́ть, гу́, жи́шь, гу́т *pf.* (*of* **∼га́ть**) **1.** (**на**+*a.*) to run against, run into. **2.** (*coll.*) to come running (*together*). **3.** (*of liquids*) to run into; to fill up; (*fig.*; *of money, etc.*) to accumulate. **4.** (*of wind*) to spring up.
набекре́нь *adv.* (*coll.*) (*of hats*) aslant, tilted; **с шля́пой н.** with one's hat on one side; **у него́ мозги́ н.** (*joc.*) he is crack-brained.
набел|и́ть(ся), ю(сь), ∼и́шь(ся) *pf. of* **бели́ть(ся) 2.**
на́бело *adv.* clean, without corrections and erasures; **переписа́ть н.** to make a fair copy of.
на́бережн|ая, ой *f.* embankment, quay.
набз|де́ть, жу́, ди́шь *pf. of* **бздеть**
набива́|ть(ся), ю(сь) *impf. of* **наби́ть(ся)**
наби́вк|а, и *f.* **1.** (*action and substance*) stuffing, padding, packing. **2.** (*text.*) printing.
набивно́й *adj.* (*text.*) printed.
набира́|ть(ся), ю(сь) *impf. of* **набра́ть(ся)**
наби́т|ый (∼, ∼а) *p.p.p. of* **∼ь** *and adj.* packed, crowded; **зал ∼ битко́м** the hall is crowded out; **н. дура́к** arrant fool.
наб|и́ть[1], **ью́, ьёшь** *pf.* (*of* **∼ива́ть**) **1.** (+*a. and i.*) to stuff (with), pack (with), fill (with); **н. тру́бку** to fill one's pipe; **н. це́ны** to knock up the prices; to bid up; **н. оско́мину** to

set one's teeth on edge (*also fig.*); **н. ру́ку на чём-н.** (*fig., coll.*) to become a practised hand at sth., become a dab hand. **2.** (*text.*) to print.

наб|и́ть[2], ью́, ьёшь *pf.*: **н. гвозде́й в сте́ну** to drive (*a number of*) nails into a wall; **н. у́ток** to bag (*a number of*) duck; **н. посу́ды** to smash (*a lot of*) crockery.

наб|и́ться, ью́сь, ьёшься *pf.* (*of* **~ива́ться**) **1.** to crowd (*into a place*); **битко́м н.** to be crowded out. **2.** (*coll.*; *+d.*) to impose o.s. (upon), inflict o.s. (upon); **н. к кому́-н. в го́сти** to invite o.s. to s.o.'s house (*etc.*).

наблюда́тел|ь, я *m.* observer, spectator.

наблюда́тельност|ь, и *f.* power of observation, observation.

наблюда́тел|ьный *adj.* **1.** (**~ен, ~ьна**) observant. **2.** observation; **н. пункт** (*mil.*) observation post.

наблюда́|ть, ю *impf.* **1.** to observe; to watch. **2.** (**за**+*i.*) to take care (of), look after. **3.** (**за** *and, obs.*, **над**+*i.*) to supervise, superintend; **н. за у́личным движе́нием** to control traffic; **н. за поря́дком** to be responsible for keeping order.

наблюде́ни|е, я *nt.* **1.** observation. **2.** supervision, superintendence.

наблю|сти́, ду́, дёшь, *past.* **~́л, ~ла́** *pf.* (*obs.*) to make an observation.

набо́б, а *m.* nabob.

на́божност|ь, и *f.* piety.

на́бож|ный (~ен, ~на) *adj.* devout, pious.

набо́йк|а, и *f.* **1.** (*text.*) printed cloth. **2.** printed pattern on cloth. **3.** heel (*of foot-wear*).

набо́йщик, а *m.* **1.** (*text.*) (linen-)printer. **2.** filler, stuffer.

на́бок *adv.* on one side, awry.

наболе́|вший *p.p. of* **~ть** *and adj.* sore, painful (*also fig.*).

набол|е́ть, е́ет *pf.* to become painful.

наболта́|ть[1], ю *pf.* (*coll.*) to mix in (*a quantity of*).

наболта́|ть[2], ю *pf.* (*coll.*) **1.** (*+a. or g.*) to talk a lot (*of nonsense, etc.*). **2.** (**на**+*a.*) to gossip (about), talk (about); **на неё ~ли** they told a lot of lies about her.

на́больш|ий, его *m.* (*dial.*) **1.** boss. **2.** head of family.

набо́р, а *m.* **1.** recruitment. **2.** levy. **3.** (*typ.*) composition, type-setting. **4.** (*typ.*) composed matter. **5.** set, collection; **н. слов** mere verbiage. **6.** decorative plate (*on harness, belt, etc.*).

набо́рн|ая, ой *f.* type-setting office.

набо́рн|ый *adj.* type-setting; **~ая доска́** galley; **~ая маши́на** typesetter (*machine*).

набо́рщик, а *m.* compositor, type-setter.

набра́сыва|ть(ся), ю(сь) *impf. of* **наброса́ть(ся)** *and* **набро́сить(ся)**

набра́|ть, наберу́, наберёшь, *past* **~л, ~ла́, ~ло** *pf.* (*of* **набира́ть**) **1.** (*+g. or a.*) to gather; to collect, assemble; **н. у́гля** to take on coal; **н. но́мер** to dial a (*telephone*) number; **н. ско́рость** to pick up, gather speed; **н. высоту́** (*aeron.*) to climb; **н. воды́ в рот** (*fig.*) to keep mum. **2.** to recruit, enrol, engage. **3.** (*typ.*) to compose, set up.

набра́|ться, наберу́сь, наберёшься, *past* **~лся, ~ла́сь ~́ло́сь** *pf.* (*of* **набира́ться**) **1.** (*usu. impers.*) to assemble, collect; to accumulate; **~ло́сь мно́го наро́ду** a large crowd collected. **2.** (*+g.; coll.*) to find, collect; to acquire; (*pej.*) to pick up; **н. хра́брости** to take courage; **н. блох** to pick up fleas.

набре|сти́, ду, дёшь, *past* **~̈л, ~ла́** *pf.* **1.** (**на**+*a.*) to come across; to happen upon; **я ~̈л на интере́сную мысль** I have hit on an interesting idea. **2.** to collect, gather; **~ло́ мно́го наро́ду** a large crowd gathered.

наброса́|ть[1], ю *pf.* (*of* **набра́сывать**) **1.** to sketch, outline, adumbrate; **н. план** to outline a plan. **2.** to jot down.

наброса́|ть[2], ю *pf.* to throw about; to throw (*in successive instalments*).

набро́|сить, шу, сишь *pf.* (*of* **набра́сывать**) to throw (on, over); **н. шаль на пле́чи** to throw a shawl over one's shoulders.

набро́|ситься, шусь, сишься *pf.* (*of* **набра́сываться**) (*in var. senses*) to fall upon; to go for; **соба́ка ~силась на меня́** the dog went for me; **н. на кого́-н. с вопро́сами** to deluge s.o. with questions.

набро́с|ок, ка *m.* sketch, draft.

набры́зга|ть, ю *pf.* (*+i. or g.*) to splash.

набрю́шник, а *m.* abdominal band.

набрю́шный *adj.* abdominal

набух|а́ть, а́ю *impf. of* **~́нуть**

набу́х|нуть, ну, нешь, *past* **~, ~ла** *pf.* (*of* **~а́ть**) to swell.

наб|ью́, ьёшь *see* **~и́ть**

нава́г|а, и *f.* (*zool.*) navaga (*a small fish of the cod family*).

наважде́ни|е, я *nt.* delusion; hallucination.

нава́к|сить, шу, сишь *pf. of* **ва́ксить**

нава́лива|ть(ся), ю(сь) *impf. of* **навали́ть(ся)**

навал|и́ть, ю́, ~́ишь *pf.* (*of* **~́ивать**) to heap, pile; to load (*also fig.*); *impers.*: **сне́гу ~и́ло по коле́но** the snow had piled up knee deep.

навал|и́ться, ю́сь, ~́ишься *pf.* (*of* **~́иваться**) (**на**+*a.*) **1.** (*coll.*) to fall (upon). **2.** to lean (on, upon); to bring all one's weight to bear (on).

нава́лк|а, и *f.* loading, lading; **в ~у** loose, unpacked.

нава́лом *adv.* piled up; **фру́ктов н.** loads of fruit.

наваля́|ть[1], ю *pf. of* **валя́ть 5.**

наваля́|ть[2], ю *pf.*: **н. во́йлока, ва́ленок** to make (*a quantity of*) felt, felt boots.

нава́р, а *m.* **1.** grease (*on the surface of soup*). **2.** (*coll.*) profit; **соли́дный н.** a fat profit.

нава́рива|ть, ю *impf. of* **навари́ть[1]**

нава́рист|ый (~, ~а) *adj.* with large fat content (*of soup*).

навар|и́ть[1], ю́, ~́ишь *pf.* (*of* **~́ивать**) to weld on.

навар|и́ть[2], ю́, ~́ишь *pf.* to cook, boil (*a quantity of*).

навева́|ть, ю *impf. of* **наве́ять**

наве́д|аться, аюсь *pf.* (*of* **~ываться**) (**к**; *coll.*) to call (on).

наведе́ни|е, я *nt.* **1.** laying; placing; **«н. мосто́в»** (*pol.*) bridge-building; **сторо́нник «~я мосто́в»** (*pol.*) bridge-builder. **2.** (*phil.*; *obs.*) induction.

наве|ду́, дёшь *see* **~сти́**

наве́дыва|ться, юсь, *impf. of* **наве́даться**

навез|ти́[1], у́, ёшь, *past* **~̈, ~ла́** *pf.* (*of* **навози́ть[1]**) (**на**+*a.*; *coll.*) to drive (on, against).

навез|ти́[2], у́, ёшь, *past* **~̈, ла́** *pf.* (*of* **навози́ть[2]**) to bring (*a quantity of*).

наве́к, *adv.* for ever.

наве́к|и = **~**

наве́л|ь, я *m.* navel orange.

наверб|ова́ть, у́ю *pf. of* **вербова́ть**

наве́рно *adv.* **1.** probably, most likely. **2.** (*obs.*) for sure; certainly, exactly.

наве́рно|е *adv.* = **~ 1.**

наверн|у́ть, у́, ёшь *pf.* (*of* **навёртывать**) **1.** to screw (on). **2.** to wind (round). **3.** (*sl.*) to scoff up (= *eat*).

наверн|у́ться, у́сь, ёшься *pf.* (*of* **навёртываться**) **1.** (*coll.*) to turn up; (*of tears*) to well up. **2.** *pass. of* **~у́ть**

наверняка́ *adv.* (*coll.*) **1.** for sure, certainly. **2.** safely, without taking risks; **бить н.** to take no chances; **держа́ть пари́ н.** to bet on a certainty.

наверста́|ть, ю *pf.* (*of* **навёрстывать**) to make up (for), catch up (with); **н. поте́рянное вре́мя** to make up for lost time; **н. упу́щенное** to repair an omission.

навёрстыва|ть, ю *impf. of* **наверста́ть**

навер|те́ть[1], чу́, ~́тишь *pf.* (*of* **~̈тывать**) to wind (round), twist (round).

навер|те́ть[2], чу́, ~́тишь *pf.* (*of* **~́чивать**) to drill (*a number of*) (*holes, etc.*).

навёртыва|ть, ю *impf. of* **наверну́ть** *and* **наверте́ть[1]**

навёртыва|ться, юсь *impf. of* **наверну́ться**

наве́рх *adv.* up, upward; upstairs; to the top.

наверху́ *adv.* above; upstairs.

наве́рчива|ть, ю *impf. of* **наверте́ть[2]**

наве́с, а *m.* **1.** penthouse; awning; **н. для автомоби́ля** carport. **2.** overhang, jutting-out part. **3.** (*sport*) lob.

навеселе́ *adv.* (*coll.*) tipsy.

наве́|сить, шу, сишь *pf.* (*of* **~шивать[1]**) **1.** (*+a. or g.*) to hang (up), suspend; **н. карти́н** to hang (*a number of*) pictures. **2.** (*sport*) to lob.

наве́ск|а[1], и *f.* hinge-plate.

наве́ск|а[2], и *f.* (*chem.*) dose by weight.

навесн|о́й *adj.*: **~а́я дверь** door on hinges; **~а́я пе́тля** hinge.

навéсный *adj.* (*mil.*): **н. огóнь** plunging fire.
наве|стѝ[1], дý, дёшь, *past* **~́л, ~лá** *pf.* (*of* **наводѝть**) (**на**+*a.*) **1.** to direct (at); to aim (at); **н. когó-н. на мысль** to suggest an idea to s.o.; **н. на след** to put on the track. **2.** to cover (with); **н. лоск, глянец** to polish, gloss, glaze. **3.** to lay, put, make; **н. порядок** to introduce order, establish order; **н. справку** to make an inquiry; **н. скуку** to bore; **н. страх** to inspire fear.
наве|стѝ[2], дý, дёшь, *past* **~́л, ~лá** *pf.* (*of* **наводѝть**) to bring (*a quantity of*).
наве|стѝть, щý, стѝшь *pf.* (*of* **~щáть**) to visit, call on.
навéт, а *m.* (*obs.*) slander, calumny.
навéтренный *adj.* windward.
навéтчик, а *m.* (*obs.*) slanderer.
навéчно *adv.* for ever; in perpetuity.
навéш|ать[1], аю *pf.* (*of* **~ивать[1]**) (+*a. or g.*) to hang (up), suspend.
навéш|ать[2], аю *pf.* (*of* **~ивать[2]**) to weigh out (*a quantity of*).
навéшива|ть[1], и *impf. of* **навéсить** *and* **навéшать[1]**
навéшива|ть[2], ю *impf. of* **навéшать[2]**
навещá|ть, ю *impf. of* **навестѝть**
навé|ять[1], ю, ешь *pf.* (*of* **~вáть**) to blow; (*fig.*; +*a.* **на**+*a.*) to cast (on, over), plunge (into); **егó расскáз ~ял грусть на слýшателей** his story cast a gloom over the audience, plunged the audience into gloom.
навé|ять[2], ю, ешь *pf.* (*of* **~вáть**) to winnow (*a quantity of*).
нáвзничь *adv.* backwards, on one's back.
навзрыд *adv.*: **плáкать н.** to sob.
навивá|ть, ю *impf. of* **навѝть**
навигáтор, а *m.* navigator.
навигац|иóнный *adj. of* **~́ия**
навигáци|я, и *f.* (*in var. senses*) navigation.
навин|тѝть, чý, тѝшь *pf.* (*of* **~́чивать**) (**на**+*a.*) to screw (on).
навѝнчива|ть, ю *impf. of* **навинтѝть**
навис|áть, áю *impf.* (*of* **~́нуть**) (**на**+*a.*, **над**) to hang (over), overhang; (*of cliffs, etc.*) to beetle; (*fig.*) to impend, threaten; **над нáми ~áет опáсность** danger threatens us, is imminent; **н. над флáнгами врагá** to hang on the enemy's flanks.
навѝслый *adj.* (*coll.*) overhanging, beetling.
навѝс|нуть, ну, нешь, *past* **~, ~ла** *pf. of* **~áть**
навѝс|ший *p.p. act. of* **~нуть** *and adj.*: **~шие брóви** beetling brows.
нав|ѝть, ью, ьёшь, *past* **~ѝл, ~илá, ~ѝло** *pf.* (*of* **~ивáть**) (+*a. or g.*) **1.** to wind (on). **2.** to load, stack (*straw, hay*).
навлекá|ть, ю *impf. of* **навлéчь**
навле|кý, чёшь, кýт *see* **~́чь**
навлé|чь, кý, чёшь, кýт, *past* **~́к, ~клá** *pf.* (*of* **~кáть**) (**на**+*a.*) to bring (on); to draw (on); **н. на себя гнев** to incur anger.
наво|дѝть, жý, ~́дишь *impf. of* **навестѝ; наводящие вопрóсы** leading questions; **наводящий, наводѝвший** 'it' (*in children's games*).
навóдк|а, и *f.* (*mil.*) laying, training; **прямóй ~ой** over open sights.
наводнéни|е, я *nt.* flood, inundation.
наводн|ѝть, ю́, ѝшь *pf.* (*of* **~ять**) (+*a. and i.*) to flood (with), inundate (with), deluge (with); (*fig.*): **н. рынок дешёвыми товáрами** to flood the market with cheap goods.
наводн|ять, яю *impf. of* **~ѝть**
навóдчик, а *m.* **1.** gun-layer. **2.** (*sl.*) tipper-off (*thieves' informant*).
навó|жу, зишь *see* **~зить**
наво|жý[1], ~́дишь *see* **~дѝть**
наво|жý[2], ~́зишь *see* **~зѝть**
навóз, а *m.* manure, dung.
навó|зить, жу, зишь *impf.* (*of* **у~**) to manure.
наво|зѝть[1,2], жý, ~́зишь *impf. of* **навезтѝ[1,2]**
наво|зѝть[3], жý, ~́зишь *pf.* (*coll.*) to get in (*a supply of*).
навóзник, а *m.* dung-beetle.
навóз|ный *adj. of* **~; н. жук** dung-beetle; **гром не из тýчи, а из ~ной кýчи** (*coll.*) his bark is worse than his bite.
навó|й, я *m.* (*text.*) weaver's beam.
нáволок|а, и *f.* pillow-case, pillow-slip.
нáволо|чка = ~ка
навоня|ть, ю, *pf.* (*coll.*; +*i.*) to stink (of).
наворáжива|ть, ю *impf. of* **наворожѝть**
наворáчива|ть, ю *impf. of* **наворотѝть**
навор|овáть, ýю *pf.* (*coll.*) to steal (*a quantity of*).
наворож|ѝть, ý, ѝшь *pf.* (*of* **наворáживать**) (*coll.*) **1.** to foretell, prophesy; **онá ~ѝла мне дóлгий век** she prophesied me a long life. **2.** to make, earn by fortune-telling. **3.** to endow with magical properties.
наворо|тѝть, чý, ~́тишь *pf.* (*of* **наворáчивать**) (*coll.*; +*a. or g.*) to heap up, pile up.
наворо|чý, ~́тишь *see* **~тѝть**
наворс|овáть, ýю *pf. of* **ворсовáть**
наворч|áть, ý, ѝшь *pf.* (*coll.*; **на**+*a.*) to grumble (at).
навостр|ѝть, ю́, ѝшь *pf.* (*coll.*) to sharpen; **н. ýши** to prick up one's ears; **н. лыжи** to take to one's heels.
навостр|ѝться, ю́сь, ѝшься *pf.* (**в**+*p. or* +*inf.*; *coll.*) to become good (at), become adept (at); **он ~ѝлся плясáть** he has become a good dancer.
навощ|ѝть, ý, ѝшь *pf. of* **вощѝть**
навр|áть[1], ý, ёшь, *past* **~áл, ~алá, ~áло** *pf.* (*coll.*) **1.** (*pf. of* **врать**) to romance, tell yarns. **2.** (**в**+*p.*) to make mistakes (in); **н. в расскáзе** to get the story wrong. **3.** (**на**+*a.*) to slander.
навр|áть[2], ý. ёшь *pf.* (*coll.*; +*a. or g.*) to tell (*a lot of*) (*sc. lies*); **н. всяких небылѝц** to tell all manner of tales.
навре|дѝть, жý, дѝшь *pf.* (+*d.*) to do much harm (to).
навряд (ли) *adv.* scarcely, hardly.
навсегдá *adv.* for ever, for good; **раз и н.** once (and) for all.
навстрéчу *adv.* to meet; towards; **пойтѝ н. комý-н.** to go to meet s.o.; (*fig.*) to meet s.o. halfway.
навыворот *adv.* (*coll.*) **1.** inside out, wrong side out. **2.** (*fig.*) wrong way round.
нáвык, а *m.* experience, skill (*in practical or manual work*).
навыкат(е) *adv.*: **глазá н.** bulging eyes.
навык|áть, áю *impf. of* **~́нуть**
навык|нуть, ну, нешь, *past* **~, ~ла** *pf.* (*of* **~áть**) (*coll.*; **к** *or* +*inf.*) to acquire the habit (of), skill (in).
навылет *adv.* (right) through; **он был рáнен н. в рýку** he was wounded by a bullet passing right through his arm.
навынос *adv.* take-away, for consumption off the premises.
навыпуск *adv.* worn outside; **брюки н.** trousers worn over boots; **рубáха н.** shirt worn outside of trousers.
навырез *adv.*: **купѝть арбýз н.** to buy a water-melon with the right to sample a section.
навытяжку *adv.*: **стоять н.** to stand at attention.
нав|ь, и *f.* (*in Russ. myth.*) ghost, spirit.
нав|ью́, ьёшь *see* **~ѝть**
навью́чива|ть, ю *impf. of* **навью́чить**
навью́ч|ить, у, ишь *pf.* (*of* **вью́чить** *and* **~ивать**) to load (up).
навя|зáть[1], жý, ~́жешь *pf.* (*of* **~́зывать**) **1.** (**на**+*a.*) to tie on (to), fasten (to). **2.** (*fig.*; +*d. and a.*) to thrust (on); to foist (on); **н. комý-н. совéт** to thrust advice on s.o.
навя|зáть[2], жý, ~́жешь *pf.* (*of* **~́зывать**) (+*a. or g.*) to knit (*a number of*).
навяз|áть[3], áет *impf. of* **~́нуть**
навя|зáться, жýсь, ~́жешься *pf.* (*of* **~́зываться**) (*coll.*; +*d.*) **1.** to thrust o.s. (upon), intrude o.s. (upon). **2.** *pass. of* **~зáть[1]**
навяз|нуть, нет, *past* **~, ~ла** *pf.* (*of* **~áть**) to stick; **это ~ло у нас в зубáх** (*fig.*) we are sick and tired of it.
навязчив|ый (~, ~а) *adj.* **1.** importunate; obtrusive. **2.** persistent; **~ая идéя** idée fixe, obsession.
навязыва|ть(ся), ю(сь) *impf. of* **навязáть(ся)**
нагадá|ть, ю *pf.* (*coll.*; +*a. or g.*) to foretell, predict.
нагá|дить, жу, дишь *pf. of* **гáдить**
нагáйк|а, и *f.* whip.
нагáн, а *m.* revolver.
нагáр, а *m.* deposit formed as result of combustion; (candle-)snuff.
нáгел|ь, я *m.* (*tech.*) wooden pin.
нагибá|ть(ся), ю(сь) *impf. of* **нагнýть(ся)**

нагишо́м *adv.* (*coll.*) stark naked.
нагла́|дить[1], **жу, дишь** *pf.* (*of* **~живать**) to smooth (out).
нагла́|дить[2], **жу, дишь** *pf.* (*of* **~живать**) to iron (*a quantity of*).
нагла́жива|ть, ю *impf. of* **нагла́дить**
нагла́зник, а *m.* **1.** eye-shade. **2.** blinker.
нагле́|ть, ю *impf.* (*of* **об~**) to become impudent, become insolent.
нагле́ц, а́ *m.* impudent fellow, insolent fellow.
на́глост|ь, и *f.* impudence, insolence, effrontery, impertinence.
наглота́|ться, юсь *pf.* (+*g.*) to swallow (*a large quantity of*).
на́глухо *adv.* tightly, hermetically; **застегну́ться н.** to do up all one's buttons.
на́гл|ый (~, ~а́, ~о) *adj.* impudent, insolent, impertinent.
нагля|де́ться, жу́сь, ди́шься *pf.* (**на**+*a.*) to see enough (of); **на э́тот вид гляжу́ — не ~жу́сь** I never tire of looking at this view.
нагля́дно *adv.* clearly, graphically; by visual demonstration.
нагля́дност|ь, и *f.* **1.** clearness. **2.** use of visual methods, use of visual aids.
нагля́д|ный (~ен, ~на) *adj.* **1.** clear; graphic, obvious; **~ное доказа́тельство** ocular demonstration. **2.** visual; **~ные посо́бия** visual aids; **н. уро́к** object-lesson.
наг|на́ть[1], **оню́, о́нишь,** *past* **~на́л, ~нала́, ~на́ло** *pf.* (*of* **~оня́ть**) **1.** to overtake, catch up (with). **2.** to make up (for). **3.** (*fig., coll.*) to inspire, arouse, occasion.
наг|на́ть[2], **оню́, о́нишь** *pf.* (+*a. or g.*) **1.** to herd together (*a number of*). **2.** to distil (*a quantity of*).
нагне|сти́, ту́, тёшь *pf.* (*of* **~та́ть**) to compress, force; (*tech.*) to supercharge.
нагнета́тел|ь, я *m.* (*tech.*) supercharger.
нагнета́тельн|ый *adj.* (*tech.*): **н. кла́пан** pressure valve; **~ая труба́** force pipe.
нагнета́|ть, ю *impf. of* **нагнести́**
нагне|ту́, тёшь *see* **~сти́**
нагное́ни|е, я *nt.* (*med.*) **1.** fester. **2.** suppuration.
нагнои́т|ься, и́тся *pf.* (*med.*) to fester, suppurate.
нагн|у́ть, у́, ёшь *pf.* (*of* **нагиба́ть**) to bend.
нагн|у́ться, у́сь, ёшься *pf.* (*of* **нагиба́ться**) to bend (down), stoop.
нагова́рива|ть, ю *impf. of* **наговори́ть**[1]
наговóр, а *m.* **1.** slander, calumny. **2.** incantation.
наговор|и́ть[1], **ю́, и́шь** *pf.* (*of* **нагова́ривать**) **1.** (*coll.*; **на**+*a.*) to slander, calumniate. **2.: н. пласти́нку** to have a recording made (of one's voice), record (one's voice). **3.** to pronounce incantations over.
наговор|и́ть[2], **ю́, и́шь** *pf.* (+*a. or g.*) to talk, say a lot (of); **н. чепухи́** to talk a lot of nonsense.
наговор|и́ться, ю́сь, и́шься *pf.* to talk o.s. out; **они́ не мо́гут н.** they cannot talk enough.
наг|о́й (~, ~а́, ~́о) *adj.* naked, nude, bare.
наголе́нный *adj.* worn, etc., on shin(s); **н. щито́к** shin-pad.
на́голо́ *adv.* bare; **остри́чь на́голо** to cut close to the skin, crop close; **с ша́шками наголо́** with drawn swords.
на́голову *adv.*: **разби́ть н.** to rout, smash.
наголода́|ться, юсь *pf.* to be half-starved.
наго́льный *adj.*: **н. тулу́п** uncovered sheepskin coat.
нагоня́|й, я *m.* (*coll.*) scolding, rating.
нагоня́|ть, ю, *impf. of* **нагна́ть**
на-гора́ *adv.* (*mining*) to the surface, to the top.
нагора́жива|ть, ю *impf. of* **нагороди́ть**
нагор|а́ть, а́ю *impf. of* **~е́ть**
нагор|е́ть[1], **и́т** *pf.* (*of* **~а́ть**) **1.** to need snuffing (*of a candle*). **2.** (+*g.*) to be used up (*of fuel*).
нагор|е́ть[2], **и́т** *pf.* (*of* **~а́ть**) (*impers.,* +*d.*; *coll.*): **тебе́ за э́то ~и́т** you'll get it hot for this.
наго́рн|ый *adj.* **1.** mountainous, hilly. **2.** (*of river bank*) high. **3.: Н~ая про́поведь** (*bibl.*) Sermon on the Mount.
нагоро|ди́ть, жу́, ~́дишь *pf.* (*of* **нагора́живать**) **1.** to build, erect (*in large quantity*). **2.** (*coll.*) to pile up, heap up. **3.** (*fig.*) to talk, write (*a lot of nonsense*); **н. вздо́ра, чепухи́** to talk a lot of nonsense.
наго́рь|е, я *nt.* table-land, plateau.
нагот|а́, ы́ *f.* nakedness, nudity.
наготове *adv.* in readiness; ready to hand; **быть н.** to hold o.s. in readiness, be on call.
наготóв|ить, лю, ишь *pf.* (+*a. or g.*) **1.** to lay in (*a supply of*). **2.** to cook (*a large quantity of*).
наготóв|иться, люсь, ишься *pf.* (*coll.*; +*g.* **на**+*a.*) to have enough (for), provide enough (for); **на них не ~ишься еды́** one cannot provide enough food for them; **он так бы́стро растёт, на него́ не ~ишься оде́жды** he is growing so fast, it is impossible to keep him in clothes.
награ́б|ить, лю, ишь *pf.* (+*a. or g.*) to amass by robbery.
награ́д|а, ы *f.* **1.** reward, recompense. **2.** award; decoration; (*in schools*) prize.
награ|ди́ть, жу́, ди́шь *pf.* (*of* **~жда́ть**) (+*a. and i.*) **1.** to reward (with). **2.** to decorate (with); to award, confer; (*fig.*) to endow (with); **н. кого́-н. о́рденом** to confer a decoration upon s.o., award s.o. a decoration; **приро́да ~ди́ла его́ вели́кими тала́нтами** nature has endowed him with great talent.
наград|но́й *adj. of* **~́а**
наградн|ы́е, ы́х *pl. only* bonus.
награжда́|ть, ю *impf. of* **награди́ть**
награждённ|ый *p.p.p. of* **награди́ть**; *as n.* **н., ~ого** *m.* recipient (*of an award*).
нагре́в, а *m.* (*tech.*) heat, heating; **пове́рхность ~а** heating surface.
нагрева́тел|ь, я *m.* (*tech.*) heater.
нагрева́тельный *adj.* (*tech.*) heating.
нагрева́|ть(ся) ю(сь) *impf. of* **нагре́ть(ся)**
нагре́|ть, ю *pf.* (*of* **~ва́ть**) **1.** to warm, heat; **н. ру́ки** (*fig.*) to feather one's nest. **2.** (*coll.*) to swindle; **они́ ~ли меня́ на пять рубле́й** they swindled me out of five roubles.
нагре́|ться[1], **юсь,** *pf.* (*of* **нагрева́ться**) to become warm, become hot; to warm up, heat up.
нагре́|ться[2], **юсь,** *pf.* (*of* **~ва́ться**) (*coll.*) to be swindled.
нагримир|ова́ть, у́ю *pf. of* **гримирова́ть**
нагроможда́|ть, ю *impf. of* **нагромозди́ть**
нагромоз|ди́ть, жу́, ди́шь *pf.* (*of* **громозди́ть** *and* **нагроможда́ть**) to pile up, heap up.
нагруб|и́ть, лю́, и́шь *pf. of* **груби́ть**
нагрубия́н|ить, ю, ишь *pf. of* **грубия́нить**
нагру́дник, а *m.* **1.** bib. **2.** breastplate.
нагру́дный *adj.* breast.
нагружа́|ть(ся), ю(сь) *impf. of* **нагрузи́ть(ся)**
нагру|зи́ть, жу́, ~́зишь *pf.* (*of* **грузи́ть** *and* **~жа́ть**) (+*a. and i.*) **1.** to load (with). **2.** (*fig.*) to burden (with).
нагру|зи́ться, жу́сь, ~́зишься *pf.* (*of* **~за́ться**) (+*i.*) to load o.s. (with), burden o.s. (with).
нагру́зк|а, и *f.* **1.** loading. **2.** load; **поле́зная н.** (*tech.*) payload, working load. **3.** (*fig.*) work; commitments, obligation(s); **парти́йная н.** party work, party obligations; **преподава́тельская н.** teaching load.
нагрязн|и́ть, ю́, и́шь *pf. of* **грязни́ть**
нагря́н|уть, у, ешь *pf.* (*coll.*) to appear unexpectedly; (**на**+*a.*) to descend (on).
нагу́л, а *m.* (*agric.*) fattening.
нагу́лива|ть, ю *impf. of* **нагуля́ть**
нагул|я́ть, я́ю *pf.* (*of* **~́ивать**) to acquire, develop (*as result of feeding, exercise, etc.*); **н. жи́ру** (*agric.*) to fatten, put on weight; **н. брюшко́** (*fig., joc.*) to develop a paunch; **н. аппети́т** to work up an appetite.
нагуля́|ться, юсь *pf.* to have had a long walk.
над *prep.*+*i.* **1.** over, above. **2.** on; at; **рабо́тать над диссерта́цией** to be working on a dissertation; **смея́ться над** to laugh at.
над... *comb. form* super-, over-.
нада|ва́ть, ю́, ёшь *pf.* (*coll.*; +*d. and a. or g.*) to give (*a large quantity of*).
надав|и́ть[1], **лю́, ~́ишь** *pf.* (*of* **~́ливать**) (**на**+*a.*) to press (on).
надав|и́ть[2], **лю́, ~́ишь** *pf.* (+*a. or g.*) **1.** to press, squeeze (*a number of*). **2.** (*coll.*) to swat (*a quantity of*).
нада́влива|ть, ю *impf. of* **надави́ть**[1]
нада́ива|ть, ю *impf. of* **надои́ть**
нада́рива|ть, ю *impf. of* **надари́ть**

надар|и́ть, ю́, и́шь *pf.* (*of* **~ивать**) (*coll.*; *+a. or g. and d.*) to present (*a large quantity of*).
надба́в|ить, лю, ишь *pf.* = **наба́вить**
надба́вк|а, и *f.* = **наба́вка**
надбавля́|ть, ю *impf. of* **надба́вить**
надбив|а́ть, ю *impf. of* **надби́ть**
надби́т|ый *p.p.p. of* **~ь** *and adj.* cracked; chipped.
над|би́ть, обью́, обьёшь *pf.* (*of* **~бива́ть**) to crack; to chip.
надбро́вный *adj.* (*anat.*) superciliary.
надвига́|ть(ся), ю(сь) *impf. of* **надви́нуть(ся)**
надви́н|уть, у, ешь *pf.* (*of* **надвига́ть**) to move, pull (up to, over).
надви́н|уться, усь, ешься *pf.* (*of* **надвига́ться**) to approach, draw near.
надво́дный *adj.* above-water; **н. борт** free-board; **н. кора́бль** surface ship.
на́двое *adv.* **1.** in two. **2.** ambiguously; **ба́бушка н. сказа́ла** (*coll.*) I wouldn't be too sure about that.
надво́рный *adj.* situated in the yard; **н. сове́тник** (*obs.*) court counsellor (*civil servant of seventh class, equivalent in rank to lieutenant-colonel*).
надвя|за́ть, жу́, ~жешь *pf.* (*of* **~зывать**) to add (*in knitting*); to add a length (*of string, thread, etc.*).
надвя́зыва|ть, ю *impf. of* **надвяза́ть**
надгорта́нник, а *m.* (*anat.*) epiglottis.
надгро́би|е, я *nt.* **1.** (*obs.*) epitaph. **2.** gravestone.
надгро́бн|ый *adj.* (placed on, over, a) grave; funeral, graveside; **~ое сло́во** graveside oration.
надгрыз|а́ть, а́ю *impf. of* **~ть**
надгры́з|ть, у́, ёшь, *past* **~, ~ла** *pf.* (*of* **~а́ть**) to nibble (at).
надда|ва́ть, ю́, ёшь *impf. of* **~ть**
надда́|ть, м, шь, ст, ди́м, ди́те, ду́т, *past* **~л, ~ла́, ~ло** *pf.* (*of* **~ва́ть**) (*coll.*; *+a. or g.*) to add, increase, enhance; **н. хо́ду** to increase the pace; **~й!** get a move on!
надду́в, а *m.* (*tech.*, *aeron.*) supercharge.
надёв|анный *p.p.p. of* **~а́ть** *and adj.* worn, used (*of clothing*).
надева́|ть, ю *impf. of* **наде́ть**
наде́жд|а, ы *f.* hope, prospect; **подава́ть ~у** to hold out hope; **подава́ть ~ы** to promise well, shape well.
надёж|ный (~ен, ~на) *adj.* reliable, trustworthy; safe.
наде́л, а *m.* allotment; land holding (*esp. after the emancipation of the serfs in 1861*).
наде́ла|ть, ю *pf.* (*+a. or g.*) **1.** to make (*a quantity of*). **2.** (*coll.*; *+g.*) to cause (*a lot of*), make (*a lot of*). **3.** (*coll.*) to do (*sth. wrong*); **что ты ~л?** what have you done?
надел|ённый *p.p.p of* **~и́ть; он ~ён больши́ми спосо́бностями** he is richly talented.
надел|и́ть, ю́, и́шь *pf.* (*of* **~я́ть**) (*+a. and i.*) to invest (with), to provide (with); (*fig.*) to endow (with).
наде́|ну, нешь *see* **~ть**
надёрг|ать, аю *pf.* (*of* **~ивать**) (*+a. or g.*) to pull, pluck (*a quantity of*).
надёргива|ть, ю *impf. of* **надёргать** *and* **надёрнуть**
надёр|нуть, ну, нешь *pf.* (*of* **~гивать**) (**на**+*a.*) to pull (on, over).
над|еру́, ерёшь *see* **~ра́ть**
наде́|ть, ну, нешь *pf.* (*of* **~ва́ть**) to put on (*clothes, etc.*).
наде́|яться, юсь, ешься *impf.* (*of* **по~**) **1.** (**на**+*a.*) to hope (for). **2.** (**на**+*a.*) to rely (on). **3.** to expect.
надзе́мный *adj.* overground.
надзира́тел|ь, я *m.* overseer, supervisor; **кла́ссный н.** (*obs.*) form-master.
надзира́|ть, ю *impf.* (**за**+*i.*) to oversee, supervise.
надзо́р, а *m.* **1.** supervision, surveillance. **2.** (*collect.*) inspectorate; **прокуро́рский н.** Directorate of Public Prosecutions.
надив|и́ться, лю́сь, и́шься *pf.* (*coll.*; *+d. or* **на**+*a.*) to admire sufficiently; **не мо́жешь н. на его́ му́жество** one cannot sufficiently admire his courage.
надира́|ть, ю *impf. of* **надра́ть**
надира́|ться, юсь *impf. of* **надра́ться**
надка́лыва|ть, ю *impf. of* **надколо́ть**
надкла́ссовый *adj.* (*pol.*) transcending class.
надко́жиц|а, ы *f.* (*bot.*) cuticle.
надколе́нн|ый *adj.*: **~ая ча́шка** knee-cap; (*anat.*) patella.
надкол|о́ть, ю́, ~ешь *pf.* (*of* **надка́лывать**) **1.** to crack. **2.** to score.
надко́стниц|а, ы *f.* (*anat.*) periosteum; **воспале́ние ~ы** (*med.*) periostitis.
надкры́льl|е, я *nt.* (*zool.*) shard, elytron; wing-case.
надку|си́ть, шу́, ~сишь *pf.* (*of* **~сывать**) to take a bite of.
надку́сыва|ть, ю *impf. of* **надкуси́ть**
надла́мыва|ть(ся), ю(сь) *impf. of* **надломи́ть(ся)**
надлежа́щий *adj.* fitting, proper; appropriate.
надлеж|и́т, *past* **~а́ло** (*impers.*, *+d. and inf.*) it is necessary, it is required; **вам н. яви́ться в де́сять часо́в** you are required to present yourself at ten o'clock.
надло́м, а *m.* **1.** crack. **2.** (*fig.*) sharp deterioration of psychological state; crack-up. **3.** violent expression of emotion.
надлом|и́ть, лю́, ~ишь *pf.* (*of* **надла́мывать**) to break partly; to crack; (*fig.*) to overtax, break down.
надлом|и́ться, лю́сь, ~ишься *pf.* (*of* **надла́мываться**) **1.** to crack (*also fig.*); **здоро́вье у него́ ~и́лось** he has had a breakdown. **2.** *pass. of* **~и́ть**
надло́м|ленный *p.p.p. of* **~и́ть** *and adj.* broken (*also fig.*).
надме́нност|ь, и *f.* haughtiness, arrogance.
надме́н|ный (~ен, ~на) *adj.* haughty, arrogant.
на́до[1] = **над**
на́до[2] *+d. and inf.* it is necessary; one must, one ought; (*+a. or g.*) there is need of; **не н.** (*i*) one need not, (*ii*) one must not; **мне н. идти́** I must go, I ought to go; **мне н. вина́** I need some wine; **так ему́ и н.** serves him right!; **н. быть** (*coll.*) probably; **что н.** (*as pred.*; *coll.*) the best there is.
на́до|бно (*obs.*) = **~**
на́добност|ь, и *f.* necessity, need; **име́ть н. в чём-н.** to require sth.
на́доб|ный (~ен, ~на) *adj.* (*obs.*) necessary, needful.
надое́д|а, ы *c.g.* (*coll.*) pain (in the neck).
надоеда́ла = **надое́да**
надоеда́|ть, ю *impf. of* **надое́сть**
надое́длив|ый (~, ~а) *adj.* boring, tiresome.
надое́|сть, м, шь, ст, ди́м, ди́те, дя́т *pf.* (*of* **~да́ть**) **1.** (*+d. and i.*) to get on the nerves (of), to pester (with), plague (with); to bore (with); **он мне до чёртиков ~л** I'm sick to death of him. **2.** (*impers.*, *+d. and inf.*): **мне,** *etc.*, **~ло** I, *etc.*, am tired (of), sick (of); **нам ~ло игра́ть в чехарду́** we are tired of playing leapfrog.
надо|и́ть, ю́, и́шь *pf.* (*of* **нада́ивать**) (*+a. or g.*) to obtain (*a quantity of milk*).
надо́|й, я *m.* (*agric.*) yield (*of milk*).
на́долб|а, ы *f.* stake; **противота́нковые ~ы** anti-tank obstacles.
надо́лго *adv.* for a long time.
надо́мник, а *m.* homeworker.
надорв|а́ть, у́, ёшь, *past* **~а́л, ~ала́, ~а́ло** *pf.* (*of* **надрыва́ть**) to tear slightly; (*fig.*) to (over)strain, overtax; **н. живо́тики (со́ смеху)** (*coll.*) to split one's sides (with laughter).
надорв|а́ться, у́сь, ёшься, *past* **~а́лся, ~ала́сь, ~а́лось** *pf.* (*of* **надрыва́ться**) **1.** to tear slightly (*intrans.*); to (over)strain o.s. **2.** to let o.s. go, let rip.
надоу́м|ить, лю, ишь *pf.* (*of* **~ливать**) (*coll.*) to advise, to give the (*required*) idea.
надоу́млива|ть, ю *impf. of* **надоу́мить**
надпа́рыва|ть, ю *impf. of* **надпоро́ть**
надпи́лива|ть, ю *impf. of* **надпили́ть**
надпил|и́ть, ю́, ~ишь *pf.* (*of* **~ивать**) to make an incision in (*by sawing*).
надпи|са́ть, шу́, ~шешь *pf.* (*of* **~сывать**) **1.** to inscribe; to superscribe. **2.** (*obs.*) to address (*an envelope, etc.*).
надпи́сыва|ть, ю *impf. of* **надписа́ть**
на́дпис|ь, и *f.* inscription; superscription; (*on medal, coin, etc.*) legend; **переда́точная н.** (*comm.*) endorsement.
надпор|о́ть, ю́, ~ешь *pf.* (*of* **надпа́рывать**) (*coll.*) to unstitch, unpick (*a few stitches*).

надпо́чечный *adj.* (*anat.*) adrenal.
над|ра́ть, еру́, ерёшь, *past* **~ра́л, ~рала́, ~ра́ло** *pf.* (*of* **~ира́ть**) (+*a. or g.*) to tear off, strip (*a quantity of*); **н. у́ши кому́-н.** to pull s.o.'s ears.
над|ра́ться, еру́сь, ерёшься, *past* **~ра́лся, ~рала́сь, ~ра́лось** *pf.* (*of* **~ира́ться**) (*coll.*) to become sozzled.
надре́з, а *m.* cut, incision; notch.
надре́|зать, жу, жешь *pf.* (*of* **~за́ть** *and* **~зывать**) to make an incision (in).
надрез|а́ть, а́ю *impf. of* **~ать**
надре́зыва|ть, ю *impf.* = **надре́за́ть**
надруга́тельств|о, а *nt.*: **(над)** outrage (upon).
надруга́|ться, юсь *pf.*: **(над)** to outrage, do violence to.
надры́в, а *m.* **1.** slight tear, rent. **2.** strain. **3.** (*fig.*) sharp deterioration of psychological state; crack-up. **4.** violent expression of emotion.
надрыва́|ть(ся), ю(сь) *impf. of* **надорва́ть(ся)**
надры́в|ный (~ен, ~на) *adj.* **1.** hysterical. **2.** heart-rending.
надса́д|а, ы *f.* (*coll.*) strain; effort.
надса|ди́ть, жу́, ~дишь *pf.* (*of* **~живать**) (*coll.*) **1.** to (over)strain. **2.** (+*d.*) to vex, distress.
надса|ди́ться, жу́сь, ~дишься *pf.* (*of* **~живаться**) (*coll.*) to (over)strain o.s.
надса́д|ный (~ен, ~на) *adj.* (*coll.*) back-breaking; heavy; **н. ка́шель** hacking cough.
надса́жива|ть(ся), ю(сь) *impf. of* **надсади́ть(ся)**
надсма́трива|ть, ю *impf.* **(за**+*i. or* **над)** to oversee, supervise; to inspect.
надсмо́тр, а *m.* supervision; surveillance.
надсмо́трщик, а *m.* overseer, supervisor; jailer.
надста́в|ить, лю, ишь *pf.* (*of* **~ля́ть**) to lengthen (*garment or part of garment*).
надста́вк|а, и *f.* added piece, extension.
надставля́|ть, ю *impf. of* **надста́вить**
надставно́й *adj.* put on.
надстра́ива|ть, ю *impf. of* **надстро́ить**
надстро́|ить, ю, ишь *pf.* (*of* **надстра́ивать**) **1.** to build on. **2.** to raise the height (of).
надстро́йк|а, и *f.* **1.** building on; raising. **2.** superstructure (*also phil.*).
надстро́чн|ый *adj.* superscript.
надтре́снут|ый (~, ~а) *adj.* cracked (*also fig.*).
надува́л|а, ы *c.g.* (*coll.*) swindler, cheat.
надува́тельский *adj.* (*coll.*) swindling, underhand.
надува́тельств|о, а *nt.* (*coll.*) swindling, cheating.
надува́|ть(ся), ю(сь) *impf. of* **наду́ть(ся)**
надувн|о́й *adj.* pneumatic; **н. матра́ц** air bed; **~а́я рези́новая ло́дка** inflatable rubber dinghy.
наду́манный *adj.* far-fetched, forced.
наду́м|ать, аю *pf.* (*coll.*) **1.** (+*inf.*) to decide (to). **2.** (*impf.* **~ывать**) to think up, make up.
наду́мыва|ть, ю *impf. of* **наду́мать**
наду́т|ый (~, ~а) *p.p.p. of* **~ь** *and adj.* (*coll.*) **1.** swollen. **2.** haughty; puffed up. **3.** sulky. **4.** (*liter.*) inflated, turgid.
наду́|ть, ю, ешь *pf.* (*of* **~ва́ть**) **1.** to inflate, blow up; to puff out; **н. велосипе́дную ка́меру** to inflate, blow up a bicycle tyre; (*impers.*; *pf. only*): **ве́тром ~ло пы́ли** the wind blew the dust up; **мне ~ло в у́хо** I have ear-ache from the draught; **н. гу́бы** (*coll.*) to pout one's lips. **2.** (*coll.*) to dupe; to swindle.
наду́|ться[1], юсь, ешься *pf.* (*of* **~ва́ться**) **1.** to fill out, swell out; **паруса́ ~лись** the sails filled out. **2.** (*fig.*, *coll.*) to be puffed up. **3.** (*fig.*, *coll.*) to pout; to sulk.
наду́|ться[2], юсь, ешься *pf.* (*coll.*; +*g.*) to swig (*a quantity of*).
наду́ш|енный *p.p.p. of* **~и́ть** *and adj.* scented, perfumed.
надуш|и́ть(ся), у́(сь), ~ишь(ся) *pf. of* **души́ть(ся)[2]**
надшива́|ть, ю *impf. of* **надши́ть**
над|ши́ть, ошью́, ошьёшь *pf.* (*of* **~шива́ть**) **1.** to lengthen (*a garment*). **2.** to stitch on (to).
надым|и́ть, лю́, и́шь *pf. of* **дыми́ть**
надыш|а́ть, у́, ~ишь *pf.* **1.** to make the air (*in a room, etc.*) warm with one's breathing. **2.** (*coll.*; **на**+*a.*) to breathe (on).
надыш|а́ться, у́сь, ~ишься *pf.* **1.** (+*i.*) to breathe in, inhale. **2.: не н.** (**на**+*a.*) to dote (on, upon).
наеда́|ться, юсь *impf. of* **нае́сться**
наедине́ *adv.* privately, in private; **н. с** (+*i.*) alone (with).
нае́|ду, дешь *see* **~хать**
нае́зд, а *m.* **1.** flying visit; **быва́ть ~ом** to pay short, infrequent visits. **2.** (*cavalry*) raid.
нае́з|дить, жу, дишь *pf.* (*of* **~живать**) **1.** to cover (*driving or riding*); **мы ~дили сто миль за два часа́** we covered a hundred miles in two hours. **2.** (*coll.*) to make (= *gain, acquire by conveying*) **н. де́сять рубле́й** to make ten roubles. **3.** (**доро́гу**, *etc.*) to use (a road, *etc.*) a good deal. **4.** to break in (*a horse*).
нае́здник, а *m.* **1.** horseman, rider; jockey; (*mil.*; *obs.*) raider. **2.** (*zool.*) ichneumon fly.
нае́здничеств|о, а *nt.* **1.** horsemanship. **2.** (*obs.*) (cavalry) raiding.
наезжа́|ть, ю *impf.* **1.** (*coll.*) to pay occasional visits. **2.** *impf. of* **нае́хать**
нае́з|женный *p.p.p. of* **~дить** *and adj.* well-trodden, beaten.
нае́зжива|ть, ю *impf. of* **нае́здить**
нае́зж|ий *adj.* (*coll.*) newly-arrived; **~ие лю́ди** new-comers.
нае́з|жу, дишь *see* **~дить**
на|ём, ~йма *m.* hire; renting; **взять в н.** to rent; **сдать в н.** to let.
наёмник, а *m.* **1.** (*hist.*) mercenary. **2.** hireling (*also fig.*).
наёмный *adj.* hired; rented.
наёмщик, а *m.* tenant, lessee.
нае́|сться, мся, шься, стся, ди́мся, ди́тесь, дя́тся, *past* **~лся, ~лась** *pf.* (*of* **~да́ться**) **1.** to eat one's fill. **2.** (+*g. or i.*) to eat (a large quantity of), stuff o.s. (with).
нае́|хать, ду, дешь *pf.* (*of* **~зжа́ть**) **1.** (**на**+*a.*) to run (into, over), collide (with); **на нас ~хал авто́бус** a bus ran into us (over us). **2.** (*coll.*) to come, arrive (*unexpectedly or in numbers*).
нажа́л|оваться, уюсь *pf.* (*coll.*; **на**+*a.*) to complain (of).
нажа́рива|ть(ся), ю(сь) *impf. of* **нажа́рить(ся)**
нажа́р|ить[1], ю, ишь *pf.* (*of* **~ивать**) (*coll.*) to overheat.
нажа́р|ить[2], ю, ишь *pf.* to roast, fry (*a quantity of*).
нажа́р|иться, юсь, ишься *pf.* (*of* **~иваться**) (*coll.*) to bask, warm o.s. (*for a long time*).
наж|а́ть[1], му́, мёшь *pf.* (*of* **~има́ть**) **1.** (+*a. or* **на**+*a.*) to press (on); **н. (на) кно́пку** to press the button. **2.** (*fig.*, *coll.*; **на**+*a.*) to put pressure (upon). **3.** (*fig.*, *coll.*) to press on, press ahead; **~мём и вы́полним э́ту рабо́ту!** let us press on and finish this job!
наж|а́ть[2], ну́, нёшь *pf.* (*of* **~ина́ть**) (+*a. or g.*) to reap, harvest (*a quantity of*).
нажда́к, а́ *m.* emery.
нажда́|чный *adj. of* **~к; ~чная бума́га** emery paper.
наж|е́чь, гу́, жёшь, гу́т, *past* **~ёг, ~гла́** *pf.* (*of* **~ига́ть**) (+*a. or g.*) to burn (*a quantity of*).
нажи́в|а[1], ы *f.* gain, profit.
нажи́в|а[2], ы *f.* = **~ка**
нажива́|ть(ся), ю(сь) *impf. of* **нажи́ть(ся)**
нажив|и́ть, лю́, и́шь *pf.* (*of* **~ля́ть**) to bait.
нажи́вк|а, и *f.* bait.
наживля́|ть, ю *impf. of* **наживи́ть**
наживн|о́й[1] *adj. only in phr.* **э́то де́ло ~о́е** (*coll.*) it'll come (with time).
наживно́й[2] *adj.* usable as bait.
нажи|ву́, вёшь *see* **~ть**
нажига́|ть, ю *impf. of* **наже́чь**
нажи́м, а *m.* **1.** pressure (*also fig.*) **2.** (*tech.*) clamp.
нажима́|ть, ю *impf. of* **нажа́ть[1]**
нажи́мист|ый (~, ~а) *adj.* (*coll.*) exacting; stubborn, insistent.
нажимн|о́й *adj.* (*tech.*) pressure; **н. винт** stop screw; **~о́е приспособле́ние** pressure mechanism.
нажина́|ть, ю *impf. of* **нажа́ть[2]**
нажира́|ться, юсь *impf. of* **нажра́ться**
наж|и́ть, иву́, ивёшь, *past* **~ил, ~ила́, ~ило** *pf.* (*of* **~ива́ть**) to acquire, gain; (*fig.*) to contract (*disease*), incur.
наж|и́ться[1], иву́сь, ивёшься, *past* **~и́лся́, ~ила́сь** *pf.* (*of* **~ива́ться**) to become rich, make a fortune.

нажи́|ться[2], **ву́сь, вёшься** *pf.* (*coll.*) to live (*somewhere*) long enough.
наж|му́, мёшь *see* **~а́ть**[1]
наж|ну́, нёшь *see* **~а́ть**[2]
нажр|а́ться, у́сь, ёшься *pf.* (*of* **нажира́ться**) (*coll.*; *+g. or i.*) to gorge o.s. (with).
наза́втра *adv.* (*coll.*) on *or* for the next day.
наза́д *adv.* **1.** back, backwards; **н.!** back!; stand back! **2.** **(тому́) н.** ago.
назади́ *adv.* (*coll.*) behind.
назализа́ци|я, и *f.* (*ling.*) nasalization.
назализи́р|овать, ую *impf. and pf.* (*ling.*) to nasalize.
наза́льный *adj.* (*ling.*) nasal.
Назаре́т, а *m.* Nazareth.
назва́нива|ть, ю *impf.* (*coll.*) to keep ringing (*on telephone, etc.*).
назва́ни|е, я *nt.* name, appellation; title (*book*).
назва́ный *adj.* sworn; adopted; (*fig.*): **он мой н. брат** he is my sworn brother.
наз|ва́ть[1], **ову́, овёшь,** *past* **~ва́л, ~вала́, ~ва́ло** *pf.* (*of* **~ыва́ть**) (*+i.*) to call; to name, designate; **они́ ~ва́ли дочь Татья́ной** they have called their daughter Tatyana; **он ~ва́л себя́ Никола́ем** he gave his name as Nicholas.
наз|ва́ть[2], **ову́, овёшь,** *past* **~ва́л, ~вала́, ~ва́ло** *pf.* (*coll.*; *+g.*) to invite (*a number of*).
наз|ва́ться[1], **ову́сь, овёшься,** *past* **~ва́лся, ~вала́сь** *pf. of* **~ыва́ться**
наз|ва́ться[2], **ову́сь, овёшься,** *past* **~ва́лся, ~вала́сь** *pf.* (*coll.*) to invite o.s.
наздра́вств|оваться, уюсь *pf.*: **на вся́кое чиха́ние не ~уешься** (*coll.*) one cannot please everyone.
назём, а *m.* (*dial.*) manure, dung.
назе́мн|ый *adj.* ground, surface; terrestrial; **~ые войска́** (*mil.*) ground troops; **~ая (по́чта)** surface mail.
на́земь *adv.* (down) to the ground.
назида́ни|е, я *nt.* (*obs.*, *now iron.*) edification; **сказа́ть что-н. в н. кому-н.** to say sth. for s.o.'s edification.
назида́тел|ьный (~ен, ~ьна) *adj.* edifying.
на́зло́ 1. *adv.* out of spite. **2.** *prep.* (*+d.*) to spite.
назнач|а́ть, а́ю *impf. of* **~́ить**
назначе́ни|е, я *nt.* **1.** fixing, setting. **2.** appointment. **3.** (*med.*) prescription. **4.** purpose. **5.** destination.
назна́ч|ить, у, ишь *pf.* (*of* **~а́ть**) **1.** to fix, set, appoint; **н. день встре́чи** to fix, appoint a day for a meeting; **н. опла́ту** to fix a rate of pay. **2.** (*+i.*) to appoint, nominate; **его́ ~или команди́ром ро́ты** he has been appointed company commander. **3.** (*med.*) to prescribe.
назо́йливост|ь, и *f.* importunity.
назо́йлив|ый (~, ~а) *adj.* importunate.
назрева́|ть, ю *impf.* (*of* **назре́ть**) **1.** to ripen, mature; to gather head. **2.** (*fig.*) to become imminent; **кри́зис ~л** a crisis was brewing.
назре́|ть, ю, ешь, *pf. of* **~ва́ть**
назу́бник, а *m.* gumshield.
назубо́к *adv.* (*coll.*): **знать н.** to know by heart.
называ́|емый *pres. part. pass. of* **~ть; так н.** so-called.
называ́|ть, ю *impf. of* **назва́ть**[1]
называ́|ться, юсь *impf.* (*of* **назва́ться**[1]) (*+i.*) **1.** to call o.s. **2.** to be called; **как ~ется э́то село́?** what is this village called? what is the name of this village?; **что ~ется** (*coll.*) as they say. **3.** (*obs.*) to give one's name.
наибо́лее *adv.* (the) most.
наибо́льший *adj.* the greatest; the largest; **о́бщий н. дели́тель** (*math.*) highest common factor.
наи́вннча|ть, ю *impf.* (*coll.*) to affect naïveté
наи́вност|ь, и *f.* naïveté (naivety).
наи́в|ный (~ен, ~на) *adj.* naïve.
наивы́сш|ий *adj.* the highest; **в ~ей сте́пени** to the utmost.
наи́гранн|ый 1. *p.p.p. of* **наигра́ть. 2.** *adj.* (*fig.*) put on, assumed; forced; **~ая весёлость** assumed gaiety.
наигра́|ть, ю *pf.* (*of* **наи́грывать**) **1.** (*coll.*) to make, acquire (*by playing*). **2.** (*coll.*) to strum. **3.: н. пласти́нку** to make a recording.
наигра́|ться, юсь *pf.* (*coll.*) to play for a long time, for long enough.
наи́грыва|ть, ю *impf. of* **наигра́ть**
на́игрыш, а *m.* **1.** folk-tune. **2.** (*theatr. sl.*) artificiality.
наизна́нку *adv.* inside out; **вы́вернуть н.** to turn inside out.
наизу́сть *adv.* by heart; from memory.
наилу́чший *adj.* (the) best.
наиме́нее *adv.* (the) least.
наименова́ни|е, я *nt.* appellation, designation.
наимен|ова́ть, у́ю *pf. of* **именова́ть**
наиме́ньш|ий *adj.* (the) least; **о́бщее ~ее кра́тное** (*math.*) lowest common multiple.
наипа́че *adv.* (*obs.*) still more; in particular.
наискосо́к *adv.* = **на́искось**
на́искось *adv.* obliquely, slantwise.
наи́ти|е, я *nt.* inspiration; **по ~ю** instinctively, intuitively.
наиху́дший *adj.* (the) worst.
найдёныш, а *m.* foundling.
найми́т, а *m.* hireling.
на|йти́[1], **~йду́, ~йдёшь,** *past* **~шёл, ~шла́** *pf.* (*of* **~ходи́ть**) (*in var. senses*) to find; to discover; **н. себе́ моги́лу, смерть** (*rhet.*) to meet one's death.
на|йти́[2], **йду́, йдёшь,** *past* **~шёл, ~шла́** *pf.* (*of* **~ходи́ть**) **1.** **(на**+*a.*) to come (across, over, upon); to come (up against); **что э́то на неё ~шло́?** what has come over her? **2.** (*impers.*, *coll.*) to gather, collect; **~шло́ мно́го наро́ду** a large crowd collected.
на|йти́сь, йду́сь, йдёшься, *past* **~шёлся, ~шла́сь** *pf.* (*of* **~ходи́ться**[1]) **1.** to be found; to turn up. **2.** not to be at a loss; **я не ~шёлся, что сказа́ть** I was at a loss for what to say.
найто́в, а *m.* (*naut.*) lashing, seizing.
найто́в|ить, лю, ишь *impf.* (*of* **об~**) (*naut.*) to lash, seize.
нака́вер|зить, жу, зишь *pf. of* **ка́верзить**
нака́з, а *m.* **1.** (*obs.*) order; instructions. **2.** mandate (*in former USSR, list of desiderata presented by electors to deputy*).
наказа́ни|е, я *nt.* **1.** punishment. **2.** (*fig.*, *coll.*) nuisance; **мне с ним (су́щее, пря́мо, про́сто) н.** he is a (perfect) nuisance to me.
нака|за́ть[1], **жу́, ~́жешь** *pf.* (*of* **~́зывать**) to punish.
нака|за́ть[2], **жу́, ~́жешь** *pf.* (*of* **~́зывать**) (*obs. or dial.*; *+d.*) to instruct, bid.
наказу́емый *adj.* (*leg.*) punishable.
нака́л, а *m.* **1.** incandescence. **2.** (*radio*) heating.
накал|ённый *p.p.p. of* **~и́ть** *and adj.* **1.** incandescent; white-hot. **2.** (*fig.*) strained, tense; **~ённая междунаро́дная обстано́вка** tense international situation.
нака́ливани|е, я *nt.* (*tech.*) incandescing.
нака́лива|ть(ся), ю(сь) *impf. of* **накали́ть(ся)**
накал|и́ть, ю́, и́шь *pf.* (*of* **~́ивать**) to heat, incandesce.
накал|и́ться, ю́сь, и́шься *pf.* (*of* **~́иваться**) to glow, incandesce.
нака́лыва|ть(ся), ю(сь) *impf. of* **наколо́ть(ся)**
наканифо́л|ить, ю, ишь *pf. of* **канифо́лить**
накану́не 1. (*adv.*) the day before. **2.** (*prep.*+*g.*) on the eve (of); **н. Рождества́ Христо́ва** on Christmas Eve.
нака́п|ать, аю *pf.* (*of* **~ывать**[1]) **1.** (*+a. or g.*) to pour by drops; **н. лека́рства** to pour out some medicine. **2.** (*+g. or i.*) to spill; **он ~ал на столе́ черни́лами (черни́л)** he has spilled ink on the table.
нака́пливать(ся) *impf.* = **накопля́ть(ся)**
нака́пыва|ть[1], **ю** *impf. of* **нака́пать**
нака́пыва|ть[2], **ю** *impf. of* **накопа́ть**
нака́рка|ть, ю *pf.* (*coll.*) to bring down (evil) by one's own prophecies.
нака́т, а *m.* layer (*of beams or planks*).
накат|а́ть[1], **а́ю** *pf.* (*of* **~́ывать**) **1.** to roll out; to roll smooth. **2.** (*coll.*) to write hurriedly; **н. письмо́** to dash off a letter.
накат|а́ть[2], **а́ю** *pf.* (*of* **~́ывать**) (*+a. or g.*) to roll (*a quantity of*).
ката́|ться, юсь *pf.* (*coll.*) to have had enough (*of driving, riding*).
нака|ти́ть, чу́, ~́тишь *pf.* (*of* **~́тывать**) **(на**+*a.*) to roll up (onto); (*impers.*, *coll.*): **на него́ ~ти́ло** he is out of his senses, he has taken leave of his senses.

нака́тыва|ть, ю *impf. of* **наката́ть** *and* **накати́ть**
накач|а́ть[1], **а́ю** *pf.* (*of* **~́ивать**) to pump up, pump full.
накача́|ть[2], **а́ю** *pf.* to pump (*a quantity of*).
накач|а́ться, а́юсь *pf.* (*of* **~́иваться**) **1.** (*coll.*) to become sozzled. **2.** *pass. of* **~а́ть**
нака́чива|ть(ся), ю(сь) *impf. of* **накача́ть(ся)**
накид|а́ть, а́ю *pf.* (*of* **~́ывать**) = **наброса́ть**[2]
наки́дк|а, и *f.* **1.** cloak, mantle; wrap. **2.** pillow-cover. **3.** increase; extra charge.
наки́дыва|ть(ся), ю(сь) *impf. of* **накида́ть** *and* **наки́нуть(ся)**
наки́|нуть, ну, нешь *pf.* (*of* **~дывать**) **1.** to throw on, throw over. **2.** (**на**+*a.*) to add (*to the price of*).
наки́|нуться, нусь, нешься *pf.* (*of* **~дываться**) (**на**+*a.*) to fall (on, upon).
накип|а́ть, а́ет *impf. of* **~е́ть**
накип|е́ть, и́т *pf.* (*of* **~а́ть**) to form a scum; to form a scale; (*fig., impers.*) to swell, boil; **в нём ~е́ла зло́ба** he is boiling with resentment.
на́кип|ь, и *f.* **1.** scum. **2.** scale, fur, coating, deposit.
накла́д, а *m.*: **быть, оста́ться в ~е** (*coll.*) to be down, come off loser.
накла́дк|а, и *f.* **1.** (*tech.*) bracket. **2.** false hair, hair-piece. **3.** (*sl.*) blunder, clanger.
накладн|а́я, о́й *f.* invoice, way-bill.
накла́дно *adv.* (*coll.*) to one's disadvantage, to one's cost.
накладн|о́й *adj.* **1.** laid on, super-imposed; **~о́е зо́лото** rolled gold; **н. карма́н** patch pocket; **~ы́е расхо́ды** overhead expenses, overheads. **2.** false; **~а́я борода́** false beard.
накла́дыва|ть, ю *impf. of* **наложи́ть**
наклеве|та́ть, щу́, ~́щешь *pf. of* **клевета́ть**
наклёвыва|ться, юсь *impf. of* **наклю́нуться**
накле́ива|ть, ю *impf. of* **накле́ить**
накле́|ить, ю, ешь *pf.* (*of* **~ивать**) to stick on, paste on.
накле́йк|а, и *f.* **1.** sticking on, pasting on. **2.** sticker.
наклепа́|ть[1], **ю** *pf.* (*of* **наклёпывать**) to rivet.
наклеп|а́ть[2], **лю́, ~́лешь** *pf. of* **клепа́ть**[2]
наклёпыва|ть, ю *impf. of* **наклепа́ть**[1]
наклик|а́ть, а́ю *impf. of* **~́ать**
накли́|кать, чу, чешь *pf.* (*of* **~ка́ть**); **н. на себя́** to bring upon o.s.; **н. беду́ (на**+*a.*) to bring disaster (upon).
накло́н, а *m.* slope, incline; declivity.
наклоне́ни|е[1], **я** *nt.* inclination.
наклоне́ни|е[2], **я** *nt.* (*gram.*) mood.
наклон|и́ть, ю́, ~́ишь *pf.* (*of* **~я́ть**) to incline, bend; to bow.
наклон|и́ться, ю́сь, ~́ишься *pf.* (*of* **~я́ться**) to stoop, bend.
накло́нност|ь, и *f.* **1.** (**к**) leaning (towards), penchant (for). **2.** inclination, propensity, proclivity; **дурны́е ~и** evil propensities.
накло́нн|ый *adj.* inclined, sloping; **~ая пло́скость** inclined plane; **кати́ться по ~ой пло́скости** (*fig.*) to go downhill, go to the dogs (*morally*).
наклон|я́ть(ся), я́ю(сь) *impf. of* **~и́ть(ся)**
наклю́н|уться, усь, ишься *pf.* (*of* **наклёвываться**) **1.** to peck its way out of the shell. **2.** (*coll.*) to turn up; **слу́чай ~ется** an occasion will present itself.
накля́узнича|ть, ю *pf. of* **кля́узничать**
накова́л|ьня, ьни, *g. pl.* **~ен** *f.* **1.** anvil. **2.** (*anat.*) incus.
нако́жный *adj.* (*med.*) cutaneous.
накола́чива|ть, ю *impf. of* **наколоти́ть**[1,2]
наколе́нник, а *m.* knee-pad.
наколе́нный *adj.* worn on the knee.
нако́лк|а, и *f.* **1.** head-dress (*fastened with pins*). **2.** (*sl.*) tip-off.
наколо|ти́ть[1], **чу́, ~́тишь** *pf.* (*of* **накола́чивать**) (*coll.*) **1.** to knock on. **2.** to knock up (*money*).
наколо|ти́ть[2], **чу́, ~́тишь** *pf.* (*of* **накола́чивать**) (+*a. or g.*) **н. гвозде́й** to drive in (*a number of*) nails; **н. посу́ды** to smash (*a quantity of*) crockery.
накол|о́ть[1], **ю́, ~́ешь** *pf.* (*of* **нака́лывать**) (+*a. or g.*) to split (*a quantity of*); **н. дров** to chop (*a quantity of*) wood.
накол|о́ть[2], **ю́, ~́ешь** *pf.* (*of* **нака́лывать**) **1.** to prick; **н. узо́р** to prick out a pattern. **2.** to pin down; **н. ба́бочку на була́вку** to pin down a butterfly. **3.** to slaughter, stick (*a number of*).
накол|о́ться, ю́сь, ~́ешься *pf.* (*of* **нака́лываться**) to prick o.s.
наконе́ц *adv.* **1.** at last; finally, in the end; **н.-то!** at last!, about time too! **2.** after all.
наконе́чник, а *m.* tip, point; ferrule; **н. стрелы́** arrow-head.
наконе́чн|ый *adj.* final; **~ое ударе́ние** (*gram.*) end-stress.
накопа́|ть, ю *pf.* (*of* **нака́пывать**) (+*a. or g.*) to dig up (*a number of*).
накопи́тел|ь, я *m.* (*comput.*) storage; **н. на ди́сках** disk drive.
накоп|и́ть, лю́, ~́ишь *pf.* (*of* **копи́ть; ~ля́ть** *and* **нака́пливать**) (+*a. or g.*) to accumulate, amass.
накоп|и́ться, лю́сь, ~́ишься *pf.* (*of* **~ля́ться** *and* **нака́пливаться**) to accumulate.
накопле́ни|е, я *nt.* accumulation.
накопля́|ть(ся), ю(сь) *impf. of* **накопи́ть(ся)**
накоп|ти́ть[1], **чу́, ти́шь** *pf. of* **копти́ть 3.**
накоп|ти́ть[2], **чу́, ти́шь** *pf.* (+*a. or g.*) to smoke (= *cure*) (*a quantity of*).
накорм|и́ть, лю́, ~́ишь *pf. of* **корми́ть**
накоротке́ *adv.*: **произвести́ ата́ку н.** to carry out a rapid attack at close range.
нако|си́ть, шу́, ~́сишь *pf.* (+*a. or g.*) to mow (down) (*a quantity of*).
нако́стн|ый *adj.* (*situated on*) bone; **~ая о́пухоль** bone tumour.
накра́пыва|ть, ет *impf.* (*impers. or* +**дождь**) to trickle, drizzle; **ста́ло н.** it began to spit (*with rain*).
накра́|сить, шу, сишь *pf.* (*of* **~шивать**) **1.** to paint. **2.** to make up.
накра́|ситься, шусь, сишься *pf. of* **кра́ситься**
накра́|сть, ду́, дёшь, *past* **~л** *pf.* (*of* **~дывать**) (+*a. or g.*) to steal (*a number of*).
накрахма́л|ить, ю, ишь *pf. of* **крахма́лить**
накра́шива|ть, ю *impf. of* **накра́сить**
накрен|и́ть, ю́, и́шь *pf.* **1.** *pf. of* **крени́ть. 2.** (*impf.* **~я́ть**) to tilt to one side, tilt.
накрен|и́ться, ю́сь, и́шься *pf.* **1.** *pf. of* **крени́ться. 2.** (*impf.* **~я́ться**) to tilt, list.
накрен|я́ть(ся), я́ю(сь) *impf. of* **~и́ть(ся)**
на́крепко *adv.* **1.** fast, tight; **закры́ть н.** to shut fast. **2.** (*coll.*) categorically; strictly; **приказа́ть н.** to give a strict injunction.
на́крест *adv.* crosswise; **сложи́ть ру́ки крест-н.** to cross one's arms.
накрич|а́ть, у́, и́шь *pf.* (**на**+*a.*) to shout (at).
накрич|а́ться, у́сь, и́шься *pf.* (*coll.*) to have shouted to one's heart's content.
накро|и́ть, ю́, и́шь *pf.* (+*a. or g.*) to cut out (*a quantity of*).
накрош|и́ть, у́, ~́ишь *pf.* (*of* **кроши́ть**) **1.** to crumble, shred (*a quantity of*). **2.** to spill crumbs.
накр|о́ю, о́ешь *see* **~ы́ть**
накро|ю́, и́шь *see* **~и́ть**
накру|ти́ть[1], **чу́, ~́тишь** *pf.* (*of* **~чивать**) to wind, turn.
накру|ти́ть[2], **чу́, ~́тишь** *pf.* **1.** to twist (*a quantity of*). **2.** (*coll.*) to do, say (*sth. complicated or unusual*).
накру́чива|ть, ю *impf. of* **накрути́ть**[1]
накрыва́|ть(ся), ю(сь) *impf. of* **накры́ть(ся)**
накр|ы́ть, о́ю, о́ешь *pf.* (*of* **~ыва́ть**) **1.** to cover; **н. (на) стол** to lay the table; **н. к у́жину** to lay supper. **2.** (*fig., coll.*) to catch; **н. на ме́сте преступле́ния** to catch red-handed.
накр|ы́ться, о́юсь, о́ешься *pf.* (*of* **~ыва́ться**) (+*i.*) to cover o.s. (with).
накто́уз, а *m.* (*naut.*) binnacle.
накуп|а́ть, а́ю *impf. of* **~и́ть**
накуп|и́ть, лю́, ~́ишь *pf.* (*of* **~а́ть**) (+*a. or g.*) to buy up (*a number or quantity of*).
наку́р|енный *p.p.p. of* **~и́ть** *and adj.* smoky, smoke-filled; **в. ко́мнате ~ено** the room is full of (tobacco) smoke.
накур|и́ть[1], **ю́, ~́ишь** *pf.* (+*i.*) to fill with smoke, with fumes.

накур|и́ть², **ю́**, **∠ишь** *pf.* (+*a. or g.*) to distil (*a quantity of*).
накур|и́ться, **ю́сь**, **∠ишься** *pf.* (*coll.*) to smoke to one's heart's content.
накуроле́|сить, **шу**, **сишь** *pf. of* **куроле́сить**
наку́т|ать, **аю** *pf.* (*of* **~ывать**) (+*a. or g.* **на**+*a.*) to put on (*clothing, etc.*); **мно́го ~али на ребёнка** the child was well wrapped up.
наку́тыва|ть, **ю** *impf. of* **наку́тать**
нала́влива|ть, **ю** *impf. of* **налови́ть**
налага́|ть, **ю** *impf. of* **наложи́ть**
нала́|дить, **жу**, **дишь** *pf.* (*of* **~живать**) **1.** to regulate, adjust; to repair, put right. **2.** to set going, arrange; **н. дела́** to get things going.
нала́|диться, **жусь**, **дишься** *pf.* (*of* **~живаться**) **1.** to go right; **рабо́та ~дилась** the work is well in hand. **2.** *pass. of* **~дить**
нала́дчик, **а** *m.* (*tech.*) adjuster.
нала́жива|ть(ся), **ю(сь)** *impf. of* **нала́дить(ся)**
налака́|ться, **юсь** *pf.* **1.: н. молока́** to lap up one's fill of milk. **2.** (*coll.*) to get drunk.
нала́ком|иться, **люсь**, **ишься** *pf.* (*coll.*; +*i.*) to have one's fill (of dainties).
на|лга́ть, **лгу́**, **лжёшь**, **лгут**, *past* **~лга́л**, **~лгала́**, **~лга́ло** *pf.* **1.** to lie, tell lies. **2.** (*impf.* **лгать 2.**) (**на**+*a.*) to slander.
нале́во *adv.* **1.** (**от**) to the left (of); **н.!** (*mil.*) left turn! **2.** (*coll.*) on the side (= *illicitly*); **рабо́тать н.** to moonlight.
налега́|ть, **ю** *impf. of* **нале́чь**
налегке́ *adv.* (*coll.*) **1.** without luggage; **путеше́ствовать н.** to travel light. **2.** lightly clad.
належ|а́ть, **у́**, **и́шь** *pf.* (*coll.*) to acquire as result of lying a long time; **н. про́лежни** develop bed-sores.
налез|а́ть[1,2], **а́ю** *impf. of* **∠ть**[1,2]
нале́з|ть¹, **у**, **ешь**, *past* **~**, **~ла** *pf.* (*of* **~а́ть¹**) to get in, get on (*in large numbers, in quantities*).
нале́з|ть², **ет** *pf.* (*of* **~а́ть²**) (*of clothing or footwear*) (**на**+*a.*) to fit, go on.
нале́п|и́ть¹, **лю́**, **∠ишь** *pf.* (*of* **лепи́ть 2.** *and* **~ля́ть**) to stick on.
налеп|и́ть², **лю́**, **∠ишь** *pf.* (+*a. or g.*) to model (*a number of*).
налеп|ля́ть, **ля́ю**, *impf. of* **~и́ть¹**
налёт¹, **а** *m.* (*in var. senses*) raid; **кавалери́йский н.** cavalry raid; **возду́шный н.** air-raid; **с ~а** (*fig.*) suddenly, without warning, without preparation; **бить с ~а** to swoop down on; **он ду́мает, что он смо́жет поби́ть реко́рд с ~а** he thinks he will be able to beat the record just like that.
налёт², **а** *m.* deposit; thin coating; (*on bronze*) patina; **зубно́й н.** dental plaque; (*fig.*) touch, soupçon; **н. в го́рле** (*med.*) patch, spot; **с ~ом иро́нии** with a touch of irony.
налет|а́ть¹, **а́ю** *impf. of* **~е́ть**
налет|а́ть², **а́ю** *pf.* to have flown (so many hours *or* miles).
нале|те́ть¹, **чу́**, **ти́шь** *pf.* (*of* **~та́ть¹**) **1.** (**на**+*a.*) to fall (upon); to swoop down (on); to fly (upon, against); to run (into) (*of vehicles*). **2.** (*of wind, storm*) to spring up.
нале|те́ть², **чу́**, **ти́шь** *pf.* (*of* **~та́ть¹**) to fly in, drift in (*in quantities, in large numbers*).
налётчик, **а** *m.* burglar, robber; raider.
на|ле́чь, **ля́гу**, **ля́жешь**, **ля́гут**, *imper.* **~ля́г**, *past* **~лёг**, **~легла́** *pf.* (*of* **~лега́ть**) (**на**+*a.*) **1.** to lean (on); to weigh down (on); to lie (upon); **н. плечо́м на дверь** to try to force the door with one's shoulder; **н. на подчинённых** (*fig.*) to come down upon one's subordinates. **2.** to apply o.s. (to), throw o.s. (into); **н. на вёсла** to ply one's oars.
нали́в, **а** *m.* **1.** pouring in. **2.** swelling, ripening; **«бе́лый н.»** *variety of apple.*
налива́|ть(ся), **ю(сь)** *impf. of* **нали́ть(ся)**
нали́вк|а, **и** *f.* fruit liqueur; **вишнёвая н.** cherry brandy.
наливн|о́й *adj.* **1.** (*tech.*) worked by water; for conveying liquids; **~о́е колесо́** overshot wheel; **~о́е су́дно** (*naut.*) tanker. **2.** ripe. juicy.
нали́м, **а** *m.* (*zool.*) burbot, eel pout.
налин|ова́ть, **у́ю** *pf. of* **линова́ть**
налип|а́ть, **а́ет** *impf. of* **∠нуть**
нали́п|нуть, **нет**, *past* **~**, **~ла** *pf.* (*of* **~а́ть**) (**на**+*a.*) to stick (to).
налито́й *adj.* **1.** juicy, ripe. **2.** fleshy, well-fleshed.
нал|и́ть, **ью́**, **ьёшь**, *past* **∠и́л**, **~ила́**, **∠и́ло** *pf.* (*of* **~ива́ть**) to pour out; (+*i.*) to fill (with); **н. бо́чку водо́й** to fill a barrel with water.
нал|и́ться, **ью́сь**, **ьёшься**, *past* **~и́лся**, **~ила́сь**, **~и́ло́сь** *pf.* (*of* **~ива́ться**) **1.** (+*i.*) to fill (with); **н. кро́вью** to become bloodshot. **2.** to ripen, become juicy. **3.** *pass. of* **~и́ть**
налицо́ *adv.* present, available, on hand.
нали́честв|овать, **ую** *impf.* to be present, be on hand.
нали́чи|е, **я** *nt.* presence; **быть, оказа́ться в ~и** to be present, be available; **при ~и** (+*g.*) in the presence (of), given.
нали́чник, **а** *m.* **1.** casing, jambs and lintel of a door *or* window. **2.** lock-plate.
нали́чност|ь, **и** *f.* **1.** amount on hand; cash-in-hand; **н. това́ров в магази́не** stock-in-trade. **2.** = **нали́чие**
нали́чн|ый *adj.* on hand, available; **~ые (де́ньги)** ready money, cash; **плати́ть ~ыми** to pay in cash, pay down; **за н. расчёт** for cash; **н. соста́в** (*mil.*) available personnel, effectives.
нало́бник, **а** *m.* (*part of a harness*) frontlet.
нало́бн|ый *adj.*: **~ая ле́нточка** headband.
налов|и́ть, **лю́**, **∠ишь** *pf.* (+*a or g.*) to catch (*a number of*).
наловч|и́ться, **у́сь**, **и́шься** *pf.* (+*inf.*) to become proficient (in), become good (at).
нало́г, **а** *m.* tax; **доба́вочный подохо́дный н.** surtax; **н. на доба́вленную сто́имость** value added tax, VAT; **необлага́емый ~ом** tax-deductible.
нало́г|овый *adj. of* **~**
налогоплате́льщик, **а** *m.* tax-payer.
наложе́ни|е, **я** *nt.* **1.** imposition; **н. аре́ста** (*leg.*) seizure; **н. швов** (*med.*) suture, stitching. **2.** (*math.*) superposition.
нало́ж|енный *p.p.p. of* **~и́ть**; **~енным платежо́м** cash on delivery (*abbr.* C.O.D.).
налож|и́ть¹, **у́**, **∠ишь** *pf.* **1.** (*impf.* **накла́дывать**) to lay in, on; to put in, on; to superimpose; to apply; **н. повя́зку** to apply a bandage; **н. на себя́ ру́ки** to lay hands on o.s. **2.** (*impf.* **накла́дывать**) to load, pack; **н. корзи́ну бельём, н. белья́ в корзи́ну** to load a basket with linen. **3.** (*impf.* **налага́ть**) (**на**+*a.*) to lay (on), impose; **н. на себя́ бре́мя** to undertake a burden; **н. штраф** to impose a fine; **н. аре́ст на чьё-н. иму́щество** (*leg.*) to seize s.o.'s property.
налож|и́ть², **у́**, **∠ишь** *pf.* (*of* **накла́дывать**) to put, lay (*a quantity of*).
нало́жниц|а, **ы** *f.* (*obs.*) concubine.
нало́|й, **я** *m.* = **анало́й**
налома́|ть, **ю** *pf.* (+*a. or g.*) to break (*a quantity of*); **н. бока́ кому́-н.** (*coll.*) to give s.o. a sound thrashing; **н. дров** (*coll., joc.*) to commit follies.
нало́па|ться, **юсь** *pf.* (*coll.*) to gorge o.s.
налощ|и́ть, **у́**, **и́шь** *pf. of* **лощи́ть**
нал|ью́, **ьёшь** *see* **~и́ть**
налюб|ова́ться, **у́юсь** *pf.* (+*i. or* **на**+*a.*) to gaze to one's heart's content (at) (*usu. with neg.*).
нал|я́гу, **я́жешь**, **я́гут** *see* **~е́чь**
наля́па|ть, **ю** *pf. of* **ля́пать**
нам *d. of* **мы**
намагни́|тить, **чу**, **тишь** *pf.* (*of* **~чивать**) to magnetize.
намагни́чива|ть, **ю** *impf. of* **намагни́тить**
нама́з, **а** *m.* (Mohammedan) prayer.
нама́|зать, **жу**, **жешь** *pf. of* **ма́зать** *and* **~зывать**
нама́|заться, **жусь**, **жешься** *pf.* **1.** (*impf.* **~зываться**) (+*i.*) to rub o.s. (with). **2.** *pf. of* **ма́заться**
нама́зыва|ть(ся), **ю(сь)** *impf. of* **нама́зать(ся)**
намал|ева́ть, **ю́ю**, **ю́ешь** *pf. of* **малева́ть**
намара́|ть, **ю** *pf. of* **мара́ть 2.**
намарин|ова́ть, **у́ю** *pf.* (+*a. or g.*) to pickle (*a quantity of*).
нама́слива|ть, **ю** *impf.* = **ма́слить**
нама́сл|ить, **ю**, **ишь** *pf. of* **~ивать** *and* **ма́слить**
наматра́цник, **а** *m.* mattress cover.
нама́тывани|е, **я** *nt.* winding, reeling.
нама́тыва|ть, **ю** *impf. of* **намота́ть**[2]
нама́чива|ть, **ю** *impf. of* **намочи́ть**
нама́|яться, **юсь**, **ешься** *pf.* (*coll.*) **1.** to be tired out. **2.** to

have had a lot of trouble.
наме́дни *adv.* (*dial.*) the other day, lately.
намёк, а *m.* **1.** hint, allusion; **то́нкий н.** gentle hint; **ко́свенный н.** innuendo; **сде́лать н.** to drop a hint; **с ~ом** (**на**+*a.*) with a suggestion (of). **2.** (*fig.*) faint resemblance.
намек|а́ть, а́ю *impf.* (*of* **~ну́ть**) (**на**+*a.*, **о**+*p.*) to hint (at), allude (to).
намек|ну́ть, ну́, нёшь *pf. of* **~а́ть**
намел|и́ть, ю́, и́ть *pf. of* **мели́ть**
наменя́|ть, ю *pf.* (+*a. or g.*) to obtain (*a quantity of*) by exchange.
намерева́|ться, юсь *impf.* (+*inf.*) to intend (to), mean (to).
наме́рен (**~а, ~о**) *adj. as pred.* **быть н.** (+*inf.*) to intend; **я н. за́втра е́хать** I intend to go tomorrow; **что вы ~ы сде́лать?** what do you intend to do?
наме́рени|е, я *nt.* intention; purpose.
наме́ренный *adj.* intentional, deliberate.
намерз|а́ть, а́ю *impf. of* **~нуть**
намёрз|нуть, ну, нешь, *past* **~, ~ла** *pf.* (*of* **~а́ть**) to freeze (on); **на ступе́ньках ~ло мно́го льда** a lot of ice had formed on the steps.
намёрз|нуться, нусь, нешься, *past* **~ся, ~лась** *pf.* (*coll.*) to get frozen.
наме́р|ить, ю, ишь *pf.* **1.** (+*a. or g.*) to measure out (*a quantity of*). **2.** to measure (*a certain quantity or distance*).
на́мертво *adv.* tightly, fast.
наме|си́ть, шу́, ~сишь *pf.* (+*a or g.*) to knead (*a quantity of*).
наме|сти́, ту́, тёшь, *past* **~л, ~ла́** *pf.* (*of* **~та́ть**[1]) (+*a. or g.*) **1.** to sweep together (*a quantity of*). **2.** to cause to drift; **~ло́ мно́го сне́гу** big snow-drifts have formed.
наме́стник, а *m.* **1.** deputy. **2.** (*hist.*) governor-general.
наме́стни|ческий *adj. of* **~к**
наме́стничеств|о, а *nt.* (*hist.*) region ruled by governor-general.
намёт[1]**, а** *m.* casting-net.
намёт[2]**, ю** *m.* (*dial.*) gallop.
намета́|ть[1]**, ю** *impf. of* **намести́**
намета́|ть[2]**, ю** *pf. of* **мета́ть**[2]
наме|та́ть[3]**, чу́, ~чешь** *pf.* (+*a. or g.*) to throw together (*a quantity of*).
наме|та́ть[4]**, чу́, ~чешь** *pf.* (*of* **~тывать**) (*coll.*) to train; **н. глаз** to acquire a (good) eye; **н. ру́ку** (**на**+*a.*) to become proficient (in).
наме́|тить[1]**, чу, тишь** *pf. of* **ме́тить**[1] *and* **~ча́ть**[1]
наме́|тить[2]**, чу, тишь** *pf.* **1.** (*impf.* **~ча́ть**[2]) to plan, project; to have in view; **н. пое́здку в Росси́ю** to plan a visit to Russia. **2.** (*impf.* **~ча́ть**[2]) to nominate; to select; **его́ ~тили кандида́том в председа́тели** he has been nominated for chairman; **н. зда́ние к разруше́нию** to designate a building for demolition. **3.** *pf. of* **ме́тить**[2]
наме́|титься, чусь, тишься *pf.* (*of* **~ча́ться**) to be outlined; to take shape.
намётк|а[1]**, и** *f.* **1.** basting, tacking. **2.** basting thread, tacking thread.
намётк|а[2]**, и** *f.* rough draft, preliminary outline.
намётыва|ть, ю *impf. of* **намета́ть**[4]
намеча́|ть[1]**, ю** *impf.* = **ме́тить**
намеча́|ть[2]**, ю** *impf. of* **наме́тить**[2]
намеча́|ться, юсь *impf. of* **наме́титься**
наме́|чу, тишь *see* **~тить**
наме|чу́, чешь *see* **~та́ть**
намеш|а́ть, а́ю *pf.* (*of* **~ивать**) (+*a. or g.* **в**+*a.*) to add (to), mix in(to).
наме́шива|ть, ю *impf. of* **намеша́ть**
на́ми *i. of* **мы**
намиби́йский *adj.* Namibian.
Нами́би|я, и *f.* Namibia.
намина́|ть, ю *impf. of* **намя́ть**
намно́го *adv.* much, far (*with comparatives*); **н. лу́чше** much better.
нам|ну́, нёшь *see* **~я́ть**
намозо́л|ить, ю, ишь *pf. of* **мозо́лить**
намок|а́ть, а́ю *impf.* (*of* **~нуть**) to become wet, get wet.
намо́к|нуть, ну, нешь, *past* **~, ~ла** *pf. of* **~а́ть**
намоло|ти́ть, чу́, ~тишь *pf.* (+*a. or g.*) to thresh (*a quantity of*).
нам|оло́ть, елю́, е́лешь *pf.* (+*a. or g.*) to grind, mill (*a quantity of*); **н. вздо́ру, чепухи́** (*coll.*) to talk a lot of nonsense.
намо́рдник, а *m.* muzzle.
намо́рщ|ить(ся), у(сь) ишь(ся) *pf. of* **мо́рщить(ся)**
намо|сти́ть, щу́, сти́шь *pf. of* **мости́ть 2.**
намота́|ть[1]**, ю** *pf. of* **мота́ть**[1]
намота́|ть[2]**, ю** *pf.* (*of* **нама́тывать**) (+*a. or g.*) to wind (*a quantity of*).
намоч|и́ть, у́, ~ишь *pf.* (*of* **нама́чивать**) **1.** to wet, moisten. **2.** to soak, steep. **3.** (*intrans.*; *coll.*) to spill water (on the floor, *etc.*).
намудр|и́ть, ю, и́шь *pf. of* **мудри́ть**
наму́сл|ить, ю, ишь *pf. of* **му́слить**
намус|о́лить *pf.* = **~лить**
наму́сор|ить, ю, ишь *pf. of* **му́сорить**
наму|ти́ть, чу́, ~ти́шь *pf.* **1.** to stir up mud; to make muddy. **2.** (*intrans.*; *fig.*, *coll.*) to make a mess; to create chaos.
наму́ч|иться, усь, ишься *pf.* (*coll.*) to be worn out; to have had a hard time.
намы́в, а *m.* (*geol.*) alluvium.
намывно́й *adj.* (*geol.*) alluvial.
намы́ливать(ся) *impf.* = **мы́лить(ся)**
намы́л|ить(ся), ю(сь), ишь(сь) *pf. of* **~ивать(ся)** *and* **мы́лить(ся)**
нам|ы́ть, о́ю, о́ешь *pf.* (+*a. or g.*) **1.** to wash (*a quantity of*). **2.** (*of a river*) to deposit.
нам|я́ть[1]**, ну́, нёшь** *pf.* (*of* **~ина́ть**) to hurt (*by pressure or friction*); to crush; **н. кому́-н. бока́, ше́ю** to give s.o. a sound thrashing.
нам|я́ть[2]**, ну́, нёшь** *pf.* (+*a. or g.*) **1.** to mash (*a quantity of*). **2.** to trample down (*a certain area of*).
нанесе́ни|е, я *nt.* **1.** drawing, plotting (*on a map*). **2.** infliction; **н. уда́ров** assault and battery.
нанес|ти́[1]**, у́, ёшь,** *past* **~, ~ла́** *pf.* (*of* **наноси́ть**) **1. (на ка́рту)** to draw, plot, (on a map). **2.** to cause; to inflict; **н. оскорбле́ние** to insult; **н. визи́т** to pay a visit. **3.** (+*a.* **на**+*a.*) to dash (against); (*impers.*): **ло́дку ~ло́ на мель** the boat struck a shoal.
нанес|ти́[2]**, у́, ёшь,** *past* **~, ~ла́** *pf.* (+*a. or g.*) **1.** to bring (*a quantity of*). **2.** to pile up (*a quantity of*); (*of sand, snow, etc.*) to drift.
нанес|ти́[3]**, ёт,** *past* **~ла́** *pf.*: **н. яи́ц** to lay (*a number of*) eggs.
нани|за́ть, жу́, ~жешь *pf. of* **низа́ть** *and* **~зывать**
нани́зыва|ть, ю *impf.* = **низа́ть**
нанима́тел|ь, я *m.* **1.** tenant. **2.** (*obs.*) employer.
нанима́|ть(ся), ю(сь) *impf. of* **наня́ть(ся)**
на́нк|а, и *f.* (*text.*) nankeen.
на́нк|овый *adj. of* **~а**
на́ново *adv.* (*coll.*) anew, afresh.
нано́с, а *m.* (*geol.*) alluvium; drift.
нано|си́ть[1]**, шу́, ~сишь** *impf. of* **нанести́**
нано|си́ть[2]**, шу́, ~сишь** *pf.* (+*a. or g.*) to bring (*a quantity of*).
нано́сный *adj.* **1.** (*geol.*) alluvial. **2.** (*fig.*, *coll.*) alien; borrowed. **3.** (*obs.*) slanderous.
на́нсук, а *m.* (*text.*) nainsook.
нанюх|аться, аюсь *pf.* (*of* **~иваться**) (+*g.*) **1.** to smell to one's heart's content; to take snuff to one's heart's content. **2.** to be intoxicated (with).
нанюхива|ться, юсь *impf. of* **нанюхаться**
на́н|ятый *p.p.p. of* **~я́ть**
на|ня́ть, найму́, наймёшь, *past* **~нял, ~няла́, ~няло** *pf.* (*of* **~нима́ть**) to rent; to hire; **н. на рабо́ту** to engage, take on.
на|ня́ться, найму́сь, наймёшься, *past* **~нялся́, ~няла́сь** *pf.* (*of* **~нима́ться**) (*coll.*) to become employed, get a job.
наобеща́|ть, ю *pf.* (+*a. or g.*) to promise (much); **н. с три ко́роба** to promise the world.

наоборо́т *adv.* **1.** back to front; **прочёсть сло́во н.** to read a word backwards. **2.** the other way round; the wrong way (round); **он всё понима́ет н.** he take everything the wrong way. **3.** on the contrary; **как раз н.** quite the contrary; **и н.** and vice versa; **я не сержу́сь, а, н., рад был, что вы пришли́** I am not angry; on the contrary, I was glad that you came.
наобу́м *adv.* without thinking; at random.
наор|а́ть, у́, ёшь *pf.* (**на**+*a.*; *coll.*) to shout (at).
нао́тмашь *adv.* **1.** with the back of the hand; **уда́рить н.** to strike a swinging blow. **2.** out from the body.
наотре́з *adv.* flatly, point-blank.
напа́да|ть, ет *pf.* to fall (*in a certain quantity*); **в тече́ние но́чи ~ло мно́го сне́га** there was a heavy fall of snow during the night.
напада́|ть, ю *impf. of* **напа́сть**
напада́ющ|ий, его *m.* (*sport*) forward.
нападе́ни|е, я *nt.* **1.** attack, assault. **2.** (*sport*) forwards, forward-line.
напа́д|ки, ок, кам *no sg.* attacks.
напа|ду́, дёшь *see* **∸сть**
напа́ива|ть¹, ю *impf. of* **напои́ть**
напа́ива|ть², ю *impf. of* **напая́ть**
напа́ко|стить, щу, стишь *pf. of* **па́костить**
напа́лм, а *m.* (*chem.*; *mil.*) napalm.
напа́лм|овый *adj. of* **~**
напа́р|ить, ю, ишь *pf.* (+*a. or g.*) to steam (*a quantity of*).
напа́рник, а *m.* fellow worker, mate.
напа́рыва|ть(ся), ю(сь) *impf. of* **напоро́ть(ся)**
напас|ти́сь, у́сь, ёшься, *past* **∸ся, ~ла́сь** *pf.* (*coll.*; *usu.* +*neg.*) to lay in, save up enough.
напа́|сть¹, ду́, дёшь, *past* **~л** *pf.* (*of* **~да́ть**) (**на**+*a.*) **1.** to attack; to descend (on). **2.** to come (over); to grip, seize; **на нас всех ~л страх** fear seized us all. **3.** to come (upon, across); **я ~л на мысль** the thought occurred to me.
напа́ст|ь², и *f.* (*coll.*) misfortune, disaster.
напа́чка|ть, ю *pf. of* **па́чкать**
напая́|ть, ю, ешь *pf.* (*of* **напа́ивать²**) to solder (onto).
напе́в, а *m.* tune, melody.
напева́|ть, ю *impf.* **1.** *impf. of* **напе́ть. 2.** to hum; to croon.
напе́в|ный (~ен, ~на) *adj.* melodious.
напека́|ть, ю *impf. of* **напе́чь¹**
на́перво *adv.* (*coll.*) at first.
наперебо́й *adv.* vying with one another.
наперевес *adv.* in a horizontal position.
наперего́нки́ *adv.* racing one another; **бе́гать н.** to race (with) one another.
напере́д *adv.* (*coll.*) **1.** in front. **2.** in advance.
наперeко́р *adv. and prep.* (+*d.*) in defiance (of), counter (to).
напере́з *adv.* (*and prep.*+*d.*) so as to cross one's path; **бежа́ть кому́-н. н.** to run to head s.o. off.
наперерыв *adv.* = **наперебо́й**
на|пере́ть, пру́, прёшь, *past* **~пёр, ~пёрла** *pf.* (*of* **~пира́ть**) (*coll.*; **на**+*a.*) to press; to put pressure (upon).
напере|хва́т *adv.* (*dial.*) **1.** = **~ре́з. 2.** = **~бо́й**
напереч ёт *adv.* **1.** through and through; every single one. **2.** *as pred.* very few, not many.
напе́рсник, а *m.* (*obs.*) confidant.
напе́рсниц|а, ы *f.* (*obs.*) **1.** confidante. **2.** mistress.
напе́рсный *adj.* (*eccl.*) pectoral.
напёрст|ок, ка *m.* thimble.
наперстя́нк|а, и *f.* (*bot.*) foxglove.
напе́рч|ить, у, ишь *pf. of* **пе́рчить**
нап|е́ть, ою́, оёшь *pf.* (*of* **~ева́ть**) **1.** to sing (*air, melody*). **2.: н. пласти́нку** to make a recording of one's voice. **3.** (*coll.*; +*d. or* **в у́ши** +*d.*) to give s.o. a piece of one's mind.
напеча́та|ть(ся), ю(сь) *pf. of* **печа́тать(ся)**
напе́|чь¹, чёт, *past* **~кло́** *pf.* (*of* **~ка́ть**) (*impers.*; *coll.*) to burn, scorch (*with the sun*); **го́лову у меня́ ~кло́** my head got scorched.
напе́|чь², ку́, чёшь, ку́т, *past* **∸к, ~кла́** *pf.* (+*a. or g.*) to bake (*a number of*); **н. расска́зов** (*fig.*, *coll.*) to concoct stories.
напива́|ться, юсь *impf. of* **напи́ться**
напи́лива|ть, ю *impf. of* **напили́ть**
напил|и́ть, ю́, ∸ишь *pf.* (*of* **∸ивать**) (+*a. or g.*) to saw (*a quantity of*).
напи́л|ок, ка *m.* (*coll.*) = **~ьник**
напи́льник, а *m.* (*tech.*) file.
напира́|ть, ю *impf.* (*coll.*; **на**+*a.*) **1.** *impf. of* **напере́ть. 2.** to emphasize, stress.
написа́ни|е, я *nt.* **1.** way of writing (*a letter of the alphabet*). **2.** spelling.
напи|са́ть, шу́, ∸шешь *pf. of* **писа́ть**
напит|а́ть, а́ю *pf.* **1.** (*impf.* **пита́ть**) to sate, satiate. **2.** (*impf.* **∸ывать**) (+*i.*) to impregnate (with).
напит|а́ться, а́юсь *pf.* **1.** (*coll.*) to sate o.s.; to take one's fill. **2.** (*impf.* **∸ываться**) (+*i.*) to be impregnated (with).
напи́т|ок, ка *m.* drink, beverage; **прохлади́тельные ~ки** soft drinks; **тонизи́рующий н.** tonic, pick-me-up.
напи́тыва|ть(ся), ю(сь) *impf. of* **напита́ть(ся)**
нап|и́ться, ью́сь, ьёшься, *past* **~и́лся, ~ила́сь, ~и́ло́сь** *pf.* (*of* **~ива́ться**) **1.** (+*g.*) to slake one's thirst (with, on); to have a drink (of). **2.** to get drunk.
напих|а́ть, а́ю *pf.* (*of* **∸ивать**) (**в**+*a.*) to cram (into), stuff (into).
напи́хива|ть, ю *impf. of* **напиха́ть**
напи́чка|ть, ю *pf. of* **пи́чкать**
напи|шу́, ∸шешь *see* **~са́ть**
напла́в|ить, лю, ишь *pf.* (+*a. or g.*) to melt, smelt (*a quantity of*).
напла́канный *adj.* tear-stained, red (with crying).
напла́|каться, чусь, чешься *pf.* **1.** to have one's cry out, have a good cry. **2.** (*coll.*) to have trouble; **он ещё ~чется** there is trouble in store for him yet.
напла́ст|анный *p.p.p. of* **~а́ть** *and adj.* sliced.
напласта́|ть, ю *pf.* (*coll.*; +*g.*) to slice, cut in slices.
напластова́ни|е, я *nt.* (*geol.*) bedding, stratification.
напла́|чу, чешь *see* **~кать**
наплева́тельский *adj.* (*coll.*) devil-may-care.
напл|ева́ть, юю́, юёшь *pf.* **1.** (+*g.*) to spit (out). **2.** (*fig.*, *coll.*; **на**+*a.*) to wash one's hands (of); **н.!** to hell with it! who cares!; **н. на него́!** damn him! to hell with him!; **мне н.!** I don't give a damn *or* toss!; I couldn't care less!
напле|сти́¹, ту́, тёшь, *past* **∸л, ~ла́** *pf.* (+*a. or g.*) to make by weaving (*a number of*); **н. вздо́ру** (*fig.*, *coll.*) to talk a lot of nonsense.
напле|сти́², ту́, тёшь, *past* **∸л, ~ла́** *pf.* (**на**+*a.*; *coll.*) to slander.
напле́чник, а *m.* shoulder strap; (*sport*) shoulder pad.
напле́чный *adj.* (worn on the) shoulder.
напло|ди́ть, жу́, ди́шь *pf.* (*coll.*) to bring forth, produce (*in great numbers*); (*joc.*) to breed.
напло|ди́ться, жу́сь, ди́шься *pf.* (*coll.*) to multiply.
напло|и́ть, ю́, и́шь *pf. of* **плои́ть**
наплы́в| а *m.* **1.** influx (*of people, etc.*). **2.** (*med.*, *bot.*) canker; excrescence.
наплыва́|ть, ю *impf. of* **наплы́ть**
наплы́|ть, ву́, вёшь, *past* **~л, ~ла́, ~ло** *pf.* (*of* **~ва́ть**) **1.** (**на**+*a.*) to run (against), dash (against). **2.** (*of incrustation, etc.*) to form.
напова́л *adv.* outright, on the spot.
наподо́бие *prep.* (+*g.*) like, resembling, in the likeness of.
напо́|енный *p.p.p. of* **~и́ть 1., 2.**
напо|ённый *p.p.p. of* **~и́ть 3.**
напо|и́ть, ю́, и́шь *pf.* (*of* **пои́ть** *and* **напа́ивать¹**) **1.** to give to drink; to water (*an animal*). **2.** to make drunk. **3.** (*poet.*) to impregnate; to fill.
напока́з *adv.* for show; **вы́ставить н.** to show off (*also fig.*).
наполз|а́ть, а́ю *impf. of* **~ти́**
наполз|ти́¹, у́, ёшь, *past* **∸, ~ла́** *pf.* (*of* **~а́ть**) (**на**+*a.*) to crawl (over, against).
наполз|ти́², у́, ёшь, *past* **∸, ~ла́** *pf.* to crawl in (*in great numbers*).
наполне́ни|е, я *nt.* filling; **пульс хоро́шего ~я** (*med.*) normal pulse.
наполни́тел|ь, я *m.* (*tech.*) filler.
напо́лн|ить, ю, ишь *pf.* (*of* **~я́ть**) to fill.

напо́лн|иться, юсь, ишься *pf.* (*of* **~я́ться**) (*+i.*) to fill (with) (*intrans.*)
наполн|я́ть(ся), я́ю(сь) *impf. of* **∠ить(ся)**
наполови́ну *adv.* half; **зал ещё н. пуст** the hall is still half empty; **де́лать де́ло н.** to do a thing by halves.
напома́|дить, жу, дишь *pf. of* **пома́дить**
напомина́ни|е, я *nt.* **1.** reminding. **2.** reminder.
напомина́|ть, ю *impf. of* **напо́мнить**
напо́мн|ить, ю, ишь *pf.* (*of* **напомина́ть**) **1.** (*+d.* **о***+p. or +d. and a.*) to remind (of); **портре́т ~ил мне о про́шлом** *or* **~ил мне про́шлое** the portrait reminded me of the past. **2.** to remind (of), recall (= *to resemble*); **он ~ил мне моего́ де́да** he reminded me of my grandfather.
напо́р, а *m.* pressure (*also fig.*); (*of water, steam, etc.*) head; **он подде́рживал меня́ с ~ом** (*coll.*) he supported me vigorously.
напо́ристост|ь, и *f.* (*coll.*) energy; push, go.
напо́рист|ый (~, ~а) *adj.* (*coll.*) energetic; pushing.
напо́р|ный *adj. of* **~** (*tech.*); **н. бак** pressure tank; **н. кла́пан** pressure valve; **н. насо́с** force pump; **~ная труба́** rising pipe, rising main.
напор|о́ть¹, ю́ ∠ешь *pf.* (*of* **напа́рывать**) (*coll.*) to tear, cut; **н. ру́ку на гвоздь** to cut one's hand on a nail.
напор|о́ть², ю́, ∠ешь *pf.* to rip (*a quantity of*); (*coll.*): **н. вздо́ру, чепухи́** to talk a lot of nonsense.
напор|о́ться, ю́сь, ∠ешься *pf.* (*of* **напа́рываться**) (**на***+a.*) **1.** to cut o.s. (on). **2.** to run (upon, against); (*fig.*) to run (into, up against).
напо́р|тить¹, чу, тишь *pf.* (*+a. or g.*) to spoil (*a quantity of*).
напо́р|тить², чу, тишь *pf.* (*+d.*) to injure, harm.
напосле́док *adv.* (*coll.*) in the end, finally, after all.
нап|ою́¹, оёшь *see* **~е́ть**
напо|ю́², и́шь *see* **~и́ть**
напр. (*abbr. of* **наприме́р**) e.g., for example.
напра́в|ить, лю, ишь *pf.* (*of* **~ля́ть**) **1.** (**на***+a.*) to direct (to, at); **н. внима́ние** to direct one's attention (to); **н. свой путь** to bend one's steps (towards); **н. уда́р** to aim a blow (at). **2.** to send; **н. заявле́ние** to send in an application. **3.** to sharpen; **н. бри́тву** to set a razor. **4.** (*coll.*): **н. рабо́ту** to organize work.
напра́в|иться, люсь, ишься *pf.* (*of* **~ля́ться**) **1.** (**к, в***+a.*, **на***+a.*) to make (for). **2.** (*coll.*) to get going, get under way (*fig.*). **3.** *pass. of* **~ить**
напра́вк|а, и *f.* setting (*of razor, etc.*)
направле́ни|е, я *nt.* **1.** (*in var. senses*) direction; **по ~ю (к)** in the direction (of), towards; **взять н. на се́вер** to make for, head for the north. **2.** (*mil.*) sector. **3.** (*fig.*) trend, tendency; **н. ума́** turn of mind; **либера́льное н.** liberal tendency. **4.** (*official*) order, warrant; directive; **н. в санато́рий** warrant for stay at, certificate approving treatment at a sanatorium. **5.** (*official*) action; effect; **дать н. де́лу** to take action on a matter.
напра́вленност|ь, и *f.* **1.** direction, tendency, trend. **2.** purposefulness.
напра́в|ленный *p.p.p. of* **~ить** *and adj.* **1.** (*radio*) directional. **2.** purposeful; unswerving.
направля́|ть, ю *impf. of* **напра́вить**
направля́|ться, юсь *impf. of* **напра́виться; ~емся в Му́рманск** we are bound for Murmansk.
направля́ющ|ая, ей *f.* (*tech.*) guide.
направля́|ющий *pres. part. act. of* **~ть** *and adj.* (*tech.*) guiding, guide; leading; **н. ва́лик, н. ро́лик** guide roller; **~ющая лине́йка, н. шабло́н** former bar; **н. сте́ржень, н. штифт** guide pin, guide bolt.
напра́во *adv.* to the right; on the right.
напрактик|ова́ться, у́юсь *pf.* (**в***+p.*; *coll.*) to acquire skill (in).
напра́слин|а, ы *f.* (*coll.*) wrongful accusation, slander.
напра́сно *adv.* **1.** vainly, in vain; to no purpose. **2.** wrong, unjustly, mistakenly; **н. вы пришли́ без де́нег** it was a mistake for you to come without money.
напра́с|ный (~ен, ~на) *adj.* **1.** vain, idle; **~ная наде́жда** vain hope. **2.** unfounded, wrongful.
напра́шива|ться, юсь *impf. of* **напроси́ться**; (*impf. only*) to arise, suggest itself; **~ется вопро́с** the question inevitably arises.
наприме́р for example, for instance.
напрока́|зить, жу, зишь *pf. of* **прока́зить**
напрока́знича|ть, ю *pf. of* **прока́зничать**
напрока́т *adv.* for hire, on hire; **взять н.** to hire; **дать, отда́ть н.** to hire out, let.
напролёт *adv.* (*coll.*) through, without a break; **рабо́тать всю ночь н.** to work the whole night through.
напроло́м *adv.* straight, regardless of obstacles (*also fig.*).
напропалу́ю *adv.* (*coll.*) regardless of the consequences; all out.
напроро́ч|ить, у, ишь *pf. of* **проро́чить**
напро|си́ться, шу́сь, ∠сишься *pf.* (*of* **напра́шиваться**) (*coll.*) to thrust o.s. upon; **н. на комплиме́нты** to fish for compliments.
напро́тив *adv. and prep.+g.* **1.** opposite; **он живёт н. (на́шего до́ма)** he lives opposite (our house). **2.** (*+d.*) in defiance (of); to contradict; **она́ всё де́лает мне н.** she does everything to spite me. **3.** on the contrary.
на́прочь *adv.* (*coll.*) completely.
нап|ру́, рёшь *see* **~ере́ть**
напру́жива|ть(ся), ю(сь) *impf. of* **напру́житься**
напру́ж|ить, у, ишь *pf.* (*of* **~ивать**) (*coll.*) to strain; to tense, tauten.
напру́ж|иться, усь, ишься *pf.* (*of* **~иваться**) (*coll.*) to become tense, become taut.
напряга́|ть(ся), ю(сь) *impf. of* **напря́чь(ся)**
напря|гу́, жёшь *see* **∠чь**
напряже́ни|е, я *nt.* **1.** tension; effort, exertion. **2.** (*phys., tech.*) strain; stress; (*elec.*) tension; voltage; **н. на зажи́мах** terminal voltage, electrode potential; **н. смеще́ния** grid bias.
напряжённост|ь, и *f.* tenseness; intensity; tension.
напряжён|ный (~, ~на) *adj.* tense, strained; intense; intensive; all-out; **~ные отноше́ния** strained relations; **~ная рабо́та** intensive work.
напрями́к *adv.* (*coll.*) **1.** straight. **2.** (*fig.*) straight out, bluntly.
напря́|чь, гу́, жёшь, гу́т, *past* **~г, ~гла́** *pf.* (*of* **~га́ть**) to tense, strain (*also fig.*); **н. все си́лы** to strain every nerve.
напря́|чься, гу́сь, жёшься, гу́ться, *past* **~гся, ~гла́сь** *pf.* **1.** to become tense. **2.** to exert o.s., strain o.s.
напу́др|ить(ся), ю(сь), ишь(ся) *pf. of* **пу́дрить(ся)**
напу́льсник, а wrist-band.
на́пуск, а *m.* **1.** letting in. **2.** (*hunting*) letting loose, slipping (*from leash*). **3.** (*in dress, blouse, etc.*) full front. **4.** (*tech.*) lap joint.
напуска́|ть(ся), ю(сь) *impf. of* **напусти́ть(ся)**
напускно́й *adj.* assumed, put on.
напу|сти́ть, щу́, ∠стишь *pf.* (*of* **~ска́ть**) **1.** (*+g.*) to let in; **н. воды́ в ва́нну** to fill a bath. **2.** to let loose, slip, set on (*hounds, etc.*). **3.** (**на себя́***+a.*) to affect, put on; **н. на себя́ ва́жность** to assume an air of importance. **4.: н. стра́ху на кого́-н.** (*coll.*) to strike fear into s.o.
напу|сти́ться, щу́сь, ∠стишься *pf.* (*of* **~ска́ться**) (*coll.*; **на***+a.*) to fly at, go for.
напу́та|ть, ю *pf.* (*coll.*; **в***+p.*) to make a mess (of), make a hash (of); to confuse, get wrong; **вы ~ли в а́дресе** you got the address wrong.
напу́тственн|ый *adj.* parting, farewell; **~ое сло́во** parting words.
напу́тстви|е, я *nt.* parting words, farewell speech.
напу́тств|овать, ую *impf. and pf.* to address, counsel (at parting); **н. до́брыми пожела́ниями** to bid farewell, wish bon voyage.
напух|а́ть, а́ет *impf. of* **∠нуть**
напу́х|нуть, нет, *past* **~, ~ла** *pf.* (*of* **~а́ть**) to swell.
напу|щу́, ∠стишь *see* **~сти́ть**
напы́ж|иться, усь, ишься *pf. of* **пы́житься**
напыл|и́ть, ю́, и́шь *pf. of* **пыли́ть**
напы́щенност|ь, и *f.* **1.** pomposity. **2.** bombast.
напы́щен|ный (~, ~на) *adj.* **1.** pompous. **2.** bombastic, high-flown.
напя́лива|ть, ю *impf. of* **напя́лить**

напя́л|ить, ю, ишь *pf.* (*of* **~ивать**) **1.** to stretch on. **2.** (*coll.*) to pull on, struggle into (*a tight garment*).
нар... *comb. form, abbr. of* **наро́дный 4.**
нараба́тыва|ть, ю *impf. of* **нарабо́тать**[2]
нарабо́та|ть[1]**, ю** *pf.* (*+a. or g.*) to make, turn out (*a quantity of*).
нарабо́та|ть[2]**, ю** *pf.* (*of* **нараба́тывать**) to make, earn.
нарабо́та|ться, юсь *pf.* (*coll.*) to have worked enough; to have tired o.s. with work.
наравне́ *adv.* (**с**+*i.*) **1.** on a level (with); **ма́льчик шёл н. с солда́тами** the small boy kept pace with the soldiers. **2.** equally (with); on an equal footing (with).
нара́д|оваться, уюсь *pf.* (*+d. or* **на**+*a.*; *usu. +neg.*) to rejoice, delight sufficiently (in); **она́ на сы́на не ~уется** she dotes on her son.
нараспа́шку *adv.* (*coll.*) unbuttoned; **у него́ душа́ н.** (*fig.*) he wears his heart upon his sleeve.
нараспе́в *adv.* in a sing-song voice; drawlingly.
нараста́ни|е, я *nt.* growth, accumulation.
нараст|а́ть, а́ю *impf. of* **~и́**
нарас|ти́, ту́, тёшь, *past* **наро́с, наросла́** *pf.* (*of* **~та́ть**) **1.** (**на**+*p.*) to grow (on), form (on); **мох наро́с на камня́х** moss has grown on the stones. **2.** to increase; (*of sound*) to swell. **3.** to accumulate.
нара|сти́ть, щу́, сти́шь *pf.* (*of* **~́щивать**) **1.** to graft (on). **2.** to lengthen; (*fig.*) to increase, augment.
нарасхва́т *adv.*: **продава́ться н.** to sell like hot cakes; **э́ту кни́гу покупа́ют н.** there is a great demand for this book.
нара́щивани|е, я *nt.* increase; build-up; **н. вооруже́ний** arms build-up.
нара́щива|ть, ю *impf. of* **нарасти́ть**
нарва́л, а *m.* (*zool.*) narwhal.
нарв|а́ть[1]**, у́, ёшь,** *past* **~а́л, ~ала́, ~а́ло** *pf.* (*+a. or g.*) **1.** to pick (*a quantity of*). **2.** to tear (*a quantity of*).
нарв|а́ть[2]**, ёт,** *past* **~а́л, ~ала́, ~а́ло** *pf.* (*of* **нарыва́ть**) to gather, come to a head (*of a boil or abscess*); **у меня́ па́лец ~а́л** *or* (*impers.*) **па́лец ~а́ло** I have a gathering on my finger.
нарв|а́ться, у́сь, ёшься, *past* **~а́лся, ~ала́сь, ~а́ло́сь** *pf.* (*of* **нарыва́ться**) (*coll.*; **на**+*a.*) to run into, run up (against).
нард, а *m.* spikenard, nard.
наре́|жу, жешь *see* **~зать**
наре́з, а *m.* **1.** (*tech.*) thread; groove (*in rifling*). **2.** (*hist., econ.*) lot, plot (*of land*).
наре́|зать[1]**, жу, жешь** *pf.* (*of* **~за́ть**) **1.** to cut into pieces; to slice; to carve. **2.** (*tech.*) to thread; to rifle. **3.** (*hist., econ.*) to allot, parcel out (*land*).
наре́|зать[2]**, жу, жешь** *pf.* (*+a. or g.*) to cut, slice (*a quantity of*).
нарез|а́ть, а́ю *impf. of* **~́ать**[1]
наре́|заться, жусь, жешься *pf.* (*of* **~за́ться**) **1.** (*coll.*) to get drunk. **2.** *pass. of* **~зать**[1]
нарез|а́ться, а́юсь *impf. of* **~́аться**
наре́зк|а, и *f.* **1.** cutting (into pieces), slicing. **2.** (*tech.*) thread; rifling.
нарезно́й *adj.* (*tech.*) threaded; rifled.
нарека́ни|е, я *nt.* censure; reprimand.
нарека́|ть, ю *impf. of* **наре́чь**
нареч|ённый *p.p.p. of* **~́ь** *and adj.* (*obs.*) betrothed; *as n.* **н., ~ённого** *m.* fiancé; **~ённая, ~ённой** *f.* fiancée.
наре́чи|е[1]**, я** *nt.* dialect.
наре́чи|е[2]**, я** *nt.* adverb.
наре́чный *adj.* adverbial.
наре́|чь, ку́, чёшь, ку́т, *past* **~̈к, ~кла́** *pf.* (*of* **~ка́ть**) (*obs.*) (*+a. and i. or d. and a.*) to name; **ма́льчика ~кли́ Серге́ем, ма́льчику ~кли́ и́мя Серге́й** they named the boy Sergei.
нарза́н, а *m.* Narzan (*kind of mineral water*).
нарза́н|ный *adj. of* **~**
нарис|ова́ть, у́ю *pf. of* **рисова́ть**
нарица́тельн|ый *adj.* **1.** (*econ.*) nominal; **~ая сто́имость** nominal cost. **2.** (*gram.*): **и́мя ~ое** common noun.
наркодел|е́ц, ьца́ *m.* drug trafficker *or* pusher.
нарко́з, а *m.* **1.** narcosis, anaesthesia. **2.** anaesthetic, drug; **ме́стный н.** local anaesthetic.
наркологи́ческий *adj.*: **н. диспансе́р** drug-abuse clinic.
нарко́м, а *m.* (*abbr. of* **наро́дный комисса́р**) (*hist.*) people's commissar.
наркома́н, а *m.* drug addict.
наркома́ни|я, и *f.* drug addiction.
наркома́т, а *m.* (*abbr. of* **наро́дный комиссариа́т**) (*hist.*) people's commissariat.
наркосиндика́т, а *m.* drug ring.
наркотизи́р|овать, ую *impf. and pf.* (*med.*) to narcotize, anaesthetize.
нарко́тик, а *m.* narcotic; drug; **торго́вля ~ами** drug trafficking.
наркоти́ческ|ий *adj.* narcotic; **~ие сре́дства** narcotics, drugs.
наро́д, а (у) *m.* (*in var. senses*) people; **англи́йский н.** the English people, the people of England; **челове́к из ~а** a man of the people; **ма́ло бы́ло ~у на ми́тинге** there were not many people at the meeting; **вы — упря́мый н.** (*coll.*) you are a stubborn lot; **как говоря́т в ~е** as the expression goes; as they say.
наро́д|ец, ца *m. dim.* (*affectionate or pej.*) *of* **~**
наро|ди́ть, жу́, ди́шь *pf.* (*+a. or g.*) to give birth to (*a number of*).
наро|ди́ться, жу́сь, ди́шься *pf.* (*of* **~жда́ться**) **1.** (*coll.*) to be born. **2.** (*fig.*) to come into being, arise.
наро́дник, а *m.* (*hist.*) narodnik, populist.
наро́дничес|кий *adj. of* **~тво**
наро́дничеств|о, а *nt.* (*hist.*) narodnik movement, populism.
наро́дност|ь, и *f.* **1.** nationality. **2.** (*sg. only*) national character; national traits.
народнохозя́йственный *adj.* pertaining to the national economy.
наро́дн|ый *adj.* **1.** national; **~ое хозя́йство** national economy; **н. поэ́т** national poet; **н. арти́ст СССР** (*designation of recipient of official honour*) national artist of the USSR. **2.** folk; **~ое иску́сство** folk art. **3.** (*pol.*) of the (*sc. common, working*) people, popular; **~ая во́ля** (*hist.*) Narodnaya volya ('The People's Will') **Н. фронт** Popular Front. **4.** *forms part of the official designation of certain Communist and former Communist states, also of certain organs of power and offices in the former USSR*; **страны ~ой демокра́тии** 'the People's Democracies'; **Кита́йская Н~ая Респу́блика** the People's Republic of China; **н. заседа́тель** assessor (*in courts*); **н. сле́дователь** examining magistrate; **н. суд** 'People's Court' (*court of first instance*); **н. судья́** judge in 'People's Court' (*elected presiding magistrate*).
народовла́сти|е, я *nt.* democracy, sovereignty of the people.
народово́л|ец, ьца *m.* (*hist.*) member of 'Narodnaya volya'.
народово́л|ьческий *adj. of* **~ец**
народонаселе́ни|е, я *nt.* population.
нарожда́|ться, юсь *impf. of* **народи́ться**
нарожде́ни|е, я *nt.* birth, springing up; **н. ме́сяца** appearance of new moon.
наро́ст, а *m.* **1.** outgrowth, excrescence; burr, tumour (*in animals and plants*). **2.** (*tech.*) incrustation, scale.
нарочи́то *adv.* deliberately, intentionally.
нарочи́т|ый (~, ~а) *adj.* deliberate, intentional.
наро́чно *adv.* **1.** on purpose, purposely. **2.** for fun, pretending.
на́рочн|ый (*obs.* **наро́чный**)**, ого** *m.* courier; express messenger, special messenger.
наро́ч|ный *adj.* = **~и́тый**
нарсу́д, а *m.* people's court.
на́рт|енный *adj. of* **~ы**
на́рт|ы, ~ *pl.* (*sg.* **~а, ~ы** *f.*) sledge (*drawn by reindeer or dogs*).
наруб|и́ть, лю́, ~́ишь *pf.* (*+a. or g.*) to chop (*a quantity of*); to cut (*a quantity of*).
нару́бк|а, и *f.* notch.
нару́жно *adv.* outwardly.
нару́жност|ь, и *f.* exterior; (outward) appearance; **н.**

обмáнчива appearances are deceptive.
нарýжн|ый *adj.* (*in var. senses*) external, exterior, outward; (*tech.*) male (*of screw thread*); **~ое (лекáрство)** medicine for external application, 'not to be taken'; **~ое спокóйствие** outward calm.
нарýжу *adv.* outside, on the outside; **вы́йти н.** to come out; (*fig.*) to come to light, transpire.
нарукáвник, а *m.* oversleeve; armlet.
нарукáвн|ый *adj.* (worn on the) sleeve; **~ая повя́зка** armband, brassard.
нарумя́н|ить(ся), ю(сь), ишь(ся) *pf. of* **румя́нить(ся)**
нарýчник, а *m.* handcuff, manacle.
нарýчн|ый *adj.* worn on the arm; **~ые часы́** wrist-watch.
наруш|áть, áю *impf. of* **~́ить**
нарушéни|е, я *nt.* breach; infringement, violation; offence (*against the law*); **н. сýточного ри́тма** jet lag.
нарушúтел|ь, я *m.* transgressor, infringer.
нарýш|ить, у, ишь *pf.* (*of* **~áть**) **1.** to break, disturb (*sleep, quiet, etc.*). **2.** to break, infringe (upon), violate, transgress.
нарцúсс, а *m.* narcissus, daffodil.
нá р|ы, ~ *no sg.* plank-bed; bunk.
нары́в, а *m.* abscess; boil.
нарывá|ть(ся), ю(сь) *impf. of* **нарвáть²(ся)**
нарывнóй *adj.* vesicatory; **н. плáстырь** poultice.
нар|ы́ть, óю, óешь *pf.* (+*a. or g.*) to dig (*a quantity of*).
нарядд¹, а *m.* attire, apparel, costume.
наря́д², а *m.* **1.** order, warrant. **2.** (*mil.*) detail (*group of soldiers*). **3.** (*mil.*) duty; **расписáние ~ов** roster; duty detail, orders.
наря|дúть¹, жý, ~́дишь *pf.* (*of* **~жáть**) **1.** (**в**+*a.*) to dress (in), array (in). **2.** (+*i.*) to dress up (as).
наря|дúть², жý, ~́дишь *pf.* (*of* **~жáть**) to detail, appoint; **н. в караýл** to put on guard; **н. слéдствие** to set up, order an inquiry.
наря|дúться¹, жýсь, ~́дишься *pf.* (*of* **~жáться**) **1.** (**в**+*a.*) to array o.s. (in). **2.** to dress up. **3.** *pass. of* **~дúть¹**
наря|дúться², жýсь, ~́дишься *pf.* (*of* **~жáться**) *pass. of* **~дúть¹**
наря́дност|ь, и *f.* elegance, smartness.
наря́д|ный¹ (~ен, ~на) *adj.* well-dressed; elegant; smart (*also of items of dress*).
наря́д|ный² *adj. of* **~²**; *as n.* **~ная, ~ной** *f.* (*coll.*) office (*where work is assigned*).
нарядý *adv.* (**с**+*i.*) side by side (with), equally (with); **дéти н. со взрóслыми** grown-ups and children alike; **н. с э́тим** at the same time.
наряжá|ть(ся), ю(сь) *impf. of* **нарядúть(ся)**
нас *a., g., and p. of* **мы**
НАСА *nt. indecl.* NASA (*abbr. of* National Aeronautics and Space Administration — *Национáльное управлéние по аэронáвтике и исслéдованию космúческого прострáнства*).
наса|дúть¹, жý, ~́дишь *pf.* (*of* **~́живать**) (+*a. or g.*) **1.** to plant (*a quantity of*). **2.** to sit (*a number of*).
наса|дúть², жý, ~́дишь *pf.* (*of* **~́живать**) to stick, pin; to haft; **н. на вéртел** to spit; **н. червякá на крючóк** to fix a worm on to a hook.
наса|дúть³, жý, ~́дишь *pf.* (*of* **~ждáть**) (*fig.*) to implant, inculcate; to propagate.
насáдк|а, и *f.* **1.** setting, fixing, putting on. **2.** attachment; **набóр ~́ок** set of attachments. **3.** (*tech.*) nozzle, mouthpiece. **4.** bait.
насажá|ть, ю *pf.* = **насадúть¹**
насаждá|ть, ю *impf. of* **насадúть³**
насаждéни|е, я *nt.* **1.** planting, plantation; (*fig.*) spreading, propagation, dissemination. **2.** (*forest*) stand; wood.
наса|ждённый *p.p.p. of* **~дúть³**
насá|женный *p.p.p. of* **~дúть¹˒²**
насáжива|ть, ю *impf. of* **насадúть¹˒²**
насáжива|ться, юсь *impf. of* **насéсть¹**
насáлива|ть, ю *impf. of* **насолúть**
насáсыва|ть, ю *impf. of* **насосáть**
насáхарива|ть, ю *impf. of* **насáхарить**
насáхар|ить, ю, ишь *pf.* (*of* **~ивать**) to sugar, sweeten (*with sugar*).
насвúстыва|ть, ю *impf.* (*coll.*) to whistle (*a tune*); (*of birds*) to pipe, twitter.
наседá|ть, ю *impf.* (*of* **насéсть²**) (**на**+*a.*) **1.** to press (*of mil. forces, crowds, etc.*). **2.** (*of dust, etc.*) to settle, collect.
насéдк|а, и *f.* **1.** brood-hen, sitting hen. **2.** (*sl.*) stool-pigeon.
насекá|ть, ю *impf. of* **насéчь**
насекóм|ое, ого *nt.* insect.
насекомоя́дный *adj.* insectivorous.
населéни|е, я *nt.* **1.** population; inhabitants. **2.** peopling, settling.
населённост|ь, и *f.* density of population.
насел|ённый *p.p.p. of* **~úть** *and adj.* **1.** populated; **н. пункт** (*official designation*) locality, place; built-up area. **2.** populous, densely populated.
насел|úть, ю́, úшь *pf.* (*of* **~я́ть**) to people, settle.
насéльник, а *m.* inhabitant.
насел|я́ть, я́ю *impf.* **1.** to inhabit. **2.** *impf. of* **~úть**
насéст, а *m.* roost, perch.
нас|éсть¹, я́дет, *past* **~éл** *pf.* (*of* **~áживаться**) to sit down (*in numbers*).
нас|есть², я́ду, я́дешь, *past* **~éл** *pf. of* **~едáть**
насéчк|а, и *f.* **1.** notching; making incisions; embossing; (*med.*) scarification. **2.** cut, incision; notch. **3.** inlay.
насé|чь, кý, чёшь, кýт, *past* **~к, ~клá** *pf.* (*of* **~кáть**) **1.** to make incisions (in, on); to notch. **2.** to emboss; to damascene.
насé|ять, ю, ешь *pf.* (+*a. or g.*) to sow (*a quantity of*).
наси|дéть, жý, дúшь *pf.* (*of* **~́живать**) **1.** to hatch. **2.** to warm (*by sitting*).
наси|дéться, жýсь, дúшься *pf.* (*coll.*) to sit long enough.
насú|женный *p.p.p. of* **~дéть; ~женное яйцó** fertilized egg; **~женное мéсто** (*fig.*) familiar spot, old haunt.
насúжива|ть, ю *impf. of* **насидéть**
наси|жý, дúшь *see* **~дéть**
насúли|е, я *nt.* violence, force.
насил|овать, ую *impf.* **1.** to coerce, constrain. **2.** (*pf.* **из~**) to rape, violate.
насúлу *adv.* (*coll.*) with difficulty, hardly.
насúльник, а *m.* **1.** user of force; aggressor. **2.** rapist.
насúльнича|ть, ю *impf.* (*coll.*) **1.** to commit acts of violence. **2.** to rape.
насúльнический *adj.* forcible, violent.
насúльно *adv.* by force, forcibly; **н. мил не бýдешь** (*prov.*) love cannot be compelled.
насúльственный *adj.* violent; forcible.
наска|зáть, жý, ~́жешь *pf.* (*coll.*; +*a. or g.*) to say, talk a lot (of); **н. новостéй** to have a lot of news to tell.
наска|кáть, чý, ~́чешь *pf.* (*of* **~́кивать**) **1.** (**на**+*a.*) to ride (into); to run (against), collide (with). **2.** to ride up, gallop up.
наскáкива|ть, ю *impf. of* **наскакáть** *and* **наскочúть**
наскандáл|ить, ю, ишь *pf. of* **скандáлить**
насквóзь *adv.* through (and through); throughout; **промóкнуть н.** to get wet through; **вúдеть (знать) когó-н. н.** (*fig.*) to see through s.o.
наскóк, а *m.* **1.** swoop; sudden attack, descent; **дéйствовать ~ом** to act on impulse; **с ~а** (*fig., coll.*) hurriedly, just like that. **2.** (*fig., coll.*) attack.
наскóлько *adv.* **1.** (*interrog.*) how much?; how far? **2.** (*rel.*) as far as, so far as; **н. мне извéстно** as far as I know, to the best of my knowledge.
нáскоро *adv.* (*coll.*) hastily, hurriedly.
наскоч|úть, ý, ~́ишь *pf.* (*of* **наскáкивать**) **1.** to run (against), collide (with); **н. на неприя́тность** (*fig.*) to get into trouble. **2.** (*fig., coll.*) to fly (at).
наскребá|ть, ю *impf. of* **наскрести́**
наскре|стú, бý, бёшь, *past* **~́б, ~блá** *pf.* (*of* **~бáть**) to scrape up, scrape together; (*fig.*): **н. дéнег на поéздку** to scrape up some money for an outing.
наскýч|ить, у, ишь *pf.* (*coll.*) **1.** (+*d.*) to bore; **мне э́то ~ило** I am sick of it. **2.** (*obs.*; +*i.*) to be bored (by), grow tired (of).
насла|дúть, жý, дúть *pf.* (*of* **~ждáть**) to delight, please.
насла|дúться, жýсь, дúшься *pf.* (*of* **~ждáться**) (+*i.*) to enjoy; to take pleasure (in), delight (in).

наслажда́|ть(ся), ю(сь) *impf. of* **наслади́ть(ся)**
наслажде́ни|е, я *nt.* enjoyment, delight.
насла́ива|ться, юсь *impf. of* **наслои́ться**
насла|сти́ть, щу́, сти́шь *pf.* (*coll.*) to make very (too) sweet.
на|сла́ть[1], шлю́, шлёшь *pf.* (*of* **~сыла́ть**) (*obs.*) to send down (*calamities, etc.*).
на|сла́ть[2], шлю́, шлёшь *pf.* (*+a. or g.*) to send (*a quantity of*).
насле́ди|е, я *nt.* legacy; heritage.
насле|ди́ть, жу́, ди́шь *pf.* (*of* **следи́ть**[2]) to leave (dirty) marks, traces.
насле́дник, а *m.* heir; legatee; (*fig.*) successor.
насле́дниц|а, ы *f.* heiress.
насле́дный *adj.* first in the line of succession; **н. принц** Crown prince.
насле́довани|е, я *nt.* inheritance.
насле́д|овать, ую *impf. and pf.* **1.** (*pf. also* **у~**) to inherit. **2.** (*+d.*) to succeed (to).
насле́дственность, и *f.* heredity.
насле́дственный *adj.* hereditary, inherited.
насле́дств|о, а *nt.* **1.** inheritance, legacy; **получи́ть в н., по ~у** to inherit. **2.** (*fig.*) heritage.
наслое́ни|е, я *nt.* **1.** (*geol.*) stratification. **2.** layer, deposit. **3.** (*fig.*) later development, extraneous feature (*of culture or individual personality*).
насло|и́ться, ю́сь, и́шься *pf.* (*of* **насла́иваться**) (**на**+*a.*) to be deposited (on), accumulate (on).
наслуж|и́ться, у́сь ~ишься *pf.* (*coll.*) to have served for long enough.
наслу́ша|ться, юсь *pf.* (*+g.*) **1.** to hear (a lot of). **2.** to hear enough, listen to long enough; **я не ~юсь э́тих пе́сен** I cannot hear enough of these songs.
наслы́шан *adj. as pred.* (*obs.*; **о**+*p.*) familiar (with) by hearsay; **мы о вас мно́го ~ы** we have heard a lot about you.
наслы́ш|аться, усь, ишься *pf.* (**о**+*p.*) to have heard a lot (about).
наслы́шк|а, и *f.*: **по ~е** (*coll.*) by hearsay.
насма́рку *adv.* (*coll.*): **пойти́ н.** to come to nothing.
на́смерть *adv.* to death; **стоя́ть н.** to fight to the last ditch; **испуга́ть н.** to frighten to death.
насмеха́тельств|о, а *nt.* (*obs.*) mockery.
насмеха́|ться, юсь *impf.* (**над**) to jeer (at), gibe (at), ridicule.
насмеш|и́ть, у́, и́шь, *pf.* (*of* **смеши́ть**) (**кого́-н.**) to make (s.o.) laugh.
насме́шк|а, и *f.* mockery, ridicule; gibe.
насме́шлив|ый (~, ~) *adj.* **1.** mocking, derisive. **2.** sarcastic.
насме́шник, а *m.* (*coll.*) scoffer.
насме|я́ться, ю́сь, ёшься *pf.* **1.** (*coll.*) to have a good laugh. **2.** (**над**) to laugh (at); **н. над чьи́ми-н. чу́вствами** to insult s.o.'s feelings.
на́сморк, а *m.* cold (*in the head*); **схвати́ть, получи́ть н.** to catch a cold; **у меня́ сде́лался на́сморк** I have caught a cold.
насмотр|е́ться, ю́сь, ~ишься *pf.* **1.** (*+g.*) to see a lot (of). **2.** (**на**+*a.*) to have looked enough (at), to see enough (of); **не н.** not to tire of looking (at).
насоба́ч|иться, усь, ишься *pf.* (*coll.*; *+inf.*) to become adept (at), become a good hand (at).
нас|ова́ть, ую́ уёшь *pf.* (*of* **~о́вывать**) (*coll.*; *+g. or a.*) to shove in, stuff in (*a quantity of*); **н. конфе́т в карма́ны** to stuff sweets into one's pockets.
насо́выва|ть, ю *impf. of* **насова́ть**
насол|и́ть[1], ю́, ~и́шь *pf.* (*of* **наса́ливать**) **1.** to salt; to put much salt (into). **2.** (*fig.*; *+d.*) to spite, injure; to do a bad turn (to).
насол|и́ть[2], ю́, ~и́шь *pf.* (*+a. or g.*) to salt, pickle (*a quantity of*).
насоло|ди́ть, жу́, ди́шь *pf. of* **солоди́ть**
насор|и́ть, ю́, и́шь *pf. of* **сори́ть**
насо́с[1], а *m.* pump.
насо́с[2], а *m.* (*disease of horses*) lampas.
насос|а́ть, у́, ёшь, *pf.* (*of* **наса́сывать**) (*+a. or g.*) **1.** to suck (*a quantity of*). **2.** to pump.
насос|а́ться, у́сь, ёшься *pf.* **1.** (*+g.*) to have sucked one's fill. **2.** (*coll.*) to get drunk.
насо́с|ный *adj. of* **~**[1]; **н. агрега́т** pumping unit; **~ная ста́нция** pumping station.
насочин|и́ть, ю́, и́шь *pf.* (*coll.*) (*+a. or g.*) to talk a lot of nonsense; to make up (a lot of falsehoods).
на́спех *adv.* hastily; carelessly.
наспле́тнича|ть, ю *pf. of* **спле́тничать**
нас|р|а́ть, у, ёшь *pf. of* **сра́ть**
наст, а *m.* thin crust of ice over snow.
наста|ва́ть, ю́, ёшь *impf. of* **~ть**
настави́тел|ьный (~ен, ~ьна) *adj.* edifying, instructive; **н. тон** didactic tone.
наста́в|ить[1], лю, ишь *pf.* (*of* **~ля́ть**) **1.** to lengthen; to put on, add on; **н. нос кому́-н.** to fool, dupe s.o.; **н. рога́ кому́-н.** to cuckold s.o. **2.** (**на**+*a.*) to aim (at), point (at); **н. револьве́р на кого́-н.** to point a revolver at s.o.
наста́в|ить[2], лю, ишь *pf.* (*of* **~ля́ть**) to edify; to exhort, admonish; **н. на путь и́стинный** to set on the right path.
наста́в|ить[3], лю, ишь *pf.* (*+a. or g.*) to set up, place (*a quantity of*).
наста́вк|а, и *f.* addition.
наставле́ни|е, я *nt.* **1.** exhortation, admonition. **2.** directions, instructions; (*mil.*) manual.
наставля́|ть, ю *impf. of* **наста́вить**
наста́вник, а *m.* **1.** (*obs.*) mentor, preceptor; **кла́ссный н.** form-master. **2.** instructor (*of apprentices*).
наста́вни|ческий *adj. of* **~к; н. тон** edifying tone.
наста́вничеств|о, а *nt.* (*obs.*) tutorship.
наставно́й *adj.* lengthened; added.
наста́ива|ть[1,2], ю, *impf. of* **настоя́ть[1,2]**
наста́ива|ться, юсь *impf. of* **настоя́ться[2]**
наста́|ть, ну, нешь *pf.* (*of* **~ва́ть**) (*of times or seasons*) to come, begin.
наста|ю́, ёшь *see* **~ва́ть**
на́стежь *adv.* wide open; **откры́ть н.** to open wide.
настели́ть = настла́ть
наст|елю́, е́лешь *see* **~ла́ть**
насте́нный *adj.* wall.
настиг|а́ть, а́ю *impf. of* **~нуть** *and* **насти́чь**
насти́гн|уть, у, ешь *pf.* = **насти́чь**
насти́л, а *m.* flooring; planking.
настила́|ть, ю *impf. of* **настла́ть**
насти́лк|а, и *f.* **1.** laying, spreading. **2.** = **насти́л**
насти́льн|ый *adj.* (*mil.*) grazing; **н. ого́нь** grazing fire; **~ая бо́мба** anti-personnel bomb.
настира́|ть, ю *pf.* (*+a. or g.*) to wash, launder (*a quantity of*).
насти́|чь, гну, гнешь, *past.* **~г, ~гла** *pf.* (*of* **~га́ть**) to overtake (*also fig.*).
наст|ла́ть, елю́, ~е́лешь *pf.* (*of* **~ила́ть**) to lay, spread; **н. пол** to lay a floor; **н. соло́му** to spread straw.
насто́|й, я *m.* infusion.
насто́йк|а, и *f.* **1.** liqueur (*prepared by maceration, not distilled*). **2.** (*pharm.*) tincture.
насто́йчив|ый (~, ~а) *adj.* **1.** persistent. **2.** urgent, insistent.
насто́лько *adv.* so; so much; **н., наско́лько** as much as.
насто́льно-изда́тельский *adj.* desktop publishing; DTP.
насто́льн|ый *adj.* **1.** table, desk; desktop; **~ая полигра́фия** desktop publishing; **~ая игра́** board game; **н. те́ннис** table tennis. **2.** (*fig.*) for constant reference, in constant use; **~ая кни́га, ~ое руково́дство** reference book; handbook, manual.
насторáжива|ть(ся), ю(сь) *impf. of* **насторожи́ть(ся)**
настороже́ *adv.*: **быть н.** to be on one's guard; to be on the qui vive.
насторо|жённый (*and* **~женный**) *p.p.p. of* **~жи́ть** *and adj.* guarded, suspicious.
насторож|и́ть, у́, и́шь *pf.* (*of* **настора́живать**) to put on one's guard; **н. слух, у́ши (н. внима́ние** *fig. only*) to prick up one's ears (*also fig.*).
насторож|и́ться, у́сь, и́шься *pf.* (*of* **настора́живаться**)

to prick up one's ears.

настоя́ни|е, я *nt.* insistence.

настоя́тел|ь, я *m.* (*eccl.*) **1.** prior, superior. **2.** senior priest (*of a church*).

настоя́тельниц|а, ы *f.* (*eccl.*) prioress, mother superior.

настоя́тел|ьный (~ен, ~ьна) *adj.* **1.** persistent; insistent. **2.** urgent, pressing.

насто|я́ть[1]**, ю́, и́шь** *pf.* (*of* **наста́ивать**) (**на**+*p.*) to insist (on); **н. на своём** to insist on having it one's own way; **он ~я́л на том, что́бы пойти́ самому́** he insisted on going himself.

насто|я́ть[2]**, ю́, и́шь** *pf.* (*of* **наста́ивать**) to draw, infuse; **н. чай** to let tea draw; **н. во́дку на ви́шнях** to prepare a liqueur from cherries.

насто|я́ться[1]**, ю́сь, и́шься** *pf.* (*coll.*) to stand a long time.

насто|я́ться[2]**, ю́сь, и́шься** *pf.* (*of* **наста́иваться**) **1.** to draw, brew (*of tea, etc.*). **2.** *pass. of* **~я́ть**[2]

настоя́щ|ий *adj.* **1.** present; this; **в ~ее вре́мя** at present, now; **~ее вре́мя** (*gram.*) the present tense; *as n.* **~ее, ~его** *nt.* the present (time); **жить ~им** to live in the present. **2.** real, genuine; veritable; **~ая цена́** fair price. **3.** (*coll., pej.*) complete, utter, absolute; **он н. дура́к** he is an absolute fool.

настрада́|ться, юсь *pf.* to suffer much.

настра́ива|ть(ся), ю(сь) *impf. of* **настро́ить(ся)**

настра́чива|ть, ю *impf. of* **настрочи́ть**[2]

настреля́|ть, ю *pf.* (+*a. or g.*) to shoot (*a quantity of*).

настри́г, а *m.* (*agric.*) **1.** shearing, clipping. **2.** clip.

настри́|чь, гу́, жёшь, гу́т, *past* **~г, ~гла** *pf.* (+*a. or g.*) (*agric.*) to shear, clip (*a number of*).

на́строго *adv.* (*coll.*) strictly.

настрое́ни|е, я *nt.* **1.** (*also* **н. ду́ха**) mood, temper, humour; **припо́днятое/пода́вленное н.** high/low spirits; **челове́к ~я** a man of moods; **быть в плохо́м** *etc.*, **~и** to be in a bad, *etc.*, mood; **н. умо́в** state of opinion, public mood. **2.** (+*inf.*) mood (for); **у меня́ нет ~я танцева́ть, я не в ~и танцева́ть** I am not in a mood for dancing; I don't feel like dancing.

настро́енност|ь, и *f.* mood, humour.

настро́|ить[1]**, ю, ишь** *pf.* (*of* **настра́ивать**) **1.** (*mus.*) to tune; to tune up, attune; **н. приёмник на сре́днюю волну́** to tune in to medium wave. **2.** (*fig.*; **на**+*a.*) to dispose (to), incline (to); to incite; **н. кого́-н. на весёлый лад** to make s.o. happy, cheer s.o. up; **н. кого́-н. (про́тив)** to incite s.o. (against).

настро́|ить[2]**, ю, ишь** *pf.* (+*a. or g.*) to build (*a quantity of*)

настро́|иться, юсь, ишься *pf.* (*of* **настра́иваться**) **1.** (**на**+*a.*) to dispose o.s. (to); (+*inf.*) to make up one's mind (to); **он ~ился на мра́чный лад** he has made himself gloomy, he had got into a gloomy mood; **я ~ился е́хать в Москву́** I made up my mind to go to Moscow. **2.** *pass. of* **~ить**[1]

настро́|й, я *m.* (*coll.*) = **настрое́ние**

настро́йк|а, и *f.* **1.** (*mus., radio*) tuning. **2.** (*radio, aeron.*) tuning call. **3.** (*tech.*): **н. станка́** tooling.

настро́йщик, а *m.* tuner.

настропал|и́ть, ю́, и́шь *pf.* (*coll.*) to incite, set on.

настроч|и́ть[1]**, у́, и́шь** *pf. of* **строчи́ть**

настроч|и́ть[2]**, у́, и́шь** *pf.* (*of* **настра́чивать**) (*coll.*) to incite, set on.

настря́па|ть, ю *pf.* **1.** (+*a. or g.*) to cook (*a quantity of*). **2.** (*fig., coll.*) to cook up.

насту|ди́ть, жу́, ~́дишь *pf.* (*of* **~́живать**) (*coll.*) to cool, make cold.

настуж|а́ть = **~́ивать**

насту́жива|ть, ю *impf. of* **настуди́ть**

насту́к|ать, аю *pf.* (*of* **~ивать**) (*coll.*) **1.** to discover by tapping. **2.** to knock out, bash out (*on typewriter*).

насту́кива|ть, ю *impf. of* **насту́кать**

наступа́тельный *adj.* (*mil.*) offensive; (*fig.*) aggressive.

наступ|а́ть[1]**, а́ю** *impf. of* **~и́ть**

наступа́|ть[2]**, ю** *adj.* (*mil.*) to advance, be on the offensive.

наступа́|ющий[1] *pres. part. act. of* **~ть**[1] *and adj.* coming.

наступа́|ющий[2] *pres. part. act. of* **~ть**[2]; *as n.* **н., ~ющего** *m.* attacker.

наступ|и́ть[1]**, лю́, ~́ишь** *pf.* (*of* **~а́ть**[1]) (**на**+*a.*) to tread (on); **медве́дь (***or* **слон) наступи́л ему́ на у́хо** he has absolutely no ear for music.

наступ|и́ть[2]**, ~́ит** *pf.* (*of* **~а́ть**[1]) (*of times or seasons*) to come, begin; to ensue; to set in (*also fig.*); **~́ит вре́мя, когда́…** there will come a time, when ….

наступле́ни|е[1]**, я** *nt.* (*mil.*) offensive; attack; **перейти́ в н.** to assume the offensive.

наступле́ни|е[2]**, я** *nt.* coming, approach.

насту́рци|я, и *f.* (*bot.*) nasturtium.

настыва́|ть, ю *impf. of* **насты́ть**

насты́|ть, ну, нешь *pf.* (*of* **~ва́ть**) (*coll.*) to become cold.

насул|и́ть, ю́, и́шь *pf.* (+*a. or g.*) (*coll.*) to promise (much.)

насу́п|ить(ся), лю(сь), ишь(ся) *pf. of* **су́пить(ся)** *and* **~ливать(ся)**

насу́пливать(ся) = **су́пить(ся)**

насупроти́в *adv. and prep.*+*g.* (*dial.*) opposite.

насурьм|и́ть(ся), лю́(сь), и́шь(ся) *pf. of* **сурьми́ть(ся)**

на́сухо *adv.* dry; **вы́тереть н.** to wipe dry.

насуш|и́ть, у́, ~́ишь *pf.* (+*a. or g.*) to dry (*a quantity of*).

насу́щност|ь, и *f.* urgency.

насу́щ|ный (~ен, ~на) *adj.* vital, urgent; **хлеб н.** daily bread (*also fig.*).

нас|ую́, уёшь *see* **~ова́ть**

насчёт *prep.*+*g.* about; as regards, concerning.

насчит|а́ть, а́ю *pf.* (*of* **~́ывать**) to count, number.

насчи́тыва|ть, ю *impf.* **1.** *impf. of* **насчита́ть. 2.** (*no pf.*) to number (= *to contain*); **э́тот го́род ~ет свы́ше ста ты́сяч жи́телей** this city has over one hundred thousand inhabitants.

насчи́тыва|ться, ется *impf.* (*impers.*) to number (= *to be, be contained*); **в на́шем селе́ ~ется не бо́лее двухсо́т жи́телей** the population of our village numbers no more than two hundred.

насыла́|ть, ю *impf. of* **насла́ть**[1]

насы́п|ать, лю, лешь *pf.* (*of* **~а́ть**) **1.** (+*a. or g.*) to pour (in, into); to fill (with); **н. муки́ в мешо́к** to pour flour into a bag; **н. мешо́к муко́й** to fill up a bag with flour. **2.** (+*a. or g.* **на**+*a.*) to spread (on); **н. песку́ на доро́жку** to spread sand on the path. **3.** to raise (*a heap or pile of sand, etc.*)

насып|а́ть, а́ю *impf. of* **~́ать**

насы́пк|а, и *f.* pouring (in), filling.

насыпно́й *adj.* poured; piled (up); **н. холм** artificial mound.

на́сып|ь, и *f.* embankment (*of rail. or road*).

насы́|тить, щу, тишь *pf.* (*of* **~ща́ть**) **1.** to sate, satiate. **2.** (*chem.*) to saturate, impregnate.

насы́|титься, щусь, тишься *pf.* (*of* **~ща́ться**) **1.** to be full; to be sated. **2.** (*chem.*) to become saturated.

насыща́|ть(ся), ю(сь) *impf. of* **насы́тить(ся)**

насыще́ни|е, я *nt.* **1.** satiety, satiation. **2.** (*chem.*) saturation.

насы́щенност|ь, и *f.* **1.** saturation. **2.** (*fig.*) richness.

насы́|щенный *p.p.p. of* **~тить** *and adj.* **1.** saturated. **2.** (*fig.*) rich.

ната́лкива|ть(ся), ю(сь) *impf. of* **натолкну́ть(ся)**

ната́плива|ть, ю *impf. of* **натопи́ть**[1]

ната́птыва|ть, ю *impf. of* **натопта́ть**

ната́ск|анный *p.p.p. of* **~ать**

натаск|а́ть[1]**, а́ю** *pf.* (*of* **~́ивать**) to train (*hounds*); (*fig., coll.*) to coach, cram.

натаск|а́ть[2]**, а́ю** *pf.* (+*a. or g.*) **1.** to bring, lay (*a quantity of*). **2.** (*coll.*) to fish out, hook (*a quantity of*); **н. из устарёвших сочине́ний** (*fig., pej.*) to fish up outdated authorities.

ната́скива|ть, ю *impf. of* **натаска́ть**[1] *and* **натащи́ть**[1]

ната́счик, а *m.* trainer (of hounds).

натащ|и́ть[1]**, у́, ~́ишь** *pf.* (*of* **ната́скивать**) to pull (on, over).

натащ|и́ть[2]**, у́, ~́ишь** *pf.* (+*a. or g.*) to bring (*a quantity of*); to pile up (*a quantity of*).

ната́|ять, ю, ешь *pf.* (+*a. or g.*) to melt (*a quantity of snow or ice*) (*also intrans.*).

натвор|и́ть, ю́, и́шь *pf.* (+*g.*; *coll., pej.*) to do, get up to; **н. вся́ких глу́постей** to get up to every sort of stupid trick; **что ты ~и́л!** what ever have you done?

на́те *int.* (*coll., addressed to more than one pers. or, politely, to one*) here (you are)!; there (you are)! (= *take it!*); **тепе́рь**

н. вам and now see what's happened.

натёк, а *m.* **1.** (*geol.*) deposit. **2.** (*coll.*) pool (*of some liquid*).

натека́|ть, ет *impf. of* **натёчь**

нате́льн|ый *adj.* worn next to the skin; **~ое бельё** (*collect.*) underclothes, body linen; **~ая фуфа́йка** vest.

на|тере́ть[1], **тру́, трёшь,** *past* **~тёр, ~тёрла** *pf.* (*of* **~тира́ть**) **1.** to rub (in, on); **н. ру́ки вазели́ном** to rub vaseline into one's hands. **2.** to polish (*floors, etc.*). **3.** to rub sore; to chafe; **н. себе́ мозо́ль** to get a corn.

на|тере́ть[2], **тру́, трёшь,** *past.* **~тёр, ~тёрла** *pf.* (*+a. or g.*) to grate, rasp (*a quantity of*).

на|тере́ться, тру́сь, трёшься, *past* **~тёрся, ~тёрлась** *pf.* (*of* **~тира́ться**) **1.** (*+i.*) to rub o.s. (with). **2.** *pass. of* **~тере́ть**

натерп|е́ться, лю́сь, ~́ишься *pf.* (*+g.; coll.*) to have endured much; to have gone through much.

натёр|тый *p.p.p. of* **~е́ть**

нате́|чь, чёт, ку́т, *past.* **~̈к, ~кла́** *pf.* (*of* **~ка́ть**) (*of liquids*) to accumulate.

натёш|иться, усь, ишься *pf.* (*coll.*) **1.** to enjoy o.s., have a good time. **2. (над)** to have a good laugh (at).

натира́ни|е, я *nt.* **1.** rubbing in. **2.** polishing (*of floors, etc.*). **3.** (*coll.*) embrocation, ointment.

натира́|ть(ся), ю(сь) *impf. of* **натере́ть(ся)**

на́тиск, а *m.* **1.** onslaught, charge, onset. **2.** pressure. **3.** (*typ.*) impress.

нати́ска|ть, ю *pf.* (*+a. or g.*) **1.** (*coll.*) to cram in, stuff in (*a quantity of*). **2.** (*coll.*) to shove (s.o.) about. **3.** (*typ.*) to impress (*a quantity of*).

на́-тка = на́те (*but addressed familiarly to one pers.*).

натк|а́ть, у́, ёшь, *past* **~а́л, ~ала́, ~а́ло** *pf.* (*+a. or g.*) to weave (*a quantity of*).

наткн|у́ть, у́, ёшь *pf.* (*of* **наты́кать**) **1.** to stick, pin. **2.** to stick, pin (*a quantity of*).

наткн|у́ться, у́сь, ёшься *pf.* (*of* **натыка́ться**) **(на+***a.***) 1.** to run (against), strike; to stumble (upon); **н. на гвоздь** to run against a nail; **н. на неожи́данное сопротивле́ние** (*fig.*) to meet with unexpected resistance. **2.** (*fig.*) to stumble (upon, across), come (across); **н. на интере́сную мысль** to stumble across an interesting idea.

НАТО *nt. indecl.* NATO (*abbr. of* North Atlantic Treaty Organization — *Организа́ция Се́вероатланти́ческого догово́ра*).

на́тов|ец, ца *m.* NATO member.

на́товский *adj. of* **НАТО**

натолкн|у́ть, у́, ёшь *pf.* (*of* **ната́лкивать**) (*+a.* **на***+a.*) **1.** to push (against), shove (against). **2.** (*fig.*) to direct, lead (into, onto); **он меня́ ~у́л на мысль** he suggested the idea to me; **н. на грех** to lead into sin.

натолкн|у́ться, у́сь ёшься *pf.* (*of* **ната́лкиваться**) **на***+a.*) to run (against); (*fig.*) to run across.

натол|о́чь, ку́, чёшь, ку́т, *past* **~о́к, ~кла́** *pf.* (*+a. or g.*) to pound, crush (*a quantity of*).

натоп|и́ть[1], **лю́, ~́ишь** *pf.* (*of* **ната́пливать**) to heat well, heat up.

натоп|и́ть[2], **лю́, ~́ишь** *pf.* (*+a. or g.*) **1.** to melt (*a quantity of*). **2.** to heat (*a quantity of*).

натоп|та́ть, чу́, ~́чешь *pf.* (*of* **ната́птывать**) (*coll.;* **в, на***+p.*) to make dirty footmarks (in, on).

наторг|ова́ть, у́ю *pf.* (*coll.*) **1.** (*+a. or g.*) to make, gain (*by commerce*). **2. (на***+a.***)** to sell (for).

нато́ре́лый *adj.* (*coll.*) skilled, expert.

нато́ре|ть, ю *pf.* (**в***+p.; coll.*) to become skilled (at, in), become expert (at, in).

наточ|и́ть, у́, ~́ишь *pf. of* **точи́ть**[1]

натоща́к *adv.* on an empty stomach.

натр, а *m.* (*chem.*) natron; **е́дкий н.** caustic soda.

натрав|и́ть[1], **лю́, ~́ишь** *pf.* (*of* **~́ливать**) (**на***+a.*) to set (*dog*) (on); (*fig.*) to stir up (against).

натрав|и́ть[2], **лю́, ~́ишь** *pf.* (*of* **~́ливать**) to etch.

натрав|и́ть[3], **лю́, ~́ишь** *pf.* (*+a. or g.*) to exterminate (*a quantity of*).

натра́влива|ть, ю *impf. of* **натрави́ть**[1,2]

натравл|я́ть = ~́ивать

натрениро́ванный *adj.* trained.

натренир|ова́ть(ся), у́ю(сь) *pf. of* **тренирова́ть(ся)**

на́три|евый *adj. of* **~й**

на́три|й, я *m.* (*chem.*) sodium.

на́трое *adv.* in three.

натро́нн|ый *adj.* (*chem.*) sodium; **~ая и́звесть** sodium carbonate.

нат|ру́, рёшь *see* **~ере́ть**

натруб|и́ть, лю́, и́шь *pf.* (*coll.*) to trumpet a good deal; **н. в у́ши кому́-н.** to din into s.o.'s ear.

натру|ди́ть, жу́, ~ди́шь *pf.* (*of* **~жи́вать**) to tire out, overwork.

натру|ди́ться, жу́сь, ~ди́шься *pf.* (*coll.*) **1.** to become tired out. **2.** to have worked long enough; to have overworked.

натру́жива|ть, ю *impf. of* **натруди́ть**

натряс|ти́, у́, ёшь, *past* **~́, ~ла́** *pf.* (*+a. or g.*) to scatter, let fall (*a quantity of*).

натряс|ти́сь, у́сь, ёшься, *past* **~́ся, ~ла́сь** *pf.* (*coll.*) **1.** to be shaken much; (*fig.*) to shake, quake much. **2.** to be scattered; to spill.

нату́г|а, и *f.* effort, strain.

на́туго *adv.* (*coll.*) tightly; **ту́го-на́туго** very tightly.

нату́жива|ть(ся), ю(сь) *impf. of* **нату́жить(ся)**

нату́ж|ить, у, ишь *pf.* (*of* **~ивать**) (*coll.*) to tense, tighten.

нату́ж|иться, усь, ишься *pf.* (*of* **~иваться**) (*coll.*) to exert all one's strength; to strain.

нату́жный *adj.* (*coll.*) strained, forced.

нату́р|а, ы *f.* **1.** (*in var. senses*) nature. **2.** (artist's) model, sitter; **рисова́ть с ~ы** to paint from life. **3.** (*econ.*) kind; **плати́ть ~ой** to pay in kind. **4.: на ~е** (*coll.*) on the spot; (*cin.*) on location.

натурализа́ци|я, и *f.* naturalization.

натурали́зм, а *m.* naturalism.

натурализ|ова́ть, у́ю *impf. and pf.* to naturalize.

натурали́ст, а *m.* (*in var. senses*) naturalist.

натуралисти́ческий *adj.* naturalistic.

натура́льно *adv.* (*obs.*) naturally, of course.

натура́льност|ь, и *f.* genuineness; naturalness.

натура́л|ьный (~ен, ~ьна) *adj.* **1.** (*in var. senses*) natural; **в ~ьную величину́** life-size. **2.** real; genuine; **н. смех** unforced laughter. **3.** (*econ.*) in kind; **н. обме́н** barter.

натури́ст, а *m.* wholefooder.

нату́рн|ый *adj.* (*art*) from life; **н. класс** life class; **~ая съёмка** (*cinema*) shooting on location, take made on location.

натуропа́т, а *m.* naturopath.

натуропа́ти|я, и *f.* naturopathy.

натуропла́т|а, ы *f.* payment in kind.

нату́рщик, а *m.* (artist's) model, sitter.

нату́рщи|ца, цы *f. of* **~к**

наты́кать = наткну́ть

натыка́|ть(ся), ю(сь) *impf. of* **наткну́ть(ся)**

натюрмо́рт, а *m.* (*art*) still life.

натюрмо́рт|ный *adj. of* **~**

натя́гива|ть(ся), ю(сь) *impf. of* **натяну́ть(ся)**

натяже́ни|е, я *nt.* pull, tension.

натя́жк|а, и *f.* (*coll.*) **1.** strained interpretation; **допусти́ть ~у** to stretch a point; **с ~ой** (*fig.*) at a stretch. **2.** = **натяже́ние**

натяжн|о́й *adj.* (*tech.*) tension; **~о́е приспособле́ние** tension device, stretcher; **н. ро́лик** tension pulley; **н. рыча́г** tension lever.

натя́нутост|ь, и *f.* tension (*also fig.*)

натя́н|утый *p.p.p. of* **~уть** *and adj.* **1.** tight. **2.** (*fig.*) strained; forced; **~утые отноше́ния** strained relations; **~утое сравне́ние** far-fetched simile.

натя|ну́ть, ну́, ~́нешь *pf.* (*of* **~́гивать**) **1.** to stretch; to draw (tight); **н. лук** to draw a bow; **н. верёвку** (*naut.*) to haul a rope taut. **2.** to pull on; **н. ша́пку на́ уши** to pull a cap over one's ears.

натя|ну́ться, ну́сь, ~́нешься *pf.* (*of* **~́гиваться**) to stretch (*intrans.*).

науга́д *adv.* at random, by guess-work.

науго́льник, а *m.* (*tech.*) (try-)square, back square; bevel, bevel square.

наудалу́ю *adv.* (*coll.*) at a venture.

наудáчу *adv.* at random; by guesswork.

нау|дúть, жý, ~́дишь *pf.* (*+a. or g.*) to hook (*a number of*).

наýк|а, и *f.* **1.** science; learning; study; scholarship; **общéственные ~и** social sciences, social studies; **прикладны́е ~и** applied science; **тóчные ~и** exact science. **2.** (*coll.*) lesson; **э́то тебé н.!** let this be a lesson to you!

нау|стúть, щý, стúшь *pf.* (*of* **~щáть**) (*obs.*) to incite, egg on.

наýськ|ать, аю *pf.* (*of* **~ивать**) (**на**+*a.*) to set (*dogs on*).

наýськива|ть, ю *impf. of* **наýськать**

наутёк *adv.*: **пустúться н.** (*coll.*) to take to one's heels.

наýтро *adv.* next morning.

науч|úть, ý, ~́ишь *pf.* (*of* **учúть**) (*+a. and d. or +inf.*) to teach; **н. когó-н. рýсскому языкý** to teach s.o. Russian; **н. когó-н. водúть машúну** to teach s.o. to drive (a car).

науч|úться, ýсь, ~́ишься *pf.* (*of* **учúться**) (*+d. or inf.*) to learn.

наýчно-исслéдовательск|ий *adj.* scientific research; **~ая рабóта** (scientific) research work.

наýчно-фантастúческий *adj.* science fiction.

наýч|ный (~ен, ~на) *adj.* scientific; **н. рабóтник** member of staff of scientific or other learned body; **~ная фантáстика** science fiction.

наýшник[1]**, а** *m.* **1.** ear-flap; ear-muff. **2.** ear-phone, head-phone.

наýшник[2]**, а** *m.* (*pej.*) informer, slanderer.

наýшнича|ть, ю *impf.* (*+d.* **на**+*a.*) to tell tales (about), inform (on, about).

наýшничеств|о, а *nt.* tale-bearing, informing.

наущá|ть, ю *impf. of* **наустúть**

нау|щý, стúшь *see* **~стúть**

нафáбр|ить, ю, ишь *pf. of* **фáбрить**

нафталúн, а *m.* (*chem.*) naphthalene, naphthaline.

нафталúн|ный *adj. of* **~**

нафталúн|овый = ~ный; н. шáрик camphor ball, moth-ball.

нахáл, а *m.* impudent, insolent fellow, cheeky fellow; smart alec(k).

нахáлк|а, и *f.* impudent, insolent woman.

нахáльнича|ть, ю *impf.* to be impudent, insolent.

нахáл|ьный (~ен, ~ьна) *adj.* impudent, impertinent; cheeky, brazen.

нахáльств|о, а *nt.* impudence, impertinence, effrontery; **имéть н.** (*+inf.*) to have the cheek (to), have the face (to).

нахам|úть, лю́, úшь *pf.* (*coll.*; *+d.*) to play s.o. a caddish trick, to speak offensively.

нахвáлива|ть, ю *impf. of* **нахвалúть**

нахвал|úть, ю́, ~́ишь *pf.* (*of* **~́ивать**) (*coll.*) to praise (highly).

нахвал|úться, ю́сь, ~́ишься *pf.* (*coll.*) **1.** to boast much. **2.** (*+i.*; *usu. +neg.*) to praise sufficiently; **я не могý им н.** I cannot speak too highly of him.

нахват|áть, áю *pf.* (*of* **~́ывать**) (*coll.*; *+a. or g.*) to pick up, get hold (of), come by.

нахват|áться, áюсь *pf.* (*of* **~́ываться**) (*coll., fig.*; *+g.*) to pick up, come by; **в солдáтах он нахватáлся арáбских слов** in the army he picked up a few words of Arabic.

нахлéбник, а *m.* **1.** (*obs.*) boarder, paying guest. **2.** parasite, hanger-on.

нахле|стáть, щý, ~́щешь *pf.* (*of* **~́стывать**) (*coll.*) to whip.

нахле|стáться, ~щýсь, ~́щешься *pf.* (*of* **~́стываться**) (*sl.*) to get sloshed (*drunk*).

нахлёстыва|ть(ся), ю(сь) *impf. of* **нахлестáть(ся)**

нахлобýчива|ть, ю *impf. of* **нахлобýчить**

нахлобýч|ить, у, ишь *pf.* (*of* **~ивать**) (*coll.*) **1.** to pull down (over one's head *or* eyes). **2.: н. комý-н.** (*fig.*) to rate s.o., give s.o. a dressing-down.

нахлобýчк|а, и *f.* **1.** (*coll.*) rating, dressing-down. **2.** (*obs.*) blow on the head.

нахлы́н|уть, ет *pf.* (**на**+*a.*) to flow, gush (over, into); (*fig.*) to surge, crowd; **~ули слёзы** tears welled (in my, her, *etc.*, eyes); **на меня́ ~ули мы́сли** thoughts crowded into my mind.

нахмýр|енный *p.p.p. of* **~ить** *and adj.* frowning, scowling.

нахмýр|ить(ся), ю(сь), ишь(ся) *pf. of* **хмýрить(ся)**

нахо|дúть, жý, ~́дишь *impf. of* **найтú**

нахо|дúться[1]**, жýсь, ~́дишься** *impf. of* **найтúсь**

нахо|дúться[2]**, жýсь ~́дишься** *impf.* to be (situated); **где ~́дится стáнция?** where is the station?

нахо|дúться[3]**, жýсь, ~́дишься** *pf.* (*coll.*) to tire o.s. by walking; to have walked long enough.

нахóдк|а, и *f.* **1.** find. **2.** (*fig., coll.*) godsend.

нахóдчивост|ь, и *f.* **1.** resource, resourcefulness. **2.** readiness, quick-wittedness.

нахóдчив|ый (~, ~а) *adj.* **1.** resourceful. **2.** ready, quick-witted.

нахождéни|е, я *nt.* **1.** finding. **2.: мéсто ~я** the whereabouts.

нахоло|дúть, жý, дúшь *pf. of* **холодúть 1.**

нахóхл|иться, юсь, ишься *pf.* (*of* **хóхлиться**) (*fig., coll.*) to bristle (up).

нахохо|тáться, чýсь, ~́чешься *pf.* (*coll.*) to have had a good laugh.

нахрáпист|ый (~, ~а) *adj.* (*coll., pej.*) high-handed.

нахрáпом *adv.* (*coll.*) unceremoniously, insolently, with a high hand.

нацарáп|ать, аю *pf.* (*of* **~ывать**) **1.** to scratch. **2.** (*fig., coll.*) to scrawl, scribble.

нацарáпыва|ть, ю *impf. of* **нацарáпать**

наце|дúть, жý, ~́дишь *pf.* (*+a. or g.*) **1.** to fill (*a vessel*) through a strainer. **2.** to pour through a strainer (*a quantity of*).

нацéлива|ть(ся), ю(сь) *impf. of* **нацéлить(ся)**

нацéл|ить, ю, ишь *pf.* **1.** (*impf.* **цéлить** *and* **~ивать**) to aim, level. **2.** (*impf.* **~ивать**) (*fig.*) to aim, direct.

нацéл|иться, юсь, ишься *pf.* (*of* **~иваться**) **1.** (**в**+*a.*) to aim (at), take aim (at). **2.** (*fig., coll.*; **на**+*a.*) to aim (at, for).

нáцело *adv.* (*coll.*) entirely, without remainder.

нацéнива|ть, ю *impf. of* **наценúть**

нацен|úть, ю́, ~́ишь *pf.* (*of* **~́ивать**) (*comm.*) to raise the price of.

нацéнк|а, и *f.* mark-up.

нацеп|úть, лю́, ~́ишь *pf.* (*of* **~ля́ть**) to fasten on; to attach (*by means of hook or pin*).

нацеп|ля́ть, ля́ю *impf. of* **~úть**

нацúзм, а *m.* Nazism.

национализáци|я, и *f.* nationalization.

национализúр|овать, ую *impf. and pf.* to nationalize.

националúзм, а *m.* nationalism.

националúст, а *m.* nationalist.

националистúческий *adj.* nationalist(ic).

национáльност|ь, и *f.* **1.** nationality (*in var. senses: the words* **н.** *and* **национáльный** *are used in reference not to the State but to the particular national groups which compose it*; *e.g.* **граждáнство — совéтское, национáльность — рýсская** (*or* **еврéйская, армя́нская**, *etc.*) citizenship — Soviet, nationality Russian (*or* Jewish, Armenian, *etc.*)); ethnic group. **2.** national character.

национáльн|ый *adj.* national (*see also* **~ость); ~ые словарú** minority-language dictionaries.

нацúст, а *m.* Nazi.

нацúстский *adj.* Nazi.

нáци|я, и *f.* nation.

нацмéн, а *m.* (*coll.*) member of a national minority.

нацмéн|ка, ки *f. of* **~**

нач... *comb. form, abbr. of* **1. начáльник. 2. начáльствующий**

нача|дúть, жý, дúшь *pf. of* **чадúть**

начáл|о, а *nt.* beginning; commencement; **в ~е четвёртого** soon after three (o'clock); **для ~а** to start with, for a start; **по ~у** at first; **положúть н.** (*+d.*) to begin, commence. **2.** origin, source; **вестú н. (от), взять н. (в**+*p.*) to originate (from, in). **3.** principle, basis; **рабóтать на нóвых ~ах** to work on a new basis; **~а матемáтики** the elements of mathematics. **4.** (*obs.*) command, authority; **быть под ~ом у когó-н.** to be under s.o.; **отдáть под н., под ~а** (*+d.*) to put under, place in the charge (of).

нача́льник, а *m.* head, chief; superior; **н. свя́зи** chief signal officer; **н. отде́ла** head of a department.
нача́льнический *adj.* overbearing, imperious.
нача́льн|ый *adj.* **1.** initial, first; **~ая ско́рость** initial speed; (*artillery*) muzzle velocity. **2.** elementary; **~ая шко́ла** primary school.
нача́льственный *adj.* overbearing, domineering.
нача́льств|о, а *nt.* **1.** (*collect.*) (the) authorities. **2.** command, direction. **3.** (*coll.*) head, boss.
нача́льствовани|е, я *nt.* command.
нача́льств|овать, ую *impf.* **(над)** to command, be in command (of).
нача́льствующий *adj.*: **н. соста́в** command personnel.
нача́тк|и, ов *no sg.* rudiments, elements.
нач|а́ть, ну́, нёшь, *past* **~́ал, ~ала́, ~́ало** *pf.* (*of* **~ина́ть**) to begin, start, commence; **н. с нача́ла** to begin at the beginning; **н. всё снача́ла** to start all over again, start afresh; **н. с того́, что он ни одного́ сло́ва не по́нял** to begin with, he did not understand a single word; **он на́чал моли́твой (***or* **с моли́твы)** he began with a prayer.
нач|а́ться, ну́сь, нёшься, *past* **~а́лся́, ~ала́сь** *pf.* (*of* **~ина́ться**) to begin, start; to break out.
начди́в, а *m.* (*abbr. of* **нача́льник диви́зии**) division commander.
начека́н|ить, ю, ишь *pf.* (*+a. or g.*) to mint (*a quantity of*).
начеку́ *adv.* on the alert, on the qui vive.
начерн|и́ть, ю́, и́шь *pf. of* **черни́ть 1.**
на́черно *adv.* roughly; **написа́ть н.** to make a rough copy.
наче́рпа|ть, ю *pf.* (*+a. or g.*) to scoop up (*a quantity of*).
начерта́ни|е, я *nt.* tracing; outline.
начерта́тельн|ый *adj. only in phr.* **~ая геоме́трия** descriptive geometry.
начерта́|ть, ю *pf.* to trace (*also fig.*); to inscribe.
начер|ти́ть, чу́, ~́чишь *pf. of* **черти́ть**[1]
начёс, а *m.* **1.** nap (*of material*). **2.** (hair dressed in) fringe; backcombing.
наче|са́ть[1]**, шу́, ~́шешь** *pf.* (*+a. or g.*) **1.** to comb, card (*a quantity of*). **2.** to backcomb.
наче|са́ть[2]**, шу́, ~́шешь** *pf.* (*of* **~̈сывать**) (*coll.*) to injure by scratching.
нач|е́сть, ту́, тёшь *pf.* (*of* **~и́тывать**) (*book-keeping*) to recover.
начёсыва|ть, ю *impf. of* **начеса́ть**[1,2]
начёт, а *m.* (*book-keeping*) recovery of unauthorized expenditure; recovery of deficit in account; **сде́лать н. на кого́-н.** to recover unauthorized expenditure from s.o.
начётист|ый (~, ~а) *adj.* (*coll.*) disadvantageous, unprofitable.
начётничеств|о, а *nt.* (*pej.*) dogmatism (*based on uncritical, mechanical reading*).
начётчик, а *m.* **1.** pers. well-read in Scriptures. **2.** (*fig. pej.*) dogmatist (*pers. basing opinions uncritically on wide but mechanical reading*).
начина́ни|е, я *nt.* undertaking.
начина́тел|ь, я *m.* originator, initiator.
начина́тельный *adj.* (*gram.*): **н. глаго́л** inceptive *or* inchoative verb.
начина́|ть(ся), ю(сь) *impf. of* **нача́ть(ся)**
начина́|ющий *pres. part. act. of* **~ть**; *as n.* **н., ~ющего** *m.* beginner.
начина́я *as prep.* **(с**+*g.***)** as (from), starting (with).
начин|и́ть[1]**, ю́, и́шь** *pf.* (*of* **~я́ть**) (*+i.*) to fill (with), stuff (with).
начин|и́ть[2]**, ю́, ~́ишь** *pf.* (*+a. or g.*) **1.** to mend (*a quantity of*). **2.: н. карандаше́й** to sharpen (*a number of*) pencils.
начи́нк|а, и *f.* (*cul.*) stuffing, filling.
начин|я́ть, я́ю *impf. of* **~и́ть**[1]
начисле́ни|е, я *nt.* additional sum; extra.
начи́сл|ить, ю, ишь *pf.* (*of* **~я́ть**) (*book-keeping*) to add (to s.o.'s account); to charge extra.
начисл|я́ть, я́ю *impf. of* **~́ить**
начи́|стить[1]**, щу, стишь** *pf.* (*of* **~ща́ть**) to polish, shine (*trans.*).
начи́|стить[2]**, щу, стишь** *pf.* (*+a. or g.*) to peel (*a quantity of*); to clean (*a quantity of*) (*vegetables, etc.*).
на́чисто *adv.* **1.** clean, fair; **переписа́ть н.** to make a fair copy (of). **2.** (*coll.*) completely, thoroughly; **н. отказа́ться** to refuse flatly. **3.** (*coll.*) openly, without equivocation.
начистоту́ *adv.* openly, without equivocation.
начист|у́ю *adv.* (*coll.*) **1.** = **~оту́. 2.** utterly, altogether.
начи́танност|ь, и *f.* (*wide*) reading; erudition.
начи́тан|ный (~, ~на) *adj.* well-read, widely-read.
начита́|ть, ю *pf.* (*+a. or g.*) to read (*a number of*).
начита́|ться, юсь *pf.* **1.** (*+g.*) to have read (*much of*). **2.** to have read one's fill.
начи́тыва|ть, ю *impf. of* **наче́сть**
начища́|ть, ю *impf. of* **начи́стить**
нач|ну́, нёшь *see* **~а́ть**
начсоста́в, а *m.* command personnel.
начу|ди́ть, жу́, ди́шь *pf.* (*coll.*) to behave oddly; **что ты там начуди́л?** what have you been up to?
наш, ~́его, *f.* **~́а, ~́ей;** *nt.* **~́е, ~́его;** *pl.* **~́и, ~́их** *possessive pron.* our(s); **~́его** (*after comp.*) we; **у них де́нег бо́льше ~́его** they have more money than we; **~́а взяла́!** (*coll.*) we've won!; **знай ~́их!** (*coll.*) that's the sort we are!; we'll show you!; **~́е вам!** (*coll.*) hello there!; **(служи́ть) и ~́им и ва́шим** (*coll.*) to run with the hare and hunt with the hounds; *as n.* **~́и, ~́их** our people, people on our side; **его́ счита́ют одни́м из ~́их** they regard him as one of us.
нашал|и́ть, ю́, и́шь *pf.* to be naughty.
нашаты́р|ный *adj. of* **~ь; н. спирт** liquid ammonia.
нашаты́р|ь, я́ *m.* (*chem.*) sal ammoniac, ammonium chloride.
нашеп|та́ть, чу́, ~́чешь *pf.* (*of* **~̈тывать**) **1.** (*+a. or g.*) to whisper (*a number of*) (*also fig.*). **2.** **(на**+*a.***)** to put a spell (upon).
нашёптыва|ть, ю *impf. of* **нашепта́ть**
наше́стви|е, я *nt.* invasion, descent.
на́шивать *freq. of* **носи́ть**
нашива́|ть, ю *impf. of* **наши́ть**[1]
наши́вк|а, и *f.* (*mil.*) stripe, chevron (*on sleeve*); tab.
нашивно́й *adj.* sewed (sewn) on.
наш|и́ть[1]**, ью́, ьёшь** *pf.* (*of* **~ива́ть**) to sew on.
наш|и́ть[2]**, ью́, ьёшь** *pf.* (*+a. or g.*) to sew (*a quantity of*).
нашлёпа|ть, ю *pf.* (*coll.*) to slap; to spank.
на|шлю́, шлёшь *see* **~сла́ть**
нашпиг|ова́ть, у́ю *pf. of* **шпигова́ть**
нашпи́лива|ть, ю *impf. of* **нашпи́лить**
нашпи́л|ить, ю, ишь *pf.* (*of* **~ивать**) (*coll.*) to pin on.
нашум|е́ть, лю́, и́шь *pf.* to make much noise; (*fig.*) to cause a sensation.
нащёлка|ть, ю *pf.* (*+a. or g.*) to crack (*a quantity of*) (*nuts, etc.*).
нащип|а́ть, лю́, ~́лешь *pf.* (*+a. or g.*) to pluck, pick (*a quantity of*).
нащу́п|ать, аю *pf.* (*of* **~ывать**) to find, discover (*by groping*).
нащу́пыва|ть, ю *impf.* (*of* **нащу́пать**) to grope (for, after); to fumble (for, after); to feel about (for) (*also fig.*); **н. по́чву** (*fig.*) to feel one's way, see how the land lies.
наэлектриз|ова́ть, у́ю *pf.* (*of* **~о́вывать**) to electrify (*also fig.*).
наэлектризо́выва|ть, ю *impf. of* **наэлектризова́ть**
ная́бednича|ть, ю *pf. of* **я́бедничать**
наяву́ *adv.* waking; in reality; **гре́зить н.** to day-dream.
ная́д|а, ы *f.* (*myth.*) naiad.
ная́рива|ть, ю *impf.* (*coll.*) to bash out (*a tune, etc., on a mus. instrument*).
не[1] not; **не..., не** neither ... nor.
не[2] *separable component of prons.* **не́кого** *and* **не́чего; мне не́ с кем разгова́ривать** I have no one to talk to; **не́ о чем бы́ло говори́ть** there was nothing to talk about.
не... *pref.* un-, in-, non-, mis-, dis-.
неавтоно́мный *adj.* (*comput.*) on-line.
неаккура́тност|ь, и *f.* **1.** carelessness; inaccuracy. **2.** unpunctuality. **3.** untidiness.
неаккура́т|ный (~ен, ~на) *adj.* **1.** careless; inaccurate. **2.** unpunctual. **3.** untidy.
неандерта́л|ец, ьца *m.* (*anthrop.*) Neanderthal man.

неандерта́льский *adj.* (*anthrop.*) Neanderthal.
неаполита́н|ец, ца *m.* Neapolitan.
неаполита́н|ка, ки *f. of* **~ец**
неаполита́нский *adj.* Neapolitan.
Неа́пол|ь, я *m.* Naples.
неаппети́т|ный (~ен, ~на) *adj.* unappetizing (*also fig.*).
небезопа́с|ный (~ен, ~на) *adj.* unsafe, insecure.
небезоснова́тел|ьный (~ен, ~ьна) *adj.* not unfounded.
небезразли́ч|ный (~ен, ~на) *adj.* not indifferent.
небезрезульта́т|ный (~ен, ~на) *adj.* not fruitless, not futile.
небезупре́ч|ный (~ен, ~на) *adj.* not irreproachable.
небезуспе́ш|ный (~ен, ~на) *adj.* not unsuccessful.
небезызве́ст|ный (~ен, ~на) *adj.* not unknown; **~но, что...** it is no secret that ....
небезынтере́с|ный (~ен, ~на) *adj.* not without interest.
небелёный *adj.* unbleached.
небережли́в|ый (~, ~а) *adj.* thriftless, improvident.
неб|еса́ *pl. of* **~о**
небескоры́ст|ный (~ен, ~на) *adj.* not disinterested.
небе́сн|ый *adj.* heavenly, celestial; **~ая импе́рия** (*hist.*) the Celestial Empire (*China*); **~ая меха́ника** (*astron.*) celestial mechanics; **~ые свети́ла** heavenly bodies; **н. свод** firmament; **Ца́рство ~ое** the Kingdom of Heaven; **~ого цве́та** sky-blue.
небесполе́з|ный (~ен, ~на) *adj.* of some use.
небеспристра́ст|ный (~ен, ~на) *adj.* not impartial.
неблагови́д|ный (~ен, ~на) *adj.* **1.** unseemly, improper. **2.** (*obs.*) unsightly.
неблагода́рност|ь, и *f.* ingratitude.
неблагода́р|ный (~ен, ~на) *adj.* **1.** ungrateful. **2.** thankless.
неблагожела́тел|ьный (~ен, ~ьна) *adj.* malevolent, ill-disposed.
неблагозву́чи|е, я *nt.* disharmony, dissonance.
неблагозву́ч|ный (~ен, ~на) *adj.* inharmonious, disharmonious.
неблагонадёж|ный (~ен, ~на) *adj.* (*hist.*) unreliable (*esp. politically*).
неблагополу́чи|е, я *nt.* trouble.
неблагополу́чно *adv.* not successfully, not favourably; **дела́ у них обстоя́т н.** their affairs are in a bad way, things are not turning out happily for them.
неблагополу́ч|ный (~ен, ~на) *adj.* unfavourable, bad; **дело име́ло н. исхо́д** the affair had a bad ending; (*impers.*): **у нас ~но** things are going badly; we are in a bad way.
неблагопристо́йност|ь, и *f.* obscenity, indecency, impropriety.
неблагопристо́|йный (~ен, ~йна) *adj.* obscene, indecent, improper.
неблагоприя́т|ный (~ен, ~на) *adj.* unfavourable, inauspicious.
неблагоразу́м|ный (~ен, ~на) *adj.* imprudent, ill-advised, unwise.
неблагоро́д|ный (~ен, ~на) *adj.* ignoble, base; **н. мета́лл** base metal.
неблагоро́дств|о, а *nt.* baseness.
неблагоскло́н|ный (~ен, ~на) *adj.* unfavourable; **(к)** ill-disposed (towards).
неблагоустро́ен|ный (~, ~на) *adj.* uncomfortable; badly planned.
нёбн|ый *adj.* **1.** (*anat.*) palatine; **~ая занаве́ска** uvula. **2.** (*ling.*) palatal.
не́б|о, а, *pl.* **~еса́, ~е́с, ~еса́м** *nt.* sky; heaven; **попа́сть па́льцем в н.** (*coll.*) to miss the point, be wide of the mark; **как н. от земли́** (as far removed) as heaven from earth, worlds apart; **жить ме́жду ~ом и землёй** not to have a roof above one's head; **под откры́тым ~ом** in the open (air); **с ~а свали́ться** (*fig., coll.*) to fall from the moon; **упа́сть с ~а на зе́млю** (*fig.*) to come down to earth; **нам н. с овчи́нку показа́лось** (*coll.*) we were frightened out of our wits.
нёб|о, а *nt.* (*anat.*) palate.
небога́т|ый (~, ~а) *adj.* **1.** of modest means. **2.** (*fig.*) modest.
небожи́тел|ь, я *m.* (*myth.*) celestial being, god.
небольш|о́й *adj.* small; not great; **о́чень ~ое расстоя́ние** a very short distance; **ты́сяча с ~и́м** a thousand odd; **де́ло ста́ло за ~и́м** one small thing is lacking.
небосво́д, а *m.* firmament; the vault of heaven.
небоскло́н, а *m.* horizon (*strictly*, sky immediately over the horizon).
небоскрёб, а *m.* (*obs.*) skyscraper.
небо́сь *adv.* (*coll.*) **1.** probably, most likely, I dare say; **ты, н., мно́го книг чита́л** I suppose you've read lots of books. **2.** (*obs.*) don't be afraid (= *не бо́йся*).
небре́жнича|ть, ю *impf.* (*coll.*) to be careless.
небре́жност|ь, и *f.* carelessness, negligence.
небре́ж|ный (~ен, ~на) *adj.* careless, negligent; slipshod; offhand.
небри́т|ый (~, ~а) *adj.* unshaven.
небыва́лый *adj.* **1.** unprecedented. **2.** fantastic, imaginary. **3.** (*coll.*) inexperienced.
небыва́льщин|а, ы *f.* **1.** (*obs.*) fable. **2.** fantastic story.
небыли́ц|а, ы *f.* fable; cock-and-bull story.
небыти|е́, я́ *nt.* non-existence.
небьющийся *adj.* unbreakable.
Нев|а́, ы́ *f.* the Neva (*river*).
неважне́цкий *adj.* (*coll.*) indifferent, so-so.
нева́жно *adv.* not too well, indifferently; **дела́ иду́т н.** things are not going too well.
нева́ж|ный (~ен, ~на́, ~но) *adj.* **1.** unimportant, insignificant. **2.** poor, indifferent.
невдалеке́ *adv.* not far away, not far off.
невдо|га́д (*dial.*) = **~мёк**
невдомёк *adv.* (*+d.*) (*coll.*): **мне бы́ло н.** it never occurred to me, I never thought of it.
неве́дени|е, я *nt.* ignorance; **пребыва́ть в блаже́нном ~и** (*iron.*) to be in a state of blissful ignorance.
неве́домо *adv.* (*coll.*; *+***что, как, когда́, куда́** *etc.*) God knows, no one knows; **он так и появи́лся, н. отку́да** he just turned up, God knows where from.
неве́дом|ый (~, ~а) *adj.* **1.** unknown. **2.** (*fig.*) mysterious.
неве́ж|а, и *c.g.* boor, lout.
неве́жд|а, ы *c.g.* ignoramus.
неве́жествен|ный (~, ~на) *adj.* ignorant.
неве́жеств|о, а *nt.* **1.** ignorance. **2.** (*coll.*) rudeness, bad manners.
неве́жливост|ь, и *f.* rudeness, impoliteness, bad manners.
неве́жлив|ый (~, ~а) *adj.* rude, impolite.
невезе́ни|е, я *nt.* (*coll.*) bad luck.
невезу́х|а, и *f.* = **невезе́ние**
невезу́ч|ий (~, а) *adj.* (*coll.*) unlucky.
невели́к|ий (~, ~а́, ~о́) *adj.* **1.** small, short. **2.** slight, insignificant.
неве́ри|е, я *nt.* unbelief; lack of faith.
неве́рност|ь, и *f.* **1.** incorrectness. **2.** disloyalty; infidelity, unfaithfulness.
неве́р|ный (~ен, ~на́, ~но) *adj.* **1.** incorrect; **~ная но́та** false note. **2.** unsteady, uncertain; **~ная похо́дка** unsteady gait; **н. слух** (*mus.*) unsure ear; **Фома́ н.** (*coll.*) a doubting Thomas. **3.** faithless, disloyal; unfaithful; **н. друг** false friend. **4.** dim, flickering (*of light*). **5.** *as n.* **н., ~ного** *m.* (*relig.*) infidel.
невероя́ти|е, я *nt. now only in phr.* **до ~я** incredibly.
невероя́тно *adv.* incredibly, unbelievably.
невероя́тност|ь, и *f.* **1.** improbability. **2.** incredibility; **до ~и** incredibly, to an unbelievable extent.
невероя́т|ный (~ен, ~на) *adj.* **1.** improbable, unlikely. **2.** incredible, unbelievable (*also fig.*); (*impers., as pred.*): **~но** it is incredible, it is unbelievable; it is beyond belief.
неве́рующ|ий *adj.* (*relig.*) unbelieving; *as n.* **н., ~его** *m.*, **~ая, ~ей** *f.* unbeliever.
невес|ёлый (~ел, ~ела́, ~ело) *adj.* joyless, mirthless; melancholy, sombre.
невесо́мост|ь, и *f.* weightlessness.
невесо́мый *adj.* **1.** (*phys.*) imponderable. **2.** weightless (*also fig.*).
неве́ст|а, ы *f.* **1.** fiancée; bride. **2.** (*coll.*) marriageable girl.
неве́стк|а, и *f.* **1.** daughter-in-law (*son's wife*). **2.** sister-in-law (*brother's wife*).

неве́сть *adv.* (*col.*; +**кто, что, ско́лько** *etc.*) God knows, goodness knows, heaven knows.
невеще́ственный *adj.* immaterial.
невзачёт, *adv.* (*coll.*): **э́то н.** it does not count.
невзго́д|а, ы *f.* adversity, misfortune.
невзира́я *prep.* (**на**+*a.*) in spite of, regardless of; **н. на ли́ца** without respect of persons.
невзнача́й *adv.* (*coll.*) by chance; unexpectedly.
невзно́с, а *m.* non-payment (*of fees, etc.*).
невзра́ч|ный (~ен, ~на) *adj.* unprepossessing, unattractive; plain.
невзыска́тел|ьный (~ен, ~ьна) *adj.* modest, undemanding.
не́видал|ь, и *f.* (*coll.*) wonder, prodigy; **вот н.!; э́ка(я) н.!** (*iron.*) that's nothing.
неви́дан|ный (~, ~а) *adj.* unprecedented.
невиди́мк|а, и *c.g and f.* **1.** *c.g.* invisible being; **сде́латься ~ой** to become invisible; **челове́к-н.** invisible man; **ша́пка-н.** cap of darkness. **2.** *f.* invisible hairpin.
неви́димост|ь, и *f.* invisibility.
неви́дим|ый (~, ~а) *adj.* invisible.
неви́д|ный (~ен, ~на) *adj.* **1.** invisible. **2.** (*coll.*) insignificant.
неви́дящ|ий *adj.* unseeing; **смотре́ть ~им взгля́дом** to look vacantly.
неви́нност|ь, и *f.* (*in var. senses*) innocence; **де́вичья н.** virginity.
неви́н|ный (~ен, ~на) *adj.* (*in var. senses*) innocent; virgin(al); **~ная же́ртва** innocent victim; **~ные удово́льствия** innocent pleasures.
невино́в|ный (~ен, ~на) *adj.* (**в**+*p.*) innocent (of); (*leg.*) not guilty; **призна́ть ~ным** to acquit.
невку́с|ный (~ен, ~на) *adj.* unpalatable.
невменя́емост|ь, и *f.* (*leg.*) irresponsibility.
невменя́ем|ый (~, ~а) *adj.* **1.** (*leg.*) irresponsible. **2.** (*coll.*) beside o.s.
невмеша́тельств|о, а *m.* (*pol.*) non-intervention, non-interference; **поли́тика ~а** (*pol.*) hands-off policy.
невмоготу́ *adv.* (*coll.*; +*d.*) unbearable (to, for), unendurable (to, for); **э́то мне н.** I can't stand it; this is more than I can stand; **ста́ло н.** it became unbearable; it became too much.
невмо́чь = **невмоготу́**
невнима́ни|е, я *nt.* **1.** inattention; carelessness. **2.** (**к**) lack of consideration (for).
невнима́тельност|ь, и *f.* inattention, thoughtlessness.
невнима́тел|ьный (~ен, ~ьна) *adj.* (*in var. senses*) inattentive, thoughtless.
невня́т|ный (~ен, ~на) *adj.* indistinct, incomprehensible.
не́вод, а, *pl.* **~а́, ~о́в** *m.* seine, sweep-net.
невозбра́н|ный (~ен, ~на) *adj.* (*obs.*) free, unrestricted.
невозвра́т|ный (~ен, ~на) *adj.* irrevocable, irretrievable.
невозвраще́н|ец, ца *m.* (*pol.*) defector.
невозвраще́ни|е, я *nt.* failure to return.
невозде́ланн|ый *adj.* uncultivated, untilled; **~ая земля́** waste land.
невозде́ржанност|ь, и *f.* intemperance; incontinence; (*fig.*) lack of self-control, lack of self-restraint.
невозде́ржан|ный (~, ~на) *adj.* intemperate; incontinent; (*fig.*) uncontrolled, unrestrained; **он ~ на язы́к** he has a loose tongue.
невозде́ржност|ь, и *f.* = **невозде́ржанность**
невозде́рж|ный (~ен, ~на) *adj.* = **невозде́ржанный**
невозмо́жност|ь, и *f.* impossibility; **до ~и** (*coll.*) to the last degree; **за ~ью** (+*g. or inf.*) owing to the impossibility (of).
невозмо́ж|ный (~ен, ~на) *adj.* **1.** impossible; (*impers., pred.*): **~но** it is impossible; *as n.* **~ное, ~ного** *nt.* the impossible. **2.** insufferable.
невозмути́м|ый (~, ~а) *adj.* **1.** imperturbable. **2.** calm, unruffled.
невознагради́м|ый (~, ~а) *adj.* **1.** irreparable. **2.** that can never be repaid.
невозобновля́емый *adj.* non-renewable.
нево́лей *adv.* (*obs.*) against one's will, forcibly.
нево́л|ить, ю, ишь *impf.* (*of* **при~**) (*coll.*) to force, compel.
нево́льник, а *m.* (*obs.*) slave.
нево́льн|ица, ицы *f. of* **~ик**
нево́льничеств|о, а *nt.* (*obs.*) slavery.
нево́льн|ичий *adj. of* **~ик; н. ры́нок** slave market; **н. труд** slave labour.
нево́льно *adv.* involuntarily; unintentionally, unwittingly.
нево́льн|ый *adj.* **1.** involuntary; unintentional. **2.** forced; **~ая поса́дка** forced landing.
нево́л|я, и *f.* **1.** bondage; captivity. **2.** (*coll.*) necessity.
невообрази́м|ый (~, ~а) *adj.* unimaginable, inconceivable; **н. шум** (*fig.*) unimaginable din.
невооружённ|ый *adj.* unarmed; **~ым гла́зом** with the naked eye.
невоспи́танност|ь, и *f.* ill breeding; bad manners.
невоспи́танный *adj.* ill-bred.
невоспламеня́ем|ый (~, ~а) *adj.* uninflammable, non-inflammable.
невосполни́м|ый (~, ~а) *adj.* irreplaceable.
невосприи́мчивост|ь, и *f.* **1.** lack of receptivity. **2.** (*med.*) immunity.
невосприи́мчив|ый (~, ~а) *adj.* **1.** unreceptive. **2.** (*med.*) (**к**) immune (to).
невостре́бованный *adj.* not called for, unclaimed.
невпопа́д *adv.* (*coll.*) out of place, inopportunely; **отвеча́ть н.** to answer irrelevantly.
невпроворо́т *adv.* (*coll.*) **1.** a lot, a great deal. **2.** too much; **э́то нам н.** it's too hard for us.
невразуми́тел|ьный (~ен, ~ьна) *adj.* unintelligible, incomprehensible.
невралги́ческий *adj.* neuralgic.
невралги́|я, и *f.* neuralgia; **н. седа́лищного не́рва** sciatica.
неврасте́ник, а *m.* neurasthenic.
неврастени́|ческий *adj. of* **~я**
неврастени́ч|ный (~ен, ~на) *adj.* neurasthenic (*pers.*).
неврастени́|я, и *f.* neurasthenia.
невреди́м|ый (~, ~а) *adj.* unharmed, intact; **цел и ~** safe and sound.
неври́т, а *m.* neuritis.
невро́з, а *m.* neurosis.
неврологи́ческий *adj.* neurological
невроло́ги|я, и *f.* neurology.
невропато́лог, а *m.* neuropathologist.
невропатоло́ги|я, и *f.* neuropathology.
невро́тик, а *m.* neurotic.
невроти́ческий *adj.* neurotic.
неврче́ни|е, я *nt.* non-delivery.
невтерпёж *adv.* (+*d.*; *coll.*) unbearable; **мне,** *etc.*, **ста́ло н.** I, *etc.*, cannot stand it any longer.
невы́год|а, ы *f.* **1.** disadvantage. **2.** loss.
невы́год|ный (~ен, ~на) *adj.* **1.** disadvantageous, unfavourable; **показа́ть себя́ с ~ной стороны́** to place o.s. in an unfavourable light, show o.s. at a disadvantage; **ста́вить в ~ное положе́ние** to place at a disadvantage. **2.** unprofitable, unremunerative; (*impers., pred.*): **~но** it does not pay.
невы́держанност|ь, и *f.* **1.** lack of self-control. **2.** inconsistency.
невы́держанный *adj.* **1.** lacking self-control. **2.** inconsistent; **н. стиль** uneven style. **3.** (*of cheese, wine, etc.*) unmatured.
невы́езд, а *m.* constant residence in one place; **дать подпи́ску о ~е** to give a written undertaking not to leave a place.
невыла́з|ный (~ен, ~на) *adj.* such that one cannot emerge from it; **~ная грязь** a veritable quagmire; **быть в ~ных долга́х** (*fig.*) to be up to the eyes in debt.
невыноси́м|ый (~, ~а) *adj.* unbearable, insufferable, intolerable.
невыполне́ни|е, я *nt.* non-fulfilment; (+*g.*) failure to carry out.
невыполни́м|ый (~, ~а) *adj.* impracticable; unrealizable.
невырази́м|ый (~, ~а) *adj.* inexpressible, beyond expression; *as n.* **«~ые, ~ых»** (*joc., euph.*) unmentionables (= *pants*).
невырази́тел|ьный (~ен, ~ьна) *adj.* inexpressive, expressionless.
невы́сказанный *adj.* unexpressed, unsaid.

невысо́к|ий (~, ~а́, ~о) *adj.* rather low; rather short; **~ого ка́чества** of poor quality; **быть ~ого мне́ния (о**+*p.*) to have a low opinion (of).
невы́ход, а *m.* failure to appear; **н. на рабо́ту** absence (from work).
невя́зк|а, и *f.* (*coll.*) discrepancy.
не́г|а, и *f.* **1.** comfort; abundance. **2.** voluptuousness, languor.
негаси́м|ый (~, ~а) *adj.* (*rhet.*) ever-burning, eternal (*of flame, etc.*); unquenchable (*also fig.*).
негати́в, а *m.* (*phot.*) negative.
негати́вный *adj.* (*in var. senses*) negative.
негашён|ый *adj.*: **~ая и́звесть** quick-lime.
не́где *adv.* (+*inf.*) there is nowhere; **н. доста́ть э́ту кни́гу** this book is nowhere to be had; **я́блоку н. упа́сть** there's not an inch of room.
неги́бкий *adj.* inflexible.
негла́сный *adj.* secret.
неглиже́ *nt. indecl.* negligée.
неглижи́р|овать, ую *impf.* (*coll., obs.*; +*i.*) to neglect, disregard.
неглубо́кий *adj.* rather shallow; (*fig.*) superficial.
неглу́п|ый (~, ~а́, ~л) *adj.* quite intelligent; **он о́чень ~** he is no fool.
него́ *a. and g. of* **он** *when governed by preps.*
него́дник, а *m.* reprobate, scoundrel; ne'er-do-well.
него́дност|ь, и *f.* worthlessness; **привести́ в н.** to put out of commission.
него́д|ный (~ен, ~на) *adj.* **1.** unfit, unsuitable. **2.** worthless, good-for-nothing; **н. чек** dud cheque.
негодова́ни|е, я *nt.* indignation.
негод|ова́ть, у́ю *impf.* (**на**+*a.*, **про́тив**) to be indignant (with).
негод|у́ющий *pres. part. act. of* **~ова́ть** *and adj.* indignant.
негодя́|й, я *m.* scoundrel, rascal.
негостеприи́мный *adj.* inhospitable.
негоциа́нт, а *m.* (*obs.*) merchant.
негр, а *m.* black (man), Negro; **америка́нский н.** Afro-American.
негра́мотност|ь, и *f.* illiteracy (*also fig.*).
негра́мот|ный (~ен, ~на) *adj.* **1.** illiterate (*also fig.*); *as n.* **н., ~ного** *m.*, **~ная, ~ной** *f.* illiterate (*pers.*). **2.** (*fig.*) crude, inexpert.
негрит|ёнок, ёнка, *pl.* **~я́та, ~я́т** *m.* black child, Negro child, piccaninny.
негрито́с, а *m.* negrito.
негритя́нк|а, и *f.* black woman, Negress.
негритя́нский *adj.* Negro.
негро́мкий *adj.* low.
не́гус, а *m.* Negus.
неда́вний *adj.* recent.
неда́вно *adv.* recently.
недалёк|ий (~, ~а́, ~л *or* **~о́)** *adj.* **1.** not far off, near; short; **на ~ом расстоя́нии** at a short distance. **2.** (*fig.*) not bright, dull-witted.
недалеко́ (*and* **недалёко**) *adv.* not far, near; **за приме́ром идти́ н.** one does not have to search far for an example.
недальнови́дност|ь, и *f.* lack of foresight, short-sightedness (*fig.*).
недальнови́д|ный (~ен, ~на) *adj.* short-sighted (*fig.*).
неда́ром *adv.* not for nothing, not without reason; not without purpose.
недви́жимост|ь, и *f.* (*leg.*) immovable property, real estate.
недви́жим|ый[1] *adj.* immovable; **~ое иму́щество = ~ость**
недви́жи́м|ый[2] **(~, ~а)** *adj.* motionless.
недвусмы́сленный *adj.* unequivocal, unambiguous.
недееспосо́б|ный (~ен, ~на) *adj.* **1.** (*leg.*) incapable. **2.** unable to function.
недействи́тельност|ь, и *f.* **1.** ineffectiveness; inefficacity. **2.** (*leg.*) invalidity; nullity.
недействи́тел|ьный (~ен, ~ьна) *adj.* **1.** (*obs.*) ineffective, ineffectual. **2.** (*leg.*) invalid; null, null and void.
неделика́т|ный (~ен, ~на) *adj.* **1.** indelicate, indiscreet. **2.** rude, coarse.
недели́мост|ь, и *f.* indivisibility.
недели́м|ый (~, ~а) *adj.* indivisible; **н. фонд** (*fig., leg.*) indivisible fund (*of a collective farm*).
неде́льный *adj.* of a week's duration; **я вы́полню э́ту рабо́ту в н. срок** I will finish this work in a week's time; **н. о́тпуск** week's leave.
неде́л|я, и *f.* week; **~ями** for weeks (at a time); **на э́той ~е** this week.
недержа́ни|е, я *nt. only in phr.* **н. мочи́** (*med.*) irretention of urine.
недёшево *adv.* (*coll.*) at a considerable price, rather dear (*also fig.*).
недисциплини́рованност|ь, и *f.* indiscipline.
недисциплини́рованный *adj.* undisciplined.
недобо́р, а *m.* arrears; shortage.
недоброжела́тел|ь, я *m.* ill-wisher.
недоброжела́тельност|ь, и *f.* malevolence, ill-will.
недоброжела́тел|ьный (~ен, ~ьна) *adj.* malevolent, ill-disposed.
недоброжела́тель|ство = ~ность
недоброка́чественност|ь, и *f.* poor quality, bad quality.
недоброка́чествен|ный (~, ~на) *adj.* of poor quality, low-grade, bad.
недобросо́вестност|ь, и *f.* **1.** bad faith; unscrupulousness, lack of scruple. **2.** carelessness.
недобросо́вест|ный (~ен, ~на) *adj.* **1.** unscrupulous. **2.** lacking in conscientiousness; careless.
недо́бр|ый *adj.* **1.** unkind; unfriendly. **2.** bad, evil; **~ая весть** bad news; **~ые лю́ди** (*obs.*) wicked men (*euph.* = *brigands*).
недове́ри|е, я *nt.* distrust; mistrust; **во́тум ~я** vote of no confidence.
недове́рчив|ый (~, ~а) *adj.* distrustful; mistrustful.
недове́с, а *m.* short weight.
недове́|сить, шу, сишь *pf.* (*of* **~шивать**) **1.** (+*g.*) to give short weight (of). **2.** to prove to be short-weight.
недове́шива|ть, ю *impf. of* **недове́сить**
недово́л|ьный (~ен, ~ьна) *adj.* (+*i.*) dissatisfied, discontented, displeased (with); *as n.* **н., ~ьного** *m.* malcontent.
недово́льств|о, а *nt.* dissatisfaction, discontent, displeasure.
недовы́работк|а, и *f.* underproduction.
недога́длив|ый (~, ~а) *adj.* slow(-witted).
недогля|де́ть, жу́, ди́шь *pf.* **1.** (+*g.*) to overlook, miss. **2.** (**за**+*i.*) not to take sufficient care (of), not to look after properly.
недоговорённост|ь, и *f.* **1.** reticence. **2.** lack of agreement.
недогру́зк|а, и *f.* underloading; (*fig.*) short time (*in factory or works*).
недода|ва́ть, ю́, ёшь *impf. of* **∠ть**
недо|да́ть, да́м, да́шь, да́ст, дади́м, дади́те, даду́т, *past* **∠дал, ~дала́, ∠дало** *pf.* (*of* **~дава́ть**) to give short; to deliver short; **он мне ∠дал три рубля́** he gave me three roubles short.
недода́ч|а, и *f.* deficiency in payment *or* supply.
недоде́ланный *adj.* unfinished.
недоде́лк|а, и *f.* incompleteness.
недодерж|а́ть, у́, ∠ишь *pf.* **1.** (*phot.*) to under-expose; to under-develop. **2.** to keep for too short a time in the necessary place.
недоде́ржк|а, и *f.* **1.** (*phot.*) under-exposure; under-development. **2.** keeping for too short a time in the necessary place.
недоеда́ни|е, я *nt.* under-nourishment, malnutrition.
недоеда́|ть, ю *impf.* to be undernourished, be underfed.
недозво́лен|ный (~, ~а) *adj.* illicit, unlawful.
недозре́лый *adj.* unripe, immature (*also fig.*).
недои́мк|а, и *f.* arrears.
недои́м|очный *adj. of* **~ка**
недои́мщик, а *m.* pers. in arrears (*in paying taxes, etc.*).
недока́зан|ный (~, ~а) *adj.* not proved, not proven.
недоказа́тельный *adj.* unconvincing, inadequate.
недоказу́емый *adj.* indemonstrable.
недоко́нчен|ный (~, ~а) *adj.* unfinished, incomplete.
недолга́ *only in phr.* **(вот) и вся н.** (*coll.*) and that is all there is to it.

недо́л|гий (~ог, ~га́, ~го) *adj.* short, brief.
недо́лго *adv.* **1.** not long; **н. ду́мая** without hesitation. **2.** (*coll.*): **н. и** (+*inf.*) one can easily; it is easy (to), it is a simple matter (to); **тут и потону́ть н.** one could easily drown here; **недо́лго и до греха́** serious trouble could easily happen.
недолгове́ч|ный (~ен, ~на) *adj.* short-lived, ephemeral.
недолёт, а *m.* (*mil.*) falling short (*of bullets, shells*).
недолю́блива|ть, ю *impf.* (+*a. or g.*; *coll.*) not to be overfond of; **они́ ~ли друг дру́га** there was no love lost between them.
недоме́рива|ть, ю *impf. of* **недоме́рить**
недоме́р|ить, ю, ишь *pf.* (*of* **~ивать**) to give short measure.
недоме́р|ок, ка *m.* undersize object.
недомога́ни|е, я *nt.* indisposition.
недомога́|ть, ю *impf.* to be indisposed, be unwell.
недомо́лвк|а, и *f.* innuendo; reservation, omission.
недомы́сли|е, я *nt.* thoughtlessness, inability to think things out.
недонесе́ни|е, я *nt.* failure to give information (*concerning crime committed or meditated*); **н. о преступле́нии** (*leg.*) misprision of felony.
недоно́с|ок, ка *m.* **1.** premature baby. **2.** (*fig., coll., pej.*) retarded *or* immature pers.
недоно́шен|ный (~, ~а) *adj.* (*med.*) premature, pre-term.
недооце́нива|ть, ю *impf. of* **недооцени́ть**
недооцен|и́ть, ю́, ~́ишь *pf.* (*of* **~́ивать**) to underestimate, underrate.
недооце́нк|а, и *f.* underestimation, underestimate.
недопечённый *adj.* half-baked.
недополуч|а́ть, а́ю *impf. of* **~и́ть**
недополуч|и́ть, у́, ~́ишь *pf.* (*of* **~а́ть**) to receive less (than one's due).
недопусти́м|ый (~, ~а) *adj.* inadmissible, intolerable.
недора́звитост|ь, и *f.* under-development, backwardness.
недора́звит|ый *adj.* under-developed, backward; **~ые стра́ны** (*pol., econ.*) under-developed countries.
недоразуме́ни|е, я *nt.* misunderstanding.
недо́рого *adv.* not dear, cheaply.
недор|ого́й (~́ог, ~ога́, ~́ого) *adj.* inexpensive; reasonable (*of price*).
недоро́д, а *m.* harvest failure.
не́доросл|ь, я *m.* **1.** (*hist.*) minor. **2.** (*fig., coll.*) young ignoramus, young oaf.
недоска́занност|ь, и *f.* understatement.
недослы́ш|ать, у, ишь *pf.* **1.** (+*a. or g.*) to fail to hear all of. **2.** (*intrans.*; *coll.*) to be hard of hearing.
недосмо́тр, а *m.* oversight.
недосмотр|е́ть, ю́, ~́ишь *pf.* **1.** (+*g.*) to overlook, miss. **2.** (**за**+*i.*) not to look after properly.
недосо́л, а *m.* insufficient salting; **н. на столе́,** *see* **пересо́л**
недос|па́ть, плю́, пи́шь *pf.* (*of* **~ыпа́ть**) not to have one's sleep out.
недоста|ва́ть, ёт, *impf.* (*of* **~́ть**) (*impers.*, +*g.*) to be missing, be lacking, be wanting; **ему́ ~ёт о́пыта** he lacks experience; **мне о́чень ~ва́ло вас** I missed you very much; **э́того ещё ~ва́ло!** that would be (*or* is) the limit!; that would be (*or* is) the last straw!
недоста́т|ок, ка *m.* **1.** (+*g. or* **в**+*p.*) shortage (of), lack (of), deficiency (in); **за ~ком** (+*g.*) for want (of); **име́ть н. в рабо́чей си́ле** to be short-handed. **2.** shortcoming, imperfection; defect; **н. зре́ния** defective eyesight.
недоста́точно *adv.* **1.** insufficiently. **2.** not enough.
недоста́точност|ь, и *f.* insufficiency; inadequacy; **витами́нная н.** vitamin deficiency.
недоста́точ|ный (~ен, ~на) *adj.* insufficient; inadequate; **н. глаго́л** (*gram.*) defective verb.
недоста́|ть, нет *pf. of* **~ва́ть**
недоста́ч|а, и *f.* (*coll.*) lack, shortage.
недостаю́щий *adj.* missing.
недостижи́м|ый (~, ~а) *adj.* unattainable.
недостове́р|ный (~ен, ~на) *adj.* not authentic, apocryphal.
недосто́|йный (~ин, ~йна) *adj.* unworthy.
недосту́пност|ь, и *f.* inaccessibility.
недосту́п|ный (~ен, ~на) *adj.* inaccessible (*also fig.*); **э́то ~но моему́ понима́нию** it is beyond my comprehension.
недосу́г, а *m.* (*coll.*) lack of time, lack of leisure; **придёт он на конце́рт? нет, ему́, мол, н.** is he coming to the concert? No, he says he is busy.
недосчит|а́ться, а́юсь *pf.* (*of* **~́ываться**) (+*g.*) to find missing, miss; to be out (in one's accounts); **он ~а́лся десяти́ рубле́й** he found he was ten roubles short; **по́сле налёта мы ~а́лись трёх бомбардиро́вщиков** after the raid we found three of our bombers were missing.
недосчи́тыва|ться, юсь *impf. of* **недосчита́ться**
недосыпа́|ть, ю *impf. of* **недоспа́ть**
недосяга́ем|ый (~, ~а) *adj.* unattainable.
недотёп|а, ы *c.g.* (*coll.*) duffer.
недотро́г|а, и *c.g.* (*coll.*) touchy pers.
недоумева́|ть, ю *impf.* to be perplexed, be at a loss; to wonder.
недоуме́ни|е, я *nt.* perplexity, bewilderment; **быть в ~и** to be in a quandary.
недоуме́нный *adj.* puzzled, perplexed.
недоу́чк|а, и *c.g.* (*coll.*) half-educated pers.
недохва́тк|а, и *f.* (*coll.*) shortage.
недочелове́к, а *m.* subhuman.
недочёт, а *m.* **1.** deficit; shortage. **2.** defect, shortcoming.
не́др|а, ~ *no sg.* **1.** depths (*of the earth*); **н. земли́** bowels of the earth; **разве́дка ~** prospecting of mineral wealth. **2.** (*fig.*) depths, heart.
недрема́нн|ый *adj.* (*obs.*) unwinking, unslumbering; **~ое о́ко** (*fig., iron.*) the unwinking eye (*sc.* of authority).
недре́млющий *adj.* unwinking, unslumbering; vigilant, watchful.
не́друг, а *m.* enemy, foe.
недружелю́б|ный (~ен, ~на) *adj.* unfriendly.
недру́жный *adj.* disunited; disjointed.
неду́г, а *m.* ailment, disease.
неду́жит|ься, ~ся *impf.* (*impers.*, +*d.*; *coll.*) to be unwell, be poorly.
неду́рно *adv.* not badly, well enough; **н.!** not bad!
недур|но́й (~ён, ~на́, ~́но) *adj.* **1.** not bad. **2.** **(собо́й)** not bad-looking.
недю́жинный *adj.* out of the ordinary, outstanding, exceptional.
неё *a. and g. of* **она́** *when governed by preps.*
неесте́ствен|ный (~, ~на) *adj.* (*in var. senses*) unnatural.
нежда́нно *adv.* (*coll.*) unexpectedly; **н.-нега́данно** quite unexpectedly.
нежда́нный *adj.* (*coll.*) unexpected.
нежела́ни|е, я *nt.* unwillingness, disinclination.
нежела́тел|ьный (~ен, ~ьна) *adj.* **1.** undesirable. **2.** unwanted; (+*d.*) contrary to the wishes (of); **н. посети́тель** unwanted visitor; **э́то бы́ло мне ~ьно** it was not what I wanted.
не́жели *conj.* (*obs.*) than.
не́женк|а, и *c.g.* (*coll.*) mollycoddle.
нежив|о́й *adj.* **1.** lifeless; **роди́ться ~ы́м** to be still-born. **2.** inanimate, inorganic. **3.** (*fig.*) dull, lifeless.
нежи́знен|ный (~, ~на) *adj.* **1.** impracticable; inapplicable. **2.** weird.
нежило́й *adj.* **1.** uninhabited. **2.** not fit for habitation; uninhabitable.
не́жит|ь[1], и *f.* (*collect.*) (*in Russ. folklore*) the spirits (*gnomes, goblins, etc.*).
не́ж|ить[2], у, ишь *impf.* to pamper, coddle; caress.
не́ж|иться, усь, ишься *impf.* to luxuriate; **н. на со́лнце** to bask in the sun.
не́жнича|ть, ю *impf.* (*coll.*) **1.** to bill and coo, canoodle. **2.** (*fig.*) to be over-indulgent.
не́жност|ь, и *f.* **1.** tenderness. **2.** delicacy. **3.** (*pl. only*) display of affection, endearments; compliments, flattery.
не́ж|ный (~ен, ~на́, ~но) *adj.* **1.** tender; affectionate; **~ные взгля́ды** tender glances. **2.** delicate (= *soft, fine*; *of colours, taste, skin, etc.*). **3.** tender, delicate; **н. пол** the weaker sex.
незабве́н|ный (~, ~на) *adj.* unforgettable.

незабу́дк|а, и *f.* (*bot.*) forget-me-not.
незабыва́ем|ый (~, ~а) *adj.* unforgettable.
незаве́ренный *adj.* uncertified.
незави́д|ный (~ен, ~на) *adj.* unenviable; poor.
незави́симо *adv.* independently; **н. от** irrespective of.
незави́симост|ь, и *f.* independence.
незави́сим|ый (~, ~а) *adj.* independent.
незави́сящ|ий *only in phr.* **по ~им от нас,** *etc.*, **обстоя́тельствам (***or* **причи́нам)** owing to circumstances beyond our, *etc.*, control.
незада́ч|а, и *f.* (*coll.*) ill-luck.
незада́члив|ый (~, ~а) *adj.* (*coll.*) unlucky, luckless.
незадо́лго *adv.* **(до, пе́ред)** shortly (before), not long (before).
незаконнорождённост|ь, и *f.* illegitimacy.
незаконнорождённый *adj.* illegitimate.
незако́нност|ь, и *f.* illegality, unlawfulness.
незако́нн|ый *adj.* illegal, illicit, unlawful; illegitimate; **~ая жена́** common-law wife.
незакономе́рност|ь, и *f.* exceptionality, exceptional character.
незакономе́р|ный (~ен, ~на) *adj.* exceptional.
незако́нченност|ь, и *f.* incompleteness unfinished state.
незако́нчен|ный (~, ~а) *adj.* incomplete, unfinished.
незамедли́тельно *adv.* without delay.
незамедли́тел|ьный (~ен, ~ьна) *adj.* immediate.
незамени́м|ый (~, ~а) *adj.* **1.** irreplaceable. **2.** indispensable.
незамерза́ющий *adj.* non-freezing; ice-free; (*tech.*) anti-freeze.
незаме́тно *adv.* imperceptibly, insensibly.
незаме́т|ный (~ен, ~на) *adj.* **1.** imperceptible. **2.** inconspicuous; insignificant.
незаму́жняя *adj.* unmarried, single, maiden; **н. же́нщина** (*leg.*) spinster.
незамыслова́т|ый (~, ~а) *adj.* simple, uncomplicated.
незапа́мятн|ый *adj.* immemorial; **с ~ых времён** from time immemorial.
незапя́тнанный *adj.* unsullied, stainless.
незарабо́танный *adj.* unearned.
незара́зный *adj.* non-contagious.
незаслу́жен|ный (~, ~на) *adj.* undeserved, unmerited.
незастро́енный *adj.* undeveloped, not built over.
незате́йлив|ый (~, ~а) *adj.* simple, plain; modest.
незатуха́ющий *adj.* (*radio*) undamped; continuous.
незауря́д|ный (~ен, ~на) *adj.* outstanding, exceptional.
не́зачем *adv.* (*+inf.*) there is no point (in), it is pointless; there is no need (to); it is no use, it is useless; **н. бо́льше ждать** there is no point in waiting any longer.
незашифро́ванный *adj.* not in cipher, not in code; en clair.
незва́ный *adj.* uninvited.
нзде́шний *adj.* **1.** (*coll.*) not of these parts; **я н.** I am a stranger here. **2.** unearthly, supernatural, mysterious; **н. мир** the other world.
нездоро́вит|ься, ~ся *impf.* (*impers.*, *+d.*) to feel unwell.
нездоро́в|ый (~, ~а) *adj.* **1.** unhealthy, morbid (*also fig.*); sickly; unwholesome; **~ая обстано́вка** unhealthy environment. **2.** *as pred.* unwell, poorly.
нездоро́вь|е, я *nt.* indisposition; ill-health.
неземно́й *adj.* **1.** (*obs.*) supernatural, unearthly. **2.** not belonging *or* pertaining to the earth.
незло́бив|ый (~, ~а) *adj.* mild, forgiving.
незлопа́мят|ный (~ен, ~на) *adj.* forgiving.
незнако́м|ец, ца *m.* stranger.
незнако́м|ка, ки *f. of* **~ец**
незнако́м|ый (~, ~а) *adj.* **1.** unknown, unfamiliar. **2.** **(с***+i.***)** unacquainted (with).
незна́ни|е, я *nt.* ignorance.
незна́чащий *adj.* insignificant, of no significance.
незначи́тел|ьный (~ен, ~ьна) *adj.* insignificant, negligible; unimportant.
незна́ющ|ий *adj.* (*+g.*) ignorant (of); **н. у́стали** indefatigable; **~ая грани́ц любо́вь** love that knows no bounds.
незре́лост|ь, и *f.* unripeness; (*fig.*) immaturity.
незре́л|ый (~, ~а) *adj.* unripe (*also fig.*); (*fig.*) immature.
незри́м|ый (~, ~а) *adj.* invisible.
незы́блем|ый (~, ~а) *adj.* unshakeable, stable.
неизбе́жност|ь, и *f.* inevitability.
неизбе́ж|ный (~ен, ~на) *adj.* inevitable, unavoidable; inescapable.
неизбы́в|ный (~ен, ~на) *adj.* unescapable, permanent.
неизве́дан|ный (~, ~на) *adj.* unexplored, unknown; not experienced before.
неизве́стност|ь, и *f.* **1.** uncertainty; **быть в ~и (о***+p.***)** to be uncertain (about), be in the dark (about). **2.** obscurity; **жить в ~и** to live in obscurity.
неизве́ст|ный (~ен, ~на) *adj.* (*in var. senses*) unknown; uncertain; **~но где, когда́** etc., no one knows where, when, *etc.* (*= somewhere, at some time, etc.*); *as n.* **н., ~ного** *m.*, **~ная, ~ной** *f.* unknown pers.; **~ное, ~ного** *nt.* (*math.*) unknown (quantity).
неизвини́тел|ьный (~ен, ~ьна) *adj.* inexcusable, unpardonable.
неизглади́м|ый (~, ~а) *adj.* indelible, ineffaceable.
нёизданный *adj.* unpublished.
неизлечи́м|ый (~, ~а) *adj.* incurable.
неизме́н|ный (~ен, ~на) *adj.* **1.** invariable, immutable. **2.** (*rhet.*) devoted, true.
неизменя́ем|ый (~, ~а) *adj.* unalterable.
неизмери́мо *adv.* immeasurably.
неизмери́мост|ь, и *f.* immeasurability; immensity.
неизмери́м|ый (~, ~а) *adj.* immeasurable; immense.
неизрече́нный *adj.* (*obs.*) ineffable.
неизъясни́м|ый (~, ~а) *adj.* inexplicable; ineffable, indescribable.
неиме́ни|е, я *nt.* absence; lack, want; **за ~ем лу́чшего** for want of sth. better.
неимове́р|ный (~ен, ~на) *adj.* incredible, unbelievable.
неиму́щий *adj.* indigent, poor.
неискорени́м|ый (~, ~а) *adj.* ineradicable.
нейскрен|ний (~ен, ~на) *adj.* insincere.
нейскренност|ь, и *f.* insincerity.
неиску́с|ный (~ен, ~на) *adj.* unskilful, inexpert.
неискушённост|ь, и *f.* inexperience, innocence.
неискушён|ный (~, ~а) *adj.* inexperienced, innocent, unsophisticated.
неисповеди́м|ый (~, ~а) *adj.* inscrutable.
неисполне́ни|е, я *nt.* non-execution, non-performance; **н. зако́на** failure to observe a law.
неисполни́м|ый (~, ~а) *adj.* impracticable; unrealizable.
неиспо́рчен|ный (~, ~а) *adj.* (*fig.*) unspoiled, innocent.
неиспо́рченност|ь, и *f.* (*fig.*) innocence.
неисправи́м|ый (~, ~а) *adj.* **1.** incorrigible. **2.** irremediable, irreparable.
неиспра́вност|ь, и *f.* **1.** disrepair. **2.** carelessness.
неиспра́в|ный (~ен, ~на) *adj.* **1.** out of order; faulty, defective. **2.** careless.
неиспы́танный *adj.* untried, untested.
неиссяка́ем|ый (~, ~а) *adj.* inexhaustible.
нёистовств|о, а *nt.* **1.** fury, frenzy. **2.** brutality, savagery.
нёистовств|овать, ую *impf.* **1.** to rage, rave. **2.** to commit brutalities.
нёистов|ый (~, ~а) *adj.* furious, frenzied; **~ые аплодисме́нты** tempestuous applause.
неистощи́м|ый (~, ~а) *adj.* inexhaustible.
неистреби́м|ый (~, ~а) *adj.* ineradicable; undying.
неисчерпа́ем|ый (~, ~а) *adj.* inexhaustible.
неисчисли́м|ый (~, ~а) *adj.* innumerable; incalculable.
ней *d., i., and p. of* **она́** *when governed by preps.*
нейзи́льбер, а *m.* German silver.
нейло́н, а *m.* nylon.
нейло́новый *adj.* nylon, made of nylon.
неймёт (*no other form in use*), *impf.*, *only in prov.* **(хоть) ви́дит о́ко, да зуб н.** there's many a slip 'twixt cup and lip.
неймётся *impf.* (*impers.*, *+d.*; *coll.*): **ему́ н.** he is set on it, there is no holding him; **ей н.** she will not sit still.
нейро́н, а *m.* (*physiol.*) neuron.
нейтрализа́тор, а *m.*: **каталисти́ческий н.** catalytic converter.

нейтрализа́ци|я, и *f.* (*in var. senses*) neutralization.
нейтрали́зм, а *m.* (*pol.*) neutralism.
нейтрализ|ова́ть, у́ю *impf. and pf.* (*in var. senses*) to neutralize.
нейтралите́т, а *m.* (*pol.*) neutrality.
нейтра́льност|ь, и *f.* (*in var. senses*) neutrality.
нейтра́л|ьный (~ен, ~ьна) *adj.* (*in var. senses*) neutral.
нейтро́н, а *m.* (*phys.*) neutron.
неказа́ст|ый (~, ~а) *adj.* (*coll.*) unprepossessing, ill-favoured.
неквалифици́рованный *adj.* unqualified; **н. рабо́чий** unskilled labourer.
не́кий *pron.* a certain; a kind of; **вас спра́шивал н. господи́н Па́влов** a (certain) Mr Pavlov was asking for you.
некле́точный *adj.* (*biol.*) non-cellular.
не́когда[1] *adv.* once, formerly; in the old days.
не́когда[2] *adv.* there is no time; **мне сего́дня н. разгова́ривать с ва́ми** I have no time to chat today.
не́кого, не́кому, не́кем, не́ о ком *pron.* (*+inf.*) there is nobody (to); **н. вини́ть** nobody is to blame; **ей не́ с кем пойти́** she has nobody to go with (her).
неколеби́мый = непоколеби́мый
некомпете́нт|ный (~ен, ~на) *adj.* not competent, unqualified.
некомпле́кт|ный (~ен, ~на) *adj.* incomplete; not up to strength.
некороно́ванный *adj.* uncrowned.
некорре́ктност|ь, и *f.* discourtesy, impoliteness.
некорре́кт|ный (~ен, ~на) *adj.* discourteous, impolite.
не́котор|ый *pron.* some; **он ~ое вре́мя не дви́гался с ме́ста** for a time he did not budge; **мы с ~ых пор живём здесь** we have been living here for some time; **~ым о́бразом** somehow, in some way; **в, до ~ой сте́пени** to some extent, to a certain extent; *as n.* **~ые, ~ых** some; some people.
некраси́в|ый (~, ~а) *adj.* **1.** plain; unsightly. **2.** (*coll.*; *of conduct, actions, etc.*) unseemly, indecorous.
некредитоспосо́бност|ь, и *f.* insolvency.
некредитоспосо́б|ный (~ен, ~на) *adj.* insolvent.
некре́п|кий (~ок, ~ка́) *adj.* rather weak.
некро́з, а *m.* (*med.*) necrosis.
некроло́г, а *m.* obituary (notice).
некрома́нти|я, и *f.* necromancy.
некро́пол|ь, я *m.* necropolis.
некру́п|ный (~ен, ~на́, ~но) *adj.* medium-sized, not large.
некры́т|ый (~, ~а) *adj.* roofless.
некста́ти *adv.* inopportunely; mal à propos; **вот н.!** what a nuisance!
некта́р, а *m.* nectar.
не́кто *pron.* someone; **н. Петро́в** one Petrov, a certain Petrov.
не́куда *adv.* (*+inf.*) there is nowhere (to); **мне н. пойти́** I have nowhere to go.
некульту́рност|ь, и *f.* **1.** low level of civilization; uncivilized ways. **2.** bad manners, boorishness.
некульту́р|ный (~ен, ~на) *adj.* **1.** uncivilized; backward. **2.** rough(-mannered), boorish. **3.** (*bot.*) uncultivated.
некуря́щ|ий *adj.* non-smoking; *as n.* **н., ~его** *m.* non-smoker; **ваго́н для ~их** non-smoking carriage.
нела́д|ный (~ен, ~на) *adj.* (*coll.*) wrong, bad; **у него́ ~но с гру́дью** there is sth. the matter with his chest; **будь он ~ен!** blast him!
нелад|ы́, о́в *no sg.* (*coll.*) **1.** discord, disagreement; **у них н.** they don't hit it off. **2.** trouble, sth. wrong.
нела́сковый *adj.* reserved, unfriendly.
нелега́льност|ь, и *f.* illegality.
нелега́л|ьный (~ен, ~ьна) *adj.* illegal; **перейти́ на ~ьное положе́ние** (*of resistance movements, etc.*) to go underground.
нелега́льщин|а, ы *f.* (*coll.*) illegal activities; illegal literature.
нелёгкая (*coll.*): **н. его́ сюда́ несёт!** what the deuce brings him here?; **куда́ их н. понесла́?** where the deuce have thy gone?
нелёг|кий (~ок, ~ка́) *adj.* **1.** difficult, not easy. **2.** heavy, not light (*also fig.*).
неле́пост|ь, и *f.* absurdity, nonsense.
неле́п|ый (~, ~а) *adj.* absurd, ridiculous.
нeléст|ный (~ен, ~на) *adj.* unflattering, uncomplimentary.
нелета́ющий *adj.* flightless.
нелету́чий *adj.* (*chem.*) non-volatile.
нелицеприя́т|ный (~ен, ~на) *adj.* (*obs.*) impartial.
нели́шний *adj.* not superfluous; not out of place.
нело́в|кий (~ок, ~ка́, ~ко) *adj.* **1.** awkward; gauche; clumsy. **2.** uncomfortable. **3.** (*fig.*) awkward; embarrassing; **~кое молча́ние** awkward silence; **~ко при нём ссыла́ться на э́то** it is awkward to refer to it in his presence; **ему́ ~ко приглаша́ть на бал незнако́мую да́му** he feels awkward about inviting a lady he does not know to the dance.
нело́вко *adv.* awkwardly; uncomfortably; **чу́вствовать себя́ н.** to feel ill at ease, feel awkward, feel uncomfortable.
нело́вкост|ь, и *f.* **1.** awkwardness, gaucherie, clumsiness (*also fig.*); **чу́вствовать н.** to feel awkward, feel uncomfortable. **2.** blunder, gaffe.
нелоги́чност|ь, и *f.* illogicality.
нелоги́ч|ный (~ен, ~на) *adj.* illogical.
нельзя́ *adv.* (*+inf.*) **1.** it is impossible; **н. не призна́ть** it is impossible not to admit, one cannot but admit. **2.** it is not allowed; **здесь н. кури́ть** smoking is not allowed here. **3.** one ought not, one should not; **н. ложи́ться (спать) так по́здно** you ought not to go to bed so late. **4.: как н.** (*+comp. adv.*) as … as possible; **как н. лу́чше** in the best possible way.
не́льм|а, ы *f.* white salmon.
нелюбе́зност|ь, и *f.* ungraciousness; discourtesy.
нелюбе́з|ный (~ен, ~на) *adj.* ungracious, unobliging; discourteous.
нелюби́м|ый (~, ~а) *adj.* unloved.
нелюб|о́вь, ви́ *f.* **(к)** dislike (for).
нелюбопы́т|ный (~ен, ~на) *adj.* **1.** incurious. **2.** uninteresting.
нелюди́м, а *m.* unsociable pers.
нелюди́м|ый (~, ~а) *adj.* unsociable.
нём *p. of* **он, оно́**
нема́ло *adv.* **1.** not a little; not a few. **2.** a good deal; considerably.
немалова́ж|ный (~ен, ~на) *adj.* of no small importance.
нема́лый *adj.* no small; considerable.
Не́ман, а *m.* the Niemen (*river*).
неме́дленно *adv.* immediately, forthwith.
неме́дленный *adj.* immediate.
неме́ркнущий *adj.* (*fig., rhet.*) unfading.
неме́тчин|а, ы *f.* (*obs.*) **1.** Germany; foreign parts. **2.** (*pej.*) German (*or* foreign) way of life.
неме́|ть, ю *impf.* (*of* **о~**) **1.** to become dumb, grow dumb. **2.** (*pf. also* **за~**) to become numb, grow numb.
не́м|ец, ца *m.* **1.** German. **2.** (*obs.*) foreigner.
неме́цк|ий *adj.* **1.** German; **~ая овча́рка** Alsatian (dog). **2.** (*obs.*) foreign.
немига́ющий *adj.* unwinking.
немилосе́рд|ный (~ен, ~на) *adj.* merciless, unmerciful (*also fig.*).
неми́лостив|ый (~, ~а) *adj.* ungracious; harsh.
неми́лост|ь, и *f.* disgrace, disfavour; **впасть в н.** to fall into disgrace.
неми́л|ый (~, ~а́, ~о) *adj.* (*folk poet.*) unloved; hated.
немину́ем|ый (~, ~а) *adj.* inevitable, unavoidable.
не́м|ка, ки *f. of* **~ец**
немно́г|ие *adj.* few, a few; *as n.* **н., ~их** few.
немно́го *adv.* **1.** (*+g.*) a little, some, not much; a few, not many; **вре́мени оста́лось н.** little time is left, time is short. **2.** a little, somewhat, slightly; **я н. уста́л** I am a little tired; **н. спустя́** not long after.
немно́г|ое, ого *nt.* few things, little.
немногосло́в|ный (~ен, ~на) *adj.* laconic, brief, terse.
немно́жко *adv.* (*coll.*) a little; a trifle, a bit.
немну́щийся *adj.* (*text.*) non-creasing, crease-resistant; 'non-iron'.

немо́жется (*impers.*, *+d.*; *coll.*): **мне,** *etc.* **н.** I, *etc.*, am unwell, poorly.
нем|о́й (~, ~а́, ~о) *adj.* 1. dumb; **~а́я а́збука** deaf-and-dumb alphabet; *as n.* **н., ~о́го** *m.* mute; **~ы́е** (*collect.*) the dumb. **2.** (*fig.*) dead, silent; **~а́я тишина́** deathly hush. **3.** (*fig.*) mute; **н. согла́сный** (*ling.*) mute consonant; **н. фильм** silent film.
немо́лчный *adj.* (*poet.*) incessant, unceasing.
немот|а́, ы́ *f.* dumbness; muteness.
не́моч|ь, и *f.* (*coll.*) illness, sickness; **бле́дная н.** (*med.*) chlorosis, green sickness; **чёрная н.** (*coll.*, *obs.*) falling sickness (*epilepsy*).
не́мощ|ный (~ен, ~на) *adj.* sick; feeble, sickly.
не́мощ|ь, и *f.* (*coll.*) sickness; feebleness.
нему́ *d. of* **он, оно́** *after preps.*
немудрён|ый (~, ~а́) *adj.* (*coll.*) simple, easy; **э́то де́ло ~ое** it is a simple matter; (*impers.*, *as pred.*): **~о́** it is no wonder.
немы́слим|ый (~, ~а) *adj.* (*coll.*) unthinkable, inconceivable.
ненави́|деть, жу, дишь *impf.* to hate, detest, loathe.
ненави́стник, а *m.* hater.
ненави́ст|ный (~ен, ~на) *adj.* hated; hateful.
не́навист|ь, и *f.* hatred, detestation.
ненагля́дный *adj.* (*coll.*) **1.** beloved. **2.** (*folk poet.*) wondrously beautiful.
ненадёванный *adj.* (*coll.*) new, not yet worn.
ненадёж|ный (~ен, ~на) *adj.* unreliable, untrustworthy; insecure.
нена́добност|ь, и *f.* uselessness; **за ~ью** as not wanted.
ненадо́лго *adv.* for a short while, not for long.
ненаме́ренно *adv.* unintentionally, unwittingly, accidentally.
ненаме́рен|ный (~, ~а) *adj.* unintentional, accidental.
ненападе́ни|е, я *nt.* non-aggression; **пакт о ~и** non-aggression pact.
ненаро́ком *adv.* (*coll.*) unintentionally, accidentally.
ненаруши́м|ый (~, ~а) *adj.* inviolable.
ненаси́л|ие, я *nt.* non-violence.
ненаси́льственный *adj.* non-violent.
нена́ст|ный (~ен, ~на) *adj.* (*of weather*) bad, foul.
ненастоя́щий *adj.* artificial; counterfeit.
нена́сть|е, я *nt.* bad, foul weather.
ненасы́т|ный (~ен, ~на) *adj.* insatiable (*also fig.*).
ненатура́л|ьный (~ен, ~ьна) *adj.* **1.** affected; not natural. **2.** artificial, imitation.
ненау́ч|ный (~ен, ~на) *adj.* unscientific.
ненорма́льност|ь, и *f.* abnormality.
ненорма́л|ьный (~ен, ~ьна) *adj.* **1.** (*in var. senses*) abnormal. **2.** mad.
нену́ж|ный (~ен, ~на́, ~но) *adj.* unnecessary; superfluous; needless.
необду́ман|ный (~, ~на) *adj.* thoughtless, precipitate.
необеспе́ченн|ый *adj.* **1.** without means; unprovided for; **~ая жизнь** precarious existence. **2.** (*+i.*) not provided (with).
необита́ем|ый (~, ~а) *adj.* uninhabited; **н. о́стров** desert island.
необозри́м|ый (~, ~а) *adj.* boundless, immense.
необосно́ванност|ь, и *f.* groundlessness.
необосно́ван|ный (~, ~на) *adj.* unfounded, groundless.
необрабо́тан|ный (~, ~а) *adj.* **1.** (*of land*) uncultivated, untilled. **2.** (*of minerals*) raw, crude. **3.** (*fig.*) unpolished; untrained.
необразо́ванност|ь, и *f.* lack of education.
необразо́ван|ный (~, ~на) *adj.* uneducated.
необрати́м|ый (~, ~а) *adj.* irreversible.
необу́здан|ный (~, ~на) *adj.* unbridled; ungovernable.
необходи́мост|ь, и *f.* necessity; **по ~и** perforce, necessarily; **това́ры пе́рвой ~и** essential goods.
необходи́м|ый (~, ~а) *adj.* necessary, essential; (*impers.*, *as pred.*): **~о** it is necessary *or* imperative.
необщи́тел|ьный (~ен, ~ьна) *adj.* unsociable.
необъясни́м|ый (~, ~а) *adj.* inexplicable, unaccountable.
необъя́т|ный (~ен, ~на) *adj.* immense, unbounded.
необыкнове́н|ный (~ен, ~на) *adj.* unusual, uncommon.
необыча́|йный (~ен, ~йна) *adj.* extraordinary, exceptional.
необы́ч|ный (~ен, ~на) *adj.* unusual; **~ные ви́ды вооруже́ний** unconventional weapons.
необяза́тел|ьный (~, ~на) *adj.* **1.** not obligatory, optional. **2.** unobliging.
неограни́чен|ный (~, ~на) *adj.* unlimited, unbounded; **~ная мона́рхия** absolute monarchy; **~ные полномо́чия** plenary powers.
неоднозна́чн|ый (~ен, ~на) *adj.* **1.** ambiguous, equivocal. **2.** complex, complicated.
неоднокра́тно *adv.* repeatedly.
неоднокра́тный *adj.* repeated.
неоднoро́дност|ь, и *f.* heterogeneity; **н. строе́ния** (*tech.*) non-uniformity of structure.
неоднoро́д|ный (~ен, ~на) *adj.* heterogeneous; dissimilar, not uniform.
неодобре́ни|е, я *nt.* disapproval, disapprobation.
неодобри́тел|ьный (~ен, ~на) *adj.* disapproving.
неодоли́м|ый (~, ~а) *adj.* invincible, insuperable.
неодушевлён|ный (~, ~на) *adj.* inanimate.
неожи́данност|ь, и *f.* **1.** unexpectedness, suddenness. **2.** surprise.
неожи́дан|ный (~, ~на) *adj.* unexpected, sudden.
неозо́йский *adj.* (*geol.*) Neozoic.
неоклассици́зм, а *m.* neoclassicism.
неоконча́тел|ьный (~ен, ~на) *adj.* inconclusive.
неоко́нченный *adj.* unfinished.
неоли́т, а *m.* (*archaeol.*) the neolithic period.
неолити́ческий *adj.* (*archaeol.*) neolithic.
неологи́зм, а *m.* neologism.
нео́н, а *m.* (*chem.*) neon.
нео́н|овый *adj. of* **~; ~овая ла́мпа** neon lamp.
неопа́с|ный (~ен, ~на) *adj.* harmless, not dangerous.
неопера́бельный *adj.* (*med.*) inoperable.
неопери́вшийся *adj.* unfledged; (*fig.*) callow.
неопису́ем|ый (~, ~а) *adj.* indescribable.
неопла́тн|ый *adj.* that cannot be repaid; **н. должни́к** insolvent debtor; **я у вас в ~ом долгу́** (*fig.*) I am eternally indebted to you.
неопо́знан|ный (~, ~а) *adj.* unidentified.
неопра́вданный *adj.* unjustified, unwarranted.
неопределённост|ь, и *f.* vagueness, uncertainty.
неопределён|ный (~ен, ~на) *adj.* **1.** indefinite; **~ное наклоне́ние, ~ная фо́рма глаго́ла** (*gram.*) infinitive; **н. член** (*gram.*) indefinite article. **2.** indeterminate; vague, uncertain; **~ное уравне́ние** (*math.*) indeterminate equation.
неопредели́м|ый (~, ~а) *adj.* indefinable.
неопроверж́им|ый (~, ~а) *adj.* irrefutable.
неопря́тност|ь, и *f.* slovenliness; untidiness, sloppiness.
неопря́т|ный (~ен, ~на) *adj.* slovenly; untidy, sloppy; dirty.
нео́пытност|ь, и *f.* inexperience.
нео́пыт|ный (~ен, ~на) *adj.* inexperienced.
неорганизо́ванност|ь, и *f.* lack of organization; disorganization.
неорганизо́ван|ный (~, ~на) *adj.* unorganized; disorganized.
неоргани́ческий *adj.* inorganic.
неосведомлённый *adj.* ill-informed.
неосе́длый *adj.* nomadic.
неосла́б|ный (~ен, ~на) *adj.* unremitting, unabated.
неосмотри́тельност|ь, и *f.* imprudence; indiscretion.
неосмотри́тел|ьный (~ен, ~ьна) *adj.* imprudent, incautious; indiscreet.
неоснова́тел|ьный (~ен, ~ьна) *adj.* **1.** unfounded, lacking foundation. **2.** (*coll.*) frivolous.
неоспори́мост|ь, и *f.* incontestability, indisputability.
неоспори́м|ый (~, ~а) *adj.* unquestionable, incontestable, indisputable.
неосторо́жност|ь, и *f.* carelessness; imprudence.
неосторо́ж|ный (~ен, ~на) *adj.* careless; imprudent, indiscreet, incautious.
неосуществи́м|ый (~, ~а) *adj.* impracticable, unrealizable.
неосяза́ем|ый (~, ~а) *adj.* impalpable, intangible.
неотврати́мост|ь, и *f.* inevitability.
неотврати́м|ый (~, ~а) *adj.* inevitable.
неотвя́з|ный (~ен, ~на) *adj.* importunate; obsessive.
неотвя́зчив|ый (~, ~а) *adj.* importunate; obsessive.

неотдели́м|ый (~, ~а) *adj.* inseparable.
неотёсан|ный (~, ~на) *adj.* **1.** unpolished. **2.** (*fig.*) uncouth.
не́откуда *adv.* there is nowhere; **мне н. э́то получи́ть** there is nowhere I can get it from.
неотло́жк|а, и *f.* (*coll.*) emergency medical service.
неотло́жност|ь, и *f.* urgency.
неотло́ж|ный (~ен, ~на) *adj.* urgent, pressing; **~ная по́мощь** first aid.
неотлу́чно *adv.* constantly, permanently.
неотлу́ч|ный (~ен, ~на) *adj.* ever-present; permanent.
неотрази́м|ый (~, ~а) *adj.* irresistible (*also fig.*); **~ые до́воды** incontrovertible arguments.
неотсту́пност|ь, и *f.* persistence; importunity.
неотсту́п|ный (~ен, ~на) *adj.* persistent; importunate.
неотчётлив|ый (~, ~а) *adj.* vague, indistinct.
неотчужда́емост|ь, и *f.* (*leg.*) inalienability.
неотчужда́ем|ый (~, ~а) *adj.* (*leg.*) inalienable.
неотъе́млем|ый (~, ~а) *adj.* inalienable; **~ое пра́во** inalienable right, imprescriptible right; **~ая часть** integral part.
неофициа́л|ьный (~ен, ~ьна) *adj.* unofficial.
неохо́т|а, ы *f.* **1.** reluctance. **2.** (*+d.*, *as pred.*): **мне,** *etc.*, **н. идти́** I, *etc.*, have no wish to go.
неохо́тно *adv.* reluctantly; unwillingly.
неоцени́м|ый (~, ~а) *adj.* inestimable, priceless, invaluable.
неощути́м|ый (~, ~а) *adj.* imperceptible.
неощути́тел|ьный (~ен, ~ьна) *adj.* imperceptible, insensible.
Непа́л, а *m.* Nepal.
непа́л|ец, ца *m.* Nepalese.
непа́льский *adj.* Nepalese.
непа́рный *adj.* odd (*not forming a pair*).
неparти́йный *adj.* **1.** non-Party; **н. большеви́к** non-Party Bolshevik (*one, not a member of the CPSU, but acting in its spirit*). **2.** unbefitting a member of the Communist Party.
непереводи́м|ый (~, ~а) *adj.* untranslatable.
непередава́ем|ый (~, ~а) *adj.* inexpressible, indescribable.
неперехо́дный *adj.* (*gram.*) intransitive.
непеча́тный *adj.* (*coll.*) unprintable.
непи́сан|ый *adj.* unwritten; **~ые пра́вила** unwritten rules.
неплатёж, а́ *m.* non-payment.
неплатёжеспосо́бност|ь, и *f.* (*fin.*) insolvency.
неплатёжеспосо́б|ный (~ен, ~на) *adj.* (*fin.*) insolvent.
неплате́льщик, а *m.* defaulter; pers. in arrears with payment (*of taxes, etc.*)
неплодоро́д|ный (~ен, ~на) *adj.* barren, sterile; infertile.
неплодотво́р|ный (~ен, ~на) *adj.* unproductive.
непло́хо *adv.* not badly, quite well.
неплох|о́й (~, ~а́, ~о) *adj.* not bad, quite good.
непобеди́м|ый (~, ~а) *adj.* invincible.
непова́дно *as pred.* (*impers.*, *+d. and inf.*; *coll.*): **что́бы н. бы́ло** to teach (s.o.) not (to do sth. again); **мальчи́шку вы́пороли, что́бы ему́ н. бы́ло кра́сть я́блоки** they gave the boy a thrashing to teach him not to steal apples again.
непови́н|ный (~ен, ~на) *adj.* innocent.
неповинове́ни|е, я *nt.* insubordination, disobedience.
неповоро́тлив|ый (~, ~а) *adj.* clumsy, awkward; sluggish, slow.
неповтори́м|ый (~, ~а) *adj.* unique.
непого́д|а, ы *f.* bad weather.
непогреши́мост|ь, и *f.* infallibility.
непогреши́м|ый (~, ~а) *adj.* infallible.
неподалёку *adv.* not far off.
непода́тлив|ый (~, ~а) *adj.* stubborn, intractable; unyielding, tenacious.
неподатно́й *adj.* exempt from capitation.
неподве́домствен|ный (~, ~на) *adj.* (*+d*) not subject to the authority (of), beyond the jurisdiction (of).
неподви́жност|ь, и *f.* immobility.
неподви́ж|ный (~ен, ~на) *adj.* motionless, immobile, immovable (*also fig.*); fixed, stationary; **~ное лицо́** immobile countenance; **н. загради́тельный ого́нь** (*mil.*) standing barrage.
неподгора́ющ|ий *adj.*: **~ая кастрю́ля** non-stick saucepan.
неподде́льност|ь, и *f.* genuineness; sincerity.
неподде́л|ьный (~ен, ~ьна) *adj.* genuine; unfeigned, sincere.
неподку́пност|ь, и *f.* incorruptibility, integrity.
неподку́п|ный (~ен, ~на) *adj.* incorruptible.
неподоба́ющий *adj.* unseemly, improper.
неподража́ем|ый (~, ~а) *adj.* inimitable.
неподсу́д|ный (~ен, ~на) *adj.* (*+d.*) not under the jurisdiction (of).
неподходя́щий *adj.* unsuitable, inappropriate.
неподчине́ни|е, я *nt.* insubordination; **н. суде́бному постановле́нию** (*leg.*) contempt of court.
непозволи́тел|ьный (~ен, ~ьна) *adj.* inadmissible, impermissible.
непознава́ем|ый (~, ~а) *adj.* (*phil.*) unknowable.
непокла́дист|ый (~, ~а) *adj.* **1.** obstinate, uncompromising. **2.** (*coll.*, *obs.*) clumsy.
непоко́|йный (~ен, ~йна) *adj.* (*coll.*) troubled; restless, disturbed.
непоколеби́м|ый (~, ~а) *adj.* steadfast, unshakeable, inflexible.
непоко́рност|ь, и *f.* recalcitrance; unruliness.
непоко́р|ный (~ен, ~на) *adj.* refractory, recalcitrant; unruly.
непокры́т|ый (~, ~а) *adj.* uncovered, bare.
непола́дк|а, и *f.* **1.** defect, fault. **2.** (*in pl.*) disagreement, quarrel.
неполнопра́вный *adj.* not possessing full rights.
неполнот|а́, ы́ *f.* incompleteness.
неполноце́нност|ь, и *f.* inferiority; **ко́мплекс ~и** inferiority complex; **психи́ческая н.** mental deficiency.
неполноце́н|ный (~ен, ~на) *adj.* inferior; substandard; **у́мственно н.** mentally deficient; **физи́чески н.** physically handicapped.
непо́л|ный (~он, ~на́, ~но) *adj.* not fully; incomplete; defective; **с тех пор прошло́ непо́лных два́дцать лет** since then not quite twenty years had passed; **~ная семья́** single-parent family; **~ное сре́днее образова́ние** incomplete secondary education (*comprising seven years' schooling*); **рабо́тать ~ную неде́лю** to work part-time.
непоме́р|ный (~ен, ~на) *adj.* excessive, inordinate.
непонима́ни|е, я *nt.* incomprehension.
непоня́тливост|ь, и *f.* slowness, dullness.
непоня́тлив|ый (~, ~а) *adj.* slow-witted, stupid, dull.
непоня́т|ный (~ен, ~на) *adj.* unintelligible, incomprehensible; (*impers.*, *as pred*): **~но** it is incomprehensible; **мне ~но, как он мог э́то сде́лать** I cannot understand how he could do it.
непопада́ни|е, я *nt.* miss (*in shooting*).
непоправи́м|ый (~, ~а) *adj.* irreparable, irremediable; irretrievable.
непоро́ч|ный (~ен, ~на) *adj.* pure, chaste; **~ное зача́тие** (*relig.*) the Immaculate Conception (*of the Virgin*).
непоря́д|ок, ка *m.* disorder; violation of order.
непоря́доч|ный (~ен, ~на) *adj.* dishonourable.
непосвящён|ный (~, ~а́) *adj.* uninitiated.
непосе́д|а, ы *c.g.* (*coll.*) fidget; rolling stone.
непосе́дливост|ь, и *f.* restlessness.
непосе́длив|ый (~, ~а) *adj.* fidgety, restless.
непосеще́ни|е, я *nt.* (*+g.*) non-attendance (at).
непоси́л|ьный (~ен, ~ьна) *adj.* beyond one's strength, excessive.
непосле́довательност|ь, и *f.* inconsistency; inconsequence.
непосле́довател|ьный (~ен, ~ьна) *adj.* inconsistent; inconsequent.
непослуша́ни|е, я *nt.* disobedience.
непослу́ш|ный (~ен, ~на) *adj.* disobedient, naughty.
непосре́дственност|ь, и *f.* spontaneity; ingenuousness.
непосре́дствен|ный (~, ~на) *adj.* **1.** immediate, direct. **2.** (*fig.*) direct; spontaneous, ingenuous.
непостижи́м|ый (~, ~а) *adj.* incomprehensible, inscrutable; **уму́ ~о** it passes understanding.
непостоя́н|ный (~ен, ~на) *adj.* inconstant, changeable.
непостоя́нств|о, а *nt.* inconstancy.
непоти́зм, а *m.* nepotism.
непотопля́ем|ый (~, ~а) *adj.* unsinkable.

непотре́б|ный (~ен, ~на) *adj.* (*obs.*) obscene, indecent; **~ные слова́** obscenities.
непотре́бств|о, а *nt.* (*obs.*) obscenity; indecent conduct.
непоча́тый *adj.* (*coll.*) untouched, not begun, entire; **н. край (*or* у́гол)** (+*g.*) a wealth (of), a whole host (of).
непочте́ни|е, я *nt.* disrespect.
непочти́тел|ьный (~ен, ~ьна) *adj.* disrespectful.
непра́вд|а, ы *f.* untruth, falsehood, lie; **все́ми пра́вдами и ~ами** by fair means or foul; by hook or by crook.
неправдоподо́би|е, я *nt.* improbability, unlikelihood.
неправдоподо́б|ный (~ен, ~на) *adj.* improbable, unlikely; implausible.
непра́вед|ный (~ен, ~на) *adj.* (*obs.*) iniquitous, unjust.
непра́вильно *adv.* **1.** irregularly. **2.** incorrectly, erroneously; *in conjunction with vv. frequently* = mis-; *e.g.*, **н. истолкова́ть** to misinterpret.
непра́вильност|ь, и *f.* **1.** irregularity; anomaly. **2.** incorrectness.
непра́вил|ьный (~ен, ~ьна) *adj.* **1.** irregular; anomalous; **н. глаго́л** irregular verb; **~ьная дробь** (*math.*) improper fraction; **~ьные черты́ лица́** irregular features. **2.** incorrect, erroneous, wrong, mistaken; **н. подхо́д (к де́лу)** wrong approach, wrong attitude.
неправоме́рност|ь, и *f.* illegality.
неправоме́р|ный (~ен, ~на) *adj.* illegal.
неправомо́чност|ь, и *f.* (*leg.*) incompetence.
неправомо́ч|ный (~ен, ~на) *adj.* (*leg.*) not competent; not entitled.
неправоспосо́бност|ь, и *f.* (*leg.*) disability, disqualification; incapacity.
неправоспосо́б|ный (~ен, ~на) *adj.* (*leg.*) disqualified.
неправот|а́, ы́ *f.* **1.** error. **2.** wrongness; injustice.
непра́в|ый (~, ~а́, ~о) *adj.* **1.** wrong, mistaken. **2.** unjust.
непревзойдённый *adj.* unsurpassed; matchless.
непредви́денный *adj.* unforeseen.
непреднаме́рен|ный (~, ~на) *adj.* unpremeditated.
непредубеждённый *adj.* unprejudiced, unbiased.
непредумы́шленный *adj.* unpremeditated.
непредусмотри́тельност|ь, и *f.* improvidence, short-sightedness.
непредусмотри́тел|ьный (~ен, ~ьна) *adj.* improvident, short-sighted.
непреклóнност|ь, и *f.* inflexibility; inexorability.
непреклóн|ный (~ен, ~на) *adj.* inflexible, unbending; inexorable, adamant.
непрелóж|ный (~ен, ~на) *adj.* **1.** immutable, unalterable. **2.** indisputable.
непреме́нно *adv.* **1.** without fail; certainly; **они́ н. приду́т за́втра** they are sure to come tomorrow. **2.** absolutely; **мне н. ну́жно поговори́ть с ним** it is absolutely essential that I speak to him.
непреме́н|ный (~ен, ~на) *adj.* indispensable; **н. секрета́рь** permanent secretary.
непреобори́м|ый (~, ~а) *adj.* insuperable; irresistible.
непреодоли́м|ый (~, ~а) *adj.* insuperable, insurmountable; irresistible; **~ая си́ла** (*leg.*) force majeure.
непререка́ем|ый (~, ~а) *adj.* unquestionable, indisputable; **н. тон** peremptory tone.
непреры́вно *adv.* uninterruptedly, continuously.
непреры́вност|ь, и *f.* continuity.
непреры́в|ный (~ен, ~на) *adj.* uninterrupted, unbroken; continuous; **~ная дробь** (*math.*) continued fraction; **н. лист** through plate (*in ship-building*); **~ная па́луба** (*naut.*) flush deck; **н. сварно́й шов** (*tech.*) line welding, continuous weld.
непреста́нно *adv.* incessantly, continually.
непреста́н|ный (~ен, ~на) *adj.* incessant, continual.
неприве́тлив|ый (~, ~а) *adj.* unfriendly, ungracious; bleak.
непривы́чк|а, и *f.* want of habit; **с ~и он бы́стро захмеле́л** being unaccustomed to strong drink, he quickly became drunk.
непривы́ч|ный (~ен, ~на) *adj.* unaccustomed, unwonted; unusual.
непригля́д|ный (~ен, ~на) *adj.* unattractive, unsightly.
непригóд|ный (~ен, ~на) *adj.* unfit, useless; unserviceable; ineligible.
неприе́млем|ый (~, ~а) *adj.* unacceptable.
непри́знанный *adj.* unrecognized, unacknowledged.
неприкаса́ем|ый, ого *m.* untouchable, Harijan.
неприка́янный *adj.* (*coll.*) restless, unable to find anything to do; **ходи́ть, броди́ть,** *etc.*, **как н.** to go about, wander about, *etc.*, like a lost soul.
неприкоснове́нност|ь, и *f.* inviolability; **дипломати́ческая н.** diplomatic immunity.
неприкоснове́н|ный (~ен, ~на) *adj.* inviolable; **н. запа́с** (*mil.*) emergency ration, iron ration; **н. капита́л** reserve capital.
неприкра́шенный *adj.* plain, unvarnished.
неприкры́т|ый *adj.* undisguised; **~ая ложь** barefaced lie.
неприли́чи|е, я *nt.* indecency, impropriety, unseemliness.
неприли́ч|ный (~ен, ~на) *adj.* indecent, improper; unseemly, unbecoming.
непримени́м|ый (~, ~а) *adj.* inapplicable.
неприме́т|ный (~ен, ~на) *adj.* **1.** imperceptible. **2.** (*fig.*) unremarkable, undistinguished.
непримири́мост|ь, и *f.* irreconcilability; intransigence.
непримири́м|ый (~, ~а) *adj.* irreconcilable; intransigent, uncompromising.
непринуждённост|ь, и *f.* unconstraint; naturalness, ease.
непринуждён|ный (~, ~на) *adj.* unconstrained; natural, relaxed, easy; spontaneous; laid-back.
неприсоедине́ни|е, я *nt.*: **поли́тика ~я** (*pol.*) policy of non-alignment.
неприсоедини́вш|ийся *adj.*: **~иеся стра́ны** non-aligned countries.
неприспосо́блен|ный (~, ~на) *adj.* **(к)** unadapted (to); maladjusted.
непристо́йност|ь, и *f.* obscenity; indecency.
непристо́|йный (~ен, ~йна) *adj.* obscene; indecent.
непристу́п|ный (~ен, ~на) *adj.* **1.** inaccessible; unassailable, impregnable. **2.** (*fig.*) inaccessible, unapproachable.
непрису́тственный *adj.* (*obs.*): **н. день** public holiday.
непритво́р|ный (~ен, ~на) *adj.* unfeigned, genuine.
неприхотли́вост|ь, и *f.* **1.** unpretentiousness; modesty. **2.** simplicity, plainness.
неприхотли́в|ый (~, ~а) *adj.* **1.** unpretentious; modest, undemanding. **2.** simple, plain; **~ая пи́ща** frugal meal.
неприча́ст|ный (~ен, ~на) *adj.* **(к)** not implicated (in), not privy (to).
неприя́знен|ный (~, ~на) *adj.* hostile, inimical.
неприя́зн|ь, и *f.* hostility, enmity.
неприя́тел|ь, я *m.* enemy; (*mil.*) the enemy.
неприя́тельский *adj.* hostile; (*mil.*) enemy
неприя́тност|ь, и *f.* unpleasantness; nuisance, annoyance, trouble.
неприя́т|ный (~ен, ~на) *adj.* unpleasant, disagreeable; annoying, troublesome.
непробу́дный *adj.* from which there is no waking; **н. сон** deep sleep; **н. пья́ница** inveterate drunkard.
непроводни́к, а́ *m.* (*phys.*) non-conductor, dielectric.
непрогля́д|ный (~ен, ~на) *adj.* (*of darkness, fog. etc.*) impenetrable; pitch-dark.
непродолжи́тел|ьный (~ен, ~ьна) *adj.* of short duration, short-lived; **в ~ьном вре́мени** shortly, in a short time.
непродукти́в|ный (~ен, ~на) *adj.* unproductive.
непрое́зжий *adj.* impassable.
непрозра́чност|ь, и *f.* opacity.
непрозра́ч|ный (~ен, ~на) *adj.* opaque.
непроизводи́тел|ьный (~ен, ~ьна) *adj.* unproductive; wasteful.
непроизво́л|ьный (~ен, ~ьна) *adj.* involuntary.
непрола́з|ный (~ен, ~на) *adj.* (*coll.*) impassable.
непромока́ем|ый (~, ~а) *adj.* waterproof; **н. плащ** mackintosh, waterproof (coat), raincoat.
непроница́емост|ь, и *f.* impenetrability; impermeability.
непроница́ем|ый (~, ~а) *adj.* **1.** impenetrable, impermeable; **(для)** impervious (to); **н. для зву́ка** sound-proof. **2.** inscrutable, impassive.
непропорциона́льност|ь, и *f.* disproportion.

непропорциона́л|ьный (~ен, ~ьна) *adj.* disproportionate.
непрости́тел|ьный (~ен, ~ьна) *adj.* unforgivable, unpardonable, inexcusable.
непротивле́ни|е, я *nt.* non-resistance.
непроходи́мо *adv.* (*coll.*) utterly, hopelessly.
непроходи́м|ый (~, ~а) *adj.* **1.** impassable. **2.** (*fig., coll.*) complete, utter; **н. дура́к** utter fool.
непро́ч|ный (~ен, ~на) *adj.* fragile, flimsy; (*fig.*) precarious, unstable.
непро́шеный *adj.* (*coll.*) unbidden, uninvited; **непро́шеное одолже́ние** an unsolicited service.
непрям|о́й (~́, ~а́, ~́о) *adj.* **1.** indirect; circuitous. **2.** (*fig., coll.*) evasive.
непутёвый *adj.* (*coll.*) good-for-nothing, useless.
непутём *adv.* (*coll.*) badly; **де́лать всё н.** to make a mess of everything.
непью́щий *adj.* non-drinking; temperate, abstemious (*in relation to alcoholic liquor*).
неработоспосо́б|ный (~ен, ~на) *adj.* unable to work, disabled.
нерабо́ч|ий *adj.* non-working; **~ее вре́мя** time off, free time.
нера́венств|о, а *nt.* inequality, disparity.
неравно́ *particle expr. anticipation of disagreeable eventuality* (*coll.*); **н. опозда́ем** suppose we are late; **н. он зайдёт, а нас до́ма не бу́дет** what if he comes while we are out.
неравноду́ш|ный (~ен, ~на) *adj.* **(к)** not indifferent (to).
неравноме́р|ный (~ен, ~на) *adj.* uneven, irregular.
неравнопра́в|ный (~ен, ~на) *adj.* not enjoying equal rights.
нера́в|ный (~ен, ~на́, ~но) *adj.* unequal.
нераде́ни|е, я *nt.* (*obs.*) = **нера́ди́вость**
нера́ди́вост|ь, и *f.* negligence, carelessness, remissness.
нера́ди́в|ый (~, ~а) *adj.* negligent, careless, remiss.
неразбери́х|а, и *f.* (*coll.*) muddle, confusion.
неразбо́рчив|ый (~, ~а) *adj.* **1.** illegible, indecipherable. **2.** (*fig.*) undiscriminating; not fastidious; **н. в сре́дствах** unscrupulous; **сексуа́льно н.** promiscuous.
неразвит|о́й (нера́звит, ~а́, ~о) *adj.* undeveloped; (intellectually) backward.
нера́звитост|ь, и *f.* lack of development; **у́мственная н.** backwardness.
неразга́данн|ый *adj.* unsolved; **~ая та́йна** unresolved mystery.
неразгово́рчив|ый (~, ~а) *adj.* taciturn, not talkative.
неразделённ|ый *adj.*: **~ая любо́вь** unrequited love.
неразделим|ый (~, ~а) *adj.* indivisible, inseparable.
неразде́л|ьный (~ен, ~ьна) *adj.* indivisible, inseparable; **~ьное иму́щество** (*leg.*) common estate.
неразличи́м|ый (~, ~а) *adj.* indistinguishable; indiscernible.
неразлу́ч|ный (~ен, ~на) *adj.* inseparable.
неразрешённый *adj* **1.** unsolved. **2.** prohibited, banned.
неразреши́м|ый (~, ~а) *adj.* insoluble.
неразры́в|ный (~ен, ~на) *adj.* indissoluble.
неразу́ми|е, я *nt.* (*obs.*) folly, foolishness.
неразу́м|ный (~ен, ~на) *adj.* unreasonable; unwise; foolish.
нераска́янный *adj.* unrepentant.
нерасположе́ни|е, я *nt.* **(к)** dislike (for), disinclination (for, to).
нерасполо́женный *adj.* **(к)** ill-disposed (towards); unwilling (to), disinclined (to).
нераспоряди́тел|ьный (~ен, ~ьна) *adj.* inefficient, unauthoritative.
нераспростране́ни|е, я *nt.* non-proliferation (*esp. of nuclear weapons*).
нерассуди́тельност|ь, и *f.* lack of common sense, want of sense.
нерассуди́тел|ьный (~ен, ~ьна) *adj.* unreasoning; lacking common sense.
нерастворим|ый (~, ~а) *adj.* insoluble.
нерасторжи́м|ый (~, ~а) *adj.* indissoluble.
нерасторо́п|ный (~ен, ~на) *adj.* sluggish, slow.
нерасчётливост|ь, и *f.* **1.** extravagance, wastefulness. **2.** improvidence.
нерасчётлив|ый (~, ~а) *adj.* **1.** extravagant, wasteful. **2.** improvident.
нерациона́л|ьный (~ен, ~ьна) *adj.* irrational.
нерв, а *m.* (*anat. and fig.*) nerve; **гла́вный н.** (*fig.*) nerve-centre; **де́йствовать кому́-н. на ~́ы** to get on s.o.'s nerves.
нерва́ци|я, и *f.* (*bot.*) nervation.
нерви́р|овать, ую *impf.* to get on s.o.'s nerves, irritate.
нерви́ческий *adj.* (*obs.*) nervous.
не́рвнича|ть, ю *impf.* to be *or* become fidgety, fret, be *or* become irritable.
нервнобольн|о́й, о́го *m.* nervous case, pers. suffering from nervous disorder.
не́рвно-паралити́ческ|ий *adj.* (*mil.*): **ОВ ~ого ти́па** nerve gas.
не́рвност|ь, и *f.* irritability, edginess.
не́рв|ный (~ен, ~на́, ~но) *adj.* **1.** (*in var. senses*) nervous; neural; **~ное волокно́** nerve-fibre; **н. припа́док** fit of nerves; **~ная систе́ма** the nervous system; **н. у́зел** (*anat.*) ganglion; **н. центр** nerve-centre. **2.** irritable, highly strung.
нерво́з|ный (~ен, ~на) *adj.* nervy, irritable.
нервотрёпк|а, и *f.* (*coll.*) rigmarole, hassle.
нервю́р|а, ы *f.* (*aeron.*) rib; **н. крыла́** wing-rib.
нереа́л|ьный (~ен, ~ьна) *adj.* **1.** unreal. **2.** impracticable.
нерегуля́р|ный (~ен, ~на) *adj.* irregular (*also mil.*).
нере́д|кий (~ок, ~ка́, ~ко) *adj.* not infrequent; not uncommon.
нере́дко *adv.* not infrequently, quite often.
не́рест, а *m.* (*zool.*) spawning.
нерести́лищ|е, а *nt.* spawning-ground.
нереши́мост|ь, и *f.* indecision.
нереши́тельност|ь, и *f.* indecision; indecisiveness; **быть в ~и** to be undecided.
нереши́тел|ьный (~ен, ~ьна) *adj.* indecisive, irresolute.
нержаве́йк|а, и *f.* (*coll.*) stainless steel.
нержаве́ющ|ий *adj.* non-rusting; **~ая сталь** stainless steel.
неро́б|кий (~ок, ~ка́, ~ко) *adj.* not timid; **он челове́к ~кого деся́тка** he is no coward.
неро́вност|ь, и *f.* **1.** unevenness, roughness. **2.** inequality; irregularity.
неро́в|ный (~ен, ~на́, ~но) *adj.* **1.** uneven, rough; **н. грунт** rough country. **2.** unequal; irregular; **н. пульс** irregular pulse; **~ён час** (*coll., obs., now* = **не ро́вен час**) who knows what may happen; one never knows.
неро́вн|я, и (*and* **неровн|я́, и́**) *c.g.* (*coll.*): **он её н.** he is not her equal.
не́рп|а, ы *f.* (*zool.*) ringed seal.
неру́дный *adj.* (*tech.*) non-metallic.
нерукотво́рный *adj.* (*relig. and poet.*) not made by hands.
неруши́м|ый (~, ~а) *adj.* inviolable, indissoluble.
неря́х|а, и *c.g.* sloven; (*coll.*) scruff; (*used of woman only*) slattern.
неря́шеств|о, а *nt.* = **неря́шливость**
неря́шливост|ь, и *f.* slovenliness, untidiness; (*coll.*) scruffiness; (*used of woman only*) sluttishness.
неря́шлив|ый (~, ~а) *adj.* **1.** slovenly, untidy; (*coll.*) scruffy; (*used of woman only*) sluttish. **2.** careless, slipshod.
несваре́ни|е, я *nt. only in phr.* **н. желу́дка** indigestion.
несве́дущ|ий (~, ~а) *adj.* **(в+***p.***)** ignorant (about), not well-informed (about).
несве́ж|ий (~, ~а́, ~е) *adj.* **1.** not fresh, stale; tainted. **2.** (*fig.*) weary, wan.
несвобо́дн|ый *adj.*: **~ое сочета́ние** (*ling.*) set phrase.
несвоевре́мен|ный (~ен, ~на) *adj.* inopportune, untimely, unseasonable.
несво́йствен|ный (~ен, ~на) *adj.* not characteristic; **э́то ему́ ~но** it is not like him.
несвя́з|ный (~ен, ~на) *adj.* disconnected, incoherent.
несгиба́емый *adj.* unbending, inflexible.
несгово́рчив|ый (~, ~а) *adj.* intractable.
несгора́емый *adj.* fire-proof, incombustible; **н. шкаф** safe.
несде́ржанный *adj.* unrestrained.
несе́ни|е, я *nt.* performance, execution.
несессе́р, а *m.* toilet-case.
несжима́ем|ый (~, ~а) *adj.* incompressible.

несказа́нный *adj.* unspeakable, ineffable.
нескла́дица|а, ы *f.* (*coll.*) nonsense.
нескла́д|ный (~ен, ~на) *adj.* **1.** incoherent. **2.** ungainly, awkward. **3.** absurd.
несклоня́ем|ый (~, ~а) *adj.* (*gram.*) indeclinable.
не́скольк|о[1], **их** *num.* some, several; a few; **в ~их слова́х** in a few words; **н. челове́к** several people.
не́сколько[2] *adv.* somewhat, rather, slightly; **они́ н. разочаро́ваны** they are rather disillusioned.
нескончáем|ый (~, ~а) *adj.* interminable, never-ending.
нескро́мност|ь, и *f.* **1.** immodesty, lack of modesty. **2.** indelicacy; indiscretion. **3.** indiscreetness.
нескро́м|ный (~ен, ~нá, ~но) *adj.* **1.** immodest; vain. **2.** indiscreet.
несло́ж|ный (~ен, ~нá, ~но) *adj.* simple, uncomplicated.
несльíхан|ный (~, ~на) *adj.* unheard-of, unprecedented.
несльíш|ный (~ен, ~на) *adj.* inaudible.
несменя́емост|ь, и *f.* irremovability (from office).
несменя́ем|ый (~, ~а) *adj.* irremovable.
несме́т|ный (~ен, ~на) *adj.* countless, incalculable, innumerable.
несмолкáем|ый (~, ~а) *adj.* ceaseless, unremitting, never-abating.
несмотря́ *prep.* (**на**+*a.*) in spite of, despite; notwithstanding; **н. ни на что** in spite of everything.
несмывáем|ый (~, ~а) *adj.* indelible, ineffaceable.
несно́с|ный (~ен, ~на) *adj.* intolerable, insupportable.
несоблюде́ни|е, я *nt.* non-observance.
несовершеннолéти|е, я *nt.* minority.
несовершеннолéтн|ий *adj.* under-age; *as n.* **н., ~его** *m.* minor.
несоверше́н|ный (~ен, ~на) *adj.* **1.** imperfect, incomplete. **2.** (*gram.*) imperfective.
несовмести́м|ый (~, ~а) *adj.* incompatible.
несогла́си|е, я *nt.* **1.** disagreement; **н. в мне́ниях** difference of opinion; **н. ме́жду двумя́ ве́рсиями** discrepancy between two versions. **2.** discord, variance. **3.** (*sg. only*) refusal.
несогла́с|ный (~ен, ~на) *adj.* **1.** (**с**+*i.*) not agreeing (with) **2.** (**с**+*i.*) inconsistent (with), incompatible (with). **3.** (**на**+*a.* *or* +*inf.*) not consenting (to), not agreeing (to); **я на э́то ~ен** I cannot agree to this. **4.** discordant.
несогласовáни|е, я *nt.* (*gram.*) non-agreement.
несогласо́ванност|ь, и *f.* lack of co-ordination, non-coordination.
несогласо́ванный *adj.* uncoordinated, not concerted.
несозву́ч|ный (~ен, ~на) *adj.* (+*d.*) dissonant; inconsonant (with).
несознáтельност|ь, и *f.* thoughtlessness; irresponsibility; (*political*) backwardness.
несознáтел|ьный (~ен, ~ьна) *adj.* **1.** irresponsible. **2.** unconscious of social obligations.
несоизмери́мост|ь, и *f.* incommensurability.
несоизмери́м|ый (~, ~а) *adj.* incommensurable, incommensurate.
несократи́мый *adj.* (*math.*) irreducible.
несокруши́м|ый (~, ~а) *adj.* indestructible; unconquerable.
несоли́д|ный (~ен, ~на) *adj.* not impressive, unimpressive, light-weight.
несо́лоно *adv. only in phr.* (*coll.*): **уйти́ н. хлебáвши** to get nothing for one's pains, go away empty-handed.
несомне́нно *adv.* undoubtedly, doubtless.
несомне́н|ный (~ен, ~на) *adj.* undoubted, indubitable, unquestionable.
несообрази́тел|ьный (~ен, ~ьна) *adj.* slow(-witted).
несообрáзност|ь, и *f.* **1.** incongruity, incompatibility. **2.** absurdity.
несообрáз|ный (~ен, ~на) *adj.* **1.** (**с**+*i.*) incongruous (with), incompatible (with). **2.** absurd.
несоответ́ствен|ный (~, ~на) *adj.* (+*d.*) incongruous (with), not corresponding (to).
несоответ́стви|е, я *nt.* lack of correspondence, disparity.
несоразме́рност|ь, и *f.* disproportion.
несоразме́р|ный (~ен, ~на) *adj.* disproportionate.
несосве́тимый = несусве́тный
несостоя́тельност|ь, и *f.* **1.** insolvency, bankruptcy. **2.** modest means. **3.** groundlessness.
несостоя́тел|ьный (~ен, ~ьна) *adj.* **1.** insolvent, bankrupt. **2.** of modest means. **3.** groundless, unsupported.
неспе́л|ый (~, ~á, ~о) *adj.* unripe.
неспе́ш|ный (~ен, ~на) *adj.* unhurried.
неспоДру́ч|ный (~ен, ~на) *adj.* (*coll.*) inconvenient, awkward.
неспоко́|йный (~ен, ~йна) *adj.* restless; uneasy.
неспосо́бност|ь, и *f.* incapacity, inability.
неспосо́б|ный (~ен, ~на) *adj.* dull, not able; (**к**+*d.*, **на**+*a.*) incapable (of); **онá ~на к му́зыке** she has no aptitude for music; **н. на ложь** incapable of a lie.
несправедли́вост|ь, и *f.* injustice, unfairness.
несправедли́в|ый (~, ~а) *adj.* **1.** unjust, unfair. **2.** incorrect, unfounded.
неспровоци́рованный *adj.* unprovoked.
неспростá *adv.* (*coll.*) not without purpose; with an ulterior motive.
несравне́нно *adv.* **1.** incomparably, matchlessly. **2.** far, by far; **н. лу́чше** far better.
несравне́н|ный (~ен, ~на) *adj.* incomparable, matchless.
несравни́м|ый (~, ~а) *adj.* **1.** incomparable; unmatched. **2.** not comparable.
нестерпи́м|ый (~, ~а) *adj.* unbearable, unendurable.
нес|ти́[1], **у́, ёшь,** *past* **≈, ~лá** *impf.* (*of* **по~**), *det.* **1.** to carry. **2.** to bear; to support. **3.** (*fig.*) to bear; to suffer; to incur; **н. убы́тки** (*fin.*) to incur losses. **4.** to perform; **н. дежу́рство** to be on duty. **5.** (*fig.*) to bear, bring; **н. ги́бель** to bring destruction. **6.** (*impers.*, *coll.*): **куда́ вас ~ёт?** wherever are you going? **7.** (*impers.*, *coll.*; +*i.*) to stink (of), reek (of); **от него́ ~ёт чесноко́м** he reeks of garlic. **8.** (*impers.*, *coll.*): **его́,** *etc.*, **~ёт** he has, *etc.*, diarrhoea. **9.** (*coll.*) (**вздор, чепуху́,** *etc.*) to talk (nonsense).
нес|ти́[2], **ёт,** *past* **≈, ~лá** *impf.* (*of* **с~**) to lay (*eggs*).
нес|ти́сь[1], **у́сь, ёшься,** *past* **≈ся, ~ла́сь** *impf.* (*of* **по~**), *det.* **1.** to rush, tear, fly; (*on water, in the air*) to float, drift; (**по**+*d.*, **вдоль; над**) to skim (along; over). **2.** (*of sounds, smells, etc.*) to spread, be diffused.
нес|ти́сь[2], **ётся,** *past* **≈ся, ~ла́сь** *impf.* (*of* **с~**) to lay (eggs) (*intrans.*).
несто́йкий *adj.* (*chem.*) unstable, non-persistent.
несто́ящий *adj.* (*coll.*) worthless, good-for-nothing.
нестроеви́к, á *m.* (*mil.*) non-combatant.
нестроево́й[1] *adj.* unfit for building purposes.
нестроево́й[2] *adj.* (*mil.*) non-combatant, administrative.
нестро́|йный (~ен, ~йнá, ~йно) *adj.* **1.** clumsily built. **2.** discordant, dissonant. **3.** disorderly.
несть (*obs.*) there is not.
несу́н, а *m.* (*coll.*) pilferer.
несурáзност|ь, и *f.* **1.** absurdity, senselessness. **2.** awkwardness.
несурáз|ный (~ен, ~на) *adj.* **1.** absurd, senseless. **2.** awkward.
несусве́т|ный (~ен, ~на) *adj.* (*coll.*) extreme, utter; unimaginable; **~ная чепухá** utter nonsense.
несу́шк|а, и *f.* (*coll.*) laying hen, hen in lay.
несуще́ствен|ный (~, ~на) *adj.* inessential, immaterial.
несу́щ|ий *pres. part. act. of* **нести́** *and adj.* (*tech.*) carrying; supporting; **н. винт** rotor (*of helicopter*); **~ая пове́рхность** lifting surface; (*aeron.*) airfoil.
несхо́д|ный (~ен, ~на) *adj.* **1.** unlike, dissimilar. **2.** (*coll.*; *of price*) unreasonable.
несчастли́в|ец, ца *m.* unlucky pers., an unfortunate.
несчастли́в|ый (~, ~а) *adj.* **1.** unfortunate, luckless. **2.** unhappy.
несчáст|ный (~ен, ~на) *adj.* **1.** unhappy; unfortunate, unlucky; **н. слу́чай** accident. **2.** *as n.* **н., ~ного** *m.* wretch; an unfortunate.
несчáсть|е, я *nt.* **1.** misfortune; **к ~ю** unfortunately. **2.** accident.
несчёт|ный (~ен, ~на) *adj.* innumerable, countless.
несъедо́бный *adj.* **1.** uneatable. **2.** inedible; **н. гриб** toadstool.
нет[1] **1.** no; not; **вы его́ ви́дели? н.** you saw him? — No; **вы не ви́дели его́? н., ви́дел** you didn't see him? Yes, I did; **н. да н., н. как н.** (*coll.*; *emph.*) absolutely not,

absolutely nothing; **н.-н. да и взгля́нет на меня́** he glanced at me from time to time. **2.** nothing, naught; **свести́ на н.** to bring to naught; **свести́сь (сойти́) на н.** to come to naught; *as n.* **н.**, **~а** *m.*; **на н. и суда́ н.** (*prov.*) what cannot be cured must be endured; **пироги́ с ~ом** (*joc.*) pie without filling; **быть в ~ях (в ~ех)** (*obs. or joc.*) to be missing, be adrift.

нет² (*+g.*) (there) is not, (there) are not; **здесь н. собо́ра** there is not a cathedral here; **у меня́ н. вре́мени** I have no time.

нетакти́ч|ный (~ен, ~на) *adj.* tactless.

нетвёрдо *adv.* **1.** unsteadily, not firmly. **2.** not definitely; **знать н.** to have a shaky knowledge of; **я н. уве́рен** I am not quite sure.

нетвёрд|ый (~, ~а́, ~о) *adj.* unsteady; shaky (*also fig.*).

не́тел|ь, и *f.* heifer.

нетерпёж, а́ *m.* (*coll.*) impatience.

нетерпели́в|ый (~, ~а) *adj.* impatient.

нетерпе́ни|е, я *nt.* impatience.

нетерпи́мост|ь, и *f.* intolerance.

нетерпи́м|ый (~, ~а) *adj.* **1.** intolerable. **2.** intolerant.

нетле́н|ный (~ен, ~на) *adj.* imperishable.

нетопы́р|ь, я́ *m.* (*zool.*) bat.

неторопли́в|ый (~, ~а) *adj.* leisurely, unhurried.

нето́чност|ь, и *f.* **1.** inaccuracy, inexactitude. **2.** error, slip.

нето́ч|ный (~ен, ~на́, ~но) *adj.* inaccurate, inexact.

нетрадицио́н|ный (~ен, ~на) *adj.* unconventional.

нетре́бовател|ьный (~ен, ~ьна) *adj.* not exacting, undemanding; unpretentious.

нетре́зв|ый (~, ~а́, ~о) *adj.* not sober, drunk; **в ~ом ви́де** in a state of intoxication.

нетро́нут|ый (~, ~а) *adj.* untouched; (*fig.*) chaste, virginal.

нетрудово́й *adj.* **1.** not derived from labour; **н. дохо́д** unearned income. **2.** not engaged in labour.

нетрудоспосо́бност|ь, и *f.* disablement, disability; incapacity for work.

нетрудоспосо́б|ный (~ен, ~на) *adj.* disabled; invalid.

не́тто *adj. indecl.* (*comm.*) net.

не́ту (*coll.*) = **нет**²

не́тях *see* **нет**¹

неубеди́тел|ьный (~ен, ~ьна) *adj.* unconvincing.

не́убранный *adj.* **1.** untidy. **2.** unharvested.

неуваже́ни|е, я *nt.* disrespect, lack of respect; (*leg.*) **н. к суду́** contempt of court.

неуважи́тел|ьный (~ен, ~ьна) *adj.* **1.** (*of cause, ground, etc.*) inadequate; not acceptable. **2.** (*obs.*) disrespectful.

неуве́ренност|ь, и *f.* uncertainty; **н. в себе́** diffidence.

неуве́рен|ный *adj.* **1.** (**~, ~а**) uncertain; **н. в себе́** diffident. **2.** (**~, ~на**) hesitating; vacillating.

неувяда́|емый (~ем, ~ема) *adj.* = **~ющий**

неувяда́ющий *adj.* (*rhet.*) unfading, everlasting.

неувя́зк|а, и *f.* (*coll.*) lack of co-ordination; misunderstanding.

неугаси́м|ый (~, ~а) *adj.* inextinguishable, unquenchable (*also fig.*).

неугомо́н|ный (~ен, ~на) *adj.* (*coll.*) indefatigable, irrepressible.

неуда́ч|а, и *f.* failure.

неуда́члив|ый (~, ~а) *adj.* unlucky.

неуда́чник, а *m.* unlucky pers., failure.

неуда́ч|ный (~ен, ~на) *adj.* unsuccessful; unfortunate; **~ное выраже́ние** unfortunate expression; **~ное нача́ло** bad start.

неудержи́м|ый (~, ~а) *adj.* irrepressible.

неудо́б|ный (~ен, ~на) *adj.* **1.** uncomfortable. **2.** (*fig.*) inconvenient; awkward; embarrassing.

неудобовари́м|ый (~, ~а) *adj.* indigestible (*also fig.*).

неудобопоня́т|ный (~ен, ~на) *adj.* unintelligible, obscure.

неудобопроизноси́м|ый (~, ~а) *adj.* **1.** unpronounceable. **2.** (*joc.*) unrepeatable (= *obscene*), risqué.

неудобочита́емый *adj.* difficult to read, obscure.

неудо́бств|о, а *nt.* **1.** discomfort; inconvenience. **2.** embarrassment.

неудо́бь *adv. now only in phr.* **н. сказу́емый** risqué.

неудовлетворе́ни|е, я *nt.* **1.** non-compliance; **н. жа́лобы** rejection of a complaint, failure to act on a complaint. **2.** dissatisfaction.

неудовлетворённост|ь, и *f.* dissatisfaction, discontent.

неудовлетворён|ный *adj.* **1.** (**~, ~на**) dissatisfied, discontented. **2.** (**~, ~а́**) unsatisfied.

неудовлетвори́тел|ьный (~ен, ~ьна) *adj.* unsatisfactory.

неудово́льстви|е, я *nt.* displeasure.

неуём|ный (~ен, ~на) *adj.* (*coll.*) irrepressible; **~ная печа́ль** uncontrollable grief.

неуже́ли *interrog. particle* really? is it possible?; **н. он так ду́мает?** does he really think that?; **н. ты не знал, что мы здесь?** did you really not know that we were here? surely you knew that we were here?

неужи́вчивост|ь, и *f.* unaccommodating nature; quarrelsome disposition.

неужи́вчив|ый (~, ~а) *adj.* unaccommodating, difficult (to get on with); quarrelsome.

неу́жто *interrog. particle* (*coll.*) = **неуже́ли**

неузнава́емост|ь, и *f.* unrecognizability; **он похуде́л до ~и** he has become so thin that you would not recognize him.

неузнава́ем|ый (~, ~а) *adj.* unrecognizable.

неукло́н|ный (~ен, ~на) *adj.* steady, steadfast; undeviating.

неуклю́жест|ь, и *f.* clumsiness, awkwardness.

неуклю́ж|ий (~, ~а, ~е) *adj.* clumsy; awkward.

неукосни́тел|ьный (~ен, ~ьна) *adj.* strict, rigorous.

неукроти́м|ый (~, ~а) *adj.* indomitable.

неулови́м|ый (~, ~а) *adj.* **1.** elusive, difficult to catch. **2.** (*fig.*) imperceptible.

неуме́л|ый (~, ~а) *adj.* clumsy; unskilful.

неуме́ни|е, я *nt.* inability; lack of skill.

неуме́ренност|ь, и *f.* **1.** immoderation. **2.** intemperance.

неуме́рен|ный (~, ~на) *adj.* **1.** immoderate; excessive. **2.** intemperate.

неуме́ст|ный (~ен, ~на) *adj.* **1.** inappropriate; misplaced, out of place. **2.** irrelevant.

неумёх|а, и *c.g.* (*coll.*) wally.

неу́м|ный (~ён, ~на́, ~но́) *adj.* foolish, silly.

неумоли́м|ый (~, ~а) *adj.* implacable; inexorable.

неумолка́ем|ый (~, ~а) *adj.* (*of sounds*) incessant, unceasing.

неумо́л|чный (~чен, ~чна) *adj.* = **~ка́емый**

неумышлен|ный (~, ~на) *adj.* unpremeditated; unintentional, inadvertent.

неупла́т|а, ы *f.* non-payment.

неупотреби́тел|ьный (~ен, ~ьна) *adj.* not in use, not current.

неуравнове́шен|ный (~, ~на) *adj.* (*psych.*) unbalanced.

неурожа́|й, я *m.* bad harvest, failure of crops.

неурожа́й|ный *adj. of* **~**; **н. год** lean year, bad harvest year.

неуро́чный *adj.* untimely.

неуря́диц|а, ы *f.* (*coll.*) **1.** disorder, mess. **2.** (*pl.*) squabbling.

неуси́дчив|ый (~, ~а) *adj.* restless, not persevering.

неуспева́емост|ь, и *f.* poor progress (*in studies*).

неуспева́ющий *adj.* backward, not making satisfactory progress.

неуста́н|ный (~ен, ~на) *adj.* tireless, unwearying.

неусто́йк|а, и *f.* **1.** (*leg.*) forfeit (*for breach of contract*). **2.** (*coll.*) failure.

неусто́йчивост|ь, и *f.* instability, unsteadiness.

неусто́йчив|ый (~, ~а) *adj.* unstable, unsteady; **~ое равнове́сие** unstable equilibrium.

неустрани́м|ый (~, ~а) *adj.* unremovable; **~ое препя́тствие** insurmountable obstacle.

неустраши́м|ый (~, ~а) *adj.* fearless, intrepid, undaunted.

неустро́ен|ный (~, ~на) *adj.* unsettled, not put in order, badly organized.

неустро́йств|о, а *nt.* disorder.

неусту́пчив|ый (~, ~а) *adj.* unyielding, uncompromising.

неусы́п|ный (~ен, ~на) *adj.* vigilant; indefatigable.

неутеши́тел|ьный (~ен, ~ьна) *adj.* not comforting, depressing; **~ьные ве́сти** distressing news.

неуте́ш|ный (~ен, ~на) *adj.* inconsolable; disconsolate.

неутоли́м|ый (~, ~а) *adj.* unquenchable; unappeasable; (*fig.*) insatiable.

неутоми́м|ый (~, ~а) *adj.* tireless, indefatigable.

не́уч, а *m.* (*coll.*) ignoramus.
неучти́вост|ь, и *f.* discourtesy, impoliteness, incivility.
неучти́в|ый (~, ~а) *adj.* discourteous, impolite, uncivil.
неую́т|ный (~ен, ~на) *adj.* bleak, comfortless.
неуязви́м|ый (~, ~а) *adj.* **1.** invulnerable. **2.** unassailable.
неф, а *m.* (*archit.*) nave.
нефи́рменный *adj.*: **н. конве́рт** plain envelope; **н. бланк** sheet of unheaded notepaper.
нефри́т[1]**, а** *m.* (*med.*) nephritis.
нефри́т[2]**, а** *m.* (*min.*) nephrite, jade.
нефте... *comb. form* oil-, petro-.
нефтево́з, а *m.* oil-tanker (*lorry*).
нефтедо́ллар, а *m.* petrodollar.
нефтеналивн|о́й *adj.* equipped for carrying oil in bulk; **~о́е су́дно** oil-tanker.
нефтено́с|ный (~ен, ~на) *adj.* oil-bearing.
нефтеперего́нный *adj.* oil-refining; **н. заво́д** oil refinery.
нефтеперераба́тывающий *adj.* oil-refining.
нефтепрово́д, а *m.* oil pipe-line.
нефтета́нкер, а *m.* oil-tanker (*ship*).
нефтехрани́лищ|е, а *nt.* oil-tank, oil reservoir.
нефт|ь, и *f.* oil, petroleum; **н.-сыре́ц** crude oil.
нефтя́ник, а *m.* oil(-industry) worker.
нефтя́нк|а, и *f.* (*coll.*) **1.** oil-engine. **2.** oil-barge.
нефтян|о́й *adj.* oil; **~а́я вы́шка** derrick; **н. фонта́н** oil-gusher.
нехва́тк|а, и *f.* (*coll.*) shortage.
нехи́т|рый (~ёр, ~ра́, ~ро́) *adj.* **1.** artless, guileless. **2.** (*coll.*) simple; uncomplicated.
нехоро́ш|ий (~, ~а́, ~о́) *adj.* bad.
нехорошо́ *adv.* badly; **чу́вствовать себя́ н.** to feel unwell.
не́хотя *adv.* **1.** reluctantly, unwillingly. **2.** inadvertently, unintentionally.
не́христ|ь, я *m.* **1.** (*obs.*) unbeliever. **2.** (*coll.*) brute, hard-hearted pers.
нецелесообра́з|ный (~ен, ~на) *adj.* inexpedient; pointless.
нецензу́р|ный (~ен, ~на) *adj.* unprintable; **~ные слова́** swear words, obscenities.
неча́янност|ь, и *f.* **1.** unexpectedness. **2.** surprise. **3.** unexpected event.
неча́янный *adj.* **1.** unexpected. **2.** accidental; unintentional.
не́чего, не́чему, не́чем, не́ о чем 1. *pron.* (*+inf.*) there is nothing (to); **мне н. чита́ть** I have nothing to read; **не́ о чем бы́ло говори́ть** there was nothing to talk about; **от н. де́лать** for want of sth. better to do, to while away the time; **н. сказа́ть!** (*coll., iron.*) indeed!; well, I declare! **2.** *as pred.* (*impers.*; *+inf.*) it's no good, it's no use; there is no need; **н. жа́ловаться** it's no use complaining; **н. и говори́ть, что...** it goes without saying that ....
нечелове́ческий *adj.* **1.** superhuman. **2.** inhuman.
нечести́в|ый (~, ~а) *adj.* impious, profane.
нече́стност|ь, и *f.* dishonesty.
нече́ст|ный (~ен, ~на́) *adj.* **1.** dishonest. **2.** dishonourable; crooked, bent; **~ная игра́** (*sport*) foul play.
не́чет, а *m.* (*coll.*) odd number.
нечёт|кий (~ок, ~ка́) *adj.* illegible; indistinct; inaccurate, slipshod.
нечётный *adj.* odd.
нечистопло́т|ный (~ен, ~на) *adj.* **1.** dirty; untidy, slovenly. **2.** (*fig.*) unscrupulous.
нечистот|а́, ы́, *pl.* **~ы, ~** *f.* **1.** dirtiness. **2.** *pl. only* sewage, garbage.
нечи́ст|ый (~, ~а́, ~о) *adj.* **1.** unclean, dirty (*also fig.*); **~ое де́ло** suspicious affair; **~ая пи́ща** (*relig.*) unclean food. **2.** impure, adulterated; **~ая поро́да** impure breed; **~ое произноше́ние** defective pronunciation. **3.** careless, inaccurate. **4.** dishonourable; dishonest; **быть ~ым на́ руку** to be light-fingered. **5.: ~ая си́ла;** *as n.* **н., ~ого** *m.* the Evil one, the Evil Spirit.
не́чист|ь, и *f.* (*collect.*; *coll.*) **1.** evil spirits. **2.** (*fig., pej.*) scum, vermin.
нечленоразде́л|ьный (~ен, ~на) *adj.* inarticulate.
не́что *pron.* (*nom. and a. cases only*) something.
нечувстви́тел|ьный (~ен, ~ьна) *adj.* **1. (к)** insensitive (to). **2.** imperceptible.
нешу́точ|ный (~ен, ~на) *adj.* grave, serious; **де́ло ~ное** it is no joke; it is no laughing matter.
неща́д|ный (~ен, ~на) *adj.* merciless.
неэвкли́дов *adj.*: **~а геоме́трия** non-Euclidean geometry.
нея́вк|а, и *f.* non-appearance, failure to appear.
неядови́тый *adj.* non-poisonous; (*chem.*) non-toxic.
нея́снос|ь, и *f.* vagueness, obscurity.
нея́с|ный (~ен, ~на́, ~но) *adj.* vague, obscure.
нея́сыт|ь, и *f.* tawny owl.
ни 1. *correlative conj.* **ни... ни** neither ... nor; **ни тот ни друго́й** neither (the one nor the other); **ни то ни сё** neither one thing nor the other; **ни ры́ба, ни мя́со** neither fish, flesh nor good red herring; **ни с того́, ни с сего́** all of a sudden; for no apparent reason; **ни за что, ни про что** for no reason at all. **2.** *particle* not a; **ни оди́н, ни одна́, ни одно́** not a, not one, not a single; **на у́лице не́ было ни (одно́й) души́** there was not a soul about; **ни ша́гу да́льше!** not a step further!; **ни гу-гу́!** (*coll.*) not a word!; mum's the word! **3.** *separable component of prons.* **никако́й, никто́, ничто́** *following preps.*; **ни в како́м (ни в ко́ем) слу́чае** on no account; **ни за что на све́те!** not for the world! **4.** (*particle, in comb. with* **как, кто, куда́** *etc.*) = -ever; **как бы мы ни стара́лись** however hard we tried; **что бы он ни говори́л** whatever he might say.
Ниага́рск|ий водопа́д, ~ого ~а *m.* (the) Niagara Falls.
ни́в|а, ы *f.* (corn-)field; **на ~е просвеще́ния** (*fig.*) in the field of education.
нивели́р, а *m.* (*tech.*) level.
нивели́р|овать, ую *impf. and pf.* (*tech. and fig.*) **1.** to level. **2.** to survey, contour.
нивелиро́вк|а, и *f.* **1.** levelling. **2.** surveying, contouring.
нивелиро́вщик, а *m.* **1.** leveller. **2.** surveyor.
нигде́ *adv.* nowhere.
Ни́гер, а *m.* **1.** Niger (*state*). **2.** the Niger (*river*).
нигери́|ец, йца *m.* Nigerian.
нигери́|йка, йки *f. of* **~ец**
нигери́йский *adj.* Nigerian.
Ниге́ри|я, и *f.* Nigeria.
нигили́зм, а *m.* nihilism.
нигили́ст, а *m.* nihilist.
нигилисти́ческий *adj.* nihilistic.
нидерла́нд|ец, ца *m.* Dutchman, Netherlander.
нидерла́ндский *adj.* Dutch, Netherlands.
Нидерла́нд|ы, ов *no sg.* the Netherlands.
нижа́йший *superl. of* **ни́зкий; ваш н. слуга́** your very humble servant.
ни́же 1. *comp. of* **ни́зкий** *and* **ни́зко. 2.** *prep.* (*+g.*) *and adv.* below, beneath.
нижеподписа́вшийся *adj.* (the) undersigned.
нижесле́дующий *adj.* following.
нижеупомя́нутый *adj.* undermentioned.
ни́жн|ий *adj.* (*in var. senses*) lower; **~ее бельё** underclothes, underwear; **~яя пала́та** Lower Chamber, Lower House; **н. чин** (*mil., obs.*) other rank, ranker; **~яя ю́бка** slip; **н. эта́ж** ground floor.
ни|жу́, ~жешь *see* **~за́ть**
низ, а, *pl.* **~ы́** *m.* **1.** bottom; ground floor. **2.** (*pl.*) lower classes. **3.** (*pl.*; *mus.*) low notes.
ни|за́ть, жу́, ~жешь *impf.* (*of* **на~**) to string, thread; **н. слова́** to speak very smoothly.
ни за что́ *adv.* in no circumstances.
низведе́ни|е, я *nt.* bringing down.
низверг|а́ть, а́ю *impf.* (*of* **~нуть**) to precipitate; (*fig.*) to overthrow.
низверг|а́ться, а́юсь *impf.* (*of* **~нуться**) **1.** to crash down. **2.** *pass. of* **~а́ть**
низве́рг|нуть(ся), ну(сь), нешь(ся), *past* **~(ся), ~ла(сь),** *pf. of* **~а́ть(ся)**
низверже́ни|е, я *nt.* overthrow.
низве|сти́, ду́, дёшь, *past* **~л, ~ла́** *pf.* (*of* **низводи́ть**) to bring down; (*fig.*) to bring low; to reduce.
низво|ди́ть, жу́, ~дишь *impf. of* **низвести́**
низи́н|а, ы *f.* low-lying area.
ни́з|кий (~ок, ~ка́, ~ко) *adj.* **1.** (*in var. senses*) low; **~кого**

происхожде́ния of humble origin. **2.** base, mean; **н. посту́пок** shabby act.
низколо́б|ый (~, ~а) *adj.* low-browed.
низкоопла́чиваемый *adj.* poorly-paid.
низкопокло́нник, а *m.* toady, crawler.
низкопокло́ннича|ть, ю *impf.* **(пе́ред)** to cringe (to), grovel (before).
низкопокло́нств|о, а *nt.* cringing, servility.
низкопро́б|ный (~ен, ~на) *adj.* **1.** base, low-grade (*of precious metals*). **2.** (*fig.*) base; inferior; rubbishy, trashy.
низкоро́сл|ый (~, ~а) *adj.* undersized, stunted.
низкосо́рт|ный (~ен, ~на) *adj.* low-grade; of inferior quality.
низлага́|ть, ю *impf. of* **низложи́ть**
низложе́ни|е, я *nt.* deposition, dethronement.
низлож|и́ть, у́, ~́ишь *pf.* (*of* **низлага́ть**) to depose, dethrone.
ни́зменност|ь, и *f.* **1.** (*geog.*) lowland (*not exceeding 200m above sea-level*). **2.** baseness.
ни́змен|ный (~, ~на) *adj.* **1.** low-lying. **2.** low; base, vile.
низово́й[1] *adj.* (*geog.*) lower; situated down stream; **н. ве́тер** wind blowing from downstream (*esp. from mouth of Volga*).
низово́й[2] *adj.* local; (*pol.*) grass-roots; **н. аппара́т** basic organization; **н. рабо́тник** worker in basic organization.
низо́в|ье, ья, *g. pl.* **~ьев** *nt.* the lower reaches (*of a river*).
низо|йти́, йду́, йдёшь, *past* **нисшёл, ~шла́** *pf.* (*of* **нисходи́ть**) (*obs.*) to descend.
ни́зом *adv.* (*coll.*) along the bottom; **е́хать н.** to take the lower road.
ни́зост|ь, и *f.* lowness; baseness, meanness.
низри́н|уть, у, ешь *pf.* (*rhet.*) to throw down, overthrow.
низри́н|уться, усь, ешься *pf.* (*rhet.*) to crash down.
ни́зш|ий *superl. of* **ни́зкий**; lowest; **~ее образова́ние** primary education; **~ие слу́жащие** the most junior employees.
НИИ- *m. indecl.* (*abbr. of* ***нау́чно-иссле́довательский институ́т***) research institute.
ника́к[1] *adv.* by no means, in no way, nowise; **он н. не мог узна́ть её а́дрес** in no way could he discover her address; **н. нельзя́** it is quite impossible; **н. нет** *respectful reply in negative to question.*
ника́к[2] *adv.* (*coll.*) it seems, it would appear; **они́, н., уже́ пришли́** they are here already, it seems.
никак|о́й *pron.* no; **не... ~о́го, ~о́й, ~и́х** no ... whatever; **я не име́ю ~о́го представле́ния (поня́тия)** I have no idea, no conception; **~и́х возраже́ний!** no objections!; **учёный он н.** (*coll.*) he is no scholar; **и ~и́х (гвозде́й)!** (*coll.*) and that's all there is to it; and that's that.
Никара́гуа *f. indecl.* Nicaragua.
никарагуа́н|ец, ца *m.* Nicaraguan.
никарагуа́н|ка, ки *f. of* **~ец**
никарагуа́нский *adj.* Nicaraguan.
ни́келевый *adj.* nickel.
никелиро́в|анный *p.p.p of* **~а́ть** and nickel-plated.
никелир|ова́ть, у́ю *impf. and pf.* to plate with nickel, nickel.
никелиро́вк|а, и *f.* nickel-plating.
ни́кел|ь, я *m.* nickel.
ни́к|нуть, ну, нешь, *past* **~, ~ла** *impf.* (*of* **по~** *and* **с~**) to droop, flag (*also fig.*).
никогда́ *adv.* never; **как н.** as never before.
нико́|й *pron.* (*obs.*) no; *now only in phrr.* **~им о́бразом** by no means, in no way; **ни в ко́ем слу́чае** on no account, in no circumstances.
никоти́н, а *m.* nicotine.
никоти́н|ный *adj. of* **~**
никоти́н|овый *adj.* = **~ный**
никто́, никого́, никому́, нике́м, ни о ком *pron.* nobody, no one; **там никого́ не́ было** there was nobody there; **н. друго́й** nobody else; **ни у кого́ нет э́того** no one has it.
никуда́ *adv.* nowhere; **э́то н. не годи́тся** (*fig.*) this won't do; it is no good at all; **н. не го́дный** good-for-nothing, worthless, useless.
никуд|ы́шный *adj.* (*coll.*) = **~а́ не го́дный.**
никчёмный *adj.* (*coll.*) useless, good-for-nothing; needless.
Нил, а *m.* the Nile (*river*).
ним *i. of* **он, оно́**; *d. of* **они́** *after preps.*
нима́ло *adv.* not in the least, not at all.
нимб, а *m.* halo, nimbus.
ни́ми *i. of* **они́** *after preps.*
ни́мф|а, ы *f.* **1.** nymph. **2.** (*pl., anat.*) labia minora. **3.** (*zool.*) pupa.
нимфома́ни|я, и *f.* nymphomania.
нимфома́нк|а, и *f.* nymphomaniac.
нио́би|й, я *m.* (*chem.*) niobium.
ниотку́да *adv.* from nowhere; **н. не сле́дует, что...** it in no way follows that ....
нипочём *adv.* (*coll.*) **1.** (*+d.*) it is nothing (to); **э́то ему́ н.** it is child's play to him; **ему́ н. провести́ це́лую ночь на заня́тиях** he thinks nothing of spending a whole night working. **2.** for nothing, dirt-cheap; **прода́ть н.** to sell for a song. **3.** never, in no circumstances.
ни́ппел|ь, я, *pl.* **~я́, ~е́й** *m.* (*tech.*) nipple.
нирва́н|а, ы *f.* nirvana.
ниско́лько 1. *adv.* not at all, not in the least; no whit; **ей от э́того бы́ло н. не лу́чше** she was none the better for it. **2.** *pron.* (*coll.*) none at all; **ско́лько вам э́то сто́ило? — н.** how much did it cost you? It cost me nothing.
ниспада́|ть, ет *impf. of* **ниспа́сть**
ниспа́|сть, ду́, дёшь, *past* **~л, ~ла** *pf.* (*of* **~да́ть**) (*obs.*) to fall, drop.
ниспо|сла́ть, шлю́, шлёшь *pf.* (*of* **~сыла́ть**) (*relig.*) to send down (*sc. from heaven*).
ниспосыла́|ть, ю *impf. of* **ниспосла́ть**
ниспроверг|а́ть, а́ю *impf.* (*of* **~́нуть**) to overthrow, overturn (*also fig.*).
ниспрове́рг|нуть, ну, нешь, *past* **~, ~ла** *pf. of* **~а́ть**
ниспроверже́ни|е, я *nt.* overthrow.
ниста́гм, а *m.* (*med.*) nystagmus.
нисхо|ди́ть, жу́, ~́дишь *impf. of* **низойти́**
нисход|я́щий *pres. part. act. of* **~и́ть** *and adj.* **1.** descending; **по ~я́щей ли́нии** in the line of descent, in a descending line. **2.** (*ling.*) falling.
нисше́стви|е, я *nt.* descending, descent.
нитеви́д|ный (~ен, ~на) *adj.* thread-like, filiform; **н. пульс** (*med.*) thready pulse.
нитево́д, а *m.* (*text.*) thread guide; **ро́лик ~а** tension bowl.
нитело́вк|а, и *f.* (*text.*) thread picker.
нитерёзк|а, и *f.* (*text.*) thread cutter.
ни́тк|а, и *f.* thread; **н. же́мчуга** string of pearls; **на живу́ю ~у** (*fig., coll.*) hastily, anyhow; **ши́то бе́лыми ~ами** (*fig., coll.*) transparent, patent, obvious; **до (после́дней) ~и обобра́ть** (*fig., coll.*) to fleece, leave without a shirt to one's back; **промо́кнуть до ~и** (*fig.*) to get soaked to the skin; **вы́тянуться в ~у** (*fig., coll.*) (*i*) to stand in line, (*ii*) to become worn to a shadow.
нито́н, а *m.* (*chem.*) niton.
ни́точк|а, и *f. dim. of* **ни́тка; по ~е разобра́ть** (*fig.*) to analyse minutely, subject to minute scrutiny; **ходи́ть по ~е** (*fig.*) to toe the line, sing small.
ни́т|очный *adj. of* **~ка; ~очное произво́дство** spinning.
нитра́т, а *m.* (*chem.*) nitrate.
нитри́р|овать, ую *impf. and pf.* (*chem.*) **1.** to nitride. **2.** to nitrate.
нитри́т, а *m.* (*chem.*) nitrite.
нитрифика́ци|я, и *f.* (*chem.*) nitrification.
нитрифици́р|овать, ую *impf. and pf.* (*chem., bot.*) to nitrify.
нитробензо́л, а *m.* (*chem.*) nitrobenzene.
нитрова́ни|е, я *nt.* (*chem.*) nitration.
нитроглицери́н, а *m.* (*chem.*) nitroglycerine.
нитроипри́т, а *m.* (*chem., mil.*) nitrogen mustard (gas).
нитроклетча́тк|а, и *f.* (*chem.*) nitrocellulose.
нитросоедине́ни|е, я *nt.* nitro-compound.
нитча́тк|а, и *f.* **1.** tape-worm. **2.** (*bot.*) hair-weed, crow-silk.
ни́тчатый *adj.* filiform.
нит|ь, и *f.* **1.** (*in var. senses*) thread; **путево́дная н.** clue; **~́и дру́жбы** bonds of friendship; **проходи́ть кра́сной ~́ью** (*fig.*) to stand out, run through (*of theme, motif*). **2.** (*bot., elec.*) filament; **н. нака́ла** (*elec.*) glow-lamp filament; (*radio*) heated filament. **3.** (*med.*) suture.

ни́тянк|а, и *f.* (*coll.*) knitted cotton glove.
ни́тяный *adj.* cotton.
них *a. and g. of* **они́** *when governed by preps.*
ниц *adv.* (*obs.*) face downwards; **пасть н.** to prostrate o.s., kiss the ground.
Ни́цц|а, ы *f.* Nice.
ничего́[1] *g. of* **ничто́**
ничего́[2] *adv.* **1.** (*also* **н. себе́**) so-so; passably, not (too) badly; all right; **ко́рмят здесь н.** the food here is not too bad; **как вы чу́вствуете себя́? — н.** how do you feel? all right. **2.** *as indecl. adj.* not (too) bad, passable, tolerable; **на́ша кварти́ра н.** our flat is not too bad; **па́рень он н.** he is not a bad chap.
нич|е́й (~ья́, ~ье́) *pron.* nobody's, no one's; **~ья́ земля́** no man's land; *as n.* **~ья́, ~ье́й** *f.* (*sport*) draw, drawn game; **сыгра́ть в ~ью** to play a drawn game, draw.
ниче́йный *adj.* (*coll.*) **1.** no man's. **2.** (*sport*) drawn.
ничко́м *adv.* prone, face downwards.
ничто́, ничего́, ничему́, ниче́м, ни о чём *pron.* **1.** nothing; **э́то ничего́ не зна́чит** it means nothing; **ниче́м не ко́нчилось** it came to nothing; **ничего́ подо́бного!** nothing of the kind!; **э́то ничего́!** it's nothing!; it doesn't matter!; **ничего́!** (*coll.*) that's all right!; never mind! **2.** nought; nil.
ничто́же *pron.* **н. сумня́ся, н. сумня́шеся** (*iron.*) without a second's hesitation.
ничто́жеств|о, а *nt.* **1.** nothingness. **2.** a nonentity, a nobody.
ничто́жност|ь, и *f.* **1.** insignificance. **2.** a nonentity, a nobody.
ничто́ж|ный (~ен, ~на) *adj.* insignificant; paltry, worthless.
ничу́ть *adv.* (*coll.*) not at all, not in the least, not a bit; **н. не быва́ло** not at all.
нич|ья́, е́й *f. see* **ниче́й**
ни́ш|а, и *f.* niche, recess; (*archit.*) bay.
нища́|ть, ю *impf.* (*of* **об~**) to grow poor, be reduced to beggary.
ни́щенк|а, и *f.* beggar-woman.
ни́щенский *adj.* beggarly.
ни́щенств|о, а *nt.* **1.** begging. **2.** beggary.
ни́щенств|овать, ую *impf.* **1.** to beg, go begging. **2.** to be destitute.
нищет|а́, ы́ *f.* **1.** destitution; indigence, poverty (*also fig.*). **2.** (*collect.*) beggars; the poor.
ни́щ|ий *adj.* **1.** destitute; indigent, poverty-stricken; **~ая бра́тия** (*folk poet.*) the poor; **н. ду́хом** poor in spirit. **2.** *as n.* **н., ~его** *m.* beggar, mendicant; pauper.
НКВД *m. indecl.* (*abbr. of* ***Наро́дный комиссариа́т вну́тренних дел***) (*hist.*) NKVD, People's Commissariat for Internal Affairs.
НЛО *m. indecl.* (*abbr. of* **неопо́знанный лета́ющий объе́кт**) UFO (*unidentified flying object*).
но[1] *conj.* **1.** but; *after concessive clause not translated or* still, nevertheless; **хотя́ он и бо́лен, но наме́рен прийти́** although he is ill, he (still) intends to come. **2.** (*coll.*) *as nt. n.* a 'but'; snag, difficulty; **тут есть одно́ «но»** there is just one snag in it.
но[2] *int.* gee up!
нова́тор, а *m.* innovator.
нова́тор|ский *adj. of* **~** *and* **~ство**
нова́торств|о, а *nt.* innovation.
Но́в|ая Гвине́|я, ~ой ~и *f.* New Guinea.
Но́в|ая Зела́нди|я, ~ой ~и *f.* New Zealand.
Но́в|ая Шотла́нди|я, ~ой ~и *f.* Nova Scotia.
нове́йший *superl. of* **но́вый**; newest; latest.
нове́лл|а, ы *f.* **1.** short story. **2.** (*in Roman law*) novel.
новелли́ст, а *m.* short story-writer.
но́веньк|ий *adj.* **1.** brand-new. **2.** *as n.* **н., ~ого** *m.* new boy; **~ая, ~ой** *f.* new girl.
новизн|а́, ы́ *f.* novelty; newness.
нови́к, а́ *m.* **1.** (*hist.*) young courtier. **2.** (*obs.*) novice.
новин|а́, ы́ *f.* (*dial.*) **1.** virgin soil. **2.** freshly-reaped corn. **3.** piece of unbleached linen.
нови́нк|а, и *f.* novelty; **мне в ~у лете́ть самолётом** it is a new experience for me to travel by plane.
нович|о́к, ка́ *m.* **1.** (**в**+*p.*) novice (at), beginner (at), tiro; (*sport*) colt. **2.** (*in school*) new boy; new girl.
новобра́н|ец, ца *m.* recruit.
новобра́чн|ая, ой *f.* bride.
новобра́чн|ые, ых *pl.* newly-weds.
новобра́чн|ый, ого *m.* bridegroom.
нововведе́ни|е, я *nt.* innovation.
нового́дний *adj.* new year's.
новогре́ческий *adj.*: **н. язы́к** Modern Greek.
новозаве́тный *adj.* of the New Testament.
новозела́нд|ец, ца *m.* New Zealander.
новозела́нд|ка, ки *f. of* **~ец**
новозела́ндский *adj.* New Zealand.
новоиспечённый *adj.* (*coll., joc.*) newly made; newly fledged.
новокаи́н, а *m.* (*pharm.*) novocaine.
новолу́ни|е, я *nt.* new moon.
новомо́д|ный (~ен, ~на) *adj.* in the latest fashion, up-to-date; (*fig., pej.*) newfangled.
новообразова́ни|е, я *nt.* new growth; new formation; (*med.*) neoplasm.
новообращённый *adj.* (*relig. and fig.*) newly converted.
новопреста́вленный *adj.* (*relig.*) the late, the late-lamented.
новоприбы́вш|ий *adj.* newly-arrived; *as n.* **н., ~его** *m.* new-comer.
новорождённ|ый *adj.* **1.** new-born; *as n.* **н., ~ого** *m.* the baby; (*med.*) neonate. **2.** *as n.* one celebrating his birthday; **поздра́вить ~ого** to wish many happy returns (*of a birthday*).
новосёл, а *m.* new settler.
новосе́ль|е, я *nt.* **1.** new home; new abode. **2.** house-warming; **справля́ть н.** to give a house-warming party.
новостро́йк|а, и *f.* **1.** erection of new buildings. **2.** newly-erected building; **шко́ла-н.** new school.
но́вост|ь, и, *g. pl.* **~е́й** *f.* **1.** news; tidings; **э́то что ещё за ~и!; вот ещё ~и!** (*coll.*) well, I like that!; did you ever! **2.** novelty.
новоте́льный *adj.* newly-calved.
новоя́вленный *adj.* (*relig. or iron.*) newly brought to light.
но́вшеств|о, а *nt.* innovation, novelty.
но́в|ый (~, ~а́, ~о) *adj.* **1.** new; novel; fresh; **соверше́нно н.** brand-new; **Н. год** new year's day; **Н. заве́т** the New Testament; **Н. свет** the New World; **что ~ого?** what's the news?; what's new? **2.** modern; recent; **~ая исто́рия** modern history; **~ые языки́** modern languages.
нов|ь, и *f.* virgin soil.
ног|а́, и́, *a.* **~у,** *pl.* **~и, ног, ~а́м** *f.* foot; leg; **вверх ~а́ми** head over heels; **без (за́дних) ног** (*coll.*) dead-beat; **в ~а́х посте́ли** at the foot of the bed; **валя́ться в ~а́х у кого́-н.** to prostrate o.s. before s.o.; **идти́ в ~у** (**с**+*i.*) to keep step (with), keep pace (with) (*also fig.*); **идти́ н. за́ ~у** (*coll.*) to plod along; **к ~е́!** (*mil.*) order arms!; **положи́ть ~у на́ ~у** to cross one's legs; **сиде́ть н. на́ ~у** to sit with legs crossed; **он не стоя́л на ~а́х** he could barely stand upright (*sc. from weakness, intoxication, etc.*); **поста́вить кого́-н. на́ ~и** (*fig.*) to set s.o. on his feet; **стать на́ ~и** (*fig.*) to stand on one's own feet; **подня́ть кого́-н. на́ ~и** to goad s.o. into action; **жить на широ́кую (большу́ю, ба́рскую) ~у** to live in (grand) style, live like a lord; **быть на коро́ткой ~е́** (**с**+*i.*) to be on a good footing (with), be intimate (with); **хрома́ть на о́бе ~и́** to be lame in both legs; (*fig., coll.*) to go badly, creak; **верте́ться у кого́-н. под ~а́ми** to get under s.o.'s feet; **сбить с ног** to knock down; **сби́ться с ~и́** to lose the step, get out of step; **дать ~у** to keep in step, get in step; **встать с ле́вой ~и́** to get out of bed on the wrong side; **со всех ног** (*coll.*) as fast as one's legs will carry one; **е́ле ~и унести́** to escape by the skin of one's teeth; **он дава́й Бог ~и** (*coll.*) he took to his heels; **ног под собо́й не слы́шать (от ра́дости)** (*coll.*) to be beside o.s. (*with joy*); **ног под собо́й не чу́вствовать (от уста́лости** *etc.*) to be barely able to stand (from tiredness, *etc*); **мое́й ~и́ у вас не бу́дет** (*coll.*) I shall not set foot in your house again; **мы — ни ~о́й туда́** (*coll.*) we never go near the place; **стоя́ть одно́й ~о́й в моги́ле** to have one foot in the grave; **протяну́ть ~и** (*coll.*) to turn up one's toes.
ноготк|и́, о́в (*bot.*) marigold.

ногот|о́к, ка́ *m. dim. of* **но́готь; мужичо́к с н.** Tom Thumb.
но́г|оть, тя, *pl.* **~ти, ~те́й** *m.* (finger-, toe-) nail.
ног|тево́й *adj. of* **~оть**
ногтое́д|а, ы *f.* (*med.*) whitlow.
нож, а́ *m.* knife; **перочи́нный н.** penknife; **разрезно́й н.** paper-knife; **н.-пила́** bread-knife; **садо́вый н.** pruning-knife; **н. в спи́ну** (*fig.*) stab in the back; **э́то мне н. о́стрый** (*fig.*) for me this is sheer hell; **без ~а́ заре́зать** to do for; **быть на ~а́х (с+*i.*)** to be at daggers drawn (with); **под ~о́м** under the knife (= *during a surgical operation*); **пристава́ть к кому́-н. с ~о́м к го́рлу** to pester s.o., importune s.o.
нож|ево́й *adj. of* **~; н. ма́стер** cutler; **~евы́е това́ры** cutlery.
но́жик, а *m.* knife.
но́жк|а, и *f.* **1.** *dim. of* **нога́; подста́вить ~у** (+*d.*) to trip up. **2.** leg (*of furniture, utensils, etc*); stem (of wine-glass). **3.** (*bot.*) stalk; stem (*of mushroom*).
но́жниц|ы, ~ *pl.* **1.** scissors, pair of scissors; shears. **2.** (*econ.*) discrepancy.
ножн|о́й *adj. of* **нога́; н. приво́д** foot drive, pedal operation, treadle drive; **н. то́рмоз** foot brake, pedal brake; **~а́я шве́йная маши́на** treadle sewing-machine.
но́ж|ны ~ен, ~нам (*and* нож|ны́, ~о́н, ~на́м) *pl.* sheath; scabbard.
ножо́вк|а, и *f.* hacksaw.
ножо́вщик, а *m.* cutler.
ножо́вый = ножево́й
ноздрева́тост|ь, и *f.* porosity, sponginess.
ноздрева́т|ый (~, ~а) *adj.* porous, spongy.
ноздр|я́, и́, *pl.* **~и, ~е́й** *f.* nostril
нока́ут, а *m.* (*sport*) knock-out.
нокаути́р|овать, ую *impf. and pf.* (*sport*) to knock out.
нокда́ун, а *m.* (*sport*) knock-down.
ноктю́рн, а *m.* (*mus.*) nocturne.
нолево́й = нулево́й
нол|ь, я́ *m.* **= нуль; ноль-ноль** *indicates timing of event at the hour exactly*; **экспре́сс в Берли́н отхо́дит в семна́дцать н.-н.** the express for Berlin departs at 17.00 hours.
нома́д, а *m.* nomad.
номенклату́р|а, ы *f.* **1.** nomenclature. **2.** list, schedule, catalogue. **3.** nomenklatura (*in the former USSR, system by which appointments to specified posts in government or economic administration were made by organs of the Communist Party*).
номенклату́р|ный *adj. of* **~а**
но́мер, а, *pl.* **~а́** *m.* **1.** number; number, issue (*of newspaper, magazine, etc.*). **2.** size; **како́й н. боти́нок вы но́сите?** what size do you take in shoes? **3.** room (*in hotel*). **4.** item on the programme, number, turn; **со́льный н.** solo (number); **эстра́дный н.** music-hall turn. **5.** (*coll.*) trick; **вы́кинуть н.** to play a trick; **вот так н.!** (*coll.*) what a funny thing! **6.** (*mil.*): **н. оруди́йного расчёта** member of a gun crew; gun number.
номерн|о́й 1. *adj. of* **но́мер**; numbered. **2.** *as n.* **н., ~о́го** *m.* boots (*in a hotel*).
номер|о́к, ка́ *m.* **1.** tally; label, ticket (*in cloakroom, etc.*). **2.** small room (*in a hotel*).
номина́л, а *m.* (*econ.*) face-value; **по ~у** at face-value.
номина́льн|ый *adj.* **1.** nominal; **~ая цена́** face value. **2.** (*tech.*) rated, indicated, nominal.
номогра́мм|а, ы *f.* (*math.*) nomogram, nomograph.
но́н|а, ы *f.* (*mus.*) ninth.
но́не *adv.* (*dial.*) **= ны́не**
нонпаре́л|ь, и *f.* (*typ.*) nonpareil.
но́нче *adv.* (*dial.*) **= ны́нче**
но́н|ы, ~ (*in Roman calendar*) nones.
нор|а́, ы́, *pl.* **~ы, ~, ~ам** *f.* burrow, hole; lair; (*of hare*) form.
Норве́ги|я, и *f.* Norway.
норве́ж|ец, ца *m.* Norwegian.
норве́ж|ка, ки *f. of* **~ец**
норве́жский *adj.* Norwegian.
норд, а *m.* (*naut.*) **1.** north. **2.** north wind.
норд-ве́ст, а *m.* (*naut.*) **1.** north-west. **2.** north-wester(-ly wind).
норд-о́ст, а *m.* (*naut.*) **1.** north-east. **2.** north-easter(-ly wind).
но́ри|я, и *f.* (*tech.*) noria, bucket chain.
но́рк|а[1]**, и** *f. dim. of* **нора́**
но́рк|а[2]**, и** *f.* **(америка́нская) н.** mink (*mustela vison*); **(европе́йская) н.** marsh-otter (*mustela lutreola*).
но́рк|овый *adj. of* **~а**[2]
но́рм|а, ы *f.* **1.** standard, norm. **2.** rate; **н. вы́работки** rate of output; **сверх ~ы** in excess of planned rate.
нормализа́ци|я, и *f.* standardization.
нормализ|ова́ть, у́ю *impf. and pf.* to standardize.
норма́л|ь, и *f.* (*math., phys.*) normal.
норма́льно *as pred.* (*coll.*) it is all right, okay, OK.
норма́льност|ь, и *f.* normality.
норма́л|ьный (~ен, ~ьна) *adj.* (*in var. senses*) normal; **н. уста́в** model regulations; **~ьная колея́** (*rail.*) standard gauge.
норма́нд|ец, ца *m.* Norman (*inhabitant of Normandy*).
Норма́нди|я, и *f.* Normandy.
норма́нд|ка, ки *f. of* **~ец**
Норма́ндск|ие острова́|а́, ~их ~о́в *no sg.* the Channel Islands.
норма́ндский *adj.* Norman.
норма́нн, а *m.* (*hist.*) Northman, Norseman.
норма́ннский *adj.* (*hist.*) Norse.
нормати́в, а *m.* (*econ.*) norm.
нормати́в|ный (~ен, ~на) *adj.* **1.** *adj. of* **~**; corresponding to norm. **2.** normative.
нормирова́ни|е, я *nt.* **1.** regulation, normalization; **н. труда́** norm-fixing, norm-setting (*in production*). **2.** rationing.
нормиро́в|анный *p.p.p. of* **~а́ть; н. рабо́чий день** fixed working hours; **~анное снабже́ние** rationing.
нормир|ова́ть, у́ю *impf. and pf.* **1.** to regulate, normalize; **н. за́работную пла́ту** to fix wages. **2.** to ration, place on the ration.
нормиро́в|ка, ки *f.* (*coll.*) **= ~а́ние**
нормиро́вщик, а *m.* regulator; **н. труда́** norm-setter.
но́ров, а *m.* **1.** (*obs.*) custom. **2.** (*coll.*) obstinacy, capriciousness; **челове́к с ~ом** difficult pers. **3.** (*of horses*) restiveness.
норови́ст|ый (~, ~а) *adj.* (*coll.*) restive; jibbing.
норов|и́ть, лю́, и́шь *impf.* (*coll.*) **1.** (+*inf.*) to strive (to), aim (at). **2.** **(в+*nom.-a.*)** to strive to become; **он ~и́т в писа́тели** he has literary aspirations.
нос, а, о ~е, на ~у́, *pl.* **~ы** *m.* **1.** nose; **у меня идёт кровь ~ом (из ~у)** my nose is bleeding; **говори́ть в н.** to speak through one's nose; **~ом к ~у** (*coll.*) face to face; **на ~у́** (*coll.*) near at hand, imminent; **заруби́ э́то себе́ на ~у́!** put that in your pipe and smoke it!; **э́то мне не по́ ~у** (*coll.*) it's not to my liking; **оста́вить с ~ом** (*coll.*) to dupe, make a fool of; **оста́ться с ~ом** (*coll.*) to be duped, be left looking a fool; **задра́ть н., подня́ть н.** (*coll.*) to cock one's nose, put on airs; **клева́ть ~ом** (*coll.*) to nod; **натяну́ть н. кому́-н.** (*coll.*) to make a fool of s.o.; **н. вороти́ть (от)** (*coll.*) to turn up one's nose (at); **пове́сить н. (на кви́нту)** (*coll.*) to be crestfallen, be discouraged; **показа́ть н.** (*coll.*) to cock a snook; **сова́ть н. не в своё де́ло** (*coll.*) to poke one's nose into other people's affairs; **ткнуть кого́-н. ~ом во что-н.** (*coll.*) to thrust sth. under s.o.'s nose; **уткну́ться ~ом во что-н.** (*coll.*) to bury one's face (o.s.) in sth. **2.** beak. **3.** (*naut.*) bow, head; prow.
носа́ст|ый (~, ~а) *adj.* big-nosed.
носа́т|ый (~, ~а) *adj.* **= носа́стый**
но́сик, а *m.* **1.** *dim. of* **нос. 2.** toe (*of a shoe*). **3.** spout.
носи́л|ки, ок *no sg.* **1.** stretcher. **2.** sedan(-chair); litter. **3.** (hand-)barrow.
носи́льн|ый *adj.* for personal wear; **~ое бельё** personal linen.
носи́льщик, а *m.* porter.
носи́тел|ь, я *m.* **1.** (*fig.*) bearer; repository. **2.: н. зара́зы** (*biol., med.*) carrier. **3.** (*chem.*) vehicle.
но|си́ть, шу́, ~сишь *impf.* **1.** *indet. of* **нести́. 2.** (*indet. only*) to carry; to bear (*also fig.*); **н. свою́ де́вичью**

фами́лию to use one's maiden name; **н. кого́-н. на рука́х** (*indet. only*) to make a fuss of s.o., make much of s.o. **3.** (*indet. only*) to wear; to carry.

но|си́ться, шу́сь, ∠сишься *impf.* **1.** *indet. of* **нести́сь; э́то ∠сится в во́здухе** (*fig.*) it is in the air, it is rumoured. **2.** (**с**+*i.*) to fuss (over), make much (of); **н. с мы́слью** to nurse an idea, be obsessed with an idea. **3.** (*intr.*) to wear; **э́та мате́рия хорошо́ ∠сится** this stuff wears well.

но́ск|а[1], **и** *f.* **1.** carrying; bearing. **2.** wearing.

но́ск|а[2], **и** *f.* laying.

но́с|кий[1] **(~ок, ~ка)** *adj.* (*of clothing, footwear*, etc.) hard-wearing, durable.

но́ск|ий[2] *adj.*: **~ая ку́рица** a good layer.

носов|о́й *adj.* **1.** *adj. of* **нос; н. плато́к** (pocket) handkerchief. **2.** (*ling.*) nasal. **3.** (*naut.*) bow, fore; **~а́я часть (су́дна)** ship's bows, fore part; **~а́я ча́шка** (*aeron.*) bow cap.

носогло́тк|а, и *f.* (*anat.*) nasopharynx.

носогло́точный *adj.* (*anat.*) nasopharyngeal.

носогре́йк|а, и *f.* (*coll.*) nose-warmer (*short pipe*).

нос|о́к[1], **ка́** *m.* **1.** toe (*of boot or stocking*). **2.** *dim.of* ~

нос|о́к[2], **ка́**, *pl.* **~ки́, ~ко́в** *m.* sock.

нозоло́ги|я, и *f.* (*med.*) nosology.

носоро́г, а *m.* rhinoceros.

носо́|чный *adj. of* **~к**[2]

ностальги́|я, и *f.* homesickness.

носу́х|а, и *f.* (*zool.*) coati.

но́счик, а *m.* carrier, porter.

но́т|а[1], **ы** *f.* **1.** (*mus.*) note. **2.** (*pl.*) (sheet) music; **игра́ть по ~ам (без нот)** to play from music (without music); **как по ~ам** (*fig.*) without a hitch, according to plan.

но́т|а[2], **ы** *f.* (diplomatic) note.

нотабе́н|а, ы *f. and* **нотабе́не** *nt. indecl.* nota bene (*abbr.* NB); **поста́вить ~у** to mark.

нотариа́льный *adj.* notarial.

нота́риус, а *m.* notary.

нота́ци|я[1], **и** *f.* (*coll.*) lecture, reprimand; **прочита́ть кому́-н. ~ю** to read s.o. a lecture.

нота́ци|я[2], **и** *f.* notation.

нотифика́ци|я, и *f.* notification.

нотифици́р|овать, ую *impf. and pf.* to notify, inform officially.

но́т|ка, ки *f. dim. of* **~а**[1]

но́тный *adj. of* **но́ты**

ноу́мен, а *m.* (*phil.*) noumenon.

ноумена́льный *adj.* (*phil.*) noumenal.

ноч|ева́ть, у́ю *impf.* (*of* **пере~**) to pass the night.

ночёвк|а, и *f.* spending the night, passing the night.

но́ч|ка, ки *f.* (*coll.*) *dim. of* **~ь**

ночле́г, а *m.* **1.** lodging for the night. **2.** = **ночёвка**

ночле́жк|а, и *f.* (*coll.*) doss-house.

ночле́жник, а *m.* **1.** (*coll.*) (overnight) visitor, guest. **2.** dosser.

ночле́|жный *adj. of* **~г; н. дом** doss-house.

ночни́к[1], **а́** *m.* night-light.

ночни́к[2], **а́** *m.* (*coll.*) night-driver; night-flier, night-flying ace.

ночн|о́е, о́го *nt.* pasturing of horses for the night.

ночн|о́й *adj.* night; nocturnal; **~а́я ба́бочка** moth; **н. горшо́к** chamber-pot; **н. сто́лик** bedside table; **~ы́е ту́фли** bedroom slippers; **~а́я фиа́лка** wild orchid.

ноч|ь, и, о ∠и, в ~и́, *pl.* **∠и, ~е́й** *f.* night; **глуха́я н.** the dead of night; **споко́йной ~и!** good-night!; **по ~а́м** (*of recurring events*) by night, at night.

но́чью *adv.* by night.

но́ш|а, и, *f.* burden.

ноше́ни|е, я *nt.* **1.** carrying. **2.** wearing.

но́шеный *adj.* worn; second-hand.

но́щно *adv. only in phr.* **де́нно и н.** (*coll.*) day and night.

но́|ю, ешь *see* **ныть**

но́ющ|ий *pres. part. act. of* **ныть; ~ая боль** ache.

ноя́бр|ь, я́ *m.* November.

ноя́бр|ьский *adj. of* ~

нрав, а *m.* **1.** disposition, temper; **быть** (+*d.*) **по ∠у** to please. **2.** (*pl.*) manners, customs, ways.

нра́в|иться, люсь, ишься *impf.* (*of* **по~**) (+*d.*) to please; **мне, ему́**, *etc.*, **~ится** I like, he likes, *etc.*; **мне о́чень ~ится э́та пье́са** I like this play very much; **она́ мне ка́к-то ~ится** I rather like her; **мы стара́емся н. вам** we try to please you; (*impers.*): **ей не ~ится ката́ться на ло́дке** she does not like going in boats.

нра́в|ный (~ен, ~на) *adj.* (*coll.*) testy, peppery.

нравоописа́тельный *adj.* descriptive of manners; **н. рома́н** novel of manners.

нравоуче́ни|е, я *nt.* **1.** moralizing; moral admonition. **2.** (*liter.*) moral.

нравоучи́тельный *adj.* moralistic, edifying.

нра́вственност|ь, и *f.* morality; morals.

нра́вствен|ный (~, ~на) *adj.* moral.

НРБ *f. indecl.* (*abbr. of* ***Наро́дная Респу́блика Болга́рия***) People's Republic of Bulgaria.

н. ст. (*abbr. of* ***но́вый стиль***) NS, New Style (*of calendar*).

НТР *f. indecl.* (*abbr. of* ***нау́чно-техни́ческая револю́ция***) scientific and technological revolution.

ну *int. and particle* **1.** well!; well ... then!; come on!; **ну, ну!** come, come!; come now! **2. (да) ну!** not really?; you don't mean to say so! **3.** *expr. surprise and pleasure or displeasure* well; what; why; **ну и...** what (a) ...!; here's ... (for you)!; there's ... (for you)!; **ну вот и..!** there you are, you see ...!; **ну, неуже́ли?!** what! really?; no? really?; **ну, пра́во!, ну, одна́ко же!** well, to be sure!; **ну и денёк!** what a day!; **ну и молоде́ц!** (*also iron.*) there's a good boy!; there's a clever chap! **4.** *indicating resumption of talk*; *expr. concession, resignation, relief, qualified recognition of point* well; **ну вот** (*in narration*) well, well then; **ну что ж, ну́ так** well then; **ну хорошо́** all right then, very well then; **ведь вы сказа́ли, что вы их увиде́ли, не пра́вда ли? — ну да, но то́лько сза́ди** but you did say you saw them, didn't you? Yes, I know, but only from behind. **5.: ну́ как** (+*fut.*) suppose, what if; **ну́ как они́ не приду́т во́-вре́мя?** suppose they don't come in time? **6.** *as pred.* (+*inf.*) to start; **он ну крича́ть** he started yelling. **7.: а ну́** (+*g.*) to hell (with)!; to the deuce (with)!; **а ну́ тебя́!** to hell with you!

нуби́йский *adj.* Nubian.

нувори́ш, а *m.* nouveau riche.

нуди́зм, а *m.* nudism, naturism.

нуди́ст, а *m.* nudist, naturist.

ну́|дить, жу, дишь *impf.* (*obs.*) **1.** to force, compel. **2.** to wear out.

ну|ди́ть, жу́, ди́шь *impf.* (*coll.*) to wear out (*with complaints, questions, etc.*).

ну́дност|ь, и *f.* tediousness.

ну́д|ный (~ен, ~на) *adj.* (*coll.*) tedious, boring.

нужд|а́, ы́, *pl.* **∠ы** *f.* **1.** want, straits; indigence. **2.** need; necessity; **в слу́чае ~ы́** if necessary, if need be; **н. всему́ нау́чит** necessity is the mother of invention; **~ы́ нет, нет ~ы́** (*coll.*) no matter!; never mind; **~ы́ нет, что здесь те́сно, зато́ нам ве́село** it doesn't matter if it's a bit crowded here so long as we enjoy ourselves. **3.** (*coll., euph.*) call of nature; **сбе́гать по ма́ленькой/большо́й ~е́** to go to the loo.

нужда́емост|ь, и *no pl., f.* (**в**+*p.*) needs (in), requirements (in).

нужда́|ться, юсь *impf.* **1.** to be in want; to be needy, hard-up. **2.** (**в**+*p.*) to need, require; to be in need (of).

ну́жник, а *m.* (*coll.*) latrine.

ну́жно (+*d.*) **1.** (*impers.*; +*inf. or* +**что́бы**) it is necessary; (one) ought, (one) should, (one) must, (one) need(s); **н. бы́ло (бы) взять такси́** you should have taken a taxi; **н., что́бы она́ реши́лась** she ought to make up her mind. **2.** (*impers.*, +*a. or g.*; *coll.*) I, *etc.*, need; **мне н. пять рубле́й** I need five roubles. **3.** *see* **ну́жный**

ну́ж|ный (~ен, ~на́, ~но, ~ны́) *adj.* necessary; requisite; (*pred. forms* +*d.*) I, *etc.*, need; **что вам ~но?** what do you need? what do you want? **о́чень (мне) ~но!** (*coll., iron.*) won't that be nice!; a fat lot of good that is!

ну́-ка *int.* now!; now then!; come!; come on!

ну́ка|ть, ю *impf.* (*coll.*) to urge; to say 'come on'.

нул|ево́й *adj. of* **~ь**; (*math.*) zero; **н. вариа́нт** (*pol.*) zero option.

нул|ь, я́ *m.* **1.** nought; zero; nil; cipher; **своди́ться к ~ю́** (*fig.*) to come to nothing, come to nought. **2.** (*fig.*) nonentity, cipher.

нумера́тор, а *m.* **1.** numerator. **2.** (*elec.*) annunciator.

нумера́ци|я, и *f.* **1.** numeration. **2.** numbering.

нумер|ова́ть, у́ю *impf.* (*of* **за~** *and* **пере~**) to number; **н. страни́цы** to paginate.

нумизма́т, а *m.* numismatist.

нумизма́тик|а, и *f.* numismatics.

нумизмати́ческий *adj.* numismatic.

ну́нци|й, я *m.* nuncio.

ну́те(-ка) *int.* well then!; come on!

ну́три|я, и *f.* (*zool.*) coypu; (*fur of coypu*) nutria.

нутроме́р, а *m.* (*tech.*) internal calipers.

нутр|о́, а́ *nt.* (*coll.*) **1.** inside, interior. **2.** (*fig.*) core, kernel. **3.** (*fig.*) instinct(s), intuition; **~о́м понима́ть** to understand intuitively; **всем ~о́м** with one's whole being; **э́то мне не по ~у́** it goes against the grain with me; **игра́ть ~о́м** (*theatr. sl.*) to live the part.

нутряно́й *adj.* internal.

ны́не *adv.* (*obs.*) **1.** now. **2.** today.

ны́нешн|ий *adj.* present; present-day; incumbent; **н. президе́нт** the incumbent president; **в ~ие времена́** nowadays.

ны́нче *adv.* (*coll.*) **1.** today; **не н. за́втра** any day now. **2.** now.

ныр|ну́ть, ну́, нёшь *pf. of* **~я́ть**

ныр|о́к[1], ка́ *m.* (*coll.*) **1.** dive. **2.** diver.

ныр|о́к[2], ка́ *m.* (*zool.*) pochard.

ныря́л|о, а *nt.* (*tech.*) plunger, plunger piston.

ныря́льщик, а *m.* diver.

ныр|я́ть, я́ю *impf.* (*of* **~ну́ть**) to dive.

ны́тик, а *m.* (*coll.*) (*coll.*) moaner, whinger.

ныть, но́ю, но́ешь *impf.* **1.** to ache. **2.** (*coll., pej.*) to moan, whinge; to make a fuss.

нытьё, я́ *nt.* (*coll., pej.*) moaning, whining.

Нью-Йо́рк, а *m.* New York.

Ньюфа́ундле́нд, а *m.* Newfoundland.

н. э. (*abbr. of* ***на́шей э́ры***) AD; **до н. э.** (*abbr. of* ***до на́шей э́ры***) BC.

НЭП, а *or* **нэп, а** *m.* (*abbr. of* ***но́вая экономи́ческая поли́тика***) (*hist.*) NEP (*New Economic Policy*).

нэ́пман, а *m.* (*pej.*) 'Nepman', profiteer (*during period of New Economic Policy*).

нэ́п|овский *adj. of* **~**

нюа́нс, а *m.* nuance, shade.

нюанси́р|овать, ую *impf. and pf.* (*mus.*) to bring out fine shades of feeling, observe nuances.

ню́ни *only in phr.* **распусти́ть н.** (*coll.*) to snivel, whimper.

ню́н|я, и *c.g.* (*coll.*) sniveller, cry-baby.

Ню́рнберг, а *m.* Nuremberg.

нюх, а *m.* scent; (*fig.*) flair.

ню́хальщик, а *m.* (*coll.*) snuff-taker.

ню́хательный *adj.*: **н. таба́к** snuff.

ню́ха|ть, ю *impf.* (*of* **по~**) to smell (at); **н. таба́к** to take snuff; **не ~л** (*+g.*) to have no experience (of); **по́роха не ~л** (*fig.*) he's still wet behind the ears; **он матема́тики и не ~л** he doesn't know the first thing about mathematics.

нюхн|у́ть, у́, ёшь *inst. pf.* (*coll.*) to take a sniff of.

ня́нч|ить, у, ишь *impf.* to nurse.

ня́нч|иться, усь, ишься *impf.* (**с**+*i.*) **1.** to (dry-)nurse. **2.** (*fig.*) to fuss (over).

ня́ньк|а, и *f.* (*coll.*) = **ня́ня; у семи́ ня́нек дитя́ без гла́зу** (*prov.*) too many cooks spoil the broth.

ня́н|я, и *f.* **1.** (dry-)nurse; **приходя́щая н.** babysitter; child-minder. **2.** (*coll.*) (hospital) nurse.

О

о[1] (об, обо) *prep.* **1.** (*+p.*) of, about, concerning; on; **о чём вы ду́маете?** what are you thinking about?; **ле́кция бу́дет о Пу́шкине** the lecture will be on Pushkin. **2.** (*+p.*) with, having; **стол о трёх но́жках** a table with three legs, three-legged table; **па́лка о двух конца́х** a two-edged weapon. **3.** (*+a.*) against; on, upon; **опере́ться о сте́ну** to lean against the wall; **споткну́ться о ка́мень** to stumble against a stone; **бок о́ бок** side by side; **рука́ о́б руку** hand in hand. **4.** (*+a. or p.*; *obs. or coll.*) (*of time*) on, at, about; **об э́ту по́ру** about his time; **о Рождестве́** about Christmas-time.

о[2] *int.* oh!

о. (*abbr. of* **о́стров**) I., Island, Isle.

о... (*also* **об...**, **обо...** *and* **объ...**) *vbl. pref. indicating*: **1.** transformation; process of becoming sth. **2.** action applied to entire surface of object *or* to series of objects.

ОАЕ *f. indecl.* (*abbr. of* ***Организа́ция африка́нского еди́нства***) OAU (*Organization of African Unity*).

оа́зис, а *m.* oasis (*also fig.*).

об *prep. see* **о[1]**

об... (*also* **обо...** *and* **объ...**) *vbl. pref.* **1.** = **о...** . **2.** indicating action *or* motion about an object.

о́ба, обо́их *m. and nt.*; **о́бе, обе́их** *f. num.* both; **гляде́ть в о., смотре́ть в о.** (*coll.*) to keep one's eyes open, be on one's guard; **обе́ими рука́ми** with both hands (*fig., coll.*); very willingly, readily.

оба́б|иться, люсь, ишься *pf.* **1.** (*of a man*) to become effeminate. **2.** (*of a woman*) to become sluttish; to become coarse.

обагр|и́ть, ю́, и́шь *pf.* (*of* **~я́ть**) to crimson, incarnadine; **о. кро́вью** to stain with blood; **о. ру́ки в крови́ (кро́вью)** to steep one's hands in blood.

обагр|и́ться, ю́сь, и́шься *pf.* (*of* **~я́ться**) to be crimsoned; **о. (кро́вью)** to be stained with blood.

обагр|я́ть(ся), я́ю(сь) *impf. of* **~и́ть(ся)**

обалдева́|ть, ю *impf. of* **обалде́ть**

обалде́лый *adj.* (*coll.*) crazed; stunned.

обалде́нный *adj.* (*sl.*) great, ace, brill.

обалде́|ть, ю *pf.* (*of* **~ва́ть**) (*coll.*) to become dulled, become crazed; to be stunned (*by surprise, etc.*).

обанкро́|титься, чусь, тишься *pf. of* **банкро́титься**

обая́ни|е, я *nt.* fascination, charm.

обая́тел|ьный (~ен, ~на) *adj.* fascinating, charming.

обва́л, а *m.* **1.** fall(ing), crumbling; collapse; caving-in. **2.** landslip; **сне́жный о.** snow-slip, avalanche.

обва́лива|ть[1](ся), ю(сь) *impf. of* **обвали́ть(ся)**

обва́лива|ть[2], ю *impf. of* **обваля́ть**

обва́лист|ый (~, ~а) *adj.* (*coll.*) liable to fall, liable to cave in.

обвал|и́ть, ю́, ~́ишь *pf.* (*of* **~́ивать[1]**) **1.** to cause to fall, cause to collapse; to crumble (*trans.*). **2.** to heap round; **о. избу́ камня́ми** to heap stones round a hut.

обвал|и́ться, ю́сь, ~́ишься *pf.* (*of* **~́иваться**) to fall, collapse, cave in; to crumble.

обвал|я́ть, я́ю *pf.* (*of* **~́ивать[2]**) (*+a.*, **в**+*p.*) to roll (in).

обва́рива|ть(ся), ю(сь) *impf. of* **обвари́ть(ся)**

обвар|и́ть, ю́, ~́ишь *pf.* (*of* **~́ивать**) **1.** to pour boiling water over. **2.** to scald.

обвар|и́ться, ю́сь, ~́ишься *pf.* (*of* **~́иваться**) **1.** to scald o.s. **2.** *pass. of* **~и́ть**

обвева́|ть, ю *impf. of* **обве́ять**

обве|ду́, дёшь *see* **~сти́**
обвез|ти́, у́, ёшь, *past* **~̈, ~ла́** *pf.* (*of* **обвози́ть**) **1.** to convey round. **2.** (*coll.*) to go the round of.
обвенча́|ть(ся), ю(сь) *pf. of* **венча́ть(ся)**[1]
оберн|у́ть, у́, ёшь *pf.* (*of* **обвёртывать**) (+*i.*) to wrap up (in).
обвер|те́ть, чу́, ~́тишь *pf.* (*of* **~̈тывать**) (+*i.*) to wrap up (in); **о. ше́ю ша́рфом** to wrap a scarf about one's neck.
обвёртыва|ть, ю *impf. of* **оберну́ть** *and* **обверте́ть**
обве́с[1]**, а** *m.* false weight, short weight.
обве́с[2]**, а** *m.*: **о. мо́стика** (*naut.*) bridge cloth, bridge dodger.
обве́|сить, шу, сишь *pf.* (*of* **~шивать**[1]) to give short weight to; to cheat (*in weighing goods*).
обве|сти́, ду́, дёшь, *past* **~̈л, ~ла́** *pf.* (*of* **обводи́ть**) **1.** to lead round, take round; **о. вокру́г па́льца** (*fig., coll.*) to twist round one's little finger. **2.** (+*i.*) to encircle (with); to surround (with); **о. рвом** to surround with a ditch; **о. взо́ром, глаза́ми** to look round (at), take in (*with one's eyes*). **3.** to outline; **о. чертёж ту́шью** to outline a sketch in ink. **4.** (*sport*) to dodge; to get past.
обве́тр|енный *p.p.p. of* **~ить** *and adj.* weather-beaten; chapped.
обве́тре|ть, ет *pf.* to become weather-beaten.
обвре́трива|ть(ся), ю(сь) *impf. of* **обве́трить(ся)**
обве́тр|ить, ю, ишь *pf.* (*of* **~ивать**) to expose to the wind; (*impers.*): **мне ~ило гу́бы** my lips are chapped.
обве́тр|иться, юсь, ишься *pf.* (*of* **~иваться**) to become weather-beaten.
обветша́лый *adj.* decrepit, decayed; dilapidated.
обветша́|ть, ю *pf. of* **ветша́ть**
обве́ш|ать, аю *pf.* (*of* **~ивать**[2]) (*coll.*; +*i.*) to hang round (with), cover (with).
обве́шива|ть[1]**, ю** *impf. of* **обве́сить**
обве́шива|ть[2]**, ю** *impf. of* **обве́шать**
обве́|ять, ю, ешь *pf.* (*of* **~ва́ть**) **1.** (+*i.*) to fan (with). **2.** (*agric.*) to winnow.
обвива́|ть(ся), ю(сь) *impf. of* **обви́ть(ся)**
обвине́ни|е, я *nt.* **1.** charge, accusation; **пу́нкты ~я** (*leg.*) counts of an indictment; **по ~ю (в**+*p.*) on a charge (of); **возвести́ на кого́-н. о.** (**в**+*p.*) to charge s.o. (with); **вы́нести о.** to find guilty. **2.** (*leg.*) the prosecution (*as a party in lawsuit*).
обвини́тел|ь, я *m.* accuser; (*leg.*) prosecutor; **госуда́рственный о.** public prosecutor.
обвини́тельн|ый *adj.* accusatory; **о. акт** (bill of) indictment; **о. пригово́р** verdict of 'guilty'; **~ая речь** speech for the prosecution, indictment.
обвин|и́ть, ю́, и́шь *pf.* (*of* **~я́ть**) **1.** (**в**+*p.*) to accuse (of), charge (with). **2.** (*leg.*) to prosecute, indict.
обвиня́ем|ый, ого *m.* (*leg.*) the accused; defendant.
обвин|я́ть, я́ю *impf. of* **~и́ть**
обвис|а́ть, а́ет *impf.* (*of* **~́нуть**) to hang, droop; to sag; to grow flabby.
обви́сл|ый *adj.* (*coll.*) flabby; hanging; **~ые усы́** drooping moustache.
обви́с|нуть, нет, *past* **~, ~ла** *pf. of* **~а́ть**
обви́|ть, обовью́, обовьёшь, *past* **~л, ~ла́ ~ло** *pf.* (*of* **~ва́ть**) to wind (round), entwine; **о. ше́ю рука́ми** to throw one's arms round s.o.'s neck.
обви́|ться, обовью́сь, обовьёшься, *past* **~лся, ~ла́сь** *pf.* (*of* **~ва́ться**) to wind round, twine o.s. round.
об-во (*abbr. of* **о́бщество**) Soc., Society.
обво́д, а *m.* **1.** enclosing, surrounding. **2.** outlining; **о. су́дна** (*naut., tech.*) line.
обво|ди́ть, жу́, ~́дишь *impf. of* **обвести́**
обводне́ни|е, я *nt.* **1.** irrigation. **2.** filling up (with water).
обводни́тельный *adj.* irrigation.
обводн|и́ть, ю́, и́шь *pf.* (*of* **~я́ть**) **1.** to irrigate. **2.** to fill up (with water).
обво́дный *adj.*: **о. кана́л** (*tech.*) by-pass.
обводн|я́ть, я́ю *impf. of* **~и́ть**
обвола́кива|ть(ся), ю(сь) *impf. of* **обволо́чь(ся)**
обволо́|чь, ку́, чёшь, ку́т, *past* **~к, ~кла́** *pf.* (*of* **обвола́кивать**) to cover; to envelop (*also fig.*).
обволо́|чься, ку́сь, чёшься, ку́тся, *past* **~кся, ~кла́сь** *pf.* (*of* **обвола́киваться**) (+*i.*; *coll.*) to become covered (with), enveloped (by, in).
обвора́жива|ть, ю *impf. of* **обворожи́ть**
обвор|ова́ть, у́ю *pf.* (*of* **~о́вывать**) (*coll.*) to rob.
обворо́выва|ть, ю *impf. of* **обворова́ть**
обворожи́тел|ьный (~ен, ~ьна) *adj.* fascinating, charming, enchanting.
обворож|и́ть, у́, и́шь *pf.* (*of* **обвора́живать**) to fascinate, charm, enchant.
обвя|за́ть[1]**, жу́, ~́жешь** *pf.* (*of* **~́зывать**) to tie round; **о. верёвкой** to cord, rope; **о. го́лову платко́м** to tie a head-scarf round one's head.
обвя|за́ть[2]**, жу́, ~́жешь** *pf.* (*of* **~́зывать**) to edge in chain-stitch.
обвя|за́ться, жу́сь, ~́зешься *pf.* (*of* **~́зываться**) **1.** (+*i.*) to tie round o.s.; **о. верёвкой** to tie a rope round o.s. **2.** *pass. of* **~за́ть**
обвя́зыва|ть(ся), ю(сь) *impf. of* **обвяза́ть(ся)**
обга́|дить, жу, дишь *pf.* (*of* **~живать**) (*vulg.*) to shit on, shit up.
обга́жива|ть, ю *impf. of* **обга́дить**
обгла́дыва|ть, ю *impf. of* **обглода́ть**
обгло́д|анный *p.p.p. of* **~а́ть; ~анная кость** picked bone, bare bone.
обгло|да́ть, жу́, ~́жешь *pf.* (*of* **обгла́дывать**) to pick, gnaw round.
обгло́д|ок, ка *m.* (*coll.*) bare bone.
обго́н, а *m.* passing.
обгон|ю́, ~́ишь *see* **обогна́ть**
обгоня́|ть, ю *impf. of* **обогна́ть**
обгор|а́ть, а́ю *impf. of* **~е́ть**
обгоре́лый *adj.* burnt; charred; scorched.
обгор|е́ть, ю́, и́шь *pf.* to be scorched; to be burnt on the surface, receive surface burns.
обгрыз|а́ть, а́ю *impf. of* **~́ть**
обгры́з|ть, у́, ёшь, *past* **~, ~ла** *pf.* (*of* **~а́ть**) to gnaw round.
обда|ва́ть(ся), ю́(сь), ёшь(ся) *impf. of* **обда́ть(ся)**
обд|а́ть, а́м, а́шь, а́ст, ади́м, ади́те, аду́т, *past* **~́ал, ~ала́, ~́ало** *pf.* (*of* **~ава́ть**) (+*i.*) **1.** to pour over; **о. кого́-н. кипятко́м** to pour boiling water over s.o. **2.** (*fig.*) to seize, cover; **о. взгля́дом презре́ния** to fix with a look of scorn; **меня́ ~́ало хо́лодом** (*impers.*) I came over cold.
обд|а́ться, а́мся, а́шься, а́стся, ади́мся, ади́тесь, аду́тся, *past* **~а́лся, ~ала́сь** *pf.* (*of* **~ава́ться**) (+*i.*) to pour over o.s.; **о. кипятко́м** to scald o.s.
обде́л|ать, аю *pf.* (*of* **~ывать**) **1.** to finish; to dress (*leather, stone, etc.*); **о. драгоце́нные ка́мни** to set precious stones. **2.** (*fig.*) to manage, arrange; **о. те́му** (*coll.*) to treat, handle a subject; **о. свои́ дели́шки** (*coll.*) to manage one's affairs with profit; **он ма́стер о. свои́ дели́шки** he is an expert at looking after number one. **3.** *euph.* = **обга́дить**
обдел|и́ть, ю́, ~́ишь *pf.* (*of* **~я́ть**) (+*a. and i.*) to do out of one's (fair) share (of); **он ~и́л сестёр насле́дством** he did his sisters out of their share of the legacy.
обде́лыва|ть, ю *impf. of* **обде́лать**
обдел|я́ть, я́ю *impf. of* **~и́ть**
обдёрга|нный *p.p.p. of* **~ть** *and adj.* (*coll.*) shabby; ragged, in rags.
обдёрг|ать, аю *pf.* (*of* **~ивать**) (*coll.*) to tear down, pull down; to trim, even up.
обдёргива|ть, ю *impf. of* **обдёргать** *and* **обдёрнуть**
обдёргива|ться, юсь *impf. of* **обдёрнуться**
обдерн|и́ть, ю́, и́шь *pf.* (*of* **~я́ть**) to turf.
обдёр|нуть, ну, нешь *pf.* (*of* **~гивать**) to adjust, pull down (*dress, skirt, etc.*).
обдёр|нуться, нусь, нешься *pf.* (*of* **~гиваться**) (*coll.*) **1.** to adjust one's dress. **2.** (*cards.*) to pull out the wrong card.
обдерн|я́ть, я́ю *impf. of* **~и́ть**
обдер|у́, ёшь *see* **ободра́ть**
обдира́л|а, ы *m.* (*coll.*) fleecer.
обдира́|ть, ю *impf. of* **ободра́ть**
обди́рк|а, и *f.* **1.** peeling; hulling; skinning, flaying. **2.** (*dial.*) groats.
обди́рный *adj.* peeled; hulled.
обдува́л|а, ы *m.* (*coll.*) cheat, trickster.

обдува́|ть, ю *impf. of* **обду́ть**
обду́манно *adv.* after careful consideration; deliberately (= *after deliberation*).
обду́манност|ь, и *f.* deliberation; deliberateness; careful planning.
обду́ман|ный 1. (**~, ~а**) *p.p.p. of* **обду́мать. 2.** (**~, ~на**) *adj.* well-considered, well-weighed, carefully thought out; **с зара́нее ~ным наме́рением** deliberately; (*leg.*) of malice prepense.
обду́м|ать, аю *pf.* (*of* **~ывать**) to consider, think over, weigh.
обду́мыва|ть, ю *impf. of* **обду́мать**
обду́|ть[1], **ю, ешь** *pf.* (*of* **~ва́ть**) to blow (on, round).
обду́|ть[2], **ю, ешь** *pf.* (*of* **~ва́ть**) (*coll.*) to cheat; to fool, dupe.
о́бе *see* **о́ба**
обе́га|ть, ю *pf.* (*of* **обега́ть**) **1.** to run (all over, all round). **2.** to run round (to see); **за неде́лю до отъе́зда нам удало́сь о. всех знако́мых** in the week before our departure we managed to look in on all our acquaintances.
обега́|ть, ю *impf. of* **обе́гать** *and* **обежа́ть**
обе́д, а *m.* **1.** dinner; **зва́ный о.** dinner-party; **сесть за о.** to sit down to dinner; **звать к ~у** to call to dinner. **2.** dinner-time (= *midday*); **пе́ред ~ом** before dinner; in the morning; **по́сле ~а** after dinner; in the afternoon.
обе́да|ть, ю *impf.* (*of* **по~**) to have dinner, dine.
обе́д|енный[1] *adj. of* **~**; **~енное вре́мя** dinner time; **о. переры́в** lunch hour, lunch break; **о. стол** dinner table.
обе́д|енный[2] *adj. of* **~ня**
обедне́|вший *p.p. act. of* **~ть** *and adj.* impoverished.
обедне́|лый *adj.* (*coll.*) = **~вший**
обедне́ни|е, я *nt.* impoverishment.
обедне́|ть, ю *pf. of* **бedне́ть**
обедн|и́ть, ю́, и́шь *pf.* (*of* **~я́ть**) to impoverish.
обе́д|ня, ни, *g. pl.* **~ен** *f.* (*eccl.*) mass; **испо́ртить ~ню кому́-н.** (*fig., coll.*) to spoil s.o.'s game, put a spoke in s.o.'s wheel.
обедн|я́ть, яю *impf. of* **~и́ть**
обе|жа́ть, гу́, жи́шь, гу́т *pf.* (*of* **~га́ть**) **1.** to run (over, round). **2.** to run (past). **3.** (*sport*) to outrun, pass.
обезбо́ливани|е, я *nt.* anaesthetization.
обезбо́лива|ть, ю *impf. of* **обезбо́лить**
обезбо́лива|ющий *pres. part. act. of* **~ть**; **~ющее сре́дство** anaesthetic.
обезбо́л|ить, ю, ишь *pf.* (*of* **~ивать**) to anaesthetize.
обезво́|дить, жу, дишь *pf.* (*of* **~живать**) to dehydrate.
обезво́|женный *p.p.p. of* **~дить** *and adj.* dehydrated.
обезво́жива|ть, ю *impf. of* **обезво́дить**
обезвре́|дить, жу, дишь *pf.* (*of* **~живать**) to render harmless; to neutralize.
обезвре́жива|ть, ю *impf. of* **обезвре́дить**
обезгла́в|ить, лю, ишь *pf.* (*of* **~ливать**) **1.** to behead, decapitate. **2.** (*fig.*) to deprive of a head, of a leader.
обезгла́влива|ть, ю *impf. of* **обезгла́вить**
обезде́неже|ть, ю *pf.* (*coll.*) to run short of money.
обездо́л|енный *p.p.p. of* **~ить** *and adj.* unfortunate, hapless.
обездо́лива|ть, ю *impf. of* **обездо́лить**
обездо́л|ить, ю, ишь *pf.* (*of* **~ивать**) to deprive of one's share.
обезжи́р|енный *p.p.p. of* **~ить** *and adj.* fatless; skimmed.
обезжи́рива|ть, ю *impf. of* **обезжи́рить**
обезжи́р|ить, ю, ишь *pf.* (*of* **~ивать**) to deprive of fat, remove fat (from); to skim.
обеззара́жива|ть, ю *impf. of* **обеззара́зить**
обеззара́жива|ющий *p.p.p of* **~ть** *and adj.* disinfectant.
обеззара́|зить, жу, зишь *pf.* (*of* **~живать**) to disinfect.
обезземе́л|енный *p.p.p. of* **~ить** *and adj.* landless, deprived of land.
обезземе́лива|ть, ю *impf. of* **обезземе́лить**
обезземе́л|ить, ю, ишь *pf.* (*of* **~ивать**) to dispossess of land.
обеззу́бе|ть, ю *pf.* (*coll.*) to lose one's teeth.
обезле́сени|е, я *nt.* deforestation.
обезле́си|ть, шь *pf.* to deforest.
обезли́чени|е, я *nt.* **1.** depersonalization. **2.** depriving of personal responsibility; removal of personal responsibility (from).
обезли́ч|енный *p.p.p. of* **~ить** *and adj.* **1.** pooled (*of working tools, etc.: assigned to and made the responsibility of no one individual user*). **2.** impersonal, multiple, group (*in which no one individual bears responsibility*); **~енное руково́дство** group management. **3.** (*econ., fin.*) not owned by a specified pers.; **~енная облига́ция** (*fin.*) bearer bond.
обезли́чива|ть, ю *impf. of* **обезли́чить**
обезли́ч|ить, у, ишь *pf.* (*of* **~ивать**) **1.** to deprive of individuality, depersonalize. **2.** to deprive of personal responsibility; to do away with personal responsibility (for). **3.** (*econ., fin.*) to remove from ownership by a specified pers.; to make available to bearer unspecified.
обезли́чк|а, и *f.* lack of personal responsibility; (*rail.*) multiple manning.
обезлю́де|ть, ю *pf.* to become depopulated.
обезобра́жива|ть, ю *impf. of* **обезобра́зить**
обезобра́|зить, жу, зишь *pf.* (*of* **~живать** *and* **безобра́зить**) to disfigure.
обезопа́|сить, шу, сишь *pf.* (**от**) to secure (against).
обезопа́|ситься, шусь, сишься *pf.* (**от**) to secure o.s., make o.s. secure (against).
обезору́жива|ть, ю *impf. of* **обезору́жить**
обезору́ж|ить, у, ишь *pf.* (*of* **~́ивать**) to disarm (*also fig.*).
обезу́ме|ть, ю *pf.* to lose one's senses, lose one's head; **о. от испу́га** to become panic-stricken.
обезья́н|а, ы *f.* monkey; ape.
обезья́н|ий *adj. of* **~а**; (*zool.*) simian; (*fig.*) ape-like.
обезья́нник, а *m.* monkey-house.
обезья́нничань|е, я *nt.* (*coll.*) aping.
обезья́ннича|ть, ю *impf.* (*of* **с~**) (*coll.*) to ape.
обел|и́ть, ю́, и́шь *pf.* (*of* **~я́ть**) (*fig.*) to whitewash; to vindicate; to prove the innocence (of).
обел|и́ться, ю́сь, и́шься *pf.* (*of* **~я́ться**) to vindicate o.s., obtain recognition of one's innocence.
обел|я́ть(ся), я́ю(сь) *impf. of* **~и́ть(ся)**
обер-... *comb. form* **1.** (*in designations of holders of rank or office*) chief-. **2.** (*coll., pej.*) arch-.
оберега́|ть(ся), ю(сь) *impf. of* **обере́чь(ся)**
обере́|чь, гу́, жёшь, гу́т, *past* **~́г, ~гла́** *pf.* (*of* **~га́ть**) (**от**) to guard (against), protect (from).
обере́|чься, гу́сь, жёшься, гу́тся, *past* **~́гся, ~гла́сь** *pf.* (*of* **~га́ться**) **1.** (**от**) to guard o.s. (from, against), protect o.s. (from) **2.** *pass. of* **~чь**
обер-конду́ктор, а *m.* chief guard (*of a train*).
оберн|у́ть, у́, ёшь *pf.* (*of* **обора́чивать**) **1.** (*impf. also* **обёртывать**) to wind (round), twist (round); **о. вокру́г па́льца** (*coll.*) to twist round one's little finger. **2.** (*impf. also* **обёртывать**) to wrap up. **3.** (*impf. also* **обёртывать**) to turn; **о. лицо́ (к)** to turn one's face (towards); **о. в свою́ по́льзу** (*fig.*) to turn to account, turn to advantage. **4.** (*coll.*) to overturn, upturn. **5.** (*comm.*) to turn over. **6.** (*coll.*) to work through, go through.
оберн|у́ться, у́сь, ёшься *pf.* (*of* **обора́чиваться**) **1.** (*impf. also* **обёртываться**) to turn; **о. лицо́м** to turn one's head. **2.** (*impf. also* **обёртываться**) to turn out; **собы́тия ~у́лись и́наче, чем мы ожида́ли** events turned out otherwise than we expected. **3.** (*coll.*) to (go and) come back; **я ~у́сь за два часа́** I shall be back in two hours. **4.** (*coll.*) to manage, get by. **5.** (*impf. also* **обёртываться**) (+*i. or* **в**+*a.*) to turn into, become (*also fig.*); **о. вампи́ром** to turn into a vampire.
о́бер-прокуро́р, а *m.* (*hist.*) chief procurator (*title of official in charge of Holy Synod set up in 1721*).
обёртк|а, и *f.* wrapper; envelope; (*of book*) (*obs.*) dust-jacket, cover.
оберто́н, а *m.* (*mus.*) overtone.
обёрт|очный *adj. of* **~ка; ~очная бума́га** wrapping paper.
обёртыва|ть(ся), ю(сь) *impf. of* **оберну́ть(ся)**
обескро́в|ить, лю, ишь *pf.* (*of* **~ливать**) to drain of blood; to bleed white; (*fig.*) to render lifeless.
обескро́в|ленный *p.p.p. of* **~ить** *and adj.* bloodless; (*fig.*) anaemic, lifeless.

обескро́влива|ть, ю *impf. of* **обескро́вить**
обескура́жива|ть, ю *impf. of* **обескура́жить**
обескура́ж|ить, у, ишь *pf.* (*coll.*) to discourage, dishearten; to dismay.
обеспа́мяте|ть, ю *pf.* **1.** to lose one's memory. **2.** to lose consciousness, become unconscious, faint.
обеспе́чени|е, я *nt.* **1.** securing, guaranteeing; ensuring. **2.** (+*i.*) providing (with), provision (of, with). **3.** guarantee; security (= *pledge*). **4.** security (= *material maintenance*); safeguard(s); **социа́льное о.** social security. **5.** (*mil.*) security; protection. **6.: програ́ммное о.** (*comput.*) software.
обеспе́ченност|ь, и *f.* **1.** (+*i.*) being provided (with), provision (of, with); **о. школ уче́бниками** the provision of schools with text-books. **2.** (material) security.
обеспе́ч|енный *p.p.p. of* **~ить** *and adj.* well-to-do; well provided for.
обеспе́чива|ть, ю *impf. of* **обеспе́чить**
обеспе́ч|ить, у, ишь *pf.* (*of* **~ивать**) **1.** to provide for. **2.** (+*i.*) to provide (with), guarantee supply (of); **о. экспеди́цию обору́дованием** to provide an expedition with equipment. **3.** to secure, guarantee; to ensure, assure. **4.** (**от**) to safeguard (from), protect (from).
обеспло́|дить, жу, дишь *pf.* (*of* **~живать**) to sterilize; to render barren.
обеспло́жива|ть, ю *impf. of* **обеспло́дить**
обеспоко́|ить(ся), ю(сь) *pf. of* **беспоко́ить(ся) 1.**
обесси́ле|ть, ю *pf.* to grow weak, lose one's strength; to collapse, break down.
обесси́лива|ть, *impf. of* **обесси́лить**
обесси́л|ить, ю, ишь *pf.* (*of* **~ивать**) to weaken.
обесcла́в|ить, лю, ишь *pf.* (*of* **бесcла́вить**) to defame.
обессме́р|тить, чу, тишь *pf.* to immortalize.
обессу́д|ить, *pf. now only used in imper.* **не ~ь(те)** (please) don't take it amiss; (please) don't be angry.
обесто́чива|ть, ю *impf. of* **обесто́чить**
обесто́ч|ить, у, ишь *pf.* (*of* **~ивать**) (*elec.*) to de-energize.
обесцве́|тить, чу, тишь *pf.* (*of* **~чивать**) to decolo(u)rize, deprive of colour; (*fig.*) to render colourless, tone down.
обесцве́|титься, чусь, тишься *pf.* (*of* **~чиваться**) to become colourless (*also fig.*).
обесцве́чива|ть(ся), ю(сь) *impf. of* **обесцве́тить(ся)**
обесце́нени|е, я *nt.* depreciation; loss of value.
обесце́н|енный *p.p.p. of* **~ить** *and adj.* depreciated.
обесце́нива|ть(ся), ю(сь) *impf. of* **обесце́нить(ся)**
обесце́н|ить, ю, ишь *pf.* (*of* **~ивать**) to depreciate, cheapen.
обесце́н|иться, юсь, ишься *pf.* (*of* **~иваться**) **1.** (*intrans.*) to depreciate, cheapen. **2.** *pass. of* **~ить**
обесче́|стить, щу, стишь *pf. of* **бесче́стить**
обе́т, а *m.* (*rhet.*) vow, promise.
обетова́нн|ый *adj.*: **~ая земля́, о. край** the Promised Land.
обеща́ни|е, я *nt.* promise; **дать, сдержа́ть о.** to give, keep a promise (*or* one's word).
обеща́|ть, ю *impf. and pf.* to promise.
обеща́|ться, юсь *impf. and pf.* (*coll.*) **1.** to promise. **2.** to give (exchange) a promise (*sc.* to marry).
обжа́ловани|е, я *nt.* appeal; **о. пригово́ра** (*leg.*) appealing against a sentence.
обжа́л|овать, ую *pf.* (*leg.*) to lodge a complaint (against); to appeal (against).
обжа́рива|ть, ю *impf. of* **обжа́рить**
обжа́р|ить, ю, ишь *pf.* (*of* **~ивать**) (*cul.*) to fry on both sides, all over.
обжа́ть[1]**, обожму́, обожмёшь** *pf.* (*of* **обжима́ть**) to press out; to wring out.
обжа́ть[2]**, обожну́, обожнёшь** *pf.* (*of* **обжина́ть**) (*dial.*) to reap (*the whole of*).
обже́чь, обожгу́, обожжёшь, обожгу́т, *past* **обжёг, обожгла́** *pf.* (*of* **обжига́ть**) **1.** to burn, scorch; **о. себе́ па́льцы** to burn one's fingers (*also fig.*). **2.** to bake (*bricks, etc.*); to calcine (lime).
обже́чься, обожгу́сь, обожжёшься, обожгу́тся, *past.* **обжёгся, обожгла́сь** *pf.* **1.** (+*i. or* **на**+*p.*) to burn o.s. (on, with); **о. горя́чим ча́ем** to scald o.s. with hot tea; **о. крапи́вой** to be stung by a nettle; **обжёгшись на молоке́, ста́нешь дуть и на́ воду** (*prov.*) a burnt child dreads the fire. **2.** (*fig., coll.*) to burn one's fingers.
обжива́|ть(ся), ю(сь) *impf. of* **обжи́ть(ся)**
обжи́г, а *m.* (*tech.*) kilning, glazing; (*of clay*) baking; (*of ores*) roasting; (*of lime*) calcining.
обжига́л|а, ы *m.* (*tech.*) kiln-worker.
обжига́тельн|ый *adj.* (*tech.*) glazing; baking; roasting; **~ая печь** kiln.
обжига́|ть(ся), ю(сь) *impf. of* **обже́чь(ся)**
обжи́м, а *m.* (*tech.*) **1.** pressing out. **2.** cap tool, snap tool, riveting set.
обжима́|ть, ю *impf. of* **обжа́ть**[1]
обжи́м|ка, ки *f.* (*tech.*) = **~; пла́тье в ~ку** (*coll.*) tight-fitting dress.
обжи́мный *adj.* (*tech.*) pressing, blooming; **о. стан** blooming mill, roughing mill.
обжина́|ть, ю *impf. of* **обжа́ть**[2]
обжира́|ться, юсь *impf. of* **обожра́ться**
обжит|о́й (*and* **~ый**) *p.p.p. of* **~ь**
обж|и́ть, иву́, ивёшь, *past* **~ил, ~ила́, ~ило** *pf.* (*of* **~ива́ть**) (*coll.*) to render habitable.
обж|и́ться, иву́сь, ивёшься, *past* **~илс́я, ~ила́сь** *pf.* (*of* **~ива́ться**) (*coll.*) to make o.s. at home, feel at home.
обжо́р|а, ы *c.g.* (*coll.*) glutton, gormandizer.
обжо́рлив|ый (~, ~а) *adj.* gluttonous.
обжо́рный *adj.* **о. ряд** (*obs.*) refreshment stall (*in market*).
обжо́рств|о, а *nt.* gluttony.
обжу́лива|ть, ю *impf. of* **обжу́лить**
обжу́л|ить, ю, ишь *pf.* (*coll.*) to cheat, swindle.
обзаведе́ни|е, я *nt.* **1.** (+*i.*) providing (with), fitting out. **2.** (*coll.*) establishment; (*collect.*) fittings, appointments, paraphernalia.
обзаве|сти́сь, ду́сь, дёшься, *past* **~лся, ~ла́сь** *pf.* (*of* **обзаводи́ться**) (+*i.*; *coll.*) to provide o.s. (with); to set up; **о. семьёй** to settle down (*to married life*); **о. хозя́йством** to set up home.
обзаво|ди́ться, жу́сь, ~дишься *impf. of* **обзавести́сь**
обзо́р, а *m.* **1.** survey, review. **2.** (*mil.*) field of view.
обзо́р|ный *adj. of* **~; ~ная ле́кция, ~ная статья́** survey.
обзыва́|ть, ю *impf. of* **обозва́ть**
обива́|ть, ю *impf. of* **оби́ть; о. (все) поро́ги** (*fig.*) to leave no stone unturned.
оби́вк|а, и *f.* **1.** upholstering. **2.** upholstery.
обивно́й *adj.* for upholstery.
оби́д|а, ы *f.* **1.** offence, injury, insult; (sense of) grievance, resentment; **быть на кого́-н. в оби́де** to bear a grudge against s.o.; **зата́ить ~у** to bear a grudge, nurse a grievance; **проглоти́ть ~у** to swallow an insult; **не дава́ть себя́ в ~у** to (be able to) stick up for o.s.; **не в ~у будь ска́зано** no offence meant. **2.** (*coll.*) annoying thing, nuisance; **кака́я о.!** what a nuisance!
оби́|деть, жу, дишь *pf.* (*of* **~жа́ть**) **1.** to offend; to hurt (the feelings of), wound. **2.** to hurt; to do damage (to); **му́хи не ~дит** (*fig.*) he would not harm a fly. **3.** (+*i.*; *following* **Бог, приро́да** *etc.*) to stint, begrudge; **приро́да не ~дела его́ тала́нтом** he has plenty of natural ability.
оби́|деться, жусь, дишься *pf.* (*of* **~жа́ться**) (**на**+*a.*) to take offence (at), take umbrage (at); to feel hurt (by), resent.
оби́д|ный (~ен, ~на) *adj.* **1.** offensive; **мне ~но** I feel hurt, it pains me. **2.** (*coll.*) annoying, tiresome; **~но** (*impers.*) it is a pity, it is a nuisance; **~но, что мы опозда́ли** it is a pity that we were late.
оби́дчивост|ь, и *f.* touchiness, susceptibility (*to offence*), sensitivity.
оби́дчив|ый (~, ~а) *adj.* touchy, susceptible (*to offence*), sensitive.
оби́дчик, а *m.* (*coll.*) offender.
обижа́|ть, ю *impf. of* **оби́деть**
обижа́|ться, юсь *impf. of* **оби́деться; не ~йтесь** don't be offended.
оби́|женный *p.p.p of* **~деть** *and adj.* offended, hurt, aggrieved; **быть ~жен (на**+*a.*) to have a grudge (against); **у него́ был о. вид** he had an aggrieved air, he looked offended; **о. Бо́гом, о. приро́дой** (*joc.*) not over-blessed (with talents); ill-starred.

оби́ли|е, я *nt.* abundance, plenty; **жить в ~и** to live in comfort.

оби́л|овать, ую *impf.* (*+i.*; *obs.*) to abound (in).

оби́л|ьный (~ен, ~ьна) *adj.* abundant, plentiful; (*+i.*) rich (in); **~ьное угоще́ние** lavish entertainment; **о. урожа́й** bumper crop; **день, о. происше́ствиями** an eventful day.

обину́ясь *only in phr.* **не о.** without a moment's hesitation.

обиня́к, а́ *m. only in phrr.* **говори́ть ~о́м, ~а́ми** to beat about the bush; **говори́ть без ~о́в** to speak plainly, speak in plain terms.

обира́л|а, ы *c.g.* (*coll.*) extortionist, bloodsucker.

обира́ловк|а, и *f.* (*coll.*) clip-joint.

обира́|ть, ю *impf. of* **обобра́ть**

обита́ем|ый (~, ~а) *adj.* inhabited; **~ая косми́ческая ста́нция** manned space station.

обита́тел|ь, я *m.* inhabitant; resident; (*of a house*) inmate; **о. морски́х глуби́н** denizen of the deep.

обита́|ть, ю *impf.* (**в**+*p.*) to live (in), dwell (in), reside (in).

оби́тел|ь, и *f.* **1.** cloister. **2.** (*fig.*; *obs.*) abode, dwelling-place.

оби́тель|ский *adj. of* ~

оби́|ть, обобью́, обобьёшь *pf.* (*of* **~ва́ть**) **1.** (**с**+*g.*) to knock (off, down from); **о. плоды́ с я́блони** to knock down fruit from an apple-tree. **2.** (*+i.*) to upholster (with), cover (with); **о. гвоздя́ми** to stud; **о. желе́зом** to bind with iron. **3.** to wear out (*the surface of, at the edges*); **о. подо́л ю́бки** to wear the hem of a skirt; **о. штукату́рку** to chip off plaster.

обихо́д, а *m.* **1.** custom, use, practice; **повседне́вный о.** everyday practice; **предме́ты дома́шнего ~а** household articles; **пусти́ть в о.** to bring into (general) use; **вы́йти из ~а** to be no longer in use, fall into disuse. **2.** (*eccl.*) ordinary; rules of church singing.

обихо́д|ный (~ен, ~на) *adj.* everyday; **~ное выраже́ние** colloquial expression.

обка́лыва|ть, ю *impf. of* **обколо́ть**

обка́п|ать, аю *pf.* (*of* **~ывать**[1]) (*+i.*) to let drops (of) fall on; to cover with drops (of).

обка́пыва|ть[1]**, ю** *impf. of* **обка́пать**

обка́пыва|ть[2]**, ю** *impf. of* **обкопа́ть**

обка́рмлива|ть, ю *impf. of* **обкорми́ть**

обкат|а́ть, а́ю *pf.* (*of* **´~ывать**) **1.** to roll. **2.** to roll smooth (*a road surface, etc.*). **3.** (*tech.*) to run in (*a new vehicle, etc.*).

обка́тк|а, и *f.* (*tech.*) running in.

обка́тыва|ть, ю *impf. of* **обката́ть**

обкла́дк|а, и *f.* (*in var. senses*) facing; **о. дёрном** turfing.

обкла́дыва|ть, *impf. of* **обложи́ть**

обкол|о́ть, ю́, ´~ешь *pf.* (*of* **обка́лывать**) **1.** to cut away (*ice, etc.*). **2.** to prick all over.

обко́м, а *m.* (*abbr. of* **областно́й комите́т**) oblast committee.

обкопа́|ть, ю *pf.* (*of* **обка́пывать**[2]) (*coll.*) to dig round.

обкорм|и́ть, лю́, ´~ишь *pf.* (*of* **обка́рмливать**) to overfeed.

обкорна́|ть, ю *pf. of* **корна́ть**

обкра́дыва|ть, ю *impf. of* **обокра́сть**

обку́р|енный *p.p.p. of* **~ить** *and adj.*; **~енная тру́бка** seasoned pipe; **~енные па́льцы** tobacco-stained fingers.

обку́рива|ть, ю *impf. of* **обкури́ть**

обкур|и́ть, ю́, ´~ишь *pf.* (*of* **´~ивать**) **1.**: **о. тру́бку** to season a pipe. **2.** to fumigate. **3.** (*coll.*) to envelop with (tobacco) smoke; to stain with tobacco.

обкус|а́ть, а́ю *pf.* (*of* **´~ывать**) to bite round; to nibble.

обку́сыва|ть, ю *impf. of* **обкуса́ть**

обл. *abbr. of* **1. о́бласть** oblast. **2. областно́й** dial., dialectal.

обл... *comb. form, abbr. of* **областно́й 1.**

обла́в|а, ы *f.* **1.** (*hunting*) battue; beating up. **2.** (*fig.*) (*police*) raid, swoop; cordon; cordoning off; round-up.

облага́емый *adj.* taxable.

облага́|ть, ю *impf. of* **обложи́ть**

облага́|ться, юсь *impf.* (*of* **обложи́ться**): **о. нало́гом** to be liable to tax, be taxable.

облагоде́тельств|овать, ую *pf.* (*obs. or iron.*) to do a great favour.

облагора́жива|ть, ю *impf. of* **облагоро́дить**

облагоро́|дить, жу, дишь *pf.* (*of* **облагора́живать**) to ennoble.

облада́ни|е, я *nt.* possession.

облада́тел|ь, я *m.* possessor.

облада́|ть, ю, *impf.* (*+i.*) to possess, be possessed (of); **о. хоро́шим здоро́вьем** to enjoy good health; **о. пра́вом** to have the right; **о. больши́м тала́нтом** to have great talents, be very talented.

обла́|зить, жу, зишь *pf.* (*coll.*) to climb round, climb all over.

о́блак|о, а, *pl.* **~а́, ~о́в** *nt.* cloud; **кучевы́е ~а́** cumuli; **пе́ристые ~а́** cirri; **слои́стые ~а́** strati; **быть, носи́ться в ~а́х** (*fig.*) to live in the clouds; **свали́ться с ~о́в** (*fig.*) to appear from nowhere.

обла́мыва|ть(ся), ю(сь) *impf. of* **облома́ть(ся)**

обла́п|ить, лю, ишь *pf.* (*of* **~ливать**) (*coll.*) to hug.

обла́плива|ть, ю *impf. of* **обла́пить**

облапо́шива|ть, ю *impf. of* **облапо́шить**

облапо́ш|ить, у, ишь *pf.* (*of* **~ивать**) (*coll.*) to cheat, swindle.

обласка́|ть, ю *pf.* to treat with affection, display much kindness towards.

областно́й *adj.* **1.** oblast; provincial; regional. **2.** (*ling.*) dialectal; regional.

о́бласт|ь, и, *g. pl.* **~е́й** *f.* **1.** (*designation of administrative division of former USSR*) oblast; province; **прие́хать из ~и** to come from oblast (*fig., coll. = from administrative centre of oblast*). **2.** region, district; belt; **о. вечнозелёных расте́ний** evergreen belt; **озёрная о.** lake district; (*in Germany*) -land; **Ре́йнская о.** the Rhineland; **Ру́рская о.** the Ruhr (*region*); **Саа́рская о.** Saarland, the Saar (*region*); **Суде́тская о.** Sudetenland. **3.** (*anat., med.*) tract; region. **4.** (*fig.*) province, field, sphere, realm, domain; **о. микробиоло́гии** the field of microbiology; **о. мифоло́гии** the realm of mythology.

обла́тк|а, и *f.* **1.** (*eccl.*) wafer, host. **2.** (*pharm.*) capsule. **3.** paper seal.

обла́т|очный *adj. of* **~ка**

облач|а́ть(ся), а́ю(сь) *impf. of* **~и́ть(ся)**

облаче́ни|е, я *nt.* **1.** (**в**+*a.*) robing (in). **2.** (*eccl.*) vestments, robes.

облач|и́ть, у́, и́шь *pf.* (*of* **~а́ть**) (**в**+*a.*) **1.** (*eccl.*) to robe (in). **2.** (*rhet. or coll., joc.*) to array (in), get up (in).

облач|и́ться, у́сь, и́шься *pf.* (*of* **~а́ться**) **1.** (*eccl.*) to robe, put on robes. **2.** (*rhet. or coll., joc.*) to array o.s.

о́блачк|о, а, *pl.* **~а́, ~о́в** *nt. dim. of* **о́блако**

о́блачност|ь, и *f.* **1.** cloudiness. **2.** (*meteor.*) cloud conditions; **о. в де́сять ба́ллов** ten tenths cloud.

о́блач|ный (~ен, ~на) *adj.* cloudy.

облега́|ть, ю *impf.* **1.** *impf. of* **обле́чь**[1]. **2.** (*of clothes*) to fit tightly; **о. фигу́ру** to outline the figure.

облега́|ющий *pres. part. act. of* **~ть** *and adj.* tight-fitting.

облегч|а́ть(ся), а́ю(сь) *impf. of* **~и́ть(ся)**

облегче́ни|е, я *nt.* **1.** facilitation. **2.** relief; **вздохну́ть с ~ем** to heave a sigh of relief.

облегч|и́ть, у́, и́шь *pf.* (*of* **~а́ть**) **1.** to facilitate. **2.** to lighten. **3.** to relieve; to alleviate; to mitigate; (*leg.*) to commute; **о. ду́шу** to relieve one's mind.

облегч|и́ться, у́сь, и́шься *pf.* (*of* **~а́ться**) **1.** to be relieved, find relief. **2.** to become easier; to become lighter. **3.** (*coll., euph.*) to relieve o.s.

обледене́лый *adj.* ice-covered.

обледене́ни|е, я *nt.* icing(-over); **пери́од ~я** Ice Age.

обледене́|ть, ю *pf.* to ice over, become covered with ice.

облез|а́ть, а́ет *impf. of* **´~ть**

обле́зл|ый *adj.* (*coll.*) shabby, bare; **~ая ко́шка** mangy cat.

обле́з|ть, ет, *past* **~, ~ла** *pf.* (*of* **~а́ть**) (*coll.*) **1.** (*of fur, etc.*) to come out, come off. **2.** to grow bare (*of fur, feathers, etc.*); to grow mangy. **3.** (*of paintwork, etc.*) to peel off.

облека́|ть(ся), ю(сь) *impf. of* **обле́чь**[2]**(ся)**

обле́нива|ться, юсь *impf. of* **облени́ться**

облен|и́ться, ю́сь, ´~ишься *pf.* (*of* **´~иваться**) to grow lazy.

облеп|и́ть, лю́, ∸ишь *pf.* (*of* **~ля́ть**) **1.** to stick (to); (*fig.*) to cling (to); to surround, throng; **нас ~и́ла ку́ча мальчи́шек** we were surrounded by a swarm of small boys. **2.** (*+a. and i.*) to paste all over (with), plaster (with); **о. сте́ну объявле́ниями** to plaster a wall with notices.
облепи́х|а, и *f.* (*bot.*) sea buckthorn (*Hippophae rhamnoides*).
облепля́|ть, ю *impf. of* **облепи́ть**
облесе́ни|е, я *nt.* afforestation.
обле|си́ть, шу́, си́шь *pf.* to afforest.
облёт, а *m.* buzzing (*by aircraft*).
облет|а́ть[1], а́ю *impf. of* **~е́ть**
облет|а́ть[2], а́ю *pf.* (*of* **∸ывать**) **1.** to fly (all round, all over); **мы ~а́ли всю Евро́пу** we have flown all over Europe; **она́ ~а́ла всех подру́г** (*fig., coll.*) she flew round to all her girl-friends. **2.** to test (*an aircraft*).
обле|те́ть, чу́, ти́шь *pf.* (*of* **~та́ть[1]**) **1.** (*+a. or* **вокру́г**) to fly (round). **2.** (*of news, rumours, etc.*) to spread (round, all over); **за полчаса́ весть о побе́де ~те́ла го́род** in half an hour the news of the victory had spread round the town. **3.** (*of leaves*) to fall.
облётыва|ть, ю *impf. of* **облета́ть[2]**
облеч|ённый *p.p.p. of* **∸ь[2]** *and adj.* **1.: о. вла́стью** invested with power. **2.** (*ling.*): **~ённое ударе́ние** circumflex accent (*as mark of perispomenon or properispomenon stress in ancient Greek*).
обл|е́чь[1], я́гу, я́жешь, я́гут, *past* **~ёг, ~егла́** *pf.* (*of* **~ега́ть**) to cover, surround, envelop (*also fig.*); **ту́чи ~егли́ го́ру** rain-clouds enveloped the mountain.
обле́|чь[2], ку́, чёшь, ку́т, *past* **∸к, ~кла́** *pf.* (*of* **~ка́ть**) (*+a.* **в***+a. or +a. and i.*) to clothe (in); to invest (with), vest (in); (*fig.*) to wrap (in), shroud (in); **о. полномо́чиями** to invest with authority, commission; **о. та́йной** to shroud in mystery; **о. свою́ мысль непоня́тными слова́ми** to wrap one's idea in unintelligible words; **о. кого́-н. дове́рием** to express confidence in s.o.
обле́|чься, ку́сь, чёшься, ку́ться, *past* **∸кся, ~кла́сь** *pf.* (*of* **~ка́ться**) (**в***+a.*) to clothe o.s. (in), dress o.s. (in); (*fig.*) to take the form (of), assume the shape (of).
облива́ни|е, я *nt.* **1.** spilling (over), pouring (over). **2.** shower-bath; sponge-down.
облива́|ть, ю *impf. of* **обли́ть**
облива́|ться, юсь *impf. of* **обли́ться; се́рдце у меня́ кро́вью ~ется** my heart bleeds.
обли́вк|а, и *f.* **1.** glazing. **2.** glaze.
обливно́й *adj.* glazed.
облигац|ио́нный *adj. of* **∸ия**
облига́ци|я, и *f.* (*fin.*) bond, debenture.
обли́з|анный *p.p.p. of* **~а́ть** *and adj.* (*fig.*) smooth.
обли|за́ть, жу́, ∸жешь *pf.* (*of* **∸зывать**) to lick (all over); to lick clean; **па́льчики ∸жешь** (*fig., coll.*) (*sc.* it is, it will be) a real treat.
обли|за́ться, жу́сь, ∸жешься *pf.* (*of* **∸зываться**) **1.** to smack one's lips (*also fig.*). **2.** (*of an animal*) to lick itself.
обли́зыва|ть, ю *impf. of* **облиза́ть; о. гу́бы** (*fig., coll.*) to smack one's lips.
обли́зыва|ться, юсь *impf. of* **облиза́ться**
о́блик, а *m.* **1.** look, aspect, appearance. **2.** (*fig.*) cast of mind, temper.
облиня́|ть, ю *pf.* (*coll.*) **1.** to fade, lose colour (*also fig.*). **2.** to moult, lose hair *or* feathers.
облип|а́ть, а́ю *impf. of* **∸нуть**
обли́п|нуть, ну, нешь, *past* **~, ~ла** *pf.* (*of* **~а́ть**) (*+i.*) to become stuck (in, with).
облисполко́м, а *m.* (*abbr. of* ***областно́й исполни́тельный комите́т***) oblast executive committee.
о́блит|ый (~, ~а́, ~о) *and* **обли́тый (~, ~а́, ~о)** *p.p.p. of* **обли́ть**; (*fig.*; *+i.*) covered (by), enveloped (in); **о. све́том луны́** bathed in moonlight.
обл|и́ть, оболью́, обольёшь, *past* **∸ил, ~ила́, ∸ило** *and* **~и́л, ~ила́, ~и́ло** *pf.* (*of* **~ива́ть**) **1.** (*p.p.p.* **∸итый**) to pour (over), sluice (over); to spill (over); **о. ска́терть вино́м** to spill wine over the table-cloth; **о. презре́нием** (*fig.*) to pour contempt (on); **о. гря́зью, о. помо́ями** (*fig., coll.*) to fling mud (at). **2.** (*p.p.p.* **~и́тый**) to glaze.
обли́|ться, оболью́сь, обольёшься, *past* **~лся, ~ла́сь, ~ло́сь** *and* **~лось** *pf.* (*of* **~ва́ться**) **1.** to have a shower-bath, douche o.s.; to sponge down; **о. холо́дной водо́й** to have a cold shower. **2.** to pour over o.s., spill over o.s.; **о. по́том** to be bathed in sweat; **о. слеза́ми** to melt into tears. **3.** *pass. of* **~ть**
облиц|ева́ть, у́ю, у́ешь *pf.* (*of* **~о́вывать**) (*+a. and i.*) to face (with), revet (with).
облицо́вк|а, и *f.* facing, revetment; lining, coating.
облицо́в|очный *adj. of* **~ка; о. кирпи́ч** facing brick, decorative tile.
облицо́выва|ть, ю *impf. of* **облицева́ть**
облич|а́ть, а́ю *impf.* (*of* **~и́ть**) **1.** to expose, unmask, denounce. **2.** (*impf. only*) to reveal, display, manifest; to point (to).
обличе́ни|е, я *nt.* exposure, unmasking, denunciation.
обличи́тел|ь, я *m.* exposer, unmasker, denouncer.
обличи́тельн|ый *adj.* denunciatory; **~ая речь, ~ая статья́** diatribe, tirade.
облич|и́ть, у́, и́шь *pf. of* **~а́ть**
обли́чь|е, я *nt.* **1.** (*coll.*) face. **2.** aspect, appearance (*also fig.*).
облобыза́|ть, ю *pf.* (*obs., joc.*) to kiss.
обложе́ни|е, я *nt.* **1.** taxation; assessment, rating. **2.** (*mil.*; *obs.*) investment.
обло́ж|енный *p.p.p. of* **~и́ть; о. язы́к** (*med.*) furred tongue.
облож|и́ть, у́, ∸ишь *pf.* **1.** (*impf.* **обкла́дывать**) to put (round); to edge; **о. больно́го поду́шками** to surround a patient with pillows; **о. сте́ну мра́мором** to face a wall with marble. **2.** (*impf.* **обкла́дывать**) to cover; (*impers.*): **круго́м ~и́ло (не́бо)** the sky is completely overcast; **го́рло у него́ ~и́ло** (*med.*) his throat is furred. **3.** (*impf.* **обкла́дывать**) to surround; **о. кре́пость** (*mil.*; *obs.*) to invest a fortress; (*hunting*) to close round, corner. **4.** (*impf.* **облага́ть**) to assess; **о. нало́гом** to tax; **о. ме́стным нало́гом** to rate. **5.** (*impf.* **обкла́дывать**) (*coll.*) to swear (at), berate.
облож|и́ться, у́сь, ∸ишься *pf.* **1.** (*impf.* **обкла́дываться**) (*+i.*) to put round o.s., surround o.s. (with). **2.** *pass. of* **~и́ть**
обло́жк|а, и *f.* (dust-)cover; folder.
обложно́й *adj.*: **о. дождь** (*coll.*) incessant rain.
облока́чиваться, юсь *impf. of* **облокоти́ться**
облоко|ти́ться, чу́сь, ∸ти́шься *pf.* (*of* **облока́чиваться**) (**на***+a.*) to lean one's elbow(s) (on, against).
обло́м, а *m.* **1.** breaking off. **2.** break. **3.** (*archit.*) profile. **4.** (*coll.*) clodhopper, bumpkin.
облома́|ть, ю, *pf.* (*of* **обла́мывать**) **1.** to break off; **о. зу́бы (обо что-н.)** (*coll.*) to come a cropper. **2.** to break (*horses*). **3.** (*fig., coll.*) to talk into, cajole.
облома́|ться, юсь, *pf.* (*of* **обла́мываться**) to break off, snap.
облом|и́ть, лю́, ∸ишь *pf.* to break off.
облом|и́ться, лю́сь, ∸ишься *pf.* = **~а́ться**
обло́мовщин|а, ы *f.* Oblomovism, chronic inertia (*as typified by the eponymous hero of I. A. Goncharov's novel 'Oblomov'*).
обло́м|ок, ка *m.* **1.** fragment. **2.** (*pl.*) débris, wreckage.
обло́мо|чный *adj. of* **~к; ~чные го́рные поро́ды** (*geol.*) disintegrated rock formations; detritus.
облоно́|о *nt. indecl.* (*abbr. of* ***областно́й отде́л наро́дного образова́ния***) oblast education department.
облуп|и́ть, лю́, ∸ишь *pf. of* **лупи́ть[1]** *and* **∸ливать**
облуп|и́ться, лю́сь, ∸ишься *pf. of* **лупи́ться** *and* **∸ливаться**
облу́п|ленный *p.p.p. of* **~и́ть** *and adj.* chipped; **знать как ~ленного** (*coll.*) to know inside out.
облу́пліва|ть, ю *impf.* (*of* **облупи́ть**) **1.** to peel; to shell (*eggs*). **2.** (*fig., coll.*) to fleece.
облу́плива|ться, юсь *impf.* (*of* **облупи́ться**) to peel (off), scale; to come off, chip (*of paint, plaster, etc.*).
облупл|я́ть(ся), я́ю(сь) *impf.* = **∸ивать(ся)**
облуч|а́ть, а́ю *impf. of* **~и́ть**
облуче́ни|е, я *nt.* (*med.*) irradiation.
облуч|и́ть, у́, и́шь *pf.* (*of* **~а́ть**) to irradiate.

облуч|о́к, ка́ *m.* coachman's seat.

облущ|и́ть, у́, и́шь *pf. of* **лущи́ть**

облы́ж|ный (~ен, ~на) *adj.* (*coll.*) false.

о́блый *adj.* (*obs.*) **1.** round. **2.** (*fig.*) portly, rotund.

облысе́|ть, ю, ешь *pf. of* **лысе́ть**

облюб|ова́ть, у́ю *pf.* (*of* **~о́вывать**) to pick, choose, select.

облюбо́выва|ть, ю *impf. of* **облюбова́ть**

обл|я́гу, я́жешь, я́гут *see* **~е́чь**[1]

обма́|зать, жу, жешь *pf.* (*of* **~зывать**) **1.** to coat (with); to putty (with). **2.** to soil (with), besmear (with); **о. себе́ ру́ки ма́слом** to cover one's hands with oil.

обма́|заться, жусь, жешься *pf.* (*of* **~зываться**) **1.** (+*i.*) to besmear o.s. (with), get o.s. covered (with). **2.** *pass. of* **~зать**

обма́зк|а, и *f.* **1.** coating; puttying.

обма́зыва|ть(ся), ю(сь) *impf. of* **обма́зать(ся)**

обма́кива|ть, ю *impf. of* **обмакну́ть**

обмак|ну́ть, ну́, нёшь, *past* **~ну́л** *pf.* (*of* **~́ивать**) to dip; **о. блин в смета́ну** to dip a pancake into sour cream.

обма́н, а *m.* fraud, deception; **о. зре́ния** optical illusion; **ввести́ в о.** to deceive; **не да́ться кому́-н. в о.** not to be taken in by s.o.

обма́нк|а, и *f.* (*min.*) blende; **рогова́я о.** hornblende; **смоляна́я о.** pitchblende.

обма́нны|й *adj.* fraudulent; **~м путём** fraudulently, by fraud.

обман|у́ть, у́, ~́ешь *pf.* (*of* **~́ывать**) to deceive; to cheat, swindle; **о. чьё-н. дове́рие** to betray s.o.'s trust; **о. чьи-н. наде́жды** to disappoint s.o.'s hopes.

обман|у́ться, у́сь, ~́ешься *pf.* (*of* **~́ываться**) to be deceived; **о. в свои́х ожида́ниях** to be disappointed in one's expectations.

обма́нчив|ый (~, ~а) *adj.* deceptive, delusive; **нару́жность ~а** appearances are deceptive.

обма́нщик, а *m.* deceiver; cheat, fraud.

обма́нываʼ|ть(ся), ю(сь) *impf. of* **обману́ть(ся)**

обмар|а́ть, а́ю *pf.* (*of* **~́ывать**) (*coll.*) to soil, dirty.

обма́рыва|ть, ю *impf. of* **обмара́ть**

обма́тыва|ть(ся), ю(сь) *impf. of* **обмота́ть(ся)**

обма́хива|ть(ся), ю(сь) *impf. of* **обмахну́ть(ся)**

обмах|ну́ть, ну́, нёшь *pf.* (*of* **~́ивать**) **1.** to fan. **2.** to dust (off); to brush (off); **о. сор со ска́терти** to brush crumbs off the cloth.

обмах|ну́ться, ну́сь, нёшься *pf.* (*of* **~́иваться**) **1.** to fan o.s. **2.** *pass. of* **~ну́ть**

обма́чива|ть(ся), ю(сь) *impf. of* **обмочи́ть(ся)**

обмеле́ни|е, я *nt.* shallowing, shoaling.

обмеле́|ть, ет *pf.* (*of* **меле́ть**) **1.** to become shallow. **2.** (*naut.*) to run aground.

обме́н, а *m.* (+*i.*) exchange (of), interchange (of); barter; **о. мне́ниями** exchange of opinions; **о. веще́ств** (*biol.*) metabolism; **в о. (за+*a.*)** in exchange (for).

обме́нива|ть(ся), ю(сь) *impf. of* **обменить(ся)** *and* **обменя́ть(ся)**

обмен|и́ть, ю́, ~́ишь *pf.* (*of* **~́ивать**) (*coll.*) to exchange (*accidentally*) to barter; to swap.

обмен|и́ться, ю́сь, ~́ишься *pf.* (*of* **~́иваться**) (+*i.*) (*coll.*) to exchange (*accidentally*).

обме́н|ный *adj. of* **~**

обмен|я́ть, я́ю *pf.* (*of* **меня́ть 2.** *and* **~́ивать**) (+*a.* **на**+*a.*) to exchange (for).

обмен|я́ться, я́юсь *pf.* (*of* **меня́ться 2.** *and* **~́иваться**) (+*i.*) to exchange; to swap; **о. взгля́дами** to exchange looks; **о. впечатле́ниями** to compare notes.

обме́р[1]**, а** *m.* measurement.

обме́р[2]**, а** *m.* false measure.

об|мере́ть, омру́, омрёшь, *past* **~́мер, ~мерла́, ~́мерло** *pf.* (*of* **~мира́ть**) (*coll.*) to faint; **о. от у́жаса** to be horror-struck; **я ~́мер** my heart stood still.

обме́рива|ть(ся), ю(сь) *impf. of* **обме́рить(ся)**

обме́р|ить[1]**, ю, ишь** *pf.* (*of* **~ивать**) to measure.

обме́р|ить[2]**, ю, ишь** *pf.* (*of* **~ивать**) to cheat in measuring; to give short measure (to).

обме́р|иться, юсь, ишься *pf.* (*of* **~иваться**) (*coll.*) to make a mistake in measuring.

обме|сти́, ту́, тёшь, *past* **~́л, ~ла́** *pf.* (*of* **~та́ть**[1]) to sweep off; to dust.

обмета́|ть[1]**, ю** *impf. of* **обмести́**

обме|та́ть[2]**, чу́, ~́чешь** *pf.* (*of* **~́тывать**) **1.** to overstitch, oversew; to whipstitch; to hem. **2.** (*impers.*; *coll.*): **у меня́ ~та́ло гу́бы** my lips are cracked (with cold sores).

обмётыва|ть, ю *impf. of* **обмета́ть**[2]

обмина́|ть, ю *impf. of* **обмя́ть**

обмира́|ть, ю *impf. of* **обмере́ть**

обмозг|ова́ть, у́ю *pf.* (*of* **~о́вывать**) (*coll.*) to think over, turn over (in one's mind).

обмозго́выва|ть, ю *impf. of* **обмозгова́ть**

обмок|а́ть, а́ю *impf. of* **~́нуть**

обмо́к|нуть, ну, нешь, *past* **~, ~ла** *pf.* (*of* **~а́ть**) (*coll.*) to get wet all over.

обмола́чива|ть, ю *impf. of* **обмолоти́ть**

обмо́лв|иться, люсь, ишься *pf.* (*coll.*) **1.** to make a slip in speaking. **2.** (+*i.*) to say; to utter; **не о. ни сло́вом** (**о**+*p.*) to say not a word (about).

обмо́лвк|а, и *f.* slip of the tongue.

обмоло́т, а *m.* (*agric.*) threshing.

обмоло|ти́ть, чу́, ~́тишь *pf.* (*of* **обмола́чивать**) (*agric.*) to thresh.

обмора́жива|ть(ся), ю(сь) *impf. of* **обморо́зить(ся)**

обморо́жени|е, я *nt.* frost-bite.

обморо́|женный *p.p.p. of* **~зить** *and adj.* frost-bitten.

обморо́|зить, жу, зишь *pf.* (*of* **обмора́живать**); **я ~зил себе́ нос, ру́ки** *etc.* my nose is, hands, *etc.*, are frost-bitten.

обморо́|зиться, жусь, зишься *pf.* (*of* **обмора́живаться**) to suffer frost-bite, be frost-bitten.

о́бморок, а *m.* fainting-fit; swoon; (*med.*) syncope; **в глубо́ком ~е** in a dead faint; **упа́сть в о.** to faint (away); to swoon.

обморо́ч|ить, у, ишь *pf. of* **моро́чить**

о́бморо|чный *adj. of* **~к**; **~чное состоя́ние** (*med.*) syncope.

обмота́|ть, ю *pf.* (*of* **обма́тывать**) (+*a. and i. or a.* **вокру́г**) to wind (round); **о. ше́ю ша́рфом, о. шарф вокру́г ше́и** to wind a scarf round one's neck.

обмота́|ться, юсь *pf.* (*of* **обма́тываться**) **1.** (+*i.*) to wrap o.s. (in). **2.** *pass. of* **~ть**

обмо́тк|а, и *f.* (*elec.*) winding.

обмо́т|ки, ок *no sg.* puttees, leg-wrappings.

обмо́т|очный *adj. of* **1. ~ка. 2. ~ки**

обмоч|и́ть, у́, ~́ишь *pf.* (*of* **обма́чивать**) to wet; **о. посте́ль** (*coll.*) to wet the bed.

обмоч|и́ться, у́сь, ~́ишься *pf.* (*of* **обма́чиваться**) to wet o.s. (*also coll.*).

обм|о́ю, о́ешь *see* **~ы́ть**

обмундирова́ни|е, я *nt.* **1.** fitting out (with uniform). **2.** uniform.

обмундир|ова́ть, у́ю *pf.* (*of* **~о́вывать**) to fit out (with uniform).

обмундир|ова́ться, у́юсь *pf.* (*of* **~о́вываться**) to fit oneself out (with uniform); to draw uniform.

обмундиро́в|ка, ки *f.* = **~а́ние**

обмундиро́в|очный *adj. of* **~ка**; **~очные де́ньги** uniform allowance.

обмундиро́выва|ть(ся), ю(сь) *impf. of* **обмундирова́ть(ся)**

обмуро́вк|а, и *f.* brick-work.

обмыва́ни|е, я *nt.* bathing, washing.

обмыва́|ть(ся), ю(сь) *impf. of* **обмы́ть(ся)**

обмы́л|ок, ка *m.* (*coll.*) remnant of a cake of soap.

обм|ы́ть, о́ю, о́ешь *pf.* (*of* **~ыва́ть**) **1.** to bathe, wash; **о. ра́ну** to bathe a wound. **2.** (*coll.*) to celebrate, drink to.

обм|ы́ться, о́юсь, о́ешься *pf.* (*of* **~ыва́ться**) **1.** to bathe, wash. **2.** *pass. of* **~ы́ть**

обмяк|а́ть, а́ю *impf.* (*of* **~́нуть**) (*coll.*) to become soft; (*fig.*) to become flabby.

обмя́к|нуть, ну, нешь, *past* **~, ~ла** *pf. of* **~а́ть**

об|мя́ть, омну́, омнёшь, *pf.* (*of* **~мина́ть**) to press down; to trample down.

обнагле́|ть, ю, ешь *pf. of* **нагле́ть**

обнадёжива|ть, ю *impf. of* **обнадёжить**

обнадёж|ить, у, ишь *pf.* (*of* **~ивать**) to give hope (to), reassure.

обнаж|а́ть(ся), а́ю(сь) *impf. of* **~и́ть(ся)**
обнаже́ни|е, я *nt.* **1.** baring, uncovering. **2.** (*fig.*) revealing. **3.** (*geol.*): **о. го́рной поро́ды** outcrop.
обнаж|ённый *p.p.p. of* **~и́ть** *and adj.* naked, bare; nude.
обнаж|и́ть, у́, и́шь *pf.* (*of* **~а́ть**) **1.** to bare, uncover; **о. го́лову** to bare one's head; **о. шпа́гу** to draw the sword. **2.** (*fig.*) to lay bare, reveal.
обнаж|и́ться, у́сь, и́шься *pf.* (*of* **~а́ться**) **1.** to bare o.s., uncover o.s. **2.** *pass. of* **~и́ть**
обнайто́в|ить, лю, ишь *pf. of* **найто́вить**
обнаро́довани|е, я *nt.* publication, promulgation.
обнаро́д|овать, ую *pf. and impf.* (*liter.*) to publish, promulgate.
обнару́жени|е, я *nt.* **1.** disclosure; displaying, revealing. **2.** discovery; detection.
обнару́жива|ть(ся), ю(сь) *impf. of* **обнару́жить(ся)**
обнару́ж|ить, у, ишь *pf.* (*of* **~ивать**) **1.** to disclose; to display, reveal; **о. свою́ ра́дость** to betray one's joy. **2.** to discover, bring to light; to detect.
обнару́ж|иться, усь, ишься *pf.* (*of* **~иваться**) **1.** to be revealed; to come to light. **2.** *pass. of* **~иваться**
обна́шива|ть, ю *impf. of* **обноси́ть**[1]
обнес|ти́[1], **у́, ёшь,** *past* **~́, ~ла́** *pf.* (*of* **обноси́ть**[2]) (+*i.*) to enclose (with); **о. и́згородью** to fence (in); **о. пери́лами** to rail in, off.
обнес|ти́[2], **у́, ёшь,** *past* **~́, ~ла́** *pf.* (*of* **обноси́ть**[3]) (+*i.*) to serve round; **~ли́ ли вы всех госте́й шампа́нским?** have you passed round the champagne to all the guests?; have all the guests had champagne?
обнес|ти́[3], **у́, ёшь,** *past* **~́, ~ла́** *pf.* (*of* **обноси́ть**[4]) (+*a. and i.*) to pass over, leave out (*in serving sth.*); **меня́ ~ли́ вино́м** I have not had (= *been offered*) wine.
обнима́|ть(ся), ю(сь) *impf. of* **обня́ть(ся)**
обни́мк|а, и *f. only in phr.* **в ~у** (*coll.*) in an embrace, embracing one another.
обнища́лый *adj.* impoverished; beggarly.
обнища́ни|е, я *nt.* impoverishment, pauperization.
обнища́|ть, ю *pf. of* **нища́ть**
обнов|и́ть, лю́, и́шь *pf.* (*of* **~ля́ть**) **1.** to renovate; to renew; to reform; to update. **2.** to repair, restore; **о. свои́ зна́ния** (*fig.*) to refresh one's knowledge; **о. свои́ си́лы** (*fig.*) to recruit (one's forces). **3.** (*coll., fig.*) to christen; to use *or* wear for the first time.
обнов|и́ться, лю́сь, и́шься *pf.* (*of* **~ля́ться**) **1.** to revive, be restored. **2.** *pass. of* **~и́ть**
обно́вк|а, и *f.* (*coll.*) new acquisition, 'new toy'; new dress.
обновле́н|ец, ца *m.* (*hist.*) 'Renovationist' (*member of 'Renovation' church in 1920s*).
обновле́ни|е, я *nt.* renovation, renewal; **вне́шнее о.** face-lift.
обновля́|ть(ся), ю(сь) *impf. of* **обнови́ть(ся)**
обно|си́ть[1], **шу́, ~́сишь** *pf.* (*of* **обна́шивать**) (*coll.*) to wear in (*new clothing or footwear*).
обно|си́ть[2,3,4], **шу́, ~́сишь** *impf. of* **обнести́**[1,2,3]
обно|си́ться, шу́сь, ~́сишься *pf.* (*coll.*) **1.** to have worn out all one's clothes; to be out at elbow. **2.** to become worn in, become comfortable (*of new clothes*).
обно́с|ки, ков *pl.* (*sg.* **~ок, ~ка** *m.*) (*coll.*) old clothes.
обню́х|ать, аю *pf.* (*of* **~ивать**) to sniff (around).
обню́хива|ть, ю *impf. of* **обню́хать**
обн|я́ть, иму́, и́мешь, *past* **~́ял, ~яла́, ~́яло** *pf.* (*of* **~има́ть**) (*in var. senses*) to embrace; to clasp in one's arms; (*fig.*) to envelop; **он шёл, ~я́в её за та́лию** he was walking with his arm round her waist; **о. взгля́дом** to survey; **о. умо́м** (*fig.*) to comprehend, take in.
обн|я́ться, иму́сь, и́мешься, *past* **~ялся́, ~яла́сь, ~яло́сь** *pf.* (*of* **~има́ться**) to embrace; to hug one another.
обо *prep.* = **о**[1]
обо... *vbl. pref.* = **о...** *and* **об...**
обобра́|ть, оберу́, оберёшь, *past* **~л, ~ла́ ~ло** *pf.* (*of* **обира́ть**) (*coll.*) **1.** to pick, gather; **о. кусты́ мали́ны** to pick raspberries. **2.** to rob; (*sl.*) to clean out.
обобра́ться, оберу́сь, оберёшься *pf.* (*coll.*; +*g.*): **не оберёшься** beyond count, innumerable.
обобщ|а́ть, а́ю *impf. of* **~и́ть**
обобще́ни|е, я *nt.* generalization.
обобществ|и́ть, лю́, и́шь *pf.* (*of* **~ля́ть**) to socialize; to collectivize.
обобществле́ни|е, я *nt.* socialization; collectivization.
обобществля́|ть, ю *impf. of* **обобществи́ть**
обобщ|и́ть, у́, и́шь *pf.* (*of* **~а́ть**) to generalize.
обобь|ю́, ёшь *see* **оби́ть**
обовши́ве|ть, ю, ешь *pf. of* **вши́веть**
обогати́тел|ь, я *m.* (*mining tech.*) **1.** concentrator; enriching agent. **2.** ore concentration specialist.
обогати́тельный *adj.* (*mining tech.*) concentrating; **о. аппара́т** ore separator.
обога|ти́ть, щу́, ти́шь *pf.* (*of* **~ща́ть**) **1.** (*in var. senses*) to enrich. **2.** (*mining tech.*) to concentrate; **о. руду́** to concentrate ore, dress ore.
обога|ти́ться, щусь, ти́шься *pf.* (*of* **~ща́ться**) **1.** to become rich; (+*i.*) to enrich o.s. (with). **2.** *pass. of* **~ти́ть**
обогаща́|ть(ся), ю(сь) *impf. of* **обогати́ть(ся)**
обогаще́ни|е, я *nt.* **1.** (*in var. senses*) enrichment. **2.** (*mining tech.*) concentration; **о. руды** ore concentration, ore dressing.
обогна́|ть, обгоню́, обго́нишь, *past* **~л, ~ла́, ~ло** *pf.* (*of* **обгоня́ть**) to pass, leave behind; to outstrip, outdistance (*also fig.*).
обогн|у́ть, у́, ёшь *pf.* (*of* **огиба́ть**) **1.** to round; to skirt; (*naut.*) to double. **2.** to bend round; **о. о́бруч вокру́г бо́чки** to hoop a barrel.
обоготворе́ни|е, я *nt.* deification, idolization.
обоготвор|и́ть, ю́, и́шь *pf.* (*of* **~я́ть**) to deify, idolize.
обоготвор|я́ть, я́ю *impf. of* **~и́ть**
обогре́в, а *m.* (*tech.*) heating.
обогрева́ни|е, я *nt.* heating, warming.
обогрева́тел|ь, я *m.* (*tech.*) heater.
обогрева́|ть(ся), ю(сь) *impf. of* **обогре́ть(ся)**
обогре́|ть, ю, ешь *pf.* (*of* **~ва́ть**) to heat, warm.
обогре́|ться, юсь, ешься *pf.* (*of* **~ва́ться**) **1.** to warm o.s.; to warm up. **2.** *pass. of* **~ть**
о́бод, а, *pl.* **~́ья, ~́ьев** *m.* rim; felloe.
obод|о́к, ка́ *m.* thin rim, thin border, fillet.
ободо́|чный *adj. of* **~к; ~чная кишка́** (*anat.*) colon.
ободра́н|ец, ца *m.* (*coll.*) ragamuffin, ragged fellow.
obо́др|анный *p.p.p. of* **~а́ть** *and adj.* ragged.
ободра́ть, обдеру́, обдерёшь *pf.* (*of* **обдира́ть**) **1.** to strip; to skin, flay; to peel; **о. кору́ с де́рева** to bark a tree. **2.** (*fig., coll.*) to fleece.
ободре́ни|е, я *nt.* encouragement, reassurance.
ободри́тел|ьный (~ен, ~ьна) *adj.* encouraging, reassuring.
ободр|и́ть, ю́, и́шь *pf.* (*of* **~я́ть**) to cheer up; to encourage, reassure.
ободр|и́ться, ю́сь, и́шься *pf.* (*of* **~я́ться**) **1.** to cheer up, take heart. **2.** *pass. of* **~и́ть**
ободр|я́ть(ся), я́ю(сь) *impf. of* **~и́ть(ся)**
обо́его, обо́ему (*no nom. or a.*), *m. and nt. num.* both; **обо́его по́ла** of both sexes.
обоепо́л|ый (~, ~а) *adj.* (*biol.*) bisexual; (*bot.*) monoecious.
обожа́ни|е, я *nt.* adoration.
обожа́тел|ь, я *m.* (*coll.*) admirer.
обожа́|ть, ю *impf.* to adore, worship.
обож|гу́, жёшь, гу́т *see* **обже́чь**
обожд|а́ть, у́, ёшь, *past* **~а́л, ~ала́, ~а́ло** *pf.* (*coll.*) to wait (for a while).
обожеств|и́ть, лю́, и́шь *pf.* (*of* **~ля́ть**) to deify, worship.
обожествле́ни|е, я *nt.* deification, worshipping.
обожествля́|ть, ю *impf. of* **обожестви́ть**
обожжённый *p.p.p. of* **обже́чь**
обожм|у́, ёшь *see* **обжа́ть**[1]
обожн|у́, ёшь *see* **обжа́ть**[2]
обожр|а́ться, у́сь, ёшься, *past* **~а́лся, ~ала́сь** *pf.* (*of* **обжира́ться**) (*coll.*) to guzzle, stuff o.s.
обо́з, а *m.* **1.** string of carts; string of sledges; **пожа́рный о.** (*collect.*) fire-fighting vehicles, fire brigade. **2.** (*mil.*) (*unit*) transport; **быть в ~е** (*fig.*) to bring up the rear, be left behind.
обозва́|ть, обзову́, обзовёшь, *past* **~л, ~ла́, ~ло** *pf.* (*of* **обзыва́ть**) (+*a. and i.*) to call; **о. кого́-н. дурако́м** to call s.o. a fool.
обозл|ённый *p.p.p. of* **~и́ть** *and adj.* embittered.

обозл|и́ть, ю, и́шь *pf.* **1.** *pf. of* **зли́ть. 2.** to embitter.
обозл|и́ться, ю́сь, и́шься *pf. of* **зли́ться**
обозна|ва́ться, ю́сь, ёшься *impf. of* **~́ться**
обозна́|ться, юсь, ешься *pf.* (*of* **~ва́ться**) (*coll.*) to take s.o. for s.o. else; to be mistaken.
обознач|а́ть, а́ю *impf.* **1.** (*no pf.*) to mean. **2.** (*pf.* **~́ить**) to mark, designate; **о. на ка́рте грани́цу** to mark a frontier on a map. **3.** (*pf.* **~́ить**) to reveal; to emphasize.
обознач|а́ться, а́юсь *impf.* (*of* **~́иться**) **1.** to appear; to reveal o.s. **2.** *pass. of* **~а́ть 2., 3.**
обозначе́ни|е, я *nt.* **1.** marking, designation. **2.** sign, symbol; **усло́вные ~я** conventional signs (*on maps, etc.*).
обозна́ч|ить, у, ишь *pf. of* **~а́ть 2., 3.**
обозна́ч|иться, усь, ишься *pf. of* **~а́ться**
обо́зник, а *m.* driver.
обо́з|ный *adj. of* **~**; *as n.* **о., ~ного** *m.* (*mil.*) driver.
обозрева́тел|ь, я *m.* author of survey, author of review; columnist (*see* **обозре́ние**); **полити́ческий о.** political correspondent (*of newspaper*).
обозрева́|ть, ю *impf. of* **обозре́ть**
обозре́ни|е, я *nt.* **1.** surveying, viewing; looking round. **2.** survey; overview. **3.** review (*periodical journal*). **4.** (*theatr.*) revue.
обозр|е́ть, ю́, и́шь *pf.* (*of* **~ева́ть**) **1.** to survey, view; to look round. **2.** (*fig.*) to survey, (pass in) review (*in print*).
обозри́м|ый (~, ~а) *adj.* visible; **в ~ом бу́дущем** in the foreseeable future.
обо́|и, ев *no sg.* wall-paper; **окле́ить ~ями** to paper.
обой|дённый *p.p.p. of* **~ти́**
обо́йм|а, ы, *g. pl.* **~** *f.* **1.** (*mil.*) cartridge clip, charger. **2.** (*tech.*) iron ring; **о. шарикоподши́пника** ball race.
обо́|йный *adj. of* **~и**
обо|йти́, йду́, йдёшь, *past* **~шёл, ~шла́** *pf.* (*of* **обходи́ть**[1]) **1.** to go round, pass; **о. фланг проти́вника** (*mil.*) to turn the enemy's flank. **2.** to make the round (of), go (all) round; (*of doctor, sentry, etc.*) to make (go) one's round(s); **слух ~шёл весь го́род** the rumour spread all over the town. **3.** to avoid; to leave out; to pass over; **о. молча́нием** to pass over in silence; **о. зако́н** to get round (evade) a law; **о. затрудне́ние** to get round a difficulty. **4.** (*coll., pej.*) to con.
обо|йти́сь, йду́сь, йдёшься, *past* **~шёлся, ~шла́сь** *pf.* (*of* **обходи́ться**) **1.** (**с**+*i.*) to treat; **пло́хо о. с кем-н.** to treat s.o. badly. **2.** (*coll.*) to cost, come to; **во ско́лько ~шёлся ваш костю́м?** how much did your suit come to? **3.** (+*i.*) to manage (with, on), make do (with, on); **о. ста рубля́ми** to make do with one hundred roubles; **без ва́шей по́мощи мы бы не ~шли́сь** without your aid we could not have managed. **4.** to turn out, end; **всё ~шло́сь благополу́чно** everything turned out all right; **как-н. ~йдётся!** things will turn out all right somehow!; things will sort themselves out!
обо́йщик, а *m.* paper-hanger; interior decorator, upholsterer.
о́бок *adv. and prep.* +*g. or d.* (*coll.*) close by; near.
обокра́|сть, обкраду́, обкрадёшь, *past* **~л, ~ла** *pf.* (*of* **обкра́дывать**) to rob.
оболва́нива|ть, ю *impf. of* **оболва́нить**
оболва́н|ить, ю, ишь *pf.* (*of* **~ивать**) (*coll.*) **1.** to rough-hew. **2.** (*fig.*) to make a fool of.
обо|лга́ть, лгу́, лжёшь, *past* **~лга́л, ~лгала́, ~лга́ло** *pf.* to slander, calumniate.
оболо́чк|а, и *f.* **1.** cover, envelope, jacket; shell; (*tech.*) casing. **2.** (*anat.*) membrane; **ра́дужная о.** iris; **рогова́я о.** cornea; **сли́зистая о.** mucous membrane. **3.** (*bot.*) coat.
обо́лтус, а *m.* (*coll.*) blockhead, booby.
обольсти́тел|ь, я *m.* (*obs.*) seducer.
обольсти́тел|ьный (~ен, ~ьна) *adj.* seductive, captivating.
оболь|сти́ть, щу́, сти́шь *pf.* (*of* **~ща́ть**) **1.** to captivate. **2.** to seduce.
оболь|сти́ться, щу́сь, сти́шься *pf.* (*of* **~ща́ться**) to be (labour) under a delusion; (+*i.*) to flatter o.s. (with).
обольща́|ть(ся), ю(сь) *impf. of* **обольсти́ть(ся)**
обольще́ни|е, я *nt.* **1.** seduction. **2.** delusion.
оболь|ю́, ёшь *see* **обли́ть**
обомле́|ть, ю, ешь *pf.* (*coll.*) to be stupefied.
обомн|у́, ёшь *see* **обмя́ть**
обомр|у́, ёшь *see* **обмере́ть**
обомше́лый *adj.* moss-grown.
обоня́ни|е, я *nt.* (*sense of*) smell; **име́ть то́нкое о.** to have a fine sense of smell.
обоня́тельный *adj.* (*anat.*) olfactory.
обоня́|ть, ю *impf.* to smell.
обора́чиваемост|ь, и *f.* (*fin., econ.*) turnover.
обора́чива|ть(ся), ю(сь) *impf. of* **оберну́ть(ся)** *and* **обороти́ть(ся)**
оборва́н|ец, ца *m.* ragamuffin, ragged fellow.
обо́рв|анный *p.p.p. of* **~а́ть** *and adj.* torn, ragged.
оборв|а́ть, у́, ёшь, *past* **~а́л, ~ала́, ~а́ло** *pf.* (*of* **обрыва́ть**) **1.** to tear off, pluck (*petals, etc.*); to strip (*a shrub of blossom, etc.*). **2.** to break; to snap. **3.** (*fig.*) to cut short, interrupt; (*coll.*) to snub.
оборв|а́ться, у́сь, ёшься, *past* **~а́лся, ~ала́сь, ~а́ло́сь** *pf.* (*of* **обрыва́ться**) **1.** to break; to snap. **2.** to (*lose one's hold of sth. and*) fall; (*of objects*) to come away. **3.** to stop suddenly, stop short, come abruptly to an end.
обо́рвыш, а *m.* (*coll.*) ragamuffin.
обо́рк|а, и *f.* frill, flounce.
оборо́н|а, ы *no pl., f.* **1.** defence. **2.** (*mil.*) defences, defensive positions.
обoрони́тельный *adj.* defensive.
оборон|и́ть, ю́, и́шь *pf.* (*of* **~я́ть**) to defend; **~и́ Бог (~и́ Бо́же, ~и́ Го́споди)!** (*obs.*) God forbid!
оборон|и́ться, ю́сь, и́шься *pf.* (*of* **~я́ться**) **(от)** to defend o.s. (from).
оборо́н|ный *adj. of* **~а**; **~ная промы́шленность** defence industry.
обороноспосо́бност|ь, и *f.* defensive capability.
обороноспосо́б|ный (~ен, ~на) *adj.* prepared for defence.
оборон|я́ть(ся), я́ю(сь) *impf. of* **~и́ть(ся)**
оборо́т, а *m.* **1.** turn; (*tech.*) revolution, rotation; **приня́ть дурно́й о.** (*fig.*) to take a bad turn. **2.** circulation; (*fin., comm., rail.*) turnover; **ввести́, пусти́ть в о.** to put into circulation. **3.** back (= *reverse side*); **смотри́ на ~е** please turn over; **взять кого́-н. в о.** (*fig., coll.*) to get at s.o. **4.** turn (of speech); **о. ре́чи** phrase, locution. **5.** (*tech.*) knee, bend (*in a pipe*).
о́борот|ень, ня *m.* werewolf.
оборо́тист|ый (~, ~а) *adj.* (*coll.*) resourceful.
оборо|ти́ть, чу́, ~́тишь *pf.* (*of* **обора́чивать**) (*coll.*) to turn.
оборо|ти́ться, чу́сь, ~́тишься *pf.* (*of* **обора́чиваться**) (*coll.*) **1.** to turn (round). **2.** (**в**+*a. or* +*i.*) to turn (into).
оборо́тлив|ый (~, ~а) *adj.* (*coll.*) resourceful.
оборо́т|ный *adj. of* **~**; **о. капита́л** (*fin., comm.*) working capital; **~ная сторона́** verso; reverse side (*also fig.*); **э ~ное** *name of letter* **'э'**.
обору́довани|е, я *nt.* **1.** equipping. **2.** equipment; **вспомога́тельное о.** (*comput.*) peripherals, add-ons.
обору́д|овать, ую *impf. and pf.* to equip, fit out; (*fig., coll.*) to manage, arrange.
обо́рыш, а *m.* (*coll.*) left-over, remnant.
обоснова́ни|е, я *nt.* **1.** basing. **2.** basis, ground.
обосно́в|анный *p.p.p. of* **~а́ть** *and adj.* well-founded, well-grounded.
обосн|ова́ть, ую́, уёшь *pf.* (*of* **~о́вывать**) to ground, base; to substantiate.
обосн|ова́ться, ую́сь, уёшься *pf.* (*of* **~о́вываться**) **1.** to settle down. **2.** *pass. of* **~ова́ть**
обосно́выва|ть(ся), ю(сь) *impf. of* **обоснова́ть(ся)**
обосо́б|ить, лю, ишь *pf.* (*of* **~ля́ть**) to isolate.
обосо́б|иться, люсь, ишься *pf.* (*of* **~ля́ться**) to stand apart, keep aloof.
обособле́ни|е, я *nt.* isolation.
обосо́бленно *adv.* apart; aloof; **жить о.** to live by o.s.
обосо́б|ленный *p.p.p. of* **~ить** *and adj.* isolated, solitary.
обособля́|ть(ся), ю(сь) *impf. of* **обосо́бить(ся)**
обостре́ни|е, я *nt.* aggravation, exacerbation; **о. боле́зни** (*med.*) acute condition.
обостр|ённый *p.p.p. of* **~и́ть** *and adj.* **1.** sharp. pointed. **2.** of heightened sensitivity; **о. слух** a keen ear. **3.** strained, tense.

обостр|и́ть, ю́, и́шь *pf.* (*of* **~я́ть**) **1.** to sharpen, intensify. **2.** to strain; to aggravate, exacerbate.

обостр|и́ться, ю́сь, и́шься *pf.* (*of* **~я́ться**) **1.** to become sharp, become pointed. **2.** (*of the senses, etc.*) to become more sensitive, become keener. **3.** to become strained; to become aggravated, become exacerbated; **боле́знь ~и́лась** (*med.*) the condition has become acute. **4.** *pass. of* **~и́ть**

обостр|я́ть(ся), я́ю(сь) *impf. of* **~и́ть(ся)**

обосца́ть (*vulg.*) *pf. of* **сцать**

оботр|у́, ёшь *see* **обтере́ть**

обо́чин|а, ы *f.* edge; side (*of road, etc.*).

обою́дност|ь, и *f.* mutuality, reciprocity.

обою́д|ный (~ен, ~на) *adj.* mutual, reciprocal; **по ~ному согла́сию** by mutual consent.

обоюдоо́стрый *adj.* double-edged, two-edged (*also fig.*).

обраба́тыва|ть, ю *impf. of* **обрабо́тать**

обраба́тыва|ющий *pres. part. act. of* **~ть** *and adj.*; **~ющая промы́шленность** manufacturing industry.

обрабо́та|ть, ю *pf.* (*of* **обраба́тывать**) **1.** to work (up); to treat, process; (*tech.*) to machine; **о. зе́млю** to work the land; **о. ра́ну** to dress a wound. **2.** to polish, perfect (*a liter. production, etc.*). **3.** (*fig., coll.*) to work upon, win round.

обрабо́тк|а, и *f.* working (up); treatment, processing; (*tech.*) machining; **о. земли́** cultivation of land.

обра́д|овать(ся), ую(сь) *pf. of* **ра́довать(ся)**

о́браз[1], **а** *m.* **1.** shape, form; appearance; **по ~у своему́ и подо́бию** (*rhet. or joc.*) in one's own image. **2.** (*liter.*) image; **мы́слить ~ами** to think in images. **3.** (*liter.*) type; figure; **о. Га́млета** the Hamlet type. **4.** mode, manner; way; **о. де́йствий** line of action, policy; **о. жи́зни** way of life, mode of life; **о. правле́ния** form of government; **по ~у пе́шего хожде́ния** (*joc.*) on foot, on Shank's mare; **обстоя́тельство ~а де́йствия** (*gram.*) adverbial modifier of manner; **каки́м ~ом?** how?; **таки́м ~ом** thus; **гла́вным ~ом** mainly, chiefly, largely; **ра́вным ~ом** equally.

о́браз[2], **а,** *pl.* **~а́** *m.* icon.

образ|е́ц, ца́ *nt.* **1.** model, pattern (*also fig.*); **ста́вить в о.** to set up as a model. **2.** specimen, sample; (*of material*) pattern.

образи́н|а, ы *f.* (*coll., pej.*) ugly mug; (*as term of abuse*) scum.

образн|о́й *adj. of* **о́браз**[2]; *as n.* **~а́я, ~о́й** *f.* **1.** icon-room. **2.** icon-maker's workshop.

о́бразност|ь, и *f.* picturesqueness; (*liter.*) figurativeness; imagery.

о́браз|ный (~ен, ~на) *adj.* picturesque, graphic; (*liter.*) figurative; employing images.

образова́ни|е[1], **я** *nt.* formation; **о. слов** word-formation; **о. па́ра** (*tech.*) production of steam.

образова́ни|е[2], **я** *nt.* education.

образо́ванност|ь, и *f.* education (= *educated state*).

образо́в|анный *p.p.p. of* **~а́ть** *and adj.*; **о. челове́к** an educated pers.

образова́тел|ьный (~ен, ~ьна) *adj.* educational; **о. ценз** educational qualification.

образ|ова́ть[1], **у́ю** *impf.* (*in pres. tense*) *and pf.* (*of* **~о́вывать**) to form; to make up.

образ|ова́ть[2], **у́ю** *pf.* (*of* **~о́вывать**) (*obs.*) to educate.

образ|ова́ться, у́ется *pf.* (*of* **~о́вываться**) **1.** to form; to arise. **2.** (*coll.*) to turn out well; **не беспоко́йтесь, всё ~у́ется!** don't worry, everything will be all right! **3.** *pass. of* **~ова́ть**

образо́выва|ть(ся), ю(сь) *impf. of* **образова́ть(ся)**

образу́м|ить, лю, ишь *pf.* (*coll.*) to bring to reason, make listen to reason.

образу́м|иться, люсь, ишься *pf.* (*coll.*) to come to one's senses, see reason.

образу́ющ|ая, ей *f.* (*math.*) generatrix.

образцо́в|ый *adj.* model; exemplary; **~ое поведе́ние** exemplary conduct; **~ое произведе́ние** masterpiece; **~ое хозя́йство** model farm.

обра́зчик, а *m.* specimen, sample; (*of material*) pattern.

обра́м|ить, лю, ишь *pf.* (*of* **~ля́ть**) to frame.

обрамле́ни|е, я *nt.* **1.** framing. **2.** frame; (*fig.*) setting.

обрамля́|ть, ю, *impf. of* **обра́мить**

обраста́ни|е, я *nt.* **1.** overgrowing. **2.** (*fig.*) accumulation, acquisition.

обраст|а́ть, а́ю *impf. of* **~и́**

обраст|и́, у́, ёшь, *past* **обро́с, обросла́** *pf.* (*of* **~а́ть**) (+*i.*) **1.** to become (be) overgrown (with); **о. гря́зью** (*coll.*) to be coated with mud. **2.** (*fig.*) to become (be) surrounded (by), become (be) cluttered (with); to acquire, accumulate; **он обро́с нену́жной ме́белью** he has surrounded himself with superfluous items of furniture.

обра́т, а *m.* skim milk.

обрати́мост|ь, и *f.* reversibility.

обрати́м|ый (~, ~а) *adj.* reversible.

обра|ти́ть, щу́, ти́шь *pf.* (*of* **~ща́ть**) (*in var. senses*) to turn; (**в**+*a.*) to turn (into); **о. внима́ние (на**+*a.*) to pay attention (to), take notice (of), notice; **о. чьё-н. внима́ние (на**+*a.*) to call, draw s.o.'s attention (to); **о. на себя́ внима́ние** to attract attention (to o.s.); **о. иму́щество в капита́л** to realize property; **о. в бе́гство** to put to flight; **о. в свою́ ве́ру** to convert (to one's faith); **о. в шу́тку** to turn into a joke.

обра|ти́ться, щу́сь, ти́шься *pf.* (*of* **~ща́ться**) **1.** to turn; to revert; **о. лицо́м к стене́** to turn (one's face) towards the wall; **о. в бе́гство** to take to flight. **2. (к)** to turn (to), appeal (to); to apply (to); to accost; **она́ не зна́ла, к кому́ о. за по́мощью** she did not know to whom to turn for help; **о. с призы́вом к кому́-н.** to appeal to s.o.; **о. к юри́сту** to take legal advice; **о. к славянове́дению** to take up Slavonic studies. **3.** (**в**+*a.*) to turn (into), become; **о. в ци́ника** to become a cynic; **о. в слух** (*fig.*) to be all ears; to prick up one's ears. **4.** (**в**+*a.*) to be converted (to).

обра́тно *adv.* **1.** back; backwards; **туда́ и о.** there and back; **пое́здка туда́ и о.** round trip; **взять о.** to take back; **идти́ о., е́хать о.** to go back; to return, retrace one's steps. **2.** conversely; inversely; **о. пропорциона́льный** inversely proportional. **3.** (*vulg.*) again.

обра́тн|ый *adj.* **1.** reverse; **о. а́дрес** sender's address; **о. биле́т** return ticket; **~ая вспы́шка** back-firing; **о. кла́пан** (*tech.*) return valve; **о. путь** return journey; **~ые растя́жки** (*aeron.*) landing wires; **име́ющий ~ую си́лу** (*leg.*) retroactive, retrospective; **о. уда́р** backfire; **о. ход** (*tech.*) reverse motion, back stroke; **~ая связь** (*elec.*) feed-back. **2.** opposite; **в ~ую сто́рону** in the opposite direction. **3.** (*math.*) inverse; **~ое отноше́ние** inverse ratio.

обраща́|ть, ю *impf. of* **обрати́ть**

обраща́|ться, юсь *impf.* **1.** *impf. of* **обрати́ться. 2.** (*physiol., econ., etc.*) to circulate. **3.** (**с**+*i.*) to treat; **пло́хо о. с кем-н.** to treat s.o. badly, maltreat s.o. **4.** (**с**+*i.*) to handle, manage (*an inanimate object*); **он, по-ви́димому, не уме́ет о. с автома́том** apparently he does not know how to handle a sub-machine-gun; **«о. осторо́жно!»** 'handle with care!'.

обраще́ни|е, я *nt.* **1. (к)** appeal (to), address (to). **2.** (**в**+*a.*) conversion (to, into); **о. в ве́ру** conversion to faith. **3.** circulation; **изъя́ть из ~я** to withdraw from circulation; **пусти́ть в о.** to put in circulation. **4.** (**с**+*i.*) treatment (of); **плохо́е о.** ill-treatment. **5.** (**с**+*i.*) handling (of), use (of). **6.** manner.

обревиз|ова́ть, у́ю *pf. of* **ревизова́ть**

обре́з[1], **а** *m.* edge; **в о.** (*coll.*; +*g.*) only just enough; **де́нег у меня́ в о.** I have not a penny to spare.

обре́з[2], **а** *m.* sawn-off gun.

обре́зани|е, я *nt.* circumcision.

обреза́ни|е, я *nt.* **1.** cutting. **2.** trimming; paring; pruning; bevelling.

обре́|зать, жу, жешь *pf.* (*of* **~зывать** *and* **~за́ть**) **1.** to clip, trim; to pare; to prune; to bevel; **о. кому́-н. кры́лья** (*fig.*) to clip s.o.'s wings. **2.** to cut; **о. себе́ па́лец** to cut one's finger. **3.** to circumcise. **4.** (*coll.*) to cut short; to snub.

обрез|а́ть, а́ю *impf. of* **∸ать**

обре́|заться, жусь, зешься *pf.* (*of* **~за́ться** *and* **~зываться**) **1.** to cut o.s. **2.** *pass. of* **~зать**

обрез|а́ться, а́юсь *impf. of* **∸аться**

обрезно́й *adj.* (*tech.*) trimming.

обре́з|ок, ка *m.* scrap; (*pl.*) ends; clippings.

обре́зыва|ть(ся), ю(сь) *impf. of* **обре́зать(ся)**
обрека́|ть, ю *impf. of* **обре́чь**
обре|ку́, чёшь, ку́т *see* **~́чь**
обремени́тел|ьный (~ен, ~ьна) *adj.* burdensome, onerous.
обремен|и́ть, ю́, и́шь *pf.* (*of* **~я́ть**) to burden.
обремен|я́ть, я́ю *impf. of* **~и́ть**
обреми́|зиться, жусь, зишься *pf.* (*obs., coll.*) to get into a mess, into difficulties.
обре|сти́, ту́, тёшь (*arch.* **обря́щу, обря́щешь**) *past* **~̈л, ~ла́** *pf.* (*of* **~та́ть**) (*rhet.*) to find; **ищи́те да обря́щете** seek and ye shall find.
обре|сти́сь, ту́сь, тёшься, *past* **~̈лся, ~ла́сь** *pf.* (*obs.*) to be found; to turn up.
обрета́|ть, ю *impf. of* **обрести́**
обрета́|ться, юсь *impf.* (*obs., coll.*) to be; to pass one's time.
обрече́ни|е, я *nt.* doom.
обречённост|ь, и *f.* being doomed; **чу́вство ~и** feeling of doom.
обреч|ённый *p.p.p. of* **~́ь** *and adj.* doomed.
обре́|чь, ку́, чёшь, ку́т, *past* **~̈к, ~кла́** *pf.* (*of* **~ка́ть**) to condemn, doom.
обреше́|тить, чу, тишь *pf.* (*of* **~чивать**) to lath.
обреше́чива|ть, ю *impf. of* **обреше́тить**
обрис|ова́ть, у́ю *pf.* (*of* **~о́вывать**) to outline, delineate, depict (*also fig.*).
обрис|ова́ться, у́юсь *pf.* (*of* **~о́вываться**) **1.** to appear (in outline); to take shape. **2.** *pass. of* **~ова́ть**
обрисо́вк|а, и *f.* outlining, delineation, depicting.
обрисо́выва|ть(ся), ю(сь) *impf. of* **обрисова́ть(ся)**
обри́т|ый *p.p.p. of* **~ь** *and adj.* shaven.
обр|и́ть, е́ю, е́ешь *pf.* to shave (off).
обр|и́ться, е́юсь, е́ешься *pf.* to shave one's head.
обро́к, а *m.* (*hist.*) quit-rent; **быть на ~е, ходи́ть по ~у** to be liable for quit-rent.
оброн|и́ть, ю́, ~́ишь *pf.* **1.** to drop (*sc. and lose*). **2.** to let drop, let fall (*a remark, etc.*).
обро́|чный *adj. of* **~к; о. крестья́нин** peasant on quit-rent.
обруб|а́ть, а́ю *impf. of* **~и́ть**
обруб|и́ть[1], лю́, ~́ишь *pf.* (*of* **~а́ть**) to chop off; to lop off; to dock.
обруб|и́ть[2], лю́, ~́ишь *pf.* (*of* **~а́ть**) to hem.
обру́б|ок, ка *m.* stump.
обруга́|ть, ю *pf.* to curse; to call names; (*coll.; of book reviews, etc.*) to tear to pieces.
обрусе́лый *adj.* Russified, Russianized.
обрусе́ни|е, я *nt.* Russification, Russianization.
обрусе́|ть, ю *pf.* to become Russified, become Russianized.
обруси́|ть, шь *pf.* to Russify, Russianize.
о́бруч, а, *pl.* **~и, ~е́й** *m.* hoop.
обруча́льн|ый *adj.*: **~ое кольцо́** wedding ring; **о. обря́д** betrothal.
обруч|а́ть(ся), а́ю(сь) *impf. of* **~и́ть(ся)**
обруче́ни|е, я *nt.* betrothal.
обруч|и́ть, у́, и́шь *pf.* (*of* **~а́ть**) to betrothe.
обруч|и́ться, у́сь, и́шься *pf.* (*of* **~а́ться**) (**с**+*i.*) to become engaged (to).
обру́шива|ть(ся), ю(сь) *impf. of* **обру́шить(ся)**
обру́ш|ить, у, ишь *pf.* (*of* **~ивать**) to bring down, rain down.
обру́ш|иться, усь, ишься *pf.* (*of* **~иваться**) **1.** to come down, collapse, cave in. **2.** (*fig.*) to come down (upon), fall (upon).
обры́в, а *m.* **1.** precipice. **2.** (*tech.*) break, rupture.
обрыва́|ть(ся), ю(сь) *impf. of* **оборва́ть(ся)**
обры́вист|ый (~, ~а) *adj.* steep, precipitous; (*fig.*) abrupt.
обры́в|ок, ка *m.* scrap; snatch (*of tune, song, etc.*); **~ки мы́слей** desultory thoughts; **~ки разгово́ра** scraps of conversation.
обры́зг|ать, аю *pf.* (*of* **~ивать**) (+*i.*) to besprinkle (with); to splash; to bespatter (with).
обры́згива|ть, ю *impf. of* **обры́згать**
обры́ска|ть, ю *pf.* (*coll.*) to go through, hunt through.
обрю́зглый *adj.* flabby, flaccid.
обрю́зг|нуть, ну, нешь, *past* **~, ~ла** *pf.* to become flabby, become flaccid.
обрю́зг|ший = **~лый**
обря́д, а *m.* rite, ceremony.
обря|ди́ть, жу́, ~́дишь *pf.* (*of* **~жа́ть**) (*coll., joc.*) (+*i.*) to get up (in), trick out (in).
обря|ди́ться, жу́сь, ~ди́шься *pf.* (*of* **~жа́ться**) (*coll., joc.*) (+*i.*) to get o.s. up (in).
обря́дност|ь, и *f.* (*collect.*) rites, ritual, ceremonial.
обря́довый *adj.* ritual, ceremonial.
обряжа́|ть(ся), ю(сь) *impf. of* **обряди́ть(ся)**
обса|ди́ть, жу́, ~́дишь *pf.* (*of* **~́живать**) to plant round; **о. кла́дбище ти́сами** to surround a cemetery with yew-trees.
обса́жива|ть, ю *impf. of* **обсади́ть**
обса́лива|ть, ю *impf. of* **обса́лить** *and* **обсоли́ть**
обса́л|ить, ю, ишь *pf.* (*of* **~ивать**) (*coll.*) to smear with grease, spill grease on.
обса́сыва|ть, ю *impf. of* **обсоса́ть**
обса́харива|ть, ю *impf. of* **обса́харить**
обса́хар|ить, ю, ишь *pf.* (*of* **~ивать**) (*coll.*) to sugar.
обсемене́ни|е, я *nt.* **1.** (*agric.*) sowing. **2.** (*bot.*) going to seed.
обсемен|и́ть, ю́, и́шь *pf.* (*of* **~я́ть**) (*agric.*) to sow (*a field*).
обсемен|и́ться, ю́сь, и́шься *pf.* (*of* **~я́ться**) **1.** (*bot.*) to go to seed. **2.** *pass. of* **~и́ть**
обсемен|я́ть(ся), я́ю(сь) *impf. of* **~и́ть(ся)**
обсервато́ри|я, и *f.* observatory.
обсерва|цио́нный *adj. of* **~́ция**
обсерва́ци|я, и *f.* observation.
обсидиа́н, а *m.* (*min.*) obsidian.
обска|ка́ть, чу́, ~́чешь *pf.* (*of* **~́кивать**) **1.** to gallop round. **2.** (*pf. only*) to outgallop.
обска́кива|ть, ю *impf. of* **обскака́ть 1.**
обскура́нт, а *m.* obscurant, obscurantist.
обскуранти́зм, а *m.* obscurantism.
обскуранти́стский *adj.* obscurantist.
обсле́довани|е, я *nt.* (+*g.*) inspection (of), inquiry (into); investigation (of); observation, tests (*in hospital*).
обсле́довател|ь, я *m.* inspector, investigator.
обсле́д|овать, ую *impf. and pf.* to inspect; to investigate; **о. больно́го** to examine a patient.
обслу́живани|е, я *nt.* service; (*tech.*) servicing, maintenance; **бытово́е о.** consumer service (*including such facilities as hairdressing, dry-cleaning, domestic utensil repairs, etc.*); **медици́нское о.** health service.
обслу́жива|ть, ю *impf. of* **обслужи́ть; о. стано́к** to mind a machine; (*naut.*): **о. ору́дия** to man the guns; **~ющий персона́л** (serving) staff; (*collect.*) assistants, attendants.
обслуж|и́ть, у́, ~́ишь *pf.* (*of* **~́ивать**) to attend (to), serve; (*tech.*) to serve; to mind, operate; **о. потреби́теля** to serve a customer.
обслюн|и́ть, ю́, и́шь *pf.* (*coll.*) to slobber all over.
обсол|и́ть, ю́ *pf.* (*of* **обса́ливать**) to salt all over.
обсос|а́ть, у́, ёшь *pf.* (*of* **обса́сывать**) **1.** to suck round (*a sweet, etc.*). **2.** (*fig., coll.*) to chew over.
обсо́х|нуть, ну, нешь, *past* **~, ~ла** *pf.* (*of* **обсыха́ть**) to dry, become dry; **у него́ молоко́ на губа́х не ~ло** (*fig.*) he is still green.
обста́в|ить, лю, ишь *pf.* (*of* **~ля́ть**) **1.** (+*i.*) to surround (with), encircle (with). **2.** (+*i.*) to furnish (with). **3.** (*fig.*) to arrange; to organize. **4.** (*coll.*) to get the better (of); to get round, cheat.
обста́в|иться, люсь, ишься *pf.* (*of* **~ля́ться**) **1.** (+*i.*) to surround o.s. (with). **2.** to establish o.s., set o.s. up (*in lodgings, etc.*). **3.** *pass. of* **~ить**
обставля́|ть(ся), ю(сь) *impf. of* **обста́вить(ся)**
обстано́вк|а, и *f.* **1.** furniture; décor (*also theatr.*). **2.** situation, conditions; environment; set-up; **боева́я о.** (*mil.*) tactical situation.
обстано́в|очный *adj. of* **~ка; ~́очная пье́са** (*theatr.*) spectacular.
обстир|а́ть, а́ю *pf.* (*of* **~́ывать**) (*coll.*) to do the washing (*for a number of*).
обсти́рыва|ть, ю *impf. of* **обстира́ть**
обстоя́тел|ьный (~ен, ~ьна) *adj.* **1.** circumstantial, detailed. **2.** (*coll.; of a pers.*) thorough, reliable.

обстоя́тельственный *adj.* (*gram.*) adverbial.
обстоя́тельств|о[1], **а** *nt.* circumstance; **смягча́ющие ~а** extenuating circumstances; **по незави́сящим от меня́ ~ам** for reasons beyond my control; **по семе́йным ~ам** due to family circumstances; **ни при каки́х ~ах** in no circumstances; **смотря́ по ~ам** depending on circumstances.
обстоя́тельств|о[2], **а** *nt.* (*gram.*) adverbial modifier.
обсто|я́ть, и́т *impf.* to be; to get on; **как ~и́т де́ло?** how is it going?; how are things going? **как ~я́т ва́ши дела́?** how are you getting on?; **всё ~и́т благополу́чно** all is well; everything is going all right; **вот как ~и́т де́ло** that is the way it is; that's how matters stand.
обстра́гива|ть, ю *impf. of* **обстрога́ть**
обстра́ива|ть(ся), ю(сь) *impf. of* **обстро́ить(ся)**
обстрека́|ть, ю *pf. of* **стрека́ть**
обстре́л, а *m.* firing, fire; **артиллери́йский о.** bombardment, shelling; **быть под ~ом** to be under fire; **попа́сть под о.** to come under fire.
обстре́лива|ть(ся), ю(сь) *impf. of* **обстреля́ть(ся)**
обстре́л|янный *p.p.p. of* **~я́ть** *and adj.* seasoned, experienced (*of soldiers, also fig.*); **~янная пти́ца** (*coll.*) old hand, pers. who has knocked around.
обстрел|я́ть, я́ю *pf.* (*of* **~ивать**) to fire (at, on); to bombard.
обстрел|я́ться, я́юсь *pf.* (*of* **~иваться**) (*coll.*) to become seasoned (by being in battle); to receive a baptism of fire.
обстрога́|ть, ю *pf.* (*of* **обстра́гивать**) to plane; to whittle.
обстро́|ить, ю, ишь *pf.* (*of* **обстра́ивать**) to build (up).
обстро́|иться, юсь, ишься *pf.* (*of* **обстра́иваться**) **1.** to be built (up); (*coll.*) to spring up. **2.** to build for o.s.
обструга́|ть, ю *pf.* = **обстрога́ть**
обструкциони́зм, а *m.* (*pol.*) obstructionism.
обструкциони́ст, а *m.* (*pol.*) obstructionist.
обстру́кци|я, и *f.* (*pol.*) obstruction; filibustering.
обступ|а́ть, а́ю *impf. of* **~и́ть**
обступ|и́ть, лю́, ~ишь *pf.* (*of* **~а́ть**) to surround; to cluster (round).
обсу|ди́ть, жу́, ~дишь *pf.* (*of* **~жда́ть**) to discuss; to consider.
обсужда́|ть, ю *impf. of* **обсуди́ть**
обсужде́ни|е, я *nt.* discussion.
обсу́шива|ть(ся), ю(сь) *impf. of* **обсуши́ть(ся)**
обсуш|и́ть, у́, ~ишь *pf.* (*of* **~ивать**) to dry (out).
обсуш|и́ться, у́сь, ~ишься *pf.* (*of* **~иваться**) to dry o.s., get dry.
обсчит|а́ть, а́ю *pf.* (*of* **~ывать**) to cheat (*in counting out money*); to shortchange.
обсчит|а́ться, а́юсь *pf.* (*of* **~ываться**) to make a mistake (*in counting*); **вы ~а́лись на шесть копе́ек** you were six kopecks out.
обсчи́тыва|ть(ся), ю(сь) *impf. of* **обсчита́ть(ся)**
обсы́п|ать, лю, лешь *pf.* (*of* **~а́ть**) (+*i.*) to strew; to sprinkle.
обсып|а́ть, а́ю *impf. of* **~ать**
обсы́п|аться, люсь, лешься *pf.* = **осы́паться**
обсыха́|ть, ю *impf. of* **обсо́хнуть**
обта́ива|ть, ю *impf. of* **обта́ять**
обта́чива|ть, ю *impf. of* **обточи́ть**
обта́|ять, ю *pf.* (*of* **~ивать**) **1.** to melt away (around). **2.** to become clear (*of ice*).
обтека́ем|ый *adj.* (*tech.*) streamlined; **~ая фо́рма** streamline form.
обтека́тел|ь, я *m.* (*aeron. tech.*) fairing.
обтека́|ть, ю *impf. of* **обте́чь**
обтер|е́ть, оботру́, оботрёшь, *past* **~**, **~ла** *pf.* (*of* **обтира́ть**) **1.** to wipe; to wipe dry. **2.** (+*i.*) to rub (with).
обтер|е́ться, оботру́сь, оботрёшься, *past* **~ся**, **~лась** *pf.* (*of* **обтира́ться**) **1.** to wipe o.s. dry, dry o.s. **2.** to sponge down. **3.** (*coll.*) to wear thin, rub (*as result of friction*). **4.** (*fig., coll.*) to adapt o.s., become acclimatized.
обтерп|е́ться, лю́сь, ~ишься *pf.* (*coll.*) to become acclimatized, become accustomed.
обтёс|анный *p.p.p. of* **~а́ть**; **гру́бо о.** rough-finished.
обте|са́ть, шу́, ~шешь *pf.* (*of* **~сывать**) to square; to rough-hew; to dress, trim. **2.** (*fig., coll.*) to teach manners (to), lick into shape.
обте|са́ться, шу́сь, ~шешься *pf.* (*of* **~сываться**) (*coll.*) to acquire (*polite*) manners, acquire polish.
обтёсыва|ть(ся) *impf. of* **обтеса́ть(ся)**
обте́|чь, ку́, чёшь, ку́т, *past* **~к**, **~кла́** *pf.* (*of* **~ка́ть**) **1.** to flow round. **2.** (*mil.*) to by-pass.
обтира́ни|е, я *nt.* **1.** sponge-down. **2.** (*coll.*) lotion.
обтира́|ть(ся), ю(сь) *impf. of* **обтере́ть(ся)**
обточ|и́ть, у́, ~ишь *pf.* (*of* **обта́чивать**) to grind; (*tech.*) to turn, machine, round off.
обто́чк|а, и *f.* (*tech.*) turning, machining, rounding off.
обтрёп|анный *p.p.p. of* **~а́ть** *and adj.* **1.** frayed. **2.** shabby.
обтреп|а́ть, лю́, ~лешь *pf.* to fray.
обтреп|а́ться, лю́сь, ~лешься *pf.* **1.** to become frayed, fray. **2.** to become shabby.
обтюра́тор, а *m.* **1.** (*anat. and tech.*) obturator. **2.** (*phot.*) shutter. **3.** (*mil.*) gas-check (*in breech of gun*).
обтюра́ци|я, и *f.* (*tech.*) obturation; stopping-up.
обтя́гива|ть, ю *impf. of* **обтяну́ть**
обтя́гивающий *adj.* skin-tight, figure-hugging.
обтя́жк|а, и *f.* **1.** cover (*for furniture*). **2.** (*aeron.*) skin. **3.**: **пла́тье в ~у** close-fitting dress.
обтя|ну́ть, ну́, ~нешь *pf.* (*of* **~гивать**) **1.** (+*i.*) to cover (*furniture*) (with). **2.** to fit close (to).
обува́|ть(ся), ю(сь) *impf. of* **обу́ть(ся)**
обу́вк|а, и *f.* (*coll.*) boots.
обувн|о́й *adj. of* **о́бувь; о. магази́н** shoe shop; **~а́я промы́шленность** boot and shoe industry.
обувщи́к, а́ *m.* boot and shoe operative.
о́був|ь, и *no pl., f.* footwear; boots, shoes.
обу́гливани|е, я *nt.* carbonization.
обу́глива|ть(ся), ю(сь) *impf. of* **обу́глить(ся)**
обу́гл|ить, ю, ишь *pf.* (*of* **~ивать**) to char; to carbonize.
обу́гл|иться, юсь, ишься *pf.* (*of* **~иваться**) to become charred, char.
обу́жива|ть, ю *impf. of* **обу́зить**
обу́з|а, ы *f.* burden; **быть ~ой для кого́-н.** to be a burden to s.o.
обузд|а́ть, а́ю *pf.* (*of* **~ывать**) to bridle, curb (*also fig.*); (*fig.*) to restrain, control; **о. свой хара́ктер** to restrain o.s.; **о. свои́ стра́сти** to curb one's passions.
обу́здыва|ть, ю *impf. of* **обузда́ть**
обу́|зить, жу, зишь *pf.* (*of* **~живать**) to make too tight.
обурева́|ть, ет *impf.* to shake; to grip; **его́ ~ют сомне́ния** he is a prey to doubts.
обуржуа́зивани|е, я *nt.* embourgeoisement.
обуржуа́|зиться, жусь, зишься *pf.* to become bourgeois, undergo embourgeoisement.
обусло́в|ить, лю, ишь *pf.* (*of* **~ливать**) **1.** to condition; (+*i.*) to make conditional (upon), stipulate (for); **он ~ил своё согла́сие предоставле́нием маши́ны** he made his consent conditional upon the provision of a car. **2.** to cause, bring about; to be the condition of.
обусло́в|иться, люсь, ишься *pf. of* **~ливаться**
обусло́влива|ть, ю *impf. of* **обусло́вить**
обусло́влива|ться, юсь *impf.* (*of* **обусло́виться**) (+*i.*) to be conditioned (by), be conditional (upon); to depend (on); **разме́р ~ется тре́бованиями** the size is conditioned by the requirements.
обу́т|ый *p.p.p. of* **~ь; оде́тый и о.** clothed and shod.
обу́|ть, ю, ешь *pf.* (*of* **~ва́ть**) **1.**: **о. кого́-н.** to put on s.o.'s boots (shoes) for him. **2.** to provide with boots *or* shoes.
обу́|ться, юсь, ешься *pf.* (*of* **~ва́ться**) **1.** to put on one's boots, shoes. **2.** to provide o.s. with boots *or* shoes.
о́бух, а (*and* **обу́х, а́)** *m.* butt, back; head (*of an axe*); (*naut.*) eye-bolt; **меня́ то́чно ~ом по голове́** (*coll.*) you could have knocked me down with a feather; **плётью ~а не перешибёшь** (*prov.*) the weakest goes to the wall.
обуч|а́ть(ся), а́ю(сь) *impf. of* **~и́ть(ся)**
обуче́ни|е, я *nt.* teaching; instruction, training; **совме́стное о. (лиц обо́его по́ла)** co-education; **о. по ме́сту рабо́ты** on-the-job *or* in-service training.
обуч|и́ть, у́, ~ишь *pf.* (*of* **учи́ть** *and* **~а́ть**) **(кого́-н. чему́-н.)** to teach (s.o. sth.); to instruct, train (in).
обуч|и́ться, у́сь, ~ишься *pf.* (*of* **учи́ться** *and* **~а́ться**) (+*d. or* +*inf.*) to learn.

обу́шный *adj. of* **о́бух**
обуш|о́к, ка́ *m.* pick (with detachable point); (*naut.*) eye-bolt.
обуя́|ть, ет *pf.* (*obs.*) to seize; to grip; **его ~л страх** fear had seized him.
обха́жива|ть, ю *impf.* (*coll.*) to cajole, try to get round.
обхва́т, а *m.* (*measurement of circumference*) girth; **в ~е** in circumference; **ме́рить в ~е** to girth.
обхва|ти́ть, чу́, ~тишь *pf.* (*of* **~тывать**) to encompass (with outstretched arms); to clasp.
обхва́тыва|ть, ю *impf. of* **обхвати́ть**
обхо́д, а *m.* **1.** (*doctor's, postman's, etc.*) round; (*guard's, policeman's*) beat; **пойти́ в о.** to go round, make (go) one's round(s). **2.** roundabout way; by-pass. **3.** (*mil.*) turning movement, wide enveloping movement. **4.** evasion, circumvention (*of law, etc.*).
обходи́тел|ьный (~ен, ~ьна) *adj.* pleasant; courteous; well-mannered.
обхо|ди́ть[1], жу́, ~дишь *impf. of* **обойти́**
обхо|ди́ть[2], жу́, ~дишь *pf.* to go all round.
обхо|ди́ться, жу́сь, ~дишься *impf. of* **обойти́сь**
обхо́дн|ый *adj.* roundabout, circuitous; **о. путь** detour; **~ым путём** in a roundabout way; **~ое движе́ние** (*mil.*) turning movement.
обхо́дчик, а *m.* (*rail.*) trackman.
обхожде́ни|е, я *nt.* manners; (**с**+*i.*) treatment (of), behaviour (towards).
обче́сться, обочту́сь, обочтёшься, *past* **обчёлся, обочла́сь** *pf.* (*coll.*) = **обсчита́ться; (их) раз, два и обчёлся** (they) can be counted on the fingers of one hand.
обчи́|стить, щу, стишь *pf.* (*of* **~ща́ть**) **1.** to clean; to brush. **2.** (*fig., coll.*) to clean out (= *to rob*).
обчи́|ститься, щусь, стишься *pf.* (*of* **~ща́ться**) **1.** to clean o.s.; to brush o.s. **2.** *pass. of* **~стить**
обчища́|ть(ся), ю(сь) *impf. of* **обчи́стить(ся)**
обша́рива|ть, ю *impf. of* **обша́рить**
обша́р|ить, ю, ишь *pf.* (*of* **~ивать**) to rummage; to ransack.
обша́рка|ть, ю *pf.* (*coll.*) to wear out (*by much walking*).
обша́рпа|нный *p.p.p. of* **~ть; ~нное зда́ние** dilapidated building.
обша́рпа|ть, ю *pf.* (*coll.*) to wear (away).
обшива́|ть, ю *impf. of* **обши́ть[1,2]**
обши́вк|а, и *f.* **1.** edging, bordering. **2.** trimming, facing. **3.** boarding, panelling; **о. фане́рой** veneering; (*tech.*) sheathing; (*naut.*) planking; **стальна́я о.** plating; **нару́жная о.** skin-plating.
обши́в|очный *adj. of* **~ка**
обши́р|ный (~ен, ~на) *adj.* extensive (*also fig.*) spacious; vast; **у него́ ~ное знако́мство** he has a very wide circle of acquaintance.
об|ши́ть[1], ошью́, ошьёшь *pf.* (*of* **~шива́ть**) **1.** to edge, border. **2.** to trim, face. **3.** to sew round (*a package*). **4.** to plank; to revet; (*tech.*) to sheathe.
об|ши́ть[2], ошью́, ошьёшь *pf.* (*of* **~шива́ть**) to sew for; to make clothes for; **она́ сама́ ~ши́ла всю семью** she has made all the family's clothes herself.
обшла́г, а́, *pl.* **~а́** *m.* cuff.
обща́|ться, юсь *impf.* (**с**+*i.*) to associate (with), mix (with).
общевойсково́|й *adj.* (*mil.*) common to all arms; **~е кома́ндование** combined command.
общедосту́п|ный (~ен, ~на) *adj.* **1.** of moderate price. **2.** (*of book, etc.*) popular.
общежите́йский *adj.* everyday, ordinary.
общежи́ти|е, я *nt.* **1.** hostel. **2.** society, community; communal life.
общеизве́ст|ный (~ен, ~на) *adj.* well-known, generally known; notorious.
общенаро́дный *adj.* common to whole people; national; public; **о. пра́здник** public holiday.
обще́ни|е, я *nt.* intercourse; relations, links; **ли́чное о.** personal contact.
общеобразова́тельны|й *adj.* of general education; **~е предме́ты** general subjects.
общепоня́т|ный (~ен, ~на) *adj.* comprehensible to all, within the grasp of all.
общепри́знан|ный (~, ~а) *adj.* universally recognized.
общепри́нят|ый (~, ~а) *adj.* generally accepted.
общераспространённый *adj.* in general use, generally used, generally found.
общесою́зн|ый *adj.* All-Union (*in former USSR, common to or valid for the entire Union*); **~ого значе́ния** of importance to the entire USSR.
обще́ственник, а *m.* social activist; pers. actively engaging in public life.
обще́ственност|ь, и *f.* **1.** (*collect.*) (the) public, the community; public opinion; **англи́йская о.** the British public. **2.** (*collect.*) community; communal organizations; **о. заво́да** factory organizations; **нау́чная о.** the scientific community, scientific circles. **3.** disposition to public work, disposition to serve the community; **дух ~и** public spirit, public-spiritedness.
обще́ственн|ый *adj.* **1.** social, public; **~ая жизнь** public life; **~ое мне́ние** public opinion; **~ые нау́ки** social sciences; **~ое пита́ние** public catering; **~ое порица́ние** public censure; **~ая рабо́та** public work, social work; **~ые рабо́ты** public works; **~ая со́бственность** public property, public ownership. **2.** voluntary, unpaid, amateur; **на ~ых нача́лах** on a voluntary basis; **~ые организа́ции** voluntary organizations.
о́бществ|о, а *nt.* **1.** (*in var. senses*) society; association; **нау́чное о.** learned body; **первобы́тное о.** primitive society; **нау́ка об ~е** social science; **быва́ть в ~е** to frequent society, be a socialite. **2.** (*econ.*) company; **акционе́рное о.** joint-stock company. **3.** company, society; **в ~е кого́-н.** in s.o.'s company; **попа́сть в дурно́е о.** to fall into bad company.
обществове́дени|е, я *nt.* social science, civics.
обществове́д|ческий *adj. of* **~ение**
общеупотреби́тел|ьный (~ен, ~ьна) *adj.* in general use.
общечелове́ческий *adj.* common to all mankind.
о́бщ|ий *adj.* general; common; **о. враг** common enemy; **~ее де́ло** common cause; **о. знако́мый** mutual acquaintance; **~ее ме́сто** commonplace; **~ее собра́ние** general meeting; **~ее согла́сие** common consent; **~ая су́мма** sum total; **о. наибо́льший дели́тель** (*math.*) the greatest common divisor; **~ее наиме́ньшее кра́тное** (*math.*) the least common multiple; **в ~ем** on the whole, in general, in sum; **в ~их черта́х** in general outline; **не име́ть ничего́ ~его (с**+*i.*) to have nothing in common (with).
о́бщи́н|а, ы *f.* community; commune.
общи́нн|ый *adj.* communal; **~ая земля́** common (land).
общип|а́ть, лю́, ~лешь *pf.* (*of* **щипа́ть 4.** *and* **~ывать**) to pluck.
общи́пыва|ть, ю *impf. of* **общипа́ть**
общи́тельност|ь, и *f.* sociability.
общи́тел|ьный (~ен, ~ьна) *adj.* sociable.
о́бщност|ь, и *f.* community; **о. интере́сов** community of interests.
общо́ *adv.* (*coll.*) generally; **он изложи́л свои́ взгля́ды сли́шком о.** he expounded his views in too general terms.
объ... *vbl. pref.* = **о...** *and* **об...**
объего́рива|ть, ю *impf. of* **объего́рить**
объего́р|ить, ю, ишь, *pf.* (*of* **~ивать**) (*coll.*) to cheat, swindle.
объеда́|ть(ся), ю(сь) *impf. of* **объе́сть(ся)**
объеде́ни|е, я *nt.* **1.** overeating. **2.** (*as prep., coll.*) sth. delicious; **то́рты э́ти — пря́мо о.** these cakes are simply delicious.
объедине́ни|е, я *nt.* **1.** unification. **2.** union, association.
объедин|ённый *p.p.p. of* **~и́ть** *and adj.* united; **Организа́ция Объединённых На́ций** United Nations (Organization).
объедини́тельный *adj.* unifying, uniting.
объедин|и́ть, ю́, и́шь *pf.* (*of* **~я́ть**) to unite; to join; **о. ресу́рсы** to pool resources; **о. уси́лия** to combine efforts.
объедин|и́ться, ю́сь, и́шься *pf.* (*of* **~я́ться**) (**с**+*i.*) to unite (with).
объедин|я́ть(ся), я́ю(сь) *impf. of* **~и́ть(ся)**
объе́д|ки, ков *pl.* (*sg.* **~ок, ~ка** *m.*) (*coll.*) leavings (*of food*), leftovers, scraps.

объéзд, а *m.* **1.** riding round, going round. **2.** circuit, detour. **3.** (*obs.*) mounted posse.
объéз|ди́ть[1]**, жу, дишь** *pf.* (*of* **~жáть**[1]) to travel over.
объéз|дить[2]**, жу, дишь** *pf.* (*of* **~жáть**[2]) to break in (*horses*).
объéздк|а, и *f.* breaking in (*of horses*).
объéздчик[1]**, а** *m.* mounted patrol; **леснóй о.** forest warden.
объéздчик[2]**, а** *m.* horse-breaker.
объезжá|ть[1]**, ю** *impf. of* **объéздить**[1] *and* **объéхать**
объезжá|ть[2]**, ю** *impf. of* **объéздить**[2]
объéзжий *adj.* roundabout, circuitous; **о. путь** detour.
объéкт, а *m.* **1.** (*in var. senses*) object. **2.** (*mil.*) objective. **3.** establishment; works; **строи́тельный о.** building site.
объекти́в, а *m.* (*opt.*) objective, object-glass, lens.
объективáци|я, и *f.* = **объективизáция**
объективизáци|я, и *f.* objectification.
объективи́зм, а *m.* **1.** (*term of Marxist philosophy*) objectivism. **2.** objectivity.
объективи́р|овать, ую *impf. and pf.* to objectify.
объекти́вност|ь, и *f.* objectivity.
объекти́в|ный (~ен, ~на) *adj.* **1.** objective. **2.** unbiased.
объéкт|ный *adj. of* **~ 1.**
объéкт|овый *adj. of* **~ 3.**
объём, а *m.* volume (*also fig.*); bulk, size, capacity.
объёмист|ый (~, ~а) *adj.* (*coll.*) voluminous, bulky.
объёмн|ый *adj.* by volume, volumetric; **о. вес** weight by volume; **о. заря́д** space charge; **~ое отношéние** volume ratio.
объé|сть, м, шь, ст, ди́м, ди́те, дя́т, *past* **~л** *pf.* (*of* **~дáть**) **1.** to eat round; to nibble. **2.** (*coll.*): **о. когó-н.** to eat s.o. out of house and home.
объé|сться, мся, шься, стся, ди́мся, ди́тесь, дя́тся, *past* **~лся** *pf.* (*of* **~дáться**) to overeat.
объé|хать, ду, дешь *pf.* (*of* **~зжáть**[1]) **1.** to go round, skirt. **2.** to overtake, pass. **3.** to travel over.
объяв|и́ть, лю́, ́~ишь *pf.* (*of* **~ля́ть**) to declare, announce; to publish, proclaim; to advertise; **о. войну́** to declare war; **о. кóнкурс** to announce a competition; **о. собрáние откры́тым** to declare a meeting open; **о. вне закóна** to outlaw.
объяв|и́ться, лю́сь, ́~ишься *pf.* (*of* **~ля́ться**) **1.** (*coll.*) to turn up, appear. **2.** (*+i.*) to announce o.s. (to be), declare o.s. (to be). **3.** *pass. of* **~и́ть**
объявлéни|е, я *nt.* **1.** declaration, announcement; notice; **о. войны́** declaration of war. **2.** advertisement; **дать о. в газéту, помести́ть о. в газéте** to put an advertisement in a paper.
объявля́|ть(ся), ю(сь) *impf. of* **объяви́ть(ся)**
объядéние (*obs.*) = **объедéние**
объяснéни|е, я *nt.* (*in var. senses*) explanation; **о. в любви́** declaration of love.
объясни́м|ый (~, ~а) *adj.* explicable, explainable.
объясни́тельный *adj.* explanatory.
объясн|и́ть, ю́, и́шь *pf.* (*of* **~я́ть**) to explain.
объясн|и́ться, ю́сь, и́шься *pf.* (*of* **~я́ться**) **1.** to explain o.s.; (**с**+*i.*) to have a talk (with); to have it out (with); **о. в любви́** (*+d.*) to make a declaration of love (to). **2.** to become clear, be explained; **тепéрь всё ~и́лось** everything is now clear.
объясн|я́ть, я́ю *impf. of* **~и́ть**
объясн|я́ться, я́юсь *impf.* **1.** *impf. of* **~и́ться. 2.** to speak; to make o.s. understood; **умéете ли вы о. по-францу́зски?** can you make yourself understood in French?; **о. жéстами и знáками** to use sign language. **3.** (*+i.*) to be explained (by), be accounted for (by); **э́тим ~я́ется егó стрáнное поведéние** that accounts for his strange behaviour.
объя́ти|е, я *nt.* embrace; **с распростёртыми ~ями** with open arms; **брóситься комý-н. в ~я** to fall into s.o.'s arms; **заключи́ть в ~я** to embrace, fold in one's arms.
объя́т|ый *p.p.p. of* **~ь; о. плáменем** enveloped in flames; **о. стрáхом** terror-stricken; **о. ду́мой** wrapped in thought.
объя́|ть, обойму́, обоймёшь (*and coll.* **обыму́, обы́мешь**) *pf.* (*obs.*) **1.** to comprehend, grasp. **2.** to seize, grip, come over; **у́жас ~л егó** terror seized him.

обывáтел|ь, я *m.* **1.** (*obs.*) inhabitant, resident. **2.** (*fig.*) philistine.
обывáтельский *adj.* **1.** (*obs.*) belonging to the local inhabitants. **2.** (*fig.*) philistine; narrow-minded.
обывáтельщин|а, ы *f.* philistinism; narrow-mindedness.
обыгр|áть, áю *pf.* (*of* **́~ывать**) **1.** to beat (*at a game*); to win; **о. когó-н. на что-н.** to win sth. of s.o. **2.** (*theatr.*) to use with (good) effect, play up; (*fig.*) to turn to advantage, turn to account. **3.** (*mus.*) to mellow (*an instrument by playing*).
обы́грыва|ть, ю *impf. of* **обыгрáть**
обыдёнкой *adv.* (*dial.*) in one day.
обы́денност|ь, и *f.* **1.** ordinariness. **2.** everyday occurrence.
обы́денн|ый *adj.* ordinary; commonplace, everyday; **~ое происшéствие** everyday occurrence.
обыдёнщин|а, ы *f.* uneventfulness; commonplaceness.
обыкновéни|е, я *nt.* habit, wont; **по ~ю** as usual; **имéть о.** (*+inf.*) to be in the habit (of).
обыкновéнно *adv.* usually, as a rule.
обыкновéн|ный (~ен, ~на) *adj.* usual; ordinary; commonplace; **~ная истóрия** everyday occurrence; **бóльше ~ного** more than usual.
óбыск, а *m.* search; **óрдер на прáво ~а** search warrant.
обы|скáть, щу́, ~щешь *pf.* (*of* **́~скивать**) to search.
обы|скáться, щу́сь, ́~щешься *pf.* (*coll.*) to carry out a search (in vain).
обы́скива|ть, ю *impf. of* **обыскáть**
обы́ча|й, я *m.* custom; (*leg.*) usage; **по ~ю** in accordance with custom; **э́то у нас в ~е** it is our custom.
обы́чно *adv.* usually; as a rule.
обы́чн|ый *adj.* usual; ordinary; **~ое прáво** (*leg.*) customary law.
обюрокрá|тить, чу, тишь *pf.* (*of* **~чивать**) (*coll.*) to make bureaucratic.
обюрокрá|титься, чусь, тишься *pf.* (*of* **~чиваться**) (*coll.*) to become a bureaucrat, become bureaucratic.
обюрокрáчива|ть(ся), ю(сь) *impf. of* **обюрокрáтить(ся)**
обя́занност|ь, и *f.* duty; responsibility; **вóинская о.** military service; **по ~и** as in duty bound; in the line of duty; **исполня́ть ~и дирéктора** to act as director; **исполня́ющий ~и дирéктора** acting director.
обя́зан|ный (~, ~а) *adj.* **1.** (*+inf.*) obliged, bound; **он ~ верну́ться** he is obliged to go back; it is his duty to go back. **2.** (*+d.*) obliged, indebted (to); **я вам óчень ~** I am very much obliged to you; **онá вам ~а своéй жи́знью** she owes her life to you; **мы э́тим ~ы Петрóву** we have Petrov to thank for this.
обязáтельно *adv.* without fail; **я о. приду́** I shall come without fail; **он о. там бу́дет** he is sure to be there, he is bound to be there.
обязáтельност|ь, и *f.* **1.** obligatoriness; binding force. **2.** (*obs.*) obligingness.
обязáтел|ьный (~ен, ~ьна) *adj.* **1.** obligatory; compulsory; binding; **~ьное обучéние** compulsory education; **~ьное постановлéние** binding decree. **2.** obliging.
обязáтельственн|ый *adj.* (*leg.*): **~ое прáво** liability law.
обязáтельств|о, а *nt.* **1.** obligation; engagement; **долговóе о.** promissory note; **взять на себя́ о.** (*+inf.*) to pledge o.s. (to), undertake (to). **2.** (*pl.*; *leg.*) liabilities.
обя|зáть, жу́, ́~жешь *pf.* (*of* **́~зывать**) **1.** to bind, oblige, commit; **о. когó-н. яви́ться в определённое врéмя** to bind s.o. to appear at a stated time. **2.** to oblige; **вы меня́ óчень ́~жете** I shall be greatly indebted to you.
обя|зáться, жу́сь, ́~жешься *pf.* (*of* **́~зываться**) to bind o.s., pledge o.s., undertake.
обя́зыва|ть, ю *impf. of* **обязáть; ни к чему́ не ~ющий** non-committal.
обя́зыва|ться, юсь *impf. of* **обязáться; не хочу́ ни пéред кéм о.** I wish to be beholden to no one.
ОВ *nt. indecl.* (*abbr. of* **отравля́ющее веществó**) (*mil.*) toxic chemical agent; **ОВ нéрвно-паралити́ческого ти́па** nerve gas.
о-в (*abbr. of* **óстров**) I., Island, Isle.
о-вá (*abbr. of* **островá**) Is, Islands, Isles.
овáл, а *m.* **1.** oval. **2.** balloon (*in comic strip, etc.*).

ова́льный *adj.* oval.
ова́ци|я, и *f.* ovation.
овдове́|вший *p.p. of* **~ть** *and adj.* widowed.
овдове́|ть, ю *pf.* to become a widow(er).
овева́|ть, ю *impf. of* **ове́ять**
ов|е́н, на́ *m.* **1.** (*obs.*) ram. **2.** (*astron.*) Aries, the Ram (*first sign of the Zodiac*).
ов|ёс, са́ *m.* oats.
ов|е́чий *adj. of* **~ца́; волк в ~е́чьей шку́ре** a wolf in sheep's clothing.
ове́чк|а, и *f. dim. of* **овца́;** (*fig.*) harmless creature.
овеществ|и́ть, лю́, и́шь *pf.* (*of* **~ля́ть**) to substantiate.
овеществля́|ть, ю *impf. of* **овеществи́ть**
ове́я|нный *p.p.p of* **~ть; о. сла́вой** covered with glory.
ове́|ять, ю, ешь *pf.* (*of* **~ва́ть**) (*+i.*) **1.** to fan. **2.** (*fig.*) to surround (with), cover (with).
ови́н, а *m.* barn (*for drying crops*).
ОВИР, а *m.* (*abbr. of* **отде́л виз и регистра́ции**) visa and registration department.
овладева́|ть, ю *impf. of* **овладе́ть**
овладе́ни|е, я *nt.* (*+i.*) mastery; mastering.
овладе́|ть, ю *pf.* (*of* **~ва́ть**) (*+i.*) **1.** to seize; to take possession (of); **о. собо́й** to get control of o.s., regain self-control; **мно́ю ~ла ра́дость** I was overcome with joy. **2.** (*fig.*) master.
о-во (*abbr. of* **о́бщество**) Soc., Society.
о́вод, а, *pl.* **~ы, ~ов** (*and* **~а́, ~о́в**) gadfly.
овощево́дств|о, а *nt.* vegetable-growing.
овощехрани́лищ|е, а *nt.* vegetable store.
о́вощ|и, е́й *pl.* (*sg.* **~, ~а** *m.*) vegetables; **вся́кому ~у своё вре́мя** (*prov.*) there is a time for everything, everything in good season.
овощно́й *adj.* vegetable; **о. магази́н** greengrocery, greengrocer's (shop); **о. стол.** vegetarian cooking.
овра́г, а *m.* ravine, gully.
овра́ж|ек[1], ка *m. dim. of* **овра́г**
овра́ж|ек[2], ка *m.* (*zool.*) gopher.
овра́жист|ый (~, ~а) *adj.* abounding in ravines.
овра́|жный *adj. of* **~г; о. песо́к** pit sand.
овсе́ц, а́ *no pl., m.* (*coll.*) *dim. of* **овёс; дать ло́шади ~а́** to give a horse his oats.
овсю́г, а́ *m.* (*bot.*) wild oats.
овся́ниц|а, ы *f.* (*bot.*) fescue.
овся́нк|а[1], и *f.* **1.** oatmeal. **2.** oatmeal porridge.
овся́нк|а[2], и *f.* (*zool.*) (yellow) bunting, yellow-hammer.
овсян|о́й *adj. of* **овёс; о. ко́лос** ear of oats; **~о́е по́ле** field of oats.
овся́н|ый *adj.* made of oats; oatmeal; **~ая ка́ша** oatmeal porridge; **~ая крупа́** oatmeal.
овуля́ци|я, и *f.* (*biol.*) ovulation.
овц|а́, ы́, *pl.* **~́ы, ове́ц, ~́ам** *f.* sheep; ewe; **заблу́дшая о.** (*fig.*) lost sheep.
овцебы́к, а *m.* musk-ox.
овцево́д, а *m.* sheep-breeder.
овцево́дств|о, а *nt.* sheep-breeding.
овча́р, а *m.* shepherd.
овча́рк|а, и *f.* sheep-dog; **неме́цкая о.** German shepherd (*dog*), Alsatian.
овча́р|ня, ни, *g. pl.* **~ен** *f.* sheep-fold.
овчи́н|а, ы *f.* sheepskin.
овчи́н|ка, ки *f. dim. of* **~а; ей не́бо с ~ку показа́лось** she was frightened out of her wits; **о. вы́делки не сто́ит** (*fig.*) the game is not worth the candle.
овчи́нный *adj.* sheepskin.
ога́р|ок, ка *m.* candle-end; *pl.* cinders; (*tech.*) skimmings, scoria.
огиба́|ть, ю *impf. of* **обогну́ть**
ОГИЗ, а *m.* (*abbr. of* **Объедине́ние госуда́рственных изда́тельств**) State Publishing Association.
оглавле́ни|е, я *nt.* table of contents.
огла|си́ть, шу́, си́шь *pf.* (*of* **~ша́ть**) **1.** to proclaim, announce; **о. резолю́цию** to read out a resolution; **о. жениха́ и неве́сту** to publish banns of marriage. **2.** to divulge, make public. **3.** to fill (*with loud cries, etc.*).
огла|си́ться, шу́сь, си́шься *pf.* (*of* **~ша́ться**) **1.** (*+i.*) to resound (with). **2.** *pass. of* **~си́ть**
огла́ск|а, и *f.* publicity; **избега́ть ~и** to shun publicity; **получи́ть ~у** to be made known, receive publicity; **преда́ть ~е** to make public, make known.
оглаша́|ть(ся), ю(сь) *impf. of* **огласи́ть(ся)**
оглаше́ни|е, я *nt.* proclaiming, publication; **не подлежи́т ~ю** confidential (*classification of document*); (*eccl.*) (publication of) banns.
оглаше́нный *adj.*: **как о.** (*coll.*) like one possessed.
огло́б|ля, ли, *g. pl.* **~ель** *f.* shaft; **поверну́ть ~ли** (*fig., coll.*) to turn back, retrace one's steps.
огло́х|нуть, ну, нешь, *past* **~, ~ла** *pf. of* **гло́хнуть 1.**
оглуп|и́ть, лю́, ~и́шь *pf.* (*of* **~ля́ть**) **1.** to fool, make a fool of; to deceive. **2.** to distort; to misrepresent.
оглупля́|ть, ю *impf.* **1.** *impf. of* **оглупи́ть. 2.** to try to fool, try to deceive.
оглуш|а́ть, а́ю *impf. of* **~и́ть**
оглуши́тел|ьный (~ен, ~ьна) *adj.* deafening.
оглуш|и́ть, у́, и́шь *pf.* **1.** *pf. of* **глуши́ть 1.. 2.** (*impf.* **~а́ть**) to deafen; to stun (*also fig.*).
огля|де́ть, жу́, ди́шь *pf.* (*of* **~́дывать**) to look round; to examine, inspect.
огля|де́ться, жу́сь, ди́шься *pf.* (*of* **~дываться**) **1.** to look round. **2.** to get used to things around one; (*fig.*) to adapt o.s., become acclimatized; **о. в темноте́** to become accustomed to the darkness.
огля́дк|а, и *f.* **1.** looking back; **бежа́ть без ~и** to run without turning one's head. **2.** care, caution; **без ~и** carelessly; **де́йствовать с ~ой** to act circumspectly.
огля́дыва|ть(ся), ю(сь) *impf. of* **огляде́ть(ся)** *and* **огляну́ть(ся)**
огля|ну́ть, ну́, ~́нешь *inst. pf.* (*of* **~́дывать**) to take a look over.
огля|ну́ться, ну́сь, ~́нешься *pf.* (*of* **~́дываться**) to turn (back) to look at sth.; to glance back.
огневи́дный *adj.* (*geol.*) igneous, plutonic.
огневи́к, а́ *m.* **1.** fire-stone. **2.** (*med.*) anthrax. **3.** (*coll.*) gunner.
огневи́ц|а, ы *f.* (*dial.*) fever.
огнев|о́й *adj. of* **ого́нь;** (*fig.*) fiery; (*geol.*) igneous, pyrogenous; **о. бой** (*mil.*) firing; **о. вал** (*mil.*) barrage; **~а́я коро́бка** fire-box; **~о́е окаймле́ние** box barrage; **~ы́е сре́дства** weapons; **~а́я то́чка** (*mil.*) weapon emplacement.
огнегаси́тельный *adj.* fire-extinguishing; **о. прибо́р** fire-extinguisher.
огнедобы́тчик, а *m.* oil industry worker.
огнеды́шащ|ий *adj.* fire-spitting; **~ая гора́** (*obs.*) volcano.
огнемёт, а *m.* (*mil.*) flame-thrower.
О́гненн|ая Земл|я́, ~ой ~и́ *f.* Tierra del Fuego.
о́гненный *adj.* fiery (*also fig.*).
огнеопа́с|ный, (~ен, ~на) *adj.* inflammable.
огнепокло́нник, а *m.* fire-worshipper.
огнепокло́нни|ческий *adj. of* **~к**
огнепокло́нничеств|о, а *nt.* fire-worship.
огнеприпа́с|ы, ов *no sg.* ammunition.
огнесто́|йкий (~ек, ~йка) *adj.* fire-proof, fire-resistant.
огнестре́льн|ый *adj.*: **~ое ору́жие** fire-arm(s); **~ая ра́на** bullet wound.
огнетуши́тел|ь, я *m.* fire-extinguisher.
огнеупо́р|ный (~ен, ~на) *adj.* fire-resistant, fire-proof; refractory; **~ная гли́на** fire-clay; **о. кирпи́ч** fire-brick.
огнеупо́ры, ов *no sg.* (*tech.*) refractory materials.
огни́в|о, а *nt.* steel (*used formerly for striking fire from flint*).
ого́ *int.* oho!
огова́рива|ть(ся), ю(сь) *impf. of* **оговори́ть(ся)**
огово́р, а *m.* slander.
оговор|и́ть[1], ю́, и́шь *pf.* (*of* **огова́ривать**) to slander.
оговор|и́ть[2], ю́, и́шь *pf.* (*of* **огова́ривать**) **1.** to stipulate (for); to fix, agree (on); **мы ~и́ли усло́вия рабо́ты** we have fixed the conditions of work. **2.** to make a reservation, make a proviso (concerning); to specify; **он ~и́л своё несогла́сие** he specified his disagreement.
оговор|и́ться, ю́сь, и́шься *pf.* (*of* **огова́риваться**) **1.** to make a reservation, make a proviso. **2.** to make a slip in speaking. **3.** *pass. of* **~и́ть**

оговóр|ка, ки *f.* **1.** reservation, proviso; **без ~ок** without reserve; **он согласи́лся, но с нéкоторыми ~ками** he agreed but made certain reservations. **2.** slip of the tongue.
оговóрщик, а *m.* (*coll.*) slanderer.
оголéни|е, я *nt.* denudation.
огол|ённый *p.p.p. of* **~и́ть** *and adj.* bare, nude; uncovered, exposed.
огол|éц, ьцá *m.* (*coll.*) lad, (young) fellow.
огол|и́ть, ю́, и́шь *pf.* (*of* **~я́ть**) to bare; to strip, uncover; **о. фланг** (*mil.*) to expose one's flank.
огол|и́ться, ю́сь, и́шься *pf.* (*of* **~я́ться**) **1.** to strip (o.s.). **2.** to become exposed. **3.** *pass. of* **~и́ть**
оголтéлый *adj.* (*coll.*) unbridled; frenzied.
огол|я́ть(ся), я́ю(сь) *impf. of* **~и́ть(ся)**
огон|ёк, ькá *m.* **1.** (small) light; **блуждáющий о.** will o' the wisp; **весёлый о.** merry twinkle; **зайти́ к комý-н. на о.** (*coll.*) to drop in on s.o. (*seeing a light in the window*). **2.** (*fig.*) zest, spirit.
ог|óнь, ня́ *m.* **1.** fire (*also fig.*); **говори́ть с ~нём** to speak with fervour; **антóнов о.** gangrene; **~нём и мечóм** with fire and sword; **меж двух ~нéй** between two fires, between the devil and the deep blue sea; **пройти́ о. и вóду** to go through fire and water; **из ~ня́ да в пóлымя** (*fig.*) out of the frying-pan into the fire. **2.** (*mil.*) fire; firing; **управлéние ~нём** fire control; **закреплённый о. в тóчку** fire on fixed lines; **отвечáть ~нём** to fire back. **3.** light; **хвостовóй о.** (*aeron.*) tail light; **опознавáтельный о.** recognition lights; **такóго человéка днём с ~нём не найдёшь** (*coll.*) you will not find another like him in a month of Sundays.
огорáжива|ть(ся), ю(сь) *impf. of* **огороди́ть(ся)**
огорóд, а *m.* kitchen-garden; **брóсить кáмешек в чей-н. о.** (*fig.*, *coll.*) to throw stones at s.o.; to make hints about s.o.
огоро|ди́ть, жý, ~ди́шь *pf.* (*of* **огорáживать**) to fence in, enclose.
огоро|ди́ться, жýсь, ~ди́шься *pf.* (*of* **огорáживаться**) **1.** to fence o.s. in. **2.** *pass. of* **~ди́ть**
огорóдник, а *m.* market-gardener.
огорóднича|ть, ю *impf.* (*coll.*) to go in for market-gardening, be a market-gardener.
огорóдничеств|о, а *nt.* market-gardening.
огорóд|ный *adj. of* **~**; **~ное хозя́йство** market-gardening, market-garden.
огорóш|ить, у, ишь *pf.* (*coll.*) to take aback, disconcert.
огорч|áть(ся), áю(сь) *impf. of* **~и́ть(ся)**
огорчéни|е, я *nt.* grief, affliction; chagrin; **быть в ~и** to be in distress.
огорчи́тел|ьный (~ен, ~ьна) *adj.* distressing.
огорч|и́ть, ý, и́шь *pf.* (*of* **~áть**) to grieve, distress, pain.
огорч|и́ться, ýсь, и́шься *pf.* (*of* **~áться**) to grieve; to be distressed, be pained; **не ~áйтесь!** cheer up!
ОГПУ *nt. indecl.* (*abbr. of* ***Объединённое госудáрственное полити́ческое управлéние***) (*hist.*) OGPU, United State Political Directorate.
огрáб|ить, лю, ишь *pf. of* **грáбить**[1]
ограблéни|е, я *nt.* robbery; burglary; **ýличное о.** mugging.
огрáд|а, ы *f.* fence.
огра|ди́ть, жý, ди́шь *pf.* (*of* **~ждáть**) **1.** (*obs.*) to enclose, fence in. **2. (от)** to guard (against, from), protect (against).
огра|ди́ться, жýсь, ди́шься *pf.* (*of* **~ждáться**) **(от)** to defend o.s. (against); to protect o.s. (against), guard o.s. (against, from).
ограждá|ть(ся), ю(сь) *impf. of* **огради́ть(ся)**
ограничéни|е, я *nt.* limitation, restriction.
ограни́ченност|ь, и *f.* limitedness, scantiness; (*fig.*) narrowness, narrow-mindedness.
ограни́ч|енный *p.p.p. of* **~ить** *and adj.* limited; **о. человéк** (*fig.*) narrow(-minded) pers., hidebound pers.
ограни́чива|ть(ся), ю(сь) *impf. of* **ограни́чить(ся)**
ограничи́тел|ь, я *m.* (*tech.*): **о. хóда** catch, stop, stop piece, arresting device.
ограничи́тельный *adj.* restrictive, limiting.
ограни́ч|ить, у, ишь *pf.* (*of* **~ивать**) to limit, restrict, cut down; **о. себя́ в расхóдах** to cut down one's expenditure; **о. орáтора врéменем** to set a speaker a time limit.
ограни́ч|иться, усь, ишься *pf.* (*of* **~иваться**) (*+i.*) **1.** to limit o.s. (to), confine o.s. (to); **он ~ился крáткой рéчью** he confined himself to a short speech. **2.** to be limited (to), be confined (to).
огребá|ть, ю *impf. of* **огрести́**; **о. дéньги** (*coll.*) to rake in money.
огре|сти́, бý, бёшь, *past* **~б, ~блá** *pf.* (*of* **~бáть**) to rake round.
огрé|ть, ю *pf.* (*coll.*) to catch a blow, fetch a blow.
огрéх, а *m.* **1.** (*agric.*) gap (*in sowing*, *ploughing*, *etc.*). **2.** (*coll.*) fault, imperfection (*in work*).
огромáд|ный (~ен, ~на) *adj.* (*coll.*, *joc.*) ginormous, humongous.
огрóм|ный (~ен, ~на) *adj.* huge; vast; enormous.
огрубéлый *adj.* coarse, hardened.
огрубé|ть, ю *pf. of* **грубéть.**
огрýз|нуть, ну, нешь, *past* **~, ~ла** *pf.* (*coll.*) to grow stout.
огрыз|áться, áюсь *impf.* (*of* **~нýться**) **(на**+*a.*) to snap (at) (*of a dog*; *also fig.*).
огрыз|нýться, нýсь, нёшься *pf. of* **~áться**
огры́з|ок, ка *m.* bit, end; **о. карандашá** (*coll.*) pencil stub, stump.
огýз|ок, ка *m.* rump.
огýлом *adv.* (*coll.*) wholesale, indiscriminately.
огýльно *adv.* without grounds; **о. обвиня́ть** to make a groundless accusation.
огýл|ьный (~ен, ~ьна) *adj.* **1.** wholesale, indiscriminate; **~ьное охáивание** wholesale disparagement. **2.** unfounded, groundless. **3.** (*obs.*) wholesale (*comm.*).
огур|éц, цá *m.* cucumber.
огурé|чный *adj. of* **~ц**; **~чная травá** (*bot.*) borage.
огýрчик, а *m. affectionate dim. of* **огурéц; как о.** (*coll.*) *of pers. of ruddy, healthy appearance.*
óд|а, ы *f.* ode.
одáлжива|ть, ю *impf. of* **одолжи́ть**
одали́ск|а, и *f.* odalisque.
одарённост|ь, и *f.* endowments, (natural) gifts, talent.
одар|ённый *p.p.p. of* **~и́ть** *and adj.* gifted, talented.
одáрива|ть, ю *impf. of* **одари́ть**
одар|и́ть, ю́, и́шь *pf.* **1.** (*impf.* **~ивать**) to give presents (to); **онá ~и́ла всех детéй игрýшками** she has given all the children toys. **2.** (*impf.* **~я́ть**) (*+i.*) to endow (with); **прирóда ~и́ла егó разнообрáзными спосóбностями** nature has endowed him with a variety of talents.
одар|я́ть, я́ю *impf. of* **~и́ть**
одевá|ть(ся), ю(сь) *impf. of* **одéть(ся)**
одёж|а, и *f.* (*coll.*) clothes.
одéжд|а, ы *f.* **1.** clothes; garments; clothing; **вéрхняя о.** outer clothing, overcoat; **мужскáя о.** menswear; **произвóдственная о.** industrial clothing, overalls; **фóрменная о.** uniform. **2.** (*tech.*) surfacing, top dressing (*of road*).
одéжк|а, и *f. dim. of* **одéжда; по ~е протя́гивай нóжки** (*prov.*) cut your coat according to the cloth.
одеколóн, а *m.* eau-de-Cologne; **цветóчный о.** flower-scented eau-de-Cologne.
одеколóн|ный *adj. of* **~**
одел|и́ть, ю́, и́шь *pf.* (*of* **~я́ть**) (*+i.*) **1.** to present (with). **2.** (*obs.*) to endow (with).
одел|я́ть, я́ю *impf. of* **~и́ть**
од|ёр, рá *m.* (*coll.*) old hack (*horse*).
одёргива|ть, ю *impf. of* **одёрнуть**
одеревенéлый *adj.* numb; (*fig.*) lifeless.
одеревенé|ть, ю *pf. of* **деревенéть**
одерж|áть, ý, ~ишь *pf.* (*of* **~ивать**) to gain; **о. верх (над)** to gain the upper hand (over), prevail (over); **о. побéду** to gain a (the) victory, carry the day.
одéржива|ть, ю *impf. of* **одержáть**
одержи́м|ый (~, ~а) *adj.* **1.** (*+i.*) possessed (by); afflicted (by); **о. стрáхом** ridden by fear; **о. навя́зчивой идéей** obsessed by an idée fixe. **2.** *as n.* **о., ~ого** *m.* one possessed, madman.
одёр|нуть, ну, нешь *pf.* (*of* **~гивать**) **1.** to pull down, straighten (*article of clothing*). **2.** (*fig.*, *coll.*) to call to order; to silence; to snub.

одесну́ю *adv.* (*obs.*) to the right; on the right hand.
одесси́т, а *m.* inhabitant of Odessa.
оде́т|ый *p.p.p. of* **~ь** *and adj.* (*+i. or* **в**+*a.*) dressed (in), clothed (in); with one's clothes on; **о. сне́гом** snow-clad; **хорошо́ о.** well-dressed.
оде́|ть, ну, нешь *pf.* (*of* **~ва́ть**) (*+i. or* **в**+*a.*) to dress (in), clothe (in).
оде́|ться, нусь, нешься *pf.* (*of* **~ва́ться**) **1.** to dress (o.s.); to clothe o.s.; **о. в вече́рнее пла́тье** to put on an evening dress. **2.** *pass. of* **~ть**
одея́л|о, а *nt.* blanket; coverlet; **о-гре́лка** electric blanket; **стёганое о.** counterpane, quilt; **лоску́тное о.** patchwork quilt.
одея́ни|е, я *nt.* garb, attire.
оди́н, одного́ *m.*; **одна́, одно́й** *f.*; **одно́, одного́** *nt.*; *pl.* **одни́, одни́х** *num. and pron.* **1.** one; **о. стол** one table; **одни́ но́жницы** one pair of scissors; **одно́** one thing; **одно́ де́ло…, друго́е де́ло…** it is one thing …, another thing …; **о. за други́м** one after the other; **одни́… други́е** some … other; **с одно́й стороны́… с друго́й (стороны́)** on the one hand … on the other hand; **одно́ вре́мя** at one time; **о. раз** once; **одни́м ро́счерком пера́** with a stroke of the pen; **одни́м сло́вом** in a word; **о.-два** one or two; **о.-еди́нственный** one and only; **о. из ты́сячи** one in a thousand; **в о. го́лос** with one voice, with one accord; **в о. прекра́сный день** one fine day, once upon a time; **все до одного́** all to a man; **одно́ к одному́** (*coll.*) moreover; one way and another; **все, как о.** one and all; **о. на о.** in private, tête-à-tête; face to face; **по одному́** one by one, one at a time; in single file. **2.** a, an; a certain; **я встре́тил одного́ моего́ бы́вшего колле́гу** I met an old colleague of mine. **3.** alone; by o.s.; **да́йте ей сде́лать э́то одно́й** let her do it by herself; **я живу́ о.** I live alone; **о.-одинёхонек, о.-одинёшенек** all by o.s. **4.** only; alone; nothing but; **он о. зна́ет доро́гу** he alone knows the way; **она́ чита́ет одни́ детекти́вные рома́ны** she reads nothing but detective stories. **5.: о., о. и тот же** the same, one and the same; **мы с ней одного́ во́зраста** she and I are the same age; **э́то одно́ и то же** it is the same thing; **мне э́то всё одно́** it is all one to me.
одина́кий *adj.* (*obs.*, *coll.*) identical.
одина́ково *adv.* equally, alike.
одина́ковост|ь, и *f.* identity (*of views, etc.*)
одина́ков|ый (~, ~а) *adj.* (**с**+*i.*) identical (with), the same (as).
одина́рный *adj.* single.
одинё|хонек, ~шенек *see* **оди́н 3.**
одиннадцатиле́тний *adj.* eleven-year-old.
оди́ннадцатый *adj.* eleventh.
оди́ннадцат|ь, и *num.* eleven.
одино́к|ий (~, ~а) *adj.* **1.** solitary; lonely; lone. **2.** *as n.* **о., ~ого** *m.* single man, bachelor; **~ая, ~ой** *f.* single woman.
одино́ко *adv.* lonely; **чу́вствовать себя́ о.** to feel lonely.
одино́честв|о, а *nt.* solitude; loneliness.
одино́чк|а, и *c.g and f.* **1.** *c.g.* lone pers.; **кустáрь-о.** craftsman working alone; **мать-о.** unmarried mother; **оте́ц-о.** single father; **жить ~ой** to live alone; **в ~у** alone, on one's own; **по ~е** one by one. **2.** *f.* (*coll.*) one-man cell, solitary confinement. **3.** *f.* single-oar (*rowing-boat*).
одино́чн|ый *adj.* **1.** individual; one-man; **~ое заключе́ние** solitary confinement. **2.** single; **о. вы́стрел** single shot; **о. ого́нь** (*mil.*) single-round firing.
одио́з|ный (~ен, ~на) *adj.* odious, offensive.
одиссе́|я, и *f.* (*fig.*) Odyssey.
одича́лый *adj.* (having gone) wild.
одича́ни|е, я *nt.* running wild.
одича́|ть, ю *pf. of* **дича́ть**
одна́жды *adv.* once; one day; **о. у́тром (ве́чером, но́чью)** one morning (evening, night).
одна́ко 1. *adv. and conj.* however; but; though. **2.** *int.* you don't say so!; not really!
одноа́ктный *adj.* (*theatr.*) one-act.
одноато́мный *adj.* monoatomic.
однобо́к|ий (~, ~а) *adj.* one-sided (*also fig.*).
однобо́ртный *adj.* single-breasted.
одновале́нтный *adj.* (*chem.*) univalent, monovalent.
одновесе́льный *adj.* one-oared.
одновре́ме́нно *adv.* simultaneously, at the same time.
одновре́ме́нност|ь, и *f.* simultaneity; synchronism.
одновре́ме́нный *adj.* simultaneous; synchronous.
одногла́зк|а, и *f.* (*zool.*) cyclops.
одногла́зый *adj.* one-eyed.
одногоди́чный *adj.* one-year, of one year's duration.
одного́д|ок, ка *m.* (**с**+*i.*; *coll.*) of the same age (as).
одного́рбый *adj.*: **о. верблю́д** dromedary, Arabian camel.
однодво́р|ец, ца *m.* (*hist.*) odnodvorets (*member of special group of smallholders in 18th-century Russia, descendants of lowest category of service class*).
одноде́вный *adj.* one-day.
однодо́льный *adj.* (*bot.*) monocotyledonous.
однодо́мный *adj.* (*bot.*) monoecious.
одноду́м, а *m.* pers. with idée fixe, obsessional.
одножи́льный *adj.* (*elec.*) single-core.
однозву́чный *adj.* monotonous.
однозна́чащий *adj.* **1.** synonymous. **2.** monosemantic.
однозна́ч|ный (~ен, ~на) *adj.* **1.** synonymous. **2.** (*ling.*) monosemantic. **3.** (*math.*) simple; **~ное число́** simple number, digit. **4.** (*fig.*) simple, straightforward.
одноимён|ный (~ен, ~на) *adj.* of the same name.
однокали́берный *adj.* of the same calibre.
однока́мерный *adj.* (*zool.*) monothalamous.
однока́шник, а *m.* (*obs.*, *coll.*) school-fellow.
однокла́ссник, а *m.* classmate.
однокле́точный *adj.* (*biol.*) unicellular.
одноклу́бник, а *m.* (*coll.*) fellow-member of club.
одноколе́йный *adj.* single-track.
одноколе́нчатый *adj.* (*tech.*) single-jointed.
однoко́лк|а, и *f.* (*coll.*) gig.
одноко́нный *adj.* one-horse.
однокопы́тный *adj.* (*zool.*) solidungular, solid-hoofed.
одноко́нтурный *adj.* (*elec.*) single-circuit.
одноко́рпусный *adj.* (*naut.*) single-hull.
однокра́тный *adj.* single; (*gram.*) instantaneous, semelfactive; **о. глаго́л** semelfactive verb.
однoку́рсник, а *m.* fellow-member of course.
однола́мповый *adj.* (*radio*) single-valve.
однoле́тний *adj.* **1.** one-year. **2.** (*bot.*) annual.
однoле́тник, а *m.* (*bot.*) annual.
однoле́т|ок, ка *m.* (**с**+*i.*) (*coll.*) of the same age (as).
однoма́стный *adj.* of one colour.
однoма́чтовый *adj.* single-masted.
однoме́стный *adj.* single-seated, single-seater.
однoмото́рный *adj.* single-engine.
однoно́гий *adj.* one-legged.
однообра́зи|е, я *nt.* monotony.
однообра́зност|ь, и *f.* = **однообра́зие**
однообра́з|ный (~ен, ~на) *adj.* monotonous.
одноо́кис|ь, и *f.* (*chem.*) monoxide.
одноо́сный *adj.* uniaxial, monoaxial.
однопала́тный *adj.* (*pol.*) unicameral, single-chamber.
однопа́лубный *adj.* one-decked.
однoплеме́нный *adj.* of the same tribe.
однoполча́н|ин, ина, *pl.* **~е, ~** *m.* comrade-in-arms (*one serving in same regiment*).
однoпо́лый *adj.* (*bot.*) unisexual.
однoпо́люсный *adj.* (*phys.*) unipolar.
однoпу́тк|а, и *f.* (*coll.*) single-track railway.
однoпу́тный *adj.* one-way.
однoро́гий *adj.* one-horned, unicornous.
однoро́дност|ь, и *f.* homogeneity, uniformity.
однoро́д|ный (~ен, ~на) *adj.* **1.** homogeneous, uniform. **2.** similar.
однoру́кий *adj.* one-handed, one-armed.
однoря́дк|а, и *f.* (*hist.*) single-breasted caftan.
однoсельча́н|ин, ина, *pl.* **~е, ~** *m.* fellow-villager.
однoсло́жно *adv.*: **говори́ть о.** to speak in monosyllables.
однoсло́жност|ь, и *f.* **1.** monosyllabism. **2.** (*fig.*) terseness, abruptness.
однoсло́ж|ный *adj.* **1.** monosyllabic. **2. (~ен, ~на)** (*fig.*) terse, abrupt.

однослóйный *adj.* single-layer; one-ply, single-ply.
односпáльн|ый *adj.*: **~ая кровáть** single bed.
одностволь́н|ый *adj.*: **~ое ружьё** single-barrelled gun.
одностворчат|ый *adj.* **1.** (*zool.*) univalve. **2. ~ая дверь** single door.
односторóнн|ий *adj.* **1.** one-sided (*also fig.*); unilateral. **2.** one-way; **~ее движéние** one-way traffic; **о. ум** (*fig.*) one-track mind.
однотáктный *adj.* (*tech.*) one-stroke, single-cycle.
однотёс, а *m.* plank nail.
однотип|ный (~ен, ~на) *adj.* of the same type, of the same kind; **о. корáбль** sister-ship.
однотóмник, а *m.* one-volume edition, omnibus volume.
однотóмный *adj.* one-volume.
однофáзный *adj.* (*elec.*) single-phase, monophase.
однофами́л|ец, ьца *m.* (**с**+*i.*) pers. bearing the same surname (as), namesake.
одноцвéтный *adj.* one-colour; (*typ.*) monochrome.
одноцили́ндровый *adj.* one-cylinder.
одночлéн, а *m.* (*math.*) monomial.
одночлéнный *adj.* (*math.*) monomial.
одношéрстный *adj.* (*of animals*) of one colour.
одноэтáжный *adj.* **1.** single-stage. **2.** one-storeyed.
одноя́дерный *adj.* mononuclear.
одноязы́ч|ный (~ен, ~на) *adj.* monolingual; unilingual.
одноя́русный *adj.* single-stage.
одобрéни|е, я *nt.* approval.
одобри́тел|ьный (~ен, ~ьна) *adj.* approving.
одóбр|ить, ю, ишь *pf.* (*of* **~я́ть**) to approve (of); **не о.** to disapprove (of).
одобр|я́ть, я́ю *impf. of* **~ить**
одолевá|ть, ю *impf. of* **одолéть**
одолé|ть, ю *pf.* (*of* **~вáть**) **1.** to overcome, conquer; **егó ~л сон** he was overcome by sleepiness; **нас ~ло зловóние** the stench overpowered us. **2.** (*fig.*) to master; to cope (with); to get through; **о. всю премýдрость** to master all the ins and outs.
одолж|áть, áю *impf. of* **~и́ть**
одолжá|ться, юсь *impf.* (*+d. or* **у**) to be obliged (to), be beholden (to); **~йтесь!** (*obs., coll.*) have some!
одолжéни|е, я *nt.* favour, service; **сдéлайте мне о.** do me a favour; **я сочтý э́то за о.** I shall esteem it, regard it as a favour.
одолж|и́ть, ý, и́шь *pf.* (*of* **одáлживать** *and* **~áть**) **1.** (*+d.*) to lend. **2.** (*coll.*; **у**) to borrow (from).
одомáшнени|е, я *nt.* domestication, taming.
одомáшн|енный *p.p.p. of* **~ить** *and adj.* domesticated.
одомáшнива|ть, ю *impf. of* **одомáшнить**
одомáшн|ить, ю, ишь *pf.* (*of* **~ивать**) to domesticate, tame.
одонтóлог, а *m.* odontologist.
одонтолóги|я, и *f.* (*med.*) odontology.
одр, á *m.* (*arch.*; *now only in certain phrr.*) bed, couch; **на смéртном ~é** on one's death-bed.
одревеснéни|е, я *nt.* lignification.
одряхлé|ть, ю *pf. of* **дряхлéть**
одувáнчик, а *m.* (*bot.*) dandelion.
одýм|аться, аюсь *pf.* (*of* **~ываться**) to change one's mind; to think better of it; to bethink o.s.
одýмыва|ться, юсь *impf. of* **одýматься**
одурáчива|ть, ю *impf. of* **одурáчить**
одурáч|ить, у, ишь *pf.* (*of* **дурáчить** *and* **~ивать**) (*coll.*) to make a fool (of), fool.
одурéлый *adj.* (*coll.*) dulled, besotted.
одурéни|е, я *nt.* stupefaction, torpor.
одурé|ть, ю *pf. of* **дурéть**
одурмáнива|ть, ю *impf. of* **одурмáнить**
одурмáн|ить, ю, ишь *pf.* (*of* **дурмáнить** *and* **~ивать**) to stupefy; (*with drug*) to drug.
óдур|ь, и *f.* (*coll.*) stupefaction, torpor; **сóнная о.** (*bot.*) deadly nightshade.
одуря́|ть, ю *impf.* (*coll.*) to stupefy; **~ющий зáпах** heavy scent.
одутловáт|ый (~, ~а) *adj.* puffy.
одухотворённост|ь, и *f.* spirituality.
одухотворённый *p.p.p. of* **одухотвори́ть** *and adj.* inspired.
одухотвор|и́ть, ю, и́шь *pf.* (*of* **~я́ть**) **1.** to inspire; to animate. **2.** to attribute soul (to) (*natural phenomena, animals, etc.*).
одухотвор|я́ть, я́ю *impf. of* **~и́ть**
одушев|и́ть, лю́, и́шь *pf.* (*of* **~ля́ть**) to animate.
одушев|и́ться, лю́сь, и́шься *pf.* (*of* **~ля́ться**) to be animated.
одушевлéни|е, я *nt.* animation.
одушевлённый *p.p.p. of* **одушеви́ть** *and adj.* animated.
одушевля́|ть(ся), ю(сь) *impf. of* **одушеви́ть(ся)**
оды́шк|а, и *f.* short breath; **страдáть ~ой** to be short-winded.
ожереб|и́ться, лю́сь, и́шься *pf. of* **жереби́ться**
ожерéль|е, я *nt.* necklace.
ожесточ|áть(ся), áю(сь) *impf. of* **~и́ть(ся)**
ожесточéни|е, я *nt.* bitterness.
ожесточённост|ь, и *f.* = **ожесточéние**
ожесточённый *p.p.p. of* **ожесточи́ть** *and adj.* bitter; embittered; hardened.
ожесточ|и́ть, ý, и́шь *pf.* (*of* **~áть**) to embitter; to harden.
ожесточ|и́ться, ýсь, и́шься *pf.* (*of* **~áться**) to become embittered; to become hardened.
ожéчь(сь) = **обжéчь(ся)**
оживáльный *adj.* (*archit.*) ogival.
оживá|ть, ю *impf. of* **ожи́ть**
ожив|и́ть, лю́, и́шь *pf.* (*of* **~ля́ть**) **1.** to revive. **2.** (*fig.*) to enliven, vivify, animate.
ожив|и́ться, лю́сь, и́шься *pf.* (*of* **~ля́ться**) **1.** to become animated, liven (up). **2.** *pass. of* **~и́ть**
оживлéни|е, я *nt.* **1.** animation, gusto. **2.** reviving; enlivening.
оживлённый *p.p.p. of* **оживи́ть** *and adj.* animated; lively.
оживля́|ть(ся), ю(сь) *impf. of* **оживи́ть(ся)**
оживотвор|и́ть, ю́, и́шь *pf. of* **животвори́ть**
ожидáни|е, я *nt.* expectation; waiting; **обманýть ~я** to disappoint; **в ~и** (*+g.*) pending; **быть в ~и** (*of a woman*; *euph.*) to be expecting; **сверх ~я** beyond expectation.
ожидá|ть, ю *impf.* (*+g.*) to wait (for); to expect, anticipate; **о. ребёнка** (*of a woman*) to be expecting a baby; **мы э́того не ~ли** we were not expecting that; **как я и ~л** just as I expected.
ожижáтел|ь, я *m.* (*tech.*) liquefier.
ожижá|ть, ю *impf.* (*tech.*) to liquefy.
ожижéни|е, я *nt.* (*chem.*) liquefaction (*of gas*); (*meteor.*) thinning; liquation.
ожирéни|е, я *nt.* obesity; **о. сéрдца** adipose heart.
ожирé|ть, ю *pf. of* **жирéть**
ож|и́ть, ивý, ивёшь, *past* **~ил, ~илá, ~ило** *pf.* (*of* **~ивáть**) to come to life, revive (*also fig.*).
ожóг, а *m.* burn; scald.
оз. (*abbr. of* **óзеро**) L., Lake.
озабó|тить, чу, тишь *pf.* (*of* **~чивать**) to trouble, worry, cause anxiety.
озабó|титься, чусь, тишься *pf.* (*of* **~чиваться**) (*+i.*) to attend (to); **о. заготóвкой тóплива** to see to the laying in of fuel.
озабóченност|ь, и *f.* preoccupation; anxiety.
озабó|ченный *p.p.p. of* **~тить** *and adj.* preoccupied; anxious, worried.
озабóчива|ть(ся), ю(сь) *impf. of* **озабóтить(ся)**
озаглáв|ить, лю, ишь *pf.* (*of* **~ливать**) to entitle; to head (*a chapter, etc.*).
озаглáвлива|ть, ю *impf. of* **озаглáвить**
озадáченност|ь, и *f.* perplexity, puzzlement.
озадáч|енный *p.p.p. of* **~ить** *and adj.* perplexed, puzzled.
озадáчива|ть, ю *impf. of* **озадáчить**
озадáч|ить, у, ишь *pf.* (*of* **~ивать**) to perplex, puzzle, take aback.
озар|и́ть, ю́, и́шь *pf.* (*of* **~я́ть**) to light up, illuminate, illumine; **улы́бка ~и́ла её лицó** a smile lit up her face; **их ~и́ло** (*fig.*) it dawned upon them.
озар|и́ться, ю́сь, и́шься *pf.* (*of* **~я́ться**) **1.** (*+i.*) to light up (with); **её лицó ~и́лось рáдостью** her face lit up with joy. **2.** *pass. of* **~и́ть**

озар|я́ть(ся), я́ю(сь) *impf. of* **~и́ть(ся)**
озвере́лый *adj.* brutal; brutalized.
озвере́|ть, ю *pf. of* **звере́ть**
озву́ч|енный *p.p.p. of* **~ить; о. фильм** sound film.
озву́чива|ть, ю *impf. of* **озву́чить**
озву́ч|ить, у, ишь *pf.* (*of* **~ивать**) (*cin.*) to add a soundtrack to.
оздорови́тел|ьный (~ен, ~ьна) *adj.* **1.** sanitary. **2.** fitness, keep-fit; **о. бег** jogging; **о. ла́герь** health camp.
оздоров|и́ть, лю́, и́шь *pf.* (*of* **~ля́ть**) to render (more) healthy, bring into a healthy state (*also fig.*); **о. ме́стность** to improve the sanitary conditions of a locality.
оздоровля́|ть, ю *impf. of* **оздорови́ть**
озелене́ни|е, я *nt.* planting with trees and gardens.
озелен|и́ть, ю́, и́шь *pf.* (*of* **~я́ть**) to plant with trees and gardens.
озелен|я́ть, я́ю *impf. of* **~и́ть**
о́земь *adv.* (*coll.*) to the ground, down.
озерк|о́, а́, *pl.* **~и́, ~о́в** *nt. dim. of* **о́зеро**
озёрный *adj. of* **о́зеро; о. райо́н** lake district.
о́зер|о, а, *pl.* **озёра, озёр** *nt.* lake; **о. Лох-Не́сс** Loch Ness.
ози́м|ый *adj.* winter; **~ая культу́ра** winter crop; **~ое по́ле** winter-field; *as n.* **~ые, ~ых** winter crops.
о́зим|ь, и *f.* winter crop.
озира́|ть, ю *impf.* (*obs.*) to view.
озира́|ться, юсь *impf.* to look round; to look back.
озло́б|ить, лю, ишь *pf.* (*of* **~ля́ть**) to embitter.
озло́б|иться, люсь, ишься *pf.* (*of* **~ля́ться**) to become embittered.
озлобле́ни|е, я *nt.* bitterness, animosity.
озло́б|ленный *p.p.p. of* **~ить** *and adj.* embittered.
озлобля́|ть(ся), ю(сь) *impf. of* **озло́бить(ся)**
ознако́м|ить, лю, ишь *pf.* (*of* **~ля́ть**) (**с**+*i.*) to acquaint (with).
ознако́м|иться, люсь, ишься *pf.* (*of* **~ля́ться**) (**с**+*i.*) to familiarize o.s. with.
ознакомля́|ть(ся), ю(сь) *impf. of* **ознако́мить(ся)**
ознаменова́ни|е, я *nt.* marking, commemoration; **в о.** (+*g.*) to mark, to commemorate, in commemoration (of).
ознамен|ова́ть, у́ю *pf.* (*of* **~о́вывать**) to mark, commemorate; to celebrate.
означа́|ть, ю *impf.* to mean, signify, stand for; **что ~ют э́ти бу́квы?** what do these letters stand for?
озна́ченный *adj.* (*obs.*) the aforesaid.
озно́б, а *m.* shivering; chill; **почу́вствовать о.** to feel shivery.
озноб|и́ть, лю́, и́шь *pf.* (*of* **~ля́ть**) (*coll.*): **я ~и́л себе́ у́ши** *etc.*, my ears, *etc.*, are frozen.
озноблю́|ть, ю *impf. of* **ознобить**
озокери́т, а *m.* (*min.*) ozocerite.
озоло|ти́ть, чу́, ти́шь *pf.* **1.** to gild. **2.** (*coll.*) to load with money.
озо́н, а *m.* ozone.
озона́тор, а *m.* (*phys.*) ozonizer.
озони́ровани|е, я *nt.* ozonization.
озони́рова|нный *p.p.p. of* **~ть** *and adj.* ozonized.
озони́р|овать, ую *impf. and pf.* to ozonize.
озо́н|ный *adj. of* **~; о. слой** ozone layer.
озонобезвре́д|ный (~ен, ~на) *adj.* ozone-friendly.
озорни́к, а́ *m.* (*coll.*) **1.** naughty child, mischievous child. **2.** mischief-maker.
озорнича́|ть, ю *impf.* (*of* **с~**) (*coll.*) **1.** (*of a child*) to be naughty, get up to mischief. **2.** (*of an adult*) to make mischief, play dirty tricks.
озорно́й *adj.* (*coll.*) mischievous, naughty.
озорств|о́, а́ *nt.* (*coll.*) mischief, naughtiness.
озя́б|нуть, ну, нешь, *past* **~, ~ла** *pf.* to be cold, be chilly; **я ~!** I am frozen!
ой (*or* **ой-ой-ой**) *int. expr. surprise, fright or pain* o; oh; ow, ouch!; oops!
о́й-ли *int.* (*coll.*) *expr. doubt* really?; is it possible?
ок. (*abbr. of* **о́коло**) approx., c., circa.
ока|за́ть, жу́, ~жешь *pf.* (*of* **~зывать**) to render, show; **о. влия́ние** (**на**+*a.*) to influence, exert influence (upon); **о. внима́ние** (+*d.*) to pay attention (to); **о. давле́ние** (**на**+*a.*) to exert pressure (upon), bring pressure to bear (upon); **о. де́йствие** (**на**+*a.*) to have an effect (upon); to take effect; **о. му́жество** (*obs.*) to display bravery; **о. по́мощь** (+*d.*) to help, give help; **о. предпочте́ние** (+*d.*) to show preference (for), prefer; **о. соде́йствие** (+*d.*) to render assistance; **о. сопротивле́ние** (+*d.*) to offer, put up resistance (to); **о. услу́гу** (+*d.*) to do, render a service; to do a good turn; **о. честь** (+*d.*) to do an honour.
ока|за́ться, жу́сь, ~жешься *pf.* (*of* **~зываться**) **1.** to turn out (to be), prove (to be); to be found (to be); **он ~за́лся отли́чным расска́зчиком** he proved to be a first-rate story-teller; **~за́лось, что она́ всё вре́мя лгала́** it turned out that she had been telling lies all the time. **2.** to find o.s.; to be found; **я ~за́лся в больни́це** I found myself in hospital; **трёх экземпля́ров не ~зало́сь** three copies were missing.
ока́зи|я, и *f.* **1.** opportunity; **посла́ть письмо́ с ~ей** to profit by an opportunity to send a letter. **2.** unexpected happening; **что за о.!** what an odd thing!; how odd!
ока́зыва|ть(ся), ю(сь) *impf. of* **оказа́ть(ся)**
окайм|и́ть, лю́, и́шь *pf.* (*of* **~ля́ть**) (+*i.*) to border (with), edge (with).
окаймля́|ть, ю *impf. of* **окайми́ть**
ока́лин|а, ы *f.* cinder; (*tech.*) scale; slag, dross.
окамене́лост|ь, и *f.* fossil.
окамене́лый *adj.* fossilized; petrified.
окамене́|ть, ю *pf. of* **камене́ть**
окант|ова́ть, у́ю *pf. of* **кантова́ть**[1]
оканто́вк|а, и *f.* mount (*for pictures, etc.*).
ока́нчива|ть(ся), ю(сь) *impf. of* **око́нчить(ся)**
о́кань|е, я *nt.* okanie (*pronunciation of unstressed* 'o' *as* 'o').
ока́пыва|ть(ся), ю(сь) *impf. of* **окопа́ть(ся)**
ока́рмлива|ть, ю *impf. of* **окорми́ть**
ока|ти́ть, чу́, ~тишь *pf.* (*of* **~чивать**) to pour (over); **о. холо́дной водо́й** to pour cold water (over) (*also fig.*).
ока|ти́ться, чу́сь, ~тишься *pf.* (*of* **~чиваться**) to pour over o.s.
о́ка|ть, ю *impf.* to pronounce unstressed 'o' as 'o' in Russ. words.
ока́чива|ть(ся), ю(сь) *impf. of* **окати́ть(ся)**
окая́нный *adj.* damned, cursed.
окая́нств|о, а *nt.* (*eccl.*) sinfulness.
окая́нств|овать, ую *pf.* (*eccl.*) to live a life of sin.
океа́н, а *m.* ocean.
Океа́ни|я, и *f.* Oceania; the South Sea Islands.
океаногра́фи|я, и *f.* oceanography.
океанографи́ческий *adj.* oceanographic.
океа́нский *adj.* ocean; oceanic; **о. парохо́д** ocean(-going) liner.
оки́дыва|ть, ю *impf. of* **оки́нуть**
оки́|нуть, ну, нешь *pf.* (*of* **~дывать**) to cast round; **о. взгля́дом, о. взо́ром** to take in at a glance; to glance over.
о́кис|ел, ла *m.* (*chem.*) oxide.
окисле́ни|е, я *nt.* (*chem.*) oxidation.
окисли́тел|ь, я *m.* (*chem.*) oxidizer, acidifier.
окисли́тельный *adj.* (*chem.*) oxidizing.
окисл|и́ть, ю́, и́шь *pf.* (*of* **~я́ть**) (*chem.*) to oxidize.
окисл|и́ться, ю́сь, и́шься *pf.* (*of* **~я́ться**) (*chem.*) **1.** to oxidize. **2.** *pass. of* **~и́ть**
окисл|я́ть(ся), я́ю(сь) *impf. of* **~и́ть(ся)**
о́кис|ь, и *f.* (*chem.*) oxide; **безво́дная о.** anhydride; **во́дная о.** hydroxide; **о. желе́за** ferric oxide; **о. ме́ди** cupric oxide; **о. углеро́да** carbon monoxide.
окказионали́зм, а *m.* (*ling.*) nonce-word.
окклюди́р|овать, ую *impf. and pf.* (*chem.*) to occlude.
окклю́зи|я, и *f.* (*chem.*) occlusion.
оккульти́зм, а *m.* occultism.
окку́льтный *adj.* occult.
оккупа́нт, а *m.* invader, occupier.
оккупа|цио́нный *adj. of* **~ция; ~цио́нная а́рмия** army of occupation.
оккупа́ци|я, и *f.* (*mil.*) occupation.
оккупи́р|овать, ую *impf. and pf.* (*mil.*) to occupy.
окла́д[1]**, а** *m.* **1.** salary scale; salary; **основно́й о.** (*mil.*) basic pay. **2.** tax, assessment.

окла́д², **а** *m.* setting, framework (*of icon*).
окла́дист|ый (~, ~а) *adj.* (*of beard*) broad and thick.
окладно́й *adj. of* **окла́д**¹; **о. лист** tax sheet.
оклеве|та́ть, щу́, ~́шешь *pf.* to slander, calumniate, defame.
окле́ива|ть, ю *impf. of* **окле́ить**
окле́|ить, ю, ишь *pf.* (*of* **~ивать**) (+*i.*) to cover (with); to glue over (with), paste over (with); **о. ко́мнату обо́ями** to paper a room.
окле́йк|а, и *f.* glueing, pasting; **о. обо́ями** papering.
о́клик, а *m.* hail, call.
оклик|а́ть, а́ю *impf. of* **~́нуть**
окли́к|нуть, ну, нешь *pf.* (*of* **~а́ть**) to hail, call (to).
окн|о́, а́, *pl.* **~́а, о́кон, ~́ам** *nt.* **1.** window; **опускно́е о.** sash window; **слухово́е о.** dormer window; **ко́мната в три ~а́** room with three windows; **о. вы́дачи** serving-hatch. **2.** (*fig.*) gap; aperture. **3.** (*school sl.*) free period.
о́к|о, а, *pl.* **о́чи, оче́й** *nt.* (*arch. or poet.*) eye; **в мгнове́ние ~а** in the twinkling of an eye; **о. за о.** an eye for an eye.
ок|ова́ть, ую́, уёшь *pf.* (*of* **~о́вывать**) to bind (*with metal*); (*fig.*) to fetter, shackle.
око́вк|а, и *f.* binding (*with metal*); nailing (*of boots*).
око́в|ы, ~ *no sg.* fetters (*also fig.*); **сбро́сить с себя́ о.** to cast off one's chains.
око́выва|ть, ю *impf. of* **окова́ть**
окола́чива|ться, юсь *impf.* (*coll.*) to lounge about, kick one's heels.
околд|ова́ть, у́ю *pf.* (*of* **~о́вывать**) to bewitch, entrance, enchant (*also fig.*).
околдо́выва|ть, ю *impf. of* **околдова́ть**
околева́|ть, ю *impf. of* **околе́ть**
околе́лый *adj.* (*coll.*; *of animals*) dead.
околёсиц|а, ы *f.* (*coll.*) nonsense, rubbish; **нести́ ~у** to talk stuff and nonsense.
околёс|ная, ной *f.* = **~ица**
околе́|ть, ю *pf.* (*of* **~ва́ть**) (*of animals and pej. of persons*) to die.
око́лиц|а, ы *f.* **1.** outskirts (of a village); **вы́ехать за ~у** to leave the confines of a village; **на ~е** on the outskirts. **2.** (*dial.*) neighbourhood. **3.** (*dial.*) roundabout route.
околи́чност|ь, и *f.* (*obs.*) circumlocution; innuendo; **говори́ть без ~ей** to speak plainly.
о́коло *prep.*+*g. and adv.* **1.** by; close (to), near; around, about; **он сиде́л о. меня́** he was sitting by me; **никого́ нет о.** there is nobody about; **где́-н. о. (э́того ме́ста)** hereabouts, somewhere here; **(что́-н.) о. э́того, о. того́** thereabouts. **2.** about; **о. полу́ночи** about midnight; **о. шести́ ме́тров** about six metres.
около́до|к, ~чный = **около́ток, около́точный**
околоплане́тный *adj.* circumplanetary.
околопло́дник, а *m.* (*bot.*) pericarp, seed vessel.
околосерде́чн|ый *adj.* **~ая су́мка** (*anat.*) pericardium.
околот|ок, ка *m.* **1.** neighbourhood. **2.** (*obs.*) ward, town district, precinct; area, sector (*of public transport*). **3.** (*obs.*) police-station. **4.** (*mil.*; *obs.*) aid post, dressing-station.
около́то|чный *adj. of* **~к; о. надзира́тель** *or as n.* **о., ~чного** *m.* (*obs.*) police-officer.
околоу́шный *adj.* (*anat.*) parotid.
околоцве́тник, а *m.* (*bot.*) perianth.
околпа́чива|ть, ю *impf. of* **околпа́чить**
околпа́ч|ить, у, ишь *pf.* (*of* **~ивать**) (*coll.*) to fool, dupe.
око́лыш, а *m.* cap-band.
око́льнич|ий, его *m.* (*hist.*) okolnichy (*in Muscovite period, member of social group with status second to that of boyars*).
око́льны|й *adj.* roundabout; **~е пути́** devious ways; **вы́ведать ~м путём** (*fig.*) to find out in a roundabout way.
окольц|ева́ть, у́ю *pf. of* **кольцева́ть 2.**
оконе́чност|ь, и *f.* extremity.
око́нн|ый *adj. of* **окно́; ~ая ра́ма** window-frame, sash; **~ое стекло́** window-pane; window-glass.
оконфу́|зить, жу, зишь *pf.* (*coll.*) to embarrass, confuse.
оконча́ни|е, я *nt.* **1.** end; conclusion, termination; **о. сро́ка** expiration; **по ~и университе́та** on graduating; **о. сле́дует** (*note to serial article, story, etc.*) to be concluded. **2.** (*gram.*) ending.
оконча́тельно *adv.* finally, definitively; completely.
оконча́тельный *adj.* final, definitive.
око́нч|ить, у, ишь *pf.* (*of* **ока́нчивать**) to finish, end; **о. шко́лу** to leave school; **о. университе́т** to graduate, go down (*from university*).
око́нч|иться, ится *pf.* (*of* **ока́нчиваться**) **1.** to finish, end, terminate; to be over. **2.** *pass. of* **~ить**
око́п, а *m.* (*mil.*) trench; entrenchment.
окопа́|ть, ю *pf.* (*of* **ока́пывать**) to dig round.
окопа́|ться, юсь *pf.* (*of* **ока́пываться**) **1.** (*mil.*) to entrench (o.s.), dig in. **2.** (*fig., iron.*) to find o.s. a soft spot, comfortable hide-out. **3.** *pass. of* **~ть**
око́п|ный *adj. of* **~; ~ная война́** trench warfare.
окора́чива|ть, ю *impf. of* **окороти́ть**
око́рк|а, и *f.* barking, bark stripping.
окорм|и́ть, лю́, ~́ишь *pf.* (*of* **ока́рмливать**) **1.** to overfeed, cram (stuff) with food. **2.** to poison with bad food.
окорна́|ть, ю *pf. of* **корна́ть**
о́коро|к, ка, *pl.* **~ка́** *m.* ham, gammon; (*of mutton, veal*) leg.
окоро|ти́ть, чу́, ти́шь *pf.* (*of* **окора́чивать**) (*coll.*) to make too short; to crop.
окостенева́|ть, ю *impf. of* **окостене́ть**
окостене́лый *adj.* ossified (*also fig.*).
окостене́|ть, ю *pf.* (*of* **костене́ть** *and* **~ва́ть**) to ossify (*also fig.*).
око́т, а *m.* (time of) having kittens (*also of time of bringing forth young of certain other animals*).
око|ти́ться, чу́сь, ти́шься *pf. of* **коти́ться**
окочене́лый *adj.* stiff with cold.
окочене́|ть, ю *pf. of* **кочене́ть**
око́ш|ко, ка, *pl.* **~ки, ~ек, ~кам** *nt. dim. of* **окно́**
окра́ин|а, ы *f.* **1.** outskirts; outlying districts. **2.** (*obs.*) *pl.* borders, marches (*of a country*).
окра́|сить, шу, сишь *pf.* (*of* **~шивать**) to paint, colour; to dye; to stain; **слегка́ о.** to tinge, tint.
окра́ск|а, и *f.* **1.** painting, colouring; dyeing; staining. **2.** colouring, coloration; colour; **защи́тная о.** (*zool.*) protective coloration. **3.** (*fig.*) tinge, tint; (*pol.*) slant; **ирони́ческая о.** ironic tinge, touch of irony; **стилисти́ческая о.** stylistic nuance; **прида́ть чему́-н. другу́ю ~у** to put a different complexion on sth.
окра́шива|ть, ю *impf. of* **окра́сить**
окре́п|нуть, ну, нешь, *past* **~, ~ла** *pf. of* **кре́пнуть**
окре́ст *prep.*+*g. and adv.* (*obs.*) around, about.
окре|сти́ть, щу́, ~́стишь *pf.* **1.** (*impf.* **крести́ть**) to baptize, christen. **2.** (*coll.*; +*a. and i.*) to nickname; **его́ ~сти́ли «медве́дем»** he was nicknamed 'the bear'.
окре|сти́ться, щу́сь, ~́стишься *pf. of* **крести́ться 1.**
окре́стност|ь, и *f.* **1.** environs. **2.** neighbourhood, vicinity.
окре́стный *adj.* **1.** neighbouring. **2.** surrounding.
окриве́|ть, ю *pf. of* **криве́ть**
о́крик, а *m.* hail; shout, cry; **гру́бый о.** harsh bellow.
окри́кива|ть, ю *impf. of* **окри́кнуть**
окри́к|нуть, ну, нешь *pf.* (*of* **~ивать**) to hail, shout (to).
окрова́в|ить, лю, ишь *pf.* (*of* **~ливать**) to stain with blood.
окрова́в|иться, люсь, ишься *pf.* (*of* **~ливаться**) to spill blood on o.s.
окрова́в|ленный *p.p.p. of* **~ить** *and adj.* blood-stained; bloody.
окрова́влива|ть(ся), ю(сь) *impf. of* **окрова́вить(ся)**
окровене́|ть, ю *pf.* (*coll.*) to become covered with blood; to become soaked in blood.
окровен|и́ть, ю́, и́шь *pf.* (*coll.*) to stain with blood.
окроп|и́ть, лю́, и́шь *pf.* (*of* **кропи́ть** *and* **~ля́ть**) to (be)sprinkle.
окропля́|ть, ю *impf. of* **окропи́ть**
окро́шк|а, и *f.* **1.** okroshka (*cold kvass soup with chopped vegetables and meat or fish*). **2.** (*fig., coll.*) hodgepodge, jumble.
о́круг, а, *pl.* **~а́** *m.* (*in former USSR, territorial division for administrative, legal, military, etc., purposes*) okrug; region, district; circuit; **вое́нный о.** military district, command; **избира́тельный о.** electoral district.
окру́г|а, и *f.* (*coll.*) neighbourhood.

округл|ённый *p.p.p. of* **~и́ть** *and adj.* rounded (*also fig.*).
округле́|ть, ю *pf. of* **кругле́ть**
округл|и́ть, ю́, и́шь *pf.* (*of* **~я́ть**) **1.** to round (off) (*also fig.*). **2.** to express in round numbers.
округл|и́ться, ю́сь, и́шься *pf.* (*of* **~я́ться**) **1.** to become rounded. **2.** to be expressed in round numbers.
окру́глост|ь, и *f.* **1.** roundedness. **2.** protuberance, bulge.
окру́гл|ый (~, ~а) *adj.* rounded, roundish.
округл|я́ть(ся), я́ю(сь) *impf. of* **~и́ть(ся)**
окруж|а́ть, а́ю *impf. of* **~и́ть**
окружа́|ющий *pres. part. act. of* **~ть** *and adj.* surrounding; **~ющая обстано́вка** surroundings; *as n.* **~ющее, ~ющего** *nt.* environment; **~ющие, ~ющих** one's associates; entourage.
окруже́ни|е, я *nt.* **1.** encirclement; **попа́сть в о.** (*mil.*) to be encircled, be surrounded. **2.** surroundings; environment; milieu; **в ~и** (*+g.*) accompanied (by); surrounded (by), in the midst (of); **он появи́лся в ~и боле́льщиков** he appeared surrounded by fans.
окруж|и́ть, у́, и́шь *pf.* (*of* **~а́ть**) (*in var. senses*) to surround; to encircle; **о. кого́-н. забо́тами** to lavish attentions on s.o.
окружко́м, а *m.* (*abbr. of* **окружно́й комите́т**) *see* **окружно́й**
окружн|о́й *adj.* **1.** *adj. of* **о́круг; о. комите́т** district committee; **о. суд** circuit court. **2.** operating (situated) about a circle; **~а́я желе́зная доро́га** circle line; **~а́я ско́рость** (*tech.*) peripheral speed.
окру́жност|ь, и *f.* **1.** circumference; circle; **име́ть де́сять ме́тров в ~и** to be ten metres in circumference; **на три ми́ли в ~и** within a radius of three miles, for three miles round. **2.** (*obs.*) neighbourhood.
окру́жн|ый *adj.* (*obs.*) **1.** = **~о́й. 2.** neighbouring.
окру|ти́ть, чу́, ~тишь *pf.* (*of* **~чивать**) **1.** (*+i.*) to wind round. **2.** (*coll.*) to marry (*see* **~ти́ться**).
окру|ти́ться, чу́сь, ~тишься *pf.* (*of* **~чиваться**) **1.** (*+i.*) to wind round o.s. **2.** (*coll.*) to get spliced (= *to get married*).
окру́чива|ть(ся), ю(сь) *impf. of* **окрути́ть(ся)**
окрыл|и́ть, ю́, и́шь *pf.* (*of* **~я́ть**) to inspire, encourage.
окрыл|я́ть, я́ю *impf. of* **~и́ть**
окры́с|иться, ишься *pf.* (**на**+*a.*; *coll.*) to snap (at).
оксиацетиле́нов|ый *adj.*: **~ая сва́рка** welding.
оксиди́р|овать, ую *impf. and pf.* (*chem.*) to oxidize.
оксидиро́вк|а, и *f.* (*chem.*) oxidation.
О́ксфорд, а *m.* Oxford.
оксфо́рд|ец, ца *m.* Oxonian.
оксфо́рдский *adj.* Oxford; Oxonian.
оксю́морон, а *m.* (*liter.*) oxymoron.
окта́в|а, ы *f.* **1.** (*mus. and liter.*) octave. **2.** (*mus.*) low bass.
окта́н, а *m.* (*chem.*) octane.
окта́нов|ый *adj.* (*chem.*) octane; **~ое то́пливо** (high-) octane fuel; **~ое число́** octane number, octane rating.
окта́эдр, а *m.* (*math.*) octahedron.
окте́т, а *m.* (*mus.*) octet.
октроир|овать, ую *impf. and pf.* to grant; to concede.
октябр|ёнок, ёнка, *pl.* **~я́та, ~я́т** *m.* (Little) Octobrist (*in former USSR, child aged 7–11 preparing for entry into Pioneers*).
октя́бр|ь, я́ *m.* October (*fig.* = *Russ. revolution of October 1917*).
октя́брь|ский *adj. of* **~**
оку́кливани|е, я *nt.* (*zool.*) pupation.
оку́клива|ться, ется *impf. of* **оку́клиться**
оку́кл|иться, ится *pf.* (*of* **~иваться**) (*zool.*) to pupate.
окули́р|овать, ую *impf. and pf.* (*hort.*) to inoculate, engraft.
окулиро́вк|а, и *f.* (*hort.*) inoculation, grafting.
окули́ст, а *m.* oculist.
окуля́р, а *m.* eye-piece, ocular.
окун|а́ть(ся), а́ю(сь) *impf. of* **~у́ть(ся)**
о́кун|евый *adj. of* **~ь**
окун|у́ть, у́, ёшь, *pf.* (*of* **~а́ть**) to dip; **о. ло́жку в па́току** to dip a spoon into the treacle.
окун|у́ться, у́сь, ёшься, *pf.* (*of* **~а́ться**) **1.** to dip (o.s.). **2.** (*fig.*; **в**+*a.*) to plunge (into), become (utterly) absorbed (in), engrossed (in); **о. в спор** to plunge into an argument; **он ~у́лся в сочине́ния Плато́на** he has become utterly absorbed in the works of Plato.
о́кун|ь, я, *pl.* **~и, ~е́й** *m.* perch (*fish*).
окуп|а́ть(ся), а́ю(сь) *impf. of* **~и́ть(ся)**
окуп|и́ть, лю́, ~ишь *pf.* (*of* **~а́ть**) to compensate, repay, make up (for); **о. расхо́ды** to cover one's outlay.
окуп|и́ться, лю́сь, ~ишься *pf.* (*of* **~а́ться**) to be compensated, be repaid; (*fig.*) to pay; to be justified, be requited, be rewarded; **затра́ченные на́ми уси́лия ~и́лись** our efforts were rewarded.
окургу́|зить, жу, зишь *pf.* (*coll.*) to cut too short.
оку́ривани|е, я *nt.* fumigation.
оку́рива|ть, ю *impf. of* **окури́ть**
окур|и́ть, ю́, ~ишь *pf.* (*of* **~ивать**) to fumigate; **о. се́рой** to sulphurate.
оку́р|ок, ка *m.* cigarette-end; cigarette stub; cigar-butt.
оку́т|ать, аю *pf.* (*of* **~ывать**) **1.** (*+i.*) to wrap up (in). **2.** (*fig.*) to shroud, cloak; **о. та́йной** to shroud in mystery.
оку́т|аться, аюсь, *pf.* (*of* **~ываться**) **1.** (*+i.*) wrap up (in). **2.** (*fig.*) to shroud, cloak; **о. та́йной** to shroud in mystery.
оку́тыва|ть(ся), ю(сь) *impf. of* **оку́тать(ся)**
оку́чива|ть, ю *impf. of* **оку́чить**
оку́ч|ить, у, ишь *pf.* (*of* **~ивать**) (*agric.*) to earth up.
ола́д|ья, ьи, *pl.* **~ий** *f.* fritter; **карто́фельная о.** potato cake.
олеа́ндр, а *m.* oleander.
оледене́лый *adj.* frozen.
оледене́|ть, ю *pf. of* **ледене́ть**
оледен|и́ть, ю́, и́шь *pf. of* **ледени́ть**
оле́йн, а *m.* (*chem.*) olein.
оле́йнов|ый *adj.* (*chem.*) olein, oleic; **~ая кислота́** oleic acid.
оленево́д, а *m.* reindeer-breeder.
оленево́дств|о, а *nt.* reindeer-breeding.
оле́н|ий *adj. of* **~ь; ~ьи рога́** antlers; **о. лиша́й, о. мох** (*bot.*) reindeer moss; **о. рог** (*chem.*) hartshorn; **о. язы́к** (*bot.*) hart's tongue.
оле́нин|а, ы *f.* venison.
оле́н|ь, я *m.* deer; **безро́гий о.** pollard; **благоро́дный о.** stag, red deer; **се́верный о.** reindeer; **кана́дский о.** wapiti.
олеогра́фи|я, и *f.* oleograph(y).
оли́в|а, ы *f.* olive; olive-tree.
оливи́н, а *m.* (min.) olivine, chrysolite.
оли́вк|а, и *f.* olive; olive-tree.
оли́вков|ый *adj.* **1.** olive; **~ая ветвь** olive branch (*fig.*; *as symbol of peace*); **~ое ма́сло** olive oil. **2.** olive-coloured.
олига́рх, а *m.* oligarch.
олигархи́ческий *adj.* oligarchical.
олига́рхи|я, и *f.* oligarchy.
олигоце́н, а *m.* (*geol.*) Oligocene (epoch).
Оли́мп, а *m.* (Mt.) Olympus (*geog. and myth.*).
олимпиа́д|а, ы *f.* **1.** Olympics. **2.** Olympiad.
олимпи́|ец, йца *m.* (*myth. and fig.*) Olympian.
олимпи́йски|й[1] *adj.* Olympic; **~е и́гры** Olympic Games, Olympics.
олимпи́йск|ий[2] *adj.* of Olympus; **~ое споко́йствие** (*fig.*) Olympian calm.
оли́ф|а, ы *f.* drying oil.
олицетворе́ни|е, я *nt.* personification; embodiment.
олицетвор|ённый *p.p.p. of* **~и́ть; он — ~ённая хи́трость** he is cunning personified.
олицетвор|и́ть, ю́, и́шь *pf.* (*of* **~я́ть**) to personify; to embody.
олицетвор|я́ть, я́ю *impf. of* **~и́ть**
о́лов|о, а *nt.* tin; **за́кись ~а** stannous oxide; **о́кись ~а** stannic oxide.
оловоно́сный *adj.* tin-bearing, stanniferous.
оловяни́стый *adj.* stannous.
оловя́нн|ый *adj.* tin; stannic; **о. ка́мень** (*min.*) tin spar, tin ore, cassiterite; **~ая кислота́** stannic acid; **о. колчеда́н** (*min.*) tin pyrites, stannite; **~ое ма́сло** (*chem*) stannic chloride; **~ая посу́да** tinware; pewter; **~ая соль** stannic salt; **~ая фо́льга** tin foil.

о́лух, а *m.* (*coll.*) blockhead, dolt, oaf; **о. царя́ небе́сного** perfect fool, complete idiot.
олу́ш|а, и *f.* (*zool.*): **се́верная о.** gannet.
О́льстер, а *m.* Ulster.
ольх|а́, и́, *pl.* **∸и** *f.* alder(-tree).
ольх|о́вый *adj. of* **~а́**
ольша́ник, а *m.* alder thicket.
оля́пк|а, и *f.* (*zool.*) dipper.
ом, а *m.* (*elec.*) ohm.
Ома́н, а *m.* Oman; **Ома́н и Маска́т** Muscat and Oman.
ома́р, а *m.* lobster.
оме́г|а, и *f.* omega; **от а́лфы до ~и** (*fig.*) from A to Z, from beginning to end.
оме́л|а, ы *f.* mistletoe.
омерзе́ни|е, я *nt.* loathing; **внуши́ть о.** (*+d.*) to inspire loathing (in).
омерзе́|ть, ю *pf.* to become loathsome; **мне э́тот пейза́ж ~л** I have come to loathe this view.
омерзи́тел|ьный (~ен, ~ьна) *adj.* loathsome, sickening; **быть в ~ьном настрое́нии** (*coll.*) to be in a foul mood.
омертве́лост|ь, и *f.* stiffness, numbness; (*med.*) necrosis, mortification.
омертве́л|ый *adj.* stiff, numb; (*med.*) necrotic; **~ая ткань** dead tissue.
омертве́ни|е, я *nt.* = **омертве́лость**
омертве́|ть, ю *pf. of* **мертве́ть 1.**
омертв|и́ть, лю́, и́шь *pf.* (*of* **~ля́ть**) **1.** to deaden. **2.** (*econ.*) to withdraw from circulation.
омёт, а *m.* stack (of straw).
омеща́нива|ться, юсь, *impf. of* **омеща́ниться**
омеща́н|иться, юсь, ишься *pf.* (*of* **~иваться**) (*coll., pej.*) to become a philistine.
оми́ческмй *adj.* (*elec.*) ohmic.
омле́т, а *m.* omelette.
омме́тр, а *m.* (*elec.*) ohmmeter.
о́мнибус, а *m.* (horse-drawn) omnibus.
омове́ни|е, я *nt.* ablution(s); (*eccl.*) lavabo.
омола́жива|ть(ся), ю(сь) *impf. of* **омолоди́ть(ся)**
омоло|ди́ть, жу́, ди́шь *pf.* (*of* **омола́живать**) to rejuvenate.
омоло|ди́ться, жу́сь, ди́шься *pf.* (*of* **омола́живаться**) to rejuvenate, rejuvenesce.
омоложе́ни|е, я *nt.* rejuvenation.
омо́ним, а *m.* (*ling.*) homonym.
омони́мик|а, и *f.* **1.** study of homonyms. **2.** (*collect.*) homonyms.
омоними́ческий *adj.* (*ling.*) homonymous.
омони́ми|я, и *f.* (*ling.*) homonymy.
омоч|и́ть, у́, ∸ишь *pf.* (*obs.*) to wet; to moisten.
омоч|и́ться, у́сь, ∸ишься *pf.* (*obs.*) to become wet; to become moist.
омрач|а́ть(ся), а́ю(сь) *impf. of* **~и́ть(ся)**
омрач|и́ть, у́, и́шь *pf.* (*of* **~а́ть**) to darken, cloud.
омрач|и́ться, у́сь, и́шься *pf.* (*of* **~а́ться**) to become darkened, become clouded (*also fig.*).
омулёвый *adj. of* **о́муль**
о́мул|ь, я, *g. pl.* **~ей** *m.* omul (*sea fish of salmon family, found also in Lake Baikal*).
о́мут, а *m.* **1.** whirlpool; (*fig.*) whirl, maelstrom. **2.** deep place (*in river or lake*); **в ти́хом ~е че́рти во́дятся** (*prov.*) still waters run deep.
омша́ник, а *m.* heated structure (*for housing bees in winter, etc.*).
омыва́|ть, ю 1. *impf. of* **омы́ть. 2.** *impf.* (*geog.*) to wash (*of seas*).
омыва́|ться, юсь *impf.* (*geog.*) to be washed; **за́падный бе́рег Ирла́ндии ~ется Атланти́ческим океа́ном** the west coast of Ireland is washed by the Atlantic.
омыле́ни|е, я *nt.* (*chem.*) saponification.
ом|ы́ть, о́ю, о́ешь *pf.* (*of* **~ыва́ть**) (*rhet., obs.*) to wash, lave; **о. кро́вью** to steep in blood.
он, его́, ему́, им, о нём *pron.* he.
она́, её, ей, ей (е́ю), о ней *pron.* she.
она́гр, а *m.* (*zool.*) onager.
онани́зм, а *m.* onanism, masturbation.
онани́р|овать, ую *impf.* to masturbate.
онани́ст, а *m.* masturbator.
ондáтр|а, ы *f.* (*animal*) musk-rat, musquash; (*fur*) musquash.
ондáтр|овый *adj. of* **~а**
ондуля́тор, а *m.* (*elec.*) undulator.
онеме́лый *adj.* **1.** dumb. **2.** numb.
онеме́|ть, ю *pf. of* **неме́ть**
онеме́чива|ть, ю *impf. of* **онеме́чить**
онеме́ч|ить, у, ишь *pf.* (*of* **~ивать**) to Germanize.
онёр, а *m.* (*cards*) honour; **со всеми́ ~ами** (*fig., joc.*) with everything it takes, with everything one could want.
они́, их, им, и́ми, о них *pron.* they.
о́никс, а *m.* onyx.
онколо́ги|я, и *f.* (*med.*) oncology.
онко́л|ь, я *m.* (*fin., comm.*) call-account.
ОНО *nt. indecl.* (*abbr. of* **отде́л наро́дного образова́ния**) education department (*of local authority*).
оно́, его́, ему́, им, о нём *pron.* **1.** it. **2.** (= **э́то**) this, that; **о. и ви́дно** that is evident. **2.** *as emph. particle* **о. коне́чно** well, of course; **вот о. что!** oh, I see!
онома́стик|а, и *f.* (*ling.*) onomastics.
онтогене́з, а *m.* (*biol.*) ontogenesis.
онтологи́ческий *adj.* (*phil.*) ontological.
отноло́ги|я, и *f.* (*phil.*) ontology.
ону́ч|а, и *f.* onucha (*sock or cloth puttee worn in boot or bast-shoe*).
о́ный *pron.* (*obs.*) that; the above-mentioned; **во вре́мя о́но** in those days; (*joc.*) in days of old.
ооли́т, а *m.* (*min.*) oolite.
ООН *f. indecl.* (*abbr. of* **Организа́ция Объединённых На́ций**) UN (*United Nations Organization*).
оо́новский *adj.* (*coll.*) UN (*United Nations*).
ООП *f. indecl.* (*abbr. of* **Организа́ция освобожде́ния Палести́ны**) PLO (*Palestine Liberation Organization*).
опада́|ть, ю *impf. of* **опа́сть**
опада́|ющий *pres. part. act. of* **~ть** *and adj.* (*bot.*) deciduous.
опа́здыва|ть, ю *impf.* **1.** *impf. of* **опозда́ть. 2.** (*impf. only*) (*coll.*) to be slow (*of clocks and watches*).
опа́ива|ть, ю *impf. of* **опои́ть**
опа́л, а *m.* opal.
опа́л|а, ы *f.* disgrace, disfavour; **быть в ~е** to be in disgrace, be out of favour.
опалесце́нци|я, и *f.* (*phys.*) opalescence.
опалесци́р|овать ую *impf. and pf.* (*phys.*) to opalesce.
опа́лива|ть(ся), ю(сь) *impf. of* **опали́ть(ся)**
опал|и́ть, ю́, и́шь *pf.* (*of* **пали́ть**[1] *and* **∸ивать**) to singe.
опал|и́ться, ю́сь, и́шься *pf.* (*of* **∸иваться**) to singe o.s.
опа́ловый *adj.* opal; opaline.
опа́луб|ить, лю, ишь *pf.* (*tech.*) to case, sheathe, tub.
опа́лубк|а, и *f.* (*tech.*) **1.** casing, lining, sheathing, tubbing; **о. кры́ши** roof-boarding. **2.** concrete mould, form.
опа́лый *adj.* (*coll.*) sunken; emaciated.
опа́льный[1] *adj.* disgraced; in disgrace, out of favour.
опа́льн|ый[2] *adj.*: **~ая маши́на** (*tech.*) cloth singeing machine.
опа́мят|оваться, уюсь *pf.* (*obs.*) to come to one's senses; to collect o.s.
опа́р|а, ы *f.* **1.** leavened dough. **2.** leaven.
опарши́ве|ть, ю *pf. of* **парши́веть**
опаса́|ться, юсь *impf.* **1.** (*+g.*) to fear, be afraid (of). **2.** (*+g. or inf.*) to beware (of); to avoid, keep off; **он ~ется алкого́ля** he does not touch alcohol; **о. сли́шком мно́го пить** to beware of drinking to excess.
опасе́ни|е, я *nt.* fear; apprehension; misgiving(s).
опа́ск|а, и *f.*: **с ~ой** (*coll.*) with caution, cautiously; warily.
опа́слив|ый (~, ~а) *adj.* (*coll.*) cautious; wary.
опа́сност|ь, и *f.* danger; peril; **вне ~и** out of danger; **смотре́ть ~и в глаза́** to look dangers in the face.
опа́с|ный (~ен, ~на) *adj.* dangerous, perilous.
опа́|сть, ду́, дёшь *pf.* (*of* **~да́ть**) **1.** (*of leaves*) to fall (off). **2.** to subside; (*of a swelling, etc.*) to go down.
опаха́л|о, а *nt.* fan.
опа|ха́ть, шу́, ∸шешь *pf.* (*of* **∸хивать**[1]) to plough round.
опа́хива|ть[1]**, ю** *impf. of* **опаха́ть**

опа́хива|ть², ю *impf. of* **опахну́ть**
опах|ну́ть, ну́, нёшь *pf.* (*of* **~́ивать²**) to fan.
ОПЕК *f. indecl.* OPEC (*abbr. of* Organization of Petroleum-Exporting Countries — *Организа́ция стран-экспортёров не́фти*).
опе́к|а, и *f.* **1.** guardianship, wardship, tutelage (*also fig.*); trusteeship; **быть под ~ой кого́-н.** to be under s.o.'s guardianship; **взять под ~у** to take as ward; (*fig.*) to take charge (of), take under one's wing; **учреди́ть ~у над кем-н.** to place s.o. in ward. **2.** (*collect.*) guardians, board of guardians; **Междунаро́дная о.** International Trusteeship. **3.** (*fig.*) care; surveillance; **вы́йти из-под ~и** to become one's own master.
опека́|емый *pres. part. pass. of* **~ть**; *as n.* **о., ~емого** *m.* ward.
опека́|ть, ю *impf.* **1.** to be guardian (to), have the wardship (of). **2.** (*fig.*) to take care (of), watch (over).
опеку́н, а́ *m.* (*leg.*) guardian, tutor; trustee.
опеку́н|ский *adj. of* **~; О. сове́т** (*obs.*) board of guardians.
опеку́нств|о, а *nt.* guardianship, tutorship.
опён|ок, ка, *pl.* **~ки, ~ков** *m.* honey agaric (*mushroom*).
о́пер|а, ы *f.* opera; **«мы́льная о.»** soap (opera); **из друго́й ~ы, не из той ~ы** (*coll.*) quite a different matter.
опера́бельный *adj.* (*med.*) operable.
операти́вност|ь, и *f.* drive; energy (*in getting things done*).
операти́в|ный *adj.* **1.** (**~ен, ~на**) energetic; efficient; **~ное руково́дство** efficient and flexible leadership. **2.** executive. **3.** (*med.*) operative; surgical; **~ное вмеша́тельство** surgical interference. **4.** (*mil.*) operation(s), operational; strategical; **~ное иску́сство** campaign tactics; **~ная сво́дка** summary of operations.
опера́тор, а *m.* **1.** operator. **2.** (*med.*) surgeon. **3.** cameraman.
опера|цио́нный *adj. of* **~́ция; ~цио́нное отделе́ние** (*in hospital*) surgical wing; **о. стол** operating-table; *as n.* **~цио́нная, ~цио́нной** *f.* theatre, operating-room.
опера́ци|я, и *f.* (*med., mil., etc.*) operation; **перенести́ ~ю** to have, undergo an operation; to be operated (upon); **сде́лать ~ю** to perform an operation.
опере|ди́ть, жу́, ди́шь *pf.* (*of* **~жа́ть**) **1.** to outstrip, leave behind. **2.** to forestall.
опережа́|ть, ю *impf. of* **опереди́ть**
опере́ни|е, я *nt.* feathering, plumage; **хвостово́е о.** (*aeron.*) tail unit.
оперённый *adj.* feathered.
опере́т|ка, ки *f.* = **~та**
опере́т|очный *adj. of* **~ка** *and* **~та**
опере́тт|а, ы *f.* musical comedy, operetta.
опере́ть, обопру́, обопрёшь, *past* **опёр, оперла́** *pf.* (*of* **опира́ть**) (**о**+*a.*) to lean (against).
опере́ться, обопру́сь, обопрёшься, *past* **опёрся, оперла́сь** *pf.* (*of* **опира́ться**) (**на**+*a.*; **о**+*a.*) to lean (on; against); **о. о подоко́нник** to lean against the window-sill; **о. на подде́ржку жены́** (*fig.*) to lean for support on one's wife.
опери́р|овать, ую *impf. and pf.* **1.** (*med.*) to operate (upon). **2.** (*mil.*) to operate, act. **3.** (+*i.*; *fin., etc.*) to operate (with), execute operations (with); (*fig.*) to use, handle; **о. недоста́точными да́нными** to operate with inadequate data.
опер|и́ть, ю́, и́шь *pf.* (*of* **~я́ть**) to feather (*an arrow*); to adorn with feathers.
опер|и́ться, ю́сь, и́шься *pf.* (*of* **~я́ться**) **1.** (*of birds*) to be fledged. **2.** (*fig.*) to stand on one's own feet.
о́перн|ый *adj.* opera; operatic; **о. певе́ц, ~ая певи́ца** opera singer; **о. теа́тр** opera-house.
опёрт|ый (~, ~á, ~о) *p.p.p. of* **опере́ть**
опер|ши́сь *past ger. of* **~е́ться; о. (на**+*a.*) leaning (on).
опер|я́ть(ся), я́ю(сь) *impf. of* **~и́ть(ся)**
опеча́л|ить(ся), ю(сь), ишь(ся) *pf. of* **печа́лить(ся)**
опеча́т|ать, аю *pf.* (*of* **~ывать**) to seal up.
опеча́т|ка, ки *f.* misprint; **спи́сок ~ок** (list of) errata.
опе́ш|ить, у, ишь *pf.* (*coll.*) to be taken aback.
опива́|ться, юсь *impf. of* **опи́ться**
опи́вк|и, ов *no sg.* (*coll.*) dregs.
о́пи|й, я *m.* opium.
о́пий|ный *adj. of* **~**
опи́лива|ть, ю *impf. of* **опили́ть**
опил|и́ть, ю́, ~́ишь *pf.* (*of* **~́ивать**) to saw; to file.
опи́л|ки, ок *no sg.* sawdust; (metal) filings.
опира́|ть(ся), ю(сь) *impf. of* **опере́ть(ся)**
описа́ни|е, я *nt.* description; account; **э́то не поддаётся ~ю** it is beyond description, it beggars description.
опи́с|анный *p.p.p. of* **~а́ть** *and adj.* (*math.*) circumscribed.
описа́тельный *adj.* descriptive.
описа́тельств|о, а *nt.* (*pej.*) (bare) description.
опи|са́ть, шу́, ~́шешь *pf.* (*of* **~́сывать**) **1.** to describe. **2.** to list, inventory; **о. иму́щество** (*leg.*) to distrain property. **3.** (*math.*) to describe, circumscribe.
опи|са́ться, шу́сь, ~́шешься *pf.* to make a slip of the pen.
опи́ск|а, и *f.* slip of the pen.
опи́сыва|ть, ю *impf. of* **описа́ть**
о́пис|ь, и *f.* list, schedule; inventory; **о. иму́щества** (*leg.*) distraint.
опи́|ться, обопью́сь, обопьёшься, *past* **~́лся, ~ла́сь, ~́ло́сь** *pf.* (*of* **~ва́ться**) (*coll.*) to drink to excess, drink o.s. stupid.
о́пиум, а *m.* opium.
о́пиум|ный *adj. of* **~**
опла́|кать, чу, чешь *pf.* (*of* **~кивать**) to mourn (over); to bewail, bemoan.
опла́кива|ть, ю *impf. of* **опла́кать**
опла́т|а, ы *f.* pay, payment; remuneration; **поча́сная о.** payment by the hour; **сде́льная о.** piece work payment.
опла|ти́ть, чу́, ~́тишь *pf.* to pay (for); **о. расхо́ды** to meet the expenses, foot the bill; **о. счёт** to settle the account, pay the bill; **о. убы́тки** to pay damages.
опла́|ченный *p.p.p. of* **~ти́ть; с ~ченным отве́том** reply-paid.
опла́чива|ть, ю *impf. of* **оплати́ть**
опла́|чу, чешь *see* **~кать**
опла|чу́, ~́тишь *see* **~ти́ть**
оплёв|анный *p.p.p. of* **~а́ть; как о.** as if in disgrace.
опл|ева́ть, юю́, юёшь *pf.* (*of* **~ёвывать**) **1.** (*coll.*) to cover with spittle. **2.** (*fig.*) to spit upon, humiliate. **3.** (*fig.*) to spurn.
оплёвыва|ть, ю *impf. of* **оплева́ть**
опле|сти́, ту́, тёшь, *past* **~̈л, ~ла́** *pf.* (*of* **~та́ть**) **1.** to twine (round); to braid; **о. буты́ль соло́мой** to wicker a bottle. **2.** (*fig., coll.*) to twist, get round.
оплета́|ть, ю *impf. of* **оплести́**
оплеу́х|а, и *f.* (*coll.*) slap in the face.
опле́ч|ье, ья, *g. pl.* **~ий** *nt.* (*obs.*) shoulder(s) (*of garment*).
оплеши́ве|ть, ю *pf. of* **плеши́веть**
оплодотворе́ни|е, я *nt.* impregnation, fecundation; fertilization.
оплодотвори́тел|ь, я *m.* (*bot.*) fertilizer.
оплодотвор|и́ть, ю́, и́шь *pf.* (*of* **~я́ть**) to impregnate (*also fig.*), fecundate; to fertilize.
оплодотвор|я́ть, я́ю *impf. of* **~и́ть**
опломбир|ова́ть, у́ю *pf. of* **пломбирова́ть**
опло́т, а *m.* (*rhet.*) stronghold, bulwark.
оплоша́|ть, ю *pf.* (*coll.*) to take a false step, blunder.
оплóшност|ь, и *f.* false step, blunder.
оплóш|ный (~ен, ~на) *adj.* (*obs.*) **1.** mistaken; **о. посту́пок** false step. **2.** blundering.
оплыва́|ть, ю *impf. of* **оплы́ть**
оплы́|ть¹, ву́, вёшь *pf.* (*of* **~ва́ть**) **1.** to become swollen, swell up. **2.** (*of a candle*) to gutter. **3.** to fall (*as a result of a landslide*).
оплы́|ть², ву́, вёшь *pf.* (*of* **~ва́ть**) to sail round; to swim round; **о. о́стров** to sail round an island; **о. о́зеро** to sail round (the edge of) a lake.
опове|сти́ть, щу́, сти́шь *pf.* (*of* **~ща́ть**) to notify, inform.
оповеща́|ть, ю *impf. of* **оповести́ть**
оповеще́ни|е, я *nt.* notification; **радиосе́тка ~я** (*mil.*) (early) warning system.
опога́н|ить, ю, ишь *pf. of* **пога́нить**
оподельдо́к, а *m.* (*med., hist.*) opodeldoc.
оподле́|ть, ю *pf. of* **подле́ть**

опо́|ек, йка *m.* calf(-leather).
опо́ечный *adj.* calf(-skin).
опозда́|вший *p.p. act. of* **~ть**; *as n.* **о., ~вшего** *m.* latecomer.
опозда́ни|е, я *nt.* being late; lateness; delay; **по́езд прибы́л без ~я** the train arrived on time; **с ~ем на де́сять мину́т** ten minutes late.
опозда́|ть, ю *pf.* (*of* **опа́здывать**) to be late; to be overdue; **о. на ле́кцию** to be late for the lecture; **о. на полчаса́** to be half an hour late; **о. с упла́той нало́гов** to be late in paying taxes.
опознава́ни|е, я *nt.* identification; **о. самолётов** aircraft recognition.
опознава́тельный *adj.* distinguishing; **о. знак** landmark, (*naut.*) beacon; (*on wings of aircraft*) marking.
опозна|ва́ть, ю́, ёшь *impf. of* **~́ть**
опозна́ни|е, я *nt.* (*leg.*) identification.
опозна́|ть, ю *pf.* (*of* **~ва́ть**) to identify.
опозо́рени|е, я *nt.* (*leg.*) defamation.
опозо́р|ить(ся), ю(сь), ишь(ся) *pf. of* **позо́рить(ся)**
опо|и́ть, ю́, и́шь *pf.* (*of* **опа́ивать**) **1.** to injure by giving too much to drink. **2.** (*obs.*) to poison (*by means of a potion*).
опо́йковый *adj.* calf(-skin).
опо́к|а[1], **и** *f.* (*tech.*) flask, mould box, casting box, box form; **литьё в ~ах** flask casting.
опо́к|а[2], **и** *f.* (*geol.*) silica clay.
ополаскивател|ь, я *m.*: **о. (для воло́с)** hair conditioner.
опола́скива|ть, ю *impf. of* **ополоска́ть** *and* **ополосну́ть**
ополз|а́ть, а́ю *impf. of* **~ти́**[1,2]
о́полз|ень, ня *m.* landslide, landslip.
о́полз|невый *adj. of* **~ень**
ополз|ти́[1], **у́, ёшь**, *past* **~́**, **~ла́** *pf.* (*of* **~а́ть**) to crawl round.
ополз|ти́[2], **ёт**, *past* **~́**, **~ла́** *pf.* (*of* **~а́ть**) to slip.
ополо|ска́ть, щу́, ~́шешь *pf.* (*of* **опола́скивать**) = **~сну́ть**
ополосн|у́ть, у́, ёшь, *pf.* (*of* **опола́скивать**) to rinse; to swill.
ополоу́ме|ть, ю *pf.* (*coll.*) to go crazy; to be beside o.s.
ополч|а́ть(ся), а́ю(сь) *impf. of* **~и́ть(ся)**
ополче́н|ец, ца *m.* militiaman; home guard.
ополче́ни|е, я *nt.* **1.** militia; home guard. **2.** (*collect.*; *hist.*) irregulars; levies.
ополче́н|ский *adj. of* **~ец** *and* **~ие**
ополч|и́ть, у́, и́шь *pf.* (*of* **~а́ть**) (**на**+*a. or* **про́тив** *obs.*) to arm (against); (*fig.*) to enlist the support of (against).
ополч|и́ться, у́сь, и́шься *pf.* (*of* **~а́ться**) (**на**+*a. or* **про́тив**) to take up arms (against); (*fig.*) to be up in arms (against); to turn (against).
ополя́ч|ить, у, ишь *pf.* to polonize.
опо́мн|иться, юсь, ишься *pf.* to come to one's senses; to collect o.s.
опо́р, а *m. only in phr.* **во весь о.** at full speed, at top speed, full tilt.
опо́р|а, ы *f.* support (*also fig.*); (*tech.*) bearing; pier (*of a bridge*); (*fig.*) buttress; **то́чка ~ы** (*phys., tech.*) fulcrum, bearing, point of rest.
опора́жнива|ть, ю *impf. of* **опоро́жнить**
опо́р|ки, ков *pl.* (*sg.* **~ок, ~ка** *m.*) down-at-heel shoes.
опо́р|ный *adj. of* **~а**; (*tech.*) bearing, supporting; **о. ка́мень** abutment stone; **~ная при́зма** fulcrum; **о. пункт** (*mil.*) strong point; **~ная сва́я** bridge pile; **о. столб** chock (block).
опоро́жн|ить, ю, ишь *pf.* (*of* **опора́жнивать**) to empty; to drain (at a draught); **о. кише́чник** to evacuate one's bowels.
опорожня́|ть, ю *impf.* = **опора́жнивать**
опоро́с, а *m.* farrow (*of sow*).
опороси́|ться, шься *pf. of* **пороси́ться**
опоро́ч|ить, у, ишь *pf. of* **поро́чить**
опосля́ *adv.* (*coll. or dial.*) afterwards.
опосре́дств|овать, ую *impf. and pf.* (*phil.*) to mediate.
опо́ссум, а *m.* (*zool.*) opossum.
опосты́ле|ть, ю *pf.* (*coll.*; +*d.*) to grow hateful (to), grow wearisome (to).
опохмел|и́ться, ю́сь, и́шься *pf.* (*of* **~я́ться**) (*coll.*) to take a hair of the dog that bit you.
опохмел|я́ться, я́юсь, *impf. of* **~и́ться**
опочива́л|ьня, ьни, *g. pl.* **~ен** *f.* (*obs.*) bedchamber.
опочива́|ть, ю *impf. of* **опочи́ть**
опочи́|ть, ю, ешь *pf.* (*of* **~ва́ть**) (*obs.*) **1.** to go to sleep. **2.** (*fig., poet.*) to pass to one's rest.
опошле́|ть, ю *pf. of* **пошле́ть**
опо́шл|ить, ю, ишь *pf.* (*of* **~я́ть**) to vulgarize, debase.
опошля́|ть, ю *impf. of* **опо́шлить**
опоя́|сать, шу, шешь *pf.* (*of* **~сывать**) **1.** to gird, engird(le). **2.** (*fig.*) to girdle.
опоя́|саться, шусь, шешься *pf.* (*of* **~сываться**) **1.** (+*i.*) to gird o.s. (with), gird on. **2.** *pass. of* **~сать**
опоя́сыва|ть(ся), ю(сь) *impf. of* **опоя́сать(ся)**
оппозиционе́р, а *m.* member of the opposition.
оппози|цио́нный *adj. of* **~́ция**
оппози́ци|я, и *f.* opposition.
оппоне́нт, а *m.* opponent; **официа́льный о.** official opponent (*at defence of dissertation, etc.*).
оппони́р|овать, ую *impf.* (+*d.*) to oppose, act as opponent (to).
оппортуни́зм, а *m.* opportunism.
оппортуни́ст, а *m.* opportunist.
оппортунисти́ческий *adj.* opportunist.
оппортунисти́ч|ный (~ен, ~на) *adj.* = **~еский**
оппортуни́ст|ский *adj. of* **~**
опра́в|а, ы *f.* setting, mounting; case; **очки́ без ~ы** rimless spectacles.
оправда́ни|е, я *nt.* **1.** justification. **2.** excuse. **3.** (*leg.*) acquittal, discharge.
оправда́тельный *adj.*: **о. пригово́р** verdict of 'not guilty'; **о. докуме́нт** voucher.
оправд|а́ть, а́ю *pf.* (*of* **~́ывать**) **1.** to justify, warrant; to vindicate; to authorize; **о. ожида́ния** to come up to expectations; **о. себя́** to justify o.s.; **о. расхо́ды** to authorize expenses. **2.** to excuse; **о. посту́пок боле́знью** to excuse an action by reason of sickness. **3.** (*leg.*) to acquit, discharge.
оправд|а́ться, а́юсь *pf.* (*of* **~́ываться**) **1.** to justify o.s.; to vindicate o.s.; **о. незна́нием** (*leg.*) to plead ignorance. **2.** to be justified; **моё предсказа́ние ~а́лось** my prediction has come true; **расхо́ды ~а́лись** the expense was worth it.
опра́вдыва|ть, ю *impf. of* **оправда́ть**
опра́вдыва|ться, юсь *impf.* **1.** *impf. of* **оправда́ться. 2.** to try to justify *or* vindicate o.s.
опра́в|ить, лю, ишь *pf.* (*of* **~ля́ть**) **1.** to put in order, set right, adjust (*dress, coiffure, etc.*). **2.** to set, mount.
опра́в|иться, люсь, ишься *pf.* (*of* **~ля́ться**) **1.** to put (one's dress, *etc.*) in order. **2.** (**от**) to recover (from). **3.** (*coll.*) to urinate.
опра́вк|а, и *f.* **1.** (*tech.*) mandrel, chuck; (riveting) drift. **2.** setting, mounting.
оправля́|ть(ся), ю(сь) *impf. of* **опра́вить(ся)**
опра́стыва|ть(ся), ю(сь) *impf. of* **опроста́ть(ся)**
опра́шива|ть, ю *impf. of* **опроси́ть**
определе́ни|е, я *nt.* **1.** definition; (*chem., phys., etc.*) determination. **2.** (*leg.*) decision. **3.** (*gram.*) attribute.
определён|ный (~ен, ~на) *adj.* **1.** definite; determinate; fixed; **о. за́работок** fixed wage; **о. член** (*gram.*) definite article. **2.** certain; **в ~ных слу́чаях** in certain cases.
определи́м|ый (~, ~а) *adj.* definable.
определи́тел|ь, я *m.* (*math.*) determinant.
определ|и́ть, ю́, и́шь *pf.* (*of* **~я́ть**) **1.** to define; to determine; to fix, appoint; **о. боле́знь** to diagnose a disease; **о. ме́ру наказа́ния** to fix a punishment; **о. расстоя́ние** to judge a distance. **2.** (*obs.*) to appoint; to allot, assign; **о. на слу́жбу** to appoint to a post; **о. пай** to assign a share.
определ|и́ться, ю́сь, и́шься *pf.* (*of* **~я́ться**) **1.** to be formed; to take shape; to be determined. **2.** (*obs.*) to find a place; **о. на слу́жбу** to take service. **3.** (*aeron.*) to obtain a fix, find one's position. **4.** *pass. of* **~и́ть**
определ|я́ть(ся), я́ю(сь) *impf. of* **~и́ть(ся)**
опресне́ни|е, я *nt.* desalination.
опресн|ённый *p.p.p. of* **~и́ть; ~ённая вода́** distilled water.

опресни́тел|ь, я *m.* (water-)distiller.
опресн|и́ть, ю́, и́шь *pf.* (*of* **~я́ть**) to distil (*salt water*); to desalinate.
опре́снок|и, ов *pl.* (*sg.* **~, ~а** *m.*) unleavened bread.
опресн|я́ть, я́ю *impf. of* **~и́ть**
опри́чник, а *m.* (*hist.*) oprichnik (*member of oprichnina*).
опри́чнин|а, ы *f.* (*hist.*) oprichnina (*special administrative élite established in Russia by Ivan IV, also the territory assigned to this élite*).
опри́чн|ый *adj. of* **~ина**
опри́чь *prep.+g.* (*obs.*) except, save.
опро́б|овать, ую *pf.* **1.** (*tech.*) to test. **2.** to sample, try.
опроверг|а́ть, а́ю *impf. of* **~́нуть**
опрове́рг|нуть, ну, нешь, *past* **~, ~ла** *pf.* (*of* **~а́ть**) to refute, disprove.
опроверже́ни|е, я *nt.* refutation; disproof; denial.
опрокидн|о́й *adj.*: **грузови́к с ~ы́м я́щиком** tip-up lorry.
опроки́дывател|ь, я *m.* (*tech.*) tipper, tipple. dumper.
опроки́дыва|ть(ся), ю(сь) *impf. of* **опроки́нуть(ся)**
опроки́|нуть, ну, нешь *pf.* (*of* **~дывать**) **1.** to overturn; to topple over. **2.** (*mil.*) to overthrow; to overrun. **3.** (*sl.*) to knock back (= *drink off*). **4.** (*fig.*) to upset; to refute.
опроки́|нуться, нусь, нешься *pf.* (*of* **~дываться**) **1.** to overturn; to topple over, tip over; to capsize. **2.** *pass. of* **~нуть**
опроме́тчив|ый (~, ~а) *adj.* precipitate, rash, hasty, unconsidered.
о́прометью *adv.* headlong.
опро́с, а *m.* (*mil., etc.*) interrogation; (*leg., etc.*) (cross-)examination; referendum; **о. обще́ственного мне́ния** opinion poll.
опро|си́ть, шу́, ~́сишь *pf.* (*of* **опра́шивать**) to interrogate; to (cross-)examine.
опро́с|ный *adj. of* **~; о. лист** questionnaire; (*leg.*) interrogatory.
опроста́|ть, ю *pf.* (*of* **опра́стывать**) (*coll.*) to empty; to remove the contents (of).
опроста́|ться, юсь *pf.* (*of* **опра́стываться**) (*coll.*) **1.** to become empty. **2.** *pass. of* **~ть. 3.** to defecate.
опро|сти́ться, щу́сь, сти́шься *pf.* (*of* **~ща́ться**) to adopt the 'simple life'.
опростоволо́|ситься, шусь, сишься *pf.* (*coll.*) to make a gaffe, blunder.
опротест|ова́ть, у́ю *pf.* (*of* **~о́вывать**) **1.: о. ве́ксель** (*fin.*) to protest a bill. **2.** (*leg.*) to appeal (against).
опротесто́выва|ть, ю *impf. of* **опротестова́ть**
опроти́ве|ть, ю *pf.* to become loathsome, become repulsive.
опроща́|ться, юсь *impf. of* **опрости́ться**
опроще́ни|е, я *nt.* adoption of the 'simple life'.
опры́ск|ать, *pf.* (*of* **~ивать**) to sprinkle; to spray.
опры́ск|аться, аюсь, *pf.* (*of* **~иваться**) **1.** to sprinkle o.s.; to spray o.s. **2.** *pass. of* **~ать**
опры́скивател|ь, я *m.* (*agric.*) sprinkler; sprayer.
опры́скива|ть(ся), ю(сь) *impf. of* **опры́скать(ся)**
опрыща́ве|ть, ю *pf. of* **прыща́веть**
опря́тност|ь, и *f.* neatness, tidiness.
опря́т|ный (~ен, ~на) *adj.* neat, tidy.
опта́нт, а *m.* (*leg.*) pers. having right of option (*of citizenship*).
оптати́вный *adj.* (*gram.*) optative.
опта́ци|я, и *f.* (*leg.*) option (*of citizenship*); **пра́во ~и** right of option (*of citizenship of one or other of two states*).
о́птик, а *m.* optician.
о́птик|а, и *f.* **1.** optics. **2.** (*collect.*) optical instruments.
оптима́льный *adj.* optimum, optimal.
оптими́зм, а *m.* optimism.
оптими́ст, а *m.* optimist.
оптимисти́ческий *adj.* optimistic.
о́птимум, а *m.* (*biol., etc.*) optimum.
опти́р|овать, ую *impf. and pf.* (*leg.*) to opt (for).
опти́ческ|ий *adj.* optic, optical; **о. обма́н** optical illusion; **~ая ось** optic axis; **~ое стекло́** optical glass, lens.
оптови́к, а́ *m.* wholesale dealer, wholesaler.
опто́вый *adj.* wholesale.
о́птом *adv.* wholesale; **о. и в ро́зницу** wholesale and retail.

опубликова́ни|е, я *nt.* publication; **о. зако́на** promulgation of a law.
опублик|ова́ть, у́ю *pf.* (*of* **публикова́ть** *and* **~о́вывать**) to publish; **о. зако́н** to promulgate a law.
опублико́выва|ть, ю *impf. of* **опубликова́ть**
о́пус, а *m.* (*mus.*) opus.
опуска́|ть(ся), ю(сь) *impf. of* **опусти́ть(ся)**
опускн|о́й *adj.* movable; **~а́я дверь** trapdoor.
опусте́лый *adj.* deserted.
опусте́|ть, ю *pf. of* **пусте́ть**
опу|сти́ть, щу́, ~́стишь *pf.* (*of* **~ска́ть**) **1.** to lower; to let down; **о. што́ры** to draw the blinds; **о. глаза́** to look down; **о. го́лову** (*fig.*) to hang one's head; **о. ру́ки** (*fig.*) to lose heart. **2.** to turn down (*collar, etc.*). **3.** to omit.
опу|сти́ться, щу́сь, ~́стишься *pf.* (*of* **~ска́ться**) **1.** to lower o.s. **2.** to sink; to fall; to go down; **о. в кре́сло** to sink into a chair; **о. на коле́ни** to go down on one's knees; **у него́ ру́ки ~сти́лись** (*fig.*) he has lost heart. **3.** (*fig.*) to sink; to let o.s. go; to go to pieces.
опустош|а́ть, а́ю *impf. of* **~и́ть**
опустоше́ни|е, я *nt.* devastation, ruin.
опустоши́тел|ьный (~ен, ~ьна) *adj.* devastating.
опустош|и́ть, у́, и́шь *pf.* (*of* **~а́ть**) to devastate, lay waste, ravage.
опу́т|ать, аю *pf.* (*of* **~ывать**) to enmesh, entangle (*also fig.*); (*fig.*) to ensnare.
опу́тыва|ть, ю *impf. of* **опу́тать**
опух|а́ть, а́ю *impf. of* **~́нуть**
опу́хлый *adj.* (*coll.*) swollen.
опу́х|нуть, ну, нешь, *past* **~, ~ла** *pf.* (*of* **~а́ть**) to swell (up).
о́пухол|ь, и *f.* swelling; (*med.*) tumour.
опуш|а́ть, а́ю *impf. of* **~и́ть**
опуш|и́ть, у́, и́шь *pf.* (*of* **~а́ть**) **1. (ме́хом)** to edge, trim (with fur). **2.** (*of hoar-frost or snow*) to powder; to cover; **бо́роду у него́ ~и́ло сне́гом** his beard was powdered with snow.
опу́шк|а¹, и *f.* edging, trimming.
опу́шк|а², и *f.* edge (*of a forest, of a wood*).
опуще́ни|е, я *nt.* **1.** lowering; letting down; **о. ма́тки** (*med.*) prolapsus (prolapse) of the uterus. **2.** omission.
опу́|щенный *p.p.p. of* **~сти́ть; как в во́ду о.** (*fig.*) crestfallen, downcast.
опыле́ни|е, я *nt.* (*bot.*) pollination; **перекрёстное о.** cross-pollination.
опы́ливател|ь, я *m.* (*agric.*) insecticide dust sprayer.
опы́лива|ть, ю *impf. of* **опыли́ть 2.**
опыли́тел|ь, я *m.* **1.** (*bot.*) pollinator. **2.** (*agric.*) = **опы́ливатель**
опыл|и́ть, ю́, и́шь *pf.* **1.** (*impf.* **~я́ть**) (*bot.*) to pollinate. **2.** (*impf.* **~́ивать**) (*agric.*) to spray with insecticide dust.
опыл|я́ть, я́ю *impf. of* **~и́ть 1.**
о́пыт, а *m.* **1.** experience; **на ~е, по ~у** by experience. **2.** experiment; test, trial; attempt.
о́пытник, а *m.* experimenter.
о́пытност|ь, и *f.* experience.
о́пыт|ный *adj.* **1. (~ен, ~на)** experienced. **2.** experimental; **узна́ть ~ным путём** to learn by means of experiment; **~ная ста́нция** experimental station.
опьяне́лый *adj.* intoxicated.
опьяне́ни|е, я *nt.* intoxication.
опьяне́|ть, ю *pf. of* **пьяне́ть**
опьян|и́ть, ю́, и́шь *pf.* (*of* **пьяни́ть** *and* **~я́ть**) to intoxicate, make drunk; **успе́х ~и́л его́** success has gone to his head.
опьян|я́ть, я́ю *impf. of* **~и́ть**
опьяня́|ющий *pres. part. act. of* **~ть** *and adj.* intoxicating.
опя́ть *adv.* again.
опя́ть-таки *adv.* (*coll.*) **1.** (and) what is more; **он холостя́к, о.-т. бога́тый челове́к** he is a bachelor, and what is more he is a rich man. **2.** but again; however; **я постуча́л ещё раз, о.-т. ничего́ не послы́шалось** I knocked again, but again there was nothing to be heard.
ора́в|а, ы *f.* (*coll.*) crowd, horde.
ора́кул, а *m.* oracle.

ора́л|о, а *nt.* (*obs. and dial.*) plough.
ора́нжевый *adj.* orange (*colour*).
оранжере́|йный *adj. of* **~я; ~йное расте́ние** hothouse plant (*also fig.*)
оранжере́|я, и *f.* hothouse, greenhouse, conservatory.
ора́р|ь, я́ *m.* (*eccl.*) stole.
ора́тор, а *m.* orator, (public) speaker.
орато́ри|я, и *f.* **1.** (*mus.*) oratorio. **2.** (*eccl.*) oratory.
ора́тор|ский *adj. of* **~**; oratorical; **~ское иску́сство** oratory.
ора́торств|овать, ую *impf.* to orate, harangue, speechify.
ор|а́ть[1], **у́, ёшь** *impf.* (*coll.*) to bawl, yell.
ор|а́ть[2], **у́, ёшь** (*also* **ю, ~ешь**) *impf.* (*dial.*) to plough.
орби́т|а, ы *f.* **1.** (*astron. and fig.*) orbit; **вы́вести на ~у** to put into orbit; **о. влия́ния** sphere of influence. **2.** (*anat.*) eye-socket; **глаза́ у него́ вы́шли из ~** (*fig.*) his eyes leaped from their sockets.
орг... *comb. form, abbr. of* **организацио́нный**
...орг *comb. form, abbr. of* **организа́тор**
орга́зм, а *m.* (*physiol.*) orgasm.
о́рган, а *m.* (*biol., pol., etc.*) organ; **исполни́тельный о.** agency; **~ы вла́сти** organs of government; **~ы** (*sc.* **госбезопа́сности**) (*coll., iron.*) 'the organs' (*of State security*); **~ы печа́ти** organs of the press; **~ы ре́чи** speech organs; **половы́е ~ы** genitals.
орга́н, а *m.* (*mus.*) organ.
организа́тор, а *m.* organizer.
организа́тор|ский *adj. of* **~**; **о. тала́нт** talent for organization.
организа|цио́нный *adj. of* **~ция**
организа́ци|я, и *f.* (*in var. senses*) organization, body; agency; **о. по оказа́нию по́мощи** aid *or* relief agency; **О. Объединённых На́ций** United Nations Organization.
органи́зм, а *m.* organism.
организо́ванност|ь, и *f.* (good) organization; orderliness.
организо́ванный *p.p.p. of* **организова́ть** *and adj.* organized; orderly, disciplined.
организ|ова́ть, у́ю *impf. and pf.* (*pf. also* **с~**) to organize.
организ|ова́ться, у́юсь *impf. and pf.* **1.** to be organized. **2.** to organize (*intrans.*).
орга́ник|а, и *f.* (*coll.*) organic chemistry.
органи́ст, а *m.* organist.
органи́ческ|ий *adj.* organic; **~ая хи́мия** organic chemistry; **~ое це́лое** integral whole.
органи́ч|ный (~ен, ~на) *adj.* organic.
орга́н|ный *adj. of* **~**; **о. конце́рт** concerto for organ.
органогра́фи|я, и *f.* (*biol.*) organography.
органотерапи́|я, и *f.* organotherapy.
орга́нчик, а *m.* **1.** *dim. of* **орга́н. 2.** musical-box.
о́рги|я, и *f.* orgy.
оргте́хник|а, и *f.* (*abbr. of* **организацио́нная те́хника**) office equipment.
орд|а́, ы́, *pl.* **~ы, ~, ~ам** *f.* (*hist. and fig.*) horde; **Золота́я о.** the Golden Horde.
ордали|я, и *f.* (*hist.*) ordeal.
о́рден[1], **а,** *pl.* **~а́, ~о́в** *m.* order; decoration; **о. Подвя́зки** Order of the Garter; **о. Почётного Легио́на** Legion of Honour; **о. Трудово́го Кра́сного Зна́мени** Order of the Red Banner of Labour.
о́рден[2], **а,** *pl.* **~ы, ~ов** *m.* **1.** order; **иезуи́тский о.** Society of Jesus; **о. тамплие́ров** Order of Knights Templars. **2.** = **о́рдер**[2]
орденоно́с|ец, ца *m.* holder of an order *or* decoration.
орденоно́сный *adj.* decorated with an order.
о́рден|ский *adj. of* **~**; **~ская ле́нта** ribbon.
о́рдер[1], **а,** *pl.* **~а́, ~о́в** *m.* order, warrant; (*leg.*) writ; **о. на о́быск** search warrant; **о. на поку́пку** coupon; **о. на кварти́ру** authorization to an apartment.
о́рдер[2], **а,** *pl.* **~ы, ~ов** *m.* (*archit.*) order; **кори́нфский о.** Corinthian order.
ордина́р, а *m.* normal level (*of water in reservoir, etc.*).
ордина́р|ец, ца *m.* (*mil.*) orderly; batman.
ордина́р|ный (~ен, ~на) *adj.* **1.** ordinary. **2.** (*obs.*) on the staff, permanent.
ордина́т|а, ы *f.* (*math.*) ordinate.
ордина́тор, а *m.* house-surgeon.
ординату́р|а, ы *f.* **1.** appointment as house-surgeon; permanent appointment (*of professor*). **2.** clinical studies (*in medical school*).
орд|ы́нский *adj. of* **~а́**
ор|ёл, ла́, *m.* eagle; **о. и́ли ре́шка?** heads or tails?
орео́л, а *m.* halo, aureole.
оре́х, а *m.* **1.** nut; **австрали́йский о.** macadamia; **америка́нский о.** Brazil nut; **гре́цкий о.** walnut; **кита́йский о.** peanut; **коко́совый о.** coconut; **лесно́й о., обыкнове́нный о.** hazel-nut; **муска́тный о.** nutmeg; **бу́дет тебе́ на ~и!; ему́ доста́лось (попа́ло) на ~и!** (*fig.*) you'll catch it!; he's caught it!; **разде́лать (отде́лать) кого́-н. под о.** (*coll.*) to give it s.o. hot. **2.** nut-tree. **3.** (*wood*) walnut; **шкаф из ~а** walnut cupboard.
оре́ховк|а, и *f.* (*zool.*) nutcracker.
оре́х|овый *adj. of* **~**; **~овое де́рево** nut-tree; (*wood*) walnut; **~овая скорлупа́** nutshell; **~ового цве́та** nut-brown; **о. шокола́д** nut chocolate.
орехоко́лк|а, и *f.* nutcrackers.
орехотво́рк|а, и *f.* (*zool.*) gall-fly.
оре́ш|ек, ка *m. dim. of* **оре́х; черни́льный о.** nut-gall.
оре́шник, а *m.* **1.** (hazel) nut-tree. **2.** hazel-grove.
оре́шниц|а, ы *f.* = **орехоко́лка**
оригина́л, а *m.* **1.** original. **2.** character, eccentric (*pers.*).
оригина́льнича|ть, ю *impf.* (*of* **с~**) (*coll.*) to put on an act, try to be clever.
оригина́л|ьный (~ен, ~ьна) *adj.* (*in var. senses*) original.
ориентали́ст, а *m.* orientalist.
ориента́льный *adj.* oriental.
ориента́ци|я, и *f.* **1.** (**на**+*a.*) orientation (toward); direction of attention (toward). **2.** (*fig.*) (**в**+*p.*) understanding (of), grasp (of); **у него́ хоро́шая о. в ю́жно-америка́нских дела́х** he has a firm grasp of South American affairs; **у меня́ нет ~и в торго́вом де́ле** I have no head for business.
ориенти́р, а *m.* (*mil.*) reference point; guiding line; **(есте́ственный) о.** landmark.
ориенти́рова|нный *p.p.p. of* **~ть** *and adj.* knowledgeable.
ориенти́р|овать, ую *impf. and pf.* **1.** to orient, orientate; (**в**+*p.*) to enlighten (concerning); **он не ~овал меня́ в экономи́ческом положе́нии** he did not put me in the picture about the economic position. **2.** (**на**+*a.*) to direct (toward).
ориенти́р|оваться, уюсь *impf. and pf.* **1.** to orient o.s.; to find one's bearings (*also fig.*); **я пло́хо ~уюсь** I have a poor sense of direction; **она́ ско́ро ~овалась в но́вой обстано́вке** (*fig.*) she soon found her feet in her new surroundings. **2.** (**на**+*a.*) to head (for), make (for); (*fig.*) to direct one's attention (to, toward); **о. на рабо́чих слу́шателей** to cater for a working-class audience.
ориентиро́вк|а, и *f.* = **ориента́ция**
ориентиро́вочно *adv.* tentatively; approximately; **гру́бо о.** as a rough guide.
ориентиро́воч|ный *adj.* **1.** position-finding. **2.** (**~ен, ~на**) tentative; rough, approximate.
орке́стр, а *m.* **1.** orchestra; band. **2.** orchestra-pit.
оркестра́нт, а *m.* member of an orchestra *or* band.
оркестрио́н, а *m.* (*obs.*) orchestrion.
оркестр|ова́ть, у́ю *impf. and pf.* to orchestrate.
оркестро́вк|а, и *f.* orchestration.
оркестро́вый *adj.* **1.** *adj. of* **орке́стр. 2.** orchestral.
оркне́|ец, йца *m.* Orcadian.
оркне́|йка, йки *f. of* **~ец**
Оркне́йск|ие о́стров|а́, ~их ~о́в *no sg.* the Orkney Islands; the Orkneys.
оркне́йский *adj.* Orcadian.
орла́н, а *m.* sea eagle.
орл|ёнок, ёнка, *pl.* **~я́та, ~я́т** *m.* eaglet.
орле́ц, а́ *m.* **1.** (*min.*) rhodonite. **2.** (*eccl.*) round hassock (*with woven design of eagle; placed under feet of officiating bishop*).
орли́ный *adj. of* **орёл**; aquiline; **о. взгляд** eagle eye; **о. нос** aquiline nose.
орли́ц|а, ы *f.* female eagle.

орло́вский *adj.* (of) Oryol.
орля́нк|а, и *f.* pitch-and-toss.
орна́мент, а *m.* ornament; ornamental design.
орнамента́льный *adj.* ornamental.
орнамента́ци|я, и *f.* ornamentation.
орнаменти́р|овать, ую *impf. and pf.* to ornament.
орнито́лог, а *m.* ornithologist; **о.-люби́тель** bird-watcher.
орнитологи́ческий *adj.* ornithological.
орнитоло́ги|я, и *f.* ornithology.
орнитопте́р, а *m.* (*aeron.*) ornithopter.
оробе́лый *adj.* timid; frightened.
оробе́|ть, ю *pf. of* **робе́ть**
орогове́|ть, ет *pf.* to become horny.
орографи́ческий *adj.* orographic(al).
орогра́фи|я, и *f.* orography.
ороси́тельный *adj.* irrigation; irrigating; **о. кана́л** irrigation canal.
оро|си́ть, шу́, си́шь *pf.* (*of* **~ша́ть**) to irrigate; to water; **о. слеза́ми** to wash with tears.
оро|ша́ть, ша́ю *impf. of* **~си́ть**
ороше́ни|е, я *nt.* irrigation; **поля́ ~я** sewage-farm.
ортодо́кс, а *m.* conformist.
ортодокса́л|ьный (~ен, ~ьна) *adj.* orthodox.
ортодо́кси|я, и *f.* orthodoxy.
ортопе́д, а *m.* orthopaedist.
ортопеди́ческий *adj.* orthopaedic.
ортопе́ди|я, и *f.* orthopaedics.
ору́ди|е, я *nt.* **1.** instrument; implement; tool (*also fig.*); **сельскохозя́йственные ~я** agricultural implements. **2.** piece of ordnance; gun; **зени́тное о.** anti-aircraft gun; **полево́е о.** field-gun; **самохо́дное о.** self-propelled gun.
оруд|и́йный *adj. of* **∠ие 2.**; **о. ого́нь** gun-fire; **о. око́п** gun-entrenchment; **~и́йная пальба́** cannonade; **о. расчёт** gun crew.
ору́д|овать, ую *impf.* (*coll.*; *+i.*) **1.** to handle. **2.** (*fig.*, *pej.*) to be active; **он там всем ~ует** he bosses the whole show.
оруже́йник, а *m.* gunsmith, armourer.
оруж|е́йный *adj. of* **∠ие**; **~е́йная пала́та** armoury; **о. ма́стер** armourer.
оруженос|ец, ца *m.* armour-bearer, sword-bearer; (*fig.*) henchman.
ору́жи|е, я *nt.* arm(s); weapons; **огнестре́льное о.** fire-arm(s); **стрелко́вое о.** small arms; **холо́дное о.** cold steel; **род ~я** arm of the service; **к ~ю!** to arms!; **бра́ться за о.** to take up arms; **подня́ть о.** (**на**+*a.*) to take up arms (against); **положи́ть о., сложи́ть о.** to lay down one's arms; **бить кого́-н. его́ же ~ем** (*fig.*) to beat s.o. at his own game.
орфографи́ческ|ий *adj.* orthographic(al); **~ая оши́бка** spelling mistake.
орфогра́фи|я, и *f.* orthography, spelling.
орфоэпи́ческий *adj.*: **о. слова́рь** pronouncing dictionary.
орфоэ́пи|я, и *f.* orthoepy; (rules of) correct pronunciation.
орхиде́|я, и *f.* (*bot.*) orchid.
оря́син|а, ы *f.* (*coll.*) rod, pole.
ос|а́, ы́, *pl.* **∠ы** *f.* wasp.
оса́д|а, ы *f.* siege; **снять ~у** to raise a siege.
оса|ди́ть¹, **жу́, ди́шь** *pf.* (*of* **~жда́ть**) to besiege, lay siege to; to beleaguer; **о. вопро́сами** to ply with questions; **о. про́сьбами** to bombard with requests.
оса|ди́ть², **жу́, ∠дишь** *pf.* (*of* **~жда́ть**) (*chem.*) to precipitate.
оса|ди́ть³, **жу́, ∠дишь** *pf.* (*of* **∠живать**) **1.** to check, halt; to force back; **о. ло́шадь** to rein in a horse. **2.** (*fig.*): **о. кого́-н.** to put s.o. in his place, take s.o. down a peg.
оса́дк|а, и *f.* **1.** set, settling (*of soil, etc.*). **2.** (*naut.*) draught; **су́дно с небольшо́й ~ой** vessel of shallow draught.
оса́д|ный *adj. of* **~а**; **~ная артилле́рия** siege artillery; **~ная война́** siege war(fare); **~ное положе́ние** state of siege.
оса́д|ок, ка *m.* **1.** (*pl.*) precipitation. **2.** sediment, deposition. **3.** (*fig.*) after-taste; **у меня́ от э́того разгово́ра был неприя́тный о.** the conversation left an unpleasant taste in my mouth.
оса́д|очный *adj. of* **~ок**; **~очные поро́ды** (*geol.*) sedimentary rocks; **о. чан** (*chem.*) precipitation tank; **~очная маши́на** (*tech.*) upsetting machine.
осажда́|ть, ю *impf. of* **осади́ть**¹·²
осажда́|ться, юсь, *impf.* **1.** (*of atmospheric precipitations*) to fall. **2.** (*chem.*) to be precipitated; to fall out.
осаждённый *p.p.p. of* **осади́ть**¹·²
оса́женный *p.p.p. of* **осади́ть**³
оса́жива|ть, ю *impf. of* **осади́ть**³
оса́нист|ый (~, ~а) *adj.* portly.
оса́нк|а, и *f.* carriage, bearing.
оса́нн|а, ы *f.* hosanna; **восклица́ть, петь ~у кому́-н.** (*fig.*) to sing s.o.'s praises.
осатане́лый *adj.* (*coll.*) possessed; diabolical, demoniacal.
ОСВ *nt. indecl.* (*abbr. of* **ограниче́ние стратеги́ческих вооруже́ний**): **перегово́ры по ОСВ** SALT (*Strategic Arms Limitation Treaty*) talks.
осва́ива|ть(ся), ю(сь) *impf. of* **осво́ить(ся)**
осведоми́тел|ь, я *m.* informant.
осведоми́тельн|ый *adj.* **1.** informative. **2.** (*giving, conveying*) information; **~ая рабо́та** information work, publicity work.
осве́дом|ить, лю, ишь *pf.* (*of* **~ля́ть**) to inform.
осве́дом|иться, люсь, ишься *pf.* (*of* **~ля́ться**) (**о**+*i.*) to inquire (about).
осведомле́ни|е, я *nt.* informing, notification.
осведомлённост|ь, и *f.* knowledge, (possession of) information; **у него́ хоро́шая о. в исла́ндских са́гах** he is very knowledgeable about the Icelandic sagas.
осведомлённый *p.p.p. of* **осве́домить** *and* (**в**+*p.*) well-informed (about), knowledgeable (about); versed (in), conversant (with).
осведом|ля́ть(ся), ля́ю(сь) *impf. of* **∠ить(ся)**
освеж|а́ть, а́ю *impf. of* **~и́ть**
освеж|ева́ть, у́ю *pf. of* **свежева́ть**
освежи́тельный *adj.* refreshing.
освеж|и́ть, у́, и́шь *pf.* (*of* **~а́ть**) **1.** to refresh; to freshen; **о. ко́мнату** to give a room an airing. **2.** (*fig.*) to refresh, revive; **о. свои́ зна́ния** to refresh one's knowledge; **о. соста́в предприя́тия** (*coll.*) to introduce fresh blood into the staff of an enterprise.
Осве́нцим, а *m.* Auschwitz.
освети́тел|ь, я *m.* **1.** pers. in charge of lighting effects. **2.** condenser (*of microscope*).
освети́тельн|ый *adj.* lighting, illuminating; **~ая бо́мба** candle bomb; **~ая раке́та** (*aeron.*) flare; **~ая сеть** lighting system; **о. снаря́д** star shell.
осве|ти́ть, щу́, ти́шь *pf.* (*of* **~ща́ть**) to light up; to illuminate, illumine; (*fig.*) to throw light on; to cover, report (*in the press*).
осве|ти́ться, щу́сь, ти́шься *pf.* (*of* **~ща́ться**) **1.** to light up; to brighten; **её лицо́ ~ти́лось улы́бкой** (*fig.*) a smile lit up her face. **2.** *pass. of* **~ти́ть**
осветли́тел|ь, я *m.* (*chem.*) clarifying agent.
осветл|и́ть, ю́, и́шь *pf.* (*of* **~я́ть**) (*chem.*) to clarify.
осветл|я́ть, я́ю *impf. of* **~и́ть**
освеща́|ть(ся), ю(сь) *impf. of* **освети́ть(ся)**
освеще́ни|е, я *nt.* light, lighting, illumination; **иску́сственное о.** artificial light(ing); **электри́ческое о.** electric light.
освещённост|ь, и *f.* (*degree of, area of*) illumination.
осве|щённый *p.p.p. of* **~ти́ть**; **о. звёздами** star-lit; **о. луно́й** moonlit; **о. свеча́ми** candle-lit.
освиде́тельств|овать, ую *pf. of* **свиде́тельствовать 3.**
освинц|ева́ть, у́ю *pf.* to lead, lead-plate.
осви|ста́ть, щу́, ∠щешь *pf.* (*of* **∠стывать**) to hiss (off), catcall; **о. актёра** to hiss an actor off the stage.
осви́стыва|ть, ю *impf. of* **освиста́ть**
освободи́тел|ь, я *m.* liberator.
освободи́тельн|ый *adj.* liberation, emancipation; **~ая война́** war of liberation.
освобо|ди́ть, жу́, ди́шь *pf.* (*of* **~жда́ть**) **1.** to free, liberate; to release, set free; to emancipate; **о. аресто́ванного** to discharge a prisoner; **о. от вое́нной слу́жбы** to exempt from military service. **2.** to dismiss; **о. от до́лжности** to relieve of one's post. **3.** to vacate; to clear, empty.

освобо|ди́ться, жу́сь, ди́шься *pf.* (*of* **~жда́ться**) **1.** **(от)** to free o.s. (of, from); to become free. **2.** *pass. of* **~ди́ть**

освобожда́|ть(ся), ю(сь) *impf. of* **освободи́ть(ся)**

освобожде́ни|е, я *nt.* **1.** liberation; release; emancipation; discharge. **2.** dismissal. **3.** vacation (*of premises, etc.*).

освобо|ждённый *p.p.p. of* **~ди́ть; о. от нало́га** tax-free, exempt from tax.

освое́ни|е, я *nt.* assimilation, mastery, familiarization; **о. но́вой те́хники** learning to handle new machinery; **о. кра́йнего се́вера** the opening up of the Far North.

осво́|ить, ю, ишь *pf.* (*of* **осва́ивать**) **1.** to assimilate, master; to cope (with); to become familiar (with). **2.** (*bot.*) to acclimatize.

осво́|иться, юсь, ишься *pf.* (*of* **осва́иваться**) **1.** **(с+***i.***)** to familiarize o.s. (with). **2.** to feel at home; **о. в но́вой среде́** to get the feel of new surroundings.

освя|ти́ть, щу́, ти́шь *pf.* **1.** (*impf.* **святи́ть**) (*eccl.*) to consecrate; to bless, sanctify. **2.** (*impf.* **~ща́ть**) (*fig.*) to sanctify, hallow.

освяща́|ть, ю *impf. of* **освяти́ть**

освя|щённый *p.p.p. of* **~ти́ть; обы́чай, о. века́ми** time-honoured custom.

ос|ево́й *adj. of* **~ь**; axial; **о. кана́л** (*elec.*) axial duct; **~ева́я ша́йба** axle tree.

оседа́ни|е, я *nt.* **1.** settling, subsidence. **2.** settlement.

оседа́|ть, ю *impf. of* **осе́сть**

осёдл|анный *p.p.p. of* **~а́ть**

оседла́|ть, ю *pf.* **1.** (*impf.* **седла́ть**) to saddle. **2.** (*mil.*; *fig.*) to establish a grip (upon); **о. доро́гу** to get astride a road.

осе́длост|ь, и *f.* settled (way of) life; **черта́ ~и** (*hist.*) the Pale of Settlement (*area to which Jews were confined in tsarist Russia*).

осе́длый *adj.* settled (*opp. nomadic*).

осека́|ться, юсь *impf. of* **осе́чься**

ос|ёл, ла́ *m.* donkey; ass (*also fig. of a human being*).

оселе́д|ец, ца *m.* top-knot (*hist.*; *long forelock left by Ukrainians on shaven head*).

осел|о́к, ка́ *m.* **1.** touchstone (*also fig.*). **2.** whetstone; oilstone; hone.

осемене́ни|е, я *nt.* (*artificial*) insemination.

осемен|и́ть, ю́, и́шь *pf.* (*of* **~я́ть**) to inseminate (*by artificial means*).

осемен|я́ть, я́ю *impf. of* **~и́ть**

осен|и́ть, ю́, и́шь *pf.* (*of* **~я́ть**) **1.** to overshadow; (*fig.*) to shield; **о. кре́стом** to make the sign of the cross (over). **2.** (*fig.*) to dawn upon, strike; **его́ ~и́ла мысль** it dawned upon him; (*impers.*): **меня́ внеза́пно ~и́ло** it suddenly occurred to me.

осен|и́ться, ю́сь, и́шься *pf.* (*of* **~я́ться**) *pass. of* **~и́ть; о. кре́стом** to cross o.s.

осе́нний *adj. of* **о́сень**; autumnal.

о́сен|ь, и *f.* autumn.

о́сенью *adv.* in autumn.

осен|я́ть(ся), я́ю(сь) *impf. of* **~и́ть(ся)**

осер|ди́ться, жу́сь, ́~дишься *pf.* **(на+***a.*; *coll.***)** to become angry (with).

осерча́|ть, ю *pf. of* **серча́ть**

ос|е́сть, я́ду, я́дешь, *past* **~е́л, ~е́ла** *pf.* (*of* **~еда́ть**) **1.** to settle, subside; to sink; to form a sediment. **2.** (*of human beings*) to settle.

осети́н, а, *g. pl.* **о.** *m.* Ossetian, Ossete.

осети́н|ка, ки *f. of* **~**

осети́нский *adj.* Ossetian.

осётр, а́ *m.* sturgeon.

осетри́н|а, ы *f.* (flesh of) sturgeon.

осетро́вый *adj. of* **осётр**

осе́чк|а, и *f.* misfire; **дать ~у** to misfire (*also fig.*).

осе́|чься, ку́сь, чёшься, ку́тся, *past* **~кся, ~клась** *pf.* (*of* **~ка́ться**) (*coll.*) **1.** to misfire (*also fig.*). **2.** to stop short (*in speaking*).

оси́лива|ть, ю *impf. of* **оси́лить**

оси́л|ить, ю, ишь *pf.* (*of* **~ивать**) **1.** to overpower. **2.** (*coll.*) to master; to manage; **о. гре́ческий алфави́т** to master the Greek alphabet; **я е́ле ~ил ещё оди́н стака́н** I was hardly able to manage another glass.

оси́н|а, ы *f.* asp(en).

оси́нник, а *m.* aspen wood.

оси́н|овый *adj. of* **~а**; **дрожа́ть как о. лист** to tremble like an aspen leaf.

ос|и́ный *adj. of* **~а́**; **~и́ное гнездо́** (*fig.*) hornets' nest; **потрево́жить ~и́ное гнездо́** to stir up a hornets' nest; **~и́ная та́лия** wasp waist.

оси́плый *adj.* hoarse, husky.

оси́п|нуть, ну, нешь, *past* **~, ~ла** *pf.* to go hoarse.

осироте́лый *adj.* orphaned.

осироте́|ть, ю *pf.* to become an orphan, be orphaned.

оска́блива|ть, ю *impf. of* **оскобли́ть**

оска́л, а *m.* bared teeth; grin.

оска́лива|ть(ся), ю(сь) *impf. of* **оска́лить(ся)**

оска́л|ить, ю, ишь *pf.* (*of* **ска́лить** *and* **~ивать**): **о. зу́бы** to bare one's teeth.

оска́л|иться, юсь, ишься *pf.* (*of* **ска́литься** *and* **~иваться**) to bare one's teeth.

оскальпи́р|овать, ую *pf. of* **скальпи́ровать**

оскандал|ить(ся), ю(сь), ишь(ся) *pf. of* **сканда́лить(ся)**

оскверне́ни|е, я *nt.* defilement; profanation.

оскверн|и́ть, ю́, и́шь *pf.* (*of* **~я́ть**) to defile; to profane.

оскверн|и́ться, ю́сь, и́шься *pf.* (*of* **~я́ться**) **1.** to defile o.s. **2.** *pass. of* **~и́ть**

оскверн|я́ть(ся), я́ю(сь) *impf. of* **~и́ть(ся)**

осклаб|иться, люсь, ишься *pf.* to grin.

оскобл|и́ть, ю́, ́~и́шь *pf.* (*of* **оска́бливать**) to scrape (off).

оско́л|ок, ка *m.* splinter, sliver; fragment.

оско́ло|чный *adj. of* **~к; ~чная бо́мба** fragmentation bomb, anti-personnel bomb.

оско́мин|а, ы *f.* bitter taste (in the mouth); **наби́ть ~у** to set the teeth on edge (*also fig.*).

оско́мист|ый (~, ~а) *adj.* (*coll.*) sour, bitter.

оскоп|и́ть, лю́, и́шь *pf.* (*of* **~ля́ть**) to castrate.

оскопля́|ть, ю *impf. of* **оскопи́ть**

оскорби́тельност|ь, и *f.* abusiveness.

оскорби́тел|ьный (~ен, ~ьна) *adj.* insulting, abusive.

оскорб|и́ть, лю́, и́шь *pf.* (*of* **~ля́ть**) to insult, offend.

оскорб|и́ться, лю́сь, и́шься *pf.* (*of* **~ля́ться**) to take offence; to be offended, be hurt.

оскорбле́ни|е, я *nt.* insult; **о. де́йствием** (*leg.*) assault and battery; **о. сло́вом** contumely; **переноси́ть ~я** to bear insults.

оскорб|лённый *p.p.p. of* **~и́ть; ~лённая неви́нность** outraged innocence.

оскорбля́|ть, ю *impf. of* **оскорби́ть**

оскоро́м|иться, люсь, ишься *pf. of* **скоро́миться**

оскрёб|ки, ков *pl.* (*sg.* **~ок, ~ка** *m.*) (*coll.*) scrapings.

оскудева́|ть, ю *impf. of* **оскуде́ть**

оскуде́лый *adj.* scarce, scanty.

оскуде́ни|е, я *nt.* scarcity; impoverishment.

оскуде́|ть, ю *pf.* (*of* **скуде́ть** *and* **~ва́ть**) to grow scarce.

ослабева́|ть, ю *impf. of* **ослабе́ть**

ослабе́лый *adj.* weakened, enfeebled.

ослабе́|ть, ю *pf.* (*of* **слабе́ть** *and* **~ва́ть**) to weaken, become weak; to slacken; to abate.

ослаби́тел|ь, я *m.* (*phot.*) clearing agent.

осла́б|ить, лю, ишь *pf.* (*of* **~ля́ть**) **1.** to weaken. **2.** to slacken, relax; to loosen; **о. внима́ние** to relax one's attention; **о. нажи́м** to slacken pressure; **о. по́яс** to loosen a belt.

ослабле́ни|е, я *nt.* weakening; slackening, relaxation; **о. напряже́ния** slackening of tension.

ослабля́|ть, ю *impf. of* **осла́бить**

осла́б|нуть, ну, нешь, *past* **~, ~ла** *pf.* = **~еть**

осла́в|ить, лю, ишь *pf.* (*of* **~ля́ть**) (*coll.*) to defame, decry; to give a bad name.

осла́в|иться, люсь, ишься *pf.* (*of* **~ля́ться**) (*coll.*) to get a bad name.

ославля́|ть(ся), ю(сь) *impf. of* **осла́вить(ся)**

осл|ёнок, ёнка, *pl.* **~я́та** *m.* foal (*of ass*).

ослепи́тел|ьный (~ен, ~ьна) *adj.* blinding, dazzling.

ослеп|и́ть, лю́, и́шь *pf.* (*of* **~ля́ть**) to blind, dazzle (*also fig.*).
ослепле́ни|е, я *nt.* **1.** blinding, dazzling. **2.** (*fig.*) blindness; **де́йствовать в ~и** to act blindly.
ослепля́|ть, ю *impf. of* **ослепи́ть**
осле́п|нуть, ну, нешь, *past* **~, ~ла** *pf. of* **сле́пнуть**
осли́злый *adj.* slimy.
осли́з|нуть, нет, *past* **~, ~ла** *pf.* to become slimy.
осли́ный *adj. of* **осёл**; ass's; (*fig.*) asinine.
осли́ц|а, ы *f.* she-ass.
О́сло *m. indecl.* Oslo.
осложне́ни|е, я *nt.* complication.
осложн|и́ть, ю́, и́шь *pf.* (*of* **~я́ть**) to complicate.
осложн|и́ться, ю́сь, и́шься *pf.* (*of* **~я́ться**) to become complicated.
осложн|я́ть(ся), я́ю(сь) *impf. of* **~и́ть(ся)**
ослуша́ни|е, я *nt.* disobedience.
ослу́ш|аться, аюсь *pf.* (*of* **~иваться**) to disobey.
ослу́шива|ться, юсь *impf. of* **ослу́шаться**
ослу́шник, а *m.* (*obs.*) disobedient pers.
ослы́ш|аться, усь, ишься *pf.* to mishear.
ослы́шк|а, и *f.* mishearing.
осма́н, а *m.* Osmanli Turk, Ottoman.
осма́нский *adj.* Osmanli, Ottoman.
осма́трива|ть(ся), ю(сь) *impf. of* **осмотре́ть(ся)**
осме́ива|ть, ю *impf. of* **осмея́ть**
осмеле́|ть, ю *pf. of* **смеле́ть**
осме́лива|ться, юс, *impf. of* **осме́литься**
осме́л|иться, юсь, ишься *pf.* (*of* **~иваться**) (+*inf.*) to dare; to take the liberty (of); **~юсь доложи́ть...** (*obs. polite formula*) I beg to report ....
осме|я́ть, ю́, ёшь *pf.* (*of* **~́ивать**) to mock, ridicule.
о́сми|й, я *m.* (*chem.*) osmium.
осмо́л, а *m.* tar-impregnated wood.
осмол|и́ть, ю́, и́шь *pf. of* **смоли́ть**
о́смос, а *m.* (*phys.*) osmosis.
осмоти́ческий *adj.* (*phys.*) osmotic.
осмо́тр, а *m.* examination, inspection; **медици́нский о.** medical (examination); checkup.
осмотр|е́ть, ю́, ~́ишь *pf.* (*of* **осма́тривать**) to examine, inspect; to look round, look over.
осмотр|е́ться, ю́сь, ~́ишься *pf.* (*of* **осма́триваться**) **1.** to look round. **2.** (*fig.*) to take one's bearings, see how the land lies. **3.** *pass. of* **~е́ть**
осмотри́тельност|ь, и *f.* circumspection.
осмотри́тел|ьный (~ен, ~ьна) *adj.* circumspect.
осмо́трщик, а *m.* inspector.
осмы́сл|енный *p.p.p. of* **~ить** *and adj.* intelligent, sensible.
осмы́слива|ть, ю *impf. of* **осмы́слить**
осмы́сл|ить, ю, ишь *pf.* (*of* **~ивать** *and* **~я́ть**) to interpret, give a meaning to; to comprehend.
осмысл|я́ть, я́ю *impf.* = **~́ивать**
осна|сти́ть, щу́, сти́шь *pf.* (*of* **~ща́ть**) (*naut.*) to rig; (*fig.*) to fit out, equip.
осна́стк|а, и *f.* (*naut.*) rigging.
оснаща́|ть, ю *impf. of* **оснасти́ть**
оснаще́ни|е, я *nt.* **1.** rigging; fitting out. **2.** equipment.
оснеж|ённый *p.p.p. of* **~и́ть** *and adj.* snow-covered.
оснеж|и́ть, у́, и́шь *pf.* (*poet.*) to cover with snow.
осно́в|а, ы *f.* **1.** base, basis, foundation; *pl.* fundamentals; **лежа́ть в ~е** (+*g.*) to be the basis (of). **2.** (*gram.*) stem. **3.** (*text.*) warp.
основа́ни|е, я *nt.* **1.** founding, foundation. **2.** (*chem., math., etc.*) base; foundation (*of building*); **о. горы́** foot of a mountain; **о. коло́нны** (*archit.*) column socle; **разру́шить до ~я** to raze to the ground; **изучи́ть до ~я** (*fig.*) to study from A to Z. **3.** (*fig.*) foundation, basis; ground, reason; **на како́м ~и вы э́то утвержда́ете?** on what grounds do you assert this?; **на ра́вных ~ях** with equal reason; **не без ~я** not without reason; **име́ть о. предполага́ть** to have reason to suppose; **с по́лным ~ем** with good reason.
основа́тел|ь, я *m.* founder.
основа́тел|ьный (~ен, ~ьна) *adj.* **1.** well-founded; just; **~ьная жа́лоба** reasonable complaint. **2.** solid, sound (*also fig.*); thorough; **~ьные до́воды** sound arguments. **3.** (*coll.*) bulky.
осн|ова́ть, ую́, уёшь *pf.* (*of* **~о́вывать**) **1.** to found. **2.** (**на**+*p.*) to base (on).
осн|ова́ться, ую́сь, уёшься *pf.* (*of* **~о́вываться**) **1.** to settle. **2.** *pass. of* **~ова́ть**
основн|о́й *adj.* fundamental, basic; principal; **~о́е значе́ние** primary meaning; **о. капита́л** (*fin.*) fixed capital; **~а́я мысль** keynote; **~ы́е цвета́** primary colours; **в ~о́м** on the whole.
осно́в|ный[1] *adj. of* **~а 3.**; **~ные ни́ти** warp threads.
осно́в|ный[2] *adj. of* **~а́ние 2.** (*chem.*); **~ные со́ли** basic salts.
основополо́жник, а *m.* founder, initiator.
осно́выва|ть, ю *impf. of* **основа́ть**
осно́выва|ться, юсь *impf.* **1.** *impf. of* **основа́ться. 2.** *impf. only* (**на**+*p.*) to base o.s. (on); to be based, founded (on); **о. на дога́дках** to base o.s. on conjecture.
осо́б|а, ы *f.* person, individual, personage; **ва́жная о.** (*iron.*) big noise, big-wig.
осо́бенно *adv.* especially; particularly; unusually; **не о.** not very, not particularly; **она́ сего́дня ве́чером о. болтли́ва** she is unusually talkative this evening; **вы лю́бите соба́к? — не о.** do you like dogs? Not very much.
осо́бенност|ь, и *f.* peculiarity; **в ~и** especially, in particular, (more) particularly.
осо́бенн|ый *adj.* (e)special, particular, peculiar; **ни́чего ~ого** nothing in particular; nothing much.
особня́к, а́ *m.* private residence; detached house.
особняко́м *adv.* by o.s.; **держа́ться о.** to keep aloof.
осо́б|ый *adj.* special; particular; peculiar; **оста́ться при ~ом мне́нии** to reserve one's own opinion; (*leg.*) to dissent; **удели́ть ~ое внима́ние** (+*d.*) to give special attention (to).
о́соб|ь, и *f.* individual.
осо́бь *indecl. adj. only in phr.* **о. статья́** (*coll.*) quite another matter.
осове́лый *adj.* (*coll.*) dazed, dreamy.
осове́|ть, ю *pf.* (*coll.*) to fall into a dazed, dreamy state.
осовреме́нива|ть, ю *impf. of* **осовреме́нить**
осовреме́н|ить, ю, ишь *pf.* (*of* **~ивать**) to bring up to date; to modernize.
осое́д, а *m.* (*zool.*) honey-buzzard.
осозна|ва́ть, ю́, ёшь *impf. of* **~́ть**
осозна́|ть, ю *pf.* (*of* **~ва́ть**) to realize.
осо́к|а, и *f.* (*bot.*) sedge.
осоко́р|ь, я *m.* (*bot.*) black poplar.
осолове́лый *adj.* (*coll.*) = **осове́лый**
осолове́|ть, ю, ешь *pf. of* **солове́ть**
о́сп|а, ы *f.* **1.** smallpox; **ве́тряная о.** chicken-pox; **коро́вья о.** cow-pox; **чёрная о.** smallpox. **2.** (*coll.*) pock-marks; vaccination marks; **лицо́ в ~е** pock-marked face.
оспа́рива|ть, ю *impf.* **1.** *impf. of* **оспо́рить. 2.** *impf. only* to contend (for); **он ~ет зва́ние чемпио́на ми́ра** he is contending for the title of world champion.
о́сп|енный *adj. of* **~а**; variolar, variolic, variolous; **о. знак** pock-mark.
о́спин|а, ы *f.* pock-mark.
оспопрививáни|е, я *nt.* vaccination.
оспо́р|ить, ю, ишь *pf.* (*of* **оспа́ривать**) to dispute, question; **о. завеща́ние** to dispute a will.
осрам|и́ть(ся), лю́(сь), и́шь(ся) *pf. of* **срами́ть(ся)**
ОССВ *no sg., indecl.* (*abbr. of* ***ограниче́ние и сокраще́ние стратеги́ческих вооруже́ний***): **перегово́ры по О.** START (*Strategic Arms Reduction Treaty*) talks.
ОСТ, а *m.* (*abbr. of* ***общесою́зный станда́рт***) All-Union standard.
ост, а *m.* (*naut.*) east.
оста|ва́ться, ю́сь, ёшься *impf. of* **оста́ться**
оста́в|ить, лю, ишь *pf.* (*of* **~ля́ть**) **1.** to leave; to abandon, give up; **о. в поко́е** to leave alone, let alone; **о. на второ́й год** (*in schools*) to keep in the same form, not move up; **~ь(те)!** stop that!; lay off! **2.** to reserve; to keep; **о. за собо́й пра́во** to reserve the right.
оставля́|ть, ю *impf. of* **оста́вить; ~ет жела́ть мно́гого** (*or* **лу́чшего**) it leaves much to be desired.

остальн|óй *adj.* the rest (of); **в ~óм** in other respects; *as n.* **~ы́е** *pl.* the others; **~óе** *nt.* the rest; **всё ~óе** everything else.
останáвлива|ть(ся), ю(сь) *impf. of* **останови́ть(ся)**
остáнк|и, ов *no sg.* remains.
останóв, а *m.* (*tech.*) stop, stopper, ratchet-gear.
останов|и́ть, лю́, ~ишь *pf.* (*of* **останáвливать**) **1.** to stop. **2.** to stop short, restrain. **3.** (**на**+*p.*) to direct (to), concentrate (on); **о. взгляд** to rest one's gaze (on); **о. внимáние** to concentrate one's attention (on).
останов|и́ться, лю́сь, ~ишься *pf.* (*of* **останáвливаться**) **1.** to stop; to come to a stop, come to a halt; **ни пéред чем не о.** (*fig.*) to stop at nothing. **2.** to stay, put up, (*coll.*) stop; **о. у знакóмых** to stay with friends. **3.** (**на**+*p.*) (*fig.*) to dwell (on) (*in a speech, lecture, etc.*); to settle (on), rest (on); **взор мáльчика ~и́лся на нóвой игрýшке** the boy's gaze rested on the new toy.
останóвк|а, и *f.* **1.** stop; stoppage; **о. за вáми** you are holding us up; **о. за ви́зами** there is a hold-up over the visas. **2.** (*bus, tram*) stop; **конéчная о.** terminus; **мне нáдо проéхать ещё однý ~у** I have to go one stop further.
останóв|очный *adj. of* **~ка**; **о. пункт** stop, stopping place.
остáт|ок, ка *m.* **1.** (*in var. senses*) remainder; rest; residue; remnant (*of material*); *pl.* remains; leavings, leftovers; **распродáжа ~ков** clearance sale. **2.** (*chem.*) residuum. **3.** (*fin., comm.*) rest, balance.
остáто|чный *adj. of* **~к**; (*chem., tech.*) residual.
остá|ться, нусь, нешься *pf.* (*of* **~вáться**) to remain; to stay; to be left (over); **о. в барыша́х** to gain, be up; **о. в долгý** to be in debt; **о. в живы́х** to survive, come through; **о. нá ночь** to stay the night; **о. при своём мнéнии** to remain of the same opinion; **о. на вторóй год (в том же клáссе)** to remain in the same form a second year; **за ним ~лось пять фýнтов** he owes five pounds; **пóсле негó ~лись женá и трóе детéй** he left a wife and three children; **от обéда ничегó не ~лось** there is nothing left over from dinner; (*impers.*): **~ётся, ~лось** (+*d.*) it remains (remained), it is (was) necessary; **нам не ~лось ничегó другóго, как согласи́ться** we had no choice but to consent; **~лось тóлько заплати́ть** it remained only to pay.
остеклене́|ть, ю *pf. of* **стеклене́ть**
остекл|и́ть, ю́, и́шь *pf.* (*of* **~я́ть**) to glaze.
остекл|я́ть, я́ю *impf. of* **~и́ть**
Остéнде *m. indecl.* Ostend.
остеóлог, а *m.* osteologist.
остеологи́ческий *adj.* osteological.
остеолóги|я, и *f.* osteology.
остеомиэли́т, а *m.* (*med.*) osteomyelitis.
остепен|и́ть, ю́, и́шь *pf.* (*of* **~я́ть**) to make staid; to calm, mellow.
остепен|и́ться, ю́сь, и́шься *pf.* (*of* **~я́ться**) to settle down; to become staid, become respectable; to mellow.
остепеня́|ть(ся), ю(сь) *impf. of* **остепени́ть(ся)**
остервенéлый *adj.* frenzied.
остервенéни|е, я *nt.* frenzy; **рабóтать с ~ем** to work like a maniac.
остервен|éть, ю *pf. of* **стервенéть**
остервен|и́ться, ю́сь, и́шься *pf.* to be frenzied.
остерегá|ть, ю *impf. of* **остерéчь**
остерегá|ться, юсь *impf.* (*of* **остерéчься**) (+*g. or inf.*) to beware (of); to be careful (of); **~йтесь собáки!** beware of the dog!; **~йся, чтóбы не упáсть!** mind you don't fall!
остерé|чь, гý, жёшь, гýт, *past* **~г, ~глá** *pf.* (*of* **~гáть**) to warn, caution.
остерé|чься, гýсь, жёшься, гýтся, *past* **~гся, ~глáсь** *pf. of* **~гáться**
остери́|я, и *f.* inn, hostelry (*in Italy*).
остзé|ец, йца *m.* (*obs.*) Baltic German.
остзéйский *adj.* (*obs.*) Baltic (German); **о. барóн** (*hist.*) 'Baltic baron'.
Ост-И́нди|я, и *f.* the East Indies.
ости́ст|ый (~, ~а) *adj.* (*bot.*) awned, bearded, aristate.
ости́т, а *m.* (*med.*) osteitis.
óстов, а *m.* **1.** frame, framework (*also fig.*); shell; hull. **2.** (*anat.*) skeleton.
остóйчивост|ь, и *f.* (*naut.*) stability.
остóйчив|ый (~, ~а) *adj.* (*naut.*) stable.
остолбенéлый *adj.* (*coll.*) dumbfounded.
остолбенé|ть, ю *pf. of* **столбенéть**
остолóп, а *m.* (*coll.*) blockhead.
осторóжно *adv.* carefully; cautiously; guardedly; gingerly; **о.!** look out! mind out!; (*on package*) 'with care'.
осторóжност|ь, и *f.* care; caution.
осторóж|ный (~ен, ~на) *adj.* careful; cautious; **бýдьте ~ны!** take care!; be careful!
осточерте́|ть, ю *pf.* (+*d.*; *coll.*) to bore; to repel; **мне э́то ~ло** I am fed up with it.
остраки́зм, а *m.* ostracism; **подвéргнуть ~у** to ostracize.
острáстк|а, и *f.* (*coll.*) warning, caution; **в ~у, для ~и** as a warning.
острекáв|ить, лю, ишь *pf. of* **стрекáвить**
остригá|ть(ся), ю(сь) *impf. of* **остри́чь(ся)**
остри|ё, я́ *nt.* **1.** point; spike; **о. кли́на** (*mil.*) spearhead of the attack. **2.** (cutting) edge; **о. кри́тики** (*fig.*) the edge of a criticism.
остр|и́ть[1]**, ю́, и́шь** *impf.* to sharpen, whet.
остр|и́ть[2]**, ю́, и́шь** *impf.* (*of* **с~**) to be witty; to make witticisms, crack jokes; **о. на чужóй счёт** to be witty at others' expense, score off others.
остри́|чь, гý, жёшь, гýт, *past* **~г, ~гла** *pf.* (*of* **стричь** *and* **~гáть**) to cut; to clip.
остри́|чься, гýсь, жёшься, гýться, *past* **~гся, ~глась** *pf.* (*of* **стри́чься** *and* **~гáться**) to cut one's hair; to have one's hair cut.
óстров, а, *pl.* **~á** *m.* island; isle.
островитя́н|ин, ина, *pl.* **~е, ~** *m.* islander.
островнóй *adj.* island; insular.
остров|óк, кá *m.* islet; **о. безопáсности** island (*in road, for pedestrians crossing*).
острóг, а *m.* **1.** (*obs.*) gaol. **2.** (*hist.*) stockaded town. **3.** (*hist.*) stockade, palisade.
острог|á, и́ *f.* fish-spear, harpoon.
остроглáз|ый (~, ~а) *adj.* (*coll.*) sharp-sighted, keen-eyed.
острогýбц|ы, ев (*tech.*) cutting nippers.
остродефици́т|ный (~ен, ~на) *adj.* extremely scarce; in extremely short supply.
острóжник, а *m.* (*obs.*) imprisoned criminal, convict.
острó|жный *adj. of* **~г**
остроконéчный *adj.* pointed.
остроли́ст, а *m.* (*bot.*) holly.
остронóс|ый (~, ~а) *adj.* sharp-nosed; (*fig.*) pointed, tapered.
острослóв, а *m.* wit.
остросюжéт|ный (~ен, ~на) *adj.* gripping, tense.
острóт|а, ы *f.* witticism, joke; **злáя о.** sarcasm; **плóская о.** stupid joke; **тóнкая о.** subtle crack.
острот|á, ы́ *f.* sharpness; keenness; acuteness; pungency, poignancy.
остроугóльник, а *m.* (*math.*) acute-angled figure.
остроугóл|ьный (~ен, ~ьна) *adj.* (*math.*) acute-angled.
остроýми|е, я *nt.* **1.** wit; wittiness. **2.** ingenuity.
остроýм|ный (~ен, ~на) *adj.* witty.
óстр|ый (~ *and* **остёр, ~á, ~о)** *adj.* sharp (*also fig.*); pointed (*also fig.*); acute; keen; **~ое воспалéние** (*med.*) acute inflammation; **~ое замечáние** pointed remark; **о. зáпах** acrid smell; **~ое зрéние** keen eyesight; **о. интерéс (к)** keen interest (in); **о. недостáток** acute shortage; **~ое положéние** critical situation; **о. сóус** piquant sauce; **о. сыр** strong cheese; **о. ýгол** (*math.*) acute angle; **он остёр на язы́к** (*coll.*) he has a sharp tongue.
остря́к, á *m.* wit.
осту|ди́ть, жý, ~дишь *pf.* (*of* **студи́ть** *and* **~жáть**) to cool.
остужá|ть, ю *impf. of* **остуди́ть**
оступ|áться, áюсь *impf. of* **~и́ться**
оступ|и́ться, лю́сь, ~ишься *pf.* (*of* **~áться**) to stumble.
осты́ва|ть, ю *impf. of* **осты́ть**
осты́|ть, ну, нешь *pf.* (*of* **~вáть**) to get cold; (*fig.*) to cool (down); **у вас чай ~л** your tea is cold.
ост|ь, и, *pl.* **~и, ~éй** *f.* (*bot.*) awn, beard.
осу|ди́ть, жý, ~дишь *pf.* (*of* **~ждáть**) **1.** to censure,

condemn. **2.** (*leg.*) to condemn, sentence; to convict.
осуждá|ть, ю *impf. of* **осуди́ть**
осуждéни|е, я *nt.* **1.** censure, condemnation. **2.** (*leg.*) conviction.
осуждённ|ый *p.p.p. of* **осуди́ть** *and adj.* condemned; convicted; *as n.* **о., ~ого** *nt.* convict, convicted pers.
осу́н|уться, усь, ешься *pf.* (*coll.*) (*of the face*) to grow thin, get pinched(-looking).
осуш|áть, áю *impf. of* **~и́ть**
осушéни|е, я *nt.* drainage.
осуш|и́тельный *adj. of* **~éние; о. канáл** drainage canal.
осуш|и́ть, ý, ∸ишь *pf.* (*of* **~áть**) to drain; to dry; **о. глазá** to dry one's eyes; **о. лугá** to drain meadows; **о. слёзы комý-н.** to console s.o.; **о. стакáн пи́ва** to drain a glass of beer.
осуществи́м|ый (~, ~а) *adj.* practicable, realizable, feasible.
осуществ|и́ть, лю́, и́шь *pf.* (*of* **~ля́ть**) to realize, bring about; to accomplish, carry out; to implement.
осуществ|и́ться, и́тся *pf.* (*of* **~ля́ться**) **1.** to be fulfilled, come true; **её дéтская мечтá ~и́лась** her childhood dream has come true. **2.** *pass. of* **~и́ть**
осуществлéни|е, я *nt.* realization; accomplishment; implementation.
осуществля́|ть(ся), ю(сь) *impf. of* **осуществи́ть**
осцилло́граф, а *m.* (*phys.*) oscillograph.
осцилля́тор, а *m.* (*phys.*) oscillator.
осчастли́в|ить, лю, ишь *pf.* (*of* **~ливать**) to make happy; to grace (*iron.*).
осчастли́влива|ть, ю *impf. of* **осчастли́вить**
осы́па|нный *p.p.p. of* **~ть; о. звёздами** star-studded, star-spangled.
осы́п|ать, лю, лешь *pf.* (*of* **~áть**) **1.** (*+a. and i.*) to strew (with); to shower (on); (*fig.*) to heap (on); **о. когó-н. брáнью** to heap abuse on s.o.; **о. поцелýями** to smother with kisses; **о. когó-н. удáрами** to rain blows on s.o. **2.** to pull down, knock down (*a heap of sand, etc.*). **3.** to shed (*foliage, etc.*).
осы́п|аться, люсь, лешься *pf.* (*of* **~áться**) to crumble; (*of leaves, etc.*) to fall.
осып|áть(ся), áю(сь) *impf. of* **∸ать(ся)**
о́сып|ь, и *f.* scree.
ос|ь, и, *pl.* **∸и, ~éй** *f.* **1.** axis; **земнáя о.** axis of the equator; **имéющий óбщую о.** coaxial. **2.** axle; (*tech.*) spindle; pin.
осьминóг, а *m.* (*zool.*) octopus.
осязáем|ый (~, ~а) *adj.* tangible; palpable.
осязáние, я *nt.* touch; **чу́вство ~я** a sense of touch.
осязáтел|ьный (~ен, ~ьна) *adj.* **1.** tactile, tactual; **~ьные óрганы** tactile organs. **2.** (*fig.*) tangible, palpable, sensible; **~ьные результáты** tangible results.
осязá|ть, ю *impf.* to feel.
от (ото) *prep.+g.* from; of; for **1.** (*indicates initial point, point of origin of action, prior of pair of termini, source, etc.*) **от цéнтра гóрода** from the centre of the town; **отплы́ть от бéрега** to put out from the shore; **от начáла до концá** from beginning to end; **от Пýшкина до Маякóвского** from Pushkin to Mayakovsky; **от девяти́ (часóв) до пяти́ (часóв)** from nine (o'clock) to five (o'clock); **дéти в вóзрасте от пяти́ до десяти́ лет** children from five to ten (years); **цéны от рубля́ и вы́ше** prices from a rouble upward; **бли́зко от гóрода** near the town; **на сéвер от Москвы́** to the north of Moscow; **врéмя от врéмени** from time to time; **день ото дня** from day to day; **от всей души́** with all one's heart; **от и́мени** (*+g.*) on behalf (of); **слóво, произведённое от лати́нского** a word derived from the Latin; **узнáть от дрýга** to learn from a friend; **я получи́л письмó от дóчери** I have received a letter from my daughter; **сын от прéжнего брáка** a son by a previous marriage; **жеребёнок от А. и Б.** a foal by A. out of B. **2.** (*indicates cause or instrumentality*) **вскри́кнуть от рáдости** to cry out for joy; **дрожáть от стрáха** to tremble with fear; **умерéть от гóлода** to die of hunger; **глазá, крáсные от слёз** eyes red with weeping. **3.** (*indicates date of document*) **вáше письмó от пéрвого áвгуста** your letter of the first of August. **4.** (*indicates use, purpose, or assignment*) **ключ от двéри** door key; **пýговица от пиджакá** coat button; **цепóчка от часóв** watch-chain; **рабóчий от станкá** machine-operative. **5.** for; against; **срéдство от сеннóй лихорáдки** remedy for hay-fever; **микстýра от кáшля** cough mixture; **защищáть глазá от сóлнца** to shield one's eyes from the sun; **застраховáть от огня́** to insure against fire.
от... (*also* **ото...** *and* **отъ...**) *vbl. pref. indicating* **1.** completion of action *or* task assigned. **2.** action *or* motion away from given point. **3.** (*vv. in form refl.*) action of negative character.
отáв|а, ы *f.* (*agric.*) after-grass, aftermath.
отáплива|ть, ю *impf. of* **отопи́ть**
отáр|а, ы *f.* large flock (*of sheep*).
отбáв|ить, лю, ишь *pf.* (*of* **~ля́ть**) to pour off.
отбавля́|ть, ю *impf. of* **отбáвить; хоть ~й** (*coll.*) more than enough.
отбарабáн|ить, ю, ишь *pf.* (*coll.*) to rattle off.
отбегá|ть, ю *impf. of* **отбежáть**
отбе|жáть, гý, жи́шь, гýт *pf.* (*of* **~гáть**) to run off.
отбел|ённый *p.p.p. of* **~и́ть; о. чугýн** chilled cast iron.
отбéлива|ть, ю *impf. of* **отбели́ть**
отбел|и́ть, ю́, ∸ишь *pf.* (*of* **∸ивать**) to bleach; (*tech.*) to blanch; to chill, refine.
отбéлк|а, и *f.* bleaching; (*tech.*) blanching; chilling, refining.
отбéльный *adj.* (*tech.*) blanching; chilling, refining.
отбивá|ть(ся), ю(сь) *impf. of* **отби́ть(ся)**
отби́вк|а, и *f.* **1.** marking out, delineation. **2.** whetting, sharpening.
отбивн|óй *adj.*: **~áя котлéта** (*cul.*) chop.
отбирá|ть, ю *impf. of* **отобрáть**
отби́ти|е, я *nt.* repulse; repelling.
отби́|ть, отобью́, отобьёшь *pf.* (*of* **~вáть**) **1.** to beat off, repulse, repel; **о. атáку** to beat off an attack; **о. мяч** (*sport*) to return a ball; **о. удáр** to parry a blow. **2.** to take (*by force*); to win over; (*coll.*): **о. у когó-н.** to take off s.o., do s.o. out of; **о. плéнных** to liberate prisoners; **о. покупáтелей** (*fig.*) to win customers; **он ~л у товáрища егó дéвушку** he has taken his friend's girl. **3.** to remove, dispel; **о. у когó-н. охóту к чемý-н.** to discourage s.o. from sth., take away s.o.'s inclination for sth. **4.** to break off, knock off; **о. нóсик у чáйника** to knock the spout off a tea-pot. **5.** to whet, sharpen. **6.: о. такт** to beat (out) time. **7.** to knock up; to damage by blows, by knocks; **о. рýку нелóвким удáром** to hurt one's hand with a clumsy blow. **8.** to mark out.
отби́|ться, отобью́сь, отобьёшься *pf.* (*of* **~вáться**) **1.** (**от**) to defend o.s. (against); to repulse, beat off. **2.** to drop behind, straggle; **о. от стáда** to stray from the herd; **о. от рук** (*coll.*) to get out of hand. **3.** to break off. **4.** *pass. of* **~ть**
отблáгове|стить, щу, стишь *pf. of* **благовести́ть 1.**
отблагодар|и́ть, ю́, и́шь *pf.* to show one's gratitude (to).
óтблеск, а *m.* reflection.
отбó|й, я *m.* **1.** repulse; repelling; **о. мячá** (*sport*) return; **~ю нет** (**от**; *coll.*) there is no getting rid (of). **2.** (*mil.*) retreat; **о. воздýшной тревóги** all-clear signal; **бить о.** to beat a retreat (*also fig.*); **труби́ть о.** to sound off. **3.** ringing off (*on telephone*); **дать о.** to ring off.
отбóйк|а, и *f.* (*tech.*) breaking, cutting.
отбóй|ный *adj.* **1.** *adj. of* **~ка; о. молотóк** miner's pick; **пневмати́ческий о. молотóк** pneumatic drill (*for coal-cutting*). **2.** *adj. of* **~ 3.**
отбомб|и́ться, лю́сь, и́шься *pf.* (*coll.*) to have dropped one's load (of bombs).
отбóр, а *m.* selection; **естéственный о.** (*biol.*) natural selection.
отбóрн|ый *adj.* choice, select(ed); picked; **~ые войскá** crack troops; **~ые выражéния** refined language; **~ая рýгань** choice swear-words.
отбóрочн|ый *adj.*: **~ая коми́ссия** selection board; **~ое соревновáние** (*sport*) knock-out competition.
отбóрщик, а *m.* **1.** grader, sorter. **2.** selector.
отбоя́рива|ться, юсь *impf.* (*of* **отбоя́риться**) (*coll.*) to try to escape, get out of.
отбоя́р|иться, юсь, ишься *pf.* (*of* **~иваться**) (*coll.*; **от**)

to escape (from), get rid (of), give the slip (to).

отбра́сыва|ть, ю *impf. of* **отбро́сить**

отбрива́|ть, ю *impf. of* **отбри́ть**

отбр|и́ть, е́ю, е́ешь *pf.* (*of* **~ива́ть**) (*coll.*) to rebuff, rebuke.

отбро́с|ы, ов *pl.* (*sg.* **~, ~а** *m.*) garbage, refuse; offal; **ведро́ для ~ов** dust-bin; **о. произво́дства** industrial waste; **о. о́бщества** (*fig.*) dregs of society.

отбро́|сить, шу, сишь *pf.* (*of* **отбра́сывать**) **1.** to throw off; to cast away; **о. тень** to cast a shadow. **2.** (*mil.*) to throw back, thrust back, hurl back. **3.** to give up, reject, discard; **о. мысль** to give up an idea.

отбуксир|ова́ть, у́ю *pf.* to tow off.

отбыва́ни|е, я *nt.* serving; **о. сро́ка наказа́ния** serving of a sentence.

отбыва́|ть, ю *impf. of* **отбы́ть**

отбы́ти|е, я *nt.* departure.

от|бы́ть[1], **бу́ду, бу́дешь,** *past* **~́был, ~была́, ~́было** *pf.* (*of* **~быва́ть**) to depart, leave.

от|бы́ть[2], **бу́ду, бу́дешь,** *past* **~́был, ~была́, ~́было** *pf.* (*of* **~быва́ть**) to serve (a period of); **о. наказа́ние** to serve one's sentence, do time (*in prison*); **о. во́инскую пови́нность** to serve one's time in the army, do (one's) military service.

отва́г|а, и *f.* courage, bravery.

отва́|дить, жу, дишь *pf.* (*of* **~живать**) **1.** (*+a.* **от**) to break (of), make to stop; **о. кого́-н. от пья́нства** to break s.o. of drunkenness. **2.** to scare away, drive off.

отва́жива|ть, ю *impf. of* **отва́дить**

отва́ж|иться, усь, ишься *pf.* (*+inf.*) to dare, venture; to have the courage (to).

отва́ж|ный (~ен, ~на) *adj.* courageous, brave.

отва́л[1], **а** *m.* **до ~а** (*coll.*) to satiety; **нае́сться до ~а** to stuff o.s.

отва́л[2], **а** *m.* **1.** mould-board (*of a plough*). **2.** (*mining*) dump; slag-heap; bank, terrace (*of open-cast mine*).

отва́л[3], **а** *m.* (*naut.*) putting off, pushing off, casting off.

отва́лива|ть(ся), ю(сь) *impf. of* **отвали́ть(ся)**

отвал|и́ть, ю́, ~́ишь *pf.* (*of* **~́ивать**) **1.** to heave off; to push aside. **2.** (*naut.*) to put off, push off, cast off. **3.** (*coll.*) to fork out, stump up (*a sum of money*).

отвал|и́ться, ю́сь, ~́ишься *pf.* (*of* **~́иваться**) **1.** to fall off, slip. **2.** *pass. of* **~и́ть**

отва́л|ьный *adj. of* **~**[2,3]; *as n.* **~ьная, ~ьной** *f.* (*coll., obs.*) farewell party.

отва́р, а *m.* broth; decoction; **ячме́нный о.** barley-water.

отва́рива|ть, ю *impf. of* **отвари́ть**

отвар|и́ть, ю́ ~́ишь *pf.* (*of* **~́ивать**) **1.** to boil (*cabbage, etc.*). **2.** (*tech.*) to unweld.

отварно́й *adj.* (*cul.*) boiled.

отве́д|ать, аю *pf.* (*of* **~ывать**) (*+a. or g.*) to taste; to try.

отве|дённый *p.p.p of* **~сти́**

отве́дыва|ть, ю *impf. of* **отве́дать**

отвез|ти́, у́, ёшь, *past* **~̈, ~ла́** *pf.* (*of* **отвози́ть**) to take (away); to cart away.

отверг|а́ть, а́ю *impf. of* **~́нуть**

отве́рг|нуть, ну, нешь, *past* **~, ~ла** *pf.* (*of* **~а́ть**) to reject, turn down; to repudiate; to spurn.

отвердева́|ть, ю *impf. of* **отверде́ть**

отверде́лост|ь, и *f.* hardening, callus.

отверде́лый *adj.* hardened.

отверде́|ть, ю *pf.* (*of* **~ва́ть**) to harden.

отве́ржен|ец, ца *m.* outcast.

отве́р|женный *p.p.p.* (*obs.*) *of* **~гнуть** *and adj.* outcast.

отверз|а́ть, а́ю *impf.* (*of* **~́ть**) (*obs., poet.*) to open.

отве́рз|ть, у, ешь, *past* **~, ~ла** *pf. of* **~а́ть**

отвер|ну́ть, ну́, нёшь, *pf.* (*of* **~̈тывать**) **1.** (*impf. also* **отвора́чивать**) to turn away, turn aside; **о. лицо́** to turn one's face away; **о. одея́ло** to turn down a blanket. **2.** to turn on (*a tap, etc.*). **3.** to unscrew. **4.** (*coll.*) to screw off, twist off; **он едва́ не ~ну́л мне ру́ку** he almost twisted my arm off.

отвер|ну́ться, ну́сь, нёшься *pf.* (*of* **~̈тываться**) **1.** (*impf. also* **отвора́чиваться**) to turn away, turn aside; **о. от кого́-н.** (*fig.*) to turn one's back upon s.o.; to send s.o. to Coventry. **2.** (*of a tap, etc.*) to come on. **3.** to come unscrewed.

отве́рсти|е, я *nt.* **1.** opening, aperture, orifice; hole; **входно́е о.** inlet; **выходно́е о., выпускно́е о.** outlet; **о. для опуска́ния моне́ты** slot; **о. решета́, о. си́та** mesh. **2.** (*zool.*) foramen; **заднепрохо́дное о.** (*anat.*) anus.

отве́рст|ый (~, ~а) *adj.* (*obs., poet.*) open.

отвер|те́ть, чу́, ~́тишь *pf.* (*of* **~̈тывать**) **1.** to unscrew. **2.** to screw off, twist off.

отверт|е́ться[1], **~́ится** *pf.* (*of* **~̈ываться**) to come unscrewed.

отвер|те́ться[2], **чу́сь, ~́тишься** *pf.* (*coll.*; **от**) to get off; to get out (of), wriggle out (of); **нам удало́сь о.** we managed to get out of it.

отвёртк|а, и *f.* screwdriver; **крестова́я о.** Phillips- (*propr.*) *or* cross-head screwdriver.

отвёртыва|ть(ся), ю(сь) *impf. of* **отверну́ть(ся)** *and* **отверте́ть(ся)**

отве́с, а *m.* **1.** (*tech.*) plumb, plummet; **груз ~а** bob. **2.** slope; **по ~у** plumb, perpendicularly.

отве́|сить, шу, сишь *pf.* (*of* **~шивать**) to weigh out; **о. фунт са́хару** to weigh out a pound of sugar; **о. покло́н** (*+d*) to make a low bow (to); **о. пощёчину** (*+d.*) (*fig., coll.*) to deal s.o. a slap in the face.

отве́сно *adv.* plumb; sheer.

отве́с|ный (~ен, ~на) *adj.* perpendicular; steep.

отве|сти́, ду́, дёшь, *past* **~̈л, ~ла́** *pf.* (*of* **отводи́ть**) **1.** to lead, take, conduct; **о. ло́шадь в коню́шню** to lead a horse to the stable. **2.** to draw aside, take aside; **о. от собла́зна** to lead out of temptation's way. **3.** to deflect; to draw off; **о. войска́** (*mil.*) to draw off one's troops; **о. во́ду (из)** to drain; **о. ду́шу** to unburden one's heart; **о. обвине́ние** to justify o.s.; **о. уда́р** to parry a blow; **он не мог о. глаз от неё** he could not take his eyes off her; **о. глаза́ кому́-н.** (*fig.*) to distract s.o.'s attention, pull the wool over s.o.'s eyes. **4.** to reject; (*leg.*) to challenge (*jurors, etc.*). **5.** to allot, assign.

отве́т, а *m.* **1.** answer, reply, response; **держа́ть о.** to answer; **в о. (на**+*a.*) in reply (to), in response (to). **2.** (*obs.*) responsibility; **быть в ~е (за**+*a.*) to be answerable (for); **призва́ть к ~у** to call to account.

ответв|и́ть, лю́, и́шь *pf.* (*of* **~ля́ть**) (*tech.*) to take off, tap, shunt.

ответв|и́ться, лю́сь, и́шься *pf.* (*of* **~ля́ться**) to branch off.

ответвле́ни|е, я *nt.* branch, offshoot (*also fig.*); branch pipe; (*elec.*) tap, shunt.

ответв|лённый *p.p.p. of* **~и́ть; ~лённая цепь** (*elec.*) branch circuit, derived circuit.

ответвля́|ть(ся), ю(сь) *impf. of* **ответви́ть(ся)**

отве́|тить, чу, тишь *pf.* (*of* **~ча́ть**) **1.** (**на**+*a.*) to answer, reply (to); **о. на письмо́** to answer a letter; **о. уро́к** to repeat one's lesson. **2.** (**на**+*a.* +*i.*) to answer (with), return; **о. на чьё-н. чу́вство** to return s.o.'s feelings. **3.** (**за**+*a.*) to answer (for), pay (for); **вы ~тите за э́ти слова́!** you will pay for these words!

отве́тн|ый *adj.* given in answer, answering; **о. вы́стрел** reply (to shots fired); **~ое чу́вство** response, reciprocation of feelings.

отве́тственност|ь, и *f.* responsibility; (*leg.*) amenability; **снять о. с кого́-н.** to relieve s.o. of responsibility; **привле́чь к ~и (за**+*a.*) to call to account, bring to book.

отве́тствен|ный (~, ~на) *adj.* **1.** responsible; **о. реда́ктор** editor-in-chief; **о. рабо́тник** executive. **2.** crucial; **о. моме́нт** crucial point.

отве́тств|овать, ую *impf. and pf.* (*obs.*) to answer, reply.

отве́тчик, а *m.* **1.** (*leg.*) defendant, respondent. **2.** (*coll.*) bearer of responsibility. **3.: телефо́нный о.** answerphone, telephone answering machine.

отвеча́|ть, ю *impf.* **1.** *impf. of* **отве́тить. 2.** (**за**+*a.*) to answer (for), be answerable (for). **3.** (*+d.*) to answer (to), meet, be up (to); **о. своему́ назначе́нию** to answer the purpose, be up to the mark; **о. тре́бованиям** to meet requirements.

отве́шива|ть, ю *impf. of* **отве́сить**

отви́лива|ть, ю *impf. of* **отвильну́ть**

отвильн|у́ть, у́, ёшь *pf.* (*of* **отви́ливать**) (*coll., pej.;* **от**) to dodge.

отвин|ти́ть, чу́, ти́шь *pf.* (*of* ~**чивать**) to unscrew.
отвин|ти́ться, чу́сь, ти́шься *pf.* (*of* ~**чиваться**) to unscrew, come unscrewed.
отви́нчива|ть(ся), ю(сь) *impf. of* **отвинти́ть(ся)**
отвис|а́ть, а́ю *impf.* (*of* ~**нуть**) to hang down, sag.
отви|се́ться, шу́сь, си́шься *pf.* (*coll.*): **дать пла́тью о.** to hang out a dress so as to remove the creases.
отви́слы|й *adj.* loose-hanging, baggy; **с ~ми уша́ми** lop-eared.
отви́с|нуть, ну, нешь, *past* ~, ~**ла** *pf. of* ~**а́ть**
отвлека́|ть(ся), ю(сь) *impf. of* **отвле́чь(ся)**
отвлека́|ющий *pres. part. act. of* ~**ть; ~ющее сре́дство** (*obs., med.*) revulsive, revulsant.
отвлече́ни|е, я *nt.* **1.** abstraction. **2.** distraction; **для ~я внима́ния** to distract attention. **3.** (*obs., med.*) revulsion, counter-irritation.
отвлечён|ный (~, ~на) *adj.* abstract; **~ная величина́** abstract quantity; **~ное и́мя существи́тельное** abstract noun.
отвле́|чь, ку́, чёшь, ку́т, *past* ~**к**, ~**кла́** *pf.* (*of* ~**ка́ть**) **1.** to distract, divert; **о. чьё-н. внима́ние** to divert s.o.'s attention. **2.** to abstract.
отвле́|чься, ку́сь, чёшься, ку́тся, *past* ~**кся**, ~**кла́сь** *pf.* (*of* ~**ка́ться**) **1.** to be distracted; **о. от те́мы** to digress; **его́ мы́сли ~кли́сь далеко́** his thoughts were far away. **2. (от)** to abstract o.s. (from).
отво́д, а *m.* **1.** leading, taking, conducting. **2.** taking aside; deflection; diversion; **о. воды́** draining off of water; **о. во́йск** withdrawal of troops; **для ~а глаз** (*coll.*) as a blind. **3.** rejection; (*leg.*) challenge; **дать о. кандида́ту** to reject a candidate. **4.** allotment, allocation; **полоса́ ~а** designated strip of land (*for building of rail., highway, etc.*). **5.** (*tech.*) pipe-bend, elbow. **6.** (*elec.*) tap, tapping; **о. тепла́** heat elimination.
отво|ди́ть, жу́, ~дишь *impf. of* **отвести́**
отво́дк|а, и *f.* (*tech.*) **1.** branch pipe. **2.** belt shifter.
отво́дн|ый *adj.* (*tech.*) branch; drain, outlet; **о. кана́л** drain; **о. кран** drain cock; **~ая труба́** branch pipe; outlet pipe, discharge pipe.
отво́д|ок, ка *m.* (*hort.*) cutting, layer.
отвод|я́щий *pres. part. act. of* ~**и́ть** *and adj.*: **о. (му́скул)** (*anat.*) abductor; **~я́щая труба́** (*tech.*) exhaust (pipe).
отво|ева́ть[1], **ю́ю, ю́ешь** *pf.* (*of* ~**ёвывать**) **(у)** to win back (from), reconquer (from).
отво|ева́ть[2], **ю́ю, ю́ешь** *pf.* (*coll.*) **1.** to fight, spend in fighting; **мы де́сять лет ~ева́ли** we have fought for ten years. **2.** to finish fighting, finish the war.
отвоёвыва|ть, ю *impf. of* **отвоева́ть**[1]
отво|зи́ть, жу́, ~зишь *impf. of* **отвезти́**
отвола́кива|ть, ю *impf. of* **отволо́чь**
отволо́|чь, ку́, чёшь, ку́т, *past* ~**к**, ~**кла́** *pf.* (*of* **отвола́кивать**) to drag away, drag aside.
отвора́чива|ть(ся), ю(сь) *impf. of* **отверну́ть(ся)** *and* **отвороти́ть(ся)**
отвор|и́ть, ю́, ~ишь *pf.* (*of* ~**я́ть**) to open; **о. кровь** (*med.; obs.*) to let blood.
отвор|и́ться, ю́сь, ~ишься *pf.* (*of* ~**я́ться**) to open.
отворо́т, а *m.* lapel; flap; top (*of boot*).
отворо|ти́ть, чу́, ~тишь *pf.* (*of* **отвора́чивать**) to turn away, turn aside; **о. взгляд** to avert one's gaze.
отворо|ти́ться, чу́сь, ~тишься *pf.* (*of* **отвора́чиваться**) to turn away, turn aside; **о. от кого́-н.** to look away from s.o.; (*fig.*) to turn one's back on s.o., cut s.o.
отвор|я́ть(ся), я́ю(сь) *impf. of* ~**и́ть(ся)**
отврати́тел|ьный (~ен, ~ьна) *adj.* repulsive, disgusting, loathsome; abominable.
отвра|ти́ть, щу́, ти́шь *pf.* (*of* ~**ща́ть**) **1.** to avert, stave off. **2.** (*obs.*) (+*a.* **от**) to deter (from), stay (from); **о. кого́-н. от преда́тельства** to deter s.o. from committing an act of treachery.
отвра́т|ный (~ен, ~на) *adj.* (*coll.*) = ~**и́тельный**
отвра|ща́ть, ща́ю *impf. of* ~**ти́ть**
отвраще́ни|е, я *nt.* aversion, disgust, repugnance; loathing; **внуши́ть о.** (+*d.*) to disgust, fill with disgust, repel; **пита́ть о. (к)** to have an aversion (for), be repelled (by), loathe.

отвык|а́ть, а́ю *impf. of* ~**нуть**
отвы́к|нуть, ну, нешь, *past* ~, ~**ла** *pf.* (*of* ~**а́ть**) **(от** *or* +*inf.*) to break o.s. (of the habit of), give up; to get out of the habit of; to grow out (of); **о. от куре́ния, о. кури́ть** to give up smoking; **о. от дурно́й привы́чки** to break o.s. of a bad habit.
отвя|за́ть, жу́, ~жешь *pf.* (*of* ~**зывать**) to untie, unfasten; to untether; (*naut.*) to unbend.
отвя|за́ться, жу́сь, ~жешься *pf.* (*of* ~**зываться**) **1.** to come untied, come loose. **2.** (*fig., coll.*; **от**) to get rid (of), shake off, get shot (of). **3.** (*fig., coll.*; **от**) to leave alone, leave in peace; stop nagging; **~жи́сь от меня́!** leave me alone!
отвя́зыва|ть(ся), ю(сь) *impf. of* **отвяза́ть(ся)**
отгад|а́ть, а́ю *pf.* (*of* ~**ывать**) to guess.
отга́дк|а, и *f.* answer (*to a riddle*).
отга́дчик, а *m.* (*coll.*) guesser, diviner.
отга́дыва|ть, ю *impf. of* **отгада́ть**
отгиба́|ть(ся), ю(сь) *impf. of* **отогну́ть(ся)**
отглаго́льный *adj.* (*gram.*) verbal.
отгла́|дить, жу, дишь *pf.* (*of* ~**живать**) to iron (out).
отгла́жива|ть, ю *impf. of* **отгла́дить**
отглода́|ть, ю *pf.* (*coll.*) to bite off.
отгова́рива|ть(ся), ю(сь) *impf. of* **отговори́ть(ся)**
отговор|и́ть, ю́, и́шь *pf.* (*of* **отгова́ривать**) **(от** *or* +*inf.*) to dissuade (from); **я ~и́л его́ е́хать** I have talked him out of going.
отговор|и́ться, ю́сь, и́шься *pf.* (*of* **отгова́риваться**) (+*i.*) to excuse o.s. (on the ground of); to plead; **о. нездоро́вьем** to plead ill-health.
отгово́рк|а, и *f.* excuse; pretext; **пуста́я о.** lame excuse, hollow pretence.
отголо́с|ок, ка *m.* echo (*also fig.*).
отго́н[1], **а** *m.* **1.** driving off. **2.** pasturing (*of cattle*).
отго́н[2], **а** *m.* (*tech.*) distillation products.
отго́нк|а[1], **и** *f.* driving off.
отго́нк|а[2], **и** *f.* distillation.
отгоня́|ть, ю *impf. of* **отогна́ть**
отгора́жива|ть(ся), ю(сь) *impf. of* **отгороди́ть(ся)**
отгоро|ди́ть, жу́, ~и́шь *pf.* (*of* **отгора́живать**) to fence off, partition off; **о. ши́рмой** to screen off.
отгоро|ди́ться, жу́сь, ~ди́шься *pf.* (*of* **отгора́живаться**) to fence o.s. off; (*fig., coll.*; **от**) to shut *or* cut o.s. off (from).
отго|сти́ть, щу́, сти́шь *pf.* (*coll.*; **у**) to have been a guest (of), have stayed (with).
отграни́чива|ть, ю *impf. of* **отграни́чить**
отграни́ч|ить, у, ишь *pf.* (*of* ~**ивать**) to delimit.
отгреба́|ть, ю *impf. of* **отгрести́**
отгре|сти́[1], **бу́, бёшь,** *past* ~**б**, ~**бла́** *pf.* (*of* ~**ба́ть**) to rake away.
отгре|сти́[2], **бу́, бёшь,** *past* ~**б**, ~**бла́** *pf.* (*of* ~**ба́ть**) to row off.
отгружа́|ть, ю *impf. of* **отгрузи́ть**
отгру|зи́ть, жу́, ~зи́шь *pf.* (*of* ~**жа́ть**) to ship, dispatch.
отгру́зк|а[1], **и** *f.* shipment, dispatching.
отгру́зк|а[2], **и** *f.* unloading.
отгрыз|а́ть, а́ю *impf. of* ~**ть**
отгры́з|ть, у́, ёшь, *past* ~, ~**ла** *pf.* (*of* ~**а́ть**) to bite off, gnaw off.
отгу́лива|ть, ю *impf. of* **отгуля́ть 2.**
отгул|я́ть, я́ю *pf.* (*coll.*) **1.** to have spent, to have finished (*holidays, leave, etc.*); **мы ~я́ли о́тпуск** our holidays are over. **2.** (*impf.* ~**ивать**) to take (time) off; **о. день** to take a day off.
отда|ва́ть[1]**(ся), ю́(сь), ёшь(ся)** *impf. of* **отда́ть(ся)**
отда|ва́ть[2], **ёт** *impf.* (*impers.*+*i.*; *coll.*) to taste (of); to smell (of); (*fig.*) to smack (of); **от него́ ~ёт во́дкой** he reeks of vodka; **э́то ~ёт суеве́рием** this smacks of superstition.
отдав|и́ть, лю́, ~ишь *pf.* to crush; **о. кому́-н. но́гу** to tread on s.o.'s foot.
отдале́ни|е, я *nt.* **1.** removal; (*fig.*) estrangement. **2.** distance; **держа́ть в ~и** to keep at a distance.
отдалённост|ь, и *f.* remoteness.
отдалён|ный (~, ~на) *adj.* distant, remote; **о. ро́дственник** distant relative; **~ное схо́дство** remote likeness.

отдал|и́ть, ю́, и́шь *pf.* (*of* **~я́ть**) **1.** to remove; (*fig.*) to estrange, alienate. **2.** to postpone, put off.
отдал|и́ться, ю́сь, и́шься *pf.* (*of* **~я́ться**) **1.** **(от)** to move away (from) (*also fig.*). **2.** (*fig.*) to digress; **о. от те́мы** to stray from the subject. **3.** *pass. of* **~и́ть**
отдал|я́ть(ся), я́ю(сь) *impf. of* **~и́ть(ся)**
отда́ни|е, я *nt.* **1.** giving back, returning; **о. че́сти** (*mil.*) saluting. **2.** (*eccl.*) keeping, observing (*of a festival*).
отда́рива|ть(ся), ю(сь) *impf. of* **отдари́ть(ся)**
отдар|и́ть, ю́, и́шь *pf.* (*of* **~́ивать**) (*coll.*) to give in return.
отдар|и́ться, ю́сь, и́шься *pf.* (*of* **~́иваться**) (*coll.*) to make a present in return, repay a gift.
отд|а́ть, а́м, а́шь, а́ст, ади́м, ади́те, аду́т, *past* **~́ал, ~ала́, ~́ало** *pf.* (*of* **~ава́ть**) **1.** to give back, return; **о. до́лжное кому́-н.** to render s.o. his due; **о. после́дний долг** (*+d.*) to pay the last honours; **о. себе́ отчёт** **(в**+*p.*) to be aware (of), realize; **не о. себе́ отчёта (в**+*p.*) to fail to realize. **2.** to give (up), devote; **о. жизнь нау́ке** to devote one's life to learning. **3.** (*+a. and d. or +a.* **за**+*a.*) to give in marriage (to), give away. **4.** **(в**+*a.*, **под**+*a.*) to give, put, place (= *hand over for certain purpose*); **о. кни́гу в переплёт** to have a book bound, send a book to be bound; **о. ма́льчика в шко́лу** to send (put) a small boy to school; **о. под стра́жу** to give into custody; **о. под суд** to prosecute. **5.** (*in comb. with certain nn.*) to give; to make (*or not requiring separate translation*); **о. покло́н** (*obs.*) to bow, make a bow; **о. прика́з** (*+d.*) to issue an order, give orders (to); **о. распоряже́ние** to give instructions; **о. честь** (*+d.*) to salute. **6.** (*coll.*) to sell, let have; **он мне э́то ~́ал за бесце́нок** he let me have it for a song. **7.** (*of a fire-arm*) to kick. **8.** (*fig.*; *impers.*): **мне ~́ало в спи́ну** I felt a twinge in my back. **9.** (*naut.*) to unbend; to let go; to cast off; **о. я́корь** to cast anchor, let go the anchor; **о. концы́!** let go!
отд|а́ться, а́мся, а́шься, а́стся, ади́мся, ади́тесь, аду́тся, *past* **~а́лся, ~ала́сь** *pf.* (*of* **~ава́ться**) **1.** (*+d.*) to give o.s. up (to), to devote o.s. (to); (*of a woman*) to give o.s. (to). **2.** to resound; to reverberate; to ring (*in one's ears*).
отда́ч|а, и *f.* **1.** return; payment, reimbursement. **2.**: **о. внаём** letting. **3.** (*naut.*) letting go; casting off. **4.** (*tech.*) efficiency, performance; output. **5.** (*mil.*) recoil, kick.
отдежу́р|ить, ю, ишь *pf.* **1.** to come off duty. **2.** to spend on duty; **о. во́семь часо́в** to have had eight hours on (duty).
отде́л, а *m.* **1.** department; **о. ка́дров** personnel department. **2.** section, part (*of book, periodical, etc.*).
отде́л|ать, аю *pf.* (*of* **~ывать**) **1.** to finish, put the finishing touches (to); to decorate; **о. пла́тье кружева́ми** to trim a dress with lace. **2.** (*coll.*) to give a dressing down.
отде́л|аться, аюсь *pf.* (*of* **~ываться**) **1.** **(от)** to get rid (of), get shot (of). **2.** (*+i.*) to escape (with), get off (with); **сча́стливо о.** to have a lucky escape; **о. цара́пиной** to get off with a scratch.
отделе́ни|е, я *nt.* **1.** separation. **2.** department, branch; **о. мили́ции** local police-station; **о. свя́зи** local post office. **3.** compartment, section; part (*of concert programme, etc.*); **о. шка́фа** pigeon-hole; **маши́нное о.** (*naut.*) engine-room. **4.** (*mil.*) section.
отдел|ённый[1] *p.p.p. of* **~и́ть**
отделён|ный[2] *adj. of* **~́ие 3.**; **о. команди́р** section commander.
отделе́нческий *adj.* department(al), branch.
отдели́м|ый (~, ~а) *adj.* separable.
отдели́тел|ь, я *m.* (*tech., chem.*) separator.
отдел|и́ть, ю́, ~́ишь *pf.* (*of* **~я́ть**) **1.** to separate, part; to detach. **2.** to separate off; **о. перегоро́дкой** to partition off. **3.** (*obs.*) to cut off (*with portion of estate, property, etc.*).
отдел|и́ться, ю́сь, ~́ишься *pf.* (*of* **~я́ться**) **1.** to separate, part; to get detached; to come apart; to come off. **2.** (*obs.*) to set up on one's own.
отде́лк|а, и *f.* **1.** finishing; trimming. **2.** finish, decoration; décor.
отде́лочник, а *m.* (interior) decorator.
отде́лыва|ть(ся), ю(сь) *impf. of* **отде́лать(ся)**
отде́льно *adv.* separately.
отде́льност|ь, и *f.*: **в ~и** taken separately, individually.
отде́льный *adj.* **1.** separate, individual. **2.** (*mil.*) independent.
отдел|я́ть(ся), я́ю(сь) *impf. of* **~и́ть(ся)**
отдёргива|ть, ю *impf. of* **отдёрнуть**
отдёр|нуть, ну, нешь *pf.* (*of* **~гивать**) **1.** to draw aside, pull aside; **о. занаве́ску** to draw back the curtain. **2.** to jerk back, withdraw.
отдира́|ть, ю *impf. of* **отодра́ть**
отдохнове́ни|е, я *nt.* (*obs.*) repose.
отдохн|у́ть, у́, ёшь *pf.* (*of* **отдыха́ть**) to rest; to have (take) a rest.
отдуба́|сить, шу, сишь *pf. of* **дуба́сить**
отдува́|ть, ю *impf. of* **отду́ть**
отдува́|ться, юсь *impf.* **1.** to pant, blow, puff. **2.** (*fig., coll.*; **за**+*a.*) to be answerable (for), take the rap (for).
отду́м|ать, аю *pf.* (*of* **~ывать**) (*coll.*) to change one's mind; **мы ~али перее́хать** we have changed our mind about moving.
отду́мыва|ть ю *impf. of* **отду́мать**
отду́|ть, ю, ешь *pf.* (*of* **~ва́ть**) **1.** (*coll.*) to blow away. **2.** to thrash soundly.
отду́шин|а, ы *f.* air-hole, (air) vent; (*fig.*) safety-valve.
отду́шник, а *m.* air-hole, (air) vent.
о́тдых, а *m.* rest; relaxation; holiday; **день ~а** day of rest, rest day.
отдыха́|ть, ю *impf.* (*of* **отдохну́ть**) to be resting; to be on holiday.
отдыха́|ющий *pres. part. of* **~ть**; *as n.* **о., ~ющего** *m.*; **~ющая, ~ющей** *f.* holiday-maker.
отдыш|а́ться, у́сь, ~́ишься *pf.* to recover one's breath.
отёк, а *m.* (*med.*) oedema; **о. лёгких** emphysema.
отека́|ть, ю *impf. of* **оте́чь**
отёл, а *m.* calving.
отел|и́ться, ю́сь, ~́ишься *pf. of* **тели́ться**
оте́л|ь, я *m.* hotel.
оте́ль|ный *adj. of* **~**
отепл|и́ть, ю́, и́шь *pf.* (*of* **~я́ть**) to protect against cold, make (*house, room, etc.*) proof against cold.
отепл|я́ть, я́ю *impf. of* **~и́ть**
от|е́ц, ца́ *m.* father (*also fig. in var. senses*); **на́ши ~цы́** (*fig.*) our (fore)fathers; **О. небе́сный** (*relig.*) the heavenly Father; **о. семе́йства** (*coll.*) paterfamilias; **~цы́ це́ркви** (*eccl., hist.*) the Fathers of the Church.
оте́ческий *adj.* fatherly, paternal.
оте́честв|енный *adj. of* **~о**; **~енная промы́шленность** home industry; **~енная война́** (*hist.*) the Patriotic War (*designation of Russ. operations against Napoleon in 1812*); **Вели́кая ~енная война́** the Great Patriotic War (*in former USSR, official designation of war of 1941–45 against Germany and her allies*).
оте́честв|о, а *nt.* native land, fatherland, home (country).
оте́|чь, ку́, чёшь, ку́т, *past* **~̈к, ~кла́** *pf.* (*of* **~ка́ть**) **1.** to swell, become swollen. **2.** (*of a candle*) to gutter.
от|жа́ть[1]**, отожму́, отожмёшь** *pf.* (*of* **~жима́ть**) **1.** to wring out. **2.** (*coll.*) to press back.
от|жа́ть[2]**, отожну́, отожнёшь** *pf.* (*of* **~жина́ть**) to finish harvesting.
от|же́чь, отожгу́, отожжёшь, *past* **~жёг, ~ожгла́** *pf.* (*of* **~жига́ть**) (*tech.*) to anneal.
отжива́|ть, ю *impf. of* **отжи́ть**
отжива́|ющий *pres. part. act. of* **~ть** *and adj.* moribund.
отжи́|вший *past part. act. of* **~ть** *and adj.* obsolete; outmoded.
о́тжиг, а *m.* (*tech.*) **1.** annealing. **2.** (glass) fritting.
отжига́|ть, ю *impf. of* **отже́чь**
отжима́|ть, ю *impf. of* **отжа́ть**[1]
отжина́|ть, ю *impf. of* **отжа́ть**[2]
от|жи́ть, живу́, живёшь, *past* **~́жил, ~жила́, ~́жило** *pf.* (*of* **~жива́ть**) to become obsolete, become outmoded; **о. свой век** to have had one's day; to go out of fashion.
отза́втрака|ть, ю *pf.* (*coll.*) to have had breakfast.
отзвон|и́ть, ю́, и́шь *pf.* **1.** to stop ringing; to stop striking (*of a clock*); **~и́л и с колоко́льни доло́й** (*coll.*) finished and done with. **2.** (*fig., coll.*) to rattle off.

о́тзвук, а *m.* echo (*also fig.*).
отзвуч|а́ть, и́т *pf.* to be heard no more.
о́тзыв, а *m.* **1.** opinion, judgement; **похва́льный о.** honourable mention. **2.** reference; testimonial; **дать хоро́ший о. о ко́м-н.** to give s.o. a good reference. **3.** review. **4.** (*mil.*) reply (*to password*).
отзы́в, а *m.* recall (*of diplomatic representative*).
отзыва́|ть, ю *impf.* **1.** *impf. of* **отозва́ть. 2.** (*+i.*) to taste (of); **о. го́речью** to have a bitter taste.
отзыва́|ться, юсь *impf.* **1.** *impf. of* **отозва́ться. 2.** (*+i.*) = **~ть**
отзывн|о́й *adj.*: **~ы́е гра́моты** letters of recall.
отзы́вчив|ый (~, ~а) *adj.* responsive.
оти́т, а *m.* (*med.*) otitis.
отка́з, а *m.* **1.** refusal; denial; repudiation; (*leg.*) rejection, nonsuit; **получи́ть о.** to be refused, be turned down; **не принима́ть ~а** to take no denial; **до ~а** to overflowing, to satiety; **по́лный до ~а** cram-full, full to capacity. **2. (от)** renunciation (of), giving up (of). **3.** (*tech.*) failure; **де́йствовать без ~а** to run smoothly. **4.** (*mus.*) natural.
отка|за́ть, жу́, ´~жешь *pf.* (*of* **´~зывать**) **1.** (*+d.* **в**+*p.*) to refuse, deny; **она́ ~за́ла ему́ в про́сьбе** she refused his request; **ему́ нельзя́ о. в тала́нте** there is no denying that he has talent; **не ~жи́те в любе́зности...** be so kind as .... **2.** (*+d.* **от**) to dismiss, discharge; **о. от до́ма** to forbid the house. **3.** (*obs.*) to leave, bequeath. **4.** (*tech.*) to fail, break down; (*coll.*) to conk out.
отка|за́ться, жу́сь, ´~жешься *pf.* (*of* **´~зываться**) **1. (от** *or +inf.*) to refuse, decline; to turn down; **о. от предложе́ния** to turn down a proposal; **о. от свое́й по́дписи** to deny one's signature; **о. от свои́х слов** to retract one's words; **о. от упла́ты до́лга** to repudiate a debt; **о. служи́ть** (*fig., coll.*) to be out of order; **мои́ часы́ ~за́лись служи́ть** my watch would not go; **не ~жу́сь** (*coll.*) I don't mind if I do; **не ~за́лся бы** (*coll.*) I wouldn't say no. **2.** to renounce, give up; to relinquish, abdicate; **о. от борьбы́** to give up the struggle.
отка́зни|к, а *m.* refusenik.
отка́зни|ца, ~цы *f. of* **~к**
отка́зыва|ть(ся), ю(сь) *impf.* (*of* **отказа́ть(ся)**): **ни в чём себе́ не о.** to deny o.s. nothing.
отка́лыва|ть(ся), ю(сь) *impf. of* **отколо́ть(ся)**
отка́пыва|ть, ю *impf. of* **откопа́ть**
отка́рмлива|ть, ю *impf. of* **откорми́ть**
отка́т, а *m.* (*mil.*) recoil.
отка|ти́ть, чу́, ´~тишь *pf.* (*of* **´~тывать**) **1.** to roll away. **2.** (*in coalmines, etc.*) to haul; to tram, truck.
отка|ти́ться, чу́сь, ´~тишься *pf.* (*of* **´~тываться**) **1.** to roll away. **2.** (*mil.*; *fig., coll.*) to roll back, be forced back.
отка́тк|а, и *f.* (*in coal-mines, etc.*) haulage; trucking.
отка́тчик, а *m.* haulage-man.
откач|а́ть, а́ю *pf.* (*of* **´~ивать**) **1.** to pump out. **2.** to resuscitate (*a pers. saved from drowning*).
отка́чива|ть, ю *impf. of* **откача́ть**
откачн|у́ть, у́, ёшь *pf.* **1.** to swing to one side. **2.** (*fig., coll.*; *impers.*) **его́ ~у́ло от бы́вших его́ собуты́льников** he has drifted away from his former drinking companions.
откачн|у́ться, у́сь, ёшься *pf.* (*coll.*) **1.** to swing to one side. **2.** (*of a pers.*) to reel back; to slump back. **3.** (*fig.*; **от**) to swing away (from), turn away (from).
отка́шл|ивать, иваю *impf. of* **~януть**
отка́шл|иваться, иваюсь *impf. of* **~яться**
отка́шл|януть, яну, янешь *pf.* (*of* **~ивать**) to hawk up.
отка́шл|яться, яюсь *pf.* (*of* **~иваться**) to clear one's throat.
отквит|а́ть, а́ю *pf.* (*of* **´~ывать**) (*coll.*; *+d.*) to settle accounts (with), give as good as one gets.
откви́тыва|ть, ю *impf. of* **отквита́ть**
откидно́й *adj.* folding, collapsible.
отки́дыва|ть(ся), ю(сь) *impf. of* **отки́нуть(ся)**
отки́|нуть, ну, нешь *pf.* (*of* **~дывать**) **1.** to throw away; to cast away (*also fig.*). **2.** to turn back, fold back.
отки́|нуться, нусь, нешься *pf.* (*of* **~дываться**) **1.** to lean back; to recline, settle back. **2.** *pass. of* **~нуть**
откла́дыва|ть, ю *impf. of* **отложи́ть**
откла́нива|ться, юсь *impf. of* **откла́няться**
откла́н|яться, яюсь *pf.* (*of* **~иваться**) (*obs.*) to take one's leave.
откле́ива|ть(ся), ю(сь) *impf. of* **откле́ить(ся)**
откле́|ить, ю, ишь *pf.* (*of* **~ивать**) to unstick.
откле́|иться, ится *pf.* (*of* **~иваться**) **1.** to come unstuck. **2.** *pass. of* **~ить**
о́тклик, а *m.* **1.** response; (*fig.*) comment. **2.** (*fig.*) echo; repercussion.
отклик|а́ться, а́юсь *impf.* (*of* **´~нуться**) **(на**+*a.*) to answer, respond (to) (*also fig.*).
откли́к|нуться, нусь, нешься *pf. of* **~а́ться**
отклоне́ни|е, я *nt.* **1.** deviation; divergence; **о. от те́мы** digression. **2.** declining, refusal. **3.** (*phys.*) deflection, declination; error; diffraction; **вероя́тное о.** probable error; **магни́тное о.** deflection of the needle; **у́гол ~я** angle of deviation.
отклон|и́ть, ю́, ´~ишь *pf.* (*of* **~я́ть**) **1.** to deflect. **2.** to decline; **о. попра́вку** to vote down an amendment; **о. предложе́ние** to decline an offer.
отклон|и́ться, ю́сь, ´~ишься *pf.* (*of* **~я́ться**) **1.** to deviate; to diverge; to swerve; **о. от те́мы** to digress. **2.** *pass. of* **~и́ть**
отключ|а́ть, а́ю *impf. of* **~и́ть**
отключ|ённый *p.p.p. of* **~и́ть** *and adj.* (*elec.*) dead; **опера́ция проводи́мая на ~ённом се́рдце** open-heart operation.
отключ|и́ть, у́, и́шь *pf.* (*of* **~а́ть**) (*elec.*) to cut off, disconnect; **о. телефо́нный аппара́т** to cut off a telephone.
отковы́рива|ть, ю *impf. of* **отковыря́ть**
отковыр|я́ть, я́ю *pf.* (*of* **´~ивать**) to pick off.
откозыря́|ть[1], ю *pf.* (*coll.*; *+d.*) to salute.
откозыря́|ть[2], ю *pf.* (*coll.*; *cards*) to play a trump in reply.
отко́л, а *m.* (*fig.*; *pol., etc.*) split; splitting, splintering, breaking away.
отко́л|е *adv.* = **~ь**
отколо|ти́ть, чу́, ´~тишь *pf.* **1.** to knock off. **2.** to beat up.
откол|о́ть, ю́, ´~ешь *pf.* (*of* **отка́лывать**) **1.** to break off; to chop off. **2.** to unpin. **3.** (*coll., pej.*): **о. глу́пость** to play a stupid trick; **о. словцо́** to make a wisecrack.
откол|о́ться, ю́сь, ´~ешься *pf.* (*of* **отка́лываться**) **1.** to break off. **2.** to come unpinned *or* undone. **3.** (*fig.*) to break away; to cut o.s. off.
отколуп|а́ть, а́ю *pf.* (*of* **´~ывать**) to pick off.
отколу́пыва|ть, ю *impf. of* **отколупа́ть**
отко́ль *adv.* (*obs.*) whence, where from.
откомандир|ова́ть, у́ю *pf.* (*of* **~о́вывать**) **1.** to detach; to post (*to new duties or establishment*). **2. (за**+*i.*) (*coll.*) to send (*to fetch*).
откомандиро́выва|ть, ю *impf. of* **откомандирова́ть**
откопа́|ть, ю *pf.* (*of* **отка́пывать**) **1.** to dig out; to exhume, disinter. **2.** (*fig., coll.*) to dig up, unearth.
отко́рм, а *m.* fattening (up).
откорм|и́ть, лю́, ´~ишь *pf.* (*of* **отка́рмливать**) to fatten (up).
отко́рм|ленный *p.p.p. of* **~и́ть** *and adj.* fat, fatted, fattened; **о. скот** fat stock.
отко́с, а *m.* slope (*esp. of rail. embankment*); **о. холма́** hillside; **пусти́ть по́езд под о.** to derail a train; **у́гол есте́ственного ~а** (*phys.*) angle of rest.
откреп|и́ть, лю́, и́шь *pf.* (*of* **~ля́ть**) **1.** to unfasten, untie. **2.** to strike off the register.
откреп|и́ться, лю́сь, и́шься *pf.* (*of* **~ля́ться**) **1.** to become unfastened. **2.** to remove one's name (*from a register, etc.*).
открепля́|ть(ся), ю(сь) *impf. of* **открепи́ть(ся)**
откре́щива|ться, юсь *impf.* (*coll.*; **от**) to disown; to refuse to have anything to do (with).
открове́ни|е, я *nt.* revelation.
открове́ннича|ть, ю *impf.* (*coll.*; **с**+*i.*) to be candid (with), be frank (with).
открове́нност|ь, и *f.* candour, frankness; bluntness, outspokenness; *pl.* (*coll.*) candid revelations.
открове́н|ный (~ен, ~на) *adj.* **1.** candid, frank; blunt, outspoken. **2.** open, unconcealed; **~ная неприя́знь** unconcealed hostility. **3.** (*coll.*; *of dress*) revealing.

откру|ти́ть, чу́, ∠тишь *pf.* (*of* **∠чивать**) to untwist; **о. кран** to turn off a tap.

откру|ти́ться, чу́сь, ∠тишься *pf.* (*of* **∠чиваться**) **1.** to come untwisted. **2.** (*coll.*; **от**) to get out (of).

откру́чива|ть(ся), ю(сь) *impf. of* **открути́ть(ся)**

открыва́лк|а, и *f.* **1.** tin- *or* can-opener. **2.** corkscrew.

открыва́|ть(ся), ю(сь) *impf. of* **откры́ть(ся)**

откры́л|ок, ка *m.* (*aeron.*) stub-wing.

откры́ти|е, я *nt.* **1.** opening. **2.** discovery.

откры́тк|а, и *f.* post-card; **о. с ви́дом** picture post-card.

откры́то *adv.* (*in var. senses*) openly; **жить о.** (*obs.*) to keep open house.

откры́т|ый *p.p.p. of* **~ь** *and adj.* (*in var. senses*) open; **в ~ую** (*cards and fig.*) showing one's hand; **на ~ом во́здухе, под ~ым не́бом** out of doors, in the open air; **с ~ыми глаза́ми** (*fig.*) with open eyes; **при ~ых двеpя́х** open to the public; **о. дом** (*fig.*) open house; **~ое заседа́ние** public sitting; **~ое мо́ре** the open sea; **~ое письмо́** (*i*) post-card, (*ii*) open letter; **~ое пла́тье** low-necked dress; **~ые го́рные рабо́ты** opencast mining; **~ая сце́на** open-air stage.

откр|ы́ть, о́ю, о́ешь *pf.* (*of* **~ыва́ть**) **1.** (*in var. senses*) to open; **о. кому́-н. глаза́ на что-н.** (*fig.*) to open s.o.'s eyes to sth.; **о. кровь** (*med.*; *obs.*) to let blood; **о. ми́тинг** to open a meeting; **о. ого́нь** (*mil.*) to open fire; **о. па́мятник** to unveil a monument; **о. счёт** to open an account. **2.** to uncover, reveal (*also fig.*); **о. грудь** to bare one's breast; **о. ду́шу** to lay bare one's heart; **о. ка́рты** (*fig.*) to show one's hand; **о. секре́т** to reveal a secret. **3.** to discover; **о. Аме́рику** (*fig., iron.*) to retail stale news. **4.** to turn on (*gas, water, etc.*).

откр|ы́ться, о́юсь, о́ешься *pf.* (*of* **~ыва́ться**) **1.** to open. **2.** to come to light, be revealed; **пе́ред на́ми ~ы́лся великоле́пный вид а** magnificent view unfolded before us. **3.** (*+d.*) to confide (in, to). **4.** *pass. of* **~ы́ть**

отксе́р|ить, ю, ишь *pf. of* **ксе́рить**

отку́да *adv.* (*interrog.*) whence, where from; (*rel.*) whence, from which; **о. вы?** where do you come from?; where are you from?; **о. вы об э́том зна́ете?** how do you come to know about it?; **о. ни возьми́сь** (*coll.*) quite unexpectedly, suddenly.

отку́да-либо *adv.* from somewhere or other.

отку́да-нибудь *adv.* = **отку́да-либо**

отку́да-то *adv.* from somewhere.

о́ткуп, а, *pl.* **~а́** *m.* (*hist.*) farming (*of revenues, etc.*); **взять на о.** to farm; **отда́ть на о.** to farm out (*also fig.*).

откуп|а́ть(ся), а́ю(сь) *impf. of* **~и́ть(ся)**

откуп|и́ть, лю́, ∠ишь *pf.* (*of* **~а́ть**) to pay up.

откуп|и́ться, лю́сь, ∠ишься *pf.* (*of* **~а́ться**) (**от**) to pay off.

отку́порива|ть, ю *impf. of* **отку́порить**

отку́пор|ить, ю, ишь *pf.* (*of* **~ивать**) to uncork; to open (*a bottle*).

отку́порк|а, и *f.* opening, uncorking.

откупщи́к, а́ *m.* tax-farmer.

отку|си́ть, шу́, ∠сишь *pf.* (*of* **∠сывать**) to bite off; to snap off (*with pincers, etc.*).

отку́сыва|ть, ю *impf. of* **откуси́ть**

отку́ша|ть, ю *pf.* (*obs.*) **1.** to have finished eating. **2.** to eat; to try (*food*); **позва́ть о.** to invite to a meal.

отлага́тельств|о, а *nt.* delay; procrastination; **де́ло не те́рпит ~а** the matter is urgent.

отлага́|ть(ся), ю(сь) *impf. of* **отложи́ть(ся)**

отлакир|ова́ть, у́ю *pf. of* **лакирова́ть**

отла́мыва|ть(ся), ю(сь) *impf. of* **отлома́ть(ся)** *and* **отломи́ть(ся)**

отлега́|ть, ю *impf. of* **отле́чь**

отлеж|а́ть, у́, и́шь *pf.* (*of* **∠ивать**): **я ~а́л но́гу** my foot has gone to sleep.

отлеж|а́ться, у́сь, и́шься *pf.* **1.** to lie up; to rest (*in bed*). **2.** to lie, be stored (*in order to season, ripen, etc.*).

отлёжива|ть(ся), ю(сь) *impf. of* **отлежа́ть(ся)**

отлеп|и́ть, лю́, ∠ишь *pf.* (*of* **~ля́ть**) (*coll.*) to unstick, take off (*sth. adhesive*).

отлеп|и́ться, ∠ится *pf.* (*of* **~ля́ться**) (*coll.*) to come unstuck, come off.

отлепля́|ть(ся), ю(сь) *impf. of* **отлепи́ть(ся)**

отлёт, а *m.* flying away; departure (*of aircraft*); **быть на ~е** to be about to leave, be on the point of departure; **держа́ть на ~е** to hold in one's outstretched hand; **держа́ться на ~е** (*coll.*) to hold o.s. aloof; to be standoffish; **дом на ~е** house standing by itself.

отлета́|ть[1], ю *pf.* **1.** to have completed a flight. **2.** (*coll.*) to have been flying (*for a given period*); **он ~л два́дцать лет** he has twenty years' flying experience.

отлет|а́ть[2], а́ю *impf. of* **~е́ть**

отле|те́ть, чу́, ти́шь *pf.* (*of* **~та́ть[2]**) **1.** to fly (away, off); (*fig.*) to fly, vanish. **2.** to rebound, bounce back. **3.** (*coll.*; *of buttons, etc.*) to come off.

отл|е́чь, я́гу, я́жешь, я́гут, *past* **~ёг, ~егла́** *pf.* (*of* **~ега́ть**) **1.** (*obs.*; **от**) to move away (from). **2.** (*coll.*; *impers.*): **у неё ~егло́ от се́рдца** she felt relieved; she felt as if a weight had been lifted from her.

отли́в[1], а *m.* ebb, ebb-tide.

отли́в[2], а *m.* tint; play of colours; **с золоты́м ~ом** shot with gold.

отлива́|ть[1], ю *impf. of* **отли́ть**

отлива́|ть[2], ет *impf.* (*+i.*) to be shot (*with a colour*).

отли́вк|а, и *f.* (*tech.*) **1.** casting, founding. **2.** cast, ingot, moulding.

отливн|о́й *adj.* (*tech.*) cast, founded, moulded; **~а́я печь** founding furnace.

отлип|а́ть, а́ет *impf. of* **∠нуть**

отли́п|нуть, нет, *past* **~, ~ла** *pf.* (*of* **~а́ть**) to come off, come unstuck.

отли́т|ый (о́тлит, ~а́, о́тлито *and* **~, ~а́ ~о)** *p.p.p. of* **~ь; в ~ом ви́де** (*tech.*) as cast.

отли́ть, отолью́, отольёшь, *past* **о́тли́л, отлила́, о́тли́ло** *pf.* (*of* **отлива́ть[1]**) **1.** (*+a. or g.*) to pour off; to pump out. **2.** (*tech.*) to cast, found. **3.** (*vulg.*) to urinate.

отлич|а́ть, а́ю *impf. of* **~и́ть**

отлич|а́ться, а́юсь *impf.* **1.** (*pf.* **~и́ться**) to distinguish o.s., excel (*also joc., iron.*). **2.** (*impf. only*) (**от**) to differ (from). **3.** (*impf. only*) (*+i.*) to be notable (for).

отли́чи|е, я *nt.* **1.** difference, distinction; **знак ~я** distinguishing feature; (*mil.*) order, decoration; **в о. от** in contradistinction to. **2.** distinction (*as grade of merit*); distinguished services; **получи́ть дипло́м с ~ем** to obtain a distinction (*in university examination, etc.*).

отличи́тельный *adj.* distinctive; distinguishing; **о. при́знак** distinguishing feature.

отлич|и́ть, у́, и́шь *pf.* (*of* **~а́ть**) **1.** to distinguish; **о. одно́ от друго́го** to tell one thing from another. **2.** to single out.

отлич|и́ться, у́сь, и́шься *pf. of* **~а́ться**

отли́чник, а *m.* **1.** pupil *or* student obtaining 'excellent' marks. **2.: о. произво́дства** exemplary worker.

отли́чно 1. *adv.* excellently; perfectly; extremely well; **о. знать** to know perfectly well; **он о. понима́ет по-ру́сски** he understands Russian perfectly. **2.** *n.*; *nt. indecl.* 'excellent' mark (*in school, etc.*).

отли́ч|ный (~ен, ~на) *adj.* **1.** (*obs.*) (**от**) different (from). **2.** excellent; perfect; extremely good; **~но!** excellent!

отло́г|ий (~, ~а) *adj.* sloping.

отло́гост|ь, и *f.* slope.

отло́|же *comp. of* **~гий**

отложе́ни|е, я *nt.* **1.** secession. **2.** sediment, precipitation; (*geol.*) deposit.

отлож|и́ть, у́, и́шь *pf.* **1.** (*impf.* **откла́дывать**) to put aside, set aside; to put away, put by; **о. на чёрный день** to put by for a rainy day. **2.** (*impf.* **откла́дывать** *and* **отлага́ть**) to put off, postpone; **о. па́ртию** to adjourn a game; **о. реше́ние** to suspend judgement; **о. в до́лгий я́щик** to shelve. **3.** (*impf.* **откла́дывать**) (*of insects*) to lay. **4.** (*impf.* **откла́дывать**) (*obs.*) to turn back, turn down. **5.** (*impf.* **откла́дывать**) to unharness. **6.** (*impf.* **отлага́ть**) (*geol.*) to deposit.

отлож|и́ться, у́сь, ∠ишься *pf.* (*of* **отлага́ться**) **1.** (*obs.*; **от**) to detach o.s. (from); to separate (from); (*pol.*) to secede. **2.** (*geol.*) to deposit; to be deposited.

отложно́й *adj.*: **о. воротни́к** turn-down collar.

отлома́|ть, ю *pf.* (*of* **отла́мывать**) to break off.

отлома́|ться, юсь *pf.* (*of* **отла́мываться**) to break off.
отлом|и́ть(ся), лю́(сь), ⁓ишь(ся) *pf.* = **⁓а́ть(ся)**
отлуп|и́ть, лю́, ⁓ишь *pf. of* **лупи́ть**[2]
отлупц|ева́ть, у́ю *pf. of* **лупцева́ть**
отлуч|а́ть(ся), а́ю(сь) *impf. of* **отлучи́ть(ся)**
отлуче́ни|е, я *nt.* (*eccl. and fig.*) excommunication.
отлуч|и́ть, у́, и́шь *pf.* (*of* **⁓а́ть**) (*obs.*; **от**) to separate *or* remove (from); **о. (от це́ркви)** (*eccl.*) to excommunicate.
отлуч|и́ться, у́сь, и́шься *pf.* (*of* **⁓а́ться**) **1.** to absent o.s. **2.** *pass. of* **⁓и́ть**
отлу́чк|а, и *f.* absence; **самово́льная о.** (*mil.*) absence without leave (*abbr.* AWOL); **быть в ⁓е** to be absent, be away.
отлы́нива|ть, ю *impf.* (*coll.*; **от**) to shirk.
отма́лчива|ться, юсь *impf. of* **отмолча́ться**
отма́тыва|ть, ю *impf. of* **отмота́ть**
отма|ха́ть[1]**, шу́, ⁓шешь** *pf.* (*of* **⁓хивать**) **1.** to stop waving. **2.: о. ру́ки** to tire one's arms by waving.
отмаха́|ть[2]**, ю** *pf.* (*coll.*) to cover (*a distance*); **за день мы ⁓ли свы́ше тридцати́ миль** in the day we covered more than thirty miles.
отма́хива|ть(ся), ю(сь) *impf. of* **отмаха́ть**[1] *and* **отмахну́ть(ся)**
отмах|ну́ть, ну́, нёшь *pf.* (*of* **⁓ивать**) (*coll.*) to wave away, brush off (*with one's hand*).
отмах|ну́ться, ну́сь, нёшься *pf.* (*of* **⁓иваться**) **(от) 1.** = **⁓ну́ть; о. от комаро́в** to brush mosquitoes off. **2.** (*fig.*) to brush aside.
отма́чива|ть, ю *impf. of* **отмочи́ть**
отмеж|ева́ть, у́ю *pf.* (*of* **⁓ёвывать**) to mark off, draw a boundary line (between).
отмеж|ева́ться, у́юсь *pf.* (*of* **⁓ёвываться**) **1. (от)** to dissociate o.s. (from); to refuse to acknowledge. **2.** *pass. of* **⁓ева́ть**
отмежёвыва|ть(ся), ю(сь) *impf. of* **отмежева́ть(ся)**
о́тмел|ь, и *f.* (sand-)bar, (sand-)bank.
отме́н|а, ы *f.* abolition; abrogation, repeal, revocation; cancellation, countermand; **о. крепостно́го пра́ва** abolition of serfdom; **о. зако́на** repeal of a law; **о. спекта́кля** cancellation of a show.
отмен|и́ть, ю́, ⁓ишь *pf.* (*of* **⁓я́ть**) to abolish; to abrogate, repeal, revoke, rescind; to cancel, countermand; (*leg.*) to disaffirm.
отме́н|ный (⁓ен, ⁓на) *adj.* excellent.
отмен|я́ть, я́ю *impf. of* **⁓и́ть**
отмер|е́ть, отомрёт, *past* **о́тмер, ⁓ла́, о́тмерло** *pf.* (*of* **отмира́ть**) to die off; (*fig.*) to die out, die away.
отмерз|а́ть, а́ет *impf. of* **⁓нуть**
отмёрз|нуть, нет, *past* **⁓, ⁓ла** *pf.* (*of* **⁓а́ть**) to freeze; **ру́ки у меня́ ⁓ли** my hands are frozen.
отме́рива|ть, ю *impf. of* **отме́рить**
отме́р|ить, ю, ишь *pf.* (*of* **⁓ивать** *and* **⁓я́ть**) to measure off.
отмер|я́ть, я́ю *impf.* = **⁓ивать**
отме|сти́, ту́, тёшь, *past* **⁓л, ⁓ла́** *pf.* (*of* **⁓та́ть**) to sweep aside (*also fig.*).
отме́стк|а, и *f.* (*coll.*) revenge; **в ⁓у** in revenge.
отмета́|ть, ю *impf. of* **отмести́**
отме́тин|а, ы *f.* mark; (*on forehead of horse, etc.*) star.
отме́|тить, чу, тишь *pf.* (*of* **⁓ча́ть**) **1.** to mark, note; to make a note (of); **о. пти́чкой** to tick off. **2.** to point to, mention, record; **о. чьи-н. по́двиги** to point to s.o.'s feats. **3.** to register (out), sign out (*departing tenant, etc.*). **4.** to celebrate, mark by celebration.
отме́|титься, чусь, тишься *pf.* (*of* **⁓ча́ться**) **1.** to sign one's name (*on a list*). **2.** to register (out), sign out (*on departure*).
отме́тк|а, и *f.* **1.** note. **2.** (*in school or examinations*) mark.
отме́тчик, а *m.* marker.
отмеча́|ть(ся), ю(сь) *impf. of* **отме́тить(ся)**
отмира́ни|е, я *nt.* dying off; dying away, fading away, withering away.
отмобилиз|ова́ть, у́ю *pf.* (*coll.*) to mobilize totally.
отмок|а́ть, а́ет *impf. of* **⁓нуть**
отмо́к|нуть, нет, *past* **⁓, ⁓ла** *pf.* (*of* **⁓а́ть**) **1.** to grow wet. **2.** to soak off.
отмолч|а́ться, у́сь, и́шься *pf.* (*of* **отма́лчиваться**) (*coll.*) to keep silent, say nothing.
отмора́жива|ть, ю *impf. of* **отморо́зить**
отморо́жени|е, я *nt.* frost-bite.
отморо́|женный *p.p.p of* **⁓зить** *and adj.* frost-bitten.
отморо́|зить, жу, зишь *pf.* (*of* **отмора́живать**) to injure by frost-bite; **я ⁓зил себе́ у́ши** my ears are frost-bitten.
отмота́|ть, ю *pf.* (*of* **отма́тывать**) to unwind.
отмоч|и́ть, у́, ⁓ишь *pf.* (*of* **отма́чивать**) **1.** to unstick by wetting. **2.** to soak, steep. **3.** (*coll.*) to do, say (*sth. ludicrous or outrageous*).
отмсти́ть = **отомсти́ть**
отмще́ни|е, я *nt.* (*obs.*) vengeance.
отмыва́|ть(ся), ю(сь) *impf. of* **отмы́ть(ся)**
отмыка́|ть(ся), ю(сь) *impf. of* **отомкну́ть(ся)**
отм|ы́ть, о́ю, о́ешь *pf.* (*of* **⁓ыва́ть**) **1.** to wash clean. **2.** to wash off, wash away.
отм|ы́ться, о́юсь, о́ешься *pf.* (*of* **⁓ыва́ться**) **1.** to wash o.s. clean. **2.** (*of dirt, etc.*) to come out, come off.
отмы́чк|а, и *f.* pass key, master key; lock-pick.
отмяк|а́ть, а́ет, *impf. of* **⁓нуть**
отмя́к|нуть, нет, *past* **⁓, ⁓ла** *pf.* (*of* **⁓а́ть**) to grow soft.
отне́кива|ться, юсь *impf.* (*coll.*) to refuse.
отнес|ти́, у́, ёшь, *past* **⁓, ⁓ла́** *pf.* (*of* **относи́ть**) **1. (в+*a.*, к)** to take (to). **2.** to carry away, carry off; (*impers.*): **ло́дку ⁓ло́ тече́нием** the boat was carried away by the current. **3.** (*coll.*) to cut off. **4. (к)** to ascribe (to), attribute (to), refer (to); **ру́копись ⁓ли́ к пя́тому ве́ку** the manuscript was believed to date from the fifth century; **мы ⁓ли́ его́ раздражи́тельность на счёт глухоты́** we put his irritability down to his deafness.
отнес|ти́сь, у́сь, ёшься, *past* **⁓ся, ⁓ла́сь** *pf.* (*of* **относи́ться**) **(к) 1.** to treat; to regard; **хорошо́ о. к кому́-н.** to treat s.o. well, be nice to s.o.; **скепти́чески о. к предположе́нию** to be sceptical about an hypothesis; **как вы ⁓ли́сь к э́той ле́кции?** what did you think of the lecture? **2.** (*obs.*) to apply (to).
отникелир|ова́ть, у́ю *pf. of* **никелирова́ть**
отнима́|ть(ся), ю(сь) *impf. of* **отня́ть(ся)**
относи́тельно 1. *adv.* relatively. **2.** *prep.* (+*g.*) concerning, about, with regard to.
относи́тельност|ь, и *f.* relativity; **тео́рия ⁓и Эйнште́йна** Einstein's Theory of Relativity.
относи́тел|ьный (⁓ен, ⁓ьна) *adj.* relative; **⁓ьное местоиме́ние** (*gram.*) relative pronoun.
отно|си́ть, шу́, ⁓сишь *impf. of* **отнести́**
отно|си́ться, шу́сь, ⁓сишься *impf.* **1.** *impf. of* **отнести́сь. 2.** *impf. only* **(к)** to concern, have to do (with), relate (to); **э́то к де́лу не ⁓сится** that's beside the point, that is irrelevant; **два ⁓сится к трём как шесть к девяти́** (*math.*) two is to three as six is to nine. **3.** *impf. only* **(к)** to date (from); **храм э́тот ⁓сится к двена́дцатому ве́ку** this church dates from the twelfth century.
отноше́ни|е, я *nt.* **1. (к)** attitude (to); treatment (of); **внима́тельное о. к ста́рым** consideration for the old; **у него́ стра́нное о. к же́нщинам** he has a strange attitude to women. **2.** relation; respect; **име́ть о. к чему́-н.** to bear a relation to sth., have a bearing on sth.; **не име́ть ⁓я (к)** to bear no relation (to), have nothing to do (with); **в ⁓и** (+*g.*), **по ⁓ю (к)** with respect (to), with regard (to); **в не́которых ⁓ях** in some respects. **3.** (*pl.*) relations; terms; **дипломати́ческие ⁓я** diplomatic relations; **быть в дру́жеских ⁓ях (с**+*i.*) to be on friendly terms (with). **4.** (*math.*) ratio; **в прямо́м (обра́тном) ⁓и** in direct (inverse) ratio. **5.** (*official*) letter, memorandum.
отны́не *adv.* (*obs.*) henceforth, henceforward.
отню́дь *adv.* by no means, not at all.
отня́ти|е, я *nt.* taking away; **о. руки́** amputation of an arm; **о. от груди́** weaning.
от|ня́ть, ниму́, ни́мешь, *past* **⁓нял, ⁓няла́, ⁓няло** *pf.* (*of* **⁓нима́ть**) **1.** to take (away); **о. от груди́** to wean; **о. жизнь у кого́-н.** to take s.o.'s life; **от шести́ о. три** to take away three from six; **э́то ⁓няло у меня́ три часа́** it took me three hours. **2.** to amputate.

от|ня́ться, ни́мется, *past* **~ня́лся, ~няла́сь** *pf.* (*of* **~нима́ться**) to be paralyzed; **у него́ ~няла́сь пра́вая рука́** he has lost the power of his right arm; **у неё ~ня́лся язы́к** she has lost the power of speech.

ото *prep.* = **от**

ото... *vbl. pref.* = **от...**

отобе́да|ть, ю *pf.* **1.** to have finished dinner. **2.** (*obs.*) to dine, have dinner.

отобража́|ть, ю *impf. of* **отобрази́ть**

отображе́ни|е, я *nt.* reflection; representation.

отобра|зи́ть, жу́, зи́шь *pf.* (*of* **~жа́ть**) to reflect; to represent.

от|обра́ть, беру́, берёшь, *past* **~обра́л, ~обрала́, ~обра́ло** *pf.* (*of* **отбира́ть**) **1.** to take (away); to seize; **о. биле́ты** to collect tickets; **о. показа́ние у свиде́теля** (*leg.*) to take a deposition from a witness. **2.** to select, pick out.

отова́рива|ть, ю *impf. of* **отова́рить**

отова́р|ить, ю, ишь *pf.* (*of* **~ивать**) to pledge goods in support of; **о. чек** to issue goods against a sale receipt.

отовсю́ду *adv.* from everywhere, from every quarter.

от|огна́ть[1]**, гоню́, го́нишь,** *past* **~огна́л, ~огнала́, ~огна́ло** *pf.* (*of* **~гоня́ть**) to drive off; to keep off; (*fig.*) to suppress.

от|огна́ть[2]**, гоню́, го́нишь,** *past* **~огна́л, ~огнала́, ~огна́ло** *pf.* (*of* **~гоня́ть**) (*chem.*) to distill (off).

отогн|у́ть, у́, ёшь *pf.* (*of* **отгиба́ть**) to bend back; to flange.

отогн|у́ться, у́сь, ёшься *pf.* (*of* **отгиба́ться**) to bend back.

отогрева́|ть(ся), ю(сь) *impf. of* **отогре́ть(ся)**

отогре́|ть, ю *pf.* (*of* **~ва́ть**) to warm.

отогре́|ться, юсь *pf.* (*of* **~ва́ться**) to warm o.s.

отодвига́|ть(ся), ю(сь) *impf. of* **отодви́нуть(ся)**

отодви́|нуть, ну, нешь *pf.* (*of* **~га́ть**) **1.** to move aside. **2.** (*fig.*) to put off, put back.

отодви́|нуться, нусь, нешься *pf.* (*of* **~га́ться**) **1.** to move aside. **2.** *pass. of* **~нуть**

от|одра́ть, деру́, дерёшь, *past* **~одра́л, ~одрала́, ~одра́ло** *pf.* (*of* **~дира́ть**) **1.** to tear off, rip off. **2.** (*coll.*) to flog; **о. кого́-н. за́ уши** to pull s.o.'s ears.

отож(д)еств|и́ть, лю́, и́шь *pf.* (*of* **~ля́ть**) to identify.

отож(д)ествля́|ть, ю *impf. of* **отож(д)естви́ть**

отожжённый *p.p.p. of* **отже́чь** *and adj.* (*tech.*) annealed.

от|озва́ть, зову́, зовёшь, *past* **~озва́л, ~озвала́, ~озва́ло** *pf.* (*of* **~зыва́ть**) **1.** to take aside. **2.** to recall (*a diplomatic representative*).

от|озва́ться, зову́сь, зовёшься, *past* **~озва́лся, ~озвала́сь, ~озва́ло́сь** *pf.* (*of* **~зыва́ться**) **1.** (**на**+*a.*) to answer; to respond (to). **2.** (**о**+*p.*) to speak (of); **рецензе́нты хорошо́ ~озвали́сь о его́ второ́й кни́ге** his second book was well received by (received good notices from) the reviewers. **3.** (**на**+*a.*) to tell (on, upon); **деторожде́ние ~озвало́сь на её здоро́вье** child-bearing has told on her health.

ото|йти́, йду́, йдёшь, *past* **~шёл, ~шла́** *pf.* (*of* **отходи́ть**[1]) **1.** to move away; to move off; (*of trains, etc.*) to leave, depart. **2.** to withdraw; to recede; (*mil.*) to withdraw, fall back; (*fig.*; **от**) to move away (from); to digress (from), diverge (from); **он далеко́ ~шёл от пре́жних взгля́дов** he has moved a long way from his earlier views. **3.** (*of stains, etc.*) to come out; (**от**) to come away (from), come off; **обо́и ~шли́ от стены́** the paper has come off (the wall). **4.** to recover (normal state); to come to o.s.; to come round; (*impers.*, *coll.*): **у меня́ ~шло́ от се́рдца** I felt better; I felt relieved. **5.** (**к**) to pass (to), go (to) (= *pass into the possession of, by inheritance, etc.*). **6.** to be lost (*in processing*). **7.** (*obs.*) to pass; **ле́то ~шло́** summer was over; **о. в ве́чность** (*rhet.*) to pass away, pass to one's eternal rest.

отол|га́ться, гу́сь, жёшься, *past* **~га́лся, ~гала́сь** *pf.* (*coll.*) to lie one's way out (*of a difficult situation*).

отологи́ческий *adj.* otological.

отоло́ги|я, и *f.* otology.

отомкн|у́ть, у́, ёшь *pf.* (*of* **отмыка́ть**) to unlock, unbolt.

отомкн|у́ться, у́сь, ёшься *pf.* (*of* **отмыка́ться**) **1.** to unlock. **2.** *pass. of* **~у́ть**

отом|сти́ть, щу́, сти́шь *pf. of* **мстить**

отопи́тел|ь, я *m.* heater.

отопи́тельный *adj.* heating; **о. сезо́н** cold season, season for fires.

отоп|и́ть, лю́, ~́шь *pf.* (*of* **ота́пливать** *and* **отопля́ть**) to heat.

отопле́н|ец, ца *m.* heating engineer.

отопле́ни|е, я *nt.* heating.

отопля́|ть, ю *impf. of* **отопи́ть**

ора́чива|ть, ю *impf. of* **оторочи́ть**

ото́рванност|ь, и *f.* isolation; loneliness; **чу́вствовать о. от цивилиза́ции** to feel cut off from civilization.

оторв|а́ть, у́, ёшь, *past* **~а́л, ~ала́, ~а́ло** *pf.* (*of* **отрыва́ть**[1]) to tear off; to tear away (*also fig.*); **о. кого́-н. от рабо́ты** to tear s.o. away from his work; **с рука́ми о.** (*coll.*) to seize with both hands.

оторв|а́ться, у́сь, ёшься, *past* **~а́лся, ~ала́сь, ~ало́сь** *pf.* (*of* **отрыва́ться**) **1.** to come off, be torn off. **2.** (*aeron.*): **о. от земли́** to take off. **3.** (*fig.*; **от**) to be cut off (from), lose touch (with); to break away (from); **о. от проти́вника** to lose contact with the enemy. **4.** (*fig.*; **от**) to tear o.s. away (from); **от э́той кни́ги я не мог о.** I could not tear myself away from this book.

оторопе́лый *adj.* (*coll.*) dumb-founded.

оторопе́|ть, ю *pf.* (*coll.*) to be struck dumb.

о́тороп|ь, и *f.* (*coll.*) confusion, fright; **меня́ о. взяла́** I was dumb-founded.

отороч|и́ть, у́, и́шь *pf.* (*of* **ора́чивать**) to edge, trim.

оторо́чк|а, и *f.* edging, trimming.

ото|сла́ть, шлю́, шлёшь *pf.* (*of* **отсыла́ть**) **1.** to send off, dispatch; **о. де́ньги** to send a remittance. **2.** (**к**) to refer (to); **о. чита́теля к предыду́щему то́му** to refer the reader to the preceding volume; **его́ ~сла́ли к заве́дующему** he was referred to the manager.

отосп|а́ться, лю́сь, и́шься, *past* **~а́лся, ~ала́сь** *pf.* (*of* **отсыпа́ться**[2]) to have a long sleep, have one's sleep out; **о. по́сле доро́ги** to sleep off a journey.

отоше́дший *p.p. of* **отойти́**

ото|шёл, шла́ *see* **~йти́**

ото|шлю́, шлёшь *see* **~сла́ть**

отоща́лый *adj.* (*coll.*) emaciated.

отоща́|ть, ю *pf. of* **тоща́ть**

отпада́|ть, ю *impf. of* **отпа́сть**

отпаде́ни|е, я *nt.* falling away; (*fig.*; **от**) defection (from).

отпа́ива|ть[1]**, ю** *impf. of* **отпая́ть**

отпа́ива|ть[2]**, ю** *impf. of* **отпои́ть**

отпа́рива|ть, ю *impf. of* **отпа́рить**

отпари́р|овать, ую *pf. of* **пари́ровать**

отпа́р|ить, ю, ишь *pf.* (*of* **~ивать**) **1.** to steam; **о. брю́ки** to press trousers through a damp cloth. **2.** to steam off.

отпа́рыва|ть, ю *impf. of* **отпоро́ть**[1]

отпа́|сть, ду́, дёшь, *past* **~л** *pf.* (*of* **~да́ть**) **1.** to fall off, drop off; to fall away. **2.** (*fig.*; **от**) to fall away (from), defect (from), drop away (from); **мно́гие чле́ны ~ли от па́ртии** many members have fallen away from the party. **3.** (*fig.*) to pass, fade; **у него́ ~ла охо́та к путеше́ствию по А́фрике** his desire to travel in Africa has passed; **вопро́с об э́том ~л** the question no longer arises.

отпа|я́ть, я́ю *pf.* (*of* **~́ивать**[1]) to unsolder.

отпева́ни|е, я *nt.* burial service.

отпева́|ть, ю *impf. of* **отпе́ть**

от|пере́ть, опру́, опрёшь, *past* **~́пер, ~перла́, ~́перло** *pf.* (*of* **~пира́ть**) to unlock; to open.

от|пере́ться[1]**, опрётся,** *past* **~пёрся, ~перла́сь** *pf.* (*of* **~пира́ться**) to open.

от|пере́ться[2]**, опру́сь, опрёшься,** *past* **~пёрся, ~перла́сь** *pf.* (*of* **~пира́ться**) (*coll.*; **от**) to deny; to disown.

отпе́т|ый *p.p.p. of* **~ь** *and adj.* (*coll.*) arrant, inveterate.

отп|е́ть, ою́, оёшь *pf.* (*of* **~ева́ть**) to read the burial service (for, over).

отпеча́т|ать, аю *pf.* **1.** (*impf.* **печа́тать**) to print (off). **2.** (*impf.* **~ывать**) to imprint; **о. па́льцы на стекле́** to leave finger-prints on glass. **3.** (*impf.* **~ывать**) to open (up).

отпеча́т|аться, ается *pf.* **1.** to leave an imprint. **2.** *pass. of* **~ать**

отпечатлé|ться, ется *pf.* (*obs.*) to leave its mark.
отпечáт|ок, ка *m.* imprint, impress (*also fig.*); **о. пáльца** finger-print.
отпечáтыва|ть(ся), ю(сь) *impf. of* **отпечáтать(ся)**
отпивá|ть, ю *impf. of* **отпúть**
отпúлива|ть, ю *impf. of* **отпилúть**
отпил|úть, ю́, ∠ишь *pf.* (*of* **∠ивать**) to saw off.
отпирáтельств|о, а *nt.* denial, disavowal.
отпирá|ть(ся), ю(сь) *impf. of* **отперéть(ся)**
отпи|сáть, шу́, ∠шешь *pf.* (*of* **∠сывать**) **1.** (*obs.*) to bequeath, leave. **2.** (*obs.*) to confiscate. **3.** (*dial.*) to notify (in writing).
отпи|сáться, шу́сь, ∠шешься *pf.* (*of* **∠сываться**) to make a (purely) formal reply.
отпúск|а, и *f.* (*pej.*) formal reply.
отпúсыва|ть(ся), ю(сь) *impf. of* **отписáть(ся)**
от|пúть, опью́, опьёшь, *past* **∠пил, ~пилá, ∠пило** *pf.* (*of* **~пивáть**) (+*a. or g.*) to take a sip (of).
отпúхива|ть(ся), ю(сь) *impf. of* **отпихну́ть(ся)**
отпих|ну́ть, ну́, нёшь *pf.* (*of* **∠ивать**) (*coll.*) to push off; to shove aside.
отпих|ну́ться, ну́сь, нёшься *pf.* (*of* **∠иваться**) (*coll.*) to push off (*esp. in a boat*).
отплáт|а, ы *f.* repayment.
отпла|тúть, чу́, ∠тишь *pf.* (*of* **∠чивать**) (+*d.*) to pay back (to); repay, requite; **о. кому́-н. той же монéтой** to pay s.o. in his own coin.
отплáчива|ть, ю *impf. of* **отплатúть**
отплёвыва|ть, ю *impf. of* **отплю́нуть**
отплёвыва|ться, юсь *impf.* to spit (*also fig., to express disgust*).
отплывá|ть, ю *impf. of* **отплы́ть**
отплы́ти|е, я *nt.* sailing, departure.
отплы́|ть, ву́, вёшь, *past* **~л, ~лá, ~ло** *pf.* (*of* **~вáть**) to sail, set sail; to swim off.
отплю́н|уть, у, ешь *pf.* (*of* **отплёвывать**) to spit (out), expectorate.
отпля|сáть, шу́, ∠шешь *pf.* **1.** to dance (*trans.*). **2.** to finish dancing.
отпля́сыва|ть, ю *impf.* (*coll.*) to dance with zest.
óтповед|ь, и *f.* reproof, rebuke.
отпо|úть, ю́, úшь *pf.* (*of* **отпáивать**[2]) **1.** to finish watering. **2.** to fatten (on liquids). **3.** (*coll.*; +*i.*) to cure by giving to drink; **о. отрáвленного молокóм** to give milk to s.o. suffering from poisoning.
отполз|áть, áю *impf. of* **~тú**
отполз|тú, у́, ёшь, *past* **∠, ~лá** *pf.* (*of* **~áть**) to crawl away.
отполир|овáть, у́ю *pf. of* **полировáть**
отпóр, а *m.* repulse; rebuff; **дать о.** (+*d.*) to repulse; **встрéтить о.** to be repulsed; to meet with a rebuff.
отпор|óть[1]**, ю́, ∠ешь** *pf.* (*of* **отпáрывать**) to rip off.
отпор|óть[2]**, ю́, ∠ешь** *pf.* (*of* **порóть**) (*coll.*) to flog, thrash.
отпотевá|ть, ю *impf. of* **отпотéть**
отпотé|ть, ю *pf.* (*of* **потéть** *and* **~вáть**) to moisten, be covered with moisture.
отпочк|овáться, у́ется *pf.* (*of* **~óвываться**) (*biol.*) to gemmate, propagate by gemmation; (*fig.*) to detach o.s.
отпочкóвыва|ться, юсь *impf. of* **отпочковáться**
отправúтел|ь, я *m.* sender.
отпрáв|ить, лю, ишь *pf.* (*of* **~лять**) to send, forward, dispatch; **о. на тот свет** to send to kingdom come; **о. естéственные потрéбности** to relieve nature.
отпрáв|иться, люсь, ишься *pf.* (*of* **~ляться**) to set out, set off, start; to leave, depart; **о. на бокову́ю** (*coll.*) to turn in, go to bed.
отпрáвк|а, и *f.* sending off, forwarding, dispatch.
отправлéни|е, я *nt.* **1.** sending. **2.** departure (*of trains, ships*). **3.** function (*of the organism*). **4.** exercise, performance; **о. обя́занностей** exercise of one's duties.
отправля́|ть, ю *impf.* **1.** *impf. of* **отпрáвить. 2.** (*impf. only*) to exercise, perform (*duties, functions*).
отправля́|ться, юсь *impf.* **1.** *impf. of* **отпрáвиться. 2.** (*fig.*; **от**) to proceed (from).
отправн|óй *adj.*: **о. пункт, ~áя тóчка** starting-point.
отпрáздн|овать, ую *pf. of* **прáздновать**
отпрáшива|ться, юсь *impf.* (*of* **отпросúться**) to ask (for) leave.
отпресс|овáть, у́ю *pf. of* **прессовáть**
отпро|сúться, шу́сь, ∠сишься *pf.* (*of* **отпрáшиваться**) **1.** to ask (for) leave. **2.** to obtain leave.
отпры́гива|ть, ю *impf. of* **отпры́гнуть**
отпры́г|нуть, ну, нешь *pf.* (*of* **~ивать**) to jump back, spring back; to jump aside, spring aside; to bounce back.
óтпрыск, а *m.* (*bot. and fig.*) offshoot, scion.
отпрягá|ть, ю *impf. of* **отпря́чь**
отпря́дыва|ть, ю *impf. of* **отпря́нуть**
отпря́|нуть, ну, нешь *pf.* (*of* **~дывать**) to recoil, start back.
отпря́|чь, гу́, жёшь, гу́т, *past* **~г, ~глá** *pf.* (*of* **~гáть**) to unharness.
отпу́гива|ть, ю *impf. of* **отпугну́ть**
отпуг|ну́ть, ну́, нёшь, *pf.* (*of* **∠ивать**) to frighten off, scare away.
óтпуск, а, в ~е *or* **в ~у́,** *pl.* **~á, ~óв** *m.* **1.** leave, holiday(s); (*mil.*) leave, furlough; **в ~е, в ~у́** on leave; **о. по болéзни** sick-leave. **2.** issue, delivery, distribution. **3.** (*tech.*) tempering, drawing.
отпускá|ть, ю *impf. of* **отпустúть**
отпускнúк, á *m.* pers. on leave, holiday-maker; soldier on leave.
отпускн|óй *adj.* **1.** *adj. of* **óтпуск 1.; ~ы́е дéньги** holiday pay; **~óе свидéтельство** authorization of leave (*of absence*); (*mil.*) leave pass. **2.** (*econ.*): **~áя ценá** selling price.
отпу|стúть, щу́, ∠стишь *pf.* (*of* **~скáть**) **1.** to let go, let off; to let out; to set free; to release; to give leave (of absence); **~стú мою́ ру́ку!** let go (of) my arm!; **о. на прáздник** to release for the holiday; **о. комплимéнт** (*coll.*) to make a compliment; **о. шу́тку** (*coll.*) to crack a joke. **2.** to relax, slacken; **о. пóвод лóшади** to give a horse its head; (*impers., coll.*): **боль ~стúло** the pain has eased. **3.** to (let) grow; **о. (себé) бóроду** to grow a beard. **4.** to issue, give out; (*in a shop, etc.*) to serve. **5.** to assign, allot. **6.** to remit; to forgive; **о. кому́-н. грехú** (*eccl.*) to give s.o. absolution. **7.** (*tech.*) to temper, draw (the temper of).
отпущéни|е, я *nt.* remission; **о. грехóв** (*eccl.*) absolution; **козёл ~я** (*coll.*) scapegoat.
отпу́щенник, а *m.* (*hist.*) freedman.
отрабáтыва|ть, ю *impf. of* **отрабóтать**
отрабóта|нный *p.p.p. of* **~ть** *and adj.* (*tech.*) worked out; waste, spent, exhaust; **о. газ** waste gas, exhaust gas.
отрабóта|ть[1]**, ю** *pf.* (*of* **отрабáтывать**) **1.** to work off (*a debt, etc.*). **2.** (*coll.*) to work (*a given length of time*). **3.** to work through, give a work-out to.
отрабóта|ть[2]**, ю** *pf.* to finish one's work.
отрабóтк|а, и *f.* working off, paying by work.
отрабóточн|ый *adj.*: **~ая систéма** statute labour, corvée.
отрáв|а, ы *f.* poison; (*fig.*) bane.
отравúтел|ь, я *m.* poisoner.
отрав|úть, лю́, ∠ишь *pf.* (*of* **~ля́ть**) to poison (*also fig.*).
отрав|úться, лю́сь, ∠ишься *pf.* (*of* **~ля́ться**) **1.** to poison o.s. **2.** *pass. of* **~úть**
отравля́|ть(ся), ю(сь) *impf. of* **отравúться**
отрáд|а, ы *f.* joy, delight; comfort.
отрáдный *adj.* gratifying, pleasing; comforting.
отражáтел|ь, я *m.* **1.** (*phys.*) reflector; (*radar*) scanner. **2.** (*in fire-arm*) ejector.
отражáтельн|ый *adj.* (*tech.*) reflecting, deflecting; **~ая заслóнка, о. лист, ~ая плитá** deflector (plate), baffle (plate).
отражá|ть(ся), ю(сь) *impf. of* **отразúть(ся)**
отражéни|е, я *nt.* **1.** reflection; reverberation. **2.** repulse, parry; warding off.
отра|зúть, жу́, зúшь *pf.* (*of* **~жáть**) **1.** to reflect (*also fig.*). **2.** to repulse, repel, parry; to ward off.
отра|зúться, жу́сь, зúшься *pf.* (*of* **~жáться**) **1.** to be reflected; to reverberate. **2.** (*fig.*; **на**+*p.*) to affect; to tell (on); **поéздка в гóры благоприя́тно ~зúлась на егó рабóте** the mountain trip had a beneficial effect on his work.

отрапорт|ова́ть, у́ю *pf.* to report.
отраслев|о́й *adj. of* **о́трасль; ~о́е объедине́ние** trade association of a branch of industry.
о́трасл|ь, и *f.* (*obs. or fig.*) branch; **о. дре́внего ро́да** scion of an ancient line; **о. промы́шленности** branch of industry.
отраст|а́ть, а́ю *impf. of* **~и́**
отраст|и́, у́, ёшь, *past* **отро́с, отросла́** *pf.* (*of* **~а́ть**) to grow.
отра|сти́ть, щу́, сти́шь *pf.* (*of* **~щивать**) to (let) grow; **о. во́лосы** to grow one's hair long; **о. брю́хо** (*coll.*) to develop a paunch.
отра́щива|ть, ю *impf. of* **отрасти́ть**
отреаги́р|овать, ую *pf.* (*coll.*) *of* **реаги́ровать 2.**
отре́бь|е, я *nt.* (*collect.*) **1.** (*obs.*) waste, refuse. **2.** (*fig.*) rabble.
отрегули́р|овать, ую *pf. of* **регули́ровать**
отредакти́р|овать, ую *pf. of* **редакти́ровать**
отре́з, а *m.* **1.** cut; **ли́ния ~а** line of the cut; perforated line; (*on document, ticket, etc.*) 'tear off here'. **2.** length (*of material*); **о. на пла́тье** dress length.
отре́занност|ь, и *f.* **(от)** lack of communication (with), being cut off (from).
отрез|а́ть, а́ю *impf. of* **~ать**
отре́|зать, жу, жешь *pf.* (*of* **~за́ть**) **1.** to cut off (*also fig.*); to divide, apportion (land); **проти́вник ~зал нам отступле́ние** the enemy had cut off our retreat. **2.** (*coll.*) to snap out.
отрезве́|ть, ю *pf. of* **трезве́ть**
отрезви́тельный *adj.* sobering (*also fig.*).
отрезв|и́ть, лю́, и́шь *pf.* (*of* **~ля́ть**) to sober (*also fig.*).
отрезв|и́ться, лю́сь, и́шься *pf.* (*of* **~ля́ться**) to become sober, sober up.
отрезвле́ни|е, я *nt.* sobering (up).
отрезвля́|ть(ся), ю(сь) *impf. of* **отрезви́ть(ся)**
отрезно́й *adj.* perforated; **о. тало́н** tear-off coupon.
отре́з|ок, ка *m.* piece, cut; section; (*hist.*) portion (*of land*); (*math.*) segment; **о. вре́мени** space (*of time*).
отрека́|ться, юсь *impf. of* **отре́чься**
отрекоменд|ова́ть, у́ю *pf.* to introduce.
отрекоменд|ова́ться, у́юсь *pf.* to introduce o.s.
отремонти́р|овать, ую *pf. of* **ремонти́ровать**
отре́пь|е, я, *pl.* **~я, ~ев** *nt.* (*collect.*) rags; **ходи́ть в о., в ~ях** to be in rags.
отрече́ни|е, я *nt.* **(от)** renunciation (of); **о. от престо́ла** abdication.
отре́|чься, ку́сь, чёшься, ку́тся, *past* **~кся, ~кла́сь** *pf.* (*of* **~ка́ться**) **(от)** to renounce, disavow, give up; **о. от престо́ла** to abdicate.
отреш|а́ть(ся), а́ю(сь) *impf. of* **~и́ть(ся)**
отрешённост|ь, и *f.* estrangement, aloofness.
отреш|и́ть, у́, и́шь *pf.* (*of* **~а́ть**) **(от)** to release (from); **о. от до́лжности** to dismiss, suspend.
отреш|и́ться, у́сь, и́шься *pf.* (*of* **~а́ться**) **(от)** to renounce, give up; **я не мог о. от мы́сли** I could not get rid of the idea.
отри́н|уть, у, ешь *pf.* (*obs.*) to reject.
отрица́ни|е, я *nt.* denial; negation.
отрица́тел|ьный (~ен, ~ьна) *adj.* (*in var. senses*) negative; (*fig.*) bad, unfavourable; **~ьное электри́чество** negative electricity; **~ьная сторона́** bad side, drawback.
отрица́|ть, ю *impf.* to deny; to disclaim; **о. вино́вность** (*leg.*) to plead not guilty.
отро́г, а *m.* (*geog.*) spur.
о́троду *adv.* (*coll.*) **1.** in age; **ему́ пять лет о.** he is five years old. **2.: не ... о.** never in one's life; never in one's born days; **я о. не вида́л ничего́ подо́бного** I have never seen the like.
отро́дь|е, я *nt.* (*coll., pej.*) race, breed; **Ха́мово о.** (*obs.*) hoi polloi.
отродя́сь *adv.* (*coll.*): **не ... о.** never in one's life; never in one's born days.
о́трок, а *m.* boy, lad; adolescent.
отрокови́ц|а, ы *f.* (*obs.*) girl, lass, maiden.
отро́ст|ок, ка *m.* **1.** (*bot.*) shoot, sprout. **2.** (*tech.*) branch, extension. **3.** (*anat.*) appendix.
о́троческий *adj.* adolescent.
о́трочеств|о, а *nt.* adolescence.
о́труб, а, *pl.* **~а́, ~о́в** *m.* (*hist.*) holding (*consolidated peasant small-holding, 1906–17*).
отру́б, а, *pl.* **~ы, ~ов** *m.* butt (*of tree*).
о́труб|и, е́й *no sg.* bran.
отруб|а́ть, а́ю *impf. of* **~и́ть**
отруб|и́ть, лю́, ~ишь *pf.* (*of* **~а́ть**) **1.** to chop off. **2.** (*fig., coll.*) to snap back.
отрубно́й *adj. of* **о́труб**
о́труб|ный *adj. of* **~и**
отру́гива|ться, юсь *impf.* (*coll.*) to return abuse.
отры́в, а *m.* **1.** tearing off. **2.** (*fig.*) alienation, isolation; loss of contact, loss of communication; **в ~е (от)** out of touch (with); **учи́ться без ~а от произво́дства** to study while continuing (normal) work; **о. от земли́** (*aeron.*) take-off; **о. от проти́вника** (*mil.*) disengagement.
отрыва́|ть[1], **ю** *impf. of* **оторва́ть**
отрыва́|ть[2], **ю** *impf. of* **отры́ть**
отрыва́|ться, юсь *impf. of* **оторва́ться**
отры́вист|ый (~, ~а) *adj.* jerky, abrupt; curt.
отрывно́й *adj.* perforated; **о. календа́рь** tear-off calendar.
отры́в|ок, ка *m.* fragment, excerpt; passage (*of book, etc.*); **о. из фи́льма** film clip.
отры́вoч|ный (~ен, ~на) *adj.* fragmentary, scrappy.
отры́гива|ть, ю *impf. of* **отрыгну́ть**
отрыг|ну́ть, ну́, нёшь *pf.* (*of* **~ивать**) (*+a. or g.*) to belch.
отры́жк|а, и *f.* **1.** belch; belching, eructation. **2.** (*fig.*) survival, throw-back.
отр|ы́ть, о́ю, о́ешь *pf.* (*of* **~ыва́ть**[2]) to dig out; to unearth (*also fig.*).
отря́д, а *m.* **1.** detachment; **передово́й о.** (*fig.*) vanguard. **2.** (*biol.*) order.
отря|ди́ть, жу́, ди́шь *pf.* (*of* **~жа́ть**) to detach, detail, tell off.
отряжа́|ть, ю *impf. of* **отряди́ть**
отряс|а́ть, а́ю *impf. of* **~ти́**
отряс|ти́, у́, ёшь, *past* **~, ~ла́** *pf.* (*of* **~а́ть**) (*obs.*) to shake off; **о. прах от ног свои́х** (*fig.*) to shake off the dust from one's feet.
отря́хива|ть(ся), ю(сь) *impf. of* **отряхну́ть(ся)**
отрях|ну́ть, ну́, нёшь *pf.* (*of* **~ивать**) to shake down, shake off; **о. снег с воротника́** to shake snow off one's collar.
отрях|ну́ться, ну́сь, нёшься *pf.* (*of* **~иваться**) to shake o.s. down.
отса|ди́ть, жу́, ~дишь *pf.* (*of* **~живать**) **1.** (*hort.*) to transplant, plant out. **2.** to seat apart. **3.** (*tech.*) to jig.
отса́дк|а, и *f.* **1.** (*hort.*) transplanting, planting out. **2.** (*tech.*) jigging.
отса́жива|ть, ю *impf. of* **отсади́ть**
отса́жива|ться, юсь *impf. of* **отсе́сть**
отсалют|ова́ть, у́ю *pf. of* **салютова́ть**
отса́сывани|е, я *nt.* suction.
отса́сывател|ь, я *m.* suction pump.
отса́сыва|ть, ю *impf. of* **отсоса́ть**
отсве́т, а *m.* reflection; reflected light.
отсве́чива|ть, ю *impf.* **1.** to be reflected; (*+i.*) to shine (with); **в ко́мнате ~л с у́лицы фона́рь** the light of the street-lamp was reflected in the room. **2.** (*coll.*) to stand (be) in the light.
отсебя́тин|а, ы *f.* (*coll.*) words of one's own; sth. of one's own devising; (*theatr.*) ad-libbing.
отсе́в, а *m.* **1.** sifting, selection. **2.** siftings, residue.
отсева́|ть, ю *impf.* = **отсе́ивать**
отсе́ива|ть(ся), ю(сь) *impf. of* **отсе́ять(ся)**
отсе́к, а *m.* **1.** (*naut., etc.*) compartment; carrel (*in library*). **2.** (*astronautics*) module.
отсека́|ть, ю *impf. of* **отсе́чь**
отсе́ле *adv.* (*obs.*) hence, from here.
отсел|и́ть, ю, и́шь *pf.* (*of* **~я́ть**) to settle out, move further out.
отсел|и́ться, ю́сь, и́шься *pf.* (*of* **~я́ться**) to settle out, move further out.
отсе́л|ь = ~е

отсел|я́ть(ся), я́ю(сь) *impf. of* **~и́ть(ся)**

отс|е́сть я́ду, я́дешь, *past* **~е́л** *pf.* (*of* **~а́живаться**) to seat o.s. apart; **(от)** to move away (from).

отсече́ни|е, я *nt.* cutting off, severance; **дать го́лову на о.** (*coll.*) to stake one's life.

отсе́чк|а, и *f.* (*tech.*) cut-off.

отсе́|чь, ку́, чёшь, ку́т, *past* **~к, ~кла́** *pf.* (*of* **~ка́ть**) to cut off, chop off, sever.

отсе́|ять, ю, ешь *pf.* (*of* **~ивать**) **1.** to sift, screen. **2.** (*fig.*) to eliminate.

отсе́|яться, юсь, ешься *pf.* (*of* **~иваться**) **1.** *pass. of* **~ять. 2.** (*fig.*) to fall off, fall away; **бо́льшая часть слу́шателей ~ялась** the greater part of the audience had fallen away.

отси|де́ть, жу́, ди́шь *pf.* (*of* **~́живать**) **1.** to stay (for); to sit out; **он ~де́л де́сять лет в тюрьме́** he has done ten years (in prison). **2.** to make numb by sitting; **я ~де́л себе́ но́гу** I have pins and needles in my leg.

отси|де́ться, жу́сь, ди́шься *pf.* (*of* **~́живаться**) (*coll.*) to sit out (a siege); (*fig., pej.*) to sit on the fence.

отси́жива|ть(ся), ю(сь) *impf. of* **отсиде́ть(ся)**

отска́блива|ть, ю *impf. of* **отскобли́ть**

отска|ка́ть, чу́, ~́чешь *pf.* (*coll.*) to gallop, cover by galloping.

отска́кива|ть, ю *impf. of* **отскочи́ть**

отскобл|и́ть, ю́, ~́ишь *pf.* (*of* **отска́бливать**) to scratch off.

отско́к, а *m.* rebound.

отскоч|и́ть, у́, ~́ишь *pf.* (*of* **отска́кивать**) **1.** to jump aside, jump away; to rebound, bounce back. **2.** (*coll.*) to come off, break off.

отскреба́|ть, ю *impf. of* **отскрести́**

отскре|сти́, бу́, бёшь, *past* **~́б, ~бла́** *pf.* (*of* **~ба́ть**) to scrape off, scratch off.

отсла́ива|ться, ется *impf. of* **отслои́ться**

отслое́ни|е, я *nt.* (*geol.*) exfoliation.

отсло|и́ться, и́тся *pf.* (*of* **отсла́иваться**) (*geol.*) to exfoliate; to scale off.

отслу́жива|ть, ю *impf. of* **отслужи́ть**

отслуж|и́ть, у́, ~́ишь *pf.* (*of* **~́ивать**) **1.** to serve; to serve one's time. **2.** (*coll.*) (*of implements, etc.*) to have served its turn, be worn out. **3.** (*eccl.*) to finish (*a service*).

отсове́т|овать, ую *pf.* (*+d. and inf.*) to dissuade (from).

отсортир|ова́ть, у́ю *pf.* (*of* **~о́вывать**) to sort (out).

отсортиро́выва|ть, ю *impf. of* **отсортирова́ть**

отсос|а́ть, у́, ёшь *pf.* (*of* **отса́сывать**) (*+a. or g.*) to suck off; to filter by suction.

отсо́х|нуть, нет, *past* **~, ~ла** *pf.* (*of* **отсыха́ть**) to dry up, to wither.

отсро́чива|ть, ю *impf. of* **отсро́чить**

отсро́ч|ить, у, ишь *pf.* (*of* **~ивать**) **1.** to postpone, delay, defer; (*leg.*) to adjourn. **2.** (*coll.*) to extend (*period of validity of a document*).

отсро́чк|а, и *f.* **1.** postponement, delay, deferment; (*leg.*) adjournment; **о. наказа́ния** respite; **дать ме́сячную ~у** to grant a month's grace. **2.** (*coll.*) extension (*of period of validity of document*).

отстава́ни|е, я *nt.* lag.

отста|ва́ть, ю́, ёшь *impf. of* **~́ть**

отста́в|ить, лю, ишь *pf.* (*of* **~ля́ть**) **1.** to set aside, put aside. **2.** (*obs.*) to dismiss, discharge. **3.** (*coll.*) to rescind; **о.!** (*mil. word of command*) as you were!

отста́вк|а, и *f.* **1.** dismissal, discharge. **получи́ть ~у у кого́-н.** to be dismissed by s.o., get the sack from s.o. **2.** resignation; retirement; **вы́йти в ~у** to resign, retire; **пода́ть в ~у** to tender one's resignation; **в ~е** retired, in retirement. **3.** (*coll.*) brush-off.

отставля́|ть, ю *impf. of* **отста́вить**

отставно́й *adj.* retired.

отста́ива|ть, ю *impf.* **1.** *impf. of* **отстоя́ть**[1] **2.** to fight, dispute; to try to vindicate; **мы бу́дем о. на́шу то́чку зре́ния** we shall dispute our point of view.

отста́ива|ться, юсь *impf. of* **отстоя́ться**

отста́лост|ь, и *f.* (*fig.*) backwardness.

отста́лый *adj.* (*fig.*) backward; **у́мственно о.** mentally retarded; **физи́чески о.** physically handicapped.

отста́|ть, ну, нешь *pf.* (*of* **~ва́ть**) **1. (от)** to fall behind, drop behind; to lag behind; (*fig.*) to be backward, be retarded; to be behind, be behindhand; **о. в рабо́те** to be behind in (with) one's work; **о. от кла́сса** to be behind (the rest of) one's class; **о. от ве́ка, о. от совреме́нности** to be behind the times. **2. (от)** to be left behind (by), become detached (from); **о. от гру́ппы** to become detached from a group; **о. от по́езда** to be left behind by the train (*sc., at a station en route*). **3. (от)** to lose touch (with); to break (with); **я ~л от всех свои́х знако́мых вое́нного вре́мени** I have lost touch with all my war-time acquaintances. **4.** (*coll.*; **от**) to give up; **о. от привы́чки** to break o.s. of a habit. **5.** (*of a clock or watch*) to be slow; **о. на полчаса́** to be half an hour slow. **6.** (*of plaster, wall-paper, etc.*) to come off. **7.** (*coll.*; **от**) to leave alone; **~нь от меня́!** leave me alone!

отста|ю́щий *pres. part. of* **~ва́ть**; *as n.* **о., ~ю́щего** *m.* backward pupil; **рабо́та с ~ю́щими** remedial work.

отстега́|ть, ю *pf.* (*of* **стега́ть**[1]) to beat, lash.

отстёгива|ть(ся), ю(сь) *impf. of* **отстегну́ть(ся)**

отстег|ну́ть, ну́, нёшь *pf.* (*of* **~́ивать**) to unfasten, undo; to unbutton.

отстег|ну́ться, нётся *pf.* (*of* **~́иваться**) to come unfastened, come undone.

отстир|а́ть, а́ю *pf.* (*of* **~́ывать**) to wash off.

отстир|а́ться, а́юсь *pf.* (*of* **~́ываться**) to wash off, come out in the wash.

отсти́рыва|ть(ся), ю(сь) *impf. of* **отстира́ть(ся)**

отсто́|й, я *m.* sediment, deposit.

отсто́йник, а *m.* settling tank; sedimentation tank; cesspool.

отсто|я́ть[1]**, ю́, и́шь** *pf.* (*of* **отста́ивать**) to defend, save; to stand up for; **о. свои́ права́** to assert one's rights.

отсто|я́ть[2]**, ю́, и́шь** *pf.* to stand through, stand out; **мы ~я́ли весь спекта́кль** we stood through the entire show.

отсто|я́ть[3]**, ю́, и́шь** *impf.* **(от)** to be ... distant (from); **ста́нция ~и́т от це́нтра го́рода на два киломе́тра** the station is two kilometres (away) from the centre of the town; **э́ти дере́вни ~я́т друг от дру́га на пять вёрст** these villages are five versts apart.

отсто|я́ться, и́тся *pf.* (*of* **отста́иваться**) **1.** (*chem.*) to settle, precipitate. **2.** (*fig.*) to settle, become stabilized, become fixed.

отстра́ива|ть(ся), ю(сь) *impf. of* **отстро́ить(ся)**

отстране́ни|е, я *nt.* **1.** pushing aside. **2.** dismissal, discharge.

отстран|и́ть, ю́, и́шь *pf.* (*of* **~я́ть**) **1.** to push aside; **о. от себя́ все забо́ты** to lay aside all one's cares. **2.** to dismiss, discharge.

отстран|и́ться, ю́сь, и́шься *pf.* (*of* **~я́ться**) **1. (от)** to move away (from); (*fig.*) to keep out of the way (of), keep aloof (from); **о. от уда́ра** to dodge a blow; **о. от до́лжности** to relinquish a post. **2.** *pass. of* **~и́ть**

отстран|я́ть(ся), я́ю(сь) *impf. of* **~и́ть(ся)**

отстре́лива|ть[1]**, ю** *impf. of* **отстрели́ть**

отстре́лива|ть[2]**, ю** *impf. of* **отстреля́ть**

отсре́лива|ться, юсь *impf. of* **отстреля́ться**[1]

отстрел|и́ть, ю́, ~́ишь *pf.* (*of* **~́ивать**[1]) to shoot off.

отстрел|я́ть, я́ю *pf.* (*of* **~́ивать**[2]) to shoot (*for commercial purposes, etc.*).

отстрел|я́ться[1]**, я́юсь** *pf.* (*of* **~́иваться**) **1.** to defend o.s. (by shooting). **2.** to return fire, fire back.

отстрел|я́ться[2]**, я́юсь** *pf.* to have finished firing; to have completed a practice (shoot).

отстрига́|ть, ю *impf. of* **отстри́чь**

отстри́|женный *p.p.p. of* **~чь**

отстри́|чь, гу́, жёшь, гу́т, *past* **~г, ~гла** *pf.* (*of* **~га́ть**) to cut off, clip.

отстр|о́ить[1]**, о́ю, о́ишь** *pf.* (*of* **~а́ивать**) to complete construction (of), finish building; to build up.

отстр|о́ить[2]**, о́ю, о́ишь** *pf.* (*of* **~а́ивать**) (*radio*) to tune out, reject (*interfering wavelength*).

отстр|о́иться[1]**, о́юсь, о́ишься** *pf.* (*of* **~а́иваться**) (*coll.*) **1.** to finish building. **2.** *pass. of* **~о́ить**[1]

отстр|о́иться[2]**, о́юсь, о́ишься** *pf.* (*of* **~а́иваться**) (*radio*) to tune out (*adjust receiver so as to avoid interference*).

отстро́йк|а, и *f.* (*radio*) tuning out.
отсту́к|ать, аю *pf.* (*of* **~ивать**) (*coll.*) to tap out; **о. мело́дию** to strum a tune; **о. на маши́нке** to bash out on a typewriter.
отсту́кива|ть, ю *impf. of* **отсту́кать**
о́тступ, а *m.* (*typ.*) break off, indention.
отступа́тельный *adj.* (*mil.*) retreat, withdrawal.
отступ|а́ть(ся), а́ю(сь) *impf. of* **~и́ть(ся)**
отступ|и́ть, лю́, ~́ишь *pf.* (*of* **~а́ть**) **1.** to step back; to recede. **2.** (*mil.*) to retreat, fall back. **3.** (*fig.*) to back down; **(от)** to go back (on); to give up; **о. от реше́ния** to go back on a decision. **4.** (*fig.*; **от**) to swerve (from), deviate (from); **о. от обы́чая** to depart from custom; **о. от те́мы** to digress. **5.** (*typ.*) to indent.
отступ|и́ться, лю́сь, ~́ишся *pf.* (*of* **~а́ться**) (*coll.*; **от**) to give up, renounce; **о. от своего́ сло́ва** to go back on one's word; **они́ все ~и́лись от него́** they have all given him up.
отступле́ни|е, я *nt.* **1.** (*mil. and fig.*) retreat. **2.** deviation; digression.
отсту́пник, а *m.* apostate; recreant.
отсту́пничеств|о, а *nt.* apostasy.
отступн|о́й *adj.*: **~ы́е де́ньги** (*or as n.* **~о́е, ~о́го** *nt.*) smart-money; indemnity, compensation.
отступ|я́ *ger. of* **~и́ть,** *as adv.* **(от)** off, away (from); **о. два-три ме́тра** two or three metres off; **немно́го о. от до́ма** a little way away from the house.
отсу́тстви|е, я *nt.* absence; (+*g.*) lack (of); **в его́ о.** in his absence; **за ~ем** (+*g.*) in the absence (of); for lack (of), for want (of); **находи́ться в ~и** to be absent; **блиста́ть свои́м ~ем** to be conspicuous by one's absence.
отсу́тств|овать, ую *impf.* to be absent; (*leg.*) to default.
отсу́тств|ующий *pres. part. of* **~овать** *and adj.* absent (*also fig.*); **о. вид** blank expression; *as n.* **о., ~ующего** *m.* absentee; **~ующие** those absent; **безве́стно о.** missing pers.
отсу́чива|ть, ю *impf. of* **отсучи́ть**
отсуч|и́ть, у́, ~́ишь *pf.* (*of* **~ивать**) (*coll.*; **рукава́** *etc.*) to roll down (*sleeves, etc.*).
отсчёт, а *m.* reading (*on an instrument*).
отсчит|а́ть, а́ю *pf.* (*of* **~́ывать**) **1.** to count out, count off; **о. пять шаго́в от до́ма** to count five paces from the house; **о. кому́-н. де́сять рубле́й** to count out ten roubles to s.o. **2.** to read off, take a reading.
отсчи́тыва|ть, ю *impf. of* **отсчита́ть**
отсыла́|ть, ю *impf. of* **отосла́ть**
отсы́лк|а, и *f.* **1.** dispatch; **о. де́нег** remittance. **2.** reference.
отсы́п|ать, лю, лешь *pf.* (*of* **~а́ть**) (+*a. or g.*) to pour off; to measure off.
отсып|а́ть, а́ю *impf. of* **~́ать**
отсы́п|аться, люсь, лешься *pf.* (*of* **~а́ться**[1]) **1.** to pour out. **2.** *pass. of* **~ать**
отсып|а́ться[1]**, а́юсь** *impf. of* **~́аться**
отсып|а́ться[2]**, а́юсь** *impf. of* **отоспа́ться**
отсыре́лый *adj.* damp.
отсыре́|ть, ю *pf. of* **сыре́ть**
отсыха́|ть, ю *impf. of* **отсо́хнуть**
отсю́да *adv.* from here; hence (*also fig.*); (*fig.*) from this; **о. сле́дует, что...** from this it follows that ....
Отта́в|а, ы *f.* Ottawa.
отта́ива|ть, ю *impf. of* **отта́ять**
отта́лкивани|е, я *nt.* (*phys.*) repulsion.
отта́лкива|ть, ю *impf. of* **оттолкну́ть**
отта́лкива|ющий *pres. part. act. of* **~ть** *and adj.* repulsive, repellent.
отта́птыва|ть, ю *impf. of* **оттопта́ть**
оттаска́|ть, ю *pf.* (*of* **таска́ть 2.**) to pull; **о. кого́-н. за́ волосы** to pull s.o.'s hair.
отта́скива|ть, ю *impf. of* **оттащи́ть**
отта́чива|ть, ю *impf. of* **отточи́ть**
оттащ|и́ть, у́, ~́ишь *pf.* (*of* **отта́скивать**) to drag aside (away), pull aside (away).
отта́|ять, ю, ешь *pf.* (*of* **~ивать**) (*trans. and intrans.*) to thaw out.
оттен|и́ть, ю́, и́шь *pf.* (*of* **~я́ть**) **1.** to shade (in). **2.** (*fig.*) to set off, make more prominent.
отте́н|ок, ка *m.* shade, nuance (*also fig.*); tint, hue; **о. значе́ния** shade of meaning; **он говори́л с ~ком иро́нии** there was a note of irony in his voice.
оттен|я́ть, я́ю *impf. of* **~и́ть**
о́ттепел|ь, и *f.* thaw.
оттер|е́ть, ототру́, ототрёшь, *past* **~́, ~́ла** *pf.* (*of* **оттира́ть**) **1.** to rub off, rub out. **2.** to restore sensation (*to parts of the body*) by rubbing. **3.** (*coll.*) to press back, push aside.
оттер|е́ться, ототру́сь, ототрёшься, *past* **~́ся, ~́лась** *pf.* (*of* **оттира́ться**) to rub out; to come out (*by rubbing*).
оттесн|и́ть, ю, и́шь *pf.* (*of* **~я́ть**) to drive back; press back; to push aside, shove aside (*also fig.*); **о. проти́вника** (*mil.*) to force the enemy back; **о. конкуре́нта** (*fig.*) to edge a competitor out.
оттесн|я́ть, я́ю *impf. of* **~и́ть**
о́ттиск, а *m.* **1.** impression. **2.** off-print, separate.
otти́скива|ть, ю *impf. of* **отти́снуть**
отти́с|нуть, ну, нешь *pf.* (*of* **~кивать**) **1.** (*coll.*) to push aside. **2.** (*coll.*) to crush. **3.** to print.
оттого́ *adv.* that is why; **о. мы и не могли́ прие́хать** that's why we couldn't come; **о... что** because; **я о. опозда́л, что мото́р не заводи́лся** I was late because the engine would not start.
отто́ле *adv.* (*obs.*) thence, from there.
оттолкн|у́ть, у́, ёшь *pf.* (*of* **отта́лкивать**) **1.** to push away, push aside. **2.** (*fig.*) to antagonize, alienate.
оттолкн|у́ться, у́сь, ёшься *pf.* (*of* **отта́лкиваться**) **1. (от)** to push off (from). **2.** (*fig.*; **от**) to dispense (with), discard.
отто́л|ь = ~е
оттома́нк|а, и *f.* ottoman.
оттоп|та́ть, чу́, ~́чешь *pf.* (*of* **отта́птывать**) (*coll.*) **1.** to hurt, damage (*by much walking*). **2.: о. кому́-н. но́гу** to tread (heavily) on s.o.'s foot.
оттопы́р|енный *p.p.p. of* **~ить** *and adj.* protruding, sticking out.
оттопы́рива|ть(ся), ю(сь) *impf. of* **оттопы́рить(ся)**
оттопы́р|ить, ю, ишь *pf.* (*of* **~ивать**) (*coll.*) to stick out; **о. ло́кти** to stick out one's elbows.
оттопы́р|иться, ится *pf.* (*of* **~иваться**) to protrude, stick out; to bulge.
отторг|а́ть, а́ю *impf. of* **~́нуть**
отто́рг|нуть, ну, нешь, *past* **~, ~ла** *pf.* (*of* **~а́ть**) to tear away, seize.
отторже́ни|е, я *nt.* tearing away; (*med.*) rejection (*of a transplanted organ*).
отточ|и́ть, у́, ~́ишь *pf.* (*of* **отта́чивать**) to sharpen, whet.
отту́да *adv.* from there.
оттуш|ева́ть, у́ю, у́ешь *pf.* (*of* **~ёвывать**) to shade (off.).
оттушёвыва|ть, ю *impf. of* **оттушева́ть**
оттяга́|ть, ю *pf.* (*coll.*) to gain by a lawsuit.
оття́гива|ть, ю *impf. of* **оттяну́ть**
оття́жк|а, и *f.* **1.** delay, procrastination. **2.** (*naut.*) guy(-rope); strut, brace, stay.
оття|ну́ть, ну́, ~́нешь *pf.* (*of* **~́гивать**) **1.** to draw out, pull away. **2.** (*mil.*) to draw off. **3.** (*coll.*) to delay; **что́бы о. вре́мя** to gain time. **4.** (*tech.*) to forge out.
оття́п|ать, аю *pf.* (*of* **~́ывать**) (*coll.*) to chop off.
оття́пыва|ть, ю *impf. of* **оття́пать**
оту́жина|ть, ю *pf.* **1.** to have had supper. **2.** (*obs.*) to have supper.
отума́нива|ть, ю *impf. of* **отума́нить**
отума́н|ить, ю, ишь *pf.* (*of* **~ивать**) **1.** to blur; to dim; **её глаза́ ~ило слеза́ми** her eyes were dimmed with tears. **2.** (*fig.*) to (be)cloud, obscure; **моё созна́ние ~ило вино́м** wine had clouded my reason.
отупе́лый *adj.* (*coll.*) stupefied, dulled.
отупе́ни|е, я *nt.* stupefaction, dullness, torpor.
отупе́|ть, ю *pf.* (*coll.*) to grow dull, sink into torpor.
отутю́жива|ть, ю *impf. of* **отутю́жить**
отутю́ж|ить, у, ишь *pf.* (*of* **~ивать**) **1.** to iron (out). **2.** (*fig., coll.*) to beat up.
оту́ч|а́ть(ся), а́ю(сь) *impf. of* **~и́ть(ся)**
оту́чива|ться, юсь *impf. of* **отучи́ться**[2]

отуч|и́ть, у́, ~́ишь *pf.* (*of* **~а́ть**) (**от** *or* +*inf.*) to break (of); **о. от груди́** to wean.

отуч|и́ться[1], **у́сь, ~́ишься** *pf.* (*of* **~а́ться**) (**от** *or* +*inf.*) to break o.s. (of).

отуч|и́ться[2], **у́сь, ~́ишься** *pf.* (*of* **~́иваться**) to have finished one's lessons; to finish learning.

отха́жива|ть, ю *impf. of* **отходи́ть**[2,3]

отха́рк|ать, аю *pf.* (*of* **~ивать**) to expectorate.

отха́ркива|ть, ю *impf. of* **отха́ркать**

отха́ркива|ться, юсь *impf. of* **отха́ркнуться**

отха́ркива|ющий *pres. part. act. of* **~ть; ~ющее (сре́дство)** (*med.*) expectorant.

отха́ркн|уть, у, ешь *pf.* to hawk up.

отха́рк|нуться, нусь, нешься *pf.* (*of* **~иваться**) **1.** (*coll.*) to clear one's throat. **2.** to come up (*as result of expectoration*).

отхва|ти́ть, чу́, ~́тишь *pf.* (*of* **~́тывать**) (*coll.*) **1.** to snip off; to chop off; **он ~ти́л себе́ па́лец топоро́м** he chopped his finger off with an axe. **2.** to perform, execute in lively fashion.

отхва́тыва|ть, ю *impf. of* **отхвати́ть**

отхлеб|ну́ть, ну́, нёшь *pf.* (*of* **~́ывать**) (*coll.*; +*a. or g.*) to take a sip (of); to take a mouthful (of).

отхлёбыва|ть, ю *impf. of* **отхлебну́ть**

отхле|ста́ть, щу́, ~́щешь *pf.* (*coll.*) to give a lashing.

отхлы́н|уть, у, ешь *pf.* to rush back, flood back (*also fig.*).

отхо́д, а *m.* **1.** departure; sailing. **2.** (*mil.*) withdrawal, retirement, falling back. **3.** (**от**) deviation (from), break (with). **4.** *see* **~ы**

отхо|ди́ть[1], **жу́, ~́дишь** *impf. of* **отойти́**

отхо|ди́ть[2], **жу́, ~́дишь** *pf.* (*of* **отха́живать**) (*coll.*) to cure, heal, nurse back to health.

отхо|ди́ть[3], **жу́, ~́дишь** *pf.* (*of* **отха́живать**) (*coll.*) to tire, hurt (*by walking*).

отхо́дн|ая, ой *f.* prayer for the dying; **справля́ть ~ую кому́-н.** (*fig.*) to write s.o. off.

отхо́дник, а *m.* (*obs.*) seasonal worker (*esp. of peasants going to cities*).

отхо́дничеств|о, а *nt.* (*obs.*) seasonal work.

отхо́дчив|ый (~, ~а) *adj.* not bearing grudges.

отхо́д|ы, ов (*tech.*) waste (products); siftings, screening; tailings.

отхо́|женный *p.p.p. of* **~ди́ть**[3]**; но́ги у меня́ ~жены** I have been walked off my feet.

отхо́ж|ий *adj.*: **о. про́мысел** seasonal work; **~ее ме́сто** (*coll.*) latrine, earth closet.

отцве|сти́, ту́, тёшь, *past* **~́л, ~ла́** *pf.* (*of* **~та́ть**) to finish blossoming, fade (*also fig.*); **она́ ~ла́** she has lost her bloom.

отцве|та́ть, та́ю *impf. of* **~сти́**

отце|ди́ть, жу́, ~́дишь *pf.* (*of* **~́живать**) to strain off, filter.

отце́жива|ть, ю *impf. of* **отцеди́ть**

отцеп|и́ть, лю́, ~́ишь *pf.* (*of* **~ля́ть**) to unhook; to uncouple.

отцеп|и́ться, лю́сь, ~́ишься *pf.* (*of* **~ля́ться**) **1.** to come unhooked; to come uncoupled. **2.** (*fig., coll.*) to leave alone; **~и́сь ты от меня́!** leave me alone!

отце́пк|а, и *f.* (*rail.*) uncoupling.

отцепля́|ть(ся), ю(сь) *impf. of* **отцепи́ть(ся)**

отцеуби́йств|о, а *nt.* parricide, patricide (*act*).

отцеуби́йц|а, ы *c.g.* parricide, patricide (*agent*).

отцо́в *adj.* one's father's.

отцо́вск|ий *adj.* one's father's; paternal; **~ое насле́дие** patrimony.

отцо́вств|о, а *nt.* paternity.

отча́ива|ться, юсь *impf. of* **отча́яться**

отча́лива|ть, ю *impf. of* **отча́лить; ~й!** (*coll.*) clear off!; beat it!

отча́л|ить, ю, ишь *pf.* (*of* **~ивать**) (*naut.*) **1.** to cast off. **2.** (*intrans.*) to push off, cast off.

отча́сти *adv.* partly.

отча́яни|е, я *nt.* despair.

отча́ян|ный (~, ~а) *adj.* despairing; (*fig., coll.; in var. senses*) desperate; **о. взор** despairing look; **о. дура́к** (*coll.*) awful fool; **о. игро́к** desperate gambler; **~ное положе́ние** desperate plight.

отча́|яться, юсь, ешься *pf.* (*of* **~иваться**) (+*inf. or* **в**+*p.*) to despair (of).

о́тче (*obs.*) *voc. of* **оте́ц; О. наш** Our Father (*the Lord's prayer*).

отчего́ *adv.* why; **вот о.** that's why.

отчего́-либо *adv.* for some reason or other.

отчего́-то *adv.* for some reason.

отчека́нива|ть, ю *impf. of* **отчека́нить**

отчека́н|ить, ю, ишь *pf.* (*of* **чека́нить** *and* **~ивать**) **1.** to coin, mint. **2.** (*fig.*) to execute clearly and distinctly; **о. слова́** to rap out (one's words).

отчёркива|ть, ю *impf. of* **отчеркну́ть**

отчерк|ну́ть, ну́, нёшь *pf.* (*of* **~́ивать**) to mark off.

отчерп|ну́ть, ну́, нёшь *pf.* (*of* **~́ывать**) (+*a. or g.*) to ladle out.

отче́рпыва|ть, ю *impf. of* **отчерпну́ть**

о́тчеств|о, а *nt.* patronymic; **как его́ по ~у** what is his patronymic?

отчёт, а *m.* account; **дать о.** (**в**+*p.*) to give an account (of), report (on); **взять де́ньги под о.** to take money on account; **отдава́ть себе́ о.** (**в**+*p.*) to be aware (of), realize.

отчётливост|ь, и *f.* **1.** distinctness; precision. **2.** intelligibility, clarity.

отчётлив|ый (~, ~а) *adj.* **1.** distinct; precise. **2.** intelligible, clear.

отчётно-вы́борн|ый *adj.*: **~ое собра́ние** meeting held to hear reports and elect new officials.

отчётност|ь, и *f.* **1.** book-keeping. **2.** accounts.

отчёт|ный *adj. of* **~; о. бланк** report card; **о. год** financial year, current year; **о. докла́д** report.

отчи́зн|а, ы *f.* (*poet.*) one's country, native land; mother country, fatherland.

о́тчий *adj.* (*obs., poet.*) paternal.

о́тчим, а *m.* step-father.

о́тчина, ы *f.* = **во́тчина**

отчисле́ни|е, я *nt.* **1.** deduction. **2.** assignment. **3.** dismissal.

отчи́сл|ить, ю, ишь *pf.* (*of* **~я́ть**) **1.** to deduct; **о. часть зарпла́ты в упла́ту подохо́дного нало́га** to deduct part of wages for income-tax payment. **2.** to assign. **3.** to dismiss; **о. в запа́с** (*mil.*) to transfer to the reserve.

отчисл|я́ть, я́ю *impf. of* **~́ить**

отчи́|стить, щу, стишь *pf.* (*of* **~ща́ть**) **1.** to clean off; to brush off. **2.** to clean up.

отчи́|ститься, щусь, стишься *pf.* (*of* **~ща́ться**) **1.** to come off, come out. **2.** to become clean.

отчит|а́ть, а́ю *pf.* (*of* **~́ывать**) (*coll.*) to read a lecture (to), tell off.

отчит|а́ться, а́юсь *pf.* (*of* **~́ываться**) (**в**+*p.*) to give an account (of), report (on); **о. пе́ред избира́телями** to report back to the electors.

отчи́тыва|ть(ся), ю(сь) *impf. of* **отчита́ть(ся)**

отчища́|ть(ся), ю(сь) *impf. of* **отчи́стить(ся)**

отчу|ди́ть, жу́, ди́шь *pf.* (*of* **~жда́ть**) (*leg.*) to alienate, estrange.

отчужда́|емый *pres. part. pass. of* **~ть** *and adj.* (*leg.*) alienable.

отчужда́|ть, ю *impf. of* **отчуди́ть**

отчужде́ни|е, я *nt.* **1.** (*leg.*) alienation. **2.** estrangement.

отчуждённост|ь, и *f.* estrangement.

отшага́|ть, ю *pf.* (*coll.*) to walk; to tramp; to trudge.

отшагн|у́ть, у́, ёшь *pf.* (*coll.*) to step aside, step back.

отшагн|у́ться, у́сь, ёшься *pf.* (**от**) **1.** to start back (from); to recoil (from). **2.** (*fig.*) to give up; to forsake; to break (with); **о. от дру́га** to give up a friend.

отшвы́рива|ть, ю *impf. of* **отшвырну́ть**

отшвыр|ну́ть, ну́, нёшь *pf.* (*of* **~́ивать**) to fling away; to throw off.

отше́льник, а *m.* hermit, anchorite; (*fig.*) recluse.

отше́льни|ческий *adj. of* **~к**

отше́льничеств|о, а *nt.* a hermit's life, a recluse's life (*also fig., iron.*).

отши́б, а *m. only in phr.* **на ~е** at a distance (*from a settlement*); **жить на ~е** (*fig.*) to live in seclusion, live a recluse's life.

отшиб|áть, áю *impf. of* **~и́ть**
отшиб|и́ть, ý, ёшь, *past* **∸, ∸ла** *pf.* (*of* **~áть**) (*coll.*) **1.** to break off; to knock off; **о. рýчку у чáйника** to knock the handle off a teapot; **у меня́ ∸ло пáмять** my memory has failed me. **2.** to hurt; **о. себé рýку** to hurt one's arm. **3.** to throw back.
отши́ть, отошью́, отошьёшь *pf.* (*coll.*) to snub, rebuff.
отшлёп|ать, аю *pf.* (*of* **~ывать**) (*coll.*) to spank.
отшлёпыва|ть, ю *impf. of* **отшлёпать**
отшлиф|овáть, ýю *pf.* (*of* **~óвывать**) to grind; to polish (*also fig.*).
отшпи́лива|ть(ся), ю(сь) *impf. of* **отшпи́лить(ся)**
отшпи́л|ить, ю, ишь *pf.* (*of* **~ивать**) to unpin, unfasten.
отшпи́л|иться, юсь, ишься *pf.* (*of* **~иваться**) to come unpinned, come unfastened.
отштукатýр|ить, ю, ишь *pf. of* **штукатýрить**
отшу|ти́ться, чýсь, ∸тишься *pf.* (*of* **∸чиваться**) to laugh off; to make a joke in reply.
отшýчива|ться, юсь *impf. of* **отшути́ться**
отщелкá|ть, ю *pf.* (*coll.*) to slang.
отщепéн|ец, ца *m.* renegade.
отщеп|и́ть, лю́, и́шь *pf.* (*of* **~ля́ть**) to chip off.
отщепля́|ть, ю *impf. of* **отщепи́ть**
отщип|áть, лю́, ∸лешь *pf.* (*of* **∸ывать**) to pinch off, nip off.
отщи́пыва|ть, ю *impf. of* **отщипáть**
отъ... *vbl. pref.* = **от...**
отъедá|ть(ся), ю(сь) *impf. of* **отъéсть(ся)**
отъéзд, а *m.* departure.
отъé з|дить, жу, дишь *pf.* (*coll.*) to have driven; to have covered (*driving, riding.*)
отъезжá|ть, ю *impf. of* **отъéхать**
отъезжá|ющий *pres. part. of* **~ть**; *as n.* **о., ~ющего** *m.* departing pers.
отъéзжий *adj.* (*obs.*) distant.
отъёмный *adj.* removable, detachable.
отъé|сть, м, шь, ст, ди́м, ди́те, дя́т, *past* **~л, ~ла** *pf.* (*of* **~дáть**) to eat off.
отъé|сться, мся, шься, стся, ди́мся, ди́тесь, дя́тся, *past* **~лся, ~лась** *pf.* (*of* **~дáться**) to put on weight; to feed well.
отъé|хать, ду, дешь *pf.* (*of* **~зжáть**) to depart.
отъя́вленный *adj.* (*coll., pej.*) thorough, inveterate, out-and-out.
от|ъя́ть, ыму́, ы́мешь *pf.* (*obs.*) = **~ня́ть**
отыгр|áть, áю *pf.* (*of* **∸ывать**) to win back.
отыгр|áться, áюсь *pf.* (*of* **∸ываться**) **1.** to win back, get back what one has lost. **2.** (*fig., coll.*) to get out (*of an awkward situation*).
оты́грыва|ть(ся), ю(сь) *impf. of* **отыгрáть(ся)**
óтыгрыш, а *m.* sum won back.
отымённый *adj.* (*ling.*) denominative.
оты|скáть, щý, ∸щешь *pf.* (*of* **∸скивать**) to find; to track down, run to earth.
оты|скáться, щýсь, ∸щешься *pf.* (*of* **∸скиваться**) to turn up, appear.
оты́скива|ть, ю *impf.* **1.** *impf. of* **отыскáть. 2.** (*impf. only*) to look for, try to find.
оты́скива|ться, юсь *impf. of* **отыскáться**
отэкзамен|овáть, ýю *pf.* to finish examining.
отяго|ти́ть, щý, ти́шь *pf.* (*of* **~щáть**) to burden.
отягощá|ть, ю *impf. of* **отяготи́ть**
отягч|áть, áю *impf. of* **~и́ть; ~áющие (винý) обстоя́тельства** aggravating circumstances.
отягч|и́ть, ý, и́шь *pf.* (*of* **~áть**) to aggravate.
отяжелéлый *adj.* heavy.
отяжелé|ть, ю *pf.* to become heavy.
офéн|ский *adj. of* **~я**
офéн|я, и *m.* (*hist.*) pedlar, huckster.
офи́т, а *m.* (*min.*) ophite.
офицéр, а *m.* officer.
офицéр|ский *adj. of* **~; ~ское собрáние** officers' mess.
офицéрств|о, а *nt.* **1.** (*collect.*) the officers. **2.** commissioned rank.
официáльн|ый *adj.* official; **~ое лицó** an official.
официáнт, а *m.* waiter.
официáнтк|а, и *f.* waitress.
официóз, а *m.* semi-official organ (*of press*).
официóз|ный (~ен, ~на) *adj.* semi-official.
оформи́тел|ь, я *m.* decorator, stage-painter.
офóрм|ить, лю, ишь *pf.* (*of* **~ля́ть**) **1.** to get up, mount, put into shape; **о. пьéсу** to design the sets for a play. **2.** to register officially, legalize; **о. вступлéние в брак** to register a marriage; **о. докумéнт** to draw up a paper. **3.** to enrol, take on the staff.
офóрм|иться, люсь, ишься *pf.* (*of* **~ля́ться**) **1.** to take shape. **2.** to be registered; to legalize one's position. **3.** to be taken on the staff, join the staff.
оформлéни|е, я *nt.* **1.** get-up; mounting; **сцени́ческое о.** staging. **2.** registration, legalization.
оформля́|ть(ся), ю(сь) *impf. of* **офóрмить(ся)**
офóрт, а *m.* etching.
офранцý|зить, жу, зишь *pf.* to Gallicize, Frenchify.
офранцý|зиться, жусь, зишься *pf.* to become Gallicized, Frenchified.
офсáйд, а *m.* (*sport*) offside.
офсéт, а *m.* (*typ.*) offset process.
офтальми́|я, и *f.* (*med.*) ophthalmia.
офтальмóлог, а *m.* ophthalmologist.
офтальмологи́ческий *adj.* ophthalmological.
офтальмолóги|я, и *f.* ophthalmology.
ох *int.* oh!; ah!
охáива|ть, ю *impf. of* **охáять**
охáльник, а *m.* (*coll.*) mischief-maker.
охáльнича|ть, ю *impf.* (*coll.*) to get up to mischief.
охáльный *adj.* mischievous.
óхань|е, я *nt.* (*coll.*) moaning, groaning.
охáпк|а, и *f.* armful; **взять в ~у** (*coll.*) to take in one's arms.
охарактериз|овáть, ýю *pf.* to characterize, describe.
óх|ать, аю *impf.* (*of* **~нуть**) to moan, groan; to sigh.
охá|ять, ю *pf.* (*of* **хáять** *and* **~ивать**) (*coll.*) to criticize, censure.
охвáт, а *m.* **1.** scope, range. **2.** inclusion. **3.** (*mil.*) outflanking, envelopment.
охва|ти́ть, чý, ∸тишь *pf.* (*of* **∸тывать**) **1.** to envelop; to enclose; **дом ~ти́ло плáменем** the house was enveloped in flames; **о. бóчку обручáми** to hoop a cask. **2.** to grip, seize; **их ~ти́л ýжас** they were seized with panic. **3.** (*+i.*) (*coll.*) to draw (in), involve (in); **о. молодёжь общéственной рабóтой** to draw young people into social work. **4.** (*fig.*) to comprehend, take in. **5.** (*mil.*) to outflank, envelop.
охвáтн|ый *adj.*: **~ое движéние** (*mil.*) flanking movement, enveloping movement.
охвáтыва|ть, ю *impf. of* **охвати́ть**
охвá|ченный *p.p.p. of* **~ти́ть; о. ýжасом** terror-stricken.
охвóстье, я *nt.* (*collect.*) **1.** chaff, husks. **2.** (*fig.*) rabble.
охладевá|ть, ю *impf. of* **охладéть**
охладéлый *adj.* (*obs.*) cold; grown cold.
охладé|ть, ю *pf.* (*of* **~вáть**) to grow cold; (*fig.*; **к**) to grow cold (towards), lose interest (in).
охлади́тел|ь, я *m.* (*tech.*) cooler, refrigerator; condenser.
охлади́тельный *adj.* cooling.
охла|ди́ть, жý, ди́шь *pf.* (*of* **~ждáть**) to cool, cool off (*also fig.*); **о. чей-н. пыл** to damp s.o.'s ardour.
охла|ди́ться, жýсь, ди́шься *pf.* (*of* **~ждáться**) to become cool, cool down (*also fig.*).
охлаждá|ть(ся), ю(сь) *impf. of* **охлади́ть(ся)**
охлаждá|ющий *pres. part. act. of* **~ть** *and adj.* cooling, refrigerating; **~ющая жи́дкость** coolant; **~ющее прострáнство** condensation chamber.
охлаждéни|е, я *nt.* **1.** cooling (off); **повéрхность ~я** cooling surface; **с воздýшным ~ем** air-cooled. **2.** (*fig.*) coolness.
охлóп|ок, ка, *pl.* **~ки, ~ков** (*and* **~ья, ~ьев**) *m.* tuft; (*sg. only.*; *collect.*) waste (*of fibrous substances*).
охмелé|ть, ю *pf.* (*of* **хмелéть**) (*coll.*) to become tight.
охмел|и́ть, ю́, и́шь *pf.* (*of* **~я́ть**) to make intoxicated (*also fig.*).

охмел|я́ть, я́ю *impf. of* **~и́ть**
о́х|нуть, ну, нешь *pf. of* **~ать**
охоло|сти́ть, щу́, сти́шь *pf.* to castrate, geld.
охора́шива|ться, юсь *impf.* (*coll.*) to smarten o.s. up.
охо́т|а[1]**, ы** *f.* hunt, hunting; chase; **о. с ружьём** shooting; **псо́вая о.** riding to hounds; **соколи́ная о.** falconry; **ти́хая о.** (wild) mushroom gathering.
охо́т|а[2]**, ы** *f.* **1.** (**к** *or* +*inf.*) desire, wish, inclination; **у него́ больше нет ~ы писа́ть** he no longer has any desire to write; **по свое́й ~е** of one's own accord; **что ему за о.!** what makes him do it!; **о. тебе́ спо́рить с ним!** (*coll.*) what makes you argue with him! **2.** heat (*in female animals*).
охо́|титься, чусь, тишься *impf.* (**на**+*a. or* **за**+*i.*) to hunt; (*fig.*; **за**+*i.*) to hunt for.
охо́тк|а, и *f.*: **в ~у** (*coll.*) with pleasure, eagerly.
охо́тник[1]**, а** *m.* hunter; sportsman; **о. за привиде́ниями** ghostbuster.
охо́тник[2]**, а** *m.* **1.** (**до** *or* +*inf.*) lover (of); enthusiast (for); **он большо́й о. до грибо́в** he is a great mushroom lover. **2.** volunteer; **есть ли ~и пойти́?** are there any volunteers? will anyone volunteer to go?
охо́тнич|ий *adj.* hunting; sporting, shooting; **о. биле́т** hunting permit; **о. до́мик** shooting-box; **~ье ружьё** fowling-piece, sporting gun; **~ья соба́ка** hound, gun-dog; **о. расска́з** (*joc.*) traveller's tale, tall story.
охо́тно *adv.* willingly, gladly, readily.
охо́ч|ий (~, ~а) *adj.* (+*inf.*; *coll.*) inclined (to), keen (to), having an urge (to).
о́хр|а, ы *f.* ochre; **кра́сная о.** raddle, ruddle.
охра́н|а, ы *f.* **1.** guarding; protection; **о. труда́** measures for protection of labour. **2.** guard; **ли́чная о.** body-guard; **погрании́чная о.** frontier guard; **в сопровожде́нии ~ы** under escort, in custody.
охране́ни|е, я *nt.* safeguarding; (*mil.*) protection; **сторожево́е о.** outposts.
охрани́тел|ь, я *m.* **1.** (*rhet.*) protector, guardian. **2.** (*obs.*) conservative.
охрани́тельный *adj.* **1.** (*leg.*) protective. **2.** (*obs.*) conservative.
охран|и́ть, ю́, и́шь *pf.* (*of* **~я́ть**) to guard, protect.
охра́нк|а, и *f.* (*coll.*) Okhranka (*Secret Police Department in tsarist Russia*).
охра́нник, а *m.* (*coll.*) **1.** guard. **2.** secret police agent; member of Okhranka.
охра́н|ный *adj. of* **~а**; **~ная гра́мота, о. лист** safe-conduct, pass; **~ная зо́на** (*mil.*) restricted area; **~ное отделе́ние** (*hist.*) Secret Police Department (*in tsarist Russia*).
охран|я́ть, я́ю *impf. of* **~и́ть**
охри́плый *adj.* (*coll.*) hoarse.
охри́п|нуть, ну, нешь, *past* **~, ~ла** *pf.* (*of* **хри́пнуть**) to become hoarse.
о́хр|ить, ю, ишь *impf.* to colour with ochre.
охроме́|ть, ю *pf.* (*of* **хроме́ть**) (*coll.*) to go lame.
оху́лк|а, и *only in phrr.* **~и на́ руку не класть (положи́ть)** to have one's wits about one; **он ~и на́ руку не поло́жит** (*coll.*) he is no fool.
оцара́па|ть, ю *pf.* (*of* **цара́пать**) to scratch.
оцара́па|ться, юсь *pf.* to scratch o.s.
оце́жива|ть, ю *impf.*: **о. комара́** (*fig.*) to strain at a gnat.
оцело́т, а *m.* (*zool.*) ocelot.
оце́нива|ть, ю *impf. of* **оцени́ть**
оцен|и́ть, ю́, ~ишь *pf.* (*of* **~ивать**) **1.** to estimate, evaluate; to appraise; **о. в де́сять рубле́й** to estimate at ten roubles. **2.** to appreciate; **о. что-н. по досто́инству** to appreciate sth. at its true value.
оце́нк|а, и *f.* **1.** estimation, evaluation; appraisal; estimate; **о. иму́щества** valuation of property; **о. обстано́вки** (*mil.*) estimate of the situation. **2.** appreciation; **дать настоя́щую ~у чему́-н.** to give sth. a proper appreciation.
оце́н|очный *adj. of* **~ка**
оце́нщик, а *m.* valuer.
оцепене́лый *adj.* torpid; benumbed.
оцепене́|ть, ю *pf. of* **цепене́ть**
оцеп|и́ть, лю́, ~ишь *pf.* (*of* **~ля́ть**) to surround; to cordon off.
оцепле́ни|е, я *nt.* **1.** surrounding; cordoning off. **2.** cordon.
оцепля́|ть, ю *impf. of* **оцепи́ть**
оцинко́в|анный *p.p.p. of* **~а́ть** *and adj.* zinc-coated, galvanized.
оцинк|ова́ть, у́ю *pf.* (*of* **~о́вывать**) to (coat with) zinc, galvanize.
оцинко́выва|ть, ю *impf. of* **оцинкова́ть**
оча́г, а́ *m.* **1.** hearth (*also fig.*); **ку́хонный о.** kitchen range; **дома́шний о.** (*fig.*) hearth, home. **2.** (*fig.*) centre, seat; nidus; **о. войны́** seat of war; **о. зара́зы** nidus of infection; **о. землетрясе́ния** earthquake centre.
оча́нк|а, и *f.* (*bot.*) euphrasy, eyebright.
очарова́ни|е, я *nt.* charm, fascination.
очарова́тел|ьный (~ен, ~ьна) *adj.* charming, fascinating.
очар|ова́ть, у́ю *pf.* (*of* **~о́вывать**) to charm, fascinate.
очаро́выва|ть, ю *impf. of* **очарова́ть**
очеви́д|ец, ца *m.* eye-witness.
очеви́дно *adv.* obviously, evidently; **вы, о., не согла́сны** you obviously do not agree.
очеви́д|ный (~ен, ~на) *adj.* obvious, evident, manifest, patent.
очелове́чива|ть(ся), ю(сь) *impf. of* **очелове́чить(ся)**
очелове́ч|ить, у, ишь *pf.* (*of* **~ивать**) to make human, humanize.
очелове́ч|иться, усь, ишься *pf.* (*of* **~иваться**) to become human.
о́чень *adv.* very; very much.
очерви́ве|ть, ю *pf. of* **черви́веть**
очередн|о́й *adj.* **1.** next; next in turn; **о. вопро́с** the next question; **о. вы́пуск** latest issue (*of a journal, etc.*); **~а́я зада́ча** the immediate task; **~о́е зва́ние** the next higher rank. **2.** periodic(al); recurrent; usual, regular; (*pej.*) routine; **~ы́е неприя́тности** the usual trouble; **о. о́тпуск** regular holidays; **~а́я эпиде́мия гриппа** periodical epidemic of influenza.
очерёдност|ь, и *f.* periodicity; regular succession; order of priority.
о́черед|ь, и, *pl.* **~и, ~е́й** *f.* **1.** turn; **пропусти́ть свою́ о.** to miss one's turn; **о. за ва́ми** it is your turn; **в свою́ о.** in one's turn; **на ~и** next (in turn); **по ~и** in turn, in order, in rotation; **в пе́рвую о.** in the first place, in the first instance. **2.** queue, line; **стоя́ть в ~и (за**+*i.*) to queue (for), stand in line (for). **3.** (*mil.*): **(пулемётная) о.** burst; **батаре́йная о.** (battery) salvo.
очерёт, а *m.* (*bot.*) bog-rush.
о́черк, а *m.* essay, sketch, study; outline; **~и ру́сской исто́рии** studies in Russ. history.
очёркива|ть, ю *impf. of* **очеркну́ть**
очерки́ст, а *m.* essayist.
очерк|ну́ть, ну́, нёшь *pf.* (*of* **~ивать**) to place a circle round.
очерко́в|ый *adj. of* **о́черк**; **~ая тема́тика** subject-matter for an essay.
очерн|и́ть, ю́, и́шь *pf. of* **черни́ть 2.**
очерстве́лый *adj.* hardened, callous.
очерстве́|ть, ю́ *pf. of* **черстве́ть 2.**
очерта́ни|е, я *nt.* outline.
очер|ти́ть, чу́, ~тишь *pf.* (*of* **~чивать**) to outline; **~тя́ го́лову** (*coll.*) without thinking, headlong.
очёрчива|ть, ю *impf. of* **очерти́ть**
очёс, а *m.* (*collect.*) = **~ки**
оче|са́ть, шу́, ~шешь *pf.* (*of* **~сывать**) to comb out.
очёс|ки, ков *pl.* (*sg.* **~ок, ~ка** *m.*) combings; flocks; **льняны́е о.** flax tow.
очёсыва|ть, ю *impf. of* **очеса́ть**
очёчник, а *m.* spectacle case.
о́чи *pl. of* **о́ко**
очи́нива|ть, ю *impf. of* **очини́ть**
очин|и́ть, ю́, ~ишь *pf.* (*of* **~ивать** *and* **чини́ть**[2]) to sharpen, point.
очи́нк|а, и *f.* sharpening; **маши́нка для ~и карандаше́й** pencil-sharpener.
очисти́тельн|ый *adj.* purifying, cleansing; **о. аппара́т** (*tech.*) purifier; rectifier; **о. бак** (sugar) clarifier, clearing pan; **о. заво́д** refinery; **~ое сре́дство** cleanser, detergent.

очи́|стить, щу, стишь *pf.* (*of* **~ща́ть**) **1.** to clean; to cleanse, purify; (*tech.*) to refine; to rectify. **2.** **(от)** to clear (of); to free; **о. почто́вый я́щик** to clear a letter-box; **о. кише́чник** to open bowels. **3.** to peel.
очи́|ститься, щусь, стишься *pf.* (*of* **~ща́ться**) **1.** to clear o.s. **2.** **(от)** to become clear (of). **3.** *pass. of* **~стить**
очи́стк|а, и *f.* **1.** cleaning; cleansing, purification; (*tech.*) refinement; rectification; **мо́края о. га́за** gas scrubbing; **о. сто́чных вод** sewage disposal; **для ~и со́вести** (*coll.*) for conscience' sake. **2.** clearance; freeing; (*mil.*) mopping-up; **о. кише́чника** evacuation of the bowels.
очи́стк|и, ов *no sg.* peelings.
очи́т|ок, ка *m.* (*bot.*) stonecrop.
очища́|ть(ся), ю(сь) *impf. of* **очи́стить(ся)**
очище́ни|е, я *nt.* cleansing; purification; **ме́сячное о.** (*obs.*) menstruation.
очи́|щенный *p.p.p. of* **~стить**; *as n.* **~щенная, ~щенной** *f.* (*coll.*) vodka.
очк|и́, о́в *no sg.* spectacles; goggles; **защи́тные о.** protective goggles.
очк|о́[1], **а́**, *pl.* **~и́, ~о́в** *nt.* **1.** (*on cards or dice*) pip. **2.** (*in scoring*) point; **дать ~о́в вперёд** to give points. **3.** hole; **смотрово́е о.** peep-hole.
очк|о́[2], **а́** *nt.*: **втере́ть кому́-н. ~и́** (*coll.*) to throw dust in s.o.'s eyes.
очковтира́тельств|о, а *nt.* (*coll.*) deception.
очко́|вый[1] *adj. of* **~**[1]; **~вая систе́ма** points system (of scoring).
очко́в|ый[2] *adj.*: **~ая змея́** cobra.
очн|у́ться, у́сь, ёшься *pf.* **1.** to wake. **2.** to come to (o.s.), regain consciousness.
о́чн|ый *adj.* **1.** (*opp.* **зао́чный**) internal (*instruction, student, etc., as opposed to* external, extra-mural). **2.:** **~ая ста́вка** (*leg.*) confrontation.
очу́вств|оваться, уюсь *pf.* **1.** to come to (o.s.), regain consciousness. **2.** (*coll.*) to have a change of heart; to repent.
очуме́лый *adj.* (*coll.*) mad, off one's head; **бежа́ть, как о.** to run like a mad thing.
очуме́|ть, ю *pf.* (*coll.*) to go mad, go off one's head.
очут|и́ться, ⁓ишься *pf.* to find o.s.; to come to be; **о. в нело́вком положе́нии** to find o.s. in an awkward position; **как вы здесь ~и́лись?** how did you come to be here?
очу́ха|ться, юсь *pf.* (*coll.*) to come to o.s.
ошале́лый *adj.* (*coll.*) crazy, crazed.
ошале́|ть, ю *pf. of* **шале́ть**
ошара́шива|ть, ю *impf. of* **ошара́шить**
ошара́ш|ить, у, ишь *pf.* (*of* **~ивать**) (*coll.*) **1.** to beat, bang. **2.** (*fig.*) to strike dumb, flabbergast.
ошварт|ова́ть, у́ю *pf.* (*naut.*) to make fast.
оше́йник, а *m.* (*animal's*) collar; **соба́чий о.** dog-collar; **противоблоши́ный о.** flea collar.
ошеломи́тельный *adj.* stunning.
ошелом|и́ть, лю́, и́шь *pf.* (*of* **~ля́ть**) to stun.
ошеломле́ни|е, я *nt.* stupefaction.
ошеломля́|ть, ю *impf. of* **ошеломи́ть**; **~ющий** stunning.
ошельм|ова́ть, у́ю *pf. of* **шельмова́ть**
ошиб|а́ться, а́юсь *impf. of* **~и́ться**
ошиб|и́ться, у́сь, ёшься, *past* **~ся, ⁓лась** *pf.* (*of* **~а́ться**) to be mistaken, make a mistake, make mistakes; to be wrong; to err, be at fault.
оши́бк|а, и *f.* mistake; error; blunder; **по ~е** by mistake.
оши́боч|ный (~ен, ~на) *adj.* erroneous, mistaken.
оши́ка|ть, ю *pf.* (*of* **ши́кать 2.**) (*coll.*) to hiss off the stage.
ошлак|ова́ть, у́ю *pf.* (*no impf.*) (*tech.*) to form slack, form clinker.
ошмёт|ки, ков *pl.* (*sg.* **~ок, ~ка** *m.*) (*coll.*) worn out shoes; rags.
ошпа́рива|ть, ю *impf. of* **ошпа́рить**
ошпа́р|ить, ю, ишь *pf.* (*of* **~ивать**) to scald.
оштраф|ова́ть, у́ю *pf. of* **штрафова́ть**
оштукату́р|ить, ю, ишь *pf. of* **штукату́рить**
ошу́юю *adv.* (*arch.*) to the left, on the left hand.
ощен|и́ться, и́тся *pf. of* **щени́ться**
още́рива|ть(ся), ю(сь) *impf. of* **още́рить(ся)**
още́р|ить, ю, ишь *pf.* (*of* **~ивать**) (*coll.*) to gnash.
ощер|иться, юсь, ишься *pf.* (*of* **~иваться**) (*coll.*) to gnash one's teeth.
ощети́нива|ться, юсь *impf. of* **ощети́ниться**
ощети́н|иться, юсь, ишься *pf.* (*of* **~иваться** *and* **щети́ниться**) to bristle up (*also fig.*).
ощи́п|анный *p.p.p. of* **~а́ть** *and adj.* (*fig., coll.*) wretched, piteous.
ощип|а́ть, лю́, ⁓лешь *pf.* (*of* **щипа́ть 4.** *and* **⁓ывать**) to pluck.
ощи́пыва|ть, ю *impf. of* **ощипа́ть**
ощу́п|ать, аю *pf.* (*of* **~ывать**) to feel; to grope about (in).
ощу́пыва|ть, ю *impf. of* **ощу́пать**
о́щуп|ь, и *f.*: **на о.** to the touch; by touch; **идти́ на о.** to grope one's way.
о́щупью *adv.* **1.** gropingly, fumblingly; by touch; **иска́ть о.** to grope for; **пробра́ться о.** to grope one's way. **2.** (*fig.*) blindly.
ощут|и́мый (~и́м, ~и́ма) *adj.* = **~и́тельный**
ощути́тел|ьный (~ен, ~ьна) *adj.* **1.** perceptible, tangible, palpable. **2.** (*fig.*) appreciable.
ощу|ти́ть, щу́, ти́шь *pf.* (*of* **~ща́ть**) to feel, sense, experience; **о. го́лод** to feel hunger; **он ~ти́л её отсу́тствие** he felt her absence.
ощуща́|ть, ю *impf. of* **ощути́ть**
ощуще́ни|е, я *nt.* **1.** (*physiol.*) sensation. **2.** feeling, sense.
оягн|и́ться, и́тся *pf. of* **ягни́ться**

П

па *nt. indecl.* (*dance*) step.
па́в|а, ы *f.* peahen.
павиа́н, а *m.* baboon.
павильо́н, а *m.* **1.** pavilion. **2.** film studio.
павли́н, а *m.* peacock.
павли́н|ий *adj. of* **~**
па́вод|ок, ка *m.* flood (*esp. resulting from melting of snow*); freshet.
па́волок|а, и *f.* (*hist.*) pavoloka (*in Kievan Russia, heavy ornamented brocade, imported as a luxury item*).
пагина́ци|я, и *f.* pagination.
па́год|а, ы *f.* pagoda.
па́голен|ок, ка *m.* (*dial.*) leg (*of boot or stocking*).
па́губ|а, ы *f.* ruin, destruction; bane.
па́губ|ный (~ен, ~на) *adj.* pernicious, ruinous; baneful; fatal.
па́дал|ь, и *f.* (*usu. collect.*) carrion.
па́дан|ец, ца *m.* faller (*fallen fruit*).
па́да|ть, ю *impf.* **1.** (*pf.* **пасть** *and* **упа́сть**) (*in var. senses*) to fall; to sink; to drop; to decline; **баро́метр ~л** the barometer was falling; **~ет снег** it is snowing; **це́ны ~ют** prices are dropping; **се́рдце у них ~ло** their spirits were sinking; **п. ду́хом** to lose heart, lose courage; **п. в о́бморок** to faint; **п. от уста́лости** to be ready to drop. **2.** (*pf.* **пасть**) (*fig.*; **на**+*a.*) to fall (on, to); **отве́тственность ~ет на вас** the responsibility falls on you. **3.** (*impf. only*) (*ling.*; *of stress or accent*) to fall, be; **ударе́ние ~ет на пе́рвый слог** the stress is on the first syllable. **4.** (*impf. only*) (*of hair, teeth, etc.*) to fall out, drop out. **5.** (*pf.* **пасть**; *of cattle*) to die.
па́да|ющий *pres. part. of* **~ть** *and adj.* (*phys.*) incident; **~ющие звёзды** shooting stars.
паде́ж, а́ *m.* (*gram.*) case.
падёж, а́ *m.* murrain, cattle plague.
паде́ж|ный *adj. of* **~**; **~ное оконча́ние** case ending.

падё́ж|ный *adj. of* ~
Па-де-Калé *m. indecl.* **1.** the Pas de Calais (= *the Strait of Dover*). **2.** the Pas-de-Calais (*French department*).
падéни|е, я *nt.* **1.** fall; drop, sinking; **морáльное п.** degradation; **п. цен** slump in prices. **2.** (*phys.*) incidence; **ýгол ~я** angle of incidence. **3.** (*geol.*) dip. **4.: п. ударéния** (*ling.*) incidence of stress.
падишáх, а *m.* padishah.
пáд|кий (~ок, ~ка) *adj.* (**на**+*a. or* **до**) having a weakness (for), having a penchant (for); susceptible (to); **п. на дéньги** mercenary; **он ~ок до слáдкого** he has a sweet tooth.
пáдуб, а *m.* holly.
падýч|ий *adj.* (*obs.*) falling; **~ая звездá** shooting star; **~ая (болéзнь)** falling sickness, epilepsy.
пáдчериц|а, ы *f.* step-daughter.
паевóй *adj. of* **пай**[1]; **п. взнос** share.
па|ёк, йкá *m.* ration.
паенакоплéни|е, я *nt.* (*econ.*) share-accumulation.
паж, á *m.* (*hist.*) page.
пáж|еский *adj. of* ~; **П. Кóрпус** Corps of Pages (*hist.*; *name of mil. school in St. Petersburg*).
пáжит|ь, и *f.* (*obs., poet.*) pasture.
паз, а, о ~́е, в ~ý, *pl.* **~ы́, ~óв** *m.* (*tech.*) groove, slot, mortise, rabbet.
па|зи́ть, жý, зи́шь *impf.* (*tech.*) to groove, mortise.
пáзух|а, и *f.* **1.** bosom; **за ~ой** in one's bosom; **держáть кáмень за ~ой** (*fig.*) to nurse a grievance, harbour a grudge; **жить как у Христá за ~ой** to live in clover. **2.** (*anat.*) sinus; **лóбные ~и** frontal sinuses. **3.** (*bot.*) axil.
пáин|ька, ьки, *g. pl.* **~ек** *c.g.* (*coll.*) good child; **будь п.!** be a good boy (girl)!; **п.-мáльчик** good (little) boy.
па|й[1]**, я,** *pl.* **~и́, ~ёв** *m.* share; **вступи́тельный п.** initial shares; **товáрищество на ~я́х** joint-stock company; **на ~я́х** (*fig., coll.*) on an equal footing, going shares.
пай-...[2] *c.g. indecl.* (*coll.*) good child; **п.-мáльчик** good (little) boy.
пáйк|а, и *f.* solder(ing).
пайкóвый *adj. of* **паёк**; rationed.
пáйщик[1]**, а** *m.* shareholder.
пáйщик[2]**, а** *m.* solderer.
пак, а *no pl., m.* pack-ice.
пакгáуз, а *m.* warehouse, storehouse; **тамóженный п.** bonded warehouse.
пакéт, а *m.* **1.** parcel, package; packet; **индивидуáльный п.** (*mil.*) individual field dressing; first-aid packet. **2.** (official) letter. **3.** paper bag.
Пакистáн, а *m.* Pakistan.
пакистáн|ец, ца *m.* Pakistani.
пакистáн|ка, ки *f. of* **~ец**
пакистáнский *adj.* Pakistani.
пáкл|я, и *f.* tow; oakum.
пак|овáть, ýю *impf.* (*of* **у~**) to pack.
пáко|стить, щу, стишь *impf.* (*coll.*) **1.** (*pf.* **за~** *and* **на~**) to soil, dirty. **2.** (*pf.* **ис~**) to spoil, mess up. **3.** (*pf.* **на~**) (+*d.*) to play dirty tricks (on).
пáкостник, а *m.* (*coll.*) **1.** dirty dog, wretch. **2.** debauchee.
пáкост|ный (~ен, ~на) *adj.* dirty, mean, foul; nasty.
пáкост|ь, и *f.* **1.** dirty trick; **дéлать ~и** (+*d.*) to play dirty tricks (on). **2.** filth. **3.** obscenity, filthy word.
пакт, а *m.* pact; **п. о ненападéнии** non-aggression pact.
пал[1]**, а** *m.* (*naut.*) bollard; pawl.
пал[2]**, а** *m.* (*dial.*) fire.
палантúн, а *m.* fur tippet, stole.
палáт|а, ы *f.* **1.** (*pl. only*; *obs.*) palace. **2.** (*obs.*) chamber, hall; **Оружéйная п.** Armoury Museum (*in Moscow*); **у негó умá п.** (*coll.*) he is as wise as Solomon. **3.** (*hospital*) ward. **4.** (*pol.*) chamber, house; **вéрхняя, ни́жняя п.** Upper, Lower Chamber; **п. лóрдов** House of Lords; **п. óбщин** House of Commons. **5.** *as name of State institutions*; **Всесою́зная кни́жная п.** All-Union Book Chamber (*national bibliographical centre in Moscow*); **П. мер и весóв** Weights and Measures Office; **Торгóвая п.** Chamber of Commerce.
палатализáци|я, и *f.* (*ling.*) palatalization.
палатализ|овáть, ýю *impf. and pf.* (*ling.*) to palatalize.
палатáльный *adj.* (*ling.*) palatal.
палáтк|а, и *f.* **1.** tent; marquee; **в ~ах** under canvas. **2.** stall, booth.
палáт|ный *adj. of* **~а**; **~ная сестрá** ward sister.
палáццо *nt. indecl.* palace (*esp. of Venetian doges*).
палáч, á *m.* hangman; executioner; (*fig.*) butcher.
палáш, á *m.* broadsword.
пáлевый *adj.* straw-coloured, pale yellow.
палёны|й *adj.* singed, scorched; **пáхнет ~м** there is a smell of burning.
палеóграф, а *m.* palaeographer.
палеографи́ческий *adj.* palaeographic.
палеогрáфи|я, и *f.* palaeography.
палеозáвр, а *m.* palaeosaurus.
палеозóйский *adj.* (*geol.*) Palaeozoic.
палеоли́т, а *m.* (*archaeol.*) palaeolithic period.
палеолити́ческий *adj.* (*archaeol.*) palaeolithic.
палеонтóлог, а *m.* palaeontologist.
палеонтологи́ческий *adj.* palaeontologic(al).
палеонтолóги|я, и *f.* palaeontology.
Палести́н|а, ы *f.* Palestine.
палести́н|ец, ца *m.* Palestinian.
палести́н|ка, ки *f. of* **~ец**
палести́нский *adj.* Palestinian.
пáлехский *adj.* (made in) Palekh (*place famed for its lacquer-work*).
пáл|ец, ьца *m.* **1.** finger; **п. ноги́** toe; **большóй п.** thumb; **указáтельный п.** forefinger, index (finger); **срéдний п.** middle finger, third finger; **безымя́нный п.** fourth finger, ring-finger; **предохрани́тельный п.** finger-stall; (*fig.*): **п. о п. не удáрить, ~ьцем не шевельнýть** (*coll.*) not to raise a finger, not to stir o.s.; **емý ~ьца в рот не клади́** (*coll.*) he is not to be trusted, he needs to be watched; **~ьцы ломáть** to tear one's hair; **смотрéть сквозь ~ьцы на что-н.** (*coll.*) to shut one's eyes to sth.; **знать что-н., как свои пять ~ьцев** (*coll.*) to have sth. at one's finger-tips; **обвести́ когó-н. вокрýг ~ьца** (*coll.*) to twist s.o. round one's (little) finger; **вы́сосать из ~ьца** (*coll.*) to fabricate, concoct; **он ~ьцем никогó не трóнет** he wouldn't hurt a fly; **попáсть ~ьцем в нéбо** (*coll.*) to be wide of the mark; **как по ~ьцам рассказáть** to recount in detail, recount circumstantially. **2.** (*tech.*) pin, peg; cam, cog, tooth.
пале|я́, и́ *f.* (*hist. liter.*) Palaea (*early Russ. liter. form, borrowed from Byzantium, comprising exposition of Old Testament texts*).
палимпсéст, а *m.* palimpsest.
палингенéз, а *m.* (*biol.*) palingenesis.
палингенéз|ис, иса *m.* = ~
палиндрóм, а *m.* palindrome.
палисáд, а *m.* **1.** paling. **2.** (*mil.*) palisade, stockade.
палисáдник, а *m.* front garden.
палисáндр, а *m.* rosewood.
палисáндр|овый *adj. of* ~
пали́тр|а, ы *f.* palette.
пал|и́ть[1]**, ю́, и́шь** *impf.* **1.** (*pf.* **с~**) to burn, scorch. **2.** (*pf.* **о~**) to singe.
пал|и́ть[2]**, ю́, и́шь** *impf.* (*coll.*) to fire (*from gun*); **~и́!** (*word of command*) fire!
пáлиц|а, ы *f.* club, cudgel.
пáлк|а, и *f.* stick; cane, staff; **п. метлы́** broom-stick; **постáвить в ~и** (*obs.*) to cane, give a caning; **встáвить комý-н. ~и в колёса** to put a spoke in s.o.'s wheel; **из-под ~и** under the lash; **п. о двух концáх** two-edged weapon; **э́то п. о двух концáх** it cuts both ways.
паллáди|й, я *m.* (*chem.*) palladium.
паллиати́в, а *m.* palliative.
паллиати́вный *adj.* palliative.
палóмник, а *m.* **1.** pilgrim (*also fig.*). **2.** (*hist. liter.*) pilgrim's tale.
палóмнича|ть, ю *impf.* to go on (a) pilgrimage.
палóмничеств|о, а *nt.* pilgrimage (*also fig.*).
пáлочк|а, и *f.* **1.** *dim. of* **пáлка**; **барабáнная п.** drumstick; **волшéбная п.** magic wand; **дирижёрская п.** conductor's baton; **п.-выручáлочка** (*children's game*) 'I spy'; **пахýчая**

п. joss-stick; **ры́бная п.** fish finger. **2.** (*med.*) bacillus.
па́лочковый *adj.* (*med.*) bacillary.
па́лочник, а *m.* (*zool.*) stick insect.
па́л|очный *adj.* *of* **~ка; ~очные уда́ры** strokes of the cane; **~очная дисципли́на** discipline of the rod.
па́лтус, а *m.* halibut, turbot.
па́луб|а, ы *f.* deck; **полётная п.** flight deck; **жила́я п.** messdeck; **шлю́почная п.** boat deck.
па́луб|ный *adj.* *of* **~а; п. груз** deck cargo.
па́лый *adj.* (*dial.*; *of cattle*) dead.
пальб|а́, ы́ *f.* firing; **пу́шечная п.** cannonade.
па́льм|а, ы *f.* palm(-tree); **коко́совая п.** coconut(-tree); **фи́никовая п.** date(-palm); **получи́ть ~у пе́рвенства** to bear the palm.
па́льм|овый *adj.* *of* **~а; ~овое де́рево** boxwood; *as n.* **~овые, ~овых** Palmaceae.
па́льник, а *m.* (*mil.*; *obs.*) linstock.
пал|ьну́ть, ьну́, ьнёшь *inst. pf.* (*of* **~и́ть**²) to fire a shot; to discharge a volley.
пальтец|о́, а́ *nt.* (*coll.*) *dim. of* **пальто́**
пальти́ш|ко, ка, *pl.* **~ки, ~ек** *nt.* (*coll.*, *pej.*) *dim. of* **пальто́**
пальто́ *nt. indecl.* (over)coat; topcoat.
пальто́|вый *adj. of* **~**
пальцеви́д|ный (~ен, ~на) *adj.* finger-shaped.
пальцево́й *adj. of* **па́лец**
пальцеобра́з|ный (~ен, ~на) *adj.* (*bot.*) digitate.
па́ль|чатый *adj.* = **~цеобра́зный**
па́льчик, а *m. dim. of* **па́лец**; *see* **ма́льчик**
па́льщик, а *m.* (*tech.*) shot-firer, blaster.
пал|я́щий *pres. part. act. of* **~и́ть**¹ *and adj.* burning, scorching.
пампа́с|овый *adj. of* **~ы; ~овая трава́** pampas grass.
пампа́с|ы, ов *no sg.* (*geog.*) pampas.
пампу́шк|а, и *f.* (*dial.*) pampushka (*kind of fritter*).
памфле́т, а *m.* lampoon.
памфлети́ст, а *m.* lampoonist.
па́мятк|а, и *f.* **1.** (commemorative) booklet. **2.** instruction, written rules. **3.** (*coll.*, *obs.*) memento.
па́мятлив|ый (~, ~а) *adj.* (*coll.*) having a retentive memory, retentive.
па́мятник, а *m.* monument; memorial; tombstone; statue; **~и пи́сьменности** literary texts.
па́мят|ный (~ен, ~на) *adj.* **1.** memorable. **2.** serving to assist the memory; **~ная доска́** memorial plate, plaque; **~ная кни́жка** notebook, memorandum book.
па́мят|овать, ую *impf.* (*obs.*; **о**+*p.*) to remember.
па́мят|ь, и *f.* **1.** memory; **у него́ кури́ная п.** he has a memory like a sieve; **на мое́й ~и** within my memory; **говори́ть на п.** to speak from memory; **вдруг мне пришло́ на п., что…** suddenly I remembered that …; **по ~и** from memory; **по ста́рой ~и** from force of habit. **2.** memory, recollection, remembrance; **ве́чная п. ему́!** may his memory live for ever! **оста́вить по себе́ до́брую п.** to leave fond memories of o.s.; **в п.** (+*g.*) in memory (of); **подари́ть на п.** to give as a keepsake. **3.** mind, consciousness; **быть без ~и** to be unconscious; **быть от кого́-н. без ~и** (*coll.*) to be head over heels in love with s.o., be crazy about s.o. **4.** (*eccl.*; +*g.*) commemoration of death (of), feast (of).
пан, а, *pl.* **~ы́** *m.* **1.** (*hist.*) Polish landowner. **2.** gentleman; **ли́бо п., ли́бо пропа́л** (*prov.*) all or nothing.
панаги́|я, и *f.* (*eccl.*) panagia (*image worn round neck by Orthodox bishops*).
Пана́м|а, ы *f.* Panama.
пана́м|а, ы *f.* panama (hat).
панамерика́нский *adj.* Pan-American.
пана́мский *adj.* Panamanian.
панаце́|я, и *f.* panacea; **п. от всех зол** (*fig.*) universal panacea.
панба́рхат, а *m.* panne (*dress material*).
панда́н, а *m.* (*obs.*) complement; **в п. (к)** to complement.
панда́н|ус, уса *m.* (*bot.*) screw-pine.
па́ндус, а *m.* (*tech.*) ramp.
панеги́рик, а *m.* panegyric, eulogy.
панегири́ст, а *m.* panegyrist, eulogist.
панегири́ческий *adj.* panegyrical, eulogistic.
пане́л|ь, и *f.* **1.** pavement, footpath. **2.** panel(ling), wainscot(ting). **3.: п. прибо́ров** instrument panel; dashboard.
пане́ль|ный *adj.* *of* **~; ~ная обши́вка** panelling, wainscotting.
па́н|и *f. indecl. of* **~**
панибра́тский *adj.* (*coll.*) familiar.
панибра́тств|о, а *nt.* (*coll.*) familiarity.
па́ник|а, и *f.* panic; **впасть в ~у** to become panic-stricken, panic.
паникади́л|о, а *nt.* (*eccl.*) chandelier.
паникёр, а *m.* panic-monger, scaremonger, alarmist.
паникёр|ский *adj. of* **~**
паникёрств|о, а *nt.* alarmism.
паникёрств|овать, ую *impf.* (*no pf.*) (*coll.*) to be panic-stricken, panic.
паник|ова́ть, у́ю *impf.* (*no pf.*) (*coll.*) to panic.
панир|ова́ть, у́ю *impf.* (*cul.*) to bread.
паниро́вк|а, и *f.* (*cul.*) breading.
паниро́вочн|ый *adj.*: **~ые сухари́** (*cul.*) breadcrumbs.
панихи́д|а, ы *f.* office for the dead; requiem; **гражда́нская п.** civil funeral.
панихи́д|ный *adj. of* **~а**; (*fig.*) funereal.
пани́ческий *adj.* **1.** panic. **2.** (*coll.*) panicky.
панк, а *m.* (*also as indecl. adj.*) punk.
па́нков|ский *adj.* = **~ый**
па́нк|овый *adj. of* **~**
па́нкреас, а *m.* (*anat.*) pancreas.
панкреати́ческий *adj.* (*anat.*) pancreatic.
па́нн|а, ы *f.* (*Polish*) young lady.
панно́ *nt. indecl.* panel.
пано́птикум, а *m.* **1.** panopticon, collection of curios. **2.** waxworks.
панора́м|а, ы *f.* **1.** (*in var. senses*) panorama. **2.** (*mil.*) panoramic sight.
панора́мный *adj.* panoramic; **п. фильм** Cinerama (*propr.*) film.
пансио́н, а *m.* **1.** boarding school. **2.** boarding-house. **3.** (full) board and lodging; **ко́мната с ~ом** room and board; **жить на ~е** to have full board and lodging, live en pension.
пансиона́т, а *m.* holiday hotel, guest-house.
пансионе́р, а *m.* **1.** boarder (*in school*). **2.** guest (*in boarding-house*).
па́н|ский *adj. of* **~**
панслави́зм, а *m.* (*hist.*) Pan-Slavism.
па́нств|о, а *nt.* (*obs.*) **1.** (*collect.*) Polish landowners. **2.** superciliousness.
пантало́н|ы, ~ *no sg.* **1.** (*obs.*) trousers. **2.** (*woman's*) drawers, knickers.
панталы́к, а (у) *m.* (*coll.*) *only in phrr.* **сбить с ~у** to drive demented; **сби́ться с ~у** to be driven demented, be at one's wit's end.
пантеи́зм, а *m.* pantheism.
пантеи́ст, а *m.* pantheist.
пантеисти́ческий *adj.* pantheistic(al).
пантео́н, а *m.* pantheon.
панте́р|а, ы *f.* panther.
панто́граф, а *m.* (*tech.*) pantograph.
пантоми́м|а, ы *f.* pantomime, mime; dumb show.
пантомими́ческий *adj.* pantomimic.
пантоми́м|ный *adj.* = **~и́ческий**
панту́ф|ли, ель *no sg.* (*obs.*) slippers.
па́нт|овый *adj. of* **~ы**
пантокри́н, а *m.* Pantocrin (*medicament prepared from antlers of young Siberian stag*).
па́нт|ы, ов *no sg.* antlers of young Siberian stag (*as used in preparation of medicament*).
па́нцирн|ый *adj.* **1.** armour-clad, iron-clad. **2.** (*zool.*) testaceous; *as n.* **~ые, ~ых** Testacea.
па́нцир|ь, я *m.* **1.** (*hist.*) coat of mail, armour. **2.** (*zool.*) test. **3.** (*obs.*) diving suit.
панъевропе́йский *adj.* Pan-European.
па́п|а¹**, ы** *m.* (*coll.*) papa, daddy.
па́п|а²**, ы** *m.*: **п. ри́мский** (the) Pope.

папа́й|я, и *f.* papaya, paw-paw.
папа́х|а, и *f.* papakha (*Caucasian fur hat*).
папа́ш|а, и *m.* (*coll.*) = **па́па**
па́перт|ь, и *f.* church-porch, parvis.
папи́зм, а *m.* papism.
папилько́тк|а, и *f.* curling-paper.
папироло́ги|я, и *f.* papyrology.
папиро́с|а, ы *f.* cigarette (*of Russ. type, with cardboard mouthpiece*).
папиро́сник, а *m.* (*coll.*) cigarette vendor.
папиро́сниц|а[1], **ы** *f.* cigarette girl.
папиро́сниц|а[2], **ы** *f.* cigarette-case.
папиро́с|ный *adj. of* **~а; ~ная бума́га** rice-paper.
папи́рус, а *m.* papyrus.
папи́рус|ный *adj.*; *of* **~**
папи́ст, а *m.* papist.
па́пк|а, и *f.* **1.** file; document case, paper-case. **2.** cardboard, pasteboard; **переплетённый в ~у** in boards.
па́поротник, а *m.* fern.
па́поротник|овый *adj. of* **~**; ferny; *as n.* **~овые, ~овых** (*bot.*) Filicinae.
па́прик|а, и *f.* paprika.
па́пский *adj.* papal; **п. престо́л** St. Peter's chair.
па́пств|о, а *nt.* papacy; papal authority.
Па́пуа *f. indecl.* Papua.
папуа́с, а *m.* Papuan.
папуа́с|ка, ки *f. of* **~**
папуа́сский *adj.* Papuan.
папье́-маше́ *nt. indecl.* papier-mâché.
пар[1], **а, о ~е, в ~у́,** *pl.* **~ы́** *m.* **1.** steam; **быть под ~а́ми** to be under steam, have steam up; **на всех ~а́х** (*fig.*) full steam ahead, at full speed; **очи́стить ~а́ми** to fumigate. **2.** exhalation.
пар[2], **а,** *pl.* **~ы́** *m.* (*agric.*) fallow; **находи́ться под ~ом** to lie fallow.
па́р|а, ы *f.* **1.** (*in var. senses*) pair; couple; **супру́жеская п.** married couple; **п. сил** (*tech.*) couple; **ходи́ть ~ами** to walk in couples; **е́хать на ~е** to drive a pair (*of horses*); **на ~у мину́т** for a couple of minutes; **п. пустяко́в!** it's child's play!; it's a mere bagatelle!; **на ~у слов** for a few words; **под ~у** to match, to make up a pair; **она́ ему́ не п.** she is no match for him; **два сапога́ п.** (*coll., pej.*) they make a pair. **2.** suit (*of clothes*). **3.** (*school sl.*) a 'two' (*out of five*).
пара́бол|а[1], **ы** *f.* (*math.*) parabola.
пара́бол|а[2], **ы** *f.* parable.
параболи́ческий[1] *adj.* (*math.*) parabolic.
параболи́ческий[2] *adj.* parabolical.
парава́н, а *m.* (*naut.*) paravane.
парагва́|ец, йца *m.* Paraguayan.
Парагва́|й, я *m.* Paraguay.
парагва́|йка, йки *f. of* **~ец**
парагва́йский *adj.* Paraguayan.
пара́граф, а *m.* paragraph.
пара́д, а *m.* **1.** parade; (*mil.*) review; **возду́шный п.** air display; fly-past; **морско́й п.** naval review; **приня́ть п.** to inspect a parade. **2.** (*coll., joc.*) ceremonial get-up; **быть в по́лном ~е** to be all tricked out, be in one's best bib and tucker; **что э́то за п. у вас?** what's the big show?
паради́гм|а, ы *f.* (*gram.*) paradigm.
пара́дно-выходн|о́й *adj.*: **~а́я фо́рма вне стро́я** (*mil.*) ceremonial walking-out dress.
пара́дност|ь, и *f.* magnificence; ostentation.
пара́д|ный (~ен, ~на) *adj.* **1.** *adj. of* **~ 1.; п. костю́м** ceremonial dress; **~ная фо́рма** full dress (uniform). **2.** gala; **п. спекта́кль** gala night. **3.** main, front; **~ная дверь** front door; **п. подъе́зд** main entrance; *as n.* **~ное, ~ного** *nt. and* **~ная, ~ной** *f.* front door.
парадо́кс, а *m.* paradox.
парадокса́л|ьный (~ен, ~ьна) *adj.* paradoxical.
парази́т, а *m.* (*biol. and fig.*) parasite.
паразита́р|ный (~ен, ~на) *adj.* parasitic(al).
паразити́зм, а *m.* (*biol. and fig.*) parasitism.
паразити́р|овать, ую *impf.* to parasitize.
паразити́ческий *adj.* (*biol. and fig.*) parasitic(al).
паразити́ный *adj.* (*biol.*) parasitic.
паразитоло́ги|я, и *f.* parasitology.
парализо́ванност|ь, и *f.* paralysis.
парализо́в|анный *p.p.p. of* **~а́ть** *and adj.* paralysed.
парализ|ова́ть, у́ю *impf. and pf.* to paralyse (*also fig.*).
парали́тик, а *m.* paralytic.
паралити́ческий *adj.* paralytic.
парали́ч, а́ *m.* paralysis; palsy.
парали́чный *adj.* paralytic; **п. больно́й** paralytic.
паралла́кс, а *m.* (*astron.*) parallax.
параллелепи́пед, а *m.* (*math.*) parallelepiped.
параллели́зм, а *m.* parallelism.
параллелогра́мм, а *m.* (*math.*) parallelogram.
паралле́л|ь, и *f.* (*in var. senses*) parallel; **провести́ п. (ме́жду)** to draw a parallel (between).
паралле́льно *adv.* (**с**+*i.*) **1.** parallel (with). **2.** simultaneously (with), at the same time(as).
паралле́льност|ь, и *f.* parallelism.
паралле́л|ьный (~ен, ~ьна) *adj.* (*in var. senses*) parallel; **~ьные бру́сья** (*sport*) parallel bars; **~ая медици́на** alternative *or* complementary medicine.
паралоги́зм, а *m.* paralogism.
парамагнети́зм, а *m.* (*phys.*) paramagnetism.
парамагни́тный *adj.* (*phys.*) paramagnetic.
пара́метр, а *m.* (*math.*) parameter.
паранндж|а́, и́ *f.* yashmak.
парано́ик, а *m.* (*med.*) paranoiac.
параноический *adj.* (*med.*) paranoid; paranoiac.
парано́й|я, и *f.* (*med.*) paranoia.
парапе́т, а *m.* parapet.
парати́ф, а *m.* paratyphoid.
пара́ф, а *m.* **1.** paraph. **2.** initials.
парафи́н, а *m.* paraffin (wax).
парафи́н|овый *adj. of* **~**
парафи́р|овать, ую *impf. and pf.* (*dipl.*) to initial.
парафра́з, а *m.* paraphrase.
парафра́з|а, ы *f.* = **~**
парафрази́р|овать, ую *impf. and pf.* to paraphrase.
пара́ш|а, и *f.* (*prison sl.*) close-stool.
парашю́т, а *m.* **1.** parachute; **на ~е** by parachute; **прыжо́к с ~ом** parachute jump. **2.** (*sport, coll.*) high cross.
парашюти́зм, а *m.* parachute jumping (*as sport*); sky-diving.
парашюти́ровани|е, я *nt.* (*aeron.*) pancaking.
парашюти́р|овать, ую *impf.* (*of* **с~**) (*aeron.*) to pancake.
парашюти́ст, а *m.* parachute jumper; sky-diver; **п.-деса́нтник** paratrooper.
парашю́т|ный *adj. of* **~**; **п. спорт** parachute jumping; sky-diving.
парвеню́ *m. indecl.* parvenu, upstart.
пардо́н 1. *int.* (I beg your) pardon. **2.** *as n., in phr.* **проси́ть ~у** to ask forgiveness.
паренхи́м|а, ы *f.* (*anat., bot.*) parenchyma.
па́рен|ый *adj.* stewed; **деше́вле ~ой ре́пы** dirt-cheap.
па́р|ень, ня, *pl.* **~ни, ~не́й** *m.* **1.** boy, lad. **2.** (*coll.*) chap, fellow.
пари́ *nt. indecl.* bet; **держа́ть п., идти́ на п.** to bet, lay a bet; **п. держу́, что...** I bet that ....
Пари́ж, а *m.* Paris.
парижа́н|ин, ина, *pl.* **~е, ~** *m.* Parisian.
парижа́н|ка, ки *f. of* **~ин**; Parisienne.
пари́жск|ий *adj.* Parisian; **~ая лазу́рь ~ая синь** Paris blue, ferric ferrocyanide.
пари́к, а́ *m.* wig.
парикма́хер, а *m.* barber; hairdresser.
парикма́херск|ая, ой *f.* barber's (shop), hairdresser's; hairdressing saloon.
пари́л|ьня, ьни, *g. pl.* **~ен** *f.* **1.** sweating-room (*in baths*). **2.** (*tech.*) steam-shop.
па́рильщик, а *m.* sweating-room attendant.
пари́р|овать, ую *impf. and pf.* (*pf. also* **от~**) to parry, counter.
парите́т, а *m.* parity.
парите́т|ный *adj. of* **~**; **на ~ных нача́лах (с**+*i.*) on a par (with), on an equal footing(with).
па́р|ить, ю, ишь *impf.* (*no pf.*) **1.** to steam. **2.** to steam out,

sweat out (*in baths, to beat about the body with a heated besom to induce perspiration*). **3.** (*cul.*) to stew. **4.** (*impers.*): **~ит** it is sultry.

пар|и́ть, ю́, и́шь *impf.* (*no pf.*) to soar, swoop, hover; **п. в облака́х** (*fig.*) to live in the clouds.

па́р|иться, юсь, ишься *impf.* **1.** (*pf.* **по~**) to steam, sweat (*in baths*). **2.** (*cul.*) to stew.

па́ри|я, и, *g. pl.* **~й** *c.g.* pariah, outcast.

парк, а *m.* **1.** park; **разби́ть п.** to lay out a park. **2.** yard, depot; (*mil.*) park, depot; **артиллери́йский п.** ordnance depot; **трамва́йный п.** tram depot. **3.** fleet; stock; pool; **автомоби́льный п.** fleet of motor vehicles; **ваго́нный п.** rolling-stock; **мирово́й п. персона́льных компью́теров** the total number of personal computers in the world.

па́рк|а[1], **и** *f.* **1.** steaming. **2.** (*cul.*) stewing.

па́рк|а[2], **и** *f.* parka (*skin jacket worn by Eskimos, etc.*).

парке́т, а *m.* parquet; parquetry; **настла́ть п.** to parquet, lay a parquet floor.

парке́тин|а, ы *f.* parquet block.

парке́т|ный *adj. of* **~**; **п. пол** parquet floor; **п. шарку́н** (*fig., coll., pej.*) socialite.

парке́тчик, а *m.* parquet floor layer.

па́р|кий (~ок, ~ка) *adj.* (*coll.*) steamy.

па́ркинг, а *m.* car park.

парк|ова́ть, у́ю *impf.* (*of* **запаркова́ть**) to park.

парк|ова́ться, у́юсь *impf.* (*of* **запаркова́ться**) to park.

парко́вочный *adj.*: **п. автома́т** *or* **счётчик** parking meter.

па́рк|овый *adj. of* **~**; **~овые культу́ры** park plants.

парла́мент, а *m.* parliament.

парламентари́зм, а *m.* parliamentarism.

парламента́ри|й, я *m.* parliamentarian.

парламента́рный *adj.* parliamentarian.

парламентёр, а *m.* (*mil.*) envoy; bearer of a flag of truce.

парламентёр|ский *adj. of* **~**; **п. флаг** flag of truce.

парла́ментский *adj.* parliamentary; **п. зако́н** Act of Parliament; **п. запро́с** interpellation.

парна́с|ец, ца *m.* (*liter.*) Parnassian.

парна́сский *adj.* (*liter.*) Parnassian.

парни́к, а́ *m.* hotbed, seed-bed; forcing bed; **в ~е́** under glass.

парник|о́вый *adj. of* **~**; **~о́вые расте́ния** hothouse plants.

парни́шк|а, и *m.* (*coll.*) boy, lad.

парн|о́й *adj.* **1.** fresh; **~о́е молоко́** milk fresh from the cow; **~о́е мя́со** fresh meat. **2.** (*coll.*) steamy.

парнокопы́тн|ые, ~ых *pl.* (*sg.* **~ое, ~ого** *nt.*) (*zool.*) Artiodactyla, artiodactyls.

па́рн|ый[1] *adj.* **1.** pair; forming a pair; twin; **п. носо́к, п. сапо́г,** *etc.*, pair, fellow (*other one of pair of socks, boots, etc.*); **~ая гре́бля** sculling. **2.** pair-horse. **3.**: **~ые ли́стья** (*bot.*) conjugate leaves.

па́рный[2] *adj.* (*coll.*) steamy.

парови́к, а́ *m.* **1.** (*tech.*) boiler. **2.** (*coll., obs.*) steam-engine. **3.** local steam-train.

парово́з, а *m.* (steam-)engine, locomotive.

парово́зник, а *m.* loco man (*engine-driver or fireman*).

парово́з|ный *adj. of* **~**; **~ная брига́да** engine crew; **~ное депо́** engine-shed.

паровозоремо́нтный *adj.* engine-repair, locomotive-repair.

паровозострое́ни|е, я *nt.* engine building, locomotive building.

паровозостро|и́тельный *adj. of* **~е́ние; п. заво́д** engine-building works.

паров|о́й[1] *adj.* **1.** *adj. of* **пар**[1]; **~а́я маши́на** steam-engine; **~о́е отопле́ние** steam heating; central heating; **~а́я пра́чечная** steam laundry. **2.** (*cul.*) steamed.

парово́й[2] *adj.* lying fallow.

паровпускн|о́й *adj.* (*tech.*): **п. кла́пан** inlet valve; **~а́я труба́** steam supply pipe.

паровыпускно́й *adj.* (*tech.*) exhaust.

парогенера́тор, а *m.* (*tech.*) steam-generator.

парод|и́йный *adj. of* **~ия**

пароди́р|овать, ую *impf. and pf.* to parody.

пароди́ст, а *m.* mimic, impressionist.

паро́ди|я, и *f.* **1.** parody. **2.** skit. **3.** travesty, caricature.

пароко́нный *adj.* two-horse.

парокси́зм, а *m.* paroxysm.

паро́л|ь, я *m.* password, countersign.

паро́м, а *m.* ferry(-boat); **п.-самолёт** flying bridge, air ferry; **перепра́вить на ~е** to ferry.

паро́мщик, а *m.* ferryman.

паронепроница́емый *adj.* steam-tight, steam-proof.

парообра́зный *adj.* vaporous.

парообразова́ни|е, я *nt.* (*phys., tech.*) steam-generation, vaporization.

пароотво́дн|ый *adj.*: **~ая труба́** (*tech.*) steam exhaust pipe, steam-escape pipe.

пароотсека́тел|ь, я *m.* steam cut-off valve.

пароперегрева́тел|ь, я *m.* (*tech.*) steam superheater.

паро-пескостру́йный *adj.*: **п. аппара́т** (*tech.*) steam sand blaster.

паропрово́д, а *m.* (*tech.*) steam pipe.

парораспредели́тел|ь, я *m.* (*tech.*) steam distributor, steam header.

парораспредели́тельн|ый *adj.*: **~ая коро́бка** (*tech.*) steam-box.

парораспыли́тел|ь, я *m.* (*tech.*) steam atomizer.

паросбо́рник, а *m.* (*tech.*) steam collector; dome (*of boiler*).

паросилов|о́й *adj.*: **~а́я устано́вка** (*tech.*) steam power plant.

паро́сский *adj.* Parian; **п. мра́мор** Parian marble.

пароструйный *adj.* steamjet.

парохо́д, а *m.* steamer; steamship; **букси́рный п.** steam tug; **колёсный п.** paddle-boat *or* steamer; **океа́нский п.** ocean liner.

парохо́дик, а *m.* (*coll.*) **1.** *dim. of* **парохо́д. 2.** toy boat.

парохо́д|ный *adj. of* **~**; **~ное о́бщество** steamship company.

парохо́дств|о, а *nt.* **1.** steam-navigation. **2.** steamship-line.

парт... *comb. form, abbr. of* **парти́йный**

па́рт|а, ы *f.* (school) desk; **сесть за ~у** to begin to learn.

партакти́в, а *m.* (*pol.*) Party activists.

партбиле́т, а *m.* (*pol.*) party(-membership) card.

партеногене́з, а *m.* (*zool.*) parthenogenesis.

парте́р, а *m.* (*theatr.*) the pit; the stalls.

парте́сн|ый *adj.*: **~ое пе́ние** (*eccl.*) part-singing.

парти́|ец, йца *m.* (*Soviet Communist*) Party-member.

партиза́н, а, *pl.* **~ы** *m.* partisan; guerrilla.

партиза́н|ить, ю, ишь *impf.* (*coll.*) to be a partisan, fight with the partisans.

партиза́н|ский *adj.* **1.** *adj. of* **~**; **~ская война́** guerrilla warfare; **~ское движе́ние** the Resistance (movement) (*e.g. against Germany during World War II*); **п. отря́д** partisan detachment. **2.** (*fig., pej.*) unplanned, haphazard.

партиза́нств|о, а *nt.* **1.** guerrilla warfare; resistance movement. **2.** (*collect.*) partisans, guerrillas.

партиза́нщин|а, ы *f.* **1.** guerrilla warfare. **2.** (*fig., pej.*) unplanned work, haphazard work.

па́ртийк|а, и *f.* (*coll.*) *dim. of* **па́ртия**

парти́йк|а, и *f. of* **парти́ец**

парти́йност|ь, и *f.* **1.** Party spirit. **2.** party membership.

парти́йн|ый *adj.* (*pol.*) **1.** party; (Communist) Party; **п. биле́т** party-(Party-)membership card; **п. стаж** length of party (Party) membership; **~ая яче́йка** Party cell. **2.** Party (*in accordance with the spirit of the CPSU*); **п. дух** Party spirit. **3.** *as n.* **п., ~ого** *m.* (*Communist*) Party member.

партикуляри́зм, а *m.* (*pol.*) particularism.

партикуля́р|ный (~ен, ~на) *adj.* (*obs.*) **1.** private; unofficial. **2.** civil; **~ное пла́тье** civilian clothes, mufti.

партиту́р|а, ы *f.* (*mus.*) score.

па́рти|я[1], **и** *f.* (*pol.*) party; the Party.

па́рти|я[2], **и** *f.* **1.** party, group. **2.** batch; lot; consignment (*of goods*). **3.** (*sport*) game; set. **4.** (*mus.*) part. **5.** (*obs.*) (good) match (*marriage*); **сде́лать хоро́шую ~ю** to make a good match.

парткабине́т, а *m.* Party educational centre.

партко́м, а *m.* Party committee.

партнёр, а *m.* partner.

партнёрств|о, а *nt.* partnership; **войти́ в п. (с+*i.*)** to go into partnership (with).

парто́рг, а *m.* (*abbr. of* **парти́йный организа́тор**) Party organizer.
парторганиза́ци|я, и *f.* Party organization.
партста́ж, а *m.* length of (Communist) Party membership.
партсъе́зд, а *m.* Party congress.
па́руб|ок, ка *m.* (*Ukrainian*) boy, lad, youth.
па́рус, а, *pl.* **~а́** *m.* sail; **идти́ под ~а́ми** to sail, be under sail; **подня́ть ~а́, поста́вить ~а́** to make sail, set sail; **на всех ~а́х** in full sail (*also fig.*).
паруси́н|а, ы *f.* canvas, sail-cloth; duck.
па́русник, а *m.* sailing vessel, sailer.
па́рус|ный *adj. of* **~; п. спорт** sailing.
парфо́рсн|ый *adj.*: **~ая езда́** circus riding.
парфюме́р, а *m.* perfumer.
парфюме́ри|я, и *f.* (*collect.*) perfumery.
парфюме́р|ный *adj. of* **~ия; п. магази́н** perfumer's shop; **~ная фа́брика** perfumery.
парце́лл|а, ы *f.* (*agric.*) parcel (of land).
парцелли́р|овать, ую *impf. and pf.* (*agric.*) to parcel (out).
парцелля́ци|я, и *f.* (*agric.*) parcelling (out).
парч|а́, и́, *g. pl.* **~е́й** *f.* brocade.
парч|о́вый *adj. of* **~а́**
парш|а́, и́ *f.* tetter, mange; scab.
парши́ве|ть, ю *impf.* (*of* **за~** *and* **о~**) to become mangy; to be covered with scabs.
парши́в|ец, ца *m.* (*coll.*) lousy fellow.
парши́в|ый (~, ~а) *adj.* **1.** mangy, scabby; **~ая овца́** (*fig.*) black sheep. **2.** (*coll.*) nasty; rotten, lousy.
пас[1]**, а** *m.* (*cards*) pass; **объяви́ть п.** to pass; *as int.* **я п.** (I) pass; **в э́том де́ле я п.** (*fig., coll.*) I'm no good at this; this is not in my line.
пас[2]**, а** *m.* (*sport*) pass; *as int.* **п. сюда́!** pass!
па́сек|а, и *f.* apiary, bee-garden.
па́се|чный *adj. of* **~ка**
па́сквил|ь, я *m.* libel, lampoon, pasquinade; squib.
па́сквильный *adj.* libellous.
пасквиля́нт, а *m.* lampoonist, slanderer.
паску́д|ный (~ен, ~на) *adj.* (*coll.*) foul, filthy.
паслён, а *m.* (*bot.*) solanum; morel; **сла́дко-го́рький п.** bitter-sweet; **чёрный п.** deadly nightshade.
паслён|овый *adj. of* **~;** *as n.* **~овые, ~овых** Solanaceae.
па́см|о, а *nt.* (*text.*) lea.
па́смур|ный (~ен, ~на) *adj.* **1.** dull, cloudy; overcast. **2.** (*fig.*) gloomy, sullen.
пас|ова́ть[1]**, у́ю** *impf.* (*of* **с~**) **1.** (*also pf. in past tense*) (*cards*) to pass. **2.** (*fig., coll.*) to give up, give in; **п. пе́ред тру́дностями** to give in to difficulties.
пас|ова́ть[2]**, у́ю** *impf. and pf.* (*sport*) to pass.
па́сок|а, и *f.* (*anat.; obs.*) lymph.
па́сочниц|а, ы *f.* (*cul.*) mould for paskha.
па́с|очный *adj. of* **~ха 3.**
паспарту́ *nt. indecl.* passe-partout.
па́спорт, а, *pl.* **~а́** *m.* **1.** passport. **2.** registration certificate (*of motor vehicle, piece of machinery, etc.*).
паспортиза́ци|я, и *f.* **1.** passport system. **2.** (*tech.*) certification.
паспорти́ст, а *m.* passport officer.
па́спорт|ный *adj. of* **~; п. стол** passport office.
пасс, а *m.* (*in hypnotism*) pass.
пасса́ж, а *m.* **1.** passage; arcade. **2.** (*mus.*) passage. **3.** (*obs., coll.*) unexpected turn (of events); **како́й п.!** What a thing to happen!
пассажи́р, а *m.* passenger; **попу́тный п.** hitchhiker.
пассажи́р|ский *adj. of* **~; ~ское движе́ние** passenger services.
пасса́т, а *m.* (*meteor.*) trade wind.
пасса́т|ный *adj. of* **~; п. ве́тер** trade wind.
пасси́в, а *m.* **1.** (*comm.*) liabilities. **2.** (*gram.*) passive voice.
пасси́вност|ь, и *f.* passiveness, passivity.
пасси́в|ный (~ен, ~на) *adj.* **1.** passive; **~ное избира́тельное пра́во** (*pol.*) eligibility. **2.** (*econ.*): **п. бала́нс** unfavourable balance.
па́сси|я, и *f.* (*obs., coll.*) passion; **бы́вшая п.** old flame.
па́ст|а, ы *f.* paste; **зубна́я п.** toothpaste.
па́стбищ|е, а *nt.* pasture.
па́стбищный *adj.* pasturable.
па́ств|а, ы *f.* (*eccl.*) flock, congregation.
пасте́л|ь, и *f.* **1.** pastel, crayon. **2.** pastel (drawing).
пасте́льный *adj.* (drawn in) pastel.
пастериза́ци|я, и *f.* pasteurization.
пастеризо́в|анный *p.p.p. of* **~а́ть** *and adj.* pasteurized.
пастериз|ова́ть, у́ю *impf. and pf.* to pasteurize.
пастерна́к, а *m.* parsnip.
пас|ти́, у́, ёшь, *past* **~, ~ла́** *impf.* (*no pf.*) to graze, pasture; to shepherd, tend.
пастил|а́, ы́, *pl.* **~ы** *f.* pastila (*sort of fruit fudge*).
пас|ти́сь, ётся, *past* **~ся, ~ла́сь** *impf.* (*no pf.*) to graze, pasture; to browse.
па́стор, а *m.* (*Protestant*) minister, pastor.
пастора́л|ь, и *f.* **1.** (*liter.*) pastoral. **2.** (*mus.*) pastorale.
пастора́льный *adj.* pastoral, bucolic.
пасту́х, а́ *m.* herdsman; shepherd; cowboy.
пасту́|шеский *adj. of* **~х; п. по́сох** shepherd's crook.
пасту́|ший *adj. of* **~х; ~шья су́мка** (*bot.*) shepherd's purse.
пасту́шк|а, и *f.* shepherdess.
пастуш|о́к, ка́ *m.* **1.** *affectionate dim. of* **пасту́х. 2.** (*poet.*) swain. **3.** (*zool.*): **водяно́й п.** water-rail.
па́стыр|ский *adj. of* **~ь;** (*eccl.*) pastoral.
па́стыр|ь, я *m.* **1.** (*obs.*) shepherd. **2.** (*eccl.*) pastor.
па|сть[1]**, ду́, дёшь,** *past* **~л, ~ла** *pf. of* **~да́ть**
паст|ь[2]**, и** *f.* mouth (*of animal*); jaws.
пастьб|а́, ы́ *f.* pasturage.
Па́сх|а, и *f.* **1.** Passover. **2.** Easter. **3. п.** (*cul.*) paskha (*sweet cream-cheese dish eaten at Easter*).
пасха́ли|я, и *f.* (*eccl.*) paschal cycle, paschal tables.
пасынк|ова́ть, у́ю *impf. and pf.* (*bot.*) to prune, remove side shoots.
па́сын|ок, ка *m.* **1.** stepson, stepchild. **2.** (*fig.*) outcast. **3.** (*bot.*) side shoot.
пасья́нс, а *m.* (*card-game*) patience; **раскла́дывать п.** to play patience.
пат[1]**, а** *m.* (*in chess*) stalemate.
пат[2]**, а** *m.* (*cul.*) paste.
Патаго́ни|я, и *f.* Patagonia.
пате́нт, а *m.* (**на**+*a.*) patent (for); licence (for); **владе́лец ~а** patentee.
патенто́в|анный *p.p.p. of* **~а́ть** *and adj.* patent; **~анное лека́рство** patent medicine.
патент|ова́ть, у́ю *impf.* (*of* **за~**) to patent, take out a patent (for).
па́тер, а *m.* Father (*in designation of Catholic priest*).
патери́к, а́ *m.* (*eccl.; liter.*) Lives of the Fathers.
пате́тик|а, и *f.* (the) pathetic element; emotionalism.
патети́ческий *adj.* **1.** enthusiastic; passionate. **2.** emotional. **3.** bombastic.
патети́ч|ный (~ен, ~на) *adj.* = **~ский**
патефо́н, а *m.* (*small, portable*) gramophone.
патефо́н|ный *adj. of* **~**
па́тин|а, ы *f.* (*archaeol., tech.*) patina.
па́тл|ы, ~ *pl.* (*sg.* **~а, ~ы** *f.*) (*coll.*) locks (*of hair*).
пат|ова́ть, у́ю *impf.* (*of* **за~**) (*in chess*) to stalemate.
па́ток|а, и *f.* treacle; syrup; **све́тлая п.** golden syrup; **чёрная п.** molasses.
пато́лог, а *m.* pathologist.
патологи́ческий *adj.* pathological.
патоло́ги|я, и *f.* pathology.
па́то|чный *adj. of* **~ка;** treacly.
патриа́рх, а *m.* (*ethnol. and eccl.*) patriarch.
патриарха́льност|ь, и *f.* patriarchal character.
патриарха́л|ьный (~ен, ~ьна) *adj.* (*ethnol. and fig.*) patriarchal.
патриарха́т, а *m.* (*ethnol.*) patriarchy.
патриа́рхи|я, и *f.* (*eccl.*) patriarchate.
патриа́ршеств|о, а *nt.* (*eccl.*) patriarchate.
патриа́р|ший *adj. of* **~х** (*eccl.*).
патрио́т, а *m.* patriot.
патриоти́зм, а *m.* patriotism.
патриоти́ческий *adj.* patriotic.
патриоти́ч|ный (~ен, ~на) *adj.* = **~еский**
патри́стик|а, и *f.* (*eccl., liter.*) patristics, patristic studies.
па́триц|а, ы *f.* (*typ.*) punch.

патрициа́нский *adj. of* **патри́ций**
патри́ци|й, я *m.* (*hist.*) patrician.
патро́н[1], **а** *m.* **1.** (*in var. senses*) patron; (*eccl.*) patron saint. **2.** boss.
патро́н[2], **а** *m.* **1.** cartridge. **2.** (*tech.*) chuck (*of drill, lathe*), holder. **3.** lamp socket, lamp holder. **4.** (*tailor's*) pattern.
патрона́ж, а *m.* home visiting (*by health service worker*).
патрона́ж|ный *adj. of* ~; **~ная сестра́** district nurse, health visitor.
патрони́р|овать, ую *impf.* to patronize.
патро́нник, а *m.* (*mil.*) (cartridge-)chamber.
патро́н|ный *adj. of* ~[2]; **~ная ги́льза** cartridge case; **п. заво́д** cartridge factory; **~ная обо́йма** charger; cartridge clip; **~ная су́мка** cartridge pouch.
патронта́ш, а *m.* bandolier, ammunition belt.
па́труб|ок, ка *m.* (*tech.*) **1.** nipple, nozzle. **2.** socket, sleeve, connection; branch pipe. **3.** boss (*of thermometer*).
патрули́р|овать, ую *impf.* (*no pf.*) (*mil.*) to patrol.
патру́л|ь, я́ *m.* patrol.
патру́ль|ный *adj. of* ~; *as n.* **п., ~ного** *m.* patrol.
па́уз|а, ы *f.* pause; interval; (*mus.*) rest.
па́уз|ок, ка *m.* (*river*) lighter.
пау́к, а́ *m.* spider.
паукообра́зн|ые, ых *pl.* (*sg.* **~ое, ~ого** *nt.*) (*zool.*) Arachnida, arachnids.
па́упер, а *m.* pauper.
паупериза́ци|я, и *f.* pauperization.
паупери́зм, а *m.* pauperism.
паути́н|а, ы *f.* cobweb, spider's web; gossamer; (*fig.*) web; **п. лжи** tissue of lies.
паути́н|ка, ки *dim. of* **~а**; **чулки́-п.** very fine stockings.
пау́|чий *adj. of* **~к**
па́фос, а *m.* **1.** pathos. **2.** (*+g.*) enthusiasm (for), zeal (for); **п. коммунисти́ческого строи́тельства** enthusiasm for the building of Communism. **3.** spirit; emotional content; **п. рома́на** the spirit of a novel. **4.** (*pej.*) (*affected*) pathos, bombast.
пах, а, о ~́е, в ~у́ *m.* (*anat.*) groin.
па́ханы|й *adj.* ploughed (up); **~е зе́мли** ploughland.
па́хар|ь, я *m.* ploughman.
па|ха́ть, шу́, ~́шешь *impf.* to plough, till.
па́х|нуть, ну, нешь, *past* ~ *or* **~нул, ~ла** *impf.* (*no pf.*) (*+i.*) to smell (of); to reek (of); **~нет лу́ком** there is a smell of onions; (*fig.*) to savour (of), smack (of); **~нет бедо́й** this means trouble; **~ло ссо́рой** a quarrel was in the air.
пахн|у́ть, ёт *pf.* (*no impf.*) (*+i.*; *coll.*) to puff, blow; **~у́л ве́тер** there was a gust of wind; (*impers.*): **~у́ло хо́лодом** there came a cold blast.
пахово́й *adj.* (*anat.*) inguinal.
па́хот|а, ы *f.* ploughing, tillage.
па́хотный *adj.* arable.
па́хт|а, ы *f.* buttermilk; **жир ~ы** butterfat.
па́хтань|е, я *nt.* **1.** churning. **2.** butter-milk.
па́хта|ть, ю *impf.* to churn.
паху́ч|ий (~, ~а) *adj.* odorous, strong-smelling.
паца́н, а *m.* (*coll.*) boy, lad.
пацие́нт, а *m.* patient.
пацифи́зм, а *m.* pacifism.
пацифи́ст, а *m.* pacifist.
па́че *adv.* (*arch.*) more; *now only in phrr.* **тем п.** the more so, the more reason; **п. ча́яния** contrary to expectation; beyond expectation.
па́чк|а, и *f.* **1.** bundle; batch; packet, pack; **п. пи́сем** bundle of letters; **п. папиро́с** packet of cigarettes; **п. книг** parcel of books. **2.** (*mil.*) (*cartridge*) clip; **стреля́ть ~ами** (*obs.*) to fire bursts. **3.** tutu.
па́чка|ть, ю *impf.* **1.** (*pf.* **за~** *and* **ис~**) to dirty, soil, stain, sully (*also fig.*); **п. ру́ки** (*fig.*) to soil one's hands; **п. чьё-н. до́брое и́мя** to sully s.o.'s good name. **2.** (*pf.* **на~**) (*coll.*) to daub.
па́чка|ться, юсь *impf.* (*of* **за~, ис~,** *and* **на~**) **1.** to make o.s. dirty; to soil o.s. **2.** to become dirty.
пачкотн|я́, и́ *f.* (*coll.*) daub.
пачку́н, а *m.* (*coll.*) **1.** sloven. **2.** dauber.
паш|а́, и́, *g. pl.* **~е́й** *m.* pasha.
па́ш|ня, ни, *g. pl.* **~ен** *f.* ploughed field.
пашо́т, а *m.*: **яйцо́-п.** poached egg.
паште́т, а *m.* pâté, pie.
паэ́ль|я, и *f.* (*cul.*) paella.
па́юсн|ый *adj.*: **~ая икра́** pressed caviar(e).
пая́льник, а *m.* soldering iron.
пая́льн|ый *adj.* soldering; **~ая ла́мпа** blow lamp; **~ая тру́бка** blowpipe, blow torch.
пая́льщик, а *m.* tinman, tinsmith.
па́яный *adj.* soldered.
пая́снича|ть, ю *impf.* (*no pf.*) (*coll.*) to clown, play the fool.
пая́|ть, ю *impf.* (*no pf.*) to solder.
пая́ц, а *m.* **1.** (*circus*) clown. **2.** (*fig., pej.*) clown.
ПВО *f. indecl.* (*abbr. of* **противовозду́шная оборо́на**) (*mil.*) anti-aircraft defences.
пеа́н[1], **а** *m.* paean.
пеа́н[2], **а** *m.* (*med.*) Pean's forceps, clamp forceps.
пев|е́ц, ца́ *m.* singer.
певи́ц|а, ы *f. of* **пе́вец**
певу́н, а́ *m.* (*coll.*) songster.
певу́ч|ий (~, ~а) *adj.* melodious.
пе́вч|ий 1. *adj.* singing; **~ая пти́ца** songbird. **2.** *as n.* **п., ~его** *m.* chorister, choirboy.
пега́нк|а, и *f.* (*zool.*) shelduck.
пе́г|ий (~, ~а) *adj.* skewbald.
пед... *comb. form, abbr. of* **педагоги́ческий**
педаго́г, а *m.* teacher; pedagogue.
педаго́гик|а, и *f.* pedagogy, pedagogics.
педагоги́ческий *adj.* pedagogic(al); educational; **п. институ́т** teachers' training college; **п. факульте́т** education department (*for training educationalists*).
педагоги́ч|ный (~ен, ~на) *adj.* sensible, wise (*in sphere of education*).
педализа́ци|я, и *f.* (*mus.*) pedalling.
педализи́р|овать, ую *impf. and pf.* **1.** (*mus.*) to pedal. **2.** (*fig.*) to harp upon.
педа́л|ь, и *f.* pedal; treadle; **брать п., нажа́ть п.** to pedal; **рабо́тать ~ью** to treadle; **нажа́ть на все ~и** (*fig., coll.*) to go flat out.
педа́ль|ный *adj. of* ~; **п. нажи́м** pedalling; **п. автомоби́ль** pedal car (*child's pedal-operated motorcar*).
педа́нт, а *m.* pedant.
педанти́зм, а *m.* pedantry.
педанти́ческий *adj.* pedantic.
педанти́чност|ь, и *f.* pedantry.
педанти́ч|ный (~ен, ~на) *adj.* = **~еский**
педву́з, а *m.* = **growинститу́т**
пе́дел|ь, я *m.* bedel.
педера́ст, а *m.* p(a)ederast, sodomite.
педера́сти|я, и *f.* p(a)ederasty, sodomy.
педиа́тр, а *m.* p(a)ediatrician.
педиатри́|я, и *f.* p(a)ediatrics.
педикю́р, а *m.* chiropody.
педикю́рш|а, и *f.* chiropodist.
пединститу́т, а *m.* teacher training college.
педо́метр, а *m.* pedometer.
педофи́л, а *m.* paedophile.
педучи́лищ|е, а *n.* (primary and preschool) teacher training college.
пе́жин|а, ы *f.* **1.** skewbaldness. **2.** patch (*on skewbald horse*).
пейза́ж, а *m.* **1.** landscape; scenery. **2.** (*art*) landscape.
пейзажи́ст, а *m.* landscape painter.
пейза́ж|ный *adj. of* ~; **~ная живо́пись** landscape painting.
пек, а *m.* (*tech.*) pitch.
пёк, пекла́ *see* **печь**[1]
пека́рн|ый *adj.* baking; **~ая печь** bakehouse oven; **~ое ремесло́** bakery trade.
пека́р|ня, ни, *g. pl.* **~ен** *f.* bakery, bakehouse.
пе́кар|ский *adj. of* **~ь**; **~ские дро́жжи** baker's yeast.
пе́кар|ь, я, *pl.* **~я́, ~е́й** *and* **~и, ~ей** *m.* baker.
Пеки́н, а *m.* Peking; Beijing.
пеклева́нник, а *m.* fine rye bread.
пеклева́нн|ый *adj.* finely ground; **~ая мука́** rye flour (of the best quality); **п. хлеб** fine rye bread.

пекл|ева́ть, ю́ю, ю́ешь *impf.* to grind fine.
пе́кл|о, а *nt.* **1.** scorching heat; **попа́сть в са́мое п.** (*fig., coll.*) to get into the thick of it. **2.** (*coll.*) hell.
пекти́н, а *m.* (*chem.*) pectin.
пекти́новы|й *adj.* (*chem.*) pectic; **~е вещества́** pectins.
пеку́, пеку́т *see* **печь**[1]
пелен|а́, ы́, *pl.* **~ы́, ~, ~а́м** *f.* shroud; **с ~** (*obs., fig.*) from the cradle; **у него́ (сло́вно) п. (с глаз) упа́ла** the scales fell from his eyes.
пелена́|ть, ю *impf.* (*of* **за~** *and* **с~**) to swaddle.
пе́ленг, а *m.* (*naut., aeron.*) bearing.
пеленга́тор, а *m.* (*naut., aeron.*) direction finder.
пеленг|и́ровать, и́рую *impf. and pf.* = **~ова́ть**
пеленг|ова́ть, ую́ *impf. and pf.* (*naut., aeron.*) to take the bearings (of), set.
пелён|ка, ки *f.* nappy; (*pl.*) swaddling clothes; **с пелёнок** (*fig.*) from the cradle.
пелери́н|а, ы *f.* cape, pelerine.
пелика́н, а *m.* pelican.
пельме́н|и, ей *pl.* (*sg.* **~ь, ~я** *m.*) (*cul.*) pelmeni (*kind of ravioli*).
пе́мз|а, ы *f.* pumice(-stone).
пе́мз|овый *adj. of* **~а**
пе́н|а, ы *f.* **1.** foam, spume; scum; froth, head (*on liquids*); **мы́льная п.** soapsuds; **говори́ть с ~ой у рта, с ~ой на уста́х** (*fig.*) to foam at the mouth. **2.** lather (*on horses*).
пена́л, а *m.* pencil-box.
пена́т|ы, ов *no sg.* (*myth. and fig.*) penates; **верну́ться к (свои́м, родны́м) ~ам** to return to one's hearth and home.
Пенджа́б, а *m.* Punjab.
пенджа́б|ец, ца *m.* Punjabi.
пенджа́б|ка, ки *f. of* **~ец**
пенджа́бский *adj.* Punjabi.
пе́ни|е, я *nt.* singing; **п. (птиц)** (birds') song; **п. петуха́** cock's crow.
пе́нист|ый (~, ~а) *adj.* foamy; frothy; **~ое вино́** sparkling wine.
пенитенциа́рный *adj.* (*leg.*) penitentiary.
пе́н|ить, ю, ишь *impf.* to froth.
пе́н|иться, ится *impf.* to foam; to froth (*intrans.*).
пеницилли́н, а *m.* penicillin.
пе́нк|а[1]**, и** *f.* (*on milk, etc.*) skin; **снять ~и (с**+*g.*) to skim; (*fig.*) to take the pickings (of).
пе́нк|а[2]**, и** *f.* (*min.*): **морска́я п.** meerschaum.
пе́нк|овый *adj. of* **~а**[2]; **~овая тру́бка** meerschaum (pipe).
пе́нни *nt. indecl.* penny.
пе́н|ный *adj.* (*obs.*) = **~истый**
пенопла́ст, а *m.* foam rubber.
пенопласт|и́ческий *adj. of* **~**
пеностекл|о́, а́ *nt.* glass fibre.
пеностек|о́льный *adj. of* **~ло́**
пе́ночк|а, и *f.* (*zool.*) warbler (*Phylloscopus*).
пенс, а *m.* penny.
пенсионе́р, а *m.* pensioner.
пенсио́нн|ый *adj. of* **пе́нсия; ~ая кни́жка** pension book; **п. во́зраст** retirement age.
пе́нси|я, и *f.* pension.
пенсне́ *nt. indecl.* pince-nez.
пента́метр, а *m.* (*liter.*) pentameter.
пе́нтюх, а *m.* (*coll.*) lout, bumpkin.
пенчингбо́л, а *m.* punchball.
пень, пня *m.* stump, stub; **стоя́ть как п.** (*coll.*) to be rooted to the ground; **вали́ть че́рез п. коло́ду** (*coll.*) to do a thing anyhow.
пеньк|а́, и́ *f.* hemp.
пенько́вый *adj.* hempen.
пеньюа́р, а *m.* peignoir.
пе́н|я, и *f.* fine.
пеня́|ть, ю *impf.* (*of* **по~**) (+*d. or* **на**+*a.*; *coll.*) to blame, reproach; **~й на себя́!** you have only yourself to blame!
пео́н[1]**, а** *m.* (*liter.*) paeon.
пео́н[2]**, а** *m.* peon.
пе́п|ел, ла *m.* ash(es).
пепели́щ|е, а *nt.* **1.** site of fire. **2.** (hearth and) home; **верну́ться на ста́рое п.** to return to one's old home.
пе́пельниц|а, ы *f.* ash-tray.
пе́пельно-се́рый *adj.* ash-grey.
пе́пельн|ый *adj.* ashy; **~ого цве́та** ash-grey.
пепси́н, а *m.* (*physiol.*) pepsin.
пепси́новый *adj.* peptic.
пепто́н, а *m.* (*physiol.*) peptone.
пер. (*abbr. of* **переу́лок**) Lane.
перва́ч, а́ *m.* (*coll.*) first-quality goods.
перве́йший *adj.* (*coll.*) the first; first-class.
пе́рвен|ец, ца *m.* first-born; (*fig.*) firstling.
пе́рвенств|о, а *nt.* first place; (*sport*) championship; **завоева́ть п. ми́ра по футбо́лу** to win the world championship at football.
пе́рвенств|овать, ую *and* **~ова́ть, ~у́ю** *impf.* (*no pf.*) to take first place; **(над)** to take precedence (of), take priority (over).
первенств|у́ющий *pres. part. act. of* **~ова́ть** *and adj.* pre-eminent; primary.
перви́нк|а, и *f.*: **в ~у** (*coll.*) for the first time; **мне не в ~у предупрежда́ть её** this is not the first time I have warned her.
перви́чност|ь, и *f.* primacy; priority.
перви́чн|ый *adj.* primary; initial; **~ая парторганиза́ция** primary Party organization; **п. пери́од боле́зни** initial period of illness; **~ые поро́ды** (*geol.*) primary rocks.
первобы́тный *adj.* (*ethnol. and fig.*) primitive; primordial; primeval.
первого́д|ок, ка *m.* (*coll.*) young of animal less than one year old.
пе́рв|ое, ого *nt.* first course (*of a meal*).
перворзда́нный *adj.* primordial; (*geol.*) primitive, primary; **п. хао́с** primordial chaos (*also fig., iron.*).
первоисто́чник, а *m.* primary source; origin.
первокатего́рник, а *m.* first-rank (first-flight) player (*esp. of chess-players*).
первокла́ссник, а *m.* pupil of the first class, first-former.
первокла́ссный *adj.* first-class, first-rate.
первоку́рсник, а *m.* first-year student, freshman.
Первома́|й, я *m.* (*coll.*) May Day.
первома́й|ский *adj. of* **~**
пе́рво-на́перво *adv.* (*coll.*) first of all.
первонача́льно *adv.* originally.
первонача́льн|ый *adj.* **1.** original. **2.** primary; initial; **~ое накопле́ние** (*econ.*) primary accumulation; **~ая причи́на** (*phil.*) first cause. **3.** elementary. **4.: ~ые чи́сла** (*math.*) prime numbers.
первоо́браз, а *m.* prototype; protoplast.
первообра́зный *adj.* prototypal; protoplastic.
первоосно́в|а, ы *f.* (*phil.*) first principle.
первооткрыва́тел|ь, я *m.* discoverer.
первоочередн|о́й *adj.* first and foremost, immediate; **~а́я зада́ча** immediate task.
первоочере́дн|ый = **~о́й**
первопеча́тник, а *m.* printing pioneer.
первопеча́тн|ый *adj.* **1.** printed early, belonging to the first years of printing; **~ые кни́ги** incunabula. **2.** first printed.
первопресто́льн|ый *adj.* (*rhet.*) being the oldest (first) capital; *as n.* **Первопресто́льная, ~ой** *f.* Moscow (*by contrast with St. Petersburg*).
первопричи́н|а, ы *f.* (*phil.*) first cause.
первопрохо́д|ец, ца *m.* (*fig., rhet.*) pioneer; pacemaker; trailblazer.
первопрохо́дческий *adj.* trail-blazing, pioneering.
первопу́т|ок, ка *m.* (*coll.*) the first sledging (*of the winter*); **е́хать по ~ку** to traverse a road after the first snowfall.
перворазря́дник, а *m.* (*sport*) first-rank player.
перворазря́дный *adj.* first-class, first-rank.
перворо́дный *adj.* (*obs.*) **1.** first-born. **2.** primal; **п. грех** (*eccl.*) original sin.
перворо́дств|о, а *nt.* **1.** (*leg.*) primogeniture. **2.** (*fig.*) primacy.
перворождённый *adj.* first-born.
первосвяще́нник, а *m.* high priest, chief priest; pontiff.
первосо́ртный *adj.* **1.** of the best quality. **2.** (*coll.*) first-class, first-rate.

первостате́йный *adj.* **1.** (*obs.*) of the first order; of consequence. **2.** (*coll.*) first-rate, first-class.
первостепе́нный *adj.* paramount, of the first order.
первоцве́т, а *m.* (*bot.*) primrose.
пе́рв|ый *adj.* (*in var. senses*) first; former; earliest; **~ое (число́ ме́сяца)** the first (of the month); **~ого января́** on the first of January; **полови́на ~ого** half past twelve; **в ~ом часу́** after twelve, past twelve, between twelve and one; **он п. вошёл** he was the first to enter; **быть ~ым, идти́ ~ым** to come first, lead; **~ое вре́мя** at first; **п. встре́чный** the first comer; **~ое де́ло, ~ым де́лом** (*coll.*) first of all, first thing; **не ~ой мо́лодости** not in one's first youth; **~ая по́мощь** first aid; **п. рейс** maiden voyage; **не ~ой све́жести** not quite fresh, stale; **~ая скри́пка** first violin; (*fig.*) first fiddle; **п. эта́ж** ground floor; **в ~ую го́лову** (*coll.*) first and foremost; **в ~ую о́чередь** in the first place; **из ~ых рук** first-hand; **на п. взгляд, с ~ого взгля́да** at first sight; **при ~ой возмо́жности** at one's earliest convenience, as soon as possible; **с ~ого ра́за** from the first; **п. блин ко́мом** (*prov.*) practice makes perfect.
перг|а́, и́ *f.* bee-bread.
перга́мен, а *m.* = **~т**
перга́мент, а *m.* parchment.
перга́мент|ный *adj. of* **~**; **~ная бума́га** oil-paper.
пер|де́ть, жу́, ди́шь *impf.* (*vulg.*) to fart.
пере... *vbl. pref. indicating* **1.** *action across or through sth.* (trans-). **2.** *repetition of action* (re-). **3.** *superiority, excess, etc.* (over-, out-). **4.** *extension of action to encompass many or all objects or cases of a given kind.* **5.** *division into two or more parts.* **6.** (*reflexives*) reciprocity of action.
переадрес|ова́ть, у́ю *pf.* (*of* **~о́вывать**) to re-address.
переадресо́выва|ть, ю *impf. of* **переадресова́ть**
перебази́р|овать, ую *pf.* (*no impf.*) to shift.
перебаллоти́р|овать, ую *pf.* (*of* **~о́вывать**) to submit to second ballot.
перебаллоти́ро́вк|а, и *f.* second ballot.
перебаллотиро́выва|ть, ю *impf. of* **перебаллоти́ровать**
перeба́рщива|ть, ю *impf. of* **переборщи́ть**
перебега́|ть, ю *impf. of* **перебежа́ть**
перебе|жа́ть, гу́, жи́шь, гу́т *pf.* (*of* **~га́ть**) **1.** **(че́рез)** to cross (running); **п. (че́рез) у́лицу** to run across the street; **п. кому́-н. доро́гу** to cross s.o.'s path. **2.** (*fig.*, *coll.*; **к**) to go over (to), desert (to).
перебе́жк|а, и *f.* (*mil.*) bound, rush.
перебе́жчик, а *m.* deserter; (*fig.*) turncoat.
перебе́лива|ть, ю *impf. of* **перебели́ть**
перебел|и́ть, ю́, и́шь *pf.* (*of* **~́ивать**) **1.** to whitewash again. **2.** to make a fair copy (of).
перебе|си́ться, шу́сь, ~́сишься *pf.* **1.** to go mad, run mad. **2.** (*coll.*) to have sown one's wild oats.
перебива́|ть(ся), ю(сь) *impf. of* **переби́ть(ся)**[1,2]
переби́вк|а, и *f.* re-upholstering.
перебинт|ова́ть[1], **у́ю** *pf.* (*of* **~о́вывать**) to change the dressing (on), put a new dressing (on).
перебинт|ова́ть[2], **у́ю** *pf.* (*of* **~о́вывать**) to dress, bandage (*all, a quantity of*).
перебинто́выва|ть, ю *impf. of* **перебинтова́ть**
перебира́|ть[1]**(ся), ю(сь)** *impf. of* **перебра́ть(ся)**
перебира́|ть[2], **ю** *impf.* **1.** to finger; **п. стру́ны** to run one's fingers over the strings; **п. чётки** to tell one's beads. **2.** (*+i.*) to move, advance (*in turn or in a regular manner*).
переб|и́ть[1], **ью́, ьёшь** *pf.* (*of* **~ива́ть**) **1.** to re-upholster. **2.** to beat up again (*pillow, feather-bed, etc.*).
переб|и́ть[2], **ью́, ьёшь** *pf.* (*of* **~ива́ть**) **1.** to interrupt. **2.** to intercept; **п. кому́-н. доро́гу** to cross s.o.'s path; **п. поку́пку** (*coll.*) to outbid for sth.
переб|и́ть[3], **ью́, ьёшь** *pf.* **1.** to kill, slay, slaughter. **2.** to beat. **3.** to break.
переб|и́ться[1], **ью́сь, ьёшься** *pf.* (*of* **~ива́ться**) to break.
переб|и́ться[2], **ью́сь, ьёшься** *pf.* (*of* **~ива́ться**) (*coll.*) to make ends meet; **п. с хле́ба на квас** to live from hand to mouth.
перебо́|й, я *m.* interruption, intermission; stoppage, hold-up; misfire (*of engine*); **пульс с ~ями** intermittent pulse.
перебо́йный *adj.* interrupted, intermittent.
переболе́|ть[1], **ю** *pf.* (*+i.*) to have had, have been down (*with an illness*); **де́ти все ~ли коклю́шем** the children have all been down with whooping-cough.
перебол|е́ть[2], **и́т** *pf.* to recover, become well again.
перебо́рк|а[1], **и** *f.* **1.** sorting out. **2.** (*tech.*) re-assembly.
перебо́рк|а[2], **и** *f.* partition; (*naut.*) bulk-head.
перебор|о́ть, ю́, ~́ешь *pf.* (*no impf.*) to master.
переборщ|и́ть, у́, и́шь *pf.* (*of* **переба́рщивать**) (**в**+*p.*; *coll.*) to go too far; to overdo it.
перебра́нива|ться, юсь *impf.* (**с**+*i.*; *coll.*) to bandy angry words (with), have words (with).
перебран|и́ться, ю́сь, и́шься *pf.* (**с**+*i.*; *coll.*) to quarrel (with), fall out (with).
перебра́нк|а, и *f.* (*coll.*) wrangle, squabble; slanging match.
перебра́сыва|ть(ся), ю(сь) *impf. of* **перебро́сить(ся)**
пере|бра́ть[1], **беру́, берёшь,** *past* **~бра́л, ~брала́, ~бра́ло** *pf.* (*of* **~бира́ть**) **1.** to sort out (*also fig.*); to look through. **2.** (*fig.*) to turn over (in one's mind). **3.** to take in excess; **п. пять очко́в** to score five extra points.
пере|бра́ть[2], **беру́, берёшь,** *past* **~бра́л, ~брала́, ~бра́ло** *pf.* (*of* **~бира́ть**) **1.** (*typ.*) to reset. **2.** (*tech.*) to (dismantle and) reassemble.
пере|бра́ться, беру́сь, берёшься, *past* **~бра́лся, ~брала́сь, ~брало́сь** *pf.* (*coll.*) **1.** to get over, cross. **2.** to move; **п. на но́вую кварти́ру** to change one's lodgings.
перебр|оди́ть, о́дит *pf.* to have fermented; to have risen.
переброса́|ть, ю *pf.* to throw one after another.
перебро́|сить, шу, сишь *pf.* (*of* **перебра́сывать**) **1.** to throw over; **п. мост че́рез ре́ку** to throw a bridge across a river. **2.** to transfer (*troops, etc.*).
перебро́|ситься, шусь, сишься *pf.* (*of* **перебра́сываться**) **1.** (*+i.*) to throw one to another; **п. не́сколькими слова́ми** (*fig.*) to exchange a few words. **2.** (*of fire, disease, etc.*) to spread.
перебро́ск|а, и *f.* transfer.
перебыва́|ть, ю *pf.* to have called, have been; **он везде́ ~л** he has been all over the world.
перева́л, а *m.* **1.** passing, crossing. **2.** (*geog.*) pass.
перева́л|ец, ьца *m.*: **ходи́ть с ~ьцем** (*coll.*) to waddle.
перева́лива|ть, ю *impf. of* **перевали́ть**
перева́лива|ться[1], **юсь** *impf. of* **перевали́ться**
перева́лива|ться[2], **юсь** *impf.* (*no pf.*) to waddle.
перевал|и́ть, ю́, ~́ишь *pf.* (*of* **~́ивать**) **1.** to transfer, shift. **2.** to cross; (*impers.*; *coll.*): **~и́ло за по́лночь** it is past midnight; **ей ~и́ло за́ сорок (лет)** she has turned forty; she is past forty.
перевал|и́ться, ю́сь, ~́ишься *pf.* (*of* **~́иваться**[1]) to roll over; to fall over; **п. на пра́вый бок** to roll over on to one's right side.
перева́лк|а, и *f.* **1.** transshipment, conveyance. **2.** transshipping point.
перева́л|очный *adj. of* **~ка**; **п. пункт** (*in var. senses*) staging post.
перева́рива|ть, ю *impf. of* **перевари́ть**
перевари́м|ый (~, ~а) *adj.* digestible.
перевар|и́ть[1], **ю́, ~́ишь** *pf.* (*of* **~́ивать**) **1.** to cook again; to boil again. **2.** (*in cooking*) to overdo.
перевар|и́ть[2], **ю́, ~́ишь** *pf.* (*of* **~́ивать**) **1.** to digest; **п. прочи́танное** (*fig.*) to digest what one has read. **2.** (*fig.*) to swallow; to bear, stand.
переве́д|аться, аюсь *pf.* (*of* **~ываться**) (*obs.*; **с**+*i.*) to demand satisfaction (from).
переве́дыва|ться, юсь *impf. of* **переве́даться**
перевез|ти́, у́, ёшь, *past* **~̈, ~ла́** *pf.* (*of* **перевози́ть**) **1.** to take across, put across. **2.** to transport, convey (*from A to B*); to (re)move (*furniture, etc.*).
переверн|у́ть, у́, ёшь *pf.* (*of* **перевёртывать** *and* **перевора́чивать**) to turn over; to invert; **п. страни́цу** to turn over the page; **п. наизна́нку** to turn inside out.
переверн|у́ться, у́сь, ёшься *pf.* (*of* **перевёртываться** *and* **перевора́чиваться**) to turn over; **~ётся в гробу́** (*joc.*) he would turn in his grave.
перевер|те́ть, чу́, ~́тишь *pf.* (*of* **~̈тывать** *and* **~́чивать**) (*coll.*) to overwind.

перевёртыва|ть(ся), ю(сь) *impf. of* **перевернýть(ся)** *and* **перевертéть**

перевéрчива|ть, ю *impf. of* **перевертéть**

перевéс, а *m.* preponderance; advantage; **численный п.** numerical superiority; **взять п.** to gain the upper hand; **п. на нáшей сторонé, в нáшу пóльзу** the odds are in our favour.

перевé|сить[1], **шу, сишь** *pf.* (*of* **~шивать**) to hang somewhere else; **п. картúну с однóй стенú на другýю** to move a picture from one wall to another.

перевé|сить[2], **шу, сишь** *pf.* (*of* **~шивать**) **1.** to weigh again. **2.** to outweigh, outbalance (*also fig.*); (*fig.*) to tip the scales.

перевé|ситься, шусь, сишься *pf.* (*of* **~шиваться**) to lean over.

переве|стú[1], **дý, дёшь,** *past* **~́л, ~лá** *pf.* (*of* **переводúть**) **1.** to take across; **п. детéй чéрез ýлицу** to escort children across the road. **2.** to transfer, move, switch, shift; **п. на другýю рабóту** to transfer to another post; **п. в слéдующий класс** to move up into the next form; **п. валюту** to transfer currency; **п. дéньги по телегрáфу** to wire money; **п. стрéлку** to shunt, switch; **п. стрéлку часóв вперёд (назáд)** to put a clock on (back). **3.** (**с**+*g.* **на**+*a.*) to translate (from into); (**в, на**+*a.*) to convert (to), express (as, in); **п. с рýсского языкá на англúйский** to translate from Russian into English; **п. в метрúческие мéры** to convert to metric units (of measurement). **4.: п. дух** to take breath. **5.** (*art*) to transfer, copy.

переве|стú[2], **дý, дёшь,** *past* **~́л, ~лá** *pf.* (*of* **переводúть**) (*coll.*) **1.** to destroy, exterminate. **2.** to spend, use up.

переве|стúсь[1], **дýсь, дёшься,** *past* **~́лся, ~лáсь** *pf.* (*of* **переводúться**) **1.** to move, be transferred. **2.** *pass. of* **~стú**[1,2]

переве|стúсь[2], **дýсь, дёшься,** *past* **~́лся, ~лáсь** *pf.* (*of* **переводúться**) (*coll.*) to come to an end; to become extinct; **к концý недéли дéньги у меня ~лúсь** by the end of the week I was spent up.

перевéш|ать[1], **аю** *pf.* (*of* **~ивать**) to weigh (*all or a quantity of*).

перевéш|ать[2], **аю** *pf.* to hang (*a number of*).

перевéшива|ть, ю *impf. of* **перевéсить** *and* **перевéшать**[1]

перевéшива|ться, юсь *impf. of* **перевéситься**

перевивá|ть, ю *impf. of* **перевúть**

перевидá|ть, ю *pf.* (*coll.*) to have seen (*also fig. = to have experienced*).

перевирá|ть, ю *impf. of* **переврáть**

перев|úть[1], **ью, ьёшь,** *past* **~úл, ~илá, ~úло** *pf.* (*of* **~ивáть**) to weave again.

перев|úть[2], **ью, ьёшь,** *past* **~úл, ~илá, ~úло** *pf.* (*of* **~ивáть**) (+*i.*) to interweave (with), intertwine (with).

перевóд[1], **а** *m.* **1.** transfer, move, switch, shift; **п. дéнег** remittance; **почтóвый п.** postal order; **п. стрéлки** shunting, switching; **п. стрéлки часóв вперёд (назáд)** putting a clock on (back). **2.** translation; version; **п. мер** conversion of measures; **синхрóнный п.** simultaneous interpreting.

перевóд[2], **а** *m.* (*coll.*) spending, using up; **пустóй п. дéнег (деньгáм)** squandering; **нет ~у** (+*d.*) there is no shortage (of), there is an inexhaustible supply (of).

перево|дúть(ся), жý(сь), ~́дишь(ся) *impf. of* **перевестú(сь)**

переводн|óй *adj. of* **перевóд**[1]; **~áя бумáга** carbon paper; transfer paper; **~áя картúнка** transfer.

перевóд|ный *adj. of* **~**[1]; **п. ромáн** novel in translation; **п. бланк** postal order form.

перевóдчик, а *m.* translator; interpreter.

перевóз, а *m.* **1.** transportation. **2.** ferry.

перево|зúть, жý, ~́зишь *impf. of* **перевезтú**

перевóзк|а, и *f.* conveyance, transportation.

перевóз|очный *adj. of* **~ка; ~очные срéдства** means of conveyance.

перевóзчик, а *m.* **1.** ferryman; boatman; removal man. **2.** (*zool.*) common sandpiper.

переволн|овáть, ýю *pf.* (*coll.*) to alarm.

переволн|овáться, ýюсь *pf.* (*coll.*) to be alarmed; to suffer prolonged anxiety.

перевооруж|áть(ся), áю(сь) *impf. of* **~úть(ся)**

перевооружéни|е, я *nt.* re-armament.

перевооруж|úть, ý, úшь *pf.* (*of* **~áть**) to re-arm.

перевооруж|úться, ýсь, úшься *pf.* (*of* **~áться**) to re-arm (*intrans.*).

перевопло|тúть, щý, тúшь *pf.* (*of* **~щáть**) to reincarnate; to transform.

перевопло|тúться, щýсь, тúшься *pf.* (*of* **~щáться**) to be reincarnated; to undergo a transformation.

перевоплощá|ть(ся), ю(сь) *impf. of* **перевоплотúть(ся)**

переворáчива|ть(ся), ю(сь) *impf. of* **перевернýть(ся)**

переворóт, а *m.* **1.** revolution; overturn; **госудáрственный п.** coup d'état. **2.** (*geol.*) cataclysm.

переворош|úть, ý, úшь *pf.* (*coll.*) **1.** to turn (over) (*also fig.*); **п. сéно** to turn hay; **п. свою пáмять** to search through one's memories. **2.** (*fig.*) to turn upside down.

перевоспитáни|е, я *nt.* re-education; rehabilitation.

перевоспит|áть, áю *pf.* (*of* **~́ывать**) to re-educate; to rehabilitate.

перевоспит|áться, áюсь *pf.* (*of* **~́ываться**) to re-educate o.s.; to be re-educated.

перевоспúтыва|ть(ся), ю(сь) *impf. of* **перевоспитáть(ся)**

перевр|áть, ý, ёшь, *past* **~áл, ~алá, ~áло** *pf.* (*of* **перевирáть**) (*coll.*) to garble, confuse; to misinterpret; **п. цитáту** to misquote.

перевыбирá|ть, ю *impf. of* **перевы́брать**

перевы́бор|ы, ов *no sg.* re-election.

перевы́б|рать, еру, ерешь *pf.* (*of* **~ирáть**) to re-elect.

перевыполнéни|е, я *nt.* over-fulfilment.

перевы́полн|ить, ю, ишь *pf.* (*of* **~я́ть**) to over-fulfil.

перевыполн|я́ть, я́ю *impf. of* **~́ить**

перевя|зáть[1], **жý, ~́жешь** *pf.* (*of* **~́зывать**) **1.** to dress, bandage. **2.** to tie up, cord.

перевя|зáть[2], **жý, ~́жешь** *pf.* (*of* **~́зывать**) to knit again.

перевя́зк|а, и *f.* dressing, bandage.

перевя́з|очный *adj. of* **~ка; п. материáл** dressing; **п. пункт** dressing station.

перевя́зыва|ть, ю *impf. of* **перевязáть**

пéревяз|ь, и *f.* **1.** (*mil., hist.*) cross-belt, shoulder-belt, baldric. **2.** (*med.*) sling; **рукá у негó былá на ~и** he had his arm in a sling.

перегáр, а *m.* (*coll.*) (*unpleasant*) residual taste of alcohol in the mouth; smell of alcohol; **от негó неслó ~ом** he reeked of alcohol

перегúб, а *m.* **1.** bend, twist; fold. **2.** (*fig.*) exaggeration; **допустúть п. в чём-н.** to carry sth. too far.

перегибá|ть(ся), ю(сь) *impf. of* **перегнýть(ся)**

перегласóвк|а, и *f.* (*ling.*) mutation.

перегля́дыва|ться, юсь *impf. of* **переглянýться**

перегля|нýться, нýсь, ~́нешься *pf.* (*of* **~́дываться**) (**с**+*i.*) to exchange glances (with).

перегн|áть, перегоню, перегóнишь, *past* **~áл, ~алá, ~áло** *pf.* (*of* **перегоня́ть**) **1.** to outdistance, leave behind; (*fig.*) to overtake, surpass. **2.** to drive (*somewhere else*; *from A to B*); **п. самолёты** to ferry planes. **3.** (*chem., tech.*) to distil, sublimate.

перегнивá|ть, ю *impf. of* **перегнúть**

перегн|úть, иёт, *past* **~úл, ~илá, ~úло** *pf.* (*of* **~ивáть**) to rot through.

перегнó|й, я *m.* humus.

перегнóй|ный *adj. of* **~; ~ная пóчва** humus.

перег|нýть, нý, нёшь *pf.* (*of* **~ибáть**) to bend; **п. пáлку** (*fig., coll.*) to go too far.

перег|нýться, нýсь, нёшься *pf.* (*of* **~ибáться**) **1.** to bend. **2.** to lean over.

переговáрива|ть, ю *impf. of* **переговорúть**[2]

переговáрива|ться, юсь *impf.* (**с**+*i.*) to exchange remarks (with).

переговор|úть[1], **ю, úшь** *pf.* (**о**+*p.*) to talk (about); to talk over, discuss; **п. по телефóну** to speak over the telephone.

переговор|úть[2], **ю, úшь** *pf.* (*of* **переговáривать**) to silence; to out-talk.

переговóрн|ый *adj.*: **~ая бýдка** telephone booth; **п. телефóнный пункт** trunk-call office.

переговóр|ы, ов *no sg.* negotiations; talks; (*mil.*) parley; **вестú**

п. (**с**+*i.*) to negotiate (with), carry on negotiations (with); (*mil.*) to parley (with); **идýт п.** negotiations are in progress.
перего́н[1], **а** *m.* driving.
перего́н[2], **а** *m.* stage (*between two rail. stations*).
перего́нк|а, и *f.* (*tech., chem.*) distillation; **сухáя п.** sublimation.
перего́н|ный *adj. of* **~ка; п. завóд** distillery; **п. куб** still.
перегоня́|ть, ю *impf. of* **перегнáть**
перегорáжива|ть, ю *impf. of* **перегороди́ть**
перегор|áть, áю *impf. of* **~éть**
перегорéлый *adj.* (*coll.*) burnt out.
перегор|éть, и́т *pf.* (*of* **~áть**) **1.** to burn out, fuse. **2.** to burn through. **3.** to rot through.
перегоро|ди́ть, жý, ~ди́шь *pf.* (*of* **перегорáживать**) to partition off.
перегорóдк|а, и *f.* **1.** partition. **2.** (*tech.*) baffle (plate). **3.** (*fig.*) barrier.
перегорóд|очный *adj. of* **~ка**
перегрéв, а *m.* overheating; (*tech.*) superheating.
перегревáтел|ь, я *m.* (*tech.*) superheater.
перегревá|ть(ся), ю(сь) *impf. of* **перегрéть(ся)**
перегрé|ть, ю *pf.* (*of* **~вáть**) **1.** to overheat. **2.** (*tech.*) to superheat.
перегрé|ться, юсь *pf.* (*of* **~вáться**) to burn (out), get burned.
перегружá|ть, ю *impf. of* **перегрузи́ть**
перегру|зи́ть[1], **жý, ~зи́шь** *pf.* (*of* **~жáть**) to overload, surcharge; **п. рабóтой** to overwork.
перегру|зи́ть[2], **жý, ~зи́шь** *pf.* (*of* **~жáть**) to load (*somewhere else; from A to B*); to transship; **п. с поéзда на парохóд** to load from a train on to a ship.
перегрýзк|а[1], **и** *f.* overload, surcharge; overloading; **п. рабóтой** overwork.
перегрýзк|а[2], **и** *f.* reloading; shifting; transfer, transshipping.
перегрýз|очный *adj. of* **~ка**[2]
перегруппир|овáть, ýю *pf.* (*of* **~óвывать**) to re-group.
перегруппирóвк|а, и *f.* re-grouping.
перегруппир|óвывать, óвываю *impf. of* **~овáть**
перегры́з|ть, ý, ёшь, *past* **~, ~ла** *pf.* (*of* **~áть**) to gnaw through, bite through.
перегры́з|ться, ýсь, ёшься, *past* **~ся, ~лась** *pf.* (*no impf.*) (**из-за**; *coll.; of dogs*) to fight (over); (*fig.*) to quarrel (over), wrangle (about).
пéред *and* **пéредо** *prep.+i.* **1.** (*of place; also fig.*) before; in front of; in the face of; **п. дворцóм** in front of the palace; **при́зрак стоя́л пéредо мнóй** the apparition stood before me; **п. опáсностью** in the face of danger. **2.** (*in relation to, as compared with*) to; **извини́ться п. кем-н.** to apologize to s.o.; **вáша истóрия ничтó п. нáшей** your story is nothing to ours. **3.** (*of time*) before; **п. обéдом** before dinner; **п. тем, как** (*conj.*) before.
перёд, пéреда, *pl.* **~á, ~óв** *m.* front, fore-part.
передa|вáть(ся), ю(сь), ёшь(ся) *impf. of* **передáть(ся)**
передá|точный *adj. of* **~ча; п. вал** (*tech.*) countershaft; **п. механи́зм** driving gear, drive; **~точная нáдпись** (*fin.*) endorsement; **~точное числó** (*tech.*) gear ratio.
передáтчик, а *m.* (*radio*) transmitter; **п. теплá** (*phys.*) heat conductor.
передá|ть[1], **м, шь, ст, ди́м, ди́те, дýт,** *past* **пéредал, ~лá, пéредало** *pf.* (*of* **~вáть**) **1.** to pass; to hand; to hand over; to transfer; **п. по наслéдству** to hand down; **п. свой правá** to make over one's rights; **п. дéло в суд** to bring a matter into court, take a matter to law, sue. **2.** to tell; to communicate; to transmit, convey; **п. по рáдио** to broadcast; **п. благодáрность** to convey thanks; **п. задáзу** to communicate infection; **п. поручéние** to deliver a message; **п. приказáние** to transmit an order; **п. привéт** to convey greetings, send one's regards; **~й(те) им (мой) привéт** give them my regards; remember me to them. **3.** to reproduce (*a sound, a thought, etc.*).
передá|ть[2], **м, шь, ст, ди́м, ди́те, дýт,** *past* **пéредал, ~лá, пéредало** *pf.* (*of* **~вáть**) to pay too much, give too much; **вы пéредали три рубля́** you have paid three roubles too many.
передá|ться, стся, дýтся, *past* **~лся, ~лáсь** *pf.* (*of* **~вáться**) **1.** to pass; to be transmitted, be communicated; to be inherited; **корь ~лáсь емý от живýщих ря́дом детéй** he picked up measles from the children next door. **2.** (+*d.; coll.*) to go over, (to).
передáч|а, и *f.* **1.** passing; transmission; communication; transfer, transference; **п. имýщества** (*leg.*) assignation; **без прáва ~и** not transferable; **Петрóву для ~и Ивановóй** (*form of address on letter*) (Mrs., Miss) Ivanova, c/o (Mr.) Petrov. **2.** parcel (*delivered to pers. in hospital or prison*). **3.** broadcast; **прямáя п.** live broadcast; **реклáмная п.** commercial, advert (*on TV or radio*). **4.** (*tech.*) drive; gear(ing); transmission; **баланси́рная п.** transmission by rocking lever; **большáя п.** high gear ratio; **зубчáтая п.** train of gears, toothed gearing; **конéчная п.** end drive; **пéрвая п.** low gear; **реверси́вная п.** reversing gear; **ремённая п.** belt drive; **червя́чная п.** worm-gear.
передвигá|ть(ся), ю(сь) *impf. of* **передви́нуть(ся)**
передвижéни|е, я *nt.* movement; (*tech.*) travel; **срéдства ~я** means of conveyance.
передви́ж|ка, ки *f.* **1.** = **~éние. 2.** *as adj.* travelling, itinerant; **библиотéка-п.** travelling library; **теáтр-п.** strolling players.
передви́жник, а *m.* (*art*) Peredvizhnik (*member of Russ. school of realist painters of second half of nineteenth century*).
передвижн|óй *adj.* **1.** movable, mobile; **п. кран** travelling crane. **2.** travelling, itinerant; **~áя вы́ставка** travelling exhibition.
передви́|нуть, ну, нешь *pf.* (*of* **~гáть**) to move, shift (*also fig.*); **п. стрéлки часóв вперёд (назáд)** to put the clock on (back); **п. срóки экзáменов** to alter the date of examinations.
передви́|нуться, нусь, нешься *pf.* (*of* **~гáться**) to move, shift; (*tech.*) to travel.
передéл, а *m.* re-partition; re-division, re-distribution; **п. земли́** re-allotment of land.
передéл|ать[1], **аю** *pf.* (*of* **~ывать**) to do anew; to alter; (*fig.*) to re-fashion, recast; **п. плáтье** to alter a dress.
передéл|ать[2], **аю** *pf.* (*coll.*) to do; **я ~ал все делá** I have done all I had to do.
передел|и́ть, ю́, ~ишь *pf.* (*of* **~я́ть**) to re-divide.
передéлк|а, и *f.* **1.** alteration; **отдáть что-н. в ~у** to have sth. altered; **попáсть в ~у** (*coll.*) to get into a pretty mess. **2.** adaptation (*of liter. work, etc.*).
передéлыва|ть, ю *impf. of* **передéлать**[1]
передел|я́ть, я́ю *impf. of* **~и́ть**
передёргива|ть(ся), ю(сь) *impf. of* **передёрнуть(ся)**
передерж|áть[1], **ý, ~ишь** *pf.* (*of* **~ивать**) **1.** to overdo; to overcook. **2.** (*phot.*) to over-expose.
передерж|áть[2], **ý, ~ишь** *pf.* (*of* **~ивать**) (*coll.*): **п. экзáмен** to take an examination again.
передéржива|ть, ю *impf. of* **передержáть**
передéржк|а[1], **и** *f.* (*phot.*) over-exposure.
передéржк|а[2], **и** *f.* (*coll.*) re-examination.
передéржк|а[3], **и** *f.* (*coll.*) cheating (*at cards*), juggling (*with facts*).
передёр|нуть, ну, нешь *pf.* (*of* **~гивать**) **1.** to pull aside. **2.** (*impers.*): **егó ~нуло от бóли** he was convulsed with pain. **3.** to cheat (*at cards*). **4.** (*fig.*) to distort, misrepresent; **п. фáкты** to juggle with facts.
передёр|нуться, нусь, нешься *pf.* (*of* **~гиваться**) (*coll.*) to flinch, wince.
перед|кóвый *adj. of* **~óк**; *as n.* **п., ~кóвого** *m.* (*mil.*) limber number.
передненёбный *adj.* (*ling.*) front palatal.
переднеприводнóй *adj.*: **п. автомоби́ль** front-wheel drive vehicle.
пéредн|ий *adj.* front; anterior; first; **~ие конéчности** fore-legs; **п. край оборóны** (*mil.*) main line of resistance; **~яя крóмка (крылá)** (*aeron.*) leading edge (of wing); **~яя лóшадь** leader; **п. план** foreground; **~яя часть** fore-part.
передни́к, а *m.* apron; pinafore.
пéредн|яя, ей *f.* ante-room; (entrance) hall, lobby.
пéредо = **пéред**

передова́я, ~о́й *f.* **1.** leading article, leader; editorial. **2.** (*mil.*) forward position.
передове́р|ить, ю, ишь *pf.* (*of* **~я́ть**) (+*d.*) to transfer trust (to); (*leg.*) to transfer power of attorney (to); **п. догово́р** to sub-contract (to).
передовер|я́ть, я́ю *impf. of* **~́ить**
передови́к, а́ *m.* **1.** leading worker (*factory worker, etc., winning distinction for display of initiative and/or exemplary work*). **2.** (*coll.*) leader-writer.
передови́ц|а, ы *f.* (*coll.*) leading article, leader; editorial.
передов|о́й *adj.* forward, headmost; foremost, advanced (*also fig.*); **~ы́е взгля́ды** advanced views; **п. отря́д** (*mil.*) advanced detachment; (*fig.*) vanguard; **~а́я статья́** leading article, leader; editorial.
передозиро́вк|а, и *f.* (*med.*) overdose.
перед|о́к, ка́ *m.* **1.** front (*of carriage, etc.*). **2.** (*mil.*; *usu. pl.*) limber.
передо́м *adv.* (*coll.*) in front.
передо́х|нуть, нет, *past* **~, ~ла** *pf.* (*no impf.*) to die off (*usu. of animals*).
передохн|у́ть, у́, ёшь *pf.* (*of* **передыха́ть**) (*coll.*) to pause for breath, take a short rest.
передра́знива|ть, ю *impf. of* **передразни́ть**
передразн|и́ть, ю́, ~́ишь *pf.* (*of* **~́ивать**) to take off, mimic.
пере|дра́ться, деру́сь, дерёшься, *past* **~дра́лся, ~драла́сь, ~дра́ло́сь** *pf.* (*no impf.*) (*coll.*) to fight, exchange blows (*of many people, etc.*).
передро́г|нуть, ну, нешь, *past* **~, ~ла** *pf.* (*no impf.*) (*coll.*) to get chilled through
передря́г|а, и *f.* (*coll.*) row, scrape.
переду́м|ать, аю *pf.* (*of* **~ывать**) **1.** to (think it over and) change one's mind; to think better of it. **2.** to do a great deal of thinking.
переду́мыва|ть, ю *impf. of* **переду́мать**
передыха́|ть, ю *impf. of* **передохну́ть**
переды́шк|а, и *f.* respite, breathing-space; breather; **не дава́я ни мину́ты ~и** without a moment's respite.
перееда́ни|е, я *nt.* overeating; surfeit.
перееда́|ть, ю *impf. of* **перее́сть**
перее́зд[1], **а** *m.* (*in var. senses*) crossing.
перее́зд[2], **а** *m.* removal.
переезжа́|ть, ю *impf. of* **перее́хать**
перее́|сть[1], **м, шь, ст, ди́м, ди́те, дя́т,** *past* **~л** *pf.* (*of* **~да́ть**) **1.** to overeat, surfeit. **2.** (*coll.*) to out-eat, surpass in eating.
перее́|сть[2], **м, шь, ст, ди́м, ди́те, дя́т,** *past* **~л** *pf.* (*of* **~да́ть**) to corrode, eat away.
перее́|хать[1], **ду, дешь** *pf.* (*of* **~зжа́ть**) **1.** to cross. **2.** to run over, knock down.
перее́|хать[2], **ду, дешь** *pf.* (*of* **~зжа́ть**) to move (*to a new place of residence*).
пережа́рива|ть, ю *impf. of* **пережа́рить**[1]
пережа́р|ить[1], **ю, ишь** *pf.* (*of* **~ивать**) to overdo, overroast.
пережа́р|ить[2], **ю, ишь** *pf.* to roast (*all or a number of*).
пережд|а́ть, у́, ёшь, *past* **~а́л, ~ала́, ~а́ло** *pf.* (*of* **пережида́ть**) to wait through; **мы ~а́ли грозу́** we waited till the storm was over.
переж|ева́ть, у́ю, уёшь *pf.* (*of* **~ёвывать**) to masticate, chew.
пережёвыва|ть, ю *impf.* **1.** *impf. of* **пережева́ть. 2.** (*fig.*) to repeat over and over again.
пережен|и́ться, ~́ится *pf.* (*coll.*) to marry; **все её бра́тья ~и́лись** all her brothers have married.
переж|е́чь, гу́, жёшь, гу́т, *past* **~ёг, ~гла́** *pf.* (*of* **~ига́ть**) **1.** to burn more than one's quota (*of fuel, etc.*). **2.** to burn through. **3.** (*tech.*) to calcine.
пережива́ни|е, я *nt.* experience; feeling.
пережива́|ть, ю *impf.* **1.** *impf. of* **пережи́ть. 2.** (*impf. only*) (*coll.*) to be upset, worry.
пережида́|ть, ю *impf. of* **пережда́ть**
пережит|о́е, о́го *nt.* one's past.
пережи́т|ок, ка *m.* survival.
пережи́|ть, ву́, вёшь, *past* **пе́режил, ~ла́, пе́режило** *pf.* (*of* **~ва́ть**) **1.** to live through; **п. жизнь** to live one's life through. **2.** to experience; to go through; to endure, suffer; **тяжело́ п. что-н.** to feel sth. keenly, take sth. hard; **она́ ещё не совсе́м ~ла́ потрясе́ния** she has still not completely got over the shock. **3.** to outlive, outlast, survive.
перезаб|ы́ть, у́ду, у́дешь *pf.* (*no impf.*) (*coll.*) to forget.
перезакла́дыва|ть, ю *impf. of* **перезаложи́ть**
перезаключ|а́ть, а́ю *impf. of* **~и́ть**
перезаключ|и́ть, у́, и́шь *pf.* (*of* **~а́ть**) to renew; **п. догово́р** to renew a contract.
перезалож|и́ть, у́, ~́ишь *pf.* (*of* **перезакла́дывать**) to pawn again, re-pawn; to remortgage.
перезаря|ди́ть, жу́, ~ди́шь *pf.* (*of* **~жа́ть**) **1.** to re-charge; to re-load. **2.** (*elec.*) to overcharge.
перезаря́дк|а, и *f.* **1.** re-charging; re-loading. **2.** (*elec.*) overcharging.
перезаряжа́|ть, ю *impf. of* **перезаряди́ть**
перезво́н, а *m.* ringing, chime.
перезим|ова́ть, у́ю *pf.* (*of* **зимова́ть**) to winter, pass the winter.
перезнако́м|ить, лю, ишь *pf.* (*coll.*; **с**+*i.*) to acquaint (with), introduce (to).
перезнако́м|иться, люсь, ишься *pf.* (*no impf.*) (*coll.*) to become acquainted (with).
перезрева́|ть, ю *impf. of* **перезре́ть**
перезре́лый *adj.* overripe; (*fig.*) passé, past one's prime.
перезре́|ть, ю *pf.* (*of* **~ва́ть**) **1.** to become overripe. **2.** (*fig.*) to be past one's prime; to have lost the bloom of youth.
переигр|а́ть[1], **а́ю** *pf.* (*of* **~́ывать**) to play again.
переигр|а́ть[2], **а́ю** *pf.* (*of* **~́ывать**) (*theatr.*; *coll.*) to overact, overdo.
переигр|а́ть[3], **а́ю** *pf.* to play, act, perform (*all or a number of*).
переи́грыва|ть, ю *impf. of* **переигра́ть**[1,2]
переизбира́|ть, ю *impf. of* **переизбра́ть**
переизбра́ни|е, я *nt.* re-election.
переиз|бра́ть, беру́, берёшь, *past* **~бра́л, ~брала́, ~бра́ло** *pf.* (*of* **~бира́ть**) to re-elect.
переизда|ва́ть, ю́, ёшь *impf. of* **~́ть**
переизда́ни|е, я *nt.* **1.** re-publication. **2.** new edition, reprint.
переизда́|ть, м, шь, ст, ди́м, ди́те, ду́т, *past* **~л, ~ла́, ~ло** *pf.* (*of* **~ва́ть**) to re-publish, reprint.
переимен|ова́ть, у́ю *pf.* (*of* **~о́вывать**) (**в**+*a.*) to rename.
переимено́выва|ть, ю *impf. of* **переименова́ть**
переи́мчив|ый (~, ~а) *adj.* (*coll.*) imitative.
переина́чива|ть, ю *impf. of* **переина́чить**
переина́ч|ить, у, ишь *pf.* (*of* **~ивать**) to alter, to modify.
пере|йти́, йду́, йдёшь, *past* **~шёл, ~шла́** *pf.* (*of* **~ходи́ть**) **1.** (+*a. or* **че́рез**) to cross; to get across, get over, go over; **п. грани́цу** to cross the frontier; **п. через мо́ст** to go across a bridge. **2.** (**в, на**+*a. or* **к**) to pass (to); to turn (to); **п. в наступле́ние** to pass to the offensive, assume the offensive; **п. в ру́ки** (+*g.*) to pass into the hands (of); **п. из рук в ру́ки** to change hands; **п. в сле́дующий класс** (*in school*) to move up; **п. в сосе́днюю ко́мнату** to go into the next room; **п. к друго́му владе́льцу** to change hands; **п. на другу́ю рабо́ту** to change one's job; **п. на произво́дство тра́кторов** to go over to making tractors; **п. на сто́рону проти́вника** to go over to the enemy. **3.** (**в**+*a.*) to turn (into); **их ссо́ра ~шла́ в дра́ку** from words they came to blows.
перека́л, а *m.* (*tech.*) overheating; overtempering.
перекале́чива|ть, ю *impf. of* **перекале́чить**
перекале́ч|ить, у, ишь *pf.* (*of* **~ивать**) to cripple, main, mutilate.
перека́лива|ть, ю *impf. of* **перекали́ть**
перекал|и́ть, ю́, и́шь *pf.* (*of* **~́ивать**) (*tech.*) to overtemper; (*coll.*) to overheat.
перека́лыва|ть, ю *impf. of* **переколо́ть**
перека́пыва|ть, ю *impf. of* **перекопа́ть**
перека́рмлива|ть, ю *impf. of* **перекорми́ть**
перека́т[1], **а** *m.* shoal.
перека́т[2], **а** *m.* roll, peal (*of thunder*).

перекати́-по́л|е, я *nt.* **1.** (*bot.*) baby's breath (*Gypsophila paniculata*). **2.** (*fig.*; *of pers.*) rolling stone.
перека|ти́ть, чу́, ~тишь *pf.* (*of* **~тывать**) to roll (*somewhere else*).
перека|ти́ться, чу́сь, ~тишься *pf.* (*of* **~тываться**) to roll (*somewhere else*).
перека́тн|ый *adj.* **1.** rolling; **голь ~ая** (*collect.*) the down-and-outs. **2.** (*geol.*) erratic.
перекач|а́ть, а́ю *pf.* (*of* **~ивать**) to pump over, pump across.
перека́чива|ть, ю *impf. of* **перекача́ть**
перека́шива|ть(ся), ю(сь) *impf. of* **перекоси́ть(ся)**
переквалифика́ци|я, и *f.* re-qualification; changing one's profession.
переквалифици́р|овать, ую *impf. and pf.* to re-qualify.
переквалифици́р|оваться, уюсь *impf. and pf.* to re-qualify; to change one's profession.
перекид|а́ть, а́ю *pf.* (*of* **~ывать**) to throw (one after another).
перекидно́й *adj.*: **п. мо́стик** footbridge; **п. календа́рь** loose-leaf *or* desk calendar.
переки́дыва|ть(ся), ю(сь) *impf. of* **перекида́ть** *and* **переки́нуть(ся)**
переки́|нуть, ну, нешь *pf.* (*of* **~дывать**) to throw (over).
переки́|нуться, нусь, нешься *pf.* (*of* **~дываться**) **1.** to leap (over). **2.** (*of fire, disease, etc.*) to spread. **3.** (*+i.*) to throw (one to another). **4.** (*obs., coll.*) (**к**) to go over (to), defect (to).
перекипя|ти́ть, чу́, ти́шь *pf.* to boil again.
перекис|а́ть, а́ет *impf. of* **~нуть**
переки́с|нуть, нет, *past* **~, ~ла** *pf.* (*of* **~а́ть**) to turn sour.
пе́рекис|ь, и *f.* (*chem.*) peroxide.
перекла́дин|а, ы *f.* **1.** cross-beam, cross-piece, transom; joist. **2.** (*sport*) horizontal bar, crossbar.
перекладн|ы́е, ы́х *pl.* (*sg.* **~а́я, ~о́й** *f.*) (*hist.*) post-horses, relay-horses; **е́хать на ~ы́х** to travel by post-chaise.
перекла́дыва|ть, ю *impf. of* **переложи́ть**
перекле́ива|ть, ю *impf. of* **перекле́ить**
перекле́|ить[1], ю, ишь *pf.* (*of* **~ивать**) to re-stick; to glue again, paste again.
перекле́|ить[2], ю, ишь *pf.* (*of* **~ивать**) to stick (*a number of*).
перекле́йк|а[1], и *f.* re-sticking.
перекле́йк|а[2], и *f.* ply-wood.
переклик|а́ться, а́юсь *impf.* (**с**+*i.*) **1.** (*pf.* **~нуться**) to call to one another. **2.** (*fig.*) to have sth. in common (with); to call up, have a ring (of).
перекли́чк|а, и *f.* **1.** roll-call, call-over. **2.** interchange, exchange (*of views, etc., on radio or in press*).
переключа́тел|ь, я *m.* (*tech.*) switch; commutator; **конта́ктный п.** stud switch, tap switch; **сенсо́рный п.** touch-sensitive control.
переключ|а́ть(ся), а́ю(сь) *impf. of* **~и́ть(ся)**
переключ|и́ть, у́, и́шь *pf.* (*of* **~а́ть**) (*tech. and fig.*; **на**+*a.*) to switch (over to); **п. ско́рость** to change gear; **п. своё внима́ние на...** to switch one's attention to....
переключ|и́ться, у́сь и́шься *pf.* (*of* **~а́ться**) (*tech. and fig.*; **на**+*a.*) to switch (over to); **заня́вшись бы́ло дре́вними языка́ми, он ~и́лся на изуче́ние совреме́нных** having started to study ancient languages, he switched (over) to studying modern; **п. на бли́жний свет** to dip one's headlights.
перек|ова́ть, ую́, уёшь *pf.* (*of* **~о́вывать**) **1.** to re-forge; to hammer again; **п. коня́** to re-shoe a horse. **2.** to hammer out, beat out; **п. мечи́ на ора́ла** to beat swords into ploughshares (*also fig.*).
перено́выва|ть, ю *impf. of* **перекова́ть**
переколо|ти́ть, чу́, ~тишь *pf.* (*coll.*) to break, smash.
перекол|о́ть[1], ю́, ~ешь *pf.* (*of* **перека́лывать**) **1.** to pin (*somewhere else*). **2.** to prick all over.
перекол|о́ть[2], ю́, ~ешь *pf.* (*of* **перека́лывать**) to chop, hew.
перекопа́|ть, ю *pf.* (*of* **перека́пывать**) **1.** to dig over again. **2.** to dig (*all of*). **3.** to dig across.
перекорм|и́ть, лю́, ~ишь *pf.* (*of* **перека́рмливать**) **1.** to overfeed, surfeit. **2.** (*pf. only*) to feed (*all of, many*).
перекóр|ы, ов *no sg.* (*coll.*) squabble.
перекоря́|ться, юсь *impf.* (*no pf.*) (*coll.*) to squabble.
переко|си́ть[1], шу́, ~сишь *pf.* (*of* **перека́шивать**) to warp; (*fig.*) to distort; (*impers.*): **~си́ло око́нную ра́му** the window-frame has warped; **от зло́бы его́ ~си́ло** his face was distorted with malice.
переко|си́ть[2], шу́, ~сишь *pf.* to mow (*all of, a large area of*).
переко|си́ться, шу́сь, ~сишься *pf.* (*of* **перека́шиваться**) to warp, be warped; (*fig.*) to become distorted.
перекоч|ева́ть, у́ю *pf.* (*of* **~ёвывать**) to migrate; to move on (*of nomads, also coll.*).
перекочёвыва|ть, ю *impf. of* **перекочева́ть**
переко́|шенный *p.p.p. of* **~си́ть** *and adj.* distorted, twisted.
перекра́ива|ть, ю *impf. of* **перекрои́ть**
перекра́|сить[1], шу, сишь *pf.* (*of* **~шивать**) to re-colour, re-paint; to re-dye.
перекра́|сить[2], шу, сишь *pf.* (*of* **~шивать**) to colour, paint; to dye.
перекра́|ситься, шусь, сишься *pf.* (*of* **~шиваться**) **1.** to change colour. **2.** (*fig.*) to become a turn-coat.
перекра́шива|ть(ся), ю(сь) *impf. of* **перекра́сить(ся)**
перекре|сти́ть[1], щу́, ~стишь *pf.* (*of* **крести́ть 3.**) to make the sign of the cross over.
перекре|сти́ть[2], щу́, ~стишь *pf.* (*of* **~щивать**) to cross.
перекре|сти́ть[3], щу́, ~стишь *pf.* (*of* **~щивать**) to baptize (*all of, a large number of*).
перекре|сти́ться[1], щу́сь, ~стишься *pf.* (*of* **крести́ться 2.**) to cross o.s.
перекре|сти́ться[2], щу́сь, ~стишься *pf.* (*of* **~щиваться**) to cross, intersect.
перекрёстн|ый *adj.* cross; **п. допро́с** cross-examination; **п. ого́нь** (*mil.*) cross-fire; **~ое опыле́ние** (*bot.*) cross-pollination; **~ая ссы́лка** cross-reference.
перекрёст|ок, ка *m.* cross-roads, crossing; **крича́ть на всех ~ках** (*coll.*) to shout from the house-tops.
перекре́щива|ть(ся), ю(сь) *impf. of* **перекрести́ть[2,3](ся)[2]**
перекри́кива|ть, ю *impf. of* **перекрича́ть**
перекри|ча́ть, чу́, чи́шь *pf.* (*of* **~кивать**) to out-voice, drown; to shout down.
перекро|и́ть, ю́, и́шь *pf.* (*of* **перекра́ивать**) to cut out again; (*fig.*) to rehash; to re-shape; **п. ка́рту ми́ра** to re-draw the map of the world.
перекрыва́|ть, ю *impf. of* **перекры́ть**
перекры́ти|е, я *nt.* **1.** (*archit.*) ceiling, overhead cover. **2.** (*tech.*) overlap(ping), damming (of a river).
перекр|ы́ть[1], о́ю, о́ешь *pf.* (*of* **~ыва́ть**) to re-cover.
перекр|ы́ть[2], о́ю, о́ешь *pf.* (*of* **~ыва́ть**) **1.** (*coll.*) to exceed; **п. реко́рд** to break a record. **2.** (*cards*) to beat; to trump. **3.** to close, cut off; to dam (*a river*).
перекувы́ркива|ть(ся), ю(сь) *impf. of* **перекувырну́ть(ся)**
перекувыр|ну́ть, ну́, нёшь *pf.* (*of* **~кивать**) (*coll.*) to upset, overturn.
перекувыр|ну́ться, ну́сь, нёшься *pf.* (*of* **~киваться**) (*coll.*) **1.** to topple over. **2.** to turn a somersault.
перекуп|а́ть[1], а́ю *impf. of* **~и́ть**
перекупа́|ть[2], ю *pf.* to bath.
перекупа́|ть[3], ю *pf.* (*coll.*) to bathe too long.
перекупа́|ться, юсь *pf.* (*coll.*) to bathe too long, stay in (the water) too long.
перекуп|и́ть, лю́, ~ишь *pf.* (*of* **~а́ть**) to buy up (*sth. sought by others*); to outbid for.
переку́пщик, а *m.* second-hand dealer.
переку́р, а *m.* (*coll.*) break (for a smoke); **пойдём на п.** let's take five.
переку́рива|ть, ю *impf. of* **перекури́ть**
перекур|и́ть, ю́, ~ишь *pf.* (*of* **~ивать**) **1.** to smoke to excess. **2.** (*coll.*) to break for a smoke.
перекуса́|ть, ю *pf.* to bite.
переку|си́ть, шу́, ~сишь *pf.* (*of* **~сывать**) **1.** to bite through. **2.** (*coll.*) to have a bite, have a snack.
переку́сыва|ть *impf. of* **перекуси́ть**

перелагá|ть, ю *impf. of* **переложи́ть**
перелáмыва|ть(ся), ю(сь) *impf. of* **переломи́ть(ся)**
перележ|áть, ý, и́шь *pf.* to lie too long.
перелез|áть, áю *impf. of* **~ть**
перелéз|ть, у, ешь, *past* **~, ~ла** *pf.* (*of* **~áть**) to climb over, get over.
перелéс|ок, ка *m.* copse, coppice.
перелéсь|е, я *nt.* (*dial.*) glade.
перелёт, а *m.* **1.** flight (*of aircraft*). **2.** migration (*of birds*). **3.** shot over the target, plus round.
перелет|áть, áю *impf. of* **~éть**
переле|тéть, чý, ти́шь *pf.* (*of* **~тáть**) **1.** (*+a. or* **чéрез**) to fly over. **2.** to fly too far; to overshoot (the mark).
перелётн|ый *adj.*: **~ая пти́ца** bird of passage (*also fig.*); migratory bird.
пере|лéчь, ля́гу, ля́жешь, ля́гут, *past* **~лёг, ~леглá** *pf.* (*no impf.*) to lie somewhere else; **п. с одногó бóка на другóй** to turn from one side to another.
перели́в, а *m.* tint, tinge; play (of colours); modulation (*of voice*).
перели́вани|е, я *nt.* **1.** decantation. **2.** (*med.*) transfusion.
перели́вá|ть[1], ю *impf. of* **перели́ть; п. из пустóго в порóжнее** (*fig.*) to mill the wind, beat the air.
переливá|ть[2], ет *impf.* (*of colours*) to play; **п. всéми цветáми рáдуги** to be iridescent.
переливá|ться[1], юсь *impf. of* **перели́ться**
переливá|ться[2], ется *impf.* (*of colours*) to play; (*of voices*) to modulate; **п. всéми цветáми рáдуги** to be iridescent.
перели́вк|а, и *f.* (*tech.*) re-casting.
перели́вчат|ый (~, ~а) *adj.* iridescent; (*of voice*) modulating; (*of silk*) shot.
перелист|áть, áю *pf.* (*of* **~ывать**) **1.** to turn over, leaf. **2.** to look through, glance at.
перели́стыва|ть, ю *impf. of* **перелистáть**
перел|и́ть[1], ью́, ьёшь, *past* **~и́л, ~илá, ~и́ло** *pf.* (*of* **~ивáть**) **1.** to pour (*somewhere else*; *from A into B*); to decant; **п. молокó из кастрю́ли в кувши́н** to pour milk from a saucepan into a jug. **2.** (*med.*) to transfuse; **п. кровь** (*+d.*) to administer a blood transfusion (to). **3.** to let overflow.
перел|и́ть[2], ью́, ьёшь, *past* **~и́л, ~илá, ~и́ло** *pf.* (*of* **~ивáть**) **1.** to re-cast. **2.** to melt down; **п. колоколá на пýшки** to melt down bells for guns.
перел|и́ться, ью́сь, ьёшься, *past* **~и́лся, ~илáсь, ~и́лóсь** *pf.* (*of* **~ивáться**) **1.** to flow (*somewhere else*; *from A to B*). **2.** to overflow, run over.
перелиц|евáть, ýю *pf.* (*of* **~óвывать**) to turn (*an article of clothing*); to have turned.
перелицóвыва|ть, ю *impf. of* **перелицевáть**
перелóв, а *m.* overfishing.
перелов|и́ть, лю́, ~ишь *pf.* to catch (*all or a number of*).
перелóг, а *m.* (*agric.*) fallow.
переложéни|е, я *nt.* (*mus.*) arrangement; transposition; **п. в стихи́** versification.
перелож|и́ть, ý, ~ишь *pf.* **1.** (*impf.* **перекла́дывать** *and* **перелагáть**) to put somewhere else; to shift, move; (*fig.*) to shift off, transfer; **п. руль** (*naut.*) to put the helm over; **п. отвéтственность на когó-н.** to shift off the responsibility on to s.o. **2.** (*impf.* **перекла́дывать**) (*+a. and i.*) to interlay (with); **п. посýду солóмой** to interlay crockery with straw. **3.** (*impf.* **перекла́дывать**) to re-set, re-lay. **4.** (*impf.* **перелагáть**) (**в, на**+*a.*) to set (to), arrange (for); to transpose; to put (into); **п. на мýзыку** to set to music; **п. в стихи́** to put into verse. **5.** (*impf.* **перекла́дывать**) (*+g.*) to put in too much; **вы ~и́ли сóли в суп** you have put too much salt in the soup.
перелóжный *adj. of* **перелóг**
перелó|й, я *m.* (*obs.*) gonorrhoea.
перелóм, а *m.* **1.** break, breaking; fracture. **2.** (*fig.*) turning point, crisis, sudden change.
переломá|ть, ю *pf.* to break (*all or a number of*).
переломá|ться, юсь *pf.* (*coll.*) to break, be broken.
перелом|и́ть, лю́, ~ишь *pf.* (*of* **перелáмывать**) **1.** to break in two; to break *or* fracture. **2.** (*fig.*) to break *or* master; **п. себя́** to master o.s.; to restrain one's feelings; **п. комý-н. вóлю** to break s.o.'s will.
перелом|и́ться, ~ится *pf.* (*of* **перелáмываться**) to break in two; to be fractured.
перелóм|ный *adj. of* **~; п. момéнт** critical moment, crucial moment.
перемá|зать[1], жу, жешь *pf.* (*of* **~зывать**) (*coll.*; *+i.*) to soil (with), make dirty (with).
перемá|зать[2], жу, жешь *pf.* (*of* **~зывать**) to re-coat (*with paint, etc.*).
перемá|заться, жусь, жешься *pf.* (*of* **~зываться**) (*coll.*) to soil o.s., besmear o.s.
перемáзыва|ть(ся), ю(сь) *impf. of* **перемáзать(ся)**
перемáлыва|ть, ю *impf. of* **перемолóть**
перемáнива|ть, ю *impf. of* **перемани́ть**
переман|и́ть, ю́, ~ишь *pf.* (*of* **~ивать**) to entice; **п. на свою́ стóрону** to win over.
перемáтыва|ть, ю *impf. of* **перемотáть**
перемáхива|ть, ю *impf. of* **перемахнýть**
перемах|нýть, нý, нёшь *pf.* (*of* **~ивать**) (*coll.*) to jump over, leap over.
перемежá|ть, ю *impf.* (*no pf.*) (*+a. and i.* or **с**+*i.*) to alternate; **он ~л угрóзы (с) лéстью** he alternated threats and blandishments.
перемежá|ться, ется *impf.* (*no pf.*) (**с**+*i.*) to alternate; **снег ~лся с грáдом** snow alternated with hail, it snowed and hailed by turns; **~ющаяся лихорáдка** (*med.*) intermittent fever, remittent (fever).
перемеж|евáть, ýю *pf.* (*of* **~ёвывать**) to re-survey.
перемежёвыва|ть, ю *impf. of* **перемежевáть**
перемéн|а, ы *f.* **1.** change, alteration; **без ~** (there is) no change. **2.** change (of clothes). **3.** (*school*) interval, break; **большáя п.** long (*sc.* midday) break.
перемен|и́ть, ю́, ~ишь *pf.* (*of* **~я́ть**) to change; **п. пози́цию** to shift one's ground (*also fig.*); **п. тон** (*fig.*) to change one's tune.
перемен|и́ться, ю́сь, ~ишься *pf.* (*of* **~я́ться**) to change; **п. местáми** to change places; **п. в лицé** to change countenance; **п. к комý-н.** to change (one's attitude) towards s.o.
перемéнн|ый *adj.* variable; **~ая величинá** (*math.*) variable (quantity); **~ая погóда** changeable weather; **п. ток** (*elec.*) alternating current (*abbr.* AC); **рабóтать от сéти ~ого тóка** to operate from AC mains supply.
перемéнчив|ый (~, ~а) *adj.* (*coll.*) changeable.
перемен|я́ть(ся), я́ю(сь) *impf. of* **~и́ть(ся)**
пере|мерéть, мрёт, *past* **пéремер, ~мерлá, пéремерло** *pf.* (*coll.*) to die (off).
перемерз|áть, áю *impf. of* **~нуть**
перемёрз|нуть, ну, нешь *pf.* (*of* **~áть**) (*coll.*) **1.** to get chilled, freeze. **2.** (*of plants*) to be nipped by the frost.
перемéрива|ть, ю *impf. of* **перемéрить**
перемéр|ить[1], ю, ишь *pf.* (*of* **~ивать**) to re-measure.
перемéр|ить[2], ю, ишь *pf.* to try on.
переме|сти́ть, щý, сти́шь *pf.* (*of* **~щáть**) to move (*somewhere else*); to transfer.
переме|сти́ться, щýсь, сти́шься *pf.* (*of* **~щáться**) **1.** to move. **2.** *pass. of* **~сти́ть**
перемé|тить[1], чу, тишь *pf.* (*of* **~чáть**) to mark again.
перемé|тить[2], чу, тишь *pf.* (*no impf.*) to mark (*a quantity of*).
переметн|ýться, ýсь, ёшься *pf.* (*no impf.*) (*coll.*) to go over, desert.
перемётн|ый *adj.*: **~ая сумá** saddle bag; **сумá ~ая** (*fig., obs.*) weathercock.
перемеш|áть, áю *pf.* (*of* **~ивать**) **1.** to (inter)mix, intermingle; **п. кáрты** to shuffle cards; **п. ýгли в пéчке** to poke the fire. **2.** (*coll.*) to mix up; (*fig.*) to confuse; **он, по-ви́димому, ~áл нáши фами́лии** he evidently got our names mixed up.
перемеш|áться, áюсь *pf.* (*of* **~иваться**) **1.** to get mixed (up); **всё у негó в головé ~áлось** he has got everything mixed up. **2.** *pass. of* **~áть**
перемéшива|ть(ся), ю(сь) *impf. of* **перемешáть(ся)**
перемещá|ть(ся), ю(сь) *impf. of* **перемести́ть(ся)**
перемещéни|е, я *nt.* **1.** transference, shift; displacement.

2. (*geol.*) dislocation, displacement. 3. (*tech.*) travel.

переме|щённый *p.p.p. of* **~сти́ть; ~щённые ли́ца** (*pol.*) displaced persons.

перемигива|ться, юсь *impf. of* **перемигну́ться**

перемиг|ну́ться, ну́сь, нёшься *pf.* (*of* **~иваться**) (*coll.*; **с**+*i.*) to wink (at); **п. ме́жду собо́й** to wink at each other.

перемина́|ться, юсь *impf.* (*no pf.*): **п. с ноги́ на́ ногу** (*coll.*) to shift from one foot to the other.

перемири|е, я *nt.* armistice, truce.

перемнож|а́ть, а́ю *impf. of* **~ить**

перемно́ж|ить, у, ишь *pf.* (*of* **~а́ть**) to multiply.

перемога́|ть, ю *impf.* (*coll.*) 1. (*pf.* **перемо́чь**) to overcome (*an illness, etc.*). 2. to try to overcome (*an illness, etc.*).

перемога́|ться, юсь *impf.* (*coll.*) to try to overcome an illness; **три дня он ~лся, но наконе́ц ему́ пришло́сь позва́ть врача́** he held out for three days, but in the end he had to call in the doctor.

перемок|а́ть, а́ю *impf. of* **~нуть**

перемо́к|нуть, ну, нешь, *past* **~, ~ла** *pf.* (*of* **~а́ть**) (*coll.*) to get drenched.

перемо́лв|ить, лю, ишь *pf.* (*no impf.*): **п. сло́во** (**с**+*i.*; *coll.*) to exchange a word (with).

перемо́лв|иться, люсь, ишься *pf.* (*no impf.*) (+*i.*; **с**+*i.*; *coll.*) to exchange words (with); **п. не́сколькими слова́ми с сосе́дом** to exchange a few words with a neighbour.

перем|оло́ть, елю́, е́лешь *pf.* (*of* **~а́лывать**) to grind, mill; (*fig.*) to pulverize.

перем|оло́ться, е́лется *pf.* (*of* **~а́лываться**) *pass. of* **~оло́ть; ~е́лется — мука́ бу́дет** (*prov.*) it will all come right in the end; time is a great healer.

перемота́|ть, ю *pf.* (*of* **перема́тывать**) 1. to wind; to reel. 2. to re-wind.

перемо́|чь, гу́, ~жешь *pf. of* **~га́ть**

перемудр|и́ть, ю́, и́шь *pf.* (*no impf.*) (*coll.*) to be too clever by half.

перему́ч|иться, усь, ишься *pf.* (*no impf.*) (*coll.*) to have suffered very much.

перемыва́|ть, ю *impf. of* **перемы́ть**

перем|ы́ть[1], **о́ю, о́ешь** *pf.* (*of* **~ыва́ть**) to wash up again.

перем|ы́ть[2], **о́ю, о́ешь** *pf.* to wash (up) (*all or a quantity of*).

перемы́чк|а, и *f.* (*tech.*) 1. straight arch. 2. cross piece; tie plate. 3. bulkhead; dam.

перенапряга́|ть(ся), ю(сь) *impf. of* **перенапря́чь(ся)**

перенапря́|чь, гу́, жёшь, *past* **~г, ~гла́** *pf.* (*of* **~га́ть**) to overstrain.

перенапря́|чься, гу́сь, жёшься, *past* **~гся, ~гла́сь** *pf.* (*of* **~га́ться**) to overstrain o.s.

перенаселе́ни|е, я *nt.* overpopulation.

перенаселённост|ь, и *f.* overpopulation; overcrowding (*in a dwelling*).

перенасел|ённый *p.p.p. of* **~и́ть** *and adj.* overpopulated; overcrowded.

перенасел|и́ть, ю́, и́шь *pf.* (*of* **~я́ть**) to overpopulate.

перенасел|я́ть, я́ю *impf. of* **~и́ть**

перенасы́|тить, щу, тишь *pf.* (*of* **~ща́ть**) (*chem.*) to supersaturate.

перенасыща́|ть, ю *impf. of* **перенасы́тить**

перенасы́|щенный *p.p.p. of* **~тить** *and adj.* (*chem.*) supersaturated.

перенесе́ни|е, я *nt.* transference, transportation.

перенес|ти́[1], **у́, ёшь,** *past* **~, ~ла́** *pf.* (*of* **переноси́ть**) 1. to carry (*somewhere else*); to transport; to transfer; **п. ого́нь** (*mil.*) to switch fire; **п. де́ло в областно́й суд** to take the matter to the oblast court; **п. столи́цу в Москву́** to move the capital to Moscow. 2.: **п. сло́во** (*typ.*) to carry over (*part of word*) to the next line. 3. to put off, postpone; to carry over.

перенес|ти́[2], **у́, ёшь,** *past* **~, ~ла́** *pf.* (*of* **переноси́ть**) to endure, bear, stand; **п. боле́знь** to have an illness; **я э́того не мог п.** I couldn't stand that.

перенес|ти́сь, у́сь, ёшься, *past* **~ся, ~ла́сь** *pf.* (*of* **переноси́ться**) 1. to be carried, be borne; (*fig.*) to be carried away (*in thought*). 2. *pass. of* **~ти́**[1]

перенима́|ть, ю *impf. of* **переня́ть**

перено́с, а *m.* 1. transfer; transportation. 2. (*typ.*) division of words; **знак ~а** hyphen.

переноси́м|ый (**~, ~а**) *pres. part. pass. of* **переноси́ть** *and adj.* bearable, endurable.

переносо|си́ть(ся), шу́(сь), ~сишь(ся) *impf. of* **перенести́(сь)**

перено́сиц|а, ы *f.* bridge of the nose.

перено́ск|а, и *f.* carrying over, transporting; carriage.

переносно́й = перено́сный 1.

перено́сный *adj.* 1. portable. 2. (*ling.*) figurative; metaphorical.

перено́счик, а *m.* carrier; **п. слу́хов** tale-bearer, rumour-monger.

переноч|ева́ть, у́ю *pf.* (*of* **ночева́ть**) to spend the night.

перенумер|ова́ть, у́ю *pf.* (*of* **нумерова́ть**) to number; **п. страни́цы** to page.

пере|ня́ть, йму́, ймёшь, *past* **пе́ренял, ~няла́, пе́реняло** *pf.* (*of* **~нима́ть**) (*coll.*) 1. to imitate, copy; **п. привы́чку** to acquire a habit; **п. чей-н. приём** to take a leaf out of s.o.'s book. 2. to intercept, bar the way (to).

переоборуд|ова́ть, у́ю *impf. and pf.* to re-equip; to refit (*ship, etc.*).

переобремен|и́ть, ю́, и́шь *pf.* (*of* **~я́ть**) to overburden.

переобремен|я́ть, я́ю *impf. of* **~и́ть**

переобува́|ть(ся), ю(сь) *impf. of* **переобу́ть(ся)**

переобу́|ть, ю, ешь *pf.* (*of* **~ва́ть**) to change s.o.'s shoes; **п. боти́нки** to change one's shoes.

переобу́|ться, юсь, ешься *pf.* (*of* **~ва́ться**) to change one's shoes, boots, *etc.*

переодева́лк|а, и *f.* changing-room.

переодева́|ть(ся), ю(сь) *impf. of* **переоде́ть(ся)**

переоде́тый *adj.*: **п. полице́йский** plain-clothes policeman.

переоде́|ть, ну, нешь *pf.* (*of* **~ва́ть**) 1. to change s.o.'s clothes; **они́ ~ли де́вочку в наря́дное пла́тье** they changed the little girl into a party frock; **п. бельё ребёнку** (*coll.*) to change a baby; **п. пла́тье** to change one's dress. 2. (+*i.*; **в**+*a.*) to dress up, disguise (as, in); **п. де́вочку ма́льчиком** to dress up a little girl as a boy.

переоде́|ться, нусь, нешься *pf.* (*of* **~ва́ться**) 1. to change (one's clothes). 2. (+*i.*, **в**+*a.*) to disguise o.s. *or* dress up (as, in); **она ~лась в ма́льчика** she disguised herself as a boy.

переосвиде́тельств|ова́ть, у́ю *impf. and pf.* (*med.*) to re-examine.

переоце́нива|ть, ю *impf. of* **переоцени́ть**

переоцен|и́ть, ю́, ~ишь *pf.* (*of* **~ивать**) 1. to overestimate, overrate; **п. свои́ си́лы** to overestimate one's strength, bite off more than one can chew. 2. to revalue, reappraise.

переоце́нк|а, и *f.* 1. overestimation. 2. revaluation, reappraisal.

перепа́д, а *m.* (*tech.*) overfall.

перепа́да|ть, ет *pf.* (*coll.*) to fall (*one after another*).

перепада́|ть, ю *impf. of* **перепа́сть**

перепа́ива|ть, ю *impf. of* **перепои́ть**

перепа́лк|а, и *f.* (*coll.*) exchange of fire, skirmish (*also fig.*).

перепа́рхива|ть, ю *impf. of* **перепорхну́ть**

перепа́|сть, дёт, *past* **~л** *pf.* (*of* **~да́ть**) (*coll.*) 1. to fall intermittently; **дождь ~дёт** there will be rain at intervals, it will be showery. 2. (*impers.*; +*d.*) to fall to one's lot.

перепа|ха́ть, шу́, ~шешь *pf.* (*of* **~хивать**) to plough (up) again; to plough over.

перепа́хива|ть, ю *impf. of* **перепаха́ть**

перепа́чка|ть, ю *pf.* to soil, make dirty (all over).

перепа́чка|ться, юсь *pf.* to make o.s. dirty (all over).

перепе́в, а *m.* repetition, rehash.

перепека́|ть, ю *impf. of* **перепе́чь**

пе́репел, а, *pl.* **~а́** *m.* (*zool.*) quail.

перепелен|а́ть, а́ю *pf.* (*of* **~ывать**): **п. ребёнка** to change a baby, change a baby's nappy.

перепелёныва|ть, ю *impf. of* **перепелена́ть**

перепели́ный *adj. of* **пе́репел**

перепёлк|а, и *f.* (*zool.*) female quail; **вирги́нская п.** bobwhite (quail).

перепеля́тник, а *m.* 1. quail-shooter. 2. (sparrow-)hawk.

перепе́рчива|ть, ю *impf. of* **перепе́рчить**

перепе́рч|ить, у, ишь *pf.* (*of* **~ивать**) to put too much pepper into.
перепеча́т|ать, аю *pf.* (*of* **~ывать**) **1.** to reprint. **2.** to type (out).
перепеча́тк|а, и *f.* **1.** reprinting; **п. воспреща́ется** copyright reserved. **2.** reprint.
перепеча́тыва|ть, ю *impf. of* **перепеча́тать**
перепе́|чь[1], **ку́, ёшь** *pf.* (*of* **~ка́ть**) to overbake.
перепе́|чь[2], **ку́, ёшь** *pf.* to bake (*all or a number of*).
перепива́|ть(ся), ю(сь) *impf. of* **перепи́ть(ся)**
перепи́лива|ть, ю *impf. of* **перепили́ть**
перепил|и́ть[1], **ю́, ~ишь** *pf.* (*of* **~ивать**) to saw in two.
перепил|и́ть[2], **ю́, ~ишь** *pf.* to saw (*all or a number of*).
перепи|са́ть[1], **шу́, ~шешь** *pf.* (*of* **~сывать**) **1.** to re-write; to re-type; **п. на́бело** to make a fair copy (of). **2.** to re-copy.
перепи|са́ть[2], **шу́, ~шешь** *pf.* (*of* **~сывать**) to make a list (of), list; **п. всех прису́тствующих** to take the names of all those present.
перепи́ск|а, и *f.* **1.** copying; typing. **2.** correspondence; **быть в ~е (с**+*i.*) to be in correspondence (with). **3.** (*collect.*) correspondence, letters.
перепи́счик, а *m.* copyist; typist.
перепи́сыва|ть, ю *impf. of* **переписа́ть**
перепи́сыва|ться, юсь *impf.* (**с**+*i.*) to correspond (with).
пе́репис|ь, и *f.* **1.** census. **2.** inventory.
переп|и́ть, ью́, ьёшь, *past* **~и́л, ~ила́, ~и́ло** *pf.* (*of* **~ива́ть**) (*coll.*) **1.** to drink excessively. **2.** to out-drink; **к. утру́ он ~и́л всех това́рищей** by morning he had drunk all his companions under the table.
переп|и́ться, ью́сь, ьёшься, *past* **~и́лся, ~ила́сь, ~и́ло́сь** *pf.* (*of* **~ива́ться**) (*coll.*) to get completely drunk.
перепла́в|ить[1], **лю, ишь** *pf.* (*of* **~ля́ть**) to smelt.
перепла́в|ить[2], **лю, ишь** *pf.* (*of* **~ля́ть**) **1.** to float; to raft. **2.** (*fig., coll.*) to convey surreptitiously.
переплавля́|ть, ю *impf. of* **перепла́вить**
перепланир|ова́ть, ую, у́ю *pf.* (*of* **~о́вывать**) **1.** to re-plan, make new plans (for), alter plan (of). **2.** to re-plan (*streets, districts, etc.*).
перепланиро́вк|а, и *f.* re-planning (*of streets, districts, etc.*).
перепланиро́выва|ть, ю *impf. of* **перепланирова́ть**
перепла́т|а, ы *f.* surplus payment.
перепла|ти́ть, чу́, ~тишь *pf.* (*of* **~чивать**) to overpay; to pay excessively.
перепла́чива|ть, ю *impf. of* **переплати́ть**
переплёвыва|ть, ю *impf. of* **переплю́нуть**
перепле|сти́[1], **ту́, тёшь**, *past* **~л, ~ла́** *pf.* (*of* **~та́ть**) **1.** to bind (*books*). **2.** (+*i.*) to interlace (with), interknit (with).
перепле|сти́[1], **ту́, тёшь**, *past* **~л, ~ла́** *pf.* (*of* **~та́ть**) to braid again, plait again.
перепле|сти́сь, тётся, *past* **~лся, ~ла́сь** *pf.* (*of* **~та́ться**) **1.** to interlace, interweave. **2.** (*fig.*) to get mixed up.
переплёт, а *m.* **1.** binding; **отда́ть кни́гу в п.** to have a book bound. **2.** binding, book-cover. **3.** transom (*of door or window*); **око́нный п.** window-sash. **4.** caning (*of a chair*). **5.** (*coll.*) mess, scrape; **попа́сть в п.** to get into a mess, get into trouble.
переплета́|ть(ся), ю(сь) *impf. of* **переплести́(сь)**
переплётн|ая, ой *f.* bindery, bookbinder's shop.
переплётчик, а *m.* bookbinder.
переплыва́|ть, ю *impf. of* **переплы́ть**
переплы́|ть, ву́, вёшь, *past* **~л, ~ла́, ~ло** *pf.* (*of* **~ва́ть**) to swim (across); to sail (across).
переплю́н|уть, у, ешь *pf.* (*of* **переплёвывать**) (*coll.*) to spit further than; (*fig.*) to do better than, surpass.
переподгота́влива|ть, ю *impf. of* **переподгото́вить**
переподгото́в|ить, лю, ишь *pf.* (*of* **переподгота́вливать**) to train anew.
переподгото́вк|а, и *f.* further training; training anew; **ку́рсы по ~е** refresher courses.
перепо|и́ть, ю́, ~и́шь *pf.* (*of* **перепа́ивать**) **1.** to give too much to drink (*to an animal*). **2.** (*coll.*) to make drunk.
перепо́|й, я *m.* excessive drinking; **у меня́ разболе́лась голова́ с ~я (с ~ю)** I had a hangover.

переполз|а́ть, а́ю *impf. of* **~ти́**
переполз|ти́, у́, ёшь, *past* **~, ~ла́** *pf.* (*of* **~а́ть**) to crawl across; to creep across.
переполне́ни|е, я *nt.* overfilling; overcrowding; **п. желу́дка** repletion.
перепо́лн|ить, ю, ишь *pf.* (*of* **~я́ть**) to overfill; to overcrowd.
перепо́лн|иться, ится *pf.* (*of* **~я́ться**) to overfill; to be overcrowded; **её се́рдце ~илось ра́достью** her heart overflowed with joy.
переполн|я́ть(ся), я́ю(сь) *impf. of* **~ить(ся)**
переполо́х, а *m.* alarm; commotion, rumpus.
переполош|и́ть, у́, и́шь *pf.* (*coll.*) to alarm; to rouse.
перепо́нк|а, и *f.* membrane; web (*of bat or water-fowl*); **бараба́нная п.** (*anat.*) ear-drum, tympanum.
перепончатокры́лы|й *adj.* (*zool.*) hymenopterous; *as n.* **~е, ~х** Hymenoptera.
перепо́нчатый *adj.* membraneous, membranous; webbed; web-footed.
перепоруч|а́ть, а́ю *impf. of* **~и́ть**
перепоруч|и́ть, у́, ~ишь *pf.* (*of* **~а́ть**) (+*d.*) to turn over (to), reassign (to); **п. веде́ние де́ла друго́му защи́тнику** to turn over one's case to another lawyer.
перепорхн|у́ть, у́, ёшь *pf.* (*of* **перепа́рхивать**) to flutter, flit (*somewhere else*; *from A to B*).
перепра́в|а, ы *f.* passage, crossing; ford.
перепра́в|ить[1], **лю, ишь** *pf.* (*of* **~ля́ть**) **1.** to convey, transport to; take across. **2.** to forward (*mail*).
перепра́в|ить[2], **лю, ишь** *pf.* (*of* **~ля́ть**) (*coll.*) to correct.
перепра́в|иться, люсь, ишься *pf.* (*of* **~ля́ться**) to cross, get across; to swim across; to sail across.
переправля́|ть(ся), ю(сь) *impf. of* **перепра́вить(ся)**
перепрева́|ть, ю *impf. of* **перепре́ть**
перепре́|ть, ю *pf.* (*of* **~ва́ть**) **1.** to rot. **2.** (*coll.*) to be overdone.
перепро́б|овать, ую *pf.* to taste (*all or a quantity of*); (*fig.*) to try.
перепрода|ва́ть, ю́, ёшь *impf. of* **~ть**
перепродав|е́ц, ца́ *m.* re-seller.
перепрода́ж|а, и *f.* re-sale.
перепрода́|ть, м, шь, ст, ди́м, ди́те, ду́т, *past* **перепро́дал, ~ла́, перепро́дало** *pf.* (*of* **~ва́ть**) to re-sell.
перепроизво́дств|о, а *nt.* overproduction.
перепры́гива|ть, ю *impf. of* **перепры́гнуть**
перепры́г|нуть, ну, нешь *pf.* (*of* **~ивать**) to jump (over).
перепря|га́ть, га́ю *impf. of* **~чь**
перепря́жк|а, и *f.* **1.** changing of horses. **2.** (*hist.*) stage (*on post-chaise route*).
перепря́|чь, гу́, жёшь, гу́т, *past* **~г, ~гла́** *pf.* (*of* **~га́ть**) **1.** to re-harness. **2.** to change (*horses*).
перепу́г, а (у) *m.* (*coll.*): **с ~у, от ~у** in one's fright.
перепуга́|ть, ю *pf.* (*no impf.*) to frighten, give a fright, give a turn.
перепуга́|ться, юсь *pf.* (*no impf.*) to get a fright.
перепуска́|ть, ю *impf. of* **перепусти́ть**
перепу|сти́ть, щу́, ~стишь *pf.* (*of* **~ска́ть**) **1.** to let flow (*from A to B*). **2.** to let go; to slacken.
перепу́т|ать, аю *pf.* (*of* **~ывать**) **1.** to entangle. **2.** (*fig.*) to confuse, mix up, muddle up.
перепу́т|аться, аюсь *pf.* (*of* **~ываться**) **1.** to get entangled. **2.** (*fig.*) to get confused, get mixed up.
перепу́тыва|ть(ся), ю(сь) *impf. of* **перепу́тать(ся)**
перепу́ть|е, я *nt.* cross-roads; **быть на п.** (*fig.*) to be at the cross-roads.
перераба́тыва|ть(ся), ю(сь) *impf. of* **перерабо́тать(ся)**
перерабо́та|ть[1], **ю** *pf.* (*of* **перераба́тывать**) **1.** (**в, на**+*a.*) to work (into), make (into); to convert (to); to treat; **п. свёклу в са́хар** to convert beet to sugar; **п. пи́щу** to digest food. **2.** to re-make; (*fig.*) to re-cast, re-shape; **п. статью́** to re-cast an article.
перерабо́та|ть[2], **ю** *pf.* (*of* **перераба́тывать**) (*coll.*) to exceed fixed hours of work, work overtime; **мы вчера́ ~ли три часа́** we did three hours overtime yesterday.
перерабо́та|ться[1], **юсь** *pf.* (*of* **перераба́тываться**) *pass. of* **~ть**

перерабо́та|ться[2], **юсь** *pf.* (*of* **перераба́тываться**) (*coll.*) to overwork.
перерабо́тк|а[1], **и** *f.* **1.** working over, treatment. **2.** re-making; (*fig.*) re-casting, re-shaping.
перерабо́тк|а[2], **и** *f.* overtime work.
перераспределе́ни|е, я *nt.* re-distribution.
перераспредел|и́ть, ю́, и́шь *pf.* (*of* **~я́ть**) to re-distribute.
перераспредел|я́ть, я́ю *impf. of* **~и́ть**
перераста́ни|е, я *nt.* **1.** outgrowing. **2.** (**в**+*a.*) growing (into), development (into). **3.** (*mil.*) escalation.
перераст|а́ть, а́ю *impf. of* **~и́**
перераст|и́, у́, ёшь, *past* **перерóс, переросла́** *pf.* (*of* **~а́ть**) **1.** to outgrow, (over)top; to outstrip (*in height, also fig.*); **трина́дцати лет она́ уже́ переросла́ отца́** at thirteen she had already outgrown her father; **п. своего́ учи́теля** to outstrip one's teacher. **2.** (*fig.*; **в**+*a.*) to grow (into), develop (into), turn (into). **3.** to be too old (for); **для де́тского са́да он перерóс** he is too old for kindergarten.
перерасхóд, а *m.* **1.** over-expenditure. **2.** (*fin.*) overdraft.
перерасхóд|овать, ую *pf.* (*no impf.*) **1.** to spend to excess. **2.** (*fin.*) to overdraw.
перерасчёт, а *m.* re-computation.
перерв|а́ть, у́, ёшь, *past* **~а́л, ~ала́, ~а́ло** *pf.* (*of* **перерыва́ть**[1]) to break, tear asunder.
перерв|а́ться, у́сь, ёшься, *past* **~а́лся, ~ала́сь, ~а́ло́сь** *pf.* (*of* **перерыва́ться**[1]) to break, come apart.
перерегистра́ци|я, и *f.* re-registration.
перерегистри́р|овать, ую *pf.* to re-register.
перерегистри́р|оваться, уюсь *pf.* **1.** to re-register. **2.** *pass. of* **~овать**
перере́|зать[1], **жу, жешь** *pf.* (*of* **~за́ть** *and* **~зывать**) **1.** to cut. **2.** (*fig.*) to cut off; **п. путь неприя́телю** to bar the enemy's way. **3.** (*geog.*) to break.
перере́|зать[2], **жу, жешь** *pf.* to kill, slaughter (*all or a number of*).
перерез|а́ть, а́ю *impf. of* **∠ать**[1]
перере́зыва|ть, ю *impf.* = **перереза́ть**
перереш|а́ть[1], **а́ю** *impf. of* **~и́ть**
перереш|а́ть[2], **а́ю** *pf.* to solve (*all or a number of problems*).
перереш|и́ть, у́, и́шь *pf.* (*of* **~а́ть**[1]) **1.** to re-solve; to decide, settle in a different way. **2.** to change one's mind, reconsider one's decision.
переро|ди́ть, жу́, ди́шь *pf.* (*of* **~жда́ть**) to regenerate.
переро|ди́ться, жу́сь, ди́шься *pf.* (*of* **~жда́ться**) **1.** (*coll.*) to be re-born. **2.** (*fig.*) to regenerate, be regenerated. **3.** (*biol. and fig.*) to degenerate.
перерожде́ни|е, я *nt.* **1.** regeneration. **2.** degeneration.
перерóст|ок, ка *m.* (*coll.*) backward child (*pupil older than his class-mates*).
переруб|а́ть, а́ю *impf. of* **~и́ть**
переруб|и́ть, лю́, ∠ишь *pf.* (*of* **~а́ть**) to chop in two; to hew asunder.
переруга́|ться, юсь *pf.* (*coll.*; **с**+*i.*) to fall out (with), fall foul (of), break (with).
переру́гива|ться, юсь *impf.* (*coll.*; **с**+*i.*) to quarrel (with), squabble (with).
переры́в, а *m.* interruption; interval, break, intermission; **обе́денный п.** dinner *or* lunch break; **п. на пять мину́т** five minutes' interval; **без ~а** without a break; **с ~ами** off and on.
перерыва́|ть[1], **ю** *impf. of* **перерва́ть**
перерыва́|ть[2], **ю** *impf. of* **переры́ть**
перерыва́|ться, юсь *impf. of* **перерва́ться**
перер|ы́ть, óю, óешь *pf.* (*of* **~ыва́ть**[2]) **1.** to dig up. **2.** (*fig., coll.*) to rummage (in).
переря|ди́ть, жу́, ∠ди́шь *pf.* (*of* **∠живать**) (+*i.*; *coll.*) to disguise (as), dress up (as).
переря|ди́ться, жу́сь, ∠ди́шься *pf.* (*of* **∠живаться**) (+*i.*; *coll.*) to disguise o.s. *or* dress up (as).
переря́жива|ть(ся), ю(сь) *impf. of* **переряди́ть(ся)**
переса|ди́ть, жу́, ∠дишь *pf.* (*of* **∠живать**) **1.** to make s.o. change his seat. **2.: п. кого́-н. че́рез что-н.** to help s.o. across sth. **3.** (*bot.*) to transplant. **4.** (*med.*) to graft.
переса́дк|а, и *f.* **1.** (*bot.*) transplantation. **2.** (*med.*) grafting; **опера́ция по ~е се́рдца** heart transplant operation. **3.** (*on rail.*) change; changing; **в Москву́ без ~и** no change for Moscow; through train to Moscow.
переса́жива|ть, ю *impf. of* **пересади́ть**
переса́жива|ться, юсь *impf. of* **пересе́сть**
переса́лива|ть, ю *impf. of* **пересоли́ть**
переда|ва́ть, ю́, ёшь *impf. of* **∠ть**
переда́|ть, м, шь, сь, ди́м, ди́те, ду́т, *past* **~л, ~ла́, ∠ло** *pf.* (*of* **~ва́ть**) **1.** to re-let; to sub-let. **2.** (*cards*) to re-deal. **3.** (*coll.*) to re-sit (*an examination*).
пересека́|ть(ся), ю(сь) *impf. of* **пересе́чь(ся)**
переселе́н|ец, ца *m.* **1.** migrant, emigrant; immigrant. **2.** settler.
переселе́ни|е, я *nt.* **1.** migration, emigration; immigration, re-settlement. **2.** move (*to new place of residence*).
переселе́н|ческий *adj. of* **~ец; ~ческая организа́ция** emigration, re-settlement organization.
пересел|и́ть, ю́, и́шь *pf.* (*of* **~я́ть**) to move; to transplant; to resettle.
пересел|и́ться, ю́сь, и́шься *pf.* (*of* **~я́ться**) to move; to migrate.
пересел|я́ть(ся), я́ю(сь) *impf. of* **~и́ть(ся)**
перес|е́сть, я́ду, я́дешь *pf.* (*of* **~а́живаться**) **1.** to change one's seat. **2.** to change (*trains, etc.*).
пересече́ни|е, я *nt.* crossing, intersection; **то́чка ~я** point of intersection.
перес|ечённый *p.p.p. of* **~е́чь**[1]; **~ечённая ме́стность** (*geog.*) broken terrain.
пересе́|чь[1], **ку́, чёшь, ку́т,** *past* **~к, ~кла́** *pf.* (*of* **~ка́ть**) **1.** to cross; to traverse; **п. у́лицу** to cross the road; **п. путь неприя́телю** (*fig.*) to cut the enemy off, bar the enemy's way. **2.** to cross, intersect.
пересе́|чь[2], **ку́, чёшь, ку́т,** *past* **~к, ~кла́** *pf.* (*of* **~ка́ть**) (*coll.*) to flog.
пересе́|чься, чётся, ку́тся, *past* **~кся, ~кла́сь** *pf.* (*of* **~ка́ться**) to cross, intersect.
переси|де́ть, жу́, ди́шь *pf.* (*of* **∠живать**) **1.** (*coll.*) to out-sit; **он ~де́л всех други́х госте́й** he outstayed all the other guests. **2.** to sit too long.
переси́жива|ть, ю *impf. of* **пересиде́ть**
переси́лива|ть, ю *impf. of* **переси́лить**
переси́л|ить, ю, ишь *pf.* (*of* **~ивать**) to overpower; (*fig.*) to overcome, master.
переска́з, а *m.* **1.** re-telling, narration. **2.** exposition.
переска|за́ть, жу́, ∠жешь *pf.* (*of* **∠зывать**) **1.** to re-tell, narrate; **~жи́(те) мне содержа́ние э́того рома́на** tell me the story of this novel (in your own words). **2.** to retail, relate; **п. слу́хи** to retail rumours.
переска́зыва|ть, ю *impf. of* **пересказа́ть**
переска́кива|ть, ю *impf. of* **перескочи́ть**
перескоч|и́ть, у́, ∠ишь *pf.* (*of* **переска́кивать**) **1.** (+*a. or* **че́рез**) to jump (over); to vault (over); (*fig.*; *in reading*) to skip (over). **2.** (*fig.*) to skip; **п. с одно́й те́мы на другу́ю** to skip from one topic to another.
пересла|сти́ть, щу́, сти́шь *pf.* (*of* **∠щивать**) to make too sweet, put too much sugar (into).
пере|сла́ть, шлю́, шлёшь *pf.* (*of* **~сыла́ть**) to send; to remit; to forward.
пересла́щива|ть, ю *impf. of* **пересласти́ть**
пересма́трива|ть, ю *impf. of* **пересмотре́ть**
пересме́ива|ть, ю *impf.* (*coll.*) to mock, make fun of.
пересме́ива|ться, юсь *impf.* (*coll.*; **с**+*i.*) to exchange smiles (with).
пересме́шк|а, и *f.* (*coll.*) mockery, banter.
пересме́шник, а *m.* **1.** (*coll.*) mocker, banterer. **2.** (*zool.*) mocking-bird.
пересмóтр, а *m.* **1.** revision. **2.** reconsideration; (*leg.*) review (*of a sentence*); re-trial.
пересмотр|е́ть[1], **ю́, ∠ишь** *pf.* (*of* **пересма́тривать**) **1.** to revise; to go over again. **2.** to re-consider; (*leg.*) to review. **3.** to go through (*in search of sth.*).
пересмотр|е́ть[2], **ю́, ∠ишь** *pf.* to have seen (*all or a quantity of*); to have gone all through.
переснима́|ть, ю *impf. of* **пересня́ть**
пересн|я́ть, иму́, и́мешь, *past* **~я́л, ~яла́, ~я́ло** *pf.* (*of*

~има́ть) 1. to photograph again, take another photo (of). **2.** to make a copy.
пересозда|ва́ть, ю́, ёшь *impf. of* **∸ть**
пересозда́|ть, м, шь, ст, ди́м, ди́те, ду́т, *past* **~л, ~ла́, ~ло** *pf.* (*of* **~ва́ть**) to re-create.
пересо́л, а *m.* excess of salt; **недосо́л на столе́, п. на спине́** (*coll.*) better too little than too much.
пересол|и́ть, ю́, ∸ишь *pf.* (*of* **переса́ливать**) **1.** to put too much salt (into). **2.** (*fig.*, *coll.*) to go too far.
пересо́х|нуть, нет, *past* **~, ~ла** *pf.* (*of* **пересыха́ть**) to dry out; to dry up, become parched.
пересп|а́ть, лю́, и́шь, *past* **~а́л, ~ала́, ~а́ло** *pf.* (*coll.*) **1.** to oversleep. **2.** to spend the night. **3.** (**с**+*i.*; *euph.*) to sleep (with).
переспе́лый *adj.* overripe.
переспо́р|ить, ю, ишь *pf.* to out-argue, defeat in argument; **его́ не ~ишь** he must have the last word.
переспра́шива|ть, ю *impf. of* **переспроси́ть**
переспро|си́ть¹, шу́, ∸сишь *pf.* (*of* **переспра́шивать**) to ask again; to ask to repeat.
переспро|си́ть², шу́, ∸сишь *pf.* to question (*all or a number of*).
перессо́р|ить, ю, ишь *pf.* (*coll.*) to set at variance.
перессо́р|иться, юсь, ишься *pf.* (*coll.*; **с**+*i.*) to quarrel (with), fall out (with).
переста|ва́ть, ю́, ёшь *impf. of* **∸ть**
переста́в|ить, лю, ишь *pf.* (*of* **~ля́ть**) to move, shift; **п. ме́бель** to re-arrange the furniture; **п. слова́ во фра́зе** to transpose the words in a sentence; **п. часы́ вперёд (наза́д)** to put the clock on (back).
переставля́|ть, ю *impf. of* **переста́вить**
переста́ива|ть, ю *impf. of* **перестоя́ть**
перестано́вк|а, и *f.* **1.** re-arrangement, transposition. **2.** (*math.*) permutation.
перестара́|ться, юсь *pf.* (*coll.*) to overdo it, put too much into it.
переста́р|ок, ка *m.* (*coll.*) pers. over age (*for given purpose*); **он мог бы ещё воева́ть — не п.** he could still fight, he is not too old.
переста́|ть, ну, нешь *pf.* (*of* **~ва́ть**) (+*inf.*) to stop, cease.
перестел|и́ть, ю́, ∸ешь *pf.* (*coll.*) = **перестла́ть**
перестила́|ть, ю *impf. of* **перестели́ть** *and* **перестла́ть**
перестир|а́ть¹, а́ю *pf.* (*of* **∸ывать**) to wash again.
перестир|а́ть², а́ю *pf.* (*no impf.*) to wash (*all or a number of*).
перести́рыва|ть, ю *impf. of* **перестира́ть¹**
перест|ла́ть, елю́, е́лешь *pf.* (*of* **~ила́ть**) to re-lay; **п. пол в ко́мнате** to re-floor a room; **п. посте́ль** to re-make a bed.
пересто|я́ть, ю́, и́шь *pf.* (*of* **переста́ивать**) stand too long.
перестрада́|ть, ю *pf.* (*no impf.*) to have suffered, have gone through.
перестра́ива|ть(ся), ю(сь) *impf. of* **перестро́ить(ся)**
перестрах|ова́ть, у́ю *pf.* (*of* **~о́вывать**) to re-insure.
перестрах|ова́ться, у́юсь *pf.* (*of* **~о́вываться**) **1.** to re-insure o.s. **2.** (*fig.*, *pej.*) to cover o.s. *or* play safe (*by seeking to transfer or share responsibility*).
перестрахо́вк|а, и *f.* **1.** re-insurance. **2.** (*fig.*, *pej.*) covering o.s.; playing safe (*esp. of editors of magazines unwilling to risk publishing controversial material*).
перестрахо́вщик, а *m.* (*pej.*) adherent of policy of 'playing safe'.
перестрахо́выва|ть(ся), ю(сь) *impf. of* **перестрахова́ть(ся)**
перестре́лива|ть, ю *impf. of* **перестреля́ть**
перестре́лива|ться, юсь *impf.* to fire (at each other), to shoot it out.
перестре́лк|а, и *f.* firing; skirmish; exchange of fire, shootout; **артиллери́йская п.** artillery duel.
перестрел|я́ть, я́ю *pf.* (*of* **∸ивать**) **1.** to shoot (down). **2.** to use up, expend (*in shooting*).
перестро́|ечный *adj. of* **~йка**
перестро́|ить, ю, ишь *pf.* (*of* **перестра́ивать**) **1.** to rebuild, reconstruct. **2.** to re-design, re-fashion, re-shape; to reorganize; **п. фра́зу** to reshape a sentence; **п. на вое́нный лад** to put on a war footing. **3.** (*mil.*) to re-form. **4.** (*mus.*, *radio*) to re-tune.
перестро́|иться, юсь, ишься *pf.* (*of* **перестра́иваться**) **1.** to re-form; to reorganize o.s.; to improve one's methods of work. **2.** (*mil.*) to re-form. **3.** (*radio*) (**на**+*a.*) to switch over (to), tune (on to); **п. на коро́ткую волну́** to switch over to short wave.
перестро́йк|а, и *f.* **1.** rebuilding, reconstruction; (*pol.*, *econ.*) perestroika. **2.** reorganization. **3.** (*mil.*) re-formation. **4.** (*mus.*, *radio*) re-tuning.
перасту́кивани|е, я *nt.* (*in prison, etc.*) communication by tapping.
перасту́кива|ться, юсь *impf.* (**с**+*i.*) (*in prison, etc.*) to communicate (with) by tapping.
переступ|а́ть, а́ю *impf.* **1.** *impf. of* **~и́ть. 2.** (*impf. only*) to move slowly; **он е́ле ~а́л (нога́ми)** his feet would hardly carry him; **п. с ноги́ на́ ногу** to shift from one foot to the other.
переступ|и́ть, лю́, ∸ишь *pf.* (*of* **~а́ть**) (+*a. or* **че́рез**) to step over; (*fig.*) to overstep; **п. поро́г** to cross the threshold; **п. зако́н** to break the law; **п. грани́цы прили́чия** to overstep the bounds of decency.
пересу́д, а *m.* (*coll.*) re-trial.
пересу́д|ы, ов *no sg.* (*coll.*) gossip.
пересу́шива|ть, ю *impf. of* **пересуши́ть¹**
пересуш|и́ть¹, у́, ∸ишь *pf.* (*of* **∸ивать**) to overdry.
пересуш|и́ть², у́, ∸ишь *pf.* (*no impf.*) to dry (*all or a quantity of*).
пересчит|а́ть¹, а́ю *pf.* (*of* **∸ывать**) **1.** to re-count; **п. ко́сти (рёбра) кому́-н.** (*fig.*, *coll.*) to give s.o. a drubbing. **2.** (**на**+*a.*) to convert (to), express (in terms of).
пересчит|а́ть², а́ю *pf.* (*no impf.*) to count.
пересчи́тыва|ть, ю *impf. of* **пересчита́ть¹**
пересыла́|ть, ю *impf. of* **пересла́ть**
пересы́лк|а, и *f.* sending; forwarding; **п. де́нег** remittance; **сто́имость ~и** postage; **п. беспла́тно** post free; carriage paid.
пересы́л|очный *adj. of* **~ка**
пересы́льн|ый *adj.* transit; **~ая тюрьма́** transit prison.
пересы́п|ать¹, лю, лешь *pf.* (*of* **~а́ть**) to pour (*dry substance*) into another container; **п. зерно́ в мешки́** to pour off grain into bags.
пересы́п|ать², лю, лешь *pf.* (*of* **~а́ть**) (+*i.*) **1.** to powder (with). **2.** (*fig.*) to (inter)lard, intersperse (with); **п. речь руга́тельствами** to lard one's speech with profanities.
пересып|а́ть, а́ю *impf. of* **∸ать**
пересыха́|ть, ет *impf. of* **пересо́хнуть**
перета́плива|ть, ю *impf. of* **перетопи́ть¹**
перетаск|а́ть, а́ю *pf.* (*of* **∸ивать**) **1.** to carry away. **2.** (*fig.*, *coll.*) to pinch, lift.
перета́скива|ть, ю *impf. of* **перетаска́ть** *and* **перетащи́ть**
перетас|ова́ть, у́ю *pf.* (*of* **~о́вывать**) to re-shuffle (*cards, also fig.*).
перетасо́выва|ть, ю *impf. of* **перетасова́ть**
перетащ|и́ть, у́, ∸ишь *pf.* (*of* **перета́скивать**) **1.** to drag over; to carry over; to move, shift; **п. сунду́к на черда́к** to move a trunk into the attic. **2.** (*fig.*, *coll.*) to win over, gain over.
перетека́|ть, ю *impf. of* **перете́чь**
пере|тере́ть, тру́, трёшь, *past* **~тёр, ~тёрла** *pf.* (*of* **~тира́ть**) **1.** to wear out, wear down; **терпе́ние и труд всё ~тру́т** (*coll.*) it's dogged does it. **2.** (**в**+*a.*) to grind (into).
пере|тере́ться, трётся, *past* **~тёрся, ~тёрлась** *pf.* (*of* **~тира́ться**) **1.** to wear out, wear through. **2.** *pass. of* **~тере́ть**
перетерп|е́ть, лю́, ∸ишь *pf.* (*coll.*) to suffer, endure.
перете́|чь, ку́, чёшь, ку́т, *past* **∸к, ~кла́** *pf.* (*of* **~ка́ть**) to overflow.
перетира́|ть(ся), ю(сь) *impf. of* **перетере́ть(ся)**
перето́лк|и, ов *no sg.* (*coll.*) tittle-tattle.
перетолк|ова́ть¹, у́ю *pf.* (*no impf.*) (*coll.*) to talk over, discuss; **на́до нам с тобо́й об э́том п.** we must talk it over.

перетолк|овáть[2], **ýю** *pf.* (*of* **~óвывать**) (*coll.*) to misinterpret.

перетолкóвыва|ть, ю *impf. of* **перетолковáть**[2]

перетоп|и́ть[1], **лю́, ~́ишь** *pf.* (*of* **перетáпливать**) to melt.

перетоп|и́ть[2], **лю́, ~́ишь** *pf.* (*coll.*) to heat; to kindle.

перетóржк|а, и *f.* re-auctioning.

перетревóж|ить, у, ишь *pf.* (*no impf.*) (*coll.*) to disturb, alarm.

перетревóж|иться, усь, ишься *pf.* (*no impf.*) (*coll.*) to be alarmed, become anxious.

пере|трý, трёшь, тёр, тёрла *see* **~терéть**

перетрý|сить, шу, сишь *pf.* (*no impf.*) (*coll.*) to have a fright; to take fright.

перетряс|áть, áю *impf. of* **~ти́**

перетряс|ти́, ý, ёшь, *past* **~́, ~лá** *pf.* (*of* **~áть**) to shake up.

перéть, пру, прёшь, *past* **пёр, пёрла** *impf.* (*coll.*) **1.** to go, make one's way; **п. сквозь толпý** to barge through the crowd. **2.** to push, press. **3.** to drag. **4.** to come out; to appear, show; **рéвность так и прёт из негó** his jealousy will out. **5.** (*pf.* **с~**) to steal, pinch.

перетя́гивани|е, я *nt.*: **п. канáта** (*sport*) tug-of-war.

перетя́гива|ть(ся), ю(сь) *impf. of* **перетянýть(ся)**

перетя|нýть[1], **нý, ~́нешь** *pf.* (*of* **~́гивать**) **1.** to pull, draw (*somewhere else*; *from A to B*); **п. лóдку к бéрегу** to pull the boat to the shore. **2.** (*fig., coll.*) to pull over, attract; **п. на свою́ стóрону** to win over, gain support of. **3.** to pull in too tight. **4.** to outbalance, outweigh.

перетя|нýть[2], **нý, ~́нешь** *pf.* (*of* **~́гивать**) to stretch again.

перетя|нýться, нýсь, ~́нешься *pf.* (*of* **~́гиваться**) to lace o.s. too tight.

переубе|ди́ть, ди́шь *pf.* (*of* **~ждáть**) to make change one's mind, over-persuade.

переубе|ди́ться, ди́шься *pf.* (*of* **~ждáться**) to change one's mind, be over-persuaded.

переубеждá|ть(ся), ю(сь) *impf. of* **переубеди́ть(ся)**

переýл|ок, ка *m.* lane, narrow street.

переупря́м|ить, лю, ишь *pf.* (*no impf.*) (*coll.*) to prove more stubborn than.

переусéрдств|овать, ую *pf.* (*no impf.*) (*coll.*) to be over-diligent, show excess of zeal.

переустрóйств|о, а *nt.* reconstruction.

переутом|и́ть, лю́, и́шь *pf.* (*of* **~ля́ть**) to overtire, overstrain; to overwork.

переутом|и́ться, лю́сь, и́шься *pf.* (*of* **~ля́ться**) to overtire o.s., overstrain o.s.; to overwork; (*pf. only*) to be run down.

переутомлéни|е, я *nt.* overstrain; overwork.

переутомля́|ть(ся), ю(сь) *impf. of* **переутоми́ть(ся)**

переуч|éсть, тý, тёшь, *past* **~ёл, ~лá** *pf.* (*of* **~и́тывать**) to take stock.

переучёт, а *m.* stock-taking.

переýчива|ть(ся), ю(сь) *impf. of* **переучи́ть(ся)**

переучи́тыва|ть, ю *impf. of* **переучéсть**

переуч|и́ть, ý, ~́ишь *pf.* (*of* **~́ивать**) to teach again.

переуч|и́ться, ýсь ~́ишься *pf.* (*of* **~́иваться**) **1.** to re-learn. **2.** (*coll.*) to study too much.

переформир|овáть, ýю *pf.* (*of* **~óвывать**) (*mil.*) to re-form.

переформирóвыва|ть, ю *impf. of* **переформировáть**

перефрази́р|овать, ую *impf. and pf.* to paraphrase.

перефразирóвк|а, и *f.* paraphrase.

перехвáлива|ть, ю *impf. of* **перехвали́ть**

перехвал|и́ть, ю́, ~́ишь *pf.* (*of* **~́ивать**) to over-praise.

перехвáт, а *m.* **1.** interception. **2.** intake, taking in (*of article of clothing*).

перехва|ти́ть, чý, ~́тишь *pf.* (*of* **~́тывать**) **1.** to intercept, catch; **я ~ти́л егó по дорóге на слýжбу** I caught him on the way to work. **2.** to take in; **п. верёвкой** to lash. **3.** (*coll.*) to take a snack; to catch up (*sth. to eat*). **4.** (*coll.*) to borrow (*for a short time*). **5.** (*coll.*) to overshoot the mark.

перехвáтчик, а *m.* (*aeron.*) interceptor.

перехвáтыва|ть, ю *impf. of* **перехвати́ть**

перехворá|ть, ю *pf.* (*no impf.*) (+*i.*) to have had; to have been down (with) (*sc.* an illness).

перехитр|и́ть, ю́, и́шь *pf.* to outwit, over-reach.

перехóд, а *m.* **1.** (*in var. senses*) passage, transition; crossing; switch(over); **подзéмный п.** underpass, subway. **2.** (*mil.*) (day's) march. **3.** (*relig.*) going over, conversion.

перехо|ди́ть[1], **жý, ~́дишь** *impf. of* **перейти́**

перехо|ди́ть[2], **жý, ~́дишь** *pf.* (*no impf.*) (*coll.*) to go all over.

перехо|ди́ть[3], **жý, ~́дишь** *pf.* (*no impf.*) (*coll.; at games*) to have one's turn again, make one's move again.

перехóдный *adj.* **1.** transitional. **2.** (*gram.*) transitive. **3.** (*tech.*) transient.

переход|я́щий *pres. part. of* **~и́ть** *and adj.* **1.** transient, transitory; **п. кýбок** (*sport*) challenge cup. **2.** intermittent. **3.** (*fin.*) brought forward, carried over.

перехóжий *adj. see* **кали́ка**

пéр|ец, ца *m.* pepper; **стручкóвый п.** capsicum; **задáть комý-н. ~цу** (*coll.*) to give it s.o. hot.

перецарáпа|ться, юсь *pf.* **1.** to scratch o.s. **2.** to scratch each other.

перецел|овáть, ýю *pf.* (*no impf.*) to kiss (*all or a number of*).

перецел|овáться, ýюсь *pf.* (*no impf.*) to kiss one another.

перецéнива|ть, ю *impf. of* **перецени́ть**

перецен|и́ть, ю́, ~́ишь *pf.* (*of* **~́ивать**) **1.** to price too high. **2.** = **переоцени́ть**

пéреч|ень, ня *m.* list; enumeration.

перечёркива|ть, ю *impf. of* **перечеркнýть**

перечерк|нýть, нý, нёшь *pf.* (*of* **~́ивать**) to cross (out), cancel.

перечер|ти́ть, чý, ~́тишь *pf.* (*of* **~́чивать**) **1.** to draw again. **2.** to copy, trace.

перечéрчива|ть, ю *impf. of* **перечерти́ть**

перече|сáться, ~́шешься *pf.* (*no impf.*) (*coll.*) **1.** to do one's hair again. **2.** to do one's hair differently.

пере|чéсть[1], **чтý, чтёшь,** *past* **~чёл, ~лá** *pf.* = **~считáть**[2]; **их мóжно по пáльцам п.** you could count them on the fingers of one hand.

пере|чéсть[2], **чтý, чтёшь,** *past* **~чёл, ~лá** *pf.* = **~читáть**

перечи́нива|ть, ю *impf. of* **перечини́ть**[1]

перечин|и́ть[1], **ю́, ~́ишь** *pf.* (*of* **~́ивать**) to mend again, repair again; **п. карандáш** to re-sharpen a pencil.

перечин|и́ть[2], **ю́, ~́ишь** *pf.* to mend, repair (*all or a number of*).

перечислéни|е, я *nt.* **1.** enumeration. **2.** (*fin.*) transferring.

перечи́сл|ить, ю, ишь *pf.* (*of* **~я́ть**) **1.** to enumerate. **2.** to transfer; **егó ~или в запáс** he has been transferred to the reserve; **п. на текýщий счёт** (*fin.*) to transfer to one's current account.

перечисл|я́ть, я́ю *impf. of* **~́ить**

перечит|áть[1], **áю** *pf.* (*of* **~́ывать**) to re-read.

перечит|áть[2], **áю** *pf.* to read (*all or a quantity of*); **он ~áл все кни́ги в библиотéке** he has read all the books in the library.

перéч|ить, у, ишь *impf.* (*no pf.*) (+*d.*; *coll.*) to contradict; to go against.

пéречниц|а, ы *f.* pepper-pot; **чёртова п.** (*vulg.*; *of cantankerous old woman*) old hag.

пéре|чный *adj. of* **~ц**

перечýвств|овать, ую *pf.* (*no impf.*) to feel, experience.

перешáгива|ть, ю *impf. of* **перешагнýть**

перешаг|нýть, нý, нёшь *pf.* (*of* **~́ивать**) to step over; **п. (чéрез) порóг** to cross the threshold.

перешé|ек, йка *m.* isthmus, neck (of land).

перешёптыва|ться, юсь *impf.* to whisper to one another.

перешиб|áть, áю *impf. of* **~и́ть**

перешиб|и́ть, ý, ёшь, *past* **~́, ~́ла** *pf.* (*of* **~áть**) (*coll.*) to break, fracture.

перешивá|ть, ю *impf. of* **переши́ть**

переши́вк|а, и *f.* altering, alteration (*of clothes*).

переш|и́ть, ью́, ьёшь *pf.* (*of* **~ивáть**) **1.** to alter; to have altered. **2.** (*tech.*) to alter (*gauge of rail., etc.*).

перештóп|ать[1], **аю** *pf.* (*of* **~ывать**) to darn over, darn again.

перештóп|ать[2], **аю** *pf.* (*no impf.*) to darn (*all or a number of*).

перештóпыва|ть, ю *impf. of* **перештóпать**

перещеголя́|ть, ю *pf.* (*no impf.*) (*coll.*) to beat, outdo, surpass.

переэкзамен|ова́ть, у́ю *pf.* (*of* **~о́вывать**) to re-examine.

переэкзамен|ова́ться, у́юсь *pf.* (*of* **~о́вываться**) to resit an examination.

переэкзамено́вк|а, и *f.* re-examination, resit.

переэкзамено́выва|ть(ся), ю(сь) *impf. of* **переэкзаменова́ть(ся)**

пе́ри *f. indecl.* (*myth.*) peri.

периге́|й, я *m.* (*astron.*) perigee.

периге́ли|й, я *m.* (*astron.*) perihelium.

перика́рд, а *m.* (*anat.*) pericardium.

перика́рд|ий *m.* = **~**

перикарди́т, а *m.* (*med.*) pericarditis.

пери́л|а, ~ *no sg.* rail(ing); handrail; banisters.

пери́метр, а *m.* (*math.*) perimeter.

пери́н|а, ы *f.* feather-bed.

пери́од, а *m.* (*in var. senses*) period; **леднико́вый п.** (*geol.*) glacial period, ice age.

периодиза́ци|я, и *f.* division into periods.

перио́дик|а, и *f.* (*collect.*) periodicals.

периоди́ческ|ий *adj.* periodic(al); recurring; **~ая дробь** recurring decimal; **п. журна́л** periodical, magazine; **~ая печа́ть** the periodical press; (*collect.*) periodicals; **~ое явле́ние** recurrent phenomenon.

периоди́чност|ь, и *f.* periodicity.

периоди́ч|ный (~ен, ~на) *adj.* periodic(al).

перипате́тик, а *m.* (*hist. phil.*) peripatetic.

перипат|ети́ческий *adj. of* **~е́тик**

перипети́|я, и *f.* (*liter.*) peripeteia; (*fig.*) reversal of fortune, upheaval.

периско́п, а *m.* periscope.

перископи́ческий *adj.* periscopic.

периста́льтик|а, и *f.* (*physiol.*) peristalsis.

перисти́л|ь, я *m.* (*archit.*) peristyle.

пе́ристо-кучево́й *adj.* (*meteor.*) cirro-cumulus.

пе́ристы|й *adj.* **1.** (*zool.*, *bot.*) pinnate. **2.** feather-like, plumose; **~е облака́** fleecy clouds; cirri.

перитони́т, а *m.* (*med.*) peritonitis.

перифери́йный *adj.* provincial.

периферийческий *adj.* peripheral.

перифери́|я, и *f.* **1.** periphery. **2.** (*collect.*) the provinces; the outlying districts. **3.** (*comput.*) peripherals, peripheral devices.

перифра́з|а, ы *f.* periphrasis.

перифрази́р|овать, ую *impf. and pf.* to use a periphrasis (for).

перифрасти́ческий *adj.* periphrastic.

пёрк|а, и *f.* (*tech.*) bit, flat bit, cutter, drill point; (flat) drill; **ло́жечная п.** shell auger.

перка́л|ь, и *f.* (*and* **~я,** *m.*) (*text.*) percale.

перколя́тор, а *m.* (coffee) percolator.

перку́сси|я, и *f.* (*med.*) percussion.

перкути́р|овать, ую *impf. and pf.* (*med.*) to percuss.

перл, а *m.* (*obs. in literal sense*; *fig.*, *rhet. and typ.*) pearl.

перламу́тр, а *m.* mother-of-pearl, nacre.

перламу́тр|овый *adj. of* **~**; **~овая пу́говица** pearl button.

пе́рлин|ь, я *m.* (*naut.*) hawser.

перло́в|ый *adj.*: **~ая крупа́** pearl barley.

перлюстра́ци|я, и *f.* censorship (*opening and inspection of correspondence*).

перлюстри́р|овать, ую *impf. and pf.* to censor (*correspondence*).

перманéнт, а *m.* permanent wave.

перманéнтный *adj.* permanent.

пе́рм|ский *adj.* Permian (*branch of Finno-Ugric ethnic and linguistic group*); **~ская систе́ма** (*geol.*) Permian formation (*from Perm, a town in the Urals*).

перна́т|ый (~, ~а) *adj.* feathered, feathery; **~ое ца́рство** 'feathered world' (*birds*).

пёр|нуть, нет (*inst. pf. of* **~де́ть**) (*vulg.*) to (give a) fart.

пер|о́, а́, *pl.* **~ья, ~ьев** *nt.* **1.** feather; **ни пу́ха, ни ~а́!** good luck! **2.** pen; **ве́чное п.** fountain-pen; **взя́ться за п.** (*fig.*) to take up the pen; **владе́ть ~о́м** to wield a skilful pen; **про́ба ~а́** (*fig.*) first attempt at writing. **3.** leaf (*of onion or garlic*). **4.** fin. **5.** blade (*of an oar*); paddle (*of wheel*).

перочи́нный *adj.*: **п. нож** pen-knife.

перпендикуля́р, а *m.* (*math.*) perpendicular; **опусти́ть п.** to drop a perpendicular.

перпендикуля́р|ный (~ен, ~на) *adj.* perpendicular.

перро́н, а *m.* platform (*at rail. station*).

перро́н|ный *adj. of* **~**; **п. биле́т** platform ticket.

перс, а *m.* Persian.

пе́рс|и, ей *no sg.* (*arch. or poet.*) breast, bosom.

перси́дский *adj.* Persian; **п. порошо́к** insect-powder.

Перси́дск|ий зали́в, ~ого ~а *m.* the Persian Gulf.

пе́рсик, а *m.* **1.** peach. **2.** peach-tree.

пе́рсик|овый *adj. of* **~**; peachy; **~овое де́рево** peach-tree.

Пе́рси|я, и *f.* Persia.

перси|я́нин, я́нина, *pl.* **~я́не, ~я́н** *m.* (*obs.*) = **перс**

перс|ия́нка, ия́нки *f. of* **~**

персо́н|а, ы *f.* person; **ва́жная п.** (*coll.*) big wig; **со́бственная п.** one's own self; **яви́ться со́бственной ~ой** (*obs. or iron.*) to appear in person; **п. гра́та** persona grata; **обе́д на́ шесть ~** dinner for six.

персона́ж, а *m.* (*liter.*) character; (*fig.*) personage.

персона́л, а *m.* personnel, staff.

персона́льный *adj.* personal; individual; **п. пенсионе́р** pers. in receipt of special pension.

персонифика́ци|я, и *f.* personification.

персонифици́р|овать, ую *impf. and pf.* to personify.

перспекти́в|а, ы *f.* **1.** (*art*) perspective. **2.** vista, prospect. **3.** (*fig.*) prospect, outlook; **что в ~е?** what is in prospect?, what are the prospects?; **име́ть ~у** to have prospects, have a future (before one).

перспекти́в|ный *adj.* **1.** (*art*) perspective. **2.** forward-looking; envisaging future development; **~ное плани́рование** (*econ.*) long-term planning. **3.** **(~ен, ~на)** having prospects; promising; **~ная молода́я балери́на** a promising young ballerina.

перст, а́ *m.* (*obs.*) finger; **оди́н, как п.** all alone.

пе́рст|ень, ня *m.* (finger-)ring; **(с печа́тью)** signet-ring.

перстневи́дный *adj.*: **п. хрящ** (*anat.*) cricoid.

перст|ь, и *f.* (*arch. or rhet.*) dust, earth.

Перу́ *f. indecl.* Peru.

перуа́н|ец, ца *m.* Peruvian.

перуа́н|ка, ки *f. of* **~ец**

перуа́нский *adj.* Peruvian; **п. бальза́м** Peru balsam.

перу́н|ы, ов *no sg.* (*obs.*, *poet.*) thunderbolts; (*fig.*) fulminations; **мета́ть п.** to fulminate.

перфе́кт, а *m.* (*gram.*) perfect (tense).

перфока́рт|а, ы *f.* punched card (*in computer programming, etc.*).

перфоле́нт|а, ы *f.* punched tape.

перфора́тор, а *m.* (*tech.*) **1.** perforator; punch. **2.** drill, boring machine.

перфора́ци|я, и *f.* (*tech.*) **1.** perforation, punching. **2.** drilling, boring.

перфори́р|овать, ую *impf. and pf.* (*tech.*) **1.** to perforate, punch. **2.** to drill, bore.

перха́|ть, ю *impf.* (*no pf.*) (*coll.*) to cough (*in trying to remove an irritation of the throat*).

перхлора́т, а *m.* (*chem.*) perchlorate.

перхо́т|а, ы *f.* (*coll.*) tickling in the throat.

пе́рхот|ь, и *f.* dandruff, scurf.

перце́пци|я, и *f.* (*phil.*) perception.

перцо́вк|а, и *f.* pepper-brandy.

перцо́вый *adj. of* **пе́рец**

перча́тк|а, и *f.* glove; gauntlet; **бро́сить ~у** (*fig.*) to throw down the gauntlet.

перчи́нк|а, и *f.* peppercorn.

пе́рч|ить, у, ишь *impf.* (*of* **на~** *and* **по~**) (*coll.*) to pepper.

першеро́н, а *m.* percheron (*breed of horse*).

перш|и́ть, и́т *impf.* (*coll.*; *impers.*): **у меня́ в го́рле ~и́т** I have a tickle in my throat.

пёрыш|ко, ка, *pl.* **~ки, ~ек, ~кам** *nt.* (*coll.*) *dim. of* **перо́; лёгкий, как п.** light as a feather.

пёс, пса *m.* (*coll.*) dog; (*astron.*): **созве́здие Большо́го Пса** Canis Major; **созве́здие Ма́лого Пса** Canis Minor;

(*coll.*): **п. знает** the devil only knows.
пе́сельник, а *m.* (*coll.*) singer.
пе́сенк|а, и *f.* song; **его́ п. спе́та** (*coll.*) he is done for; he has had it.
пе́сенник, а *m.* **1.** song-book. **2.** (chorus) singer. **3.** song-writer.
пе́с|енный *adj. of* **~ня**
песе́т|а, ы *f.* peseta.
пес|е́ц, ца́ *m.* polar fox; **бе́лый, голубо́й п.** white, blue fox (fur).
пёс|ий *and* **пе́сий** *adj. of* **~; пе́сья звезда́** (*astron.*) Sirius, the Dog Star.
пёсик, а *m.* (*coll.*) *dim. of* **пёс**; doggie.
песка́р|ь, я́ *m.* gudgeon (*fish*).
пескостру́йный *adj.* (*tech.*) sand-blast.
песнопе́в|ец, ца *m.* **1.** (*obs. rhet.*) singer; psalmist. **2.** (*poet.*) poet, bard.
песнопе́ни|е, я *nt.* **1.** (*eccl.*) psalm; canticle. **2.** (*poet.*) poetry, poesy.
песн|ь, и, *g. pl.* **~ей** *f.* **1.** (*obs.*) song; **П. ~ей** the Song of Songs, Song of Solomon. **2.** (*liter.*) canto, book.
пе́с|ня, ни, *g. pl.* **~ен** *f.* song; air; **до́лгая п.** (*fig., coll.*) a long story; **э́та п. стара́** (*coll.*) it's the same old story; **тяну́ть всё ту же ~ню** (*coll.*) to harp on one string; **п. спе́та = пе́сенка спе́та**
пес|о́к, ка́ *m.* **1.** sand; **золото́й п.** gold dust; **са́харный п.** granulated sugar; **стро́ить на ~ке́** (*fig.*) to build on sand; **как п. морско́й, как ~ку́ морско́го** (numerous) as the sands of the sea. **2.** (*pl.*) sands; **зыбу́чие ~ки́** quicksands. **3.** (*med.*) gravel.
песо́чник, а *m.* (*zool.*) sand-piper.
песо́чниц|а, ы *f.* **1.** sand-box; sand-pit. **2.** sanding apparatus. **3.** sugar bowl.
песо́чн|ый *adj.* **1.** *adj. of* **песо́к**; sandy; **~ые часы́** sand-glass, hour-glass. **2.** (*cul.*) short; **~ое пече́нье** shortbread, shortcake.
пессими́зм, а *m.* pessimism.
пессими́ст, а *m.* pessimist.
пессимисти́ческий *adj.* pessimistic.
пессимисти́ч|ный (~ен, ~на) *adj.* = **~еский**
пест, а́ *m.* pestle; **п., знай свою́ сту́пу** (*prov.*) cobbler, stick to your last; **как п. в ло́жках** a square peg in a round hole.
пе́стик[1], **а** *m.* (*bot.*) pistil.
пе́стик[2], **а** *m. dim. of* **пест**
пе́ст|овать, ую *impf.* (*of* **вы́~**) **1.** (*obs.*) to nurse. **2.** (*fig.*) to cherish, foster.
пестр|е́ть[1], **е́ет** *impf.* (*no pf.*) **1.** to become many-coloured. **2.** (*+i.*) to be gay (with); **корабли́ ~е́ли фла́гами** the ships were gay with bunting. **3.** to show colourfully, make a brave show (*of objects of different colours*).
пестр|е́ть[2], **и́т** *impf.* (*no pf.*) **1.** (*of many-coloured objects*) to strike the eye (*also fig.*); **его́ и́мя ~и́т в газе́тах** (*coll.*) he is always getting his name in the papers. **2.** (*coll.*) to be too gaudy, be flashy. **3.** (*+i.*) to abound (in), be rich (in); **письмо́ ~и́т оши́бками** the letter bristles with mistakes.
пестр|и́ть, ю́, и́шь *impf.* (*no pf.*) **1.** to make gaudy; to make colourful. **2.** (*impers.*): **у меня́ ~и́ло в глаза́х** I was dazzled (*sc.* by the colours).
пестрот|а́, ы́ *no pl., f.* diversity of colours; (*fig.*) mixed character.
песту́шк|а, и *f.* **1.** speckled trout. **2.** (*zool.*) lemming.
пёстр|ый (~, ~а́, ~о *and* **~о́)** *adj.* **1.** motley, variegated, many-coloured, parti-coloured. **2.** (*fig., coll.*) mixed; **п. соста́в населе́ния** mixed population. **3.** (*fig.*) florid; pretentious, mannered; **п. слог** florid style.
пестрядёвый *adj. of* **пе́стрядь**
пе́стряд|ь, и *f.* a coarse, coloured, cotton fabric.
пестў́н, а́ *m.* (*obs.*) mentor.
пес|цо́вый *adj. of* **~е́ц**
песча́ник, а *m.* (*geol.*) sandstone.
песча́нк|а, и *f.* (*zool.*) sanderling.
песча́н|ый *adj.* sandy; **~ая коса́** sandbar; **п. холм** dune.
песчи́нк|а, и *f.* grain of sand.
пета́рд|а, ы *f.* **1.** (*hist. mil.*) petard. **2.** detonating cartridge (*as alarm signal on rail.*). **3.** fire-cracker.
петербу́ргский = санкт-петербу́ргский
петербуржа́нка = санкт-петербуржа́нка
петербу́ржец = санкт-петербу́ржец
пети́т, а *m.* (*typ.*) brevier.
петифу́р, а *m.* (*cul.*) petit four.
пети́ци|я, и *f.* petition.
петли́ц|а, ы *f.* **1.** buttonhole. **2.** tab (*on uniform collar*).
пе́т|ля, ли, *g. pl.* **~ель** *f.* **1.** loop; **мёртвая п.** (*aeron.*) loop; **сде́лать мёртвую ~лю** to loop the loop. **2.** (*fig.*) noose; **он досто́ин ~ли** he deserves to hang; **лезть в ~лю** to put one's neck into the noose, take risks needlessly; **наде́ть ~лю на ше́ю** to hang a millstone about one's neck. **3.** buttonhole; **мета́ть ~ли** to work buttonholes, buttonhole; (*fig., joc.*) (*i*) to conceal one's tracks, (*ii*) to confuse the issue. **4.** stitch; **спусти́ть ~лю** to drop a stitch; to ladder one's stocking. **5.** hinge; **дверь соскочи́ла с ~ель** the door has come off its hinges.
петля́|ть, ю *impf.* (*coll.*) to dodge.
петрифика́ци|я, и *f.* petrification; fossilization.
петро́граф, а *m.* petrographer.
петрогра́фи|я, и *f.* petrography.
петроле́йный *adj.* (*chem.*) petroleum.
петру́шк|а[1], **и** *f.* parsley.
петру́шк|а[2], **и** *m. and f.* **1.** *m.* Punch. **2.** *m.* Punch-and-Judy show. **3.** *f.* (*fig., coll.*) foolishness, absurdity; **кака́я-то п. получи́лась** an absurd thing happened; **брось валя́ть ~у!** stop being a fool!
пету́н|ия, ии *f.* (*bot.*) petunia.
пету́н|ья, ьи, *g. pl.* **~ий** *f.* = **~ия**
пету́х, а́ *m.* **1.** cock; **инде́йский п.** turkey-cock; **фаза́н-п.** cock-pheasant; **до ~о́в** before cock-crow; **встать с ~а́ми** to rise with the lark; **пусти́ть ~а́** (*mus. sl.*) to let out a squeak (*on a high note*); **пусти́ть кра́сного ~а́** to set fire, commit act of arson. **2.** *fig., of an irascible pers.*
пету́х|а, и *m.* (*coll., pej.*) queer, poof(ter).
пету́|ший *adj. of* **~х; п. гре́бень** cockscomb.
петуши́ный *adj. of* **пету́х; п. бой** cockfight(-ing); **п. го́лос** (*fig.*) squeaky voice.
петуш|и́ться, у́сь, и́шься *impf.* (*of* **вс~**) (*coll.*) to ride the high horse; to take umbrage.
петуш|о́к, ка́ *m.* **1.** cockerel; **идти́ ~ко́м** (*coll., joc.*) to strut. **2.** (*elec.*) commutator lug, commutator riser.
пе́т|ый *p.p.p. of* **~ь**; (*coll.*): **п. дура́к** perfect fool.
петь, пою́, поёшь *impf.* (*of* **про~** *and* **с~**) to sing (*also of birds and, fig., of inanimate objects*); to chant, intone; **п. ба́сом** to have a bass voice; **п. ве́рно, фальши́во** to sing in tune, out of tune; **п. вполго́лоса** to hum; **п. другу́ю пе́сню** to sing another tune; **п. Ла́заря** (*coll., pej.*) to bemoan one's fate, grumble, complain; **п. сла́ву** (*+d.*) to sing the praises (of).
пехо́т|а, ы *f.* infantry, foot; **морска́я п.** (the) marines.
пехоти́н|ец, ца *m.* infantryman.
пехо́тный *adj.* infantry.
печа́л|ить, ю, ишь *impf.* (*of* **о~**) to grieve, sadden.
печа́л|иться, юсь, ишься *impf.* (*of* **о~**) to grieve, be sad.
печа́л|ь, и *f.* grief, sorrow; **кака́я п.!** how sad!; **не твоя́ п.** it's no concern of yours; **тебе́ что за п.?** what has that to do with you?
печа́льник, а *m.* (*obs., now iron.*) one who feels for others, sympathizer.
печа́л|ьный (~ен, ~ьна) *adj.* **1.** sad, mournful, doleful; wistful. **2.** grievous; **п. коне́ц** dismal end, bad end; **~ьные результа́ты** unfortunate results; **оста́вить по себе́ ~ьную па́мять** to leave a bad reputation.
печа́тани|е, я *nt.* printing.
печа́та|ть, ю *impf.* (*of* **на~**) to print; to type.
печа́та|ться, юсь *impf.* (*of* **на~**) **1.** to write (*for a journal, etc.*); to have (literary compositions, etc.) published; **тридцати́ лет он ещё нигде́ не ~лся** at thirty he had not yet had anything published. **2.** to be at the printer's, be in the press.
печа́тк|а, и *f.* signet.
печа́тник, а *m.* printer.

печа́тн|ый *adj.* **1.** printing; **~ое де́ло** printing; **п. лист** quire, printer's sheet; **п. стано́к** printing-press. **2.** printed; in the press; **~ая кни́га** printed book (*opp. manuscript*); **п. о́тзыв о но́вом рома́не** press comment on a new novel. **3.: писа́ть по ~ому, ~ыми бу́квами** to (write in) print; to write in block capitals.

печа́т|ь[1], **и** *f.* seal, stamp (*also fig.*); **госуда́рственная п.** State Seal, Great Seal; **наложи́ть п. (на+**a.**)** to affix a seal (to); **носи́ть п.** (+*g.*) to have the seal (of), bear the stamp (of); **п. го́ря** the stamp of grief; **на мои́х уста́х п. молча́ния** my lips are sealed.

печа́ть[2], **и** *f.* **1.** print(ing); **быть в ~и** to be in print, be at the printer's; **вы́йти из ~и** to appear, come out, be published; **подписа́ть к ~и** to send to press; **«подпи́сано к ~и»** 'passed for printing'. **2.** print, type; **ме́лкая п.** small print; **кру́пная п.** large print; **убо́ристая п.** close print. **3.** (the) press; **свобо́да ~и** freedom of the press; **име́ть благоприя́тные о́тзывы в ~и** to have a good press.

пече́ни|е, я *nt.* baking.

печёнк|а, и *f.* **1.** liver (*of animal, as food*). **2.** (*coll.*) liver; **сиде́ть (у кого́-н.) в ~ах** to plague (s.o.).

печёночник, а *m.* (*bot.*) liverwort.

печён|очный *adj. of* **~ка** *and* **пе́чень**; hepatic.

печёный *adj.* (*cul.*) baked.

пе́чен|ь, и *f.* liver; **воспале́ние ~и** (*med.*) hepatitis, inflammation of the liver.

пече́нь|е, я *nt.* pastry; biscuit; **минда́льное п.** macaroon.

пе́чк|а, и *f.* stove; **танцева́ть от ~и** (*coll., iron.*) to begin again from the beginning.

печни́к, а́ *m.* stove-setter; stove-repairer.

печ|но́й *adj. of* **~ь**[2]; **п. агрега́т** furnace unit; **п. газ** furnace gas; **п. ка́мень** ovenstone; **~но́е отопле́ние** stove heating; **~на́я труба́** chimney, flue.

печь[1], **пеку́, печёшь, пеку́т,** *past* **пёк, пекла́** *impf.* (*of* **ис~́**) to bake; **со́лнце пекло́** there was a scorching sun.

печь[2], **и, о ~́и, в ~и́,** *pl.* **~́и, ~е́й** *f.* **1.** stove; oven; **сверхвысокочасто́тная п.** microwave oven. **2.** (*tech.*) furnace, kiln, oven; **до́менная п.** blast-furnace; **кремацио́нная п.** incinerator.

пе́чься[1], **печётся, пеку́тся,** *past* **пёкся, пекла́сь** *impf.* (*of* **ис~́**) to bake; to broil (*in the sun*).

пе́чься[2], **пеку́сь, печёшься, пеку́тся,** *past* **пёкся, пекла́сь** *impf.* (*no pf.*) (**о**+*p.*) to take care (of), care (for), look after.

пешедра́лом *adv.* (*coll.*) = **пешко́м**

пешехо́д, а *m.* pedestrian.

пешехо́дн|ый *adj.* pedestrian; **п. мост** foot-bridge; **~ая тропа́** footpath.

пе́ш|ечный *adj. of* **~ка**

пе́ш|ий *adj.* **1.** pedestrian; **по о́бразу ~его хожде́ния** on Shanks' mare. **2.** (*mil.*) unmounted, foot.

пе́шк|а, и *f.* (*in chess, also fig.*) pawn.

пешко́м *adv.* on foot.

пеще́р|а, ы *f.* cave, cavern; grotto.

пеще́рист|ый (~, ~а) *adj.* **1.** with many caves. **2.** (*anat.*) cavernous.

пеще́р|ный *adj. of* **~а**; **п. челове́к** (*archaeol.*) cave-dweller, cave-man, troglodyte.

ПЗУ *nt. indecl.* (*abbr. of* ***постоя́нное запомина́ющее устро́йство***) (*comput.*) ROM (*read-only memory*).

пи *nt. indecl.* (*math.*) pi (π).

пиани́но *nt. indecl.* (upright) piano.

пиани́ссимо *adv.* (*mus.*) pianissimo.

пиани́ст, а *m.* pianist.

пиа́но *adv.* (*mus.*) piano.

пиано́л|а, ы *f.* (*mus.*) pianola.

пиа́стр, а *m.* piastre.

пива́|ть, ю *impf.* (*coll.*) *freq. of* **пить**

пивн|а́я, о́й *f.* alehouse; pub.

пив|но́й *adj. of* **~́о**; **~ны́е дро́жжи** brewer's yeast; **~на́я кру́жка** beer mug.

пи́в|о, а *nt.* beer; **све́тлое п.** pale ale; **тёмное п.** brown ale; **~а не сва́ришь с ним** (*fig., coll.*) he's an awkward customer.

пивова́р, а *m.* brewer.

пивоваре́ни|е, я *nt.* brewing.

пивова́ренн|ый *adj.*: **п. заво́д** brewery; **~ая промы́шленность** brewing.

пи́галиц|а, ы *f.* (*zool.*) lapwing, peewit; (*fig., coll.*) puny pers.

пигме́|й, я *m.* pygmy (*also fig.*).

пигме́нт, а *m.* pigment.

пигмента́ци|я, и *f.* pigmentation.

пигме́нтный *adj.* pigmental, pigmentary.

пиджа́к, а́ *m.* jacket, coat.

пиджа́|чный *adj. of* **~к**; **п. костю́м, ~чная па́ра** (lounge-)suit.

пи́дор, а *m.* (*coll.*) homo, poof.

пидора́с, а *m.* (*coll., pej.*) queer, poofter.

пиете́т, а *m.* respect, reverence.

пижа́м|а, ы *f.* pyjamas.

пижо́н, а *m.* (*coll.*) fop; (*sl., pej.*) twit.

пизд|а́, ы́ *f.* (*vulg.*) cunt.

пии́т, а *m.* (*arch.*) poet.

пик[1], **а** *m.* (*geog.*) peak; spire; pinnacle.

пик[2], **а 1.** *m.* peak (*of work, traffic, etc.*); **п. нагру́зки** (*elec.*) peak load. **2.** *adj. indecl.* **часы́ пик** rush-hour.

пи́к|а[1], **и** *f.* pike, lance.

пи́к|а[2], **и** *f.* (*cards*) spade; **да́ма ~** the queen of spades; **пойти́ ~ой** to play a spade.

пи́к|а[3], **и** *f. only in phr.* **сде́лать что-н. в ~у кому́-н.** to do a thing to spite s.o.

пика́нтност|ь, и *f.* piquancy, savour, zest.

пика́нт|ный (~ен, ~на) *adj.* piquant (*also fig.*), savoury; (*fig.*) juicy; spicy; **п. анекдо́т** risqué story.

пика́п, а *m.* pick-up (van).

пике́[1] *nt. indecl.* (*text.*) piqué.

пике́[2] *nt. indecl.* (*aeron.*) dive; **перейти́ в п.** to go into a dive.

пике́|йный *adj. of* **~**[1]

пике́т[1], **а** *m.* picket (picquet, piquet).

пике́т[2], **а** *m.* (*card-game*) piquet.

пикети́р|овать, ую *impf.* to picket.

пике́тчик, а *m.* picket.

пики́ровани|е, я *nt.* (*aeron.*) dive, diving.

пики́рованный *adj.* (*obs.*) piqued, in pique.

пики́р|овать, ую *impf. and pf.* (*pf. also* **с~**) (*aeron.*) to dive, swoop.

пикир|ова́ть, у́ю *impf. and pf.* (*agric.*) to thin out.

пики́р|оваться, уюсь *impf.* (*no pf.*) (**с**+*i.*) to exchange caustic remarks, cross swords.

пикиро́вк|а[1], **и** *f.* (*agric.*) thinning.

пикиро́вк|а[2], **и** *f.* (*coll.*) altercation, slanging-match.

пикиро́вщик, а *m.* dive-bomber.

пики́р|ующий *pres. part of* **~овать** *and adj.*; **п. бомбардиро́вщик** dive-bomber.

пи́кколо *nt. indecl.* piccolo.

пикни́к, а́ *m.* picnic.

пи́кн|уть, у, ешь *pf.* (*coll.*) to let out a squeak; (*fig.*) to make a sound (of protest); **попро́буй то́лько п.** (*with implied threat*) one sound out of you!; **п. не сметь** not to dare utter a word; **он п. не успе́л** before he could say knife.

пи́к|овый *adj.* **1.** *adj. of* **~а**[2]; **~овая да́ма** queen of spades; **~овая масть** spades. **2.** (*fig., coll.*) awkward; unfavourable; **попа́сть в ~овое положе́ние** to get into a pretty mess; **оста́ться при ~овом интере́се** to get nothing for one's pains.

пикра́т, а *m.* (*chem.*) picrate.

пикри́новый *adj.* (*chem.*) picric.

пиксафо́н, а *m.* liquid tar soap.

пикт, а *m.* (*hist.*) Pict.

пиктографи́ческий *adj.* pictographic.

пиктогра́фи|я, и *f.* pictography.

пи́кул|и, ей *no sg.* pickles.

пи́кш|а, и *f.* haddock.

пил|а́, ы́, *pl.* **~́ы, ~** *f.* **1.** saw; **ажу́рная п.** jig-saw; **ле́нточная п.** band-saw; **лучко́вая п.** sash saw, bow saw; **механи́ческая п.** frame-saw; **попере́чная п.** cross-cut saw; **столя́рная п.** buck-saw. **2.** (*fig.*) nagger.

пила́в, а *m.* (*cul.*) pilaff, pilau, pilaw.

пила́-ры́ба, пилы́-ры́бы *f.* saw-fish.
пилёный *adj.* sawn; **п. лес** timber; **п. са́хар** lump sugar.
пилигри́м, а *m.* pilgrim.
пили́ка|ть, ю *impf.* (*coll.*) to scrape, strum (*on a fiddle, etc.*).
пил|и́ть, ю́, ~́ишь *impf.* **1.** to saw. **2.** (*fig., coll.*) to nag (at).
пи́лк|а, и *f.* **1.** sawing. **2.** fret-saw. **3.** nail-file.
пи́ллерс, а *m.* (*naut.*) deck stanchion.
пиломатериа́л|ы, ов *no sg.* saw-timber.
пило́н, а *m.* (*archit.*) pylon.
пилообра́зный *adj.* serrated, notched.
пилора́м|а, ы *f.* power-saw bench.
пило́т, а *m.* pilot; **п.-сме́ртник** suicide pilot; **налёт ~ов-сме́ртников** kamikaze attack.
пилота́ж, а *m.* pilotage; **вы́сший п.** aerobatics.
пилоти́р|овать, ую *impf.* to pilot; to man.
пило́тк|а, и *f.* (*mil.*) forage cap.
пиль *int.* (*command to hounds*) take!
пи́льщик, а *m.* sawyer, wood-cutter.
пилю́л|я, и *f.* pill (*also fig.*); **проглоти́ть ~ю** (*fig.*) to swallow the pill; **позолоти́ть ~ю** to gild the pill.
пиля́стр|а, ы *f.* (*archit.*) pilaster.
пим|ы́, о́в *pl.* (*sg.* **~, ~а́** *m.*) pimy (**1.** *deer-skin boots worn in northern regions of former USSR.* **2.** *dial. name for valenki*).
пинакоте́к|а, и *f.* picture gallery.
пина́|ть, ю *impf. of* **пнуть**
пингви́н, а *m.* penguin.
пинг-по́нг *m.* ping-pong.
пине́тк|а, и *f.* (*baby's*) bootee.
пи́ни|я, и *f.* Italian pine.
пин|о́к, ка́ *m.* (*coll.*) kick.
пи́нт|а, ы *f.* pint.
пинце́т, а *m.* pincers, tweezers.
пи́нчер, а *m.* (*breed of dog*) pinscher.
пио́н, а *m.* (*bot.*) peony.
пионе́р, а *m.* (*in var. senses*) pioneer; **(ю́ный) пионе́р** (Young) Pioneer (*in former USSR, member of Communist children's organization*).
пионервожа́т|ый, ого *m.* (*and* **~ая, ~ой** *f.*) Pioneer leader.
пионе́ри|я, и *f.* (*collect.; coll.*) Pioneers.
пионе́р|ский *adj. of* **~**
пиоре́|я, и *f.* (*med.*) pyorrhoea.
пипе́тк|а, и *f.* pipette; medicine dropper; reservoir (*of fountain-pen*).
пи-пи́ (*baby talk*): **сде́лать п.** to do a wee(-wee).
пир, а, о ~́е, в ~у́, *pl.* **~ы́** *m.* feast, banquet; **п. горо́й, п. на весь мир** sumptuous feast; **в чужо́м ~у́ похме́лье,** *see* **похме́лье**
пирами́д|а, ы *f.* pyramid.
пирамида́льный *adj.* pyramidal; **п. то́поль** Lombardy poplar.
пирамидо́н, а *m.* (*pharm.*) pyramidon, amidopyrine; headache tablets.
пира́нь|я, и *f.* (*zool.*) piranha.
пира́т, а *m.* pirate; **возду́шный п.** air pirate, skyjacker.
пира́тский *adj.* piratic(al).
пира́тств|о, а *nt.* piracy.
Пирене́|и, -ев *no sg.* the Pyrenees.
пирене́йский *adj.* Pyrenean.
пири́т, а *m.* (*min.*) pyrites.
пир|ова́ть, у́ю *impf.* to feast, banquet; to celebrate with feasting.
пирови́нн|ый *adj.*: **~ая кислота́** (*chem.*) pyrotartaric acid.
пиро́г, а́ *m.* pie; tart; **п. с мя́сом** meat pie; **возду́шный п.** soufflé; **сва́дебный п.** wedding cake; **ешь п. с гриба́ми, держи́ язы́к за зуба́ми** (*prov.*) keep your breath to cool your porridge.
пиро́г|а, и *f.* pirogue.
пирогравю́р|а, ы *f.* pyrogravure, poker-work.
пиро́жник, а *m.* pastry-cook.
пиро́жн|ое, ого *nt.* **1.** (*collect.*) pastries; (fancy) cake, pastry. **2.** (*obs.*) sweet.
пирож|о́к, ка́ *m.* pasty, patty, pie.
пироксили́н, а *m.* pyroxylin, gun-cotton.
пироксили́н|овый *adj. of* **~; ~овая ша́шка** slab of gun-cotton.
пиро́метр, а *m.* (*phys., tech.*) pyrometer.
пиросе́рн|ый *adj.*: **~ая кислота́** (*chem.*) pyrosulphuric acid.
пироте́хник|а, и *f.* pyrotechnics.
пиротехни́ческий *adj.* pyrotechnic.
пирри́хи|й, я *m.* (*liter.*) pyrrhic (foot).
пи́рров *adj.*: **~а побе́да** Pyrrhic victory.
пиру́шк|а, и *f.* (*coll.*) carousal; binge.
пируэ́т, а *m.* pirouette.
пи́ршеств|о, а *nt.* feast, banquet.
пи́ршеств|овать, ую *impf.* to feast, banquet.
писа́к|а, и *m.* (*coll.*) scribbler, quill-driver.
писа́ни|е, я *nt.* **1.** writing. **2.** writing, screed; **(свяще́нное) п.** Holy Scripture, Holy Writ.
пи́сан|ый *adj.* written, manuscript; **~ая краса́вица** a picture (of beauty); **говори́ть как по-~ому** to speak as from the book; **носи́ться с чем-н. как (дура́к) с ~ой то́рбой** to fuss over sth. like a child with a new toy.
писарско́й *adj. of* **пи́сарь**
пи́сар|ь, я, *pl.* **~я́** *m.* (*obs.*) clerk.
писа́тел|ь, я *m.* writer, author.
писа́тель|ский *adj. of* **~; п. труд** writing, literary work.
пи́са|ть, ю *impf.* (*vulg.*) to piss.
пи|са́ть, шу́, ~́шешь *impf.* (*of* **на~**) **1.** to write; **п. на маши́нке** to type; **п. про́зой, стиха́ми** to write prose, verse; **п. дневни́к** to keep a diary; **п. под дикто́вку** to take dictation; **не про нас ~́сано** (*coll.*) (*i*) it is Greek to us, (*ii*) it is not (intended, meant) for us; **дурака́м зако́н не ~́сан** (*coll.*) fools rush in where angels fear to tread; **~ши́ пропа́ло** it is as good as lost. **2.** (*+i.*) to paint (in); **п. портре́ты ма́слом** to paint portraits in oils.
пи|са́ться, шу́сь, ~́шешься *impf.* **1.** to spell, be spelled; **как ~́шется э́то сло́во?** how do you spell this word? **2.** (*impers.; +d.*) to feel an inclination for writing; **мне сего́дня не ~́шется** I don't feel like writing today. **3.** (*+i.; obs.*) to style o.s.; to sign o.s.; **он ~́шется торго́вцем** he styles himself a merchant. **4.** *pass. of* **~са́ть**
пис|е́ц, ца́ *m.* **1.** (*obs.*) clerk. **2.** (*hist.*) scribe.
писк, а *m.* peep; chirp; squeak; (*of chicks*) cheep.
пискли́в|ый (~, ~а) *adj.* squeaky.
пискля́в|ый (~, ~а) *adj.* (*coll.*) = **пискли́вый**
пи́скн|уть, у, ешь *inst. pf.* (*of* **пища́ть**) (*coll.*) to give a squeak; **то́лько ~и у меня́!** (*with implied threat*) one squeak out of you!
пископн|я́, и́ *f.* (*coll.*) squeaking; chirruping.
писку́н, а́ *m.* (*coll.*) **1.** squeaker. **2.** whiner.
писсуа́р, а *m.* urinal.
пистоле́т, а *m.* pistol; **п.-пулемёт** sub-machine-gun.
писто́н, а *m.* **1.** (percussion) cap. **2.** (*mus.*) piston.
писто́н|ный *adj. of* **~; ~ное ружьё** percussion musket.
писцо́вы|й *adj. of* **писе́ц; ~е кни́ги** (*hist.*) cadastres.
писчебума́жны|й *adj.*: **п. магази́н** stationer's (shop); **~е принадле́жности** stationery.
пи́сч|ий *adj.*: **~ая бума́га** writing paper; **п. материа́л** writing materials.
письмена́, письмён, ~м *no sg.* characters, letters; **дре́вние еги́петские п.** ancient Egyptian characters.
пи́сьменно *adv.* in writing, in written form; **изложи́ть п.** to set down in writing, put down on paper.
пи́сьменност|ь, и *f.* **1.** literature; (*collect.*) literary texts. **2.** the written language.
пи́сьменн|ый *adj.* **1.** writing; **п. прибо́р** desk set; **п. стол** writing-table, bureau. **2.** written; **в ~ом ви́де, в ~ой фо́рме** in writing, in written form; **п. знак** letter; **п. о́тзыв** written testimonial; **п. экза́мен** written examination.
письм|о́, а́, *pl.* **~́а, пи́сем, ~́ам** *nt.* **1.** letter; **заказно́е п.** registered letter; **це́нное п.** registered letter (with statement of value); **поздрави́тельное п.** letter of congratulation; **п.-секре́тка** letter-card. **2.** writing; **иску́сство ~а́** art of writing. **3.** script; hand(-writing); **ара́бское п.** Arabic script; **ме́лкое п.** small hand.

письмо́вник, а *m.* (*hist.*) manual of letter-writing (*containing specimen letters*).
письмоводи́тел|ь, я *m.* (*obs.*) clerk.
письмоно́с|ец, ца *m.* postman.
пита́ни|е, я *nt.* **1.** nourishment, nutrition; feeding; **недоста́точное п.** malnutrition; **обще́ственное п.** public catering; **уси́ленное п.** high-calorie diet, nourishing diet. **2.** (*tech.*) feed, feeding; **резервуа́р ~я** feed tank. **3.** (*elec.*) power supply.
пита́тел|ь, я *m.* (*tech.*) feeder.
пита́тельност|ь, и *f.* nutritiousness, food value.
пита́тел|ьный (~ен, ~ьна) *adj.* **1.** nourishing, nutritious; supplying nutriment; **п. пункт** refreshment place (*kiosk, etc.*); **~ьная среда́** (*biol.*) culture medium; (*fig.*) breeding-ground; **~ьное вещество́** nutrient. **2.** (*anat.*) alimentary. **3.** (*tech.*) feed, feeding; **~ьная труба́** feed pipe, supply pipe.
пита́|ть, ю *impf.* (*of* **на~**) **1.** to feed; to nourish (*also fig.*); to sustain; **п. больно́го** to feed a patient; **п. наде́жду** to nourish the hope; **п. отвраще́ние (к)** to have an aversion (for); **п. привя́занность** to be attached (to), cultivate an attachment (to). **2.** (*tech.*) to feed, supply; **п. го́род электроэне́ргией** to supply a city with electricity.
пита́|ться, юсь *impf.* (*+i.*) to feed (on), live (on); **хорошо́ п.** to be well fed, eat well; **п. наде́ждами** to live on hope.
пит-бу́л|ь, я *m.* pit bull terrier.
пите́йн|ый *adj.* (*obs.*): **п. дом, ~ое заведе́ние** public house.
питека́нтроп а *m.* (*anthrop.*) pithecanthropus, Java man.
Пи́тер, а *n.* (*coll.*) St. Petersburg.
пи́тер|ский *adj. of* **П~**
пито́м|ец, ца *m.* **1.** foster-child, nursling; charge. **2.** pupil; alumnus.
пито́мник, а *m.* nursery (*for plants or animals*; *also fig.*); **древе́сный п.** arboretum.
пито́н, а *m.* python.
пить, пью, пьёшь, *past* **пил, пила́, пи́ло** *impf.* (*of* **вы́~**) to drink; to have, take (*liquids*); **мне п. хо́чется** I am thirsty; **п. за** (*+a.*), **за здоро́вье** (*+g.*) to drink to, to the health (of); **п. го́рькую, п. мёртвую** (*coll.*) to drink hard; **как п. дать** (*coll.*) for sure; as sure as eggs is eggs; **как п. дать придёт** he will come for sure.
пить|ё, я́ *nt.* **1.** drinking. **2.** drink, beverage.
питьев|о́й *adj.* drinkable; **~а́я вода́** drinking water; **~а́я со́да** household soda.
пифагоре́|ец, йца *m.* Pythagorean.
пифагоре́йский *adj.* Pythagorean.
пифаго́ров *adj.*: **~а теоре́ма** Pythagoras' theorem.
пи́фи|я, и *f.* (*hist.*) the Pythian, Pythoness.
пих|а́ть, а́ю *impf.* (*of* **~ну́ть**) (*coll.*) **1.** to push; to elbow, jostle. **2.** to shove, cram; **п. ве́щи в чемода́н** to cram things into a suitcase.
пиха́|ться, юсь *impf.* (*coll.*) to push; to elbow, shove; to jostle one another.
пих|ну́ть, ну́, нёшь *pf. of* **~а́ть**
пи́хт|а, ы *f.* fir(-tree) (*Abies*); **европе́йская п.** silver fir (*Abies alba, Abies pectinata*).
пи́хт|овый *adj. of* **~а**
пи́цц|а, ы *f.* pizza.
пиццери́|я, и *f.* pizza parlour, pizzeria.
пиццика́то = пиччика́то
пи́чка|ть, ю *impf.* (*of* **на~**) (*coll.*) to stuff, cram (*also fig.*)
пичу́г|а, и *f.* (*coll.*) bird.
пичу́жк|а, и *f.* (*coll.*) = **пичу́га**
пиччика́то (*mus.*) **1.** *adv.* **2.** *n: indecl. nt.* pizzicato.
пи́шущ|ий *pres. part. act. of* **писа́ть** *and adj.*; **п. э́ти стро́ки** the present writer; **~ая бра́тия** (*coll.*) the literary fraternity; **~ая маши́нка** typewriter.
пи́щ|а, и *no pl., f.* food; **п. для ума́** food for thought; mental pabulum; **дава́ть ~у слу́хам** to feed rumours.
пища́л|ь, и *f.* (*hist.*) (h)arquebus.
пищ|а́ть, у́, и́шь *impf.* (*of* **пи́скнуть**) **1.** to squeak; (*of chicks, etc.*) to cheep, peep. **2.** (*fig., coll.*) to whine; to sing (*of kettle, etc.*).
пище... *comb. form, abbr. of* **пищево́й**
пищеваре́ни|е, я *nt.* digestion; **расстро́йство ~я** indigestion, dyspepsia.
пищевари́тельный *adj.* digestive; **п. кана́л** alimentary canal.
пищеви́к, а́ *m.* food industry worker.
пищево́д, а *m.* (*anat.*) oesophagus, gullet.
пищ|ево́й *adj. of* **~а**; **~евы́е проду́кты** foodstuffs; eatables; **~ева́я промы́шленность** food industry.
пищекомбина́т, а *m.* catering combine.
пи́щик, а *m.* **1.** (*hunting*) pipe for luring birds. **2.** (*mus.*) reed. **3.** buzzer.
пия́вк|а, и *f.* leech; **ста́вить ~и** (*med.*) to apply leeches; **пристава́ть как п.** (*fig., coll.*) to stick like a leech.
пл. (*abbr. of* **пло́щадь**) Sq., Square.
плав, а *m.*: **на ~у́** afloat.
пла́вани|е, я *nt.* **1.** swimming; **худо́жественное п.** synchronized swimming. **2.** sailing; navigation; **су́дно да́льнего ~я** ocean-going ship; **отпра́виться в п., пусти́ться в п.** to put out to sea.
пла́вательн|ый *adj.* swimming; natatorial, natatory; **п. бассе́йн** swimming pool; **~ая перепо́нка** (*of birds, bats*) web; (*of tortoise*) flipper; **п. пузы́рь** (fish-)sound, swimming-bladder.
пла́ва|ть, ю *impf.* **1.** *indet. of* **плыть; ме́лко п.** (*fig., coll.*) to be a shallow pers. **2.** to float (*have the property of floating*).
плавба́з|а, ы *f.* (*abbr. of* **пла́вучая ба́за**) factory ship.
пла́в|ень, ня *m.* (*tech.*) flux, fusing agent.
плави́к, а́ *m.* (*min.*) fluorspar.
плавико́в|ый *adj. of* **плави́к; ~ая кислота́** (*chem.*) hydrofluoric acid; **п. шпат** (*min.*) fluorspar.
плави́льник, а *m.* (*tech.*) crucible.
плави́льн|ый *adj.* (*tech.*) melting, smelting; **п. горн** smelting hearth; **п. жар** fusion temperature; **~ая печь** smelting furnace; **п. ти́гель** crucible, melting pot.
плави́л|ьня, ьни, *g. pl.* **~ен** *f.* foundry, smeltery.
плави́льщик, а *m.* founder, smelter.
пла́в|ить, лю, ишь *impf.* to melt; smelt; to fuse.
пла́в|иться, ится *impf.* to melt; to fuse (*intrans.*).
пла́вк|а, и *f.* fusing; fusion.
пла́в|ки, ок *no sg.* swimming trunks.
пла́вк|ий *adj.* fusible; **п. предохрани́тель, п. ште́псель, ~ая про́бка** (*elec.*) fuse; **~ая про́волока** fuse wire.
пла́вкост|ь, и *f.* fusibility.
плавле́ни|е, я *nt.* melting, fusion; **то́чка ~я** melting point.
пла́вленый *adj.*: **п. сыр** processed cheese.
пла́вн|и, ей *no sg.* (*reed-covered*) flats (*on lower reaches of rivers Dnieper, Kuban, etc.*).
плавни́к, а́ *m.* fin; flipper; **брюшно́й п.** abdominal fin; **грудно́й п.** thoracic fin; **спинно́й п.** dorsal fin; **хвостово́й п.** caudal fin.
плавн|о́й *adj.*: **~а́я сеть** drift net.
пла́вност|ь, и *f.* smoothness; facility.
пла́в|ный (~ен, ~на) *adj.* **1.** smooth; **~ная речь** flowing speech; **п. сти́х** rhythmical verse. **2.** (*ling.*) liquid.
плаву́н, а́ *m.* (*geol.*) quick ground.
плавун|е́ц, ца́ *m.*: **жук-п.** (*zool.*) water-tiger.
плаву́нчик, а *m.* (*zool.*) phalarope.
плаву́чест|ь, и *f.* buoyancy.
плаву́ч|ий *adj.* **1.** floating; **~ая льди́на** ice-floe; **п. мая́к** lightship, light-vessel; **~ая бурова́я устано́вка** sea drilling rig. **2.** buoyant.
плагиа́т, а *m.* plagiarism.
плагиа́тор, а *m.* plagiarist.
плаз, а *m.* (*shipbuilding*) loft.
пла́зм|а, ы *f.* (*biol. and phys.*) plasma.
пла́кальщик, а *m.* (*hired*) mourner, mute.
плака́т, а *m.* placard; poster, bill.
плакати́ст, а *m.* poster artist.
плака́т|ный *adj. of* **~; ~ные кра́ски** poster paints.
пла́|кать, чу, чешь *impf.* **1.** to weep, cry; **п. навзры́д** to sob; **хоть ~чь!** it is enough to make you weep!; **~кали де́нежки!** (*coll.*) the money has simply vanished (*sc.* has been spent)! **2.** to weep (for), cry (for); to mourn.
пла́|каться, чусь, чешься *impf.* (*of* **по~**) (**на**+*a.*) to complain (of), lament; **п. на свою́ судьбу́** to bemoan one's fate.
плакир|ова́ть, у́ю *impf. and pf.* (*tech.*) to plate.

плакиро́вк|а, и *f.* (*tech.*) plating.
пла́кс|а, ы *c.g.* (*coll.*) cry-baby.
плакси́в|ый (~, ~а) *adj.* (*coll.*) whining; (*fig.*) piteous, pathetic; **п. ребёнок** cry-baby; **п. тон** pathetic tone.
плаку́н-трав|а́, ы́ *f.* (*bot.*) purple loosestrife (*Lythrum salicaria*).
плаку́ч|ий *adj.* weeping; **~ая и́ва** weeping willow.
пламегаси́тел|ь, я *m.* (*mil.*) **1.** flash eliminator, flash-hider. **2.** flash extinguisher, anti-flash charge.
пламене́|ть, ю *impf.* (*poet.*) to flame, blaze; **п. стра́стью** to burn with passion.
пла́менник, а *m.* **1.** (*poet.*) torch, flambeau. **2.** (*bot.*) phlox.
пла́менност|ь, и *f.* ardour.
пла́менн|ый *adj.* **1.** flaming, fiery; (*fig.*) ardent, burning. **2.** (*tech.*) **~ая труба́** flue; **~ая печь** flame furnace, reverbatory furnace; **п. у́голь** bituminous coal.
пла́мен|ь, и *m.* (*obs.*, *poet.*) = **пла́мя**
пла́м|я, ени *nt.* flame; fire, blaze; **вспы́хнуть ~енем** to burst into flame.
план, а *m.* **1.** (*in var. senses*) plan; scheme; **уче́бный п.** curriculum; **по ~́у** according to plan. **2.** plane (*also fig.*); **пере́дний п.** foreground; **за́дний п.** background; **кру́пный п.** close-up (*in filming*); (*fig.*): **вы́двинуть на пе́рвый п.** to bring to the forefront; **отодви́нуть на за́дний п.** to put on the back burner.
планёр, а *m.* (*aeron.*) glider; **п. самолёта** airframe.
планери́зм, а *m.* gliding.
планери́ст, а *m.* glider-pilot.
планёр|ный *adj. of* **~**; **п. спорт** gliding.
плане́т|а, ы *f.* **1.** planet; **больши́е ~ы** major planets; **ма́лые ~ы** minor planets. **2.** (the) planet (= *Earth*). **3.** (*obs.*, *coll.*) (bad) fortune.
планета́ри|й, я *m.* planetarium.
плане́т|ный *adj. of* **~а**; planetary.
планиме́тр, а *m.* (*surveying*) planimeter.
планиметр|и́ческий *adj.* **1.** *of* **~́**. **2.** *of* **~́ия**
планиме́три|я, и *f.* (*math.*) plane geometry.
плани́ровани|е[1]**, я** *nt.* planning; **п. городо́в** town-planning.
плани́ровани|е[2]**, я** *nt.* (*aeron.*) gliding; glide.
плани́р|овать[1]**, ую** *impf.* (*of* **за~**) to plan.
плани́р|овать[2]**, ую** *impf.* (*of* **с~**) (*aeron.*) to glide (down).
планир|ова́ть, у́ю *impf.* (*of* **рас~**) to lay out (*a park, etc.*).
планиро́вк|а, и *f.* laying out; lay-out.
планиро́вщик, а *m.* workman engaged in laying out (*park, etc.*).
планисфе́р|а, ы *f.* (*astron.*) planisphere.
пла́нк|а, и *f.* lath, slat.
планкто́н, а *m.* (*biol.*) plankton.
планкто́н|ный *adj. of* **~**
планови́к, а́ *m.* planner.
пла́новост|ь, и *f.* planned character; development according to plan.
пла́нов|ый *adj.* **1.** planned, systematic; **~ое хозя́йство** planned economy. **2.** planning; **~ая коми́ссия** planning commission.
планоме́рност|ь, и *f.* systematic character, planned character.
планоме́р|ный (~ен, ~на) *adj.* systematic, planned, regular.
планта́ж, а *m.* deep ploughing.
планта́тор, а *m.* planter.
планта́ци|я, и *f.* plantation.
планша́йб|а, ы *f.* (*tech.*) face plate.
планше́т, а *m.* **1.** (*surveying*) plane-table; **огнево́й п.** (*mil.*) artillery board. **2.** map-case. **3.** busk (*of corset*).
планши́р, а *m.* (*naut.*) gunwale, top strake.
планши́р|ь, я *m.* = **~**
пласт, а́ *m.* layer; sheet; (*archit.*) course; (*geol.*) stratum, bed; **лежа́ть ~о́м** to lie motionless; to be on one's back.
пласта́|ть, ю *impf.* to cut in layers.
пла́стик, а *m.* plastic (*material*).
пла́стик|а, и *f.* **1.** (*collect.*) the plastic arts. **2.** eurhythmics.
пластили́н, а *m.* Plasticine (*propr.*).
пласти́н|а, ы *f.* plate.
пласти́нк|а, и *f.* **1.** (*in var. senses*) plate; **граммофо́нная п.** gramophone record; **чувстви́тельная п.** (*phot.*) sensitive plate. **2.** (*bot.*) blade, lamina.
пласти́нчатый *adj.* lamellar, lamellate.
пласти́ческ|ий *adj.* plastic; **~ая ма́сса** plastic; **~ая хирурги́я** plastic surgery.
пласти́чност|ь, и *f.* plasticity.
пласти́ч|ный *adj.* **1.** plastic; supple, pliant. **2.** **(~ен, ~на)** rhythmical; fluent, flowing; **~ное движе́ние те́ла** rhythmical movement of the body; **п. жест** flowing gesture.
пластма́сс|а, ы *f.* (*abbr. of* **пласти́ческая ма́сса**) plastic.
пластма́сс|овый *adj. of* **~а**
пласт|ова́ть, у́ю *impf.* **1.** to lay in layers. **2.** to cut in layers.
пласту́н, а́ *m.* (*hist.*) dismounted Cossack.
пласту́н|ский *adj. of* **~**; **переполза́ние по-~ски** (*mil.*) the leopard crawl.
пла́стыр|ь, я *m.* **1.** (*med.*) plaster; **вытяжно́й п.** drawing plaster; **ли́пкий п.** sticking plaster. **2.** (*naut.*) collision mat.
плат, а *m.* (*obs.*) = **~о́к**
пла́т|а, ы *f.* **1.** pay; salary; **за́работная п.** wages. **2.** payment, charge; fee; **входна́я п.** entrance fee; **п. за прое́зд** fare.
плата́н, а *m.* plane(-tree), platan.
плата́|ть, ю *impf.* (*of* **за~**) (*coll.*) to patch.
платёж, а *m.* payment; **нало́женным ~о́м** cash on delivery; **прекрати́ть ~и́** suspend payment(s).
платёжеспосо́бност|ь, и *f.* solvency.
платёжеспосо́б|ный (~ен, ~на) *adj.* solvent.
платёж|ный *adj. of* **~**; **п. бала́нс** balance of payments; **~ная ве́домость** pay-sheet; pay-roll; **п. день** pay-day.
пла́тельщик, а *m.* payer.
пла́тин|а, ы *f.* (*min.*) platinum.
пла́тин|овый *adj. of* **~а**
пла|ти́ть, чу́, ~́тишь *impf.* (*of* **за~**) **1.** to pay; **п. дань** (+*d.*) to pay tribute (to); **п. нали́чными** to pay in cash, pay in ready money; **п. нату́рой** to pay in kind. **2.** (*fig.*; +*i.* **за**+*a.*) to pay back, return; **п. кому́-н. услу́гой за услу́гу** to make it up to s.o., return a favour; **п. кому́-н. взаи́мностью** to reciprocate s.o.'s love.
пла|ти́ться, чу́сь, ~́тишься *impf.* (*of* **по~**) (+*i.* **за**+*a.*) to pay (with for); **п. жи́знью за свои́ оши́бки** to pay for one's mistakes with one's life.
пла́тн|ый *adj.* **1.** paid; requiring payment, chargeable; **~ая доро́га** toll road; **~ое ме́сто** paid seat. **2.** paying; **п. посети́тель** paying guest.
плато́ *nt. indecl.* plateau.
плат|о́к, ка́ *m.* shawl; kerchief; **носово́й п.** (pocket) handkerchief.
платони́зм, а *m.* Platonism.
плато́ник, а *m.* Platonist.
платони́ческий *adj.* (*phil.*) Platonic; (*fig.*) platonic.
платфо́рм|а, ы *f.* **1.** platform (*of rail. station*). **2.** (open) goods truck. **3.** (*fig.*, *pol.*) platform.
пла́ть|е, я, *g. pl.* **~ев** *nt.* **1.** clothes, clothing; **ве́рхнее п.** outer garments. **2.** dress, gown, frock; **вече́рнее п.** evening dress.
плат|яно́й *adj. of* **~́ье**; **п. шкаф** wardrobe; **~яна́я щётка** clothes-brush.
плау́н, а́ *m.* (*bot.*) lycopodium, wolf's-claw, club-moss.
плафо́н, а *m.* **1.** (*archit.*) plafond. **2.** shade (*for lamp suspended from ceiling*).
пла́х|а, и *f.* block; (*hist.*) executioner's block; **взойти́ на ~у** to mount the scaffold.
плац, а, о ~́е, на ~у́ *m.* (*mil.*) parade-ground; **уче́бный п.** drill square.
плацда́рм, а *m.* **1.** (*mil.*) bridgehead; beachhead. **2.** (*pol.*; *fig.*) base.
плаце́нт|а, ы *f.* (*anat.*) placenta.
плацка́рт|а, ы *f.* reserved seat *or* berth ticket.
плацка́рт|ный *adj. of* **~а**; **п. ваго́н** carriage with numbered reserved seats; **~ное ме́сто** reserved seat.
плац-пара́д, а *m.* (*mil.*) parade ground.
плач, а *m.* **1.** weeping, crying. **2.** (*ceremonial*) wailing; keening. **3.** lament.
плаче́в|ный (~ен, ~на) *adj.* **1.** mournful, sad; **име́ть п. вид** to be a sorry sight. **2.** (*fig.*) lamentable, deplorable, sorry; **в ~ном состоя́нии** in a sad state, in a sorry plight.

плашко́ут, а *m.* (*naut.*) lighter.
плашко́утный *adj.*: **п. мост** pontoon bridge.
плашмя́ *adv.* flat; flatways; prone; **упа́сть п.** to fall flat; **уда́рить са́блей п.** to strike with the flat of the sword.
плащ, а́ *m.* **1.** cloak. **2.** mackintosh, raincoat; waterproof cape.
плащани́ц|а, ы *f.* (*eccl.*) shroud of Christ.
плащ-пала́тк|а, и *f.* ground sheet.
плебе́|й, я *m.* (*hist.*) plebeian.
плебе́йский *adj.* plebeian.
плебисци́т, а *m.* plebiscite.
плебс, а *m.* (*collect.*; *hist.*) plebs.
плев|а́, ы́ *f.* (*anat.*) membrane, film, coat; **де́вственная п.** hymen; **лёгочная п.** pleura.
плева́тельниц|а, ы *f.* spittoon.
плева́ть, плюю́, плюёшь *impf.* (*of* **плю́нуть**) **1.** to spit; to expectorate; **п. в потоло́к** (*fig.*, *joc.*) to idle, fritter away the time. **2.** (**на**+*a.*; *coll.*) to spit (upon); not to care a rap about; **им п. на всё** they don't give a damn about anything.
плева́ться, плюю́сь, плюёшься *impf.* (*coll.*) to spit.
пле́вел, а *m.* (*bot.*) darnel, cockle; weed.
плев|о́к, ка́ *m.* **1.** spit(tle). **2.** (*med.*) sputum.
плёвр|а, ы *f.* (*anat.*) pleura.
плеври́т, а *m.* (*med.*) pleurisy.
плёв|ый *adj.* (*coll.*) **1.** worthless; rubbishy; **п. челове́к** good-for-nothing. **2.** trifling, trivial; **де́ло ~ое** trifling matter.
плед, а *m.* rug; plaid.
плеер, а *m.* personal stereo, Walkman (*propr.*).
пле́йер = пле́ер
плейстоце́н, а *m.* (*geol.*) Pleistocene.
плейстоце́н|овый *adj. of* ~
племенно́й *adj.* **1.** tribal. **2.** pedigree; **п. скот** pedigree cattle, bloodstock.
пле́м|я, ени, *pl.* **~ена́, ~ён, ~ена́м** *nt.* **1.** tribe. **2.** breed; **на п.** for breeding. **3.** (*fig.*) tribe; breed, stock; **пти́чье п.** (*joc.*) the feathered tribe.
племя́нник, а *m.* nephew.
племя́нниц|а, ы *f.* niece.
плен, а, о ~е, в ~у́ *m.* captivity; **быть в ~у́** to be in captivity; **взять в п.** to take prisoner; **попа́сть в п. (к)** to be taken prisoner (by).
плена́рный *adj.* plenary.
плене́ни|е, я *nt.* (*obs.*) capture; captivity.
плени́тельност|ь, и *f.* fascination.
плени́тел|ьный (~ен, ~ьна) *adj.* captivating, fascinating, charming.
плен|и́ть, ю́, и́шь *pf.* (*of* **~я́ть**) **1.** (*obs.*) to take prisoner, take captive. **2.** (*fig.*) to captivate, fascinate, charm.
плен|и́ться, ю́сь, и́шься *pf.* (*of* **~я́ться**) (+*i.*) to be captivated (by), be fascinated (by).
плёнк|а, и *f.* (*in var. senses*) film; pellicle.
пле́нник, а *m.* (*obs. or fig.*) prisoner, captive.
пле́нн|ый *adj.* captive; *as n.* **п., ~ого** *m.* captive, prisoner.
плён|очный *adj. of* **~ка**; filmy.
пле́нум, а *m.* plenum, plenary session.
плен|я́ть(ся), я́ю(сь) *impf. of* **~и́ть(ся)**
плеона́зм, а *m.* (*liter.*) pleonasm.
плеонасти́ческий *adj.* (*liter.*) pleonastic.
плёс, а *m.* reach (*of river*); stretch (*of river or lake*).
пле́сенный *adj.* mouldy, musty.
пле́сен|ь, и *f.* mould.
плеск, а *m.* splash; **п. вёсел** plash of oars; **п. волн** lapping of waves.
пле|ска́ть, щу́, ~щешь *impf.* (*of* **~сну́ть**) to splash; to plash; to lap; **п. о бе́рег** to lap against the shore; **п. на кого́-н. водо́й** to splash s.o. (with water).
пле|ска́ться, щу́сь, ~щешься *impf.* to splash; to lap.
пле́снев|еть, еет *impf.* (*of* **за~**) to grow mouldy, grow musty.
плес|ну́ть, ну́, нёшь *pf. of* **~ка́ть**
пле|сти́, ту́, тёшь, *past* **~л, ~ла́** *impf.* (*of* **с~**) to braid, plait; to weave, tat; **п. вено́к** to make a wreath; **п. корзи́ну** to make a basket; **п. небыли́цы** (*coll.*, *pej.*) to spin yarns; **п. паути́ну** to spin a web; **п. се́ти** to net; **п. вздор, п. чепуху́** (*coll.*, *pej.*) to talk rubbish.
пле|сти́сь, ту́сь, тёшься, *past* **~лся, ~ла́сь** *impf.* (*coll.*) to drag o.s. along, trudge; **п. в хвосте́** (*fig.*) to lag behind.
плете́ни|е, я *nt.* **1.** braiding, plaiting; **п. слове́с** (*iron.*) verbiage. **2.** wicker-work.
плетёнк|а, и *f.* **1.** (wicker) basket. **2.** hurdle.
плетён|ый *adj.* wattled, wicker; **~ая корзи́нка** wicker basket.
плет|е́нь, ня́ *m.* hurdle; wattle fencing.
плётк|а *f.* lash.
плет|ь, и, *pl.* **~и, ~е́й** *f.* lash.
плечев|о́й *adj.* (*anat.*) humeral; **~а́я кость** humerus.
пле́чик|и, ов *no sg.* (*coll.*) (coat-)hanger.
пле́чик|о, а, *pl.* **~и, ~ов** *nt.* **1.** shoulder-strap. **2.** *dim. of* **плечо́**
плечи́ст|ый (~, ~а) *adj.* broad-shouldered.
плеч|о́, а́, *pl.* **~и, ~, ~а́м** *nt.* **1.** shoulder; **ле́вое, пра́вое п. вперёд!** (*mil.*) right wheel, left wheel!; **всё э́то у меня́ за ~а́ми** (*fig.*) all that is behind me; **~о́м к ~у́** shoulder to shoulder; **взять на́ ~и** to shoulder; **на п.!** (*mil.*) slope arms!; **на ~а́х проти́вника** on top of, on the heels of the enemy; **име́ть го́лову на ~а́х** to have a good head on one's shoulders; **вы́нести на свои́х ~а́х** to bear (the full brunt of); **э́то ему́ не по ~у́** he is not up to it; **с ~а́** straight from the shoulder; **(сло́вно) гора́ с мои́х ~ свали́лась** that's a weight off my mind; **с ~ доло́й!** that's done, thank goodness; **с чужо́го ~а́** (*of clothing*) worn, second-hand; **пожа́ть ~а́ми** to shrug one's shoulders. **2.** (*anat.*) upper arm, humerus. **3.** (*tech.*) arm.
плеши́ве|ть, ю *impf.* (*of* **о~**) to grow bald.
плеши́в|ый (~, ~а) *adj.* bald.
плеши́н|а, ы *f.* bald patch.
плеш|ь, и *f.* bald patch; bare patch.
плея́д|ы, ~ *pl.* (*sg.* **~а, ~ы** *f.*) **1. П.** (*astron.*) Pleiades. **2.** (*sg.*; *fig.*) Pleiad; galaxy.
пли *int.* (*see* **пали́ть**) (*mil.*; *obs.*) fire!
пли́нтус, а *m.* **1.** plinth. **2.** skirting board.
плиоце́н, а *m.* (*geol.*) Pl(e)iocene.
плис, а *m.* velveteen.
пли́с|овый *adj. of* ~
плиссе́ *indecl.* **1.** *adj.* pleated; **ю́бка п.** pleated skirt. **2.** *n.*; *nt.* pleat(s).
плиссир|ова́ть, у́ю *impf.* (*no pf.*) to pleat.
плиссиро́вк|а, и *f.* pleating.
плит|а́, ы́, *pl.* **~ы** *f.* **1.** plate, slab; flag-(stone); **моги́льная п.** gravestone, tombstone; **мра́морная п.** marble slab. **2.** stove; cooker.
пли́тк|а, и *f.* **1.** *dim. of* **плита́**; tile, (thin) slab; **кра́ски в ~ах** solid water-colours; **п. шокола́да** bar of chocolate. **2.** stove; cooker.
плитня́к, а́ *m.* flagstone.
пли́т|очный *adj. of* **~ка**; **п. пол** tiled floor.
пли́ц|а, ы *f.* **1.** bailer. **2.** (*obs.*) blade (*of paddle-wheel*).
плов, а *m.* (*cul.*) = **пила́в**
плов|е́ц, ца́ *m.* swimmer; **п. на доске́** surfer.
плову́чий *adj.* = **плаву́чий**
плод, а́ *m.* **1.** fruit (*also fig.*); **приноси́ть п.** to bear fruit; **запре́тный п.** (*fig.*) forbidden fruit. **2.** (*biol.*) foetus.
пло|ди́ть, жу́, ди́шь *impf.* (*of* **рас~**) to produce, procreate; to engender (*also fig*).
пло|ди́ться, жу́сь, ди́шься *impf.* (*of* **рас~**) to multiply; to propagate.
пло́дный *adj.* **1.** (*biol.*) fertile. **2.** fertilized.
плодови́тост|ь, и *f.* fruitfulness, fertility, fecundity.
плодови́т|ый (~, ~а) *adj.* fruitful, prolific (*also fig.*); fertile, fecund; **п. писа́тель** prolific writer.
плодово́дств|о, а *nt.* fruit-growing.
плодово́д|ческий *adj. of* **~ство**
плодо́в|ый *adj. of* **плод**; **~ое де́рево** fruit-tree; **п. сад** orchard.
плодоли́стик|а, и *m.* (*bot.*) carpel.
плодоно́жк|а, и *f.* (*bot.*) fruit stem.
плодоно|си́ть, ~сит *impf.* (*no pf.*) to bear fruit.
плодоно́с|ный (~ен, ~на) *adj.* fruit-bearing, fruitful.
плодоо́вощ|и, е́й *no sg.* fruit and vegetables.
плодоовощно́й *adj.* fruit and vegetable.

плодоро́ди|е, я *nt.* fertility, fecundity.
плодоро́д|ный (~ен, ~на) *adj.* fertile, fecund.
плодосме́нн|ый *adj.*: **~ая систе́ма** (*agric.*) rotation of crops.
плодотво́р|ный (~ен, ~на) *adj.* fruitful.
плодоя́д|ный (~ен, ~на) *adj.* frugivorous.
плоён|ый *adj.* (*obs.*) pleated; **~ые во́лосы** waved hair.
пло|и́ть, ю́, и́шь *impf.* (*of* **на~**) (*obs.*) to pleat; to wave (*hair*).
пло́мб|а, ы *f.* **1.** (*lead*) stamp, seal. **2.** stopping, filling (*for tooth*); **ста́вить ~у в зуб** to stop, fill a tooth.
пломби́р, а *m.* 'plombières' (*ice cream with candied fruit*).
пломбир|ова́ть, у́ю *impf.* **1.** (*pf.* **о~**) to seal. **2.** (*pf.* **за~**) to stop, fill (*a tooth*).
пло́с|кий (~ок, ~ка́, ~ко) *adj.* **1.** flat; plane; **~кая грудь** flat chest; **~кая пове́рхность** plane surface; **~кая стопа́** (*med.*) flat-foot. **2.** (*fig.*) trivial, tame; **~кая шу́тка** feeble joke.
плоского́рь|е, я *nt.* plateau; tableland.
плоскогру́д|ый (~, ~а) *adj.* flat-chested.
плоскогу́бц|ы, ев *no sg.* pliers.
плоскодо́нк|а, и *f.* flat-bottomed boat; punt.
плоскодо́нный *adj.* flat-bottomed.
плоскостно́й *adj.* plane.
плоскосто́пи|е, я *nt.* (*med.*) flat-foot, flat feet.
пло́скост|ь, и, *pl.* **~и, ~е́й** *f.* **1.** flatness. **2.** plane (*also fig.*); **накло́нная п.** inclined plane; **кати́ться по накло́нной ~и** (*fig.*) to go downhill. **3.** platitude, triviality.
плот, а́ *m.* raft.
плотв|а́, ы́ *f.* (*fish*) roach.
плоти́н|а, ы *f.* dam; weir; dike, dyke.
плотне́|ть, ю *impf.* (*of* **по~**) to grow stout.
пло́тник, а *m.* carpenter.
пло́тнича|ть, ю *impf.* to work as a carpenter.
пло́тничеств|о, а *nt.* carpentry.
пло́тничный *adj.* carpentering.
пло́тно *adv.* **1.** close(ly), tightly; **п. заколоти́ть дверь** to board up, nail up a door. **2.**: **п. пое́сть** to have a square meal, eat heartily.
пло́тност|ь, и *f.* **1.** thickness; compactness; solidity, strength; **п. населе́ния|** density of population. **2.** (*phys.*) density.
пло́т|ный (~ен, ~на́, ~но) *adj.* **1.** thick; compact; dense (*also phys.*); **п. ого́нь** (*mil.*) heavy fire. **2.** solid, strong; (*of a pers.*; *coll.*) thick-set, solidly built. **3.** tightly-filled. **4.** (*coll.*; *of a meal*) square, hearty.
плотово́д, а *m.* rafter, raftsman (*floating timber on rafts*).
плотовщи́к, а́ *m.* rafter, raftsman (*floating timber or ferrying passengers on rafts*).
плотоя́д|ный (~ен, ~на) *adj.* **1.** carnivorous. **2.** lustful; voluptuous.
пло́тский *adj.* (*arch.*) carnal, fleshly.
плот|ь, и *f.* flesh; **во ~и́** in the flesh; **п. от ~и** flesh of one's flesh; **п. и кровь** (one's) flesh and blood; **облéчь в п. и кровь** to embody; **кра́йняя п.** (*anat.*) foreskin, prepuce.
пло́хо 1. *adv.* bad(ly); ill; **п. вести́ себя́** to behave badly; **п. обраща́ться (с+*i.*)** to ill-treat, ill-use; **чу́вствовать себя́ п.** to feel unwell, feel bad; **п. па́хнуть** to smell bad; **п. ко́нчить** (*coll.*) to come to a bad end; **п. лежа́ть** (*coll.*) to lie in temptation's way; **п.-п.** (*coll.*) at (the very) least. **2.** *n.*; *nt. indecl.* bad mark; **я опя́ть получи́л п. по а́лгебре** I have got a bad mark in algebra again.
плохова́то *adv.* (*coll.*) rather badly, not too well.
плохова́т|ый (~, ~а) *adj.* (*coll.*) rather bad, not too good.
плох|о́й (~, ~а́, ~о) *adj.* (*in var. senses*) bad; poor; **~а́я пого́да** bad weather; **~о́е настрое́ние** bad mood, low spirits; **п. рабо́тник** a poor workman; **~о́е пищеваре́ние** poor digestion; **~о́е утеше́ние** poor consolation; **с ним шу́тки ~и** he is not one to be trifled with; *as pred.* **ему́ о́чень ~о** he is very bad; he is in a very bad way.
плоша́|ть, ю *impf.* (*of* **с~**) (*coll.*) to make a mistake, slip up.
пло́шк|а, и *f.* **1.** (*coll.*) flat dish, saucer. **2.** lampion.
площа́дк|а, и *f.* **1.** ground, area; **де́тская п.** children's playground; **спорти́вная п.** sports ground; **строи́тельная п.** building site; **те́ннисная п.** tennis court; **киносъёмочная п.** (*film*) set; **п. для игры́ в го́льф** golf course *or* links. **2.** landing (*on staircase*). **3.** platform; **пускова́я п.** launching pad (*of rocket*).
площадн|о́й *adj.* vulgar, coarse; **~а́я брань** Billingsgate language.
пло́щад|ь, и, *pl.* **~и, ~е́й** *f.* **1.** (*math.*) area. **2.** area; space; **жила́я п.** living space, floor-space; **посевна́я п.** sown area, area under crops. **3.** square; **база́рная п.** market-place.
пло́|ще *comp. of* **~ский** *and* **~ско**
плуг, а, *pl.* **~и́** *m.* plough.
плуга́р|ь, я́ *m.* ploughman.
плугово́й *adj. of* **плуг**
плу́нжер, а *m.* (*tech.*) plunger.
плут, а́ *m.* **1.** cheat, swindler, knave. **2.** (*joc.*) rogue.
плута́|ть, ю *impf.* (*coll.*) to stray.
плути́шк|а, и *m.* (*coll.*) little rogue, mischievous imp.
плу́тн|и, ей *pl.* (*sg.* **~я, ~и** *f.*) (*coll.*) cheating, swindling; tricks.
плутова́т|ый (~, ~а) *adj.* cunning.
плут|ова́ть, у́ю *impf.* (*of* **на~** *and* **с~**) (*coll.*) to cheat, swindle.
плуто́вк|а, и *f. of* **плут, плути́шка**
плутовск|о́й *adj.* **1.** knavish; **~и́е приёмы** knavish tricks. **2.** (*coll.*) roguish, mischievous. **3.** (*liter.*) picaresque.
плутовств|о́, а́ *nt.* cheating; trickery, knavery.
плутокра́т, а́ *m.* plutocrat.
плутократи́ческий *adj.* plutocratic.
плутокра́ти|я, и *f.* plutocracy.
плыву́н, а́ *m.* = **плаву́н**
плыву́чий *adj.* flowing, deliquescent.
плы|ть, ву́, вёшь, *past* **~л, ~ла́, ~ло** *impf.* (*det. of* **пла́вать**) **1.** to swim; to float; **п. сто́я** to tread water; **п. кому́-н. в ру́ки** (*fig.*, *coll.*) to drop into s.o.'s lap; **всё ~ло пе́ред мои́ми глаза́ми** everything was swimming before my eyes. **2.** to sail; **п. на вёслах** to row; **п. под паруса́ми** to sail, go under sail; **п. по тече́нию** to go down stream; (*fig.*) to go with the stream; **п. про́тив тече́ния** to go up stream; (*fig.*) to go against the stream; **п. по во́ле волн** to drift.
плювио́метр, а *m.* pluviometer.
плюга́в|ый (~, ~а) *adj.* (*coll.*) shabby, mean; despicable.
плюма́ж, а *m.* plume (*on hat*).
плю́н|уть, у, ешь *pf. of* **плева́ть; п. не́куда** no room to swing a cat.
плюрали́зм, а *m.* (*phil. & pol.*) pluralism.
плюралисти́ческий *adj.* (*phil. & pol.*) pluralistic.
плюра́льный *adj.*: **п. во́тум** (*leg.*) plural vote.
плюс, а *m.* **1.** plus; *as connective in math. expressions* **два п. два равно́ четырём** two plus two equals four. **2.** (*fig.*, *coll.*) advantage; **э́тот прое́кт не без ~ов** this scheme has some advantages.
плюс|на́, ны́, *pl.* **~ны, ~ен, ~нам** *f.* (*anat.*) metatarsus.
плюс|ова́ть, у́ю *impf.* (*tech.*) to dip, immerse.
плю́с|овый *adj. of* **~; п. гандика́п** (*sport*) plus handicap.
плю́х|ать(ся), аю(сь) *impf. of* **~нуть(ся)**
плю́х|нуть, ну, нешь *pf.* (*of* **~ать**) (*coll.*) to flop (down), plump (down); **п. в кре́сло** to flop into an arm-chair.
плю́х|нуться, нусь, нешься *pf.* (*of* **~аться**) = **~нуть**
плюш, а *m.* plush.
плю́ш|евый *adj. of* **~**
плю́шк|а, и *f.* (*coll.*) bun.
плющ, а́ *m.* ivy; **вью́щийся п.** tree ivy.
плющи́льн|ый *adj.* (*tech.*) flattening, laminating; **п. мо́лот** planing hammer, flatter; **п. стано́к** flatting mill, rolling mill; **~ая маши́на** upsetting machine.
плю́щ|ить, у, ишь *impf.* (*of* **с~**) (*tech.*) to flatten, laminate.
пляж, а *m.* beach.
пляс, а *no pl.*, *m.* (*coll.*) dance; **пусти́ться в п.** to break into a dance.
пля́ск|а, и *f.* dance; dancing (*esp. folk-dancing*); **п. свято́го Ви́та** (*med.*) St. Vitus's dance, chorea.
пля|са́ть, шу́, ~шешь *impf.* (*of* **с~**) to dance.
плясов|о́й *adj.* dancing; *as n.* **~а́я, ~о́й** *f.* dance tune.
плясу́н, а́ *m.* (*coll.*) dancer; **кана́тный п.** rope-dancer.

пневмáтик, а *m.* pneumatic tire.
пневмáтик|а, и *f.* pneumatics.
пневматúческий *adj.* pneumatic.
пневмокóкк, а *m.* (*med.*) pneumococcus.
пневмокостю́м, а *m.* pressure suit.
пневмонú|я, и *f.* pneumonia.
пневмотóракс, а *m.* (*med.*) pneumothorax.
пнúст|ый (~, ~а) *adj. of* **пень**
ПНР *f. indecl.* (*abbr. of* ***Пóльская Нарóдная Респýблика***) Polish People's Republic.
пнуть, пну, пнёшь *pf.* (*of* **пинáть**) (*coll.*) to kick.
по *prep.* **I.** *+d.* **1.** on; along; **идтú по травé** to walk on the grass; **спустúться по верёвке** to come down on a rope; **éхать по ýлице** to go along the street; **идтú по следáм** (*+g.*) to follow in the tracks (of); **хлóпнуть по спинé** to slap on the back; **по всемý, по всей** all over. **2.** round, about (*or not translated*); **ходúть по магазúнам** to go round the shops; **ходúть по кóмнате** to pace the room; **разместúть войскá по гóроду** to quarter troops about the town. **3.** by, on, over (*sc. some means of communication*); **по вóздуху** by air; **по желéзной дорóге** by rail, by train; **по пóчте** by post; **по рáдио** on the wireless, over the radio; **по телефóну** on, over the telephone; **передáть по рáдио** to broadcast. **4.** according to; by; in accordance with; **по прáву** by right(s); **по расписáнию** according to schedule; **по статьé закóна** according to the letter of the law; **женúться по любвú** to marry for love; **звать по úмени** to call by first name; **рабóтать по плáну** to work according to plan; **сýдя по результáтам** judging by results; **по мне** in my opinion, in my view, as far as I am concerned; **жить по срéдствам** to live within one's means; **по Платóну** according to Plato. **5.** by, in (= *in respect of*); **по профéссии** by profession; **по положéнию** by one's position; ex officio; **по происхождéнию он армянúн** he is an Armenian by descent, he is of Armenian origin; **лýчший по кáчеству** better in quality; **товáрищ по орýжию** comrade-in-arms; **товáрищ по шкóле** school-mate; **рóдственник по мáтери** a relative on one's mother's side. **6.** at, on, in (= *in the field of*); **чемпиóн по шáхматам** champion at chess, chess champion; **лéкции по европéйской истóрии** lectures on European history; **специалúст по ядерной фúзике** specialist in (on) nuclear physics. **7.** by (reason of); on account of; from; **по болéзни** on account of sickness; **по рассéянности** from absent-mindedness; **егó простúли по мóлодости лет** he was pardoned by reason of his youth; **по счастлúвому стечéнию обстоятельств** by a happy conjunction of circumstances. **8.** (*indicating the object of an action or feeling*) at, for (*or not translated*); **стрелять по протúвнику** to fire at the enemy; **охóта по крýпному звéрю** big game hunting; **скучáть по дéтям** to miss one's children; **тоскá по дóму, по рóдине** homesickness; **по áдресу** (*+g.*) to the address (of); **это по егó áдресу** (*fig.*) this is meant for him. **9.** (*in temporal phrr.*) on; in; **по понедéльникам** on Mondays; **по прáздникам** on holidays; **онá рабóтает по утрáм** she works (in the) mornings; **я не видáл её по цéлым недéлям** I did not see her for weeks at a time; **он приéдет по веснé** he will come in the spring.

II. *+d. or a. of cardinal num. forms distributive num.* (*+d., but also +a., esp. in coll. usage*) **по одномý (однóй); по пятú, по шестú,** *etc.*; **по одúннадцати,** *etc.*; **по двадцатú,** *etc.*; **по ста; по пятúсот,** *etc.*; **по полторá (полторы́)**; (*+a.*) **пó два (две), пó три, по четы́ре, по двéсти, по трúста, по четы́реста; дáйте им по** (*sc.* **одномý) я́блоку** give them an apple each; **мы получúли по три фýнта** we received three pounds each; **по рублю́ штýка** one rouble each; **по дéсять (десятú) рублéй штýка** ten roubles each; **пó два, пó двое** in twos, two by two.

III. *+a.* **1.** to, up to; **по пóяс в водé** up to the waist in water; **зáнят по гóрло** up to one's eyes in work; **пó уши в долгáх** up to one's ears in debt; **пó уши влюблён** head over heels in love; **по сегóдня** up to today; **по пéрвое мáя** up to (and including) the first of May; **по сю (ту) стóрону** on this (that) side. **2.** (*following vv. of motion; coll.*) for (= *to fetch, to get*); **идтú пó воду** to go for water.

IV. *+p.* **1.** on, after; **по истечéнии срóка** on expiry of the term set; **по окончáнии рабóты** after work; **по прибы́тии** on arrival; **по рассмотрéнии** on examination. **2.** (*after vv. of grieving, mourning, etc.*) for; **плáкать по мýже** to mourn (for) one's husband; **носúть трáур по ком-н.** to be in mourning for s.o. **3.: по нём,** *etc.*, as he, *etc.*, likes, is used.
по- *+d. of adj. or ending* **...ски** *forms adv. indicating* **1.** *manner of action, conduct, etc., as* **жить по-стáрому** to live in the old style; **рабóтать по-товáрищески** to work in a comradely fashion. **2.** *use of given language, as* **говорúть по-рýсски** to speak Russian. **3.** *accordance with opinion or wish, as* **по-мóему** in my opinion; **пусть бýдет по-вáшему** (let it be) as you wish.
по...[1] *as vbl. pref.* **1.** *forms pf. aspect.* **2.** *indicates action of short duration or of incomplete character, as* **порабóтать** to do a little work; **поспáть** to have a sleep. **3.** (*+suff.* **...ыва..., ...ива...**) *indicates action repeated at intervals or of indet. duration, as* **позвáнивать** to keep ringing.
по...[2] *pref. modifying comp. adj. or adv., as* **погрóмче** a little louder.
...пó *in cpd. words, abbr. of* ***потребúтельское óбщество***
п. о. (*abbr. of* ***почтóвое отделéние***) PO, Post Office.
поаккóрдн|ый *adj.*: **~ая плáта** piece-work rate.
побагровé|ть, ю *pf. of* **багровéть**
побáива|ться, юсь *impf.* (*+g. or inf.*; *coll.*) to be rather afraid.
побáлива|ть, ю *impf.* (*coll.*) to ache a little; to ache on and off.
по-бáрски *adv.* like a lord.
побасёнк|а, и *f.* (*coll.*) tale, story.
побéг[1]**, а** *m.* flight; escape.
побéг[2]**, а** *m.* (*bot.*) sprout, shoot; sucker; set; graft.
побéга|ть, ю *pf.* to run a little, have a run.
побегýшк|и: быть у когó-н. на ~ах (*coll.*) to run errands for s.o.; (*fig.*) to be at s.o.'s beck and call.
побéд|а, ы *f.* victory; **крýпная п.** landslide (victory); **войнá до пóлной ~ы** total war; **одержáть ~у** to gain a victory.
победúтел|ь, я *m.* victor, conqueror; (*sport*) winner.
побед|úть, úшь *pf.* (*of* **побеждáть**) to conquer, vanquish; to defeat, win a victory (over); (*fig.*) to master, overcome.
побéдный *adj.* victorious, triumphant; **п. гол** winning goal; winner.
победонóс|ный (~ен, ~на) *adj.* victorious, triumphant.
побежáлост|ь, и *f.* (*chem., tech.*) iridescence; **цвет ~и** oxide tint.
побе|жáть, гý, жúшь, гýт *pf.* **1.** *pf. of* **бежáть. 2.** to break into a run.
побеждá|ть, ю *impf. of* **победúть**
побéжк|а, и *f.* pace, gait.
побелé|ть, ю *pf. of* **белéть**
побел|úть, ю, ~úшь *pf. of* **белúть 1.**
побéлк|а, и *f.* whitewashing.
поберéжный *adj.* coastal.
поберéжь|е, я *nt.* coast, seaboard, littoral.
поберé|чь, гý, жёшь, гýт, *past* **~г, ~глá** *pf.* (*coll.*) to look after, take care (of); **п. здорóвье** to take care of one's health; **~гú мой вéщи до моегó возвращéния** look after my things until I come back.
поберé|чься, гýсь, жёшься, гýться, *past* **~гся, ~глáсь** *pf.* to take care of o.s.; **~гúсь!** mind out!
побесéд|овать, ую *pf.* to have a (little) talk, have a chat.
побеспокó|ить, ю, ишь *pf. of* **беспокóить 2.; позвóльте вас п.** may I trouble you?
побеспокó|иться, юсь, ишься *pf.* **1.** *pf. of* **беспокóиться 2.. 2.** to be rather worried.
побирá|ться, юсь *impf.* (*coll.*) to beg, live by begging.
побирýшк|а, и *c.g.* (*coll.*) beggar.
поб|úть, ью, ьёшь *pf.* **1.** *pf. of* **бить 1., 2.; п. рекóрд** to break a record. **2.** (*of rain, hail, etc.*) to beat down; (*of frost*) to nip. **3.** to break, smash (*a number of*). **4.** to kill (*a number of*).
поб|úться, ьётся *pf.* **1.** *pf. of* **бúться. 2.** to break.
поблагодар|úть, ю, úшь *pf. of* **благодарúть**
поблáжк|а, и *f.* indulgence; allowance(s); **дéлать ~у** (*+d.*)

to indulge, make allowance(s) (for).
побледне́|ть, ю *pf. of* **бледне́ть**
поблёклый *adj.* faded; withered.
поблёк|нуть, ну, нешь, *past* ~, **~ла** *pf. of* **блёкнуть**
поблёскива|ть, ю *impf.* to gleam.
побли́зости *adv.* near at hand, hereabout(s); **п. (от)** near (to).
побож|и́ться, у́сь, и́шься *pf. of* **божи́ться**
побо́|и, ев *no sg.* beating, blows; **терпе́ть п.** to take a beating.
побо́ищ|е, а *nt.* slaughter, carnage; bloody battle; **ледо́вое п.** *see* **ледо́вый**
поболта́|ть, ю *pf.* (*coll.*) to have a chat.
побо́рник, а *m.* champion, upholder.
побор|о́ть, ю́, ~́ешь *pf.* to overcome; to fight down; to beat (*in wrestling*).
побо́р|ы, ов *pl.* (*sg.* ~, **~а** *m.*) requisitions; extortion.
побо́чн|ый *adj.* side; secondary; collateral; **п. эффе́кт** side effect; **п. насле́дник** collateral heir; **п. проду́кт** by-product; **~ая рабо́та** side-line; **п. сын** natural son.
побо|я́ться, ю́сь, и́шься *pf.* (+*g. or inf.*) to be afraid; **он хоте́л возрази́ть да ~я́лся** he wanted to raise an objection but did not venture to.
побран|и́ть, ю́, и́шь *pf.* to give a scolding, tick off.
побран|и́ться, ю́сь, и́шься *pf.* (**с**+*i.*; *coll.*) to have a quarrel, have words (with).
побрата́|ться, юсь *pf. of* **брата́ться**
побрати́м, а *m.* **1.** (*obs.*) sworn brother. **2.** twin(ned) town.
побрати́мств|о, а *nt.* (*obs.*) sworn brotherhood.
по-бра́тски *adv.* like a brother; fraternally.
по|бра́ть, беру́, берёшь, *past* **~бра́л, ~брала́, ~бра́ло** *pf.* (*coll.*) to take (a quantity of); **чёрт тебя́ ~бери́, чёрт бы тебя́ ~бра́л!** the devil take you!
побре́зга|ть, ю *pf. of* **бре́згать; не ~йте!** (*coll.*; *polite form of invitation*) make yourself free!
побре|сти́, ду́, дёшь, *past* **~́л, ~ла́** *pf.* to plod.
побр|и́ть(ся), е́ю(сь) *pf. of* **бри́ть(ся)**
побро|ди́ть[1]**, жу́, ~́дишь** *pf.* to wander for some time.
побро|ди́ть[2]**, жу́, ~́дишь** *pf.* to ferment for some time.
поброса́|ть, ю *pf.* **1.** to throw up; to throw about. **2.** to desert, abandon.
побря́к|ать, аю *pf.* (*of* **~ивать**) (+*i.*; *coll.*) to rattle.
побря́кива|ть, ю *impf. of* **побря́кать**
побряку́шк|а, и *f.* (*coll.*) trinket; rattle.
побуди́тельн|ый *adj.* stimulating; **~ая причи́на** motive, incentive; **~ые сре́дства** stimulants.
побу|ди́ть[1]**, жу́, ~́дишь** *pf.* **1.** to try to wake. **2.** to wake, rouse.
побу|ди́ть[2]**, жу́, ~ди́шь** *pf.* (*of* **~жда́ть**) (**к** *or* +*inf.*) to induce (to), impel (to), prompt (to), spur (to); **что ~би́ло вас уйти́?** what made you go?
побу́дк|а, и *f.* (*mil.*) reveille.
побужда́|ть, ю *impf. of* **побуди́ть**
побужде́ни|е, я *nt.* motive; inducement; incentive; **по со́бственному ~ю** of one's own accord.
побуре́|ть, ю *pf. of* **буре́ть**
побыва́льщин|а, ы *f.* (*obs.*) narration; true story.
побыва́|ть, ю *pf.* **1.** to have been, have visited; **он ~л всю́ду** he has been everywhere; **в про́шлом году́ мы ~ли в Норве́гии и в Шве́ции** last year we were in Norway and Sweden. **2.** (*coll.*) to look in, visit; **мне на́до п. в конто́ре** I have to look in at the office.
побы́вк|а, и *f.* leave, furlough; **прие́хать домо́й на ~у** to come home on leave.
по|бы́ть, бу́ду, бу́дешь, *past* **~́был, ~была́, ~́было** *pf.* to stay (*for a short time*); **мы ~́были в Ло́ндоне два дня** we stayed in London for two days.
пова́|дить, жу, дишь *pf.* (*of* **~живать**[1]) (*coll.*) to accustom; to train.
пова́|диться, жусь, дишься *pf.* (+*inf.*; *coll.*, *pej.*) to get into the habit (of); to take to going (somewhere).
пова́дк|а, и *f.* (*coll.*) habit.
пова́дливост|ь, и *f.* (*coll.*) susceptibility; amenableness.
пова́длив|ый (~, ~а) *adj.* (*coll.*) susceptible; amenable.
пова́дно *only in phr.* **что́бы не́ было п.** (+*d.*) (in order) to teach not to do so (again).
пова́жива|ть[1]**, ю** *impf. of* **пова́дить**
пова́жива|ть[2]**, ю** *impf.* (*coll.*) to take from time to time.
повал|и́ть[1]**, ю́, ~́ишь** *pf. of* **вали́ть**[1]
повал|и́ть[2]**, ю́, ~́ишь** *pf.* to begin to throng, begin to pour; **дым ~и́л из трубы́** smoke began to belch from the chimney; **снег ~и́л хло́пьями** snow began to fall in flakes.
пова́льно *adv.* without exception.
пова́льн|ый *adj.* general, mass; **п. о́быск** general search; **~ая боле́знь** epidemic.
пова́нива|ть, ет *impf.* (*coll.*) to smell slightly.
пова́пленный *adj. only in phr.* **гроб п.** (*fig.*) whited sepulchre.
по́вар, а, *pl.* **~а́** *m.* cook; **п.-ма́стер** master chef.
пова́ренн|ый *adj.* culinary; **~ая кни́га** cookery-book; **~ая соль** common salt, table salt (*sodium chloride*).
повар|ёнок, ёнка, *pl.* **~я́та, ~я́т** *m.* (*coll.*) kitchen-boy.
поварёшк|а, и *f.* (*coll.*) ladle, strainer.
повари́х|а, и *f. of* **по́вар**
пова́рнича|ть, ю *impf.* (*coll.*) to cook, be a cook.
пова́р|ня, ни, *g. pl.* **~ен** *f.* (*obs.*) kitchen.
поварско́й *adj. of* **по́вар**
по-ва́шему *adv.* **1.** in your opinion. **2.** as you wish.
пове́д|ать, аю *pf.* (*of* **~ывать**) to relate, communicate; **п. та́йну** to disclose a secret.
поведе́ни|е, я *nt.* conduct, behaviour.
пове́дыва|ть, ю *impf. of* **пове́дать**
повез|ти́, у́, ёшь, *past* **~́, ~ла́** *pf. of* **везти́**
повелева́|ть, ю *impf.* **1.** (+*i.*, *obs.*) to command, rule. **2.** (+*d. and inf.*) to enjoin; **так ~ет мне со́весть** thus my conscience enjoins.
повеле́ни|е, я *nt.* (*obs.*) command, injunction.
повел|е́ть, ю́, и́шь *pf.* to order, command.
повели́тел|ь, я *m.* (*obs.*, *rhet.*) sovereign, master.
повели́тельниц|а, ы *f.* (*obs.*, *rhet.*) sovereign, mistress, lady.
повели́тел|ьный (~ен, ~ьна) *adj.* imperious, peremptory; authoritative; **п. жест** imperious gesture; **п. тон** peremptory tone; **~ьное наклоне́ние** (*gram.*) imperative mood.
повенча́|ть(ся), ю(сь) *pf. of* **венча́ть(ся)**[1]
поверг|а́ть, а́ю *impf. of* **~́нуть**
пове́рг|нуть, ну, нешь, *past* ~, **~ла** *pf.* (*of* **~а́ть**) **1.** (*obs.*) to throw down, lay low; **боле́знь ~ла его́ в посте́ль** the illness has prostrated him. **2.** (**в**+*a.*) to plunge (into); **п. в отча́яние, уны́ние** to plunge into despair, depression.
пове́р|енный *p.p.p. of* **~ить**[2]; *as n.* **п., ~енного** *m.* **1.** (*also* **~енная, ~енной** *f.*) confidant(e). **2.** attorney; **прися́жный п.** (*obs.*) barrister; **п. в дела́х** chargé d'affaires.
пове́р|ить[1]**, ю, ишь** *pf. of* **ве́рить**
пове́р|ить[2]**, ю, ишь** *pf.* (*of* **~я́ть**) **1.** to check (up); to verify. **2.** (+*d.*) to confide (to), entrust (to); **п. кому́-н. та́йну** to confide a secret to s.o.
пове́рк|а, и *f.* **1.** check, check-up; checking up, verification; (*math.*) proof. **2.** (*mil.*) roll-call; **п. карау́лов** turning-out of the guard.
повер|ну́ть, ну́, нёшь *pf.* (*of* **~́тывать**) to turn; (*fig.*) to change; **п. разгово́р** to change the subject (*of a conversation*).
повер|ну́ться, ну́сь, нёшься *pf.* (*of* **~́тываться**) to turn; **п. круго́м** to turn round, turn about; **п. спино́й (к)** to turn one's back (upon); **п. на я́коре** to swing at anchor; **п. к лу́чшему** to take a turn for the better.
пове́р|очный *adj. of* **~ка; ~очные испыта́ния** tests.
пове́рстн|ый *adj.* (*measured*) by versts; **~ая пла́та** payment by the verst.
пове́ртыва|ть(ся), ю(сь) *impf. of* **поверну́ть(ся)**
пове́рх *prep.*+*g.* over, above; on top of; **смотре́ть п. очко́в** to look over the top of one's spectacles.
пове́рхностност|ь, и *f.* superficiality.
пове́рхностн|ый *adj.* **1.** surface, superficial; **~ная зака́лка** (*tech.*) case hardening; **~ное натяже́ние** (*tech.*) surface tension; **п. разря́д** (*elec.*) surface discharge; **~ная ра́на** superficial injury; **~ное унаво́живание** (*agric.*) top

dressing. **2.** (**~ен, ~на**) (*fig.*) superficial; shallow; perfunctory.
пове́рхност|ь, и *f.* surface.
по́верху *adv.* on the surface, on top.
пове́р|ье, ья, *g. pl.* **~ий** *nt.* popular belief, superstition.
повер|я́ть, я́ю *impf. of* **~и́ть**
пове́с|а, ы *m.* (*coll.*) rake, scapegrace.
повеселе́|ть, ю *pf.* to cheer up, become cheerful.
повесел|и́ть(ся), ю́(сь), и́шь(ся) *pf. of* **весели́ть(ся)**
по-весе́ннему *adv.* as in spring.
пове́|сить(ся), шу(сь), сишь(ся) *pf. of* **ве́шать(ся)**[1]
пове́снича|ть, ю *impf.* (*coll.*) to lead a wild life.
повествова́ни|е, я *nt.* narrative, narration.
повествова́тельный *adj.* narrative.
повеств|ова́ть, у́ю *impf.* (**о**+*p.*) to narrate, recount, relate.
пове|сти́[1], **ду́, дёшь,** *past* **~л, ~ла́** *pf. of* **вести́ 1.**
пове|сти́[2], **ду́, дёшь,** *past* **~л, ~ла́** *pf.* (*of* **поводи́ть**[1]) (+*i.*) to move; **п. бровя́ми** to raise one's eye-brows; **он и бро́вью не ~л** he did not turn a hair.
пове|сти́сь, ду́сь, дёшься, *past* **~лся, ~ла́сь** *pf. of* **вести́сь; уж так ~ло́сь** (*coll.*) such is the custom.
пове́стк|а, и *f.* **1.** notice, notification; **п. на заседа́ние** notice of meeting; **п. в суд** summons, writ, subpoena; **п. дня** agenda, order of the day; **на ~е дня** on the agenda (*also fig.*). **2.** signal; bugle call.
по́вест|ь, и, *pl.* **~и, ~е́й** *f.* story, tale.
пове́три|е, я *nt.* (*coll.*) epidemic, infection (*also fig.*); **п. на дифтери́т** diphtheria epidemic.
пове́т|ь, и *f.* (*dial.*) loft (*in peasant hut*).
пове́шени|е, я *nt.* hanging.
пове́|шенный *p.p.p. of* **~сить**; *as n.* **п., ~шенного** *m.* hanged man.
пове́|ять, ет *pf.* **1.** to begin to blow; to blow softly. **2.** (*impers.*, +*i.*) to breathe (of); (*fig.*) to begin to be felt; **~яло прохла́дой** there came a breath of fresh air.
повздо́р|ить, ю, ишь *pf. of* **вздо́рить**
повзросле́|ть, ю *pf.* to grow up.
повива́льн|ый *adj.* (*obs.*) obstetric; **~ая ба́бка** midwife; **~ое иску́сство** midwifery.
повида́|ть, ю *pf.* (*coll.*) to see.
повида́|ться, юсь *pf. of* **вида́ться**
по-ви́димому *adv.* apparently, to all appearance, seemingly.
пови́дл|о, а *nt.* jam.
повили́к|а, и *f.* (*bot.*) dodder.
повин|и́ться, ю́сь, и́шься *pf. of* **вини́ться**
пови́нн|ая, ой *f.* confession, acknowledgement of guilt; **принести́ ~ую, яви́ться с ~ой** to give o.s. up; to plead guilty; to acknowledge one's guilt, own up.
пови́нност|ь, и *f.* duty, obligation; **доро́жная п.** compulsory road maintenance; **во́инская п.** compulsory military service, conscription.
пови́н|ный (**~ен, ~на**) *adj.* **1.** guilty. **2.** (*obs.*) obliged, bound.
повин|ова́ться, у́юсь *impf.* (*in past tense also pf.*) (+*d.*) to obey.
повинове́ни|е, я *nt.* obedience.
повис|а́ть, а́ю *impf. of* **~нуть**
пови|се́ть, шу́, си́шь *pf.* to hang for a time.
пови́с|нуть, ну, нешь, *past* **~, ~ла** *pf.* (*of* **~а́ть**) **1.** (**на**+*p.*) to hang (by). **2.** to hang down, droop; **п. в во́здухе** (*fig.*) to hang in mid-air; (*of a joke*) to fall flat.
повиту́х|а, и *f.* (*coll.*) midwife.
повлажне́|ть, ю *pf. of* **влажне́ть**
повле́|чь, ку́, чёшь, ку́т, *past* **~к, ~кла́** *pf.* (**за собо́й**) to entail, bring in one's train; **п. за собо́й неприя́тные после́дствия** to have unpleasant consequences.
повлия́|ть, ю *pf. of* **влия́ть**
по́вод[1], **а,** *pl.* **~ы** *m.* (**к**) occasion, cause, ground (for, of); **п. к войне́** casus belli; **дать п.** (+*d.*) to give occasion (to), give cause (for); **дать п. к напа́дкам** to lay o.s. open; **без вся́кого ~а** without cause; **по ~у** (+*g.*) apropos (of), as regards, concerning; **по како́му ~у?** in what connection? why?
по́вод[2], **а, о ~е, на ~у́,** *pl.* **~а́, ~ов** *or* **~ья, ~ьев** *m.* rein; **быть у кого́-н. на ~у́** (*fig.*) to be under s.o.'s thumb.
пово|ди́ть[1], **жу́, ~дишь** *impf. of* **повести́**[2]
пово|ди́ть[2], **жу́, ~дишь** *pf.* to make go; **п. ло́шадь** to walk a horse.
повод|о́к, ка́ *m.* (dog's) lead.
поводы́р|ь, я́ *m.* (*coll.*) leader, guide.
пово́зк|а, и *f.* **1.** vehicle, conveyance. **2.** (*unsprung*) carriage.
пово́йник, а *m.* (*obs.*) povoynik (*kind of kerchief worn on the head by married Russ. peasant woman*).
пово́лжский *adj.* situated on the Volga.
повора́чива|ть(ся), ю(сь) *impf. of* **повороти́ть(ся); ~йся!, ~йтесь!** (*coll.*) get a move on! look sharp!
поворож|и́ть, у́, и́шь *pf. of* **ворожи́ть**
поворо́т, а *m.* turn(ing); **огни́ ~а** direction indicator lamps (*of car*); (*fig.*) turning-point; **п. реки́** bend; **пе́рвый п. напра́во** the first turning to the right; **на ~е доро́ги** at the turn of the road; **п. к лу́чшему** turn for the better.
поворо|ти́ть(ся), чу́(сь), ~тишь(ся) *pf. of* **повора́чивать(ся)** to turn.
поворо́тливост|ь, и *f.* **1.** nimbleness, agility, quickness. **2.** (*tech., naut.*) manoeuvrability, handiness.
поворо́тлив|ый (**~, ~а**) *adj.* **1.** nimble, agile, quick. **2.** (*tech., naut.*) manoeuvrable, handy.
поворо́тн|ый *adj.* rotary, rotating, revolving; (*fig.*) turning; **п. кран** slewing crane, swing crane; **п. круг** turn-table; **п. крюк** shackle hook; **п. мост** swing bridge; **п. резе́ц** swing tool; **~ое сиде́нье** swivel seat; **~ые сала́зки** swivel carriage; **п. моме́нт, п. пункт** turning-point.
повре|ди́ть, жу́, ди́шь *pf.* **1.** *pf. of* **вреди́ть. 2.** (*pf. of* **~жда́ть**) to damage; to injure, hurt; **п. себе́ но́гу** to hurt one's leg.
повре|ди́ться, жу́сь, ди́шься *pf.* (*of* **~жда́ться**) to be damaged; to be injured; **п. в уме́** (*coll.*) to become mentally deranged.
поврежда́|ть(ся), ю(сь) *impf. of* **повреди́ть(ся)**
поврежде́ни|е, я *nt.* damage, injury.
повре|ждённый *p.p.p. of* **~ди́ть; п. в уме́** (*coll.*) mentally deranged.
повремен|и́ть, ю́, и́шь *pf.* (*coll.*) to wait a little; (**с**+*i.*) to delay (over).
повреме́нн|ый *adj.* **1.** periodical. **2.** reckoned on time basis; **~ая опла́та** payment by time (*by the hour, etc.*); **~ая рабо́та** time-work (*work paid by the hour, etc.*).
повседне́вно *adv.* daily, every day.
повседне́вност|ь, и *f.* daily occurrence.
повседне́вн|ый *adj.* daily; everyday; **~ая рабо́та** daily task; **п. слу́чай** everyday occurrence.
повсеме́стно *adv.* everywhere, in all parts.
повсеме́ст|ный (**~ен, ~на**) *adj.* universal, general.
повска|ка́ть, ~чет *pf.* to jump up one after another.
повска́кива|ть, ет *pf.* = **повскака́ть**
повста́н|ец, ца *m.* insurgent, rebel.
повста́нческий *adj.* insurgent, rebel.
повстреча́|ть, ю *pf.* (*coll.*) to meet, run into.
повстреча́|ться, юсь *pf.* (+*d.* or **с**+*i.*) to meet, run into; **мне ~лся знако́мый, я ~лся с знако́мым** I met an acquaintance.
повсю́ду *adv.* everywhere.
повто́р, а *m.* replay.
повторе́ни|е, я *nt.* **1.** repetition; reiteration; **кра́ткое п.** recapitulation. **2.** recurrence. **3.** revision (*of school work*).
повтори́тельный *adj.* recapitulatory; **п. курс** refresher course.
повтор|и́ть, ю́, и́шь *pf.* (*of* **~я́ть**) **1.** to repeat; to reiterate. **2.** to revise (*school work*).
повтор|и́ться, ю́сь, и́шься *pf.* (*of* **~я́ться**) **1.** to repeat o.s. **2.** to recur. **3.** *pass. of* **~и́ть**
повто́рный *adj.* repeated; recurring.
повтор|я́ть(ся), я́ю(сь) *impf. of* **~и́ть(ся)**
повыси́тельный *adj.* (*elec.*) step-up.
повы́|сить, шу, сишь *pf.* (*of* **~ша́ть**) **1.** to raise, heighten; **п. вдвое́, втрое́** to double, treble; **п. в пять раз,** *etc.*, to raise five-fold, *etc.*; **п. давле́ние** to increase pressure; **п. го́лос** to raise one's voice (*also fig., in anger*). **2.** to promote, prefer, advance; **п. кого́-н. по слу́жбе** to give s.o. promotion.
повы́|ситься, шусь, сишься *pf.* (*of* **~ша́ться**) **1.** to rise;

to improve; **п. в чьём-н. мне́нии** to rise in s.o.'s estimation; **на́ши а́кции ~сились** our shares have gone up; (*fig.*) our stock has risen. **2.** to be promoted, receive advancement.
повыша́|ть(ся), ю(сь) *impf. of* **повы́сить(ся)**
повы́ше *comp. adj. and adv.* a little higher (up); a little taller.
повыше́ни|е, я *nt.* rise, increase; **п. по слу́жбе** advancement, promotion, preferment.
повы́|шенный *p.p.p. of* **~сить** *and adj.* heightened; increased; **~шенное настрое́ние** state of excitement; **~шенная температу́ра** high temperature; **~шенная чувстви́тельность** heightened sensibility.
повя|за́ть[1], **жу́, ~жешь** *pf.* (*of* **~зывать**) to tie; **п. га́лстук** to tie a tie; **п. го́лову платко́м** to tie a scarf on one's head.
повя|за́ть[2], **жу́, ~жешь** *pf.* to do a little knitting, knit for a while.
повя|за́ться, жу́сь, ~жешься *pf.* (*of* **~зываться**) (*+i.*) to tie o.s. (with); **п. (платко́м)** to tie a scarf on one's head.
повя́зк|а, и *f.* **1.** band; fillet. **2.** bandage.
повя́зыва|ть(ся), ю(сь) *impf. of* **повяза́ть(ся)**
погада́|ть, ю *pf. of* **гада́ть**
пога́н|ец, ца *m.* (*coll.*) rascal.
пога́н|ить, ю, ишь *impf.* (*of* **о~**) (*coll.*) to pollute, defile.
пога́н|ка, ки *f.* **1.** = **~ый гриб. 2.** (*zool.*) grebe. **3.** *f. of* **~ец**
пога́н|ый (~, ~а) *adj.* **1.** foul, unclean; **п. гриб** non-edible mushroom, toadstool; **~ая пи́ща** (*relig.*) unclean food; **~ое ведро́** garbage can, refuse pail. **2.** (*coll.*) foul, filthy, vile; **~ое настрое́ние** foul mood. **3.** (*obs.*) non-Christian.
по́ган|ь, и *f.* (*collect.*; *pej.*) filth; dregs.
погаса́|ть, ю *impf.* to go out, be extinguished.
пога|си́ть, шу́, ~сишь *pf.* (*of* **гаси́ть** *and* **~ша́ть**) to liquidate, cancel; **п. долг** to clear off a debt; **п. ма́рку** to cancel a stamp.
пога́с|нуть, ну, нешь, *past* **~, ~ла** *pf. of* **га́снуть**
погаша́|ть, ю *impf. of* **погаси́ть**
пога́|шенный *p.p.p. of* **~си́ть** *and adj.* used (*of postage stamps, etc.*); cashed.
погиб|а́ть, а́ю *impf. of* **~нуть**
поги́бел|ь, и *f.* (*obs.*) ruin, perdition; **согну́ться в три ~и** to be hunched up; (*fig.*) to be reduced to submission, be cowed.
поги́бельный *adj.* (*obs.*) ruinous, fatal.
поги́б|нуть, ну, нешь, *past* **~, ~ла** *pf.* (*of* **ги́бнуть** *and* **~а́ть**) to perish; (*naut. and fig.*) to be lost; **кора́бль ~ со всей кома́ндой** the ship was lost with all hands.
поги́б|ший *p.p. of* **~нуть** *and adj.* (*obs.*) lost, ruined.
погла́|дить[1], **жу, дишь** *pf. of* **гла́дить**
погла́|дить[2], **жу, дишь** *pf.* to do a little ironing.
погла́жива|ть, ю *impf.* to stroke (*every so oft., from time to time*).
поглазе́|ть, ю *pf. of* **глазе́ть**
погло|ти́ть, щу́, ~тишь *pf.* (*of* **~ща́ть**) to swallow up, take up, absorb (*also fig.*); **п. во́ду** to absorb water; **п. чьё-н. внима́ние** to engross s.o.; **п. рома́н** to devour a novel.
поглоща́емост|ь, и *f.* absorbability.
поглоща́|ть, ю *impf. of* **поглоти́ть**
поглупе́|ть, ю *pf. of* **глупе́ть**
погля|де́ть, жу́, ди́шь *pf.* **1.** *pf. of* **гляде́ть. 2.** to have a look. **3.** to look for a while.
погля|де́ться, жу́сь, ди́шься *pf. of* **гляде́ться**
погля́дыва|ть, ю *impf.* **1.** (**на**+*a.*) to cast looks, glance (at, upon); to look from time to time (at). **2.** (**за**+*i.*; *coll.*) to keep an eye (on).
по|гна́ть, гоню́, го́нишь, *past* **~гна́л, ~гнала́, ~гна́ло** *pf.* to drive; to begin to drive.
по|гна́ться, гоню́сь, го́нишься, *past* **~гна́лся, ~гнала́сь, ~гна́ло́сь** *pf.* (**за**+*i.*) to run (after); to start in pursuit (of), give chase; (*fig.*) to strive (after, for); **п. за эффе́ктами** to strive for effect.
погни́|ть, ю, ёшь, *past* **~л, ~ла́, ~ло** *pf.* to rot, decay, moulder.
погн|у́ть, у́, ёшь *pf.* to bend.
погн|у́ться, ётся *pf.* to bend (*intrans.*).
погнуша́|ться, юсь *pf. of* **гнуша́ться**
погова́рива|ть, ю *impf.* (**о**+*p.*) to talk (of); **~ют** there is talk (of); it is rumoured; **~ют о его́ жени́тьбе** there is talk of his marrying; it is rumoured that he is getting married.
поговор|и́ть, ю́, и́шь *pf.* to have a talk.
погово́рк|а, и *f.* (*proverbial*) saying, by-word; **войти́ в ~у** to become a by-word, become proverbial.
пого́д|а, ы *f.* weather; **кака́я бы ни была́ п.** rain or shine, wet or fine; **э́то не де́лает ~ы** that is not what counts, this does not affect the matter; **ждать у мо́ря (***or* **у́ моря) ~ы** to wait for sth. to turn up.
пого|ди́ть, жу́, ди́шь *pf.* (*coll.*) to wait a little; **~ди́те!** wait a moment! one moment!; **немно́го ~дя́** a little later.
пого́д|ки, ков *pl.* (*sg.* **~ок, ~ка** *m.*) brothers or sisters born at a year's interval; **мы с ней п.** there is a year's difference between us.
пого́дный[1] *adj.* annual, yearly.
пого́д|ный[2] *adj. of* **~а**
пого́жий *adj.* fine, lovely (*of weather*).
поголо́вно *adv.* one and all; (all) to a man.
поголо́вн|ый *adj.* general, universal; **п. нало́г** poll-tax, capitation(-tax); **~ое ополче́ние** levy in mass; **~ая пе́репись** universal census.
поголо́вь|е, я *nt.* (number of) live-stock.
поголубе́|ть, ю *pf. of* **голубе́ть**
пого́н[1], **а** *m.* (*mil.*) **1.** shoulder-strap. **2.** (rifle-)sling.
пого́н[2], **а** *m.* distillate, fraction.
пого́нный *adj.* linear.
пого́нщик, а *m.* driver, teamster; **п. му́лов** muleteer.
пого́н|я, и *f.* pursuit, chase.
погоня́|ть[1], **ю** *impf.* to urge on, drive (*also fig.*).
погоня́|ть[2], **ю** *pf.* to drive (*for a certain time*).
погор|а́ть, а́ю *impf. of* **~е́ть**[1]
погоре́л|ец, ьца *m.* one who has lost all his possessions in a fire; fire victim.
погор|е́ть[1], **ю́, и́шь** *pf.* (*of* **~а́ть**) **1.** to lose all one's possessions in a fire. **2.** to burn down; to be burnt out.
погор|е́ть[2], **ю́, и́шь** *pf.* to burn for a while.
погоряч|и́ться, у́сь, и́шься *pf.* to get heated (*fig.*), get worked up.
пого́ст, а *m.* (*obs.*) **1.** country churchyard. **2.** pogost (*country church together with cemetery and clergy house and adjacent buildings*).
пого|сти́ть, щу́, сти́шь *pf.* (**у**) to stay for a while (at, with).
погран... *comb. form* frontier(-).
пограни́чник, а *m.* frontier-guard.
пограни́чно-пропускно́й *adj.*: **п. пункт** border control post.
пограни́чн|ый *adj.* frontier; boundary; **п. столб** boundary post; **~ая стра́жа** frontier guards.
по́греб, а, *pl.* **~а́** *m.* cellar (*also fig.*); **ви́нный п.** wine-cellar; **порохово́й п.** powder-magazine (*also fig.*).
погреба́льн|ый *adj.* funeral; **п. звон** knell; **~ое пе́ние** dirge.
погреба́|ть, ю *impf. of* **погрести́**[1]
погребе́ни|е, я *nt.* burial, interment.
погреб|е́ц, ца́ *m.* (*obs.*) provisions hamper.
погрему́шк|а, и *f.* rattle.
погре|сти́[1], **бу́, бёшь,** *past* **~ёб, ~бла́** *pf.* (*of* **~ба́ть**) to bury.
погре|сти́[2], **бу́, бёшь,** *past* **~ёб, ~бла́** *pf.* to row a little.
погре́|ть, ю *pf.* to warm.
погре́|ться, юсь *pf.* to warm o.s.
погреш|а́ть, а́ю *impf. of* **~и́ть**
погреш|и́ть, у́, и́шь *pf.* (*of* **~а́ть**) (**про́тив**) to sin (against); to err.
погре́шност|ь, и *f.* error, mistake, inaccuracy; **треуго́льник ~и** (*naut.*) cocked hat.
погро|зи́ть, жу́, зи́шь *pf. of* **грози́ть 2.**
погро|зи́ться, жу́сь, зи́шься *pf. of* **грози́ться**
погро́м, а *m.* pogrom, massacre.
погро́м|ный *adj. of* **~**
погро́мщик, а *m.* pers. organizing *or* taking part in a pogrom.
погромых|а́ть, а́ю *pf.* (*of* **~ивать**) (*of thunder*) to rumble intermittently.

погромы́хива|ть, ю *impf. of* **погромыхáть**
погружá|ть(ся), ю(сь) *impf. of* **погрузи́ть(ся); ~емый нагревáтель** immersion heater.
погружéни|е, я *nt.* sinking, submergence; immersion; (*of a submarine*) dive, diving.
погру́|женный *and* **~жённый** *p.p.p. of* **~зи́ть; п. в вóду** immersed (in water); **п. в размышлéния** deep in thought; **п. в себя́** wrapped up in o.s.
погру|зи́ть, жу́, ~зи́шь *pf.* (*of* **~жáть**) **1.** (**в**+*a.*) to dip (into), plunge (into), immerse; to submerge; to duck. **2.** *pf. of* **грузи́ть 2.**
погру|зи́ться, жу́сь, ~зи́шься *pf.* **1.** (**в**+*a.*) to sink (into), plunge (into); (*of a submarine*) to submerge, dive; (*fig.*) to be plunged (in); to be absorbed (in), be buried (in), be lost (in); **п. в темнотý** to be plunged into darkness; **п. в чтéние** to be absorbed in reading; **п. в размышлéния** to be deep in thought. **2.** *pf. of* **грузи́ться**
погру́зк|а, и *f.* loading; lading, shipment.
погру́зочно-разгру́зочный *adj.* loading-and-unloading.
погру́зочный *adj.* loading; **п. жёлоб** loading chute.
погряз|áть, áю *impf. of* **~нуть**
погря́з|нуть, ну, нешь, *past* **~, ~ла** *pf.* (*of* **~áть**) (**в**+*p.*) to be stuck (in); to be bogged down (in); to wallow (in) (*also fig.*); **п. в долгáх** to be up to one's eyes in debt.
погуб|и́ть, лю́, ~ишь *pf. of* **губи́ть**
погу́дк|а, и *f.* (*coll.*) tune, melody; **стáрая п. на нóвый лад** (*fig.*) the same tune in a new setting, the (same) old story.
погу́лива|ть, ю *impf.* (*coll.*) **1.** to walk up and down. **2.** to go on the spree from time to time.
погуля́|ть, ю *pf. of* **гуля́ть**
погусте́|ть, ет *pf. of* **густéть**
под[1]**, а, о ~е, на ~у́** *m.* hearth(-stone); sole (of furnace).
под[2] (*also* **подо**) *prep.* **1.** (+*a. and i.*) under; **постáвить п. стол** to put under the table; **находи́ться п. столóм** to be under the table; **п. арéстом** under arrest; **п. ви́дом** (+*g.*) under, in the guise (of); **п. влия́нием** (+*g.*) under the influence (of); **п. вопрóсом** open to question; **пóд гору** downhill; **п. замкóм** under lock and key; **п. землёй** underground; **быть п. ружьём** to be under arms; **взять когó-н. пóд руку** to take s.o.'s arm; **п. рукóй** (close) at hand, to hand; **отдáть п. суд** to prosecute; **п. услóвием** on condition. **2.** (+*a. and i.*) in the environs of, near; **жить п. Москвóй** to live near Moscow; **поéхать на дáчу п. Москвý** to go to a dacha near Moscow; **би́тва п. Бородинóм** the battle of Borodino. **3.** (+*i.*) occupied by, used as; (+*a.*) for; (to serve) as; **помещéние под шкóлой** premises occupied by a school; **отвести́ помещéние п. шкóлу** to earmark premises for a school; **бáнка п. варéнье** jam jar; **пóле п. пшени́цей** wheat-field. **4.** (+*a.*) towards (*of time*); on the eve of; **п. вéчер** towards evening; **п. Нóвый год** on New Year's Eve; **емý п. пятьдеся́т (лет)** he is getting on for fifty. **5.** (+*a.*) to (the accompaniment of); **танцевáть п. граммофóнные пласти́нки** to dance to gramophone records; **писáть п. диктóвку** to write from dictation. **6.** (+*a.*) in imitation of; **э́то сдéлано п. орéх** it is imitation walnut; **он пи́шет п. Тургéнева** he writes in imitation of (*the style of*) Turgenev. **7.** (+*a.*) on (= *in exchange for*); **п. залóг** on security; **п. распи́ску** on receipt. **8.** (+*i.*) (*meant, etc.*) by; **что нáдо понимáть п. э́тим выражéнием?** what is meant by this expression?; **что п. э́тим подразумевáется?** what is implied by this? **9.** (+*i.*; *cul.*) in, with; **ры́ба п. бешамéлью** fish cooked in white sauce; **говя́дина п. хрéном** beef with horse-radish.
под...[1] (*also* **подо...** *and* **подъ...**) *as vbl. pref. indicates* **1.** *action from beneath or affecting lower part of sth., as* **подчеркнýть** to underline. **2.** *motion upwards, as* **подня́ть** to raise. **3.** *motion towards, as* **подъéхать** to approach. **4.** *action carried out or event occurring in slight degree, as* **подкрáсить** to touch up; **поджи́ть** to begin to heal up. **5.** *supplementary action, as* **подрабóтать** to earn additionally. **6.** *underhand action, as* **подкупи́ть** to bribe.
под...[2] (*also* **подо...** *and* **подъ...**) *as pref. of nn. and adjs.* under-, sub-.
подавáльщик, а *m.* **1.** waiter. **2.** supplier. **3.** (*sport; in game of lapta*) pitcher.
подавáльщиц|а, ы *f.* waitress.
пода|вáть(ся), ю́(сь), ёшь(ся) *impf. of* **подáть(ся)**
подав|и́ть[1]**, лю́, ~ишь** *pf.* (*of* **~ля́ть**) **1.** to suppress, put down; to repress; **п. восстáние** to put down a rising; **п. стон** to stifle a groan. **2.** (*fig.*) to depress; to crush, overwhelm. **3.** (*mil.*) to neutralize.
подав|и́ть[2]**, лю́, ~ишь** *pf.* (*no impf.*) **1.** (*coll.*) to press, trample (*a quantity of*). **2.** to press, squeeze for a time.
подав|и́ться, лю́сь, ~ишься *pf. of* **дави́ться**
подавлéни|е, я *nt.* **1.** suppression; repression. **2.** (*mil.*) neutralization.
подáвленност|ь, и *f.* depression; blues.
подáв|ленный *p.p.p. of* **~и́ть** *and adj.* **1.** suppressed; **п. стон** muffled groan. **2.** depressed, dispirited.
подáвлива|ть, ю *impf.* to exert slight pressure.
подавля́|ть, ю *impf. of* **подави́ть**[1]
подавля́|ющий *pres. part. act. of* **~ть** *and adj.* overwhelming; overpowering; **~ющее большинствó** overwhelming majority.
подáвно *adv.* so much the more, all the more.
подáгр|а, ы *f.* gout, podagra.
подáгрик, а *m.* gouty pers., sufferer from gout.
подагри́ческий *adj.* gouty.
подáльше *adv.* (*coll.*) a little farther.
подар|и́ть, ю́, ~ишь *pf. of* **дари́ть**
подáр|ок, ка *m.* present, gift; **получи́ть в п.** to receive as a present.
подáтел|ь, я *m.* bearer (*of a letter, etc.*); **п. прошéния** petitioner.
подáтливост|ь, и *f.* **1.** pliancy, pliability. **2.** (*fig.*) complaisance.
подáтлив|ый (~, ~а) *adj.* **1.** pliant, pliable. **2.** (*fig.*) complaisant.
податн|óй *adj.* (*hist.*) tax, duty; **п. инспéктор** assessor of taxes; **~áя систéма** taxation; *as n.* **п., ~óго** *m.* = **п. инспéктор**
пóдат|ь, и, *pl.* **~и, ~éй** *f.* (*hist.*) tax, duty, assessment.
по|дáть, дáм, дáшь, дáст, дади́м, дади́те, дадýт *past* **~дал, ~далá, ~дало** *pf.* (*of* **~давáть**) **1.** (*in var. senses*) to give; to proffer; **п. гóлос** to vote; **п. знак** to give a sign; **п. пóмощь** to lend a hand, proffer aid; **п. примéр** to set an example; **п. рýку** (+*d.*) to offer one's hand; **п. сигнáл** to give the signal; **~дáйте ей пальтó** help her on with her coat. **2.** to serve (*food*); **п. на стол** to serve up; **обéд ~дан** dinner is served. **3.** to bring up (*train or other conveyance*); **слéдующий пóезд ~дадýт на э́ту платфóрму** the next train will come in at this platform. **4.** to put, move, turn; **п. лóшадь в галóп** to put a horse into a gallop. **5.** (*sport*): **п. мяч** to serve. **6.** to serve, forward, present, hand in (*application, complaint, etc.*); **п. апелля́цию** to appeal; **п. жáлобу** to lodge a complaint; **п. заявлéние** to hand in an application; **п. телегрáмму** to send a telegram; **п. в отстáвку** to tender one's resignation; **п. в суд (на**+*a.*) to bring an action (against). **7.** (*liter., theatr.*) to present, display. **8.** (*tech.*) to feed.
по|дáться, дáмся, дáшься, дáстся, дади́мся, дади́тесь, дадýтся, *past* **~дáлся, ~далáсь, ~далóсь** *pf.* (*of* **~давáться**) **1.** to move; **п. назáд** to draw back; **п. в стóрону** to move aside. **2.** (*coll.*) to give way, yield (*also fig.*); to cave in, collapse. **3.** (**на**+*a.*; *coll.*) to make (for), set out (for).
подáч|а, и *f.* **1.** giving, presenting; **п. гóлоса** voting; **п. заявлéния** sending in of application. **2.** (*sport*) service, serve. **3.** (*tech.*) feed, feeding, supply; (*chem.*) introduction; **высотá ~и** lift (*of pump*); **корóбка ~и** gear-box, feed unit.
подáчк|а, и *f.* (*coll.*) **1.** sop; crumb. **2.** (*fig.*) tip.
подая́ни|е, я *nt.* charity, alms; dole.
подбáв|ить, лю, ишь *pf.* (*of* **~ля́ть**) (+*a. or g.*) to add; **п. сáхару в кóфе** to put (more) sugar in coffee; **п. рóму в чай** to lace tea with rum.
подбáвк|а, и *f.* addition.
подбавля́|ть, ю *impf. of* **подбáвить**
подбáлтыва|ть, ю *impf. of* **подболтáть**
подбегá|ть, ю *impf. of* **подбежáть**

подбе|жа́ть, гу́, жи́шь, гу́т *pf.* (*of* **~га́ть**) **(к)** to run up (to), come running up (to).

подберёзовик, а *m.* brown mushroom (*Boletus scaber*).

подбива́|ть, ю *impf. of* **подби́ть**

подби́вк|а, и *f.* **1.** lining. **2.** re-soling.

подбира́|ть(ся), ю(сь) *impf. of* **подобра́ть(ся)**

подби́т|ый *p.p.p. of* **~ь; п. ва́той** wadded; **п. ме́хом** fur-lined; **п. глаз** black eye.

под|би́ть, обью́, обьёшь *pf.* (*of* **~бива́ть**) **1.** (+*i.*) to line (with). **2.** to re-sole. **3.** to injure; to bruise; **п. кому́-н. глаз** to give s.o. a black eye. **4.** (*mil.*) to put out of action, knock out; **п. самолёт** to shoot down a plane. **5.** (+*inf. or* **на**+*a.*; *coll.*) to incite (to), instigate (to).

подбодр|и́ть, ю́, и́шь *pf.* (*of* **~я́ть**) (*coll.*) to cheer up, encourage.

подбодр|и́ться, ю́сь, и́шься *pf.* (*of* **~я́ться**) to cheer up, take heart.

подбодр|я́ть(ся), я́ю(сь) *impf. of* **~и́ть(ся)**

подбо́йк|а, и *f.* **1.** lining. **2.** re-soling. **3.** (*tech.*) swage.

подболта́|ть, ю *pf.* (*of* **подба́лтывать**) (+*a. or g.*) to mix in, stir in; **п. молока́ в суп** to stir milk into soup.

подбо́р, а *m.* **1.** selection, assortment; **(как) на п.** choice, well-matched. **2.: в п.** (*typ.*) run on.

подбо́рк|а, и *f.* set, selection (*esp. a section of related news items under a single heading in a newspaper*).

подборо́д|ок, ка *m.* chin.

подбоче́нива|ться, юсь *impf. of* **подбоче́ниться**

подбоче́нившись *adv.* with one's arms akimbo, with one's hands on one's hips.

подбоче́н|иться, юсь, ишься *pf.* (*of* **~иваться**) to place one's arms akimbo.

подбра́сыва|ть, ю *impf. of* **подбро́сить**

подбро́|сить, шу, сишь *pf.* (*of* **подбра́сывать**) **1.** to throw up, toss up; **(под)** to throw (under); **п. моне́ту** to toss up. **2.** (+*a. or g.*) to throw in, throw on; **п. резе́рвы** (*mil.*) to throw in one's reserves; **п. дров в печь** to throw more wood on the fire. **3.** to place surreptitiously; **п. младе́нца** to abandon a baby.

подбрю́шник, а *m.* belly-band (*of horse*).

подва́л, а *m.* **1.** cellar; basement. **2.** (*in newspaper*) feuilleton.

подва́лива|ть, ю *impf. of* **подвали́ть**

подвал|и́ть, ю́, ~ишь *pf.* (*of* **~ивать**) **1.** (*coll.*) (+*a. or g.*) to heap up. **2.** (+*a. or g.*) (*coll.*) to add; (*impers.*): **наро́ду ~и́ло** still more people came. **3.** (*naut.*; **к**) to come in (to), steam in (to).

подва́л|ьный *adj. of* **~; п. эта́ж** basement.

подва́рива|ть, ю *impf. of* **подвари́ть**

подвар|и́ть, ю́, ~ишь *pf.* (*of* **~ивать**) (*coll.*) **1.** (+*g.*) to boil in addition. **2.** to heat up again.

подва́хтенны|й *adj.*: **~е матро́сы** (*naut.*) watch below.

подве́домствен|ный (~, ~на) *adj.* (+*d.*) dependent (on), within the jurisdiction (of).

подвез|ти́, у́, ёшь, *past* **~, ~ла́** *pf.* (*of* **подвози́ть**) **1.** to bring, take (with one); to give a lift (*on the road*). **2.** (+*a. or g.*) to bring up, transport. **3.** (*coll.*): **мне,** *etc.*, **~ло́,** *etc.*, have had a stroke of luck.

подвене́чн|ый *adj.*: **~ое пла́тье** wedding dress.

подверг|а́ть(ся), а́ю(сь) *impf. of* **~нуть(ся)**

подве́рг|нуть, ну, нешь, *past* **~, ~ла** *pf.* (*of* **~а́ть**) (+*d.*) to subject (to); to expose (to); **п. испыта́нию** to put to the test; **п. наказа́нию** to impose a penalty (upon); **п. опа́сности** to expose to danger, endanger; **п. сомне́нию** to call in question; **п. штра́фу** to fine.

подве́рг|нуться, нусь, нешься, *past* **~ся, ~лась** *pf.* (*of* **~а́ться**) **1.** (+*d.*) to undergo. **2.** *pass. of* **~нуть**

подве́рженност|ь, и *f.* (+*d.*) liability (to), susceptibility (to).

подве́ржен|ный (~, ~а) *adj.* (+*d.*) subject (to), liable (to); susceptible (to).

подвер|ну́ть, ну́, нёшь *pf.* (*of* **~тывать**) **1.** to screw up a little; **п. винт** to tighten a screw. **2.** to tuck in, tuck up; **п. одея́ло** to tuck in a blanket; **п. брю́ки** to tuck up one's trousers. **3.** to twist, sprain; **п. но́гу** to sprain one's ankle.

подвер|ну́ться, ну́сь, нёшься *pf.* (*of* **~тываться**) **1.** to be twisted, sprained; **нога́ у меня́ ~ну́лась** I have sprained my ankle. **2.** (*fig., coll.*) to turn up, crop up; **он кста́ти ~ну́лся** he turned up just at the right moment. **3.** *pass. of* **~ну́ть**

подвёртыва|ть(ся), ю(сь) *impf. of* **подверну́ть(ся)**

подве́с, а *m.* (*tech.*) suspension; hanger.

подвесе́льный *adj.* at the oars.

подве́|сить, шу, сишь *pf.* (*of* **~шивать**) to hang up, suspend.

подве́|ситься, шусь, сишься *pf.* (*of* **~шиваться**) **(на**+*p.*) to hang (on to, on by), be suspended (from).

подве́ск|а, и *f.* **1.** hanging up, suspension. **2.** pendant; **п. для ключе́й** key fob; **се́рьги с ~ами** drop ear-rings. **3.** (*tech.*) hanger; suspension bracket, suspension clip.

подвесно́й *adj.* hanging, suspended, pendant; overhead; **п. конве́йер** overhead conveyer; **п. мост** suspension bridge; **п. мото́р** outboard motor.

подве́с|ок, ка *m.* pendant.

подве|сти́, ду́, дёшь, *past* **~л, ~ла́** *pf.* (*of* **подводи́ть**) **1.** to lead up, bring up; to extend; **п. резе́рвы** to bring up reserves. **2. (под**+*a.*) to place (under); **п. фунда́мент** to under-pin; **п. дом под кры́шу** to roof a house; **п. ми́ну под мост** to mine a bridge; **п. про́чную ба́зу под свои́ до́воды** to place one's arguments on a sound footing; **п. бро́ви** to pencil one's eyebrows. **3.** to subsume; to put together; **п. бала́нс** (+*g.*) to balance; **п. ито́ги** to reckon up; to sum up (*also fig.*); **он ~л ва́ши гру́бые слова́ под оскорбле́ние** he took your rude words as an insult. **4.** (*coll.*) to let down; to put in a spot. **5.** (*impers.*; *coll.*): **у меня́ живо́т ~ло́** I feel pinched (with hunger).

подве́тренн|ый *adj.* leeward; **п. борт** (*naut.*) lee side; **бе́рег с ~ой стороны́** lee shore.

подве́шива|ть(ся), ю(сь) *impf. of* **подве́сить(ся)**

подвздо́шный *adj.* (*anat.*) iliac.

подвива́|ть(ся), ю(сь) *impf. of* **подви́ть(ся)**

по́двиг, а *m.* exploit, feat; heroic deed; **боево́й п.** feat of arms; **герои́ческий п.** epic of heroism.

подвига|ть, ю *pf.* (+*i.*) to move a little.

подвига́|ть(ся), ю(сь) *impf. of* **подви́нуть(ся)**

подви́гн|уть, у, ешь *pf.* **(на**+*a.*) (*rhet., obs.*) to rouse (to).

подви́д, а *m.* (*biol.*) subspecies.

подви́жник, а *m.* **1.** (*relig.*) ascetic; zealot. **2.** (*fig.*) zealot, devotee; hero; **п. нау́ки** pers. utterly devoted to (*the cause of*) learning.

подви́жничеств|о, а *nt.* **1.** (*relig.*) asceticism. **2.** selfless devotion (*to a cause*); heroic conduct; endeavour.

подвижн|о́й *adj.* **1.** (*in var. senses*) mobile; movable; (*tech.*) travelling; **п. блок** travelling block; **п. го́спиталь** mobile hospital; **~ы́е и́гры** outdoor games; **п. кран** travelling crane; **п. масшта́б** sliding scale; **п. пра́здник** (*eccl.*) movable feast; **~о́е равнове́сие** (*chem.*) mobile equilibrium; **п. соста́в** (*rail.*) rolling stock. **2.** lively; agile; **~о́е лицо́** mobile features.

подви́жност|ь, и *f.* **1.** mobility. **2.** liveliness; agility.

подви́жный *adj.* mobile; lively; agile.

подviза́|ться, юсь *impf.* (*rhet. or iron.*) to work, act; to pursue an occupation; **п. на юриди́ческом по́прище** to follow the law; **п. на сце́не** to tread the boards.

подвин|ти́ть, чу́, ти́шь *pf.* (*of* **~чивать**) **1.** to screw up, tighten. **2.** (*fig., coll.*) to urge, goad.

подви́|нуть, ну, нешь *pf.* (*of* **~га́ть**) **1.** to move; to push. **2.** (*fig.*) to advance, push forward.

подви́|нуться, нусь, нешься *pf.* (*of* **~га́ться**) **1.** to move. **2.** (*fig.*) to advance, progress.

подви́нчива|ть, ю *impf. of* **подвинти́ть**

под|ви́ть, овью́, овьёшь, *past* **~ви́л, ~вила́, ~ви́ло** *pf.* (*of* **~вива́ть**) to curl slightly, frizz.

под|ви́ться, овью́сь, овьёшься, *past* **~ви́лся, ~вила́сь, ~ви́лось** *pf.* (*of* **~вива́ться**) to curl one's hair slightly, frizz one's hair.

подвла́ст|ный (~ен, ~на) *adj.* (+*d.*) subject to, dependent on.

подво́д, а *m.* (*tech.*) supply, feed, admission; (*elec.*) lead, feeder.

подво́д|а, ы *f.* cart.

подво|ди́ть, жу́, ~дишь *impf. of* **подвести́**

подво́дник, а *m.* (*naut.*) submariner.
подводн|о́й *adj.* **~а́я труба́** (*tech.*) feed pipe.
подво́дн|ый[1] *adj.* submarine; under-water; **п. загради́тель** mine-layer; **п. ка́бель** submarine cable; **п. ка́мень** reef, rock; **~ая ло́дка** submarine; **~ое тече́ние** undercurrent.
подво́д|ный[2] *adj. of* **~а; ~ная пови́нность** (*hist.*) obligation to provide transport.
подво́дчик, а *m.* carter.
подво́з, а *m.* transport; supply.
подво|зи́ть, жу́, ~́зишь *impf. of* **подвезти́**
подво́|й, я *m.* (*bot.*) wilding.
подво́рн|ый *adj.* household; **~ая пе́репись** census of (*peasant*) households; **~ая по́дать** (*hist.*) hearth-money, chimney-money; **п. спи́сок** list of homesteads.
подворотнич|о́к, ка́ *m.* undercollar (*of soldier's tunic*).
подворо́т|ня, ни, *g. pl.* **~ен** *f.* **1.** space between gate and ground. **2.** board attached to bottom of gate.
подво́р|ье, ья, *g. pl.* **~ий** *nt.* (*obs.*) **1.** town house (*daughter church in town, usu. with hostel attached, belonging to monastery*). **2.** town residence, town house (*belonging to pers. normally residing elsewhere*).
подво́х, а *m.* (*coll.*) dirty trick; **устро́ить п. кому́-н.** to play s.o. a dirty trick.
подвыпи|вший *p.p. of* **~ть** *and adj.* (*coll.*) slightly tight.
подвы́п|ить, ью, ьешь *pf.* (*coll.*) to become slightly tight.
подвя|за́ть, жу́, ~́жешь *pf.* (*of* **~́зывать**) to tie up; to keep up.
подвя́зк|а, и *f.* garter; (*stocking*) suspender.
подвя́зыва|ть, ю *impf. of* **подвяза́ть**
подга́|дить, жу, дишь *pf.* (*coll.*) **1.** to spoil the effect (of), make a mess (of). **2.** (+ *d.*) to play a dirty trick (on).
подгиба́|ть(ся), ю(сь) *impf. of* **подогну́ть(ся)**
подгла́зь|е, я *nt.* bag under the eyes.
подгля|де́ть, жу́, ди́шь *pf.* (*of* **~́дывать**) (**в**+*a.*; *coll.*) to peep (at); to spy (on), watch furtively.
подгля́дыва|ть, ю *impf. of* **подгляде́ть**
подгнива́|ть, ю *impf. of* **подгни́ть**
подгни́|ть, ю́, ёшь, *past* **~л, ~ла́, ~ло** *pf.* (*of* **~ва́ть**) to begin to rot, rot slightly.
подгова́рива|ть, ю *impf. of* **подговори́ть**
подговор|и́ть, ю́, и́шь *pf.* (*of* **подгова́ривать**) (**на**+*a. or* +*inf.*) to put up (to), incite (to), instigate (to).
подголо́вник, а *m.* head-rest.
подголо́с|ок, ка *m.* **1.** (*mus.*) second part, supporting voice. **2.** (*coll., pej.*) yes-man.
подгоня́|ть, ю *impf. of* **подогна́ть**
подгор|а́ть, а́ю *impf. of* **~е́ть**
подгоре́лый *adj.* slightly burnt.
подгор|е́ть, и́т *pf.* (*of* **~а́ть**) to burn slightly.
подго́рный *adj.* lowland.
подгоро́дный *adj.* situated in the outskirts of a town.
подгота́влива|ть(ся), ю(сь) *impf. of* **подгото́вить(ся)**
подготови́тельн|ый *adj.* preparatory; **~ая рабо́та** spade-work.
подгото́в|ить, лю, ишь *pf.* (*of* **подгота́вливать** *and* **~ля́ть**) (**для, к**) to prepare (for); **п. по́чву** (*fig.*) to pave the way.
подгото́в|иться, люсь, ишься *pf.* (*of* **подгота́вливаться** *and* **~ля́ться**) (**к**) to prepare (for), get ready (for).
подгото́вк|а, и *f.* **1.** (**к**) preparation (for), training (for); **артиллери́йская п.** artillery preparation, preparatory bombardment. **2.** (**в**+*p. or* **по**+*d.*) grounding (in), schooling (in).
подгото́вленност|ь, и *f.* preparedness.
подготовля́|ть(ся), ю(сь) *impf. of* **подгото́вить(ся)**
подгреба́|ть, ю *impf. of* **подгрести́**
подгре|сти́[1]**, бу́, бёшь,** *past* **~̈б, ~бла́** *pf.* (*of* **~ба́ть**) to rake up.
подгре|сти́[2]**, бу́, бёшь,** *past* **~̈б, ~бла́** *pf.* (*of* **~ба́ть**) (**к**) to row up (to).
подгру́д|ок, ка *m.* dewlap.
подгру́пп|а, ы *f.* sub-group.
подгу́зник, а *m.* nappy, diaper, pilch.
подгуля́|ть, ю *pf.* (*coll.*) **1.** to take a drop too much, be slightly under the weather. **2.** (*joc.*) to be rather bad, be rather poor, be pretty poor; **обе́д немно́го ~л** the dinner was pretty poor.

подда|ва́ть(ся), ю(сь), ёшь(ся) *impf. of* **подда́ть(ся)**
поддавк|и́, о́в *no sg.*: **игра́ть в п.** to play at give-away (*to play draughts according to convention that winner is the first player to lose all his pieces*).
подда́кива|ть, ю *impf.* (*of* **подда́кнуть**) (+*d.*; *coll.*) to say yes (to), assent (to); (*also pej.*).
подда́к|нуть, ну, нешь *pf. of* **~ивать**
по́дданн|ый *p.p.p. of* **подда́ть**; *as n.* **п., ~ого** *m., and* **~ая, ~ой** *f.* subject, national.
по́дданств|о, а *nt.* citizenship, nationality.
под|да́ть, да́м, да́шь, да́ст, дади́м, дади́те, даду́т, *past* **~́дал, ~дала́, ~́дало** *pf.* (*of* **~дава́ть**) **1.** to strike; to kick. **2.** (*at draughts, etc.*) to give away. **3.** (+*g.*; *coll.*) to add, increase; **п. жа́ру** to add fuel to the fire; **п. па́ру** to increase steam; **п. га́зу** to get a move on.
под|да́ться, да́мся, да́шься, да́стся, дади́мся, дади́тесь, даду́тся, *past* **~да́лся, ~дала́сь** *pf.* (*of* **~дава́ться**) **1.** (+*d.*) to yield (to), give way (to), give in (to); **дверь не ~дала́сь** the door would not give; **п. искуше́нию** to yield to temptation; **не п. описа́нию** to beggar description; **п. отча́янию** to give way to despair; **п. угро́зам** to give in to threats. **2.** (*coll.*) to give o.s. up.
поддева́|ть, ю *impf. of* **подде́ть**
поддёвк|а, и *f.* poddyovka (*man's light tight-fitting coat*).
подде́л|ать, аю *pf.* (*of* **~ывать**) to counterfeit, falsify, fake; to forge; to fabricate; **п. по́дпись** to forge a signature.
подде́л|аться, аюсь *pf.* (*of* **~ываться**) **1.** (**под**+*a.*) to imitate, put on. **2.** (**к**; *coll.*) to ingratiate o.s. (with).
подде́лк|а, и *f.* falsification; forgery; counterfeit; imitation, fake; **п. под же́мчуг** imitation pearls.
подде́лывател|ь, я *m.* forger; counterfeiter, falsifier.
подде́лыва|ть(ся), ю(сь) *impf. of* **подде́лать(ся)**
подде́льн|ый *adj.* false, counterfeit; forged; sham, spurious; **~ые драгоце́нности** imitation jewellery; **~ая моне́та** counterfeit coin; **п. па́спорт** forged passport.
поддёргива|ть, ю *impf. of* **поддёрнуть**
поддержа́ни|е, я *nt.* maintenance; **п. ми́ра** peacekeeping; **во́йска́ по ~ю ми́ра** peacekeeping force.
поддерж|а́ть, у́, ~́ишь *pf.* (*of* **~́ивать**) **1.** to support (*also fig.*); to back (up), second; **мора́льно п.** to give moral support; **п. резолю́цию** to second a resolution. **2.** to keep up, maintain; **п. ого́нь** to keep up the fire; **п. разгово́р** to keep up a conversation; **п. регуля́рное сообще́ние** to maintain a regular service; **п. отноше́ния** (**с**+*i.*) to keep in touch (with).
подде́ржива|ть, ю *impf.* **1.** *impf. of* **поддержа́ть. 2.** (*impf. only*) to bear, support.
подде́ржк|а, и *f.* **1.** (*in var. senses*) support; backing; seconding; **огнева́я п.** (*mil.*) fire support; covering fire. **2.** support, prop, stay.
поддёр|нуть, ну, нешь *pf.* (*of* **~гивать**) to pull up.
подде́|ть, ну, нешь *pf.* (*of* **~ва́ть**) **1.** (**под**+*a.*; *coll.*) to put on under, wear under; **~нь(те) сви́тер под ку́ртку** put a sweater on under your jacket. **2.** to hook; to catch up. **3.** (*fig., coll.*) to catch out.
поддо́нник, а *m.* saucer (*placed under flowerpot*).
поддра́знива|ть, ю *impf. of* **поддразни́ть**
поддразн|и́ть, ю́, ~́ишь *pf.* (*of* **~́ивать**) (*coll.*) to tease.
поддува́л|о, а *nt.* ash-pit (*of stove, furnace*).
поддува́|ть, ю *impf.* **1.** to blow (*from underneath*). **2.** to blow slightly.
по-де́довски *adv.* (*coll.*) as of old.
поде́йств|овать, ую *pf. of* **де́йствовать 2.**
подека́дно *adv.* every ten days.
поде́ла|ть, ю *pf.* (*no impf.*) (*coll.*) **1.** to do; **ничего́ не ~ешь** there is nothing to be done; it can't be helped; **ничего́ не могу́ с ни́ми п.!** I can't do anything with them. **2.** to make, build.
подел|и́ть(ся), ю́(сь), ~́ишь(ся) *pf. of* **дели́ть(ся)**
поде́лк|а, и *f.* **1.** odd job. **2.** article; **~и из де́рева** wood articles.
подело́м *adv.* (*coll.*): **п. ему́,** *etc.*, it serves him, *etc.*, right.
поде́лыва|ть *impf.* (*coll.*) *only used in question* **что ~ешь? что ~ете?** how are you getting on?
подёнк|а, и *f.* (*zool.*) ephemeron, ephemera.

подённо *adv.* by the day.
подённ|ый *adj.* by the day; **~ая опла́та** pay by the day; **~ая рабо́та** day-labour, time-work.
подёнщик, а *m.* day-labourer, time-worker.
подёнщин|а, ы *f.* work paid by the day, day-labour.
подёнщиц|а, ы *f.* woman hired by the day.
подёрг|ать, аю *pf. of* **~ивать**
подёргивани|е, я *nt.* twitch(ing), jerk.
подёргива|ть, ю *impf.* **1.** (*impf. of* **подёргать**) (+*a. or* **за**+*a.*) to pull (at), tug (at). **2.** (*impf. only*) (+*i.*) to twitch.
подёргива|ться, юсь *impf.* to twitch.
подержа́ни|е, я *nt.* **на п.** for temporary use; **взять на п.** to borrow; **дать на п.** to lend.
подёржанный *adj.* second-hand.
подерж|а́ть, у́, ~ишь *pf.* to hold for some time; to keep for some time.
подерж|а́ться, у́сь, ~ишься *pf.* **1.** (**за**+*a.*) to hold (on to) for some time. **2.** to hold (out), last, stand.
подёрн|уть, ет *pf.* to cover, coat; (*impers.*): **реку́ ~уло льдом** the river was coated with ice.
подёрн|уться, ется *pf.* (+*i.*) to be covered (with).
подешеве́|ть, ет *pf. of* **дешеве́ть**
поджа́рива|ть(ся), ю(сь) *impf. of* **поджа́рить(ся)**
поджа́рист|ый (~, ~а) *adj.* brown, browned; crisp.
поджа́р|ить, ю, ишь *pf.* (*of* **~ивать**) to fry, roast, grill (slightly); **п. хлеб** to toast bread.
поджа́р|иться, юсь, ишься *pf.* (*of* **~иваться**) **1.** to fry, roast (slightly). **2.** *pass. of* **~ить**
поджа́рк|а, и *f.* (*cul.*; *coll.*) grilled or fried piece of beef.
поджа́р|ый (~, ~а) *adj.* (*coll.*) lean, wiry, sinewy.
под|жа́ть, ожму́, ожмёшь *pf.* (*of* **~жима́ть**) to draw in; **п. гу́бы** to purse one's lips; **п. хвост** to have one's tail between one's legs (*also fig.*); **сиде́ть ~жа́в но́ги** to sit cross-legged.
поджелу́дочн|ый *adj.*: **~ая железа́** (*anat.*) pancreas.
под|же́чь, ожгу́, ожжёшь, ожгу́т, *past* **~жёг, ~ожгла́** *pf.* (*of* **~жигать**) **1.** to set fire (to), set on fire (*with criminal intent or otherwise*). **2.** (*coll.*) to burn slightly.
поджива́|ть, ю *impf. of* **поджи́ть**
поджига́тел|ь, я *m.* **1.** incendiary. **2.** (*fig.*) instigator; **п. войны́** warmonger; war hawk.
поджига́тельский *adj.* inflammatory.
поджига́тельств|о, а *nt.* **1.** incendiarism. **2.** (*fig.*) instigation; **п. войны́** warmongering.
поджига́|ть, ю *impf. of* **подже́чь**
поджида́|ть, ю *impf.* to wait (for); to lie in wait (for).
поджи́л|ки, ок *no sg.* knee tendons; **у меня́ от стра́ха п. затрясли́сь** (*fig., coll.*) I was shaking in my shoes; I was quaking with fear.
поджима́|ть, ю *impf. of* **поджа́ть**
подж|и́ть, ивёт, *past* **~и́л, ~ила́, ~и́ло** *pf.* (*of* **~ива́ть**) to heal (up); (*of a cut*) to close (up).
поджо́г, а *m.* arson.
подзаб|ы́ть, у́ду, у́дешь *pf.* (*coll.*) to forget partially; **я ~ы́л ру́сский язы́к** my Russian is a little rusty.
подзаголо́в|ок, ка *m.* sub-title, sub-heading.
подзадо́рива|ть, ю *impf. of* **подзадо́рить**
подзадо́р|ить, ю, ишь *pf.* (*of* **~ивать**) (*coll.*) to egg on, set on.
подзаты́льник, а *m.* (*coll.*) clip (on the back of the head).
подзащи́тн|ый, ого *m.* (*leg.*) client.
подземе́л|ье, ья, *g. pl.* **~ий** *nt.* cave; dungeon.
подзе́мк|а, и *f.* (*coll.*) underground (railway), tube.
подзе́мн|ый *adj.* underground, subterranean; **~ая (городска́я) желе́зная доро́га** underground (railway), tube; **~ые рабо́ты** underground workings; **п. толчо́к** earthquake shock; tremor.
подзерка́льник, а *m.* looking-glass table, dressing-table with looking-glass.
подзо́л, а *m.* (*agric.*) podzol (*sterile greyish-white soil, deficient in salts*).
подзо́лист|ый (~, ~а) *adj.* (*agric.*) containing podzol.
подзо́р, а *m.* **1.** cornice (*of Russ. wood building*). **2.** edging, trimming.
подзо́рн|ый *adj.*: **~ая труба́** spy-glass, telescope.
подзу|ди́ть, жу́, ~дишь *pf.* (*of* **~живать**) (*coll.*) to egg on, set on.
подзу́жива|ть, ю *impf. of* **подзуди́ть**
подзыва́|ть, ю *impf. of* **подозва́ть**
поди́[1] (*coll.*) = **пойди́** (*imper. of* **пойти́**); **п. сюда́!** come here!
поди́[2] (*coll.*) **1.** probably; I dare say; I shouldn't wonder; *or translated* must (be), is sure (to be); **ты, п., уста́ла** you must be tired; **он, п., забы́л** he has probably forgotten; **они́, п., прие́дут** I dare say they'll be there. **2.** *particle expr. amazement, incredulity, etc.* (*also* **на́ п.**); **п. ты, ра́зве он э́то сказа́л?** go on, he never said that?; impossible! he couldn't have said that!; **он на́чал так руга́ться, что на́ п.** he began to swear so, you can't imagine; **вот п. ж ты** just imagine; well, who would have thought it possible. **3.** *particle+imper.* just try; **п. удержи́ его́** just try to stop him.
подив|и́ть, лю́, и́шь *pf.* (*no impf.*) (*coll., obs.*) to cause to marvel, astonish.
подив|и́ться, лю́сь, и́шься *pf. of* **диви́ться**
подира́|ть, ет *impf.*: **моро́з по ко́же ~ет** (*coll.*) it makes one's flesh creep; it gives one the creeps.
подка́лыва|ть, ю *impf. of* **подколо́ть**
подка́пыва|ть(ся), ю(сь) *impf. of* **подкопа́ть(ся)**
подкарау́лива|ть, ю *impf.* (*of* **подкарау́лить**) **1.** to catch. **2.** (*impf. only*) to be on the watch (for), lie in wait (for).
подкарау́л|ить, ю, ишь *pf. of* **подкарау́ливать**
подка́рмлива|ть, ю *impf. of* **подкорми́ть**
подка|ти́ть, чу́, ~тишь *pf.* (*of* **~тывать**) **1.** to roll. **2.** (*coll.*; *of a carriage, etc.*) to roll up, drive up. **3.** (*coll.*): **у меня́ ком ~ти́л к го́рлу** I felt a lump rise in my throat.
подка|ти́ться, чу́сь, ~тишься *pf.* (*of* **~тываться**) (**под**+*a.*) to roll (under).
подка́тыва|ть(ся), ю(сь) *impf. of* **подкати́ть(ся)**
подкач|а́ть, а́ю *pf.* (*of* **~ивать**) (*coll.*) to make a mess (of things); to let one down.
подка́чива|ть, ю *impf. of* **подкача́ть**
подка́чк|а, и *f.* (*phys.*) pump.
подка́шива|ть(ся), ю(сь) *impf. of* **подкоси́ть(ся)**
подка́шлива|ть, ю *impf.* (*coll.*) to cough (*intentionally, to draw attention, etc.*).
подка́шлян|уть, у, ешь *pf.* to give a cough.
подки́дыва|ть, ю *impf. of* **подки́нуть**
подки́дыш, а *m.* foundling.
подки́|нуть, ну, нешь *pf.* (*of* **~дывать**) = **подбро́сить**
подки́сл|енный *p.p.p. of* **~и́ть** *and adj.* (*chem.*) acidified, acidulous.
подкисл|и́ть, ю́, и́шь *pf.* (*of* **~я́ть**) (*chem.*) to acidify.
подкисл|я́ть, я́ю *impf. of* **~и́ть**
подкла́дк|а, и *f.* **1.** lining; **на шёлковой ~е** silk-lined. **2.** (*fig., coll.*) the inside, the secret (of); **мы обнару́жили ~у э́того собы́тия** we have discovered what lay behind this event.
подкладно́|й *adj.* put under; **~е су́дно** bed-pan.
подкла́д|очный *adj. of* **~ка; п. материа́л** lining (material).
подкла́дыва|ть, ю *impf. of* **подложи́ть**
подкла́сс, а *m.* (*biol.*) sub-class.
подкле́ива|ть, ю *impf. of* **подкле́ить**
подкле́|ить, ю, ишь *pf.* (*of* **~ивать**) **1.** (**под**+*a.*) to glue (under), paste (under). **2.** to glue up, paste up. **3.** *pf. of* **кле́ить 2.**
подкле́йк|а, и *f.* glueing, pasting.
подключ|а́ть(ся), а́ю(сь) *impf. of* **~и́ть(ся)**
подключ|и́ть, у́, и́шь *pf.* (*of* **~а́ть**) (*coll.*) **1.** (*tech.*) to link up, connect up. **2.** (*fig.*) to attach; **его́ ~и́ли ко второ́му ку́рсу** he has been attached to the second year.
подключ|и́ться, у́сь, и́шься *pf.* (*of* **~а́ться**) (*coll.*) **1.** (*tech. and fig.*) *pass. of* **~и́ть. 2.** (*fig.*) to settle down; to get the hang of things.
подключи́чный *adj.* (*anat.*) subclavian, subclavicular.
подко́в|а, ы *f.* (horse-)shoe.
подк|ова́ть, ую́, уёшь *pf.* (*of* **кова́ть** *and* **~о́вывать**) **1.** to shoe. **2.** (**в**+*p.*; *fig., coll.*) to ground (in), give a grounding (in).
подко́выва|ть, ю *impf. of* **подкова́ть**

подковы́рива|ть, ю *impf. of* **подковырну́ть**
подковы́рк|а, и *f.* (*coll.*) catch; attempt to catch out.
подковыр|ну́ть, ну́, нёшь *pf.* (*of* **~ивать**) **1.** to pick (*a sore, etc.*). **2.** (*fig., coll.*) to catch out.
подко́жный *adj.* subcutaneous, hypodermic.
подколе́нный *adj.* (*anat.*) popliteal.
подколо́дн|ый *adj.*: **змея́ ~ая** (*fig., coll.*) snake in the grass.
подкол|о́ть, ю́, ~ешь *pf.* (*of* **подка́лывать**) **1.** to pin up. **2.** to chop up. **3.** to attach, append (*to a document or file*).
подкоми́сси|я, и *f.* sub-committee.
подкомите́т, а *m.* sub-committee.
подконтро́льный *adj.* under control.
подко́п, а *m.* **1.** undermining. **2.** underground passage. **3.** (*fig., coll.*) intrigue(s), underhand plotting.
подкопа́|ть, ю *pf.* (*of* **подка́пывать**) to undermine, sap.
подкопа́|ться, юсь *pf.* (*of* **подка́пываться**) (**под**+*a.*) **1.** to undermine, sap; (*of animals*) to burrow (under). **2.** (*fig., coll.*) to intrigue (against).
подкорм|и́ть, лю́, ~ишь *pf.* (*of* **подка́рмливать**) **1.** to feed up; to fatten (*livestock*). **2.** (*agric.*) to add fertilizer to.
подко́рмк|а, и *f.* **1.** feeding; fattening. **2.** additional fertilization.
подко́с, а *m.* (*tech.*) strut, brace, angle brace.
подко|си́ть, шу́, ~сишь *pf.* (*of* **подка́шивать**) **1.** to cut down. **2.** to fell, lay low (*also fig.*); **э́то оконча́тельно ~си́ло (меня́, его́,** *etc.*) that was the last straw.
подкос|и́ться, ~ится *pf.* (*of* **подка́шиваться**) to give way, fail one.
подкра́дыва|ться, юсь *impf. of* **подкра́сться**
подкра́|сить, шу, сишь *pf.* (*of* **~шивать**) to tint, colour; to touch up (*make-up, etc.*).
подкра́|ситься, шусь, сишься *pf.* (*of* **~шиваться**) to touch up one's make-up.
подкра́|сться, ду́сь, дёшься *pf.* (*of* **~дываться**) (**к**) to steal up (to), sneak up (to).
подкра́шива|ть(ся), ю(сь) *impf. of* **подкра́сить(ся)**
подкреп|и́ть, лю́, и́шь *pf.* (*of* **~ля́ть**) **1.** to support. **2.** (*fig.*) to support, back; to confirm, corroborate; **п. пригово́р ссы́лкой на прецеде́нты** to support a judgement by reference to precedent. **3.** to fortify, recruit (*with food and/or drink*); **п. себя́ пе́ред доро́гой** to fortify o.s. for a journey. **4.** (*mil.*) to reinforce.
подкреп|и́ться, лю́сь, и́шься *pf.* (*of* **~ля́ться**) **1.** to fortify o.s. (*with food and/or drink*). **2.** *pass. of* **~и́ть**
подкрепле́ни|е, я *nt.* **1.** confirmation, corroboration. **2.** sustenance. **3.** (*mil.*) reinforcement.
подкрепля́|ть(ся), ю(сь) *impf. of* **подкрепи́ть(ся)**
подкузьм|и́ть, лю́, и́шь *pf.* (*coll.*) to do a bad turn; to do (down).
подкула́чник, а *m.* (*pej.*) kulak's henchman, kulak's man.
по́дкуп, а *m.* bribery; graft.
подкуп|а́ть, а́ю *impf. of* **~и́ть**
подкуп|и́ть, лю́, ~ишь *pf.* (*of* **~а́ть**) **1.** to bribe; to suborn. **2.** (*fig.*) to win over; **всех нас ~и́ла её доброта́** her kindness won all our hearts.
подла́|диться, жусь, дишься *pf.* (*of* **~живаться**) (**к**; +*coll.*) **1.** to adapt o.s. (to), fit in (with). **2.** to humour; to make up (to).
подла́жива|ться, юсь *impf. of* **подла́диться**
подла́мыва|ться, ется *impf. of* **подломи́ться**
по́дле *prep.*+*g.* by the side of, beside.
подлёдный *adj.* under the ice.
подлеж|а́ть, у́, и́шь *impf.* (+*d.*) to be liable (to), be subject (to); **п. ве́дению кого́-н.** to be within s.o.'s competence; **э́тот дом ~и́т сно́су** this house is to be pulled down; **п. суду́** to be indictable; **«не ~и́т оглаше́нию»** (*classification of document*) 'Confidential'; **не ~и́т сомне́нию** it is beyond doubt; it is not open to question.
подлежа́щ|ее, его *nt.* (*gram.*) subject.
подлежа́|щий *pres. part. act. of* **~ть** *and adj.* (+*d.*) liable (to), subject (to); **п. обложе́нию сбо́ром** dutiable; **не п. обложе́нию сбо́ром** exempt from duty, duty-free; **не п. оглаше́нию** confidential, private; off-the-record.
подлез|а́ть, а́ю *impf. of* **~ть**
подле́з|ть, у, ешь *pf.* (*of* **~а́ть**) (**под**+*a.*) to crawl (under), creep (under).
подле́кар|ь, я *m.* (*obs.*) doctor's assistant.
подле́с|ок, ка *m.* undergrowth.
подлет|а́ть, а́ю *impf. of* **~е́ть**
подле|те́ть, чу́, ти́шь *pf.* (*of* **~та́ть**) (**к**) to fly up (to); (*fig.*) to run up (to), rush up (to).
подле́|ть, ю, ешь *impf.* (*of* **о~**) (*coll.*) to grow mean; to become a scoundrel.
подле́ц, а́ *m.* scoundrel, villain, rascal.
подле́чива|ть(ся), ю(сь) *impf. of* **подлечи́ть(ся)**
подлеч|и́ть, у́, ~ишь *pf.* (*of* **~ивать**) (*coll.*) to treat.
подлеч|и́ться, у́сь, ~ишься *pf.* (*of* **~иваться**) (*coll.*) to take medical treatment.
подлива́|ть, ю *impf. of* **подли́ть**
подли́вк|а, и *f.* sauce, dressing; gravy.
подливн|о́й *adj.*: **~о́е колесо́** (*tech.*) undershot wheel.
подли́з|а, ы *c.g.* (*coll.*) lickspittle, toady.
подли|за́ть, жу́, ~жешь *pf.* (*of* **~зывать**) to lick up.
подли|за́ться, жу́сь, ~жешься *pf.* (*of* **~зываться**) (**к**; *coll.*) to lick s.o.'s boots; to suck up (to).
подли́зыва|ть(ся), ю(сь) *impf. of* **подлиза́ть(ся)**
по́длинник, а *m.* original (*opp. copy*).
по́длинно *adv.* really; genuinely; **п. хоро́ший фильм** a really good film.
по́длинност|ь, и *f.* authenticity.
по́длин|ный (~ен, ~на) *adj.* **1.** genuine; authentic; original; **его́ ~ные слова́** his very words; his own words; **«с ~ным ве́рно»** 'certified true copy'. **2.** true, real; **п. учёный** a true scholar.
подлипа́ла = подли́за
под|ли́ть, олью́, ольёшь, *past* **~ли́л, ~лила́, ~ли́ло** *pf.* (*of* **~лива́ть**) (+*a. or g.* **в**+*a.*) to add (to); **п. ма́сла в ого́нь** (*fig.*) to add fuel to the fire.
по́длича|ть, ю *impf.* to act meanly; to behave like a scoundrel, cad.
подло́г, а *m.* forgery.
подло́дк|а, и *m.* submarine; sub.
подлож|и́ть, у́, ~ишь *pf.* (*of* **подкла́дывать**) **1.** (**под**+*a.*) to lay under; to line; **п. ва́ту** to wad. **2.** (+*a. or g.*) to add; **~и́те дрова́** *or* **дров** put some more wood on. **3.** to put furtively; **п. свинью́ кому́-н.** to play a dirty trick on s.o.
подло́ж|ный (~ен, ~на) *adj.* false, spurious; counterfeit, forged.
подлоко́тник, а *m.* elbow-rest; arm (*of chair*).
подлом|и́ться, ~ится *pf.* (*of* **подла́мываться**) (**под**+*i.*) to break (under).
по́длост|ь, и *f.* **1.** meanness, baseness. **2.** mean trick, low-down trick.
подлу́нный *adj.* sublunar.
по́дл|ый (~, ~а́, ~л) *adj.* mean, base, ignoble.
подма́|зать, жу, жешь *pf.* (*of* **~зывать**) to grease, oil; (*fig., coll.*) to grease s.o.'s palm.
подма́|заться, жусь, жешься *pf.* (*of* **~зываться**) **1.** to touch up one's make-up. **2.** (**к**) to curry favour (with), make up (to).
подма́зыва|ть(ся), ю(сь) *impf. of* **подма́зать(ся)**
подмал|ева́ть, ю́ю, ю́ешь *pf.* (*of* **~ёвывать**) to tint, colour; to touch up.
подмалёвыва|ть, ю *impf. of* **подмалева́ть**
подманда́тн|ый *adj.* (*pol.*) mandated; **~ая террито́рия** mandated territory.
подма́нива|ть, ю *impf. of* **подмани́ть**
подман|и́ть, ю́, ~ишь *pf.* (*of* **~ивать**) to call (to), to beckon.
подмасте́рь|е, я, *g. pl.* **~ев** *m.* apprentice.
подма́хива|ть, ю *impf. of* **подмахну́ть**
подмах|ну́ть, ну́, нёшь *pf.* (*of* **~ивать**) (*coll.*) to scribble a signature to; to sign (hastily and negligently).
подма́чива|ть, ю *impf. of* **подмочи́ть**
подме́н, а *m.* substitution (*of sth. false for sth. real*).
подме́н|а, ы *f.* = **~**
подме́нива|ть, ю *impf. of* **подмени́ть**

подмен|и́ть, ю́, ~ишь *pf.* (*of* **~ивать** *and* **~я́ть**) (*+a. and i.*) to substitute (for) (*intentionally*); **кто́-то на вечери́нке ~и́л мне шля́пу** s.o. at the party took my hat (and left his instead).

подмен|я́ть, я́ю *impf. of* **~и́ть**

подмерз|а́ть, а́ет *impf. of* **~нуть**

подмёрз|нуть, нет, *past* **~, ~ла** *pf.* (*of* **~а́ть**) to freeze slightly.

подме|си́ть, шу́, ~сишь *pf.* (*of* **~шивать**[1]) to add, mix in.

подме|сти́, ту́, тёшь, *past* **~л, ~ла́** *pf.* (*of* **~та́ть**[1]) to sweep.

подмета́|ть[1]**, ю** *impf. of* **подмести́**

подме|та́ть[2]**, чу́, ~чешь** *pf.* (*of* **~тывать**) to baste, tack.

подме́|тить, чу, тишь *pf.* (*of* **~ча́ть**) to notice.

подмётк|а, и *f.* sole; **в ~и кому́-н. не годи́ться** (*coll.*) not to be fit to hold a candle to s.o.

подмётн|ый *adj.*: **~ое письмо́** (*obs.*) anonymous letter.

подмётыва|ть, ю *impf. of* **подмета́ть**[2]

подмеча́|ть, ю *impf. of* **подме́тить**

подмеш|а́ть, а́ю *pf.* (*of* **~ивать**[2]) to stir in.

подме́шива|ть[1]**, ю** *impf. of* **подмеси́ть**

подме́шива|ть[2]**, ю** *impf. of* **подмеша́ть**

подми́гива|ть, ю *impf. of* **подмигну́ть**

подмиг|ну́ть, ну́, нёшь *pf.* (*of* **~ивать**) (*+d.*) to wink (at).

подмина́|ть, ю *impf. of* **подмя́ть**

подмо́г|а, и *f.* (*coll.*) help, assistance; **идти́ на ~у** (*+d.*) to come to the aid (of), lend a hand.

подмок|а́ть, а́ю *impf. of* **~нуть**

подмо́к|нуть, ну, нешь, *past* **~, ~ла** *pf.* (*of* **~а́ть**) to get slightly wet.

подмора́жива|ть, ет *impf. of* **подморо́зить**

подморо́женный *adj.* frost-bitten, frozen (slightly).

подморо́з|ить, ит *pf.* (*of* **подмора́живать**) to freeze; **к ве́черу ~ило** towards evening it began to freeze.

подмоско́вн|ый *adj.* (situated) near Moscow; *as n.* **~ая ~ой** *f.* (*obs.*) estate near Moscow.

подмо́стк|и, ов *no sg.* **1.** scaffolding, staging. **2.** (*theatr.*) stage; boards.

подмо́ч|енный *p.p.p. of* **~и́ть** *and adj.* **1.** slightly wet, damp. **2.** damaged (*also fig.*); **~енная репута́ция** tarnished reputation.

подмоч|и́ть, у́, ~ишь *pf.* (*of* **подма́чивать**) **1.** to wet slightly, damp. **2.** to damage by exposing to damp.

подмы́в, а *m.* washing away, undermining.

подмыва́|ть, ю *impf.* **1.** *impf. of* **подмы́ть. 2.** (*impers.*) to urge; **меня́ так и ~ет** (*+inf.*) I feel an urge (to); I can hardly keep (from).

подм|ы́ть, о́ю, о́ешь *pf.* (*of* **~ыва́ть**) **1.** to wash. **2.** to wash away, undermine.

подмы́ш|ечный *adj. of* **~ки**

подмы́шк|а, и *f.* arm-pit (*of article of clothing*).

подмы́ш|ки, ек *no sg.* arm-pits (*see also* **мы́шка**[2]).

подмы́шник, а *m.* dress-preserver *or* -shield.

под|мя́ть, омну́, омнёшь *pf.* (*of* **~мина́ть**) to crush; to trample down.

поднадзо́р|ный (~ен, ~на) *adj.* under surveillance, under supervision.

поднаж|а́ть, му́, мёшь *pf.* (**на**+*a.*; *coll.*) to press, put pressure (on); to chivvy.

поднача́льный *adj.* (*obs., now joc. only*) subordinate.

подна́чива|ть, ю *impf. of* **подна́чить**

подна́ч|ить, у, ишь *pf.* (*of* **~ивать**) (*coll.*) to egg on.

поднебе́сн|ая, ой *f.* (*folk poet.*) the earth.

поднебе́сь|е, я *nt.* (*folk poet.*) the heavens.

поднево́л|ьный (~ен, ~ьна) *adj.* **1.** dependent; subordinate. **2.** forced; **п. труд** forced labour.

поднес|ти́, у́, ёшь, *past* **~, ~ла́** *pf.* (*of* **подноси́ть**) **1.** (**к**) to take (to), bring (to). **2.** (*+d. and a.*) to present (with); to take (as a present); to treat (to); **п. кому́-н. буке́т цвето́в** to present s.o. with a bouquet; **~и́ ему́ рю́мку коньяку́** take him, treat him to a (glass of) brandy.

подне́сь *adv.* (*obs.*) to this day, up to now.

по́дниз|ь, и *f.* (*obs.*) string (*of beads, etc.*).

поднима́|ть(ся), ю(сь) *impf. of* **подня́ть(ся)**; **~й вы́ше!** (*coll.*) try again!

поднов|и́ть, лю́, и́шь *pf.* (*of* **~ля́ть**) to renew, renovate.

подновля́|ть, ю *impf. of* **поднови́ть**

подного́тн|ая, ой *f.* (*coll.*) the whole truth, all there is to know; the ins and outs, the tricks of the trade; **он зна́ет про них всю ~ую** he knows all (there is to know) about them.

подно́жи|е, я *nt.* **1.** foot (*of an inanimate object, mountain, etc.*). **2.** pedestal.

подно́жк|а[1]**, и** *f.* step, footboard.

подно́жк|а[2]**, и** *f.* (*in wrestling*) backheel; **дать кому́-н. ~у** to trip s.o. up.

подно́жн|ый *adj.*: **п. корм** pasture, pasturage; **быть на ~ом корму́** to be at grass; **пусти́ть на п. корм** to put to grass.

подно́с, а *m.* tray; salver; **ча́йный п.** tea-tray.

подноси́тел|ь, я *m.* giver, donor.

подно|си́ть, шу́, ~сишь *impf. of* **поднести́**

подно́ск|а, и *f.* transporting, bringing up.

подно́счик, а *m.* **1.** carrier; **п. патро́нов** ammunition carrier. **2.** innkeeper's assistant, drinks server.

подноше́ни|е, я *nt.* **1.** presenting, giving. **2.** present, gift; **цвето́чные ~я** floral tributes.

подня́ти|е, я *nt.* raising; rise; rising; **п. за́навеса** curtain-rise; **голосова́ть ~ем рук** to vote by show of hands.

под|ня́ть, ниму́, ни́мешь, *past* **~нял, ~няла́, ~няло** *pf.* (*of* **~нима́ть**) **1.** (*in var. senses*) to raise; to lift; to hoist; **п. ка́рту** to colour a map; **п. настрое́ние** (*+g.*) to cheer up, raise the spirits (of); **п. ору́жие** to take up arms; **п. паруса́** to raise sail, set sail; **п. ру́ку (на**+*a.*) to lift up one's hand (against); **п. флаг** to hoist a flag; (*naut.*) to make the colours; **п. целину́** to open up virgin lands, break fresh ground; **п. шерсть** to bristle up; **п. я́корь** to weigh anchor; **п. на во́здух** to blow up; **п. на́ смех** to make a laughing-stock (of). **2.** to pick up; **п. пе́тли** to pick up stitches. **3.** to rouse, stir up; **п. восста́ние** to stir up rebellion; **п. ссо́ру** to pick a quarrel; **п. на́ ноги** to rouse, get up. **4.** (*fig.*) to improve; to enhance; **п. де́ло** (*coll.*) to cope with an affair, manage an affair successfully.

под|ня́ться, ниму́сь, ни́мешься, *past* **~ня́лся́, ~няла́сь** *pf.* (*of* **~нима́ться**) **1.** (*in var. senses*) to rise; to go up; to get up; **п. на́ ноги** to rise to one's feet; **п. в ата́ку** to go in to the attack; **п. в гало́п** to break into a gallop. **2.** (**на**+*a.*) to climb, ascend, go up. **3.** to arise; to break out, develop; **~няла́сь ссо́ра** a quarrel arose; **~няла́сь дра́ка** a fight started. **4.** (*econ.*; *fig.*) to improve; to recover.

подо *prep.* = **под**[2]

подо...[1] *as vbl. pref.* = **под...**[1]

подо...[2] *as pref. of nn. and adjs.* = **под...**[2]

подоба́|ть, ет *impf.* (*impers.*; *+d. and inf.*) to become, befit; **как ~ет** as befits one; **не ~ет** it does not do.

подоба́|ющий *pres. part. act. of* **~ть** *and adj.* proper, fitting.

подо́би|е, я *nt.* **1.** likeness; **по своему́ о́бразу и ~ю** in one's own image. **2.** (*math.*) similarity.

подо́блачный *adj.* under the clouds.

подо́бно *adv.* (*+d.*) like; **п. верблю́ду** like a camel; **п. тому́, как** just as.

подо́б|ный (~ен, ~на) *adj.* like; similar; **~ное поведе́ние** such behaviour; **~ные треуго́льники** (*math.*) similar triangles; **я никогда́ не встреча́л ~ного дурака́** I have never met such a fool; **ничего́ ~ного!** (*coll.*) nothing of the kind!; **и тому́ ~ное** (*abbr.* **и т. п.**) and so on, and such like.

подобостра́сти|е, я *nt.* servility.

подобостра́ст|ный (~ен, ~на) *adj.* servile.

подо́бранност|ь, и *f.* neatness, tidiness.

подо́бр|анный *p.p.p. of* **~а́ть** *and adj.* neat, tidy.

под|обра́ть, беру́, берёшь, *past* **~обра́л, ~обрала́, ~обра́ло** *pf.* (*of* **~бира́ть**) **1.** to pick up; **п. коло́сья** to glean. **2.** to tuck up; to take up; **п. во́лосы** to put up one's hair. **3.** to select, pick; **п. деся́тников** to pick foremen; **п. ключ к замку́** to fit a key to a lock; **п. дже́мпер под цвет костю́ма** to choose a jumper to match a suit.

под|обра́ться, беру́сь, берёшься, *past* **~обра́лся, ~обрала́сь, ~обра́ло́сь** *pf.* (*of* **~бира́ться**) **1.** (**к**) to steal up (to), approach stealthily. **2.** to make o.s. tidy. **3.** *pass. of* **~обра́ть**

подобре́|ть, ю *pf. of* **добре́ть**[1]
по-добрососе́дски: жить п. (**с**+*i.*) to have good-neighbourly relations (with ...).
подобру́-поздоро́ву *adv.* (*coll.*) in good time, while the going is good.
подо́вый *adj.* baked in the hearth.
подо́г, а́ *m.* (*dial.*) stick.
под|огна́ть, гоню́, го́нишь, *past* **~огна́л, ~огнала́, ~огна́ло** *pf.* (*of* **~гоня́ть**) **1.** (**к**) to drive (to). **2.** (*coll.*) to drive on, urge on, hurry. **3.** (**к**) to adjust (to), fit (to).
под|огну́ть, огну́, огнёшь *pf.* (*of* **~гиба́ть**) to tuck in; to bend under.
под|огну́ться, огну́сь, огнёшься *pf.* (*of* **~гиба́ться**) to bend; **коле́ни у него́ ~огну́лись** he was bent, doubled up (*from fatigue, etc.*).
подогре́в, а *m.* (*tech.*) heating; **предвари́тельный п.** pre-heating.
подогрева́тел|ь, я *m.* (*tech.*) heater.
подогрева́тельный *adj.* (*tech.*) heating.
подогрева́|ть, ю *impf. of* **подогре́ть**
подогре́|ть, ю *pf.* (*of* **~ва́ть**) to warm up, heat up; (*fig.*) to rouse.
пододвига́|ть, ю *impf. of* **пододви́нуть**
пододви́|нуть, ну, нешь *pf.* (*of* **~га́ть**) (**к**) to move up (to), push up (to).
пододея́льник, а *m.* quilt cover, blanket cover, duvet cover.
подожд|а́ть, у́, ёшь, *past* **~а́л, ~ала́, ~а́ло** *pf.* (+*a. or g.*) to wait (for).
под|озва́ть, зову́, зовёшь, *past* **~озва́л, ~озвала́, ~озва́ло** *pf.* (*of* **~зыва́ть**) to call up; to beckon.
подозрева́|емый *pres. part. pass. of* **~ть** *and adj.* suspected; suspect.
подозрева́|ть, ю *impf.* (*no pf.*) to suspect (*s.o. or that sth. is the case*); **я ~ю его́ в преступле́нии** I suspect him of a crime; **я ~ю, что он соверши́л преступле́ние** I suspect that he has committed a crime.
подозре́ни|е, я *nt.* suspicion; **оста́ться вне ~й** to remain above suspicion; **по ~ю** (**в**+*p.*) on suspicion (of); **быть под ~ем, на ~и** to be under suspicion.
подозри́тельно *adv.* suspiciously; **вести́ себя́ п.** to behave suspiciously; **смотре́ть п.** (**на**+*a.*) to regard with suspicion.
подозри́тельност|ь, и *f.* suspiciousness.
подозри́тел|ьный (~ен, ~ьна) *adj.* **1.** suspicious; suspect; shady, fishy; **~ьного ви́да** suspicious-looking; **п. субъе́кт** shady character. **2.** suspicious (= *mistrustful*).
подо|и́ть, ю́, ~и́шь *pf. of* **дои́ть**
подо́йник, а *m.* milk-pail.
подо|йти́, йду́, йдёшь, *past* **~шёл, ~шла́** *pf.* (*of* **подходи́ть**) **1.** (**к**) to approach (*also fig.*); to come up (to), go up (to); **по́езд ~шёл к ста́нции** the train pulled in to the station; **джу́нгли ~шли́ к са́мому поселе́нию** the jungle came right up to the settlement; **крити́чески п. к вопро́су** to approach a question critically, adopt a critical approach to a question. **2.** (+*d.*) to do (for); to suit; to fit; **э́тот пиджа́к о́чень мне ~йдёт** this coat will suit me very well; **э́то сло́во не ~йдёт в да́нном конте́ксте** this word will not do in the context under consideration; **ва́ше кре́сло едва́ ли ~йдёт к сти́лю ко́мнаты** your chair will hardly go with the room.
подоко́нник, а *m.* window-sill.
подо́л, а *m.* **1.** hem (*of skirt*); **держа́ться за чей-н. п.** to cling to s.o.'s skirts. **2.** (*dial.*) lower part, lower slopes; foot (*of hill*).
подо́лгу *adv.* for long; for hours, days, weeks, months, *etc.*; **мы с ним п. болта́ли** he and I used to chat by the hour; **они́ п. к нам не заходи́ли** they have not been in to see us for ages.
подоль|сти́ться, щу́сь, сти́шься *pf.* (**к**; *coll.*) to worm o.s. into s.o.'s favour, into s.o.'s good graces.
подольща́|ться, юсь *impf. of* **подольсти́ться**
по-дома́шнему *adv.* simply; without ceremony; **оде́т п.** (dressed) in clothes worn about the house.
подо́н|ки, ков *pl.* (*sg.* **~ок, ~ка** *m.*) dregs (*also fig.*); (*fig.*) scum; riff-raff.
подопе́чн|ый *adj.* under wardship; **~ая террито́рия** (*pol.*) trust territory.
подопле́к|а, и *f.* (*coll.*) the real (*opp. the ostensible, apparent*) state of affairs; the real cause, the underlying cause; **знать ~у переме́ны отноше́ний** to know the real cause of a volte-face.
подо́пытный *adj.* experimental; **п. кро́лик** (*fig.*) guinea-pig.
подорв|а́ть, у́, ёшь, *past* **~а́л, ~ала́, ~а́ло** *pf.* (*of* **подрыва́ть**[1]) **1.** to blow up; to blast. **2.** (*fig.*) to undermine; to sap; to damage severely; **п. чей-н. авторите́т** to undermine s.o.'s authority; **п. здоро́вье** to sap one's health.
подо́рлик, а *m.* (*zool.*) spotted eagle.
подорожа́|ть, ю *pf. of* **дорожа́ть**
подоро́жн|ая, ой *f.* (*hist.*) order for (fresh) post-horses.
подоро́жник, а *m.* **1.** (*bot.*) plantain. **2.** (*coll.*) provisions taken on a journey. **3.** (*obs.*) highwayman. **4.** (*zool.*): **лапла́ндский п.** Lapland bunting.
подоро́жный *adj.* on the road, along the road; **п. столб** milestone.
подоси́новик, а *m.* (*bot.*) orange-cap boletus (*mushroom*) (*Boletus versipellis*).
подо|сла́ть, шлю́, шлёшь *pf.* (*of* **подсыла́ть**) to send, dispatch (*secretly, on a secret mission*).
подосно́в|а, ы *f.* real cause, underlying cause.
подоспева́|ть, ю *impf. of* **подоспе́ть**
подоспе́|ть, ю *pf.* (*of* **~ва́ть**) (*coll.*) to arrive, appear (in time).
под|остла́ть, стелю́, сте́лешь *pf.* (*of* **~стила́ть**) (**под**+*a.*) to lay (under), stretch (under).
подотде́л, а *m.* section, subdivision.
подоткн|у́ть, у́, ёшь *pf.* (*of* **подтыка́ть**) to tuck in, tuck up; **п. простыню́** to tuck in a sheet; **п. ю́бку** to tuck up one's skirt.
подотря́д, а *m.* (*biol.*) sub-order.
подотчёт|ный (~ен, ~на) *adj.* **1.** (+*d.*) accountable (to). **2.** (*fin.*) on account; **~ная су́мма** sum paid out on account; imprest.
подо́хн|уть, у, ешь *pf.* (*of* **до́хнуть** *and* **подыха́ть**) **1.** (*of animals*) to die. **2.** (*coll.*; *of human beings*) to peg out, kick the bucket.
подохо́дный *adj.*: **п. нало́г** income tax.
подо́шв|а, ы *f.* **1.** sole (*of foot or boot*). **2.** foot (*of slope*). **3.** (*tech.*) base.
подо́шв|енный *adj. of* **~а**
подпада́|ть, ю *impf. of* **подпа́сть**
подпа́ива|ть, ю *impf. of* **подпои́ть**
подпа́лин|а, ы *f.* burnt place, scorch-mark; **ло́шадь с ~ой** dappled horse.
подпал|и́ть, ю́, и́шь *pf.* (*of* **~ивать**) (*coll.*) **1.** to singe, scorch. **2.** to set on fire.
подпа́рыва|ть(ся), ю(сь) *impf. of* **подпоро́ть(ся)**
подпа́с|ок, ка *m.* herdsboy.
подпа́|сть, ду́, дёшь, *past* **~л** *pf.* (*of* **~да́ть**) (**под**+*a.*) to fall (under); **п. под чьё-н. влия́ние** to fall under s.o.'s influence.
подпа|ха́ть, жу́, ~шешь *pf.* (*of* **~хивать**) to plough a little.
подпа́хива|ть[1]**, ю** *impf. of* **подпаха́ть**
подпа́хива|ть[2]**, ет** *impf.* (*coll.*) to stink a little.
подпева́л|а, ы *c.g.* (*coll.*) yes-man.
подпева́|ть, ю *impf.* (+*d.*) to join (in singing); to take up a song; (*fig.*) to echo.
под|пере́ть, опру́, опрёшь, *past* **~пёр, ~пёрла** *pf.* (*of* **~пира́ть**) to prop up.
подпи́лива|ть, ю *impf. of* **подпили́ть**
подпил|и́ть, ю́, ~ишь *pf.* (*of* **~ивать**) **1.** to saw; to file. **2.** to saw a little off; to file down.
подпи́л|ок, ка *m.* file.
подпира́|ть, ю *impf. of* **подпере́ть**
подписа́вш|ий, его *m.* signatory.
подписа́ни|е, я *nt.* signing.
подпи|са́ть, шу́, ~шешь *pf.* (*of* **~сывать**) **1.** to sign. **2.** to add (*to sth. written*); **п. ещё одно́ подстро́чное примеча́ние** to add another footnote. **3.** to subscribe (= *include in list of subscribers*); **п. кого́-н. на журна́л** to take out a magazine subscription for s.o.

подпи|са́ться, шу́сь, ∠шешься *pf.* (*of* **∠сываться**) **1.** (**под**+*i.*) to sign, put one's name (to); (*fig.*) to subscribe (to). **2.** (**на**+*a.*) to subscribe (to, for); **п. на журна́л** to subscribe to, take out a subscription for a magazine.

подпи́ск|а, и *f.* **1.** subscription. **2.** engagement; written undertaking; signed statement; **дать ~у о невы́езде** to give a written undertaking not to leave a place.

подписн|о́й *adj.* subscription; **п. лист** subscription list; **~а́я цена́** the price of subscription.

подпи́счик, а *m.* (**на**+*a.*) subscriber (to).

по́дпис|ь, и *f.* **1.** signature; **поста́вить свою́ п.** (**под**+*i.*) to put one's signature (to, beneath), affix one's signature (to); **за ~ью** (+*g.*) signed (by); **за ~ью и печа́тью** signed and sealed. **2.** caption; inscription.

подплыва́|ть, ю *impf. of* **подплы́ть**

подплы́|ть, ву́, вёшь, *past* **~л, ~ла́ ~ло** *pf.* (*of* **~ва́ть**) (**к**) to swim up (to); to sail up (to).

подпо|и́ть, ю́, ∠и́шь *pf.* (*of* **подпа́ивать**) (*coll.*) to make tipsy.

по́дпол, а *m.* (*dial.*) cellar.

подполз|а́ть, а́ю *impf. of* **~ти́**

подполз|ти́, у́, ёшь, *past* **∠, ~ла́** *pf.* (*of* **~а́ть**) (**к**) to creep up (to); (**под**+*a.*) to creep (under).

подполко́вник, а *m.* lieutenant-colonel.

подпо́ль|е, я *nt.* **1.** cellar. **2.** (*fig.*) underground work; (the) underground (organization); **уйти́ в п.** to go underground.

подпо́льный *adj.* **1.** under the floor. **2.** (*fig.*) underground; secret, clandestine.

подпо́льщик, а *m.* member of an underground organization.

подпо́р, а *m.* (*tech.*) head (*of water*).

подпо́р|а, ы *f.* prop, support; brace, strut.

подпо́рк|а, и *f.* = **подпо́ра**

подпо́р|ный *adj. of* **~а; ~ная сте́нка** breast-wall; (*naut.*) bulkhead.

подпор|о́ть, ю́, ∠ешь *pf.* (*of* **подпа́рывать**) to rip; to unpick, unstitch.

подпор|о́ться, ∠ется *pf.* (*of* **подпа́рываться**) to rip; to come unpicked, come unstitched.

подпору́чик, а *m.* (*hist.*) second lieutenant.

подпо́чв|а, ы *f.* subsoil, substratum.

подпо́чвенн|ый *adj.* subsoil; subterranean; **~ая вода́** underground water; **п. слой** pan.

подпоя́|сать, шу, шешь *pf.* (*of* **~сывать**) to belt; to gird (on).

подпоя́|саться, шусь, шешься *pf.* (*of* **~сываться**) to belt o.s.; to gird o.s.; to put on a belt, girdle.

подпоя́сыва|ть(ся), ю(сь) *impf. of* **подпоя́сать(ся)**

подпра́в|ить, лю, ишь *pf.* (*of* **~ля́ть**) to rectify; to touch up, retouch.

подправля́|ть, ю *impf. of* **подпра́вить**

подпру́г|а, и *f.* saddle-girth, belly-band.

подпры́гива|ть, ю *impf. of* **подпры́гнуть**

подпры́г|нуть, ну, нешь *pf.* (*of* **~ивать**) to leap up, jump up; to bob up and down.

подпуска́|ть, ю *impf. of* **подпусти́ть**

подпу|сти́ть, шу́, ∠стишь *pf.* (*of* **~ска́ть**) **1.** to allow to approach; **п. на расстоя́ние вы́стрела** to allow to come within range. **2.** (+*a.* *or* *g.*; *coll.*) to add in. **3.** (*coll.*) to get in, put in (*a sarcasm, a witticism, etc.*).

подпя́тник, а *m.* (*tech.*) step bearing.

подраба́тыва|ть, ю *impf. of* **подрабо́тать**

подрабо́та|ть, ю *pf.* (*of* **подраба́тывать**) (*coll.*) **1.** (+*a.* *or g.*) to earn additionally. **2.** to work up.

подра́внива|ть, ю *impf. of* **подровня́ть**

подра́гива|ть, ю *impf.* (*coll.*) to shake, tremble intermittently.

подража́ни|е, я *nt.* imitation.

подража́тел|ь, я *m.* imitator.

подража́тел|ьный (~ен, ~ьна) *adj.* imitative.

подража́тельств|о, а *nt.* (*pej.*) imitativeness.

подража́|ть, ю *impf.* (*no pf.*) (+*d.*) to imitate.

подразде́л, а *m.* subsection.

подразделе́ни|е, я *nt.* **1.** subdivision. **2.** (*mil.*) sub-unit, element.

подраздел|и́ть, ю́, и́шь *pf.* (*of* **~я́ть**) to subdivide.

подраздел|я́ть, я́ю *impf. of* **~и́ть**

подразумева́|ть, ю *impf.* to imply, entail, mean.

подразумева́|ться, ется *impf.* to be implied, be entailed, be meant; **что ~ется под э́тим выраже́нием?** what is meant by this expression?; **(само́ собо́й) ~ется** it is understood, it goes without saying.

подра́мник, а *m.* stretcher (*frame for canvas*).

подра́м|ок, ка *m.* = **~ник**

подра́н|ок, ка *m.* (*hunting*) wounded game; winged bird.

подраст|а́ть, а́ю *impf. of* **~и́; ~а́ющее поколе́ние** the rising generation.

подраст|и́, у́, ёшь, *past* **подро́с, подросла́** *pf.* to grow (a little).

подра|сти́ть, щу́, сти́шь *pf.* (*of* **∠щивать**) to grow; to breed; **п. цыпля́т** to keep chickens.

по|дра́ть(ся), деру́(сь), дерёшь(ся), *past* **~дра́л(ся), ~драла́(сь), ~дра́ло́(сь)** *pf. of* **дра́ть(ся)**

подра́щива|ть, ю *impf. of* **подрасти́ть**

подрёберный *adj.* (*anat.*) sub-costal.

подре́|зать, жу, жешь *pf.* (*of* **~за́ть**) **1.** to cut; to clip, trim; to prune, lop; **п. коло́ду** (*cards; sl.*) to cut the pack; **п. кому́-н. кры́лья** (*fig.*) to clip s.o.'s wings. **2.** (+*g.*) to cut off in addition; **п. хле́ба** to cut some more bread.

подреза́|ть, ю *impf. of* **подре́зать**

подрем|а́ть, лю́, ~лешь *pf.* to have a nap; to doze.

подреше́тник, а *m.* counter-lathing.

подрис|ова́ть, у́ю *pf.* (*of* **~о́вывать**) **1.** to retouch, touch up. **2.** to add, put in (*on a painting, photograph, etc.*).

подрисо́выва|ть, ю *impf. of* **подрисова́ть**

подро́бно *adv.* minutely, in detail; at (great) length.

подро́бност|ь, и *f.* **1.** detail; **вдава́ться в ~и** to go into detail; **рассказа́ть, не вдава́ясь в ~и** to relate without going into detail; **во всех ~ях** in every detail; **до мельча́йших ~ей** to the minutest detail. **2.** minuteness.

подро́б|ный (~ен, ~на) *adj.* detailed, minute.

подровня́|ть, ю *pf.* (*of* **подра́внивать**) to level, even; to trim.

подро́ст|ок, ка *m.* juvenile; teenager; youth; young girl.

подруб|а́ть, а́ю *impf. of* **~и́ть**

подруб|и́ть[1], лю́, ∠ишь *pf.* (*of* **~а́ть**) to hew.

подруб|и́ть[2], лю́, ∠ишь *pf.* (*of* **~а́ть**) to hem.

подру́г|а, и *f.* (*female*) friend; **п. по шко́ле** school-friend; **п. жи́зни** helpmate (*sc. one's wife*).

по-дру́жески *adv.* in a friendly way; as a friend.

подруж|и́ться, у́сь, и́шься *pf. of* **дружи́ться**

подру́жк|а, и *f.* *affectionate dim. of* **подру́га; п. неве́сты** bridesmaid.

подру́лива|ть, ю *impf. of* **подрули́ть**

подрул|и́ть, ю́, и́шь *pf.* (*of* **∠ивать**) (**к**; *aeron.*) to taxi up (to).

подрумя́нива|ть(ся), ю(сь) *impf. of* **подрумя́нить(ся)**

подрумя́н|ить, ю, ишь *pf.* (*of* **~ивать**) **1.** to rouge; to touch up with rouge. **2.** to make ruddy, make rosy; **моро́з ~ил им щёки** the frost brought a flush to their cheeks. **3.** (*cul.*) to brown.

подрумя́н|иться, юсь, ишься *pf.* (*of* **~иваться**) **1.** to apply rouge, use rouge. **2.** to become ruddy, become rosy; to flush, become flushed. **3.** (*cul.*) to brown.

подру́чн|ый *adj.* **1.** at hand, to hand; improvised, makeshift; **~ые сре́дства** improvised means. **2.** *as n.* **п., ~ого** *m.* assistant, mate; **п. водопрово́дчика** plumber's mate.

подры́в, а *m.* undermining; (*fig.*) injury, detriment; **п. самолю́бия** a blow to one's pride; **п. здоро́вья** sapping of health; **п. торго́вли** injury to trade.

подрыва́|ть[1], ю *impf. of* **подорва́ть**

подрыва́|ть[2], ю *impf. of* **подры́ть**

подрывни́к, а́ *m.* (*mil.*) member of demolition squad.

подрывн|о́й *adj.* blasting, demolition; (*fig.*) undermining, subversive; **~а́я рабо́та** blasting, demolition work; **~а́я де́ятельность** subversive activities.

подр|ы́ть, о́ю, о́ешь *pf.* (*of* **~ыва́ть[2]**) to undermine, sap.

подря́д[1] *adv.* in succession; running; on end; **три го́да п.** three years running; **не́сколько дней п. шёл дождь** it rained for days on end.

подря́д[2], а *m.* contract; **по ~у** by contract; **взять п. на**

постро́йку плоти́ны to contract for the building of a dam; сдать п. (на+*a.*) сдать с ~а to put out to contract.

подря|ди́ть, жу́, ди́шь *pf.* (*of* ~жа́ть) (*coll.*) to hire.

подря|ди́ться, жу́сь, ди́шься *pf.* (*of* ~жа́ться) (*coll.*) **1.** to contract, undertake. **2.** *pass. of* ~ди́ть

подря́д|ный *adj. of* ~²; ~ная рабо́та work done by contract.

подря́дчик, а *m.* contractor.

подряжа́|ть(ся), ю(сь) *impf. of* подряди́ть(ся)

подря́сник, а *m.* cassock.

подса́д, а *m.* (*forestry*) plantation.

подса|ди́ть¹, жу́, ∠дишь *pf.* (*of* ∠живать) **1.** to help (to) sit down; п. кого́-н. на ло́шадь to help s.o. mount a horse. **2.** (к) to place next (to); меня́ ~ди́ли к глухо́й да́ме I was placed next to a deaf lady. **3.** to fit in (*extra people in a compartment, etc.*).

подса|ди́ть², жу́, ∠дишь *pf.* (*of* ∠живать) (+*a. or g.*) to plant some more.

подсадн|о́й *adj.*: ~я у́тка decoy duck.

подса́жива|ть, ю *impf. of* подсади́ть

подса́жива|ться, юсь *impf. of* подсе́сть

подса́лива|ть, ю *impf. of* подсоли́ть

подса́чива|ть, ю *impf. of* подсочи́ть

подсве́чник, а *m.* candlestick.

подсви́стыва|ть, ю *impf.* (+*d.*) to whistle as accompaniment to.

подсева́|ть, ю *impf. of* подсе́ять

подсе́д, а *m.* (*disease of horses*) malanders, mallenders.

подседе́льник, а *m.* girth, belly-band.

подсе́к|а, и *f.* (*hist., agric.*) slash-burn clearing.

подсека́|ть, ю *impf. of* подсе́чь

подсе́кци|я, и *f.* sub-section.

под|се́сть, ся́ду, ся́дешь, *past* ~се́л *pf.* (*of* ~са́живаться) (к) to sit down (near, next to), take a seat (near, next to).

подсе́|чь, ку́, чёшь, ку́т, *past* ~к, ~кла́ *pf.* (*of* ~ка́ть) **1.** to hew; to hack (down). **2.** hook, strike (*a fish*).

подсе́|ять, ю, ешь *pf.* (*of* ~ва́ть) (+*a. or g.*) to sow (*in addition*); to undersow.

подси|де́ть, жу́, ди́шь *pf.* (*of* ∠живать) **1.** lie in wait (for). **2.** (*fig., coll.*) to scheme, intrigue (against).

подси́живани|е, я *nt.* (*coll.*) scheming, intriguing.

подси́жива|ть, ю *impf. of* подсиде́ть

подси́нива|ть, ю *impf. of* подсини́ть

подсин|и́ть, ю́, и́шь *pf.* (*of* ∠ивать) to blue, apply blueing to.

подска́блива|ть, ю *impf. of* подскобли́ть

подска|за́ть, жу́, ∠жешь *pf.* (*of* ∠зывать) (+*d.*) to prompt (*also fig.*); to suggest.

подска́зк|а, и *f.* prompting.

подска́зчик, а *m.* (*coll.*) prompter.

подска́зыва|ть, ю *impf. of* подсказа́ть

подска|ка́ть, чу́, ∠чешь *pf.* (*of* ~кивать¹) (к) to come galloping up (to).

подска́кива|ть¹, ю *impf. of* подскака́ть

подска́кива|ть², ю *impf. of* подскочи́ть

подскобл|и́ть, ю́, ∠и́шь *pf.* (*of* подска́бливать) to scrape off.

подскоч|и́ть, у́, ∠ишь *pf.* (*of* подска́кивать²) **1.** (к) to run up (to), come running (to). **2.** to jump up, leap up; п. от ра́дости to jump with joy; це́ны ~и́ли prices soared.

подскреба́|ть, ю *impf. of* подскрести́

подскре|сти́, бу́, бёшь, *past* ∻б, ~бла́ *pf.* (*of* ~ба́ть) to scrape; to scrape clean.

подсла|сти́ть, щу́, сти́шь *pf.* (*of* ∠щивать) to sweeten, sugar.

подсла́щива|ть, ю *impf. of* подсласти́ть

подсле́дственный *adj.* (*leg.*) under investigation.

подслепова́т|ый (~, ~а) *adj.* weak-sighted.

подслу́жива|ться, юсь *impf. of* подслужи́ться

подслуж|и́ться, у́сь, ∠ишься *pf.* (*of* ∠иваться) (к; *coll.*) to fawn (upon), cringe (before); to worm o.s. into the favour (of).

подслу́ш|ать, аю *pf.* (*of* ~ивать) to overhear; to eavesdrop (on).

подслу́шива|ть, ю *impf. of* подслу́шать

подсма́трива|ть, ю *impf. of* подсмотре́ть

подсме́ива|ться, юсь *impf.* (над) to laugh (at), make fun (of).

подсме́н|а, ы *f.* next shift; relief.

подсмотр|е́ть, ю́, ∠ишь *pf.* (*of* подсма́тривать) to spy.

подсне́жник, а *m.* (*bot.*) snowdrop.

подсо́бк|а, и *f.* (*coll.*) box-room.

подсо́бн|ый *adj.* subsidiary, supplementary; secondary; auxiliary; ancillary; ~ое предприя́тие subsidiary enterprise; п. проду́кт by-product; п. рабо́чий ancillary worker.

подсо́выва|ть, ю *impf. of* подсу́нуть

подсозна́ни|е, я *nt.* the subconscious.

подсозна́тел|ьный (~ен, ~ьна) *adj.* subconscious.

подсол|и́ть, ю́, ∠и́шь *pf.* (*of* подса́ливать) to add more salt (to), put more salt (into).

подсо́лнечник, а *m.* sunflower.

подсо́лнечн|ый¹ *adj. of* ~ик; ~ое ма́сло sunflower oil.

подсо́лнечн|ый² *adj.* in the sun; ~ая сторона́ the sunny side; *as n.* ~ая, ~ой *f.* (*obs.*) the universe.

подсо́лнух, а *m.* (*coll.*) **1.** sunflower. **2.** sunflower-seeds.

подсо́х|нуть, ну, нешь *pf.* (*of* подсыха́ть) to get dry, dry out a little.

подсоч|и́ть, у́, и́шь *pf.* (*of* подса́чивать) to tap (*trees, for resin or sap*).

подсо́чк|а, и *f.* tapping.

подспо́рь|е, я *nt.* (*coll.*) help, support; служи́ть больши́м ~ем to be a great help.

подспу́дн|ый *adj.* latent; unused; secret, hidden; ~ые си́лы latent strength; ~ые мы́сли secret thoughts.

подста́в|а, ы *f.* (*obs.*) relay (*of horses*).

подста́в|ить, лю, ишь *pf.* (*of* ~ля́ть) **1.** (под+*a.*) to put (under), place (under); п. го́лову под струю́ воды́ из кра́на to put one's head under a tap; п. но́жку кому́-н. to trip s.o. up (*also fig.*). **2.** (+*d.*) to bring up (to), put up (to); to hold up (to); п. кому́-н. стул to offer s.o. a seat. **3.** (*fig.*) to expose, lay bare; п. ферзя́ под уда́р (*chess*) to expose one's queen. **4.** (*math.*) to substitute.

подста́вк|а, и *f.* stand; support, rest, prop; coaster.

подставля́|ть, ю *impf. of* подста́вить

подставн|о́й *adj.* false; substitute; ~о́е лицо́ dummy, figure-head, man of straw; ~ы́е свиде́тели suborned witnesses.

подстака́нник, а *m.* glass-holder (*for use in drinking Russ. tea*).

подстано́вк|а, и *f.* (*math.*) substitution.

подста́нци|я, и *f.* sub-station.

подстёгива|ть, ю *impf. of* подстегну́ть

подстег|ну́ть¹, ну́, нёшь *pf.* (*of* ∻ивать) to fasten underneath.

подстег|ну́ть², ну́, нёшь *pf.* (*of* ∻ивать) to whip up, urge forward, urge on (*also fig.*).

подстерега́|ть, ю *impf. of* подстере́чь

подстере́|чь, гу́, жёшь, гу́т, *past* ∻г, ~гла́ *pf.* (*of* ~га́ть) to be on the watch (for), lie in wait (for); п. моме́нт to seize an opportunity.

подстила́|ть, ю *impf. of* подостла́ть

подсти́лк|а, и *f.* bedding; litter.

подстора́жива|ть, ю *impf.* (*of* подсторожи́ть) to be on the watch for.

подсторож|и́ть, у́, и́шь *pf. of* подстора́живать

подстра́ива|ть, ю *impf. of* подстро́ить

подстрека́тел|ь, я *m.* instigator; firebrand.

подстрека́тельский *adj.* inflammatory.

подстрека́тельств|о, а *nt.* instigation, incitement, setting-on.

подстрек|а́ть, а́ю *impf. of* ~ну́ть

подстрек|ну́ть, ну́, нёшь *pf.* (*of* ~а́ть) **1.** (к) to instigate (to), incite (to), set on (to). **2.** to excite; п. любопы́тство to excite one's curiosity.

подстре́лива|ть, ю *impf. of* подстрели́ть

подстрел|и́ть, ю́, ∠ишь *pf.* (*of* ∠ивать) to wound (*by a shot*); to wing.

подстрига́|ть(ся), ю(сь) *impf. of* подстри́чь(ся)

подстри́|женный *p.p.p. of* ~чь; ко́ротко ~женные во́лосы (closely) cropped hair.

подстри́|чь, гу́, жёшь, гу́т, *past* **~г, ~гла** *pf.* (*of* **~га́ть**) to cut; to clip, trim; to prune; **п. бо́роду** to trim one's beard; **п. но́гти** to cut one's nails.

подстри́|чься, гу́сь, жёшься, гу́ться, *past* **~гся, ~глась** *pf.* (*of* **~га́ться**) to trim one's hair; to have a hair-trim.

подстро́|ить, ю, ишь *pf.* (*of* **подстра́ивать**) **1.** (**к**) to build on (to); **п. фли́гель к до́му** to build on a wing to a house. **2.** to tune (up). **3.** (*fig.*, *coll.*) to contrive; (*pej.*) to arrange; **п. шу́тку** (*+d.*) to play a trick (on); **э́то де́ло ~ено** it's a put-up job.

подстро́чник, а *m.* word-for-word translation.

подстро́чн|ый *adj.*: **п. перево́д** word-for-word translation; **~ое примеча́ние** footnote.

по́дступ, а *m.* (*geog.*; *fig.*) approach; **да́льние ~ы к го́роду** the distant approaches to the city; **к нему́ и ~а нет** he is quite inaccessible.

подступ|а́ть(ся), а́ю(сь) *impf. of* **~и́ть(ся)**

подступ|и́ть, лю́, ~ишь *pf.* (*of* **~а́ть**) (**к**) to approach, come up (to), come near; **слёзы ~и́ли к её глаза́м** tears came to her eyes.

подступ|и́ться, лю́сь, ~ишься *pf.* (*of* **~а́ться**) (**к**) to approach; **к нему́ не ~ишься** he is quite inaccessible; **к э́тому мне не п.** it is quite beyond my means.

подсуди́м|ый, ого *m.* (*leg.*) defendant; the accused; prisoner at the bar; **скамья́ ~ых** the dock, the bar.

подсу́дност|ь, и *f.* jurisdiction; cognizance.

подсу́д|ный (~ен, ~на) *adj.* (*+d.*) under, within the jurisdiction (of); within the competence (of); cognizable (to).

подсу́м|ок, ка *m.* (*mil.*) cartridge pouch.

подсу́н|уть, у, ешь *pf.* (*of* **подсо́вывать**) **1.** (**под**+*a.*) to shove (under). **2.** (*+d. and a.*; *coll.*) to slip (into); to palm off (on, upon); **они́ мне ~ули не ту кни́гу** they palmed off the wrong book on me.

подсу́шива|ть, ю *impf. of* **подсуши́ть**

подсуш|и́ть, у́, ~ишь *pf.* (*of* **~ивать**) to dry a little.

подсчёт, а *m.* calculation; count.

подсчит|а́ть, а́ю *pf.* (*of* **~ывать**) to count up, reckon up; to calculate.

подсчи́тыва|ть, ю *impf. of* **подсчита́ть**

подсыла́|ть, ю *impf. of* **подосла́ть**

подсы́п|ать, лю, лешь *pf.* (*of* **~а́ть**) (*+a. or g.*) to add, pour in.

подсыха́|ть, ю *impf. of* **подсо́хнуть**

подта́ива|ть, ет *impf. of* **подта́ять**

подта́лкива|ть, ю *impf. of* **подтолкну́ть**

подта́плива|ть, ю *impf. of* **подтопи́ть**

подта́скива|ть, ю *impf. of* **подтащи́ть**

подтас|ова́ть, у́ю *pf.* (*of* **~о́вывать**) to shuffle unfairly; (*fig.*) to garble, juggle (with); **п. фа́кты** to juggle with facts.

подтасо́вк|а, и *f.* unfair shuffling; (*fig.*) garbling, juggling.

подтасо́выва|ть, ю *impf. of* **подтасова́ть**

подта́чива|ть, ю *impf. of* **подточи́ть**

подтащ|и́ть, у́, ~ишь *pf.* (*of* **подта́скивать**) (**к**) to drag up (to).

подта́|ять, ет *pf.* (*of* **~ивать**) to thaw a little, melt a little.

подтверди́тельн|ый *adj.* confirmatory; **посла́ть ~ое письмо́** to send a letter to confirm.

подтвер|ди́ть, жу́, ди́шь *pf.* (*of* **~жда́ть**) to confirm; to corroborate, bear out; **п. получе́ние чего́-н.** to acknowledge receipt of sth.

подтвержда́|ть, ю *impf. of* **подтверди́ть**

подтвержде́ни|е, я *nt.* confirmation; corroboration.

подтёк, а *m.* bruise.

подтека́|ть, ет *impf.* **1.** *impf. of* **подте́чь. 2.** (*impf. only*) to leak; to be leaking.

подте́кст, а *m.* subtext, concealed meaning; **угада́ть п.** to read between the lines.

подтексто́вк|а, и *f.* **1.** words (*of song or other vocal music*). **2.** composition of words (*for vocal music*).

под|тере́ть, отру́, отрёшь, *past* **~тёр, ~тёрла** *pf.* (*of* **~тира́ть**) to wipe (up).

подте́|чь, чёт, ку́т, *past* **~к, ~кла́** *pf.* (*of* **~ка́ть**) (**под**+*a.*) to flow (under), run (under).

подтира́|ть, ю *impf. of* **подтере́ть**

подтолкн|у́ть, у́, ёшь *pf.* (*of* **подта́лкивать**) **1.** to push slightly; **п. ло́ктем** to nudge. **2.** (*fig.*) to urge on.

подтоп|и́ть, лю́, ~ишь *pf.* (*of* **подта́пливать**) (*coll.*) to heat a little.

подточ|и́ть, у́, ~ишь *pf.* (*of* **подта́чивать**) **1.** to sharpen slightly, give an edge (to). **2.** to eat away, gnaw; to undermine (*also fig.*); **тюре́мное заключе́ние ~и́ло его́ здоро́вье** imprisonment has undermined his health.

подтру́нива|ть, ю *impf. of* **подтруни́ть**

подтрун|и́ть, ю́, и́шь *pf.* (*of* **~ивать**) (**над**) to chaff, tease.

подтуш|ева́ть, у́ю *pf.* (*of* **~ёвывать**) to shade slightly.

подтушёвыва|ть, ю *impf. of* **подтушева́ть**

подтыка́|ть, ю *impf. of* **подоткну́ть**

подтя́гива|ть(ся), ю(сь) *impf. of* **подтяну́ть(ся)**

подтя́ж|ки, ек *no sg.* braces, suspenders.

подтя́нутост|ь, и *f.* smartness.

подтя́н|утый *p.p.p. of* **~у́ть** *and adj.* smart.

подтя|ну́ть, ну́, ~нешь *pf.* (*of* **~гивать**) **1.** to tighten. **2.** (**к**) to pull up (to), haul up (to); **п. ло́дку к бе́регу** to haul up a boat on shore. **3.** (*mil.*) to bring up, move up. **4.** (*fig.*, *coll.*) to take in hand, pull up, chase up.

подтя|ну́ться, ну́сь, ~нешься *pf.* (*of* **~гиваться**) **1.** to gird o.s. more tightly; **п. по́ясом** to tighten one's belt. **2.** to pull o.s. up (*on gymnastic apparatus, etc.*). **3.** (*mil.*) to move up, move in. **4.** (*fig.*, *coll.*) to pull o.s. together, take o.s. in hand.

поду́ма|ть, ю *pf.* **1.** *pf. of* **ду́мать; п. (то́лько), ~й(те) (то́лько)!** just think!; **~ешь** (*as iron. int.*; *coll.*) I say!; what do you know?; **~ешь, кака́я блестя́щая мысль!** I say, what a brain-wave!; **и не ~ю!** I wouldn't think of it!; I wouldn't dream of it; **мо́жно п.** one might think. **2.** to think a little, for a while.

поду́мыва|ть, ю *impf.* (**о**+*p. or +inf.*; *coll.*) to think (of, about); **п. об отъе́зде, п. уе́хать** to think of leaving.

по-дура́цки *adv.* (*coll.*) foolishly, like a fool.

подура́ч|иться, усь, ишься *pf.* (*coll.*) to fool about, play the fool.

подурне́|ть, ю *pf. of* **дурне́ть**

поду́ськ|ать, аю *pf.* (*of* **~ивать**) (*coll.*) to set on; (*fig.*) to egg on; **п. соба́ку на кого́-н.** to set a dog on s.o.

поду́скива|ть, ю *impf. of* **поду́ськать**

поду́|ть, ю, ешь *pf.* **1.** *pf. of* **дуть 1.. 2.** to begin to blow.

поду́чива|ть(ся), ю(сь) *impf. of* **подучи́ть(ся)**

подуч|и́ть, у́, ~ишь *pf.* (*of* **~ивать**) **1.** (*+a. and d.*) to teach, instruct (in); **п. кого́-н. стрельбе́** to give s.o. a few lessons in shooting. **2.** to learn. **3.** (*inf.*; *coll.*) to prompt (to), egg on (to), put up (to).

подуч|и́ться, у́сь, ~ишься *pf.* to learn (a little more, a little better).

поду́шечк|а, и *f.* **1.** *dim. of* **поду́шка; п. для була́вок** pincushion. **2.** sweet, bon-bon.

подуш|и́ть, у́, ~ишь *pf.* to spray with perfume.

подуш|и́ться, у́сь, ~ишься *pf.* to spray o.s. with perfume, put some perfume on.

поду́шк|а, и *f.* **1.** pillow; cushion; **п. для штемпеле́й** ink-pad. **2.** (*tech.*) cushion; bolster.

поду́шн|ый *adj.*: **~ая по́дать** (*hist.*) poll-tax, capitation.

подфа́рник, а *m.* (*tech.*) fender lamp, sidelight.

подхали́м, а *m.* toady, lickspittle.

подхалима́ж, а *m.* (*coll.*) toadying, bootlicking, grovelling.

подхали́мнича|ть, ю *impf.* (*coll.*) to toady.

подхали́мств|о, а *nt.* = **подхалима́ж**

подхва|ти́ть, чу́, ~тишь *pf.* (*of* **~тывать**) (*in var. senses*) to catch (up); to pick up; to take up; **п. су́мку** to catch up one's bag; **п. мяч** to catch a ball; **п. на́сморк** to catch, pick up a cold; **п. пе́сню** to catch up a melody, join in a song.

подхва́тыва|ть, ю *impf. of* **подхвати́ть**

подхлест|ну́ть, ну́, нёшь *pf.* (*of* **~ывать**) to whip up (*also fig.*, *coll.*).

подхлёстыва|ть, ю *impf. of* **подхлестну́ть**

подхо́д, а *m.* (*in var. senses*) approach; **у него́ непра́вильный п. к де́лу** he has the wrong approach to the matter.

подхо́д|ец, ца *m.* (*coll.*) approach; **говори́ть с ~цем** to make reservations, speak in a roundabout way.

подхо|ди́ть, жу́, ~́дишь *impf. of* **подойти́**
подход|я́щий *pres. part. of* **~и́ть** *and adj.* suitable, proper, appropriate; **п. моме́нт** the right moment.
подцеп|и́ть, лю́, ~́ишь *pf.* (*of* **~ля́ть**) to hook on, couple on; (*fig., joc.*) to pick up; **п. ваго́н-рестора́н к по́езду** to attach a restaurant car to a train; **п. на́сморк** to pick up a cold.
подцепля́|ть, ю *impf. of* **подцепи́ть**
подча́с *adv.* sometimes, at times.
подча́с|ок, ка *m.* relief sentry.
подчелюстно́й *adj.* (*anat.*) sub-maxillary.
подчёркива|ть, ю *impf. of* **подчеркну́ть**
подчерк|ну́ть, ну́, нёшь *pf.* (*of* **~́ивать**) **1.** to underline; to score under. **2.** (*fig.*) to emphasize, stress, accentuate.
подчине́ни|е, я *nt.* **1.** subordination; submission, subjection; **быть в ~и (у)** to be subordinate (to). **2.** (*gram.*) subordination.
подчинённост|ь, и *f.* subordination.
подчин|ённый 1. *p.p.p. of* **~и́ть**; (+*d.*) under, under the command (of). **2.** *adj.* subordinate; **~ённое госуда́рство** tributary state; *as n.* **п., ~ённого** *m.* subordinate.
подчини́тельный *adj.* (*gram.*) subordinative.
подчин|и́ть, ю́, и́шь *pf.* (*of* **~я́ть**) (+*d.*) to subordinate (to), subject (to); to place (under), place under the command (of); **п. свое́й во́ле** to bend to one's will.
подчин|и́ться, ю́сь, и́шься *pf.* (*of* **~я́ться**) (+*d.*) to submit (to); **п. прика́зу** to obey an order.
подчин|я́ть(ся), я́ю(сь) *impf. of* **~и́ть(ся)**
подчи́|стить, щу, стишь *pf.* (*of* **~ща́ть**) to rub out, erase.
подчи́стк|а, и *f.* rubbing out, erasure.
подчисту́ю *adv.* (*coll.*) completely, without remainder; **мы съе́ли всё п.** we left our plates clean.
подчи́тчик, а *m.* (*typ.*) copy-holder.
подчища́|ть, ю *impf. of* **подчи́стить**
подше́фник, а *m.* dependent (*pers. or institution*).
подше́фный *adj.* aided, assisted; (+*d.*) under the patronage (of), sponsored by, supported (by).
подшиб|а́ть, а́ю *impf. of* **~и́ть**
подшиб|и́ть, у́, ёшь, *past* **~́, ~́ла** *pf.* (*of* **~а́ть**) to knock; **п. кому́-н. глаз** to give s.o. a black eye.
подши́б|ленный *p.p.p. of* **~и́ть; п. глаз** black eye.
подшива́|ть, ю *impf. of* **подши́ть**
подши́вк|а, и *f.* **1.** hemming; lining; soling. **2.** hem. **3.** filing (*of papers*); **п. газе́ты** newspaper file.
подши́пник, а *m.* (*tech.*) bearing; bush; **обыкнове́нный п.** journal bearing; **ро́ликовый п.** roller bearing; **ша́риковый п.** ball bearing.
подши́пник|овый *adj. of* **~; п. сплав** Babbitt; **п. щит** bearing housing.
под|ши́ть, ошью́, ошьёшь *pf.* (*of* **~шива́ть**) **1.** to sew underneath; to hem; to line; to sole. **2.** to file (*papers*).
подшле́мник, а *m.* cap comforter.
подшта́нник|и, ов *no sg.* (*coll.*) drawers.
подшто́п|ать, аю *pf.* (*of* **~ывать**) to darn.
подшто́пыва|ть, ю *impf. of* **подшто́пать**
подшу|ти́ть, чу́, ~́тишь *pf.* (*of* **~́чивать**) **(над)** to chaff, mock (at); to play a trick (on).
подшу́чива|ть, ю *impf. of* **подшути́ть**
подъ...[1] *as vbl. pref.* = **под...**[1]
подъ...[2] *as pref. of nn. and adjs.* = **под...**[2]
подъеда́|ть, ю *impf. of* **подъе́сть**
подъе́зд, а *m.* **1.** porch, entrance, doorway. **2.** approach(es).
подъезд|но́й *adj. of* **~ 2.; ~на́я алле́я** drive; **~на́я доро́га** access road; **п. путь** spur track.
подъе́зд|ный *adj. of* **~ 1.**
подъезжа́|ть, ю *impf. of* **подъе́хать**
подъём, а *m.* **1.** lifting; raising; **п. фла́га** hoisting of colours; **п. затону́вшего су́дна** salvaging of a sunken vessel; **п. паро́в** ploughing up. **2.** ascent. **3.** (*aeron.*) climb. **4.** rise, upgrade slope. **5.** (*fig.*) raising, development; rise; **промы́шленный п.** boom, upsurge; **круто́й п. произво́дства** a sharp rise in production; **на ~е** on the up and up, on the upgrade. **6.** (*fig.*) élan; enthusiasm, animation; **говори́ть с больши́м ~ом** to speak with great animation; **лёгок на п.** quick on one's toes, quick off the mark; **тяжёл на п.** sluggish, slow to start. **7.** instep. **8.** rising time; (*mil.*) reveille. **9.** (*tech.*) lever, hand screw, jack.
подъёмник, а *m.* lift, elevator, hoist.
подъёмн|ый *adj.* **1.** lifting; **п. кран** crane, jenny, derrick; **~ая маши́на** lift; **п. механи́зм, ~ое устро́йство** lifting device, hoist; **~ое окно́** sash window. **2.: п. мост** drawbridge, bascule bridge. **3.: ~ые (де́ньги)** travelling expenses (*when moving house*).
подъ|е́сть, е́м, е́шь е́ст, еди́м, еди́те, едя́т, *past* **~е́л** *pf.* (*of* **~еда́ть**) (*coll.*) **1.** to eat up, finish off. **2.** to eat through, eat into.
подъе́|хать, ду, дешь *pf.* (*of* **~зжа́ть**) **(к) 1.** to drive up (to), draw up (to). **2.** (*coll.*) to call (on). **3.** (*fig., coll.*) to get round.
подъязы́чный *adj.* (*anat.*) sub-lingual.
подъяре́мн|ый *adj.* yoked; **~ое живо́тное** beast of burden; **~ая жизнь** (*fig.*) a life under the yoke, enslavement.
подья́ч|ий, его *m.* (*hist.*) scrivener, clerk, government official (*in Muscovite Russia*).
подыгр|а́ть, а́ю *pf.* (*of* **~́ывать**) (+*d.*; *coll.*) **1.** (*mus.*) to accompany; to vamp. **2.** (*theatr.*) to play up (to). **3.** (*cards*) to play into s.o.'s hand.
подыгр|а́ться, а́юсь *pf.* (*of* **~́ываться**) **(к;** *coll.*) to get round.
поды́грыва|ть, ю *impf. of* **подыгра́ть**
поды́грыва|ться, юсь *impf.* **1.** *impf. of* **подыгра́ться. 2.** (*impf. only*) to try to get round.
подыма́|ть(ся), ю(сь) *impf.* (*coll.*) = **поднима́ть(ся)**
поды|ска́ть, щу́, ~́щешь *pf.* (*of* **~́скивать**) to seek out, find.
поды́скива|ть, ю *impf.* **1.** *impf. of* **подыска́ть. 2.** (*impf. only*) to seek, try to find.
подыто́жива|ть, ю *impf. of* **подыто́жить**
подыто́ж|ить, у, ишь *pf.* (*of* **~ивать**) to sum up.
подыха́|ть, ю *impf. of* **подо́хнуть**
подыш|а́ть, у́, ~́ишь *pf.* to breathe; **вы́йти п. све́жим во́здухом** to go out for a breath of fresh air.
поеда́|ть, ю *impf. of* **пое́сть**
поеди́н|ок, ка *m.* duel, single combat.
поедо́м *adv.*: **п. есть кого́-н.** (*coll.*) to make s.o.'s life a misery (by nagging).
по́езд, а, *pl.* **~а́** *m.* **1.** train; **~ом** by train; **п. да́льнего сле́дования** long-distance train; **п. прямо́го сообще́ния** through train. **2.** (*obs.*) convoy, procession (*of vehicles*); **сва́дебный п.** wedding procession.
пое́з|дить, жу, дишь *pf.* to travel about.
пое́здк|а, и *f.* journey; trip, excursion, outing, tour; **ознакоми́тельная п.** fact-finding tour.
по́ездник, а *m.* (*coll.*) commuter (*by rail*).
поезд|но́й *adj. of* **по́езд; ~на́я брига́да** train crew.
поезжа́й(те): *used as imper. of* **е́хать** *and* **пое́хать**
поезжа́н|ин, ина, *pl.* **~е, ~** *m.* (*obs.*) member of wedding procession.
поёмн|ый *adj.* under water at flood times; **~ые луга́** water-meadows.
поёный *adj.* (*agric.*) udder-fed.
по|е́сть, е́м, е́шь, е́ст, еди́м, еди́те, едя́т, *past* **~е́л** *pf.* (*of* **~еда́ть**) **1.** to eat (up). **2.** to eat a little; to take some food, have a bite. **3.** (*of rodents, insects, etc.*) to eat, devour.
пое́|хать, ду, дешь *pf.* (*of* **е́хать**) to go (*in or on a vehicle or on an animal*); to set off, depart; **~хали!** (*coll.*) come on!; come along!; let's go!; **ну, ~хал!** (*coll.*) now he's off!
пожале́|ть, ю *pf. of* **жале́ть**
пожа́л|овать, ую *pf. of* **жа́ловать; добро́ п.!** welcome!; **~уйте** *formula of polite request*; **~уйте сюда́!** would you mind coming here?; this way, please!; **~уйте в столо́вую!** dinner (supper, *etc.*) is served!
пожа́л|оваться, уюсь *pf. of* **жа́ловаться**
пожа́луй *adv.* perhaps; very likely; it may be; if you like; **мы, п., пое́дем** we shall very likely go; **п., ты прав** you may be right; **по мне п.** (*coll.*) it's all right by me.
пожа́луйста *particle* **1.** please; **переда́йте мне, п., каранда́ш** will you please pass me a pencil; **сади́тесь, п.** please sit down. **2.** (*polite expr. of consent*) certainly!, by all means!, with pleasure! (*or not translated*); **мо́жно посмотре́ть э́ти**

снúмки? — **п.** may I look at these photos? Certainly; **передáйте мне, п., кнúгу.** — **п.** would you mind passing me the book? — There you are. **3.** (*polite acknowledgement of thanks*) don't mention it; not at all.

пожáр, а *m.* fire; conflagration; **как на п. бежáть** (*coll.*) to run like hell; **не на п.!** (*coll.*) hold your horses!; there's no hurry!

пожáрищ|е[1], а *m.* (*coll.*) big fire.

пожáрищ|е[2], а *nt.* site of a fire.

пожáрник, а *m.* fireman.

пожáр|ный *adj. of* ~; **~ная комáнда** fire-brigade; **п. кран** fire-cock; **~ная машúна** fire-engine; **п. насóс** fire-pump; **в ~ном порядке** (*coll., joc.*) hastily, in slapdash fashion; **на всякий п. слýчай** (*coll., joc.*) in case of dire need; *as n.* **п., ~ного** *m.* fireman.

пожáти|е, я *nt.*: **п. рукú** handshake.

по|жáть[1], жму, жмёшь *pf.* (*of* **~жимáть**) press, squeeze; **п. рýку** (+*d.*) to shake hands (with); **п. плечáми** to shrug one's shoulders.

по|жáть[2], жну, жнёшь *pf.* (*of* **~жинáть**) to reap (*also fig.*); **п. слáву** to win renown; **п. плоды́ чужóго трудá** (*fig.*) to reap where one has not sown; **что посéешь, то и ~жнёшь** (*prov.*) one must reap as one has sown.

по|жáться, жмýсь, жмёшься *pf.* (*of* **~жимáться**) to shrink up, huddle up.

пож|евáть, уЮ, уЁшь *pf.* (*of* **~ёвывать**) to chew, masticate.

пожёвыва|ть, ю *impf. of* **пожевáть**

пожелáни|е, я *nt.* wish, desire.

пожелá|ть, ю *pf. of* **желáть**

пожелтéлый *adj.* yellowed; gone yellow.

пожелтé|ть, ю *pf. of* **желтéть**

пожен|úть, ю́, ∠ишь *pf. of* **женúть**

пожен|úться, ∠имся *pf.* (*pl. used only*; *of man and woman*) to get married.

пожéртвовани|е, я *nt.* donation, offering.

пожéртв|овать, ую *pf. of* **жéртвовать**

по|жéчь, жгу́, жжёшь, жгут, *past* **~жёг, ~жглá** *pf.* to burn up; to destroy by fire.

пожúв|а, ы *f.* (*coll.*) gain, profit.

поживá|ть, ю *impf.* to live; **как (вы) ~ете?** how are you (getting on)?; **стáли онú жить-п. да добрá наживáть** they lived happily ever after.

пожив|úться, лю́сь, úшься *pf.* (+*i.*; *coll.*) to live (off), profit (by); **п. на счёт другóго** to make good at another's expense.

пожú|вший *p.p. act. of* **~ть** *and adj.* (*usu. pej.*) experienced.

пожидé|ть, ю *pf.* (*coll.*) (*of liquids*) to become thinner, become more dilute.

пожúзненн|ый *adj.* life; for life; **~ое заключéние** life imprisonment; **~ая рéнта** life annuity.

пожилóй *adj.* middle-aged; elderly.

пожимá|ть(ся), ю(сь) *impf. of* **пожáть[1](ся)**

пожинá|ть, ю *impf. of* **пожáть[2]**

пожирá|ть, ю *impf. of* **пожрáть; п. глазáми** to devour with one's eyes.

пожúтк|и, ов *no sg.* (*coll.*) belongings; (one's) things; goods and chattels; **со всéми ~ами** bag and baggage.

по|жúть, живу́, живёшь, *past* **∠жил, ~жилá, ∠жило** *pf.* **1.** to live (*for a time*); to stay; **мы ∠жили три гóда в Кúеве** we lived for three years in Kiev; **я там ~живу́ недéли две** I shall stay there about a couple of weeks. **2.** (*coll.*) to live it up, live fast; **п. в своё удовóльствие** to live for pleasure; **~живём-увúдим** we shall see what we shall see.

пожм|у́, ёшь *see* **пожáть[1]**

пожн|у́, ёшь *see* **пожáть[2]**

пóж|ня, ни, *g. pl.* **~ен** *f.* (*dial.*) stubble(-field).

пожр|áть, у́, ёшь, *past* **~áл, ~алá, ~áло** *pf.* (*of* **пожирáть**) to devour; (*coll.*) to gobble up.

пóз|а, ы *f.* pose, attitude, posture; (*fig.*) pose; **принять, какýю-н. ~у** to strike an attitude, adopt a pose; **принять ~у велúкого учёного** to pose as a great scholar; **э́то тóлько п.** it is a mere pose.

позабáв|ить, лю, ишь *pf.* to amuse a little.

позабáв|иться, люсь, ишься *pf.* to amuse o.s. a little.

позабó|титься, чусь, тишься *pf. of* **забóтиться**

позабывá|ть, ю *impf. of* **позабы́ть**

позаб|ы́ть, у́ду, у́дешь *pf.* (*of* **~ывáть**) (+*a. or* **о**+*p.*; *coll.*) to forget (about).

позавúд|овать, ую *pf. of* **завúдовать**

позáвтрака|ть, ю *pf. of* **зáвтракать**

позавчерá *adv.* the day before yesterday.

позавчерá|шний *adj. of* ~

позадú[1] *adv.* (*of place*; *fig. of time*) behind; **остáвить п.** to leave behind; **наихýдшие временá остáлись п.** the worst times are behind, are past.

позадú[2] *prep.*+*g.* behind.

позаимств|овать, ую *pf. of* **заимствовать**

позапрóшлый *adj.* before last; **п. год** the year before last.

позáр|иться, юсь, ишься *pf. of* **зáриться**

по|звáть, зову́, зовёшь, *past* **~звáл, ~звалá, ~звáло** *pf. of* **звать**

по-звéрски *adv.* brutally, like a beast.

позволéни|е, я *nt.* permission, leave; **с вáшего ~я** with your permission, by your leave; **с ~я сказáть** if one may say so; **э́тот, с ~я сказáть, вождь** (*iron.*) this apology for a leader; this, if one may so call him, leader.

позволúтел|ьный (~ен, ~ьна) *adj.* permissible.

позвóл|ить, ю, ишь *pf.* (*of* **~ять**) (+*d. of pers. and inf.*, +*a. of inanimate object*) to allow, permit; **éсли доктора́ ~ят мне поéхать, я увúжу вас в Москвé** if the doctors allow me to travel, I shall see you in Moscow; **п. себé** (+*inf.*) to permit o.s., venture, take the liberty (of); (+*a.*) to be able to afford; **п. себé сдéлать замечáние** to venture a remark; **п. себé поéздку в Парúж** to be able to afford a trip to Paris; **п. себé вóльность (с**+*i.*) to take liberties (with); **~ь(те)** (*i*) *polite form of request* **~ьте представить дóктора X.** allow me to introduce Doctor X., (*ii*) *expr. of disagreement or objection* **~ьте, что э́то знáчит?** excuse me, what does that mean?

позвол|я́ть, я́ю *impf. of* **∠ить**

позвон|úть(ся), ю́(сь), úшь(ся) *pf. of* **звонúть(ся)**

позвон|óк, кá *m.* (*anat.*) vertebra.

позвонóчник, а *m.* (*anat.*) spine, backbone, spinal column, vertebral column.

позвонóчн|ый *adj.* (*anat.*) vertebral; **п. столб** spinal column, vertebral column; *as n.* **~ые, ~ых** (*zool.*) vertebrates.

поздн|ée *comp. of* **∠ий** *and* **∠о** later; **придú не п. пятú часóв** come by five o'clock at latest.

позднéйший *adj.* later, latest.

пóздн|ий *adj.* late; tardy; **до ~ей нóчи** until late at night, late into the night; **~о** it is late.

пóздно *adv.* late.

поздорóва|ться, юсь *pf. of* **здорóваться**

поздоровé|ть, ю *pf. of* **здоровéть**

поздорóв|иться, ится *pf. only in phr.* (*coll.*): **не ~ится емý,** *etc.* **(от)** much good will it do him, *etc.*

поздравúтел|ь, я *m.* bearer of congratulations, well-wisher.

поздравúтельн|ый *adj.* congratulatory; **~ая кáрточка** greetings card.

поздрáв|ить, лю, ишь *pf.* (*of* **~лять**) **(с**+*i.*) to congratulate (on, upon); **п. когó-н. с днём рождéния** to wish s.o. many happy returns of the day; **п. когó-н. с Нóвым гóдом** to wish s.o. a happy New Year.

поздравлéни|е, я *nt.* congratulation.

поздравля́|ть, ю *impf. of* **поздрáвить**

позёвыва|ть, ю *impf.* (*coll.*) to yawn (from time to time).

позеленé|ть, ю *pf. of* **зеленéть 1.**

позелен|úть, ю́, úшь *pf. of* **зеленúть**

позём, а *m.* (*dial.*) manure.

поземéльный *adj.* land; **п. налóг** land-tax.

позёмк|а, и *f.* blizzard accompanied by ground wind.

позёр, а *m.* poseur; pseud.

пóз|же *comp. of* **~дний** *and* **~дно**; later (on).

по-зúмнему *adv.* as in winter, as for winter; **одéт п.** (dressed) in winter clothes.

позúр|овать, ую *impf.* (+*d.*) to sit (to), pose (for); (*fig.*) to pose.

позити́в, а *m.* (*phot.*) positive.
позитиви́зм, а *m.* (*phil.*) positivism.
позитиви́ст, а *m.* (*phil.*) positivist.
позити́в|ный (~ен, ~на) *adj.* (*in var. senses*) positive.
позитро́н, а *m.* (*phys.*) positron, positive electron.
позицио́нн|ый *adj. of* **пози́ция; ~ая война́** trench warfare.
пози́ци|я, и *f.* (*in var. senses*) position; stand; **вы́годная п.** advantage-ground; **выжида́тельная п.** wait-and-see attitude; **заня́ть ~ю** (*mil.*) to take up a position; (*fig.*) to take one's stand; **с ~и си́лы** from (a position of) strength.
позла|ти́ть, щу́, ти́шь *pf.* (*of* **~ща́ть**) (*obs. or fig.*) to gild.
позлаща́|ть, ю *impf. of* **позлати́ть**
позл|и́ть, ю́, и́шь *pf.* to tease a little.
познава́емост|ь, и *f.* (*phil.*) cognoscibility.
познава́ем|ый (~, ~а) *pres. part. pass. of* **познава́ть** *and adj.* cognizable, knowable.
познава́тельный *adj.* cognitive; **п. проце́сс** cognition.
позна|ва́ть, ю́, ёшь *impf. of* **~́ть**
позна|ва́ться, ю́сь, ёшься *impf.* (*no pf.*) to become known; **друзья́ ~ю́тся в беде́** (*prov.*) a friend in need is a friend indeed.
познако́м|ить(ся), лю(сь), ишь(ся) *pf. of* **знако́мить(ся).**
познако́м|ленный *p.p.p. of* **~ить**
позна́ни|е, я *nt.* **1.** (*phil.*) cognition; **тео́рия ~я** theory of knowledge, epistemology. **2.** (*pl.*) knowledge.
позна́|ть, ю *pf.* (*of* **~ва́ть**) to get to know; to become acquainted with; (*phil.*) to cognize; **п. го́ре** to become acquainted with grief; **п. же́нщину** (*euph.*) to know a woman.
позоло́т|а, ы *f.* gilding, gilt.
позоло|ти́ть, чу́, ти́шь *pf. of* **золоти́ть**
позо́р, а *m.* shame, disgrace; infamy, ignominy; **быть ~ом (для)** to be a disgrace (to); **вы́ставить на п.** to put to shame; **покры́ть себя́ ~ом** to disgrace o.s.; to cover o.s. with ignominy.
позо́р|ить, ю, ишь *impf.* (*of* **о~**) to disgrace, defame, discredit.
позо́р|иться, юсь, ишься *impf.* (*of* **о~**) to disgrace o.s.
позо́рищ|е, а *nt.* (*coll.*) shameful event, disgrace.
позо́р|ный (~ен, ~на) *adj.* shameful, disgraceful; infamous, ignominious; **п. столб** pillory; **поста́вить к ~ному столбу́** (*fig.*) to pillory.
позуме́нт, а *m.* galoon, braid; **золото́й п.** gold braid, gold lace.
позы́в, а *m.* (*physiological*) urge, call; **п. на рво́ту** urge to be sick, (feeling of) nausea.
позыва́|ть, ет *impf.* (*impers.*) to feel an urge, feel a need; **меня́ ~ет на рво́ту** I feel an urge to be sick.
позывн|о́й *adj.* **п. сигна́л** (*radio*) call sign; *as n.* **~ы́е, ~ы́х** call sign; (*naut.*) ship's number; **подня́ть ~ы́е** to make the ship's number.
поигра́|ть, ю *pf.* to have a game, play a little.
пои́грыва|ть, ю *impf.* (*coll.*) to play now and then.
пои́л|ец, ьца *m.*: **п. и корми́лец** (*obs.*) bread-winner.
пои́лк|а, и *f.* **1.** feeding-trough; feeding-bowl. **2.** feeding-vessel (*for invalids*).
поимённо *adv.* by name; **вызыва́ть п.** to call over (*the roll of*).
поимённый *adj.* nominal; **п. спи́сок** list of names, nominal roll.
поимен|ова́ть, у́ю *pf.* to name, call out by name.
по́имк|а, и *f.* catching, capture; **п. на ме́сте преступле́ния** catching in the act, catching red-handed.
поиму́щественный *adj.*: **п. нало́г** property tax.
по-ино́му *adv.* differently, in a different way.
поинтерес|ова́ться, у́юсь *pf.* (*+i.*) to be curious (about); to display interest (in); **он ~ова́лся узна́ть, кто вы** he was curious to find out who you are.
по́иск, а *m.* **1.** (*pl.*) search; **в ~ах** (*+g.*) in search (of), in quest (of). **2.** (*mil.*) (reconnaissance) raid.
пои|ска́ть, щу́, ~́щешь *pf.* to look for, search for; **~щи́те хороше́нько** have a good look.
пои́стине *adv.* indeed, in truth.
по|и́ть, ю́, ~́ишь *impf.* (*of* **на~**) to give to drink; to water (*cattle*); **п. ребёнка** to feed a baby (*at the breast*); **п. вино́м** to treat to wine; **п. и корми́ть семью́** to maintain the family, be the family bread-winner.
по|ищу́, и́щешь *see* **~иска́ть**
пой|ду́, дёшь *see* **~ти́**
по́йл|о, а *nt.* swill, mash; **п. для свине́й** hog-wash, pig-swill.
по́йм|а, ы, *g. pl.* **~** *f.* flood-lands; water-meadow.
пойма́|ть, ю *pf. of* **лови́ть**
пойм|у́, ёшь *see* **поня́ть**
по́йнтер, а *m.* (*dog*) pointer.
пой|ти́, ду́, дёшь, *past* **пошёл, пошла́** *pf.* **1.** *pf. of* **идти́** *and* **ходи́ть; пошёл!** off you go!; **пошёл вон!** be off!; off with you!; **уж е́сли на то пошло́** if it comes to that; for that matter; **(так) не ~дёт** (*coll.*) that won't work; that won't wash. **2.** to begin to (be able to) walk. **3.** (*coll.*) to begin. **4. (в+***a.***)** to take after; **он пошёл в отца́** he takes after his father.
пока́[1] *adv.* for the present, for the time being; **п. что** (*coll.*) in the meanwhile; **п. ещё, п.-то ещё** (*coll.*) not for a while yet; **э́то п. всё** that is all for now; **э́то п. оста́вьте** leave it for the time being; **не беспоко́йтесь, п.-то ещё он появи́тся** don't worry, he won't turn up for a while yet; **ну, п.!** (*coll.*) cheerio!; bye-bye!
пока́[2] *conj.* **1.** while; **нам на́до попроси́ть его́, п. он тут** we must ask him while he is here. **2.: п. не** until, till, before; **не на́до уходи́ть, п. она́ не придёт** we must not go until she comes; **п. ещё не по́здно** before it's too late.
пока́з, а *m.* showing, demonstration; (*fig.*) portrayal; **п. но́вого фи́льма** showing of a new film.
показа́ни|е, я *nt.* **1.** testimony, evidence. **2.** (*leg.*) deposition; affidavit; **дава́ть п.** to testify, bear witness, make a deposition. **3.** reading (*on an instrument*).
пока́з|анный *p.p.p. of* **~а́ть** *and adj.* **1.** (*obs. or coll.*) fixed, appointed; **в ~анное вре́мя** at the time appointed. **2.** (*med.*) indicated.
показа́тел|ь, я *m.* **1.** (*math.*) exponent, index. **2.** index; (*fig.*) showing; **ка́чественные ~и** qualitative indices; **дать хоро́шие ~и, доби́ться хоро́ших ~ей** to make a good showing.
показа́тел|ьный (~ен, ~ьна) *adj.* **1.** significant; instructive, revealing; **о́чень ~ьное заявле́ние** a very significant pronouncement. **2.** model; demonstration; **п. проце́сс** show-trial; **п. уро́к** demonstration lesson, object-lesson; **~ьное хозя́йство** model farm. **3.** (*math.*) exponential.
пока|за́ть, жу́, ~́жешь *pf.* (*of* **~́зывать**) **1.** to show; to display, reveal; **п. себя́** to prove o.s. *or* one's worth; **он ~за́л себя́ хоро́шим ора́тором** he has shown himself to be a good speaker; **п. свои́ зна́ния** to display one's knowledge; **они́ ~за́ли де́вочку врачу́** they took the little girl to the doctor; **он ~за́л вид, что се́рдится** he feigned anger; **п. това́р лицо́м** (*fig., coll.*) to display o.s. in a favourable light. **2.** (*of instruments*) to show, register, read. **3. (на+***a.***)** to point (at, to); **п. кому́-н. на дверь** (*fig., coll.*) to show s.o. the door. **4.** (*leg.*) to testify, give evidence.
пока|за́ться, жу́сь, ~́жешься *pf.* **1.** *pf. of* **каза́ться. 2.** (*pf. of* **~́зываться**) to show o.s.; to appear; to come in sight; **из-за облако́в ~за́лась луна́** the moon appeared from behind the clouds; **п. врачу́** to see a doctor. **3.** *pass. of* **~за́ть**
показно́й *adj.* for show; ostentatious.
показу́х|а, и *f.* (*coll.*) show; **э́то сплошна́я п.** it's all put on, just for show.
пока́зыва|ть(ся), ю(сь) *impf. of* **показа́ть(ся)**
по-како́вски *adv.* (*coll.*) in what language?
пока́лыва|ть, ю *impf.* to prick occasionally; (*impers.*): **у меня́ ~ет в боку́** I have an occasional stitch in my side.
покаля́ка|ть, ю *pf. of* **каля́кать**
пока́мест *adv. and conj.* (*coll.*) = **пока́**
покара́|ть, ю *pf. of* **кара́ть**
score
поката́|ть[1]**, ю** *pf.* to roll.
поката́|ть[2]**, ю** *pf.* to take for a drive; **п. дете́й** to take children out.
поката́|ться, юсь *pf.* to go for a drive; **п. на ло́дке** to go out boating.
пока|ти́ть, чу́, ~́тишь *pf.* **1.** *pf. of* **кати́ть. 2.** to start (rolling), set rolling.

пока|ти́ться, чу́сь, ∠тишься *pf.* **1.** *pf. of* **кати́ться; п. со́ смеху** (*coll.*) to roar with laughter. **2.** to start rolling.
пока́тост|ь, и *f.* slope, incline; declivity.
пока́т|ый (~, ~а) *adj.* sloping; slanting; **п. лоб** retreating forehead.
покача́|ть, ю *pf.* to rock, swing (for a time); **п. ребёнка на качéлях** to give a child a swing; **п. голово́й** to shake one's head.
покача́|ться, юсь *pf.* to rock, swing (for a time); to have a swing.
пока́чива|ться, юсь *impf.* to rock slightly; **идти́ ~ясь** to walk unsteadily.
покачн|у́ть, у́, ёшь *pf.* to shake.
покачн|у́ться, у́сь, ёшься *pf.* **1.** to sway, totter, give a lurch. **2.** (*fig., coll.*) to totter, go downhill.
пока́шлива|ть, ю *impf.* to have a slight cough; to cough intermittently.
пока́шля|ть, ю *pf.* to cough.
покая́ни|е, я *nt.* **1.** (*eccl.*) confession. **2.** penitence, repentance; **принести́ п.** (**в**+*p.*) to repent (of); **отпусти́ть ду́шу на п.** (*obs. or coll.*) to let go in peace.
покая́нный *adj.* penitential.
пока́|яться, юсь, ешься *pf. of* **ка́яться**
покварта́льно *adv.* by the quarter, per quarter, every quarter.
поквита́|ться, юсь *pf.* (**с**+*i.*; *coll.*) to be quits (with); to get even (with); **тепе́рь мы с ва́ми ~лись** now we're quits; **я ещё с ним ~юсь** I'll get even with him yet.
по́кер, а *m.* (*card-game*) poker.
по́кер|ный *adj. of* ~
покива́|ть, ю *pf.* to nod (*several times*).
покида́|ть, ю *impf. of* **поки́нуть**
поки́нут|ый *p.p.p. of* **~ь** *and adj.* deserted; abandoned.
поки́|нуть, ну, нешь *pf.* (*of* **~да́ть**) to leave; to desert, abandon, forsake.
поклада́я *only in phr.* **не п. рук** indefatigably.
покла́дист|ый (~, ~а) *adj.* complaisant, obliging.
покла́ж|а, и *f.* (*coll.*) load; luggage.
поклёп, а *m.* (*coll.*) slander, calumny; **взвести́ п.** (**на**+*a.*) to slander, cast aspersions (on).
покли́|кать, чу, чешь *pf.* (*coll.*) to call (to).
покло́н, а *m.* **1.** bow; **сде́лать п.** to bow (*in greeting*); **класть ~ы** to bow (*in prayer*); **идти́ на п., идти́ с ~ом к кому́-н.** to go cap in hand to s.o. **2.** (*fig.*) greeting; **посла́ть ~ы** to send one's compliments, send one's kind regards.
поклоне́ни|е, я *nt.* worship.
поклон|и́ться, ю́сь, ∠ишься *pf. of* **кла́няться**
покло́нник, а *m.* admirer, worshipper.
покло́ня́|ться, юсь *impf.* (+*d.*) to worship.
покля́|сться, ну́сь, нёшься *pf. of* **кля́сться**
поко́вк|а, и *f.* (*tech.*) forging; forged piece.
поко́ем *adv.* (*obs.*) in the shape of the letter **п.**
поко́|ить, ю, ишь *impf.* (*obs.*) to tend, cherish.
поко́|иться, юсь, ишься *impf.* **1.** (**на**+*p.*) to rest (on, upon), repose (on, upon), be based (on, upon); **п. на дога́дке** to be based on conjecture. **2.** (*of the dead*) to lie; **здесь ~ится прах** (+*g.*) here lies (the body of).
поко́|й[1], **я** *m.* rest, peace; **ве́чный п.** (*fig., poet.*) eternal rest; **оста́вить в ~е** to leave in peace; **уйти́ на п., удали́ться на п.** to retire; **то́чка ~я** (*phys.*) point of rest, fulcrum; **у́гол ~я** (*phys.*) angle of repose.
поко́|й[2], **я** *m.* (*obs.*) room, chamber.
поко́йник, а *m.* the deceased.
поко́йницк|ая, ой *f.* mortuary.
поко́йницкий *adj.* (*coll.*) corpse-like.
поко́|йный[1] **(~ен, ~йна)** *adj.* **1.** calm, quiet; **бу́дьте ~йны** don't be alarmed; don't (you) worry. **2.** comfortable; restful; **~йной но́чи!** good night!
поко́йн|ый[2] *adj.* (the) late; **п. коро́ль** the late king; *as n.* **п., ~ого** *m.*, **~ая, ~ой** *f.* the deceased.
поколеб|а́ть, ∠лю, ∠лешь *pf. of* **колеба́ть**
поколеб|а́ться, ∠люсь, ∠лешься *pf.* **1.** *pf. of* **колеба́ться. 2.** to waver for a time, hesitate for a time.
поколе́ни|е, я *nt.* generation; **из ~я в п.** from generation to generation.
поколо|ти́ть(ся), чу́(сь), ∠тишь(ся) *pf. of* **колоти́ть(ся)**
поко́нч|ить, у, ишь *pf.* (**с**+*i.*) **1.** to finish off; to finish (with), be through (with), have done (with); **с э́тим ~ено** that's done with. **2.** to put an end (to); to do away (with); **п. с собо́й** to put an end to one's life; to do away with o.s.; **п. жизнь самоуби́йством** to commit suicide.
покоре́ни|е, я *nt.* subjugation, subdual; **п. во́здуха** conquest of the air.
покори́тел|ь, я *m.* subjugator; **п. серде́ц** lady-killer.
покор|и́ть, ю́, и́шь *pf.* (*of* **~я́ть**) to subjugate, subdue; **п. чьё-н. се́рдце** to win s.o.'s heart.
покор|и́ться, ю́сь, и́шься *pf.* (*of* **~я́ться**) (+*d.*) to submit (to); to resign o.s. (to); **п. свое́й у́части** to resign o.s. to one's lot.
покорм|и́ть(ся), лю́(сь), ∠ишь(ся) *pf. of* **корми́ть(ся)**
поко́рн|ейший *superl. of* **~ый; ваш п. слуга́** (*polite formula in concluding letter*; *obs.*) your most humble servant; **~ейшая про́сьба** most humble petition.
поко́рно *adv.* humbly; submissively, obediently; **п. благодарю́** (*coll.*) thank you; **благодарю́ п.** (*iron.*; *expr. refusal and/or astonishment*) thank you (very much)!; **благодарю́ п., я уж лу́чше пешко́м** thank you, I would rather walk.
поко́рност|ь, и *f.* submissiveness, obedience.
поко́р|ный (~ен, ~на) *adj.* **1.** (+*d.*) submissive (to), obedient; **п. судьбе́** resigned to one's fate. **2.** (*in conventional expressions of politeness*; *obs.*) humble, obedient; **ваш п. слуга́** your obedient servant; **слуга́ п.!** (*coll., iron.*) no, thank you!; I'm not having any!
покоро́б|ить(ся), лю(сь), ишь(ся) *pf. of* **коро́бить(ся)**
поко́рств|овать, ую *impf.* (+*d.*; *obs.*) to submit (to); to be submissive (to), be obedient (to).
покор|я́ть(ся), я́ю(сь) *impf. of* **~и́ть(ся)**
поко́с, а *m.* **1.** mowing, haymaking; **второ́й п.** aftermath. **2.** meadow(-land).
покоси́|вшийся *p.p. of* **~ться** *and adj.* rickety, crazy, ramshackle.
поко|си́ться, шу́сь, си́шься *pf. of* **коси́ться**
покра́ж|а, и *f.* **1.** theft. **2.** stolen goods.
покра́п|ать, лет *pf.* (*of rain*) to spit.
покра́пыва|ть, ет *impf.*; (*impers.*): **~л дождь, ~ло** it was spitting with rain off and on.
покра́|сить, жу, сишь *pf. of* **кра́сить**
покра́ск|а, и *f.* painting, colouring.
покрасне́|ть, ю *pf. of* **красне́ть 1.**
покрив|и́ть(ся), лю́(сь), и́шь(ся) *pf. of* **криви́ть(ся)**
покри́кива|ть, ю *impf.* (**на**+*a.*; *coll.*) to shout (at).
покро́в[1], **а** *m.* **1.** cover; covering; hearse-cloth, pall; (*fig.*) cloak, shroud, pall; **ко́жный п.** (*anat.*) integument; **по́чвенный п.** top-soil; **сне́жный п.** blanket of snow; **твёрдый п.** (*biol.*) crust, incrustation; **под ~ом но́чи** under cover of night. **2.** (*obs.*) coverlet; blanket. **3.** (*fig., obs.*) protection; **взять под свой п.** to take under one's protection.
Покро́в[2], **а́** *m.* (*eccl.*) (Feast of) the Protection, Protective Veil (of the Virgin).
покрови́тел|ь, я *m.* patron, protector.
покрови́тельниц|а, ы *f.* patroness, protectress.
покрови́тельственн|ый *adj.* **1.** (*in var. senses*) protective; **~ая систе́ма** (*econ.*) protectionism; **п. тари́ф** (*econ.*) protective tariff; **~ая окра́ска** (*zool.*) protective colouring. **2.** condescending, patronizing.
покрови́тельств|о, а *nt.* protection, patronage; **О́бщество ~а живо́тным** Society for the Prevention of Cruelty to Animals; **под ~ом** (+*g.*) under the patronage (of), under the auspices (of).
покрови́тельств|овать, ую *impf.* (+*d.*) to protect, patronize.
покро́в|ный *adj. of* **~**; (*anat.*) integumentary; **~ные культу́ры, ~ные расте́ния** (*agric.*) cover crops; **~ное стёклышко** cover glass (*of microscope*).
покро́|й, я *m.* cut (*of garment*); **все на оди́н п.** (*fig.*) all in the same style.
покро́мк|а, и *f.* selvedge.
покрош|и́ть, у́, ∠ишь *pf.* (+*a. or g.*) to crumble; to crumb; to mince, chop.

покругле́|ть, ю *pf. of* **кругле́ть**
покруж|и́ть, у́, ~́ишь *pf.* (*coll.*) **1.** to circle several times. **2.** to roam, wander (*for some time*).
покрупне́|ть, ю *pf. of* **крупне́ть**
покрыва́л|о, а *nt.* **1.** coverlet, bedspread, counterpane. **2.** shawl; veil. **3.** cover; **нефтяно́е п.** oil-slick.
покрыва́|ть(ся), ю(сь) *impf. of* **покры́ть(ся)**
покры́ти|е, я *nt.* **1.** covering; **п. доро́ги** road surfacing; **п. кры́ши** roofing. **2.** covering, discharge, payment; **п. расхо́дов** defrayment of expenses.
покр|ы́ть, о́ю, о́ешь *pf.* (*of* **крыть** *and* **~ыва́ть**) **1.** to cover; **п. кры́шей** to roof; **п. кра́ской** to coat with paint; **п. ла́ком** to varnish, lacquer; **п. позо́ром** to cover with shame; **п. себя́ сла́вой** to cover o.s. with glory; **п. та́йной** to shroud in mystery. **2.** to meet, pay off; **п. расхо́ды** to cover expenses, defray expenses. **3.** to drown (*sound*). **4.** to shield, cover up (for); to hush up. **5.** to cover (*distance*). **6.** (*cards*) to cover. **7.** (*coll.*) to curse, swear (at). **8.** (*zool., of stallion, bull, etc.*) to cover.
покр|ы́ться, о́юсь, о́ешься *pf.* (*of* **~ыва́ться**) to cover o.s.; to get covered.
покры́шк|а, и *f.* **1.** cover(ing); **ни дна ни ~и,** *see* **дно. 2.** tyre-cover, (outer) tyre.
поку́да *adv. and conj.* (*coll.*) = **пока́**
покум|и́ться, лю́сь, и́шься *pf. of* **куми́ться**
покупа́тел|ь, я *m.* buyer, purchaser; customer, client.
покупа́тельн|ый *adj.* purchasing; **~ая спосо́бность** (*econ.*) purchasing power.
покупа́тель|ский *adj. of* **~**
покупа́|ть[1], ю *impf. of* **купи́ть**
покупа́|ть[2], ю *pf.* to bathe; to bath.
покупа́|ться, юсь *pf.* to bathe, have a bathe; to have, take a bath.
поку́пк|а, и *f.* **1.** buying; purchasing, purchase. **2.** (*object purchased*) purchase; **вы́годная п.** bargain; **де́лать ~и** to go shopping.
покуп|но́й *adj.* **1.** bought, purchased (*opp. home-made or received as a gift*). **2.** = **~а́тельный; ~на́я цена́** purchase price.
покупщи́к, а́ *m.* (*obs.*) buyer, purchaser.
поку́рива|ть, ю *impf.* (*coll.*) to smoke (a little, from time to time).
покур|и́ть, ю́, ~́ишь *pf.* **1.** *pf. of* **кури́ть. 2.** to have a smoke; **дава́й ~́им** let's have a smoke.
покуса́|ть, ю *pf.* to bite; to sting.
поку|си́ться, шу́сь, си́шься *pf.* (*of* **~ша́ться**) (**на**+*a.*) **1.** to attempt, make an attempt (upon); **п. на свою́ жизнь** to make an attempt upon one's own life; **п. на самоуби́йство** to attempt suicide. **2.** to encroach (on, upon); **п. на чьи-н. права́** to encroach on s.o.'s rights.
поку́ша|ть, ю *pf. of* **ку́шать**
покуша́|ться, юсь *impf. of* **покуси́ться**
покуше́ни|е, я *nt.* attempt; **п. на жизнь** (+*g.*) (*or* **на**+*a.*) attempt upon the life (of).
пол[1], а, о ~́е, на ~у́, *pl.* **~ы́** *m.* floor.
пол[2], а *m.* sex; **обо́его ~́а** of both sexes.
пол... *comb. form, abbr. of* **полови́на**; half (*as in* **полчаса́** half an hour; **полдеся́того** half past nine; **полдю́жины** half a dozen, *etc.*)
пол|а́, ы́, *pl.* **~́ы** *f.* skirt, flap, lap; **из-под ~ы́** on the sly, under cover; **торгова́ть из-под ~ы́** to sell under the counter.
полага́|ть[1], ю *impf.* (*obs.*) to lay, place.
полага́|ть[2], ю *impf.* to suppose, think; **~ют, что он умира́ет** he is believed to be dying; **на́до п.** it is to be supposed; one must suppose.
полага́|ться, юсь *impf.* **1.** *impf. of* **положи́ться. 2.** (*impers.*): **~ется** one is supposed (to); **так ~ется** it is the custom; **не ~ется** it is not done; **здесь ~ется снима́ть шля́пу** one is supposed to take off one's hat here. **3. ~ется** (+*d.*) to be due (to); **нам э́то ~ется** it is our due; we have a right to it.
пола́|дить, жу, дишь *pf.* (**с**+*i.*) to come to an understanding (with); to get on (with).
пола́ком|ить(ся), лю(сь), ишь(ся) *pf. of* **ла́комить(ся)**
пола́т|и, ей *no sg.* sleeping-bench (*on high raised platform in Russ. peasant hut*).
по́лб|а, ы *f.* (*bot.*) spelt, German wheat.
полбеды́ *f.* (*coll.*) a small loss, a minor misfortune; **э́то ещё п.** it is not so very serious.
по́лб|енный *adj. of* **~а**
полве́ка, полуве́ка *m.* half a century.
полго́да, полуго́да *m.* half a year, six months; **с п., о́коло полуго́да** for about six months.
полго́ря = полбеды́
по́лдень, полу́дня *and* **по́лдня** *m.* **1.** noon, midday; **за п.** (*or* **за́ полдень**) past noon; **к полу́дню** towards noon; **вре́мя до полу́дня** forenoon; **вре́мя по́сле полу́дня** afternoon. **2.** (*obs.*) south.
полдне́вный *adj. of* **по́лдень**
по́лдник, а *m.* (afternoon) snack (*light meal between dinner and supper*).
по́лдничa|ть *impf.* (*coll.*) to have an (afternoon) snack.
полдоро́г|и *f.* half-way; **встре́титься на ~е** to meet half-way; **останови́ться на ~е** to stop half-way (*also fig.*).
по́л|е, я, *pl.* **~я́, ~е́й** *nt.* **1.** (*in var. senses*) field; **спорти́вное п.** playing field, sports ground; **п. би́твы, п. бра́ни** (*obs.*), **п. сраже́ния** battle-field; **п. де́ятельности** sphere of action; **п. зре́ния** field of vision; **оди́н в п. не во́ин** (*prov.*) the voice of one man is the voice of no one. **2.** (*art*) ground; (*heraldry*) field. **3.** (*pl.*) margin; **заме́тки на ~ях** notes in the margin. **4.** (*pl.*) brim (*of hat*).
полеве́ни|е, я *nt.* (*pol.*) leftward movement.
полеве́|ть, ю *pf. of.* **леве́ть**
полёвк|а, и *f.* field-vole.
полево́дств|о, а *nt.* field-crop cultivation.
полев|о́й *adj.* (*in var. senses*) field; **~а́я артилле́рия** field artillery; **п. бино́кль** field glasses; **п. го́спиталь** field hospital; **~а́я мышь** field-mouse; **~а́я су́мка** (*mil.*) map case; **~ы́е цветы́** wild flowers; **п. шпат** (*min.*) feldspar.
полега́ни|е, я *nt.* (*agric.*) lodging (*of crops*).
полега́|ть, ю *impf. of* **поле́чь 3.**
полего́ньку *adv.* (*coll.*) by easy stages.
полегча́|ть, ет *pf. of* **легча́ть; больно́му ~ло** the patient is feeling better; **у меня́ на душе́ ~ло** I feel a load off my mind.
поле́гче *comp. of* **лёгкий** *and* **легко́ 1.** (*somewhat, a little*) lighter. **2.** a little easier, a little less difficult; **п.!** take it easy!, ease up a bit!, not so fast!
полеж|а́ть, у́, и́шь *pf.* to lie down (*for a while*).
полёжива|ть, ю *impf.* (*coll.*) to lie down (*off and on*).
поле́з|ный (~́ен, ~на) *adj.* useful; helpful; wholesome, health-giving; **~ное де́йствие** efficiency, duty (*of a machine*); **~ная жила́я пло́щадь** actual living space; **~ная лошади́ная си́ла** effective horsepower, working horsepower; **~ная нагру́зка** (*tech.*) working load, pay-load; **э́то лека́рство о́чень ~но от ка́шля** this medicine is very good for coughs; **чем могу́ быть ~ен?** can I help you?
поле́з|ть, у, ешь, *past* **~, ~ла** *pf.* **1.** *pf. of* **лезть. 2.** to start to climb.
полемизи́р|овать, ую *impf.* (**с**+*i.*) to carry on polemics (with).
поле́мик|а, и *f.* polemic(s); dispute, controversy; **вступи́ть в ~у** (**с**+*i.*) to enter into polemics (with).
полеми́ст, а *m.* polemicist, controversialist.
полеми́ческий *adj.* polemic(al), controversial.
полеми́ч|ный (~ен, ~на) *adj.* polemical.
поле́нива|ться, юсь *impf.* (*coll.*) to be rather lazy.
полен|и́ться, ю́сь, ~́ишься *pf.* (+*inf.*) to be too lazy to.
поле́ниц|а, ы *c.g.* (*folk poet.*) hero, heroine.
поле́нниц|а, ы *f.* pile (*of logs*); stack (*of firewood*).
поле́н|о, а, *pl.* **~ья, ~ьев** log, billet.
поле́сь|е, я *nt.* wooded locality; woodlands.
полёт, а *m.* flight; flying; **бре́ющий п.** hedge-hopping; **высо́тный п.** altitude flying; **пики́рующий п.** diving; **слепо́й п.** blind flying; **фигу́рный п.** aerobatics; **вид с пти́чьего ~а** bird's-eye view; **п. фанта́зии** flight of fancy; **пти́ца высо́кого ~а** (*fig., oft. iron.*) bigwig.
полета́|ть, ю *pf.* to fly (*for a while*), do some flying.
поле|те́ть, чу́, ти́шь *pf.* **1.** *pf. of* **лете́ть. 2.** to start to fly;

to fly off. **3.** (*fig., coll.*) to fall, go headlong.
по-ле́тнему *adv.* as in summer, as for summer; **одёт п.** (dressed) in summer clothes.
полеч|и́ть, у́, ~́ишь *pf.* to treat (*for a while*).
полеч|и́ться, у́сь, ~́ишься *pf.* to undergo treatment (*for a while*).
пол|е́чь, я́гу, я́жешь, я́гут, *past* **~ёг, ~егла́** *pf.* **1.** to lie down (*in numbers*). **2.** (*fig.*) to fall, be killed (*in numbers*). **3.** (*impf.* **~ега́ть**) (*agric.*) to be lodged (*of standing crops*).
по́лз|ать, аю *impf.*, *indet. of* **~ти́; п. в нога́х у кого́-н.** (*fig.*) to grovel at s.o.'s feet.
ползко́м *adv.* crawling, on all fours.
полз|ти́, у́, ёшь, *past* **~, ~ла́** *impf.* **1.** to crawl, creep (along); **по́езд ~** the train was crawling. **2.** to ooze (out). **3.** (*fig., coll.; of rumour, etc.*) to spread. **4.** (*coll.; of fabric*) to fray, ravel out. **5.** (*of soil*) to slip, collapse.
ползу́н, а́ *m.* (*tech.*) slide-block, slider, runner.
ползун|о́к, ка́ *m.* **1.** (*coll.*) toddler. **2.** *pl.* (*coll.*) rompers, romper suit.
ползу́ч|ий *adj.* creeping; **~ие расте́ния** (*bot.*) creepers.
поли... *comb. form* poly-.
полиа́ндри|я, и *f.* polyandry.
полиартри́т, а *m.* (*med.*) polyarthritis.
поли́в|а, ы *f.* glaze.
полива́|ть(ся), ю(сь) *impf. of* **поли́ть(ся)**
поливитами́н|ы, ов *no sg.* multivitamins.
поли́вк|а¹, и *f.* watering.
поли́вк|а², и *f.* gravy.
поливн|о́й *adj.* requiring irrigation; requiring watering; **~ы́е зе́мли** irrigation area.
поли́в|очный *adj. of* **~ка¹; ~очная жи́дкость** cooling mixture, coolant; **~очная маши́на** watering machine.
полига́ми|я, и *f.* polygamy.
полигло́т, а *m.* polyglot.
полиго́н, а *m.* (*mil.*) (artillery *or* bombing) range; **испыта́тельный п.** proving ground, testing area; **уче́бный п.** training ground.
полиграфи́ст, а *m.* printing trades worker.
полиграфи́ческ|ий *adj.* **1.** polygraphic; **~ое произво́дство** printing. **2.: п. отде́л** non-specialist section (*of library*).
полиграфи́|я, и *f.* **1.** (*tech.*) polygraphy; printing trades. **2.** non-specialist section (*of library, in which books are classified by authors' names only, without regard to subject-matter*).
поликли́ник|а, и *f.* **1.** polyclinic, clinic; health centre. **2.** outpatients' department (*of hospital*).
полилове́|ть, ю *pf. of* **лилове́ть**
полиме́р, а *m.* (*chem.*) polymer.
полимериза́ци|я, и *f.* (*chem.*) polymerization.
полиморфи́зм, а *m.* polymorphism.
полиморфи́ческий *adj.* polymorphic, polymorphous.
полимо́рфный *adj.* polymorphous.
полинези́|ец, йца *m.* Polynesian.
полинези́|йка, йки *f. of* **~ец**
полинези́йский *adj.* Polynesian.
Полине́зи|я, и *f.* Polynesia.
полиненасы́щенн|ый *adj.*: **~ые жиры́** polyunsaturated fats.
полино́м, а *m.* (*math.*) polynomial.
полиня́лый *adj.* faded, discoloured.
полиня́|ть, ет *pf. of* **линя́ть**
полиомиели́т, а *m.* (*med.*) poliomyelitis, infantile paralysis.
поли́п, а *m.* **1.** (*zool.*) polyp. **2.** (*med.*) polypus.
поли́п|ный *adj. of* **~**
полирова́льн|ый *adj.* polishing; **~ая бума́га** sandpaper; **п. стано́к** buffing machine.
полир|ова́ть, у́ю *impf.* (*of* **от~**) to polish.
поliро́вк|а, и *f.* polish(ing); buffing.
полиро́вочный *adj.* polishing; buffing.
полиро́вщик, а *m.* polisher.
по́лис, а *m.* policy; **страхово́й п.** insurance policy.
полисеманти́зм, а *m.* (*ling.*) polysemy.
полисеманти́ческий *adj.* (*ling.*) polysemantic.
полисеми́|я, и *f.* (*ling.*) polysemy.
полисинтети́ческий *adj.* (*ling.*) polysynthetic.
полисме́н, а *m.* policeman; constable.
полиспа́ст, а *m.* block and tackle; pulley block; tackle block.
поли́стный *adj.* per sheet.
полит... *comb. form, abbr. of* **полити́ческий**
политбюро́ *nt. indecl.* the Politburo (*executive organ of the Central Committee of the CPSU*).
политгра́мот|а, ы *f.* elementary course of political education.
политеи́зм, а *m.* polytheism.
политеи́ст, а *m.* polytheist.
политеисти́ческий *adj.* polytheistic.
политехниза́ци|я, и *f.* introduction of polytechnic education.
полите́хник, а *m.* student of polytechnic.
полите́хникум, а *m.* polytechnic (school).
политехни́ческий *adj.* polytechnic(al).
политзаключённ|ый, ого *m.* political prisoner.
поли́тик, а *m.* **1.** politician. **2.** student of politics; expert on political questions. **3.** (*fig., coll.*) politician, political figure.
поли́тик|а, и *f.* **1.** policy; **п. на гра́ни войны́** 'brinkmanship'; **провести́ ~у** to carry out a policy. **2.** politics; **п. си́лы** power politics; **говори́ть о ~е** to talk politics.
политика́н, а *m.* (*pej.*) politician, intriguer.
политика́нств|о, а *nt.* intrigue.
политика́нств|овать, ую *impf.* to intrigue, be an intriguer.
политинформа́тор, а *m.* political information officer.
политипа́ж, а *m.* (*typ.*) polytype.
полити́ческ|ий *adj.* political; **п. де́ятель** political figure, politician; **~ие нау́ки** political science; **~ая эконо́мия** political economy; **по ~им соображе́ниям** for political reasons.
полити́ч|ный (~ен, ~на) *adj.* (*coll.*) politic.
политкаторжа́н|ин, ина, *pl.* **~е, ~** *m.* political convict (*in pre-1917 Russia*).
политкруж|о́к, ка́ *m.* political study circle.
полито́лог, а *m.* political scientist.
политоло́ги|я, и *f.* political science.
политпросве́т, а *m.* (*formed from abbr. of* **полити́ческий** *and* **просвети́тельный**) political education.
политрабо́тник, а *m.* political worker.
политру́к, а *m.* (*abbr. of* **полити́ческий руководи́тель**) political instructor (*in former USSR, in units of armed forces*).
политуправле́ни|е, я *nt.* Political Administration.
политу́р|а, ы *f.* polish, varnish.
политучёб|а, ы *f.* political education; study of current affairs.
политшко́л|а, ы *f.* political school.
пол|и́ть, ью́, ьёшь, *past* **~́л, ~ила́, ~́йло** *pf.* (*of* **~ива́ть**) **1.** (*+a. and i.*) to pour (on, upon); **п. что-н. водо́й** to pour water on sth.; **п. цветы́** to water the flowers. **2.** to begin to pour.
пол|и́ться, ью́сь, ьёшься, *past* **~и́лся, ~ила́сь, ~и́ло́сь** *pf.* (*of* **~ива́ться**) **1.** (*+i.*) to pour over o.s. **2.** to begin to flow.
политэконо́м, а *m.* (*coll.*) political economist.
политэконо́ми|я, и *f.* political economy.
политэмигра́нт, а *m.* political refugee.
полифони́ческий *adj.* polyphonic.
полифони́|я, и *f.* (*mus.*) polyphony.
полихлорвини́л, а *m.* PVC (*polyvinyl chloride*).
полицейме́йстер, а *m.* (*hist.*) chief of police.
полице́йск|ий *adj.* police; **п. уча́сток** police-station; *as n.* **п., ~ого** *m.* policeman, police-officer.
поли́ци|я, и *f.* police; **сыскна́я п.** criminal investigation department.
поли́чн|ое, ого *nt.*: **пойма́ть с ~ым** to catch red-handed.
полишине́л|ь, я *m.* Punch(inello); **секре́т ~я** open secret.
полиэ́др, а *m.* (*math.*) polyhedron.
полиэтиле́н, а *m.* polythene.
полк, а́, о ~е́, в ~у́ *m.* regiment; **авиацио́нный п.** group (*in air force*); **на́шего ~у́ при́было** (*coll.*) our numbers have grown; our ranks have swollen.

по́лк|а[1], **и** *f.* **1.** shelf; **кни́жная п.** bookshelf. **2.** (*in rail. sleeping-car*) berth.
по́лк|а[2], **и** *f.* weeding.
полко́вник, а *m.* colonel.
полково́д|ец, ца *m.* (*not denoting specific mil. rank*) captain, commander; military leader; warlord.
полково́й *adj.* regimental.
поллюта́нт, а *m.* pollutant.
поллю́ци|я, и *f.* (*physiol.*) spermatorrhoea, nocturnal emission.
полмиллио́на *m.* half a million.
полмину́ты *f.* half a minute.
полне́йший *adj.* sheer, uttermost.
полне́|ть, ю *impf.* (*of* **по~**) to grow stout, put on weight.
полнёхон|ький (~ек, ~ька) *adj.* (*coll.*) brim-full, crammed, packed.
полн|и́ть, ю́, и́шь *impf.* (*coll.*) to overfill; **э́то пла́тье её ~и́т** this dress makes her look fat.
по́лно[1] *adv.* brim-full, full to the brim; **сли́шком п.** too full.
по́лно[2] *adv.* (*coll.*) **1.** enough (of that)!; that will do!; **п. ворча́ть!** stop grumbling! **2.** you don't mean that; you don't mean to say so.
полно́ *adv.* (+*g.*) (*coll.*) lots; **в ко́мнате полно́ наро́ду** the room is packed with people.
полнове́сност|ь, и *f.* **1.** full weight. **2.** (*fig.*) soundness.
полнове́с|ный (~ен, ~на) *adj.* **1.** of full weight, full-weight. **2.** (*fig.*) sound.
полновла́сти|е, я *nt.* sovereignty.
полновла́ст|ный (~ен, ~на) *adj.* sovereign; **п. хозя́ин** sole master.
полново́д|ный (~ен, ~на) *adj.* deep.
полново́дь|е, я *nt.* high water.
полногла́си|е, я *nt.* (*ling.*) full vocalism, pleophony.
полнозву́ч|ный (~ен, ~на) *adj.* sonorous.
полнокро́ви|е, я *nt.* (*med.*) plethora.
полнокро́в|ный (~ен, ~на) *adj.* **1.** (*med.*) plethoric. **2.** (*fig.*) full-blooded, sanguineous.
полнолу́ни|е, я *nt.* full moon.
полнометра́жный *adj.*: **п. фильм** feature-length film.
полномо́чи|е, я *nt.* authority, power, plenary powers; commission; (*leg.*) proxy; **чрезвыча́йные ~я** emergency powers; **срок ~й** term of office; **превыше́ние ~й** exceeding one's commission; **дать ~я** (+*d.*) to empower; **име́ть ~я вы́ступить от и́мени** (+*g.*) to have authority to speak (for); **предъяви́ть свои́ ~я** (**на**+*a.*) to show one's authority (to, for).
полномо́ч|ный (~ен, ~на) *adj.* plenipotentiary; **п. представи́тель** plenipotentiary.
полнопра́ви|е, я *nt.* full rights; competency.
полнопра́в|ный (~ен, ~на) *adj.* enjoying full rights; competent; **п. член** full member.
полноро́дный *adj.* (*leg.*) full (*brother or sister, as opposed to half-brother, half-sister*).
по́лностью *adv.* fully, in full; completely, utterly; **п. верну́ть долг** to pay a debt in full; **п. утверди́ть ме́ру** to approve a measure in its entirety.
полнот|а́, ы́ *no pl., f.* **1.** fullness, completeness; plenitude; **от ~ы́ се́рдца, души́** in the fullness of one's heart; **п. вла́сти** absolute power. **2.** stoutness, corpulence; plumpness.
по́лноте *int.* (*coll.*) enough!; come come!
полноце́нност|ь, и *f.* full value.
полноце́н|ный (~ен, ~на) *adj.* **1.** of full value. **2.** (*fig.*) of value; **~ная рабо́та** work done in accordance with requirements.
полно́чи *f. indecl.* half the (a) night.
полно́чный *adj.* **1.** midnight. **2.** (*obs.*) northern.
по́лночь, по́лночи *and* **полу́ночи** *f.* **1.** midnight; **за́ п.** after midnight. **2.** (*obs.*) north.
по́л|ный (~он, ~на́, ~́но́) *adj.* **1.** (+*g. or i.*) full (of); complete, entire, total; absolute; **в состоя́нии ~ного безу́мия** stark mad; **п. биле́т** whole ticket (*opp. child's ticket of half fare*); **~ным го́лосом** at the top of one's voice; **сказа́ть ~ным го́лосом** (*fig.*) to say outright; **жить ~ной жи́знью** to live a full life; **~ное затме́ние** total eclipse; **п. карма́н** (+*g.*) a pocketful (of); **~ная незави́симость** complete independence, full sovereignty; **~ное ничто́жество** a complete nonentity; **п. пансио́н** full board and lodging; **п. поко́й** absolute rest; **~ное собра́ние сочине́ний** complete works; **п. ход вперёд!** full speed ahead!; **идти́ ~ным хо́дом** to be in full swing; **~ная ча́ша** (*fig.*) plenty; **в ~ной ме́ре** fully, in full measure; **в ~ном расцве́те сил** in one's prime; **они́ пришли́ в ~ном соста́ве** they came in full force; **на ~ном ходу́** at full speed; **он пи́шет с ~ным зна́нием де́ла** he writes with a complete grasp of his subject. **2.** stout, portly; plump.
полны́м-полно́ *adv.* chock-full, chock-a-block, jam-packed; **в авто́бусе бы́ло п.-п наро́ду** the bus was jam-packed with people.
по́ло *nt indecl.* (*sport*) polo; **во́дное п.** water polo.
пол-оборо́та *m. indecl.* half-turn; **п. нале́во, напра́во** (*mil.*) left, right incline.
поло́в|а, ы *f.* chaff.
полови́к, а́ *m.* mat, matting floor-covering; door-mat.
полови́н|а, ы *f.* **1.** half; middle; **два с ~ой** two and a half; **п. шесто́го** half past five; **в ~е девятна́дцатого ве́ка** in the middle of the nineteenth century; **на ~е доро́ги** halfway; **п. две́ри** leaf of a door. **2.** (*obs.*) apartment, rooms, wing.
полови́нк|а, и *f.* **1.** half. **2.** leaf (*of door*).
полови́нн|ый *adj.* half; **п. окла́д** half-pay; **заплати́ть за что-н. в ~ом разме́ре** to pay half-price for sth.
полови́нчатост|ь, и *f.* half-heartedness; indeterminateness.
полови́нчат|ый (~, ~а) *adj.* **1.** halved; half-and-half; **п. кирпи́ч** half-brick; **п. чугу́н** mottled iron. **2.** (*fig.*) half-hearted; undecided; indeterminate; **~ое реше́ние** compromise decision.
полови́ц|а, ы *f.* floor board.
поло́вник[1], **а** *m.* (*hist.*) share-cropper.
поло́вник[2], **а** *m.* (*dial.*) ladle.
полово́дь|е, я *nt.* flood, high water (*at time of spring thaw*).
полов|о́й[1] *adj.* floor; **~а́я тря́пка** floorcloth; **~а́я щётка** broom.
полов|о́й[2] *adj.* sexual; **~о́е бесси́лие** impotence; **~о́е влече́ние** sexual attraction; **~а́я зре́лость** puberty; **~ы́е о́рганы** genitals, sexual organs; **~а́я связь** sexual intercourse.
полов|о́й[3], **о́го** *m.* (*obs.*) waiter.
поло́вый *adj.* pale yellow, sandy.
по́лог, а *m.* bed-curtain; **под ~ом но́чи** (*poet.*) under cover of night.
поло́гий *adj.* gently sloping.
поло́гост|ь, и *f.* slope, declivity.
положе́ни|е, я *nt.* **1.** position; whereabouts. **2.** position; posture; attitude; **в сидя́чем ~и** in a sitting position. **3.** (*in var. senses*) position; condition, state; situation; status, standing; circumstances; **семе́йное п.** marital status; **социа́льное п.** social status; **вое́нное п.** martial law; **перевести́ на ми́рное п.** to transfer to a peace-time footing; **оса́дное п.** state of siege; **чрезвыча́йное п.** state of emergency; **п. веще́й** state of affairs; **при тако́м ~и дел** as things stand, things being as they are; **хозя́ин ~я** master of the situation; **быть на высоте́ ~я** to be up to the mark, be on top of the situation; **выходи́ть из ~я** to find a way out; **войти́ в чьё-н. п.** to understand s.o.'s position; **челове́к с ~ем** a man of high position; **быть в стеснённом ~и** to be in straightened, reduced circumstances; **быть на нелега́льном ~и** to be in hiding; **быть в (интере́сном) ~и** (*coll.*, *euph.*) to be in the family way, be expecting. **4.** regulations, statute; **по ~ю** according to the regulations. **5.** thesis; tenet; clause, provisions (*of an agreement, etc.*).
поло́ж|енный *p.p.p. of* **~и́ть** *and adj.* agreed, determined; **в п. час** at a time agreed.
поло́жим let us assume; **он, п., всё ви́дел** he saw everything, let us assume; **п., что он всё ви́дел** assuming that he saw everything. (*Also in expressions indicating doubt or dissent.*)
положи́тельно *adv.* **1.** positively; favourably; **п. отве́тить**

(*i*) to answer in the affirmative, (*ii*) to give a favourable answer; to agree, consent; **отнести́сь п. (к)** to take a favourable view (of), look favourably (upon). **2.** (*coll.*) positively, completely, absolutely; **она́ п. ничего́ не понима́ет** she understands absolutely nothing.

положи́тел|ьный (~ен, ~ьна) *adj.* **1.** (*in var. senses*) positive; **~ьная сте́пень сравне́ния** (*gram.*) positive degree; **~ьная филосо́фия** positive philosophy, positivism; **п. электри́ческий заря́д** positive electric charge. **2.** affirmative; **п. отве́т** affirmative reply. **3.** favourable; possessing good qualities; **п. геро́й** (*liter.*) positive hero; **~ьная оце́нка** favourable reception. **4.** (*coll.*) complete, absolute; **п. дура́к** complete fool.

полож|и́ть, у́, ~́ишь *pf.* **1.** *pf. of* **класть; п. жизнь** to lay down one's life; **п. ору́жие** to lay down one's arms. **2.** (*+inf.*; *obs.*) to decide; to agree. **3.** (*coll.*, *obs.*) to propose, offer; to fix; **они́ ~и́ли ему́ хоро́шее жа́лованье** they have offered him a good salary.

полож|и́ться, у́сь, ~́ишься *pf.* (*of* **полага́ться**) (**на**+*a.*) to rely (upon), count (upon); to pin one's hopes (upon).

по́лоз[1], **а,** *pl.* **поло́зья, поло́зьев** *m.* (sledge) runner.

по́лоз[2], **а** *m.* grass-snake.

пол|о́к[1], **ка́** *m.* (*in Russ. steam bath*) sweating shelf.

пол|о́к[2], **ка́** *m.* dray.

поло́льник, а *m.* hoe.

поло́льщик, а *m.* weeder.

полома́|ть, ю *pf.* to break.

полома́|ться, юсь *pf. of* **лома́ться**

поло́мк|а, и *f.* breakage; breakdown.

поломо́йк|а, и *f.* (*coll.*) charwoman.

поло́н, а *m.* (*arch.*) captivity.

полоне́з, а *m.* polonaise.

полониза́ци|я, и *f.* Polonization.

полонизи́р|овать, ую *impf. and pf.* to Polonize.

полони́зм, а *m.* (*ling.*) polonism.

поло́ни|й, я *m.* (*chem.*) polonium.

полон|и́ть, ю́, и́шь *pf.* (*arch.*) to take captive.

полоро́ги|й *adj.* horned; *pl. as n.* **~е, ~х** horned ruminant mammals.

полос|а́, ы́, *a.* **по́лосу́,** *pl.* **по́лосы, поло́с, ~а́м** *f.* **1.** stripe; streak; **мате́рия (с) бе́лыми и голубы́ми ~а́ми** material in blue and white stripes. **2.** (*in var. senses*) strip; (*of iron, etc.*) band, flat bar. **3.** wale, weal. **4.** region; zone, belt; strip; **ниче́йная п.** no man's land; **оборони́тельная п.** defence zone; **песча́ная п.** sandy strip; **чернозёмная п.** black-earth belt. **5.** (*agric.*: *obs.*) patch, strip. **6.** period; phase; **~о́й, ~а́ми** (*as adv. of time*) in patches; **п. хоро́шей пого́ды** spell of fine weather; **п. неуда́ч** run of bad luck; **мра́чная п. нашла́ на него́** he is going through a bad patch. **7.** (*typ.*) type page.

полоса́тик, а *m.* (*zool.*) rorqual.

полоса́т|ый (~, ~а) *adj.* striped, stripy.

поло́ск|а, и *f. dim. of* **полоса́; в ~у** striped.

полоска́ни|е, я *nt.* **1.** rinse, rinsing; gargling. **2.** gargle.

полоска́тельниц|а, ы *f.* slop-basin.

полоска́тельн|ый *adj.*: **~ая ча́шка** slop-basin.

поло|ска́ть, щу́, ~́щешь *impf.* (*of* **вы́~**) to rinse; **п. го́рло** to gargle.

поло|ска́ться, щу́сь, ~́щешься *impf.* **1.** to paddle. **2.** (*of a flag, sail, etc.*) to flap.

полосн|у́ть, у́, ёшь *pf.* (*no impf.*) (*coll.*) to slash.

поло́сный *adj.* (*typ.*) full page.

полос|ова́ть, у́ю *impf.* **1.** (*pf.* **рас~**) (*tech.*) to make into bars. **2.** (*pf.* **ис~**) (*coll.*) to flog, scourge, welt.

полосов|о́й *adj.* (*tech.*) band, strip, bar; **~о́е желе́зо** bar-iron.

по́лост|ь[1], **и,** *g. pl.* **~е́й** *f.* (*anat.*) cavity; **брюшна́я п.** abdominal cavity.

по́лост|ь[2], **и,** *g. pl.* **~е́й** *f.* travelling rug.

полоте́н|це, ца, *g. pl.* **~ец** *nt.* towel; **мохна́тое п.** Turkish towel; **посу́дное п.** tea-towel; **п. на ва́лике** roller towel.

полотёр, а *m.* floor-polisher.

полотёрн|ый *adj.* floor-polishing; **~ая щётка** brush, broom.

поло́тнищ|е, а *nt.* **1.** (*of material*) width; panel; **п. пала́тки** tent section, ground sheet; **па́рус в пять ~** sail of five panels. **2.** flat (part), blade.

полот|но́, на́, *pl.* **~́на, ~́ен, ~́нам** *nt.* **1.** linen; **бле́дный как п.** white as a sheet. **2.** (*art*) canvas (*fig.* = *painting*). **3.**: **железнодоро́жное п.** permanent way. **4.** (*tech.*) web; blade; **п. пилы́** saw blade, saw web.

полотня́ный *adj.* linen.

полот|о́к, ка́ *m.* (*obs.*) half of a (smoked, dried, *or* salted) bird or other game.

пол|о́ть, ю́, ~́ешь *impf.* (*of* **вы́~**) to weed.

полоу́ми|е, я *nt.* craziness.

полоу́м|ный (~ен, ~на) *adj.* (*coll.*) half-witted, crazy.

полпи́в|о, а *nt.* (*obs.*, *coll.*) light beer.

полпре́д, а *m.* (*abbr. of* **полномо́чный представи́тель**) (ambassador) plenipotentiary.

полпути́ *m. indecl.*: **на п.** half-way; **верну́ться с п.** to turn back half-way; **останови́ться на п.** (*fig.*) to stop half-way.

полсло́в|а, на ~е *nt.*: **п. от него́ не услы́шишь** you cannot get a word out of him; **мо́жно вас на п.?** may I have a word with you?; may I speak to you for a minute?

полтерге́йст, а *m.* poltergeist.

полти́н|а, ы *f.* (*coll.*) = **~ник; два с ~ой** two roubles fifty kopecks.

полти́нник, а *m.* **1.** fifty kopecks. **2.** fifty-kopeck piece.

полтора́, полу́тора *m. and nt.* one and a half; **в п. ра́за бо́льше** half as much again; **ни два ни п.** neither one thing nor the other.

полтора́ста, полу́тораста *num.* a hundred and fifty.

полтор|ы́ *f.* = **~а́; п. ты́сячи** one and a half thousand.

полу... *comb. form* half-, semi-, demi-.

полуба́к, а *m.* (*naut.*) forecastle; top-gallant forecastle.

полубессозна́тельный *adj.* semi-unconscious.

полубо́г, а *m.* demigod.

полуботи́н|ки, ок *pl.* (*sg.* **~ок, ~ка** *m.*) shoes.

полува́ттный *adj.* (*elec.*) half-watt.

полувое́нный *adj.* paramilitary.

полугла́сн|ый, ого *m.* (*ling.*) semivowel.

полуго́ди|е, я *nt.* half-year, six months.

полугоди́чный *adj.* half-yearly; of six months' duration; **~е ку́рсы** six-months courses.

полугодова́лый *adj.* six-month(s)-old.

полугодово́й *adj.* half-yearly, six-monthly; **п. отчёт** half-yearly report.

полугра́мотный *adj.* semi-literate.

полугра́ци|я, и *f.* pantie-girdle.

полу́д|а, ы *f.* tinning; tin plate.

полу́денный *adj.* **1.** midday. **2.** (*obs.*, *poet.*) southern.

полу|ди́ть, жу́, ~́дишь *pf. of* **луди́ть**

полужёсткий *adj.* (*tech.*) semi-rigid.

полужив|о́й (~́, ~а́, ~́о) *adj.* half dead; more dead than alive.

полузащи́т|а, ы *f.* (*collect.*; *sport*) half-backs, midfield players; **центр ~ы** centre half.

полузащи́тник, а *m.* (*sport*) half-back, midfield player.

полуи́м|я, ени, *pl.* **~ена́, ~ён, ~ена́м** *nt.* (*obs.*, *coll.*) pet name, diminutive (*of personal name*) (*e.g.* Volodya *for* Vladimir, Nadya *for* Nadezhda).

полукафта́н, а *m.* short caftan.

полуке́д|ы, ов *or* **~** *no sg.* gym shoes; sneakers; plimsolls.

полукомбина́ци|я, и *f.* half-slip, waist petticoat.

полукро́вк|а, и *f.* half-breed, first-hybrid.

полукру́г, а *m.* semicircle.

полукру́глый *adj.* semicircular.

полукру́жны|й *adj.*: **~е кана́лы** (*anat.*) semicircular canals.

полулеж|а́ть, у́, и́шь *impf.* to recline.

полумгл|а́, ы́ *f.* mist, half-light (*before sunrise or sunset*); gloaming.

полуме́р|а, ы *f.* half-measure.

полумёртв|ый (~, ~а́) *adj.* half-dead.

полуме́сяц, а *m.* half moon; crescent.

полуме́сячный *adj.* fortnightly; of a fortnight's duration.

полумра́к, а *m.* semi-darkness, shade.

полунаго́й *adj.* half-naked.

полу́ндра *int.* (*naut.*) stand from under!

полуноск|и́, о́в *no sg.* ankle socks.

полуно́чни|к, а *m.* (*coll.*) nightbird.
полуно́чни|ца, ы *f. of* **~к**
полуно́чнича|ть, ю *impf.* (*coll.*) to burn the midnight oil.
полу́но́чный *adj.* **1.** midnight. **2.** (*obs., poet.*) northern.
полуоборо́т, а *m.* half-turn.
полуоде́т|ый (~, ~а) *adj.* half-dressed, half-clothed.
полуосвещённый *adj.* half-lit.
полуо́стров, а *m.* peninsula.
полуостровно́й *adj.* peninsular.
полуотво́рен|ный (~, ~а) *adj.* half-open; ajar.
полуоткры́т|ый (~, ~а) *adj.* half-open; ajar.
полупальто́ *nt indecl.* shorty overcoat.
полупереxо́д, а *m.* (*mil.*) half day's march.
полуподва́льный *adj.*: **п. эта́ж** semi-basement.
полупокло́н, а *m.* slight bow.
полупроводни́к, а́ *m.* (*phys.*) semi-conductor, transistor.
полупроводнико́вый *adj.* transistor(ized).
полупья́н|ый (~, ~а́, ~о) *adj.* half tight, tipsy.
полуразру́шен|ный (~, ~а) *adj.* tumbledown, dilapidated.
полуро́т|а, ы *f.* (*mil.*) half-company.
полусве́т[1], **а** *m.* twilight.
полусве́т[2], **а** *m.* demi-monde.
полусерьёзный *adj.* half-serious; half in joke.
полусло́в|о, а *nt.*: **оборва́ть кого́-н. на ~е** to cut s.o. short; **останови́ться на ~е** to stop short, stop in the middle of a sentence; **поня́ть с ~а** to be quick on the uptake.
полусме́рт|ь, и *f.*: **до ~и** (*fig., coll.*) to death; **изби́ть кого́-н. до ~и** to beat s.o. within an inch of his life; **испуга́ться до ~и** to be frightened to death.
полус|о́н, на́ *m.* half sleep; somnolence, drowsiness.
полусо́нный *adj.* half asleep; dozing.
полуспу́щенный *adj.*: **п. флаг** flag at half-mast.
полуста́н|ок, ка *m.* (*rail.*) halt.
полусти́ши|с, я *nt.* hemistich.
полуте́н|ь, и, о ~и, в ~и́ *f.* penumbra.
полуто́н, а, *pl.* **~ы** *and* **~а́** *m.* **1.** (*mus.*) semitone. **2.** (*art*) half-tint.
полуто́нк|а, и *f.* (*coll.*) ten-hundredweight lorry.
полуторато́нк|а, и *f.* (*coll.*) thirty-hundredweight lorry.
полу́торн|ый *adj.* of one and a half; **в ~ом разме́ре** half as much again.
полутьм|а́, ы́ *f.* semi-darkness; twilight.
полууста́в, а *m.* (*palaeog.*) semi-uncial.
полуфабрика́т, а *m.* semi-finished product; prepared raw material (*esp. of foodstuffs*).
полуфина́л, а *m.* (*sport*) semi-final.
полуфина́л|ьный *adj. of* **~; ~ьные встре́чи** semi-finals.
получасово́й *adj.* of half an hour's duration; half-hourly.
получа́тел|ь, я *m.* recipient.
получ|а́ть(ся), а́ю(сь) *impf. of* **~и́ть(ся)**
получе́ни|е, я *nt.* receipt; **распи́ска в ~и** receipt; **по ~и** on receipt, on receiving.
получ|и́ть, у́, ~ишь *pf.* (*of* **~а́ть**) to get, receive, obtain; **п. замеча́ние** to receive a reprimand; **п. на́сморк** to catch a cold; **п. обра́тно** to recover, get back; **п. огла́ску** to become known, receive publicity; **п. паёк** to draw rations; **п. призна́ние** to obtain recognition; **п. прика́з** to receive an order; **п. примене́ние** to come into use, effect; **п. удово́льствие** to derive pleasure.
получ|и́ться, ~ится *pf.* (*of* **~а́ться**) **1.** to come, arrive, turn up; **~и́лась посы́лка** a parcel has come. **2.** to turn out, prove, be; **результа́ты ~и́лись нева́жные** the results are poor; **~и́лось, что он был прав** it turned out that he was right, he proved right. **3.** *pass. of* **~и́ть**
полу́чк|а, и *f.* (*coll.*) **1.** receipt. **2.** pay (packet), sum paid.
полу́чше *adv.* rather better, a little better.
полуша́ри|е, я *nt.* hemisphere; **~я головно́го мо́зга** cerebral hemispheres.
полушёпот, а *m.* **говори́ть ~ом** to speak in undertones.
полуше́рст|ь, и *f.* wool mixture.
полу́шк|а, и *f.* (*obs.*) quarter-kopeck piece; **не име́ть ни ~и** to be penniless.
полушто́ф, а *m.* (*obs.*) half-shtof (*see* **што́ф**[1]).
полушу́б|ок, ка *m.* (knee-length) sheepskin coat, sheepskin jacket.
полушутя́ *adv.* half in joke.
полцены́ *f. indecl.*: **за п.** at half price; for half its value.
полчаса́, получа́са *m.* half an hour.
по́лчищ|е, а *nt.* horde; (*fig.*) mass, flock.
полшага́ *m. indecl.* half-pace.
по́л|ый *adj.* **1.** hollow. **2.: ~ая вода́** flood-water.
по́лымя *nt.* (*dial.*) flame; **из огня́ да в п.** (*prov.*) out of the frying-pan into the fire.
полы́н|ный *adj. of* **~ь; ~ная во́дка** absinthe.
полы́н|ь, и *f.* wormwood.
полын|ья́, ьи́, *g. pl.* **~е́й** *f.* polynya (*unfrozen patch of water in the midst of ice*).
полысе́|ть, ю *pf. of* **лысе́ть**
полыха́|ть, ет *impf.* to blaze.
по́льз|а, ы *f.* use; advantage, benefit, profit; **кака́я от э́того п.?** what good will it do?; what use is it?; **что ~ы говори́ть об э́том?** what's the use of talking about it?; **извлека́ть из чего́-н. ~у** to benefit from sth; to profit by sth.; **принести́ ~у** (+*d.*) to be of benefit (to); **для ~ы** (+*g.*) for the benefit (of); **в ~у** (+*g.*) in favour (of), on behalf (of); **до́воды в ~у чего́-н.** arguments in favour; **э́то говори́т не в ва́шу ~у** it does not speak well for you; it is not to your credit; **два-ноль в ~у Дина́мо** (*sport*) 2–0 to Dynamo.
по́льзовани|е, я *nt.* use; **многокра́тного ~я** reusable; **о́бщего ~я** in general use; **пра́во ~я** (*leg.*) right of user, usufruct; **находи́ться в чьём-н. ~и** (*leg.*) to be in s.o.'s use.
по́льзовател|ь, я *m.* user; **коне́чный п.** end-user.
по́льз|овать, ую *impf.* (*obs.*) to treat.
по́льз|оваться, уюсь *impf.* (+*i.*) **1.** to make use (of), utilize. **2.** (*pf.* **вос~**) to profit (by); **п. слу́чаем** to take an opportunity. **3.** to enjoy; **п. дове́рием** (+*g.*) to enjoy the confidence (of); **п. креди́том** to possess credit; **п. права́ми** to enjoy rights; **п. уваже́нием** to be held in respect; **п. успе́хом** to have success, be a success.
по́льк|а[1], **и** Pole, Polish woman.
по́льк|а[2], **и** *f.* polka.
по́льск|ий *adj.* Polish; *as n.* (*obs.*) **п., ~ого** *m.* polonaise.
поль|сти́ть(ся), щу́(сь), сти́шь(ся) *pf. of* **льсти́ть(ся)**
По́льш|а, и *f.* Poland.
полюб|и́ть, лю́, ~ишь *pf.* to come to like, grow fond (of); to fall in love (with).
полюб|и́ться, лю́сь, ~ишься *pf.* (*coll.*) (+*d.*) to catch the fancy (of); to become attractive (to); **она́ мне сра́зу же ~и́лась** I was immediately attracted by her, I took an immediate liking to her.
полюб|ова́ться, у́юсь *pf. of* **любова́ться; ~у́йся, ~у́йтесь (на**+*a.*; *coll., iron.*) just look; **~у́йся на э́того дурака́!** just look at that fool!
полюбо́вно *adv.* amicably; **реши́ть, ко́нчить де́ло п.** to come to an amicable agreement.
полюбо́вный *adj.* amicable.
полюбопы́тств|овать, ую *pf. of* **любопы́тствовать**
по-людски́ *adv.* (*coll.*) as others do, in the accepted manner; **жить п.** to live as other people do; to live like a (normal) human being.
по́люс, а *m.* (*geog., phys., and fig.*) pole; **Се́верный п.** North Pole; **они́ — два ~а** they are poles apart.
по́люсный *adj.* (*phys.*) polar; **п. зажи́м** (*elec.*) pole terminal.
поля́к, а *m.* Pole.
поля́н|а, ы *f.* glade, clearing.
поляриза́тор, а *m.* (*phys.*) polarizer.
поляризацио́нный *adj.* (*phys.*) polarizing.
поляриза́ци|я, и *f.* (*phys.*) polarization.
поляриз|ова́ть, у́ю *impf. and pf.* (*phys.*) to polarize.
поля́рник, а *m.* polar explorer, member of polar expedition.
поля́рност|ь, и *f.* (*phys.*) polarity.
поля́рн|ый *adj.* **1.** polar, arctic; **~ая звезда́** Pole-star, North star; **се́верный п. круг** Arctic Circle. **2.** (*fig.*) polar, diametrically opposed.
поля́чк|а, и *f.* (*obs.*) = **по́лька**[1]
пом. (*abbr. of* **помо́щник**) assistant.
пом... *comb. form, abbr. of* **помо́щник**
помава́|ть, ю *impf.* (*obs.*) (+*i.*) to wave, brandish.
пома́д|а, ы *f.* pomade; **губна́я п.** lipstick.

помá|дить, жу, дишь *impf.* (*of* **на~**) (*obs.*) to pomade; **п. вóлосы** to grease one's hair; **п. гýбы** to put lipstick on.
помáдк|а, и *f.* (*collect.*) fruit candy.
помáд|ный *adj. of* **~а; п. карандáш** lipstick.
помáзани|е, я *nt.* (*eccl.*) anointing (*of monarch at coronation*).
помáзанник, а *m.* (*eccl.*) anointed sovereign.
помá|зать, жу, жешь *pf.* **1.** *pf. of* **мáзать**[1]. **2.** (*eccl.*) to anoint.
помá|заться, жусь, жешься *pf. of* **мáзаться**
помаз|óк, кá *m.* small brush (*shaving brush, brush for painting throat, etc.*).
помалéньку *adv.* (*coll.*) **1.** gradually, gently; **рабóтать п.** to take one's time over one's work, take things easily. **2.** in a small way, modestly; **жить п.** to live modestly. **3.** tolerably, so-so.
помáлкива|ть, ю *impf.* (*coll.*) to hold one's tongue, keep mum.
по-мальчи́шески *adv.* in a boyish way, like a boy.
поман|и́ть, ю́, ~ишь *pf. of* **мани́ть**
помáрк|а, и *f.* blot; pencil mark; correction.
пома|хáть, шý, ~шешь *pf.* (*+i.*) to wave (*for a while, a few times*).
помáхива|ть *impf.* (*+i.*) to wave, brandish, swing (*from time to time*); **собáка ~ла хвостóм** the dog would wag his tail.
помбýх, а *m.* (*abbr. of* ***помóщник бухгáлтера***) assistant book-keeper.
помéдл|ить, ю, ишь *pf.* (**с**+*i.*; *coll.*) to linger (over).
помел|ó, á, *pl.* **~ья, ~ьев** *nt.* mop; (*witch's*) broomstick.
помéньше *comp. of* **мáленький** *and* **мáло** somewhat smaller, a little smaller; somewhat less, a little less.
поменя́|ть(ся), ю(сь) *pf. of* **меня́ть(ся) 2.**
померáн|ец, ца *m.* **1.** Seville *or* sour orange (*fruit*). **2.** sour orange (*tree*).
померáн|цевый *adj. of* **~ец; ~цевые цветы́** orange-blossom.
по|мерéть, мрý, мрёшь, *past* **~мер, ~мерлá, ~мерло** *pf.* (*of* **~мирáть**) (*coll.*) to die; **п. сó смеху** to split one's sides (with laughing).
померéщ|иться, усь, ишься *pf. of* **мерéщиться**
помёрз|нуть, ну, нешь, *past* **~, ~ла** *pf.* to be frost-bitten; (*of flowers, etc.*) to be killed by frost.
помéр|ить(ся), ю(сь), ишь(ся) *pf. of* **мéрить(ся)**
помéрк|нуть, ну, нешь, *past* **~, ~ла** *pf. of* **мéркнуть**
помертвéлый *adj.* deadly pale; (*fig.*) lifeless, deathly; gloomy.
помертвé|ть, ю *pf. of* **мертвéть**
помести́тельност|ь, и *f.* spaciousness; capaciousness.
помести́тел|ьный (~ен, ~ьна) *adj.* spacious, roomy; capacious.
поме|сти́ть, щý, сти́шь *pf.* (*of* **~щáть**) **1.** to lodge, accommodate; to put up; **мы могли́ бы их п. в свобóдную кóмнату** we could put them into the spare room. **2.** to place, locate; (*fin.*) to invest; **п. объявлéние в газéте** to put an advertisement in a paper; **п. на пéрвой страни́це** to carry on the front page; **п. сбережéния в сберкáссу** to put one's savings in a savings bank.
поме|сти́ться, щýсь, сти́шься *pf.* (*of* **~щáться**) **1.** to find room; to put up; (*of things*) to go in; **в э́тот я́щик мои́ вéщи не ~стя́тся** my things will not go into this drawer. **2.** *pass. of* **~сти́ть**
помéстн|ый[1] *adj.*: **~ое дворя́нство** landed gentry; **п. строй** (*hist.*) estate system of land tenure.
помéстный[2] *adj.* (*obs.*) local; **п. собóр** (*hist.*, *eccl.*) local council.
помéст|ье, ья, *g. pl.* **~ий** *nt.* (*hist.*) estate.
пóмес|ь, и *f.* **1.** cross-breed, hybrid; cross; mongrel; **п. терьéра и овчáрки, п. терьéра с овчáркой** a cross between a terrier and a sheepdog. **2.** (*fig.*) mixture, hotchpotch.
помéсячно *adv.* by the month; monthly, per month.
помéсячный *adj.* monthly.
помёт, а *m.* **1.** dung, excrement; droppings. **2.** litter, brood; (*of piglets*) farrow.
помéт|а, ы *f.* **1.** mark, note; **сдéлать ~ы на поля́х** to make notes in the margin. **2.** (*in a dictionary*) style tag; usage label.
помé|тить, чу, тишь *pf.* (*of* **~чáть**) to mark; to date; **п. гáлочкой** to tick; **я ~тил письмó 2-м января́** I dated my letter the 2nd of January.
помéх|а, и *f.* **1.** hindrance; obstacle; encumbrance; **быть ~ой** (*+d.*) to hinder, impede, stand in the way (of). **2.** (*pl. only*) (*radio*) interference.
помечá|ть, ю *impf. of* **помéтить**
помéшан|ный (~, ~а) *adj.* **1.** mad, crazy; insane; *as n.* **п., ~ного** *m.* madman; **~ная, ~ной** *f.* madwoman. **2.** (**на**+*p.*; *fig.*, *coll.*) mad (on, about), crazy (about); **они́ ~ы на бри́дже** they are mad about bridge.
помешáтельств|о, а *nt.* **1.** madness, craziness; lunacy, insanity. **2.** (**на**+*p.*; *fig.*, *coll.*) craze (for).
помешá|ть[1,2]**, ю** *pf. of* **мешáть**[1,2]
помешá|ться, юсь *pf.* **1.** to go mad, go crazy. **2.** (**на**+*p.*; *fig.*, *coll.*) to become mad (on, about), become crazy (about).
помещá|ть, ю *impf. of* **помести́ть**
помещá|ться, юсь *impf.* **1.** (*impf. only*) to be; to be located, be situated; to be housed; **где ~ется ваш кабинéт?** where is your office? **2.** (*impf. only*): **на э́том стадиóне ~ется сéмьдесят ты́сяч человéк** this stadium holds seventy thousand people. **3.** *impf. of* **помести́ться**
помещéни|е, я *nt.* **1.** placing, location; investment. **2.** room, lodging, apartment; premises; **жилóе п.** housing, accommodation.
помéщик, а *m.* (*hist.*) landowner.
помéщи|чий *adj. of* **~к; ~п. дом** manor-house.
помзáв, а *m.* (*abbr. of* ***помóщник завéдующего***) assistant manager.
помидóр, а, *g. pl.* **~ов** *m.* tomato.
помидóр|ный *adj. of* **~**
поми́ловани|е, я *nt.* (*leg.*) pardon, forgiveness; **прóсьба о ~и** appeal (for pardon).
поми́л|овать, ую *pf.* to pardon, forgive, spare; **~уй!, ~уйте!** *as int. expr. disagreement or protest* (*coll.*) pardon me!; excuse me!; for pity's sake!; **Гóсподи, ~уй!** (*petition in liturgy*) Lord, have mercy (upon us)!
поми́мо *prep.+g.* **1.** apart from; besides; **п. всегó прóчего** apart from anything else; **п. други́х соображéний** other considerations apart. **2.** without the knowledge (of), unbeknown (to); **всё э́то реши́лось п. меня́** all this was decided without my knowledge.
поми́н, а *m.* **1.** (*coll.*) mention; **лёгок на ~е** talk of the devil (and he is sure to appear); **егó и в ~е нет** there is no trace of him; **об э́том и ~у нé было** there was not so much as a mention of it. **2.** (*eccl.*) prayer (*for the dead or for sick persons*).
поминáльны|й *adj.* **п. обéд** funeral repast; **~е обря́ды** funeral rites, last rites.
поминáни|е, я *nt.* (*eccl.*) **1.** prayer (for the dead *or* for sick persons). **2.** list of names of dead and sick persons.
поминá|ть, ю *impf. of* **помянýть; не ~й(те) меня́ ли́хом!** remember me kindly!; **а егó ~й, как звáли!** (*coll.*) he just vanished into thin air.
поми́н|ки, ок *no sg.* funeral repast, funeral banquet, wake.
поминовéни|е, я *nt.* (*eccl.*) prayer for the dead *and/or* for the sick; remembrance (of the dead *and/or* the sick) in prayer.
поминýтно *adv.* every minute; (*fig.*, *coll.*) continually, constantly.
поминýтн|ый *adj.* **1.** occurring every minute; (*fig.*, *coll.*) continual, constant. **2.** by the minute.
помирá|ть, ю *impf. of* **померéть**
помир|и́ть(ся), ю́(сь), и́шь(ся) *pf. of* **мири́ть(ся)**
помнáч, а *m.* (*abbr. of* ***помóщник начáльника***) assistant chief.
пóмн|ить, ю, ишь *impf.* (*+a. or* **о**+*p.*) to remember; **не п. себя́ (от)** to be beside o.s. (with).
пóмн|иться, ится *impf.* (*impers.+d.*) I, *etc.*, remember; **мне ещё ~ится день пожáра** I still remember the day of the fire; **наскóлько мне ~ится** as far as I can remember;

~ится, э́то произошло́ в декабре́ as I remember, it happened in December.
помно́гу *adv.* (*coll.*) in plenty, in large quantities; in large numbers.
помнож|а́ть, а́ю *impf. of* **~́ить**
помно́ж|ить, у, ишь *pf.* (*of* **мно́жить** *and* **~а́ть**) to multiply; **п. два на́ три** to multiply two by three.
помога́|ть, ю *impf. of* **помо́чь**
пом|огу́, о́жешь, о́гут *see* **~о́чь**
по-мо́ему *adv.* **1.** in my opinion; to my mind, to my way of thinking. **2.** in conformity with my wishes, as I would have it.
помо́|и, ев *no sg.* slops; **обли́ть кого́-н. ~ями** (*fig., coll.*) to fling mud at s.o.
помо́й|ка, ки, *g. pl.* **помо́ек** *f.* rubbish heap, rubbish dump; cesspit.
помо́|йный *adj. of* **~и; ~йное ведро́** slop-pail; **~йная я́ма** refuse pit; cesspit.
помо́л, а *m.* grinding; **мука́ кру́пного, ме́лкого ~а** coarse-ground, fine-ground flour.
помо́лв|ить, лю, ишь *pf.* (+*a.* **с**+*i.*, *or* +*a.* **за**+*a.*; *obs.*) to betrothe (to); to announce the engagement (of); **её ~или с Ива́ном** *or* **за Ива́на** she is engaged to Ivan, her engagement to Ivan is announced.
помо́лвк|а, и *f.* betrothal, engagement; **объяви́ть ~у** to announce an engagement.
помо́лв|ленный *p.p.p. of* **~ить; быть ~ленным с кем-н.** to be engaged to s.o.
помол|и́ться, ю́сь, ~́ишься *pf.* **1.** *pf. of* **моли́ться. 2.** to spend some time in prayer.
помоло́ги|я, и *f.* pomology.
помолоде́|ть, ю *pf. of* **молоде́ть**
помолч|а́ть, у́, и́шь *pf.* to be silent for a while.
помо́р, а *m.* coast-dweller (*esp. of Russ. inhabitants of coasts of White Sea*).
помор|и́ть, ю́, и́шь *pf. of* **мори́ть**[1]
помо́р|ка, ки *f. of* **~**
помо́рник, а *m.* (*zool.*) skua.
поморо́|зить, жу, зишь *pf. of* **моро́зить**
помо́р|ский *adj. of* **~** *and* **~ье**
помо́рщ|иться, усь, ишься *pf. of* **мо́рщиться**
помо́рь|е, я *nt.* seaboard, coastal region; **балти́йское п.** Pomorze, Pomerania (*Southern coast of Baltic Sea*); **се́верное п.** White Sea Coast.
поморя́н|ин, ина, *pl.* **~е, ~** *m.* (*ethnol.*) Pomeranian (*member of West Slavonic tribes inhabiting Baltic seaboard*).
помо́ст, а *m.* dais; platform, stage, rostrum; scaffold.
по́моч|и, ей *no sg.* **1.** leading strings; **быть, ходи́ть на ~а́х** (*fig.*) to be in leading strings. **2.** braces.
помоч|и́ться, у́сь, ~́ишься *pf. of* **мочи́ться**
по́моч|ь, и *f.* **1.** (*obs.*) = **по́мощь. 2.** (*obs.*) mutual aid (*afforded one another by villagers*).
помо́|чь, гу́, жешь, гут, *past* **~г, ~гла́** *pf.* (*of* **~га́ть**) **1.** (+*d.*) to help, aid, assist; to succour; **~ги́(те) ей наде́ть пальто́** help her on with her coat. **2.** to relieve, bring relief; **инъе́кции ~гли́ от бо́ли** the injections relieved the pain.
помо́щник, а *m.* **1.** help, helper; helpmate, helpmeet. **2.** assistant; aide; mate; **п. дире́ктора** assistant director; **п. капита́на** (*naut.*) mate; **п. машини́ста** engine-driver's mate; **п. судьи́** (*sport*) linesman.
по́мощ|ь, и *f.* help, aid, assistance; succour; relief; **оказа́ть п.** to help, render assistance; **отказа́ть в ~и** to refuse aid; **пода́ть ру́ку ~и** (+*d.*) to lend a hand, lend a helping hand; **позва́ть на п.** to call for help; **прийти́ на п.** (+*d.*) to come to the aid (of); **на п.!** help!; **с ~ью** (+*g.*), **при ~и** (+*g.*) with the help (of), by means (of); **без посторо́нней ~и** unaided, single-handed; **ско́рая п.** ambulance; **каре́та ско́рой ~и** (*obs.*) ambulance; **п. на дому́** home visiting (*by doctors to patients*); **пе́рвая п.** first aid; **п. иностра́нным госуда́рствам** foreign aid.
по́мп|а[1]**, ы** *f.* pomp, state.
по́мп|а[2]**, ы** *f.* pump.
помпе́зност|ь, и *f.* pomposity.
помпе́зный *adj.* pompous.
Помпе́|й, я *m.* Pompey.
помпо́н, а *m.* pompon.
помрач|а́ть(ся), а́ет(ся) *impf. of* **~и́ть(ся)**
помраче́ни|е, я *nt.* darkening, obscuring; **п. зре́ния** loss of sight; **уму́ п.** (*of unusual event or object*) it takes one's breath away.
помрач|и́ть, и́т *pf.* (*of* **~а́ть**) (*obs.*) to darken, obscure, cloud.
помрач|и́ться, и́тся *pf.* (*of* **~а́тся**) to grow dark, become obscured, become clouded.
помрачне́|ть, ю *pf. of* **мрачне́ть**
помре́ж, а *m.* (*abbr. of* **помо́щник режиссёра**) (*theatr.*) assistant producer; (*cin.*) assistant director.
пому|ти́ть(ся), чу́, ти́шь, ти́т(ся) *pf. of* **му́тить(ся)**
пому́ч|ить, у, ишь *pf.* to make suffer, torment.
пому́ч|иться, усь, ишься *pf.* to suffer (*for a while*); **п. с зада́чей** to torment o.s. over a problem.
помч|а́ть, у́, и́шь *pf.* **1.** to begin to whirl, rush. **2.** (*coll.*) = **~а́ться**
помч|а́ться, у́сь, и́шься *pf.* to begin to rush, begin to tear along.
помыка́|ть, ю *impf.* (+*i.*; *coll.*) to order about.
по́мыс|ел, ла *m.* thought; intention, design; **благи́е ~лы** good intentions.
помы́сл|ить, ю, ишь *pf.* (*of* **помышля́ть**) (**о**+*p.*) to think (of, about), contemplate; **об э́том и п. мы не сме́ли** we dared not even dream of it.
пом|ы́ть(ся), о́ю(сь), о́ешь(ся) *pf. of* **мыть(ся)**
помышле́ни|е, я *nt.* (*obs.*) thought; intention, design; **он оста́вил вся́кое п. о жени́тьбе** he has put aside any idea of marriage.
помышля́|ть, ю *impf. of* **помы́слить**
помя́н|утый *p.p.p. of* **~у́ть; не тем будь ~ут (~ута, ~уты)** (*expr. of regret at speaking ill of a pers.*) God forgive him (her, them)!; may it not be remembered against him (her, them)!
помян|у́ть, у́, ~́ешь *pf.* (*of* **помина́ть**) **1.** to mention, make mention (of); **п. добро́м кого́-н.** to speak well of s.o.; **~и́ моё сло́во** (*coll.*) mark my words. **2.** to pray (for), remember in one's prayers (*pray for repose of the dead or recovery of the sick*). **3.** to give a funeral banquet (for, in memory of).
помя́т|ый *p.p.p. of* **~ь** *and adj.* (*coll.*) flabby, baggy.
пом|я́ть, ну́, нёшь *pf.* to rumple slightly; to crumple slightly.
пом|я́ться[1]**, ну́сь, нёшься** *pf. of* **мя́ться**[1]
пом|я́ться[2]**, ну́сь, нёшься** *pf.* (*coll.*) to vacillate, hum and ha (*for a while*).
пона... *vbl. pref. indicating action performed gradually or by instalments.*
по-над *prep.*+ *i.* (*dial.*) along, by.
понаде́|яться, юсь, ешься *pf.* (**на**+*a.*; *coll.*) to count (upon), rely (on); **нельзя́ на него́ п.** you cannot rely on him.
пона́доб|иться, люсь, ишься *pf.* to be, become necessary; **е́сли ~ится** if necessary.
понапра́сну *adv.* (*coll.*) in vain.
понаслы́шке *adv.* (*coll.*) by hearsay.
по-настоя́щему *adv.* in the right way, properly.
поначáлу *adv.* (*coll.*) at first, in the beginning.
по-на́шему *adv.* **1.** in our opinion. **2.** as we would wish.
понёв|а, ы (*dial.*) homespun skirt (*of checked or striped pattern*).
понево́ле *adv.* willy-nilly; against one's will.
понеде́льник, а *m.* Monday.
понеде́льно *adv.* by the week, per week; weekly.
понеде́льный *adj.* weekly.
поне́же *conj.* (*arch.*) because, since.
понемно́гу *adv.* **1.** little, a little at a time. **2.** little by little.
понемно́жку *adv.* = **понемно́гу**; (*in answer to question* **как пожива́ете?**) (doing) all right.
понес|ти́, у́, ёшь, *past* **~̈,** **~ла́** *pf.* **1.** *pf. of* **нести́. 2.** (*of horses*) to bolt.
понес|ти́сь, у́сь, ёшься, *past* **~̈ся, ~ла́сь** *pf.* **1.** *pf. of* **нести́сь. 2.** to rush off, tear off, dash off.
по́ни *m. indecl.* pony.

понижа́|ть(ся), ю(сь) *impf. of* **пони́зить(ся)**
пони́же *adv.* rather lower; rather shorter.
пониже́ни|е, я *nt.* fall, drop; lowering; reduction; **п. давле́ния** drop in pressure; **п. зарпла́ты** wage-cut; **п. цен** reduction, fall in prices; **п. по слу́жбе** demotion; **игра́ть на п.** (*fin.*) to speculate for a fall, sell short, bear.
понизи́тельный *adj.* (*elec.*) step-down.
пони́|зить, жу, зишь *pf.* (*of* **~жа́ть**) to lower; to reduce; **п. го́лос** to lower one's voice; **п. по слу́жбе** to demote.
пони́|зиться, жусь, зишься *pf.* (*of* **~жа́ться**) to fall, drop, sink, go down.
понизо́вь|е, я *nt.* lower reaches.
по́низу *adv.* low; along the ground.
поника́|ть, ю *impf. of* **пони́кнуть**
пони́к|нуть, ну, нешь, *past* **~, ~ла** *pf.* (*of* **ни́кнуть** *and* **~а́ть**) to droop, flag, wilt; **п. голово́й** to hang one's head.
понима́ни|е, я *nt.* **1.** understanding, comprehension; **э́то вы́ше моего́ ~я** it is past my comprehension, it is beyond me. **2.** interpretation, conception; **но́вое п. исто́рии** a new interpretation of history; **в моём ~и** as I see it.
понима́|ть, ю *impf.* (*of* **поня́ть**) **1.** to understand; to comprehend; to realize; **~ю!** I see! **2.** to interpret; **непра́вильно п.** to misunderstand; **как вы ~ете э́тот посту́пок?** what do you make of this action? **3.** (*impf. only*) (*+a. or* **в***+p.*) to be a (good) judge (of), know (about); **я ничего́ не ~ю в му́зыке** I know nothing about music.
по-но́вому *adv.* in a new fashion; **нача́ть жить п.** to start life afresh, turn over a new leaf.
поножо́вщин|а, ы *f.* (*coll.*) knife-fight; knifing.
понома́р|ь, я́ *m.* sexton, sacristan.
поно́с, а *m.* diarrhoea; **крова́вый п.** bloody flux.
поно|си́ть[1], шу́, ~сишь *impf.* to abuse, revile.
поно|си́ть[2], шу́, ~сишь *pf.* **1.** to carry (*for a while*). **2.** to wear (*for a while*).
поно́ск|а, и *f.* **1.** object carried by a dog between its teeth. **2.** carrying; **обучи́ть соба́ку ~е** to train a dog to carry things.
поно́сный *adj.* (*obs.*) abusive, defamatory.
поно́|шенный *p.p.p. of* **~си́ть[2]** *and adj.* worn, shabby, threadbare; **п. вид** (*fig.*) haggard appearance, worn look.
понра́в|иться, люсь, ишься *pf. of* **нра́виться**
понтёр, а *m.* (*cards*) punter.
понти́р|овать, ую *impf.* (*of* **с~**) (*cards*) to punt.
понто́н, а *m.* **1.** pontoon. **2.** pontoon bridge.
понтонёр, а *m.* pontoneer, pontonier.
понто́н|ный *adj. of* **~; ~ный мост** pontoon bridge.
понуди́тельный *adj.* impelling, pressing; coercive.
пону́|дить, жу, дишь *pf.* (*of* **~жда́ть**) to force, compel, coerce; to impel; **его́ ~дили к реше́нию** he was forced into a decision.
понужда́|ть, ю *impf. of* **пону́дить**
понука́|ть, ю *impf.* (*coll.*) to urge on, goad.
пону́р|ить, ю, ишь *pf.*: **п. го́лову** to hang one's head.
пону́р|иться, юсь, ишься *pf.* to hang one's head.
пону́рый *adj.* downcast, depressed.
по́нчик, а *m.* doughnut.
поны́не *adv.* (*obs.*) up to the present, until now.
понюха|ть, ю *pf. of* **ню́хать**
понюшк|а, и *f.*: **п. табаку́** pinch of snuff; **ни за ~у табаку́** (*fig., coll.*) for nothing, to no purpose.
поня́ти|е, я *nt.* **1.** concept. **2.** notion, idea; **у него́ о́чень сму́тное п. о геогра́фии** he has very confused notions about geography; **име́ть п.** (**о***+p.*) to have an idea (about, of); **~я не име́ю!** (*coll.*) I've no idea!; I haven't a clue!; **где нахо́дится центр го́рода? — не име́ю ни мале́йшего ~я!** where is the city centre? I haven't the faintest idea! **3.** (*usu. pl.*) notions; level (of understanding); **счита́ться с ~ями слу́шателей** to take into account one's audience level.
поняти́йный *adj.* conceptual.
поня́тливост|ь, и *f.* comprehension, understanding.
поня́тлив|ый (~, ~а) *adj.* quick (in the uptake).
поня́тност|ь, и *f.* clearness, intelligibility; perspicuity.
поня́т|ный (~ен, ~на) *adj.* **1.** understandable; **~но, что...** it is understandable that...; it is natural that...; **~но** (*coll.*) of course, naturally; **я, ~но, не мог согласи́ться** of course, I could not consent; **~ное де́ло** (*coll.*) of course, naturally. **2.** clear, intelligible; perspicuous; **~но?** (*coll.*) (do you) see?; is that clear?; **~но!** (*coll.*) I see!; I understand!; quite!
понят|о́й, о́го *m.* witness (*at an official search, etc.*).
пон|я́ть, пойму́, поймёшь, *past* **~ял, ~яла́, ~яло** *pf.* (*of* **~има́ть**) to understand; to comprehend; to realize; **п. намёк** to take a hint; **дать п.** to give to understand.
пообе́да|ть, ю *pf. of* **обе́дать**
пообеща́|ть, ю *pf.* (*of* **обеща́ть**) to promise.
пообжи́|ться, ву́сь, вёшься *pf.* (*coll.*) to get accustomed to one's new surroundings.
по́одаль *adv.* at some distance, a little way away.
поодино́чке *adv.* one at a time, one by one.
посмотр|е́ться, ю́сь, ~ишься *pf.* (*coll.*) to take a look round; (*fig.*) to feel one's feet.
поочерёдно *adv.* in turn, by turns.
поочерёдный *adj.* taken in turn, proceeding by turns.
поощре́ни|е, я *nt.* encouragement; incentive, spur.
поощри́тел|ьный (~ен, ~ьна) *adj.* encouraging.
поощр|и́ть, ю́, и́шь *pf.* (*of* **~я́ть**) to encourage; to give an incentive (to), give a spur (to).
поощр|я́ть, я́ю *impf. of* **~и́ть**
поп[1], а́ *m.* (*coll.*) priest; **како́в п., тако́в и прихо́д** (*prov.*) like master, like man.
поп[2], а́ *m.* pin (*in game of gorodki*); **поста́вить на ~а́** (*coll.*) to place upright.
поп-... *comb. form* pop-.
по́п|а, ы *f.* (*coll.*) (*baby's*) bottom.
попада́ни|е, я *nt.* hit (*on target*); **прямо́е п.** direct hit.
попа́да|ть, ет *pf.* to fall (*of a number of objects*).
попада́|ть(ся), ю(сь) *impf. of* **попа́сть(ся)**
попадь|я́, и́ *f.* (*coll.*) priest's wife.
попа́|ло, как п. *etc., see* **~сть**
поп-анса́мбл|ь, я *m.* pop group.
попа́рно *adv.* in pairs, two by two.
попа́|сть, ду́, дёшь, *past* **~л** *pf.* (*of* **~да́ть**) **1.** (**в***+a.*) to hit; **п. в цель** to hit the target; **не п. в цель** to miss; **пу́ля ~ла ему́ в лоб** the bullet hit him in the forehead; **п. ни́ткой в ушко́ иглы́** to get a thread through a needle; **п. па́льцем в не́бо** (*coll.*) to be wide of the mark. **2.** (**в***+a.*) to get (to), find o.s. (in); (**на***+a.*) to hit (upon), come (upon); **п. в Ло́ндон** to get to London; **п. на по́езд** to catch a train; **п. домо́й** to get home; **п. в плен** to be taken prisoner; **п. кому́-н. в ру́ки** to fall into s.o.'s hands; **п. под суд** to be brought to trial; **не туда́ п.** to get the wrong number (*on telephone*); **п. на рабо́ту** to land a job; **п. впроса́к** to put one's foot into it; **п. в беду́** to get into trouble, come to grief; **п. в са́мую то́чку** to hit the nail on the head; (*impers.*; *coll.*): **ему́ ~ло** he caught it (hot); **ему́ ~дёт!** he'll catch it! **3.** (*coll.*): **~ло** *gives indef. force to certain prons. and advs.*: **как ~ло** anyhow; helter-skelter; **что ~ло** any old thing; **где ~ло** anywhere; **он э́то сде́лал чем ~ло** he made it with whatever came to hand.
попа́|сться, ду́сь, дёшься, *past* **~лся** *pf.* (*of* **~да́ться**) **1.** to find o.s.; **он мне ~лся навстре́чу на у́лице** I ran into him in the street; **э́то письмо́ мне ~лось соверше́нно случа́йно** I came across the letter quite by chance; **п. кому́-н. на глаза́** to catch s.o.'s eye; **что ~дётся** anything; **пе́рвый ~вшийся** the first comer, the first pers. one happens to meet. **2.** to be caught; (**в***+a.*) to get (into); **п. в кра́же** to be caught stealing; **п. с поли́чным** to be taken red-handed; **п. на у́дочку** to swallow the bait, fall for the bait (*also fig.*); **п. в`беду́** to get into trouble; **смотри́, бо́льше не ~ди́сь!** don't let me catch you again!
попа́хива|ть, ет *impf.* (*coll.*) (*+i.*) to smell slightly (of).
поп-ед|а́, ы́ *f.* = **поп-ку́хня**
попённ|ый *adj.*: **~ая опла́та** payment by number of trees cut down.
попеня́|ть, ю *pf. of* **пеня́ть**
попере́к *adv. and prep.+g.* across; **разре́зать п.** to cut across; **положи́те их п.** lay them crosswise; **де́рево упа́ло п. доро́ги** the tree fell across the road; **стоя́ть у кого́-н. п. доро́ги** to be in s.o.'s way; **стать кому́-н. п. го́рла** to stick in s.o.'s throat; **вдоль и п.** far and wide; **знать что-н.**

вдоль и п. to know sth. inside out, know all the ins and outs of sth.

попереме́нно *adv.* in turn, by turns.

попере́чин|а, ы *f.* cross-beam, cross-piece, cross-bar; boom jib (*of crane*).

попере́чник, а *m.* diameter; **шесть ме́тров в ~е** six metres in diameter, six metres across.

попере́чн|ый *adj.* transverse, diametrical, cross-; (*aeron.*) dihedral; **~ая ба́лка** cross-beam, cross-tie; **~ая пила́** cross-cut saw; **~ая си́ла** transverse force; **п. разре́з, ~ое сече́ние** cross-section; **(ка́ждый) встре́чный и п.** anybody and everybody; (every) Tom, Dick, and Harry.

поперхн|у́ться, у́сь, ёшься *pf.* (+*i.*) to choke (over).

попе́рч|ить, у, ишь *pf. of* **пе́рчить**

попече́ни|е, я *nt.* care; charge; **быть на ~и** (+*g.*) to be in the charge (of); **оста́вить дете́й на п. отца́** to leave children in care of their father; **отложи́ть п. о чём-н.** to cease caring about sth.

попечи́тел|ь, я *m.* **1.** guardian, trustee. **2.** (*hist.*) warden, administrator (*of educational or similar institution or district*).

попечи́тель|ный *adj.* **1.** (*obs.*) solicitous. **2.** *adj. of* **~ство; п. сове́т** board of guardians.

попечи́тельств|о, а *nt.* **1.** guardianship, trusteeship. **2.** (*hist.*) board of guardians.

попива́|ть, ю *impf.* (*coll.*) to have a little drink (of); **стать п.** to take to drink.

попира́|ть, ю *impf. of* **попра́ть**

попи́скива|ть, ю *impf.* to cheep, give a cheep.

попи́сыва|ть, ю *impf.* (*coll.*) to write (*from time to time*); (*of a literary man*; *iron.*) to do a bit of writing.

по́пито *p.p.p. of* **попи́ть** (*coll.*); **нема́ло бы́ло п.** a fair quantity was drunk.

по|пи́ть, пью, пьёшь, *past* **≃пил, ~пила́, ≃пи́ло** *pf.* to have a drink.

по́пк|а[1]**, и** *m.* (*coll.*) parrot; Polly.

по́пк|а[2]**, и** *f.* (*coll.*) = **по́па**

поп-ку́хн|я, и *f.* (*coll.*) junk food.

попла́ва|ть, ю *pf.* to have, take a swim.

поплав|ко́вый *adj. of* **~о́к; ~ко́вая ка́мера** float chamber (*of carburettor*); **п. кран** ballcock.

поплав|о́к, ка́ *m.* **1.** float. **2.** (*coll.*) floating restaurant.

попла́|кать, чу, чешь *pf.* to cry (*a little, for a while*); to shed a few tears.

попла|ти́ться, чу́сь, ≃тишься *pf. of* **плати́ться**

попл|ева́ть, юю́, юёшь *pf.* (*coll.*) to spit (*a few times*).

поплёвыва|ть, ю *impf.* (*coll.*) to spit (*at intervals*).

попле|сти́сь, ту́сь, тёшься, *past* **≃лся, ~ла́сь** *pf.* (*coll.*) to push off; to drag o.s. along; **я тепе́рь ~ту́сь домо́й** I shall push off home now.

попли́н, а *m.* (*text.*) poplin.

попли́н|овый *adj. of* **~**

поплотне́|ть, ю *pf. of* **плотне́ть**

поплы́|ть, ву́, вёшь, *past* **~л, ~ла́, ~ло** *pf.* to strike out, start swimming.

попля|са́ть, шу́, ≃шешь *pf.* (*coll.*) to have a bit of dancing; **ты у меня́ ≃шешь!** (*coll.*) you'll pay for this!; you'll catch it!

поп-му́зык|а, и *f.* pop (music).

попо́вич, а *m.* (*coll.*) son of a priest.

попо́в|на, ны, *g. pl.* **~ен** *f.* (*coll.*) daughter of a priest.

попо́вник, а *m.* (*bot.*) marguerite, white ox-eye.

попо́вский *adj. of* **поп**[1]

попо́вщин|а, ы *f.* **1.** (*coll., pej.*) religious superstition. **2.** popovshchina (*movement in part of the Russ. Old Believer sect, retaining role of priests*).

попо́йк|а, и *f.* (*coll.*) drinking-bout.

попола́м *adv.* in two, in half; half-and-half; **раздели́ть п.** to divide in two, divide in half, halve; **дава́йте заплати́м п.** let's go halves; **ви́ски п. с водо́й** whisky and water half-and-half.

по́полз|ень, ня *m.* (*zool.*) nuthatch.

поползнове́ни|е, я *nt.* **1.** feeble impulse; half-formed intention; **я име́л п. вы́сказать своё мне́ние, но в конце́ концо́в сдержа́лся** I had half a mind to say what I thought but in the end I restrained myself. **2.** (**на**+*a.*) pretension(s) (to).

пополз|ти́, у́, ёшь, *past* **попо́лз, ~ла́** *pf.* to begin to crawl.

пополне́ни|е, я *nt.* **1.** replenishment; re-stocking; **п. горю́чим** re-fuelling. **2.** (*mil.*) reinforcement; **п. поте́рь** replacement of casualties.

пополне́|ть, ю *pf. of* **полне́ть**

попо́лн|ить, ю, ишь *pf.* (*of* **~я́ть**) to replenish, supplement, fill up; to re-stock; (*mil.*) to reinforce; **п. горю́чим** to re-fuel; **п. свои́ зна́ния** to supplement one's knowledge.

попо́лн|иться, ится *pf.* (*of* **~я́ться**) **1.** to increase. **2.** *pass. of* **~ить**

пополн|я́ть(ся), я́ю, я́ет(ся) *impf. of* **≃ить(ся)**

пополу́дни *adv.* in the afternoon, post meridiem; **в два часа́ п.** at 2 p.m.

пополу́ночи *adv.* after midnight, ante meridiem; **в два часа́ п.** at 2 a.m.

попо́мн|ить, ю, ишь *pf.* (*coll.*) **1.** to remember; **~и(те) моё сло́во** mark my words. **2.** (+*d.*) to remind; **я тебе́ э́то ~ю!** I'll get even with you!

попо́н|а, ы *f.* horse-cloth.

попо́тч|евать, ую *pf. of* **по́тчевать**

поп-пев|е́ц, ца́ *m.* pop singer.

поправе́|ть, ю *pf. of* **праве́ть**

поправи́м|ый (~, ~а) *adj.* reparable, remediable.

попра́в|ить, лю, ишь *pf.* (*of* **~ля́ть**) **1.** to mend, repair. **2.** to correct, set right, put right. **3.** to adjust, set straight; **п. причёску** to tidy one's hair. **4.** to improve, better; **п. своё здоро́вье** to restore one's health; **де́ла п. нельзя́** the matter cannot be mended.

попра́в|иться, люсь, ишься *pf.* (*of* **~ля́ться**) **1.** to correct o.s. **2.** to get better, recover; **я совсе́м ~ился** I am completely recovered. **3.** to put on weight; to look better; **он о́чень ~ился** he has put on a lot of weight; he looks much better. **4.** to improve.

попра́вк|а, и *f.* **1.** mending, repairing. **2.** correction; amendment; **п. к резолю́ции** amendment to a resolution; **внести́ ~и в законопрое́кт** to amend a bill. **3.** adjustment. **4.** recovery; **де́ло идёт на ~у** things are improving; things are on the mend.

поправле́ни|е, я *nt.* **1.** correction, correcting. **2.** recovery; improvement; **он вы́ехал на Кавка́з для ~я здоро́вья** he has gone to the Caucasus for his health.

поправля́|ть(ся), ю(сь) *impf. of* **попра́вить(ся)**

попра́вочный *adj.* correction; **п. коэффицие́нт** (*phys.*) correction factor.

попр|а́ть, у́, ёшь *pf.* (*of* **попира́ть**) to trample (upon); (*fig.*) to flout.

по-пре́жнему *adv.* as before; as usual.

попрёк, а *m.* reproach.

попрек|а́ть, а́ю *impf.* (*of* **~ну́ть**) (+*a. and i. or* +*a.* **за**+*a.*) to reproach (with); **п. кого́-н. гру́бостью** *or* **за гру́бость** to reproach s.o. with rudeness.

попрек|ну́ть, ну́, нёшь *pf. of* **~а́ть**

по́прищ|е, а *nt.* field; walk of life, profession; **вое́нное п.** soldiering; **литерату́рное п.** the world of letters; **вступи́ть на но́вое п.** to embark on a new career.

по-прия́тельски *adv.* as a friend; in a friendly manner.

попро́б|овать, ую *pf. of* **про́бовать**

попро|си́ть(ся), шу́(сь), ≃сишь(ся) *pf. of* **проси́ть(ся)**

по́просту *adv.* (*coll.*) simply; without ceremony; **п. говоря́** to put it bluntly.

попроша́йк|а, и *c.g.* **1.** (*obs.*) beggar. **2.** (*coll., pej.*) cadger.

попроша́йнича|ть, ю *impf.* **1.** (*obs.*) to beg. **2.** (*coll., pej.*) to cadge.

попроша́йничеств|о, а *nt.* **1.** (*obs.*) begging. **2.** (*coll., pej.*) cadging.

попроща́|ться, юсь *pf.* (**с**+*i.*) to take leave (of), say good-bye (to).

попру́[1] *see* **попра́ть**

попру́[2] *see* **попере́ть**

попры́гива|ть, ю *impf.* (*coll.*) to hop about.

попрыгу́н (*oblique cases not used*) *m.* (*coll., joc.*) fidget.

попрыгу́нь|я, ьи *f. of* **~**

попры́ска|ть, ю *pf.* (+*i.*) to sprinkle (with).

попря́|тать, чу, чешь *pf.* (*coll.*) to hide.

попря́|таться, чусь, чешься *pf.* (*coll.*) to hide (o.s.); **п.**

от дождя́ to take cover from the rain.
попуга́|й, я *m.* parrot.
попуга́йнича|ть, ю *impf.* (*coll.*) to parrot.
попуга́йчик, а *m.* parakeet; **волни́стый п.** budgerigar; budgie.
попуга́|ть, ю *pf.* (*coll.*) to scare, put the wind up a little.
попу́гива|ть, ю *impf.* (*coll.*) to give a scare (*from time to time*).
попу́дно *adv.* (*obs.*) by the pood (*see* **пуд**).
попу́др|ить, ю, ишь *pf.* to powder.
попу́др|иться, юсь, ишься *pf.* to powder one's face.
популяриза́тор, а *m.* popularizer.
популяриза́ци|я, и *f.* popularization.
популяризи́р|овать, ую *impf. and pf.* to popularize.
популяриз|ова́ть, у́ю *impf. and pf.* = **~и́ровать**
популя́рност|ь, я *f.* popularity.
популя́р|ный (~ен, ~на) *adj.* popular.
попурри́ *nt indecl.* (*mus.*) pot-pourri.
попусти́тел|ь, я *m.* (*pej.*) one who tolerates (*dishonest practices, etc.*).
попусти́тельств|о, а *nt.* (*pej.*) tolerance, toleration, permissiveness; connivance; **при ~е** (*+g.*) with the connivance (of).
попусти́тельств|овать, ую *impf.* (*+d.*) (*pej.*) to tolerate, put up (with); to connive (at); **почему́ она́ ~ует его́ пья́нству?** why does she put up with his drunkenness?
по-пусто́му *adv.* (*coll.*) in vain, to no purpose.
по́пусту *adv.* (*coll.*) = **по-пусто́му**
попу́та|ть, ет *pf.* (*coll., joc.*) to beguile; **чёрт ~л** it's the devil's work.
попу́тно *adv.* on one's way; at the same time; (*fig.*) in passing; incidentally; **мо́жно п. заме́тить, что...** it may be observed in passing that ....
попу́тн|ый *adj.* **1.** accompanying; following; passing; **п. ве́тер** fair wind, favourable wind; **идти́ с ~ым ве́тром** (*naut.*) to sail free; **~ая струя́** back-eddy, backwash. **2.** (*fig.*) passing, incidental; **п. вопро́с** incidental question; **~ое замеча́ние** passing remark.
попу́тчик, а *m.* fellow-traveller (*also fig., pol.*).
попуще́ни|е, я *nt.* (*obs.*) **1.** (*pej.*) tolerance; connivance. **2.** calamity.
попыта́|ть, ю *pf.* (*+a. or g.; coll.*) to try (out); **п. сча́стья** to try one's luck.
попыта́|ться, юсь *pf. of* **пыта́ться**
попы́тк|а, и *f.* attempt, endeavour; **предприня́ть ~у** to make an attempt; **~и сближе́ния** (*pol.*) approaches.
попы́хива|ть, ю *impf.* (*coll.*) to let out puffs; **п. тру́бкой, п. из тру́бки** to puff away at a pipe.
попя́|титься, чусь, тишься *pf. of* **пя́титься**
попя́тн|ый *adj.* (*obs.*) backward; **идти́ на п.** *or* **на ~ую** (*coll.*) to go back on one's word.
по́р|а, ы *f.* pore.
пор|а́, ы *a.* **~̀у** *f.* **1.** time, season; **весе́нняя п.** springtime; **осе́нняя п.** autumn; **вече́рней ~о́й** of an evening; **в ~̀у** opportunely, at the right time; **не в ~̀у** inopportunely, at the wrong time; **вы прие́хали в са́мую ~̀у** you came just at the right time; **в ту ~̀у** then, at that time; **в ~е́** (*coll.*) in one's prime; **до ~ы́, до вре́мени** for the time being; **до каки́х ~?** till when?, till what time?; **до каки́х ~ вы оста́нетесь здесь?** how long will you be here?; **до сих ~** till now, up to now, hitherto; (*obs.*) up to here, up to this point; **до сей ~ы́** to this day; **на пе́рвых ~а́х** at first; **с да́вних ~** long, for a long time, for ages; **с каки́х ~?, с кото́рых ~?** since when?; **с тех ~, как...** (ever) since ...; **с э́тих ~** since then, since that time. **2.** *as pred.* it is time; **давно́ п.** it is high time; **п. спать!** (it is) bedtime!
порабо́та|ть, ю *pf.* to do some work, put in some work.
поработи́тел|ь, я *m.* enslaver.
порабо|ти́ть, щу́, ти́шь *pf.* (*of* **~ща́ть**) to enslave; (*fig.*) to enthral(l).
порабоща́|ть, ю *impf. of* **поработи́ть**
порабоще́ни|е, я *nt.* enslavement; enthralment.
поравня́|ться, юсь *pf.* (**с***+i.*) to come up (to), come alongside.
пораде́|ть, ю *pf. of* **раде́ть**
пора́д|овать, ую *pf.* **1.** *pf. of* **ра́довать. 2.** to give pleasure for a while, make happy for a while.
пора́д|оваться, уюсь *pf.* **1.** *pf. of* **ра́доваться. 2.** to be happy for a while.
поража́|ть(ся), ю(сь) *impf. of* **порази́ть(ся)**
поражéн|ец, ца *m.* defeatist.
пораже́ни|е, я *nt.* **1.** defeat; **не име́ть ~й** (*sport*) to be unbeaten. **2.** (*mil.*) hitting (*the target, the objective*). **3.** (*med.*) affection; lesion. **4. п. в права́х** (*leg.*) disfranchisement.
пораже́нческий *adj.* defeatist.
пораже́нчеств|о, а *nt.* defeatism.
порази́тел|ьный (~ен, ~ьна) *adj.* striking; staggering, startling.
пора|зи́ть, жу́, зи́шь *pf.* (*of* **~жа́ть**) **1.** to defeat; to rout. **2.** (*mil.*) to hit, strike; **п. кинжа́лом** to stab with a dagger. **3.** (*med.*) to affect, strike. **4.** (*fig.*) to strike; to stagger; to startle; **меня́ ~зи́л её мра́чный вид** I was struck by her gloomy appearance; **нас ~зи́ли све́дения об их помо́лвке** we were staggered by the news of their engagement.
пора|зи́ться, жу́сь, зи́шься *pf.* (*of* **~жа́ться**) **1.** to be staggered, be startled, be astounded. **2.** *pass. of* **~зи́ть**
по-ра́зному *adv.* differently, in different ways.
порайо́нный *adj.* (by) area.
пора́н|ить, ю, ишь *pf.* to wound; to injure; to hurt.
пора́н|иться, юсь, ишься *pf.* to injure o.s.; to hurt o.s.
пораст|а́ть, а́ет *impf. of* **~и́**
пораст|и́, ёт, *past* **поро́с, поросла́** *pf.* (*+i.*) to become overgrown (with).
порв|а́ть, у́, ёшь, *past* **~а́л, ~ала́, ~а́ло** *pf.* **1.** to tear slightly. **2.** (*impf.* **порыва́ть**) (**с***+i.; fig.*) to break (with); to break off (with); **она́ давно́ ~ала́ с ним** she broke with him long ago; **п. дипломати́ческие сноше́ния** to break off diplomatic relations.
порв|а́ться, ётся, *past* **~а́лся, ~ала́сь, ~а́ло́сь** *pf.* **1.** to break (off), snap. **2.** to tear slightly. **3.** (*impf.* **порыва́ться**[1]) (*fig.*) to be broken (off).
поредé|ть, ет *pf. of* **реде́ть**
поре́з, а *m.* cut.
поре́|зать, жу, жешь *pf.* **1.** to cut; **п. себе́ па́лец** to cut one's finger. **2.** (*+a. or g.*) to cut (*a quantity of*); **п. хле́ба** to cut some bread. **3.** (*+a. or g.*) to kill, slaughter (a number of).
поре́|заться, жусь, жешься *pf.* to cut o.s.
поре́|й, я *m.* leek.
порекоменд|ова́ть, у́ю *pf. of* **рекомендова́ть**
пореш|и́ть, у́, и́шь *pf.* **1.** (*coll.*) to make up one's mind. **2.** (*obs.*) to decide, finish, settle; **вот мы ~и́ли де́ло** now we have settled the matter. **3.** (*fig., coll.*) to finish off, do away (with), do for.
поржаве́|ть, ет *pf. of* **ржаве́ть**
по́ристост|ь, и *f.* porosity.
по́рист|ый (~, ~а) *adj.* porous.
порица́ни|е, я *nt.* blame, censure; reproof, reprimand; **досто́йный ~я** reprehensible; **вы́разить п.** (*+d.*) to censure, pass a vote of censure (on); **вы́нести обще́ственное п.** (*+d.*) to reprimand publicly, administer a public reprimand.
порица́тел|ьный (~ен, ~ьна) *adj.* disapproving; reproving.
порица́|ть, ю *impf.* to blame; to censure.
по́рк|а[1]**, и** *f.* unstitching, unpicking, undoing, ripping.
по́рк|а[2]**, и** *f.* (*coll.*) flogging, thrashing; whipping, lashing.
порно́граф *m.* pornographer.
порнографи́ческий *adj.* pornographic.
порногра́фи|я, и *f.* pornography.
порножурна́л, а *m.* pornographic *or* girlie magazine.
порномагази́н, а *m.* sex shop.
порнофи́льм, а *m.* blue movie, skinflick.
по́ровну *adv.* equally, in equal parts; **раздели́ть п.** to divide equally, into equal parts.
поро́г, а *m.* **1.** threshold (*also fig.*); **переступи́ть п.** to cross the threshold; **обива́ть ~и у кого́-н.** to haunt s.o.'s threshold, pester s.o.; **я их на п. не пущу́** they shall not set foot on my threshold, they shall not darken my door; **п. бе́дности** poverty line; **стоя́ть на ~е сме́рти** to be at death's

door; **светово́й п.** (*physiol.*) visual threshold; **слухово́й п., п. слы́шимости** (*physiol.*) threshold of audibility. **2.** (*geog.*) rapids. **3.** (*tech.*) baffle (plate), dam, altar (*of furnace*).
поро́д|а, ы *f.* **1.** breed, race, strain, species; (*fig.*) kind, sort, type; **коро́ва джерсе́йской ~ы** Jersey cow; **они́ как раз одно́й и той же ~ы** they are of exactly the same type. **2.** (*obs.*) breeding. **3.** (*geol.*) rock; **го́рная п.** rock; layer, bed, stratum; **материко́вая п.** bed-rock; matrix, gauge; **пуста́я п.** barren rock, dead rock.
поро́дистост|ь, и *f.* (pure) breeding.
поро́дист|ый (~, ~а) *adj.* pure-breed; thoroughbred, pedigree.
поро|ди́ть, жу́, ди́шь *pf.* (*of* **~жда́ть**) (*obs.*) to give birth (to), beget; (*fig.*) to raise, generate, engender, give rise (to); **его́ отсу́тствие ~ди́ло мно́го то́лков** his absence produced a crop of rumours.
породнённост|ь, и *f.* twinning (*of cities or towns*).
породн|ённый *p.p.p. of* **~и́ть; ~ённые города́** linked cities, twinned cities.
породн|и́ть(ся), ю́(сь), и́шь(ся) *pf. of* **родни́ть(ся)**
поро́дный *adj.* (*agric.*) pedigree.
порожда́|ть, ю *impf. of* **породи́ть**
порожде́ни|е, я *nt.* result, outcome; (*rhet.*) fruit, handiwork.
поро́жист|ый (~, ~а) *adj.* full of rapids.
поро́жний *adj.* (*coll.*) empty; **п. ход** (*tech.*) idling.
порожня́к, а́ *m.* empties (*empty wagons on rail.*).
порожняко́вый *adj.*: **п. соста́в = порожня́к**
порожняко́м *adv.* (*coll.*) empty, without a load.
по́рознь *adv.* separately, apart.
порозове́|ть, ю *pf. of* **розове́ть**
поро́й (*and* поро́ю) *adv.* at times, now and then.
поро́к, а *m.* **1.** vice. **2.** defect; flaw, blemish; **~и ре́чи** defects of speech; **п. се́рдца** heart disease, heart trouble.
пороло́н, а *m.* foam rubber.
поропла́ст, а *m.* foam plastic.
порос|ёнок, ёнка, *pl.* **~я́та, ~я́т** *m.* piglet; (*cul.*) sucking-pig.
порос|и́ться, и́тся *impf.* (*of* **о~**) to farrow.
по́росл|ь, и *f.* verdure, shoots.
порося́тин|а, ы *f.* sucking-pig (*meat*).
порос|я́чий *adj. of* **~ёнок**
поро́тно *adv.* (*mil.*) by companies.
пор|о́ть[1]**, ю́, ~ешь** *impf.* (*of* **рас~**) to unstitch, unpick, undo, rip; **п. вздор, ерунду́, чушь** (*coll.*) to talk nonsense; **п. горя́чку** (*coll.*) to be in a (tearing) hurry; **не́чего п. горя́чку** there's no hurry.
пор|о́ть[2]**, ю́, ~ешь** *impf.* (*of* **вы́~**) (*coll.*) to flog, thrash; to whip, lash; to give a flogging, thrashing, *etc.*
пор|о́ться, ~ется *impf.* (*of* **рас~**) **1.** to come unstitched, come undone; to rip. **2.** *pass. of* **~о́ть**[1]
по́рох, а (у), *pl.* **~а́, ~о́в** *m.* gun-powder; powder; **он как п.** he is hot-blooded; **ему́ ~а не хвата́ет** (*coll.*) he has not got it in him, he is not up to it; **п. да́ром тра́тить** to spend one's wits to no purpose; **держа́ть п. сухи́м** (*fig.*) to keep one's powder dry; **ни синь ~а** (*coll.*) not a trace; **~ом па́хнет** (*fig.*) there's a smell of gunpowder in the air; there is trouble brewing; **он ~а не вы́думает** (*coll.*) he will not set the Thames on fire.
пороховни́ц|а, ы *f.* powder-flask.
порохово́й *adj. of* **по́рох; п. заво́д** powder-mill; **п. по́греб** powder-magazine.
поро́ч|ить, у, ишь *impf.* (*of* **о~**) **1.** to discredit; **п. чьи-н. вы́воды** to discredit s.o.'s conclusions. **2.** to cover with shame, bring into disrepute; to defame, denigrate, blacken, smear; **п. чью-н. репута́цию** to blacken s.o.'s reputation.
поро́чност|ь, и *f.* **1.** viciousness, depravity. **2.** fallaciousness.
по́р|очный *adj. of* **~ка**
поро́ч|ный (~ен, ~на) *adj.* **1.** vicious, depraved; wanton **2.** faulty, defective; fallacious; **п. круг** vicious circle.
поро́ш|а, и *f.* newly-fallen snow.
пороши́нк|а, и *f.* grain of powder
порош|и́ть, и́т *impf.* (*of snow*) to fall in powdery form; (*impers.*): **~и́ло** it was snowing slightly; a light snow was falling.
порош|ко́вый *adj. of* **~о́к**
порошкообра́з|ный (~ен, ~на) *adj.* powder-like, powdery.
порош|о́к, ка́ *m.* powder; **стира́льный п.** washing-powder; **кра́сящий п.** toner; **стере́ть в п.** to grind into dust; (*fig., coll.*) to make mincemeat (of).
поро́ю = поро́й
по́рск|ать, аю *impf. of* **~нуть**
порск|а́ть, а́ю *impf.* (*of* **~ну́ть**) to set on (*hounds*).
по́рск|нуть, ну, нешь *pf.* (*of* **~ать**) (*dial.*) **1.** to snort (*with laughter*). **2.** to flee, dash off.
порск|ну́ть, ну́, нёшь *pf. of* **~а́ть**
порт[1]**, а, о ~е, в ~у́,** *pl.* **~ы́, ~о́в** *m.* port; harbour; **вое́нный п.** naval port, naval dockyard; **возду́шный п.** airport; **морско́й п.** seaport.
порт[2]**, а** *m.* (*naut.*) port(hole).
По́рт|а, ы *f.* (*hist.*) The (Sublime *or* Ottoman) Porte.
порта́л, а *m.* **1.** (*archit.*) portal. **2.** (*tech.*) gantry (*of crane*).
порта́л|ьный *adj. of* **~; п. кран** gantry crane.
портати́вност|ь, и *f.* portability, portableness.
портати́в|ный (~ен, ~на) *adj.* portable; **~ная радиоустано́вка, п. приёмник-переда́тчик** portable radio set, walkie-talkie.
портве́йн, а *m.* port (*wine*).
по́ртер, а *m.* porter, stout.
по́ртерн|ая, ой *f.* (*obs.*) pub, bar, ale-house.
по́ртик, а *m.* portico.
по́р|тить, чу, тишь *impf.* (*of* **ис~**) **1.** to spoil, mar; to damage; **п. своё зре́ние** to ruin one's eyesight; **п. кому́-н. удово́льствие** to mar s.o.'s pleasure; **п. механи́зм** to damage the works; **не ~тите себе́ не́рвы** don't take it to heart; don't worry. **2.** to corrupt.
по́р|титься, чусь, тишься *impf.* (*of* **ис~**) **1.** to deteriorate; (*of foodstuffs*) to go bad; (*of teeth*) to decay; to rot; **не п. от жары́** to be heatproof; **отноше́ния ста́ли п.** relations have begun to deteriorate. **2.** to get out of order. **3.** to become corrupt.
порт|ки́, ко́в *or* **~о́к** *no sg.* (*coll.*) = **~ы́**
портмоне́ *nt indecl.* (*obs.*) purse.
портни́х|а, и *f.* dressmaker.
портно́вский *adj.* tailor's, tailoring.
портн|о́й, о́го *m.* tailor.
портня́ж|ить, у, ишь *impf.* (*coll.*) to be a tailor.
портня́жнича|ть, ю *impf.* (*coll.*) = **портня́жить**
портня́жн|ый *adj.* tailor's, sartorial; **~ое де́ло** tailoring.
портови́к, а́ *m.* docker.
порто́вый *adj. of* **порт; п. го́род** port; **п. рабо́чий** docker.
портомо́|йня, йни, *g. pl.* **~ен** *f.* (*obs.*) wash-house.
по́рто-фра́нко *nt indecl.* (*econ.*) free port.
портпле́д, а *m.* hold-all.
портре́т, а *m.* portrait; likeness; **п. во весь рост** full-length portrait; **поясно́й п.** half-length portrait; **он — живо́й п. своего́ отца́** he is the image of his father.
портрети́ст, а *m.* portrait-painter, portraitist.
портре́т|ный *adj. of* **~; ~ная галере́я** portrait gallery.
портсига́р, а *m.* cigarette-case; cigar-case.
португа́л|ец, ьца *m.* Portuguese.
Португа́ли|я, и *f.* Portugal.
португа́л|ка, ки *f. of* **~ец**
португа́льский *adj.* Portuguese.
портула́к, а *m.* (*bot.*) purslane.
портупе́й-ю́нкер, а *m.* (*mil., hist.*) **1.** senior cadet. **2.** junior ensign (*in pre-revolutionary Russ. cavalry*).
портупе́|я, и *f.* (*mil.*) sword-belt; waist-belt; shoulder-belt.
портфе́л|ь, я *m.* **1.** brief-case; portfolio; **п.-диплома́т** attaché case. **2.** (*fig.*) portfolio; **мини́стр без ~я** Minister without Portfolio; **он получи́л п. мини́стра просвеще́ния** he has been made Minister of Education.
портше́з, а *m.* sedan(-chair).
порт|ы́, ов *no sg.* (*coll.*) trousers.
портье́ *m. indecl.* (*hotel*) porter, doorman.
портье́р|а, ы *f.* portière, door-curtain.
портя́нк|а, и *f.* foot binding (*worn instead of sock or stocking*); puttee.
поруб|и́ть, лю́, ~ишь *pf.* **1.** to chop down (*all or a large number of*). **2.** to do a bit of chopping.
пору́бк|а, и *f.* tree-felling, wood-chopping.

поруб́щик, а *m.* wood-stealer.
поруга́ни|е, я *nt.* profanation, desecration; **отда́ть на п.** to profane, desecrate.
пору́ганн|ый *adj.* profaned, desecrated; **~ая честь** outraged honour.
поруга́|ть, ю *pf.* (*coll.*) to scold, swear (at).
поруга́|ться, юсь *pf.* **1.** to swear, curse. **2.** (**c**+*i.*; *coll.*) to fall out (with).
пору́к|а, и *f.* bail; guarantee; surety; **кругова́я п.** collective guarantee; **взять на ~и** (*i*) to bail (out), go bail (for), (*ii*) to take on probation; **отпусти́ть на ~и** to accept bail (for), release on bail, put on probation.
по-ру́сски *adv.* (in) Russian; **говори́ть п.** to speak Russian.
поруч|а́ть, а́ю *impf. of* **~и́ть**
поруче́йник, а *m.* (*zool.*) marsh sandpiper.
поруче́н|ец, ца *m.* special messenger.
поруче́ни|е, я *nt.* commission, errand; message; mission; **дать п.** to give a commission, charge; **по ~ю** (+*g.*) on the instructions (of); on behalf (of); per procurationem (per pro., p.p.).
по́руч|ень, ня *m.* handrail.
пору́чик, а *m.* (*obs.*) lieutenant.
поручи́тел|ь, я *m.* **1.** guarantee, guarantor. **2.** warrantor, bail, surety.
поручи́тельств|о, а *nt.* guarantee; bail.
поруч|и́ть, у́, ~ишь *pf.* (*of* **~а́ть**) to charge, commission; to entrust; to instruct; **он ~и́л мне переда́ть вам де́ньги** he charged me to hand you the money; **ма́льчика ~и́ли тата́рской ня́не** the little boy has been entrusted to the care of a Tartar nannie.
поруч|и́ться, у́сь, ~ишься *pf. of* **руча́ться**
порфи́р, а *m.* (*min.*) porphyry.
порфи́р|а, ы *f.* (the) purple (*as Roman emperor's or other monarch's robe*).
порфи́р|ный *adj.* **1.** *adj. of* **~**. **2.** (*obs.*) purple.
порх|а́ть, а́ю *impf.* (*of* **~ну́ть**) to flutter, flit, fly about.
порх|ну́ть, ну́, нёшь *pf. of* **~а́ть**
порцио́н, а *m.* ration; **полево́й п.** (*mil.*; *obs.*) field ration allowance.
порцио́н|ный *adj.* **1.** à la carte. **2.** *adj. of* **~**; **~ные де́ньги** (*mil.*; *obs.*) ration allowance.
по́рци|я, и *f.* portion; (*of food*) helping; **две ~и ды́ни** two portions of melon, melon for two, melon twice.
по́рч|а, и *f.* **1.** spoiling; damage; wear and tear; **п. отноше́ний** deterioration of relations. **2.** corruption. **3.** (*dial.*) wasting disease (*in popular belief caused by magic spells*); **навести́ ~у на кого́-н.** to put the evil eye on s.o.
по́рченый *adj.* (*coll.*) **1.** spoiled; (*of foodstuffs*) bad; damaged, out of order, unserviceable. **2.** (*dial.*) bewitched, under the evil eye.
по́рш|ень, ня *m.* (*tech.*) piston; plunger, sucker (*of pump*).
порш|нево́й *adj. of* **~ень; ~нево́е кольцо́** piston ring; **~нева́я маши́на** reciprocating engine; **п. приво́д** piston drive; **п. самолёт** piston aircraft (*opp. jet aircraft*); **п. сте́ржень** piston rod.
поры́в[1], **а** *m.* **1.** gust; rush. **2.** (*fig.*) fit, gust; uprush, upsurge; **благоро́дный п.** noble impulse; **п. гне́ва** fit of temper; **под влия́нием ~а** on an impulse, on the spur of the moment.
поры́в[2], **а** *m.* breaking, snapping.
порыва́|ть, ю *impf. of* **порва́ть**
порыва́|ться[1], **юсь** *impf. of* **порва́ться**
порыва́|ться[2], **юсь** *impf.* **1.** to make jerky movements. **2.** (+*inf.*) to try, endeavour.
поры́висто *adv.* fitfully, by fits and starts.
поры́вистост|ь, и *f.* impetuosity, violence.
поры́вист|ый (~, ~а) *adj.* **1.** gusty. **2.** jerky. **3.** (*fig.*) impetuous, violent; fitful.
порыже́лый *adj.* (*coll.*) reddish-brown (*as result of fading*).
порыже́|ть, ю *pf. of* **рыже́ть**
пор|ы́ться, о́юсь, о́ешься *pf.* (**в**+*p.*; *coll.*) to rummage (in, among); **п. в па́мяти** to give one's memory a jog.
по-ры́царски *adv.* in a chivalrous manner.
порябе́|ть, ю *pf. of* **рябе́ть**
поря|ди́ться, жу́сь, ди́шься *pf. of* **ряди́ться**
поря́дков|ый *adj.* ordinal; **~ое числи́тельное** ordinal numeral.
поря́дком *adv.* (*coll.*) **1.** pretty, rather; **мне п. надое́л э́тот фильм** I found it a rather boring film. **2.** properly, thoroughly; **он не объясни́л п., как туда́ попа́сть** he did not explain properly how to get there.
поря́длив|ый (~, ~а) *adj.* neat, orderly.
поря́д|ок, ка *m.* (*in var. senses*) order. **1.** = *correct state or arrangement*; **навести́ п.** (**в**+*a.*) to introduce order (in); **привести́ в п.** to put in order; **привести́ себя́ в п.** to tidy o.s. up, set o.s. to rights; **призва́ть, к ~ку** to call to order; **следи́ть за ~ком** to keep order; **всё в ~ке!** everything is all right!; it's quite all right!; all correct!; OK!; **э́то в ~ке веще́й** it is in the order of things, it is quite natural; **не в ~ке** out of order, not right; **у него́ кише́чник ещё не в ~ке** his bowels are not right yet; there is still sth. the matter with his bowels; **для ~ка** (*i*) to maintain order, (*ii*) to preserve the conventions; **к ~ку!** (*at a meeting*) order!; **взять сло́во к ~ку веде́ния собра́ния** to rise to a point of order. **2.** = *sequence*; **алфави́тный п.** alphabetical order; **после́довательный п.** sequence; **де́ло идёт свои́м ~ком** things are taking their (regular, normal) course; **по ~ку** in order, in succession; **п. дня** agenda, order of business, order of the day; **стоя́ть в ~ке дня** to be on the agenda. **3.** manner, way; procedure; **в ~ке** (+*g.*) by way (of), on the basis (of); **в администрати́вном ~ке** administratively; **в обяза́тельном ~ке** without fail; **в спе́шном ~ке** quickly; **в устано́вленном ~ке** in accordance with established procedure; **зако́нным ~ком** legally; **пресле́довать суде́бным ~ком** to prosecute; **п. вы́боров** election procedure; **п. голосова́ния** voting procedure, method of voting. **4.** (*mil.*) = *formation*; **боево́й п.** battle order. **5.** (*pol.*) = *system*, *régime*; **ста́рый п.** the old order; **устано́вленный п.** the established order. **6.** (*pl.*) customs, usages, observances.
поря́дочно *adv.* **1.** decently; honestly; respectably; **они́ поступи́ли вполне́ п.** they acted perfectly decently. **2.** (*coll.*) fairly, pretty; a fair amount; **она́ п. уста́ла** she was pretty tired; **мы п. вы́пили** we had a fair amount to drink. **3.** (*coll.*) fairly well, quite decently; **он поёт п.** he sings quite decently; he has quite a decent voice.
поря́дочност|ь, и *f.* decency; honesty, probity.
поря́доч|ный (~ен, ~на) *adj.* **1.** decent; honest; respectable; **~ные лю́ди** respectable people, decent folk. **2.** (*coll.*) fair, considerable, decent; **они́ живу́т на ~ном расстоя́нии отсю́да** they live a fair distance from here; **он уже́ накопи́л ~ную су́мму** he has already saved up a decent sum; **п. дохо́д** a respectable income; **он — п. плут** he is pretty much of a rogue.
пос. (*abbr. of* **посёлок**) settlement.
поса́д, а *m.* **1.** (*hist.*) trading quarter (*situated outside city wall*). **2.** (*obs.*) suburb.
поса|ди́ть, жу́, ~дишь *pf. of* **сади́ть** *and* **сажа́ть**
поса́дк|а, и *f.* **1.** planting. **2.** embarkation; boarding (*train, bus, etc.*); (*mil.*) entrainment; embussing. **3.** (*aeron.*) landing; alighting (*on water*); **вы́нужденная п.** forced landing. **4.** seat (*manner of sitting in saddle*).
поса́дник, а *m.* (*hist.*) posadnik (*governor of medieval Russ. city-state, appointed by prince or elected by citizens*).
поса́дничеств|о, а *nt.* (*hist.*) office of posadnik.
поса́дни|чий *adj. of* **~к**
поса́дочн|ый *adj.* **1.** planting. **2.** (*aeron.*) landing; **~ые огни́** flare path; **~ая площа́дка** landing ground; **п. пробе́г** landing run; **~ая фа́ра** landing light.
поса́д|ский *adj. of* **~**; **~ские лю́ди** (*hist.*) tradespeople; *as n.* **п., ~ского** *m.* (*obs.*) inhabitant of suburb.
посажа́|ть, ю *pf.* (*coll.*) **1.** (+*a. or g.*) to seat (*a number of*). **2.** (+*g.*) to do a bit of planting.
поса́|женный *p.p.p. of* **~ди́ть**
посаже́нный *adj.* by the sazhen (*see* **саже́нь**); by the fathom.
посажёный *adj.* proxy (*for parent of bride or bridegroom at wedding ceremony*), sponsor.
поса́пыва|ть, ю *impf.* (*coll.*) to snuffle; to breathe heavily (*in sleep*).

посáсыва|ть, ю *impf.* (*coll.*) to suck (at).
посáхар|ить, ю, ишь *pf. of* **сáхарить**
посвáта|ть(ся), ю(сь) *pf. of* **свáтать(ся)**
посвежé|ть, ю *pf. of* **свежéть**
посве|тúть, чý, ⁓тишь *pf.* **1.** to shine for a while. **2.** (*+d.*) to hold a light (for); **я тебé ⁓чý до углá переýлка** I will light you to the corner of the lane.
посветлé|ть, ю *pf. of* **светлéть**
пóсвист, а *m.* whistle; whistling.
посви|стáть, щý, ⁓щешь *pf.* to whistle (to, up).
посви|стéть, щý, стúшь *pf.* to whistle, give a whistle.
посвúстыва|ть, ю *impf.* to whistle (*softly, from time to time*).
по-своéму *adv.* in one's own way; **дéлайте п., поступáйте п.** have it your own way.
по-свóйски *adv.* (*coll.*) **1.** in one's own way; **он всегдá поступáет п.** he always pleases himself. **2.** in a familiar way, as between friends.
посвятúтельный *adj.* dedicatory.
посвя|тúть, щý, тúшь *pf.* (*of* **⁓щáть**) **1.** (*+a.* **в**+*a.*) to let (into), initiate (into); **мы вас ⁓тúм в нáшу тáйну** we will let you into our secret. **2.** (*+a. and d.*) to devote (to), give up (to); to dedicate (to); **п. себя наýке** to devote o.s. to (the cause of) learning; **он ⁓тúл пéрвую кнúгу своéй мáтери** he dedicated his first book to his mother. **3.** (*+a.* **в**+*nom.-a.*) to ordain, consecrate; **п. в дья́коны** to ordain deacon; **п. в епúскопы** to consecrate bishop; **п. в ры́цари** to knight, confer a knighthood (upon).
посвящá|ть, ю *impf. of* **посвятúть**
посвящéни|е, я *nt.* **1.** initiation. **2.** (*in liter. work*) dedication. **3.** ordination; consecration; **п. в ры́цари** knighting.
посéв, а *m.* **1.** sowing. **2.** crops; **плóщадь ⁓ов** sown area, area under crops.
посевн|óй *adj.* sowing; **⁓áя плóщадь** sown area, area under crops; *as n.* **⁓áя, ⁓óй** *f.* sowing campaign.
поседéлый *adj.* grown grey, grizzled.
поседé|ть, ю *pf. of* **седéть**
посейчáс *adv.* (*coll.*) up to now, up to the present.
поселéн|ец, ца *m.* **1.** settler. **2.** deportee.
поселéни|е, я *nt.* **1.** settling. **2.** settlement. **3.** deportation; **отпрáвить на п.** to deport.
посел|úть, ю́, úшь *pf.* (*of* **⁓я́ть**) **1.** to settle; to lodge. **2.** to inspire, arouse, engender; **п. враждý мéжду друзья́ми** to engender enmity between friends.
посел|úться, ю́сь, úшься *pf.* (*of* **⁓я́ться**) to settle, take up residence, make one's home.
посел|кóвый *adj. of* **⁓ок**
посёл|ок, ка *m.* **1.** settlement (*of urban type*); (*new*) housing estate; **трущóбный п.** shantytown. **2.** (*in former USSR, name of administrative unit*) settlement.
посел́ян|ин, ина, *pl.* **⁓е, ⁓** *m.* (*obs.*) peasant.
посел|я́ть(ся), я́ю(сь) *impf. of* **⁓úть(ся)**
посемý *adv.* (*obs.*) therefore.
посеребр|ённый *p.p.p. of* **⁓úть** *and adj.* silver-plated.
посеребр|úть, ю́, úшь *pf. of* **серебрúть**
посередú *adv. and prep.+g.* (*coll.*) = **⁓не**
посередúне *adv. and prep.+g.* in the middle (of), half way along.
посерé|ть, ю *pf. of* **серéть**
посессиóнный *adj.* (*hist.*) possessional.
посéсси|я, и *f.* (*hist., leg.*) leasehold landed property.
посетúтел|ь, я *m.* visitor; caller; guest; **ежеднéвный п. пивнóй** habitué of a bar, regular.
посетúтель|ский *adj. of* **⁓**
посе|тúть, щý, тúшь *pf.* (*of* **⁓щáть**) to visit, call on; **п. лéкции** to attend lectures; **п. музéй** to see a museum.
посéт|овать, ую *pf. of* **сéтовать**
посé|чься, чётся, кýтся *pf. of* **сéчься**
посещáемост|ь, и *f.* attendance; **плохáя п.** poor attendance.
посещá|ть, ю *impf. of* **посетúть**
посещéни|е, я *nt.* visiting; visit.
посé|ять, ю *pf. of* **сéять**
посивé|ть, ю *pf. of* **сивéть**
посидéл|ки, ок *no sg.* (*obs.*) young people's gathering (*for recreation on winter evenings*).
поси|дéть, жý, дúшь *pf.* to sit (*for a while*); **п. вечерóк в гостя́х** to spend an evening at friends.
посúл|ьный (⁓ен, ⁓ьна) *adj.* within one's powers, feasible; **⁓ьная задáча** feasible task; **оказáть ⁓ьную пóмощь** to do what one can to help; **э́то не былá ⁓ьная для негó рабóта** he was not up to the work.
посинéлый *adj.* gone blue.
посинé|ть, ю *pf. of* **синéть**
поска|кáть[1], чý, ⁓чешь *pf. of* **скакáть**
поска|кáть[2], чý, ⁓чешь *pf.* to hop, jump.
поскользн|ýться, ýсь, ёшься *pf.* to slip.
поскóльку *conj.* **1.** so far as, as far as; **никтó не звонúл, п. мне извéстно** no one has rung as far as I know; **мы путешéствуем постóльку, п. позволя́ют срéдства** we travel (just) as much as we can afford. **2.** in so far as, since; so long as; **п. вы готóвы подписáть, готóв и я** so long as you are ready to sign, I am too.
поскóнный *adj.* hempen.
пóскон|ь, и *f.* **1.** (*bot.*) hemp-plant. **2.** (*obs.*) home-spun hempen sacking.
поскорée *adv.* somewhat quicker; *int.* **⁓!** quick!; make haste!
поскрёбк|и, ов *no sg.* scrapings, leftovers (*of food*).
поскуп|úться, лю́сь, úшься *pf. of* **скупúться**
послаблéни|е, я *nt.* indulgence.
послáн|ец, ца *m.* messenger, envoy.
послáни|е, я *nt.* **1.** message. **2.** (*liter.*) epistle; **Послáния** (*bibl.*) the Epistles.
послáнник, а *m.* envoy, minister; **чрезвычáйный п. и полномóчный минúстр** envoy extraordinary and minister plenipotentiary.
пóсл|анный *p.p.p. of* **⁓áть**; *as n.* **п., ⁓анного** *m.* messenger, envoy.
по|слáть, шлю́, шлёшь *pf.* (*of* **⁓сылáть**) **1.** to send, dispatch; **п. за дóктором** to send for the doctor; **п. по пóчте** to post; **п. поклóн** to send one's regards; **п. когó-н. к чёрту** (*fig., coll.*) to send s.o. to the devil. **2.** (*sport, etc.*) to move (*part of the body*).
пóсле *adv. and prep.+g.* after; afterwards, later (on); (*after a neg.*) since; **п. войны́** after the war; **мы с ним не видáлись п. войны́** he and I have not seen one another since the war; **он пришёл п. всех** he came last; **п. всегó** after all, when all is said and done; **п. чегó** whereupon.
после... *comb. form* post-.
послевоéнный *adj.* post-war.
послéд, а *m.* (*anat.*) placenta.
после|дúть, жý, дúшь *pf.* (**за**+*i.*) to look (after), see (to).
послéдк|и, ов *no sg.* (*coll.*) remnants, leftovers.
послéдн|ий *adj.* **1.** last; final; **(в) ⁓ее врéмя, за ⁓ее врéмя** lately, of late, latterly, recently; **(в) п. раз** for the last time; **до ⁓его врéмени** until very recently; **до ⁓ей крáйности** to the very uttermost. **2.** (the) latest; **⁓ие извéстия** the latest news; **⁓яя мóда** the latest fashion. **3.** the latter. **4.** (*coll.*) worst, lowest; **⁓ие временá** (*obs.*) bad times, hard times; **⁓ее дéло** the end; **э́то ужé ⁓ее дéло!** it's the end!; it's the very limit!; **⁓яя кáпля** the drop to fill the cup; the last straw; **ругáться ⁓ими словáми** to use foul language. **5.** *as n.* **⁓ее, ⁓его** *nt.* the last; the uttermost.
послéдовател|ь, я *m.* follower.
послéдовательност|ь, и *f.* **1.** succession, sequence; **п. времён** (*gram.*) sequence of tenses; **в стрóгой ⁓и** in strict sequence. **2.** consistency.
послéдовател|ьный (⁓ен, ⁓ьна) *adj.* **1.** successive, consecutive. **2.** consistent, logical.
послéд|овать, ую *pf. of* **слéдовать**
послéдстви|е, я *nt.* consequence, sequel; after-effect; (*pl.*) aftermath; **чревáтый ⁓ями** fraught, pregnant with consequences; **остáвить жáлобу без ⁓й** to take no action on a complaint.
послéдующий *adj.* subsequent, succeeding, following, ensuing; (*math.*) consequent.
послéдыш, а *m.* **1.** (*coll.*) last-born child, youngest child (*in a family*). **2.** (*fig., pej.*) belated follower.

послеза́втра *adv.* the day after tomorrow.
послеза́втра|шний *adj. of* ~
послело́г, а *m.* (*gram.*) postposition.
послеобе́денный *adj.* after-dinner.
послеоктя́брьский *adj.* post-October (*occurring or having occurred since the 1917 Russ. Revolution*).
послереволюцио́нный *adj.* post-revolutionary.
послеродово́й *adj.* post-natal.
послесло́ви|е, я *nt.* postface; concluding remarks.
послеуда́рный *adj.* (*ling.*) post-tonic.
посло́виц|а, ы *f.* proverb, saying; **войти́ в ~у** to become proverbial.
посло́вичный *adj.* proverbial.
послуж|и́ть^1, у́, ~́ишь *pf. of* **служи́ть**
послуж|и́ть^2, у́, ~́ишь *pf.* to serve (*for a while*).
послужно́й *adj.*: **п. спи́сок** service record.
послуша́ни|е, я *nt.* **1.** obedience. **2.** (*eccl.*) work of penance; **назна́чить кому́-н. п.** to impose a penance on s.o.
послу́ша|ть(ся), ю(сь) *pf. of* **слу́шать(ся)**
по́слушник, а *m.* novice, lay brother.
по́слушниц|а, ы *f.* novice, lay sister.
послу́ш|ный (~ен, ~на) *adj.* obedient, dutiful.
послы́ш|ать, у, ишь *pf.* (*obs.*) to hear.
послы́ш|аться, усь, ишься *pf. of* **слы́шаться**
послюн|и́ть, ю́, и́шь *pf. of* **слюни́ть**
посма́трива|ть, ю *impf.* (**на**+*a.*) to look (at) from time to time; **п. на часы́** to consult one's watch from time to time; to watch the clock; **~й(те)!** keep an eye out!
посме́ива|ться, юсь *impf.* to chuckle, laugh softly; **п. в кула́к** to laugh up one's sleeve.
посме́нно *adv.* in turns, by turns; by shifts.
посме́нн|ый *adj.* by turns, in shifts; **~ая рабо́та** shift work.
посме́ртный *adj.* posthumous.
посме́|ть, ю *pf. of* **сметь**
посме́шищ|е, а *nt.* laughing-stock, butt.
посмея́ни|е, я *nt.* mockery, ridicule; **отда́ть кого́-н. на п.** to make a laughing-stock of s.o.
посмотр|е́ть(ся), ю́(сь), ~́ишь(ся) *pf. of* **смотре́ть(ся)**
посмугле́|ть, ю *pf. of* **смугле́ть**
поснима́|ть, ю *pf.* (*coll.*) to take off, take away (all *or* a number of); **пора́ нам п. все рожде́ственские украше́ния** it is time we took down all the Christmas decorations.
по-соба́чьи *adv.* like a dog.
посо́би|е, я *nt.* **1.** (*financial*) aid, help, relief, assistance; allowance, benefit; **п. безрабо́тным** unemployment benefit, the dole; **~я матеря́м** family allowances; **п. по боле́зни** sick benefit, sick pay; **п. по нетрудоспосо́бности** disablement allowance. **2.** textbook; (educational) aid; **нагля́дные ~я** visual aids; **учё́бные ~я** educational supplies; school text-books.
пособ|и́ть, лю́, и́шь *pf.* (*of* **~ля́ть**) (*coll.*) to aid; to relieve; **п. го́рю** to assuage grief.
пособля́|ть, ю *impf. of* **пособи́ть**
посо́бник, а *m.* accomplice; abettor.
посо́бничеств|о, а *nt.* (+*g.*) complicity (in); aiding and abetting.
посо́ве|ститься, щусь, стишься *pf. of* **со́веститься**
посове́т|овать(ся), ую(сь) *pf. of* **сове́товать(ся)**
посоде́йств|овать, ую *pf. of* **соде́йствовать**
пос|о́л^1, ла́ *m.* ambassador.
посо́л^2, а *m.* salting.
посол|и́ть, ю́, ~́ишь *pf. of* **соли́ть**
посолове́лый *adj.* bleary, bleared.
посолове́|ть, ю *pf. of* **солове́ть**
по́солонь *adv.* (*obs.*) with the sun, clockwise.
посо́льс|кий *adj.* **1.** ambassadorial, ambassador's. **2.** *adj. of* **~тво; п. автомоби́ль** embassy car. **3.: П. прика́з** (*hist.*) Embassies' Department (*in Muscovite Russia*).
посо́льств|о, а *nt.* embassy.
по-сосе́дски *adv.* in a neighbourly way.
посо́тенно *adv.* by the hundred, by hundreds.
по́сох, а *m.* **1.** staff, crook. **2.** (*bishop's*) crozier.
посо́х|нуть, ну, нешь, *past* **~, ~ла** *pf.* to wither, become withered.

посош|о́к, ка́ *m.* **1.** *dim. of* **по́сох. 2.** (*coll.*, *joc.*) one for the road (*final drink before departure*).
посп|а́ть, лю́, и́шь, *past* **~а́л, ~ала́, ~а́ло** *pf.* to have a sleep, have a nap, snooze.
поспева́|ть^1, ет *impf. of* **поспе́ть^1**
поспева́|ть^2, ет *impf. of* **поспе́ть^2**
поспекта́кльн|ый *adj.*: **~ая опла́та** (*theatr.*) pay by the performance, pay per night.
поспе́|ть^1, ет *pf.* (*of* **~ва́ть^1**) (*coll.*) **1.** to ripen. **2.** (*of food in preparation*) to be done.
поспе́|ть^2, ю *pf.* (*of* **~ва́ть^2**) (*coll.*) to have time; (**к, на**+*a.*) to be in time (for); (**за**+*i.*) to keep up (with), keep pace (with); **~ли ли вы?** were you in time?, did you make it?; **она́ е́ле-е́ле ~ла на по́езд** she just caught the train; **мы не могли́ п. за ни́ми** we could not keep up with them.
поспеша́|ть, ю *impf.* (*coll.*) to hurry.
поспе́шеств|овать, ую *impf.* (+*d.*; *arch.*) to help, assist.
поспеш|и́ть, у́, и́шь *pf. of* **спеши́ть; ~и́шь, люде́й насмеши́шь** (*prov.*) more haste, less speed.
поспе́шно *adv.* in a hurry, hurriedly, hastily; **п. отступи́ть** to beat a hasty retreat; **п. уйти́** to hurry off, hurry away.
поспе́шност|ь, и *f.* haste.
поспе́ш|ный (~ен, ~на) *adj.* hasty, hurried.
поспле́тнича|ть, ю *pf.* to have a gossip; to tattle, talk scandal.
поспо́р|ить^1, ю, ишь *pf.* **1.** *pf. of* **спо́рить. 2.** (**с**+*i.*) to contend (with). **3.** to bet, have a bet.
поспо́р|ить^2, ю, ишь *pf.* to argue (*for a while*).
посрам|и́ть, лю́, и́шь *pf.* (*of* **~ля́ть**) to disgrace.
посрам|и́ться, лю́сь, и́шься *pf.* (*of* **~ля́ться**) to disgrace o.s., cover o.s. with shame.
посрамле́ни|е, я *nt.* disgrace.
посрамля́|ть(ся), ю(сь) *impf. of* **посрами́ть(ся)**
посреди́ *adv. and prep.*+*g.* in the middle (of), in the midst (of); **п. у́лицы** in the middle of the street; **п. толпы́** in the midst of the crowd.
посреди́не *adv.* = **посереди́не**
посре́дник, а *m.* **1.** mediator, intermediary; go-between. **2.** (*comm.*) middle-man. **3.** (*mil.*) umpire (*on manoeuvres*).
посре́днича|ть, ю *impf.* to act as a go-between, mediate, come in between.
посре́днический *adj.* intermediary, mediatory.
посре́дничеств|о, а *nt.* mediation.
посре́дственно 1. *adv.* so-so, not outstandingly well, not all that well; **он п. игра́ет в те́ннис** he is not particularly good at tennis. **2.** *n.*; *nt. indecl.* fair, satisfactory (*as examination mark*); **я сдал экза́мен по фи́зике на п.** I got a 'fair' in physics.
посре́дственност|ь, и *f.* mediocrity (*also = mediocre pers.*).
посре́дствен|ный (~, ~на) *adj.* **1.** mediocre, middling. **2.** (*of school marks, etc.*) fair, satisfactory.
посре́дств|о, а *nt.* mediation; **при ~е, че́рез п.** (+*g.*) by means of, through the instrumentality of; thanks to.
посре́дством *prep.*+*g.* by means of; by dint of; with the aid of.
посре́дствующий *adj.* intermediate; connecting.
поссо́р|ить(ся), ю(сь), ишь(ся) *pf. of* **ссо́рить(ся)**
пост^1, а́, о ~е́, на ~у́, *pl.* **~ы́** *m.* (*in var. senses*) post; **наблюда́тельный п.** observation post; **быть на своём ~у́, стоя́ть на ~у́** to be at one's post; (*of policeman*) to be on one's beat; (*of traffic controller*) to be on point-duty; **занима́ть высо́кий п.** to hold a high post; **расста́вить ~ы́** (*mil.*) to post sentries.
пост^2, а́, о ~е́, в ~у́ *m.* **1.** fasting; (*fig.*, *coll.*) abstinence. **2.** (*eccl.*) fast; **Вели́кий п.** Lent.
поста́в, а, *pl.* **~а́, ~о́в** *m.* **1.** pair of mill-stones. **2.** (*dial.*) loom; piece of canvas.
постав|е́ц, ца́ *m.* (*obs. or dial.*) **1.** provisions hamper. **2.** sideboard, dresser.
поста́в|ить^1, лю, ишь *pf. of* **ста́вить**
поста́в|ить^2, лю, ишь *pf.* (*of* **~ля́ть**) to supply, purvey.
поста́вк|а, и *f.* supply; delivery; **ма́ссовая п.** bulk delivery.
поставщи́к, а́ *m.* supplier, purveyor, provider; caterer; outfitter.
постаме́нт, а *m.* pedestal, base.

постана́влива|ть, ю *impf.* = **постановля́ть**

постанов|и́ть, лю́, ~́ишь *pf.* (*of* **постана́вливать** *and* **~ля́ть**) to decide, resolve; to decree, enact, ordain.

постано́вк|а, и *f.* **1.** erection, raising. **2.** (*in var. senses*) putting, placing, setting; arrangement, organization; **п. вопро́са** formulation of a question; **у неё хоро́шая п. головы́** she holds her head well; **п. го́лоса** (*mus.*) voice training; **п. па́льцев** (*mus.*) fingering; finger training; **п. рабо́ты** arrangement of work. **3.** (*theatr.*) staging, production; **вчера́ мы ви́дели «Ча́йку» Че́хова в но́вой ~е** yesterday we saw a new production of Chekhov's 'Seagull'.

постановле́ни|е, я *nt.* **1.** decision, resolution; **вы́нести п.** to pass a resolution. **2.** decree, enactment; **изда́ть п.** to issue a decree.

постано́в|очный *adj. of* **~ка 3.**; **~очная пье́са** play suitable for staging; play effective in stage production; **~очные эффе́кты** (stage) effects.

постано́вщик, а *m.* producer (*of play*), stage-manager; director (*of film*).

постара́|ться, юсь *pf. of* **стара́ться**

постаре́|ть, ю *pf. of* **старе́ть**

по-ста́рому *adv.* **1.** as before. **2.** as of old.

постате́йный *adj.* by paragraphs, paragraph-by-paragraph, clause-by-clause.

постел|и́ть, ю́, ~́ишь *pf.* (*coll.*) = **постла́ть**

посте́л|ь, и *f.* **1.** bed; **лечь в п.** to get into bed; **лежа́ть в ~и** to be in bed; **встать с ~и** to get out of bed; **постла́ть п.** to make up a bed; **прико́ванный к ~и** bed-ridden. **2.** (*geol., tech.*) bed; bottom.

посте́ль|ный *adj. of* **~**; **~ное бельё** bed-clothes; **~ные принадле́жности** bedding; **п. режи́м** confinement to bed; **коме́дия ~ного содержа́ния** (*coll.*) bedroom comedy.

постепе́нно *adv.* gradually, little by little.

постепе́нност|ь, и *f.* gradualness; **п. разви́тия** gradual development.

постепе́н|ный (~ен, ~на) *adj.* gradual.

постепе́новщин|а, ы *f.* (*pol., pej.*) gradualism.

постесня́|ться, юсь *pf. of* **стесня́ться**

постиг|а́ть, а́ю *impf. of* **~́нуть** *and* **пости́чь**

пости́гнуть = **пости́чь**

постиже́ни|е, я *nt.* comprehension, grasp.

постижи́м|ый (~, ~а) *adj.* comprehensible.

постила́|ть, ю *impf. of* **постла́ть**

пости́лк|а, и *f.* **1.** spreading, laying. **2.** bedding; litter.

пости́л|очный *adj. of* **~ка**; **~очная соло́ма** bed-straw.

постира́|ть, ю *pf.* **1.** (*coll.*) to wash. **2.** to do some washing.

по|сти́ться, щу́сь, сти́шься *impf.* to fast, keep the fast.

пости́|чь, гну, гнешь, *past* **~г** *and* (*obs.*) **~гнул, ~гла** *pf.* (*of* **~га́ть**) **1.** to comprehend, grasp. **2.** to overtake, befall, strike; **их ~гло ещё одно́ несча́стье** yet another misfortune has befallen them.

пост|ла́ть, елю́, е́лешь, *past* **~ла́л, ~лала́, ~ла́ло** *pf.* (*of* **стлать** *and* **~ила́ть**) to spread, lay; **п. ковёр** to lay a carpet (down); **п. посте́ль** to make one's bed; **как ~е́лешь, так и поспи́шь** (*prov.*) as you make your bed, so must you lie.

по́стник, а *m.* faster, pers. observing fast.

по́стнича|ть, ю *impf.* to fast.

по́стничеств|о, а *nt.* fasting.

по́ст|ный (~ен, ~на́, ~но) *adj.* **1.** Lenten; **п. день** (*eccl.*) fast-day; **~ная еда́** Lenten fare; **п. обе́д** meatless dinner (*comprising fish and/or vegetables*); **п. са́хар** boiled sweets. **2.** (*coll.*; *of meat*) lean. **3.** (*fig., coll., joc.*) glum. **4.** (*fig., coll., joc.*) pious, sanctimonious.

постов|о́й *adj. of* **пост**[1]; **~а́я бу́дка** sentry-box; **п. милиционе́р** militia-man on point-duty; **~а́я слу́жба** sentry duty; *as n.* **п., ~о́го** *m.* = **п. милиционе́р**

посто́й[1], **~те** (*coll.*) stop!; wait (a minute)!

посто́|й[2], **я** *m.* billeting, quartering; **поста́вить на п.** to billet, quarter; **свобо́ден от ~я** exempt from billeting.

посто́льку *conj.* (*in main clause, following* **поско́льку** *in subordinate clause*) to that extent (*or not translated*); **поли́тика п. поско́льку** (*fig.*) wait-and-see policy; policy of sitting on the fence.

посторон|и́ться, ю́сь, ~́ишься *pf. of* **сторони́ться**

посторо́нн|ий *adj.* **1.** extraneous, outside; **~ие вопро́сы** side issues; **без ~ей по́мощи** unassisted, single-handed; **~ие соображе́ния** extraneous considerations; **~ее те́ло** foreign body. **2.** strange; *as n.* **п., ~его** *m.* stranger; outsider; **«~им вход запрещён»** 'unauthorized persons not admitted'.

постоя́л|ец, ьца *m.* (*obs.*) lodger; (*in hotel, etc.*) guest.

постоя́лый *adj.*: **п. двор** (*obs.*) coaching inn.

постоя́нн|ая, ой *f.* (*math.*) constant; **п. вре́мени** time constant.

постоя́нно *adv.* constantly, continually, perpetually, always.

постоя́н|ный *adj.* **1.** constant, continual; **п. ка́шель** continual cough; **п. посети́тель** constant visitor. **2.** constant; permanent, invariable; **п. а́дрес** permanent address; **~ная а́рмия** regular army; **~ная величина́** (*math.*) constant; **п. жи́тель** permanent resident; **п. капита́л** (*econ.*) constant capital; **~ное напряже́ние** (*elec.*) direct-current voltage; **п. ого́нь** (*naut.*) fixed light; **п. ток** (*elec.*) direct current. **3. (~ен, ~на)** (*of personal, moral qualities, etc.*) constant, steadfast, unchanging; **она́ далеко́ не ~на во вку́сах** she is far from constant in her tastes.

постоя́нств|о, а *nt.* constancy; permanency.

посто|я́ть[1], **ю́, и́шь** *pf.* to stand (*for a while*).

посто|я́ть[2], **ю́, и́шь** *pf.* (**за**+*a.*) to stand up (for).

постпаке́т, а *m.* mail packet.

пострада́|вший *p.p. of* **~ть**; *as n.* **п., ~вшего** *m.* victim.

пострада́|ть, ю *pf. of* **страда́ть**

постра́ни́чный *adj.* paginal, by the page, per page.

постра́нств|овать, ую *pf.* to do some travelling.

постраща́|ть, ю *pf. of* **страща́ть**

постре́л, а *m.* (*coll.*) little imp, little rascal.

постре́лива|ть, ю *impf.* to fire intermittently, at intervals.

постреля́|ть, ю *pf.* **1.** to spend some time shooting, do some shooting. **2.** (+*a. or g.*; *coll.*) to shoot, bag (*a number of*).

по́стриг, а *m.* taking of monastic vows; (*of a woman*) taking the veil.

пострига́|ть(ся), ю(сь) *impf. of* **постри́чь(ся)**[2]

постри́жен|ец, ца *m.* one who has taken monastic vows.

постриже́ни|е, я *nt.* admission to monastic vows, tonsure; taking of monastic vows.

постри́женик, а *m.* = **постри́женец**

постри́жен|ка, ки *f. of* **~ец** *and* **~ик**

постри́|чь[1], **гу́, жёшь, гу́т,** *past* **~г, ~гла** *pf.* to clip, trim.

постри́|чь[2], **гу́, жёшь, гу́т,** *past* **~г, ~гла** *pf.* (*of* **~га́ть**) to make a monk (nun), admit to monastic vows.

постри́|чься[1], **гу́сь, жёшься, гу́тся,** *past* **~гся, ~глась** *pf.* to have a (hair-)trim.

постри́|чься[2], **гу́сь, жёшься, гу́тся,** *past* **~гся, ~глась** *pf.* (*of* **~га́ться**) to take monastic vows; to take the veil (*of a woman*).

построе́ни|е, я *nt.* **1.** (*in var. senses*) construction. **2.** (*mil.*) formation.

постро́|ечный *adj. of* **~йка**

постро́|ить(ся), ю(сь), ишь(ся) *pf. of* **стро́ить(ся)**

постро́йк|а, и *f.* **1.** (*action*) building, erection, construction. **2.** (*edifice*) building. **3.** building-site.

постро́мк|а, и *f.* trace (*part of harness*).

постро́чный *adj.* by the line, per line.

постскри́птум, а *m.* postscript.

посту́ка|ть, ю *pf.* to knock (*for a while*).

посту́кива|ть, ю *impf.* to knock (*from time to time*), tap, patter; **ходи́ть, ~я па́лочкой** to walk tapping with one's stick.

постула́т, а *m.* (*math., phil.*) postulate.

постули́р|овать, ую *impf. and pf.* to postulate.

поступа́тельно-возвра́тный *adj.* (*tech.*) reciprocating.

поступа́тельн|ый *adj.* forward, advancing; **~ое движе́ние** forward movement; (*tech.*) translation; **п. ход** step forward, onward march.

поступ|а́ть(ся), а́ю(сь) *impf. of* **~и́ть(ся)**

поступ|и́ть, лю́, ~́ишь *pf.* (*of* **~а́ть**) **1.** to act; **в да́нных обстоя́тельствах он пра́вильно ~и́л** in the circumstances he acted rightly, did right; **они́ с ним пло́хо ~и́ли** they have treated him badly. **2.** (**в, на**+*a.*) to enter, join; **п. в**

шко́лу to go to school, enter school; **п. в университе́т** to enter the university; **п. на рабо́ту** to start work; **п. на вое́нную слу́жбу** to join up, enlist. **3.** (*of inanimate objects*) to come through, come in; to be forthcoming; to be received; **~ила жа́лоба** a complaint has been received, has come in; **~ило ли его́ заявле́ние?** has his application come through, been received?; **де́ло ~ило в суд** the matter was taken to court, came up before the court; **~ило 1/XII** (*of an article submitted to a periodical, etc.*) Received 1 December; **п. в прода́жу** to be on sale, come on the market; **п. в произво́дство** to go into production.

поступ|и́ться, лю́сь, ~́ишься *pf.* (*of* **~а́ться**) (*+i.*) to waive, forgo; to give up; **п. свои́ми права́ми** to waive one's rights.

поступле́ни|е, я *nt.* **1.** entering, joining; **п. на вое́нную слу́жбу** enlisting, joining up. **2.** receipt; (*book-keeping*) entry; **п. изве́стий** receipt of news; **п. дохо́дов** revenue return.

посту́п|ок, ка *m.* action; act, deed; (*pl., collect.*) conduct, behaviour.

по́ступ|ь, и *f.* gait; step, tread; **ме́рная п.** measured tread.

постуч|а́ть(ся), у́(сь), и́шь(ся) *pf. of* **стуча́ть(ся)**

постфа́ктум *adv.* post factum, after the event.

посты|ди́ть, жу́, ди́шь *pf.* (*coll.*) to reprimand slightly, pull up.

посты|ди́ться, жу́сь, ди́шься *pf. of* **стыди́ться; ~ди́тесь!** you ought to be ashamed (of yourself)!

посты́д|ный (~ен, ~на) *adj.* shameful.

посты́л|ый (~, ~а) *adj.* (*coll.*) hateful, repellent.

посу́д|а, ы *f.* **1.** (*collect.*) crockery; plates and dishes, service; **гли́няная п., фая́нсовая п.** earthenware; **жестяна́я п.** tinware; **ку́хонная п.** kitchen utensils; **жаропро́чная п.** bakeware; **стекля́нная п.** glassware; **фарфо́ровая п.** china; **ча́йная п.** tea-service; **би́тая п. два ве́ка живёт** (*prov.*) creaking doors hang the longest. **2.** (*coll.*) vessel, crock.

посуда́ч|ить, у, ишь *pf.* (*coll.*) to gossip.

посу́дин|а, ы *f.* **1.** vessel, crock. **2.** (*coll.*) (*naut.*) old tub.

посу|ди́ть, жу́, ~́дишь *pf.* (*obs.*) to judge, consider; **~ди́ сам** judge for yourself.

посу́дник, а *m.* **1.** dishwasher. **2.** (*coll.*) dresser.

посу́д|ный *adj. of* **~а; п. магази́н** china-shop; **~ное полоте́нце** dish-cloth, tea-towel; **п. шкаф** dresser, china cupboard.

посудомо́йк|а, и *f.* dishwashing machine.

посу́л, а *m.* **1.** (*coll.*) promise. **2.** (*obs.*) bribe.

посул|и́ть, ю́, и́шь *pf. of* **сули́ть**

посу́точно *adv.* by the day, for every 24 hours.

посу́точн|ый *adj.* 24-hour, round-the-clock; **у них ~ое дежу́рство** they have a 24-hour spell of duty; they have 24 hours on; **~ая опла́та** pay by the day.

по́суху *adv.* (*coll.*) on dry land.

посца́ть (*vulg.*) *pf. of* **сцать**

посчастли́в|иться, ится *pf.* (*impers.+d.*) to have the luck (to); to be lucky enough (to); **ей ~илось побы́ть в Пари́же** she had the luck to stay in Paris.

посчита́|ть, ю *pf.* to count (up).

посчита́|ться, юсь *pf.* **1.** (**с**+*i.*; *coll.*) to get even (with). **2.** *pf. of* **счита́ться**

посыла́|ть, ю *impf. of* **посла́ть**

посы́лк|а[1], **и** *f.* **1.** sending. **2.** parcel; **п.-бо́мба** parcel bomb. **3.** errand; **быть на ~ах (у)** to run errands (for).

посы́лк|а[2], **и** *f.* (*phil.*) premise; **больша́я, ма́лая п.** major, minor premise.

посы́лочный *adj.* parcel; **~ая фи́рма** mail-order firm.

посы́льн|ый *adj.* **1.** dispatch; **~ое су́дно** dispatch-boat. **2.** *as n.* **п., ~ого** *m.* messenger.

посып|а́ть, а́ю *impf. of* **~́ать**

посы́п|ать, лю, лешь *pf.* (*of* **~а́ть**) (*+i.*) to strew (with); to sprinkle (with); **п. гра́вием** to gravel; **п. со́лью** to sprinkle with salt, to salt.

посы́п|аться, лется *pf.* to begin to fall; (*fig.*) to rain, pour down; **~ались ли́стья** the leaves had begun to fall; **несча́стья ~ались на них** misfortunes came upon them thick and fast.

посяга́тельств|о, а *nt.* (**на**+*a.*) encroachment (on, upon), infringement (of); **п. на свобо́ду** infringement of liberty.

посяг|а́ть, а́ю *impf. of* **~ну́ть**

посяг|ну́ть, ну́, нёшь *pf.* (*of* **~а́ть**) (**на**+*a.*) to encroach (on, upon), infringe (on, upon); **п. на чью-н. жизнь** to make an attempt on s.o.'s life.

пот, а, о ~́е, в ~у́, *pl.* **~ы́, ~о́в** *m.* sweat, perspiration; **весь в ~у́** all of a sweat, bathed in sweat; **облива́ясь ~́ом** dripping with sweat; **в ~́е лица́** by the sweat of one's brow; **~́ом и кро́вью** with blood and sweat; **труди́ться до седьмо́го (четвёртого) ~́а** (*coll.*) to sweat one's guts out; **вогна́ть кого́-н. в п., согна́ть семь ~о́в с кого́-н.** (*coll.*) to work s.o. to the bone, make s.o. sweat blood.

потаённый *adj.* = **потайно́й**

потайно́й *adj.* secret; (*tech.*) countersunk, flush; hidden, concealed; **п. микрофо́н** hidden microphone; **п. ход** secret passage.

потака́|ть, ю *impf.* (*no pf.*) (*+d.*; *coll.*) to indulge; **п. же́нщине в капри́зах, п. капри́зам же́нщины** to indulge a woman's whims.

пота́л|ь, и *f.* Dutch gold, brass leaf.

пота́ль|ный *adj. of* **~**

потанц|ева́ть, у́ю *pf.* to dance (*for a while*), do some dancing.

потаска́|ть, ю *pf.* (*coll.*) to pinch, filch (*all or a number of*).

потаску́н, а *m.* (*coll.*) lecher, rake.

потаску́х|а, и *f.* (*coll.*) strumpet, trollop.

потаску́шк|а, и *f.* = **потаску́ха**

потасо́вк|а, и *f.* (*coll.*) **1.** brawl, fight. **2.** beating, hiding; **зада́ть кому́-н. ~у** to give s.o. a hiding. **3.** *pl.* (*fig.*) tight spot(s).

пота́тчик, а *m.* (*coll.*) indulger.

пота́чк|а, и *f.* indulgence.

пота́ш, а́ *m.* potash.

потащ|и́ть, у́, ~́ишь *pf.* to begin to drag.

потащ|и́ться, у́сь, ~́ишься *pf.* to begin to drag o.s., begin slowly to make one's way.

по-тво́ему *adv.* **1.** in your opinion. **2.** as you wish; as you advise; **пусть бу́дет п.** have it your own way; just as you think.

потво́рств|о, а *nt.* indulgence, pandering.

потво́рств|овать, ую *impf.* (*+d.*) to show indulgence (towards), pander (to).

потво́рщик, а *m.* panderer.

потёк, а *m.* stain; damp patch.

потём|ки, ок *no sg.* darkness.

потемне́ни|е, я *nt.* darkening; dimness.

потемне́|ть, ю *pf. of* **темне́ть**

поте́ни|е, я *nt.* sweating, perspiration.

потенциа́л, а *m.* (*phys. and fig.*) potential; **ра́зность ~ов** potential difference; **вое́нный п.** war potential.

потенциа́л|ьный (~ен, ~ьна) *adj.* potential.

потенцио́метр, а *m.* (*elec.*) potentiometer.

поте́нци|я, и *f.* potentiality.

потепле́ни|е, я *nt.* getting warmer; **наступи́ло п.** a warm spell set in.

потепле́|ть, ет *pf. of* **тепле́ть**

по|тере́ть, тру́, трёшь, *past* **~тёр, ~тёрла** *pf.* to rub.

по|тере́ться, тру́сь, трёшься, *past* **~тёрся, ~тёрлась** *pf. of* **тере́ться**

потерпе́|вший *p.p. act. of* **~ть**; *as n.* **п., ~вшего** *m.* victim; survivor; **п. от пожа́ра** fire victim; **п. кораблекруше́ние** ship-wrecked pers., shipwreck survivor.

потерп|е́ть, лю́, ~́ишь *pf.* **1.** to be patient (*for a while*). **2.** to suffer, tolerate, stand (for); **я не ~лю́ никако́й на́глости** I won't stand for any cheek. **3.** to suffer, undergo; **п. кораблекруше́ние** to be shipwrecked; **п. пораже́ние** to sustain a defeat, be defeated; **п. убы́тки** to suffer losses.

потёртост|ь, и *f.* place sore from rubbing.

потёр|тый *p.p.p. of* **~е́ть** *and adj.* (*coll.*) **1.** shabby, threadbare. **2.** (*fig.*) washed-out.

поте́р|я, и *f.* loss; waste; *pl.*; (*mil.*) losses; **п. вре́мени** waste of time; **спи́сок ~ь** (*mil.*) casualty list; **~и уби́тыми и ра́неными** losses in killed and wounded.

поте́р|янный *p.p.p. of* **~я́ть** *and adj.* (*fig.*) lost; **у неё был**

п. вид she had a lost expression; **он — челове́к п.** he is done for.
потеря́|ть(ся), ю(сь) *pf. of* **теря́ть(ся)**
потесн|и́ть, ю, и́шь *pf. of* **тесни́ть**
потесн|и́ться, ю́сь, и́шься *pf.* to make room; to sit closer, stand closer, move up (*so as to make room for others*).
поте́|ть, ю *impf.* **1.** (*pf.* **вс~**) to sweat, perspire. **2.** (*pf.* **за~** *and* **от~**) to mist over, become covered with steam. **3.** (*impf. only*) (**над;** *fig.*) to sweat (over), toil (over).
поте́ха, и *f.* (*coll.*) fun, amusement; **устро́ить что-н. для ~и** to do sth. for fun; **вот п.!** what fun!; **и пошла́ п.!** now the fun has begun!
поте́|чь, ку́, чёшь, ку́т, *past* **~к, ~кла́** *pf.* to begin to flow.
потеша́|ть, ю *impf.* to amuse.
потеша́|ться, юсь *impf.* **1.** to amuse o.s. **2.** **(над)** to laugh (at), mock (at), make fun (of).
поте́ш|ить, у, ишь *pf.* **1.** *pf. of* **те́шить. 2.** to amuse (for a while).
поте́ш|иться, усь, ишься *pf.* **1.** *pf. of* **те́шиться. 2.** to amuse o.s. (*for a while*), have a bit of fun.
поте́ш|ный *adj.* **1.** (**~ен, ~на**) (*coll.*) funny, amusing. **2.** (*obs.*) (done, contrived) for fun, for amusement; **п. полк** (*hist.*) 'poteshny' regiment, 'toy-soldiers' (*regiment of boy-soldiers formed by Peter the Great*). **3.** *as n.* (*pl.*) **~ные, ~ных = п. полк**
поти́р, а *m.* (*eccl.*) chalice.
потира́|ть, ю *impf.* to rub (*from time to time*); **п. ру́ки от ра́дости** to rub one's hands with joy.
потихо́ньку *adv.* (*coll.*) **1.** slowly. **2.** softly, noiselessly. **3.** on the sly, secretly.
потли́вост|ь, и *f.* disposition to sweat, perspire.
потли́в|ый (~, ~а) *adj.* sweaty; subject to sweating.
потни́к, а́ *m.* sweat-cloth, saddle-cloth.
по́т|ный (~ен, ~на́, ~но) *adj.* **1.** sweaty, damp with perspiration; **~ные ру́ки** clammy hands. **2.** (*of glass, etc.*) misty, covered with steam.
потов|о́й *adj. of* **пот; ~ы́е же́лезы** sweat glands; **п. жир** wool yolk, suint.
потого́нн|ый *adj.*: **~ое (сре́дство)** (*med.*) sudorific, diaphoretic; **~ая систе́ма труда́** sweated labour system.
пото́к, а *m.* **1.** (*in var. senses*) stream; flow; **го́рный п.** mountain stream; **людско́й п.** stream of people; **проходи́ть несконча́емым ~ом** to file past in an endless stream; **п. слов** flow of words; **скос ~а** (*aeron.*) downwash; **лить ~и слёз** to weep in floods; **отда́ть на п. и разграбле́ние** (*hist.*) to give over to wholesale pillage. **2.** production line. **3.** (*in education*) stream, group.
потолка́|ться, юсь *pf.* (*coll.*) to knock about.
потолк|ова́ть, у́ю *pf.* (**с**+*i.*; *coll.*) to have a talk (with).
потол|о́к, ка́ *m.* ceiling (*also aeron.*); **взять что-н. с ~ка́** (*joc.*) to make sth. up.
потоло́|чный *adj. of* **~к**; (*fig., joc.*) chance, random; **~чные доказа́тельства** unfounded arguments.
потолсте́|ть, ю *pf. of* **толсте́ть**
пото́м *adv.* afterwards; later (on); then, after that; **мы п. придём** we shall come later; **ну, что вы сде́лали п.?** well, what did you do then?
пото́м|ок, ка *m.* descendant; scion; *pl.* offspring, progeny.
пото́мственный *adj.* hereditary; **он п. серебряных дел ма́стер** he comes of a family of silversmiths.
пото́мств|о, а *nt.* (*collect.*) posterity, descendants.
потому́ 1. *adv.* that is why; **я был в отпуску́, п. я и не знал об э́том** I was on leave, that is why I did not know about it. **2.** *conj.* **п. что; п.... что** because, as; **я не знал об э́том, п. что был в отпуску́** I did not know about it because I was on leave; **я п. не знал об э́том, что был в отпуску́** (*division of conj. alters emphasis*) the reason I did not know about it was that I was on leave.
потон|у́ть, у́, ~ешь *pf. of* **тону́ть**
пото́п, а *m.* flood, deluge; **всеми́рный п.** (*bibl.*) the Flood, the Deluge; **до ~а** (*fig., joc.*) before the Flood.
потопа́|ть, ю *impf.* = **тону́ть**
потоп|и́ть[1]**, лю, ~ишь** *pf.* to heat (*for a while*).
потоп|и́ть[2]**, лю́, ~ишь** *pf.* (*of* **~ля́ть**) to sink.
потопле́ни|е, я *nt.* sinking.
потоп|та́ть, чу́, ~чешь *pf. of* **топта́ть**
потора́плива|ть, ю *impf.* (*coll.*) to hurry up, urge on.
потора́плива|ться, юсь *impf.* (*coll.*) to hurry, make haste; **~йтесь!** get a move on!
поторг|ова́ться, у́юсь *pf.* (*coll.*) to bargain (for a while), haggle.
потороп|и́ть(ся), лю́(сь), ~ишь(ся) *pf. of* **торопи́ть(ся)**
пото́|чный *adj. of* **~к; ~чная ли́ния** production line; **ма́ссовое ~чное произво́дство** mass production.
потра́в|а, ы *f.* damage (*caused to crops by cattle*).
потрав|и́ть, лю́, ~ишь *pf. of* **трави́ть**[1] **4.**
потра́|тить(ся), чу(сь), тишь(ся) *pf. of* **тра́тить(ся)**
потра́ф|ить, лю, ишь *pf.* (*of* **~ля́ть**) (+*d. or* **на**+*a.*; *coll.*) to please, satisfy; **им не ~ишь** there's no pleasing them.
потрафля́|ть, ю *impf. of* **потра́фить**
потре́б|а, ы *f.* (*obs.*) need, want.
потреби́тел|ь, я *m.* consumer, user.
потреби́тельн|ый *adj.* consumption; **~ая сто́имость** (*econ.*) use value.
потреби́тель|ский *adj. of* **~; ~ская коопера́ция** (*collect.*) consumers' co-operatives.
потреб|и́ть, лю́, и́шь *pf. of* **~ля́ть**
потребле́ни|е, я *nt.* consumption, use; **това́ры широ́кого ~я** consumer goods; **чрезме́рное п.** overconsumption.
потребля́|ть, ю *impf.* (*of* **потреби́ть**) to consume, use.
потре́бност|ь, и *f.* need, want, necessity, requirement; **жи́зненные ~и** the necessities of life; **физи́ческая п.** physical need; **испы́тывать п. в чём-н.** to feel a need for sth.; **кака́я у вас п. в кни́гах?** what are your requirements for books?
потре́б|ный (~ен, ~на) *adj.* necessary, required, requisite.
потре́б|овать(ся), ую(сь) *pf. of* **тре́бовать(ся)**
потрево́ж|ить(ся), у(сь), ишь(ся) *pf. of* **трево́жить(ся)**
потрёп|анный *p.p.p. of* **~а́ть** *and adj.* **1.** shabby; ragged, tattered; **~анные брю́ки** frayed trousers; **~анная кни́га** a tattered book. **2.** battered. **3.** (*fig.*) worn, seedy.
потреп|а́ть(ся), лю́, ~лет(ся) *pf. of* **трепа́ть(ся)**
потре́ска|ться, ется *pf. of* **тре́скаться**
потре́скива|ть, ю *impf.* to crackle.
потро́га|ть, ю *pf.* to touch, run one's hand over (*to get the feel of sth.*); **п. па́льцем** to finger.
потрох|а́, о́в *no sg.* pluck (*animal viscera*); **жа́реные п.** haslet(s); **гуси́ные п.** goose giblets; **свины́е п.** pig's fry; **со все́ми ~а́ми** (*fig., joc.*) lock, stock, and barrel.
потрош|и́ть, у́, и́шь *impf.* (*of* **вы~**) to disembowel, clean; to draw (*fowl*).
потру|ди́ться, жу́сь, ~дишься *pf.* **1.** to take some pains; to do some work. **2.** **~ди́сь, ~ди́тесь** (+*inf.*) (*official or joc. injunction*) be so kind as (to); **~ди́тесь зайти́ ко мне за́втра** be so kind as to call on me tomorrow; **~ди́сь, ~ди́тесь вы́йти!** kindly leave the room!
потряс|а́ть, а́ю *impf. of* **~ти́**
потряса́|ющий *pres. part. act. of* **~ть** *and adj.* (*coll.*) staggering, stupendous, tremendous.
потрясе́ни|е, я *nt.* shock.
потряс|ти́[1]**, у́, ёшь,** *past* **~, ~ла́** *pf.* (*of* **~а́ть**) **1.** to shake; to rock; **п. во́здух кри́ками** to rend the air with shouts; **п. до основа́ния** to rock to its foundations. **2.** (+*i.*) to brandish, shake; **п. кулако́м** to shake one's fist. **3.** (*fig.*) to shake; to stagger, stun.
потряс|ти́[2]**, у́, ёшь,** *past* **~, ~ла́** *pf.* to shake (*a little, a few times*).
потря́хива|ть, ю *impf.* (+*i.*) to shake (*a little, from time to time*); to jolt.
потя́г|а, и *f.* **1.** muscular contraction; **родовы́е ~и** birth-pangs. **2.** (*fig.*) (*vain, unsuccessful*) attempt; **~и на остроу́мие** attempts to be funny.
потя́п|ить, лю, ишь *pf.* (*of* **~ля́ть**) to lower, cast down; **~я взор** with downcast eyes.
потуп|и́ть, лю́, ~ишь *pf.* to blunt.
потя́п|иться, люсь, ишься *pf.* (*of* **~ля́ться**) to look down, cast down one's eyes.
потупля́|ть(ся), ю(сь) *impf. of* **потя́пить(ся)**
по-туре́цки *adv.* in Turkish; in the Turkish fashion; **сиде́ть п.** to sit cross-legged.

потускне́лый *adj.* tarnished; (*fig.*) lack-lustre.
потускне́|ть, ю *pf. of* **тускне́ть**
потусторо́нний *adj.*: **п. мир** the other world.
потуха́ни|е, я *nt.* extinction.
потух|а́ть, а́ю *impf. of* **~́нуть**
поту́х|нуть, ну, нешь, *past* **~, ~ла** *pf.* (*of* **ту́хнуть**^{1} *and* **~а́ть**) to go out; (*fig.*) to die out.
поту́х|ший *p.p. act. of* **~нуть** *and adj.* extinct; (*fig.*) lifeless, lack-lustre; **п. вулка́н** extinct volcano.
потучне́|ть, ю *pf. of* **тучне́ть**
потуш|и́ть^1**, у́, ~́ишь** *pf. of* **туши́ть**
потуш|и́ть^2**, у́, ~́ишь** *pf.* to stew (*for a while*); to leave to stew.
по́тч|евать, ую *impf.* (*of* **по~**) (+*i.*; *coll.*) to regale (with), treat (to), entertain (to).
потяга́|ться, юсь *pf. of* **тяга́ться**
потя́гивани|е, я *nt.* stretching o.s.
потя́гива|ть, ю *impf.* (*coll.*) **1.** to pull (*a little*); to tug (at), give a tug; **п. папиро́су** to draw at a cigarette. **2.** to sip; to have a swig (of).
потя́гива|ться, юсь *impf. of* **потяну́ться**
потяго́т|а, ы *f.* (*coll.*) = **потя́гивание**
потян|у́ть, у́, ~́ешь *pf.* to begin to pull.
потян|у́ться, у́сь, ~́ешься *pf.* (*of* **тяну́ться** *and* **потя́гиваться**) to stretch o.s.
поу́жина|ть, ю *pf. of* **у́жинать**
поумне́|ть, ю *pf. of* **умне́ть**
поуро́чно *adv.* **1.** by the piece. **2.** by the lesson.
поуро́чн|ый *adj.* **1.** by the piece; **~ая опла́та** piece-work payment. **2.** by the lesson.
поутру́ *adv.* (*coll.*) in the morning.
поуча́|ть, ю *impf.* **1.** (*obs.*) to teach, instruct. **2.** (*coll., iron.*) to preach (at), lecture.
поуче́ни|е, я *nt.* (*liter.*) exhortation, homily; (*coll., iron.*) preaching; sermon, sermonizing.
поучи́тел|ьный (~ен, ~ьна) *adj.* instructive.
поуч|и́ть, у́, ~́ишь *pf.* **1.** to do a bit of teaching. **2.** (+*a. and d.*) to give a bit of instruction (in); to give a few tips (on).
поуч|и́ться, у́сь, ~́ишься *pf.* to study (*for a while*); to do a bit of studying.
пофарт|и́ть, и́т *pf.* (*of* **фарти́ть**) (*impers.*+*d.*; *sl.*) to be lucky, be in luck; **нам ~и́ло** we were in luck.
пофор|си́ть, шу́, си́шь *pf.* (+*i.*; *coll.*) to show off, parade.
поха́бник, а *m.* (*coll.*) foul-mouthed pers.
поха́бнича|ть, ю *impf.* (*of* **с~**) (*coll.*) to use foul language, use obscenities.
поха́б|ный (~ен, ~на) *adj.* (*coll.*) obscene, bawdy, smutty.
поха́бщин|а, ы *f.* (*coll.*) obscenity, bawdiness, smuttiness.
поха́жива|ть, ю *impf.* (*coll.*) **1.** to pace; to stroll. **2.** to come, go (*from time to time*).
похвал|а́, ы́ *f.* praise; **отозва́ться с ~о́й (о**+*p.*) to praise, speak favourably (of).
похва́лива|ть, ю *impf.* (*coll.*) to praise; to pay repeated tributes to.
похвал|и́ть(ся), ю́(сь), ~́ишь(ся) *pf. of* **хвали́ть(ся)**
похвальб|а́, ы́ *f.* (*coll.*) bragging, boasting.
похва́л|ьный (~ен, ~ьна) *adj.* **1.** praiseworthy, laudable, commendable. **2.** laudatory; **~ьная гра́мота, п. лист** (*obs.*) certificate of merit; (school) certificate of good conduct and progress; **~ьное сло́во** eulogy, encomium, panegyric.
похваля́|ться, юсь *impf.* (+*i.*; *coll.*) to boast (of, about), brag (about).
похва́рыва|ть, ю *impf.* (*coll.*) to be frequently unwell, be subject to indisposition.
похва́ста|ть(ся), ю(сь) *pf. of* **хва́стать(ся)**
похе́р|ить, ю, ишь *pf.* (*coll.*) to cross out, cancel.
похити́тел|ь, я *m.* thief; kidnapper; abductor; hijacker.
похи́|тить, щу, тишь *pf.* (*of* **~ща́ть**) to steal; to kidnap; to abduct, carry off; to hijack.
похища́|ть, ю *impf. of* **похи́тить**
похище́ни|е, я *nt.* theft; kidnapping; abduction; hijacking.
похлёбк|а, и *f.* soup, broth, skilly.
похло́па|ть, ю *pf.* to slap, clap (a few times).
похлопо|та́ть, чу́, ~́чешь *pf. of* **хлопота́ть**
похме́ль|е, я *nt.* hangover; 'the morning after the night before'; **быть с ~я** to have a hangover; **в чужо́м пиру́ п.** unpleasantness suffered through no fault of one's own.
похо́д^1**, а** *m.* **1.** march; (*naut.*) cruise; **вы́ступить в п.** to take the field, get on the march; **в ~е** (*naut.*) cruising, on cruise; **на ~е** on the march. **2.** (*mil.*; *fig.*) campaign; **кресто́вый п.** crusade. **3.** walking tour, hike.
похо́д^2**, а** *m.* (*coll.*) overweight.
похода́тайств|овать, ую *pf. of* **хода́тайствовать**
похо|ди́ть^1**, жу́, ~́дишь** *impf.* (**на**+*a.*) to resemble, bear a resemblance (to), be like.
похо|ди́ть^2**, жу́, ~́дишь** *pf.* to walk (*for a while*).
похо́дк|а, и *f.* gait, walk, step.
похо́д|ный *adj. of* **~**^{1}; **п. го́спиталь** field hospital; **~ное движе́ние** march; **~ная жизнь** camp life; **~ная коло́нна** column of route; **~ная крова́ть** camp-bed; **~ная ку́хня** mobile kitchen, field kitchen; **~ная пе́сня** marching song; **п. поря́док** marching order; **~ная ра́ция** walkie-talkie set; **~ное снаряже́ние** field kit; **п. строй** march formation; **~ная фо́рма** marching order, field dress.
по́ходя *adv.* (*coll.*) **1.** as one goes along; on the march; **мы е́ли п.** we ate as we went along. **2.** (*fig.*) in passing; in an offhand manner.
похожде́ни|е, я *nt.* adventure, escapade; **любо́вное п.** (love) affair.
похо́ж|ий (~, ~а) *adj.* resembling, alike; (**на**+*a.*) like; **он ~ на де́да** he is like his grandfather; **они́ о́чень ~и друг на дру́га** they are very much alike; **э́то на неё не ~е** (*fig.*) that's not like her; **э́то на Пе́тю ~е!** just like Petya!; that's Petya all over!; **он не ~ на самого́ себя́** he is not himself; **э́то ни на что́ не ~е** (*fig., pej.*) it's like nothing on earth; it is unheard of. **2.** (*coll.*): **~е** it appears, it would appear; **~е на то, что...** it looks as if ...; **он, ~е, бо́лен** it would appear he is ill.
по-хозя́йски *adv.* thriftily; **израсхо́довать насле́дство п.** to spend a legacy wisely.
похолода́ни|е, я *nt.* fall of temperature, cold spell, cold snap.
похолода́|ть *pf. of* **холода́ть**
похолоде́|ть, ю *pf. of* **холоде́ть**
похорон|и́ть, ю́, ~́ишь *pf. of* **хорони́ть**
похоро́нн|ый *adj.* **1.** funeral; **~ое бюро́** undertaker's, funeral parlour; **п. звон** (funeral) knell; **п. марш** dead march. **2.** (*fig., coll.*) funereal.
по́хор|оны, о́н, она́м *no sg.* funeral; burial.
по-хоро́шему *adv.* in an amicable way.
похороше́|ть, ю *pf. of* **хороше́ть**
похотли́вост|ь, и *f.* lustfulness, lewdness, lasciviousness.
похотли́в|ый (~, ~а) *adj.* lustful, lewd, lascivious.
похотни́к, а́ *m.* (*anat.*) clitoris.
по́хот|ь, и *f.* lust.
похохо|та́ть, чу́, ~́чешь *pf.* to laugh (*a little, for a while*); to have a laugh.
похрабре́|ть, ю *pf. of* **храбре́ть**
похра́пыва|ть, ю *impf.* (*coll.*) to snore (softly, gently).
похристо́с|оваться, уюсь *pf. of* **христо́соваться.**
похуде́|ть, ю *pf. of* **худе́ть**
похул|и́ть, ю́, и́шь *pf.* (*obs.*) to curse, abuse.
поцара́па|ть, ю *pf.* to scratch slightly
поцара́па|ться, юсь *pf.* to get slightly scratched.
поца́рств|овать, ую *pf.* to reign (*for some time*).
поцел|ова́ть(ся), у́ю(сь) *pf. of* **целова́ть(ся)**
поцелу́|й, я *m.* kiss.
поцеремо́н|иться, юсь, ишься *pf. of* **церемо́ниться**
почасово́й *adj.* by the hour.
поча́т|ок, ка *m.* **1.** (*bot.*) ear; spadix; **п. кукуру́зы** corn-cob. **2.** (*text.*) cop.
поч|а́ть, ну́, нёшь, *past* **~́ал, ~ала́, ~́ало** *pf.* (*of* **~ина́ть**) (*obs. or dial.*) to begin.
по́чв|а, ы *f.* **1.** soil, ground, earth. **2.** (*fig.*) ground, basis, footing; **на ~е** (+*g.*) owing (to), because (of); **вы́бить ~у из-под чьих-н. ног** to cut the ground from under s.o.'s feet, take the wind out of s.o.'s sails; **зонди́ровать ~у** to explore the ground; **подгото́вить ~у** to prepare the

ground, pave the way; **стоя́ть на твёрдой ~е, не теря́ть ~ы под нога́ми** to be on firm ground; **его́ утвержде́ния не име́ют под собо́й никако́й ~ы** his assertions have no foundation.

по́чвенник, а *m.* (*hist.*) member of 'back-to-the-soil' movement.

по́чвенничеств|о, а *nt.* (*hist.*) 'back-to-the-soil' movement.

по́чв|енный *adj. of* **~а**

почвове́д, а *m.* soil scientist.

почвове́дени|е, я *nt.* soil science.

почвоутомле́ни|е, я *nt.* (*agric.*) exhaustion of soil, soil depletion.

почём[1] *interrog. and rel. adv.* (*coll.*) how much; **п. сего́дня я́блоки?** how much are apples today?; **узна́ть, п. фунт ли́ха** (*coll.*) to fall upon hard times, plumb the depths of misfortune.

почём[2] *interrog. adv.* (*only used with parts of v.* **знать** *coll.*) how?; **п. знать?** who knows?; who can tell?; how is one to know?; **п. я зна́ю, кто ей э́то рассказа́л?** how should I know who told her about it?

почему́ 1. *interrog. and rel. adv.* why; **п. вы так ду́маете?** why do you think that?; **я зна́ю и́стинную причи́ну, п. он так ду́мает** I know the real reason why he thinks that. **2.** *as conj.* (and) so; (and) that's why; **она́ простуди́лась, п. и оста́лась до́ма** she has caught a cold, (and) so she has stayed at home.

почему́-либо = почему́-нибудь

почему́-нибудь *adv.* for some reason or other.

почему́-то *adv.* for some reason.

по́черк, а *m.* hand(writing).

почеркове́д, а *m.* graphologist.

почерне́лый *adj.* darkened.

почерне́|ть, ю *pf. of* **черне́ть**

почерп|а́ть, а́ю *impf. of* **~ну́ть**

почерп|ну́ть, ну́, нёшь *pf.* (*of* **~а́ть**) **1.** (*+a. or g.*) to draw. **2.** (*fig.*) to get; **п. све́дения** to glean, pick up information.

почерстве́|ть, ю *pf. of* **черстве́ть**

поче|са́ть(ся), шу́(сь), ~́шешь(ся) *pf. of* **чеса́ть(ся)**

по́чест|ь, и *f.* honour; **возда́ть ~и, оказа́ть ~и** (*+d.*) to do honour (to), render homage (to).

по|че́сть, чту́, чтёшь, *past* **~чёл, ~чла́** *pf.* (*of* **~чита́ть**[1]) (*obs.*) to consider, think; **он ~чёл свои́м до́лгом вы́ступить** he considered it his duty to speak.

почёсыва|ть, ю *impf.* (*coll.*) to scratch (*from time to time*).

почёт, а *m.* honour; respect, esteem; **быть в ~е у кого́-н., по́льзоваться ~ом у кого́-н.** to stand high in s.o.'s esteem; to be highly thought of by s.o.; **п. и уваже́ние!** (*coll.*) my compliments!

почёт|ный *adj.* **1.** honoured, respected, esteemed; **п. гость** guest of honour. **2.** honorary; **~ное зва́ние** honorary title; **п. член** honorary member. **3.** **(~ен, ~на)** honourable; doing honour; **п. карау́л** guard of honour; **~ное ме́сто** place of honour; **п. мир** honourable peace.

по́ч|ечный[1] *adj. of* **~ка**[1]

по́чечный[2] *adj.* (*anat., med.*) nephritic; renal; **~ые ка́мни** gall-stones; **~ая лоха́нка** calix (of kidney).

почечу́|й, я *m.* (*obs.*) piles.

почива́л|ьня, ьни, *g. pl.* **~ен** *f.* (*obs.*) bed-chamber.

почива́|ть, ю *impf.* (*obs.*) **1.** to sleep. **2.** *impf. of* **почи́ть**

почи́|вший *p.p. of* **~ть**; *as n.* **п., ~вшего** *m.*, **~вшая, ~вшей** *f.* the deceased.

почи́н, а *m.* **1.** initiative; **взять на себя́ п.** to take the initiative; **по со́бственному ~у** on one's own initiative. **2.** beginning, start; (*comm.*) first sale of day.

почин|и́ть, ю́, ~ишь *pf.* (*of* **чини́ть**[1] *and* **~я́ть**) to repair, mend.

почи́нк|а, и *f.* repairing, mending; **отда́ть что́-н. в ~у** to have sth. repaired, mended.

почи́н|ок, ка *m.* (*dial.*) **1.** forest clearing. **2.** small or new settlement.

почин|я́ть, я́ю *impf. of* **~и́ть**

почи́|стить(ся), щу(сь), стишь(ся) *pf. of* **чи́стить(ся)**

почита́й *adv.* (*dial.*) **1.** almost; nigh on. **2.** it seems; very likely.

почита́ни|е, я *nt.* **1.** honouring; (*+g.*) respect (for). **2.** reverence, worship.

почита́тел|ь, я *m.* admirer; worshipper.

почита́|ть[1], **ю** *impf. of* **поче́сть**

почита́|ть[2], **ю** *impf.* **1.** to honour, respect, esteem. **2.** to revere.

почита́|ть[3], **ю** *pf.* **1.** to read (a little, for a while). **2.** (*coll.*) to read.

почи́тыва|ть, ю *impf.* (*coll.*) to read (now and then).

почи́|ть, ю, ешь *pf.* (*of* **~ва́ть**) (*rhet.*) to rest, take one's rest; (*fig.*) to pass away, pass to one's rest; **п. на ла́врах** to rest on one's laurels.

почи́ще *adv.* **1.** cleaner. **2.** (*fig., coll.*) better; stronger, more vividly; **он вы́разился п. остальны́х** he expressed himself more vividly than the others.

по́чк|а[1], **и** *f.* **1.** (*bot.*) bud. **2.** (*bot., zool.*) gemma.

по́ч|ка[2], **ки** *f.* **1.** (*anat.*) kidney; **воспале́ние ~ек** nephritis; **иску́сственная п.** (*med.*) kidney machine. **2.** (*pl.*; *cul.*) kidneys.

почкова́ни|е, я *nt.* (*biol.*) budding; gemmation.

почк|ова́ться, у́ется *impf.* (*biol.*) to bud; to gemmate.

по́чк|овый *adj. of* **~а**[1]

по́чт|а, ы *f.* **1.** post; **возду́шная п.** air mail; **спе́шная п.** special delivery, express delivery; **электро́нная п.** e-mail; **посла́ть по ~е, ~ой** to send by post, post; **с у́тренней (с вече́рней) ~ой** by the morning (evening) post; **с обра́тной ~ой** by return (of post). **2.** (the) post, (the) mail; **пришла́ ли п.?** has the post come? **3.** post office; **рабо́тники ~ы** postal workers.

почтальо́н, а *m.* postman.

почта́мт, а *m.* head post office (*of city or town*); **гла́вный п.** General Post Office.

почте́ни|е, я *nt.* respect, esteem; deference; **относи́ться с ~ем (к)** to treat with respect; **с соверше́нным ~ем** (*epistolary formula*) respectfully yours; **моё п.!** (*coll.*) my compliments!

почте́н|ный (~ен, ~на) *adj.* **1.** honourable; respectable, estimable; venerable; **~ная рабо́та** estimable work; **п. во́зраст** venerable age. **2.** (*fig., coll.*) considerable, respectable; **труд ~ных разме́ров** a work of respectable dimensions.

почти́ *adv.* almost, nearly; **п. ничего́** next to nothing; **п. что = п.**

почти́тельност|ь, и *f.* respect, deference.

почти́тел|ьный (~ен, ~ьна) *adj.* **1.** respectful, deferential. **2.** (*fig., coll.*) considerable, respectable.

по|чти́ть, чту́, чти́шь *pf.* to honour; **п. чью-н. па́мять встава́нием** to stand in s.o.'s memory.

почтме́йстер, а *m.* (*obs.*) postmaster.

почто́ *adv.* (*obs.*) why; what for.

почтови́к, а́ *m.* postal worker.

почто́во-телегра́фн|ый *adj.* post and telegraph; **~ое учрежде́ние** postal and telecommunications establishment.

почт|о́вый *adj. of* **~́а; ~о́вая бума́га** note-paper; **п. ваго́н** mail-van; **п. го́лубь** carrier-pigeon, homing pigeon; **п. и́ндекс** post-code, Zip code; **~о́вая ка́рточка** postcard; **~о́вая ма́рка** (postage) stamp; **~о́вое отделе́ние** post-office; **п. перево́д** postal order; **п. по́езд** mail train; **~о́вые расхо́ды** postage; **п. я́щик** letter-box, pillar-box; **е́хать на ~о́вых** (*hist.*) to travel by post-chaise.

поч|ту́[1], **тёшь** *see* **~е́сть**

поч|ту́[2], **ти́шь** *see* **~ти́ть**

почу́вств|овать, ую *pf. of* **чу́вствовать**

почу́д|иться, ится *pf. of* **чу́диться**

почу́|ять, ю *pf. of* **чу́ять**

пошаба́ш|ить, у, ишь *pf. of* **шаба́шить**

поша́лива|ть, ю *impf.* (*coll.*) **1.** to be naughty; to act up; to play up (*from time to time*) (*also fig.*); **се́рдце у меня́ ~ет** my heart plays me up; I have trouble with my heart (*from time to time*); **моя́ маши́на ~ет** my car is acting up. **2.** (*fig.*) to engage in robbery; **в э́том райо́не ~ют** your wallet isn't safe in these parts.

пошал|и́ть, ю́, и́шь *pf.* to play pranks, get up to mischief (*for a while*).

поша́р|ить, ю, ишь *pf. of* **ша́рить**

пошатн|у́ть, у́, ёшь *pf.* to shake (*also fig.*); **п. чью-н. ве́ру** to shake s.o.'s faith; (*impers.*): **меня́ ~у́ло** I was shaken.

пошатн|у́ться, у́сь, ёшься *pf.* **1.** to shake; to totter, reel, stagger; **он ~у́лся и упа́л** he staggered and fell. **2.** (*fig.*) to be shaken; **её здоро́вье ~у́лось** her health has cracked.
поша́тыва|ться, юсь *impf.* to totter, reel, stagger.
пошеве́лива|ть, ю *impf.* (*coll.*) to stir (*from time to time*).
пошеве́лива|ться, юсь *impf.* (*coll.*) to stir, budge (*from time to time*); **ну, ~йся!** come on!, get a move on!
пошевел|и́ть(ся), ю́(сь), ~и́шь(ся) *pf. of* **шевели́ть(ся)**
пошевельн|у́ть(ся), у́(сь), ёшь(ся) *pf.* = **пошевели́ть(ся)**
по́шевн|и, ей *no sg.* (*dial.*) (wide) sledge.
пош|ёл, ла́ *see* **пойти́**
пошеп|та́ть, чу́, ~чешь *pf.* to say in a whisper; to talk in whispers (*for a while*).
пошеп|та́ться, чу́сь, ~чешься *pf.* (*coll.*) to converse in whispers.
пошехо́н|ец, ца *m.* Gothamite; bumpkin (*from* **Пошехо́нье** *place popularized by Saltykov-Shchedrin as symbol of backwardness*)
поши́б, а *m.* (*coll.*) manners; ways.
поши́вк|а, и *f.* sewing.
поши́вочн|ый *adj.* sewing; **~ая мастерска́я** (sewing) workshop.
пошле́|ть, ю *impf.* (*of* **о~**) (*coll.*) to become commonplace, become vulgar.
по́шлин|а, ы *f.* duty; customs; **ввозна́я п., и́мпортная п.** import duty; **э́кспортная п.** export duty; **ге́рбовая п.** stamp-duty; **суде́бная п.** costs, legal expenses; **тамо́женная п.** customs; **обложи́ть ~ой** to impose duty (on).
по́шлин|ный *adj. of* **~а**
по́шлост|ь, и *f.* **1.** vulgarity, commonness. **2.** triviality; triteness, banality; **говори́ть ~и** to utter banalities, talk commonplaces.
по́шл|ый (~, ~а́, ~о) *adj.* **1.** vulgar, common; **у него́ о́чень ~ые вку́сы** he has very vulgar tastes. **2.** commonplace, trivial; trite, banal; **~ая по́весть** banal story.
пошля́к, а́ *m.* (*coll.*) vulgar pers., common pers.
пошля́тин|а, ы *f.* (*coll.*) **1.** vulgarity; vulgar action. **2.** triviality; triteness, banality.
пошту́чно *adv.* by the piece.
пошту́чн|ый *adj.* by the piece; **~ая опла́та** piecework payment.
пошум|е́ть, лю́, и́шь *pf.* to make a bit of a noise.
пошу|ти́ть, чу́, ~тишь *pf. of* **шути́ть**
поща́д|а, ы *f.* mercy; **без ~ы** without mercy; **не дать ~ы** to give no quarter; **проси́ть ~ы** to ask for mercy, cry quarter.
поща|ди́ть, жу́, ди́шь *pf. of* **щади́ть**
пощеко|та́ть, чу́, ~чешь *pf. of* **щекота́ть**
пощёлкивани|е, я *nt.* clicking.
пощёлкива|ть, ю *impf.* (*+i.*) to click; **п. па́льцами** to snap one's fingers.
пощёчин|а, ы *f.* box on the ear; slap in the face (*also fig.*); **дать ~у** (*+d.*) to slap in the face.
пощип|а́ть, лю́, ~лешь *pf.* **1.** (*+a. or g.*) to nibble. **2.** (*coll.*) to pull out, pull up. **3.** (*fig., joc.*) to pinch (from), rob. **4.** (*fig., joc.*) to pick holes in; to tear a strip off.
пощи́пыва|ть, ю *impf.* (*coll.*) to pinch (*from time to time*).
пощу́па|ть, ю *pf. of* **щу́пать**
поэ́зи|я, и *f.* poetry.
поэ́м|а, ы *f.* poem (*usu. of large proportions*).
поэ́т, а *m.* poet.
поэта́пный *adj.* phased.
поэте́сс|а, ы *f.* poetess.
поэтизи́р|овать, ую *impf. and pf.* to poeticize, wax poetic (about).
поэ́тик|а, и *f.* **1.** poetics; theory of poetry. **2.** poetic manner, poetic style; **п. Пу́шкина** Pushkin's (poetic) manner.
поэти́ческ|ий *adj.* (*in var. senses*) poetic(al); **~ая во́льность** poetic licence.
поэти́ч|ный (~ен, ~на) *adj.* (*fig.*) poetic(al).
поэ́тому *adv.* therefore, and so.
по|ю́[1]**, ёшь** *see* **петь**
по|ю́[2]**, ~и́шь** *see* **пои́ть**
появ|и́ться, лю́сь, ~ишься *pf.* (*of* **~ля́ться**) to appear, make one's appearance; to show up; to heave in sight; **луна́ ~и́лась из-за облако́в** the moon emerged from behind the clouds.
появле́ни|е, я *nt.* appearance.
появля́|ться, юсь *impf. of* **появи́ться**
поя́рковый *adj.* felt.
поя́р|ок, ка *no pl., m.* lamb's wool.
по́яс, а, *pl.* **~а́, ~о́в** *m.* **1.** belt, girdle; waistband; **спаса́тельный п.** lifebelt; **заткну́ть за́ п.** (*coll.*) to outdo. **2.** (*fig.*) waist; **кла́няться в п.** to bow from the waist; **по п.** up to the waist, waist-deep, waist-high. **3.** (*pl.* **~ы**) (*geog., econ.*) zone, belt; **поля́рный п.** frigid zone; **тропи́ческий п.** torrid zone.
поясне́ни|е, я *nt.* explanation, elucidation.
поясни́тельный *adj.* explanatory, elucidatory.
поясн|и́ть, ю́, и́шь *pf.* (*of* **~я́ть**) to explain, elucidate.
поясни́ц|а, ы *f.* waist, loins; small of the back; **боль, простре́л в ~е** lumbago.
поясни́чный *adj.* (*anat.*) lumbar.
поясн|о́й *adj.* **1.** *adj. of* **по́яс 1.**; **п. реме́нь** (waist-)belt. **2.** to the waist, waist-high; **~а́я ва́нна** hip-bath; **п. покло́н** bow from the waist; **п. портре́т** half-length portrait. **3.** (*geog., econ.*) zonal; **~о́е вре́мя** zone time; **п. тари́ф** zonal tariff; **~о́е распределе́ние** zoning.
поясн|я́ть, я́ю *impf. of* **~и́ть**
пр. *abbr. of* **1. прое́зд** Passage. **2. проспе́кт** Avenue. **3. про́чее: и ~** etc., etcetera, and so on.
праба́б|ка, ки *f.* = **~ушка**
праба́бушк|а, и *f.* great-grandmother.
пра́вд|а, ы *f.* **1.** truth; the truth; **э́то и́стинная п.** (*coll.*) it's the simple truth; **су́щая п.** the honest truth; **э́то п.** it is true; it is the truth; **по ~е сказа́ть, ~у говоря́** to tell the truth; truth to tell; **ва́ша п.** you are right; **что п., то п.** there's no denying the truth; **все́ми ~ами и непра́вдами** by fair means or foul; **п. глаза́ ко́лет** (*prov.*) home truths are hard to swallow. **2.** justice; **иска́ть ~ы** to seek justice. **3.** (*hist.*) law, code of laws; **Сали́ческая п.** the Salic Law. **4.: п.?** is that so?; indeed?; really?; **п. (ли)?** is it so?; is it true?; **п. ли, что он умира́ет?** is it true that he is dying?; **не п. ли?** *in interrog. sentences indicates that affirmative answer is expected*; **вы погаси́ли свет, не п. ли?** you (did) put out the light, didn't you? **5.** (*as concessive conj.*) true; **п., я ему́ не написа́л, но я вот-во́т собира́лся позвони́ть** true I had not written to him, but I was on the point of ringing.
правди́вост|ь, и *f.* **1.** truth; veracity. **2.** truthfulness; uprightness.
правди́в|ый (~, ~а) *adj.* **1.** true; veracious; **п. расска́з** true story. **2.** truthful; upright; **п. отве́т** honest answer.
правди́ст, а *m.* (*coll.*) pers. employed on production of newspaper 'Pravda'.
правдоподо́би|е, я *nt.* verisimilitude; probability, likelihood; plausibility.
правдоподо́б|ный (~ен, ~на) *adj.* probable, likely; plausible.
пра́ведник, а *m.* righteous man; upright pers., moral pers.; **спать сном ~а** to sleep the sleep of the just.
пра́ведн|ица, ицы *f. of* **~ик**
пра́вед|ный (~ен, ~на) *adj.* **1.** righteous; upright. **2.** just.
правёж, а́ *m.* (*hist.*) flogging (*of insolvent debtor*); **поста́вить кого́-н. на п.** to have s.o. flogged.
праве́|ть, ю *impf.* (*of* **по~**) (*pol.*) to become more conservative, swing to the right.
пра́вил|о, а *nt.* **1.** rule; regulation; **граммати́ческие ~а** grammatical rules; **тройно́е п.** (*math.*) the rule of three; **~а вну́треннего распоря́дка** the regulations (*of an establishment*); **~а у́личного движе́ния** traffic regulations, Highway Code; **как п.** as a rule; **по всем ~ам** according to all the rules. **2.** rule, principle; **взять за п.** to make it a rule; **взять себе́ за п.** (*+inf.*) to make a point (of).
прави́л|о, а *nt.* **1.** (*tech.*) reversing rod, guide-bar; (*mil.*) traversing handspike. **2.** boot-tree. **3.** (*hunting*) tail, brush. **4.** (*obs.*) helm, rudder.
пра́вильно *adv.* **1.** rightly; correctly; **п. ли иду́т ва́ши часы́?** is your watch right? **2.** regularly.

пра́вильност|ь, и *f.* **1.** rightness; correctness. **2.** regularity.
пра́вил|ьн|ый (~ен, ~ьна) *adj.* **1.** right, correct; **п. отве́т** the right answer; **~ьное реше́ние** sound decision; **~ьная дробь** proper fraction; **~ьно** (*as pred.*) it is correct; **~ьно!** that's right!, exactly!, just so! **2.** (*in var. senses*) regular; **~ьное движе́ние поездо́в** regular train service(s); **~ьное соотноше́ние** just proportion; **~ьное спряже́ние** (*gram.*) regular conjugation; **~ьные черты́ лица́** regular features. **3.** (*math.*) rectilineal, rectilinear.
прави́л|ьный *adj.* **1.** *adj. of* **~о. 2.** (*tech.*) correcting, levelling, straightening; **~ьная маши́на** levelling machine.
прави́тел|ь, я *m.* **1.** ruler. **2.** (*obs.*) manager, head; **п. дел** head clerk, first secretary.
прави́тельственн|ый *adj.* governmental; government; **~ое реше́ние** governmental decision; **~ое учрежде́ние** government establishment.
прави́тельств|о, а *nt.* government.
пра́в|ить¹, лю, ишь *impf.* (*no pf.*) (*+i.*) **1.** to rule (over), govern. **2.** to drive; **п. маши́ной** to drive a car; **п. рулём** to steer.
пра́в|ить², лю, ишь *impf.* (*no pf.*) **1.** to correct; **п. корректу́ру** to read, correct proofs. **2.** to set (*metal tools*).
пра́вк|а, и *f.* **1.** correcting; **п. корректу́ры** proof correcting, proof-reading. **2.** setting (*of metal tools*).
правле́н|ец, ца *m.* (*coll.*) board member.
правле́ни|е, я *nt.* **1.** governing, government; **о́браз ~я** form of government. **2.** board (*of directors, of management, etc.*), governing body; **быть чле́ном ~я** to be on the board.
пра́вленый *adj.* corrected; **п. экземпля́р** fair copy.
пра́внук, а *m.* great-grandson.
пра́внучк|а, и *f.* great-granddaughter.
пра́в|о¹, а, *pl.* **~а́** *nt.* **1.** law; **гражда́нское п.** civil law; **обы́чное п.** common law, customary law; **уголо́вное п.** criminal law; **изучи́ть п.** to study law, read for the law. **2.** right; **(води́тельские) ~а́** driving licence; **п. ве́то** (right of) veto; **п. го́лоса, избира́тельное п.** the vote, suffrage; **лиши́ть ~а го́лоса** to disfranchise; **~а́ гражда́нства** civic rights; **п. да́вности** (*leg.*) prescriptive right; **п. убе́жища** asylum, right of sanctuary; **п. на насле́дство** right of inheritance; **по ~у** by rights; **с по́лным ~ом** rightfully; **быть в ~е** (*+inf.*) to have the right (to), be entitled (to); **воспо́льзоваться свои́м ~ом (на+*a.*)** to exercise one's right (to); **восстанови́ться в ~а́х** to be rehabilitated; **вступи́ть в свои́ ~а́** to come into one's own; **име́ть п. (на+*a.*)** to have the right (to), be entitled (to).
пра́во² *adv.* (*coll.*) really, truly, indeed; **я, п., не зна́ю, куда́ де́лась** I really do not know where she has got to.
правобере́жный *adj.* situated on the right bank, right-bank.
правове́д, а *m.* **1.** lawyer, jurist. **2.** (*obs.*) student, graduate of law school.
правове́дени|е, я *nt.* (*obs.*) jurisprudence, science of law.
правове́рност|ь, и *f.* orthodoxy.
правове́р|ный (~ен, ~на) *adj.* (*relig.*) **1.** orthodox. **2.** *as n.* **п., ~ного** *m.* true believer (*esp. of Moslems*); **~ные** the faithful.
правови́к, а́ *m.* (*coll.*) jurist.
правов|о́й *adj.* **1.** legal, of the law; **п. контра́кт** legal contract. **2.** lawful, rightful; **~о́е госуда́рство** (*pol.*) state functioning in accordance with (constitutional) law, *Rechtsstaat*.
правоме́р|ный (~ен, ~на) *adj.* lawful, rightful.
правомо́чи|е, я *nt.* competence.
правомо́ч|ный (~ен, ~на) *adj.* competent.
правонаруше́ни|е, я *nt.* infringement of the law, offence.
правонаруши́тел|ь, я *m.* infringer of the law, offender, delinquent; **ю́ный п.** juvenile delinquent.
правоохрани́тельн|ый *adj.* law-enforcement; **~ые о́рганы** law-enforcement agencies.
правописа́ни|е, я *nt.* spelling, orthography.
правопоря́д|ок, ка *m.* law and order.
правосла́ви|е, я *nt.* (*relig.*) Orthodoxy.
правосла́вн|ый *adj.* (*relig.*) orthodox; **~ая це́рковь** Orthodox Church; *as n.* **п., ~ого** *m.*, **~ая, ~ой** *f.* member of the Orthodox Church.
правоспосо́бност|ь, и *f.* (*leg.*) (legal) capacity.
правоспосо́б|ный, (~ен, ~на) *adj.* (*leg.*) capable.
правосу́ди|е, я *nt.* justice; **отправля́ть п.** to administer the law.
правот|а́, ы́ *f.* rightness; (*leg.*) innocence; **доказа́ть свою́ ~у́** to prove one's case.
правофланго́вый *adj.* right-flank, right-wing.
пра́в|ый¹ *adj.* **1.** right; right-hand; (*naut.*) starboard; **п. борт** starboard side; **~ая ло́шадь** off(-side) horse; **~ая рука́** (*fig.*) right hand, right-hand man; **~ая сторона́** right side, off side. **2.** (*pol.*) right-wing, right; **~ая па́ртия** party of the right.
пра́в|ый² (~, ~а́, ~о, ~ы́) *adj.* **1.** right, correct; **вы не совсе́м ~ы** you are not quite right. **2.** righteous, just; **~ое де́ло** a just cause. **3.** (*leg.*) innocent, not guilty.
пра́в|ящий *pres. part. act. of* **~ить** *and adj.* ruling; **~ящая верху́шка** ruling clique; **~ящие кла́ссы** the ruling classes.
Пра́г|а, и *f.* Prague.
прагмати́зм, а *m.* (*phil.*) pragmatism.
прагма́тик, а *m.* (*phil.*) pragmatist.
прагмати́ческ|ий *adj.* pragmatic; **~ая са́нкция** (*hist.*) pragmatic sanction.
пра́дед, а *m.* **1.** great-grandfather. **2.** (*pl.*) ancestors, forefathers.
праде́довск|ий *adj. of* **пра́дед; ~ие времена́** ancestral times.
праде́душк|а, и *m. dim. of* **пра́дед**
пра́жский *adj.* Prague.
пра́зднеств|о, а *nt.* festival, solemnity; festivities.
пра́здник, а *m.* **1.** (public) holiday; (religious) feast, festival; **по ~ам** on high days and holidays; **с ~ом!** compliments of the season; **бу́дет и на на́шей у́лице п.** (*fig.*) our day will come. **2.** festive occasion, occasion for celebration; **по слу́чаю ~а** to celebrate the occasion.
пра́здничн|ый *adj.* holiday; festive; **п. день** red-letter day, holiday; **п. наря́д** holiday attire; **~ое настрое́ние** festive mood.
пра́зднovани|е, я *nt.* celebration.
пра́здн|овать, ую *impf.* (*of* **от~**) to celebrate.
празднoсло́ви|е, я *nt.* idle talk, empty talk.
пра́здност|ь, и *f.* **1.** idleness, inactivity. **2.** emptiness.
праздношата́ни|е, я *nt.* (*coll.*) idling, lounging.
пра́зд|ный (~ен, ~на) *adj.* **1.** idle, inactive; **~ная жизнь** a life of idleness. **2.** idle, empty; **~ное любопы́тство** idle curiosity; **п. разгово́р** empty talk. **3.** idle, vain, useless; **~ные попы́тки** idle attempts.
пра́ктик, а *m.* **1.** practical worker; **он хоро́ший п., но слаб в теорети́ческих зна́ниях** he is a good practical worker but his theoretical knowledge is weak. **2.** practical pers.
пра́ктик|а, и *f.* **1.** (*in var. senses*) practice; **на ~е** in practice; **вам нужна́ ещё разгово́рная п.** you need more conversational practice; **у на́шего врача́ больша́я п.** our doctor has a large practice. **2.** practical work.
практика́нт, а *m.* probationer; student engaged in practical work.
практик|ова́ть, у́ю *impf.* **1.** to practise, apply in practice. **2.** (*intrans.*; *of a doctor or lawyer*) to practise.
практик|ова́ться, у́юсь *impf.* **1.** (*pf.* **на~**) **(в+*p.*)** to practise, have practice (in); **п. в игре́ на скри́пке** to practise the violin; **п. в ру́сском языке́** to practise speaking Russian. **2.** *pass. of* **~ова́ть; э́тот приём бо́льше не ~у́ется** this method is no longer used.
пра́ктикум, а *m.* practical work.
практици́зм, а *m.* **1.** practicalness; (*slightly pej.*) savoir-faire. **2.** (*in pol. philosophy of Lenin, etc.*) over-emphasis of practice (*opp. theory*).
практи́ческ|ий *adj.* (*in var. senses*) practical; **~ие заня́тия** practical training; **~ая медици́на** applied medicine; **~ая рабо́та** practical work.
практи́чност|ь, и *f.* practicalness; efficiency.
практи́ч|ный (~ен, ~на) *adj.* practical; efficient; **п. челове́к** practical pers.; **п. спо́соб** efficient method.
прама́тер|ь, и *f.* (*rhet.*) the first mother; mother of the human race.
пра́от|ец, ца *m.* forefather; **отпра́виться к ~цам** (*joc.*) to be gathered to one's forefathers.

пра́порщик, а *m.* **1.** (*in tsarist army*) ensign. **2.** (*in Russian army*) warrant officer.
прароди́тел|ь, я *m.* primogenitor.
праславя́нский *adj.* (*ling.*) Common Slavonic.
пра́сол, а *m.* (*obs.*) cattle-dealer; fish- and meat-wholesaler.
прах, а *no pl., m.* **1.** (*obs. or rhet.*) dust, earth; **обрати́ть в п., поверѓнуть в п.** to reduce to dust, to ashes; **отрясти́ п. с ног** (*fig.*) to shake the dust from one's feet; **пойти́ ~́ом, рассы́паться ~́ом** to go to rack and ruin; **п. и суета́** a hollow sham; **разби́ть, разнести́ в пух и п.,** *see* **пух. 2.** ashes, remains; **здесь поко́ится п.** (+*g.*) here lies; **мир ~́у его́** may he rest in peace. **3.: п. его́ возьми́!** may he rot!
пра́чечн|ая, ой *f.* laundry; wash-house; **п.-автома́т, автомати́ческая п.** launderette, washeteria.
пра́чк|а, и *f.* laundress.
пращ|а́, и́, *g. pl.* **~е́й** *f.* sling (*weapon*).
пра́щур, а *m.* ancestor, forefather.
праязы́к, а́ *m.* (*ling.*) parent language.
пре...[1] *adj. pref. indicating superl. degree* very, most, exceedingly.
пре...[2] *vbl. pref. indicating action in extreme degree or superior measure* sur-, over-, out- (*cf.* **пере...**).
преа́мбул|а, ы *f.* preamble.
пребыва́ни|е, я *nt.* stay, sojourn; **ме́сто постоя́нного ~я** permanent residence, permanent address; **п. в до́лжности, п. на посту́** tenure of office, period of office.
пребыва́|ть, ю *impf.* **1.** to be; to abide, reside; **п. в отсу́тствии** to be absent. **2.** to be (*in a state of*); **п. в неве́дении** to be in the dark; **п. в уны́нии** to be in the dumps; **п. у вла́сти** to be in power.
превали́р|овать, ую *impf.* to prevail.
превенти́вн|ый *adj.* preventive; **~ая война́** preventive war.
превзо|йти́, йду́, идёшь, *past* **~шёл, ~шла́** *pf.* (*of* **превосходи́ть**) (**в**+*p. or* +*i.*) to surpass (in); to excel (in); **п. всех в мета́нии ди́ска** to excel in discus-throwing; **п. все ожида́ния** to exceed expectations; **п. самого́ себя́** to surpass o.s.; **п. чи́сленностью** to outnumber.
превозмога́|ть, ю *impf. of* **превозмо́чь**
превозмо́|чь, гу́, ~́жешь, ~́гут, *past* **~г, ~гла́** *pf.* (*of* **~га́ть**) to overcome, surmount.
превознес|ти́, у́, ёшь, *past* **~̈, ~ла́** *pf.* (*of* **превозноси́ть**) to extol.
превозно|си́ть, шу́, ~́сишь *impf. of* **превознести́**
превозно|си́ться, шу́сь, ~́сишься *impf.* to put on airs; to have a high opinion of o.s.
превосходи́тельный *adj.* having the title of excellency.
превосходи́тельств|о, а *nt.* (*as title*) Excellency.
превосхо|ди́ть, жу́, ~́дишь *impf. of* **превзойти́**
превосхо́д|ный (~ен, ~на) *adj.* **1.** superlative; superb, outstanding. **2.** (*obs.*) superior; **~ные си́лы** superior forces. **3.: ~ная сте́пень** (*gram.*) superlative degree.
превосхо́дств|о, а *nt.* superiority; **чи́сленное п.** numerical superiority; **я́вное п.** marked superiority; **п. в во́здухе** (*mil.*) air superiority.
превосход|я́щий *pres. part. of* **~и́ть** *and adj.* superior.
превра|ти́ть, щу́, ти́шь *pf.* (*of* **~ща́ть**) (**в**+*a.*) to convert (into), turn (to, into), reduce (to); to transmute; **п. я́рды в ме́тры** to convert yards into metres; **п. в ка́мень** to turn to stone; **п. в у́голь** to carbonize; **п. в шу́тку** to turn into a joke.
превра|ти́ться, щу́сь, ти́шься *pf.* (*of* **~ща́ться**) (**в**+*a.*) to turn (into), change (into); **п. в слух** to be all ears.
превра́тно *adv.* wrongly; **п. истолкова́ть** to misinterpret.
превра́тност|ь, и *f.* **1.** wrongness, falsity. **2.** vicissitude; **~и судьбы́** vicissitudes of fate, reversals of fortune.
превра́т|ный (~ен, ~на) *adj.* **1.** wrong, false; **у него́ бы́ло ~ное поня́тие о том, что произошло́** he had a false impression of what happened. **2.** changeful, inconstant, perverse; **~ная судьба́** perverse fate.
превраща́|ть(ся), ю(сь) *impf. of* **преврати́ть(ся)**
превраще́ни|е, я *nt.* transformation, conversion; transmutation; metamorphosis.
превы́|сить, шу, сишь *pf.* (*of* **~ша́ть**) to exceed; **п. власть, п. полномо́чия** to exceed one's authority; **п. свой креди́т в ба́нке** to overdraw (one's account).
превыша́|ть, ю *impf. of* **превы́сить**
превы́ше *adv.* (*obs.*) far above; **п. всего́** above all.
превыше́ни|е, я *nt.* exceeding, excess; **п. вла́сти** exceeding one's authority; **п. своего́ креди́та в ба́нке** overdrawing; **зада́ние бы́ло вы́полнено с ~ем** the task was accomplished and to spare.
прегра́д|а, ы *f.* bar, barrier; obstacle.
прегра|ди́ть, жу́, ди́шь *pf.* (*of* **~жда́ть**) to bar, obstruct, block; **п. путь кому́-н.** to bar s.o.'s way.
преграждá|ть, ю *impf. of* **прегради́ть**
прегреш|а́ть, а́ю *impf. of* **~и́ть**
прегреше́ни|е, я *nt.* sin, transgression.
прегреш|и́ть, у́, и́шь *pf.* (*of* **~а́ть**) (*obs.*) to sin, transgress.
пред[1]**, а** *n.* (*sl.*) = **председа́тель**
пред[2] *prep.* = **пе́ред**
пред...[1] *pref.* pre-, fore-, ante-.
пред...[2] *comb. form, abbr. of* **председа́тель**
...пред *comb. form, abbr. of* **представи́тель**
преда|ва́ть(ся), ю́(сь), ёшь(ся) *impf. of* **преда́ть(ся)**
преда́ни|е[1]**, я** *nt.* legend, tradition.
преда́ни|е[2]**, я** *nt.* handing over, committing; **п. забве́нию** burying in oblivion; **п. земле́** committing to the earth; **п. сме́рти** putting to death; **п. суду́** bringing to trial.
пре́данност|ь, и *f.* devotion.
пре́дан|ный (~, ~на) *p.p.p. of* **преда́ть** *and adj.* (+*d.*) devoted (to); **п. друг** staunch friend, faithful friend; **п. Вам** (*epistolary formula*) yours faithfully, yours truly.
преда́тел|ь, я *m.* traitor, betrayer; **оказа́ться ~ем** to turn traitor.
преда́тельниц|а, ы *f.* traitress.
преда́тельск|ий *adj.* traitorous, perfidious; treacherous (*also fig.*); **~ая пого́да** treacherous weather; **п. румя́нец** telltale blush.
преда́тельств|о, а *nt.* treachery, betrayal, perfidy.
пре|да́ть, да́м, да́шь, да́ст, дади́м, дади́те, даду́т, *past* **~́дал, ~дала́, ~́дало** *pf.* (*of* **~дава́ть**) **1.** (+*d.*) to hand over (to), commit (to); **п. гла́сности** to make known, make public; **п. забве́нию** to bury in oblivion; **п. земле́** to commit to the earth; **п. огню́** to commit to the flames; **п. огню́ и мечу́** to give over to fire and sword; **п. суду́** to bring to trial. **2.** to betray.
пре|да́ться, да́мся, да́шься, да́стся, дади́мся, дади́тесь, даду́тся, *past* **~да́лся, ~дала́сь** *pf.* (*of* **~дава́ться**) (+*d.*) **1.** to give o.s. up (to); **п. мечта́м** to fall into a reverie, lapse into day-dreams; **п. отча́янию** to give way to despair; **п. поро́кам** to indulge in vices; **п. страстя́м** to abandon o.s. to one's passions. **2.** (*obs.*) to entrust o.s. (to); to put o.s. in the hands (of); **п. врагу́** to go over to the enemy.
предба́нник, а *m.* dressing-room (*in a bath-house*).
предваре́ни|е, я *nt.* **1.** (*obs.*) forewarning, telling beforehand. **2.** forestalling; **п. равноде́нствия** (*astron.*) precession (of the equinox); **п. впу́ска па́ра** (*tech.*) pre-admission of steam. **3.** (*tech.*) lead.
предвари́лк|а, и *f.* (*coll.*) lock-up (*place of detention before trial*).
предвари́тельно *adv.* beforehand; as a preliminary; **п. нагре́ть** to preheat.
предвари́тельн|ый *adj.* preliminary; prior; **~ое заключе́ние** (*leg.*) imprisonment before trial; **~ая кома́нда** (*mil.*) preparatory command; **п. нагре́в** (*tech.*) pre-heating; **~ые переговóры** preliminary talks, pour-parlers; **~ая прода́жа биле́тов** advance sale of tickets, advance booking; **~ое сле́дствие** (*leg.*) preliminary investigation, inquest; **по ~ому соглаше́нию** by prior arrangement; **~ое усло́вие** prior condition, prerequisite; **п. экза́мен** preliminary examination.
предвар|и́ть, ю́, и́шь *pf.* (*of* **~я́ть**) **1.** (*obs.*) to forewarn, tell beforehand. **2.** to forestall, anticipate.
предвар|я́ть, я́ю *impf. of* **~и́ть**
предве́сти|е, я *nt.* presage, portent.
предве́стник, а *m.* forerunner, precursor; herald, harbinger; presage, portent.
предве́ч|ный (~ен) *adj.* (*theol.; epithet of God*) everlasting; existing from before time.

предвещá|ть, ю *impf.* (*no pf.*) to betoken, foretoken, foreshadow, herald, presage, portend; **тýчи ~ли грозý** the clouds betokened a storm; **э́то ~ет хорóшее** this bodes well, this augurs well.

предвзя́тост|ь, и *f.* preconception; prejudice, bias.

предвзя́т|ый (~, ~а) *adj.* preconceived; prejudiced, biased.

предви́дени|е, я *nt.* foresight, prevision; foreseeing, foreknowledge.

предви́|деть, жу, дишь *impf.* (*no pf.*) to foresee.

предви́д|еться, ится *impf.* (*no pf.*) to be foreseen; to be expected.

предвку|си́ть, шý, ~́сишь *pf.* (*of* **~шáть**) to look forward (to), anticipate (with pleasure).

предвкушá|ть, ю *impf. of* **предвкуси́ть**

предвкушéни|е, я *nt.* (pleasurable) anticipation.

предводи́тел|ь, я *m.* leader; **п. дворя́нства** (*hist.*) marshal of the nobility (*in tsarist Russia*: *representative of nobility of province or district, elected to manage their affairs and represent their interests in local government organs*).

предводи́тельств|о, а *nt.* **1.** leadership; **под ~ом** (*+g.*) under the leadership (of), under the command (of). **2.** (*hist.*) office of marshal of the nobility.

предводи́тельств|овать, ую *impf.* (*+i.*) to lead, be the leader (of).

предводи́тельш|а, и *f.* (*hist.*; *coll.*) wife of marshal of the nobility.

предвоéнный *adj.* **1.** preceding the outbreak of war. **2.** pre-war.

предвозве|сти́ть, щý, сти́шь *pf.* (*of* **~щáть**) to foretell.

предвозвéстник, а *m.* herald; harbinger, precursor.

предвозвещá|ть, ю *impf. of* **предвозвести́ть**

предвосхи́|тить, щý, тишь *pf.* (*of* **~щáть**) to anticipate; **п. пригово́р** to anticipate the verdict.

предвосхищá|ть, ю *impf. of* **предвосхи́тить**

предвосхищéни|е, я *nt.* anticipation.

предвы́борн|ый *adj.* (pre-)election; **~ая кампáния** election campaign; **~ое собрáние** (pre-)election meeting.

предгóр|ье, ья, *g. pl.* **~ий** *nt.* foothills.

предгрозов|óй *adj.*: **~áя мóлния** lightning before a storm.

предгрóзь|е, я *nt.* time before a storm (*also fig.*).

преддвéри|е, я *nt.* threshold (*also fig.*); **в ~и** (*+g.*) on the threshold (of).

предéл, а *m.* (*in var. senses*) limit; bound, boundary; end; (*pl.*) range; **в ~ах** (*+g.*) within, within the limits (of), within the bounds (of); **за ~ами** (*+g.*) outside, beyond the bounds (of); **в ~ах гóрода, городскóй черты́** within the city, within the bounds of the city; **в ~ах досягáемости** within striking distance; **в ~ах гóда** within the year; **за ~ами страны́** outside the country; **вы́йти за ~ы гóрода** to go outside the city boundary; **вы́йти за ~ы** (*+g.*) to overstep the limits (of), exceed the bounds (of); **э́то за ~ами мои́х сил** it is beyond my power; **родны́е ~ы** (*arch. or poet.*) one's native borders; **п. желáний** summit, pinnacle of (one's) desires; **~ы колебáния температýры** temperature range; **п. насыщéния** saturation point; **п. прóчности** (*tech.*) breaking point; **положи́ть п.** (*+d.*) to put an end (to), terminate.

предéл|ьный *adj.* **1.** *adj. of* **~**; **н. вóзраст** age-limit; **~ьная ли́ния** boundary line; **п. срок** time-limit, deadline; **п. ýгол** critical angle. **2.** maximum; utmost; **~ьное напряжéние** (*tech.*) breaking point, pressure limit; **~ьная скóрость** maximum speed; **с ~ьной я́сностью** with the utmost clarity. **3.** (*chem.*) saturated.

предержá́щ|ий *only in phr.* **влáсти ~ие** (*obs. or iron.*) the powers that be.

предзакáтный *adj.* before sunset.

предзнаменовáни|е, я *nt.* omen, augury.

предзнамен|овáть, ýю *impf.* to bode, augur, portend.

предикáт, а *m.* (*phil. and gram.*) predicate.

предикати́вный *adj.* (*gram.*) predicative; **п. член** predicate.

предикáци|я, и *f.* (*phil. and gram.*) predication.

предислóви|е, я *nt.* preface, foreword; **без ~й** without more ado; **прóсим без ~й!** don't beat about the bush!

предкры́л|ок, ка *m.* (*aeron.*) stat.

предлагá|ть, ю *impf. of* **предложи́ть**

предлежáни|е, я *nt.* (*med.*): **ягоди́чное п. плодá** breech delivery *or* presentation.

предлóг[1]**, а** *m.* pretext; **под ~ом** (*+g.*) on the pretext (of), on a plea (of); **под различными ~ами** on various pretexts; **п. для ссóры** an excuse for a quarrel.

предлóг[2]**, а** *m.* (*gram.*) preposition.

предложéни|е[1]**, я** *nt.* **1.** offer; proposition; proposal (of marriage); **п. пóмощи** offer of assistance; **сдéлать п. комý-н.** to propose (marriage) to s.o.; **приня́ть п.** to accept an offer; to accept a proposal (of marriage). **2.** (*at meeting, etc.*) proposal, motion; suggestion; **внести́ п.** to introduce a motion; **отклони́ть п.** to turn down a proposal. **3.** (*econ.*) supply; **закóн спрóса и ~я** law of supply and demand.

предложéни|е[2]**, я** *nt.* **1.** (*gram.*) sentence; **глáвное п.** main clause; **придáточное п.** subordinate clause; **услóвное п.** conditional sentence; **ввóдное п.** parenthesis, parenthetic clause. **2.** (*phil.*) proposition.

предлож|и́ть, ý, ~́ишь *pf.* (*of* **предлагáть**) **1.** to offer; **п. свои́ услýги** to offer one's services, come forward; **п. рýку (и сéрдце) комý-н.** (*obs.*) to make a proposal of marriage to s.o. **2.** to propose; to suggest; **п. резолю́цию** to move a resolution; **п. тост** to propose a toast; **п. чью-н. кандидатýру** to propose s.o. for election; **п. когó-н. в председáтели** to propose s.o. for chairman; **п. внимáнию** to call attention (to); **мы ~и́ли ей обрати́ться к врачý** we suggested that she should see a doctor; **они́ ~и́ли нам вмéсте с ни́ми поéхать на бéрег мóря** they have invited us to go with them to the seaside *or* they have suggested that we might go with them to the seaside. **3.** to put, set, propound; **п. вопрóс** to put a question; **п. задáчу** to set a problem; **п. нóвую теóрию** to propound a new theory. **4.** to order, require; **им ~и́ли освободи́ть кварти́ру** they have been ordered to vacate their apartment.

предлóжный *adj.* (*gram.*) prepositional; **п. падéж** prepositional case.

предмáйский *adj.* pre-May Day (*taking place in the period immediately preceding May Day*).

предмéст|ье, ья, *g. pl.* **~ий** *nt.* suburb.

предмéт, а *m.* **1.** object; article, item; (*pl.*) goods; **~ы домáшнего обихóда** household goods, domestic utensils; **~ы пéрвой необходи́мости** necessities; **~ы ширóкого потреблéния** consumer goods. **2.** subject, topic, theme; (*+g.*) object (of); **п. насмéшек** object of ridicule, butt; **п. спóра** point at issue; **п. (любви́)** (*obs.*) object of one's affections; **какóй п. вáшего исслéдования?** what is the subject of your research? **3.** (*school*) subject; **онá сдалá экзáмен по пяти́ ~ам** she passed the examination in five subjects. **4.: мéстный п.** (*mil.*) (ground) feature. **5.** object (= *purpose*); **на п.** (*+g.*) with the object (of); **на сей п.** (*official or joc.*) to this end, with this object; **имéть в ~е** (*obs.*) to have in view.

предмéтник, а *m.* (*teachers' sl.*) specialist.

предмéт|ный *adj. of* **~**; **п. урóк** object-lesson; **п. каталóг** subject catalogue; **п. указáтель** subject index; **п. стóлик** stage (*of microscope*).

предмóстн|ый *adj.*: **п. плацдáрм, ~ое укреплéние** bridgehead.

предназнач|áть, áю *impf. of* **~́ить**

предназначéни|е, я *nt.* **1.** earmarking. **2.** (*obs.*) destiny.

предназнáч|ить, у, ишь *pf.* (*of* **~áть**) (**для,** *or* **на**+*a.*) to destine (for), intend (for), mean (for); to earmark (for), set aside (for); **бóмбу ~или для императóра** the bomb was intended for the emperor; **мы ~или э́ти дéньги на покýпку автомоби́ля** we set aside this money to buy a car.

преднамéренно *adv.* by design, deliberately.

преднамéренност|ь, и *f.* premeditation.

преднамéрен|ный (~, на) *adj.* premeditated; aforethought; deliberate.

предначертáни|е, я *nt.* outline, plan, design; **п. судьбы́** predestination.

предначéрт|анный *p.p.p. of* **~áть; п. судьбóй** predestined.

предначертá|ть, ю *pf.* to plan beforehand; to foreordain.

предо = пред

предобéденный *adj.* before-dinner, preprandial.

пре́д|ок, ка *m.* forefather, ancestor; (*pl.*) forbears.
предокт́ябрьский *adj.* pre-October (*taking place during the period immediately preceding the Russ. Revolution of October 1917 or its anniversary*).
предоперацио́нный *adj.* (*med.*) pre-operative.
предопределе́ни|е, я *nt.* **1.** predetermining. **2.** predestination.
предопредел|и́ть, ю́, и́шь *pf.* (*of* **~я́ть**) to predetermine; to predestine, foreordain.
предопредел|я́ть, я́ю *impf. of* **~и́ть**
предоста́в|ить, лю, ишь *pf.* (*of* **~ля́ть**) **1.** to let; to leave; **нам ~или сами́м реши́ть де́ло** the decision was left to us; we were left to decide the matter for ourselves; **п. кого́-н. самому́ себе́** to leave s.o. to his own devices, to his own resources. **2.** to give, grant; **п. креди́т** to give credit; **п. пра́во** to concede a right; **п. возмо́жность** to afford an opportunity, give a chance; **п. кому́-н. сло́во** to let s.o. have the floor, call upon s.o. to speak; **они́ ~или ко́мнату в на́ше распоряже́ние** they have put a room at our disposal.
предоставля́|ть, ю *impf. of* **предоста́вить; ~ю сло́во това́рищу X** (*formula of chairman introducing speaker at meeting*) I call upon Comrade X to speak.
предостерега́|ть, ю *impf. of* **предостере́чь**
предостереже́ни|е, я *nt.* warning, caution.
предостере́|чь, гу́, жёшь, гу́т, *past* **~̀г, ~гла́** *pf.* (*of* **~га́ть**) **(от)** to warn (against), caution (against), put on one's guard (against).
предосторо́жност|ь, и *f.* **1.** (*no pl.*) caution; **ме́ры ~и** precautionary measures, precautions. **2.** precaution.
предосуди́тельност|ь, и *f.* reprehensibility, blameworthiness.
предосуди́тел|ьный (~ен, ~ьна) *adj.* wrong, reprehensible, blameworthy.
предотвра|ти́ть, щу́, ти́шь *pf.* (*of* **~ща́ть**) to prevent, avert; to stave off; **п. войну́** to avert a war; **п. опа́сность** to stave off danger.
предотвраща́|ть, ю *impf. of* **предотврати́ть**
предотвраще́ни|е, я *nt.* prevention, averting; staving off.
предохране́ни|е, я *nt.* **(от)** protection (against), preservation (from).
предохрани́тел|ь, я *m.* guard, safety device; safety catch; **(пла́вкий) п.** (*elec.*) safety fuse, cut-out; **п. от обледене́ния** (*aeron.*) de-icer.
предохрани́тельн|ый *adj.* **1.** preservative; preventive; **~ые ме́ры** precautionary measures, precautions; **~ая приви́вка** preventive inoculation. **2.** (*tech.*) safety; protective; **п. кла́пан** safety-valve; **~ая коро́бка** fuse box; **~ые очки́** safety goggles; **~ая плита́** (*radio*) baffle plate; **п. ште́псель** fuse; **п. щит** guard shield, fender.
предохран|и́ть, ю́, и́шь *pf.* (*of* **~я́ть**) **(от)** to preserve, protect (from, against).
предохран|я́ть, я́ю *impf. of* **~и́ть**
предписа́ни|е, я *nt.* order, injunction; (*pl.*) directions, instructions; (*med., etc.*) prescription; **п. суда́** court order; **согла́сно ~ю** by order.
предпи|са́ть, шу́, ~̀шешь *pf.* (*of* **~̀сывать**) **1.** (*+inf.*) to order, direct, instruct (to). **2.** to prescribe (*a cure, a diet, etc.*); **врач ~са́л ей курс инъе́кций** the doctor prescribed for her, put her on a course of injections.
предпи́сыва|ть, ю *impf. of* **предписа́ть**
предплече́|ье, ья, *g. pl.* **~ий** *nt.* (*anat.*) forearm.
предплу́жник, а *m.* (*agric.*) coulter.
предплюс|на́, ны́, *pl.* **~̀ны, ~̀ен** *f.* (*anat.*) tarsus.
предполага́емый *pres. part. pass. of* **предполага́ть** *and adj.* proposed.
предполага́|ть, ю *impf.* **1.** *impf. of* **предположи́ть. 2.** (*impf. only*) to intend, propose; to contemplate; **мы ~ем оста́вить дете́й у ба́бушки** we propose to leave the children at their grandmother's; **он как бу́дто ~ет жени́ться** apparently he is contemplating marrying. **3.** (*impf. only*) to presuppose; **успе́х в э́том де́ле ~ет хоро́шую пого́ду** the success of this business presupposes good weather.
предполага́|ться, ется *impf.* **1.** *pass. of* **~ть. 2.** (*impers.*): **~ется** it is proposed, it is intended; **~ется проложи́ть отсю́да автостра́ду** it is proposed to build a motorway from here.
предположе́ни|е, я *nt.* **1.** supposition, assumption. **2.** intention; **у меня́ п. жени́ться** I am thinking of marrying.
предположи́тельно *adv.* **1.** supposedly, presumably. **2.** (*in parenthesis*) probably; **мы прие́дем в Ло́ндон, п., к десяти́ часа́м** we shall be in London probably by ten o'clock.
предлположи́тельн|ый *adj.* conjectural; hypothetical; estimated; **э́то ещё лишь ~о** this is still only hypothetical.
предполож|и́ть, у́, ~̀ишь *pf.* (*of* **предполага́ть**) to suppose, assume; to conjecture, surmise; **~̀им, что он опозда́л на по́езд** (let us) suppose he missed the train.
предпо́ль|е, я (*mil.*) forward defensive positions.
предполя́рный *adj.* sub-arctic.
предпо|сла́ть, шлю́, шлёшь *pf.* (*of* **~сыла́ть**) (*+d. and a.*) to preface (with); **дире́ктор шко́лы ~сла́л вы́говору не́сколько о́бщих замеча́ний** the headmaster prefaced the ticking-off with a few general remarks.
предпосле́дн|ий *adj.* penultimate, last but one, next to last; one from the bottom (*on list*); **Ва́ше ~ее письмо́** your last letter but one; **п. слог** penultimate syllable.
предпосыла́|ть, ю *impf. of* **предпосла́ть**
предпосы́лк|а, и *f.* **1.** prerequisite, precondition. **2.** (*phil.*) premise.
предпоч|е́сть, ту́, тёшь, *past* **~ёл, ~ла́** *pf.* (*of* **~ита́ть**) to prefer; **п. говя́дину бара́нине** to prefer beef to mutton; **я ~ёл бы идти́ пешко́м** I would rather walk, go on foot.
предпочита́|ть, ю *impf. of* **предпоче́сть**
предпочте́ни|е, я *nt.* preference; predilection; **оказа́ть п., отда́ть п.** (*+d.*) to show a preference (for), give preference.
предпочти́тельно *adv.* **1.** rather. preferably. **2.** **(пе́ред;** *obs.*) in preference (to).
предпочти́тел|ьный (~ен, ~ьна) *adj.* preferable.
предпра́зднична|ый *adj.* holiday (*taking place in the period immediately preceding a holiday*); **~ое настрое́ние** holiday mood; **~ая суета́** holiday rush.
предприи́мчивост|ь, и *f.* enterprise.
предприи́мчив|ый (~, ~а) *adj.* enterprising.
предпринима́тел|ь, я *m.* owner (of a firm *or* business); employer; entrepreneur.
предпринима́тель|ский *adj. of* **~**
предпринима́тельств|о, а *no pl., nt.* (private) business undertakings; **свобо́дное п.** free enterprise.
предпринима́|ть, ю *impf. of* **предприня́ть**
предпри|ня́ть, му́, ~̀мешь, *past* **~̀нял, ~няла́, ~̀няло** *pf.* (*of* **~нима́ть**) to undertake; (*mil., etc.*) to launch; **п. ата́ку** to launch an attack; **п. шаги́** to take steps.
предприя́ти|е, я *nt.* **1.** undertaking, enterprise; business; **риско́ванное п.** risky undertaking, venture. **2.** (*econ.*) enterprise, concern, business; works; **ме́лкое п.** small business; **фабри́чно-заводско́е п.** (industrial) works.
предрасполага́|ть, ю *impf. of* **предрасположи́ть**
предрасположе́ни|е, я *nt.* **(к)** predisposition (to); (*med.*) diathesis.
предрасполо́ж|енный *p.p.p. of* **~и́ть; (к)** predisposed (to).
предраспол ож|и́ть, у́, ~̀ишь *pf.* (*of* **предрасполага́ть**) **(к)** to predispose (to).
предрассве́тн|ый *adj.* occurring before dawn; **~ая мгла** early morning mist; **~ые су́мерки** false dawn; **п. хо́лод** the chill of approaching dawn.
предрассу́д|ок, ка *m.* prejudice; **закосне́лый в ~ках** steeped in prejudice.
предрека́|ть, ю *impf. of* **предре́чь**
предре́|чь, ку́, чёшь, ку́т, *past* **~̀к, ~кла́** *pf.* (*of* **~ка́ть**) (*obs.*) to foretell.
предреш|а́ть, а́ю *impf. of* **~и́ть**
предреш|и́ть, у́, и́шь *pf.* (*of* **~а́ть**) **1.** to decide beforehand. **2.** to predetermine.
предродово́й *adj.* antenatal.
председа́тел|ь, я *m.* chairman; president.
председа́тель|ский *adj. of* **~; ~ское ме́сто** the chair (*at a meeting*); **заня́ть ~ское ме́сто** to take the chair.
председа́тельств|о, а *nt.* chairmanship; presidency.

председа́тельств|овать, ую *impf.* to be in the chair, preside.

председа́тельств|ующий *pres. part. act. of* **~овать**; *as n.* **п., ~ующего** *m.* chairman.

предсе́рди|е, я *nt.* (*anat.*) auricle.

предсказа́ни|е, я *nt.* prediction; forecast, prophecy; prognostication.

предсказа́тел|ь, я *m.* foreteller, forecaster; soothsayer.

предска|за́ть, жу́, ∸жешь *pf.* (*of* **∸зывать**) to foretell, predict; to forecast, prophesy; to prognosticate.

предска́зыва|ть, ю *impf. of* **предсказа́ть**

предсме́ртн|ый *adj.* occurring before death; **~ое жела́ние** dying wish; **~ые страда́ния** death-agony; **п. час** one's last hour.

предста|ва́ть, ю́, ёшь *impf. of* **∸ть**

представи́тел|ь, я *m.* **1.** representative; (+*g.*) spokesman (for); **полномо́чный п.** plenipotentiary. **2.** (*bot.*, *etc.*) specimen.

представи́тельност|ь, и *f.* imposingness; imposing appearance, presence.

представи́тельный[1] *adj.* (*pol.*, *leg.*) representative.

представи́тел|ьный[2] **(~ен, ~ьна)** *adj.* imposing.

представи́тельств|о, а *nt.* **1.** representation, representing. **2.** (*collect.*) representation, representatives; **дипломати́ческое п.** diplomatic representatives; **торго́вое п.** trade delegates. **3.** (*pol.*, *leg.*) election of, sending of representatives (*to organs of government*).

предста́в|ить, лю, ишь *pf.* (*of* **~ля́ть**) **1.** to present; **п. тру́дности** to offer difficulty; **п. интере́с** to be of interest, have interest. **2.** to produce, submit; **п. доказа́тельства** to produce evidence; **п. спи́сок чле́нов ассоциа́ции** to submit a list of members of an association. **3.** (+*a. and d.*) to introduce (to), present (to). **4. (к)** to recommend (for), put forward (for); **п. кого́-н. к о́рдену** to recommend s.o. for a decoration. **5.: п. себе́** to imagine, fancy, picture, conceive; **~ь(те) себе́, кака́я э́то была́ доса́да!** (just) imagine what a nuisance that was! **6.** to represent, display; **п. что́-то в смешно́м ви́де** to hold sth. up to ridicule. **7.** (*theatr.*) to perform; to play.

предста́в|иться, люсь, ишься *pf.* (*of* **~ля́ться**) **1.** to present itself, occur, arise; **на́шим глаза́м ~илась мра́чная карти́на** a gloomy picture rose before our eyes; **~ился слу́чай пое́хать в Москву́** a chance arose to go to Moscow; **я им сообщу́, как то́лько ~ится возмо́жность** I will inform them as soon as an opportunity arises. **2.** (*impers.*+*d.*) to seem (to); **э́то тебе́ то́лько ~илось** you only imagined it, it was just your imagination. **3.** (+*d.*) to introduce o.s. (to). **4.** (+*i.*) to pretend (to be); to pass o.s. off (as); **п. больны́м** to feign sickness.

представле́ни|е, я *nt.* **1.** presentation; **п. но́вого сотру́дника** introduction of a new colleague; **п. про́пуска** presentation of a permit. **2.** (written) declaration, statement; representation; **~я бы́ли сде́ланы всем прави́тельствам** representations have been made to all the governments. **3.** (*theatr.*) performance. **4.** (*psych.*) representation. **5.** idea, notion, conception; **дать п. (о**+*p.*) to give an idea (of); **я не име́ю ни мале́йшего ~я** I have not the faintest idea, remotest conception.

представля́|ть ю *impf.* **1.** *impf. of* **предста́вить. 2.** (*impf. only*) to represent; **он ~ет США в ООН** he represents the USA at the UN. **3.: п. собо́й** to represent, be; to constitute; **э́то ~ет собо́й исключе́ние** this constitutes an exception.

представля́|ться, юсь *impf. of* **предста́виться**

предста́тел|ь, я *m.* (*obs.*) protector; champion.

предста́тельн|ый *adj.*: **~ая железа́** (*anat.*) prostate (gland).

предста́|ть, ну, нешь *pf.* (*of* **~ва́ть**) **(пе́ред)** to appear (before); **п. пе́ред судо́м** to appear in court.

предсто|я́ть, и́т *impf.* to be in prospect, lie ahead, be at hand; to be in store; **~я́ла суро́вая зима́** a hard winter lay ahead; **нам ~и́т мно́го неприя́тностей** we are in for a lot of trouble, there is a lot of trouble in store for us; **ему́ ~и́т предста́вить диссерта́цию к пе́рвому ию́ня** he has to submit his dissertation by the first of June.

предстоя́|щий *pres. part. of* **~ть** *and adj.* coming, forthcoming; impending, imminent; **~щие вы́боры** the forthcoming elections; **она́ страши́лась ~щего медици́нского осмо́тра** she was dreading the impending medical (examination).

предте́ч|а, и *c.g.* forerunner, precursor; **Иоа́нн п.** John the Baptist.

предубе|ди́ть, ди́шь *pf.* (*of* **~жда́ть**) (*obs.*) to prejudice, bias.

предубежда́|ть, ю *impf. of* **предубеди́ть**

предубежде́ни|е, я *nt.* prejudice, bias.

предубе|ждённый *p.p.p. of* **~ди́ть** (*obs.*) *and adj.* prejudiced, biased.

предуве́дом|ить, лю, ишь *pf.* (*of* **~ля́ть**) to inform beforehand, give advance notice; to warn, forewarn; **вам сле́довало п. их о ва́шем прие́зде** you should have warned them that you were coming.

предуведомле́ни|е, я *nt.* warning, forewarning; notice in advance.

предуведомля́|ть, ю *impf. of* **предуве́домить**

предугад|а́ть, а́ю *pf.* (*of* **∸ывать**) to guess (in advance).

предуга́дыва|ть, ю *impf. of* **предугада́ть**

предуда́рный *adj.* (*ling.*) pre-tonic.

предумы́шленност|ь, и *f.* premeditation.

предумы́шленный *adj.* premeditated, aforethought.

предупреди́тельност|ь, и *f.* courtesy; attentiveness.

предупреди́тел|ьный *adj.* **1.** preventive, precautionary. **2. (~ен, ~ьна)** courteous; attentive; obliging.

предупре|ди́ть, жу́, ди́шь *pf.* (*of* **~жда́ть**) **1. (о**+*p.*) to let know beforehand (about), notify in advance (about), warn (about); to give notice (of, about); **надлежи́т п. экскурсово́да о жела́нии посети́ть за́мок** notice is to be given to the guide if it is wished to visit the castle; **п. за неде́лю об увольне́нии** to give a week's notice (*of dismissal*). **2.** to prevent, avert; **п. ава́рию** to prevent an accident. **3.** to anticipate; to forestall; **п. замеча́ние** to anticipate a remark; **я как раз э́то хоте́л сказа́ть, но вы ~ди́ли меня́** that is just what I was about to say, but you took the words out of my mouth.

предупрежда́|ть, ю *impf. of* **предупреди́ть**

предупрежде́ни|е, я *nt.* **1.** notice; notification. **2.** prevention. **3.** anticipating; forestalling. **4.** warning; **получи́ть вы́говор с ~ем** (*leg.*) to be dismissed with a caution.

предусма́трива|ть, ю *impf. of* **предусмотре́ть**

предусмотр|е́ть, ю́, ∸ишь *pf.* (*of* **предусма́тривать**) to envisage, foresee; to stipulate (for), provide (for), make provision (for); **п. все возмо́жности** to provide for every eventuality.

предусмотри́тельност|ь, и *f.* foresight, prudence.

предусмотри́тел|ьный (~ен, ~ьна) *adj.* prudent; provident; far-sighted; **~ная поли́тика** far-sighted policy.

предустано́вленный *adj.* (*obs.*) pre-established, predetermined.

преду́тренний *adj.* occurring immediately before morning; **п. час** the hour before dawn.

предчу́встви|е, я *nt.* presentiment; foreboding, misgiving, premonition.

предчу́вств|овать, ую *impf.* to have a presentiment (of, about), have a premonition (of, about); **я ~овал, что вы сего́дня появи́тесь** I had a feeling that you would turn up today.

предше́ственник, а *m.* predecessor; forerunner, precursor.

предше́ств|овать, ую *impf.* (+*d.*) to go in front (of); to precede; **её сме́рти ~овала дли́тельная боле́знь** her death was preceded by a long illness.

предше́ств|ующий *pres. part. act. of* **~овать** *and adj.* previous; foregoing; *as n.* **~ующее, ~ующего** *nt.* the foregoing.

предъяви́тел|ь, я *m.* bearer; **п. и́ска** plaintiff, claimant; **чек на ~я** cheque payable to bearer.

предъяв|и́ть, лю́, ∸ишь *pf.* (*of* **~ля́ть**) **1.** to show, produce, present; **п. биле́т** to show one's ticket; **п. доказа́тельства** to produce evidence, present proofs. **2.** (*leg.*, *etc.*) to bring (forward); **п. иск (к)** to bring a suit (against); **п. обвине́ние** (+*d.* **в**+*p.*) to charge (with), bring an accusation (against of); **ему́ ~и́ли обвине́ние в поджо́ге** he is charged with arson; **п. пра́во (на**+*a.*) to lay claim (to), raise a claim (to); **п. тре́бование (к)** to lay claim (to); **п. высо́кие**

тре́бования (к) to make big demands (of, on).

предъявле́ни|е, я *nt.* **1.** showing, producing, presentation; **вход разреша́ется по ~и удостовере́ния ли́чности** entry is permitted on presentation of identity card. **2.** (*leg., etc.*) bringing; **п. и́ска** bringing of a suit; **п. обвине́ния (в+*p.*)** accusation (of), charge (of); **п. пра́ва** assertion of a claim.

предъявля́|ть, ю *impf. of* **предъяви́ть**

предыду́щ|ий *adj.* previous, preceding; *as n.* **~ее, ~его** *nt.* the foregoing; **из ~его сле́дует** from the foregoing it follows.

предыстори́ческий *adj.* prehistoric.

предысто́ри|я, и *f.* prehistory.

прее́мник, а *m.* successor.

прее́мственност|ь, и *f.* succession; continuity.

прее́мствен|ный (~, ~на) *adj.* successive.

прее́мств|о, а *nt.* succession.

пре́жде 1. *adv.* (*opp.* **пото́м**) before; first; **п. чем** *as conj.* before; **на́до бы́ло ду́мать об э́том п.** you should have thought about it before; **ты до́лжен дое́сть ка́шу, п. чем взять ды́ню** you must eat up your kasha before you have any melon. **2.** *adv.* (*opp.* **тепе́рь**) formerly, in former times; before; **п. он учи́л в интерна́те** he taught in a boarding-school before. **3.** *prep.+g.* before; **они́ пришли́ п. нас** they arrived before us; **п. всего́** first of all, to begin with; first and foremost.

преждевре́менно *adv.* prematurely; before one's time.

преждевре́менност|ь, и *f.* prematurity, untimeliness.

преждевре́мен|ный (~ен, ~на) *adj.* premature, untimely; **~ные ро́ды** (*med.*) premature birth.

пре́жн|ий *adj.* previous, former; **в ~ее вре́мя** in the old days, in former times.

презе́нт, а *m.* (*obs. or joc.*) present.

презента́бел|ьный (~ен, ~ьна) *adj.* presentable.

презента́ци|я, и *f.* presentation; launch; **п. това́ра** sales presentation; **п. кни́ги** book launch.

презент|ова́ть, у́ю *impf. and pf.* (*obs. or joc.*) to present.

презервати́в, а *m.* **1.** contraceptive. **2.** (*med.*; *obs.*) prophylactic.

презервати́вный *adj.* (*med.*) prophylactic, preventive.

презерва́ци|я, и *f.* preservation.

президе́нт, а *m.* president.

президе́нт|ский *adj. of* **~**; **~ские вы́боры** presidential elections.

президе́нтств|о, а *nt.* presidency.

прези́диум, а *m.* presidium.

презира́|ть, ю *impf.* **1.** (*impf. only*) to despise, hold in contempt. **2.** (*pf.* **презре́ть**) to disdain; **п. опа́сность** to scorn danger.

презре́ни|е, я *nt.* disdain, contempt, scorn.

презре́н|ный (~, ~на) *adj.* contemptible, despicable; **п. мета́лл** (*coll.*) filthy lucre.

презр|е́ть, ю́, и́шь *pf. of* **презира́ть**

презри́тел|ьный (~ен, ~ьна) *adj.* contemptuous, scornful, disdainful.

презу́мпци|я, и *f.* (*phil., leg.*) presumption.

преиму́щественно *adv.* mainly, chiefly, principally.

преиму́щественн|ый *adj.* **1.** primary, prime, principal. **2.** preferential, priority. **3.** (*leg.*) preferential; **~ое пра́во** preference; **~ое пра́во на поку́пку** pre-emption.

преиму́честв|о, а *nt.* **1.** advantage; **име́ть п. (пе́ред)** to possess, have an advantage (over); **получи́ть п. (пе́ред)** to gain an advantage (over); **они́ име́ют то п., что у них телефо́н** they have the advantage of being on the telephone. **2.** preference; **по ~у** for the most part, chiefly. **3.** (*leg.*) privilege.

преиспо́дн|яя, ей *f.* (*obs.*) the nether regions, the underworld, inferno.

преиспо́лн|енный *p.p.p. of* **~ить** *and adj.* (*+g. or i.*) filled (with), full (of); **п. опа́сности** fraught with danger; **п. реши́мости** firmly resolved.

преиспо́лн|ить, ю, ишь *pf.* (*of* **~я́ть**) (*+g. or i.*) to fill (with).

преиспо́лн|иться, юсь, ишься *pf.* (*of* **~я́ться**) (*+g. or i.*) to be filled (with), become full (of).

преисполн|я́ть(ся), я́ю(сь) *impf. of* **~ить(ся)**

прейскура́нт, а *m.* price-list; bill of fare.

пре|йти́, йду́, йдёшь, *past* **~шёл, ~шла́** *pf.* (*of* **~ходи́ть**) (*obs.*) **1.** to cross. **2.** to pass, have passed.

преклоне́ни|е, я *nt.* **(пе́ред)** admiration (for), worship (for).

преклон|и́ть, ю́, и́шь *pf.* (*of* **~я́ть**) to incline, bend; to lower; **п. го́лову** to bow (one's head) (*in token of respect or worship*); **п. коле́на** to genuflect.

преклон|и́ться, ю́сь, и́шься *pf.* (*of* **~я́ться**) **(пе́ред) 1.** to bow down (before), bend down (before). **2.** (*fig.*) to admire, worship.

прекло́нный *adj.* **п. во́зраст** old age, declining years.

преклон|я́ть(ся), я́ю(сь) *impf. of* **~и́ть(ся)**

прекосло́ви|е, я *nt.* (*obs.*) contradiction; **без вся́кого ~я** without contradiction.

прекосло́в|ить, лю, ишь *impf.* (*+d.*) to contradict.

прекра́сно *adv.* **1.** excellently; perfectly well; **они́ п. зна́ют, что э́то воспрещено́** they know perfectly well that it is forbidden. **2.** *as int.* excellent!; splendid!

прекрасноду́ши|е, я *nt.* (*iron.*) starry-eyed idealism.

прекрасноду́ш|ный (~ен, ~на) *adj.* (*iron.*) starry-eyed.

прекра́с|ный (~ен, ~на) *adj.* **1.** beautiful, fine; **п. пол** the fair sex; **ра́ди ~ных глаз** pour les beaux yeux; **в оди́н п. день** one fine day, once upon a time; *as n.* **~ное, ~ного** *nt.* (*phil.*) the beautiful. **2.** excellent, capital, first-rate.

прекра|ти́ть, щу́, ти́шь *pf.* (*of* **~ща́ть**) to stop, cease, discontinue; to put a stop (to), put an end (to); to break off, sever, cut off; **п. войну́** to end the war; **п. вое́нные де́йствия** to cease hostilities; **п. знако́мство (с+*i.*)** to break (it off) (with), give up; **п. обсужде́ние вопро́са** to drop the subject; **п. ого́нь** (*mil.*) to cease fire; **п. платежи́** to suspend, stop payments; **п. подпи́ску** to discontinue a subscription, stop subscribing; **п. пода́чу га́за** to cut off the gas (supply); **п. пре́ния** to close a debate; **п. рабо́ту** to leave off work, down tools; **п. рабо́тать** to stop work(ing); **п. сноше́ния (с+*i.*)** to sever relations (with).

прекра|ти́ться, ти́тся *pf.* (*of* **~ща́ться**) **1.** to cease, end. **2.** *pass. of* **~ти́ть**

прекраща́|ть(ся), ю, ет(ся) *impf. of* **прекрати́ть(ся)**

прекраще́ни|е, я *nt.* stopping, ceasing, cessation, discontinuance; **п. вое́нных де́йствий** cessation of hostilities; **п. огня́** cease-fire; **п. платеже́й** suspension of payments; **п. пре́ний** closure of a debate.

прела́т, а *m.* prelate.

преле́ст|ный (~ен, ~на) *adj.* charming, delightful, lovely.

пре́лест|ь, и *f.* charm, fascination; **кака́я п.!** how lovely!; **~и жи́зни в дере́вне** the delights of living in the country; **езда́ в автомоби́ле уже́ потеря́ла п. новизны́** the novelty of driving had already worn off.

прелимина́ри|и, ев *no sg.* (*dipl.*) preliminaries.

прелимина́рный *adj.* (*dipl.*) preliminary.

прелом|и́ть, лю́, ⁓ишь *pf.* (*of* **~ля́ть**) **1.** (*phys.*) to refract. **2.** (*fig.*) to interpret, put a construction (upon).

прелом|и́ться, ⁓ится *pf.* (*of* **~ля́ться**) **1.** (*phys.*) to be refracted. **2.** (*fig.*) to be interpreted; to take on a different aspect; **в свете́ но́вых све́дений исто́рия ~и́лась по-ино́му** in the light of new information a different construction was put upon the affair.

преломле́ни|е, я *nt.* **1.** (*phys.*) refraction. **2.** (*fig.*) interpretation, construction.

преломля́емост|ь, и *f.* (*phys.*) refrangibility.

преломля́|емый *pres. part. pass. of* **~ть** *and adj.* (*phys.*) refractable, refrangible.

преломля́|ть(ся), ю, ет(ся) *impf. of* **преломи́ть(ся)**

преломля́|ющий *pres. part. act. of* **~ть** *and adj.* (*phys.*) refractive, refracting.

пре́л|ый (~, ~а) *adj.* rotten, fusty.

прел|ь, и *f.* rot, mouldiness, mould.

прель|сти́ть, щу́, сти́шь *pf.* (*of* **~ща́ть**) **1.** to attract; **его́ ~сти́ла перспекти́ва повы́шенной зарпла́ты** he was attracted by the prospect of higher wages. **2.** to lure, entice; **п. обеща́ниями** to lure with promises.

прель|сти́ться, щу́сь, сти́шься *pf.* (*of* **~ща́ться**) (*+i.*) to be attracted (by); to be tempted (by), fall (for); **мы**

~стúлись предложéнием сóбственной квартúры we fell for the offer of having accommodation of our own.

прельщá|ть(ся), ю(сь) *impf. of* **прельстúть(ся)**

прелюбодé|й, я *m.* (*obs.*) adulterer.

прелюбодéйств|овать, ую *impf.* (*obs.*) to commit adultery.

прелюбодеянú|е, я *nt.* (*obs.*) adultery.

прелю́ди|я, и *f.* (*mus. and fig.*) prelude.

премиáльн|ый *adj. of* **прéмия; ~ая систéма** bonus system; **п. фонд** bonus funds; *as n.* (*pl.*) **~ые, ~ых** bonus.

премúн|уть, у, ешь *pf. only with neg.* (+*inf.*) not to fail (to); **я не ~у зайтú к вам** I shall not fail to call in to see you.

премировáни|е, я *nt.* awarding of a prize; awarding of a bonus.

премирóв|анный *p.p.p. of* **~áть** *and adj.* prize-winning, prize; **п. проéкт пáмятника** prize-winning design for a monument; **п. бык** prize bull; *as n.* **п., ~анного** *m.* prize-winner.

премир|овáть, у́ю *impf. and pf.* to award a prize (to); to give a bonus (to).

прéми|я, и *f.* **1.** prize; bonus; bounty, gratuity; **Нóбелевская п.** Nobel Prize; (*cin.*): **п. Óскара** Oscar. **2.** (*fin.*) premium; **страховáя п.** premium, insurance.

премнóго *adv.* (*obs.*) very much, extremely.

прему́дрост|ь, и *f.* wisdom; **~и** (*iron.*) subtleties.

прему́др|ый (~, ~а) *adj.* (very) wise, sage.

премьéр, а *m.* **1.** prime minister, premier. **2.** (*theatr.*) leading actor, lead.

премьéр|а, ы *f.* (*theatr.*) première, first night, opening night.

премьéр-минúстр, а *m.* prime minister, premier.

премьéрш|а, и *f.* (*theatr.*) leading lady, lead.

пренебрегá|ть, ю *impf. of* **пренебрéчь**

пренебрежéни|е, я *nt.* **1.** scorn, contempt, disdain; **обнару́жить, вы́казать своё п. (к)** to show one's contempt (for); **говорúть с ~ем (о+*p.*)** to disparage, speak slightingly (of). **2.** neglect, disregard; **п. своúми обя́занностями** neglect of one's duties, dereliction of duty.

пренебрежúтельност|ь, и *f.* scorn.

пренебрежúтел|ьный (~ен, ~ьна) *adj.* scornful, slighting, disdainful.

пренебрé|чь, гу́, жёшь, гу́т, *past* **~̈г, ~глá** *pf.* (*of* **~гáть**) (+*i.*) **1.** to scorn, despise; **п. опáсностью** to scorn danger; **п. совéтом** to scorn advice. **2.** to neglect, disregard.

прéни|е, я *nt.* rotting.

прéни|я, й *no sg.* debate; discussion; **судéбные п.** pleadings; **откры́ть, прекратúть п.** to open, close a debate.

преобладáни|е, я *nt.* predominance.

преобладá|ть, ет *impf.* to predominate; to prevail.

преобладá|ющий *pres. part. act. of* **~ть** *and adj.* predominant; prevalent.

преображá|ть, ю *impf. of* **преобразúть**

преображéни|е, я *nt.* **1.** transformation. **2.** (*relig.*) the Transfiguration.

преобра|зúть, жу́, зúшь *pf.* (*of* **~жáть**) to transform, transfigure.

преобразовáни|е, я *nt.* **1.** transformation. **2.** reform; reorganization.

преобразовáтел|ь, я *m.* **1.** reformer; reorganizer. **2.** (*phys., tech.*) transformer.

преобраз|овáть, у́ю *pf.* (*of* **~óвывать**) **1.** to transform (*also phys., tech.*). **2.** to reform, reorganize.

преобразóвыва|ть, ю *impf. of* **преобразовáть**

преодолевá|ть, ю *impf. of* **преодолéть**

преодолé|ть, ю *pf.* (*of* **~вáть**) to overcome, get over; **п. препя́тствия** to surmount obstacles; **п. тру́дности** to get over difficulties; **п. отставáние** to make up lee-way.

преодолúм|ый (~, ~а) *adj.* surmountable; **э́то затруднéние ~о** this difficulty is not insuperable.

преосвящéнн|ый *adj.* **1.** (*title of bishop*) Right Reverend. **2.** (*eccl.*) pre-consecrated; **~ые дары́** reserved sacrament.

преосвящéнств|о, а *nt.*: **егó п.** (*title of bishop*) his Grace.

препарáт, а *m.* (*chem., pharm.*) preparation.

препарáтор, а *m.* laboratory assistant.

препарúр|овать, ую *impf. and pf.* (*chem., pharm.*) to prepare, make a preparation (of).

препинáни|е, я *nt.*: **знáки ~я** (*gram.*) stops, punctuation marks.

препирáтельств|о, а *nt.* altercation, wrangling, squabbling.

препирá|ться, юсь *impf.* (**с**+*i.*; *coll.*) to wrangle (with), squabble (with).

преподавáни|е, я *nt.* teaching, tuition, instruction.

преподавáтел|ь, я *m.* teacher; (*in university or other higher education institution*) lecturer, instructor; **п.-предмéтник** subject teacher.

преподавáтель|ский *adj. of* **~; п. состáв** teaching staff.

препода|вáть, ю́, ёшь *impf.* to teach; **п. хúмию** to teach, be a lecturer in chemistry.

преподá|ть, м, шь, ст, дúм, дúте, ду́т, *past* **препóдал, ~лá, препóдало** *pf.* (*obs.*) to give (*advice, a lesson, etc.*).

преподнесéни|е, я *nt.* presentation.

преподнес|тú, у́, ёшь, *past* **~̈, ~лá** *pf.* (*of* **преподносúть**) (+*a. and d.*) to present (with), make a present (of to); **он ~̈ нам неприя́тную нóвость** he brought us a piece of bad news; **п. что-н. комý-н. в готóвом вúде** (*fig.*) to hand sth. to s.o. on a plate.

преподно|сúть, шу́, ~́сишь *impf. of* **преподнестú**

преподóби|е, я *nt.*: **егó п.** (*title of priest*) his Reverence, the Reverend.

преподóбный *adj.* (*title of canonized monks*) Saint; Venerable.

препóн|а, ы *f.* (*obs.*) obstacle, impediment.

препоруч|áть, áю *impf. of* **~úть**

препоруч|úть, у́, ~́ишь *pf.* (*of* **~áть**) (*obs.*) to entrust, commit.

препоя́|сать, шу, шешь *pf.* (*obs.*) to gird; **п. свои чрéсла** (*fig., rhet.*) to gird up one's loins.

препроводúтельный *adj.* accompanying (*document, etc.*).

препрово|дúть, жу́, дúшь *pf.* (*of* **~ждáть**) to send, forward, dispatch.

препровождá|ть, ю *impf. of* **препроводúть**

препровождéни|е[1], я *nt.* forwarding, dispatching.

препровождéни|е[2], я *nt.* passing; **для ~я врéмени** to pass the time.

препя́тстви|е, я *nt.* **1.** obstacle, impediment, hindrance; **чинúть комý-н. ~я** to put obstacles in s.o.'s way. **2.** (*sport*) obstacle; **бег с ~ями, скáчки с ~ями** steeple-chase; **взять п.** to clear an obstacle; (*fig.*) to clear a hurdle; **сбить п.** to bring down an obstacle.

препя́тств|овать, ую *impf.* (*of* **вос~**) (+*d.*) to hinder, impede, hamper; to stand in the way (of); **непогóда ~овала их свидáниям** bad weather interfered with their rendezvous.

прерв|áть, у́, ёшь, *past* **~áл, ~алá, ~áло** *pf.* (*of* **прерывáть**) to break off, sever; to interrupt, to cut short; **п. заня́тия** to interrupt one's studies; **п. молчáние** to break a silence; **п. орáтора** to interrupt a speaker; **п. дипломатúческие отношéния** to break off *or* sever diplomatic relations; **п. переговóры** to break off negotiations; to suspend talks; **п. рабóту** to take a break; **п. рабóту на канúкулы** (*of parliament, etc.*) to go into recess; **п. разговóр** to interrupt a conversation; **нас ~áли** (*of telephone conversation*) we have been cut off.

прерв|áться, ёшься, *past* **~áлся, ~алáсь, ~áлось** *pf.* (*of* **прерывáться**) **1.** to be interrupted; **переговóры ~áлись** conversations have been broken off, have broken down. **2.** (*of a voice, from emotion*) to break.

пререкáни|е, я *nt.* altercation, wrangle, argument; **вступúть в п. с кем-н.** to start an argument with s.o.

пререкá|ться, юсь *impf.* (**с**+*i.*) to argue (with).

прéри|я, и *f.* prairie.

прерогатúв|а, ы *f.* prerogative.

прерывáтел|ь, я *m.* (*radio*) interrupter; (*elec.*) (circuit) breaker, cut-out.

прерывá|ть(ся), ю(сь) *impf. of* **прервáть(ся)**

прерывá|ющийся *pres. part. of* **~ться; ~ющимся гóлосом** with a catch in one's voice.

преры́висто *adv.* in a broken way; **говорúть п.** to speak in a staccato way; **дышáть п.** to gasp.

преры́вист|ый (~, ~а) *adj.* broken, interrupted, intermittent; **п. ток** (*tech.*) intermittent current.

пресви́тер, а *m.* (*eccl.*) **1.** presbyter. **2.** (*in Presbyterian Church*) èlder.
пресвитериа́нский *adj.* (*relig.*) Presbyterian.
пресвитериа́нств|о, а *nt.* (*relig.*) Presbyterianism.
пресека́|ть(ся), ю, ет(ся) *impf. of* **пресе́чь(ся)**
пресече́ни|е, я *nt.* **1.** interruption, cutting off. **2.** (*liter.*; *obs.*) caesura.
пресе́|чь, ку́, чёшь, ку́т, *past* **~к, ~кла** *pf.* (*of* **~ка́ть**) to cut short, stop; **п. в ко́рне** to nip in the bud.
пресе́|чься, чётся, ку́тся, *past* **~кся, ~кла́сь** *pf.* (*of* **~ка́ться**) **1.** to stop. **2.** (*of a voice, from emotion*) to break. **3.** *pass. of* **~чь**
пресле́довани|е, я *nt.* **1.** pursuit, chase. **2.** persecution, victimization; **ма́ния ~я** persecution complex. **3.** (*leg.*): **суде́бное п.** prosecution.
пресле́довател|ь, я *m.* persecutor.
пресле́д|овать, ую *impf.* **1.** to pursue, chase, be after; (*fig.*) to haunt; **подозре́ние ~ует меня́** a suspicion haunts me. **2.** (*fig.*) to strive (for, after), pursue; **п. цель** to pursue an end. **3.** to persecute, torment; to victimize. **4.** (*leg.*) to prosecute.
пресловýтый *adj.* notorious; (*iron.*) famous, celebrated.
пресмыка́тельств|о, а *nt.* grovelling, crawling.
пресмыка́|ться, юсь *impf.* **1.** (*obs.*) to creep, crawl. **2.** (**пе́ред**; *fig.*) to grovel (before), cringe (before), lick the boots (of).
пресмыка́ющ|ееся, егося *nt.* reptile.
пресново́дный *adj.* freshwater.
пре́с|ный (~ен, ~на́, ~но) *adj.* **1.** (*of water*) fresh, sweet. **2.** unsalted; **п. хлеб** unleavened bread. **3.** (*of food*) flavourless, tasteless; (*fig.*) insipid, vapid, flat; **~ные остро́ты** feeble jokes.
преспоко́йно *adv.* (*coll.*) **1.** very quietly. **2.** calmly, coolly.
преспоко́|йный (~ен, ~йна) *adj.* (*coll.*) very quiet; very peaceful.
пресс, а *m.* press; punch.
пре́сс|а, ы *f.* (*collect.*) the press.
пресс-атташе́ *m. indecl.* press attaché.
пресс-бюро́ *nt. indecl.* press department.
пресс-конфере́нци|я, и *f.* press conference.
пресс|ова́ть, у́ю *impf.* (*of* **с~**) to press, compress.
прессо́вк|а, и *f.* pressing, compressing.
прессовщи́к, а́ *m.* presser, press operator.
пресс-папье́ *nt. indecl.* **1.** paper-weight. **2.** blotter.
преста́в|иться, люсь, ишься *pf.* (*obs.*) to pass away.
преставле́ни|е, я *nt.* (*obs.*) passing (away).
престаре́л|ый *adj.* aged; advanced in years; **дом ~ых** old people's home.
престидижита́тор, а *m.* juggler, prestidigitator.
прести́ж, а *m.* prestige; **поте́ря ~а** loss of face; **охраня́ть свой п.** to save one's face.
престо́л, а *m.* **1.** throne; **вступи́ть на п.** to come to the throne, mount the throne; **отре́чься от ~а** to abdicate; **све́ргнуть с ~а** to dethrone. **2.** (*eccl.*) altar, communion table. **3.** (*eccl.*): **Па́пский п.** Holy See, See of Rome.
престолонасле́ди|е, я *nt.* succession to the throne.
престолонасле́дник, а *m.* successor to the throne.
престо́л|ьный *adj. of* **~**; **п. го́род** capital (city); **п. пра́здник** patron saint's day, patronal festival.
преступ|а́ть, а́ю *impf. of* **~и́ть**
преступ|и́ть, лю́, ~́ишь *pf.* (*of* **~а́ть**) to transgress, trespass (against); **п. зако́н** to violate the law.
преступле́ни|е, я *nt.* crime, offence; (*leg.*) felony; transgression; **госуда́рственное п.** treason; **уголо́вное п.** criminal offence; **п. по до́лжности** (*leg.*) malfeasance; **соста́в ~я** (*leg.*) corpus delicti.
престу́пник, а *m.* criminal, offender; (*leg.*) felon; **вое́нный п.** war criminal.
престу́пност|ь, и *f.* **1.** criminality. **2.** (*collect.*) crime; **рост ~и** increase in crime.
престу́п|ный (~ен, ~на) *adj.* criminal; (*leg.*) felonious.
пресуществле́ни|е, я *nt.* (*relig.*) transubstantiation.
пресы́|тить, щу, тишь *pf.* (*of* **~ща́ть**) (*obs.*) (*+i.*) to satiate (with); to surfeit (on), sate (with).
пресы́|титься, щусь, тишься *pf.* (*of* **~ща́ться**) (*+i.*) to be satiated (with); be surfeited (with), have had a surfeit (of).
пресыща́|ть(ся), ю(сь) *impf. of* **пресы́тить(ся)**
пресыще́ни|е, я *nt.* satiety; surfeit; **до ~я** to satiety.
пресы́щенност|ь, и *f.* satiety; surfeit.
пресы́|щенный *p.p.p. of* **~тить** *and adj.* satiated; surfeited, sated, replete.
претворе́ни|е, я *nt.* conversion; transubstantiation (*esp. relig.*); **п. в жизнь** realization, putting into practice.
претвор|и́ть, ю́, и́шь *pf.* (*of* **~я́ть**) **1.** (**в**+*a.*) to turn (into), change (into), convert (into); to transubstantiate (*esp. relig.*). **2.**: **п. в жизнь, п. в де́ло** to realize, carry out, put into practice.
претвор|и́ться, и́тся *pf.* (*of* **~я́ться**) **1.** (**в**+*a.*) to turn (into), become; **вода́ ~и́лась в вино́** the water was turned into wine. **2.**: **п. в жизнь** to be realized, come true; **моя́ мечта́ ~и́лась в жизнь** my dream has come true.
претвор|я́ть(ся), я́ю, я́ет(ся) *impf. of* **~и́ть(ся)**
претенде́нт, а *m.* (**на**+*a.*) **1.** claimant (to, upon), aspirant (to); candidate (for); contestant; **он п. на ру́ку принце́ссы** he aspires to the hand of the princess. **2.** pretender (to); **п. на престо́л** pretender to the throne.
претенд|ова́ть, у́ю *impf.* (**на**+*a.*) to pretend (to), have pretensions (to); to aspire (to); to lay claim (to); **он ~у́ет на до́лжность мини́стра иностра́нных дел** he aspires to the position of Minister of Foreign Affairs.
прете́нзи|я, и *f.* **1.** claim; **име́ть ~ю (на**+*a.*) to claim, lay claim (to), make claims (on); **заяви́ть ~ю** to lodge a claim; **отклони́ть ~ю** to reject a claim. **2.** pretension; **челове́к с ~ями, без ~й** a pretentious, an unpretentious pers.; **у него́ нет никаки́х ~й на остроу́мие** he has no pretensions to wit; **быть в ~и на кого́-н.** to have a grudge, grievance against s.o.
претенцио́зност|ь, и *f.* pretentiousness, affectation.
претенцио́з|ный (~ен, ~на) *adj.* pretentious, affected.
претерпева́|ть, ю *impf. of* **претерпе́ть**
претерп|е́ть, лю́, ~́ишь *pf.* (*of* **~ева́ть**) to undergo; to suffer, endure; **план ~е́л измене́ния** the plan has undergone changes; **п. лише́ния** to endure privations.
прет|и́ть, и́т *impf.* (*+d.*) to sicken; **от э́той пи́щи мне ~и́т** I am nauseated by this food.
преткнове́ни|е, я *nt.*: **ка́мень ~я** stumbling-block.
пре́тор, а *m.* (*hist.*) praetor.
преториа́н|ец, ца *m.* (*hist.*) praetorian (guard).
преториа́нский *adj.* (*hist.*) praetorian.
пре|ть, ю *impf.* **1.** (*pf.* **со~́**) to rot. **2.** (*impf. only*) to become damp (*of ground, in spring, from warmth of atmosphere*). **3.** (*pf.* **у~́**) to stew. **4.** (*pf.* **взо~́**) (*coll.*) to sweat, perspire.
преувеличе́ни|е, я *nt.* exaggeration; overstatement.
преувели́чива|ть, ю *impf. of* **преувели́чить**
преувели́ч|ить, у, ишь *pf.* (*of* **~ивать**) to exaggerate; to overstate.
преуменьш|а́ть, а́ю *impf. of* **~́ить**
преуменьше́ни|е, я *nt.* underestimation; understatement.
преуме́ньш|ить, ~́у, ~́ишь *pf.* (*of* **~а́ть**) to underestimate, minimize; to belittle; to understate; **п. опа́сность** to underestimate the danger; **п. чью-н. по́мощь** to belittle s.o.'s assistance.
преуспева́|ть, ю *impf.* **1.** *impf. of* **преуспе́ть. 2.** (*impf. only*) to thrive, prosper, flourish.
преуспева́|ющий *pres. part. act. of* **~ть** *and adj.* successful, prosperous.
преуспе́|ть, ю *pf.* (*of* **~ва́ть**) (**в**+*p.*) to succeed (in), be successful (in); **п. в жи́зни** to get on in life.
преуспея́ни|е, я *nt.* (*obs. or iron.*) success.
префе́кт, а *m.* prefect.
префекту́р|а, ы *f.* prefecture.
префера́нс, а *m.* preference (*card-game*).
пре́фикс, а *m.* (*gram.*) prefix.
префи́кс *adj. indecl.*: **платёж п.** (*comm.*) payment made before term appointed, prior payment.
префикса́льный *adj.* (*gram.*) with a prefix.
префикса́ци|я, и *f.* (*gram.*) addition of prefix (*to a v., etc.*).
прехо|ди́ть, жу́, ~́дишь *impf. of* **прейти́**
преходя́щий *adj.* transient.
прецеде́нт, а *m.* precedent; **установи́ть п.** to establish a precedent.

прецéсси|я, и *f.* (*astron.*) precession.
прецизиóнный *adj.* (*tech.*) precision; **п. прибóр** precision instrument.
при *prep.+p.* **1.** (*of local proximity*) by, at; in the presence of; **при дорóге** by the road(-side); **бúтва при Бородинé** the battle of Borodino; **письмó бы́ло подпúсано при мне** the letter was signed in my presence; **не нáдо так выражáться при дéтях** you should not use such language in front of the children. **2.** attached to, affiliated to, under the auspices of (*usu. not translated*); **он рабóтает при университéте** he is attached to the university; **военврáч при батальóне** battalion medical officer. **3.** (*indicating possession, presence of object(s) mentioned*) by, with; about, on; **у негó нé было при себé дéнег** he had no money on him; **есть ли у вас при себé перочúнный нож?** do you have a pen-knife about you?; **быть при orýжии** to have arms about one, be armed. **4.** with (= *taking into account the attribute, etc., referred to*); for, notwithstanding; **при такúх талáнтах он должнó быть далекó пойдёт** with such talent he ought to go far; **при желáнии всегó мóжно добúться** where there's a will there's a way; **при всех егó достóинствах, он мне не нрáвится** for all his virtues, I do not like him; **при всём том** (*i*) with it all, moreover, (*ii*) for all that. **5.** in the time of, in the days of; under (*sc.* the rule of); during; **при Ивáне Грóзном** during the reign of, in the time of Ivan the Terrible; **при Ромáновых** under the Romanovs; **при мне бы́ло не так** in my day it was not like this. **6.** (*indicating accompanying circumstances*) by; **при дневнóм свéте** by daylight; **при свéте лáмпы** by lamplight. **7.** (*referring to action on occasion unspecified*) when; on; in case of; **при перехóде чéрез ýлицу** when crossing the street; **при слýчае** when the occasion arises, at convenience; **при анáлизе** on analysis; **при малярúи** in case of malaria; **при услóвии** under the condition (that). **8.** with (= *by means of, thanks to*); **при пóмощи рыбакóв нам удалóсь оттолкнýть лóдку** with the aid of the fishermen we succeeded in pushing the boat off.
при...¹ *vbl. pref. indicating* **1.** *completion of action or motion up to given terminal point, as* **приéхать** to arrive. **2.** *action of attaching, as* **пристрóить** to build on. **3.** *direction of action towards speaker, as* **пригласúть** to invite. **4.** *direction of action from above downward, as* **придавúть** to press down. **5.** *incompleteness or tentativeness of action, as* **приоткры́ть** to open slightly. **6.** *exhaustiveness of action, as* **приучúть** to train. **7.** (*+suffix.* **...ыва...**, **...ива...**) *accompaniment, as* **припля́сывать** to dance (to a tune).
при...² *as pref. of nn. and adjs.* (*esp. geog.*) *indicates juxtaposition or proximity, as* **приозéрье** lake-side; **прибрéжный, примóрский** coastal.
прибáв|ить, лю, ишь *pf.* (*of* **~ля́ть**) **1.** (*+a. or g.*) to add; **п. (в вéсе)** to put on (weight); **за три мéсяца онá ~ила дéсять фýнтов** she put on ten pounds in three months. **2.** (*+g.*) to increase, augment; **п. жáлованья** to increase a salary, give a rise; **п. шáгу** to quicken, hasten one's steps; **п. хóду** (*coll.*) to put on speed. **3.** (**в**+*p.*) to lengthen, widen (*part of an item of clothing*); **нáдо п. в рукавáх** the sleeves need to be lengthened. **4.** (*fig., coll.*) to lay *or* pile it on (= *exaggerate*).
прибáв|иться, ится *pf.* (*of* **~ля́ться**) **1.** to increase; (*of water*) to rise; (*of the moon*) to wax; **п. в вéсе** to put on weight; **день ~ился** the days are getting longer; (*impers.*): **воды́ ~илось** the water has risen; **нарóду ~илось** the crowd has grown. **2.** *pass. of* **~ить**
прибáвк|а, и *f.* **1.** addition, augmentation. **2.** increase, supplement; **получúть ~у** to get a rise.
прибавлéни|е, я *nt.* **1.** addition, augmentation; **п. семéйства** addition to the family; **сказáть в п.** to say in addition, add. **2.** supplement, appendix. **3.** (*fig., coll.*) embroidery (= *exaggeration*).
прибавля́|ть(ся), ю, ет(ся) *impf. of* **прибáвить(ся)**
прибáвочн|ый *adj.* **1.** additional. **2.** (*econ.*) surplus; **~ая стóимость** surplus value.
прибáлт, а *m.* Balt.
прибалтúйский *adj.* Baltic (= *adjacent to the Baltic Sea*).
Прибáлтик|а, и *f.* the Baltic States.
прибáлт|ка, ки *f. of* **~**
прибаýтк|а, и *f.* humorous catchphrase, facetious saying.
прибегá|ть¹**, ю** *impf. of* **прибéгнуть**
прибегá|ть²**, ю** *impf. of* **прибежáть**
прибéг|нуть, ну, нешь, *past* **~, ~ла** *pf.* (*of* **~áть**¹) **(к)** to resort (to), have resort (to); to fall back (on); **п. к сúле** to resort to force.
прибедн|úться, ю́сь, úшься *pf.* (*of* **~я́ться**) (*coll.*) **1.** to pretend to be poorer than one is, feign poverty. **2.** to show false modesty.
прибедн|я́ться, я́юсь *impf. of* **~úться**
прибе|жáть, гý, жúшь, гýт *pf.* (*of* **~гáть**²) to come running.
прибéжищ|е, а *nt.* refuge; **послéднее п.** (*fig.*) last resort; **найтú п.** (**в**+*p.*) to take refuge (in).
приберегá|ть, ю *impf. of* **приберéчь**
приберé|чь, гý, жёшь, гýт, *past* **~г, ~глá** *pf.* (*of* **~гáть**) to save up.
прибивá|ть, ю *impf. of* **прибúть**¹
прибирá|ть(ся), ю(сь) *impf. of* **прибрáть(ся)**
приб|úть¹**, ью́, ьёшь** *pf.* (*of* **~ивáть**) **1.** to nail, affix with nails; **п. флаг к дрéвку** to nail a flag to a pole. **2.** to lay, flatten; **град ~úл посéвы** the hail has laid the corn. **3.** (*usu. impers.*) to throw up; **труп ~úло к бéрегу** a body was washed ashore.
приб|úть²**, ью́, ьёшь** *pf. of* **бить 1.**
прибл. (*abbr. of* **приблизúтельно**) approx., approximately.
приближá|ть, ю *impf. of* **приблúзить**
приближá|ться, юсь *impf.* **1.** *impf. of* **приблúзиться. 2.** (*impf. only*) to approximate; **п. к úстине** to approximate to the truth.
приближéни|е, я *nt.* **1.** approach; approaching, drawing near. **2.** (*math.*) approximation.
приближённост|ь, и *f.* proximity.
приближённый¹ *adj.* approximate, rough; **п. мéтод** (*math.*) method of approximation.
приближённ|ый²**, ого** *m.* (*obs.*) retainer, pers. in attendance; (*pl.*) retinue.
приблизúтельно *adv.* approximately, roughly.
приблизúтельност|ь, и *f.* approximateness.
приблизúтел|ьный (~ен, ~ьна) *adj.* approximate, rough.
приблú|зить, жу, зишь *pf.* (*of* **~жáть**) **1.** to bring nearer, move nearer; **п. кнúгу к глазáм** to bring a book nearer one's eyes. **2.** to hasten, advance; **я намéрен п. мой отъéзд** I intend to hasten my departure; **~зили егó призы́в в áрмию** the date of his call-up has been advanced.
приблú|зиться, жусь, зишься *pf.* (*of* **~жáться**) **(к)** to approach, draw near; to draw nearer (to), come nearer (to).
приблýдный *adj.* (*coll.; of animals*) stray.
прибó|й, я *m.* surf, breakers.
прибóр, а *m.* **1.** instrument, device, apparatus, appliance, gadget. **2.** set; **брúтвенный п.** shaving things; **камúнный п.** set of fire-irons; **пúсьменный п.** desk-set; **столóвый п.** cover; **накры́ть стол на шесть ~ов** to lay (places) for six; **туалéтный п.** toilet set, washing things; **чáйный п.** tea-service. **3.** fittings; **печнóй п.** stove fittings.
прибóр|ный *adj. of* **~**; **~ная доскá** dashboard; (*aeron.*) instrument panel.
приборостроéни|е, я *nt.* instrument-making.
при|брáть, берý, берёшь, *past* **~брáл, ~бралá, ~брáло** *pf.* (*of* **~бирáть**) **1.** to clear up, clean up, tidy (up); **п. постéль** to make a bed; **п. кóмнату, п. в кóмнате** to do a room; **п. на столé** to clear the table; **п. когó-н. к рукáм** to take s.o. in hand; **п. что-н. к рукáм** to lay one's hands on sth. **2.** to put away; **~берú игрýшки — порá спать!** put your toys away, it's time for bed!
при|брáться, берýсь, берёшься, *past* **~брáлся, ~бралáсь, ~брáлóсь** *pf.* (*of* **~бирáться**) to tidy o.s. up; to have a clear-up of one's things.
прибрéжн|ый *adj.* **1.** coastal, littoral; **~ые островá** offshore islands; **~ая полосá** coastal strip. **2.** riverside; riverain, riparian.
прибрéжь|е, я *nt.* littoral; coastal strip.
прибре|стú, дý, дёшь, *past* **~́л, ~лá** *pf.* (*coll.*) to come trudging (along); **п. домóй** to crawl home.

прибывá|ть, ю *impf. of* **прибы́ть**
при́был|ь, и *f.* **1.** profit, gain (*also fig.*); return; **валовáя п.** gross profit; **чи́стая п.** net profit; **какáя мне в э́том п.?** (*coll.*) what do I get out of it? **2.** increase, rise; **п. населéния** increase of population; **водá идёт на п.** the water is rising. **3.** (*tech.*) riser; **п. отли́вки** head of casting, lost head.
при́быльност|ь, и *f.* profitability, lucrativeness.
при́быль|ный *adj.* **1.** profitable, lucrative. **2.** *adj. of* ~ **3.**; **п. конéц** deadhead.
прибы́ти|е, я *nt.* arrival.
при|бы́ть[1], **бу́ду, бу́дешь,** *past* **~был, ~былá, ~было** *pf.* (*of* **~бывáть**) to arrive; (*of a train, etc.*) to get in; **пóезд ~был** the train is in; **пóчта ~былá** the post has come.
при|бы́ть[2], **бу́дет,** *past* **~был, ~былá, ~было** *pf.* (*of* **~бывáть**) (*coll.*) to increase, grow; (*of water*) to rise, swell; (*of the moon*) to wax; **водá ~былá** the water has risen; **нáшего полку́ ~было** our numbers have grown.
привáд|а, ы *f.* lure, bait (*put out to catch birds or fish*).
привá|дить, жу, дишь *pf.* (*of* **~живать**) **1.** to train (*a bird, etc., by putting out food*). **2.** **(к)** to attract (to), predispose (towards).
привáжива|ть, ю *impf. of* **привáдить**
привáл, а *m.* **1.** halt, stop. **2.** stopping-place.
привáлива|ть, ю *impf. of* **привали́ть**
привал|и́ть, ю́, ~ишь *pf.* (*of* **~ивать**) **1.** to lean, rest; **п. дровá к забóру** to pile logs against the fence. **2.** (*of a vessel*) to come alongside. **3.** (*fig., coll.*) to turn up; **на матч ~и́ло мнóго нарóду** people flocked to the match; **счáстье нам ~и́ло** fortune smiled on us.
привáрива|ть, ю *impf. of* **привари́ть**
привар|и́ть, ю́, ~ишь *pf.* (*of* **~ивать**) **1.** **(к)** to weld on (to). **2.** (*+a. or g.*) to boil some more, cook some more.
привáрк|а, и *f.* welding.
привáр|ок, ка *m.* (*mil. and coll.*) **1.** (*collect.*) victuals, rations. **2.** cooked food, hot meal.
привáт-доцéнт, а *m.* privat-docent (*unestablished university lecturer*).
привáт-доцентýр|а, ы *f.* **1.** post of privat-docent. **2.** (*collect.*) the privat-docents.
приватизáци|я, и *f.* privatization.
приватизи́р|овать, ую *impf. & pf.* to privatize.
привáтный *adj.* (*obs.*) private.
приведéни|е, я *nt.* **1.** bringing; **п. к прися́ге** administration of oath, swearing in. **2.** putting; **п. в движéние** setting in motion; **п. в исполнéние** carrying out, putting into effect; **п. в поря́док** putting in order. **3.** (*math.*) reduction; **п. к óбщему знаменáтелю** reduction to a common denominator. **4.** adduction, adducing; **п. примéров** adducing of instances.
привез|ти́, у́, ёшь, *past* **~, ~лá** *pf.* (*of* **привози́ть**) to bring (*not on foot*).
приверéдлив|ый (~, ~а) *adj.* fastidious, pernickety; squeamish.
приверéдник, а *m.* fastidious pers.; squeamish pers.
приверéднича|ть, ю *impf.* to be hard to please; to be fastidious; to be squeamish.
привéржен|ец, ца *m.* adherent; follower.
привéрженност|ь, и *f.* adherence; attachment, devotion.
привéржен|ный (~, ~а) *adj.* **(к)** attached (to), devoted (to).
приверн|у́ть, у́, ёшь *pf.* (*of* **привёртывать**) **1.** to screw tight, tighten, clamp. **2.** to turn down; **п. фити́ль** to turn a wick down.
привер|тéть, чу́, ~тишь *pf.* (*of* **~тывать**) to screw tight, tighten, clamp.
привёртыва|ть, ю *impf. of* **приверну́ть** *and* **привертéть**
привéс, а *m.* additional weight.
привé|сить, шу, сишь *pf.* (*of* **~шивать**) to hang up, suspend.
привéс|ок, ка *m.* (*coll.*) **1.** makeweight. **2.** (*fig.*) appendage.
приве|сти́, ду́, дёшь, *past* **~л, ~лá** *pf.* (*of* **приводи́ть**) **1.** to bring; to lead, take; **он ~л с собóй невéсту** he has brought his fiancée (with him); **п. когó-н. к прися́ге** to administer the oath to s.o., swear s.o. in; **~л Бог сви́деться!** (*obs.*) we were meant to meet again! **2.** **(к;** *fig.*) to lead (to), bring (to), conduce (to), result (in); **э́то к добру́ не ~дёт** no good will come of it; **её поведéние ~лó меня́ к заключéнию, что онá душéвно расстрóена** her behaviour led me to the conclusion that she is out of her mind. **3.** (**в**+*a.*) to put, set (*or translated by v. corresponding to n. governed by* **в**); **п. в бéшенство** to throw into a rage, drive mad; **п. в движéние, в дéйствие** to set in motion, set going; **п. затруднéние** to cause difficulties, put in a difficult position; **п. в изумлéние** to astonish, astound; **п. в исполнéние** to carry out, carry into effect, put into effect; **п. приговóр в исполнéние** to execute a sentence; **п. в хорóшее настроéние** to put in a good mood; **п. в негóдность** to put out of commission; **п. в отчáяние** to reduce to despair; **п. в поря́док** to put in order, tidy (up); to arrange, fix; **п. в у́жас** to horrify; **п. в чу́вство** to bring to, bring round. **4.** **(к;** *math.*) to reduce (to). **5.** to adduce, cite; **п. доказáтельства** to adduce proofs; **п. примéр** to give an example, cite an instance; **п. цитáту (из)** to make a quotation (from), quote.
приве|сти́сь, дётся, *past* **~лóсь** *pf.* (*of* **приводи́ться**) (*impers.+d.; coll.*) to happen, chance; to be one's lot; **мне ~лóсь там быть тогдá, когдá они́ проезжáли** I happened to be there when they drove past; **ему́ ~лóсь быть свидéтелем преступлéния** it was his lot to be a witness of the crime.
привéт, а *m.* greeting(s); regards; **горя́чий п.** (one's) warmest regards; **передáть п., слать п.** to send one's regards; **моя́ женá шлёт вам п.** my wife sends her regards, asks to be remembered to you; **передáйте п. вáшим коллéгам** remember me to your colleagues, my regards to your colleagues; **с сердéчным ~ом** (*epistolary formula*) yours sincerely; **п. из Москвы́!** greetings from Moscow!; **он с~ом** (*coll.*) he's crackers.
привéтливост|ь, и *f.* affability; cordiality.
привéтлив|ый (~, ~а) *adj.* affable; cordial.
привéтственн|ый *adj.* salutatory; welcoming; **~ая речь** speech of welcome.
привéтстви|е, я *nt.* **1.** greeting, salutation. **2.** speech of welcome.
привéтств|овать, ую *impf.* **1.** (*in past tense also pf.*) to greet, salute, hail; to welcome. **2.** (*fig.*) to welcome; **п. предложéние** to welcome a suggestion. **3.** (*also pf.*) (*mil.*) to salute.
привé|шенный *p.p.p. of* **~сить; у негó язы́к хорошó ~шен** (*coll.*) he has a ready tongue.
привéшива|ть, ю *impf. of* **привéсить**
прививá|ть(ся), ю, ет(ся) *impf. of* **приви́ть(ся)**
приви́вк|а, и *f.* **1.** **(от, прóтив;** *med.*) inoculation (against); vaccination. **2.** (*bot.*) inoculation, grafting, engrafting.
приви́в|очный *adj. of* **~ка**
привидéни|е, я *nt.* ghost, spectre; apparition.
приви́|деться, дится *pf. of* **ви́деться 2.**
привилегирóванност|ь, и *f.* privilege(s).
привилегирóванн|ый *adj.* privileged; **~ое положéние** privileged position.
привилéги|я, и *f.* privilege.
привин|ти́ть, чу́, ти́шь *pf.* (*of* **~чивать**) to screw on.
приви́нчива|ть, ю *impf. of* **привинти́ть**
привирá|ть, ю *impf. of* **приврáть**
приви́ти|е, я *nt.* inculcation.
прив|и́ть, ью́, ьёшь, *past* **~и́л, ~илá, ~и́ло** *pf.* (*of* **~ивáть**) (*+a. and d.*) **1.** (*med.*) to inoculate (with); **п. комý-н. óспу** to vaccinate s.o. against smallpox. **2.** (*bot.*) to graft, engraft (upon); to inoculate (with); (*fig.*) to implant (in). **3.** (*fig.*) to inculcate (in); to cultivate (in), foster (in); **п. комý-н. вкус к стихáм** to inculcate in s.o. a taste for poetry; **п. нóвую мóду** to set a new fashion.
прив|и́ться, ьётся, *past* **~и́лся, ~илáсь** *pf.* (*of* **~ивáться**) **1.** (*of an inoculation or graft*) to take. **2.** (*fig.*) to become established, find acceptance, catch on; **э́ти взгля́ды ~или́сь не всю́ду** these views did not find universal acceptance; **мóда носи́ть цветны́е чулки́ не ~илáсь у нас** the fashion for coloured stockings did not catch on here.
при́вкус, а *m.* after-taste; smack (*also fig.*); **егó словá имéли п. нáглости** his words smacked of insolence.
привлекáтельност|ь, и *f.* attractiveness.

привлека́тел|ьный (~ен, ~ьна) *adj.* attractive; fetching; **~ьная улы́бка** winning smile.

привлека́|ть, ю *impf. of* **привле́чь**

привлече́ни|е, я *nt.* attraction.

привле́|чь, ку́, ёшь, ку́т, *past* **~к, ~кла́** *pf.* (*of* **~ка́ть**) **1.** to draw, attract; **п. внима́ние** to attract attention; **кри́ки ~кли́ нас к ра́неному** cries drew us to the wounded man. **2.** to draw in; **п. на свою́ сто́рону** to win over (*to one's side*); **п. к рабо́те** to recruit, enlist the services (of). **3.** (*leg.*) to have up; **п. к суду́** to sue (in court), take to court; to bring to trial, put on trial; **п. к отве́тственности (за+*a.*)** to make answer (for), make answerable (for), call to account (for); **п. к уголо́вной отве́тственности** to institute criminal proceedings (against).

привнес|ти́, у́, ёшь, *past* **~, ~ла́** *pf.* (*of* **привноси́ть**) to introduce, insert; **п. элеме́нт коми́зма в де́ло** to introduce an element of comedy into proceedings.

привно|си́ть, шу́, ~сишь *impf. of* **привнести́**

приво́д[1], **а** *m.* (*leg.*) bringing to court (*of accused or witness for questioning*); taking into custody; **постановле́ние о ~е** warrant for arrest.

при́во́д[2], **а** *m.* (*tech.*) drive, driving gear; **кулачко́вый п.** cam drive; **ремённый п.** belt drive; **ручно́й п.** hand gear; **червя́чный п.** worm gear.

приво|ди́ть(ся), жу́(сь) ~дишь(ся) *impf. of* **привести́(сь)**

приво́дк|а, и *f.* (*typ.*) registration.

приводне́ни|е, я *nt.* splash-down.

приводн|и́ться, ю́сь, и́шься *pf.* (*of* **~я́ться**) to land, come down on water.

приводн|о́й *adj.* (*tech.*) driving; **п. вал** driving shaft; **п. механи́зм** driving gear; **~а́я радиоста́нция** homing wireless set; **~а́я цепь** sprocket chain, chain drive.

приводн|я́ться, я́юсь *impf. of* **~и́ться**

приво|жу́[1], **~дишь** *see* **~ди́ть**

приво|жу́[2], **~зишь** *see* **~зи́ть**

приво́з, а *m.* **1.** bringing, supply; import, importation. **2.** (*coll.*) load.

приво|зи́ть, жу́, ~зишь *impf. of* **привезти́**

привозно́й *adj.* imported.

приво́зн|ый = ~о́й

приво́|й, я *m.* (*agric.*) graft.

привола́кива|ть, ю *impf. of* **приволочи́ть** *and* **приволо́чь**

привола́кива|ться, юсь *impf. of* **1. приволочи́ться** *and* **приволо́чься. 2. приволокну́ться**

приволокн|у́ться, у́сь, ёшься *pf.* (*of* **привола́киваться**) (**за+*i.***; *coll.*) to flirt (with).

приволоч|и́ть(ся), у́(сь), и́шь(ся) *pf.* = **~ь(ся)**

приволо́|чь, ку́, чёшь, ку́т, *past* **~к, ~кла́** *pf.* (*of* **привола́кивать**) (*coll.*) to drag (over).

приволо́|чься, ку́сь, чёшься, ку́тся, *past* **~кся, ~кла́сь** *pf.* (*of* **привола́киваться**) (*coll.*) to drag o.s.

приво́ль|е, я *nt.* **1.** free space; **степны́е ~я** 'wide open spaces' of the steppe. **2.** freedom.

приво́льн|ый *adj.* free; **~ая жизнь** free and easy life.

привора́жива|ть, ю *impf. of* **приворожи́ть**

приворож|и́ть, у́, и́шь *pf.* (*of* **привора́живать**) (*obs. or fig.*) to bewitch, charm.

приворо́тн|ый *adj.*: **~ое зе́лье** (*folk poet.*) love-philtre.

привра́тник, а *m.* **1.** doorman, porter. **2.** (*anat.*) pylorus.

привр|а́ть, у́, ёшь, *past* **~а́л, ~ала́, ~а́ло** *pf.* (*of* **привира́ть**) (*coll.*) to make up; to exaggerate.

привска́кива|ть, ю *impf. of* **привскочи́ть**

привскоч|и́ть, у́, ~ишь *pf.* (*of* **привска́кивать**) to start, jump up.

привста|ва́ть, ю́, ёшь *impf. of* **~ть**

привста́|ть, ну, нешь *pf.* (*of* **~ва́ть**) to rise, stand up (*for a moment*); to half-rise; **когда́ судья́ вошёл, все ~ли** when the judge entered everyone stood up.

привходя́щ|ий *adj.*: **~ие обстоя́тельства** attendant circumstances.

привык|а́ть, а́ю *impf. of* **~нуть**

привы́к|нуть, ну, нешь, *past* **~, ~ла** *pf.* (*of* **~а́ть**) (**к** *or+inf.*) **1.** to get accustomed (to), get used (to); **она́ ско́ро ~ла к его́ храпе́нию** she soon got used to his snoring. **2.** to get into the habit (of), get into the way (of); **он ~ руга́ться** he has got into the habit of swearing.

привы́чк|а, и *f.* habit; **войти́ в ~у** to become a habit; **вы́работать в себе́ ~у** to form a habit; **име́ть ~у (к)** to be accustomed (to); to be in the habit (of), be given (to); **приобрести́ ~у** (*+inf.*) to get into the habit (of), fall into the habit (of); **э́то не в на́ших ~ах** it is not our habit, not our practice.

привы́чност|ь, и *f.* habitualness.

привы́ч|ный (~ен, ~на) *adj.* **1.** habitual, usual, customary. **2. (к)** accustomed (to), used (to); **он челове́к п.** he is a man of habit, of set habits.

привя́занност|ь, и *f.* **1. (к)** attachment (to); affection (for, towards). **2.** (*fig.*) (object of) attachment, object of affection; **ста́рая п.** old flame.

привя́з|анный *p.p.p. of* **~а́ть** *and adj.* **(к)** attached (to).

привя|за́ть, жу́, ~жешь *pf.* (*of* **~зывать**) **(к) 1.** to tie (to), bind (to), fasten (to), attach (to), secure (to); **п. козу́** to tether a goat. **2. (к себе́;** *fig.*) to attach (to o.s.), get a hold (over the affections of).

привя|за́ться, жу́сь, ~жешься *pf.* (*of* **~зываться**) **(к) 1.** to become attached (to); **она́ о́чень к вам ~за́лась** she has become very attached to you. **2.** to attach o.s. (to); **на доро́ге како́й-то ни́щий ~за́лся к нам** a beggar attached himself to us on the road. **3.** (*coll.*) to pester, bother.

привязно́й *adj.* fastened, secured; **п. аэроста́т** captive balloon, balloon on bearings; **п. реме́нь** seat-belt (*in cars, etc.*).

привя́зчивост|ь, и *f.* **1.** capacity for giving affection; susceptibility to affection. **2.** disposition to annoy, pester, bother.

привя́зчив|ый (~, ~а) *adj.* **1.** affectionate; susceptible (*to affection*), given to forming attachments easily. **2.** importunate, annoying, given to pestering.

при́вяз|ь, и *f.* tic; lead, leash; tether; **на ~и** on a leash; **посади́ть соба́ку на п.** to put a dog on a leash.

прига́р, а *m.* (*coll.*) burnt place, burnt part (*of cooked food*).

при́гар|ь, и *f.* taste of burning; **молоко́ с ~ью** milk tasting burned.

пригвožда́|ть, ю *impf. of* **пригвозди́ть**

пригвоз|ди́ть, жу́, ди́шь *pf.* (*of* **пригвожда́ть**) **(к)** to nail (to); (*fig.*) to pin (down); **п. к ме́сту** to root to the spot; **п. к позо́рному столбу́** to pillory; **п. взгля́дом** to fix with a look.

пригиба́|ть(ся), ю(сь) *impf. of* **пригну́ть(ся)**

пригла́|дить, жу, дишь *pf.* (*of* **~живать**) to smooth.

пригла́|диться, жусь, дишься *pf.* (*of* **~живаться**) to smooth one's hair.

пригла́жива|ть(ся), ю(сь) *impf. of* **пригла́дить(ся)**

пригласи́тельный *adj.* conveying an invitation; **п. биле́т** invitation card.

пригла|си́ть, шу́, си́шь *pf.* (*of* **~ша́ть**) **1.** to invite, ask; **п. на обе́д** to invite, ask to dinner; **п. на та́нцы** to ask to a dance; **п. кого́-н. на та́нец** to ask s.o. to dance, ask s.o. for a dance; **п. в го́сти** to invite, ask round. **2.** to call (*a doctor, etc.*). **3.** to offer; **его́ ~си́ли на рабо́ту в но́вой шко́ле** he has been offered a job in a new school.

приглаша́|ть, ю *impf. of* **пригласи́ть**

приглаше́ни|е, я *nt.* **1.** invitation; **по ~ю** by invitation; **разосла́ть ~я** to send out invitations. **2.** offer (*of employment*).

приглуш|а́ть, а́ю *impf. of* **~и́ть**

приглуш|и́ть, у́, и́шь *pf.* (*of* **~а́ть**) to damp down; to muffle, deaden (*sound*); to choke, damp (a fire).

пригля|де́ть, жу́, ди́шь *pf.* (*of* **~дывать**) (*coll.*) **1.** to choose; to find, look out; **п. себе́ удо́бную кварти́ру** to look o.s. out convenient lodgings. **2. (за+*i.*)** to look after; **п. за детьми́** to look after children.

пригля|де́ться, жу́сь, ди́шься *pf.* (*of* **~дываться**) (*coll.*) **1. (к)** to look closely (at), scrutinize. **2. (к)** to get accustomed (to), get used (to); **п. к темноте́** to get accustomed to darkness. **3.** (*+d.*) to tire, bore; **мне ~де́лись кинофи́льмы о вое́нных де́йствиях** I am tired of war-films.

пригля́дыва|ть(ся), ю(сь) *impf. of* **пригляде́ть(ся)**

приглян|у́ться, у́сь, ~́ешься *pf.* (*+d.*; *coll.*) to take one's fancy, attract; **она́ сра́зу ~у́лась ему́** he was attracted by her instantly.

при|гна́ть[1], **гоню́, го́нишь,** *past* **~гна́л, ~гнала́, ~гна́ло** *pf.* (*of* **~гоня́ть**) to drive home, bring in (*cattle*).

при|гна́ть[2], **гоню́, го́нишь,** *past* **~гна́л, ~гнала́, ~гна́ло** *pf.* (*of* **~гоня́ть**) to fit, adjust, joint.

пригн|у́ть, у́, ёшь *pf.* (*of* **пригиба́ть**) to bend down, bow.

пригн|у́ться, у́сь, ёшься *pf.* (*of* **пригиба́ться**) to bend down, bow.

growth

пригова́рива|ть[1], **ю** *impf.* (*coll.*) to keep saying, keep repeating (*as accompaniment to given action*).

пригова́рива|ть[2], **ю** *impf. of* **приговори́ть**

пригово́р, а *m.* sentence; verdict; **вы́нести п.** to pass sentence; to bring in a verdict.

приговор|и́ть, ю́, и́шь *pf.* (*of* **пригова́ривать**[2]) (**к**) to sentence (to), condemn (to); **п. к пожи́зненному заключе́нию** to sentence to imprisonment for life.

приго|ди́ться, жу́сь, ди́шься *pf.* (*+d.*) to prove useful (to); to come in useful, come in handy; to stand in good stead.

приго́дност|ь, и *f.* fitness, suitableness.

приго́д|ный (~ен, ~на) *adj.* (**к**) fit (for), suitable (for), good (for); useful; **ни к чему́ не п.** good-for-nothing, worthless.

приго́ж|ий (~, ~а) *adj.* (*folk poet.*) **1.** comely. **2.** (*of weather*) fine.

приголу́б|ить, лю, ишь *pf.* (*of* **голу́бить** *and* **~ливать**) (*folk poet.*) to caress, fondle.

приголу́блива|ть, ю *impf. of* **приголу́бить**

приго́н, а *m.* **1.** driving home, bringing in. **2.** drove, herd.

приго́нк|а, и *f.* fitting, adjusting, jointing; **п. часте́й** (*tech.*) assembling.

пригоня́|ть, ю *impf. of* **пригна́ть**

пригор|а́ть, а́ет *impf. of* **~е́ть**

пригоре́лый *adj.* burnt.

пригор|е́ть, и́т *pf.* (*of* **~а́ть**) to be burnt; **молоко́ ~е́ло** the milk is burnt.

при́город, а *m.* **1.** suburb. **2.** (*hist.*) subject town; small town.

при́городн|ый *adj.* suburban; **~ое движе́ние** (*rail.*) local service(s); **п. по́езд** local train.

пригóр|ок, ка *m.* hillock, knoll.

при́го́рш|ня, ни, *g. pl.* **~ен** *and* **~ней** *f.* handful; **пить во́ду ~нями** to drink water from cupped hands; **ме́рить по́лными ~нями** to give good measure; **хвата́ть по́лными ~нями** to seize with both hands.

пригорю́нива|ться, юсь *impf. of* **пригорю́ниться**

пригорю́н|иться, юсь, ишься *pf.* (*of* **~иваться**) (*folk poet.*) to become sad.

пригота́влива|ть(ся), ю(сь) *impf.* = **приготовля́ть(ся)**

приготови́тельный *adj.* preparatory.

пригото́в|ить, лю, ишь *pf.* (*of* **пригота́вливать** *and* **~ля́ть**) to prepare; **п. обе́д** to cook, prepare a dinner; **п. роль** to learn (up) a part; **п. ру́копись к набо́ру** to prepare a manuscript for setting-up; **п. кому́-н. сюрпри́з** to prepare a surprise for s.o.

пригото́в|иться, люсь, ишься *pf.* (*of* **пригота́вливаться** *and* **~ля́ться**) (*+inf.*) to prepare (to); (**к**) to prepare (o.s.) (for).

приготовле́ни|е, я *nt.* preparation; **без ~я** off-hand, extempore.

приготовля́|ть(ся), ю(сь) *impf. of* **пригото́вить(ся)**

пригреба́|ть(ся), ю(сь) *impf. of* **пригрести́(сь)**

пригрева́|ть, ю *impf. of* **пригре́ть**

пригре́|зиться, жусь, зишься *pf. of* **гре́зиться**

пригре|сти́, бу́, бёшь, *past* **~́б, ~бла́** *pf.* (*of* **~ба́ть**) (*coll.*) **1.** to rake up. **2.** (**к**) to row (towards).

пригре|сти́сь, бу́сь, бёшься, *past* **~́бся, ~бла́сь** *pf.* (*of* **~ба́ться**) (*coll.*) = **~сти́ 2.**

пригре́|ть, ю *pf.* (*of* **~ва́ть**) **1.** to warm. **2.** (*fig.*) to cherish; to give shelter (to), take to one's care; **п. змею́ на груди́** to cherish a snake in one's bosom.

пригро|зи́ть, жу́, зи́шь *pf. of* **грози́ть 1.**

пригу́б|ить, лю, ишь *pf.* to take a sip (of), taste.

прида|ва́ть, ю́, ёшь *impf. of* **прида́ть**

придав|и́ть, лю́, ~́ишь *pf.* (*of* **~́ливать**) to press; to press down, weigh down (*also fig.*); to squeeze.

прида́влива|ть, ю *impf. of* **придави́ть**

прида́ни|е, я *nt.* adding, giving, imparting; **для ~я хра́брости** to give courage; **для ~я зако́нной си́лы** (*+d.*; *leg.*) for the enforcing (of).

прида́н|ое, ого *nt.* **1.** dowry; trousseau. **2.** layette.

прида́т|ок, ка *m.* appendage, adjunct.

прида́точн|ый *adj.* **1.** additional, supplementary. **2.** (*gram.*) subordinate; **~ое предложе́ние** subordinate clause. **3.** (*bot.*) adventitious.

прида́|ть, м, шь, ст, ди́м, ди́те, ду́т, *past* **при́дал, ~ла́, при́дало** *pf.* (*of* **~ва́ть**) **1.** to add; (*mil.*) to attach. **2.** to increase, strengthen; **п. бо́дрости** (*+d.*) to hearten, put heart (into); **п. ду́ху** (*+d.*) to inspire, encourage. **3.** (*+a. and d.*) to give (to), impart (to); (*fig.*) attach (to); **п. вкус** to impart relish (to), give piquancy (to); **п. лоск** to give a polish, impart lustre (to); **п. водонепроница́емость** to waterproof; **п. значе́ние** to attach importance (to).

прида́ч|а, и *f.* **1.** adding; (*mil.*) attaching. **2.** addition, supplement; **в ~у** into the bargain, in addition.

придвига́|ть(ся), ю(сь) *impf. of* **придви́нуть(ся)**

придви́|нуть, ну, нешь *pf.* (*of* **~га́ть**) to move (up), draw (up); **~нь(те) кре́сло к пе́чке** draw your chair up to the stove.

придви́|нуться, нусь, нешься *pf.* (*of* **~га́ться**) to move up, draw near.

придво́рн|ый *adj.* court; **п. врач** court physician; **п. поэ́т** poet laureate; **п. шут** court jester; *as n.* **п., ~ого** *m.* courtier.

приде́л, а *m.* (*eccl.*) side-altar; side-chapel.

приде́л|ать, аю *pf.* (*of* **~ывать**) (**к**) to fix (to), attach (to).

приде́лыва|ть, ю *impf. of* **приде́лать**

придерж|а́ть, у́, ~́ишь *pf.* (*of* **~́ивать**) to hold back (*also fig.*); **п. това́р** to hold back goods; **п. язы́к** to hold one's tongue.

приде́ржива|ть, ю *impf. of* **придержа́ть**

приде́ржива|ться, юсь *impf.* **1.** (**за**+*a.*) to hold on (to); **п. за по́ручень** to hold on to the rail. **2.** (*+g.*) to hold (to), keep (to) (*also fig.*); (*fig.*) to stick (to), adhere (to); **п. пра́вой стороны́** to keep to the right; **п. догово́ра** to adhere to an agreement; **п. мне́ния** to hold the opinion, be of the opinion; **п. те́мы** to stick to the subject; **он ~ется рю́мочки** (*coll.*) he is fond of the bottle.

приди́р|а, ы *c.g.* (*coll.*) caviller, fault-finder.

придира́|ться, юсь *impf. of* **придра́ться**

приди́рк|а, и *f.* (*coll.*) cavil, captious objection; (*pl.*) fault-finding, nagging, carping.

приди́рчивост|ь, и *f.* captiousness.

приди́рчив|ый (~, ~а) *adj.* captious, fault-finding, carping, nagging.

придоро́жный *adj.* roadside, wayside.

при|дра́ться, деру́сь, дерёшься, *past* **~дра́лся, ~драла́сь, ~дра́ло́сь** *pf.* (*of* **~дира́ться**) (**к**) **1.** to find fault (with), cavil (at), carp (at); to nag (at), pick (on); **п. к кому́-н. из-за пустяко́в** to find fault with s.o. over trifles. **2.** (*coll.*) to seize (on, upon); **п. к слу́чаю** to seize (upon) an opportunity.

приду́м|ать, аю *pf.* (*of* **~ывать**) to think (of), think up, devise, invent; **п. отгово́рку** to think up an excuse; **п. развлече́ние** to devise an entertainment.

приду́мыва|ть, ю *impf. of* **приду́мать**

придурковáтост|ь, и *f.* (*coll.*) silliness, daftness, imbecility.

придурковáт|ый (~, ~а) *adj.* (*coll.*) simple(-minded), daft, dopey; **п. взгляд** dopey expression.

при́дур|ь, и *f.*: **с ~ью** (*coll.*) a bit crazy, a bit daft.

придуш|и́ть, у́, ~́ишь *pf.* (*coll.*) to strangle, smother.

придыха́ни|е, я *nt.* (*ling.*) aspiration.

придыха́тельн|ый *adj.* (*ling.*) aspirate; *as n.* **п., ~ого** *m.* aspirate.

при|ду́ *see* **~йти́**

приеда́|ться, юсь *impf. of* **прие́сться**

прие́зд, а *m.* arrival, coming; **с ~ом!** welcome!

приезжа́|ть, ю *impf. of* **прие́хать**

приезжа́ющ|ий *pres. part. of* **приезжа́ть**; *as n.* **п., ~его** *m.*, **~ая, ~ей** *f.* newcomer, (new) arrival; **гости́ница для ~их** hotel.

прие́зж|ий *adj.* newly arrived; passing through; **~ая тру́ппа** troupe on tour; *as n.* **п., ~его** *m.*, **~ая, ~ей** *f.* newcomer; (*in hotel, etc.*) visitor; **~ие лю́ди** strangers (*opp. local inhabitants*).

приём, а *m.* **1.** receiving; reception; **часы́ ~а** (reception) hours, calling hours; (*of a doctor*) surgery (hours). **2.** reception, welcome; **оказа́ть кому́-н. раду́шный п.** to accord s.o. a hearty welcome. **3.** admittance (*to membership of association, party, etc.*). **4.** reception (= *formal party*). **5.** dose. **6.** go; motion, movement; **в оди́н п.** at one go; **вы́пить стака́н в два ~а** to drain a glass in two draughts; **испо́лнить кома́нду в три ~а** to execute a command in three movements. **7.** method, way, mode; device, trick (*also pej.*); (*sport*) hold, grip; **лече́бный п.** method of treatment; **жу́льнический п.** a rogue's trick, a cad's trick. **8.** (*mil.*) position; (*pl.*; *collect.*) manual; **п. «в ру́ку»** 'trail arms' position; **руже́йные ~ы** manual of the rifle; **~ы с ору́жием** manual of arms.

приёмк|а, и *f.* **1.** formal acceptance (*of building, etc., on completion of construction*). **2.** quality control (*procedure or organization*).

прие́млемост|ь, и *f.* acceptability; admissibility.

прие́млем|ый (~, ~а) *adj.* acceptable; admissible.

приёмн|ая, ой *f.* **1.** waiting-room. **2.** drawing-room; reception room.

приёмник[1], а *m.* wireless (set), radio (set), receiver.

приёмник[2], а *m.* reception centre (*for orphaned children, etc.*).

приёмн|ый *adj.* **1.** receiving; reception; **п. день** visiting day; at home day; **~ые часы́** (reception) hours, calling hours; (*of a doctor*) surgery (hours); **п. поко́й** casualty ward; **п. жёлоб** hopper; **~ое отве́рстие** intake, inlet. **2.** relating to admittance, entrance; **~ая коми́ссия** selection committee, selection board; **п. экза́мен** entrance examination. **3.** foster, adoptive; **п. оте́ц** foster-father; **~ая мать** foster-mother; **п. сын** adopted son, foster-son.

приёмо-переда́точный *adj.* (*radio*) two-way.

приёмочн|ый *adj.* reception; acceptance; **п. пункт** reception centre; **п. акт** acceptance certificate, inspection certificate; **~ое испыта́ние** acceptance test, official test.

приёмщик, а *m.* examiner, inspector (*of goods at a factory*).

приёмыш, а *m.* adopted child, foster-child.

при|е́сться, е́стся, едя́тся, *past* **~е́лся, ~е́лась** *pf.* (*of* **~еда́ться**) (+*d.*; *coll.*) to pall (on), tire, bore; **мне ~е́лась э́та рабо́та** I am fed up with this work.

прие́|хать, ду, дешь *pf.* (*of* **~зжа́ть**) to arrive, come (*not on foot*).

прижа́т|ый *p.p.p. of* **~ь; быть ~ым к стене́** (*fig.*) to have one's back to the wall.

приж|а́ть, му́, мёшь *pf.* (*of* **~има́ть**) **1. (к)** to press (to), clasp (to); **п. к земле́** (*mil.*) to pin down; **п. к груди́** to clasp to one's bosom; **п. к стене́** (*fig.*) to drive into a corner; **п. у́ши** (*of a horse*) to lay back its ears. **2.** (*fig.*) to press, bring pressure to bear (upon); **п. до́лжников** to press one's debtors.

приж|а́ться, му́сь, мёшься *pf.* (*of* **~има́ться**) **1. (к)** to press o.s. (to, against); to cuddle up (to), snuggle up (to), nestle up (to); **п. к стене́** to flatten o.s. against the wall. **2.** *pass. of* **~а́ть**

при|же́чь, жгу́, жжёшь, жгу́т, *past* **~жёг, ~жгла́** *pf.* (*of* **~жига́ть**) to cauterize, sear.

прижива́л|ка, ки *f. of* **~щик**

прижива́льщик, а *m.* **1.** (*hist.*) dependant. **2.** (*fig.*) hanger-on, sponger, parasite.

прижива́|ть(ся), ю(сь) *impf. of* **прижи́ть(ся)**

прижига́ни|е, я (*med.*) cauterization, searing.

прижига́|ть, ю *impf. of* **приже́чь**

прижи́зненный *adj.* occurring during one's lifetime.

прижима́|ть(ся), ю(сь) *impf. of* **прижа́ть(ся)**

прижи́мист|ый (~, ~а) *adj.* (*coll.*) close-fisted, tight-fisted, stingy.

прижи́мк|а, и *f.* (*fig.*, *coll.*) pressure; clamping down.

приж|и́ть, иву́, ивёшь, *past* **~ил, ~ила́, ~ило** *pf.* (*of* **~ива́ть**) (*coll.*) to beget (*usu. of extra-marital unions*).

приж|и́ться, иву́сь, ивёшься, *past* **~и́лся, ~ила́сь** *pf.* (*of* **~ива́ться**) **1.** to settle down, get acclimatized. **2.** (*of plants*) to take root, strike root.

приз[1], а, *pl.* **~ы́** *m.* prize; **переходя́щий п.** challenge prize; **получи́ть п.** to win a prize; **присуди́ть п.** (+*d.*) to award a prize (to).

приз[2], а *m.* (*naut.*, *leg.*) prize.

призаду́м|аться, аюсь *pf.* (*of* **~ываться**) to become thoughtful, become pensive.

призаду́мыва|ться, юсь *impf. of* **призаду́маться**

приза|ня́ть, йму́, ймёшь, *past* **~нял, ~няла́, ~няло** *pf.* (*coll.*) to borrow.

призва́ни|е, я *nt.* vocation, calling; **сле́довать своему́ ~ю** to follow one's vocation; **чу́вствовать п. к духо́вному са́ну** to have a vocation to go into the church; **хиру́рг по ~ю** a surgeon by vocation.

при|зва́ть, зову́, зовёшь, *past* **~зва́л, ~звала́, ~зва́ло** *pf.* (*of* **~зыва́ть**) to call, summon; to call upon, appeal; **п. на по́мощь** to call for help; **п. на вое́нную слу́жбу** to call up (*for mil. service*), call to the colours; **п. к поря́дку** to call to order; **п. прокля́тия на чью-н. го́лову** to call down curses on s.o.'s head.

при|зва́ться, зову́сь, зовёшься, *past* **~зва́лся, ~звала́сь, ~звало́сь** *pf.* (*of* **~зыва́ться**) **1.** to be called up. **2.** *pass. of* **~зва́ть**

при́звук, а *m.* additional sound.

призе́мист|ый (~, ~а) *adj.* stocky, squat; thickset.

приземле́ни|е, я *nt.* (*aeron.*) landing, touch-down.

приземл|и́ть, ю, и́шь *pf.* (*of* **~я́ть**) (*aeron.*) to land, bring in to land.

приземл|и́ться, ю́сь, и́шься *pf.* (*of* **~я́ться**) (*aeron.*) to land, touch down.

приземля́|ть(ся), ю(сь) *impf. of* **приземли́ть(ся)**

призёр, а *m.* prize-winner, prizeman.

при́зм|а, ы *f.* prism; **сквозь ~у** (+*g.*; *fig.*) in the light (of).

призмати́ческий *adj.* prismatic.

призна|ва́ть(ся), ю́(сь), ёшь(ся) *impf. of* **призна́ть(ся)**

при́знак, а *m.* sign; indications; **п. боле́зни** symptom; **служи́ть ~ом** (+*g.*) to be a sign (of); **обнару́живать ~и** (+*g.*) to show signs (of); **име́ются все ~и того́, что** there is every indication that; **не подава́ть ~ов жи́зни** to show no sign of life; **по ~у** (+*g.*) on the basis (of).

призна́ни|е, я *nt.* **1.** confession, declaration; admission, acknowledgement; **нево́льное п.** involuntary admission; **п. вины́** avowal of guilt; **п. в любви́** declaration of love; **по о́бщему ~ю** by general admission. **2.** recognition; **п. де-фа́кто** (*leg.*, *pol.*) de facto recognition; **получи́ть п.** to obtain, win recognition; **получи́ть всео́бщее п.** to be generally recognized.

при́зн|анный *p.p.p. of* **~а́ть** *and adj.* acknowledged, recognized.

призна́тельност|ь, и *f.* gratitude.

призна́тел|ьный (~ен, ~ьна) *adj.* grateful.

призна́|ть, ю *pf.* (*of* **~ва́ть**) **1.** to recognize; to spot, identify; **вы меня́ не ~ли?** did you not recognize me?; **я ~л в нём иностра́нца по оде́жде** I spotted him as a foreigner by his dress. **2.** (*leg.*, *pol.*) to recognize; **п. прави́тельство** to recognize a government. **3.** to admit, own, acknowledge; **п. вину́, п. себя́ вино́вным** (*leg.*) to plead guilty; **п. свою́ оши́бку** to admit one's mistake; **п. себя́ побеждённым** to acknowledge defeat. **4.** to deem, vote; **п. ну́жным** to deem (it) necessary; **п. недействи́тельным** to declare invalid, nullify; **п. (не)вино́вным** to find (not) guilty; **п. неуда́чным** to vote a failure.

призна́|ться, юсь *pf.* (*of* **~ва́ться**) **(в**+*p.*) to confess (to), own (to); **п. в любви́** to make a declaration of love; **п. в преступле́нии** to confess to a crime; **на́до п., что** it must be admitted that, the truth is that; **п. (сказа́ть)** to tell the truth; **п., и фами́лии его́ не зна́ю** to tell the truth I don't even know his name.

призов|о́й *adj. of* **приз; ~ы́е де́ньги** prize-money; **~о́е су́дно** (*naut.*, *leg.*) prize.

призо́р, а *m.*: **без ~а** (*coll.*) untended, neglected.

при́зрак, а *m.* spectre, ghost, phantom, apparition; **гоня́ться за ~ами** to catch at shadows.

при́зрачност|ь, и *f.* illusoriness.

при́зрач|ный (~ен, ~на) *adj.* **1.** spectral, ghostly, phantasmal. **2.** (*fig.*) illusory, imagined; **~ная опа́сность** imagined danger.

призрева́|ть, ю *impf. of* **призре́ть**

призре́ни|е, я *nt.* care, charity; **дом ~я бе́дных** almshouse, poor people's home.

призр|е́ть, ю́, ~и́шь *pf.* (*of* **~ева́ть**) to support by charity.

призы́в, а *m.* **1.** call, appeal; **откли́кнуться на чей-н. п.** to respond to s.o.'s call. **2.** slogan; **первома́йские ~ы** May Day slogans. **3.** (*mil.*) call-up, conscription. **4.** (*collect.*; *mil.*) levy; (group of) conscripts, draft; **ле́нинский п.** (*hist.*) 'The Lenin enrolment' (*mass enrolment of new members of CPSU following death of V. I. Lenin*).

призыва́|ть(ся), ю(сь) *impf. of* **призва́ть(ся)**

призывни́к, а́ *m.* man called up for military service; man due for call-up.

призывно́й *adj.* call-up; **п. во́зраст** call-up age; **п. уча́сток** reception unit.

призы́вный *adj.* invocatory; inviting; **п. клич** call.

при́иск, а *m.* mine (*for precious metals*); **золоты́е ~и** gold-field(s).

приискáни|е, я *nt.* finding.

приискáтел|ь, я *m.* miner, mine worker.

при|иска́ть, ищу́, и́щешь *pf.* (*of* **~и́скивать**) to find.

прии́скива|ть, ю *impf.* (*coll.*) **1.** *impf. of* **приискáть. 2.** (*impf. only*) to look for, hunt for; **мы ~ем кварти́ру без ме́бели** we are looking for unfurnished accommodation.

приисково́й *adj. of* **при́иск**

при|йти́, ду́, дёшь, *past* **~шёл, ~шла́** *pf.* (*of* **~ходи́ть**) (*in var. senses*) to come; to arrive; **п. пе́рвым** to come in first; **п. в восто́рг (от)** to go into raptures (over); **п. в плохо́е настрое́ние** to get into a bad mood; **п. в у́жас** to be horrified; **п. в я́рость** to fly into a rage; **п. в го́лову кому́-н., на ум кому́-н.** to occur to s.o., strike s.o., cross one's mind; **мысль ~шла́ мне в го́лову** the idea occurred to me; **п. в себя́, п. в чу́вство** to come round, regain consciousness; (*fig.*) to come to one's senses; **п. к концу́** to come to an end; **п. к заключе́нию, п. к убежде́нию** to come to the conclusion, arrive at a conclusion; **п. к соглаше́нию** to come to an agreement.

при|йти́сь, ду́сь, дёшься, *past* **~шёлся, ~шла́сь** *pf.* (*of* **~ходи́ться**) **1.** (**по**+*d.*) to fit; **ковёр ~шёлся как раз по разме́рам спа́льни** the carpet fitted the bedroom floor just right; **п. кому́-н. по вку́су, по нра́ву** to be to s.o.'s taste, liking; **га́лстук ~шёлся мне по вку́су** the tie was just what I wanted. **2.** (**на**+*a.*; *of dates, days or occasions*) to fall (on); **Па́сха ~шла́сь на 28-ое ма́рта** Easter fell on the 28th of March. **3.** (*impers.*+*d.*) to have (to); **нам ~шло́сь подожда́ть ещё два часа́** we had to wait another two hours; **ей ~дётся неме́дленно верну́ться в Москву́** she will have to return to Moscow immediately. **4.** (*impers.*+*d.*) to happen (to), fall to the lot (of); **мне ~шло́сь быть ря́дом в тот моме́нт, когда́ он упа́л в о́бморок** I happened to be standing by when he fainted; **им ту́го ~шло́сь** they had a rough time; **как ~дётся** (*coll.*) anyhow, at haphazard. **5.** (*impers.*; **на**+*a.* *or* **с**+*g.*; *coll.*) to be owing (to, from); **на ка́ждого ~шло́сь по фу́нту** they got a pound each; **с вас ~дётся де́сять рубле́й** there is ten roubles to come from you.

прика́з, а *m.* **1.** order, command; **по ~у** by order; **п. по войска́м** order of the day; **п. о выступле́нии** (*mil.*) marching orders; **отда́ть п.** to give an order, issue an order. **2.** (*hist.*) office, department.

приказа́ни|е, я *nt.* order, command, injunction.

прика|за́ть, жу́, ~жешь *pf.* (*of* **~зывать**) (+*d.*) to order, command; to give orders; to direct; **п. до́лго жить** (*coll.*) to pass on, depart this life; **что ~жете?** what do you wish?, what can I do for you?; **как ~жете** as you please, as you wish; **как ~жете понима́ть э́то?** how am I supposed to take this?; what do you mean by this?

прика́з|ный 1. *adj. of* **~ 1.**; **в ~ном поря́дке** in the form of an order. **2.** *adj.* (*hist.*) departmental; **п. язы́к** chancery language (*opp. literary language*); *as n.* **п., ~ного** *m.* clerk, scribe. **3.** *as n.* (*obs.*) petty official.

прика́зчик, а *m.* (*obs.*) **1.** shop-assistant, salesman. **2.** steward, bailiff.

прика́зыва|ть, ю *impf. of* **приказа́ть**

прика́лыва|ть, ю *impf. of* **приколо́ть**

прика́нчива|ть, ю *impf. of* **прико́нчить**

прикарма́нива|ть, ю *impf. of* **прикарма́нить**

прикарма́н|ить, ю, ишь *pf.* (*of* **~ивать**) (*coll.*) to pocket.

прика́рмлива|ть, ю *impf.* **1.** *impf. of* **прикорми́ть. 2.** (*impf. only*) to give additional food (*during the weaning period*).

прикаса́|ться, юсь *impf. of* **прикосну́ться**

прика|ти́ть, чу́, ~тишь *pf.* (*of* **~тывать**) **1.** (**к**) to roll up (to). **2.** (*coll.*) to roll up, turn up.

прика́тыва|ть, ю *impf. of* **прикати́ть**

прики́дыва|ть(ся), ю(сь) *impf. of* **прики́нуть(ся)**

прики́|нуть, ну, нешь *pf.* (*of* **~дывать**) **1.** to throw in, add. **2.** to estimate (approximately); **п. на веса́х** to weigh; **п. в уме́** (*fig.*) to weigh (up), ponder.

прики́|нуться, нусь, нешься *pf.* (*of* **~дываться**) (+*i.*; *coll.*) to pretend (to be), feign; **п. больны́м** to pretend to be ill, feign illness; **п. лисо́й** to fawn, toady; **п. раска́явшимся** to feign repentance; **он ~нулся, что не ви́дит меня́** he pretended that he could not see me.

прикла́д[1], **а** *m.* butt, butt-stock (*of firearm*).

прикла́д[2], **а** *m.* trimmings (*used by tailor or boot-maker*).

прикла́дк|а, и *f.* levelling (*of rifle*); position; **п. лёжа, п. с коле́на, п. сто́я** lying, kneeling, standing position (*with rifle in hand*).

прикладн|о́й *adj.* applied; **~о́е иску́сство** applied art(s); **~а́я фи́зика** applied physics.

прикла́дыва|ть(ся), ю(сь) *impf. of* **приложи́ть(ся)**

прикле́ива|ть(ся), ю(сь) *impf. of* **прикле́ить(ся)**

прикле́|ить, ю, ишь *pf.* (*of* **~ивать**) to stick; to glue; to paste; to affix; **п. ма́рку** to stick on a stamp; **п. афи́шу к стене́** to stick (up) a bill on a wall.

прикле́|иться, ится *pf.* (*of* **~иваться**) (**к**) to stick (to), adhere (to).

приклеп|а́ть, а́ю *pf.* (*of* **~ывать**) to rivet.

приклёпк|а, и *f.* riveting.

приклёпыва|ть, ю *impf. of* **приклепа́ть**

приклон|и́ть, ю́, ~ишь *pf.*; **п. го́лову** to lay one's head; **у него́ не́где п. го́лову** he has nowhere to lay his head; **п. слух, п. у́хо** (*obs.*) to listen intently.

приключ|а́ть(ся), а́ю, а́ет(ся) *impf. of* **~и́ть(ся)**

приключе́ни|е, я *nt.* adventure.

приключе́нческий *adj.* adventure; **п. рома́н** adventure story.

приключе́нчеств|о, а *nt.* adventure literature.

приключ|и́ть, у́, и́шь *pf.* (*of* **~а́ть**) (*tech.*) to connect up.

приключ|и́ться, и́тся *pf.* (*of* **~а́ться**) (*coll.*) to happen, occur.

прикноп|и́ть, лю́, ~ишь *pf.* to pin up (*with a drawing pin*).

прико́в|анный *p.p.p. of* **~а́ть**; **п. к посте́ли** bed-ridden, confined to one's bed.

прик|ова́ть, ую́, уёшь *pf.* (*of* **~о́вывать**) **1.** (**к**) to chain (to). **2.** (*fig.*) to chain; to rivet; **на́ше внима́ние ~ова́ла к себе́ их блестя́щая фо́рма** our attention was riveted on their gorgeous uniforms; **страх ~ова́л нас к ме́сту** fear rooted us to the spot.

прико́выва|ть, ю *impf. of* **прикова́ть**

прико́л, а *m.* stake; **пала́точный п.** tent-peg; **стоя́ть на ~е** (*naut.*) to be laid up, be idle.

прикола́чива|ть, ю *impf. of* **приколоти́ть**

приколо|ти́ть, чу́, ~тишь *pf.* (*of* **прикола́чивать**) to nail, fasten with nails.

прикол|о́ть, ю́, ~ешь *pf.* (*of* **прика́лывать**) **1.** to pin, fasten with a pin. **2.** (*coll.*) to stab, transfix; **п. штыко́м** to bayonet.

прикомандир|ова́ть, у́ю *pf.* (*of* **~о́вывать**) (**к**) to attach (to), second (to).

прикомандиро́выва|ть, ю *impf. of* **прикомандирова́ть**

прико́нч|ить, у, ишь *pf.* (*of* **прика́нчивать**) (*coll.*) **1.** to use up. **2.** (*fig.*) to finish off.

прикоп|и́ть, лю́, ∸ишь *pf.* (*+a. or g.*; *coll.*) to save (up), put by.
прико́рм, а *m.* **1.** lure, bait (*for birds or fish*). **2.** additional food.
прикорм|и́ть, лю́, ∸ишь *pf.* (*of* **прика́рмливать**) to lure (*by putting out food*).
прико́рм|ка, ки *f.* = ~
прикорн|у́ть, у́, ёшь *pf.* (*coll.*) **(к)** to lean up (against), prop o.s. up (against) (*with a view to taking a nap*); **п. на дива́не** to curl up on the sofa.
прикоснове́ни|е, я *nt.* **1.** touch; **то́чка ~я** point of contact. **2.** (*sg. only*) concern; **я не име́ю никако́го ~я к э́тому де́лу** this affair is no concern of mine, is nothing to do with me.
прикоснове́нност|ь, и *f.* **(к)** concern (in), involvement (in).
прикоснове́н|ный (~, ~на) *adj.* **(к)** concerned (in), involved (in), implicated (in); **он был ~ к убийству** he was implicated in a murder.
прикосн|у́ться, у́сь ёшься *pf.* (*of* **прикаса́ться**) **(к)** to touch (lightly).
прикра́с|а, ы *f.* (*usu. pl.*) (*coll.*) embellishment; **без ~** unvarnished, unadorned; **рассказа́ть без ~** to give a straightforward account.
прикра́|сить, шу, сишь *pf.* (*of* **~шивать**) to embellish, embroider (*in speech*).
прикра́шива|ть, ю *impf. of* **прикра́сить**
прикрепи́тельный *adj.*: **п. тало́н** registration card (*document certifying that customer is registered with stated retailer for supply of provisions, etc.*).
прикреп|и́ть, лю́, и́шь *pf.* (*of* **~ля́ть**) **(к) 1.** to fasten (to). **2.** (*fig.*) to attach (to); **п. де́тский сад к больни́це** to attach a kindergarten to a hospital.
прикреп|и́ться, лю́сь, и́шься *pf.* (*of* **~ля́ться**) **(к) 1.** to register (at, with). **2.** *pass. of* **~и́ть**
прикрепле́ни|е, я *nt.* **1.** fastening. **2.** (*fig.*) attachment; **п. к земле́** (*hist.*) attaching to the soil (*as serf*). **3.** registration.
прикрепля́|ть(ся), ю(сь) *impf. of* **прикрепи́ть(ся)**
прикри́кива|ть, ю *impf. of* **прикри́кнуть**
прикри́к|нуть, ну, нешь *pf.* (*of* **~ивать**) **(на+*a.*)** to shout (at), raise one's voice (at).
прикру|ти́ть, чу́, ∸тишь *pf.* (*of* **∸чивать**) **1. (к)** to tie (to), bind (to), fasten (to). **2.** (*coll.*) to turn down (a wick).
прикру́чива|ть, ю *impf. of* **прикрути́ть**
прикрыва́|ть(ся), ю(сь) *impf. of* **прикры́ть(ся)**
прикры́ти|е, я *nt.* cover; escort; (*fig.*) screen, cloak; **под ~ем** (*+g.*) under cover (of), screened (by); **артиллери́йское п.** artillery cover; **п. истреби́телями** fighter cover, fighter escort.
прикр|ы́ть, о́ю, о́ешь *pf.* (*of* **~ыва́ть**) **1.** (*+i.*) to cover (with); to screen; **п. кастрю́лю кры́шкой** to put the lid on a saucepan. **2.** to protect, shelter, shield; **п. глаза́ руко́й** to shade, shield one's eyes (with one's hand); **п. наступле́ние артилле́рией** to cover an attack with an artillery barrage. **3.** (*fig.*) to cover (up), conceal, screen; **п. своё неве́жество** to conceal one's ignorance. **4.** (*coll.*) to close down, wind up.
прикр|ы́ться, о́юсь, о́ешься *pf.* (*of* **~ыва́ться**) **1.** (*+i.*) to cover o.s. (with); (*fig.*) to use as a cover, take refuge (in), shelter (behind); **он ~ы́лся положе́нием иностра́нца** he took refuge in the fact of being a foreigner. **2.** (*coll.*) to close down, go out of business. **3.** *pass. of* **~ы́ть**
прикуп|а́ть, а́ю *impf. of* **~и́ть**
прикуп|и́ть, лю́, ∸ишь *pf.* (*of* **~а́ть**) (*+a. or g.*) to buy (*some more*).
прику́пк|а, и *f.* additional purchase.
прику́рива|ть, ю *impf. of* **прикури́ть**
прикур|и́ть, ю́, ∸ишь *pf.* (*of* **∸ивать**) **(у кого́-н.)** to get a light (*from s.o.'s cigarette*).
прику́с, а *m.* bite.
прику|си́ть, шу́, ∸сишь *pf.* (*of* **∸сывать**) to bite; **п. (себе́) язы́к** to bite one's tongue; (*fig., coll.*) to hold one's tongue, keep one's mouth shut.
прику́сыва|ть, ю *impf. of* **прикуси́ть**
прила́в|ок, ка *m.* counter; **рабо́тник ~ка** counter hand, salesman, (shop) assistant.
прилага́|емый *pres. part. pass. of* **~ть** *and adj.* accompanying; enclosed; subjoined; **п. почто́вый перево́д** the enclosed postal order.
прилага́тельн|ый *adj.*: **и́мя ~ое** (*or as n.* **~ое, ~ого** *nt.*) adjective.
прилага́|ть, ю *impf. of* **приложи́ть**
прила́|дить, жу, дишь *pf.* (*of* **~живать**) **(к)** to fit (to), adjust (to).
прила́жива|ть, ю *impf. of* **прила́дить**
приласка́|ть, ю *pf.* to caress, fondle, pet.
приласка́|ться, юсь *pf.* **(к)** to snuggle up (to).
прилгн|у́ть, у́, ёшь *pf.* (*coll.*) to insert fabrications (*into a narrative*).
прилега́|ть, ет *impf.* **(к) 1.** (*pf.* **приле́чь**[1]) to fit. **2.** (*no pf.*) to adjoin, be adjacent (to), border (upon); **сад ~ет к те́ннисному ко́рту** the garden adjoins the tennis court.
прилега́|ющий *pres. part. of* **~ть** *and adj.* **1.** close-fitting, tight-fitting. **2. (к)** adjoining, adjacent (to), contiguous (to).
прилежа́ни|е, я *nt.* diligence, industry, assiduousness; application.
прилежа́щий *adj.* (*math.*) adjacent, adjoining, contiguous.
приле́ж|ный (~ен, ~на) *adj.* diligent, industrious, assiduous.
прилеп|и́ть, лю́, ∸ишь *pf.* (*of* **~ля́ть**) **(к)** to stick (to, on).
прилеп|и́ться, лю́сь, ∸ишься *pf.* (*of* **~ля́ться**) **1. (к)** to stick (to, on). **2.** *pass. of* **~и́ть**
прилепля́|ть(ся), ю(сь) *impf. of* **прилепи́ть(ся)**
прилёт, а *m.* arrival (*by air*).
прилет|а́ть, а́ю *impf. of* **~е́ть**
приле|те́ть, чу́, ти́шь *pf.* (*of* **~та́ть**) **1.** to arrive (*by air*), fly in. **2.** (*fig., coll.*) to fly, come flying.
при|ле́чь[1], **ля́жет, ля́гут,** *past* **~лёг, ~легла́** *pf. of* **~лега́ть**
при|ле́чь[2], **ля́гу, ля́жешь, ля́гут,** *past* **~лёг, ~легла́** *pf.* **1.** to lie down (*for a short while*). **2.** (*of standing crops*) to be laid flat.
прили́в, а *m.* **1.** flow, flood (*of tide*); rising tide; (*fig.*) surge, influx; **волна́ ~а** tidal wave; **п. и отли́в** ebb and flow; **п. негодова́ния** (up)surge of indignation. **2.** (*med.*) congestion; **п. кро́ви** rush of blood; (*fig.*) **п. эне́ргии** burst of energy. **3.** (*tech.*) boss, lug; (*naut.*) cleat.
прилива́|ть, ет *impf. of* **прили́ть**
прили́вный *adj.* tidal.
прили́з|анный *p.p.p. of* **~а́ть; ~анные во́лосы** smarmed-down hair.
прили|за́ть, жу́, ∸жешь *pf.* (*of* **∸зывать**) to lick smooth.
прили́зыва|ть, ю *impf. of* **прилиза́ть**
прилип|а́ть, а́ет *impf. of* **∸нуть**
прили́п|нуть, нет, *past* **~, ~ла** *pf.* (*of* **~а́ть**) **(к)** to stick (to), adhere (to).
прили́пчив|ый (~, ~а) *adj.* (*coll.*) **1.** sticking, adhesive. **2.** (*fig.*) boring, tiresome. **3.** (*of diseases*) catching.
прили́стник, а *m.* (*bot.*) stipule.
при|ли́ть, льёт, *past* **~ли́л, ~лила́, ~ли́ло** *pf.* (*of* **~лива́ть**) **(к)** to flow (to); (of blood) to rush (to); **кровь ~лила́ к её щека́м** blood rushed to her cheeks.
прили́честв|овать, ует *impf.* (*+d.*; *obs.*) to befit, become.
прили́чи|е, я *nt.* decency, propriety; decorum; **соблюда́ть ~я** to observe the decencies, the proprieties.
прили́ч|ный (~ен, ~на) *adj.* **1.** decent, proper; decorous, seemly; **п. анекдо́т** a clean story. **2.** (*+d.*; *obs.*) fitting; appropriate (to). **3.** (*coll.*) decent, tolerable, fair; **~ная зарпла́та** a decent wage.
приложе́ни|е, я *nt.* **1.** application; **п. я́дерной фи́зики к констру́кции подво́дных ло́док** the application of nuclear physics to the design of submarines. **2.** affixing; apposition; **п. печа́ти** affixing of a seal. **3.** enclosure (*of document, etc., with letter*). **4.** supplement (*to newspaper, periodical, etc.*). **5.** appendix (*to a book*). **6.** (*gram.*) apposition.
прилож|и́ть, у́, ∸ишь *pf.* **1.** (*impf.* **прикла́дывать**) **(к)** to put (to), hold (to); **п. ру́ку ко лбу** to put one's hand to one's head; **п. ру́ку** to put one's hand (to), take a hand (in); to add one's signature (to). **2.** (*impf.* **прикла́дывать** *and* **прилага́ть**) to add, join; to enclose; to affix; **п. к заявле́нию характери́стику** to enclose a testimonial with an application; **п. печа́ть** to affix a seal. **3.** (*impf.* **прилага́ть**) to apply; **п. си́лу** to apply force; **п. все уси́лия**

to strain every effort; **п. всё стара́ние** to do one's best, try one's hardest.

прилож|и́ться, у́сь, ∸ишься *pf.* (*of* **прикла́дываться**) **1.** (+*i.*, **к**) to put (*one's ear, eye, or mouth*) (to); **п. гла́зом к замо́чной сква́жине** to put one's eye to the keyhole; **п. (губа́ми)** to kiss. **2.** to take aim. **3.** *pass. of* **~и́ть; остально́е ∸ится** the rest will come.

прилуне́ни|е, я *nt.* (*aeron.*) Moon landing, moonfall.

прилун|и́ться, ю́сь, и́шься *pf.* to land on the Moon.

прильн|у́ть, у́, ёшь *pf. of* **льнуть**

при́м|а, ы *f.* (*mus.*) **1.** tonic. **2.** first string, top string. **3.** first violin.

при́ма-балери́на, при́мы-балери́ны *f.* prima ballerina.

примадо́нн|а, ы *f.* prima donna.

примá|заться, жусь, жешься *pf.* (*of* **~зываться**) (**к**; *coll.*, *pej.*) to attach o.s. (to), get in (with).

примá́зыва|ться, юсь *impf. of* **примá́заться**

примáнива|ть, ю *impf. of* **примани́ть**

приман|и́ть, ю́, ∸ишь *pf.* (*of* **∸ивать**) (*coll.*) to lure; to decoy; to entice, allure.

примáнк|а, и *f.* bait, lure; (*fig.*) enticement, allurement.

примáс, а *m.* (*eccl.*) primate.

примáт[1], **а** *m.* (*phil.*) primacy; pre-eminence.

примáт[2], **а** *m.* (*zool.*) primate.

примáчива|ть, ю *impf. of* **примочи́ть**

примелькá|ться, юсь *pf.* (*coll.*) to become familiar; **её лицó мне óчень ~лось** her face is very familiar to me.

применéни|е, я *nt.* application; use; **п. к мéстности** (*mil.*) use of ground, adaptation to terrain; **нáши мéтоды получи́ли ширóкое п.** our methods have been widely adopted; **в ~и (к)** in application (to).

примени́мост|ь, и *f.* applicability.

примени́м|ый (~, ~а) *adj.* applicable, suitable.

примени́тельно *adv.* **(к)** conformably (to), in conformity (with); as applied (to).

примен|и́ть, ю́, ∸ишь *pf.* (*of* **~я́ть**) to apply; to employ, use; **п. свои́ знáния** to apply one's knowledge; **п. на прáктике** to put into practice.

примен|и́ться, ю́сь, ∸ишься *pf.* (*of* **~я́ться**) (**к**) to adapt o.s. (to), conform (to).

примéр, а *m.* **1.** example, instance; **привести́ п.** to give an example; **привести́ в п.** to cite as an example; **поясни́ть ~ом** to illustrate by means of an example; **к ~у** (*coll.*) by way of illustration, for example. **2.** example; model; **брать п. с когó-н., слéдовать чьему́-н. ~у** to follow s.o.'s example; **подавáть п.** to set an example; **показáть п.** to give an example, give the lead; **для ~а** as an example; **по ~у** (+*g.*) after the example (of), on the pattern (of); **не в п.** (+*d.*; *coll.*) unlike; (+*comp.*) far more, by far; **не в п. прóчим** unlike the others; **онá сегóдня игрáет не в п. лу́чше, чем игрáла на той недéле** her playing today is better by far than it was last week.

примерз|áть, áю *impf. of* **∸нуть**

примёрз|нуть, ну, нешь, *past* **~, ~ла** *pf.* (*of* **~áть**) **(к)** to freeze (to).

примéр|ить, ю, ишь *pf.* (*of* **мéрить 2.** *and* **~я́ть**) to try on, to fit.

примéр|иться, юсь, ишься *pf.* (*of* **~я́ться**) (*coll.*) to contrive.

примéрк|а, и *f.* trying on; fitting.

примéрно *adv.* **1.** in exemplary fashion; **п. вести́ себя́** to be an example. **2.** approximately, roughly.

примéр|ный (~ен, ~на) *adj.* **1.** exemplary, model; **п. перевóд** a model version. **2.** approximate, rough; **~ная ци́фра** ball-park figure.

примéрочн|ая, ой *f.* fitting-room.

пример|я́ть(ся), я́ю(сь) *impf. of* **∸ить(ся)**

при́мес|ь, и *f.* admixture; dash; (*fig.*) touch; **без ~ей** unadulterated; **молокó с ~ью кóфе** milk with a dash of coffee.

примéт|а, ы *f.* sign, token; mark; **имéть на ~е** to have one's eye (on); **быть на ~е** to be before the eye, be the centre of attention.

примет|áть, áю *pf.* (*of* **∸ывать**) to tack (on), stitch (on).

примé|тить, чу, тишь *pf.* (*of* **~чáть**) to notice, perceive.

примéтливост|ь, и *f.* power(s) of observation.

примéтлив|ый (~, ~а) *adj.* (*coll.*) observant.

примéтно *adv.* perceptibly, visibly, noticeably; **он п. похудéл** he has grown perceptibly thinner.

примéт|ный (~ен, ~на) *adj.* **1.** perceptible, visible, noticeable. **2.** conspicuous, prominent.

примётыва|ть, ю *impf. of* **приметáть**

примечáни|е, я *nt.* **1.** note, footnote; **снабди́ть ~ями** to annotate. **2.** (*pl.*) comment(s), commentary.

примечáтельност|ь, и *f.* noteworthiness.

примечáтел|ьный (~ен, ~ьна) *adj.* noteworthy, notable, remarkable.

примечá|ть, ю *impf.* **1.** *impf. of* **примéтить. 2.** (*impf. only*) (**за**+*i.*; *coll.*) to keep an eye (on); **~й за ним, а то он доéст все конфéты** keep an eye on him, or else he'll finish off all the sweets.

примеш|áть, áю *pf.* (*of* **∸ивать**) (+*a. or g.*) to add, admix; (*tech.*) to alloy.

примéшива|ть, ю *impf. of* **примешáть**

приминá|ть, ю *impf. of* **примя́ть**

примирéн|ец, ца *m.* (*pej.*) conciliator, compromiser.

примирéни|е, я *nt.* reconciliation.

примирéнческий *adj.* (*pej.*) compromising.

примирéнчеств|о, а *nt.* (*pej.*) conciliatoriness, spirit of compromise, appeasement.

примир|и́мый (~и́м, ~и́ма) *pres. part. pass. of* **~и́ть** *and adj.* reconcilable.

примири́тел|ь, я *m.* reconciler, conciliator, peace-maker.

примири́тел|ьный (~ен, ~ьна) *adj.* conciliatory.

примир|и́ть, ю́, и́шь *pf.* (*of* **~я́ть**) to reconcile; to conciliate; **п. супру́гов** to reconcile a husband and wife; **п. когó-н. с необходи́мостью бóльших жертв** to reconcile s.o. to the necessity for great sacrifices.

примир|и́ться, ю́сь, и́шься *pf.* (*of* **~я́ться**) (**с**+*i.*) **1.** to be reconciled (to), make it up (with). **2.** to reconcile o.s. (to); **п. с неудóбствами** to reconcile o.s. to, accept discomforts.

примир|я́ть(ся), я́ю(сь) *impf. of* **~и́ть(ся)**

примити́в, а *m.* **1.** (*art*) primitive. **2.** primitive artefact; specimen, *etc.*, in rude, undeveloped state. **3.** (*coll.*) primitive pers.

примитиви́зм, а *m.* (*art*) primitivism.

примити́в|ный (~ен, ~на) *adj.* primitive; rude, crude.

примкн|у́ть, у́, ёшь *pf.* (*of* **примыкáть**) (**к**) **1.** to fix (to), attach (to); **п. штыки́!** fix bayonets! **2.** (*fig.*) to join, attach o.s. (to); to side (with).

примóлкн|уть, у, ешь *pf.* (*coll.*) to fall silent.

примóрский *adj.* seaside; maritime; **п. курóрт** seaside resort.

примóрь|е, я *nt.* littoral, seaside.

примо|сти́ть, щу́, сти́шь *pf.* (*coll.*) to find room (for), stick (*in a crowded place or inconvenient surroundings*).

примо|сти́ться, щу́сь, сти́шься *pf.* (*coll.*) to find room for o.s.; to perch o.s. (*in a crowded place or inconvenient surroundings*).

примоч|и́ть, у́, ∸ишь *pf.* (*of* **примáчивать**) to bathe, moisten; **п. себé глаз** to bathe one's eye.

примóчк|а, и *f.* wash, lotion; embrocation; **свинцóвая п.** Goulard (water); **п. для глаз** eye-lotion.

при́мул|а, ы *f.* primula, primrose.

при́мус, а *m.* Primus (*propr.*)(-stove).

при́мус|ный *adj. of* **~; ~ная игóлка** Primus (*propr.*) pricker.

примч|áть, у́, и́шь *pf.* (*coll.*) **1.** to bring in a hurry, hurry along with. **2.** = **~áться**

примч|áться, у́сь, и́шься *pf.* to come tearing along.

примыкáни|е, я *nt.* **1.** contiguity. **2.** (*gram.*) agglutination.

примыкá|ть, ю *impf.* **1.** *impf. of* **примкну́ть. 2.** (*impf. only*) (**к**) to adjoin, border (upon), abut (upon).

примыкá|ющий *pres. part. act. of* **~ть** *and adj.* affiliated.

при|мя́ть, мну́, мнёшь *pf.* (*of* **~минáть**) to crush, flatten; to trample down, tread down.

принадлеж|áть, у́, и́шь *impf.* **1.** (+*d.*) to belong (to); to appertain (to); **п. по прáву** to belong by right, belong rightfully; **ему́ ~и́т честь э́того откры́тия** to him belongs the credit for this discovery. **2.** **(к)** to belong (to), be a member (of); **п. к аэроклу́бу** to belong to a flying club.

принадлéжност|ь, и *f.* **1.** **(к)** belonging (to), membership (of); **п. к ассоциáции** membership of an association. **2.** (*obs.*) property. **3.** **по ~и** to the proper quarter, through the proper channels. **4.** (*pl.*) accessories, appurtenances; equipment; outfit, tackle; **бри́твенные ~и** shaving tackle; **туалéтные ~и** toiletries; **канцеля́рские ~и** office equipment; **~и костю́ма** accessories (*gloves, handbag, etc.*).

прина|лéчь, ля́гу, ля́жешь, ля́гут, *past* **~лёг, ~леглá** *pf.* (**на**+*a.*; *coll.*) **1.** to rest lightly (upon). **2.** to apply o.s. (to), go (at, to) with a will; **п. на вёсла** to ply one's oars vigorously, pull vigorously.

принаря|ди́ть, жу́, ~ди́шь *pf.* (*of* **~жáть**) (*coll.*) to dress up, deck out.

принаря|ди́ться, жу́сь, ~ди́шься *pf.* (*of* **~жáться**) (*coll.*) to doll *or* get o.s. up; to get dolled up.

принаряжá|ть(ся), ю(сь) *impf. of* **принаряди́ть(ся)**

принево́лива|ть, ю *impf. of* **принево́лить**

принево́л|ить, ю, ишь *pf.* (*of* **~ивать**) (+*inf.*; *coll.*) to force (to), make; **они́ ~или его́ жени́ться** they made him marry.

принес|ти́, у́, ёшь, *past* **~, ~лá** *pf.* (*of* **приноси́ть**) **1.** to bring (*also fig.*); to fetch; **п. обрáтно** to bring back; **~лá тебя́** *etc.*, **нелёгкая!** why the devil did you, *etc.*, have to turn up?; **п. благодáрность** to express gratitude, tender thanks; **п. жáлобу** (**на**+*a.*) to bring, lodge a complaint (against); **п. счáстье** to bring luck; **п. в жéртву** to sacrifice. **2.** to bear, yield; to bring in; **п. плоды́** to bear fruit, yield fruit; **нáша ко́шка ~лá шесть котя́т** our cat had six kittens; **п. большо́й дохо́д** to bring in big revenue, show a large return; **п. по́льзу** to be of use, be of benefit.

принес|ти́сь, у́сь, ёшься, *past* **~ся, ~лáсь** *pf.* (*of* **приноси́ться**) (*coll.*) **1.** to come tearing along. **2.** *pass. of* **~ти́**; (*of sounds, etc.*) to be borne along.

принижá|ть, ю *impf. of* **прини́зить**

принижéни|е, я *nt.* disparagement, belittling, depreciation.

прини́|женный *p.p.p. of* **~зить** *and adj.* humbled, submissive.

прини́|зить, жу, зишь *pf.* (*of* **~жáть**) **1.** to humble, humiliate. **2.** to disparage, belittle, depreciate; **п. значéние морско́го фло́та** to belittle the importance of the Navy.

приник|áть, áю *impf. of* **~нуть**

прини́к|нуть, ну, нешь, *past* **~, ~ла** *pf.* (*of* **~áть**) (**к**) to press o.s. (against), press o.s. close (to); to nestle up (against); **п. у́хом к замо́чной сквáжине** to put one's ear to the keyhole.

принимá|ть, ю *impf.* **1.** *impf. of* **приня́ть**. **2.** (*impf. only*) to be 'at home', entertain; to receive (*guests, visitors, patients*); **они́ ~ют по четвергáм** they are 'at home' on Thursdays; **онá чáсто ~ет** she does a lot of entertaining; **до́ктор Петро́в сего́дня не ~ет** Doctor Petrov does not see patients today. **3.** to deliver (*at birth of child*).

принимá|ться, юсь *impf. of* **приня́ться**

принорáвлива|ть(ся), ю(сь) *impf. of* **приноро́вить(ся)**

приноров|и́ть, лю́, и́шь *pf.* (*of* **принорáвливать**) (*coll.*) to fit, adapt, adjust; **п. переéзд на но́вую квартиру к лéтним кани́кулам** to arrange a move to new lodgings to fit in with the summer holidays.

приноров|и́ться, лю́сь, и́шься *pf.* (*of* **принорáвливаться**) (**к**; *coll.*) to adapt o.s. (to), accommodate o.s. (to).

прино|си́ть(ся), шу́(сь), ~сишь(ся) *impf. of* **принести́(сь)**

приношéни|е, я *nt.* gift, offering.

при́нтер, а *m.* (*comput.*) printer; **(крáско)стру́йный п.** ink-jet printer; **лáзерный п.** laser printer; **иго́льчатый** *or* **то́чечный п.** dot-matrix printer.

принуди́тел|ьный (~ен, ~ьна) *adj.* **1.** compulsory, forced, coercive; **~ьные рабо́ты** forced labour, hard labour; **п. сбор** levy. **2.** (*tech.*) forced; positive; **~ьное движéние** positive motion; **~ьная перемéна хо́да** positive reversing; **~ьная подáча** forced feed; positive feed.

прину́|дить, жу, дишь *pf.* (*of* **~ждáть**) to force, compel, coerce, constrain.

принуждá|ть, ю *impf. of* **прину́дить**

принуждéни|е, я *nt.* compulsion, coercion, constraint; **по ~ю** under compulsion, under duress.

принуждённост|ь, и *f.* constraint; stiffness.

принуждённый *p.p.p. of* **прину́дить** *and adj.* constrained, forced; **п. смех** forced laughter.

принц, а *m.* prince (*other than a Russ.* **князь**).

принцéсс|а, ы *f.* princess.

при́нцип, а *m.* principle; **в ~е** in principle, theoretically; **из ~а** on principle.

принципáл, а *m.* (*obs.*) principal, head.

принципáт, а *m.* (*hist.*) principate.

принципиáльно *adv.* **1.** on principle; on a question of principle. **2.** in principle.

принципиáльност|ь, и *f.* adherence to principle(s).

принципиáл|ьный (~ен, ~ьна) *adj.* **1.** of principle; based on, guided by principle; **п. вопро́с** question of principle; **п. человéк** man of principle; **~ьное разноглáсие** disagreement on a question of principle; **имéть ~ьное значéние** to be a matter of principle; **подня́ть вопро́с на ~ьную высоту́** to make a question a matter of principle. **2.** in principle; general; **они́ дáли ~ьное соглáсие** they consented in principle.

принню́х|аться, аюсь *pf.* (*of* **~иваться**) (**к**; *coll.*) to get used to the smell (of).

принню́хива|ться, юсь *impf. of* **принню́хаться**

приня́ти|е, я *nt.* **1.** taking; taking up, assumption; **п. пи́щи** taking of food; **п. прися́ги** taking of the oath; **п. постá** taking up a post. **2.** acceptance. **3.** admission, admittance; **п. граждáнства** naturalization.

при́нят|ый *p.p.p. of* **приня́ть; ~о** it is accepted, it is usual; **не ~о** it is not done.

при|ня́ть, му́, ~мешь, *past* **~нял, ~нялá, ~няло** *pf.* (*of* **~нимáть**) **1.** (*in var. senses*) to take; to accept; **п. вáнну** to take, have a bath; **п. граждáнство** to be naturalized; **п. бритáнское граждáнство** to take British citizenship, become a British citizen; **п. крещéние** to be baptized; **п. лекáрство** to take medicine; **п. мéры** to take measures; **п. мéры предосторо́жности** to take precautions; **п. монáшество** to take monastic vows, become a monk; to take the veil; **п. намéрение** to form the intention; **п. подáрок** to accept a present; **п. прися́гу** to take the oath; **п. решéние** to take, reach, come to a decision; **п. товáры** to take receipt of goods; **~ми́те моё сочу́вствие** accept my condolences; **п. учáстие (в**+*p.*) to take part (in); participate (in), partake (in, of); **п. христиáнство** to adopt, embrace Christianity; **п. во внимáние, п. в расчёт, п. к свéдению** to take into consideration, take into account, take cognizance (of); **не п. во внимáние, не п. к свéдению** to disregard; **не п. в расчёт** to discount, fail to take account of; **п. в шу́тку** to take as a joke; **п. всерьёз** to take seriously; **п. за прáвило** to make it a rule; **п. (бли́зко) к сéрдцу** to take, lay to heart; **п. что-н. на свой счёт** to take sth. as referring to o.s.; **п. что-н. на себя́** to take upon o.s.; **п. на себя́ обязáтельство** to assume an obligation, take on a commitment; **п. на себя́ труд** (+*inf.*) to undertake the labour (of); **п. под распи́ску** to sign for. **2.** to take up (*a post, a command, etc.*); to take over; **п. но́вое назначéние** to take up a new appointment; **п. комáндование** (+*i.*) to take command (of), assume command (of, over); **п. диви́зию** to take up command of a division; **п. духо́вный сан** to take holy orders; **п. делá (от)** to take over duties (from). **3.** to accept; **п. бой** to accept battle; **п. зако́н** to pass a law; **п. законопроéкт** to approve a bill; **п. оправдáния** to accept excuses; **п. предложéние** to accept an offer; to accept a proposal; **п. резолю́цию** to pass, adopt, carry a resolution; **п. совéт** to take advice; **п. как до́лжное** to accept as one's due, take as a matter of course. **4.** **(в, на**+*a.*) to admit (to); to accept (for); **п. в пáртию** to admit to a party; **п. в шко́лу** to admit to, accept for a school; **п. на слу́жбу** to accept for a job; **п. в граждáнство** to grant citizenship. **5.** (*see also* **~нимáть**) to receive; **п. больны́х, гостéй, делегáцию** to receive patients, guests, a delegation; **они́ ~няли нас раду́шно** they gave us a warm welcome, a cordial reception; **п. в штыки́** (*coll.*) to meet with the point of the bayonet. **6.** to assume, take (on); **п. весёлый вид** to assume an air of gaiety; **болéзнь ~нялá серьёзный харáктер** the illness assumed a grave character; **перегово́ры**

~няли **благоприя́тный оборо́т** the talks took a favourable turn. **7.** (+*a.* **за**+*a.*) to take (for); **по акце́нту я ~нял вас за шотла́ндца** I took you for a Scotsman by your accent. **8.** to move; **п. в сто́рону** (*mil.*) to execute a side step; **~ми́ к стороне́!** stand aside!; make way! **9.** (*coll.*) to remove, take away; **~ми́те ру́ки прочь!** take your hands off!

при|ня́ться, му́сь, ~мешься, *past* **~нялся́, ~няла́сь** *pf.* (*of* **~нима́ться**) **1.** (+*inf.*) to begin; to start. **2.** (**за**+*a.*) to set (to), get down (to); **п. за рабо́ту** to set to work; **п. за чте́ние** to get down to reading. **3.** (**за**+*a.*; *coll.*) to take in hand. **4.** (*of plants*) to strike root, take root; (*of injections*) to take.

приободр|и́ть, ю́, и́шь *pf.* (*of* **~я́ть**) to cheer up, encourage, hearten.

приободр|и́ться, ю́сь, и́шься *pf.* (*of* **~я́ться**) to cheer up, feel more cheerful, feel happier.

приободр|я́ть(ся), я́ю(сь) *impf. of* **~и́ть(ся)**

приобре|сти́, ту́, тёшь, *past* **~л, ~ла́** *pf.* (*of* **~та́ть**) to acquire, gain; **п. о́пыт** to gain experience; **п. меланхоли́ческий вид** to acquire a melancholy look; **п. но́вое значе́ние** to acquire a new significance.

приобрета́|ть, ю *impf. of* **приобрести́**

приобрете́ни|е, я *nt.* **1.** acquisition, acquiring. **2.** acquisition, gain; (*fig., coll.*) bargain, 'a find'.

приобщ|а́ть(ся), а́ю(сь) *impf. of* **~и́ть(ся)**

приобщ|и́ть, у́, и́шь *pf.* (*of* **~и́ть**) **1.** (**к**) to introduce (to), associate (with); **п. приёмного сы́на к семе́йной жи́зни** to introduce an adopted son to family life. **2.** to join, attach; **п. к де́лу** to file. **3.** (*eccl.*) to administer the sacrament (to), communicate.

приобщ|и́ться, у́сь, и́шься *pf.* (*of* **~а́ться**) **1.** (**к**) to join (in); **п. к обще́ственной жи́зни** to join in social life. **2.** (*eccl.*) to communicate (*intrans.*).

приоде́|ть, ну, нешь *pf.* (*coll.*) to dress up, deck out.

приоде́|ться, нусь, нешься *pf.* (*coll.*) to dress up; to get o.s. up.

приозёрный *adj.* lakeside, lakeland.

прио́р, а *m.* (*eccl.*) prior.

приорите́т, а *m.* priority.

приоса́нива|ться, юсь *impf. of* **приоса́ниться**

приоса́н|иться, юсь, ишься *pf.* (*coll.*) to assume a dignified air.

приостана́влива|ть(ся), ю(сь) *impf. of* **приостанови́ть(ся)**

приостанов|и́ть, лю́, ~ишь *pf.* (*of* **приостана́вливать**) to call a halt (to), suspend, check; **п. исполне́ние пригово́ра** to suspend sentence.

приостанов|и́ться, лю́сь, ~ишься *pf.* (*of* **приостана́вливаться**) to halt, come to a halt; **выступа́я с ре́чью, п.** to pause in making a speech.

приостано́вк|а, и *f.* halt, suspension; **п. исполне́ния пригово́ра** suspension of sentence; **п. рабо́т** stoppage (of work).

приотвор|и́ть, ю́, ~ишь *pf.* (*of* **~я́ть**) to open slightly, half-open; **п. дверь** to set a door ajar.

приотвор|и́ться, ~ится *pf.* (*of* **~я́ться**) to open slightly, half-open.

приотвор|я́ть(ся), я́ю(сь) *impf. of* **~и́ть(ся)**

приоткрыва́|ть(ся), ю(сь) *impf. of* **приоткры́ть(ся)**

приоткр|ы́ть(ся), о́ю(сь), о́ешь(ся) *pf.* = **приотвори́ть(ся)**

приохо́|тить, чу, тишь *pf.* (**к**; *coll.*) to give a taste (for).

приохо́|титься, чусь, тишься *pf.* (**к**; *coll.*) to acquire a taste (for), take (to).

припада́|ть, ю *impf.* **1.** *impf. of* **припа́сть**[1]. **2.** (*impf. only*) to be slightly lame; **п. на ле́вую но́гу** to be lame in the left leg.

припа́д|ок, ка *m.* fit; attack; paroxysm; **не́рвный п.** attack of nerves; **серде́чный п.** heart attack; **эпилепти́ческий п.** epileptic fit; **п. бе́шенства** paroxysm of rage.

припа́дочн|ый *adj.* subject to fits; **~ые явле́ния** fits; *as n.* **п., ~ого** *m.* epileptic.

припа́ива|ть, ю *impf. of* **припая́ть**

припа́йк|а, и *f.* soldering; brazing.

припа́рк|а, и *f.* (*med.*) poultice; fomentation; **приложи́ть ~у** (+*d.*) to poultice, foment.

припас|а́ть, а́ю *impf. of* **~ти́**

припас|ти́, у́, ёшь, *past* **~, ~ла́** *pf.* (*of* **~а́ть**) (+*a.* *or g.*; *coll.*) to store, lay in, lay up; **п. консе́рвов** to lay in tinned food.

припа́|сть[1]**, ду́, дёшь,** *past* **~л** *pf.* (*of* **~да́ть**) (**к**) to press o.s. (to), fall down (before); **п. к чьим-н. нога́м** to prostrate o.s. before s.o.; **п. у́хом** to press one's ear (to).

припа́|сть[2]**, дёт,** *past* **~л** *pf.* (*coll., obs.*) to appear, show itself.

припа́с|ы, ов *no sg.* stores, supplies; **боевы́е п.** ammunition; **вое́нные п.** munitions; **съестны́е п.** provisions, victuals.

припа́хива|ть, ет *impf.* (*coll.*) to stink.

припая́|ть, ю *pf.* (*of* **припа́ивать**) (**к**) to solder (to); to braze (to); (*fig., coll.*): **ему́ ~ли пять лет** he was sentenced to five years.

припе́в, а *m.* refrain, burden.

припева́|ть, ю *impf.* to hum; **жить ~ючи** (*coll.*) to be in clover; to live the life of Riley.

припёк[1]**, а** *m.* surplus (*excess in weight of loaf when baked over that of flour used*).

припёк[2]**, а** *m.*: **на ~е** (*coll.*) right in the sun, exposed to the full heat of the sun.

припёк|а, и *f.*: **сбо́ку п.** (*coll.*) for no reason at all.

припека́|ть, ет *impf.* (*coll.*) (*of the sun*) to be very hot.

при|пере́ть, пру́, прёшь, *past* **~пёр, ~пёрла** *pf.* (*of* **~пира́ть**) **1.** (**к**) to press (against); **п. стул к две́ри, п. дверь сту́лом** to put a chair against the door; **п. кого́-н. к сте́нке** (*fig., coll.*) to drive s.o. into a corner, put s.o. in a spot. **2.** (*coll.*) to set ajar. **3.** (*sl.*) to barge in, roll up.

припеча́т|ать, аю *pf.* (*of* **~ывать**) (*coll.*) to seal; **п. сургучо́м** to apply sealing-wax (to).

припеча́тыва|ть, ю *impf. of* **припеча́тать**

припира́|ть, ю *impf. of* **припере́ть**

припи|са́ть, шу́, ~шешь *pf.* (*of* **~сывать**) **1.** to add (*to sth. written*). **2.** (**к**) to attach (to), register (at). **3.** (+*d.*) to attribute (to); to ascribe (to); to put down (to), impute (to); **п. стихотворе́ние Эсхи́лу** to attribute a poem to Aeschylus; **п. неуда́чу ле́ности** to put a failure down to laziness.

припи́ск|а, и *f.* **1.** addition; postscript; **п. к завеща́нию** (*leg.*) codicil. **2.** attaching, registration; **порт ~и** (*naut.*) port of registration.

приписно́й *adj.* attached; on the establishment.

припи́сыва|ть, ю *impf. of* **приписа́ть**

припла́т|а, ы *f.* additional payment.

припла|ти́ть, чу́, ~тишь *pf.* (*of* **~чивать**) to pay in addition.

припла́чива|ть, ю *impf. of* **приплати́ть**

приплe|сти́, ту́, тёшь, *past* **~л, ~ла́** *pf.* (*of* **~та́ть**) **1.** to plait in. **2.** (*fig., coll.*) to drag in; **ра́зве бы́ло необходи́мо п. моё и́мя?** was it really necessary to drag my name in?

приплe|сти́сь, ту́сь, тёшься, *past* **~лся, ~ла́сь** *pf.* to drag o.s. along.

приплета́|ть, ю *impf. of* **приплести́**

припло́д, а *m.* issue, increase (*of animals*).

приплыва́|ть, ю *impf. of* **приплы́ть**

приплы́|ть, ву́, вёшь, *past* **~л, ~ла́, ~ло** *pf.* (*of* **~ва́ть**) to swim up; to sail up; **п. к бе́регу** to reach the shore.

приплю́снут|ый *p.p.p. of* **~ь** *and adj.*: **п. нос** flat nose.

приплю́сн|уть, у, ешь *pf.* (*of* **приплю́щивать**) to flatten.

приплюс|ова́ть, у́ю *pf.* (*of* **~о́вывать**) (*coll.*) to add on.

приплюсо́выва|ть, ю *impf. of* **приплюсова́ть**

приплю́щива|ть, ю *impf. of* **приплю́снуть**

припля́сыва|ть, ю *impf.* to dance, hop, trip, skip; **идти́ ~я по тротуа́ру** to trip along the pavement.

приподнима́|ть(ся), ю(сь) *impf. of* **приподня́ть(ся)**

припо́днятост|ь, и *f.* elation; animation.

припо́дн|ятый *p.p.p. of* **~я́ть** *and adj.* elated; animated; uplifted.

приподн|я́ть, иму́, и́мешь, *past* **~ял, ~яла́, ~яло** *pf.* (*of* **~има́ть**) to raise slightly; to lift slightly.

приподн|я́ться, иму́сь, и́мешься, *past* **~я́лся, ~яла́сь** *pf.* (*of* **~има́ться**) to raise o.s. (a little); **п. на ло́кте** to raise o.s. on one's elbow; **п. на цы́почках** to stand on tiptoe; **п. на носки́** to rise on one's toes.

припо́|й, я *m.* solder; **кре́пкий п.** brazing solder.

приполз|áть, áю *impf. of* **~тú**
приполз|тú, ý, ёшь, *past* **~, ~лá** *pf.* (*of* **~áть**) to creep up, crawl up.
приполя́рный *adj.* polar.
припоминá|ть, ю *impf. of* **припóмнить**
припóм|нить, ню, нишь *pf.* (*of* **~инáть**) **1.** to remember, recollect, recall; **смýтно п.** to have a hazy recollection (of). **2.** (+*d.*) to remind; **я э́то тебé ~ню!** (*coll.*) you won't forget this!; I'll get even with you for this!
припрáв|а, ы *f.* relish, condiment, flavouring, seasoning, dressing; **п. к салáту** salad dressing.
припрáв|ить[1]**, лю, ишь** *pf.* (*of* **~ля́ть**) (+*i.*) to season (with), flavour (with), dress (with).
припрáв|ить[2]**, лю, ишь** *pf.* (*of* **~ля́ть**) (*typ.*) to make ready.
припрáвк|а, и *f.* (*typ.*) making ready.
приправля́|ть, ю *impf. of* **припрáвить**
припры́гива|ть, ю *impf.* (*coll.*) to hop, skip.
припря́|тать, чу, чешь *pf.* (*of* **~тывать**) (*coll.*) to secrete, put by (*for further use*).
припря́тыва|ть, ю *impf. of* **припря́тать**
припýгива|ть, ю *impf. of* **припугнýть**
припуг|нýть, нý, нёшь *pf.* (*of* **~ивать**) (*coll.*) to intimidate, scare.
припýдрива|ть(ся), ю(сь) *impf. of* **припýдрить(ся)**
припýдр|ить, ю, ишь *pf.* (*of* **~ивать**) **1.** to powder. **2.** (*tech.*) to dust.
припýдр|иться, юсь, ишься *pf.* (*of* **~иваться**) to powder o.s.
прúпуск, а *m.* (*tech.*) allowance, margin; **п. на усáдку** shrinkage allowance; **остáвить п. (на**+*a.*) to allow (for).
припускá|ть, ю *impf. of* **припустúть**
припу|стúть, щý, ~стишь *pf.* (*of* **~скáть**) **1. (к)** to put (to) (*for coupling or feeding*); **п. телёнка к корóве** to put a calf to the cow. **2.** (*tailoring*) to let out. **3.** (*coll.*) to urge on. **4.** (*coll.*) to quicken one's pace. **5.** (*coll.*; *of rain*) to come down harder.
припýт|ать, аю *pf.* (*of* **~ывать**) **1.** to tie on, fasten. **2. (к;** *fig., coll.*) to drag in (to), implicate (in).
припýтыва|ть, ю *impf. of* **припýтать**
припух|áть, áет *impf. of* **~нуть**
припýхлост|ь, и *f.* (slight) swelling.
припýхлый *adj.* (slightly) swollen.
припýх|нуть, нет, *past* **~, ~ла** *pf.* (*of* **~áть**) to swell up a little.
прирабáтыва|ть, ю *impf. of* **приработáть**
приработá|ть, ю *pf.* (*of* **прирабáтывать**) to earn extra, earn in addition.
прúработ|ок, ка *m.* extra earnings, additional earnings.
прирáвнива|ть, ю *impf. of* **приравня́ть**
приравн|я́ть, я́ю *pf.* (*of* **~ивать**) **(к)** to equate (with); to place on the same footing (as).
прираст|áть, áю *impf. of* **~ú**
прираст|ú, ý, ёшь, *past* **прирóс, приросл**á *pf.* (*of* **~áть**) **1. (к)** to adhere (to); (*of a graft*) to take; **п. к мéсту, п. к землé** (*fig.*) to become rooted to the spot, to the ground. **2.** to increase; to accrue.
приращéни|е, я *nt.* **1.** increase, increment. **2.** (*ling.*) augment.
приревн|овáть, ýю *pf.* **(к)** to be jealous (of); **онá ~овáла мýжа к своéй прия́тельнице** she was jealous of her husband's interest in her friend.
прирез|áть, áю *impf. of* **~ать**[2]
прирé|зать[1]**, жу, жешь** *pf.* (*of* **~зывать**) (*coll.*) to kill; to cut the throat (of).
прирé|зать[2]**, жу, жешь** *pf.* (*of* **~зáть** *and* **~зывать**) to add on; **п. учáсток к óгороду** to add on a piece to a garden.
прирéз|ок, ка *m.* additional piece.
прирéзыва|ть, ю *impf. of* **прирéзать**
прирéльсовый *adj.* (*rail.*) track-side.
прирéчный *adj.* riverside, riverain.
прирóд|а, ы *f.* **1.** nature; **мёртвая п.** the inorganic world; **закóн ~ы** law of nature; **отдáть долг ~е** (*i*) (*rhet.*) to pay the debt to nature, (*ii*) (*coll., euph.*) to answer a call of nature. **2.** nature, character; **от ~ы** by nature, congenitally; **по ~е** by nature, naturally; **э́то в ~е вещéй** it is in the nature of things.
прирóдн|ый *adj.* **1.** natural; **~ые богáтства** natural resources; **п. газ** natural gas. **2.** born; **п. англичáнин** an Englishman by birth. **3.** inborn, innate; **п. ум** native wit.
природобезврéд|ный (~ен, ~на) *adj.* environment-friendly.
природовéд, а *m.* natural historian, naturalist.
природовéдени|е, я *nt.* natural history.
природосберегáющий *adj.* environment-friendly.
прирождённый *adj.* **1.** inborn, innate. **2.** a born; **п. лгун** a born liar.
прирóст, а *m.* increase, growth.
прирóст|ок, ка *m.* (*bot.*; *coll.*) growth, excrescence.
прирубéжный *adj.* situated near the frontier, near the border.
прируч|áть, áю *impf. of* **~úть**
приручéни|е, я *nt.* taming, domestication.
прируч|úть, ý, úшь *pf.* (*of* **~áть**) to tame (*also fig.*); to domesticate.
присáжива|ться, юсь *impf. of* **присéсть**
присáлива|ть, ю *impf. of* **присолúть**
присáсыва|ться, юсь *impf. of* **присосáться**
присвáива|ть, ю *impf. of* **присвóить**
прúсвист, а *m.* **1.** whistle. **2.** sibilance, hissing in one's speech.
присвúстыва|ть, ю *impf.* **1.** to whistle. **2.** to sibilate.
присвоéни|е, я *nt.* **1.** appropriation; **незакóнное п.** misappropriation. **2.** awarding, conferment.
присвó|ить, ю, ишь *pf.* (*of* **присвáивать**) **1.** to appropriate; **незакóнно п. срéдства** to misappropriate funds. **2.** (+*a. and d.*) to give, award, confer; **п. úмя** (+*d. and g.*) to name (after); **емý ~или стéпень дóктора** he has been given the degree of Doctor, a doctorate has been conferred upon him; **москóвскому метрó ~ено úмя Лéнина** the Moscow Underground was named after Lenin.
приседáни|е, я *nt.* **1.** squatting. **2.** (*obs.*) curts(e)y.
приседá|ть, ю *impf. of* **присéсть**
присéст, а *m.*: **в одúн п., за одúн п.** (*coll.*) at one sitting, at a stretch.
при|сéсть, ся́ду, ся́дешь, *past* **~сéл** *pf.* **1.** (*impf.* **~сáживаться**) to sit down, take a seat. **2.** (*impf.* **~седáть**) to squat; (*in fright*) to cower. **3.** (*impf.* **~седáть**) to curts(e)y, drop curts(e)ys.
прúсказк|а, и *f.* (*story-teller's*) introduction; flourish, embellishment (*of a story*).
приска|кáть, чý, ~чешь *pf.* **1.** to come galloping, arrive at a gallop; (*fig., coll.*) to rush, tear. **2.** to hop, come hopping.
прискóрби|е, я *nt.* sorrow, regret; **к моемý ~ю** to my regret; **мы с глубóким ~ем извещáем о смéрти** (+*g.*) (*formula of obituary notices*) we announce with deep regret the death (of).
прискóрб|ный (~ен, ~на) *adj.* regrettable, lamentable, deplorable.
прискýч|ить, у, ишь *pf.* (+*d.*; *coll.*) to bore, tire, weary.
при|слáть, шлю, шлёшь *pf.* (*of* **~сылáть**) to send, dispatch.
прислóвь|е, я *nt.* **1.** (*coll.*) saying (*introduced into a speech, etc.*). **2.** (*gram.*; *obs.*) inseparable particle (*e.g.* **-то, -ка**).
прислон|úть, ю́, ~úшь *pf.* (*of* **~я́ть**) **(к)** to lean (against), rest (against).
прислон|úться, ю́сь, ~úшься *pf.* (*of* **~я́ться**) **(к)** to lean (against), rest (against).
прислон|я́ть(ся), я́ю(сь) *impf. of* **~úть(ся)**
прислýг|а, и *f.* **1.** maid, servant. **2.** (*collect.*; *obs.*) servants, domestics. **3.** (*mil.*) crew; **орудúйная п.** gun crew.
прислýжива|ть, ю *impf.* (+*d.*; *obs.*) to wait (upon), attend.
прислýжива|ться, юсь *impf. of* **прислужúться**
прислуж|úться, ýсь, ~ишься *pf.* (*of* **~иваться**) **(к;** *obs.*) to worm o.s. into the favour (of), fawn (upon), cringe (to).
прислýжник, а *m.* **1.** (*obs.*) servant. **2.** (*coll.*) lickspittle; underling.
прислýжничеств|о, а *nt.* subservience, servility.
прислýш|аться, аюсь *pf.* (*of* **~иваться**) **(к) 1.** to listen (to). **2.** (*fig.*) to listen (to), lend an ear (to); to heed, pay attention (to); **п. к чьемý-н. совéту** to listen to s.o.'s advice.

3. (*coll.*) to accustom one's ear (to), become accustomed to the sound (of); **мы уже́ ~ались к ночно́му у́личному движе́нию** we are now accustomed to the (noise of) traffic at night.

прислу́шива|ться, юсь *impf. of* **прислу́шаться**

присма́трива|ть(ся), ю(сь) *impf. of* **присмотре́ть(ся)**

присмире́|ть, ю *pf.* to grow quiet.

присмо́тр, а *m.* care, looking after, tending; supervision, surveillance; **п. за детьми́** child-minding.

присмотр|е́ть, ю́, ~ишь *pf.* (*of* **присма́тривать**) **1.** (**за**+*i.*) to look after, keep an eye (on); to supervise, superintend; **п. за ребёнком** to mind the baby. **2.** (*coll.*) to look for; **п. себе́ рабо́ту** to look for a job. **3.** *pf. only* to find.

присмотр|е́ться, ю́сь, ~ишься *pf.* (*of* **присма́триваться**) (**к**) **1.** to look closely (at); **п. к кому́-н.** to size s.o. up, take s.o.'s measure. **2.** to get accustomed (to), get used (to).

присн|и́ться, ю́сь, и́шься *pf. of* **сни́ться**

приснопа́мятный *adj.* (*rhet.*) memorable, unforgettable.

при́сн|ый *adj.* **1.** (*obs. or eccl.*) eternal, everlasting. **2.** *as n.* **~ые, ~ых** (*coll.*) associates; **ты и твой ~ые** you and your gang; you and your mates.

присове́т|овать, ую *pf.* = **посове́товать**

присовокуп|и́ть, лю́, и́шь *pf.* (*of* **~ля́ть**) to add; to say in addition; **п. бума́гу к де́лу** to file a paper.

присовокупля́|ть, ю *impf. of* **присовокупи́ть**

присоедине́ни|е, я *nt.* **1.** addition. **2.** (*pol.*) annexation, joining. **3.** (**к**) joining, associating o.s. (with), adhesion (to). **4.** (*elec.*) connection.

присоедини́тельный *adj.* (*gram.*) connective.

присоедин|и́ть, ю́, и́шь *pf.* (*of* **~я́ть**) **1.** to add; to join. **2.** (*pol.*) to annex, join. **3.** (*elec.*) to connect.

присоедин|и́ться, ю́сь, и́шься *pf.* (*of* **~я́ться**) (**к**) **1.** to join; **пора́ нам п. к остальны́м** it is time we joined the others. **2.** (*fig.*) to join, associate o.s. (with); **п. к мне́нию** to subscribe to an opinion.

присоедин|я́ть(ся), я́ю(сь) *impf. of* **~и́ть(ся)**

присол|и́ть, ю́, ~и́шь *pf.* (*of* **приса́ливать**) (*coll.*) to salt, add a pinch of salt (to).

присос|а́ться, у́сь, ёшься *pf.* (*of* **приса́сываться**) (**к**) to stick (to), attach o.s. (to) by suction; (*fig.*, *pej.*) to fasten on (to).

присосе́|диться, жусь, дишься *pf.* (**к**; *coll.*) to sit down next (to).

присо́ск|а, и *f.* (*biol.*, *zool.*) sucker.

присо́х|нуть, нет, *past* **~, ~ла** *pf.* (*of* **присыха́ть**) (**к**) to adhere (in drying) (to); to stick (to), dry (on).

приспева́|ть, ю *impf. of* **приспе́ть**

приспе́|ть, ю *pf.* (*of* **~ва́ть**) (*coll.*; *of time*) to come, draw nigh, be ripe.

приспе́шник, а *m.* stooge, myrmidon.

приспи́ч|ить, ит *pf.* (*impers.*+*d. and inf.*; *coll.*) to feel, have an urge (to), to be impatient (to); **им ~ило уходи́ть** they were impatient to be off.

приспоса́блива|ть(ся), ю(сь) *impf.* = **приспособля́ть(ся)**

приспосо́б|ить, лю, ишь *pf.* (*of* **~ля́ть**) to fit, adjust, adapt, accommodate; **п. шко́лу под больни́цу** to adapt a school as a hospital.

приспосо́б|иться, люсь, ишься *pf.* (*of* **~ля́ться**) **1.** (**к**) to adapt *or* accommodate o.s. (to). **2.** *pass. of* **~ить**

приспособле́н|ец, ца *m.* time-server.

приспособле́ни|е, я *nt.* **1.** adaptation, accommodation; **п. к кли́мату** acclimatization. **2.** device, contrivance, contraption; appliance, gadget.

приспосо́бленност|ь, и *f.* fitness, suitability.

приспособле́нческий *adj.* time-serving.

приспособле́нчеств|о, а *nt.* time-serving.

приспособля́емост|ь, и *f.* adaptability.

приспособля́|ть(ся), ю(сь) *impf. of* **приспосо́бить(ся)**

приспуска́|ть, ю *impf. of* **приспусти́ть**

приспу|сти́ть, щу́, ~стишь *pf.* (*of* **~ска́ть**) to lower a little; **п. флаг** to lower a flag to half-mast; (*naut.*) to half-mast the colours.

приспу́|щенный *p.p.p. of* **~сти́ть; ~щенные фла́ги** flags at half-mast.

при́став, а, *pl.* **~а́** *m.* (*hist.*) police-officer; **станово́й п.** district superintendent of police; **суде́бный п.** bailiff.

пристава́ни|е, я *nt.* pestering, bothering; **сексуа́льные ~я** sexual harassment.

приста|ва́ть, ю́, ёшь *impf. of* **приста́ть**

приста́в|ить, лю, ишь *pf.* (*of* **~ля́ть**) **1.** (**к**) to put (to, against), place (to, against), set (to, against), lean (against); **п. ле́стницу к стене́** to put a ladder against the wall. **2.** to add (*a piece of material*, *etc.*). **3.** (**к**) to appoint to look after; **п. проводника́ к иностра́нным тури́стам** to appoint a guide to look after foreign tourists.

приста́вк|а, и *f.* (*gram.*) prefix.

приставля́|ть, ю *impf. of* **приста́вить**

приставн|о́й *adj.* added, attached; **~а́я ле́стница** step ladder

приста́вочный *adj.* (*gram.*) **1.** of a prefix. **2.** having a prefix.

при́стально *adv.* fixedly, intently; **п. смотре́ть** (**на**+*a.*) to look fixedly, intently (at); to stare (at), gaze (at).

при́стал|ьный (~ен, ~ьна) *adj.* fixed, intent; **п. взгляд** fixed, intent look; stare, gaze; **с ~ьным внима́нием** intently.

приста́нищ|е, а *nt.* refuge, shelter, asylum.

пристанцио́нный *adj.* station.

при́стан|ь, и, *pl.* **~и, ~е́й** *f.* **1.** landing-stage, jetty; pier; wharf. **2.** (*obs.*) refuge, asylum. **3.** (*fig.*, *poet.*) haven.

приста́|ть, ну, нешь *pf.* (*of* **~ва́ть**) **1.** (**к**) to stick (to), adhere (to). **2.** (**к**) to join; to attach o.s. (to); **п. к гру́ппе экскурса́нтов** to join a party of excursionists; **ко мне ~ла чужа́я соба́ка** s.o.'s dog attached itself to me. **3.** (**к**; *fig.*, *coll.*; *of infectious disease*) to be passed on (to); **к де́тям ~ла ве́тряная о́спа** the children have picked up chickenpox. **4.** (**к**) to pester, bother, badger; **п. с предложе́ниями** to pester with suggestions. **5.** (**к**; *naut.*) to put in (to), come alongside. **6.** *pf. only* (*impers.*+*d.*; *coll.*) to befit; **не ~ло тебе́ так говори́ть** you ought not to speak like that. **7.** *pf. only* (+*d.*; *coll.*) to become, suit.

пристёгива|ть, ю *impf. of* **пристегну́ть**

пристег|ну́ть, ну́, нёшь *pf.* (*of* **~ивать**) **1.** to fasten; to button up. **2.** (*fig.*, *coll.*) to drag in.

пристежн|о́й *adj.* fastening (*opp. sewn on*); **руба́шка с ~ы́м воротничко́м** shirt with separate collar.

присто́йност|ь, и *f.* decency, propriety, decorum.

присто́|йный (~ен, ~йна) *adj.* decent, proper, decorous, becoming, seemly.

пристра́ива|ть(ся), ю(сь) *impf. of* **пристро́ить(ся)**

пристра́сти|е[1], **я** *nt.* (**к**) **1.** weakness (for), predilection (for), passion (for); **у неё п. к верхово́й езде́** she has a passion for riding. **2.** partiality (for, towards), bias (towards); **вы́казать п.** to show partiality.

пристра́сти|е[2], **я** *nt.*: **допро́с с ~ем** (*hist. and fig.*, *joc.*) interrogation under torture.

пристра|сти́ть, щу́, сти́шь *pf.* (**к**; *coll.*) to give one an impulse (to), make keen (on); **его́ докла́д ~сти́л меня́ к заня́тиям по исто́рии И́ндии** his talk made me keen on studying the history of India.

пристра|сти́ться, щу́сь, сти́шься *pf.* (**к**) to take (to), to conceive a liking (for).

пристра́стност|ь, и *f.* partiality, bias.

пристра́ст|ный (~ен, ~на) *adj.* partial, biased.

пристра́чива|ть, ю *impf. of* **пристрочи́ть**

пристращ|а́ть, а́ю *pf.* (*of* **~ивать**) (*coll.*) to intimidate.

пристра́щива|ть, ю *impf. of* **пристраща́ть**

пристре́лива|ть, ю *impf. of* **пристрели́ть** *and* **пристреля́ть**

пристре́лива|ться, юсь *impf. of* **пристреля́ться**

пристрел|и́ть, ю́, ~ишь *pf.* (*of* **~ивать**) to shoot (down).

пристре́лк|а, и *f.* (*mil.*) adjustment (of fire), ranging; fire for adjustment; **п. ви́лки** bracketing for range; **п. репе́ра** registration; **вести́ ~у** to find the range.

пристре́лочн|ый *adj.* (*mil.*) ranging; registering; **п. ориенти́р** registration point; **~ое ору́дие** registration gun; **п. снаря́д** projectile with spotting charge.

пристре́льный *adj.* (*mil.*): **п. ого́нь** straddling fire.

пристре́л|янный *p.p.p. of* **~я́ть** *and adj.* (*mil.*) adjusted.

пристрел|я́ть, я́ю *pf.* (*of* **~ивать**) (*mil.*) to adjust.

пристрел|я́ться, я́юсь *pf.* (*of* **~иваться**) (*mil.*) to adjust fire; to find the range.

пристро́|ить, ю, ишь *pf.* (*of* **пристра́ивать**) **1. (к)** to add (*to a building*), build on (to). **2.** (*coll.*) to place, settle, fix up; **п. кого́-н. на слу́жбу** to settle s.o. in a job. **3. (к;** *mil.*) to join up (with), form up (with).

пристро́|иться, юсь, ишься *pf.* (*of* **пристра́иваться**) **1.** (*coll.*) to be placed, be settled, be fixed up, get a place; **он ~ился в конто́ру** he has got a place in an office. **2. (к;** *mil.*) to join up (with), form up (with); (*aeron.*) to take up formation (with).

пристро́йк|а, и *f.* annexe, extension; outhouse; lean-to.

пристроч|и́ть, у́, ~́ишь *pf.* (*of* **пристра́чивать**) **(к)** to sew on (to).

пристру́нива|ть, ю *impf. of* **пристру́нить**

пристру́н|ить, ю, ишь *pf.* (*of* **~ивать**) (*coll.*) to take in hand.

присту́кива|ть, ю *impf. of* **присту́кнуть**

присту́к|нуть[1]**, ну, нешь** *pf.* (*of* **~ивать**) (*+i.*; *coll.*) to tap; **п. каблука́ми** to tap one's heels.

присту́к|нуть[2]**, ну, нешь** *pf.* (*of* **~ивать**) to club to death; to kill (*with a blow*).

при́ступ, а *m.* **1.** (*mil.*) assault, storm; **пойти́ на п.** to go in to the assault; **взять ~ом** to take by storm. **2.** fit, attack; bout, touch; **п. бо́ли** pang; paroxysm; **п. гне́ва** fit of temper; **п. гри́ппа** bout of influenza; **п. ка́шля** fit, bout of coughing. **3.** (*fig., coll.*) access; **к нему́ ~у нет** he is inaccessible, unapproachable; **к э́той мате́рии ~у нет** this material is out of the question (= *is too expensive*).

приступ|а́ть(ся), а́ю(сь) *impf. of* **~и́ть(ся)**

приступ|и́ть, лю́, ~́ишь *pf.* (*of* **~а́ть**) **(к) 1.** (*obs.*) to approach; (*fig.*) to importune, pester. **2.** to set about, get down (to), start; **п. к де́лу** to set to work, get down to business.

приступ|и́ться, лю́сь, ~́ишься *pf.* (*of* **~а́ться**) **(к;** *coll.*) to approach, accost, go up (to); **к нему́ не ~́ишься, нельзя́ п.** he is inaccessible, unapproachable.

присту́п|ок, ка *m.* (*coll.*) step.

присты|ди́ть, жу́, ди́шь *pf. of* **стыди́ть**

пристя́жк|а, и *f.* **1.: в ~е** (*of a horse*) in traces. **2.** trace-horse, outrunner.

пристяжн|а́я, о́й *f.* trace-horse, outrunner.

прису|ди́ть, жу́, ~́дишь *pf.* (*of* **~жда́ть**) **1.** (*+a.* **к** *or +a. and d.*) to sentence (to), condemn (to); **п. кого́-н. к заключе́нию, п. заключе́ние кому́-н.** to sentence s.o. to imprisonment; **п. к штра́фу, п. штраф** (*+d.*) to fine, impose a fine (on). **2.** (*leg.*; *coll.*) to award. **3.** (*+d.*) to award, adjudge (to); to confer (on); **ему́ ~ди́ли сте́пень до́ктора** a doctorate has been conferred on him.

присужда́|ть, ю *impf. of* **присуди́ть**

присужде́ни|е, я *nt.* awarding, adjudication; conferment.

прису́тственн|ый *adj.* (*obs.*): **п. день** working-day; **~ое ме́сто** office, work-place; **~ые часы́** office hours, business hours.

прису́тстви|е, я *nt.* **1.** presence; **в ~и дете́й** in the presence of the children, in front of the children; **п. ду́ха** presence of mind. **2.** (*obs.*) business (of the day). **3.** (*obs.*) office.

прису́тств|овать, ую *impf.* **(на**+*p.*) to be present (at), attend, assist (at).

прису́тств|ующий *pres. part. act. of* **~овать** *and adj.* present; *as n.* **~ующие, ~ующих** those present; **о ~ующих не говоря́т** present company (always) excepted.

прису́щ|ий (~, ~а) *adj.* (*+d.*) inherent (in); characteristic, distinctive; **~ая ей ще́дрость** the generosity characteristic of her; **неприя́тные ~ие положе́нию после́дствия** the disagreeable consequences inherent in the situation.

присчит|а́ть, а́ю *pf.* (*of* **~́ывать**) to add on.

присчи́тыва|ть, ю *impf. of* **присчита́ть**

присыла́|ть, ю *impf. of* **присла́ть**

присы́п|ать, лю, лешь *pf.* (*of* **~а́ть**) **1.** (*+a. or g.*) to add some more, pour some more. **2.** (*+a. and i.*) to sprinkle (with), dust (with).

присып|а́ть, а́ю *impf. of* **~́ать**

присы́пк|а, и *f.* **1.** sprinkling, dusting. **2.** powder.

присыха́|ть, ю *impf. of* **присо́хнуть**

прися́г|а, и *f.* oath; oath of allegiance; **ло́жная п.** perjury; **дать ~у** to swear; **приня́ть ~у** to take the oath; **привести́ к ~е** to swear in, administer the oath (to); **под ~ой** on oath, under oath.

присяг|а́ть, а́ю *impf.* (*of* **~ну́ть**) **(в**+*p.*) to swear (to); to take one's oath, swear an oath; **п. в ве́рности** (*+d.*) to swear allegiance (to).

присяг|ну́ть, ну́, нёшь *pf. of* **~а́ть**

прися́жн|ый *adj.* **1.** (*leg.*; *obs.*) sworn; **п. пове́ренный** barrister; **п. заседа́тель** juror, juryman; *as n.* **п., ~ого** *m.* = **п. заседа́тель; суд ~ых** jury. **2.** (*coll.*) born, inveterate; **п. ворчу́н** born grumbler.

прита|и́ться, ю́сь, и́шься *pf.* to hide; to conceal o.s.

прита́птыва|ть, ю *impf.* **1.** *impf. of* **притопта́ть. 2.** *impf. only* (*coll.*) to tap (with) one's heels.

прита́скива|ть, ю *impf. of* **притащи́ть**

притач|а́ть, а́ю *pf.* (*of* **~́ивать**) **(к)** to stitch (to), sew on (to).

прита́чива|ть, ю *impf. of* **притача́ть**

притащ|и́ть, у́, ~́ишь *pf.* (*of* **прита́скивать**) to bring, drag, haul.

притащ|и́ться, у́сь, ~́ишься *pf.* (*coll.*) to drag o.s.

притвор|и́ть, ю́, ~́ишь *pf.* (*of* **~я́ть**) to set ajar; to leave not quite shut.

притвор|и́ться[1]**, ~́ится** *pf.* (*of* **~я́ться**) to be ajar, to be not quite shut.

притвор|и́ться[2]**, ю́сь, и́шься** *pf.* (*of* **~я́ться**) (*+i.*) to pretend (to be); to feign, simulate; to sham; **п. больны́м** to pretend to be ill, feign illness; **п. безразли́чным** to feign indifference.

притво́р|ный (~ен, ~на) *adj.* pretended, feigned, affected, sham; **~ное неве́жество** feigned ignorance; **~ные слёзы** crocodile tears.

притво́рств|о, а *nt.* pretence; sham; dissembling.

притво́рщик, а *m.* **1.** pretender, sham. **2.** dissembler, hypocrite.

притвор|я́ть(ся), я́ю(сь) *impf. of* **~и́ть(ся)**

притека́|ть, ю *impf. of* **прите́чь**

при|тере́ть, тру́, трёшь, *past* **~тёр, ~тёрла** *pf.* (*of* **~тира́ть**) **1.** to rub in lightly. **2.** (*tech.*) to grind in, lap.

притерп|е́ться, лю́сь, ~́ишься *pf.* **(к;** *coll.*) to get accustomed (to), get used (to).

притёр|тый *p.p.p. of* **~е́ть** *and adj.*; **~тая про́бка** ground-in stopper (*of bottle*); **~тое стекло́** ground glass.

притесне́ни|е, я *nt.* oppression.

притесни́тел|ь, я *m.* oppressor.

притесни́тел|ьный (~ен, ~ьна) *adj.* oppressive.

притесн|и́ть, ю́, и́шь *pf.* (*of* **~я́ть**) to oppress, keep down.

притесн|я́ть, я́ю *impf. of* **~и́ть**

прите́|чь, чёт, ку́т, *past* **~́к, ~кла́** *pf.* (*of* **~ка́ть**) to flow in, pour in (*also fig.*); **выраже́ния соболезнова́ния ~кли со всех сторо́н** messages of sympathy poured in from all sides.

притира́|ть, ю *impf. of* **притере́ть**

прити́скива|ть, ю *impf. of* **прити́снуть**

прити́с|нуть, ну, нешь *pf.* (*of* **~кивать**) (*coll.*) to press, squeeze; **п. па́лец две́рью** to pinch one's finger in the door.

притих|а́ть, а́ю *impf. of* **~́нуть**

прити́х|нуть, ну, нешь, *past* **~, ~ла** *pf.* (*of* **~а́ть**) to quiet down, grow quiet, hush; (*fig.*) to pipe down, sing small.

приткн|у́ть, у́, ёшь *pf.* (*of* **притыка́ть**) (*coll.*) to stick; **~и свой ве́щи куда́ хо́чешь** stick your things anywhere you like.

приткн|у́ться, у́сь, ёшься *pf.* (*coll.*) to perch o.s.; to find room for o.s.; **мне бы́ло не́где п.** I could not find a spare inch.

прито́к, а *m.* **1.** (*geog.*) tributary. **2.** inflow, influx (*also fig.*); intake; **п. све́жего во́здуха** supply of fresh air; **п. но́вых ка́дров** (*fig.*) intake of fresh blood.

при́толок|а, и *f.* lintel.

прито́м *conj.* (and) besides; **он был там не раз и п. прекра́сно зна́ет язы́к** he has been there several times, (and) besides he knows the language extremely well.

притом|и́ть, лю́, и́шь *pf.* (*coll.*) to tire.

притом|и́ться, лю́сь, и́шься *pf.* (*coll.*) to get tired.

прито́н, а *m.* den, haunt; **воровско́й п.** den of thieves;

игóрный п. gambling-den, gambling-hell.
притóп|нуть, ну, нешь *pf.* (*of* **~ывать**) to stamp one's foot; **п. каблукáми** to tap one's heels.
притоп|тáть, чý, ~чешь *pf.* (*of* **притáптывать**) to tread down.
притóпыва|ть, ю *impf. of* **притóпнуть**
притoрáчива|ть, ю *impf. of* **приторочи́ть**
при́торност|ь, и *f.* sickly sweetness, excessive sweetness.
при́тор|ный (~ен, ~на) *adj.* sickly sweet, luscious, cloying (*also fig.*); **~ная улы́бка** unctuous smile.
притoроч|и́ть, ý, и́шь *pf.* (*of* **приторáчивать**) to strap.
притрáгива|ться, юсь *impf. of* **притрóнуться**
притрóн|уться, усь, ешься *pf.* (*of* **притрáгиваться**) (**к**) to touch; **они́ не ~улись к ýжину** they have not touched their supper.
притул|и́ться, ю́сь, и́шься *pf.* (*coll.*) to find room for o.s.; to find shelter.
притуп|и́ть, лю́, ~ишь *pf.* (*of* **~ля́ть**) to blunt, dull, take the edge of; (*fig.*) to dull, deaden.
притуп|и́ться, лю́сь, ~ишься *pf.* (*of* **~ля́ться**) to become blunt; (*fig.*) to become dull.
притупля́|ть(ся), ю(сь) *impf. of* **притупи́ть(ся)**
притуш|и́ть, ý, ~ишь *pf.* (*coll.*) to damp (*a fire*); **п. фáры** to dip lights.
при́тч|а, и *f.* parable; **что за п.?** (*coll.*) what is the meaning of all this?; what an extraordinary thing!; **п. во язы́цех** (*joc.*) the talk of the town.
притыкá|ть, ю *impf. of* **приткнýть**
притягáтельност|ь, и *f.* attractiveness.
притягáтел|ьный (~ен, ~ьна) *adj.* attractive, magnetic.
притя́гива|ть, ю *impf. of* **притянýть**
притяжáтельный *adj.* (*gram.*) possessive.
притяжéни|е, я *nt.* (*phys.*) attraction; **закóн земнóго ~я** law of gravity.
притязáни|е, я *nt.* claim, pretension; **имéть ~я (на+***a.***)** to have claims (to, on).
притязáтел|ьный (~ен, ~ьна) *adj.* demanding, exacting.
притязá|ть, ю *impf.* (**на+***a.*) to lay claim (to).
притя́н|утый *p.p.p. of* **~уть; п. зá уши, п. зá вóлосы** (*fig.*) far-fetched.
притя|нýть, нý, ~нешь *pf.* (*of* **~гивать**) **1.** to drag (up), pull (up); **п. зá уши, зá вóлосы доказáтельства** to adduce far-fetched arguments. **2.** (*fig.*) to draw, attract; **п. как магни́т** to attract like a magnet. **3.** (*coll.*) to summon; **п. к отвéту** to call to account; **п. к судý** to have up, sue.
приуготóв|ить, лю, ишь *pf.* (*of* **~ля́ть**) (*obs.*) to prepare, have in store (*usu. fig.*).
приуготовля́|ть, ю *impf. of* **приуготóвить**
приудáр|ить, ю, ишь (*of* **~я́ть**) **1.** to deal a light blow. **2.** (*fig., coll.*) to get cracking. **3.** (**за+***i.*; *fig., coll.*) to go (after), pursue (= *begin courting*).
приудар|я́ть, я́ю *impf. of* **~ить**
приукрá|сить, шу, сишь *pf.* (*of* **~шивать**) (*coll.*) to adorn; (*fig.*) to embellish, embroider.
приукрáшива|ть, ю *impf. of* **приукрáсить**
приуменьш|áть, áю *impf. of* **~и́ть**
приумéньш|ить, ~ý, ~и́шь *pf.* (*of* **~áть**) to diminish, lessen, reduce.
приумнож|áть(ся), áю(сь) *impf. of* **~ить(ся)**
приумножéни|е, я *nt.* increase, augmentation.
приумнóж|ить, у, ишь *pf.* (*of* **~áть**) to increase, augment, multiply.
приумнóж|иться, ится *pf.* (*of* **~áться**) to increase, multiply.
приумóлк|нуть, ну, нешь, *past* **~, ~ла** *pf.* (*coll.*) to fall silent (*for a while*).
приун|ы́ть, óю, óешь *pf.* (*coll.*) to become depressed, become gloomy.
приурóчива|ть, ю *impf. of* **приурóчить**
приурóч|ить, у, ишь *pf.* (*of* **~ивать**) (**к**) to time (for, to coincide with); **~или издáние кни́ги к прибы́тию áвтора** publication of the book was timed to coincide with the author's arrival.
приусáдебный *adj.* adjoining the farm(-house); **п. учáсток (колхóзника)** personal plot (belonging to collective farmer).
приути́х|нуть, ну, нешь, *past* **~, ~ла** *pf.* to quiet down; (*of a storm*) to abate; (*of wind*) to fall, drop.
приуч|áть(ся), áю(сь) *impf. of* **~и́ть(ся)**
приуч|и́ть, ý, ~ишь *pf.* (*of* **~áть**) (**к** *or* **+***inf.*) to train (to), school (to, in); to inure, accustom; **п. когó-н. к дисципли́не** to inculcate discipline in s.o.; **п. когó-н. купáться в холóдной водé** to school s.o. to taking cold baths.
приуч|и́ться, ýсь, ~ишься *pf.* (*of* **~áться**) (**+***inf.*) to train *or* school *or* discipline o.s. (to); to become inured (to); to accustom o.s. (to).
прифран|ти́ться, чýсь, ти́шься *pf.* (*coll.*) to dress up, put on one's best bib and tucker.
прифронтов|óй *adj.* (*mil., pol.*) front, front-line; **~ы́е госудáрства** front-line states.
прихвáрыва|ть, ю *impf.* (*coll.*) to be unwell off and on.
прихвастн|ýть, ý, ёшь *pf.* (*coll.*) to boast a little, brag a little.
прихва|ти́ть, чý, ~тишь *pf.* (*of* **~тывать**) (*coll.*) **1.** to catch up, seize up (= *to take*; *to get*). **2.** to tie up, fasten. **3.** (*of frost*) to touch, nip.
прихвáтыва|ть, ю *impf. of* **прихвати́ть**
прихворн|ýть, ý, ёшь *pf.* (*coll.*) to be indisposed, be unwell.
при́хвост|ень, ня *m.* (*coll.*) hanger-on, stooge.
прихлебáтел|ь, я *m.* (*coll.*) sponger.
прихлебáтельств|о, а *nt.* (*coll.*) sponging.
прихлебн|ýть, ý, ёшь *pf.* to take a sip.
прихлёбыва|ть, ю *impf.* (*coll.*) to sip.
прихлóп|нуть, ну, нешь *pf.* (*of* **~ывать**) (*coll.*) **1.** to slam. **2.** to squeeze, pinch; **п. пáлец двéрью** to pinch one's finger in the door. **3.** (*sl.*) to kill.
прихлóпыва|ть, ю *impf.* **1.** *impf. of* **прихлóпнуть. 2.** *impf. only* to clap.
прихлы́н|уть, у, ешь *pf.* (**к**) to rush (towards), surge (towards).
прихóд[1]**, а** *m.* coming, arrival; advent.
прихóд[2]**, а** *m.* receipts; **п. и расхóд** credit and debit.
прихóд[3]**, а** *m.* (*eccl.*) parish; **какóв поп, такóв и п.** (*prov.*) like master, like man.
прихо|ди́ть, жý, ~дишь *impf. of* **прийти́**
прихо|ди́ться, жýсь, ~дишься *impf.* **1.** *impf. of* **прийти́сь. 2.** *impf. only* (**+***d. and i.*) to be (*in a given degree of relationship to*); **я ей ~жýсь дя́дей** I am her uncle; **они́ нам ~дятся рóдственниками** they are related to us.
прихóд|ный *adj. of* **~**[2]; **~ная кни́га** receipt-book.
прихóд|овать, ую *impf.* (*of* **за~**) (*book-keeping*) to enter (*of pers. receiving sum from client, customer, etc.*).
прихóдо-расхóдн|ый *adj.* credit and debit; **~ая кни́га** account-book.
прихóдский *adj.* parochial; parish; **п. свящéнник** parish priest; parson, vicar, rector.
приход|я́щий *pres. part. act. of* **~и́ть** *and adj.* non-resident; **п. больнóй** outpatient; **~я́щая домрабóтница** daily maid, charwoman; **п. учени́к** day-boy.
прихожáн|ин, ина, *pl.* **~е** *m.* parishioner.
прихóж|ая, ей *f.* (entrance) hall, lobby; antechamber.
прихорáшива|ться, юсь *impf.* (*coll.*) to doll *or* smarten o.s. up.
прихотли́вост|ь, и *f.* capriciousness, fastidiousness, whimsicality.
прихотли́в|ый (~, ~а) *adj.* **1.** capricious, fastidious, whimsical. **2.** fanciful, intricate (*of pattern, etc.*).
при́хот|ь, и *f.* whim, caprice, whimsy, fancy.
прихрáмыва|ть, ю *impf.* to limp, hobble.
прицéл, а *m.* **1.** back-sight; **опти́ческий п.** telegraphic sight; **п. для бомбометáния** bomb sight; **взять на п.** to take aim (at), aim (at), point (at). **2.** aiming.
прицéлива|ться, юсь *impf. of* **прицéлиться**
прицéл|иться, юсь, ишься *pf.* (*of* **~иваться**) to take aim, take sight.
прицéл|ьный *adj. of* **~; ~ьная бомбардирóвка** precision bombing; **~ьная колóдка** back-sight bed; **~ьная ли́ния** line of sight; **п. огóнь** aimed fire; **~ьная плáнка** back-sight leaf; **~ьные приспособлéния** sighting device; back-

sight; **п. хомýтик** back-sight slide.
прицéнива|ться, юсь *impf. of* **прицени́ться**
прицен|и́ться, ю́сь, ~́ишься *pf.* (*of* **~́иваться**) (**к**; *coll.*) to ask the price (of).
прицéп, а *m.* trailer.
прицеп|и́ть, лю́, ~́ишь *pf.* (*of* **~ля́ть**) (**к**) **1.** to hitch (to), hook on (to); to couple (to); **п. вагóны к паровóзу** to couple trucks to a locomotive. **2.** (*coll.*) to pin on (to), fasten (to), tack (to), tag on (to).
прицеп|и́ться, лю́сь, ~́ишься *pf.* (*of* **~ля́ться**) (**к**) **1.** to stick (to), cling (to). **2.** (*fig., coll.*) to pester; to nag (at).
прицéпк|а, и *f.* **1.** hitching, hooking on; coupling. **2.** (*coll.*) pestering; nagging. **3.** (*coll.*) chaser.
прицепля́|ть(ся), ю(сь) *impf. of* **прицепи́ть(ся)**
прицепнóй *adj.*: **п. вагóн** trailer; **п. инвентáрь** (*agric.*) tractor-drawn implements.
причáл, а *m.* **1.** mooring, making fast. **2.** mooring line. **3.** berth, moorage; **у ~ов** at its, her moorings.
причáлива|ть, ю *impf. of* **причáлить**
причáл|ить, ю, ишь *pf.* (*of* **~ивать**) **1.** (**к**) to moor (to). **2.** (*intrans.*) to moor.
причáл|ьный *adj. of* **~**; **п. канáт** mooring line.
причáсти|е[1], **я** *nt.* (*gram.*) participle.
причáсти|е[2], **я** *nt.* (*eccl.*) **1.** communion; the Eucharist. **2.** making one's communion, communicating.
прича|сти́ть, щý, сти́шь *pf.* (*of* **~щáть**) (*eccl.*) to give communion.
прича|сти́ться, щýсь, сти́шься *pf.* (*of* **~щáться**) (*eccl.*) to receive communion, make one's communion, communicate.
причáст|ный[1] (**~ен, ~на**) *adj.* (**к**) participating (in), concerned (in), connected (with), involved (in); privy (to); **быть ~ным (к)** to participate (in), be concerned (in), connected (with), be involved (in); to be privy (to); **быть ~ным к теáтру** to be connected with the theatre; **быть ~ным к покушéнию на жизнь короля́** to be privy to an attempt on the life of the king.
причáстный[2] *adj.* (*gram.*) participial.
причáст|ный[3] *adj. of* **~ие**[2]; **~ное винó** communion wine.
причащá|ть(ся), ю(сь) *impf. of* **причасти́ть(ся)**
причащéни|е, я *nt.* (*eccl.*) receiving communion, making one's communion, communicating.
причём *conj.* **1.** moreover, and (*or translated by means of participial clause*); **бы́ло óчень темнó, п. я плóхо ориенти́руюсь в э́той мéстности** it was very dark and I don't know this area well. **2.** while (*+participial clause*); despite the fact that; **он реши́л поéхать, п. отдавáл себé отчёт в опáсности** he decided to go, while recognizing the danger.
приче|сáть, шý, ~́шешь *pf.* (*of* **~́сывать**) to comb; **п. когó-н.** to do s.o.'s hair; to brush, comb s.o.'s hair.
приче|сáться, шýсь, ~́шешься *pf.* (*of* **~́сываться**) to do one's hair; to brush, comb one's hair; to have one's hair done.
причёск|а, и *f.* haircut; hair style, hair-do, coiffure.
при|чéсть, чтý, чтёшь, *past* **~чёл, ~члá** *pf.* (*of* **~чи́тывать**) **1.** (*coll.*) to add on. **2.** (*obs.*) to number, reckon.
причёсыва|ть(ся), ю(сь) *impf. of* **причесáть(ся)**
причéтник, а *m.* (*eccl.*) junior deacon.
причи́н|а, ы *f.* cause; reason; **уважи́тельная п.** good cause, good reason; **по той и́ли инóй ~е** for some reason or other, for one reason or another; **по той простóй ~е, что** for the simple reason that; **по ~е** (*+g.*) by reason (of), on account (of), owing (to) because (of).
причин|и́ть, ю́, и́шь *pf.* (*of* **~я́ть**) to cause; to occasion.
причи́нност|ь, и *f.* causality.
причи́нн|ый *adj.* causal, causative; **~ая связь** causation; **~ое мéсто** (*coll.*) privy parts.
причин|я́ть, я́ю *impf. of* **~и́ть**
причи́сл|ить, ю, ишь *pf.* (*of* **~я́ть**) (**к**) **1.** to add on (to). **2.** to reckon (among), number (among), rank (among); **егó ~или к сáмым вы́дающимся матемáтикам** he was ranked among the foremost mathematicians. **3.** to attach (to).
причисл|я́ть, я́ю *impf. of* **~́ить**
причитáни|е, я *nt.* (ritual) lamentation; **похорóнные ~я** keen, keening.
причитá|ть, ю *impf.* (**по**+*p.*) to lament (for), keen (over); to bewail.
причитá|ться, ется *impf.* (*+d.*; **с**+*g.*) to be due (to; from); **вам ~ется два рубля́** there is two roubles due to you, you have two roubles to come; **с вас ~ется два рубля́** you have two roubles to pay.
причи́тыва|ть, ю *impf. of* **причéсть**
причмóкива|ть, ю *impf. of* **причмóкнуть**
причмóк|нуть, ну, нешь *pf.* (*of* **~ивать**) to smack one's lips.
причт, а *m.* (*collect.*) the clergy of a parish.
причýд|а, ы *f.* caprice, whim, whimsy, fancy; oddity, vagary; **человéк с ~ами** crank, odd pers., queer pers.
причýд|иться, ится *pf. of* **чýдиться**
причýдливост|ь, и *f.* **1.** oddity, queerness; quaintness, fantasticality. **2.** (*coll.*) capriciousness, whimsicality.
причýдлив|ый (~, ~а) *adj.* **1.** odd, queer; quaint, fantastical. **2.** (*coll.*) capricious, whimsical.
причýдник, а *m.* (*coll.*) crank, odd pers., queer pers.
пришварт|овáть, ýю *pf.* (*of* **~óвывать**) (**к**) to moor (to), make fast (to).
пришварт|овáться, ýюсь *pf.* (*of* **~óвываться**) (**к**) to moor (to), tie up (at).
пришвартóвыва|ть(ся), ю(сь) *impf. of* **пришвартовáть(ся)**
пришéл|ец, ьца *m.* newcomer, stranger.
пришепётыва|ть, ю *impf.* (*coll.*) to lisp slightly.
пришéстви|е, я́ *nt.* (*obs.*) advent, coming; **до вторóго ~я** (*joc.*) till doomsday.
пришиб|и́ть, ý ёшь, *past* **~́, ~́ла** *pf.* (*coll.*) **1.** to strike dead. **2.** (*fig.*) to knock out, break (= *to dispirit*).
приши́б|ленный *p.p.p. of* **~и́ть** *and adj.* (*coll.*) broken; crest-fallen.
пришивá|ть, ю́ *impf. of* **приши́ть**
пришивнóй *adj.* sewn on; **п. воротничóк** attached collar.
приш|и́ть, ью́, ьёшь *pf.* (*of* **~ивáть**) **1.** to sew on. **2.** to nail on. **3.** (*+a.* **к** *or +a. and d.*; *fig., coll.*) to pin (on), pin an accusation (of on).
пришкóльный *adj.* (adjoining a) school.
при́шлый *adj.* newly come, arrived; strange, alien.
пришпи́лива|ть, ю *impf. of* **пришпи́лить**
пришпи́л|ить, ю, ишь *pf.* (*of* **~ивать**) to pin.
пришпóрива|ть, ю *impf. of* **пришпóрить**
пришпóр|ить, ю, ишь *pf.* (*of* **~ивать**) to spur; to put, set spurs (to).
прищёлкива|ть, ю *impf. of* **прищёлкнуть**
прищёлк|нуть, ну, нешь *pf.* (*of* **~ивать**): **п. кнутóм** to crack the whip; **п. пáльцами** to snap one's fingers.
прищем|и́ть, лю́, и́шь *pf.* (*of* **~ля́ть**) to pinch, squeeze; **п. себé пáлец двéрью** to pinch one's finger in the door.
прищемля́|ть, ю *impf. of* **прищеми́ть**
прищеп|и́ть лю́, и́шь *pf.* (*of* **~ля́ть**) (*bot.*) to graft.
прищепля́|ть, ю *impf. of* **прищепи́ть**
прищéпк|а, и *f.* (clothes-)peg.
прищéп|ок, ка *m.* = **~ка**
прищýрива|ть(ся), ю(сь) *impf. of* **прищýрить(ся)**
прищýр|ить, ю, ишь *pf.* (*of* **~ивать**); **п. глазá** = **~иться**
прищýр|иться, юсь, ишься *pf.* (*of* **~иваться**) to screw up one's eyes.
прию́т, а *m.* **1.** shelter, refuge. **2.** (*obs.*) asylum; **дéтский п.** orphanage, orphan-asylum; **роди́льный п.** maternity home, lying-in hospital.
прию|ти́ть, чý, ти́шь *pf.* to shelter, give refuge.
прию|ти́ться, чýсь, ти́шься *pf.* to take shelter.
прия́знен|ный (~, ~на) *adj.* (*obs.*) friendly, amicable.
прия́зн|ь, и *f.* (*obs.*) friendliness, good-will.
прия́тел|ь, я *m.* friend.
прия́тельниц|а, ы *f.* **1.** (female) friend. **2.** girl-friend, lady-friend.
прия́тельский *adj.* friendly, amicable.
прия́т|ный (~ен, ~на) *adj.* nice, pleasant, agreeable, pleasing; **п. на вид** nice-looking, gratifying to the eye; **п. на вкус** palatable, tasty; (*impers., pred.*): **~но** it is pleasant; it is nice.
при|я́ть, мý, ~́мешь *pf.* (*obs.*) = **~ня́ть**
про *prep.+a.* **1.** about; **мы говори́ли про вас** we were talking

about you. **2.** (*coll.*) for; **это не про нас** this is not for us. **3.: про себя** to o.s.; **я подумал про себя** I thought to myself; **прочти письмо вслух, а не про себя!** read the letter aloud, not to yourself!
про...[1] *vbl. pref. indicating* **1.** *action through, across or past object, as* **прострелить** to shoot through; **проехать** to pass (by). **2.** *overall or exhaustive action, as* **прогреть** to warm thoroughly. **3.** *duration of action throughout given period of time, as* **просидеть всю ночь** sit up all night. **4.** *loss or failure, as* **проиграть** to lose (*a game*).
про...[2] *as pref. of nn. and adjs.* pro-.
проанализир|овать, ую *pf. of* **анализировать**
проб|а, ы *f.* **1.** trial, test; try-out; assay; audition, screen-test; **п. голоса** voice test; **п. сил** trial of strength; **взять на ~у** to take on trial. **2.** sample. **3.** standard (*measure of purity of gold*); **золото 56-ой ~ы** 14 carat gold; **золото 96-ой ~ы** pure gold, 24 carat gold. **4.** hallmark.
пробавля|ться, юсь *impf.* (*coll.*) to subsist (on), make do (on).
пробалтыва|ть(ся), ю(сь) *impf. of* **проболтать(ся)**
проба|сить, шу, сишь *pf.* (*coll.*) to speak in a bass, deep voice.
пробег, а *m.* **1.** (*sport*) run, race; **лыжный п.** ski-run. **2.** run, mileage, distance covered; **суточный п. паровоза** 24 hours' run for a locomotive; **находиться в ~е** to be working, be operating.
пробега|ть, ю *pf.* (*coll.*) to run about (*for a certain time*).
пробега|ть, ю *impf. of* **пробежать**
пробе|жать, гу, жишь, гут *pf.* (*of* **~гать**) **1.** to pass (running), run past, run by; to run through; to run along; **п. пальцами по клавиатуре** to run one's fingers over the keyboard. **2.** to run; to cover; **поезд ~жал шестьдесят миль ровно в час** the train covered sixty miles in exactly one hour. **3.** (*fig.*) to run, flit (over, down, across); **холод ~жал по её спине** a chill ran down her spine. **4.** (*fig., coll.*) to run through, look through, skim.
пробе|жаться, гусь, жишься, гутся *pf.* to run, take a run.
пробел, а *m.* **1.** blank, gap; hiatus; lacuna; **заполнить ~ы** to fill in the blanks. **2.** (*fig.*) deficiency, gap; **~ы в знаниях** gaps in one's knowledge.
пробива|ть(ся), ю(сь) *impf. of* **пробить(ся)**
пробивк|а, и *f.* **1.** holing, piercing; punching. **2.** caulking.
пробивн|ой *adj.* **1.** piercing, punching; **~ая сила** penetrating power (*of missile*); **п. станок** (*tech.*) punch. **2.** (*elec.*) disruptive. **3.** (*coll.*) go-ahead, go-getting.
пробира|ть(ся), ю(сь) *impf. of* **пробрать(ся)**
пробирк|а, и *f.* test-tube.
пробирн|ый *adj.* testing; assaying; **п. камень** touchstone; **~ое клеймо** hallmark; **п. металл** test metal; **~ая палата** assay office; **~ая склянка** test-tube.
пробир|овать, ую *impf.* to test, assay.
пробирщик, а *m.* assayer, assay-master.
про|бить[1], **бью, бьёшь,** *past* **~бил, ~била, ~било** *pf. of* **бить 9.**
про|бить[2], **бью, бьёшь,** *past* **~бил, ~била, ~било** *pf.* (*of* **~бивать**) to make a hole (in); to hole, pierce; to punch; **п. корабль** to hole a ship; **п. стену** to breach a wall; **п. шину** to puncture a tyre; **п. путь, дорогу** to open the way (*also fig.*); **п. себе дорогу** (*fig.*) to carve one's way.
про|биться[1], **бьюсь, бьёшься** *pf.* (*of* **~биваться**) **1.** to fight, force, make one's way through; to break, strike through; **п. с трудом** to struggle along; **п. сквозь толпу** to fight one's way through the crowd. **2.** (*of plants*) to shoot, show, push up.
про|биться[2], **бьюсь, бьёшься** *pf.* **(над)** to struggle (with) (*for a certain time*).
пробк|а, и *f.* **1.** cork (*substance*). **2.** cork; stopper; plug; **глуп как п.** daft as a brush. **3.** (*elec.*) fuse. **4.** (*fig.*) traffic jam; congestion.
пробков|ый *adj.* cork; subereous, suberic; **п. дуб** cork-oak; **~ая кислота** suberic acid; **п. пояс** cork jacket, lifejacket.
проблем|а, ы *f.* problem.
проблематик|а, и *f.* (*collect.*) problems.
проблематический *adj.* problematic(al).
проблематичност|ь, и *f.* problematical character.
проблематич|ный (~ен, ~на) *adj.* = **~еский**
проблеск, а *m.* flash; ray, gleam (*also fig.*); **п. надежды** ray of hope.
проблескива|ть, ю *impf. of* **проблеснуть**
проблес|нуть, ну, нёшь *pf.* (*of* **~кивать**) to flash, gleam.
проблужда|ть, ю *pf.* to wander, rove, roam (*for a certain time*).
пробный *adj.* **1.** trial, test, experimental; **п. камень** touchstone; **п. ковш** assay spoon; **п. полёт** test flight; **п. спирт** proof spirit; **п. шар** ballon d'essai; **п. экземпляр** specimen copy. **2.** hallmarked.
проб|овать, ую *impf.* (*of* **по~**) **1.** to test; **п. пищу** to taste, try food. **2.** (*+inf.*) to try (to), attempt (to), endeavour (to).
пробода|ть[1], **ет** *pf.* to gore.
пробода|ть[2], **ет** *impf.* (*med.*) to perforate, puncture.
прободени|е, я *nt.* (*med.*) perforation.
пробоин|а, ы *f.* hole (*esp. caused by missile*); **получить ~у** to be holed.
пробо|й, я *m.* **1.** clamp, hasp, holdfast. **2.** (*elec.*) spark-over.
пробойник, а *m.* (*tech.*) punch.
проболе|ть[1], **ю** *pf.* to be ill (*for a certain time*).
пробол|еть[2], **ит** *pf.* to hurt (*for a certain time*).
проболта|ть, ю *pf.* (*of* **пробалтывать**) (*coll.*) **1.** to play for time by talking. **2.** to blab (out).
проболта|ться[1], **юсь** *pf.* (*of* **пробалтываться**) (*coll.*) to blab, blurt out a secret, let the cat out of the bag.
проболта|ться[2], **юсь** *pf.* (*coll.*) to idle, loaf.
пробор, а *m.* parting (*of the hair*); **прямой п.** parting in the middle; **косой п.** parting at one side; **делать (себе) п.** to part one's hair.
пробормо|тать, чу, ~чешь *pf. of* **бормотать**
пробочник, а *m.* (*coll.*) corkscrew.
пробрасыва|ть, ю *impf. of* **пробросить**
про|брать, беру, берёшь, *past* **~брал, ~брала, ~брало** *pf.* (*of* **~бирать**) **1.** to penetrate; **мороз ~брал меня до костей** I was chilled to the marrow; **их ~брал страх** fear had struck them; **его ничем не ~берёшь** he cannot be got at. **2.** (*coll.*) to scold, rate. **3.** (*agric.*) to clear, weed.
про|браться, берусь, берёшься, *past* **~брался, ~бралась, ~бралось** *pf.* (*of* **~бираться**) **1.** to fight, force one's way. **2.** to steal (through, past); **п. ощупью** to feel one's way; **п. на цыпочках** to tiptoe (through).
пробро|дить, жу, ~дишь *pf.* to wander (*for a certain time*).
пробро|сить, шу, сишь *pf.* (*of* **пробрасывать**) (*coll.*) **1.** to count up (*on an abacus*). **2.** to overcount (by).
пробст, а *m.* (*eccl.*) provost (*in Lutheran Church, clergyman in charge of principal church in town*).
пробу|дить, жу, ~дишь *pf.* (*of* **будить** *and* **~ждать**) to wake; to awaken, rouse, arouse (*also fig.*).
пробу|диться, жусь, ~дишься *pf.* (*of* **~ждаться**) to wake up, awake (*also fig.*).
пробужда|ть(ся), ю(сь) *impf. of* **пробудить(ся)**
пробуждени|е, я *nt.* waking up, awakening.
пробурав|ить, лю, ишь *pf.* (*of* **~ливать**) to bore, drill, perforate.
пробуравлива|ть, ю *impf. of* **пробуравить**
пробурч|ать, у, ишь *pf. of* **бурчать**
проб|ыть, уду, удешь, *past* **~ыл, ~ыла** *pf.* to stay, remain; to be (*for a certain time*); **он ~ыл у нас три недели** he stayed with us for three weeks.
провал, а *m.* **1.** downfall. **2.** (*geog.*) gap; funnel. **3.** failure; **п. памяти** failure of memory; **какой п.!** what a flop!
провалива|ть, ю *impf.* **1.** *impf. of* **провалить**. **2. ~й!** (*coll.*) clear off!; beat it!; hop it!
провалива|ться, юсь *impf. of* **провалиться**
провал|ить, ю, ~ишь *pf.* (*of* **~ивать**) **1.** to cause to collapse, knock down. **2.** (*fig., coll.*) to ruin, make a mess (of); **п. роль** (*theatr.*) to ruin a part. **3.** (*fig.*) to reject; **п. кандидата на экзамене** to fail a candidate in an examination; **п. законопроект** to kill a bill.

провал|и́ться, ю́сь, ~́ишься *pf.* (*of* **~́иваться**) **1.** to collapse, come down, fall through; **потоло́к ~и́лся** the ceiling has come down. **2.** (*fig., coll.*) to fail, miscarry; (*in an examination*) to fail, be ploughed; **по́лностью п.** to be a complete, utter failure. **3.** (*coll.*) to disappear, vanish; **он как сквозь зе́млю ~и́лся** he vanished into thin air; **я гото́в был сквозь зе́млю ~и́ться** I wished the earth could swallow me up; **п. мне на э́том ме́сте, е́сли...** I'll be damned if ....

Прова́нс, а *m.* Provence.

провансá́л|ец, ца *m.* Provençal.

провансá́л|ка, ки *f. of* **~ец**

провансá́л|ь, я *m.* mayonnaise, salad dressing.

провансá́льский *adj.* Provençal.

прова́нск|ий *adj.*: **~ое ма́сло** olive oil, salad-oil.

прова́рива|ть *impf. of* **провари́ть**

провар|и́ть, ю́, ~́ишь *pf.* (*of* **~́ивать**) to boil thoroughly.

прове́д|ать, аю *pf.* (*of* **~ывать**) (*coll.*) **1.** to come to see, call on. **2.** (**о**+*p.*) to find out (about), learn (of, about).

проведе́ни|е, я *nt.* **1.** leading, taking, piloting. **2.** building; installation. **3.** carrying out, through; conducting; **п. кампа́нии** (*mil. and fig.*) conduct of a campaign; **п. в жизнь** putting into effect, implementation.

прове́дыва|ть, ю *impf. of* **прове́дать**

провез|ти́, у́, ёшь, *past* **~̈, ~ла́** *pf.* (*of* **провози́ть**) **1.** to convey, transport; **п. контраба́ндой** to smuggle. **2.** to bring (with one).

провентили́р|овать, ую *pf. of* **вентили́ровать**

прове́р|енный *p.p.p. of* **~ить** *and adj.* proved, of proved worth.

прове́р|ить, ю, ишь *pf.* (*of* **~я́ть**) **1.** to check (up on); to verify; to audit; **п. биле́ты** to examine tickets; **п. ка́ссу** to check the till; **п. чью-н. рабо́ту** to check up on s.o.'s work; **п. тетра́ди** to correct exercise-books. **2.** to test; **п. свои́ си́лы** to try one's strength.

прове́рк|а, и *f.* **1.** checking; examination; verification; check-up; **п. исполне́ния** work check-up; **п. нали́чия** stock-taking, inventory-making; **п. счето́в** audit(ing); **п. бо́я ору́жия** (*mil.*) checking the zero of a weapon; **п. управле́ния огнём** (*mil.*) verification of fire. **2.** testing.

провер|ну́ть, ну́, нёшь *pf.* (*of* **~̈тывать**) (*coll.*) **1.** to bore, perforate, pierce. **2.** to crank (*a motor*). **3.** (*fig.*) to rush through (*discussion of a question, etc.*).

прове́рочн|ый *adj.* checking, verifying; **~ая рабо́та** test paper.

провер|те́ть, чу́, ~́тишь *pf.* (*of* **~̈тывать**) (*coll.*) to bore, perforate, pierce.

провёртыва|ть, ю *impf. of* **проверну́ть** *and* **проверте́ть**

прове́рщик, а *m.* checker, inspector.

провер|я́ть, я́ю *impf. of* **~́ить**

прове́с[1]**, а** *m.* short weight.

прове́с[2]**, а** *m.* sag; dip (*of wire*).

прове́|сить[1]**, шу, сишь** *pf.* (*of* **~шивать**) to give short weight.

прове́|сить[2]**, шу, сишь** *pf.* (*of* **~шивать**) to dry in the open, air.

прове́|сить[3]**, шу, сишь** *pf.* (*of* **~шивать**) (*tech.*) to plumb.

прове|сти́, ду́, дёшь, *past* **~̈л, ~ла́** *pf.* (*of* **проводи́ть**[1]) **1.** to lead, take; **п. су́дно** (*naut.*) to pilot a vessel. **2.** to build; to install; **п. железнодоро́жную ве́тку** to build a branch line; **п. водопрово́д** to lay on water; **п. электри́чество** to install electricity. **3.** to carry out, carry on; to conduct, hold; **п. о́пыты** to carry out tests; **п. заседа́ние** to conduct a meeting; **п. рефо́рмы** to carry out reforms; **п. бесе́ду** to give a talk. **4.** to carry through; to carry, pass, get through (*a resolution, a bill, etc.*); to implement (*a decision, etc.*); **им не удало́сь п. законопрое́кт че́рез Пала́ту ло́рдов** they did not succeed in getting the bill through the House of Lords; **п. иде́ю в жизнь** to put an idea into effect, implement an idea. **5.** to advance, put forward (*an idea, etc.*). **6.** (*book-keeping*) to register; **п. по кни́гам** to book; **п. по ка́ссе** to register, ring up on the till. **7.** to draw (*a line, etc.*); **п. грани́цу** to draw a boundary-line. **8.** (+*i.*) to pass over, run over; **она́ ~ла́ руко́й по лбу** she passed her hand over her forehead. **9.** to spend, pass (*time*); **что́бы п. вре́мя** to pass the time; **как вы ~ли́ вре́мя?** (*addressed to pers. on return from holiday, etc.*) did you have a good time?, what sort of time did you have? **10.** (*coll.*) to take in, trick, fool; **меня́ не ~дёшь** you can't fool me.

прове́трива|ть(ся), ю(сь) *impf. of* **прове́трить(ся)**

прове́тр|ить, ю, ишь *pf.* (*of* **~ивать**) to air; to ventilate.

прове́тр|иться, юсь, ишься *pf.* (*of* **~иваться**) **1.** to have an airing; (*fig., coll.*) to have a change of scene. **2.** *pass. of* **~ить**

прове́шива|ть, ю *impf. of* **прове́сить**

провиа́нт, а *m.* provisions, victuals.

прови́дени|е, я *nt.* foresight, forecast.

провиде́ни|е, я *nt.* (*relig.*) Providence.

прови́|деть, жу, дишь *impf.* to foresee.

прови́д|ец, ца *m.* (*obs., rhet.*) seer, prophet.

провиз|ио́нный *adj. of* **~́ия; п. магази́н** provision shop.

прови́зи|я, и *no pl., f.* provisions; **снабди́ть ~ей** to cater (for); to provision, victual.

прови́зор, а *m.* (*qualified*) pharmaceutical chemist.

провизо́р|ный (~ен, ~на) *adj.* provisional; temporary.

провин|и́ться, ю́сь, и́шься *pf.* (**в**+*p.*) to be guilty (of); to commit an offence; **п. пе́ред кем-н.** to wrong s.o., do s.o. an injury; **в чём мы ~и́лись?** what have we done wrong?

прови́нност|ь, и *f.* (*coll.*) fault; offence.

провинциа́л, а *m.* provincial (*pers.*).

провинциали́зм, а *m.* provincialism.

провинциа́льност|ь, и *f.* provinciality.

провинциа́л|ьный (~ен, ~ьна) *adj.* provincial (*also fig.*).

прови́нци|я, и *f.* **1.** province. **2.** the provinces (*opp. capital or other centre*); **жить в глухо́й ~и** to live in the depths of the country.

провира́|ться, юсь *impf. of* **провра́ться**

провис|а́ть, а́ет *impf. of* **~́нуть**

прови́с|нуть, нет *pf.* (*of* **~а́ть**) to sag.

про́вод, а, *pl.* **~а́** *m.* wire, lead, conductor; **возду́шный п.** aerial conductor; **заземля́ющий п.** earth(-wire); **п. с пу́щенным то́ком** live wire.

проводи́мост|ь, и *f.* (*elec.*) conductivity, conduction; **акти́вная п., ва́ттная п.** conductance; **уде́льная п.** specific conductivity.

прово|ди́ть[1]**, жу́, ~́дишь** *impf.* **1.** *impf. of* **провести́. 2.** *impf. only* (*phys., elec.*) to conduct, be a conductor.

прово|ди́ть[2]**, жу́, ~́дишь** *pf.* (*of* **~жа́ть**) to accompany; to see off; **п. на по́езд** to see off (on the train); **п. кого́-н. домо́й** to take, see s.o. home; **п. кого́-н. до двере́й** to see s.o. to the door; **п. поко́йника** to attend a funeral; **п. глаза́ми** to follow with one's eyes.

прово́дк|а, и *f.* **1.** leading, taking. **2.** building; installation. **3.** (*collect.*; *elec.*) wiring, wires.

проводни́к[1]**, а́** *m.* **1.** guide. **2.** (*of train*) conductor; guard.

проводни́к[2]**, а́** *m.* **1.** (*phys., elec.*) conductor. **2.** (*fig.*) bearer; transmitter.

проводни́|ца, цы *f. of* **~к**[1]

проводн|о́й *adj. of* **про́вод; ~а́я связь** telegraphic communication (*opp. radio*).

про́вод|ы, ов *no sg.* seeing-off; send-off.

провожа́т|ый, ого *m.* guide, escort.

провожа́|ть, ю *impf. of* **проводи́ть**[2]

прово́з, а *m.* carriage, conveyance, transport; **пла́та за п.** payment for carriage.

провозве|сти́ть, щу́, сти́шь *pf.* (*of* **~ща́ть**) (*obs.*) **1.** to prophesy. **2.** to proclaim.

провозвеща́|ть, ю *impf. of* **провозвести́ть**

провозгла|си́ть, шу́, си́шь *pf.* (*of* **~ша́ть**) to proclaim; **п. ло́зунг** to advance a slogan; **п. тост** to propose a toast; **п. тост за кого́-н.** to propose s.o.'s health; **его́ ~си́ли королём** he was proclaimed king.

провозглаша́|ть, ю *impf. of* **провозгласи́ть**

провозглаше́ни|е, я *nt.* proclamation; declaration.

прово|зи́ть, жу́, ~́зишь *impf. of* **провезти́**

прово|зи́ться[1]**, жу́сь, ~́зишься** *pf.* **1.** (*coll.*) to play about (*for a certain time*). **2.** (**с**+*i.*) to spend (*a certain time*) (over, in seeing to); **я ~зи́лся це́лый ме́сяц с получе́нием ви́зы** I spent a whole month over obtaining the visa.

прово|зи́ться², **жу́сь, ~́зишься** *impf. pass., of* **~зи́ть**
провозоспосо́бност|ь, и *f.* (*rail.*) carrying capacity
провока́тор, а *m.* **1.** agent provocateur. **2.** (*fig.*) instigator, provoker.
провокацио́нный *adj.* provocative.
провока́ци|я, и *f.* provocation.
про́волок|а, и *f.* wire; **колю́чая п.** barbed wire.
про́волочк|а, и *f. dim. of* **про́волока**; short wire, fine wire.
проволо́чк|а, и *f.* (*coll.*) delay, procrastination.
про́воло|чный *adj. of* **~ка; ~чное загражде́ние** wire entanglement; **~чная сеть** wire netting.
провоня́|ть, ет *pf.* (+*i.*; *coll.*) to stink (of).
прово́рност|ь, и *f.* = **прово́рство**
прово́р|ный (~ен, ~на) *adj.* **1.** quick, swift, expeditious. **2.** agile, nimble, adroit, dexterous.
провор|ова́ться, у́юсь *pf.* (*coll.*) to be caught stealing, embezzling.
проворо́н|ить, ю, ишь *pf.* (*coll.*) to miss, let slip, lose; **п. свою́ о́чередь** to miss one's turn; **п. ме́сто** to lose one's place.
прово́рств|о, а *nt.* **1.** quickness, swiftness. **2.** agility, nimbleness, adroitness, dexterity.
проворч|а́ть, у́, и́шь *pf.* to mutter.
провоци́р|овать, ую *impf. and pf.* (*pf. also* **с~**) to provoke.
провр|а́ться, у́сь, ёшься, *past* **~а́лся, ~ала́сь, ~ало́сь** *pf.* (*of* **провира́ться**) (*coll.*) to give o.s. away; to slip up (*in lying*).
провя́л|ить, ю, ишь *pf. of* **вя́лить**
прогад|а́ть, а́ю *pf.* (*of* **~́ывать**) (*coll.*) to miscalculate.
прога́дыва|ть, ю *impf. of* **прогада́ть**
прогаз|ова́ть, у́ю *pf.* (*coll.*) to run up (*an engine*).
прога́лин|а, ы *f.* glade.
проги́б, а *m.* (*tech.*) caving in, sagging, flexure, deflection; camber; **стрела́ ~а** sag, sagging; depth of camber.
прогиба́|ть(ся), ю(сь) *impf. of* **прогну́ть(ся)**
прогла́|дить¹, **жу, дишь** *pf.* (*of* **~живать**) to iron (out).
прогла́|дить², **жу, дишь** *pf.* to iron (*for a certain time*).
прогла́жива|ть, ю *impf. of* **прогла́дить**¹
прогла́тыва|ть, ю *impf. of* **проглоти́ть; говори́ть, ~я слова́** to swallow one's words.
прогло|ти́ть, чу́, ~́тишь *pf.* (*of* **прогла́тывать**) to swallow (*also fig.*); **п. оскорбле́ние** to swallow, pocket an insult; **п. язы́к** to lose one's tongue; **п. кни́гу** to devour a book; **язы́к ~́тишь** it makes your mouth water.
прогля|де́ть¹, **жу́, ди́шь** *pf.* (*of* **~́дывать**) to look through, glance through; **п. глаза́** (*coll.*) to wear one's eyes out.
прогля|де́ть², **жу́, ди́шь** *pf.* to overlook.
прогля́дыва|ть, ю *impf. of* **прогляде́ть** *and* **прогляну́ть**
прогля|ну́ть, ~́нет *pf.* (*of* **~́дывать**) to show (up, through), peep (out, through); to be perceptible; **со́лнце ~ну́ло из-за облако́в** the sun peeped out from behind the clouds; **в её взгля́де ~ну́ла тоска́** there was a touch of wistfulness in her look.
про|гна́ть, гоню́, го́нишь, *past* **~гна́л, ~гнала́, ~гна́ло** *pf.* (*of* **~гоня́ть**) **1.** to drive away (*also fig.*); (*fig.*) to banish; **п. с глаз доло́й** to banish from one's sight; **п. забо́ты** to banish care. **2.** to drive (through); **п. коро́в в по́ле** to drive the cows into the field; **п. кого́-н. сквозь строй** (*hist.*) to make s.o. run the gauntlet. **3.** (*coll.*) to sack, fire.
прогне́ва|ть, ю *pf.* (*obs.*) to anger, incense.
прогне́ва|ться, юсь *pf.* (*obs.*) (**на**+*a.*) to become angry (with).
про́гнев|ить, лю, ишь *pf. of* **гневи́ть**
прогнива́|ть, ю *impf. of* **прогни́ть**
прогн|и́ть, ию́, иёшь, *past* **~и́л, ~ила́, ~и́ло** *pf.* (*of* **~ива́ть**) to rot through.
прогно́з, а *m.* prognosis; forecast; **п. пого́ды** weather forecast.
прогн|у́ть, у́, ёшь *pf.* (*of* **прогиба́ть**) to cause to cave in, cause to sag.
прогн|у́ться, у́сь, ёшься *pf.* (*of* **прогиба́ться**) to cave in, sag.
проговА́рива|ть(ся), ю(сь) *impf. of* **проговори́ть(ся)**
проговор|и́ть, ю́, и́шь *pf.* (*of* **прогова́ривать**) **1.** to say, pronounce, utter; **п. сквозь зу́бы** to mutter; **он ни сло́ва не ~и́л** he did not utter a word. **2.** to speak, talk (*for a certain time*); **они́ ~и́ли три часа́ подря́д** they talked for three hours on end.
проговор|и́ться, ю́сь, и́шься *pf.* (*of* **прогова́риваться**) to blab (out), talk; to let the cat out of the bag.
проголода́|ть, ю *pf.* to starve, go hungry.
проголода́|ться, юсь *pf.* to get hungry, grow hungry.
проголос|ова́ть, у́ю *pf. of* **голосова́ть**
прого́н¹, **а** *m.* **1.** (*archit.*) purlin; (*of a bridge*) bearer, baulk. **2.** (*archit.*) well, well-shaft (*for a staircase*).
прого́н², **а** *m.* (*dial.*) cattle track.
прого́н³, **а** *m.* (*theatr. sl.*) run-through (= *first full rehearsal of play in order of scenes*).
прого́н|ный *adj. of* **~ы; ~ные (де́ньги)** (*obs.*) travelling allowance.
прого́н|ы, ов *no sg.* (*obs.*) fare (*for journey by post-chaise*).
прогоня́|ть, ю *impf. of* **прогна́ть**
прогор|а́ть, а́ю *impf. of* **~е́ть**¹
прогор|е́ть¹, **ю́, и́шь** *pf.* (*of* **~а́ть**) **1.** to burn through; to burn to a cinder. **2.** (*coll.*) to go bankrupt, go bust.
прогор|е́ть², **ю́, и́шь** *pf.* to burn (*for a certain time*).
прого́рклост|ь, и *f.* rancidity, rankness.
прого́рклый *adj.* rancid, rank.
прого́рк|нуть, ну, нешь, *past* **~, ~ла** *pf. of* **го́ркнуть**
просо|сти́ть, щу́, сти́шь *pf.* to stay.
програ́мм|а, ы *f.* programme; schedule; (*comput.*) program; **обслу́живающая п.** (*comput.*) utility (program); **театра́льная п.** play-bill; **учёбная п.** syllabus; curriculum; **п. ска́чек** race-card; **п. спорти́вных состяза́ний** fixture list.
программи́р|овать, ую *impf.* (*of* **за~**) to programme.
программи́ст, а *m.* (computer) programmer.
програ́мм|ный *adj.* **1.** *adj. of* **~а; ~ная му́зыка** programme music; **~ное обеспе́чение** (*comput.*) software. **2.** (*tech.*) programmed, automatically operated.
прогрева́|ть(ся), ю(сь) *impf. of* **прогре́ть(ся)**
прогре́сс, а *m.* progress.
прогресси́вк|а, и *f.* (*abbr. of* ***прогресси́вная опла́та***) (*coll.*) payment on sliding scale (*for completion of piece-work in excess of plan*).
прогресси́в|ный (~ен, ~на) *adj.* (*in var. senses*) progressive.
прогресси́р|овать, ую *impf.* to progress, make progress; (*of an illness*) to grow progressively worse.
прогре́сси|я, и *f.* (*math.*) progression.
прогре́|ть, ю *pf.* (*of* **~ва́ть**) to heat, warm thoroughly; **п. мото́р** to warm up an engine.
прогре́|ться, юсь *pf.* (*of* **~ва́ться**) to get thoroughly warmed; (*of an engine, etc.*) to warm up.
прогрохо|ти́ть, чу́, ти́шь *pf. of* **грохоти́ть**
прогу́л, а *m.* absence (from work); absenteeism; truancy.
прогу́лива|ть, ю *impf.* **1.** *impf. of* **прогуля́ть**¹. **2.** *impf. only* to walk; **п. ло́шадь** to walk a horse.
прогу́лива|ться, юсь *impf.* **1.** *impf. of* **прогуля́ться. 2.** *impf. only* to stroll, saunter.
прогу́лк|а, и *f.* **1.** walk; stroll; ramble; **п. для моцио́на** constitutional. **2.** outing; **п. в экипа́же, п. в автомоби́ле** drive; **п. в ло́дке** row; **п. под паруса́ми** sail; **п. верхо́м** ride.
прогу́л|очный *adj. of* **~ка; ~очная зо́на** pedestrian precinct; **~очная ло́дка** pleasure-boat (*opp. racing-craft*).
прогу́л|ьный *adj. of* **~; ~ьное вре́мя** time off work (*without good cause*).
прогу́льщик, а *m.* absentee; truant.
прогуля́|ть¹, **ю** *pf.* (*of* **прогу́ливать**) **1.** to be absent from work (*without good cause*); to play truant. **2.** to miss; **п. обе́д** to miss one's dinner (*as result of failing to appear at right time*); **п. уро́ки** to skip lessons, bunk off school.
прогуля́|ть², **ю** *pf.* to walk; to stroll.
прогуля́|ться, юсь *pf.* (*of* **прогу́ливаться**) to take a walk, stroll.
прод... *comb. form, abbr. of* **продово́льственный**
прода|ва́ть, ю́, ёшь *impf. of* **~́ть**
прода|ва́ться, ю́сь, ёшься *impf.* **1.** (*impf. only*) to be on

sale, be for sale; **дом ~ётся** the house is for sale; **~ётся мотоци́кл** (*formula of advertisement of sale*) 'motor-cycle for sale'. **2.** (*impf. only*) to sell; **дёшево п.** to sell cheap, go cheap; **его́ но́вый рома́н хорошо́ ~ётся** his new novel is selling well. **3.** *impf. of* **∸ться**

продав|е́ц, ца́ *m.* **1.** seller; vendor. **2.** salesman, shop-assistant.

продав|и́ть, лю́, ∸ишь *pf.* (*of* **∸ливать**) to break (through); to crush.

прода́влива|ть, ю *impf. of* **продави́ть**

продавщи́ц|а, ы *f.* **1.** seller; vendor. **2.** saleswoman, shop-assistant, shop-girl.

прода́ж|а, и *f.* sale, selling; **опто́вая п.** wholesale; **п. в ро́зницу** retail; **п. с торго́в** auction sale, public sale; **пусти́ть в ~у** to put on sale; **пойти́ в ~у** to be offered for sale, be on the market, be up for sale; **поступи́ть в ~у** to be on sale, be on the market; **нет в ~е** is not on sale, is not obtainable; (*of a book*) is out of print.

прода́жност|ь, и *f.* mercenariness, venality.

прода́ж|ный *adj.* **1.** to be sold, for sale; **~ная цена́** sale price. **2.** **(~ен, ~на)** (*fig.*) mercenary, venal; corrupt; bent; **~ная душа́** mercenary creature; **~ная же́нщина** streetwalker.

прода́лблива|ть, ю *impf. of* **продолби́ть**

прода́|ть, м, шь, ст, ди́м, ди́те, ду́т, *past* **про́дал, ~ла́, про́дало** *pf.* (*of* **~ва́ть**) **1.** to sell; **п. о́птом** to sell wholesale; **п. в ро́зницу** to sell retail; **п. с торго́в** to auction; **п. в креди́т** to sell on credit, on tick; **п. себе́ в убы́ток** to sell at a loss. **2.** (*fig., pej.*) to sell, sell out.

прода́|ться, мся, шься, стся, ди́мся, ди́тесь, ду́тся, *past* **~лся, ~ла́сь** *pf.* (*of* **~ва́ться**) to sell o.s.

продвига́|ть(ся), ю(сь) *impf. of* **продви́нуть(ся)**

продвиже́ни|е, я *nt.* **1.** advancement. **2.** (*mil.; fig.*) progress, advance.

продви́|нуть, ну, нешь *pf.* (*of* **~га́ть**) **1.** to move forward, push forward. **2.** (*fig.*) to promote, further, advance; **п. по слу́жбе** to promote, give promotion; **п. де́ло** to expedite a matter.

продви́|нуться, нусь, нешься *pf.* (*of* **~га́ться**) **1.** to advance (*also fig.*); to move on, move forward; to push on, push forward; to forge ahead; **п. вперёд** (*mil. and fig.*) to gain ground, make headway, make an advance. **2.** to be promoted, receive promotion, receive advancement. **3.** *pass. of* **~нуть**

продева́|ть, ю *impf. of* **проде́ть**

продежу́р|ить, ю, ишь *pf.* to be on duty (*for a certain time*).

продеклами́р|овать, ую *pf. of* **деклами́ровать**

проде́л|ать, аю *pf.* (*of* **~ывать**) **1.** to make (*an aperture, a way through, etc.*). **2.** to do, perform, accomplish; **п. бо́льшую рабо́ту** to accomplish a great work.

проде́лк|а, и *f.* trick; prank, escapade; **моше́нническая п.** dirty trick, swindle, fraud.

проде́лыва|ть, ю *impf. of* **проде́лать**

продемонстри́р|овать, ую *pf. of* **демонстри́ровать**

продёрг|ать, аю *pf.* (*of* **~ивать**) (*agric.*) to thin (out), weed (out).

продёргива|ть, ю *impf. of* **продёргать** *and* **продёрнуть**

продерж|а́ть, у́, ∸ишь *pf.* to hold (*for a certain time*); to keep (*for a certain time*); **его́ ~а́ли два ме́сяца в больни́це** he was kept in hospital for two months.

продерж|а́ться, у́сь, ∸ишься *pf.* to hold out.

продёр|нуть, ну, нешь *pf.* (*of* **~гивать**) (*coll.*) **1.** to pass, run; **п. ни́тку в иго́лку** to thread a needle. **2.** (*fig.*) to tear to shreds, pull to pieces (= *to criticize severely*).

проде́|ть, ну, нешь *pf.* (*of* **~ва́ть**) to pass, run; **п. ни́тку в иго́лку** to thread a needle.

продефили́р|овать, ую *pf. of* **дефили́ровать**

продешев|и́ть, лю́, и́шь *pf.* (*coll.*) to sell too cheap.

продикт|ова́ть, у́ю *pf. of* **диктова́ть**

продира́|ть(ся), ю(сь) *impf. of* **продра́ть(ся)**

продлева́|ть, ю *impf. of* **продли́ть**

продле́ни|е, я *nt.* extension, prolongation

продл|ённый *p.p.p. of* **~и́ть; шко́ла с ~ённым днём** extended-day school.

продл|и́ть, ю́, и́шь *pf.* (*of* **~ева́ть**) to extend, prolong; **п. о́тпуск** to extend leave; **п. срок де́йствия ви́зы** to extend a visa.

продл|и́ться, ю́сь, и́шься *pf. of* **дли́ться**

продма́г, а *m.* (*abbr. of* **продово́льственный магази́н**) grocer's (shop).

проднало́г, а *m.* (*hist.*) tax in kind.

продово́льств|енный *adj. of* **~ие; ~енная ка́рточка** ration book, ration card, food-card; **п. магази́н** grocery (store), provision store; **~енные райо́ны** food-producing areas; **п. склад** food store; (*mil.*) ration store, ration dump; **~енное снабже́ние** food supply; **~енные това́ры** food-stuffs.

продово́льстви|е, я *nt.* food-stuffs, provisions; (*mil.*) rations; **но́рма ~я** ration scale.

продолб|и́ть, лю́, и́шь *pf.* (*of* **прода́лбливать**) to make a hole (in), chisel through.

продолгова́тост|ь, и *f.* oblong form.

продолгова́т|ый (~, ~а) *adj.* oblong; **п. мозг** (*anat.*) medulla oblongata.

продолжа́тел|ь, я *m.* continuer, successor.

продолж|а́ть, а́ю *impf.* **1.** to continue, go on, proceed; **п. свою́ рабо́ту** to continue, go on with one's work; **п. рабо́тать** to continue to work, go on working. **2.** *impf. of* **∸ить**

продолж|а́ться, а́ется *impf.* (*of* **∸иться**) to continue, last, go on, be in progress; **восста́ние ~а́ется уже́ второ́й год** the insurrection is now in its second year.

продолже́ни|е, я *nt.* **1.** continuation; sequel; **п. сле́дует** to be continued. **2.** extension, prolongation; continuation; **п. ли́нии** extension of a line; **забо́р слу́жит ~ем стены́** the fence serves as a continuation of the wall. **3.: в п.** (*+g.*) in the course (of), during, for, throughout; **в п. го́да** throughout the year; **в п. почти́ двух лет я ни ра́зу её не вида́л** during almost two years I did not see her once.

продолжи́тельност|ь, и *f.* duration, length.

продолжи́тел|ьный (~ен, ~ьна) *adj.* long; prolonged, protracted.

продо́лж|ить, у, ишь *pf.* (*of* **~а́ть**) to extend, prolong.

продо́лж|иться, усь, ишься *pf. of* **~а́ться**

продо́льн|ый *adj.* longitudinal, lengthwise, linear; (*naut.*) fore-and-aft; **~ая ось** longitudinal axis; **~ая перебо́рка** (*naut.*) fore-and-aft bulkhead; **~ая пила́** rip-saw; **п. разре́з** longitudinal section.

продохн|у́ть, у́, ёшь *pf.* (*coll.*) to breathe freely.

продразвёрстк|а, и *f.* (*hist.*) requisitioning of farm produce.

про|дра́ть, деру́, дерёшь, *past* **~дра́л, ~драла́, ~дра́ло** *pf.* (*of* **~дира́ть**) (*coll.*) to tear; to wear holes (in); **п. глаза́** to open one's eyes.

про|дра́ться, деру́сь, дерёшься, *past* **~дра́лся, ~драла́сь, ~драло́сь** *pf.* (*of* **~дира́ться**) (*coll.*) **1.** to tear; to wear into holes; **у меня́ ло́кти ~дра́лись** my coat is out at the elbows. **2.** to squeeze through, force one's way through.

продрем|а́ть, лю́, ∸лешь *pf.* to doze (*for a certain time*).

продро́г|нуть, ну, нешь, *past* **~, ~ла** *pf.* to be chilled to the marrow.

продува́ни|е, я *nt.* = **проду́вка**

продува́тельный *adj.* = **проду́вочный**

продува́|ть, ю *impf.* **1.** *impf. of* **проду́ть. 2.** (*impf. only*) to blow (*from all sides*); **прия́тно ~л ветеро́к** there was a pleasant breeze.

продува́|ться, юсь *impf. of* **проду́ться**

проду́вк|а, и *f.* (*tech.*) blowing through, blowing off; scavenging.

продувн|о́й[1] *adj.* (*tech.*) = **∸очный**

продувн|о́й[2] *adj.* (*coll.*) crafty, sly, roguish; **~а́я бе́стия** rogue.

проду́в|очный *adj. of* **~ка; п. во́здух** scavenging air; **п. кла́пан** blow valve, blow-off valve; **п. насо́с** scavenging pump; **~очная труба́** blow-off pipe, blast pipe.

проду́кт, а *m.* **1.** product; **побо́чный п.** by-product; **~ы сгора́ния** (*chem.*) products of combustion. **2.** *pl.* produce;

provisions, food-stuffs; **моло́чные ~ы** dairy produce; **натура́льные ~ы** wholefoods; **~ы се́льского хозя́йства** farm produce.

продукти́вно *adv.* productively; with a good result, to good effect.

продукти́вност|ь, и *f.* productivity.

продукти́в|ный (~ен, ~на) *adj.* (*in var. senses*) productive; (*fig.*) fruitful; **п. скот** productive livestock; **п. су́ффикс** (*ling.*) productive suffix.

продукто́вый *adj.* food, provision; **п. магази́н** grocery (store), provision store.

проду́кци|я, и *f.* production, output.

продума|нный *p.p.p. of* **~ть** *and adj.* well thought-out, considered; **~нное реше́ние** a considered decision.

проду́м|ать, аю *pf.* (*of* **~ывать**) to think over; to think out.

проду́мыва|ть, ю *impf. of* **проду́мать**

проду́|ть, ю, ешь *pf.* (*of* **~ва́ть**) **1.** to blow through; (*tech.*) to blow through, blow off, blow out; to scavenge. **2.** (*impers.+a.*) to be in a draught; **придви́ньте стул, а то вас ~ет** bring your chair up, or else you will be in a draught. **3.** (*coll.*) to lose (*at games*).

проду́|ться, юсь, ешься *pf.* (*of* **~ва́ться**) (*coll.*) to lose (*at games*).

проду́шин|а, ы *f.* air-hole, vent.

продыря́в|ить, лю, ишь *pf.* (*of* **~ливать**) to make a hole (in), pierce.

продыря́в|иться, люсь, ишься *pf.* (*of* **~ливаться**) to become full of holes.

продыря́влива|ть(ся), ю(сь) *impf. of* **продыря́вить(ся)**

проеда́|ть(ся), ю(сь) *impf. of* **прое́сть(ся)**

прое́зд, а *m.* **1.** passage, thoroughfare; **«~а нет!»** 'no thoroughfare!' **2.** journey.

прое́з|дить[1], жу, дишь *pf.* (*of* **~жа́ть**) **1.** to exercise (*a horse, etc.*). **2.** (*coll.*) to spend on a journey, in travelling; **мы ~дили сто рубле́й** we got through a hundred roubles on the journey.

прое́з|дить[2], жу, дишь *pf.* to spend (*a certain time*) driving, riding, travelling; **они́ ~дили тро́е су́ток** they had travelled for three days and nights.

прое́з|диться, жусь, дишься *pf.* (*coll.*) to have spent all one's money on a journey, in travelling.

проездн|о́й *adj.* travelling; **п. биле́т** ticket; **~а́я пла́та** fare; *as n.* **~ы́е, ~ы́х** travelling expenses.

прое́здом *adv.* en route, in transit, while passing through.

проезжа́|ть, ю *impf. of* **прое́здить** *and* **прое́хать**

прое́зж|ий *adj.*: **~ая доро́га** thoroughfare, public road; **~ие лю́ди** passers-by; *as n.* **п., ~его** *m.* passer-by.

прое́кт, а *m.* **1.** project, scheme, design. **2.** draft; **п. догово́ра** draft treaty.

проекти́вн|ый *adj.* **~ая геоме́трия** descriptive geometry, projecting geometry.

проекти́ровани|е, я *nt.* projecting, planning, designing; **автоматизи́рованное п.** CAD, computer-aided design.

проекти́р|овать[1], ую *impf.* **1.** (*pf.* **за~** *and* **с~**) to project, plan, design; **п. но́вый теа́тр** to design a new theatre. **2.** *impf. only* (*fig.*) to plan; **мы ~уем уе́хать весно́й** we plan to go away in the spring.

проекти́р|овать[2], ую *impf.* (*math.*) to project.

проектиро́вк|а, и *f.* = **проекти́рование**

проектиро́вщик, а *m.* planner, designer.

прое́ктн|ый *adj.* **1.** planning, designing; **~ое бюро́** planning office. **2.** designed; **~ая мо́щность** (*tech.*) rated capacity; **~ая ско́рость** designed speed.

проекцио́нный *adj.*: **п. фона́рь** projector, magic lantern.

прое́кци|я, и *f.* **1.** (*math.*) projection; **вертика́льная п.** vertical projection, front view; elevation; **горизонта́льная п.** horizontal projection, plan view. **2.** projection (*on to a screen*).

проём, а *m.* (*archit.*) aperture; embrasure; **дверно́й п.** doorway.

прое́|сть, м, шь, ст, ди́м, ди́те, дя́т, *past* **~л** *pf.* (*of* **~да́ть**) **1.** to eat through; to corrode. **2.** (*coll.*) to spend on food.

прое́|сться, мся, шься, стся, ди́мся, ди́тесь, дя́тся *past* **~лся** *pf.* (*of* **~да́ться**) (*coll.*) to spend all one's money on food.

прое́|хать, ду, дешь *pf.* (*of* **~зжа́ть**) **1.** to pass (by, through); to drive (by, through), ride (by, through). **2.** to pass, go past (*inadvertently or by mistake*). **3.** to go, do, make, cover (*a certain distance*).

прое́|хаться, дусь, дешься *pf.* (*coll.*) to go for an outing; **п. на чей-н. счёт, п. по чьему́-н. а́дресу** (*joc.*) to take it out of s.o., have a laugh at s.o.'s expense.

прожа́р|енный *p.p.p. of* **~ить** *and adj.* (*cul.*) well-done.

прожа́рива|ть(ся), ю(сь) *impf. of* **прожа́рить(ся)**

прожа́р|ить, ю, ишь *pf.* (*of* **~ивать**) to fry, roast thoroughly.

прожа́р|иться, юсь, ишься *pf.* (*of* **~иваться**) **1.** to fry, roast thoroughly. **2.** *pass. of* **~ить**

прожд|а́ть, у́, ёшь, *past* **~а́л, ~ала́, ~а́ло** *pf.* (*+a. or g.*) to wait (for), spend (*a certain time*) waiting (for).

прож|ева́ть, ую́, уёшь *pf.* (*of* **~ёвывать**) to chew well, masticate well.

прожёвыва|ть, ю *impf. of* **прожева́ть**

проже́кт, а *m.* **1.** (*obs.*) = **прое́кт. 2.** (*coll., iron.*) (hair-brained) scheme.

прожектёр, а *m.* (*iron.*) schemer.

прожектёрств|о, а *nt.* (*iron.*) (hair-brained) scheming.

прожектёрств|овать, ую *impf.* (*iron.*) to scheme, go in for hair-brained schemes.

проже́ктор, а, *pl.* **~ы** *and* **~а́** *m.* searchlight; **п. залива́ющего све́та** floodlight projector.

прожектори́ст, а *m.* searchlight operator.

проже́ктор|ный *adj. of* **~**

про́желт|ь, и *f.* yellow tint.

про|же́чь, жгу́, жжёшь, жгу́т, *past* **~жёг, ~жгла́** *pf.* (*of* **~жига́ть**) **1.** to burn through; **п. дыру́ в чём-н.** to burn a hole in sth. **2.** to burn, leave alight (*for a certain time*).

про|жжённый *p.p.p. of* **~же́чь** *and adj.* (*coll.*) arch, double-dyed; **п. плут** arch-scoundrel.

прожива́|ть, ю *impf.* **1.** to live, reside. **2.** *impf. of* **прожи́ть**

прожива́|ться, юсь *impf. of* **прожи́ться**

прожига́тел|ь, я *m.*: **п. жи́зни** fast liver.

прожига́|ть[1], ю *impf. of* **проже́чь**

прожига́|ть[2], ю *impf.*: **п. жизнь** to lead a fast life, live fast.

прожи́лк|а, и *f.* (*in var. senses*) vein.

прожи́ти|е, я *nt.* living, livelihood; **хвата́ет ли у них де́нег на п.?** have they enough to live on?

прожи́точный *adj.* necessary, sufficient to live on; **п. ми́нимум** living wage, subsistence wage.

про|жи́ть, живу́, живёшь, *past* **~́жил, ~жила́, ~́жило** *pf.* (*of* **~жива́ть**) **1.** to live; **он ~́жил сто лет** he lived to be a hundred (*years of age*). **2.** to spend; **мы ~́жили ме́сяц а́вгуст на берегу́ мо́ря** we spent the month of August at the seaside. **3.** to spend, run through (*money*); **в оди́н год я ~́жил насле́дство** in a year I had run through the legacy.

про|жи́ться, живу́сь, живёшься, *past* **~жи́лся, ~жила́сь** *pf.* (*of* **~жива́ться**) (*coll.*) to have spent all one's money, be spent up.

прожо́рливост|ь, и *f.* voracity, voraciousness, gluttony.

прожо́рлив|ый (~, ~а) *adj.* voracious, gluttonous.

прожужж|а́ть, у́, и́шь *pf.* to buzz, drone, hum; **п. у́ши кому́-н.** (*coll.*) to keep dinning sth. into s.o.'s ears, drone on at s.o.

про́з|а, ы *f.* prose; **п. жи́зни** the prosaic side of life.

прозаи́зм, а *m.* prosaic expression (*in poetry*).

проза́ик, а *m.* prose-writer, prosaist.

прозаи́ческий *adj.* **1.** prose; **п. перево́д** prose translation. **2.** prosaic; matter-of-fact; prosy.

прозаи́чност|ь, и *f.* **1.** matter-of-factness; prosiness. **2.** (*fig.*) dullness, flatness.

прозаи́ч|ный (~ен, ~на) *adj.* **1.** prosaic; matter-of-fact; prosy. **2.** (*fig.*) common-place, humdrum.

прозакла́дыва|ть, ю *impf. and pf.* (*coll.*) **1.** to stake, wager. **2.** (*obs.*) to lose (*in betting*).

прозва́ни|е, я *nt.* nickname, sobriquet; **по ~ю** nicknamed, otherwise known as.

про|зва́ть, зову́, зовёшь, *past* **~зва́л, ~звала́, ~́зва́ло**

pf. (*of* **~зыва́ть**) to nickname, name.
про́звищ|е, я *nt.* nickname, sobriquet.
прозвон|и́ть, ю́, и́шь *pf.* **1.** to ring out, peal. **2.** to ring for, announce by ringing; **~и́ли обе́д, ~и́ли обе́дать** the bell (gong, *etc.*) went for dinner.
прозвуч|а́ть, и́т *pf. of* **звуча́ть**
прозева́|ть[1], **ю** *pf. of* **зева́ть 3.**; (*coll.*) to miss.
прозева́|ть[2], **ю** *pf.* to yawn (*for a certain time*).
прозе́ктор, а *m.* prosector, dissector.
прозе́кторск|ая, ой *f.* dissecting-room.
прозели́т, а *m.* proselyte.
прозим|ова́ть, у́ю *pf. of* **зимова́ть**
прозна́|ть, ю *pf.* (+*a. or* о+*p.*; *coll.*) to find out (about), hear (about).
прозоде́жд|а, ы *f.* (*abbr. of* ***произво́дственная оде́жда***) working clothes; overalls.
прозорли́вост|ь, и *f.* sagacity, perspicacity, intuition.
прозорли́в|ый (~, ~а) *adj.* sagacious, perspicacious.
прозра́чност|ь, и *f.* transparence, transparency.
прозра́ч|ный (~ен, ~на) *adj.* transparent (*also fig.*); limpid, pellucid; **п. намёк** transparent hint.
прозрева́|ть, ю *impf. of* **прозре́ть**
прозре́ни|е, я *nt.* **1.** recovery of sight. **2.** (*fig.*) insight.
прозр|е́ть, ю́, и́шь *pf.* (*of* **~ева́ть**) **1.** to recover one's sight. **2.** (*fig.*) to begin to see clearly; **ту́т-то я и ~е́л** my eyes were opened; I saw the light.
прозыва́|ть, ю *impf. of* **прозва́ть**
прозыва́|ться, юсь *impf.* to be nicknamed, have a nickname.
прозяба́ни|е, я *nt.* vegetation (*also fig.*).
прозяба́|ть, ю *impf.* to vegetate (*also fig.*).
прозя́б|нуть, ну, нешь, *past* **~, ~ла** *pf.* (*coll.*) to be chilled.
проигр|а́ть[1], **а́ю** *pf.* (*of* **≁ывать**) to lose (= *to be defeated, etc.*); **п. фигу́ру** to lose a piece (*at chess*); **п. суде́бный проце́сс** to lose a case; **мы ничего́ не ~а́ли, прие́хав авто́бусом** we lost nothing in coming by bus; **п. в чьём-н. мне́нии** to sink in s.o.'s estimation.
проигр|а́ть[2], **а́ю** *pf.* (*of* **≁ывать**) to play (through, over); **п. конце́рт на патефо́нных пласти́нках** to play through a concerto on gramophone records; **п. магнитофо́нную ле́нту** to play over a tape (*on a tape recorder*).
проигр|а́ть[3], **а́ю** *pf.* to play (*for a certain time*).
проигр|а́ться, а́юсь *pf.* (*of* **≁ываться**) to lose all one's money (*at gambling*).
прои́грыватель|ь, я *m.* record-player; turntable; **п. компакт-ди́сков** CD player.
прои́грыва|ть(ся), ю(сь) *impf. of* **проигра́ть(ся)**
про́игрыш, а *m.* loss; **оста́ться в ~е** to be the loser, come off loser
произведе́ни|е, я *nt.* **1.** work, production; **и́збранные ~я Л. Н. Толсто́го** selected works of L. N. Tolstoy; **ме́лкие ~я** minor works. **2.** (*math.*) product.
произве|сти́, ду́, дёшь, *past* **≁л, ~ла́** *pf.* (*of* **производи́ть**) **1.** to make; to carry out; to execute; **п. вы́стрел** to fire a shot; **п. о́пыты** to carry out experiments; **п. платёж** to effect payment; **п. сле́дствие** to hold an inquest; **п. смотр** (+*d.*) to hold a review (of), review; **п. съёмку кинофи́льма** to shoot a film; **п. уче́ние** (*mil.*) to drill, train. **2.** to give birth (to); **п. на свет** to bring into the world. **3.** (*fig.*) to cause, produce; **п. впечатле́ние (на**+*a.*) to make, create an impression (on, upon); **п. сенса́цию** to cause, make a sensation. **4.** (**в**+*nom.-a.*) to promote (to, to the rank of); **его́ ~ли́ в подполко́вники** he has been promoted (to the rank of) lieutenant-colonel.
производи́тел|ь[1], **я** *m.* **1.** producer; **ме́лкие ~и** small producers. **2.** sire; **жеребе́ц-п.** stud-horse; **бык-п.** breeding bull.
производи́тел|ь[2], **я** *m.*: **п. рабо́т** clerk of the works.
производи́тельност|ь, и *f.* productivity, output, productiveness.
производи́тел|ьный (~ен, ~ьна) *adj.* productive; efficient.
произво|ди́ть, жу́, ≁дишь *impf.* **1.** *impf. of* **произвести́. 2.** *impf. only* to produce. **3.** *impf. only* (*ling.*) to derive.
произво́дн|ый *adj.* derivative, derived; **~ое сло́во** derivative; *as n.* **~ая, ~ой** *f.* (*math.*) derivative.
произво́дственник, а *m.* production worker.
произво́дств|енный *adj. of* **~о; ~енное зада́ние** production target, production quota; **~енное обуче́ние** industrial training; **~енная пра́ктика** practical training; **~енное совеща́ние** production conference; **п. стаж** industrial work record, industrial experience.
произво́дств|о, а *nt.* **1.** production, manufacture; **изде́ржки ~а** production costs; **сре́дства ~а** means of production; **изде́лия куста́рного, фабри́чного ~а** hand-made, factory-made goods; **япо́нского ~а** Japanese-made; **рабо́тать на ~е** to work on production. **2.** factory, works; **пойти́ на п.** to go to work at a factory. **3.** carrying-out, execution. **4. (в**+*nom.-a.*) promotion (to, to the rank of).
производ|я́щий *pres. part. act. of* **~и́ть** *and adj.* (*econ.*) producing, producer.
произво́л, а *m.* **1.** arbitrariness; **оста́вить на п. судьбы́** to leave to the mercy of fate. **2.** arbitrary rule.
произво́льно *adv.* **1.** arbitrarily. **2.** at will.
произво́льност|ь, и *f.* arbitrariness.
произво́л|ьный (~ен, ~ьна) *adj.* arbitrary.
произнесе́ни|е, я *nt.* pronouncing; utterance, delivery.
произнес|ти́, у́, ёшь, *past* **≁, ~ла́** *pf.* (*of* **произноси́ть**) **1.** to pronounce; to articulate. **2.** to pronounce, say, utter; **п. пригово́р** to pronounce sentence; **п. речь** to deliver a speech; **он не ≁ ни сло́ва** he did not utter a word.
произноси́тельн|ый *adj.* (*ling.*) articulatory; **п. аппара́т** articulatory apparatus; **~ые тру́дности англи́йского языка́** the difficulties of English pronunciation.
произно|си́ть, шу́, ≁сишь *impf. of* **произнести́**
произноше́ни|е, я *nt.* pronunciation; articulation.
произо|йти́, йду́, йдёшь, *past* **~шёл, ~шла́** *pf.* (*of* **происходи́ть**) **1.** to happen, occur, take place. **2. (от, из-за)** to spring (from), arise (from), result (from); **ава́рия ~шла́ от небре́жности** the crash resulted from carelessness. **3. (из, от)** to come (from, of), descend (from), be descended (from).
произраста́ни|е, я *nt.* growth, growing, sprouting.
произраст|а́ть, а́ет *impf. of* **~и́**
произраст|и́, ёт, *past* **произро́с, произросла́** *pf.* (*of* **~а́ть**) to grow, sprout, spring up.
проиллюстри́р|овать, ую *pf.* (*of* **иллюстри́ровать**) to illustrate.
проинструкти́р|овать, ую *pf.* (*of* **инструкти́ровать**) to instruct, give instructions (to).
проинтервьюи́р|овать, ую *pf.* (*of* **интервьюи́ровать**) to interview.
проинформи́р|овать, ую *pf.* (*of* **информи́ровать**) to inform.
прои|ска́ть, щу́, ≁щешь *pf.* to look (for), search (for), spend (*a certain time*) in search (of).
про́иск|и, ов *no sg.* intrigues; machinations, underhand plotting.
проистека́|ть, ю *impf. of* **происте́чь**
происте́|чь, ку́, чёшь, ку́т, *past* **≁к, ~кла́** *pf.* (*of* **~ка́ть**) **(из, от)** to spring (from), result (from).
происхо|ди́ть, жу́, ≁дишь *impf.* **1.** *impf. of* **произойти́. 2.** *impf. only* to go on, be going on; **что тут ≁дит?** what is going on here?
происхожде́ни|е, я *nt.* (*in var. senses*) origin; provenance; parentage, descent, extraction, birth; **п. ви́дов** (*biol.*) origin of species; **он по ~ю армяни́н** he is an Armenian by birth; he is of Armenian extraction.
происше́стви|е, я *nt.* event, incident, happening, occurrence; accident; **отде́л~й** (*in newspaper*) local news.
пройдо́х|а, и *c.g.* (*coll.*) creeper; scoundrel, rascal.
про́йм|а, ы *f.* armhole.
про|йти́, йду́, йдёшь, *past* **~шёл, ~шла́** *pf.* (*of* **~ходи́ть**[1]) **1.** to pass (by, through); to go (by, through); **п. ми́мо** to pass by, go by, go past; (+*g.*; *fig.*) to overlook, disregard; **п. по́лем** to go by, through the field(s); **п. торже́ственным ма́ршем** to march past; **п. молча́нием** to pass over in silence; **п. по мосту́** to cross a bridge; **п. в жизнь** to be put into effect. **2.** to pass, go past (*inadvertently or by mistake*). **3.** to go, do, make, cover (*a certain distance*); **п.**

две ты́сячи миль за неде́лю to do two thousand miles in a week. **4.** (*of news, rumours, etc.*) to travel, spread. **5.** (*of rain, etc.*) to fall. **6.** (*of time*) to pass, elapse, go, go by; **~шёл це́лый год** a whole year had passed; **не ~шло́ шести́ ме́сяцев, как он верну́лся** not six months had passed before he returned. **7.** to be over; to pass (off), abate, let up; **~шло́ ле́то** summer was over; **боль ~шла́** the pain passed (off); **дождь ~шёл** the rain abated. **8.** (+*a. or* **че́рез**) to pass, go through, get through; **де́ло ~шло́ мно́го инста́нций** the case went through many instances; **его́ пье́са снача́ла не ~шла́ че́рез цензу́ру** his play at first did not pass the censorship; **э́то не ~йдёт** (*coll.*) it won't work. **9.** to go, go off; **как ~шёл ваш докла́д?** how did your lecture go?; **заседа́ние ~шло́ уда́чно** the meeting went off successfully. **10.** (**в**+*nom.-a.*) to become, be made; to be placed (on), be taken (on); **он ~шёл в доце́нты** he has been made a reader, he has received a readership; **она́ ~шла́ в штат** she has been taken on the staff. **11.** (*coll.*) to do, take; **п. хи́мию** to do chemistry; **мы уже́ ~шли́ вое́нную слу́жбу** we have already done military service; **п. ку́рс лече́ния** to take a course of treatment.

про|йти́сь, йду́сь, йдёшься, *past* **~шёлся, ~шла́сь** *pf.* (*of* **~ха́живаться**) **1.** to walk up and down, stroll; to take a stroll; **п. по ко́мнате** to pace up and down the room. **2.** (*coll.*) to dance. **3.** (**по**+*d.*; *coll.*) to run (over), go (over); **п. по кла́вишам** to run one's fingers over the keys. **4.: п. на чей-н. счёт, п. по чьему́-н. а́дресу** (*coll.*) to have a fling at s.o., give s.o. a bad write-up.

прок, а (у) *m.* (*coll.*) use, benefit; **что в э́том ∸у?** what is the good of it?; **из э́того не бу́дет ∸у** no good will come of this.

прокажённ|ый *adj.* leprous; *as n.* **п., ~ого** *m.*, **~ая, ~ой** *f.* leper.

прока́з|а[1]**, ы** *f.* leprosy.

прока́з|а[2]**, ы** *f.* mischief, prank, trick.

прока́|зить, жу, зишь *impf.* (*of* **на~**) (*coll.*) to be up to mischief, play pranks.

прока́злив|ый (~, ~а) *adj.* mischievous.

прока́зник, а *m.* mischief-maker; prankster.

прока́знича|ть, ю *impf.* (*of* **на~**) = **прока́зить**

прока́лива|ть, ю *impf. of* **прокали́ть**

прокал|и́ть, ю́, и́шь *pf.* (*of* **∸ивать**) (*tech.*) to temper, anneal; to calcine, fire.

прока́лк|а, и *f.* (*tech.*) tempering.

прока́лыва|ть, ю *impf. of* **проколо́ть**

проканите́л|ить(ся), ю(сь), ишь(ся) *pf. of* **каните́лить(ся)**

прока́пчива|ть, ю *impf. of* **прокопти́ть**

прока́пыва|ть, ю *impf. of* **прокопа́ть**

прокарау́л|ить[1]**, ю, ишь** *pf.* (*coll.*) to let slip, let go (*by carelessness, inattention*) while on guard; **он ~ил аресто́ванного** he let the prisoner escape.

прокарау́л|ить[2]**, ю, ишь** *pf.* to be on guard (*for a certain time*); to guard, watch (*for a certain time*).

прока́т[1]**, а** *m.* (*tech.*) **1.** rolling. **2.** rolled iron.

прока́т[2]**, а** *m.* hire.

прокат|а́ть[1]**, а́ю** *pf.* (*of* **∸ывать**) **1.** to spread flat with a roller. **2.** (*tech.*) to roll, laminate.

прокат|а́ть[2]**, а́ю** *pf.* to take out (*for a drive, etc.*) (*for a certain time*).

прокат|а́ться[1]**, а́юсь** *pf.* (*of* **∸ываться**) (*tech.*) to roll out.

прокат|а́ться[2]**, а́юсь** *pf.* to go out (*for a drive, etc.*) (*for a certain time*).

прока|ти́ть, чу́, ∸тишь *pf.* (*of* **∸тывать**) **1.** to take out; to take for a drive, ride. **2.** to roll. **3.** to roll by, past. **4.** (*coll.*) to slate. **5.: п.,** (*obs.*) **п. на вороны́х** to blackball.

прока|ти́ться, чу́сь, ∸тишься *pf.* (*of* **∸тываться**) **1.** to roll (*also fig., of thunder, etc.*). **2.** to go for a drive, go for a spin.

прока́тк|а, и *f.* (*tech.*) rolling, lamination.

прока́тн|ый[1] *adj.* (*tech.*) rolling; **~ое желе́зо** rolled iron; **п. стан** rolling mill.

прока́тный[2] *adj.* hired, let out on hire.

прока́тчик, а *m.* rolling mill operative.

прока́тыва|ть(ся), ю(сь) *impf. of* **прокатáть(ся)**[1] *and* **прокати́ть(ся)**

прока́шлива|ть(ся), ю(сь) *impf. of* **прока́шлять(ся)**

прока́шл|ять, яю *pf.* **1.** to cough. **2.** (*impf.* **~ивать**) to cough up.

прока́шл|яться, яюсь *pf.* (*of* **~иваться**) to clear one's throat.

прокип|е́ть, и́т *pf.* to boil thoroughly, sufficiently.

прокипя|ти́ть, чу́, ти́шь *pf.* to boil thoroughly, sufficiently.

прокис|а́ть, а́ет *impf. of* **∸нуть**

прокѝс|нуть, нет *pf.* (*of* **~а́ть**) to turn (sour).

прокла́дк|а, и *f.* **1.** laying; building, construction; **п. доро́ги** road building; breaking a road; **п. трубопрово́да** pipe laying. **2.** (*tech.*) washer, gasket; packing, padding.

прокладн|о́й *adj.* packing; **кни́га с ~ы́ми листа́ми** book with blank sheets (*for notes*).

прокла́дыва|ть, ю *impf. of* **проложи́ть**

прокламáци|я, и *f.* (political) leaflet.

проклами́р|овать, ую *impf. and pf.* to proclaim.

прокле́ива|ть, ю *impf. of* **прокле́ить**

прокле́|ить, ю, ишь *pf.* (*of* **~ивать**) to paste, glue; to size.

проклина́|ть, ю *impf.* **1.** *impf. of* **прокля́сть. 2.** (*coll.*) to curse, swear at.

прокл|я́сть, яну́, янёшь, *past* **∸ял, ~яла́, ∸яло** *pf.* (*of* **~ина́ть**) to curse, damn.

прокля́ти|е, я *nt.* **1.** damnation; **преда́ть ~ю** to consign to perdition. **2.** curse; imprecation. **3.** *as int.* **п.!** curse it!; damn it!; damnation!

про́кл|ятый *p.p.p. of* **~я́сть; будь я ~ят, е́сли...** I'm damned if ...; I'll be damned if ...; **будь он ~ят!** damn him!; curse him!

прокля́тый *adj.* accursed, damned; (*coll.*) damnable, confounded.

проковы́рива|ть, ю *impf. of* **проковыря́ть**

проковыр|я́ть, я́ю *pf.* (*of* **∸ивать**) to pick a hole (in).

проко́л, а *m.* **1.** puncture. **2.** pricking, piercing. **3.** (*coll.*) endorsement (*on driving licence*).

прокол|о́ть, ю́, ∸ешь *pf.* (*of* **прока́лывать**) **1.** to prick, pierce; to perforate; **п. навы́в** to lance a boil; **п. ши́ну** to puncture a tyre. **2.** to run through (*with a bayonet, etc.*).

прокомментир|овать, ую *pf.* to comment (upon).

прокомпости́р|овать, ую *pf. of* **компости́ровать**

проконопа́|тить, чу, тишь *pf. of* **конопа́тить**

проконспекти́р|овать, ую *pf. of* **конспекти́ровать**

проко́нсул, а *m.* (*hist.*) proconsul.

проконсульти́р|овать(ся), ую(сь) *pf. of* **консульти́ровать(ся)**

проконтроли́р|овать, ую *pf. of* **контроли́ровать**

прокопа́|ть, ю *pf.* (*of* **прока́пывать**) **1.** to dig. **2.** to dig through.

прокопа́|ться, юсь *pf.* (*coll., pej.*) to dawdle, mess about (*for a certain time*).

прокопте́лый *adj.* (*coll.*) sooty, soot-caked.

прокоп|ти́ть, чу́, ти́шь *pf.* (*of* **прока́пчивать**) **1.** to smoke, cure in smoke. **2.** (*coll.*) to foul with smoke, soot.

прoко́рм, а *m.* nourishment, sustenance.

прокорм|и́ть(ся), лю́(сь), ∸ишь(ся) *pf. of* **корми́ть(ся)**

прокорректи́р|овать, ую *pf. of* **корректи́ровать**

проко́с, а *m.* swath.

прокра́дыва|ться, юсь *impf. of* **прокра́сться**

прокра́|сить, шу, сишь *pf.* (*of* **~шивать**) to paint over, cover with paint.

прокра́|сться, ду́сь, дёшься *pf.* (*of* **~дываться**) to steal; **п. ми́мо** to steal by, past.

прокра́шива|ть, ю *impf. of* **прокра́сить**

прокрич|а́ть, у́, и́шь *pf.* **1.** to shout, cry; to give a shout, raise a cry. **2.** (**о**+*p.*; *coll.*) to trumpet; **п. у́ши кому́-н. о чём-н.** to din sth. into s.o.'s ears.

прокру́стов *adj.*: **~о ло́же** (*myth. and fig.*) bed of Procrustes.

прокурату́р|а, ы *f.* office of public prosecutor.

проку́рива|ть, ю *impf. of* **прокури́ть**

прокур|и́ть, ю́, ∸ишь *pf.* (*of* **∸ивать**) (*coll.*) **1.** to spend on smoking. **2.** to fill with tobacco smoke.

прокуро́р, а *m.* public prosecutor; procurator; investigating magistrate; counsel for the prosecution (*in criminal cases*);

речь ~а speech for the prosecution.
прокуро́р|ский *adj. of* ~; **н. надзо́р** powers of procurator; **довести́ до све́дения ~ского надзо́ра** to inform the procurator's office.
проку́с, а *m.* bite.
проку|си́ть, шу́, ≁сишь *pf.* (*of* **≁сывать**) to bite through.
проку́сыва|ть, ю *impf. of* **прокуси́ть**
проку|ти́ть, чу́, ≁тишь *pf.* (*of* **≁чивать**) (*coll.*) **1.** to squander, dissipate. **2.** to go on the spree, go on the binge.
проку|ти́ться, чу́сь, ≁тишься *pf.* (*of* **≁чиваться**) (*coll.*) to dissipate one's money.
проку́чива|ть(ся), ю(сь) *impf. of* **прокути́ть(ся)**
пролага́|ть, ю *impf. of* **проложи́ть**
прола́з|а, ы *c.g.* (*coll.*) creeper; scoundrel, rascal.
прола́мыва|ть(ся), ю(сь) *impf. of* **пролома́ть(ся)** *and* **проломи́ть(ся)**
пролега́|ть, ет *impf.* to lie, run; **доро́га ~ла вдоль бе́рега кана́ла** the path lay by the canal.
пролеж|а́ть, у́, и́шь *pf.* (*of* **≁ивать**) to lie; to spend (*a certain time*) lying; **она́ всю зи́му ~а́ла в посте́ли** she spent the whole winter in bed; **посы́лка неде́лю ~а́ла на по́чте** the parcel lay for a week in the post office.
про́леж|ень, ня *m.* (*med.*) bedsore.
пролёжива|ть, ю *impf. of* **пролежа́ть**
пролез|а́ть, а́ю *impf. of* **≁ть**
проле́з|ть, у, ешь, *past* **~, ~ла** *pf.* (*of* **~а́ть**) **1.** to get through, climb through. **2.** (**в**+*a.*; *fig., coll., pej.*) to worm o.s. (into, on to); **он ~в чле́ны комите́та** he has wormed his way on to the committee.
пролёт[1], **а** *m.* flight.
пролёт[2], **а** *m.* **1.** (*archit.*) bay; **п. мо́ста** span. **2.** stair-well. **3.** (*coll.*) stage (*distance between stations on rail.*).
пролетариа́т, а *m.* proletariat.
пролетариза́ци|я, и *f.* proletarianization.
пролетаризи́р|овать, ую *impf. and pf.* to proletarianize.
пролета́ри|й, я *m.* proletarian; **~и всех стран, соединя́йтесь!** workers of the world, unite!
пролета́рский *adj.* proletarian.
пролет|а́ть[1], **а́ю** *impf. of* **~е́ть**
пролет|а́ть[2], **а́ю** *pf.* to fly (*for a certain time*).
проле|те́ть, чу́, ти́шь *pf.* (*of* **~та́ть**[1]) **1.** to fly, cover (*a certain distance*). **2.** to fly (by, through, past) (*also fig.*); **кани́кулы ~те́ли** the holidays flew (by). **3.** (*fig.*) to flash, flit; **у неё в голове́ ~те́ла мысль** a thought flashed through her mind.
пролётк|а, и *f.* droshky, (horse-)cab.
пролётн|ый *adj.*: **~ая пти́ца** bird of passage.
проли́в, а *m.* (*geog.*) strait, sound.
пролива́|ть, ю *impf. of* **проли́ть**
проливно́й *adj.*: **п. дождь** pouring rain, pelting rain; **шёл п. дождь** it was pouring.
проли́ти|е, я *nt.* shedding; **п. кро́ви** bloodshed.
прол|и́ть, ью́, ьёшь, *past* **≁ил, ~ила́, ≁ило** *pf.* (*of* **~ива́ть**) to spill, shed; **п. чью-н. кровь** to shed s.o.'s blood; **п. слёзы** (**по**+*d. or p.*, **о**+*p.*) to shed tears (over); **п. свет** (**на**+*a.*; *fig.*) to shed light (on).
про́лог, а *m.* (*liter.*) calendar (*collection of saints' lives, homilies, etc., arranged in order of the calendar*).
проло́г, а *m.* prologue.
проложи́ть, у́, ≁ишь *pf.* (*of* **прокла́дывать**) **1.** (*impf. also* **пролага́ть**) to lay; to build, construct; **п. доро́гу** to build, break a road; (*fig.*) to pave the way; **п. себе́ доро́гу че́рез толпу́** to hack one's way through the crowd; **п. курс** (*naut., aeron.*) to lay a course; **п. путь** (*fig.*) to pave the way; **п. но́вые пути́** (*fig.*) to pioneer, blaze new trails. **2.** (**ме́жду** *or* +*a. and i.*) to interlay; to insert (between); **п. кни́гу бе́лыми листа́ми** to interleave a book; **п. соло́му ме́жду стекля́нными изде́лиями, п. стекля́нные изде́лия соло́мой** to insert straw between items of glassware.
проло́м, а *m.* **1.** breach, break; gap. **2.** (*med.*) fracture.
пролома́|ть, ю *pf.* (*of* **прола́мывать**) to break (through); **п. лёд** to break the ice.
пролома́|ться, ется *pf.* (*of* **прола́мываться**) to break.
пролом|и́ть, лю́, ≁ишь *pf.* (*of* **прола́мывать**) to break (through); **п. дыру́** to make a hole; **п. себе́ че́реп** to fracture one's skull.
пролом|и́ться, ≁ится *pf.* (*of* **прола́мываться**) to break (down), give way; **береги́тесь! по́ручень ~и́лся** look out! the handrail has given way.
пролонга́ци|я, и *f.* (*leg., fin.*) prolongation.
пролонги́р|овать, ую *impf. and pf.* (*leg., fin.*) to prolong.
пром... *comb. form, abbr. of* **промы́шленный**
прома́|зать[1], **жу, жешь** *pf.* (*of* **~зывать**) to smear thoroughly; to oil thoroughly.
прома́|зать[2], **жу, жешь** *pf. of* **ма́зать 5.**
прома́ргива|ть, ю *impf. of* **проморга́ть**
промарин|ова́ть, у́ю *pf.* (*of* **маринова́ть**) (*coll.*) to delay (intentionally), hold up, shelve (*for a certain time*).
прома́сл|енный *p.p.p. of* **~ить** *and adj.* oiled, greased; oily, greasy; **~енная бума́га** oil-paper.
прома́слива|ть, ю *impf. of* **прома́слить**
прома́сл|ить, ю, ишь *pf.* (*of* **~ивать**) to oil, treat with oil, grease.
прома́тыва|ть(ся), ю(сь) *impf. of* **промота́ть(ся)**
про́мах, а *m.* miss; (*fig.*) slip, blunder; **дать п.** to be unlucky; **он ма́лый не п.** (*coll.*) he's nobody's fool.
прома́хива|ться, юсь *impf. of* **промахну́ться**
промах|ну́ться, ну́сь, нёшься *pf.* (*of* **≁иваться**) to miss, miss the mark; (*at billiards*) to miscue; (*fig., coll.*) to miss the mark, be wide of the mark; to make a mistake; to miss an opportunity.
прома́чива|ть, ю *impf. of* **промочи́ть**
промедле́ни|е, я *nt.* delay; procrastination.
промéдл|ить, ю, ишь *pf.* to delay, dally; to procrastinate.
проме́ж *prep.* (+*g. or i.*) (*coll.*) between; among; **п. нас** between ourselves.
проме́жност|ь, и *f.* (*anat.*) perineum.
промежу́т|ок, ка *m.* interval; space; **п. вре́мени** period, space, stretch of time; interim.
промежу́точный *adj.* intermediate (*also fig.*); intervening; interim.
промелькн|у́ть, у́, ёшь *pf.* **1.** to flash; (*of time*) to fly by; **п. в голове́** to flash through one's mind. **2.** to be faintly perceptible; **в его́ слова́х ~у́ло разочарова́ние** there was a shade of disappointment in his words.
проме́нива|ть, ю *impf. of* **променя́ть**
промен|я́ть, я́ю *pf.* (*of* **≁ивать**) (**на**+*a.*) **1.** to exchange (for), trade (for), barter (for). **2.** to change (for).
проме́р, а *m.* **1.** measurement; survey; sounding. **2.** error in measurement.
промерз|а́ть, а́ю *impf. of* **≁нуть**
промёрзлый *adj.* frozen.
промёрз|нуть, ну, нешь, *past* **~, ~ла** *pf.* (*of* **~а́ть**) to freeze through.
проме́рива|ть, ю *impf. of* **проме́рить**
проме́р|ить, ю, ишь *pf.* (*of* **~ивать** *and* **~я́ть**) **1.** to measure; to survey; to sound. **2.** (*pf. only*) to make an error in measurement.
промер|я́ть, я́ю *impf.* = **≁ивать**
проме|си́ть, шу́, ≁сишь *pf.* (*of* **≁шивать**) to stir well, thoroughly; to knead well, thoroughly.
проме́шива|ть, ю *impf. of* **промеси́ть**
проме́шка|ть, ю *pf.* (*coll.*) to linger, dawdle.
промина́|ть(ся), ю(сь) *impf. of* **промя́ть(ся)**
промкомбина́т, а *m.* industrial combine.
промо́зглый *adj.* dank.
промо́ин|а, ы *f.* pool, gully (*formed by flood, rain, etc.*).
промока́тельн|ый *adj.*: **~ая бума́га** blotting-paper.
промок|а́ть[1], **а́ю** *impf.* **1.** *impf. of* **≁нуть. 2.** *impf. only* to let water through, not be waterproof; **э́ти боти́нки ~а́ют** these boots are not waterproof. **3.** *impf. only* to absorb ink.
промок|а́ть[2], **а́ю** *impf. of* **~ну́ть**
промока́шк|а, и *f.* (*coll.*) blotting-paper.
промо́к|нуть, ну, нешь *pf.* (*of* **~а́ть**[1]) to get soaked, get drenched; **п. до косте́й** to get soaked to the skin.
промок|ну́ть, ну, нёшь *pf.* (*of* **~а́ть**[2]) (*coll.*) to blot.
промо́лв|ить, лю, ишь *pf.* to say, utter.
промолч|а́ть, у́, и́шь *pf.* to keep silent, say nothing, hold one's peace.

проморга́|ть, ю *pf.* (*of* **прома́ргивать**) (*coll.*) to miss, overlook; **п. удо́бный слу́чай** to miss an opportunity, let a chance slip.

промор|и́ть, ю́, и́шь *pf.* (*coll.*) **1. (го́лодом)** to starve (*for a certain time*). **2.** to impose privations (upon) (*for a certain time*).

промота́|ть, ю *pf.* (*of* **мота́ть**[2] *and* **прома́тывать**) to squander.

промота́|ться, юсь *pf.* (*of* **прома́тываться**) (*coll.*) to squander one's money, dissipate one's substance.

промоч|и́ть, у́, ~́ишь *pf.* (*of* **прома́чивать**) to get wet (through); to soak, drench; **п. но́ги** to get one's feet wet; **п. го́рло, п. гло́тку** (*coll.*) to wet one's whistle.

промтова́р|ный *adj. of* **~ы; п. магази́н** manufactured goods shop.

промтова́р|ы, ов *no sg.* manufactured goods (*collect. name of manufactured consumer goods other than foodstuffs*).

прому|де́ть, жу́, ди́шь *pf. of* **муде́ть**

промфинпла́н, а *m.* (*abbr. of* ***промы́шленно-фина́нсовый план***) industrial and financial plan.

промч|а́ться, у́сь, и́шься *pf.* **1.** to tear (by, past, through); **п. стрело́й** to dart (by, past), flash (by, past). **2.** (*fig.*; *of time*) to fly (by).

промыва́ни|е, я *nt.* washing (out); (*med.*) bathing, irrigation; (*tech.*) scrubbing.

промыва́|ть, ю *impf. of* **промы́ть**

промы́вк|а, и *f.* washing, flushing.

про́мыс|ел, ла *m.* **1.** hunting, catching; **охо́тничий п.** hunting; game-shooting; **пушно́й п.** trapping; **ры́бный п.** fishing. **2.** trade, business; **го́рный п.** mining; **куста́рный п.** handicraft industry, cottage industry; **отхо́жий п.** seasonal work; **пушно́й п.** fur trade. **3.** *pl.* works; **го́рные ~лы** mines; **золоты́е ~лы** gold-fields, gold-mines; **нефтяны́е ~лы** oil-fields; **соляны́е ~лы** salt-mines, salt-works.

про́мысл, а *m.* (*relig.*) Providence.

промы́сл|ить, ю, ишь *pf.* (*of* **промышля́ть**) (*coll.*) to get, come by.

промысло́ви́к, а́ *m.* **1.** hunter. **2.** miner.

промысло́в|ый *adj.* **1.** *adj. of* **про́мысел 1.; ~ая избу́шка** shooting-box, hunter's (trapper's, *etc.*) hut; **~ые пти́цы** game-birds; **~ое свиде́тельство** licence. **2.** *adj. of* **про́мысел 2., 3.; ~ая коопера́ция** traders' co-operative (*organization*), producers' co-operative; **п. нало́г** business tax; **~ая ры́ба** marketable fish.

пром|ы́ть, о́ю, о́ешь *pf.* (*of* **~ыва́ть**) **1.** to wash well, thoroughly; **п. мозги́** (*+d.*) to brain-wash. **2.** (*med.*) to bathe; **п. желу́док** to irrigate the stomach. **3.** (*tech.*) to wash; to scrub (*gas*); **п. зо́лото** to pan out gold; **п. руду́** to jig ore.

промы́шленник, а *m.* manufacturer, industrialist.

промы́шленност|ь, и *f.* industry.

промы́шленный *adj.* industrial.

промышля́|ть, ю *impf.* **1.** *impf. of* **промы́слить. 2.** (*+i.*) to earn one's living (by). **3.** to hunt; to trade (in).

промя́мл|ить, ю, ишь *pf. of* **мя́млить 1.**

про|мя́ть, мну́, мнёшь *pf.* (*of* **~мина́ть**) **1.** to break (through), crush. **2.** (*coll.*) to give a shaking-up; **п. но́ги** to stretch one's legs.

про|мя́ться, мну́сь, мнёшься *pf.* (*of* **~мина́ться**) (*coll.*) to stretch one's legs.

прона́шива|ть(ся), ю(сь) *impf. of* **проноси́ть(ся)**[1]

пронес|ти́, у, ёшь, *past* **~́, ~ла́** *pf.* (*of* **проноси́ть**[3]) **1.** to carry (by, past, through). **2.** (*impers.*; *coll.*) to have a motion; to open one's bowels. **3. ~ло́!** the danger is over!

пронес|ти́сь, у́сь, ёшься, *past* **~́ся, ~ла́сь** *pf.* (*of* **проноси́ться**[2]) **1.** to rush (by, past, through); (*of clouds*) to scud (past). **2.** (*fig.*) to fly by. **3.** (*of rumours*, *etc.*) to spread.

пронз|а́ть, а́ю *impf. of* **~и́ть**

пронзи́тел|ьный (~ен, ~ьна) *adj.* penetrating; piercing; (*of sounds*) shrill, strident; **п. взгляд** penetrating glance; **~ьным го́лосом** in a shrill voice; **п. крик** piercing shriek.

прон|зи́ть, жу́, зи́шь *pf.* (*of* **~за́ть**) to pierce, run through, transfix; **п. взгля́дом** to pierce with a glance.

прони|за́ть, жу́, ~́жешь *pf.* (*of* **~́зывать**) to pierce; to permeate, penetrate; (*fig.*) to run through; **свет ~за́л темноту́** the light pierced the darkness; **одна́ иде́я ~за́ла все его́ произведе́ния** one idea ran through all his works.

прони́зыва|ть, ю *impf. of* **пронза́ть**

прони́зыва|ющий *pres. part. act. of* **~ть** *and adj.* piercing, penetrating.

проник|а́ть, а́ю *impf. of* **~́нуть**

проникнове́ни|е, я *nt.* **1.** penetration. **2.** = **проникнове́нность**

проникнове́нност|ь, и *f.* feeling; heartfelt conviction; **говори́ть с ~ью** to speak with feeling.

проникнове́н|ный (~ен, ~на) *adj.* full of feeling; heartfelt.

прони́кнут|ый (~, ~а) *adj.* (*+i.*) imbued (with), instinct (with), full (of).

прони́к|нуть, ну, нешь, *past* **~, ~ла** *pf.* (*of* **~а́ть**) **(в+***a.***)** to penetrate (*also fig.*); **(че́рез)** to percolate (through); **п. в чьи-н. наме́рения** to fathom s.o.'s designs; **п. в суть де́ла** to get to the bottom of the matter.

пронима́|ть, ю *impf. of* **проня́ть**

проница́емост|ь, и *f.* penetrability, permeability, perviousness.

проница́ем|ый (~, ~а) *adj.* permeable, pervious; **п. для све́та** pellucid.

проница́тельност|ь, и *f.* penetration; perspicacity; insight, acumen, shrewdness.

проница́тел|ьный (~ен, ~ьна) *adj.* perspicacious; acute, shrewd; penetrating, piercing; **п. взор** penetrating gaze.

проница́|ть, ю *impf.* (*obs.*) to penetrate.

проно|си́ть[1]**, шу́, ~́сишь** *pf.* (*of* **прона́шивать**) to wear out, wear to shreds.

проно|си́ть[2]**, шу́, ~́сишь** *pf.* to wear (*for a certain time*).

проно|си́ть[3]**, шу́, ~́сишь** *impf. of* **пронести́**

проно|си́ться[1]**, ~́сится** *pf.* (*of* **прона́шиваться**) to wear through, wear to shreds.

проно|си́ться[2]**, шу́сь, ~́сишься** *impf. of* **пронести́сь**

проны́р|а, ы *c.g.* (*coll.*) pushful pers.; sly-boots; intriguer.

проны́рлив|ый (~, ~а) *adj.* pushful, pushing.

проню́х|ать, аю *pf.* (*of* **~ивать**) (*coll.*) to smell out, nose out, get wind (of).

пронюхива|ть, ю *impf. of* **пронюхать**

про|ня́ть, йму́, ймёшь, *past* **~́нял, ~няла́, ~́няло** *pf.* (*of* **~нима́ть**) (*coll.*) **1.** to penetrate, strike through. **2.** (*fig.*) to get at; **ничем не ~ймёшь** you can't get through to him.

прообраз, а *m.* prototype.

пропага́нд|а, ы *f.* propaganda; propagation.

пропаганди́р|овать, ую *impf.* to engage in propaganda (for); to propagandize.

пропаганди́ст, а *m.* propagandist.

пропаганди́ст|ский *adj. of* **~**

пропада́|ть, ю *impf. of* **пропа́сть**

пропа́ж|а, и *f.* **1.** loss. **2.** lost object, missing object.

пропа́лыва|ть, ю *impf. of* **прополо́ть**

пропа́н, а *m.* propane.

про́паст|ь, и *f.* **1.** precipice (*also fig.*); abyss; **на краю́ ~и** (*fig.*) on the brink of a precipice. **2.** (*coll.*) a mass (of), masses (of); **у него́ п. де́нег** he has masses of money; **наро́ду бы́ло п.** there were swarms of people; **бы́ло их до ~и** there were scores of them.

пропа́|сть ду́, дёшь, *past* **~л** *pf.* (*of* **~да́ть**) **1.** to be missing; to be lost; **п. бе́з вести** (*mil.*) to be missing; **пиши́ ~ло** (*coll.*) it is as good as lost. **2.** to disappear, vanish; **куда́ вы ~ли?** where did you vanish to?; **очарова́ние ~ло** the glamour faded away. **3.** to be lost, be done for; (*of flowers*, *etc.*) to die; **тепе́рь мы ~ли!** now we're done for!; **~ди́ про́падом!** (*coll.*) the devil take it! **4.** to be wasted; **п. да́ром** to go for naught, go to waste; **всё у́тро и без того́ ~ло** the whole morning was wasted as it was.

пропа|ха́ть[1]**, шу́, ~́шешь** *pf.* (*of* **~́хивать**) to plough thoroughly.

пропа|ха́ть[2]**, шу́, ~́шешь** *pf.* to plough (*for a certain time*).

пропа́хива|ть, ю *impf. of* **пропаха́ть**[1]

пропа́х|нуть, ну, нешь, *past* **~, ~ла** *pf.* to become permeated with the smell (of).

пропа́шк|а, и *f.* (*agric.*) tilling between rows.

пропа́шник, а *m.* (*agric.*) cultivator, furrow plough.

пропашн|о́й *adj.*: **~ы́е культу́ры** crops requiring tilling between rows; **п. тра́ктор** tractor-cultivator.
пропа́щ|ий *adj.* (*coll.*) hopeless; good-for-nothing; **он п. челове́к** he's a hopeless case; **э́то ~ее де́ло** it's a bad job.
пропеде́втик|а, и *f.* propaedeutics; preliminary study.
пропедевти́ческий *adj.* propaedeutic; **п. курс** introductory course.
пропека́|ть(ся), ю(сь) *impf. of* **пропе́чь(ся)**
пропе́ллер, а *m.* propeller.
проп|е́ть¹, ою́, оёшь *pf.* **1.** *pf. of* **петь. 2.: п. го́лос** (*coll.*) to lose one's voice (*from singing*); to sing o.s. hoarse.
проп|е́ть², ою́, оёшь *pf.* to sing (*for a certain time*).
пропеча́т|ать, аю *pf.* (*of* **~ывать**) (*coll.*) to expose (*in the press*).
пропеча́тыва|ть, ю *impf. of* **пропеча́тать**
пропе́|чь, ку́, чёшь, ку́т, *past* **~́к, ~кла́** *pf.* (*of* **~ка́ть**) to bake well, thoroughly.
пропе́|чься, ку́сь, чёшься, ку́тся, *past* **~́кся, ~кла́сь** *pf.* (*of* **~ка́ться**) to bake well, get baked through.
пропива́|ть(ся), ю(сь) *impf. of* **пропи́ть(ся)**
пропи́л, а *m.* (saw-)kerf, slit, notch.
пропи́лива|ть, ю *impf. of* **пропили́ть**
пропил|и́ть, ю́, ~́ишь *pf.* (*of* **~́ивать**) to saw through.
пропи|са́ть, шу́, ~́шешь *pf.* (*of* **~́сывать**) **1.** to prescribe. **2.** to register; **п. па́спорт** to stamp a passport. **3.** (+*d.*; *coll.*) to give it hot, tear off a strip.
пропи|са́ться, шу́сь, ~́шешься *pf.* (*of* **~́сываться**) to register (*intrans.*).
пропи́ск|а, и *f.* **1.** registration; **п. па́спорта** stamping of a passport. **2.** residence permit.
прописн|о́й *adj.* **1.** (*of letters of the alphabet*) capital; **писа́ться с п. бу́квы** to be written with a capital letter. **2.** commonplace, trivial; **~а́я и́стина** truism; **~а́я мора́ль** copy-book ethics.
пропи́сыва|ть(ся), ю(сь) *impf. of* **прописа́ть(ся)**
про́пис|ь, и *f.* **1.** *usu. pl.* sample(s) of writing. **2.** (*fig., pej.*) copy-book maxim; **жить по ~ям** to live according to the copy-book.
про́писью *adv.* in words, in full; **написа́ть число́ п.** to write out a number in words, in full.
пропита́ни|е, я *nt.* subsistence, sustenance; **зарабо́тать себе́ на п.** to earn one's living.
пропит|а́ть, а́ю *pf.* (*of* **~́ывать**) **1.** to keep, provide (for). **2.** (+*i.*) to impregnate (with), saturate (with), soak (in), steep (in); **п. ма́слом** to oil.
пропит|а́ться, а́юсь *pf.* (*of* **~́ываться**) **1.** (+*i.*) to become saturated (with), become steeped (in). **2.** *pass. of* **~а́ть**
пропи́тк|а, и *f.* (*tech.*) impregnation.
пропи́тыва|ть(ся), ю(сь) *impf. of* **пропита́ть(ся)**
про|пи́ть, пью́, пьёшь, *past* **~́пил, ~пила́, ~́пило** *pf.* (*of* **~пива́ть**) **1.** to spend on drink, squander on drink. **2.** (*coll.*) to ruin (*through excessive drinking*).
про|пи́ться, пью́сь, пьёшься, *past* **~пи́лся, ~пила́сь, ~пи́ло́сь** *pf.* (*of* **~пива́ться**) (*coll.*) to ruin o.s. (*through excessive drinking*).
пропих|а́ться, а́юсь *pf.* = **~ну́ться**
пропи́хива|ть(ся), ю(сь) *impf. of* **пропихну́ть(ся)**
пропих|ну́ть, ну́, нёшь *pf.* (*of* **~́ивать**) (*coll.*) to shove through, force through.
пропих|ну́ться, ну́сь, нёшься *pf.* (*of* **~́иваться**) (*coll.*) to shove, force one's way through.
пропла́ва|ть, ю *pf.* to swim (*for a certain time*); to sail (*for a certain time*).
пропла́|кать, чу, чешь *pf.* to cry, weep (*for a certain time*); **п. глаза́** (*coll.*) to cry one's eyes out.
пропле́сневе|ть, ет *pf.* to go mouldy all through.
проплы́в, а *m.* (*swimming*) race, heat.
проплыва́|ть, ю *impf. of* **проплы́ть**
проплы́|ть, ву́, вёшь, *past* **~л, ~ла́, ~ло** *pf.* (*of* **~ва́ть**) **1.** to swim (by, past, through); to sail (by, past, through); to float, drift (by, past, through); (*fig., joc.*) to sail (by, past). **2.** to cover (*a certain distance*).
пропове́дник, а *m.* **1.** preacher. **2.** (+*g.*; *fig.*) advocate (of).
пропове́д|овать, ую *impf.* **1.** to preach. **2.** (*fig.*) to advocate, propagate.
про́поведь, и *f.* **1.** sermon; homily. **2.** (+*g.*; *fig.*) advocacy (of), propagation (of).
пропо́йный *adj.* (*coll.*) drunken, besotted.
пропо́йц|а, ы *m.* (*coll.*) drunkard.
пропола́скива|ть, ю *impf. of* **прополоска́ть**
пропалз|а́ть, а́ю *impf. of* **~ти́**
пропалз|ти́, у́, ёшь, *past* **~, ~ла́** *pf.* (*of* **~а́ть**) to creep, crawl (by, past, through).
про́полис, а *m.* propolis.
прополк|а, и *f.* weeding.
прополо|ска́ть, щу́, ~́щешь *pf.* (*of* **пропола́скивать**) to rinse, swill; **п. го́рло** to gargle.
пропол|о́ть, ю́, ~́ешь *pf.* (*of* **пропа́лывать**) to weed.
пропорциона́льност|ь, и *f.* proportionality; proportion; **обра́тная п.** inverse proportion.
пропорциона́л|ьный (~ен, ~ьна) *adj.* **1.** proportional; proportionate; **~ьное представи́тельство** proportional representation; **сре́днее ~ьное** (*math.*) the mean proportional. **2.** well-proportioned.
пропо́рци|я, и *f.* proportion; ratio.
пропоте́лый *adj.* sweat-soaked.
пропоте́|ть, ю *pf.* **1.** to sweat thoroughly. **2.** to be soaked in sweat.
про́пуск, а *m.* **1.** *no pl.* admission. **2.** (*pl.* **~и** and **~а́**) pass, permit. **3.** (*pl.* **~а́**) (*mil.*) password. **4.** (*pl.* **~и**) (+*g.*) non-attendance (at), absence (from). **5.** (*pl.* **~и**) blank, gap.
пропуска́|ть, ю *impf.* **1.** *impf. of* **пропусти́ть. 2.** *impf. only* to let pass; **п. во́ду** to leak; **не п. воды́** to be waterproof; **э́та бума́га ~ет черни́ла** this paper absorbs ink.
пропускн|о́й *adj.*: **~а́я бума́га** blotting-paper; **~а́я спосо́бность** capacity.
пропу|сти́ть, щу́, ~́стишь *pf.* (*of* **~ска́ть**) **1.** to let pass, let through; to make way (for); to let in, admit; to take, have a capacity (of), **п. на перро́н** to let on to the platform; **вы́ставка ~сти́ла пять миллио́нов посети́телей** the exhibition had five million visitors; **п. ми́мо уше́й** to give no ear (to), pay no heed (to). **2. (че́рез)** to run (through), pass (through); **п. че́рез фильтр** to filter. **3.** to omit, leave out; (*in reading*) to skip. **4.** to miss; to let slip; **п. ле́кцию** to miss a lecture, cut a lecture; **п. удо́бный слу́чай** to miss an opportunity. **5.** (*coll.*) to drink.
пропылесо́с|ить, ю, ишь *pf. of* **пылесо́сить**
пропых|те́ть, чу́, ти́шь *pf. of* **пыхте́ть**
проpа́б, а *m.* (*abbr. of* ***производи́тель рабо́т***) clerk of the works, work superintendent.
прораба́тыва|ть, ю *impf. of* **прорабо́тать¹**
прорабо́та|ть¹, ю *pf.* (*of* **прораба́тывать**) (*coll.*) **1.** to work (at), study; to get up, mug up. **2.** to slate, pick holes (in).
прорабо́та|ть², ю *pf.* to work (*for a certain time*).
прорабо́тк|а, и *f.* **1.** study, studying, getting up. **2.** slating.
прора́н, а *m.* (*tech.*) passage (*through dam while under construction*).
прораста́ни|е, я *nt.* germination; sprouting.
прораст|а́ть, а́ет *impf. of* **~и́**
прораст|и́, ёт, *past* **проро́с, проросла́** *pf.* (*of* **~а́ть**) to germinate, sprout, shoot (*of plant*).
про́рв|а, ы *f.* (*coll.*) **1.** (+*g.*) a mass (of); masses (of), heaps (of). **2.** glutton.
прорв|а́ть, у́, ёшь, *past* **~а́л, ~ала́, ~а́ло** *pf.* (*of* **прорыва́ть**) **1.** to break through; to tear, make a rent (in), make a hole (in); **п. блока́ду** to run the blockade; **п. ли́нию оборо́ны проти́вника** to break through the enemy's defence line; (*impers.*): **~а́ло плоти́ну** the dam has burst; **я ~а́л носо́к** I have a hole in my sock. **2.** (*impers.*; *coll.*) to lose patience.
прорв|а́ться, у́сь, ёшься, *past* **~а́лся, ~ала́сь, ~ало́сь** *pf.* (*of* **прорыва́ться**) **1.** to break, burst (open). **2.** to tear. **3.** to break (out, through); to force one's way (through).
проре|ди́ть, жу́, ди́шь *pf.* (*of* **~́живать**) (*agric.*) to thin out.
проре́жива|ть, ю *impf. of* **проре́ди́ть**
проре́з, а *m.* cut; slit, notch; **ме́лкий п.** nick.

проре́|зать, жу, жешь *pf.* (*of* **~зывать** *and* **~за́ть**) to cut through (*also fig.*).

проре́|заться, жется *pf.* (*of* **ре́заться, ~зываться** *and* **~за́ться**) (*of teeth*) to cut, come through; **у неё уже́ ~зались зу́бы** she has already cut her teeth.

прорез|а́ть(ся), а́ю(сь) *impf. of* **~́ать(ся)**

прорези́нива|ть, ю *impf. of* **прорези́нить**

прорези́н|ить, ю, ишь *pf.* (*of* **~ивать**) to rubberize.

проре́зывани|е, я *nt.*: **п. зубо́в** teething, dentition.

проре́зыва|ть(ся), ю(сь) *impf. of* **проре́зать(ся)**

про́рез|ь, и *f.* opening, aperture.

прoréктор, а *m.* pro-rector.

прорепети́р|овать, ую *impf. of* **репети́ровать**

проре́х|а, и *f.* **1.** rent, tear. **2.** (*in garment*) slit; **застегну́ть ~у (брюк)** to do up one's flies. **3.** (*fig., coll.*) gap, deficiency.

прорецензи́р|овать, ую *pf. of* **рецензи́ровать**

проржа́ве|ть, ет *pf.* to rust through.

прорис|ова́ть, у́ю *pf.* (*of* **~о́вывать**) to trace clearly.

прорисо́выва|ть, ю *impf. of* **прорисова́ть**

прорица́ни|е, я *nt.* (*obs.*) soothsaying, prophecy.

прорица́тел|ь, я *m.* (*obs.*) soothsayer, prophet.

прорица́|ть, ю *impf.* (*obs.*) to prophesy.

проро́к, а *m.* prophet.

пророн|и́ть, ю́, ~́ишь *pf.* to utter, breathe, drop (*a word, a sound, etc.*); **он не ~и́л ни зву́ка** he did not utter a sound.

проро́ческий *adj.* prophetic, oracular.

проро́честв|о, а *nt.* prophecy, oracle.

проро́честв|овать, ую *impf.* (**о**+*p.*) to prophesy.

проро́ч|ить, у, ишь *impf.* (*of* **на~**) to prophesy, predict.

проруб|а́ть, а́ю *impf. of* **~и́ть**

проруб|и́ть, лю́, ~́ишь *pf.* (*of* **~а́ть**) to hack through, cut through, hew through.

про́руб|ь, и *f.* ice-hole.

прору́х|а, и *f.* (*coll.*) blunder, mistake.

проры́в, а *m.* **1.** break; (*mil.*) break-through, breach. **2.** (*fig.*) hitch, hold-up; **по́лный п.** breakdown.

прорыва́|ть[1], ю *impf. of* **прорва́ть**

прорыва́|ть[2], ю *impf. of* **проры́ть**

прорыва́|ться[1], юсь *impf. of* **прорва́ться**

прорыва́|ться[2], ю *impf. of* **проры́ться**

прор|ы́ть, о́ю, о́ешь *pf.* (*of* **~ыва́ть**[2]) to dig through.

прор|ы́ться, о́юсь, о́ешься *pf.* (*of* **~ыва́ться**[2]) to dig one's way through, burrow through.

проса|ди́ть[1], жу́, ~́дишь *pf.* (*of* **~́живать**) (+*i.*; *coll.*) to stick (into); **п. но́гу гвоздём** to get a nail into one's foot.

проса|ди́ть[2] жу́, ~́дишь *pf.* (*of* **~́живать**) (*coll.*) to squander, lose.

проса́жива|ть, ю *impf. of* **просади́ть**

проса́лива|ть[1], ю *impf. of* **проса́лить**

проса́лива|ть[2], ю *impf. of* **просоли́ть**

проса́л|ить, ю, ишь *pf.* (*of* **~ивать**[1]) to grease.

проса́чивани|е, я *nt.* **1.** percolation; oozing, exudation. **2.** (*fig.*) leakage; infiltration.

проса́чива|ться, юсь *impf. of* **просочи́ться**

просва́та|ть, ю *pf.* (*of bride-to-be's parents*) to promise in marriage.

просве́рлива|ть, ю *impf. of* **просверли́ть**

просверл|и́ть, ю́, и́шь *pf.* (*of* **~́ивать**) to drill, bore; to perforate, pierce.

просве́т, а *m.* **1.** shaft of light; (*fig.*) ray of hope. **2.** (*archit.*) light; aperture, opening.

просвети́тел|ь, я *m.* **1.** educator, teacher. **2.** (*hist.*) representative of the Enlightenment.

просвети́тельн|ый *adj.* educational; **~ая филосо́фия** (*hist.*) philosophy of the Enlightenment.

просвети́тель|ский *adj. of* **~**

просвети́тельств|о, а *nt.* educational activities, cultural activities.

просве|ти́ть[1], щу́, ти́шь *pf.* (*of* **~ща́ть**) to educate; to enlighten.

просве|ти́ть[2], чу́, ~́тишь *pf.* (*of* **~́чивать**[1]) (*med.*) to X-ray.

просветле́ни|е, я *nt.* **1.** (*of weather*) clearing up, brightening up. **2.** (*fig.*) lucid interval.

просветл|ённый *p.p.p. of* **~и́ть** *and adj.* (*fig.*) clear, lucid.

просветле́|ть, ю *pf.* **1.** (*of weather*) to clear up, brighten up. **2.** (*fig.*) to brighten; **п. от ра́дости** to light up with joy. **3.** (*fig.*; *of consciousness, etc.*) to become lucid.

просветл|и́ть, ю́, и́шь *pf.* (*of* **~я́ть**) to clarify.

просветл|я́ть, я́ю *impf. of* **~и́ть**

просве́чива|ть[1], ю *impf. of* **просвети́ть**[2]

просве́чива|ть[2], ю *impf.* **1.** to be translucent. **2.** (**че́рез, сквозь**) to be visible (through), show (through), appear (through); to shine (through); **шрам ~л че́рез её чуло́к** the scar showed through her stocking.

просвеща́|ть, ю *impf. of* **просвети́ть**[1]

просвеще́н|ец, ца *m.* educationalist.

просвеще́ни|е, я *nt.* **1.** education, instruction; **наро́дное п.** public education. **2.** enlightenment; **эпо́ха П~я** (*hist.*) the Age of the Enlightenment.

просвещённост|ь, и *f.* enlightenment, culture.

просве|щённый *p.p.p. of* **~ти́ть**[1] *and adj.* enlightened; educated, cultured; **~щённое мне́ние** expert opinion; **п. челове́к** educated pers.

просвир|а́, ы́, *pl.* **про́свиры, про́свир, про́свира́м** *f.* (*eccl.*) (communion) bread; host.

просви́р|ня, ни, *g. pl.* **~ен** *f.* woman making communion bread.

просвирня́к, а́ *m.* (*bot.*) marsh mallow.

просви|сте́ть, щу́, сти́шь *pf.* **1.** to whistle; **п. мело́дию** to whistle a tune. **2.** to give a whistle; to whistle (by, past); **~сте́ла над голово́й пу́ля** a bullet whistled overhead.

про́сед|ь, и *f.* streak(s) of grey; **во́лосы с ~ью** greying hair, hair touched with grey.

просе́ива|ть, ю *impf. of* **просе́ять**

про́сек|а, и *f.* cutting (*in a forest*).

просёл|ок, ка *m.* country road, cart-track.

просемина́р, а *m.* (*in higher educational institutions*) beginners' class, beginners' seminar.

просемина́ри|й, я *m.* (*obs.*) = **просемина́р**

просе́|ять, ю, ешь *pf.* (*of* **~ивать**) to sift, riddle, screen; **~янный игро́к** (*sport*) seed.

просигнализи́р|овать, ую *pf. of* **сигнализи́ровать**

проси|де́ть[1], жу́, ди́шь *pf.* (*of* **~́живать**) to sit (*for a certain time*); **п. ночь у посте́ли больно́го** to sit up all night with a patient.

проси|де́ть[2], жу́, ди́шь *pf.* (*of* **~́живать**) to wear out the seat (of); to wear into holes (*by sitting*).

проси́жива|ть, ю *impf. of* **просиде́ть**

про́син|ь, и *f.* (*coll.*) bluish tint.

проси́тел|ь, я *m.* applicant; suppliant; petitioner.

проси́тельный *adj.* pleading.

про|си́ть, шу́, ~́сишь *impf.* (*of* **по~**) **1.** (+*a. of pers. asked*; +*a. or g. of thing sought, or* **о**+*p.*) to ask (for), beg; **~шу́ (вас)** please; **п. кого́-н. о по́мощи** to ask s.o. for help, ask s.o.'s assistance; **п. вре́мени на размышле́ние** to ask for time to think (sth.) over; **п. разреше́ния** to ask permission; **п. сове́та** to ask (for) advice; **п. извине́ния у кого́-н.** to beg s.o.'s pardon, apologize to s.o.; **п. ми́лостыню** to beg, go begging; **~шу́ поко́рнейше** (*coll., obs., as expr. of surprise*) if you please. **2.** (**за**+*a.*) to intercede (for). **3.** to invite; **вас ~́сят к столу́** please to take your places at the table; **«~́сят не кури́ть»** 'no smoking'.

про|си́ться, шу́сь, ~́сишься *impf.* (*of* **по~**) **1.** (+*inf. or* **в**+*a.*, **на**+*a.*) to ask (for); to apply (for); **п. в о́тпуск** to apply for leave. **2.** (*of children and household pets*) to want to go (*sc. to relieve o.s.*). **3.** (*fig., coll.*) to ask (for); **п. с языка́** to be on the tip of one's tongue; **зака́т так и ~си́лся на карти́ну** the sunset was just asking to be painted.

просия́|ть, ю *pf.* **1.** (*of the sun*) to begin to shine. **2.** (**от**) to beam (with), light up (with); **она́ ~ла от сча́стья** she beamed with joy; **лицо́ у него́ ~ло** his face lit up.

проска|ка́ть, чу́, ~́чешь *pf.* to gallop (by, past, through).

проска́кива|ть, ю *impf. of* **проскочи́ть**

проска́льзыва|ть, ю *impf. of* **проскользну́ть**

просквоз|и́ть, и́т *pf.* (*impers.*; *coll.*): **меня́, *etc.*, ~и́ло** I, *etc.*, have caught cold from being in a draught.

просклоня́|ть, ю *pf. of* **склоня́ть**[2]

проскользн|у́ть, у́, ёшь *pf.* (*of* **проска́льзывать**) (*coll.*) to slip in, creep in (*also fig.*); **~у́ло мно́го оши́бок** many errors have crept in.

проскоч|и́ть, у́, ~́ишь *pf.* (*of* **проска́кивать**) **1.** to rush by, tear by. **2.** **(че́рез)** to slip (through). **3.** **(сквозь, ме́жду)** to fall (through, between); **п. ме́жду па́льцами** to fall through one's fingers. **4.** (*fig., coll.*) to slip in, creep in; **~и́ло не́сколько оши́бок** a few errors crept in.

проскрип|е́ть, лю́, и́шь *pf.* **1.** *pf. of* **скрипе́ть**. **2.** (*coll.*) to creak along.

проскрипцио́нный *adj.*: **п. спи́сок** (*hist.*) proscription list; black list.

проскри́пци|я, и *f.* (*hist.*) proscription.

проскурня́к, а́ *m.* (*bot.*) marsh mallow.

проскуча́|ть, ю *pf.* to have a dull, boring time; **мы ~ли всю неде́лю** we had a dull week.

прosла́б|ить, ит *pf. of* **сла́бить**

просла́в|ить, лю, ишь *pf.* (*of* **~ля́ть**) to glorify; to bring glory (to), bring fame (to); to make famous, make illustrious.

просла́в|иться, люсь, ишься *pf.* (*of* **~ля́ться**) (+*i.*) to become famous (for), become renowned (for); **он ~ился остро́тами** he became famous for his witticisms.

прославле́ни|е, я *nt.* glorification; apotheosis.

просла́в|ленный *p.p.p. of* **~ить** *and adj.* famous, renowned, celebrated, illustrious.

прославля́|ть(ся), ю(сь) *impf. of* **просла́вить(ся)**

просла́ива|ть, ю *impf. of* **прослои́ть**

просле|ди́ть, жу́, ди́шь *pf.* (*of* **~́живать**) **1.** to track (down). **2.** to trace (through); to trace back, retrace; **п. разви́тие па́пства** to trace the development of the papacy.

просле́д|овать, ую *pf.* to proceed, go in state.

просле́жива|ть, ю *impf. of* **проследи́ть**

просле|зи́ться, жу́сь, зи́шься *pf.* to shed a few tears.

просло|и́ть, ю́, и́шь *pf.* (*of* **просла́ивать**) (+*i.*) to interlay (with), sandwich (with).

просло́йк|а, и *f.* **1.** layer, stratum (*also fig.*). **2.** (*geol.*) seam, streak.

прослуж|и́ть, у́, ~́ишь *pf.* **1.** to work, serve (*for a certain time*); **он ~и́л три го́да на Да́льнем Восто́ке** he served for three years in the Far East. **2.** to be in use, serve; **э́то пальто́ ~́ит мне ещё оди́н год** this coat will last me another year.

прослу́ш|ать, аю *pf.* **1.** (*impf.* **слу́шать**) to hear (through); **п. курс ле́кций** to attend a course of lectures. **2.** (*impf.* **~ивать**) (*med.*) to listen to; **п. чьё-н. се́рдце** to listen to s.o.'s heart. **3.** (*impf.* **~ивать**) (*coll.*) to miss, not to catch; **прости́те, я ~ал, что вы сказа́ли** I am sorry, I did not catch what you said.

прослу́шива|ть, ю *impf. of* **прослу́шать**

просл|ы́ть, ву́, вёшь, *past* **~л, ~ла́, ~́ло** *pf.* (+*i.*) to pass (for), be reputed.

прослы́ш|ать, у, ишь *pf.* (*coll.*) to find out, hear; **я то́лько что ~ал о ва́шем несча́стном слу́чае** I have only just heard about your accident.

просма́лива|ть, ю *impf. of* **просмоли́ть**

просма́трива|ть, ю *impf. of* **просмотре́ть**

просмол|и́ть, ю́, и́шь *pf.* (*of* **просма́ливать**) to tar; to coat, impregnate with tar; (*naut.*) to pay.

просмо́тр, а *m.* survey; view, viewing; **п. докуме́нтов** examination of papers; **закры́тый п.** private view; **предвари́тельный п.** preview.

просмотр|е́ть, ю́, ~́ишь *pf.* (*of* **просма́тривать**) **1.** to survey; to view. **2.** to look over, look through; to glance over, glance through; to run over; **п. ру́копись** to glance through a manuscript; **п. партиту́ру** to run over the score. **3.** to overlook, miss.

прос|ну́ться, ну́сь, нёшься *pf.* (*of* **~ыпа́ться**[1]) to wake up, awake.

про́с|о, а *nt.* millet.

просо́выва|ть(ся), ю(сь) *impf. of* **просу́нуть(ся)**

просоди́ческий *adj.* (*liter.*) prosodic, prosodial.

просо́ди|я, и *f.* (*liter.*) prosody.

просол|и́ть, ю́, ~́ишь *pf.* (*of* **проса́ливать**[2]) to salt; **п. мя́со** to corn meat.

просо́х|нуть, ну, нешь, *past* **~, ~ла** *pf.* (*of* **просыха́ть**) to get dry, dry out.

просоч|и́ться, и́тся *pf.* (*of* **проса́чиваться**) **1.** to percolate; to filter; to leak, ooze; to seep out. **2.** (*fig.*) to filter through; to leak out; **~и́лись све́дения о пораже́нии** news of the defeat filtered through.

просп|а́ть[1]**, лю́, и́шь**, *past* **~а́л, ~ала́, ~а́ло** *pf.* (*of* **просыпа́ть**[2]) **1.** to oversleep. **2.** to miss, pass (*due to being asleep*).

просп|а́ть[2]**, лю́, и́шь**, *past* **~а́л, ~ала́, ~а́ло** *pf.* to sleep (*for a certain time*).

просп|а́ться, лю́сь, и́шься, *past* **~а́лся, ~ала́сь, ~а́лось** *pf.* (*coll.*) to sleep o.s. sober; sleep it off (*sc. one's drunkenness*).

проспе́кт[1]**, а** *m.* avenue.

проспе́кт[2]**, а** *m.* **1.** prospectus. **2.** summary, résumé.

проспирт|ова́ть, у́ю *pf.* (*of* **~о́вывать**) to alcoholize.

проспирто́выва|ть, ю *impf. of* **проспиртова́ть**

проспо́рива|ть, ю *impf. of* **проспо́рить**[1]

проспо́р|ить[1]**, ю, ишь** *pf.* (*of* **~ивать**) to lose (*in a wager*).

проспо́р|ить[2]**, ю, ишь** *pf.* to argue (*for a certain time*).

проспряга́|ть, ю *pf. of* **спряга́ть**

просро́ч|енный *p.p.p. of* **~ить** *and adj.* overdue.

просро́чива|ть, ю *impf. of* **просро́чить**

просро́ч|ить, у, ишь *pf.* (*of* **~ивать**) to exceed the time limit; **п. о́тпуск** to overstay one's leave; **п. платёж** to fail to pay in time.

просро́чк|а, и *f.* delay; expiration of a time limit; **п. в предъявле́нии и́ска** (*leg.*) non-claim.

проста́в|ить, лю, ишь *pf.* (*of* **~ля́ть**) **1.** to put down (in writing), state, fill in; **п. да́ту (в, на**+*p.*) to date. **2.** (*coll.*) to stake and lose (*at cards, etc.*).

проставля́|ть, ю *impf. of* **проста́вить**

проста́ива|ть, ю *impf. of* **простоя́ть**

проста́к, а́ *m.* simpleton.

проста́т|а, ы *f.* (*anat.*) prostate, prostatic gland.

простег|а́ть, а́ю *pf.* (*of* **~̈ивать**) to quilt.

простёгива|ть, ю *impf. of* **простега́ть**

просте́йш|ий *superl. of* **просто́й**; *pl. as n.* **~ие, ~их** (*zool.*) protozoa.

простéн|ок, ка *m.* (*archit.*) pier.

про́стенький *adj.* (*coll.*) quite simple; plain, unpretentious.

прос|тере́ть, тру́, трёшь, *past* **~тёр, ~тёрла** *pf.* (*of* **~тира́ть**[1]) **1.** to extend, hold out, reach out; **п. ру́ку** to hold out one's hand. **2.** (*fig.*) to raise, stretch; **они́ сли́шком далеко́ ~тёрли свои́ тре́бования** they raised their demands too high.

прос|тере́ться, трётся, *past* **~тёрся, ~тёрлась** *pf.* (*of* **~тира́ться**[1]) to stretch, extend; **п. на со́тни миль** to stretch for hundreds of miles.

простира́|ть[1]**, ю** *impf. of* **простере́ть**

простира́|ть[2]**, ю** *pf.* to wash (*for a certain time*).

простир|а́ть[3]**, а́ю** *pf.* (*of* **~́ывать**) (*coll.*) to wash well, thoroughly.

простира́|ться, юсь *impf. of* **простере́ться**

простирн|у́ть, у́, ёшь *pf.* (*coll.*) to give a wash.

прости́рыва|ть, ю *impf. of* **простира́ть**[3]

прости́тел|ьный (~ен, ~ьна) *adj.* pardonable, excusable, justifiable.

проституи́р|овать, ую *impf. and pf.* to prostitute.

проститу́тк|а, и *f.* prostitute.

проститу́ци|я, и *f.* prostitution.

про|сти́ть, щу́, сти́шь *pf.* (*of* **~ща́ть**) **1.** to forgive, pardon; **п. грехи́** to forgive sins; **~сти́те (меня́)!** excuse me!; I beg your pardon! **2.** to remit; **п. долг кому́-н.** to remit s.o.'s debt. **3.** **~сти́(те)!** (*obs.*) good-bye!; farewell!; **сказа́ть после́днее ~сти** to say the last farewell.

про|сти́ться, щу́сь, сти́шься *pf.* (*of* **~ща́ться**) **(с**+*i.*) to say good-bye (to), take one's leave (of), bid farewell.

про́сто *adv.* simply; **п. по привы́чке** from mere habit, purely out of habit; **п. так** for no particular reason; **э́то п. невероя́тно** it is simply incredible; **я п. не зна́ю** I really don't know.

простова́тост|ь, и *f.* simplicity, simple-mindedness.

простова́т|ый (~, ~а) *adj.* simple, simple-minded.

простоволо́с|ый (~, ~а) *adj.* bare-headed, with head uncovered.

простоду́ши|е, я *nt.* open-heartedness; simple-heartedness, simple-mindedness; ingenuousness, artlessness.

простоду́ш|ный (~ен, ~на) *adj.* open-hearted; simple-hearted, simple-minded; ingenuous, artless.

прост|о́й[1] (~, ~а́, ~́о) *adj.* **1.** simple; easy; **вам ~́о критикова́ть** it is easy for you, all very well for you to criticize. **2.** simple (= *unitary*); **~о́е предложе́ние** (*gram.*) simple sentence; **~о́е те́ло** (*chem.*) simple substance, element; **~о́е число́** (*math.*) prime number. **3.** simple; ordinary; **~ы́м гла́зом** with the naked eye; **п. наро́д** the common people; **~о́е письмо́** non-registered letter. **4.** simple, plain; unaffected, unpretentious; **~ы́е лю́ди** ordinary people; homely people; **~ы́е мане́ры** unaffected manners; **п. о́браз жи́зни** plain living. **5.** mere; **~о́е любопы́тство** mere curiosity; **п. сме́ртный** a mere mortal; **по той ~о́й причи́не, что** for the simple reason that.

просто́|й[2], я *m.* standing idle, enforced idleness; stoppage; **пла́та за п.** demurrage.

простоква́ш|а, и *f.* sour milk, yoghurt.

простолюди́н, а *m.* man of the common people.

про́сто-на́просто *adv.* (*coll.*) simply.

простонаро́д|ный (~ен, ~на) *adj.* of the common people.

простонаро́дь|е, я *nt.* the common people.

простон|а́ть, у́, ~́ешь *pf.* **1.** to utter a groan, moan. **2.** to groan, moan (*for a certain time*).

просто́р, а *m.* **1.** spaciousness; space, expanse; **степны́е ~ы** the expanses of the steppe(s). **2.** freedom, scope; elbow-room; **дать п.** (*+d.*) to give scope, give free range, give full play.

простор́ечи|е, я *nt.* popular speech; **в ~и** in common parlance.

простор́еч|ный (~ен, ~на) *adj. of* **~ие**

просто́р|ный (~ен, ~на) *adj.* spacious, roomy; (*of clothing*) ample; **здесь ~но** there is plenty of room here, there is ample space here.

простосерде́чи|е, я *nt.* simple-heartedness; frankness; openness.

простосерде́ч|ный (~ен, ~на) *adj.* simple-hearted; frank; open.

простот|а́, ы́ *f.* (*in var. senses*) simplicity; **по ~е́ серде́чной** in one's innocence.

простофи́л|я, и *c.g.* (*coll.*) duffer, ninny.

просто|я́ть, ю́, и́шь *pf.* (*of* **проста́ивать**) **1.** to stay, stand (*for a certain time*); **по́езд ~я́л на запасно́м пути́ всю ночь** the train stood in a siding all night. **2.** to stand idle, lie idle. **3.** to stand, last.

простра́нност|ь, и *f.* **1.** extensiveness, extent. **2.** diffuseness, prolixity; verbosity.

простра́н|ный (~ен, ~на) *adj.* **1.** extensive, vast. **2.** diffuse, prolix; verbose.

простра́нственный *adj.* spatial.

простра́нств|о, а *nt.* space; expanse; **возду́шное п.** air space; **закры́тое возду́шное п.** no-fly zone; **безвозду́шное п.** (*phys.*) vacuum; **вре́дное п.** (*tech.*) clearance; **мёртвое п.** (*mil.*) dead ground; **пусто́е п.** void; **боя́знь ~а** (*med.*) agoraphobia.

простра́ци|я, и *f.* prostration (*mental and physical exhaustion*).

простра́чива|ть, ю *impf. of* **прострочи́ть**

простре́л, а *m.* (*coll.*) lumbago.

простре́лива|ть, ю *impf.* **1.** *impf. of* **прострелять. 2.** *impf. only* (*mil.*) to rake, sweep with fire. **3.** *impf. only* (*mil.*) to cover, have covered.

простре́лива|ться, юсь *impf.* (*mil.*) **1.** to be exposed to fire. **2.** *pass. of* **~ть**

прострел|и́ть, ю́, ~́ишь *pf.* (*of* **~́ивать**) to shoot through.

простроч|и́ть, у́, ~́ишь *pf.* (*of* **простра́чивать**) to stitch; to back-stitch.

просту́д|а, ы *f.* (chest) cold; chill; **схвати́ть ~у** (*coll.*) to catch (a) cold, catch a chill.

просту|ди́ть, жу́, ~́дишь *pf.* (*of* **~жа́ть**) to let catch cold.

просту|ди́ться, жу́сь, ~́дишься *pf.* (*of* **~жа́ться**) to catch (a) cold; to catch, take a chill.

просту́дный *adj.* catarrhal.

простужа́|ть(ся), ю(сь) *impf. of* **простуди́ть(ся)**

просту́|женный *p.p.p. of* **~ди́ть** *and adj.*; **я вновь ~жен** I have caught another cold.

просту́к|ать, аю *pf.* (*of* **~ивать**) (*med.*) to tap.

просту́кива|ть, ю *impf. of* **просту́кать**

проступ|а́ть, а́ет *impf. of* **~и́ть**

проступ|и́ть, ~́ит *pf.* (*of* **~а́ть**) to appear, show through, come through; **сыры́е пя́тна ~и́ли на стена́х** damp patches have appeared on the walls; **пот ~и́л у него́ на лбу** perspiration stood out on his forehead.

просту́п|ок, ка *m.* fault; breach of manners; (*leg.*) misdemeanour.

простыва́|ть, ю *impf. of* **просты́ть**

просты́н|ный *adj. of* **~я́**; **~ное полотно́** sheeting.

простын|я́, и́, *pl.* **про́стыни, ~́ь, ~я́м** *f.* sheet.

просты́|ть, ну, нешь *pf.* (*of* **~ва́ть**) **1.** to get cold; to cool; **и след ~л** (*+g.*; *coll.*) not a trace (of). **2.** (*coll.*) to catch cold.

просу́н|уть, у, ешь *pf.* (*of* **просо́вывать**) (**в**+*a.*) to push (through, in), shove (through, in), thrust (through, in).

просу́н|уться, усь, ешься *pf.* (*of* **просо́вываться**) to push through, force one's way through.

просу́шива|ть(ся), ю(сь) *impf. of* **просуши́ть(ся)**

просуш|и́ть, у́, ~́ишь *pf.* (*of* **~́ивать**) to dry thoroughly, properly.

просуш|и́ться, у́сь, ~́ишься *pf.* (*of* **~́иваться**) to (get) dry.

просу́шк|а, и *f.* drying.

просуществ|ова́ть, у́ю *pf.* to exist (*for a certain time*); to last, endure.

просфор|а́, ы́ *f.* (*eccl.*) (communion) bread; host.

просце́ниум, а *m.* (*theatr.*) proscenium.

просчёт, а *m.* **1.** counting (up), reckoning (up). **2.** error (*in counting, reckoning*).

просчит|а́ть, а́ю *pf.* (*of* **~́ывать**) **1.** to count (up), reckon (up). **2.** to count out, give in error; **вы ~а́ли пятьдеся́т рубле́й** you have given fifty roubles too much.

просчит|а́ться, а́юсь *pf.* (*of* **~́ываться**) **1.** to make an error in counting; to be out in counting; to go wrong; **мы ~а́лись на два́дцать рубле́й** we are out by twenty roubles. **2.** (*fig.*) to miscalculate.

просчи́тыва|ть(ся), ю(сь) *impf. of* **просчита́ть(ся)**

про́сып, а *m.*: **без ~у** (*coll.*) without waking, without stirring.

просы́п|ать, лю, лешь *pf.* (*of* **~а́ть[1]**) to spill.

просып|а́ть[1], а́ю *impf. of* **~́ать**

просып|а́ть[2], а́ю *impf. of* **проспа́ть**

просы́п|аться, лется *pf.* (*of* **~а́ться[2]**) to spill, get spilled.

просып|а́ться[1], а́юсь *impf. of* **просну́ться**

просып|а́ться[2], а́ю *impf. of* **~́аться**

просыха́|ть, ю *impf. of* **просо́хнуть**

про́сьб|а, ы *f.* **1.** request; **обраща́ться с ~ой** to make a request; **удовлетвори́ть ~у** to comply with a request; **у меня́ к вам п.** I have a favour to ask you; **по мое́й ~е** at my request; **«п. не кури́ть!»** 'no smoking, please!' **2.** (*obs.*) application, petition; **пода́ть ~у об отста́вке** to send in one's resignation.

прося́нк|а, и *f.* (*zool.*): **овся́нка-п.** cornbunting.

просяно́й *adj.* millet.

прота́лин|а, ы *f.* thawed patch (*of earth*).

прота́лкива|ть, ю *impf. of* **протолкну́ть**

прота́лкива|ться, юсь *impf. of* **протолка́ться** *and* **протолкну́ться**

протанц|ева́ть, у́ю *pf.* **1.** to dance; **п. вальс** to dance a waltz, do a waltz. **2.** to dance (*for a certain time*).

прота́плива|ть, ю *impf. of* **протопи́ть**

прота́птыва|ть, ю *impf. of* **протопта́ть**

протара́н|ить, ю, ишь *pf.* (*of* **тара́нить**) **1.** (*mil.*) to ram. **2.** (*fig.*) to break through, smash.

прота́скива|ть, ю *impf. of* **протащи́ть**

прота́чива|ть, ю *impf. of* **проточи́ть**

протащ|и́ть, у́, ~́ишь *pf.* (*of* **прота́скивать**) **1.** to pull (through, along), drag (through, along), trail. **2.** (*coll., pej.*) to insinuate, work in.

прота́|ять, ю, ешь *pf.* to thaw through.

протеже́ *c.g. indecl.* protégé; (*used of woman only*) protégée.
протежи́р|овать, ую *impf.* (*+d.*) to favour; to pull strings (for).
проте́з, а *m.* prosthetic appliance; artificial limb; **зубно́й п.** false tooth, denture.
протези́р|овать, ую *impf. and pf.* to equip with a prosthetic appliance; to make a prosthetic appliance.
проте́зн|ый *adj.* prosthetic; **~ая мастерска́я** orthopaedic workshop.
протеи́н, а *m.* (*chem.*) protein.
протека́|ть, ю *impf.* **1.** *impf. of* **проте́чь. 2.** *impf. only* (*of a river or stream*) to flow, run. **3.** *impf. only* to leak, be leaky.
проте́ктор, а *m.* **1.** (*pol.*) power exercising protectorate **2.** (*obs.*) protector, patron. **3.** (*tech.*) protector, protective device; **двойно́й п.** double tread (*of pneumatic tyre*).
протектора́т, а *m.* protectorate.
протекциони́зм, а *m.* **1.** (*pol., econ.*) protectionism. **2.** (*coll.*) favouritism.
протекциони́ст, а *m.* protectionist.
проте́кци|я, и *f.* patronage, influence; **оказа́ть кому́-н. ~ю** to use one's influence on s.o.'s behalf, pull strings for s.o.
проте́|кший *p.p. act. of* **~чь** *and adj.* past, last.
про|тере́ть, тру́, трёшь, *past* **~тёр, ~тёрла** *pf.* (*of* **~тира́ть**) **1.** to rub a hole (in); to wear into holes. **2.** to rub through, grate; **п. че́рез си́то** to rub through a sieve. **3.** to rub over, wipe over. **4.: п. глаза́** (*coll.*) to rub one's eyes.
про|тере́ться, трётся, *past* **~тёрся, ~тёрлась** *pf.* (*of* **~тира́ться**) to wear through, wear into holes.
протерп|е́ть, лю́, ~ишь *pf.* to wait, last out, to endure, stand.
протесн|и́ться, ю́сь, и́шься *pf.* to push one's way (through), elbow one's way (through), barge (through).
проте́ст, а *m* **1.** protest; remonstrance; **заяви́ть п.** to make a protest; **пода́ть п.** to enter, register a protest. **2.: п. ве́кселя** (*fin., comm.*) protest of a promissory note. **3.** (*leg.*) objection; **принести́ п.** to bring an objection.
протеста́нт[1], **а** *m.* protester, objector.
протеста́нт[2], **а** *m.* (*relig.*) Protestant.
протестанти́зм, а *m.* = **протеста́нтство**
протеста́нтский *adj.* (*relig.*) Protestant.
протеста́нтств|о, а *nt.* (*relig.*) Protestantism.
протест|ова́ть, у́ю *impf.* **(про́тив)** to protest (against), object (to).
проте́|чь, чёт, ку́т, *past* **~к, ~кла́** *pf.* (*of* **~ка́ть**) **1.** to ooze, seep. **2.** (*of time*) to elapse, pass; **кани́кулы бы́стро ~кли́** the holidays flew by. **3.** (*of an illness, etc.*) to take its course.
про́тив *prep.+g.* **1.** (*in var. senses*) against; **п. тече́ния** against the current; **не найдётся ли у вас что-н. п. головно́й бо́ли?** do you happen to have anything for a headache?; **за и п.** for and against, pro and con; **име́ть что-н. п.** to have sth. against; to mind, object; **вы ничего́ не име́ете п. того́, что я курю́?** do you mind my smoking?; **вы ничего́ не бу́дете име́ть п., е́сли я закурю́?** will you mind if I smoke? **2.** opposite; facing; **друг п. дру́га** facing one another; **останови́тесь, пожа́луйста, п. це́ркви** please stop opposite the church. **3.** contrary to; **п. на́ших ожида́ний** contrary to our expectations. **4.** (*coll.*) as against; in proportion to; according to; **в э́том году́ п. про́шлого** this year as against last (year); **де́сять ша́нсов п. одного́** ten to one; **ка́ждому п. потре́бностей его́** to each according to his needs.
про́тив|ень, ня *m.* griddle.
противи́тельный *adj.* (*gram.*) adversative.
проти́в|иться, люсь, ишься *impf.* (*of* **вос~**) (*+d.*) to oppose; to resist, stand up (against).
про́тивник, а *m.* **1.** opponent, adversary, antagonist; **п. вивисе́кции** antivivisectionist; **п. войны́** war resister; **п. коммуни́зма** anticommunist. **2.** (*collect.; mil.*) the enemy.
про́тивно[1] *adv.* in a disgusting way.
проти́вно[2] *prep.+d.* against; contrary to; **поступа́ть п. свое́й со́вести** to go against one's conscience.
проти́вн|ый[1] *adj.* **1.** opposite; contrary; **п. ве́тер** contrary wind, head wind; **~ое мне́ние** a contrary opinion; **в ~ом слу́чае** otherwise; **доказа́тельство от ~ого** the rule of contraries. **2.** opposing, opposed; **~ые сто́роны** opposing sides.
проти́в|ный[2] **(~ен, ~на)** *adj.* nasty, offensive, disgusting; unpleasant, disagreeable; **п. за́пах** nasty smell; **он мне ~ен** I find him offensive; **мне ~но припомина́ть э́то происше́ствие** I find it disagreeable to recollect the event.
противо... *comb. form* anti-, contra-, counter-.
противоалкого́льный *adj.* temperance; **п. зако́н** prohibition.
противобо́рств|о, а *nt.* struggle; (*pol.*) confrontation.
противобо́рств|овать, ую *impf.* (*+d.; obs.*) to oppose; to fight (against).
противове́с, а *m.* (*tech. and fig.*) counterbalance, counterpoise.
противовозду́шн|ый *adj.* anti-aircraft; **~ая оборо́на** air defence.
противога́з, а *m.* gas-mask, respirator.
противога́зов|ый *adj.* anti-gas; **~ая су́мка** gas-mask case.
противоде́йстви|е, я *nt.* opposition, counteraction.
противоде́йств|овать, ую *impf.* (*+d.*) to oppose, counteract.
противодетони́рующий *adj.*: **п. материа́л** (*tech.*) anti-knock compound.
противоесте́ствен|ный (~, ~на) *adj.* unnatural.
противозако́нност|ь, и *f.* illegality.
противозако́н|ный (~ен, ~на) *adj.* unlawful; (*leg.*) illegal.
противозача́точн|ый *adj.* contraceptive; **~ые сре́дства** contraceptives.
противозени́тный *adj.*: **п. мане́вр** (*aeron.*) evasive action.
противоипри́тный *adj.* anti-mustard-gas.
противокисло́тный *adj.* acid-proof.
противолежа́щий *adj.* (*math.*) opposite; **п. у́гол** alternate angle.
противолихора́дочн|ый *adj.* (*med.*) anti-febrile; **~ое сре́дство** febrifuge.
противоло́дочный *adj.* (*naut.*) anti-submarine.
противоми́нн|ый *adj.* (*naut.*) anti-mine-and-torpedo; **~ая артилле́рия** secondary armament.
противообледени́тель = **антиобледени́тель**
противообще́ственный *adj.* antisocial.
противооткáтн|ый *adj.* (*mil.*) anti-recoil; **~ые устро́йства** recoil mechanism.
противопехо́тн|ый *adj.* (*mil.*): **~ая ми́на** antipersonnel mine.
противоподло́дочный *adj.* (*naut.*) anti-submarine.
противопожа́рн|ый *adj.* anti-fire; **~ая дверь** fire door; **~ые ме́ры** fire-prevention measures.
противопоказа́ни|е, я *nt.* **1.** (*leg.*) contradictory evidence. **2.** (*med.*) contra-indication.
противопока́занный *adj.* (*med.*) contra-indicated.
противополага́|ть, ю *impf. of* **противополо́жить**
противоположе́ни|е, я *nt.* opposition.
противополож|и́ть, у́, ~ишь *pf.* (*of* **противополага́ть**) (*+d.*) to oppose (to).
противополо́жност|ь, и *f.* **1.** opposition; contrast; **в п.** (*+d.*) as opposed (to), by contrast (with). **2.** opposite, antipode, antithesis; **по́лная п.** complete antithesis; **пряма́я п.** exact opposite.
противополо́ж|ный (~ен, ~на) *adj.* **1.** opposite. **2.** opposed, contrary; **диаметра́льно п.** diametrically opposed.
противопоста́в|ить, лю, ишь *pf.* (*of* **~ля́ть**) (*+d.*) **1.** to oppose (to). **2.** to contrast (with), set off (against).
противопоставле́ни|е, я *nt.* (*+d.*) **1.** opposing (to), opposition (to). **2.** contrasting (with), setting off (against).
противопоставля́|ть, ю *impf. of* **противопоста́вить**
противоправи́тельственный *adj.* anti-government(al).
противоприга́рный *adj.* non-stick.
противораке́тн|ый *adj.* (*mil.*) anti-missile; **~ая раке́та** anti-missile missile.
противоречи́вост|ь, и *f.* contradictoriness; discrepancy.
противоречи́в|ый (~, ~а) *adj.* contradictory; discrepant, conflicting; **~ые сообще́ния** conflicting reports.

противоре́чи|е, я *nt.* **1.** contradiction; inconsistency; **~я в показа́ниях** contradictions in evidence. **2.** contrariness; defiance; **дух ~я** spirit of defiance, contrariness; **вы э́то де́лаете про́сто из ду́ха ~я** you are doing it simply out of contrariness. **3.** conflict, clash; **кла́ссовые ~я** conflicts of class interests; **находи́ться в ~и (с+*i.*)** to be at variance (with), conflict (with).

противоре́ч|ить, у, ишь *impf.* (+*d.*) **1.** to contradict; **п. самому́ себе́** to contradict o.s.; **он всё ~ил ма́тери** he was always contradicting his mother. **2.** to be at variance (with), conflict (with), run counter (to), be contrary (to); **э́то ~ит действи́тельности** it is contrary to the facts; **их показа́ния ~ат одно́ друго́му** their evidence is conflicting.

противосамолётный *adj.* (*mil.*) anti-aircraft.

противоснаря́дный *adj.* (*mil.*) shell-proof.

противостолбня́чный *adj.* (*med.*) anti-tetanus.

противостоя́ни|е, я *nt.* **1.** (*astron.*) opposition. **2.** (*pol.*) confrontation.

противосто|я́ть, ю́, и́шь *impf.* (+*d.*) **1.** to resist, withstand. **2.** to countervail. **3.** (*astron.*) to be in opposition.

противота́нков|ый *adj.* anti-tank; anti-mechanized; **~ая лову́шка** tank trap; **~ое ружьё** anti-tank rifle.

противото́к, а *m.* (*tech.*) counter-current, counterflow.

противоуго́нный *adj.* anti-theft.

противохими́ческий *adj.* (*mil.*) anti-gas.

противоцинго́тный *adj.* (*med.*) anti-scorbutic.

противочу́мный *adj.* (*med.*) anti-plague.

противошу́м|ы, ов *no sg.* earplugs.

противоя́ди|е, я *nt.* antidote.

протира́|ть(ся), ю(сь) *impf. of* **протере́ть(ся)**

прoти́рк|а, и *f.* cleaning rag.

проти́ск|аться, аюсь *pf.* (*of* **~иваться**) to push one's way through, elbow one's way through.

проти́скива|ть, ю *impf. of* **проти́снуть**

проти́скива|ться, юсь *impf. of* **проти́скаться**

проти́с|нуть, ну, нешь *pf.* (*of* **~кивать**) to push through, shove through.

проти́с|нуться, нусь, нешься *pf.* = **~каться**

проткн|у́ть, у́, ёшь *pf.* (*of* **протыка́ть**) to pierce; to transfix; to spit, skewer.

протодья́кон, а *m.* (*eccl.*) archdeacon.

протозо́а *pl. indecl.* (*zool.*) Protozoa.

протоиере́|й, я *m.* (*eccl.*) archpriest.

протоисто́ри|я, и *f.* prehistory.

прото́к, а *m.* **1.** channel. **2.** (*anat.*) duct.

протоко́л, а *m.* **1.** minutes, record of proceedings; report; **вести́ п.** to take the minutes, record the minutes; **занести́ в п.** to enter in the minutes. **2.** (*leg.*) statement; charge-sheet; **п. дозна́ния, п. допро́са** examination record; **соста́вить п.** to draw up a report. **3.** (*dipl.*) protocol.

протоколи́зм, а *m.* dry, factual exposition.

протоколи́р|овать, ую *impf. and pf.* (*pf. also* **за~**) to minute; to record.

протоко́л|ьный *adj. of* **~**; **п. отде́л** protocol department; **п. стиль** (*fig.*) officialese (= *dry, factual style of exposition, not long-winded jargon*).

протолка́|ться, юсь *pf.* (*of* **прота́лкиваться**) (*coll.*) **1.** to force, jostle one's way (through). **2.** to lounge about.

протолкн|у́ть, у́, ёшь *pf.* (*of* **прота́лкивать**) to push through, press through; (*fig.*): **п. де́ло** to push a matter forward.

протолкн|у́ться, у́сь, ёшься *pf.* = **протолка́ться**

прото́н, а *m.* (*phys.*) proton.

прото́н|ный *adj. of* **~**

протоп|и́ть, лю́, ~ишь *pf.* (*of* **прота́пливать**) to heat thoroughly.

протопла́зм|а, ы *f.* (*biol.*) protoplasm.

протопо́п, а *m.* (*obs.*) archpriest.

протоп|та́ть, чу́, ~чешь *pf.* (*of* **прота́птывать**) **1.** to beat, make (*by walking*); **п. тропи́нку** to make a path. **2.** to wear out (*footwear*).

проторг|ова́ть, у́ю *pf.* (*coll.*) to lose (*in trading*).

проторг|ова́ться, у́юсь *pf.* (*coll.*) to have losses (*in trading*); to be ruined (*in trade, in business*).

протор|ённый *p.p.p. of* **~и́ть** *and adj.* beaten, well-trodden; **~ённая доро́жка** beaten track.

про́тор|и, ей *no sg.* (*obs.*) expenses.

протор|и́ть, ю́, и́шь *pf.* (*of* **~я́ть**) to beat; **п. путь** to blaze a trail.

протор|я́ть, я́ю *impf. of* **~и́ть**

прототи́п, а *m.* prototype.

прото́ч|енный *p.p.p. of* **~и́ть; п. червя́ми** worm-eaten.

проточ|и́ть, у́, ~ишь *pf.* (*of* **прота́чивать**) **1.** to gnaw through, eat through. **2.** (*of running water*) to wash. **3.** to turn (*on a lathe*).

прото́чн|ый *adj.* flowing, running; **~ая вода́** running water; **п. пруд** pond fed by springs.

протра́в|а, ы *f.* (*chem.*) mordant; pickle, dip.

протрави́тел|ь, я *m.* **1.** (*tech.*) mordanting machine, pickling machine. **2.** (*chem.*) mordant.

протрав|и́ть[1]**, лю́, ~ишь** *pf.* (*of* **~ливать** *and* **~ля́ть**) (*tech.*) **1.** to treat with a mordant; to pickle, dip. **2.** to etch.

протрав|и́ть[2]**, лю́, ~ишь** *pf.* (*in hunting*) to fail to catch, let go.

протра́влива|ть, ю *impf. of* **протрави́ть**[1]

протравл|я́ть, я́ю *impf.* = **~ивать**

протра́л|ить, ю, ишь *pf. of* **тра́лить**

протрезв|и́ть, лю́, и́шь *pf.* (*of* **~ля́ть**) to sober.

протрезв|и́ться, лю́сь, и́шься *pf.* (*of* **~ля́ться**) to sober up, get sober.

протрезвля́|ть(ся), ю(сь) *impf. of* **протрезви́ть(ся)**

протубера́н|ец, ца *m.* (*astron.*) solar prominence; solar flare.

протур|и́ть, ю́, ~и́шь *pf.* (*coll.*) to drive away, chuck out.

протух|а́ть, а́ю *impf. of* **~нуть**

протýх|нуть, ну, нешь, *past* **~, ~ла** *pf.* (*of* **~а́ть**) to become foul, rotten; to go bad.

протýх|ший *p.p. act. of* **~нуть** *and adj.* foul, rotten; (*of food*) bad, tainted.

протыка́|ть, ю *impf. of* **проткну́ть**

протя́гива|ть(ся), ю(сь) *impf. of* **протяну́ть(ся)**

протяже́ни|е, я *nt.* **1.** extent, stretch; distance, expanse, area; **на большо́м ~и** over a wide area; **на всём ~и (+*g.*)** along the whole length (of), all along. **2.** space (*of time*); **на ~и (+*g.*)** during, for the space (of).

протяжённост|ь, и *f.* extent, length.

протяжён|ный (~, ~на) *adj.* extensive.

протя́жност|ь, и *f.* slowness; **п. ре́чи** drawl.

протя́ж|ный (~ен, ~на) *adj.* long drawn-out; **~ное произноше́ние** drawl.

протя|ну́ть, ну́, ~нешь *pf.* (*of* **~гивать**) **1.** to stretch; to extend. **2.** to stretch out, extend, hold out, reach out; **п. ру́ку** to hold out one's hand; **п. ру́ку по́мощи** to extend a helping hand; **п. табаке́рку** to proffer a snuff-box; **п. но́ги** (*fig., coll.*) to turn up one's toes. **3.** to protract. **4.** to drawl out. **5.** (*pf. only*) to last; **больно́й недо́лго ~нет** the patient won't last long. **6.** (*hunting*) to fly over (*of birds*).

протя|ну́ться, ну́сь, ~нешься *pf.* (*of* **~гиваться**) **1.** to stretch out; to reach out; **п. на дива́не** to stretch out on the sofa. **2.** to extend, stretch, reach. **3.** *pf. only* to last, go on.

проу́л|ок, ка *m.* (*coll.*) lane.

проу́чива|ть, ю *impf. of* **проучи́ть**[1]

проуч|и́ть[1]**, у́, ~ишь** *pf.* (*of* **~ивать**) (*coll.*) to teach, give a good lesson; **я его́ ~у́!** I'll teach him!

проуч|и́ть[2]**, у́, ~ишь** *pf.* to study, learn up (*for a certain time*).

проуч|и́ться, у́сь, ~ишься *pf.* to spend (*a certain time*) in study.

проу́шин|а, ы *f.* lug; staple.

проф... *comb. form, abbr. of* **1. профессиона́льный. 2. профсою́зный**

профа́н, а *m.* **1.** (*in relation to a given field of knowledge*) layman. **2.** ignoramus.

профана́ци|я, и *f.* profanation.

профани́р|овать, ую *impf. and pf.* to profane.

профбиле́т, а *m.* trade-union card.

профершпи́л|иться, юсь, ишься *pf.* (*coll.*) to lose all one's money, be ruined.

профессиона́л, а *m.* professional.

профессионали́зм, а *m.* **1.** professionalism. **2.** (*ling.*) specialist term.

профессиона́льн|ый *adj.* **1.** professional, occupational; **п. диплома́т** career diplomat; **~ое заболева́ние** occupational disease; **~ое образова́ние** vocational training; **~ая ориента́ция** career guidance; **п. риск** occupational hazard; **п. секре́т** trade secret; **п. сою́з** trade union. **2.** professional (*opp. amateur*).

профе́сси|я, и *f.* profession, occupation, trade; **по ~и** by profession, by trade.

профе́ссор, а, *pl.* **~а́** *m.* professor.

профе́ссорск|ий *adj.* **1.** professorial. **2.** *as n.* **~ая ~ой** *f.* staff common room.

профе́ссорств|о, а *nt.* professorship, (university) chair.

профе́ссорств|овать, ую *impf.* to be a professor, have a (university) chair.

профессу́р|а, ы *f.* **1.** professorship, (university) chair. **2.** (*collect.*) the professors.

профила́ктик|а, и *f.* **1.** (*med.*) prophylaxis. **2.** (*collect.*) preventive measures, precautions.

профилакти́ческий *adj.* **1.** (*med.*) prophylactic. **2.** preventive, precautionary.

профилакто́ри|й, я *m.* dispensary.

про́фил|ь, я *m.* **1.** profile; side-view; (*fig.*) outline; **в п.** in profile, half-faced. **2.** section; **попере́чный п.** cross-section; **п. крыла́** (*aeron.*) airfoil. **3.** type; **шко́лы ра́зного ~я** schools of various types.

про́филь|ный *adj.* *of* **~**; **~ное желе́зо** section iron; **п. резе́ц, п. фре́зер** (*tech.*) profile cutter, forming tool.

профильтр|ова́ть, у́ю *pf. of* **фильтрова́ть**

профин|ти́ть, чу́, ти́шь *pf.* (*coll.*) to squander.

профитро́л|ь, я *m.* (*cul.*) profiterole.

профко́м, а *m.* (*abbr. of* ***профсою́зный комите́т***) trade-union committee.

профконсульта́нт, а *m.* careers adviser.

профо́рг, а *m.* (*abbr. of* ***профсою́зный организа́тор***) trade-union organizer.

профо́рм|а, ы *f.* form, formality; **чи́стая п.** pure, mere formality; **для ~ы, ра́ди ~ы** for form's sake, as a matter of form.

профрабо́т|а, ы *f.* trade-union work.

профрабо́тник, а *m.* trade-union official.

профсою́з, а *m.* trade union.

профсою́зный *adj.* trade-union.

профтехшко́л|а, ы *f.* (*abbr. of* ***профессиона́льно-техни́ческая шко́ла***) trade school.

профшко́л|а, ы *f.* trade-union school.

проха́жива|ться, юсь *impf. of* **пройти́сь**

прохва|ти́ть, чу́, ~́тишь *pf.* (*of* **~́тывать**) (*coll.*) **1.** (*of cold, draught, etc.*) to penetrate; **меня́ ~ти́ло на сквозняке́** I caught a chill from being in a draught. **2.** to bite through. **3.** (*fig.*) to tear to pieces.

прохва́тыва|ть, ю *impf. of* **прохвати́ть**

прохвора́|ть, ю *pf.* (*coll.*) to be ill (*for a certain time*); to be laid up (*for a certain time*).

прохво́ст, а *m.* (*coll.*) scoundrel.

прохла́д|а, ы *f.* coolness.

прохла́д|ец, ца *m.*: **с ~цем** (*coll.*) without making much effort; listlessly.

прохлади́тельн|ый *adj.* refreshing, cooling; **~ые напи́тки** soft drinks.

прохла|ди́ться, жу́сь, ди́шься *pf.* (*coll.*) to cool off.

прохла́д|ный (~ен, ~на) *adj.* **1.** cool; fresh; (*impers., pred.*): **~но** it is cool, it is fresh. **2.** (*fig.*) cool; **отноше́ния у них ста́ли ~ными** there has been a cooling-off between them.

прохла́д|ца, цы *f.* = **~ец**

прохлажда́|ться, юсь *impf.* (*coll.*) to take it easy.

прохо́д, а *m.* **1.** (*in var. senses*) passage; **пра́во ~а** right of way; **не дава́ть ~а** (*+d.*) to give no peace, pester; **мне от него́ ~а нет** I cannot get rid of him, shake him off. **2.** passageway; gangway, aisle; **кры́тый п.** covered way. **3.** (*anat.*) duct; **за́дний п.** anus; **слухово́й п.** acoustic duct.

проходи́м|ец, ца *m.* rogue, rascal.

проходи́мост|ь, и *f.* **1.** (*of roads, etc.*) passability. **2.** (*anat.*) permeability. **3.** (*of motor, etc., transport*) cross-country ability.

проходи́м|ый (~, ~а) *adj.* passable.

прохо|ди́ть[1], жу́, ~́дишь *impf.* **1.** *impf. of* **пройти́. 2.** *impf. only* **(че́рез)** to lie (through), go (through), pass (through); **кана́л ~́дит че́рез джу́нгли** the canal passes through jungle.

прохо|ди́ть[2], жу́, ~́дишь *pf.* to walk (*for a certain time*); **мы ~ди́ли весь день** we have spent the whole day walking.

прохо́дк|а, и *f.* (*mining*) working; sinking (*of shaft*); drift.

проходн|о́й *adj. of* **прохо́д**; passage; **~а́я бу́дка** entrance check-point, entrance lodge; **~а́я ко́мната** inter-communicating room, room giving access into another; **~а́я конто́ра** entrance-gate office; **~о́е свиде́тельство** (*hist.*) travel permit, travel document (*issued by police to deportees*).

прохо́дчик, а *m.* (*mining*) shaft sinker; drifter.

прохожде́ни|е, я *nt.* passing, passage; **п. торже́ственным ма́ршем** (*mil.*) march past.

прохо́ж|ий *adj.* passing, in transit; *as n.* **п., ~его** *m.*, **~ая, ~ей** *f.* passer-by.

процвета́ни|е, я *nt.* prosperity, well-being; flourishing, thriving.

процвета́|ть, ю *impf.* to prosper, flourish, thrive.

проце|ди́ть, жу́, ~́дишь *pf.* (*of* **~́живать**) to filter, strain.

процеду́р|а, ы *f.* **1.** procedure. **2.** (*usu. pl.*) treatment.

проце́жива|ть, ю *impf. of* **процеди́ть**

проце́нт, а *m.* **1.** percentage; rate (per cent); **сто ~ов** one hundred per cent; **ба́нковский учётный п.** bank rate; **просты́е, сло́жные ~ы** (*math.*) simple, compound interest; **рабо́тать на ~ах** to work on a percentage basis. **2.** interest; **разме́р ~а** rate of interest.

проце́нт|ный *adj. of* **~**; interest-bearing; **~ное отноше́ние** percentage; **~ные бума́ги** interest-bearing securities; **~ные облига́ции** interest-bearing bonds.

проце́сс, а *m.* **1.** process. **2.** (*leg.*) trial; legal action, legal proceedings; lawsuit; cause, case; **вести́ п. (с+*i.*)** to be at law (with). **3.** (*med.*) active condition; **п. в лёгких** active pulmonary tuberculosis.

проце́сси|я, и *f.* procession.

проце́ссор, а *m.* (*comput.*) processor.

процессуа́льн|ый *adj. of* **проце́сс 2.**; **~ые но́рмы** legal procedure.

процити́р|овать, ую *pf. of* **цити́ровать**

прочёркива|ть, ю *impf. of* **прочеркну́ть**

прочерк|ну́ть, ну́, нёшь *pf.* (*of* **~́ивать**) to strike through, draw a line through.

прочер|ти́ть, чу́, ~́тишь *pf.* (*of* **~́чивать**) to draw.

проче́рчива|ть, ю *impf. of* **прочерти́ть**

проче|са́ть, шу́, ~́шешь *pf.* (*of* **~́сывать**) **1.** to comb out thoroughly. **2.** (*mil.; fig.*) to comb.

прочёск|а, и *f.* screening (*as a security measure*).

про|че́сть, чту́, чтёшь, *past* **~чёл, ~чла́** *pf.* = **~чита́ть**

прочёсыва|ть, ю *impf. of* **прочеса́ть**

прочёт, а *m.* (*coll.*) error (*in counting*).

про́ч|ий *adj.* other; **и ~ее (*abbr.* и пр., и проч.)** etcetera, and so on; **~ие** (the) others; **ме́жду ~им** by the way; **поми́мо всего́ ~его** in addition.

прочи́|стить, щу, стишь *pf.* (*of* **~ща́ть**) to clean; to cleanse thoroughly; **п. тру́бку** to clean a pipe.

прочита́|ть[1], ю *pf. of* **чита́ть**

прочита́|ть[2], ю *pf.* to read (*for a certain time*).

прочи́тыва|ть, ю *impf.* (*coll.*) to read through, peruse.

про́ч|ить, у, ишь *impf.* **(в+*a.*)** to intend (for), destine (for); **его́ ~или в свяще́нники** he was intended for the church.

прочища́|ть, ю *impf. of* **прочи́стить**

про́чно *adv.* firmly, soundly, solidly, well.

про́чност|ь, и *f.* firmness, soundness, stability, solidity; durability; endurance; **п. на изги́б** (*tech.*) bending strength; **п. на изно́с** (*tech.*) resistance to wear; **п. на разры́в** (*tech.*) tensile strength; **п. на уда́р** (*tech.*) resistance to shock, impact value; **запа́с ~и, коэффицие́нт ~и** safety factor, safety margin.

про́ч|ный (~ен, ~на́, ~но) *adj.* firm, sound, stable, solid; durable, lasting; **~ные зна́ния** sound knowledge; **~ная кра́ска** fast dye; **~ное сча́стье** lasting happiness; **~ная ткань** durable fabric.
прочте́ни|е, я *nt.* reading; perusal; **по ~и** (+*g.*) on reading.
прочу́вствова|нный *p.p.p. of* **~ть** *and adj.* full of emotion; heart-felt.
прочу́вств|овать, ую *pf.* **1.** to feel deeply, acutely, keenly. **2.** to experience, go through. **3.** to feel, get the feel (of); **п. свою́ роль** to get the feel of one's part.
прочь *adv.* **1.** away, off; **(поди́) п.!** go away!; be off!; **(пошёл) п. отсю́да!** get out of here!; **п. с глаз мои́х!** get out of my sight!; **п. с доро́ги!** (get) out of the way!, make way!; **ру́ки п.!** hands off! **2.** *as pred.* averse (to); **не п.** (+*inf.*; *coll.*) to have no objection (to); not to be averse (to); **я не п. пойти́ туда́** I have no objection to going there; I am quite willing to go there; **он не п. вы́пить стака́нчик** he is not averse to taking a drop.
проше́дш|ий *p.p. act. of* **пройти́** *and adj.* past; last; **~им ле́том** last summer; **~ее вре́мя** (*gram.*) past tense; *as n.* **~ее, ~его** *nt.* the past.
проше́ни|е, я *nt.* application, petition; **пода́ть п.** to submit an application, forward a petition.
прошеп|та́ть, чу́, ~́чешь *pf. of* **шепта́ть**
проше́стви|е, я *nt.*: **по ~и** (+*g.*) after the lapse (of), after the expiration (of); **по ~и сро́ка** after the expiration of the term.
прошиб|а́ть, а́ю *impf. of* **~и́ть**
прошиб|и́ть, у́, ёшь, *past* **~́, ~́ла** *pf.* (*of* **~а́ть**) (*coll.*) **1.** to break through. **2.: его́ ~́ пот** he broke into a sweat; **её ~́ла слеза́** she shed a tear.
прошива́|ть, ю *impf. of* **проши́ть**
проши́вк|а, и *f.* **1.** insertion (*on linen, etc.*). **2.** (*tech.*) broach, broaching bit.
прош|и́ть, ью́, ьёшь *pf.* (*of* **~ива́ть**) **1.** to sew, stitch. **2.** (*tech.*) to broach.
прошлого́дний *adj.* last year's; of last year.
про́шл|ый *adj.* **1.** past; bygone, former; **э́то де́ло ~ое** it's a thing of the past; *as n.* **~ое, ~ого** *nt.* the past; **далёкое ~ое** the distant past; **отойти́ в ~ое** to become a thing of the past. **2.** last; **в ~ом году́** last year; **на ~ой неде́ле** last week.
прошля́п|ить, лю, ишь *pf.* (*coll.*) to blunder, slip up.
прошмы́гива|ть, ю *impf. of* **прошмыгну́ть**
прошмыг|ну́ть, ну́, нёшь *pf.* (*of* **~́ивать**) (*coll.*) to slip (by, past, through).
прошнур|ова́ть, у́ю *pf. of* **шнурова́ть 2.**
прошпакл|ева́ть, ю́ю, ю́ешь *pf.* (*of* **~ёвывать**) to putty; (*naut.*) to caulk.
прошпаклёвыва|ть, ю *impf. of* **прошпаклева́ть**
прошτра́ф|иться, люсь, ишься *pf.* (*coll.*) to be at fault.
проштуди́р|овать, ую *pf. of* **штуди́ровать**
прошум|е́ть, лю́, и́шь *pf.* **1.** to roar past. **2.** (*fig.*) to become famous.
проща́й(те) good-bye!; farewell!; adieu!
проща́льн|ый *adj.* farewell, parting; valedictory; **~ая пиру́шка** farewell party; **~ые слова́** parting words.
проща́ни|е, я *nt.* farewell; parting, leave-taking; **на п.** at parting.
проща́|ть(ся), ю(сь) *impf. of* **прости́ть(ся)**
про́ще *comp. of* **просто́й** *and* **про́сто**; simpler; plainer; easier.
прощелы́г|а, и *c.g.* (*coll.*) knave, rogue.
проще́ни|е, я *nt.* forgiveness, pardon; absolution; **проси́ть ~я у кого́-н.** to ask s.o.'s pardon; **прошу́ ~я!** I beg your pardon!; (I am) sorry!
прощу́п|ать, аю *pf.* (*of* **~ывать**) **1.** to feel; to detect (*by feeling*). **2.** (*fig.*, *coll.*) to sound (out).
прощу́пыва|ть, ю *impf. of* **прощу́пать**
проэкзамен|ова́ть(ся), у́ю(сь) *pf. of* **экзаменова́ть(ся)**
прояви́тел|ь, я *m.* (*phot.*) developer.
проявл|и́ть, лю́, ~́ишь *pf.* (*of* **~ля́ть**) **1.** to show, display, manifest, reveal; **п. забо́ту (о**+*p.*) to show concern (for, about), take trouble (about); **п. интере́с (к)** to show interest (in); **п. себя́** to show one's worth; **п. себя́** (+*i.*) to show o.s., prove (to be); **он ~и́л себя́ пре́данным колле́гой** he proved to be a loyal colleague. **2.** (*phot.*) to develop.
прояв|и́ться, ~́ится *pf.* (*of* **~ля́ться**) **1.** to show (itself), reveal itself, manifest itself. **2.** *pass. of* **~и́ть**
проявле́ни|е, я *nt.* display, manifestation; **при пе́рвом ~и** (+*g.*) at the first sign(s) of.
проявля́|ть(ся), ю(сь) *impf. of* **прояви́ть(ся)**
проя́сне|ть, ет *pf.* (*of the sky*) to clear; (*impers.*): **~ло** it cleared up.
проясне́|ть, ет *pf.* to brighten (up); **лицо́ ма́льчика вдруг ~ло** the boy's face suddenly brightened up.
проясн|и́ться, и́тся *pf.* (*of* **~я́ться**) (*of weather and fig.*) to clear (up); **днём ~и́лось** in the afternoon it cleared up.
проясн|я́ться, я́ется *impf. of* **~и́ться**
пруд, а́, в ~у́, *pl.* **~ы́** *m.* pond.
пру|ди́ть, жу́, ~́дишь *impf.* (*of* **за~**) to dam (up); **хоть пруд ~ди́** (*coll.*) in abundance; **де́нег у них — хоть пруд ~ди́** they are rolling in money.
прудово́й *adj. of* **пруд**
пружи́н|а, ы *f.* spring; **гла́вная п.** mainspring (*also fig.*); **боева́я п.** (*mil.*) mainspring, firing pin spring; **п.-волосо́к** hairspring.
пружи́нистост|ь, и *f.* springiness, elasticity.
пружи́нист|ый (~, ~а) *adj.* springy, elastic.
пружи́н|ить, ю, ишь *impf.* **1.** (*trans.*) to tense. **2.** (*intrans.*) to be elastic, possess spring; **хорошо́ п.** to be well sprung.
пружи́нк|а, и *f.* **1.** (*of watch or clock*) mainspring; hairspring. **2.** loop, coil (*contraceptive device*).
пружи́н|ный *adj. of* **~а; ~ные весы́** spring scales, spring balance; **п. матра́ц** spring mattress; **~ная рессо́ра** coil spring.
руса́к, а́ *m.* (*coll.*) cockroach.
прусса́к, а́ *m.* Prussian.
прусса́|чка, чки *f. of* **~к**
Пру́сси|я, и *f.* Prussia.
пру́сск|ий *adj.* Prussian; **~ая си́няя (кра́ска)** Prussian blue.
прут, а-а́ *m.* **1.** (*pl.* **~́ья, ~́ьев**) twig; switch; **и́вовый п.** withe, withy. **2.** (*pl.* **~ы́, ~о́в**) (*tech.*) bar.
пру́тик, а *m. dim. of* **прут; волше́бный п.** dowsing rod.
прутко́в|ый *adj.* rod-shaped; **~ое желе́зо** (*tech.*) rod iron, wire rod.
пры́гал|ка, ки (*also pl.* **~ки, ~ок**) *f.* (*coll.*) skipping-rope.
пры́гани|е, я *nt.* jumping, leaping; skipping.
пры́г|ать, аю *impf.* (*of* **~нуть**) **1.** to jump, leap, spring; to bound; **п. на одно́й ноге́** to hop on one leg; **п. со скака́лкой** to skip; **п. с упо́ром** to vault; **п. с шесто́м** (*sport*) to pole-vault; **п. от ра́дости** to jump with, for joy. **2.** to bounce.
пры́г|нуть, ну, нешь *pf. of* **~ать**
прыгу́н, а́ *m.* **1.** (*sport*) jumper; **п. в во́ду** diver. **2.** (*coll.*) fidget, restless pers.
прыжко́в|ый *adj.*: **~ая вы́шка** diving board.
прыж|о́к, ка́ *m.* **1.** jump, leap, spring; caper; **де́лать ~ки́** to caper, cut capers. **2.** (*sport*) jump; **~ки́** jumping; **акробати́ческие ~ки́** tumbling; **~ки́ на бату́те** trampolining; **~ки́ в во́ду** diving; **~ки́ с парашю́том** parachute jumping, sky-diving; **п. в высоту́** high jump; **п. в длину́** long jump; **п. с упо́ром** vault(ing); **п. с шесто́м** pole-vault; **п. с ме́ста** standing jump; **п. с разбе́га** running jump.
пры́ска|ть, ю *impf. of* **пры́снуть**
пры́ска|ться, юсь *impf.* (*of* **по~**) (+*i.*; *coll.*) to (be)sprinkle *or* spray o.s. (with).
пры́с|нуть, ну, нешь *pf.* (*of* **~кать**) (*coll.*) **1.** (+*i.*) to (be)sprinkle (with); to spray (with). **2.** to spurt, gush; **(со́ смеху)** (*fig.*) to burst out laughing.
пры́т|кий (~ок, ~ка́, ~ко) *adj.* quick, lively, sharp.
пры́т|ь, и *f.* (*coll.*) **1.** speed; **во всю п.** at full speed, as fast as one's legs can carry one. **2.** quickness, liveliness, go; **отку́да у него́ така́я п.?** where does he get his energy from?
прыщ, а́ *m.* pimple; (*med.*) pustule; **лицо́ в ~а́х** pimply face.
прыща́ве|ть, ю *impf.* (*of* **о~**) to become covered in pimples.

прыща́в|ый (~, ~а) *adj.* pimply, pimpled.
прыщева́т|ый (~, ~а) *adj.* somewhat pimply.
прюне́л|евый *adj. of* **~ь**
прюне́л|ь, и *f.* (*text.*) prunella.
пря́да|ть, ю *impf.* (*obs. or dial.*): **п. уша́ми** (*of, or in the manner of, a horse*) to move its ears.
пряде́ни|е, я *nt.* spinning.
пря́деный *adj.* spun.
пряди́льн|ый *adj.* spinning; **п. стано́к** spinning loom; **~ая фа́брика** spinning mill.
пряди́л|ьня, ьни, *g. pl.* **~ен** *f.* (*obs.*) spinning mill.
пряди́льщик, а *m.* spinner.
пряд|ь, и *f.* **1.** lock (*of hair*). **2.** strand.
пря́ж|а, и *no pl., f.* yarn, thread; **шерстяна́я п.** woollen yarn, worsted.
пря́жк|а, и *f.* buckle, clasp.
пря́лк|а, и *f.* distaff; spinning-wheel.
прям|а́я, о́й *f.* **1.** straight line; **провести́ ~у́ю** to draw a straight line; **расстоя́ние по ~о́й** distance as the crow flies. **2.** (*sport*) straight; **фи́нишная п.** home straight (*athletics*); home stretch (*horse- or motor-racing*); **да́льняя п.** back straight *or* stretch.
прямёхонько *adv.* (*coll.*) straight, directly.
прямизн|а́, ы́ *f.* straightness.
прямико́м *adv.* (*coll.*) straight; across country.
пря́мо *adv.* **1.** straight (on); **п.!** (*mil. word of command*) forward!; **иди́те п.!** (go) straight on!; **держа́ться п.** to hold o.s. straight *or* erect. **2.** straight, directly; **п. к де́лу** to the point; **попа́сть п. в цель** to hit the bull's eye (*also fig.*); **смотре́ть п. в глаза́ кому́-н.** to look s.o. straight in the face; **п. со шко́льной скамьи́** (*fig.*) straight from school. **3.** (*fig.*) straight; frankly, openly, bluntly; **сказа́ть что-н. кому́-н. п. в лицо́** to say sth. to s.o.'s face; **мы ему́ п. сказа́ли, что э́то ему́ не уда́стся** we told him straight that he would not succeed. **4.** (*coll.*) real; really; **он п. идио́т** he is a real idiot; **я п. не зна́ю, что с ней ста́ло** I really don't know what has become of her.
прямоду́ши|е, я *nt.* directness, straightforwardness.
прямоду́ш|ный (~ен, ~на) *adj.* direct, straightforward.
прямое́зжий *adj.* (*folk poet.*) straight.
прям|о́й (~, ~а́, ~́о) *adj.* **1.** straight; upright, erect; **~а́я кишка́** (*anat.*) rectum; **п. пробо́р** parting in the middle; **п. уго́л** (*math.*) right angle; **п. у́зел** reef knot; **п. ход** forward stroke (*of engine*). **2.** (*of means of communication, etc.*) through; direct; **по́езд ~о́го сообще́ния** through train; **п. про́вод** direct (*telephone*) line. **3.** (*in var. senses*) direct; **~ые вы́боры** direct elections; **~о́е дополне́ние** (*gram.*) direct object; **~а́я наво́дка** (*mil.*) direct laying; **~о́й наво́дкой** over open sights; **п. нало́г** direct tax; **п. насле́дник** heir in a direct line, direct heir; **п. нача́льник** immediate superior; **~о́е попада́ние** (*mil.*) direct hit; **~а́я противополо́жность** direct opposite, exact opposite; **~а́я речь** (*gram.*) direct speech, oratio recta; **п. смысл сло́ва** the literal sense of a word. **4.** (*of character*) straightforward. **5.** (*coll.*) real; **п. убы́ток** sheer loss; **п. расчёт пойти́ самому́** it is really worth while going o.s.
прямокры́л|ые, ых *pl.* (*zool.*) Orthoptera.
прямолине́йност|ь, и *f.* straightforwardness.
прямолине́|йный (~ен, ~на) *adj.* **1.** rectilinear. **2.** (*fig.*) straightforward; direct.
прямот|а́, ы́ *f.* straightforwardness; plain dealing.
прямото́чный *adj.* (*tech.*) uniflow, direct-flow; **п. котёл** continuously operating boiler; **п. дви́гатель** (*aeron.*) ram jet engine.
прямоуго́льник, а *m.* (*math.*) rectangle.
прямоуго́льный *adj.* right-angled; rectangular; **п. треуго́льник** right-angled triangle.
пря́ник, а *m.* spice cake; gingerbread; **медо́вый п.** honey-cake; (*fig., see* **хлыст**[1]).
пря́ни|чный *adj. of* **~к**
пря́ност|ь, и *f.* spice.
пря́|нуть, ну, нешь *pf.* (*obs.*) to jump aside.
пря́ный *adj.* spicy (*also fig.*); (*of smells*) heady.
пря|сть[1], **ду́, дёшь,** *past* **~л, ~́ла́, ~́ло** *impf.* (*of* **с~**) to spin.
пря|сть[2], **ду́, дёшь** *impf.* = **~́дать**
пря́|тать, чу, чешь *impf.* (*of* **с~**) to hide, conceal; to put away.
пря́|таться, чусь, чешься *impf.* (*of* **с~**) to hide; to conceal o.s.; to take refuge.
пря́т|ки, ок *no sg.* hide-and-seek; **игра́ть в п.** to play hide-and-seek.
пря́х|а, и *f.* spinner.
псалмопе́в|ец, ца *m.* psalmodist.
псал|о́м, ма́ *m.* psalm.
псало́мщик, а *m.* (*eccl.*) (psalm-)reader; sexton.
псалты́р|ь, и *f. and* (*coll.*) **п., ~я́** *m.* (*eccl.*) Psalter.
пса́р|ня, ни, *g. pl.* **~ен** *f.* kennel.
псар|ь, я́ *m.* huntsman (*pers. in charge of hounds*).
псевдо... *comb. form* pseudo-.
псевдогеро́ический *adj.* (*liter.*) mock-heroic.
псевдони́м, а *m.* pseudonym; pen-name; alias.
пси́н|а, ы *f.* (*coll.*) **1.** dog's flesh. **2.** dog's smell, doggy smell. **3.** dog.
пси́ный *adj.* dog's; doggy.
псих, а *m.* (*abbr. of* **психопа́т**) (*coll.*) loony, nutcase; headbanger.
психасте́ник, а *m.* (*med.*) psychasthenic.
психастени́ческий *adj.* (*med.*) psychasthenic.
психастени́|я, и *f.* (*med.*) psychasthenia.
психбольни́ц|а, ы *f.* mental hospital.
психиа́тр, а *m.* psychiatrist.
психиатри́ческ|ий *adj.* psychiatric(al); **~ая лече́бница** mental hospital.
психиатри́|я, и *f.* psychiatry.
пси́хик|а, и *f.* state of mind; psyche; psychology; **нездоро́вая п.** unhealthy state of mind; **вре́дно де́йствовать на ~у** to have a harmful effect on the psyche; **п. лётчиков-истреби́телей** the psychology of fighter-pilots.
психи́чески *adv.* mentally, psychically, psychologically; **п. больно́й** mentally diseased; *as n.* **п. больно́й, п. больно́го** *m.* mental patient, mental case.
психи́ческ|ий *adj.* mental, psychical; **~ая боле́знь** mental illness, mental disease; **~ая ата́ка** (*mil.*) psychological attack.
психоана́лиз, а *m.* psychoanalysis.
психоанали́тик, а *m.* psychoanalyst.
психоаналити́ческий *adj.* psychoanalytic(al).
псих|ова́ть, у́ю *impf.* (*coll.*) **1.** to behave like a madman; to feign insanity. **2.** to be upset, hysterical; to have a (nervous) breakdown.
психо́з, а *m.* mental illness; (*med.*) psychosis; **вое́нный п.** war hysteria.
психо́лог, а *m.* psychologist.
психологи́зм, а *m.* (*phil.*) psychologism.
психологи́ческий *adj.* psychological.
психоло́ги|я, и *f.* psychology.
психоневро́з, а *m.* (*med.*) psychoneurosis.
психопа́т, а *m.* psychopath; (*coll.*) lunatic.
психопатологи́ческий *adj.* psychopathological.
психопатоло́ги|я, и *f.* psychopathology.
психотерапе́вт, а *m.* psychotherapist.
психотерапи́|я, и *f.* psychotherapy.
психоте́хник|а, и *f.* vocational psychology.
психофи́зик|а, и *f.* psychophysics.
психофизиоло́ги|я, и *f.* psychophysiology.
психофизи́ческий *adj.* psychophysical.
псо́в|ый *adj.*: **~ая охо́та** the chase, hunting (*with hounds*).
псориа́з, а *m.* psoriasis.
пта́шк|а, и *f.* little bird; birdie; **ра́нняя п.** (*fig.*) early bird.
птен|е́ц, ца́ *m.* nestling; fledg(e)ling (*also fig.*).
птерода́ктил|ь, я *m.* pterodactyl.
пти́ц|а, ы *f.* bird; **боло́тная п.** wader; **водопла́вающие ~ы** waterfowl; **дома́шняя п.** (*collect.*) poultry; **перелётная п.** bird of passage; **хи́щные ~ы** birds of prey; **ва́жная п.** (*fig., coll.*) big noise; **обстре́лянная п., стре́ляная п.** (*fig., coll.*) old hand.
птицево́д, а *m.* poultry farmer, poultry breeder.
птицево́дств|о, а *nt.* poultry farming, poultry-keeping.
птицево́дческий *adj.* poultry-farming, poultry-keeping.

птицело́в, а *m.* fowler.
птицело́вств|о, а *nt.* fowling.
птицефе́рм|а, ы *f.* poultry farm.
пти́ч|ий *adj. of* **пти́ца; п. двор** poultry-yard; **~ье молоко́** (*coll., joc.*) pigeon's milk; **вид с ~ьего полёта** bird's-eye view; **жить на ~ьих права́х** to live from hand to mouth.
пти́чк|а[1], **и** *f. dim. of* **пти́ца**
пти́чк|а[2], **и** *f.* tick; **ста́вить ~у** to tick.
пти́чник[1], **а** *m.* poultry-yard, hen-run; hen-house.
пти́чник[2], **а** *m.* poultryman.
птомаи́н, а *m.* (*chem.*) ptomaine.
ПТУ *nt. indecl.* (*abbr. of* ***профессиона́льно-техни́ческое учи́лище***) vocational technical school.
пуа́нт, а *m.*: **на ~ах** (*theatr.*) on the tips of the toes (*also fig.*).
пу́блик|а, и *f.* (*collect.*) (the) public; (*in theatres, etc.*) (the) audience.
публика́ци|я, и *f.* **1.** publication. **2.** advertisement, notice; **помести́ть ~ю в газе́те** to place an advertisement in a newspaper; **п. о сме́рти** obituary notice.
публик|ова́ть, у́ю *impf.* (*of* **о~**) to publish.
публици́ст, а *m.* publicist; commentator on current affairs.
публици́стик|а, и *f.* social and political journalism; writing on current affairs.
публицисти́ческий *adj.* publicistic.
публи́чно *adv.* publicly; in public; openly.
публи́чност|ь, и *f.* publicity.
публи́чн|ый *adj.* public; **~ая библиоте́ка** public library; **п. дом** brothel; **~ая же́нщина** prostitute; **~ое пра́во** public law; **~ые торги́** auction, public sale.
пу́гал|о, а *nt.* scarecrow.
пу́ган|ый *adj.* (*coll.*) scared; **~ая воро́на (и) куста́ бои́тся** (*prov.*) the burnt child dreads the fire; once bitten twice shy.
пуга́|ть, ю *impf.* (*of* **ис~**) **1.** to frighten, scare. **2.** to intimidate; (*+i.*) to threaten (with).
пуга́|ться, юсь *impf.* (*of* **ис~**) (*+g.*) to be frightened (of), be scared (of); to take fright (at); (*of a horse*) to shy (at).
пуга́ч, а́ *m.* **1.** toy-pistol. **2.** (*zool.*) screech owl.
пугли́вост|ь, и *f.* fearfulness, timorousness, timidity.
пугли́в|ый (~, ~а) *adj.* fearful, timorous; timid.
пугн|у́ть, у́, ёшь *pf.* to give a fright, give a scare.
пу́говиц|а, ы *f.* button; **застегну́ться на все ~ы** to have all one's buttons done up; **держа́ть за ~у** (*coll.*) to buttonhole.
пу́гови|чный *adj. of* **~ца; ~чное произво́дство** button-making.
пу́говк|а, и *f.* (*small*) button.
пуд, а, *pl.* **~ы́, ~о́в** *m.* pood (*old Russ. measure of weight, equivalent to 16.38 kilograms*).
пу́дел|ь, я, *pl.* **~и, ~ей** *or* **~я́, ~е́й** *m.* poodle.
пу́динг, а *m.* pudding.
пудлингова́ни|е, я *nt.* (*tech.*) puddling.
пудлинг|ова́ть, у́ю *impf. and pf.* (*tech.*) to puddle.
пу́длингов|ый *adj.* (*tech.*) puddling, puddled; **~ое желе́зо** puddle iron; **~ая печь** puddling furnace.
пудови́к, а́ *m.* **1.** one-pood bag. **2.** one-pood weight.
пудово́й *adj.* one pood in weight.
пу́др|а, ы *f.* powder; **са́харная п.** castor sugar.
пу́дрениц|а, ы *f.* powder-case, powder-compact.
пу́дреный *adj.* powdered.
пу́др|ить, ю, ишь *impf.* (*of* **на~**) to powder.
пу́др|иться, юсь, ишься *impf.* (*of* **на~**) to use powder, powder one's face.
пуза́н, а́ *m.* (*coll.*) pers. with a paunch.
пуза́т|ый (~, ~а) *adj.* (*coll.*) big-bellied, pot-bellied.
пу́з|о, а *nt.* (*coll.*) belly, paunch.
пузыр|ёк, ька́ *m.* **1.** phial, vial. **2.** bubble; bleb.
пузы́р|иться, ится *impf.* **1.** (*coll.*) to bubble; to effervesce. **2.** (*coll.*) to pout, sulk.
пузы́рник, а *m.* (*bot.*) senna-pod.
пузы́рчат|ый (~, ~а) *adj.* (*coll.*) covered with bubbles; blebby.
пузы́р|ь, я́ *m.* **1.** bubble; **мы́льный п.** soap-bubble; **пуска́ть мы́льные ~и́** to blow bubbles. **2.** blister. **3.** (*anat.*) bladder; **жёлчный п.** gall-bladder; **мочево́й п.** (urinary) bladder; **пла́вательный п.** (fish-) sound, swimming-bladder. **4.** air-bladder; **п. со льдом** ice-bag. **5.** (*coll.*) kid, kiddy.
пук, а, *pl.* **~и́** *m.* bunch, bundle; tuft; **п. цвето́в** bunch of flowers; **п. соло́мы** wisp of straw.
пу́к|ать, аю *impf.* (*of* **~нуть**) (*coll.*) to fart.
пу́к|нуть, ну, нешь *pf. of* **~ать**
пул|ево́й *adj. of* **~я**
пулемёт, а *m.* machine-gun; **ручно́й п.** light machine-gun; **станко́вый п.** heavy machine-gun.
пулемёт|ный *adj. of* **~; ~ная ле́нта** (machine-gun) cartridge belt; **~ная огнева́я то́чка** machine-gun emplacement.
пулемётчик, а *m.* machine-gunner.
пулесто́йкий *adj.* bullet-proof.
пуло́вер, а *m.* pullover.
пульвериза́тор, а *m.* pulverizer, atomizer, sprayer.
пульвериза́ци|я, и *f.* pulverization, spraying.
пульверизи́р|овать, ую *impf. and pf.* to pulverize, spray.
пу́льк|а[1], **и** *f. dim. of* **пу́ля**
пу́льк|а[2], **и** *f.* (*cards*) pool.
пу́льп|а, ы *f.* (*anat.*) pulp.
пульс, а *m.* pulse; pulse rate; **бие́ние ~а** pulsation, beating of the pulse; **счита́ть п.** to take the pulse; **щу́пать п.** to feel the pulse.
пульса́ци|я, и *f.* pulsation, pulse.
пульси́р|овать, ую *impf.* **1.** to pulse, pulsate; to beat, throb. **2.** (*tech.*) to pulse, pulsate.
пульсо́метр, а *m.* (*tech.*) pulsometer, vacuum pump.
пульт, а *m.* **1.** desk, stand; **дирижёрский п.** conductor's stand. **2.** (*in power station, etc.*) control panel; (*on aerodrome, etc.*) (traffic) control panel.
пу́л|я, и *f.* bullet; **лить, отлива́ть ~и** (*fig., coll.*) to tell lies.
пуля́рк|а, и *f.* fatted fowl.
пу́м|а, ы *f.* puma, cougar; mountain-lion.
пуни́ческий *adj.* (*hist.*) Punic.
пункт, а *m.* **1.** point; spot; **наблюда́тельный п.** observation post; **населённый п.** inhabited locality; built-up area; **опо́рный п.** (*mil.*) strong point; **исхо́дный п., нача́льный п.** starting point; **коне́чный п.** terminus, terminal; **кульминацио́нный п.** culmination, climax. **2.** (*centre operating special services*) point; centre; **медици́нский п.** (*mil.*) dressing-station, aid post; **перегово́рный п.** (*collect.*) public (telephone) call-boxes; **призывно́й п.** recruiting centre; **ссыпно́й п.** grain-collecting centre. **3.** point; paragraph, item; plank (*of pol. programme*); **по ~ам** point by point; **соглаше́ние из трёх ~ов** a three-point agreement. **4.** (*typ.*) full point.
пу́нктик, а *m.* (*coll.*) **1.** *dim. of* **пункт. 2.** (*fig.*) eccentricity, peculiarity; **он — челове́к с ~ом** he is a bit odd.
пункти́р, а *m.* dotted line.
пункти́рн|ый *adj.*: **~ая ли́ния** dotted line.
пунктуа́льност|ь, и *f.* punctuality.
пунктуа́л|ьный (~ен, ~ьна) *adj.* punctual.
пунктуа́ци|я, и *f.* punctuation.
пу́нкци|я, и *f.* (*med.*) puncture.
пу́ночк|а, и *f.* (*zool.*) snow-bunting.
пунсо́н, а *m.* (*tech.*) punch, die, stamp.
пунцо́вый *adj.* crimson.
пунш, а *m.* punch (*drink*).
пу́нш|евый *adj. of* **~**
пуп, а́ *m.* navel; (*anat.*) umbilicus; **п. земли́** the hub of the universe.
пупови́н|а, ы *f.* (*anat.*) umbilical cord; navel-string.
пуп|о́к, ка́ *m.* **1.** navel. **2.** (*of birds*) gizzard.
пупо́чн|ый *adj.* (*anat.*) umbilical; **~ая гры́жа** umbilical hernia.
пупы́рыш|ек, ка *m.* (*coll.*) pimple.
пург|а́, и́ *no pl., f.* snow-storm, blizzard.
пури́зм, а *m.* purism.
пури́ст, а *m.* purist.
пурита́н|ин, ина, *pl.* **~е, ~** *m.* Puritan.
пурита́нский *adj.* Puritan; (*fig.*) puritanical.
пурита́нств|о, а *nt.* Puritanism.

пу́рпур, а *m.* purple.
пурпу́рный *adj.* purple.
пурпу́р|овый *adj.* = **~ный; ~овая кислота́** (*chem.*) purpuric acid.
пуск, а *m.* starting (up); setting in motion.
пуска́й *particle and conj.* (*coll.*) = **пусть**
пуска́|ть(ся), ю(сь) *impf. of* **пусти́ть(ся)**
пусков|о́й *adj.* starting; **п. пери́од** starting period, initial phase (*of working of factory, etc.*); **~а́я рукоя́тка** starting crank; **~о́е устро́йство** starter; **~а́я площа́дка** (rocket) launching platform.
пустельг|а́, и́ *f. and c.g.* **1.** *f.* (*zool.*) kestrel; staniel, windhover. **2.** *c.g.* (*coll.*) good-for-nothing.
пусте́|ть, ет *impf.* (*of* **о~**) to (become) empty; to become deserted.
пу|сти́ть, щу́, ~́стишь *pf.* (*of* **~ска́ть**) **1.** to let go; **п. на во́лю** to set free; **п. кро́вь кому́-н.** to bleed s.o. **2.** to let; to allow, permit; **п. кого́-н. в о́тпуск** to let s.o. go on leave; **нас не ~сти́ли в пала́ту** they would not let us into the ward; **~сти́те соба́ку на двор** let the dog go out. **3.** to let in, allow to enter; **не п.** to keep out; **п. по предъявле́нии биле́та** to allow to enter on showing a ticket; **п. жильцо́в** to take in lodgers; **п. козла́ в огоро́д** (*prov.*) to set a cat among the pigeons. **4.** to start, set in motion, set going; to set working; **п. во́ду** to turn on water; **п. волчо́к** to spin a top; **п. заво́д** to start up a factory; **п. змея́** to fly a kite; **п. слух** to start a rumour; **п. фейерве́рк** to let off fireworks; **п. фонта́н** to set a fountain playing; **п. часы́** to start a clock. **5.** to set, put; to send; **п. себе́ пу́лю в лоб** to blow out one's brains, put a bullet through one's head; **п. в обраще́ние** to put in circulation; **п. ло́шадь во весь опо́р** to give a horse his head; **п. в прода́жу** to offer, put up for sale; **п. в произво́дство** to put in production; **п. в ход** to start, launch, set going, set in train; **п. в ход все сре́дства** to move heaven and earth; **п. кора́бль ко дну** to send a ship to the bottom; **п. по́ миру** to ruin utterly; **п. по́езд под отко́с** to derail a train; **п. по́ле под пар** to put a field to lie fallow. **6.** (*+a. or i.*) to throw, shy; **п. ка́мнем в окно́** to throw a stone at a window; **п. пыль в глаза́** to cut a dash, show off. **7.** (*bot.*) to put forth, put out; **п. ко́рни** to take root (*also fig.*); **п. ростки́** to shoot, sprout. **8.** (*coll.*; *in painting*) to put on; to touch up; **п. каёмку лило́вым** to put violet on the border.
пу|сти́ться, щу́сь, ~́стишься *pf.* (*of* **~ска́ться**) (**в**+*a. or +inf.*; *coll.*) **1.** to set out, start; **п. в путь** to set out, get on the way. **2.** to begin, start; to set to; **п. в оправда́ния** to start making excuses; **п. в пляс** to break into a dance.
пустобрёх, а *m.* (*coll.*) chatterbox, windbag.
пустова́т|ый (~, ~а) *adj.* **1.** rather empty. **2.** fatuous.
пуст|ова́ть, у́ю *impf.* to be empty, stand empty; to be tenantless, be uninhabited; (*of land*) to lie fallow.
пустоголо́в|ый (~, ~а) *adj.* empty-headed.
пустозво́н, а *m.* (*coll.*) idle talker, windbag.
пустозво́н|ить, ю, ишь *impf.* (*coll.*) to engage in idle talk.
пустозво́нств|о, а *nt.* (*coll.*) idle talk.
пуст|о́й (~, ~а́, ~́о) *adj.* **1.** empty; void; hollow; tenantless, uninhabited; deserted; **~о́е ме́сто** blank space; **~а́я поро́да** (*geol.*) barren rock, waste rock, dead rock; **на п. желу́док** on an empty stomach; **с ~ы́ми рука́ми** empty-handed; **чтоб тебе́ ~́о бы́ло!** (*coll.*) I wish you at the bottom of the sea!, the devil take you! **2.** (*fig.*) idle; shallow; futile, frivolous; **~а́я болтовня́** idle talk; **п. челове́к** shallow pers. **3.** (*fig.*) vain, ungrounded; **~а́я зате́я** vain enterprise; **~ы́е мечты́** castles in the air; **~а́я отгово́рка** lame excuse; **~ы́е слова́** mere words; **~ы́е угро́зы** empty threats, bluster.
пустоме́л|я, и *c.g.* (*coll.*) idle talker, windbag.
пустопоро́жний *adj.* (*coll.*) empty, vacant.
пустосло́в, а *m.* (*coll.*) idle talker, windbag.
пустосло́ви|е, я *nt.* (*coll.*) idle talk, verbiage.
пустосло́в|ить, лю, ишь *impf.* (*coll.*) to engage in idle talk.
пустот|а́, ы́, *pl.* **~́ы** *f.* **1.** emptiness; void; (*phys.*) vacuum. **2.** (*fig.*) shallowness; futility, frivolousness.
пустоте́лый *adj.* hollow.
пустоцве́т, а *m.* barren flower (*also fig.*).
пу́стош|ь, и *f.* waste (plot of) land, waste ground.
пусты́нник, а *m.* hermit, anchorite.
пусты́н|ный (~ен, ~на) *adj.* **1.** uninhabited; **п. о́стров** desert island. **2.** deserted.
пу́стын|ь, и *f.* hermitage, monastery.
пусты́н|я, и *f.* desert, wilderness.
пусты́р|ь, я́ *m.* waste land, vacant plot (of land).
пусты́шк|а, и *f.* (*coll.*) **1.** baby's dummy. **2.** hollow object; (*fig.*) shallow pers., hollow man.
пусть 1. *particle* let; **п. бу́дет так!** so be it!; **п. она́ сама́ реши́т** let her decide herself; **п.** x **ра́вен 3** (*math.*) let x = 3. **2.** *as conj.* though, even if; **п. им бу́дет проти́вно, но я до́лжен вы́сказать своё мне́ние** even if they don't like it, I must express my opinion. **3.** *particle* (*coll.*) all right, very well.
пустя́к, а́ *m.* trifle; bagatelle; **су́щий п.** a mere bagatelle; **спо́рить из-за ~о́в** to split hairs; **па́ра ~о́в!** (*coll.*) child's play!; **~и́!** (*i*) it's nothing!; never mind!; (*ii*) nonsense!; rubbish!
пустяко́вый *adj.* trifling, trivial.
пустя́чный *adj.* = **пустяко́вый**
путá́н|а, ы *f.* (*coll.*) tart, whore.
пу́таник, а *m.* muddle-head (*pers.*)
пу́таниц|а, ы *f.* muddle, confusion; mess, tangle.
пу́таный *adj.* **1.** muddled, confused; confusing. **2.** (*coll.*) muddle-headed.
пу́та|ть, ю *impf.* (*of* **с~**) **1.** to tangle (*a thread, etc.*). **2.** to confuse, muddle; **он всё ~л слу́шателей примене́нием анало́гий** he always muddled his audience by his use of analogy. **3.** to confuse, mix up; **ты ещё ~ешь на́ши имена́** you are still mixing our names up. **4.** (*pf.* **в~**) (**в**+*a.*; *coll.*) to implicate (in), mix up (in).
пу́та|ться, юсь *impf.* (*of* **с~**) **1.** to get tangled. **2.** (*of thoughts*) to get confused. **3.** to get mixed up, get muddled; **п. в расска́зе** to give a muddled account; **п. в показа́ниях** to contradict o.s. in one's evidence. **4.** (*pf.* **в~**) (**в**+*a.*; *coll.*) to get mixed up (in); **п. в тёмные дели́шки** to get mixed up in shady business. **5.** *impf. only* (*coll.*) to mooch about. **6.** (**с**+*i.*; *coll.*) to get mixed up (with), get entangled (with); to carry on (with) (*a pers. of the opposite sex*).
путёвк|а, и *f.* **1.** pass, authorization; **сде́лать зая́вку на ~у в санато́рий** to apply for a place in a sanatorium; **п. в жизнь** a start in life. **2.** place in a tourist group; **я купи́л ~у в Чехослова́кию** I have booked a place on a tour of Czechoslovakia. **3.** schedule of duties (*of public transport workers*).
путеводи́тел|ь, я *m.* guide, guide-book.
путево́дн|ый *adj.* guiding; **~ая звезда́** guiding star; (*fig.*) lodestar.
путев|о́й *adj.* travelling, itinerary; **~ы́е заме́тки** travel notes; **~а́я ка́рта** road-map; **п. ко́мпас** (*naut.*) steering compass; **п. обхо́дчик, п. сто́рож** (*rail.*) permanent way man; **~а́я ско́рость** (*aeron.*) absolute speed, ground speed.
путе́|ец, йца *m.* (*coll.*) **1.** railway engineer. **2.** railwayman, railman.
путём[1] *prep.* (*+g.*) by means of, by dint of.
путём[2] *adv.* (*coll.*) properly; coherently; **он ничего́ п. не уме́ет объясни́ть** he cannot explain anything coherently.
путеме́р, а *m.* pedometer.
путеобхо́дчик, а *m.* (*rail.*) permanent way man.
путепрово́д, а *m.* **1.** (*on roads*) overpass, flyover; underpass. **2.** (*rail.*) overbridge.
путеше́ственник, а *m.* traveller.
путеше́стви|е, я *nt.* **1.** journey; trip; (*on the sea*) voyage; cruise. **2.** *pl.* (*liter.*) travels.
путеше́ств|овать, ую *impf.* to travel, go on travels; (*on the sea*) to voyage.
пути́н|а, ы *f.* fishing season.
пу́тлищ|е, а *nt.* stirrup strap.
пу́тник, а *m.* traveller, wayfarer.
пу́тн|ый *adj.* (*coll.*) sensible; **из него́ ничего́ ~ого не вы́йдет** you'll never make a man of him.
путч, а *m.* (*pol.*) putsch.
пу́ты, пут *no sg.* **1.** hobble. **2.** (*fig.*) fetters, chains, trammels.

пут|ь, и́, *i.* **ём, о ~и́,** *pl.* **~и́, ~е́й, ~я́м** *m.* **1.** way, track, path; (*aeron.*) track; (*astron.*) race; (*fig.*) road, course; **во́дный п.** water-way; **морски́е ~и́** shipping-routes, sea-lanes; **са́нный п.** sledge-track; **тылово́й п.** (*mil.*) line of retreat; **~и́ сообще́ния** communications; **жи́зненный п.** (*fig.*) life; **на пра́вильном ~и́** on the right track; **друго́го, ино́го ~и́ нет** there are no two ways about it; **сби́ться с (ве́рного) ~и́** to lose one's way; (*fig.*) to go astray; **стоя́ть попере́к ~и́ кому́-н.** (*fig.*) to stand in s.o.'s path. **2.** (*rail.*) track; **запа́сный п.** siding. **3.** journey; voyage; **в ~и́** on one's way, en route; **в четырёх днях ~и́ (от)** four days' journey (from); **на обра́тном ~и́** on the way back; **по ~и́** on the way; **нам с ва́ми по ~и́** we are going the same way; **держа́ть п.** (**на**+*a.*) to head (for), make (for); **счастли́вого ~и́!** bon voyage! **4.** *pl.* (*anat.*) passage, duct; **дыха́тельные ~и́** respiratory tract. **5.** (*fig.*) way, means; **каки́м ~ём?** how?, in what way?; **ми́рным ~ём** amicably, peaceably; **око́льным ~ём, око́льными ~я́ми** in, by a roundabout way; **найти́ ~и́ и сре́дства** to find ways and means; **пойти́ по ~и́** (+*g.*) to take the path (of). **6.** (*coll.*) use, benefit; **без ~и́** in vain, uselessly.

пуф, а *m.* **1.** pouf(fe). **2.** canard, hoax.

пух, а, о ~е, в ~у́ *m.* down; fluff; **в п. и прах** (*coll.*) completely, utterly; **разряди́ться в п. и прах** to put on all one's finery; **разби́ть в п. и прах** to put to complete rout; **ни ~а, ни пера́!** (*coll.*) good luck!

пу́хл|ый (~, ~а́, ~о) *adj.* chubby, plump.

пухля́к, а́ *m.* (*zool.*) willow tit.

пу́х|нуть, ну, нешь, *past* **~, ~ла** *impf.* to swell.

пухови́к, а́ *m.* feather-bed.

пухо́вк|а, и *f.* powder-puff.

пухо́вый *adj.* downy.

пучегла́зи|е, я *nt.* (*med.*) exophthalmus.

пучегла́з|ый (~, ~а) *adj.* goggle-eyed, lobster-eyed.

пучи́н|а, ы *f.* gulf, abyss (*also fig.*); the deep.

пу́ч|ить, у, ишь *impf.* (*coll.*) **1.** (*pf.* **вс~**) to become swollen; (*impers.*): **у него́ живо́т ~ит** he is troubled with wind. **2.** (*pf.* **вы́~**): **п. глаза́** to goggle.

пу́чност|ь, и *f.* (*radio*) antinode, loop.

пуч|о́к, ка́ *m* **1.** bunch, bundle; (*bot.*) fascicle; **п. луче́й** (*phys.*) pencil (of rays); **п. се́на** wisp of hay; **п. цвето́в** bunch of flowers. **2.** (*coll.*) bun (*hair-do*).

пу́ш|ечный *adj.* *of* **~ка**[1]; **п. ого́нь** gunfire, cannon fire; **~ечное мя́со** cannon-fodder.

пуши́нк|а, и *f.* bit of fluff; **п. сне́га** snow-flake.

пуши́ст|ый (~, ~а) *adj.* fluffy, downy.

пуш|и́ть, у́, и́шь *impf.* (*of* **рас~**) **1.** to fluff up. **2.** (*coll.*) to swear at.

пу́шк|а[1], **и** *f.* gun, cannon; **стреля́ть из пу́шек по воробья́м** (*prov.*) to swat a fly with a sledgehammer.

пу́шк|а[2], **и** *f.* (*coll.*) lying, lies; **на ~у взять кого́-н.** to trick s.o.; **получи́ть на ~у** (*i*) to obtain by a trick, (*ii*) to get for nothing.

пушка́р|ь, я́ *m.* **1.** (*hist.*) cannon-founder. **2.** (*obs., coll.*) gunner.

пушкини́ст, а *m.* Pushkin scholar.

пушкинове́дени|е, я *nt.* Pushkin studies.

пушни́н|а, ы *f.* (*collect.*) furs, fur-skins, pelts.

пушно́й *adj.* **1.** fur-bearing; **п. зверь** (*collect.*) fur-bearing animals. **2.** fur; **п. про́мысел** fur trade; **п. това́р** furs.

пуш|о́к, ка́ *m.* **1.** fluff. **2.** (*on fruit*) bloom.

пу́щ|а, и *f.* dense forest, virgin forest.

пу́ще *adv.* (*coll.*) more; **п. всего́** most of all.

пу́щ|ий *adj.* *only in phr.* **для ~ей ва́жности** for greater show.

пуэрторика́н|ец, ца *m.* Puerto Rican.

пуэрторика́н|ка, ки *f.* *of* **~ец**

пуэрторика́нский *adj.* Puerto Rican.

Пуэ́рто-Ри́ко *nt. indecl.* Puerto Rico.

Пфальц, а *m.* the Palatinate (*in Germany*).

ПХВ *m. indecl.* (*abbr.*) = **полихлорвини́л**

Пхенья́н, а *m.* Pyongyang.

пчел|а́, ы́, *pl.* **~ы** *f.* bee; **рабо́чая п.** worker bee.

пчел|и́ный *adj.* *of* **~а́**; **п. воск** beeswax; **~и́ная ма́тка** queen bee; **п. рой** swarm of bees; **п. у́лей** beehive.

пчелово́д, а *m.* bee-keeper, bee-master, apiarist.

пчелово́дств|о, а *nt.* bee-keeping, apiculture.

пчелово́дческий *adj.* bee-keeping.

пче́льник, а *m.* bee-garden, apiary.

пшени́ц|а, ы *f.* wheat; **ярова́я п.** spring wheat; **ози́мая п.** winter wheat.

пшени́чный *adj.* wheaten.

пшённик, а *m.* millet-pudding.

пшён|ный *adj.* *of* **~о́**

пшен|о́, а́ *nt.* millet.

пшик, а *m.* (*coll.*) nothing; **око́нчиться ~ом** (*fig.*) to fizzle out, come to nought; **оста́лся оди́н п.** nothing was left.

пыж, а́ *m.* wad (*used in loading fire-arm from muzzle*).

пы́жик, а *m.* young deer; fur of young deer.

пы́жиковый *adj.* deerskin.

пы́ж|иться, усь, ишься *impf.* (*of* **на~**) (*coll.*) **1.** to be puffed up, strut. **2.** to go all out.

пыл, а, о ~е, в ~у́ *m.* **1.** (*dial.*) heat; **пирожки́ с ~у** hot pasties. **2.** (*fig.*) heat, ardour; **ю́ный п.** youthful ardour; **в ~у́ сраже́ния** in the heat of the battle.

пыла́|ть, ю *impf.* **1.** to blaze, flame. **2.** (*fig.*; *of the face*) to glow. **3.** (+*i.*; *fig.*) to burn (with); **п. стра́стью** to be afire with passion.

пылесо́с, а *m.* vacuum cleaner, Hoover (*propr.*).

пылесо́с|ить, ю, ишь *impf.* (*of* **про~**) to vacuum-clean, hoover.

пыли́нк|а, и *f.* speck of dust.

пыл|и́ть, ю́, и́шь *impf.* **1.** (*pf.* **на~**) to raise dust. **2.** (*pf.* **за~**) to cover with dust, make dusty.

пыл|и́ться, ю́сь, и́шься *impf.* (*of* **за~**) to get dusty, get covered with dust.

пы́л|кий (~ок, ~ка́, ~ко *adj.* ardent, passionate, fervent; fervid; **~кое воображе́ние** fervid imagination; **~кая речь** impassioned speech.

пы́лкост|ь, и *f.* ardour, passion, fervency.

пыл|ь, и, о ~и, в ~и́ *f.* dust; **водяна́я п.** spray; **у́гольная п.** coal-dust; slack; **смести́ п. (с**+*g.*) to dust.

пы́льник[1], **а** *m.* (*bot.*) anther.

пы́льник[2], **а** *m.* dust-coat.

пы́л|ьный (~ен, ~ьна́, ~ьно) *adj.* **1.** dusty; **~ная тря́пка** (*coll.*) duster. **2.: п. котёл** (*agric.*) dust bowl.

пыльц|а́, ы́ *f.* (*bot.*) pollen.

пыре́|й, я *m.* (*bot.*) couch-grass.

пырн|у́ть, у́, ёшь *pf.* (*coll.*) to jab; **п. ножо́м** to thrust a knife (into); **п. рога́ми** to butt.

пыта́|ть, ю *impf.* **1.** to torture (*also fig.*); (*fig.*) to torment. **2.** (*coll.*) to try (for); **п. сча́стье** to try one's luck.

пыта́|ться, юсь *impf.* (*of* **по~**) to try, attempt, endeavour.

пы́тк|а, и *f.* torture, torment (*also fig.*); **ору́дие ~и** instrument of torture.

пытли́вост|ь, и *f.* inquisitiveness.

пытли́в|ый (~, ~а) *adj.* inquisitive; **п. взгляд** a searching look.

пы́|хать, шу, шешь *impf.* **1. (жа́ром)** to blaze. **2.** (*fig.*): **п. гне́вом** to blaze with anger; **п. здоро́вьем** to be a picture of health.

пых|те́ть, чу́, ти́шь *impf.* to puff, pant.

пы́шк|а, и *f.* **1.** bun; doughnut. **2.** (*fig., coll.*) chubby child; plump woman.

пы́шност|ь, и *f.* splendour, magnificence.

пы́ш|ный (~ен, ~на́, ~но) *adj.* **1.** splendid, magnificent. **2.** fluffy; light; luxuriant; **~ные во́лосы** fluffy hair; **п. пиро́г** light pie; **~ные рукава́** puffed sleeves.

пьедеста́л, а *m.* pedestal (*also fig.*); **вознести́ на п.** (*fig.*) to place on a pedestal.

пьезо́метр, а *m.* (*tech.*) piezometer.

пье́ксы, пьекс *no sg.* ski boots.

пье́с|а, ы *f.* **1.** (*theatr.*) play. **2.** (*mus.*) piece.

пьяне́|ть, ю, ешь *impf.* (*of* **о~**) to get drunk, get intoxicated.

пьян|и́ть, ю́, и́шь *impf.* (*of* **о~**) to make drunk, intoxicate (*also fig.*); (*fig.*) to go to one's head.

пья́ниц|а, ы *c.g.* drunkard; tippler, toper; **го́рький п.** hard drinker, sot.

пья́нк|а, и *f.* (*coll.*) drinking-bout, binge, booze-up.

пья́нств|о, а *nt.* drunkenness; hard drinking.
пья́нств|овать, ую *impf.* to drink hard, drink heavily.
пья́н|ый (~, ~á, ~о) *adj.* **1.** drunk; drunken; tipsy, tight; intoxicated; **по ~ой ла́вочке, с ~ых глаз** (*coll.*) one over the eight; *as n.* **п., ~ого** *m.* (a) drunk. **2.** heady, intoxicating.
пэр, а *m.* peer.
пюпи́тр, а *m.* desk, reading-desk; **но́тный п.** music-stand.
пюре́ *nt. indecl.* (*cul.*) purée; **карто́фельное п.** mashed potatoes.
пяд|ь, и, *pl.* **~и, ~е́й** *f.* span; **ни ~и не уступи́ть** (*fig.*) not to yield an inch; **будь он семи́ ~е́й во лбу** (*fig.*) be he a Solomon.
пя́л|ить, ю, ишь *impf.*: **п. глаза́ (на+***a.*; *coll.*) to stare (at).
пя́л|ьцы, ец *no sg.* tambour; lace-frame.
пяст|ь, и *f.* (*anat.*) metacarpus.
пят|á, ы́, *pl.* **~ы, ~, ~а́м** *f.* **1.** heel; **ахилле́сова п.** Achilles' heel; **ходи́ть за кем-н. по ~а́м** to follow on s.o.'s heels, tread on s.o.'s heels; **под ~о́й** (*+g.*; *fig.*) under the heel (of); **с, от головы́ до́ ~** from top to toe, all over, altogether. **2.** (*tech.*) abutment; **п. сво́да** skewback.
пята́к, á *m.* (*coll.*) five-copeck piece.
пятач|о́к[1], **ка́** *m.* (*coll.*) = **пята́к; аэродро́м с п.** pocket handkerchief aerodrome.
пятач|о́к[2], **ка́** *m.* (*coll.*) snout.
пятери́чный *adj.* fivefold, quintuple.
пятёрк|а, и *f.* **1.** (*number*) five. **2.** five, 'A' (*highest mark in Russ. educational marking system*). **3.** (*coll.*) five-rouble note. **4.** (*cards*) five; **козырна́я п.** five of trumps.
пятерн|я́, и́, *g. pl.* **~е́й** *f.* (*coll.*) five fingers; palm with fingers extended.
пя́тер|о, ы́х *num.* five.
пятиалты́нн|ый, ого *m.* (*coll.*) fifteen-kopeck piece.
пятибо́р|ец, ца *m.* pentathlete.
пятибо́рь|е, я *nt.* (*sport*) pentathlon; **совреме́нное п.** modern pentathlon.
пятигра́нник, а *m.* (*math.*) pentahedron.
пятигра́нный *adj.* (*math.*) pentahedral.
пятиднве́рн|ый *adj.*: **~ая маши́на** hatchback.
пятидесятиле́ти|е, я *nt.* **1.** fifty years. **2.** fiftieth anniversary; fiftieth birthday.
пятидесятиле́тний *adj.* **1.** fifty-year, of fifty years. **2.** fifty-year-old.
пятидеся́тник, а *m.* **1.** (*hist.*) 'man of the fifties' (*member of group of Russ. intelligentsia active during the 1850s*). **2.** (*relig.*) Pentecostalist.
Пятидеся́тниц|а, ы *f.* (*eccl.*) Pentecost.
пятидеся́т|ый *adj.* fiftieth; **~ые го́ды** the fifties; **п. но́мер** number fifty; **~ая страни́ца** page fifty.
пятидне́вк|а, и *f.* five-day period; five-day week.
пятикла́ссник, а *m.* fifth-form pupil, fifth-former.
Пятикни́жи|е, я *nt.* (*eccl., liter.*) Pentateuch.
пятиконе́чн|ый *adj.*: **~ая звезда́** five-pointed star.
пятикра́тный *adj.* fivefold, quintuple.
пятиле́ти|е, я *nt.* **1.** five years. **2.** fifth anniversary.
пятиле́тк|а, и *f.* **1.** five years. **2.** (*econ.*) five-year plan. **3.** five-year-old; **де́вочка-п.** five-year-old girl.
пятиле́тний *adj.* **1.** five-year; **п. план** (*econ.*) five-year plan. **2.** five-year-old.
пятиме́сячный *adj.* **1.** five-month. **2.** five-months-old.
пятинеде́льный *adj.* **1.** five-week. **2.** five-week-old.
пятио́кис|ь, и *f.* (*chem.*) pentoxide.
пятипо́ль|е, я *nt.* (*agric.*) five-field crop rotation.
пятисло́жный *adj.* pentasyllabic.
пятисло́йный *adj.* five-ply.
пятисо́тенный *adj.* five-hundred-rouble.
пятисотле́ти|е, я *nt.* **1.** five centuries. **2.** quincentenary.
пятисо́тый *adj.* five-hundredth.
пятисто́пный *adj.* (*liter.*) pentameter; **п. ямб** iambic pentameter.
пятито́нк|а, и *f.* (*coll.*) five-ton lorry.
пятиты́сячный *adj.* five-thousandth.
пя́|тить, чу, тишь *impf.* (*of* **по~**) to back, move back.
пя́|титься, чусь, тишься *impf.* (*of* **по~**) to back, move backward(s); (*of a horse*) to jib.
пятиуго́льник, а *m.* (*math.*) pentagon.
пятиуго́льный *adj.* pentagonal.
пятиэта́жный *adj.* five-storied.
пя́тк|а, и *f.* heel (*also of sock or stocking*); **лиза́ть кому́-н. ~и** to lick s.o.'s boots; **показа́ть ~и** to show a clean pair of heels; **удира́ть так, что то́лько ~и сверка́ют** to take to one's heels, show a clean pair of heels; **у меня́ душа́ в ~и ушла́** my heart sank to my boots.
пятнадцатиле́тний *adj.* **1.** fifteen-year. **2.** fifteen-year-old.
пятна́дцатый *adj.* fifteenth.
пятна́дцат|ь, и *num.* fifteen.
пятна́|ть, ю *impf.* (*of* **за~**) **1.** to spot, stain, smirch (*also fig.*). **2.** (*coll.*) to catch (*at tag*).
пятна́ш|ки, ек *no sg.* (*coll.*) (*children's game*) tag.
пятни́ст|ый (~, ~а) *adj.* spotted, dappled; **п. оле́нь** spotted deer.
пя́тниц|а, ы *f.* Friday; **по ~ам** on Fridays, every Friday; **у него́ семь ~ на неде́ле** he keeps changing his mind.
пят|но́, на́, *pl.* **~на, ~ен, ~нам** *nt.* **1.** (*in var. senses*) spot; patch; blot; stain; **роди́мое п.** birth-mark; **со́лнечные ~на** (*astron.*) sun-spots; **тёмное п.** (*astron.*) nebula; **выводи́ть ~на** to remove stains. **2.** (*fig.*) blot, stain; stigma, blemish.
пя́тныш|ко, ка, *pl.* **~ки, ~ек, ~кам** *nt.* speck.
пят|о́к, ка́ *m.* (*+g.*; *coll.*) five (*similar objects*).
пя́т|ый *adj.* fifth; **глава́ ~ая** chapter five; **~ая коло́нна** fifth column; **п. но́мер** number five, size five; **~ое число́ (ме́сяца)** the fifth (*day of the month*); **в ~ом часу́** after four (o'clock), past four; **рассказа́ть из ~ого в деся́тое** to tell a story in snatches.
пят|ь, и́, ью́ *num.* five.
пятьдеся́т, пяти́десяти, пятью́десятью *num.* fifty.
пятьсо́т, пятисо́т, пятиста́м *num.* five hundred.
пя́тью *adv.* five times.

Р

р. *abbr. of* **1. река** R., River. **2. рубль** r., rouble(s).
раб, á *m.* slave (*also fig.*); bondsman.
раб... *comb. form, abbr. of* **рабо́чий**, *adj.* **1.**
раб|á, ы *f.* slave; bondwoman, bondmaid.
рабко́р, а *m.* (*abbr. of* ***рабо́чий корреспонде́нт***) worker correspondent.
раблезиа́нский *adj.* (*liter.*) Rabelaisian.
рабовладе́л|ец, ьца *m.* slave-owner.
рабовладе́льческий *adj.* slave-holding, slave-owning.
раболе́пи|е, я *nt.* servility.
раболе́п|ный (~ен, ~на) *adj.* servile.
раболе́пств|о, а *nt.* servility.
раболе́пств|овать, ую *impf.* **(пе́ред)** to fawn (on), cringe (to).
рабо́т|а, ы *f.* **1.** work, working; functioning, running; **лёгкая, тяжёлая р.** (*tech.*) light, heavy duty; **едини́ца ~ы** (*phys.*) unit of work; **режи́м ~ы, усло́вия ~ы** (*tech.*) operating conditions, working conditions; **обеспе́чить норма́льную ~у** (*+g.*) to ensure normal functioning (of). **2.** (*in var. senses*) work; labour; **дома́шняя р.** homework; **ка́торжные ~ы** (*obs.*) penal servitude; **лепна́я р.** stucco work, plaster work; mouldings; **принуди́тельные ~ы** forced labour; **сельскохозя́йственные ~ы** agricultural work; **совме́стная р.** collaboration; **у́мственная р.** mental work, brain-work; **взять в ~у** (*coll.*) to take to task. **3.** work, job; **постоя́нная р.** regular work; **случа́йная р.** casual work, odd job(s); **иска́ть ~у** to look for a job; **поступи́ть**

на ~у to go to work; снять с ~ы to lay off, dismiss; быть без ~ы, не име́ть ~ы to be out of work. 4. work, workmanship.

рабо́та|ть, ю *impf.* 1. (на+*a.*; над) to work (for; on); р. сверхуро́чно to work overtime; р. сде́льно to do piece-work; вре́мя ~ет на нас time is on our side; он ~ет над но́вым рома́ном he is working on a new novel. 2. to work, run, function; не р. not to work, be out of order; р. на не́фти to run on oil. 3. (*of an institution, etc.*) to be open; галере́я не ~ет по воскресе́ньям the gallery is not open on Sundays. 4. (+*i.*) to work, operate; р. вёслами to ply the oars; р. локтя́ми (*coll.*) to elbow; р. рычаго́м to operate a lever.

рабо́та|ться, ется *impf.* (*impers.*; *coll.*): сего́дня хорошо́ ~ется work is going well today; вчера́ мне не ~лось I didn't feel like working yesterday; I couldn't get on with my work yesterday.

рабо́тник, а *m.* worker; workman; hand, labourer; нау́чный р. member of staff of scientific and/or learned institution; р. иску́сства pers. working in the arts, in the artistic world; р. наро́дного образова́ния educationalist; р. у́мственного труда́ brain worker; р. физи́ческого труда́ manual worker.

рабо́тниц|а, ы *f.* (woman-)worker; дома́шняя р. domestic servant, (house)maid; home help.

рабо́тн|ый *adj.*: р. дом (*obs.*) workhouse; ~ые лю́ди (*hist.*) workers, working men.

работода́тел|ь, я *m.* employer.

работома́н, а *m.* workaholic.

работома́н|ка, ки *f.* *of* ~

работорго́в|ец, ца *m.* slave-trader, slaver.

работорго́вл|я, и *f.* slave-trade.

работоспосо́бност|ь, и *f.* capacity for work, efficiency.

работоспосо́б|ный (~ен, ~на) *adj.* 1. able-bodied. 2. hardworking.

работя́г|а, и *c.g.* (*coll.*) hard worker; slogger.

работя́щий *adj.* (*coll.*) hard-working, industrious.

рабо́ч|ий¹, его *m.* worker; working man; workman; hand, labourer; ~ие (*collect.*; *as social class*) the workers; подённый р. day-labourer; сезо́нный р. seasonal worker; сельскохозя́йственный р. farm labourer, agricultural worker; р. от станка́ factory worker, bench-worker.

рабо́ч|ий² *adj.* 1. worker's, working-class; ~ее движе́ние working-class movement; р. класс the working class; ~ая молодёжь young workers; р. по́езд workmen's train. 2. work, working; ~ая кома́нда (*mil.*) fatigue party, work party; ~ая ло́шадь draught-horse; р. мураве́й worker ant; ~ая пчела́ worker bee; ~ие ру́ки hands; ~ая си́ла (*i*) (*collect.*) manpower, labour force, (*ii*) labour; р. скот draught animals. 3. working; ~ее вре́мя working time, working hours; р. день working day; р. костю́м, ~ее пла́тье working clothes; ~ее ме́сто operator's position; ~ая характери́стика (*tech.*) performance, performance curve. 4. (*tech.*) working, driving; ~ее давле́ние working pressure, effective pressure; ~ее колесо́ driving wheel; rotor wheel (*of turbine*); р. ход working stroke; р. чертёж working drawing.

рабселько́р, а *m.* (*abbr. of* рабо́че-се́льский корреспонде́нт) worker-peasant correspondent.

ра́б|ский *adj.* 1. *adj. of* ~; р. труд slave labour. 2. (*fig.*) servile.

ра́бств|о, а *nt.* slavery, servitude; отме́на ~а abolition of slavery.

рабфа́к, а *m.* (*hist.*) (*abbr. of* рабо́чий факульте́т) 'rabfak'; workers' school (*educational establishment in existence during the first years after the Russ. Revolution, set up to prepare workers and peasants for higher education*).

рабфа́ков|ец, ца *m.* 'rabfak' student.

рабфа́к|овский *adj.* *of* ~

рабы́н|я, и, *g. pl.* ~ь *f.* slave, bondwoman, bondmaid.

равви́н, а *m.* rabbi.

равели́н, а *m.* (*mil., hist.*) ravelin.

равенду́к, а *m.* (*text.*) duck.

ра́венств|о *nt.* equality; parity; знак ~а (*math.*) sign of equality, equals sign.

равио́ли *nt. and pl. indecl.* ravioli.

равне́ни|е, я *nt.* 1. dressing, alignment; р. нале́во!, р. напра́во! (*mil. words of command*) left dress!, right dress! 2. (на+*a.*) emulation (of).

равни́н|а, ы *f.* plain.

равни́н|ный *adj.* *of* ~а; р. жи́тель plainsman; ~ная ме́стность flat country.

равно́¹ *adv.* 1. alike, in like manner. 2. *as conj.* р. как (и), а р. и as well as; and also, as also; (*after neg.*) nor; золото́й брасле́т, р. как и други́е её драгоце́нности, пропа́л a gold bracelet, as well as other jewellery of hers, had disappeared.

равно́² *nt. pred. form of* ра́вный. 1. (*math.*) make(s), equals, is; три плюс три р. шести́ three plus three equals six. 2.: всё р. it is all the same, it makes no difference; *as adv.* all the same; всё р., что it is just the same as, it is equivalent to; мне всё р. I don't mind; it's all the same, all one to me; я всё р. вам позвоню́ I will ring you all the same; не всё ли р.? what difference does it make?; what's the difference?; what does it matter?

равно... *comb. form* equi-, iso-.

равнобе́дренный *adj.* (*math.*) isosceles.

равновели́к|ий (~, ~а) *adj.* (*math.*) equivalent; (*phys.*) isometric, equigraphic; ~ие треуго́льники equivalent triangles.

равнове́си|е, я *nt.* equilibrium (*also fig.*); balance, equipoise; душе́вное р. mental equilibrium; полити́ческое р. balance of power; вы́вести из ~я to disturb the equilibrium (of), upset the balance (of); привести́ в р. to balance; сохраня́ть р. to keep one's balance.

равноде́йствующ|ая, ей *f.* (*math., phys.*) resultant (force).

равноде́нственный *adj.* equinoctial, equidiurnal.

равноде́нстви|е, я *nt.* equinox; весе́ннее, осе́ннее р. vernal, autumnal equinox; то́чка ~я equinoctial point.

равноду́ши|е, я *nt.* indifference.

равноду́ш|ный (~ен, ~на) *adj.* (к) indifferent (to).

равнозна́чащий *adj.* equivalent, equipollent.

равнозна́ч|ный (~ен, ~на) *adj.* = ~ащий

равноме́рност|ь, и *f.* evenness; uniformity.

равноме́р|ный (~ен, ~на) *adj.* even; (*phys., tech.*) uniform; ~ное распределе́ние even distribution.

равноо́сный *adj.* (*math., phys.*) equiaxial.

равноотстоя́щий *adj.* (*math.*) equidistant.

равнопра́ви|е, я *nt.* equality (of rights), possession of equal rights.

равнопра́в|ный (~ен, ~на) *adj.* possessing, enjoying equal rights.

равноси́л|ьный (~ен, ~ьна) *adj.* 1. of equal strength; equally matched. 2. (+*d.*) equal (to), equivalent (to), tantamount (to); э́то ~ьно изме́не it is tantamount to treachery; it amounts to treachery.

равносторо́нний *adj.* (*math.*) equilateral.

равноуго́льный *adj.* (*math.*) equiangular.

равноуско́ренный *adj.* (*phys., tech.*) uniformly accelerated.

равноце́н|ный (~ен, ~на) *adj.* of equal value, of equal worth; equivalent.

ра́в|ный (~ен, ~на́, ~но́) *adj.* equal; ~ным о́бразом equally, likewise; при про́чих ~ных усло́виях other things being equal; ему́ нет ~ного he has no equal, there is no match for him.

равня́|ть, ю *impf.* (*of* с~) 1. to make even; to treat equally; р. счёт (*sport*) to equalize. 2. (с+*i.*; *coll.*) to compare (with), treat as equal (to).

равня́|ться, юсь *impf.* (*of* с~) 1. (по+*d.*) (*mil.*) to dress; ~йсь! (*word of command*) right dress!; р. в заты́лок to cover off. 2. (с+*i.*; *coll.*) to compete (with), compare (with), match; по пода́че никто́ не мог р. с ним (*sport*) in serving no one could compete with him. 3. *impf. only* (+*d.*) to equal, be equal (to); (*fig.*) to be equivalent (to), be tantamount (to), amount (to); два́жды пять ~ется десяти́ twice five is ten.

рагу́ *nt. indecl.* (*cul.*) ragout; кита́йское р. chop suey.

рад (~а, ~о) *pred. adj.* (+*d.*; +*inf.*; что) glad (of; to; that); я был о́чень р. слу́чаю поговори́ть с ни́ми I was very glad of the opportunity to talk to them; о́чень р.

(познако́миться с ва́ми)! (*acknowledgement of introduction*) very pleased to meet you!; **р. стара́ться!** (*i*) (*coll.*) gladly!; with pleasure!; (*ii*) (*obs.*; *soldiers' acknowledgement of commendation*) very good, sir!; **и не р., сам не р.** (*coll.*) I, *etc.*, regret it; I, *etc.*, am sorry; **и не р., что пошёл** I'm sorry I went; **р. не р.** (*coll.*) willy-nilly; like it or not; **р.-радёшенек** (*coll.*) pleased as Punch, chuffed.
ра́д|а, ы *f.* rada (= *council*; *popular assembly in Ukraine, Byelorussia, Lithuania and Poland at var. times in history*).
рада́р, а *m.* radar.
рада́р|ный *adj. of* ~
раде́ни|е, я *nt.* (*obs.*) **1.** zeal. **2.** (*relig.*) rites (*of some Russ. sects*).
раде́|ть, ю, ешь *impf.* (*obs.*) **1.** (*pf.* **по~**) (+*d.*) to oblige; (**о**+*p.*) to be concerned (about). **2.** *impf. only* (*relig.*; *of some Russ. sects*) to carry out rites.
ра́дж|а, и *m.* rajah.
ра́ди *prep.*+*g.* for the sake of; **чего́ р.?** what for?; **шу́тки р.** for fun; **р. Бо́га, р. всего́ свято́го** (*coll.*) for God's sake, for goodness' sake.
радиа́льный *adj.* (*math.*, *tech.*) radial.
радиа́тор, а *m.* radiator.
радиацио́нный *adj.* radiation.
радиа́ци|я, и *f.* radiation.
ра́диев|ый *adj.* radium; **~ая ка́псула** radium seed.
ра́ди|й, я *m.* (*chem.*) radium.
радика́л[1], а *m.* (*math.*, *chem.*) radical.
радика́л[2], а *m.* (*pol.*) radical.
радикали́зм, а *m.* (*pol.*) radicalism.
радика́льност|ь, и *f.* **1.** (*pol.*) radicalism. **2.** radical nature, drastic nature, sweeping character.
радика́л|ьный (~ен, ~ьна) *adj.* **1.** (*pol.*) radical. **2.** radical, drastic, sweeping; **~ьные измене́ния** sweeping changes; **~ьные ме́ры** drastic measures; **~ьное сре́дство** drastic remedy.
ра́дио *nt. indecl.* **1.** radio, wireless; **по р.** by radio, over the air; **переда́ть по р.** to broadcast; **слу́шать р.** to listen in. **2.** radio, wireless set; **провести́ р.** to install a radio, wireless set. **3.** (*coll.*) public address system, tannoy (system).
радиоакти́вност|ь, и *f.* (*chem.*, *phys.*) radio-activity.
радиоакти́в|ный (~ен, ~на) *adj.* (*chem.*, *phys.*) radio-active; **~ное загрязне́ние, ~ное зараже́ние** radio-active contamination; **р. изото́п** radio-active isotope, radio-isotope; **~ные оса́дки** radio-active fall-out; **р. ряд** radio-active family, radio-active series, disintegration series, decay chain; **р. яд** radio-active poison, radiation poison.
радиоаппара́т, а *m.* radio set.
радиобесе́д|а, ы *f.* phone-in.
радиобиологи́ческий *adj.* radio-biological.
радиобиоло́ги|я, и *f.* radio-biology.
радиовеща́ни|е, я *nt.* broadcasting.
радиовеща́тельн|ый *adj.* broadcasting; **~ая ста́нция** broadcasting station, transmitter.
радиоволн|а́, ы́ *f.* radio-wave.
радиогра́мм|а, ы *f.* radio-telegram, wireless message.
радио́граф, а *m.* radiographer.
радиографи́ческий *adj.* radiographic.
радиогра́фи|я, и *f.* radiography.
радиожурнали́ст, а *m.* broadcaster.
радиозо́нд, а *m.* radio-sounding apparatus.
радио́л|а, ы *f.* radiogram.
радио́лог, а *m.* radiologist.
радиологи́ческ|ий *adj.* radiological; **~ая устано́вка** radiological unit.
радиоло́ги|я, и *f.* radiology.
радиолока́тор, а *m.* radio-location set; radar set.
радиолок|ацио́нный *adj. of* **~а́ция**
радиолока́ци|я, и *f.* radio-location, radar.
радиолюби́тел|ь, я *m.* radio amateur, 'ham'; wireless enthusiast.
радиома́чт|а, ы *f.* radio-mast, wireless mast.
радиомая́к, а́ *m.* radio-beacon.
радиомо́ст, а *m.* satellite (radio) link-up.
радиопе́ленг, а *m.* radio directional bearing.
радиопеленга́тор, а *m.* radio direction finder.
радиопеленга́ци|я, и *f.* radio homing.
радиопереда́тчик, а *m.* (wireless) transmitter.
радиопереда́ча, и *f.* transmission, broadcast.
радиоперекли́чк|а, и *f.* radio link-up.
радиоперехва́т, а *m.* radio interception; radio intercept.
радиополуко́мпас, а *m.* radio compass.
радиопостано́вк|а, и *f.* radio show.
радиоприбо́р, а *m.* wireless (set), radio (set).
радиоприёмник, а *m.* (wireless) receiver; wireless (set), radio (set).
радиору́бк|а, и *f.* (*naut.*, *aeron.*) radio room, radio cabin.
радиосвя́з|ь, и *f.* wireless communication.
радиосе́т|ь, и *f.* radio network.
радиослу́шател|ь, я *m.* (radio) listener.
радиоста́нци|я, и *f.* radio station, broadcasting station.
радиотелегра́ф, а *m.* radio telegraph.
радиотелеграфи́|я, и *f.* radio-telegraphy, wireless telegraphy.
радиотелефо́н, а *m.* radio-telephone.
радиотерапи́|я, и *f.* radio-therapy.
радиоте́хник, а *m.* radio mechanic.
радиоте́хник|а, и *f.* radio engineering.
радио|техни́ческий *adj. of* **~те́хника**
радиотрансляцио́нный *adj.* broadcasting.
радиоу́з|ел, ла́ *m.* radio relay centre.
радиоуправля́емый *adj.* remote-controlled.
радиофика́ци|я, и *f.* installation of radio.
радиофици́р|овать, ую *impf. and pf.* to install radio (in), equip with radio.
радиохими́ческий *adj.* radiochemical.
радиохи́ми|я, и *f.* radiochemistry.
ради́р|овать, ую *impf. and pf.* to radio.
ради́ст, а *m.* wireless operator, radio operator; (*naut.*) telegraphist.
ра́диус, а *m.* radius.
ра́д|овать, ую *impf.* (*of* **об~**) to gladden, make glad, make happy; **р. се́рдце** to rejoice the heart.
ра́д|оваться, уюсь *impf.* (*of* **об~**) (+*d.*) to be glad (at), be happy (at), rejoice (in).
ра́дост|ный (~ен, ~на) *adj.* glad, joyous, joyful; **~ное изве́стие** glad tidings, good news.
ра́дост|ь, и *f.* gladness, joy; **р. жи́зни** joie de vivre; **не чу́вствовать себя́ от ~и** to be beside o.s. with joy; **на ~ях** (+*g.*, *coll.*) in celebration (of), to celebrate; **с ~ью** with pleasure, gladly; **моя́ р., р. моя́** my darling.
ра́дуг|а, и *f.* rainbow.
ра́дужно *adv.* cheerfully; **р. смотре́ть (на**+*a.*) to look on the bright side (of).
ра́дужн|ый *adj.* **1.** iridescent, opalescent; **~ая оболо́чка (гла́за)** (*anat.*) iris. **2.** cheerful; optimistic; **~ые наде́жды** high hopes; **~ое настрое́ние** high spirits.
раду́ши|е, я *nt.* cordiality.
раду́ш|ный (~ен, ~на) *adj.* cordial; **р. приём** hearty welcome; **р. хозя́ин** kind host.
ра|ёк, йка́ *m.* (*theatr.*; *obs.*) gallery; the gods.
раж, а *m.* (*coll.*) rage, passion; **войти́ в р., прийти́ в р.** to fly into a rage.
раз[1], а, *pl.* **~ы́, ~** *m.* **1.** time; occasion; **оди́н р., ка́к-то р.** once; **два ~́а** twice; **мно́го р.** many times; **ещё р.** once again, once more; **не р.** more than once; time and again; **ни ~́у** not once, never; **р. навсегда́** once (and) for all; **р. в день** once a day; **вся́кий р.** every time, each time; **вся́кий р., когда́** whenever; **ино́й р.** sometimes, now and again; **во второ́й р.** for the second time; **в друго́й р.** another time, some other time; **в са́мый р.** (*coll.*) at the right moment; just right; **до друго́го ~́а** till another time; **р. за ~́ом** time after time; **на э́тот р.** this time, on this occasion, for (this) once; **с пе́рвого ~́а** from the very first; **во́т тебе (и) р.!** (*coll.*) well, I never!; **как р.** just, exactly; **как р. то** the very thing. **2.** (*num.*) one.
раз[2] *adv.* once, one day.
раз[3] *conj.* if; since; **р. вы бу́дете во Фра́нции, не смо́жете ли вы прие́хать и сюда́?** if you are going to be in France, can't you come here too?
раз... (*also* **разо..., разъ...** *and* **рас...)** *vbl. pref. indicating* **1.** *division into parts* (dis-, un-). **2.** *distribution*, *direction*

of action in different directions (dis-). **3.** *action in reverse* (un-). **4.** *termination of action or state.* **5.** *intensification of action.*

разбави́тел|ь, я *m.* thinner.

разба́в|ить, лю, ишь *pf.* (*of* **~ля́ть**) to dilute.

разбавля́|ть, ю *impf. of* **разба́вить**

разбаза́ривани|е, я *nt.* (*coll.*) squandering.

разбаза́рива|ть, ю *impf. of* **разбаза́рить**

разбаза́р|ить, ю, ишь *pf.* (*of* **~ивать**) (*coll.*) to squander.

разба́лива|ться, юсь *impf. of* **разболе́ться**

разба́лтыва|ть(ся), ю(сь) *impf. of* **разболта́ть(ся)**

разбе́г, а *m.* run, running start; **пры́гнуть с ~у** to take a running jump; **нырну́ть с ~у** to take a running dive; **прыжо́к с ~у** running jump; **р. при взлёте** (*aeron.*) take-off run.

разбега́|ться, юсь *impf. of* **разбежа́ться**

разбе|жа́ться, гу́сь, жи́шься, гу́тся *pf.* (*of* **~га́ться**) **1.** to take a run, run up. **2.** to scatter, disperse; **р. по места́м** to run to one's places, (*mil.*) to one's stations, posts. **3.** (*of thoughts, etc.*) to be scattered; **глаза́ у меня́ ~жа́лись** I was dazzled.

разбере|ди́ть, жу́, ди́шь *pf. of* **береди́ть**

разбива́|ть(ся), ю(сь) *impf. of* **разби́ть(ся)**

разби́вк|а, и *f.* **1.** laying out (*of a garden, etc.*). **2.** (*typ.*) spacing (out).

разбинт|ова́ть, у́ю *pf.* (*of* **~о́вывать**) to remove a bandage (from).

разбинт|ова́ться, у́юсь *pf.* (*of* **~о́вываться**) **1.** to remove one's bandage(s). **2.** (*of a bandage*) to come off, come undone. **3.** to come unbandaged; **нога́ у меня́ ~ова́лась** the bandage has come off my leg.

разбинто́выва|ть(ся), ю(сь) *impf. of* **разбинтова́ть(ся)**

разбира́тельств|о, а *nt.* (*leg.*) examination, investigation; **суде́бное р.** court examination.

разбира́|ть, ю *impf.* **1.** *impf. of* **разобра́ть. 2.** (*impf. only*) to be fastidious; **не ~я** indiscriminately.

разбира́|ться, юсь *impf. of* **разобра́ться**

разбитно́й *adj.* (*coll.*) bright, sprightly; sharp.

разби́т|ый *p.p.p. of* **~ь** *and adj.* (*coll.*) jaded, down.

раз|би́ть, обью́, обьёшь *pf.* (*of* **~бива́ть**) **1.** (*impf. also* **бить**) to break, smash; **р. вдре́безги** to smash to smithereens. **2.** to divide (up); to break up, break down; **р. на гру́ппы** to divide up into groups; **р. компле́кт** to break a set. **3.** to lay out, mark out; **р. ко́лышками** to peg out; **р. ла́герь** to pitch a camp. **4.** to damage severely, hurt badly; to fracture; **р. кому́-н. нос в кровь** to make s.o.'s nose bleed. **5.** to beat, defeat, smash (*also fig.*); **р. чьи-н. до́воды** to destroy s.o.'s arguments. **6.** (*typ.*) to space (out).

раз|би́ться, обью́сь, обьёшься *pf.* (*of* **~бива́ться**) **1.** to break, get broken, get smashed. **2.** to divide; to break up. **3.** to hurt o.s. badly; to smash o.s. up.

разбла́гове|стить, щу, стишь *pf. of* **бла́говестить**

разблоки́р|овать, ую *pf.* (*mil.*) to lift the blockade (of).

разбогате́|ть, ю, ешь *pf. of* **богате́ть**

разбо́|й, я *m.* robbery, brigandage; **морско́й р.** piracy.

разбо́йник, а *m.* **1.** robber, brigand; **морско́й р.** pirate; **р. с большо́й доро́ги** highwayman. **2.** (*joc.*; *affectionate form of address to child, etc.*) scamp!; scallywag!

разбо́йнича|ть, ю *impf.* to rob, plunder.

разбо́йни|чий *adj. of* **~к; р. прито́н** den of thieves.

разболе́|ться¹, юсь, ешься *pf.* (*of* **разба́ливаться**) (*coll.*) to become ill; **он совсе́м ~лся** his health has completely cracked.

разбол|е́ться², и́тся *pf.* (*of* **разба́ливаться**) to begin to ache badly.

разбо́лт|анный *p.p.p. of* **~а́ть¹** *and adj.* (*fig.*) disorderly.

разболта́|ть¹, ю *pf.* (*of* **разба́лтывать**) **1.** to shake up, stir up. **2.** to loosen.

разболта́|ть², ю *pf.* (*of* **разба́лтывать**) (*coll.*) to blab out, give away.

разболта́|ться, юсь *pf.* (*of* **разба́лтываться**) **1.** to mix (*as result of stirring*). **2.** to come loose, work loose. **3.** (*fig.*) to get out of hand; to come unstuck.

разбомб|и́ть, лю́, и́шь *pf.* (*no impf.*) to destroy by bombing.

разбо́р, а *m.* **1.** stripping, dismantling. **2.** buying up. **3.** sorting out. **4.** investigation; **р. де́ла** (*leg.*) trial, hearing (*of a case*). **5.** (*gram.*) parsing; analysis. **6.** critique. **7.** selectiveness; **без ~у** indiscriminately, promiscuously; **с ~ом** discriminatingly, fastidiously. **8.** sort, quality; **пе́рвого, второ́го ~а** first, second quality.

разбо́рк|а, и *f.* **1.** sorting out. **2.** stripping, dismantling, taking to pieces.

разбо́рный *adj.* collapsible.

разбо́рчивост|ь, и *f.* **1.** fastidiousness; scrupulousness. **2.** legibility.

разбо́рчив|ый (~, ~а) *adj.* **1.** fastidious, exacting; discriminating; scrupulous. **2.** legible.

разбран|и́ть, ю́, и́шь *pf.* (*coll.*) to berate; to blow up.

разбран|и́ться, ю́сь, и́шься *pf.* (**с**+*i.*; *coll.*) to fall out (with); to quarrel (with), squabble (with).

разбра́сывател|ь, я *m.* (*agric.*) spreader.

разбра́сыва|ть, ю *impf. of* **разброса́ть**

разбра́сыва|ться, юсь *impf.* **1.** *impf. of* **разброса́ться. 2.** (*fig.*) to dissipate one's energies; to try to do too much at once.

разбреда́|ться, юсь *impf. of* **разбрести́сь**

разбре|сти́сь, ду́сь, дёшься, *past* **~̈лся, ~ла́сь** *pf.* (*of* **~да́ться**) to disperse; to straggle; **р. по дома́м** to disperse and go home.

разбро́д, а *m.* disorder.

разброни́р|овать, ую *pf.* to cancel reservation (of), de-reserve.

разбро́санност|ь, и *f.* **1.** sparseness; scattered nature. **2.** (*fig.*) disconnectedness, incoherence.

разбро́с|анный *p.p.p. of* **~а́ть** *and adj.* **1.** sparse, scattered; straggling. **2.** (*fig.*) disconnected, incoherent.

разброса́|ть, ю *pf.* (*of* **разбра́сывать**) to throw about; to scatter, spread, strew; **р. наво́з** to spread manure; **р. де́ньги на ве́тер** to squander one's money.

разброса́|ться, юсь *pf.* (*of* **разбра́сываться**) to throw o.s. *or* one's things about.

разбры́з|гать, жу, жешь *pf.* (*of* **~гивать**) to splash; to spray.

разбры́згивател|ь, я *m.* sprinkler.

разбры́згива|ть, ю *impf. of* **разбры́згать**

разбу|ди́ть, жу́, ~̍дишь *pf. of* **буди́ть**

разбух|а́ть, а́ет *impf. of* **~̍нуть**

разбу́х|нуть, нет, *past* **~, ~ла** *pf.* (*of* **~а́ть**) to swell (*also fig.*).

разбуш|ева́ться, у́юсь *pf.* **1.** (*of a storm*) to rage; to blow up; (*of the sea*) to run high. **2.** (*coll.*) to fly into a rage.

разбуя́н|иться, юсь, ишься *pf.* (*coll.*) to fly into a rage.

разва́жнича|ться, юсь *pf.* (*coll.*) to put on airs.

разва́л, а *m.* **1.** breakdown, disintegration, disruption; disorganization. **2.** flea market, open-air bazaar.

разва́л|ец, ьца *m.* (*coll.*): **ходи́ть с ~ьцем** to shamble; **рабо́тать с ~ьцем** to go slow.

разва́лива|ть(ся), ю(сь) *impf. of* **развали́ть(ся)**

разва́лин|а, ы *f.* **1.** *pl.* ruins; **гру́да ~** a heap of debris; **лежа́ть в ~ах** to be in ruins; **преврати́ть в ~ы** to reduce to ruins. **2.** (*fig., coll.*; *of a pers.*) wreck, ruin.

развал|и́ть, ю́, ~̍ишь *pf.* (*of* **~̍ивать**) **1.** to pull down (*a building, etc.*). **2.** (*fig.*) to mess up.

развал|и́ться, ю́сь, ~̍ишься *pf.* (*of* **~̍иваться**) **1.** to fall down, tumble down, collapse. **2.** (*fig.*) to go to pieces, fall to pieces, break down. **3.** (*coll.*) to lounge, sprawl.

разва́л|ьца, ьцы *f.* = **~ец**

разва́рива|ть(ся), ю(сь) *impf. of* **развари́ть(ся)**

развар|и́ть, ю́, ~̍ишь *pf.* (*of* **~̍ивать**) to boil soft.

развар|и́ться, ю́сь, ~̍ишься *pf.* (*of* **~̍иваться**) to be boiled soft; **р. в ка́шу** to be boiled to a pulp.

разварно́й *adj.* boiled.

ра́зве 1. *interrog. particle, neutral or indicating that neg. answer is expected*; +*neg. indicates that affirmative answer is expected* **р. они́ все вместя́тся в э́ту маши́ну?** will they (really) all get in this car?; **р. ты не знал, что он ру́сский?** didn't you know that he is Russian?; surely you knew that he is Russian? **2.** *interrog. particle, expr. hesitation about course of action to be followed* (+*inf.*; *coll.*)

р. отложи́ть нам пое́здку? perhaps we had better postpone the trip?; **р. поговори́ть вам с её отцо́м?** perhaps you should have, mightn't it be a good thing to have a talk with her father? **3. р. (что), р. (то́лько)** *as adv.* only; perhaps; *as conj.* except that, only; **кро́ме р.** (+*g.*) except perhaps, with the possible exception (of); **он вы́глядит так же как всегда́, р. что похуде́л** he looks the same as ever, except that he has lost weight. **4.** *conj.* (*obs.*) unless.

развева́|ть, ю *impf.* **1.** *impf. of* **разве́ять. 2.** *impf. only* to blow about; **ве́тер ~л зна́мя** the banner was flapping, streaming in the wind.

развева́|ться, юсь *impf.* **1.** *impf. of* **разве́яться. 2.** *impf. only* to fly, flutter; **с ~ющимися знамёнами** with banners flying.

разве́д... *comb. form, abbr. of* **разве́дывательный**

разве́д|ать, аю *pf.* (*of* **~ывать**) **1.** (**о**+*p.*; *coll.*) to find out (about), ascertain. **2.** (*mil.*) to reconnoitre. **3.** (**на**+*a.*; *geol.*) to prospect (for); *pf. only* to locate; **р. на нефть** to prospect for oil.

разведе́ни|е¹, я *nt.* breeding, rearing; cultivation.

разведе́ни|е², я *nt.* opening, swinging open (*of a bascule bridge or draw-bridge*).

разведённ|ый *p.p.p. of* **развести́** *and adj.* divorced; *as n.* **р., ~ого** *m.*, **~ая, ~ой** *f.* divorcee.

разве́дк|а, и *f.* **1.** (*geol., etc.*) prospecting. **2.** (*mil.*) reconnaissance; **звукова́я р.** sound ranging; **опти́ческая р.** flash ranging; **р. бо́ем** reconnaissance in force; **р. в глубину́** reconnaissance in depth. **3.** (*mil.*) reconnaissance party. **4.** secret service, intelligence service.

разве́дочн|ый *adj.* (*geol.*) prospecting, exploratory; **~ая сква́жина** test well.

разве́дчик¹, а *m.* **1.** (*mil.*) scout. **2.** secret-service agent; intelligence officer. **3.** (*geol.*) prospector.

разве́дчик², а *m.* reconnaissance aircraft.

разве́дывательн|ый *adj.* (*mil.*) **1.** reconnaissance; **р. бой** probing attack; reconnaissance in force; **р. дозо́р** reconnaissance patrol; **р. отря́д** reconnaissance detachment. **2.** intelligence; **р. отде́л** intelligence section; **~ая рабо́та** intelligence work, secret-service work; **~ая слу́жба** Intelligence Service (*corresponding to Intelligence Corps in Br. Army*).

разве́дыва|ть, ю *impf. of* **разве́дать**

развез|ти́¹, у́, ёшь, *past* **≃, ~ла́** *pf.* (*of* **развози́ть**) to convey, deliver.

развез|ти́², у́, ёшь, *past* **≃, ~ла́** *pf.* (*of* **развози́ть**) (*coll.*) **1.** to exhaust, wear out; (*impers.*): **от жары́ нас ~ло́** we were exhausted from the heat. **2.** to make impassable, make unfit for traffic; (*impers.*): **доро́гу ~ло́ от дожде́й** the road was made impassable by rain.

разве́ива|ть(ся), ю(сь) *impf. of* **разве́ять(ся)**

развенч|а́ть, а́ю *pf.* (*of* **≃ивать**) **1.** to dethrone. **2.** (*fig.*) to debunk.

разве́нчива|ть, ю *impf. of* **развенча́ть**

разверз|а́ть(ся), а́ю(сь) *impf. of* **≃нуть(ся)**

разве́рз|нуть, ну, нешь, *past* **~, ~ла** *pf.* (*of* **~а́ть**) (*obs., poet.*) to open wide.

разве́рз|нуться, нусь, нешься, *past* **~ся, ~лась** *pf.* (*of* **~а́ться**) (*obs., poet.*) to open wide, yawn, gape.

развёрн|утый *p.p.p. of* **~у́ть** *and adj.* **1.** extensive, large-scale, all-out. **2.** detailed; **~утая програ́мма** detailed programme, comprehensive programme. **3.** (*mil.*) deployed; **р. строй** extended line formation.

развер|ну́ть, ну́, нёшь *pf.* (*of* **≃тывать** *and* **развора́чивать**) **1.** to unfold; to unroll; to unwrap; to unfurl; **р. ковёр** to unroll a carpet; **р. зна́мя** to unfurl a banner. **2.** (*mil.*) to deploy. **3.** (**в**+*a.*; *mil.*) to expand (into); **р. батальо́н в полк** to expand a battalion into a regiment. **4.** (*fig.*) to show, display. **5.** (*fig.*) to develop; to expand; **р. аргумента́цию** to develop a line of argument; **р. торго́влю** to expand trade. **6.** to turn; to swing (about, around). **7.** (*tech.*) to ream, broach. **8.** (*radar*) to scan.

развер|ну́ться, ну́сь, нёшься *pf.* (*of* **≃тываться** *and* **развора́чиваться**) **1.** to unfold; to unroll; to come unwrapped. **2.** (*mil.*) to deploy. **3.** (**в**+*a.*, *mil.*) to expand (into), be expanded (into). **4.** (*fig.*) to show *or* display o.s. **5.** (*fig.*) to develop; to spread; to expand. **6.** to turn, swing (about, around); (*naut.*) to slew (about).

раверст|а́ть, а́ю *pf.* (*of* **≃ывать**) to distribute, allot, apportion.

развёрстк|а, и *f.* allotment, apportionment.

развёрстыва|ть, ю *impf. of* **разверста́ть**

разве́р|стый *p.p.p. of* **~знуть** *and adj.* (*obs., poet.*) open, yawning, gaping; **~стая пасть** gaping maw.

развер|те́ть, чу́, ≃тишь *pf.* (*of* **≃чивать**) **1.** to unscrew. **2.** (*tech.*) to ream.

развёртк|а¹, и *f.* **1.** (*math.*) development, evolvement. **2.** (*tech.*) reaming. **3.** (*radar*) scanning.

развёртк|а², и *f.* (*tech.*) reamer, broach bit.

развёртывани|е, я *nt.* **1.** unfolding; unrolling; unwrapping. **2.** (*mil.*) deployment. **3.** (*fig.*) development, expansion.

развёртыва|ть(ся), ю(сь) *impf. of* **разверну́ть(ся)**

развёрчива|ть, ю *impf. of* **разверте́ть**

разве́с, а *m.* weighing out.

развесел|и́ть, ю́, и́шь *pf.* to cheer up, amuse.

развесел|и́ться, ю́сь, и́шься *pf.* to cheer up.

развесёлый *adj.* (*coll.*) merry, gay.

разве́сист|ый (~, ~а) *adj.* branchy; **р. кашта́н** spreading chestnut; **~ая клю́ква** myth, fable (*of credulous travellers' tales*).

разве́|сить¹, шу, сишь *pf.* (*of* **~шивать**) to weigh out.

разве́|сить², шу, сишь *pf.* (*of* **~шивать**) **1.** to hang. **2.** to spread (*branches*); **р. у́ши** (*fig., coll.*) to listen open-mouthed.

разве́|сить³, шу, сишь *pf.* (*of* **~шивать**) to hang.

развесно́й *adj.* sold by weight.

разве|сти́¹, ду́, дёшь, *past* **≃л, ~ла́** *pf.* (*of* **разводи́ть**) **1.** to take, conduct; **р. дете́й по дома́м** to take the children to their homes; **р. войска́ по кварти́рам** to disperse troops to their billets; **р. часовы́х** to post sentries. **2.** (*in var. senses*) to part, separate; **р. мост** to raise a bridge, swing a bridge open; **р. пилу́** to set a saw; **р. рука́ми** to spread one's hands (*in a gesture of helplessness*). **3.** to divorce. **4.** to dilute, to dissolve; **р. порошо́к водо́ю, в воде́** to dissolve powder in water.

разве|сти́², ду́, дёшь, *past* **≃л, ~ла́** *pf.* (*of* **разводи́ть**) **1.** to breed, rear; to cultivate; **р. сад** to plant a garden; **р. парк** to lay out a park. **2.** to start (*a source of heat or power*); **р. костёр** to make a camp fire; **р. ого́нь** to light a fire, kindle a fire; **р. пары́** to raise steam, get up steam. **3.** (*fig., coll.*; *pej.*) to start; **р. чепуху́** to start talking nonsense.

разве|сти́сь¹, ду́сь, дёшься, *past* **≃лся, ~ла́сь** *pf.* (*of* **разводи́ться**) (**с**+*i.*) to divorce, be divorced (from).

разве|сти́сь², ду́сь, дёшься, *past* **≃лся, ~ла́сь** *pf.* (*of* **разводи́ться**) to breed, multiply.

развет|ви́ться, и́тся *pf.* (*of* **~ля́ться**) to branch; to fork; to ramify.

разветвле́ни|е, я *nt.* **1.** branching; ramification; forking. **2.** branch; fork (*of road, etc.*); **р. не́рва** (*anat.*) radicle.

разветвля́|ться, юсь *impf. of* **разветви́ться**

разве́ш|ать, аю *pf.* (*of* **~ивать**) to hang.

разве́шива|ть, ю *impf. of* **разве́сить** *and* **разве́шать**

разве́|ять, ю, ишь *pf.* **1.** (*impf.* **~ивать**) to scatter, disperse; (*fig.*) to dispel; **р. миф** to shatter a myth. **2.** (*impf.* **~ва́ть**) to cause to flutter.

разве́|яться, юсь, ешься *pf.* (*of* **~иваться** *and* **~ва́ться**) to disperse; (*fig.*) to be dispelled.

развива́|ть(ся), ю(сь) *impf. of* **разви́ть(ся)**

разви́лин|а, ы *f.* fork, bifurcation.

разви́лист|ый (~, ~а) *adj.* forked.

развин|ти́ть, чу́, ти́шь *pf.* (*of* **≃чивать**) to unscrew.

развин|ти́ться, чу́сь, ти́шься *pf.* (*of* **≃чиваться**) **1.** to come unscrewed. **2.** (*fig.*) to come unstuck.

разви́нченност|ь, и *f.* (*coll.*) unbalance.

разви́н|ченный *p.p.p. of* **~ти́ть** *and adj.* (*coll.*) **1.** unstrung, unstuck. **2.** (*of gait*) unsteady, lurching.

разви́нчива|ть(ся), ю(сь) *impf. of* **развинти́ть(ся)**

разви́ти|е, я *nt.* **1.** (*in var. senses*) development; evolution; **р. бо́я** (*mil.*) progress of battle. **2.** (*intellectual*) maturity.

развит|óй (ра́звит, ~á, ра́звито) *adj.* **1.** developed. **2.** (intellectually) mature; adult.
разви́т|ый (~, ~á, ~о) *p.p.p. of* **~ь**
раз|ви́ть[1], **овью́, овьёшь,** *past* **~ви́л, ~вила́, ~ви́ло** *pf.* (*of* **~вива́ть**) to unwind, untwist.
раз|ви́ть[2], **овью́, овьёшь,** *past* **~ви́л, ~вила́, ~ви́ло** *pf.* (*of* **~вива́ть**) (*in var. senses*) to develop; **р. мускулату́ру** to develop one's muscles; **р. мысль** to develop an idea; **р. ско́рость** to gather, pick up speed.
раз|ви́ться[1], **овью́сь, овьёшься,** *past* **~ви́лся, ~вила́сь** *pf.* (*of* **~вива́ться**) to untwist; (*of hair*) to come uncurled, lose its curl.
раз|ви́ться[2], **овью́сь, овьёшься,** *past* **~ви́лся, ~вила́сь** *pf.* (*of* **~вива́ться**) (*in var. senses*) to develop.
развлека́тел|ьный (~ен, ~ьна) *adj.* entertaining; **~ьное чте́ние** light reading.
развлека́|ть(ся), ю(сь) *impf. of* **развле́чь(ся)**
развлече́ни|е, я *nt.* entertainment; amusement; diversion.
развле́|чь, ку́, чёшь, ку́т, *past* **~́к, ~кла́** *pf.* (*of* **~ка́ть**) to entertain, amuse; to divert.
развле́|чься, ку́сь, чёшься, ку́тся, *past* **~́кся, ~кла́сь** *pf.* (*of* **~ка́ться**) **1.** to have a good time; to amuse o.s. **2.** to be diverted, be distracted.
разво́д[1], **а** *m.* divorce; **дать р. кому́-н.** to give s.o. a divorce, agree to a divorce; **проце́сс о ~е** divorce suit, divorce proceedings; **они́ в ~е** they are divorced.
разво́д[2], **а** *m.* (*mil.*): **р. карау́лов** guard mounting; **р. часовы́х** posting of sentries.
разво́д[3], **а** *m.* breeding; **оста́вить на р.** to keep for breeding.
разво|ди́ть(ся), жу́(сь), ~́дишь(ся) *impf. of* **развести́(сь)**
разво́дк|а[1], **и** *f.* separation; **р. мо́ста** raising of a bridge, swinging a bridge open; **р. пилы́** saw setting.
разво́дк|а[2], **и** *f.* (*tech.*) saw set.
разводн|о́й *adj.*: **р. ключ** adjustable spanner, monkey wrench; **р. мост** drawbridge.
разво́д|ы, ов *no sg.* **1.** design, pattern. **2.** stains; **черни́льные р.** ink-stains.
разво́дь|е, я, *g. pl.* **~ев** *nt.* **1.** (*dial.*) spring floods. **2.** patch of ice-free water.
разводя́щ|ий, его *m.* (*mil.*) corporal of the guard; guard commander.
разво|ева́ться, ю́юсь, ю́ешься *pf.* (*coll.*) to bluster.
разво́з, а *m.* conveyance.
разво|зи́ть, жу́, ~́зишь *impf. of* **развезти́**
разво|зи́ться, жу́сь, ~́зишься *pf.* (*coll.*) (*of children*) to kick up a din.
разво́зк|а, и *f.* **1.** conveying; delivery. **2.** (*coll.*) delivery cart.
разволн|ова́ть, у́ю *pf.* to excite, agitate.
разволн|ова́ться, у́юсь *pf.* to get excited, get agitated.
развора́чива|ть, ю *impf. of* **разверну́ть** *and* **развороти́ть**
развора́чива|ться, юсь *impf. of* **разверну́ться**
развор|ова́ть, у́ю *pf.* (*of* **~о́вывать**) to loot, clean out.
разворо́выва|ть, ю *impf. of* **разворова́ть**
разворо́т, а *m.* **1.** (*aeron., etc.*) turn; (*of motor transport*) U-turn. **2.** (*coll.*) development; **р. торго́вли** growth of trade.
разворо|ти́ть, чу́, ~́тишь *pf.* (*of* **развора́чивать**) **1.** to make havoc (of); to knock to pieces. **2.** to smash up, break up.
разворош|и́ть, у́, и́шь *pf.* to turn upside down, scatter.
развра́т, а *m.* debauchery, depravity, dissipation.
развратител|ь, я *m.* debaucher, seducer, corrupter.
развра|ти́ть, щу́, ти́шь *pf.* (*of* **~ща́ть**) **1.** to debauch, corrupt. **2.** (*fig.*) to deprave.
развра|ти́ться, щу́сь, ти́шься *pf.* (*of* **~ща́ться**) to become corrupted, become depraved; to go to the bad.
развра́тник, а *m.* debauchee, profligate, libertine.
развра́тнича|ть, ю *impf.* to indulge in debauchery, lead a depraved life.
развра́тност|ь, и *f.* depravity, profligacy; corruptness.
развра́т|ный (~ен, ~на) *adj.* debauched, depraved, profligate; corrupt.
развраща́|ть(ся), ю(сь) *impf. of* **разврати́ть(ся)**
развращённост|ь, и *f.* corruptness.
развра|щённый *p.p.p. of* **~ти́ть** *and adj.* corrupt.
разв|ы́ться, о́юсь, о́ешься *pf.* (*coll.*) to begin to howl, set up a howl.
развью́чива|ть, ю *impf. of* **развью́чить**
развью́ч|ить, у, ишь *pf.* (*of* **~ивать**) to unload, unburden.
развя|за́ть, жу́, ~́жешь *pf.* (*of* **~́зывать**) to untie, unbind, undo; to unleash; **р. кому́-н. ру́ки** to untie s.o.'s hands (*also fig.*); **р. войну́** to unleash war.
развя|за́ться, жу́сь, ~́жешься *pf.* (*of* **~́зываться**) **1.** to come untied, come undone; **у него́ ~за́лся язы́к** (*fig.*) his tongue has been loosened. **2.** (**с**+*i.*; *fig.*) to have done (with), be through (with).
развя́зк|а, и *f.* **1.** (*liter.*) denouement. **2.** outcome, issue, upshot; **счастли́вая р.** happy ending; **де́ло идёт к ~е** things are coming to a head. **3.**: **р. движе́ния, кольцева́я (тра́нспортная) р.** (traffic) roundabout.
развя́з|ный (~ен, ~на) *adj.* (unduly) familiar; free-and-easy.
развя́зыва|ть(ся), ю(сь) *impf. of* **развяза́ть(ся)**
разгад|а́ть, а́ю *pf.* (*of* **~́ывать**) **1.** to guess the meaning (of); **р. зага́дку** to solve a riddle; **р. сны** to interpret dreams; **р. шифр** to break a cipher. **2.** to guess, divine; **р. челове́ка** to size a pers. up, get to the bottom of a pers.
разга́дк|а, и *f.* solution (*of a riddle, etc.*).
разга́дыва|ть, ю *impf. of* **разгада́ть**
разга́р[1], **а** *m.*: **в ~е** (+*g.*) at the height (of); **в по́лном ~е** in full swing; **в ~е бо́я** in the heat of the battle.
разга́р[2], **а** *m.* erosion (*of firearm barrel*).
разгиба́|ть(ся), ю(сь) *impf. of* **разогну́ть(ся); не ~я спины́** without a let-up; **~ющий му́скул** (*anat.*) extensor.
разгильдя́|й, я *m.* (*coll.*) sloven; sloppy individual.
разгильдя́йнича|ть, ю *impf.* (*coll.*) to be slovenly, be sloppy; to be slipshod.
разглаго́льствовани|е, я *nt.* (*coll.*) big talk, lofty phrases.
разглаго́льств|овать, ую *impf.* (*coll.*) to hold forth, expatiate; to talk big, use lofty phrases.
разгла́|дить, жу, дишь *pf.* (*of* **~живать**) to smooth out; to iron out, press; (*tech.*) to planish.
разгла́|диться, дится *pf.* (*of* **~живаться**) **1.** to become smoothed out. **2.** *pass. of* **~дить**
разгла́жива|ть(ся), ет(ся) *impf. of* **разгла́дить(ся)**
разгла|си́ть, шу́, си́шь *pf.* (*of* **~ша́ть**) **1.** to divulge, give away, let out. **2.** (**о**+*p.*; *coll.*) to trumpet, broadcast.
разглаша́|ть, ю *impf. of* **разгласи́ть**
разглаше́ни|е, я *nt.* divulging, (unauthorized) disclosure; **р. вое́нной та́йны** divulging of military secrets.
разгля|де́ть, жу́, ди́шь *pf.* to make out, discern, descry.
разгля́дыва|ть, ю *impf.* to examine closely, scrutinize.
разгне́ва|ть, ю *pf.* to anger, incense.
разгне́ва|ться, юсь *pf. of* **гне́ваться**
разгова́рива|ть, ю *impf.* (**с**+*i.*) to talk (to, with), speak (to, with), converse (with); **переста́ньте р.!** stop talking!; **они́ друг с дру́гом не ~ют** they are not on speaking terms.
разгов|е́ться, е́юсь, е́ешься *pf.* (*of* **~ля́ться**) to break a (period of) fast.
разговля́|ться, юсь *impf. of* **разгове́ться**
разгово́р, а (у) *m.* talk, conversation; **кру́пный р.** high words; **перемени́ть р.** to change the subject; **об э́том и ~у быть не мо́жет** there can be no question about it; **об э́том бы́ло мно́го ~ов** there was a great deal of talk about it; **без ~ов!** and no argument!
разговор|и́ть, ю́, и́шь *pf.* (*coll.*) to dissuade.
разговор|и́ться, ю́сь, и́шься *pf.* **1.** (**с**+*i.*) to get into conversation (with). **2.** to warm to one's theme; **заста́вить кого́-н. р.** to get s.o. talking.
разгово́рник, а *m.* phrase-book.
разгово́р|ный *adj.* **1.** colloquial; **р. язы́к** spoken language. **2.**: **~ная бу́дка** telephone booth; **р. уро́к** conversation class.
разгово́рчивост|ь, и *f.* talkativeness, loquacity.
разгово́рчив|ый (~, ~а) *adj.* talkative, loquacious.
разго́н, а *m.* **1.** dispersal; dissolution; **р. собра́ния** breaking up of a meeting. **2.** **быть в ~е** (*coll.*) to be out. **3.** (*sport*) run, running start; **прыжо́к с ~а** running jump. **4.** distance (*between similar objects*). **5.** (*typ.*) space.
разго́нист|ый (~, ~а) *adj.* (*coll.*; *of handwriting or type*) spaced-out.
разгоня́|ть(ся), ю(сь) *impf. of* **разогна́ть(ся)**

разгора́жива|ть, ю *impf. of* **разгороди́ть**
разгор|а́ться, а́ется *impf. of* **~е́ться**
разгор|е́ться, и́тся *pf.* (*of* **~а́ться**) **1.** to flame up, flare up. **2.** (*fig.*) to flare up; **~е́лся спор** a heated argument developed; **стра́сти ~е́лись** feeling ran high, passions rose; **глаза́ у неё ~е́лись на бриллиа́нтовое кольцо́** (*coll.*) she hankered after, she set her heart on a diamond ring. **3.** (*fig.*) to flush.
разгоро|ди́ть, жу́, ~ди́шь *pf.* (*of* **разгора́живать**) to partition off.
разгоряч|и́ть, у́, и́шь *pf. of* **горячи́ть**
разгоряч|и́ться, у́сь, и́шься *pf.* (*of* **горячи́ться**) (**от**) to be flushed (with); **р. от вина́** to be flushed with wine.
разгра́б|ить, лю, ишь *pf.* to plunder, pillage, loot.
разграбле́ни|е, я *nt.* plunder, pillage.
разгра|ди́ть, жу́, ди́шь *pf.* (*of* **~жда́ть**) (*mil.*) to remove obstacles (from); to clear (*of mines*).
разгражда́|ть, ю *impf. of* **разгради́ть**
разгражде́ни|е, я *nt.* (*mil.*) removal of obstacles.
разграниче́ни|е, я *nt.* **1.** demarcation, delimitation. **2.** differentiation.
разграни́чива|ть, ю *impf. of* **разграни́чить**
разграничи́тельн|ый *adj.*: **~ая ли́ния** line of demarcation, dividing line.
разграни́ч|ить, у, ишь *pf.* (*of* **~ивать**) **1.** to delimit, demarcate. **2.** to differentiate, distinguish.
разграф|и́ть, лю́, и́шь *pf.* (*of* **графи́ть** *and* **~ля́ть**) to rule (*in squares, columns, etc.*).
разграфле́ни|е, я *nt.* ruling.
разграфля́|ть, ю *impf. of* **разграфи́ть**
разгреба́|ть, ю *impf. of* **разгрести́**
разгре|сти́, бу́, бёшь, *past* **~̈б, ~бла́** *pf.* (*of* **~ба́ть**) to rake (aside, away); to shovel (aside, away).
разгро́м, а *m.* **1.** crushing defeat, utter defeat, rout; knock-out blow. **2.** (*coll.*) havoc, devastation; **карти́на ~а** scene of devastation; **в кварти́ре был по́лный р.** there was complete chaos in the flat.
разгром|и́ть, лю́, и́шь *pf. of* **громи́ть**
разгружа́|ть(ся), ю(сь) *impf. of* **разгрузи́ть(ся)**
разгру|зи́ть, жу́, ~зи́шь *pf.* (*of* **~жа́ть**) **1.** to unload. **2.** (**от**; *fig., coll.*) to relieve (of); **р. от доба́вочных обя́занностей** to relieve of extra commitments.
разгру|зи́ться, жу́сь, ~зи́шься *pf.* (*of* **~жа́ться**) **1.** to unload. **2.** (**от**; *fig., coll.*) to be relieved (of).
разгру́зк|а, и *f.* **1.** unloading. **2.** (*fig., coll.*) relieving, affording relief.
разгрузн|о́й *adj.*: **~о́е су́дно** (*naut.*) lighter.
разгру́зочн|ый *adj.* unloading; **~ые рабо́ты** unloading operations; **~ое су́дно** (*naut.*) lighter.
разгруппир|ова́ть, у́ю *pf.* (*of* **~о́вывать**) to divide into groups, group.
разгруппиро́выва|ть, ю *impf. of* **разгруппирова́ть**
разгрыза́|ть, ю *impf. of* **разгры́зть**
разгры́з|ть, у́, ёшь, *past* **~, ~ла** *pf.* (*of* **~а́ть**) to crack (*with one's teeth*); **р. оре́х** to crack a nut.
разгу́л, а *m.* **1.** revelry, debauch. **2.** (+*g.*; *fig.*) raging (of); wild outburst (of); **р. антисемити́зма** a wild outburst of anti-semitism.
разгу́лива|ть, ю *impf.* **1.** to stroll about, walk about. **2.** *impf. of* **разгуля́ть**
разгу́лива|ться, юсь *impf. of* **разгуля́ться**
разгу́ль|е, я *nt.* (*coll.*) merry-making.
разгу́л|ьный (~ен, ~ьна) *adj.* (*coll.*) loose, wild, rakish; **вести́ ~ьную жизнь** to lead a wild life.
разгул|я́ть, я́ю *pf.* (*of* **~ивать**) (*coll.*) **1.** to amuse so as to keep awake. **2.** to dispel; **р. чью-н. хандру́** to dispel s.o.'s gloom.
разгул|я́ться, я́юсь *pf.* (*of* **~иваться**) (*coll.*) **1.** to spread o.s.; to have free scope. **2.** (*of children*) to wake up, stop feeling sleepy. **3.** (*of weather*) to clear up, improve; **день ~я́лся** it has turned out a fine day.
разда|ва́ть(ся), ю́(сь), ёшь(ся) *impf. of* **разда́ть(ся)**
раздав|и́ть, лю́, ~ишь *pf.* (*of* **~ливать**) **1.** to crush; to squash. **2.** (*fig.*) to crush, overwhelm. **3.** (*coll.*) to down, sink (*alcoholic beverages*).

разда́влива|ть, ю *impf. of* **раздави́ть**
разда́рива|ть, ю *impf. of* **раздари́ть**
раздар|и́ть, ю́, ~ишь *pf.* (*of* **~ивать**) (+*d.*) to give away (to), make a present of.
разда́точн|ый *adj.* distributing, distribution; **~ая ве́домость** list of those due to receive (*gifts, money, etc.*); **р. пункт** distribution centre.
разда́тчик, а *m.* distributor, dispenser.
разда́|ть[1]**, м, шь, ст, ди́м, ди́те, ду́т,** *past* **ро́здал, ~ла́, ро́здало** *pf.* (*of* **~ва́ть**) to distribute, give out, serve out, dispense; **р. ми́лостыню** to dispense charity; **р. кни́ги** to give out books.
разда́|ть[2]**, м, шь, ст, ди́м, ди́те, ду́т,** *past* **ро́здал, ~ла́, ро́здало** *pf.* (*of* **~ва́ть**) (*coll.*) to stretch (*footwear*); to enlarge, widen, let out (*clothing*).
разда́|ться[1]**, мся, шься, стся, ди́мся, ди́тесь, ду́тся,** *past* **~лся, ~ла́сь, ~ло́сь** *pf.* (*of* **~ва́ться**) to be heard; to resound; to ring (out); **~лся вы́стрел** a shot rang out; **~лся стук (в дверь)** a knock at the door was heard.
разда́|ться[2]**, мся, шься, стся, ди́мся, ди́тесь, ду́тся,** *past* **~лся, ~ла́сь, ~ло́сь** *pf.* (*of* **~ва́ться**) (*coll.*) **1.** to make way. **2.** to stretch, expand. **3.** to put on weight.
разда́ч|а, и *f.* distribution.
раздва́ива|ть(ся), ю(сь) *impf. of* **раздвои́ть(ся)**
раздвига́|ть(ся), ю(сь) *impf. of* **раздви́нуть(ся)**
раздвижно́й *adj.* expanding; sliding; **р. за́навес** (*theatr.*) draw curtain; **р. стол** leaf table, expanding table.
раздви́|нуть, ну, нешь *pf.* (*of* **~га́ть**) to move apart, slide apart; **р. занаве́ски** to draw back the curtains; **р. стол** to extend a table, insert a leaf into a table.
раздви́|нуться, нется *pf.* (*of* **~га́ться**) to move apart, slide apart; **за́навес ~нулся** the curtain was drawn back; (*in theatre*) the curtain rose; **толпа́ ~нулась** the crowd made way.
раздвое́ни|е, я *nt.* division into two, bifurcation; **р. ли́чности** (*med.*) split personality.
раздво́|енный (*and* **раздвоённый**) *p.p.p. of* **~и́ть** *and adj.* **1.** forked; bifurcated; **~енное копы́то** cloven hoof; **~енное созна́ние** split mind. **2.** (*bot.*) dichotomous, furcate.
раздво|и́ть, ю́, и́шь *pf.* (*of* **раздва́ивать**) to divide into two; to bisect.
раздво|и́ться, ю́сь, и́шься *pf.* (*of* **раздва́иваться**) to bifurcate, fork, split, become double.
раздева́лк|а, и *f.* (*coll.*) cloak-room.
раздева́льный *adj.* (*for*) undressing.
раздева́л|ьня, ьни, *g. pl.* **~ен** *f.* = **~ка**
раздева́ни|е, я *nt.* undressing.
раздева́|ть(ся), ю(сь) *impf. of* **разде́ть(ся)**
разде́л, а *m.* **1.** division; partition; allotment. **2.** section, part (*of book, etc.*).
разде́л|ать, аю *pf.* (*of* **~ывать**) to dress, prepare; **р. гря́дки** to prepare (flower-)beds (*for sowing*); **р. под дуб** to grain in imitation of oak; **р. кого́-н. под оре́х** (*coll.*) to give it s.o. hot.
разде́л|аться, аюсь *pf.* (*of* **~ываться**) (**с**+*i.*) **1.** to be through (with); to settle (accounts) (with); **р. с долга́ми** to pay off debts. **2.** (*fig.*) to settle accounts (with), get even (with).
разделе́ни|е, я *nt.* division; **р. труда́** division of labour.
раздели́м|ый (~, ~а) *adj.* divisible.
раздели́тельн|ый *adj.* **1.** dividing, separating; **~ая черта́** dividing line. **2.** (*phil., gram.*) disjunctive; (*gram.*) distributive; **р. сою́з** disjunctive conjunction; **~ое местоиме́ние** distributive pronoun.
раздел|и́ть, ю́, ~ишь *pf.* (*of* **~я́ть**) **1.** to divide. **2.** to separate, part. **3.** to share.
раздел|и́ться, ю́сь, ~ишься *pf.* (*of* **~я́ться**) **1.** (**на**+*a.*) to divide (into); to be divided; **нам придётся р. на две гру́ппы** we shall have to divide into two groups; **мне́ния ~и́лись** opinions were divided. **2.** to separate, part company. **3.** *pf. only* (**на**+*a.*) to be divisible (by); **число́ со́рок де́вять ~ится на семь** forty-nine is divisible by seven.
разде́льн|ый *adj.* **1.** separate; **~ое обуче́ние** separate education for boys and girls. **2.** (*of pronunciation*) clear, distinct.

раздел|я́ть, я́ю *impf. of* **~и́ть; р. чьи-н. взгля́ды** to share s.o.'s views.
раздел|я́ться, я́юсь *impf. of* **~и́ться**
раздёрг|ать, аю *pf.* (*of* **~ивать**) (*coll.*) to tear up.
раздёргива|ть, ю *impf. of* **раздёргать** *and* **раздёрнуть**
раздёр|нуть, ну, нешь *pf.* (*of* **~гивать**) to draw apart, pull apart; **р. занаве́ски** to draw back the curtains.
разде́т|ый *p.p.p. of* **~ь** *and adj.* **1.** unclothed. **2.** poorly clothed, ill-clad.
разде́|ть, ну, нешь *pf.* (*of* **~ва́ть**) to undress.
разде́|ться, нусь, нешься *pf.* (*of* **~ва́ться**) to undress, strip; to take off one's things.
раздира́|ть, ю *impf.* **1.** *impf. of* **разодра́ть. 2.** *impf. only* (*fig.*) to rend, tear, lacerate, harrow.
раздира́|ться, ю, ет(ся) *impf. of* **разодра́ться**
раздира́|ющий *pres. part. act. of* **~ть** *and adj.*; **р. (ду́шу)** heart-rending, heart-breaking, harrowing.
раздобре́|ть, ю *pf. of* **добре́ть**[2]
раздо́бр|иться, юсь, ишься *pf.* (*coll.*) to become generous, become kind.
раздобыва́|ть, ю *impf. of* **раздобы́ть**
раздо|бы́ть, бу́ду, бу́дешь, *past* **~бы́л** *pf.* (*of* **~быва́ть**) (*coll.*) get, procure, come by, get hold of; **р. де́нег** to raise money, come by some money.
раздо́ль|е, я *nt.* **1.** expanse. **2.** (*fig.*) freedom, liberty; **им р.** they are quite free to do as they please.
раздо́л|ьный (~ен, ~ьна) *adj.* free.
раздо́р, а *m.* discord, dissension; **я́блоко ~а** apple of discord, bone of contention; **се́ять р.** to breed strife.
раздоса́д|овать, ую *pf.* to vex.
раздраж|а́ть(ся), а́ю(сь) *impf. of* **~и́ть(ся)**
раздража́|ющий *pres. part. act. of* **~ть** *and adj.* irritating, annoying, exasperating; *as n.* **~ющее, ~ющего** *nt.* irritant.
раздраже́ни|е, я *nt.* irritation.
раздражи́тел|ь, я *m.* (*med.*) irritant.
раздражи́тельност|ь, и *f.* irritability; shortness of temper.
раздражи́тел|ьный (~ен, ~ьна) *adj.* irritable; short of temper, short-tempered.
раздраж|и́ть, у́, и́шь *pf.* (*of* **~а́ть**) **1.** to irritate, annoy, exasperate, put out. **2.** (*med.*) to irritate.
раздраж|и́ться, у́сь, и́шься *pf.* (*of* **~а́ться**) **1.** to get irritated, get annoyed. **2.** (*med.*) to become inflamed.
раздразн|и́ть, ю́, ~ишь *pf.* **1.** to tease. **2.** to stimulate; **р. чей-н. аппети́т** to whet s.o.'s appetite.
раздроб|и́ть, лю́, и́шь *pf.* **1.** *pf. of* **дроби́ть. 2.** (*impf.* **~ля́ть**) (**в**+*a.*; *math.*) to turn (into), reduce (to); **р. гра́ммы в сантигра́ммы** to turn grams into centigrams.
раздроб|и́ться, и́тся *pf. of* **дроби́ться**
раздробле́ни|е, я *nt.* **1.** breaking, smashing to pieces. **2.** (*math.*) reduction.
раздро́б|ленный (*and* **раздроблённый**) *p.p.p. of* **~и́ть** *and adj.* **1.** (*of a bone*) shattered. **2.** (*fig.*) small-scale; fragmented.
раздробля́|ть, ю *impf. of* **раздроби́ть**
раздруж|и́ться, у́сь, и́шься *pf.* (*coll.*) to break it off (with), to break off friendly relations (with).
раздува́льный *adj.*: **р. мех** (*tech.*) bellows.
раздува́|ть(ся), ю(сь) *impf. of* **разду́ть(ся)**
разду́м|ать, аю *pf.* (*of* **~ывать**) to change one's mind; (+*inf.*) to decide not (to); **я ~ал подава́ть заявле́ние на э́то ме́сто** I decided not to apply for that job; I changed my mind about applying for that job.
разду́м|аться, аюсь *pf.* (**о**+*p.*; *coll.*) to be absorbed in thinking (about).
разду́мыва|ть, ю *impf.* **1.** *impf. of* **разду́мать. 2.** *impf. only* (**о**+*p.*) to ponder (on, over), consider; **я давно́ ~ю, купи́ть ли маши́ну и́ли нет** for a long time I have been considering whether or not to buy a car; **не ~я** without a moment's thought.
разду́мь|е, я *nt.* **1.** meditation; thought, thoughtful mood; **в глубо́ком р.** deep in thought. **2.** hesitation; **меня́ взяло́ р.** I can't make up my mind.
разду́т|ый *p.p.p. of* **~ь** *and adj.* (*fig., coll.*) exaggerated; inflated; **~ые шта́ты** inflated staffs.
разду́|ть, ю, ешь *pf.* (*of* **~ва́ть**) **1.** to blow; to fan; **р. пла́мя** (*fig.*) to fan the flames. **2.** to blow (out); **р. щёки** to blow out one's cheeks; (*impers.*): **у него́ ~ло щёку** his cheek is swollen. **3.** (*fig., coll.*) to exaggerate; to inflate, swell; **р. поте́ри** to exaggerate losses. **4.** to blow about; (*impers.*): **~ло бума́ги по́ полу** the papers had blown all over the floor.
разду́|ться, юсь, ешься *pf.* (*of* **~ва́ться**) to swell.
раздуш|и́ть, у́, ~ишь *pf.* (*coll.*) to drench in perfume.
разева́|ть, ю *impf. of* **рази́нуть**
разжа́лоб|ить, лю, ишь *pf.* to move (to pity).
разжа́лоб|иться, люсь, ишься *pf.* to be moved to pity.
разжа́ловани|е, я *nt.* demotion, degrading.
разжа́лова|нный *p.p.p. of* **~ть**; *as n.* **р., ~нного** *m.* (*mil.*) demoted, degraded officer.
разжа́л|овать, ую *pf.* (*mil.*) to demote, degrade; **р. в солда́ты** to reduce to the ranks.
раз|жа́ть, ожму́, ожмёшь *pf.* (*of* **~жима́ть**) to unclasp; to release, unfasten, undo; **р. кула́к** to unclench one's fist; **р. ру́ки** to unclasp one's hands.
раз|жа́ться, ожмётся *pf.* (*of* **~жима́ться**) to come loose; to relax.
разж|ева́ть, ую́, уёшь *pf.* (*of* **~ёвывать**) **1.** to chew, masticate; (*fig., coll.*) to chew over. **2.** (*fig.*) to spell out.
разжёвыва|ть, ю *impf. of* **разжева́ть**
раз|же́чь, ожгу́, ожжёшь, ожгу́т, *past* **~жёг, ~ожгла́** *pf.* (*of* **~жига́ть**) **1.** to kindle. **2.** (*fig.*) to kindle, rouse, stir up; **р. стра́сти** to arouse passion.
разжи́в|а, ы *f.* (*coll.*) gain, profit.
разжива́|ться, юсь *impf. of* **разжи́ться**
разжига́ни|е, я *nt.* kindling (*also fig.*).
разжига́|ть, ю *impf. of* **разже́чь**
разжи|ди́ть, жу́, ди́шь *pf.* (*of* **~жа́ть**) to dilute, thin.
разжижа́|ть, ю *impf. of* **разжиди́ть**
разжиже́ни|е, я *nt.* dilution, thinning; rarefaction.
разжима́|ть(ся), ет(ся) *impf. of* **разжа́ть(ся)**
разжире́|ть, ю *pf. of* **жире́ть**
разж|и́ться, иву́сь, ивёшься, *past* **~и́лся, ~ила́сь** *pf.* (*of* **~ива́ться**) (*coll.*) **1.** to get rich, make a pile. **2.** (+*i.*) to come by, get hold of.
разаво́д, а *m.*: **на р.** (*coll.*) for breeding.
раззадо́рива|ть(ся), ю(сь) *impf. of* **раззадо́рить(ся)**
раззадо́р|ить, ю, ишь *pf.* (*of* **~ивать**) (*coll.*) to stir up, excite.
раззадо́р|иться, юсь, ишься *pf.* (*of* **~иваться**) (*coll.*) to get excited, get worked up.
раззва́нива|ть, ю *impf. of* **раззвони́ть**
раззвон|и́ть, ю́, и́шь *pf.* (*of* **раззва́нивать**) (**о**+*p.*; *coll.*) to trumpet, proclaim (from the housetops).
раззнако́м|ить, лю, ишь *pf.* to alienate.
раззнако́м|иться, люсь, ишься *pf.* (**с**+*i.*) to break off one's acquaintance (with), break (with).
раззуд|е́ться, и́тся *pf.* (*coll.*) to begin to itch (*also fig.*).
раззя́в|а, ы *c.g.* = **рази́ня**
рази́н|уть, у, ешь *pf.* (*of* **разева́ть**) (*coll.*) to open wide (*the mouth*); to gape; **слу́шать, ~ув рот** to listen open-mouthed.
рази́н|я, и *c.g.* (*coll.*) scatter-brain.
рази́тел|ьный (~ен, ~ьна) *adj.* striking; **р. приме́р** striking example.
ра|зи́ть[1]**, жу́, зи́шь** *impf.* to strike, smite, hit.
раз|и́ть[2]**, и́т** *impf.* (*impers.*+*i.*; *coll.*) to reek (of), stink (of); **из ко́мнаты ~и́ло чесноко́м** the room reeked of garlic.
разлага́|ть(ся), ю(сь) *impf. of* **разложи́ть(ся)**
разла́д, а *m.* **1.** disorder. **2.** discord, dissension.
разла́|дить, жу, дишь *pf.* (*of* **~живать**) to derange; (*coll.*) to mess up.
разла́|диться, дится *pf.* (*of* **~живаться**) to get out of order; (*coll.*) to go wrong.
разла́ком|ить, лю, ишь *pf.* (+*i.*; *coll.*) to give s.o. a taste (for).
разла́ком|иться, люсь, ишься *pf.* (+*i.*; *coll.*) to get a taste (for).
разла́мыва|ть(ся), ю, ет(ся) *impf. of* **разлома́ть(ся)** *and* **разломи́ть(ся)**
разлёжива|ться, юсь *impf.* (*coll., pej.*) to lie about.

разлез|а́ться, а́ется *impf. of* **∸ться**
разле́з|ться, ется, *past* **~ся, ~лась** *pf.* (*of* **~а́ться**) (*coll.*) to come to pieces; to come apart at the seams; to fall apart.
разле́нива|ться, юсь *impf. of* **разлени́ться**
разлен|и́ться, ю́сь, ∸ишься *pf.* (*of* **∸иваться**) (*coll.*) to become sunk in sloth.
разлеп|и́ть, лю́, ∸ишь *pf.* (*of* **~ля́ть**) to unstick.
разлеп|и́ться, ∸ится *pf.* (*of* **~ля́ться**) to come unstuck.
разлепля́|ть(ся), ю(сь), ет(ся) *impf. of* **разлепи́ть(ся)**
разлёт, а *m.* (*of birds*) flying away, departure.
разлет|а́ться, а́юсь *impf. of* **~е́ться**
разле|те́ться, чу́сь, ти́шься *pf.* (*of* **~та́ться**) **1.** to fly away; to scatter (*in the air*). **2.** (*coll.*) to smash, shatter; **ста́туя ~те́лась вдре́безги** the statue smashed to smithereens. **3.** (*fig., coll.*) to vanish, be shattered; **её мечта́ ~те́лась** her dream was shattered; **все на́ши наде́жды ~те́лись** all our hopes were dashed. **4.** (*coll.*) to rush.
разл|е́чься, я́гусь, я́жешься, *past* **~ёгся, ~егла́сь** *pf.* (*coll.*) to sprawl; to stretch o.s. out.
разли́в, а *m.* **1.** bottling. **2.** flood; overflow.
разлива́ни|е, я *nt.* pouring out.
разлива́нн|ый *adj. only in phr.* **~ое мо́ре** (*joc.*) oceans, lashings (*usu. of alcoholic beverages*).
разлива́тельн|ый *adj.*: **~ая ло́жка** ladle.
разлива́|ть(ся), ю, ет(ся) *impf. of* **разли́ть(ся)**
разли́вк|а, и *f.* **1.** bottling. **2.** (*tech.*) teeming, casting.
разливн|о́й *adj.* on tap, on draught; **~о́е вино́** wine from the wood.
разли́вочн|ый *adj.* (*tech.*) teeming, casting; **~ая маши́на** casting machine, liquid filling machine.
разлин|ова́ть, у́ю *pf.* (*of* **~о́вывать**) to rule (*paper, etc.*).
разлино́выва|ть, ю *impf. of* **разлинова́ть**
разли́ти|е, я *nt.* overflow; **р. же́лчи** (*med.*) bilious attack.
раз|ли́ть, олью́, ольёшь, *past* **~ли́л, ~лила́, ~ли́ло** *pf.* (*of* **~лива́ть**) **1.** to pour out; **р. по буты́лкам** to bottle; **р. чай** to pour out tea. **2.** to spill; **р. водо́й** to pour water (over), douse, drench; **их водо́й не ~ольёшь** (*coll.*) they are thick as thieves. **3.** (*fig.*) to pour out, spread, broadcast.
раз|ли́ться, ольётся, *past* **~ли́лся, ~лила́сь** *pf.* (*of* **~лива́ться**) **1.** to spill; **суп ~ли́лся по ска́терти** the soup has spilled over the table-cloth. **2.** to overflow; **река́ ~лила́сь** the river has overflowed, has burst its banks. **3.** (*med.*): **у него́ ~лила́сь жёлчь** he had a bilious attack. **4.** (*fig.*) to spread; **по её лицу́ ~лила́сь улы́бка** a smile spread across her face.
различ|а́ть, а́ю *impf. of* **~и́ть**
различа́|ться, юсь *impf.* to differ.
разли́чи|е, я *nt.* distinction; difference; **де́лать р. (ме́жду)** to make distinctions (between); **без ~я** without distinction; **зна́ки ~я** (*mil.*) badges of rank.
различи́тельный *adj.* distinctive; **р. при́знак** distinctive, distinguishing feature.
различ|и́ть, у́, и́шь *pf.* (*of* **~а́ть**) **1.** to distinguish; to tell the difference (between). **2.** to discern, make out.
разли́ч|ный (~ен, ~на) *adj.* **1.** different; **у нас бы́ли ~ные мне́ния** our opinions differed. **2.** various, diverse; **~ные лю́ди** all manner of people; **по ~ным соображе́ниям** for various reasons.
разложе́ни|е, я *nt.* **1.** breaking down; (*chem.*) decomposition; (*math.*) expansion; (*phys.*) resolution. **2.** decomposition, decay; putrefaction. **3.** (*fig.*) demoralization; disintegration.
разложи́|вшийся *p.p. act. of* **~ться** *and adj.* **1.** decomposed, decayed. **2.** (*fig.*) demoralized.
разлож|и́ть¹, у́, ∸ишь *pf.* (*of* **раскла́дывать**) **1.** to put away; **р. свои́ ве́щи по я́щикам** to put away one's things in their respective drawers. **2.** to lay out, to spread (out); to (lay and) make (*a fire*); **р. ого́нь** to make a fire; **р. ска́терть** to spread a table-cloth; **р. складну́ю крова́ть** to put up a camp bed. **3.** to distribute, apportion; **р. при́быль** to distribute, share out profits.
разлож|и́ть², у́, ∸ишь *pf.* (*of* **разлага́ть**) **1.** to break down; (*chem.*) to decompose; (*math.*) to expand; (*phys.*) to resolve; **р. вещество́ на составны́е ча́сти** to break a substance down into its component parts; **р. число́ на мно́жители** to factorize a number. **2.** (*fig.*) to break down, demoralize.
разлож|и́ться¹, у́сь, ∸ишься *pf.* (*of* **раскла́дываться**) (*coll.*) to arrange one's things, put one's things out.
разлож|и́ться², у́сь, ∸ишься *pf.* (*of* **разлага́ться**) **1.** (*chem.*) to decompose; (*math.*) to expand. **2.** to decompose, rot, decay; **труп уже́ ~и́лся** the body has already decomposed. **3.** (*fig.*) to become demoralized; to disintegrate, crack up, go to pieces.
разло́м, а *m.* **1.** breaking. **2.** break.
разлома́|ть, ю *pf.* (*of* **разла́мывать**) to break (in pieces); **р. дом** to pull down a house.
разлома́|ться, ется *pf.* (*of* **разла́мываться**) to break (in pieces); to break up.
разлом|и́ть, лю́, ∸ишь *pf.* (*of* **разла́мывать**) **1.** to break (in pieces). **2.** (*impers.; coll.*): **меня́ всего́ ~и́ло** every bone in my body aches.
разлом|и́ться, ∸иться *pf.* (*of* **разла́мываться**) to break in pieces.
разлу́к|а, и *f.* **1.** separation; **жить в ~е (с+*i.*)** to live apart (from), be separated (from). **2.** parting; **час ~и** hour of parting.
разлуч|а́ть(ся), а́ю(сь) *impf. of* **~и́ть(ся)**
разлуч|и́ть, у́, и́шь *pf.* (*of* **~а́ть**) (+*a.* **с**+*i.*) to separate (from), part (from), sever (from).
разлуч|и́ться, у́сь, и́шься *pf.* (*of* **~а́ться**) (**с**+*i.*) to separate, part (from).
разлюб|и́ть, лю́, ∸ишь *pf.* to cease to love, stop loving; to cease to like, like no longer.
размагни́|тить, чу, тишь *pf.* (*of* **~чивать**) (*tech.*) to demagnetize.
размагни́|титься, чусь, тишься *pf.* (*of* **~чиваться**) **1.** (*tech.*) to become demagnetized. **2.** (*fig., coll.*) to lose one's grip; to become unbalanced.
размагни́чива|ть(ся), ю(сь) *impf. of* **размагни́тить(ся)**
разма́|зать, жу, жешь *pf.* (*of* **~зывать**) **1.** to spread, smear; **р. варе́нье по всему́ лицу́** to get jam all over one's face. **2.** (*coll.*) to pad out, amplify (*a narration*).
разма́|заться, жется *pf.* (*of* **~зываться**) to spread; to get smeared.
размазн|я́, и́, *g. pl.* **~е́й** *f. and c.g.* (*coll.*) **1.** *f.* thin gruel, thin porridge; (*fig.*) slush. **2.** *c.g.* (*fig.*) ninny, wishy-washy pers.
разма́зыва|ть(ся), ю, ет(ся) *impf. of* **разма́зать(ся)**
разма́ива|ть(ся), ю(сь) *impf. of* **размая́ть(ся)**
размал|ева́ть, ю́ю, ю́ешь *pf.* (*of* **~ёвывать**) (*coll.*) to daub.
размалёвыва|ть, ю *impf. of* **размалева́ть**
разма́лыва|ть, ю *impf. of* **размоло́ть**
разма́рива|ть(ся), ю(сь) *impf. of* **размори́ть(ся)**
разма́тыва|ть(ся), ю, ет(ся) *impf. of* **размота́ть(ся)**
разма́х, а *m.* **1.** sweep; **со всего́ ~у** with all one's might; **уда́рить с ~у** to strike with all one's might. **2.** span; **р. кры́льев** (*aeron.*) wing-span, wing-spread. **3.** (*tech.*) swing, amplitude (*of pendulum*). **4.** (*fig*) scope, range, sweep, scale; **широ́кий р.** wide range, grand scale; **у них широ́кий р. жи́зни** they live in style, they do things in a big way.
разма́хива|ть, ю *impf.* (+*i.*) to swing; to brandish; **р. рука́ми** to gesticulate.
разма́хива|ться, юсь *impf. of* **размахну́ться**
размах|ну́ться, ну́сь, нёшься *pf.* (*of* **∸иваться**) **1.** to swing one's arm (*to strike or as if to strike*). **2.** (*fig., coll.*) to do things in a big way; (*pej.*) to bite off more than one can chew.
разма́чива|ть, ю *impf. of* **размочи́ть**
разма́шисто *adv.* sweepingly, boldly; **писа́ть р.** to write a bold hand; **р. грести́** to row with vigorous strokes.
разма́шист|ый (~, ~а) *adj.* sweeping; **р. жест** sweeping gesture; **р. по́черк** bold hand; **р. стиль** (*fig.*) happy-go-lucky style.
разма́|ять, ю, ешь *pf.* (*of* **~ивать**) (*coll.*) to keep awake, prevent from sleeping.
разма́|яться, юсь, ешься *pf.* (*of* **~иваться**) (*coll.*) to become wakeful, cease to feel sleepy.
размежева́ни|е, я *nt.* demarcation, delimitation.

размеж|ева́ть, у́ю, у́ешь *pf.* (*of* **~ёвывать**) to divide out, delimit (*also fig.*); **р. сфе́ры влия́ния** to delimit spheres of influence.

размеж|ева́ться, у́юсь, у́ешься *pf.* (*of* **~ёвываться**) **1.** to fix the boundaries; (*fig.*) to delimit the functions, spheres of action. **2.** (*fig.*) to break off relations.

размежёвыва|ть(ся), ю(сь) *impf. of* **размежева́ть(ся)**

размельч|а́ть, а́ю *impf. of* **~и́ть**

размельч|и́ть, у́, и́шь *pf.* (*of* **~а́ть**) to divide into particles; to pulverize.

разме́н, а *m.* exchange; **р. де́нег** changing of money.

разме́нива|ть(ся), ю(сь) *impf. of* **разменя́ть(ся)**

разме́нн|ый *adj.*: **~ая моне́та** small change.

размен|я́ть, я́ю *pf.* (*of* **~ивать**) to change; **р. сторублёвку** to change a hundred-rouble note.

размен|я́ться, я́юсь *pf.* (*of* **~иваться**) (*coll.*) **1.** (*+i.*) to exchange; **р. пе́шками** (*in chess*) to exchange pawns. **2.** (*fig.*) to dissipate one's talents.

разме́р, а *m.* **1.** dimensions; **воро́нка ~ом в де́сять квадра́тных ме́тров** a crater measuring ten square metres. **2.** size; (*pl.*) measurements; **како́й ваш р.?** what size do you take? **3.** rate, amount; **получа́ть зарпла́ту в ~е десяти́ рубле́й в день** to be paid at the rate of ten roubles per day. **4.** scale, extent; (*pl.*) proportions; **в широ́ких ~ах** on a large scale; **увели́читься до огро́мных ~ов** to assume enormous proportions. **5.** metre (*of verse*); (*mus.*) measure.

разме́р|енный *p.p.p. of* **~ить** *and adj.* measured; **~енная похо́дка** measured tread.

разме́р|ить, ю, ишь *pf.* (*of* **~я́ть**) to measure off; **р. свои́ си́лы** (*fig.*) to measure one's strength.

размер|я́ть, я́ю *impf. of* **~ить**

разме|си́ть, шу́, ~сишь *pf.* (*of* **~шивать**) to knead.

разме|сти́, ту́, тёшь, *past* **~л, ~ла́** *pf.* (*of* **~та́ть**[1]) **1.** to sweep clean; **р. доро́жку** to clear a path. **2.** to shovel, sweep away.

разме|сти́ть, щу́, сти́шь *pf.* (*of* **~ща́ть**) **1.** to place, accommodate; to stow; **р. делега́тов по гости́ницам** to accommodate the delegates in hotels; **р. войска́ по кварти́рам** to quarter troops. **2.** to distribute; **р. заём** to float a loan.

разме|сти́ться, щу́сь, сти́шься *pf.* (*of* **~ща́ться**) **1.** to take one's seat. **2.** *pass. of* **~сти́ть**

размета́|ть[1]**, ю** *impf. of* **размести́**

разме|та́ть[2]**, чу́, ~чешь** *pf.* (*of* **~тывать**) to scatter, disperse.

разме|та́ться, чу́сь, ~чешься *pf.* **1.** (*coll.*) to toss (*in sleep or delirium*). **2.** to sprawl.

разме́|тить, чу, тишь *pf.* (*of* **~ча́ть**) to mark; **р. курси́вный шрифт** to mark italics.

разме́точн|ый *adj.* (*tech.*): **~ая плита́** layout block; **~о-сверли́льный стано́к** jig borer.

разме́тчик, а *m.* marker.

размётыва|ть, ю *impf. of* **размета́ть**[2]

размеча́|ть, ю *impf. of* **разме́тить**

размеш|а́ть, а́ю *pf.* (*of* **~ивать**) to stir.

разме́шива|ть, ю *impf. of* **размеси́ть** *and* **размеша́ть**

размеща́|ть(ся), ю(сь) *impf. of* **размести́ть(ся)**

размеще́ни|е, я *nt.* **1.** placing, accommodation; distribution, disposal, allocation; siting; **р. гру́за** stowage; **р. войск по кварти́рам** quartering, billeting of troops; **р. вооружённых сил** stationing of armed forces; **р. промы́шленности** location of industry. **2.** (*fin.*) placing, investment; **р. за́йма** floating a loan.

размина́|ть(ся), ю(сь) *impf. of* **размя́ть(ся)**

размини́ровани|е, я *nt.* (*mil.*) mine clearing.

размини́р|овать, ую *pf.* to clear of mines.

разми́нк|а, и *f.* (*sport*) limbering-up; knock-up, knocking-up; warm-up.

размин|у́ться, у́сь, ёшься *pf.* (*coll.*) **1.** (**с**+*i.*) to pass (*without meeting*); to miss; **когда́ я вошёл, никого́ не́ было; мы, должно́ быть, ~у́лись с ним на доро́ге** when I went in there was no one there; we must have passed one another on the road. **2.** (*of letters*) to cross. **3.** to (be able to) pass; **на э́том уча́стке доро́ги маши́нам нельзя́ р.** it is impossible for cars to pass on this part of the road.

размнож|а́ть(ся), а́ю, ает(ся) *impf. of* **~ить(ся)**

размноже́ни|е, я *nt.* **1.** reproduction in quantity; duplicating; mimeographing. **2.** (*biol.*) reproduction, propagation.

размно́ж|ить, у, ишь *pf.* (*of* **~а́ть**) **1.** to multiply (copies of), manifold, duplicate; to mimeograph. **2.** to breed, rear.

размно́ж|иться, ится *pf.* (*of* **~а́ться**) **1.** (*biol.*) to propagate itself; to breed; to spawn. **2.** *pass. of* **~ить**

размозж|и́ть, у́, и́шь *pf.* to smash.

размок|а́ть, а́ет *impf. of* **~нуть**

размо́к|нуть, нет, *past* **~, ~ла** *pf.* (*of* **~а́ть**) to get soaked; to get sodden.

размо́л, а *m.* **1.** grinding. **2.** quality (*of ground grain*); **мука́ кру́пного, ме́лкого ~а** coarse, coarse-ground flour; fine, finely ground flour.

размо́лвк|а, и *f.* tiff, disagreement.

раз|моло́ть, мелю́, ме́лешь *pf.* (*of* **разма́лывать**) to grind.

размора́жива|ть(ся), ю(сь) *impf. of* **разморо́зить(ся)**

размор|и́ть, и́т *pf.* (*of* **разма́ривать**) (*coll.*) to exhaust; (*impers.*): **её ~и́ло на со́лнце** the sun was too much for her.

размор|и́ться, ю́сь, и́шься *pf.* (*of* **разма́риваться**) (*coll.*) to be worn out.

разморо́|зить, жу, зишь *pf.* (*of* **размора́живать**) to unfreeze, defreeze; to defrost.

разморо́|зиться, жусь, зишься *pf.* (*of* **размора́живаться**) to become unfrozen, de-frozen; to become defrosted.

размота́|ть, ю *pf.* (*of* **разма́тывать**) to unwind, uncoil, unreel.

размота́|ться, ется *pf.* (*of* **разма́тываться**) to unwind, uncoil, unreel; to come unwound.

размоч|и́ть, у́, ~ишь *pf.* (*of* **разма́чивать**) to soak, steep.

размусо́лива|ть, ю *impf. of* **размусо́лить**

размусо́л|ить, ю, ишь *pf.* (*of* **~ивать**) (*coll.*) **1.** to slobber all over **2.** (*fig.*) to relate in a drivelling fashion.

размы́в, а *m.* wash-out, erosion.

размыва́|ть, ю *impf. of* **размы́ть**

размыка́ни|е, я *nt.* (*elec.*) breaking, break, disconnection.

размы́ка|ть, ю *pf.* (*coll.*) to shake off; **р. го́ре** (*poet.*) to shake off one's grief.

размыка́|ть, ю *impf. of* **разомкну́ть**

размы́сл|ить, ю, ишь *pf.* (*of* **размышля́ть**) (**о**+*p.*) to reflect (on, upon), meditate (on, upon), ponder (over), muse (on, upon), turn over in one's mind.

разм|ы́ть, о́ю, о́ешь *pf.* (*of* **~ыва́ть**) to wash away, (*geol.*) to erode.

размышле́ни|е, я *nt.* reflection, meditation, thought; **тяжёлые ~я** brooding; **по зре́лом ~и** on second thoughts, on reflection; **быть погружённым в ~я** to be lost in thought.

размышля́|ть, ю *impf. of* **размы́слить**

размягч|а́ть(ся), а́ю(сь) *impf. of* **~и́ть(ся)**

размягче́ни|е, я *nt.* softening; **р. мо́зга** (*med.*) softening of the brain.

размягч|и́ть, у́, и́шь *pf.* (*of* **~а́ть**) to soften.

размягч|и́ться, у́сь, и́шься *pf.* (*of* **~а́ться**) to soften, grow soft.

размя́к|нуть, ну, нешь, *past* **~, ~ла** *pf. of* **мя́кнуть**

раз|мя́ть, омну́, омнёшь *pf.* (*of* **мять** *and* **~мина́ть**) **1.** to knead; to mash (*potatoes, etc.*). **2.: р. но́ги** (*coll.*) to stretch one's legs.

раз|мя́ться, омну́сь, омнёшься *pf.* (*of* **~мина́ться**) **1.** to grow soft (*as result of kneading*). **2.** (*coll.*) to stretch one's legs; (*sport*) to limber up, loosen up.

разна́шива|ть(ся), ю, ет(ся) *impf. of* **разноси́ть(ся)**[1]

разне́жива|ть(ся), ю(сь) *impf. of* **разне́жить(ся)**

разне́ж|ить, у, ишь *pf.* (*of* **~ивать**) (*coll.*) to appeal to the tender feelings (of).

разне́ж|иться, усь, ишься *pf.* (*of* **~иваться**) (*coll., pej.*) to grow soft, become too soft.

разнемо́|чься, гу́сь, ~жешься, ~гутся, *past* **~гся, ~гла́сь** *pf.* (*coll.*) to become ill, be taken ill.

разнес|ти́, у́, ёшь, *past* **~, ~ла́** *pf.* (*of* **разноси́ть**[2]) **1.** to carry, convey; to take round; **р. газе́ты** to deliver newspapers; **р. слух** to spread a rumour. **2.** to enter, note

down; **р. цита́ты на ка́рточки** to note down quotations on cards. **3.** to smash, break up. **4.** to scatter, disperse. **5.** (*coll.*) to cause to swell; (*impers.*): **его́ щёку ~ло́** his cheek is swollen. **6.** (*fig., coll.*) to blow up.
разнес|ти́сь, ётся, *past* **~ся, ~ла́сь** *pf.* (*of* **разноси́ться**[2]) **1.** to spread. **2.** to resound.
разнима́|ть, ю *impf. of* **разня́ть**
ра́зн|иться, юсь, ишься *impf.* to differ.
ра́зниц|а, ы *f.* difference; disparity; **кака́я р.?** (*coll.*) what difference does it make?
разнобо́|й, я *m.* lack of co-ordination; difference, disagreement.
разнове́с, а *m.* (*collect.*) set of weights.
разнови́дност|ь, и *f.* variety.
разновреме́нный *adj.* taking place at different times.
разногла́си|е, я *nt.* **1.** difference, disagreement; **р. во взгля́дах** difference of opinion. **2.** discrepancy; **р. в показа́ниях** conflicting evidence.
разноголо́сиц|а, ы *f.* discordance, dissonance (*also fig., coll.*); **р. во мне́ниях** dissent.
разноголо́сый *adj.* discordant.
разнокали́берный *adj.* **1.** (*mil.*) of different calibres. **2.** (*fig., coll.*) mixed, heterogeneous.
разнома́стный *adj.* **1.** of different colours. **2.** (*cards*) of different suits.
разномы́сли|е, я *nt.* difference of opinion(s).
разнообра́зи|е, я *nt.* variety, diversity; **для ~я** for a change.
разнообра́|зить, жу, зишь *impf.* to vary, diversify.
разнообра́зност|ь, и *f.* = **разнообра́зие**
разнообра́з|ный (~ен, ~на) *adj.* various, varied, diverse.
разноплеме́нный *adj.* of different races, tribes.
разнорабо́ч|ий, его *m.* unskilled labourer.
разноречи́в|ый (~, ~а) *adj.* contradictory, conflicting.
разноре́чи|е, я *nt.* (*obs.*) contradiction.
разноро́дност|ь, и *f.* heterogeneity.
разноро́д|ный (~ен, ~на) *adj.* heterogeneous.
разно́с, а *m.* **1.** carrying; delivery (*of mail, etc.*). **2.** (*fig., coll.*) blowing-up.
разно|си́ть[1]**, шу́, ~сишь** *pf.* (*of* **разна́шивать**) to wear in (*footwear*).
разно|си́ть[2]**, шу́, ~сишь** *impf. of* **разнести́**
разно|си́ться[1]**, ~сится** *pf.* (*of* **разна́шиваться**) (*of footwear*) to become comfortable.
разно|си́ться[2]**, ~сится** *impf. of* **разнести́(сь)**
разно́ск|а, и *f.* delivery.
разносклоня́емый *adj.* (*gram.*) irregularly declined.
разно́сн|ый[1] *adj.*: **~ая кни́га** delivery book; **~ая торго́вля** street-trading, street-hawking.
разно́сн|ый[2] *adj.* (*coll.*) abusive; **~ая реце́нзия** scathing review; **~ые слова́** swear-words.
разносо́л, а *m.* (*cul.*) **1.** (*obs.*) pickle(s). **2.** (*pl. only*) (*coll.*) dainties, delicacies.
разноспряга́емый *adj.* (*gram.*) irregularly conjugated.
разносторо́н|ний *adj.* **1.** (*math.*) scalene. **2.** (**~ен, ~ня**) (*fig.*) many-sided; versatile; **~нее образова́ние** all-round education.
разносторо́нност|ь, и *f.* versatility.
ра́зност|ь, и *f.* **1.** (*math.*) difference. **2.** difference, diversity; **ра́зные ~и** (*coll.*) this and that.
разно́счик, а *m.* pedlar, hawker; barrow boy.
разнохара́ктер|ный (~ен, ~на) *adj.* diverse, varied.
разноцве́тный *adj.* of different colours; many-coloured, variegated, motley.
разночи́н|ец, ца *m.* (*hist.*) raznochinets (*in 19th century, Russ. intellectual not of gentle birth*).
разночи́н|ный *adj. of* **~ец**
разночте́ни|е, я *nt.* (*philol.*) variant reading.
разношёрст|ный (~ен, ~на) *adj.* **1.** (*of animals*) with coats of different colour. **2.** (*fig., coll.*) mixed; ill-assorted.
разношёрст|ый *adj.* = **~ный**
разноязы́чный *adj.* polyglot.
разну́зд|анный *p.p.p. of* **~а́ть** *and adj.* unbridled, unruly.
разнузд|а́ть, а́ю *pf.* (*of* **~ывать**) to unbridle.
разну́здыва|ть, ю *impf. of* **разнузда́ть**

ра́зн|ый *adj.* **1.** different, differing. **2.** various, diverse; **~ого ро́да** of various kinds; *as n.* **~ое, ~ого** *nt.* (*on agenda of meeting, etc.*) any other business.
разню́х|ать, аю *pf.* (*of* **~ивать**) (*coll.*) to smell out (*also fig.*); (*fig.*) to nose out, ferret out.
разню́хива|ть, ю *impf. of* **разню́хать**
раз|ня́ть, ниму́, ни́мешь, *past* **~ня́л (*and* ро́знял), ~няла́, ~ня́ло (*and* ро́зняло)** *pf.* (*of* **~нима́ть**) **1.** to take to pieces, dismantle, disjoint. **2.** to part, separate (*persons fighting*).
разо... *vbl. pref.* = **раз...**
разоби́|деть, жу, дишь *pf.* (*coll.*) to offend greatly; to put s.o.'s back up properly.
разоби́|деться, жусь, дишься *pf.* (*coll.*) to take offence.
разоблач|а́ть(ся), а́ю(сь) *impf. of* **~и́ть(ся)**
разоблаче́ни|е, я *nt.* exposure, unmasking.
разоблачи́тел|ь, я *m.* unmasker.
разоблач|и́ть, у́, и́шь *pf.* (*of* **~а́ть**) **1.** (*eccl. or joc.*) to disrobe, divest. **2.** (*fig.*) to expose, unmask.
разоблач|и́ться, у́сь, и́шься *pf.* (*of* **~а́ться**) **1.** (*eccl. or joc.*) to disrobe. **2.** (*fig.*) to be exposed, be unmasked.
раз|обра́ть, беру́, берёшь, *past* **~обра́л, ~обрала́, ~обра́ло** *pf.* (*of* **~бира́ть**) **1.** to take to pieces, strip, dismantle; **р. дом** to pull down a house. **2.** to buy up, take. **3.** to sort out. **4.** to investigate, look into; **р. де́ло** (*leg.*) to hear a case. **5.** (*gram.*) to parse; to analyse. **6.** to make out, understand; **я не могу́ р. его́ по́черк** I cannot make out his handwriting; **мы не мо́жем р., в чём де́ло** we cannot understand what it is all about. **7.** (*fig., coll.*) to fill (with), seize (with); **её ~обрала́ ре́вность** she was filled with jealousy.
раз|обра́ться, беру́сь, берёшься, *past* **~обра́лся, ~обрала́сь, ~обра́ло́сь** *pf.* (*of* **~бира́ться**) **1.** (*coll.*) to unpack. **2.** (**в**+*p.*) to investigate, look into; to understand; **р. в пчелово́дстве** to know about bee-keeping; **я в нём не ~обра́лся** I could not make him out.
разобщ|а́ть(ся), а́ю(сь) *impf. of* **~и́ть(ся)**
разобще́ни|е, я *nt.* disconnection, uncoupling.
разобщённо *adv.* apart, separately; **де́йствовать р.** to act independently.
разобщи́тел|ь, я *m.* (*tech.*) disconnector.
разобщ|и́ть, у́, и́шь *pf.* (*of* **~а́ть**) **1.** to separate; (*fig.*) to estrange, alienate. **2.** (*tech.*) to disconnect, uncouple, disengage.
разобщ|и́ться, у́сь, и́шься *pf.* (*of* **~а́ться**) **1.** (*tech.*) to become disconnected. **2.** *pass. of* **~и́ть**
ра́зов|ый *adj.* valid for one occasion (only); **~ого по́льзования** disposable.
раз|огна́ть, гоню́, го́нишь, *past* **~огна́л, ~огнала́, ~огна́ло** *pf.* (*of* **~гоня́ть**) **1.** to drive away; to disperse; (*fig.*) to dispel; **р. демонстра́цию** to break up a demonstration; **р. го́ре** to dispel grief. **2.** (*coll.*) to drive at high speed, race. **3.** (*typ.*) to space.
раз|огна́ться, гоню́сь, го́нишься, *past* **~огна́лся, ~огнала́сь, ~огна́ло́сь** *pf.* (*of* **~гоня́ться**) to gather speed; to gather momentum.
разогн|у́ть, у́, ёшь *pf.* (*of* **разгиба́ть**) to unbend, straighten; **р. спи́ну** to straighten one's back.
разогн|у́ться, у́сь, ёшься *pf.* (*of* **разгиба́ться**) to straighten o.s. up.
разогре́в, а *m.* (*tech.*) initial heating; firing (*of furnace*).
разогрева́ни|е, я *nt.* warming-up.
разогрева́|ть(ся), ю(сь) *impf. of* **разогре́ть(ся)**
разогре́|ть, ю *pf.* (*of* **~ва́ть**) to warm up.
разогре́|ться, юсь *pf.* (*of* **~ва́ться**) to warm up, grow warm.
разоде́т|ый *p.p.p. of* **~ь** *and adj.* dressed up; **весь р.** all dressed up, in one's best bib and tucker.
разоде́|ть, ну, нешь *pf.* (*coll.*) to dress up.
разоде́|ться, нусь, нешься *pf.* (*coll.*) to dress up; **р. в пух и прах** to be dressed to kill.
разодолж|а́ть, а́ю *impf. of* **~и́ть**
разодолж|и́ть, у́, и́шь *pf.* (*of* **~а́ть**) (*coll.*) to give a nasty surprise.
раз|одра́ть, деру́, дерёшь, *past* **~одра́л, ~одрала́, ~одра́ло** *pf.* (*of* **~дира́ть**) to tear up.

раз|одра́ться, дерётся, *past* **~одра́лся, ~одрала́сь, ~одра́ло́сь** *pf.* (*of* **~дира́ться**) (*coll.*) to tear.
разозл|и́ть, ю́, и́шь *pf.* (*of* **злить**) to make angry, enrage.
разозл|и́ться, ю́сь, и́шься *pf.* (*of* **зли́ться**) to get angry, get in a rage.
раз|ойти́сь, ойду́сь, ойдёшься, *past* **~ошёлся, ~ошла́сь** *pf.* (*of* **расходи́ться**) **1.** to go away; to disperse; **толпа́ ~ошла́сь** the crowd broke up; **ту́чи ~ошли́сь** the clouds dispersed. **2.** (**c**+*i.*) to part (from), separate (from), to get divorced (from); **мы ~ошли́сь друзья́ми** we parted friends; **он ~ошёлся с жено́й** he has separated from his wife. **3.** to branch off, diverge; to radiate. **4.** to pass (*without meeting*). **5.** (**c**+*i.*) to be at variance (with), conflict (with); **р. во мне́нии с кем-н.** to disagree with s.o. **6.** to dissolve; to melt. **7.** to be sold out; to be spent; (*of a book*) to be out of print; **все де́ньги ~ошли́сь** all the money has been spent. **8.** (*coll.*) to gather speed. **9.** (*coll.*) to let o.s. go; to fly off the handle; **бу́ря ~ошла́сь** the storm raged.
раз|о́к, ка́ *m.* (*coll.*) *dim. of* **~; ещё р.** once more; **р. друго́й** once or twice.
ра́зом *adv.* (*coll.*) at once, at one go.
разо́мкн|утый *p.p.p. of* **~у́ть** *and adj.*; **р. строй** (*mil.*) open order.
разомкн|у́ть, у́, ёшь *pf.* (*of* **размыка́ть**) to open, unfasten; (*tech.*) to break, disconnect.
разомле́|ть, ю *pf.* (*coll.*) to languish, grow languid.
разонра́в|иться, люсь, ишься *pf.* (*coll.*; +*d.*) to cease to please, lose its attraction (for).
разопрева́|ть, ю *impf. of* **разопре́ть**
разопре́|ть, ю *pf.* (*of* **~ва́ть**) **1.** to become soft (*in cooking*). **2.** (*coll.*) to be worn out, done in (*from heat*).
разо́р, а *m.* (*coll.*) ruin, destruction.
разор|а́ться, у́сь, ёшься *pf.* (*coll.*) to become uproarious, raise a hullabaloo.
разорв|а́ть, у́, ёшь, *past* **~а́л, ~ала́, ~а́ло** *pf.* (*of* **разрыва́ть**[1]) **1.** to tear (to pieces); **р. кого́-н. на ча́сти** (*fig.*, *coll.*) to wear s.o. out (*with requests, entreaties, etc.*). **2.** (*impers.*) to blow up, burst; **котёл ~а́ло** the boiler has burst. **3.** (*fig.*) to break (off), sever; **р. дипломати́ческие сноше́ния** to break off diplomatic relations.
разорв|а́ться, ётся, *past* **~а́лся, ~ала́сь, ~а́ло́сь** *pf.* (*of* **разрыва́ться**) **1.** to break, snap; to tear, become torn. **2.** to blow up, burst; to explode, go off. **3.** (*coll.*; *usu.*+*neg.*) to be everywhere at once; **я не могу́ р.** I can't be everywhere at once; I can't do half a dozen things at once; **хоть ~и́сь!** hold hard!, give us a chance!
разоре́ни|е, я *nt.* destruction, ravage; ruin.
разори́тел|ьный (~ен, ~ьна) *adj.* ruinous; wasteful.
разор|и́ть, ю́, и́шь *pf.* (*of* **~я́ть**) **1.** to destroy, ravage. **2.** to ruin, bring to ruin.
разор|и́ться, ю́сь, и́шься *pf.* (*of* **~я́ться**) to ruin o.s.; to be ruined.
разоруж|а́ть(ся), а́ю(сь) *impf. of* **~и́ть(ся)**
разоруже́ни|е, я *nt.* disarmament.
разоруж|и́ть, у́, и́шь *pf.* (*of* **~а́ть**) to disarm; (*naut.*) to dismantle, unrig.
разоруж|и́ться, у́сь, и́шься *pf.* (*of* **~а́ться**) to disarm.
разор|я́ть(ся), я́ю(сь) *impf. of* **~и́ть(ся)**
разо|сла́ть, шлю́, шлёшь *pf.* (*of* **рассыла́ть**) **1.** to send round, distribute, circulate; **р. листо́вки** to distribute leaflets. **2.** to send out, dispatch.
разосп|а́ться, лю́сь, и́шься, *past* **~а́лся, ~ала́сь, ~а́лось** *pf.* (*coll.*) to be fast asleep; to oversleep.
разостла́ть (*and* **расстели́ть**), **расстелю́, расстéлешь** *pf.* (*of* **расстила́ть**) to spread (out), lay.
разостла́|ться (*and* **расстели́ться**), **рассте́лется** *pf.* (*of* **расстила́ться**) to spread; **тума́н ~лся по всей сте́пи** fog spread over the whole steppe.
разохо́|тить, чу, тишь *pf.* (**к, на**+*a.*; *coll.*) to stimulate (to), arouse an inclination (to, for).
разохо́|титься, чусь, тишься *pf.* (+*inf.*; *coll.*) to take a liking (to), feel an inclination (for); **сперва́ он не хоте́л танцева́ть, а тепе́рь ~тился** he did not want to go to the dance at first, but now he is keen to go.
разочарова́ни|е, я *nt.* disappointment.
разочаро́в|анный *p.p.p. of* **~а́ть** *and adj.* disappointed, disillusioned.
разочар|ова́ть, у́ю *pf.* (*of* **~о́вывать**) to disappoint.
разочар|ова́ться, у́юсь *pf.* (*of* **~о́вываться**) (**в ком-н., в чём-н.**) to be disappointed (in s.o., with sth.).
разочаро́выва|ть(ся), ю(сь) *impf. of* **разочарова́ть(ся)**
разраба́тыва|ть, ю *impf. of* **разрабо́тать**
разрабо́та|ть, ю *pf.* (*of* **разраба́тывать**) **1.** (*agric.*) to cultivate. **2.** (*mining*) to work, exploit. **3.** to work out, work up; to develop; to elaborate; **р. вопро́с** to work up a subject; **р. го́лос** to develop a voice; **р. ме́тоды** to devise methods; **р. пла́ны** to work out plans.
разрабо́тк|а, и *f.* **1.** (*agric.*) cultivation. **2.** (*mining*) working, exploitation; **откры́тая р.** open-cast mining. **3.** field; pit, working; **р. сла́нца** slate quarry. **4.** working out, working up; elaboration.
разра́внива|ть, ю *impf. of* **разровня́ть**
разража́|ться, юсь *impf. of* **разрази́ться**
разра|зи́ться, жу́сь, зи́шься *pf.* (*of* **~жа́ться**) (*of a storm, etc.*) to break out, burst out; **р. слеза́ми** to burst into tears; **р. сме́хом** to burst out laughing.
разраст|а́ться, а́ется *impf. of* **~и́сь**
разраст|и́сь, ётся, *past* **разро́сся, разросла́сь** *pf.* (*of* **~а́ться**) to grow (up) (*also fig.*); to spread; to grow thickly; **де́ло разросло́сь** the business has grown; **но́вый посёлок разро́сся** a new estate has grown up.
разрев|е́ться, у́сь, ёшься *pf.* (*coll.*) to raise a howl, start howling.
разре|ди́ть, жу́, ди́шь *pf.* (*of* **~жа́ть**) **1.** to thin out, weed out. **2.** to rarefy.
разрежа́|ть, ю *impf. of* **разреди́ть**
разре|жённый *p.p.p. of* **~ди́ть** *and adj.* (*phys.*) rarefied, rare; **~жённый во́здух** rarefied air.
разре́з, а *m.* **1.** cut; slit. **2.** section; **попере́чный р.** cross-section; **продо́льный р.** longitudinal section; **р. глаз** shape of one's eyes. **3.** (*fig.*, *coll.*) point of view; **в ~е** (+*g.*) from the point of view (of), in the context (of).
разре́|зать, жу, жешь *pf.* (*of* **~за́ть**) to cut; to slit.
разрез|а́ть, а́ю *impf. of* **~ать**
разрезн|о́й *adj.* **1.** cutting; **р. нож** paper-knife; **~а́я пила́** rip saw. **2.** slit, with slits; **~а́я ю́бка** slit skirt.
разреш|а́ть, а́ю *impf. of* **~и́ть**
разреш|а́ться, а́юсь *impf.* **1.** *impf. of* **~и́ться. 2.** *impf. only* to be allowed; **здесь кури́ть не ~а́ется** no smoking (is allowed here).
разреше́ни|е, я *nt.* **1.** permission; **с ва́шего ~я** with your permission, by your leave. **2.** permit, authorization; **р. на въезд** entry permit. **3.** solution (*of a problem*). **4.** settlement (*of a dispute*). **5.** (*med.*) resolution; **р. от бре́мени** (*obs.*) delivery.
разреши́м|ый (~, ~а) *adj.* solvable.
разреш|и́ть, у́, и́шь *pf.* (*of* **~а́ть**) **1.** (+*d.*) to allow, permit; **~и́те пройти́** allow me to pass; do you mind letting me pass? **2.** to authorize; **р. кни́гу к печа́ти** to authorize the printing of a book. **3.** (**от**; *obs.*) to release (from); (*eccl.*) to absolve (from), give dispensation (from); **р. кого́-н. от обяза́тельства** to release s.o. from an obligation; **р. от поста́** to give dispensation from a fast. **4.** to solve (*a problem*). **5.** to settle; **р. сомне́ния** to resolve doubts.
разреш|и́ться, у́сь, и́шься *pf.* (*of* **~а́ться**) **1.** to be solved. **2.** to be settled. **3. (от бре́мени)** (+*i.*; *obs.*) to be delivered (of); **она́ ~и́лась де́вочкой** she was delivered of a girl.
разрис|ова́ть, у́ю *pf.* (*of* **~о́вывать**) **1.** to cover with drawings. **2.** (*fig.*) to paint a picture (of).
разрисо́выва|ть, ю *impf. of* **разрисова́ть**
разровня́|ть, ю *pf.* (*of* **разра́внивать**) to level.
разро́зн|енный *p.p.p. of* **~ить** *and adj.* **1.** uncoordinated. **2.** odd; **р. компле́кт** broken set, set made up of odd parts; **~енные тома́** odd volumes.
разро́знива|ть, ю *impf. of* **разро́знить**
разро́зн|ить, ю, ишь *pf.* (*of* **~ивать**) to break a set (of).
разруб|а́ть, а́ю *impf. of* **~и́ть**
разруб|и́ть, лю́, ~ишь *pf.* (*of* **~а́ть**) to cut, cleave; **р. го́рдиев у́зел** to cut the Gordian knot.
разруга́|ть, ю *pf.* (*coll.*) to berate; to blow up.

разругá|ться, юсь *pf.* (**с**+*i.*; *coll.*) to quarrel (with).
разрумя́нива|ть(ся), ю(сь) *impf. of* **разрумя́нить(ся)**
разрумя́н|ить, ю, ишь *pf.* (*of* **~ивать**) **1.** to rouge. **2.** to flush, redden; **морóз ~ил её щёки** the frost brought a flush to her cheeks.
разрумя́н|иться, юсь, ишься *pf.* (*of* **~иваться**) **1.** to put rouge on. **2.** to blush; to be flushed.
разрýх|а, и *f.* ruin, collapse; **привестú хозя́йство к ~е** to dislocate the economy.
разруш|áть(ся), áю, áет(ся) *impf. of* **~ить(ся)**
разрушéни|е, я *nt.* destruction; (*pl.*) havoc.
разрушúтел|ьный (~ен, ~ьна) *adj.* destructive.
разрýш|ить, у, ишь *pf.* (*of* **~áть**) **1.** to destroy; to demolish, wreck; to ruin (*also fig.*). **2.** (*fig.*) to frustrate, blast, blight; **р. чьи-н. надéжды** to blight s.o.'s hopes.
разрýш|иться, ится *pf.* (*of* **~áться**) **1.** to go to ruin, collapse; **все их плáны ~ились** all their plans have fallen to the ground. **2.** *pass. of* **~ить**
разры́в, а *m.* **1.** (*in var. senses*) break; gap; rupture, severance; breach; **р. лúнии фрóнта** (*mil.*) breach in the front line; **р. дипломатúческих отношéний** rupture, severance of diplomatic relations; **р. мéжду поколéниями** generation gap; **мéжду нúми произошёл р.** they have broken it off. **2.** (*shell*) burst, explosion.
разрывá|ть[1], **ю** *impf. of* **разорвáть**
разрывá|ть[2], **ю** *impf. of* **разры́ть**
разрывá|ться, юсь *impf. of* **разорвáться**
разрывнóй *adj.* explosive, bursting.
разр|ы́ть, óю, óешь *pf.* (*of* **~ывáть**[2]) **1.** to dig up. **2.** (*fig., coll.*) to turn upside-down, rummage through.
разрыхлéни|е, я *nt.* loosening.
разрыхл|úть, ю́, úшь *pf.* (*of* **~я́ть**) to loosen; to hoe.
разрыхл|я́ть, я́ю *impf. of* **~úть**
разря́д[1], **а** *m.* discharge.
разря́д[2], **а** *m.* category, rank; sort; (*sport*) class, rating; **пéрвого ~а** first-class.
разря|дúть[1], **жý, ~дишь** *pf.* (*of* **~жáть**) (*coll.*) to dress up.
разря|дúть[2], **жý, дúшь** *pf.* (*of* **~жáть**) **1.** (*elec.*) to discharge; **р. атмосфéру** (*fig.*) to relieve tension, clear the air. **2.** to unload (*a fire-arm*). **3.** (*typ.*) to space out.
разря|дúться[1], **жýсь, ~дишься** *pf.* (*of* **~жáться**) to dress up; to doll o.s. up.
разря|дúться[2], **дúтся** *pf.* (*of* **~жáться**) **1.** (*elec.*) to run down; (*fig.*) to clear, ease; **атмосфéра ~дúлась** the atmosphere has become less tense. **2.** *pass. of* **~дúть**[2]
разря́дк|а, и *f.* **1.** discharging; unloading; **р. напряжённости** (*pol.*) lessening of tension, détente. **2.** (*typ.*) letter-spacing.
разря́дник[1], **а** *m.* (*elec.*) discharger; spark-gap.
разря́дник[2], **а** *m.* (*sport*) player with official rating.
разря́д|ный *adj. of* **~**[1]; **~ная ёмкость, ~ная мóщность** discharge capacity.
разряжá|ть(ся), ю(сь) *impf. of* **разрядúть(ся)**
разубе|дúть, жý, дúшь *pf.* (*of* **~ждáть**) (**в**+*p.*) to dissuade (from), argue (out of); **мы их ~дúли** we have made them change their mind.
разубе|дúться, жýсь, дúшься *pf.* (*of* **~ждáться**) (**в**+*p.*) to change one's mind (about), change one's opinion (about).
разубеждá|ть(ся), ю(сь) *impf. of* **разубедúть(ся)**
разувá|ть(ся), ю(сь) *impf. of* **разýть(ся)**
разуверéни|е, я *nt.* dissuasion.
разувéр|ить, ю, ишь *pf.* (*of* **~я́ть**) (**в**+*p.*) to undermine faith (in); to argue (out of).
разувéр|иться, юсь, ишься *pf.* (*of* **~я́ться**) (**в**+*p.*) to lose faith (in).
разузна|вáть, ю́, ёшь *impf.* **1.** *impf. of* **разузнáть**. **2.** *impf. only* to make inquiries (about).
разузнá|ть, ю *pf.* (*of* **~вáть**) to find out.
разукрá|сить, шу, сишь *pf.* (*of* **~шивать**) to adorn; to decorate; to embellish.
разукрá|ситься, шусь, сишься *pf.* (*of* **~шиваться**) to adorn *or* decorate o.s.
разукрáшива|ть(ся), ю(сь) *impf. of* **разукрáсить(ся)**
разукрупн|úть, ю́, úшь *pf.* (*of* **~я́ть**) to break up into smaller units.
разукрупн|úться, úтся *pf.* (*of* **~я́ться**) to break up into smaller units.
разукрупн|я́ть(ся), я́ю, я́ет(ся) *impf. of* **~úть(ся)**
рáзум, а *m.* reason; mind, intellect; **у негó ум за р. зашёл** (*coll.*) he is, was at his wit's end.
разумéни|е, я *nt.* **1.** (*obs.*) understanding. **2.** opinion, viewpoint; **по моемý ~ю** to my mind, as I see it.
разумé|ть, ю *impf.* **1.** (*obs.*) to understand. **2.** (**под**) to understand (by), mean (by).
разумé|ться, ется *impf.* to be understood, be meant; **под э́тим ~ется...** by this is meant ...; (**сáмо собóй**) **~ется** it stands to reason; it goes without saying, of course; **он, ~ется, не знал, что вы ужé пришлú** he, of course, did not know that you were already here.
разýмник, а *m.* (*coll.*) clever chap, clever boy.
разýм|ный (~ен, ~на) *adj.* **1.** possessing reason. **2.** judicious, intelligent. **3.** reasonable; **э́то (вполнé) ~но** it is (perfectly) reasonable, that makes (good) sense.
разý|ть, ю, ешь *pf.* (*of* **~вáть**); **р. когó-н.** to take s.o.'s shoes off.
разý|ться, юсь, ешься *pf.* (*of* **~вáться**) to take one's shoes off.
разухáбист|ый (~, ~а) *adj.* (*coll.*) **1.** rollicking. **2.** (*pej.*) free-and-easy.
разýчива|ть(ся), ю(сь) *impf. of* **разучúть(ся)**
разуч|úть, ý, ~ишь *pf.* (*of* **~ивать**) to learn (up); **р. роль** to learn, study one's part.
разуч|úться, ýсь, ~ишься *pf.* (*of* **~иваться**) (+*inf.*) to forget (how to), lose the art (of); **я ~úлся ходúть на лы́жах** I have forgotten how to ski.
разъ... *vbl. pref.* = **раз...**
разъедá|ть(ся), ю(сь) *impf. of* **разъéсть(ся)**
разъединéни|е, я *nt.* **1.** separation. **2.** (*elec.*) disconnection, breaking.
разъединúтел|ь, я *m.* (*elec.*) disconnecting switch, cut out switch.
разъедин|úть, ю́, úшь *pf.* (*of* **~я́ть**) **1.** to separate. **2.** (*elec.*) to disconnect, break; **нас ~úли** we were cut off (*on telephone*).
разъедин|úться, ю́сь, úшься *pf.* (*of* **~я́ться**) **1.** to separate, part. **2.** *pass. of* **~úть**
разъедин|я́ть(ся), я́ю(сь) *impf. of* **~úть(ся)**
разъéзд, а *m.* **1.** departure; dispersal. **2.** (*pl.*) travel, journeyings. **3.** (*mil.*) mounted patrol. **4.** section of double track (*on single-line rail.*); station, halt (*on single-line rail.*).
разъездн|óй *adj.*: **р. агéнт** (*obs.*) traveller, travelling representative; **~ы́е дéньги** travelling expenses; **р. путь** (*rail.*) siding.
разъезжá|ть, ю *impf.* to drive (about, around), ride (about, around); to travel; **р. по делáм слýжбы** to travel about on business.
разъезжá|ться, юсь *impf. of* **разъéхаться**
разъé|сть, ст, дя́т, *past* **~л** *pf.* (*of* **~дáть**) to eat away; to corrode (*also fig.*); **егó ~ли сомнéния** he was consumed with doubts.
разъé|сться, мся, шься, стся, дúмся, дúтесь, дя́тся, *past* **~лся** *pf.* (*of* **~дáться**) (*coll.*) to get fat (*from good living*).
разъé|хаться, дусь, дешься *pf.* (*of* **~зжáться**) **1.** to depart; to disperse; **приéхавшие на пóхороны ~хались** the mourners have departed. **2.** to separate, cease living together. **3.** to (be able to) pass; **тут грузовикáм нельзя́ р.** it is impossible for lorries to pass here. **4.** to pass one another (*without meeting*), miss one another. **5.** (*coll.*) to slide apart. **6.** (*coll.*) to fall to pieces, fall apart.
разъяр|úть, ю́, úшь *pf.* (*of* **~я́ть**) to infuriate, rouse to fury.
разъяр|úться, ю́сь, úшься *pf.* (*of* **~я́ться**) to become furious, get into a fury.
разъяр|я́ть(ся), я́ю(сь) *impf. of* **~úть(ся)**
разъяснéни|е, я *nt.* explanation, elucidation; interpretation.
разъяснúтельный *adj.* explanatory, elucidatory.
разъя́сн|ить, ит *pf.* (*coll.*) (*impers.*) to clear up (*of the weather*).
разъясн|úть, ю́, úшь *pf.* (*of* **~я́ть**) to explain, elucidate; to interpret.

разъя́сн|иться, ится *pf.* = **~ить**
разъясн|и́ться, и́тся *pf.* (*of* **~я́ться**) to become clear, be cleared up.
разъясн|я́ть(ся), я́ю, я́ет(ся) *impf. of* **~и́ть(ся)**
разыгр|а́ть, а́ю *pf.* (*of* **~ывать**) **1.** to play (through); to perform; **р. дурака́** to play the fool. **2.** to draw (*a lottery, etc.*); to raffle. **3.** (*coll.*) to play a trick (on), play a practical joke (on).
разыгр|а́ться, а́юсь *pf.* (*of* **~ываться**) **1.** to be carried away by a game, by play. **2.** (*of a pianist, an actor, etc.*) to warm up. **3.** (*of wind or sea*) to rise; to get up; (*of a storm*) to break; (*fig.*; *of feelings*) to run high.
разы́грыва|ть(ся), ю(сь) *impf. of* **разыгра́ть(ся) 2., 3.**
разыска́ни|е, я *nt.* **1.** hunting down, searching out. **2.** (piece of) research.
разы|ска́ть, щу́, ~щешь *pf.* to find (after searching).
разы|ска́ться, щу́сь, ~щешься *pf.* **1.** (*impf.* **~скива́ться**) to be sought for. **2.** to turn up, be found.
разы́скива|ть, ю *impf.* to hunt, search for.
разы́скива|ться, юсь *impf. of* **разыска́ться; р. поли́цией** to be wanted by the police.
ра|й, я, о ~е, в ~ю́ *m.* (*bibl.*) paradise; (Garden of) Eden; **земно́й р., р. земно́й** (*fig.*) earthly paradise.
рай... *comb. form, abbr. of* **райо́нный**
райко́м, а *m.* (*abbr. of* ***райо́нный комите́т***) rayon *or* district committee.
райо́н, а *m.* **1.** region; area; zone. **2.** (*designation of administrative division of former USSR*) rayon *or* raion; district.
райони́ровани|е, я *nt.* **1.** division into districts. **2.** earmarking for a given area; zoning.
райони́р|овать, ую *impf. and pf.* **1.** to divide into districts. **2.** to earmark for a given area; to zone.
райо́н|ный *adj. of* **~**
ра́й|ский *adj. of* **~**; (*fig.*) heavenly; **~ская пти́ца** bird of paradise.
райсове́т, а *m.* rayon *or* district soviet.
рак, а *m.* **1.** (*zool.*) crawfish, crayfish; **кра́сный как р.** red as a lobster; **показа́ть, где ~и зиму́ют** (*coll.*) to give it s.o. hot; **знать, где ~и зиму́ют** (*coll.*) to know a thing or two, know what's what. **2.** (*med.*) cancer; (*bot.*) canker. **3. Р.** (*astrol., astron.*) Crab, Cancer; **тро́пик ~а** (*geog.*) Tropic of Cancer.
ра́к|а, и *f.* (*eccl.*) shrine (*of a saint*).
раке́т|а¹, ы *f.* **1.** (air-)rocket; flare; **пусти́ть ~у** to let off a rocket. **2.** (*mil.*) rocket, ballistic missile; **зени́тная р.** surface-to-air missile; **крыла́тая р.** cruise missile; **межконтинента́льная р.** inter-continental ballistic missile (ICBM). **3.** (*outer-space*) rocket; **р.-носи́тель** launch vehicle. **4.** (*coll.*) hydrofoil (*vessel*).
раке́т|а², ы *f.* = **~ка**
раке́т|ка, ки *f.* (*sport*) racket.
раке́тниц|а, ы *f.* rocket projector; Very pistol, signal pistol.
раке́тный¹ *adj.* rocket(-powered), jet; **р. дви́гатель** rocket engine, jet engine.
раке́т|ный² *adj. of* **~а²**
ракетодро́м, а *m.* rocket launch site.
раке́тчик, а *m.* **1.** rocket signaller. **2.** missile specialist.
раки́т|а, ы *f.* (*bot.*) brittle willow.
раки́тник, а *m.* broom (*bush*); broom plantation.
ра́ковин|а, ы *f.* **1.** shell; **ушна́я р.** (*anat.*) aural cavity. **2.** sink; wash-basin. **3.** (*in metal*) blister, bubble; **уса́дочная р.** air hole, blow hole.
ра́к|овый *adj. of* **~**; (*med.*) cancerous; **~овая о́пухоль** cancerous tumour.
ракообра́зн|ые, ых *pl.* (*sg.* **~ое, ~ого** *nt.*) (*zool.*) Crustacea.
ракообра́зный *adj.* (*zool.*) cancroid.
раку́рс, а *m.* (*art*) foreshortening; **в ~е** foreshortened.
раку́шечник, а *m.* (*geol.*) coquina, shell rock.
раку́шк|а, и *f.* cockle-shell; mussel.
ра́лли *nt. indecl.* rally.
ралли́ст, а *m.* rallyist, rally driver.
ра́м|а, ы *f.* **1.** frame; **око́нная р.** window-frame, sash; **вста́вить в ~у** to frame. **2.** chassis, carriage.
рамаза́н, а *m.* (*relig.*) Ramadan.
рам|ена́, ён, ена́м *no sg.* (*arch. or poet.*) shoulders.
ра́мен|ь, и *f.* (*dial.*) coniferous forest.
ра́мен|ье, ья *nt.* = **~ь**
ра́мк|а, и *f.* frame; **в ~е** framed; **без ~и** unframed; **объявле́ние о сме́рти в тра́урной ~е** black-bordered obituary announcement.
ра́м|ки, ок (*pl. only*) framework; limits; **в ~ках** (*+g.*) within the framework (of), within the limits (of); **вы́йти за р.** (*+g.*) to exceed the limits (of).
ра́м|ный *adj. of* **~а**
ра́м|очный *adj. of* **~ка; ~очная анте́нна** loop aerial, frame aerial.
ра́мп|а, ы *f.* (*theatr.*) footlights.
ра́н|а, ы *f.* wound.
ранг, а *m.* class, rank.
ранго́ут, а *m.* (*naut.*) masts and spars.
ранго́ут|ный *adj. of* **~; ~ное де́рево** (*naut.*) spar.
раpermanentево́й *adj. of* **ра́на**
ра́нее *adv.* = **ра́ньше**
ране́ни|е, я *nt.* **1.** wounding. **2.** wound; injury.
ра́нен|ый *adj.* wounded; injured; *as n.* **р., ~ого** *m.* injured man; (*involving weapon*) wounded man; casualty; *pl.* the injured; the wounded.
ране́т, а *m.* rennet (*variety of apple*).
ра́н|ец, ца *m.* knapsack, haversack; satchel; (*mil.*) pack.
ранжи́р, а *m.*: **по ~у** (*coll.*) in order of size.
ра́н|ить, ю, ишь *impf. and pf.* to wound; to injure.
ра́нн|ий *adj.* early; **~им у́тром** early in the morning; **~яя пти́чка** (*fig.*) early bird; **с ~его де́тства** from early childhood; **с ~их лет** from (one's) earliest years.
ра́но¹ *pred.* it is early; **ещё р. ложи́ться спать** it is too early for bed.
ра́но² *adv.* early; **р. и́ли по́здно** sooner or later.
рант, а, о ~е, на ~у́ *m.* welt; **сапоги́ на ~у́** welted boots.
ранть́е *m. indecl.* rentier.
ран|ь, и *f.* (*coll.*) early hour; **куда́ ты направля́ешься в таку́ю р.?** where are you bound for at this ungodly hour?
ра́ньше *adv.* **1.** earlier; **как мо́жно р.** as early as possible; as soon as possible. **2.** before; **до Ло́ндона он не дое́дет р. ве́чера** he will not reach London before evening. **3.** first (of all). **4.** before, formerly; **р. мы жи́ли в дере́вне** we used to live in the country.
рапи́д, а *m.* (*phot.*) slow motion.
рапи́р|а, ы *f.* foil.
ра́порт, а *m.* report.
рапорт|ова́ть, у́ю *impf. and pf.* to report.
РАПП, а *m.* (*abbr. of* ***Росси́йская ассоциа́ция пролета́рских писа́телей***) (*hist.*) Russian Proletarian Writers' Association.
рапс, а *m.* (*bot.*) rape.
рапсо́ди|я, и *f.* (*mus.*) rhapsody.
рарите́т, а *m.* rarity, curiosity.
рас... *vbl. pref.* = **раз...**
ра́с|а, ы *f.* race.
раси́зм, а *m.* racism, racialism.
раси́ст, а *m.* racist, racialist.
раска́ива|ться, юсь *impf. of* **раска́яться**
раскал|ённый *p.p.p. of* **~и́ть** *and adj.* scorching, burning hot; **р. добела́** white-hot; **р. до́красна́** red-hot.
раскал|и́ть, ю́, и́шь *pf.* (*of* **~я́ть**) to bring to a great heat; **р. добела́** to make white-hot; **р. до́красна́** to make red-hot.
раскал|и́ться, ю́сь, и́шься *pf.* (*of* **~я́ться**) to glow, become hot; **р. добела́** to become white-hot; **р. до́красна́** to become red-hot.
раска́лыва|ть(ся), ю(сь) *impf. of* **расколо́ть(ся)**
раскал|я́ть(ся), я́ю(сь) *impf. of* **~и́ть(ся)**
раска́пыва|ть, ю *impf. of* **раскопа́ть**
раска́рмлива|ть, ю *impf. of* **раскорми́ть**
раскасси́р|овать, ую *pf.* (*mil.*) to disband; (*fig.*) to wind up, liquidate.
раска́т, а *m.* roll, peal; **р. гро́ма** peal of thunder.
раскат|а́ть, а́ю *pf.* (*of* **~ывать**) **1.** to unroll. **2.** to roll (out); to smooth out; to level; **р. те́сто** to roll out dough.
раскат|а́ться, а́юсь *pf.* (*of* **~ываться**) **1.** to unroll. **2.** to roll out.

раска́тист|ый (~, ~а) *adj.* rolling, booming; **р. смех** peal(s) of laughter.

раска|ти́ть, чу́, ~́тишь *pf.* (*of* **~́тывать**) **1.** to set rolling. **2.** to roll away.

раска|ти́ться, чу́сь, ~́тишься *pf.* (*of* **~́тываться**) **1.** to gather momentum. **2.** to roll away.

раска́тыва|ть, ю *impf.* **1.** *impf. of* **раската́ть** *and* **раскати́ть. 2.** (*coll.*) to drive (about, around), ride (about, around).

раска́тыва|ться, юсь *impf. of* **раската́ть(ся)** *and* **раскати́ть(ся)**

раскач|а́ть, а́ю *pf.* (*of* **~́ивать**) **1.** to swing; to rock. **2.** to loosen, shake loose. **3.** (*fig., coll.*) to shake up, stir up.

раскач|а́ться, а́юсь *pf.* (*of* **~́иваться**) **1.** to swing (o.s.); to rock (o.s.). **2.** to shake loose. **3.** (*fig., coll.*) to bestir o.s., get into the swing of.

раска́шля|ться, юсь *pf.* to have a fit of coughing.

раска́яни|е, я *nt.* repentance.

раска́|яться, юсь *pf.* (*of* **ка́яться** *and* **~иваться**) (**в**+*p.*) to repent (of).

расквартирова́ни|е, я *nt.* quartering, billeting.

расквартир|ова́ть, у́ю *pf.* (*of* **~о́вывать**) to quarter, billet.

расквартиро́выва|ть, ю *impf. of* **расквартирова́ть**

расква́|сить, шу, сишь *pf.* (*of* **~шивать**) (*coll.*) to punch (*and draw blood from*); **р. кому́-н. нос** to give s.o. a bloody nose.

расква́шива|ть, ю *impf. of* **расква́сить**

расквита́|ться, юсь *pf.* (**с**+*i.*; *coll.*) to settle accounts (with) (*also fig.*); (*fig.*) to get even (with).

раскида́ть, а́ю *pf.* (*of* **~́ывать**) to scatter; to throw about.

раски́дист|ый (~, ~а) *adj.* branchy, spreading.

раскидно́й *adj.* folding.

раски́дыва|ть, ю *impf. of* **раскида́ть** *and* **раски́нуть**

раски́дыва|ться, юсь *impf. of* **раски́нуться**

раски́|нуть, ну, нешь *pf.* (*of* **~дывать**) **1.** to stretch (out); **р. ру́ки** to stretch one's arms. **2.** to spread (out); to set up; **р. шатёр** to pitch a tent. **3.: р. умо́м** to consider, think over.

раски́|нуться, нусь, нешься *pf.* (*of* **~дываться**) **1.** to spread out, stretch out; **по всему́ скло́ну холма́ ~нулось вое́нное кла́дбище** the entire side of the hill was occupied by a military cemetery. **2.** (*coll.*) to sprawl.

раскис|а́ть, а́ю *impf. of* **~́нуть**

раскисле́ни|е, я *nt.* (*chem.*) deoxidization.

раскисл|и́ть, ю́, и́шь *pf.* (*of* **~я́ть**) (*chem.*) to deoxidize, reduce.

раскисл|я́ть, я́ю *impf. of* **~и́ть**

раски́с|нуть, ну, нешь, *past* **~, ~ла** *pf.* (*of* **~а́ть**) **1.** to rise (*from fermentation*). **2.** (*fig., coll.*) to become limp.

раскла́дк|а, и *f.* apportionment; going shares.

раскладу́шк|а, и *f.* (*coll.*) folding bed, divan bed.

раскладн|о́й *adj.* folding; **~а́я крова́ть** camp-bed.

раскла́дыва|ть(ся), ю(сь) *impf. of* **разложи́ть(ся)**[1]

раскла́нива|ться, юсь *impf. of* **раскла́няться**

раскла́н|яться, яюсь *pf.* (*of* **~иваться**) **1.** to exchange bows (*on meeting or leave-taking*). **2.** to take leave (of).

раскле́ива|ть(ся), ю(сь) *impf. of* **раскле́ить(ся)**

раскле́|ить, ю, ишь *pf.* (*of* **~ивать**) **1.** to unstick. **2.** to stick, paste (*in various places*).

раскле́|иться, юсь, ишься *pf.* (*of* **~иваться**) **1.** to come unstuck. **2.** (*fig., coll.*) to fall through, fail to come off; **сде́лка ~илась** the deal fell through. **3.** (*fig., coll.*) to feel seedy, be off colour; **он совсе́м ~ился** he has gone to pieces.

раскле́йк|а, и *f.* sticking, pasting.

раскле́йщик, а *m.* bill-sticker.

расклеп|а́ть, а́ю *pf.* (*of* **~̈ывать**) to unrivet, unclench.

расклёпыва|ть, ю *impf. of* **расклепа́ть**

раск|ова́ть, ую́, уёшь *pf.* (*of* **~о́вывать**) **1.** to unchain, unfetter, to unshoe (*a horse*). **2.** to hammer out, flatten; (*tech.*) to upset, jump (up).

раск|ова́ться, ую́сь, уёшься *pf.* (*of* **~о́вываться**) **1.** (*of a horse*) to cast a shoe. **2.** to free o.s. (*from fetters*).

раско́выва|ть(ся), ю(сь) *impf. of* **раскова́ть(ся)**

расковыр|я́ть, я́ю *pf.* (*of* **~́ивать**) to pick open; to scratch raw.

раско́ка|ть, ю *pf.* (*coll.*) to drop and break.

раско́л, а *m.* **1.** (*relig., hist.*) schism, dissent. **2.** (*pol., etc.*) split, division.

расკола́чива|ть, ю *impf. of* **расколоти́ть**

расколо|ти́ть, чу́, ~́тишь *pf.* (*of* **расмола́чивать**) **1.** to unnail; to prise open. **2.** to stretch (*footwear*). **3.** (*coll.*) to break; to smash (*crockery, etc.; fig., the enemy*).

раскол|о́ть, ю́, ~́ешь *pf.* **1.** *pf. of* **коло́ть**[1]. **2.** (*impf.* **раска́лывать**) (*fig.*) to disrupt, break up.

раскол|о́ться, ю́сь, ~́ешься *pf.* (*of* **раска́лываться**) to split (*also fig.*).

раско́льник, а *m.* **1.** (*relig., hist.*) schismatic, dissenter. **2.** (*pol.; fig.*) splitter.

раско́льническ|ий *adj.* **1.** (*relig., hist.*) schismatic, dissenting. **2.: ~ая та́ктика** (*pol.*) splitting tactics.

раскопа́|ть, ю *pf.* (*of* **раска́пывать**) to dig up, unearth (*also fig.*); (*archaeol.*) to excavate.

раско́пк|а, и *f.* digging up; *pl.* (*archaeol.*) excavations.

раскорм|и́ть, лю́, ~́ишь *pf.* (*of* **раска́рмливать**) to fatten.

раскоря́к|а, и *c.g.* (*coll.*) bow-legged pers.; **ходи́ть ~ой** to walk bow-legged.

раско́с, а *m.* (*tech.*) cross stay, diagonal strut, angle brace.

раско́сый *adj.* (*of eyes*) slanting.

раскоше́лива|ться, юсь *impf. of* **раскоше́литься**

раскоше́л|иться, юсь, ишься *pf.* (*of* **~иваться**) (*coll.*) to loosen one's purse-strings, to fork out.

раскра́дыва|ть, ю *impf. of* **раскра́сть**

раскра́ива|ть, ю *impf. of* **раскрои́ть**

раскра́|сить, шу, сишь *pf.* (*of* **~шивать**) to paint, colour.

раскра́ск|а, и *f.* **1.** painting, colouring. **2.** colours, colour scheme.

раскрасне́|ться, юсь *pf.* to flush, go red (in the face).

раскра́|сть, ду́, дёшь, *past* **~л** *pf.* (*of* **~дывать**) to loot, clean out.

раскрепо|сти́ть, щу́, сти́шь *pf.* (*of* **~ща́ть**) to set free, liberate, emancipate.

раскрепо|сти́ться, щу́сь, сти́шься *pf.* (*of* **~ща́ться**) **1.** to free *or* liberate o.s. **2.** *pass. of* **~сти́ть**

раскрепоща́|ть(ся), ю(сь) *impf. of* **раскрепости́ть(ся)**

раскрепоще́ни|е, я *nt.* liberation, emancipation; **р. же́нщины** emancipation of women.

раскритик|ова́ть, у́ю *pf.* to criticize severely, slate.

раскрич|а́ться, у́сь, и́шься *pf.* **1.** to start shouting, start crying. **2.** (**на**+*a.*) to shout (at), bellow (at).

раскро|и́ть, ю́, и́шь *pf.* (*of* **раскра́ивать**) **1.** to cut out (*material*). **2.** (*fig., coll.*) to cut open; **р. кому́-н. че́реп** to split s.o.'s skull.

раскрош|и́ть(ся), у́(сь), ~́ишь(ся) *pf. of* **кроши́ть(ся)**

раскру|ти́ть, чу́, ~́тишь *pf.* (*of* **~́чивать**) to untwist, untwine, undo.

раскру|ти́ться, ти́тся *pf.* (*of* **~́чиваться**) to come untwisted, come undone.

раскру́чива|ть(ся), ю, ет(ся) *impf. of* **раскрути́ть(ся)**

раскрыва́|ть(ся), ю(сь) *impf. of* **раскры́ть(ся)**

раскры́ти|е, я *nt.* **1.** opening. **2.** exposure, disclosing.

раскр|ы́ть, о́ю, о́ешь *pf.* (*of* **~ыва́ть**) **1.** to open (wide); **р. зо́нтик** to put up an umbrella; **р. кни́гу** to open a book; **р. ско́бки** to open brackets. **2.** to expose, bare. **3.** to reveal, disclose, lay bare; to discover; **р. секре́т** to disclose a secret; **р. свои́ ка́рты** (*fig.*) to show one's cards *or* one's hand.

раскр|ы́ться, о́юсь, о́ешься *pf.* (*of* **~ыва́ться**) **1.** to open; **лепестки́ то́лько что ~ы́лись** the petals have only just opened. **2.** to uncover o.s. **3.** to come out; to come to light.

раскуда́х|таться, чусь, чешься *pf.* (*coll.*) to set up a cackling.

раскула́чивани|е, я *nt.* dispossession of the kulaks, dekulakization.

раскула́чива|ть, ю *impf. of* **раскула́чить**

раскула́ч|ить, у, ишь *pf.* (*of* **~ивать**) to dispossess the kulaks, dekulakize.

раскуме́ка|ть, ю *pf.* (*coll.*) to learn, find out.

раскуп|а́ть, а́ю *impf. of* **~и́ть**
раскуп|и́ть, лю́, ~ишь *pf.* (*of* **~а́ть**) to buy up.
раску́порива|ть(ся), ю, ет(ся) *impf. of* **раску́порить(ся)**
раску́пор|ить, ю, ишь *pf.* (*of* **~ивать**) to uncork, open.
раску́пор|иться, ится *pf.* (*of* **~иваться**) to open, come uncorked.
раску́порк|а, и *f.* uncorking, opening.
раску́рива|ть(ся), ю, ет(ся) *impf. of* **раскури́ть(ся)**
раскур|и́ть, ю́, ~ишь *pf.* (*of* **~ивать**) **1.** to puff at (*a pipe or cigarette*). **2.** to light up.
раскур|и́ться, ~ится *pf.* (*of* **~иваться**) (*of a pipe or cigarette*) to draw.
раску|си́ть, шу́, ~сишь *pf.* (*of* **~сывать**) **1.** to bite through. **2.** (*pf. only*) to get to the core, heart (of); **р. кого́-н.** to see through s.o., rumble s.o.
раску́сыва|ть, ю *impf. of* **раскуси́ть**
раску́т|ать, аю *pf.* (*of* **~ывать**) to unwrap.
раску́т|аться, аюсь *pf.* (*of* **~ываться**) to unwrap o.s.
раску|ти́ться, чу́сь, ~тишься *pf.* (*coll.*) to take to going on drinking-bouts.
раску́тыва|ть(ся), ю(сь) *impf. of* **раску́тать(ся)**
ра́совый *adj.* racial.
распа́д, а *m.* **1.** disintegration, break-up; (*fig.*) collapse. **2.** (*chem.*) decomposition, dissociation.
распада́|ться, ется *impf. of* **распа́сться**
распа́ива|ть(ся), ю(сь), ет(ся) *impf. of* **распая́ть(ся)**
распак|ова́ть, у́ю *pf.* (*of* **~о́вывать**) to unpack.
распак|ова́ться, у́юсь *pf.* (*of* **~о́вываться**) **1.** (*of a parcel, etc.*) to come undone. **2.** (*coll.*) to unpack (one's things).
распако́выва|ть(ся), ю(сь) *impf. of* **распакова́ть(ся)**
распал|и́ть, ю́, и́шь *pf.* (*of* **~я́ть**) **1.** to make burning hot. **2.** (*fig.*) to inflame; **р. гне́вом** to incense.
распал|и́ться, ю́сь, и́шься *pf.* (*of* **~я́ться**) **1.** to get burning hot. **2.** (*+i.*; *fig.*) to burn (with); **р. гне́вом** to be incensed.
распал|я́ть(ся), я́ю(сь) *impf. of* **~и́ть(ся)**
распа́р, а *m.* (*tech.*) bosh, body (*of blast furnace*).
распа́рива|ть(ся), ю(сь) *impf. of* **распа́рить(ся)**
распа́р|ить, ю, ишь *pf.* (*of* **~ивать**) **1.** to steam out; to stew well. **2.** to cause to sweat.
распа́р|иться, юсь, ишься *pf.* (*of* **~иваться**) **1.** to steam out; to be well stewed. **2.** to break into a sweat.
распа́рыва|ть(ся), ю, ет(ся) *impf. of* **распоро́ть(ся)**
распа́|сться, дётся, *past* **~лся** *pf.* (*of* **~да́ться**) **1.** to disintegrate, fall to pieces; (*fig.*) to break up; to collapse; **коали́ция ~лась** the coalition broke up. **2.** (*chem.*) to decompose, dissociate.
распа|ха́ть, шу́, ~шешь *pf.* (*of* **~хивать**) to plough up.
распа́хива|ть, ю *impf. of* **распаха́ть** *and* **распахну́ть**
распа́хива|ться, юсь *impf. of* **распахну́ться**
распах|ну́ть, ну́, нёшь *pf.* (*of* **~ивать**) to open wide; to fling open, throw open; **широко́ р. две́ри** (*+d.*) to open wide the doors (to) (*also fig.*).
распах|ну́ться, ну́сь, нёшься *pf.* (*of* **~иваться**) **1.** to open wide; to fly open, swing open. **2.** to throw open one's coat.
распа́шк|а, и *f.* ploughing up.
распашно́й[1] *adj.* (*obs.*; *of clothing*) worn open, unfastened.
распашн|о́й[2] *adj.*: **~о́е весло́** paddle; **~а́я гре́бля** paddling.
распашн|о́й[3] *adj.* (*dial.*) for ploughing up; **~а́я земля́** ploughland.
распашо́нк|а, и *f.* (*baby's*) vest.
распа|я́ть, я́ю *pf.* (*of* **~ивать**) to unsolder.
распа|я́ться, я́ется *pf.* (*of* **~иваться**) to come unsoldered.
распева́|ть, ю *impf.* **1.** *impf. of* **распе́ть. 2.** to sing for a certain time.
распека́|ть, ю *impf. of* **распе́чь**
распелен|а́ть, а́ю *pf.* (*of* **~ывать**) to unswaddle.
распере́ть, разопру́, разопрёшь, *past* **распёр, распёрла** *pf.* (*of* **распира́ть**) (*coll.*) to burst open, cause to burst.
распетуш|и́ться, у́сь, и́шься *pf.* (*coll.*) to get into a paddy; to have one's hackles up.
расп|е́ть, ою́, оёшь *pf.* (*of* **~ева́ть**) **1.** to sing through. **2.** to practise (*one's voice*).
расп|е́ться, ою́сь, оёшься *pf.* (*coll.*) **1.** (*of a singer*) to warm up. **2.** to sing away.
распеча́т|ать, аю *pf.* (*of* **~ывать**) **1.** to unseal; **р. письмо́** to open a letter. **2.** to print out.
распеча́т|аться, ается *pf.* (*of* **~ываться**) to come unsealed, to come open.
распеча́тк|а, и *f.* printout.
распеча́тыва|ть(ся), ю, ет(ся) *impf. of* **распеча́тать(ся)**
распе́|чь, ку́, чёшь, ку́т, *past* **~к, ~кла́** *pf.* (*of* **~ка́ть**) (*coll.*) to blow up.
распива́|ть, ю *impf. of* **распи́ть**
распи́вочно *adv.*: **прода́жа пите́й р.** sale of liquor for consumption on the premises.
распи́вочн|ый *adj.* (*obs.*) for consumption on the premises; *as n.* **~ая, ~ой** *f.* (*obs.*) tavern, bar.
распи́л, а *m.* saw cut.
распи́лива|ть, ю *impf. of* **распили́ть**
распил|и́ть, ю́, ~ишь *pf.* (*of* **~ивать**) to saw up.
распи́лк|а, и *f.* sawing.
распило́вк|а, и *f.* = **распи́лка**
распина́|ть, ю *impf. of* **распя́ть**
распина́|ться, юсь *impf.* (**за кого́-н.**; *coll.*) to put o.s. out (*sc. on s.o.'s behalf*).
распира́|ть, ю *impf. of* **распере́ть**
расписа́ни|е, я *nt.* time-table, schedule; **боево́е р.** (*mil.*) order of battle; (*naut.*) battle stations; **по ~ю** according to time-table, according to schedule.
распи|са́ть, шу́, ~шешь *pf.* (*of* **~сывать**) **1.** to enter; to note down; **р. счета́ по кни́гам** to enter bills in the account-book. **2.** to assign, allot. **3.** to paint. **4.** (*fig., coll.*) to paint a picture (of).
распи|са́ться, шу́сь, ~шешься *pf.* (*of* **~сываться**) **1.** to sign (one's name); (**в**+*p.*) to sign (for); **прочти́те э́ту бума́гу и ~ши́тесь** read this paper and sign your name; **р. в получе́нии заказно́го паке́та** to sign for a registered letter. **2.** (*coll.*) to register one's marriage. **3.** (**в**+*p.*; *fig.*) to acknowledge, testify (to); **р. в со́бственном неве́жестве** to acknowledge one's own ignorance.
распи́ск|а[1]**, и** *f.* painting.
распи́ск|а[2]**, и** *f.* receipt; **р. в получе́нии** (*+g.*) receipt (for); **письмо́ с обра́тной ~ой** letter with advice of delivery; **сдать письмо́ под ~у** to make s.o. sign for a letter.
расписно́й *adj.* painted, decorated.
распи́сыва|ть(ся), ю(сь) *impf. of* **расписа́ть(ся)**
рас|пи́ть, разопью́, разопьёшь, *past* **~пи́л** (*and* **ро́спил**), **~пила́, ~пи́ло** (*and* **ро́спило**) *pf.* (*of* **~пива́ть**) (*coll.*) to drink up; **р. бу́тылку** (**с кем-н.**) to split a bottle (with s.o.).
распих|а́ть, а́ю *pf.* (*of* **~ивать**) (*coll.*) **1.** to push aside. **2.** to shove; **р. я́блоки по карма́нам** to stuff apples into one's pockets.
распи́хива|ть, ю *impf. of* **распиха́ть**
распла́в|ить, лю, ишь *pf.* (*of* **~ля́ть**) to melt, fuse.
распла́в|иться, ится *pf.* (*of* **~ля́ться**) to melt, fuse (*intrans.*).
расплавле́ни|е, я *nt.* melting, fusion.
расплавля́|ть(ся), ю, ет(ся) *impf. of* **распла́вить(ся)**
распла́|каться, чусь, чешься *pf.* to burst into tears.
распланир|ова́ть, у́ю *pf. of* **плани́ровать**
распласт|а́ть, а́ю *pf.* (*of* **~ывать**) **1.** to split, divide into layers. **2.** to spread; **р. кры́лья** to spread one's wings.
распласт|а́ться, а́юсь *pf.* (*of* **~ываться**) to sprawl.
распла́стыва|ть(ся), ю(сь) *impf. of* **распласта́ть(ся)**
распла́т|а, ы *f.* payment; (*fig.*) retribution; **час ~ы** day of reckoning.
распла|ти́ться, чу́сь, ~тишься *pf.* (*of* **~чиваться**) **1.** (**с**+*i.*) to pay off; to settle accounts (with), get even (with) (*also fig.*); **р. с долга́ми** to pay off one's debts; **р. по ста́рым счета́м** to pay off old scores. **2.** (**за**+*a.*; *fig.*) to pay (for).
распла́чива|ться, юсь *impf. of* **расплати́ться**
расплe|ска́ть, щу́, ~щешь *pf.* (*of* **~скивать**) to spill.
расплe|ска́ться, щу́сь, ~щешься *pf.* (*of* **~скиваться**) **1.** to spill. **2.** *pass. of* **~ска́ть**
расплёскива|ть(ся), ю(сь) *impf. of* **расплеска́ть(ся)**

распле|сти́, ту́, тёшь, *past* **~л, ~ла́** *pf.* (*of* **~та́ть**) to untwine, untwist, unweave, undo, to unplait.
распле|сти́сь, тётся, *past* **~лся, ~ла́сь** *pf.* (*of* **~та́ться**) to untwine, untwist; to come undone; to come unplaited.
расплета́|ть(ся), ю, ет(ся) *impf. of* **расплести́(сь)**
расплo|ди́ть(ся), жу́(сь), ди́шь(ся) *pf. of* **плоди́ть(ся)**
расплыва́|ться, ется *impf. of* **расплы́ться**
расплы́вчат|ый (~, ~а) *adj.* dim, ndistinct; diffuse, vague; **~ые очерта́ния** dim outlines; **р. стиль** woolly style.
расплы́|ться, вётся, *past* **~лся, ~ла́сь** *pf.* (*of* **~ва́ться**) **1.** to run; **черни́ла ~лись** the ink has run. **2.** (*coll.*) to spread; to run to fat; **р. в улы́бку** to break into a smile.
расплю́щива|ть(ся), ю, ет(ся) *impf. of* **расплю́щить(ся)**
расплю́щ|ить, у, ишь *pf.* (*of* **~ивать**) to flatten out, hammer out.
расплю́щ|иться, ится *pf.* (*of* **~иваться**) to become flat.
распознава́|емый *pres. part. pass. of* **~ть** *and adj.* recognizable, identifiable.
распознава́ни|е, я *nt.* recognition, identification.
распозна|ва́ть, ю́, ёшь *impf. of* **~ть**
распозна́|ть, ю, ешь *pf.* (*of* **~ва́ть**) to recognize, identify; **р. боле́знь** to diagnose an illness.
располага́|ть[1], **ю** *impf.* **1.** (*+i.*) to dispose (of), have at one's disposal, have available; **р. вре́менем** to have time available; **р. больши́ми сре́дствами** to dispose of ample means. **2.** (*+inf.*; *obs.*) to intend, propose.
располага́|ть[2], **ю** *impf. of* **расположи́ть**
располага́|ться, юсь *impf. of* **расположи́ться**[1]
располага́|ющий *pres. part. act. of* **~ть** *and adj.* prepossessing.
располз|а́ться, а́юсь *impf. of* **~ти́сь**
располз|ти́сь, у́сь ёшься, *past* **~ся, ~ла́сь** *pf.* (*of* **~а́ться**) **1.** to crawl (away). **2.** (*of clothing, etc.*; *coll.*) to come unravelled; to tear, give at the seams.
расположе́ни|е, я *nt.* **1.** disposition, arrangement; **р. по кварти́рам** (*mil.*) billeting; **р. не́рвов** (*bot.*) nervation; **р. слов** word-order. **2.** situation, location; **р. на ме́стности** (*mil.*) location on the ground. **3.** favour, liking; sympathies; **по́льзоваться чьим-н. ~ем** to enjoy s.o.'s favour, be liked by s.o., be in s.o.'s good books; **чу́вствовать к кому́-н. р.** to be favourably disposed towards s.o. **4.** **(к)** disposition (to), inclination (to, for); tendency (to), propensity (to); bias (towards), penchant (for); **у неё р. к бронхи́ту** she has a tendency to bronchitis, she is inclined to be bronchial. **5. р. (ду́ха)** disposition, mood, humour; **быть в плохо́м ~и ду́ха** to be in a bad mood; **у меня́ нет ~я танцева́ть** I am not in the mood for dancing.
располо́жен|ный (~, ~а) *p.p.p. of* **расположи́ть** *and pred adj.* **1.** **(к)** well disposed (to, towards). **2.** **(к** *or +inf.*) disposed (to), inclined (to); in the mood (for); **я не ~ к отвлечённому размышле́нию** I am not disposed to, am not in the mood for abstract speculation; **я не о́чень ~ сего́дня рабо́тать** I don't feel much like working today.
располож|и́ть, у́, ~ишь *pf.* (*of* **располага́ть**[2]) **1.** to dispose, arrange, set out; **р. свои́ войска́** to dispose, station one's troops. **2.** to win over, gain; **р. кого́-н. к себе́, в свою́ по́льзу** to gain s.o.'s favour.
располож|и́ться[1], **у́сь, ~ишься** *pf.* (*of* **располага́ться**) to take up position; to settle *or* compose o.s.; to make o.s. comfortable; **р. спать** to settle o.s. to sleep.
располож|и́ться[2], **у́сь, ~ишься** *pf.* (*+inf.*; *obs.*) to resolve, make up one's mind.
распо́р, а *m.* (*tech.*) thrust.
распо́рк|а, и *f.* (*tech.*) cross-bar, strut, tie-beam, tie-rod, spreader bar.
распор|о́ть, ю́, ~ешь *pf.* (*of* **поро́ть**[1] *and* **распа́рывать**) to unstitch, unpick, undo, rip.
распор|о́ться, ~ется *pf.* (*of* **поро́тся** *and* **распа́рываться**) to come unstitched, come undone, rip.
распоряди́тел|ь, я *m.* manager; master of ceremonies.
распоряди́тельност|ь, и *f.* good management; efficiency; **отсу́тствие ~и** mismanagement.
распоряди́тел|ьный (~ен, ~ьна) *adj.* capable; efficient; **р. челове́к** a good organizer.
распоря|ди́ться, жу́сь, ди́шься *pf.* (*of* **~жа́ться**) **1.** (о+*p. or +inf.*) to order; to see (that); **мы ~ди́мся о проведе́нии э́того реше́ния** we will see that this decision is implemented; **я ~жу́сь возмести́ть вам расхо́ды** I will see that you are reimbursed for the expenses. **2.** (*+i.*) to manage; to deal (with); **разреши́ть кому́-н. р. по своему́ усмотре́нию** to give s.o. a free hand; **как р. э́тими деньга́ми?** what is to be done with this money?; how should this money be used?
распоря́д|ок, ка *m.* order; routine; **пра́вила вну́треннего ~ка (в учрежде́нии, на фа́брике,** *etc.*) (office, factory, *etc.*) regulations; **р. дня** the daily routine.
распоряжа́|ться, юсь *impf.* **1.** *impf. of* **распоряди́ться. 2.** *impf. only* to give orders, be in charge; to be the boss; **р. как у себя́ до́ма** to behave as though the place belongs to one.
распоряже́ни|е, я *nt.* **1.** order; instruction, direction; **до осо́бого ~я** until further notice. **2.** disposal, command; **быть в ~и кого́-н.** to be at s.o.'s disposal; **име́ть в своём ~и** to have at one's disposal, command.
распоя́|сать, шу, шешь *pf.* (*of* **~сывать**) to ungird.
распоя́|саться, шусь, шешься *pf.* (*of* **~сываться**) **1.** to take off one's belt; to ungird o.s. **2.** (*fig., coll., pej.*) to throw aside all restraint; to let o.s. go.
распоя́сыва|ть(ся), ю(сь) *impf. of* **распоя́сать(ся)**
распра́в|а, ы *f.* **1.** (*hist.*) punishment, execution; **твори́ть суд и ~у** to administer justice and mete out punishment. **2.** violence; reprisal; **крова́вая р.** massacre; **кула́чная р.** fist-law; **коро́ткая р.** short shrift; **у нас с ни́ми р. коротка́** we'll give them short shrift; we'll make short work of them.
распра́в|ить, лю, ишь *pf.* (*of* **~ля́ть**) **1.** to straighten; to smooth out; **р. морщи́ны** to smooth out wrinkles. **2.** to spread, stretch; **р. кры́лья** to spread one's wings (*also fig.*).
распра́в|иться[1], **ится** *pf.* (*of* **~ля́ться**) to get smoothed out.
распра́в|иться[2], **люсь, ишься** *pf.* (*of* **~ля́ться**) **(с** *+i.*) to deal (with), make short work (of), give short shrift; **р. без суда́** to take the law into one's own hands.
расправля́|ть(ся), ю(сь) *impf. of* **распра́вить(ся)**
распределе́ни|е, я *nt.* distribution; allocation, assignment; **р. нало́гов** assessment of taxes; **р. войск** (*mil.*) order of battle.
распредели́тел|ь, я *m.* **1.** distributor; retailer; **закры́тый р.** retail establishment closed to persons not registered. **2.** (*elec.*) distributor; spreader.
распредели́тельн|ый *adj.* distributive, distributing; **~ая доска́, р. щит** (*tech.*) switchboard; **р. вал** (*tech.*) cam shaft; **р. кла́пан** (*tech.*) regulating valve; **~ая коро́бка** (*elec.*) switch box, junction box, panel box.
распредел|и́ть, ю́, и́шь *pf.* (*of* **~я́ть**) to distribute; to allocate, allot, assign; **р. своё вре́мя** to allocate one's time.
распредел|и́ться, и́тся *pf.* (*of* **~я́ться**) **1.** to divide up, split up. **2.** *pass. of* **~и́ть**
распредел|я́ть(ся), я́ю(сь) *impf. of* **~и́ть(ся)**
распрекра́с|ный (~ен, ~на) *adj.* (*coll.*) beautiful, fine, splendid.
распрода|ва́ть, ю́, ёшь *impf. of* **~ть**
распрода́ж|а, и *f.* sale; clearance sale, bargain sale.
распрода́|ть, м, шь, ст, ди́м, ди́те, ду́т, *past* **распро́дал, ~ла́, распро́дало** *pf.* (*of* **~ва́ть**) to sell off; to sell out; **биле́ты распро́даны** all the tickets are sold.
распростер|е́ть, *fut. tense not used, past* **~, ~ла** *pf.* (*of* **распростира́ть**) to stretch out, extend.
распростер|е́ться, *fut. tense not used, past* **~ся, ~лась** *pf.* (*of* **распростира́ться**) **1.** to stretch o.s. out; to prostrate o.s. **2.** (*fig.*) to spread.
распростёр|тый *p.p.p. of* **~е́ть** *and adj.* **1.** outstretched; **встре́тить с ~тыми объя́тиями** to receive with outstretched arms. **2.** prostrate, prone.
распростира́|ть(ся), ю(сь) *impf. of* **распростере́ть(ся)**
распро|сти́ться, щу́сь, сти́шься *pf.* **(с** *+i.*) to take final leave (of); **р. с мечто́й** to bid farewell to one's dream(s).
распростране́ни|е, я *nt.* spreading, diffusion; dissemination; **р. зара́зы** spreading of infection; **име́ть большо́е р.** to be widely practised.
распространённост|ь, и *f.* prevalence; diffusion.

распростран|ённый *p.p.p. of* **~и́ть** *and adj.* **1.** widespread, prevalent; **широко́ р.** widely-distributed. **2.: ~ённое предложе́ние** (*gram.*) extended sentence.

распространи́тел|ь, я *m.* spreader.

распространи́тельн|ый *adj.* extended; (excessively) wide; **~ое толкова́ние прика́за** a wide interpretation of an injunction.

распростран|и́ть, ю́, и́шь *pf.* (*of* **~я́ть**) **1.** to spread, diffuse; to disseminate, propagate; to popularize; **р. слух** to spread a rumour; **р. но́вое уче́ние** to disseminate a new doctrine. **2.** to extend; **р. де́йствие зако́на на всех** to extend the application of a law to all. **3.** to give off, give out (*a smell*).

распростран|и́ться, ю́сь, и́шься *pf.* (*of* **~я́ться**) **1.** to spread; to extend; (*of a law, etc.*) to apply. **2.** (**о**+*p.*; *coll.*) to enlarge (on), expatiate (on), dilate (on).

распростран|я́ть(ся), я́ю(сь) *impf. of* **~и́ть(ся)**

распроща́|ться, юсь *pf.* (**с**+*i.*; *coll.*) = **распрости́ться**

распры́ска|ть, ю *pf.* (*coll.*) to spray about; to use up (in spraying).

ра́спр|я, и, *g. pl.* **~ей** *f.* quarrel, feud.

распряга́|ть(ся), ю(сь) *impf. of* **распря́чь(ся)**

распрям|и́ть, лю́, и́шь *pf.* (*of* **~ля́ть**) to straighten, unbend.

распрям|и́ться, лю́сь, и́шься *pf.* (*of* **~ля́ться**) to straighten o.s. up.

распрямля́|ть(ся), ю(сь) *impf. of* **распрями́ть(ся)**

распря́|чь, гу́, жёшь, гу́т, *past* **~г, ~гла́** *pf.* (*of* **~га́ть**) to unharness.

распря́|чься, жётся, гу́тся, *past* **~гся, ~гла́сь** *pf.* (*of* **~га́ться**) to get unharnessed.

распублик|ова́ть, у́ю *pf.* (*of* **~о́вывать**) to publish, to promulgate.

распублико́выва|ть, ю *impf. of* **распубликова́ть**

распуг|а́ть, а́ю *pf.* (*of* **~́ивать**) to scare away, frighten away.

распуска́|ть(ся), ю(сь) *impf. of* **распусти́ть(ся)**

распу|сти́ть, щу́, ~́стишь *pf.* (*of* **~ска́ть**) **1.** to dismiss; to disband; **р. парла́мент** to dissolve parliament; **р. кома́нду** (*naut.*) to pay off a crew; **р. на кани́кулы** to dismiss for the holidays. **2.** to let out; to relax; **р. во́лосы** to let one's hair down; **р. знамёна** to unfurl banners; **р. паруса́** to set sail. **3.** (*fig.*) to allow to become undisciplined, allow to get out of hand; to spoil. **4.** to dissolve; to melt. **5.** (*coll.*) to spread, put out (*rumours, etc.*).

распу|сти́ться, щу́сь, ~́стишься *pf.* (*of* **~ска́ться**) **1.** (*bot.*) to open, blossom out, come out. **2.** to come loose; **чуло́к у неё ~сти́лся** her stocking had come down. **3.** (*fig.*) to become undisciplined, get out of hand, let o.s. go. **4.** to dissolve; to melt.

распу́т|ать, аю *pf.* (*of* **~ывать**) **1.** to untangle, disentangle; to unravel. **2.** to untie, loose (*an animal*). **3.** (*fig.*) to disentangle, unravel; to puzzle out.

распу́т|аться, аюсь *pf.* (*of* **~ываться**) **1.** to get disentangled, come undone. **2.** (*fig., coll.*) to get disentangled, be cleared up. **3.** (**с**+*i.*; *coll.*) to rid o.s. (of), shake off.

распу́тиц|а, ы *f.* time (*during spring and autumn*) of bad roads.

распу́тник, а *m.* profligate, libertine.

распу́тнича|ть, ю *impf.* to lead a dissolute life.

распу́т|ный (~ен, ~на) *adj.* dissolute, dissipated, debauched.

распу́тств|о, а *nt.* dissipation, debauchery, profligacy, libertinism.

распу́тыва|ть(ся), ю(сь) *impf. of* **распу́тать(ся)**

распу́ть|е, я *nt.* crossroads; **быть на р.** (*fig.*) to be at the crossroads, be at the parting of the ways.

распух|а́ть, а́ю *impf. of* **~́нуть**

распу́х|нуть, ну, нешь, *past* **~, ~ла** *pf.* (*of* **~а́ть**) **1.** to swell up. **2.** (*fig., coll.*) to swell, become inflated.

распуш|и́ть, у́, и́шь *pf. of* **пуши́ть**

распу́щенност|ь, и *f.* **1.** lack of discipline. **2.** dissoluteness, dissipation.

распу́|щенный *p.p.p. of* **~сти́ть** *and adj.* **1.** undisciplined; **р. ребёнок** spoiled child. **2.** dissolute, dissipated.

распыле́ни|е, я *nt.* **1.** spraying; atomization. **2.** dispersion, scattering; **р. средств** dissipation of resources.

распыли́тел|ь, я *m.* spray(er), atomizer, pulverizer.

распыл|и́ть, ю́, и́шь *pf.* (*of* **~я́ть**) **1.** to spray; to atomize; to pulverize. **2.** (*fig.*) to disperse, scatter; **р. си́лы** to scatter one's forces.

распыл|и́ться, и́тся *pf.* (*of* **~я́ться**) **1.** to disperse, to get scattered. **2.** *pass. of* **~и́ть**

распыл|я́ть(ся), я́ю(сь) *impf. of* **~и́ть(ся)**

распя́лива|ть, ю *impf. of* **распя́лить**

распя́л|ить, ю, ишь *pf.* (*of* **~ивать**) to stretch (*on a frame*).

распя́ти|е, я *nt.* **1.** crucifixion. **2.** cross, crucifix.

расп|я́ть, ну́, нёшь *pf.* (*of* **~ина́ть**) to crucify.

расса́д|а, ы *no pl., f.* seedlings.

расса|ди́ть, жу́, ~́дишь *pf.* (*of* **~́живать**) **1.** to seat, offer seats. **2.** to separate, seat separately. **3.** to transplant, plant out.

расса́дк|а, и *f.* transplanting, planting out.

расса́дник, а *m.* **1.** seed-plot. **2.** (*fig.*) hotbed, breeding-ground.

расса́жива|ть, ю *impf. of* **рассади́ть**

расса́жива|ться, юсь *impf. of* **рассе́сться**[1]

расса́сывани|е, я *nt.* (*med.*) resolution, resorption.

расса́сыва|ться, юсь *impf. of* **рассоса́ться**

рассве|сти́, тёт, *past* **~ло́** *pf.* (*of* **~та́ть**) to dawn; **уже́ ~ло́** it was already light; **соверше́нно ~ло́** it was broad daylight.

рассве́т, а *m.* dawn, daybreak.

рассвета́|ть, ет *impf. of* **рассвести́; ~ет** day is breaking.

рассвирепе́|ть, ю *pf.* (*of* **свирепе́ть**) to become savage; to turn nasty.

рассе́да́|ться, юсь *impf. of* **рассе́сться**[2]

расседл|а́ть, а́ю *pf.* (*of* **~́ывать**) to unsaddle.

рассе́ивани|е, я *nt.* dispersion; dispersal, scattering, dissipation.

рассе́ива|ть(ся), ю(сь) *impf. of* **рассе́ять(ся)**

рассека́|ть, ю *impf. of* **рассе́чь**

рассекре́|тить, чу, тишь *pf.* (*of* **~чивать**) **1.** to declassify, remove from secret list. **2.** to deny access to secret documents; to take off secret work.

рассекре́чива|ть, ю *impf. of* **рассекре́тить**

расселе́ни|е, я *nt.* **1.** settling (*in a new place*). **2.** separation; settling apart.

рассе́лин|а, ы *f.* cleft, fissure.

рассел|и́ть, ю́, и́шь *pf.* (*of* **~я́ть**) **1.** to settle (*in a new place*). **2.** to separate; to settle apart.

рассел|и́ться, ю́сь, и́шься *pf.* (*of* **~я́ться**) **1.** to settle (*in a new place*). **2.** to separate, settle separately.

рассел|я́ть(ся), я́ю(сь) *impf. of* **~и́ть(ся)**

рассер|ди́ть, жу́, ~́дишь *pf.* to anger, make angry.

рассер|ди́ться, жу́сь, ~́дишься *pf.* (**на**+*a.*) to get, become angry (with).

рассе́р|женный *p.p.p. of* **~ди́ть** *and adj.* angry.

рассерча́|ть, ю *pf.* (*coll.*) to get angry.

рас|се́сться[1]**, ся́дусь, ся́дешься,** *past* **~се́лся** *pf.* (*of* **~са́живаться**) **1.** to take one's seat. **2.** (*coll.*) to sprawl.

рас|се́сться[2]**, ся́дется,** *past* **~се́лся** *pf.* (*of* **~седа́ться**) to crack.

рассе́|чь, ку́, чёшь, ку́т, *past* **~к, ~кла́** *pf.* (*of* **~ка́ть**) **1.** to cut through; to cleave (*also fig.*). **2.** to cut (badly); **я ~к себе́ па́лец** I have cut my finger badly.

рассе́яни|е, я *nt.* diffusion; dispersion; **р. тепла́** (*phys.*) dissipation of heat, thermal dispersion; **р. све́та** (*phys.*) diffusion of light.

рассе́янност|ь, и *f.* **1.** diffusion; dispersion; dissipation. **2.** absent-mindedness, distraction.

рассе́я|нный *p.p.p. of* **~ть** *and adj.* **1.** diffused; dissipated; **р. свет** (*phys.*) diffused light. **2.** scattered, dispersed; **~нное населе́ние** scattered population. **3.** absent-minded; **р. взгляд** vacant look. **4.** (*fig.*) dissipated.

рассе́|ять, ю, ешь *pf.* (*of* **~ивать**) **1.** to sow broadcast, scatter. **2.** (*fig.*) to place (about), establish (about), dot (about). **3.** to disperse, scatter; (*fig.*) to dispel; **р. чьи-н. сомне́ния** to dispel s.o.'s doubts.

рассе́|яться, юсь, ешься *pf.* (*of* **~иваться**) **1.** to disperse, scatter; **толпа́ ~ялась** the crowd dispersed; **неприя́тельский отря́д ~ялся** the enemy detachment scattered; **тума́н**

~ялся the fog cleared; **её горе ~ялось** her grief passed; **р. как дым** to vanish into thin air, into smoke. **2.** to divert o.s., distract o.s.; **ему надо р.** he needs a break.

расси|деться, жусь, дишься *pf.* (*of* ~**живаться**) (*coll.*) to sit for a long time.

рассижива|ться, юсь *impf. of* **рассидеться**

рассказ, а *m.* **1.** account, narrative. **2.** story, tale.

расска|зать, жу, ~жешь *pf.* (*of* ~**зывать**) to tell, narrate, recount.

рассказчик, а *m.* story-teller, narrator.

рассказыва|ть, ю *impf. of* **рассказать**

расслабева|ть, ю *impf. of* **расслабеть**

расслабе|ть, ю *pf.* (*of* ~**вать**) to weaken, grow weak; to tire; to grow limp.

расслаб|ить, лю, ишь *pf.* (*of* ~**лять**) to weaken, enfeeble; to enervate.

расслаб|ленный *p.p.p. of* ~**ить** *and adj.* weak; limp.

расслабля|ть, ю *impf. of* **расслабить**

расслаб|нуть, ну, нешь, *past* ~, ~**ла** *pf.* (*coll.*) = ~**еть**

расслав|ить, лю, ишь *pf.* (*of* ~**лять**) (*coll.*) **1.** to praise to the skies. **2.** to shout from the house-tops.

расславля|ть, ю *impf. of* **расславить**

расслаива|ть(ся), ю, ет(ся) *impf. of* **расслоить(ся)**

расследовани|е, я *nt.* investigation, examination; (*leg.*) inquiry; **назначить р.** (+*g.*) to order an inquiry (into); **произвести р.** (+*g.*) to hold an inquiry (into).

расслед|овать, ую *impf. and pf.* to investigate, look into, hold an inquiry (into).

расслоени|е, я *nt.* stratification (*also fig.*); exfoliation.

рассло|ить, ю, ишь *pf.* (*of* **расслаивать**) to divide into layers, stratify (*also fig.*).

рассло|иться, ится *pf.* (*of* **расслаиваться**) to become stratified (*also fig.*); to exfoliate, flake off.

расслойк|а, и *f.* **1.** stratification. **2.** (*geol.*) stratum.

расслуша|ть, ю *pf.* (*obs.*) to listen properly (to).

расслыш|ать, у, ишь *pf.* to catch; **я не ~ал вас** I didn't catch what you said.

рассматрива|ть, ю *impf.* **1.** *impf. of* **рассмотреть**. **2.** *impf. only* to regard (as), consider; **мы ~ем это как обман** we regard it as a fraud. **3.** *impf. only* to scrutinize, examine.

рассмеш|ить, у, ишь *pf.* to make laugh, set laughing.

рассме|яться, юсь, ёшься *pf.* to burst out laughing.

рассмотрени|е, я *nt.* examination, scrutiny; consideration; **представить на р.** to submit for consideration; **быть на ~и** to be under consideration; **оставить жалобу без ~я** to reject a complaint; **передать дело на новое р.** to submit a case for re-consideration.

рассмотр|еть, ю, ~ишь *pf.* (*of* **рассматривать**) **1.** to descry, discern, make out; **мы с трудом ~ели надпись на памятнике** we had difficulty in making out the inscription on the monument. **2.** to examine, consider; **р. заявление** to consider an application.

расс|овать, ую, уёшь *pf.* (*of* ~**овывать**) (*coll.*) to shove (about), stuff (about); **р. свои вещи по чемоданам** to stuff one's things into suitcases.

рассовыва|ть, ю *impf. of* **рассовать**

рассол, а *m.* **1.** brine. **2.** (*cul.*) pickle.

рассольник, а *m.* rassolnik (*meat or fish soup with pickled cucumbers*).

рассор|ить, ю, ишь *pf.* to set at variance, set at loggerheads.

рассор|ить, ю, ишь *pf.* (*coll.*) to drop (over); **р. окурки по полу** to litter the floor with cigarette-butts.

рассор|иться, юсь, ишься *pf.* (**с**+*i.*) to fall out (with), fall foul (of).

рассортир|овать, ую *pf.* (*of* ~**овывать**) to sort out.

рассортировк|а, и *f.* sorting out.

рассортировыва|ть, ю *impf. of* **рассортировать**

рассос|аться, ётся *pf.* (*of* **рассасываться**) (*med.*) to resolve.

рассох|нуться, нется, *past* ~**ся**, ~**лась** *pf.* (*of* **рассыхаться**) to crack.

расспрашива|ть, ю *impf. of* **расспросить**

расспрос, а *m.* question, questioning; **надоесть ~ами** to pester with questions.

расспро|сить, шу, ~сишь *pf.* (*of* **расспрашивать**) to question; **р. кого-н. о дороге** to ask s.o. the way.

рассредоточени|е, я *nt.* (*mil.*) dispersion, dispersal.

рассредоточива|ть, ю *impf. of* **рассредоточить**

рассредоточ|ить, у, ишь *pf.* (*of* ~**ивать**) (*mil.*) to disperse.

рассрочива|ть, ю *impf. of* **рассрочить**

рассроч|ить, у, ишь *pf.* (*of* ~**ивать**) to spread (*over a period*); **р. выплату долга** to allow payment of a debt by instalments; **р. издание энциклопедии на десять лет** to spread the publication of an encyclopaedia over (a period of) ten years.

рассрочк|а, и *f.* instalment system; **в ~у** by, in instalments; **купить с ~ой платежа** to purchase by instalments, on the hire-purchase system; **предоставить ~у** to grant the right to pay by instalments.

расставани|е, я *nt.* parting; **при ~и** on parting.

расста|ваться, юсь, ёшься *impf. of* **расстаться**

расстав|ить, лю, ишь *pf.* (*of* ~**лять**) **1.** (*impf. also* **расстанавливать**) to place, arrange; **р. часовых** to post sentries; **р. шахматы** to set out chess-men. **2.** to move apart; **р. ноги** to stand with one's legs apart. **3.** (*tailoring*) to let out.

расставк|а, и *f.* (*tailoring*) letting out.

расставля|ть, ю *impf. of* **расставить**

расстанавлива|ть, ю *impf. of* **расставить**

расстановк|а, и *f.* **1.** placing, arrangement; **р. знаков препинания** punctuation. **2.** pause; spacing; **говорить с ~ой** to speak without haste, speak slowly and deliberately.

расста|ться, нусь, нешься *pf.* (*of* ~**ваться**) (**с**+*i.*) **1.** to part (with); to leave; **~немся друзьями** let us part friends. **2.** to give up; **р. с мыслью** to put the thought out of one's head.

расстега|й, я *m.* open-topped pasty.

расстёгива|ть(ся), ю(сь) *impf. of* **расстегнуть(ся)**

расстег|нуть, ну, нёшь *pf.* (*of* ~**ивать**) to undo, unfasten; to unbutton; to unhook, unclasp, unbuckle.

расстег|нуться, нусь, нёшься *pf.* (*of* ~**иваться**) **1.** to come undone, become unfastened; to become unbuttoned; to become unhooked. **2.** to undo one's coat, unbutton one's coat; to undo one's buttons.

расстел|иться, ю(сь), ~ишь(ся) *pf.* = **разостлать(ся)**

расстила|ть, ю *impf. of* **разостлать**

расстила|ться, юсь *impf.* **1.** *impf. of* **разостлаться**. **2.** *impf. only* to extend, unfold; **перед нашими глазами ~лась величественная панорама гор** before our eyes unfolded a magnificent mountain panorama.

расстояни|е, я *nt.* distance, space, interval; **на близком ~и (от)** at a short distance (from), a short way away (from); **на далёком ~и** in the far distance, a great way off; **на ~и пушечного выстрела** within gunshot; **на ~и человеческого голоса** within hail; **они живут на ~и двух миль от ближайшего соседа** they live two miles from their nearest neighbour; **держать кого-н. на ~и** to keep s.o. at arm's length; **держаться на ~и** to keep one's distance, hold aloof.

расстраива|ть(ся), ю(сь) *impf. of* **расстроить(ся)**

расстрел, а *m.* **1.** (military) execution; **приговорить к ~у** to sentence to be shot. **2.** shooting up.

расстрелива|ть, ю *impf. of* **расстрелять**

расстрел|ять, яю *pf.* (*of* ~**ивать**) **1.** to shoot, execute by shooting. **2.** to shoot up; to fire upon at close range. **3.** to use up (*in firing*).

расстриг|а, и *m.* unfrocked priest, unfrocked monk.

расстрига|ть, ю *impf. of* **расстричь**

расстри|чь, гу, жёшь, гут, *past* ~**г**, ~**гла** *pf.* (*of* ~**гать**) (*eccl.*) to unfrock.

расстро|енный *p.p.p. of* ~**ить** *and adj.* disordered, deranged; **р. вид** downcast appearance.

расстро|ить, ю, ишь *pf.* (*of* **расстраивать**) **1.** to disorder, derange; to throw into confusion; to unsettle; to upset; **р. желудок** to cause indigestion; **р. замыслы** to thwart schemes; **р. своё здоровье** to ruin one's health; **р. чьи-н. планы** to upset s.o.'s plans; **р. ряды противника** to break the enemy's ranks; **р. свадьбу** to break an engagement; **р. хозяйство** to shatter the economy. **2.** to upset, put out. **3.** (*mus.*) to put out of tune, untune.

расстро́|иться, юсь, ишься *pf.* (*of* **расстра́иваться**) **1.** to fall into confusion, fall apart; (*fig.*) to fall to the ground, fall through; **все на́ши пла́ны ~ились** all our plans have fallen through. **2.** (**от**) to be upset (over, about), be put out (about). **3.** (*mus.*) to become out of tune.

расстро́йств|о, а *nt.* **1.** disorder; derangement; confusion; **р. желу́дка** stomach disorder, stomach upset; (*coll.*) diarrhoea; **р. пищеваре́ния** indigestion; **р. ре́чи** speech defect; **внести́ р.** (**в**+*a.*), **привести́ в р.** to throw into confusion, derange, disorganize; **дела́ пришли́ в р.** things are in a sad state. **2.** (*coll.*) upset; **привести́ в р.** to upset, put out; **быть в ~е** to be upset, be put out.

расступ|а́ться, а́ется *impf. of* **~и́ться**

расступ|и́ться, ~ится *pf.* (*of* **~а́ться**) to part, make way; **толпа́ ~и́лась** the crowd parted; **земля́ ~и́лась** (*poet.*) the earth opened.

расстыко́вк|а, и *f.* (*of space vehicles*) undocking.

рассуди́тельност|ь, и *f.* reasonableness; good sense.

рассуди́тел|ьный (~ен, ~ьна) *adj.* reasonable; sober-minded; sensible.

рассу|ди́ть, жу́, ~дишь *pf.* **1.** to judge (between), arbitrate (between); **~ди́те нас** settle our dispute, be an arbiter between us; **р. спор** to settle a dispute. **2.** to think, consider; to decide; **нам на́до р., как сообщи́ть ей э́ти но́вости** we have to think how to break this news to her; **мы ~ди́ли, что пришло́ вре́мя верну́ться домо́й** we decided that the time had come to return home.

рассу́д|ок, ка *m.* **1.** reason; intellect; **го́лос ~ка** the voice of reason; **в по́лном ~ке** in full possession of one's faculties; **лиши́ться ~ка** to lose one's reason, go out of one's mind. **2.** common sense, good sense.

рассу́доч|ный (~ен, ~на) *adj.* **1.** rational, of the reason. **2.** governed by the reason (*to exclusion of feelings*); **~ная любо́вь** intellectual love.

рассужда́|ть, ю *impf.* **1.** to reason. **2.** (**о**+*p.*) to discuss, debate; to argue (about); to discourse (on); **р. на каку́ю-н. те́му** to discuss a topic.

рассужде́ни|е, я *nt.* **1.** reasoning. **2.** (*usu. pl.*) discussion, debate; argument; discourse; **без ~й** without argument, without arguing. **3.** (*obs.*) dissertation. **4.**: **в ~и** (+*g.*; *obs.*) with regard to, as regards.

рассу́чива|ть(ся), ю, ет(ся) *impf. of* **рассучи́ть(ся)**

рассуч|и́ть, у́, ~ишь *pf.* (*of* **~ивать**) to untwist; to undo; **р. рукава́** to roll one's sleeves down.

рассуч|и́ться, ~ится *pf.* (*of* **~иваться**) to untwist; to come undone.

рассчи́т|анный *p.p.p. of* **~а́ть** *and adj.* **1.** calculated, deliberate; **~анная гру́бость** calculated rudeness. **2.** (**на**+*a.*) intended (for), meant (for), designed (for); **кни́га, ~анная на широ́кого чита́теля** a book intended for the general public; **автостра́да, ~анная на бы́строе движе́ние** motorway designed for fast traffic.

рассчит|а́ть, а́ю *pf.* (*of* **~ывать**) **1.** to calculate, compute; (*tech.*) to rate; **не р. свои́х сил** to overrate one's strength. **2.** to dismiss, sack. **3.** (*mil.*) to number off, order to number.

рассчит|а́ться, а́юсь *pf.* (*of* **~ываться**) **1.** (**с**+*i.*) to settle accounts (with), reckon (with). **2.** (*mil.*) to number; **по поря́дку номеро́в ~а́йсь!** (*word of command*) number!

рассчи́тыва|ть, ю *impf.* **1.** *impf. of* **рассчита́ть** *and* **расче́сть. 2.** *impf. only* (**на**+*a.*) to calculate (on, upon), count (on, upon), reckon (on, upon); (+*inf.*) to expect (to), hope (to); **р. на многочи́сленную пу́блику** to count on a large attendance; **мы ~ли ко́нчить рабо́ту в э́том году́** we were hoping to finish the work this year. **3.** *impf. only* (**на**+*a.*) to count (on, upon), rely (on, upon), depend (upon).

рассчи́тыва|ться, юсь *impf. of* **рассчита́ться** *and* **расче́сться**

рассыла́|ть, ю *impf. of* **разосла́ть**

рассы́лк|а, и *f.* distribution, delivery.

рассы́льн|ый *adj.*: **~ая кни́га** delivery book; *as n.* **р., ~ого** *m.* delivery man, errand-boy.

рассы́п|ать, лю, лешь *pf.* (*of* **~а́ть**) to spill; to strew, scatter; **р. в цепь** (*mil.*) to draw up in extended line.

рассы́п|аться, люсь, лешься *pf.* (*of* **~а́ться**) **1.** to spill, scatter. **2.** to spread out, deploy; **р. в цепь** (*mil.*) to extend. **3.** to crumble; to go to pieces, disintegrate (*also fig.*). **4.** (**в**+*p.*) to be profuse (in); **р. в благода́рностях** to be profuse in the expression of thanks; **р. в похвала́х** (+*d.*) to shower praises (upon).

рассып|а́ть(ся), а́ю(сь) *impf. of* **~ать(ся)**

рассыпн|о́й *adj.* **1.** (sold) loose, (sold) by the piece; **~ы́е папиро́сы** cigarettes sold loose. **2.**: **р. строй** (*mil.*) extended order.

рассы́пчат|ый (~, ~а) *adj.* friable; (*cul.*) short, crumbly; **~ое пече́нье** shortbread.

рассыха́|ться, юсь *impf. of* **рассо́хнуться**

расталкива|ть, ю *impf. of* **растолка́ть**

раста́плива|ть(ся), ю, ет(ся) *impf. of* **растопи́ть(ся)**

раста́птыва|ть, ю *impf. of* **растопта́ть**

растаск|а́ть, а́ю *pf.* (*of* **~ивать**) **1.** to take away, remove (*little by little, bit by bit*). **2.** to pilfer, filch.

раста́скива|ть, ю *impf. of* **растаска́ть** *and* **растащи́ть**

растас|ова́ть, у́ю *pf.* (*of* **~о́вывать**) (*coll.*) to shuffle (*cards*).

растасо́выва|ть, ю *impf. of* **растасова́ть**

растафа́ри *c.g. & adj. indecl.* Rastafarian; Rasta.

раста́чива|ть, ю *impf. of* **расточи́ть**[2]

растащ|и́ть, у́, ~ишь *pf.* (*of* **раста́скивать**) **1.** to part, separate, drag asunder. **2.** = **растаска́ть**

раста́|ять, ю, ешь *pf. of* **та́ять**

раство́р[1], **а** *m.* (extent of) opening, span; **р. две́ри** doorway; **р. окна́** extent to which a window is opened; **р. ци́ркуля** spread of a pair of compasses.

раство́р[2], **а** *m.* **1.** (*chem.*) solution. **2.** (*tech.*) mortar; **строи́тельный р.** grout.

растворе́ни|е, я *nt.* solution, dissolution.

раствори́мост|ь, и *f.* (*chem.*) solubility

раствори́м|ый (~, ~а) *adj.* (*chem.*) soluble; **р. в воде́** water-soluble; **р. ко́фе** instant coffee.

раствори́тел|ь, я *m.* (*chem.*) solvent.

раствор|и́ть[1], **ю́, ~ишь** *pf.* (*of* **~я́ть**) to open.

раствор|и́ть[2], **ю́, и́шь** *pf.* (*of* **~я́ть**) to dissolve.

раствор|и́ться[1], **~ится** *pf.* (*of* **~я́ться**) to open.

раствор|и́ться[2], **и́тся** *pf.* (*of* **~я́ться**) to dissolve.

раствор|я́ть(ся), я́ю(сь) *impf. of* **~и́ть(ся)**

растека́|ться, юсь *impf. of* **расте́чься**

расте́ни|е, я *nt.* plant; **одноле́тнее р.** annual; **многоле́тнее р.** perennial; **ползу́чее р.** creeper.

растениево́д, а *m.* plant-grower.

растениево́дств|о, а *nt.* plant-growing.

растере́ть, разотру́, разотрёшь, *past* **растёр, растёрла** *pf.* (*of* **растира́ть**) **1.** to grind; **р. в порошо́к** to grind to powder; (*chem.*) to triturate. **2.** (**по**+*d.*) to rub (over), spread (over). **3.** to rub, massage.

растере́ться, разотру́сь, разотрёшься, *past* **растёрся, растёрлась** *pf.* (*of* **растира́ться**) **1.** to become powdered, turn into powder; (*chem.*) to become triturated. **2.** (+*i.*) to rub o.s. briskly (with).

растерз|а́ть, а́ю *pf.* (*of* **~ывать**) **1.** to tear to pieces. **2.** (*fig.*, *poet.*) to lacerate; to harrow.

расте́рзыва|ть, ю *impf. of* **растерза́ть**

расте́рива|ть(ся), ю(сь) *impf. of* **растеря́ть(ся)**

расте́рянност|ь, и *f.* confusion, perplexity, dismay.

расте́р|янный *p.p.p. of* **~я́ть** *and adj.* confused, perplexed, dismayed; **р. взгляд** look of dismay.

растер|я́ть, я́ю *pf.* (*of* **~ивать**) to lose (little by little).

растер|я́ться, я́юсь *pf.* (*of* **~иваться**) **1.** to get lost. **2.** to lose one's head.

расте́|чься, чётся, ку́тся, *past* **~кся, ~кла́сь** *pf.* (*of* **~ка́ться**) **1.** to spill; to run. **2.** (*fig.*) to spread; **по её лицу́ ~кла́сь улы́бка** a smile spread over her face.

раст|и́, у́, ёшь, *past* **рос, росла́** *impf.* **1.** (*biol.*, *bot.*) to grow; (*of children*) to grow up; **он рос на Украи́не** he grew up in (the) Ukraine. **2.** (*fig.*) to grow, increase. **3.** (*fig.*) to advance, develop; to grow in stature.

растира́ни|е, я *nt.* **1.** grinding. **2.** (*med.*) massage.

растира́|ть(ся), ю(сь) *impf. of* **растере́ть(ся)**

расти́ск|ать, аю *pf.* (*of* **~ивать**) (*coll.*) to shove (in).

расти́скива|ть, ю *impf. of* **расти́скать** *and* **расти́снуть**

расти́с|нуть, ну, нешь *pf.* (*of* **~кивать**) (*coll.*) to unclench.
расти́тельност|ь, и *f.* **1.** vegetation; verdure; **лишённый ~и** barren. **2.** hair (*on face or body*).
расти́тельн|ый *adj.* vegetable; **~ое ма́сло** vegetable oil; **р. мир, ~ое ца́рство** the vegetable kingdom; **~ая пи́ща** vegetable diet; **жить ~ой жи́знью** (*fig.*, *iron.*) to vegetate.
ра|сти́ть, щу́, сти́шь *impf.* **1.** to raise, bring up; to train; **р. дете́й** to raise children. **2.** to grow, cultivate; **р. бо́роду** to grow a beard.
растлева́|ть, ю *impf. of* **растли́ть**
растле́ни|е, я *nt.* **1.** seduction (*of minors*). **2.** (*fig.*) corruption; decay, decadence.
растле́нный *adj.* corrupt; decadent.
растли́тел|ь, я *m.*: **р. малоле́тних дете́й** child molester.
растл|и́ть, ю́, и́шь *pf.* (*of* **~ева́ть**) **1.** to seduce (*minors*). **2.** (*fig.*) to corrupt.
растолка́|ть, ю *pf.* (*of* **раста́лкивать**) **1.** to push asunder, apart. **2.** to shake (*in order to awaken*).
растолкн|у́ть, у́, ёшь *pf.* (*coll.*) to push asunder, part forcibly.
растолк|ова́ть, у́ю *pf.* (*of* **~о́вывать**) to explain.
растолко́выва|ть, ю *impf. of* **растолкова́ть**
растол|о́чь, ку́, чёшь, ку́т, *past* **~о́к, ~окла́** *pf. of* **толо́чь**
растолсте́|ть, ю *pf.* to grow stout, put on weight.
растоп|и́ть[1]**, лю́, ~ишь** *pf.* (*of* **раста́пливать**) to light, kindle.
растоп|и́ть[2]**, лю́, ~ишь** *pf.* (*of* **раста́пливать**) to melt; to (cause to) thaw.
растоп|и́ться[1]**, ~ится** *pf.* (*of* **раста́пливаться**) to begin to burn.
растоп|и́ться[2]**, ~ится** *pf.* (*of* **раста́пливаться**) to melt.
растóпк|а, и *f.* **1.** lighting, kindling. **2.** (*collect.*) kindling (wood).
растоп|та́ть, чу́, ~чешь *pf.* (*of* **раста́птывать**) to trample, stamp (on), crush.
растопы́рива|ть, ю *impf. of* **растопы́рить**
растопы́р|ить, ю, ишь *pf.* (*of* **~ивать**) to spread wide, open wide.
расторг|а́ть, а́ю *impf. of* **~нуть**
расто́рг|нуть, ну, нешь, *past* **~, ~ла** *pf.* (*of* **~а́ть**) to cancel, dissolve, annul, abrogate (*a contract or agreement*); **р. брак** to dissolve a marriage.
расторг|ова́ть, у́ю *pf.* (*of* **~о́вывать**) (*coll.*) to sell out.
расторг|ова́ться, у́юсь *pf.* (*of* **~о́вываться**) (*coll.*) **1.** to begin to do a brisk trade. **2.** to have sold out.
расторже́ни|е, я *nt.* cancellation, dissolution, annulment, abrogation.
растормош|и́ть, у́, и́шь *pf.* (*coll.*) **1.** to tug (*in order to awaken*). **2.** (*fig.*) to stir up, spur to activity.
расторо́п|ный (~ен, ~на) *adj.* (*coll.*) quick, prompt, smart; efficient.
расточ|а́ть, а́ю *pf.* (*of* **~и́ть**[1]) **1.** to waste, squander, dissipate. **2.** (*fig.*) to lavish, shower; **р. похвалы́** (+*d.*) to lavish praises (on, upon).
расточи́тел|ь, я *m.* squanderer, waster, spendthrift.
расточи́тел|ьный (~ен, ~ьна) *adj.* extravagant, wasteful.
расточ|и́ть[1]**, у́, и́шь** *pf.* (*of* **~а́ть**)
расточ|и́ть[2]**, у́, ~ишь** *pf.* (*of* **раста́чивать**) (*tech.*) to bore (out).
расто́чк|а, и *f.* (*tech.*) boring.
растрав|и́ть, лю́, ~ишь *pf.* (*of* **~ля́ть**) to irritate; **р. ра́ну** (*fig.*) to rub salt in a wound; **р. ста́рое го́ре** (*fig.*) to reopen an old wound.
растравля́|ть, ю *impf. of* **растрави́ть**
растранжи́р|ить, ю, ишь *pf. of* **транжи́рить**
растра́т|а, ы *f.* **1.** spending; waste, squandering. **2.** embezzlement, peculation.
растра́|тить, чу, тишь *pf.* (*of* **~чивать**) **1.** to spend; to waste, squander, dissipate; **р. си́лы** to dissipate one's energies; **р. своё вре́мя** to fritter away one's time. **2.** to embezzle, peculate.
растра́тчик, а *m.* embezzler, peculator.
растра́чива|ть, ю *impf. of* **растра́тить**
растрево́ж|ить, у, ишь *pf.* (*coll.*) to alarm, agitate; to put the wind up; **р. мураве́йник** to stir up an ant-hill.
растрево́ж|иться, усь, ишься *pf.* (*coll.*) to get the wind up.
растрезво́н|ить, ю, ишь *pf. of* **трезво́нить**
растрёп|а, ы *c.g.* (*coll.*) sloven, scruff; tousle-head.
растрёп|анный *p.p.p. of* **~а́ть** *and adj.* tousled, dishevelled; tattered; **быть в ~анных чу́вствах** (*coll.*) to be confused, be mixed up.
растреп|а́ть, лю́, ~лешь *pf.* **1.** to disarrange; **р. во́лосы кому́-н.** to tousle s.o.'s hair. **2.** to tatter, tear (*a book, etc.*).
растреп|а́ться, ~лется *pf.* **1.** to get disarranged, get dishevelled. **2.** to get tattered, get torn.
растре́ск|аться, ается *pf.* (*of* **~иваться**) to crack; (*of skin*) to chap.
растре́скива|ться, ется *impf. of* **растре́скаться**
растро́га|ть, ю *pf.* to move, touch; **р. кого́-н. до слёз** to move s.o. to tears.
растро́га|ться, юсь *pf.* to be (deeply) moved, touched.
растру́б, а *m.* funnel-shaped opening, bell, bell-mouth; socket (*of pipe*); **с ~ом** bell-shaped, bell-mouthed; **брю́ки с ~ами** bell-bottomed trousers; **соедине́ние ~ом** bell-and-spigot joint.
раструб|и́ть, лю́, и́шь *pf.* (+*a. or* **о**+*p.*; *coll.*) to trumpet.
растряс|ти́, у́, ёшь, *past* **~, ~ла́** *pf.* **1.** to strew (*hay, etc.*). **2.** (*coll.*) to shake (*in order to awaken*). **3.** (*impers.*) to jolt about. **4.** (*coll.*) to squander.
растуш|ева́ть, у́ю, у́ешь *pf.* (*of* **~ёвывать**) to shade.
растушёвк|а, и *f.* **1.** shading. **2.** stump (*for softening pencil-marks, etc., in drawing*).
растушёвыва|ть, ю *impf. of* **растушева́ть**
растя́гива|ть(ся), ю(сь) *impf. of* **растяну́ть(ся); ~ющиеся носки́** stretch socks.
растяже́ни|е, я *nt.* tension; stretch, stretching; (*med.*) strain, sprain.
растяжи́мост|ь, и *f.* tensility, tensile strength; extensibility; expansibility.
растяжи́м|ый (~, ~а) *adj.* tensile; extensible; expansible; **~ое поня́тие** loose concept.
растя́жк|а, и *f.* **1.** stretching, extension, lengthening out. **2.** (*aeron.*) bracing wire, anti-drag wire.
растя́нутост|ь, и *f.* **1.** long-windedness, prolixity. **2.** (*mil.*) extension, stretching out.
растя́н|утый *p.p.p. of* **~у́ть** *and adj.* **1.** long-winded, prolix. **2.** stretched; **р. фронт** (*mil.*) extended front.
растя|ну́ть, ну́, ~нешь *pf.* (*of* **~гивать**) **1.** to stretch (out). **2.** (*med.*) to strain, sprain; **р. себе́ му́скул** to pull a muscle; **р. себе́ свя́зку** to strain a ligament. **3.** to stretch too far; (*fig.*) to prolong, drag out; **р. расска́з** to drag out, spin out a story; **р. слова́** to drawl.
растя|ну́ться, ну́сь, ~нешься *pf.* (*of* **~гиваться**) **1.** to stretch (out), lengthen out. **2.** to stretch too far; (*fig.*) to be prolonged, drag out; **обсужде́ние его́ докла́да ~ну́лось на полтора́ часа́** discussion of his lecture dragged out for an hour and a half. **3.** to stretch o.s. out, sprawl. **4.** *pf. only* (*coll.*) to measure one's length, go head-long.
растя́п|а, ы *c.g.* (*coll.*) muddler, bungler.
расфас|ова́ть, у́ю *pf.* (*of* **~о́вывать**) to pack up, parcel up.
расфасо́вк|а, и *f.* packing, parcelling.
расфасо́выва|ть, ю *impf. of* **расфасова́ть**
расформирова́ни|е, я *nt.* breaking up; (*mil.*) disbandment.
расформир|ова́ть, у́ю *pf.* (*of* **~о́вывать**) to break up; (*mil.*) to disband.
расформиро́выва|ть, ю *impf. of* **расформирова́ть**
расфран|ти́ться, чу́сь, ти́шься *pf.* (*coll.*) to dress up.
расфранчённый *adj.* (*coll.*) dressed up to the nines; overdressed.
расфурфы́р|иться, юсь, ишься *pf.* (*coll.*, *pej.*) to dress flashily.
расха́жива|ть, ю *impf.* to walk, pace; **р. по ко́мнате** to pace up and down a room.
расхва́лива|ть, ю *impf. of* **расхвали́ть**
расхвал|и́ть, ю́, ~ишь *pf.* (*of* **~ивать**) to lavish, shower praise (on, upon).
расхва́рыва|ться, юсь *impf. of* **расхвора́ться**

расхва́ста|ться, юсь *pf.* (**о**+*p.*; *coll.*) to boast extravagantly (of, about); to shoot a line (about).

расхват|а́ть, а́ю *pf.* (*of* ~ывать) to snatch, seize (*with the object of purchasing, etc.*).

расхва́тыва|ть, ю *impf. of* **расхвата́ть**

расхвора́|ться, юсь *pf.* (*of* **расхва́рываться**) to fall ill; **она́ не на шу́тку ~лась** she is seriously ill.

расхити́тел|ь, я *m.* plunderer.

расхи́|тить, щу, тишь *pf.* (*of* **~ща́ть**) to plunder, misappropriate.

расхища́|ть, ю *impf. of* **расхи́тить**

расхище́ни|е, я *nt.* plunder, plundering, misappropriation.

расхлеб|а́ть, а́ю *pf.* (*of* ~ывать) **1.** to eat up (*without leaving anything*). **2.** (*fig.*) to disentangle.

расхлёбыва|ть, ю *impf. of* **расхлеба́ть; завари́л ка́шу, тепе́рь сам и ~й** (*coll.*) you got yourself into this mess, now get yourself out of it.

расхля́банност|ь, и *f.* **1.** looseness; instability. **2.** (*fig.*) slackness; laxity, lack of discipline.

расхля́банн|ый *adj.* (*coll.*) **1.** loose, unstable; **~ое здоро́вье** tottering health; **~ая похо́дка** unstable gait, slouching. **2.** (*fig.*) lax, undisciplined.

расхля́ба|ться, юсь *pf.* (*coll.*) **1.** to come loose, work loose. **2.** (*fig.*) to go to pieces.

расхо́д, а *m.* **1.** expense; (*pl.*) expenses, outlay, cost; **накладны́е ~ы** overhead expenses, overheads; **де́ньги на карма́нные ~ы** pocket-money; **ввести́ в ~ы** to put to expense; **взять на себя́ ~ы** to bear the expenses. **2.** (*in var. senses*) expenditure, consumption; **р. горю́чего** fuel consumption. **3.** (*book-keeping*) expenditure, outlay; **прихо́д и р.** income and expenditure; **списа́ть в р.** to write off; (*fig., coll.*) to liquidate; **быть в ~е** (*fig., coll.*) to be absent, be missing. **4.: вы́вести в р.** (*coll.*) to shoot.

расхо|ди́ться, жу́сь, ~дишься *impf. of* **разойти́сь**

расхо́д|ный *adj. of* **~; ~ная кни́га** expenses book, housekeeping book.

расхо́довани|е, я *nt.* expense, expenditure.

расхо́д|овать, ую *impf.* (*of* **из~**) **1.** to spend, expend. **2.** to use up, consume.

расхо́д|оваться, уюсь *impf.* (*of* **из~**) **1.** (*coll.*) to spend; to lay out money. **2.** *pass. of* **~овать**

расхожде́ни|е, я *nt.* divergence; **р. во мне́ниях** difference of opinion.

расхола́жива|ть, ю *impf. of* **расхолоди́ть**

расхоло|ди́ть, жу́, ди́шь *pf.* (*of* **расхола́живать**) to damp the ardour (of).

расхо|те́ть, чу́, ~чешь, ти́м, ти́те, тя́т *pf.* (+*inf.*; *coll.*) to cease to want.

расхо|те́ться, ~чется *pf.* (*impers.*+*d.*; *coll.*) to cease to want; **мне ~те́лось есть** I no longer want to eat.

расхохо|та́ться, чу́сь, ~чешься *pf.* to burst out laughing; to start roaring with laughter.

расхрабр|и́ться, ю́сь, и́шься *pf.* (*coll.*) to screw up one's courage, pluck up courage.

расцара́п|ать, аю *pf.* (*of* **~ывать**) to scratch (all over).

расцара́п|аться, аюсь *pf.* (*of* **~ываться**) to scratch o.s.

расцара́пыва|ть(ся), ю(сь) *impf. of* **расцара́пать(ся)**

расцве|сти́, ту́, тёшь, *past* **~л, ~ла́** *pf.* (*of* **~та́ть**) to bloom; to blossom (out) (*also fig.*); (*fig.*) to flourish; **не дать чему́-н. р.** (*fig.*) to nip sth. in the bud; **его́ лицо́ ~ло́ улы́бкой** his face was wreathed in smiles.

расцве́т, а *m.* bloom, blossoming (out); (*fig.*) flourishing; flowering, heyday; **в ~е сил** in the prime of life, in one's prime, in one's heyday.

расцвета́|ть, ю *impf. of* **расцвести́**

расцве|ти́ть, чу́, ти́шь *pf.* (*of* ~чивать) **1.** to paint in bright colours. **2.** to deck, adorn; **р. фла́гами** (*naut.*) to dress.

расцве́тк|а, и *f.* colours; coloration, colouring; **нас порази́ла я́ркая р. обстано́вки в их кварти́ре** we were struck by the bright colours of the furnishings in their flat.

расцве́чивани|е, я *nt.* (*naut.*) dressing.

расцве́чива|ть, ю *impf. of* **расцвети́ть**

расцел|ова́ть, у́ю *pf.* to kiss, smother with kisses.

расцел|ова́ться, у́юсь *pf.* to exchange kisses.

расце́нива|ть, ю *impf. of* **расцени́ть**

расцен|и́ть, ю́, ~ишь *pf.* (*of* ~ивать) **1.** to estimate, assess, value. **2.** (*fig.*) to rate, assess; to regard, consider; **как вы ~или его́ игру́?** what did you think of his acting?

расце́нк|а, и *f.* **1.** valuation. **2.** price. **3.** (wage-)rate.

расце́н|очный *adj. of* **~ка; ~очно-конфли́ктная коми́ссия** rates and disputes tribunal.

расцеп|и́ть, лю́, ~ишь *pf.* (*of* **~ля́ть**) to uncouple, unhook; to disengage, release.

расцеп|и́ться, ~ится *pf.* (*of* **~ля́ться**) to come uncoupled, come unhooked.

расцепле́ни|е, я *nt.* uncoupling, unhooking; disengaging, release; **механи́зм ~я** release gear.

расцепля́|ть(ся), ю, ет(ся) *impf. of* **расцепи́ть(ся)**

расча́лк|а, и *f.* (*tech., aeron.*) brace, bracing wire.

расчер|ти́ть, чу́, ~тишь *pf.* (*of* ~чивать) to rule, line.

расче́рчива|ть, ю *impf. of* **расчерти́ть**

расче|са́ть, шу́, ~шешь *pf.* (*of* ~сывать) **1.** to comb; to card. **2.** to scratch.

расче|са́ться, шу́сь, ~шешься *pf.* (*of* ~сываться) (*coll.*) **1.** to comb one's hair. **2.** to scratch o.s.

расчёск|а, и *f.* **1.** combing. **2.** comb.

расче́сть, разочту́, разочтёшь, *past* **расчёл, разочла́** *pf.* (*of* **рассчи́тывать**) **1.** to calculate, compute. **2.** to dismiss, sack.

расче́сться, разочту́сь, разочтёшься, *past* **расчёлся, разочла́сь** *pf.* (*of* **рассчи́тывать(ся)** (**с**+*i.*) to settle accounts (with).

расчёсыва|ть(ся), ю(сь) *impf. of* **расчеса́ть(ся)**

расчёт[1], а *m.* **1.** calculation (*also tech.*); computation; estimate, reckoning; **из ~а** (+*g.*) on the basis (of), at a rate (of); **распредели́ть тантье́му из ~а чи́стой при́был и** to distribute a bonus on the basis of net profits; **из ~а трёх проце́нтов годовы́х** at three per cent per annum; **приня́ть в р.** to take into account, consideration; **не принима́ть в р.** to leave out of account; **не принима́емый в р.** negligible; **по мои́м ~ам** by my reckoning; **э́то не входи́ло в мои ~ы** I had not reckoned with that, I had not bargained for that; **ошиби́ться в свои́х ~ах** to be out in one's reckoning, miscalculate. **2.** (*coll.*) gain, advantage; **нет ~а** (+*inf.*) it is not worth while, there is nothing to be gained. **3.** (**с**+*i.*) settling (with); **нали́чный р.** cash payment; **безнали́чный р.** payment by written order, by cheque; **быть в ~е** (**с**+*i.*) to be quits (with), be even (with). **4.** dismissal, discharge; **дать р.** (+*d.*) to dismiss, sack; **получи́ть р.** to be dismissed, get the sack; **взять р.** to leave one's work, hand in notice.

расчёт[2], а *m.* (*mil.*) crew, team, detachment; **оруди́йный р.** gun crew.

расчётливост|ь, и *f.* economy, thrift.

расчётлив|ый (~, ~а) *adj.* economical, thrifty; careful.

расчётн|ый *adj.* **1.** calculation, computation; **~ое ме́сто** (*navigation*) dead reckoning position; **~ая оши́бка** error in computation; **~ая табли́ца** calculation table. **2.** pay, accounts; **р. бала́нс** balance of payments; **~ая ве́домость** pay-roll, pay-sheet; **р. день** pay-day; **~ая кни́жка** pay-book; **р. отде́л** accounts department. **3.** (*tech.*) rated, calculated, designed; **~ая величина́** rating; **~ая мо́щность** rated capacity; **~ая ско́рость** rated speed.

расчётчик, а *m.* estimator, designer.

расчи́сл|ить, ю, ишь *pf.* (*of* **~я́ть**) to calculate, compute, reckon.

расчисл|я́ть, я́ю *impf. of* **~ить**

расчи́|стить, щу, стишь *pf.* (*of* **~ща́ть**) to clear.

расчи́|ститься, стится *pf.* (*of* **~ща́ться**) **1.** (*of the sky*) to clear. **2.** *pass. of* **~стить**

расчи́стк|а, и *f.* clearing.

расчиха́|ться, юсь *pf.* to sneeze repeatedly.

расчища́|ть(ся), ю, ет(ся) *impf. of* **расчи́стить(ся)**

расчлене́ни|е, я *nt.* **1.** dismemberment; partition. **2.** (*mil.*) development; dispersal; deployment; extension.

расчлен|ённый *p.p.p. of* **~и́ть** *and adj.*; **р. поря́док** (*mil.*) dispersed formation; **р. строй** (*mil.*) extended order, open order formation.

расчлен|и́ть, ю́, и́шь *pf.* (*of* **~я́ть**) **1.** to dismember; to partition; to break up, divide. **2.** (*mil.*) to develop; to disperse; to deploy; to extend.

расчлен|я́ть, я́ю *impf. of* **~и́ть**
расчу́вств|оваться, уюсь *pf.* (*coll.*) to be deeply moved.
расчу́ха|ть, ю *pf.* (*coll.*) to nose out; (*fig.*) to scent, sense; **он ~л, в чём де́ло** he sensed what was the matter.
расшал|и́ться, ю́сь, и́шься *pf.* to get up to mischief, start playing about.
расша́рк|аться, аюсь *pf.* (*of* **~иваться**) (*obs.*) to bow, scraping one's feet; (*fig.*) to bow and scrape.
расша́рива|ться, юсь *impf. of* **расша́ркаться**
расша́танност|ь, и *f.* shakiness; shattered condition.
расша́т|анный *p.p.p. of* **~а́ть** *and adj.* shaky; rickety; tottering; **~анные не́рвы** shattered nerves.
расшат|а́ть, а́ю *pf.* (*of* **~́ывать**) **1.** to shake loose; to make rickety. **2.** (*fig.*) to shatter; to impair; **э́тот уда́р ~а́л её здоро́вье** the blow shattered her health; **р. дисципли́ну** to impair discipline.
расшат|а́ться, а́юсь *pf.* (*of* **~́ываться**) **1.** to get loose; to become rickety. **2.** (*fig.*) to go to pieces, crack up.
расша́тыва|ть(ся), ю(сь) *impf. of* **расшата́ть(ся)**
расшвы́рива|ть, ю *impf. of* **расшвыря́ть**
расшвыр|я́ть, я́ю *pf.* (*of* **~́ивать**) to throw about, throw left and right, send flying.
расшеве́лива|ть, ю *impf. of* **расшевели́ть**
расшевел|и́ть, ю́, и́шь *pf.* (*of* **~́ивать**) to stir, shake; (*fig.*) to stir, rouse.
расшевел|и́ться, ю́сь, и́шься *pf.* to begin to stir; (*fig.*) to rouse o.s.
расшиб|а́ть(ся), а́ю(сь) *impf. of* **расшиби́ть(ся)**
расшиб|и́ть, у́, ёшь, *past* **~́, ~́ла** *pf.* (*of* **~а́ть**) (*coll.*) **1.** to hurt; to knock, stub; **р. па́лец ноги́ об ка́мень** to stub one's toe on a rock. **2.** to break up, smash to pieces.
расшиб|и́ться, у́сь, ёшься, *past* **~́ся, ~́лась** *pf.* (*of* **~а́ться**) (*coll.*) to hurt o.s., knock o.s.
расши́в|а, ы *f.* rasshiva (*large flat-bottomed sailing-boat in use on Volga and Caspian Sea*).
расшива́|ть, ю *impf. of* **расши́ть**
расшивно́й *adj.* embroidered.
расшире́ни|е, я *nt.* **1.** broadening, widening, expansion, extension. **2.** (*phys.*) expansion. **3.** (*med.*) dilation, dilatation; distension; **р. се́рдца** dilation of the heart; **р. вен** varicose veins.
расши́р|енный *p.p.p. of* **~ить** *and adj.* broadened, expanded; enlarged; dilated; more extensive, more comprehensive; **~енная програ́мма** more extensive programme; **~енные зрачки́** dilated pupils; **с ~енными глаза́ми** wide-eyed; **~енное воспроизво́дство** (*phys.*) breeding.
расшири́тел|ь, я *m.* (*tech.*) dilator; reamer.
расшири́тельн|ый *adj.* broad, extended; **~ое толкова́ние** broad interpretation.
расши́р|ить, ю, ишь *pf.* (*of* **~я́ть**) to broaden, widen; to enlarge; to expand; to extend; **р. чей-н. кругозо́р** to broaden s.o.'s outlook, mind; **р. сфе́ру влия́ния** to extend a sphere of influence.
расши́р|иться, юсь, ишься *pf.* (*of* **~я́ться**) **1.** to broaden, widen, gain in breadth; to extend. **2.** (*phys.*) to expand, dilate.
расшир|я́ть(ся), я́ю(сь) *impf. of* **~́ить(ся)**
расши́ть[1], **разошью́, разошьёшь** *pf.* (*of* **расшива́ть**) to embroider.
расши́ть[2], **разошью́, разошьёшь** *pf.* (*of* **расшива́ть**) to undo, unpick.
расшифр|ова́ть, у́ю *pf.* (*of* **~о́вывать**) to decipher, decode; (*fig.*) to interpret.
расшифро́вк|а, и *f.* deciphering, decoding; **р. аэрофото-сни́мков** (*mil.*) interpretation of aerial photographs.
расшифро́вщик, а *m.* decoder.
расшифро́выва|ть, ю *impf. of* **расшифрова́ть**
расшнур|ова́ть, у́ю *pf.* (*of* **~о́вывать**) to unlace.
расшнур|ова́ться, у́юсь *pf.* (*of* **~о́вываться**) **1.** to come unlaced, come undone. **2.** to unlace o.s. (*from a corset, etc.*).
расшнуро́выва|ть(ся), ю(сь) *impf. of* **расшнурова́ть(ся)**
расшум|е́ться, лю́сь, и́шься *pf.* (*coll.*) to get noisy, kick up a din.
расще́др|иться, юсь, ишься *pf.* (*coll., also iron.*) to have a fit of generosity.
расще́лин|а, ы *f.* cleft, crevice.
расщёлкива|ть, ю *impf. of* **расщёлкнуть**
расщёлк|нуть, ну, нешь *pf.* (*of* **~ивать**) to crack open.
расще́п, а *m.* split.
расщеп|и́ть, лю́, и́шь *pf.* (*of* **~ля́ть**) **1.** to split, splinter. **2.** (*phys.*) to split; (*chem.*) to break up.
расщеп|и́ться, и́тся *pf.* (*of* **~ля́ться**) to split, splinter.
расщепле́ни|е, я *nt.* **1.** splitting, splintering. **2.** (*phys.*) splitting, fission; (*chem.*) break-up, disintegration; **р. ядра́** nuclear fission.
расщепля́|ть(ся), ю, ет(ся) *impf. of* **расщепи́ть(ся)**
расщепля́|ющийся *pres. part. of* **~ться** *and adj.* (*phys.*) fissile, fissionable.
ра́та|й, я *m.* (*folk poet.*) ploughman.
ратификацио́нн|ый *adj.*: **~ые гра́моты** (*dipl.*) instruments of ratification.
ратифика́ци|я, и *f.* (*dipl.*) ratification.
ратифици́р|овать, ую *impf. and pf.* (*dipl.*) to ratify.
ра́тник, а *m.* **1.** (*arch.*) warrior. **2.** (*obs.*) militiaman.
ра́тный *adj.* (*obs. or poet.*) martial, warlike; **р. по́двиг** feat of arms.
ра́т|овать, ую *impf.* (*obs.*) (**за**+*a.*) to fight (for), stand up (for); (**про́тив**) to declaim (against), inveigh (against).
ра́туш|а, и *f.* **1.** (*esp. in Poland and the Baltic States*) town hall. **2.** (*hist.*) town council.
рат|ь, и *f.* (*arch. or poet.*) **1.** host, army. **2.** war; battle; **идти́ на р.** to go into battle.
ра́унд, а *m.* (*sport*) round.
ра́ут, а *m.* (*obs.*) rout; reception.
рафина́д, а *m.* lump sugar.
рафина́д|ный *adj. of* **~; р. заво́д** sugar refinery.
рафинёр, а *m.* (*tech.*; *of paper*) refiner.
рафини́рованност|ь, и *f.* refinement.
рафини́рова|нный *p.p.p. of* **~ть** *and adj.* (*fig.*) refined.
рафини́р|овать, ую *impf. and pf.* to refine.
раха́т-луку́м, а *m.* Turkish delight.
рахи́т, а *m.* (*med.*) rachitis, rickets.
рахи́тик, а *m.* sufferer from rachitis, rickets.
рахити́чный *adj.* (*med.*) rachitic, rickety.
раце́|я, и *f.* (*coll., iron.*) sermon, lecture; **чита́ть, кому́-н. ~ю** to read s.o. a lecture.
рацио́н, а *m.* ration, food allowance.
рационализа́тор, а *m.* rationalizer.
рационализа́тор|ский *adj. of* **~; ~ское предложе́ние** rationalization proposal, proposal for improving production methods.
рационализа́ци|я, и *f.* rationalization, improvement.
рационализи́р|овать, ую *impf. and pf.* to rationalize, improve.
рационали́зм, а *m.* (*phil.*) rationalism.
рационали́ст, а *m.* rationalist.
рационалисти́ческий *adj.* rationalistic.
рационалисти́ч|ный (~ен, ~на) *adj.* rational.
рациона́льно *adv.* rationally; efficiently; **р. испо́льзовать** to make efficient use (of), make good use (of).
рациона́л|ьный (~ен, ~ьна) *adj.* **1.** rational; efficient; **~ьная дие́та** balanced diet; **~ьное пита́ние** sound nutrition. **2.** (*math.*) rational.
ра́ци|я, и *f.* portable radio transmitter, walkie-talkie set.
ра́чий *adj. of* **рак; ра́чьи глаза́** goggle eyes.
рачи́тельност|ь, и *f.* (*obs.*) zealousness; assiduity.
рачи́тел|ьный (~ен, ~ьна) *adj.* (*obs.*) zealous; assiduous.
ра́шкул|ь, я *m.* (*art*) charcoal-pencil.
ра́шпил|ь, я *m.* (*tech.*) rasp, rasp file; grater.
рван|у́ть, у́, ёшь *pf.* **1.** to jerk; to tug (at); **р. кого́-н. за рука́в** to tug s.o. by the sleeve. **2.** to start with a jerk, get off with a jerk; **вдруг ~у́л ве́тер** suddenly a wind got up.
рван|у́ться, у́сь, ёшься *pf.* to rush, dash, dart.
рва́н|ый *adj.* torn; lacerated; **~ые башмаки́** broken shoes; **~ая ра́на** (*med.*) lacerated wound, laceration.
рван|ь, и *no pl.*, *f.* **1.** rags; broken footwear. **2.** (*coll.*) scoundrel, scamp; (*collect.*) riff-raff.
рвать[1], **рву, рвёшь**, *past* **рвал, рвала́, рва́ло** *impf.* **1.** to tear; to rend; to rip; **р. в клочки́** to tear to pieces; **р. на себе́ во́лосы** to tear one's hair; **р. и мета́ть** to rant and

rave. **2.** to pull out, tear out; **р. зýбы** to pull out teeth; **р. из рук у когó-н.** to snatch out of s.o.'s hands; **р. с кóрнем** to uproot. **3.** to pick, pluck; **р. цветы́** to pick flowers. **4.** to blow up. **5.** (*fig.*) to break off, sever; **р. отношéния с кем-н.** to break off relations with s.o.

рвать[2], **рвёт**, *past* **рвáлó** *impf.* (*of* **вы́рвать**[2]) (*impers.*; *coll.*) to vomit, throw up, be sick.

рвá|ться[1], **рвётся**, *past* **~лся**, **~лáсь**, **~лóсь** *impf.* **1.** to break; to tear. **2.** to burst, explode.

рвá|ться[2], **рвусь**, **рвёшься**, *past* **~лся**, **~лáсь**, **~лóсь** *impf.* to strain (to, at); to be bursting (to); **р. в бой** to be bursting to go into action; **р. в дрáку** to be spoiling for a fight; **р. на свобóду** to be dying to be free; **р. с привязи** to strain at the leash.

рвач, **á** *m.* (*coll.*) self-seeker, grabber.

рвáческий *adj.* (*coll.*) self-seeking, grabbing.

рвáчеств|о, **а** *nt.* (*coll.*) self-seeking, grabbing.

рвéни|е, **я** *nt.* zeal, fervour, ardour.

рвóт|а, **ы** *f.* **1.** vomiting, retching. **2.** vomit.

рвóтн|ый *adj.* vomitive, emetic; **р. кáмень** nux vomica; **р. кóрень** ipecacuanha; **~ое срéдство** (*also as n.* **~ое**, **~ого** *nt.*) emetic.

рде|ть, **ю** *impf.* (*of sth. red*) to glow.

реабилитáци|я, **и** *f.* rehabilitation.

реабилитúр|овать, **ую** *impf. and pf.* to rehabilitate.

реабилитúр|оваться, **уюсь** *impf. and pf.* **1.** to vindicate o.s. **2.** *pass. of* **~овать**

реагéнт, **а** *m.* (*chem.*) reagent.

реагúр|овать, **ую** *impf.* (**на**+*a.*) **1.** to react (to). **2.** (*pf.* **от~**) to react(to), (*fig.*) respond (to).

реактúв, **а** *m.* (*chem.*) reagent.

реактúвност|ь, **и** *f.* (*physiol.*) reactivity.

реактúвн|ый *adj.* **1.** (*chem.*, *phys.*) reactive: **~ая бумáга** (*chem.*) reagent paper, test-paper; **~ая катýшка** (*elec.*) reactive coil, choke coil, inductance coil. **2.** (*tech.*, *aeron.*) jet propulsion; jet(-propelled); **р. двúгатель** jet engine; **р. самолёт** jet-propelled aircraft.

реáктор, **а** *m.* (*phys.*, *tech.*) reactor, pile; **р. для двúгателей** propulsion reactor; **р. на бы́стрых нейтрóнах** fast (neutron) reactor; **р.-размножúтель**, **р. с расширенным воспроизвóдством я́дерного горю́чего** breeder reactor, breeder plant.

реакционéр, **а** *m.* (*pol.*) reactionary.

реакциóн|ный (**~ен**, **~на**) *adj.* (*pol.*) reactionary.

реáкци|я, **и** *f.* (*chem.*, *phys.*, *pol.*; *fig.*) reaction; (*pol.*, *collect.*) reactionaries.

реáл[1], **а** *m.* (*hist.*) real (*Spanish coin*).

реáл[2], **а** *m.* (*typ.*) composing frame.

реализáци|я, **и** *f.* realization (= (*i*) *implementation*, (*ii*) *sale*).

реалúзм, **а** *m.* (*in var. senses*) realism.

реализ|овáть, **ýю** *impf. and pf.* to realize (= (*i*) *to implement*, (*ii*) *to sell*); **р. цéнные бумáги** to realize securities.

реалúст, **а** *m.* (*in var. senses*) realist.

реалистúческий *adj.* **1.** (*art*, *liter.*, *etc.*) realist. **2.** realistic.

реалистúч|ный (**~ен**, **~на**) *adj.* = **~еский 2.**

реáли|я, **и** *f.* realia.

реáльност|ь, **и** *f.* **1.** reality. **2.** practicability.

реáл|ьный (**~ен**, **~ьна**) *adj.* **1.** real. **2.** realizable, practicable, workable; **р. план** workable plan. **3.** realistic; practical; **вестú ~ьную полúтику** to pursue a realistic policy; **~ьная зáработная плáта** real wages; **~ьное учúлище** (*obs.*) modern school (*non-classical secondary school*).

ребён|ок, **ка** (*as pl.* **ребя́та**, **ребя́т** *and* **дéти**, **детéй**) *m.* child, infant; **груднóй р.** baby, babe-in-arms.

рёберный *adj.* (*anat.*) costal.

ребóрд|а, **ы** *f.* flange.

ребрúст|ый (**~**, **~а**) *adj.* **1.** having prominent ribs. **2.** (*tech.*) ribbed; costate; finned.

ребр|ó, **á**, *pl.* **~а**, **рёбер**, **~ам** *nt.* **1.** (*anat.*, *tech.*) rib; (*tech.*) fin; **нúжние ~а** short ribs; **пересчитáть комý-н. ~а** (*coll.*) to give s.o. a drubbing. **2.** edge, verge; **постáвить ~óм** to place edgewise, place on its side; **постáвить вопрóс ~óм** to put a question point-blank.

рéбус, **а** *m.* rebus.

ребя́та, **ребя́т** (*coll.*) **1.** (*sg.* **ребёнок** *m.*) children. **2.** (*of adults*) boys, lads.

ребятúш|ки, **ек**, **кам** *no sg.* (*coll.*) children, kids.

ребя́ческий *adj.* **1.** of a child, childish. **2.** (*fig.*) childish, infantile, puerile.

ребя́честв|о, **а** *nt.* childishness, puerility.

ребя́чий *adj.* (*coll.*) childish.

ребя́ч|иться, **усь**, **ишься** *impf.* (*coll.*) to behave like a child, behave childishly.

рёв, **а** *m.* **1.** roar; bellow, howl; **р. вéтра** the howling of the wind. **2.** (*coll.*) howl (*of a child*, *etc.*); **поднять р.** to raise a howl.

рев... *comb. form*, *abbr. of* **революциóнный**

ревáнш, **а** *m.* revenge; (*sport*) return match.

реваншúзм, **а** *m.* (*pol.*) revanchism.

реваншúст, **а** *m.* (*pol.*) revanchist, revenge-seeker.

ревéн|ный *adj. of* **~ь**; **р. порошóк** gregory-powder.

ревéн|ь, **я́** *m.* rhubarb.

реверáнс, **а** *m.* (*obs.*) curts(e)y; **сдéлать р.** to curts(e)y, drop a curts(e)y.

реверберáци|я, **и** *f.* (*tech.*) reverberation.

рéверс, **а** *m.* **1.** reverse (*of coin*, *etc.*). **2.** (*tech.*) reversing gear. **3.** (*obs.*) caution-money (*deposit required to be paid by young officers on marrying*).

реверсúвный *adj.* (*tech.*) reversing, reversible.

ревéрси|я, **и** *f.* **1.** (*leg.*) reversion. **2.** (*biol.*) reversion (to type). **3.** (*tech.*) reversing.

рев|éть, **ý**, **ёшь** *impf.* **1.** to roar; to bellow, howl. **2.** (*coll.*) to howl; **ревмя́ р.** to set up a fearful howl.

ревизионúзм, **а** *m.* (*pol.*) revisionism.

ревизионúст, **а** *m.* (*pol.*) revisionist.

ревизиóнн|ый *adj.*: **~ая комúссия** inspection commission; auditing commission.

ревúзи|я, **и** *f.* **1.** inspection; audit. **2.** revision. **3.** (*hist.*) census.

ревиз|овáть, **ýю** *impf. and pf.* **1.** (*pf. also* **об~**) to inspect. **2.** to revise.

ревизóр, **а** *m.* inspector.

ревкóм, **а** *m.* (*abbr. of* **революциóнный комитéт**) revolutionary committee.

ревматúзм, **а** *m.* rheumatism; rheumatics; **суставнóй р.** rheumatic fever.

ревмáтик, **а** *m.* rheumatic.

ревматúческий *adj.* rheumatic; **р. артрúт** rheumatoid arthritis.

рев|мя́ *see* **~éть**

ревнúв|ец, **ца** *m.* jealous man.

ревнúв|ый (**~**, **~а**) *adj.* jealous.

ревнúтел|ь, **я** *m.* (*+g.*; *obs.*) adherent (of), enthusiastic supporter (of).

ревн|овáть, **ýю** *impf.* to be jealous; **р. когó-н.** (**к**) to be jealous because of s.o.'s attachment (to), begrudge s.o.'s attachment (to); **онá ~овáла мýжа к егó рабóте** she was jealous of her husband's work.

рéвност|ный (**~ен**, **~на**) *adj.* zealous, earnest, fervent.

рéвност|ь, **и** *f.* **1.** jealousy. **2.** (*obs.*) zeal, earnestness, fervour.

револьвéр, **а** *m.* revolver, pistol; **шестизаря́дный р.** six-shooter.

револьвéр|ный *adj.* **1.** *adj. of* **~**. **2.** (*tech.*): **~ная головка** capstan head; **р. станóк** capstan lathe, turret lathe.

револьвéрщик, **а** *m.* capstan, turret lathe operator.

революционéр, **а** *m.* revolutionary.

революционизúр|овать, **ую** *impf. and pf.* **1.** to spread revolutionary ideas (among, in). **2.** to revolutionize.

революционизúр|оваться, **уюсь** *impf. and pf.* **1.** to become permeated with revolutionary ideas. **2.** to be revolutionized.

революциóн|ный (**~ен**, **~на**) *adj.* revolutionary.

революци|я, **и** *f.* (*pol. and fig.*) revolution.

ревýн, **á** *m.* (*zool.*; *coll.*) howler.

ревю́ *nt. indecl.* revue.

регáли|я, **и** *f.* (*hist.*) state monopoly.

регáли|и, **й** *pl.* (*sg.* **~я**, **~и** *f.*) regalia.

ре́гби *nt. indecl.* Rugby (football), rugger; **люби́тельское р.** rugby union; **профессиона́льное р.** rugby league.
рег|би́йный *adj. of* **~би**
ре́гги *nt. indecl.* = **рэ́ггей**
регенерати́вный *adj.* (*tech.*) regenerative.
регенера́ци|я, и *f.* (*tech.*) regeneration.
ре́гент, а *m.* **1.** regent. **2.** (*mus.*) precentor.
ре́гентств|о, а *nt.* regency.
регио́н, а *m.* region, area.
региона́льный *adj.* regional.
реги́стр, а *m.* (*in var. senses*) register.
регистра́тор, а *m.* registrar.
регистрату́р|а, ы *f.* registry.
регистра́ци|я, и *f.* registration.
регистри́р|овать, ую *impf. and pf.* (*pf. also* **за~**) to register, record.
регистри́р|оваться, уюсь *impf. and pf.* (*pf. also* **за~**) **1.** to register (o.s.). **2.** to register one's marriage. **3.** *pass. of* **~овать**
регла́мент, а *m.* **1.** regulations; standing orders. **2.** (*at a meeting*) time-limit; **установи́ть р.** to fix a time-limit.
регламента́ци|я, и *f.* regulation.
регламенти́р|овать, ую *impf. and pf.* to regulate.
регла́н, а *m.* raglan (*coat*).
регресси́в|ный (~ен, ~на) *adj.* regressive.
регресси́р|овать, ую *impf.* to regress.
регули́ровани|е, я *nt.* **1.** regulation, control. **2.** adjustment.
регули́р|овать, ую *impf.* **1.** (*pf.* **у~**) to regulate; to control; **р. у́личное движе́ние** to control traffic. **2.** (*pf.* **от~**) to adjust; **р. мото́р** to tune an engine.
регулиро́вщик, а *m.* traffic-controller.
ре́гул|ы, ~ *no sg.* (*obs.*) menses, menstruation.
регуля́рност|ь, и *f.* regularity.
регуля́р|ный (~ен, ~на) *adj.* regular; **~ные войска́** regular troops, regulars.
регуля́тор, а *m.* (*tech.*) regulator; governor; (*pl.*) controls (*on TV, etc.*).
ред. *abbr. of* **1. реда́ктор** Ed., Editor. **2. реда́кция** Editorial Office.
ред... *comb. form, abbr. of* **редакцио́нный**
редакти́ровани|е, я *nt.* editing.
редакти́р|овать, ую *impf.* **1.** (*pf.* **от~**) to edit (*a manuscript, etc.*). **2.** (*impf. only*) to be editor of (*a journal, etc.*). **3.** (*pf.* **с~**) to word.
реда́ктор, а *m.* **1.** editor; **гла́вный р., отве́тственный р.** editor-in-chief. **2.: р. те́кстов, те́кстовый р.** word-processor (*software*).
реда́кторский *adj.* editorial.
реда́кторств|о, а *nt.* editorship.
реда́кторств|овать, ую *impf.* (*coll.*) to be (an) editor.
редакцио́нн|ый *adj.* editorial, editing; **~ая коми́ссия** drafting committee.
реда́кци|я, и *f.* **1.** editorial staff. **2.** editorial office. **3.** editing; **под ~ей** (+*g.*) edited (by). **4.** wording.
реде́|ть, ю *impf.* (*of* **по~**) to thin, thin out; **~ющие во́лосы** thinning hair.
реди́с, а *no pl., m.* radish(es).
реди́ск|а, и *f.* radish.
ре́д|кий (~ок, ~ка́, ~ко) *adj.* **1.** thin, sparse; **~кие во́лосы** thin hair; **~кие зу́бы** widely spaced teeth; **р. лес** sparse wood; **~кая ткань** flimsy fabric. **2.** rare; uncommon; **~кая кни́га** rare book; **~кая красота́** rare beauty; **он — р. подража́тель** he is a rare mimic.
ре́дко *adv.* **1.** sparsely; far apart. **2.** rarely, seldom.
редколе́сь|е, я *nt.* sparse growth of trees.
редколле́ги|я, и *f.* editorial board.
ре́дкост|ный (~ен, ~на) *adj.* rare; uncommon.
ре́дкост|ь, и *f.* **1.** thinness, sparseness. **2.** rarity; **на р.** uncommonly; **на р. проница́тельный челове́к** a pers. of rare discernment; **не р., что** not uncommonly; **не р., что он проси́живает ночь за кни́гой** it is not unusual for him to sit up all night reading. **3.** rarity, curiosity, curio.
реду́ктор, а *m.* **1.** (*tech.*) reducing gear. **2.** (*chem.*) reducing agent.
реду́кци|я, и *f.* (*in var. senses*) reduction.
реду́т, а *m.* (*mil., hist.*) redoubt.
редуци́рова|нный *p.p.p. of* **~ть** *and adj.* (*ling.*) reduced.
редуци́р|овать, ую *impf. and pf.* (*in var. senses*) to reduce.
ре́дьк|а, и *f.* radish; **надое́ло э́то мне ху́же го́рькой ~и** I am sick and tired of it.
редюи́т, а *m.* (*mil.*) reduit.
рее́стр, а *m.* list, roll, register.
ре́|же *comp. of* **~дкий** *and* **~дко**
режи́м, а *m.* **1.** (*pol.*) régime. **2.** routine; procedure; (*med.*) regimen; (*tech.*) mode of operation; **шко́льный р.** school routine; **р. пита́ния** diet; **р. безопа́сности** safety measures; **р. эконо́мии** policy of economy. **3.** conditions; (*tech.*) working conditions, operating conditions; **р. реки́** habits of a river. **4.** (*tech.*) rate; **р. набо́ра высоты́** (*aeron.*) rate of climb.
режи́мный *adj.* secret, classified.
режиссёр, а *m.* (*theatr.*) producer; (*cin.*) director.
режиссёр|ский *adj. of* **~**
режисси́р|овать, ую *impf.* (*theatr.*) to produce, stage; (*cin.*) to direct.
режиссу́р|а, ы *f.* (*theatr.*) **1.** producing; profession of producer. **2.** production. **3.** (*collect.*) producers.
ре́жущ|ий *pres. part. act. of* **ре́зать** *and adj.* cutting, sharp; **~ая кро́мка** cutting edge, blade; **р. уда́р** slash.
реза́к, а́ *m.* **1.** chopping-knife, chopper; pole-axe. **2.** slaughterman.
ре́зан|ый *adj.* **1.** cut; **р. хлеб** cut loaf. **2.** (*sport*) slice, sliced; **~ая пода́ча** (*tennis*) slice service; **р. уда́р** slice.
ре́|зать, жу, жешь *impf.* **1.** *impf. only* to cut; to slice. **2.** *impf. only* (*med.*) to operate, open; (*coll., joc.*) to carve. **3.** *impf. only* to cut (= *to have the power of cutting*); **э́ти но́жницы бо́льше не ~жут** these scissors do not cut any longer. **4.** (*pf.* **за~**) to kill; to slaughter; to knife. **5.** *impf. only* (**по**+*d.*) to carve (on), engrave (on). **6.** *impf. only* to cut (into); to cause sharp pain; **реме́нь ~зал его́ плечо́** the strap was cutting into his shoulder; **у меня́ ~зало в желу́дке** I had griping pains in the stomach; **р. глаза́** to irritate the eyes; **р. слух** to pain the ear, grate upon the ears. **7.** (*coll.*) to speak bluntly; **р. пра́вду в глаза́** to speak the truth boldly. **8.** *impf. only* to pass close (to), shave; **р. корму́** (*naut.*) to pass close astern. **9.** (*pf.* **с~**) (*sport*) to slice, cut, chop.
ре́|заться, жусь, жешься *impf.* **1.** (*pf.* **про~**) (*of teeth*) to cut, come through; **у него́ уже́ ~жутся зу́бы** he is already teething, cutting teeth. **2.** *impf. only* to play furiously.
резв|и́ться, лю́сь, и́шься *impf.* to sport, gambol, caper, romp.
ре́звост|ь, и *f.* **1.** sportiveness, playfulness, friskiness. **2.** (*sport; of a horse*) speed; **показа́ть хоро́шую р.** to show a good time.
ре́зв|ый (~, ~а́, ~о) *adj.* **1.** sportive, playful, frisky. **2.** (*sport; of a horse*) fast.
резед|а́, ы́ *f.* (*bot.*) mignonette.
резе́кци|я, и *f.* (*med.*) resection.
резе́рв, а *m.* (*mil., etc.*) reserve(s); **име́ть в ~е** to have in reserve; **перевести́ в р.** (*mil.*) to transfer to the reserve.
резерва́ци|я, и *f.* reservation.
резерви́р|овать, ую *impf. and pf.* to reserve.
резерви́ст, а *m.* (*mil.*) reservist.
резе́рвный *adj.* (*mil. and fin.*) reserve; (*comput.*) back-up; **~ая ко́пия** back-up copy.
резервуа́р, а *m.* reservoir, vessel, tank.
рез|е́ц, ца́ *m.* **1.** (*tech.*) cutter; cutting tool; chisel. **2.** (*tooth*) incisor.
резиде́нт, а *m.* (*dipl., etc.*) resident (*esp. of member of Intelligence Service operating in foreign country*).
резиде́нци|я, и *f.* residence.
рези́н|а, ы *f.* (india-)rubber.
рези́нк|а, и *f.* **1.** (india-)rubber, eraser. **2.** (piece of) elastic. **3.** rubber band. **4.** chewing-gum.
рези́нов|ый *adj.* **1.** rubber; **~ая промы́шленность** rubber industry; **~ые сапоги́** wellingtons, gum boots; **~ая тесьма́, ле́нта** rubber band. **2.** elastic.
рези́нщик, а *m.* worker in rubber industry.
ре́зк|а, и *f.* cutting.

ре́з|кий (~ок, ~ка́, ~ко) *adj.* sharp; harsh; abrupt; **р. ве́тер** sharp wind, cutting wind; **р. го́лос** shrill voice; **р. за́пах** strong smell; **~кое измене́ние** abrupt change, sudden switch; **~кие мане́ры** abrupt manners; **р. свет** strong, harsh light; **~кие слова́** sharp words; **~кое увеличе́ние** dramatic increase; **~кие черты́ лица́** sharp features.

ре́зкост|ь, и *f.* **1.** sharpness; harshness; abruptness. **2.** sharp words, harsh words; **наговори́ть ~ей** to use harsh words.

резн|о́й *adj.* carved, fretted; **~а́я рабо́та** (*archit.*) carving, fretwork.

резн|я́, и́ *f.* slaughter, butchery, carnage.

резолюти́вн|ый *adj.* containing conclusions, containing a resolution; **в ~ой фо́рме** in the form of a resolution.

резолю́ци|я, и *f.* **1.** resolution; **вы́нести, приня́ть ~ю** to pass, adopt, approve, carry a resolution. **2.** instructions (*on a document*); **наложи́ть ~ю** to append instructions.

резо́н, а *m.* (*coll.*) **1.** reason, basis; **в э́том есть свой р.** there is a reason for this. **2.** reasoning, argument; **они́ не хоте́ли слу́шать никаки́х ~ов** they would not listen to any argument.

резона́нс, а *m.* **1.** (*phys.*) resonance. **2.** (*fig.*) echo, response; **дать, име́ть р.** to have repercussions.

резонёр, а *m.* arguer, moralizer.

резонёрств|овать, ую *impf.* to argue, moralize.

резони́р|овать, ую *impf.* to resound.

резо́н|ный (~ен, ~на) *adj.* reasonable.

результа́т, а *m.* result; outcome; **~ы обсле́дования** findings; **дать ~ы** to yield results; **в ~е** (*+g.*) as a result (of).

результати́вный *adj.* successful.

ре́з|че *comp. of* **~кий** *and* **~ко**

ре́зчик, а *m.* engraver, carver.

рез|ь, и *f.* colic; gripe.

резьб|а́, ы́ *f.* **1.** carving, fretwork. **2.** (*tech.*) thread(ing).

резюме́ *nt. indecl.* summary, résumé.

резюми́р|овать, ую *impf. and pf.* to sum up, summarize, recapitulate.

рейд[1]**, а** *m.* (*naut.*) road(s), roadstead.

рейд[2]**, а** *m.* **1.** (*mil.*) raid. **2.** 'swoop' (*by group of journalists, to investigate alleged malpractice, grievance, etc.*); special (*journalistic*) assignment.

ре́йдер, а *m.* (*naut.*) (commerce) raider.

ре́йк|а, и *f.* **1.** lath. **2.: зубча́тая р.** (*tech.*) rack; **переда́ча зубча́той ~ой** rack and pinion gear. **3.** (*surveyor's*) rod, pole.

Ре́йкьявик, а *m.* Reykjavik.

Рейн, а *m.* the Rhine (*river*).

рейнве́йн, а *m.* hock.

ре́йнск|ий *adj.* Rhine, Rhenish; **~ое (вино́)** Rhine wine, hock.

рейс, а *m.* trip, run (*of public transport vehicle*); voyage, passage; flight; **но́мер ~а** flight number; **пе́рвый р.** maiden voyage, maiden trip.

рейсфе́дер, а *m.* **1.** drawing-pen, mapping pen. **2.** pencil-holder.

рейсши́н|а, ы *f.* T-square.

ре́йтинг, а *m.* rating (*in opinion poll*).

рейту́з|ы, ~ *no sg.* **1.** (riding-)breeches. **2.** (*women's or children's*) pantaloons, knickers. **3.** tights.

рейх, а *m.* Reich; **тре́тий р.** Third Reich.

река́, ре́ку́, реки́, *pl.* **ре́ки, рек, ре́ка́м, ре́ка́ми, ре́ка́х** *f.* river; **ли́ться,** *etc.*, **реко́й** (*fig.*) to pour, flood.

ре́квием, а *m.* (*eccl. and mus.*) requiem.

реквизи́р|овать, ую *impf. and pf.* to requisition, commandeer.

реквизи́т, а *m.* (*theatr.*) properties, props.

реквизи́тор, а *m.* (*theatr.*) property-man.

реквизи́ци|я, и *f.* requisition, commandeering.

рекла́м|а, ы *f.* **1.** advertising, publicity; **крикли́вая р.** hype. **2.** advertisement.

реклама́ци|я, и *f.* claim for replacement (*of defective goods, etc.*).

реклами́р|овать, ую *impf. and pf.* to advertise, publicize; to boost, push; **крикли́во р.** to hype.

реклами́ст, а *m.* **1.** composer of advertisements. **2.** (*coll., pej.*) one given to self-advertisement.

рекла́мный *adj.* publicity.

рекламода́тел|ь, я *m.* advertiser.

рекогносци́р|овать, ую *impf. and pf.* (*mil.*) to reconnoitre.

рекогносциро́вк|а, и *f.* (*mil.*) reconnaissance; reconnoitring.

рекогносциро́вочный *adj.* reconnaissance.

рекоменда́тельн|ый *adj.*: **р. о́тзыв** recommendation, testimonial; **~ое письмо́** letter of recommendation; **р. спи́сок книг** list of recommended books.

рекоменда́ци|я, и *f.* recommendation.

рекоменд|ова́ть, у́ю *impf. and pf.* **1.** (*pf. also* **по~** *and* **от~**) to recommend; to speak well for; **э́то его́ не о́чень ~у́ет** this does not speak too well for him. **2.** (*pf. also* **по~**) (*+inf.*) to recommend, advise; **я вам ~у́ю посове́товаться с до́ктором** I recommend you to see a doctor.

рекоменд|ова́ться, у́юсь *impf. and pf.* **1.** (*pf. also* **от~**) to introduce o.s. **2.** *pass. of* **~ова́ть; не ~у́ется** it is not recommended; it is not advisable.

реконструи́р|овать, ую *impf. and pf.* to reconstruct.

реконструкти́вный *adj.*: **р. пери́од** period of reconstruction.

реконстру́кци|я, и *f.* reconstruction.

реко́рд, а *m.* record; **поби́ть р.** to break a record; **установи́ть р.** to set up, establish a record.

рекорди́ст, а *m.* (*agric.*) champion.

реко́рдный *adj.* record, record-breaking.

рекордсме́н, а *m.* record-holder; record-breaker; **р. ми́ра** world record-holder.

рекордсме́н|ка, ки *f. of* **~**

ре́крут, а *m.* (*hist.*) recruit.

рекрути́р|овать, ую *impf. and pf.* to recruit.

рекру́т|ский *adj. of* **~; р. набо́р** recruiting, recruitment.

ректифика́т, а *m.* rectified spirit.

ректифика́ци|я, и *f.* (*tech.*) rectification.

ректифици́р|овать, ую *impf. and pf.* (*tech.*) to rectify.

ре́ктор, а *m.* rector, vice-chancellor, principal (*head of a university*).

реле́ *nt. indecl.* (*tech.*) relay

реле́|йный *adj. of* **~**

религиове́дени|е, я *nt.* religious studies.

религио́зност|ь, и *f.* religiosity; piety, piousness.

религио́з|ный *adj.* **1.** of religion, religious; **~ные во́йны** (*hist.*) Wars of Religion; **р. обря́д** religious ceremony. **2.** **(~ен, ~на)** religious; pious.

рели́ги|я, и *f.* religion.

рели́кви|я, и *f.* relic.

рели́кт, а *m.* relic; survival.

рели́кт|овый *adj. of* **~**; surviving.

релье́ф, а *m.* (*art and geol.*) relief.

релье́фно *adv.* in relief, boldly; **р.-то́чечный шрифт** Braille (script).

релье́ф|ный (~ен, ~на) *adj.* relief, raised, bold; **~ная рабо́та** embossed work; **~ная ка́рта** relief map.

рельс, а, *g. pl.* **~ов** *m.* rail; **сойти́ с ~ов** to be derailed, go off the rails; **поста́вить на ~ы** (*fig.*) to get going, launch.

ре́льс|овый *adj. of* **~; р. путь** railway, track.

релятиви́зм, а *m.* (*phil.*) relativity.

реля́ци|я, и *f.* (*mil.*; *obs.*) communiqué, report.

рема́рк|а, и *f.* (*theatr.*) stage direction.

ремённ|ый *adj.* belt; **~ая переда́ча** (*tech.*) belt-drive.

рем|е́нь, ня́ *m.* strap; belt; thong; **р. безопа́сности** seat belt; **поясно́й р.** (*mil.*) (waist-)belt; **привязно́й р.** seat-belt; **руже́йный р.** rifle sling; **р. для пра́вки бритв** (razor) strop.

реме́сленник, а *m.* **1.** artisan, craftsman. **2.** (*fig., pej.*) hack. **3.** pupil of trade school.

реме́сленнический *adj.* (*pej.*) hack-working, mechanical.

реме́сленничеств|о, а *nt.* **1.** workmanship, craftsmanship. **2.** (*pej.*) hack-work.

реме́сленн|ый *adj.* **1.** handicraft; trade; **~ое учи́лище** trade school, industrial school. **2.** (*fig., pej.*) mechanical, stereotyped.

ремес|ло́, ла́, *pl.* **~́ла, ~́ел** *nt.* **1.** handicraft; trade. **2.** profession.

ремеш|о́к, ка́ *m.* small strap; wristlet.

реми́з, а *m.* (*cards*) fine; **поста́вить р.** to pay a fine.

ремилитариза́ци|я, ую *f.* remilitarization.

ремилитаризи́р|овать, ую *impf. and pf.* to remilitarize.

ремилитариз|ова́ть, у́ю *impf. and pf.* to remilitarize.

реминисце́нци|я, и *f.* reminiscence.

ремо́нт, а *m.* **1.** repair(s); maintenance; **капита́льный р.** overhaul, refit, major repairs; **космети́ческий р.** face-lift; **теку́щий р.** maintenance, routine repairs; **закры́т на р.** closed for repairs; **в ~е** under repair. **2.** (*mil.*) remount (service).

ремонтёр, а *m.* (*mil.*; *obs.*) remount officer.

ремонти́р|овать, ую *impf. and pf.* **1.** (*pf. also* **от~**) to repair; to refit, recondition, overhaul. **2.** (*mil.*) to remount.

ремо́нт|ный *adj. of* **~**; **~ная лету́чка** mobile repair shop; **~ная мастерска́я** repair shop; **~ная ло́шадь** (*mil.*) remount.

ренега́т, а *m.* renegade.

ренега́тств|о, а *nt.* desertion; apostasy.

ренет, а *m.* rennet (*apple*).

ренкло́д, а *m.* greengage.

реноме́ *nt. indecl.* reputation.

рено́нс, а *m.* (*cards*) revoke.

ре́нт|а, ы *f.* **1.** rent; **земе́льная р.** ground-rent. **2.** income (*from investments, etc.*); **ежего́дная р.** annuity; **госуда́рственная р.** (income from) government securities.

рента́бел|ьный (~ен, ~ьна) *adj.* paying, profitable.

рентге́н, а *m.* X-ray treatment, X-rays.

рентгениза́ци|я, и *f.* X-raying.

рентгенизи́р|овать, ую *impf. and pf.* to X-ray.

рентге́нов *adj.*: **~ы лучи́** X-rays.

рентге́новск|ий *adj.* X-ray; **р. кабине́т** X-ray room; **~ие лучи́** X-rays; **р. сни́мок** X-ray photograph.

рентгеногра́мм|а, ы *f.* X-ray photograph, radiograph, röntgenogram.

рентгеногра́фи|я, и *f.* radiography.

рентгено́лог, а *m.* radiologist.

рентгеноло́ги|я, и *f.* radiology.

рентгенотерапи́|я, и *f.* X-ray therapy.

Реомю́р, а *m.* Réaumur; **10° по ~у** 10° Réaumur.

реорганиза́ци|я, и *f.* reorganization.

реорганиз|ова́ть, у́ю *impf. and pf.* to reorganize.

реоста́т, а *m.* (*elec.*) rheostat.

ре́п|а, ы *f.* turnip; **дешёвле па́реной ~ы** (*coll.*) dirt-cheap.

репар|ацио́нный *adj. of* **~а́ция**

репара́ци|я, и *f.* reparation.

репатриа́нт, а *m.* repatriate.

репатриа́ци|я, и *f.* repatriation.

репатрии́р|овать, ую *impf. and pf.* to repatriate.

репатрии́р|оваться, уюсь *impf. and pf.* to repatriate o.s.

репе́йник, а *m.* **1.** (*bot.*) burdock. **2.** Velcro.

репелле́нт, а *m.* insect repellent.

репе́р, а *m.* **1.** (*surveying*) bench-mark, datum mark. **2.** (*mil.*) registration mark, registration point.

репертуа́р, а *m.* (*theatr. and fig.*) repertoire.

репети́р|овать, ую *impf.* **1.** (*pf.* **про~** *and* **с~**) (*theatr.*) to rehearse. **2.** *impf. only* to coach.

репети́тор, а *m.* coach (*tutor*).

репетицио́нный *adj.* rehearsal.

репети́ци|я, и *f.* **1.** rehearsal; **генера́льная р.** dress rehearsal. **2.** repeater mechanism (*in watch*); **часы́ с ~ей** repeater.

ре́пиц|а, ы *f.* dock (*of horse's tail*).

ре́плик|а, и *f.* **1.** rejoinder, retort; heckling comment; **подава́ть ~и ора́тору** to heckle a speaker. **2.** (*theatr.*) cue; **пода́ть ~у** to give the cue.

репол́ов, а *m.* (*zool.*) linnet.

репорта́ж, а *m.* reporting; account, piece of reporting.

репортёр, а *m.* reporter.

репортёрств|овать, ую *impf.* to report, be a reporter.

репресса́л|ии, ий *pl.* (*sg.* **~ия, ~ии** *rare f.*) (*pol.*) reprisals.

репресси́в|ный (~ен, ~на) *adj.* repressive.

репресси́р|овать, ую *impf. and pf.* to subject to repression.

репре́сси|я, и *f.* punitive measure.

репри́нт, а *m.* reprint.

репри́нтн|ый *adj.*: **~ое изда́ние** reprint.

репрогра́фи|я, и *f.* reprographics.

репроду́ктор, а *m.* loud-speaker.

репроду́кци|я, и *f.* reproduction (*of a picture, etc.*).

репс, а *m.* (*text.*) rep(p), reps.

репти́ли|я, и *f.* **1.** reptile. **2.** (*pej.*) mercenary pers., mercenary newspaper, *etc.*

репти́л|ьный (~ен, ~ьна) *adj.* (*pej.*) mercenary, venal.

репута́ци|я, и *f.* reputation, name; **по́льзоваться хоро́шей ~ей** to have a good reputation, name; **по́льзоваться ~ей** (+*g.*) to have a reputation, name (for); **спасти́ свою́ ~ю** to save one's face.

ре́пчатый *adj.* turnip-shaped; **р. лук** (common) onion.

ресни́ц|а, ы *f.* eyelash.

ресни́чк|а, и *f.* **1.** *dim. of* **ресни́ца. 2.** *pl.* (*biol.*) cilia.

ресни́чный *adj.* (*biol.*) ciliary.

респекта́бельност|ь, и *f.* respectability.

респекта́бел|ьный (~ен, ~ьна) *adj.* respectable.

респира́тор, а *m.* respirator.

респу́блик|а, и *f.* republic.

республика́н|ец, ца *m.* republican.

республика́нский *adj.* **1.** republican. **2.** of (situated in, *etc.*) a constituent republic of the former USSR.

рессо́р|а, ы *f.* spring (*of vehicle*).

рессо́рный *adj.* spring; sprung.

реставра́тор, а *m.* restorer.

реставра́ци|я, и *f.* restoration.

реставри́р|овать, ую *impf. and pf.* to restore.

рестора́н, а *m.* restaurant; **р. бы́строго обслу́живания** fast-food restaurant.

рестора́тор, а *m.* (*obs.*) restaurateur, restaurant-keeper.

ресу́рс, а *m.* resource; **де́нежные ~ы у них ничто́жны** their financial resources are negligible; **после́дний р.** the last resort.

ретив|о́е, о́го *nt.* (*folk poet.*) heart.

рети́вост|ь, и *f.* zeal, ardour.

рети́в|ый (~, ~а) *adj.* (*coll.*) zealous, ardent.

рети́н|а, ы *f.* (*anat.*) retina.

ретир|ова́ться, у́юсь *impf. and pf.* **1.** (*obs.*) to retire, withdraw. **2.** (*iron.*) to make off.

рето́рси|я, и *f.* (*pol.*) retortion.

рето́рт|а, ы *f.* (*chem.*) retort.

ретрогра́д, а *m.* retrograde pers., reactionary.

ретрогра́д|ный (~ен, ~на) *adj.* retrograde, backward, reactionary.

ретрораке́т|а, ы *f.* retro-rocket (*on space craft*).

ретроспекти́в|ный (~ен, ~на) *adj.* retrospective; **р. взгляд** backward glance.

ретушёр, а *m.* retoucher.

ретуши́р|овать, ую *impf. and pf.* (*pf. also* **от~**) to retouch.

ре́туш|ь, и *f.* retouching.

рефера́т, а *m.* **1.** synopsis, abstract (*of a book, dissertation, etc.*). **2.** paper, essay.

рефере́ндум, а *m.* referendum.

рефере́нт, а *m.* **1.** reader of a paper; seminar leader, colloquium leader. **2.** assessor (*of thesis, book, etc.*).

рефери́р|овать, ую *impf. and pf.* to abstract, make a synopsis of.

рефле́кс, а *m.* reflex; **усло́вный р., безусло́вный р.** conditioned, unconditioned reflex.

рефле́кси|я, и *f.* reflection; introspection.

рефлексоло́ги|я, и *f.* (*physiol.*) study of reflexes.

рефлексотерапе́вт, а *m.* reflexologist.

рефлекти́в|ный (~ен, ~на) *adj.* (*physiol.*) reflex.

рефле́ктор, а *m.* reflector.

рефлекто́рный *adj.* (*physiol., astron.*) reflex.

рефо́рм|а, ы *f.* reform.

реформа́тор, а *m.* reformer.

реформа́торский *adj.* reformative, reformatory.

реформа́|тский *adj. of* **Р~ция; ~тская це́рковь** Reformed Church.

Реформа́ци|я, и *f.* (*hist.*) Reformation.

реформи́зм, а *m.* (*pol.*) reformism.

реформи́р|овать, ую *impf. and pf.* to reform.
реформи́ст, а *m.* (*pol.*) reformist.
рефра́ктор, а *m.* (*phys., astron.*) refractor.
рефра́кци|я, и *f.* (*phys., astron.*) refraction.
рефре́н, а *m.* (*liter.*) refrain, burden.
рефрижера́тор, а *m.* **1.** (*tech.*) refrigerator; condenser, cooler. **2.** refrigerator van, ship.
рехн|у́ться, у́сь, ёшься *pf.* (*coll.*) to go mad, go off one's head.
рецензе́нт, а *m.* reviewer.
рецензи́р|овать, ую *impf.* (*of* **про~**) to review, criticize.
реце́нзи|я, и *f.* **1.** review; (*theatr.*) notice; **р. на кни́гу, р. о кни́ге** book review; **дать на ~ю** to send for review. **2.** (*philol.*) recension.
реце́пт, а *m.* **1.** (*med.*) prescription. **2.** (*cul.*) recipe; (*fig.*) method, way, practice; **поступи́ть по ста́рому ~у** to follow the old practice.
рецепту́р|а, ы *f.* (*med.*) principles of prescription-writing.
рециди́в, а *m.* **1.** (*med., etc.*) recurrence; relapse. **2.** (*leg.*) repeated commission (*of offence*).
рецидиви́зм, а *m.* (*leg.*) recidivism.
рецидиви́ст, а *m.* (*leg.*) recidivist.
рециркули́р|овать, ую *impf. and pf.* to recycle.
рециркуля́ци|я, и *f.* recycling.
речев|о́й *adj.* speech; vocal; **р. аппара́т** organs of speech, vocal organs; **~ы́е на́выки** speech habits.
рече́ни|е, я *nt.* (*obs.*) set phrase; saying; (*ling.*) locution.
речи́ст|ый (~, ~а) voluble, garrulous.
речитати́в, а *m.* (*mus.*) recitative.
ре́чк|а, и *f.* small river; rivulet.
речн|о́й *adj.* river; riverine, fluvial; **р. вокза́л** river (steamer and bus) station; **~о́е сообще́ние** river communication; **~ы́е пути́ сообще́ния** inland waterways; **~о́е судохо́дство** river navigation; **р. трамва́й** river bus, water bus.
реч|ь, и *f.* **1.** speech; **дар ~́и** faculty of speech, gift of speech. **2.** enunciation, speech, way of speaking; **горта́нная р.** guttural speech; **отчётливая р.** distinct enunciation. **3.** style of speaking, language; **делова́я р.** business language. **4.** discourse; **о чём была́ р.?** what was the topic of discussion?, what was it all about?; **р. идёт о том, где сле́дует назна́чить ме́сто встре́чи** the question is where to fix the meeting-place; **е́сли р. идёт о сре́дствах** if it is a question of funds, with regard to funds; **не об э́том р.** that is not the point; **о пое́здке за грани́цу не мо́жет быть в э́том году́ и ~́и** a trip abroad is out of the question this year; **завести́ р.** (**о**+*p.*) to lead, turn the conversation (towards); **р. несомне́нно зайдёт о вопро́сах рели́гии** the conversation will undoubtedly turn to religion. **5.** speech; oration; address; **вступи́тельная р.** opening address; **засто́льная р.** after-dinner speech; **защити́тельная р.** speech for the defence; **торже́ственная р.** oration; **вы́ступить с ~́ью** to make a speech. **6.** (*gram.*) speech; **пряма́я р.** direct speech, oratio recta; **ко́свенная р.** indirect speech, oratio obliqua; **ча́сти ~́и** parts of speech.
реш|а́ть(ся), а́ю(сь) *impf. of* **~и́ть(ся)**
реша́|ющий *pres. part. act. of* **~ть** *and adj.* decisive, deciding; key, conclusive; **р. го́лос** deciding vote, casting vote; **р. фа́ктор** decisive factor; (*tech.*) determinant.
реше́ни|е, я *nt.* **1.** decision; **приня́ть р.** to take a decision, make up one's mind. **2.** decree, judg(e)ment; decision, verdict; **зао́чное р.** judg(e)ment by default; **вы́нести р.** to deliver a judg(e)ment; to pass a resolution; **отмени́ть р.** to revoke a decision; (*leg.*) to quash a sentence. **3.** solution; answer (*to a problem*).
реше́тин|а, ы *f.* lath.
решётк|а, и *f.* **1.** grating; grille, railing; lattice; trellis; fender, fireguard; **за ~ой** (*fig., coll.*) behind bars (= *in prison*); **посади́ть за ~у** to put behind bars. **2.** (fire-)grate. **3.** (*coll.*) tail (*of coin*).
реше́тник[1], **а** *m.* (*collect.*) lathing.
реше́тник[2], **а** *m.* sieve-maker.
решет|о́, а́, *pl.* **~̈а** *nt.* sieve.
решётчат|ый (*and* **реше́тчатый)** *adj.* lattice, latticed; trellised; **~ая ба́лка, ~ая фе́рма** lattice girder; **~ая констру́кция** lattice-work; **р. люк** grating.
реши́мост|ь, и *f.* resolution, resoluteness.
реши́тельно *adv.* **1.** resolutely. **2.** decidedly, definitely; **р. отказа́ться** to refuse flatly; **я р. про́тив э́того прое́кта** I am definitely opposed to this scheme. **3.** absolutely; **э́то мне р. всё равно́** it makes absolutely no difference to me; **мы р. не зна́ли, куда́ мы попа́ли** we had absolutely no idea where we had got to; **его́ жда́ли на вокза́ле р. все** practically everyone was at the station to meet him.
реши́тельност|ь, и *f.* resolution, resoluteness, determination.
реши́тел|ьный (~ен, ~ьна) *adj.* **1.** resolute, determined; decided; firm; **р. вид** resolute air; **~ьные ме́ры** strong measures, drastic measures; **р. тон** firm tone. **2.** definite; **р. отве́т** definite reply. **3.** decisive; crucial; **р. моме́нт** crucial point; **~ьная побе́да** sweeping victory. **4.** (*coll.*) absolute, blatant; **р. дура́к** absolute fool.
реш|и́ть, у́, и́шь *pf.* (*of* **~а́ть**) **1.** (*+inf. or +a.*) to decide, determine; to make up one's mind; **р. де́ло в чью-н. по́льзу** to decide a case in s.o.'s favour; **р. чью-н. у́часть** to decide s.o.'s fate. **2.** to solve; to settle; **р. зада́чу** to solve a problem; to accomplish a task.
реш|и́ться, у́сь, и́шься *pf.* (*of* **~а́ться**) **1.** (**на**+*a. or +inf.*) to make up one's mind (to), decide (to), determine (to), resolve (to); to bring o.s. (to). **2.** (*+g.; coll.*) to lose, be deprived (of).
ре́шк|а, и *f.* (*coll.*) tail (*of coin*); **орёл и́ли р.?** heads or tails?
реэвакуа́ци|я, и *f.* re-evacuation.
реэвакуи́р|овать, ую *impf. and pf.* to re-evacuate.
ре́|ять, ю, ешь *impf.* **1.** to soar, hover. **2.** to flutter.
рж|а, и *f.* (*obs.*) = **ржа́вчина**
ржаве|ть, ет *impf.* (*of* **за~** *and* **по~**) to rust.
ржа́вост|ь, и *f.* rustiness.
ржа́вчин|а, ы *f.* **1.** rust. **2.** (*bot.*) mildew.
ржа́вый *adj.* rusty.
ржа́ни|е, я *nt.* neighing.
ржа́нк|а, и *f.* (*zool.*) plover; **р. глу́пая** dotterel; **золоти́стая р.** golden plover.
ржано́й *adj.* rye.
рж|ать, у, ёшь *impf.* to neigh; (*coll.*) laugh loudly.
риа́л, а *m.* rial (*Iranian monetary unit*).
Ривье́р|а, ы *f.* the Riviera.
Ри́г|а, и *f.* Riga.
ри́г|а, и *f.* threshing barn.
ри́гел|ь, я *m.* (*tech.*) cross-bar, collar-beam.
ригори́зм, а *m.* rigorism.
ригористи́ческий *adj.* rigorist.
ри́дер, а *m.* (microfiche) reader.
ридикю́л|ь, я *m.* (*obs.*) handbag.
ри́жский *adj.* (of) Riga.
ри́з|а, ы *f.* **1.** (*eccl.*) chasuble. **2.** (*on icons*) riza. **3.** (*obs., poet.*) raiment, garments; **напи́ться до положе́ния ~** to drink o.s. insensible.
ри́зниц|а, ы *f.* (*eccl.*) vestry, sacristy.
рикоше́т, а *m.* ricochet, rebound; **~ом** at the rebound (*also fig.*).
рикошети́р|овать, ую *impf.* to ricochet.
ри́кш|а, и *f.* rickshaw, jinricksha.
Рим, а *m.* Rome.
ри́млян|ин, ина, *pl.* **~е, ~** *m.* Roman.
ри́мск|ий *adj.* Roman; **па́па р.** the Pope; **р. нос** roman nose; **~ое пра́во** Roman law; **~ая свеча́** roman candle; **~ие ци́фры** roman numerals.
ринг, а *m.* (*sport*) ring.
ри́н|уться, усь, ешься *pf.* to dash, dart.
Ри́о-Гра́нде *f. indecl.* the Rio Grande.
Ри́о-де-Жане́йро *m. indecl.* Rio de Janeiro.
рис, а *m.* rice; paddy.
рис. (*abbr. of* **рису́нок**) fig., figure.
риск, а *m.* risk; **на свой (страх и) р.** at one's own risk, at one's peril; **с ~́ом (для)** at the risk (of); **с повы́шенным ~ом** high-risk; **пойти́ на р.** to run risks, take chances; **р. — благоро́дное де́ло** (*prov.*) nothing venture, nothing gain.
рискн|у́ть, у́, ёшь *pf.* (*+inf.*) to take the risk (of), venture (to).
риско́ванност|ь, и *f.* riskiness.

рискóван|ный (~, ~на) *adj.* **1.** risky; **~ная игрá** gamble; **~ное предприя́тие** risky business, venture. **2.** risqué.
риск|овáть, у́ю *impf.* **1.** to run risks, take chances. **2.** (*+i.*) to risk; (*+inf.*) to risk, take the risk (of); **р. головóй** to risk one's neck; **ничéм не р.** to run no risk; **не хотéть ничéм р.** to take no chances; **р. опоздáть на пóезд** to risk missing the train.
рисовáльн|ый *adj.* drawing; **~ое перó** lettering pen.
рисовáльщик, а *m.* graphic artist; draughtsman; **я óчень плохóй р.** I am no good at drawing, no draughtsman.
рисовáни|е, я *nt.* drawing.
рис|овáть, у́ю *impf.* (*of* **на~**) **1.** to draw; **р. акварéлью** to paint in water-colours; **р. с натýры** to draw, paint from life. **2.** (*fig.*) to depict, paint, portray.
рис|овáться, у́юсь *impf.* **1.** to be silhouetted; to appear, present o.s.; **воéнная жизнь ~овáлась емý чи́стым кошмáром** he saw life in the army as a pure nightmare. **2.** (*pej.*) to pose, act. **3.** *pass. of* **~овáть**
рисóвк|а, и *f.* (*pej.*) posing, acting.
рисовóдств|о, а *nt.* rice-growing.
ри́сов|ый *adj.* rice; **~ая кáша** rice pudding; **~ое пóле** rice-field, paddy-field.
ристáлищ|е, а *nt.* (*obs.*) stadium; hippodrome.
рисýн|ок, ка *m.* **1.** drawing; illustration; (*in scientific work, article, etc.*) figure; pattern, design; outline; **акварéльный р.** water-colour painting. **2.** drawing, draughtsmanship (*opp. use of colour*).
рисýнчатый *adj.* patterned, ornamented.
ритм, а *m.* rhythm.
ри́тмик|а, и *f.* **1.** (*liter.*) rhythm system. **2.** eurhythmics.
ритми́ческий *adj.* rhythmic(al).
ритми́чност|ь, и *f.* rhythm.
ритми́ч|ный (~ен, ~на) *adj.* rhythmic(al); **~ная рабóта** smooth functioning.
ри́тор, а *m.* **1.** (*hist.*) teacher of rhetoric. **2.** (*obs.*) rhetorician, orator.
ритóрик|а, и *f.* rhetoric.
ритори́ческий *adj.* rhetorical; **р. вопрóс** rhetorical question.
ритуáл, а *m.* ritual; ceremonial.
ритуáльный *adj.* ritual.
риф[1]**, а** *m.* reef; **корáлловый р.** coral reef.
риф[2]**, а** *m.* (*naut.*) reef; **брать ≁ы** to reef.
рифлéни|е, я *nt.* (*tech.*) channelling, grooving, fluting, corrugating.
рифлён|ый *adj.* (*tech.*) chequered, channelled, grooved, fluted, corrugated; **~ое желéзо** corrugated iron.
ри́фм|а, ы *f.* rhyme.
рифм|овáть, у́ю *impf.* (*of* **с~**) **1.** to rhyme. **2.** to select in order to make rhyme.
рифм|овáться, у́юсь *impf.* to rhyme.
рифмóвк|а, и *f.* rhyming, rhyme system.
рифмоплёт, а *m.* (*pej.*) rhymer, rhymester.
рици́н, а *m.* **1.** (*bot.*) castor plant. **2.** (*med.*) castor oil.
рици́н|овый *adj. of* **~; ~овое мáсло** castor oil.
рия́л, а *m.* riyal (*Saudi Arabian currency unit*).
р-н (*abbr. of* **райóн**) rayon, raion.
рóббер, а *m.* (*cards*) rubber.
робé|ть, ю *impf.* (*of* **о~**) to be timid; to quail; **не ~й(те)!** don't be afraid!
рóб|кий (~ок, ~кá, ~ко) *adj.* timid, shy.
рóбост|ь, и *f.* timidity, shyness.
рóбот, а *m.* robot.
робо(то)тéхник|а, и *f.* robotics.
рóбче *comp. of* **рóбкий**
ров, рва, о рве, во рву *m.* ditch; **крепостнóй р.** moat, fosse; **противотáнковый р.** anti-tank ditch.
ровéсник, а *m.* pers. of the same age; **мы с ним ~и** we are of the same age.
рóвно *adv.* **1.** regularly, evenly. **2.** exactly; (*of time*) sharp; **р. пять рублéй** five roubles exactly; **р. в час** at one o'clock sharp; on the stroke of one. **3.** (*coll.*) absolutely; **онá р. ничегó не знáет** she knows absolutely nothing. **4.** (*coll.*) exactly like, just like.
рóвност|ь, и *f.* regularity, evenness.
рóв|ный (~ен, ~нá, ~но) *adj.* **1.** flat, even, level; **~ная повéрхность** plane surface. **2.** regular, even; equable; **р. пульс** regular pulse; **р. харáктер** even temper, equable temperament. **3.** exact, even; equal; **р. счёт** even account, exact money; **для ~ного счёта** to make it even; to bring to a round figure; **~ным счётом ничегó** (*coll.*) precisely nothing; **не ~ен час,** *see* **нерóвный**
рóвня, рóвни́ *c.g.* equal, match; **он ей не р.** he is not her equal, he is no match for her.
ровня́|ть, ю *impf.* (*of* **с~**) to even, level; **р. с землёй** to raze to the ground.
ровня́|ться, юсь *impf.* (*of* **с~**) **1.** to become even, become level. **2.** (**по**+*d.*) to attain to the level (of).
рог, а, *pl.* **~á, ~óв** *m.* **1.** horn; antler; **р. изоби́лия** horn of plenty, cornucopia; **брать быкá за ~á** (*coll.*) to take the bull by the horns; **настáвить ~á** (*+d.*; *coll.*) to cuckold; **согнýть в барáний р.** (*coll.*) to make knuckle under; **сломи́ть ~á** (*+d.*; *coll.*) to bring to one's knees. **2.** bugle, horn; **альпи́йский р.** alpenhorn; **охóтничий р.** hunting-horn.
рогáлик, а *m.* crescent-shaped roll, croissant.
рогáст|ый (~, ~а) *adj.* (*coll.*) large-horned.
рогáтин|а, ы *f.* bear-spear.
рогáтк|а, и *f.* **1.** turnpike; *pl.* chevaux-de-frise. **2.** (*boy's*) catapult.
рогáт|ый (~, ~а) *adj.* **1.** horned; **крýпный р. скот** cattle; **мéлкий р. скот** small cattle, sheep and goats. **2.** (*coll.*) cuckolded.
рогáч, á *m.* **1.** stag. **2.** stag-beetle.
рогови́ц|а, ы *f.* (*anat.*) cornea.
рогов|óй *adj.* horn; horny; corneous; **~ы́е очки́** horn-rimmed spectacles; **~áя оболóчка глáза** (*anat.*) cornea; **~áя мýзыка** music for horn; **~áя обмáнка** (*min.*) hornblende.
рогóж|а, и *f.* bast mat, matting.
рогóз, а *m.* (*bot.*) reed mace.
рогонóс|ец, ца *m.* (*coll., joc.*) cuckold.
рогýлк|а, и *f.* (*cul.*) croissant.
род, а, о ≁е, в ~ý, *pl.* **~ы́, ~óв** *m.* **1.** family, kin, clan; **человéческий р.** mankind, human race; **без ≁у, без плéмени** without kith or kin. **2.** birth, origin, stock; generation; **он ≁ом из Ирлáндии** he is an Irishman by birth, a native of Ireland; **из ≁а в р.** from generation to generation; **емý на ~ý напи́сано** (*+inf.*) he was preordained (to); **ей дéсять лет óт ~у** she is ten years of age. **3.** (*biol.*) genus. **4.** sort, kind; **литератýрный р.** literary genre; **р. войск** arm of the service; **вся́кого ≁а** of all kinds, all kind of; **такóго ≁а** of such a kind, such; **в э́том ≁е** of this sort; **что-то в э́том ≁е** sth. of the kind; sth. to that effect; **в нéкотором ≁е** in some sort, to some extent; **в своём ≁е** in one's own way; **своегó ≁а** a kind of; in one's own way; **он своегó ≁а гéний** he is a genius in his own way. **5.** (*gram.*) gender.
родáнист|ый *adj.* (*chem.*) thiocyanate (of), sulphocyanate (of); **~ая кислотá** thiocyanic acid, sulphocyanic acid.
роддóм, а *m.* (*abbr. of* **роди́льный дом**) maternity home.
родези́|ец, йца *m.* Rhodesian.
родези́|йка, йки *f. of* **~ец**
родези́йский *adj.* Rhodesian.
Родéзи|я, и *f.* Rhodesia.
родéо *nt. indecl.* rodeo.
рóди|й, я *m.* (*chem.*) rhodium.
роди́льниц|а, ы *f.* woman recently confined.
роди́льн|ый *adj.*: **р. дом** maternity home, lying-in hospital; **~ая горя́чка** puerperal fever; **~ое отделéние** delivery room.
роди́мчик, а *m.* (*coll.*) convulsions (*of mother or child about time of birth*).
роди́м|ый *adj.* **1.** own; native. **2.: ~ое пятнó** birth-mark. **3.** (*as form of address*) (my) dear.
рóдин|а, ы *f.* native land, mother country; home, homeland; **вернýться на ~у** to return home; **тоскá по ~е** home-sickness, nostalgia.
рóдинк|а, и *f.* birth-mark.
роди́н|ы, ~ *no sg.* (*obs.*) celebration of birth of child.

роди́тел|и, ей *no sg.* parents.
роди́тел|ь, я *m.* (*obs.*) father.
роди́тельниц|а, ы *f.* (*obs.*) mother.
роди́тельный *adj.* (*gram.*) genitive.
роди́тельский *adj.* parental, parents'; paternal; **р. комите́т** parents' committee.
ро|ди́ть, жу́, ди́шь, *past* **~ди́л, ~дила́, ~ди́ло** *impf. and pf.* **1.** (*impf. also* **рожа́ть**) to bear, give birth (to); **в чём мать ~дила́** (*joc.*) in one's birthday suit. **2.** (*impf. also* **рожда́ть**) (*fig.*) to give birth, rise (to).
ро|ди́ться, жу́сь, ди́шься, *past* **~ди́лся, ~дила́сь, ~ди́ло́сь** *impf. and pf.* **1.** (*impf. also* **рожда́ться**) to be born; **р. преподава́телем** to be a born teacher. **2.** (*impf. also* **рожда́ться**) (*fig.*) to arise, come into being. **3.** to spring up, thrive; **кукуру́за у нас ~дила́сь хорошо́** we had a good maize-crop.
ро́дич, а *m.* (*coll.*) relation, relative.
родни́к, а́ *m.* spring.
роднико́в|ый *adj. of* **родни́к; ~ая вода́** spring water.
родн|и́ть, ю́, и́шь *impf.* to make related, link.
родн|и́ться, ю́сь, и́шься *impf.* (*of* **по~**) (**с**+*i.*) to become related (with).
родничо́|к[1]**, ка́** *m. dim. of* **родни́к**
роднич|о́к[2]**, ка́** *m.* (*anat.*) fontanel(le).
родн|о́й *adj.* **1.** own (*by blood relationship in direct line*); **р. брат** one's brother (*opp. cousin, etc.*); *as n.* **~ы́е, ~ы́х** relations, relatives, one's people; **в кругу́ ~ы́х** in the family circle; with one's people. **2.** native; home; intimate, familiar; **~а́я страна́, ~а́я земля́** native land; **р. го́род** home town; **р. язы́к** mother tongue. **3.** (*as form of address*) (my) dear.
родн|я́, и́ *f.* **1.** (*collect.*) relations, relatives, kinsfolk. **2.** relation, relative.
родови́тост|ь, и *f.* blood; high birth, good birth.
родови́т|ый (~, ~а) *adj.* high-born, well-born, of the blood.
родов|о́й[1] *adj.* **1.** (*ethnol.*) clan. **2.** ancestral, patrimonial; **~о́е име́ние, ~о́е иму́щество** patrimony. **3.** (*biol.*) generic. **4.** (*gram.*) gender.
родов|о́й[2] *adj.* birth, labour; **~ы́е схва́тки** birth throes, labour.
родовспомога́тельн|ый *adj.*: **~ое учрежде́ние** maternity home.
рододе́ндрон, а *m.* (*bot.*) rhododendron.
родонача́льник, а *m.* ancestor, forefather; (*fig.*) father.
Ро́дос, а *m.* Rhodes.
родосло́вн|ая, ой *f.* genealogy, pedigree.
родосло́вн|ый *adj.* genealogical; **~ое де́рево** family tree; **~ая кни́га** family register; stud-book; **~ая табли́ца** genealogical table.
ро́дственник, а *m.* relation, relative; **ближа́йший р.** next of kin.
ро́дственност|ь, и *f.* **1.** connection, tie. **2.** familiarity, intimacy.
ро́дствен|ный (~, ~на) *adj.* **1.** kindred, related; **~ные отноше́ния** blood relations; **~ные свя́зи** kinship ties. **2.** kindred, related, allied; **~ные наро́ды** related peoples; **~ные языки́** cognate languages. **3.** familiar, intimate.
родств|о́, а́ *nt.* **1.** relationship, kinship (*also fig.*); **кро́вное р.** blood relationship, blood tie, consanguinity; **быть в ~е́** (**с**+*i.*) to be related (to); **не по́мнящий ~а́** (*in official documents*; *obs.*) ancestry unknown. **2.** (*collect., coll.*) relations, relatives.
ро́д|ы, ов *no sg.* birth; childbirth, delivery, lying-in; **в ~ах** in labour; **стимуля́ция ~ов** induction (of labour).
рое́ни|е, я *nt.* swarming (*of bees, etc.*).
ро́ж|а[1]**, и** *f.* (*coll.*) mug (= *face*).
ро́ж|а[2]**, и** *f.* (*med.*) erysipelas.
рожа́|ть, ю *impf. of* **роди́ть**
рожда́емост|ь, и *f.* birth-rate.
рожда́|ть(ся), ю(сь) *impf. of* **роди́ть(ся)**
рожде́ни|е, я *nt.* **1.** birth; **день ~я** birthday; **ме́сто ~я** birth-place; **глухо́й от ~я** deaf from birth. **2.** birthday.
рождённый *p.p.p. of* **роди́ть**; (+*inf.*) born (to), destined (to).
рожде́ственск|ий *adj.* Christmas; **р. дед** Father Christmas, Santa Claus; **~ая ёлка** Christmas-tree; **р. пост** Advent; **р. соче́льник** Christmas Eve.
Рождеств|о́, а́ *nt.* Christmas; the Nativity; **на Р.** at Christmas(-time).
роже́ни́ц|а, ы *f.* woman in childbirth.
роже́чник, а *m.* horn-player; bugler.
ро́жист|ый *adj.* (*med.*) erysipelatous; **~ое воспале́ние** erysipelas.
рож|о́к, ка́ *m.* **1.** small horn. **2.** (*mus.*) horn, clarion; bugle; **францу́зский р.** French horn. **3.** ear-trumpet. **4.** feeding-bottle; **корми́ть с ~ка́** to bottle-feed. **5.** (**га́зовый**) (gas-)burner, (gas-)jet. **6.** shoe-horn.
рож|о́н, на́ *m.*: **лезть, идти́ на р.** (*coll.*) to kick against the pricks; **про́тив ~на́ пере́ть** (*coll.*) to swim against the tide; **како́го ещё ~на́ на́до?** (*coll.*) what the hell more do you need?
рожь, ржи *f.* rye.
ро́з|а, ы *f.* **1.** rose; rose-tree, rose-bush. **2.** (*archit.*) rose-window, rosace.
роза́ри|й, я *m.* rosarium, rose-garden.
ро́звальн|и, ей *no sg.* rozvalni (*low, wide sledge*).
ро́з|га, ги, *g. pl.* **~ог** *f.* **1.** birch (rod); **наказа́ть ~гой** to birch. **2.** *pl.* blows of the birch; **дать ~ог** to give the birch.
ро́зговень|е, я *nt.* (*eccl.*) first meal after fast.
ро́здых, а *m.* (*coll.*) pause (*from work*), breather.
розео́л|а, ы *f.* (*med.*) roseola.
розе́тк|а, и *f.* **1.** rosette. **2.** (*elec.*) socket; wall-plug. **3.** jam-dish. **4.** candle-ring (*glass, metal, or china ring on candlestick to collect wax*). **5.** (*archit.*) rose-window.
розмари́н, а *m.* (*bot.*) rosemary.
ро́зниц|а, ы *f.* retail; **торгова́ть в ~у** to engage in retail trade.
ро́зничный *adj.* retail; **р. торго́вец** retailer.
ро́зно *adv.* (*coll.*) apart, separately.
розн|ь, и *f.* **1.** difference; **челове́к челове́ку р.** there are no two people alike; there are people and people. **2.** disagreement, dissension.
розова́т|ый (~, ~а) *adj.* pinkish.
розове́|ть, ю *impf.* (*of* **по~**) to turn pink.
розовощёкий *adj.* pink-cheeked, rosy-cheeked.
ро́зов|ый (~, ~а) *adj.* **1.** *adj. of* **ро́за; ~ое де́рево** rosewood; **р. куст** rose-bush; **~ое ма́сло** attar of roses. **2.** pink, rose-coloured. **3.** (*fig.*) rosy; **смотре́ть сквозь ~ые очки́** to view through rose-coloured spectacles.
ро́зыгрыш, а *m.* **1.** drawing (*of a lottery, etc.*). **2.** (*sport*) playing off (*of a cup-tie, etc.*). **3.** (*sport*) draw, drawn game. **4.** practical joke.
ро́зыск, а *m.* **1.** search. **2.** (*leg.*) inquiry; **Уголо́вный р.** Criminal Investigation Department.
ро|и́ться, и́тся *impf.* (*of bees, etc.*) to swarm; (*fig.*; *of thoughts*) to crowd.
рой, ро́я, *pl.* **рои́** *m.* swarm (*of bees, etc.*).
рок[1]**, а** *m.* fate.
рок[2]**, а** *m.* rock (*var. of popular music*); **тяжёлый р.** hard rock.
рок- *comb. form* rock.
рока́д|а, ы *f.* (*mil.*) belt road, lateral road.
рока́дный *adj.* (*mil.*) belt, lateral.
рокир|ова́ть(ся), у́ю(сь) *impf. and pf.* (*chess*) to castle.
рокиро́вк|а, и *f.* (*chess*) castling; (*mil.*; *fig.*) lateral troop movement.
рок-му́зык|а, и *f.* rock music.
рок-н-ро́лл, а *m.* rock 'n' roll.
роков|о́й *adj.* **1.** fateful; fated; **~а́я краса́вица** femme fatale. **2.** fatal.
рококо́ *nt. indecl.* rococo.
ро́кот, а *m.* roar, rumble.
роко|та́ть, чу́, ~чешь *impf.* to roar, rumble.
ро́лик, а *m.* **1.** roller, castor. **2.** (*elec.*) (porcelain) cleat. **3.** *pl.* roller skates. **4.: рекла́мный р.** (*cin.*) trailer.
ро́ликовый *adj. of* **~; ~овая доска́** skateboard; **р. подши́пник** roller bearing.
роликодро́м, а *m.* roller-skating rink.
ро́лкер, а *m.* ro-ro (*roll-on roll-off*) ship
ро́ллер, а *m.* (*child's*) scooter.
ро́ллинг, а *m.* **1.** skateboard. **2.** skateboarding.

рол|ь, и, *pl.* **~и, ~е́й** *f.* (*theatr.*) role (*also fig.*); part; **в ~и** (+*g.*) in the role (of); **игра́ть р.** (+*g.*) to take the part (of), play, act; (*fig.*) to matter, count, be of importance; **э́то не игра́ет ~и** it is of no importance, it does not count; **вы́держать свою́ р.** (*fig.*) to keep up one's part.
ром, а *m.* rum.
рома́н, а *m.* **1.** novel; romance. **2.** (*coll.*) love affair; romance.
романи́ст[1], **а** *m.* novelist.
романи́ст[2], **а** *m.* Romance philologist.
романи́ческий *adj.* romantic.
рома́нс, а *m.* (*mus.*) romance.
рома́нск|ий *adj.* Romance, Romanic; **р. стиль** (*archit.*) Romanesque; **~ие языки́** Romance languages.
романти́зм, а *m.* romanticism.
рома́нтик, а *m.* (*in var. senses*) romantic; romanticist.
рома́нтик|а, и *f.* romance; **р. медици́нских иссле́дований** the romance of medical research.
романти́ческий *adj.* romantic.
романти́чност|ь, и *f.* romantic quality.
романти́ч|ный (~ен, ~на) *adj.* = **~еский**
рома́шк|а, и *f.* (*bot. and pharm.*) camomile.
рома́шк|овый *adj. of* **~а; р. чай** camomile tea.
ромб, а *m.* (*math.*) rhomb(us); (*mil.*) diamond formation; (*aeron.*) box of four.
ромби́ческий *adj.* (*math.*) rhombic.
роме́йский *adj.* (*hist.*) Romaic, of East Rome.
ро́мовый *adj. of* **ром**
ромште́кс, а *m.* rump steak.
Ро́н|а, ы *f.* the Rhone (*river*).
ро́ндо *nt. indecl.* (*mus.*) rondo.
рондо́ *nt. indecl.* (*liter.*) rondeau, rondel.
роня́|ть, ю *impf.* (*of* **урони́ть**) **1.** to drop, let fall; **р. слёзы** to shed tears; **р. сло́во** to let fall a word. **2.** *impf. only* to shed; **р. ли́стья** to shed its leaves; **р. опере́ние** to moult. **3.** (*fig.*) to injure, discredit; **р. себя́ в обще́ственном мне́нии** to drop in public estimation.
ро́пот, а *m.* murmur, grumble.
роп|та́ть, щу́, ~щешь *impf.* to murmur, grumble.
рос, ла́ *see* **расти́**
рос|а́, ы́, *pl.* **~ы** *f.* dew; **то́чка ~ы́** dew-point; **медо́вая р.** (*bot.*) honey dew; **до ~ы́** first thing (in the morning); **по ~е́** while the dew is still on the ground.
роси́нк|а, и *f.* dewdrop; **(ни) ма́ковой ~и во рту не́ было** neither food nor drink has passed (my) lips.
роси́ст|ый (~, ~а) *adj.* dewy.
роско́шеств|о, а *nt.* **1.** extravagant taste, exotic taste. **2.** extravagance.
роско́шеств|овать, ую *impf.* to luxuriate, live in luxury.
роско́ш|ный (~ен, ~на) *adj.* **1.** luxurious, sumptuous. **2.** (*coll.*) luxuriant, splendid.
ро́скош|ь, и *f.* **1.** luxury. **2.** luxuriance; splendour.
ро́слый *adj.* tall, strapping.
ро́сный[1] *adj.*: **р. ла́дан** benzoin, benjamin.
ро́с|ный[2] *adj.* (*dial.*) *of* **~а́**
росома́х|а, и *f.* (*zool.*) wolverene, glutton.
ро́спис|ь, и *f.* **1.** list, inventory. **2.** painting; **р. стен** wall-painting(s), mural(s).
ро́спуск, а *m.* dismissal; (*mil.*) disbandment; **р. парла́мента** dissolution of Parliament; **р. на кани́кулы** breaking up for the holidays.
росси́йский *adj.* Russian.
Росси́|я, и *f.* Russia.
ро́ссказн|и, ей *no sg.* (*coll.*) old wives' tale, cock-and-bull story.
ро́ссып|ь, и *f.* **1.** scattering; **грузи́ть зерно́ ~ью** to load grain loose. **2.** (*pl.*; *min.*) deposit, placer.
рост, а *m.* **1.** growth (*also fig.*); (*fig.*) increase, rise. **2.** height, stature; **~ом** in height; **он ~ом с вас** he is (of) your height; **высо́кого ~а** tall; **во весь р.** full length; (*fig.*) in all its magnitude; **встать во весь р.** to stand upright, stand up straight. **3.** (*obs.*) interest; **дать де́ньги в р.** to lend money on interest.
ро́стбиф, а *m.* roast beef.
ростовщи́к, а́ *m.* usurer, money-lender.
ростовщи́ческий *adj.* usurious.
ростовщи́честв|о, а *nt.* usury, money-lending.
рост|о́к, ка́ *m.* sprout, shoot; **пусти́ть ~ки́** to sprout, put out shoots.
ростр, а *m.* (*hist.*) beak (*of war-galley*), rostrum.
ро́стр|а, ы *f.* (*hist.*) rostrum.
ростра́льный *adj.* (*archit.*) rostral.
ро́стр|ы, ~ *no sg.* (*naut.*) booms.
ро́счерк, а *m.* flourish; **одни́м ~ом пера́** with a stroke of the pen.
рося́нк|а, и *f.* (*bot.*) sundew.
рот, рта, о рте́, во рту́ *m.* mouth; **дыша́ть ртом** to breathe through one's mouth; **у меня́ пять ртов в семье́** I have five mouths to feed in my family; **не брать в р.** (+*g.*) not to touch; **она́ мя́са в р. не брала́** she would never touch meat; **рази́нуть р.** to stand agape, be open-mouthed; **не сметь рта раскры́ть** not to dare to open one's mouth; **зажа́ть, за́ткнуть р. кому́-н.** to stop s.o.'s mouth, shut s.o. up; **смотре́ть в р. кому́-н.** to hang on s.o.'s words; **хлопо́т по́лон р.** (*coll.*) to have one's hands full.
ро́т|а, ы *f.* (*mil.*) company.
рота́тор, а *m.* duplicator, duplicating machine.
ротаци́зм, а *m.* (*ling.*) rhotacism.
ротацио́нн|ый *adj.*: **~ая маши́на** (*typ.*) rotary press.
рота́ци|я, и *f.* **1.** = **~о́нная маши́на. 2.** (*agric.*) rotation.
ротве́йлер, а *m.* Rottweiler.
ро́тмистр, а *m.* (*mil.*) captain (*of cavalry in tsarist Russ. army*).
ро́т|ный *adj. of* **~а;** *as n.* **р., ~ного** *m.* company commander.
ротозе́|й, я *m.* (*coll.*) scatter-brain, gaper.
ротозе́йнича|ть, ю *impf.* (*coll.*) to be scatter-brained.
ротозе́йств|о, а *nt.* (*coll.*) scatter-brainedness.
рото́нд|а, ы *f.* **1.** (*archit.*) rotunda. **2.** (*lady's*) cloak.
ротоно́г|ие, их *pl.* (*sg.* **~ое, ~ого** *nt.*) (*zool.*) Stomatopoda.
ро́тор, а *m.* (*tech.*) rotor.
ро́хл|я, и, *g. pl.* **~ей** *c.g.* (*coll.*) dawdler.
ро́щ|а, и *f.* small wood, grove.
ро́щиц|а, ы *f. dim. of* **ро́ща**
рояли́ст, а *m.* royalist.
рояли́стский *adj.* royalist.
роя́л|ь, я *m.* piano; grand piano; **кабине́тный р.** baby grand; **игра́ть на ~е** to play the piano; **у ~я** at the piano.
РСФСР *f. indecl.* (*abbr. of* ***Росси́йская Сове́тская Федерати́вная Социалисти́ческая Респу́блика***) RSFSR (*Russian Soviet Federal Socialist Republic*).
РТС *f. indecl.* (*abbr. of* ***ремо́нтно-техни́ческая ста́нция***) (*agric.*) repairs and engineering station.
рту́тн|ый *adj.* mercury, mercurial; **р. выпрями́тель** (*elec.*) mercury arc rectifier, mercury vapour rectifier; **~ая ла́мпа** (*elec.*) mercury vapour lamp, mercury arc lamp; **~ая мазь** (*pharm.*) mercury ointment; **~ое отравле́ние** (*med.*) mercurialism, mercury poisoning; **р. столб** mercury (column).
рту́т|ь, и *f.* mercury, quicksilver.
руба́к|а, и *m.* (*coll.*) fine swordsman.
руба́н|ок, ка *m.* (*tech.*) plane.
руба́х|а, и *f.* shirt; **р.-па́рень** (*coll.*) straight-forward fellow.
руба́шк|а, и *f.* **1.** shirt; **ни́жняя р., нате́льная р.** petticoat, vest, singlet; **ночна́я р.** night-shirt, night-dress; **роди́ться в ~е** to be born with a silver spoon in one's mouth; **своя́ р. бли́же к те́лу** (*prov.*) charity begins at home. **2.** colour (*of animal's coat*). **3.** back (*of playing cards*). **4.** (*tech.*) jacket, casing, lining.
рубе́ж, а́ *m.* **1.** boundary, border(line); **за ~о́м** abroad. **2.** (*mil.*) line; **р. ата́ки** assault position.
руб|е́ц[1], **ца́** *m.* **1.** scar, cicatrice; weal. **2.** hem, seam.
руб|е́ц[2], **ца́** *m.* **1.** (*zool.*) paunch (*ruminant's first stomach*). **2.** (*cul.*) tripe.
руби́ди|й, я *m.* (*chem.*) rubidium.
руби́льник, а *m.* (*elec.*) knife-switch.
руби́н, а *m.* ruby.
руби́новый *adj.* ruby; ruby(-coloured).
руб|и́ть, лю́, ~ишь *impf.* **1.** to fell (*trees*). **2.** to hew, chop, hack. **3.** (*cul.*) to mince, chop up. **4.** to put up, erect (*of logs*).
руб|и́ться, лю́сь, ~ишься *impf.* to fight (with cold steel).
ру́бищ|е, а *no pl., nt.* rags, tatters.

рýбк|а[1], **и** *f.* **1.** felling. **2.** hewing, chopping, hacking. **3.** mincing, chopping up.
рýбк|а[2], **и** *f.* (*naut.*) deck house, deck cabin; **боевáя р.** conning tower; **кормовáя р.** roundhouse; **рулевáя р.** wheel-house; **штýрманская р.** chart house.
рублёвк|а, и *f.* (*coll.*) one-rouble note.
рубл|ёвый *adj.* **1.** *adj. of* **~ь. 2.** one rouble (*in price*).
рýблен|ый *adj.* **1.** minced, chopped; **~ая капýста** chopped cabbage; **~ое мя́со** minced meat, hash; **~ые котлéты** rissoles. **2.** of logs; **~ая избá** log hut, log cabin.
рубл|ь, я́ *m.* rouble.
рýбрик|а, и *f.* **1.** rubric, heading. **2.** column (*of figures*).
рубц|евáться, ýется *impf.* (*of* **за~**) to cicatrize.
рýбчатый *adj.* ribbed.
рýбчик, а *m.* **1.** *dim. of* **рубéц**[1]. **2.** rib (*on material*).
рýган|ь, и *f.* abuse, bad language, swearing.
ругáтел|ь, я *m.* habitual user of bad language.
ругáтельн|ый *adj.* abusive; **~ые словá** bad language, swear-words.
ругáтельств|о, а *nt.* oath, swear-word.
ругá|ть, ю *impf.* (*of* **вы́~** *and* **из~**) **1.** to curse, swear (at), abuse. **2.** to tear to pieces, lash (= *criticize severely*).
ругá|ться, юсь *impf.* **1.** to curse, swear, use bad language; **р. как извóзчик** to swear like a trooper. **2.** to swear at one another, abuse one another.
ругн|ýть(ся), ý(сь), ёшь(ся) *pf.* to swear.
руд|á, ы́, *pl.* **∸ы** *f.* ore; **желéзная р.** iron-ore, iron-stone.
рудимéнт, а *m.* rudiment.
рудиментáрный *adj.* rudimentary.
рудни́к, á *m.* mine, pit.
руднкóвый *adj. of* **рудни́к**
рудни́|чный *adj. of* **~к; р. газ** fire-damp; **~чная стóйка** pit prop; **~чная лáмпа** miner's lamp, Davy lamp.
рýд|ный *adj. of* **~á; ~ная жи́ла** vein; **~ное месторождéние** ore deposit.
рудокóп, а *m.* miner.
рудонóс|ный (~ен, ~на) *adj.* ore-bearing.
рудоподъёмник, а *m.* ore lift.
рудопромы́вочный *adj.* ore-washing.
ружéйник, а *m.* gunsmith.
ружéйн|ый *adj. of* **ружьё; р. вы́стрел** rifle-shot; **р. мáстер** armourer, gunsmith; **~ые приёмы** manual of the rifle.
руж|ьё, ья́, *pl.* **∸ья, ∸ей, ∸ьям** *nt.* (hand-)gun, rifle; **дробовóе р.** shot-gun; **охóтничье р.** fowling-piece, sporting gun; **противотáнковое р.** anti-tank rifle; **стать в р.** to fall in; **в р.!** (*mil. command*) to arms!; **быть под ~ьём** to be under arms; **призвáть под р.** to call to arms, call to the colours.
руи́н|а, ы *f.* ruin (*usu. pl.*).
рук|á, и́, *a.* **∸у,** *pl.* **∸и, ~, ~áм** *f.*

I. 1. hand; arm; **подáть ∸у** (*+d.*) to offer one's hand; **пожáть ∸у** (*+d.*), **здорóваться зá ~у** (**с**+*i.*) to shake hands (with); **∸и вверх!** hands up!; **~áми не трóгать!** please, do not touch!; **вести́ зá ~у** to lead by the hand; **взя́ться зá ~у** to join hands, link arms; **из ~ в ∸и** from hand to hand; **взять нá ~и** to take in one's arms; **держáть на ~áх** to hold in one's arms; **р. óб ~у** hand in hand; **написáть от ~и́** to write out by hand; **взять когó-н. пóд ~у** to take s.o.'s arm; **идти́ с кем-н. пóд ~у** to walk arm in arm with s.o.; walk with s.o. on one's arm. **2.** hand, handwriting; signature; **приложи́ть ∸у** to affix one's signature. **3.** side, hand; **на лéвой ~é** on the left; **по прáвую ∸у** at the right hand. **4.** *pl.* hands (*fig. = power, possession*); **взять в свои́ ∸и** to take into one's own hands; **взять (себя́) в ∸и** to take (o.s.) in hand; **держáть в свои́х ~áх** to have in one's clutches, have under one's thumb; **попáсться в ∸и комý-н.** to fall into s.o.'s hands; **прибрáть к ~áм** to appropriate; **быть в хорóших ~áх** to be in good hands; **скóлько у вас на ~áх инострáнной валю́ты?** how much foreign currency have you on you?; **свобóда ~** a free hand; **в сóбственные ∸и** (*on cover of letter, etc.*) 'personal'. **5.** (*fig.*) hand (*of pers. giving or receiving proposal of marriage*); **проси́ть ~и́ у когó-н.** to ask s.o.'s hand in marriage. **6.** (*fig.*) hand; source, authority; **из пéрвых, вторы́х ~** at first, second hand; **узнáть из вéрных ~** to have on good authority. **7.** (*g. sg.*; *coll., obs.*) sort, kind, quality; **срéдней ~и́** of medium quality; **большóй ~и́ негодя́й** a scoundrel of the first order.

II. (*fig.*; *in var. senses*) hand; **отдáть в ∸и комý-н.** to hand over to s.o. in pers.; **игрáть (на роя́ле) в четы́ре ~и́** to play duets (on the piano); **передáть дéло в чьи-н. ∸и** to put a matter in s.o.'s hands; **перейти́ в другíе ∸и, из ~ в ∸и** to change hands; **сон в ∸у** the dream has come true; **вали́ться из ~** *see* **вали́ться; из ~ вон (плóхо)** (*coll.*) thoroughly bad, quite useless; **вы́дать нá ~и** to hand out; **имéть на ~áх** to have on one's hands; **умерéть на чьих-н. ~áх** to die in s.o.'s arms; **мáстер на все ∸и** Jack of all trades; **э́то бýдет им нá ~у** that will serve their purpose; it will be playing into their hands; **нá ~у нечи́ст** (*coll.*) dishonest, underhand; **на скóрую ∸у** off-hand; **быть свя́занным по ~áм и ногáм** to be bound hand and foot; **дать комý-н. по ~áм** (*coll.*) to give a rap over the knuckles; **удáрить по ~áм** to strike a bargain; **по ~áм!** it's a bargain!, done!; **говори́ть комý-н. пóд ~у** to distract s.o. by talking; **под ~óй** at hand, to hand; **под пья́ную ∸у** under the influence (of drink); **с ~ долóй** off one's hands; **сбыть с ~** to get off one's hands; **э́то тебé не сойдёт с ~** (*coll.*) you won't get away with it; **греть ∸и (на**+*p.*) to make a good thing (out of); **дать вóлю ~áм** (*coll.*) to bring one's fists into play; **дать ∸у на отсечéние** to swear; **э́то дéло чужи́х ~** this is s.o. else's doing; **живóй ~óй** rapidly; **как ~óй сня́ло** it has vanished as if by magic; **ломáть ∸и** to wring one s hands; **махнýть ~óй (на**+*a.*) to give up as lost; **наби́ть ∸у** to get one's hand in; **наложи́ть на себя́ ∸и** to lay hands on o.s.; **не поднимáется р.** (*+inf.*) one cannot bring o.s. (to); **мне не р.** (*+inf.*) I have no call (to), it does not suit me (to); **приложи́ть ∸у (к)** to put one's hand (to), take a hand (in) (*see also* **I. 2.**); **развязáть ∸и** (*+d.*) to give a free hand; **р. у негó не дрóгнет** (*+inf.*) he will not scruple (to); **∸и у меня́ не дохóдят до э́того** it is beyond me; I've no time to do it; **∸и прочь!** hands off!; **~óй подáть** a stone's throw away, but a step; **умы́ть ∸и (в**+*p.*) to wash one s hands (of); **у меня́ ∸и чéшутся** (*+inf.*) my fingers are itching (to); I itch (to).
рукáв, á, *pl.* **~á** *m.* **1.** sleeve; **спустя́ ~á** (*coll.*) in a slipshod manner. **2.** branch, arm (*of river*). **3.** (*tech.*) hose; **пожáрный р.** fire-hose.
рукави́ц|а, ы *f.* mitten; gauntlet; **держáть в ежóвых ~ах** to rule with a rod of iron.
рукáвчик, а *m.* **1.** *dim. of* **рукáв. 2.** cuff.
рукоби́ть|е, я *nt.* (*obs.*) shaking hands on a bargain.
рукоблýди|е, я *nt.* masturbation.
рукоблýдник, а *m.* masturbator.
рукоблýднича|ть, ю *impf.* to indulge in masturbation.
рукóвéд, а *m.* palmist, chiromancer.
руковéдени|е, я *nt.* palmistry, chiromancy.
руководи́тел|ь, я *m.* **1.** leader; manager; **клáссный р.** (*in school*) form monitor. **2.** instructor; guide; **наýчный руководи́тель** supervisor of studies.
руково|ди́ть, жý, ди́шь *impf.* (*+i.*) to lead; to guide; to direct, manage.
руково|ди́ться, жýсь, ди́шься *impf.* (*+i.*) to follow; to be guided (by).
руковóдств|о, а *nt.* **1.** leadership; guidance; direction. **2.** guiding principle, guide; **р. к дéйствию** guide to action. **3.** handbook, guide, manual; **р. по эксплуатáции** instructions for use. **4.** (*collect.*) (the) leadership, leaders; governing body.
руковóдств|оваться, уюсь *impf.* (*+i.*) to follow; to be guided (by).
руковод|я́щий *pres. part. act. of* **~и́ть** *and adj.* leading; guiding; high-level, senior; **~я́щая статья́** editorial, leader; **р. комитéт** steering committee.
рукодéли|е, я *nt.* **1.** needlework. **2.** (*pl.*) hand-made wares.
рукодéльниц|а, ы *f.* needlewoman.
рукодéльнича|ть, ю *impf.* to do needlework.
рукокры́л|ые, ых *pl.* (*sg.* **~ое, ~ого** *nt.*) (*zool.*) Cheiroptera.
рукомóйник, а *m.* wash-stand, wash-hand-stand.
рукопáшн|ая, ой *f.* hand-to-hand fight(-ing).

рукопа́шный *adj.* hand-to-hand.
рукопи́сный *adj.* manuscript; **р. шрифт** cursive, italics.
ру́копис|ь, и *f.* manuscript
рукоплеска́ни|е, я *nt.* applause, clapping.
рукопле|ска́ть, щу́, ~́щешь *impf.* (+*d.*) to applaud, clap.
рукопожа́ти|е, я *nt.* handshake; **обменя́ться ~ями (с**+*i.*) to shake hands (with).
рукотво́р|ный (~ен, ~на) *adj.* man-made, artificial.
рукоя́тк|а, и *f.* **1.** handle; hilt; haft, helve; shaft; **по ~у** up to the hilt. **2.** crank, crank handle.
рула́д|а, ы *f.* (*mus.*) roulade, run.
рулев|о́й *adj. of* **руль; ~о́е колесо́** steering wheel; **~а́я коло́нка** steering column; **р. механи́зм, ~о́е устро́йство** steering gear; *as n.* **р., ~о́го** *m.* **1.** helmsman. **2.** (*sport*) cox(swain); **дво́йка без ~о́го** coxless pair.
рулёжк|а, и *f.* (*aeron.*) taxiing.
руле́т, а *m.* (*cul.*) **1** roll; **мясно́й р.** meat loaf. **2.** boned gammon.
руле́тк|а, и *f.* **1.** tape-measure. **2.** roulette; **игра́ть в ~у** to play roulette.
рул|и́ть, ю́, и́шь *impf.* (*aeron.*) to taxi.
руло́н, а *m.* roll.
рул|ь, я́ *m.* rudder; helm (*also fig.*); (steering-)wheel; handle-bars; **р. высоты́** (*aeron.*) elevator; **р. поворо́та** (*aeron.*) rudder; **пра́вить ~ём, сиде́ть за ~ём, быть на ~е́, стоя́ть на ~е́** to steer; **стать за р.** to take the helm; **ле́во руля́** port the helm; **стоя́ть на ~е́** (*fig.*) to be at the helm; **без ~я́ и без ветри́л** (*fig.*) without any sense of purpose.
румб, а *m.* (*naut.*) (compass) point.
ру́мпел|ь, я *m.* (*naut.*) tiller.
румы́н, а *m.* Romanian.
Румы́ни|я, и *f.* Romania, Rumania.
румы́н|ка, ки *f. of* **~**
румы́нский *adj.* Romanian.
румя́н|а, ~ *no sg.* rouge; blusher.
румя́н|ец, ца *m.* (high) colour; flush; blush.
румя́н|ить, ю, ишь *impf.* **1.** (*pf.* **за~**) to redden (*also fig.*); to cause to glow. **2.** (*pf.* **на~**) to rouge.
румя́н|иться, юсь, ишься *impf.* **1.** (*pf.* **за~**) to redden; to glow; to flush. **2.** (*pf.* **на~**) to use rouge.
румя́н|ый (~, ~а) *adj.* rosy, ruddy, rubicund.
ру́н|а, ы *f.* (*philol.*) rune.
рунду́к, а́ *m.* (*obs.*) locker, bin.
руни́ст|ый (~, ~а) *adj.* (*obs.*) fleecy.
руни́ческий *adj.* (*philol.*) runic.
рун|о́¹, а́, *pl.* **~́а** *nt.* (*obs. or poet.*) fleece; **золото́е р.** (*myth.*) the Golden Fleece.
рун|о́², а́, *pl.* **~́а** *and* **~́ья** *nt.* (*dial.*) school (*of fish*).
ру́пи|я, и *f.* rupee.
ру́пор, а *m.* megaphone, speaking-trumpet; loud hailer; (*fig.*) mouthpiece.
Рур, а *m.* the Ruhr (*river*).
руса́к¹, а́ *m.* (grey) hare.
руса́к², а́ *m.* (*coll.*) Russian.
руса́лк|а, и *f.* mermaid.
руса́л|очий *adj. of* **~ка**
руси́зм, а *m.* (*ling.*) Russianism, Russ(ic)ism.
руси́н, а *m.* Ruthenian.
руси́н|ка, ки *f. of* **~**
руси́нский *adj.* Ruthenian.
руси́ст, а *m.* Russianist.
руси́стик|а, и *f.* Russian philology.
русифика́тор, а *m.* Russifier, Russianizer.
русифика́ци|я, и *f.* Russification, Russianization.
русифици́р|овать, ую *impf. and pf.* to russify, russianize.
ру́сл|о, а, *g. pl.* **~** *nt.* **1.** (river-)bed, channel; **измени́ть р. реки́** to change the course of a river. **2.** (*fig.*) channel, course; **мои́ дела́ пошли́ по но́вому ~у** my affairs have taken a new turn.
русоволо́с|ый (~, ~а) *adj.* having light-brown hair.
ру́сск|ая, ой *f.* **1.** *f. of* **~ий** *as n.* **2.** russkaya (*Russ. folk-dance*).
ру́сск|ий *adj.* Russian (*also as n.* **р., ~ого** *m.*).
ру́с|ый (~, ~а) *adj.* light-brown.
Рус|ь, и́ *f.* (*hist.*) Rus, Russia.
руте́ни|й, я *m.* (*chem.*) ruthenium.
рути́л, а *m.* (*min.*) rutile.
рути́н|а, ы *f.* (*pej.*) routine; rut, groove.
рутинёр, а *m.* slave to routine, pers. in a rut, in a groove.
рутинёр|ский *adj. of* **~; ~ские взгля́ды** rigid views.
рутинёрств|о, а *nt.* slavery to routine.
рути́н|ный *adj. of* **~а**
ру́хляд|ь, и *f.* (*collect.*; *coll.*) junk, lumber.
ру́хн|уть, у, ешь *pf.* to crash down, tumble down, collapse; (*fig.*) to crash, fall to the ground.
руча́тельств|о, а *nt.* guaranty, warrant; guarantee; **с ~ом** guaranteed.
руча́|ться, юсь *impf.* (*of* **поручи́ться**) (**за**+*a.*) to warrant, guarantee, certify; to answer (for), vouch (for); **р. голово́й** (**за**+*a.*) to stake one's life (on); **я не могу́ за него́ р.** I cannot vouch for him.
руче|ёк, йка́ *m. dim. of* **ручéй**
руч|е́й, ья́ *m.* **1.** brook, stream; **~ьи́ слёз** floods of tears. **2.** (*tech.*) groove, calibre, pass (*of roller*).
ру́чк|а, и *f.* **1.** *dim. of* **рука́**. **2.** handle; arm (*of chair*); **р. две́ри** door-handle, door-knob; **дойти́ до ~и** (*fig., coll.*) to reach the end of one's tether. **3.** penholder; pen; **автомати́ческая р.** fountain-pen.
ручни́к, а́ *m.* (*tech.*) bench hammer.
ручн|о́й *adj.* **1.** hand; arm; manual; **~а́я грана́та** hand grenade; **~а́я кладь** hand luggage; **~а́я пила́** hand-saw; **~о́е полоте́нце** hand towel; **~а́я прода́жа** counter sale; **~а́я прода́жа лека́рств** sale of medicines without prescription; **р. пулемёт** light machine-gun; **~а́я рабо́та** handwork; **~а́я теле́жка** hand-cart; **р. труд** manual labour; **~ы́е часы́** wrist watch. **2.** tame.
ру́ш|ить¹, у, ишь *impf.* to pull down.
ру́ш|ить², у, ишь *impf.* to husk.
ру́ш|иться, усь, ишься *impf. and pf.* to fall in, collapse; (*fig.*) to fall to the ground.
ры́б|а, ы *f.* fish; (*pl., astron.*) Pisces; **ни р., ни мя́со** neither fish, flesh nor fowl; **чу́вствовать себя́ как р. в воде́** to feel in one's element; **би́ться как р. об лёд** to struggle desperately.
рыба́к, а́ *m.* fisherman.
рыба́лк|а, и *f.* **1.** (*coll.*) fishing; fishing trip; **идти́ на ~у** to go fishing. **2.** (*dial.*) fishing spot. **3.** (*dial.*) seagull.
ры́ба́р|ь, я (~я́) *m.* (*obs.*) = **рыба́к**
рыба́|цкий *adj. of* **~к; р. посёлок** fishing village.
рыба́|чий *adj. of* **~к; ~чья ло́дка** fishing-boat.
рыба́ч|ить, у, ишь *impf.* to fish.
рыба́чк|а, и *f.* **1.** fisherwoman. **2.** fisherman's wife.
рыбёшк|а, и *f.* (*coll.*) small fry.
ры́бий *adj.* **1.** fish; piscine; **р. жир** cod-liver oil; **р. клей** isinglass, fish-glue. **2.** fish-like, fishy.
ры́бник, а *m.* **1.** fishmonger, fish vendor. **2.** fish marketer.
ры́бн|ый *adj.* fish; **~ые консе́рвы** tinned fish; **~ая ло́вля** fishing; **р. магази́н** fish-shop, fishmonger's; **р. про́мысел** fishery; **р. ры́нок** fish market; **р. садо́к** fish-pond.
рыбово́д, а *m.* fish-breeder.
рыбово́дств|о, а *nt.* fish-breeding.
рыбово́дческ|ий *adj.*: **~ая фе́рма** fish farm.
рыбозаво́д, а *m.* fish-factory; **плаву́чий р.** fish-factory ship.
рыбоконсе́рвный *adj.*: **р. заво́д** fish cannery.
рыболо́в, а *m.* fisherman; angler.
рыболове́цкий *adj.* fishing.
рыболо́вн|ый *adj.* fishing; **~ые принадле́жности, ~ая снасть** fishing tackle; **р. райо́н** fishing-ground, fishery.
рыболо́вств|о, а *nt.* fishing, fishery (*as branch of economy*).
рыбопито́мник, а *m.* fish hatchery.
рыбопромы́шленност|ь, и *f.* fishing industry.
рыботорго́в|ец, ца *m.* fishmonger.
рыботорго́вк|а, и *f.* fishwife.
рыбохо́д, а *m.* fish-run (*in dam*).
рыв|о́к, ка́ *m.* **1.** jerk. **2.** (*sport*) dash, burst, spurt; **фи́нишный р.** (*sport*) finishing kick.
рыг|а́ть, а́ю *impf.* (*of* **~ну́ть**) to belch.
рыг|ну́ть, ну́, нёшь *pf. of* **~а́ть**
рыда́|ть, ю *impf.* to sob.

рыдва́н, а *m.* (*hist.*) large coach.
рыжева́т|ый (~, ~а) *adj.* reddish; rust-coloured.
рыжеволо́с|ый (~, ~а) *adj.* red-haired.
рыже́|ть, ю *impf.* (*of* **по~**) to turn reddish.
ры́ж|ий (~, ~а́, ~е) *adj.* **1.** red, red-haired, ginger; (*of a horse*) chestnut. **2.** of faded red-brown colour. **3.** *as n.* **р., ~его** *m.* circus clown; **я что, р.?** (*coll.*) why leave me out?
ры́жик[1]**, а** *m.* saffron milk-cap (*mushroom*).
ры́жик[2]**, а** *m.* (*coll.*) 'Ginger', 'Sandy' (*pet name for red-haired child, or for dog, etc., with red coat*).
рыка́|ть, ю *impf.* to roar.
ры́л|о, а *nt.* **1.** snout (*of pig, etc.*). **2.** (*coll.*) snout, mug.
ры́л|ьце, ьца, *g. pl.* **~ец** *nt.* **1.** *dim. of* **~о**; (*dial.*) spout; **у него́ р. в пуху́** he has been at the jam-pot. **2.** (*bot.*) stigma.
рым, а *m.* (*naut.*) (mooring-)ring, eyebolt.
ры́нд|а[1]**, ы** *f.* (*hist.*) rynda (*bodyguard of tsars in Muscovite period*).
ры́нд|а[2]**, ы** *f.* ship's bell.
ры́н|ок, ка *m.* **1.** market(-place). **2.** (*econ.*) market.
ры́но|чный *adj. of* **~к; р. день** market-day; **~чная торго́вля** marketing; **по ~чной цене́** at the market price.
рыса́к, а́ *m.* trotter.
ры́с|ий *adj.* lynx; **~ьи глаза́** (*fig.*) lynx eyes.
рыси́ст|ый *adj.*: **~ые испыта́ния** trotting races; **~ая ло́шадь** trotter.
рыс|и́ть, и́шь *impf.* to trot.
ры́|скать, щу, щешь *impf.* **1.** to rove, roam. **2.** (**по**+*d.*) to scour, ransack (*in search of sth.*); **р. по ска́лам** to scour the cliffs; **р. по карма́нам** to ransack one's pockets. **3.** (*naut.*) to gripe, yaw.
рысц|а́, ы́ *f.* jog-trot; **е́хать ~о́й** to go at a jog-trot.
рыс|ь[1]**, и, о ~́и, на ~и́** *f.* trot; **кру́пная р.** round trot; **на ~я́х** at a trot.
рыс|ь[2]**, и** *f.* lynx.
ры́сью *adv.* at a trot.
ры́твин|а, ы *f.* rut, groove.
рыть, ро́ю, ро́ешь *impf.* to dig; to burrow; to root up; **р. око́пы** to dig trenches; **р. зе́млю копы́том** to paw the ground (*also fig.*).
рыть|ё, я́ *nt.* digging.
ры́ться, ро́юсь, ро́ешься *impf.* (**в**+*p.*) to dig (in); (*fig.*) to rummage (in), ransack, burrow (in).
рыхле́|ть, ю *impf.* (*of* **по~**) to become friable.
рыхл|и́ть, ю́, и́шь *impf.* to loosen; to make friable.
ры́хл|ый (~, ~а́, ~о) *adj.* **1.** friable; mellow (*of soil*); loose; porous. **2.** (*fig.*) podgy.
ры́цар|ский *adj.* **1.** *adj. of* **~ь; р. поеди́нок** joust; **р. рома́н** tale of chivalry. **2.** (*fig.*) chivalrous.
ры́царств|о, а *nt.* **1.** (*collect.*; *hist.*) knights. **2.** knighthood; **получи́ть р.** to receive a knighthood. **3.** (*fig.*) chivalry.
ры́цар|ь, я *m.* knight; **стра́нствующий р.** knight errant.
рыча́г, а́ *m.* lever; (*fig.*) key factor, linchpin; **переводно́й р.** switch lever; **р. управле́ния** control lever; **де́йствие ~а́** leverage.
рыча́|жный *adj. of* **~г; ~жные весы́** beam balance; **р. мо́лот** sledge hammer.
рыча́ни|е, я *nt.* growl, snarl.
рыч|а́ть, у́, и́шь *impf.* to growl, snarl.
рья́ност|ь, и *f.* zeal.
рья́н|ый (~, ~а) *adj.* zealous.
ре́ггей *m. indecl.* reggae.
рюкза́к, а́ *m.* rucksack, knapsack; backpack.
рюкза́чник, а *m.* backpacker.
рю́мк|а, и *f.* wine-glass.
рю́мочк|а, и *f. dim. of* **рю́мка; та́лия ~ой, в ~у** (*coll.*) wasp waist.
ряби́н|а[1]**, ы** *f.* **1.** rowan-tree, mountain ash, service-tree. **2.** rowan-berry, ashberry.
ряби́н|а[2]**, ы** *f.* (*coll.*) pit, pock; **лицо́ с ~ами** pocked-marked face.
ряби́нник, а *m.* (*zool.*) fieldfare.
ряби́новк|а, и *f.* rowan-berry vodka.
ряби́н|овый *adj. of* **~а**
ряб|и́ть, и́т *impf.* **1.** to ripple. **2.** (*impers.*): **у меня́ ~и́т в глаза́х** I am dazzled.
ряб|о́й (~, ~а́, ~́о) *adj.* **1.** pitted, pock-marked. **2.** speckled.
ряб|о́к, ка́ *m.* (*zool.*) sandgrouse.
ря́бчик, а *m.* (*zool.*) hazel-grouse, hazel-hen.
ряб|ь, и *f.* **1.** ripple(s). **2.** dazzle.
ря́вк|ать, аю *impf.* (*of* **~нуть**) (**на**+*a.*; *coll.*) to bellow (at), roar (at).
ря́вк|нуть, ну, нешь *pf. of* **~ать**
ряд, а, в ~́е *and* **в ~у́,** *pl.* **~ы́, ~о́в** *m.* **1.** (*in var. senses*) row; line; **пе́рвый р., после́дний р.** (*theatr.*) front row, back row; **р. за ~́ом** row upon row; **из ~́а вон выходя́щий** outstanding, extraordinary, out of the common (run); **стоя́ть в одно́м ~у́** (**с**+*i.*) to rank (with). **2.** (*mil.*) file, rank; **непо́лный р.** blank file; **~ы́ вздвой!** (*command*) form fours!; **в ~а́х а́рмии** in the ranks of the army; **в пе́рвых ~а́х** in the first ranks; (*fig.*) in the forefront. **3.** series (*also math.*); number; **в це́лом ~́е слу́чаев** in a number of cases.
ря|ди́ть[1]**, жу́, ~́дишь** *impf.* (+*i.*) to dress up (as), get up (as).
ря|ди́ть[2]**, жу́, ~́дишь** *impf.* (*obs.*) **1.** to ordain, lay down the law. **2.** to contract.
ря|ди́ться[1]**, жу́сь, ~́дишься** *impf.* **1.** (*coll.*) to dress up. **2.** (+*i.*) to dress up (as), disguise o.s. (as).
ря|ди́ться[2]**, жу́сь, ~́дишься** *impf.* (*of* **по~**) (*obs.*) **1.** (**с**+*i.*) to bargain (with). **2.** (+*inf.*) to undertake (to), contract (to).
рядко́м *adv.* = **ря́дом**
рядов|о́й[1] *adj.* **1.** ordinary, common. **2.** (*mil.*): **р. соста́в** rank and file; men, other ranks; *as n.* **р., ~о́го** *m.* private (soldier).
рядов|о́й[2] *adj.* (*agric.*): **~а́я се́ялка** seed drill; **р. посе́в** sowing in drills.
ря́дом *adv.* **1.** alongside, side by side; (**с**+*i.*) next to; **он сиди́т р. с премье́р-мини́стром** he is sitting next to the Prime Minister. **2.** near, close by, just by, next door; **э́то совсе́м р.** it is a stone's throw away; **он жил р. с бо́йней** he lived next door to the slaughterhouse. **3.: сплошь и р.** more often than not; pretty often.
ря́дышком *adv.* (*coll.*) = **ря́дом**
ряж, а *m.* (*tech.*) crib(-work).
ряжев|о́й *adj. of* **ряж; ~а́я плоти́на** crib-dam.
ря́жен|ый *adj.* dressed up, disguised; *as n.* **р., ~ого** *m.*; **~ая, ~ой** *f.* mummer.
ря́с|а, ы *f.* cassock.
ря́ск|а, и *f.* (*bot.*) duckweed.
ря́шк|а, и *f.* (*coll.*) mug (= *face*).

С

С (*abbr. of* **се́вер**) N, North.
с *prep.*

I. +*g.* **1.** (*in var. senses*) from; off; **с ю́го-восто́ка** from the South-East; **с Во́лги** from the Volga; **с Кавка́за** from the Caucasus; **с ты́ла** from the rear; **с головы́ до ног** from head to foot; **со сна** half awake; **с пе́рвого взгля́да** at first sight; **шум со спорти́вной площа́дки** the noise from the playing-field; **по́шлина с табака́** duty on tobacco; **перево́д с ру́сского** translation from Russian; **сда́ча с рубля́** change of a rouble; **верну́ться с рабо́ты** to return from work; **убра́ть посу́ду со стола́** the clear the things from the table; **упа́сть с ками́нной по́лки** to fall off the mantelpiece; **уста́ть с доро́ги** to be tired after a journey; **ходи́ть с туза́** to lead with the ace; **снять с кого́-н. фотогра́фию** to take s.o.'s photograph; **взять приме́р с**

кого́-н. to follow s.o.'s example; **дово́льно с тебя́!** that's enough from you! **ско́лько с меня́?** how much do I owe? **2.** for, from, with; **с ра́дости** for joy; **со стыда́** for shame, with shame. **3.** on, from; **с ле́вой стороны́ от желе́зной доро́ги** on the left-hand side of the railway; **с одно́й, с друго́й стороны́** on the one, on the other hand; **с како́й то́чки зре́ния?** from what point of view? **4.** with (= *on the basis of*); **с разреше́ния дире́ктора шко́лы** with the headmaster's permission; **с ва́шего согла́сия** with your consent. **5.** by, with (= *by means of*); **взять с бо́ю** to take by storm; **писа́ть с большо́й бу́квы** to write with a capital letter. **6.** (*of time*) from, since; as from; **с девяти́ (часо́в) до пяти́** from nine (o'clock) till five; **с де́тства** from childhood; **с утра́** since morning; **мы с ней не ви́делись с января́** I have not seen her since January; **они́ бу́дут в Москве́ с двадца́того числа́** they will be in Moscow from the twentieth; **с 1850 по 1900** from 1850 to 1900.

II. *+a.* **1.: я бу́ду там с год** I shall be there about a year; **мы прошли́ с ми́лю** we walked about a mile. **2.** the size of; **с дом** the size of a house; **на́ша до́чка ро́стом с ва́шу** our daughter is about the same height as yours; **ма́льчик с па́льчик** Tom Thumb.

III. *+i.* **1.** (*in var. senses*) with; and; **с удово́льствием** with pleasure; **мы с ва́ми** you and I; **он с сестро́й** he and his sister. **2.** (*indicates possession*) **хлеб с ма́слом** bread and butter; **челове́к со стра́нностями** queer, peculiar pers. **3.** by, on (= *by means of*); **получи́ть с пе́рвой по́чтой** to receive by first post; **я прие́хал с экспре́ссом** I came on the express. **4.** with (= *with the passage of*); **с года́ми** with the years; **с ка́ждым днём** every day. **5.** with (*or not translated*) (= *in regard to, as regards*); **как обстои́т у вас с рабо́той?** how is the work going? **что с ва́ми?** what is the matter with you?; what's up? **у неё пло́хо с се́рдцем** her heart is bad; **как у вас с деньга́ми?** how are you off for money?

с. *abbr. of* **село́** village.

с... (*also* **со...** *and* **съ...**) *vbl. pref. indicating* **1.** *unification, movement from various sides to a point, as* **свари́ть** to weld. **2.** *movement or action made in a downward direction, as* **спусти́ться** to descend. **3.** *removal of sth. from somewhere, as* **сорва́ть** to tear off.

СА *f. indecl.* (*abbr. of* **Сове́тская А́рмия**) Soviet Army.

саа́м, а *m.* Lapp, Laplander.

саа́м|ка, ки *f. of* ~

саа́мский *adj.* Lappish.

Саа́р, а *m.* the Saar (*river*).

са́бельный *adj.* sabre.

сабз|а́, ы́ *f.* sultanas.

са́б|ля, ли, *g.pl.* ~**ель** *f.* sabre

сабота́ж, а *m.* sabotage.

сабота́жник, а *m.* saboteur

сабота́жнича|ть, ю *impf.* (*coll.*) to engage in sabotage.

саботи́р|овать, ую *impf. and pf.* to sabotage.

сабу́р, а *m.* (*pharm.*) juice of aloe leaves.

са́ван, а *m.* shroud, cerement; **сне́жный с.** blanket of snow.

сава́нн|а, ы *f.* (*geog.*) savannah.

савра́сый *adj.* (*of horses*) light brown with black mane and tail.

са́г|а, и *f.* saga.

сагити́р|овать, ую *pf.* **1.** *pf. of* **агити́ровать. 2.** (*pf. only*) to win over.

са́го *nt. indecl.* (*bot.*) sago.

са́го|вый *adj. of* ~; ~**вая ка́ша** sago pudding.

сад, а, о ~́**е, в** ~**у́,** *pl.* ~**ы́** *m.* garden; **фрукто́вый с.** orchard; **зоологи́ческий с.** zoological gardens, zoo; **де́тский с.** kindergarten.

сади́зм, а *m.* sadism.

сади́ст, а *m.* sadist.

сади́стский *adj.* sadistic.

са|ди́ть¹, жу́, ~́**дишь** *impf.* (*of* **по**~) to plant.

са|ди́ть², жу́, ~́**дишь** *impf.* (*coll.*) **1.** to slap. **2.** (*fig.*) to hurtle; to dash; to stream.

са|ди́ться, жу́сь, ди́шься *impf.* (*of* **сесть**); ~**ди́(те)сь!** (*polite request*) sit down!; take a seat!

са́дн|ить, ит *impf.* (*impers.; coll.*) to smart, burn.

садо́вник, а *m.* gardener.

садово́д, а *m.* gardener; horticulturist.

садово́дств|о, а *nt.* **1.** gardening; horticulture. **2.** horticultural establishment.

садово́дческий *adj.* horticultural.

сад|о́вый *adj.* **1.** *adj. of* ~. **2.** garden, cultivated (*opp. wild*).

сад|о́к, ка́ *m.* place for keeping live creatures; **кро́личий с.** rabbit-hutch; **ры́бный с.** fish-pond; **живоры́бный с.** fish-well (*in river vessel or barge*); **с. для птиц** bird-cage.

садо-мазохи́зм, а *m.* sado-masochism.

са́ж|а, и *f.* soot, lamp-black.

сажа́|ть, ю *impf.* (*of* **посади́ть**) **1.** to plant. **2.** to seat; to set, put; to offer a seat; **с. пти́цу в кле́тку** to cage a bird; **с. хлеб в печь** to put bread into the oven; **с. в тюрьму́** to put into prison, imprison, jail; **с. ку́рицу на я́йца** to set a hen on eggs; **с. на хлеб и на во́ду** to put on bread and water; **с. под аре́ст** to put under arrest.

са́жен|ец, ца *m.* seedling; sapling.

сажё́н|ки, ок *no sg.* overarm stroke (*in swimming*).

саже́нный (*and* **сажённый**) *adj.* (*coll.*) huge, enormous.

са́женый *adj.* planted.

са́жен|ь, и, *pl.* ~**и, са́жен** *and* **саже́не́й** *f.* sazhen (*old Russ. measure of length, equivalent to 2.13 metres*); **морска́я с.** Russian fathom (*1.83 metres*).

саза́н, а *m.* wild carp (*Cyprinus carpo*).

сайг|а́, и *f.* (*zool.*) saiga.

са́йк|а, и *f.* (*bread*) roll.

сак, а *m.* (*obs.*) **1.** bag. **2.** (*woman's*) sack-coat.

саквоя́ж, а *m.* travelling-bag, grip.

саке́ *nt. indecl.* sake.

са́кл|я, и, *g. pl.* ~**ей** *f.* saklya (*Caucasian mountain hut*).

сакримента́л|ьный (~**ен,** ~**ьна)** *adj.* sacramental; sacred.

сакс, а *m.* (*hist.*) Saxon.

сакса́ул, а *m.* (*bot.*) haloxylon.

саксо́н|ец, ца *m.* Saxon.

Саксо́ни|я, и *f.* Saxony.

саксо́н|ка, ки *f. of* ~**ец**

саксо́нский *adj.* Saxon; **с. фарфо́р** Dresden (*or* Meissen) china.

саксофо́н, а *m.* saxophone.

сала́з|ки, ок *no sg.* **1.** hand sled, toboggan. **2.** (*tech.*) slide, slide rails; **с. станка́** sliding carriage.

салама́ндр|а, ы *f.* salamander.

салама́т|а, ы *f.* (*obs. or dial.*) (*cul.*) salamata (*kind of porridge*).

сала́т, а *m.* **1.** lettuce. **2.** salad.

сала́тник, а *m.* salad-dish, salad-bowl.

сала́тниц|а, ы *f.* = **сала́тник**

сала́т|ный *adj. of* ~; ~**ного цве́та** light green.

са́линг, а *m.* (*naut.*) cross-trees.

са́л|ить, ю, ишь *impf.* to grease.

салици́л, а *m.* (*chem.*) salicylate.

салици́лк|а, и *f.* (*chem.*) salicylic acid.

салици́ловый *adj.* salicylic.

са́л|ки, ок *pl.* (*sg.* ~**ка,** ~**ки** *f.*) **1.** (*children's game*) tag, touch. **2.** (*sg.*) 'it' (*in this game*); **кто у нас** ~**ка?** who is 'it'?

са́л|о, а *nt.* **1.** fat, lard; suet; **ко́жное с.** sebum. **2.** tallow. **3.** thin broken ice (*on surface of water*); slush.

сало́н, а *m.* **1.** salon; **автомоби́льный с.** motorcar showroom; motor show; **да́мский с.** beauty parlour. **2.** saloon.

сало́н-ваго́н, а *m.* saloon car, saloon carriage.

сало́н|ный *adj. of* ~; ~**ные бесе́ды** small talk; ~**ное воспита́ние** high society upbringing.

сало́п, а *m.* (*obs.*) (*woman's*) coat.

салопи́йский *adj.* (*geol.*) Salopian.

сало́пниц|а, ы *f.* (*coll., obs.*) **1.** slut. **2.** scandalmonger.

салото́пенный *adj.* tallow-melting.

салты́к *only in phr.* (*coll., obs.*): **на свой с.** in one's own fashion, in one's own way.

салфе́тк|а, и *f.* serviette, (table-)napkin; **бума́жная с.** tissue.

салфе́т|очный *adj. of* ~**ка;** ~**очное полотно́** diaper-cloth, damask.

Сальвадо́р, а *m.* El Salvador.

сальвадо́р|ец, ца *m.* Salvadorean.

сальвадо́р|ка, ки *f. of* ~**ец**

сальвадо́рский *adj.* Salvadorean.
са́льдо *nt. indecl.* (*book-keeping*) balance.
са́льник, а *m.* **1.** (*anat.*) epiploon. **2.** (*tech.*) stuffing box, (packing) gland.
са́льност|ь, и *f.* obscenity, bawdiness.
са́льн|ый *adj.* **1.** tallow; **~ая свеча́** tallow candle. **2.** (*anat.*) sebaceous; **~ая железа́** sebaceous gland. **3.** greasy. **4.** obscene, bawdy; **с. анекдо́т** bawdy story, dirty joke.
са́льто-морта́ле *nt. indecl.* somersault.
салю́т, а *m.* (*mil.*, *naut.*) salute.
салют|ова́ть, у́ю *impf. and pf.* (*pf. also* **от~**) (*+d.*) to salute.
сам[1], **самого́** *m.*; **сама́, само́й,** *a.* **самоё (***and* **саму́)** *f.*; **~о́, самого́** *nt.*; *pl.* **са́ми, сами́х** *refl. pron.* myself, yourself, himself, *etc.*; **с. по себе́** in itself, per se; by o.s., unassisted; **с. собо́й** of itself, of its own accord; **он с. не свой** he is not himself; **с. себе́ хозя́ин** one's own master; **она́ — сама́ доброта́** she is kindness itself.
сам[2], **самого́** *m.* (*coll.*) boss, chief.
сам- *comb. form* (*dial.*) **1.** (*of harvest yield*) *x* times what was sown; *x*fold; **с.дру́г** double *or* twice what was sown; **с.трете́й** three times what was sown. **2.** (*of people*): **с.дру́г** (together) with another pers.; **с.се́мь** (together) with six others (*i.e. speaker is reckoned as one*).
сама́н, а *m.* adobe.
сама́н|ный *adj. of* **~**; **с. кирпи́ч** adobe (brick).
самаритя́н|ин, ина, *pl.* **~е, ~** *m.* (*bibl.*, *hist.*) Samaritan.
са́мбо *nt. indecl.* (*abbr. of* **самооборо́на без ору́жия**) unarmed combat.
самбу́к, а *m.* (*cul.*) fruit purée.
сам|е́ц, ца́ *m.* male (*of species*).
самизда́т, а *m.* (*coll.*) samizdat.
са́мк|а, и *f.* female (*of species*).
само... *comb. form* self-, auto-.
Само́а *nt. indecl.* Samoa.
самоана́лиз, а *m.* self-examination, introspection.
самоа́н|ец, ца *m.* Samoan.
самоа́н|ка, ки *f. of* **~ец**
самоа́нский *adj.* Samoan.
самобичева́ни|е, я *nt.* **1.** self-flagellation. **2.** (*fig.*) self-reproach.
самобы́тност|ь, и *f.* originality.
самобы́т|ный (~ен, на) *adj.* original.
самова́р, а *m.* samovar.
самовла́сти|е, я *nt.* absolute power, despotism.
самовла́ст|ный (~ен, ~на) *adj.* **1.** absolute. **2.** (*fig.*) despotic, autocratic.
самовлюблённост|ь, и *f.* narcissism.
самовлюблённый *adj.* narcissistic.
самовнуше́ни|е, я *nt.* auto-suggestion.
самовозгора́ни|е, я *nt.* spontaneous combustion, spontaneous ignition.
самовозгора́|ться, ется *impf.* to ignite spontaneously.
самово́ли|е, я *nt.* licence.
самово́л|ьный (~ен, ~ьна) *adj.* **1.** wilful, self-willed. **2.** unauthorized; **~ьная отлу́чка** (*mil.*) absence without leave.
самовоспламене́ни|е, я *nt.* spontaneous ignition.
самовосхвале́ни|е, я *nt.* self-praise, self-glorification.
самовя́з, а *m.* tying (*opp. made-up*) tie.
самого́н, а *m.* home-distilled vodka, hooch.
самого́н|ка, ки *f.* = **~**
самодви́жущийся *adj.* self-propelled.
саморде́йствующий *adj.* self-acting, automatic.
самоде́лк|а, и *f.* (*coll.*) home-made product.
самоде́л|ьный (~ен, ~ьна) *adj.* **1.** home-made. **2.** self-made.
самоде́льщик, а *m.* (*coll.*) do-it-yourselfer, DIY enthusiast.
самодержа́ви|е, я *nt.* autocracy.
самодержа́в|ный (~ен, ~на) *adj.* autocratic.
самоде́рж|ец, ца *m.* autocrat.
самоде́ятельност|ь, и *f.* **1.** initiative, spontaneous action. **2.** amateur performance, amateur talent activities (*theatricals, music, etc.*); **ве́чер ~и** amateurs' night.
самоде́ятельный *adj.* **1.** amateur. **2.** (*econ.*) self-employed.
самодисципли́н|а, ы *f.* self-discipline.
самодовле́ющий *adj.* self-sufficing, self-sufficient.
самодово́л|ьный (~ен, ~ьна) *adj.* self-satisfied, smug, complacent.
самодово́льств|о, а *nt.* self-satisfaction, smugness, complacency.
самоду́р, а *m.* petty tyrant, wilful pers.
самоду́рств|о, а *nt.* petty tyranny, wilfulness.
самое́д, а *m.* (*ethnol.*, *obs.*) Samoyed.
самозабве́ни|е, я *nt.* selflessness.
самозаводя́щийся *adj.* self-winding.
самозаготóвк|а, и *f.* laying in of one's own supplies.
самозажига́ющийся *adj.* self-igniting.
самозака́лк|а, и *f.* (*tech.*) air-hardened steel.
самозарожде́ни|е, я *nt.* (*biol.*) spontaneous generation.
самозаря́дный *adj.* self-loading.
самозащи́т|а, ы *f.* self-defence; **я уби́л его́ в ~е** I killed him in self-defence.
самозва́н|ец, ца *m.* impostor, pretender.
самозва́нный *adj.* false, self-styled.
самозва́нств|о, а *nt.* imposture.
самоинду́кци|я, и *f.* (*phys.*) self-induction.
самока́т, а *m.* **1.** (*mil.*, *obs.*) bicycle. **2.** (*child's*) scooter.
самока́тчик, а *m.* (*mil.*, *obs.*) bicyclist.
самокри́тик|а, и *f.* self-criticism.
самокрити́ч|ный (~ен, ~на) *adj.* containing self-criticism.
самокру́тк|а[1], **и** *f.* (*coll.*) roll-up, roll-your-own (= *hand-rolled cigarette*).
самокру́тк|а[2], **и** *f.* (*obs.*, *coll.*) secret marriage, elopement.
самолёт, а *m.* aeroplane, aircraft.
самолёт|ный *adj of* **~**; **~ная радиоста́нция** airborne radio set.
самолётовожде́ни|е, я *nt.* air navigation.
самолётовы́лет, а *m.* sortie (*of aircraft*).
самолётострое́ни|е, я *nt.* aircraft construction.
самолёт-снаря́д, самолёта-снаря́да *m.* flying bomb.
самоли́чно *adv.* (*coll.*) oneself; **сде́лать что-н. с.** to do sth. by o.s.; **я с. ви́дел э́то** I saw it with my own eyes.
самоли́чн|ый *adj.* (*coll.*) personal; **~ое прису́тствие** attendance in pers.
самолюби́в|ый (~, ~а) *adj.* proud, haughty.
самолю́би|е, я, *nt.* pride, self-esteem; **ло́жное с.** false pride; **щади́ть чьё-н. с.** to spare, respect s.o.'s pride.
самомне́ни|е, я *nt.* conceit, self-importance; **он с бо́льшим ~ем** he has a high opinion of himself.
самонаблюде́ни|е, я *nt.* (*psych.*) introspection.
самонаде́янност|ь, и *f.* (*pej.*) conceit, arrogance.
самонаде́ян|ный (~, ~на) *adj.* (*pej.*) conceited, arrogant.
самонazва́ни|е, я *nt.* native name, own name; **ро́мэни — с. цыга́н** 'Romany' is the gypsies' own name for themselves.
самообвине́ни|е, я *nt.* self-accusation.
самооблада́ни|е, я *nt.* self-control, self-possession, composure.
самообложе́ни|е, я *nt.* voluntary rate-paying.
самообма́н, а *m.* self-deception.
самообольще́ни|е, я *nt.* self-deception; **пребыва́ть в ~и** to live in a fool's paradise.
самооборо́н|а, ы *f.* self-defence.
самообразова́ни|е, я *nt.* self-education.
самообслу́живани|е, я *nt.* self-service.
самоокупа́емост|ь, и *f.* ability to pay its way (*without subsidy*).
самоокупа́ющийся *adj.* paying its way.
самооплодотворе́ни|е, я *nt.* (*biol.*) self-fertilization.
самоопределе́ни|е, я *nt.* self-determination.
самоопредел|и́ться, ю́сь, и́шься *pf.* (*of* **~я́ться**) (*pol.*) to define one's position.
самоопредел|я́ться, я́юсь *impf. of* **~и́ться**
самоопроки́дывающийся *adj.* self-tipping; **с. грузови́к** tip-up lorry.
самоопыле́ни|е, я *nt.* (*bot.*) self-fertilization.
самоотверже́ни|е, я *nt.* = **самоотве́рженность**
самоотве́рженност|ь, и *f.* selflessness.
самоотве́ржен|ный (~, ~на) *adj.* selfless, self-sacrificing.
самоотво́д, а *m.* withdrawal (*of candidature*), refusal to accept (*nomination for an office, etc.*).
самоотрече́ни|е, я *nt.* self-denial, (self-)abnegation, enunciation.

самооце́нк|а, и *f.* self-appraisal.
самоочеви́дный *adj.* self-evident.
самопи́с|ец, ца *m.*: **бортово́й с.** (*aeron.*) flight recorder.
самопи́шущ|ий *adj.* (self-)recording, (self-)registering; **с. прибо́р** recording instrument; **~ее перо́** fountain-pen.
самопоже́ртвовани|е, я *nt.* self-sacrifice.
самопозна́ни|е, я *nt.* (*phil.*) self-knowledge.
самопо́мощ|ь, и *f.* self-help, mutual aid.
самопроизво́льност|ь, и *f.* spontaneity
самопроизво́л|ьный (~ен, ~ьна) *adj.* spontaneous.
самопря́лк|а, и *f.* (treadle) spinning-wheel.
самопу́ск, а *m.* (*tech.*) self-starter.
саморазгружа́ющ|ийся *adj.* self-unloading; **~аяся ба́ржа** hopper(-barge).
саморазоблаче́ни|е, я *nt.* self-exposure.
саморегули́рующий *adj.* self-regulating.
саморекла́м|а, ы *f.* self-advertisement.
саморо́дный *adj.* (*min.*) native, virgin.
саморо́д|ок *m.* (*min.*) native metal, native ore; nugget; (*fig.*) pers. without education but possessing natural talents; **компози́тор-с.** born composer, natural composer.
самоса́д, а *m.* home-grown tobacco.
самоса́дочн|ый *adj.*: **~ая соль** lake-salt; **~ое о́зеро** salt lake.
самосва́л, а *m.* tip-up (lorry), dump truck.
самосма́зк|а, и *f.* (*tech.*) self-lubrication, automatic lubrication.
самосожже́ни|е, я *nt.* self-immolation.
самосозна́ни|е, я *nt.* (self-)consciousness.
самосохране́ни|е, я *nt.* self-preservation.
самости́йник, а *m.* Ukrainian separatist.
самостоя́тельно *adv.* independently; on one's own.
самостоя́тельност|ь, и *f.* independence.
самостоя́тел|ьный (~ен, ~ьна) *adj.* (*in var. senses*) independent; **~ьное госуда́рство** independent state; **с. учёный труд** work of original scholarship.
самостре́л[1], а *m.* (*hist.*) arbalest, cross-bow.
самостре́л[2], а *m.* pers. with self-inflicted wound (*designed to escape onerous military duty, etc.*).
самостре́льный *adj.* self-firing, automatic.
самосу́д, а *m.* lynch law, mob law
самотёк, а *m.* drift (*also fig.*); (*tech.*) gravity feed; **пусти́ть де́ло на с.** to let things slide.
самотёком *adv.* **1.** (*tech.*) by gravity. **2.** haphazard; of its own accord; **идти́ с.** to drift.
самотё|чный *adj. of* **~к; ~чное ороше́ние** natural irrigation.
самоторможе́ни|е, я *nt.* self-braking.
самоуби́йственный *adj.* suicidal (*also fig.*).
самоуби́йств|о, а *nt.* suicide; **конча́ть ~ом, поко́нчить жизнь ~ом** to commit suicide.
самоуби́йц|а, ы *c.g.* suicide (*agent*).
самоуваже́ни|е, я *nt.* self-esteem.
самоуве́ренност|ь, и *f.* self-confidence, self-assurance.
самоуве́рен|ный (~, ~на) *adj.* self-confident, self-assured.
самоуни(чи)же́ни|е, я *nt.* self-abasement, self-disparagement.
самоуплотне́ни|е, я *nt.* **1.** voluntary giving up of part of one's dwelling space. **2.** (*tech.*) self-packing.
самоуплотн|и́ться, ю́сь, и́шься *pf.* (*of* **~я́ться**) to give up voluntarily part of one's dwelling space.
самоуплотн|я́ться, я́юсь *impf. of* **~и́ться**
самоуправле́ни|е, я *nt.* self-government; **ме́стное с.** local government.
самоуправля́ющийся *adj.* self-governing.
самоупра́вно *adv.* arbitrarily; **поступа́ть с.** to take the law into one's own hands.
самоупра́вный *adj.* arbitrary.
самоупра́вств|о, а *nt.* arbitrariness.
самоуспокое́ни|е, я *nt.* complacency.
самоуспоко́енност|ь, и *f.* = **самоуспокое́ние**
самоустана́вливающийся *adj.* (*tech.*) self-adjusting, self-aligning.
самоустран|и́ться, ю́сь, и́шься *pf.* (*of* **~я́ться**) **(от)** to get out (of), dodge.
самоустран|я́ться, я́юсь *impf.* **1.** *impf. of* **~и́ться. 2.** *impf. only* **(от)** to try to get out (of), try to dodge.
самоучи́тел|ь, я *m.* self-instructor, manual for self-tuition; **с. англи́йского языка́** English self-taught.
самоу́чк|а, и *c.g.* self-taught pers.
самохва́льств|о, а *nt.* self-advertisement.
самохо́д, а *m.* (*tech.*) self feed, self-act travel.
самохо́дк|а, и *f.* self-propelled gun.
самохо́дный *adj.* self-propelled.
самоцве́т, а *m.* semi-precious stone, gem.
самоцве́т|ный *adj.*: **с. ка́мень = ~**
самоце́л|ь, и *f.* end in itself.
самочи́нный *adj.* arbitrary, unauthorized.
самочу́встви|е, я *nt.* general state; **у него́ плохо́е с.** he feels bad; **как ва́ше с.?** how do you feel?; (*in general, not restricted to sick persons*) how are you (keeping)?
саму́м, а *m.* simoom.
самура́|й, я *m.* samurai.
самши́т, а *m.* box(-tree).
са́м|ый *pron.* **1.** (*in conjunction with nn., esp. denoting points of time or place, and with* **тот** *and* **э́тот**) the very, right; **в ~ое вре́мя** at the right time; **с ~ого нача́ла** from the very outset, right from the start; **с ~ого утра́** ever since the morning, since first thing; **в ~ом углу́** right in the corner; **до ~ого ве́рха** to the very top, right to the top; **до ~ого Владивосто́ка** right to, all the way to Vladivostok; **в с. раз** (*coll.*) just right; **в~ом де́ле** indeed; **в ~ом де́ле?** indeed?, really?; **на ~ом де́ле** actually, in (actual) fact; **тот с. челове́к, кото́рый...** the very man who...; **на э́том ~ом ме́сте** on this very spot (*but* **э́тот с.** *is oft. purely pleonastic, being roughly equivalent to coll. Eng.*'*this here*'). **2.: тот же с. (кото́рый, что); тако́й же с. (как)** the same (as); **э́тот же с.** the same. **3.** *forms superl. of adjs.; also expr. superl. in conjunction with certain nn. denoting degree of quantity or quality*; **с. глу́пый** the stupidest, the most stupid; **~ые пустяки́** the merest trifles; **погоди́те ~ую ма́лость!** wait just one moment!; just a second!
сан, а *m.* dignity, office; **высо́кий с.** high office; **духо́вный с.** holy orders, the cloth; **быть посвящённым в духо́вный с.** to be ordained; **из уваже́ния к ва́шему ~у** out of respect for your cloth.
сан... *comb. form, abbr. of* **санита́рный**
санато́ри|й, я *m.* sanatorium.
санато́р|ный *adj. of* **~ий; с. режи́м** sanatorium regimen.
санато́р|ский *adj. of* **~ий; с. слу́жащий** sanatorium attendant.
сангви́н, а *m.* (*art*) sanguine.
сангви́н|а, ы *f.* = **~**
сангви́ник, а *m.* sanguine pers.
сангвини́ческий *adj.* sanguine.
санда́л, а *m.* sandal-wood tree.
сандале́т|ы, ~ *no sg.* (*woman's*) sandals.
санда́ли|я, и *f.* sandal.
санда́ловый *adj.* sandal-wood.
са́н|и, е́й *no sg.* sledge, sleigh; **е́хать в, на ~я́х** to drive in a sledge.
санита́р, а *m.* hospital attendant, hospital orderly; (*mil.*) medical orderly.
санитари́|я, и *f.* sanitation.
санита́рн|ый *adj.* **1.** medical; hospital; **~ое дово́льствие** medical supplies; **~ая каре́та, ~ая маши́на** ambulance; **~ая кни́жка** (*mil.*) health record; **с. по́езд** hospital train; **~ая полева́я су́мка** (*mil.*) first-aid kit; **с. самолёт** ambulance plane; **~ая слу́жба** health service, medical service; **~ое су́дно** hospital ship; **~ая часть** (*mil.*) medical unit; **с. я́щик** first-aid box. **2.** sanitary; sanitation; **с. врач** sanitary inspector; **с. день** (room-)cleaning day (*in university hostels, etc.*); **~ые пра́вила** sanitary regulations; **с. у́зел** lavatory; sanitary unit.
са́н|ки, ок *no sg.* **1.** = **~и. 2.** toboggan.
Санкт-Петербу́рг, а *m.* St. Petersburg.
санкт-петербу́ргский *adj.* St. Petersburg.
санкт-петербу́рж|анка, а́нки *f. of* **~ец**
санкт-петербу́рж|ец, ца *m.* St. Petersburger.
санкциони́р|овать, ую *impf. and pf.* to sanction.
са́нкци|я, и *f.* **1.** sanction, approval. **2.** *pl.* (*pol., econ.*) sanctions.

са́н|ный *adj. of* ~**и; с. путь** sleigh-road.
сановит|ый (~, ~а) *adj.* **1.** of exalted rank. **2.** (*fig.*) imposing.
сано́вник, а *m.* dignitary, high official.
сано́вный *adj.* of exalted rank.
са́ноч|ки, ек *no sg. affectionate dim. of* **са́нки; лю́бишь ката́ться, люби́ и с. вози́ть** (*prov.*) you must take the rough with the smooth.
санскри́т, а *m.* Sanscrit.
санскрито́лог, а *m.* Sanscrit scholar.
санскри́тский *adj.* Sanscrit.
санте́хник|а, и *f.* sanitary engineering; **магази́н** ~**и** plumbing supplies shop, plumber's merchant.
санте́хник, а *m.* sanitary engineer.
сантигра́мм, а *m.* centigram.
санти́м, а *m.* centime.
сантиме́нт|ы, ов *no sg.* (*coll.*) sentimentality; **развести́ с.** to sentimentalize.
сантиме́тр, а *m.* **1.** centimetre. **2.** tape-measure.
сантони́н, а *m.* (*pharm.*) santonin.
сану́з|ел, ла́ *m. see* **санита́рный**
Сан-Франци́ско *m. indecl.* San Francisco.
сап[1]**, а** *m.* (*med.*) glanders.
сап[2]**, а** *m.* (*coll.*) stertorous breathing.
са́п|а, ы *f.* (*mil.*) sap; **ти́хой** ~**ой** on the sly, on the quiet.
сапёр, а *m.* (*mil.*) sapper; pioneer.
сапёр|ный *adj. of* ~; ~**ные рабо́ты** field engineering; ~**ная ро́та** engineer company; pioneer company.
сапно́й *adj.* (*med.*) glanderous.
сапо́г, а́, *g.pl.* **сапо́г** *m.* (high-)boot; top-boot, jackboot; **два** ~**а́ па́ра** they make a pair.
сапо́жник, а *m.* shoemaker, bootmaker, cobbler.
сапо́жнича|ть, ю *impf.* to be a shoemaker.
сапо́жн|ый *adj.* boot, shoe; ~**ая ва́кса, с. крем** blacking, shoe-polish; ~**ое ремесло́** shoemaking; ~**ая щётка** shoe-brush.
сапфи́р, а *m.* sapphire.
сапфи́ческий *adj.* (*liter.*) sapphic.
сараба́нд|а, ы *f.* (*mus.*) saraband.
Сара́ев|о, а *nt.* Sarajevo.
сара́|й, я *m.* shed; (*fig.*; *of uncomfortable room or dwelling*) barn; **каре́тный с.** coach-house; **сенно́й с.** hay-loft; **с. для дров** wood-shed.
саранч|а́, и *no pl., f.* locust(s).
сарафа́н, а *m.* sarafan (*Russ. peasant women's dress, without sleeves and buttoning in front*); tunic dress.
сараци́н, а *m.* (*hist.*) Saracen.
сарде́льк|а, и *f.* polony, saveloy.
сарди́н|а, ы *f.* sardine, pilchard; ~**ы в ма́сле** (tinned) sardines.
сарди́н|ец, ца *m.* Sardinian.
Сарди́ни|я, и *f.* Sardinia.
сарди́н|ка, ки *f.*= ~**а**
сарди́нский *adj.* Sardinian.
сардони́ческий *adj.* sardonic.
са́рж|а, и *f.* (*text.*) serge.
сарка́зм, а *m.* sarcasm.
саркасти́ческий *adj.* sarcastic.
саркофа́г, а *m.* sarcophagus.
сарма́тский *adj.* (*hist.*) Sarmatian.
сарпи́нк|а, и *f.* (*text.*) printed calico.
сары́ч, а́ *m.* (*zool.*) buzzard.
сатан|а́, ы́ *m.* Satan.
сатани́нский *adj.* Satanic.
сателли́т, а *m.* **1.** (*astron.*; *fig.*) satellite. **2.** (*tech.*) planet pinion (*of gear*), planet wheel.
сати́н, а *m.* (*text.*) sateen.
сатине́т, а *m.* (*text.*) satinet(te).
сатини́р|овать, ую *impf. and pf.* to satin.
сати́н|овый *adj. of* ~
сати́р, а *m.* (*myth.*) satyr.
сати́р|а, ы *f.* satire.
сати́рик, а *m.* satirist.
сатири́ческий *adj.* satirical.
сатра́п, а *m.* satrap.
сатра́пи|я, и *f.* satrapy.
сатура́тор, а *m.* soda-fountain.
сатурна́л|ии, ий *no sg.* (*hist.*) saturnalia.
сау́дов|ец, ца *m.* Saudi.
сау́дов|ка, ки *f. of* ~**ец**
Сау́довск|ая Ара́ви|я, ~**ой** ~**и** *f.* Saudi Arabia.
сау́довский *adj.* Saudi.
са́ун|а, ы *f.* sauna.
сафа́ри *nt. indecl.* safari; **«с.» зоопа́рк** safari park.
сафья́н, а *m.* morocco (leather).
сафья́новый *adj.* morocco (leather).
Сахали́н, а *m.* Sakhalin.
са́хар, а (у) *m.* sugar; **свеклови́чный с.** beet sugar; **тростнико́вый с.** cane sugar; **моло́чный с.** (*chem.*) milk sugar, lactose.
Саха́р|а, ы *f.* the Sahara (*desert*).
сахари́н, а *m.* saccharin(e).
са́харист|ый (~, ~а) *adj.* sugary; saccharine.
са́хар|ить, ю, ишь *impf.* (*of* **по**~) to sugar, sweeten.
са́харниц|а, ы *f.* sugar-basin.
са́хар|ный *adj. of* ~; (*fig.*) sugary; ~**ная боле́знь** (*med.*) diabetes; ~**ная глазу́рь** icing; ~**ная голова́** sugar-loaf; **с. заво́д** sugar-refinery; ~**ная кислота́** (*chem.*) saccharic acid; **с. песо́к** granulated sugar; ~**ная пу́дра** icing sugar; ~**ная свёкла** sugar-beet; **с. тростни́к** sugar-cane.
сахароваре́ни|е, я *nt.* sugar refining.
сахарозаво́дчик, а *m.* (*obs.*) sugar manufacturer, owner of a sugar-refinery.
сахаро́з|а, ы *f.* (*chem.*) saccharose, sucrose.
сачк|ова́ть, у́ю *impf.* (*coll.*) to skive, loaf.
сач|о́к[1]**, ка́** *m.* net; **с. для ры́бы** landing-net; **с. для ба́бочек** butterfly-net.
сач|о́к[2]**, ка́** *m.* (*coll.*) skiver, loafer.
сба́в|ить, лю, ишь *pf.* (*of* ~**ля́ть**) (**с**+*g.*) to take off (from), deduct (from); **с. с цены́** to reduce the price; **с. в ве́се** to lose weight; **с. газ** (*tech.*) to throttle back; **с. спе́си кому́-н.** (*coll.*) to take s.o. down a peg; **с. тон** (*fig.*) to change one's tune.
сбавля́|ть, ю *impf. of* **сба́вить**
сбаланси́р|овать, ую *pf. of* **баланси́ровать**
сба́лтыва|ть, ю *impf. of* **сболта́ть**
сбе́га|ть, ю *pf.* (**за**+*i.*; *coll.*) to run (for), run to fetch; ~**й за до́ктором!** run for a doctor!
сбега́|ть(ся), ю(сь) *impf. of* **сбежа́ть(ся)**
сбе|жа́ть, гу́, жи́шь гу́т *pf.* (*of* ~**га́ть**) **1.** (**с**+*g.*) to run down (from); **с. с ле́стницы** to run downstairs. **2.** to run away. **3.** (**с**+*g.*; *fig.*) to disappear, vanish; **хму́рое выраже́ние** ~**жа́ло с его́ лица́** the frown vanished from his face.
сбе|жа́ться, жи́тся, гу́тся *pf.* (*of* ~**га́ться**) to come running; to gather, collect.
сбер... *comb. form, abbr. of* **сберега́тельный**
сберба́нк, а *m.* = **сберка́сса**
сберега́тельн|ый *adj.*: ~**ая ка́сса** savings bank; ~**ая кни́жка** savings-bank book.
сберега́|ть, ю *impf. of* **сбере́чь**
сбереже́ни|е, я *nt.* **1.** economy; **с. сил** (*mil.*) economy of force. **2.** (*pl.*) savings.
сбере́|чь, гу́, жёшь, гу́т, *past* ~̈**г,** ~**гла́** *pf.* (*of* ~**га́ть**) **1.** to save, preserve; to protect; **с. шу́бу от мо́ли** to protect a fur coat from moth. **2.** to save, save up, put aside.
сберка́сс|а, ы *f.* savings bank.
сберкни́жк|а, и *f.* savings book.
сбива́лк|а, и *f.* (*cul.*) (egg-)whisk.
сбива́|ть, ю *impf. of* **сбить**
сбива́|ться, юсь *impf.* **1.** *impf. of* **сби́ться. 2.** *impf. only* (**на**+*a.*) to resemble; to remind one (of).
сби́вчивост|ь, и *f.* inconsistency, contradictoriness.
сби́вчив|ый (~, ~а) *adj.* inconsistent, contradictory.
сби́т|ень, ня *m.* (*hist.*) sbiten (*hot drink made with honey and spices*).
сби́т|ый *p.p.p. of* ~**ь** *and adj.*: ~**ые сли́вки** whipped cream.
сбить, собью́, собьёшь *pf.* (*of* **сбива́ть**) **1.** to bring down, knock down; to knock off, dislodge; **с. самолёт** to bring

down, shoot down an aircraft; **с. противника с позиций** to dislodge the enemy from his positions; **с. цену** to beat down the price; **с. спесь с кого-н.** to bring s.o. down a peg. **2.** to put out; to distract; to deflect; **с. с такта** to throw out of time; **с. кого-н. с толку** to muddle s.o., to confuse s.o.; **с. кого-н. с дороги** to misdirect s.o.; **с. с пути истинного** (*fig.*) to lead s.o. astray. **3.** to wear down, tread down; **с. каблуки** to wear one's shoes down at the heels. **4.** to knock together; **с. ящик из досок** to knock together a box out of planks. **5.** (*impf. also* **бить**) to churn; to beat up, whip, whisk.

сбиться, собьюсь, собьёшься *pf.* (*of* **сбиваться**) **1.** to be dislodged; to slip; **твоя шляпа сбилась набок** your hat is crooked, skew-whiff; **с. с ног** (*coll.*) to be run off one's legs, off one's feet. **2.** to be deflected; to go wrong; **с. в вычислениях** to be out in one's calculations; **с. в показаниях** to be inconsistent in one's testimony, contradict o.s. in one's evidence; **с. с дороги, с. с пути** to lose one's way; to go astray (*also fig.*); **с. с ноги** to lose the step; **с. со счёта** to lose count; **с. с такта** to get out of time. **3.** to become worn down; to become blunt. **4.: с. в кучу, с. толпой** to bunch, huddle.

сближа|ть(ся), ю(сь) *impf. of* **сблизить(ся)**

сближение, я *nt.* **1.** rapprochement. **2.** (*mil.*) approach, closing in. **3.** intimacy.

сбли|зить, жу, зишь *pf.* (*of* **~жать**) to bring together, draw together.

сбли|зиться, жусь, зишься *pf.* (*of* **~жаться**) **1.** to draw together, converge. **2.** (**с**+*i.*) to become good friends (with). **3.** (*mil.*) to approach, close in.

сбо|й[1], **я** *m.* (*collect.*) head, legs, and entrails (of animal; *as meat*).

сбо|й[2], **я** *m.* failure, shortcoming.

сбоку *adv.* from one side; on one side; **вид с.** side-view; **смотреть на кого-н. с.** to look sideways at s.o.

сболта|ть, ю *pf.* (*of* **сбалтывать**) to stir up, shake up, mix up; **с. лекарство** to shake (a bottle of) medicine.

сбор, а *m.* **1.** collection; **с. урожая** harvest(-carrying); **с. налогов** tax collection; **с. подписей** collection of signatures. **2.** dues; duty; takings, returns; **гербовый с.** stamp-duty; **портовый с.** harbour dues; **таможенный с.** customs duty; **полный с.** (*theatr.*) full house; **делать хорошие ~ы** (*theatr.*) to play to full houses, get good box-office returns. **3.** assemblage, gathering; **быть в ~е** to be assembled, be in session. **4.** (*mil.*) assembly (= *signal to assemble*). **5.** (*mil.*) (periodical) training; **лагерный с.** camp; **учебный с.** refresher course. **6.** (*pl.*) preparations.

сборищ|е, а *nt.* assemblage, mob.

сборк|а, и *f.* **1.** (*tech.*) assembling, assembly, erection. **2.** (*in dress, etc.*) gather; **в ~ах, со ~ами** with gathers.

сборник[1], **а** *m.* **1.** collection (*of stories, articles, etc.*). **2.** (*tech.*) storage tank, receptacle.

сборник[2], **а** *m.* (*sport, coll.*) member of representative team.

сборн|ый *adj.* **1.** that can be taken to pieces, detachable; **с. дом** prefabricated house. **2.** mixed, combined; **~ая команда** (*sport*) combined team, representative team. **3.** (*mil.*) assembly; **с. пункт** assembly point, rallying point. **4.: с. лист** (*typ.*) preliminary sheets ('prelims').

сборочный *adj.* (*tech.*) assembly; **с. конвейер** assembly belt; **с. цех** assembly shop.

сборчатый *adj.* gathered, with gathers.

сборщик, а *m.* **1.** collector; **с. налогов** tax-collector. **2.** (*tech.*) assembler, fitter, mounter.

сбрасыва|ть(ся), ю(сь) *impf. of* **сбросить(ся)**

сбрива|ть, ю *impf. of* **сбрить**

сбрить, сбрею, сбреешь *pf.* (*of* **сбривать**) to shave off.

сброд, а *no pl., m.* (*collect.*) riff-raff, rabble.

сбродн|ый *adj.* (*coll.*) assembled by chance; **~ая компания** motley assembly, chance collection of people.

сброс, а *m.* **1.** (*tech.*) overflow disposal (system). **2.** (*geol.*) fault, break. **3.** dropping, shedding. **4.** (*cards*) discard.

сбро|сить, шу, сишь *pf.* (*of* **сбрасывать**) **1.** to throw down; to drop; **с. бомбы** to drop bombs; **с. на парашюте** to drop by parachute. **2.** to throw off (*also fig.*); to cast off, shed; **с. с себя одеяло** to throw off a blanket; **с. иго** to throw off the yoke. **3.** (*cards*) to throw away, discard.

сбро|ситься, шусь, сишься *pf.* (*of* **сбрасываться**) (**с**+*g.*) to leap (off, from).

сброшюр|овать, ую *pf. of* **брошюровать**

сбру|я, и *f.* (*collect.*) harness.

сбыва|ть(ся), ю(сь) *impf. of* **сбыть(ся)**

сбыт, а *no pl., m.* (*econ., comm.*) sale; **рынок ~а** (seller's) market; **хороший с.** good sales; **найти себе хороший с.** to sell well.

сбытовой *adj.* (*econ., comm.*) selling, marketing.

сбыточный *adj.* (*obs.*) possible, feasible.

сбытчик, а *m.*: **с. наркотиков** drug dealer *or* trafficker.

сбыть[1], **сбуду, сбудешь,** *past* **сбыл, сбыла, сбыло** *pf.* (*of* **сбывать**) **1.** to sell, market. **2.** (*coll.*) to get rid (of), rid o.s. (of); (*comm.*) to dump, push off; **с. с рук** to get off one's hands.

сбыть[2], **сбудет,** *past* **сбыл, сбыла, сбыло** *pf.* (*of* **сбывать**) (*of level of water*) to fall.

сбыться, сбудется, *past* **сбылся, сбылась** *pf.* (*of* **сбываться**) **1.** to come true, be realized. **2.** (*obs.*) to happen; **что сбудется с ней?** what will become of her?

св. (*abbr. of* **святой**) St, Saint.

свадебный *adj.* wedding; nuptial; **с. подарок** wedding present.

свад|ьба, ьбы, *g. pl.* **~еб** *f.* wedding; **справлять ~ьбу** to celebrate a wedding.

Свазиленд, а *m.* Swaziland.

свайнобойный *adj.* pile-driving.

свайн|ый *adj.* pile; **~ые постройки** pile-dwellings.

сваливa|ть(ся), ю(сь) *impf. of* **свалить(ся)**

свал|ить[1], **ю, ~ишь** *pf.* (*of* **валить**[1] *and* **~ивать**) **1.** to throw down, bring down; to overthrow; to lay low. **2.** to heap up, pile up; **с. вину (на**+*a.*) to lump the blame (on).

свал|ить[2], **~ит** *pf.* (*coll.*) to sink, drop, fall, abate.

свал|иться, юсь, ~ишся *pf.* (*of* **валиться** *and* **~иваться**) to fall (down), collapse; **с. как снег на голову** to come like a bolt from the blue.

свалк|а, и *f.* **1.** dump; scrap heap. **2.** (*coll.*) scuffle, fight; **общая с.** free-for-all, mêlée.

свалочн|ый *adj. of* **свалка; ~ое место** dump, scrap heap (*also fig.*).

сваля|ть, ю *pf. of* **валять 3., 4.**

сваля|ться, ется *pf.* to get tangled.

сварива|ть(ся), ю(сь) *impf. of* **сварить(ся)**

свар|ить, ю, ~ишь *pf.* **1.** *pf. of* **варить. 2.** (*impf.* **~ивать**) (*tech.*) to weld.

свар|иться, юсь, ~ишься *pf.* **1.** *pf. of* **вариться. 2.** (*impf.* **~иваться**) (*tech.*) to weld (together).

сварк|а, и *f.* (*tech.*) welding; **с. в притык** butt welding; **с. в цепь** chain welding; **с. по шву, с. со швом** seam welding; **с. с токами** spot welding.

сварлив|ый (~, ~а) *adj.* peevish, shrewish; **~ая женщина** shrew.

сварной *adj.* (*tech.*) welded; **с. шов** welded joint.

сварочн|ый *adj.* (*tech.*) welding; **~ая горелка** welding torch, burner; **~ое железо** weld iron, wrought iron; **~ая сталь** weld steel, puddled steel.

сварщик, а *m.* welder.

свастик|а, и *f.* swastika.

сват, а *m.* **1.** matchmaker. **2.** son-in-law's father; daughter-in-law's father.

свата|ть, ю *impf.* (*of* **по~**) **1.** (*pf. also* **со~**) (+*a. and d.*) to propose as husband; (*also* +*a.* **за**+*a.*) to propose as wife; to (try to) marry off (to); to (try to) arrange a match (between); **ему, за него ~ют какую-то немецкую барышню** they are trying to arrange a match for him with a German girl; they are trying to marry him off to a German girl. **2.** to ask in marriage.

свата|ться, юсь *impf.* (*of* **по~**) (**к; за**+*a.*) to woo, court; to ask, seek in marriage.

свать|я, и *f.* son-in-law's mother; daughter-in-law's mother.

свах|а, и *f.* matchmaker.

сва|я, и *f.* pile.

сведени|е, я *nt.* **1.** piece of information; (*pl.*) information, intelligence; **по полученным ~ям** according to information

received. **2.** knowledge; attention, consideration, notice; **дойти́ до чьего́-н. ~я** to come to s.o.'s notice; **довести́ до чье́го-н. ~я** to bring to s.o.'s notice, inform s.o.; **приня́ть к ~ю** to take into consideration, take cognizance (of). **3.** (*pl.*) knowledge; **у него́ бо́льшие ~я по исто́рии Росси́и** he is very knowledgeable about the history of Russia. **4.** report, minute; **отчётные ~я** returns; **предста́вить с.** to present a report.
сведе́ни|е, я *nt.* **1.** reduction; **с. счётов** settling of accounts. **2.** (*med.*) contraction, cramp.
све́дущ|ий (~, ~а) *adj.* (**в**+*p.*) knowledgeable (about); versed (in), experienced (in); **~ие ли́ца** experts, persons in the know.
свеж|ева́ть, у́ю *impf.* (*of* **о~**) to skin, dress.
свежезаморо́женный *adj.* fresh-frozen, chilled.
свежеиспечённый *adj.* newly-baked; (*fig.*, *coll.*) raw, newly-fledged.
свежепросо́льный *adj.* fresh-salted.
све́жест|ь, и *f.* freshness; coolness; **не пе́рвой ~и** (*coll.*) past its (*fig.*, *joc.*; one's) best.
свеже́|ть, ю *impf.* (*of* **по~**) **1.** to become cooler; (*of the wind*) to freshen (up), blow up. **2.** to freshen up, acquire a glow of health.
све́ж|ий (~, ~а́, ~о́, ~и) *adj.* (*in var. senses*) fresh; **~ее бельё** clean underclothes; **с. ве́тер** fresh wind, fresh breeze; **на ~ем во́здухе** in the fresh air; **~ие но́вости** recent news; **~ая ры́ба** fresh fish; **со ~ими си́лами** with renewed strength; **с. цвет лица́** fresh complexion; **~о́ в па́мяти** fresh in one's memory; (*impers.*, *as pred.*): **~о́** it is fresh, it is blowing up.
свез|ти́, у́, ёшь, *past* **~**, **~ла́** *pf.* (*of* **свози́ть**[1]) **1.** to take, convey; **его́ ~ли́ в больни́цу** he has been taken to hospital. **2.** to take down. **3.** to take away, clear away.
свёкл|а, ы *f.* beet, beetroot; **кормова́я с.** mangel-wurzel; **са́харная с.** sugar-beet, white beet; **столо́вая с.** red beet.
свеклови́ц|а, ы *f.* sugar-beet.
свеклови́|чный *adj.* *of* **~ца; с. са́хар** beet-sugar.
свеклово́дств|о, а *nt.* (sugar-)beet raising.
свеклоса́харный *adj.* sugar-beet; beet-sugar.
свеклосовхо́з, а *m.* State (sugar-)beet farm.
свеко́льник, а *m.* **1.** beetroot soup. **2.** beetroot leaves.
свеко́льный *adj.* *of* **свёкла**
свёк|ор, ра *m.* father-in-law (*husband's father*).
свекро́в|ь, и *f.* mother-in-law (*husband's mother*).
свербёж, а́ *m.* (*coll.*) itch, irritation.
сверб|е́ть, и́т *impf.* (*coll.*) to itch, irritate.
сверг|а́ть, а́ю *impf.* *of* **~нуть**
све́рг|нуть, ну, нешь, *past* **~**, **~ла** *pf.* (*of* **~а́ть**) to throw down, overthrow; **с. с престо́ла** to dethrone.
сверже́ни|е, я *nt.* overthrow; **с. с престо́ла** dethronement.
све́р|зиться, хусь, зишься *pf.* (**с**+*g.*; *coll.*) to tumble (off, from).
све́р|ить, ю, ишь *pf.* (*of* **~я́ть**) (+*a.* **с**+*i.*) to collate (with); to check (against); **с. часы́** to check one's watch; **с. корректу́ру с ру́кописью** to check proofs against a manuscript.
све́р|иться, юсь, ишься *pf.* (*of* **~я́ться**) (**с**+*i.*) to check (with).
све́рк|а, и *f.* collation.
сверка́ни|е, я *nt.* sparkling, twinkling; glitter; glare.
сверка́|ть, ю *impf.* to sparkle, twinkle; to glitter; to gleam.
сверкн|у́ть, у́, ёшь *pf.* to flash (*also fig.*); **у меня́ в голове́ ~у́ла мысль** a thought flashed through my mind.
сверли́льный *adj.* (*tech.*) boring, drilling; **с. стано́к** boring machine, drilling machine, drill.
сверл|и́ть, ю, и́шь *impf.* **1.** (*tech.*) to bore, drill; **с. зуб** to drill a tooth. **2.** to bore through. **3.** (*fig.*; *of mental or physical pain*) to nag (at), gnaw (at); **его́ ~и́ла мысль об уби́том** the image of the murdered man nagged at him; **у меня́ ~и́т в у́хе** I have a nagging earache.
сверл|о́, а́, *pl.* **~а** *nt.* (*tech.*) borer, drill, auger.
сверло́вщик, а *m.* borer, driller.
сверл|я́щий *pres. part. act.* *of* **~ить** *and adj.*; **~я́щая боль** nagging, gnawing pain.
сверн|у́ть, у́, ёшь *pf.* (*of* **свёртывать** *and* **свора́чивать**) **1.** to roll (up); **с. ковёр** to roll up the carpet; **с. папиро́су** to roll a cigarette; **с. паруса́** to furl sails; **с. ше́ю кому́-н.** to wring s.o.'s neck. **2.** (*fig.*) to reduce, contract, curtail, cut down; **с. шта́ты** to axe the establishment. **3.** to turn; **с нале́во** to turn to the left; **с. с доро́ги** to turn off the road; **с. на пре́жнее** (*fig.*) to revert (*to former topic of conversation, etc.*).
сверн|у́ться, у́сь, ёшься *pf.* (*of* **свёртываться** *and* **свора́чиваться**) **1.** to roll up, curl up; to coil up; (*of petals or leaves*) to fold; **с. клубко́м** to roll o.s. up into a ball. **2.** to curdle, coagulate, turn. **3.** (*fig.*) to contract. **4.** *pass. of* **~уть**
сверста́|ть, ю *pf.* *of* **верста́ть**[1]
све́рстник, а *m.* pers. of the same age; **мы с ним ~и** he and I are the same age.
свёрт|ок, ка *m.* package, parcel, bundle.
свёртывани|е, я *nt.* **1.** rolling (up). **2.** curdling, turning; coagulation. **3.** (*fig.*) reduction, curtailment, cutting down; **с. произво́дства** production cutting, cuts.
свёртыва|ть(ся), ю(сь) *impf.* *of* **сверну́ть(ся)**
сверх *prep.*+*g.* **1.** over, above, on top of. **2.** (*fig.*) above, beyond; over and above; in excess of; **с. пла́на** in excess of the plan, over and above the plan; **с. сил** beyond one's strength; **с. (вся́кого) ожида́ния** beyond (all) expectation; **с. всего́** to crown all, on top of everything; **с. того́** moreover, besides.
сверх... *comb. form* super-, supra-, extra-, over-, preter-.
сверхзвуково́й *adj.* (*phys.*, *aeron.*) supersonic.
сверхкомпле́ктный *adj.* supernumerary.
сверхмо́щный *adj.* (*tech.*) super-power, extra-high-power.
сверхнациона́льный *adj.* supranational.
сверхно́в|ый *adj.*: **~ая (звезда́)** (*astron.*) super-nova.
сверхпла́новый *adj.* over and above the plan.
сверхпри́был|ь, и *f.* excess profit.
сверхпроводи́мост|ь, и *f.* (*elec.*) super-conductivity.
сверхскоростно́й *adj.* super-high-speed.
сверхсме́тный *adj.* above-estimate, extra-budget.
сверхсрочнослу́жащ|ий, его *m.* (*mil.*) man re-engaging after completion of statutory military service.
сверхсро́чн|ый *adj.* (*mil.*): **~ая слу́жба** additional service (*voluntarily undertaken after completion of statutory period*); **с. военнослу́жащий** = **~ослу́жащий**
све́рху *adv.* **1.** from above (*also fig.*); from the top; **с. до́низу** from top to bottom; **директи́ва с.** a directive from above; **смотре́ть на кого́-н. с. вниз** (*fig.*) to look down on s.o. **2.** on the surface.
сверхуро́чн|ый *adj.* overtime; **~ая рабо́та** overtime; *as n.* **~ые, ~ых** (*payment for*) overtime.
сверхчелове́к, а *m.* superman, overman.
сверхчелове́ческий *adj.* superhuman.
сверхчувстви́тельный *adj.* supersensitive.
сверхшта́тный *adj.* supernumerary.
сверхъесте́ственный *adj.* supernatural, preternatural.
сверч|о́к, ка́ *m.* (*zool.*) cricket; **всяк с. знай свой шесто́к** (*prov.*) the cobbler should stick to his last.
сверша́|ть(сь), ю(сь) *impf.* = **соверша́ть(ся)**
сверш|и́ть(ся), у́(сь), и́шь (ся) *pf.* = **соверши́ть(ся)**; **~и́лось!** it has come to pass! it has come off!
све́рщик, а *m.* collator.
свер|я́ть(ся), я́ю(сь) *impf.* *of* **~ить(ся)**
свес, а *m.* overhang.
све́|сить, шу, сишь *pf.* (*of* **~шивать**) **1.** to let down, lower; **сиде́ть, ~сив но́ги** to sit with one's legs dangling. **2.** to weigh.
све́|ситься, шусь, сишься *pf.* (*of* **~шиваться**) to lean over; to hang over, overhang; **с. че́рез пери́ла** to lean over the banisters.
све|сти́, ду́, дёшь, *past* **~л, ~ла́** *pf.* (*of* **своди́ть**[1]) **1.** to take; **с. дете́й в шко́лу** to take the children to school; **с. в моги́лу** to send to the grave, be the death (of). **2.** (**с**+*g.*) to take down (from, off); **с. кого́-н. с пьедеста́ла** to take s.o. off his pedestal; **с. с ума́** to drive mad. **3.** to take away; to lead off; **с. коро́ву с доро́ги** to take a cow off the road; **с. разгово́р на другу́ю те́му** to lead the conversation onto a different subject. **4.** to remove; **с. пятно́** to remove, get

out a stain. **5.** to bring together; to put together; to unite; **с. ста́рых друзе́й** to bring old friends together; **судьба́ ~ла́ их** fate threw them together; **с. да́нные в табли́цу** to tabulate data; **с. концы́ с конца́ми** to make (both) ends meet. **6.: с. дру́жбу (с+***i.***)**, **с. знако́мство (с+***i.***)** to make friends (with). **7. (к, на+***a.***)** to reduce (to), bring (to); **с. на нет** to bring to naught; **с. к са́мому необходи́мому** to reduce to the barest essentials; **с. расска́з к немно́гим слова́м** to condense a story to a few words. **8.** to trace, transfer. **9.** to cramp, convulse; **у меня́ ~ло́ но́гу** I have cramp in my foot.

све|сти́сь, дётся, *past* **~лся, ~ла́сь** *pf.* (*of* **своди́ться**) **1. (к, на+***a.***)** to come (to), reduce (to); **с. на нет** to come to naught. **2.** (*of a transfer*) to come off.

свет[1], **а** *m.* **1.** light (*also fig.*); **лу́нный с.** moonlight; **заже́чь с.** to put, turn the light on; **в два ~а** with two rows of windows; **в ~е (+***g.***)** in the light (of); **предста́вить в невы́годном ~е** to represent in an unfavourable light; **на с.** when placed in the light; **на ~у́** in the light; **при ~е (+***g.***)** by the light (of); **при ~е свечи́** by candlelight; **стоя́ть про́тив ~а** to stand in the light. **2.** daybreak; **чем с.** first thing (in the morning); **чуть с.** at daybreak, at first light; **ни с., ни заря́** before dawn; (*iron.*) at the crack of dawn. **3.** (*pl. only* **~а́**; *art*) lights; **~а́ и те́ни** lights and shades.

свет[2], **а** *m.* **1.** world (*also fig.*); **ста́рый, но́вый с.** the Old, the New World; **тот с.** the next, the other world; **коне́ц ~а** doomsday, the end of the world; **стра́ны ~а** the cardinal points (*of the compass*); **произвести́ на с.** to bring into the world; **(по)яви́ться на с.** to come into the world; **вы́пустить в с.** to bring out (= *to publish*); **его́ нет на ~е** he has departed this life; **ни за что на ~е** not for the world; **на чём с. стои́т** like nothing on earth, like hell; for all one is, was worth. **2.** society, beau monde; **вы́сший с.** the upper ten; **мо́дный с.** the fashionable set, the smart set.

света́|ть, ет *impf.*; (*impers.*): **~ет** it is dawning, it is getting light, day is breaking.

светёлк|а, и *f.* (*obs.*) attic.

свети́л|о, а *nt.* luminary (*also fig.*); **небе́сные ~а** heavenly bodies.

свети́льник, а *m.* **1.** lamp. **2.** (*obs.*) lampion.

свети́льный *adj.* illuminating.

свети́л|ьня, ьни, *g. pl.* **~ен** *f.* wick.

све|ти́ть, чу́, ~тишь *impf.* **1.** to shine. **2. (+***d.***)** to give light; to shine a light (for); **он ~ти́л нам в тунне́ле** he lit us through the tunnel.

све|ти́ться, чу́сь, ~ти́шься *impf.* to shine, gleam; **в окне́ ~тится огонёк** there is a light in the window; **в его́ глаза́х ~ти́лась безжа́лостность** there was a hard glint in his eye(s).

светле́йший *adj.* (*obs.*) (his, her) Highness (*as title of princes, etc.*).

светле́|ть, у *impf.* (*of* **по~**) to brighten (*also fig.*); (*of weather*) to clear up, brighten up.

светли́ц|а, ы *f.* (*obs.*) front room.

све́тло... *comb. form* light-.

све́тлост|ь, и *f.* **1.** brightness (*also fig.*); lightness. **2.: его́,** *etc.*, **с.** (*title of dukes and archbishops*) his, *etc.*, Grace.

све́т|лый (~ел, ~ла́, ~ло) *adj.* **1.** (*in var. senses*) light; bright; light-coloured; **~лые во́лосы** light hair; **с. день** bright day; **с. шрифт** (*typ.*) light-face; **на дворе́ ~ло́** it is daylight; **~ло́ вам, и́ли хоти́те, что́бы я заже́г свет?** can you see, or do you want me to put the light on? **2.** (*fig.*) bright, radiant, joyous; pure, unclouded; **~лое бу́дущее** radiant future; **~лая ли́чность** good pers., good soul; **~лой па́мяти** of blessed memory. **3.** (*fig.*) lucid, clear; **он — ~лая голова́** he has a lucid mind, a good head; **~лые мину́ты** lucid intervals. **4.** (*eccl.*) Easter; **~лая неде́ля** Easter week.

светлы́н|ь, и *f.* brightness (*of moonlight and/or starlight*).

светля́к, а *m.* glow-worm; fire-fly.

светобоя́зн|ь, и *f.* (*med.*) photophobia.

светов|о́й *adj. of* **свет**[1]; **с. ба́кан** light buoy; **~а́я волна́** light wave; **~а́я рекла́ма** illuminated signs; **с. сигна́л** light signal, flare; **с. эффе́кт** (*theatr.*) lighting effect; **~о́е явле́ние** luminous phenomenon.

светодио́д, а *m.* light-emitting diode, LED.

светоза́р|ный (~ен, ~на) *adj.* (*poet.*) shining, flashing; radiant.

светозвукоспекта́кл|ь, я *m.* son et lumière.

светокопирова́льный *adj.* photostatting; blueprinting.

светоко́пи|я, и *f.* Photostat (*propr.*); blueprint.

светолече́ни|е, я *nt.* (*med.*) phototherapy.

светомаскиро́вк|а, и *f.* black-out.

светонепроница́емый *adj.* light-proof.

светопреставле́ни|е, я *nt.* **1.** the end of the world, doomsday. **2.** (*fig., coll.*) chaos.

светосигнализа́ци|я, и *f.* (*mil.*) lamp signalling.

светосигна́льн|ый *adj.* (*mil.*) signal-lamp; **~ая связь** lamp communication.

светоси́л|а, ы *f.* (*phys.*) illumination; candlepower.

светосто́|йкий (~ек, ~йка) *adj.* (*chem.*) stable in light; fast to light.

светоте́н|ь, и *f.* (*art*) chiaroscuro.

светоте́хник|а, и *f.* lighting engineering.

светофи́льтр, а *m.* light filter.

светофо́р, а *m.* traffic lights; light signal.

све́точ, а *m.* **1.** (*obs.*) torch, lamp. **2.** (*fig.*) light, luminary; torch-bearer.

светочувстви́тельност|ь, и *f.* photo-sensitivity; speed (*of film*).

светочувстви́тел|ьный (~ен, ~ьна) *adj.* photo-sensitive.

све́тск|ий *adj.* **1.** society, fashionable; **~ая жизнь** high life; **с. челове́к** man of the world, man about town. **2.** (*obs.*) genteel, refined; **~ие мане́ры** genteel manners. **3.** temporal, lay, secular; worldly; **~ая власть** temporal power.

све́тскост|ь, и *f.* good manners, good breeding.

свет|я́щийся *pres. part. of* **~и́ться** *and adj.* luminous, luminescent, fluorescent, phosphorescent.

свеч|а́, и́, *i.* **~о́й,** *pl.* **~и, ~е́й, ~а́м** *f.* **1.** candle; taper; **жечь ~у́ с двух концо́в** to burn the candle at both ends. **2.: зажига́тельная с., запа́льная с.** sparking-plug. **3.** lamp candle-power; **ла́мпочка в пятьдеся́т ~е́й** lamp of fifty candle-power. **4.** (*sport*) lob.

свече́ни|е, я *nt.* luminescence, fluorescence; phosphorescence.

све́чк|а, и *f.* **1.** candle. **2.** (*med.*) suppository.

свеч|но́й *adj. of* **~а́**; **с. ога́рок** candle-end.

све́ша|ть, ю *pf.* to weigh.

све́шива|ть(ся), ю(сь) *impf. of* **све́сить(ся)**

свива́льник, а *m.* swaddling-bands, swaddling-clothes.

свива́|ть, ю *impf.* **1.** *impf. of* **свить. 2.** *impf. only* to swaddle.

свида́ни|е, я *nt.* meeting; reunion; appointment; rendezvous; date; **назна́чить с. (на+***a.***)** to make an appointment (for), make a date (for); **до ~я!** good-bye!; **до ско́рого ~я!** see you soon!

свиде́тел|ь, я *m.* witness; bystander; **с. обвине́ния, защи́ты** witness for the prosecution, for the defence; **с. Иего́вы** Jehovah's Witness; **призва́ть кого́-н. в ~и** to call s.o. to witness; **вы́звать кого́-н. ~ем, в ка́честве ~я** (*leg.*) to subpoena as a witness.

свиде́тель|ский *adj. of* **~**

свиде́тельств|о, а *nt.* **1.** evidence; testimony. **2.** certificate; **метри́ческое с.** birth certificate; **с. о бра́ке** certificate of marriage, marriage lines; **с. о прода́же** bill of sale.

свиде́тельств|овать, ую *impf.* **1. (о+***p.***, +***a. or* **+что)** (*leg.*) to give evidence (concerning); to testify (to) (*also fig.*); (*fig.*) to show, attest, be evidence (of); **письмо́ э́то ~ует о его́ беста́ктности** this letter is evidence of his tactlessness. **2.** (*pf.* **за~**) to witness; to attest, certify; **с. ко́пию** to certify a copy; **с. по́дпись** to witness a signature; **с. почте́ние (+***d.***)** to pay one's respects (to), present one's compliments (to). **3.** (*pf.* **о~**) to examine, inspect; **с. больно́го** to examine a patient.

свиде́тельств|оваться, ую́сь *impf.* **1.** *pass. of* **~овать. 2.** (+*i. or d.*; *obs.*) to call to witness.

сви́|деться, жусь, дишься *pf.* **(с+***i.***;** *coll.***)** to meet; to see one another.

свилева́т|ый (~, ~а) *adj.* knotty, gnarled.

свил|ь, и *f.* **1.** knot (*in wood*). **2.** waviness (*flaw in glass*).
свина́рк|а, и *f.* pig-tender.
свина́рник, а *m.* pigsty.
свина́р|ня, ни, *g. pl.* **~ен** *f.* = **~ник**
свин|е́ц, ца́ *m.* lead (*also fig.* = *bullet*); **о́кись ~ца́** lead oxide.
свини́н|а, ы *f.* pork.
сви́н|ка[1], ки *f. dim. of* **~ья́; морска́я с.** guinea-pig.
сви́нк|а[2], и *f.* (*med.*) mumps.
сви́нк|а[3], и *f.* (*tech.*) pig, ingot, bar; **чугу́н в ~ах** pig iron.
свиново́д, а *m.* pig-breeder.
свиново́дств|о, а *nt.* pig-breeding.
свиново́д|ческий *adj. of* **~ство**
свин|о́й *adj. of* **~ья́; ~а́я ко́жа** pigskin; **~о́е ры́ло** snout; **~а́я котле́та** pork chop; **~о́е мя́со** pork; **~о́е са́ло** lard.
свинома́тк|а, и *f.* sow.
свинопа́с, а *m.* swineherd.
свинофе́рм|а, ы *f.* pig-farm, piggery.
сви́нский *adj.* (*coll.*) swinish; **с. посту́пок** swinish trick.
сви́нств|о, а *nt.* (*coll.*) swinishness; swinish trick.
свин|ти́ть, чу́, ти́шь *pf.* (*of* **~чивать**) **1.** to screw together. **2.** to unscrew.
сви́нтус, а *m.* (*coll., joc.*) swine, rogue.
свинц|ева́ть, у́ю *impf.* (*tech.*) to plate with lead.
свинцо́в|ый *adj.* lead; leaden; leaden-coloured; **~ые бели́ла** white lead; **с. блеск** (*min.*) galena; **~ая дробь** lead shot; **~ая кислота́** plumbic acid; **~ое отравле́ние** lead-poisoning; **~ая примо́чка** Goulard water; **~ая руда́** lead-ore; **с. су́рик** red lead, minium; **с. у́ксус** vinegar of lead; **с. шлак** lead dross, lead scoria.
сви́нчива|ть, ю *impf. of* **свинти́ть**
свин|ья́, ьи́, *pl.* **~ьи, ~ей** *f.* **1.** pig, swine; hog; sow; **морска́я с.** porpoise. **2.** (*fig.*) swine; cad; **вести́ себя́ ~ьёй** to behave caddishly; **подложи́ть ~ью́** (*+d.*; *coll.*) to play a dirty trick (on).
свире́л|ь, и *f.* (reed-)pipe.
свирепе́|ть, ю *impf.* to grow fierce, grow savage.
свире́пост|ь, и *f.* fierceness, ferocity, savageness; truculence.
свире́пств|овать, ую *impf.* to rage.
свире́п|ый *adj.* fierce, ferocious, savage; truculent; **~ая эпиде́мия** violent epidemic.
свиристе́л|ь, я *m.* (*zool.*) waxwing.
свис|а́ть, а́ю *impf.* (*of* **~нуть**) to hang down, droop, dangle; to trail.
сви́с|нуть, ну, нешь *pf. of* **~а́ть**
свист, а *m.* whistle; whistling; (*of birds*) singing, piping, warbling; hiss, hissing; **с. в карма́не** (*coll., joc.*) empty pockets.
сви|ста́ть, щу́, ~щешь *impf.* to whistle; (*of birds*) to sing, pipe, warble; **с. в свисто́к** to blow a whistle; **с. всех наве́рх** (*naut.*) to pipe all hands on deck.
сви|сте́ть, щу́, сти́шь *impf.* to whistle; to hiss; **ищи́ ~щи** (*coll.*) you can whistle for it; **с. в кула́к** to whistle for it.
сви́стн|уть, у, ешь *pf.* **1.** to give a whistle. **2.** (*coll.*) to slap, smack; **с. по́ уху** to clip on the ear. **3.** (*coll.*) to sneak (off with).
свист|о́к, ка́ *m.* whistle.
свистопля́ск|а, и *f.* (*coll.*) pandemonium, bedlam; **подня́ть ~у** to let all hell loose.
свисту́льк|а, и *f.* penny whistle, tin whistle.
свисту́н, а́ *m.* whistler.
сви́т|а, ы *f.* **1.** suite, retinue. **2.** (*geol.*) suit, series, set.
сви́тер, а *m.* sweater; **спорти́вный с.** sweatshirt.
сви́т|ок, ка *m.* roll, scroll.
свить, совью́, совьёшь, *past* **свил, свила́, сви́ло** *pf.* (*of* **вить** *and* **свива́ть**) to twist, wind.
сви́ться, совью́сь, совьёшься, *past* **сви́лся, свила́сь** *pf.* (*of* **ви́ться**) to roll up, curl up, coil.
свихн|у́ть, у́, ёшь *pf.* to dislocate, sprain; **с. себе́ ше́ю** (*fig., coll.*) to come a cropper; **с. с ума́** to go off one's head.
свихн|у́ться, у́сь, ёшься *pf.* (*coll.*) **1.** to go off one's head. **2.** to go astray, go off the rails.
свищ, а́ *m.* **1.** (*tech.*) flaw; (*in metals*) honeycomb. **2.** (*in wood*) knot hole. **3.** (*med.*) fistula.
свия́з|ь, и *f.* (*zool.*) wigeon.
свобо́д|а, ы *f.* freedom, liberty; **с. во́ли** free will; **с. рук** a free hand; **с. сло́ва** freedom of speech; **с. собра́ний** freedom of assembly; **с. со́вести** liberty of conscience; **с. торго́вли** free trade; **вы́пустить на ~у** to set free, set at liberty; **предоста́вить по́лную ~у де́йствий** (*+d.*) to give a free hand, give carte blanche; **на ~е** (*i*) at leisure, (*ii*) at large.
свобо́дно *adv.* **1.** freely; easily, with ease; fluently; **дыша́ть с.** to breathe freely; **она́ с. говори́т на пяти́ языка́х** she speaks five languages fluently. **2.** (*of clothing*) loose, loosely.
свобо́д|ный (~ен, ~на) *adj.* **1.** free (= *at liberty*). **2.** free (= *unhampered, unrestrained*); easy; **с. до́ступ** easy access; **с. уда́р** (*sport*) free kick; **с. от недоста́тков** free from defects; **челове́к ~ной профе́ссии** professional man. **3.** free (= *disengaged*); vacant; spare; **~ное вре́мя** free time, time off; spare time; **~ное ме́сто** vacant place, vacant seat; **вы ~ны сего́дня ве́чером?** will you be free this evening? **4.** free(-and-easy). **5.** (*of clothing*) loose, loose-fitting; flowing. **6.** (*chem.*) free, uncombined.
свободолюби́в|ый (~, ~а) *adj.* freedom-loving.
свободолю́би|е, я *nt.* love of freedom.
свободомы́сли|е, я *nt.* free-thinking.
свободомы́слящ|ий *adj.* free-thinking; *as n.* **с., ~его** *m.* free-thinker.
свод[1], а *m.* code; collection (*of documents, manuscripts, etc.*); **с. зако́нов** code of laws.
свод[2], а *m.* arch, vault; **небе́сный с.** the firmament, the vault of heaven.
сво|ди́ть[1], жу́, ~дишь *impf. of* **свести́**
сво|ди́ть[2], жу́, ~дишь *pf.* to take (*and bring back*); **вчера́ мы ~ди́ли дете́й в кино́** we took the children to the cinema yesterday.
сво|ди́ться, жу́сь, ~дишься *impf. of* **свести́сь**
сво́дк|а, и *f.* summary, résumé; report; **операти́вная с.** (*mil.*) summary of operations; **с. пого́ды** weather forecast, weather report.
сво́дник, а *m.* procurer, pander, pimp.
сво́днича|ть, ю *impf.* to procure, pander.
сво́дничеств|о, а *nt.* procuring, pandering, pimping.
сво́дн|ый *adj.* **1.** composite, combined; collated; **~ая афи́ша теа́тров** theatre guide (*bill listing all current productions*); **с. отря́д** (*mil.*) combined force; **~ая табли́ца** summary table, index. **2.** step-; **с. брат** step-brother.
сво́дн|я, и *f.* (*coll.*) procuress.
сво́дчатый *adj.* arched, vaulted.
своевла́ст|ный (~ен, ~на) *adj.* despotic.
своево́ли|е, я *nt.* self-will, wilfulness.
своево́льнича|ть, ю *impf.* to be self-willed, be wilful.
своево́л|ьный (~ен, ~ьна) *adj.* self-willed, wilful.
своевре́менно *adv.* in good time; opportunely.
своевре́мен|ный (~ен, ~на) *adj.* timely, opportune, well-timed.
своекоры́сти|е, я *nt.* self-interest.
своекоры́ст|ный (~ен, ~на) *adj.* self-interested, self-seeking.
своеко́штный *adj.* (*obs.*) (fee-)paying.
своенра́ви|е, я *nt.* wilfulness, waywardness, capriciousness.
своенра́в|ный (~ен, ~на) *adj.* wilful, wayward, capricious.
своеобра́зи|е, я *nt.* originality; peculiarity.
своеобра́з|ный (~ен, ~на) *adj.* original; peculiar, distinctive.
сво|зи́ть[1], жу́, ~зишь *impf. of* **свезти́**
сво|зи́ть[2], жу́, ~зишь *pf.* to take (*and bring back*); **мы ~зи́ли дете́й в цирк** we took the children to the circus.
свой *possessive adj.* one's (my, your, his, *etc., in accordance with subject of sentence or clause*), one's own; **у них с. дом** they have a house of their own; **своё варе́нье** one's own, home-made jam; **свои́ войска́** friendly troops; **кри́кнуть не свои́м го́лосом** to give a frenzied scream; **умере́ть свое́й сме́ртью** to die a natural death; **в своё вре́мя** (*i*) at one time, in my, his, etc., time, (*ii*) in due time, in due course; **в своём ро́де** in one's own way; **он не в своём уме́** he is not right in the head; **на свои́х на двои́х** on Shanks' mare, pony; **она́ сама́ не своя́** she is

not herself; **он у нас с. челове́к** he's one of us; he's quite at home here; *as n.* **свои́** one's (own) people; **своё** one's own; **доби́ться своего́** to get one's own way; to hold one's own; **получи́ть своё** to get one's own back.

сво́йственник, а *m.* relation, relative by marriage; **он мне с.** he is related to me by marriage.

сво́йствен|ный (~ *and* ~ен, ~на) *adj.* (+*d.*) characteristic (of).

сво́йств|о, а *nt.* property, quality, attribute, characteristic.

свойств|о́, а *nt.* relationship by marriage, affinity; **быть в ~е́ с кем-н.** to be related to s.o. by marriage.

свола́кива|ть, ю *impf. of* **своло́чь**

сволочно́й *adj.* (*coll.*) worthless, rubbishy.

сво́лоч|ь, и, *g. pl.* **~е́й** *f.* (*coll.*) **1.** (*as term of abuse*) scum, swine. **2.** (*collect.*) riff-raff, dregs.

своло́|чь, ку́, чёшь, ку́т, *past* **~к, ~кла́** *pf.* (*of* **свола́кивать**) (*coll.*) **1.** to drag off. **2.** (*fig.*) to knock off.

сво́р|а, ы *f.* **1.** leash; (*fig.*) pair (*of greyhounds*). **2.** (*collect.*) pack (*of hounds*); (*fig.*) gang.

свора́чива|ть, ю *impf. of* **сверну́ть** *and* **свороти́ть**

свор|ова́ть, у́ю *pf. of* **ворова́ть**

своро|ти́ть, чу́, ~́тишь *pf.* (*of* **свора́чивать**) (*coll.*) **1.** to dislodge, displace, shift. **2.** to turn, swing (*also trans.*); **с. с доро́ги** to turn off the road; **с. с ума́** to go off one's head. **3.** to twist, dislocate; to break.

своя́к, а́ *m.* brother-in-law (*husband of wife's sister*).

своя́чениц|а, ы *f.* sister-in-law (*wife's sister*).

СВЧ-печ|ь, и *f.* (*abbr. of* **сверхвысокочасто́тная печь**) microwave (oven).

свык|а́ться, а́юсь *impf. of* **~́нуться**

свы́к|нуться, нусь, нешься, *past* **~ся, ~лась** *pf.* (*of* **~а́ться**) (**с**+*i.*) to get used (to), accustom o.s. (to).

свысока́ *adv.* (*pej.*) in a haughty manner, condescendingly; **обраща́ться с кем-н. с.** to condescend to, patronize s.o.

свы́ше 1. *adv.* from above; (*relig.*) from on high. **2.** *prep.*+*g.* over, more than; beyond; **с. ты́сячи самолётов уча́ствовало в налёте** over a thousand planes took part in the raid; **э́то с. мои́х сил** it is beyond me.

свя́з|анный *p.p.p. of* **~а́ть** *and adj.* **1.** constrained; **~анная речь** halting utterance. **2.** (*chem.*) combined, bound.

свя|за́ть, жу́, ~́жешь *pf.* (*of* **вяза́ть** *and* **~́зывать**) **1.** to tie; to bind (*also fig.*); **с. в у́зел** to bundle (up); **с. по рука́м и нога́м** to tie, bind hand and foot (*also fig.*); **с. обеща́нием** to bind by promise; **с. свою́ судьбу́ (с**+*i.*) to throw in one's lot (with). **2.** (*fig.*) to connect, link; **быть (те́сно) ~́занным, ~́зано (с**+*i.*) to be (closely) connected (with), be bound up (with), be tied up (with). **3. (быть) ~́зано (с**+*i.*; *fig.*) to involve, entail; **э́то предприя́тие бу́дет ~́зано с огро́мными расхо́дами** this undertaking will involve huge expense. **4.** to connect, associate; **не́которые ~за́ли эпиде́мию с. плохи́м водоснабже́нисм** some connected the epidemic with the bad water-supply.

свя|за́ться, жу́сь, ~́жешься *pf.* (*of* **~́зываться**) **(с**+*i.*) **1.** to get in touch (with), communicate (with); **с. по ра́дио** to establish a radio link. **2.** (*coll.*, *pej.*) to get involved (with), get mixed up (with).

связи́ст, а *m.* **1.** (*mil.*) signaller; member of Signal Corps. **2.** postal *and/or* telecommunications worker.

свя́зк|а, и *f.* **1.** sheaf, bunch; **с. бума́г** sheaf of papers; **с. ключе́й** bunch of keys. **2.** (*anat.*) cord; ligament; copula; **голосовы́е ~и** vocal cords. **3.** (*gram.*) copula.

связн|о́й *adj.* (*mil.*) liaison, communication; **с. самолёт** liaison aircraft; **~а́я соба́ка** messenger dog; *as n.* **с., ~о́го** *m.* messenger, runner, orderly.

свя́зный *adj.* connected, coherent.

свя́зочный *adj.* (*anat.*) ligamentous.

свя́зу́ющий *adj.* connecting, linking.

свя́зыва|ть, ю *impf. of* **связа́ть**

свя́зыва|ться, юсь *impf.* **1.** *impf. of* **связа́ться. 2.** *impf. only* (**с**+*i.*) to have to do (with); **не ~йся с ни́ми** don't have anything to do with them.

связ|ь, и, о ~́и, в ~́й *f.* **1.** connection; **причи́нная с.** (*phil.*) causation; **в ~и́ с э́тим** in this connection. **2.** link, tie, bond; **дру́жеские ~́и** friendly relations, ties of friendship; **с. Великобрита́нии с содру́жеством на́ций** the link between Great Britain and the Commonwealth; **потеря́ть с. (с**+*i.*) to lose touch (with). **3.** (*sexual*) liaison, association; **вступи́ть в с. (с**+*i.*) to form an association (with). **4.** (*pl.*) connections, contacts; **у него́ мно́го влия́тельных ~́ей в Москве́** he has many influential connections in Moscow. **5.** communication; (*mil.*) intercommunication; signals; liaison; **возду́шная с.** aerial communication; **с. по ра́дио** radio communication; **с. с во́здухом** (*mil.*) ground-air communication; **с. с землёй** (*mil.*) air-ground communication. **6.** (*sg. only*) (postal and tele-) communications; **Министе́рство ~́и** Ministry of Communications; **отделе́ние ~́и** (branch) post office; **рабо́тник ~и** post office worker. **7.** (*tech.*) tie, stay, brace, strut; (*elec.*) coupling.

святе́йшеств|о, а *nt.*: **его́ с.** (*title of Patriarchs and of the Pope*) His Holiness.

святе́йший *adj.* most holy (*pertaining to the Patriarchs and synod of the Orthodox Church, also to the Pope*); **с. патриа́рх** His Holiness the Patriarch; **с. престо́л** the papal throne.

святи́лищ|е, а *nt.* sanctuary.

святи́тел|ь, я *m.* prelate.

свя|ти́ть, чу́, ти́шь *impf.* (*of* **о~**) to consecrate; to bless, sanctify.

свя́т|ки, ок *no sg.* Christmas-tide.

свя́то *adv.* piously; religiously; **с. бере́чь** to treasure; **с. чтить** to hold sacred.

свя́т|о́й (~, ~а́, ~́о) *adj.* **1.** holy; sacred (*also fig.*); **~а́я вода́** holy water; **с. долг** sacred duty; **с. дух** the Holy Ghost, the Holy Spirit; **~а́я (неде́ля)** Holy Week; **~а́я ~ы́х** holy of holies, sanctum. **2.** saintly. **3.** (*fig.*) pious. **4.** *preceding name, or as n.* **с., ~о́го** *m.*, **~а́я, ~о́й** *f.* saint; **причи́слить к ли́ку ~ы́х** (*eccl.*) to canonize.

свя́тост|ь, и *f.* holiness; sanctity.

святота́т|ец, ца *m.* pers. committing sacrilege.

святота́тственный *adj.* sacrilegious.

святота́тств|о, а *nt.* sacrilege.

святота́тств|овать, ую *impf.* to commit sacrilege.

свя́т|очный *adj. of* **~ки; с. расска́з** Christmas tale.

святош|а, и *c.g.* sanctimonious pers.

свя́тц|ы, ев *no sg.* (church) calendar.

святы́н|я, и *f.* **1.** (*eccl.*) object of worship; sacred place. **2.** (*fig.*) sacred object.

свяще́нник, а *m.* priest (*of Orthodox Church*); clergyman.

свяще́ннический *adj.* priestly; sacerdotal.

священноде́йстви|е, я *nt.* **1.** religious rite. **2.** (*fig.*) solemn performance (of ceremony, duties, *etc.*).

священноде́йств|овать, ую *impf.* **1.** to perform a religious rite. **2.** (*fig.*) to do sth. with solemnity, with pomp.

священнослужи́тел|ь, я *m.* clergyman (*priest or deacon*).

свяще́н|ный (~ен, ~на) *adj.* holy; sacred (*also fig.*); **~ное писа́ние** Holy Writ, Scripture; **С. сою́з** (*hist.*) the Holy Alliance.

свяще́нств|о, а *nt.* priesthood (*also collect.*).

с. г. (*abbr. of* **сего́ го́да**) of this year.

сгиб, а *m.* **1.** bend. **2.** (*anat.*) flexion.

сгиба́ем|ый (~, ~а) *adj.* flexible, pliable.

сгиба́|ть(ся), ю(сь) *impf. of* **согну́ть(ся)**

сги́н|уть, у, ешь *pf.* (*coll.*) to disappear, vanish; **~ь с глаз мои́х!** out of my sight!

сгла́|дить, жу, дишь *pf.* (*of* **~живать**) **1.** to smooth out. **2.** (*fig.*) to smooth over, soften.

сгла́|диться, дится *pf.* (*of* **~живаться**) **1.** to become smooth. **2.** (*fig.*) to be smoothed over, be softened; to diminish, abate.

сгла́жива|ть(ся), ю(сь) *impf. of* **сгла́дить(ся)**

сглаз, а (у) *m.* (*coll.*) the evil eye.

сгла́|зить, жу, зишь *pf.* to put the evil eye (on, upon); (*fig.*, *coll.*) to endanger the success (of) (*an undertaking, etc., by forecasting the outcome*); **что́бы не с.!** touch wood!

сглуп|и́ть, лю́, и́шь *pf. of* **глупи́ть**

сгнива́|ть, ю *impf. of* **сгнить**

сгни|ть, ю́, ёшь *pf.* (*of* **гнить** *and* **~ва́ть**) to rot, decay.

сгно|и́ть, ю́, и́шь *pf. of* **гнои́ть**

сгова́рива|ть(ся), ю(сь) *impf. of* **сговори́ть(ся)**

сго́вор, а *m.* **1.** (*obs.*) betrothal. **2.** (*usu. pej.*) agreement, compact, deal.
сговор|и́ть, ю́, и́шь *pf.* (*of* **сгова́ривать**) (*obs.*) to give consent to the marriage (of); to betroth.
сговор|и́ться, ю́сь, и́шься *pf.* (*of* **сгова́риваться**) (**с**+*i.*) **1.** to arrange (with), make an appointment (with); **мы ~и́лись встре́титься с ни́ми при вхо́де в парк** we arranged to meet them at the entrance to the park. **2.** to come to an arrangement (with), reach an understanding (with).
сгово́рчивост|ь, и *f.* compliancy, tractability.
сгово́рчив|ый (~, ~а) *adj.* compliant, complaisant, tractable.
сгон, а *m.* driving; herding, rounding-up.
сго́нк|а, и *f.* rafting, floating.
сго́нный *adj.* **1.** rounding up; rounded up; **~ая рабо́та** rounding up, herding. **2.** rafting, floating.
сго́нщик, а *m.* **1.** herdsman, drover. **2.** (lumber-)rafter.
сгоня́|ть, ю *impf. of* **согна́ть**
сгора́ни|е, я *nt.* combustion; **дви́гатель вну́треннего ~я** internal-combustion engine.
сгор|а́ть, а́ю *impf.* **1.** *impf. of* **~е́ть. 2.** (**от**; *fig.*) to burn (with); **с. от стыда́, любопы́тства** to burn with shame, curiosity.
сго́рб|ить(ся), лю(сь), ишь(ся) *pf. of* **го́рбить(ся)**
сго́рб|ленный *p.p.p. of* **~ить** *and adj.* crooked, bent; hunchbacked.
сгор|е́ть, ю́, и́шь *pf.* (*of* **~а́ть**) **1.** to burn down; to be burnt out, down; **наш дом ~е́л** our house was burnt down. **2.** (*of fuel*) to be consumed, be used up; **за год у нас ~е́ло три це́нтнера у́гля** in the year we burned three hundredweight of coal. **3.** (*fig., coll.*) to burn o.s. out.
сгоряча́ *adv.* in the heat of the moment; in a fit of temper.
сгреба́|ть, ю *impf. of* **сгрести́**
сгре|сти́, бу́, бёшь, *past* **~́б, ~бла́** *pf.* (*of* **~ба́ть**) **1.** to rake up, rake together. **2.** (**с**+*g.*) to shovel (off, from); **с. снег с кры́ши** to shovel snow off the roof.
сгруд|и́ться, и́тся *pf.* (*coll.*) to crowd, mill, bunch.
сгружа́|ть, ю *impf. of* **сгрузи́ть**
сгру|зи́ть, жу́, ~́зишь *pf.* (*of* **~жа́ть**) to unload.
сгруппир|ова́ть(ся), у́ю(сь) *pf. of* **группирова́ть(ся)**
сгрыза́|ть, ю *impf. of* **сгрызть**
сгрыз|ть, у́, ёшь, *past* **~, ~́ла** *pf.* (*of* **~а́ть**) to chew (up).
сгуб|и́ть, лю́, ~́ишь *pf.* (*coll.*) to ruin.
сгу|сти́ть, щу́, сти́шь *pf.* (*of* **~ща́ть**) to thicken; to condense; **с. кра́ски** (*fig.*) to lay it on thick.
сгу|сти́ться, сти́тся *pf.* (*of* **~ща́ться**) to thicken; to condense; to clot.
сгу́ст|ок, ка *m.* clot; **с. кро́ви** clot of blood.
сгуща́|ть(ся), ю, ет(ся) *impf. of* **сгусти́ть(ся)**
сгуще́ни|е, я *nt.* thickening, condensation; clotting.
сгу|щённый *p.p.p. of* **~сти́ть** *and adj.*; **~щённое молоко́** condensed milk, evaporated milk.
сда́брива|ть, ю *impf. of* **сдо́брить**
сда|ва́ть, ю́, ёшь *impf. of* **сдать; с. экза́мен** to take, sit an examination.
сда|ва́ться[1]**, ю́сь, ёшься** *impf. of* **~́ться**[1]
сда|ва́ться[2]**, ётся** *impf.* (*impers., coll.*) it seems; **мне ~ётся** it seems to me; I think.
сдав|и́ть, лю́, ~́ишь *pf.* (*of* **~́ливать**) to squeeze.
сда́влива|ть, ю *impf. of* **сдави́ть**
сда́точн|ый *adj.* delivery; **~ая квита́нция** receipt; **с. пункт** delivery point.
сда́тчик, а *m.* deliverer.
сдать[1]**, сдам, сдашь, сдаст, сдади́м, сдади́те, сдаду́т,** *past* **сдал, сдала́, сда́ло** *pf.* (*of* **сдава́ть**) **1.** to hand over, pass; **с. дела́ прее́мнику** to hand over to one's successor; **с. бага́ж на хране́ние** to deposit, leave one's luggage; **с. в архи́в** (*fig., coll.*) to give up as a bad job, write off. **2.** to let, let out, hire out; **с. в аре́нду** to lease. **3.** to give change; **с. пятьдеся́т копе́ек** to give fifty kopecks change. **4.** to surrender, yield, give up; **с. пе́рвенство** (*sport*) to yield first place. **5.** to pass (*an examination, examination subject, etc.*); **он сдал то́лько лати́нь** he only passed in Latin. **6.** to deal (*cards*).
сдать[2]**, сдам, сдашь, сдаст, сдади́м, сдади́те, сдаду́т** *pf.* (*of* **сдава́ть**) **1.** to give out, give way; **мото́р сдал** the engine gave out. **2.** to be weakened, be in a reduced state.
сда́|ться[1]**, мся, шься, стся, дн́мся, ди́тесь, ду́тся,** *past* **~лся** *pf.* (*of* **~ва́ться**[1]) to surrender, yield; (*chess*) to resign; **с. на про́сьбы** to yield to entreaties.
сда́|ться[2]**,** *not used in fut.*, **~лся, ~ла́сь** *pf.* (*coll.*) to be necessary; **на что нам ~ли́сь их сове́ты?** what need had we of advice from them?
сда́ч|а, и *f.* **1.** handing over. **2.** letting out, hiring out; **с. в аре́нду** leasing. **3.** surrender. **4.** change; **три рубля́ ~и** three roubles change; **с. с рубля́** change from one rouble; **дать ~и** (*+d.*; *fig., coll.*) to give as good as one got. **5.** (*cards*) deal; **ва́ша с.** it is your deal.
сдва́ива|ть, ю *impf. of* **сдвои́ть**
сдвиг, а *m.* **1.** displacement; (*geol.*) fault, dislocation; (*tech.*) shear; **с. фа́з** (*elec.*) phase shift. **2.** (*fig.*) change (for the better), improvement.
сдвига́|ть(ся), ю(сь) *impf. of* **сдви́нуть(ся)**
сдвижн|о́й *adj.* movable; **~а́я ма́чта** (*naut.*) telescopic mast.
сдви́нут|ый *p.p.p. of* **~ь** *and adj.*; **с. по фа́зе** (*elec.*) out of phase.
сдви́|нуть, ну, нешь *pf.* (*of* **~га́ть**) **1.** to shift, move, displace; **его́ с ме́ста не ~нешь** he won't budge; **с. с ме́ста** (*fig.*) to get moving, set in motion. **2.** to move together, bring together; **с. бро́ви** to knit one's brows.
сдви́|нуться, нусь, нешься *pf.* (*of* **~га́ться**) **1.** to move, budge; **с. с ме́ста** (*fig.*) to progress; **де́ло не ~нулось с ме́ста** no headway has been made. **2.** to come together.
сдво|и́ть, ю, и́шь *pf.* (*of* **сдва́ивать**) to double.
сде́ла|ть(ся), ю(сь) *pf. of* **де́лать(ся)**
сде́лк|а, и *f.* transaction, deal, bargain; **войти́ в ~у** (**с**+*i.*) to strike a bargain (with); **заключи́ть ~у** to conclude a bargain, do a deal.
сде́льно *adv.* by the job.
сде́льн|ый *adj.* piecework; **~ая опла́та** payment by the piece, by the job; **~ая рабо́та** piecework.
сде́льщик, а *m.* piece-worker.
сде́льщин|а, ы *f.* piece-work.
сдёргива|ть, ю *impf. of* **сдёрнуть**
сде́ржанно *adv.* with restraint, with reserve.
сде́ржанност|ь, и *f.* restraint, reserve.
сде́ржан|ный *p.p.p. of* **сдержа́ть** *and* **(~, ~на)** *adj.* restrained, reserved.
сдерж|а́ть[1]**, у́, ~́ишь** *pf.* (*of* **~́ивать**) **1.** to hold (back); to hold in check, contain; **с. проти́вника** to hold the enemy in check. **2.** (*fig.*) to keep back, restrain; **с. слёзы** to suppress tears.
сдерж|а́ть[2]**, у́, ~́ишь** *pf.* (*of* **~́ивать**) to keep (*a promise, etc.*); **с. сло́во** to keep one's word.
сдерж|а́ться, у́сь, ~́ишься *pf.* (*of* **~́иваться**) to control o.s.; to restrain o.s., contain o.s.; to check o.s.
сде́ржива|ть(ся), ю(сь) *impf. of* **сдержа́ть(ся)**
сдёр|нуть, ну, нешь *pf.* (*of* **~гивать**) to pull off.
сдира́|ть, ю *impf. of* **содра́ть**
сдо́б|а, ы *f.* **1.** (*cul.*) shortening. **2.** (fancy) cake, bun (*also collect*).
сдо́бн|ый *adj.* (*cul.*) rich, short; **~ая бу́лка** bun; **~ое те́сто** fancy pastry.
сдо́бр|ить, ю, ишь *pf.* (*of* **сда́бривать**) (*+i.*) to flavour (with), spice (with); to add to taste.
сдоброва́ть *only in phr.* **ему́** *etc.*, **не с.** (*coll.*) it will be a bad look out for him, *etc.*
сдо́хн|уть, у, ешь *pf.* (*of* **сдыха́ть**) (*of cattle, also coll. of people*) to die.
сдре́йф|ить, лю, ишь *pf. of* **дре́йфить**
сдруж|и́ть, у́, и́шь *pf.* to bring together, unite in friendship.
сдруж|и́ться, у́сь, и́шься *pf.* (**с**+*i.*) to become friends (with).
сдува́|ть, ю *impf. of* **сдуть**
сду́ру *adv.* (*coll.*) stupidly, not thinking what one was doing; **он с. забы́л ключ до́ма** he stupidly left his key at home.
сду|ть, ~́ю, ~́ешь *pf.* (*of* **~ва́ть**) **1.** to blow away, blow off. **2.** (**с**+*g.*, **у**; *school sl.*) to crib (from).
сдыха́|ть, ю *impf. of* **сдо́хнуть**

се *particle* (*arch.*) lo, behold.
сё, сего́ *pron.* this (*arch. exc. in certain set phrr.*; *see* **тот**).
сеа́нс, а *m.* **1.** (*in cinema, etc.*) performance, showing, house; **после́дний с.** the last showing, the last house. **2.** sitting; **написа́ть чей-н. портре́т в двена́дцать ~ов** to paint s.o.'s portrait in twelve sittings.
СЕАТО *nt. indecl.* SEATO (*abbr. of* South-East Asia Treaty Organization — *Организа́ция догово́ра Юго-Восто́чной А́зии*).
себе́[1] *see* **себя́**
себе́[2] *particle* (*coll.*) *modifying v. or pron. and usu. containing hint of reproach*; **он с. идёт вперёд** he just goes ahead; **а они́ с. молча́ли** and they just kept their mouths shut; **он о́чень с. на уме́** he is very crafty, wily; **ничего́ с.** not bad; **так с.** so-so.
себесто́имост|ь, и *f.* (*econ.*) cost (*of manufacture*); cost price; **прода́ть по ~и** to sell at cost price.
себя́, себе́, собо́й (собо́ю), о себе́ *refl. pron.* oneself; myself, yourself, himself, *etc.*; **собо́ю** in appearance; **хоро́ш собо́ю** nice-looking; **прийти́ в с. (от)** to get over; to come to one's senses; **не в себе́** not o.s.; **от с.** (*i*) away from o.s., outwards, (*ii*) for o.s., on one's own behalf; **рабо́та не по себе́** work that is beyond one; **ка́к-то не по себе́** not quite o.s.; **чита́ть про с.** to read to o.s.; **у с.** at home, at one's (own) place.
себялю́б|ец, ца *m.* egoist.
себялюби́в|ый (~, ~а) *adj.* egoistical, selfish.
себялю́би|е, я *nt.* self-love, egoism.
сев, а *m.* sowing.
се́вер, а *m.* north.
се́率вернее *adv.* (*+g.*) to the north (of).
се́верн|ый *adj.* north, northern; northerly; **с. оле́нь** reindeer; **~ое сия́ние** northern lights, Aurora Borealis.
Се́верн|ый Ледови́т|ый океа́н, ~ого ~ого ~а *m.* the Arctic Ocean.
Се́верн|ый Поля́рн|ый круг, ~ого ~ого ~а *m.* the Arctic Circle.
се́веро-восто́к, а *m.* north-east.
се́веро-восто́чный *adj.* north-east, north-eastern.
се́веро-за́пад, а *m.* north-west.
се́веро-за́падный *adj.* north-west, north-western.
северя́н|ин, ина, *pl.* **~е, ~** *m.* northerner.
севооборо́т, а *m.* rotation of crops.
севр, а *m.* Sèvres (*porcelain*).
се́вр|ский *adj. of* **~**
севрю́г|а, и *f.* stellate sturgeon (*Acipenser stellatus*).
сегме́нт, а *m.* segment.
сегмента́ци|я, и *f.* segmentation.
сего́дня *adv.* today; **с. ве́чером** this evening, tonight; **не с.-за́втра** any day now.
сего́дня|шний *adj. of* **~**; **с. день** today; **~шняя газе́та** today's paper.
седа́лищ|е, а *nt.* (*anat.*) seat, buttocks.
седа́лищн|ый *adj.* (*anat.*) sciatic; **воспале́ние ~ого не́рва** (*med.*) sciatica.
седе́льник, а *m.* saddler.
седе́льн|ый *adj. of* **седло́; ~ая лука́** saddle-bow.
седе́|ть, ю *impf.* (*of* **по~**) to go grey, turn grey.
седе́|ющий *pres. part. act. of* **~ть** *and adj.* grizzled, greying.
седи́л|ь, я *m.* cedilla.
седин|а́, ы́, *pl.* **~́ы, ~́** *f.* **1.** grey hair(s). **2.** grey streak (*in fur*).
седла́|ть, ю *impf.* (*of* **о~**) to saddle.
сед|ло́, ла́, *pl.* **~̈ла, ~̈ел** *nt.* saddle.
седлови́н|а, ы *f.* **1.** arch, saddle (*of back of animal*). **2.** (*geog.*) col, saddle.
седоборо́д|ый (~) *adj.* grey-bearded.
седовла́с|ый (~, ~а) *adj.* grey-haired.
седоволо́с|ый (~, ~а) *adj.* = **седовла́сый**
сед|о́й (~, ~а́, ~́о) *adj.* (*of hair*) grey, gray; hoary; grey-haired; flecked with white; **~а́я старина́** hoary antiquity.
седо́к, а *m.* **1.** fare (*passenger*). **2.** rider, horseman.
седьм|о́й *adj.* seventh; **быть на ~о́м не́бе** to be in the seventh heaven; **одна́ ~а́я** one seventh.
сеза́м, а *m.* (*bot.*) sesame; **с., откро́йся!** open sesame!
сезо́н, а *m.* season.
сезо́нник, а *m.* seasonal worker.
сезо́нн|ый *adj.* seasonal; **с. биле́т** season ticket; **~ые рабо́ты** seasonal work.
сей *m.*, **сия́** *f.*, **сие́** *nt.*, *pl.* **сии́** *pron.* this; **сию́ мину́ту** this (very) minute; at once, instantly; **сего́ го́да** of this year; **сего́ ме́сяца** (*abbr.* **с. м.**) of this month; **ва́ше письмо́ от 16-го с. м.** (*formula of official correspondence*) your letter of the 16th inst.; **до сих пор** up to now, till now, hitherto; (*obs.*) up to here, up to this point; **на с. раз** this time, for this once; **о сю по́ру** (*obs.*) at the present time; **по сю по́ру** (*obs.*) up to now, up to the present; **под сим ка́мнем поко́ится** here lies; **при сём прилага́ется** (there is) enclosed herewith; herewith please find.
сейм, а *m. m.* (*hist., representative assembly*) diet; (*in Poland*) the Sejm.
се́йн|а, ы *f.* seine.
се́йнер, а *m.* seiner.
сейсми́ческий *adj.* seismic.
сейсмо́граф, а *m.* seismograph.
сейсмогра́фи|я, и *f.* seismography.
сейсмологи́ческий *adj.* seismological.
сейсмоло́ги|я, и *f.* seismology.
сейсмо́метр, а *m.* seismometer.
сейсмоопа́с|ный (~ен, ~на) *adj.* earthquake-prone.
сейсмосто́йкий *adj.* earthquake-proof.
сейф, а *m.* safe.
сейча́с *adv.* **1.** now, at present, at the (present) moment; **они́ с. в Аме́рике** they are in America at present. **2.** just, just now (= *in the immediate past*); **она́ с. вы́шла** she has just gone out. **3.** presently, soon; **с. же** at once, immediately; **с.!** in a minute!; half a minute! **4.** (*coll.*) straight away, immediately; **с. бы́ло ви́дно, что ему́ э́то не нра́вилось** it was immediately apparent that he did not like it.
Сейше́льск|ие остров|а́, ~их ~о́в *no sg.* the Seychelles (*islands*).
сек. (*abbr. of* **секу́нда**) sec., second(s).
се́канс, а *m.* (*math.*) secant.
сека́тор, а *m.* secateurs.
секве́стр, а *m.* **1.** (*leg.*) sequestration; **наложи́ть с. (на+*a.*)** to sequestrate. **2.** (*med.*) sequestrum.
секвестр|ова́ть, у́ю *impf. and pf.* (*leg.*) to sequestrate.
секи́р|а, ы *f.* pole-axe; hatchet, axe.
секре́т[1], **а** *m.* **1.** secret; **по ~у** secretly, confidentially, in confidence; **под больши́м ~ом** in strict confidence; **с. полишине́ля** open secret. **2.** hidden mechanism. **3.** (*mil.*) listening post.
секре́т[2], **а** *m.* (*physiol.*) secretion.
секретариа́т, а *m.* secretariat.
секрета́рский *adj.* secretarial; secretary's.
секрета́рств|о, а *nt.* secretaryship; secretarial duties.
секрета́рств|овать, ую *impf.* to be a secretary, act as secretary.
секрета́р|ша, ши *f.* (*coll.*) *f. of* **~ь 1.**
секрета́р|ь, я́ *m.* **1.** (*administrative assistant*) secretary; **ли́чный с.** private secretary, personal secretary; **2.** (*official*) **генера́льный с.** secretary-general; **непреме́нный с.** permanent secretary.
секре́тнича|ть, ю *impf.* (*coll.*) **1.** to be secretive; to keep things secret, keep things dark. **2.** to converse in confidential tones.
секре́тно *adv.* secretly, in secret; **сообщи́ть с.** to tell in confidence; (*on documents, etc.*) 'secret', 'confidential'; **соверше́нно с.** 'top secret'.
секре́тност|ь, и *f.* secrecy.
секре́т|ный (~ен, ~на) *adj.* secret; confidential; **с. замо́к** combination lock; **с. прика́з** secret order; **с. сотру́дник** secret agent, undercover agent.
секрето́рный *adj.* (*physiol.*) secretory.
секре́ци|я, и *f.* (*physiol.*) secretion.
секс, а *m.* sex; **с. вне бра́ка** extramarital sex.
сексапи́льност|ь, и *f.* sex appeal.
сексапи́л|ьный (~ен, ~ьна) *adj.* sexy.
сексо́т, а *m.* (*abbr. of* **секре́тный сотру́дник**) secret agent, undercover agent.

се́кст|а, ы *f.* (*mus.*) sixth.
секста́нт, а *m.* sextant.
сексте́т, а *m.* (*mus.*) sextet.
сексуа́льност|ь, и *f.* sexuality.
сексуа́л|ьный (~ен, ~ьна) *adj.* sexual.
се́кт|а, ы *f.* sect.
секта́нт, а *m.* sectarian; member of a sect.
секта́нтский *adj.* sectarian.
секта́нтств|о, а *nt.* sectarianism.
се́ктор, а *m.* **1.** (*math., mil.*) sector; **с. обстре́ла** (*mil.*) sector of fire, zone of fire; **с. Га́за** the Gaza Strip. **2.** (*fig.*) section, part, zone, sphere; (*econ.*) sector; **с. ка́дров** personnel section; **госуда́рственный с. хозя́йства** State(-owned) sector of economy.
секуляриза́ци|я, и *f.* secularization.
секуляриз|ова́ть, у́ю *impf. and pf.* to secularize.
секу́нд|а, ы *f.* (*of time*) second; **сию́ ~у!** just a moment!
секунда́нт, а *m.* (*in a duel or in boxing*) second.
секу́нд|ный *adj. of* **~а**; **~ная стре́лка** second hand.
секундоме́р, а *m.* stop-watch.
секу́щ|ая, ей *f.* (*math.*) secant.
секци|о́нный *adj.* **1.** sectional; modular. **2.** *adj. of* **~я²**; **с. зал** dissection-room.
секцио́нн|ая, ой *f.* dissection-room.
се́кци|я¹, и *f.* **1.** section. **2.** unit (*of furniture*).
се́кци|я², и *f.* dissection.
селадо́н, а *m.* (*obs.*) ladies' man, womanizer.
сел|ево́й *adj. of* **~ь**
селёдк|а, и *f.* herring.
селёдочниц|а, ы *f.* herring-dish.
селёд|очный *adj. of* **~ка**
селезёнк|а, и *f.* (*physiol.*) spleen; **воспале́ние ~и** (*med.*) splenitis.
се́лез|ень, ня *m.* drake.
селекти́вност|ь, и *f.* (*radio*) selectivity.
селе́ктор, а *m.* intercom.
селекцио́нный *adj.* (*agric.*) selection.
селекци|я, и *f.* (*agric.*) selection, breeding.
селе́ни|е, я *nt.* settlement.
селени́стый *adj.* (*chem.*) selenious; selenide (of).
селени́т¹, а *m.* (*min.*) selenite.
селени́т², а *m.* Moon-man (*in science fiction*).
селе́новый *adj.* (*chem.*) selenium, selenic.
сели́тебный *adj.* built-up; (allocated for) building, development.
сели́тр|а, ы *f.* (*chem.*) saltpetre, nitre; **кали́йная с.** potassium nitrate.
сели́тр|яный *adj. of* **~а**; **~яная кислота́** nitric acid.
сел|и́ть, ю́ и́шь *impf.* (*of* **по~**) to settle.
сели́тьб|а, ы *f.* **1.** developed land. **2.** settlement.
сел|и́ться, ю́сь, и́шься *impf.* (*of* **по~**) to settle.
сел|о́, а́, *pl.* **~а** *nt.* village; **на ~е́** (*collect.*) in the country; **ни к ~у́, не к го́роду** (*coll.*) for no reason at all; neither here nor there.
сел|ь, я *m.* (seasonal) mountain torrent.
сель... *comb. form, abbr. of* **се́льский**
сельдере́|й, я *m.* celery.
сельд|ь, и, *pl.* **~и, ~е́й** *f.* herring; **как ~и в бо́чке** (*coll.*) like sardines (*of a crowd*).
сельд|яно́й *adj. of* **~ь**
селько́р, а *m.* (*abbr. of* **се́льский корреспонде́нт**) rural correspondent.
сельпо́ *nt. indecl.* (*abbr. of* **се́льское потреби́тельское о́бщество**) village (general) store, village shop.
се́льск|ий *adj.* **1.** country, rural; **~ая ме́стность** rural area; countryside; **~ое хозя́йство** agriculture, farming. **2.** village.
сельскохозя́йственный *adj.* agricultural, farming.
сельсове́т, а *m.* village soviet.
се́льтерск|ий *adj.*: **~ая вода́** seltzer water.
сельхоз... *comb. form, as abbr. of* **сельскохозя́йственный**
селян|и́н, и́на, *pl.* **~е, ~** *m.* (*obs.*) peasant, villager.
селя́н|ка¹, ки *f. of* **~и́н**
селя́нк|а², и *f.* (*cul.*) hot-pot; **сбо́рная с.** (*fig.*) hotchpotch, hodgepodge.
сема́нтик|а, и *f.* **1.** semantics. **2.** meanings (*of a particular word*).
семанти́ческий *adj.* semantic.
семасиологи́ческий *adj.* semasiological.
семасиоло́ги|я, и *f.* semasiology.
семафо́р, а *m.* (*rail. and naut.*) semaphore, signal-post; **с. откры́т** the signal is down.
семафо́р|ить, ю *impf.* to semaphore.
сёмг|а, и *f.* salmon.
семе́йн|ый *adj.* **1.** family; domestic; **с. ве́чер** family party; **с. круг** family circle; **по ~ым обстоя́тельствам** for domestic reasons; **о́тпуск по ~ым обстоя́тельствам** (*mil.*) compassionate leave. **2.** having a family; **с. челове́к** family man.
семе́йственност|ь, и *f.* **1.** attachment to family life. **2.** (*pej.*) nepotism; use of 'influence'.
семе́йственн|ый *adj.* **1.** attached to family life. **2.** (*fig., pej.*) conducted by 'arrangement', by 'influence'; **~ые отноше́ния** 'old boy system'.
семе́йств|о, а *nt.* family.
семена́ *see* **се́мя**
семен|и́ть, ю́, и́шь *impf.* to mince (*of gait*).
семен|и́ться, и́тся *impf.* (*agric.*) to seed.
семенни́к, а́ *m.* **1.** (*biol.*) testicle. **2.** (*bot.*) pericarp; **~и́ трав** grass seeds.
семенн|о́й *adj.* **1.** seed; **с. карто́фель** seed potato. **2.** (*biol.*) seminal, spermatic; **~а́я нить** spermatozoon.
семенево́дств|о, а *n* seed-growing.
семенево́д|ческий *adj. of* **~ство**
семери́чный *adj.* septenary.
семёрк|а, и *f.* **1.** seven; number seven (*bus, tram, etc.*). **2.: с. треф** *etc.* (*cards*) the seven of clubs, *etc.* **3.** group of seven persons.
семерно́й *adj.* sevenfold, septuple.
се́мер|о, ы́х *num.* (*collect.*) seven.
семе́стр, а *m.* term, semester.
се́меч|ко, ка, *pl.* **~ки, ~ек** *nt.* **1.** *dim. of* **се́мя. 2.** (*pl.*) sunflower seeds.
сёмжин|а, ы *f.* salmon (*flesh*).
семивёрстн|ый *adj.* of seven versts; **~ые сапоги́** seven-league boots.
семидесятиле́ти|е, я *nt.* **1.** seventy years. **2.** seventieth anniversary; seventieth birthday.
семидесятиле́тний *adj.* **1.** seventy-year, of seventy years. **2.** seventy-year-old.
семидеся́т|ый *adj.* seventieth; **~ые го́ды** the seventies; **с. но́мер** number seventy; **страни́ца ~ая** page seventy.
семи́к, а́ *m.* (*eccl.*) feast of seventh Thursday after Easter.
семикла́ссник, а *m.* seventh form pupil.
семикра́тный *adj.* sevenfold, septuple.
семиле́ти|е, я *nt.* **1.** seven years; seven-year period. **2.** seventh anniversary.
семиле́тк|а, и *f.* **1.** seven-year school. **2.** (*econ.*) seven-year plan. **3.** (*coll.*) child of seven.
семиле́тний *adj.* **1.** seven-year; septennial. **2.** seven-year-old.
семиме́сячный *adj.* **1.** seven-month. **2.** seven-month-old.
семими́льн|ый *adj.* of seven miles, seven-mile; **идти́ ~ыми шага́ми** (*fig.*) to make gigantic strides.
семина́р, а *m.* seminar.
семина́ри|й, я *m.* seminar.
семинари́ст, а *m.* seminarist.
семина́ри|я, и *f.* seminary, training college; **духо́вная с.** theological college; **учи́тельская с.** (*obs.*) teachers' training college.
семина́р|ский *adj. of* **~** *and* **~ия**
семинеде́льный *adj.* **1.** seven-week. **2.** seven-week-old.
семисо́тый *adj.* seven-hundredth.
семисто́пный *adj.*: **с. ямб** iambic heptameter.
семи́т, а *m.* Semite.
семити́ческий *adj.* Semitic.
семи́т|ский = **~и́ческий**
семито́лог, а *m.* Semitologist.
семитоло́ги|я, и *f.* Semitology.
семиты́сячный *adj.* seven-thousandth.
семиуго́льник *m.* (*math.*) heptagon.

семиуго́льный *adj.* heptagonal.
семичасово́й *adj.* **1.** seven-hour, of seven hours' duration. **2.** seven o'clock.
семнадцатиле́тний *adj.* **1.** seventeen-year. **2.** seventeen-year-old.
семна́дцатый *adj.* seventeenth.
семна́дцат|ь, и *f., num.* seventeen.
сёмужий *adj.* salmon.
сем|ь, и́, *i.* **~ью́** *num.* seven.
се́мьдесят, семи́десяти, семью́десятью *num.* seventy.
семьсо́т, семисо́т, семиста́м, семьюста́ми, о семиста́х *num.* seven hundred.
се́мью *adv.* seven times.
сем|ья́, ьи́, *pl.* **~́ьи ~е́й, ~́ьям** *f.* family; **члены королевской ~и́** the royals.
семьяни́н, а, *pl.* **~ы** *m.* family man.
се́м|я, ени, *pl.* **~ена́, ~я́н, ~ена́м** *nt.* **1.** (*bot. and fig.*) seed; **пойти́ в ~ена́** to go to seed, run to seed; **~ена́ раздо́ра** seeds of discord. **2.** semen, sperm.
семядо́л|я, и, *g. pl.* **~ей** *f.* (*bot.*) seed-lobe, cotyledon.
семяизлия́ни|е, я *nt.* (*physiol.*) ejaculation.
семяпо́чк|а, и *f.* (*bot.*) seed-bud.
Се́н|а, ы *f.* the Seine (*river*).
сена́т, а *m.* senate.
сена́тор, а *m.* senator.
сена́торский *adj.* senatorial.
сена́т|ский *adj. of* ~
сенберна́р, а *m.* St. Bernard (*dog*).
Сенега́л, а *m.* Senegal.
сенега́л|ец, ца *m.* Senegalese.
сенега́л|ка, ки *f. of* **~ец**
сенега́льский *adj.* Senegalese.
се́н|и, е́й *no sg.* (entrance-)hall, vestibule.
сенни́к, а́ *m.* **1.** hay-mattress. **2.** (*dial.*) hayloft.
сенн|о́й[1] *adj.* hay; **~а́я лихора́дка** hay fever.
сен|но́й[2] *adj. of* **~́и; ~на́я де́вушка** (*obs.*) maid.
се́н|о, а *nt.* hay.
сенова́л, а *m.* hay-loft, mow.
сенозаготов|ки, ок *pl.* (*sg.* **~ка, ~ки** *f.*) State hay purchases.
сеноко́с, а *m.* **1.** hay-mowing, haymaking. **2.** haymaking (*time*). **3.** hayfield
сенокоси́лк|а, и *f.* (hay-)mowing machine.
сеноко́сный *adj.* haymaking.
сеноубо́рк|а, и *f.* hay harvesting, haymaking.
сенсацио́н|ный (~ен, ~на) *adj.* sensational.
сенса́ци|я, и *f.* sensation.
сенсибилиза́тор, а *m.* (*phot.*) sensitizer.
сенсибилиза́ци|я, и *f.* (*phot.*) sensitization.
сенсо́рный *adj.* (*physiol.*) sensory.
сенсуали́зм, а *m.* (*phil.*) sensationalism.
сенсуали́ст, а *m.* (*phil.*) sensationalist.
сенсуа́льный *adj.* (*phil.*) sensational.
сентенцио́зный *adj.* sententious.
сенте́нци|я, и *f.* maxim.
сентиментали́зм *m.* sentimentalism (*also hist., liter.*).
сентиментали́ст, а *m.* sentimentalist.
сентимента́льнича|ть, ю *impf.* **1.** to be sentimental, sentimentalize. **2.** (**с**+*i.*) to be soft (with).
сентимента́льност|ь, и *f.* sentimentality.
сентимента́л|ьный (~ен, ~ьна) *adj.* sentimental.
сентя́бр|ь, я́ *m.* September; **смотре́ть ~ём** (*coll.*) to look glum.
сентя́бр|ьский *adj. of* ~
се́н|цы, цев *no sg., dim. of* **~и**
сен|ь, и, о ~́и, в ~и́ *f.* (*obs. or poet.*) canopy; **под ~́ью** (+*g.*) under the protection (of).
сеньо́р, а *m.* **1.** (*hist.*) seigneur, seignior. **2.** señor, senhor.
сепарати́вный *adj.* (*pol.*) separatist.
сепарати́зм, а *m.* (*pol.*) separatism.
сепарати́ст, а *m.* (*pol.*) separatist.
сепара́тный *adj.* (*pol.*) separate; **с. ми́рный догово́р** separate peace treaty.
сепара́тор, а *m.* (*agric.*) separator.
се́пи|я, и *f.* **1.** sepia. **2.** sepia drawing; sepia photograph.
се́псис, а *m.* (*med.*) sepsis, septicaemia.
септе́т, а *m.* (*mus.*) septet(te).
септи́ческий *adj.* (*med.*) septic.
се́р|а, ы *f.* **1.** (*chem.*) sulphur, brimstone; **двуо́кись ~ы** sulphur dioxide. **2.** ear-wax.
сера́л|ь, я *m.* seraglio.
серб, а *m.* Serb, Serbian.
Се́рби|я, и *f.* Serbia.
сербия́нк|а, и *f.* (*obs.*) = **се́рбка**
се́рб|ка, ки *f. of* ~
сербохорва́тский *adj.* = **сербскохорва́тский**
се́рбский *adj.* Serbian.
сербскохорва́тский *adj.* Serbo-Croat(ian); **с. язы́к** Serbo-Croat(ian).
серва́нт, а *m.* sideboard; dumb-waiter.
серви́з, а *m.* service, set; **столо́вый с.** dinner service.
сервир|ова́ть, у́ю *impf. and pf.* **1.: с. стол** to lay a table. **2.** to serve; **с. за́втрак** to serve breakfast.
сервиро́вк|а, и *f.* **1.** laying. **2.** (*collect.*) table appointments (*crockery and table linen*).
се́рвис, а *m.* (consumer) service.
сервомото́р, а *m.* (*tech.*) servo-motor.
серде́чник[1], **а** *m.* (*tech.*) core; strand (*of cable*).
серде́чник[2], **а** *m.* (*coll.*) **1.** heart specialist. **2.** sufferer from heart disease.
серде́чник[3], **а** *m.* (*bot.*) cuckoo-flower, ladies' smock (*Cardamine*).
серде́чност|ь, и *f.* cordiality; warmth.
серде́ч|ный (~ен, ~на) *adj.* **1.** of the heart (*also fig.*); (*anat.*) cardiac; **~ная боле́знь** heart disease; **с. припа́док** heart attack; **~ное сре́дство, ~ное лека́рство** cardiac; **~ные дела́** love affairs. **2.** cordial, hearty, heartfelt, sincere; **~ная благода́рность** heartfelt gratitude, hearty thanks; **оказа́ть с. приём** (+*d.*) to extend a cordial welcome (to); **~ное согла́сие** (*hist.*) Entente cordiale. **3.** warm, warm-hearted.
серди́т|ый *adj.* **1.** (**на**+*a.*) angry (with, at, about), cross (with, about); irate. **2.** (*fig., coll., of tobacco, mustard, etc.*) strong. **3.: дёшево и ~о** (*coll.*) cheap but good; a good bargain.
сер|ди́ть, жу́, ~́дишь *impf.* (*of* **рас~**) to anger, make angry.
сер|ди́ться, жу́сь, ~́дишься *impf.* (*of* **рас~**) (**на**+*a.*) to be angry (with, at, about), be cross (with, about).
сердобо́ли|е, я *nt.* soft-heartedness.
сердобо́льнича|ть, ю *impf.* (*coll., iron.*) to be (too) soft-hearted.
сердобо́л|ьный (~ен, ~ьна) *adj.* (*coll.*) soft-hearted.
сердоли́к, а *m.* (*min.*) cornelian, sard.
сердоли́к|овый *adj. of* ~
се́рд|це, ца, *pl.* **~ца́, ~е́ц** *nt.* (*in var. senses*) heart; **золото́е с.** heart of gold; **в ~ца́х** in (a fit of) temper; **с глаз доло́й, из ~ца вон** (*prov.*) out of sight, out of mind; **приня́ть (бли́зко) к ~цу** to take to heart; **от всего́ ~ца** from the bottom of one's heart, wholeheartedly; **у меня́ отлегло́ от ~ца** I felt relieved; **по́ ~цу** (*coll.*) to one's liking; **с ~цем** testily, crossly; **с. замира́нием ~ца** with a sinking heart; **име́ть с. (на**+*a.*; *coll.*) to be cross (with); **с. боли́т** (+*inf.*) it pains one, one's heart bleeds; **у него́ не лежи́т с. (к)** he has no inclination (to, for).
сердцебие́ни|е, я *nt.* palpitation; (*med.*) tachycardia.
сердцеве́д, а *m.* student of human nature, reader of the human heart.
сердцеви́д|ный (~ен, ~на) *adj.* heart-shaped; (*bot.*) cordate.
сердцеви́н|а, ы *f.* core, pith, heart (*also fig.*).
сердцее́д, а *m.* (*coll.*) lady-killer.
сере́бреник, а *m.* = **сре́бреник**
серебрёный *adj.* silver-plated.
серебри́ст|ый (~, ~а) *adj.* silvery; **с. то́поль** silver poplar.
серебр|и́ть, ю́, и́шь *impf.* (*of* **по~**) to silver, silver-plate.
серебр|и́ться, и́тся *impf.* **1.** to silver, become silvery. **2.** *pass. of* **~и́ть**
серебр|о́, а́ *nt.* **1.** silver. **2.** (*collect.*) silver; **столо́вое с.** silver, plate; **сда́ча ~о́м** change in silver.
серебронос|ный (~ен, ~на) *adj.* argentiferous.

серéбряник, а *m.* silversmith.
серéбрян|ый *adj.* silver; **с. блеск** (*min.*) silver glance; **~ая свáдьба** silver wedding.
середи́н|а, ы *f.* middle, midst; **золотáя с.** the golden mean; **держáться ~ы, знать ~у** (*fig.*) to observe the mean.
середи́нный *adj.* middle, mean, intermediate.
серёдк|а, и *f.* (*coll.*) middle, centre; **с. на половинку** neither one thing nor another.
середня́к, á *m.* **1.** peasant of average means (*classified as intermediate between* **кулáк** *and* **бедня́к**). **2.** (*fig., coll.*) middling pers., undistinguished pers.
серёжк|а *f.* **1.** ear-ring. **2.** (*bot.*) catkin, amentum.
серенáд|а, ы *f.* serenade.
сéренький *adj.* grey (*also fig.*); (*fig.*) dull, drab.
серé|ть, ю *impf.* **1.** (*pf.* **по~**) to turn grey, go grey. **2.** (*impf. only*) to show grey.
сержáнт, а *m.* sergeant.
сери́йный *adj.* (*tech., econ.*) serial.
сéристый *adj.* (*chem.*) sulphureous.
сéри|я, и *f.* series; (*of film*) part; **кинофи́льм в нéскольких ~ях** film in several parts; **с. бомб** (*mil.*) bomb train.
сермя́г|а, и *f.* sermyaga (*coarse, undyed cloth or caftan of this material*).
сéрн|а, ы *f.* (*zool.*) chamois.
серни́стый *adj.* (*chem.*) sulphureous; sulphide (of); **с. аммóний** ammonium sulphide; **~ое желéзо** ferrous sulphide.
сернoки́сл|ый *adj.* (*chem.*) sulphate (of); **~ая соль** sulphate.
сéрн|ый *adj.* sulphuric; **~ая кислотá** sulphuric acid; **с. цвет** flowers of sulphur.
серовáт|ый (~, ~а) *adj.* greyish.
сероводорóд, а *m.* (*chem.*) hydrogen sulphide, sulphuretted hydrogen.
сероглáз|ый (~, ~а) *adj.* grey-eyed.
серозём, а *m.* (*agric.*) grey earth.
серóзный *adj.* (*physiol.*) serous.
сероуглерóд, а *m.* (*chem.*) carbon bisulphide.
серп, á *m.* sickle, reaping-hook; **с. луны́** crescent moon.
серпанти́н, а *m.* **1.** paper streamer. **2.** hairpin-bend road (*in mountainous terrain*).
серпенти́н, а *m.* (*min.*) serpentine.
серпови́дный *adj.* crescent(-shaped).
серсó *nt. indecl.* hoopla.
сертификáт, а *m.* certificate.
сéрум, а *m.* (*med.*) serum.
сéрфинг, а *m.* surfing.
сёрфинг = сéрфинг
серфинги́ст, а *m.* surfer.
серчá|ть, ю *impf.* (*of* **о~**) (*coll.*) to be angry, be cross.
сéр|ый (~, ~á, ~о) *adj.* **1.** grey; **с. в я́блоках** dappled. **2.** (*fig.*) grey, dull; drab; **с. день** grey day. **3.** (*fig.*) dull, dim (= *uneducated*).
серьг|á, и́, *pl.* **∠и, серёг, ~áм** *f.* **1.** ear-ring. **2.** (*tech.*) link. **3.** (*naut.*) slip rope.
серьёзно *adv.* seriously; earnestly; in earnest; **с.?** seriously?; really?
серьёзност|ь, и *f.* seriousness; earnestness; gravity.
серьёз|ный (~ен, ~на, ~но) *adj.* serious; earnest; grave.
сессиóнный *adj.* sessional.
сéсси|я, и *f.* session, sitting; (*leg.*) term.
сестр|á, ы́, *pl.* **∠ы, сестёр, ∠ам** *f.* **1.** sister; **двою́родная с.** (first) cousin. **2.: медици́нская с., с. милосéрдия** (*obs.*) nurse; **стáршая с.** (*nursing*) sister; **с.-хозя́йка** (*hospital*) matron.
сестрёнк|а, и *f.* little sister.
сéстрин *adj.* sister's.
сéстринский *adj.* nurse's; nursing.
сестри́ц|а, ы *f. affectionate dim. of* **сестрá**
сесть[1]**, ся́ду, ся́дешь,** *past* **сел, сéла** *pf.* (*of* **сади́ться**) **1.** to sit down; **с. за стол** to sit down to table; **с. обéдать** to sit down to dinner; **с. в вáнну** to get into the bath; **с. рабóтать** to get down to work; **с. в калóшу, с. в лу́жу** (*coll.*) to get into a mess, into a fix. **2.** (**в, на+***a.*) to board, take; **с. на пóезд** to board a train; **с. на лóшадь** to mount a horse. **3.** to alight, settle, perch; (*of an aircraft*) to land. **4.** (*of the heavenly bodies*) to set. **5.: с. в тюрьму́** to go to prison, jail.
сесть[2]**, ся́дет,** *past* **сел** *pf.* (*of* **сади́ться**) to shrink.
сет, а *m.* (*sport*) set.
сетевóй *adj.* net, netting, mesh.
сéтк|а, и *f.* **1.** net, netting; (luggage) rack; **с. для головы́** hair-net; **игрáть у ~и** (*tennis*) to play at net. **2.** (*coll.*) string-bag. **3.** (*geog.*) grid; (*collect.*) co-ordinates. **4.** (*radio*) grid. **5.** scale (*of charges, etc.*).
сéт|овать, ую *impf.* (*of* **по~**) **1.** (**на+***a.*) to complain (of), cry out (upon). **2.** (**о+***p.*) to lament, mourn.
сéточный *adj.* **1.** net. **2.** (*radio*) grid.
сéттер, а *m.* setter (*dog*).
сетчáтк|а, и *f.* (*anat.*) retina.
сетчатокры́л|ые, ых *pl.* (*sg.* **~ое, ~ого** *nt.*) (*zool.*) Neuroptera.
сéтчат|ый *adj.* netted, network; reticular; **~ая мáйка** string vest; **~ые чулки́** fishnet stockings; **~ая оболóчка глáза** (*anat.*) retina.
сет|ь, и, о ∠и, в ∠и *and* **~и́,** *pl.* **∠и, ~éй** *f.* **1.** net (*also fig.*); **расстáвить ∠и комý-н.** to set a trap for s.o. **2.** network; circuit, system; **локáльная с.** (*comput.*) local area network, LAN.
Сеу́л, а *m.* Seoul.
сéч|а, и *f.* (*obs.*) battle.
сечéни|е, я *nt.* **1.** cutting; **кéсарево с.** Caesarean birth, operation. **2.** section; **живóе с.** cross section.
сéчк|а, и *f.* **1.** chopper, vegetable-cutting knife. **2.** chopped straw, chaff.
Сеч|ь[1]**, и** *f.* (*hist.*) (Cossack) host.
сечь[2]**, секу́, сечёшь, секу́т,** *past* **сек, секлá** *impf.* **1.** (*impf. only*) to cut to pieces. **2.** (*pf.* **вы́~**, *past* **сек, сéкла**) to beat, flog.
сé|чься, чётся, ку́тся, *past* **~кся, ~клась** *impf.* (*of* **по~**) (*of hairs*) to split; (*of fabric*) to cut.
сéялк|а, и *f.* (*agric.*) sowing-machine, seed drill.
сéяльщик, а *m.* sower.
сéян|ец, ца *m.* seedling.
сéятел|ь, я *m.* sower (*also fig., rhet.*); disseminator.
сé|ять, ю, ешь *impf.* (*of* **по~**) **1.** to sow (*also fig.*); **с. раздóр** to sow the seeds of dissension. **2.** (*fig., coll.*) to throw about; **с. дéньги** to throw one's money about.
сжáл|иться, юсь, ишься *pf.* (**над**) to take pity (on).
сжáти|е, я *nt.* **1.** pressing, pressure; grasp, grip. **2.** compression, condensation; **кáмера ~я** compression chamber.
сжáтост|ь, и *f.* **1.** compression. **2.** conciseness.
сжáт|ый *p.p.p. of* **~ь**[1] *and* **~ь**[2] *and adj.* **1.** compressed (*air, gas*). **2.** (*fig.*) condensed, compact, concise; **~ое изложéние** exposition in condensed form.
сжать[1]**, сожму́, сожмёшь** *pf.* (*of* **сжимáть**) to squeeze; to compress (*also fig.*); to grip; **с. гу́бы** to compress one's lips; **с. зу́бы** to grit one's teeth; **с. кулаки́** to clench one's fists; **с. в объя́тиях** to hug; **с. изложéние** to compress an exposition.
сжать[2]**, сожну́, сожнёшь** *pf. of* **жать**[2]
сжá|ться, сожму́сь, сожмёшься *pf.* (*of* **сжимáться**) **1.** to tighten, clench. **2.** to shrink, contract; **её душá ~лась** her heart sank.
сж|евáть, ую́, уёшь *pf.* to chew up.
сжечь, сожгу́, сожжёшь, сожгу́т, *past* **сжёг, сожглá** *pf.* (*of* **жечь** *and* **сжигáть**) to burn (up, down); to cremate; **с. свои́ корабли́** (*fig.*) to burn one's boats.
сживá|ть(ся), ю(сь) *impf. of* **сжи́ть(ся)**
сжигá|ть, ю *impf. of* **сжечь**
сжи|ди́ть, жу́, ди́шь *pf.* (*of* **~жáть**) (*chem.*) to liquefy.
сжижá|ть, ю *impf. of* **сжиди́ть**
сжижéни|е, я *nt.* (*chem.*) liquation, liquefaction.
сжи́женный *adj.* (*chem.*) liquefied.
сжим, а *m.* clip, grip, clamp.
сжимáемост|ь, и *f.* compressibility, condensability.
сжимá|ть(ся), ю(сь) *impf. of* **сжáть**[1]**(ся)**
сжи|ть, ву́, вёшь, *past* **~л, ~лá, ∠ло** *pf.* (*of* **~вáть**) (*coll.*) to force out, edge out; **с. сó свету** to be the death (of).
сжи́|ться, ву́сь, вёшься, *past* **~лся, ~лáсь** *pf.* (*of* **~вáться**) (**с+***i.*) to get used (to), get accustomed (to); **с. с**

ро́лью (*theatr.*) to identify o.s. with a part.
сжу́льнича|ть, ю *pf. of* **жу́льничать**
сза́ди *adv. and prep.+g.* **1.** *adv.* from behind; behind; from the end; from the rear; **вид с.** rear view; **тре́тий ваго́н с.** the third coach from the rear. **2.** *prep.+g.* behind.
сзыва́|ть, ю *impf. of* **созва́ть**
Сиа́м, а *m.* Siam.
сиа́м|ец, ца *m.* Siamese.
сиа́м|ка, ки *f. of* **~ец**
сиа́мский *adj.* Siamese.
сибари́т, а *m.* sybarite.
сибари́тский *adj.* sybaritic.
сибари́тств|о, а *nt.* sybaritism.
сибари́тств|овать, ую *impf.* to lead the life of a sybarite.
сибиля́нт, а *m.* (*ling.*) sibilant.
сибирея́звенный *adj.* (*med.*) anthrax.
сиби́рк|а, и *f.* **1.** (*obs.*) sibirka (*waist-length caftan*). **2.** (*coll., obs.*) clink (= *prison*). **3.** (*hist.*) sibirka (*paper money issued in Siberia during the Civil War, 1918–20*). **4.** (*coll.*) = **сиби́рская я́зва**
сиби́рный *adj.* (*coll., obs.*) hard, severe.
сиби́рск|ий *adj.* Siberian; **~ая ко́шка** Persian cat; **~ая я́зва** (*med.*) anthrax.
Сиби́р|ь, и *f.* Siberia.
сибиря́к, а́ *m.* Siberian.
сибиря́|чка, чки *f. of* **~к**
сиве́|ть, ю *impf.* (*of* **по~**) to turn grey.
си́вк|а, и *f.* dark grey (horse).
сивк|о́, а́ *m.* = **~а**
сивола́пый *adj.* (*coll.*) rough, clumsy.
сиву́х|а, и *f.* raw vodka.
сиву́ч, а *m.* (*zool.*) Steller's sea lion.
сиву́шн|ый *adj.*: **~ое ма́сло** fusel oil.
си́в|ый (~, ~а́, ~о) *adj.* **1.** (*of horses*) grey; **бред ~ой кобы́лы** (*coll.*) raving nonsense. **2.** (*of hair*) grey, greying.
сиг, а́ *m.* whitefish (*freshwater fish of salmon family*).
сиган|у́ть, у́, ёшь *pf.* (*coll.*) to leap.
сига́р|а, ы *f.* cigar.
сигаре́т|а, ы *f.* **1.** cigarette (*without mouthpiece*). **2.** small cigar.
сигаре́т|ный *adj. of* **~а**
сига́рк|а, и *f.* (*coll.*) (home-made) cigarette (*of shag rolled in newspaper*), roll-up.
сига́р|ный *adj. of* **~а**
сига́рочниц|а, ы *f.* cigar box.
сигна́л, а *m.* signal; **вызовно́й с.** call signal; **пожа́рный с.** fire-alarm; **с. бе́дствия** distress signal; **с. возду́шной трево́ги** air-raid alarm; **с. на трубе́** trumpet-call; **с. на рожке́, с. на го́рне** bugle-call.
сигнализа́тор, а *m.* (*tech.*) signalling apparatus.
сигнализа́ци|я, и *f.* signalling.
сигнализи́р|овать, ую *impf. and pf.* **1.** (*pf. also* **про~**) to signal. **2.** (*+a. or* **о**+*p.*; *fig.*) to give warning (of).
сигна́л|ьный *adj. of* **~**; **~ьная бу́дка** signal-box; **~ьная ла́мпа** signal lamp; **с. пистоле́т** Very pistol, signal pistol, flare gun; **~ьное поло́тнище** signal panel, marking panel; **~ьная тормозна́я верёвка** communication cord.
сигна́льщик, а *m.* signaller, signal-man.
сигнату́р|а, ы *f.* **1.** (*pharm.*) label. **2.** (*typ.*) signature.
СИД *m.* (*indecl.*) (*abbr. of* ***светоизлуча́ющий дио́д***) LED (*light-emitting diode*).
сиде́л|ец, ьца *m.* (*obs.*) salesman; shop-walker.
сиде́лк|а, и *f.* (sick-)nurse.
сиде́ни|е, я *nt.* sitting.
си́д|ень, ня *m.* (*coll.*) stay-at-home; **сиде́ть ~нем** to be a stay-at-home.
сиде́нь|е, я *nt.* seat.
сидери́т, а *m.* (*min.*) siderite.
си|де́ть, жу́, ди́шь *impf.* **1.** to sit; **с., поджа́в но́ги** to sit cross-legged; **с. верхо́м** to be on horseback; **с. на ко́рточках** to squat; **с. на насе́сте** to roost, perch; **с. на я́йцах** to sit (on eggs), brood; **с. у мо́ря, ждать пого́ды** (*coll.*) to wait for sth. to turn up; **вот где ~ди́т кто-н., что-н.** (*coll.*) that's where all the trouble lies; that's the source of all the trouble. **2.** to be; **с. (в тюрьме́)** to be in prison, serve a term of imprisonment; **с. под аре́стом** to be under arrest; **с. без де́ла** to have nothing to do; **с. за кни́гой** to be (engaged in) reading. **3.** (*of a vessel*) to draw (*water*); **с. глубоко́** to be deep in the water, draw much water. **4.** (**на**+*p.*; *of clothing*) to fit, sit (on).
сид|е́ться, и́тся *impf.* (*impers.+d.*): **ему́,** *etc.*, **не ~и́тся до́ма** he, *etc.*, can't bear staying at home; **ей не ~и́тся на ме́сте** she can't keep still.
Си́дне|й, я *m.* Sydney.
сидр, а *m.* cider.
сидя́ч|ий *adj.* **1.** sitting; **в ~ей по́зе** in a sitting posture. **2.** (*fig.*) sedentary; **с. о́браз жи́зни** sedentary life. **3.** (*zool.*) sessile.
сие́ *see* **сей**
сие́н|а, ы *f.* sienna; **жжёная с.** burnt sienna.
сиени́т, а *m.* (*min.*) syenite.
сизиги́йный *adj.*: **с. прили́в** spring tide.
сизиги́|я, и *f.* (*astron.*) syzygy.
сизи́фов *adj.*: **~ труд** labour of Sisyphus.
сизоворо́нк|а, и *f.* (*zool.*) roller.
си́з|ый (~, ~а́, ~о) *adj.* blue-grey, dove-coloured.
сиккати́в, а *m.* (*tech.*) siccative.
сикомо́р, а *m.* (*bot.*) sycamore.
сикх, а *m.* Sikh.
си́кхский *adj.* Sikh.
си́л|а, ы *f.* **1.** strength, force; **в ~у** (*+g.*) on the strength (of), by virtue (of), because (of); **быть в ~ах** (*+inf.*) to have the strength (to), have the power (to); **изо всех ~, что есть ~ы** with all one's might; **крича́ть изо всех ~** to shout at the top of one's voice; **от ~ы** (*coll.*) at most; **сверх ~, свы́ше~, не по ~ам** beyond one's power(s); outside one's competence; **че́рез ~у** beyond one's powers; **рабо́тать че́рез ~у** to overwork; **~ой** by force; **с по́мощью гру́бой ~ы** by brute force; **свои́ми ~ами** unaided; **~ою веще́й** through force of circumstances; **~ою** (*+g. or* **в**+*a.*) to the strength (of); **с. во́ли** will-power; **с. ду́ха** strength of mind; **с. привы́чки** force of habit; **в ~у привы́чки** by force of habit. **2.** (*phys., tech.*) force, power; **жива́я с.** kinetic energy; **лошади́ная с.** horse-power; **подъёмная с.** (*aeron.*) lift; **с. све́та в свеча́х** candle-power; **с. тя́ги** tractive force; **с. тя́жести, с. притяже́ния** force of gravity. **3.** (*leg. and fig.*) force; **име́ющий ~у** valid; **в ~е** in force, valid; **войти́, вступи́ть в ~у** to come into force; take effect; **оста́ться в ~е** to remain valid; (*fig.*) to hold good. **4.** (*pl.*; *mil.*) forces; **вооружённые ~ы** armed forces; **вое́нно-возду́шные ~ы** air force(s); **сухопу́тные ~ы** land forces, ground forces. **5.** (*coll.*) point, essence; **с. в том, что** the crux of the matter is that. **6.** (*coll.*) quantity, multitude.
сила́ч, а́ *m.* strong man.
силика́т, а *m.* (*min.*) silicate.
си́л|иться, юсь, ишься *impf.* to try, make efforts.
сили́ци|й, я *m.* (*chem.*) silicium.
силко́м *adv.* (*coll.*) by (main) force.
силлаби́ческий *adj.* (*liter.*) syllabic.
Си́лли: остров|а́ С., ~о́в С. *no sg.* the Scilly Isles; the Scillies.
силлоги́зм, а *m.* (*phil.*) syllogism.
силови́к, а́ *m.* power-plant worker.
силов|о́й *adj.* power; **~а́я ли́ния** (*phys.*) line of force; **~о́е по́ле** (*phys.*) field of force; **с. про́вод** (*elec.*) power-line; **~а́я ста́нция** power-station, power-house; **~а́я устано́вка** power-plant.
си́лой *adv.* (*coll.*) by (main) force.
сил|о́к, ка́ *m.* noose, snare.
силоме́р, а *m.* dynamometer.
си́лос, а *m.* (*agric.*) **1.** silo. **2.** silage.
силосова́ни|е, я *nt.* siloing.
силос|ова́ть, у́ю *impf. and f.* to silo, ensile.
силосоре́зк|а, и *f.* silage cutter.
силури́йский *adj.* (*geol.*) Silurian.
силу́эт, а *m.* silhouette.
си́льно *adv.* **1.** strongly; violently; **с. ска́зано** that's going too far; that's putting it too strongly. **2.** very much, greatly; badly; **с. нужда́ться в чём-н** to want sth. badly.

сильнодействующий *adj.* virulent; drastic.
сил|ьный (~ен *and* **~ён, ~ьна, ~ьно, ~ьны)** *adj.* (*in var. senses*) strong; powerful; **~ьная воля** strong will; **с. довод** powerful argument; **~ьное желание** intense desire; **с. запах** strong smell; **с. мороз** hard frost; **~ьная речь** impressive speech; **он не ~ён в языках** he is not good at languages; languages are not his strong suit.
сильф, а *m.* (*myth.*) sylph.
сильфид|а, ы *f.* (*myth. and fig.*) sylph.
симбиоз, а *m.* (*biol.*) symbiosis.
символ, а *m.* symbol; emblem; **с. веры** (*relig.*) creed.
символизаци|я, и *f.* symbolization.
символизир|овать, ую *impf.* to symbolize.
символизм, а *m.* symbolism.
символик|а, и *f.* symbolism.
символист, а *m.* symbolist.
символист|ский *adj. of* ~
символический *adj.* symbolic(al).
символичност|ь, и *f.* symbolical character.
символич|ный (~ен, ~на) *adj.* = **~еский**
симметрический *adj.* symmetrical.
симметричност|ь, и *f.* symmetry.
симметрич|ный (~ен, ~на) *adj.* = **~еский**
симметри|я, и *f.* symmetry.
симони|я, и *f.* (*hist.*) simony.
симпатизир|овать, ую *impf.* **1.** (*+d.*) be in sympathy (with), sympathize (with). **2.** (**с**+*i.*, *obs.*) to accord (with).
симпатическ|ий *adj.* (*physiol.*, *etc.*) sympathetic; **~ая нервная система** sympathetic nervous system; **~ие чернила** invisible ink.
симпатич|ный (~ен, ~на) *adj.* likeable, attractive, nice.
симпати|я, и *f.* **1.** (**к**) liking (for); **чувствовать ~ю к кому-н.** to take a liking to s.o., be drawn to s.o. **2.** (*fig.*, *coll.*) loved one, object of one's affections.
симптом, а *m.* symptom.
симптоматик|а, и *f.* (*med.*) study of symptoms.
симптоматический *adj.* **1.** symptomatic. **2.** (*med.*) eliminating symptoms, palliative.
симптоматич|ный (~ен, ~на) *adj.* = **~еский**
симулир|овать, ую *impf. and pf.* to simulate, feign, sham.
симулянт, а *m.* simulator; malingerer.
симуляци|я, и *f.* simulation.
симфонический *adj.* symphonic; **с. оркестр** symphony orchestra.
симфони|я, и *f.* **1.** symphony. **2.** (*eccl.*, *liter.*) concordance.
синагог|а, и *f.* synagogue.
Сина|й, я *m.* Sinai.
Сингапур, а *m.* Singapore.
сингал, а *m.* Sin(g)halese.
сингал|ец, ца *m.* = **сингал**
сингал|ка, ки *f. of* ~
сингальский *adj.* Sin(g)halese.
сингапур|ец, ца *m.* Singaporean.
сингапур|ка, ки *f. of* **~ец**
сингапурский *adj.* Singaporean.
синдетикон, а *m.* seccotine.
синдикализм, а *m.* (*pol.*) syndicalism.
синдикалист, а *m.* (*pol.*) syndicalist.
синдикалистский *adj.* (*pol.*) syndicalist, syndicalistic.
синдикат, а *m.* (*econ.*) syndicate.
синдицир|овать, ую *impf. and pf.* (*econ.*) to syndicate.
синев|а, ы *f.* blue colour; **с. небес** the blue of the sky; **с. под глазами** dark patches under the eyes.
синеват|ый (~, ~а) *adj.* bluish.
синеглаз|ый (~, ~а) *adj.* blue-eyed.
синедрион, а *m.* (*hist.*) sanhedrin; (*joc.*) meeting.
синекдох|а, и *f.* (*liter.*) synecdoche.
синекур|а, ы *f.* sinecure.
синел|ь, и *f.* chenille.
синерод, а *m.* (*chem.*) cyanogen.
синеродист|ый *adj.* (*chem.*) cyanous; cyanide (of); **~ая кислота** cyanic acid.
синеродный *adj.* (*chem.*) cyanic; cyanide (of).
сине|ть, ю *impf.* **1.** (*pf.* **по~**) to turn blue, become blue. **2.** (*impf. only*) to show blue.
син|ий (~ь, ~я, ~е) *adj.* (dark) blue; **с. чулок** (*fig.*) bluestocking.
синильн|ый *adj.*: **~ая кислота** (*chem.*) prussic acid, hydrocyanic acid.
син|ить, ю, ишь *impf.* (*of* **по~**) **1.** to paint blue. **2.** to rinse in blue, blue.
синиц|а, ы *f.* tit, titmouse, tomtit.
синклит, а *m.* (*joc.*) council, synod.
синкоп|а, ы *f.* (*mus. and ling.*) syncope.
синкретизм, а *m.* syncretism.
синод, а *m.* synod.
синодальный *adj.* synodal.
синодический *adj.* (*astron.*) synodic(al).
синод|ский *adj.* = **~альный**
синолог, а *m.* sinologist.
синологи|я, и *f.* sinology.
синоним, а *m.* synonym.
синонимик|а, и *f.* **1.** study of synonyms. **2.** (*collect.*) synonyms.
синоними|я, и *f.* synonymy, synonymity.
синоптик, а *m.* weather forecaster, weather-chart maker.
синоптик|а, и *f.* weather forecasting.
синоптическ|ий *adj.* synoptical; **~ая карта** weather-chart.
синтаксис, а *m.* syntax.
синтаксический *adj.* syntactical.
синтез, а *m.* synthesis.
синтезатор, а *m.* synthesizer.
синтезир|овать, ую *impf. and pf.* to synthesize.
синтетический *adj.* synthetic.
синус[1], а *m.* (*math.*) sine.
синус[2], а *m.* (*anat.*) sinus.
синусоид|а, ы *f.* (*math.*) sinusoid.
синхронизатор, а *m.* (*tech.*) synchronizer.
синхронизаци|я, и *f.* synchronization.
синхронизир|овать, ую *impf. and pf.* to synchronize.
синхронизм, а *m.* synchronism.
синхронист, а *m.* simultaneous interpreter.
синхронический *adj.* synchronic.
синхрони|я, и *f.* synchronism.
синхронный *adj.* synchronous.
син|ь, и *f.* blue colour.
синьг|а, и *f.* (*zool.*) common scoter.
синьк|а, и *f.* **1.** blue, blueing. **2.** blueprint.
синьор, а *m.* signor.
синьор|а, ы *f.* signora.
синьорин|а, ы *f.* signorina.
синюх|а, и *f.* (*med.*) cyanosis.
синяк, а *m.* bruise; **с. под глазом** black eye; **~и под глазами** shadows, dark patches under the eyes; **избить до ~ов** to beat black and blue.
сионизм, а *m.* Zionism.
сионист, а *m.* Zionist.
сионистский *adj.* Zionist.
сипа|й, я *m.* sepoy.
сип|еть, лю, ишь *impf.* **1.** to make hoarse sounds; to speak hoarsely. **2.** (*impers.*) to be hoarse; **у него в горле ~ит** he is hoarse.
сиплый *adj.* hoarse, husky.
сипн|уть, у, ешь *impf.* (*coll.*) to become hoarse, become husky.
сипух|а, и *f.* (*zool.*) barn owl.
сирен|а, ы *f.* (*in var. senses*) siren.
сиреневый *adj.* lilac; lilac-coloured.
сирен|ь, и *f.* lilac.
сиречь *particle* (*arch.*) that is to say.
сири|ец, йца *m.* Syrian.
сири|йка, йки *f. of* **~ец**
сирийский *adj.* Syrian.
Сири|я, и *f.* Syria.
сирокко *m. indecl.* sirocco.
сироп, а *m.* syrup.
сирот|а, ы, *pl.* **~ы** *c.g.* orphan; **казанская с.** (*fig.*, *coll.*) pers. with 'hard luck story'.
сироте|ть, ю *impf.* to be orphaned.
сиротлив|ый (~, ~а) *adj.* lonely; (*fig.*) lost, stray.

сиро́т|ский *adj. of* **~а́; с. дом** orphanage; **~ская зима́** mild winter.
сиро́тств|о, а *nt.* orphanhood.
си́р|ый (~, ~а́, ~о) *adj.* (*obs.*) **1.** orphaned. **2.** (*fig.*) lonely.
систе́м|а, ы *f.* **1.** (*in var. senses*) system; **стать ~ой, войти́ в ~у** to become the rule. **2.** type; **пулемёт но́вой ~ы** machine-gun of a new type.
систематиза́ци|я, и *f.* systematization.
систематизи́р|овать, ую *impf. and pf.* to systematize.
системати́к|а, и *f.* **1.** systematization. **2.** (*biol.*) taxonomy.
системати́ческий *adj.* systematic; methodical.
системати́чност|ь, и *f.* systematic character; system.
системати́ч|ный (~ен, ~на) *adj.* systematic; methodical.
си́стол|а, ы *f.* (*med.*) systole.
си́с|ька, ьки, *g. pl.* **~ек** *f.* (*coll.*) nipple; tit.
си́т|ец, ца *m.* cotton (print); calico (print); chintz.
си́теч|ко, ка, *pl.* **~ки, ~ек** *nt. dim. of* **си́то; ча́йное с.** tea-strainer.
си́тник[1]**, а** *m.* = **си́тный хлеб**
си́тник[2]**, а** *m.* (*bot.*) rush.
си́тн|ый *adj.* (*obs.*) sifted; **с. хлеб** loaf made of sifted flour; *as n.* **с., ~ого** *m.* = **с. хлеб**
си́т|о, а *nt.* sieve; bolter.
ситро́ *nt. indecl.* fruit-flavoured mineral water.
ситуа́ци|я, и *f.* situation.
си́т|цевый *adj. of* **~ец**
ситценабивно́й *adj.* (*text.*) printing.
ситцепеча́тани|е, я *nt.* (*text.*) printing.
си́филис, а *m.* (*med.*) syphilis.
сифили́тик, а *m.* syphilitic.
сифилити́ческий *adj.* syphilitic.
сифо́н, а *m.* siphon.
сицили́|ец, йца *m.* Sicilian.
сицили́|йка, йки *f. of* **~ец**
сицили́йский *adj.* Sicilian.
Сици́ли|я, и *f.* Sicily.
сиюмину́т|ный (~ен, ~на) *adj.* present, current.
сия́ни|е, я *nt.* radiance; **се́верное с.** northern lights, Aurora Borealis.
сия́тельств|о, а *nt.*: **его́,** *etc.*, **с.** (*title of princes and counts*) his, *etc.*, Highness.
сия́|ть, ю *impf.* to shine, beam; to be radiant.
скабрёзност|ь, и *f.* scabrousness; **говори́ть ~и** to use scabrous language.
скабрёз|ный (~ен, ~на) *adj.* scabrous.
сказ, а *m.* **1.** tale; **вот тебе́ и весь с.** (*coll.*) that's the long and the short of it. **2.** (*Russ. liter.*) skaz (= *first-pers. narrative*).
сказа́ни|е, я *nt.* story, tale, legend.
сказан|у́ть, у́, ёшь *pf.* (*coll.*) to blurt (out); **ну и ~у́л словцо́!** that's a fine thing to say!
ска|за́ть, жу́, ~́жешь *pf.* **1.** *pf. of* **говори́ть; ~жи́(те)!** (*coll., iron.*) I say!; **как с.** how shall I put it?; **лу́чше с., верне́е с., точне́е с.** or rather; **не́чего с.!** well, to be sure!; **~́зано — сде́лано** (*coll.*) no sooner said than done. **2.** to interpose, object; **ничего́ не ~́жешь, он прав** there is no gainsaying it, he is right.
ска|за́ться[1]**, жу́сь, ~́жешься** *pf.* (*of* **~́зываться**) (*coll.*) **1.** (*+d.*) to inform; to give notice, give warning; **они́ уе́хали не ~за́вшись** they went away without (giving) warning. **2.** (*+i.*) to proclaim o.s.; **с. больны́м** to report sick.
ска|за́ться[2]**, жу́сь, ~́жешься** *pf.* (*of* **~́зываться**) (**на**+*p.*, **в**+*p.*) to tell (on); **бомбёжка ~за́лась на её не́рвах** the bombing told on her nerves; **в э́том посту́пке я́вно ~за́лась его́ некульту́рность** this act just showed his lack of manners.
сказа́тел|ь, я *m.* folk-tale narrator, story-teller.
ска́зк|а, и *f.* **1.** tale, story; **волше́бная с.** fairy-tale; **с. про бе́лого бычка́** (*coll.*) the same old story. **2.** (*coll.*) (tall) story, fib.
ска́зочник, а *m.* story-teller.
ска́зочн|ый *adj.* fairytale; fabulous, fantastic; **~ая страна́** fairyland; **~ое бога́тство** fabulous wealth.
сказу́ем|ое, ого *nt.* (*gram.*) predicate.
ска́зыва|ться, юсь *impf. of* **сказа́ться**
скак *m. only found in p. sg.*: **на всём ~у́** at full tilt.
скака́лк|а, и *f.* skipping-rope.
ска|ка́ть, чу́, ~́чешь *impf.* **1.** to skip, jump; **с. на одно́й ноге́** to hop. **2.** to gallop.
скаков|о́й *adj.* race, racing; **~а́я доро́жка** racecourse; **~а́я ло́шадь** racehorse.
скаку́н, а́ *m.* fast horse, racer.
ска́л|а, ы *f.* (*obs.*) scale.
скал|а́, ы́, *pl.* **~́ы** *f.* rock face, crag; **(отве́сная) с.** cliff; **подво́дная с.** reef.
скаламбу́р|ить, ю, ишь *pf. of* **каламбу́рить**
Скали́ст|ые го́р|ы, ~ых ~ *no sg.* the Rocky Mountains; the Rockies.
скали́ст|ый (~, ~а) *adj.* rocky.
ска́л|ить, ю, ишь *impf.* (*of* **о~**); **с. зу́бы** to show one's teeth, bare one's teeth; (*impf. only*) (*fig. pej.*) to grin, laugh.
ска́лк|а, и *f.* (*cul.*) rolling-pin; beater.
скалола́з, а *m.* rock-climber.
ска́лыва|ть, ю *impf. of* **сколо́ть**
скальд, а *m.* (*hist., liter.*) scald, skald.
скальки́р|овать, ую *pf. of* **кальки́ровать**
скалькули́р|овать, ую *pf. of* **калькули́ровать**
ска́льн|ый *adj.* (*geol.*) rock, rocky; **~ые рабо́ты** rock excavations.
ска́льпел|ь, я *m.* scalpel.
скальпи́р|овать, ую *impf. and pf.* (*pf. also* **о~**) to scalp.
скаме́ечк|а, и *f.* small bench; **с. для ног** footstool.
скаме́йк|а, и *f.* bench.
скам|ья́, ьи́, *pl.* **~́ьи, ~е́й** *f.* bench; **с. подсуди́мых** (*leg.*) the dock; **на шко́льной ~ье́** during one's schooldays; **со шко́льной ~ьи́** straight from school.
сканда́л, а *m.* **1.** scandal; disgrace; **како́й с.!** what a scandal!, how scandalous! **2.** brawl; rowdy scene.
скандализи́р|овать, ую *impf. and pf.* to scandalize.
скандали́ст, а *m.* brawler; trouble-maker; rowdy.
сканда́л|ить, ю, ишь *impf.* **1.** (*pf.* **на~**) (*coll.*) to brawl; to start a row. **2.** (*pf.* **о~**) to scandalize.
сканда́л|иться, юсь, ишься *impf.* (*of* **о~**) to disgrace o.s.
сканда́л|ьный (~ен, ~ьна) *adj.* **1.** scandalous. **2.** (*coll.*) rowdy; **с. челове́к** = **~и́ст. 3.** scandal; **~ьная хро́ника** scandal column, page (*of newspaper*).
ска́нди|й, я *m.* (*chem.*) scandium.
скандина́в, а *m.* Scandinavian.
скандина́в|ец, ца *m.* = **скандина́в**
Скандина́ви|я, и *f.* Scandinavia.
скандина́в|ка, ки *f. of* **~**
скандина́вский *adj.* Scandinavian.
сканди́ровани|е, я *nt.* (*liter.*) scansion.
сканди́р|овать, ую *impf. and pf.* to declaim, recite (*stressing individual syllables of words*).
ска́нер, а *m.* (*comput., med.*) scanner.
скан|ь, и *f.* (*art*) filigree.
ска́плива|ть(ся), ю(сь) *impf. of* **скопи́ть(ся)**
скапу́|ститься, щусь, стишься *pf.* (*sl.*) to fold up, pack up; to peg out.
ска́пыва|ть, ю *impf.* (*of* **скопа́ть**) to shovel away, level with a spade.
скарабе́|й, я *m.* scarab.
скарб, а *m.* (*coll.*) goods and chattels; **со всем ~́ом** bag and baggage.
ска́ред, а *m.* (*coll.*) stingy pers., miser.
ска́реднича|ть, ю *impf.* (*coll.*) to be stingy.
ска́ред|ный (~ен, ~на) *adj.* (*coll.*) stingy, miserly, niggardly.
скарифика́тор, а *m.* **1.** (*agric.*) scarifier. **2.** (*med.*) scarificator.
скарифици́р|овать, ую *impf.* (*agric.*) to scarify.
скарлати́н|а, ы *f.* (*med.*) scarlet fever, scarlatina.
скарлати́н|ный *adj. of* **~а**
ска́рмлива|ть, ю *impf. of* **скорми́ть**
скат[1]**, а** *m.* slope, incline; pitch (*of a roof*).
скат[2]**, а** *m.* (*tech.*) wheelbase.
скат[3]**, а** *m.* (*zool.*) ray, skate; **электри́ческий с.** electric ray.
скат|а́ть, а́ю *pf.* (*of* **~́ывать**) **1.** to roll (up); **с. па́рус** to furl a sail. **2.** (**за**+*i.*; *coll.*) to run to fetch. **3.** (*school sl.*) to crib.

ска́терт|ь, и, *pl.* **~и, ~е́й** *f.* table-cloth; **~ью доро́га!** (*coll.*) good riddance!

ска|ти́ть, чу́, ~́тишь *pf.* (*of* **~́тывать**) to roll down.

ска|ти́ться, чу́сь, ~́тшься *pf.* (*of* **~́тываться**) to roll down; (*fig., pej.*) to slip, slide.

ска́тк|а, и *f.* **1.** (*mil.*) greatcoat roll. **2.** rolling.

ска́тный *adj.* (*folk poet., of a pearl*) large, round, and even.

ска́тыва|ть, ю *impf. of* **ската́ть** *and* **скати́ть**

ска́тыва|ться, юсь *impf. of* **скати́ться**

ска́ут, а *m.* (boy) scout.

скафа́ндр, а *m.* protective suit (*of divers, astronauts, etc.*).

ска́чк|а, и *f.* **1.** gallop, galloping. **2.** (*pl.*) horse-race; race meeting, the races; **с. с препя́тствиями** steeplechase.

скачкообра́з|ный (~ен, ~на) *adj.* spasmodic; uneven.

скач|о́к, ка́ *m.* **1.** jump, leap, bound; **~ка́ми** by leaps. **2.** (*fig.*) a great advance, leap forward.

ска́шива|ть, ю *impf. of* **скоси́ть**

ска́щива|ть, ю *impf. of* **скости́ть**

СКВ *f. indecl.* (*abbr. of* **свобо́дно конверти́руемая валю́та**) hard currency, freely convertible currency.

сква́жин|а, ы *f.* slit, chink; **бурова́я с.** (*tech.*) bore-hole; **замо́чная с.** key-hole.

сква́жистый *adj.* porous.

сквалы́г|а, и *c.g.* (*coll.*) miser, skinflint.

сквер, а *m.* public garden.

скве́рн|а, ы *no pl.* (*collect.*; *obs.*) pollution; filth.

скве́рно *adv.* badly; **с. чу́вствовать себя́** to feel bad, feel poorly; **с. поступи́ть с кем-н.** to treat s.o. badly.

сквернословв, а *m.* foul-mouthed pers.

скверносло́ви|е, я *nt.* foul language.

скверносло́в|ить, лю, ишь *impf.* to use foul language.

скве́р|ный (~ен, ~на́, ~но) *adj.* nasty, foul; bad; **~ная пого́да** foul weather; (*impers.*): **мне ~но** I feel bad.

сквита́|ться, юсь *pf.* (**с**+*i.*; *coll.*) to be quits (with), be even (with).

сквоз|и́ть, и́т *impf.* **1.** (*impers.*): **~и́т** there is a draught. **2.** (*obs.*) to be transparent, show light through. **3.** to show through, be seen through (*also fig.*); **синева́ небе́с ~и́ла меж ветвя́ми** the blue of the sky could be seen through the branches; **в его́ слова́х ~и́ла жа́лость к себе́** there was a hint of self-pity in his words.

сквозн|о́й *adj.* **1.** through; **с. ве́тер** draught; **~о́е движе́ние** through traffic; **с. по́езд** through train. **2.** all-round. **3.** transparent.

сквозня́к, а́ *m.* draught.

сквозь *prep.*+*a.* through.

сквор|е́ц, ца́ *m.* starling.

скворе́чник, а *m.* starling-house (*wooden box affixed to pole or on tree adjoining house*).

скворе́ч|ница, ницы *f.* = **~ник**

скворе́ч|ня, ни, *g. pl.* **~ен** *f.* = **~ник**

сквош, а *m.* (*sport*) squash.

скеле́т, а *m.* skeleton.

ске́псис, а *m.* scepticism.

ске́птик, а *m.* sceptic.

скептици́зм, а *m.* scepticism.

скепти́ческий *adj.* sceptic.

скепти́ч|ный (~ен, ~на) *adj.* sceptical.

ске́рцо *nt. indecl.* (*mus.*) scherzo.

ске́тинг-ри́нг, а *m.* roller-skating rink.

скетч, а *m.* (*theatr.*) sketch.

скид|а́ть¹, а́ю *impf.* (*coll.*) to throw off.

скид|а́ть², а́ю *pf.* (*of* **~́ывать²**) (*coll.*) to throw off.

ски́дк|а, и *f.* **1.** rebate, reduction, discount; **со ~ой (в**+*a.*) with a reduction (of), at a discount (of). **2.** (**на**+*a.*; *fig.*) allowance(s) (for); **сде́лать ~у на во́зраст** to make allowances for age.

ски́дыва|ть¹, ю *impf. of* **ски́нуть**

ски́дыва|ть², ю *impf. of* **скида́ть²**

ски́|нуть, ну, нешь *pf.* (*of* **~́дывать¹**) **1.** (*coll.*) to throw off, down; **с. с себя́ оде́жду** to throw off one's clothes. **2.** (*coll.*) to knock off (*from price*).

скип, а *m.* (*tech.*) skip.

ски́петр, а *m.* sceptre.

скипида́р, а *m.* turpentine.

скипида́р|ный *adj. of* **~**

скирд, а́, *pl.* **~ы́** *m.* stack, rick.

скирд|а́, ы́, *pl.* **~́ы, ~, ~а́м** *f.* = **~**

скирд|ова́ть, у́ю *impf.* (*of* **за~**) to stack.

скис|а́ть, а́ю *impf. of* **~́нуть**

ски́с|нуть, ну, нешь, *past* **~, ~ла** *pf.* (*of* **~а́ть**) to go sour, turn sour.

скит, а́, о ~е́, в ~у́ *m.* (*small and secluded*) monastery.

скита́л|ец, ьца *m.* wanderer.

скита́льческий *adj.* wandering.

скита́льчеств|о, а *nt.* wandering.

скита́|ться, юсь *impf.* to wander; **с. по све́ту** to be a globe-trotter.

скиф¹, а *m.* (*hist.*) Scythian.

скиф², а *m.* skiff.

ски́фский *adj.* (*hist.*) Scythian.

склад¹, а *m.* **1.** storehouse; (*mil.*) depot; **тамо́женный с.** bonded warehouse; **това́рный с.** warehouse. **2.** store; **с. боеприпа́сов** (*mil.*) ammunition dump.

склад², а *m.* **1.** stamp, mould; **с. ума́** cast of mind, mentality. **2.** (*coll.*) logical connection; **ни ~́у, ни ла́ду** neither rhyme nor reason.

склад³, а, *pl.* **~ы́** *m.* syllable; **чита́ть по ~а́м** to read haltingly, spell out.

скла́д|ень, ня *m.* **1.** hinged icon. **2.** (*obs.*) folding object.

склади́р|овать, ую *impf. and pf.* to store.

скла́дк|а, и *f.* **1.** fold; pleat, tuck; crease; **ю́бка в ~у** pleated skirt; **с. на брю́ках** trouser crease. **2.** wrinkle. **3.** (*geol.*) fold; **с. ме́стности** natural feature, accident of terrain.

скла́дно *adv.* smoothly, coherently.

складн|о́й *adj.* folding, collapsible; **~а́я крова́ть** camp bed; **с. нож** pocket knife.

скла́д|ный (~ен, ~на́, ~но) *adj.* **1.** (*coll.*; *of human beings or animals*) well-knit, well-built. **2.** (*coll.*) well-made. **3.** (*of speech*) well-rounded, smooth, coherent; **с. расска́з** well-put-together story.

скла́дочн|ый *adj.* storage, warehousing; **~ое ме́сто** store-room, lumber-room.

склад|ско́й *adj.* = **~́очный**

скла́дчатый *adj.* (*geol.*) plicated, folded.

скла́дчин|а, ы *f.* clubbing, pooling; **устро́ить ~у** to club together, pool one's resources; **купи́ть автомоби́ль в ~у** to club together to buy a car.

скла́дыва|ть(ся), ю(сь) *impf. of* **сложи́ть(ся)**

скле́ива|ть(ся), ю(сь), ет(ся) *impf. of* **скле́ить(ся)**

скле́|ить, ю, ишь *pf.* (*of* **~ивать**) to stick together; to glue together, paste together.

скле́|иться, ится *pf.* (*of* **~иваться**) to stick together (*intrans.*).

скле́йк|а, и *f.* glueing together, pasting together.

склеп, а *m.* burial vault, crypt.

склеп|а́ть, а́ю *pf.* (*of* **~́ывать**) to rivet.

склёпк|а, и *f.* riveting.

склёпыва|ть, ю *impf. of* **склепа́ть**

склеро́з, а *m.* (*med.*) sclerosis; **рассе́янный** *or* **мно́жественный с.** multiple sclerosis.

склероти́ческий *adj.* (*med.*) sclerotic, sclerous.

скли́|кать, чу, чешь *pf. of* **~ка́ть**

склик|а́ть, а́ю *impf.* (*of* **~́ать**) (*coll.*) to call together.

скло́к|а, и *f.* squabble; row.

склон, а *m.* slope; **на ~́е лет** in one's declining years.

склоне́ни|е, я *nt.* **1.** (*math.*) inclination; (*astron.*) declination; **с. ко́мпаса** variation of the compass; **у́гол ~я** angle of declination; **круг ~я свети́ла** hour-circle of a celestial body. **2.** (*gram.*) declension.

склон|и́ть, ю́, ~́ишь *pf.* (*of* **~я́ть¹**) **1.** to incline, bend, bow; **с. го́лову (пе́ред)** (*fig.*) to bow one's head (to, before). **2.** (*fig.*) to incline; to win over, gain over.

склон|и́ться, ю́сь, ~́ишься *pf.* (*of* **~я́ться¹**) **1.** to bend, bow. **2.** (**к**; *fig.*) to give in (to), yield (to).

скло́нност|ь, и *f.* (**к**) inclination (to, for); disposition (to); susceptibility (to); bent (for); penchant (for).

скло́н|ный (~ен, ~на́, ~но) *adj.* (**к**) inclined (to), disposed (to), susceptible (to), given (to), prone (to).

склоня́|емый *pres. part. pass. of* **~ть**² *and adj.* (*gram.*) declinable.
склон|я́ть¹, **я́ю** *impf. of* **~и́ть**
склон|я́ть², **я́ю** *impf.* (*of* **про~**) (*gram.*) to decline.
склон|я́ться¹, **я́юсь** *impf. of* **~и́ться**
склон|я́ться², **я́ется** *impf.* (*gram.*) to be declined.
скло́чник, а *m.* (*coll.*) squabbler, trouble-maker.
скло́чнича|ть, ю *impf.* (*coll.*) to squabble; to cause rows.
скло́ч|ный (~ен, ~на) *adj.* (*coll.*) troublesome, trouble-making.
скля́нк|а, и *f.* **1.** phial; bottle. **2.** (*naut.*; *obs.*) hour-glass. **3.** (*naut.*) bell (= *one half-hour*); **шесть скля́нок** six bells.
скоб|а́, ы́, *pl.* **~́ы, ~а́м** *f.* cramp(-iron), clamp; staple; catch, fastening; (*naut.*) shackle.
ско́бел|ь, я *m.* adze, scraper(-knife), drawing-knife.
ско́бк|а¹, **и** *f.* **1.** *dim. of* **скоба́**. **2.** (*mark of punctuation, also math.*) bracket; *pl. also* parentheses; **фигу́рные ~и** braces; **заключи́ть в ~и** to parenthesize; **в ~ах** in brackets; (*fig.*) in parenthesis, by the way, incidentally.
ско́бк|а², **и** *f.*: **стри́чься в ~у** to have one's hair cut in a fringe.
скобл|и́ть, ю́, ~́ишь *impf.* to scrape, plane.
ско́бочн|ый *adj. of* **скоба́** *and* **ско́бка; ~ая маши́на** stapler, stapling machine.
скобян|о́й *adj.*: **с. това́р, ~ые изде́лия** hardware.
ско́в|анный 1. *p.p.p. of* **~а́ть; с. льда́ми** ice-bound. **2.** *adj.* constrained.
скова́|ть, скую́, скуёшь *pf.* (*of* **ско́вывать**) **1.** to forge, hammer out. **2.** to forge together. **3.** to chain; to fetter, bind (*also fig.*). **4.** (*mil.*; *fig.*) to pin down, hold, contain. **5.** (*of frost or ice*) to lock; **моро́з ~л ре́ку** the river was frozen over.
сковород|а́, ы́, *pl.* **ско́вороды, сковоро́д, ~а́м** *f.* **1.** frying-pan. **2.** (*tech.*) pan.
ско́векород|ень, ня *m.* (*tech.*) dovetail (joint); **вя́зка ~нем, соедине́ние ~нем** dove-tailing.
сковоро́дк|а, и *f.* (*coll.*) frying-pan.
ско́выва|ть, ю *impf. of* **скова́ть**
сковы́рива|ть, ю *impf. of* **сковырну́ть**
сковыр|ну́ть, ну́, нёшь *pf.* (*of* **~́ивать**) **1.** to pick off, scratch off. **2.** (*coll.*) to knock over, push over.
скок, а *m.* galloping; **во весь с.** at full gallop, at full tilt.
скола́чива|ть, ю *impf. of* **сколоти́ть**
ско́л|ок, ка *m.* **1.** chip. **2.** pricked pattern. **3.** (*fig.*) copy.
сколо|ти́ть, чу́, ~́тишь *pf.* (*of* **скола́чивать**) **1.** to knock together, knock up. **2.** (*fig., coll.*) to put together, knock up; **с. состоя́ние** to knock up a fortune.
скол|о́ть¹, **ю́, ~́ешь** *pf.* (*of* **ска́лывать**) to split off, chop off.
скол|о́ть², **ю́, ~́ешь** *pf.* (*of* **ска́лывать**) to pin together.
сколь *adv.* how.
скольже́ни|е, я *nt.* sliding, slipping; **с. зву́ка** (*mus., ling.*) glide; **с. на крыло́** (*aeron.*) side-slip.
сколь|зи́ть, жу́, зи́шь *impf.* to slide, slip; to glide; **с. глаза́ми** (**по**+*d.*) to cast one's eye (over).
ско́льз|кий (~ок, ~ка́, ~ко) *adj.* slippery (*also fig.*); **~́кое положе́ние** tricky position; **говори́ть на ~кую те́му** to be on slippery ground.
скользн|у́ть, у́, ёшь *pf.* to slide, slip; **с. в дверь** to slip through the door.
скольз|я́щий *pres. part. act. of* **~и́ть** *and adj.* sliding; **с. гра́фик рабо́ты** flexitime; **~я́щая шкала́** sliding scale; **с. у́зел** slip-knot.
ско́лько *interrog. and rel. adv.* **1.** how much; how many; **с. сто́ит?** how much does it cost?; **с. вам лет?** how old are you?; **с. вре́мени?** what time is it?; **с. душе́ уго́дно** to one's heart's content; **с. раз я тебе́ об э́том напомина́л!** how many times have I reminded you about it!; **с. лет, с. зим!** (*coll.*) what ages it has been (since we met)! **2.** = **наско́лько**
ско́лько-нибудь *adv.* any; **есть у вас при себе́ с.-н. де́нег?** have you any money on you?
скома́нд|овать, ую *pf. of* **кома́ндовать**
скомбини́р|овать, ую *pf. of* **комбини́ровать**
ско́мка|ть, ю *pf. of* **ко́мкать**
скоморо́х, а *m.* **1.** (*hist.*) skomorokh (*wandering minstrel-cum-clown*). **2.** (*fig.*) buffoon, clown.
скоморо́шеств|о, а *nt.* buffoonery.
скоморо́шнича|ть, ю *impf.* to play the buffoon.
скомпили́р|овать, ую *pf. of* **компили́ровать**
скомпон|ова́ть, у́ю *pf. of* **компонова́ть**
скомпромети́р|овать, ую *pf. of* **компромети́ровать**
сконструи́р|овать, ую *pf. of* **конструи́ровать**
сконфу́|женный *p.p.p. of* **~зить** *and adj.* confused, abashed, disconcerted.
сконфу́|зить(ся), жу(сь), зишь(ся) *pf. of* **конфу́зить(ся)**
сконцентри́р|овать, ую *pf. of* **концентри́ровать**
сконча́ни|е, я *nt.* **1.** (*obs.*) end, termination **2.** end, decease, passing.
сконча́|ться, юсь *pf.* to pass away (= *to die*).
скоп, а *m.* (*obs.*) pile, accumulation.
скоп|а́, ы́ *f.* (*zool.*) osprey.
скопа́|ть, ю *pf. of* **ска́пывать**
скоп|е́ц, ца́ *m.* eunuch.
скопидо́м, а *m.* (*coll.*) hoarder, miser.
скопидо́мнича|ть, ю *impf.* (*coll.*) to be a hoarder, miser.
скопидо́мств|о, а *nt.* (*coll.*) hoarding; miserliness.
скопи́р|овать, ую *pf. of* **копи́ровать**
скоп|и́ть¹, **лю́, ~́ишь** *pf.* (*of* **ска́пливать**) (+*a. or g.*) to save (up); to amass, pile up.
скоп|и́ть², **лю́, и́шь** *impf.* to castrate.
скоп|и́ться, ~́ится *pf.* (*of* **ска́пливаться**) **1.** to accumulate, pile up. **2.** (*of people*) to gather, collect.
ско́пищ|е, а *nt.* (*pej.*) crowd, assemblage, throng.
скопле́ни|е, я *nt.* **1.** accumulation. **2.** crowd; concentration, conglomeration.
скопн|и́ть, ю́, и́шь *pf. of* **копни́ть**
ско́пом *adv.* (*coll.*) in a crowd, in a bunch, en masse.
ско́пческий *adj.* of a eunuch.
скорб|е́ть, лю́, и́шь *impf.* (**о**+*p.*) to grieve (for, over), mourn (for, over), lament.
ско́рб|ный (~ен, ~на) *adj.* sorrowful, mournful, doleful.
скорбу́т, а *m.* (*med.*) scurvy.
скорбу́тный *adj.* (*med.*) scorbutic.
скорб|ь, и, *pl.* **~́и, ~е́й** *f.* sorrow, grief.
скор|е́е (*and* **~е́й) 1.** *comp. of* **~ый** *and* **~́о; как мо́жно с.** as soon as possible. **2.** *adv.* rather, sooner; **с. всего́** most likely, most probably.
скорлуп|а́, ы́, *pl.* **~́ы** *f.* shell; **с. оре́ха** nutshell; **замкну́ться в свою́ ~у́** to retire into one's shell.
скорм|и́ть, лю́, ~́ишь *pf.* (*of* **ска́рмливать**) (+*d.*) to feed (to).
скорня́жн|ый *adj.*: **~ое де́ло** furriery; **с. това́р** furs.
скорня́к, а́ *m.* furrier, fur-dresser.
ско́ро *adv.* **1.** quickly, fast. **2.** soon; **с. весна́!** spring will soon be here!; **как с., коль с.** (*conj.*) as soon as.
скоро́б|иться, люсь, ишься *pf. of* **коро́биться**
скорогово́рк|а, и *f.* **1.** patter. **2.** tongue-twister.
скоро́м|иться, люсь, ишься *impf.* (*of* **о~**) to break a fast, eat meat during a fast.
скоро́мник, а *m.* (*coll.*) **1.** pers. failing to observe fast. **2.** lewd pers.
скоро́м|ный (~ен, ~на) *adj.* **1.** (*of food*) forbidden to be consumed during fast (*viz. meat dishes or dishes containing milk products*); **~ные дни** meat days; **~ное ма́сло** animal (*opp. vegetable*) fat; *as n.* **~ное, ~ного** *nt.* dishes containing meat and/or milk products. **2.** (*obs.*) lewd.
скоропали́тел|ьный (~ен, ~ьна) *adj.* (*coll.*) hasty, rash.
скоропеча́тный *adj.*: **с. стано́к** (*typ.*) engine press.
скорописный *adj.* cursive.
ско́ропис|ь, и *f.* **1.** cursive (hand). **2.** (*obs.*) shorthand.
скороподъёмност|ь, и *f.* (*aeron.*) rate of climb.
скоропо́ртящийся *adj.* perishable.
скоропости́жн|ый *adj.*: **~ая смерть** sudden death.
скоропреходя́щий *adj.* transient, transitory.
скоропе́л|ый (~, ~а) *adj.* **1.** early; fast-ripening. **2.** (*fig., coll.*) premature; hasty; **с. вы́вод** hasty conclusion.
скоростни́к, а́ *m.* high-speed worker; high-speed performer.
скоростно́й *adj.* high-speed; **с. авто́бус** express bus.
скоростре́льный *adj.* rapid-firing, quick-firing.

ско́рост|ь, и, *pl.* **~и, ~е́й** *f.* **1.** speed; velocity; rate; **дозво́ленная с. (езды́)** speed-limit; **со ~ью тридцати́ миль в час** at thirty miles per hour; **с. подъёма** (*aeron.*) rate of climb; **с. све́та** velocity of light. **2. коро́бка ~е́й** (*tech.*) gear-box; **перейти́ на другу́ю с.** to change gear. **3.** (*rail.*) category of transit; **ма́лой ~ью** by (slow) goods train; **большо́й ~ью** by fast goods train; **отпра́вить груз пассажи́рской ~ью** to send a consignment by passenger train. **4.: в ~и** (*coll.*) soon; in the near future.

скоросшива́тел|ь, я *m.* loose-leaf binder.

скорота́|ть, ю *pf. of* **корота́ть**

скороте́ч|ный (~ен, ~на) *adj.* **1.** (*obs.*) transient, short-lived. **2.** (*med.*) fulminant; **~ная чахо́тка** galloping consumption.

скорохо́д, а *m.* **1.** (*obs.*) footman. **2.** fast runner; **конькобе́жец-с.** high-speed skater.

скорпио́н, а *m.* scorpion; **С.** Scorpio (*sign of zodiac*).

скорч|и́ть, у, ишь *pf. of* **ко́рчить**

ско́р|ый (~, ~а́, ~о) *adj.* **1.** quick, fast; rapid; **с. по́езд** fast train; **~ая по́мощь** ambulance (service); **на ~ую ру́ку** off-hand, in rough-and-ready fashion. **2.** near, forthcoming, impending; **в ~ом бу́дущем** in the near future; **в ~ом вре́мени** shortly, before long; **до ~ого (свида́ния)!** see you soon!

скос[1], **а** *m.* (*agric.*) mowing.

скос[2], **а** *m.* slant, splay, chamfer, taper; **у́гол ~а** angle of taper.

ско|си́ть[1], **шу́, ~сишь** *pf.* (*of* **коси́ть**[1] *and* **ска́шивать**) to mow.

ско|си́ть[2], **шу́, си́шь** *pf.* (*of* **коси́ть**[2] *and* **ска́шивать**) to squint.

ско|сти́ть, щу́, сти́шь *pf.* (*of* **ска́щивать**) (*coll.*) to strike off, knock off; **с. три рубля́ с цены́** to knock three roubles off the price.

скот, а́ *m.* **1.** (*collect.*) cattle; livestock. **2.** (*fig., coll.*) swine, beast.

скоти́н|а, ы *f.* **1.** (*collect.*) cattle; livestock. **2.** (*also m.*) (*fig., coll.*) swine, beast.

скоти́нк|а, и *f. dim. of* **скоти́на; се́рая с.** (*coll.*) simple soldiery.

ско́тник, а *m.* herd, herdsman; cowman.

ско́т|ный *adj. of* **~; с. двор** cattle-yard.

скотобо́|ец, йца *m.* slaughterer.

скотобо́|йня, йни, *g. pl.* **~ен** *f.* slaughter-house.

скотово́д, а *m.* cattle-breeder.

скотово́дств|о, а *nt.* cattle-breeding, cattle-raising.

скотово́дческий *adj.* cattle-breeding.

скотокра́дств|о, а *nt.* cattle-stealing, cattle rustling.

скотоло́жств|о, а *nt.* bestiality.

скотопригóнный *adj.*: **с. двор** stock-yard.

скотопромы́шленник, а *m.* cattle-dealer.

скотопромы́шленност|ь, и *f.* cattle-dealing, cattle-trade.

скотопромы́шленн|ый *adj. of* **~ость**

ско́тский *adj.* brutal, brutish, bestial.

скотств|о́, а́ *nt.* brutality, brutishness, bestiality.

скотч, а *m.* (*coll.*) adhesive tape; sellotape (*propr.*).

скра́дыва|ть, ю *impf.* to conceal, make less evident.

скра́|сить, шу, сишь *pf.* (*of* **~шивать**) (*fig.*) to smooth over, to relieve, take the edge off; **он мно́го чита́л, что́бы с. своё одино́чество** he read a lot to relieve his loneliness.

скра́шива|ть, ю *impf. of* **скра́сить**

скребко́вый *adj.* (*tech.*) scraping, scraper.

скребни́ц|а, ы *f.* curry-comb, horsecomb.

скреб|о́к, ка́ *m.* scraper.

скре́жет, а *m.* gnashing, gritting (*of teeth*).

скреже|та́ть, щу́, ~щешь *impf.* **(зуба́ми)** to gnash, grit one's teeth.

скре́п|а, ы *f.* **1.** (*tech.*) tie, clamp, brace. **2.** counter-signature, authentication; **ко́пия за ~ой секретаря́** copy countersigned by the secretary.

скре́пер, а *m.* (*tech.*) earth-moving machine.

скреп|и́ть, лю́, и́шь *pf.* (*of* **~ля́ть**) **1.** to fasten (together), make fast; to pin (together), to clamp, brace; **~я́ се́рдце** reluctantly, grudgingly. **2.** to countersign, authenticate, ratify.

скре́пк|а, и *f.* paper-clip.

скрепле́ни|е, я *nt.* **1.** fastening; clamping. **2.** (*tech.*) tie, clamp.

скрепля́|ть, ю *impf. of* **скрепи́ть**

скре|сти́, бу́, бёшь, *past* **~б, ~бла́** *impf.* **1.** to scrape; to scratch, claw. **2.** (*impers.; fig., coll.*) to nag, goad; **у неё ~бло́ на се́рдце** she felt a nagging anxiety.

скре|сти́сь, бу́сь, бёшься, *past* **~бся, ~бла́сь** *impf.* to scratch, make a scratching noise.

скре|сти́ть, щу́, сти́шь *pf.* (*of* **~щивать**) **1.** to cross; **с. мечи́, с. шпа́ги (с+***i.***)** to cross swords (with) (*also fig.*). **2.** (*biol.*) to cross, interbreed.

скрест|и́ться, и́тся *pf.* (*of* **скре́щиваться**) **1.** to cross; (*fig.*) to clash. **2.** (*biol.*) to cross, interbreed.

скреще́ни|е, я *nt.* crossing; intersection.

скре́щивани|е, я *nt.* **1.** crossing. **2.** (*biol.*) crossing, interbreeding.

скре́щива|ть(ся), ю, ет(ся) *impf. of* **скрести́ть(ся)**

скрив|и́ть(ся), лю́(сь), и́шь(ся) *pf. of* **криви́ть(ся)**

скрижа́л|ь, и *f.* tablet, table (*with sacred text inscribed upon it*); **~и** (*fig., arch.*) annals, memorials, records.

скрип, а *m.* squeak, creak; crunch.

скрипа́ч, а́ *m.* violinist.

скрип|е́ть, лю́, и́шь *impf.* **1.** to squeak, creak; to crunch. **2.** (*coll., joc.*) to be just alive, just keep going.

скрипи́чный *adj.* violin; **с. ма́стер** violin-maker; **с. ключ** treble clef, G clef; **с. конце́рт** violin concerto.

скри́пк|а, и *f.* violin; **пе́рвая с.** first violin; (*fig., coll.*) first fiddle.

скри́пн|уть, у, ешь *pf.* to squeak, creak.

скрипу́чий *adj.* (*coll.*) squeaky, creaking; **с. го́лос** rasping voice; **с. снег** crunching snow.

скро|и́ть, ю́, и́шь *pf. of* **крои́ть**

скро́мник, а *m.* modest man.

скро́мнича|ть, ю *impf.* to be overmodest.

скро́мност|ь, и *f.* modesty.

скро́м|ный (~ен, ~на́, ~но) *adj.* (*in var. senses*) modest; **по моему́ ~ному мне́нию** in my humble opinion.

скру́пул, а *m.* (*measure of weight*) scruple.

скрупулёзност|ь, и *f.* scrupulousness, scrupulosity.

скрупулёз|ный (~ен, ~на) *adj.* scrupulous.

скру|ти́ть, чу́, ~тишь *pf.* (*of* **крути́ть** *and* **~чивать**) **1.** to twist; to roll. **2.** to bind, tie up.

скру́чива|ть, ю *impf. of* **скрути́ть**

скрыва́|ть, ю *impf. of* **скрыть**

скрыва́|ться, юсь *impf.* **1.** *impf. of* **скры́ться. 2.** *impf. only* to lie in hiding; to lie low.

скры́тнича|ть, ю *impf.* (*coll.*) to be secretive, be reticent.

скры́т|ный (~ен, ~на) *adj.* reticent, secretive.

скры́т|ый *p.p.p. of* **~ь** *and adj.* secret, concealed; latent (*also phys.*); **с. смысл** hidden meaning; **~ая теплота́** (*phys.*) latent heat.

скр|ыть, о́ю, о́ешь *pf.* (*of* **~ыва́ть**) **(от)** to hide (from), conceal (from); **не с. того́, что** to make no secret of the fact that; **с. от кого́-н. неприя́тные изве́стия** to keep bad news from s.o.

скр|ы́ться, о́юсь, о́ешься *pf.* (*of* **~ыва́ться**) **(от) 1.** to hide (o.s.) (from); to go into hiding. **2.** to steal away (from), escape, give the slip. **3.** to disappear, vanish.

скрю́ч|ить, у, ишь *pf. of* **крю́чить**

скрю́ч|иться, усь, ишься *pf.* to bend (*intrans.*); to hunch o.s. up.

скря́г|а, и *c.g.* miser, skinflint.

скря́жнича|ть, ю *impf.* (*coll.*) to be a miser, be a skinflint.

скуде́л|ь, и *f.* (*arch.*) **1.** potter's clay. **2.** pot, vessel.

скуде́ль|ный *adj.* **1.** *adj. of* **~. 2.** (*fig.*) frail, fragile; **сосу́д с.** (*eccl. or rhet.*) weak vessel.

скуде́|ть, ю *impf.* (*of* **о~**) to grow scanty, run short; **(+***i.***)** to be short (of).

ску́д|ный (~ен, ~на́, ~но) *adj.* **1.** scanty, poor; slender, meagre; scant; **с. обе́д** meagre repast; **~ные све́дения** scant information; **~ные сре́дства** slender means **2. (+***i.***)** poor (in), short (of).

ску́дост|ь, и *f.* scarcity; poverty.

скудоу́ми|е, я *nt.* feeble-mindedness.

скудоу́м|ный (~ен, ~на) *adj.* feeble-minded.

ску́к|а, и *f.* boredom, tedium; **кака́я с.!** what a bore!
скул|а́, ы́, *pl.* **~ы** *f.* cheek-bone.
скула́ст|ый (~, ~а) *adj.* with high cheek-bones, with prominent cheek-bones.
скул|и́ть, ю́, и́шь *impf.* (*of a dog*) to whine, whimper (*also fig.*).
скулово́й *adj.* (*anat.*) malar.
ску́льптор, а *m.* sculptor.
скульпту́р|а, ы *f.* sculpture.
скульпту́рный *adj.* sculptural; (*fig.*) statuesque.
ску́мбри|я, и *f.* mackerel; scomber.
скунс, а *m.* skunk.
скуп|а́ть, а́ю *impf. of* **~и́ть**
скуперд|я́й, я *m.* (*coll.*) miser, skinflint.
скуп|е́ц, ца́ *m.* miser, skinflint.
скуп|и́ть, лю́, ~ишь *pf.* (*of* **~а́ть**) to buy up; to corner.
скуп|и́ться, лю́сь, и́шься *impf.* (*of* **по~**) (*+inf. or* **на**+*a.*) to stint, grudge, skimp; to be sparing (of); **с. на де́ньги** to be close-fisted; **не с. на похвалы́** not to stint one's praise.
ску́пк|а, и *f.* buying up; cornering.
скуп|но́й *adj. of* **~ка**
ску́по *adv.* sparingly.
скуп|о́й (~, ~а́, ~о) *adj.* **1.** stingy, miserly, niggardly; **с. на похвалы́** chary of praise; **с. на слова́** sparing of words. **2.** (*fig.*) inadequate; **с. свет** inadequate illumination.
ску́пост|ь, и *f.* stinginess, miserliness, niggardliness.
ску́п|очный *adj. of* **~ка**
ску́пщик, а *m.* buyer-up; **с. кра́деного** fence.
ску́тер, а *m.* outboard-motor boat.
скуфе́йк|а, и *f. dim. of* **скуфья́**
скуфь|я́, и́ *f.* (*clerical*) skull-cap, calotte.
скуча́|ть, ю *impf.* **1.** to be bored. **2.** (**по**+*d. or p.*) to miss, yearn (for).
ску́ченност|ь, и *f.* density, congestion; **с. населе́ния** overcrowding.
ску́ченный *adj.* dense, congested.
ску́чива|ть(ся), ю(сь) *impf. of* **ску́чить(ся)**
ску́ч|ить, у, ишь *pf.* (*of* **~ивать**) to crowd (together).
ску́ч|иться, усь, ишься *pf.* (*of* **~иваться**) to flock, cluster; to crowd together, huddle together.
ску́ч|ный (~ен, ~на́, ~но) *adj.* **1.** boring, depressing, tedious, dull. **2.** bored; **с. взгляд** look of boredom; *as pred.* **мне,** *etc.*, **~но** I, *etc.*, am bored, depressed.
ску́ша|ть, ю *pf. of* **ку́шать**
слабе́|ть, ю *impf.* (*of* **о~**) to weaken, grow weak(er), (*of wind, etc.*) to slacken, drop.
слабин|а́, ы́ *no pl., f.* **1.** (*in a rope, etc.*) slack; **вы́брать ~у́** (*naut.*) to haul in the slack. **2.** (*coll.*) weak spot, weak point.
слаби́тельн|ый *adj.* (*med.*) laxative, purgative; *as n.* **~ое, ~ого** *nt.* laxative, purgative.
сла́б|ить, ит *impf.* (*of* **про~**) **1.** (*impers.*): **его́ ~ит** he has diarrhoea. **2.** to purge, act as a laxative.
сла́б|нуть, ну, нешь, *past* **~, ~ла** *impf.* (*of* **о~**) (*coll.*) **1.** to weaken, grow weak(er). **2.** to become slack.
слабоалкого́льный *adj.* low-alcohol.
слабово́ли|е, я *nt.* weak will.
слабово́ль|ный (~ен, ~ьна) *adj.* weak-willed.
слабогру́д|ый (~, ~а) *adj.* weak-chested.
слабоду́ши|е, я *nt.* faint-heartedness.
слабоду́ш|ный (~ен, ~на) *adj.* faint-hearted.
слабора́звитый *adj.* (*econ.*) under-developed.
слабоси́ли|е, я *nt.* weakness, feebleness, debility.
слабоси́ль|ный (~ен, ~ьна) *adj.* **1.** weak, feeble. **2.** (*tech.*) low-powered.
сла́бост|ь, и *f.* **1.** weakness, feebleness; debility. **2.** (**к**) weakness (for); foible; **чу́вствовать с. (к)** to have a weakness (for).
слабото́чный *adj.* (*tech.*) low-current.
слабоу́ми|е, я *nt.* feeble-mindedness, imbecility; **ста́рческое с.** senile dementia.
слабоу́м|ный (~ен, ~на) *adj.* feeble-minded, imbecile; mentally deficient.
слабохара́ктер|ный (~ен, ~на) *adj.* characterless, of weak character.
сла́б|ый (~, ~а́, ~о) *adj.* (*in var. senses*) weak; feeble; slack, loose; (*fig.*) poor; **~ое здоро́вье** delicate health; **~ое ме́сто, ~ая сторона́** weak point, weak place; **~ая наде́жда** faint hope, slender hope; **~ое оправда́ние** lame excuse; **с. пол** the weaker sex; **с. результа́т** poor result.
сла́в|а, ы *f.* **1.** glory; fame; **во ~у** (*+g.*) to the glory (of); **на ~у** (*coll.*) wonderfully well, excellently; (*as int.*, *+d.*) hurrah (for)!; **с. Бо́гу** thank God, thank goodness. **2.** fame, name, repute, reputation; **до́брая с.** good name; **дурна́я с.** infamy. **3.** (*coll.*) rumour.
сла́вильщик, а *m.* (*obs.*) wait, carol-singer.
слави́ст, а *m.* Slavist, Slavicist.
слави́стик|а, и *f.* Slavistics; Slavonic *or* Slavic studies.
сла́в|ить, лю, ишь *impf.* **1.** to celebrate, hymn, sing the praises (of); **с. Христа́** to go carol-singing. **2.** (*coll.*) to give a bad name.
сла́в|иться, люсь, ишься *impf.* (*+i.*) to be famous (for), be famed (for), be renowned (for); to have a reputation (for).
сла́вк|а, и *f.* (*zool.*) warbler.
сла́в|ный (~ен, ~на́, ~но) *adj.* **1.** glorious; famous, renowned. **2.** (*coll.*) nice, splendid; **с. ма́лый** good chap, nice chap.
славосло́ви|е, я *nt.* **1.** (*eccl.*) doxology; gloria. **2.** glorification, eulogy.
славосло́в|ить, лю, ишь *impf.* to eulogize, extol, overpraise.
славяни́зм, а *m.* (*ling.*) **1.** Slavism, Slavicism (*in a non-Slavonic language*). **2.** Slavonicism (*in Russian*).
славян|и́н, и́на, *pl.* **~е, ~** *m.* Slav.
славянове́д, а *m.* Slavist, Slavicist.
славянове́дени|е, я *nt.* Slavistics; Slavonic *or* Slavic studies.
славянофи́л, а *m.* Slavophil(e).
славянофи́л|ьский *adj. of* **~** *and* **~ьство**
славянофи́льств|о, а *nt.* Slavophilism.
славя́нский *adj.* Slavonic; Slavic; Slav.
славя́нств|о, а *nt.* (*collect.*) the Slavonic peoples.
слага́ем|ое, ого *nt.* **1.** (*math.*) item. **2.** (*fig.*) component.
слага́|ть(ся), ю(сь) *impf. of* **сложи́ть(ся)**
слад, а (у) *m.*, *now only in phr.* **с ним,** *etc.*, **~у нет** (*coll.*) he, *etc.*, is unmanageable, is out of hand.
сла́ден|ький (~ек, ~ька) *adj.* (*coll.*) sweetish; (*fig.*) sugary, honeyed; **~ькая улы́бка** sugary smile.
сла́|дить, жу, дишь *pf.* (*of* **~живать**) **1.** (*coll.*) to arrange. **2.** (**с**+*i.*) to cope (with), manage, handle; **он про́сто не уме́л с. с подчинёнными** he simply did not know how to handle his subordinates.
сла́д|кий (~ок, ~ка́, ~ко) *adj.* **1.** sweet (*also fig.*); **~кое мя́со** (*cul.*) sweetbread; **для меня́ э́то не ~ко** (*of food*) it is not sweet enough for me; *as n.* **~кое, ~кого** *nt.* sweet (course), dessert. **2.** (*fig., pej.*) sugary, sugared, honeyed.
сладкое́жк|а, и *c.g.* (*coll.*) (pers. with) sweet tooth.
сладкозву́ч|ный (~ен, ~на) *adj.* (*obs.*) mellifluous.
сладкоречи́в|ый (~, ~а) *adj.* smooth-spoken, smooth-tongued.
сла́дост|ный (~ен, ~на) *adj.* (*obs.*) sweet, delightful.
сладостра́сти|е, я *nt.* voluptuousness.
сладостра́стник, а *m.* voluptuary.
сладостра́ст|ный (~ен, ~на) *adj.* voluptuous.
сла́дост|ь, и *f.* **1.** sweetness. **2.** (*coll.*) sweetening. **3.** (*pl.*) sweets, sweetmeats.
сла́женност|ь, и *f.* co-ordination, harmony, order.
сла́|женный *p.p.p. of* **~дить** *and adj.* (well-)coordinated, harmonious, orderly.
сла́жива|ть, ю *impf. of* **сла́дить**
сла́|зить, жу, зишь *pf.* (*coll.*) to go; **с. в подва́л за дрова́ми** to go down to the cellar for logs.
слайд, а *m.* slide, transparency.
слайдпрое́ктор, а *m.* slide projector.
сла́лом, а *m.* (*sport*) slalom.
сла́н|ец, ца *m.* (*min.*) shale, schist; slate; **гли́нистый с.** argillaceous schist; **горю́чий с., нефтено́сный с.** oil shale, bituminous shale.
сла́нцев|ый *adj.* schistose, schistous; slate, slaty; shale; **~ое ма́сло** shale oil; **с. пласт** schist.
сла|сти́ть, щу́, сти́шь *impf.* (*of* **по~**) to sweeten.

сластолю́б|ец, ца *m.* voluptuary.
сластолюби́в|ый (~, ~а) *adj.* voluptuous.
сластолю́би|е, я *nt.* voluptuousness.
сласт|ь, и, *pl.* **~́и, ~е́й** *f.* **1.** (*pl.*) sweets, sweetmeats. **2.** (*fig.*) delight, pleasure; **что за с. гуля́ть одному́?** what fun is there in going out alone?
слать, шлю, шлёшь *impf.* to send; **с. приве́т** to send greetings.
слаща́в|ый (~, ~а) *adj.* (*liter. and fig.*) sugary, sickly-sweet.
сла́ще *comp. of* **сла́дкий**
сле́ва *adv.* **(от)** on the left (of), to the left (of); **с. напра́во** from left to right.
слег|а́, и́, *pl.* **~́и, ~, ~а́м** *f.* beam.
слегка́ *adv.* lightly, gently; slightly, somewhat; **с. суту́литься** to stoop slightly; **с. гла́дить** to stroke gently.
след[1]**, а (у),** *pl.* **~ы́, ~о́в** *m.* **1.** track; trail, footprint, footstep; **верну́ться по свои́м ~а́м** to retrace one's steps; **замести́ свой ~ы́** to cover up one's tracks; **идти́ по чьим-н. ~а́м** (*fig.*) to follow in s.o.'s footsteps. **2.** (*fig.*) trace, sign, vestige; **~́а нет его́** there is no trace of it; **~ы́ о́спы** pockmarks. **3.** sole (*of the foot*).
след[2]**: не с.** (*coll.*) = **не ~́ует**
сле|ди́ть[1]**, жу́, ди́шь** *impf.* **(за**+*i.*) **1.** to watch; to track; to shadow; **с. глаза́ми за полётом мяча́** to follow (with one's eyes) the flight of a ball. **2.** (*fig.*) to follow; to keep up (with); **с. за междунаро́дными собы́тиями** to keep up with international affairs. **3.** to look after; to keep an eye (on); **с. за детьми́** to look after children; **с. за поря́дком** to keep order; **с. за тем, что́бы** to see to it that.
сле|ди́ть[2]**, жу́, ди́шь** *impf.* (*of* **на~**) **(на**+*p.*) to mark; to leave traces (on), leave footmarks, footprints (on).
сле́довани|е, я *nt.* movement, proceeding; **по́езд да́льнего ~я** long-distance train; **во вре́мя ~я по́езда** while the train is moving; **на всём пути́ ~я** all along the line, throughout the entire journey; **по пути́ ~я во́йск** (*mil.*) along the line of march.
сле́довател|ь, я *m.* investigator.
сле́довательно *conj.* consequently, therefore, hence.
сле́д|овать[1]**, ую** *impf.* (*of* **по~**) **1. (за**+*i.*) to follow, go after; **с. за кем-н. по пята́м** to follow hard on s.o.'s heels. **2.** (+*d.*) to follow; **с. отцу́** to follow in one's father's footsteps. **3.** (+*d.*) to follow; to comply (with); **с. пра́вилам** to conform to the rules; **с. при́хоти** to follow a whim. **4.** (*impf. only*) **(до, в**+*a.*) to be bound (for); **э́тот по́езд ~ует в Варша́ву** this train is (bound) for Warsaw. **5.** (*impf. only*) to follow; to result; **из э́того ~ует, что мы оши́блись** it follows from this that we were mistaken.
сле́д|овать[2]**, ует** *impf.* (*impers.*) **1.** (+*d. and inf.*) ought, should; **вам ~ует обрати́ться к ре́ктору** you should approach the rector; **не ~ует забыва́ть** it should not be forgotten; **куда́ ~ует** to the proper quarter; **как и ~овало ожида́ть** as was to be expected; **как ~ует** as it should be, properly, well and truly, good and proper. **2.** (+*d.* **с**+*g.*) to be owed, be owing; **ско́лько вам ~ует с меня́?** how much do I owe you?; **с вас ~ует де́сять рубле́й** you have ten roubles to pay.
сле́дом *adv.* **(за**+*i.*) immediately (after, behind); **идти́ с. за кем-н.** to follow s.o. close(ly).
следопы́т, а *m.* pathfinder, tracker.
сле́дств|енный *adj. of* **~ие; ~енная коми́ссия** committee of inquiry; **с. материа́л** evidence; **~енные о́рганы** investigation agencies.
сле́дстви|е[1]**, я** *nt.* consequence, result; **причи́на и с.** cause and effect.
сле́дстви|е[2]**, я** *nt.* (*leg.*) investigation; **суде́бное с.** inquest.
сле́дуем|ый *adj.* (+*d.*) due (to); **отда́ть ка́ждому ~ое** to give each his due.
сле́д|ующий *pres. part. act. of* **~овать** *and adj.* following, next; **на с. день** next day; **на ~ующей неде́ле** next week; **постано́влено ~ующее** it has been resolved as follows.
слеж|а́ться, и́тся *pf.* (*of* **~̈иваться**) to become caked; to deteriorate in storage.
слёжива|ться, ется *impf. of* **слежа́ться**
сле́жк|а, и *f.* shadowing; **установи́ть ~у за кем-н.** to have s.o. shadowed.
слез|а́, ы, *pl.* **~̈ы, ~̈, ~а́м** *f.* tear; **крокоди́ловы ~̈ы** crocodile tears; **довести́ до ~̈** to reduce to tears; **э́то до ~̈ оби́дно** it is enough to make one weep.
слеза́|ть, ю *impf. of* **слезть**
слез|и́ться, и́тся *impf.* to water; **её глаза́ ~и́лись** her eyes were watering.
слезли́в|ый (~, ~а) *adj.* **1.** given to crying. **2.** tearful, lachrymose.
слёзно *adv.* (*coll.*) tearfully, with tears in one's eyes; (*fig.*) humbly, plaintively.
слёзн|ый *adj.* **1.** (*anat.*) lachrymal; **~ая железа́** lachrymal gland; **с. прото́к** lachrymal duct, tear duct. **2.** (*fig., coll.*) humble, plaintive; **~ая про́сьба** humble petition.
слезоотделе́ни|е, я *nt.* tear-shedding; (*med.*) epiphora.
слезотече́ни|е, я *nt.* = **слезоотделе́ние**
слезоточи́в|ый (~, ~а) *adj.* **1.: ~ые глаза́** running eyes. **2.** lachrymatory; **с. газ** tear-gas.
слез|ть, у, ешь, *past* **~, ~́ла** *pf.* (*of* **~а́ть**) **(с**+*g.*) **1.** to come down (from), get down (from); to dismount (from). **2.** to alight (from), get off; **с. с трамва́я** to get off a tram. **3.** (*of paint or skin*) to come off, peel.
сленг, а *m.* slang.
сленги́зм, а *m.* slang word *or* expression.
сле́нговый *adj.* slang.
слеп|е́нь, ня́ *m.* gadfly, horse-fly.
слеп|е́ц, ца́ *m.* blind man.
слеп|и́ть[1]**, лю́, и́шь** *impf.* to blind; to dazzle.
слеп|и́ть[2]**, лю́, ~́ишь** *pf. of* **лепи́ть**
слеп|и́ть[3]**, лю́, ~́ишь** *pf.* (*of* **~ля́ть**) **1.** to stick together. **2.** to make by sticking together.
слеп|и́ться, ~́иться *pf.* (*of* **~ля́ться**) to stick together.
слепля́|ть(ся), ю(сь) *impf. of* **слепи́ть**[3]**(ся)**
сле́п|нуть, ну, нешь, *past* **~, ~ла** *and* **~́нул, ~́нула** *impf.* to become blind, go blind.
сле́по *adv.* **1.** (*fig.*) blindly; **с. повинова́ться** to obey blindly. **2.** indistinctly.
слеп|о́й (~, ~а́, ~́о) *adj.* **1.** blind (*also fig.*); **с. на оди́н глаз** blind in one eye; **~а́я кишка́** blind gut, caecum; **с. ме́тод маши́нописи** touch-typing; **с. полёт** blind flying; **~о́е пятно́** (*anat.*) blind spot; *as n.* **с., ~о́го** *m.* blind pers.; (*pl., collect.*) the blind. **2.** indistinct.
сле́п|ок, ка *m.* mould, copy.
слепорождённый *adj.* blind from birth.
слепот|а́, ы *f.* blindness (*also fig.*).
слепы́ш, а́ *m.* mole-rat.
слеса́рн|ый *adj.* metal-work, metal worker's; **~ое де́ло** metal work; **~ая (мастерска́я)** metal workshop.
слеса́р|ня, ни, *g. pl.* **~ен** *f.* metal workshop.
сле́сар|ь, я, *pl.* **~и, ~ей** *and* **~я́, ~е́й** *m.* metal worker; locksmith.
слёт, а *m.* **1.** flying together. **2.** gathering, meeting; rally.
слётанност|ь, и *f.* (*of aircrews*) co-ordination.
слета́|ть[1]**, ю** *pf.* **1.** to fly (*there and back*). **2.** (*fig., coll.*) to fly, dash, nip.
слет|а́ть[2]**, а́ю** *impf. of* **~е́ть**
слета́|ться[1]**, юсь** *pf.* to achieve co-ordination in flying.
слет|а́ться[2]**, а́юсь** *impf. of* **~е́ться**
сле|те́ть, чу́, ти́шь *pf.* (*of* **~та́ть**[2]) **(с**+*g*). **1.** to fly down (from). **2.** (*coll.*) to fall down, fall off; **с. с ло́шади** to fall from a horse. **3.** to fly away.
слет|е́ться, и́ться *pf.* (*of* **~а́ться**[2]) to fly together; (*of birds*) to congregate.
слечь, сля́гу, сля́жешь, *past* **слёг, слегла́** *pf.* to take to one's bed.
слив, а *m.* **1.** pouring away; discharge. **2.** sink, drain.
сли́в|а, ы *f.* **1.** plum. **2.** plum-tree.
слива́|ть(ся), ю(сь) *impf. of* **сли́ть(ся)**
сли́в|ки, ок *no sg.* cream (*also fig.*); **снима́ть с.** (**с**+*g.*) to skim the cream (off); **с. о́бщества** the cream of society.
сливн|о́й *adj.* **1.** poured together. **2.** overflow, waste; **~а́я труба́** overflow pipe. **3.** collection (*of milk and other fluid products*); **сдать молоко́ на с. пункт** to deliver milk to the collection point.

сли́в|овый *adj. of* **~а; с. джем** plum jam.
сли́вочник, а *m.* cream-jug.
сли́вочн|ый *adj.* cream; creamy; **~ое ма́сло** butter; **~ое моро́женое** ice-cream.
сливя́нк|а, и *f.* plum brandy, slivovitz; sloe-gin.
сли|за́ть, жу́, ~́жешь *pf.* (*of* **~́зывать**) **1.** to lick off. **2.** (*fig., coll.*) to copy; **он э́то с меня́ слиза́л** he got that idea from me.
сли́зист|ый (~, ~а) *adj.* mucous; mucilaginous, slimy; **~ая оболо́чка** (*anat.*) mucous membrane.
слизня́к, а́ *m.* **1.** slug. **2.** (*pej., coll.*) pathetic, worthless, helpless pers.
сли́зыва|ть, ю *impf. of* **слиза́ть**
слиз|ь, и *f.* mucus; mucilage, slime.
слимо́н|ить, ю, ишь *pf. of* **лимо́нить**
слиня́|ть, ет *pf.* **1.** to moult; to slough (off). **2.** (*coll.*) to fade (*of colours*).
слип|а́ться, а́ется *impf. of* **~́нуться**
сли́п|нуться, нется, *past* **~ся, ~лась** *pf.* (*of* **~а́ться**) to stick together.
сли́тно *adv.* together.
сли́тн|ый *adj.* joint, united, continuous; **~ое написа́ние слов** omission of hyphen from words.
сли́т|ок, ка *m.* ingot, bar; **зо́лото в ~ках** gold bullion.
слить, солью́, сольёшь, *past* **слил, слила́, сли́ло** *pf.* (*of* **слива́ть**) **1.** to pour out, pour off. **2.** to pour together; (*fig.*) to fuse, merge, amalgamate; **с. два концéрна** to amalgamate two concerns.
сли́ться, солью́сь, сольёшься, *past* **сли́лся, слила́сь** *pf.* (*of* **слива́ться**) **1.** to flow together. **2.** (*fig.*) to blend, mingle; to merge, amalgamate.
слич|а́ть, а́ю *impf. of* **~и́ть**
сличе́ни|е, я *nt.* collation, checking.
сличи́тельн|ый *adj.* checking; **~ая ве́домость** check-list.
слич|и́ть, у́, и́шь *pf.* (*of* **~а́ть**) (**с**+*i.*) to collate (with), check (with, against).
сли́шком *adv.* too; too much; **э́то с.!** this is too much!
слия́ни|е, я *nt.* **1.** confluence. **2.** (*fig.*) blending, merging, amalgamation; merger.
слобод|а́, ы́, *pl.* **сло́боды, слобо́д, ~а́м** *f.* **1.** (*hist.*) sloboda (*settlement exempted from normal State obligations*). **2.** (*obs.*) suburb.
слобожа́н|ин, ина, *pl.* **~е, ~** *m.* (*hist.*) inhabitant of sloboda.
слова́к, а *m.* Slovak.
Слова́ки|я, и *f.* Slovakia.
слова́рный *adj.* **1.** lexical; **с. соста́в языка́** vocabulary; **с. фонд** word stock. **2.** lexicographic(al), dictionary.
слова́р|ь, я́ *m.* **1.** dictionary; glossary, vocabulary (*to particular text*); **отраслево́й с.** specialist dictionary; **толко́вый с.** (defining) dictionary; **уче́бный с.** learner's dictionary; **энциклопеди́ческий с.** encyclopedia; **с. географи́ческих назва́ний** gazetteer. **2.** (*collect.*) vocabulary; lexis.
слова́цкий *adj.* Slovak, Slovakian.
слова́|чка, чки *f. of* **~к**
слове́н|е, ~ *no sg.* (*obs.*) the Slavs.
слове́н|ец, ца *m.* Slovene.
Слове́ни|я, и *f.* Slovenia.
слове́н|ка, ки *f. of* **~ец**
слове́нский *adj.* Slovene, Slovenian.
слове́сник, а *m.* **1.** philologist; student of philology. **2.** language and literature teacher.
слове́сност|ь, и *f.* **1.** literature. **2.** (*obs.*) philology.
слове́сн|ый *adj.* **1.** verbal, oral; **с. прика́з** verbal order. **2.** literary. **3.** (*obs.*) philological; **~ые нау́ки** philology.
слове́ч|ко, ка, *pl.* **~ки, ~ек** *nt.*, (*coll.*) *dim. of* **сло́во; мо́дное с.** buzz-word; **замо́лвить с. за кого́-н.** to put in a word for s.o.
сло́вник, а *m.* glossary; word-list, selection of words (*for inclusion in a dictionary*).
сло́вно *conj.* **1.** as if. **2.** like, as.
сло́в|о, а, *pl.* **~а́** *nt.* **1.** (*in var. senses*) word; **заимствованное с.** loanword; **други́ми ~а́ми** in other words; **одни́м ~ом** in a word; **с. в с.** word for word; **с. за́ с.** little by little; **к ~у (пришло́сь, сказа́ть)** by the way, by the by; **на ~а́х** (*i*) by word of mouth, (*ii*) in word; **ве́рить на́ с. кому́-н. в чём-н.** to take s.o.'s word for sth.; **челове́к ~а** a man of his word; **игра́ ~** play on words; **~ нет** (*coll.*) it goes without saying; **~ нет, как тут ду́рно па́хнет** there is an indescribably nasty smell. **2.** speech, speaking; **дар ~а** talent for speaking; **свобо́да ~а** freedom of speech. **3.** speech, address; **заключи́тельное с.** concluding remarks; **надгро́бное с.** funeral oration; **дать, предоста́вить с.** (+*d.*) to give the floor, to ask, call upon to speak; **пе́рвое с. принадлежи́т това́рищу X** I call upon Comrade X to open the discussion; **вам принадлежи́т реша́ющее с.** (*fig.*) the final say rests with you. **4.** (*liter.*; *hist.*) lay, tale.
словоблу́ди|е, я *nt.* (mere) verbiage, phrase-mongering.
словоизверже́ни|е, я *nt.* (*iron.*) spate of words.
словоизмене́ни|е, я *nt.* (*ling.*) inflection, accidence.
словоли́тный *adj.* type-founding.
словоли́т|ня, ни, *g. pl.* **~ен** *f.* type foundry.
сло́вом *adv.* in a word, in short.
словообразова́ни|е, я *nt.* (*ling.*) word-formation.
словообразова́тельный *adj.* word-forming.
словоохо́тливост|ь, и *f.* talkativeness, loquacity.
словоохо́тлив|ый (~, ~а) *adj.* talkative, loquacious.
словопре́ни|е, я *nt.* (*obs.*) debate.
словопроизво́дный *adj.* (*ling.*) productive.
словопроизво́дств|о, а *nt.* (*ling.*) derivation.
словосочета́ни|е, я *nt.* combination of words; **усто́йчивое с.** set phrase.
словотво́рчеств|о, а *nt.* creation of words.
словоупотребле́ни|е, я *nt.* use of words, usage.
словц|о́, а́ *nt.* (*coll.*) word; **для кра́сного ~а́** for effect, in order to be witty.
слог[1]**, а,** *pl.* **~́и, ~о́в** *m.* syllable
слог[2]**, а** *m.* style.
слогов|о́й *adj.* **1.** syllabic; **~а́я а́збука** syllabary. **2.** syllable-forming.
слогообразу́ющий *adj.* syllable-forming.
слое́ни|е, я *nt.* stratification.
слоёный *adj.*: **с. пиро́г** puff-pastry pie; **с. дете́ктор** (*phys.*) sandwich detector.
сложе́ни|е, я *nt.* **1.** adding; composition; (*math.*) addition; **с. сил** (*phys.*) composition of forces. **2.** build, constitution; **кре́пкого ~я** of strong build, sturdily-built.
сло́ж|енный *p.p.p. of* **~и́ть**
сложён|ный (~, ~а́) *adj.* formed, built; **хорошо́ с.** well built, of fine physique.
сложи́|вшийся *p.p. of* **~ться; впо́лне́ с.** fully developed, fully formed.
слож|и́ть[1]**, у́, ~́ишь** *pf.* **1.** (*impf.* **скла́дывать**) to put (together), lay (together); to pile, heap, stack; **с. свои́ ве́щи в сунду́к** to pack one's things in a trunk. **2.** (*impf.* **скла́дывать**) to add (up). **3.** (*impf.* **скла́дывать**) to fold (up); **с. вдвое́** to fold in two; **с. ру́ки** to give up the struggle; **~а́ ру́ки** with arms folded; (*fig.*) idle. **4.** (*impf.* **слага́ть**) to make up, compose; **с. пе́сню** to compose a song.
слож|и́ть[2]**, у́, ~́ишь** *pf.* **1.** (*impf.* **скла́дывать**) to take off, put down, set down; **с. груз** to set down a load. **2.** (*impf.* **слага́ть**) (**с**+*g.*; *fig.*) to lay down; to relieve (of); **с. го́лову** (*rhet.*) to lay down one's life; **с. ору́жие** to lay down one's arms; **с. с себя́ обя́занности** to resign; **с. наказа́ние** to remit a punishment.
слож|и́ться[1]**, у́сь, ~́ишься** *pf.* (*of* **скла́дываться**) (**с**+*i.*) to club together (with); to pool one's resources.
слож|и́ться[2]**, у́сь, ~́ишься** *pf.* (*of* **скла́дываться**) to form, turn out; to take shape; to arise; **обстоя́тельства ~и́лись не осо́бенно благоприя́тно** circumstances did not turn out particularly favourably; **у меня́ ~и́лось убежде́ние** the conviction has grown up in me.
сложноподчинённ|ый *adj.*: **~ое предложе́ние** (*gram.*) complex sentence.
сложносокращённ|ый *adj.* compounded of abbreviations; **~ое сло́во** acronym.
сложносочинённ|ый *adj.*: **~ое предложе́ние** (*gram.*) compound sentence.
сло́жност|ь, и *f.* complication; complexity; **в о́бщей ~и** all in all, in sum.

сложноцве́тн|ые, ых *pl.* (*sg.* **~ое, ~ого** *nt.*) (*bot.*) Compositae.

сло́ж|ный (~ен, ~на́, ~но) *adj.* **1.** compound; complex, multiple; **~ное предложе́ние** (*gram.*) compound *or* complex sentence; **~ные проце́нты** compound interest; **~ное сло́во** compound (word); **~ное число́** complex number; **с. эфи́р** (*phys.*) ester. **2.** complicated, complex, intricate; sophisticated.

слои́ст|ый (~, ~а) *adj.* stratified; lamellar; flaky, foliated; (*min.*) schistose, schistous; **~ые облака́** strati.

сло|и́ть, ю́, и́шь *impf.* to stratify; to make in layers.

сло|й, я, *pl.* **~и́** *m.* layer; stratum (*also fig.*); coat(ing) (*of paint*), film; **все ~и́ населе́ния** all sections of the population.

сло́йк|а, и *f.* puff-pastry.

слом, а *m.* pulling down, demolition, breaking up; **пойти́ на с.** to be scrapped.

слома́|ть(ся), ю(сь) *pf. of* **лома́ть(ся)**

слом|и́ть, лю́, ~́ишь *pf.* to break, smash (*fig.*) to overcome; **~я́ го́лову** (*coll.*) like mad, at breakneck speed.

слом|и́ться, лю́сь, ~́ишься *pf.* to break.

слон, а́ *m.* **1.** elephant; **де́лать из му́хи ~а́** to make mountains out of mole-hills; **~а́ не приме́тить** to miss the point. **2.** (*chess*) bishop.

слон|ёнок, ёнка, *pl.* **~я́та, ~я́т** *m.* elephant calf.

слони́х|а, и *f.* she-elephant, cow-elephant.

слоно́вост|ь, и *f.* (*med.*) elephantiasis.

слоно́в|ый *adj. of* **слон**; elephantine; **~ая боле́знь = ~ость; ~ая бума́га** ivory paper; **~ая кость** ivory.

слоня́|ться, юсь *impf.* (*coll.*) to loiter about, mooch about.

слуг|а́, и́, *pl.* **~́и, ~** *m.* **1.** servant. **2.** man, manservant.

служа́к|а, и *m.* (*coll.*) campaigner; old hand, veteran.

служа́нк|а, и *f.* maid, maidservant, housemaid.

слу́жащ|ий, его *m.* employee; white-collar worker, office worker.

слу́жб|а, ы *f.* **1.** (*in var. senses*) service; work; employment; **действи́тельная с.** (*mil.*) active service, service with the colours; **идти́ на ~у** to go to work; **быть на ~е у кого́-н.** to be in s.o.'s employ, work for s.o.; **по дела́м ~ы** on official business; **сослужи́ть кому́-н. ~у** to do s.o. a good turn, stand s.o. in good stead; **не в ~у, а в дру́жбу** (*coll.*) as a favour. **2.** (special) service; **с. движе́ния** (*rail.*) traffic management; **с. пути́** (*rail.*) track maintenance; **с. свя́зи** (*mil.*) signals service; **~ы ты́ла** (*mil.*) supply services. **3.** *pl.* (*obs.*) outbuildings.

служби́ст, а *m.* (*coll.*) red-tape-monger; martinet.

служе́бн|ый *adj.* **1.** *adj. of* **слу́жба**; office; official; work; **~ое вре́мя** office hours, working hours; **~ое де́ло** official business; **с. наря́д** duty roster; **~ая пое́здка** business trip; **в ~ом поря́дке** in the line of duty; **~ое прави́тельство** (*pol.*) caretaker government; **с. просту́пок** dereliction of duty; **с. путь** official channels; **с. стаж** seniority; **~ая характери́стика** service record. **2.** auxiliary; secondary; **~ое сло́во** (*gram.*) connective word.

служе́ни|е, я *nt.* service, serving.

служи́в|ый, ого *m.* (*coll., obs.*) soldier.

служи́л|ый *adj.* (*hist.*) service; **~ые лю́ди, ~ое сосло́вие** service class (*pers. bound by obligations of service, esp. mil. service, to the Muscovite Russ. state*).

служи́тел|ь, я *m.* **1.** (*obs.*) servant, attendant. **2.** votary, devotee; **с. ку́льта** priest, minister.

служ|и́ть, у́, ~́ишь *impf.* (*of* **по~**) **1.** (+*d.*) to serve, devote o.s. (to). **2.** (+*i.*) to serve (as); to work (as), be employed (as), be; **с. в а́рмии** to serve in the Army; **он ~́ит дипломати́ческим курье́ром** he is (employed as) a diplomatic courier; **с. доказа́тельством** (+*g.*) to serve as evidence (of). **3.** *impf. only* (+*i. or* **для**) to serve (for), do (for), be used (for); **гости́ная ~́ит нам и спа́льней** our sitting-room serves also for a bedroom. **4.** to be in use, do duty, serve; **мой ста́рый пластма́ссовый плащ ещё ~́ит** my old plastic mac(k)intosh is still in use. **5.** (*eccl.*) to celebrate; to conduct, officiate (at); **с. обе́дню** to celebrate mass. **6.** *impf. only* (*of a dog*) to (sit up and) beg.

слу́жк|а, и *m.* (*eccl.*) lay brother.

слука́в|ить, лю, ишь *pf. of* **лука́вить**

слуп|и́ть, лю́, ~́ишь *pf. of* **лупи́ть**

слух, а *m.* **1.** hearing, ear; **абсолю́тный с.** absolute pitch; **игра́ть по ~́у, на с.** to play by ear; **она́ вся обрати́лась в с.** she was all ears. **2.** rumour; hearsay; **есть с., что** it is rumoured that; **ни ~́у ни ду́ху** (**о**+*p.*) (*coll.*) not a word has been heard (of).

слуха́ч, а́ *m.* monitor.

слухов|о́й *adj.* acoustic, auditory, aural; **с. аппара́т** hearing aid; **с. нерв** (*anat.*) auditory nerve; **~о́е окно́** dormer(-window); **с. рожо́к, ~а́я тру́бка** ear-trumpet.

слу́ча|й, я *m.* **1.** case; **во вся́ком ~е** in any case, anyhow, anyway; **ни в ко́ем ~е** in no circumstances; **в лу́чшем, ху́дшем ~е** at best, at worst; **в проти́вном ~е** otherwise; **в тако́м ~е** in that case; **в ~е чего́** (*coll.*) if anything crops up; **на вся́кий с.** to be on the safe side, just in case; **на кра́йний с.** in case of special emergency; **по ~ю** (+*g.*) by reason (of), on account (of), on the occasion (of); **купи́ть по ~ю** (*coll.*) to buy secondhand. **2.** event, incident, occurrence; **несча́стный с.** accident. **3.** opportunity, occasion, chance; **упусти́ть удо́бный с.** to miss an opportunity; **при ~е** when an opportunity offers; **при ~е я ему́ сообщу́** I will inform him when I have the chance; **стихи́ на с.** occasional verse; **от ~я к ~ю** occasionally. **4.** chance.

случа́йно *adv.* **1.** by chance, by accident, accidentally; **не с. он прие́хал как раз вчера́** it was no accident that he came yesterday; **я с. подслу́шал их разгово́р** I happened to overhear their conversation. **2.** by any chance; **вы, с., не ви́дели моего́ зо́нтика?** have you by any chance seen my umbrella?

случа́йност|ь, и *f.* chance; **по счастли́вой ~и** by a lucky chance, by sheer luck.

случа́|йный (~ен, ~йна) *adj.* **1.** accidental, fortuitous; **~йная встре́ча** chance meeting; **~йное уби́йство** (*leg.*) homicide by misadventure. **2.** chance, casual, incidental; **с. за́работок** casual earnings.

случ|а́ть, а́ю *impf. of* **~и́ть**

случ|а́ться, а́ется *impf. of* **~и́ться**

случ|и́ть, у́, и́шь *pf.* (*of* **~а́ть**) (**с**+*i.*) (*of animals*) to couple (with), pair (with), mate (with).

случ|и́ться[1]**, и́тся** *pf.* (*of* **~а́ться**) (*of animals*) to couple, pair, mate.

случ|и́ться[2]**, и́тся** *pf.* (*of* **~а́ться**) **1.** to happen, come about, come to pass, befall; **что бы ни ~и́лось** whatever happens, come what may. **2.** (*impers.*; +*d. and inf.*) to happen; **мне ~и́лось попа́сть в Москву́** I happened to land up in Moscow. **3.** (*coll.*) to turn up, show up; **~и́лось у меня́ как раз пять рубле́й** I happened to have just five roubles on me.

слу́чк|а, и *f.* coupling, pairing, mating.

слу́шани|е, я *nt.* **1.** audition; hearing; **с. ле́кции** attendance at a lecture. **2.** (*leg.*) hearing.

слу́шател|ь, я *m.* **1.** hearer, listener; (*pl.*; *collect.*) audience. **2.** student.

слу́ша|ть, ю *impf.* (*of* **по~**) **1.** to listen (to), hear; **с. ле́кцию** to attend a lecture; **~й(те)!** (*coll.*) listen!, look here!; **~ю!** at your service!; very good!; (*on telephone*) hello! **2.** to attend lectures (on), go to lectures (on). **3.** to listen (to), obey. **4.** (*leg.*) to hear.

слу́ша|ться, юсь *impf.* (*of* **по~**) ((*obs.*)+*g.*) **1.** to listen (to), obey; **с. руля́** (*naut.*) to answer the helm; **~юсь!** (*mil.*) yes, sir! (*indicating readiness to carry out order*). **2.** *pass. of* **~ть**

слуш|о́к, ка́ *m.* (*coll.*) rumour.

слы|ть, ву́, вёшь, *past* **~л, ~ла́, ~́ло** *impf.* (*of* **про~**) (+*i. or* **за**+*a.*) to have a reputation (for), be said (to); to pass (for); **он ~вёт безде́льником, за безде́льника** he has a reputation for being an idler.

слыха́ть *no pres., impf.* **1.** to hear; **что у вас с.?** (*coll.*) what news have you of yourself?; tell us what you have been up to!; **ничего́ не с.** nothing can be heard. **2.** *as adv.* (*coll.*) apparently, it seems; **ты, с., пи́шешь но́вый рома́н** we hear you are writing a new novel.

слы́ш|ать, у, ишь *impf.* (*of* **у~**) **1.** to hear; **~ишь, ~ите** (*coll.*) do you hear? (*emph. command or direction*). **2.**

(*impf. only*) to have the sense of hearing; **не с.** to be hard of hearing. **3.** to notice; to feel, sense. **4.** (*coll.*) to smell.
слы́ш|аться, ится *impf.* (*of* **по~**) to be heard; to be audible.
слы́шимост|ь, и *f.* audibility.
слы́шим|ый (~, ~а) *adj.* audible.
слы́шно[1] *adv.* audibly.
слы́шно[2] *as pred., impers.* **1.** one can hear; **бы́ло с., как она́ рыда́ла** one could hear her sobbing; **нам никого́ не́ было с.** we could not hear anyone. **2.** (*coll.*); **что с.?** what news?, any news?; **о них ничего́ не с.** nothing has been heard of them. **3.** (*coll.*) it is said, they say, it is rumoured; **она́, с., бере́менна** they say she is pregnant.
слы́ш|ный (~ен, ~на́, ~но) *adj.* audible.
слю́биться *see* **стерпе́ться**
слюд|а́, ы́ *f.* mica.
слюдяно́й *adj.* mica, micaceous.
слюн|а́, ы́ *f.* saliva.
слю́н|и, е́й *no sg.* (*coll.*) slobber, spittle; **пусти́ть с.** to slobber, drivel; **распусти́ть с.** (*coll.*) to dither, become a ditherer.
слюн|и́ть, ю́, и́шь *impf.* **1.** (*pf.* **по~**) to wet with saliva. **2.** (*pf.* **за~**) to slobber over.
слю́н|ки, ок *no sg., dim. of* **~и; от э́того с. теку́т** it makes one's mouth water.
слюноотделе́ни|е, я *nt.* salivation.
слюнотече́ни|е, я *nt.* (*med.*) excessive salivation; (*fig., pej.*) sentimentalism.
слюнтя́|й, я *m.* (*coll.*) ditherer.
слюня́в|ить, лю, ишь *impf.* (*coll.*) to slobber over.
слюня́вчик, а *m.* (*baby's*) bib.
слюня́вый *adj.* (*coll.*) dribbling, drivelling.
сля́котный *adj.* slushy.
сля́кот|ь, и *f.* slush.
сля́мз|ить, ю, ишь *pf. of* **ля́мзить**
см (*abbr. of* **сантиме́тр**) cm, centimetre(s).
с. м. (*abbr. of* **сего́ ме́сяца**) (*comm.*) inst. (= *of the current month*).
см. (*abbr. of* **смотри́**) see, *vide*.
сма́|зать, жу, жешь *pf.* (*of* **~зывать**) **1.** to oil, lubricate; to grease; **с. йо́дом** to paint with iodine. **2.** (*fig., coll.*) to grease the palm (of), grease the wheels (of). **3.** to smudge; to rub off. **4.** (*fig., coll.*) to slur (over). **5.** (*fig., coll.*) to bash, dot.
сма́|заться, жусь, жешься *pf.* (*of* **~зываться**) **1.** to grease o.s. **2.** (*of paint, etc.*) to become smudged; to come off.
сма́зк|а, и *f.* **1.** oiling, lubrication; greasing. **2.** oil, lubricant; grease.
смазли́в|ый (~, ~а) *adj.* (*coll.*) pretty.
смазн|о́й *adj.*: **~ы́е сапоги́** blacked boots.
сма́зочн|ый *adj. of* **сма́зка; ~ая кана́вка** (*tech.*) lubricating groove, oil groove; **~ая коро́бка** oil can; **~ое ма́сло** lubricating oil; **с. материа́л, ~ое сре́дство** lubricant.
сма́зчик, а *m.* greaser.
сма́зывани|е, я *nt.* **1.** oiling, lubrication; greasing. **2.** (*fig.*) slurring over.
сма́зыва|ть(ся), ю(сь) *impf. of* **сма́зать(ся)**
смак, а *m.* (*coll.*) relish, savour (*also fig.*); **со ~ом** with relish, with gusto.
смак|ова́ть, у́ю *impf.* (*coll.*) to savour; to eat, drink with relish; to relish (*also fig.*).
сма́л|ец, ьца *m.* lard.
сма́льт|а, ы *f.* smalt.
сма́нива|ть, ю *impf. of* **смани́ть**
сман|и́ть, ю́, ~ишь *pf.* (*of* **~ивать**) to entice, lure.
смара́гд, а *m.* (*obs.*) emerald.
смара́гд|овый *adj. of* **~**
смастер|и́ть, ю́, и́шь *pf. of* **мастери́ть**
сма́тыва|ть, ю *impf. of* **смота́ть**
сма́тыва|ться, юсь *impf. of* **смота́ться**
сма́хива|ть[1]**, ю** *impf. of* **смахну́ть**
сма́хива|ть[2]**, ю** *impf.* (**на**+*a.*; *coll.*) to look like, resemble.
смах|ну́ть, ну́, нёшь *pf.* (*of* **~ивать**[1]) to brush (away, off), flick (away, off), whisk (away, off), flap (away, off); **с. пыль** (**с**+*g.*) to dust.
сма́чива|ть, ю *impf. of* **смочи́ть**
сма́ч|ный (~ен, ~на́, ~но) *adj.* (*coll.*) **1.** savoury, tasty. **2.** (*fig., pej.*) fruity; **~ная ру́гань** colourful language.
смеж|а́ть, а́ю *impf. of* **~и́ть**
смеж|и́ть, у́, и́шь *pf.* (*of* **~а́ть**) (*obs. or poet.*); **с. глаза́** to close one's eyes.
сме́жник, а *m.* factory producing parts for use by another.
сме́жност|ь, и *f.* contiguity.
сме́ж|ный (~ен, ~на) *adj.* adjacent, contiguous, adjoining, neighbouring; **~ные ко́мнаты** interconnecting rooms; **~ные поня́тия** closely-related concepts; **с. у́гол** (*math.*) adjacent angle.
смека́лист|ый (~, ~а) *adj.* (*coll.*) sharp, keen-witted.
смека́лк|а, и *f.* (*coll.*) native wit, mother wit; nous; sharpness.
смек|а́ть, а́ю *impf.* (*of* **~ну́ть**) (*coll.*) to see the point (of), grasp; **~а́ешь, в чём де́ло?** do you get it?; do you see the point?
смек|ну́ть, ну́, нёшь *pf. of* **~а́ть**
смеле́|ть, ю *impf.* (*of* **о~**) to grow bold(er).
сме́ло *adv.* **1.** boldly; **я могу́ с. сказа́ть** I can safely say; **с.!** don't be afraid!, have a try! **2.** easily, with ease; **в э́том за́ле с. поместя́тся пятьсо́т челове́к** this hall will hold five hundred with ease.
сме́лост|ь, и *f.* boldness, audacity, courage; **взять на себя́ с.** (+*inf.*) to take the liberty (of), make bold (to).
сме́л|ый (~, ~а́, ~о) *adj.* bold, audacious, courageous, daring.
смельча́к, а́ *m.* (*coll.*) bold spirit; dare-devil.
сме́н|а, ы *f.* **1.** changing, change; replacement; **с. карау́ла** changing of the guard; **идти́ на ~у** (+*d.*) to come to take the place (of), come to relieve. **2.** (*collect.*) replacements; successors; (*mil.*) relief; **гото́вить себе́ ~у** to prepare successors (*to take one's place, to take over*). **3.** shift; **у́тренняя, дневна́я, вече́рняя с.** morning, day, night shift; **рабо́тать в три ~ы** to work in three shifts, work a three-shift system. **4.** change (*of linen, etc.*).
смен|и́ть, ю́, ~ишь *pf.* (*of* **~я́ть**[1]) **1.** to change; to replace; (*mil.*) to relieve; **с. бельё** to change linen; **с. заве́дующего** to replace the manager; **с. карау́л** to relieve the guard; **с. ши́ны** to change tyres; **с. гнев на ми́лость** to temper justice with mercy. **2.** to replace, relieve, succeed (s.o.).
смен|и́ться, ю́сь, ~ишься *pf.* (*of* **~я́ться**) **1.** to hand over; (*mil.*) to be relieved; **с. с дежу́рства** to go off duty. **2.** (+*i.*) to give place (to); **дневно́й зно́й ~и́лся прохла́дой ве́чера** the day's heat gave way to the coolness of evening.
сме́нност|ь, и *f.* shift system, shiftwork.
сме́нн|ый *adj.* **1.** shift; **с. ма́стер** shift foreman; **~ая рабо́та** shift work. **2.** (*tech.*) changeable; **~ое колесо́** spare wheel.
сме́нщик, а *m.* relief (worker); *pl.* (*collect.*) new shift.
сменя́|емый *pres. part. pass. of* **~ть**[1] *and adj.* removable, interchangeable.
смен|я́ть[1]**, я́ю** *impf. of* **~и́ть**
смен|я́ть[2]**, я́ю** *pf.* (**на**+*a.*; *coll.*) to exchange (for).
смен|я́ться, я́юсь *impf. of* **смени́ться**
смерд, а *m.* (*hist.*) peasant farmer.
смер|де́ть, жу́, ди́шь *impf.* (*obs.*) to stink.
смерз|а́ться, а́ется *impf. of* **~нуться**
смёрз|нуться, нется, *past* **~ся, ~лась** *pf.* (*of* **~а́ться**) to freeze together.
сме́р|ить, ю, ишь *pf.* (*coll.*) to measure; **с. взгля́дом** to look (s.o.) up and down, measure at a glance.
смерк|а́ться, а́ется *impf.* (*of* **~нуться**) to get dark; **~а́лось** it was getting dark, twilight was falling.
сме́рк|нуться, нется *pf. of* **~а́ться**
смерте́льно *adv.* **1.** mortally; **с. ра́неный** mortally wounded. **2.** (*coll.*) extremely, terribly; **с. уста́ть** to be dead tired, be dead-beat.
смерте́л|ьный (~ен, ~ьна) *adj.* **1.** mortal, deadly; **с. уда́р** mortal blow. **2.** (*coll.*) extreme, terrible.
сме́ртник, а *m.* prisoner sentenced to death.
сме́ртност|ь, и *f.* mortality, death-rate.
сме́рт|ный (~ен, ~на) *adj.* **1.** mortal; *as n.* **с., ~ного** *m.* mortal; **просто́й с.** ordinary mortal. **2.** death; **с. бой** fight to the death; **с. грех** (*eccl.*) mortal sin; **семь ~ных грехо́в** (*liter.*) the Seven Deadly Sins; **~ная казнь** capital punishment, death penalty; **~ное ло́же** deathbed; **на ~ном**

одре́ on one's deathbed; **с. пригово́р** death sentence; (*fig.*) death-warrant; **с. час** last hour(s). **3.** (*fig.*) deadly, extreme.

смертоно́с|ный (~ен, ~на) *adj.* death-dealing, mortal, fatal, lethal; **с. уда́р** mortal blow.

смертоуби́йств|о, а *nt.* (*obs.*) murder.

смерт|ь, и, *pl.* **~и, ~е́й** *f.* **1.** death, decease; **ве́рная с.** certain death; **умере́ть голо́дной ~ью** to starve to death; **умере́ть свое́й ~ью** to die a natural death; **до́ ~и** (*fig., coll.*) to death; **я уста́л до́ смерти** I'm dead tired; **боро́ться не на жизнь, а на с.** to fight to the death; **разби́ть на́ с.** (*coll.*) to smash to bits; **свиде́тельство о ~и** death certificate; **быть при́ ~и** to be dying; **двум ~я́м не быва́ть, одно́й не минова́ть** you only die once. **2.: с. как** *as adv.* (*coll.*) awfully, terribly; **ему́,** *etc.*, **с. как хо́чется** (+*inf.*) he, *etc.*, is dying (for); **мне с. как хо́чется купа́ться** I'm dying for a bathe.

смерч, а *m.* **1.** waterspout. **2.** sand-storm, tornado.

смеси́тельный *adj.* (*tech.*) mixing.

сме|си́ть, шу́, ~сишь *pf. of* **меси́ть**

сме|сти́, ту́, тёшь, *past* **~л, ~ла́** *pf.* (*of* **~та́ть**[2]) **1.** to sweep off, sweep away; **с. кро́шки со стола́** to sweep crumbs off the table; **с. с лица́ земли́** to wipe off the face of the earth. **2.** to sweep into, together.

сме|сти́ть, щу́; сти́шь *pf.* (*of* **~ща́ть**) **1.** to displace, remove, move. **2.** (*fig.*) to remove, dismiss (*from one's post*).

сме|сти́ться, щу́сь, сти́шься *pf.* (*of* **~ща́ться**) to change position, become displaced.

смес|ь, и *f.* (*in var. senses*) mixture; blend, miscellany, medley.

сме́т|а, ы *f.* (*fin.*) estimate.

смета́н|а, ы *f.* soured (cultured) cream.

смет|а́ть[1]**, а́ю** *pf.* (*of* **мета́ть** *and* **~ывать**) to tack (together).

смета́|ть[2]**, ю** *pf. of* **смести́**

смётк|а, и *f.* (*coll.*) quickness (on the uptake); gumption.

сме́тлив|ый (~, ~а) *adj.* quick (on the uptake).

сме́т|ный *adj. of* **~а; ~ные ассигно́вки** budget allowances.

смётыва|ть, ю *impf. of* **смета́ть**[1]

сме|ть, ю *impf.* (*of* **по~**) to dare; to make bold; **не ~й(те)!** don't you dare!

смех, а (у) *m.* laughter; laugh; **разрази́ться ~ом** to burst out laughing; **меня́ разбира́л с.** I couldn't help laughing; **без ~у** joking apart, in earnest; **в с., на́ с., ~а ра́ди** for a joke, for fun, in jest, jokingly; **нам не до ~у** we are in no mood for laughter; **с. да и то́лько** (*coll.*) one can't but laugh.

смехот|а́, ы́ *f.* (*coll.*) matter for laughter; **э́то пря́мо с.!** this is simply ludicrous!

смехотво́р|ный (~ен, ~на) *adj.* laughable, ludicrous, ridiculous.

сме́ш|анный *p.p.p. of* **~а́ть** *and adj.* mixed; combined; **~анное акционе́рное о́бщество** joint-stock company; **~анная опера́ция** (*mil.*) combined operation; **телефо́н ~анного по́льзования** party-line; **~анная поро́да** crossbreed; **~анное число́** (*math.*) mixed number.

смеш|а́ть, а́ю *pf.* (*of* **меша́ть**[2] *and* **~ивать**) **1.** (**с**+*i.*) to mix (with), blend (with). **2.** to lump together. **3.** to confuse, mix up.

смеш|а́ться, а́юсь *pf.* (*of* **~иваться**) **1.** to mix, to (inter)blend, blend in; to mingle; **с. с толпо́й** to mingle in the crowd. **2.** to become confused, get mixed up.

смеше́ни|е, я *nt.* **1.** mixture, blending, merging. **2.** confusion, mixing up; **с. поня́тий** confusion of ideas.

сме́шива|ть(ся), ю(сь) *impf. of* **смеша́ть(ся)**

смеш|и́ть, у́, и́шь *impf.* to make laugh.

смешли́вост|ь, и *f.* risibility.

смешли́в|ый (~, ~а) *adj.* risible; easily amused.

смеш|но́й (~о́н, ~на́) *adj.* **1.** funny, droll; *as pred.* **~но́** it is funny, it makes one laugh; **вам ~но́?** do you find it funny? **2.** absurd, ridiculous, ludicrous; **э́то — ~но́е предложе́ние** this is an absurd suggestion; **до ~но́го** to the point of absurdity.

смеш|о́к, ка́ *m.* (*coll.*) chuckle; giggle.

смеща́|ть(ся), ю(сь) *impf. of* **смести́ть(ся)**

смеще́ни|е, я *nt.* **1.** displacement, removal. **2.** (*geol.*) slip, heave, upheaval, dislocation. **3.** (*radio*) bias.

сме|я́ться, ю́сь, ёшься *impf.* **1.** to laugh; **с. шу́тке** to laugh at a joke. **2.** (**над**) to laugh (at), mock (at), make fun (of). **3.** to joke, say in jest.

сми́л|оваться, уюсь *pf.* to have mercy, take pity.

смире́ни|е, я *nt.* humbleness, humility, meekness.

смире́нник, а *m.* humble pers., meek pers.

смире́нност|ь, и *f.* humility.

смире́н|ный (~, ~на) *adj.* humble, meek.

смири́тельн|ый *adj.* **~ая руба́шка** straitjacket.

смир|и́ть, ю́, и́шь *pf.* (*of* **~я́ть**) to restrain, subdue.

смир|и́ться, ю́сь, и́шься *pf.* (*of* **~я́ться**) to submit; to resign o.s.

сми́рно *adv.* quietly; **с.!** (*mil. word of command*) attention!

сми́р|ный (~ен, ~на́, ~но) *adj.* quiet; submissive.

смир|я́ть(ся), я́ю(сь) *impf. of* **~и́ть(ся)**

см. на об. (*abbr. of* **смотри́ на оборо́те**) PTO (= *please turn over*), see over.

смог, а *m.* smog.

смодели́р|овать, ую *pf. of* **моделировать**

смо́кв|а, ы *f.* fig.

смо́кинг, а *m.* dinner-jacket.

смоко́вниц|а *f.* fig-tree.

смол|а́, ы́, *pl.* **~ы** *f.* resin; pitch, tar; rosin; **иску́сственная с.** synthetic resin.

смолёный *adj.* resined; tarred, pitched.

смоли́ст|ый (~, ~а) *adj.* resinous.

смол|и́ть, ю́, и́шь *impf.* (*of* **вы́~** *and* **о~**) to resin; to tar, pitch.

смолк|а́ть, а́ю *impf. of* **~нуть**

смо́лк|нуть, ну, нешь, *past* **~, ~ла** *pf.* (*of* **~а́ть**) to fall silent; (*of sound*) to cease.

смо́лоду *adv.* from, in one's youth.

смолоку́р, а *m.* tar-extractor.

смолокуре́ни|е, я *nt.* extraction of tar.

смолоку́р|ня, ни, *g. pl.* **~ен** *f.* tar-works.

смоло|ти́ть, чу́, ~тишь *pf. of* **молоти́ть**

смоло́ть, смелю́, сме́лешь *pf. of* **моло́ть**

смолч|а́ть, у́, и́шь *pf.* to hold one's tongue.

смоль *only in phr.* **чёрный как с.** jet-black.

смол|яно́й *adj. of* **~а́; ~яна́я бо́чка** tar barrel; **с. ка́мень** pitchstone; **~яна́я кислота́** resin acid; **с. клей** resin sizing; **~яно́е ма́сло** resin oil; **с. соста́в** resinous compound.

смонти́р|овать, ую *pf. of* **монти́ровать**

сморгн|у́ть, у́, ёшь *pf.* (*coll.*): **гла́зом не с.** not to turn a hair, not to bat an eyelid.

сморка́|ть, ю *impf.* (*of* **вы́~**): **с. нос** to blow one's nose.

сморка́|ться, юсь *impf.* (*of* **вы́~**) to blow one's nose.

сморо́дин|а, ы *no pl., f.* **1.** currant; currant bush. **2.** (*collect.*) currants; **кра́сная, чёрная с.** redcurrants, blackcurrants.

сморо́дин|ный *adj. of* **~а**

сморч|о́к, ка́ *m.* **1.** morel (*mushroom*). **2.** (*fig., coll.; of pers.*) shrimp.

смо́рщ|енный *p.p.p. of* **~ить** *and adj.* wrinkled.

смо́рщ|ить(ся), у(сь), ишь(ся) *pf. of* **мо́рщить(ся)**

смота́|ть, ю *pf.* (*of* **сма́тывать**) to wind, reel; (*coll.*): **с. у́дочки** to take to one's heels, make off, clear out.

смота́|ться, юсь *pf.* (*of* **сма́тываться**) (*coll.*) **1.** to dash (there and back). **2.** to take to one's heels, make off.

смотр, а *m.* **1.** (**на ~у́,** *pl.* **~ы́**) review, inspection; **произвести́ с.** (+*d.*) to review, inspect. **2.** (**на ~е,** *pl.* **~ы**) public showing; **с. худо́жественной самоде́ятельности** amateur arts' festival.

смотр|е́ть, ю́, ~ишь *impf.* (*of* **по~**) **1.** (**на**+*a.*, **в**+*a.*) to look (at); **с. в окно́** to look out of the window; **с. в глаза́, в лицо́** (+*d.*) to look in the face; **с. в о́ба** (*coll.*) to keep one's eyes open, be on one's guard; **с. сквозь па́льцы** (**на**+*a.*; *coll.*) to make light (of), wink (at). **2.** to see; to watch; to look through; **с. чемпиона́т по те́ннису** to see a tennis championship; **с. телеви́дение** to watch television. **3.** to examine; to review, inspect; **с. больно́го** to inspect a patient. **4.** (**за**+*i.*) to look (after); to be in charge (of), supervise; **с. за поря́дком** to keep order. **5.** (**на**+*a.*; *coll.*) to follow the example (of). **6.** *impf. only* (**в**+*a.*, **на**+*a.*) to look (on to, over); **о́кна в мое́й ко́мнате ~ят в сад** my windows look on to the garden. **7.** *impf. only* (+*i.*; *coll.*) to look (like); **он ∠ит простако́м** he looks a simple fellow. **8.: ~и́(те)!** mind!, take care!; **~и́те не опозда́йте!** mind you are not late!; **~и́те, что́бы на́шим гостя́м бы́ло удо́бно** see that our guests are comfortable. **9.: ~я́ (где, как,** *etc.*) it depends (where, how, *etc.*); **~я́ (по**+*d.*) depending (on), in accordance (with).

смотр|е́ться, ю́сь, ∠ишься *impf.* (*of* **по~**) **1.** to look at o.s.; **с. в зе́ркало** to look at o.s. in the looking-glass. **2.** *pass. of* **~е́ть**

смотри́н|ы, ~ *no sg.* (*hist.*) smotriny (*Russ. folk-rite of inspection of prospective bride*).

смотри́тел|ь, я *m.* supervisor; (*in museum, etc.*) keeper, custodian.

смотров|о́й *adj.* **1.** (*mil.*) review. **2.: ~о́е окно́** inspection window; **~о́е отве́рстие** sighting aperture (*of gun sight*); **~а́я щель** vision slit (*in tank*).

смоч|и́ть, у́, ∠ишь *pf.* (*of* **сма́чивать**) to damp, wet, moisten.

смо|чь, гу́, ∠жешь, *past* **~г, ~гла́** *pf. of* **мочь**[1]

смоше́ннича|ть, ю *pf. of* **моше́нничать**

смрад, а *m.* stink, stench.

смра́д|ный (~ен, ~на) *adj.* stinking.

смугле́|ть, ю *impf.* to become dark-complexioned.

смуглоли́ц|ый (~, ~а) *adj.* dark-complexioned.

сму́гл|ый (~, ~а́, ~о) *adj.* dark-complexioned.

смугля́нк|а, и *f.* dark-complexioned woman, girl.

сму́т|а, ы *f.* (*obs.*) disturbance, sedition; **се́ять ~у** to sow discord.

сму|ти́ть, щу́, ти́шь *pf.* (*of* **~ща́ть**) **1.** to embarrass, confuse. **2.** to disturb, trouble; **с. чей-н. поко́й** to disturb s.o.'s peace and quiet.

сму|ти́ться, щу́сь, ти́шься *pf.* (*of* **~ща́ться**) to be embarrassed, be confused.

сму́т|ный (~ен, ~на́, ~но) *adj.* **1.** vague; confused, dim, muffled; **~ные воспомина́ния** dim recollections. **2.** disturbed, troubled; **~ное вре́мя** (*hist.*) Time of Troubles (*1605–13*).

смутья́н, а *m.* (*coll.*) trouble-maker.

сму́шк|а, и *f.* astrakhan.

сму́шковый *adj.* astrakhan.

смуща́|ть(ся), ю(сь) *impf. of* **смути́ть(ся)**

смуще́ни|е, я *nt.* embarrassment, confusion.

сму|щённый *p.p.p. of* **~ти́ть** *and adj.* embarrassed, confused.

смыв, а *m.* (*geol.*) wash-out.

смыва́|ть(ся), ю(сь) *impf. of* **смы́ть(ся)**

смыка́|ть(ся), ю(сь) *impf. of* **сомкну́ть(ся)**

смысл, а *m.* **1.** sense, meaning; purport; **прямо́й, перено́сный с.** literal, metaphorical sense; **в изве́стном ∠е** in a sense; **в по́лном ∠е сло́ва** in the true sense of the word; **в ∠е** (+*g.*) as regards. **2.** sense, point; **име́ть с.** to make sense; **нет никако́го ∠а** (+*inf.*) there is no sense (in), there is no point (in). **3.** (good) sense; **здра́вый с.** common sense.

смы́сл|ить, ю, ишь *impf.* (**в**+*p.*; *coll.*) to understand.

смыслов|о́й *adj. of* **смысл; ~ы́е отте́нки** shades of meaning.

смыть, смо́ю, смо́ешь *pf.* (*of* **смыва́ть**) **1.** to wash off; (*fig.*) to clear, wipe away; (*mil.*) to wipe out. **2.** to wash away; **с. волно́й с су́дна** to wash overboard.

смы́ться, смо́юсь, смо́ешься *pf.* (*of* **смыва́ться**) **1.** to wash off, come off. **2.** (*fig., coll.*) to slip away.

смы́чк|а, и *f.* union; linking.

смыч|ко́вый *adj. of* **~о́к**

смы́чный *adj.* (*ling.*) occlusive; stop.

смыч|о́к, ка́ *m.* (*mus.*) bow.

смышлён|ый (~, ~а) *adj.* (*coll.*) clever, bright.

смягч|а́ть(ся), а́ю(сь) *impf. of* **~и́ть(ся)**

смягча́|ющий 1. *pres. part. act. of* **~ть; ~ющие вину́ обстоя́тельства** extenuating circumstances. **2.** *adj.* (*med.*) emollient.

смягче́ни|е, я *nt.* **1.** softening. **2.** mollification; mitigation; extenuation. **3.** (*ling.*) palatalization.

смягч|и́ть, у́, и́шь *pf.* (*of* **~а́ть**) **1.** (*impf. also* **мягчи́ть**) to soften. **2.** to mollify; to ease, alleviate; to assuage; **с. боль** to alleviate pain; **с. гнев** to assuage anger; **с. наказа́ние** to mitigate a punishment; **с. напряже́ние** to ease tension. **3.** (*ling.*) to palatalize.

смягч|и́ться, у́сь, и́шься *pf.* (*of* **~а́ться**) **1.** to soften, become soft, grow softer. **2.** to be mollified; to relent, relax; to grow mild; to ease (off). **3.** *pass. of* **~и́ть**

смяте́ни|е, я *nt.* confusion, disarray; commotion.

смяте́н|ный (~, ~а) *adj.* (*obs.*) troubled, perturbed.

смять, сомну́, сомнёшь *pf.* (*of* **мять**) **1.** to crumple; to rumple; **с. пла́тье** to crush a dress. **2.** (*mil.*) to crush.

смя́ться, сомнётся *pf.* (*of* **мя́ться**[1]) to get creased; to get crumpled.

снаб|ди́ть, жу́, ди́шь *pf.* (*of* **~жа́ть**) (+*i.*) to supply (with), furnish (with), provide (with).

снабжа́|ть, ю *impf. of* **снабди́ть**

снабже́н|ец, ца *m.* supplier, provider.

снабже́ни|е, я *nt.* supply, supplying, provision.

снабже́н|ческий *adj. of* **~ие**

сна́добь|е, ья, *g. pl.* **~ий** *nt.* (*coll.*) drug.

сна́йпер, а *m.* sniper; sharp-shooter.

снару́жи *adv.* on the outside; from (the) outside.

снаря́д, а *m.* **1.** projectile, missile; shell; **управля́емый с.** guided missile. **2.** contrivance, machine, gadget; **гимнасти́ческие ~ы** gymnastic apparatus. **3.** (*collect.*) tackle, gear; **рыболо́вный с.** fishing tackle.

снаря|ди́ть, жу́, ди́шь *pf.* (*of* **~жа́ть**) to equip, fit out.

снаря|ди́ться, жу́сь, ди́шься *pf.* (*of* **~жа́ться**) to equip o.s., get ready.

снаря́дн|ый *adj.* **1.** shell, projectile; ammunition; **с. по́греб** shell-room, (ammunition) magazine. **2.: ~ая гимна́стика** (*sport*) apparatus work.

снаряжа́|ть(ся), ю(сь) *impf. of* **снаряди́ть(ся)**

снаряже́ни|е, я *nt.* equipment, outfit; **ко́нское с.** harness.

снаст|ь, и, *pl.* **∠и, ~е́й** *f.* **1.** (*collect.*) tackle, gear. **2.** (*usu. pl.*) rigging.

снача́ла *adv.* **1.** at first, at the beginning. **2.** all over again.

сна́шива|ть, ю *impf. of* **сноси́ть**

СНГ *nt. indecl.* (*abbr. of* ***Содру́жество незави́симых госуда́рств***) CIS (*Commonwealth of Independent States*).

снег, а, *pl.* **~а́** *m.* snow; **мо́крый с.** sleet; **как с. на́ голову** like a bolt from the blue.

снеги́р|ь, я́ *m.* bullfinch; **пусти́ть ~я́** (*coll.*) to make s.o.'s nose bleed.

снегов|о́й *adj.* snow; **~а́я ли́ния** snow-line.

снегозадержа́ни|е, я *nt.* (*agric.*) retention of snow on fields (*as protection against drought and frost*).

снегозащи́тн|ый *adj.*: **~ое огражде́ние, с. щит** snow-fence.

снегоочисти́тел|ь, я *m.* snow-plough.

снегопа́д, а *m.* snow-fall.

снегосту́пы, ов *pl.* (*sport*) snow-shoes.

снегота́ялк|а, и *f.* snow-melter.

снегоубо́рочн|ый *adj.* snow-removal; **~ая маши́на** snow-plough.

снегохо́д, а *m.* snow-tractor (*tracked vehicle used by Antarctic expeditions*).

Снегу́рочк|а, и *f.* (*folklore*) Snow Maiden.

снеда́|ть, ю *impf.* to consume, gnaw; **~емый за́вистью** consumed with envy.

снед|ь, и *f.* (*obs. or dial.*) food, eatables.

снежи́нк|а, и *f.* snow-flake.

сне́жн|ый *adj.* snow; snowy; **~ая ба́ба** snow man; **с. зано́с, с. сугро́б** snow-drift; **~ая зима́** snowy winter; **сне́жная белизна́** snow-whiteness.

снеж|о́к, ка́ *m.* **1.** light snow. **2.** snowball; **игра́ть в ~ки́** to play snowballs, have a snowball fight.

снес|ти́[1]**, у́, ёшь,** *past* **∠, ~ла́** *pf.* (*of* **сноси́ть**) **1.** to take; **с. письмо́ на по́чту** to take a letter to the post. **2.** to fetch down, bring down; **с. сунду́к с чердака́** to fetch down a trunk from the attic. **3.** (*usu. impers.*) to carry away; to blow off, take off; **урага́ном ~ло́ кры́шу** a hurricane took the roof off. **4.** to demolish, take down, pull down. **5.** to cut off, chop off; **с. го́лову кому́-н.** to chop s.o.'s head off. **6.** (*cards*) to throw away.

снес|ти́[2], **у́, ёшь** *pf.* (*of* **сноси́ть**) to bring together, pile up.
снес|ти́[3], **у́, ёшь** *pf.* (*of* **сноси́ть**) to bear, endure, suffer, stand, put up (with).
снес|ти́[4], **у́, ёшь** *pf.* (*of* **нести́**[2]) to lay (eggs).
снес|ти́сь[1], **у́сь, ёшься**, *past* **~ся, ~ла́сь** *pf.* (*of* **сноси́ться**) (**с**+*i.*) to communicate (with).
снес|ти́сь[2], **ётся** *pf. of* **нести́сь**[2]
снет|о́к, ка́ *m.* (*fish*) smelt, sparling.
снижа́|ть(ся), ю(сь) *impf. of* **сни́зить(ся)**
сниже́ни|е, я *nt.* **1.** lowering, reduction; **с. зарпла́ты** wage cut. **2.** (*aeron.*) loss of height; **идти́ на с.** to reduce height.
сни́|зить, жу, зишь *pf.* (*of* **~жа́ть**) **1.** to bring down, lower. **2.** (*fig.*) to bring down, lower, reduce; **с. себесто́имость** to cut production costs; **с. стиль** (*liter.*) to deflate one's style; **с. тон** to sing small; **с. по до́лжности** to reduce, demote.
сни́|зиться, жусь, зишься *pf.* (*of* **~жа́ться**) **1.** to descend, come down; (*of an aircraft*) to lose height. **2.** (*fig.*) to fall, sink, come down; **це́ны ~зились** prices have come down.
снизо|йти́, йду́, йдёшь, *past* **~шёл, ~шла́** *pf.* (*of* **снисходи́ть**) (**к**) to condescend (to); **с. к чьей-н. про́сьбе** to deign to grant s.o.'s request.
сни́зу *adv.* from below (*pol.*; *also fig.*); from the bottom; **с. вверх** upwards; **с. до́верху** from top to bottom.
сни́к|нуть, ну, нешь *pf. of* **ни́кнуть**
снима́|ть(ся), ю(сь) *impf. of* **снять(ся)**
сни́м|ок, ка *m.* photograph, photo, print.
сни|ска́ть, щу́, ~щешь *pf.* (*of* **сни́скивать**) (*obs.*) to gain, get, win; **с. чьё-н. расположе́ние** to win s.o.'s approval.
сни́скива|ть, ю *impf. of* **сниска́ть**
снисходи́тельност|ь, и *f.* **1.** condescension **2.** indulgence, tolerance, leniency, forbearance.
снисходи́тел|ьный (~ен, ~ьна) *adj.* **1.** condescending. **2.** indulgent, tolerant, lenient, forbearing.
снисхо|ди́ть, жу́, ~дишь *impf. of* **снизойти́**
снисхожде́ни|е, я *nt.* indulgence, leniency; **име́ть с. (к)** to be lenient (towards); **заслу́живает ~я** (*leg. formula*) recommended for mercy.
сни́|ться, снюсь, сни́шься *impf.* (*of* **при~**) (+*d.*) to dream; **ей ~лось, что** she dreamed that; **мне ~лся лев** I dreamed about a lion.
сноб, а *m.* snob.
сноби́зм, а *m.* snobbery.
сно́ва *adv.* again, anew, afresh.
снова́льный *adj.* (*text.*) warping.
снова́льщик, а *m.* (*text.*) warper.
снова́ть[1], **сную́, снуёшь** *impf.* to scurry about, dash about.
снова́ть[2], **сную́, снуёшь** *impf.* (*text.*) to warp.
сновиде́ни|е, я *nt.* dream.
сногсшиба́тел|ьный (~ен, ~ьна) *adj.* (*coll.*, *joc.*) stunning.
сноп, а́ *m.* sheaf; **с. луче́й** shaft of light; **с. траекто́рий** (*mil.*) cone of fire.
сноповяза́лк|а, и *f.* (*agric.*) binder.
сноповяза́льн|ый *adj.*: **~ая маши́на = сноповяза́лка**
сноровис́т|ый (~, ~а) *adj.* (*coll.*) quick, smart, clever.
сноро́вк|а, и *f.* skill, knack.
снос[1], **а** *m.* **1.** demolition, pulling down; **дом назна́чен на с.** the house is to be pulled down. **2.** drift; **у́гол ~а** (*aeron.*) angle of drift.
снос[2], **а (у)** *m.* wear; **тако́й мате́рии ~у нет** this material won't wear out; **не знать ~у** to wear well, be very hard-wearing.
снос[3]: **быть на ~ях** (*coll.*; *of a pregnant woman*) to be near her time.
сно|си́ть[1], **шу́, ~сишь** *pf.* (*of* **сна́шивать**) to wear out.
сно|си́ть[2], **шу́, ~сишь** *pf.* (*coll.*) to take (*and bring back*); **ему́ не с. головы́** it will cost him dear, he will pay for it.
сно|си́ть[3], **шу́, ~сишь** *impf. of* **снести́**[1,2,3]
сно|си́ться, шу́сь, ~сишься *impf. of* **снести́сь**[1]
сно́ск|а, и *f.* footnote.
сно́сно *adv.* (*coll.*) tolerably, so-so.
сно́с|ный (~ен, ~на) *adj.* (*coll.*) tolerable; fair, reasonable.
снотво́р|ный (~ен, ~на) *adj.* soporific (*also fig.*); **~ное сре́дство** soporific, sleeping draught, tablet.
снох|а́, и́, *pl.* **~и** *f.* (father's) daughter-in-law.
сноше́ни|е, я *nt.* (*usu. pl.*) intercourse; relations, dealings; **дипломати́ческие ~я** diplomatic relations; **име́ть ~я (с**+*i.*) to have dealings (with); to have (sexual) intercourse (with).
сну|ю́, ёшь *see* **снова́ть**
сню́ха|ться, юсь *pf.* (*coll.*) **1.** to get to know one another by scent. **2.** (*pej.*) to come to terms, come to an understanding.
сня́ти|е, я *nt.* **1.** taking down; **с. урожа́я** gathering in the harvest. **2.** removal; **с. запре́та** lifting of a ban; **с. с рабо́ты** dismissal, the sack. **3.** taking, making; **с. ко́пии** copying.
снят|о́й *adj.*: **~о́е молоко́** skimmed milk.
сня|ть, сниму́, сни́мешь, *past* **~л, ~ла́, ~ло** *pf.* (*of* **снима́ть**) **1.** to take off; to take down; **с. шля́пу** to take one's hat off; **с. карти́ну** to take down a picture; **с. кора́бль с мели** to refloat a ship; **с. сли́вки с молока́** to skim milk, take the cream off milk; **с. пье́су** to take a play off; **с. урожа́й** to gather in the harvest; **с. оса́ду** to raise a siege; **с. с себя́** to divest o.s. (of); **с. с себя́ отве́тственность** to decline responsibility. **2.** (*fig.*) to remove; to withdraw, cancel; **с. взыска́ние** to remit a punishment; **с. запре́т** to lift a ban; **с. предложе́ние** to withdraw a motion; **с. с рабо́ты** to discharge, sack; **с. с учёта** to strike off the register; **с. с фро́нта** to withdraw from the front. **3.** (*mil.*) to pick off. **4.** to take, make; to photograph, make a photograph (of); **с. ко́пию (с**+*g.*) to copy, make a copy (of); **с. ме́рку с кого́-н.** to take s.o.'s measurements; **с. план** to make a plan; **с. показа́ние** to take (down) evidence; **с. показа́ние га́зового счётчика** to read a gas-meter; **с. фильм** to shoot a film. **5.** to take, rent (*a house, etc.*); **с. в аре́нду** to take on lease. **6.** (*cards*) to cut.
сня́|ться, сниму́сь, сни́мешься, *past* **~лся, ~ла́сь** *pf.* (*of* **снима́ться**) **1.** to come off. **2.** to move off; **с. с я́коря** to weigh anchor; to get under way (*also fig.*). **3.** to have one's photograph taken.
со *prep.* = **с**
со... *vbl. pref.* = **с...**
соа́втор, а *m.* co-author.
соа́вторств|о, а *nt.* co-authorship.
соба́к|а, и *f.* dog; **дворо́вая с.** watchdog; **морска́я с.** dogfish; **охо́тничья с.** gun dog, hound; **с.-поводы́рь** guide-dog; **служе́бная с.** guard dog, patrol dog; **с.-ище́йка** bloodhound; **с. на се́не** (*coll.*) dog in the manger; **уста́ть как с.** to be dog-tired; **ве́шать ~ (на**+*a.*; *coll.*) to call names, pull to pieces; **вот где с. зары́та!** so that's the crux of the matter!; so that's what's at the bottom of it!; **как ~ нере́занных** (+*g.*; *coll.*) any amount (of); **~у съесть (на**+*p.*; *coll.*) to have at one's fingertips, know inside out.
собаково́д, а *m.* dog-breeder.
собаково́дств|о, а *nt.* dog-breeding.
соба́|чий *adj. of* **~ка**; canine; **~чья жизнь** dog's life; **с. хо́лод** intense cold.
соба́чк|а[1], **и** *f.* little dog, doggie.
соба́чк|а[2], **и** *f.* **1.** trigger. **2.** (*tech.*) catch, trip, arresting device; pawl (*of ratchet*).
соба́чник, а *m.* (*coll.*) dog-lover.
собезья́ннича|ть, ю *pf. of* **обезья́нничать**
СОБЕС, а *or* **собе́с, а** *m.* (*abbr. of* **(отде́л) социа́льного обеспе́чения**) **1.** social security. **2.** social security department (*of local authority*).
собесе́дник, а *m.* collocutor, interlocutor; **он — заба́вный с.** he is amusing company.
собесе́довани|е, я *nt.* conversation, discussion, interlocution.
собира́тел|ь, я *m.* collector.
собира́тельный *adj.* (*gram.*) collective.
собира́тельств|о, а *nt.* collecting.
собира́|ть, ю *impf. of* **собра́ть**
собира́|ться, юсь *impf.* **1.** (*impf. of* **собра́ться**). **2.** (+*inf.*) to intend (to), be about (to), be going (to); **я ~лся позвони́ть вам** I was going to ring you up.
соблаговол|и́ть, ю́, и́шь *pf.* (+*inf.*; *obs.*) to deign (to),

condescend (to); **наконéц онá ~́ила ответить** finally she deigned to reply.

соблáзн, а *m.* temptation.

соблазни́тел|ь, я *m.* **1.** tempter. **2.** seducer.

соблазни́тельниц|а, ы *f.* temptress.

соблазни́тел|ьный (~ен, ~ьна) *adj.* **1.** tempting; alluring; seductive. **2.** suggestive, corrupting.

соблазн|и́ть, ю́, и́шь *pf.* (*of* **~я́ть**) **1.** to tempt. **2.** to seduce, entice.

соблазн|я́ть, я́ю *impf. of* **~и́ть**

соблюдá|ть, ю *impf. of* **соблюсти́**

соблюдéни|е, я *nt.* observance; maintenance; **с. обы́чая** observance of a custom; **с. поря́дка** maintenance of order.

соблю|сти́, ду́, дёшь, *past* **~́л, ~лá** *pf.* (*of* **~дáть**) to keep (to), stick to; to observe; **с. закóн** to observe a law; **с. срóки** to keep to schedule.

собóй *see* **себя́**

соболéзновани|е, я *nt.* sympathy, condolence.

соболéзн|овать, ую *impf.* (+*d.*) to sympathize (with), condole (with).

собóл|ий, ья, ье *adj. of* **сóболь; с. мех** sable.

собо|ли́ный *adj.* sable; **~ли́ные брóви** (*poet.*) sable brows.

сóбол|ь, я, *pl.* **~я́, ~éй** *and* **~и, ~ей** *m.* **1.** sable. **2.** (*pl.* **~я́, ~éй**) sable (fur).

собóр, а *m.* **1.** (*hist.*) council, synod, assembly; **вселéнский с.** ecumenical council; **зéмский с.** Assembly of the Land (*in Muscovite Russia*). **2.** cathedral.

собóрност|ь, и *f.* collectivism; (*eccl., phil.*) conciliarism.

собóр|ный *adj. of* **~**

собóровани|е, я *nt.* (*eccl.*) extreme unction.

собóр|овать, ую *impf. and pf.* (*eccl.*) to administer extreme unction (to), anoint.

собóр|оваться, уюсь *impf. and pf.* (*eccl.*) to receive extreme unction.

собóю = собóй, *see* **себя́**

собрáни|е, я *nt.* **1.** meeting, gathering; **óбщее с.** general meeting; **с. правлéния** board meeting. **2.** assembly; **учреди́тельное с.** constituent assembly. **3.** collection; **с. закóнов** code (of laws); **с. сочинéний** collected works; **пóлное с. сочинéний** complete works.

сóбр|анный *p.p.p. of* **~áть** *and adj.*; **с. человéк** precise, accurate, self-disciplined pers.

собрáт, а, *pl.* **~ья, ~ьев** *m.* colleague; **с. по орýжию** brother-in-arms; **с. по ремеслý** fellow-worker, colleague.

собр|áть, соберý, соберёшь, *past* **~áл, ~лá, ~áло** *pf.* (*of* **собирáть**) **1.** to gather, collect, pick; **с. цветы́** to pick flowers; **с. свéдения** to collect information. **2.** to assemble, muster; to convoke, convene; **с. войскá** to muster troops; **с. всё своё мýжество** to muster up one's courage; **с. послéдние си́лы** to make a last effort. **3.** (*tech.*) to assemble, mount. **4.** to obtain, poll (*stated number or percentage of votes*). **5.** to prepare, make ready, equip; **с. когó-н. в дорóгу** to equip s.o. for a journey; **с. на стол** to lay the table. **6.** (*dressmaking*) to gather, make gathers (in), take in.

собр|áться, соберýсь, соберёшься, *past* **~áлся, ~алáсь, ~áлóсь** *pf.* (*of* **собирáться**) **1.** to gather, assemble, muster; to be amassed. **2.** (**в**+*a.*) to prepare (for), make ready (for); **с. в гóсти** to get ready to go away (*to visit s.o.*). **3.** (+*inf.*) to intend (to), be about (to), be going (to). **4.** (**с**+*i.*, *fig.*) to collect; **с. с дýхом** (*i*) to get one's breath, (*ii*) to pluck up one's courage; to pull o.s. together; **с. с мы́слями** to collect one's thoughts; **с. с си́лами** to summon up one's strength, brace o.s., nerve o.s. **5.: с. в комóк** to hunch up.

сóбственник, а *m.* owner, proprietor; **земéльный с.** landowner.

сóбственнический *adj.* possessive, proprietary.

сóбственно 1. *adv.* strictly; **с. говоря́** strictly speaking, properly speaking, as a matter of fact; **он, с. (говоря́), был прав** strictly speaking he was right. **2.** *particle* proper; **егó не интересýет с. медици́на** he is not interested in medicine proper.

собственнорýчно *adv.* with one's own hand.

собственнорýчн|ый *adj.* done, made, written with one's own hand(s); **~ая пóдпись** autograph.

сóбственност|ь, и *f.* **1.** property. **2.** possession, ownership; **приобрести́ в с.** to become the owner (of).

сóбственн|ый *adj.* **1.** (one's) own; proper; **~ыми глазáми** with one's own eyes; **в ~ые рýки** (*inscription on envelope, etc.*) 'personal'; **чýвство ~ого достóинства** proper pride, self-respect; **~ой персóной** in person; **и́мя ~ое** (*gram.*) proper name. **2.** true, proper; **в ~ом смы́сле** in the true sense. **3.** (*tech.*) natural; internal; **~ое сопротивлéние** internal resistance; **~ая скóрость** actual speed; **~ая частотá** (*radio*) natural frequency.

собуты́льник, а *m.* (*coll.*) drinking companion, boon companion.

собы́ти|е, я *nt.* event; **текýщие ~я** current affairs.

сов... *comb. form, abbr. of* **совéтский**

сов|á, ы́, *pl.* **~́ы** *f.* owl.

совáть, сую́, суёшь *impf.* (*of* **сýнуть**) to shove, thrust, poke; **с. рýки в кармáны** to stick one's hands in one's pockets; **с. монéту комý-н. в рýку** to slip a coin into s.o.'s hand; **с. нос, с. ры́ло (в**+*a.*) (*coll.*) to poke one's nose (into), pry (into).

совáться, сую́сь, суёшься *impf.* (*of* **сýнуться**) (*coll.*) **1.** to push, strain; **не знáвши брóду, не сýйся в вóду** (*prov.*) look before you leap. **2.** (**в**+*a.*; *fig.*) to butt (in), poke one's nose (into).

сов|ёнок, ёнка, *pl.***~я́та, ~я́т** *m.* owlet.

соверш|áть(ся), áю, áет(ся) *impf. of* **~и́ть(ся)**

совершéни|е, я *nt.* accomplishment, fulfilment; perpetration.

совершéнно *adv.* **1.** perfectly. **2.** absolutely, utterly, completely, totally, perfectly; **с. вéрно!** quite right!; perfectly true!; quite so!

совершеннолéти|е, я *nt.* majority; **дости́гнуть ~я** to come of age, attain one's majority.

совершеннолéтний *adj.* of age.

совершéн|ный[1] **(~ен, ~на)** *adj.* **1.** perfect. **2.** (*coll.*) absolute, utter, complete, total, perfect; **с. идиóт** absolute idiot.

совершённый[2] *adj.* (*gram.*) perfective.

совершéнств|о, а *nt.* perfection; **в ~е** perfectly, to perfection.

совершéнств|овать, ую *impf.* (*of* **у~**) to perfect; to develop, improve.

совершéнств|оваться, уюсь *impf.* (*of* **у~**) (**в**+*p.*) to perfect o.s. (in); to improve.

соверш|и́ть, ý, и́шь *pf.* (*of* **~áть**) **1.** to accomplish, carry out; to perform; to commit, perpetrate; **с. оши́бку** to make a mistake; **с. преступлéние** to commit a crime. **2.** to complete, conclude; **с. сдéлку** to complete a transaction, make a deal.

соверш|и́ться, и́тся *pf.* (*of* **~áться**) (*liter.*) **1.** to happen. **2.** to be accomplished, be completed.

сóве|стить, щу, стишь *impf.* to shame, put to shame.

сóве|ститься, щусь, стишься *impf.* (*of* **по~**) (+*g. or inf.*; *obs.*) to be ashamed (of).

сóвестлив|ый (~, ~а) *adj.* conscientious.

сóвестно *as pred.* (+*d. and inf.*) to be ashamed; **емý бы́ло с. проси́ть дéнег** he was ashamed to ask for money; **как вам не с.!** you ought to be ashamed of yourself!

сóвест|ь, и *f.* conscience; **чи́стая, нечи́стая с.** clear, guilty conscience; **со спокóйной ~ью** with a clear conscience; **для очи́стки ~и** to clear one's conscience; **по ~и (говоря́)** to be honest; **свобóда ~и** freedom of worship; **угрызéния ~и** pangs of conscience; **рабóтать на ~** to work conscientiously.

совéт[1]**, а** *m.* advice, counsel; (*leg.*) opinion.

совéт[2]**, а** *m.* **1.** Soviet, soviet. **2.** council; **С. Безопáсности** Security Council. **3.** council, conference; **воéнный с.** council of war.

совéт[3]**, а** *m.* (*arch.*) concord, harmony.

совéтник, а *m.* **1.** adviser. **2.** (*title of office*) councillor.

совéт|овать, ую *impf.* (*of* **по~**) (+*d.*) to advise.

совéт|оваться, уюсь *impf.* (*of* **по~**) (**с**+*i.*) to consult, ask advice (of), seek advice (from).

советóлог, а *m.* Sovietologist.

советолóги|я, и *f.* Sovietology.

сове́тск|ий *adj.* **1.** Soviet, of the Soviet Union; **~ая власть** Soviet rule *or* power; **с. наро́д** the Soviet people. **2.** soviet (= *of local soviets*); **~ие рабо́тники** officials of the soviets; **~ое строи́тельство** development of the soviets.
Сове́тск|ий Сою́з, ~ого ~а *m.* the Soviet Union.
сове́тчик, а *m.* adviser, counsellor.
совеща́ни|е *nt.* conference, meeting; **с. на верха́х** summit conference.
совеща́тельный *adj.* consultative, deliberative.
совеща́|ться, юсь *impf.* **1.** (**о**+*p.*) to deliberate (on, about), consult (on, about). **2.** (**с**+*i.*) to confer (with), consult.
сов|и́ный *adj. of* **~á**; owlish.
совко́вый *adj.* (*sl., pej.*) Soviet.
совлада́|ть, ю *pf.* (**с**+*i.*; *coll.*) to control; **с. с собо́й** to control o.s.
совладе́л|ец, ьца *m.* joint owner, joint proprietor.
совладе́ни|е, я *nt.* joint ownership.
совмести́мост|ь, и *f.* compatibility.
совмести́м|ый (~, ~а) *adj.* compatible.
совмести́тел|ь, я *m.* pers. holding more than one office, combining jobs; pluralist.
совмести́тельств|о, а *nt.* holding of more than one office; pluralism; **рабо́тать по ~у** to hold more than one office, combine jobs.
совмести́тельств|овать, ую *impf.* to hold more than one office, combine jobs.
совме|сти́ть, щу́, сти́шь *pf.* (*of* **~ща́ть**²) to combine.
совме|сти́ться, сти́тся *pf.* (*of* **~ща́ться**) **1.** to coincide. **2.** to be combined, combine.
совме́стно *adv.* in common, jointly.
совме́стн|ый *adj.* joint, combined; **~ые де́йствия** concerted action; (*mil.*) combined operations; **~ое заседа́ние** joint sitting; **~ое обуче́ние** co-education; **~ое предприя́тие** joint venture; **~ая рабо́та** team-work.
совмеща́|ть¹, **ю** *impf.* to hold more than one office, combine jobs.
совмеща́|ть²**(ся), ю(сь)** *impf. of* **совмести́ть(ся)**
совми́н, а *m.* (*abbr. of* **сове́т мини́стров**) Council of Ministers.
совнарко́м, а *m.* (*abbr. of* **сове́т наро́дных комисса́ров**) (*hist.*) Council of People's Commissars.
совнархо́з, а *m.* (*abbr. of* **сове́т наро́дного хозя́йства**) (*hist.*) Economic Council (*central or regional economic management board in USSR*).
сов|о́к, ка́ *m.* shovel, scoop; **садо́вый с.** trowel; **с. для му́сора** dustpan.
совокуп|и́ть, лю́, и́шь *pf.* (*of* **~ля́ть**) to combine, unite.
совокуп|и́ться, лю́сь, и́шься *pf.* (*of* **~ля́ться**) (**с**+*i.*) to copulate (with).
совокупле́ни|е, я *nt.* copulation.
совокупля́|ть(ся), ю(сь) *impf. of* **совокупи́ть(ся)**
совоку́пно *adv.* in common, jointly.
совоку́пност|ь, и *f.* aggregate, sum total; totality; **в ~и** in the aggregate; **по ~и** (+*g.*) on the basis (of), on the strength (of).
совоку́пн|ый *adj.* joint, combined, aggregate; **~ые уси́лия** combined efforts.
совою́ющий *adj.* co-belligerent.
совпада́|ть, ю *impf. of* **совпа́сть**
совпаде́ни|е, я *nt.* coincidence.
совпа́|сть, ду́, дёшь, *past* **~л** *pf.* (*of* **~да́ть**) **1.** (**с**+*i.*) to coincide (with); **части́чно с.** to overlap. **2.** to agree, concur, tally; **их показа́ния не ~ли** their evidence did not agree.
сovратите́л|ь, я *m.* perverter, seducer.
совра|ти́ть, щу́, ти́шь *pf.* (*of* **~ща́ть**) to pervert, seduce; **с. с пути́ и́стинного** to lead astray.
совра|ти́ться, щусь, ти́шься *pf.* (*of* **~ща́ться**) to go astray.
совр|а́ть, у́, ёшь, *past* **~а́л, ~ала́, ~а́ло** *pf. of* **врать**
совраща́|ть(ся), ю(сь) *impf. of* **соврати́ть(ся)**
совраще́ни|е, я *nt.* perverting, seducing, seduction.
совреме́нник, а *m.* contemporary.
совреме́нност|ь, и *f.* **1.** contemporaneity. **2.** the present (time).
совреме́н|ный (~ен, ~на) *adj.* **1.** (+*d.*) contemporaneous (with), of the time (of); **~ные Ива́ну Гро́зному поня́тия** ideas of the time of Ivan the Terrible. **2.** contemporary, present-day; modern; up-to-date; state-of-the-art; **~ная англи́йская литерату́ра** modern English literature.
совсе́м *adv.* quite, entirely, completely, altogether; **с. не** not at all, not in the least; **с. не то** nothing of the kind.
совхо́з, а *m.* sovkhoz, State farm.
совхо́з|ный *adj. of* **~**
согбе́н|ный (~, ~на) *adj.* (*obs.*) bent, stooping.
согла́си|е, я *nt.* **1.** consent; assent; **с ва́шего ~я** with your consent; **с о́бщего ~я** by common consent; **дать своё с.** to give one's consent. **2.** agreement; **в ~и** (**с**+*i.*) in accordance (with). **3.** accord; concord, harmony.
согласи́тельн|ый *adj.* conciliatory; **~ая коми́ссия** conciliation commission.
согла|си́ть, шу́, си́шь *pf.* (*of* **~ша́ть**) to reconcile.
согла|си́ться, шу́сь, си́шься *pf.* (*of* **~ша́ться**) **1.** (**на**+*a. or* +*inf.*) to consent (to), agree (to). **2.** (**с**+*i.*) to agree (with), concur (with).
согла́сно *adv.* **1.** in accord, in harmony, in concord; **петь с.** to sing in harmony. **2.** *as prep.* (+*d. or* **с**+*i.*) in accordance (with); according (to); **с. догово́ру** in accordance with the treaty, under the treaty.
согла́сност|ь, и *f.* harmony, harmoniousness.
согла́с|ный¹ **(~ен, ~на)** *adj.* **1.** (**на**+*a.*) agreeable (to); **они́ не́ были ~ны на на́ши усло́вия** they would not agree to our conditions. **2.** (**с**+*i.*) in agreement (with), concordant (with); **быть ~ным** to agree (with); **~ен, ~на, ~ны?** do you agree? **3.** harmonious, concordant.
согла́с|ный² *adj.* (*gram.*) consonant(al); *as n.* **с., ~ого** *m.* consonant.
согласова́ни|е, я *nt.* **1.** co-ordination; concordance, agreement. **2.** (*gram.*) concord, agreement; **с. времён** sequence of tenses.
согласо́ванност|ь, и *f.* co-ordination; **с. во вре́мени** synchronization.
согласо́в|анный *p.p.p. of* **~а́ть** *and adj.* coordinated; **~анные де́йствия** concerted action; **с. текст** agreed text.
соглас|ова́ть, у́ю *pf.* (*of* **~о́вывать**) (**с**+*i.*) **1.** to co-ordinate (with). **2. с. что-н. с кем-н.** to submit sth. to s.o.'s approval; to come to an agreement with s.o. about sth. **3.** (*gram.*) to make agree (with).
соглас|ова́ться, у́ется *impf. and pf.* (**с**+*i.*) **1.** to accord (with), to conform (to). **2.** (*gram.*) to agree (with).
согласо́выва|ть, ю *impf. of* **согласова́ть**
соглаша́тел|ь, я *m.* (*pol.*; *pej.*) compromiser; appeaser.
соглаша́тель|ский *adj. of* **~**; **~ская поли́тика** policy of compromise, appeasement policy.
соглаша́тельств|о, а *nt.* (*pol.*; *pej.*) compromise, appeasement.
соглаша́|ть(ся), ю(сь) *impf. of* **согласи́ть(ся)**
соглаше́ни|е, я *nt.* **1.** agreement, understanding. **2.** agreement, covenant; **заключи́ть с.** to conclude an agreement.
соглята́та|й, я *m.* (*obs.*) spy.
согна́|ть¹**, сгоню́, сго́нишь,** *past* **~л, ~ла́, ~ло** *pf.* (*of* **сгоня́ть**) to drive away.
согна́|ть²**, сгоню́, сго́нишь,** *past* **~л, ~ла́, ~ло** *pf.* (*of* **сгоня́ть**) to drive together, round up.
согн|у́ть, у́, ёшь *pf.* (*of* **гнуть** *and* **сгиба́ть**) to bend, curve, crook.
согн|у́ться, у́сь, ёшься *pf.* (*of* **гну́ться** *and* **сгиба́ться**) to bend, bow (down); to stoop.
согражда́ни́н, а, *pl.* **сограждане, сограждан** fellow-citizen.
согрева́тельный *adj.*: **с. компре́сс** (*med.*) hot compress.
согрева́|ть(ся), ю(сь) *impf. of* **согре́ть(ся)**
согре́|ть, ю *pf.* (*of* **~ва́ть**) to warm, heat.
согре́|ться, юсь *pf.* (*of* **~ва́ться**) to get warm; to warm o.s.
согреш|а́ть, а́ю *impf. of* **~и́ть**
согреше́ни|е, я *nt.* sin, trespass.
согреш|и́ть, у́, и́шь *pf.* (*of* **~а́ть**) (**про́тив**) to sin (against), trespass (against).
со́д|а, ы *f.* soda, sodium carbonate; **питьева́я с.** household soda.
соде́йстви|е, я *nt.* assistance, help; good offices.

соде́йств|овать, ую *impf. and pf.* (*pf. also* **по~**) (+*d.*) to assist, help; to further, promote; to make (for), contribute (to); **с. успе́ху предприя́тия** to contribute to the success of an undertaking.

содержа́ни|е, я *nt.* **1.** maintenance, upkeep, keeping; allowance; (*animal*) housing; **де́нежное с.** money allowance, financial support; **с. под аре́стом** custody; **быть на ~и у кого́-н.** to be kept, supported by s.o. **2.** pay; **окла́д ~я** rate of pay; **о́тпуск с сохране́нием ~я** holiday(s) with pay. **3.** content; **куби́ческое с.** volume; **с больши́м ~ем** (+*g.*) rich (in). **4.** matter, substance; content; **фо́рма и с.** form and content. **5.** content(s); plot (*of a novel, etc.*). **6.** table of contents.

содержа́нк|а, и *f.* (*obs.*) kept woman.

содержа́тел|ь, я *m.* (*obs.*) landlord (*of an inn, etc.*).

содержа́тел|ьный (~ен, ~ьна) *adj.* rich in content; **~ьное письмо́** interesting letter.

содерж|а́ть, у́, ~́ишь *impf.* **1.** to keep, maintain, support; **с. семью́** to keep a family. **2.** to keep, have (*a business, enterprise, etc.*); **с. магази́н** to keep a shop. **3.** (**в**+*p.*) to keep (*in a given state*); **с. в испра́вности** to keep going, in working order; **с. в поря́дке** to keep in order; **с. в та́йне** to keep (as a) secret; **с. под аре́стом** to keep under arrest. **4.** to contain; **его́ перево́д ~́ит мно́го оши́бок** his translation contains many mistakes.

содерж|а́ться, у́сь, ~́ишься *impf.* **1.** to be kept, be maintained. **2.** to be kept, be; **с. под аре́стом** to be under arrest. **3.** (**в**+*p.*) to be contained (by); **в э́той руде́ ~́ится ура́н** this ore contains uranium.

содержи́м|ое, ого *nt.* contents.

соде́|ять, ю, ешь *pf.* (*obs. or rhet.*) to commit, carry out.

соде́|яться, ется *pf.* (*obs. or joc.*) to happen.

со́дов|ый *adj.* soda; **~ая вода́** soda (water).

содокла́д, а *m.* supplementary report, supplementary paper.

содокла́дчик, а *m.* reader of supplementary report or paper.

содо́м, а *m.* (*coll.*) uproar, row; **подня́ть с.** to raise hell.

содра́|ть, сдеру́, сдерёшь, *past* **~л, ~ла́, ~ло** *pf.* (*of* **сдира́ть**) **1.** to tear off, strip off; **с. ко́жу** (**с**+*g.*) to skin, flay; **с. кору́** (**с**+*g.*) to bark. **2.** *pf. only* (*fig., coll.*) to fleece; **с. с кого́-н. втри́дорога** to make s.o. pay through the nose.

содрога́ни|е, я *nt.* shudder.

содрог|а́ться, а́юсь *impf. of* **~ну́ться**

содрог|ну́ться, ну́сь, нёшься *pf.* (*of* **~а́ться**) to shudder, shake, quake.

содру́жеств|о, а *nt.* **1.** concord; **рабо́тать в те́сном ~е** (**с**+*i.*) to work in close co-operation (with). **2.** community, commonwealth; **Брита́нское с. на́ций** the British Commonwealth.

со́евый *adj.* soya; **с. творо́г** tofu.

соедине́ни|е, я *nt.* **1.** joining, conjunction, combination. **2.** (*tech.*) joint, join, junction. **3.** (*chem.*) compound. **4.** (*mil.*) formation.

Соединённ|ое Короле́вств|о, ~ого ~а *nt.* United Kingdom.

Соединённ|ые Шта́т|ы (Аме́рики), ~ых ~ов (А.) *no sg.* United States (of America).

соедин|ённый *p.p.p. of* **~и́ть** *and adj.* united, joint.

соедини́тельн|ый *adj.* connective, connecting; **с. брус** draw bar; **~ое звено́** connecting link; **~ая коро́бка** (*elec.*) junction box; **~ые ско́бки** (*typ.*) brace; **с. сою́з** (*gram.*) copulative conjunction; **~ая ткань** (*biol.*) connective tissue; **~ая тя́га** coupling rod.

соедин|и́ть, ю́, и́шь *pf.* (*of* **~я́ть**) **1.** to join, unite. **2.** to connect, link; **с. по телефо́ну** to put through. **3.** (*chem.*) to combine.

соедин|и́ться, ю́сь, и́шься *pf.* (*of* **~я́ться**) **1.** to join, unite. **2.** (*chem.*) to combine. **3.** *pass. of* **~и́ть**

соедин|я́ть(ся), я́ю(сь) *impf. of* **~и́ть(ся)**

сожале́ни|е, я *nt.* **1.** (**о**+*p.*) regret (for); **к на́шему ~ю** to our sorrow, regrettably; **к ~ю** unfortunately. **2.** (**к**) pity (for).

сожале́|ть, ю *impf.* (**о**+*p. or* +**что**) to regret, deplore.

сожже́ни|е, я *nt.* burning; cremation; **с. на костре́** burning at the stake; **преда́ть ~ю** to commit to the flames.

сожи́тел|ь, я *m.* **1.** room-mate. **2.** lover.

сожи́тельниц|а, ы *f.* **1.** room-mate. **2.** mistress.

сожи́тельств|о, а *nt.* **1.** living together, lodging together. **2.** (*fig.*) living together, cohabitation.

сожи́тельств|овать, ую *impf.* (**с**+*i.*) **1.** to live (with), lodge (with); to live together. **2.** (*fig.*) to live (with); to live together, cohabit.

сожр|а́ть, у́, ёшь, *past* **~а́л, ~ала́, ~а́ло** *pf. of* **жрать**

созва́нива|ться, юсь *impf. of* **созвони́ться**

созва́|ть, созову́, созовёшь, *past* **~л, ~ла́, ~ло** *pf.* **1.** (*impf.* **сзыва́ть**) to gather; to invite. **2.** (*impf.* **созыва́ть**) to call (together), summon; to convoke, convene; **с. ми́тинг** to call a meeting.

созве́зди|е, я *nt.* constellation.

созвон|и́ться, ю́сь, и́шься *pf.* (*of* **созва́ниваться**) **1.** (**с**+*i.*; *coll.*) to speak on the telephone (to). **2.** (**о**+*p.*; *coll.*) to arrange (sth.) on the phone; **мы с тобо́й созвони́мся об э́том** we'll arrange that over the telephone.

созву́чи|е, я *nt.* **1.** (*mus.*) accord, consonance. **2.** (*liter.*) assonance.

созву́ч|ный (~ен, ~на) *adj.* **1.** harmonious. **2.** (+*d.*) consonant (with), in keeping (with); **произведе́ние, созву́чное эпо́хе** a work in keeping with the times.

созда|ва́ть(ся), ю́, ёт(ся) *impf. of* **~́ть(ся)**

созда́ни|е, я *nt.* **1.** creation, making. **2.** creation, work. **3.** creature.

созда́тел|ь, я *m.* **1.** creator; founder, originator. **2.** the Creator.

созда́|ть, м, шь, ст, ди́м, ди́те, ду́т, *past* **со́зда́л, ~ла́, со́зда́ло** *pf.* (*of* **~ва́ть**) (*in var. senses*) to create; to found, originate; to set up, establish; **с. впечатле́ние** to create the impression, give the impression; **с. иллю́зию** to create an illusion.

созда́|ться, стся, ду́тся, *past* **~лся, ~ла́сь** *pf.* (*of* **~ва́ться**) to be created; to arise, spring up; **~ло́сь неприя́тное положе́ние** a disagreeable situation arose; **у нас ~ло́сь впечатле́ние, что** we gained the impression that.

созерца́ни|е, я *nt.* contemplation.

созерца́тел|ь, я *m.* contemplative pers.; passive observer.

созерца́тел|ьный (~ен, ~ьна) *adj.* contemplative, meditative.

созерца́|ть, ю *impf.* to contemplate.

созида́ни|е, я *nt.* creation.

созида́тел|ь, я *m.* creator.

созида́тел|ьный (~ен, ~ьна) *adj.* creative, constructive.

созида́|ть, ю *impf.* (*no pf.*) to build up.

созна|ва́ть, ю́, ёшь *impf.* **1.** *impf. of* **~́ть.** **2.** to be conscious (of), realize; **я́сно с.** to be alive (to); **он ещё не ~ёт, что он сде́лал** he still does not realize what he has done.

созна|ва́ться, ю́сь, ёшься *impf. of* **~́ться**

созна́ни|е, я *nt.* **1.** (*in var. senses*) consciousness; **кла́ссовое с.** class-consciousness; **потеря́ть с.** to lose consciousness; **прийти́ в с.** to regain, recover consciousness. **2.** recognition, acknowledgement; **с. до́лга** sense of duty. **3.** confession.

созна́тельност|ь, и *f.* **1.** awareness; intelligence, acumen; **полити́ческая с.** political awareness, political sense. **2.** deliberateness.

созна́тел|ьный (~ен, ~ьна) *adj.* **1.** conscious; politically conscious. **2.** intelligent; **у него́ ~ьное отноше́ние к собы́тиям** he has an intelligent attitude to events. **3.** deliberate.

созна́|ть, ю *pf.* (*of* **~ва́ть**) to recognize, acknowledge; **с. свою́ оши́бку** to recognize one's mistake.

созна́|ться, юсь *pf.* (*of* **~ва́ться**) (**в**+*p.*) to confess (to); (*leg.*) to plead guilty; **нельзя́ не с.** it must be confessed.

созорнича́|ть, ю *pf. of* **озорнича́ть**

созрева́|ть, ю *impf. of* **созре́ть**

созре́|ть, ю *pf.* (*of* **~ва́ть**) to ripen, mature.

созы́в, а *m.* calling, summoning; convocation; **с. заседа́ния** calling of a meeting; **Верхо́вный Сове́т СССР девя́того ~а** ninth USSR Supreme Soviet (*i.e. ninth four-year term since adoption of new Soviet Constitution in 1936*).

созыва́|ть, ю *impf. of* **созва́ть**
соизво́л|ить, ю, ишь *pf.* (*of* **~я́ть**) (*+inf.*; *obs.*) to deign (to), be pleased (to).
соизвол|я́ть, я́ю *impf. of* **~ить**
соизмери́мост|ь, и *f.* commensurability.
соизмери́м|ый (~, ~а) *adj.* commensurable.
соиска́ни|е, я *nt.* competition; **диссерта́ция на с. до́кторской сте́пени** doctoral dissertation.
соиска́тел|ь, я *m.* (*+g.*) competitor (for).
со́йк|а, и, *g. pl.* **со́ек** *f.* (*zool.*) jay.
со|йти́[1], **йду́, йдёшь,** *past* **~шёл, ~шла́** *pf.* (*of* **сходи́ть**) **1.** to go down, come down; to descend, get off, alight; **с. с ле́стницы** to go downstairs; **с. с ло́шади** to dismount; **с. на не́т** to come to naught. **2.** to leave; **с. с доро́ги** to get out of the way, step aside; **с. с ре́льсов** to be derailed, come off the rails; **снег ~шёл** the snow has melted; **с. со сце́ны** to leave the stage; (*fig.*) to quit the stage; **с. с ума́** to go mad, go off one's head. **3.** (*of paint, skin, etc.*) to come off.
со|йти́[2], **йду́, йдёшь** *pf.* (*of* **сходи́ть**) **1.** (**за**+*a.*) to pass (for), be taken (for). **2.** (*coll.*) to pass, go off; **~шло́ благополу́чно** it went off all right; **~йдёт и так** it will do as it is; **э́то ~шло́ ему́ с рук** he got away with it.
со|йти́сь, йду́сь, йдёшься, *past* **~шёлся, ~шла́сь** *pf.* (*of* **сходи́ться**) **1.** to meet; to come together, gather. **2.** (**с**+*i.*) to meet, take up (with), become friends (with); to become (*sexually*) intimate (with). **3.** (*+i.*, **в**+*p. or* **на**+*p.*) to agree (about); **с. в цене́** to agree about a price; **с. хара́ктером** to get on, hit it off; **они́ не ~шли́сь хара́ктерами** they could not get on. **4.** (*fig.*) to agree, tally; **счета́ не ~шли́сь** the figures did not tally.
сок, а (у), о ~е, в *and* **на ~у́** *m.* juice; **желу́дочный с.** (*physiol.*) gastric juice; (*coll.*) **в (по́лном) ~у́** in the prime of life; **вари́ться в со́бственном ~у́** to keep o.s. to o.s.
соквартира́нт, а *m.* flat-sharer, lodgings-sharer.
соковыжима́лк|а, и *f.* juicer.
со́кол[1], **а** *m.* falcon (*also fig., rhet.; of air aces*); **гол как соко́л** (*coll.*) as poor as a church mouse.
со́кол[2], **а** *m.* **1.** = **~о́к. 2.** (*tech.*) poker, slice bar. **3.** (*dial.*) battering-ram.
соколи́н|ый *adj. of* **со́кол**[1]; **~ая охо́та** falconry; **~ые о́чи** (*poet.*) hawk eyes.
сокол|о́к, ка́ *m.* (*plasterer's*) hawk.
соко́льник, а *m.* (*hist.*) falconer.
соко́льнич|ий, его *m.* (*hist.*) falconer (*boyar in charge of falconry*).
сократи́м|ый (~, ~а) *adj.* **1.** (*math.*) able to be cancelled. **2.** (*physiol.*) contractile.
сокра|ти́ть, щу́, ти́шь *pf.* (*of* **~ща́ть**) **1.** to shorten; to curtail; to abbreviate; to abridge. **2.** to reduce, cut down; **с. расхо́ды** to cut down expenses, retrench; **с. шта́ты** to reduce the establishment, cut down the staff. **3.** to dismiss, discharge, lay off. **4.** (*math.*) to cancel.
сокра|ти́ться, ти́тся *pf.* (*of* **~ща́ться**) **1.** grow shorter. **2.** to decrease, decline. **3.** (*coll.*) to cut down (*on expenses*). **4.** (**на**+*a.*; *math.*) to be cancelled (by). **5.** (*physiol.*) to contract.
сокраща́|ть(ся), ю(сь) *impf. of* **сократи́ть(ся)**
сокраще́ни|е, я *nt.* **1.** shortening. **2.** abridgement; **с ~ями** abridged, in abridged form. **3.** abbreviation. **4.** reduction, cutting down; curtailment; **с. вооруже́ний** (*mil.*) arms build-down; **с. шта́тов** staff reduction; **уво́лить по ~ю шта́тов** to dismiss on grounds of redundancy. **5.** (*math.*) cancellation. **6.** (*physiol.*) contraction; **с. се́рдца** systole.
сокращённо *adv.* briefly; in abbreviated form.
сокра|щённый *p.p.p. of* **~ти́ть** *and adj.* brief; **~щённое сло́во** abbreviation, contraction.
сокрове́нност|ь, и *f.* secrecy.
сокрове́н|ный (~, ~на) *adj.* secret, concealed; **~ные мы́сли** innermost thoughts.
сокро́вищ|е, а *nt.* treasure; **ни за каки́е ~а** not for the world.
сокро́вищниц|а, ы *f.* treasure-house, treasury, storehouse, depository (*also fig.*); **с. иску́сства** treasure-house of art.
сокруш|а́ть, а́ю *impf. of* **~и́ть**
сокруша́|ться, юсь *impf.* (**о**+*p.*) to grieve (for, over); to be distressed (about).
сокруше́ни|е, я *nt.* **1.** smashing, shattering. **2.** (*obs.*) grief, distress.
сокрушённый *p.p.p. of* **~и́ть** *and adj.* grief-stricken.
сокруши́тел|ьный (~ен, ~ьна) *adj.* shattering; **нанести́ с. уда́р** (*+d.*) to deal, strike a crippling blow.
сокруш|и́ть, у́, и́шь *pf.* (*of* **~а́ть**) **1.** to shatter, smash. **2.** (*fig.*) to shatter; to distress.
сокры́ти|е, я *nt.* concealment; **с. кра́деного** receiving of stolen goods.
сокр|ы́ть, о́ю, о́ешь *pf.* (*obs.*) to hide, conceal, cover up.
сокр|ы́ться, о́юсь, о́ешься *pf.* (*obs.*) to hide; to conceal o.s.
со|лга́ть, лгу́, лжёшь, лгу́т, *past* **~лга́л, ~лгала́, ~лга́ло** *pf. of* **лгать**
солда́т, а, *g. pl.* **~** *m.* soldier; **служи́ть в ~ах** (*obs.*) to soldier, be a soldier.
солда́тик, а *m.* **1.** *dim. of* **солда́т. 2.** toy soldier; **игра́ть в ~и** to play soldiers.
солда́тк|а, и *f.* soldier's wife.
солдатн|я́, и́ *f.* (*collect.*; *pej.*) soldiery.
солда́т|ский *adj. of* **~**; **~ская кни́жка** soldier's pay book; **~ская ла́вка** canteen.
солда́тчин|а, ы *f.* **1.** (*hist.*) levy. **2.** military service; soldiering.
солдафо́н, а *m.* (*coll.*) crude, loud-mouthed soldier.
солева́р, а *m.* salt-worker.
солеваре́ни|е, я *nt.* salt production.
солева́р|енный (*and* **~ный**) *adj. of* **~е́ние; с. заво́д** salt-works.
солева́р|ня, ни, *g. pl.* **~ен** *f.* salt-works, saltern.
соле́ни|е, я *nt.* salting; pickling.
солено́ид, а *m.* (*elec.*) solenoid.
солён|ый *adj.* **1.** salt; **~ое о́зеро** salt lake. **2.** (**со́лон, солона́, со́лоно**) salty; **у меня́ во рту́ со́лоно** I have a salt taste in my mouth. **3.** salted; pickled; **с. огуре́ц** pickled cucumber; *as n.* **~ое, ~ого** *nt.* pickles. **4.** (*fig., coll.*) salty, spicy; **с. анекдо́т** spicy story. **5.** (*short forms only*) (*fig.*) hot; **ему́ со́лоно пришло́сь** he got it hot; **в Пари́же им со́лоно доста́лось** Paris was their undoing; Paris became too hot for them; **верну́ться не со́лоно хлеба́вши** to come home empty-handed.
соле́нь|е, я *nt.* salted food(s); pickles.
солеци́зм, а *m.* solecism.
соле|я́, и́ *f.* (*eccl.*) solium.
солидариза́ци|я, и *f.* making common cause.
солидаризи́р|оваться, уюсь *impf. and pf.* (**с**+*i.*) to express one's solidarity (with), make common cause (with), identify o.s. (with); **с. с чьим-н. мне́нием** to express one's agreement with s.o.'s opinion.
солида́рно *adv.* (*leg.*) collectively, jointly.
солида́рност|ь, и *f.* **1.** solidarity; **из ~и (с**+*i.*) in sympathy (with); **ста́чка ~и** sympathetic strike. **2.** (*leg.*) collective, joint responsibility.
солида́р|ный *adj.* **1.** (**~ен, ~на**) (**с**+*i.*) at one (with), in sympathy (with). **2.** (*leg.*) solidary.
соли́д|ный (~ен, ~на) *adj.* **1.** solid, strong, sound; **~ные зна́ния** sound knowledge. **2.** (*fig.*) solid, sound; reliable, respectable; **с. челове́к** a solid man; **с. журна́л** respectable magazine. **3.** (*coll.*) respectable, sizable; **~ная су́мма** tidy sum. **4.** middle-aged; **челове́к ~ных лет** a middle-aged man.
соли́ст, а *m.* soloist.
солите́р, а *m.* (*min.*) solitaire (diamond).
солитёр, а *m.* tapeworm.
сол|и́ть, ю́, ~и́шь *impf.* (*of* **по~**) **1.** to salt. **2.** to pickle; **с. мя́со** to corn meat.
со́лк|а, и *f.* salting; pickling.
со́лнечн|ый *adj.* **1.** sun; solar; **~ая ва́нна** sun-bath; **~ая вспы́шка** (*astron.*) solar flare; **~ое затме́ние** solar eclipse; **с. луч** sunbeam; **~ая пане́ль** solar panel; **~ые пя́тна** (*astron.*) sun-spots; **с. свет** sunlight, sunshine; **~ая систе́ма** solar system; **~ое сплете́ние** (*anat.*) solar plexus; **с. уда́р** (*med.*) sunstroke; **~ые часы́** sun-dial. **2.** sunny.

со́лнц|е, а *nt.* sun; **го́рное с.** artificial sunlight, sun-lamp; **ло́жное с.** (*astron.*) parhelion; **на с.** in the sun; **гре́ться на с.** to sun o.s., bask in the sun; **по ~у** by the sun; with the sun, clockwise; **про́тив ~а** against the sun, anticlockwise.
солнцепёк, а *m.*: **на ~е** right in the sun, in the full blaze of the sun.
солнцестоя́ни|е, я *nt.* solstice.
со́ло 1. *adv.* **2.** *n.*; *nt. indecl.* solo.
солов|е́й, ья́ *m.* nightingale; **восто́чный с.** thrush-nightingale.
солове́|ть, ю, ешь *impf.* (*of* **о~**) (*coll.*) to become drowsy.
соло́вый *adj.* light bay.
солов|ьи́ный *adj. of* **~е́й**
со́лод, а *m.* malt.
солоди́л|ьня, ьни, *g. pl.* **~ен** *f.* malthouse.
соло|ди́ть, жу́, ди́шь *impf.* (*of* **на~**) to malt.
соло́дк|а, и *f.* liquorice.
солодко́вый *adj. of* **соло́дка; с. ко́рень** (*pharm.*) liquorice.
солодо́венный *adj.*: **с. заво́д** malt-house.
соложе́ни|е, я *nt.* malting.
соло́м|а, ы *f.* straw; thatch; **крыть ~ой** to thatch.
соло́менн|ый *adj.* **1.** straw; **~ая вдова́** grass widow; **~ая кры́ша** thatch, thatched roof; **~ая шля́па** straw hat. **2.** straw-coloured; **~ые во́лосы** straw-coloured hair.
соло́минк|а, и *f.* straw; **хвата́ться за ~у** to catch, clutch at a straw.
соло́мк|а, и *f.* **1.** *dim. of* **соло́ма. 2.** match-stick; **спи́чечная с.** (*collect.*) matchwood. **3.** (*collect.*) straw packing. **4.** stick (of toffee). **5.** (*collect.*) stick-like biscuits.
соломоре́зк|а, и *f.* (*agric.*) chaff-cutter.
солони́н|а, ы *f.* salted beef, corned beef.
соло́нк|а, и *f.* salt-cellar.
со́лоно *see* **солёный**
солонча́к, а́ *m* **1.** saline soil. **2.** salt-marsh.
со́лоп, а *m.* (*vulg.*) dick, willy.
сол|ь¹, и, *pl.* **~и, ~е́й** *f.* **1.** salt; **го́рькая с.** Epsom salts; **ка́менная с.** rock-salt; **ню́хательная с.** smelling salts; **пова́ренная с.** common salt, sodium chloride; **столо́вая с.** table-salt. **2.** (*fig.*) salt, spice; point; **с. земли́** the salt of the earth; **вот в чём вся с.** that's the whole point; **мно́го ~и съесть (с кем-н.)** to spend a long time together (with s.o.).
соль² *nt. indecl.* (*mus.*) so(h), sol; G; **с.-дие́з** G sharp; **с.-бемо́ль** G flat; **ключ с.** treble clef, G clef.
со́ль|ный 1. *adj. of* **~о; с. но́мер** solo; **~ная па́ртия** solo part. **2.** *adj. of* **~ь²; с. ключ** treble clef.
сольфе́джио *nt. indecl.* (*mus.*) solfeggio, sol-fa, solmization; **петь с.** to sol-fa, solmizate.
соля́нк|а, ~и *f.* solyanka (*a sharp-tasting Russ. soup of vegetables and meat or fish*).
солян|о́й *adj.* salt, saline; **~а́я кислота́** (*chem.*) hydrochloric acid; **~ы́е ко́пи** salt-mines; **с. раство́р** saline solution, brine.
солянoки́слый *adj.* (*chem.*) hydrochloric.
соля́ри|й, я *m.* solarium.
сом, а́ *m.* sheat-fish.
Сомали́ *nt. indecl.* Somalia.
сомали́|ец, йца *m.* Somali.
сомали́|йка, йки *f. of* **~ец**
сомали́йский *adj.* Somali.
сомати́ческий *adj.* somatic.
со́мкн|утый *p.p.p. of* **~у́ть** *and adj.*; **с. строй** (*mil.*) close order.
сомкн|у́ть, у́, ёшь *pf.* (*of* **смыка́ть**) to close; **с. глаза́** to close one's eyes; **с. ряды́** (*mil.*) to close the ranks; **~и́сь!** (*mil. word of command*) close order, march!
сомкн|у́ться, ётся *pf.* (*of* **смыка́ться**) to close (up).
Со́мм|а, ы *f.* the Somme (*river*).
сомна́мбул|а, ы *c.g.* sleep-walker, somnambulist.
сомнамбули́зм, а *m.* sleep-walking, somnambulism.
сомнева́|ться, юсь *impf.* **1.** (**в**+*p.*) to doubt; to question; **я не ~юсь в его́ че́стности** I do not question his integrity. **2.** to worry; **мо́жете не с., всё бу́дет в поря́дке** you need not worry, everything will be all right.
сомне́ни|е, я *nt.* doubt; uncertainty; **без (вся́кого) ~я, вне ~я** without (any) doubt, beyond doubt; **не подлежи́т ни мале́йшему ~ю, что** there cannot be the slightest doubt that.
сомни́тел|ьный (~ен, ~ьна) *adj.* **1.** doubtful, questionable; **~ьно** it is doubtful, it is open to question. **2.** dubious; equivocal; **с. комплиме́нт** dubious compliment; **~ьные дела́** shady dealings.
сомно́жител|ь, я *m.* (*math.*) factor.
сон, сна *m.* **1.** sleep; **ве́чный с.** (*fig.*) eternal rest; **во сне, сквозь с.** in one's sleep; **на с. гряду́щий** at bedtime, the last thing; **со сна** half awake; **у меня́ сна ни в одно́м глазу́** (*coll.*) I am not in the least sleepy. **2.** dream; **ви́деть во сне** to dream, have a dream (about).
сонасле́дник, а *m.* co-heir.
сона́т|а, ы *f.* (*mus.*) sonata.
сонати́н|а, ы *f.* (*mus.*) sonatina.
соне́т, а *m.* sonnet.
сонли́в|ец, ца *m.* (*obs., coll.*) sleepyhead.
сонли́вост|ь, и *f.* sleepiness, drowsiness; somnolence.
сонли́в|ый (~, ~а) *adj.* sleepy, drowsy; somnolent.
сонм, а *m.* (*arch. or joc.*) assembly, throng; (*fig.*) swarm.
со́нмищ|е, а *nt.* = **сонм**
со́нник, а *m.* book of dream interpretations.
со́нн|ый *adj.* **1.** sleepy, drowsy (*also fig.*); somnolent, slumberous; **~ая арте́рия** (*anat.*) carotid artery; **~ая боле́знь** (*med.*) (*i*) sleeping sickness (*morbus dormitivus*), (*ii*) sleepy sickness (*encephalitis lethargica*); **~ое ца́рство** the land of Nod; **у них сейча́с ~ое ца́рство** they are all asleep. **2.** sleeping, soporific; **~ые ка́пли** sleeping-draught.
соно́рный *adj.* (*ling.*) sonorous; sonant.
со́н|я, и *f. and c.g.* **1.** *f.* dormouse. **2.** *c.g.* (*coll.*) sleepyhead.
соображá|ть, ю *impf.* **1.** *impf. of* **сообрази́ть. 2.** *impf. only* **хорошо́, пло́хо с.** to be quick, slow on the uptake.
соображе́ни|е, я *nt.* **1.** consideration, thought; **приня́ть в с.** to take into consideration; **поступа́ть без ~я** to act without thinking. **2.** understanding, grasp. **3.** consideration, reason; notion, idea; **по фина́нсовым ~ям** for financial reasons; **вы́сказать свой ~я** to express one's views.
сообрази́тельност|ь, и *f.* quickness, quick-wittedness.
сообрази́тел|ьный (~ен, ~ьна) *adj.* quick-witted, quick, sharp, bright.
сообра|зи́ть, жу́, зи́шь *pf.* (*of* **~жа́ть**) **1.** to consider, ponder, think out; to weigh (the pros and cons of). **2.** to understand, grasp. **3.** (*coll.*) to think up, arrange.
сообра́зно *adv.* (**с**+*i.*) in conformity (with).
сообра́зност|ь, и *f.* conformity.
сообра́з|ный (~ен, ~на) *adj.* (**с**+*i.*) conformable (to), in conformity (with); **э́то ни с чем не ~но** it makes no sense at all.
сообраз|ова́ть, у́ю *impf. and pf.* (**с**+*i.*) to conform (to), make conformable (to), adapt (to); **с. расхо́ды с дохо́дами** to adapt expenditure to income.
сообраз|ова́ться, у́юсь *impf. and pf.* (**с**+*i.*) to conform (to), adapt o.s. (to).
сообща́ *adv.* together, jointly.
сообщ|а́ть, а́ю *impf. of* **~и́ть**
сообщ|а́ться, а́юсь *impf.* **1.** *impf. of* **~и́ться. 2.** *impf. only* (**с**+*i.*) to communicate (with), be in communication (with).
сообще́ни|е, я *nt.* **1.** communication, report; **сро́чное** *or* **э́кстренное с.** news flash; **по после́дним ~ям** according to latest reports; **проче́сть с., сде́лать с.** to read a communication (*at a meeting of a learned society, etc.*). **2.** communication; **возду́шное с.** aerial communication; **прямо́е с.** through connection; **пути́ ~я** communications (*rail, road, canal, etc.*).
соо́бществ|о, а *nt.* association, fellowship; community; **в ~е (с**+*i.*) in association (with), together (with).
сообщ|и́ть, у́, и́шь *pf.* (*of* **~а́ть**) **1.** (+*a. or* **о**+*p.*) to communicate, report, inform, announce; **с. после́дние изве́стия** to communicate the latest news; **по ра́дио ~и́ли о заключе́нии ми́рного догово́ра** the conclusion of a peace treaty has been announced on the radio; **нам ~и́ли,**

что вас призва́ли на вое́нную слу́жбу we were told that you had been called up. **2.** to impart; **с. материа́лу огнеупо́рность** to make a material fireproof.
сообщ|и́ться, и́тся *pf.* (*of* **~а́ться**) to be communicated, communicate itself.
соо́бщник, а *m.* accomplice, confederate; partner (*in crime*); (*leg.*) accessory.
соо́бщничеств|о, а *nt.* complicity.
соору|ди́ть, жу́, ди́шь *pf.* (*of* **~жа́ть**) to build, erect.
сооруже́ни|е, я *nt.* **1.** building, erection. **2.** building, structure; **вое́нные ~я** military installations; **оборони́тельные ~я** (*mil.*) defensive works, defences.
соотве́тственно *adv.* **1.** accordingly, correspondingly. **2.** (*+d.*) according (to), in accordance (with), in conformity (with), in compliance (with).
соотве́тствен|ный (~, ~на) *adj.* (*+d.*) corresponding (to).
соотве́тстви|е, я *nt.* accordance, conformity, correspondence; **в ~и (с***+i.***)** in accordance (with); **привести́ в с. (с***+i.***)** to bring into line (with).
соотве́тств|овать, ую *impf.* (*+d.*) to correspond (to, with), conform (to), be in keeping (with); **с. действи́тельности** to correspond to the facts; **с. тре́бованиям** to meet the requirements; **с. це́ли** to answer the purpose.
соотве́тств|ующий *pres. part. act. of* **~овать** *and adj.* **1.** (*+d.*) corresponding (to). **2.** proper, appropriate, suitable; **поступа́ть ~ующим о́бразом** to act accordingly.
сооте́чественник, а *m.* compatriot, fellow-countryman.
соотнес|ти́, у́, ёшь, *past* **~̈, ~ла́** *pf.* (*of* **соотноси́ть**) to correlate.
соотноси́тел|ьный (~ен, ~ьна) *adj.* correlative.
соотно|си́ть, шу́, ~сишь *impf. of* **соотнести́**
соотно|си́ться, ~́сится *impf.* to correspond.
соотноше́ни|е, я *nt.* correlation, ratio; **с. сил** correlation of forces, alignment of forces.
сопа́тк|а, и *f.* (*coll.*) snout, hooter.
сопе́рник, а *m.* rival.
сопе́рнича|ть, ю *impf.* to be rivals; (**с***+i.*) to compete (with), vie (with).
сопе́рничеств|о, а *nt.* rivalry.
соп|е́ть, лю́, и́шь *impf.* to breathe heavily and noisily through the nose.
со́пк|а, и *f.* **1.** knoll, hill, mound. **2.** (*in Far East*) volcano.
соплеме́нник, а *m.* fellow-tribesman.
соплеме́нный *adj.* related, of the same tribe.
сопли́в|ый (~, ~а) *adj.* (*coll.*) snotty.
соп|ло́, а́, *pl.* **~́ла, ~́ел** *nt.* (*tech.*) nozzle.
сопл|я́, и́, *pl.* **~́и, ~́е́й** *f.* **1.** (nose-)drip; (*pl.*) snivel, snot. **2.** (*coll., pej.*) = **сопля́к**
сопля́к, а́ *m.* (*coll., pej.*) **1.** whimperer, sniveller. **2.** spineless creature; milksop.
соподчине́ни|е, я *nt.* co-ordination.
соподчинён|ный (~, ~а́) *adj.* (*gram.*) coordinative.
сопостави́м|ый (~, ~а) *adj.* comparable.
сопоста́в|ить, лю, ишь *pf.* (*of* **~ля́ть**) (**с***+i.*) to compare (with), confront (with).
сопоставле́ни|е, я *nt.* comparison, confrontation.
сопоставля́|ть, ю *impf. of* **сопоста́вить**
сопра́но *indecl.* (*mus.*) **1.** *nt.* soprano (*voice*). **2.** *f.* soprano (*singer*).
сопреде́л|ьный (~ен, ~ьна) *adj.* contiguous; (*fig.*) kindred, related.
сопре́|ть, ю *pf. of* **преть**
соприкаса́|ться, юсь *impf.* (*of* **соприкосну́ться**) (**с***+i.*) **1.** to adjoin, be contiguous (to). **2.** (*fig.*) to come into contact (with).
соприкоснове́ни|е, я *nt.* contiguity; (*mil. and fig.*) contact; **име́ть с. (с***+i.***)** to come into contact (with).
соприкосн|у́ться, у́сь, ёшься *pf. of* **соприкаса́ться**
сопричáстност|ь, и *f.* complicity, participation.
сопричáст|ный (~ен, ~на) *adj.*: **быть с. (к)** to be implicated (in), be a participant (in).
сопроводи́тел|ь, я *m.* escort.
сопроводи́тел|ьный *adj.* accompanying; **~ое письмо́** covering letter.
сопрово|ди́ть, жу́, ди́шь *pf. of* **~жда́ть**
сопровожда́|ть, ю *impf.* (*of* **сопроводи́ть**) (*in var. senses*) to accompany; to escort; to convey.
сопровожде́ни|е, я *nt.* accompaniment; escort, convoy; **в ~и (***+g.***)** accompanied (by); escorted (by); **звуково́е с.** soundtrack.
сопротивле́ни|е, я *nt.* resistance, opposition; (*phys., tech.*) strength; (*elec.*) resistance, impedance; **движе́ние С~я** (*pol., hist.*) the Resistance; **оказа́ть с.** to offer, put up resistance; **с. материа́лов** (study of) strength of materials; **с. разры́ву** tensile strength; **идти́ по ли́нии наиме́ньшего ~я** to take the line of least resistance.
сопротивля́емост|ь, и *f.* capacity to resist; (*elec.*) resistivity.
сопротивля́|ться, юсь *impf.* (*+d.*) to resist, oppose.
сопряжён|ный (~, ~а́) *adj.* **1.** (**с***+i.*) linked (with), attended (by), entailing; **ваш прое́кт ~ с больши́м ри́ском** your scheme entails great risk. **2.** (*math., chem., tech.*) conjugate; bilateral.
сопу́тств|овать, ую *impf.* (*+d.*) to accompany; **~ующие обстоя́тельства** attendant circumstances, concomitants.
сор, а *m.* litter, dust; **не выноси́ть ~́а из избы́** not to wash one's dirty linen in public.
соразме́р|ить, ю, ишь *pf.* (*of* **~я́ть**) (**с***+i.*) to make commensurate (with), balance (with), match (with).
соразме́рност|ь, и *f.* proportionality.
соразме́р|ный (~ен, ~на) *adj.* proportionate, commensurate; balanced; of the same order.
соразмер|я́ть, я́ю *impf. of* **~ить**
сора́тник, а *m.* companion-in-arms, comrade-in-arms.
сорван|е́ц, ца́ *m.* (*coll.*; *of a child*) a terror; (*of a girl*) tomboy.
сорв|а́ть, у́, ёшь, *past* **~а́л, ~ала́, ~а́ло** *pf.* (*of* **срыва́ть**) **1.** to tear off, break off, tear away, tear down; to pick, pluck; **с. ве́тку** to break off a branch; **ве́тер ~а́л с меня́ шля́пу** the wind took my hat off; **с. ма́ску с кого́-н.** to unmask s.o. **2.** (*coll.*) to get, extract; **с. с кого́-н. де́сять рубле́й** to get ten roubles out of s.o. **3.** (**на***+p.*) to vent (upon); **с. гнев на ком-н.** to vent one's anger upon s.o. **4.** to smash, wreck, ruin, spoil; **с. вра́жеские пла́ны** to foil, frustrate the enemy's plans; **с. рабо́ту** to upset work; **с. забасто́вку** to break a strike; **с. банк** (*cards*) to break the bank.
сорв|а́ться, у́сь, ёшься, *past* **~а́лся, ~ала́сь, ~ало́сь** *pf.* (*of* **срыва́ться**) **1.** to break away, break loose; **с. с пе́тель** to come off its hinges, come unhinged; **с. с ме́ста** (*coll.*) to dart off; **с. с це́пи** (*fig., coll.*) to break out, break loose; **с. с языка́** to escape one's lips. **2.** to fall, come down; **с. с колоко́льни** to fall from the belfry. **3.** (*coll.*) to fall through, fall to the ground, miscarry.
сорвиголов|а́, ы́, *pl.* **сорвиго́ловы, сорвиголо́в, сорвиголова́м** *c.g.* (*coll.*) daredevil; desperado.
сорганиз|ова́ть, у́ю *pf. of* **организова́ть**
со́рго *nt. indecl.* (*bot.*) sorghum; **с. ка́фрское** kaf(f)ir (corn).
соревнова́ни|е, я *nt.* **1.** (*sport*) competition, contest; event; **кома́ндное с.** team event; **отбо́рочные ~я** elimination contests; **с. на пе́рвенство ми́ра** world championship. **2.** competition, emulation; **социалисти́ческое с.** socialist emulation.
соревн|ова́ться, у́юсь *impf.* (**с***+i.*) to compete (with, against), contend (with); to engage in competition.
соревн|у́ющийся *pres. part. of* **~ова́ться**; *as n.* **с., ~у́ющегося** *m.* competitor, contender.
сорогина́льнича|ть, ю *pf. of* **оригина́льничать**
сори́нк|а, и *f.* mote; speck of dust.
сор|и́ть, ю́, и́шь *impf.* (*of* **на~**) (*+a. or i.*) to litter; to throw about (*also fig.*); to make a mess; **с. в ко́мнате оку́рками** to litter a room with cigarette butts; **с. деньга́ми** to throw one's money about.
со́рн|ый *adj.* **1.** *adj. of* **сор; ~ое ведро́** refuse pail; **с. я́щик** dustbin. **2. ~ое расте́ние, ~ая трава́** weed; **~ая трава́** (*collect.*) weeds.
сорня́к, а́ *m.* weed.
соро́дич, а *m.* **1.** relative, kinsman. **2.** fellow-countryman; pers. from same part of country.
со́рок *all other cases* **а́,** *num. forty*; **с. ~о́в** (*obs.*) a multitude, a great number.

соро́к|а, и *f.* magpie; **с. на хвосте́ принесла́** (*joc.*; *of sth. learned from an unrevealed source*) a little bird told me, us, *etc.*
сорокале́ти|е, я *nt.* **1.** forty years. **2.** fortieth anniversary, fortieth birthday.
сорокале́тний *adj.* **1.** forty-year, of forty years. **2.** forty-year-old.
сороков|о́й *adj.* fortieth; **~ы́е го́ды** the forties; **с. но́мер** number forty; **~а́я страни́ца** page forty.
сороконо́жк|а, и *f.* centipede.
сорокопу́т, а *m.* (*zool.*) shrike.
сорокоу́ст, а *m.* (forty days') prayers for the dead.
соро́чк|а, и *f.* **1.** shirt; blouse; camisole; **ночна́я с.** night-shirt, night-dress. **2.** reverse (*of playing-card*). **3.** (*med.*) caul; **роди́ться в ~е** to be born with a silver spoon in one's mouth. **4.** jacket, cover.
сорт, а, *pl.* **~а́** *m.* **1.** grade, quality; brand: **вы́сший с.** best quality; **пе́рвого ~а** first grade, first quality; first-rate. **2.** sort, kind, variety.
сорта́мент = сортиме́нт
сортиме́нт, а *m.* (*tech.*) assortment.
сорти́р, а *m.* (*coll.*) loo.
сортир|ова́ть, у́ю *impf.* to sort, assort, grade; **с. по разме́рам** to size.
сортиро́вк|а, и *f.* **1.** sorting, grading, sizing. **2.** (*agric.*) separator.
сортиро́вочн|ая, ой *f.* marshalling yard.
сортиро́вочный *adj.* sorting.
сортиро́вщик, а *m.* sorter.
со́ртност|ь, и *f.* grade, quality.
со́ртный *adj.* of high quality.
сортов|о́й *adj.* high-grade, of high quality; **~о́е желе́зо** section iron, profile iron, shaped iron; **с. стан** jobbing mill, shape mill.
соса́ни|е, я *nt.* sucking, suction.
соса́тельный *adj.* sucking.
сос|а́ть, у́, ёшь *impf.* to suck.
сосва́та|ть, ю *pf. of* **сва́тать**
сосе́д, а, *pl.* **~и, ~ей** *m.* neighbour; **с. по кварти́ре** flatmate; **с. по купе́** (*rail.*) fellow passenger.
сосе́д|ить, ишь *impf.* (**с**+*i.*) to neighbour.
сосе́дн|ий *adj.* neighbouring; adjacent, next; **с. дом** the house next door; **~яя ко́мната** the next room.
сосе́д|ский *adj. of* **~**; **~ские де́ти** the neighbours' children, the children next door.
сосе́дств|о, а *nt.* neighbourhood, vicinity; **по ~у** (+*g.*) in the neighbourhood (of), in the vicinity (of); **мы с ни́ми живём по ~у** we (and they) are neighbours.
соси́ск|а, и *f.* sausage; frankfurter.
со́ск|а, и *f.* (*baby's*) dummy.
соска́блива|ть, ю *impf. of* **соскобли́ть**
соска́кива|ть, ю *impf. of* **соскочи́ть**
соска́льзыва|ть, ю *impf. of* **соскользну́ть**
соскобл|и́ть, ю, ~и́шь *pf.* (*of* **соска́бливать**) to scrape off.
соско́к, а *m.* (*gymnastics*) dismount.
соскользн|у́ть, у́, ёшь *pf.* (*of* **соска́льзывать**) to slip off, slide off; to slide down, glide down.
соскоч|и́ть, у́, ~ишь *pf.* (*of* **соска́кивать**) **1.** to jump off, leap off; to jump down, leap down; **с. с крова́ти** to jump out of bed; **с. с трамва́я** to jump off a tram. **2.** to come off; **с. с пе́тель** to come off its hinges. **3.** (**с**+*g.*; *coll.*) to disappear (from), leave; **хмель ~и́л с него́** he sobered up.
соскреба́|ть, ю *impf. of* **соскрести́**
соскре|сти́, бу́, бёшь, *past* **~б, ~бла́** *pf.* (*of* **~ба́ть**) to scrape away, off.
соску́ч|иться, усь, ишься *pf.* **1.** to become bored. **2.** (**по**+*p.*, *preceding sg. nn.*; **по**+*d.*, *preceding pl. nn.*) to miss; **с. по дере́вне** to miss the country; **с. по друзья́м** to miss one's friends.
сослага́тельный *adj.* (*gram.*) subjunctive.
со|сла́ть, шлю́, шлёшь *pf.* (*of* **ссыла́ть**) to exile, banish, deport.
со|сла́ться[1]**, шлю́сь, шлёшься** *pf.* (*of* **ссыла́ться**) (**на**+*a.*) **1.** to refer (to), allude (to), cite, quote. **2.** to plead, allege; **с. на недомога́ние** to plead indisposition.
со|сла́ться[2]**, шлю́сь, шлёшься** *pf.* (*of* **ссыла́ться**) *pass. of* **~сла́ть**
со́слепа *adv.* (*coll.*) due to poor sight.
со́слеп|у *adv.* = **~а**
сосло́ви|е, я *nt.* **1.** estate; **дворя́нское с.** the nobility; the gentry; **духо́вное с.** the clergy; **купе́ческое с.** the merchants. **2.** corporation, professional association.
сосло́в|ный *adj. of* **~ие; ~ная мона́рхия** limited monarchy; **~ное представи́тельство** (*hist.*) representation of the estates; **с. предрассу́док** class prejudice.
сослужи́в|ец, ца *m.* colleague, fellow-employee.
сослуж|и́ть, у́, ~ишь *pf.*: **с. кому́-н. слу́жбу** to do s.o. a good turn, stand s.o. in good stead.
сосн|а́, ы́, *pl.* **~ы, со́сен** *f.* pine(-tree); **заблуди́ться в трёх ~ах,** *see* **заблуди́ться**
сосно́в|ый *adj.* pine; pinewood; deal; **с. бор** pine forest; **~ая ме́бель** deal furniture; **~ая смола́** pine tar.
сосн|у́ть, у́, ёшь *pf.* (*coll.*) to have, take a nap.
сосня́к, а́ *m.* pine forest.
сос|о́к, ка́ *m.* nipple, teat.
сосо́ч|ек, ка *m.* **1.** *dim. of* **сосо́к. 2.** (*anat.*) papilla.
сосредото́чени|е, я *nt.* (*mil., etc.*) concentration.
сосредото́ченност|ь, и *f.* (degree of) concentration.
сосредото́ч|енный *p.p.p. of* **~ить** *and adj.* concentrated; (*tech.*) lumped, centred; **с. взгляд** fixed stare; **~енное внима́ние** rapt attention; **~енная нагру́зка** (*tech.*) point load; **с. ого́нь** (*mil.*) concentrated fire, convergent fire.
сосредото́чива|ть(ся), ю(сь) *impf. of* **сосредото́чить(ся)**
сосредото́ч|ить, у, ишь *pf.* (*of* **~ивать**) to concentrate; to focus; **с. внима́ние** (**на**+*p.*) to concentrate one's attention (on, upon).
сосредото́ч|иться, усь, ишься *pf.* (*of* **~иваться**) **1.** (**на**+*p.*) to concentrate (on, upon). **2.** *pass. of* **~ить**
соста́в, а *m.* **1.** composition, make-up; structure; **социа́льный с.** social structure; **хими́ческий с.** (*i*) chemical composition, (*ii*) chemical compound; **входи́ть в с.** (+*g.*) to form part (of); **с. преступле́ния** (*leg.*) corpus delicti. **2.** staff; membership, composition, strength; **ли́чный с.** personnel; **нали́чный с.** available personnel; **с. (актёров)** cast; (*mil.*) effectives; **офице́рский с.** the officers; **в по́лном ~е** with its full complement; in, at full strength; **в ~е** (+*g.*) numbering, consisting (of), amounting (to); **делега́ция в ~е тридцати́ челове́к** a delegation of thirty (persons); **входи́ть в с.** (+*g.*) to become a member (of). **3.** train; **подвижно́й с.** rolling-stock.
состави́тел|ь, я *m.* compiler, author; **с. поездо́в** train maker-up.
соста́в|ить[1]**, лю, ишь** *pf.* (*of* **~ля́ть**) **1.** to put together, make up; **с. винто́вки в ко́злы** (*mil.*) to pile arms, stack arms; **с. по́езд** to make up a train; **с. посу́ду** to stack crockery. **2.** to compose, make up, draw up; to compile; to form, construct; **с. библиоте́ку** to form a library; **с. мне́ние** to form an opinion; **с. предложе́ние** to construct a sentence; **с. прое́кт** to draw up a draft; **с. слова́рь** to compile a dictionary; **с. спи́сок** to make a list. **3.** to be, constitute, make; **э́то не ~ит исключе́ния из пра́вила** this will not constitute an exception to the rule; **с. чьё-н. сча́стье** to make s.o.'s happiness. **4.** to form, make, amount to, total; **с. в сре́днем** to average; **расхо́ды ~или пятьсо́т фу́нтов** expenditure amounted to five hundred pounds. **5.: с. себе́** to make (for o.s.); **с. себе́ и́мя** to make a name for o.s.
соста́в|ить[2]**, лю, ишь** *pf.* (*of* **~ля́ть**) to take down, put down; **с. я́щик на пол** to put a drawer down on the floor.
соста́в|иться, ится *pf.* (*of* **~ля́ться**) to form, be formed, come into being.
составля́|ть(ся), ю(сь) *impf. of* **соста́вить(ся)**
составн|о́й *adj.* **1.** compound, composite; **~а́я кни́жная по́лка** sectional book-shelf. **2.** component; **~а́я часть** component, constituent.
соста́р|ить(ся), ю(сь) *pf. of* **ста́рить(ся)**
состоя́ни|е, я *nt.* **1.** state, condition; position; **в хоро́шем, плохо́м ~и** in good, bad condition; **прийти́ в него́дное с.** to be past repair; **с. войны́** state of war; **быть в ~и войны́**

(с+*i.*) to be at war (with); **с. пого́ды** state of the weather, weather conditions; **быть в ~и** (+*inf.*) to be able (to), be in a position (to). **2.** (*obs.*) status, condition; **гражда́нское с.** civil status. **3.** fortune; **нажи́ть с.** to make a fortune.
состоя́тельност|ь[1], **и** *f.* **1.** solvency. **2.** wealth.
состоя́тельност|ь[2], **и** *f.* justifiability, strength (*of an argument, etc.*).
состоя́тел|ьный[1] **(~ен, ~ьна)** *adj.* **1.** solvent. **2.** well-off, well-to-do.
состоя́тел|ьный[2] **(~ен, ~ьна)** *adj.* well-grounded; **не вполне́ с. до́вод** lame argument.
состо|я́ть, ю́, и́шь *impf.* **1. (из)** to consist (of), comprise, be made up (of); **кварти́ра ~и́т из трёх ко́мнат** the flat consists of three rooms; **име́ние ~и́т преиму́щественно из торфяно́го боло́та** the estate is largely made up of a peatbog. **2.** (в+*p.*) to consist (in), lie (in), be; **ра́зница ~и́т в том, что** the difference is that; **в чём ~я́т на́ши обя́занности?** what are our duties? **3.** to be; **с. чле́ном о́бщества** to be a member of a society; **с. в до́лжности заве́дующего** to occupy the post of director; **с. на вооруже́нии** (*mil.*) to be part of standard equipment; **с. на своём иждиве́нии** to keep o.s.; **с. под судо́м** to be awaiting trial; **с. при посо́льстве** to be attached to the embassy.
состо|я́ться, и́тся *pf.* to take place; **визи́т не ~я́лся** the visit did not take place; **изда́ние не ~я́лось** the edition was never printed.
состра́гива|ть, ю *impf. of* **сострога́ть**
сострада́ни|е, я *nt.* compassion, sympathy.
сострада́тел|ьный (~ен, ~ьна) *adj.* compassionate, sympathetic.
сострада́|ть, ю *impf.* (+*d.*; *obs.*) to feel pity (for).
сострига́|ть, ю *impf. of* **состри́чь**
состр|и́ть, ю́, и́шь *pf. of* **остри́ть**
состри́|чь, гу́, жёшь, гу́т, *past* **~г, ~гла** *pf.* (*of* **~га́ть**) to shear, clip off.
сострога́|ть, ю *pf.* (*of* **состра́гивать**) to plane off.
состро́|ить, ю, ишь *pf. of* **стро́ить 3.; с. грима́су, с. ро́жу** (*coll.*) to make a face.
соструга́|ть, ю *pf.* = **сострога́ть**
состря́па|ть, ю *pf. of* **стря́пать**
состык|ова́ть(ся), у́ю(сь) *pf. of* **стыкова́ть(ся)**
состяза́ни|е, я *nt.* **1.** competition, contest; match; **с. в пла́вании** swimming contest; **с. по фехтова́нию** fencing match; **с. в остроу́мии** battle of wits. **2.** (*leg.*) controversy.
состяза́тельный *adj.* (*leg.*) controversial.
состяза́|ться, юсь *impf.* (с+*i.*) to compete (with), contend (with).
сосу́д, а *m.* (*in var. senses*) vessel; **кровено́сные ~ы** blood vessels.
сосу́дистый *adj.* (*anat.*, *biol.*) vascular.
сосу́льк|а, и *f.* icicle.
сосуществова́ни|е, я *nt.* co-existence; **ми́рное с.** (*pol.*) peaceful co-existence.
сосуществ|ова́ть, у́ю *impf.* to co-exist.
сос|у́щий *pres. part. act. of* **~а́ть** *and adj.* (*zool.*) suctorial.
сосцеви́д|ный (~ен, ~на) *adj.* mammiform, mammilliform.
сосчита́|ть, ю *pf. of* **счита́ть**
сосчита́|ться, юсь *pf.* (с+*i.*) to settle accounts (with), get even (with) (*also fig.*).
сотворе́ни|е, я *nt.* creation, making; **с. ми́ра** the creation of the world.
сотвор|и́ть, ю́, и́шь *pf. of* **твори́ть**
со́тенн|ая, о́й *f.* (*coll.*) hundred-rouble note.
со́тенный *adj.* (*coll.*) worth a hundred roubles.
со́тк|а, и *f.* hundredth part.
сотк|а́ть, у́, ёшь, *past* **~а́л, ~ала́, ~а́ло** *pf. of* **ткать**
со́тник, а *m.* (*hist.*) sotnik (*lieutenant of Cossack troops*).
со́т|ня, ни, *g. pl.* **~ен** *f.* **1.** a hundred (*esp. a hundred roubles*). **2.** (*hist.*) sotnya, company (*mil. unit, originally of a hundred men*); **каза́чья с.** Cossack squadron.
сотова́рищ, а *m.* associate, partner.
сотови́д|ный (~ен, ~на) *adj.* honeycomb.
со́т|овый *adj.* **1.** *adj. of* **~ы; с. мёд** comb-honey. **2.** (*tech.*; *fig.*) honeycomb; **~овая кату́шка** honeycomb coil.
сотрапе́зник, а *m.* (*obs.*) table-companion.
сотру́дник, а *m.* **1.** collaborator. **2.** employee, official; **нау́чный с.** research officer, research fellow, research assistant (*of a learned body or scientific institution*); **с. посо́льства** embassy official. **3.** contributor (*to a newspaper, journal, etc.*).
сотру́днича|ть, ю *impf.* **1.** (с+*i.*) to collaborate (with). **2.** (в+*p.*) to contribute (to); **с. в газе́те** to contribute to a newspaper; to work on a newspaper.
сотру́дничеств|о, а *nt.* collaboration, co-operation.
сотряс|а́ть(ся), а́ю(сь) *impf. of* **~ти́(сь)**
сотрясе́ни|е, я *nt.* shaking; **с. мо́зга** (*med.*) concussion.
сотряс|ти́, у́, ёшь, *past* **~́, ~ла́** *pf.* (*of* **~а́ть**) to shake.
сотряс|ти́сь, у́сь, ёшься, *past* **~́ся, ~ла́сь** *pf.* (*of* **~а́ться**) to shake, tremble.
со́т|ы, ов *no sg.* honeycombs; **мёд в ~ах** honey in combs.
со́т|ый *adj.* hundredth; **с. год** the year one hundred; **с. но́мер** number one hundred; *as n.* **~ая, ~ой** *f.* (a) hundredth.
со́ул, а *m.*: **(му́зыка) с.** soul music.
соумы́шленник, а *m.* accomplice.
со́ус, а *m.* sauce; gravy; dressing.
со́усник, а *m.* sauce-boat, gravy-boat.
соуча́ств|овать, ую *impf.* (в+*p.*) to participate (in), take part (in).
соуча́сти|е, я *nt.* participation; complicity.
соуча́стник, а *m.* participator; accomplice; **с. преступле́ния, с. в преступле́нии** (*leg.*) accessory to a crime.
соучени́к, а́ *m.* schoolmate, schoolfellow.
соф|а́, ы́, *pl.* **~́ы** *f.* sofa.
софи́зм, а *m.* sophism, sophistry.
софи́ст, а *m.* sophist.
софи́стик|а, и *f.* sophistry.
софисти́ческий *adj.* sophistic(al).
Софи́|я, и *f.* Sofia.
сох|а́, и́, *pl.* **~́и** *f.* (*wooden*) plough (*also old land measure*).
соха́т|ый (~, ~а) *adj.* (*dial.*) with branching antlers; *as n.* **с., ~ого** *m.* elk.
со́х|нуть, ну, нёшь, *past* **~, ~ла** *impf.* **1.** to dry, get dry; to become parched. **2.** to wither; (*fig.*) to pine.
сохране́ни|е, я *nt.* **1.** preservation; conservation; care, custody, charge; **зако́н ~я эне́ргии** law of conservation of energy; **отда́ть кому́-н. на с.** to give into s.o.'s charge. **2.** retention; **о́тпуск с ~ем содержа́ния** holiday(s) with pay.
сохран|и́ть, ю́, и́шь *pf.* (*of* **~я́ть**) **1.** to preserve, keep; to keep safe; **с. ве́рность** (+*d.*) to remain faithful, loyal (to), keep, stand by; **с. на па́мять** to keep as a souvenir. **2.** to keep, retain, reserve; **с. хладнокро́вие** to keep cool, keep one's head; **с. за собо́й пра́во** to reserve the right.
сохран|и́ться, ю́сь, и́шься *pf.* (*of* **~я́ться**) **1.** to remain (intact); to last out, hold out; **здоро́вье у неё ~и́лось до девяно́ста лет** her health lasted out right up to her ninetieth year; **он хорошо́ ~и́лся** he is well preserved. **2.** *pass. of* **~и́ть**
сохра́нно *adv.* safely, intact.
сохра́нност|ь, и *f.* **1.** safety, undamaged state; **радиоприёмник пришёл в по́лной ~и** the radio arrived quite intact. **2.** safe keeping.
сохра́н|ный (~ен, ~на) *adj.* safe; undamaged.
сохран|я́ть(ся), я́ю(сь) *impf. of* **~и́ть(ся)**
соц... *comb. form, abbr. of* **1. социа́льный. 2. социалисти́ческий**
соцве́ти|е, я *nt.* (*bot.*) inflorescence.
соцдо́говор, а *m.* socialist emulation agreement.
социа́л-демокра́т, а *m.* social democrat.
социа́л-демократи́ческий *adj.* social democratic.
социа́л-демокра́ти|я, и *f.* social democracy.
социализа́ци|я, и *f.* socialization.
социализи́р|овать, ую *impf. and pf.* to socialize.
социали́зм, а *m.* socialism.
социали́ст, а *m.* socialist.
социалисти́ческий *adj.* socialist.

социали́ст-революционе́р, а *m.* (*hist.*) socialist revolutionary.

социа́л-революцио́нный *adj.* (*hist.*) socialist revolutionary.

социа́льно-бытово́й *adj.* social, welfare.

социа́льн|ый *adj.* (*in var. senses*) social; **~ое обеспе́чение** social security; **~ое положе́ние** social status; **~ая психоло́гия** social psychology.

социогра́фи|я, и *f.* descriptive sociology.

социо́лог, а *m.* sociologist.

социологи́ческий *adj.* sociological.

социоло́ги|я, и *f.* sociology.

соцреали́зм, а *m.* socialist realism.

соцсоревнова́ни|е, я *nt.* socialist emulation.

соцстра́х, а *m.* (*abbr. of* **социа́льное страхова́ние**) social insurance.

соч. (*abbr. of* **сочине́ния**) works (*of creative artist*).

соче́льник, а *m.* (*eccl.*) **рожде́ственский с.** Christmas Eve; **креще́нский с.** Twelfth-night, eve of the Epiphany.

сочета́ни|е, я *nt.* combination.

сочета́|ть, ю *impf. and pf.* (**c**+*i.*) to combine (with); **с. бра́ком** (*obs.*) to marry (to), wed (to).

сочета́|ться, юсь *impf. and pf.* **1.** to combine; **в ней ~лся ум с красото́й** she combined intelligence and good looks. **2.** (**c**+*i.*) to harmonize (with), go (with); to match. **3.: с. бра́ком** (**c**+*i.*; *obs.*) to contract matrimony (with).

сочине́ни|е, я *nt.* **1.** composing. **2.** (*literary*) work; **и́збранные ~я Го́голя** selected works of Gogol. **3.** (*school*) composition, essay. **4.** (*gram.*) co-ordination.

сочини́тел|ь, я *m.* **1.** (*obs.*) writer, author. **2.** (*coll.*) story-teller, fabricator.

сочини́тельный *adj.* (*gram.*) coordinative.

сочини́тельств|о, а *nt.* **1.** (*obs.*) writing. **2.** (*pej.*) scribbling, hack-writing. **3.** (*coll.*) fabrication.

сочин|и́ть, ю́, и́шь *pf.* (*of* **~я́ть**) **1.** to compose (*a liter. or mus. work*); to write. **2.** to make up, fabricate.

сочин|я́ть, я́ю *impf.* **1.** *impf. of* **~и́ть**. **2.** (*obs.*) to write, be a writer.

соч|и́ть, у́, и́шь *impf.* to ooze (out), exude.

соч|и́ться, и́тся *impf.* to ooze (out), exude, trickle; **с. кро́вью** to bleed.

сочле́н, а *m.* fellow member.

сочлене́ни|е, я *nt.* (*anat. and tech.*) articulation, joint, coupling.

сочлен|и́ть, ю, и́шь *pf.* (*of* **~я́ть**) to join.

сочлен|я́ть, я́ю *impf. of* **~и́ть**

со́чност|ь, и *f.* juiciness, succulence.

со́ч|ный (~ен, ~на́, ~но) *adj.* **1.** juicy (*also fig.*); succulent. **2.** (*fig.*) rich; lush; **с. го́лос** fruity voice; **~ная расти́тельность** lush vegetation.

сочу́вственност|ь, и *f.* sympathy.

сочу́вствен|ный (~, ~на) *adj.* sympathetic.

сочу́встви|е, я *nt.* sympathy; **вы́звать с.** to gain sympathy.

сочу́вств|овать, ую *impf.* (+*d.*) to sympathize (with), feel (for).

сочу́вств|ующий *pres. part. act. of* **~овать** *and adj.* sympathetic; *as n.* **с., ~ующего** *m.* sympathizer.

со́шк|а, и *f.* **1.** *dim. of* **соха́; ме́лкая с.** (*coll.*) small fry. **2.** (*mil.*) bipod.

сошни́к, а́ *m.* **1.** ploughshare. **2.** (*mil.*) trail spade (*of gun carriage*).

со́|шный *adj. of* **~ха́**

сощу́рива|ть(ся), ю(сь) *impf. of* **сощу́рить(ся)**

сощу́р|ить, ю, ишь *pf.* (*of* **щу́рить** *and* **~ивать**); **с. глаза́** to screw up one's eyes.

сощу́р|иться, юсь, ишься *pf.* (*of* **щу́риться** *and* **~иваться**) to screw up one's eyes.

сою́з[1]**, а** *m.* **1.** alliance, union; agreement; **заключи́ть с.** (**c**+*i.*) to conclude an alliance (with). **2.** union; league; **профессиона́льный с.** trade union; **Сове́тский С.** the Soviet Union.

сою́з[2]**, а** *m.* (*gram.*) conjunction.

сою́зк|а, и *f.* vamp (*of footwear*).

сою́зник, а *m.* ally.

сою́знический *adj.* ally's.

сою́зно-республика́нский *adj.* Union-Republic (*in administration of former USSR*).

сою́зн|ый[1] *adj.* **1.** allied; **~ые держа́вы** allied powers; (*hist.*) the Allies. **2.** (*of the former USSR*) Union; **~ое гражда́нство** citizenship of the USSR.

сою́з|ный[2] *adj. of* **~**[2]

со́|я, и *f.* soya bean.

спаге́тти *nt. and pl. indecl.* spaghetti.

спад, а *m.* **1.** (*econ.*) slump, recession. **2.** abatement.

спада́|ть, ю *impf. of* **спасть**

спазм, а *m.* spasm.

спа́зм|а, ы *f.* = **~**

спа́ива|ть[1]**, ю** *impf. of* **спои́ть**

спа́ива|ть[2]**, ю** *impf. of* **спая́ть**

спа|й, я *m.* (*tech.*) (soldered) joint.

спа́йк|а, и *f.* **1.** soldering; soldered joint. **2.** (*anat.*) commissure. **3.** (*fig.*) cohesion; union.

спал|и́ть, ю, и́шь *pf. of* **пали́ть**[1]

спа́льник, а *m.* (*coll.*) sleeping-bag.

спа́льн|ый *adj.* sleeping; **с. ваго́н** sleeping-car; **~ое ме́сто** berth, bunk; **с. мешо́к** sleeping-bag; **~ые принадле́жности** bedding.

спа́л|ьня, ьни, *g. pl.* **~ен** *f.* **1.** bedroom; **с.-гости́ная** bed-sitting room. **2.** bedroom suite.

спань|ё, я́ *nt.* sleep(ing).

спарашюти́р|овать, ую *pf. of* **парашюти́ровать**

спа́р|енный *p.p.p. of* **~ить** *and adj.* paired, coupled; **~енная езда́** (*rail.*) double-manning; **с. пулемёт** coaxial machine-gun; **~енная устано́вка** (*mil.*) combination gun mount.

спа́рж|а, и *f.* asparagus.

спа́рива|ть(ся), ю(сь) *impf. of* **спа́рить(ся)**

спа́р|ить, ю, ишь *pf.* (*of* **~ивать**) **1.** to couple, pair, mate (*animals*). **2.** to pair off (*to work together*).

спа́р|иться, юсь, ишься *pf.* (*of* **~иваться**) **1.** (*of animals*) to couple, pair, mate. **2.** to pair off (*to work together*).

Спа́рт|а, ы *f.* Sparta.

спартакиа́д|а, ы *f.* sports and/or athletics meeting; sports day.

спарта́н|ец, ца *m.* Spartan.

спарта́н|ка, ки *f. of* **~ец**

спарта́нский *adj.* Spartan.

спа́рхива|ть, ю *impf. of* **спорхну́ть**

спа́рыва|ть, ю *impf. of* **споро́ть**

Спас, а *m.* (*relig.*) the Saviour.

спаса́ни|е, я *nt.* rescuing, life-saving.

спаса́тел|ь, я *m.* **1.** (*at sea*) lifeguard, lifesaver; rescuer; (*pl.*) rescue party *or* team. **2.** lifeboat.

спаса́тельн|ый *adj.* rescue, life-saving; **с. круг, с. по́яс** lifebelt; **~ая ло́дка** lifeboat; **~ая экспеди́ция** rescue party.

спаса́|ть(ся), ю(сь) *impf. of* **спасти́(сь)**

спасе́ни|е, я *nt.* **1.** rescuing, saving. **2.** rescue, escape; salvation.

спаси́бо *particle* thanks; thank you; **с. и на том** that's sth. at least, we must be thankful for small mercies; *as n.* thanks; **большо́е вам с.** thank you very much, many thanks; **сде́лать что-н. за (одно́) с.** (*coll.*) to do sth. for love.

спаси́тел|ь, я *m.* **1.** rescuer, saver. **2.** (*relig.*) the Saviour.

спаси́тел|ьный (~ен, ~ьна) *adj.* saving; salutary; **с. вы́ход, ~ьное сре́дство** means of escape.

спас|ова́ть, у́ю *pf. of* **пасова́ть**[1]

спас|ти́, у́, ёшь, *past* **~,** **~ла́** *pf.* (*of* **~а́ть**) to save; to rescue; **с. положе́ние** to save the situation.

спас|ти́сь, у́сь, ёшься, *past* **~ся, ~ла́сь** *pf.* (*of* **~а́ться**) **1.** to save o.s., escape. **2.** (*relig.*) to be saved, save one's soul.

спа|сть, ду́, дёшь, *past* **~л** *pf.* (*of* **~да́ть**) **1.** (**c**+*i.*) to fall down (from); **с. с го́лоса** (*coll.*) to lose one's voice; **с. с лица́** (*coll.*) to become thin in the face; **с. с те́ла** (*coll.*) to lose weight. **2.** to abate; (*of water*) to fall.

спа|ть, сплю, спишь, *past* **~л, ~ла́, ~ло** *impf.* to sleep, be asleep; **с. мёртвым сном** to be fast asleep; **лечь с.** to go to bed; **пора́ с.** it is bedtime; **с. и ви́деть** (*fig.*) to dream (of); **с. с** (+*i.*) to sleep with (*euph.*).

спá|ться, спи́тся, *past* **~лóсь** *impf.* (*impers.*, *+d.*): **мне не спи́тся** (*i*) I cannot sleep, I cannot get to sleep, (*ii*) I am not sleepy; **ей плóхо ~лóсь** she did not sleep well.
спáянност|ь, и *f.* cohesion, unity.
спа|я́ть, я́ю *pf.* (*of* **~ивать**[2]) **1.** to solder together, weld. **2.** (*fig.*) to weld together.
СПБ, СПб (*abbr. of* **Санкт-Петербу́рг**) St. Petersburg.
спевá|ться, юсь *impf. of* **спéться**
спéвк|а, и *f.* (choir) practice, rehearsal.
спекá|ться, юсь *impf. of* **спéчься**
спектáкл|ь, я *m.* (*theatr.*) performance; show.
спектр, а *m.* (*phys.*) spectrum.
спектрáльный *adj.* (*phys.*) spectral, spectrum.
спектроскóп, а *m.* (*phys.*) spectroscope.
спектроскопи́|я, и *f.* (*phys.*) spectroscopy.
спекули́р|овать, ую *impf.* **1.** (+*i. or* **на**+*p.*) to speculate (in); to profiteer (in); to gamble (on). **2.** (**на**+*p.*; *fig.*) to gamble (on), reckon (on); to profit (by).
спекуля́нт, а *m.* speculator, profiteer.
спекуляти́вн|ый *adj.* speculative; **по ~ым цéнам** at speculative prices.
спекуля́ци|я[1], **и** *f.* **1.** (+*i.*, **с**+*i.*, or **на**+*p.*) speculation (in); profiteering; **с. на инострáнной валю́те** speculation in foreign currency. **2.** (**на**+ *f.*; *fig.*) gamble (on).
спекуля́ци|я[2], **и** *f.* (*phil.*) speculation.
спеленá|ть, ю *pf. of* **пеленáть**
спелеóлог, а *m.* **1.** speleologist. **2.** (**спортсмéн-**)**с.** caver, potholer.
спéл|ый (~, ~á, ~о) *adj.* ripe.
спéнсер, а *nt.* (*obs.*) spencer (*short woollen jacket*).
сперва́ *adv.* (*coll.*) at first; first.
спéреди *adv. and prep.+g.* in front (of); at the front, from the front.
спер|éть[1], **сопрёт,** *past* **~, ~ла** *pf.* (*of* **спирáть**) (*coll.*) to press; **у меня́ дыхáнье ~ло** it took my breath away.
спер|éть[2], **сопру́, сопрёшь,** *past* **~, ~ла** *pf.* (*of* **перéть 5.**) (*coll.*) to filch, pinch.
спéрм|а, ы *f.* sperm.
сперматозóид, а *m.* (*biol.*) spermatozoon.
спермацéт, а *m.* (*pharm.*) spermaceti.
спёр|тый *p.p.p. of* **~éть**[1] *and adj.* close, stuffy.
спеси́в|ец, ца *m.* arrogant, conceited pers.
спеси́вост|ь, и *f.* arrogance, conceit, haughtiness, loftiness.
спеси́в|ый (~, ~а) *adj.* arrogant, conceited, haughty, lofty, stuck-up.
спес|ь, и *f.* arrogance, conceit, haughtiness, loftiness; **сбить с. с когó-н.** to take s.o. down a peg.
спе|ть[1], **ет** *impf.* to ripen.
спеть[2], **спою́, споёшь** *pf. of* **петь**
спéться, спою́сь, споёшься *pf.* **1.** (*impf.* **спевáться**) (*of a choir*) to practise, rehearse. **2.** *pf. only* (*coll.*) to get on, agree, see eye to eye.
спех, а (у) *m.* (*coll.*) hurry; **что за с.?** what's the hurry?; **мне не к ~у** I'm in no hurry.
спец, а *m.* (*coll.*) = **специали́ст**
спец... *comb. form, abbr. of* **специáльный**
специализáци|я, и *f.* specialization.
специализи́рова|нный *p.p.p. of* **~ть** *and adj.* specialized.
специализи́р|овать, ую *impf. and pf.* to assign a specialization (to); to earmark for a special role.
специализи́р|оваться, уюсь *impf. and pf.* (**в**+*p. or* **по**+*d.*) to specialize (in).
специали́ст, а *m.* (**в**+*p. or* **по**+*d.*) specialist (in), expert (in).
специáльно *adv.* specially, especially.
специáльност|ь, и *f.* **1.** speciality, special interest. **2.** profession; trade.
специáл|ьный *adj.* **1.** special, especial; **с. корреспондéнт** special correspondent; **пóезд ~ьного назначéния** special (train); **со ~ьной цéлью** with the express purpose. **2.** (**~ен, ~ьна**) specialist; **~ьное образовáние** specialist education; **с. тéрмин** technical term.
специ́фик|а, и *f.* specific character.
спецификáци|я, и *f.* specification.
специфици́р|овать, ую *impf. and pf.* to specify.
специфи́ческий *adj.* specific.
спéци|я, и *f.* spice.
спецкóр, а *m.* (*abbr. of* **специáльный корреспондéнт**) special correspondent.
спецку́рс, а *m.* special course.
спецóвк|а, и *f.* (*coll.*) = **спецодéжда**
спецодéжд|а, ы *f.* working clothes, overalls.
спецхрáн, а *m.* (*abbr. of* **специáльное храни́лище**) restricted-access collection (*of politically sensitive materials*).
спé|чься, чётся, ку́тся, *past* **~кся, ~клáсь** *pf.* (*of* **~кáться**) **1.** (*of blood*) to coagulate, curdle. **2.** (*of coal*) to cake, clinker.
спéшива|ть(ся), ю(сь) *impf. of* **спéшить(ся)**
спéш|ить, у, ишь *pf.* (*of* **~ивать**) to dismount.
спеш|и́ть, у́, и́шь *impf.* (*of* **по~**) **1.** to hurry, be in a hurry; to make haste, hasten; (**с**+*i.*) to hurry up (with), get a move on (with); **с. домóй** to be in a hurry to get home; **дéлать не ~á** to do in leisurely style, take one's time over. **2.** (*of a timepiece*) to be fast; **вáши часы́ ~áт на чéтверть часá** your watch is a quarter of an hour fast.
спéш|иться, усь, ишься *pf.* (*of* **~иваться**) to dismount.
спéшк|а, и *f.* hurry, haste, rush.
спéшност|ь, и *f.* hurry, haste.
спéш|ный (~ен, ~на) *adj.* urgent, pressing; **с. закáз** rush order; **~ное письмó** express letter; **~ная пóчта** express delivery; **в ~ном поря́дке** quickly.
спивá|ться, юсь *impf. of* **спи́ться**
СПИД, а *m.* (*abbr. of* **синдрóм приобретённого иммýнного дефици́та**) (*med.*) AIDS (*acquired immune deficiency syndrome*).
спидвé|й, я *m.* speedway (racing).
спидóметр, а *m.* speedometer.
спики́р|овать, ую *pf. of* **пики́ровать**
спи́лива|ть, ю *impf. of* **спили́ть**
спил|и́ть, ю́, ~ишь *pf.* (*of* **~ивать**) to saw down; to saw off.
спин|á, ы́, *a.* **~у,** *pl.* **~ы** *f.* back; **за ~óй у когó-н.** (*fig.*) behind s.o.'s back; **гнуть ~у (пéред)** to cringe (to), kowtow (to); **нож в ~у, удáр в ~у** (*fig.*) stab in the back; **узнáть на сóбственной ~é** to learn from (one's own) bitter experience.
спи́нк|а, и *f.* **1.** *dim. of* **спинá. 2.** back (*of article of furniture or clothing*).
спи́ннинг, а *m.* (*sport*) **1.** spinning (*fishing technique*). **2.** spoon-bait.
спиннинги́ст, а *m.* fisherman employing spinning technique.
спиннóй *adj.* spinal; **с. мозг** spinal cord; **с. хребéт** spinal column.
спинномозгов|óй *adj.*: **~áя жи́дкость** (*anat.*) spinal fluid.
спирáл|ь, и *f.* spiral.
спирáльный *adj.* spiral, helical.
спирá|ть, ет *impf. of* **сперéть**[1]
спири́т, а *m.* spiritualist, spiritist.
спирити́зм, а *m.* spiritualism, spiritism.
спирити́ческий *adj.* spiritualistic, spiritistic; **с. сеáнс** (spiritualistic) seance.
спиритуали́зм, а *m.* (*phil.*) spiritualism.
спиритуали́ст, а *m.* (*phil.*) spiritualist.
спирохéт|а, ы *f.* (*biol.*) spirochaete.
спирт, а *m.* alcohol, spirit(s); **безвóдный с.** absolute alcohol; **древéсный с.** wood alcohol.
спиртн|óй *adj.* alcoholic, spirituous; **~ы́е напи́тки** alcoholic drinks, spirits; *as n.* **~óе, ~óго** *nt.* = **~ы́е напи́тки**
спиртóвк|а, и *f.* spirit-lamp.
спиртов|óй *adj.* alcoholic, spirituous; **~ы́е крáски** (*text.*) spirit colours.
спиртомéр, а *m.* alcoholometer.
спи|сáть, шу́, ~шешь *pf.* (*of* **~сывать**) **1.** (**с**+*i.*) to copy from. **2.** (**у**) to copy (off), crib (off). **3.** to write off. **4.: с. с корабля́** (*naut.*) to transfer, post (*from a ship*).
спи|сáться, шу́сь, ~шешься *pf.* (*of* **~сываться**) (**с**+*i.*) **1.** to settle by letter, arrange by letter. **2.** to exchange letters. **3.: с. с корабля́** (*naut.*) to leave ship.

спи́с|ок, ка *m.* **1.** manuscript copy. **2.** list; roll; **именно́й с.** nominal roll; **с. избира́телей** voters' list, electoral roll; **с. опеча́ток** errata; **с. уби́тых и ра́неных** casualty list; **с. ли́чного соста́ва** (*mil.*) muster-roll. **3.** record; **послужно́й с., трудово́й с.** service record.
спи́сыва|ть(ся), ю(сь) *impf. of* **списа́ть(ся)**
спито́й *adj.* (*coll.*; *of hot beverages*) weak, watered down to excess; **с. чай** weak tea.
спи́|ться, сопью́сь, сопьёшься, *past* **∸лся́, ~ла́сь, ∸ло́сь** *pf.* (*of* **~ва́ться**) to become a drunkard, take to drink; **с. с кру́гу** (*coll.*) to go to seed through drink.
спи́хива|ть, ю *impf. of* **спихну́ть**
спих|ну́ть, ну́, нёшь *pf.* (*of* **∸ивать**) to push aside, shove aside; to push down.
спи́ц|а, ы *f.* **1.** knitting needle. **2.** spoke; **после́дняя с. в колесни́це** mere cog in the machine; **пя́тая с. в колесни́це** minor character.
спич, а *m.* speech, address.
спи́чечниц|а, ы *f.* **1.** match-box. **2.** match-box stand.
спи́ч|ечный *adj. of* **~ка; ~ечная коро́бка** match-box.
спи́чк|а, и *f.* match.
сплав[1]**, а** *m.* (*tech.*) alloy; fusion.
сплав[2]**, а** *m.* (timber) floating.
спла́в|ить[1]**, лю, ишь** *pf.* (*of* **~ля́ть**) (*tech.*) to alloy, melt, fuse.
спла́в|ить[2]**, лю, ишь** *pf.* (*of* **~ля́ть**) **1.** to float (*timber*); to raft. **2.** (*coll.*) to send packing, shake off.
спла́в|иться, ится *pf.* (*of* **~ля́ться**) to fuse together, coalesce.
сплавля́|ть(ся), ю, ет(ся) *impf. of* **спла́вить(ся)**
спла́вщик[1]**, а** *m.* (*tech.*) melter.
спла́вщик[2]**, а** *m.* (timber-)floater, rafter.
сплани́р|овать, ую *pf. of* **плани́ровать**[2]
спла́чива|ть(ся), ю(сь) *impf. of* **сплоти́ть(ся)**
сплёвыва|ть, ю *impf. of* **сплю́нуть**
сплёскива|ть, ю *impf. of* **сплесну́ть**
сплес|ну́ть, ну́, нёшь *pf.* (*of* **∸кивать**) to splash (down).
спле|сти́, ту́, тёшь, *past* **∸л, ~ла́** *pf.* (*of* **плести́** *and* **~та́ть**) to weave, plait, interlace.
сплета́|ть, ю *impf. of* **сплести́**
сплете́ни|е, я *nt.* **1.** interlacing; **с. лжи** tissue of lies; **с. обстоя́тельств** combination of circumstances. **2.** (*anat.*) plexus.
сплётник, а *m.* gossip, scandalmonger.
сплётниц|а, ы *f. of* **сплётник**
сплётнича|ть, ю *impf.* (*of* **на~**) to gossip, tittle-tattle; to talk scandal.
сплёт|ня, ни, *g. pl.* **~ен** *f.* gossip, tittle-tattle; piece of scandal.
сплеча́ *adv.* **1.** straight from the shoulder (*also fig.*). **2.** (*fig., coll.*) on the spot, on the spur of the moment.
сплo|ти́ть, чу́, ти́шь *pf.* (*of* **спла́чивать**) **1.** to join. **2.** (*fig.*) to unite, rally; **с. ряды́** to close the ranks.
сплo|ти́ться, чу́сь, ти́шься *pf.* (*of* **спла́чиваться**) to unite, rally; to close the ranks.
сплох|ова́ть, у́ю *pf.* (*coll.*) to make a blunder, slip up.
сплочённост|ь, и *f.* cohesion, unity.
спло|чённый *p.p.p. of* **~ти́ть** *and adj.* **1.** unbroken. **2.** united, firm; **~чённые ряды́** serried ranks.
сплоша́|ть, ю *pf. of* **плоша́ть**
сплошн|о́й *adj.* **1.** unbroken, continuous; **с. лёд** solid mass of ice, ice-field; **с. лес** dense forest; **~а́я ма́сса** solid mass. **2.** all-round, complete; **~а́я гра́мотность** universal literacy. **3.** (*fig., coll.*) sheer, solid, complete and utter, unreserved; **с. восто́рг** sheer joy; **~а́я чепуха́** utter rubbish.
сплошь *adv.* **1.** all over, throughout; without a break; **её но́ги бы́ли с. покры́ты комари́ными уку́сами** her legs were covered all over with gnat bites; **с. и (да) ря́дом** (*coll.*) nearly always; pretty often. **2.** (*coll.*) completely, utterly; without exception.
сплут|ова́ть, у́ю *pf. of* **плутова́ть**
сплыва́|ть(ся), ет(ся) *impf. of* **сплы́ть(ся)**
сплы|ть, вёт, *past* **~л, ~ла́, ∸ло** *pf.* (*of* **~ва́ть**) (*coll.*) **1.** to be carried away (*by a current of water, by a flood*); **бы́ло да ∸ло** it was a short-lived joy; it's all over. **2.** to overflow, run over.
сплы́|ться, вётся, *past* **~лся, ~ла́сь** *pf.* (*of* **~ва́ться**) (*coll.*) to run (together), merge, blend.
сплю́н|уть, у, ешь *pf.* (*of* **сплёвывать**) **1.** to spit. **2.** (*coll.*) to spit out.
сплю́сн|уть, у, ешь *pf.* = **сплю́щить**
сплю́шк|а, и *f.* (*zool.*) scops owl.
сплю́щива|ть(ся), ю(сь) *impf. of* **сплю́щить(ся)**
сплю́щ|ить, у, ишь *pf.* (*of* **плю́щить** *and* **~ивать**) to flatten, laminate.
сплю́щ|иться, ится *pf.* (*of* **~иваться**) to become flat.
спля|са́ть, шу́, ∸шешь *pf.* to dance.
сподви́жник, а *m.* (*rhet.*) associate; comrade-in-arms.
сподо́б|ить, ит *pf.* (*impers.+inf.*; *obs. or joc.*) to manage (to), come (to), contrive (to); **как э́то тебя́ ~ило упа́сть в реку́?** how did you manage to fall in the river?
сподо́б|иться, люсь, ишься *pf.* (*+g. or +inf.*; *obs or joc.*) to be honoured (with), have the honour (of).
сподру́чник, а *m.* **1.** (*obs.*) assistant, right-hand man. **2.** (*pej.*) myrmidon.
сподру́ч|ный[1] **(~ен, ~на)** *adj.* (*coll.*) easy; convenient, handy.
сподру́чн|ый[2]**, ого** *m.* = **~ик**
спозара́нку *adv.* (*coll.*) very early (in the morning).
спо|и́ть, ю́, и́шь *pf.* (*of* **спа́ивать**[1]) **1.** to give to drink. **2.** to accustom to drinking; to make a drunkard (of).
споко́|йный (~ен, ~йна) *adj.* **1.** quiet; calm, tranquil; placid, serene; **~йное мо́ре** calm sea; **с. о́браз жи́зни** quiet life; **~йная со́весть** clear conscience; **~йная улы́бка** serene smile; **бу́дьте ~йны!** don't worry!, rest assured!; **~йной но́чи!** good night! **2.** quiet, composed. **3.** comfortable; **~йное кре́сло** easy chair.
споко́йстви|е, я *nt.* **1.** quiet, tranquillity; calm, calmness. **2.** order; **наруше́ние обще́ственного ~я** breach of the peace, breach of public order. **3.** composure, serenity; **с. ду́ха** peace of mind.
споко́н: с. ве́ку, с. веко́в (*coll.*) from time immemorial.
спола́скива|ть, ю *impf. of* **сполосну́ть**
спольз|а́ть, а́ю *impf. of* **~ти́**
сполз|ти́, у́, ёшь, *past* **~, ~ла́** *pf.* (*of* **~а́ть**) **1.** (**с+*g.***) to climb down (from). **2.** (**в+*a.*, к**; *fig., coll.*) to slip (into), fall away (into).
сполна́ *adv.* completely, in full; **де́ньги полу́чены с.** 'money received in full'.
сполосн|у́ть, у́, ёшь *pf.* (*of* **спола́скивать**) to rinse (out).
спо́лох|и, ов *no sg.* (*dial.*) **1.** northern lights. **2.** lightning.
спондеи́ческий *adj.* (*liter.*) spondaic.
сponде́|й, я *m.* (*liter.*) spondee.
спо́нсор, а *m.* sponsor, backer.
сponта́нност|ь, и *f.* spontaneity.
спонта́нный *adj.* spontaneous.
спонти́р|овать, ую *pf. of* **понти́ровать**
спор, а *m.* **1.** argument; controversy; debate; **зате́ять с.** to start an argument; **∸у нет** indisputably, undoubtedly; there's no denying. **2.** (*leg.*) dispute.
спо́р|а, ы *f.* (*biol.*) spore.
спорaди́ческий *adj.* sporadic.
спора́нги|й, я *m.* (*biol.*) sporangium, spore-case.
спо́р|ить, ю, ишь *impf.* (*of* **по~**) **(о+*p.*) 1.** to argue (about); to dispute (about), debate; **с. о слова́х** to quibble over words; **о вку́сах не ~ят** tastes differ. **2.** to dispute; **с. о насле́дстве** to dispute a legacy. **3.** to bet (on), have a bet (on).
спор|и́ться, и́тся *impf.* (*coll.*) to succeed, go well; **у него́ всё ~и́тся** he never puts a foot wrong.
спо́р|ный (~ен, ~на) *adj.* disputable, debatable, questionable; disputed, at issue; **с. вопро́с** moot point, vexed question; **с. мяч** (*in basketball*) jump ball, held ball; **~ное насле́дство** disputed legacy.
спор|о́ть, ю́, ∸ешь *pf.* (*of* **спа́рывать**) to unstitch, take off (*by cutting stitches*).
спорт, а *m.* sport; **автомоби́льный с.** motor sports; **автомоде́льный с.** car modelling; **бату́тный с.** trampolining; **дельтаплане́рный с.** hang-gliding; **ко́нный с.** equestrianism.

спорти́вн|ый *adj.* sports, sporting; casual (*of clothing*); **с. зал** gymnasium; **с. инвента́рь** sports goods, sports kit; **~ая площа́дка** sports ground, playing-field; **~ые состяза́ния** sports, sporting competitions.

спортсме́н, а *m.* sportsman.

спортсме́нк|а, и *f.* **1.** sportswoman. **2.** (*coll.*) gym-shoe.

спортсме́нский *adj.* sportsmanlike.

спорхн|у́ть, у́, ёшь *pf.* (*of* **спа́рхивать**) to flutter off; to flutter away.

спо́рщик, а *m.* debater, wrangler.

спо́р|ый (~, ~а́, ~о) *adj.* (*coll.*) successful, profitable; **~ая рабо́та** good work.

спорын|я́, и́ *f.* (*bot.*) ergot, spur.

спо́соб, а *m.* way, mode, method; means; **таки́м ~ом** in this way; **сле́дующим ~ом** as follows; **с. употребле́ния лека́рства** 'directions for use' of a medicine.

спосо́бност|ь, и *f.* **1.** (*usu. pl.*; **к**) ability (for), talent (for), aptitude (for), flair (for); **челове́к с больши́ми ~ями** pers. of great abilities; **с. к языка́м** facility for languages, linguistic ability. **2.** capacity; **покупа́тельная с.** purchasing power; purchasing capacity; **пропускна́я с.** capacity.

спосо́б|ный (~ен, ~на) *adj.* **1.** able, talented, gifted, clever; **с. к матема́тике** good at mathematics, with a gift for mathematics. **2.** (**на**+ *a. or +inf.*) capable (of), able (to); **они́ ~ны на всё** they are capable of anything.

спосо́бств|овать, ую *impf.* (*of* **по~**) (*+d.*) **1.** to assist. **2.** to be conducive (to), further, promote, make (for); **с. успе́ху бра́ка** to make for the success of a marriage.

споткн|у́ться, у́сь, ёшься *pf.* (*of* **спотыка́ться**) **1.** (**о**+*a.*) to stumble (against, over). **2.** (**на**+*p. or* **о**+*a.*; *fig., coll.*) to get stuck (on); **в перево́де я ~у́лся на сло́ве „наро́дность"** in my translation I got stuck on the word **наро́дность**.

спотыка́|ться, юсь *impf. of* **споткну́ться**

спохва|ти́ться, чу́сь, ~́тишься *pf.* (*of* **~́тываться**) (*coll.*) to remember suddenly, think suddenly; **я написа́л бы́ло вам на ста́рый а́дрес, но ~ти́лся во́ время** I was on the point of writing to you at your old address but remembered just in time (*sc.* that you had moved).

спра́ва *adv.* (**от**) to the right (of).

справедли́вост|ь, и *f.* **1.** justice; equity, fairness; **по ~и (говоря́)** in (all) fairness, by rights; **отда́ть с.** (*+d.*) to do justice (to). **2.** truth, correctness.

справедли́в|ый (~, ~а) *adj.* **1.** (*in var. senses*) just; equitable, fair; **с. судья́** impartial judge; **~ая война́** just war. **2.** justified, true, correct; **на́ши подозре́ния оказа́лись ~ыми** our suspicions proved to be justified.

спра́в|ить[1]**, лю, ишь** *pf.* (*of* **~ля́ть**) (*coll.*) to celebrate; **с. сва́дьбу** to celebrate one's wedding.

спра́в|ить[2]**, лю, ишь** *pf.* (*of* **~ля́ть**) (**себе́**; *coll.*) to get, procure, acquire.

спра́в|иться[1]**, люсь, ишься** *pf.* (*of* **~ля́ться**) (**с**+*i.*) **1.** to cope (with), manage; **с. с зада́чей** to cope with a task, be equal to a task. **2.** to manage, deal (with), get the better (of); **я с ним ~люсь!** I'll deal with him!

спра́в|иться[2]**, люсь, ишься** *pf.* (*of* **~ля́ться**) (**о**+*p.*) to ask (about), inquire (about); **об э́том вам сле́дует с. в бухгалте́рии** you must inquire about this in the accounts department; **с. в словаре́** to look up (*a word*) in the dictionary, consult a dictionary.

спра́вк|а, и *f.* **1.** information; **навести́ ~у (о**+*p.*) to inquire (about); **обрати́ться за ~ой (в**+*a.*, **к**) to apply for information (to). **2.** certificate; **с. с ме́ста рабо́ты** reference.

справля́|ть(ся), ю(сь) *impf. of* **спра́вить(ся)**

спра́вочник, а *m.* reference book, handbook, vade-mecum, guide; **телефо́нный с.** telephone directory.

спра́вочн|ый *adj.* inquiry, information; **~ое бюро́, с. стол** inquiries office, information bureau; **~ая кни́га = ~ик**

спра́шива|ть, ю *impf. of* **спроси́ть**

спра́шива|ться, юсь *impf.* **1.** *impf. of* **спроси́ться. 2.** *impf. only* **~ется** the question is, arises.

спресс|ова́ть, у́ю *pf. of* **прессова́ть**

спринт, а *m.* (*sport*) sprint.

спри́нтер, а *m.* (*sport*) sprinter.

спринц|ева́ть, у́ю *impf.* to syringe.

спринцо́вк|а, и *f.* **1.** syringing. **2.** syringe.

спрова́|дить, жу, дишь *pf.* (*of* **~живать**) (*coll.*) to show out, show the door, send on his way.

спрова́жива|ть, ю *impf. of* **спрова́дить**

спровоци́р|овать, ую *pf. of* **провоци́ровать**

спроекти́р|овать, ую *pf. of* **проекти́ровать**[1]

спрос, а *m.* **1.** (*econ.*) demand; (**на**+*a.*) demand (for), run (on); **с. и предложе́ние** supply and demand; **по́льзоваться больши́м ~́ом** to be much in demand. **2.: без ~́а (~́у)** (*coll.*) without permission; without asking leave.

спро|си́ть, шу́, ~́сишь *pf.* (*of* **спра́шивать**) **1.** (**о**+*p.*) to ask (about), inquire (about). **2.** (*+a. or g.*) to ask (for); to ask to see, desire to speak (to); **с. рези́нку** to ask for a rubber; **с. сове́та** to ask (for) advice; **~си́те хозя́йку** ask to see the landlady. **3.** (**с**+*g.*) to make answer (for), make responsible (for).

спро|си́ться, шу́сь, ~́сишься *pf.* (*of* **спра́шиваться**) **1.** (*+g. or* **у**) to ask permission (of). **2.** (*impers.*): **~́сится с него́,** *etc.*, he, *etc.*, will be answerable.

спросо́нок *adv.* (*coll.*) being only half-awake.

спроста́ *adv.* (*coll.*) without reflection; off the reel.

спрут, а *m.* octopus.

спры́гива|ть, ю *impf. of* **спры́гнуть**

спры́г|нуть, ну, нешь *pf.* (*of* **~ивать**) (**с**+*g.*) to jump off (from), leap off (from); to jump down (from), leap down (from).

спры́скива|ть, ю *impf. of* **спры́снуть**

спры́с|нуть, ну, нешь *pf.* (*of* **~кивать**) **1.** to sprinkle. **2.** (*coll.*) to celebrate, drink (to); **с. сде́лку** to wet a bargain.

спряга́|ть[1]**, ю** *impf.* (*of* **про~**) (*gram.*) to conjugate.

спряга́|ть[2]**, ю** *impf. of* **спрячь**

спряга́|ться, ется *impf.* (*gram.*) to conjugate, be conjugated.

спряже́ни|е, я *m.* (*gram.*) conjugation.

спря|сть, ду́, дёшь, *past* **~л, ~ла́, ~́ло** *pf. of* **прясть**

спря́|тать(ся), чу(сь), чешь(ся) *pf. of* **пря́тать(ся)**

спря|чь, гу́, жёшь, гу́т, *past* **~г, ~гла́** *pf.* (*of* **~га́ть**) to harness together.

спу́гива|ть, ю *impf. of* **спугну́ть**

спуг|ну́ть, ну́, нёшь *pf.* (*of* **~́ивать**) to frighten off, scare off.

спуд, а *m.* (*arch.*) bushel; *now only used in phrr.* (*i*) **под ~́ом** under a bushel; **держа́ть под ~́ом** (*fig.*) to hide under a bushel, keep back; (*ii*) **из-под ~́а** from hiding; **вы́тащить, извле́чь из-под ~́а** to bring into the light of day, put to use.

спуск, а *m.* **1.** lowering, hauling down; **с. корабля́** launch(ing). **2.** descent, descending. **3.** release; draining. **4.** slope, descent. **5.** (*in fire-arms*) trigger. **6.** (*typ.*) imposition. **7.** (*coll.*) quarter; **не дава́ть ~́у** (*+d.*) to give no quarter, not to let off.

спуска́|ть, ю *impf. of* **спусти́ть; не с. глаз (с**+*g.*) not to take one's eyes (off), keep one's eyes glued (on); not to let out of one's sight.

спуска́|ться, юсь *impf. of* **спусти́ться**

спускн|о́й *adj.* drain; **с. кран** drain-cock; **~а́я труба́** drain-pipe.

спусков|о́й *adj.* trigger; **с. крючо́к** trigger; **с. механи́зм** trigger mechanism, trigger guard group; **~а́я скоба́** trigger guard.

спу|сти́ть, щу́, ~́стишь *pf.* (*of* **~ска́ть**) **1.** to let down, lower; to haul down; **с. кора́бль (на во́ду)** to launch a ship; **с. флаг** to lower a flag; (*naut.*) to haul down the ensign; (*fig.*) to strike the colours; **~стя́ рукава́** (*coll.*) in a slipshod fashion, carelessly; **с. с ле́стницы** (*fig., coll.*) to kick downstairs. **2.** to let go, let loose, release; **с. куро́к** to pull, release the trigger; **с. затво́р** (*phot.*) to release the shutter; **с. пе́тлю** to drop a stitch; **с. соба́ку с при́вязи** to unleash a dog. **3.** to let out, drain; **с. во́ду из бассе́йна для пла́вания** to drain a swimming-bath; **с. во́ду в убо́рной** to flush a water closet. **4.** to send down, send out; **с. директи́ву в райсове́ты** to send down a directive to the district soviets. **5.** (*of objects inflated with air*) to go down; **одна́ из за́дних шин ~сти́ла** one of the back tyres has gone down. **6.** (*coll.*) to pardon, let off, let go, let pass. **7.** (*coll.*) to lose (*weight*). **8.** (*coll.*) to lose, throw away, squander; **за оди́н ве́чер он ~сти́л в ка́рты всю полу́чку** he lost the whole of his pay-packet at cards in an evening.

спу|сти́ться, щу́сь, ~́стишься *pf.* (*of* **~ска́ться**) **1.** to descend; to come down, go down; to go downstream; (*of darkness*) to fall; **с. с ле́стницы** to come downstairs; **~сти́лась мгла** a mist came down; **на её чулке́ ~сти́лась пе́тля** she has laddered her stocking. **2.** *pass. of* **~сти́ть**

спустя́ *prep.+a.* after; later; **с. де́сять дней** after ten days; **с. год** a year later.

спу́та|ть(ся), ю(сь) *pf. of* **пу́тать(ся)**

спу́тник, а *m.* **1.** (travelling) companion; fellow-traveller. **2.** concomitant. **3.** (*astron.*) satellite; **иску́сственный с. земли́** artificial earth satellite, sputnik.

спу́щенный *p.p.p. of* **спусти́ть** *and adj.* (*of a flag*) at half-mast.

спья́на *adv.* in a state of drunkenness, in one's cups.

спья́н|у *adv.* = **~а**

спя́|тить, чу, тишь *pf.*: **с. с ума́** (*coll.*) to go barmy, go off one's rocker.

спя́чк|а, и *f.* **1.** (*of animals*) hibernation. **2.** (*coll.*) sleepiness, lethargy.

ср. (*abbr. of* ***сравни́***) cf., compare.

сраба́тыва|ться, юсь *impf. of* **срабо́таться**

срабо́танност|ь[1], и *f.* harmony in work, harmonious team-work.

срабо́танност|ь[2], и *f.* wear.

срабо́танный *adj.* worn (out).

срабо́та|ть, ю *pf.* (*coll.*) **1.** to make. **2.** (*+i.*) to work, operate.

срабо́та|ться[1], юсь *pf.* to achieve harmony in work, work well together.

срабо́та|ться[2], ется *pf.* to wear out.

сравне́ни|е, я *nt.* **1.** comparison; **по ~ю (с+*i.*)** by comparison (with), as compared (with), as against; **вне ~я** beyond comparison; **не идёт в с. (с+*i.*)** it cannot be compared (with). **2.** (*liter.*) simile.

сра́внива|ть, ю *impf. of* **сравни́ть** *and* **сравня́ть**

сравни́тельно *adv.* **1. (с+*i.*)** by comparison (with). **2.** comparatively.

сравни́тел|ьный *adj.* comparative; **~ая сте́пень** (*gram.*) comparative (degree).

сравн|и́ть, ю́, и́шь *pf.* (*of* **~́ивать**) **(с+*i.*)** to compare (to, with).

сравн|и́ться, ю́сь, и́шься *pf.* **(с+*i.*)** to compare (with), come up (to), touch; **в зна́нии А́рктики никто́ не мо́жет с ним с.** for a knowledge of the Arctic no one can touch him.

сравн|я́ть, я́ю *pf.* (*of* **равня́ть** *and* **~́ивать**) to make even; **с. счёт** (*sport*) to equalize, bring the score level.

сравня́|ться, юсь *pf. of* **равня́ться**

сража́|ть, ю *impf. of* **срази́ть**

сража́|ться, юсь *impf.* (*of* **срази́ться**) **(с+*i.*)** to fight; to join battle (with).

сраже́ни|е, я *nt.* battle, engagement; **дать с.** to give battle.

сра|зи́ть, жу́, зи́шь *pf.* (*of* **~жа́ть**) **1.** (*obs.*) to slay, strike down, fell. **2.** (*fig.*) to overwhelm, crush; **её ~зи́ла весть о катастро́фе в ша́хте** she was crushed by the news of the pit disaster.

сра|зи́ться, жу́сь, зи́шься *pf. of* **~жа́ться**

сра́зу *adv.* **1.** at once. **2.** straight away, right away; straight off.

срам, а *m.* **1.** shame; **како́й с.!** for shame! **2.** (*coll.*) privy parts.

срам|и́ть, лю́, и́шь *impf.* (*of* **о~**) to shame, put to shame.

срам|и́ться, лю́сь, и́шься *impf.* (*of* **о~**) to cover o.s. with shame.

срамни́к, а́ *m.* (*coll.*) shameless pers.

срамн|о́й *adj.* **1.** (*coll.*) shameless. **2.: ~ы́е гу́бы** (*anat.*) labia; **~а́я часть** (*obs.*) privy parts.

срамот|а́, ы́ *f.* (*coll.*) shame.

сраста́ни|е, я *nt.* (*physiol., med.*) growing together, inosculation; (*of bones*) knitting.

сраст|а́ться, а́ется *impf. of* **~и́сь**

сраст|и́сь, ётся, *past* **сро́сся, сросла́сь** *pf.* (*of* **~а́ться**) (*physiol., med.*) to grow together, inosculate; (*of bones*) to knit.

сра|сти́ть, щу́, сти́шь *pf.* (*of* **~́щивать**) **1.** to join, joint. **2.** to splice.

ср|ать, у, ёшь *impf.* (*of* **насра́ть**) (*vulg.*) to shit.

сраще́ни|е, я *nt.* union.

сра́щивани|е, я *nt.* **1.** joining; splicing. **2.** (*fig.*) fusion, merging.

сра́щива|ть, ю *impf. of* **срасти́ть**

сре́бреник, а *m.* silver coin, piece of silver; **прода́ть за три́дцать ~ов** to sell for thirty pieces of silver.

сребролю́б|ец, ца *m.* (*obs.*) money-grubber.

сребролюби́в|ый (~, ~а) *adj.* (*obs.*) money-grubbing.

сребролю́би|е, я *nt.* (*obs.*) greed for money.

среброно́с|ный (~ен, ~на) *adj.* argentiferous.

сред|а́[1], ы, *a.* **~у́,** *pl.* **~́ы** *f.* **1.** environment, surroundings; milieu; (*biol.*) habitat; **в на́шей ~е́** in our midst, among us. **2.** (*phys.*) medium.

сред|а́[2], ы́, *a.* **~́у,** *pl.* **~́ы, ~а́м** *f.* Wednesday; **по ~а́м** on Wednesday, every Wednesday.

средакти́р|овать, ую *pf. of* **редакти́ровать**

среди́ *prep.+g.* **1.** among, amongst; amidst; **с. них** among them, in their midst. **2.** in the middle (of); **с. бе́ла дня** in broad daylight.

Средизе́мн|ое мо́р|е, ~ого ~я *nt.* the Mediterranean (Sea).

средиземномо́рский *adj.* Mediterranean.

среди́н|а, ы *f.* (*obs.*) middle.

среди́нн|ый *adj.* middle; **~ое отклоне́ние** (*mil.*) probable error (*in artillery firing*).

сре́дне *adv.* (*coll.*) middling, so-so.

среднеазиа́тский *adj.* Central Asian (*in context of former USSR*).

среднеанглийский *adj.*: **с. язы́к** Middle English.

средневеко́вый *adj.* medieval.

средневеко́вь|е, я *nt.* the Middle Ages.

среднегодово́й *adj.* average annual.

среднекали́берный *adj.* (*mil.*) medium(-calibre).

среднеме́сячный *adj.* average monthly.

среднесу́точный *adj.* average daily.

среднеязы́чный *adj.* (*ling.*) medio-lingual.

сре́дн|ий *adj.* **1.** middle; medium; **с. бомбардиро́вщик** medium bomber; **~ие века́** the Middle Ages; **~яя исто́рия** history of the Middle Ages; **с. зало́г** (*gram.*) middle voice; **~их лет** middle-aged; **~его ро́ста** of medium height; **~ее у́хо** (*anat.*) middle-ear. **2.** mean, average; **~ее вре́мя** mean time; **с. за́работок** average earnings; **~яя оши́бка** mean error, standard deviation; **~ее пропорциона́льное** (*math.*) the mean proportional; *as n.* **~ее, ~его** *nt.* mean, average; **в ~ем** on average; **вы́ше ~его** above (the) average. **3.** (*coll.*) middling, average; **~ие спосо́бности** average abilities. **4.** (*in education*) secondary; **~яя шко́ла** secondary school. **5.: с. род** (*gram.*) neuter (gender). **6.** (*aeron.*) waist, belly; **с. стрело́к** waist gunner.

сре́дник, а *m.* centre panel (*of icon*).

средосте́ни|е, я *nt.* **1.** (*anat.*) mediastinum. **2.** (*fig.*) partition, barrier.

средото́чи|е, я *nt.* focus, centre point.

сре́дств|о, а *nt.* **1.** means; facilities; **~а передвиже́ния** means of conveyance; **~а сообще́ния** means of communication; **~а к существова́нию** means of subsistence; **пусти́ть в ход все ~а** to move heaven and earth. **2. (от)** remedy (for); **с. от ка́шля** cough medicine, sth. for a cough; **с. от насеко́мых** insecticide; **с. от поте́ния** antiperspirant. **3.** (*pl.*) resources; credits. **4.** (*pl.*) means; **челове́к со ~ами** man of means; **жить не по ~ам** to live beyond one's means.

средь *prep.+g.* = **среди́**

срез, а *m.* **1.** cut; microscopic section. **2.** (*tech.*) shear, shearing; **пло́скость ~́а** shear plane. **3.** (*sport*) slice, slicing.

сре́|зать, жу, жешь *pf.* **1.** (*impf.* **~за́ть**) to cut off; **с. у́гол** (*fig.*) to cut off a corner; **с. на экза́мене** (*school sl.*) to plough. **2.** (*impf.* **ре́зать**) (*sport*) to slice, cut, chop.

среза|ть, ю *impf. of* **срéзать**
срé|заться, жусь, жешься *pf.* (*of* **~зáться**) (*school sl.*) to fail, be ploughed.
срезá|ться, юсь *impf. of* **срéзаться**
срепетúр|овать, ую *pf. of* **репетúровать**
срéтени|е, я *nt.* **1.** (*arch. or poet.*) meeting. **2. С.** (*eccl.*) Candlemas Day; Feast of the Purification.
срис|овáть, ýю *pf.* (*of* **~óвывать**) to copy.
срисóвыва|ть, ю *impf. of* **срисовáть**
сровня́|ть, ю *pf. of* **ровня́ть**
сроднú *adv.* akin; **быть, приходúться с.** (*+d.*) to be related (to).
сродн|úть, ю́, úшь *pf.* (**с**+*i.*) to link (with).
сродн|úться, ю́сь, úшься *pf.* (**с**+*i.*) to become closely linked (with); to get used (to); **с. с рабóтой** to get the hang of a job.
срóд|ный (~ен, ~на) *adj.* (*+d. or* **с**+*i.*) related (to).
сродств|ó, á *nt.* relationship, affinity; **химúческое с.** chemical affinity.
срóду *adj.* (*coll.*) in one's life; **с. я не видáл такóй огрóмной кóшки** never in all my born days have I seen such a huge cat.
срок, а (у) *m.* **1.** time, period; term; **мéсячный с.** period of one month; **в кратчáйший с.** in the shortest possible time; **с. воéнной слýжбы** call-up period; **с. дéйствия** period of validity; **с. полномóчий** term of office; **с. рабóты** life (*of machine, etc.*); **по истечéнии ~а** when the time is up, when the time expires; **продлúть с. вúзы** to extend a visa; **~ом до трёх мéсяцев** within three months; **дáй(те) с.** (*coll.*) wait a minute!, give us time!; **ни óтдыху, ни ~у не давáть** (*+d.*) to give no peace. **2.** date, term; **крáйний с.** closing date; **с. арéнды** term of lease; **с. дáвности** (*leg.*) prescription; **с. платежá** date of payment; **с. хранéния** shelf life; **пропустúть с. платежá** to fail to pay by the date fixed; **в укáзанный с., к установлéнному ~у** by the date fixed, by a specified date; **в с., к ~у** in time, to time.
срóст|ок, ка *m.* joint, splice.
срóчно *adv.* urgently; quickly.
срóчност|ь, и *f.* urgency; hurry; **что за с.?** what's the hurry?
срóч|ный (~ен, ~нá, ~но) *adj.* **1.** urgent, pressing; **с. закáз** rush order. **2.** at a fixed date; for a fixed period; **~ная слýжба** (*mil.*) service for a fixed period. **3.** periodic, routine; **~ное донесéние** (*mil.*) routine report.
СРР *f. indecl.* (*abbr. of* ***Социалистúческая Респýблика Румы́ния***) Socialist Republic of Romania.
сруб, а *m.* **1.** felling; **на с.** for timber. **2.** frame(work), shell (*of an izba, well, etc.*). **3.** (*hist.*) framework.
сруб|áть, áю *impf. of* **~úть**
сруб|úть, лю́, ~ишь *pf.* (*of* **~áть**) **1.** to fell, cut down. **2.** to build (*of logs*).
срыв, а *m.* disruption; derangement, frustration; **с. переговóров** break-down of talks; **с. рабóты** derangement of work, stoppage.
срывá|ть[1], ю *impf. of* **сорвáть**
срывá|ть[2], ю *impf. of* **срыть**
срывá|ться, юсь *impf. of* **сорвáться**
срыть, срóю, срóешь *pf.* (*of* **срывáть[2]**) to raze, level to the ground.
ся́ду *adv.* (*coll.*) running; **два рáза с.** twice running.
ссáдин|а, ы *f.* scratch, abrasion.
сса|дúть[1], жý, ~дишь *pf.* (*of* **~живáть**) (*coll.*) to scratch.
сса|дúть[2], жý, ~дишь *pf.* (*of* **~живáть**) **1.** to help down, help to alight; **с. когó-н. с лóшади** to help s.o. down from a horse. **2.** to put off, make get off (*from public transport*).
ссáжива|ть, ю *impf. of* **ссадúть**
сселя́|ться, ется *impf. of* **ссéсться**
ссел|úть, ю́, úшь *pf.* (*of* **~я́ть**) to settle collectively.
ссел|я́ть, я́ю *impf. of* **~úть**
ссé|сться, ся́дется, *past* **~лся, ~лась** *pf.* (*of* **~дáться**) (*coll.*) **1.** (*of materials*) to shrink. **2.** (*of milk*) to turn.
ссóр|а, ы *f.* **1.** quarrel; falling-out; **онú в ~е друг с дрýгом** they have fallen out. **2.** slanging-match.
ссóр|ить, ю, ишь *impf.* (*of* **по~**) to cause to quarrel, cause to fall out.
ссóр|иться, юсь, ишься *impf.* (*of* **по~**) (**с**+*i.*) to quarrel (with), fall out (with).
ссóх|нуться, нется, *past* **~ся, ~лась** *pf.* (*of* **ссыхáться**) **1.** to shrink, shrivel, warp. **2.** to harden out, dry out.
ССР *f. indecl.* (*abbr. of* ***Совéтская Социалистúческая Респýблика***) Soviet Socialist Republic.
СССР *m. indecl.* (*abbr. of* ***Сою́з Совéтских Социалистúческих Респýблик***) USSR (*Union of Soviet Socialist Republics*).
ссýд|а, ы *f.* loan, grant.
ссу|дúть, жý, ~дишь *pf.* (*of* **~жáть**) (*+a. and i. or +d. and a.*) to lend, loan.
ссýд|ный *adj. of* **~а; с. процéнт** interest on a loan.
ссýдо-сберегáтельн|ый *adj.*: **~ая кáсса** savings bank.
ссужá|ть, ю *impf. of* **ссудúть**
ссутýл|ить(ся), ю(сь), ишь(ся) *pf. of* **сутýлить(ся)**
ссуч|úть, ý, ~ишь *pf. of* **сучúть**
ссылá|ть(ся), ю(сь) *impf. of* **сослáть(ся)**
ссы́лк|а[1], и *f.* exile, banishment; deportation.
ссы́лк|а[2], и *f.* reference.
ссы́л|очный *adj. of* **~ка[2]; ~очное примечáние** reference note.
ссыльнопоселéн|ец, ца *m.* (*hist.*) deportee, convict settler (*ex-convict obliged by court order to settle in remote area after completing prison sentence*).
ссы́льн|ый, ого *m.* exile.
ссып|áть, áю *impf. of* **~ать**
ссы́п|ать, лю, лешь *pf.* (*of* **~áть**) to pour.
ссыпнóй *adj.*: **с. пункт** grain-collecting station.
ссыхá|ться, ется *impf. of* **ссóхнуться**
ст. *abbr. of* **1. статья́** Art., Article (*of law, etc.*). **2. столéтие** C, century.
стабилизáтор, а *m.* (*tech.*) stabilizer; (*aeron.*) tail-plane.
стабилизáци|я, и *f.* stabilization.
стабилизúр|овать, ую *impf. and pf.* to stabilize.
стабилизúр|оваться, уюсь *impf. and pf.* to become stable.
стабилиз|овáть(ся), ýю(сь) *impf. and pf.* = **~úровать(ся)**
стабúльност|ь, и *f.* stability.
стабúл|ьный (~ен, ~ьна) *adj.* stable, firm; **с. учéбник** standard text-book.
стáв|ень, ня, *g. pl.* **~ней** *m.* shutter (*on window*).
стáв|ить, лю, ишь *impf.* (*of* **по~**) **1.** to put, place, set; to stand; to station; **с. цветы́ в вáзу** to put flowers in a vase; **с. буты́лки в ряд** to stand bottles in a row; **с. гóлос комý-н.** to train s.o.'s voice; **с. диáгноз** to diagnose; **с. рекóрд** to set up, create a record; **с. тóчку** to put a full stop; **с. тóчки на „и"** to dot one's 'i's' (and cross one's 't's'); **с. часы́** to set a clock; **с. самовáр** to put a samovar on; **с. в винý что-н. комý-н.** to accuse s.o. of sth.; **с. в извéстность** to let know, inform; **с. когó-н. в нелóвкое положéние** to put s.o. in an awkward position; **с. в тупúк** to nonplus; **с. в ýгол** to stand in the corner; **с. что-н. в упрёк комý-н.** to reproach s.o. with sth.; **ни во что не с.** to hold of no account; **с. за прáвило** to make it a rule; **с. когó-н. на колéни** to force s.o. to his knees; **с. когó-н. на мéсто** to put s.o. in his place; **с. пéред совершúвшимся фáктом** to present with a fait accompli. **2.** to put up, erect; to install; **с. пáмятник** to erect a monument; **с. телефóн** to install the telephone. **3.** (*coll.*) to put in, install; **с. нóвого глáвного инженéра** to put in a new chief engineer; **с. когó-н. в архиерéи** to make s.o. a bishop. **4.** to apply, put on; **с. горчúчник** to apply a mustard plaster; **с. комý-н. термóметр** to take s.o.'s temperature. **5.** to put, present; to put on, stage; **с. резолю́цию** to put a resolution; **с. мелодрáму** to stage a melodrama. **6.** (**на**+*a.*) to place, stake (*money on*); **с. на лóшадь** to back a horse.
стáвк|а[1], и *f.* **1.** rate; **с. зарплáты** wage rate; **~и налóга** tax rates. **2.** stake; **дéлать ~у (на**+*a.*) to stake (on); (*fig.*) to count (on), gamble (on).
стáвк|а[2], и *f.* (*mil.*) headquarters; **с. главнокомáндующего** General Headquarters.
стáвк|а[3], и *f.*: **óчная с.** (*leg.*) confrontation.
стáвленник, а *m.* protégé.
стáвлен|ый *adj.*: **~ая грáмота** (*eccl.*) certificate of ordination.
стáвн|я, и *f.* = **стáвень**

стадиа́льный *adj.* taking place by stages.
стадио́н, а *m.* stadium.
ста́ди|я, и *f.* stage.
ста́дност|ь, и *f.* herd instinct, gregariousness.
ста́дный *adj.* gregarious; **с. инсти́нкт** herd instinct.
ста́д|о, а, *pl.* **~á** *nt.* herd; flock.
стаж, а *m.* **1.** length of service; record. **2. (испыта́тельный) с.** probation; **проходи́ть с.** to work on probation.
стажёр, а *m.* **1.** probationer. **2.** stazher (*student on special course not leading to degree*).
стажи́р|овать, ую *impf.* to work on probation.
ста́ива|ть, ю *impf. of* **стоя́ть**
ста́йер, а *m.* (*sport*) long-distance runner.
стака́н, а *m.* **1.** glass, tumbler, beaker. **2.** (*mil.*) body (*of projectile*).
стакка́то (*mus.*) **1.** *adv.* **2.** *n.*; *nt. indecl.* staccato.
сталагми́т, а *m.* stalagmite.
сталакти́т, а *m.* stalactite.
сталева́р, а *m.* steel founder.
сталелите́йный *adj.*: **с. заво́д** steel mill, steel works.
сталелите́йщик, а *m.* steel founder.
сталепрока́тный *adj.*: **с. заво́д, с. стан** steel-rolling mill.
ста́линск|ий *adj.* Stalin's, of Stalin; **~ая пре́мия** (*hist.*) Stalin Prize.
ста́лкива|ть(ся), ю(сь) *impf. of* **столкну́ть(ся)**
ста́ло быть *conj.* (*coll.*) consequently, therefore, accordingly.
стал|ь, и *f.* steel; **нержаве́ющая с.** stainless steel.
стальн|о́й *adj.* steel; **~о́го цве́та** steel-blue; **~ы́е во́лосы** iron-grey hair; **~а́я во́ля** iron will; **~ы́е не́рвы** nerves of steel.
Стамбу́л, а *m.* Istanbul.
стаме́ск|а, и *f.* (*tech.*) chisel.
стан[1], а *m.* figure, torso.
стан[2], а *m.* **1.** camp (*also fig.*); **в ~́е врага́** in the enemy's camp. **2.** (*hist.*) (police) district (*from 1837*).
стан[3], а *m.* (*tech.*) mill.
станда́рт, а *m.* (*in var. senses*) standard.
стандартиза́ци|я, и *f.* standardization.
стандартиз|ова́ть, у́ю *impf. and pf.* to standardize.
станда́рт|ный (~ен, ~на) *adj.* standard.
стани́н|а, ы *f.* (*tech.*) mounting, bed (plate); **бокова́я с.** side plate, cheek; **с. лафе́та** cheek, side plate of gun-carriage.
станио́л|ь, я *m.* tin foil.
стани́ц|а[1], ы *f.* stanitsa (*large Cossack village*).
стани́ц|а[2], ы *f.* (*obs.*) flock.
стани́чник, а *m.* (*Cossack*) inhabitant of stanitsa.
стани́|чный *adj. of* **~ца[1]**
станко́в|ый *adj.* **1.** *adj. of* **стано́к; с. пулемёт** (*mil.*) heavy machine-gun. **2.: ~ая жи́вопись** easel (*opp. mural*) painting.
станкострое́ни|е, я *nt.* machine-tool construction.
станов|и́ться, лю́сь, ~́ишься *impf. of* **стать**
становле́ни|е, я *nt.* (*phil.*) coming-to-be, coming into being; **в проце́ссе ~я** in the making.
станово́й[1] *adj.* main, chief, basic; **с. хребе́т** (*fig.*) backbone.
станов|о́й[2] *adj. of* **стан[2]; с. при́став** (*hist.*) district police-officer; *as n.* **с., ~о́го** *m.* = **с. при́став**
стан|о́к[1], ка́ *m.* **1.** (*tech.*) machine-tool, machine; bench; **печа́тный с.** printing-press; **столя́рный с.** joiner's bench; **тка́цкий с.** loom; **тока́рный с.** lathe; **рабо́чий от ~ка́** bench worker. **2.** (*mil.*) mount, mounting.
стан|о́к[2], ка́ *m.* stall (*for one horse*).
стано́чник, а *m.* machine operator, machine minder.
станс, а *m.* (*liter.*) stanza.
станцио́нный *adj. of* **ста́нция; с. зал** waiting-room; **с. смотри́тель** (*obs.*) postmaster.
ста́нци|я, и *f.* (*in var. senses*) station; **гидроэлектри́ческая с.** hydro-electric power station; **межплане́тная с.** interplanetary station; **телефо́нная с.** telephone exchange; **с. снабже́ния** (*mil.*) railhead.
ста́пел|ь, я *m.* (*naut.*) building slip(s), stocks; **на ~е, на ~ях** on the stocks.
ста́плива|ть, ю *impf. of* **стопи́ть**
ста́птыва|ть(ся), ю(сь) *impf. of* **стопта́ть(ся)**
стара́ни|е, я *nt.* effort, endeavour; diligence; **приложи́ть с.** to make an effort; **приложи́ть все ~я** to do one's utmost, do one's best.
стара́тел|ь, я *m.* gold prospector, gold-digger.
стара́тельност|ь, и *f.* application, assiduity, diligence, painstakingness.
стара́тел|ьный (~ен, ~ьна) *adj.* assiduous, diligent, painstaking.
стара́|ться, юсь *impf.* (*of* **по~**) to try, endeavour, seek; to make an effort; **с. изо всех сил** to do one's utmost, try one's hardest.
стар|е́е (*and* (*obs.*) **ста́ре)** *comp. of* **~ый**
старе́йшин|а, ы *m.* **1.** (*hist., ethnol.*) elder. **2.: Сове́т ~** Council of Elders (*of former USSR Supreme Soviet*).
старе́|ть, ю *impf.* (*of* **по~**) to grow old, age.
ста́р|ец, ца *m.* **1.** elder, (venerable) old man. **2.** elderly monk. **3.** spiritual adviser.
стари́к, а́ *m.* old man.
старика́н, а *m.* (*coll.*) old boy, old chap.
старика́шк|а, а *m.* (*coll., pej.*) old man, old chap.
старико́вский *adj. of* **стари́к**; senile.
ста́рин|а, ы *f.* (*liter.*) bylina.
старин|а́[1], ы́ *f.* **1.** antiquity, olden times; **в ~у́** in olden times, in days of old. **2.** (*collect.*) antiques.
старин|а́[2], ы́ *m.* (*coll.*) old fellow, old chap.
стари́нк|а *f.* (*coll.*) old fashion, old custom(s); **держа́ться ~и** to keep up the old customs; **по ~е** in the old fashion, in the old way.
стари́нный *adj.* **1.** ancient, old; antique; **с. обы́чай** time-honoured custom. **2.** old, of long standing; **с. друг** old friend.
ста́р|ить, ю, ишь *impf.* (*of* **со~**) to age; to make look old(er).
ста́р|иться, юсь, ишься *impf.* (*of* **со~**) to age; to grow old, age.
ста́риц|а, ы *f.* **1.** elderly nun. **2.** old bed (*of river*).
старич|о́к, ка́ *m.* **1.** little old man. **2.** (*sport*) 'veteran' (*competitor in contest for age-group 35 and over*).
старове́р, а *m.* **1.** (*relig.*) Old Believer. **2.** (*fig., joc.*) conservative, laudator temporis acti.
староде́вний *adj.* ancient.
стародо́вност|ь, и *f.* antiquity.
старожи́л, а *m.* old inhabitant, old resident.
старозаве́т|ный (~ен, ~на) *adj.* **1.** (*of persons*) old-fashioned, conservative. **2.** (*pej.*) old, antiquated; **~ные взгля́ды** antiquated views.
старомо́д|ный (~ен, ~на) *adj.* old-fashioned, outmoded; out-of-date.
старообра́з|ный (~ен, на) *adj.* old-looking.
старообря́д|ец, ца *m.* (*relig.*) Old Believer.
старообря́д|ческий *adj. of* **~ец** *and* **~чество**
старообря́дчеств|о, а *nt.* (*relig.*) Old Belief.
старопеча́тн|ый *adj.*: **~ые кни́ги** early printed books (*books published in Russia before the 18th century*).
старору́сский *adj.* old Russian.
старосве́тский *adj.* old-world; old-fashioned.
старославя́нский *adj.* (*ling.*) Old Church Slavonic.
ста́рост|а, ы *m.* (*elected*) head; senior (man); **се́льский с.** (*hist.*) village headman, elder; **церко́вный с.** churchwarden; **с. кла́сса** (*in school*) form prefect, monitor; **с. ку́рса** (*in college, etc.*) senior student of year.
ста́рост|ь, и *f.* old age; **на ~и лет, под с.** in one's old age.
старт, а *m.* **1.** (*sport*) start; **дать с.** to start; **на с.!** on your marks! **2.** (*aeron.*) take-off point; **взять с.** to take off.
ста́ртер *and* (*coll.*) **стартёр, а** *m.* (*sport and tech.*) starter.
старт|ова́ть, у́ю *impf. and pf.* **1.** (*sport*) to start. **2.** (*aeron.*) to take off.
ста́ртовый *adj.* starting.
стару́х|а, и *f.* old woman, old lady.
стару́|шечий *adj. of* **~ха**; old-womanish.
стару́шк|а, и *f.* (little) old lady, old woman.
ста́рческий *adj.* old man's; senile.
ста́рше *comp. of* **ста́рый; она́ с. меня́ на три го́да** she is three years older than me.
старшекла́ссник, а *m.* senior (pupil).
старшеку́рсник, а *m.* senior student.

ста́рш|ий *adj.* **1.** elder; *as n.* **~ие, ~их** (one's) elders. **2.** oldest, eldest. **3.** senior, superior; chief, head; **с. врач** head physician; **~ая медсестра́** sister; *as n.* **с., ~его** *m.* chief; (*mil.*) man in charge, senior man. **4.** senior, upper, higher; **~ая ка́рта** higher card; **с. класс** (*in school*) higher form.

старшин|а́, ы́ *m.* **1.** (*mil.*) sergeant-major; (*naut.*) petty officer. **2. войсково́й с.** (*hist.*) lieutenant-colonel (*of Cossack troops*). **3.** leader, senior representative (*of social group, professional organization, etc.*); **с. дипломати́ческого ко́рпуса** doyen of the diplomatic corps; **с. присяжных заседа́телей** foreman of the jury.

старшинств|о́, а́ *nt.* seniority; **по ~у́** by seniority.

ста́р|ый (~, ~а́, ~́о) *adj.* (*in var. senses*) old; **с. стиль** the Old Style (*of the Julian calendar*); **~ая де́ва** old maid, spinster; **по ~ой па́мяти** for old times' sake; from force of habit; *as n.* **~ые, ~ых** the old, old people; **~ое, ~ого** *nt.* the old, the past; **кто ~ое помя́нет, тому́ глаз вон** (*prov.*) let bygones be bygones.

старь|ё, я́ *nt.* (*collect.*; *coll.*) old things, old clothes.

старьёвщик, а *m.* old-clothes dealer; junk dealer.

ста́скива|ть, ю *impf. of* **стащи́ть**

стас|ова́ть, у́ю *pf. of* **тасова́ть**

ста́тик|а, и *f.* statics.

стати́ст, а *m.* (*theatr.*) super, extra, mute.

стати́стик, а *m.* statistician.

стати́стик|а, и *f.* statistics.

статисти́ческий *adj.* statistical.

стати́ческий *adj.* static.

ста́т|ный (~ен, ~на) *adj.* stately.

ста́тор, а *m.* (*tech.*) stator.

ста́точн|ый *adj.*: **~ое ли де́ло** (*coll., obs.*) is it possible?; can it be?

статс-да́м|а, ы *f.* lady-in-waiting.

ста́тский *adj.* **1.** (*obs.*) = **шта́тский. 2.** (*hist.*; *as part of titles of ranks in tsarist Russ. civil service*) State; **с. сове́тник** Councillor of State.

статс-секрета́р|ь, я́ *m.* Secretary of State.

ста́тус-кво́ *m. indecl.* status quo.

стату́т, а *m.* statute.

статуэ́тк|а, и *f.* statuette, figurine.

ста́ту|я, и *f.* statue.

стать[1]**, ста́ну, ста́нешь** *pf.* (*of* **станови́ться**) **1.** to stand; **с. на коле́ни** to kneel; **с. в о́чередь** to queue (up); **с. в по́зу** to strike an attitude; **с. на цы́почки** to stand on tip-toe; **с. на чью-н. сто́рону** to take s.o.'s side, stand up for s.o.; **с. на защи́ту угнетённых** to stand up for the oppressed. **2.** to take up position; **с. ла́герем** to camp, encamp; **с. в карау́л** to mount guard; **с. на рабо́ту** to start work; **с. на я́корь** to anchor, come to anchor. **3.** to stop, come to a halt; **мои́ часы́ ста́ли** my watch has stopped; **река́ ста́ла** the river has frozen over; **за чем де́ло ста́ло?** (*coll.*) what's holding things up?; what's the hitch? **4. (в+*a.*; *coll.*)** to cost; **во что бы то ни ста́ло** at any price, at all costs. **5.** (*impers.*; *coll.*) to suffice; **с него́ э́то ста́нет** it is what one might expect of him.

стать[2]**, ста́ну, ста́нешь** *pf.* (*of* **станови́ться**) **1.** (+*inf.*) to begin (to), start; **она́ ста́ла говори́ть во сне** she began talking in her sleep; **он, слов нет, ста́нет ворча́ть** he will start grousing, it goes without saying. **2.** (+*i.*) to become, get, grow; **он стал машини́стом** he became an engine-driver; **ста́ло темно́** it got dark; **ей ста́ло лу́чше** she was better; she had got better. **3. (с+*i.*)** to become (of), happen (to); **что с ни́ми ста́ло?** what has become of them? **4.: не с.** (*impers.*+*g.*) to cease to be; to disappear, be gone; **её отца́ давно́ не ста́ло** her father passed away long ago.

стат|ь[3]**, и,** *pl.* **~́и, ~е́й** *f.* **1.** figure, build; (*pl.*) points (*of a horse*). **2.** character, type; **быть под с.** (+*d.*) to be (well) matched (with).

стат|ь[4]**, и** *f.* (*coll., obs.*) need, necessity; **к э́той ме́стности нам не привыка́ть с.** this area is familiar ground to us; **с како́й ~́и?** (*coll.*) why?, what for?

ста́|ться, нется *pf.* (*coll.*) to happen, become; **что с на́ми ~нется?** what will become of us?; **мо́жет с.** perhaps, it may be; **вполне́ мо́жет с.** it is quite possible.

стат|ья́, ьи́, *g. pl.* **~е́й** *f.* **1.** article; **передова́я с.** leading article, leader, editorial. **2.** clause; item; (dictionary) entry; **с. догово́ра** clause of a treaty; **расхо́дная с.** debit item; **э́то осо́бая с.** that is another matter. **3.** (*coll.*) matter, job; **э́то не бу́дет хи́трая с.** that will not be difficult. **4.** (*naut.*) class, rating; **матро́с пе́рвой ~ьи́** able seaman; **старшина́ пе́рвой ~ьи́** chief petty officer. **5.** (*pl.*) points (*of a horse*).

стафилоко́кк, а *m.* (*med., biol.*) staphylococcus.

стаха́нов|ец, ца *m.* (*hist.*) Stakhanovite.

стаха́новский *adj.* (*hist.*) Stakhanovite.

стациона́р, а *m.* permanent establishment; **(лече́бный) с.** hospital.

стациона́рн|ый *adj.* **1.** stationary; **с. объе́кт** (*mil.*) stationary target. **2.** permanent, fixed; **~ая библиоте́ка** permanent library; **~ая устано́вка** (*mil.*) fixed mount. **3.: с. больно́й** in-patient; **~ое лече́ние** hospitalization.

стационе́р, а *m.* (*naut.*) station ship, guard ship.

ста́чечник, а *m.* striker.

ста́ч|ечный *adj. of* **~ка**[1]

ста́чива|ть, ю *impf. of* **сточи́ть**

ста́чк|а[1]**, и** *f.* strike; **свобо́да ста́чек** freedom to strike.

ста́чк|а[2]**, и** *f.*: **войти́ в ~у (с+*i.*;** *coll., pej.*) to come to terms (with), make a compact (with).

стащ|и́ть, у́, ~́ишь *pf.* (*of* **ста́скивать**) **1.** to drag off, pull off; to drag down. **2.** (*coll.*) to pinch, swipe, whip.

ста́|я, и *f.* (*of birds*) flock, flight; (*of fish*) school, shoal; (*of dogs or wolves*) pack; (*of lions*) pride.

ста́|ять, ет *pf.* (*of* **~ивать**) to melt.

ствол, а́ *m.* **1.** (*of tree*) trunk; stem; bole. **2.** (*of firearm*) barrel. **3.** (*anat.*) tube, pipe. **4.** (*mining*) shaft.

стволов|о́й, о́го *m.* (*in mine*) hanger-on; cager.

стволо́вый *adj. of* **ствол**

ство́льн|ый *adj.* barrel; **~ая гру́ппа** barrel assembly; **с. кожу́х** barrel housing.

створ, а *m.* **1.** = **~ка. 2.** range, alignment.

ство́рк|а, и *f.* leaf, fold; door, gate, shutter (*one of a pair*).

створо́ж|иться, ится *pf.* to curdle.

ство́рчатый *adj.* folding; valved.

стеари́н, а *m.* stearin.

стеари́н|овый *adj. of* **~; ~овая свеча́** stearin candle.

сте́б|ель, ля, *pl.* **~ли, ~ле́й** *m.* stem, stalk.

стебе́льчатый *adj.*: **с. шов** feather stitch.

стёганк|а, и *f.* (*coll.*) quilted jacket.

стёган|ый *adj.* quilted; **~ое одея́ло** quilt.

стега́|ть[1]**, ю** *impf.* (*of* **от~** *and* **стегну́ть**) to whip, lash.

стега́|ть[2]**, ю** *impf.* (*of* **вы~**) to quilt.

стег|ну́ть, ну́, нёшь *pf. of* **~а́ть**[1]

стёжк|а[1]**, и** *f.* quilting.

стёжк|а[2]**, и** *f.* (*dial.*) path.

стеж|о́к, ка́ *m.* stitch.

стез|я́, и́, *g. pl.* **~е́й** *f.* (*rhet.*) path, way.

стек, а *m.* riding-crop.

стека́|ть(ся), ю(сь) *impf. of* **сте́чь(ся)**

стеклене́|ть, ет *impf.* (*of* **о~**) to become glassy.

стек|ло́, ла́, *pl.* **~́ла, ~́ол** *nt.* glass; *pl.* lenses (*for spectacles*); **ла́мповое с.** lamp-chimney; **око́нное с.** window-pane; **пере́днее с.** wind-screen.

стеклова́т|а, ы *f.* fibreglass.

стеклови́д|ный (~ен, ~на) *adj.* **1.** glassy. **2.** (*anat.*) hyaline, hyaloid; **~ное те́ло** hyaloid (membrane).

стекловолокн|о́, а́ *nt.* fibreglass.

стеклоду́в, а *m.* glass-blower.

стеклоду́вный *adj.* glass-blowing.

стёклыш|ко, ка, *pl.* **~ки, ~ек, ~кам** *nt.* **1.** *dim. of* **стекло́. 2.** piece of glass.

стекля́нн|ый *adj.* **1.** glass; **~ая бума́га** glass-paper; **~ые изде́лия** glassware. **2.** (*fig.*) glassy.

стекля́рус, а *m.* (*collect.*) bugles (*tube-shaped glass beads*).

стеко́льный *adj.* glass; vitreous; **с. заво́д** glass-works, glass-factory.

стеко́льщик, а *m.* glazier.

стел|и́ть(ся), ю́(сь), ~́ешь(ся) *impf.* = **стлать(ся)**

стелла́ж, а́ *m.* **1.** shelves. **2.** rack, stand.

сте́льк|а, и *f.* insole, sock; **пьян как с.** (*coll.*) drunk as a lord.

сте́льная *adj.*: **с. коро́ва** calver, in-calf cow.

стемне́|ть, ю *pf. of* **темне́ть**

стен|а́, ы́, *a.* **~у,** *pl.* **~ы, ~а́м** *f.* wall (*also fig.*); **обнести́ ~о́й** to wall in; **жить с. в ~у** (**с**+*i.*) to live right on top (of); **в ~а́х** (+*g.*) within the precincts (of); **в четырёх ~а́х** within four walls; **лезть на́ ~у** (*coll.*) to climb up the wall; **как об ~у горо́х** (*coll.*) pointless, useless.

стена́|ть, ю *impf.* (*obs.*) to groan, moan.

стенгазе́т|а, ы *f.* (*abbr. of* ***стенна́я газе́та***) wall newspaper.

стенд, а *m.* **1.** stand (*at exhibition, etc.*). **2.** testing ground.

сте́ндер, а *m.* stand-pipe.

сте́нк|а, и *f.* **1.** wall; **гимнасти́ческая с.** wall-bars. **2.** (*anat., etc.*) side, wall. **3.** (*furniture*) wall unit.

стенн|о́й *adj.* wall; mural; **~а́я жи́вопись** mural painting.

стенобитный *adj.*: **с. тара́н** battering-ram.

стенограмм|а, ы *f.* shorthand report.

стено́граф, а *m.* stenographer.

стенографи́р|овать, ую *impf. and pf.* to take down in shorthand.

стенографи́ст, а *m.* = **стено́граф**

стенографи́ст|ка, ки *f. of* **~**

стенографи́ческий *adj.* stenographic, shorthand.

стенографи́|я, и *f.* stenography, shorthand.

сте́нопис|ь, и *f.* mural (painting).

сте́ньг|а, и *f.* (*naut.*) topmast.

степе́н|ный (~ен, ~на) *adj.* **1.** staid, steady. **2.** middle-aged.

сте́пен|ь, и, *g. pl.* **~е́й** *f.* **1.** degree, extent; **в вы́сшей ~и** in the highest degree; **до изве́стной ~и, до не́которой ~и** to some degree, to some extent, to a certain extent; **~и сравне́ния** (*gram.*) degrees of comparison. **2.** (*math.*) power; **возвести́ в тре́тью с.** to raise to the third power. **3. (учёная) с.** (*academic*) degree.

степ|но́й *adj. of* **~ь**

степня́к, а́ *m.* **1.** inhabitant of steppe. **2.** steppe horse.

степ|ь, и, о ~и, в ~и́, *pl.* **~и, ~е́й** *f.* steppe.

сте́рв|а, ы *f.* **1.** (*obs.*) dead animal, carrion. **2.** (*vulg.*; *as term of abuse*) shit, stinker.

стервене́|ть, ю *impf.* (*of* **о~**) (*coll.*) to become furious, get mad.

стерв|е́ц, еца́ *m.* = **~а 2.**

стервя́тник, а *m.* carrion-crow (*also fig., of enemy aircraft in World War II*).

стерео... *comb. form* stereo-.

стереодальноме́р *m.* (*mil.*) stereoscopic range-finder.

стереокино́ *nt. indecl.* stereoscopic cinema.

стереоме́три|я, и *f.* stereometry, solid geometry.

стереоско́п, а *m.* stereoscope.

стереоскопи́ческий *adj.* stereoscopic.

стереоти́п, а *m.* stereotype.

стереоти́пн|ый *adj.* **1.** stereotype. **2.** (*fig.*) stereotyped; **~ая фра́за** stock phrase.

стереотруб|а́, ы́ *f.* stereoscopic telescope; (*mil.*) battery commander's telescope.

стереофони́ческий *adj.* stereophonic.

стереохи́ми|я, и *f.* stereochemistry.

стер|е́ть, сотру́, сотрёшь, *past* **~, ~ла** *pf.* (*of* **стира́ть**[1]) **1.** to rub out, erase; to wipe off; **с. с лица́ земли́** to wipe off the face of the earth. **2.** to rub sore. **3.** to grind (down).

стер|е́ться, сотрётся, *past* **~ся, ~лась** *pf.* (*of* **стира́ться**[1]) **1.** to rub off; (*fig.*) to fade; **с. в па́мяти** to sink into oblivion. **2.** to become worn down.

стере́|чь, гу́, жёшь, гу́т, *past* **~г, ~гла́** *impf.* **1.** to guard, watch (over). **2.** to watch (for).

сте́рж|ень, ня *m.* **1.** (*tech.*) pivot; shank, rod; **поршнево́й с.** piston rod. **2.** (*fig.*) core.

стержнев|о́й *adj.* pivoted; **~а́я анте́нна** rod aerial; **с. вопро́с** key question.

стерилиза́тор, а *m.* sterilizer.

стерилиза́ци|я, и *f.* sterilization.

стерилиз|ова́ть, у́ю *impf. and pf.* to sterilize.

стери́льност|ь, и *f.* sterility.

стери́л|ьный (~ен, ~ьна) *adj.* sterile; germ-free.

сте́рлинг, а *m.* (*fin.*) sterling; **фунт ~ов** pound sterling.

сте́рлинг|овый *adj. of* **~**; **~овая зо́на** sterling area.

сте́рляд|ь, и *f.* (*zool.*) sterlet.

стерн|ь, и *f.* **1.** harvest-field. **2.** (*collect.*) stubble.

стерн|я́, и́ *f.* = **~ь**

стеро́ид, а *m.* steroid.

стерп|е́ть, лю́, ~ишь *pf.* to bear, suffer, endure.

стерп|е́ться, ~ишься *pf.* (**с**+*i.*; *coll.*) to get used (to), accept; **~ится — слю́бится** you will like it when you get used to it.

стёр|тый *p.p.p. of* **~е́ть** *and adj.* worn, effaced.

стесне́ни|е, я *nt.* constraint; **без вся́ких ~й** quite uninhibitedly.

стесн|ённый *p.p.p. of* **~и́ть** *and adj.* **~ённые обстоя́тельства** straitened circumstances.

стесни́тельност|ь, и *f.* **1.** shyness; inhibition(s). **2.** difficulty, inconvenience.

стесни́тел|ьный (~ен, ~ьна) *adj.* **1.** shy; inhibited. **2.** difficult, inconvenient.

стесн|и́ть, ю́, и́шь *pf.* (*of* **~я́ть**) to constrain; to hamper; to inhibit.

стесн|и́ться, ю́сь, и́шься *pf.* (*of* **тесни́ться**) to crowd together.

стесн|я́ть, я́ю *impf. of* **~и́ть**

стесня́|ться, юсь *impf.* (*of* **по~**) (+*inf.*) to feel too shy (to), be ashamed (to); (+*g.*) to feel shy (before, of); **не ~йтесь!** don't be shy!

стетоско́п, а *m.* (*med.*) stethoscope.

стече́ни|е, я *nt.* confluence; **с. наро́да** concourse; **с. обстоя́тельств** coincidence.

сте|чь, чёт, ку́т, *past* **~к, ~кла́** *pf.* (*of* **~ка́ть**) to flow down.

сте́|чься, чётся, ку́тся, *past* **~кся, ~кла́сь** *pf.* (*of* **~ка́ться**) to flow together; to gather, throng.

сти́бр|ить, ю, ишь *pf. of* **ти́брить**

стивидо́р, а *m.* stevedore.

стил|ево́й *adj. of* **~ь; ~евы́е катего́рии** stylistic categories.

стиле́т, а *m.* stiletto.

стилиза́ци|я, и *f.* stylization.

стилиз|ова́ть, у́ю *impf. and pf.* to stylize.

стили́ст, а *m.* stylist.

стили́стик|а, и *f.* (*study of*) style, stylistics.

стилисти́ческий *adj.* stylistic.

стил|ь, я *m.* (*in var. senses*) style; **но́вый с.** New Style (*Gregorian calendar*); **ста́рый с.** Old Style (*Julian calendar*).

сти́л|ьный (~ен, ~ьна) *adj.* stylish; **~ьная ме́бель** period furniture.

стиля́г|а, и *c.g.* stilyaga (*young pers. given to uncritical display of extravagant fashions in dress and manners*).

сти́мул, а *m.* stimulus, incentive.

стимули́р|овать, ую *impf. and pf.* to stimulate.

стипендиа́т, а *m.* grant-aided student, scholarship holder.

стипе́нди|я, и *f.* grant, scholarship.

стира́льн|ый *adj.* washing; **~ая маши́на** washing machine.

стира́|ть[1]**, ю** *impf. of* **стере́ть**

стира́|ть[2]**, ю** *impf.* (*of* **вы́~**) to wash, launder.

стира́|ться[1]**, юсь** *impf. of* **стере́ться**

стира́|ться[2]**, ется** *impf.* to wash; **хорошо́ с.** to wash well.

сти́рк|а, и *f.* washing, laundering; **отда́ть в ~у** to send to the wash, send to the laundry.

сти́скива|ть, ю *impf. of* **сти́снуть**

сти́с|нуть, ну, нешь *pf.* (*of* **~кивать**) to squeeze; **с. зу́бы** to clench one's teeth; **с. в объя́тиях** to hug.

стих[1]**, а́** *m.* **1.** verse; line (*of poetry*); **бе́лый с.** blank verse; **во́льный с.** free verse; **разме́р ~а́** metre. **2.** (*pl.*) verses; poetry.

стих[2] *m. indecl.* (*coll.*) mood; **на него́ угрю́мый с. нашёл** he was in a gloomy mood.

стих[3] *see* **~нуть**

стиха́р|ь, я́ *m.* (*eccl.*) surplice, alb.

стих|а́ть, а́ю *impf. of* **~нуть**

стихи́йност|ь, и *f.* spontaneity.

стихи́|йный (~ен, ~йна) *adj.* **1.** elemental; **~йное бе́дствие** natural calamity. **2.** (*fig.*) spontaneous, uncontrolled.

стихи́р|а, ы *f.* hymn, canticle.

стихи́|я, и *f.* element; **борьба́ со ~ями** struggle with the elements; **быть в свое́й ~и** to be in one's element.

сти́х|нуть, ну, нешь, *past* **~, ~ла** *pf.* (*of* **~а́ть**) to abate, subside; to die down; to calm down.

стихове́дени|е, я *nt.* (study of) prosody.
стихоплёт, а *m.* (*coll.*) rhymester, versifier.
стихосложе́ни|е, я *nt.* versification; prosody.
стихотворе́ни|е, я *nt.* poem.
стихотво́р|ец, ца *m.* (*obs.*) poet.
стихотво́рн|ый *adj.* in verse form; **с. разме́р** metre; **~ая речь** poetic diction.
стихотво́рчеств|о, а *nt.* poetry-writing.
стиш|о́к, ка́ *m.* (*coll.*) verse, rhyme.
стлать, стелю́, сте́лешь *impf.* (*of* **по~**) to spread; **с. посте́ль** to make a bed; **с. ска́терть** to lay a table-cloth.
стла́ться, сте́лется *impf.* to spread; **с. по земле́** (*of mists, smoke, etc.*) to creep; to hang about.
сто[1], **ста,** *pl.* **ста, сот, стам, ста́ми, стах** *num.* hundred; **не́сколько сот рубле́й** several hundred roubles; **на все сто** (*coll.*) in first-rate fashion.
сто[2] *nt. indecl.* (*hist.*) merchant guild.
стог, а, *pl.* **~а́** *m.* (*agric.*) stack, rick.
стогова́ни|е, я *nt.* (*agric.*) stacking.
стогра́дусный *adj.* centigrade.
стоеро́сов|ый *adj. only in phrr.* (*coll.*): **дуби́на ~ая!, дура́к (болва́н) с.!** damned fool!
сто́ик, а *m.* (*phil. and fig.*) stoic.
сто́имост|ь, и *f.* **1.** cost; **с. перево́зки** carriage. **2.** (*econ.*) value; **менова́я с.** exchange value; **приба́вочная с.** surplus value.
сто́|ить, ю, ишь *impf.* **1.** to cost (*also fig.*); **ско́лько ~ит э́то пла́тье?** how much is this dress?; **отсю́да до грани́цы ~ит сто рубле́й** from here to the frontier costs one hundred roubles; **до́рого с.** to cost dear; **э́то ему́ ничего́ не ~ило** it cost him nothing. **2.** (*+g.*) to be worth; to deserve; (*impers.*): **~ит** it is worth while; **~ит посмотре́ть э́тот фильм** this film is worth seeing; **~ит ли он её?** is he worthy of her?; does he deserve her?; **не ~ит того́** (*coll.*) it is not worth while; **не ~ит (благода́рности)** don't mention it. **3.: ~ит то́лько** (*impers.+inf.*) one has only (to); **~ит то́лько упомяну́ть её и́мя, (как) он вы́йдет из себя́** you have only to mention her name for him to fly off the handle.
стоици́зм, а *m.* (*phil. and fig.*) stoicism.
стои́ческий *adj.* (*phil.*) stoic; (*fig.*) stoical.
сто́йбищ|е, а *nt.* nomad camp.
сто́йк|а, и *f.* **1.** (*sport*) stand, stance; **с. на рука́х** hand-stand. **2.** (*hunting*) set; **сде́лать ~у** to point. **3.** (*tech.*) support, prop; stanchion, upright; (*aeron*) strut. **4.** bar, counter.
сто́|йкий (~ек, ~йка́, ~йко) *adj.* **1.** firm, stable; (*phys., chem.*) stable; (*of poisonous substances*) persistent. **2.** (*fig.*) stable; steadfast, staunch, steady.
сто́йкост|ь, и *f.* **1.** firmness, stability. **2.** (*fig.*) steadfastness, staunchness; determination.
сто́йл|о, а *nt.* stall.
сто́йло|вый *adj. of* **~**; **~вое содержа́ние скота́** keeping cattle stalled.
стойма́ *adv.* upright.
сток, а *m.* **1.** flow; drainage, outflow. **2.** drain, gutter; sewer.
Стокго́льм, а *m.* Stockholm.
сто́кер, а *m.* (*tech.*) (mechanical) stoker.
стокра́т *adv.* (*obs.*) a hundred times, an hundredfold.
стокра́тный *adj.* hundredfold, centuple.
сто́л, а *m.* **1.** table; **пи́сьменный с.** writing-table, desk; **сесть за с.** to sit down to table; **за ~о́м** at table. **2.** board; cooking, cuisine; **диети́ческий с.** invalid dietary; **ры́бный с.** fish diet; **«шве́дский» с.** smörgasbord; **держа́ть с.** (*obs.*) to provide board; **с. и кварти́ра** board and lodging. **3.** department; office, bureau; **с. ли́чного соста́ва** personnel department; **с. нахо́док** lost property office. **4.** (*hist.*) throne.
столб, а́ *m.* post, pole, pillar, column; **телегра́фный с.** telegraph pole; **пыль ~о́м** a cloud of dust; **стоя́ть ~о́м** (*coll.*) to stand rooted to the ground.
столбене́|ть, ю *impf.* (*of* **о~**) (*coll.*) to be rooted to the ground.
столб|е́ц, ца́ m. **1.** column (*in dictionary, newspaper, etc.*). **2.** (*pl.*) parchment roll.
сто́лбик, а *m.* **1.** *dim. of* **столб; с. рту́ти** mercury (column). **2.** (*bot.*) style.
столбня́к, а́ *m.* **1.** (*med.*) tetanus. **2.** (*coll.*) stupor; **на неё нашёл с.** she was stunned.
столбов|о́й *adj. of* **столб**; (*fig., coll.*) main, chief; **с. дворяни́н** (*hist.*) member of long-established family of (Russian) gentry; **~а́я доро́га** high road, highway (*also fig.*).
столе́ти|е, я *nt.* **1.** century. **2.** centenary.
столе́тн|ий *adj.* **1.** of a hundred years' duration; **~яя война́** the Hundred Years' War. **2.** a hundred years old; centennial; **~яя годовщи́на** centenary; **с. стари́к** centenarian.
столе́тник, а *m.* (*bot.*) agave.
сто́л|ик, а *m. dim. of* **~**; **ни́зкий с.** coffee table.
столи́ц|а, ы *f.* capital; metropolis.
столи́|чный *adj. of* **~ца; с. го́род** capital (city).
столкнове́ни|е, я *nt.* collision; (*mil. and fig.*) clash; **вооружённое с.** armed conflict, hostilities; **с. интере́сов** clash of interests.
столкн|у́ть, у́, ёшь *pf.* (*of* **ста́лкивать**) **1.** to push off, push away; **с. ло́дку в во́ду** to push a boat off (into the water). **2.** to cause to collide; to knock together. **3.** (*coll.*) to bring together.
столкн|у́ться, у́сь, ёшься *pf.* (*of* **ста́лкиваться**) **1.** (**c**+*i.*) to collide (with), come into collision (with) (*also fig.*); (*fig.*) to clash (with), conflict (with); **здесь на́ши интере́сы ~у́лись** our interests clashed at this point. **2.** (**c**+*i.*; *fig., coll.*) to run (into), bump (into); **с. со ста́рым ученико́м** to bump into an old pupil.
столк|ова́ться, у́юсь *pf.* (*of* **~о́вываться**) (**c**+*i.*; *coll.*) to come to an agreement (with).
столко́выва|ться, юсь *impf. of* **столкова́ться**
стол|ова́ться, у́юсь *impf.* to have meals, receive board; to mess; **он ~у́ется у друзе́й** he has meals with friends.
столо́в|ая, ой *f.* **1.** dining-room; dining-hall; mess. **2.** dining-room(s); canteen.
столоверче́ни|е, я *nt.* (*coll., iron.*) table-turning.
столо́в|ый *adj.* **1.** table; **~ое вино́** table wine; **~ая ло́жка** table-spoon; **с. прибо́р** cover; **~ое серебро́** (*collect.*) silver, plate; **~ая соль** table-salt. **2.** feeding, catering, messing; **~ые де́ньги** dinner money; (*mil.*) ration allowance, messing allowance; **~ые расхо́ды** catering expenses; (*mil.*) messing expenses. **3.: ~ые го́ры** (*geog.*) mesa, tableland.
столонача́льник, а *m.* (*obs.*) head of a 'desk' (*in civil service*).
стол|о́чь, ку́, чёшь, ку́т, *past* **~о́к, ~кла́** *pf.* (*of* **толо́чь**) to pound, grind.
столп, а́ *m.* (*arch. or fig.*) pillar, column; **~ы́ о́бщества** pillars of society.
столп|и́ться, и́тся *pf.* to crowd.
столпотворе́ни|е, я *nt.*: **вавило́нское с.** babel.
столь *adv.* so; **э́то не с. ва́жно** it is of no particular importance.
сто́лько *adv.* so much; so many; **ещё с. же** as much again, as many again; **не с. ... ско́лько** not so much ... as; **где ты был с. вре́мени?** where have you been all this time?; **сто́лько-то** so much, some.
сто́льник, а *m.* (*hist.*) stolnik (*Russ. courtier inferior in rank to boyar*).
сто́льный *adj.*: **с. го́род, с. град** (*hist.*) capital (city).
столя́р, а́ *m.* joiner.
столя́рнича|ть, ю *impf.* to be a joiner.
столя́рн|ый *adj.* joiner's; **~ое де́ло** joinery; **с. клей** carpenter's glue.
стоматоло́ги|я, и *f.* stomatology.
стон, а *m.* moan, groan.
стон|а́ть, у́, ~ешь *and* **~а́ю, ~а́ешь** *impf.* to moan, groan (*also fig.*).
стоп *int.* stop!; **сигна́л с.** stop signal.
стоп|а́[1], **ы́** *f.* **1.** (*pl.* **~ы́**) foot (*also fig.*); **напра́вить свои́ ~ы́** to direct, bend one's steps; **идти́ по чьим-н. ~а́м** to follow in s.o.'s footsteps. **2.** (*pl.* **~ы**) (*liter.*) foot.
стоп|а́[2], **ы́,** *pl.* **~ы** *f.* **1.** ream. **2.** pile, heap.
стоп|а́[3], **ы́,** *pl.* **~ы** *f.* (*obs.*) winebowl.
стоп|и́ть, лю́, ~ишь *pf.* (*of* **ста́пливать**) **1.** to fuse, melt. **2.** (*of* **топи́ть**) (*coll.*) to heat.

сто́пк|а¹, и *f.* pile, heap.
сто́пк|а², и *f.* small drinking vessel.
сто́пор, а *m.* **1.** (*tech.*) stop, catch, locking device. **2.** (*naut.*) stopper.
сто́пор|ить, ю, ишь *impf.* (*tech.*) to stop, lock; (*fig.*, *coll.*) to bring to a standstill.
сто́пор|иться, ится *impf.* (*coll.*) to come to a standstill.
сто́пор|ный *adj. of* ~; **с. кла́пан** stop-valve; **с. кран** stopcock; **с. механи́зм** stop gear, locking device; **~ное приспособле́ние, ~ное устро́йство** lock, catch; **с. у́зел** (*naut.*) stopper-knot.
стопоходя́щий *adj.* (*zool.*) plantigrade.
стопроце́нтный *adj.* hundred per cent.
стоп-сигна́л, а *m.* brake-light (*on car*).
стоп|та́ть, чу́, ~́чешь *pf.* (*of* **ста́птывать**) **1.** to wear down (*footwear*). **2.** (*coll.*) to trample.
стоп|та́ться, ~́чется *pf.* (*of* **ста́птываться**) to wear down, be worn down (*of footwear*).
сторг|ова́ть(ся), у́ю(сь) *pf. of* **торгова́ть(ся)**
стори́цею *adv.* (*obs.*) a hundredfold; **возда́ть с.** (+*d.*) to return a hundredfold, repay with interest.
сто́рож, а, *pl.* **~а́, ~е́й** *m.* watchman, guard; **ночно́й с.** night-watchman.
сторожеви́к, а́ *m.* patrol-boat.
сторожев|о́й *adj.* watch; **~а́я бу́дка** sentry-box; **~а́я вы́шка** watch-tower; **с. кора́бль** escort vessel; **с. пёс** watch-dog; **с. пост** sentry post; **~ы́е огни́** (*naut.*) warning lights.
сторож|и́ть, у́, и́шь *impf.* **1.** to guard, watch, keep watch (over). **2.** to lie in wait (for).
сторожи́х|а, и *f.* **1.** female watchman. **2.** watchman's wife.
сторо́жк|а, и *f.* lodge.
сторо́ж|кий (~ек, ~ка) *adj.* (*coll.*) watchful (*of animals and fig.*).
сторож|о́к, ка́ *m.* (*tech.*) **1.** catch. **2.** tongue, cock (*of scales*).
сторон|а́, ы́, *a.* **сто́рону,** *pl.* **сто́роны, сторо́н, ~а́м** *f.* **1.** (*in var. senses*) side; quarter; hand (*also fig.*); feature, aspect; **в сто́рону** (*theatr.*) aside; **шу́тки в сто́рону** (*coll.*) joking aside; **в ~е́** aside; **держа́ться в ~е́** to keep aloof; **на ~е́** (*coll.*) elsewhere, not on the spot; **он рабо́тает на ~е́** he does not work on the spot; **продава́ть на́ сторону** sell on the black market; **по ту сто́рону** (+*g.*) across, on the other side (of), on the far side (of); **с пра́вой, с ле́вой ~ы́** on the right, left side; **с. како́й ~ы́ ве́тер?** from what quarter is the wind blowing?; **с мое́й ~ы́** for my part; **э́то о́чень любе́зно с ва́шей ~ы** it is very kind of you; **со ~ы́** (+*g.*) (*indicating line of descent*) on the side of; **дед со ~ы́ ма́тери** maternal grandfather; **с одно́й ~ы..., с друго́й ~ы́** on the one hand ..., on the other hand; **узна́ть ~о́й** to find out indirectly. **2.** side, party; **вы на чьей ~е́?** whose side are you on?; **взять чью-н. сто́рону** to take s.o.'s part, side with s.o.; **Высо́кие Догова́ривающиеся Сто́роны** (*dipl.*) the High Contracting Parties. **3.** land, place; parts; **на чужо́й ~е́** in foreign parts.
сторон|и́ться, ю́сь, ~́ишься *impf.* (*of* **по~**) **1.** to stand aside, make way. **2.** (+*g.*) to shun, avoid.
сторо́нний *adj.* **1.** strange, foreign; **с. наблюда́тель** detached observer. **2.** indirect.
сторо́нник, а *m.* supporter, adherent, advocate; **с. ми́ра** peace campaigner.
стоск|ова́ться, у́юсь *pf.* (**по**+*p.*, **о**+*p.*) to pine (for), yearn (for).
сточ|и́ть, у́, ~́ишь *pf.* (*of* **ста́чивать**) to grind off.
сто́чн|ый *adj.* sewage, drainage; **~ые во́ды** sewage; **~ая труба́** sewer pipe.
стошн|и́ть, и́т *pf.* (*impers.*) to be sick, vomit; **меня́ ~и́ло** I was sick.
сто́я *adv.* upright.
стоя́к, а́ *m.* **1.** post, stanchion, upright. **2.** stand-pipe, rising pipe. **3.** chimney.
стоя́лый *adj.* stagnant; stale, old.
стоя́ни|е, я *nt.* standing.
стоя́нк|а, и *f.* **1.** stop; parking; **«с. запрещена́!»** 'no parking!'; **во вре́мя ~и (по́езда) на ста́нции** while the train is standing at a station. **2.** stopping place, halting place; parking space; moorage; **с. автомаши́н, автомоби́льная с.** car park; **с. такси́** taxi-rank. **3.** (*archaeol.*) site.
сто|я́ть, ю́, и́шь *impf.* **1.** to stand; **с. в о́череди** to stand in a queue; **с. на коле́нях** to kneel; **с. на четвере́ньках** to be on all fours. **2.** to be, be situated, lie; **село́ ~и́т на возвы́шенности** the village is situated on rising ground; **стака́ны ~я́т в шкафу́** the glasses are in the cupboard; **с. во главе́** (+*g.*) to be at the head (of), head; **с. на часа́х** to stand guard; **с. на я́коре** to be at anchor; **с. над душо́й у кого́-н.** (*coll.*) to plague s.o., worry the life out of s.o.; **с. у вла́сти** to be in power, be in office; **с. у прича́ла** (*naut.*) to lie alongside, be moored; **с. у руля́** to be at the helm. **3.** (*of weather conditions, etc.*) to be; to continue; **~и́т моро́з** there is a frost; **~я́ла хоро́шая пого́да** the weather continued fine; **а́кции ~я́т высоко́** shares continue high. **4.** to stay, put up; (*mil.*) to be stationed; **с. на кварти́рах, по кварти́рам** (*mil.*) to be billeted; **с. ла́герем** to be encamped, be under canvas. **5.** (**за**+*a.*) to stand up (for); (**на**+*p.*) to stand (on), insist (on); **с. горо́й за кого́-н.** (*coll.*) to stand up for s.o. with all one's might, be wholeheartedly behind s.o.; **с. на чьей-н. то́чке зре́ния** to share s.o.'s point of view. **6.** to stop; to come to a halt, come to a standstill; **мои́ часы́ ~я́т** my watch has stopped; **рабо́та ~и́т** work has come to a standstill; **~й(те)!** stop!; halt!
стоя́ч|ий *adj.* **1.** standing; upright, vertical; **с. воротничо́к** stand-up collar; **~ая ла́мпа** standard lamp; **~ая труба́** stand-pipe. **2.** stagnant.
сто́|ящий *pres. part. act. of* **~ить** *and adj.* deserving; worth-while.
стр. *abbr. of* **1. страни́ца** p., page. **2. страни́цы** pp., pages.
страв|и́ть, лю́, ~́ишь *pf.* (*of* **~́ливать** *and* **~ля́ть**) **1.** to set on (*to fight*); **с. одного́ с други́м** to play off one against another. **2.** to use up in feeding (*cattle*). **3.** (*of cattle*) to spoil (*by eating and trampling*). **4.** to remove by chemical means. **5.** (*naut.*) to let steam. **6.** (*naut.*) to veer, pay out (rope).
стра́влива|ть, ю *impf. of* **страви́ть**
стравля́|ть, ю *impf.* = **стра́вливать**
стра́гива|ть(ся), ю(сь) *impf. of* **стро́нуть(ся)**
страд|а́, ы́, *pl.* **~́ы** *f.* hard work at harvest-time; period of hard work; (*fig.*) toil, drudgery.
страда́л|ец, ьца *m.* sufferer.
страда́льческ|ий *adj.* full of suffering; **с. вид** an air of suffering, a martyr's air; **~ая жизнь** life of suffering.
страда́ни|е, я *nt.* suffering.
страда́тельн|ый¹ *adj.* suffering; **~ое лицо́** sufferer.
страда́тельный² *adj.* (*gram.*) passive.
страда́|ть, ю *and* (*arch.*) **стра́жду, стра́ждешь** *impf.* **1.** *impf. only* (+*i.*) to suffer (from); to be subject (to); **с. бессо́нницей** to suffer from insomnia. **2.** *impf. only* (**от**) to suffer (from), be in pain (with); **с. от зубно́й бо́ли** to have (a) toothache; **с. от любви́** to be in love. **3.** *impf. only* **с. за кого́-н.** to feel for s.o. **4.** *impf. only* (**по**+ *d. or p.*; *coll.*) to miss; to long (for), pine (for). **5.** (*pf.* **по~**) to suffer; **с. за ве́ру** to suffer for one's faith; **с. от за́сухи** to suffer from the drought; **с. от бомбёжки** to be a victim of bombing; **с. по свое́й вине́** to suffer through one's own fault. **6.** *impf. only* (*coll.*) to be weak, be poor; to be at a low ebb; **у неё па́мять ~ет** she has a poor memory.
стра́д|ный 1. *adj. of* **~а́**; **~ная пора́** busy period. **2.** (*obs.*) suffering.
страж, а *m.* **1.** (*obs.*, *now only rhet.*) guard, custodian. **2.: с. ми́ра** peacekeeper.
стра́ж|а, и *f.* guard, watch; **пограни́чная с.** (*obs.*) frontier guard(s); **быть, стоя́ть на ~е** (+*g.*) to guard; **под ~ей** under arrest, in custody; **взять, заключи́ть под ~у** to take into custody.
стра́ждущ|ий *pres. part. act.* (*obs.*) *of* **страда́ть**; **~ее челове́чество** suffering humanity.
стра́жник, а *m.* (*obs.*) **1.** police constable (*in rural areas*). **2.: берегово́й с.** coastguard; **лесно́й с.** forest warden.
страз, а *m.* paste (*jewel*); strass.

стран|а́, ы́, *pl.* **~ы** *f.* **1.** country; land. **2.: с. све́та** cardinal point (*of compass*).
страни́ц|а, ы *f.* page (*also fig., rhet.*).
стра́нник, а *m.* wanderer (*esp.* religious pilgrim).
стра́нниц|а, ы *f. of* **стра́нник**
стра́нно *adv.* **1.** strangely, in a strange way. **2.** *as pred.* it is strange, funny, odd, queer.
странноприи́мный *adj.* (*obs.*) hospitable to strangers; **с. дом** almshouse, old people's home.
стра́нност|ь, и *f.* **1.** strangeness. **2.** oddity, eccentricity; **за ним води́лись ~и** he was an odd pers.; he had his quirks.
стра́н|ный (~ен, ~на́, ~но) *adj.* strange; funny, odd, queer.
странове́дени|е, я *nt.* **1.** regional geography. **2.** regional studies.
стра́нстви|е, я *nt.* (*obs.*) wandering, journeying, travelling.
стра́нствовани|е, я *nt.* wandering, journeying, travelling.
стра́нств|овать, ую *impf.* to wander, travel.
стра́нств|ующий *pres. part. act. of* **~овать** *and adj.*; **с. актёр** strolling player; **с. ры́царь** knight-errant.
Страсбу́рг, а *m.* Strasbourg.
страстн|о́й *adj.* of Holy Week; **~а́я неде́ля** Holy Week; **~а́я пя́тница** Good Friday; **С. четве́рг** Maundy Thursday.
стра́стност|ь, и *f.* passion.
стра́ст|ный (~ен, ~на́, ~но) *adj.* passionate; impassioned; ardent; **он — с. авиамодели́ст** he is mad about making model aircraft.
страстоцве́т, а *m.* passion flower.
страст|ь[1], **и,** *g. pl.* **~е́й** *f.* **1. (к)** passion (for); **до ~и** (*coll.*) passionately; **люби́ть до ~и** to be passionately fond (of); **со ~ью** with fervour; **у неё с. к о́перам Мо́царта** she is mad about Mozart's operas. **2.: ~и Христо́вы** (*relig.*) the Passion; **Стра́сти по Матфе́ю** (*title of oratorio*) St Matthew Passion. **3.** (*coll.*) horror; **расска́зывать (про) вся́кие ~и** to recount all manner of horrors.
страсть[2] *adv.* (*coll.*) **1. (как, како́й)** awfully, frightfully; **мне с. как хо́чется ви́деть э́тот фильм** I want awfully to see this film; **она́ с. кака́я на́глая** she is frightfully brazen. **2.** an awful lot, a terrific number.
стратаге́м|а, ы *f.* stratagem.
страте́г, а *m.* strategist.
стратеги́ческий *adj.* strategic.
страте́ги|я, и *f.* strategy; **с. измо́ра проти́вника** strategy of attrition.
стратифика́ци|я, и *f.* stratification.
стратона́вт, а *m.* stratosphere flier.
стратоста́т, а *m.* stratosphere balloon.
стратосфе́р|а, ы *f.* stratosphere.
стратосфе́рный *adj.* stratospheric.
стра́ус, а *m.* ostrich.
стра́ус|овый *adj. of* **~; ~овое перо́** ostrich feather.
страх[1], **а** *m.* **1.** fear; terror; **с. Бо́жий, с. Госпо́день** the fear of God; **с. пе́ред неизве́стностью** fear of the unknown; **держа́ть в ~е** to keep in awe; **под ~ом сме́рти** on pain of death; **~а ра́ди** for fear, from fear; **со ~ом и тре́петом** with fear and trembling; **у ~а глаза́ велики́** fear hath a hundred eyes. **2.** (*pl.*) terrors. **3.** risk, responsibility; **на свой с.** at one's own risk.
страх[2] *adv.* (*coll.*) **(как)** terribly; **им с. хо́чется побыва́ть во Фра́нции** they want terribly to go to France.
страх... *comb. form, abbr. of* **страхово́й**
страхка́сс|а, ы *f.* insurance office.
страхова́ни|е, я *nt.* insurance; **с. жи́зни** life insurance; **с. от несча́стных слу́чаев** insurance against accidents; **с. от огня́** fire insurance.
страхова́тел|ь, я *m.* insurant.
страх|ова́ть, у́ю *impf.* **1.** (*pf.* **за~**) **(от)** to insure (against); **с. себя́ (от** *fig.*) to insure (against), safeguard o.s. (against). **2.** (*sport*) to stand by (*in case of accident*).
страх|ова́ться, у́юсь *impf.* (*of* **за~**) **(от)** to insure o.s. (against) (*also fig.*).
страхови́к, а́ *m.* (*coll.*) insurance man.
страхо́вк|а, и *f.* **1.** insurance. **2.** (*fig., coll.*) insurance, guarantee.
страхово́й *adj.* insurance; **с. по́лис** insurance policy.
страхо́вщик, а *m.* insurer.
страше́нный *adj.* (*coll.*) terrible.
страши́лищ|е, а *m. and nt.* fright (*object inspiring fear*); (*coll.*) monster; scarecrow.
страш|и́ть, у́, и́шь *impf.* to frighten, scare.
страш|и́ться, у́сь, и́шься *impf.* (*+g.*) to be afraid (of), fear.
стра́шно *adv.* **1.** terribly, awfully. **2.** *as pred.* it is terrible; it is terrifying; **нам бы́ло с.** we were terrified.
стра́ш|ный (~ен, ~на́, ~но) *adj.* terrible, awful, dreadful, frightful, fearful; terrifying, frightening; **с. расска́з** terrifying story; **с. сон** bad dream; **с. шум** (*coll.*) awful din; **С. суд** the Day of Judgement, Doomsday.
страща́|ть, ю *impf.* (*of* **по~**) (*coll.*) to frighten, scare.
стре́ж|ень, ня *m.* channel, main stream (*of river*).
стреж|нево́й *adj. of* **~ень; ~невы́е во́ды** channel, navigable waters (*of a river*).
стрека́в|ить, лю, ишь *impf.* (*of* **о~**) (*dial.*) to sting (*with a nettle*).
стрека́|ть, ю *impf.* (*dial.*) **1.** (*pf.* **об~**) = **~вить. 2.** (*coll.*) to take to one's heels, run for it.
стрека́ч, а́ *m. now only in phr.* **(за)да́ть ~а́** (*coll.*) to take to one's heels, run for it.
стрекоз|а́, ы́, *pl.* **~ы** *f.* dragon-fly (*also of a fidgety or lively girl*).
стре́кот, а *m.* chirr (*of grasshoppers*); (*fig.*) rattle, chatter (*of machine-gun fire, etc.*).
стрекота́ни|е, я *nt.* chirring; (*fig.*) rattle, chatter.
стреко|та́ть, чу́, ~чешь *impf.* to chirr (*of grasshoppers*); (*fig.*) to rattle, chatter (*of machine-guns, etc.*).
стрел|а́, ы́, *pl.* **~ы** *f.* **1.** arrow (*also fig.*); (*fig.*) shaft, dart; **пусти́ть ~у́** to shoot an arrow; **мча́ться ~о́й** to fly like an arrow from the bow. **2.** (*bot.*) shaft. **3.** (*archit.*) rise; **с. (подъёма) сво́да** rise of vault. **4.** (*tech.*) arm (*of crane*), boom, jib; (*pl.*; *naut.*) sheer-legs. **5.: с. мо́ста** cantilever. **6.: с. проги́ба** (*tech.*) sag.
стрел|е́ц, ьца́ *m.* **1.** (*hist.*) strelets (*in Muscovite Russia in the 16th and 17th centuries; member of military corps instituted by Ivan the Terrible and enjoying special privileges*). **2. С.** (*astron.*) Sagittarius (*constellation*).
стреле́ц|кий *adj. of* **~ 1.**
стре́лк|а, и *f.* **1.** pointer, indicator; hand (*of clock or watch*); needle (*of compass, etc.*). **2.** arrow (*on diagram, etc.*). **3.** (*rail.*) point(s), switch; **перевести́ ~у** to change the points. **4.** (*geog.*) spit. **5.** shoot, blade (*of grass, etc.*).
стрелко́в|ый *adj.* **1.** rifle, shooting; small arms; **~ое мастерство́** marksmanship; **~ое ору́жие** small arms; **с. спорт** shooting; **с. тир** rifle range. **2.** (*mil.*) rifle, infantry; **с. батальо́н** rifle battalion, infantry battalion; **~ые войска́** infantry; **с. око́п** fire trench; **~ая цепь** riflemen in extended fire positions.
стрелови́дност|ь, и *f.* (*aeron.*) angle (*of wing*); **самолёт с изменя́емой ~ью крыла́** variable geometry aircraft.
стреловид|ный (~ен, ~на) *adj.* arrow-shaped; (*bot., zool.*) sagittate; **~ное крыло́** (*aeron.*) swept-back wing; **с. шов че́репа** (*med.*) sagittate suture of skull.
стрел|о́к, ка́ *m.* **1.** shot; **иску́сный с., отли́чный с.** good shot, marksman. **2.** (*mil.*) rifleman; (*aeron.*) gunner.
стрелокры́лый *adj.*: **с. самолёт** swing-wing airplane.
стре́лочник, а *m.* (*rail.*) pointsman, switchman; **с. винова́т** (*iron.*) the little man is always blamed, muggins!
стре́лочниц|а, ы *f. of* **стре́лочник**
стре́л|очный *adj. of* **~ка 3.**
стрельб|а́, ы́, *pl.* **~ы** *f.* shooting, firing; shoot; **руже́йная с.** rifle fire, small arms fire; **уче́бная с.** practice shoot; **с. на пораже́ние** fire for effect; **с. по ка́рте** predicted shoot, shooting by the map; **с. по пло́щади** area shoot, zone fire.
стре́льбищ|е, а *nt.* shooting range, target range.
стрельн|у́ть, у́, ёшь *pf.* (*coll.*) **1.** to fire a shot. **2.** (*impers.*): **у меня́ ~у́ло в у́хе** I had a stab of pain in my ear. **3.** to rush away. **4.** (*sl.*) to cadge.
стре́льчат|ый *adj.* **1.** (*archit.*) lancet. **2.** arched, pointed; **~ые бро́ви** arched eyebrows.
стре́лян|ый *adj.* (*coll.*) **1.** shot; **~ая дичь** shot game (*opp. killed by strangling*). **2.** that has been under fire; **он — солда́т с.** he has had his baptism of fire; **с. воробе́й** old

hand. **3.** used, fired, spent; **~ая ги́льза** used cartridge, empty case.

стреля́|ть, ю *impf.* **1.** (**в**+*a.*, **по**+*d.*) to shoot (at), fire (at); **хорошо́ с.** to be a good shot; **с. из револьве́ра, из ружья́** to fire a revolver, a gun; **с. в цель** to shoot at a target; **с. по самолёту** to fire at an aeroplane; **с. из пу́шек по воробья́м** (*coll.*) to use a sledgehammer to smash walnuts. **2.** to shoot (= *to hunt, kill by shooting*); **с. куропа́ток** to go partridge-shooting. **3.: с. глаза́ми** (*coll.*) to dart glances (at); to make eyes (at). **4.** (*sl.*) to cadge. **5.** (*impers.*) to have a shooting pain. **6.** to produce a sharp sound; **с. кнуто́м** crack a whip.

стреля́|ться, юсь *impf.* **1.** (*coll.*) to shoot o.s. **2.** to fight a duel (with firearms). **3.** *pass. of* **~ть 2.**

стремгла́в *adv.* headlong.

стрем|енно́й *adj.* = **~я́нный**

стреми́тел|ьный (~ен, ~ьна) *adj.* swift, headlong; impetuous.

стрем|и́ть, лю́, и́шь *impf.* to urge.

стрем|и́ться, лю́сь, и́шься *impf.* **1.** (*obs.*) to rush, speed, charge. **2.** (**к**) to strive (for), seek, aspire (to); (*+inf.*) to strive (to), try (to); **с. к соверше́нству** to strive for perfection.

стремле́ни|е, я *nt.* (**к**) striving (for), aspiration (to).

стремни́н|а, ы *f.* **1.** rapid (*in a river*). **2.** (*obs.*) precipice.

стремни́н|ный *adj. of* **~а 2.**

стремни́ст|ый (~, ~а) *adj.* (*obs.*) steep, precipitous.

стре́м|я, я, *g., d. and p.* **~ени,** *i.* **~енем,** *pl.* **~ена́, ~я́н, ~ена́м** *nt.* **1.** stirrup; **е́хать стре́мя в стре́мя** ride side by side (*on horseback*). **2.** (*anat.*) stirrup-bone, stapedial bone, stapes.

стремя́нк|а, и *f.* step-ladder, steps.

стремя́нн|ый *adj. of* **стре́мя**; *as n.* (*hist.*) **с., ~ого** *m.* groom.

стре́нг|а, и *f.* (*naut., tech.*) strand (*of cable*).

стрено́ж|ить, у, ишь *pf. of* **трено́жить**

стре́пет, а *m.* (*zool.*) little bustard.

стрептоко́кк, а *m.* (*biol., med.*) streptococcus.

стрептоко́кк|овый *adj. of* **~**

стрептомици́н, а *m.* (*med.*) streptomycin.

стресс, а *m.* (*psych.*) stress.

стрех|а́, и́, *pl.* **~и** *f.* eaves.

стреч|о́к, ка́ *m. now only in phr.* **(за)да́ть ~ка́** (*coll.*) to take to one's heels, run for it.

стрига́льн|ый *adj.*: **~ая маши́на** (*text.*) cloth-shearing machine.

стрига́льщик, а *m.* (*text. and agric.*) shearer.

стрига́льщиц|а, ы *f. of* **стрига́льщик**

стригу́н, а́ *m.* yearling (foal).

стригун|о́к, ка́ *m.* = **стригу́н**

стригу́щий *pres. part. act. of* **стричь; с. лиша́й** (*med.*) ring-worm.

стриж, а́ *m.* (*zool.*) martin, swift; **берегово́й с.** sand-martin; **ка́менный с.** stone-martin.

стри́женый *adj.* **1.** short-haired, close-cropped. **2.** (*of hair*) short; (*of sheep*) sheared; (*of tree*) clipped.

стри́жк|а, и *f.* **1.** hair-cutting; shearing; clipping. **2.** cut, hair-style, hair-do.

стри́мер, а *m.* (*comput.*) tape-streamer.

стри́нгер, а *m.* (*naut., aeron.*) stringer.

стрихни́н, а *m.* (*med.*) strychnine.

стри|чь, гу́, жёшь, гу́т, *past* **~г, ~гла** *impf.* (*of* **о~**) **1.** to cut, clip (*hair or nails*). **2.: с. кого́-н.** to cut s.o.'s hair; **с. ове́ц** to shear sheep; **с. пу́деля** to clip a poodle; **с. всех под одну́ гребёнку** to treat all alike, reduce all to the same level. **3.** (*coll.*) to cut into pieces, into strips.

стри|чься, гу́сь, жёшься, гу́тся, *past* **~гся, ~глась** *impf.* (*of* **о~**) **1.** to cut one's hair; to have one's hair cut. **2.** to have one's hair cut short, wear one's hair short. **3.** *pass. of* **~чь**

стробоско́п, а *m.* (*phys.*) stroboscope.

строга́л|ь, я́ *m.* (*coll.*) = **~ьщик**

строга́льный *adj.* (*tech.*): **с. стано́к** planing machine, planer; **с. резе́ц** planer cutter.

строга́льщик, а *m.* plane operator, planer.

строга́|ть, ю *impf.* (*of* **вы́~**) (*tech.*) to plane, shave.

стро́г|ий (~, ~а́, ~о) *adj.* (*in var. senses*) strict; severe; **~ая дие́та** strict diet; **~ие ме́ры** strong measures; **с. пригово́р** severe sentence; **под ~им секре́том** in strict confidence; **в ~ом смы́сле сло́ва** in the strict sense of the word; **с. стиль** severe, austere style; **~ие черты́ лица́** regular features.

стро́го *adv.* strictly; severely; **с. говоря́** strictly speaking; **«с. воспреща́ется»** 'strictly forbidden'.

стро́го-на́строго *adv.* (*coll.*) very strictly.

стро́гост|ь, и *f.* **1.** (*in var. senses*) strictness; severity. **2.** (*pl.*) (*coll.*) strong measures.

строеви́к, а́ *m.* combatant soldier.

строево́й[1] *adj.* building; **с. лес** timber.

строев|о́й[2] *adj.* (*mil.*) **1.** combatant, line; **с. офице́р** officer serving in line; **~а́я слу́жба** (front-)line service, combatant service; **~а́я часть** line unit. **2.** drill; **~а́я подгото́вка** drill; **с. уста́в** drill regulations, drill manual; **с. шаг** ceremonial step.

строе́ни|е, я *nt.* **1.** building, structure. **2.** (*fig.*; *in var. senses*) structure, composition; (*biol.*) texture; **с. земно́й коры́** (*geol.*) structure of the earth's crust.

строжа́йший *superl. of* **стро́гий**

стро́же *comp. of* **стро́гий** *and* **стро́го**

строи́тел|ь, я *m.* **1.** builder (*also fig.*). **2.** (*eccl.*) Father Superior (*in some monasteries*).

строи́тельн|ый *adj.* building, construction; **~ая брига́да** construction gang; **~ое иску́сство** civil engineering; architecture; **с. лес** building timber; **~ая площа́дка** building site; **с. раство́р** lime mortar.

строи́тельств|о, а *nt.* **1.** building, construction (*also fig.*); **доро́жное с.** road-building, road-making; **жили́щное с.** house-building; **зелёное с.** laying out of parks, *etc.*; **хозя́йственное с.** building up of the economy. **2.** building site, construction project. **3.** (*fig.*) organization, structuring

стро́|ить, ю, ишь *impf.* **1.** (*pf.* **по~**) to build, construct; **с. плоти́ну** to build a dam; **с. но́вую жизнь** to make a new life; **с. возду́шные за́мки** to build castles in the air. **2.** (*pf.* **по~**) (*maths., etc.*) to construct; to formulate; to express; **с. многоуго́льник** to construct a polygon; **с. у́гол** to plot an angle; **с. фра́зу** to construct a sentence; **с. мысль** to express a thought. **3.** (*pf.* **со~**) (*in phrr. denoting facial expressions, etc.*) to make; **с. гла́зки** to make eyes; **с. грима́сы, с. ро́жу** to make, pull faces; **с. из себя́ дурака́** to make a fool of o.s. **4.** (**на**+*p.*) to base (on). **5.** (*impf. only*): **с. пла́ны** to make plans, plan; **с. себе́ иллю́зии** to create illusions for o.s. **6.** (*pf.* **по~**) (*mil.*) to draw up, form (up).

стро́|иться, юсь, ишься *impf.* (*of* **по~**) **1.** to build (*a house, etc.*) for o.s. **2.** (*mil.*) to draw up, form up; **стро́йся!** (*mil.*) fall in! **3.** *pass. of* **~ить**

стро|й, я, о ~е, в ~ю́, *pl.* **~и, ~ев** *m.* **1.** system, order, régime; **обще́ственный с.** social system, social order; **феода́льный с.** feudal system. **2.** (*ling.*) system, structure. **3.** (*mus.*) pitch. **4.** (*pl.* **~и́, ~ёв**) (*mil., naut., aeron.*) formation; **развёрнутый с.** (extended) line; **разо́мкнутый с.** extended order; **со́мкнутый с.** close order; **расчленённый с.** deployed formation; **с. пе́ленга** (*naut.*) line of bearing; **с. фро́нта** (*naut.*) line abreast; **в ко́нном ~ю́** mounted; **в пе́шем ~ю́** dismounted. **5.** (*mil.*) unit in formation; **пе́ред ~ем** in front of the ranks. **6.** (*mil. and fig.*) service, commission; **ввести́ в с.** to put into commission; **вы́вести из ~я** to disable; to put out of action; **вступи́ть в с.** to come into service, come into operation; **вы́йти из ~я** to be disabled; to become unserviceable; **оста́ться в ~ю́** (*mil.*) to remain in the ranks; (*fig.*) to remain at one's post.

строй... *comb. form, abbr. of* **строи́тельный**

стро́йк|а, и *f.* **1.** building, construction. **2.** building-site.

стройматериа́л|ы, -ов *no sg.* building *or* construction materials.

стро́йност|ь, и *f.* **1.** proportion. **2.** (*mus., etc.*) harmony; balance; order.

стро́|йный (~ен, ~йна́, ~йно) *adj.* **1.** (*of the human figure*) well-proportioned; (*of a woman*) shapely, having a good figure; svelte. **2.** (*mus., etc.*) harmonious; well-balanced; orderly; well put together.

строк|а́, и́, *pf.* **∠и, ~, ~а́м** *f.* line; **кра́сная с., абза́цная с.** (*typ.*) break line; **с. в ~у́** line by line; **нача́ть с но́вой ~и́** to begin a new paragraph; **чита́ть ме́жду ~** to read between the lines.

стро́н|уть, у, ешь *pf.* (*of* **стра́гивать**) (*coll.*) to move out, shift.

стро́н|уться, усь, ешься *pf.* (*of* **стра́гиваться**) (*intrans.*; *coll.*) to move (out).

стро́нци|й, я *m.* (*chem.*) strontium.

строп, а *m.* sling (rope); shroud line (*of parachute*).

стропи́л|о, а *nt.* rafter, truss, beam.

строптив|ец, ца *m.* obstinate pers.

строптивост|ь, и *f.* obstinacy, refractoriness.

строптив|ый (~, ~а) *adj.* obstinate, refractory; shrewish.

строф|а́, ы́, *pl.* **∠ы, ~, ~а́м** *f.* (*liter.*) stanza, strophe.

строфа́нт, а *m.* (*bot. and pharm.*) strophanthus

строфи́ческий *adj.* (*liter.*) strophic.

строчёный *adj.* stitched.

строч|и́ть, у́, ∠и́шь *impf.* (*of* **на~**[1]) **1.** to stitch. **2.** (*coll.*) to scribble, dash off. **3.** (*coll.*) to bang away (*with automatic weapons*).

стро́чк|а[1], **и** *f.* stitch.

стро́чк|а[2], **и** *f.* = **строка́; списа́ть ~у в ~у** to copy out verbatim.

строчн|о́й *adj.*: **~а́я бу́ква** small letter, lower-case letter; **писа́ть с ~о́й бу́квы** to write a small letter.

струбци́н|а, ы *f.* (*tech.*) (screw) clamp, cramp.

струг[1], **а** *m.* (*tech.*) plane.

струг[2], **а** *m.* (*obs.*) boat.

стру́жк|а, и *f.* shaving, filing; **снять ~у с кого́-н.** (*sl.*) to tear s.o. off a strip.

стру|и́ть, и́т *impf.* to pour, shed.

стру|и́ться, и́тся *impf.* to stream, flow.

стру́йно-черни́льный *adj.*: **с. при́нтер** inkjet printer.

структу́р|а, ы *f.* structure.

структурали́зм, а *m.* (*ling.*) structuralism.

структурали́ст, а *m.* (*ling.*) structuralist.

структу́рный *adj.* structural; structured.

струн|а́, ы́, *pl.* **∠ы** *f.* string (*of mus. instrument, tennis racket, etc.*); **сла́бая с.** weak point.

стру́н|ка, ки *f. dim. of* **~а́; вы́тянуться в ~ку, стать в ~ку** to stand at attention; **ходи́ть по ~ке (у, пе́ред)** to be at the beck and call (of), dance attendance (on).

стру́нник, а *m.* player on stringed instrument.

стру́нный *adj.* (*mus.*): **с. инструме́нт** stringed instrument; **с. орке́стр** string orchestra.

струп, а, *pl.* **∠ья, ∠ьев** *m.* scab.

стру́|сить, шу, сишь *pf. of* **тру́сить**

стручко́вый *adj.* leguminous; **с. пе́рец** capsicum; **с. горо́шек** peas in the pod.

струч|о́к, ка́ *m.* pod.

стру|я́, и́, *pl.* **∠и** *f.* **1.** jet, spurt, stream; current (*of air*); **бить ~ёй** to spurt. **2.** (*fig.*) spirit; impetus; **внести́ све́жую ~ю (в+*a.*)** to infuse a fresh spirit (into). **3.** (*obs., poet.*) water.

стря́па|ть, ю *impf.* (*of* **со~**) (*coll.*) to cook; (*fig.*) to cook up, concoct.

стряпн|я́, и́ *f.* (*coll.*) cooking; (*fig., pej.*) concoction.

стряпу́х|а, и *f.* (*coll.*) cook.

стря́пч|ий, его *m.* **1.** (*hist.*) officer of tsar's household (*in Muscovite Russia*). **2.** (*hist.*) scrivener, attorney. **3.** (*obs.*) solicitor.

стряс|а́ть, а́ю *impf. of* **~ти́**

стряс|ти́, у́, ёшь, *past* **~, ~ла́** *pf.* (*of* **~а́ть**) to shake off, shake down.

стряс|ти́сь, ётся, *past* **∠ся, ~ла́сь** *pf.* **(над, с+*i.*;** *coll.*) to befall; **беда́ ~ла́сь с на́ми** a disaster befell us.

стря́хива|ть, ю *impf. of* **стряхну́ть**

стрях|ну́ть, ну́, нёшь *pf.* (*of* **∠ивать**) to shake off.

ст. ст. (*abbr. of* **ста́рый стиль**) OS, Old Style (*of calendar*).

студене́|ть, ет *impf.* (*coll.*) to thicken, acquire the consistency of jelly.

студени́ст|ый (~, ~а) *adj.* jelly-like.

студе́нт, а *m.* student, undergraduate; **с.-ме́дик** medical student; **с.-юри́ст** law student.

студе́нт|ка, ки *f. of* **~**

студе́нческ|ий *adj. of* **студе́нт; с. коллекти́в** the student body; **~ое общежи́тие** student hostel, hall of residence.

студе́нчеств|о, а *nt.* **1.** (*collect.*) students. **2.** student days.

студён|ый (~, ~а) *adj.* (*coll.*) very cold, bitter, freezing; *as pred.* **~о** it is freezing.

сту́д|ень, ня *m.* galantine; aspic; (meat- *or* fish-)jelly.

студи́|ец, йца *m.* (*coll.*) student (*of art school, drama school, music school, etc.*).

студи́|йка, йки *f. of* **~ец**

студи́йн|ый *adj. of* **сту́дия; ~ая радиопереда́ча** studio broadcast.

сту|ди́ть, жу́, ∠дишь *impf.* (*of* **о~**) to cool.

сту́ди|я, и *f.* **1.** (*artist's or broadcasting*) studio, workshop. **2.** (*art, drama, music, etc.*) school.

сту́ж|а, и *f.* severe cold, hard frost.

стук[1], **а** *m.* knock; tap; thump; **с. в дверь** knock at the door; **с. колёс** rumble of wheels; **с. копы́т** clatter of hooves; **с.! с.!** (*onomat.*) knock!, knock!

стук[2] (*coll.*) *as pred.* = **∠нул**

сту́к|ать(ся), аю(сь) *impf. of* **~нуть(ся)**

стука́ч, а́ *m.* (*sl.*) stool-pigeon (= *informer*).

сту́к|нуть, ну, нешь *pf.* (*of* **~ать**) **1.** to knock; to bang; to tap; to rap; **с. в дверь** to knock, to bang; tap, rap at (on) the door; **с. кулако́м по́ столу** to bang one's fist on the table. **2.** to bang, hit, strike; **с. кого́-н. по спине́** to bang s.o. on the back. **3.** (*sl.*) to do in, do for (= *to kill*). **4.** (*sl.*) to knock back, down (= *to drink*). **5.** *pf. only* (*impers.+d.*; *coll.*): **ему́ пятьдеся́т ско́ро ∠нет** he will soon be fifty. **6.** (*coll.*): **ему́ вдруг ~нуло в го́лову** he suddenly had a bright idea.

сту́к|нуться, нусь, нешься *pf.* (*of* **∠аться**) **(о, обо+*a.*)** to knock o.s. (against), bang o.s. (against), bump o.s. (against).

стукотн|я́, и́ *f.* (*coll.*) knocking, banging, tapping, rapping.

стул, а, *pl.* **∠ья, ∠ьев** *m.* **1.** chair; **сиде́ть ме́жду двух ∠ьев** to fall between two stools. **2.** (*med.*) stool.

сту́лик, а *m.* small chair.

стульча́к, а́ *m.* (lavatory) seat.

сту́льчик, а *m.* stool.

сту́п|а, ы *f.* mortar.

ступ|а́ть, а́ю *impf. of* **~и́ть; ~а́й(те) сюда́!** come here!; **~а́й(те)!** be off!, clear out!

ступе́нчатый *adj.* stepped, graduated, graded.

ступ|е́нь, е́ни *f.* **1.** (*g. pl.* **~е́ней**) step (*of stairs*); rung (*of ladder*). **2.** (*g. pl.* **~ене́й**) stage, grade, level, phase.

ступе́нь|ка, ки *f.* = **~ 1.**

ступ|и́ть, лю́, ∠ишь *pf.* (*of* **~а́ть**) to step, take a step; to tread; **тяжело́ с.** to tread heavily; **с. че́рез поро́г** to cross the threshold.

ступи́ц|а, ы *f.* nave, hub (*of a wheel.*).

ступн|я́, и́, *pl.* **~и́, ~е́й** *f.* **1.** foot. **2.** sole (*of foot*).

стуч|а́ть, у́, и́шь *impf.* **1.** (*pf.* **по~**) to knock; to bang; to tap; to rap; (*of teeth*) to chatter. **2.** *impf.* (*3rd pers. only*) to hammer, pulse, thump, pound; **~и́т в виска́х** blood hammers in the temples; **се́рдце у неё ~а́ло** her heart was pounding.

стуч|а́ться, у́сь, и́шься *impf.* (*of* **по~**) **(в+*a.*)** to knock (at); **с. в дверь** to knock at the door (*also fig.*).

стуш|ева́ть, у́ю *pf.* (*of* **~ёвывать**) **1.** (*art*) to shade off. **2.** (*fig., coll.*) to smooth over, efface.

стуш|ева́ться, у́юсь *pf.* (*of* **~ёвываться**) **1.** (*art*) to shade off. **2.** (*coll.*) to retire into the background; to efface o.s. **3.** to be covered with confusion.

стушёвыва|ть(ся), ю(сь) *impf. of* **стушева́ть(ся)**

стыд, а́ *m.* shame; **к на́шему ~у́** to our shame; **сгоре́ть со ~а́** to burn with shame; **с. и срам!** for shame!; it's a sin and a shame!

сты|ди́ть, жу́, ди́шь *impf.* (*of* **при~**) to shame, put to shame.

сты|ди́ться, жу́сь, ди́шься *impf.* (*of* **по~**) **(+*g.*)** to be ashamed (of).

стыдли́в|ый (~, ~а) *adj.* bashful.

сты́дно *as pred.* it is a shame; **ему́**, *etc.*, **с.** he, *etc.*, is ashamed; **как тебе́ не с.!** you ought to be ashamed of yourself!
сты́дный *adj.* shameful.
стык, а *m.* **1.** (*tech.*) joint, junction, butt. **2.** (*mil.*) meeting-point of flanks of adjacent units. **3.** (*fig.*) junction, meeting-point; **с. доро́г** road junction; **на ∠е двух веко́в** at the turn of the century.
стык|ова́ть, у́ю *impf.* (*of* **со~**) (*tech.*) to join.
стык|ова́ться, у́юсь *impf.* (*of* **со~**) (*tech.*) to join (*intrans.*); (*of space vehicles*) to dock, rendezvous.
стыко́вк|а, и *f.* (*of space vehicles*) docking, rendezvous.
стыков|о́й *adj. of* **стык 1.**; (*rail.*): **~а́я накла́дка** fish-plate; **~о́е соедине́ние, с. шов** butt-weld, butt-joint.
сты́н|уть, у, ешь, *past* **стыл, сты́ла** *impf.* **1.** to cool, get cool. **2.** to become frozen over. **3.** (*fig.*): **кровь ~ет в жи́лах** one's blood freezes.
стыть = сты́нуть
сты́чк|а, и *f.* **1.** skirmish, clash. **2.** (*coll.*) squabble.
стюарде́сс|а, ы *f.* stewardess; (*on aeroplane*) air hostess.
стяг, а *m.* (*rhet.*) banner.
стя́гива|ть(ся), ю(сь) *impf. of* **стяну́ть(ся)**
стяжа́тел|ь, я *m.* grasping pers., pers. on the make; money-grubber.
стяжа́тел|ьный (~ен, ~ьна) *adj.* greedy, grasping, on the make.
стяжа́|ть, ю *impf. and pf.* **1.** to gain, win. **2.** (*impf. only*) to seek, court; **с. сла́ву** to court fame.
стя|ну́ть[1], **ну́, ∠нешь** *pf.* (*of* **∠гивать**) **1.** to tighten; to pull together; **с. на себе́ по́яс** to tighten one's belt; **с. шине́ль ремнём** to strap in a greatcoat. **2.** (*mil.*) to gather, assemble (*trans.*). **3.** (*impers., coll.*) to have cramp; **но́гу у меня́ ~ну́ло** I have cramp in my legs.
стя|ну́ть[2], **ну́, ∠нешь** *pf.* (*of* **∠гивать**) **1.** to pull off. **2.** (*coll.*) to pinch, steal.
стя|ну́ться, ну́сь, ∠нешься *pf.* (*of* **∠гиваться**) **1.** to tighten (*intrans.*). **2.** to gird o.s. tightly. **3.** (*mil.*) to gather, assemble (*intrans.*).
су *nt. indecl.* sou (*French coin*).
суахи́ли *m. indecl.* Swahili.
субалте́рн-офице́р, а *m.* (*obs.*) subaltern.
субаре́нд|а, ы *f.* sub-lease.
субарендá́тор, а *m.* sub-tenant.
суббо́т|а, ы *f.* Saturday; **Вели́кая с.** Holy Saturday.
суббо́т|ний *adj. of* **~а**
суббо́тник, а *m.* subbotnik (*in former USSR, voluntary unpaid work on days off, originally esp. on Saturdays*).
субве́нци|я, и *f.* grant, subsidy, subvention.
сублима́т, а *m.* (*chem.*) sublimate.
сублима́ци|я, и *f.* (*chem.*) sublimation.
сублими́р|овать, ую *impf. and pf.* (*chem.*) to sublimate, sublime.
субмари́н|а, ы *f.* (*naut.*; *obs.*) submarine.
субордина́ци|я, и *f.* (system of) seniority.
субре́тк|а, и *f.* soubrette.
субсиди́р|овать, ую *impf. and pf.* to subsidize.
субси́ди|я, и *f.* subsidy, grant(-in-aid).
субстантиви́р|овать, ую *impf. and pf.* (*ling.*) to substantivize.
субста́нци|я, и *f.* (*phil.*) substance.
субстра́т, а *m.* **1.** (*phil.*) substance. **2.** (*biol., geol., and ling.*) substratum.
субти́льност|ь, и *f.* tenuousness; delicateness; frailty.
субти́л|ьный (~ен, ~ьна) *adj.* (*coll.*) tenuous; delicate; frail; (*obs.*) subtle, delicate.
субти́тр, а *m.* subtitle (*in film*).
субтро́пик|и, ов *no sg.* subtropics.
субтропи́ческий *adj.* subtropical.
субъе́кт, а *m.* **1.** (*phil., gram.*) subject; (*phil.*) the self, the ego. **2.** (*med., leg.*) subject; **истери́чный с.** hysterical subject. **3.** (*coll.*) fellow, character, type; **подозри́тельный с.** suspicious character.
субъективи́зм, а *m.* **1.** (*phil.*) subjectivism. **2.** subjectivity.
субъективи́ст, а *m.* (*phil.*) subjectivist.
субъективисти́ческий *adj.* (*phil.*) subjectivist.
субъекти́вност|ь, и *f.* subjectivity.
субъекти́в|ный (~ен, ~на) *adj.* subjective.
субъе́кт|ный *adj. of* **~**
сувени́р, а *m.* souvenir.
сувере́н, а *m.* (*pol., leg.*) sovereign.
суверените́т, а *m.* (*pol., leg.*) sovereignty.
сувере́нный *adj.* (*pol., leg.*) sovereign.
суво́ров|ец, ца *m.* pupil of Suvorov military school.
сугли́нистый *adj.* loamy; argillaceous.
сугли́н|ок, ка *m.* loam, loamy soil.
сугро́б, а *m.* snow-drift.
сугу́бо *adv.* especially, particularly; exclusively.
сугу́б|ый (~, ~а) *adj.* **1.** (*obs.*) double, two-fold. **2.** especial, particular; exclusive.
суд, а́ *m.* **1.** court, law-court; **с. Бо́жий** (*hist.*) trial by single combat *or* by ordeal; **с. че́сти** court of honour; **зал ~а́** court-room; **заседа́ние ~а́** sitting of the court; **се́ссия ~а́** court session; **на ~е́** in court; **Междунаро́дный Суд** International Court of Justice. **2.** (*fig.*) court; trial, legal proceedings; **с. да де́ло** (*coll.*) hearing (of a case); (*fig.*) long-drawn-out proceedings; **вы́звать в с.** to summons, subpoena; **пода́ть в с. на кого́-н.** to bring an action against s.o.; **отда́ть под с., преда́ть ~у́** to prosecute; **быть под ~о́м** to be on trial; **на тебя́ и ~а́ нет** no one can blame you. **3.** (*collect.*) the judges; the bench. **4.** judgement, verdict; **отда́ть на с. пото́мства** to submit to the verdict of posterity.
суда́к, а́ *m.* pike-perch (*fish*).
Суда́н, а *m.* (the) Sudan.
суда́н|ец, ца *m.* Sudanese.
суда́н|ка, ки *f.* **1.** *f. of* **~ец. 2.** = **~ская трава́**
суда́нск|ий *adj.* Sudanese; **~ая трава́** Sudan grass (*Sorghum halepense*).
суда́рын|я, и *f.* (*obs.*; *mode of address*) madam, ma'am.
су́дар|ь, я *m.* (*obs.*; *mode of address*) sir.
суда́ч|ить, у, ишь *impf.* (*coll.*) to gossip, tittle-tattle.
суде́бник, а *m.* (*hist.*) code of laws.
суде́бн|ый *adj.* judicial; legal; forensic; **~ые изде́ржки** costs; **с. исполни́тель** officer of the court; **~ая медици́на** forensic medicine; **~ая оши́бка** miscarriage of justice; **~ая пала́та** (*hist.*) (regional) appellate court; **~ым поря́дком, в ~ом поря́дке** in legal form; **с. при́став** (*obs.*) bailiff; **~ое разбира́тельство** legal proceedings, hearing of a case; **~ое реше́ние** court decision, court order; **с. сле́дователь** investigator; coroner; **~ое сле́дствие** investigation in court, inquest.
суде́йск|ая, ой *f.* **1.** judge's room; judge's quarters. **2.** referees' room.
суде́йск|ий *adj.* **1.** judge's; *as n.* (*obs.*) **с., ~ого** *m.* officer of the court. **2.** (*sport*) referee's, umpire's; **с. свисто́к** referee's whistle.
суде́йств|о, а *nt.* (*sport*) refereeing, umpiring; judging.
судёныш|ко, ка, *pl.* **~ки, ~ек** *nt.* (*coll.*) tub (*vessel, ship*).
суди́лищ|е, а *nt.* (*obs. or joc.*) court of law.
суди́мост|ь, и *f.* (*leg.*) conviction(s); **снять с кого́-н. с.** to expunge s.o.'s previous convictions.
су|ди́ть, жу́, ∠дишь *impf.* **1.** to judge; to form an opinion; **наско́лько мы могли́ с.** as far as we could judge; **~ди́те са́ми** judge for yourself; **∠дя (по+***d.***)** judging (by), to judge (from); **∠дя по всему́** to all appearances; **с. да (и) ряди́ть** (*coll.*) to lay down the law, expatiate. **2.** (*leg.*) to try. **3.** to judge, pass judgement (upon); **не ~ди́те их стро́го** don't be hard on them. **4.** (*sport*) to referee, umpire. **5.** (*also pf.*) to predestine, preordain; **но Бог ~ди́л ино́е** but God decreed a different fate.
су|ди́ться, жу́сь, ∠дишься *impf.* (**с+***i.*) to be at law (with).
су́д|но[1], **на,** *pl.* **~а́, ~о́в** *nt.* vessel, craft; **с. на возду́шной поду́шке** hovercraft; **с. на подво́дных кры́льях** hydrofoil.
су́д|но[2], **на,** *pl.* **~на, ~ен** *nt.* chamber-pot; **подкладно́е с.** bed-pan.
су́дный *adj.* (*obs.*) **1.** court; judicial. **2.: С. день** (*relig.*) Day of Judgement.
судове́рф|ь, и *f.* shipyard.
судовладе́л|ец, ьца *m.* shipowner.

судоводи́тел|ь, я *m.* navigator.
судовожде́ни|е, я *nt.* navigation.
судов|о́й *adj.* ship's; marine; **~а́я кома́нда** ship's crew; **~о́е свиде́тельство** ship's certificate of registry.
судоговоре́ни|е, я *nt.* (*leg.*) pleading(s).
суд|о́к, ка́ *m.* **1.** sauce-boat, gravy-boat. **2.** cruet(-stand). **3.** (*usu. pl.*) set of dishes with covers (*for carrying food*).
судомо́йк|а, и *f.* kitchen-maid, scullery maid, washer-up.
судопроизво́дств|о, а *nt.* legal proceedings.
судоремо́нт, а *m.* ship repair.
судоремо́нт|ный *adj. of* ~
су́дорог|а, и *f.* cramp, convulsion, spasm.
су́дорож|ный (~ен, ~на) *adj.* convulsive, spasmodic (*also fig.*).
судострое́ни|е, я *nt.* shipbuilding.
судострои́тел|ь, я *m.* shipbuilder, shipwright.
судострои́тельный *adj.* shipbuilding.
судоустро́йств|о, а *nt.* judicial system.
судохо́д|ный (~ен, ~на) *adj.* **1.** navigable; **с. кана́л** shipping canal. **2.: ~ная компа́ния** shipping company.
судохо́дств|о, а *nt.* navigation, shipping.
суд|ьба́, ьбы́, *pl.* **~́ьбы, ~́еб, ~́ьбам** *f.* fate, fortune, destiny, lot; **~́ьбы страны́** the fortunes of the country; **благодари́ть ~ьбу́** to thank one's lucky stars; **искуша́ть ~ьбу́** to tempt fate, tempt providence; **каки́ми ~ьба́ми?** (*coll.*) fancy meeting you here!; how did you get here?; **не с. нам** (+*inf.*) we are not fated (to).
судьби́н|а, ы *f.* (*folk., poet.*) fate, lot.
суд|ья́, ьи́, *pl.* **~́ьи, ~е́й, ~́ьям** *m.* **1.** judge; **миров**о́й **с.** (*obs.*) Justice of the Peace; **трете́йский с.** arbitrator; **я вам не с.** who am I to judge you? **2.** (*sport*) referee, umpire; **с. на ли́нии** linesman.
су́д|я *see* **~и́ть**
суд|я́ *pres. ger. of* **~и́ть**
суеве́р, а *m.* superstitious pers.
суеве́ри|е, я *nt.* superstition.
суеве́р|ный (~ен, ~на) *adj.* superstitious.
суесло́ви|е, я *nt.* (*obs.*) idle talk.
сует|а́, ы́ *f.* **1.** vanity; **с. суе́т** vanity of vanities. **2.** bustle, fuss.
суе|ти́ться, чу́сь, ти́шься *impf.* to bustle, fuss.
суетли́в|ый (~, ~а) *adj.* fussy, bustling.
су́етност|ь, и *f.* vanity.
су́ет|ный (~ен, ~на) *adj.* vain, empty.
суетн|я́, и́ *f.* fuss, bustle.
сужде́ни|е, я *nt.* opinion; judgement (*in logic*).
суждён|ный (~, ~а́) *p.p.p. of* **суди́ть; нам бы́ло ~о́ встре́титься** we were fated to meet.
су́жен|ая, ой *f.* (*folk poet.*) intended (*bride*).
су́жен|ый, ого *m.* (*folk poet.*) intended (*bridegroom*).
су́жива|ть(ся), ю, ет(ся) *impf. of* **су́зить(ся)**
су́|зить, жу, зишь *pf.* (*of* **~живать**) to narrow (*trans.*).
су́|зиться, зится *pf.* (*of* **~живаться**) to narrow (*intrans*), get narrow; to taper.
сук, а́, о ~е́, на ~у́, *pl.* **~и́, ~о́в** *and* **су́чья, су́чьев** *m.* **1.** bough. **2.** knot (*in wood*).
су́к|а, и *f.* bitch (*also as term of abuse*).
су́к|ин *adj. of* **~а; с. сын** (*as term of abuse*) son of a bitch.
сук|но́, на́, *pl.* **~́на, ~́он** *nt.* (heavy, coarse) cloth; **положи́ть под с.** (*fig.*) to shelve.
сукнова́л, а *m.* fuller.
сукнова́льн|ый *adj.* fulling; **~ая гли́на** fuller's earth.
сукнова́льн|я, и *f.* fullery, fulling mill.
сукова́т|ый (~, ~а) *adj.* with many twigs; (*of planks*) knotty.
суко́нк|а, и *f.* piece of cloth, rag.
суко́нн|ый *adj.* **1.** cloth; **~ая фа́брика** cloth mill. **2.** (*fig.*) rough, clumsy, crude; **с. язы́к** rough tongue, clumsy way of speaking; **~ое ры́ло** (*obs.*) merchant.
су́кровиц|а, ы *f.* **1.** (*physiol.*) lymph, serum. **2.** (*med.*) ichor, pus.
сулем|а́, ы́ *f.* (*chem., med.*) corrosive sublimate, mercuric chloride.
сулем|о́вый *adj. of* **~а́**
суле|я́, и́ *f.* (*obs.*) flask.
сул|и́ть, ю́, и́шь *impf.* (*of* **по~**) to promise; **с. золоты́е го́ры** to promise the earth; **э́то не ~и́т ничего́ хоро́шего** this does not bode well.
султа́н[1], а *m.* sultan.
султа́н[2], а *m.* plume (*on headdress, etc.*).
султана́т, а *m.* sultanate.
султа́н|ский *adj. of* **~[1]**
султа́нш|а, и *f.* sultana (*sultan's wife*).
сульфа́т, а *m.* (*chem.*) sulphate.
сульфи́д, а *m.* (*chem.*) sulphide.
сульфо... *comb. form* (*chem.*) sulpho-.
сум|а́, ы́ *f.* bag, pouch; **с. перемётная** (*fig.*) weathercock; **пусти́ть с ~о́й** to ruin, reduce to beggary; **ходи́ть с ~о́й** to beg, go a-begging.
сумасбро́д, а *m.* madcap.
сумасбро́д|ка, ки *f. of* ~
сумасбро́|дить, жу, дишь *impf.* (*coll.*) to behave wildly, extravagantly.
сумасбро́днича|ть, ю *impf.* (*coll.*) = **сумасбро́дить**
сумасбро́д|ный (~ен, ~на) *adj.* wild, extravagant.
сумасбро́дств|о, а *nt.* wild, extravagant behaviour.
сумасше́дш|ий *adj.* **1.** mad; *as n.* **с., ~его** *m.* madman, lunatic; **~ая, ~ей** *f.* madwoman; **бу́йный с.** raving, violent lunatic; **объяви́ть кого́-н. ~им** to certify s.o. **2.: с. дом** (*coll.*) lunatic asylum, madhouse. **3.** (*fig.*) mad, lunatic; **~ая ско́рость** lunatic speed; **э́то бу́дет сто́ить ~их де́нег** it will cost the earth.
сумасше́стви|е, я *nt.* madness, lunacy.
сумасше́ств|овать, ую *impf.* (*coll.*) to act like a madman.
сумато́х|а, и *f.* confusion, chaos, turmoil, hurly-burly.
сумато́шлив|ый (~, ~а) *adj.* (*coll.*) given to fussing.
сумато́ш|ный (~ен, ~на) *adj.* = **~ливый**
Сума́тр|а, ы *f.* Sumatra.
суматри́йский *adj.* Sumatran.
сумбу́р, а *m.* confusion, chaos.
сумбу́р|ный (~ен, ~на) *adj.* confused, chaotic.
су́меречник, а *m.* crepuscular animal.
су́супмереч|ный (~ен, ~на) *adj.* **1.** twilight, dusk. **2.** (*zool.*) crepuscular.
су́мер|ки, ек *no sg.* twilight, dusk.
су́мернича|ть, ю *impf.* (*coll.*) to sit in the twilight.
суме́|ть, ю *pf.* (*of* **уме́ть**) (+*inf.*) to be able (to), manage (to).
су́мк|а, и *f.* **1.** bag, handbag; satchel; **с.-паке́т** paper bag; **поясна́я с.** waist *or* hip-pouch; bum-bag. **2.** (*biol.*) pouch.
су́мм|а, ы *f.* sum; **вся с., о́бщая с.** sum total; **в ~е** all in all.
сумма́р|ный (~ен, ~на) *adj.* **1.** total. **2.** summary.
сумми́р|овать, ую *impf.* **1.** to sum up. **2.** to summarize.
су́мнича|ть, ю *pf. of* **у́мничать**
сумня́ся *only in phr.* (*obs. or joc.*) **ничто́же с., ничто́же сумня́шеся** without a second's hesitation, not batting an eyelid.
су́мрак, а *m.* dusk, twilight.
су́мрач|ный (~ен, ~на) *adj.* gloomy (*also fig.*); murky.
су́мчат|ый *adj.* **1.** (*zool.*) marsupial. **2.: ~ые грибы́** (*bot.*) Ascomycetes.
сумя́тиц|а, ы *f.* confusion, chaos.
сунду́к, а́ *m.* trunk, box, chest.
су́н|уть(ся), у(сь), ешь(ся) *pf. of* **сова́ть(ся)**
суп, а, *pl.* **~ы́** *m.* soup.
суперарби́тр, а *m.* chief arbitrator.
суперобло́жк|а, и *f.* dust-cover, jacket (*of book*).
суперфосфа́т, а *m.* (*chem.*) superphosphate.
су́пес|ный *adj. of* **~ь**
су́пес|ок, ка *m.* = **~ь**
супеча́ный *adj.* = **су́песный**
су́пес|ь, и *f.* sandy soil, sandy loam.
супи́н, а *m.* (*ling.*) supine.
су́п|ить, лю, ишь *impf.* (*of* **на~**): **с. бро́ви** to knit one's brows, frown.
су́п|иться, люсь, ишься *impf.* (*of* **на~**) = **су́пить бро́ви**
супов|о́й *adj. of* **суп; ~а́я ло́жка** soup ladle; **~а́я ми́ска** soup tureen.
супо́н|ь, и *f.* hame-strap.

супорóс(н)ая *adj.*: **с. свинья́** sow in farrow.
супостáт, а *m.* (*arch., or rhet.*) adversary, foe; Satan.
супрoти́в (*coll.*) **1.** *prep.+g.* against. **2.** *adv. and prep.+g.* opposite.
супру́г, а *m.* **1.** husband, spouse. **2.** (*pl.*) husband and wife, married couple.
супру́г|а, и *f.* wife, spouse.
супру́жеский *adj.* conjugal, matrimonial.
супру́жеств|о, а *nt.* conjugal state, matrimony, wedlock.
супря́г|а, и *f.* (*dial.*) **1.** yoke (*of draught cattle*). **2.** joint tilling of land. **3.: в ~е (с+*i.*)** together (with).
сургу́ч, á *m.* sealing-wax.
сургу́ч|ный *adj. of* **~**
сурди́нк|а, и *f.* (*mus.*) mute, sordine; **под ~у** (*coll.*) on the quiet.
суре́пиц|а, ы *f.* (*bot.*) **1.** cole-seed, rape. **2.** charlock.
суре́п|ный *adj. of* **~ица; ~ное мáсло** rape-oil, colza oil.
су́рик, а *m.* (*chem.*) minium, red lead.
су́рик|овый *adj. of* **~**
суро́вост|ь, и *f.* severity, sternness.
суро́в|ый (~, ~а) *adj.* **1.** (*in var. senses*) severe, stern; rigorous; bleak. **2.** (*text.*) unbleached, brown; **~ое полотно́** crash; brown Holland.
сур|óк, кá *m.* marmot; **спать как с.** to sleep like a log.
суррогáт, а *m.* substitute.
суррогáтный *adj.* substitute, ersatz.
сурьм|á, ы́ *f.* **1.** (*chem.*) antimony. **2.** hair-dye (*containing antimony*), kohl.
сурьм|и́ть, лю́, и́шь *impf.* (*of* **на~**) (*obs.*) to dye, darken (*hair, eye-brows, etc.*).
сурьм|и́ться, лю́сь, и́шься *impf.* (*of* **на~**) (*obs.*) to dye, darken one's hair, eye-brows, etc.
сурьмянóй *adj.* antimony.
сурьмя́н|ый *adj.* = **~óй**
сусáл|ить, ю, ишь *impf.* (*obs.*) to tinsel.
сусáл|ь, и *f.* (*obs.*) tinsel.
сусáльн|ый *adj.* **1.** tinsel; **~ое зóлото** gold leaf. **2.** (*fig., coll.*) sugary.
су́слик, а *m.* (*zool.*) gopher.
сусл|и́ть, ю, ишь *impf.* (*of* **за~**) (*coll.*) to beslobber; to spatter.
су́сл|о, а *nt.* **1.: виногрáдное с.** must; **пивнóе с.** wort. **2.** grape-juice.
сусóл|ить, ю, ишь *impf.* (*of* **за~**) (*coll.*) = **сусли́ть**
суспензóри|й, я *m.* (*sport*) jock-strap.
сустáв, а *m.* (*anat.*) joint, articulation; **неподви́жность ~ов** (*med.*) anchylosis.
суставнóй *adj. of* **сустáв**
сутáн|а, ы *f.* soutane.
сутенёр, а *m.* souteneur, ponce.
су́т|ки, ок *no sg.* twenty-four hours; twenty-four-hour period; **цéлые с.** for days and nights.
су́толок|а, и *f.* commotion, hubbub, hurly-burly; **предпрáздничная с.** pre-holiday rush.
су́точ|ный *adj.* **1.** twenty-four-hour; daily; round-the-clock; **~ые дéньги** per diem subsistence allowance; *as n.* **~ые, ~ых = ~ые дéньги. 2.: с. цыплёнок** day-old chick.
суту́л|ить, ю, ишь *impf.* (*of* **с~**) to stoop.
суту́лост|ь, и *f.*: **с. фигу́ры** round shoulders, stoop.
суту́л|ый (~, ~а) *adj.* round-shouldered, stooping.
сут|ь[1], **и** *f.* essence; **с. дéла** the heart, crux of the matter; **по ~и дéла** as a matter of fact, in point of fact.
сут|ь[2] (*arch.*) *3rd pers. pl. pres. of* **быть; э́то не с. вáжно** (*coll.*) this is not so important.
сутя́г|а, и *c.g.* (*coll., obs.*) litigious pers.
сутя́жнича|ть, ю *impf.* (*obs.*) to engage in (malicious) litigation.
сутя́жн|ый *adj.* (*obs.*) litigious; **~ое дéло** malicious litigation.
суфи́зм, а *m.* Sufism.
суфи́ст, а *m.* Sufi.
суфлé *nt. indecl.* (*cul.*) soufflé.
суфлёр, а *m.* (*theatr.*) prompter.
суфлёр|ский *adj. of* **~; ~ская бу́дка** prompt-box.
суфли́р|овать, ую *impf.* (*+d.*) (*theatr.*) to prompt.
суфражи́зм, а *m.* suffragette movement.
суфражи́стк|а, и *f.* suffragette.
су́ффикс, а *m.* (*gram.*) suffix.
суффиксáльный *adj. of* **су́ффикс**
сухáрниц|а, ы *f.* biscuit dish; biscuit barrel.
сухáр|ь, я́ *m.* **1.** rusk. **2.** (*fig., coll.*) dried-up pers.
сух|áя, óй *f.* (*sport*) whitewash (*game in which loser fails to score a single point*); **сдéлать ~у́ю комý-н.** to whitewash s.o.
сухмéн|ь, и *f.* (*dial.*) **1.** dry weather, drought. **2.** dry soil.
су́хо *adv.* **1.** drily; coldly; **нас при́няли с.** we were received coldly. **2.** *as pred.* it is dry; **на у́лице с.** it is dry out of doors; **у меня́ в гóрле с.** my throat is parched.
суховáт|ый (~, ~а) *adj.* dryish.
суховé|й, я *m.* hot dry wind.
суховéй|ный *adj. of* **~**
суходóл, а *m.* waterless valley.
сухожи́ли|е, я *nt.* (*anat.*) tendon, sinew.
сухожи́л|ьный *adj. of* **~ие**
сух|óй (~, ~á, ~о) *adj.* **1.** dry; dried-up; arid; **~и́е дровá** dry firewood; **~óе ру́сло реки́** dried-up river-bed; **~и́м путём** by land, overland; **вы́йти ~и́м из воды́** to come out unscathed. **2.** (*of foodstuffs, etc.*) dry, dried; **~óе молокó** dried milk. **3.** (*of part of body*) dried-up, withered (*also fig.; of persons*). **4.** (*in var. senses*) dry (= *unconnected with, opp. to liquid*); **с. док** dry-dock; **с. закóн** (*hist.*) 'dry law' (*e.g. in USA*); **с. кáшель** dry cough; **~áя мóлния** summer lightning; **~áя перегóнка** dry, destructive distillation; **с. тумáн** fog of dust, smoke, *etc.*; **с. элемéнт** (*elec.*) dry pile. **5.** (*fig.*) dry (= *dull, boring*). **6.** (*fig.*) chilly, cold; **с. приём** chilly reception.
сухолюби́в|ый (~, ~а) *adj.* (*bot.*) xerophilous.
сухомя́тк|а, и *f.* (*coll.*) dry food (*without any beverage*).
сухопáрник, а *m.* (*tech.*) steam dome.
сухопáр|ый (~, ~а) *adj.* (*coll.*) lean, skinny.
сухопу́тн|ый *adj.* land (*opp. marine, air*); **~ые си́лы** (*mil.*) ground forces.
сухору́к|ий (~, ~а) *adj.* without the use of one arm; having a withered arm.
сухостó|й[1], **я** *m.* (*collect.*) dead wood, dead standing trees.
сухостó|й[2], **я** *m.* period before calving (*when cow ceases to give milk*).
су́хост|ь, и *f.* **1.** (*in var. senses*) dryness; aridity. **2.** (*fig.*) chilliness, coldness.
сухот|á, ы́ *f.* **1.** dryness; **у меня́ в гóрле с.** my throat is parched. **2.** dry spell (*of weather*). **3.** (*folk poet.; dial.*) longing, yearning.
сухóтк|а, и *f.* **1.** (*dial.*) wasting, emaciation. **2.: с. спиннóго мóзга** (*med.*) dorsal tabes, locomotor ataxia.
сухóточный *adj.* (*med.*) tabetic.
сухофру́кт|ы, ов *no sg.* dried fruits.
сухощáв|ый (~, ~а) *adj.* lean, skinny.
сухоядéни|е, я *nt.* dry food.
сучёный *adj.* twisted.
суч|и́ть, у́, ~ишь *impf.* (*of* **с~**) **1.** to twist, spin; to throw (*silk*). **2.** (*cul.*) to roll out (*dough*).
сучковáт|ый (~, ~а) *adj.* knotty; gnarled.
суч|óк, кá *m.* **1.** twig. **2.** knot (*in wood*); **без ~кá, без задóринки** (*coll.*) without a hitch.
су́ш|а, и *f.* (dry) land (*opp. sea*).
су́ше *comp. of* **сухóй** *and* **су́хо**
сушéни|е, я *nt.* **1.** drying. **2.** (*coll.*) dried fruit.
сушёный *adj.* dried.
суши́лк|а, и *f.* **1.** drying apparatus, dryer; **напóльная с.** airer; clothes horse. **2.** drying-room. **3.** (*cul.*) drying rack.
суши́льный *adj.* (*tech.*) drying; **с. барабáн** desiccator.
суши́л|ьня, ьни, *g. pl.* **~ен** *f.* drying-room.
суш|и́ть, у́, ~ишь *impf.* to dry (out, up); **с. вёсла** (*naut.; not fig.*) to rest on one's oars.
суш|и́ться, у́сь, ~ишься *impf.* to dry (*intrans.*), get dry.
су́шк|а, и *f.* **1.** drying. **2.** (*cul.*) dry (*ring-shaped*) cracker.
суш|ь, и *f.* **1.** dry spell (*of weather*). **2.** dry place. **3.** dry object.
существéн|ный (~, ~на) *adj.* essential, vital; material; important; **~ное замечáние** remark of material

significance; **~ная попра́вка** important amendment; **игра́ть ~ную роль** to play a vital part.
существи́тельн|ое *adj.*, *only in phr.* **и́мя с.** *or as n.* **с., ~ого** *nt.* noun, substantive.
существ|о́, а́ *nt.* **1.** essence; **по ~у́** in essence, essentially; **говори́ть по ~у́** to speak to the point; **не по ~у́** off the point, beside the point. **2.** being, creature; **люби́мое с.** loved one; **нигде́ не́ было ви́дно ни одного́ живо́го ~а́** there was nowhere a living creature in sight.
существова́ни|е, я *nt.* existence; **сре́дства к ~ю** livelihood; **отрави́ть кому́-н. (всё) с.** to make s.o.'s life a misery.
существ|ова́ть, у́ю *impf.* to exist (= (*i*) to be, be in existence, (*ii*) to live, subsist).
су́щ|ий *adj.* **1.** (*obs.*) existing. **2.** (*coll.*) real; absolute, utter, downright; **с. ад** absolute hell; **~ие пустяки́** utter rubbish.
су́щност|ь, и *f.* essence; **с. де́ла** the point; **в ~и** in essence, at bottom; **в ~и говоря́** really and truly.
Суэ́ц, а *m.* Suez.
Суэ́цк|ий кана́л, ~ого ~а *m.* the Suez Canal.
суя́гная *adj.*: **с. овца́** ewe in yean.
сфабрик|ова́ть, у́ю *pf. of* **фабрикова́ть**
сфа́гновый *adj.* sphagnum.
сфа́гнум, а *m.* (*bot.*) sphagnum, bog-moss.
сфальц|ева́ть, у́ю *pf. of* **фальцева́ть**
сфальши́в|ить, лю, ишь *pf. of* **фальши́вить**
сфантази́р|овать, ую *pf. of* **фантази́ровать**
сфе́р|а, ы *f.* **1.** (*in var. senses*) sphere; realm; **с. влия́ния** (*pol.*) sphere of influence; **вы́сшие ~ы** the upper crust, influential circles; **быть в свое́й ~е** to be on one's own ground. **2.** (*mil.*) zone, area; **с. огня́** zone of fire.
сфери́ческий *adj.* spherical.
сферо́ид, а *m.* (*math.*) spheroid.
сфероида́льный *adj.* (*math.*) spheroidal.
сфинкс, а *m.* sphinx.
сфи́нктер, а *m.* (*anat.*) sphincter.
сформир|ова́ть(ся), у́ю(сь) *pf. of* **формирова́ть(ся)**
сформ|ова́ть, у́ю *pf. of* **формова́ть**
сформули́р|овать, ую *pf. of* **формули́ровать**
сфотографи́р|овать(ся), ую(сь) *pf. of* **фотографи́ровать(ся)**
СФРЮ *f. indecl.* (*abbr. of* ***Социалисти́ческая Федерати́вная Респу́блика Югосла́вия***) Socialist Federal Republic of Yugoslavia.
с.-х. (*abbr. of* **сельскохозя́йственный**) agricultural.
схва|ти́ть, чу́, ~тишь *pf.* **1.** *pf. of* **хвата́ть**[1]. **2.** (*impf.* **~тывать**) (*coll.*) to catch (*a cold, etc.*). **3.** (*impf.* **~тывать**) (*coll.*) to grasp, comprehend; **с. смысл** to grasp the meaning, catch on. **4.** (*impf.* **~тывать**) (*tech.*) to clamp together.
схва|ти́ться, чу́сь, ~тишься *pf.* **1.** *pf. of* **хвата́ться. 2.** (*impf.* **~тываться**) (**с**+*i.*) to grapple (with), come to grips (with) (*also fig.*). **3.** (*impf.* **~тываться**) (**с**+*g.*; *coll.*) to leap (out of, from).
схва́тк|а, и *f.* **1.** skirmish, fight, encounter. **2.** (*coll.*) squabble.
схва́т|ки, ок *no sg.* contractions (*of muscles*); fit, spasm; **родовы́е с.** labour, birth pangs.
схва́тыва|ть(ся), у(сь) *impf. of* **схвати́ть(ся)**
схе́м|а, ы *f.* **1.** diagram, chart; **с. обстано́вки** situation map; **с. ориенти́ров** range card. **2.** sketch, outline, plan; **с. рома́на** plan of a novel. **3.** (*elec., radio*) circuit.
схематизи́р|овать, ую *impf. and pf.* to present in sketchy form, over-simplify.
схемати́зм, а *m.* sketchiness, over-simplification; employment of ready-made categories.
схемати́ческий *adj.* **1.** diagrammatic, schematic. **2.** sketchy, over-simplified.
схемати́ч|ный (~ен, ~на) *adj.* sketchy, over-simplified.
схи́зм|а, ы *f.* (*eccl.*) schism.
схизма́тик, а *m.* (*eccl.*) schismatic.
схизмати́ческий *adj.* (*eccl.*) schismatic.
схи́м|а, ы *f.* (*eccl.*) schema (*strictest monastic rule in Orthodox Church*).
схи́мник, а *m.* (*eccl.*) monk having taken vows of schema.
схи́мниц|а, ы *f.* (*eccl.*) nun having taken vows of schema.
схи́мничес|кий *adj. of* **~тво**
схи́мничеств|о, а *nt.* (*eccl.*) profession and practice of schema.
схитр|и́ть, ю, и́шь *pf. of* **хитри́ть**
схлы́н|уть, у, ешь *pf.* **1.** (*of waves*) to break and flow back. **2.** (*of a crowd*) to break up; to dwindle. **3.** (*of emotions*) to subside.
сход[1]**, а** *m.* **1.** coming off, alighting. **2.** descent.
сход[2]**, а** *m.* (*obs.*) gathering, assembly.
схо|ди́ть[1]**, жу́, ~дишь** *impf. of* **сойти́**
схо|ди́ть[2]**, жу́, ~дишь** *pf.* **1.** to go (*and come back*); (**за**+*i.*) to go to fetch; **с. посмотре́ть** to go to see; **~ди́ за до́ктором!** go and fetch a doctor! **2.** *pf. of* **ходи́ть 11.**
схо|ди́ться, жу́сь, ~дишься *impf. of* **сойти́сь**
схо́дк|а, и *f.* (*obs.*) gathering, assembly.
схо́дн|и, ей *pl.* (*sg.* **~я, ~и** *f.*) gangway, gang-plank.
схо́д|ный (~ен, ~на́, ~но) *adj.* **1.** similar. **2.** (*coll.*) reasonable, fair (*of prices, etc.*).
схо́дств|о, а *nt.* likeness, similarity, resemblance.
схо́дств|овать, ую *impf.* (**с**+*i.*; *obs.*) to resemble.
схо́жест|ь, и *f.* likeness, similarity.
схо́ж|ий (~, ~а) *adj.* like, similar.
схола́ст, а *m.* scholastic.
схола́стик, а *m.* = **схола́ст**
схола́стик|а, и *f.* scholasticism.
схоласти́ческий *adj.* scholastic (*of scholasticism*).
схорон|и́ть(ся), ю́(сь), ~ишь(ся) *pf. of* **хорони́ть(ся)**
сца́па|ть, ю *pf.* (*coll.*) to catch hold (of), lay hold (of).
сцара́п|ать, аю *pf.* (*of* **~ывать**) to scratch off.
сцара́пыва|ть, ю *impf. of* **сцара́пать**
сц|ать, у, ишь, *3rd pers. pl.* **ат, ут** *impf.* (*of* **обосца́ть** *and* **посца́ть**) (*vulg.*) to piss.
сце|ди́ть, жу́, ~дишь *pf.* (*of* **~живать**) to pour off, strain off. decant.
сце́жива|ть, ю *impf. of* **сцеди́ть**
сце́н|а, ы *f.* **1.** (*theatr.*) stage, boards (*also fig.*); **ста́вить на ~е** to stage, put on the stage; **сойти́ со ~ы** to go off the scene, make one's exit (*also fig.*). **2.** (*theatr., liter.*) scene. **3.** (*coll.*) scene; **устра́ивать ~ы** to make scenes.
сцена́ри|й, я *m.* **1.** scenario. **2.** film script; (**по**+*d.*) screen version (of).
сценари́ст, а *m.* scenario writer; script writer.
сцена́риус, а *m.* (*theatr.*; *obs.*) producer's assistant.
сцени́ческ|ий *adj.* stage; **~ая рема́рка** stage direction; **с. шёпот** stage whisper.
сцени́ч|ный (~ен, ~на) *adj.* suitable for the theatre, effective on the stage; **э́та пье́са не ~на** this play is not good theatre.
сцено́граф, а *m.* (*theatr.*) set designer.
сцеп, а *m.* **1.** coupling; drawbar. **2.** couple (*two goods trucks, agric. implements, etc., coupled together*).
сцеп|и́ть, лю́, ~ишь *pf.* (*of* **~ля́ть**) to couple.
сцеп|и́ться, лю́сь, ~ишься *pf.* (*of* **~ля́ться**) **1.** to be coupled. **2.** (**с**+*i.*; *coll.*) to grapple (with), come to grips (with).
сце́пк|а, и *f.* coupling.
сцепле́ни|е, я *nt.* **1.** coupling. **2.** (*phys.*) adhesion; cohesion. **3.** (*tech.*) clutch; **выключе́ние ~я** clutch release. **4.** (*fig.*) accumulation; **с. обстоя́тельств** chain of events.
сцепля́|ть(ся), ю(сь) *impf. of* **сцепи́ть(ся)**
сцепн|о́й *adj.* (*tech.*) coupling; **~о́е ды́шло, с. шату́н** coupling rod; **с. крюк, ~а́я тя́га** drawbar.
сце́пщик, а *m.* (*rail.*) coupler.
сча́лива|ть, ю *impf. of* **сча́лить**
сча́л|ить, ю, ишь *pf.* (*of* **~ивать**) to lash together.
счастли́в|ец, ца *m.* lucky man.
счастли́виц|а, ы *f.* lucky woman.
счастли́вчик, а *m.* (*coll.*) = **счастли́вец**
сча́стливо *adv.* happily; with luck; **с. отде́латься (от)** to have a lucky escape (from); **счастли́во (остава́ться)!** good luck!
счастли́в|ый (сча́стли́в, ~а) *adj.* **1.** happy. **2.** lucky, fortunate. **3.** successful; **~ого пути́!, ~ого пла́вания!** bon voyage!

сча́сть|е, я *nt.* **1.** happiness. **2.** luck, good fortune; **к ~ю, на с., по ~ю** luckily, fortunately; **на на́ше с.** luckily for us; **попыта́ть ~я** to try one's luck.
счерп|а́ть, а́ю *pf.* (*of* **~ывать**) to skim (off).
сче́рпыва|ть, ю *impf. of* **счерпа́ть**
счер|ти́ть, чу́, ~тишь *pf.* (*of* **~чивать**) (*coll.*) to copy, run off.
сче́рчива|ть, ю, *impf. of* **счерти́ть**
сче́сть(ся), сочту́(сь), сочтёшь(ся), *past* **счёл(ся), сочла́(сь)** *impf. of* **счита́ть(ся)**[1]
счёт, а (у), *pl.* **~ы** *and* **~а́** *m.* **1.** *sg. only* counting, calculation, reckoning; **вести́ с.** (*+d.*) to keep count (of); **потеря́ть с.** (*+d.*) to lose count (of); **он не в с.** he does not count; **в два ~а** in a jiffy, in a trice; **без ~у, ~у нет** countless, without number. **2.** *sg. only* (*sport*) score. **3.** (*pl.* **~а́**) bill, account; **пода́ть с.** to present a bill. **4.** (*pl.* **~а́**) (*book-keeping*) account; **откры́ть с.** to open an account; **за с.** (*+g.*) at the expense (of); **на с.** on account; **на с.** (*+g.*) at the account (of), to the account (of). **5.** (*fig.*) account, expense; **в с.** (*+g.*) on the strength (of); **в коне́чном ~е, в после́днем ~е** in the end; **за с.** (*+g.*) at the expense (of); owing (to); **на свой с.** on one's own account; **на чужо́й с.** at others' expense; **на э́тот с.** (*i*) on this score, (*ii*) in this respect, in this department; **предъяви́ть с.** to present a claim; **приня́ть на свой с.** to take as referring to o.s.; **быть на хоро́шем, дурно́м ~у́** to be in good, bad (repute); to stand well, badly; **име́ть на своём ~у́** to have to one's credit; **сбро́сить со ~ов** to dismiss, rule out. **6. ~ы** (*no sg.*; *fig.*) accounts, score(s); **ста́рые ~ы** old scores; **свести́ ~ы (с**+*i.*) to settle a score (with), get even (with). **7.** *see* **~ы**
счётн|ый *adj.* **1.** counting, calculating, computing; **~ая лине́йка** slide-rule; **~ая маши́на** calculator, calculating machine. **2.** accounts, accounting; **с. рабо́тник** accounts clerk; **~ая часть** accounts department.
счетово́д, а *m.* accountant; accounts clerk, ledger clerk.
счетово́дн|ый *adj.* accounting; **~ая кни́га** account book.
счетово́дств|о, а *nt.* accounting.
счётчик[1]**, а** *m.* teller; counter (*pers.*).
счётчик[2]**, а** *m.* meter; counter (*instrument*); **га́зовый с.** gas meter; **с. километра́жа** milometer; **с. магни́тной ле́нты** tape counter.
счётчиц|а, ы *f. of* **счётчик**[1]
счёт|ы[1]**, ов** *no sg.* abacus, counting frame.
счёт|ы[2] *see* **~ 6.**
счисле́ни|е, я *nt.* **1.** numeration, counting; **систе́ма ~я** (*math.*) scale of notation. **2.: с. пути́** (*naut.*) dead reckoning.
счи́|стить, щу, стишь *pf.* (*of* **~ща́ть**) to clean off; to clear away.
счи́|ститься, стится *pf.* (*of* **~ща́ться**) (*of dirt, etc.*) to come off.
счи́тан|ный (~, ~а) *p.p.p. of* **счита́ть; остаю́тся ~ные дни (до)** one can count the days (until).
счита́|ть[1]**, ю** *impf.* (*of* **счесть**) **1.** (*pf. also* **со~**) to count; to compute, reckon; **с. до ста** to count up to a hundred; **не ~я** not counting; **с. звёзды, с. мух** (*coll.*) to be dreaming. **2.** (*+i. or* **за**+*a.*) to count, consider, think; to regard (as); **я ~ю его́ надёжным наблюда́телем, я ~ю его́ за надёжного наблюда́теля** I consider him a reliable observer; **с. ну́жным, с. за ну́жное** to consider it necessary; **с. за сча́стье** to count it one's good fortune. **3. (что)** to consider (that), hold (that); **они́ ~ют, что я не в состоя́нии об э́том суди́ть** they consider that I am not in a position to be a judge of this.
счит|а́ть[2]**, а́ю** *pf.* (*of* **~ывать**) (**с**+*i.*) to compare (with), check (against).
счита́|ться[1]**, юсь** *impf.* (*of* **сче́сться**) (**с**+*i.*) to settle accounts (with) (*also fig.*).
счита́|ться[2]**, юсь** *impf.* (*no pf.*) **1.** (*+i.*) to be considered, be thought, be reputed; to be regarded (as); **он ~ется первокла́ссным собесе́дником** he is considered a first-rate conversationalist. **2.** (**с**+*i.*) to consider, take into consideration, to take into account, reckon (with); **с ше́фом ещё на́до с.** the boss has still to be reckoned with.
счи́тк|а, и *f.* **1.** comparison, checking; **с. гра́нок с ру́кописью** comparison of proofs with manuscript. **2.** (*theatr.*) reading (*of a part in a play*).
счи́тыва|ть, ю *impf. of* **счита́ть**[2]
счища́|ть(ся), ю(сь) *impf. of* **счи́стить(ся)**
США *no sg., indecl.* (*abbr. of* **Соединённые Шта́ты Аме́рики**) USA (*United States of America*).
сшиб|а́ть(ся), а́ю(сь) *impf. of* **~и́ть(ся)**
сшиб|и́ть, у́, ёшь, *past* **~, ~ла** *pf.* (*of* **~а́ть**) (*coll.*) to knock off; **с. с ног** to knock down, knock over; **с. с кого́-н. спесь** to take s.o. down a peg.
сшиб|и́ться, у́сь, ёшься, *past* **~ся, ~лась** *pf.* (*of* **~а́ться**) (*coll.*) **1.** to collide; to come to blows. **2.** *pass. of* **~и́ть**
сшива́|ть, ю *impf. of* **сшить**
сшить, сошью́, сошьёшь *pf.* **1.** *pf. of* **шить. 2.** (*impf.* **сшива́ть**) to sew together; (*med.*) to suture.
съ... *vbl. pref.* = **с...**
съеда́|ть, ю *impf.* to eat (up).
съеде́ни|е, я *nt., only in phr.* **отда́ть на с.** (*+d.*) to put at the mercy (of).
съедо́б|ный (~ен, ~на) *adj.* **1.** edible; **с. гриб** edible mushroom. **2.** eatable, nice.
съёжива|ться, юсь *impf. of* **съёжиться**
съёж|иться, усь, ишься *pf.* (*of* **ёжиться** *and* **~иваться**) to huddle up; to shrivel, shrink.
съезд[1]**, а** *m.* **1.** congress; conference, convention. **2.** arrival, gathering.
съезд[2]**, а** *m.* descent.
съе́з|дить, жу, дишь *pf.* **1.** to go (*and come back*); **с. в Ри́гу** (*vulg.*) to spew (*when drunk*). **2.** (*coll.*) to bash.
съе́здовский *adj.* congress.
съезжа́|ть(ся), ю(сь) *impf. of* **съе́хать(ся)**
съе́зж|ая, ей *f.* (*obs.*) cell (*in police station*).
съе́зж|ий *adj.* (*obs.*) **1.** of assembly; **~ая изба́** assembly house. **2.: с. наро́д** assembled multitude.
съел *see* **съесть**
съём, а *m.* removal.
съёмк|а, и *f.* **1.** removal. **2.** survey, surveying; plotting. **3.** (*phot.*) exposure; shooting.
съёмный *adj.* detachable, removable.
съём|очный *adj. of* **~ка; ~очная гру́ппа** film-crew; **с. люк** camera hatch (*in aircraft*); **~очная площа́дка** film-set; **~очные рабо́ты** surveying.
съёмщик, а *m.* **1.** tenant, lessee. **2.** surveyor.
съёмщиц|а, ы *f. of* **съёмщик**
съестн|о́й *adj.* food; **~ы́е припа́сы** food supplies, provisions; **~ы́е проду́кты** foodstuffs, victuals; *as n.* **~о́е, ~о́го** *nt.* = **~ы́е припа́сы**
съе|сть, м, шь, ст, ди́м, ди́те, дя́т, *past* **~л, ~ла** *pf. of* **есть**[1]; **с. соба́ку (на**+*p.*; *coll.*) to have at one's finger-tips, know inside out.
съе́|хать, ду, дешь *pf.* (*of* **~зжа́ть**) **1.** to go down, come down. **2.: с. на́ берег** (*naut.*) to go ashore. **3.** to move (*house*). **4.** (*fig., coll.*) to come down, slip. **га́лстук у тебя́ ~хал на́бок** your tie is on one side. **5.** (*fig., coll.*) to come down (= *to lower one's price*).
съе́|хаться, дусь, дешься *pf.* (*of* **~зжа́ться**) **1.** to meet. **2.** to arrive, gather, assemble.
съехи́днича|ть, ю *pf. of* **ехи́дничать**
съязв|и́ть, лю́, и́шь *pf. of* **язви́ть**
сы́воротк|а, и *f.* **1.** whey. **2.** (*biol., med.*) serum.
сы́ворот|очный *adj. of* **~ка**; serous.
сы́гранност|ь, и *f.* team-work.
сыгра́|ть, ю *pf. of* **игра́ть; с. шу́тку (с**+*i.*) to play a practical joke (on).
сыгра́|ться, юсь *pf.* to achieve team-work; to play well together.
сы́змала *adv.* (*coll.*) from a child, ever since one was a child.
сы́знова *adv.* (*coll.*) anew, afresh; **нача́ть с.** to make a fresh start, begin all over again.
сымпровизи́р|овать, ую *pf. of* **импровизи́ровать**
сын, а, *pl.* **~овья́, ~ове́й** *and* **~ы́, ~о́в** *m.* **1.** (*pl.* **~овья́**) son. **2.** (*pl.* **~ы́**) (*fig., rhet.*) son, child; **с. своего́ вре́мени** child, product of one's time.
сыни́шк|а, и *m.* (*coll.*) *dim. of* **сын**
сыно́вний *adj.* filial.

сын|óк, кá *m. dim. of* ~; (*as mode of address*) sonny.
сы́п|ать, лю, лешь *impf.* **1.** to pour, strew. **2.** (*+a. or i.; fig., coll.*) to pour forth; **с. жáлобами** to pour forth complaints; **с. деньгáми** to squander money.
сы́п|аться, лется *impf.* **1.** to fall; to pour out, run out; to scatter; **мукá ~алась из мешкá** flour poured out of the bag. **2.** (*of sounds, etc.; coll.*) to pour forth (*intrans.*), rain down; **удáры ~ались грáдом** blows were raining down, falling thick and fast. **3.** (*of plaster, etc.*) to flake off. **4.** (*of fabrics*) to fray out.
сыпнóй *adj.*: **с. тиф** (*med.*) typhus, spotted fever.
сыпнотифóзный *adj.*: **с. больнóй** typhus patient.
сыпня́к, á *m.* (*coll.*) = **сыпнóй тиф**
сыпу́ч|ий (~, ~а) *adj.* friable, free-flowing; **с. грунт** shifting ground; **с. песóк** quicksand; **~ие телá** dry substances; **мéры ~их тел** dry measures.
сып|ь, и *f.* (*med.*) rash, eruption.
сыр, а, *pl.* **~ы́** *m.* cheese; **как с. в мáсле катáться** (*coll.*) to live on the fat of the land.
сыр-бóр *now only in phr.* **вот откýда с. загорéлся** (*coll.*) that was the spark that set the forest on fire.
сырé|ть, ю *impf.* (*of* **от~**) to become damp.
сыр|éц, цá *m.* product in raw state; **кирпи́ч-с.** adobe; **шёлк-с.** raw silk.
сы́рник, а *m.* curd fritter.
сы́р|ный *adj. of* ~; caseous; **~ная недéля** Shrovetide.
сы́ро *as predicate* it is damp.
сыровáр, а *m.* cheese-maker.
сыроварéни|е, я *nt.* cheese-making.
сыровáр|ня, ни, *g. pl.* **~ен** *f.* cheese dairy, creamery.
сыровáт|ый (~, ~а) *adj.* **1.** dampish. **2.** not quite ripe. **3.** (*cul.*) underdone, undercooked.
сыродéльный *adj.* cheese-processing.
сыроéжк|а, и *f.* russula (*mushroom*).
сыр|óй (~, ~á, ~о) *adj.* **1.** damp. **2.** raw, uncooked; **~áя водá** unboiled water; **~óе мя́со** raw meat. **3.** green, unripe. **4.** raw; unfinished; **~ы́е материáлы** raw materials. **5.** (*coll.*) fat, podgy.
сыр|óк, кá *m.* cheese curds.
сыромя́тн|ый *adj.* dressed, tawed; **~ая кóжа** rawhide.
сы́ромят|ь, и *f.* tawed leather.
сы́рост|ь, и *f.* dampness, humidity.
сыр|цóвый *adj. of* **~éц**; **~цóвая стáль** natural steel.
сырь|ё, я́ *no pl., nt.* raw material(s).
сырьев|óй *adj. of* **сырьё**; **~áя бáза** raw material supply.
сырьём *adv.* (*coll.*) raw; **есть моркóвь с.** to eat carrots raw.
сыск, а *m.* (*obs.*) investigation, detection (*of criminals*).
сы|скáть, щу́, ~щешь *pf.* (*coll.*) to find.
сы|скáться, щу́сь, ~щешься *pf.* (*coll.*) to be found, come to light.
сыск|нóй *adj. of* ~; **~нáя поли́ция** (*obs.*) criminal investigation department.
сытé|ть, ю *impf.* (*coll.*) to become fuller.
сы́тно *adv.* well; **с. позáвтракать** to have a good breakfast.
сы́т|ный (~ен, ~нá, ~но) *adj.* (*of a meal*) substantial, copious; **~ное мéсто** (*fig., joc., obs.*) fat job.
сы́тост|ь, и *f.* satiety, repletion.
сы́т|ый (~, ~á, ~о) *adj.* **1.** satisfied, replete, full; **я ~ по гóрло** I have eaten my fill, I am full up. **2.** fat; **с. скот** fat stock.
сыч, á *m.* little owl (*Athene noctua*); **~óм сидéть** (*coll.*) to look glum.
сычу́г, á *m.* (*anat.*) abomasum, rennet bag.
сычу́жин|а, ы *f.* rennet.
сы́щик, а *m.* detective.
сы́щиц|а, ы *f. of* **сы́щик**
СЭВ, а *m.* (*abbr. of* ***Совет Экономи́ческой Взаимопóмощи***) COMECON (*Council for Mutual Economic Assistance*).
сэконóм|ить, лю, ишь *pf. of* **экономить**
сэр, а *m.* sir.
сюдá *adv.* here, hither.
сюжéт, а *m.* subject; topic.
сюжéт|ный *adj. of* ~
сюзерéн, а *m.* (*hist.*) suzerain.
сюзерéн|ный *adj. of* ~
сюи́т|а, ы *f.* (*mus.*) suite.
сюрпри́з, а *m.* surprise.
сюрреали́зм, а *m.* surrealism.
сюрреали́ст, а *m.* surrealist.
сюрту́к, á *m.* frock-coat.
сюсю́ка|ть, ю *impf.* to lisp.
сяк *adv.* (*coll.*): **и так и с.,** *see* **так**
сям *adv.*: **и там и с., ни там ни с.,** *see* **там**

Т

т (*abbr. of* **тóнна**) t., ton(s), tonne(s).
т. *abbr. of* **1. товáрищ** Comrade. **2. том** vol., volume.
табáк, á (у́) *m.* **1.** tobacco-plant. **2.** tobacco; **ню́хательный т.** snuff; **дéло — т.!** (*coll.*) things are in a bad way.
табакá *indecl., only in phr.* (*cul.*): **цыплёнок т.** chicken tabak (*chicken flattened and grilled on charcoal*).
табакéрк|а, и *f.* snuff-box.
табаковóд, а *m.* tobacco-grower.
табаковóдств|о, а *nt.* tobacco-growing.
табаковóд|ческий *adj. of* **~ство**
табакомáн, а *m.* chain smoker.
табáн|ить, ю, ишь *impf.* to back water (*in rowing*).
табáчник, а *m.* **1.** tobacco-worker. **2.** (*obs.*) tobacco-user.
табáчниц|а, ы *f. of* **табáчник**
табáчный *adj.* **1.** tobacco; **т. кисéт** tobacco-pouch; **т. лист** tobacco leaf. **2.**: **т. цвéт** snuff colour.
тáбел|ь, я *m.* **1.** table; **т. о рáнгах** (*hist.*) Table of Ranks (*introduced by Peter the Great*). **2.** time-board (*in factory, etc.*). **3.** number (*removed on arrival at work and replaced on leaving*).
тáбель|ный *adj. of* ~; **~ная доскá** time-board; **~ные часы́** time-clock.
тáбельщик, а *m.* timekeeper.
тáбельщиц|а, ы *f. of* **тáбельщик**
тáбес, а *m.* (*med.*) tabes.
таблéтк|а, и *f.* tablet, pill; **т. аспири́на** an aspirin.
табли́ц|а, ы *f.* table; plate (*with illustrations or diagrams*); **т. умножéния** multiplication table; **~ы логари́фмов** logarithm tables; **т. Менделéева** (*chem.*) periodic table; **т. прили́вов** tide table; **электрóнная т.** (*comput.*) spreadsheet; **т. стрельбы́** (*mil.*) firing tables; **т. вы́игрышей** prize-list; **т. (рóзыгрыша) пéрвенства** (*sport*) (score-)table; **пéрвый, послéдний в ~е** top, bottom of the table; **внести́ в ~у** to tabulate.
табли́чный *adj.* **1.** tabular. **2.** standard, as per the tables.
таблó *indec., nt.* indicator board, scoreboard (*with neon-lit figures*).
табльдóт, а *m.* table d'hôte.
тáбор, а *m.* **1.** camp. **2.** Gypsy encampment.
тáбор|ный *adj.* **1.** *adj. of* ~. **2.** Gypsy.
табу́ *nt. indecl.* taboo.
табу́н, á *m.* herd (*usu. of horses, also of reindeer and some other animals*).
табу́н|ный *adj. of* ~
табу́нщик, а *m.* horse-herd.
табурéт, а *m.* = **~ка**
табурéт|ка, ки *f.* stool.
тавéрн|а, ы *f.* tavern, inn.
тáволг|а, и *f.* (*bot.*) meadow-sweet.
тавóт, а *m.* (*tech.*) axle grease, lubricating grease.
тавóтниц|а, ы *f.* (*tech.*) grease gun, grease cup.
таврёный *adj.* branded.

тавр|и́ть, ю́, и́шь *impf.* (*of* **за~**) to brand.
тавр|о́, а́, *pl.* **~а, ~, ~а́м** *nt.* brand (*on cattle, etc.*).
тавро́|вый *adj.* **1.** *adj. of* **~**. **2.** (*tech.*) T-shaped; **~вая ба́лка** T-beam.
тавтологи́ческий *adj.* tautological.
тавтоло́ги|я, и *f.* tautology.
тага́н, а́ *m.* trivet.
таджи́к, а *m.* Tadzhik.
Таджикиста́н, а *m.* Tadzhikistan.
таджи́кский *adj.* Tadzhik.
таджи́|чка, чки *f. of* **~к**
таёжник, а *m.* taiga dweller.
таёжный *adj. of* **тайга́**
таз[1]**, а, в ~у́,** *pl.* **~ы́** *m.* basin; wash-basin; washing-up bowl.
таз[2]**, а, в ~е** *and* **в ~у́,** *pl.* **~ы́** *m.* (*anat.*) pelvis.
тазобе́дренный *adj.* (*anat.*) hip, coxal; **т. суста́в** hip joint.
та́зовый *adj.* (*anat.*) pelvic.
Таила́нд, а *m.* Thailand.
таила́нд|ец, ца *m.* Thai.
таила́нд|ка, ки *f. of* **~ец**
таи́нственност|ь, и *f.* mystery.
таи́нствен|ный (~, ~на) *adj.* **1.** mysterious; enigmatic. **2.** secret. **3.** secretive; **т. вид** secretive look.
та́инств|о, а *nt.* **1.** (*relig.*) sacrament. **2.** (*obs.*) mystery, secret.
Таи́ти *m. indecl.* Tahiti.
та|и́ть, ю́, и́шь *impf.* to hide, conceal (*emotion, etc.*); to harbour; **т. в себе́** to be fraught (with); **т. зло́бу (про́тив)** to harbour a grudge (against); **не́чего греха́ т.** it must be owned.
та|и́ться, ю́сь, и́шься *impf.* **1.** (*coll.*) to be (in) hiding, lurk. **2.** (*fig.*) to lurk, be lurking; **что за э́тим ~и́тся?** what lies behind this? **3.** (*coll.*) to hold back (= *to decline to reveal*).
таитя́н|ин, ина, *pl.* **~е, ~** *m.* Tahitian.
таитя́н|ка, ки *f. of* **~ин**
таитя́нский *adj.* Tahitian.
Тайбэ́|й, я *m.* Taipei.
Тайва́н|ь, я *m.* Taiwan.
тайва́нский *adj.* Taiwanese.
тайг|а́, и́ *f.* (*geog.*) taiga.
тайко́м *adv.* in secret, surreptitiously, by stealth; on the quiet, on the sly; behind s.o.'s back.
тайм, а *m.* (*sport*) half, period (*of game*).
таймéн|ь, я *m.* salmon-trout.
та́йн|а, ы *f.* **1.** mystery. **2.** secret; **держа́ть в ~е** to keep secret, keep dark; **храни́ть ~у** to keep a secret; **не т., что** it is no secret that.
тайни́к, а́ *m.* hiding-place; cache; **в ~а́х души́** in the inmost recesses of the heart.
тайнобра́чн|ый *adj.* (*bot.*) cryptogamous, cryptogamic; *as n.* **~ые, ~ых** Cryptogamia.
тайнопи́сный *adj.* cryptographic.
та́йнопис|ь, и *f.* cryptographic writing.
та́йн|ый *adj.* secret; clandestine; **т. аге́нт** undercover agent; **~ое голосова́ние** secret ballot; **т. коммуни́ст** crypto-Communist; **т. сове́т** (*hist.*) Privy Council.
та́йский *adj.* Thai.
тайфу́н, а *m.* typhoon.
так 1. *adv.* so; thus, in this way, like this; in such a way; **т. мно́го** so many; **мы сде́лали т.** this is what we did, we did as follows; **т. бы (и)...** (*expr. strong desire to do sth.*; *coll.*) how I, *etc.*, should like ...; **т. во́т** (*in proceeding with narration after digression*) and so, so then; **т. же** in the same way; **т. и быть** (*coll.*) all right, right you are, right-ho; **т. и есть** (*coll.*) so it is; **т. и зна́й(те)** (*expr. warning*; *coll.*) get this clear; **т. ему́** *etc.*, **и на́до** serves him, *etc.*, right; **т. или ина́че** (*i*) in any event, whatever happens, (*ii*) one way or another; **т. называ́емый** so-called; **т. себе́** so-so, middling, not too good; **т. сказа́ть** so to speak; **за т.** (*coll.*) for nothing; **и т.** even so; as it is, as it stands; **и т. да́лее** and so on, and so forth; **и т. и сяк** this way and that; **когда́ т.** (*coll.*) if so; **(не) т. ли?** isn't it so? **2.** *adv.* as it should be; **не т.** amiss, wrong; **т. ли я говорю́?** am I right?; **что́-то бы́ло не совсе́м т.** sth. was amiss, sth. was not quite right. **3.** *adv.* just like that (= *without further action or consequences*); **боле́знь не пройдёт т.** the illness will not pass just like that; **т. ему́ э́то не пройдёт** he won't get away with it like that. **4.** *adv.*: **т. (то́лько), про́сто т.** for no special reason, for no reason in particular; just for fun, for the sake of it; **т. како́й-то, т. како́й-н.** (*coll., pej.*) some sort of. **5.** *particle* (*in answer to a question*) nothing in particular, nothing special; **что тебе́ не понра́вилось там? — т., о́бщее положе́ние** what did you not like there? — Nothing in particular, just the set-up in general. **6.: т. и** (*as emph. particle*) simply, just; **её глаза́ т. и сверка́ли гне́вом** her eyes were simply blazing with anger; **я т. и забы́л принести́ кни́гу** I clean forgot, I have gone and forgotten to bring the book. **7.** *conj.* then (*or not translated*); **ты не спро́сишь его́, т. я спрошу́** if you won't ask him, then I will; **е́хать, т. е́хать** if we are going, let's go; **не сего́дня, т. за́втра** if not today, then tomorrow. **8.** *conj.* so; **т. вы зна́ете друг дру́га?** so you know one another? **9.: т. как** *conj.* as, since. **10.** *affirmative or emph. particle* yes; **т. то́чно** (*in mil. parlance*) yes.
та́ка|ть, ю *impf.* (*coll.*) to rattle, chatter (*of machine-gun fire, etc.*).
такела́ж, а *m.* (*naut.*) rigging.
такела́жник, а *m.* rigger, scaffolder.
такела́жн|ый *adj.* **1.** (*naut.*) rigging. **2.** scaffolding; **~ые рабо́ты** erection of scaffolding.
та́кже *adv.* also, too, as well; (*after neg.*) or, nor.
-таки *particle* (*coll.*) however, though; **всё-т.** nevertheless; **опя́ть-т.** again.
тако́в *m.*, **~а́** *f.*, **~о́** *nt.*, *pl.* **~ы́,** *pron.* such; **все они́ ~ы́** they are all the same; **~ы́ на́ши све́дения** so we are informed; **и был т.** (*coll.*) and that was the last we saw of him.
таков|о́й *adj.* **1.** (*obs.*) such; **е́сли ~ы́е име́ются** if any. **2.: как т.** as such.
тако́вский *adj.* (*coll.*) of such a kind.
так|о́й *pron.* **1.** such; so; **т. же** the same; **он т. до́брый!** he is such a kind man; **~о́е пальто́ мне ну́жно** I need a coat like that; **~и́м о́бразом** thus, in this way; **в ~о́м слу́чае** in that case; **до ~о́й сте́пени** to such an extent. **2.** (*coll.*) a kind of; **бли́нчик т.** a kind of pancake. **3.: кто он т.?** who is he?; **что э́то ~о́е?** what is this?; **что ~о́е „кисе́ль"?** what is 'kissel'?; **что ~о́е** what's that?; what did you say?; **что ж тут ~о́го?** what is there so wonderful about that?; **куда́ ~о́е он пошёл?** (*coll.*) wherever has he gone?
тако́й-сяко́й *pron.* (*coll.*) (a) so-and-so.
тако́й-то *pron.* so-and-so; such-and-such.
та́кс|а[1]**, ы** *f.* statutory price; tariff; **по чёрной ~е** at the black-market rate.
та́кс|а[2]**, ы** *f.* dachshund.
такса́тор, а *m.* **1.** price-fixer; valuer. **2.** afforestation inspector.
такса́ци|я, и *f.* **1.** price-fixing; valuation. **2.** afforestation inspection.
такси́ *nt. indecl.* taxi.
та́ксик, а *m. dim. of* **та́кса**[2]
такси́р|овать, ую *impf. and pf.* to fix the price (of), price.
такси́ст, а *m.* taxi-driver.
таксо́метр, а *m.* (taxi)meter; 'clock'.
таксомото́р, а *m.* taxi.
таксомото́р|ный *adj. of* **~**; **т. парк** fleet of taxis.
таксомото́рщик, а *m.* taxi-driver.
таксофо́н, а *m.* automatic telephone.
так-ся́к *adv. as pred.* (*coll.*) it is tolerable, it is passable.
такт[1]**, а** *m.* **1.** (*mus., etc.*) time; measure; bar; **отбива́ть т.** to beat time; **в т.** in time. **2.** (*tech.*) stroke (*of engine*).
такт[2]**, а** *m.* tact.
та́к-таки *particle* (*coll.*) after all; really.
та́ктик, а *m.* tactician.
та́ктик|а, и *f.* tactics.
такти́ческий *adj.* tactical.
такти́чност|ь, и *f.* tact.
такти́ч|ный (~ен, ~на) *adj.* tactful.
та́к-то *adv.* (*coll.*) so; **он не т. скро́мен** he's not all that humble; **т. так** that's as it may be.

та́кт|овый *adj. of* ~¹; **~овая черта́** bar.
тала́н, а *m.* (*folklore*) luck, good fortune.
тала́нт, а *m.* **1.** talent, gift(s). **2.** man of talent, gifted pers. **3.** (*hist.*) talent (*ancient coin and measure*).
тала́нтливост|ь, и *f.* talent, gifts.
тала́нтлив|ый (~, ~а) *adj.* talented, gifted.
та́лер, а *m.* thaler (*coin*).
та́л|и, ей *no sg.* block and tackle.
талидоми́д, а *m.* (*pharm.*) thalidomide.
талисма́н, а *m.* talisman, charm, mascot.
та́ли|я¹, и *f.* waist; **пла́тье в ~ю** dress fitting at the waist; **обня́ть кого́-н. за ~ю** to put one's arm round s.o.'s waist.
та́ли|я², и *f.* two packs of playing cards.
та́лли|й, я *m.* (*chem.*) thallium.
Та́ллин, а *m.* Tallin(n).
талму́д, а *m.* (*relig.*) Talmud.
талмуди́ст, а *m.* Talmudist; (*fig.*) pedant, doctrinaire.
талмуди́стский *adj.* Talmudistic; (*fig.*) pedantic, doctrinaire.
талмуди́ческий = талмуди́стский
тало́н, а *m.* coupon; stub (*of cheques, etc.*); **т. на обе́д** luncheon voucher; **поса́дочный т.** boarding pass; landing card.
тало́нчик, а *m. dim. of* **тало́н**
та́лреп, а *m.* (*naut.*) lanyard; **винтово́й т.** turn-buckle.
та́л|ый *adj.* thawed, melted; **~ая вода́** water from melted snow.
тальк, а *m.* talc; talcum powder.
та́льк|овый *adj. of* ~; **т. сла́нец** (*min.*) talc schist.
тальни́к, а́ *m.* willow.
там *adv.* **1.** there; **т. же** in the same place; (*in footnotes, etc.*) ibidem; **и т. и сям** here, there and everywhere. **2.** (*coll.*) later, by and by. **3.** *as particle* (*coll.*) *expr. disregard, indifference, etc.*, **вся́кие т. глу́пости говори́т** he talks all kinds of nonsense; **како́е т.!** nothing of the kind!; not a bit of good!; **чего́ т.!** go on!; go ahead!
тамад|а́, ы́ *m.* master of ceremonies, toast-master.
та́мбур¹, а *m.* **1.** (*archit.*) tambour. **2.** lobby. **3.** platform (*of rail. carriage*).
та́мбур², а *m.* chain-stitch.
тамбу́р, а *m.* (*mus.*) **1.** tambourine. **2.** (*obs.*) tambour (= *drum*).
тамбури́н, а *m.* **1.** tambourine. **2.** tambourin.
тамбурмажо́р, а *m.* (*mil.*; *obs.*) drum major.
та́мбур|ный *adj. of* ~²; **т. шов** chain-stitch.
тамизда́т, а *m.* 'tamizdat' (*publication abroad*).
тами́л, а *m.* Tamil.
тами́л|ка, ки *f. of* ~
тами́льский *adj.* Tamil.
тамо́женник, а *m.* customs official.
тамо́женн|ый *adj.* customs; **~ые по́шлины, ~ые сбо́ры** customs (*duties*).
тамо́жн|я, и *f.* custom-house.
та́мошн|ий *adj.* (*coll.*) of that place; **~ие жи́тели** the local inhabitants.
тампо́н, а *m.* (*med.*) tampon, plug; **гигиени́ческий т.** sanitary towel *or* pad.
тампона́ж, а *m.* (*tech.*) tamping.
тампона́ци|я, и *f.* (*med.*) tamponade.
тампони́р|овать, ую *impf. and pf.* (*med.*) to tampon, plug.
тамта́м, а *m.* tom-tom.
та́нгенс, а *m.* (*math.*) tangent.
тангенциа́льный *adj.* (*math.*) tangential.
та́нго *nt. indecl.* tango.
та́н|ец, ца *m.* **1.** dance; dancing; **уро́ки ~цев** dancing lessons; **т. живота́** belly-dance; **исполни́тельница ~ца живота́** belly-dancer. **2.** (*pl.*) a dance, dancing; **пойти́ на ~цы** to go to a dance, go dancing.
Танже́р, а *m.* Tangier.
танзани́йский *adj.* Tanzanian.
Танза́ни|я, и *f.* Tanzania.
тани́н, а *m.* tannin.
танк¹, а *m.* (*mil.*) tank.
танк², а *m.* container (*for transportation of liquids*).
та́нкер, а *m.* (*naut.*) tanker.
танке́тк|а¹, и *f.* tankette, small tank.
танке́тк|а², и *f.* (*coll.*) (*ladies'*) wedge-heeled shoe, slipper.
танки́ст, а *m.* member of tank crew.
та́нковый *adj.* tank, armoured.
танкодро́м, а *m.* tank training area.
танкострое́ни|е, я *nt.* tank-building, tank construction.
танк-парово́з, а *m.* (*rail.*) tank (engine).
танта́л, а *m.* (*chem.*) tantalum.
тантье́м|а, ы *f.* bonus.
танцева́льный *adj.* dancing; **т. ве́чер** a dance, party with dancing.
танц|ева́ть, у́ю *impf.* to dance.
танцкла́сс, а *m.* (*obs.*) school of dancing; dancing-classes.
танцме́йстер, а *m.* (*obs.*) dancing-master.
танцо́вщик, а *m.* (ballet) dancer.
танцо́вщиц|а, ы *f. of* **танцо́вщик**
танцо́р, а *m.* dancer.
танцо́рк|а, и *f. of* **танцо́р**
танцу́льк|а, и *f.* (*coll.*) dance, hop.
тапёр, а *m.* ballroom pianist.
тапёрш|а, и *f. of* **тапёр**
тапио́к|а, и *f.* tapioca.
тапи́р, а *m.* tapir.
та́почк|а, и *f.* (*coll.*) slipper; **спорти́вная т.** sports shoe, gym shoe, plimsoll.
та́р|а, ы *f.* **1.** packing, packaging. **2.** (*comm.*) tare.
тараба́н|ить, ю, ишь *impf.* (*coll.*) to clatter.
тараба́рск|ий *adj.* **1.** (*obs.*) cryptographic. **2.: ~ая гра́мота** (*coll.*) double Dutch.
тараба́рщин|а, ы *f.* (*coll.*) double Dutch, gibberish.
тарака́н, а *m.* cockroach.
тарака́н|ий *adj. of* ~
тара́н, а *m.* **1.** (*hist.*) battering ram. **2.** (*mil.*) ram; ramming.
тара́н|ить, ю, ишь *impf.* (*of* **про~**) to ram.
тара́н|ный *adj.* **1.** *adj. of* ~. **2.: ~ная кость** (*anat.*) astragalus.
таранта́с, а *m.* tarantass (*springless carriage*).
таранте́лл|а, ы *f.* tarantella.
таран|ти́ть, чу́, ти́шь *impf.* (*coll.*) to jabber, natter.
тара́нтул, а *m.* tarantula.
тара́н|ь, и *f.* sea-roach (*Rutilus rutilus Heckeli*).
тарара́м, а *m.* (*coll.*) row, racket, hullabaloo.
тарара́х|ать, аю *impf. of* **~нуть**
тарара́х|нуть, ну, нешь *pf.* (*of* **~ать**) (*coll.*) to bang; to crash.
тарата́йк|а, и *f.* cabriolet, gig.
тарато́р|а, ы *c.g.* (*coll.*) chatterbox, gabbler.
тарато́р|ить, ю, ишь *impf.* (*coll.*) to jabber, natter; to gabble.
тарах|те́ть, чу́, ти́шь *impf.* (*coll.*) to rattle, rumble.
тара́щ|ить, у, ишь *impf.* **т. глаза́ (на+*a.*)** to goggle (at).
тарбага́н, а *m.* Siberian marmot.
таре́лк|а, и *f.* **1.** plate; **глубо́кая т.** soup-plate; **быть не в свое́й ~е** to be not quite o.s. **2.** (*tech.*) plate, disc. **3.** (*pl.*) cymbals.
таре́л|очный *adj. of* **~ка**; **т. бу́фер** plate buffer; **~очная ми́на** (*mil.*) flat anti-tank mine; **~очная печь** (*tech.*) revolving hearth.
таре́льчат|ый *adj.* (*tech.*) plate, disc; **т. кла́пан** disc valve; **~ая му́фта** plate coupling; **т. то́рмоз** disc brake.
тари́ф, а *m.* tariff, rate.
тарифика́ци|я, и *f.* tariffing.
тарифици́р|овать, ую *impf. and pf.* to tariff.
тари́ф|ный *adj. of* ~
тарта́ни|е, я *nt.* (*tech.*) (oil-)bailing.
тартарары́: провали́ться в т. (*coll.*) I'll be damned.
тарти́нк|а, и *f.* slice of bread and butter.
тарха́н, а *m.* (*hist.*) landowner enjoying special privileges.
тарха́н|ный *adj. of* ~
та́ры-ба́ры *pl. indecl.* (*coll.*) tittle-tattle.
таска́|ть, ю *impf.* (*indet. of* **тащи́ть**) **1.** *see* **тащи́ть. 2.** (*pf.* **от~**) (*coll.*) to pull (*as punishment*); **т. кого́-н. за́ во́лосы** to pull s.o.'s hair. **2.** (*coll.*) to wear.
таска́|ться, юсь *impf.* (*indet. of* **тащи́ться**) **1.** *see* **тащи́ться. 2.** (*coll., pej.*) to roam about; to hang about.
тасма́н|ец, ца *m.* Tasmanian.

Тасма́ни|я, и *f.* Tasmania.
тасма́н|ка, ки *f. of* **~ец**
тасма́нский *adj.* Tasmanian.
тас|ова́ть, у́ю *impf.* (*of* **с~**) to shuffle (*cards in a pack*).
тасо́вк|а, и *f.* shuffle, shuffling (*of playing cards*).
ТАСС *m.* (*indecl.*) (*abbr. of* ***Телегра́фное аге́нтство Сове́тского Сою́за***) TASS (*Telegraph Agency of the Soviet Union*).
татарв|а́, ы *f.* (*collect.*, *obs.*, *pej.*) the Ta(r)tars.
тата́р|ин, ина, *pl.* **~ы, ~** *m.* Ta(r)tar.
тата́р|ка[1]**, ки** *f. of* **~ин**
тата́рк|а[2]**, и** *f.* spring onion.
тата́рник, а *m.* thistle.
тата́рский *adj.* Ta(r)tar.
тату́ир|овать, ую *impf. and pf.* to tattoo.
тату́ир|оваться, уюсь *impf. and pf.* to tattoo o.s.; to have o.s. tattooed.
татуиро́вк|а, и *f.* tattooing.
тат|ь, я *m.* (*arch.*) thief, robber.
тафт|а́, ы *f.* taffeta.
тахикарди́|я, и *f.* (*med.*) tachycardia.
Та́хо *f. indecl.* the Tagus (*river*).
тахо́метр, а *m.* tachometer.
тахт|а́, ы́ *f.* ottoman.
тача́нк|а, и *f.* cart (*used in Ukraine and Caucasus*).
тача́|ть, ю *impf.* (*of* **вы́~**) to stitch.
та́чк|а, и *f.* wheelbarrow.
Ташке́нт, а *m.* Tashkent.
тащ|и́ть, у́, ~́ишь *impf.* (*det. of* **таска́ть**) **1.** to pull; to drag, lug; to carry. **2.** (*coll.*) to take; (*fig.*) to drag off; **т. кого́-н. в кино́** to drag s.o. off to the cinema. **3.** to pull out. **4.** (*coll.*) to pinch, swipe.
тащ|и́ться, у́сь, ~́ишься *impf.* (*det. of* **таска́ться**) **1.** to drag o.s. along. **2.** to drag, trail.
та́яни|е, я *nt.* thaw, thawing.
та́|ять, ю, ешь *impf.* (*of* **рас~**) **1.** to melt; to thaw; **~ет** it is thawing. **2.** (*fig.*) to melt away, dwindle, wane; **на́ши запа́сы ~ют** our stocks are dwindling; **его́ си́лы ~яли** his strength was ebbing. **3.** (**от**; *fig.*) to melt (with), languish (with). **4.** (*impf. only*) to waste away.
Тбили́си *m. indecl.* Tbilisi.
твар|ь, и *f.* creature; (*collect.*) creatures; all creation (*also pej.*); **вся́кой ~́и по па́ре** (*coll.*) all sorts and kinds of people.
тверде́ни|е, я *nt.* hardening.
тверде́|ть, ю *impf.* to harden, become hard.
твер|ди́ть, жу́, ди́шь *impf.* **1.** (+*a. or* **о**+*p.*) to repeat, say over and over again. **2.** to memorize, learn by rote.
твёрдо *adv.* hard; firmly, firm.
твердока́менный *adj.* (*rhet.*) steadfast, staunch.
твердоло́б|ый (~, ~а) *adj.* **1.** thick-skulled. **2.** (*pol.*) diehard.
твёрдост|ь, и *f.* hardness; (*fig.*) firmness.
твёрд|ый (~, ~а́, ~о) *adj.* **1.** hard. **2.** firm; solid; **т. грунт** firm soil; **т. переплёт** stiff binding; **~ое те́ло** (*phys.*, *chem.*) solid; **фи́зика ~ого те́ла** solid state physics. **3.** (*fig. in var. senses*) firm; stable; steadfast; **~ое зада́ние** specified task; **~ые зна́ния** sound knowledge; **~ое реше́ние** firm decision; **т. срок** fixed time-limit; **~ые це́ны** stable, fixed prices. **4.** (*ling.*) hard; **т. знак** hard sign (*name of Russian letter* **'ъ'**).
тверды́н|я, и *f.* (*obs.*) stronghold (*also fig.*).
тверд|ь, и *f.* (*arch.*): **т. земна́я** the earth; **т. небе́сная** the firmament, the heavens.
твид, а *m.* tweed.
тви́д|овый *adj. of* **~**
тво|й, его́ *m.*, **~я́, ~е́й** *f.*, **~ё, ~его́** *nt.*, *pl.* **~и́, ~и́х** *possessive pron.* your, yours (thy, thine); **~его́** (*after comp. adv.*; *coll.*) than you; **я зна́ю лу́чше ~его́** I know better than you; **что т.** (*coll.*) just like; **гора́ — что т. Эльбру́с** the mountain is just like Mount Elbruz; *as n.* **~и́, ~и́х** your people.
творе́ни|е, я *nt.* **1.** creation; work. **2.** creature, being.
твор|е́ц, ца́ *m.* creator.
твори́л|о[1]**, а** *nt.* hatch; aperture; water-gate (*in dam*).
твори́л|о[2]**, а** *nt.* lime-pit.
твори́тельный *adj.*: **т. паде́ж** (*gram.*) instrumental case.
твор|и́ть[1]**, ю, и́шь** *impf.* (*of* **со~**) **1.** to create. **2.** to do; to make; **т. добро́** to do good; **т. суд и распра́ву** (*obs.*) to deal out justice; **т. чудеса́** to work wonders.
твор|и́ть[2]**, ю́, и́шь** *impf.* (*obs.*) to knead; **т. и́звесть** to slake lime.
твор|и́ться[1]**, и́тся** *impf.* (*coll.*) to happen, go on; **что тут ~и́тся?** what is going on here?
твор|и́ться[2]**, и́тся** *impf.*, *pass. of* **~и́ть**[2]
творо́г, а́ *and* **тво́рог, а** *m.* curds, cottage cheese; **со́евый т.** tofu.
творо́жист|ый (~, ~а) *adj.* curdled, clotted.
творо́жник, а *m.* curd pancake.
творо́жн|ый *adj.* curd; **~ая ма́сса** curds; **т. сыро́к** cottage cheese.
тво́рческ|ий *adj.* creative; **~ая си́ла** creative power, creativeness; **т. путь Толсто́го** Tolstoy's career as a writer.
тво́рчеств|о, а *nt.* **1.** creation; creative work. **2.** (*collect.*) works.
ТВЧ *nt. indecl.* (*abbr. of* ***телеви́дение высо́кой чёткости***) HDTV (*high-definition television*).
т. е. (*abbr. of* **то есть**) i.e., that is, viz.
теа́тр, а *m.* **1.** (*in var. senses*) theatre; **т. вое́нных де́йствий** (*mil.*) theatre of operations; **анатоми́ческий т.** dissecting-room. **2.** (*fig.*) the stage; **т. ма́лых форм** variety theatre. **3.** (*collect.*) (the) plays; **т. Шекспи́ра** the plays of Shakespeare.
театра́л, а *m.* theatre-goer, playgoer; drama-lover.
театрализа́ци|я, и *f.* adaptation for the stage.
театрализ|ова́ть, у́ю *impf. and pf.* to adapt for the stage.
театра́л|ьный (~ен, ~ьна) *adj.* **1.** theatre; theatrical; **т. зал** auditorium; **~ьная ка́сса** box-office; **~ьная шко́ла** drama school. **2.** (*fig.*) theatrical, stagy.
театрове́дени|е, я *nt.* drama study.
тевто́н, а *m.* Teuton.
тевто́нский *adj.* Teutonic.
Тегера́н, а *m.* Teh(e)ran.
Те́жу *f. indecl.* = **Та́хо**
те́з|а, ы *f.* = **~ис 1.**
теза́урус, а *m.* thesaurus.
те́зис, а *m.* **1.** thesis, proposition, point; **вы́двинуть т.** to advance a thesis. **2.** thesis (*in Hegelian philosophy*).
тёзк|а, и *c.g.* namesake; **мы с ва́ми ~и** you and I share the same name.
тезоимени́тств|о, а *nt.* (*obs.*) name-day (*esp. of member of Tsar's family*).
теи́зм, а *m.* theism.
теи́ст, а *m.* theist.
теисти́ческий *adj.* theistic.
теки́н|ец, ца *m.* Tekke (*Turkoman people*).
теки́н|ка, ки *f. of* **~ец**
теки́нский *adj.*: **т. ковёр** Turkoman carpet.
текст, а *m.* **1.** text. **2.** words, libretto.
тексти́л|ь, я *no pl.*, *m.* (*collect.*) textiles.
тексти́льный *adj.* textile.
тексти́льщик, а *m.* textile worker.
тексти́льщи|ца, цы *f. of* **~к**
текстови́к, а́ *m.* librettist.
тексто́лог, а *m.* textual critic.
текстоло́ги|я, и *f.* textual study, textual criticism.
текстуа́л|ьный (~ен, ~ьна) *adj.* **1.** verbatim, word-for-word. **2.** (*philol.*) textual.
текто́ник|а, и *f.* (*geol.*) tectonics.
тектони́ческий *adj.* (*geol.*) tectonic.
теку́чест|ь, и *f.* **1.** (*phys.*) fluidity. **2.** fluctuation, instability; **т. рабо́чей си́лы** fluctuation of manpower, labour fluidity.
теку́ч|ий (~, ~а) *adj.* **1.** (*phys.*) fluid. **2.** fluctuating, unstable.
теку́щ|ий *pres. part. act. of* **течь** *and adj.* **1.** current; of the present moment; **в ~ем году́** in the current year; **2-го числа́ ~его ме́сяца** the second instant; **~ие собы́тия** current events, current affairs; **т. счёт** rent account. **2.** routine, ordinary; **~ие дела́** routine business; **т. ремо́нт** routine repairs.

тел. (*abbr. of* **телефо́н**) tel., telephone.
теле... *comb. form* tele-.
телеавтома́т, а *m.* video games machine.
телевеща́ни|е, я *nt.* television broadcasting.
телеви́дени|е, я *nt.* television, TV; **за́мкнутое т.** closed-circuit TV.
телевизио́нный *adj.* television.
телеви́зи|я, и *f.* = **телеви́дение**
телеви́зор, а *m.* television set; **т. цветно́го, чёрно-бе́лого изображе́ния** colour, black-and-white television set.
телеви́зор|ный *adj. of* ~
теле́г|а, и *f.* cart, wagon.
телегра́мм|а, ы *f.* telegram.
телегра́ф, а *m.* **1.** telegraph. **2.** telegraph office.
телеграфи́р|овать, ую *impf. and pf.* to telegraph, wire.
телеграфи́ст, а *m.* telegraphist.
телеграфи́ст|ка, ки *f. of* ~
телеграфи́|я, и *f.* telegraphy.
телегра́фн|ый *adj.* telegraph; telegraphic; **т. а́дрес** telegraphic address; **~ая ле́нта** ticker-tape; **т. стиль** telegraphic style, telegraphese; **т. столб** telegraph-pole.
теле́жк|а, и *f.* **1.** small cart, hand-cart. **2.** bogie, trolley. **3.** (*hist.*) post-chaise.
теле́|жный *adj. of* **~га; ~жное колесо́** cartwheel.
тележурна́л, а *m.* current affairs programme (*on TV*).
телезри́тел|ь, я *m.* (television) viewer.
телеизмере́ни|е, я *nt.* telemetry.
те́лекс, а *m.* telex.
телема́н, а *m.* TV addict.
телемарафо́н, а *m.*: **(благотвори́тельный) т.** telethon.
телеметри́ческий *adj.* telemetric.
телеметри́|я, и *f.* telemetry.
телемеха́ник|а, и *f.* telemechanics, remote control.
телемо́ст, а *m.* satellite (TV) link-up.
тел|ёнок, ёнка, *pl.* **~я́та, ~я́т** *m.* calf.
телеобъекти́в, а *m.* (*phot.*) telescopic lens, telephoto lens.
телеологи́ческий *adj.* teleological.
телеоло́ги|я, и *f.* teleology.
телепати́ческий *adj.* telepathic.
телепа́ти|я, и *f.* telepathy.
телепереда́ч|а, и *f.* television transmission; **пряма́я т.** live television coverage.
телес|а́, теле́с, ~а́м *no sg.* (*coll., joc.*) frame (*of a stout pers.*).
телеско́п, а *m.* telescope.
телескопи́ческий *adj.* telescopic; **т. прице́л** telescopic sight (*of firearm*).
телескопи́|я, и *f.* telescopy.
телеско́п|ный *adj. of* ~
теле́сн|ый *adj.* **1.** bodily; corporal; somatic; physical; **~ое наказа́ние** corporal punishment; **~ого цве́та** flesh-coloured. **2.** corporeal.
телесту́ди|я, и *f.* television studio.
телесуфлёр, а *m.* teleprompter, Autocue (*propr.*).
телеуправле́ни|е, я *nt.* remote control.
телефа́кс, а *m.* (tele)fax (machine).
телефика́ци|я, и *f.* equipping with television.
телефо́н, а *m.* **1.** telephone; **автомоби́льный т.** car phone; **дополни́тельный т.** extension; **позвони́ть по ~у** (*+d.*) to telephone, phone, ring up; **вы́зов по ~у** telephone call; **т. дове́рия** confidential telephone; **т.-автома́т** public telephone, public call-box; **т.-отве́тчик** answerphone. **2.** (*coll.*) telephone number.
телефони́р|овать, ую *impf. and pf.* to telephone.
телефони́ст, а *m.* telephone operator, telephonist.
телефони́ст|ка, ки *f. of* ~
телефо́н|ный *adj. of* ~
телефоногра́мм|а, ы *f.* telephoned telegram.
телефотогра́фи|я, и *f.* telephotography.
тел|е́ц, ьца́ *m.* **1.** (*obs.*) calf; **золото́й т.** the golden calf. **2.** **Т.** (*astron.*) Taurus.
теле́це́нтр, а *m.* television centre.
телешпарга́лк|а, и *f.* Autocue (*propr.*), 'idiot board'.
те́лик, а *m.* (*coll.*) (the) telly, the (goggle-)box.
тел|и́ться, ~́ится *impf.* (*of* **о~**) to calve.
тёлк|а, и *f.* **1.** heifer. **2.** (*sl.*) bird, bit of crumpet.
теллу́р, а *m.* (*chem.*) tellurium.
те́л|о, а, *pl.* **~а́, ~, ~а́м** *nt.* (*in var. senses*) body; (*coll.*): **быть в ~е** to be stout; **войти́ в т.** to put on weight; **спасть с ~а** to grow thin; **держа́ть в чёрном ~е** to ill-treat, maltreat.
телогре́йк|а, и *f.* (*woman's*) padded jacket (*usu. sleeveless*).
телодвиже́ни|е, я *nt.* movement, motion.
тел|о́к, ка́ *m.* (*coll.*) calf.
телосложе́ни|е, я *nt.* build, frame.
телохрани́тел|ь, я *m.* bodyguard.
Тель-Ави́в, а *m.* Tel Aviv.
те́льник, а *m.* (knitted) vest.
те́л|ьный *adj.* (*coll.*) *of* **~о; ~ьного цве́та** flesh-coloured.
тельня́шк|а, и *f.* (*coll.*) (*sailor's*) striped vest.
теля́тин|а, ы *f.* veal.
теля́тник[1], **а** *m.* calf-house.
теля́тник[2], **а** *m.* calf-herd.
теля́ч|ий *adj.* **1.** *adj. of* **телёнок; ~ья ко́жа** calf(skin). **2.** (*cul.*) veal. **3.**: **т. восто́рг** (*coll.*) foolish raptures; **~ьи не́жности** (*coll.*) sloppy sentimentality.
тем 1. *i. sg. m. and nt., d. pl. of* **тот. 2.** *conj.* (so much) the; **чем вы́ше, т. лу́чше** the taller, the better; **т. лу́чше** so much the better; **т. бо́лее, что** the more so as, especially as; **т. не ме́нее** none the less, nevertheless.
те́м|а, ы *f.* **1.** subject, topic, theme; **перейти́ к друго́й ~е** to change the subject; **сочине́ние на ~у Наполео́новских войн** a work on the subject of the Napoleonic Wars. **2.** (*mus.*) theme; **т. с вариа́циями** theme and variations.
тема́тик|а, и *f.* (*collect.*) subject-matter, themes, subjects.
темати́ческий *adj.* **1.** *adj. of* **тема́тика; т. план** plan of subjects, plan of subject-matter (*e.g. of forthcoming publications*). **2.** (*mus.*) thematic.
тембр, а *m.* timbre.
те́мбр|овый *adj. of* ~
теменн|о́й *adj.* (*anat.*) sincipital; **~а́я кость** parietal bone.
те́мен|ь, и *f.* (*coll.*) darkness.
Те́мз|а, ы *f.* the Thames (*river*).
те́ми *i. pl. of* **тот**
темля́к, а́ *m.* (*mil.*) sword-knot.
тёмн|ая, ой *f.* (*obs.*) (*police*) cell, lock-up.
темне́|ть, ю *impf.* **1.** (*pf.* **по~**) to grow *or* become dark; to darken. **2.** (*pf.* **с~**): **~ет** (*impers.*) it gets dark; it is getting dark. **3.** (*impf. only*) to show up darkly.
темне́|ться, ется *impf.* to show up darkly.
темн|и́ть, ю́, и́шь *impf.* to darken; to make darker.
темни́ц|а, ы *f.* (*obs.*) dungeon.
темно́ *as pred.* it is dark; **у меня́ в глаза́х ста́ло т.** everything went dark before my eyes.
темно... *comb. form* dark-.
темноко́жий *adj.* dark-skinned, swarthy.
темноси́ний *adj.* dark blue; navy blue.
темнот|а́, ы́ *f.* **1.** dark, darkness; **в ~е́** in the dark; **до ~ы́** before dark, before it gets dark; **с ~о́й** under cover of dark(ness). **2.** (*coll.*) ignorance; backwardness.
тём|ный (~ен, ~на́, ~но́) *adj.* **1.** dark; **~ное пятно́** (*fig.*) dark stain, blemish; **~ная вода́** (*med.*) amaurosis; **~на́ вода́ во о́блацех** the matter is wrapped in mystery. **2.** obscure, vague; **~ное ме́сто** (*philol.*) obscure passage; **~ное пятно́** obscure place. **3.** sombre. **4.** shady, fishy, suspicious; **~ное де́ло** shady business. **5.** ignorant, benighted.
темп, а *m.* **1.** (*mus.*) tempo. **2.** (*fig.*) tempo; rate, speed, pace; **заме́длить т.** to slacken one's pace; **ускор́ить т.** to accelerate.
те́мпер|а, ы *f.* **1.** distemper (*paint*). **2.** tempera (*painting*).
темпера́мент, а *m.* temperament; **челове́к с ~ом** energetic pers., spirited pers.
темпера́мент|ный (~ен, ~на) *adj.* energetic; spirited, vigorous.
температу́р|а, ы *f.* **1.** temperature; **т. кипе́ния** boiling-point; **т. замерза́ния** freezing-point; **крива́я ~ы** temperature curve; **ме́рить кому́-н. ~у** to take s.o.'s temperature. **2.** (*coll.*) (heightened) temperature; **ходи́ть с ~ой** to go about with a temperature.

температу́р|ить, ю, ишь *impf.* (*coll.*) to have a temperature.
температу́р|ный *adj. of* **~а; ~ная крива́я** temperature curve; **т. шов** (*tech.*) heat crack, expansion joint.
темпера́ци|я, и *f.* (*mus.*) temperament.
темпери́р|овать, ую *impf. and pf.* (*mus.*) to temper.
тем|ь, и *f.* (*coll.*) dark, darkness.
те́м|я, ени *no pl., nt.* (*anat.*) sinciput; crown, top of the head.
тенденцио́з|ный (~ен, ~на) *adj.* (*pej.*) tendentious, biased.
тенде́нци|я, и *f.* **1. (к)** tendency (to, towards); **у него́ т. (к)** he has a tendency (to), he tends (to). **2.** (*pej.*) bias; **с ~ей** tendentious, biased.
те́ндер, а *m.* **1.** (*rail.*) tender. **2.** (*naut.*) cutter.
те́ндер|ный *adj. of* **~**
тенев|о́й *adj.* shady (*also fig.*); **~а́я сторона́** shady side; (*fig.*) bad side, seamy side.
тенелюби́в|ый (~, ~а) *adj.* (*bot.*) requiring shade.
Тенери́фе *m. indecl.* Tenerife.
тенёт|а, ~ *no sg.* snare.
тени́ст|ый (~, ~а) *adj.* shady.
те́ннис, а *m.* tennis.
теннеси́ст, а *m.* tennis-player.
теннеси́ст|ка, ки *f. of* **~**
те́ннистк|а, и *f.* (*coll.*) tennis shirt, short-sleeved shirt.
те́ннисн|ый *adj.* tennis; **т. корт, ~ая площа́дка** tennis-court.
те́нор, а, *pl.* **~а́, ~о́в** *m.* (*mus.*) tenor.
теноро́вый *adj. of* **те́нор**
тент, а *m.* awning.
тен|ь, и, в ~и́, *pl.* **~и, ~е́й** *f.* **1.** shade; **сиде́ть в ~и́** to sit in the shade; **держа́ться в ~и́** (*fig.*) to keep in the background. **2.** shadow; **дава́ть т.** to cast a shadow; **от него́ оста́лась одна́ т.** he is but a shadow of his former self; **навести́ т.** (*coll.*) to confuse the issue. **3.** shadow, phantom, ghost; **бле́ден, как т.** pale as a ghost. **4.** (*fig.*) shadow, particle, vestige, atom; **нет ни ~и сомне́ния** there is not a shadow of doubt; **в его́ расска́зе нет ни ~и пра́вды** there is not a particle of truth in his story. **5.** suspicion; **бро́сить т. на кого́-н.** to cast suspicion on s.o.
теого́ни|я, и *f.* theogony.
теодице́|я, и *f.* theodicy.
теодоли́т, а *m.* theodolite.
теократи́ческий *adj.* theocratic.
теокра́ти|я, и *f.* theocracy.
теологи́ческий *adj.* theological.
теоло́ги|я, и *f.* theology.
теоре́м|а, ы *f.* theorem.
теоретизи́р|овать, ую *impf.* to theorize.
теоре́тик, а *m.* theorist.
теорети́ческий *adj.* theoretical.
теорети́ч|ный (~ен, ~на) *adj.* (*pej.*) theoretical, abstract, abstruse.
тео́ри|я, и *f.* theory.
теософи́ческий *adj.* theosophical.
теосо́фи|я, и *f.* theosophy.
тепе́решн|ий *adj.* (*coll.*) present; **~ие лю́ди** people (of) today; **в ~ее вре́мя** at the present time, nowadays.
тепе́рь *adv.* now; nowadays, today.
тёпленьк|ий *adj.* (*coll.*) (nice and) warm; **~ое месте́чко** cushy job.
тепле́|ть, ет *impf.* (*of* **по~**) to get warm.
те́пл|иться, ится *impf.* to flicker, glimmer (*also fig.*); **~ится наде́жда** there is still a glimmer of hope, a ray of hope.
тепли́ц|а, ы *f.* greenhouse, hothouse, conservatory.
тепли́|чный *adj. of* **~ца; ~чное расте́ние** hothouse plant (*also fig.*).
тепло́[1] *adv.* **1.** warmly. **2.** *as pred.* it is warm.
тепл|о́[2], **а́** *nt.* heat; warmth; **де́сять гра́дусов ~а́** ten degrees (*Celsius*) above zero; **держа́ть в ~е́** to keep (in the) warm.
теплово́з, а *m.* diesel locomotive.
теплово́зный *adj.* diesel.
теплов|о́й *adj.* heat; thermal; **т. дви́гатель** heat-engine; **~а́я едини́ца** heat unit, thermal unit; **т. ожо́г** flashburn; **т. уда́р** (*med.*) heat stroke; **~а́я электроста́нция** thermal electric power station; **~а́я эне́ргия** heat energy, thermal energy.
теплоёмкост|ь, и *f.* (*phys.*) heat capacity, thermal capacity; **уде́льная т.** specific heat.
теплокро́вный *adj.* (*zool.*) warm-blooded.
теплолюби́в|ый (~, ~а) *adj.* (*bot.*) heat-loving.
тепломе́р, а *m.* (*phys.*) calorimeter.
теплообме́н, а *m.* (*phys.*) heat exchange.
теплопрово́д, а *m.* hot-water system.
теплопрово́дност|ь, и *f.* heat conductivity.
теплопрово́дный *adj.* heat-conducting.
теплопрозра́чный *adj.* (*phys.*) diathermic.
теплосто́йкий *adj.* heat-proof, heat-resistant.
теплот|а́, ы́ *f.* **1.** (*phys.*) heat; **едини́ца ~ы́** thermal unit. **2.** warmth (*also fig.*); **душе́вная т.** warm-heartedness.
теплотво́рност|ь, и *f.* (*phys.*) heating value, calorific value.
теплотво́рн|ый *adj.* (*phys.*) calorific; **~ая спосо́бность = ~ость**
теплоте́хник, а *m.* heating engineer.
теплоте́хник|а, и *f.* heating engineering.
теплофика́ци|я, и *f.* introduction of a heating system.
теплофици́р|овать, ую *impf. and pf.* to introduce a heating system (in).
теплохо́д, а *m.* motor ship.
теплоцентра́л|ь, и *f.* heating plant.
теплу́шк|а, и *f.* (*coll.*) heated goods van (*for transportation of human beings*).
тёп|лый (~ел, ~ла́, ~ло́, ~лы) *adj.* **1.** (*in var. senses*) warm; **~лая оде́жда** warm clothing; **~лые кра́ски** warm colours; **~лое месте́чко** (*coll.*) cushy job. **2.** warmed, heated. **3.** (*fig.*) warm, cordial; kindly, affectionate; **т. приём** warm welcome. **4.** heartfelt. **5.** (*coll.*) roguish; **~лая компа́ния** bunch of rogues.
теплы́н|ь, и *f.* (*coll.*) warm weather.
тепля́к, а́ *m.* temporary covered and heated enclosure on building site.
терапе́вт, а *m.* therapeutist.
терапевти́ческий *adj.* therapeutic.
терапи́|я, и *f.* therapy; **интенси́вная т.** intensive care.
тератоло́ги|я, и *f.* (*biol.*) teratology.
те́рби|й, я *m.* (*chem.*) terbium.
тереби́льщик, а *m.* flax-puller.
тереб|и́ть, лю́, и́шь *impf.* **1.** to pull (at), pick (at). **2.: т. лён** to pull flax. **3.** (*fig., coll.*) to pester, bother.
те́рем, а, *pl.* **~а́** *m.* (*hist.*) (tower-)chamber; tower.
тере́ть, тру, трёшь, *past* **тёр, тёрла** *impf.* **1.** to rub. **2.** to grate, grind. **3.** to rub, chafe.
тере́ться, трусь, трёшься, *past* **тёрся, тёрлась** *impf.* **1.** to rub o.s.; **(о, обо**+*a.*) to rub (against). **2.** **(о́коло;** *fig., coll.*) to hang (about, round). **3.** **(среди́;** *fig., coll.*) to mix (with), hobnob (with).
терза́|ть, ю *impf.* **1.** to tear to pieces; to pull about. **2.** to torment, torture; **меня́ ~ли сомне́ния** I was a prey to doubts.
терза́|ться, юсь *impf.* (+*i.*) to suffer; to be a prey (to).
тёрк|а, и *f.* (*cul.*) grater.
те́рмин, а *m.* term.
терминологи́ческий *adj.* terminological.
терминоло́ги|я, и *f.* terminology.
терми́т[1], **а** *m.* (*chem.*) thermite.
терми́т[2], **а** *m.* (*zool.*) termite.
терми́т|ный *adj. of* **~**[1]
терми́ческ|ий *adj.* (*phys., tech.*) thermic, thermal; **~ая обрабо́тка** thermal treatment.
термобигуди́ *no sg. indecl.* heated hair rollers.
термодина́мик|а, и *f.* thermodynamics.
термодинами́ческий *adj.* thermodynamic.
термо́метр, а *m.* thermometer; **т. Це́льсия** centigrade thermometer; **поста́вить т. кому́-н.** to take s.o.'s temperature.
термообрабо́тк|а, и *f.* (*tech.*) heat treatment, thermal treatment.

термопа́р|а, ы *f.* (*phys.*) thermocouple.
те́рмос, а *m.* thermos (flask).
термоста́т, а *m.* thermostat.
термоэлектри́ческий *adj.* thermoelectrical; **т. столб** thermopile.
термоэлектро́нный *adj.* thermionic.
термоя́дерный *adj.* thermonuclear.
те́рм|ы, ~ *no sg.* (*hist.*) thermae, (hot) baths.
тёрн, а *m.* (*bot.*) **1.** blackthorn. **2.** sloe(s).
те́рни|е, я *nt.* (*obs.*) **1.** prickly plant. **2.** prickle, thorn.
терно́вник, а *m.* (*bot.*) blackthorn.
терно́в|ый *adj.* **1.** *adj. of* **тёрн** *and* **~ник**. **2.** thorny, prickly; **т. вене́ц** crown of thorns.
тернослі́в, а *m.* damson.
тернослі́ва, ы *f.* = **тернослі́в**
терпели́вост|ь, и *f.* patience.
терпели́в|ый (~, ~а) *adj.* patient.
терпе́ни|е, я *nt.* patience; endurance, perseverance; **вы́вести из ~я** to exasperate; **вы́йти из ~я** to lose patience; **запасти́сь, вооружи́ться ~ем** to summon up patience, have patience.
терпенти́н, а *m.* turpentine.
терпенти́н|ный *adj. of* ~
терпенти́н|овый *adj.* = **~ный**
терп|е́ть, лю́, ~ишь *impf.* **1.** (*pf.* **по~**) to suffer, undergo; **т. пораже́ние** to suffer a defeat, be defeated. **2.** to bear, endure, stand; **мы не могли́ бо́льше т. тако́го хо́лода** we could bear the cold no longer. **3.** to have patience. **4.** to tolerate, suffer, put up (with); **не (мочь) т.** to be unable to bear, endure, stand, support; **т. не могу́** I can't stand it; I hate it; **вре́мя ~ит** there is plenty of time; **вре́мя не ~ит** there is no time to be lost, time is getting short; **де́ло не ~ит** the matter is urgent; **де́ло не ~ит отлага́тельства** the matter brooks no delay.
терп|е́ться, ~ится *impf.* (*impers.*): **ему́,** *etc.*, **не ~ится** (+*inf.*) he, *etc.*, is impatient (to).
терпи́мост|ь, и *f.* tolerance; indulgence; **дом ~и** (*obs.*, *euph.*) brothel.
терпи́м|ый (~, ~а) *adj.* **1.** tolerant; indulgent, forbearing. **2.** tolerable, bearable, supportable.
те́рп|кий (~ок, ~ка́) *adj.* astringent; tart, sharp.
те́рпкост|ь, и *f.* astringency; tartness, sharpness, acerbity.
те́рпн|уть, ет *impf.* (*of* **за~**) (*coll.*) to grow numb.
терпу́г, а́ *m.* (*tech.*) rasp.
террако́т|а, ы *f.* terracotta.
террако́т|овый *adj. of* **~а**
терра́ри|й, я *m.* terrarium.
терра́риум, а *m.* = **терра́рий**
терра́с|а, ы *f.* (*in var. senses*) terrace.
террасир|овать, ую *impf. and pf.* to terrace.
территориа́льн|ый *adj.* territorial; **~ая а́рмия** territorial army; **~ые во́ды** territorial waters.
террито́ри|я, и *f.* territory, confines; area.
терро́р, а *m.* terror.
терроризи́р|овать, ую *impf. and pf.* to terrorize.
террори́зм, а *m.* terrorism; **возду́шный т.** skyjacking, air piracy.
терроризова́ть, у́ю *impf. and pf.* = **~и́ровать**
террори́ст, а *m.* terrorist; **возду́шный т.** skyjacker, air pirate.
террористи́ческий *adj.* terrorist.
террори́ст|ка, ки *f. of* ~
тёрт|ый (~, ~а) *p.p.p. of* **тере́ть** *and adj.* (*full form only*) **1.** ground; grated. **2.** (*fig.*, *coll.*) hardened, experienced; **т. кала́ч** old stager, old hand.
терце́т, а *m.* **1.** (*mus.*) terzetto. **2.** (*liter.*) tercet, triplet.
терци́н|а, ы *f.* (*liter.*) terza rima.
те́рци|я, и *f.* **1.** (*mus.*) mediant; third; **больша́я т.** major third; **ма́лая т.** minor third. **2.** (*math.*) third (= *one sixtieth of a second*). **3.** (*typ.*) 16-point type.
терье́р, а *m.* terrier (*dog.*).
теря́|ть, ю *impf.* (*of* **по~**) (*in var. senses*) to lose; **т. наде́жду** to lose hope; **не т. головы́** to keep one's head; **т. си́лу** to become invalid; **т. си́лу за да́вностью** (*leg.*) to be lost by limitation; **т. по́чву под нога́ми** to feel the ground slipping away from under one's feet; **т. вре́мя на что-н.** to waste time on sth.; **т. в ве́се** to lose weight; **т. в чьём-н. мне́нии** to sink in s.o.'s estimation; **не т. из виду** to keep in sight; (*fig.*) to remember, bear in mind; **нам не́чего т.** we have nothing to lose.
теря́|ться, юсь *impf.* (*of* **по~**) **1.** to get lost; to disappear, vanish. **2.** to fail, decline, decrease, weaken; **па́мять у него́ ~ется** his memory is failing, is going. **3.** to pass unnoticed; to fail to attract notice; **ре́плика не ~лась** the retort did not pass unnoticed. **4.** to lose one's self-possession; to become flustered; **~юсь, ума́ не приложу́** I am at my wits' end. **5.**: **т. в дога́дках, т. в предположе́ниях** to be lost in conjecture.
тёс, а (у) *m.* (*collect.*) boards, planks.
теса́к, а́ *m.* **1.** broadsword; cutlass. **2.** chopper, hatchet.
те|са́ть, шу́, ~шешь *impf.* **1.** to cut, hew. **2.** to trim, square.
тесёмк|а, и *f.* tape, ribbon, lace, braid.
тесём|очный *adj. of* **~ка**
тесёмчатый *adj.* tape-like; **т. глист** tape-worm.
теси́н|а, ы *f.* board, plank.
тес|ло́, ла́, *pl.* **~ла, ~ел** *nt.* adze.
тесни́н|а, ы *f.* gorge, ravine.
тесн|и́ть, ю́, и́шь *impf.* **1.** (*pf.* **по~**) to press, crowd. **2.** to squeeze, constrict; (*of clothing*) to be too tight; **мне грудь ~и́т** I have a tightness in my chest.
тесн|и́ться, ю́сь, и́шься *impf.* **1.** (*pf.* **по~**) to press through, push a way through. **2.** (*pf.* **с~**) to crowd, cluster, jostle one another (*also fig.*; *of thoughts, etc.*).
те́сно *adv.* **1.** closely (*also fig.*); tightly; narrowly; **идти́ т. в ряд** to march shoulder to shoulder; **быть т. свя́зано (с+*i.*)** to be closely linked (with). **2.** *as pred.* it is crowded, it is cramped; it is (too) tight; **в трамва́е бы́ло о́чень т.** the tram was very crowded; **мне т. под мы́шками** it feels tight in the arm-pits.
теснот|а́, ы́ *f.* **1.** crowded state; narrowness, narrow dimensions; tightness; closeness. **2.** crush, squash; **жить в ~е́** to live cooped up; **в ~е́, да не в оби́де** the more the merrier.
те́с|ный (~ен, ~на́, ~но) *adj.* **1.** crowded, cramped; **мир ~ен!** it's a small world. **2.** narrow; **т. прохо́д** narrow passage. **3.** (too) tight. **4.** close, compact; **~ные ряды́** close ranks. **5.** (*fig.*) close, tight; **~ная дру́жба** close friendship. **6.** (*fig.*, *obs.*) hard, difficult; **~ные обстоя́тельства** straitened circumstances. **7.**: **в ~ном смы́сле сло́ва** in the narrow sense of the word.
тесо́вый *adj.* board, plank.
те́ст|о, а *nt.* **1.** dough; pastry; **т. для блино́в** batter. **2.** paste; viscous mass.
тестообра́з|ный (~ен, ~на) *adj.* doughy, dough-like, paste-like.
тест|ь, я *m.* father-in-law (*wife's father*).
тесьм|а́, ы́ *f.* tape, ribbon, lace, braid (*as adornment or for tying sth.*).
тётеньк|а, и *f.* (*affectionate form of* **тётя**, *also used by children in addressing an unknown woman*) aunty.
те́терев, а, *pl.* **~а́, ~о́в** *m.* (*zool.*) black grouse (blackcock); **глухо́й т.** (*i*) capercailzie, (*ii*) (*coll.*) deaf pers.
тетёрк|а, и *f.* grey-hen (*fem. of black grouse*).
тетёр|я, и *f.* **1.** (*dial.*) = **те́терев. 2.** (*coll.*, *joc.*) chap, fellow; **глуха́я т.** deaf pers.; **лени́вая т.** lazybones; **со́нная т.** sleepyhead.
тетив|а́, ы́ *f.* **1.** bowstring. **2.** taut rope. **3.** (*tech.*) string-board, stringer.
тётк|а, и *f.* **1.** aunt. **2.** (*as term of address to any elderly woman*; *coll.*) ma, lady.
тетра́д|ка, ки *f.* = **~ь**
тетра́д|ь, и *f.* **1.** exercise book; copy-book; **т. для рисова́ния** drawing-book; sketch-book. **2.**: **т. пи́счей бума́ги** packet of notepaper. **3.** part, fascicle (*of publication*). **4.** quire (*of manuscript*).
тетрало́ги|я, и *f.* tetralogy.
тетра́эдр, а *m.* (*math.*) tetrahedron.
тётушк|а, и *f.* (*affectionate form of* **тётка**) aunty.
тёт|я, и, *g. pl.* **~ей** *f.* **1.** aunt. **2.** (*used by children to any unknown woman*) lady. **3.** (*joc.*) woman.

те́фтел|и, ей *no sg.* (*cul.*) meat-balls.
тех *g., a., p. pl. of* **тот**
тех... *comb. form, abbr. of* **техни́ческий**
техми́нимум, а *m.* required minimum of technical knowledge.
техна́р|ь, я́ *m.* service engineer; 'techie'.
те́хник, а *m.* **1.** technician; **зубно́й т.** dental mechanic. **2.** technically qualified pers.
те́хник|а, и *f.* **1.** engineering; technics, technology; **вычисли́тельная т.** computer science. **2.** technique, art; **э́то — де́ло ~и** it is a matter of technique; **т. стихосложе́ния** the technique of versification; **овладе́ть ~ой** to master the art. **3.** (*collect.*) technical devices; **т. безопа́сности** safety devices. **4.** (*mil.*) matériel.
те́хникум, а *m.* technical college, training college.
техници́зм, а *m.* preoccupation with technical aspect of sth.
техни́чески *adv.* technically.
техни́ческ|ий *adj.* **1.** (*in var. senses*) technical; engineering; **~ие нау́ки** engineering sciences; **т. персона́л** technical staff; **т. реда́ктор,** *see* **техре́д; т. те́рмин** technical term; **~ие усло́вия** specifications. **2.** (*mil*) maintenance; **~ое обслу́живание** maintenance. **3.: ~ие культу́ры** (*agric.*) industrial crops. **4.: ~ая ско́рость** (*tech.*) maximum speed. **5.** assistant, subordinate (= *not having powers of decision*); **т. сотру́дник** junior member of staff.
технокра́т, а *m.* technocrat.
технократи́ческий *adj.* technocratic.
техно́лог, а *m.* technologist.
технологи́ческий *adj.* technological.
техноло́ги|я, и *f.* technology; **высокосло́жная т.** high technology.
техноро́к, а *m.* (*abbr. of* **техни́ческий руководи́тель**) technical director.
техосмо́тр, а *m.* (*abbr. of* **техни́ческий осмо́тр**) check-up (*of motor vehicle*); **листо́к ~а** ≃ MOT (*Ministry of Transport*) certificate (*of roadworthiness*).
техре́д, а *m.* (*abbr. of* **техни́ческий реда́ктор**) technical editor, copy editor.
тече́ни|е, я *nt.* **1.** flow. **2.** (*fig.*) course; **с ~ем вре́мени** in the course of time, in time. **3.** current, stream (*also fig.*); **по ~ю, про́тив ~я** with the stream. against the stream (*also fig.*). **4.** (*fig.*) trend, tendency. **5.: в т.** (*+g.*) during, in the course (of).
те́чк|а, и *f.* heat (*in animals*).
теч|ь[1]**, и** *f.* leak; **дать т.** to spring a leak; **заде́лать т.** to stop a leak.
течь[2]**, теку́, течёшь, теку́т,** *past* **тёк, текла́** *impf.* **1.** to flow (*also fig.*); to stream; (*fig.*; *of time*) to pass; **у тебя́ кровь течёт и́з носу** your nose is bleeding; **у него́ и́з носу течёт** his nose is running; **у меня́ слю́нки текли́** my mouth was watering. **2.** to leak, be leaky.
те́ш|ить, у, ишь *impf.* (*of* **по~**) **1.** to amuse, entertain. **2.** to gratify, please.
те́ш|иться, усь, ишься *impf.* (*of* **по~**) **1.** (*+i*) to amuse o.s. (with), play (with); **чем бы дитя́ ни ~илось, лишь бы не пла́кало** anything for a quiet life. **2. (над)** to make fun (of).
тёшк|а, и *f.* tyoshka (*abdomen of fish as foodstuff*).
тёщ|а, и *f.* mother-in-law (*wife's mother*).
тиа́р|а, ы *f.* tiara.
Тибе́т, а *m.* Tibet.
тибе́т|ец, ца *m.* Tibetan.
тибе́т|ка, ки *f. of* **~ец**
тибе́тский *adj.* Tibetan.
Тибр, а *m.* the Tiber (*river*).
ти́бр|ить, ю, ишь *impf.* (*of* **с~**) (*coll.*) to pinch, snaffle.
ти́г|ель, ля *m.* (*tech.*) crucible.
ти́гель|ный *adj. of* **~**
Тигр, а *m.* the Tigris (*river*).
тигр, а *m.* tiger.
тигр|ёнок, ёнка, *pl.* **~я́та, ~я́т** *m.* tiger cub.
тигри́ц|а, ы *f.* tigress.
тигро́в|ый *adj. of* **тигр; ~ая шку́ра** tiger-skin.
тик[1]**, а** *m.* (*med.*) tic.
тик[2]**, а** *m.* tick, ticking (*material*).
тик[3]**, а** *m.* (*bot.*) teak.
ти́кань|е, я *nt.* tick, ticking (*of a clock*).
ти́ка|ть, ю *impf.* (*coll.*) to tick.
ти́ккер, а *m.* (*radio*) ticker.
ти́ковый[1] *adj. of* **тик**[2]
ти́ков|ый[2] *adj. of* **тик**[3]**; ~ое де́рево** teak tree, teak wood.
тик-та́к *onomat.* tick-tock.
ти́льд|а, ы *f.* (*typ.*) tilde, swung dash.
ти́мберс, а *m.* (*naut.*) beam, timber.
тимиа́н = тимья́н
тимо́л, а *m.* (*chem.*) thymol.
тимофе́евк|а, и *f.* (*bot.*) timothy-grass.
тимпа́н, а *m.* **1.** (*mus.*) timbrel. **2.** (*archit.*) tympanum.
тимья́н, а *m.* (*bot.*) thyme.
ти́н|а, ы *no pl., f.* slime, mud; mire (*also fig.*).
ти́нистый *adj.* slimy, muddy.
тинкту́р|а, ы *f.* tincture.
тип, а *m.* **1.** (*in var. senses*) type; model. **2.** (*coll.*) fellow, character; **стра́нный т.** odd character.
типа́ж, а́ *m.* (*liter., art*) type.
типиза́ци|я, и *f.* typification.
типизи́р|овать, ую *impf. and pf.* to typify.
ти́пик[1]**, а** *m.* (*eccl.*) typicon (*manual of Orthodox Church containing order of services*).
ти́пик[2]**, а** *m.* (*coll., pej.*) = **тип 2.**
типи́ческий *adj.* **1.** typical (= *constituting a type*). **2.** model, standard.
типи́чност|ь, и *f.* typicalness, typical nature.
типи́ч|ный (~ен, ~на) *adj.* typical (= *characteristic*).
типов|о́й *adj.* model; standard; **~а́я моде́ль** standard model; **~о́е изде́лие** standard product.
типо́граф, а *m.* **1.** printer. **2.** printing-house owner. **3.** printing machine.
типогра́фи|я, и *f.* printing-house, printing-office, press.
типогра́фск|ий *adj.* typographical; **~ое иску́сство** typography.
типогра́фщик, а *m.* (*obs.*) printer.
типолитогра́фи|я, и *f.* typolithography.
типолитогра́фский *adj.* typolithographical.
типологи́ческий *adj.* typological.
типоло́ги|я, и *f.* typology.
типу́н, а́ *m.* pip (*disease of birds*); **т. тебе́ на язы́к!** keep your trap shut!
тир[1]**, а** *m.* shooting-range; shooting gallery.
тир[2]**, а** *m.* (*naut.*) pitch, tar.
тира́д|а, ы *f.* tirade; sally.
тира́ж, а́ *m.* **1.** drawing (*of loan or lottery*); **вы́йти в т.** to be drawn; (*fig.*) to retire from the scene, take a back seat. **2.** circulation; edition; print run; **т. э́той газе́ты полтора́ миллио́на** this newspaper has a circulation of a million and a half; **т. в сто ты́сяч экземпля́ров** an edition of a hundred thousand copies.
тира́н, а *m.* tyrant.
тира́н|ить, ю, ишь *impf.* to tyrannize (over), torment.
тирани́ческий *adj.* tyrannical.
тирани́|я, и *f.* (*hist. and fig.*) tyranny.
тира́нств|о, а *nt.* tyranny.
тира́нств|овать, ую *impf.* **(над)** to tyrannize (over).
тире́ *nt. indecl.* dash.
тир|ова́ть, у́ю *impf.* (*naut.*) to pitch, tar.
тиро́л|ец, ца *m.* Tyrolese, Tyrolean.
Тиро́л|ь, я *m.* the Tyrol, the Tirol.
тиро́л|ька, ьки *f. of* **~ец**
тиро́льский *adj.* Tyrolese, Tyrolean.
тис, а *m.* yew(-tree).
ти́ска|ть, ю *impf.* (*of* **ти́снуть**) **1.** to press, squeeze. **2.** (*typ.*) to pull.
тиск|и́, о́в *no sg.* (*tech.*) vice; **зажа́ть в т.** to grip in a vice; **в ~а́х** (*+g.*) in the grip (of), in the clutches (of).
тисне́ни|е, я *nt.* **1.** stamping, printing. **2.** imprint; design.
тиснёный *adj.* stamped, printed; **т. шрифт** raised (Braille) type.
ти́с|нуть, ну, нешь *pf. of* **~кать**
ти́с|овый *adj. of* **~**

тита́н[1], **а** *m.* (*myth. and fig.*) titan.
тита́н[2], **а** *m.* (*chem.*) titanium.
тита́н[3], **а** *m.* boiler.
титани́ческий *adj.* titanic.
тита́н|овый *adj. of* ~[2]; titanic.
ти́тл|о, а *nt.* **1.** (*obs.*) title; **под ~ом** entitled. **2.** (*philol.*) titlo (*diacritic in ancient and medieval texts*).
ти́тло|вый *adj. of* ~; **т. знак** titlo.
титр[1], **а** *m.* (*cin.*) caption, credit.
титр[2], **а** *m.* (*chem.*) titre.
титрова́ни|е, я *nt.* (*chem.*) titration.
титр|ова́ть, у́ю *impf. and pf.* (*chem.*) to titrate.
ти́тул, а *m.* **1.** (*in var. senses*) title. **2.** title-page.
титуло́в|анный *p.p.p. of* **~а́ть** *and adj.* titled.
титу́л|ова́ть, у́ю *impf. and pf.* to style, call by one's title.
ти́тул|ьный *adj.* **1.** *of* ~; **т. лист** title-page. **2.: ~ьные спи́ски** itemised lists (*of approved building projects*).
титуля́рный *adj.*: **т. сове́тник** (*hist.*) titular counsellor (*civil servant of 9th grade in tsarist Russia*).
тиу́н, а *m.* (*hist.*) tiun (*title of various officials in mediaeval Russia*).
тиф, а *m.* typhus; **брюшно́й т.** typhoid (fever); **сыпно́й т.** typhus, spotted fever.
ти́фдрук, а *m.* (*typ.*) mezzotint.
тифлопедаго́гик|а, и *f.* methods of teaching the blind.
тифо́зн|ый *adj.* typhus; typhoid; **~ая лихора́дка** typhoid fever; *as n.* **т., ~ого** *m.* typhus patient.
ти́х|ий (~, ~а́, ~о) *adj.* **1.** quiet; (*of sounds*) low, soft, gentle, faint; **т. го́лос** low voice. **2.** silent, noiseless; still; **~ая ночь** still night. **3.** (*fig.*) quiet, calm; gentle; still; **~ая жизнь** quiet life; **т. нрав** gentle disposition; **~ая пого́да** calm weather; **в ~ом о́муте че́рти во́дятся** (*prov.*) still waters run deep. **4.** slow, slow-moving; **т. ход** slow speed, slow pace; **~ая торго́вля** slack trade.
Ти́х|ий океа́н, ~ого ~а *m.* the Pacific Ocean; the Pacific.
ти́хо[1] *adv.* **1.** quietly; softly, gently; **т. постуча́ть** to knock gently. **2.** silently, noiselessly. **3.** (*fig.*) quietly, calmly; still; **сиде́ть т.** to sit still; **т.** gently!, careful! **4.** slowly; **дела́ иду́т т.** things are slack.
ти́хо[2] *as pred.* **1.** it is quiet, there is not a sound; **ста́ло т.** it became quiet, the noise died away. **2.** (*fig.*) it is quiet; it is calm; **на душе́ у меня́ ста́ло т.** my mind is at rest. **3.** (*comm.*) it is slack; **с хло́пком т.** cotton is slack.
тихомо́лком *adv.* (*coll.*) quietly, without a sound.
тихо́нько *adv.* (*coll.*) quietly; softly, gently.
тихо́н|я, и, *g. pl.* **~ей** *c.g.* demure pers.; prig; **прики́дываться ~ей, смотре́ть ~ей** to look as if butter would not melt in one's mouth.
тихоокеа́н|ец, ца *m.* sailor of Pacific fleet.
тихоокеа́нский *adj.* Pacific.
тихохо́д, а *m.* (*zool.*) sloth.
тихохо́д|ный (~ен, ~на) *adj.* slow.
ти́ше 1. *comp. of* **ти́хий** *and* **ти́хо. 2. т.!** (*i*) (be) quiet!, silence! (*ii*) gently!; careful!
тишин|а́, ы́ *f.* quiet, silence; stillness; **нару́шить ~у́** to break the silence; **соблюда́ть ~у́** to keep quiet.
тишко́м *adv.* (*coll.*) quietly; imperceptibly.
тиш|ь, и, в ~и́ *f.* quiet, silence; stillness; **т. да гладь** peace and quiet.
т. к. (*abbr. of* **так как**) as, since.
тка́н|евый *adj. of* **~ь 1., 2.**
тка́ный *adj.* woven.
тка́н|ь, и *f.* **1.** fabric, cloth; **льняны́е ~и** linen(s); **шёлковые ~и** silks. **2.** (*anat.*) tissue. **3.** (*fig.*) substance, essence; **т. расска́за** gist of a story.
ткань|ё, я́ *nt.* **1.** weaving. **2.** woven fabrics, cloth.
тканьёвый *adj.* woven.
ткать, тку, ткёшь, *past* **ткал, ткала́, тка́ло** *impf.* (*of* **со~**) to weave; **т. паути́ну** to spin a web.
тка́цк|ий *adj.* weaver's, weaving; **~ое де́ло** weaving; **т. стано́к** loom; **т. челно́к** shuttle.
ткач, а́ *m.* weaver.
тка́честв|о, а *nt.* weaving.
ткачи́х|а, и *f. of* **ткач**
ткн|у́ть(ся), у́(сь), ёшь(ся) *pf. of* **ты́кать(ся)**
тлен, а *m.* (*obs.*) decay.
тле́ни|е, я *nt.* **1.** decay, decomposition, putrefaction. **2.** smouldering.
тле́н|ный (~ен, ~на) *adj.* (*obs.*) liable to decay.
тлетво́р|ный (~ен, ~на) *adj.* **1.** putrefactive; putrid. **2.** (*fig.*) pernicious, noxious.
тле́|ть, ет *impf.* **1.** to rot, decay, decompose, putrefy; to moulder. **2.** to smoulder (*also fig.*); **ещё ~ет наде́жда** there is still a glimmer of hope.
тле́|ться, ется *impf.* to smoulder.
тл|я, и, *g. pl.* **~ей** *f.* **1.** plant-louse, aphis. **2.** (*fig., pej.*) louse.
тмин, а *m.* **1.** caraway. **2.** (*collect.*) caraway-seeds.
тми́н|ный *adj. of* ~; **~ная во́дка** kümmel.
то[1] *pron.* (*nom. and a. sg. nt. of* **тот**) that; **то, что...** the fact that ...; **то, что́** that which; **то был, была́, бы́ло** that was; **то бы́ли** those were; **то́ есть** that is (to say); **то бишь** that is to say; **то ли де́ло** (*coll.*) what a difference, how different (= *how much better*); **а то,** *see* **а; (да) и то** and that, at that; **там лишь оди́н мужчи́на, и то восьмидесятиле́тний стари́к** there is only one man there, and that an old man of eighty.
то[2] *conj.* **1.** (*in apodosis of conditional sentence*) then (*or not translated*); **е́сли вас там не бу́дет, то и я не пойду́** if you won't be there, (then) I shan't go either. **2.: то..., то** now ..., now; **то тут, то там** now here, now there. **3.: не то..., не то** either ... or; whether ... or; half ..., half; **не то по глу́пости, не то по зло́бе** either through stupidity or through malice; **не то удивле́ние, не то доса́да** half surprise, half annoyance. **4.: не то, что́бы..., но** it is not, it was not that ... (but); **не то, что́бы я не хоте́л слу́шать радиопереда́чу, но я про́сто забы́л о ней** it was not that I did not want to hear the broadcast: I simply forgot about it. **5.: то и де́ло, то и знай** (*coll.*) time and again; incessantly, perpetually.
-то[1] *emph. particle* (*in coll. Russ. oft. merely adds familiar tone*) just, precisely, exactly (*or not translated*); **в то́м-то и де́ло** that's just it; **чего́ же ва́м-то боя́ться?** what have *you* to be afraid of?; **вот ведь беда́-то где!** that's where the whole trouble lies.
-то[2] *particle forming indef. prons and advs.* (**кто́-то, како́й-то, когда́-то,** *etc.*).
т. о. (*abbr. of* ***таки́м о́бразом***) thus, in this way.
тобо́й, тобо́ю *i. of* **ты**
тов. (*abbr. of* **това́рищ**) Comrade.
това́р, а *m.* goods; wares; article; commodity; **~ы широ́кого потребле́ния** consumer goods; **показа́ть т. лицо́м** (*coll.*) to show sth. to good effect.
това́рищ, а *m.* **1.** comrade; friend; companion; colleague; **т. де́тства** childhood friend; **т. по несча́стью** fellow-sufferer, companion in distress; **т. по ору́жию** comrade-in-arms; **т. по рабо́те** colleague; mate; **т. по шко́ле** school-friend. **2.** (*as style and as term of address in former USSR*) Comrade. **3.** person; **э́тот т. прие́хал из Москвы́** this man has come from Moscow; **вот т. из Министе́рства** here is the man from the ministry. **4.** (*obs.*) assistant, deputy, vice-; **т. председа́теля** vice-president.
това́рищеск|ий *adj.* **1.** comradely; friendly; **с ~им приве́том** (*epistolary formula*) with fraternal greetings. **2.** of equals; **т. суд** Comrades' Court (*tribunal of fellow-citizens or fellow-workers — before 1917, of fellow-members of a profession — empowered to pass censure in cases of misconduct*). **3.** (*sport*) friendly, unofficial; **~ое состяза́ние, ~ая встре́ча** friendly (match).
това́риществ|о, а *nt.* **1.** comradeship, fellowship; **чу́вство ~а** feeling of solidarity. **2.** company; association, society; **т. на пая́х** joint-stock company. **3.** companionship, partnership.
това́рк|а, и *f.* (*coll., obs.*) friend.
това́рност|ь, и *f.* (*econ.*) marketability.
това́рн|ый *adj.* **1.** goods; **т. знак** trade mark; **т. склад** warehouse. **2.** (*rail.*) goods, freight; **т. ваго́н** goods truck; **т. парк** goods yard; **т. соста́в** goods train. **3.** (*econ.*) commodity; **~ая проду́кция** commodity output; **~ое хозя́йство** commodity economy. **4.** (*econ.*) marketable; **~ое зерно́** marketable grain.

товарове́д, а *m.* commodity researcher.
товарове́дени|е, я *nt.* commodity research.
товарообме́н, а *m.* (*econ.*) barter.
товарооборо́т, а *m.* commodity circulation.
товароотправи́тел|ь, я *nt.* consignor, forwarder of goods.
това́ро-пассажи́рский *adj.*: **т.-п. по́езд** mixed goods and passenger train.
товарополуча́тел|ь, я *m.* consignee.
товаропроводя́щ|ий *adj.*: **~ая сеть** commodity distribution network.
то́г|а, и *f.* (*hist.*) toga; **ряди́ться в ~у** (+*g.*) (*rhet.*) to don the garb (of), array o.s. (as).
тогда́ 1. *adv.* then (= (*i*) at that time, (*ii*) in that case). **2.: когда́..., т.** (*conj.*) when; **когда́ решу́сь, т. тебе́ напишу́** I will write to you when I have decided. **3.: т. как** (*conj.*) whereas, while.
тогда́шний *adj.* (*coll.*) of that time, of those days; the then.
того́[1] *int.* (*filling pause in utterance*) er ..., um ...
того́[2] *as pred.* you know (*coll., euph.* = (*i*) abnormal, simple, (*ii*) drunk, (*iii*) mediocre); **к десяти́ часа́м он был совсе́м т.** by ten o'clock he was completely — you know.
того́[3] *g. sg. m. and nt. of* **тот**
тожде́ственност|ь, и *f.* identity.
тожде́ствен|ный (~, ~на) *adj.* identical, one and the same.
то́ждеств|о, а *nt.* identity.
то́же[1] *adv.* also, as well, too.
то́же[2] *particle* (*coll., iron.*) *expr. disapproval of s.o.'s conduct or scepticism with regard to s.o.'s pretensions to knowledge, etc.*: **ты т. хоро́ш!** you're a fine one, I must say; **т. знато́к нашёлся!** since when is he an expert!; as if he were an expert!
тоже́ственност|ь, и *f.* = **тожде́ственность**
тоже́ственный *adj.* = **тожде́ственный**
то́жеств|о, а *nt.* = **то́ждество**
ток[1], **а** *m.* (*in var. senses*) current; **т. высо́кого напряже́ния** (*elec.*) high-tension current; **т. подогре́ва** (*radio*) heater current; **т. уте́чки** leakage current; **переме́нный т.** alternating current; **постоя́нный т.** direct current.
ток[2], **а, о ~е, на ~у́,** *pl.* **~а́, ~о́в** *m.* (*birds'*) mating-place.
ток[3], **а, о ~е́, на ~у́,** *pl.* **~а́** *and* **~и, ~о́в** *m.* threshing-floor.
ток[4], **а** *m.* toque.
тока́|й, я *m.* Tokay (wine).
тока́йск|ое, ого *nt.* = **тока́й**
тока́рн|ый *adj.* (*tech.*) turning; **~ая мастерска́я** turnery; **т. резе́ц** lathe tool; **т. стано́к** lathe; **автомати́ческий т. стано́к** engine lathe; **т. цех** turning shop; *as n.* **~ая, ~ой** *f.* = **~ая мастерска́я.**
то́кар|ь, я, *pl.* **~и** *and* **~я́** *m.* turner, lathe operator.
То́кио *m. indecl.* Tokyo.
токка́т|а, ы *f.* (*mus.*) toccata.
то́кмо *adv.* (*arch. or coll.*) only.
ток|ова́ть, у́ет *impf.* (*of birds*) to utter the mating-call.
токоприёмник, а *m.* (*elec.*) current collector, trolley (*of elec. locomotive, trolleybus, etc.*).
токсикологи́ческий *adj.* toxicological.
токсиколо́ги|я, и *f.* toxicology.
токсикома́н, а *m.* glue sniffer, solvent abuser.
токсикома́ни|я, и *f.* glue sniffing, solvent abuse.
токси́н, а *m.* (*med.*) toxin.
токси́ческий *adj.* toxic.
тол, а *m.* (*chem.*) tolite.
то́л|евый *adj. of* **~ь**
толи́к|а, и *f.* (*coll.*): **ма́лая т., не́которая т.** a little, a small quantity; a few.
толк[1], **а (у)** *m.* **1.** sense; understanding; **бе́з ~у** senselessly, wildly; **с ~ом** sensibly, intelligently; **сбить с ~у** to confuse, muddle; **взять в т.** (*coll.*) to understand, grasp, get, see; **от него́ ~у не добьёшься** you'll get no sense out of him. **2.** (*coll.*) use, profit; **из э́того не вы́йдет ~у** nothing will come of it; **понима́ть, знать т. (в**+*p.*) to know what one is talking about (in), know one's onions (in). **3.** (*obs.*) persuasion (= *sect, grouping*).
толк[2] *as pred.* (*coll.*) = **~ну́л**
толка́тел|ь, я *m.* **1.** (*tech.*) pusher, push rod, tappet. **2.: т. ядра́** (*sport*) shot-putter.
толк|а́ть, а́ю *impf.* (*of* **~ну́ть**) **1.** to push, shove; to jog; **т. ло́ктем** to nudge. **2.** (*sport*) **т. шта́нгу** to weight-lift; **т. ядро́** to put the shot. **3.** (**на**+*a.*) to push (into), incite (to), instigate (to).
толк|а́ться, а́юсь *impf.* **1.** (*impf. only*) to push (one another). **2.** (*pf.* **~ну́ться**): **т. в дверь** to knock on the door. **3.** (*pf.* **~ну́ться**) (**к**) to try to see, try to get access (to). **4.** (*impf. only*) (*coll.*) to knock about.
толка́ч, а́ *m.* **1.** (*rail.*) pusher. **2.** pestle, pounder. **3.** (*fig., coll.*) pusher, go-getter, fixer (*in industrial enterprises*).
то́лк|и, ов *pl.* talk; rumours, gossip; **иду́т т. о том, что** it is said that, it is rumoured that.
толк|ну́ть, ну́, нёшь *pf. of* **~а́ть**
толк|ну́ться, ну́сь, нёшься *pf. of* **~а́ться 2., 3.**
толкова́ни|е, я *nt.* **1.** interpretation; exegesis. **2.** (*pl.*) commentary.
толкова́тел|ь, я *m.* interpreter, commentator, expounder.
толк|ова́ть, у́ю *impf.* **1.** to interpret; **ло́жно т. чьи-н. слова́** to misinterpret, misconstrue s.o.'s words. **2.** (+*d.*; *coll.*) to explain (to); **ско́лько ему́ ни ~у́й, он ничего́ не понима́ет** it's a waste of time trying to explain things to him. **3.** (*coll.*) to talk; to say; **т. де́ло** to talk sense; **он всё своё ~у́ет** he keeps on about the same thing; **~у́ют, бу́дто** people say that, they say that.
толко́в|ый (~, ~а) *adj.* **1.** intelligent, sensible. **2.** intelligible, clear. **3.** (*full form only*) **т. слова́рь** explanatory dictionary.
то́лком *adv.* (*coll.*) **1.** plainly, clearly; **поговори́ть т.** to talk straight. **2.** seriously, in all seriousness.
толкотн|я́, и́ *f.* (*coll.*) crush, scrum, squash; crowding.
тол|ку́, ку́т *see* **~о́чь**
толку́чий *adj.*: **т. ры́нок** (*coll.*) flea market.
толку́ч|ка, ки *f.* (*coll.*) **1.** crush, scrum, squash; crowded place. **2.** = **~ий ры́нок**
толма́ч, а́ *m.* (*obs.*) interpreter.
то́л|овый *adj. of* **~**
толокн|о́, а́ *nt.* oat flour.
толокня́нк|а, и *f.* (*bot.*) bearberry (*Arctostaphylos*).
толокн|о́нный *adj. of* **~но́; т. лоб** blockhead.
тол|о́чь, ку́, чёшь, ку́т, *past* **~о́к, ~кла́** *impf.* (*of* **рас~** *and* **с~**) to pound, crush; **т. во́ду в сту́пе** to beat the air, mill the wind.
тол|о́чься, ку́сь, чёшься, ку́тся, *past* **~о́кся, ~кла́сь** *impf.* (*coll.*) to knock about; to gad about; (*fig.*) to swarm.
толп|а́, ы́, *pl.* **~ы** *f.* crowd; throng; multitude.
толп|и́ться, и́тся *impf.* to crowd; to throng; to cluster.
толсте́нный *adj.* (*coll.*) very fat.
толсте́|ть, ю *impf.* (*of* **по~**) to grow fat, grow stout; to put on weight.
толст|и́ть, и́т *impf.* (*coll.*) to make (look) fat; **хлеб о́чень ~и́т** bread is very fattening; **шу́ба её о́чень ~и́ла** the fur coat made her look very fat.
толстобрю́х|ий (~, ~а) *adj.* (*coll.*) fat-bellied.
толстове́д, а *m.* Tolstoy scholar.
толсто́в|ец, ца *m.* Tolstoyan.
толсто́вк|а[1], **и** *f. of* **толсто́вец**
толсто́вк|а[2], **и** *f.* tolstovka (*long belted blouse*).
толсто́вств|о, а *nt.* Tolstoyism.
толстогу́б|ый (~, ~а) *adj.* thick-lipped.
толстоко́ж|ий (~, ~а) *adj.* **1.** thick-skinned (*also fig.*). **2.** (*zool.*) pachydermatous; **~ее живо́тное** pachyderm.
толстомо́рдый *adj.* (*coll.*) fat-faced.
толстогу́з|ый (~, ~а) *adj.* pot-bellied (*hist., esp. as term of abuse applied to merchants*).
толстосте́нный *adj.* (*tech.*) thick-walled.
толстосу́м, а *f.* (*obs., coll.*) money-bags.
толсту́х|а, и *f.* (*coll.*) fat woman; fat girl.
толсту́шк|а, и *f. affectionate form of* **толсту́ха**
то́лст|ый (~, ~а́, ~о) *adj.* **1.** fat; stout, corpulent; **т. нос** big nose. **2.** thick; heavy; stout; **т. слой** thick layer; **~ая бума́га** thick paper; **т. про́вод** heavy-gauge wire; **т. журна́л** 'fat magazine' (= *literary monthly, etc.*); **~ая кишка́** (*anat.*) large intestine.

толстя́к, а́ *m.* fat man; fat boy.
толуо́л, а *m.* (*chem.*) toluene.
толче́ни|е, я *nt.* pounding, crushing.
толчёный *adj.* pounded, crushed; ground.
тол|чёт *see* **~о́чь**
толче|я́[1], **и́** *f.* (*coll.*) crush, scrum, squash.
толче|я́[2], **и́** *f.* (*tech.*) mill.
толч|о́к[1], **ка́** *m.* **1.** push, shove; (*sport*) put. **2.** jolt, bump; (earthquake) shock, tremor. **3.** (*fig.*) push, shove; incitement, stimulus; **дать т. к эконо́мике** to kick-start the economy; **послужи́ть мо́щным ~ко́м (к)** to serve as a powerful spur (to).
толчо́к[2] = **толку́чий ры́нок**
то́лщ|а, и *f.* **1.** thickness; **т. сне́га** depth of snow. **2.: в ~е наро́да** in the (thick of the) people.
то́лще *comp. of* **то́лстый**
толщин|а́, ы́ *f.* **1.** fatness, stoutness, corpulence. **2.** thickness.
тол|ь, я *m.* (tarred) roofing paper.
то́лько 1. *adv.* only, merely; solely; alone; just; **не т...., но и** not only ..., but also; **поду́май(те) т.!** just think!; **т. и всего́, да и т.** (*coll.*) that's all; (and) that's that; **т. что не** (*coll.*) the only thing lacking (is, was); **она́ и бога́та и краси́ва, т. что не благоразу́мна** she has money and looks, the only thing she lacks is sense; **не т. что** (*coll.*) not to mention, let alone; **т. за после́дние пять лет...** in the last five years alone .... **2.: т. что** (*adv. and conj.*) just, only just; **он т. что позвони́л** he has just rung up; **т. что мы доехали до ста́нции, про́било шесть** we had just reached the station when it struck six. **3.** *conj.* (**+как, лишь**) as soon as; one has only to ...; **т. ска́жешь, я уйду́** you have only to say (the word) and I will go. **4.** *conj.* only, but; **с удово́льствием, т. не сего́дня** with pleasure, only not today. **5.: т. бы** (*+inf.*) (*particle*) if only; **т. бы получи́ть о нём ве́сточку** if only we could hear news of him. **6.** *particle intensifying interrog. prons. and advs.*: **заче́м т.?** why on earth?, whatever for?; **кого́ т. он не зна́ет?** whom does he *not* know?; **где т. они́ не быва́ли?** where have they *not* been?
то́лько-то́лько *adv.* (*coll.*) only just.
том, а, *pl.* **~а́,** **~о́в** *m.* volume.
томага́вк, а *m.* tomahawk.
тома́т, а *m.* **1.** tomato. **2.** tomato purée.
тома́тный *adj.* tomato; **т. сок** tomato juice.
то́мик, а *m. dim. of* **том**
томи́льн|ый *adj.* (*tech.*): **т. коло́дец** soaking pit; **~ая печь** soaking furnace.
томи́тел|ьный (~ен, ~на) *adj.* wearisome, tedious, wearing; tiresome, trying; agonizing; **т. зной** trying heat; **~ьное ожида́ние** agonizing suspense; tedious wait; **~ьная ску́ка** deadly boredom.
том|и́ть, лю́, и́шь *impf.* (*of* **ис~**) **1.** to tire, wear, weary; to torment; to wear down; **т. в тюрьме́** to leave to languish in prison; **меня́ ~и́т жа́жда** I am parched. **2.** (*cul.*) to stew; to braise. **3.** (*tech.*) to render malleable.
том|и́ться, лю́сь, и́шься *impf.* **1.** to pine; to languish; **т. жа́ждой** to be parched with thirst; **т. ожида́нием** to be in an agony of suspense; **т. в плену́, в тюрьме́** to languish in captivity. **2.** *pass. of* **~и́ть**
томле́ни|е, я *nt.* **1.** languor. **2.** (*tech.*) malleablizing, cementation.
томлён|ый *adj.* **1.** (*cul.*) stewed; braised. **2.** (*tech.*) malleablized; **~ая сталь** converted steel, cement steel.
то́мност|ь, и *f.* languor.
то́м|ный (~ен, ~на́) *adj.* languid, languorous.
томпа́к, а́ *m.* tombac (*copper and zinc alloy*).
тон, а, *pl.* **~ы** *and* **~а́** *m.* **1.** (*pl.* **~ы**) (*mus. and fig.*) tone; **~ом вы́ше, ни́же** a tone higher, lower; **хоро́ший, дурно́й т.** good, bad form; **зада́ть т.** to set the tone; **перемени́ть т.** to change one's tone; **попа́сть в т.** to hit the right note. **2.** (*pl.* **~а́**) (colour) tone, tint.
тона́льност|ь, и *f.* (*mus.*) key.
то́ненький *adj.* thin; slender, slim.
тонзу́р|а, ы *f.* tonsure.
тонизи́р|овать, ую *impf. and pf.* (*physiol.*) to tone up.
то́ник, а *m.* tonic (water).
то́ник|а, и *f.* (*mus.*) tonic, keynote.
тонин|а́, ы *f.* fineness.
тони́ческий[1] *adj.* (*mus., liter.*) tonic.
тони́ческий[2] *adj.* (*physiol., med*) tonic.
то́н|кий (~ок, ~ка́, ~ко) *adj.* **1.** thin; slender, slim; **т. ло́мтик** thin slice; **~кая кишка́** (*anat.*) small intestine. **2.** fine; delicate; refined; dainty; **~кое бельё** fine linen; **т. за́пах** delicate perfume; **~кая рабо́та** fine workmanship; **т. у́жин** dainty supper; **~кие черты́ лица́** refined features. **3.: т. го́лос** thin voice. **4.** (*fig.*) subtle, delicate; fine, nice; **т. вопро́с** nice point; **т. знато́к** connoisseur; **т. кри́тик** shrewd critic; **~кая лесть** subtle flattery; **т. намёк** gentle hint; **~кое разли́чие** subtle, fine, nice distinction; **т. ум** subtle intellect. **5.** (*of the senses*) keen. **6.: т. сон** light sleep. **7.** (*coll., pej.*) sharp; crafty, sly.
то́нко *adv.* **1.** thinly. **2.** subtly, delicately, finely, nicely.
тонковолокни́ст|ый (~, ~а) *adj.* fine-fibred.
тонкозерни́ст|ый (~, ~а) *adj.* fine-grained.
тонкоко́ж|ий (~, ~а) *adj.* thin-skinned.
тонколистов|о́й *adj.* (*tech.*) sheet; **~о́е желе́зо** sheet iron; **т. стан** sheet rolling mill.
тонконтро́л|ь, я *m.* (*radio*) tone control.
тонкопряди́льн|ый *adj.*: **~ая маши́на** fine-spinning frame.
тонкору́нный *adj.* fine-fleeced.
тонкосте́нный *adj.* (*tech.*) thin-walled.
то́нкост|ь, и *f.* **1.** thinness; slenderness, slimness. **2.** fineness. **3.** subtlety. **4.** nice point, nicety, subtle point; **до ~ей** to a nicety; **вдава́ться в ~и** to split hairs.
тонкосуко́нный *adj.* (*text.*) fine cloth.
тонкошёрстный *adj.* fine-wool, fine woollen.
тонкошёрст|ый = **~ный**
тонме́йстер, а *m.* (*radio*) sound director.
то́нн|а, ы *f.* (*metric*) ton, tonne.
тонна́ж, а *m.* tonnage.
тонне́ль = **тунне́ль**
то́нн|ый (~а, ~о) *adj.* (*coll., iron.*) (*obs.*) grand; comme il faut.
то́нус, а *m.* (*physiol., med.*) tone.
тон|у́ть, у́, ~ешь *impf.* **1.** (*pf.* **по~**) to sink, go down. **2.** (*pf.* **у~**) to drown. **3.** (*pf.* **у~**) (**в**+*p.*) to sink (in); to be lost (in); to be hidden (in, by), be covered (in, by); **т. в поду́шках** to sink in the pillows; **т. в дела́х** to be up to one's eyes in work; **надгро́бный па́мятник ~ет в высо́кой траве́** the tomb-stone is hidden from view by the long grass.
тонфи́льм, а *m.* sound film; (*radio*) recording.
то́ньше *comp. of* **то́нкий** *and* **то́нко**
то́н|я, и *f.* **1.** fishery, fishing-ground. **2.** haul (*of fish*).
топ *as pred.* (*coll.*) = **~нул**
топа́з, а *m.* (*min.*) topaz.
топа́з|овый *adj. of* **~**
то́п|ать, аю *impf.* **1.** (*pf.* **~нуть**) to stamp; **т. нога́ми** to stamp one's feet. **2.** (*impf. only*) (*coll.*) to go, walk.
топинамбу́р, а *m.* Jerusalem artichoke.
топ|и́ть[1], **лю́, ~ишь** *impf.* **1.** to stoke (*a boiler, a stove, etc.*). **2.** to heat.
топ|и́ть[2], **лю́, ~ишь** *impf.* **1.** to melt (down), render. **2.: т. молоко́** to bake milk.
топ|и́ть[3], **лю́, ~ишь** *impf.* **1.** (*pf.* **по~**) to sink. **2.** (*pf.* **у~**) to drown; (*fig., coll.*) to wreck, ruin; **т. го́ре в вине́** to drown one's sorrows in drink.
топ|и́ться[1], **~ится** *impf.* (*of a stove, etc.*) to burn, be alight.
топ|и́ться[2], **~ится** *impf.* **1.** to melt. **2.** *pass of* **~и́ть**[2]
топ|и́ться[3], **лю́сь, ~ишься** *impf.* (*of* **у~**) to drown o.s.
то́пк|а[1], **и** *f.* **1.** stoking. **2.** heating. **3.** furnace; (*on locomotive*) fire-box.
то́пк|а[2], **и** *f.* melting (down).
то́п|кий (~ок, ~ка́, ~ко) *adj.* boggy, marshy, swampy.
топлён|ый *adj.* melted; **~ое молоко́** baked milk.
то́плив|ный *adj. of* **~о**; **~ная нефть** fuel oil.
то́плив|о, а *nt.* fuel; **жи́дкое т.** fuel oil; **твёрдое т.** solid fuel.
то́п|нуть, ну, нешь *pf. of* **~ать**
топо́граф, а *m.* topographer.

топографи́ческий *adj.* topographical.
топогра́фи|я, и *f.* topography.
то́пол|евый *adj. of* **~ь**
то́пол|ь, я, *pl.* **~и** *and* **~я́** *m.* poplar; **пиромида́льный т.** Lombardy poplar.
топони́ми|ка, ки *f.* (*collect.*) place-names (*of a region*).
топони́ми|я, и *f.* toponymy.
топо́р, а́ *m.* axe; **хоть т. ве́шай** (*of close atmosphere*; *coll.*) you could cut it with a knife.
топо́рик, а *m.* hatchet.
топори́щ|е[1], **а** *nt.* axe-handle, axe helve.
топори́щ|е[2], **а** *nt.* large axe.
топо́р|ный (~ен, ~на) *adj.* clumsy, crude; uncouth.
топо́рщ|ить, ит *impf.* (*coll.*) to bristle.
топо́рщ|иться, ится *impf.* (*coll.*) **1.** to bristle (*intrans.*). **2.** to puff up.
то́пот, а *m.* tread; tramp; **ко́нский т.** clatter of horses' hoofs.
топо|та́ть, чу́, ~́чешь *impf.* (*coll.*) to stamp; (*of horses*) to clatter.
то́почн|ый *adj.* furnace; **~ая коро́бка** fire-box; **~ое простра́нство** combustion chamber; **~ая труба́** furnace flue.
то́псел|ь, я *m.* (*naut.*) topsail.
топ|та́ть, чу́, ~́чешь *impf.* **1.** to trample (down). **2.** to make dirty (*with one's feet*). **3.** to trample out (*grapes, etc.*); **т. гли́ну** to knead clay.
топ|та́ться, чу́сь, ~́чешься *impf.* to stamp; **т. на ме́сте** to mark time (*also fig.*).
Топты́гин, а *m.* (*joc.*) Bruin.
топча́к, а́ *m.* treadmill.
топча́н, а́ *m.* trestle-bed.
топы́р|ить, ю, ишь *impf.* (*coll.*) to bristle; to spread wide.
топы́р|иться, ится *impf.* (*coll.*) to bristle (*intrans.*).
топ|ь, и *f.* bog, marsh, swamp.
то́р|а, ы *f.* (*relig.*) Torah, Pentateuch.
то́рб|а, ы *f.* bag; **носи́ться (с+*i.*) как (дура́к) с пи́саной ~ой** (*coll.*) to make a great song and dance (about).
торг[1], **а, о ~́е, на ~у́,** *pl.* **~и́** *m.* **1.** trading; bargaining, haggling. **2.** (*obs.*) market. **3.** (*pl.*) auction; **прода́ть с ~о́в** to sell by auction. **4.** (*pl.*) tender.
торг[2], **а** *m.* (*abbr. of* ***торго́вая организа́ция***) trading organization.
торг... *comb. form, abbr. of* **торго́вый**
...торг *comb. form, abbr. of* **1. торг**[2]. **2. торго́вля**
торга́ш, а́ *m.* (*pej.*) **1.** (small) tradesman. **2.** mercenary-minded pers.
торга́ш|еский *adj. of* **~**
торга́шество, а *nt.* **1.** small trading. **2.** mercenary-mindedness.
торг|ова́ть, у́ю *impf.* **1.** (*impf. only*) (+*i.*) to trade (in), deal (in), sell. **2.** (*impf. only*) (*of a shop or business*) to be open. **3.** (*pf.* **с~**) (*coll.*) to bargain (for).
торг|ова́ться, у́юсь *impf.* **1.** (*pf.* **с~**) (**с**+*i.*) to bargain (with), haggle (with). **2.** (*impf. only*) (*coll.*) to argue.
торго́в|ец, ца *m.* merchant; trader, dealer; tradesman; **т. нарко́тиками** drug trafficker *or* pusher.
торго́вк|а, и *f.* market-woman, stall-holder; woman street-trader.
торго́вл|я, и *f.* trade, commerce; **посы́лочная т.** mail-order.
торго́во-посы́лочн|ый *adj.*: **~ая фи́рма** mail-order firm.
торго́в|ый *adj.* trade, commercial; mercantile; **т. бала́нс** balance of trade; **т. дом** business house, firm; **~ая пала́та** chamber of commerce; **т. представи́тель** trade representative; **~ая сеть** (*collect.*) shops; **~ая то́чка** shop; **~ое су́дно** merchant ship; **т. флот** merchant navy, mercantile marine.
торгпре́д, а *m.* (*abbr. of* ***торго́вый представи́тель***) trade representative.
торгпре́дств|о, а *nt.* (*abbr. of* ***торго́вое представи́тельство***) trade delegation.
торгфло́т, а *m.* merchant navy.
тореадо́р, а *m.* toreador.
тор|е́ц, ца́ *m.* **1.** butt-end, face (*of beam, plank*). **2.** wooden paving-block. **3.** pavement of wooden blocks.
торже́ственност|ь, и *f.* solemnity.
торже́ствен|ный (~, ~на) *adj.* **1.** ceremonial; festive; gala; **т. въезд** ceremonial entry; **т. день** red-letter day; **~ная оде́жда** ceremonial attire. **2.** solemn; **~ная кля́тва** solemn vow; **т. слу́чай** solemn occasion.
торжеств|о́, а́ *nt.* **1.** celebration; (*pl.*) festivities, rejoicings. **2.** triumph (= *victory*). **3.** triumph, exultation; **сказа́ть с ~о́м** to say triumphantly; to say gloatingly.
торжеств|ова́ть, у́ю *impf.* **1.** to celebrate; **т. побе́ду** to celebrate a victory; (*fig.*) to be victorious. **2. (над)** to triumph (over); to exult (over).
торжеств|у́ющий *pres. part. act. of* **~ова́ть** *and adj.* triumphant, exultant.
то́ржищ|е, а *nt.* (*obs.*) market, bazaar.
то́ри *m. indecl.* (*pol.*) Tory.
то́ри|й, я *m.* (*chem.*) thorium.
торкре́т, а *m.*: **т.(-бето́н)** (*tech.*) gunite.
торма́шк|и: вверх т., вверх ~ами (*coll.*) head over heels, upside down, topsy-turvy.
торможе́ни|е, я *nt.* **1.** (*tech.*) braking. **2.** (*psych.*) inhibition.
то́рмоз, а *m.* **1.** (*pl.* **~а́**) brake; **т. отка́та** (*mil.*) recoil brake; **т. нака́та** (*mil.*) counter-recoil brake. **2.** (*pl.* **~ы**) (*fig.*) brake; drag, hindrance, obstacle.
тормо|зи́ть, жу́, зи́шь *impf.* (*of* **за~**) **1.** (*tech.*) to brake, apply the brake (to). **2.** (*fig.*) to hamper, impede, be a drag (on), be an obstacle in the way (of). **3.** (*psych.*) to inhibit.
тормозн|о́й *adj.* (*tech.*) brake, braking; **т. башма́к** brake-shoe; **~а́я площа́дка** (*railw.*) brake-platform; **~а́я раке́та** retro-rocket.
тормош|и́ть, у́, и́шь *impf.* (*coll.*) **1.** to pull about. **2.** (*fig.*) to pester, plague.
то́рн|ый *adj.* smooth, even; **пойти́ по ~ой доро́ге** (*fig.*) to stick to the beaten track.
торова́т|ый (~, ~а) *adj.* (*coll.*) liberal, generous.
торок|а́, о́в *no sg.* saddle-bow straps.
тороп|и́ть, лю́, ~́ишь *impf.* (*of* **по~**) **1.** to hurry, hasten; to press; **меня́ ~́ят с оконча́нием рабо́ты** I am being pressed to finish my work. **2.** to precipitate.
тороп|и́ться, лю́сь, ~́ишься *impf.* (*of* **по~**) to hurry, be in a hurry, hasten.
торопли́во *adv.* hurriedly, hastily; in a hurry, in haste.
торопли́вост|ь, и *f.* hurry, haste.
торопли́в|ый (~, ~а) *adj.* hurried, hasty.
торопы́г|а, и *c.g.* (*coll.*) pers. always in a hurry.
торо́с, а *m.* ice-hummock.
торо́сист|ый (~, ~а) *adj.* hummocky; **т. лёд** pack ice.
торпе́д|а, ы *f.* torpedo.
торпеди́р|овать, ую *impf. and pf.* to torpedo.
торпеди́ст, а *m.* (*mil., naut.*) torpedo artificer.
торпе́дник, а *m.* (*mil., naut.*) member of MTB crew.
торпе́д|ный *adj. of* **~а; т. аппара́т** torpedo-tube; **т. ка́тер** motor torpedo boat (*abbr.* MTB).
торпедоно́с|ец, ца *m.* **1.** torpedo bomber. **2.** torpedo bomber pilot.
торпедоно́сный *adj.* (*naut., aeron.*) torpedo-carrying.
торс, а *m.* trunk; torso.
торт, а *m.* cake.
торф, а *m.* peat.
торфобрике́т, а *m.* (a) peat, peat briquette.
торфодобы́ч|а, и *f.* peat-extraction, peat-cutting.
торфоразрабо́т|ки, ок *no sg.* peatbog.
торфяни́к, а́ *m.* **1.** peatbog. **2.** peat-cutter.
торфяни́ст|ый (~, ~а) *adj.* peaty.
торфян|о́й *adj.* peat; **~о́е боло́то** peatbog; **т. мох** (*bot.*) peatmoss.
торц|ева́ть, у́ю *impf.* to pave with wood blocks.
торцо́в|ый *adj. of* **торе́ц; ~ая мостова́я** wood pavement.
торч|а́ть, у́, и́шь *impf.* **1.** to stick up, stick out; to stand on end. **2.** (*coll.*) to hang about, stick around; **т. пе́ред чьи́ми-н. глаза́ми** to be under s.o.'s feet; **он ~и́т це́лый день при бассе́йне для пла́вания** he hangs about at the swimming-pool the entire day.
торчко́м *adv.* (*coll.*) on end, sticking up.
торч|мя́ = ~ко́м

торше́р, а *m.* standard lamp.
тоск|а́, и́ *f.* **1.** melancholy; anguish; pangs; **у неё т. на се́рдце** she is sick at heart; **т. любви́** pangs of love. **2.** depression; ennui, boredom; **одна́ т., сплошна́я т.** a frightful bore; **навести́ ~у́ (на+***a.*) to depress, bore; **т. берёт** (*coll.*) it makes one sick, it is sickening. **3. (по+***d. or p.*) longing (for); yearning (for), nostalgia (for); **т. по ро́дине** home-sickness.
тоскли́в|ый (~, ~а) *adj.* **1.** melancholy; depressed, miserable. **2.** dull, dreary, depressing; **~ая пого́да** depressing weather.
тоск|ова́ть, у́ю *impf.* **1.** to be melancholy, be depressed, be miserable. **2. (по+***d. or p.*) to long (for), yearn (for), pine (for), miss.
тост[1]**, а** *m.* toast; **провозгласи́ть, предложи́ть, т. (за+***a.*) to toast, drink (to); to propose a toast (to).
тост[2]**, а** *m.* piece of toast; **т. с сы́ром** Welsh rarebit.
то́стер, а *m.* toaster.
тот *m.*, **та** *f.*, **то** *nt.*, *pl.* **те**, *pron.* **1.** (*opp.* **э́тот**) that; (*pl.*) those; **мне бо́льше нра́вится та карти́на** I like that picture better; **в тот раз** on that occasion; **в то вре́мя** then, at that time, in those days; **в том слу́чае** in that case. **2.** (*opp.* **э́тот**) the former; (*replacing 3rd pers. sg. pron.*) he; she; it; **я пе́редал корректу́ру профе́ссору, тот до́лжен был вам верну́ть её** I passed the proofs on to the professor, he was supposed to return them to you. **3.** (*opp.* **э́тот**) the other; the opposite; **на той стороне́** on the other side; **по ту сто́рону (+***g.*) beyond, on the other side (of); **с того́ бе́рега** from the other shore. **4.** (*opp.* **сей** *in certain set phrr.*) that, the other; **то да сё** one thing and another; **ни то ни сё** neither one thing nor another; **поговори́ть о том, о сём** to talk about this and that, about one thing and another; **ни с того́ ни с сего́** for no reason at all; without rhyme or reason. **5.** (*opp.* **друго́й, ино́й**) the one; **и тот и друго́й** both; **ни тот ни друго́й** neither; **не тот, так друго́й** if not one, then the other. **6.: тот..., (кото́рый)** the ... (which); **тот, (кто)** the one (who), the pers. (who); **тот фильм кото́рый вы ви́дели вчера́** the film (which) you saw yesterday; **та, кто но́сит ту́фли на высо́ких каблука́х** the one wearing high-heeled shoes; **тот факт, что** the fact that (*see also* **то**[1]). **7.: тот (же), тот (же) са́мый** the same; **одно́ и то же** one and the same thing, the same thing over again; **в то же са́мое вре́мя** at the same time, on the other hand; **он тепе́рь не тот** he is not the man he was. **8.** the right; **не тот** the wrong; **э́то не та дверь** that's the wrong door; **э́то тот но́мер?** is this the (right) room?; **э́то Федо́т, да не тот** that's a horse of another colour. **9.** *+preps. forms the following conjs.*: **для того́, что́бы** in order that, in order to; **до того́, что** (*i*) until, (*ii*) to such an extent that; **ме́жду тем, как** whereas; **несмотря́ на то, что** in spite of the fact that; **пе́ред тем, как** before; **по́сле того́, как** after; **по ме́ре того́, как** in proportion as; **с тем, что́бы** (*i*) in order to, with a view to, (*ii*) on condition that, provided that. **10.** *forms part of var. adv. phrr. and particles* (*see also* **то**[1]): **вме́сте с тем** at the same time; **к тому́ же** moreover; **кро́ме того́** besides; **ме́жду тем, тем вре́менем** meanwhile; **со всем тем** notwithstanding all this; **тем са́мым** hereby; **тому́ наза́д** ago; **и тому́ подо́бное (и т. п.)** and so forth; **того́ и гляди́** any minute now; before you know where you are; **и без того́** as it is; **(да) и то сказа́ть** and indeed; **не без того́** that's about it; it can't altogether be denied.
тоталитари́зм, а *m.* (*pol.*) totalitarianism.
тоталита́рный *adj.* (*pol.*) totalitarian.
тота́льный *adj.* total.
тоте́м, а *m.* totem.
тотеми́зм, а *m.* totemism.
то́-то *particle* (*coll.*) **1.** *emph. point of utterance*: **(вот) то́-то, (вот) то́-то и оно́, (вот) то́-то и есть** that's just it; precisely, exactly. **2.** *in exclamations, expr. emotion or emotional judgement*: **то́-то прекра́сно!** there, isn't that lovely! **3.** *expr. reproach, or recalls warning or threat conveyed in previous utterance*: **ну, то́-то же!** there you are, you see!; well, what did I tell you!
то́тчас *adv.* at once; immediately (*also of spatial relations*).
тоха́рский *adj.* (*ling.*) Tokharian.
точёный *adj.* **1.** sharpened. **2.** (*tech.*) turned. **3.** (*fig.*; *of bodily features*) finely-moulded, chiselled.
то́чечн|ый *adj.* **1.** consisting of points. **2.: ~ая сва́рка** (*tech.*) spot welding.
точи́лк|а, и *f.* (*coll.*) steel, knife-sharpener; pencil-sharpener.
точи́л|о, а *nt.* whetstone, grindstone.
точи́льный *adj.* grinding, sharpening; **т. ка́мень** whetstone, grindstone; **т. материа́л** abrasive; **т. реме́нь** strop; **т. стано́к** grinding lathe.
точи́льщик, а *m.* grinder.
точ|и́ть[1]**, у́, ~ишь** *impf.* **1.** (*pf* **на~**) to sharpen; to grind; to whet, hone; **т. зу́бы на кого́-н.** to have a grudge against s.o. **2.** (*impf. only*) to turn (*on a lathe*).
точ|и́ть[2]**, у́, ~ишь** *impf.* to eat away, gnaw away; to corrode; (*fig.*) to gnaw (at), prey (upon).
точ|и́ть[3]**, у́, ~ишь** *impf.* (*obs.*) to secrete; **т. слёзы** to shed tears.
точ|и́ться[1]**, ~ится** *impf.*, *pass. of* **~и́ть**[1,2]
точ|и́ться[2]**, ~ится** *impf.* (*obs.*) to ooze.
то́чк|а[1]**, и** *f.* **1.** spot, dot; **бе́лое пла́тье в ро́зовых ~ах** white dress with pink spots; **„і" с ~ой** *name of letter* 'і' *in old Russ. orthography*; **ста́вить ~и на „и"** to dot one's 'i's' (and cross one's 't's'). **2.** (*gram*) full stop; **т. с запято́й** semicolon; **поста́вить ~у** to place a full stop; (*fig.*) to finish, come to the end. **3.** (*mus.*) dot. **4.** (*math.*, *phys.*, *tech.*) point; **т. опо́ры** fulcrum, point of support; (*fig.*) rallying-point; **мёртвая т.** dead point, dead centre; (*fig.*) dead stop, standstill; **дойти́ до мёртвой ~и** to come to a standstill, to a full stop. **5.** (*mil.*) point; **т. встре́чи, т. попада́ния** point of impact; **т. наво́дки** aiming point; **т. прице́ливания** point of aim. **6.: т. замерза́ния, кипе́ния, плавле́ния** freezing, boiling, melting point; **т. росы́** dew-point. **7.** (*fig.*) point; **т. зре́ния** point of view; **т. соприкоснове́ния** point of contact, meeting-ground; **горя́чая т.** trouble spot; **т. в ~у** (*coll.*) exactly; to the letter, word for word; **попа́сть в (са́мую) ~у** (*coll.*) to hit the nail on the head; **до ~и** (*coll.*) to the limit, to the extreme point; **дойти́ до ~и** (*coll.*) to come to the end of one's tether.
то́чк|а[2]**, и** *f.* **1.** sharpening; grinding; whetting; stropping. **2.** (*tech.*) turning (*on a lathe*).
то́чно[1] *adv.* **1.** exactly, precisely; punctually; **т. переписа́ть** to make an exact copy; **приходи́те, пожа́луйста, т. в час** please, come at one o'clock sharp, punctually at one. **2.: т. так** just so, exactly, precisely; **т. тако́й (же)** just the same. **3.** indeed.
то́чно[2] *particle* (*coll.*) yes; true; **так т.** (*in mil. parlance*) yes.
то́чно[3] *conj.* as though, as if; like; **он там стоя́л т. окамене́лый** he stood there as if turned to stone.
то́чност|ь, и *f.* exactness; precision; accuracy; punctuality; **в ~и** exactly, precisely; accurately; to the letter; **вы́числить с ~ью до...** to calculate to within ...; **с приближённой ~ью** approximately; **с ~ью часово́го механи́зма** like clockwork.
то́ч|ный (~ен, ~на́, ~но) *adj.* exact, precise; accurate; punctual; **~ная бомбардиро́вка** precision bombing; **~ные нау́ки** exact sciences; **т. перево́д** accurate translation; **т. прибо́р** precision instrument; **~ная устано́вка** sensitive adjustment; **т. челове́к** punctual pers.
то́чь-в-то́чь *adv.* (*coll.*) exactly; to the letter; word for word; **он — т.-в-т. оте́ц** he is the spit and image of his father.
тошн|и́ть, и́т *impf.* (*impers.*): **меня́,** *etc.*, **~и́т** I, *etc.*, feel sick; **меня́ от э́того ~и́т** (*fig.*) it makes me sick, it sickens me.
то́шно *as pred.* (*coll.*) **1. мне,** *etc.*, **т.** I, *etc.*, feel sick; (*fig.*) I, *etc.*, feel wretched, awful. **2.** (*+inf.*) it is sickening, it makes one sick, it is nauseating.
тошнот|а́, ы́ *f.* sickness, nausea (*also fig.*); **испы́тывать ~у́** to feel sick; **у́тренняя т.** morning sickness; **мне э́то надое́ло до ~ы́** I am sick to death of it.
тошнотво́р|ный (~ен, ~на) *adj.* sickening, sick-making, nauseating (*also fig.*).

то́ш|ный (~ен, ~на́, ~но) *adj.* (*coll.*) **1.** tiresome, tedious. **2.** sickening, nauseating.

тоща́|ть, ю *impf.* (*of* **о~**) (*coll.*) to become thin.

то́щ|ий (~, ~а́, ~е) *adj.* **1.** gaunt, emaciated; scraggy, skinny. **2.** empty; **на т. желу́док** on an empty stomach; **т. карма́н** (*fig.*) empty pocket. **3.** poor (= *with low content of some substance*); **~ее мя́со** lean meat; **~ая по́чва** poor soil; **т. сыр** skim-milk cheese; **т. у́голь** hard coal.

тпру *int.* (*to horses*) wo!; whoa!; **ни т., ни ну** (*fig., coll.*) he, *etc.*, won't budge.

трав|а́, ы́, *pl.* **~ы** *f.* grass; (a) grass, herb; **лека́рственные ~ы** medicinal herbs; **морска́я т.** sea-weed; **со́рная т.** weed; **т. ~о́й, как т.** (*coll.*) it has no taste at all; **хоть т. не расти́** (*coll.*) (everything else) can go to hell.

травене́|ть, ет *impf.* (*of* **за~**) to become overgrown (with grass).

тра́верз, а *m.* (*naut.*) beam; **на ~е** on the beam, abeam.

тра́верс, а *m.* **1.** (*mil.*) traverse; **ты́льный т.** parados. **2.** (*tech.*) traverse, cross-beam, cross-arm; cross member, transverse member; cross head.

тра́верс|а, ы *f.* = **~ 2.**

травести́ *nt. indecl.* travesty.

трави́нк|а, и *f.* blade of grass.

трав|и́ть[1], лю́, ~ишь *impf.* **1.** (*pf.* **вы́~**) to exterminate, destroy (*by poisoning*). **2.** (*coll.*) to poison. **3.** (*pf.* **вы́~**) to etch. **4.** (*pf.* **по~**) (*of cattle, etc.*) to trample down; to damage (*crops, etc.*). **5.** (*pf.* **за~**) to hunt; (*fig.*) to persecute, torment; to badger; to worry the life out of.

трав|и́ть[2], лю́, ~ишь *impf.* (*naut.*) to pay out, ease out, slacken out; (*of anchor chain*) to veer.

трав|и́ться[1], лю́сь, ~ишься *impf.* (*coll.*) to poison o.s.

трав|и́ться[2], лю́сь, ~ишься *impf., pass. of* **~и́ть[1,2]**

тра́в|ка[1], ки *f. dim of* **~а́**

тра́вк|а[2], и *f.* (*naut.*) paying out.

травле́ни|е, я *nt.* **1.** extermination, destruction. **2.** etching.

тра́вленый[1] *adj.* etched.

тра́вленый[2] *adj.* hunted; **т. зверь** (*fig., coll.*) old hand.

тра́вл|я, и *f.* hunting; (*fig.*) persecution, tormenting; badgering.

тра́вм|а, ы *f.* (*med.*) trauma, injury; **психи́ческая т.** (*psych.*) shock, trauma.

травмати́зм, а *m.* (*med.*) traumatism; (*collect.*) injuries; **произво́дственный т.** industrial injuries.

травмати́ческий *adj.* (*med., psych.*) traumatic.

травматологи́ческий *adj.*: **т. пункт** casualty (department).

тра́вник[1], а *m.* (*coll.*) herbalist.

тра́вник[2], а *m.* (*zool.*) redshank.

травни́к[3], а *m.* **1.** (*obs.*) herb-tea, herb-water. **2.** (*hist., liter.*) herbal. **3.** (*obs.*) herbarium.

травокоси́лк|а, и *f.* lawn mower.

траволече́ни|е, я *n.* herbal medicine.

траво́по́ль|е, я *nt.* grassland agriculture, ley farming.

травопо́ль|ный *adj. of* **~е**; **т. севооборо́т** grassland crop rotation.

травосе́яни|е, я *nt.* fodder-grass cultivation.

травосто́|й, я *m.* (*collect.*; *agric.*) grass, herbage.

травоя́дный *adj.* herbivorous.

травяни́ст|ый (~, ~а) *adj.* **1.** grass; herbaceous. **2.** grassy. **3.** (*coll.*) tasteless, insipid.

травян|о́й *adj.* **1.** grass; herbaceous; **т. покро́в** grass, herbage; **~ы́е расте́ния** grasses, herbs; **~ы́е уго́дья** grasslands. **2.** grassy; **т. за́пах** grassy smell; **т. цвет** grass-green. **3.: ~а́я насто́йка** herb-tea, herb-water.

трагеди́йный *adj.* (*theatr.*) tragic.

траге́ди|я, и *f.* tragedy.

траги́зм, а *m.* tragic element.

тра́гик, а *m.* **1.** tragic actor. **2.** tragedian.

трагиком́еди|я, и *f.* tragicomedy.

трагикоми́ческий *adj.* tragicomic.

траги́ческ|ий *adj.* (*in var. senses*) tragic; **т. актёр** tragic actor; **~ое зре́лище** tragic sight; **приня́ть т. оборо́т** to take a tragic turn.

траги́чност|ь, и *f.* tragedy, tragic nature, tragic character.

траги́ч|ный (~ен, ~на) *adj.* tragic (= *sad, terrible*; *not in theatr. sense*).

традицио́нност|ь, и *f.* traditional character.

традицио́н|ный (~ен, ~на) *adj.* traditional; conventional.

тради́ци|я, и *f.* tradition.

траекто́ри|я, и *f.* trajectory.

трак, а *m.* track (*of caterpillar tractor*).

тракт, а *m.* **1.** high road, highway; **почто́вый т.** (*obs.*) post road; **желу́дочно-кише́чный т.** (*anat.*) alimentary canal. **2.** route.

тракта́т, а *m.* **1.** treatise. **2.** treaty.

тракти́р, а *m.* (*obs.*) inn, eating-house.

тракти́р|ный *adj. of* **~**

тракти́рщик, а *m.* (*obs.*) innkeeper.

тракти́рщиц|а, ы *f. of* **тракти́рщик**

тракт|ова́ть, у́ю *impf.* **1.** (**о**+*p.*) to treat (of), discuss. **2.** to interpret (*a part in a play, etc.*).

тракт|ова́ться, у́ется *impf.* to be treated, be discussed; **о чём ~у́ется в э́том рома́не?** what is the subject of this novel?

тракто́вк|а, и *f.* treatment; interpretation; **э́то любопы́тная т. вопро́са** this is a curious treatment of the subject.

тра́ктор, а *m.* tractor; **т. на колёсном ходу́, колёсный т.** wheeler tractor; **т. на гу́сеничном ходу́, гу́сеничный т.** caterpillar tractor.

тракториза́ци|я, и *f.* introduction of tractors.

трактори́ст, а *m.* tractor driver.

трактори́ст|ка, ки *f. of* **~**

тра́ктор|ный *adj. of* **~**; **т. парк** fleet of tractors; **на ~ной тя́ге** tractor-drawn.

тракторострое́ни|е, я *nt.* tractor-making.

тракторострои́тельный *adj.*: **т. заво́д** tractor works.

трал, а *m.* **1.** trawl. **2.** (*mil.*) mine-sweep.

тра́лени|е, я *nt.* **1.** trawling. **2.** mine-sweeping.

тра́лер, а *m.* (*obs.*) trawler.

тра́л|ить, ю, ишь *impf.* **1.** to trawl. **2.** (*mil.*) to sweep.

тра́ловый *adj.* **1.** trawling; **т. лов** trawling. **2.** (*mil.*) mine-sweeping.

тра́л|ьный = **~овый**

тра́льщик, а *m.* **1.** trawler. **2.** (*mil.*) mine-sweeper.

трамб|ова́ть, у́ю *impf.* to ram.

трамбо́вк|а, и *f.* **1.** ramming. **2.** rammer, beetle.

трамва́|й, я *m.* **1.** tramway, tram-line. **2.** tram(-car); **речно́й т.** river bus.

трамва́й|ный *adj. of* **~**; **т. ваго́н** tram-car; **~ные ре́льсы** tram-lines.

трамва́йщик, а *m.* tram worker.

трампа́рк, а *m.* **1.** tram depot. **2.** tram fleet.

трампли́н, а *m.* (*sport and fig.*) spring-board; jumping-off place, ski-jump.

транжи́р, а *m.* (*coll.*) spendthrift, squanderbug.

транжи́р|а, ы *c.g.* = **~**

транжи́р|ить, ю, ишь *impf.* (*of* **рас~**) (*coll.*) to blow, squander.

транзи́т, а *m.* transit; **пойти́ ~ом** to go as transit goods.

транзи́т|ный *adj. of* **~**; **~ная ви́за** transit visa; **~ная та́кса** transit dues.

транквилиза́тор, а *m.* tranquillizer.

транс, а *m.* trance.

транс... *pref.* trans-.

трансаге́нтств|о, а *nt.* (*abbr. of* **тра́нспортное аге́нтство**) removal company.

трансатланти́ческий *adj.* transatlantic.

Трансва́ал|ь, я *m.* the Transvaal.

трансгре́сси|я, и *f.* (*geol.*) transgression.

Трансильва́ни|я, и *f.* Transylvania.

трансильва́нский *adj.* Transylvanian.

транскриби́р|овать, ую *impf. and pf.* to transcribe.

транскри́пци|я, и *f.* transcription.

трансли́р|овать, ую *impf. and pf.* to broadcast, transmit (*by radio*); to relay.

транслитера́ци|я, и *f.* transliteration.

трансляцио́нн|ый *adj.* (*radio*) relaying; **~ая сеть** relaying system, relay network; **т. у́зел** relaying station.

трансля́ци|я, и *f.* broadcast, transmission; relay.

трансмисс|ио́нный *adj. of* **~ия**
трансми́сси|я, и *f.* (*tech.*) transmission.
транспара́нт, а *m.* **1.** black-lined paper (*placed under unruled writing-paper*). **2.** transparency; banner.
трансплантáци|я, и *f.* (*med.*) transplantation.
транспози́ци|я, и *f.* transposition.
транспони́р|овать, ую *impf. and pf.* (*mus.*) to transpose.
транспониро́вк|а, и *f.* (*mus.*) transposition.
тра́нспорт, а *m.* **1.** transport. **2.** transportation, conveyance. **3.** consignment. **4.** (*mil.*) train, transport. **5.** (*naut.*) transport, supply ship; troopship.
транспо́рт, а *m.* (*book-keeping*) carrying forward.
транспорта́бел|ьный (~ен, ~ьна) *adj.* transportable, mobile.
транспортёр, а *m.* **1.** (*tech.*) conveyor. **2.** (*mil.*) carrier.
транспорти́р, а *m.* protractor.
транспорти́ровать[1], **ую** *impf. and pf.* to transport.
транспорти́р|овать[2], **ую** *impf. and pf.* (*book-keeping*) to carry forward.
транспортиро́вк|а, и *f.* transport, transportation.
тра́нспортник, а *m.* **1.** transport worker. **2.** transport plane.
тра́нспорт|ный *adj. of* **~**; **~ная ве́домость** (*mil.*) table of movements; **т. парк** transport pool; **т. самолёт** transport plane; (*mil.*) troop-carrier; **~ное су́дно** = **~ 5.**
транссексуали́ст, а *m.* transsexual.
транссиби́рск|ий *adj.* Trans-Siberian; **~ая магистра́ль** the Trans-Siberian Railway.
трансформа́тор[1], **а** *m.* (*elec.*) transformer.
трансформа́тор[2], **а** *m.* **1.** quick-change actor. **2.** conjuror, illusionist.
трансформа́ци|я, и *f.* transformation.
трансформи́р|овать, ую *impf. and pf.* to transform.
трансцендента́льный *adj.* (*phil.*) transcendental.
трансценде́нт|ный (~ен, ~на) *adj.* (*phil., math.*) transcendental.
транше́|йный *adj. of* **~я**
транше́|я, и *f.* (*mil.*) trench.
трап, а *m.* (*naut.*) ladder; (*aeron.*) gangway.
тра́пе́з|а, ы *f.* **1.** dining-table (*esp. in a monastery*). **2.** meal; **дели́ть ~у (с+*i.*)** to share a meal (with). **3.** refectory.
тра́пез|ный *adj. of* **~а**; *as n.* **~ная, ~ной** *f.* refectory.
трапециеви́д|ный (~ен, ~на) *adj.* **1.** trapeziform, trapezoid. **2.** tapered; **~ное крыло́** (*aeron.*) tapered wing.
трапе́ци|я, и *f.* **1.** (*math.*) trapezium. **2.** trapeze.
тра́сс|а, ы *f.* **1.** line, course; direction; **возду́шная т.** airway. **2.** route. **3.** plan, draft, sketch.
трасса́нт, а *m.* (*fin.*) drawer.
трасса́т, а *m.* (*fin.*) drawee.
трасси́р|овать, ую *impf. and pf.* to mark out, trace.
трасси́р|ующий *pres. part. act. of* **~овать** *and adj.* (*mil.*) tracer; **~ующая пу́ля** tracer bullet.
тра́т|а, ы *f.* expenditure; **пуста́я т. вре́мени** waste of time.
тра́|тить, чу, тишь *impf.* (*of* **ис~** *and* **по~**) to spend, expend, use up; to waste.
тра́|титься, чусь, тишься *impf.* (*of* **ис~** *and* **по~**) (**на+*a.***; *coll.*) to spend one's money (on), spend up (on).
тра́тт|а, ы *f.* (*fin.*) bill of exchange.
тра́улер, а *m.* trawler; **т. с кормовы́м тра́лением** stern-trawler.
тра́ур, а *m.* mourning; **облёчься в т.** to go into mourning.
тра́урн|ый *adj.* **1.** mourning; funeral; **т. марш** funeral march, dead march; **~ая повя́зка** (mourning) crape band; **~ое ше́ствие** funeral procession. **2.** mournful, sorrowful; funereal.
трафаре́т, а *m.* **1.** stencil; **раскра́сить, расписа́ть по ~у** to stencil. **2.** engraved inscription. **3.** (*fig.*) conventional, stereotyped pattern; cliché; **мы́слить по ~у** to think along conventional lines.
трафаре́тност|ь, и *f.* conventionality; stereotyped character.
трафаре́т|ный *adj.* **1.** stencilled; **т. рису́нок** stencil drawing. **2. (~ен, ~на)** (*fig.*) conventional, stereotyped; trite, hackneyed.
тра́ф|ить, лю, ишь *impf.* (*coll.*) to please, oblige.
трах *int.* bang! (*also as pred.* = **~нул**)
тра́х|ать, аю *impf. of* **~нуть**
тра́х|аться, аюсь *impf. of* **~нуться**
трахеи́т, а *m.* (*med.*) tracheitis.
трахе́йный *adj.* (*anat.*) tracheal.
трахеотоми́|я, и *f.* (*med.*) tracheotomy.
трахе́|я, и *f.* (*anat.*) trachea, windpipe.
тра́х|нуть, ну, нешь *pf.* (*of* **~ать**) (*coll.*) **1.** to bang, crash; **т. кого́-н. по спине́** to bang s.o. on the back; **т. из ружья́** to loose off with a gun. **2.** (*vulg.*) to screw, hump.
тра́х|нуться, нусь, нешься *pf.* (*of* **~аться**) (*vulg.*) to screw, hump.
трахо́м|а, ы *f.* (*med.*) trachoma.
тре́б|а[1], **ы** *f.* occasional religious rite (*christening, marriage, funeral, etc.*).
тре́ба[2] *as pred.* (*dial.*) it is necessary.
тре́бник, а *m.* prayer-book; breviary (*containing order of service of all ceremonies and rites except the Eucharist and the ordination of priests*).
тре́бовани|е, я *nt.* **1.** demand, request; **по ~ю** on demand, by request; **остано́вка по ~ю** request stop; **по ~ю (+*g.*)** at the request (of), at the instance (of); **по ~ю суда́** by order of the court. **2.** demand, claim; **согласи́ться на чьи-н. ~я** to agree to s.o.'s demands; **вы́двинуть т.** to put in a claim. **3.** requirement, condition; **отвеча́ть ~ям** to meet requirements. **4.** (*pl.*) aspirations; needs. **5.** requisition, order; **т. на то́пливо** fuel requisition.
тре́бовател|ьный (~ен, ~ьна) *adj.* **1.** demanding, exacting; particular. **2.: ~ьная ве́домость** requisition sheet, order form.
тре́б|овать, ую *impf.* (*of* **по~**) **1.** (+*g. or* +**что́бы**) to demand, request, require; **т. извине́ния у кого́-н.** to demand an apology from s.o.; **они́ ~уют, что́бы мы извини́лись** they demand that we apologize. **2.** (*impf. only*) (+*g.* **от**) to expect (from), ask (of); **вы ~уете сли́шком мно́го от ва́ших ученико́в** you expect too much from your pupils. **3.** (*pf.* **по~**) (+*g.*) to require, need, call (for); **т. неме́дленного реше́ния** to require an immediate decision. **4.** to send for, call, summon; **её ~уют к умира́ющему де́ду** she is being summoned to her dying grandfather's bedside.
тре́б|оваться, уется *impf.* (*of* **по~**) **1.** to be needed, be required; **на э́то ~уется мно́го вре́мени** it takes a lot of time; **~уется приходя́щая домрабо́тница** 'daily woman required'; **что и ~овалось доказа́ть** (*math.*) Q.E.D. (*abbr. of* quod erat demonstrandum). **2.** *pass. of* **~овать**
требух|а́, и́ *no pl., f.* **1.** entrails; (*cul.*) offal, tripe. **2.** (*fig., coll.*) tripe, rubbish.
трево́г|а, и *f.* **1.** alarm, anxiety; uneasiness, disquiet. **2.** alarm, alert; **возду́шная т.** air-raid warning, alert; **пожа́рная т.** fire-alarm; **бить ~у** to sound the alarm (*also fig.*).
трево́ж|ить, у, ишь *impf.* **1.** (*of* **вс~**) to alarm; to disturb; worry, trouble. **2.** (*pf.* **по~**) to disturb, interrupt; **нас всё вре́мя ~ат посети́тели** we are continually disturbed by callers. **3.** to annoy, bait; **не т.** to leave alone. **4.: т. ра́ну** to re-open a wound.
трево́ж|иться, усь, ишься *impf.* **1.** to worry, be anxious, be alarmed, be uneasy. **2.** (*pf.* **по~**) to worry o.s., trouble o.s., put o.s. out; **не ~ьтесь!** don't bother (yourself)!
трево́ж|ный (~ен, ~на) *adj.* **1.** worried, anxious, uneasy, troubled. **2.** alarming, disturbing, disquieting; **~ные слу́хи** alarming reports. **3.** alarm; **т. звоно́к** alarm (bell).
треволне́ни|е, я *nt.* (*now coll., joc.*) agitation, disquiet.
тригла́вый *adj.* **1.** with three cupolas. **2.** (*poet.*) three-headed.
тред-юнио́н, а *m.* trade union.
тред-юниони́зм, а *m.* trade-unionism.
тред-юниони́ст, а *m.* trade unionist.
тре́звенник, а *m.* teetotaller, abstainer.
тре́звеническ|ий *adj.* temperance; **~ое движе́ние** temperance movement.
трезве́|ть, ю *impf.* (*of* **о~**) to sober (up), become sober.
трезво́н, а *m.* **1.** peal (of bells). **2.** (*coll., joc.*) rumours, gossip. **3.** (*coll., pej.*) row, shindy; **подня́ть т., зада́ть ~у** to kick up a row.

трезво́н|ить, ю, ишь *impf.* **1.** to ring (a peal). **2.** (**о**+*p.*; *coll.*) to noise abroad; **т. по всему́ го́роду** to proclaim from the housetops.
тре́звост|ь, и *f.* **1.** soberness, sobriety (*also fig.*). **2.** abstinence; temperance.
трезву́чи|е, я *nt.* (*mus.*) triad.
тре́зв|ый (~, ~а́, ~о) *adj.* **1.** sober (*also fig.*); **име́ть т. взгляд на собы́тия** to take a sober view of events. **2.** teetotal, abstinent.
трезу́б|ец, ца *m.* trident.
трек, а *m.* (*sport*) track.
трекля́тый *adj.* (*coll.*) accursed.
трел|ь, и *f.* (*mus.*) trill, shake; warble.
трелья́ж, а *m.* **1.** trellis. **2.** three-leaved mirror.
тре́моло *nt. indecl.* (*mus.*) tremolo.
трен, а *m.* (*obs.*) train (*of dress*).
тренажёр, а *m.* training apparatus; **гребно́й т.** rowing machine; **лётный т.** flight simulator.
тре́нер, а *m.* (*sport*) trainer, coach.
тре́нер|ский *adj. of* ~
тре́нзел|ь, я, *pl.* **~и** *and* **~я́** *m.* snaffle.
тре́ни|е, я *nt.* **1.** friction, rubbing. **2.** (*pl.*) (*fig.*) friction.
трени́р|ова́ть, у́ю *impf.* (*of* **на~**) to train, coach.
трени́р|ова́ться, у́юсь *impf.* (*of* **на~**) to train o.s., coach o.s.; to be in training.
трениро́вк|а, и *f.* training, coaching.
трениро́вочный *adj.* training; practice.
трено́г|а, и *f.* tripod.
трено́гий *adj.* three-legged.
трено́ж|ить, у, ишь *impf.* (*of* **с~**) to hobble.
трено́жник, а *m.* tripod.
тре́нька|ть, ю *impf.* (*coll.*) to strum.
трепа́к, а́ *m.* trepak (*Russ. folk-dance*).
трепа́л|о, а *nt.* (*tech.*) swingle, scutcher.
трепа́льный *adj.* scutching.
трепа́льщик, а *m.* scutcher.
трепа́н, а *m.* (*med.*) trepan.
трепана́ци|я, и *f.* (*med.*) trepanation.
трепа́нг, а *m.* (*zool.*) trepang.
трепа́ни|е, я *nt.* scutching.
трепани́р|овать, ую *impf. and pf.* (*med.*) to trepan.
трёпаный *adj.* **1.** (*of flax, etc.*) scutched. **2.** torn, tattered. **3.** dishevelled.
треп|а́ть, лю́, ∸лешь *impf.* **1.** (*impf. only*) to scutch, swingle (*flax, hemp, etc.*). **2.** (*pf.* **по~**) to pull about; (*of the wind*) to blow about; to dishevel, tousle; **т. кого́-н. за во́лосы** to pull s.o.'s hair; **т. чьи-н. во́лосы** to tousle s.o.'s hair; **т. языко́м** (*coll.*) to prattle, blather; **т. чьи-н. не́рвы** to get on s.o.'s nerves; **его́ ∸лет лихора́дка** he is feverish; **т. чьё-н. и́мя** to bandy s.o.'s name about. **3.** (*pf.* **по~**) (*coll.*) to tear; to wear out. **4.** (*pf.* **по~**) to pat.
треп|а́ться, лю́сь, ∸лешься *impf.* **1.** (*pf.* **по~**) to tear, fray; to wear out. **2.** (*impf. only*) to flutter, blow about. **3.** (*impf. only*) **т. по земле́** to trail along the ground. **4.** (*impf. only*) (*coll., pej.*) to go round; to hang out. **5.** (*impf. only*) (**с**+*i.*; *fig., coll.*) to go (with) (*s.o. of the opposite sex*). **6.** (*impf. only*) (*coll.*) to blather, talk rubbish; to play the fool.
трепа́ч, а́ *m.* (*coll.*) blatherskite, bletherer.
тре́пет, а *m.* trembling, quivering (*from fear, etc. or from pleasurable sensation*); **быть в ~е** to be a-tremble, be in a dither.
трепе|та́ть, щу́, ∸щешь *impf.* **1.** to tremble, quiver; to flicker; to palpitate. **2.** (*fig.*) to tremble; to thrill, palpitate; **т. за челове́чество** to tremble for humanity; **т. от восто́рга** to thrill with joy; **т. при мы́сли** (**о**+*p.*) to tremble at the thought (of). **3.** (**пе́ред** *or* (*obs.*) +*a.*; *fig.*) to tremble (before).
тре́петный *adj.* **1.** trembling; flickering; palpitating. **2.** anxious. **3.** timid.
трёпк|а, и *f.* **1.** scutching. **2.** (*coll.*) dressing-down, scolding. **3.:** **т. не́рвов** nervous strain.
трепыха́|ться, юсь *impf.* (*coll.*) to flutter, quiver.
треск, а *m.* **1.** crack, crash; crackle, crackling; **т. руже́йных вы́стрелов** crackle of gun-fire; **т. огня́** crackling of a fire; **т. лома́ющихся су́чьев** snapping of twigs; **т. мото́ра** popping of an engine; **с ∸ом провали́ться** (*fig., coll.*) to come a crasher, flop. **2.** (*fig., coll.*) noise, fuss.
треск|а́, и́ *f.* cod.
тре́ска|ть, ю *impf.* (*coll.*) to guzzle.
тре́ска|ться¹, ется *impf.* (*of* **по~**) to crack; to chap.
тре́ска|ться², юсь *impf. of* **тре́снуться**
треск|о́вый *adj. of* **~а́; т. жир** cod-liver oil.
трескотн|я́, и́ *f.* (*coll.*) **1.** crackle, crackling; chirring (*of grasshoppers*). **2.** (*fig.*) chatter, blather.
треску́ч|ий (~, ~а) *adj.* **1.** (*pej.*) highfalutin(g), high-flown. **2.:** **т. моро́з** hard frost, ringing frost.
тре́сн|уть, у, ешь *pf.* **1.** to snap, crackle, pop. **2.** to crack; to chap; (*fig., coll.*) to crash, flop; **хоть ∸и** (*coll.*) for the life of me. **3.** (+*i.* **по**+*d. or* +*a.* **по**+*d.*; *coll.*) to bring down with a crash (on); to hit, bang; **т. кулако́м по столу́** to bang one's fist on the table; **т. кого́-н. по заты́лку** to bang s.o. on the back of the head.
тре́с|нуться, нусь, нешься *pf.* (*of* **~каться²**) (+*i.* **о**+*a.*; *coll.*) to bang (against); **т. голово́й о две́рцу шка́фа** to bang one's head against the door of a cupboard.
трест, а *m.* (*econ.*) trust (*in former USSR, a group of industrial or commercial enterprises with centralized direction*).
трест|а́, ы́ *f.* flax *or* hemp straw.
трести́р|овать, ую *impf. and pf.* to combine into a trust.
тре́ст|овский *adj. of* ~
трете́йск|ий *adj.* arbitration; **~ое реше́ние конфли́кта** arbitration; **т. суд** arbitration tribunal; **т. судья́** arbitrator.
тре́т|ий, ья, ье *adj.* **1.** third; **глава́ ~ья** chapter three; **т. но́мер** number three; **полови́на ~его** half past two; **в ~ьем часу́** between two and three; **~его дня** the day before yesterday; **до ~их петухо́в** until dawn; **~ье лицо́** (*gram.*) third pers.; **Т~ье отделе́ние** (*hist.*) Third Section (*of the Imperial Chancellery, responsible for political police, 1826–1904*); **~ье сосло́вие** (*hist.*) third estate; **~ья сторона́** third party; **т. такт** (*tech.*) power stroke; **из ~их рук** indirectly; **увольне́ние по ~ьему пу́нкту** (*hist.*) summary dismissal. **2.** *as n.* **~ье, ~ьего** *nt.* sweet, dessert.
трети́р|овать, ую *impf.* to slight.
трети́чный *adj.* (*geol., chem., etc.*) tertiary, ternary.
трет|ь, и, *pl.* **∸и, ~е́й** *f.* third.
третьёводни *adv.* (*dial.*) the day before yesterday.
третьекла́ссник, а *m.* third-former.
третьекла́ссный *adj.* third-class (*also fig.*).
третьеочередно́й *adj.* of third-rate importance.
третьесо́ртный *adj.* third-rate.
третьестепе́нный *adj.* **1.** insignificant, minor. **2.** mediocre, third-rate.
треуго́лк|а, и *f.* cocked hat.
треуго́льник, а *m.* triangle.
треуго́льный *adj.* three-cornered, triangular.
треу́х, а *m.* (*obs.*) 'three-eared' cap (*cap with ear-flaps and back flap*).
треф, а *m.* tref foods (= *foods forbidden by Jewish dietary law*).
тре́ф|а, ы *f.* (*cards*) **1.** *see* **~ы. 2.** (*coll.*) a club.
трефно́й *adj.* (*of food*) tref, non-kosher.
тре́фовый *adj.* (*cards*) of clubs.
тре́ф|ы, ~ *pl.* (*sg.* **~а, ~ы** *f.*) (*cards*) clubs; **да́ма ~** queen of clubs.
трёх... *comb. form* three-, tri-.
трёхвале́нтный *adj.* (*chem.*) trivalent.
трёхвёрст|ка, ки *f.* = **~ная ка́рта**
трёхвёрстн|ый *adj.* **1.** three versts in length. **2.:** **~ая ка́рта** map on scale of three versts to an inch.
трёхгоди́чный *adj.* three-year.
трёхгодова́лый *adj.* three-year-old.
трёхголо́с(н)ый *adj.* (*mus.*) three-part.
трёхгра́нный *adj.* three-edged; (*math.*) trihedral.
трёхдне́вн|ый *adj.* three-day; **~ая лихора́дка** tertian ague.
трёхдюймо́вк|а, и *f.* **1.** (*obs.*) three-inch field-gun. **2.** three-inch board.
трёхдюймо́вый *adj.* three-inch.
трёхзна́чный *adj.* three-digit, three-figure.

трёхколёсный *adj.* three-wheeled; **т. велосипе́д** tricycle.
трёхле́ти|е, я *nt.* **1.** period of three years. **2.** third anniversary.
трёхле́тний *adj.* **1.** three-year. **2.** three-year-old. **3.** (*bot.*) triennial.
трёхле́т|ок, ка *m.* three-year-old (*animal*).
трёхлине́й|ка, ки *f.* = **~ная винто́вка**
трёхлине́йн|ый *adj.* of three eighths of an inch calibre; **~ая винто́вка** .375 rifle.
трёхли́стный *adj.* (*bot.*) trifoliate.
трёхме́рный *adj.* three-dimensional.
трёхме́стный *adj.* three-seater.
трёхме́сячный *adj.* **1.** three-month; quarterly. **2.** three-month-old.
трёхнеде́льный *adj.* **1.** three-week. **2.** three-week-old.
трёхо́сный *adj.* triaxial.
трёхпа́л|ый *adj.* (*zool.*) tridactylous; **~ая ча́йка** kittywake.
трёхпо́ль|е, я *nt.* (*agric.*) three-field system.
трёхпо́ль|ный *adj. of* **~е**
трёхпроце́нтный *adj.* three per cent.
трёхрублёвк|а, и *f.* (*coll.*) three-rouble note.
трёхсло́жный *adj.* trisyllabic.
трёхсло́йный *adj.* three-layered; three-ply.
трёхсотле́ти|е, я *nt.* **1.** three hundred years. **2.** tercentenary.
трёхсотле́тний *adj.* **1.** of three hundred years. **2.** tercentennial.
трёхсо́тый *adj.* three-hundredth.
трёхство́льный *adj.* three-barrelled.
трёхство́рчатый *adj.* three-leaved.
трёхсторо́нний *adj.* **1.** three-sided; (*math.*) trilateral. **2.** tripartite.
трёхто́нк|а, и *f.* (*coll.*) three-ton lorry.
трёхфа́зный *adj.* (*elec.*) three-phase.
трёхходов|о́й *adj.* **1.** (*tech.*) three-way, three-pass. **2.**: **~а́я зада́ча** (*chess*) three-move problem.
трёхцве́тный *adj.* three-coloured; tricolour(ed); (*phot.*) trichromatic.
трёхчасово́й *adj.* **1.** three-hour. **2.** three o'clock.
трёхчле́н, а *m.* (*math.*) trinomial.
трёхчле́н|ный *adj. of* **~**
трёхъязы́чный *adj.* trilingual.
трёхэта́жный *adj.* three-storeyed.
трёшк|а, и *f.* (*coll.*) three-rouble note.
трёшниц|а, ы *f.* = **трёшка**
трещ|а́ть, у́, и́шь *impf.* **1.** to crack; (*fig.*) to crack up; **у меня́ голова́ ~и́т** I have a splitting headache; **т. по всем швам** (*fig.*) to go to pieces. **2.** to crackle; (*of furniture*) to creak; (*of grasshoppers*) to chirr; **~а́т моро́зы** there is a ringing frost. **3.** (*coll.*) to jabber, chatter.
тре́щин|а, ы *f.* crack, split (*also fig.*); cleft, fissure; chap (*of skin*); **дать ~у** to crack, split; (*fig.*) to show signs of cracking.
трещо́тк|а, и *f. and c.g.* **1.** *f.* rattle. **2.** *c.g.* (*fig., coll.*) chatterbox. **3.** *f.* (*tech.*) ratchet-drill.
три, трёх, трём, тремя́, о трёх *num.* three.
триа́д|а, ы *f.* triad.
триангуля́ци|я, и *f.* (*math., geod.*) triangulation.
триа́совый *adj.* (*geol.*) Triassic.
трибра́хи|й, я *m.* (*liter.*) tribrach.
трибу́н, а *m.* (*hist. or rhet.*) tribune.
трибу́н|а, ы *f.* **1.** platform, rostrum; tribune. **2.** stand (*at sports stadiums*).
трибуна́л, а *m.* tribunal.
тривиа́льност|ь, и *f.* triviality, banality; triteness.
тривиа́л|ьный (~ен, ~ьна) *adj.* trivial, banal; trite, hackneyed.
триглиф, а *m.* (*archit.*) triglyph.
тригонометри́ческий *adj.* trigonometric(al).
тригономе́три|я, и *f.* trigonometry.
тридевя́т|ый *adj.*: **в ~ом ца́рстве = за три́девять земе́ль**
три́девять: за т. земе́ль (*in legends and fig., coll.*) at the other end of the world.
тридцатиле́ти|е, я *nt.* **1.** thirty years. **2.** thirtieth anniversary.
тридцатиле́тний *adj.* **1.** thirty-year. **2.** thirty-year-old.
тридца́т|ый *adj.* thirtieth; **~ые го́ды** the thirties.
три́дцат|ь, и́, *i.* **ью** *num.* thirty.
три́дцатью *adv.* thirty times.
триеди́ный *adj.* (*theol. and fig.*) triune.
трие́р, а *m.* (*agric.*) separator, grader, sifter; grain cleaner.
три́жды *adv.* three times, thrice.
тризм, а *m.* (*med.*) lockjaw, trismus.
три́зн|а, ы *f.* (*hist.*) funeral feast.
трико́ *nt. indecl.* **1.** tricot (*woollen fabric*). **2.** tights; leotard, body stocking. **3.** (*women's stockinet*) knickers, pants.
трико́вый *adj.* tricot.
трикота́ж, а *m.* **1.** stockinet, jersey. **2.** (*collect.*) knitted wear, knitted garments.
трикота́жн|ый *adj.* stockinet, jersey; knitted; **~ые изде́лия** knitted wear; **~ая фа́брика** knitted goods factory.
триктра́к, а *m.* backgammon.
трили́стник, а *m.* (*bot.*) trefoil.
триллио́н, а *m.* trillion.
трило́ги|я, и *f.* trilogy.
тримара́н, а *m.* trimaran.
триме́стр, а *m.* term (*at educational establishment*).
триме́тр, а *m.* (*liter.*) trimeter.
три́ммер, а *m.* (*aeron. and elec.*) trimmer.
тринадцатиле́тний *adj.* **1.** thirteen year. **2.** thirteen-year-old.
трина́дцатый *adj.* thirteenth.
трина́дцат|ь, и *num.* thirteen.
трино́м, а *m.* (*math.*) trinomial.
три́о *nt. indecl.* (*mus.*) trio.
трио́д, а *m.* (*radio*) triode.
трио́д|ь, и *f.* (*eccl.*) service-book; **по́стная т.** book containing liturgy from Septuagesima to Easter; **цветна́я т.** book containing liturgy from Easter to All-Saints' week.
триоле́т, а *m.* (*liter.*) triolet.
трио́л|ь, и *f.* (*mus.*) triplet.
трип, а *m.* velveteen.
трипла́н, а *m.* triplane.
три́плекс, а *m.* triplex (*safety glass*).
три́ппер, а *m.* (*med.*) gonorrhoea.
трипси́н, а *m.* (*biol.*) trypsin.
триpе́м|а, ы *f.* trireme.
три́сел|ь, я *m.* (*naut.*) trysail.
триста, трёхсо́т, трёмста́м, тремяста́ми, трёхста́х *num.* three hundred.
трито́н, а *m.* (*zool.*) triton.
триумвира́т, а *m.* triumvirate.
триу́мф, а *m.* triumph; **с ~ом** triumphantly, in triumph.
триумфа́льный *adj.* triumphal.
триумфа́тор, а *m.* triumpher; victor.
трифто́нг, а *m.* triphthong.
трихи́н|а, ы *f.* trichina (*parasitical worm*).
трихино́з, а *m.* (*med.*) trichinosis.
троака́р, а *m.* (*med.*) trocar.
тро́гател|ьный (~ен, ~ьна) *adj.* touching; moving, affecting.
тро́га|ть[1], ю *impf.* (*of* **тро́нуть**) **1.** to touch. **2.** to disturb, trouble; **не ~й его́!** don't disturb him!; leave him be! **3.** to touch, move, affect; **т. до слёз** to move to tears.
тро́га|ть[2], ю *impf.* (*of* **тро́нуть**) (*coll.*) to start; **ну ~й!** go ahead!; get going!
тро́га|ться[1], юсь *impf.* (*of* **тро́нуться[1]**) *pass. of* **~ть[1]**; to be touched, moved, be affected.
тро́га|ться[2], юсь *impf. of* **тро́нуться[2]**
троглоди́т, а *m.* troglodyte (*also fig. of a pers.*).
тро́е, трои́х *num.* (*preceding m. nn. denoting living beings and pluralia tantum*) three; **т. су́ток** seventy-two hours.
троебо́рь|е, я *nt.* (*sport*) triathlon.
троекра́тный *adj.* thrice-repeated.
троепе́рсти|е, я *nt.* (*eccl.*) making the sign of the cross with three fingers.
тро|и́ть, ю́, и́шь *impf.* **1.** (*obs.*) to treble. **2.** to divide into three.
тро|и́ться, и́тся *impf.* **1.** to be trebled. **2.** to appear treble.
Тро́иц|а, ы *f.* **1.** (*theol.*) Trinity. **2.** (*eccl.*) Trinity; Whitsun(day). **3.** (*coll.*) trio.

Тро́ицын *adj.*: **Т. день** Trinity; Whitsun(day).
тро́йк|а, и *f.* **1.** three. **2.** (*school mark*) three (*out of five*). **3.** (*cards*) the three (*of a suit*). **4.** troika. **5.** (*coll.*) three-piece suit. **6.** No. 3 bus, tram, *etc.* **7.** three-man commission.
тройни́к, а́ *m.* **1.** object *or* measure containing three units. **2.** (*tech.*) tee; T-joint, T-pipe, T-bend. **3.** (*elec.*) branch box, T-junction box.
тройни́чный *adj.* **1.** triple. **2.** (*anat.*) trigeminal, trifacial.
тройн|о́й *adj.* triple, threefold, treble; **т. кана́т** three-ply rope; **~о́е пра́вило** (*math.*) the rule of three; **в ~о́м разме́ре** threefold, treble.
тро́йн|я, и *f.* triplets.
тро́йственн|ый *adj.* triple; **~ое согла́сие** (*hist.*) Triple Entente (*of England, France and Russia, concluded in 1907*).
трок, а *m.* surcingle.
тролле́|й, я *m.* (*tech.*) trolley.
тролле́йбус, а *m.* trolleybus.
тролле́йбус|ный *adj. of* ~
тромб, а *m.* (*med.*) clot of blood.
тромбо́з, а *m.* (*med.*) thrombosis.
тромбо́н, а *m.* trombone.
тромбони́ст, а *m.* trombonist.
тромбофлеби́т, а *m.* (*med.*) thrombo-phlebitis.
трон, а *m.* throne.
тро́нк|а, и *f.* (*dial.*) sheep-bell.
тро́н|ный *adj. of* ~; **т. зал** throne-room; (*parl.*) **~ная речь** King's *or* Queen's speech.
тро́|нуть, ну, нешь *pf. of* **~гать**
тро́|нуться[1], **нусь, нешься** *pf.* **1.** *pf. of* **~гаться**[1]. **2.** (*pf. only*) (*fig., coll.*) to be touched (= *to lose one's mind*); **он немно́го ~нулся** he is a bit touched, he is a bit cracked.
тро́|нуться[2], **нусь, нешься** *pf.* (*of* **~гаться**[2]) **1.** to start, set out; **т. с ме́ста** to make a move, get going; **по́езд ~нулся** the train started; **лёд ~нулся** the ice has begun to break (*also fig.*). **2.** (*coll.*) to go bad.
троп, а *m.* (*liter.*) trope.
троп|а́, ы́, *pl.* **~́ы, ~, ~а́м** *f.* path.
тропа́р|ь, я́ *m.* (*eccl.*) anthem (*for festival or saint's day*); troparion.
тро́пик, а *m.* (*geog.*) **1.** tropic; **т. Ра́ка** tropic of Cancer; **т. Козеро́га** tropic of Capricorn. **2.** (*pl.*) the tropics.
тропи́нк|а, и *f.* path.
тропи́ческ|ий *adj.* tropical; **~ая лихора́дка** jungle fever; **т. по́яс** torrid zone.
тропосфе́р|а, ы *f.* (*meteor.*) troposphere.
трос, а *m.* rope, cable, hawser.
тро́стинк|а, и *f.* thin reed.
тростни́к, а́ *m.* reed; rush; **са́харный т.** sugar-cane.
тростнико́вый *adj.* reed; **т. са́хар** cane-sugar.
тро́сточк|а, и *f.* = **трость**
трост|ь, и, *pl.* **~́и, ~е́й** *f.* cane, walking-stick.
троти́л, а *m.* (*chem., mil.*) trinitrotoluene (*abbr.* TNT), trinitrotoluol, trotyl.
тротуа́р, а *m.* pavement.
трофе́|й, я *m.* trophy (*also fig.*); (*pl.*) spoils of war, booty; captured material.
трофе́йн|ый *adj.* (*mil.*) captured; **~ая пу́шка** captured gun; **~ое отделе́ние** captured (enemy) matériel section.
трохеи́ческий *adj.* (*liter.*) trochaic.
трохе́|й, я *m.* (*liter.*) trochee.
троцки́зм, а *m.* Trotskyism.
троцки́ст, а *m.* Trotskyite, Trotskyist.
троцки́стский *adj.* Trotskyite, Trotskyist.
трою́родн|ый *adj.*: **т. брат, ~ая сестра́** second cousin; **т. племя́нник** second cousin once removed (*son of second cousin*).
троя́кий *adj.* threefold, triple.
троя́ко *adv.* in three (different) ways.
троя́нский *adj.*: **т. конь** Trojan horse.
труб|а́, ы́, *pl.* **~́ы** *f.* **1.** (*in var. senses*) pipe; conduit; tube; **т. орга́на** organ-pipe; **подзо́рная т.** telescope. **2.** chimney-flue; funnel, smoke-stack. **3.** (*mus.*) trumpet; **игра́ть на ~е́** to play the trumpet. **4.** (*anat.*) tube; duct. **5.** *as symbol of failure or ruin*: **де́ло т.** (*coll.*) things are in a bad way; it's a wash-out; **вы́лететь в ~у́** (*coll.*) to go bust, go smash; **пусти́ть в ~у́** to blow, squander. **6.** brush (*fox's tail*).
трубаду́р, а *m.* troubadour.
труба́ч, а́ *m.* trumpeter; trumpet-player.
труб|и́ть, лю́, и́шь *impf.* **1.** (**в**+*a.*; *mus.*) to blow. **2.** (*of trumpets, etc.*) to sound; to blare. **3.** to sound (*by blast of trumpet, etc.*); **т. сбор** (*mil.*) to sound assembly. **4.** (**о**+*p.*; *coll.*) to trumpet, proclaim from the house-tops.
тру́бк|а, и *f.* **1.** tube; pipe; **сверну́ть ~ой** to roll up. **2.** (tobacco-)pipe; **наби́ть ~у** to fill a pipe. **3.** (*mil., etc.*) fuse; **т. уда́рного де́йствия** instantaneous fuse; **т. с замедли́телем** delayed action fuse. **4.** (*telephone*) receiver.
трубкозу́б, а *m.* (*zool.*) aardvark.
тру́бный *adj.* trumpet; **т. сигна́л** trumpet-call; **т. глас** (*relig., liter.*) the last trump.
труболите́йный *adj.* pipe-casting, tube-casting.
трубопрово́д, а *m.* pipe-line; piping, tubing; manifold.
трубопрока́тный *adj.* (*tech.*) tube-rolling.
трубочи́ст, а *m.* chimney-sweep.
тру́бочн|ый *adj. of* **тру́бка; т. таба́к** pipe tobacco; **~ая гли́на** pipeclay.
тру́бчатый *adj.* tubular.
труве́р, а *m.* (*hist., liter.*) trouvère.
труд, а́ *m.* **1.** labour, work; **лю́ди ~а́** the workers. **2.** difficulty, trouble; **взять на себя́ т., дать себе́ т.** (+*inf.*) to take the trouble (to); **не сто́ит ~а́** it is not worth the trouble; **с ~о́м** with difficulty, hardly. **3.** (scholarly) work; (*pl., in titles of scholarly periodicals, etc.*) transactions.
тру|ди́ться, жу́сь, ~́дишься *impf.* to toil, labour, work; **не ~ди́тесь!** (please) don't trouble.
тру́дно *as pred.* it is hard, it is difficult; **т. сказа́ть** it is hard to say; **т. мне суди́ть** it is hard for me to tell.
трудновоспиту́ем|ый (~, ~а) *adj.* **т. ребёнок** difficult child.
труднодосту́п|ный (~ен, ~на) *adj.* difficult of access
труднопроходи́мый *adj.* difficult (to traverse).
тру́дност|ь, и *f.* difficulty; obstacle.
тру́д|ный (~ен, ~на́, ~но) *adj.* **1.** (*in var. senses*) difficult, hard; arduous. **2.** difficult, awkward. **3.** (*coll., of illness*) serious, grave; **т. больно́й** patient seriously ill.
трудови́к, а́ *m.* (*hist.*) Trudovik (*member of Labour group in Russ. Duma, 1906–1917*).
трудов|о́й *adj.* **1.** labour, work; **т. день** day's work; **~а́я кни́жка** work-book, work record; **т. ко́декс** Labour Code; **т. коллекти́в** work force; **~а́я пови́нность** labour conscription; **~о́е уве́чье** industrial disablement. **2.** working; living on one's own earnings; **т. наро́д** working people. **3.** earned; hard-earned.
трудого́лик, а *m.* (*coll.*) workaholic.
трудод|е́нь, ня́ *m.* (*hist.*) work-day (*unit of payment on collective farms*).
трудоём|кий (~ок, ~ка) *adj.* labour-consuming; labour-intensive.
трудолюби́в|ый (~, ~а) *adj.* hard-working, industrious.
трудолю́би|е, я *nt.* industry; liking for hard work.
трудосберега́ющий *adj.* labour-saving.
трудоспосо́бност|ь, и *f.* ability to work, capacity for work.
трудоспосо́б|ный (~ен, ~на) *adj.* able-bodied; capable of working.
трудотерапи́|я, и *f.* occupational therapy.
трудоустро́йств|о, а *nt.* placing in a job; resettlement (*of demobilized servicemen in civilian occupations*).
труд|я́щийся *pres. part. of* **~и́ться** *and adj.* working; *as n.* **~я́щиеся, ~я́щихся** the working people, the workers.
тру́женик, а *m.* toiler.
тру́жени|ческий *adj. of* **~к; ~ческая жизнь** life of toil.
трун|и́ть, ю, и́шь *impf.* (**над**; *coll.*) to make fun (of), mock.
труп, а *m.* dead body, corpse; carcass.
тру́п|ный *adj. of* ~; **т. за́пах** putrid smell; **~ное разложе́ние** putrefaction; **т. яд** ptomaine; **отравле́ние ~ным я́дом** ptomaine poisoning.
тру́пп|а, ы *f.* troupe, company.
трус[1], **а** *m.* coward; **~́а пра́здновать** (*coll.*) to show the white feather.
трус[2], **а** *m.* (*arch.*) earthquake.

тру́сик|и, ов *no sg.* **1.** shorts. **2.** swimming trunks. **3.** (under)pants.
тру́|сить, шу, сишь *impf.* (*of* **с~**) **1.** to be a coward; to funk; to have cold feet. **2.** (**перед** *or* +*a.*) to be afraid (of), be frightened (of).
тру|си́ть[1], **шу́, си́шь** *impf.* to shake out, scatter.
тру|си́ть[2], **шу́, си́шь** *impf.* to trot, jog.
труси́х|а, и *f. of* **трус**[1]
трусли́в|ый (~, ~а) *adj.* **1.** cowardly. **2.** faint-hearted, timorous; apprehensive.
тру́сост|ь, и *f.* cowardice.
трусц|а́, ы́ *f.* (*coll.*) jog-trot; **бег ~о́й** (*sport*) jogging.
трус|ы́, о́в *no sg.* = **~ики**
трут, а *m.* tinder; amadou.
тру́т|ень, ня *m.* drone (*also fig.*).
тру́тник, а *m.* tinder-fungus, punk.
трутови́к, а́ *m.* (*bot.*) polyporus, tree-fungus.
трух|а́, и́ *f.* dust (*of rotted wood*); hay-dust; (*fig.*) trash.
трухля́ве|ть, ет *impf.* to moulder.
трухля́в|ый (~, ~а) *adj.* mouldering; rotten.
трущо́б|а, ы *f.* **1.** overgrown place (*in forest, etc.*). **2.** (*fig.*) hole, out-of-the-way place. **3.** slum. **4.** (*coll.*) thieves' den.
трын-трава́ *as pred.* (+*d.*; *coll.*) it makes no odds; it's all the same.
трюк, а *m.* **1.** feat, stunt; **рекла́мный т.** advertising gimmick. **2.** (*fig., pej.*) trick.
трюка́ч, а́ *m.* **1.** crafty, wily pers. **2.** stuntman.
трюка́чес|кий *adj. of* **~тво; т. приём** crafty trick, stunt.
трюка́честв|о, а *nt.* (*pej.*) craft, wiliness.
трю́к|овый *adj. of* **~ 1.; т. но́мер** turn.
трюм, а *m.* (*naut.*) hold.
трю́м|ный *adj. of* **~; ~ая вода́** bilge-water.
трюмо́ *nt. indecl.* **1.** cheval-glass, pier-glass. **2.** (*archit.*) pier.
трю́фел|ь, я, *pl.* **~и, ~е́й** *m.* truffle.
тряпи́ц|а, ы *f.* (*coll.*) rag.
тряпи́чник, а *m.* (*obs.*) rag-and-bone man *or* merchant; rag-picker.
тряпи́чный *adj.* **1.** rag. **2.** (*coll., pej.*) soft, spineless.
тря́пк|а, и *f.* **1.** rag; duster. **2.** (*pl., coll.*) finery, glad rags. **3.** (*coll., pej.*) milksop, spineless creature.
тряпь|ё, я́ *nt.* (*collect.*) rags; (*coll.*) clothes, things.
тряси́н|а, ы *f.* quagmire.
тря́ск|а, и *f.* shaking, jolting.
тря́с|кий (~ок, ~ка) *adj.* **1.** shaky, jolty. **2.** bumpy.
трясогу́зк|а, и *f.* (*zool.*) wagtail.
тряс|ти́, у́, ёшь, *past* **~, ~ла́** *impf.* **1.** to shake; **т. кому́-н. ру́ку** to shake s.o.'s hand. **2.** to shake out. **3.** to cause to shake, cause to shiver (*usu. impers.*); **его́ ~ла́ лихора́дка** he was in the grip of a fever; **её ~ло́ от стра́ха** she was trembling with fear. **4.** (+*i.*) to swing; to shake; **т. гри́вой** (*of an animal*) to toss its mane. **5.** (*coll.*) to jolt, be jolty.
тряс|ти́сь, у́сь, ёшься, *past* **~ся, ~ла́сь** *impf.* **1.** to shake; to tremble, shiver; **т. от сме́ха** to shake with laughter; **т. от хо́лода** to shiver with cold. **2.** (*coll.*) to bump along, jog along; to be jolted. **3.** (**над**; *coll.*) to watch (over) (= *to fear to lose*); **они́ ~у́тся над ка́ждой копе́йкой** they watch every penny.
тряхн|у́ть, у́, ёшь *pf.* **1.** to shake. **2.: т. старино́й** (*coll.*) to hark back to days of yore; revive the customs of the (good) old days; **т. мо́лодостью** (*coll.*) to hark back to (the days of) one's youth. **3.** (+*i.*; *coll.*) to make free (with); **т. мошно́й, карма́ном** to throw one's money about; to open one's purse-strings.
тсс *int.* ssh!; (s)hush!
тт. *abbr. of* **1.** ***това́рищи*** Comrades. **2.** ***тома́*** vols; volumes.
туале́т, а *m.* **1.** dress; toilet. **2.** toilet, dressing; **соверша́ть т.** (*obs.*) to make one's toilet, dress. **3.** dressing-table. **4.** lavatory, toilet; **obще́ственный т.** public convenience.
туале́т|ный *adj. of* **~; ~ная бума́га** toilet-paper; **~ное мы́ло** toilet-soap; **~ные принадле́жности** toilet articles; **т. сто́лик** dressing-table.
туале́тчик, а *m.* lavatory attendant.
туале́тчиц|а, ы *f. of* **туале́тчик**
ту́б|а[1], **ы** *f.* (*mus.*) tuba.
ту́б|а[2], **ы** *f.* tube.
туберкулёз, а *m.* tuberculosis; **т. лёгких** pulmonary tuberculosis, consumption.
туберкулёзник, а *m.* (*coll.*) **1.** tuberculosis specialist. **2.** tubercular (patient); consumptive.
туберкулёз|ный *adj. of* **~; т. больно́й** tubercular (patient); consumptive; **~ная па́лочка** tuberculosis bacillus; *as n.* **т., ~ного** *m.* = **т. больно́й**
тубeróз|а, ы *f.* (*bot.*) tuberose.
тууви́н|ец, ца *m.* Tuvinian.
туви́н|ка, ки *f. of* **~ец**
туви́нский *adj.* Tuvinian.
ту́го *adv.* **1.** tight(ly), taut; **т. наби́ть чемода́н** to pack a suitcase tight; **т. натяну́ть** to stretch tight, taut. **2.** with difficulty; **т. продвига́ться вперёд** to make slow progress. **3.** *as pred.* **т. приходи́ться** (+*d.*; *coll.*) to have difficulties, be in a (tight) spot; **с деньга́ми у нас т.** we are in a tight spot financially.
тугоду́м, а *m.* (*coll.*) slow-witted pers.
туг|о́й (~, ~а́, ~о) *adj.* **1.** tight; taut; **т. у́зел** tight knot; **т. воротничо́к** tight collar. **2.** tightly-filled; **т. кошелёк** tightly-stuffed purse. **3.: т. на́ ухо** hard of hearing. **4.** (*fig., coll.*) tight, close (*with money*); **т. на распла́ту** close-fisted. **5.** (*fig., coll.*) difficult; **дела́ у них ~и́е** they are in a (tight) spot.
тугопла́в|кий (~ок, ~ка) *adj.* (*tech.*) refractory.
тугоу́здый *adj.* (*of a horse*) hard-mouthed.
ту́грик, а *m.* tugrik (*unit of currency in Mongolia*).
туда́ *adv.* there, thither; that way; to the right place; **т. и обра́тно** there and back; **биле́т т. и обра́тно** return ticket; **не т.!** not that way!; **ни т. ни сюда́** neither one way nor the other; **вы не т. попа́ли** (*on telephone*) you have got the wrong number; **т. ему́ и доро́га** (*coll.*) it serves him right; **т. же** (*coll.*) the same, likewise, following suit (*of s.o. attempting sth. of which he is neither capable or to which he has not the right; also as int.*).
туда́-сюда́ *adv.* (*coll.*) **1.** hither and thither. **2.** *as pred.* it will do, it will pass muster.
ту́|евый *adj. of* **~я**
ту́ер, а *m.* (*naut.*) chain-tug.
ту́же *comp. of* **туго́й** *and* **ту́го**
туж|и́ть, у́, ~ишь *impf.* (**о, по**+*p.*; *coll.*) to grieve (for).
ту́ж|иться, усь, ишься *impf.* (*coll.*) to make an effort.
тужу́рк|а, и *f.* (*man's*) double-breasted jacket.
туз[1], **а́** *m.* **1.** (*cards*) ace; **пойти́ с ~а́** to lead an ace; **т. к ма́сти** (*coll.*) just the job. **2.** (*coll.*) bigwig, big pot; big shot.
туз[2], **а** *m.* two-oar dinghy.
тузе́м|ец, ца *m.* native.
тузе́м|ка, ки *f. of* **~ец**
тузе́мный *adj.* native, indigenous.
ту|зи́ть, жу́, зи́шь *impf.* (*of* **от~**) (*coll.*) to punch; to pummel.
тук[1], **а** *m.* **1.** (*obs.*) fat. **2.** (*pl.*) mineral fertilizers.
тук[2] *as pred.* = **~нул**
ту́к|ать, аю *impf.* (*of* **~нуть**) (*coll.*) to bash, bonk.
ту́к|нуть, ну, нешь *pf. of* **~ать**
ту́к|нуться, нусь, нешься *pf.* (**о**+*a.*; *coll.*) to bang o.s. (against, on).
ту́ковый *adj.* fertilizer.
тук-ту́к *int.* (*coll.*) rat-tat (*also as pred.*).
ту́лли|й, я *m.* (*chem.*) thulium.
ту́ловищ|е, а *nt.* trunk; torso.
тулумба́с, а *m.* **1.** big drum, bass drum. **2.** (*coll., joc.*) punch; **дать кому́-н. ~а** to punch s.o.
тулу́п, а *m.* sheepskin (*or* hareskin) coat.
тул|ья́, ьи́, *g. pl.* **~е́й** *f.* crown (*of headgear*).
туляреми́|я, и *f.* (*med.*) tularaemia.
тума́к[1], **а́** *m.* (*coll.*) cuff, punch.
тума́к[2], **а́** *m.* tunny(-fish).
тума́н, а *m.* fog; mist, haze; **у него́ был т. в глаза́х** there was a mist before his eyes; **у меня́ т. в голове́** (*fig.*) I see no light, I am groping in the dark; **напусти́ть ~у** (*coll.*) to obscure the issue.
тума́н|ить, ит *impf.* to dim, cloud, obscure (*also fig.*).

тумáн|иться, ится *impf.* **1.** to grow misty, grow hazy; to become enveloped in mist. **2.** (*fig.*, *coll.*) to be in a fog, be befogged.
тумáнно *as pred.* it is foggy, it is misty.
тумáнност|ь, и *f.* **1.** fog, mist. **2.** (*astron.*) nebula. **3.** haziness, obscurity.
тумáн|ный (~ен, ~на) *adj.* **1.** foggy; misty; hazy; **~ная полосá** fog patch. **2.** (*fig.*) dull, lacklustre. **3.** (*fig.*) hazy, obscure, vague. **4.** (*obs.*): **~ные картúны** (magic) lantern slides.
тýмб|а, ы *f.* **1.** curbstone; post; **причáльная т.** (*naut.*) bollard. **2.** pedestal. **3.** advertisement hoarding (*of cylindrical shape*). **4.** (*fig.*, *joc.*; *of a pers.*) lump.
тýмбочк|а, и *f.* **1.** bedside table. **2.** *dim. of* **тýмба**
тунг, а *m.* tung-tree.
тýнг|овый *adj. of* ~; **~овое мáсло** tung-oil.
тýндр|а, ы *f.* (*geog.*) tundra.
тýндр|еный *adj.* = **~овый**
тýндр|овый *adj. of* **~а**
тун|éц, цá *m.* tunny(-fish).
тунеяд|ец, ца *m.* parasite, sponger.
тунеядств|о, а *nt.* parasitism, sponging.
тунеядств|овать, ую *impf.* to be a parasite; to sponge.
Тунúс, а *m.* **1.** Tunisia. **2.** Tunis.
тунúс|ец, ца *m.* Tunisian.
тунúс|ка, ки *f. of* **~ец**
тунúсский *adj.* Tunisian.
туннéл|ь, я *m.* tunnel; subway.
туннéль|ный *adj. of* ~
тупé|й, я *m.* (*obs.*) tuft of hair.
тупé|ть, ю *impf.* (*of* **о~**) to become blunt; to grow dull.
тýпик, а *m.* (*zool.*) puffin.
тупúк, á *m.* **1.** blind alley, cul-de-sac. **2.** (*rail.*) siding. **3.** (*fig.*) impasse, deadlock; **зайтú в т.** to reach a deadlock. **4.: постáвить в т.** to stump, nonplus; **стать в т.** to be stumped, be nonplussed, be at a loss.
туп|úть, лю́, ~ишь *impf.* to blunt.
туп|úться, ~ится *impf.* to become blunt.
тупúц|а, ы *c.g.* (*coll.*) dolt, blockhead, dimwit; duffer.
тупоголóв|ый (~, ~а) *adj.* (*coll.*) dim-witted.
туп|óй (~, ~á, ~о) *adj.* **1.** blunt. **2.: т. ýгол** (*math.*) obtuse angle. **3.** (*fig.*) dull (*pain*, *sensation*, *etc.*). **4.** (*fig.*) vacant, stupid, meaningless; **~áя улы́бка** vacant smile. **5.** (*fig.*) dull, obtuse; slow; dim; **т. ум** dull wits. **6.** (*fig.*) blind, unquestioning; **~áя покóрность** blind submission.
тупоконéчн|ый *adj.* blunt-pointed; **~ая пýля** blunt-nosed bullet.
туполóб|ый (~, ~а) *adj.* (*coll.*) dull, dim-witted.
тупонóс|ый (~, ~а) *adj.* blunt-nosed (*also fig.*).
тýпост|ь, и *f.* **1.** bluntness. **2.** (*fig.*) vacancy. **3.** (*fig.*) dullness, slowness.
тупоýми|е, я *nt.* dullness, obtuseness.
тупоýм|ный (~ен, ~на) *adj.* dull, obtuse.
тур^1, а *m.* **1.** turn (*in a dance*). **2.** (*at sports and games*; *also fig.*) round.
тур^2, а *m.* (*obs.*) gabion.
тур^3, а *m.* (*zool.*) **1.** aurochs. **2.** Caucasian goat (*Capra caucasia*).
тур|á, ы́ *f.* (*chess*) castle, rook.
турбáз|а, ы *f.* tourist centre.
турбúн|а, ы *f.* (*tech.*) turbine.
турбúнный *adj.* turbine.
турбовинтовóй *adj.* (*tech.*, *aeron.*) turbo-prop.
турбовóз, а *m.* turbine locomotive.
турбогенерáтор, а *m.* (*tech.*) turbo-alternator.
турбореактúвный *adj.* (*tech.*, *aeron.*) turbo-jet.
турéл|ь, и *f.* (*mil.*) (gun-)turret; ring mount(ing).
турéцк|ий *adj.* Turkish; **т. барабáн** big drum, bass drum; **~ие бобы́** haricot beans; **т. горóх** chick pea; **~ая мýзыка** (*mus.*, *obs.*) percussion instruments; **~ая пшенúца** (*obs.*) maize; **гол, как т. святóй** (*coll.*) poor as a church mouse; **~ое седлó** (*anat.*) sella turcica.
турúзм, а *m.* tourism; outdoor pursuits; **вóдный т.** boating; **гóрный т.** mountaineering.
тýрий *adj. of* **тур^3**
турúст, а *m.* tourist; hiker.
туристúческ|ий *adj.* tourist; **т. похóд** walking tour; **~ие путешéствия** travels.
турúстск|ий *adj.* tourist; **~ая бáза** tourist centre.
тур|úть, ю́, úшь *impf.* (*coll.*) to throw out, chuck out.
туркмéн, а, *g. pl.* **т.** *m.* Turkmen.
Туркменистáн, а *m.* Turkmenistan.
туркмéн|ка, ки *f. of* ~
туркмéнский *adj.* Turkmen.
тýрман, а *m.* tumbler-pigeon; **полетéть ~ом** (*coll.*) to fall down head over heels.
турнé *nt. indecl.* tour (*esp. of troupe of artistes or of sportsmen*).
турнéпс, а *m.* swede.
турнúк, á *m.* (*sport*) horizontal bar.
турникéт, а *m.* **1.** turnstile. **2.** (*med.*) tourniquet.
турнúр, а *m.* tournament (*at chess*, *etc.*, *also hist.*)
турн|ýть, ý, ёшь *pf.* (*coll.*) to chuck out.
турнюр, а *m.* bustle.
тýр|ок, ка, *g. pl.* **т.** *m.* Turk.
турпáн, а *m.* (*zool.*) scoter.
турýс|ы, ов *no sg.* (*coll.*) idle gossip; **т. на колёсах** nonsense, rubbish, twaddle.
турухтáн, а *m.* (*zool.*) ruff (*Philomachus pugnax*).
Тýрци|я, и *f.* Turkey.
тур|чáнка, чáнки *f. of* **~ок**
тýскл|ый (~, ~á, ~о) *adj.* **1.** dim, dull; matt; tarnished. **2.** wan; lacklustre. **3.** (*fig.*) dim, dull; colourless; tame; **т. гóлос** flat voice; **т. стиль** colourless style.
тускнé|ть, ет *impf.* (*of* **по~**) **1.** to grow dim, grow dull; to tarnish; to grow wan, lose its lustre. **2.** (**пéред;** *fig.*) to pale (before, by the side of).
тусóвк|а, и *f.* (*coll.*) get-together, do.
тут *adv.* **1.** here; **кто т.?** who's there?; **и всё т.** (*coll.*) and that's it, and that was that; **т. как т.** (*coll.*) there he is, there they are. **2.** now; **т. же** there and then.
тýтовник, а *m.* **1.** mulberry (tree). **2.** mulberry grove.
тýтов|ый *adj.* mulberry; **~ое дéрево** mulberry (tree); **т. шелкопряд** silkworm.
тýт-то *adv.* (*coll.*) **1.** right here. **2.** there and then. **3.: не т.-то бы́ло!** nothing of the sort!; far from it!
туф, а *m.* (*geol.*, *min.*) tufa; tuff.
тýфл|я, и *f.* shoe; slipper.
тýф|овый *adj. of* ~
тухлúнк|а, и *f.* (*coll.*) bad smell.
тýхл|ый (~, ~á, ~о) *adj.* rotten, bad; **~ое мя́со** tainted meat.
тухля́тин|а, ы *f.* (*coll.*) bad food; tainted meat.
тýх|нуть^1, нет, *past* **~, ~ла** *impf.* (*of* **по~**) (*of source of light or heat*) to go out.
тýх|нуть^2, нет, *past* **~, ~ла** *impf.* to go bad, become rotten.
тýч|а, и *f.* **1.** (rain) cloud; storm cloud (*also fig.*); **не из ~и гром** a bolt from the blue; **~и собрались, навúсли (над)** (*fig.*) the clouds are gathering (over). **2.** *as symbol of sombre appearance or gloomy mood*: **смотрéть ~ей** to look black, scowl, lour; **сидéть т.-~ей** to be in a black mood. **3.** cloud, swarm, host; **т.-~ей** in a swarm.
туч|евóй *adj. of* **~а**
тýчк|а, и *f. dim. of* **тýча**
тучнé|ть, ю *impf.* (*of* **по~**) **1.** to grow stout, grow fat. **2.** (*of soil*) to become fertile.
тýчност|ь, и *f.* **1.** fatness, stoutness, obesity, corpulence. **2.** (*of soil*) richness, fertility.
тýч|ный (~ен, ~нá, ~но) *adj.* **1.** fat, stout, obese, corpulent. **2.** (*of soil*) rich, fertile. **3.** (*of grass*) succulent.
туш, а *m.* (*mus.*) flourish.
тýш|а, и *f.* **1.** carcass. **2.** (*fig.*; *of a fat man*) hulk.
тушé *nt. indecl.* **1.** (*mus.*) touch. **2.** (*fencing*) touché.
туш|евáть, ýю *impf.* (*of* **за~**) to shade.
тушёвк|а, и *f.* shading.
тушёный *adj.* (*cul.*) braised, stewed.
туш|úть^1, ý, ~ишь *impf.* (*of* **по~**) **1.** to extinguish, put out. **2.** (*fig.*) to suppress, stifle, quell.
туш|úть^2, ý, ~ишь *impf.* (*cul.*) to braise, stew.
тушкáнчик, а *m.* jerboa.

туш|ь, и *f.* Indian ink; **т. (для ресни́ц)** mascara.
ту́|я, и *f.* (*bot.*) thuya.
т.ч.: в ~ (*abbr. of* **в том числе́**) incl., including.
тчк (*abbr. of* **то́чка**) stop (*in telegram*).
тща́ни|е, я *nt.* (*obs.*) zeal, assiduity.
тща́тельност|ь, и *f.* thoroughness, carefulness; care.
тща́тел|ьный (~ен, ~ьна) *adj.* thorough, careful; painstaking.
тщеду́ши|е, я *nt.* feebleness, frailty; debility.
тщеду́ш|ный (~ен, ~на) *adj.* feeble, frail, weak; puny.
тщесла́ви|е, я *nt.* vanity, vainglory.
тщесла́в|ный (~ен, ~на) *adj.* vain, vainglorious.
тщет|а́, ы́ *f.* vanity.
тще́тно *adv.* vainly, in vain.
тще́тност|ь, и *f.* futility, vainness.
тще́т|ный (~ен, ~на) *adj.* vain, futile; unavailing.
тщ|и́ться, усь, и́шься *impf.* (+*inf.*; *obs.*) to try (to), endeavour (to).
ты, тебя́, тебе́, тобо́й (*and* **тобо́ю), о тебе́** *2nd pers. sg. pers. pron.* you; thou; **быть „на ты" (с+*i*), говори́ть „ты"** (+*d*) to be on familiar terms (with).
ты|ка́ть[1], **чу, чешь** *impf.* (*of* **ткнуть) 1.** (+*i.* **в**+*a. or* +*a.* **в**+*a.*) to stick (into) (*also fig.*); to poke (into); to prod; to jab (into); **т. була́вкой во что-н.** to stick a pin into sth.; **т. па́лкой** to prod with a stick; **т. ко́лья в зе́млю** to stick stakes into the ground; **т. (свой) нос (в**+*a.*; *fig.*, *pej.*) to stick, poke one's nose (into); **т. в нос кому́-н. чем-н.** (*fig.*, *coll.*) to cast sth. in s.o.'s teeth; **т. кого́-н. но́сом во что-н.** (*fig.*, *coll.*) to rub s.o.'s nose in sth. **2.: т. па́льцем (на**+*a.*; *coll.*) to point (at), poke one's finger (at).
ты́ка|ть[2], **ю** *impf.* (*coll.*) to address as **„ты"**; be on familiar terms (with).
ты́|каться, чусь, чешься *impf.* (*of* **ткну́ться**) (*coll.*) **1.** (**в**+*a.*) to knock (against, into). **2.** to rush about, fuss about.
тыкв|а, ы *f.* pumpkin, gourd.
ты́кв|енный *adj. of* **~а**; *as n.* **~енные, ~енных** (*bot.*) gourd family, Cucurbitaceae.
тыл, а, о ~е, в ~у́, *pl.* **~ы́** *m.* **1.** back, rear. **2.** (*mil.*) rear; home front; **напа́сть с ~а** to attack in the rear. **3.** (*pl.*; *mil.*) rear services, rear organizations. **4.** the (whole) country (*opp. front or frontier areas*), the interior.
тылови́к, а́ *m.* (*mil.*) man serving in the rear.
тылов|о́й *adj.* (*mil.*) rear; **~а́я часть** service element (*of unit*); **т. го́спиталь** base hospital.
ты́льн|ый *adj.* **1.** back, rear; **~ая пове́рхность руки́** back of the hand. **2.** (*mil.*) rear; **~ая заста́ва, ~ая часть** rear party; **т. тра́верс** parados.
тын, а *m.* paling; palisade, stockade.
ты́сяцк|ий, ого *m.* **1.** (*hist.*) captain, leader. **2.** (*obs. or dial.*) master of ceremonies (*at peasant wedding ceremony*).
ты́сяч|а, и, *i.* **~ей** *and* **~ью** *num. and n.*, *f.* thousand; **в ~у раз** a thousand times (*also fig.*).
тысячеле́ти|е, я *nt.* **1.** a thousand years; millennium. **2.** thousandth anniversary.
тысячеле́тний *adj.* thousand-year; millennial.
ты́сячник, а *m.* (*coll.*) **1.** record-breaking worker (*with production figures of so many thousand units*). **2.** pers. with capital amounting to thousands.
ты́сячн|ый *adj.* **1.** thousandth; *as n.* **~ая ~ой** *f.* thousandth. **2.** of many thousands. **3.** worth a thousand, many thousand roubles.
тычи́нк|а, и *f.* (*bot.*) stamen.
тыч|о́к, ка́ *m.* **1.** sharp object sticking up; **быть, сиде́ть на ~ке́** (*i*) to be in an uncomfortable position, (*ii*) (*fig.*) to be conspicuously perched. **2.** (*tech.*) bond-stone; header. **3.** hit, prod, jab.
тьм|а[1], **ы** *no pl.*, *f.* darkness (*also fig.* = *ignorance*); **т. еги́петская, т. кроме́шная** outer darkness (*bibl.*), pitch darkness.
тьм|а[2], **ы,** *g. pl.* **тем** *f.* **1.** (*arch.*) ten thousand. **2.** (*coll.*) host, swarm, multitude; **т.-тьму́щая** countless multitudes.
тьфу *int.* (*coll.*) pah!; **т. про́пасть!** confound it!
тюбете́йк|а, и tyubeteyka (*embroidered skull-cap worn in Central Asia*).
тю́бик, а *m.* tube (*of toothpaste, etc.*).
тюк, а́ *m.* bale, package.
тю́к|ать, аю *impf.* (*of* **~нуть**) (*coll.*) to chop, hack.
тю́к|нуть, ну, нешь *pf. of* **~ать**
тю́левый *adj.* (*text.*) tulle.
тюле́невый *adj.* sealskin.
тюле́н|ий *adj. of* **~ь; т. про́мысел** sealing, seal-fishery.
тюле́н|ь, я *m.* **1.** (*zool.*) seal. **2.** (*fig.*, *coll.*) clumsy clot.
тюл|ь, я *m.* (*text.*) tulle.
тюльпа́н, а *m.* **1.** tulip. **2.** (*obs.*) (glass) lamp-shade.
тюльпа́н|ный *adj. of* **~; ~ное де́рево** tulip-tree.
тюни́к|а, и *f.* **1.** (*obs.*) over-skirt. **2.** ballerina's dress.
тюрба́н, а *m.* turban.
тюр|е́мный *adj. of* **~ьма́; ~е́мное заключе́ние** imprisonment; **т. смотри́тель** prison governor.
тюрк, а *m.* (*ethnol.*) Turki (*member of ethnic group having Turkic language*).
тю́ркский *adj.* (*ethnol.*, *ling.*) Turkic.
тюр|ьма́, ьмы́, *pl.* **~ьмы, ~ем** *f.* **1.** prison; jail, gaol; **заключи́ть в ~ьму́** to put into prison, imprison, jail; **сиде́ть в ~ьме́** to be in prison. **2.** imprisonment.
тю́р|я, и *f.* (*cul.*) tyurya (*a pulp of bread and milk, water, or kvass*).
тю́тельк|а, и *f.*: **т. в ~у** (*coll.*) to a T.
тю́тька|ться, юсь *impf.* (**с**+*i.*; *coll.*, *pej.*) to nursemaid.
тю-тю́ *as pred.* (*coll.*, *joc.*) it's all gone; we've (you've, they've) had it.
тютю́н, а́ *m.* (*dial.*) shag (tobacco).
тюфя́к, а́ *m.* **1.** mattress (*filled with straw, hay, etc.*). **2.** (*fig.*, *coll.*) flabby fellow.
тюфя́|чный *adj. of* **~к**
тя́вк|ать, аю *impf.* (*of* **~нуть**) to yap, yelp.
тя́вк|нуть, ну, нешь *pf. of* **~ать**
тяг, у *m.*: **дать ~у** (*coll.*) to take to one's heels, show a clean pair of heels.
тя́г|а[1], **и** *f.* **1.** traction; locomotion; **си́ла ~и** tractive force; **на ко́нной ~е** horse-drawn. **2.** (*collect.*) locomotives. **3.** (*aeron.*) thrust. **4.** (*in boiler chimney, etc.*) draught; **регуля́тор ~и** damper. **5. (к, на**+*a.*; *fig.*) pull (towards), attraction (towards), thirst (for), craving (for), taste (for); bent (for), inclination (to, for); **т. к зна́нию** thirst for knowledge; **он испы́тывает си́льную ~у к Восто́ку** he is strongly drawn towards the East.
тя́г|а[2], **и** *f.* flight (*esp.* of woodcock) at mating-season, *etc.*
тяга́|ть, ю *impf.* (*coll.*) to pull (up, out); **т. лён** to pull flax.
тяга́|ться, юсь *impf.* (*of* **по~**) (**с**+*i.*) **1.** (*obs.*) to be at law (with). **2.** to have a tug-of-war (with). **3.** (*coll.*) to contend (with), vie (with), measure one's own strength (with).
тяга́ч, а́ *m.* tractor (*for pulling train of trailers*).
тя́гл|о[1], **а** *nt.* (*collect.*) draught animals.
тя́гл|о[2], **а,** *g. pl.* **тя́гол** *nt.* (*hist.*) **1.** tax, impost. **2.** household (*as unit for tax assessment*). **3.** dues (*corvée, quit-rent, etc.*). **4.** strip of land (*worked by one household*).
тя́гловый[1] *adj.* = **тя́глый**
тя́гловый[2] *adj.* (*hist.*) taxed, liable to tax.
тя́глый *adj.* draught (*of cattle*).
тя́гов|ый *adj.* traction, tractive; **т. кана́т** hauling rope; **т. крюк** trace hook, towing hook, drawbar hook; **т. сте́ржень** drawbar; **~ая си́ла** tractive force.
тягоме́р, а *m.* (*tech.*) draught gauge; suction gauge; blast meter.
тя́гост|ный (~ен, ~на) *adj.* **1.** burdensome, onerous. **2.** painful, distressing; **~ное зре́лище** painful spectacle.
тя́гост|ь, и *f.* **1.** weight, burden; **быть кому́-н. в т.** to be a burden to s.o., weigh on s.o. **2.** fatigue.
тягот|а́, ы́, *pl.* **тя́готы** *f.* weight, burden.
тяготе́ни|е, я *nt.* **1.** (*phys.*) gravity, gravitation; **зако́н (всеми́рного) ~я** law of gravity. **2. (к)** attraction (towards), taste (for); bent (for), inclination (to, for); **т. к детекти́вным рома́нам** taste for detective stories.
тяготе́|ть, ю *impf.* **1. (к)** (*phys.*) to gravitate (towards). **2. (к)** (*fig.*) to gravitate (towards), be drawn (by, towards), be attracted (by, towards). **3. (над)** to hang (over), threaten; **стра́шный рок ~ет над на́ми** a terrible fate hangs over us.

тяго|ти́ть, щу́, ти́шь *impf.* to burden, be a burden (on, to); to lie heavy (on), oppress.

тяго|ти́ться, щу́сь, ти́шься *impf.* to be weighed down, oppressed.

тягу́чест|ь, и *f.* **1.** malleability, ductility. **2.** viscosity.

тягу́ч|ий (~, ~а) *adj.* **1.** malleable, ductile. **2.** viscous. **3.** (*fig.*) slow, leisurely, unhurried.

тягча́йш|ий *superl. of* **тя́жкий; ~ее преступле́ние** very serious crime.

тяж, а́ *m.* **1.** (*tech.*) drawing rod; **т. то́рмозного ва́ла** brake rod. **2.** shaft brace.

тя́жб|а, ы *f.* **1.** (*obs.*) (civil) suit, lawsuit; litigation. **2.** (*fig., coll.*) competition, rivalry.

тя́ж|ебный *adj. of* **~ба 1.**

тяжел|е́е *comp. of* **~̈ый** *and* **~о́**

тяжеле́|ть, ю *impf.* **1.** to become heavier; to put on weight. **2.** to become heavy with sleep (*of eyes*).

тяжело́[1] *adv.* **1.** heavily. **2.** seriously, gravely. **т. бо́лен** seriously ill. **3.** with difficulty.

тяжело́[2] *as pred.* **1.** it is hard; it is painful, it is distressing. **2. ему́,** *etc.*, **т.** he, *etc.*, feels miserable, wretched.

тяжелоатле́т, а *m.* weight-lifter; athlete competing in weight-lifting and/or wrestling.

тяжелоатлети́ческ|ий *adj.*: **~ое состяза́ние** meeting, competition comprising weight-lifting and/or wrestling.

тяжелове́с[1]**, а** *m.* (*sport*) heavyweight.

тяжелове́с[2]**, а** *m.* (*min.*) Siberian topaz.

тяжелове́с|ный (~ен, ~на) *adj.* **1.** heavily-loaded; **т. соста́в** heavy goods train. **2.** (*fig., pej.*) heavy, ponderous; clumsy, unwieldy; heavy-handed; **~ная остро́та** ponderous witticism.

тяжелово́з, а *m.* **1.** heavy draught-horse. **2.** heavy lorry.

тяжелоду́м, а *m.* (*coll.*) slow-witted pers.

тяжёл|ый (~, ~а́) *adj.* **1.** (*in var. senses*) heavy; **т. чемода́н** heavy suitcase; **~ая артилле́рия** heavy artillery; **~ая атле́тика** (*sport*) weight-lifting and/or wrestling; **~ая вода́** (*chem.*) heavy water; **~ое дыха́ние** heavy breathing; **~ая промы́шленность** heavy industry; **~ое то́пливо** heavy fuel (*oil, petrol*); **т. шаг** heavy step, tread. **2.** *expr. idea of excessive, disagreeable heaviness*: **т. во́здух** close air; **т. за́пах** oppressive, strong smell; **~ая пи́ща** heavy, indigestible food. **3.** hard, difficult; **~ая зада́ча** hard task; **~ые ро́ды** difficult confinement. **4.** slow; **т. ум** slow brain, wits; **т. на подъём** hard to move, sluggish. **5.** heavy, severe; **~ые поте́ри** heavy casualties; **~ое наказа́ние** severe punishment; **т. уда́р** severe blow. **6.** (*of illness, etc.*) serious, grave, bad; seriously ill; **~ое ране́ние** serious injury, wound. **7.** heavy, hard, painful; **~ое чу́вство** heavy heart; misgivings; **~ые времена́** hard times; **~ая обя́занность** painful duty; **т. день** bad, hard day. **8.** (*of character*) difficult. **9.** (*of liter. style, etc.*) heavy, ponderous, unwieldy.

тя́жест|ь, и *f.* **1.** (*phys.*) gravity; **центр ~и** centre of gravity (*also fig.*); (*fig.*) gravamen. **2.** weight, heavy object; **подня́тие ~ей** (*sport*) weight-lifting. **3.** weight, heaviness; **вся т. чего́-н.** (*fig.*) the whole weight, the brunt of sth.; **т. ули́к** weight of evidence. **4.** difficulty. **5.** heaviness, severity.

тя́ж|кий (~ек, ~ка́, ~ко) *adj.* **1.** (*fig.*) heavy, hard. **2.** severe; serious, grave; **~кая боле́знь** dangerous illness; **~кое преступле́ние** grave crime; **т. уда́р** severe blow. **3.: пусти́ться во все ~кие** (*coll.*) to plunge into dissipation.

тяжкоду́м, а *m.* (*coll.*) slow-witted pers.

тя́жущийся *adj.* litigant.

тяну́льный *adj.* (*tech.*) stretching.

тян|у́ть, у́, ~́ешь *impf.* **1.** to pull, draw; to haul; to drag; **т. на букси́ре** to tow; **т. кого́-н. за рука́в** to pull s.o. by the sleeve, tug at s.o.'s sleeve; **т. кого́-н. за́ душу** to torment s.o.; **т. ля́мку** (*coll.*) to drudge, toil. **2.** (*tech.*) to draw (*wire*). **3.** to lay; to put up (*wire, cable, etc.*); **т. телефо́нную ли́нию** to lay a telephone cable. **4.: т. жре́бий** to draw lots. **5.** (*fig.*) to draw, attract; **меня́,** *etc.* **~́ет** I long, I want; **его́ ~́ет домо́й** he wants to go home; **меня́ ~́ет ко сну** I feel sleepy; **нас ~́ет на юг** we are drawn towards, attracted by the South; **меня́ ~́ет купа́ться** I'm dying for a swim. **6.** to drawl, drag out; **т. слова́** to drawl; **т. но́ту** to sustain a note. **7.** to drag out, protract, delay; **т. с отве́том** to delay one's answer, delay over answering. **8.** to weigh (*intrans.*). **9.** to draw up; to take in, suck in; **т. в себя́ во́здух** to inhale deeply; **т. че́рез соло́минку** to suck through a straw. **10. (из, с)** to extract (from); to extort (from), squeeze (out of); **т. все си́лы из кого́-н.** to exhaust all the strength from s.o. **11.** (*of a chimney, etc.*) to draw; **пе́чь пло́хо ~́ет** the stove is not drawing well. **12.** *impers.*, *+i.*; *of a stream of air, of a smell*: **~́ет хо́лодом из-под две́ри** there is a draught coming from beneath the door; **от поле́й ~у́ло за́пахом се́на** a smell of hay was wafted from the fields. **13.** (*usu. impers.*) to press, be tight; **~́ет в плеча́х** it feels tight in the shoulders.

тян|у́ться, у́сь, ~́ешься *impf.* **1.** (*of rubber, etc.*) to stretch. **2.** (*pf.* **по~**) to stretch out, stretch o.s. **3.** (*of landscape features, etc.*) to stretch, extend; **по ту сто́рону на со́тни киломе́тров ~́ется тайга́** on that side for hundreds of kilometres stretches the taiga. **4.** (*of time*) to drag on; to crawl, hang heavy. **5.** (*coll.*) to last out, hold out; **запа́сы ещё ~́нутся** supplies are still holding out. **6. (к)** to reach (for), reach out (for); to strive (after); **т. к сла́ве** to strive after fame. **7. (за**+*i.*; *fig., coll.*) to try to keep up (with), try to equal. **8.** to move one after the other. **9.** (*of clouds, smoke, etc.*) to drift.

тяну́чк|а, и *f.* toffee, caramel.

тя́н|ущий *pres. part. act. of* **~у́ть** *and adj.*; **~ущая боль** nagging, persistent pain.

тя́п|ать, а́ю *impf.* (*of* **~нуть**) (*coll.*) **1.** to hit; to chop (at), hack (at). **2.** to grab, snatch; (*fig.*) to pinch. **3.** to knock back (= *to drink off*).

тя́пк|а, и *f.* chopper.

тяп-ля́п *adv. or as pred.* (*coll.*) anyhow (*of careless, slipshod work*).

тя́п|нуть, ну, нешь *pf. of* **~ать**

тя́т|я, и *m.* (*dial.*) dad, daddy.

У

у[1] *int.* (*expr. reproach or fear*) oh.

у[2] *prep.+g.* **1.** by; at; **у окна́** by the window; **у воро́т** at the gate; **у мо́ря** by the sea; **у роя́ля** at the piano; **у руля́** at the helm (*also fig.*); **у вла́сти** in power. **2.** at; with (*oft.* = *French 'chez'*); **у нас** (*i*) at our place, with us, (*ii*) in our country; **у себя́** at one's (own) place, at home; **я был у парикма́хера** I was at the hairdresser's; **она́ учи́лась у знамени́того испа́нского скрипача́** she was taught by a celebrated Spanish violinist; **он шьёт костю́м у хоро́шего портно́го** he is having a suit made by a good tailor; **ты у меня́ смотри́!** (you) watch out! **3.** *expr. relationship of possession, of part to whole, etc.*: **зуб у меня́ боли́т** my tooth aches; **ши́на у пере́днего колеса́ ло́пнула** there is a puncture in (the tyre of) the front wheel; **мать у неё больна́** her mother is ill. **4.** (*indicating source, place of origin, etc., of sth. obtained*) from, of; **я за́нял де́сять рубле́й у сосе́да** I borrowed ten roubles from a neighbour; **спроси́те у него́ о́ттиск** ask him to let you have an offprint; **он вы́играл у меня́ три па́ртии в ша́хматы** he won three games of chess from me. **5.: у меня́,** *etc.*, I, *etc.*, have; **у них великоле́пный дог** they have a magnificent Great Dane; **есть у вас радиоприёмник?** have you a wireless?; **у меня́ к вам ма́ленькая про́сьба** I have a small favour to ask of you.

у... *vbl. pref. indicating* **1.** *movement away from a place, as* **улете́ть** to fly away. **2.** *insertion in sth., as* **умести́ть** to put in. **3.** *covering of sth. all over, as* **усе́ять** to strew. **4.**

reduction, curtailment, etc., as **уба́вить** to reduce. **5.** *achievement of aim sought, as* **уговори́ть** to persuade; *with adj. roots forms vv. expr. comp. degree, as* **ускóрить** to accelerate.

Уайт: ó-в У., ~а У. *m.* the Isle of Wight.

уба́в|ить, лю, ишь *pf.* (*of* **~ля́ть**) **1.** (*+a. or g.*) to reduce, lessen, diminish; **у. ход** to reduce speed; **у. рука́в** to shorten a sleeve. **2.: у. в ве́се** to lose weight.

уба́в|иться, ится *pf.* (*of* **~ля́ться**) to diminish, decrease; **дни ~ились** the days are shorter; **воды́ ~илось** the water(-level) has fallen.

убавля́|ть(ся), ю(сь) *impf. of* **уба́вить(ся)**

убаю́к|ать, аю *pf.* (*of* **~ивать**) to lull (*also fig.*).

убаю́кива|ть, ю *impf. of* **убаю́кать**

убега́|ть, ю *impf. of* **убежа́ть**

убеди́тельност|ь, и *f.* persuasiveness, cogency.

убеди́тел|ьный (~ен, ~ьна) *adj.* **1.** convincing, persuasive, cogent; **быть ~ьным** to carry conviction. **2.** pressing; earnest; **~ьная про́сьба** pressing request, earnest entreaty.

убе|ди́ть, *1st pers. sg. not used,* **ди́шь** *pf.* (*of* **~жда́ть**) **1.** (**в**+*p.*) to convince (of). **2.** (*+inf.*) to persuade (to), prevail on (to).

убе|ди́ться, *1st pers. sg. not used,* **ди́шься** *pf.* (*of* **~жда́ться**) **1.** (**в**+*p.*) to make certain (of), satisfy o.s. (of). **2.** *pass. of* **~жда́ть**

убе|жа́ть, гу́, жи́шь, гу́т *pf.* (*of* **~га́ть**) **1.** to run away, run off, make off. **2.** to escape. **3.** (*coll.*) to boil over.

убежда́|ть(ся), ю(сь) *impf. of* **убеди́ть(ся)**

убежде́ни|е, я *nt.* **1.** persuasion, attempt to persuade; **путём ~я** by means of persuasion. **2.** conviction, belief.

убеждённо *adv.* with conviction.

убеждённост|ь, и *f.* conviction.

убеждён|ный *p.p.p. of* **убеди́ть** *and adj.* **1. (~, ~а́)** (**в**+*p.*) convinced (of), persuaded (of); **я в э́том соверше́нно ~** I am absolutely convinced of this. **2.** convinced, confirmed; staunch, stalwart; **у. пацифи́ст** convinced pacifist; **у. сторо́нник** staunch supporter.

убе́жищ|е, а *nt.* **1.** refuge, asylum; sanctuary; **иска́ть ~а** to seek refuge, asylum; **пра́во ~а** a right of asylum. **2.** (air-raid, *etc.*) shelter; (*mil.*) dug-out.

убел|ённый *p.p.p. of* **~и́ть; у. сединóй, седи́нами** hoary with age.

убел|и́ть, ю́, и́шь *pf.* to whiten.

уберега́|ть(ся), ю(сь) *impf. of* **убере́чь(ся)**

убере́|чь, гу́, жёшь, гу́т, *past* **~̈г, ~гла́** *pf.* (*of* **~га́ть**) (**от**) to protect (against), guard (against), keep safe (from), preserve (from); **у. шу́бу. от мо́ли** to protect a fur coat against moth.

убере́|чься, гу́сь, жёшься, гу́тся, *past* **~̈гся, ~гла́сь** *pf.* (*of* **~га́ться**) (**от**) to protect o.s. (against), guard (*intrans.*) (against).

убива́|ть, ю *impf. of* **уби́ть**

убива́|ться, юсь *impf.* **1.** (*impf. only*) (**о**+*p.*; *coll.*) to grieve (over). **2.** *impf. of* **уби́ться**

уби́йствен|ный (~, ~на) *adj.* **1.** (*obs.*) death-dealing; **~ная стрела́** deadly arrow. **2.** (*fig., coll.*) killing, murderous; **у. кли́мат** killing climate; **у. взгляд** murderous look.

уби́йств|о, а *nt.* murder; assassination.

уби́йц|а, ы *c.g.* murderer; assassin; killer.

убира́|ть(ся), ю(сь) *impf. of* **убра́ть(ся); ~йся!** clear off!, beat it!, hop it!

убира́|ющийся *pres. part. of* **~ться; ~ющееся шасси́** (*aeron.*) retractable undercarriage.

уби́т|ый (~, ~а) 1. *p.p.p. of* **~ь; неприя́тель потеря́л две ты́сячи ~ыми** the enemy lost two thousand killed; *as n.* **у., ~ого** *m.* dead man; **спать как у.** to sleep like a log; **молча́ть, как у.** to be silent as the grave; **ходи́ть, как у.** to be dazed (with grief, *etc.*). **2.: у. Бо́гом** (*coll.*) simple, dumb. **3.** *adj.* (*fig.*) crushed, broken.

уб|и́ть, ью́, ьёшь *pf.* (*of* **~ива́ть**) **1.** to kill; to murder; to assassinate; **хоть ~е́й** (*coll.*) for the life of me, to save my life; **у. бобра́,** *see* **бобр. 2.** (*fig.*) to kill, finish; to break, smash; **её отка́з ~и́л его́** her refusal finished him; **у. чьи-н. наде́жды** to smash s.o.'s hopes. **3.** (*coll.*) to expend; to waste; **у. вре́мя** to kill time; **у. мо́лодость** to waste one's youth. **4.** (*cards; coll.*) to cover.

уб|и́ться, ью́сь, ьёшься *pf.* (*of* **~ива́ться**) **1.** (*coll.*) to hurt o.s., bruise o.s. **2.** *pass. of* **~и́ть**

ублаготвор|и́ть, ю́, и́шь *pf.* (*of* **~я́ть**) (*obs. or coll., joc.*) to satisfy.

ублаготвор|я́ть, я́ю *impf. of* **~и́ть**

ублаж|а́ть, а́ю *impf. of* **~и́ть**

ублаж|и́ть, у́, и́шь *pf.* (*of* **~а́ть**) (*coll.*) to indulge; to gratify.

ублю́д|ок, ка *m.* mongrel (*also fig.*).

ублю́дочный *adj.* **1.** mongrel, cross-bred. **2.** (*fig., pej.*) compromise; half-hearted.

убо́г|ий (~, ~а) *adj.* **1.** poverty-stricken, beggarly (*also fig.*); wretched, squalid; **~ое воображе́ние** poverty-stricken imagination; **~ое жили́ще** wretched habitation; *as n.* **у., ~ого** *m.* pauper, beggar. **2.** (*obs.*) crippled; *as n.* **у., ~ого** *m.*, **~ая, ~ой** *f.* cripple.

убо́гост|ь, и *f.* poverty, penury (*also fig.*); wretchedness, squalor.

убо́жеств|о, а *nt.* **1.** (*obs.*) physical disability; infirmity. **2.** (*fig.*) poverty; lack of distinction; mediocrity; **у. иде́й** poverty of ideas.

убо́|й, я *m.* slaughter (*of livestock*); **корми́ть на у.** to fatten (*livestock*); (*fig.*) to feed up, stuff with food.

убо́йност|ь, и *f.* (*mil.*) effectiveness, destructive power (*of missile, weapon*).

убо́йн|ый *adj.* **1.: у. скот** livestock for slaughter. **2.** (*mil.*) killing, destructive, lethal; **~ая диста́нция** killing range; **~ая мо́щность** destructive power.

убо́р, а *m.* **1.** (*obs.*) dress, attire. **2.: головно́й у.** headgear, head-dress.

убо́рист|ый (~, ~а) *adj.* close, small (*of handwriting, etc.*)

убо́рк|а, и *f.* **1.** harvesting, reaping, gathering in; picking. **2.** (*mil.*) collection, removal (*of casualties from field of battle*). **3.** clearing up, tidying up.

убо́рн|ая, ой *f.* **1.** (*theatr.*) dressing-room. **2.** lavatory; public convenience.

убо́рочн|ый *adj.* harvest(ing); **~ая маши́на** harvester.

убо́рщик, а *m.* cleaner.

убо́рщиц|а, ы *f.* cleaner (*in offices, etc.*); char(woman), charlady.

убра́нств|о, а *nt.* furniture, appointments; (*poet.*) attire.

убра́|ть, уберу́, уберёшь, *past* **~л, ~ла́, ~ло** *pf.* (*of* **убира́ть**) **1.** to remove, take away; **у. с доро́ги** to put out of the way (*also fig.*); **у. со стола́** to clear the table. **2.** (*fig., coll.*) to kick out, chuck out; to sack; **у. кого́-н. из ко́мнаты** to chuck s.o. out of the room. **3.** to put away; to store; **у. я́корь** to stow the anchor. **4.** to harvest, reap, gather in. **5.** to clear up, tidy up; **у. ко́мнату** to do a room; **у. посте́ль** to make the bed. **6.** to decorate, adorn.

убра́|ться, уберу́сь, уберёшься, *past* **~лся, ~ла́сь, ~̈ло́сь** *pf.* (*of* **убира́ться**) **1.** (*coll.*) to clear up, tidy up, clean up. **2.** (*obs. or poet.*) to attire o.s. **3.** (*coll.*) to clear off, beat it.

убыва́|ть, ю *impf. of* **убы́ть**

у́был|ь, и *f.* **1.** diminution, decrease; subsidence (*of water*); **идти́ на у.** to decrease; to subside, fall, go down, recede. **2.** (*mil.*) losses, casualties.

убы́стр|ить, ю, ишь *pf.* (*of* **~я́ть**) to speed up; to hasten.

убыстр|я́ть, я́ю *impf. of* **~и́ть**

убы́т|ок, ка *m.* **1.** loss; **терпе́ть, нести́ ~ки** to incur losses; **в у., с ~ком** at a loss; **быть в ~ке** to lose, be down. **2.** (*pl.*) damages; **взыска́ть ~ки** to claim damages; **компенси́ровать ~ки** to pay damages; **определи́ть ~ки** to assess damages.

убы́точно *adv.* at a loss.

убы́точ|ный (~ен, ~на) *adj.* unprofitable; **~ная торго́вля** trading at a loss.

убы́ть, убу́ду, убу́дешь, *past* **у́был, убыла́, у́было** *pf.* (*of* **убыва́ть**) **1.** to decrease, diminish; (*of water*) to subside, fall, go down; (*of the moon*) to wane, be on the wane (*also fig.*). **2. тебя́,** *etc.*, **не убу́дет (от;** *coll.*) you, *etc.*, won't be any the worse (for); nothing will happen to you, *etc.* (as a result of). **3.** to go away, leave; **у. в командиро́вку** to go away on business; **у. в о́тпуск** to go

on leave; **у. по боле́зни** to go sick.
уважа́|емый *pres. part. pass. of* **~ть** *and adj.* respected; (*in opening formal letter*) dear.
уважа́|ть, ю *impf.* to respect, esteem.
уваже́ни|е, я *nt.* respect, esteem; **внуша́ть у.** to command respect; **пита́ть глубо́кое у. к кому́-н.** to have a profound respect for s.o.; **из ~я (к)** out of respect (for), in deference (to); **с уваже́нием** (*in letters*) yours sincerely.
уважи́тельност|ь, и *f.* **1.** validity. **2.** respectfulness.
уважи́тел|ьный (~ен, ~ьна) *adj.* **1.** valid; **~ьная причи́на** valid cause, good reason. **2.** respectful, deferential.
ува́ж|ить, у, ишь *pf.* **1.** to comply (with). **2.** (*coll.*) to humour.
ува́л, а *m.* steep slope.
у́вал|ень, ьня *m.* (*coll.*) bumpkin, clodhopper.
ува́лист|ый (~, ~а) *adj.* steeply-sloping.
ува́рива|ться, ется *impf. of* **увари́ться**
увар|и́ться, ~́ится *pf.* (*of* **~́иваться**) (*coll.*) **1.** to be thoroughly cooked. **2.** to boil away.
уведоми́тельн|ый *adj.*: **~ое письмо́** letter of advice, notice.
уве́дом|ить, лю, ишь *pf.* (*of* **~ля́ть**) to inform, notify.
уведомле́ни|е, я *nt.* information, notification.
уведомля́|ть, ю *impf. of* **уве́домить**
увез|ти́, у́, ёшь, *past* **~̈, ~ла́** *pf.* (*of* **увози́ть**) **1.** to take (away); to take with one. **2.** to abduct, kidnap.
увекове́чива|ть, ю *impf. of* **увекове́чить**
увекове́ч|ить, у, ишь *pf.* (*of* **~ивать**) **1.** to immortalize. **2.** to perpetuate.
увеличе́ни|е, я *nt.* **1.** increase; augmentation; extension. **2.** magnification (*by means of an optical instrument*); (*phot.*) enlargement.
увели́чива|ть(ся), ю(сь) *impf. of* **увели́чить(ся)**
увеличи́тельн|ый *adj.* **1.** magnifying; **~ое стекло́** magnifying glass; **у. аппара́т** (*phot.*) enlarger. **2.** (*gram.*) augmentative.
увели́ч|ить, у, ишь *pf.* (*of* **~ивать**) **1.** to increase; to augment; to extend; to enhance. **2.** to magnify; (*phot.*) to enlarge.
увели́ч|иться, ится *pf.* (*of* **~иваться**) to increase, grow, rise.
увенч|а́ть, а́ю *pf.* (*of* **венча́ть 1., 2.** *and* **~́ивать**) to crown.
увенч|а́ться, а́ется *pf.* (*of* **~́иваться**) (*+i.*; *fig., rhet.*) to be crowned (with); **у. успе́хом** to be crowned with success.
уве́нчива|ть(ся), ю(сь) *impf. of* **увенча́ть(ся)**
увере́ни|е, я *nt.* assurance; protestation.
уве́ренност|ь, и *f.* **1.** confidence; **у. в себе́** self-confidence. **2.** confidence, certitude, certainty; **мо́жно с ~ью сказа́ть** one can say with confidence, it is safe to say; **я был в по́лной ~и, что пойдёт дождь** I was quite certain that it would rain.
уве́рен|ный (~, ~на) *adj.* **1.** confident, sure; **~ная рука́** sure hand. **2.** *as pred.* **(~, ~а)** confident, sure, certain; **быть ~ным** to be sure, be certain; **бу́дь(те) ~(ы)!** you may be sure; you may rely on it.
уве́р|ить, ю, ишь *pf.* (*of* **~я́ть**) to assure; to convince, persuade.
уве́р|иться, юсь, ишься *pf.* (*of* **~я́ться**) to assure o.s., satisfy o.s.; to become convinced.
увер|ну́ться, ну́сь, нёшься *pf.* (*of* **~̈тываться**) **(от)** to dodge; to evade (*also fig.*); **у. от прямо́го отве́та** to avoid giving a direct answer.
уве́р|овать, ую *pf.* **(в**+*a.*) to come to believe (in).
увёртк|а, и *f.* dodge, evasion; subterfuge; (*pl.*) wiles.
увёртлив|ый (~, ~а) *adj.* evasive, shifty.
увёртыва|ться, юсь *impf. of* **уверну́ться**
увертю́р|а, ы *f.* (*mus.*) overture.
увер|я́ть(ся), я́ю(сь) *impf. of* **~́ить(ся)**
увеселе́ни|е, я *nt.* entertainment, amusement.
увесели́тельн|ый *adj.* pleasure, entertainment, amusement; **~ая пое́здка** pleasure-trip, jaunt.
увесел|и́ть, ю́, и́шь *pf.* (*of* **~я́ть**) to entertain, amuse.
увесел|я́ть, я́ю *impf. of* **~и́ть**
уве́сист|ый (~, ~а) *adj.* (*coll.*) weighty; **у. уда́р** heavy blow (*also fig.*).
уве|сти́, ду́, дёшь, *past* **~̈л, ~ла́** *pf.* (*of* **уводи́ть**) **1.** to take (away); to take with one. **2.** (*coll.*) to carry off, lift, walk off with (= *to steal*).
уве́т, а *m.* (*obs.*) = **увеща́ние**
уве́ч|ить, у, ишь *impf.* to maim, mutilate, cripple.
уве́чн|ый *adj.* maimed, mutilated, crippled; *as n.* **у., ~ого** *m.*, **~ая, ~ой** *f.* cripple.
уве́чь|е, я *nt.* maiming, mutilation.
уве́ш|ать, аю *pf.* (*of* **~ивать**) to cover (*with objects suspended*); **у. стену карти́нами** to cover a wall with pictures.
уве́шива|ть, ю *impf. of* **уве́шать**
увеща́ни|е, я *nt.* exhortation, admonition.
увеща́|ть, ю *impf.* (*obs.*) = **увещева́ть**
увещева́|ть, ю *impf.* to exhort, admonish.
увива́|ть, ю *impf. of* **уви́ть**
увива́|ться, юсь *impf.* **(за**+*i.*; *coll., pej.*) to hang round; to try to get round.
увида́|ть, ю *pf.* (*of* **вида́ть**) (*coll.*) to see.
увида́|ться, юсь *pf.* (*coll.*) to see one another.
уви́|деть, жу, дишь *pf.* **1.** *pf. of* **ви́деть. 2.** to catch sight of.
уви́|деться, жусь, дишься *pf. of* **ви́деться**
уви́лива|ть, ю *impf.* **(от) 1.** *impf. of* **увильну́ть. 2.** (*impf. only*) to try to get out (of).
увильн|у́ть, у́, ёшь *pf.* (*of* **уви́ливать**) **(от**; *coll.*) **1.** to dodge. **2.** (*fig.*) to evade, shirk; get out (of); **у. от отве́та** to get out of replying.
ув|и́ть, ью, ьёшь, *past* **~и́л, ~ила́, ~и́ло** *pf.* (*of* **~ива́ть**) to twine all over.
увлажни́тел|ь, я *m.*: **у. во́здуха** humidifier.
увлажн|и́ть, ю́, и́шь *pf.* (*of* **~я́ть**) to moisten, damp, wet.
увлажн|я́ть, я́ю *impf. of* **~и́ть**
увлажня́ющий *adj.*: **у. крем** moisturizer, moisturizing cream.
увлека́тел|ьный (~ен, ~ьна) *adj.* fascinating; absorbing.
увлека́|ть(ся), ю(сь) *impf. of* **увле́чь(ся)**
увлече́ни|е, я *nt.* **1.** animation. **2.** (*+i.*) passion (for); enthusiasm (for), keenness (on); crush (on). **3.** (object of) passion; **планери́зм — его́ у.** gliding is his passion; he is mad about gliding; **ста́рое у.** old flame.
увле́|чь, ку́, чёшь, ку́т, *past* **~̈к, ~кла́** *pf.* (*of* **~ка́ть**) **1.** to carry along. **2.** (*fig.*) to carry away, distract. **3.** to captivate, fascinate. **4.** to entice, allure.
увле́|чься, ку́сь, чёшься, ку́тся, *past* **~̈кся, ~кла́сь** *pf.* (*of* **~ка́ться**) (*+i.*) **1.** to be carried away (by); to become keen (on), become mad (about); **ора́тор ~̈кся** the speaker got carried away; **она́ ~кла́сь ездо́й верхо́м** she is mad about riding. **2.** to become enamoured (of), become keen (on), fall (for).
уво́д, а *m.* **1.** taking away; **у. войск** withdrawal of troops. **2.** (*coll.*) carrying off; lifting (= *stealing*); **жени́тьба ~ом** (*obs.*) elopement.
уво|ди́ть, жу́, ~́дишь *impf. of* **увести́**
уво́з, а *m.* (*coll.*) abduction; carrying off, lifting; **жени́тьба ~ом** (*obs.*) elopement.
уво|зи́ть, жу́, ~́зишь *pf. of* **увезти́**
уволаќива|ть, ю *impf. of* **уволо́чь**
уво́л|ить, ю, ишь *pf.* (*of* **~ьня́ть**) **1.** to discharge, dismiss; to sack, fire; **у. в отста́вку** to retire, pension off; **у. в запа́с** (*mil.*) to transfer to the reserve; **у. в о́тпуск** to give a holiday, grant leave (of absence). **2.** (*pf. only*) **(от**; *obs.*) to spare; **~ьте нас от подро́бного расска́за** spare us the details.
уво́л|иться, юсь, ишься *pf.* (*of* **~ьня́ться**) **1.** to retire; (*mil.*) to leave the service, get one's discharge; **у. в отста́вку** to retire, go into retirement. **2.** *pass. of* **~ить**
увол|о́чь, оку́, очёшь, оку́т, *past* **~о́к, ~окла́** *pf.* (*of* **~а́кивать**) (*coll.*) **1.** to drag away; **е́ле но́ги у.** to have a narrow escape. **2.** to carry off, make off with.
увольне́ни|е, я *nt.* discharge, dismissal; retiring, pensioning off; **у. в запа́с** (*mil.*) transfer to the reserve; **предупрежде́ние об ~и** notice (of dismissal).
увольни́тельн|ый *adj.* discharge, dismissal; **у. биле́т, ~ая запи́ска** (*mil.*) leave-pass.

увольня́|ть(ся), ю(сь) *impf. of* **уво́лить(ся)**
увор|ова́ть, у́ю *pf.* (*coll.*) to pinch, swipe.
уврач|ева́ть, у́ю *pf. of* **врачева́ть**
увуля́рный *adj.* (*ling.*) uvular.
увы́ *int.* alas!
увяда́|ть, ю *impf. of* **увя́нуть**
увя|за́ть[1], **жу́, ∽жешь** *pf.* (*of* **∽зывать**) **1.** to tie up; to pack up. **2.** to co-ordinate.
увяз|а́ть[2], **а́ю** *impf. of* **∽нуть**
увя|за́ться, жу́сь, ∽жешься *pf.* (*of* **∽зываться**) (*coll.*) **1.** to pack. **2.** (**за кем-н.**) to dog (s.o.'s footsteps).
увя́зк|а, и *f.* **1.** tying up, roping, strapping. **2.** co-ordination. **3.** (*pol.*) linkage.
увя́з|нуть, ну, нешь, *past* **∽, ∽ла** *pf.* (*of* **∽а́ть**[2]) (**в**+*p.*) to get stuck (in); to get bogged down (in) (*also fig.*).
увя́зыва|ть, ю *impf. of* **увяза́ть**[1]
увя́зыва|ться, юсь *impf. of* **увяза́ться**
увя́|нуть, ну, нешь *pf.* (*of* **∽да́ть**) to fade, wither, wilt, droop (*also fig.*).
угад|а́ть[1], **а́ю** *pf.* (*of* **∽ывать**) to guess (right), divine.
угад|а́ть[2], **а́ю** *pf.* (**в**+*a.*; *coll.*) to get (into), fall (into).
уга́дыва|ть, ю *impf. of* **угада́ть**[1]
Уга́нд|а, ы *f.* Uganda.
уга́нд|ец, ца *m.* Ugandan.
уга́нд|ка, ки *f. of* **∽ец**
уга́ндский *adj.* Ugandan.
уга́р[1], **а** *m.* **1.** carbon monoxide fumes, charcoal fumes. **2.** carbon monoxide poisoning; **у них у.** they are suffering from carbon monoxide poisoning. **3.** (*fig.*) ecstasy, intoxication; **в ∽е** (+*g.*) carried away (by); **в ∽е страсте́й** in the heat of passion.
уга́р[2], **а** *m.* (*tech., text.*) waste (*from metal smelting, etc., or from cotton spinning*).
уга́рно *as pred.*: **здесь у.** there is a smell of fumes here.
уга́рный[1] *adj.* full of (monoxide) fumes; (*tech.*): **у. газ** coal-gas, carbon monoxide.
уга́рный[2] *adj.* (*tech., text.*) waste.
угас|а́ть, а́ет *impf.* **1.** *impf. of* **∽нуть. 2.** (*impf. only*) to die down (*of a fire and fig.*); **си́лы у него́ ∽а́ли** his strength was failing.
уга́с|нуть, нет *pf.* (*of* **∽а́ть**) to go out.
углево́д, а *m.* (*chem.*) carbohydrate.
углеводоро́д, а *m.* (*chem.*) hydrocarbon.
углевыжига́тельн|ый *adj.*: **∽ая печь** charcoal kiln.
угледобы́ч|а, и *f.* coal extraction.
углежже́ни|е, я *nt.* charcoal burning.
углежо́г, а *m.* charcoal-burner.
углекислот|а́, ы́ *f.* (*chem.*) carbonic acid, carbon dioxide.
углеки́слый *adj.* (*chem.*) carbonate (of); **у. газ** carbonic acid gas; **у. аммо́ний** ammonium carbonate.
углеко́п, а *m.* (*obs.*) coal-miner, collier.
углепромы́шленност|ь, и *f.* coal-mining, coal industry.
углеро́д, а *m.* (*chem.*) carbon.
углеро́дист|ый *adj.* (*chem.*) carbonaceous; carbide (of); **∽ое желе́зо** iron carbide.
углова́т|ый (∽, ∽а) *adj.* **1.** angular. **2.** (*fig., coll.*) awkward.
углов|о́й *adj.* **1.** (*math., phys., tech.*) angle; angular; **∽а́я ско́рость** angular velocity; **∽а́я частота́** angular frequency. **2.** angle; corner; **у. дом** corner house, house on the corner; *as n.* **у., ∽о́го** *m.* (*sport*) corner; **пода́ть у.** to take a corner.
угломе́р, а *m.* **1.** (*tech.*) goniometer, azimuth instrument, protractor, clinometer. **2.** (*mil.*) deflection.
углуб|и́ть, лю́, и́шь *pf.* (*of* **∽ля́ть**) **1.** to deepen, make deeper. **2.** to drive in deeper, sink deeper. **3.** (*fig.*) to extend; **у. свой зна́ния** to extend one's knowledge.
углуб|и́ться, лю́сь, и́шься *pf.* (*of* **∽ля́ться**) **1.** to deepen, become deeper. **2.** (*fig.*) to become intensified. **3.** (**в**+*a.*) to go deep (into); to delve deeply (into) (*also fig.*); **у. в ко́рень веще́й** to go to the root of the matter. **4.** (**в**+*a.*; *fig.*) to become absorbed (in); **у. в кни́гу.** to become absorbed in a book; **у. в себя́** to become introspective.
углубле́ни|е, я *nt.* **1.** deepening. **2.** (*fig.*) extending; intensification; **для ∽я свои́х зна́ний** in order to extend one's knowledge. **3.** (*geog.*) hollow, depression, dip. **4.** (*naut.*) draught (*of a vessel*).
углубля́|ть(ся), ю(сь) *impf. of* **углуби́ть(ся)**
угль, у́гля *m.* (*arch. or poet.*) = **у́голь**
угля|де́ть, жу́, ди́шь *pf.* (*coll.*) **1.** to espy, spot. **2.** (**за**+*i.*) to look after; **не у.** (**за**+*i.*) to fail to take proper care (of).
угна́|ть, угоню́, уго́нишь, *past* **∽л, ∽ла́, ∽ло** *pf.* (*of* **угоня́ть**) **1.** to drive away. **2.** (*coll.*) to send off, dispatch. **3.** (*coll.*) to steal, lift.
угна́|ться, угоню́сь, уго́нишься, *past* **∽лся, ∽ла́сь, ∽ло́сь** *pf.* (**за**+*i.*) to keep pace (with); to keep up (with) (*also fig., coll.*).
угнезд|и́ться, и́шься *pf.* (*coll.*) to nestle, settle down (*in a confined space*).
угнета́тел|ь, я *m.* oppressor.
угнета́тельский *adj.* oppressive.
угнета́|ть, ю *impf.* **1.** to oppress. **2.** to depress, dispirit.
угнете́ни|е, я *nt.* **1.** oppression. **2.** depression; **быть в ∽и** to be depressed.
угнетённост|ь, и *f.* depression, low spirits.
угнетённ|ый *adj.* **1.** oppressed. **2.** depressed; **быть в ∽ом состоя́нии** to be depressed, be in low spirits.
угова́рива|ть, ю *impf.* **1.** *impf. of* **уговори́ть. 2.** (*impf. only*) to try to persuade, urge.
угова́рива|ться, юсь *impf. of* **уговори́ться**
угово́р, а *m.* **1.** persuasion. **2.** agreement, compact; **с ∽ом...** on condition ...; with the proviso ....
уговор|и́ть, ю́, и́шь *pf.* (*of* **угова́ривать**) (+*inf.*) to persuade (to), induce (to); to talk (into).
уговор|и́ться, ю́сь, и́шься *pf.* (*of* **угова́риваться**) (+*inf.*) to arrange (to), agree (to).
уго́д|а, ы *f.*: **в ∽у** (+*d.*) to please.
уго|ди́ть[1], **жу́, ди́шь** *pf.* (*of* **∽жда́ть**) (+*d. or* **на**+*a.*) to please, oblige.
уго|ди́ть[2], **жу́, ди́шь** *pf.* (*coll.*) **1.** (**в**+*a.*) to fall (into), get (into); to bang (against); **у. в западню́** to fall into a trap; **у. в тюрьму́** to land up in prison. **2.** (+*d.* **в**+*a.*) to hit (in, on), get (in, on); **у. кому́-н. в глаз ка́мнем** to hit s.o. in the eye with a stone.
уго́длив|ый (∽, ∽а) *adj.* obsequious.
уго́дник, а *m.* **1.** (*coll.*) pers. anxious to please. **2.**: **свято́й у.** saint.
уго́днича|ть, ю *impf.* (**пе́ред**; *coll.*) to cringe (to).
уго́дничеств|о, а *nt.* subservience, servility.
уго́дно 1. *as pred.* (+*d.*) **что вам у.?** what would you like?, what can I do for you?; **как вам у.** as you wish, as you please; please yourself; **ско́лько душе́ у.** to one's heart's content; **не у. ли вам?** (*i*) (*as polite invitation*) would you like?, (*ii*) (*iron.*; *expr. request*) would you be good enough, would you mind; **не у. ли** (*iron.*) if you please. **2.** *forms indef. prons. and advs.*: **кто у.** anyone (you like), whoever you like; **что у.** anything (you like); whatever you like; **ско́лько у.** as much as you like; any amount.
уго́д|ный (∽ен, ∽на) *adj.* pleasing, welcome.
уго́д|ье, ья, *g. pl.* **∽ий** *nt.* **1.** object or area of economic significance; **лесны́е ∽ья** forests; **полевы́е ∽ья** arable land; **ры́бные ∽ья** fishing-ground. **2.** (*obs.*) advantage, favourable side, good point.
угожда́|ть, ю *impf. of* **угоди́ть**[1]
у́г|ол, ла́, об ∽ле́, в ∽лу́ *m.* **1.** (**в ∽ле́**) (*math., phys.*) angle; **у. встре́чи** angle of impact; angle of incidence; **у. засе́чки** angle of intersection; **у. зре́ния** visual angle; (*fig.*) point of view; **у. пока́тости** angle of slope, gradient; **под ∽ло́м** (**в**+*a.*) at an angle (of); **под прямы́м ∽ло́м** at right angles. **2.** corner; **в ∽лу́** in the corner; **на ∽лу́** at the corner; **за ∽ло́м** round the corner; **поста́вить в у.** to put in the corner, make stand in the corner; **из-за ∽ла́** (from) round the corner; (*fig.*) on the sly, behind s.o.'s back; **загна́ть в у.** drive into a corner; **сре́зать у.** to cut off a corner. **3.** part of a room. **4.** place; **име́ть свой у.** to have a place of one's own; **глухо́й у., медве́жий у.** remote part, godforsaken spot.
угол|ёк, ька́ *m.* small piece of coal.
уголо́вник, а *m.* (*coll.*) criminal.
уголо́вн|ый *adj.* criminal; **∽ое де́ло** criminal case; **у. ко́декс** criminal code; **∽ое пра́во** criminal law; **у. престу́пник** criminal; **у. ро́зыск** Criminal Investigation Department.

угол|о́к, ка́ *m. dim. of* **у́гол**; corner; **у. приро́ды** nature study corner; **живо́й у.** pets' corner; **кра́сный у.** recreation and reading room.

у́голь, угля́ *m.* **1.** (*pl.* **у́гли, угле́й**) coal; **ка́менный у.** coal; **бу́рый у.** lignite; **древе́сный у.** charcoal. **2.** (*pl.* **у́гли, у́глей** *and* **~я, ~ев**) a coal; piece of coal; **сиде́ть как на ~ях** to be on thorns. **3.** (*art*) charcoal.

уго́льник, а *m.* **1.** set square. **2.** (*tech.*) corner iron; **стыково́й у.** angle bracket.

у́гольн|ый *adj.* **1.** coal; **у. бассе́йн** coal-field; **у. райо́н** coal-mining area. **2.** carbon; **~ая дугова́я ла́мпа** carbon arc lamp. **3.** (*chem.*) carbonic; **~ая кислота́** carbonic acid.

уго́льный *adj.* (*coll.*) corner.

у́гольщик[1], **а** *m.* **1.** coal-miner, collier. **2.** charcoal-burner.

у́гольщик[2], **а** *m.* collier (*ship*).

угомо́н, а (у) *m.* (*coll.*) peace (and quiet); **на них ~у нет** they give one no peace; **не знать ~у** to have no peace.

угомон|и́ть, ю́, и́шь *pf.* (*coll.*) to calm.

угомон|и́ться, ю́сь, и́шься *pf.* (*coll.*) to calm down.

уго́н, а *m.* **1.** driving away. **2.** (*coll.*) lifting, stealing; hijacking; **у. маши́ны** car theft. **3.** (*rail.*) creep (*of lines*).

уго́нщик, а *m.* thief; hijacker; **у. маши́ны** car thief; **у.-лиха́ч** joyrider; **у. самолёта** skyjacker.

угоня́|ть, ю *impf. of* **угна́ть**

угора́зд|ить, ит *pf.* (*+inf.*, *usu. impers.*; *coll.*) to urge, make; **как э́то его́ ~ило жени́ться на ней?** what on earth made him marry her?

угор|а́ть, а́ю *impf. of* **~е́ть**

угоре́лый *adj.* **1.** (*obs.*) poisoned by charcoal fumes. **2.: как у.** like a madman, like one possessed.

угор|е́ть[1], **ю́, и́шь** *pf.* (*of* **~а́ть**) **1.** to be poisoned by charcoal fumes, get carbon monoxide poisoning. **2.** (*coll.*) to be mad, be crazy; **что ты, ~е́л?** are you out of your mind?

угор|е́ть[2], **ю́, и́шь** *pf.* (*of* **~а́ть**) to burn away, burn down.

уго́рский *adj.* (*ethnol.*, *ling.*) Ugrian.

у́г|орь[1], **ря́** *m.* eel; **живо́й как у.** as lively as a cricket.

у́г|орь[2], **ря́** *m.* blackhead.

уго|сти́ть, щу́, сти́шь *pf.* (*of* **~ща́ть**) (*+i.*) to entertain (to), treat (to); **у. кого́-н. обе́дом** to have s.o. to dinner.

угото́ван|ный *p.p.p. as pred. adj.* (*obs.*) prepared, in store; **им ~о све́тлое бу́дущее** a splendid future is in store for them.

угото́в|ить, лю, ишь *pf.* (*obs.*) to prepare.

угоща́|ть, ю *impf. of* **угости́ть**

угоще́ни|е, я *nt.* **1.** (*+i.*) entertaining (to, with), treating (to). **2.** refreshments; fare.

угр, а *m.* (*ethnol.*) Ugrian (*member of ethnic group comprising Hungarians*, *Ostyaks and Voguls*).

угрева́т|ый (~, ~а) *adj.* covered with blackheads; pimply.

угро́б|ить, лю, ишь *pf.* (*sl.*) **1.** to do in. **2.** (*fig.*) to ruin, wreck; **у. чью-н. репута́цию** to ruin s.o.'s reputation.

угрожа́|ть, ю *impf.* to threaten.

угрожа́|ющий *pres. part. act. of* **~ть** *and adj.* threatening, menacing; **~ющая катастро́фа** impending disaster.

угро́з|а, ы *f.* threat, menace; **под ~ой** (*+g.*) under threat (of); **поста́вить под ~у** to threaten, endanger, imperil, jeopardize.

угро́зыск, а *m.* (*abbr. of* **уголо́вный ро́зыск**) Criminal Investigation Department (*abbr.* CID).

у́гро-фи́нский *adj.* Finno-Ugrian.

угрызе́ни|е, я *nt.* pangs; **~я со́вести** remorse; **чу́вствовать ~я со́вести** to feel pangs of conscience.

угрю́м|ый (~, ~а) *adj.* sullen, morose, gloomy.

уда́в, а *m.* (*zool.*) boa, boa constrictor.

уда|ва́ться, ётся *impf. of* **~́ться**

удав|и́ть, лю́, ~́ишь *pf.* to strangle.

удав|и́ться, лю́сь, ~́ишься *pf.* (*of* **дави́ться 2.**) to hang o.s.

уда́вк|а, и *f.* running knot, half hitch, timber hitch.

удавле́ни|е, я *nt.* strangling, strangulation.

уда́вленник, а *m.* (*coll.*) pers. who has hanged himself; victim of strangling.

удале́ни|е, я *nt.* **1.** removal; **у. аппе́ндикса** appendectomy; **у. зу́ба** extraction of a tooth. **2.** sending away; **у. с по́ля** (*sport*) sending off the field. **3.** moving off.

удалённост|ь, и *f.* remoteness, distance.

удал|ённый *p.p.p. of* **~и́ть** *and adj.* remote.

удал|е́ц, ьца́ *m.* daring pers.

удал|и́ть, ю́, и́шь *pf.* (*of* **~я́ть**) **1.** to remove; **у. зуб** to extract a tooth. **2.** to remove, send away; **у. с рабо́ты** to dismiss, sack; **у. с по́ля** (*sport*) to send off (the field). **3.** to move away.

удал|и́ться, ю́сь, и́шься *pf.* (*of* **~я́ться**) **1.** to move off, move away; **поспе́шно у.** beat a hasty retreat. **2.** to leave, withdraw, retire; **у. на поко́й** to retire to a quiet life; **у. от о́бщества** to withdraw from society.

удал|о́й (уда́л, ~а́, уда́ло) *adj.* daring, bold.

у́дал|ь, и *f.* daring, boldness.

удальств|о́, а́ *nt.* (*coll.*) = **у́даль**

удал|я́ть(ся), я́ю(сь) *impf. of* **~и́ть(ся)**

уда́р, а *m.* **1.** (*in var. senses*) blow; stroke; **одни́м ~ом** at one stroke; **нанести́ у.** to strike a blow; **у. в спи́ну** (*fig.*) stab in the back; **у. гро́ма** thunder-clap; **у. гро́ма средь я́сного не́ба** bolt from the blue. **2.** stroke (*sound*); **~ы пу́льса** stroke of the pulse. **3.** (*mil.*) blow; attack; thrust; **у. в штыки́** bayonet charge; **у. с во́здуха** air strike; **под ~ом** exposed (to attack). **4.: быть в ~е** (*coll.*) to be in good form; **не быть в ~е** to be off one's stroke. **5.** (*med.*) stroke, seizure; **со́лнечный у.** sun-stroke.

ударе́ни|е, я *nt.* **1.** (*ling.*) stress, accent; (*fig.*) stress, emphasis; **поста́вить у.** to stress, accent; **сде́лать у. (на**+*p.* *or* **на**+*a.*) to stress, emphasize. **2.** stress(-mark).

уда́р|енный *p.p.p. of* **~ить** *and adj.* (*ling.*) stressed, accented.

уда́р|ить, ю, ишь *pf.* (*of* **~я́ть** *and*, *in some senses*, *of* **бить**) **1.** (*+a.* **по**+*d.* *or* **в**+*a.*) to strike; to hit; **у. кого́-н. по лицу́** to slap s.o.'s face; **у. кулако́м по́ столу** to bang on the table with one's fist; **мо́лния ~ила в де́рево** the tree was struck by lightning. **2.** (**в**+*a.* *or* +*a.*) to strike; to sound; to beat; **у. в бараба́н** to beat a drum; **у. в наба́т, у. трево́гу** to sound the alarm; **часы́ ~или по́лночь** the clock struck midnight; **у. в смычки́** (*mus.*) to strike up. **3.: у. в го́лову** (*of blood*) to rush to one's head; (*of wine*, *etc.*) to go to one's head. **4.** (**на**+*a.* *or* **по**+*d.*) (*mil.*) to strike (against), attack. **5.** (**по**+*d.*) to strike (at), hit (at); to combat; **у. по кумовству́** to combat nepotism; **у. по карма́ну** (*coll.*) to hit one's pocket, set one back. **6.** (*of weather conditions*, *etc.*; *coll.*) to strike; to set in; **ну и моро́зец ~ил** the frosts have really set in. **7.: у. по рука́м** to strike a bargain. **8.: па́лец о па́лец не у.** (*coll.*) not to raise, lift a finger.

уда́р|иться, юсь, ишься *pf.* (*of* **~я́ться**) **1.** (**о**+*a.* *or* **в**+*a.*) to strike (against), hit; **у. о подво́дный ка́мень** to strike a reef. **2.** (**в**+*a.* *or* +*inf.*) to break (into); **у. в бе́гство, у. бежа́ть** to break into a run; **у. в слёзы** to burst into tears. **3.** (**в**+*a.*) to become addicted (to), become keen (on). **4.: у. в кра́йность** to run to an extreme; **у. из одно́й кра́йности в другу́ю** to run from one extreme to another.

уда́рник[1], **а** *m.* **1.** shock-worker, udarnik. **2.** (*mil.*) member of striking force.

уда́рник[2], **а** *m.* (*in fire-arm*) striker, firing pin; (*in detonator*) plunger.

уда́рник[3], **а** *m.* (*mus.*) percussionist.

уда́рниц|а, ы *f. of* **уда́рник**[1]

уда́рн|ый *adj.* **1.** (*tech. and mil.*) percussive; percussion; **~ая возду́шная волна́** blast wave; **у. ка́псюль** percussion cap; **~ая ми́на** (*naut.*) contact mine; **~ая сва́рка** percussive welding; **~ая си́ла** striking power, force of impact; **~ая тру́бка** percussion tube, percussion primer. **2.** (*mus.*) percussion. **3.** (*mil.*) striking, shock; **~ая гру́ппа** striking force, main attack force; **~ые ча́сти** shock troops. **4.** shock(-working); **~ая рабо́та** shock work; **~ые те́мпы** accelerated tempo (*of work*). **5.** urgent; **~ое зада́ние** urgent task, rush job; **в ~ом поря́дке** with great dispatch.

удар|я́ть(ся), я́ю(сь) *impf. of* **~́ить(ся)**

уда́|ться, стся, ду́тся, *past* **~лся, ~ла́сь** *pf.* (*of* **~ва́ться**) **1.** to succeed, be a success, be successful, work (well); **опера́ция ~ла́сь** the operation was a success. **2.** (*impers.*+*d. and inf.*) to succeed, manage; **мне не ~ло́сь**

прису́тствовать на их сва́дьбе I did not manage to attend their wedding.

уда́ч|а, и *f.* success; good luck, good fortune; **жела́ть ~и** to wish good luck; **им всегда́ у.** they are always lucky.

уда́чливост|ь, и *f.* success, luck.

уда́члив|ый (~, ~а) *adj.* successful, lucky.

уда́чник, а *m.* (*coll.*) lucky pers.

уда́ч|ный (~ен, ~на) *adj.* **1.** successful. **2.** felicitous, apt, good; **у. перево́д** felicitous translation; **у. оборо́т** apt turn of phrase; **у. вы́бор** happy choice.

удва́ива|ть, ю *impf. of* **удво́ить**

удвое́ни|е, я *nt.* doubling, redoubling; (*ling.*) reduplication.

удво́|енный *p.p.p. of* **~ить** *and adj.* doubled, redoubled; (*ling.*) reduplicated; (*of letter of the alphabet*) double.

удво́|ить, ю, ишь *pf.* (*of* **удва́ивать**) to double, redouble; (*ling.*) to reduplicate; **у. свои́ уси́лия** to redouble one's efforts.

уде́л, а *m.* **1.** lot, destiny; **доста́ться в у. кому́-н.** to fall to one's lot. **2.** (*hist.*) appanage principality (*in Kievan Russia*). **3.** (*hist.*) crown domain, crown landed property.

удел|и́ть, ю́, и́шь *pf.* (*of* **~я́ть**) to give, spare, devote; **у. часть из полу́чки на что-н.** to give up part of one's wage-packet for sth.; **у. вре́мя чему́-н.** to spare the time for sth.; **нам на́до у. внима́ние э́тому вопро́су** we must give the matter thought.

уде́льн|ый[1] *adj.* (*phys.*) specific; **у. вес** specific gravity; (*fig.*) proportion, share; **~ая мо́щность** horse power per pound of weight.

уде́льн|ый[2] *adj.* (*hist.*) **1.** appanage; **у. князь** appanage prince (*in Kievan Russia*); **у. пери́од** period of appanage principalities. **2.** crown; **~ые зе́мли** crown lands, crown domains.

удел|я́ть, я́ю *impf. of* **~и́ть**

у́держ, у *m.*: **без ~у** (*coll.*) uncontrollably, unrestrainedly, without restraint; **пла́кать без ~у** to weep uncontrollably; **~у нет ему́, на него́** (*coll.*) there's no holding him; **~у не знать** (*coll.*) to be immoderate, know no bounds.

удержа́ни|е, я *nt.* **1.** keeping, holding, retention. **2.** deduction; **у. из зарпла́ты** money stopped from wages.

удерж|а́ть, у́, ~́ишь *pf.* (*of* **~́ивать**) **1.** to hold, hold on to, not let go. **2.** to keep, retain; **у. своё ме́сто в чемпиона́те** to retain one's place in a championship competition; **у. в па́мяти** to retain in one's memory. **3.** to hold back, keep back, restrain; **у. лошаде́й** to hold horses back; **у. кого́-н. от опроме́тчивого посту́пка** to restrain s.o. from a headstrong action. **4.** to keep down, suppress; **у. слёзы** to stifle one's tears. **5.** to deduct, keep back; **у. из зарпла́ты** to stop from wages.

удерж|а́ться, у́сь, ~́ишься *pf.* (*of* **~́иваться**) **1.** to hold one's ground, hold on, hold out; to stand firm; **у. на нога́х** to remain on one's feet. **2.** **(от)** to keep (from), refrain (from); **у. от собла́зна** to resist a temptation; **мы не могли́ у. от сме́ха** we couldn't help laughing.

уде́ржива|ть(ся), ю(сь) *impf. of* **удержа́ть(ся)**

удесятер|и́ть, ю́, и́шь *pf.* (*of* **~я́ть**) to increase tenfold.

удесятер|и́ться, и́тся *pf.* (*of* **~я́ться**) to increase (*intrans.*) tenfold.

удесятер|я́ть(ся), я́ю, я́ет(ся) *impf. of* **~и́ть(ся)**

удешев|и́ть, лю́, и́шь *pf.* (*of* **~ля́ть**) to reduce the price (of).

удешев|и́ться, и́тся *pf.* (*of* **~ля́ться**) to become cheaper.

удешевле́ни|е, я *nt.* reduction of prices.

удешевля́|ть(ся), ю, ет(ся) *impf. of* **удешеви́ть(ся)**

удиви́тельно *adv.* **1.** astonishingly, surprisingly. **2.** wonderfully, marvellously. **3.** very, extremely.

удиви́тел|ьный (~ен, ~ьна) *adj.* **1.** astonishing, surprising, amazing; **~ьно** (*as pred.*) it is astonishing, it is surprising, it is amazing; it is funny; **не ~ьно, что** no wonder that. **2.** wonderful, marvellous.

удив|и́ть, лю́, и́шь *pf.* (*of* **~ля́ть**) to astonish, surprise, amaze.

удив|и́ться, лю́сь, и́шься *pf.* (*of* **~ля́ться**) (*+d.*) to be astonished (at), be surprised (at), be amazed (at); to marvel (at).

удивле́ни|е, я *nt.* astonishment, surprise, amazement; **к моему́ вели́кому ~ю** to my great surprise; **на у.** (*as pred.*; *coll.*) excellent(ly), splendid(ly), marvellous(ly); **приём вы́шел на у.** the reception went off splendidly.

удивля́|ть(ся), ю(сь) *impf. of* **удиви́ть(ся)**

удил|а́, уди́л, ~а́м *no sg.* bit; **закуси́ть у.** to take the bit between one's teeth (*also fig.*).

уди́лищ|е, а *nt.* fishing-rod.

уди́льн|ый *adj.*: **~ые принадле́жности** fishing tackle.

уди́льщик, а *m.* angler.

уди́льщиц|а, ы *f. of* **уди́льщик**

удира́|ть, ю *impf. of* **удра́ть**

уди́ть, ужу́, у́дишь *impf.*: **у. ры́бу** to fish, angle.

уди́ться, у́дится *impf.* (*of fish*) to bite.

удлине́ни|е, я *nt.* lengthening; **у. сро́ка** extension (of time).

удлин|и́ть, ю́, и́шь *pf.* (*of* **~я́ть**) to lengthen; to extend, prolong.

удлин|и́ться, и́тся *pf.* (*of* **~я́ться**) to become longer; to be extended, be prolonged.

удлин|я́ть(ся), я́ю(сь) *impf. of* **~и́ть(ся)**

удму́рт, а *m.* Urdmurt.

удму́рт|ка, ки *f. of* **~**

удму́ртский *adj.* Urdmurt.

удо́бно[1] *adv.* **1.** comfortably. **2.** conveniently.

удо́бно[2] *as pred.* **1.** (*+d.*) to feel, be comfortable; to be at one's ease; **нам здесь вполне́ у.** we are very comfortable here. **2.** (*+d.*) it is convenient (for), it suits; **у. ли вам сра́зу же прие́хать?** is it convenient for you to come at once? **3.** it is proper, it is in order; **у. ли зада́ть тако́й вопро́с?** is it proper to ask such a question?

удо́б|ный (~ен, ~на) *adj.* **1.** comfortable; cosy. **2.** convenient, suitable, opportune; **по́льзоваться ~ным слу́чаем** to take an opportunity. **3.** proper, in order.

удобовари́м|ый (~, ~а) *adj.* digestible.

удобоисполни́м|ый (~, ~а) *adj.* easy to carry out; **~ая про́сьба** a simple request.

удобообтека́емый *adj.* streamlined.

удобопоня́т|ный (~ен, ~на) *adj.* comprehensible, intelligible.

удобопроизноси́м|ый (~, ~а) *adj.* easy to pronounce.

удобочита́ем|ый (~, ~а) *adj.* easy to read; legible.

удобре́ни|е, я *nt.* (*agric.*) **1.** fertilization. **2.** fertilizer.

удо́бр|ить, ю, ишь *pf.* (*of* **~я́ть**) to fertilize, manure.

удобр|я́ть, я́ю *impf. of* **~́ить**

удо́бств|о, а *nt.* **1.** comfort. **2.** convenience; **кварти́ра со все́ми ~ами** flat with all conveniences.

удовлетворе́ни|е, я *nt.* satisfaction, gratification; **тре́бовать ~я у кого́-н.** to demand satisfaction from s.o.; **отмеча́ть с ~ем** to note with satisfaction.

удовлетворённост|ь, и *f.* satisfaction, contentment.

удовлетвор|ённый *p.p.p. of* **~и́ть** *and adj.* satisfied, contented.

удовлетвори́тельно **1.** *adv.* satisfactorily. **2.** *n.*; *nt. indecl.* 'satisfactory', 'fair' (*as school mark*).

удовлетвори́тельный (~ен, ~ьна) *adj.* satisfactory.

удовлетвор|и́ть, ю́, и́шь *pf.* (*of* **~я́ть**) **1.** to satisfy; to give satisfaction (to); to comply (with); **у. запро́сы** to satisfy requirements; **у. про́сьбу** to comply with a request. **2.** (*+d.*) to answer, meet; **у. тре́бованиям** to answer requirements. **3.** (*+i.*) to supply (with), furnish (with); **у. провиа́нтом** to victual.

удовлетвор|и́ться, ю́сь, и́шься *pf.* (*of* **~я́ться**) **1.** (*+i.*) to content o.s. (with), be satisfied (with). **2.** *pass. of* **~и́ть**

удовлетвор|я́ть(ся), я́ю(сь) *impf. of* **~и́ть(ся)**

удово́льстви|е, я *nt.* **1.** (*sg. only*) pleasure; **доста́вить у.** (*+d.*) to give pleasure. **2.** amusement; **мно́го ~й** a lot of fun.

удово́льств|оваться, уюсь *pf. of* **дово́льствоваться**

удо́д, а *m.* (*zool.*) hoopoe.

удо́|й, я *m.* **1.** yield of milk. **2.** milking.

удо́йлив|ый (~, ~а) *adj.* yielding much milk; **~ая коро́ва** good milker.

удо́йност|ь, и *f.* yield of milk; milking capacity.

удо́й|ный *adj.* **1.** *adj. of* **~**. **2.** = **~ливый**

удорожа́ни|е, я *nt.* rise in price(s).

удорож|а́ть, а́ю *impf. of* **~и́ть**

удорож|и́ть, у́, и́шь *pf.* (*of* **~а́ть**) to raise the price (of).
удоста́ива|ть(ся), ю(сь) *impf. of* **удостои́ть(ся)**
удостовере́ни|е, я *nt.* **1.** certification, attestation; **в у.** (+*g.*) in witness (of). **2.** certificate; **у. ли́чности** identity card, ID; **у. пра́ва вожде́ния автомоби́ля** driving licence; **у. о сме́рти** death certificate.
удостове́р|ить, ю, ишь *pf.* (*of* **~я́ть**) to certify, attest, witness; **у. по́дпись** to witness a signature; **у. ли́чность кого́-н.** to identify s.o.
удостове́р|иться, юсь, ишься *pf.* (*of* **~я́ться**) (**в**+*p.*) to make sure (of), to assure o.s. (of); **у. в по́длинности докуме́нта** to assure o.s. of the genuineness of a document.
удостовер|я́ть(ся), я́ю(сь) *impf. of* **~́ить(ся)**
удосто́|ить, ю, ишь *pf.* (*of* **удоста́ивать**) **1.** (+*a. and g.*) to award (to), confer (on); **у. кого́-н. Но́белевской пре́мии** to award s.o. a Nobel prize. **2.** (+*i.*; *usu. iron.*) to favour (with), vouchsafe; **у. улы́бкой** to favour with a smile.
удосто́|иться, юсь, ишься *pf.* (*of* **удоста́иваться**) (+*g.*) **1.** to receive, be awarded (*an honour, a prize, etc.*). **2.** (*usu. iron.*) to be favoured (with), be vouchsafed.
удосу́жива|ться, юсь *impf. of* **удосу́житься**
удосу́ж|иться, усь, ишься *pf.* (*of* **~иваться**) (+*inf.*; *coll.*) to find time (to), to manage.
удочер|и́ть, ю́, и́шь *pf.* (*of* **~я́ть**) to adopt (*as a daughter*).
удочер|я́ть, я́ю *impf. of* **~и́ть**
у́дочк|а, и *f.* (fishing-)rod (*also in fig., coll. phrr.*); **заки́нуть ~у** to cast a line; to put a line out (= *to try to discover sth.*); **пойма́ть, подде́ть на ~у** to catch out; **попа́сться на ~у** to swallow the bait.
удра́|ть, удеру́, удерёшь, *past* **~л, ~ла́, ~ло** *pf.* (*of* **удира́ть**) (*coll.*) to make off; to do a bunk, flit.
удруж|и́ть, у́, и́шь *pf.* (+*d.*; *coll.*) to do a good turn (*also iron.* = *to do a bad turn*).
удруч|а́ть, а́ю *impf. of* **~и́ть**
удручённост|ь, и *f.* depression, despondency.
удруч|и́ть, у́, и́шь *pf.* (*of* **~а́ть**) to depress, dispirit.
уду́м|ать, аю *pf.* (*of* **~ывать**) (*coll.*) to think up.
уду́мыва|ть, ю *impf. of* **уду́мать**
удуш|а́ть, а́ю *impf. of* **~и́ть**
удуше́ни|е, я *nt.* smothering, suffocation; asphyxiation.
удуш|и́ть, у́, ~́ишь *pf.* (*of* **~а́ть**) to smother, stifle, suffocate; to asphyxiate.
уду́шлив|ый (~, ~а) *adj.* stifling, suffocating; asphyxiating; **~ая жара́** stifling heat; **у. газ** asphyxiating gas.
уду́шь|е, я *nt.* asthma; asphyxia.
уедине́ни|е, я *nt.* solitude; seclusion.
уединённост|ь, и *f.* solitariness, seclusion.
уединён|ный (~, ~на) *p.p.p. of* **уедини́ть** *and adj.* solitary, secluded; lonely.
уедин|и́ть, ю́, и́шь *pf.* (*of* **~я́ть**) to seclude, set apart.
уедин|и́ться, ю́сь, и́шься *pf.* (*of* **~я́ться**) (**от**) to retire (from), withdraw (from); to go off (by o.s.); **у. в свою́ ко́мнату** to retire to one's room.
уедин|я́ть(ся), я́ю(сь) *impf. of* **~и́ть(ся)**
уе́зд, а *m.* (*hist.*) uyezd (*administrative unit*).
уе́зд|ный *adj. of* **~**; **у. го́род** chief town of uyezd.
уе́ть, уебу́, уебёшь, *past* **уёб, уебли́** *pf.* (*of* **еть** *and* **еба́ть**) (*vulg.*) to fuck.
уе́хать, уе́ду, уе́дешь, *imper.* **уезжа́й(те)** *pf.* (*of* **уезжа́ть**) to go away, leave, depart.
уж[1], **а́** *m.* grass-snake.
уж[2] **1.** *adv.* = **уже́. 2.** *emph. particle* (*coll.*) to be sure, indeed, certainly; **уж он узна́ет** he is sure to find out; **уж мы иска́ли, иска́ли** we searched all over the place. **3.** *particle emph. certain prons. and advs.* very; **э́то не так уж сло́жно** it's not so very complicated; it's not all that complicated.
ужа́л|ить, ю, ишь *pf. of* **жа́лить**
ужа́рива|ться, ется *impf. of* **ужа́риться**
ужа́р|иться, ится, *pf.* (*of* **~иваться**) (*coll.*) **1.** to be thoroughly roasted, fried. **2.** to roast away, be roasted up, shrink.
у́жас, а *m.* **1.** horror, terror; **внуши́ть у.** (+*d.*) to inspire with horror, horrify; **навести́ у.** (**на**+*a.*) to instil terror (into); **объя́тый ~ом** horror-struck, terror-stricken; **к моему́ ~у** to my horror. **2.** (*usu. pl.*) horror; **~ы оса́ды** the horrors of a siege. **3.** *as pred.* (*coll.*) it is awful, it is terrible. **4.: у. (как)** *as adv.* (*coll.*) awfully, terribly; **у. как гро́мко** awfully loud.
ужас|а́ть(ся), а́ю(сь) *impf. of* **~ну́ть(ся)**
ужа́сно[1] *adv.* **1.** horribly, terribly; **у. себя́ чу́вствовать** to feel awful. **2.** (*coll.*) awfully, terribly, frightfully; **он у. пло́хо игра́ет** he plays terribly badly.
ужа́сно[2] *as pred.* (*coll.*) it is awful, it is terrible, it is ghastly.
ужас|ну́ть, ну́, нёшь *pf.* (*of* **~а́ть**) to horrify, terrify.
ужас|ну́ться, ну́сь, нёшься *pf.* (*of* **~а́ться**) to be horrified, be terrified.
ужа́с|ный (~ен, ~на) *adj.* (*in var. senses*) awful, terrible, ghastly, frightful; **у. вид** awful sight; **у. на́сморк** awful cold.
у́же *comp. of* **у́зкий** *and* **у́зко**
уже́ 1. *adv.* already; now; by now; **у. не** no longer; **они́ у. при́были** they are here already; **он, должно́-быть, у. уе́хал** he must have gone by now; **она́ у. не ребёнок** she is no longer a child. **2.** *emph. particle* = **уж; э́то у. друго́е де́ло** that's quite a different matter.
уже́ли, уже́ль *adv.* (*obs.*) = **неуже́ли**
уже́ни|е, я *nt.* fishing, angling.
ужива́|ться, юсь *impf. of* **ужи́ться**
ужи́вчив|ый (~, ~а) *adj.* easy to get on with.
ужи́мк|а, и *f.* grimace.
у́жин, а *m.* supper.
у́жина|ть, ю *impf.* (*of* **по~**) to have supper.
ужи́|ться, ву́сь, вёшься, *past* **~лся, ~ла́сь** *pf.* (*of* **~ва́ться**) (**с**+*i.*) to get on (with); **мы с ней так и не ~ли́сь** she and I simply couldn't get on.
ужо́ *adv.* (*coll.*) **1.** later, by and by. **2.** *as threat*: **у. тебе́!** just you wait!; **я тебя́ у. проучу́!** just you wait — I'll show you!
ужо́вый *adj. of* **уж**[1]
узаконе́ни|е, я *nt.* **1.** legalization, legitimization. **2.** statute.
узако́нива|ть, ю *impf. of* **узако́нить**
узако́н|ить, ю, ишь *pf.* (*of* **~ивать** *and* **~я́ть**) to legalize, legitimize.
узакон|я́ть, я́ю *impf.* = **~́ивать**
узбе́к, а *m.* Uzbek.
Узбекиста́н, а *m.* Uzbekistan.
узбе́кский *adj.* Uzbek.
узбе́|чка, чки *f. of* **~к**
узд|а́, ы, *pl.* **~́ы** *f.* bridle (*also fig.*); **держа́ть в ~** to keep in check, restrain.
узде́чк|а, и *f.* **1.** bridle. **2.** (*anat.*) fraenum.
уздцы́: под у. by the bridle.
у́з|ел, ла́ *m.* **1.** knot (*also fig. and naut. measurement of speed*); bend, hitch; **завяза́ть у.** to tie a knot; **завяза́ть ~ло́м** to knot; **у. противоре́чий** knot of contradictions. **2.** junction; centre; **у. доро́г** road junction; **промы́шленный у.** industrial centre; **у. сопротивле́ния** (*mil.*) centre of resistance. **3.: не́рвный у.** (*anat.*) nerve-centre, ganglion. **4.** (*bot.*) node. **5.** (*tech.*) group, assembly. **6.** bundle, pack.
узел|о́к, ка́ *m.* **1.** small knot. **2.** (*bot.*) nodule. **3.** small bundle.
у́з|кий (~ок, ~ка́, ~ко) *adj.* **1.** narrow; **~кая колея́** (*rail.*) narrow gauge; **~кое ме́сто** (*fig.*) bottleneck. **2.** tight. **3.** (*fig.*) narrow, limited; **в ~ком смы́сле сло́ва** in the narrow sense of the word. **4.** (*fig.*) narrow, narrow-minded; **у. челове́к** narrow-minded pers.
узкова́т|ый (~, ~а) *adj.* rather narrow; rather tight.
узкого́рлый *adj.* (*of a vessel*) narrow-necked.
узкоколе́йный *adj.* narrow-gauge.
узколо́б|ый (~, ~а) *adj.* **1.** having a narrow forehead. **2.** (*fig.*) narrow-minded.
узли́ст|ый (~, ~а) *adj.* knotty; nodose.
узлова́т|ый (~, ~а) *adj.* knotty; nodose; gnarled.
узлов|о́й *adj.* **1.** junction; **~а́я ста́нция** (*rail.*) junction. **2.** main, principal, central, key; **у. вопро́с** central question. **3.** (*bot.*) nodal.
узна|ва́ть, ю́, ёшь *impf. of* **~́ть**
узна́|ть, ю *pf.* (*of* **~ва́ть**) **1.** to recognize. **2.** to get to know; become familiar with. **3.** to learn, find out.

у́зник, а *m.* (*obs. or rhet.*) prisoner.
у́зниц|а, ы *f. of* **у́зник**
узо́р, а *m.* pattern, design.
узо́р|ный *adj.* **1.** *adj. of* ~. **2.** decorated with a pattern, design.
узо́рчат|ый (~, ~а) *adj.* decorated with a pattern, design.
у́зост|ь, и *f.* narrowness (*also fig.*); tightness.
узр|е́ть, ю́, ~ишь *pf.* **1.** *pf. of* **зреть**[2]. **2.** (*fig.*) to see; to take (as); **она́ ~е́ла в моём замеча́нии оби́ду** she took my remark as an insult.
узурпа́тор, а *m.* usurper.
узурпа́ци|я, и *f.* usurpation.
узурпи́р|овать, ую *impf. and pf.* to usurp.
у́зус, а *m.* (*leg.*) usage.
у́з|ы, ~ *no sg.* (*fig.*) bonds, ties.
уйгу́р, а *m.* Uighur.
уйгу́р|ка, ки *f. of* ~
уйгу́рский *adj.* Uighur.
уй|ду́, дёшь *see* **~ти́**
у́йм|а, ы *no pl., f.* (*coll.*) lots (of), masses (of), heaps (of).
уйм|у́, ёшь *see* **уня́ть**
уй|ти́, ду́, дёшь, *past* **ушёл, ушла́** *pf.* (*of* **уходи́ть**) **1.** to go away, go off, leave; **у. из ко́мнаты** to leave the room; **у. ни с чем** to go away empty-handed; **у. в монасты́рь** to go into a monastery. **2. (от, из)** to escape (from), get away (from); to evade. **3. (от, из, с)** to retire (from), give up; **у. от поли́тики** to retire from politics; **у. от жи́зни** to retire from life; **у. из жи́зни** to pass away (= *to die*); **у. со сце́ны** to quit the stage. **4. (в+*a.*)** to sink (into); (*fig.*) to bury o.s. (in); **у. в себя́** to retire into one's shell. **5.** to be used up, be spent. **6.** (*of time, youth, etc.*) to pass away, slip away. **7.** (*coll.*) to boil over; to spill. **8.** (*obs.*) to pass, out-distance. **9. (вперёд)** (*of a timepiece*) to gain, be fast.
ука́з, а *m.* **1.** decree; edict, ukase. **2.** *as pred.* (*+neg.*) (it is) not an order, not obligatory; **ты мне не у.** I'm not obliged to do as *you* say.
указа́ни|е, я *nt.* **1.** indication, pointing out. **2.** instruction, direction; **дать ~я** to give instructions.
ука́з|анный *p.p.p. of* **~а́ть** *and adj.* fixed, appointed, stated; **на ~анном ме́сте** at the place appointed.
указа́тел|ь, я *m.* **1.** indicator; marker; (*comput.*) cursor; **у. направле́ния** road sign; **у. (возду́шной) ско́рости** airspeed indicator; **у. оборо́тов** (*tech.*) revolution counter; **у. кольца́ угломе́ра** azimuth scale index; **у. у́ровня воды́** water gauge. **2.** index; **у. со́бственных имён** index of proper names. **3.** guide, directory.
указа́тельн|ый *adj.* **1.** indicating; **~ая пласти́нка** dial; **~ая стре́лка** pointer; **у. па́лец, у. перст** forefinger, index finger; **у. столб** road sign. **2.: ~ое местоиме́ние** (*gram.*) demonstrative pronoun.
ука|за́ть, жу́, ~жешь *pf.* (*of* **~зывать**) **1.** to show, indicate. **2. (на+*a.*)** to point (at, to); (*fig.*) to point out; **у. на оши́бку** to point out a mistake. **3.** to explain; to give directions. **4.** (*obs. or coll.*) to give orders.
ука́зк|а, и *f.* **1.** pointer, fescue. **2.** (*coll., pej.*) orders; **по чужо́й ~е** at s.o. else's bidding.
ука́з|ный *adj.* (*obs.*) **1.** *adj. of* ~. **2.** established by decree.
указу́ющий *adj.*: **у. перст** (*obs.*) forefinger, index finger.
ука́зчик, а *m.* (*coll.*) pers. who gives orders; **ты нам не у.** you can't give us orders.
ука́зыва|ть, ю *impf. of* **указа́ть**
ука́лыва|ть, ю *impf. of* **уколо́ть**
украу́л|ить, ю, ишь *pf.* (*coll.*) to guard, watch.
укат|а́ть, а́ю *pf.* (*of* **~ывать**[1]) **1.** to roll (out); **у. доро́гу** to roll, make smooth a road. **2.** (*coll.*) to wear out, tire out.
укат|а́ться, а́ется *pf.* (*of* **~ываться**[1]) (*of a road surface, etc.*) to become smooth.
ука|ти́ть, чу́, ~тишь *pf.* (*of* **~тывать**[2]) **1.** to roll away. **2.** (*coll.*) to drive off.
ука|ти́ться, чу́сь, ~тишься *pf.* (*of* **~тываться**[2]) to roll away (*intrans.*).
ука́тыва|ть(ся)[1]**, ю, ет(ся)** *impf. of* **уката́ть(ся)**
ука́тыва|ть(ся)[2]**, ю(сь)** *impf. of* **укати́ть(ся)**
укач|а́ть, а́ю *pf.* (*of* **~ивать**) **1.** to rock to sleep. **2.** (*of motion of sea or of means of transport*) to make sick; (*impers.*): **меня́ ~а́ло на парохо́де** the motion of the boat made me sick; I was sea-(sick) on the boat.
ука́чива|ть, ю *impf. of* **укача́ть**
укип|а́ть, а́ю *impf. of* **~е́ть**
укип|е́ть, лю́, и́шь *pf.* (*of* **~а́ть**) (*coll.*) to boil away.
укла́д, а *m.* structure; **у. жи́зни** style of life; **обще́ственно-экономи́ческий у.** social and economic structure.
укла́дк|а, и *f.* **1.** packing; stacking, piling; stowing. **2.** laying (*of rails, sleepers, pipes, etc.*).
укла́дчик, а *m.* **1.** packer. **2.** layer (*of rails, sleepers, etc.*).
укла́дыва|ть, ю *impf. of* **уложи́ть**
укла́дыва|ться[1]**, юсь,** *impf. of* **уложи́ться**
укла́дыва|ться[2]**, юсь,** *impf. of* **уле́чься**
укле́йк|а, и *f.* (*zool.*) bleak.
укло́н, а *m.* **1.** slope, declivity; inclination; gradient. **2.** (*fig.*) bias, tendency. **3.** (*pol.*) deviation.
уклоне́ни|е, я *nt.* deviation; **у. от те́мы** digression; **у. от вое́нной слу́жбы** evasion of military service.
уклони́зм, а *m.* (*pol.*) deviationism.
уклони́ст, а *m.* (*pol.*) deviationist.
уклон|и́ть, ю́, ~ишь *pf.* (*of* **~я́ть**) to turn, fend off.
уклон|и́ться, ю́сь, ~ишься *pf.* (*of* **~я́ться**) **1. (от)** to avoid; to evade; **у. от уда́ра** to dodge a blow; **у. от прямо́го отве́та** to avoid giving a direct answer. **2.** to turn off, turn aside.
укло́нчив|ый (~, ~а) *adj.* **1.** evasive. **2.** (*obs.*) meek; compliant.
уклон|я́ть(ся), я́ю(сь) *impf. of* **~и́ть(ся)**
уклю́чин|а, ы *f.* rowlock.
укоко́ш|ить, у, ишь *pf.* (*sl.*) to bump off.
уко́л, а *m.* **1.** prick; jab. **2.** (*mil.*) thrust. **3.** injection, 'jab'.
укол|о́ть, ю́, ~ешь *pf.* (*of* **ука́лывать**) **1.** to prick. **2.** (*fig.*) to sting, wound; **у. чьё-н. самолю́бие** to touch s.o.'s pride.
укомплектова́ни|е, я *nt.* bringing up to strength.
укомплекто́в|анный *p.p.p. of* **~а́ть** *and adj.* complete, at full strength.
укомплект|ова́ть, у́ю *pf.* (*of* **комплектова́ть** *and* **~о́вывать**) **1.** to complete; to bring up to (full) strength; to man. **2.** (*+i.*) to equip (with), furnish (with).
укомплкето́выва|ть, ю *impf. of* **укомплектова́ть**
уко́р, а *m.* reproach; **~ы со́вести** pangs of conscience.
укора́чива|ть, ю *impf. of* **укороти́ть**
укорене́ни|е, я *nt.* **1.** implanting, inculcation. **2.** taking root, striking root.
укорен|и́ть, ю́, и́шь *pf.* (*of* **~я́ть**) to implant, inculcate.
укорен|и́ться, ю́сь, и́шься *pf.* (*of* **~я́ться**) to take, strike root (*also fig.*).
укорен|я́ть(ся), я́ю(сь) *impf. of* **~и́ть(ся)**
укори́зн|а, ы *f.* reproach.
укори́зненный *adj.* reproachful.
укор|и́ть, ю́, и́шь *pf.* (*of* **~я́ть**) (*+a.* **в**+*p.*) to reproach (with).
укоро|ти́ть, чу́, ти́шь *pf.* (*of* **укора́чивать**) to shorten.
укор|я́ть, я́ю *impf. of* **~и́ть**
уко́с[1]**, а** *m.* hay-harvest, hay crop.
уко́с[2]**, а** *m.* = **~ина**
уко́син|а, ы *f.* (*tech.*) strut, brace; cantilever; (crane) jib.
укра́дкой *adv.* stealthily, furtively, by stealth.
Украи́н|а, ы *f.* (the) Ukraine.
украи́н|ец, ца *m.* Ukrainian.
украи́н|ка[1]**, ки** *f. of* **~ец**
украи́нк|а[2]**, и** *f.* Ukrainka (*variety of winter wheat*).
украи́нский *adj.* Ukrainian.
укра́|сить, шу, сишь *pf.* (*of* **~ша́ть**) to adorn, decorate, ornament (*also fig.*).
укра́|ситься, шусь, сишься *pf.* (*of* **~ша́ться**) **1.** *pass. of* **~сить**. **2.** to adorn o.s.
укра́|сть, ду́, дёшь, *past* **~л** *pf.* (*of* **красть**) to steal.
украша́|ть(ся), ю(сь) *impf. of* **укра́сить(ся)**
украше́ни|е, я *nt.* **1.** adorning, decoration. **2.** adornment, decoration, ornament.
укреп|и́ть, лю́, и́шь *pf.* (*of* **~ля́ть**) **1.** to strengthen; to reinforce; to make fast. **2.** (*mil.*) to fortify. **3.** (*fig.*) to fortify, brace. **4.** (*fig.*) to strengthen; to enhance; **у. дисципли́ну** to tighten up discipline.

укреп|и́ться, лю́сь, и́шься *pf.* (*of* **~ля́ться**) **1.** to become stronger. **2.** (*mil.*) to fortify one's position. **3.** (*fig.*) to become firmly established.
укрепле́ни|е, я *nt.* **1.** strengthening, reinforcing. **2.** (*mil.*) fortification; work.
укреп|лённый *p.p.p. of* **~и́ть** *and adj.* (*mil.*) fortified.
укрепля́|ть(ся), ю(сь) *impf. of* **укрепи́ть(ся)**
укрепля́ющ|ее, его *nt.* tonic, restorative.
укро́м|ный (~ен, ~на) *adj.* secluded; sheltered; cosy.
укро́п, а *m.* (*bot.*) dill (*Anethum graveolens*); **воло́шский у.** fennel (*Foeniculum vulgare*); **морско́й у.** samphire (*Crithmum maritimum*).
укро́п|ный *adj. of* **~**; **~ное ма́сло** dill oil.
укроти́тел|ь, я *m.* (animal-)tamer.
укро|ти́ть, щу́, ти́шь *pf.* (*of* **~ща́ть**) **1.** to tame. **2.** to curb, subdue, check; **в. свои́ стра́сти** to curb one's passions.
укро|ти́ться, щу́сь, ти́шься *pf.* (*of* **~ща́ться**) **1.** to become tame. **2.** to calm down, die down.
укроща́|ть(ся), ю(сь) *impf. of* **укроти́ть(ся)**
укрупне́ни|е, я *nt.* enlargement, extension; amalgamation (*of collective farms, etc.*).
укрупн|и́ть, ю́, и́шь *pf.* (*of* **~я́ть**) to enlarge, extend; to amalgamate.
укрупн|я́ть, я́ю *impf. of* **~и́ть**
укрыва́тел|ь, я *m.* (*leg.*) concealer, harbourer; **у. кра́деного** receiver (of stolen goods).
укрыва́тельств|о, а *nt.* (*leg.*) concealment, harbouring; **у. кра́деного** receiving (of stolen goods).
укрыва́|ть(ся), ю(сь) *impf. of* **укры́ть(ся)**
укры́ти|е, я *nt.* (*mil., etc.*) cover, concealment; shelter; **у. от огня́** cover (from fire); **у. от взо́ров** concealment; **стреля́ть из ~й** to fire from covered positions.
укры́т|ый *p.p.p. of* **~ь** *and adj.* (*mil.*) concealed, covered.
укр|ы́ть, о́ю, о́ешь *pf.* (*of* **~ыва́ть**) **1.** to cover (up). **2.** to conceal, harbour; to give shelter; to receive (*stolen goods*); **у. уби́йцу** to harbour a murderer; **у. от дождя́** to give shelter from the rain.
укр|ы́ться, о́юсь, о́ешься *pf.* (*of* **~ыва́ться**) **1.** to cover o.s. (up). **2.** to take cover; to seek shelter. **3.** to escape notice; **от меня́ не ~ы́лось** it has not escaped my notice.
у́ксус, а (у) *m.* vinegar.
у́ксусник, а *m.* vinegar-cruet.
у́ксусниц|а, ы *f.* = **у́ксусник**
уксуснокисл|ый *adj.* (*chem.*) acetate (of); **~ая соль** acetate.
у́ксусн|ый *adj.* **1.** *adj. of* **у́ксус**. **2.** acetic; **~ая кислота́** acetic acid; **~ая плёнка** flower of vinegar; **~ая эссе́нция** vinegar essence.
уку́порива|ть, ю *impf. of* **уку́порить**
уку́пор|ить, ю, ишь *pf.* (*of* **~ивать**) **1.** to cork (up). **2.** (*coll.*) to pack (up), crate.
уку́порк|а, и *f.* **1.** corking. **2.** packing, crating.
уку́с, а *m.* bite; sting.
уку|си́ть, шу́, ~сишь *pf.* to bite; to sting; **кака́я му́ха его́ ~си́ла?** (*coll.*) what's bitten him?; what's got into him?
уку́т|ать, аю *pf.* (*of* **~ывать**) **(в+*a.*)** to wrap up (in).
уку́т|аться, аюсь *pf.* (*of* **~ываться**) to wrap o.s. up.
уку́тыва|ть(ся), ю(сь) *impf. of* **уку́тать(ся)**
ул. (*abbr. of* **у́лица**) St., Street; Rd., Road.
ула́влива|ть, ю *impf. of* **улови́ть**
ула́|дить, жу, дишь *pf.* (*of* **~живать**) **1.** to settle, arrange. **2.** (*obs.*) to reconcile.
ула́жива|ть, ю *impf. of* **ула́дить**
ула́мыва|ть, ю *impf. of* **улома́ть**
ула́н, а, *g. pl.* **~ов** (*and in collect. sense* **ула́н**) *m.* (*mil.*) uhlan; lancer.
Ула́н-Ба́тор, а *m.* Ulan-Bator.
ула́н|ский *adj. of* **~**
улеж|а́ть, у́, и́шь *pf.* (*coll.*) to lie down.
у́л|ей, ья *m.* (bee)hive.
улепет|ну́ть, ну́, нёшь *pf. of* **~ывать**
улепётыва|ть, ю *impf.* (*of* **улепетну́ть**) (*coll.*) to make off, bolt; **~й!** hop it!
уле|сти́ть, щу́, сти́шь *pf.* (*of* **~ща́ть**) (*coll.*) to butter up, chat up.
улет|а́ть, а́ю *impf. of* **~е́ть**
уле|те́ть, чу́, ти́шь *pf.* (*of* **~та́ть**) **1.** to fly (away). **2.** (*fig.*) to fly; to vanish; **вре́мя ~те́ло** the time had flown by.
улету́чива|ться, юсь *impf. of* **улету́читься**
улету́ч|иться, усь, ишься *pf.* (*of* **~иваться**) **1.** to evaporate, volatilize. **2.** (*coll.*) to vanish, disappear.
ул|е́чься, я́гусь, я́жешься, я́гутся, *past* **~ёгся, ~егла́сь** *pf.* **1.** (*impf.* **укла́дываться**[2]) to lie down. **2.** (*impf.* **укла́дываться**[2]) to find room (*lying down*). **3.** (*of dust, etc.*) to settle. **4.** (*fig.*) to subside; to calm down; **ве́тер ~ёгся** the wind dropped.
улеща́|ть, ю *impf. of* **улести́ть**
улизн|у́ть, у́, ёшь *pf.* (*coll.*) to slip away, steal away.
ули́к|а, и *f.* (piece of) evidence.
ули́тк|а, и *f.* **1.** (*zool.*) snail; (*pl.*) Gastropoda. **2.** (*anat.*) cochlea.
у́лиц|а, ы *f.* street; (*fig.*; *pej.*) 'the streets'; **на ~е** (*i*) in the street, (*ii*) out (of doors), outside; **оказа́ться на ~е** (*fig.*) to find o.s. in the street; **бу́дет и на на́шей ~е пра́здник** our day will come; **с ~ы** from out of doors; **челове́к с ~ы** anyone (who happens to be about).
улич|а́ть, а́ю *impf. of* **~и́ть**
улич|и́ть, у́, и́шь *pf.* (*of* **~а́ть**) **(в+*p.*)** to establish the guilt (of).
у́личн|ый *adj.* street (*also fig., pej.*); **у. бой** street fighting; **~ая де́вка** (*coll.*) streetwalker; **~ая пре́сса** gutter press.
уло́в, а *m.* catch (*of fish*).
улов|и́мый *pres. part. pass. of* **~и́ть** *and adj.* perceptible; audible.
улови́тел|ь, я *m.* (*tech.*) detector, locator.
улов|и́ть, лю́, ~ишь *pf.* (*of* **ула́вливать**) **1.** (*tech.*) to catch, pick up, locate (*a sound wave, etc.*). **2.** to detect, perceive; **у. но́тку нетерпе́ния в чьём-н. го́лосе** to detect a note of impatience in s.o.'s voice. **3.** (*coll.*) to seize (*an opportunity, etc.*).
уло́вк|а, и *f.* trick, ruse, subterfuge.
уложе́ни|е, я *nt.* (*leg.*) code (*esp. hist., of the Russ. Law Code of 1649*).
улож|и́ть, у́, ~ишь *pf.* (*of* **укла́дывать**) **1.** to lay; **у. в посте́ль** to put to bed; **у. в гроб** (*fig.*) to be the death (of). **2.** to pack; to stow; to pile, stack. **3.** (+*i.*) to cover (with), lay (with). **4.** to lay (*rails, sleepers, etc.*). **5.** (*pf. only*) (*coll.*) to dispatch (= *to kill*).
улож|и́ться, у́сь, ~ишься *pf.* (*of* **укла́дываться**[1]) **1.** to pack (up). **2.** **(в+*a.*)** to go (in), fit (in); **шу́ба не ~ится в э́тот чемода́н** a fur coat won't go into that case. **3.** **(в+*a.*;** *coll.*) to keep (within), confine o.s. (to); **у. в стипе́ндию** to manage *or* get by on a scholarship; **у. в полчаса́** to confine o.s. to half an hour. **4.: у. в голове́, в созна́нии** to sink in, go in.
улома́|ть, ю *pf.* (*of* **ула́мывать**) (*coll.*) to talk round; (+*inf.*) to talk into, prevail upon (to).
у́лочк|а, и *f. dim. of* **у́лица**
улу́с, а *m.* ulus (= (*i*) *settlement or nomad camp in some parts of Siberia*, (*ii*) *administrative division of former Yakut Autonomous Soviet Socialist Republic, etc.*).
улуч|а́ть, а́ю *impf. of* **~и́ть**
улуч|и́ть, у́, и́шь *pf.* (*of* **~а́ть**) (*coll.*) to find, seize, catch; **у. моме́нт для разгово́ра** to find a moment for a talk; **у. удо́бный слу́чай** to seize an opportunity.
улучш|а́ть(ся), а́ю(сь) *impf. of* **~ить(ся)**
улучше́ни|е, я *nt.* improvement, amelioration.
улу́чш|ить, у, ишь *pf.* (*of* **~а́ть**) to improve; to ameliorate, make better; to better.
улу́чш|иться, усь, ишься *pf.* (*of* **~а́ться**) to improve; to get better.
улыб|а́ться, а́юсь *impf.* (*of* **~ну́ться**) **1.** to smile. **2.** (+*d.*; *fig.*) to smile (upon). **3.** (*impf. only*) (+*d.*; *coll.*) to please; **зада́ча э́та мне во́все не ~а́ется** I don't like the idea of this task at all.
улы́бк|а, и *f.* smile.
улыб|ну́ться, ну́сь, нёшься *pf.* **1.** *pf. of* **~а́ться**. **2.** (*coll.*) to fail to materialize; to fall through; to vanish, disappear; **на́ша но́вая кварти́ра ~ну́лась** our new flat failed to materialize; our hopes of a new flat were dashed.

улы́бчив|ый (~, ~а) *adj.* (*coll.*) smiling; happy.
ультимати́в|ный (~ен, ~на) *adj.* categorical, having the nature of an ultimatum.
ультима́тум, а *m.* ultimatum.
ультра... *comb. form* ultra-
ультразвуково́й *adj.* (*phys., aeron.*) supersonic.
ультракоро́тк|ий *adj.* (*radio*) ultra-short; **~ие во́лны** VHF (*abbr. of* very high frequency) waveband.
ультрамари́н, а *m.* ultramarine.
ультрафиоле́товый *adj.* ultra-violet.
улюлю́ка|ть, ю *impf.* **1.** (*hunting*) to halloo. **2.** (*coll., pej.*) to whoop (in mockery).
ум, а́ *m.* mind, intellect; wits; **склад ~а́** mentality; **~а́ не приложу́** (*coll.*) it's beyond me; I give up; **у меня́ ум за ра́зум захо́дит** (*coll.*) I am at my wits' end; **быть без ~а́ (от)** to be out of one's mind (about), be mad, crazy (about); **(счита́ть,** *etc.***) в ~е́** (to count, *etc.*) in one's head; **в уме́ ли ты?** (*coll.*) are you in your right mind?; **и в ~е́ у меня́ не́ было** (*coll.*) the thought never even entered my head; **взя́ться за ум** (*coll.*) to come to one's senses; **э́то у меня́ из ~а́ нейдёт** (*coll.*) I can't get it out of my head; **прийти́ на ум** (*+d.*) (*coll.*) to occur to one, cross one's mind; **быть на ~е́** (*coll.*) to be on one's mind; **от большо́го ~а́** (*coll., iron.*) in one's infinite wisdom; **свести́ с ~а́** (*coll.*) to drive mad; (*fig.*) to make wild (*with delight, admiration*), send; **сойти́ с ~а́** to go mad; (**по**+*d. or p., fig.*) to go crazy (about); **с ~о́м** (*coll.*) sensibly, intelligently; **с ума́ сойти́!** (*coll.*) incredible!
умале́ни|е, я *nt.* belittling, disparagement.
умал|и́ть, ю́, и́шь *pf.* (*of* **~я́ть**) **1.** (*obs.*) to decrease, lessen. **2.** to belittle, disparage.
умалишённ|ый *adj.* mad, lunatic; *as n.* **у., ~ого** *m.*; **~ая, ~ой** *f.* madman; lunatic; madwoman; **дом ~ых** lunatic asylum.
ума́лчива|ть, ю *impf. of* **умолча́ть**
умал|я́ть, я́ю *impf. of* **~и́ть**
ума́слива|ть, ю *impf. of* **ума́слить**
ума́сл|ить, ю, ишь *pf.* (*of* **~ивать**) (*coll.*) to butter up.
ума|сти́ть, щу́, сти́шь *pf.* (*of* **~ща́ть**) (*obs.*) to anoint.
умаща́|ть, ю *impf. of* **умасти́ть**
ума́|ять, ю *pf.* (*coll.*) to tire out.
у́мбр|а, ы *f.* umber.
уме́л|ец, ьца *m.* skilled craftsman.
уме́л|ый *adj.* able, skilful; capable; **у. рабо́тник** able workman; **~ая поли́тика** astute policy.
уме́ни|е, я *nt.* ability, skill; know-how.
уменьша́ем|ое, ого *nt.* (*math.*) minuend.
уменьш|а́ть(ся), а́ю(сь) *impf. of* **~́ить(ся)**
уменьше́ни|е, я *nt.* reduction, diminution, decrease, lessening, abatement; **у. ско́рости** deceleration.
уменьши́тельн|ый *adj.* **1.** diminishing. **2.** (*gram.*) diminutive. **3.: ~ое и́мя** pet name (*as* Kolya *for* Nikolai).
уме́ньш|ить, ~́у, ~́ишь *pf.* (*of* **~а́ть**) to reduce, diminish, decrease, lessen; **у. ход** to reduce speed; **у. це́ны** to reduce prices; **у. расхо́ды** to cut down expenditure.
уме́ньш|иться, ~́усь, ~́ишься *pf.* (*of* **~а́ться**) **1.** to diminish, decrease, drop, dwindle; to abate. **2.** *pass. of* **~ить**
уме́ренност|ь, и *f.* moderation, moderateness; temperance.
уме́р|енный *p.p.p. of* **~ить** *and adj.* **1. (~ен, ~енна)** moderate (*pol.; also fig.*); **у. аппети́т** moderate appetite; **~енная поли́тика** moderate policy. **2.** (*geog., meteor.*) temperate; moderate; **у. по́яс** temperate zone; **у. ве́тер** moderate breeze (*on Beaufort scale*).
умер|е́ть, умру́, умрёшь, *past* **у́мер, ~ла́, у́мерло** *pf.* (*of* **умира́ть**) to die; **у. есте́ственной, наси́льственной сме́ртью** to die a natural, a violent death; **у. от, со ску́ки** to be bored to death.
уме́р|ить, ю, ишь *pf.* (*of* **~я́ть**) to moderate, to restrain.
уме́р|иться, юсь, ишься *pf.* (*of* **~я́ться**) **1.** to become more moderate; to abate, die down. **2.** *pass. of* **~ить**
умер|тви́ть, щвлю́, тви́шь *pf.* (*of* **~щвля́ть**) to kill, destroy (*also fig.*); to mortify; **у. все свои́ тво́рческие побужде́ния** to stifle all one's creative impulses.
умерщвле́ни|е, я *nt.* killing, destruction (*also fig.*); mortification.
умерщвля́|ть, ю *impf. of* **умертви́ть**
умер|я́ть(ся), я́ю(сь) *impf. of* **~́ить(ся)**
уме|сти́ть, щу́, сти́шь *pf.* (*of* **~ща́ть**) to get in, fit in, find room (for); **она́ не могла́ у. все поку́пки в су́мку** she could not get all her purchases into her bag.
уме|сти́ться, щу́сь, сти́шься *pf.* (*of* **~ща́ться**) to go in, fit in, find room.
уме́стно[1] *adv.* appropriately; opportunely.
уме́стно[2] *as pred.* it is appropriate, it is in order, it is proper, it is not out of place; **у. бы́ло бы сде́лать намёк** it would not be out of place to drop a hint.
уме́ст|ный (~ен, ~на) *adj.* appropriate; pertinent, to the point; opportune, timely; **у. вопро́с** pertinent question; **ва́ше предложе́ние вполне́ ~но** your suggestion is quite in order.
уме́|ть, ю *impf.* (*of* **с~**) (*+inf.*) to be able (to), know how (to).
умеща́|ть(ся), ю(сь) *impf. of* **умести́ть(ся)**
уме́ючи *adv.* (*coll.*) skilfully.
умиле́ни|е, я *nt.* emotion; tenderness; **прийти́ в у.** to be moved; **лить слёзы ~я** to shed tears of emotion, weep with emotion.
умили́тел|ьный (~ен, ~ьна) *adj.* moving, touching, affecting.
умил|и́ть, ю́, и́шь *pf.* (*of* **~я́ть**) to move, touch.
умил|и́ться, ю́сь, и́шься *pf.* (*of* **~я́ться**) to be moved, be touched.
умилосе́рд|ить, ишь *pf.* to propitiate, mollify.
уми́лостив|ить, лю, ишь *pf.* = **умилосе́рдить**
уми́л|ьный (~ен, ~ьна) *adj.* **1.** touching, affecting; **~ьное ли́чико** nice face. **2.** (*pej.*) ingratiating, smarmy.
умил|я́ть(ся), я́ю(сь) *impf. of* **~и́ть(ся)**
умина́|ть, ю *impf. of* **умя́ть**
умира́ни|е, я *nt.* dying.
умира́|ть, ю *impf. of* **умере́ть**
умир|и́ть, ю́, и́шь *pf.* (*of* **~я́ть**) (*obs.*) to calm.
умиротворе́ни|е, я *nt.* pacification; conciliation; appeasement.
умиротворён|ный (~, ~на) *adj.* tranquil; contented.
умиротвор|и́ть, ю́, и́шь *pf.* (*of* **~я́ть**) to pacify; to appease.
умиротвор|я́ть, я́ю *impf. of* **~и́ть**
умир|я́ть, я́ю *impf. of* **~и́ть**
умла́ут, а *m.* (*ling.*) umlaut.
умн|е́е *comp. of* **~ый** *and* **~о**
умне́|ть, ю *impf.* (*of* **по~**) to grow wiser.
у́мник, а *m.* **1.** good boy; (*coll.*) clever pers. **2.** (*iron.*) know-all, smart alec, clever Dick.
у́мниц|а, ы *f. and c.g.* (*coll.*) **1.** *f.* good girl. **2.** *c.g.* clever pers.
у́мнича|ть, ю *impf.* (*of* **с~**) (*coll.*) **1.** (*iron.*) to show off one's intelligence. **2.** (*pej.*) to try to be clever.
у́мно[1] *adv.* cleverly, wisely; sensibly.
у́мно[2] *as pred.* it is wise; it is sensible.
умнож|а́ть(ся), а́ю(сь) *impf. of* **~́ить(ся)**
умноже́ни|е, я *nt.* **1.** increase, rise. **2.** (*math.*) multiplication.
умно́жител|ь, я *m.*: **у. частоты́** (*radio*) frequency multiplier.
умно́ж|ить, у, ишь *pf.* (*of* **мно́жить** *and* **~а́ть**) **1.** to increase, augment. **2.** (*math.*) to multiply.
умно́ж|иться, усь, ишься *pf.* (*of* **мно́житься** *and* **~а́ться**) **1.** to increase, multiply (*intrans.*). **2.** *pass. of* **~ить**
у́м|ный (~ён, ~на́, ~но) *adj.* clever, wise, intelligent; sensible.
умозаключ|а́ть, а́ю *impf. of* **~и́ть**
умозаключе́ни|е, я *nt.* deduction; conclusion, inference.
умозаключ|и́ть, у́, и́шь *pf.* (*of* **~а́ть**) to deduce; to conclude, infer.
умозре́ни|е, я *nt.* (*phil.*) speculation.
умозри́тел|ьный (~ен, ~ьна) *adj.* (*phil.*) speculative.
умоисступле́ни|е, я *nt.* delirium; **де́йствовать в ~и** to act while the balance of one's mind is disturbed.
умол|и́ть, ю́, и́шь *pf.* (*of* **~я́ть**) to move by entreaties.
у́молк: без ~у (*to talk, etc.*) unceasingly, incessantly.
умолк|а́ть, а́ю *impf. of* **~́нуть**

умо́лк|нуть, ну, нешь, *past* **~, ~ла** *pf.* (*of* **~а́ть**) to fall silent, lapse into silence; (*of noises*) to cease, stop.
умоло́т, а *m.* (*agric.*) yield (*of threshed grain*).
умолча́ни|е, я *nt.* **1.** passing over in silence, failure to mention, suppression. **2.** (*liter.*) aposiopesis.
умолча́|ть, ю *pf.* (*of* **ума́лчивать**) (о+*p.*) to pass over in silence, fail to mention, suppress, hush up.
умол|я́ть, я́ю *impf.* **1.** *impf. of* **~и́ть. 2.** to entreat, implore.
умоля́|ющий *pres. part. act of* **~ть** *and adj.* imploring, pleading, suppliant.
умонастрое́ни|е, я *nt.* mood, disposition; mentality.
умопомеша́тельств|о, а *nt.* derangement of mind.
умопомраче́ни|е, я *nt.* (*obs.*) derangement of mind; fit of insanity; **до ~я** (*coll.*) stupendously, tremendously.
умопомрачи́тел|ьный (~ен, ~ьна) *adj.* (*coll.*) stupendous, tremendous, terrific.
умо́р|а, ы *f.* **1.** (*dial.*) exhaustion. **2.** *as pred.* (*coll.*) it's hilarious; it's a scream.
умори́тельн|о[1] *adv. of* **~ый**
умори́тельно[2] *as pred.* = **умо́ра 2.**
умори́тел|ьный (~ен, ~ьна) *adj.* (*coll.*) hilarious.
умор|и́ть, ю́, и́шь *pf.* (*of* **мори́ть**[1]) (*coll.*) **1.** to kill; (*fig.*) to be the death (of); **у. кого́-н. со́ смеху** to make s.o. die of laughing. **2.** to tire out, exhaust.
у́мственн|о *adv. of* **~ый; у. отста́лый** retarded, backward.
у́мственн|ый *adj.* mental, intellectual; **у. бага́ж** mental equipment, store of knowledge; **у. труд** brainwork; **рабо́тник ~ого труда́** brainworker.
у́мствовани|е, я *nt.* (*pej.*) theorizing, philosophizing.
у́мств|овать, ую *impf.* (*pej.*) to theorize, philosophize.
умудр|и́ть, ю́, и́шь *pf.* (*of* **~я́ть**) to teach, make wiser.
умудр|и́ться, ю́сь, и́шься *pf.* (*of* **~я́ться**) (*coll.*) to contrive, manage (*also, iron., to do sth. which might easily have been avoided*).
умудр|я́ть(ся), я́ю(сь) *impf. of* **~и́ть(ся)**
умфо́рмер, а *m.* (*elec.*) transformer.
умч|а́ть, у́, и́шь *pf.* to whirl, hurtle away.
умч|а́ться, у́сь, и́шься *pf.* **1.** to whirl, hurtle away (*intrans.*). **2.** (*fig.*) to fly away.
умыва́льн|ая, ой *f.* wash-room.
умыва́льник, а *m.* wash-(hand-)stand; wash-basin.
умыва́льн|ый *adj.* wash, washing; **~ая ко́мната** wash-room; **у. таз** wash-basin.
умыва́|ть(ся), ю(сь) *impf. of* **умы́ть(ся)**
умыка́ни|е, я *nt.* (*ethnol.*) abduction (*of bride from her parents*).
у́мыс|ел, ла *m.* design, intention; **со злым ~лом** with malicious intent; (*leg.*) of malice prepense.
умы́сл|ить, ю, ишь *pf.* (*of* **умышля́ть**) (+*inf.*) to intend, design; (+*a.*) to plan, plot.
ум|ы́ть, о́ю, о́ешь *pf.* (*of* **~ыва́ть**) to wash; **у. ру́ки** to wash one's hands (*also fig.*).
ум|ы́ться, о́юсь, о́ешься *pf.* (*of* **~ыва́ться**) to wash (o.s.).
умы́шленно *adv.* purposely, intentionally.
умы́|шленный *p.p.p. of* **~слить** *and adj.* intentional, deliberate, premeditated.
умышля́|ть, ю *impf. of* **умы́слить**
умягч|а́ть, а́ю *impf. of* **~и́ть**
умягч|и́ть, у́, и́шь *pf.* (*of* **~а́ть**) to soften; to mollify.
умя́ть, умну́, умнёшь *pf.* (*of* **умина́ть**) **1.** to knead well. **2.** (*coll.*) to press down; to tread down. **3.** (*sl.*) to stuff down (= *to eat*).
унава́живать = **унаво́живать**
унаво́жива|ть, ю *impf. of* **унаво́зить**
унаво́|зить, жу, зишь *pf.* (*of* **наво́зить** *and* **~живать**) to manure.
унасле́д|овать, ую *pf. of* **насле́довать 1.**
унди́н|а, ы *f.* undine, water-sprite.
унес|ти́, у́, ёшь, *past* **~́, ~ла́** *pf.* (*of* **уноси́ть**) **1.** to take away. **2.** (*coll.*) to carry off, make off with. **3.** to carry away, remove; (*impers.*): **ло́дку ~ло́ тече́нием** the boat was carried away by the current; **~и́ ты моё го́ре!** (*int. expr. disapproval*) heaven help us! **4.** (*fig.*) to carry (*in thought*).
унес|ти́сь, у́сь, ёшься, *past* **~́ся, ~ла́сь** *pf.* (*of* **уноси́ться**) **1.** to whirl away (*intrans.*). **2.** (*fig.*) to fly away, fly by; **го́ды ~ли́сь** the years flew by. **3.** (*fig.*) to travel (*in thought*).
униа́т, а *m.* (*relig.*) member of Uniat(e) Church.
униа́тский *adj.* (*relig.*) Uniat(e).
универма́г, а *m.* (*abbr. of* **универса́льный магази́н**) department store.
универса́л, а *m.* **1.** all-round craftsman. **2.** (*geod.*) theodolite.
универса́л|ьный (~ен, ~ьна) *adj.* **1.** universal; all-round; **~ьное сре́дство** panacea; **у. магази́н** department store; **~ьные зна́ния** encyclopaedic knowledge. **2.** many-sided; versatile; **~ьное образова́ние** many-sided education; **у. челове́к** versatile pers.; all-rounder. **3.** (*tech.*) multi-purpose, all-purpose; **у. инструме́нт** (*astron. and geod.*) theodolite; **у. ключ** universal wrench; **~ьное пита́ние** (*elec.*) mains-or-battery power supply.
универса́м, а *m.* (*abbr. of* **универса́льный магази́н самообслу́живания**) supermarket.
университе́т, а *m.* university; **у. культу́ры** 'university of culture' (*institution providing lecture courses, etc., on general and political topics for adults*); **поступи́ть в у.** to enter, go up to university; **око́нчить у.** to graduate (from a university).
университе́т|ский *adj. of* **~**
унижа́|ть(ся), ю(сь) *impf. of* **уни́зить(ся)**
униже́ни|е, я *nt.* humiliation, degradation, abasement.
уни́жен|ный *p.p.p. of* **уни́зить** *and adj.* (**~, ~на**) humble.
унижён|ный (~, ~на) *adj.* oppressed, degraded.
уни|за́ть, жу́, ~́жешь *pf.* (*of* **~́зывать**) (+*i.*) to cover (with), stud (with).
унизи́тел|ьный (~ен, ~ьна) *adj.* humiliating, degrading.
уни́|зить, жу, зишь *pf.* (*of* **~жа́ть**) to humble, humiliate; to lower, degrade.
уни́|зиться, жусь, зишься *pf.* (*of* **~жа́ться**) to debase o.s., demean o.s.; **у. до шантажа́** to stoop to blackmail.
уни́зыва|ть, ю *impf. of* **униза́ть**
уника́л|ьный (~ен, ~ьна) *adj.* unique.
у́никум, а *m.* unique object (*of its kind*).
унима́|ть(ся), ю(сь) *impf. of* **уня́ть(ся)**
унисо́н, а *m.* (*mus. and phys.*) unison; **в у.** in unison; (*fig.*) in unison, in concert.
унита́з, а *m.* lavatory pan.
унита́рный *adj.* unitary; **у. патро́н** (*mil.*) fixed round.
унифика́ци|я, и *f.* unification; standardization.
унифици́р|овать, ую *impf. and pf.* to unify; to standardize.
унифо́рм|а, ы *f.* **1.** (*obs.*) uniform. **2.** (*collect.*) circus staff (*in the ring*).
униформи́ст, а *m.* circus hand (*in the ring*).
уничижа́|ть, ю *impf.* (*obs.*) to disparage.
уничиже́ни|е, я *nt.* disparaging, disparagement.
уничижи́тел|ьный (~ен, ~ьна) *adj.* **1.** (*obs.*) disparaging. **2.** (*gram.*) pejorative.
уничтож|а́ть, а́ю *impf. of* **~́ить**
уничтожа́|ющий *pres. part. act. of* **~ть** *and adj.* destructive; **у. взгляд** murderous look; **~ющее замеча́ние** scathing comment.
уничтоже́ни|е, я *nt.* **1.** destruction, annihilation; extermination, obliteration; **многокра́тное у.** (*mil.*) overkill. **2.** abolition, elimination.
уничто́ж|ить, у, ишь *pf.* (*of* **~а́ть**) **1.** to destroy, annihilate; to wipe out; to exterminate, obliterate; **у. си́лы проти́вника** to wipe out the enemy's forces. **2.** to abolish; to do away with, eliminate; to cancel (out); **у. крепостно́е пра́во** to abolish serfdom. **3.** (*fig.*) to crush, make mincemeat (of), tear to shreds (*with an argument, etc.*).
у́ни|я, и *f.* (*hist., eccl.*) union (*esp. of the act of 1596 by which the Uniat(e) Church was set up*).
уно́с, а *m.* **1.** taking away, carrying away. **2.** (*obs.*) pair (*of a team of horses*).
уно|си́ть(ся), шу́(сь), ~́сишь(ся) *impf. of* **унести́(сь)**
у́нтер, а *m.* = **~-офице́р**
у́нтер-офице́р, а *m.* non-commissioned officer (*abbr.* NCO).
унт|ы́, о́в *pl.* (*sg.* **~, ~а́** *m.*) (*and* **у́нт|ы, ~,** *sg.* **~а, ~ы** *f.*) high boots (*of inverted pelt or goatskin*).

у́нци|я, и *f.* ounce (*measure*).

унывá|ть, ю *impf.* to be depressed, be dejected.

уны́л|ый (~, ~а) *adj.* **1.** (*of persons*) depressed, dejected, despondent, downcast. **2.** (*of thoughts, looks, etc.*) melancholy, doleful, cheerless.

уны́ни|е, я *nt.* depression, dejection, despondency; **впасть в у.** to become depressed; **навести́ у.** to depress.

уня́|ть, уйму́, уймёшь, *past* **~л, ~ла́, ~ло** *pf.* (*of* **унима́ть**) **1.** to calm, soothe, pacify; **у. деру́щихся** to stop a fight. **2.** (*coll.*) to stop, check; **у. пожа́р,** to stop a fire. **3.** to suppress (*feelings*).

уня́|ться, уйму́сь, уймёшься, *past* **~лся, ~ла́сь** *pf.* (*of* **унима́ться**) **1.** to calm down. **2.** (*coll.*) to stop, abate, die down; **кровотече́ние ~ло́сь** the bleeding has stopped.

упа́|вший *past. part. act. of* **~сть** *and adj.* fallen; (*of voice or tone*) weak (*from emotion or fear*).

упа́д: до ~у to the point of exhaustion, till one drops.

упада́|ть, ю *impf.* (*obs.*) to fall.

упа́д|ок, ка *m.* **1.** decline (*of pol. system, culture, etc.*); **в. состоя́нии ~ка** on the decline. **2.** decline, decay, collapse (*of physical or spiritual faculties*); **у. ду́ха** depression; **у. сил** breakdown.

упа́дочнический *adj.* decadent.

упа́дочничеств|о, а *nt.* decadence.

упа́доч|ный (~ен, ~на) *adj.* **1.** *adj. of* **упа́док 1.**; decadent. **2.** depressive; **~ное настрое́ние** depression.

упак|ова́ть, у́ю *pf.* (*of* **пакова́ть** *and* **~о́вывать**) to pack (up), wrap (up), bale.

упако́вк|а, и *f.* **1.** packing (*action*), wrapping, baling. **2.** packing (*material*), package.

упако́вочн|ый *adj.* packing; **~ая клеть** packing crate; **у. материа́л** packing material; *as n.* **~ая, ~ой** *f.* packing-house.

упако́вщик, а *m.* packer.

упако́выва|ть, ю *impf. of* **упакова́ть**

упа́рива|ть, ю *impf. of* **упа́рить**

упа́р|ить, ю, ишь *pf.* (*of* **~ивать**) to boil down, concentrate.

упас|ти́, у́, ёшь, *past* **~́, ~ла́** *pf.* (*coll.*) to save, preserve; **~и́ Бог, Бо́же ~и́** (*i*) (*expr. warning not to do sth.*) God preserve you!; heaven help you!, (*ii*) (*expr. vigorous denial*) good God, no!; God forbid!

упа́|сть, ду́, дёшь, *past* **~л** *pf.* (*of* **па́дать 1.**) (*in var. senses*) to fall.

упёк[1]**, а** *m.* loss of weight in baking.

упёк[2] *see* **упе́чь**

упека́|ть, ю *impf. of* **упе́чь**

упер|е́ть, упру́, упрёшь, *past* **~́, ~́ла** *pf.* (*of* **упира́ть**) **1.** (*a.* **в**+*a.*) to rest (against), prop (against), lean (against); **у. ле́стницу в сте́ну** to rest a ladder against the wall; **у. глаза́ в кого́-н.** (*coll.*) to fasten one's gaze upon s.o. **2.** (*sl.*) to pinch, swipe.

упер|е́ться, упру́сь, упрёшься, *past* **~́ся, ~́лась** *pf.* (*of* **упира́ться**) **1.** (+*i.* **в**+*a.*) to rest (against), prop (against), lean (against); **у. ло́ктем в стол** to rest one's elbow on the table; **у. нога́ми в зе́млю** to dig one's heels in the ground. **2.** (**в**+*a.*; *coll.*) to come up (against), bump (into) (*an obstacle*). **3.** (*coll.*) to jib; (*fig.*) to dig one's heels in.

упе́|чь, ку́, чёшь, ку́т, *past* **~́к, ~кла́** *pf.* (*of* **~ка́ть**) **1.** to bake thoroughly. **2.** (*coll.*) to drag off (*against one's will*); **у. под суд** to drag into court, through the courts.

упива́|ться, юсь *impf. of* **упи́ться**

упира́|ть, ю *impf.* **1.** *impf. of* **упере́ть. 2.** (*impf. only*) (**на**+*a.*; *coll.*) to stress, insist (on).

упира́|ться, юсь *impf.* **1.** *impf. of* **упере́ться. 2.** (*impf. only*) (**в**+*a.*; *coll.*) to come up (against), be held up (by), be stuck (on account of); **прое́кт экспеди́ции ~ется в недоста́ток де́нег** the plan for an expedition is held up for want of funds.

упи|са́ть[1]**, шу́, ~́шешь** *pf.* (*of* **~́сывать**) to get in, fit in (*sth. written*); **у. всё письмо́ на одно́м листе́** to get the whole letter on one sheet (*of paper*).

упи|са́ть[2]**, шу́, ~́шешь** *pf.* (*of* **~́сывать**) (*coll.*) to get through, consume (= *to eat up*).

упи|са́ться, ~́шется *pf.* (*of* **~́сываться**) (*of sth. written*) to go in, fit in.

упи́сыва|ть(ся), ю(сь) *impf. of* **уписа́ть(ся)**

упи́танност|ь, и *f.* nutritional state.

упи́тан|ный *p.p.p. of* **упита́ть** *and adj.* **(~, ~на)** well-fed; fattened, fatted; plump.

упит|а́ть, а́ю *pf.* (*of* **~́ывать**) to fatten (up).

упи́тыва|ть, ю *impf. of* **упита́ть**

упи́|ться, упью́сь, упьёшься, *past* **~лся, ~ла́сь** *pf.* (*of* **~ва́ться**) (+*i.*) **1.** (*coll.*) to get drunk (on). **2.** (*fig.*) to revel (in), be intoxicated (by) (*sights and sounds, etc.*).

упла́т|а, ы *f.* payment, paying; **в ~у** on account, in payment; **подлежа́щий ~е** payable.

упла|ти́ть, чу́, ~́тишь *pf.* (*of* **~́чивать**) to pay; **у. чле́нский взнос** to pay a (membership) subscription; **у. по счёту** to pay a bill, settle an account.

упла́тный *adj.* relating to payment.

упле|сти́, ту́, тёшь, *past* **~́л, ~ла́** *pf.* (*of* **~та́ть**) (*coll.*) to tuck in (to).

уплета́|ть, ю *impf. of* **уплести́**

уплотне́ни|е, я *nt.* **1.** consolidation, concentration, compression; packing (in); **у. кварти́ры** reduction of space per pers. in living accommodation; **у. рабо́чего дня** tightening up time-schedules to increase amount of work done. **2.** (*tech.*) sealing, luting. **3.** (*med.*) hardening (*of skin*).

уплотн|и́ть, ю́, и́шь *pf.* (*of* **~я́ть**) **1.** to consolidate, concentrate, compress; to pack (in); **у. кварти́ру** to reduce space per pers. in living accommodation, increase number of occupants per flat; **у. рабо́чий день** to plan the working day to increase amount of work done. **2.** (*tech.*) to seal, lute.

уплотн|и́ться, ю́сь, и́шься *pf.* (*of* **~я́ться**) **1.** (*med.*) to harden. **2.** (+*i.*) to take in, give up part of one's accommodation (to). **3.** to condense, thicken; (*of fuel in combustion*) to sinter, clinker.

уплотн|я́ть(ся), я́ю(сь) *impf. of* **~и́ть(ся)**

уплыва́|ть, ю *impf. of* **уплы́ть**

уплы́|ть, ву́, вёшь, *past* **~л, ~ла́, ~ло** *pf.* (*of* **~ва́ть**) **1.** to swim away; to sail, steam away. **2.** to be lost to sight. **3.** (*fig., coll.*) to fly away, pass, elapse; **нема́ло вре́мени ~ло** much water has flowed beneath the bridges. **4.** (*fig., coll.*) to vanish, ebb; **наде́жда ~ла́** hope faded.

упова́ни|е, я *nt.* (*obs.*) hope; **возлага́ть все ~я (на**+*a.*) to set all one's hopes (upon).

упова́|ть, ю *impf.* (**на**+*a.*) to put one's trust (in); (+*inf.*) to hope to.

уподо́б|ить, лю, ишь *pf.* (*of* **~ля́ть**) to liken.

уподо́б|иться, люсь, ишься *pf.* (*of* **~ля́ться**) (+*d.*) **1.** to become like. **2.** (*ling.*) to become assimilated (to).

уподобле́ни|е, я *nt.* **1.** likening, comparison. **2.** (*ling.*) assimilation.

уподобля́|ть(ся), ю(сь) *impf. of* **уподо́бить(ся)**

упое́ни|е, я *nt.* ecstasy, rapture, thrill; **с ~ем** ecstatically.

упоённый *part. as adj.* (+*i.*) intoxicated (with), thrilled (by), in raptures (about, over).

упои́тел|ьный (~ен, ~ьна) *adj.* intoxicating, ravishing.

упокое́ни|е, я *nt.* rest, repose; **ме́сто ~я** resting-place (= *grave*).

упоко́|ить, ю, ишь *pf.* (*obs.*) to lay to rest (= *to bury*).

упоко́|иться, юсь, ишься *pf.* (*obs.*) to find repose; to find one's resting-place (= *to be buried*).

уполз|а́ть, а́ю *impf. of* **~ти́**

уполз|ти́, у́, ёшь, *past* **~́, ~ла́** *pf.* (*of* **~а́ть**) to creep, crawl away.

уполномо́ч|енный *p.p.p. of* **~ить**; *as n.* **у., ~енного** *m.* plenipotentiary, representative, pers. authorized.

уполномо́чива|ть, ю *impf. of* **уполномо́чить**

уполномо́чи|е, я *nt.* authorization; **подписа́ть докуме́нт по ~ю кого́-н.** to sign a document on s.o.'s authority.

уполномо́ч|ить, у, ишь *pf.* (*of* **~ивать**) to authorize, empower.

уполо́вник, а *m.* (*dial.*) ladle.

упомина́ни|е, я *nt.* mentioning; (**о**+*p.*) mention (of), reference (to).

упомина́|ть, ю *impf. of* **упомяну́ть**

упо́мн|ить, ю, ишь *pf.* (*coll.*) to remember.

упомян|у́ть, у́, ∽ешь *pf.* (*of* **упомина́ть**) (+*a. or* **о**+*p.*) to mention, refer (to).
упо́р, а *m.* **1.** rest, prop, support; (*tech.*) stay, brace. **2.** (*tech.*) stop, lug; arresting device. **3.: в у.** (*mil.*) point-blank (*also fig.*); **сказа́ть кому́-н. в у.** to tell s.o. point-blank, flat(ly); **смотре́ть на кого́-н. в у.** to stare straight at s.o. **4.: сде́лать у.** (**на**+*a. or p.*) to lay special stress (on).
упо́р|ный (∼ен, ∼на) *adj.* **1.** stubborn, unyielding, obstinate; dogged, persistent; sustained; **у. челове́к** stubborn pers.; **у. ка́шель** persistent cough; **∼ная оборо́на** sustained defence. **2.** (*tech.*) supporting; **у. като́к** bogie wheel; **у. подши́пник** thrust bearing. **3.** (*tech.*) stop; **у. болт** stop; **у. рыча́г** stop lever.
упо́рств|о, а *nt.* stubbornness, obstinacy; doggedness, persistence.
упо́рств|овать, ую *impf.* to be stubborn, unyielding; (**в**+*p.*) to persist (in).
упорхн|у́ть, у́, ёшь *pf.* to fly, flit away.
упоря́дочива|ть(ся), ю(сь) *impf. of* **упоря́дочить(ся)**
упоря́доч|ить, у, ишь *pf.* (*of* **∼ивать**) to regulate, put in (good) order, set to rights.
упоря́доч|иться, ится *pf.* (*of* **∼иваться**) to come right.
употреби́тельност|ь, и *f.* (frequency of) use.
употреби́тел|ьный (∼ен, ∼ьна) *adj.* (widely-)used; common, generally accepted, usual; **у. эвфеми́зм** widely-used euphemism.
употреб|и́ть, лю́, и́шь *pf.* (*of* **∼ля́ть**) (*in var. senses*) to use; to make use (of); to take (*drink, medicine, etc.*); **у. все уси́лия** to make every effort, do one's utmost; **у. чьё-н. дове́рие во зло** to abuse s.o.'s confidence.
употребле́ни|е, я *nt.* use; application; **спо́соб ∼я** directions for use (*of medicine, etc.*); **для вну́треннего ∼я** to be taken internally; **не для вну́треннего ∼я** not to be taken; **вы́йти из ∼я** to go out of use, fall into disuse; **вы́шедший из ∼я** out of use, obsolete.
употребля́|ть, ю *impf. of* **употреби́ть**
упра́в|а, ы *f.* **1.** (*coll.*) control. **2.** (*coll.*) justice, satisfaction; **иска́ть ∼ы** to seek justice; **найти́ на кого́-н. ∼у** to obtain satisfaction from s.o. **3.** (*hist.*) office, board, authority; **у. благочи́ния** police headquarters.
управде́л, а *m.* (*coll.*) = **управдела́ми**
управдела́ми *m. indecl.* (*abbr. of* **управля́ющий дела́ми**) office manager.
управдо́м, а *m.* (*abbr. of* **управля́ющий до́мом**) house-manager.
управи́тел|ь, я *m.* (*obs.*) manager, bailiff, steward.
упра́в|иться, люсь, ишься *pf.* (*of* **∼ля́ться**) (**с**+*i.*; *coll.*) **1.** to cope (with), manage. **2.** to deal (with) (= *to get the better of*).
управле́н|ец, ца *m.* (*coll.*) manager, executive.
управле́ни|е, я *nt.* **1.** management, administration; direction; **у. госуда́рством** government; **орке́стр под ∼ем Мрави́нского** orchestra conducted by Mravinsky. **2.** (*tech.*) control; driving; piloting; steering; **у. на расстоя́нии** remote control; **у. по ра́дио** radio control; **у. автомоби́лем** driving (a car); **теря́ть у.** to get out of control. **3.** government; **о́рганы ме́стного ∼я** local government organs. **4.** (*governmental organ*) administration, authority, directorate, board; **гла́вное у. ры́бного хозя́йства** chief administration of fisheries. **5.** (*tech.*) controls; steering; **щит ∼я** control panel. **6.** (*gram.*) government.
управле́н|ческий *adj. of* **∼ие 3., 4.; у. аппара́т** government apparatus.
управл|я́емый *pres. part. pass. of* **∼я́ть** *and adj.* **у. снаря́д** guided missile.
управля́|ть, ю *impf.* (+*i.*) **1.** to manage, administer, direct, run; to govern; to be in charge (of); **у. канцеля́рией** to manage an office. **2.** (*tech.*) to control, operate (*a machine*); to drive (*a car, etc.*); to pilot; to steer; **у. су́дном** (*naut.*) to navigate a vessel; **у. весло́м** to row. **3.** (*gram.*) to govern.
управл|я́ющий *pres. part. act. of* **∼я́ть** *and adj.* control, controlling; **у. вал** (*tech.*) camshaft; *as n.* **у., ∼я́ющего** *m.* manager; bailiff, steward; **у. по́ртом** harbour master.
упражне́ни|е, я *nt.* exercise.
упражня́|ть, ю *impf.* to exercise, train; **у. му́скулы** to exercise one's muscles; **у. па́мять** to train one's memory.
упражня́|ться, юсь *impf.* (**в**+*p.*, **на**+*p.*, **с**+*i.*) to practise, train (at); **у. в стрельбе́ в цель** to practise marksmanship.
упраздне́ни|е, я *nt.* abolition; cancellation, annulment.
упраздн|и́ть, ю, и́шь *pf.* (*of* **∼я́ть**) to abolish; to cancel, annul.
упраздн|я́ть, я́ю *impf. of* **∼и́ть**
упра́шива|ть, ю *impf. of* **упроси́ть**
упрева́|ть, ю *impf. of* **упре́ть**
упре|ди́ть, жу́, ди́шь *pf.* (*of* **∼жда́ть**) (*obs.*) **1.** to warn. **2.** to forestall, anticipate.
упрежда́|ть, ю *impf. of* **упреди́ть**
упрежда́ющий *adj.* (*mil.*) pre-emptive; **у. уда́р** pre-emptive strike.
упрежде́ни|е, я *nt.* **1.** (*obs.*) warning. **2.** (*obs.*) forestalling, anticipation. **3.** (*mil.*) range correction, lead (*for firing at moving target*).
упрёк, а *m.* reproach, reproof; **бро́сить у. кому́-н.** to reproach, reprove s.o.; **ста́вить кому́-н. что-н. в у.** to hold sth. against s.o.
упрек|а́ть, а́ю *impf.* (*of* **∼ну́ть**) to reproach, reprove; (**в**+*p.*) to accuse (of), charge (with).
упрек|ну́ть, ну́, нёшь *pf. of* **∼а́ть**
упре́|ть, ю *pf.* (*of* **∼ва́ть**) (*coll.*) **1.** to be well stewed. **2.** to be covered with sweat.
упро|си́ть, шу́, ∼сишь *pf.* (*of* **упра́шивать**) **1.** to beg, entreat. **2.** (*pf. only*) to prevail upon.
упро|сти́ть, щу́, сти́шь *pf.* (*of* **∼ща́ть**) **1.** to simplify; (**до**) to reduce (to). **2.** (*pej.*) to oversimplify.
упро|сти́ться, сти́тся *pf.* (*of* **∼ща́ться**) to become simpler, be simplified.
упро́чени|е, я *nt.* strengthening, consolidation; fixing, securing.
упро́чива|ть(ся), ю(сь) *impf. of* **упро́чить(ся)**
упро́ч|ить, у, ишь *pf.* (*of* **∼ивать**) **1.** to strengthen, consolidate; to fix, secure; to establish firmly, place on firm foundations. **2.** (**за**+*i.*) to grant permanent possession (to), leave (to); **у. за кем-н. всё своё состоя́ние** to leave one's entire estate to s.o. **3.** (**за**+*i.*) to ensure; **его́ Пе́рвая симфо́ния ∼ила за ним репута́цию выдаю́щегося компози́тора** his First Symphony ensured his reputation as an outstanding composer.
упро́ч|иться, усь, ишься *pf.* (*of* **∼иваться**) **1.** to be strengthened, consolidated; to become firmer; to be firmly established; **на́ше положе́ние ∼илось** our position is firmly established. **2.** to establish o.s. (firmly), settle o.s. **3.** (**за**+*i.*) (*of property, etc.*) to be settled (upon). **4.** (**за**+*i.*) to be ensured; to become firmly attached (to); **за ним ∼илась сла́ва ко́мика** his name as a comic actor was made; **про́звище ∼илось за ней** the nickname stuck to her.
упроща́|ть(ся), ю(сь) *impf. of* **упрости́ть(ся)**
упроще́н|ец, ца *m.* (*coll.*) oversimplifier.
упроще́ни|е, я *nt.* simplification.
упрощённост|ь, и *f.* **1.** simplified character. **2.** oversimplification.
упро|щённый *p.p.p. of* **∼сти́ть** *and adj.* **1.** simplified. **2.** oversimplified.
упроще́нческий *adj.* (*pej.*) oversimplified.
упроще́нчеств|о, а *nt.* (*pej.*) oversimplification.
упру́г|ий (∼, ∼а) *adj.* **1.** elastic, resilient; **∼ая похо́дка** springy gait. **2.** (*phys.*) expansible, extensible (*of gases*).
упру́гост|ь, и *f.* **1.** elasticity, resilience; spring, bound; **преде́л ∼и** (*phys.*) elastic limit. **2.** (*phys.*) expansibility, extensibility.
упру́|же *comp. of* **∼гий**
упря́жк|а, и *f.* **1.** team, relay (*of horses, dogs, etc.*). **2.** harness, gear. **3.** (*obs., coll.*) shift, stint.
упряжн|о́й *adj.* draught; **∼а́я ло́шадь** draught-horse, carriage-horse; **∼а́я тя́га** draw-bar.
у́пряж|ь, и *f.* harness, gear.
упря́м|ец, ца *m.* (*coll.*) obstinate pers.
упря́м|иться, люсь, ишься *impf.* to be obstinate; (**в**+*p.*) to persist (in).
упря́миц|а, ы *f. of* **упря́мец**
упря́мств|о, а *nt.* obstinacy, stubbornness.

упря́мств|овать, ую *impf.* = **упря́миться**
упря́м|ый (~, ~а) *adj.* **1.** obstinate, stubborn. **2.** persistent.
упря́|тать, чу, чешь *pf.* (*of* **~тывать**) **1.** to hide, conceal. **2.** (*fig.*, *coll.*) to put away, banish.
упря́|таться, чусь, чешься *pf.* (*of* **~тываться**) (*coll.*) to hide (*intrans.*)
упря́тыва|ть(ся), ю(сь) *impf.* *of* **упря́тать(ся)**
упуска́|ть, ю *impf.* *of* **упусти́ть**
упу|сти́ть, щу́, ~́стишь *pf.* (*of* **~ска́ть**) **1.** to let go, let slip, let fall; **у. пово́дья** to let the reins go. **2.** (*fig.*) to let go, let slip; to miss; to lose; **у. возмо́жность** to miss an opportunity; **у. и́з виду** to overlook, fail to take account (of). **3.** (*coll.*) to neglect.
упуще́ни|е, я *nt.* **1.** omission. **2.** (careless) slip; negligence; **у. по слу́жбе** neglect of duty, dereliction of duty.
упы́р|ь, я́ *m.* (*coll.*) vampire; ghoul; bloodsucker.
упятер|и́ть, ю́, и́шь *pf.* (*of* **~я́ть**) to increase fivefold.
упятер|я́ть, я́ю *impf.* *of* **~и́ть**
ура́ *int.* hurrah!; hurray! (*exclamation* (*i*) *expr. exultation or approbation*, (*ii*) *of troops going in to attack*); **на у.** (*i*) (*mil.*) by storm, (*ii*) (*iron.*) by luck (= *without due preparation*).
ура́- *comb. form* blind, unthinking (*e.g.* **ура́-патриоти́зм, а** *m.* jingoism).
уравне́ни|е, я *nt.* **1.** equalization. **2.** (*math.*) equation; **у. пе́рвой сте́пени** simple equation.
ура́внива|ть¹, ю *impf.* *of* **уравня́ть**
ура́внива|ть², ю *impf.* *of* **уровня́ть**
уравни́ловк|а, и *f.* (*coll.*, *pej.*) egalitarianism; **у. в опла́те труда́** wage-levelling.
уравни́тел|ь, я *m.* **1.** equalizer, leveller; regulator; **у. хо́да** governor. **2.** (*pol.*) egalitarian.
уравни́тельн|ый *adj.* (*in var. senses*) equalizing, levelling; **~ая переда́ча** (*tech.*) differential gear.
уравнове́|сить, шу, сишь *pf.* (*of* **~шивать**) **1.** to balance; (*tech.*) to equilibrate. **2.** (*fig.*) to counterbalance; to neutralize.
уравнове́шенност|ь, и *f.* (*fig.*) balance, steadiness, composure.
уравнове́|шенный *p.p.p.* *of* **~сить** *and adj.* (*fig.*) balanced, steady, composed.
уравнове́шивани|е, я *nt.* balancing; (*tech.*) equilibration.
уравнове́шива|ть, ю *impf.* *of* **уравнове́сить**
уравня́|ть, ю *pf.* (*of* **ура́внивать¹**) to equalize, make equal, make level.
ураган, а *m.* hurricane; (*fig.*) storm.
урага́н|ный *adj.* *of* **~**; **у. ого́нь** (*mil.*) drum-fire.
уразумева́|ть, ю *impf.* *of* **уразуме́ть**
уразуме́|ть, ю *pf.* (*of* **~ва́ть**) to comprehend.
Ура́л, а *m.* the Urals.
ура́льский *adj.* (*geog.*) Ural(s).
ура́н, а *m.* **1. У.** (*astron.*) Uranus. **2.** (*chem.*) uranium.
уранини́т, а *m.* (*min.*) uraninite, pitchblende.
ура́новый *adj.* uranium, uranic.
урв|а́ть, у́, ёшь, *past* **~а́л, ~ала́, ~а́ло** *pf.* (*of* **урыва́ть**) (*coll.*) to snatch (*also fig.*), grab; **у. мину́ту-две для бесе́ды** to snatch a minute or two for a chat.
урв|а́ться, у́сь, ёшься, *past* **~а́лся, ~ала́сь, ~а́ло́сь** *pf.* (*of* **урыва́ться**) (*coll.*) to break loose; (*fig.*) to get away, snatch a free minute.
урду́ *m. indecl.* Urdu (*language*).
урегули́ровани|е, я *nt.* regulation; settlement, adjustment.
урегули́р|овать, ую *pf.* (*of* **регули́ровать**) to regulate; to settle, adjust; **у. спо́рную пробле́му** to settle a dispute.
уре́з, а *m.* (*coll.*) reduction, cut.
уре́|зать, жу, жешь *pf.* (*of* **~за́ть** *and* **~зывать**) **1.** (*coll.*) to cut off; to shorten. **2.** to cut down, reduce; to axe; **у. шта́ты** to cut down the staff.
урез|а́ть, а́ю *impf.* *of* **~́ать**
урезо́нива|ть, ю *impf.* *of* **урезо́нить**
урезо́н|ить, ю, ишь *pf.* (*of* **~ивать**) (*coll.*) to make to see reason, bring to reason.
уре́зыва|ть ю *impf.* = **уреза́ть**
урем|а́, ы́ (*and* **урём|а, ы**) *f.* (*dial.*) woods along a river.
уреми́ческий *adj.* (*med.*) uraemic.
уреми́|я, и *f.* (*med.*) uraemia.
уре́тр|а, ы *f.* (*anat.*) urethra.
урети́т, а *m.* (*med.*) urethritis.
уретроско́п, а *m.* (*med.*) urethroscope.
ури́льник, а *m.* (*obs.*) chamber-pot.
ури́н|а, ы *f.* (*med.*) urine.
у́рк|а, и *c.g.* (*prison sl.*) 'urka' (*criminal serving time, as opposed to political prisoner*).
у́рн|а, ы *f.* **1.** urn. **2.: избира́тельная у.** ballot-box. **3.** refuse bin, litter receptacle.
у́ров|ень, ня *m.* **1.** (*in var. senses*) level, plane; standard; **у. мо́ря** sea level; **высота́ над ~нем мо́ря** altitude above sea level; **в у.** (**с**+*i.*) (*i*) level (with), at the height (of); flush (with), (*ii*) (*fig.*) abreast (of), in pace (with); **на ~не земли́** at ground level; **быть на ~не** to satisfy requirements; **совеща́ние на высо́ком ~не** (*pol.*) high-level conference. **2.** (*tech.*) level, gauge.
уровнеме́р, а *m.* (*tech.*) water-level.
уровня́|ть, ю *pf.* (*of* **ура́внивать²**) to level, make even.
уро́д, а *m.* **1.** freak, monster; deformed pers. **2.** ugly pers.; (*morally*) depraved pers.
уро́дин|а, ы *c.g.* (*coll.*) = **уро́д**
уро|ди́ть, жу́, ди́шь *pf.* (*coll.*) to bear, bring forth.
уро|ди́ться, жу́сь, ди́шься *pf.* **1.** (*of crops*, *etc.*) to ripen; (*of a human being*) to be born. **2.** (**в**+*a.*; *coll.*) to take after.
уро́дливост|ь, и *f.* **1.** deformity. **2.** ugliness.
уро́длив|ый (~, ~а) *adj.* **1.** deformed, misshapen. **2.** ugly. **3.** (*fig.*) ugly, bad; abnormal; faulty; distorting, distorted; **~ое воспита́ние** bad upbringing; **у. перево́д** faulty translation.
уро́д|овать, ую *impf.* (*of* **из~**) **1.** to deform, disfigure, mutilate. **2.** to make ugly. **3.** (*fig.*) to distort.
уро́д|ский *adj.* (*coll.*) **1.** *adj.* *of* **~**. **2.** distorted.
уро́дств|о, а *nt.* **1.** deformity; disfigurement. **2.** ugliness. **3.** (*fig.*) abnormality.
урожа́|й, я *m.* **1.** harvest; crop, yield; **собра́ть у.** to gather in the harvest. **2.** bumper crop, abundance (*also fig.*, *coll.*); **в э́том году́ был урожа́й на детекти́вные рома́ны** this year there has been a bumper crop of detective stories.
урожа́йност|ь, и *f.* productivity (*of crops*), (level of) yield.
урожа́|йный (~ен, ~йна) *adj.* **1.** *adj.* *of* **~й. 2.** producing high yield, productive; **у. год** good year (*for a crop*).
урождённ|ый *p.p.p.* *of* **уроди́ть** *and adj.* **1. ~ая** (*before maiden name*) née. **2.** (*obs.*) inborn, born.
уроже́н|ец, ца *m.* (+*g.*) native (of).
уроже́н|ка, ки *f.* *of* **~ец**
уро́к, а *m.* **1.** lesson (*also fig.*); **брать ~и** (+*g.*) to have, take lessons, tuition (in); **дава́ть ~и** (+*g.*) to teach, give lessons, give tuition (in); **дать кому́-н. у.** (*fig.*) to teach s.o. a lesson; **жить на ~е** (*obs.*) to be, earn one's living as a (private) tutor. **2.** homework; lesson, task; **зада́ть у.** to set homework; **отвеча́ть у.** to repeat one's lesson. **3.** (*obs.*) task, work.
уро́лог, а *m.* (*med.*) urologist.
урологи́ческий *adj.* (*med.*) urological.
уроло́ги|я, и *f.* (*med.*) urology.
уро́н, а *no pl.*, *m.* losses, casualties; **нанести́ у.** to inflict casualties.
урон|и́ть, ю́, ~́ишь *pf.* **1.** *pf.* *of* **роня́ть. 2.** (*obs.*, *coll.*) to ruin, cause to collapse.
уро́чищ|е, а *nt.* (*geog.*) **1.** natural boundary. **2.** isolated terrain feature (*e.g. wood in swamp country*).
уро́чн|ый *adj.* **1.** (*obs.*) fixed, agreed; **~ая рабо́та** piece-work; **~ая цена́** fixed price. **2.** usual, established.
уругва́|ец, йца *m.* Uruguayan.
Уругва́|й, я *m.* Uruguay.
уругва́|йка, йки *f.* *of* **~ец**
уругва́йский *adj.* Uruguayan.
урча́ни|е, я *nt.* rumbling; **у. в желу́дке** (*coll.*) tummy-rumbling.
урч|а́ть, у́, и́шь *impf.* to rumble.
урыва́|ть(ся), ю(сь) *impf.* *of* **урва́ть(ся)**
уры́вками *adv.* (*coll.*) in snatches, by fits and starts; at odd moments.

урывоч|ный (~ен, ~на) *adj.* (*coll.*) fitful; occasional.
урюк, а (у) *no pl.*, *m.* (*collect.*) dried apricots.
урюк|овый *adj. of* ~
уряд, а *m.* (*obs.*) **1.** rule; customs, observances. **2.** rank.
уря|дить, жу, ~дишь *pf.* (*of* **~жать**) (*obs.*) to arrange, put in order.
урядник, а *m.* (*hist.*) **1.** Cossack NCO (= *non-commissioned officer; in tsarist Russ. army*). **2.** village constable.
уряжа|ть, ю *impf. of* **урядить**
ус, а *m.* **1.** (*see also* **~ы**) moustache hair; **и в ус (себе) не дуть** (*coll.*) not to give a damn; **мотать (себе) на ус** (*coll.*) to take good note (of). **2.** whisker (*of an animal*). **3.** antenna, feeler (*of an insect*). **4.** (*bot.*) tendril; awn. **5.**: **китовый ус** whalebone, baleen.
усад|ебный *adj. of* **~ьба; у. быт** life of country gentry.
уса|дить, жу, ~дишь *pf.* (*of* **~живать**) **1.** to seat, help sit down; to make sit down; **у. в тюрьму** (*coll.*) to throw into jail; **у. в печь** (*coll.*) to put into the oven. **2.** (**за**+*a. or* +*inf.*) to set (to, at); **у. кого-н. за рояль** to set s.o. to (play at) the piano. **3.** (+*i.*) to plant (with). **4.** (+*i.*) to cover (with); **стена, ~женная пятнами** a wall covered with stains.
усадк|а, и *f.* shrinking; shrinkage; contraction.
усадьб|а, ы, *g. pl.* ~ *and* **усадеб** *f.* **1.** (*hist.*) country estate; country seat. **2.** farmstead; farm centre (*in former USSR, of collective or State farm*).
усажива|ть, ю *impf. of* **усадить**
усажива|ться, юсь *impf. of* **усесться**
усаст|ый (~) *adj.* (*coll.*) with a big moustache.
усат|ый (~, ~а) *adj.* **1.** moustached; with a big moustache. **2.** (*of animals*) whiskered.
усахар|ить, ю, ишь *pf.* (*coll.*) **1.** to sugar plentifully. **2.** to win over by flattery. **3.** (*obs.*) to beat to death.
усач, а *m.* **1.** (*coll.*) man with a (big) moustache. **2.** barbel (*fish*). **3.** Capricorn beetle (*Agapanthia dahli*).
усваива|ть, ю *impf. of* **усвоить**
усвоени|е, я *nt.* mastering; assimilation.
усво|ить, ю, ишь *pf.* (*of* **усваивать**) **1.** to adopt, acquire (*a habit, etc.*); to imitate; **у. чужой выговор** to pick up s.o. else's accent. **2.** to master (= *to learn*); to assimilate; **у. правила уличного движения** to master the traffic regulations. **3.** (+*d.*; *obs.*) to inculcate (in). **4.** to assimilate (*food, medicine, etc.*).
усвояемост|ь, и *f.* **1.** comprehensibility; **хорошая у.** ease of comprehension, easiness. **2.** (*chem.*) assimilability.
усеива|ть, ю *impf. of* **усеять**
усека|ть, ю *impf. of* **усечь**
усекновени|е, я *nt.* (*relig.*): **у. главы** beheading (*of St. John Baptist*).
усерди|е, я *nt.* zeal; diligence, painstakingness.
усерд|ный (~ен, ~на) *adj.* zealous, diligent, painstaking.
усердств|овать, ую *impf.* to be zealous; to take pains.
усе|сться, усядусь, усядешься, *past* **~лся, ~лась** *pf.* (*of* **усаживаться**) **1.** to take a seat; to settle (down). **2.** (**за**+*a. or* +*inf.*) to set (to), settle down (to); **у. за карты** to settle down to (a game of) cards.
усеч|ённый *p.p.p. of* **~ь** *and adj.* (*math.*) truncated.
усе|чь, ку, чёшь, кут, *past* **~к, ~кла** *pf.* (*of* **~кать**) to cut off, truncate.
усе|ять, ю, ешь *pf.* (*of* **~ивать**) (+*i.*) **1.** to sow (with). **2.** to cover (with), dot (with), stud (with), litter (with), strew (with); **лицо, ~янное веснушками** face covered with freckles; **берег моря, ~янный медузами** sea-shore littered with jelly-fish.
уси|деть, жу, дишь *pf.* **1.** to keep one's place, remain sitting; **он так волновался, что еле мог у.** he was so excited that he could hardly sit still. **2.** (*coll.*) to hold down a job, keep a job. **3.** (*sl.*) to guzzle; to knock back (*drink*).
усидчивост|ь, и *f.* assiduity.
усидчив|ый (~, ~а) *adj.* assiduous; painstaking.
усик, а *m.* **1.** (*pl.*) small moustache. **2.** (*bot.*) tendril; awn; runner (*of strawberry, etc.*). **3.** (*zool.*) antenna, feeler.
усилени|е, я *nt.* **1.** strengthening; reinforcement. **2.** intensification; aggravation; (*radio*) amplification.
усил|енный *p.p.p. of* **~ить** *and adj.* **1.** reinforced; **~енное питание** high-caloric diet. **2.** intensified, increased; **~енная работа** high pressure of work. **3.** earnest, urgent, importunate; **~енные просьбы** earnest entreaties.
усилива|ть, ю *impf. of* **усилить**
усилива|ться, юсь *impf.* **1.** *impf. of* **усилиться. 2.** (+*inf.*; *obs.*) to try (to), make an effort (to).
усили|е, я *nt.* effort; exertion; **приложить все ~я** to make every effort, spare no effort.
усилител|ь, я *m.* **1.** (*tech.*) booster. **2.** (*radio*) amplifier. **3.** (*chem.*) active filler (*of rubber*).
усилительный *adj.* **1.** (*tech.*) booster. **2.** (*radio*) amplifying.
усил|ить, ю, ишь *pf.* (*of* **~ивать**) **1.** to strengthen, reinforce. **2.** to intensify, increase, heighten; to aggravate; (*radio*) to amplify.
усил|иться, ится *pf.* (*of* **~иваться**) to become stronger; to intensify, increase (*intrans.*); to become aggravated; (*of sound*) to swell, grow louder.
усильный *adj.* (*obs.*) earnest, urgent, importunate.
уска|кать, чу, ~чешь *pf.* **1.** to bound away; (*coll.*) to skip off, slip off. **2.** to gallop off.
ускольз|ать, аю *impf. of* **~нуть**
ускольз|нуть, ну, нёшь *pf.* (*of* **~ать**) **1.** to slip off. **2.** (*coll., of a pers.*) to slip off, steal away; to get away. **3.** (*fig.*) to disappear; to escape; **у. от внимания** to escape one's notice. **4.** (**от**; *coll.*) to evade, avoid; **у. от прямого ответа** to avoid giving a direct answer.
ускорени|е, я *nt.* acceleration; speeding up.
ускор|енный *p.p.p. of* **~ить** *and adj.* accelerated; rapid; hasty; crash; **у. аллюр** increased gait; **~енная программа** crash programme.
ускорител|ь, я *m.* (*tech.*) accelerator.
ускор|ить, ю, ишь *pf.* (*of* **~ять**) **1.** to quicken; to speed up, accelerate; **у. шаг** to quicken one's pace. **2.** to hasten; to precipitate.
ускор|иться, ится *pf.* (*of* **~яться**) **1.** to quicken; to accelerate. **2.** *pass of* **~ить**
ускор|ять, яю *impf. of* **~ить**
ускор|яться, яется *impf. of* **~иться**
уславливаться = условливаться
услад|а, ы *f.* (*obs.*) joy, delight; enjoyment.
усладител|ьный (~ен, ~ьна) *adj.* (*obs.*) pleasing, delightful.
усла|дить, жу, дишь *pf.* (*of* **~ждать**) (*obs. or poet.*) **1.** to delight, charm. **2.** to soften, mitigate.
усла|диться, жусь, дишься *pf.* (*of* **~ждаться**) (+*i.*; *obs. or poet.*) to delight (in).
услажда|ть(ся), ю(сь) *impf. of* **усладить(ся)**
усла|стить, щу, стишь *pf.* (*of* **~щать**) to sweeten.
услать, ушлю, ушлёшь *pf.* (*of* **усылать**) to send away, dispatch; **у. на каторгу** (*coll.*) to send away to (do) hard labour.
услаща|ть, ю *impf. of* **усластить**
усле|дить, жу, дишь *pf.* (**за**+*i.*) **1.** to keep an eye (on), mind. **2.** to follow; **у. за ходом рассказа** to follow a story.
услови|е, я *nt.* **1.** condition; clause, term; stipulation, proviso; **поставить ~ем** to make it a condition, stipulate; **под ~ем, что; при ~и, что; с ~ем, что** on condition that, provided that, providing. **2.** (*obs.*) agreement; **заключить у.** to conclude an agreement. **3.** (*pl.*) conditions; **~я погоды** weather conditions; **~я приёма** (*radio*) reception; **при прочих равных ~ях** other things being equal.
услов|иться, люсь, ишься *pf.* (*of* **~ливаться**) to agree, settle; to arrange, make arrangements; **мы ~ились о месте свидания** we agreed on a meeting-place.
условленный *adj.* agreed, fixed, stipulated; **в у. час** at the hour agreed.
условлива|ться, юсь *impf. of* **условиться**
условност|ь, и *f.* **1.** conditional character. **2.** convention, conventionality.
услов|ный *adj.* **1.** conventional; agreed, prearranged; **у. знак** conventional sign; **~ное название** code name; **у. жест** conventional gesture. **2.** (**~ен, ~на**) conditional; **у. приговор** (*leg.*) suspended sentence; **~ное согласие** conditional consent. **3.** (**~ен, ~на**) relative. **4.** theoretical; **~ное топливо** ideal fuel, comparison fuel. **5.** (*gram.*)

conditional. **6.: у. рефлéкс** (*physiol.*) conditioned reflex.
усложнéни|е, я *nt.* complication.
усложн|ённый *p.p.p. of* **~и́ть** *and adj.* complicated.
усложн|и́ть, ю́, и́шь *pf.* (*of* **~я́ть**) to complicate.
усложн|и́ться, и́тся *pf.* (*of* **~я́ться**) to become complicated.
усложн|я́ть, я́ю *impf. of* **~и́ть**
усложн|я́ться, я́ется *impf. of* **~и́ться**
услу́г|а, и *f.* **1.** service; good turn; **до́брые ~и** (*dipl.*) good offices; **оказа́ть ~у** to do a service; **предложи́ть свои́ ~и** to offer one's services; **к ва́шим ~ам** at your service. **2.** (*pl.*) service(s); **ко́мната со всеми ~ами** room with service; **коммуна́льные ~и** public utilities. **3.** (*collect.*; *obs.*) servants, domestics.
услужéни|е, я *nt.* (*obs.*) service; **быть в ~и (у)** to be in service (with); (*fig.*; *iron.*) to be a lackey (of).
услу́жива|ть, ю *impf.* (*obs.*) **1.** *impf. of* **услужи́ть. 2.** to serve, act as a servant.
услуж|и́ть, у́, ~ишь *pf.* (*of* **~ивать**) (*+d.*) to do a service, good turn.
услу́жлив|ый (~, ~а) *adj.* obliging.
услыха́ть = **услы́шать**
услы́ш|ать, у, ишь *pf.* (*of* **слы́шать**) **1.** to hear. **2.** (*coll.*) to perceive, sense; (*of animals*) to scent.
усма́трива|ть, ю *impf. of* **усмотрéть**
усмех|а́ться, а́юсь *impf. of* **~ну́ться**
усмех|ну́ться, ну́сь, нёшься *pf.* (*of* **~а́ться**) to smile; to grin.
усмéшк|а, и *f.* smile, grin.
усмирéни|е, я *nt.* suppression, putting down; pacification.
усмир|и́ть, ю́, и́шь *pf.* (*of* **~я́ть**) **1.** to pacify; to calm, quieten; (*fig.*) to tame. **2.** to suppress, put down (*a mutiny, etc.*).
усмир|я́ть, я́ю *impf. of* **~и́ть**
усмотрéни|е, я *nt.* discretion, judgement; **предоста́вить чьему́-н. ~ю, на чьё-н. у.** to leave to s.o.'s discretion; **поступи́ть по своему́ ~ю** to use one's own discretion, act as one thinks best.
усмотр|éть, ю́, ~ишь *pf.* (*of* **усма́тривать**) **1. (за**+*i.*) to keep an eye (on). **2.** (*coll.*) to perceive, observe. **3. (в**+*p.*) to see (in); to regard (as), interpret (as); **у. угро́зу в заявлéнии** to interpret the statement as a threat.
усна|сти́ть, щу́, сти́шь *pf.* (*of* **~ща́ть**) (*+i.*; *coll.*) **1.** to rig (*a boat*). **2.** (*fig.*) to adorn (with); to stuff (with), lard (with); **у. речь ци́фрами** to stuff a speech with figures.
уснаща́|ть, ю *impf. of* **усласти́ть**
усн|у́ть, у́, ёшь *pf.* **1.** to go to sleep, fall asleep (*also fig.*); **у. вéчным сном, навéки** (*rhet.*) to pass on to one's eternal rest. **2.** (*of fish*) to die.
усо́биц|а, ы *f.* (*hist.*) intestine strife.
усовершéнствовани|е, я *nt.* **1.** finishing, qualifying; **ку́рсы ~я** finals course(s). **2.** improvement, development, refinement.
усовершéнствов|анный *p.p.p. of* **~ать** *and adj.* **1.** finished, complete (*education, etc.*). **2.** improved (*model of machine, etc.*)
усовершéнств|овать(ся), ую(сь) *pf. of* **совершéнствовать(ся)**
усо́ве|стить, щу, стишь *pf.* (*of* **~щивать**) to appeal to the conscience (of); to make ashamed.
усо́ве|ститься, щусь, стишься *pf.* (*of* **~щиваться**) to be sorry, be conscience-stricken.
усо́вещива|ть(ся), ю(сь) *impf. of* **усо́вестить(ся)**
усомн|и́ться, ю́сь, и́шься *pf.* **(в**+*p.*) to doubt.
усо́пш|ий *adj.* (*obs.*) deceased; *as n.* **у., ~его** *m.*, **~ая, ~ей** *f.* the deceased.
усо́х|нуть, ну, нешь, *past* **~, ~ла** *pf.* (*of* **усыха́ть**) to dry up, dry out.
успева́емост|ь, и *f.* progress (*in studies*).
успева́|ть, ю *impf.* **1.** *impf. of* **успéть. 2.** (*impf. only*) **(в**+*p. or* **по**+*d.*) to make progress (in), get on well (in, at) (*of studies*).
успéется *impers., pf.* (*coll.*) there's plenty of time; there is no (need to) hurry.
успéни|е, я *nt.* (*eccl.*) **1.** death, passing. **2. У.** (Feast of) the Dormition, Assumption (of the Virgin).
успéн|ский *adj. of* **~ие 2.**
успé|ть, ю *pf.* (*of* **~ва́ть**) **1.** to have time; to manage; **у. написа́ть** to have time to write; **у. на заседа́ние** to be in time for the meeting; **у. к по́езду** to manage to catch the train; **не у. сдéлать что-н., как...** not to have time to do sth. before .... **2. (в**+*p.*) to succeed (in), be successful (in).
успéх, а *m.* **1.** success; **имéть большо́й у.** to be a great success; **по́льзоваться ~ом** to be a success; **с тем же ~ом** equally well, with the same result. **2.** (*pl.*) success, progress; **как ва́ши ~и?** how are you getting on? **дéлать ~и (в**+*p.*) to make progress (in), get on (at).
успéшност|ь, и *f.* success; progress.
успéш|ный (~ен, ~на) *adj.* successful.
успока́ива|ть(ся), ю(сь) *impf. of* **успоко́ить(ся)**
успока́ив|ающий *pres. part. act. of* **~ать** *and adj.* sedative; **~ающее срéдство** sedative.
успокоéни|е, я *nt.* **1.** calming, quieting, soothing; (*med.*) sedation. **2.** calm; peace, tranquillity.
успоко́енност|ь, и *f.* calmness; tranquillity.
успокои́тел|ьный (~ен, ~ьна) *adj.* calming, soothing; reassuring; *as n.* **~ьное, ~ьного** *nt.* sedative.
успоко́|ить, ю, ишь *pf.* (*of* **успока́ивать**) **1.** to calm, quiet, soothe; to reassure, set at rest, set one's mind at rest. **2.** to assuage, deaden (*pain, etc.*); **у. чьи-н. подозрéния** to still s.o.'s suspicions. **3.** (*coll.*) to reduce to order, control; **у. детéй** to make children be quiet.
успоко́|иться, юсь, ишься *pf.* (*of* **успока́иваться**) **1.** to calm down; to compose o.s. **2. (на дости́гнутом)** to rest content (with what has been achieved). **3.** (*of pain, etc.*) to abate; (*of the sea*) to become still; (*of the wind*) to drop. **4.** *pass. of* **~ить**
уст|а́, ~, ~а́м *no sg.* (*obs. or poet.*) mouth, lips; **вложи́ть в чьи-н. у.** (*fig.*) to put into s.o.'s mouth; **из ~ в у.** by word of mouth; **узна́ть из пéрвых, вторы́х ~** to learn at first, second hand; **э́то у всех на ~а́х** everyone's talking about it; **твои́ми бы ~а́ми мёд пить** if only you were right.
уста́в[1]**, а** *m.* regulations, rules, statutes; (*mil.*) service regulations; (*monastic*) rule; **у. университéта** university statutes; **У. КПСС** Rules of the CPSU (*Communist Party of the Soviet Union*); **У. ООН** UN (*United Nations*) Charter.
уста́в[2]**, а** *m.* (*palaeog.*) uncial (writing).
уста|ва́ть, ю́, ёшь *impf. of* **~ть; не ~ва́я** (*as adv.*) incessantly, uninterruptedly.
уста́в|ить, лю, ишь *pf.* (*of* **~ля́ть**) (*coll.*) **1.** to set, arrange, dispose; **у. мéбель в ко́мнате** to arrange furniture about the room. **2.** (*+i.*) to cover (with), fill (with), pile (with); **у. стол буты́лками** to cover a table with bottles. **3. (глаза́,** *etc.* **на**+*a.*) to direct, fix (one's gaze, *etc.*, upon).
уста́в|иться, люсь, ишься *pf.* (*of* **~ля́ться**) (*coll.*) **1.** to find room, go in. **2. (на**+*a.*) to fix one's gaze (upon), stare (at). **3.** (*obs.*) to become fixed, become steady.
уставля́|ть(ся), ю(сь) *impf. of* **уста́вить(ся)**
уста́вный[1] *adj.* regulation, statutory, prescribed.
уста́в|ный[2] *adj. of* **~**[2]
уста́лост|ь, и *f.* fatigue, tiredness, weariness; **у. метáлла** (*tech.*) metal fatigue; **испыта́ние на у.** fatigue test.
уста́лый *adj.* tired, weary, fatigued.
у́стал|ь, и *f.* (*obs. or coll.*) = **~ость; без ~и** tirelessly, untiringly, unceasingly.
устана́влива|ть(ся), ю(сь) *impf. of* **установи́ть(ся)**
установ|и́ть, лю́, ~ишь *pf.* (*of* **устана́вливать**) **1.** to place, put, set up; (*tech.*) to install, mount, rig up. **2. (на**+*a.*; **по**+*d.*) to adjust, regulate, set (to; by); **у. часы́ по ра́дио** to set one's watch by the radio. **3.** to establish, institute; **у. связь (с**+*i.*; *mil.*) to establish communication (with). **4.** to fix, prescribe, establish; **у. сро́ки о́тдыха** to fix holidays. **5.** to secure, obtain; **у. тишину́** to secure quiet. **6.** to establish, determine; to ascertain; **у. причи́ну ава́рии** to establish the cause of a crash.
установ|и́ться, лю́сь, ~ишься *pf.* (*of* **устана́вливаться**) **1.** (*coll.*) to take position, dispose o.s. **2.** to be settled, be established; to set in; **~и́лся обы́чай** it has become a custom; **пого́да ~и́лась** the weather has become settled. **3.** (*of character, etc.*) to be formed, be fixed.

установк|а, и *f.* **1.** placing, putting, setting up, arrangement; (*tech.*) installation, mounting, rigging. **2.** adjustment, regulation, setting; **у. взрывателя** fuse setting. **3.** (*tech.*) plant, unit, installation. **4.** aim, purpose; **иметь ~у (на+***a.***)** to aim (at). **5.** directions, directive.

установлени|е, я *nt.* **1.** (*in var. senses*) establishment. **2.** (*obs.*) statute; institution.

установ|ленный *p.p.p. of* **~ить** *and adj.* established, fixed, prescribed, regulation; **в ~ленном порядке** in prescribed manner; **в ~ленной форме** in due form, in accordance with set form.

установ|очный *adj.* **1.** (*tech.*) *adj. of* **~ка 1., 2.; у. винт** adjusting screw; **у. кронштейн** mounting bracket. **2.** *adj. of* **~ка 5.; у. вопрос** fundamental question.

установщик, а *m.* fitter, mounter; (*mil.*) (instrument) setter.

устарева|ть, ю *impf. of* **устареть**

устаре|вший *past. part. act. of* **~ть** *and adj.* obsolete.

устарелый *adj.* obsolete; antiquated, out of date.

устаре|ть, ю *pf.* (*of* **~вать**) **1.** (*obs.*) to grow old. **2.** to become obsolete; to become antiquated, out of date.

уста|ть, ну, нешь *pf.* (*of* **~вать**) to become tired; **я ~л** I am tired.

устерега|ть, ю *impf. of* **устеречь**

устере|чь, гу, жёшь, гут, *past* **~г, ~гла** *pf.* (*of* **~гать**) (**от**; *coll.*) to guard (against); to keep watch over.

устила|ть, ю *impf. of* **устлать**

устлать, устелю, устелешь *pf.* (*of* **устилать**) (+*i.*) to cover (with); to pave (with).

устно *adv.* orally, by word of mouth.

устн|ый *adj.* oral, verbal; **~ая речь** spoken language; **~ая словесность** oral literature; **у. экзамен** oral (examination).

усто|й[1]**, я** *m.* **1.** (*tech.*) abutment, buttress, pier (*of bridge*). **2.** foundation, support. **3.** (*pl.*; *fig.*) foundations, bases.

усто|й[2]**, я** *m.* (*coll.*) thickened layer on surface of liquid; **у. молока** cream.

устойчивост|ь, и *f.* stability, steadiness, firmness.

устойчив|ый (~, ~а) *adj.* stable, steady, firm (*also fig.*); **~ая валюта** stable currency; **~ая погода** settled weather; **~ое соединение** (*chem.*) stable compound.

усто|ять, ю, ишь *pf.* **1.** to keep one's balance, remain standing. **2.** (*fig.*) to stand one's ground. **3.** to resist, hold out; **у. перед соблазном** to resist a temptation.

усто|яться, ится *pf.* **1.** (*esp. of liquids*) to settle. **2.** (*coll.*; *of beer, etc.*) to have stood (*sufficient time*). **3.** (*coll.*) to become fixed, become permanent.

устраива|ть(ся), ю(сь) *impf. of* **устроить(ся)**

устранени|е, я *nt.* removal, elimination, clearing.

устран|ить, ю, ишь *pf.* (*of* **~ять**) **1.** to remove, eliminate, clear; **у. преграды** to remove obstacles. **2.** to remove (*from office*), dismiss.

устран|иться, юсь, ишься *pf.* (*of* **~яться**) **1.** to resign, retire, withdraw. **2.** *pass. of* **~ить**

устран|ять(ся), яю(сь) *impf. of* **~ить(ся)**

устраш|ать(ся), аю(сь) *impf. of* **~ить(ся)**

устраша|ющий *pres. part. act. of* **~ть** *and adj.* frightening, appalling.

устрашени|е, я *nt.* **1.** frightening; **средство ~я** (*mil., pol.*) deterrent. **2.** fright, fear.

устраш|ить, у, ишь *pf.* (*of* **~ать**) to frighten, scare, inspire fear (in).

устраш|иться, усь, ишься *pf.* (*of* **~аться**) to be afraid, take fright, be scared.

устрем|ить, лю, ишь *pf.* (*of* **~лять**) **(на+***a.***)** **1.** (*obs.*) to throw (*troops, etc.*) (against). **2.** to direct (to, at); **у. глаза на что-н.** to fasten one's gaze upon sth.

устрем|иться, люсь, ишься *pf.* (*of* **~ляться**) **1.** (**на**+*a.*) to rush (upon, at); to head (for). **2.** (**на**+*a.*; **к**) to be directed (at, towards), be fixed (upon), be concentrated (on); (*of a pers.*) to concentrate (on).

устремлени|е, я *nt.* **1.** rush. **2.** striving, aspiration.

устремлённост|ь, и *f.* tendency.

устремля|ть(ся), ю(сь) *impf. of* **устремить(ся)**

устриц|а, ы *f.* oyster.

устри|чный *adj. of* **~ца; ~чная раковина** oyster shell; **у. завод** oyster farm.

устроени|е, я *nt.* **1.** arranging, organization. **2.** (*obs.*) apparatus, mechanism.

устроител|ь, я *m.* organizer.

устро|ить, ю, ишь *pf.* (*of* **устраивать**) **1.** to make, construct. **2.** to arrange, organize; to establish; **у. концерт** to arrange a concert. **3.** (*fig., coll.*) to make, cause, create; **у. скандал** to make a scene. **4.** to settle, order, put in (good) order. **у. свой дела** to put one's affairs in order. **5.** to place, fix up; to get, secure; **у. кого-н. на работу** to fix s.o. up with work, find s.o. a job. **у. кому-н. комнату** (*coll.*) to get s.o. a room. **6.** (*impers.*; *coll.*) to suit, be convenient (to, for).

устро|иться, юсь, ишься *pf.* (*of* **устраиваться**) **1.** to work out (well); to come right. **2.** to manage, make arrangements. **3.** to settle down, get settled. **4.** to get fixed up (*in a job*); **он ~ился на железную дорогу кочегаром** he has got a job on the railway as a fireman.

устройств|о, а *nt.* **1.** arrangement, organization. **2.** (mode of) construction; layout; (*tech.*) working principle(s). **3.** apparatus, mechanism, device; **запоминающее у.** (*comput.*) storage (device), memory; **постоянное запоминающее у.** (*comput.*) ROM (*read-only memory*). **4.** structure, system; **общественное у.** social structure.

уступ, а *m.* **1.** shelf, ledge (*of wall or cliff*); spur (*of hill*); terrace; (*geol.*) bench; **расположенный ~ами** terraced. **2.** (*mil.*) echelon formation (*of artillery*).

уступ|ать, аю *impf. of* **~ить**

уступительный *adj.* (*gram.*) concessive.

уступ|ить, лю, ~ишь *pf.* (*of* **~ать**) **1.** (+*d.*) to let have, give up (to); to cede (to); to concede (to); **у. кому-н. место** to give up one's place to s.o.; **у. дорогу** (+*d.*) to make way (for), let pass. **2.** (+*d.*) to yield (to), give in (to). **3.** (+*d.*) to be inferior (to); **как забавник, он никому не ~ит** as an entertainer he is second to none. **4.** (*coll.*) to let have (= *to sell*). **5.** (*coll.*) to take off, knock off (= *to reduce the price by*).

уступк|а, и *f.* **1.** concession, compromise; **сделать ~и** to make concessions, compromise. **2.** reduction (*of price*).

уступчат|ый (~, ~а) *adj.* ledged, stepped, terraced.

уступчивост|ь, и *f.* pliancy; compliance, tractability.

уступчив|ый (~, ~а) pliant, pliable; compliant, tractable.

усты|дить, жу, дишь *pf.* to shame, put to shame.

усты|диться, жусь, дишься *pf.* (+*g.*) to be ashamed (of); to feel embarrassed (for).

усть|е, я, *g. pl.* **~ев** *nt.* **1.** mouth, estuary (*of a river*). **2.** mouth, orifice (*of furnace, pipe, etc.*)

устье|вый (*and* **устьевой**) *adj. of* **~**

устьиц|е, а *nt.* **1.** *dim. of* **устье. 2.** (*bot.*) stoma.

усугуб|ить, ~лю, ~ишь *pf.* (*of* **~лять**) to increase; to intensify; to aggravate.

усугубля|ть, ю *impf. of* **усугубить**

усуш|аться, ается *impf. of* **~иться**

усуш|иться, ~ится *pf.* (*of* **~аться**) **1.** (*coll.*) to shrink (*in drying*). **2.** to lose weight (*in drying*).

усушк|а, и *f.* **1.** (*coll.*) shrinkage (*in drying*). **2.** (*comm.*) wastage, loss of weight (*through drying*).

ус|ы, ов *pl.* (*sg.* **ус, а** *m.*) moustache (*see also* **ус**); **мы, etc. сами с ~ами** (*coll.*) we, *etc.*, weren't born yesterday.

усыла|ть, ю *impf. of* **услать**

усыновител|ь, я *m.* (*leg.*) adopter, adoptive father.

усыновительниц|а, ы *f.* (*leg.*) adoptive mother.

усынов|ить, лю, ишь *pf.* (*of* **~лять**) to adopt.

усыновлени|е, я *nt.* adoption.

усыновля|ть, ю *impf. of* **усыновить**

усыпальниц|а, ы *f.* burial-vault.

усып|ать, лю, лешь *pf.* (*of* **~ать**) (+*i.*) to strew (with), scatter (with); (*fig.*) to cover (with).

усып|ать, аю *impf. of* **~ать**

усыпител|ьный (~ен, ~ьна) *adj.* soporific (*also fig.*); **~ьное средство** sleeping-draught.

усып|ить, лю, ишь *pf.* (*of* **~лять**) **1.** to put to sleep (*by means of narcotics, etc.*); to lull to sleep. **2.** (*fig.*) to lull; to weaken, undermine, neutralize; **у. совесть** to lull one's conscience; **у. боль** to deaden pain. **3.** to put (*an animal*) to sleep.

усыпле́ни|е, я *nt.* **1.** putting to sleep; lulling (to sleep). **2.** (*obs.*) sleep.
усыпля́|ть, ю *impf. of* **усыпи́ть**
усыха́|ть, ю *impf. of* **усо́хнуть**
у́ська|ть, ю *impf.* (*hunting and fig.*; *coll.*) to set on.
ута́ива|ть, ю *impf. of* **утаи́ть**
ута|и́ть, ю́, и́шь *pf.* (*of* **~́ивать**) **1.** to conceal; to keep to o.s., keep secret. **2.** to appropriate.
ута́йк|а, и *f.* (*coll.*) **1.** concealment; **без ~и** frankly, openly. **2.** appropriation.
ута́птыва|ть, ю *impf. of* **утопта́ть**
ута́скива|ть, ю *impf. of* **утащи́ть**
утащ|и́ть, у́, ~́ишь *pf.* (*of* **ута́скивать**) **1.** to drag away, off (*also fig.*); **у. кого́-н. в кино́** (*coll.*) to drag s.o. off to the cinema. **2.** (*coll.*) to walk off with (= *to steal*).
у́твар|ь, и *no pl.*, *f.* (*collect.*) utensils, equipment.
утверди́тел|ьный (~ен, ~ьна) *adj.* affirmative.
утвер|ди́ть, жу́, ди́шь *pf.* (*of* **~жда́ть**) **1.** (*obs.*) to fix, secure. **2.** to establish (*securely*, *firmly*); **у. диктату́ру** to establish a dictatorship; **у. за кем-н. пра́во на име́ние** to establish s.o.'s right to an estate. **3.** (**в**+*p.*) to confirm (in) (*intention*, *opinion*, *etc.*) **4.** to approve; to confirm; to sanction, ratify; **у. пове́стку дня** to approve an agenda; **у. завеща́ние** to prove a will; **у. кого́-н. в до́лжности** to confirm s.o.'s tenure of an office.
утвер|ди́ться, жу́сь, ди́шься *pf.* (*of* **~жда́ться**) **1.** to gain a foothold, gain a firm hold (*also fig.*); to become firmly established. **2.** (**в**+*p.*) to be confirmed in (*one's resolve*, *etc.*); **у. в мы́сли** to become firmly convinced.
утвержда́|ть, ю *impf.* **1.** *impf. of* **утверди́ть**. **2.** (*impf. only*) to assert, affirm, hold, maintain, claim, allege.
утвержда́|ться, юсь *impf. of* **утверди́ться**
утвержде́ни|е, я *nt.* **1.** assertion, affirmation, claim, allegation. **2.** approval; confirmation; ratification; (*leg.*) probate. **3.** establishment.
утека́|ть, ю *impf. of* **уте́чь**
ут|ёнок, ёнка, *pl.* **~я́та, ~я́т** *m.* duckling.
утепле́ни|е, я *nt.* warming, heating.
утепл|ённый *p.p.p. of* **~и́ть** *and adj.* heated; insulated.
утепли́тел|ь, я *m.* (*tech.*) **1.** heater. **2.** insulator (*building material*).
утепл|и́ть, ю́, и́шь *pf.* (*of* **~я́ть**) to warm, heat.
утепл|я́ть, я́ю *impf. of* **~и́ть**
утер|е́ть, утру́, утрёшь, *past* **~̈, ~̈ла** *pf.* (*of* **утира́ть**) to wipe (off); to wipe dry; **у. пот со лба** to wipe the sweat off one's brow; **у. кому́-н. нос** (*coll.*) to score off s.o.
утер|е́ться, утру́сь, утрёшься, *past* **~̈ся, ~̈лась** *pf.* (*of* **утира́ться**) to wipe o.s.; to dry o.s.
утерп|е́ть, лю́, ~́ишь *pf.* to restrain o.s.
уте́р|я, и *f.* loss.
утеря́|ть, ю *pf.* to lose, mislay; to forfeit.
утёс, а *m.* cliff, crag.
утёсист|ый (~, ~а) *adj.* steep, precipitous.
утесне́ни|е, я *nt.* oppression.
утесн|и́ть, ю́, и́шь *pf.* (*of* **~я́ть**) **1.** (**в**+*a.*; *coll.*) to stuff (into), squeeze (into). **2.** (*obs.*) to oppress, persecute.
утесн|я́ть, я́ю *impf. of* **~и́ть**
уте́х|а, и *f.* (*coll.*) **1.** pleasure; delight; **для ~и** for fun. **2.** comfort, consolation.
уте́чк|а, и *f.* leak, leakage (*also fig.*); loss, wastage, dissipation; **у. га́за** gas escape; **«у. умо́в»** brain drain.
уте́|чь, ку́, чёшь, ку́т, *past* **~̈к, ~кла́** *pf.* (*of* **~ка́ть**) **1.** to flow away; to leak; (*of gas, etc.*) to escape; **мно́го воды́ ~кло́** (*fig.*) much water has flowed (*under the bridges*). **2.** (*of time*) to pass, go by. **3.** (*coll.*) to run away.
утеш|а́ть(ся), а́ю(сь) *impf. of* **~́ить(ся)**
утеше́ни|е, я *nt.* comfort, consolation.
утеши́тел|ь, я *m.* comforter.
утеши́тел|ьный (~ен, ~ьна) *adj.* comforting, consoling.
уте́ш|ить, у, ишь *pf.* (*of* **~а́ть**) to comfort, console.
уте́ш|иться, усь, ишься *pf.* (*of* **~а́ться**) **1.** to console o.s. **2.** (+*i.*) to take comfort (in).
утилизацио́нный *adj.*: **у. заво́д** salvage factory, by-products factory; **у. цех** salvage department.
утилиза́ци|я, и *f.* **1.** utilization. **2.** salvaging; melting-down (*of scrap, etc., for re-use*).
утилизи́р|овать, ую *impf. and pf.* to utilize.
утилитари́зм, а *m.* utilitarianism.
утилитари́ст, а *m.* utilitarian.
утилита́рност|ь, и *f.* utilitarian attitude.
утилита́рный *adj.* utilitarian.
ути́л|ь, я *no pl.*, *m.* (*collect.*) salvage, utility waste (*metal scrap*, *waste paper*, *etc.*).
ути́ль|ный *adj. of* **~**; **~ное желе́зо** scrap iron.
утильсырь|ё, я́ *no pl.*, *nt.* (*collect.*) = **ути́ль; сбо́рщик ~я́** salvage collector.
ути́льщик, а *m.* salvage collector.
ути́ный *adj. of* **у́тка 1.**
утира́льник, а *m.* (*coll.*) hand-towel.
утира́|ть(ся), ю(сь) *impf. of* **утере́ть(ся)**
ути́рк|а, и *f.* **1.** (*coll.*) wiping (off). **2.** (*dial.*) handkerchief; hand-towel.
утих|а́ть, а́ю *impf. of* **~́нуть**
ути́х|нуть, ну, нешь, *past* **~, ~ла** *pf.* (*of* **~а́ть**) **1.** to become quiet, still; (*of sounds*) to cease, die away. **2.** to abate, subside, slacken; (*of wind*) to drop. **3.** to become calm, calm down.
утихоми́рива|ть(ся), ю(сь) *impf. of* **утихоми́рить(ся)**
утихоми́р|ить, ю, ишь *pf.* (*of* **~ивать**) (*coll.*) to calm down; to pacify, placate.
утихоми́р|иться, юсь, ишься *pf.* (*of* **~иваться**) (*coll.*) to calm down; to abate, subside.
у́тк|а, и *f.* **1.** duck. **2.** canard, false report; **пусти́ть ~у** to start a canard. **3.** bedpan.
уткн|у́ть, у́, ёшь *pf.* (*coll.*) to bury; to fix; **у. нос в кни́гу** to bury o.s. in a book; **у. глаза́ (в**+*a.*) to fix one's gaze (upon), stare steadily (at).
уткн|у́ться, у́сь, ёшься *pf.* (**в**+*a.*; *coll.*) **1.** to bury o.s. (in), one's head (in); **у. в па́пку** to bury one's head in a file. **2.** to bump (into), come to rest (upon), come up (against); **ло́дка ~у́лась в бе́рег** the boat bumped into the bank.
утконо́с, а *m.* (*zool.*) duck-billed platypus.
утле́гар|ь, я *m.* (*naut.*) jib-boom.
у́тлый *adj.* **1.** frail; unsound, unseaworthy. **2.** poor, wretched.
ут|о́к, ка́ *m.* (*text.*) woof, weft.
утол|и́ть, ю́, и́шь *pf.* (*of* **~я́ть**) **1.** to quench, slake (*thirst*); to satisfy (*hunger*). **2.** to relieve, alleviate, soothe.
утол|сти́ть, щу́, сти́шь *pf.* (*of* **~ща́ть**) to thicken, make thicker.
утол|сти́ться, щу́сь, сти́шься *pf.* (*of* **~ща́ться**) to become thicker.
утолща́|ть(ся), ю(сь) *impf. of* **утолсти́ть(ся)**
утолще́ни|е, я *nt.* **1.** thickening. **2.** thickened part, bulge; (*tech.*) reinforcement, rib, boss.
утол|щённый *p.p.p. of* **~сти́ть** *and adj.* reinforced.
утол|я́ть, я́ю *impf. of* **~и́ть**
утоми́тел|ьный (~ен, ~ьна) *adj.* **1.** wearisome, tiring, fatiguing. **2.** tiresome; tedious.
утом|и́ть, лю́, и́шь *pf.* (*of* **~ля́ть**) to tire, weary, fatigue.
утом|и́ться, лю́сь, и́шься *pf.* (*of* **~ля́ться**) to get tired.
утомле́ни|е, я *nt.* tiredness, weariness, fatigue.
утом|лённый *p.p.p. of* **~и́ть** *and adj.* tired, weary, fatigued.
утомля́|ть(ся), ю(сь) *impf. of* **утоми́ть(ся)**
утон|у́ть, у́, ~́ешь *pf.* (*of* **тону́ть** *and* **утопа́ть**) **1.** to drown, be drowned, sink. **2.** (**в**+*p.*; *fig.*) to be lost (in).
утонч|а́ть(ся), а́ю(сь) *impf. of* **~и́ть(ся)**
утончённост|ь, и *f.* refinement.
утонч|ённый *p.p.p. of* **~и́ть** *and adj.* refined; exquisite, subtle.
утонч|и́ть, у́, и́шь *pf.* (*of* **~а́ть**) **1.** to make thinner; to taper. **2.** (*fig.*) to refine, make refined.
утонч|и́ться, у́сь, и́шься *pf.* (*of* **~а́ться**) **1.** to become thinner; to taper (*intrans.*). **2.** (*fig.*) to become refined.
утопа́|ть, ю *impf.* **1.** *impf. of* **утону́ть**. **2.** (*impf. only*) (**в**+*p.*; *fig.*) to roll (in), wallow (in).
утопи́зм, а *m.* Utopianism.
утопи́ст, а *m.* Utopian.
утоп|и́ть, лю́, ~́ишь *pf.* (*of* **топи́ть**) **1.** to drown. **2.** (*fig.*, *coll.*) to ruin. **3.** to bury, embed, countersink.

утоп|и́ться, лю́сь, ∸ишься *pf.* (*of* **топи́ться**) to drown o.s.
утопи́ческий *adj.* Utopian.
уто́пи|я, и *f.* Utopia.
уто́пленник, а *m.* drowned man.
уто́пленниц|а, ы *f. of* **уто́пленник**
уто́п|ленный *p.p.p. of* **~и́ть** *and adj.* (*tech.*) built-in; **~ленная голо́вка** countersink.
утоп|та́ть, чу́, ∸чешь *pf.* (*of* **ута́птывать**) to trample down, pound.
у́точк|а, и *f. dim. of* **у́тка; ходи́ть ~ой** to waddle along.
уточне́ни|е, я *nt.* more precise definition, amplification, elaboration.
уточн|и́ть, ю́, и́шь *pf.* (*of* **~я́ть**) to make more precise, define more precisely; to amplify, elaborate.
уто́чный *adj. of* **уто́к**
уточн|я́ть, я́ю *impf. of* **~и́ть**
утра́ива|ть, ю *impf. of* **утро́ить**
утрамб|ова́ть, у́ю *pf.* (*of* **~о́вывать**) to ram, tamp (*road material, etc.*).
утрамб|ова́ться, у́ется *pf.* (*of* **~о́вываться**) **1.** to become flat, level (*also fig.*). **2.** *pass. of* **~ова́ть**
утрамбо́выва|ть(ся), ю(сь) *impf. of* **утрамбова́ть(ся)**
утра́т|а, ы *f.* (*in var. senses*) loss; **у. трудоспосо́бности** disablement.
утра́|тить, чу, тишь *pf.* (*of* **~чивать**) to lose.
утра́чива|ть, ю *impf. of* **утра́тить**
у́тренн|ий *adj.* morning, early; **~ие за́морозки** morning frost; **~яя заря́** dawn, daybreak; (*mil.*) reveille.
у́тренник, а *m.* **1.** morning frost. **2.** morning performance, matinée.
у́трен|я, и *f.* (*eccl.*) matins.
у́тречком *adv.* (*coll.*) in the morning.
утри́р|овать, ую *impf. and pf.* to exaggerate; to overplay.
утриро́вк|а, и *f.* exaggeration.
у́тр|о, а (до ~а́, с ~а́), *d.* **у (к ~у́)**, *pl.* **~а, ~, ~ам (по ~а́м)** *nt.* **1.** morning; **в семь часо́в ~а́** at 7 a.m.; **с ~а́** early in the morning; **с ~а́ до ве́чера** from morn till night; **до́брое у.!, с до́брым ~ом!** good morning! **2.** (*obs.*) morning performance, matinée.
утро́б|а, ы *f.* **1.** womb. **2.** (*coll.*) belly; **напиха́ть свою́ ~у** to stuff one's belly. **3.: ~ой** (*coll.*) by instinct.
утро́бист|ый (~, ~а) *adj.* (*coll.*) big-bellied.
утро́бный *adj.* **1.** uterine, foetal; **у. плод** foetus; **у. пери́од разви́тия** period of gestation. **2.** internal; (*of sounds*) deep, hollow; **у. смех** belly-laugh.
утро́|ить, ю, ишь *pf.* (*of* **утра́ивать**) to treble.
у́тром *adv.* in the morning; **сего́дня у.** this morning.
утру|ди́ть, жу́, ди́шь *pf.* (*of* **~жда́ть**) to trouble, to tire.
утру|ди́ться, жу́сь, ди́шься *pf.* (*of* **~жда́ться**) (*coll.*) to trouble o.s., take trouble.
утружда́|ть(ся), ю(сь) *impf. of* **утруди́ть(ся)**
утру́ск|а, и *f.* (*comm.*) spillage.
утряс|а́ть, а́ю *impf. of* **~ти́**
утряс|ти́, у́, ёшь *pf.* (*of* **~а́ть**) (*coll.*) **1.** to shake down. **2.** to shake up, give a shaking. **3.** to settle; **у. вопро́с** to have a matter out.
утучн|и́ть, ю́, и́шь *pf.* (*of* **~я́ть**) **1.** to fatten. **2.** to enrich, manure (*soil*).
утучн|я́ть, я́ю *impf. of* **~и́ть**
утуш|а́ть, а́ю *impf. of* **~и́ть**
утуш|и́ть, у́, ∸ишь *pf.* (*of* **~а́ть**) (*coll.*) **1.** to put out, extinguish. **2.** (*fig.*) to suppress.
уты́к|ать, аю *pf.* (*of* **~а́ть** *and* **~ивать**) (*coll.*) **1.** to stick (in) all over. **2.** to stop up, caulk.
утык|а́ть, а́ю *impf. of* **∸ать**
уты́кива|ть, ю *impf.* = **утыка́ть**
утю́г, а́ *m.* (*flat*) iron.
утю́ж|ить, у, ишь *impf.* (*of* **вы́~**) **1.** to iron, press. **2.** (*coll.*) to smooth. **3.** (*coll.*) to beat; to lambast (*also fig.*).
утю́жк|а, и *f.* ironing, pressing.
утя́гива|ть, ю *impf. of* **утяну́ть**
утяжели́тел|ь, я *m.* (*tech.*) weighting compound.
утяжел|и́ть, ю́, и́шь *pf.* (*of* **~я́ть**) to make heavier, increase the weight (of).
утяжел|и́ться, и́тся *pf.* (*of* **~я́ться**) to become heavier.
утяжел|я́ть(ся), я́ю, я́ет(ся) *impf. of* **~и́ть(ся)**
утян|у́ть, у́, ∸ешь *pf.* (*of* **утя́гивать**) to drag away, off.
утя́тин|а, ы *f.* (*cul.*) duck.
уф *int.* (*expr.* (i) *relief*, (ii) *fatigue, physical discomfort, etc.*) ooh!; ee!; gosh!; phew!; **уф, жа́рко!** phew, it's hot!
уфи́ст, а *m.* ufologist.
ух *int.* **1.** (*expr. various strong feelings*) ooh!; gosh! **2.** bang!
ух|а́, и́ *f.* ukha (*fish-soup*).
уха́б, а *m.* pot-hole, pit (*in road*).
уха́бист|ый (~, ~а) *adj.* full of pot-holes; bumpy.
ухажёр, а *m.* (*coll.*) ladies' man; admirer.
уха́жива|ть, ю *impf.* (**за**+*i.*) **1.** to nurse, tend; to look after. **2.** to court (*a woman*); to pay court (to), make advances (to). **3.** to make up (to), try to get round.
у́харский *adj.* (*coll.*) smart, 'fancy'; dashing; rakish.
у́харств|о, а *nt.* (*coll.*) bravado.
у́хар|ь, я *m.* (*coll.*) 'lad', smart fellow; dashing fellow.
у́ха|ть(ся), ю(сь) *impf. of* **у́хнуть(ся)**
ухва́т, а *m.* **1.** oven fork. **2.** (*tech.*) clip.
ухва́тист|ый (~, ~а) *adj.* (*coll.*) adroit, sure, strong.
ухва|ти́ть, чу́, ∸тишь *pf.* **1.** to lay hold (of); (*fig.*) to seize. **2.** (*fig., coll.*) to grasp.
ухва|ти́ться, чу́сь, ∸тишься *pf.* (**за**+*a.*) **1.** to grasp, lay hold (of); **у. за ве́тку** to grasp a branch. **2.** (*coll.*) to set (to, about); **у. за но́вую рабо́ту** to get stuck in to a new job. **3.** (*fig., coll.*) to seize; to jump (at); to take up; **у. за предложе́ние** to jump at an offer.
ухва́тк|а, и *f.* (*coll.*) **1.** grip. **2.** (*fig.*) grasp; (a) skill; trick. **3.** manner.
ухитр|и́ться, ю́сь, и́шься *pf.* (*of* **~я́ться**) (+*inf.*; *coll.*) to manage (to), contrive (to).
ухитр|я́ться, я́юсь *impf. of* **~и́ться**
ухищре́ни|е, я *nt.* contrivance, shift, device, trick, dodge.
ухищрённый *adj.* cunning, artful.
ухищря́|ться, юсь *impf.* to contrive; to resort to contrivance.
ухло́п|ать, аю *pf.* (*of* **~ывать**) (*coll.*) **1.** to kill, do for. **2.** to squander.
ухло́пыва|ть, ю *impf. of* **ухло́пать**
ухмы́лк|а, и *f.* (*coll.*) smirk, grin.
ухмыльн|у́ться, у́сь, ёшься *pf.* (*of* **ухмыля́ться**) (*coll.*) to smirk, grin.
ухмыл|я́ться, я́юсь *impf. of* **~ьну́ться**
у́хн|уть, у, ешь *pf.* (*of* **у́хать**) (*coll.*) **1.** to cry out (*from surprise, pleasure, pain, fatigue, etc.*); (*of owls*) to hoot. **2.** to crash, bang, rumble; to ring out with a bang; **вдруг ~ул гром** there was a sudden crash of thunder; **слы́шно бы́ло как ~ула бо́мба** the thud of a bomb (exploding) could be heard. **3.** to slip, fall; to come a cropper (*also fig.*). **4.** (*fig.*) to come to grief; to go for a Burton. **5.** to drop. **6.** to lose, squander, spend up. **7.** to bang, slap; **у. кулако́м по столу́** to bang one's fist on the table.
у́хн|уться, усь, ешься *pf.* (*of* **у́хаться**) (*coll.*) to fall with a bang.
у́х|о, а, *pl.* **у́ши, уше́й** *nt.* **1.** ear; **нару́жное у.** auricle; **сре́днее у.** middle ear; **воспале́ние ~а** (*med.*) otitis; **у́ши вя́нут (от)** (*coll.*) it makes one sick to hear; **и ~ом не вести́** not to listen (= *to pay no heed*); **кра́ем ~а слу́шать** to listen with half an ear; **прожужжа́ть, прокрича́ть кому́-н. у́ши** to talk s.o.'s head off; **у. в у.** (**с**+*i.*) level (with), alongside; **дать, зае́хать, съе́здить кому́-н. в у.** (*coll.*) to box s.o.'s ear; **дуть, петь в у́ши кому́-н.** to whisper (= *to pass on scandal*) to s.o.; **во все у́ши слу́шать** to be all ears; **за́ уши тащи́ть кого́-н.** (*fig.*) to give s.o. a leg-up; **пропусти́ть ми́мо уше́й** (*coll.*) to turn a deaf ear (to), pay no heed (to); **говори́ть кому́-н. на́ у.** to have a word in s.o.'s ear, have a private word with s.o.; **по́ уши** up to one's eyes (*in work, etc.*), over head and ears, head over heels (*in love, etc.*). **2.** ear-flap, ear-piece (*of cap, etc.*). **3.** (*tech.*) ear, lug, hanger.
уховёртк|а, и *f.* (*zool.*) earwig.
ухо́д[1], **а** *m.* going away, leaving, departure; withdrawal; **вы́йти ~ом (за́муж), взять ~ом (жену́)** (*obs.*) to marry in secret, elope with.

ухóд[2], **а** *m.* (**за**+*i.*) nursing, tending, looking after; care (of); maintenance.
ухо|дúть[1], **жý, ∸дишь** *impf.* **1.** *impf. of* **уйтú. 2.** *impf. only* to stretch, extend.
ухо|дúть[2], **жý, ∸дишь** *pf.* (*coll.*) **1.** to wear out, tire out. **2.** to remove, rid o.s. (of); to do in.
ухо|дúться, жýсь, ∸дишься *pf.* (*coll.*) **1.** to be worn out, be tired out. **2.** to calm down; to be rested.
ухорéз, а *m.* (*coll.*) desperate fellow.
ухудш|áть(ся), áю, áет(ся) *impf. of* **∸ить(ся)**
ухудшéни|е, я *nt.* worsening, deterioration.
ухýдш|енный *p.p.p. of* **~ить** *and adj.* inferior.
ухýдш|ить, у, ишь *pf.* (*of* **~áть**) to make worse, worsen, deteriorate.
ухýдш|иться, ится *pf.* (*of* **~áться**) to become worse, worsen, deteriorate (*intrans.*).
уцелé|ть, ю *pf.* to remain intact, escape destruction; to remain alive, survive; to remain at liberty, escape.
уцен|ённый *p.p.p. of* **~úть** *and adj.* reduced(-price).
уцéнива|ть, ю *impf. of* **уценúть**
уцен|úть, ю́, ∸ишь *pf.* (*of* **∸ивать**) to reduce the price (of).
уцеп|úть, лю́, ∸ишь *pf.* (*coll.*) to catch hold (of), grasp, seize.
уцеп|úться, лю́сь, ∸ишься *pf.* (**за**+*a.*) **1.** to catch hold (of), grasp, seize. **2.** (*fig.*, *coll.*) to jump (at).
учáств|овать, ую *impf.* **1.** (**в**+*p.*) to take part (in), participate (in). **2.** (**в**+*p.*) to have a share (in), have shares (in); **у. в акционéрном óбществе** to have shares in a (joint-stock) company. **3.** (+*d.*; *obs.*) to sympathize (with), extend sympathy (to).
учáств|ующий *pres. part. act. of* **~овать**; *as n.* **у., ~ующего** *m.* participant.
учáсти|е, я *nt.* **1.** taking part, participation; **при ~и, с ~ем** (+*g.*) with the participation (of), with assistance (of), including, featuring; **принимáть у.** (**в**+*p.*) to take part (in), participate (in), take a hand (in). **2.** share, sharing. **3.** sympathy, concern; **принимáть у. в ком-н.** to extend sympathy to s.o., display concern for s.o.
уча|стúть, щý, стúшь *pf.* (*of* **~щáть**) to make more frequent.
участ|úться, úтся *pf.* (*of* **учащáться**) to become more frequent; (*of pulse*) to quicken.
участкóв|ый *adj. of* **учáсток; у. уполномóченный** divisional inspector (*of police*); **у. прúстав** (*hist.*) = **у. уполномóченный** (*in tsarist Russia*); *as n.* **у., ~ого** *m.* = **у. уполномóченный, у. прúстав.**
учáстлив|ый (~, ~а) *adj.* sympathetic.
учáстник, а *m.* (+*g.*) participant (in), member (of); **у. состязáния** participant in a competition, competitor; **у. литератýрного кружкá** member of a literary society.
учáст|ок, ка *m.* **1.** (*of land*) plot, strip; lot, parcel. **2.** part, section, portion; length (*of road*, *etc.*); (*rail.*) division. **3.** (*mil.*) sector (*area occupied by one regiment of Army*); area, zone; **у. глáвного удáра** area of main strike; **у. прорыва** breakthrough area. **4.** district, area, zone (*as administrative unit*); **избирáтельный у.** (*i*) electoral district, ward, (*ii*) polling station. **5.** (*fig.*) field, sphere (*of activity*). **6.** (*hist.*) (*i*) police division, district; (*ii*) police-station.
ýчаст|ь, и *f.* lot, fate, portion.
учá|ть, учнý, учнёшь, *past* **~л, ~лá, ~ло** *pf.* (*coll.*) to begin.
учащá|ть(ся), ю, ет(ся) *impf. of* **участúть(ся)**
уча|щённый *p.p.p. of* **~стúть** *and adj.* quickened; faster; **у. пульс** quickened pulse.
учáщ|ийся *pres. part. of* **учúться**; *as n.* **у., ~егося** *m.* student; pupil.
учёб|а, ы *f.* **1.** studies; studying, learning; **за ~ой** at one's studies. **2.** drill, training.
учéбник, а *m.* text-book; manual, primer.
учéбно... *comb. form, abbr. of* **учéбный**
учéбн|ый *adj.* **1.** educational; school; **~ое врéмя** school-hours, instruction, term-time; **у. год** academic year, school year; **~ое заведéние** educational institution; **у. план** curriculum; **у. предмéт** subject; **~ая часть** instructional side (*of school*); **завéдующий ~ой чáстью** director of studies. **2.** (*mil.*) training, practice; **у. патрóн** dummy cartridge (*used in training*); **~ое пóле** training ground; **у. самолёт** training aircraft, trainer; **у. сбор** training period; **~ая стрельбá** practice shoot; **~ое сýдно** training ship.
учéни|е, я *nt.* **1.** learning; studies; apprenticeship. **отдáть в у.** (+*d.*) to apprentice (to). **2.** teaching, instruction. **3.** (*mil.*) exercise; (*pl.*) training. **4.** teaching, doctrine.
ученúк, á *m.* **1.** pupil; **у.-лётчик** student pilot. **2.** apprentice. **3.** disciple, follower.
ученúц|а, ы *f. of* **ученúк**
ученú|ческий *adj.* **1.** *adj. of* **~к. 2.** raw, crude, immature.
ученúчеств|о, а *nt.* **1.** period spent as a pupil, student. **2.** apprenticeship. **3.** rawness, immaturity.
учёност|ь, и *f.* learning, erudition (*also iron.*).
учён|ый (~, ~а) *adj.* **1.** learned, erudite; (*coll.*) educated. **2.** scholarly; academic; **~ая статья́** scholarly article; **~ая стéпень** (university) degree. **3.** *forms part of title of certain academic posts and institutions in former USSR*: **у. секретáрь** academic secretary; **у. совéт** academic council. **4.** (*of animals*) trained, performing. **5.** *as n.* **у., ~ого** *m.* scholar; scientist; academic.
уч|éсть, учтý, учтёшь, *past* **~ёл, ~лá** *pf.* (*of* **~úтывать**) **1.** to take into account, consideration; to allow (for); to bear in mind. **2.** to take stock (of), make an inventory (of). **3.** (*fin.*) to discount.
учёт, а *m.* **1.** stock-taking, inventory-making; reckoning, calculation; **вестú у.** (+*g.*) to take stock (of). **2.** taking into account; **без ~а** (+*g.*) disregarding. **3.** registration; **взять на у.** to register; **встать, стать на у.** to be registered; **состоя́ть на ~е** to be on the books; **снять с ~а** to strike off the register, take off the books. **4.** (*fin.*) discount, discounting.
учетвер|úть, ю́, úшь *pf.* (*of* **~я́ть**) to quadruple.
учетвер|я́ть, я́ю *impf. of* **~úть**
учётно-вóинский *adj.*: **у.-в. докумéнт** (*mil.*) discharge papers (*also* document indicating military service-liability status).
учётно-медицúнск|ий *adj.*: **~ая кáрточка** medical record, medical card.
учётн|ый *adj.* **1.** registration; **~ая кáрточка** registration form; **~ое отделéние** records section. **2.** (*fin.*) discount; **у. процéнт, ~ая стáвка бáнковского процéнта** rate of discount; bank rate.
учётчик, а *m.* tally clerk.
учúлищ|е, а *nt.* school, college (*institution providing specialist instruction at secondary level*); **воéнное у.** military school; **ремéсленное у.** trade school.
учúлищ|ный *adj. of* **~е**
учин|úть, ю́, úшь *pf.* (*of* **~я́ть**) to make, commit; **у. скандáл** (*coll.*) to make a scene.
учин|я́ть, я́ю *impf. of* **~úть**
учúтел|ь, я *m.* **1.** (*pl.* **~я́**) teacher. **2.** (*pl.* **~и**) (*fig.*) teacher, master (= *authority*).
учúтельниц|а, ы *f. of* **учúтель**
учúтельный *adj.* (*obs.*) **1.** skilled in teaching. **2.** edifying, instructive.
учúтель|ский *adj. of* **~**; *as n.* **~ская, ~ской** *f.* teachers' common room, staff (common) room.
учúтыва|ть, ю *impf. of* **учéсть**
уч|úть, ý, ∸ишь *impf.* **1.** (*pf.* **вы́~, на~** *and* **об~**) (+*a. and d. or +inf.*) to teach; **у. когó-н. немéцкому языкý** to teach s.o. German; **у. игрáть на скрúпке** to teach to play the violin. **2.** to be a teacher. **3.** (**что**) (*of a theory*, *etc.*) to teach (that), say (that). **4.** (*pf.* **вы́~**) (+*a.*) to learn; to memorize.
уч|úться, ýсь, ∸ишься *impf.* **1.** (*pf.* **вы́~, на~** *and* **об~**) (+*d. or +inf.*) to learn, study. **2.** to be a student; **у. в шкóле** to go to, be at school. **3.** (**на когó-н.**; *coll.*) to study (to be, to become), learn (to be); **он ∸ится на перевóдчика** he is studying to be an interpreter.
учредúтел|ь, я *m.* founder.
учредúтельн|ый *adj.* constituent; **~ое собрáние** (*pol.*) constituent assembly.
учре|дúть, жý, дúшь *pf.* (*of* **~ждáть**) to found, establish, set up; to introduce, institute.

учрежда́|ть, ю *impf. of* **учреди́ть**
учрежде́ни|е, я *nt.* **1.** founding, establishment (*action*), setting up; introduction. **2.** establishment, institution (*object*).
учрежде́н|ческий *adj. of* **∼ие 2.**
учти́вост|ь, и *f.* civility, courtesy.
учти́в|ый (∼, ∼а) *adj.* civil, courteous.
учу́|ять, ю, ешь *pf.* (*coll.*) to smell, nose out; (*fig.*) to sense.
уша́нк|а, и *f.* (*coll.*) cap with ear-flaps.
уша́ст|ый (∼, ∼а) *adj.* (*coll.*) big-eared.
уша́т, а *m.* tub (*carried on pole slung through handles*).
у́ши *see* **у́хо**
уши́б, а *m.* **1.** injury; knock; bruise; (*med.*) contusion. **2.** injured place.
ушиб|а́ть(ся), а́ю(сь) *impf. of* **∼и́ть(ся)**
ушиб|и́ть, у́, ёшь, *past* **∼́, ∼́ла** *pf.* (*of* **∼а́ть**) **1.** to injure (*by knocking*); to bruise. **2.** (*fig.*, *coll.*) to hurt, shock.
ушиб|и́ться, у́сь, ёшься, *past* **∼́ся, ∼́лась** *pf.* (*of* **∼а́ться**) to hurt o.s., give o.s. a knock; to bruise o.s.
ушива́|ть, ю *impf. of* **уши́ть**
уш|и́ть, ью́, ьёшь *pf.* (*of* **∼ива́ть**) (*dressmaking*) to take in.
ушка́н, а *m.* (*dial.*) hare.
у́шк|о, а, *pl.* **∼и, у́шек** *nt. dim. of* **у́хо; у него́ ∼и на маку́шке** he is on the qui-vive.
ушк|о́, а́, *pl.* **∼и́, ∼о́в** *nt.* **1.** (*tech.*) eye, lug. **2.** tab, tag (*of boot*). **3.** eye (*of needle*). **4.** (*pl.*) (*cul.*) noodles.
ушку́|й, я *m.* (*hist.*) flat-bottomed boat (*propelled by sail or oars*).
ушку́йник, а *m.* (*hist.*) river-pirate.
ушни́к, а́ *m.* (*coll.*) ear-specialist.
ушн|о́й *adj.* ear, aural; **∼а́я боль** ear-ache; **у. врач** ear-specialist; **∼а́я ра́ковина** (*anat.*) auricle; **∼а́я се́ра** ear-wax.
уще́лист|ый (∼, ∼а) *adj.* abounding in ravines.
уще́л|ье, ья, *g. pl.* **∼ий** *nt.* ravine, gorge, canyon.
ущем|и́ть, лю́, и́шь *pf.* (*of* **∼ля́ть**) **1.** to pinch, jam, nip; **у. себе́ па́лец две́рью** to pinch one's finger in the door. **2.** (*fig.*) to limit; to encroach (upon). **3.** (*fig.*) to wound, hurt; **у. чьё-н. самолю́бие** to hurt s.o.'s pride.
ущемле́ни|е, я *nt.* **1.** pinching, jamming, nipping; **у. гры́жи** (*med.*) strangulation of hernia. **2.** (*fig.*) limitation. **3.** (*fig.*) wounding, hurting; frustration.
ущемля́|ть, ю *impf. of* **ущеми́ть**
ущем|лённый *p.p.p. of* **∼и́ть** *and adj.* (*fig.*) wounded, hurt; frustrated.
уще́рб, а *m.* **1.** detriment; loss; damage, injury; **без ∼а (для)** without prejudice (to); **в у.** (*+d.*) to the detriment (of), to the prejudice (of). **2.** weakening, decline. **3.: на ∼е** (*of the moon*) on the wane; (*fig.*) on the decline.
ущерб|и́ть, лю́, и́шь *pf.* **1.** to injure, damage. **2.** (*fig.*) to limit.
уще́рбный *adj.* (*of the moon*) waning; (*fig.*) on the decline.
ущипн|у́ть, у́, ёшь *pf.* to pinch, tweak.
Уэ́льс, а *m.* Wales.
уэ́льс|ец, ца *m.* Welshman.
уэ́льский *adj.* Welsh.
ую́т, а *m.* comfort, cosiness.
ую́т|ный (∼ен, ∼на) *adj.* comfortable, cosy.
уязви́м|ый (∼, ∼а) *adj.* vulnerable (*also fig.*); **∼ое ме́сто** (*fig.*) weak spot, sensitive spot.
уязв|и́ть, лю́, и́шь *pf.* (*of* **∼ля́ть**) to wound, hurt.
уязвля́|ть, ю *impf. of* **уязви́ть**
уясне́ни|е, я *nt.* explanation, elucidation.
уясн|и́ть, ю́, и́шь *pf.* (*of* **∼я́ть**) **1. (себе́)** to understand, make out. **2.** (*obs.*) to explain.
уясн|я́ть, я́ю *impf. of* **∼и́ть**

Ф

фа *nt. indecl.* (*mus.*) fa(h); F.
фаб... *comb. form, abbr. of* **фабри́чный**
фабза́уч, а *m.* (*abbr. of* **фабри́чно-заводско́е учи́лище**) factory workshop-school.
фа́брик|а, и *f.* factory, mill.
фа́брика-ку́хня, фа́брики-ку́хни *f.* (*large-scale*) canteen, municipal restaurant.
фабрика́нт, а *m.* (*obs.*) manufacturer, factory-owner, mill-owner.
фабрика́т, а *m.* finished product.
фабрика́ци|я, и *f.* fabrication (*also fig.*).
фабрик|ова́ть, у́ю *impf.* **1.** (*obs.*) to manufacture, make. **2.** (*pf.* **с∼**) (*fig.*, *coll.*) to fabricate, forge.
фа́бр|ить, ю, ишь *impf.* (*of* **на∼**) (*obs.*) to dye (*moustache or beard*).
фабри́чно-заводско́й (*and* **ф.-заво́дский)** *adj.* factory, works, industrial.
фабри́чн|ый *adj.* **1.** factory; industrial, manufacturing; **ф. го́род** manufacturing town; **∼ая ма́рка** trade mark; **∼ое произво́дство** manufacturing; *as n.* **ф., ∼ого** *m.*, **∼ая, ∼ой** *f.* factory worker. **2.** factory-made.
фа́бул|а, ы *f.* (*liter.*) plot, story.
фавн, а *m.* (*myth.*) faun.
фаво́р, а *m.* (*obs.*): **быть в ∼е (у), по́льзоваться ∼ом (у)** to be in favour (with); **быть не в ∼е у кого́-н.** to be in s.o.'s bad books.
фавори́т, а *m.* favourite (*also sport*).
фаворити́зм, а *m.* favouritism.
фаго́т, а *m.* (*mus.*) bassoon.
фаготи́ст, а *m.* bassoon-player.
фагоци́т, а *m.* (*biol.*) phagocyte.
фа́з|а, ы *f.* (*in var. senses*) phase; stage.
фаза́н, а *m.* pheasant.
фаза́н|ий *adj. of* **∼**
фаза́них|а, и *f.* hen pheasant.
фа́зис, а *m.* phase.
фа́зн|ый *adj.* (*tech.*) phase; **∼ая обмо́тка** phase winding.
фа́з|овый *adj.* = **∼ный; (***phys.*, *tech.***) ф. сдвиг** phase shift; **∼овая ско́рость** phase velocity; **ф. у́гол** phase angle.
фазотро́н, а *m.* (*phys.*) synchro-cyclotron.
фай, фа́я *m.* (*text.*) faille.
файдеши́н, а *m.* (*text.*) faille de Chine.
...фа́к *comb. form, abbr. of* **факульте́т**
фа́кел, а *m.* torch, flare; **ф.-ло́цман** pilot flame.
фа́кел|ьный *adj. of* **∼; ∼ьное ше́ствие** torch-light procession.
фа́кельщик, а *m.* **1.** torch-bearer. **2.** (*fig.*, *pej.*) incendiary, fire-bug.
факи́р, а *m.* fakir.
фа́кс, а *m.* fax; **посла́ть по ∼у** to fax.
факси́миле *indecl.* **1.** *adj.* **2.** *n.*; *nt.* facsimile.
факс|ими́льный *adj. of* **∼; ф. аппара́т** fax (machine).
факт, а *m.* **1.** fact; **соверши́вшийся ф.** fait accompli; **показа́ть на ∼́ах** to show proof; **факт, что** (*coll.*) it is a fact that; **ф. остаётся ∼́ом** the fact remains.
факти́чески *adv.* in fact, actually; practically, virtually, to all intents and purposes.
факти́ческ|ий *adj.* actual; real; virtual; **∼ие да́нные** the facts.
факти́ч|ный (∼ен, ∼на) *adj.* factual, authentic.
фактографи́ч|ный (∼ен, ∼на) *adj.* factual, based on fact, authentic.

фактогра́фи|я, и *f.* factual account.
фа́ктор, а *m.* factor.
факто́ри|я, и *f.* trading station.
факту́р|а, ы *f.* **1.** (*arts and liter.*) style; manner of execution; texture. **2.** (*comm.*) invoice, bill.
факту́р|ный *adj. of* **~а**
факультати́в|ный (~ен, ~на) *adj.* optional.
факульте́т, а *m.* faculty, department (*of higher education institution*).
факульте́т|ский *adj. of* **~**
фал, а *m.* (*naut.*) halyard.
фала́нг|а, и *f.* **1.** (*hist.*; *fig.*) phalanx. **2.** (*pol.*) Falange. **3.** (*anat.*) phalanx, phalange.
фаланги́ст, а *m.* (*pol.*) Falangist.
фалансте́р, а *m.* (*pol. phil.*) phalanstery.
фа́лд|а, ы *f.* tail, skirt (*of coat*).
фа́лин|ь, я *m.* (*naut.*) painter.
фалли́ческий *adj.* phallic.
фалло́пиев *adj.*: **~а труба́** (*med.*) Fallopian tube.
фа́ллос, а *m.* phallus.
фалре́п, а *m.* (*naut.*) side-rope, side-boy.
фальсифика́тор *m.* falsifier; forger.
фальсифика́ци|я, и *f.* **1.** falsification; forging. **2.** adulteration. **3.** forgery, fake, counterfeit.
фальсифици́р|овать, ую *impf. and pf.* **1.** to falsify; to forge. **2.** to adulterate.
фальц, а *m.* **1.** (*tech.*) rabbet; groove. **2.** (*typ.*) fold (*of printed sheet*).
фальцго́бел|ь, я *m.* (*tech.*) fillister, rabbeting plane.
фальц|ева́ть, у́ю *impf.* (*of* **с~**) **1.** (*tech.*) to rabbet, groove. **2.** to fold, crease.
фальце́т, а *m.* (*mus.*) falsetto.
фальцо́ванн|ый *adj.*: **~ая бума́га** (*comput.*) fan-fold paper.
фальцо́вочный *adj.* (*tech.*) rabbeting, grooving; **ф. стано́к** rabbeting machine.
фальшбо́рт, а *m.* (*naut.*) bulwark, rails.
фальши́в|ить, лю, ишь *impf.* **1.** to be a hypocrite; to act insincerely. **2.** (*pf.* **с~**) (*mus.*) to sing, play out of tune.
фальши́вк|а, и *f.* (*coll.*) forged document.
фальшивомоне́тчик, а *m.* counterfeiter, coiner (*of false money*).
фальши́в|ый (~, ~а) *adj.* **1.** false; spurious; forged, fake; artificial, imitation; **ф. докуме́нт** forged document; **~ые зу́бы** false teeth; **ф. же́мчуг** imitation pearl. **2.** false; hypocritical, insincere; **ф. комплиме́нт** insincere compliment; **попа́сть в ~ое положе́ние** to put o.s. into a false position. **3.** (*mus.*) false (= *out of tune*). **4.** (*naut.*) temporary, jury-; **~ая ма́чта** jury-mast.
фальшки́л|ь, я *m.* (*naut.*) false keel.
фальш|ь, и *f.* **1.** deception, trickery. **2.** falsity; hypocrisy, insincerity. **3.** (*mus.*) singing, playing out of tune.
фами́ли|я, и *f.* **1.** surname; **двойна́я ф.** double-barrelled surname. **2.** family, kin.
фами́льный *adj.* family.
фамилья́рнича|ть, ю *impf.* (*coll.*) to be (too) familiar.
фамилья́рност|ь, и *f.* (excessive) familiarity; unceremoniousness.
фамилья́р|ный (~ен, ~на) *adj.* (excessively) familiar; unceremonious, off-hand.
фанабе́ри|я, и *f.* (*coll.*) arrogance, bumptiousness.
фана́т, а *m.* (*coll.*) freak, fan, devotée; **музыка́льный ф.** music freak.
фанати́зм, а *m.* fanaticism.
фана́тик, а *m.* fanatic.
фанати́ческий *adj.* fanatical.
фанати́ч|ный (~ен, ~на) *adj.* fanatic(al).
фане́р|а, ы *f.* **1.** veneer. **2.** plywood.
фане́р|ный *adj. of* **~а; ф. лист** plywood sheet; **~ная рабо́та** veneering.
фа́нз|а́, ы-ы́ *f.* fanza (*peasant domicile in China or Korea*).
фанз|а́, ы́ *f.* (*text.*) foulard.
фа́нов|ый *adj.* waste, sewage; **~ая труба́** waste pipe.
фант, а *m.* forfeit (*in game 'forfeits'*); **игра́ть в ~ы** to play forfeits.
фантазёр, а *m.* dreamer, visionary.
фантази́р|овать, ую *impf.* **1.** (*impf. only*) to dream, indulge in fantasies. **2.** (*pf.* **с~**) to make up, dream up. **3.** (*impf. only*) to improvise (*on piano, etc.*).
фанта́зи|я, и *f.* **1.** fantasy; imagination; **бога́тая ф.** fertile imagination. **2.** fantasy, fancy; **предава́ться ~ям** to indulge in fantasies. **3.** fabrication. **4.** (*coll.*) fancy, whim. **5.** (*mus.*) fantasia.
фантасмаго́ри|я, и *f.* phantasmagoria.
фанта́ст, а *m.* **1.** fantasy-monger; pers. with powerful imagination; dreamer, visionary. **2.** writer, artist treating the fantastic.
фанта́стик|а, и *f.* **1.** the fantastic; (*collect.*; *liter.*) fantastic tales. **2.** fantasy, fiction (*opp. reality*); **нау́чная ф.** science fiction; sci-fi.
фантасти́ческий *adj.* **1.** fantastical. **2.** (*in var. senses*) fantastic; fabulous; imaginary.
фантасти́ч|ный (~ен, ~на) *adj.* = **~еский**
фанто́м, а *m.* phantom.
фанто́мный *adj.* **1.** (*physiol.*) imaginary, false. **2.** (*elec.*) phantom.
фанфа́р|а, ы *f.* (*mus.*) **1.** bugle. **2.** fanfare.
фанфаро́н, а *m.* (*coll.*) braggart.
фанфаро́н|ить, ю, ишь *impf.* (*coll.*) to brag.
фанфаро́нств|о, а *nt.* (*coll.*) bragging.
ФАО *f. indecl.* FAO (*abbr. of* Food and Agriculture Organization — *Продово́льственная и сельскохозя́йственная организа́ция Объединённых На́ций*).
фа́р|а, ы *f.* headlight (*on motor vehicle, locomotive, etc.*); **поса́дочные ~ы** landing lights (*on aircraft*).
фара́д|а, ы *f.* (*elec.*) farad.
фарао́н, а *m.* **1.** (*hist.*) Pharaoh (*also nickname for policeman*). **2.** faro (*card-game*).
фарао́нов *adj.* Pharaoh's; **~а мышь** (*zool.*) ichneumon.
фарва́тер, а *m.* (*naut.*) fairway, channel; **плыть, быть в чьём-н. ~е** (*fig.*) to follow s.o.'s lead, side with s.o.
Фаренге́йт, а *m.* Fahrenheit (thermometer); **80° по ~у** 80° Fahrenheit.
фаре́р|ец, ца *m.* Faeroese, Faeroe Islander.
фаре́р|ка, ки *f. of* **~ец**
Фаре́рск|ие остров|а́, ~их ~о́в *no sg.* the Faeroe Islands; the Faeroes.
фаре́рский *adj.* Faeroese.
фаринги́т, а *m.* (*med.*) pharyngitis.
фарисе́|й, я *m.* Pharisee (*also fig.*).
фарисе́йский *adj.* pharisaical (*also fig.*).
фарисе́йств|о, а *nt.* pharisaism.
фарисе́йств|овать, ую *impf.* to act pharisaically.
фармазо́н, а *m.* (*coll., obs.*) freemason.
фармако́лог, а *m.* pharmacologist.
фармакологи́ческий *adj.* pharmacological.
фармаколо́ги|я, и *f.* pharmacology.
фармакопе́|я, и *f.* pharmacopoeia.
фармаце́вт, а *m.* pharmaceutical chemist.
фармаце́втик|а, и *f.* pharmaceutics.
фармацевти́ческий *adj.* pharmaceutical.
фармаци́|я, и *f.* pharmacy.
фарс, а *m.* (*theatr.*) farce (*also fig.*).
фарт, а *m.* (*sl.*) luck.
фарт|и́ть, и́т *impf.* (*of* **по~**) (*impers.+d.*; *sl.*) to be in luck.
farто́вый *adj.* (*sl.*) **1.** lucky. **2.** fine, smashing.
фа́ртук, а *m.* **1.** apron. **2.** carriage-rug.
фарфо́р, а *m.* **1.** porcelain, china. **2.** (*collect.*) china.
фарфо́р|овый *adj. of* **~; ~овая гли́на** china clay, kaolin; **~овая посу́да** china(-ware).
фарцо́вщик, а *m.* (*sl.*) dealer, trafficker (*in goods or currency illegally bought from foreigners*).
фарш, а *m.* (*cul.*) force-meat; sausage-meat; stuffing.
фарширо́в|анный *p.p.p. of* **~а́ть** *and adj.* (*cul.*) stuffed, farci.
фаршир|ова́ть, у́ю *impf.* (*of* **за~**) (*cul.*) to stuff.
фас, а *m.* **1.** front, façade; **в ф.** en face. **2.** (*mil.*) face (*of salient*); **ф. про́волочного загражде́ния** straight leg of barbed-wire entanglement.
фаса́д, а *m.* façade, front.
фасе́т, а *m.* facet.

фасе́т|очный *adj. of* ~; **~очные глаза́** (*zool.*) compound eyes.
фа́ск|а, и *f.* (*tech.*) face, facet; (bevel) edge.
фас|ова́ть, у́ю *impf.* (*comm.*) to prepack (*in measured quantities*).
фасо́вк|а, и *f.* (*comm.*) prepacking.
фасо́вочн|ый *adj.* (*comm.*) (pre)packing, packaging; *as n.* **~ая, ~ой** *f.* packing department.
фасо́л|евый *adj. of* **~ь**
фасо́л|ь, и *f.* haricot bean, French bean; **туре́цкая ф.** runner beans.
фасо́н, а *m.* **1.** cut (*of dress, etc.*); fashion, style; **не ф.** (*coll.*) it's not done. **2.** (*coll.*) style, manner, way. **3.** (*coll.*) swank, showing off; **держа́ть ф.** to swank, show off.
фасо́нист|ый (~, ~а) *adj.* (*coll.*) fashionable, stylish.
фасо́нн|ый *adj.* (*tech.*) **1.** fashioned, shaped; **~ое желе́зо** shaped iron, profile iron, section iron. **2.** form(ing), shape, shaping; **~ая накова́льня** die block; **~ая обрабо́тка** profiling; **ф. резе́ц** form tool, shaper tool; **~ая фрезеро́вка** form milling.
фат, а *m.* fop.
фат|а́, ы́ *f.* (*bridal*) veil.
фатали́зм, а *m.* fatalism.
фатали́ст, а *m.* fatalist.
фаталисти́ческий *adj.* **1.** fatalistic. **2.** fatal.
фата́льност|ь, и *f.* fatality, fate.
фата́л|ьный (~ен, ~ьна) *adj.* **1.** fatal, fated. **2.** resigned (to one's fate); **ф. вид** resigned appearance.
фатова́т|ый (~, ~а) *adj.* foppish.
фа́тум, а *m.* fate.
фа́ун|а, ы *f.* fauna.
фаустпатро́н, а *m.* (*mil.*) 'panzer-faust' (*bazooka-type weapon*).
фахве́рк, а *m.* frame building.
фахве́рковый *adj.* frame-built.
фашизи́р|овать, ую *impf. and pf.* to run on Fascist lines; to impose Fascism (upon).
фашизи́р|оваться, уюсь *impf. and pf.* **1.** to become Fascist. **2.** *pass. of* **~овать**
фаши́зм, а *m.* Fascism.
фаши́н|а, ы *f.* fascine, faggot.
фаши́н|ный *adj. of* ~; **ф. нож** fascine-cutting knife.
фаши́ст, а *m.* Fascist.
фаши́стский *adj.* Fascist.
фаэто́н, а *m.* phaeton.
фая́нс, а *m.* faience, pottery, glazed earthenware.
фая́нс|овый *adj. of* ~
ФБР *nt. indecl.* (*abbr. of* **Федера́льное бюро́ рассле́дований**) FBI (*Federal Bureau of Investigation*).
февра́л|ь, я́ *m.* February.
февра́ль|ский *adj. of* ~
федерали́зм, а *m.* federalism.
федерали́ст, а *m.* federalist.
федера́льный *adj.* federal.
федерати́вный *adj.* federative, federal.
федера́ци|я, и *f.* federation.
феери́ческий *adj.* **1.** (*theatr.*) (based on a) fairytale. **2.** fairy-like; magical.
фее́ри|я, и *f.* **1.** play, ballet, *etc.*, based on a fairytale. **2.** magical sight.
фейерве́рк, а *m.* firework(s).
фейерве́ркер, а *m.* (*hist.*) bombardier (*non-commissioned artillery officer in tsarist Russ. army*).
фека́л|ии, ий *pl.* (*sg.* **~ия, ~ии** *f.*) faeces.
фека́льный *adj.* faecal.
фелла́х, а *m.* fellah.
фельдма́ршал, а *m.* field-marshal.
фельдфе́бел|ь, я *m.* (*hist.*) sergeant-major.
фе́льдшер, а, *pl.* **~а́** *m.* doctor's assistant, medical attendant (*med. practitioner lacking graduate qualification*).
фельдшери́ц|а, ы *f. of* **фе́льдшер**
фе́льдшер|ский *adj. of* ~
фельдъе́гер|ский *adj. of* **~ь**; **~ская связь** communication by courier.
фельдъе́гер|ь, я *m.* (*hist.*) courier, special messenger.

фельето́н, а *m.* feuilleton; satirical article.
фельетони́ст, а *m.* feuilletonist; composer of satirical articles.
фельето́н|ный *adj. of* ~
фелю́г|а, и *f.* (*naut.*) felucca.
фемини́зм, а *m.* feminism.
фемини́ст, а *m.* feminist.
фемини́ст|ка, ки *f. of* ~
фемини́стский *adj.* feminist.
фен, а *m.* (hair-)drier.
фён, а *m.* föhn (*wind*).
фе́никс, а *m.* **1.** (*mythol.*) phoenix. **2.** (*obs.*) marvel, prodigy.
фено́л, а *m.* (*chem.*) phenol, carbolic acid.
феноло́ги|я, и *f.* (*biol.*) phenology.
фено́мен, а *m.* phenomenon; phenomenal occurrence, pers.
феноменали́зм, а *m.* (*phil.*) phenomenalism.
феномена́л|ьный (~ен, ~ьна) *adj.* phenomenal.
феноменоло́ги|я, и *f.* (*phil.*) phenomenology.
фе́нхел|ь, я *m.* (*bot.*) fennel.
фео́д, а *m.* (*hist.*) feud, fief.
феода́л, а *m.* (*hist.*) feudal lord.
феодали́зм, а *m.* feudalism.
феода́льный *adj.* feudal.
фе́рз|евый *adj. of* **~ь**
ферз|ь, я́, *pl.* **~и́, ~е́й** *m.* (*chess*) queen.
фе́рм|а[1], ы *f.* farm.
фе́рм|а[2], ы *f.* (*tech.*) girder.
ферма́т|а, ы *f.* (*mus.*) fermata.
фе́рм|енный *adj. of* **~а**[2]; lattice.
ферме́нт, а *m.* (*biol., chem.*) ferment.
ферменти́р|овать, ую *impf.* to ferment.
фе́рмер, а *m.* farmer.
фе́рмер|ский *adj. of* ~; **ф. дом** farm-house.
фе́рмерств|о, а *nt.* **1.** (*private*) farming. **2.** (*collect.*) farmers.
фе́рмер|ша, ши *f.* (*coll.*) **1.** *f. of* ~. **2.** farmer's wife.
фе́рм|овый *adj. of* **~а**[2]
Фермопи́л|ы, ~ *no sg.* (*hist.*) Thermopylae.
фермуа́р, а *m.* (*obs.*) **1.** clasp (*on necklace, purse, etc.*). **2.** necklace.
фернамбу́к, а *m.* (*bot.*) Brazil wood (*Caesalpinia brasiliensis*).
феронье́рк|а, и *f.* (*obs.*) frontlet, coronet.
ферроспла́в, а *m.* ferro-alloy.
ферт, а *m.* **1.** old name of letter **'ф'**; **~ом стоя́ть** to stand with arms akimbo. **2.** (*coll.*) fop; smug pers.; **~ом гляде́ть** to look smug; **~ом ходи́ть** to strut about.
феру́л|а, ы *f.* **1.** (*obs.*) ruler, ferula (*as instrument of punishment in school*). **2.** surveillance.
фе́ряз|ь, и *f.* (*hist.*) feryaz (*loose tunic formerly worn by Russians*).
фес, а *m.* (*and* **фе́ск|а, и** *f.*) fez.
фестива́л|ь, я *m.* festival.
фесто́н, а *m.* (*dressmaking*) scallops (*decoration on fabrics*).
фети́ш, а *m.* fetish.
фетишизи́р|овать, ую *impf.* to make a fetish (of).
фетиши́зм, а *m.* fetishism.
фетиши́ст, а *m.* fetishist.
фетр, а *m.* felt.
фе́тр|овый *adj. of* ~
фефё́л|а, ы *f.* (*coll.*) slattern.
фе́фер, а (у) *m. only in phrr.* (*coll.*) **зада́ть, показа́ть ~у** (*+d.*) to give it hot (to).
фехтова́льный *adj.* fencing.
фехтова́льщик, а *m.* fencer; **ф. рапи́рой** foil fencer; **ф. шпа́гой** épée fencer.
фехтова́ни|е, я *nt.* fencing.
фехт|ова́ть, у́ю, *impf.* to fence.
фешене́бел|ьный (~ен, ~ьна) *adj.* (*obs.*) fashionable.
фе́|я, и *f.* fairy.
фи *int.* fie!; pah!
фиа́л, а *m.* phial; (*poet.*) goblet, beaker.
фиа́лк|а, и *f.* violet.
фиа́лк|овый *adj. of* **~а**; **ф. ко́рень** orris-root; *as n.* **~овые, ~овых** (*bot.*) Violaceae.
фиа́ско *nt. indecl.* failure; **потерпе́ть ф.** to be a flop.

фибергла́с, а *m.* fibreglass.
фибергла́с|овый *adj. of* ~
фи́бр|а, ы *f.* **1.** (*anat., bot.*) fibre (*also fig.*); **все́ми ~ами души́** in every fibre (of one's being). **2.** fibre (*leather-substitute material*).
фи́бр|овый *adj. of* **~а 2.**
фибро́зный *adj.* (*anat., bot.*) fibrous.
фиброли́т, а *m.* fibreboard.
фиброли́т|овый *adj. of* ~
фибро́м|а, ы *f.* (*med.*) fibroma.
фиви́йский *adj.* Theban.
Фи́в|ы, ~ *no sg.* (*hist.*) Thebes.
фи́г|а, и *f.* **1.** fig(-tree). **2.** (*coll.*) = **ку́киш**
фигаро́ *nt. indecl.* bolero (*short jacket*).
фи́гли-ми́гли, фи́глей-ми́глей *no sg.* (*coll.*) tricks.
фигля́р, а *m.* **1.** (*obs.*) (circus) acrobat; clown. **2.** poseur; (*pej.*) actor.
фигля́р|ить, ю, ишь *impf.* (*coll.*) to put on an act.
фигля́рнича|ть, ю *impf.* = **фигля́рить**
фи́г|овый *adj. of* **~а; ~овое де́рево** fig tree; **ф. листо́к** fig-leaf (*also fig.* = *pretence*).
фигу́р|а, ы *f.* **1.** (*in var. senses*) figure. **2.** (*cards*) court-card, picture-card. **3.** chess-man (*excluding pawns*).
фигура́л|ьный (~ен, ~ьна) *adj.* **1.** figurative, metaphorical. **2.** (*of liter. style*) ornate, involved.
фигура́нт, а *m.* (*theatr.*) **1.** figurant (*in ballet*). **2.** super, extra.
фигури́р|овать, ую *impf.* to figure, appear.
фигури́ст, а *m.* figure skater.
фигури́ст|ка, ки *f. of* ~
фигу́р|ка, ки *f.* **1.** *dim. of* **~а. 2.** figurine, statuette.
фигу́рн|ый *adj.* **1.** figured; ornamented; irregularly shaped. **2.: ф. резе́ц** (*tech.*) form tool. **3.: ~ое ката́ние на конька́х** figure skating; **ф. пилота́ж** aerobatics.
фидеи́зм, а *m.* (*phil.*) fideism.
Фи́джи *nt. indecl.* Fiji.
фиджи́|ец, йца *m.* Fijian.
фиджи́|йка, йки *f. of* **~ец**
фиджи́йский *adj.* Fijian.
фи́жм|ы, ~ *no sg.* farthingale.
физ... *comb. form, abbr. of* **физи́ческий**
фи́зик, а *m.* physicist.
фи́зик|а, и *f.* physics.
физио́лог, а *m.* physiologist.
физиологи́ческий *adj.* physiological.
физиоло́ги|я, и *f.* physiology.
физионо́ми|я, и *f.* physiognomy (*also joc.*).
физиотерапе́вт, а *m.* physiotherapist.
физиотерапи́|я, и *f.* physiotherapy.
физи́ческ|ий *adj.* **1.** physical; **~ая культу́ра** physical training, gymnastics; **ф. труд** manual labour. **2.** *adj. of* **фи́зика; ф. кабине́т** physics laboratory.
физкульту́р|а, ы *f.* physical training (*abbr.* PT); physical education (*abbr.* PE); **уро́к ~ы** PE class; **лече́бная ф.** exercise therapy, remedial gymnastics.
физкульту́рник, а *m.* athlete, sportsman.
физкульту́рни|ца, цы *f. of* **~к**
физкульту́рн|ый *adj.* gymnastic; athletic, sports; **ф. зал** gymnasium; **~ая подгото́вка** physical training.
фикс[1]**, а** *m.* **1.** fixed price. **2.** fixed sum.
фикс[2]**, а** *m.* (*coll.*) gold crown (*on tooth*).
фикса́ж, а *m.* (*phot.*) fixing solution, fixer.
фиксати́в, а *m.* (*art*) fixative.
фикса́тор, а *m.* (*tech.*) **1.** stop; index pin. **2.** fixing solution.
фиксату́ар, а *m.* fixative, hair-grease.
фикси́р|овать, ую *impf. and pf.* (*pf. also* **за~**) **1.** to record (*in writing, etc.*). **2.** (*in var. senses*) to fix; **ф. день свида́ния** to fix a date to meet, make a date.
фикти́в|ный (~ен, ~на) *adj.* fictitious.
фи́кус, а *m.* (*bot.*) ficus.
фи́кци|я, и *f.* fiction.
филантро́п, а *m.* philanthropist.
филантропи́ческий *adj.* philanthropic.
филантро́пи|я, и *f.* philanthropy.
филармо́ни|я, и *f.* philharmonic society.
филатели́ст, а *m.* philatelist, stamp collector.
филатели́|я, и *f.* philately.
филе́[1] *nt. indecl.* (*cul.*) **1.** sirloin. **2.** fillet (*of meat or fish*).
филе́[2] *nt. indecl.* (*dressmaking*) drawn-thread work.
филе́|й, я *m.* = ~[1]
филе́|йный *adj. of* ~[1,2]
филёнк|а, и *f.* panel, slat.
филёр, а *m.* detective, sleuth.
филиа́л, а *m.* branch (*of an institution*).
филиа́л|ьный *adj. of* ~; **~ьное отделе́ние** branch (office).
филигра́нный *adj.* **1.** filigree. **2.** (*fig.*) meticulous.
филигра́н|ь, и *f.* **1.** filigree. **2.** water-mark.
фи́лин, а *m.* eagle owl (*Bubo bubo*).
фили́ппик|а, и *f.* philippic.
филиппи́н|ец, ца *m.* Filipino.
филиппи́н|ка, ки *f. of* **~ец**
филиппи́нский *adj.* Philippine; Filipino.
Филиппи́н|ы, ~ *no sg.* the Philippines.
фили́стер, а *m.* philistine
фили́стер|ский *adj. of* ~
фили́стерств|о, а *nt.* philistinism.
филогене́з, а *m.* (*biol.*) phylogenesis.
фило́лог, а *m.* philologist, student of language and literature.
филологи́ческий *adj.* philological; **ф. факульте́т** faculty of languages and literature.
филоло́ги|я, и *f.* philology; study of language and literature.
филомени́ст, а *m.* phillumenist (*collector of matchbox labels*).
фило́н, а *m.* (*coll.*) idler, loafer.
фило́н|ить, ю, ишь *impf.* (*coll.*) to idle, loaf.
фило́соф, а *m.* philosopher.
филосо́фи|я, и *f.* philosophy.
филосо́фский *adj.* philosophic(al).
филосо́фств|овать, ую *impf.* to philosophize.
филфа́к, а *m.* (*abbr. of* **филологи́ческий факульте́т**) faculty of languages and literature.
филфа́ков|ец, ца *m.* (*coll.*) languages and literature student.
фильдеко́с, а *m.* Lisle thread.
филье́р|а, ы *f.* (*tech.*) draw plate; die; spinneret.
фи́лькин *adj.*: **~а гра́мота** invalid, crudely-written, obscure document.
фильм, а *m.* (*cin.*) film; **приключе́нческий ф.** thriller.
фи́льм|а, ы *f.* (*obs.*) = ~
фильмоте́к|а, и *f.* film library.
фильтр, а *m.* filter.
фильтра́т, а *m.* filtrate.
фильтра́ци|я, и *f.* filtration.
фильтрова́льный *adj.*: **ф. насо́с** filter pump; **ф. слой** filter-bed.
фильтр|ова́ть, у́ю *impf.* (*of* **про~**) **1.** to filter. **2.** (*fig., coll.*) screen, check.
фимиа́м, а *m.* incense; **кури́ть ф.** (*+d.*) to praise to the skies, sing the praises (of).
фин... *comb. form, abbr. of* **фина́нсовый**
фина́л, а *m.* **1.** finale. **2.** (*sport*) final.
фина́льный *adj.* final; **ф. акко́рд** (*mus.*) final chord; **ф. матч** (*sport*) final.
финанси́р|овать, ую *impf. and pf.* to finance.
финанси́ст, а *m.* **1.** financier. **2.** financial expert.
фина́нсовый *adj.* financial; **ф. год** fiscal year; **ф. отде́л** finance department.
фина́нс|ы, ов *no sg.* **1.** finance(s). **2.** (*coll.*) money.
фи́ник, а *m.* date (*fruit*).
финики́йский *adj.* Phoenician.
Финики́|я, и *f.* Phoenicia.
финики́ян|ин, ина, *pl.* **~е,** ~ *m.* Phoenician.
финики́ян|ка, ки *f. of* **~ин**
фи́ник|овый *adj. of* ~; **~овая па́льма** date-palm.
фининспе́ктор, а *m.* inspector of finance(s).
фини́фтевый *adj.* (*obs.*) enamelled.
фини́фт|ь, и *f.* (*obs.*) enamel.
фини́фт|яный = **~евый**
фи́ниш, а *m.* (*sport*) **1.** finish; finishing post. **2.** final lap.
фи́нишер, а *m.* (*naut.*) batsman (*on aircraft carrier*).

финиши́р|овать, ую *impf. and pf.* (*sport*) to finish, come in.
фи́ниш|ный *adj. of* ~; **~ная ле́нточка** finishing tape.
фи́нк|а[1], **и** *f. of* **финн**
фи́нк|а[2], **и** *f.* **1.** Finnish knife. **2.** Finnish cap (*round, flat cap with fur band*). **3.** Finnish pony. **4.** = **фи́нна**
Финля́нди|я, и *f.* Finland.
финля́ндский *adj.* Finnish.
финн, а *m.* Finn.
фи́нн|а, ы *f.* (*zool.*) pork tapeworm.
финно́з, а *m.* measles (*disease of swine*).
фи́нно-уго́рский *adj.* (*ling.*) Finno-Ugric.
финотде́л, а *m.* finance department.
фи́нский *adj.* Finnish, Finnic; **ф. зали́в** Gulf of Finland; **ф. нож** Finnish knife.
финт, а *m.* (*sport*) feint.
фин|ти́ть, чу́, ти́шь *impf.* (*coll.*) to be crafty, resort to ruses.
финтифа́нт|ы, ов *no sg.* (*coll., obs.*) **1.: вы́делывать, выки́дывать ф.** to display finesse. **2.** trifles.
финтифлю́шк|а, и *f.* (*coll.*) **1.** bagatelle. **2.** (*pl.*) trifles. **3.** flibbertigibbet.
фиоле́товый *adj.* violet.
фио́рд, а *m.* (*geog.*) fiord, fjord.
фиориту́р|а, ы *f.* (*mus.*) grace(-note).
фи́рм|а, ы *f.* **1.** (*econ.*) firm. **2.** (*obs.*) sign, mark, signature; **под ~ой** (+*g.*) under the sign (of). **3.** (*coll.*) appearance, pretext. **4.** (*sl.*) foreigner; foreign goods.
фи́рм|енный *adj. of* **~а 1.; ~енная этике́тка** proprietary label; **ф. бланк** letterhead.
фирн, а *m.* (*geog.*) névé, glacier snow.
фисгармо́ни|я, и *f.* (*mus.*) harmonium.
фиск, а *m.* fisc.
фиска́л, а *m.* (*hist.*) fiscal, finance inspector; (*coll.*) sneak, tale-bearer.
фиска́л|ить, ю, ишь *impf.* (*coll.*) to (be a) sneak.
фиска́льный *adj.* (*leg.*) fiscal.
фиста́шк|а, и *f.* pistachio(-tree).
фиста́шков|ый *adj.* **1.** pistachio; **ф. лак** mastic varnish; **~ая смола́** mastic. **2.** pistachio-green.
фи́стул|а́[1], **ы-ы́** *f.* (*med.*) fistula.
фистул|а́[2], **ы́** *f.* **1.** (*mus.*) pipe, flute. **2.** falsetto.
фити́л|ь, я́ *m.* **1.** wick; fuse. **2.** (*naut. sl.*) rocket (= *reprimand*); **вста́вить ф.** (+*d.*) to give a rocket to.
фито... *comb. form* (*biol.*) phyto-.
фитю́льк|а, и *f.* (*coll.*) little thing; (*of a pers.*) midget.
фи́ф|а, ы *f.* bimbo, flibbertigibbet (*coll.*).
фи́шк|а, и *f.* **1.** counter, chip (*for scoring, recording stake, etc., in games*). **2.** (*sl.*) face.
флаг, а *m.* flag; **вы́кинуть ф.** to put out a flag; **держа́ть (свой) ф.** (**на**+*p.*; *naut.*) to sail (in), be (in); **спусти́ть ф.** to lower a flag; **оста́ться за ~ом** (*sport; fig.*) to fail to make the distance; **под ~ом** (+*g.*) (*i*) flying the flag (of), (*ii*) (*fig.*) under the guise (of).
фла́гдук, а *m.* (*naut.*) bunting.
фла́гман, а *m.* (*naut.*) **1.** flag-officer. **2.** flag-ship; (*aeron.*) leader's plane of bomber squadron. **3.** (*fig.*) leader.
фла́гман|ский *adj. of* ~; **ф. кора́бль** = ~ **2.**
флаг-офице́р, а *m.* flag-officer.
флагшто́к, а *m.* flagstaff.
флажко́в|ый *adj. of* **флажо́к; ~ая сигнализа́ция** flag signalling.
фла́жный *adj.* flag.
флаж|о́к, ка́ *m.* (*small*) flag; signal flag.
флажоле́т, а *m.* (*mus.*) flageolet.
флако́н, а *m.* (scent-)bottle, flask.
флама́нд|ец, ца *m.* Fleming.
флама́нд|ка, ки *f. of* **~ец**
флама́ндский *adj.* Flemish.
флами́нго *m. indecl.* flamingo.
фланг, а *m.* (*mil.*) flank; wing.
фланго́в|ый *adj.* (*mil.*) flank; **ф. охва́т** flanking movement, envelopment; *as n.* **ф., ~ого** *m.* flank man.
флане́левк|а, и *f.* (*coll.*) flannel (*sailor's blouse*).
флане́левый *adj.* flannel.
флане́л|ь, и *f.* flannel.
фланёр, а *m.* flâneur, idler.
фла́н|ец, ца *m.* (*tech.*) flange.
флани́р|овать, ую *impf.* (*coll.*) to idle; to mooch.
фланки́р|овать, ую *impf. and pf.* (*mil.*) to flank.
фла́н|цевый *adj. of* **~ец**
фла́тов|ый *adj.*: **~ая бума́га** (*typ.*) flat paper.
флеби́т, а *m.* (*med.*) phlebitis.
фле́гм|а, ы *f.* **1.** (*fig.*) phlegm. **2.** (*coll.*) phlegmatic pers.
флегма́тик, а *m.* phlegmatic pers.
флегмати́ч|ный (~ен, ~на) *adj.* phlegmatic.
фле́йт|а, ы *f.* flute.
флейти́ст, а *m.* flautist.
фле́йт|овый *adj. of* **~а**
фле́кси|я, и *f.* (*ling.*) inflection.
флекти́вный *adj.* (*ling.*) inflected.
флёр, а *m.* crêpe; **наки́нуть ф.** (**на**+*a.*; *fig.*) to draw a veil (over).
флёрдора́нж, а *m.* orange blossom.
флибустье́р, а *m.* filibuster.
фли́гел|ь, я, *pl.* **~я́, ~е́й** *m.* **1.** wing (*of building*). **2.** outhouse, outbuilding.
фли́гель-адъюта́нт, а *m.* (*hist.*) aide-de-camp.
флирт, а *m.* flirtation.
флирт|ова́ть, у́ю *impf.* (**с**+*i.*) to flirt (with).
флома́стер, а *m.* felt-tip *or* fibre-tipped pen; felt-tip; marker (pen).
фло́р|а, ы *f.* flora.
флоренти́йский *adj.* Florentine.
флоренти́н|ец, ца *m.* Florentine.
флоренти́н|ка, ки *f. of* **~ец**
Флоре́нци|я, и *f.* Florence.
Флори́д|а, ы *f.* Florida.
флори́ст, а *m.* specialist in study of flora.
флори́стик|а, и *f.* (study of) flora.
флот, а *m.* **1.** fleet; **вое́нно-морско́й ф.** navy. **2.: возду́шный ф.** air force.
флота́ци|я, и *f.* (*min.*) flotation.
флоти́ли|я, и *f.* flotilla.
флотово́д|ец, ца *m.* naval commander.
фло́тск|ий *adj.* naval; *as n.* **ф., ~ого** *m.* sailor.
флуоресце́нци|я, и *f.* fluorescence.
флуоресци́р|овать, ует *impf.* (*phys.*) to fluoresce; **~ующий** fluorescent.
флэт, а *m.* (*sl.*) flat, 'pad'.
флюга́рк|а, и *f.* **1.** (*naut.*) pennant; distinguishing plate (*of boat*). **2.** (*chimney*) cowl. **3.** weather-vane.
флю́гер, а, *pl.* **~а́** *m.* **1.** weather-vane; weathercock (*also of a pers.*). **2.** (*mil.; obs.*) pennant.
флюи́д|ы, ов *pl.* (*sg.* **~, ~а** *m.*) ectoplasm; (*fig.*) emanations.
флюс[1], **а,** *pl.* **~ы** *m.* dental abscess, gumboil.
флюс[2], **а,** *pl.* **~ы́** *m.* (*tech.*) flux.
фля́г|а, и *f.* **1.** flask; (*mil.*) water bottle. **2.** churn.
фля́жк|а, и *f. dim. of* **фля́га**
фля́к, а *m.* (*gymnastics*) flic(k)-flac(k).
...фо́ *comb. form, abbr. of* **фина́нсовый отде́л**
фойе́ *nt. indecl.* foyer.
фок, а *m.* (*naut.*) **1.** foresail. **2.** foremast.
фок- *pref.* (*naut.*) fore-.
фока́льный *adj.* (*phys.*) focal.
фок-ма́чт|а, ы (*naut.*) foremast.
фокстерье́р, а *m.* fox-terrier.
фокстро́т, а *m.* foxtrot.
фо́кус[1], **а** *m.* (*math., phys., med., and fig.*) focus.
фо́кус[2], **а** *m.* **1.** (conjuring) trick; **пока́зывать ~ы** to do conjuring tricks. **2.** trick, secret (*of mechanism, etc.*); **в то́м-то и ф.** that's the whole point; that's just it. **3.** (*coll.*) whim, caprice.
фокуси́р|овать, ую *impf.* (*phys., phot.*) to focus.
фо́кусник, а *m.* **1.** conjurer, juggler. **2.** (*coll.*) rogue, tricky customer.
фо́кусича|ть, ю *impf.* **1.** (*obs.*) to do conjuring tricks. **2.** (*coll.*) to play tricks.
фо́кусный *adj.* (*phys., phot.*) focal.
фолиа́нт, а *m.* folio.

Фолкле́ндск|ие острова́, ~их ~о́в *no sg.* the Falkland Islands; the Falklands.
фолли́кул, а *m.* (*anat.*) follicle.
фольва́рк, а *m.* farm (*in West Russia, Poland, and Lithuania*).
фо́льг|а, и *f.* foil.
фолькло́р, а *m.* folklore.
фольклори́ст, а *m.* student of folklore.
фо́мк|а, и *f.* (*coll.*) jemmy.
фон, а *m.* background (*also fig.*).
фона́рик, а *m.* small lamp; torch, flash-light.
фона́р|ный *adj. of* **~ь; ф. столб** lamppost.
фона́рщик, а *m.* (*obs.*) **1.** lamplighter. **2.** torch-bearer.
фона́р|ь, я́ *m.* **1.** lantern; lamp; light. **2.** (*archit.*) light; skylight; **ф. каби́ны** (*aeron.*) cockpit canopy. **3.** (*coll.*) black eye.
фонд, а *m.* **1.** (*fin.*) fund; stock, reserves, resources; **валю́тный ф.** currency reserves; **земе́льный ф.** available land; **золото́й ф.** gold reserves; **о́бщий ф.** pool. **2.** (*pl.*) (*fin.*) stocks; (*fig.*) stock; **~ы его́ повы́сились** his stock has risen. **3.** fund, foundation (*in former USSR, organization serving as channel for State subsidies to writers, artists, etc.*). **4.** archive.
фо́нд|овый *adj. of* **~; ~овая би́ржа** stock exchange.
фоне́м|а, ы *f.* (*ling.*) phoneme.
фонендоско́п, а *m.* (*med.*) phonendoscope.
фоне́тик|а, и *f.* phonetics.
фонети́ст, а *m.* phonetician.
фонети́ческий *adj.* phonetic.
фони́р|овать, ую *impf. and pf.* (*sl.*) to 'bug'.
фони́ческий *adj.* **1.** phonic. **2.: ф. аппара́т** (*mil.*) telephone with voice frequency signalling.
фоно́граф, а *m.* phonograph.
фоноло́ги|я, и *f.* phonemics.
фоноте́к|а, и *f.* gramophone record library, sound recording library.
фонта́н, а *m.* fountain; (*fig.*) stream; **нефтяно́й ф.** oil gusher; **бить ~ом** to gush forth.
фонтани́р|овать, ует *impf.* to gush forth.
фо́р|а, ы *f.*: **дать ~у** (+*d.*) to give odds, give a start (*in a game*).
фо́рвард, а *m.* (*sport.*; *obs.*) forward.
фордеви́нд, а *m.* (*naut.*) following wind; **идти́ на ф.** to run before the wind.
форе́йтор, а *m.* (*obs.*) postilion.
форе́л|ь, и *f.* trout.
фо́рзац, а *m.* fly-leaf (*of a book*).
фо́ринт, а *m.* forint (*Hungarian currency unit*).
фо́рм|а, ы *f.* **1.** (*in var. senses*) form; **по ~е, ... по содержа́нию** in form, ... in content; **по (всей) ~е** in due form, properly. **2.** shape; (*pl.*) contours (*of human body*). **3.** (*tech.*) mould, cast; **отли́ть в ~у** to mould, cast. **4.** uniform. **5.: быть в ~е** (*coll.*) to be in (good) form.
формали́зм, а *m.* formalism (*pej. in Marxist criticism of bourgeois art, etc.*).
формали́н, а *m.* formalin.
формали́ст, а *m.* formalist.
формали́стик|а, и *f.* **1.** formalism. **2.** formalities.
формальдеги́д, а *m.* (*chem.*) formaldehyde.
форма́льност|ь, и *f.* formality.
форма́л|ьный (~ен, ~ьна) *adj.* (*in var. senses*) formal; **~ьное доказа́тельство** formal proof; **~ьная ло́гика** formal logic.
фор-ма́рс, а *m.* (*naut.*) foretop.
форма́т, а *m.* size, format.
форма́ци|я, и *f.* **1.** structure; stage (of development). **2.** stamp, mentality. **3.** (*geol.*) formation.
фо́рменк|а, и *f.* (*coll.*) (*sailor's*) duck blouse.
фо́рменный *adj.* **1.** uniform. **2.** (*obs.*) formal. **3.** (*coll.*) proper, regular, positive.
формирова́ни|е, я *nt.* **1.** forming; organizing. **2.** (*mil.*) unit, formation.
формир|ова́ть, у́ю *impf.* (*of* **с~**) to form; to organize; **ф. хара́ктер** to form character; **ф. батальо́н** to raise a battalion; **ф. по́езд** to make up a train.
формир|ова́ться, у́юсь *impf.* (*of* **с~**) **1.** to form, shape, develop (*intrans.*). **2.** *pass. of* **~ова́ть**
форм|ова́ть, у́ю *impf.* (*of* **с~**) to form, shape; to model; (*tech.*) to mould, cast.
формо́вк|а, и *f.* forming, shaping; (*tech.*) moulding, casting.
формо́вочн|ый *adj.* (*tech.*) moulding, casting; **~ая гли́на** foundry loam; **~ые черни́ла** (foundry) blacking.
формо́вщик, а *m.* moulder.
фо́рмул|а, ы *f.* formula; formulation.
формули́р|овать, ую *impf. and pf.* (*pf. also* **с~**) to formulate.
формулиро́вк|а, и *f.* **1.** formulation. **2.** formula.
формуля́р, а *m.* **1.** (*obs.*) record of service. **2.** (*tech.*) logbook (*of installation, machine, etc.*). **3.** library card (*card inserted in book recording details thereof*); reader's record card (*card kept by library for each reader, recording details of books loaned*).
форпо́ст, а *m.* (*mil.*) advanced post; outpost (*also fig.*).
форс, а (у) *m.* (*coll.*) swank; **для ~а** to show off; **сбить кому́-н. ф.** to take s.o. down a peg.
форси́ров|анный *p.p.p. of* **~ать** *and adj.* forced; accelerated; **ф. марш** forced march.
форси́р|овать, ую *impf. and pf.* **1.** to force; to speed up. **2.** (*mil.*) to force (*a crossing of*).
фор|си́ть, шу́, си́шь *impf.* (*coll.*) to swank, show off.
форс-мажо́р, а *m.* force majeur.
форсу́нк|а, и *f.* (*tech.*) sprayer, atomizer, jet; fuel injector.
форт, а, о ~е, в ~у́, *pl.* **~ы́** *m.* (*mil.*) fort.
фо́ртел|ь, я *m.* (*coll.*) trick, stunt.
фортепьяни́ст, а *m.* (*obs.*) pianist.
фортепья́нный *adj.* piano; **ф. конце́рт** piano concerto.
фортепья́но *nt. indecl.* piano.
фортификацио́нный *adj.* fortification.
фортифика́ци|я, и *f.* fortification.
фо́рточк|а, и *f.* fortochka (*small hinged pane for ventilation in window of Russ. houses*).
фо́рум, а *m.* forum.
форшла́г, а *m.* (*mus.*) grace-note.
форшма́к, а́ *m.* (*cul.*) forshmak (*baked hashed meat or herring with sliced potatoes and onions*).
форште́в|ень, ня *m.* (*naut.*) stem.
фосге́н, а *m.* (*chem.*) phosgene.
фосфа́т, а *m.* (*chem.*) phosphate.
фо́сфор, а *m.* (*chem.*) phosphorus.
фосфоресце́нци|я, и *f.* phosphorescence.
фосфоресци́р|овать, ую *impf.* to phosphoresce; **~ующая кра́ска** luminous paint.
фо́сфорист|ый *adj.* (*chem.*) phosphorous; **~ая бро́нза** phosphor bronze.
фосфори́ческий *adj.* phosphoric.
фосфорноки́слый *adj.* (*chem.*) phosphate (*of*).
фо́сфорный *adj.* (*chem.*) phosphorous, phosphoric.
фота́ри|й, я *m.* (*med.*) radiation therapy room.
фо́то *nt. indecl.* (*coll.*) photo.
фото... *comb. form* photo-.
фотоальбо́м, а *m.* photograph album.
фотоаппара́т, а *m.* camera.
фотобума́г|а, и *f.* photographic paper.
фотогени́ч|ный (~ен, ~на) *adj.* photogenic.
фотограмметри́ческий *adj.* photogrammetric.
фотограмме́три|я, и *f.* photogrammetry, photographic survey.
фото́граф, а *m.* photographer.
фотографи́р|овать, ую *impf.* (*of* **с~**) to photograph.
фотографи́р|оваться, уюсь *impf.* (*of* **с~**) to be photographed, have one's photo taken.
фотографи́ческ|ий *adj.* photographic; **~ая плёнка** photographic film.
фотогра́фи|я, и *f.* **1.** photography. **2.** photograph. **3.** photographer's studio.
фотодешифро́вщик, а *m.* aerial photograph interpreter.
фотодонесе́ни|е, я *nt.* (*mil.*) intelligence photograph.
фотока́рточк|а, и *f.* photograph.
фотокомпозицио́нный *adj.*: **ф. портре́т** photofit.
фотокопирова́льный *adj.*: **ф. аппара́т** photocopier.

фотоко́пи|я, и *f.* photostat (copy).
фотола́мп|а, ы *f.* **1.** dark room lamp. **2.** (*elec.*) photoelectric cell.
фотолюби́тел|ь, я *m.* amateur photographer.
фото́н, а *m.* (*phys.*) photon.
фотонабо́р, а *m.* photo typesetting.
фотонабо́рный *adj.*: **ф. аппара́т** phototypesetter; photo-typesetting machine.
фотообъекти́в, а *m.* (camera) lens.
фотоохо́т|а, ы *f.* wildlife photography.
фотоохо́тник, а *m.* wildlife photographer.
фоторепорта́ж, а *m.* picture story.
фоторепортёр, а *m.* press photographer.
фото-ро́бот, а *m.* identikit (picture).
фотоси́нтез, а *m.* (*bot.*) photosynthesis.
фотоста́т, а *m.* photostat (apparatus).
фототе́к|а, и *f.* photograph library, photograph collection.
фотоувеличи́тел|ь, я *m.* photographic enlarger.
фотохро́ник|а, и *f.* news in pictures.
фотоэлеме́нт, а *m.* (*elec.*) photoelectric cell.
фо́фан, а *m.* (*coll.*) dim-wit.
фрагме́нт, а *m.* fragment; detail (*of painting, etc.*); **ф. фи́льма** film clip.
фрагмента́р|ный (~ен, ~на) *adj.* fragmentary.
фра́ер, а *m.* (*sl.*) **1.** trendy chap, guy. **2.** boy-friend.
фра́з|а, ы *f.* **1.** sentence. **2.** phrase.
фразеологи́зм, а *m.* (*ling.*) idiom, idiomatic expression.
фразеологи́ческий *adj.* phraseological; **ф. оборо́т** idiom.
фразеоло́ги|я, и *f.* **1.** phraseology. **2.** mere verbiage.
фразёр, а *m.* phrase-monger.
фрази́р|овать, ую *impf.* **1.** to use empty phrases. **2.** (*mus.*) to observe the phrasing (of).
фрак, а *m.* tail-coat, tails.
фраки́|ец, йца *m.* Thracian.
фраки́йский *adj.* Thracian.
Фра́ки|я, и *f.* Thrace.
фракту́р|а, ы *f.* (*typ.*) Gothic type, black letter.
фракциони́р|овать, ую *impf. and pf.* (*chem.*) to fractionate.
фракцио́нност|ь, и *f.* (*pol.*) fractionalism.
фракцио́нный[1] *adj.* (*pol.*) fractional; factional.
фракцио́нный[2] *adj.* (*chem.*) fractional.
фра́кци|я[1], **и** *f.* (*pol.*) fraction; faction, group.
фра́кци|я[2], **и** *f.* (*chem.*) fraction.
фраму́г|а, и *f.* upper part of window *or* door; casement.
франк[1], **а** *m.* (*hist.*) Frank.
франк[2], **а** *m.* franc.
франки́р|овать, ую *impf. and pf.* to prepay, pay the postage (of).
франциро́вк|а, и *f.* prepayment.
франкмасо́н, а *m.* freemason.
франкмасо́н|ский *adj. of* ~
фра́нко- *comb. form* (*comm.*) free, prepaid; **ф.-борт, ф.-су́дно** free on board.
фра́нковый *adj.* costing, worth a franc.
франкоязы́чный *adj.* francophone.
фра́нкский *adj.* (*hist.*) Frankish.
франт, а *m.* dandy.
фран|ти́ть, чу́, ти́шь *impf.* (*coll.*) to play the dandy, dress foppishly.
франти́х|а, и *f. of* **франт**
франтова́т|ый (~, ~а) *adj.* (*coll.*) **1.** dandyish. **2.** fussy, pernickety.
франтовско́й *adj.* dandyish, dandified.
франтовств|о́, а́ *nt.* dandyism.
Фра́нци|я, и *f.* France.
францу́женк|а, и *f.* Frenchwoman.
францу́з, а *m.* Frenchman.
францу́зский *adj.* French; **ф. ключ** (*tech.*) monkey wrench.
фраппи́р|овать, ую *impf. and pf.* (*obs.*) to shock.
фрахт, а *m.* freight.
фрахт|ова́ть, у́ю *impf.* (*of* **за~**) to charter.
фра́чн|ый *adj. of* **фрак**; *as n.* **ф., ~ого** *m.* (*obs.*) pers. not wearing uniform (*i.e. not in Government service*).
ФРГ *f. indecl.* (*abbr. of* **Федерати́вная Респу́блика Герма́нии**) FRG (*Federal Republic of Germany*).

фрега́т, а *m.* **1.** (*naut.*) frigate. **2.** frigate-bird.
фрез|а́, ы́ *f.* (*tech.*) mill, milling cutter, cutter; **ф.-бараба́н** drum shredder (*for cutting peat*).
фре́зер, а *m.* = **фре́за**
фре́зерный *adj.* (*tech.*) milling; **ф. стано́к** milling machine; **ф. торф** peat cut with drum shredder.
фрезер|ова́ть, у́ю *impf. and pf.* (*tech.*) to mill, cut.
фрезеро́вк|а, и *f.* (*tech.*) milling, cutting.
фрезеро́вщик, а *m.* milling-machine operator.
фре́йлин|а, ы *f.* (*hist.*) maid of honour.
френо́лог, а *m.* phrenologist.
френологи́ческий *adj.* phrenological.
френоло́ги|я, и *f.* phrenology.
френч, а *m.* service jacket.
фре́ск|а, и *f.* fresco.
фриво́льност|ь, и *f.* frivolity.
фриво́л|ьный (~ен, ~ьна) *adj.* frivolous.
фриз, а *m.* (*archit.*) frieze.
фрикаде́льк|а, и *f.* meat-ball, fish-ball (*in soup*).
фрикасе́ *nt. indecl.* fricassee.
фрикати́вный *adj.* (*ling.*) fricative.
фрикцио́н, а *m.* (*tech.*) friction clutch.
фрикцио́нн|ый *adj.* (*tech.*) friction; **~ое колесо́** friction wheel, adhesion wheel.
фриц, а *m.* (*sl.*) Jerry (= *German soldier*).
фри́ц|евский *adj. of* ~
фро́нд|а, ы *f.* (*hist.*) Fronde (*also fig.*).
фрондёр, а *m.* (*hist.*) Frondeur (*also fig.*).
фронди́р|овать, ую *impf.* to express discontent.
фронт, а, *pl.* **~́ы, ~о́в** *m.* (*mil.*; *fig.*) front; **на два ~́а** on two fronts; **стать во ф.** to stand to attention.
фронта́льн|ый *adj.* frontal; **~ая ата́ка** frontal attack.
фронтиспи́с, а *m.* (*archit.*, *typ.*) frontispiece.
фронтови́к, а́ *m.* front-line soldier.
фронтов|о́й *adj.* (*mil.*) front(-line); **~а́я полоса́** zone of action of a front; **~ы́е пи́сьма** letters from the front.
фронто́н, а *m.* (*archit.*) pediment.
фрукт, а *m.* **1.** fruit. **2.** (*coll.*, *pej.*) fellow, type.
фрукто́вый *adj.* fruit; **ф. нож** fruit knife; **ф. сад** orchard; **ф. са́хар** fruit sugar, fructose.
фруктое́д, а *m.* (*coll.*) fruitarian.
фр|я, и *f.* (*coll.*) personage.
фря́жский *adj.* (*obs.*) western European, foreign.
фтор, а *m.* (*chem.*) fluorine.
фторирова́ни|е, я *nt.* (*med.*) fluoridation.
фто́ристый *adj.* fluorine; fluoride (of).
фу *int.* **1.** (*expr. contempt, revulsion, etc.*) ugh! **2.** (*expr. fatigue, etc.*) oh!; ooh! **3.: фу́ ты** (*expr. surprise or annoyance*) my word!; my goodness!
фу́г|а, и *f.* (*mus.*) fugue.
фуга́н|ок, ка *m.* (*tech.*) smoothing-plane.
фуга́с, а *m.* (*mil.*) landmine, fougasse.
фуга́ск|а, и *f.* (*coll.*) **1.** landmine. **2.** high-explosive bomb.
фуга́с|ный *adj.* **1.** *adj. of* ~. **2.** high-explosive; **~ная бо́мба** high-explosive bomb.
фуг|ова́ть, у́ю *impf.* (*tech.*) to joint, mortise.
фуже́р, а *m.* tall wineglass.
фузе́|я, и *f.* (*hist.*) flint-lock rifle.
фу́к|ать, аю *impf. of* **~нуть**
фу́к|нуть, ну, нешь *pf.* (*of* **~ать**) (*coll.*) **1.** to blow; to blow out. **2.** to snort. **3.** (*at draughts*) to huff. **4.** (*sl.*) to chuck out.
фу́кси|я, и *f.* fuchsia.
фуля́р, а *m.* (*text.*) foulard.
фунда́мент, а *m.* foundation, base (*also fig.*); substructure; seating (*of boiler, etc.*).
фундамента́л|ьный (~ен, ~ьна) *adj.* **1.** solid, sound; (*fig.*) thorough(-going). **2.** main, basic; **~ьная библиоте́ка** main library.
фунди́рованный *adj.* (*fin.*) funded, consolidated.
фуникулёр, а *m.* funicular (railway), cable railway.
функциона́льный *adj.* functional.
функциони́р|овать, ую *impf.* to function.
фу́нкци|я, и *f.* (*in var. senses*) function.
фунт[1], **а** *m.* **1.** (*obs.*) pound (*Russ. measure of weight, equivalent to 409.5 grams*). **2.** pound (*imperial measure of*

weight, equivalent to 453.6 grams).
фунт², а *m.* (*fin.*): **ф. (сте́рлингов)** pound (sterling).
фу́нтик, а *m.* (*cone-shaped*) paper bag.
фу́ра, ы *f.* (baggage-)wagon.
фура́ж, а́ *m.* forage, fodder.
фуражи́р, а *m.* **1.** fodder storeman. **2.** (*mil.*) forager.
фуражи́р|овать, ую *impf.* (*mil.*) to forage.
фуражиро́вк|а, и *f.* (*mil.*) foraging.
фура́жк|а, и *f.* peak-cap; (*mil.*) service cap.
фура́ж|ный *adj. of* ~; **~ное зерно́** fodder grain; **~ная да́ча** forage ration.
фурго́н, а *m.* **1.** van; estate car. **2.** caravan.
фу́ри|я, и *f.* **1.** (*myth.*) Fury. **2.** (*fig.*) fury, termagant, virago.
фу́рман, а *m.* (*obs.*) driver.
фу́рм|енный *adj. of* **~а; ~енная коро́бка** tuyère box, blast box (*in cupola furnace*).
фурниту́р|а, ы *f.* accessories.
фуру́нкул, а *m.* (*med.*) furuncle.
фурункулёз, а *m.* (*med.*) furunculosis.
фурьери́зм, а *m.* (*pol., phil.*) Fourierism.
фут, а *m.* **1.** foot (*measure of length*). **2.** foot rule.
футбо́л, а *m.* football, soccer.
футболи́ст, а *m.* football-player, footballer.
футбо́лк|а, и *f.* (*coll.*) sweatshirt.
футбо́л|ьный *adj. of* ~; **~ьные бу́тсы** football boots; **ф. мяч** football.
футер|ова́ть, у́ю *impf.* (*tech.*) to line, fettle.
футеро́вк|а, и *f.* (*tech.*) (brick-)lining, fettling.
футля́р, а *m.* case; container; (*tech.*) casing, housing; **ф. для очко́в** spectacle-case; **ф. телеви́зора** TV (*television*) cabinet.
фу́товый *adj.* one-foot.
футури́зм, а *m.* futurism.
футури́ст, а *m.* futurist.
футуристи́ческий *adj.* futuristic.
футшто́к, а *m.* (*naut.*) tide-gauge; sounding rod.
фуфа́йк|а, и *f.* jersey.
фуфу́: на ф. (*coll.*) anyhow, carelessly.
фьорд = фио́рд
фы́рк|ать, аю *impf.* (*of* **~нуть**) **1.** to snort (*also fig., of a machine*). **2.** (*coll.*) to chuckle. **3.** (*coll.*) to grouse.
фы́рк|нуть, ну, нешь *pf. of* **~ать**
фюзеля́ж, а *m.* (*aeron.*) fuselage.

X

хаба́р, а *m.* (*and* **~а́, ~ы́** *f.*) (*coll., obs.*) bribe.
ха́вбек, а *m.* (*sport.*; *obs.*) half(-back).
хавро́нь|я, и *f.* (*coll.*) sow.
хаджи́ *m. indecl.* Hadji (*title of Mohammedan pilgrim who has been to Mecca*).
ха́живать *pres. tense not used, impf.* (*coll.*) *freq. of* **ходи́ть**
хайл|о́, а́, *pl.* **~а** *nt.* **1.** (*coll.*) aperture. **2.** (*sl.*) gob.
хака́с, а *m.* Khakas (*indigenous inhabitant of Khakas Autonomous Oblast in Siberia*).
хака́с|ка, ки *f. of* ~
хака́сский *adj.* Khakas.
ха́ки *indecl.* **1.** *adj.* **2.** *n.*; *nt.* khaki.
хала́т, а *m.* **1.** dressing-gown. **2.** overall; **до́кторский х.** doctor's smock. **3.** (*oriental*) robe.
хала́тност|ь, и *f.* carelessness, negligence.
хала́т|ный *adj.* **1.** *adj. of* ~. **2.** (**~ен, ~на**) careless, negligent.
халв|а́, ы́ *f.* (*cul.*) halva.
халде́|й, я *m.* Chaldean.
халде́й|ский *adj. of* ~
хали́ф, а *m.* (*hist.*) caliph.
халифа́т, а *m.* (*hist.*) caliphate.
халту́р|а, ы *f.* (*coll.*) **1.** pot-boiler; (*collect.*) hack-work. **2.** extra work; money made on the side.
халту́р|ить, ю, ишь *impf.* (*coll.*) **1.** to turn out pot-boilers; to do hack-work. **2.** to make money on the side (*by doing extra work*).
халту́р|ный *adj. of* **~а**
халту́рщик, а *m.* (*coll.*) **1.** pers. turning out pot-boilers; hack(-worker). **2.** pers. making money on the side (*by extra work*).
халу́п|а, ы *f.* peasant house (*in Ukraine and Byelorussia*).
халцедо́н, а *m.* (*min.*) chalcedony.
хам, а *m.* (*coll.*) boor, lout.
хамелео́н, а *m.* chameleon (*also fig.*).
хам|и́ть, лю́, и́шь *impf.* (+*d.*) to be rude (to).
хамс|а́, ы́ *f.* khamsa (*small fish of anchovy family*).
ха́мский *adj.* (*coll.*) boorish, loutish.
ха́мств|о, а *nt.* (*coll.*) boorishness, loutishness.
хан, а *m.* khan.
хандр|а́, ы́ *f.* depression.
хандр|и́ть, ю́, и́шь *impf.* to be depressed.
ханж|а́, и́, *g. pl.* **~е́й** *c.g.* sanctimonious pers.; canting hypocrite.
ха́нжеск|ий (*and* **~о́й)** *adj.* sanctimonious; hypocritical.
ханжеств|о́, а́ *nt.* sanctimoniousness; hypocrisy.
ханж|и́ть, у́, и́шь *impf.* (*coll.*) to display sanctimoniousness; to play the hypocrite.
Хано́|й, я *m.* Hanoi.
ха́н|ский *adj. of* ~
ха́нств|о, а *nt.* khanate.
ханты́ *c.g. indecl.* Khanty (*formerly Ostyak(s), inhabitant(s) of Khanty-Mansi National Region*).
ханты́йский *adj.* Khanty.
ха́ос, а *m.* (*myth.*) Chaos.
хао́с, а *m.* chaos (*disorder*).
хаоти́ческий *adj.* chaotic.
хаоти́чност|ь, и *f.* chaotic character; state of chaos.
хаоти́ч|ный (~ен, ~на) *adj.* = **~еский**
ха́п|ать, аю *impf. of* **~нуть**
ха́п|нуть, ну, нешь *pf.* (*of* **~ать**) (*coll.*) **1.** to seize, grab. **2.** (*fig.*) to nab, pinch, scrounge.
хапу́г|а, и *c.g.* (*coll.*) thief, scrounger.
хара́ктер, а *m.* **1.** character, personality, nature, disposition (*of a human being*); **они́ не сошли́сь ~ами** they could not get on (together); **э́то не в его́ ~е** it's not like him. **2.** (strong) character; **челове́к с ~ом** determined pers., strong character. **3.** character, nature, type; **х. рабо́ты** type of work.
характериз|ова́ть, у́ю *impf. and pf.* **1.** to describe. **2.** to characterize, be characteristic (of).
характериз|ова́ться, у́юсь *impf.* (+*i.*) to be characterized (by), feature.
характери́стик|а, и *f.* **1.** description. **2.** reference; **х. с ме́ста пре́жней слу́жбы** reference from former place of work. **3.** (*math.*) characteristic (*of logarithm*). **4.** (*tech.*) characteristic curve; performance graph.
характе́рно *as pred.* it is characteristic; it is typical.
хара́ктерный *adj.* (*obs. or coll.*) having a strong character; strong-willed; temperamental.
характе́р|ный (~ен, ~на) *adj.* **1.** characteristic; typical; **э́то для него́ ~но** it is typical of him. **2.** distinctive. **3.** (*theatr.*) character; **х. актёр** character actor.
хариджа́н, а *m.* Harijan, untouchable.
ха́риус, а *m.* (*zool.*) grayling, umber.
ха́ркань|е, я *nt.* (*coll.*) expectoration.
ха́рк|ать, аю *impf.* (*of* **~нуть**) (*coll.*) to spit, expectorate; **х. кро́вью** to spit blood.
ха́рк|нуть, ну, нешь *pf. of* **~ать**
ха́рти|я, и *f.* charter.
харче́вн|я, и *f.* (*obs.*) eating-house.
харч|и́, е́й *pl.* (*sg.* ~, **~а** *m.*) (*coll.*) grub.
харчо́ *nt. indecl.* kharcho (*Caucasian mutton soup*).

ха́р|я, и *f.* (*sl.*) mug (= *face*).
хаси́дский *adj.* (*relig.*) Hasidic.
ха́т|а, ы *f.* **1.** peasant house (*in Southern Russia, Ukraine, and Byelorussia*; **моя́ х. с кра́ю** it's no concern of mine; that's your, their, *etc.*, funeral. **2.** (*sl.*) 'pad'.
ха́хал|ь, я *m.* (*sl.*) fancy man.
ха́|ять, ю, ешь *impf.* (*of* **о~**) (*coll.*) to play down, run down, knock (*fig.*).
хвал|а́, ы́ *f.* praise; **х. Бо́гу!** thank God!
хвале́б|ный (~ен, ~на) *adj.* laudatory, eulogistic, complimentary.
хвалёный *adj.* (*iron.*) much-vaunted, celebrated.
хвал|и́ть, ю́, ~ишь *impf.* (*of* **по~**) to praise, compliment.
хвал|и́ться, ю́сь, ~ишься *impf.* (*of* **по~**) (*+i.*) to boast (of).
хва́стать *impf.* = **~ся**
хва́ста|ться, юсь *impf.* (*of* **по~**) (*+i.*) to boast (of).
хвастли́в|ый (~, ~а) *adj.* boastful.
хвастовств|о́, а́ *nt.* boasting, bragging.
хвасту́н, а́ *m.* (*coll.*) boaster, braggart.
хват, а *m.* (*coll.*) dashing blade.
хват|а́ть[1]**, а́ю** *impf.* (*of* **~и́ть**[1] *and* **схвати́ть**) **1.** to snatch, seize, catch hold (of); to grab, grasp; **х. что попа́ло** to seize up whatever comes to hand. **2.** (*impf. only*) (*coll.*) to bite (*of fish*). **3.** (*impf. only*) (*coll.*) to pick up (= *to detain*).
хват|а́ть[2]**, а́ет** *impf.* (*of* **~и́ть**[2]) *impers.* **1.** (*+g.*) to suffice, be sufficient, enough; to last out; **у меня́**, *etc.*, **не ~а́ет** I, *etc.*, am short (of); **вре́мени не ~а́ло** there was not long enough; **у нас не ~а́ет де́нег** we have not enough money; **э́того ещё не ~а́ло!** that's all we, *etc.* need! **2.** (*+g.* **на**+*a.*) to be up to, be capable (of); **его́ не ~а́ет на тако́й посту́пок** he is not up to such an act.
хват|а́ться, а́юсь *impf.* (*of* **~и́ться** *and* **схвати́ться**) (**за**+*a.*) **1.** to snatch (at), catch (at), pluck (at); **х. за соло́минку** to reach for a straw; **х. за́ ум** to come to one's senses. **2.** to take up, try out.
хва|ти́ть[1]**, чу́, ~тишь** *pf.* (*coll.*) **1.** *pf. of* **~та́ть**[1]. **2.** to drink up, knock back; **х. ли́шнего** to have one too many. **3.** to suffer, endure. **4.** to stick one's neck out; to blurt out; **х. че́рез край** to go too far. **5.** (*in var. senses*) to strike; to hit; to smash; **его́ ~ти́л уда́р** he has had a stroke; (*impers.*): **моро́зом ~ти́ло посе́в** the frost hit the crops. **6.** to strike up, start up; **х. плясову́ю** to strike up a tune for dancing.
хват|и́ть[2]**, ~ит** *pf.* (*of* **~а́ть**[2]); **~ит!** that will do!; that's enough!; **с меня́ ~ит!** I've had enough!; **~ит тебе́ хны́кать!** that's enough of your whining!
хва|ти́ться, чу́сь, ~тишься *pf.* **1.** *pf. of* **~та́ться. 2.** (*+g.*; *coll.*) to notice the absence (of), remember (*that one has left behind*); **по́здно ~ти́лись!** you thought of it too late! **3.** (**о**+*a.*; *coll.*) to hit, bump (into).
хва́тк|а, и *f.* **1.** grasp, grip, clutch. **2.** (*coll.*) method, technique. **3.** skill.
хва́т|кий (~ок, ~ка́, ~ко) *adj.* (*coll.*) **1.** strong (*of hands, grip, etc.*); tenacious. **2.** skilful, crafty.
хвать (*coll.*) *used in place of various forms of* **хвати́ть**[1] *and* **хвати́ться 2.** (*also as int.*); **я х. его́ за воротни́к** I grabbed him by the collar; **я чуть бы́ло не сел на по́езд, а — х.! — биле́та нет** I was just about to board the train when suddenly I found I had not got my ticket.
хво́йн|ый *adj.* **1.** *adj. of* **хво́я; х. покро́в** covering of (pine) needles; **х. дёготь** pine-tar. **2.** coniferous; *as n.* **~ые, ~ых** (*bot.*) conifers.
хвора́|ть, ю *impf.* (*coll.*) to be ill, sick.
хво́рост, а (у) *m.* (*collect.*) **1.** brushwood. **2.** (*cul.*) (pastry) straws, twiglets.
хворости́н|а, ы *f.* stick, switch (*for driving cattle, etc.*).
хво́рост|ь, и *f.* (*coll.*) illness, ailment.
хворостяно́й *adj. of* **хво́рост 1.**
хво́р|ый (~, ~а́, ~о) *adj.* (*coll.*) ill, sick.
хвор|ь, и *f.* (*coll.*) illness, ailment.
хвост, а́ *m.* **1.** tail (*also fig.*; *of aircraft, comet, etc.*); tail-feathers; **маха́ть ~о́м** to wag one's tail; **задра́ть х.** to get on one's high horse; **поджа́ть х.** to draw in one's horns; **показа́ть х.** (*coll.*) to show a clean pair of heels; **(и) в х. и в гри́ву** (*coll.*) neck and crop. **2.** (*fig.*) tail, rear, end, tail-end; **х. по́езда** rear (coaches) of train; **быть, плести́сь в ~е́** to get behind, lag behind. **3.** (*coll.*) train (*of dress*); **наступи́ть на х. кому́-н.** (*coll.*) to tread on s.o.'s toes. **4.** (*coll.*) throng, following. **5.** (*coll.*) queue, line; **х. за хле́бом** bread queue. **6.** (*coll.*) unfinished portion (*of work, etc.*). **7.** (*tech.*) shank, shaft (*of tool*). **8.** (*pl.*) (*min.*) tails, tailings.
хвоста́т|ый (~, ~а) *adj.* **1.** having a tail; caudate. **2.** having a large tail.
хвости́зм, а *m.* (*pol.*) 'tailism' (*limitation of revolutionary aims to those intelligible to backward masses*).
хво́стик, а *m. dim. of* **хвост; с ~ом** and a little more; **сто с ~ом** a hundred odd.
хвости́ст, а *m.* **1.** (*pol.*) 'tailist' (*see* **хвости́зм**). **2.** (*coll.*) student failing to obtain required number of passes in examination.
хвостов|о́й *adj. of* **хвост; ~а́я ве́на** (*anat.*) caudal vein; **х. ого́нь** (*aeron.*) tail light; **~о́е опере́ние** (*aeron.*) tail unit; **х. патро́н** (*mil.*) ignition charge, cartridge.
хвостоко́л, а *m.* (*zool.*) stingray.
хвощ, а́ *m.* (*bot.*) horse-tail, mare's tail (*Equisetum*).
хво́|я, и *f.* **1.** needle(s) (*of conifer*). **2.** (*collect.*) branches (*of conifer*).
Хе́льсинки *m. indecl.* Helsinki.
хе́льсинкский *adj.* Helsinki.
хе́рес, а (у) *m.* sherry.
хе́р|ить, ю, ишь *impf.* (*coll., obs.*) to cross out.
херн|я́, и́ *f.* (*euph.*) = **хуйня́**
херуви́м, а *m.* cherub.
херуви́м|ский *adj.* **1.** *adj. of* **~. 2.** (*coll.*) cherubic.
хе́ттский *adj.* (*hist. and ling.*) Hittite.
хиба́р|а, ы *f.* (*coll.*) shack, hovel.
хиба́р|ка, ки *f. dim. of* **~а**
хи́жин|а, ы *f.* shack, hut.
хиле́|ть, ю *impf.* (*of* **за~**) (*coll.*) to become weak, sickly.
хи́л|ый (~, ~а́, ~о) *adj.* weak, sickly; puny; decrepit.
хим... *comb. form, abbr. of* **хими́ческий**
химвойск|а́, ~ *no sg.* chemical warfare troops.
химе́р|а, ы *f.* **1.** chimera. **2.** (*archit.*) gargoyle.
химери́ческий *adj.* chimerical.
химиза́ци|я, и *f.* 'chemicalization' (*intensified development of chemical industry and utilization of its products*).
хими́зм, а *m.* chemistry (= *chemical composition*).
хи́мик, а *m.* **1.** chemist. **2.** chemical industry worker.
химика́л|ии, ий *no sg.* chemicals.
химика́т|ы, ов *pl.* (*sg.* **~, ~а** *m.*) = **химика́лии**
химиотерапи́|я, и *f.* chemotherapy.
хими́ческ|ий *adj.* **1.** chemical; **х. каранда́ш** indelible pencil; **~ие препара́ты** chemicals; **~ая чи́стка (оде́жды)** dry-cleaning; **х. элеме́нт** chemical element. **2.** chemistry; **х. кабине́т** chemistry laboratory. **3.** (*mil.*) chemical warfare, gas; **~ая бо́мба** gas bomb; **~ая война́** chemical warfare; **~ое подразделе́ние** chemical warfare unit.
хи́ми|я, и *f.* chemistry.
химчи́стк|а, и *f.* dry-cleaning.
хи́нди *m. indecl.* Hindi (*language*).
хини́н, а *m.* cinchona, quinine.
хи́нн|ый *adj.* cinchona; **~ое де́рево** cinchona (*tree*); **~ая ко́рка** Peruvian bark.
хин|ь, и *f.*: **идёт ~ью** (*coll.*; *obs.*) it is in vain, to no purpose.
хире́|ть, ю *impf.* (*of* **за~**) to grow sickly; (*of plants*) to wither; (*fig.*) to decay.
хирома́нт, а *m.* chiromancer, palmist.
хирома́нти|я, и *f.* chiromancy, palmistry.
хиропра́ктик, а *m.* chiropractor.
Хиро́сим|а, ы *f.* Hiroshima.
хирото́ни|я, и *f.* (*eccl.*) consecration, ordination (*to bishopric, priesthood, diaconate*).
хиру́рг, а *m.* surgeon.
хирурги́ческ|ий *adj.* surgical; **~ие но́жницы** forceps; **~ая сестра́** theatre nurse.
хирурги́|я, и *f.* surgery.
хити́н, а *m.* (*biol.*) chitin.
хити́новый *adj.* (*biol.*) chitinous.
хито́н, а *m.* tunic.
хитре́ц, а́ *m.* cunning pers.; (*coll.*) slyboots.

хитрец|а́, ы́ *f.* (*coll.*) cunning, guile; **говори́ть с ~о́й** to speak disingenuously.
хитри́нк|а, и *f.* = **хитреца́**
хитр|и́ть, ю́, и́шь *impf.* (*of* **с~**) to use cunning, guile; to dissemble.
хитросплете́ни|е, я *nt.* **1.** cunning trick, stratagem. **2.** (*pl.*) fanciful construction; hair-splitting.
хитросплетённый *adj.* intricate, contrived.
хи́трост|ь, и *f.* **1.** cunning, guile, craft, wiles. **2.** ruse, stratagem. **3.** (*coll.*) skill, resource. **4.** (*coll.*) intricacy, subtlety.
хитроу́ми|е, я *nt.* cunning; resourcefulness.
хитроу́м|ный (~ен, ~на) *adj.* **1.** cunning; resourceful. **2.** intricate, complicated.
хи́т|рый (~ёр, ~ра́, ~ро) *adj.* **1.** cunning, sly, crafty, wily. **2.** (*coll.*) skilful, resourceful. **3.** (*coll.*) intricate, subtle; complicated.
хихи́к|ать, аю *impf.* (*of* **~нуть**) to giggle, titter, snigger.
хихи́к|нуть, ну, нешь *pf. of* **~ать**
хище́ни|е, я *nt.* theft; embezzlement, misappropriation.
хи́щник, а *m.* **1.** beast, bird of prey. **2.** (*fig.*) plunderer, despoiler.
хи́щнический *adj.* **1.** *adj. of* **хи́щник. 2.** predatory, rapacious. **3.** destructive; injurious (*to the economy*).
хи́щничеств|о, а *nt.* **1.** preying. **2.** predatoriness. **3.** injurious exploitation of natural resources. **4.** embezzlement, misappropriation.
хи́щ|ный (~ен, ~на) *adj.* **1.** predatory; **~ные зве́ри, пти́цы** beasts, birds of prey. **2.** rapacious, grasping, greedy.
хлад, а *m.* (*obs. or poet.*) cold.
хладнокро́ви|е, я *nt.* coolness, composure, presence of mind, sang-froid.
хладнокро́в|ный (~ен, ~на) *adj.* cool, composed.
хладноло́мкий *adj.* (*tech.*) cold-short, brittle at atmospheric temperature.
хла́д|ный (~ен, ~на) *adj.* (*obs. or poet.*) cold.
хладосто́|йкий (~ек, ~йка) *adj.* (*tech.*) cold-resistant; **х. соста́в** anti-freeze.
хлам, а *m.* (*collect.*) rubbish, trash.
хлами́д|а, ы *f.* **1.** (*hist.*) chlamys. **2.** (*coll.*) long, loose-fitting garment.
хлеб, а, *pl.* **~ы** *and* **~а́** *m.* **1.** (*sg. only*) bread (*also fig.*); **х. насу́щный** daily bread; **добыва́ть х.** (*fig.*) to win one's bread; **отби́ть у кого́-н. х.** to take the bread out of s.o.'s mouth; **перебива́ться с ~а на квас** to live from hand to mouth. **2.** (*pl.* **~ы**) loaf. **3.** (*pl.* **~а́**) bread-grain; (*pl.*) corn, crops; cereals. **4.** (*pl.* **~а́**) (*coll.*) food; **жить на ~а́х у кого́-н.** (*i*) to board with s.o., (*ii*) to be dependent on s.o., live off s.o.; **идти́ на ~а́ к кому́-н.** to become dependent on s.o.
хлеба́|ть, ю *impf.* **1.** to gulp (down). **2.** (*coll.*) to eat, drink (*liquids*) with a spoon.
хле́б|ец, ца *m.* small loaf.
хле́бин|а, ы *f.* bee-bread.
хле́бник, а *m.* (*obs.*) baker.
хле́бниц|а, ы *f.* bread-plate; bread-basket.
хлебн|у́ть, у́, ёшь *pf.* (*coll.*) **1.** to drink down. **2.** (*+g.*) to go through, endure, experience.
хле́бн|ый *adj.* **1.** *adj. of* **хлеб 1.; ~ые дро́жжи** baker's yeast; **~ые запа́сы** bread supplies; **х. магази́н** baker's shop; **~ое де́рево** bread-fruit tree. **2.** *adj. of* **хлеб 3.; х. амба́р** granary; **~ое вино́** (*obs.*) vodka; **~ые зла́ки** bread-grains, cereals; **х. спирт** grain alcohol, ethyl alcohol. **3.** rich (*in grain*), abundant; grain-producing. **4.** (*coll.*) lucrative, profitable.
хлёбов|о, а *nt.* (*coll.*) gruel.
хлебозаво́д, а *m.* bread-baking plant, bakery.
хлебо|заготови́тельный *adj. of* **~загото́вка**
хлебозаготóвк|а, и *f.* (State) grain procurement.
хлебозаку́пк|а, и *f.* (State) grain-purchase.
хлеб|о́к, ка́ *m.* (*coll.*) mouthful (*of liquid food*).
хлебопа́шеств|о, а *nt.* (*obs.*) tillage, cultivation, arable farming.
хлебопа́ш|ец, ца *m.* (*obs.*) tiller of the soil.
хлебопа́шный *adj.* ploughing; arable.
хлебопёк, а *m.* baker.
хлебопека́рный *adj.* baking.
хлебопека́рн|я, и *f.* bakery, bake-house.
хлебопоста́вк|а, и *f.* grain delivery (*to State*).
хлеборо́б, а *m.* peasant (engaged in arable farming); (*rhet.*) corn-producer.
хлеборо́д|ный (~ен, ~на) *adj.* rich (in grain crops), abundant; **х. год** good year (for grain crops).
хлебосо́л, а *m.* hospitable pers.
хлебосо́л|ьный (~ен, ~ьна) *adj.* hospitable.
хлебосо́льств|о, а *nt.* hospitality.
хлеботорго́в|ец, ца *m.* corn-merchant, grain-merchant.
хлеботорго́вл|я, и *f.* corn-trade.
хлебоубо́рк|а, и *f.* (corn-)harvest.
хлебоубо́рочный *adj.* harvest(ing); **х. комба́йн** combine harvester.
хле́б-со́ль, хле́ба-со́ли bread and salt (*offered to guest as symbol of hospitality*); hospitality.
хлев, а, в ~е *or* **в ~у́,** *pl.* **~а́** *m.* cow-house, cattle-shed, byre; (*fig., coll.*) pig-sty.
хлестако́вщин|а, ы *f.* shameless bragging (*in the manner of Khlestakov, hero of N.V. Gogol's comedy* 'The Government Inspector').
хле|ста́ть, щу́, ~щешь *impf.* (*of* **~стну́ть**) **1.** (*+a. or* **по**+*d.*) to lash; to whip. **2.** (*of rain, etc.*) to lash (down), beat (down), pour; to stream, gush. **3.** (*coll.*) to swill (= *to drink in large quantities*).
хлёст|кий (~ок, ~ка́, ~ко) *adj.* **1.** biting. **2.** (*fig.*) biting, scathing; trenchant. **3.** (*of sounds, etc.*) sharp. **4.** (*coll.*) lively, gay.
хлест|ну́ть, ну́, нёшь *pf. of* **~а́ть**
хлёст|че *comp. of* **~кий**
хле́ще *comp. of* **хлёсткий**
хли́па|ть, ю *impf.* (*coll.*) to sob.
хли́п|кий (~ок, ~ка́, ~ко) *adj.* (*coll.*) **1.** rickety, shaky. **2.** (*fig.*) weak, fragile. **3.** watery, slushy.
хлобы|ста́ть, щу́, ~щешь *impf.* (*of* **~стну́ть**) (*coll.*) to lash.
хлобыст|ну́ть, ну́, нёшь *inst. pf. of* **~а́ть**
хлоп[1] *int.* bang! (*as pred.; stands for pres. and past tenses of* **~ать, ~нуть** *and* **~аться**).
хлоп[2]**, а** *m.* (*coll.*) bang, clatter.
хло́па|ть, ю *impf.* (*of* **хло́пнуть**) **1.** (*+i. or* **по**+*d.*) to bang; to slap; **х. кали́ткой** to bang the gate; **х. кого́-н. по спине́** to slap s.o. on the back; **х. глаза́ми** (*i*) to look blank, (*ii*) to be at a loss what to say (*in answer to a question*); **х. уша́ми** (*coll.*) to look dumb. **2.** (**в ладо́ши**) (*+d.*) to clap, applaud. **3.** (*coll.*) to shoot. **4.** (*coll.*) to knock back (= *to drink*).
хло́па|ться, юсь *impf.* (*of* **хло́пнуться**) (*coll.*) to flop down.
хло́п|ец, ца *m.* (*coll. or dial.*) lad.
хлопково́д, а *m.* cotton-grower.
хлопково́дств|о, а *nt.* cotton-growing.
хлопково́дческий *adj.* cotton-growing.
хло́пков|ый *adj.* cotton; **~ое ма́сло** cotton-seed oil; **~ые очёски** cotton waste; **~ая пря́жа** cotton yarn.
хлопкопряди́льный *adj.* cotton-spinning.
хлопкоро́б, а *m.* cotton-grower.
хлопкоубо́рочный *adj.* cotton-picking.
хло́п|нуть(ся), ну(сь), нешь(ся) *pf. of* **~ать(ся)**
хло́п|ок, ка *m.* cotton; **х.-сыре́ц** raw cotton.
хлоп|о́к, ка́ *m.* **1.** clap. **2.** bang.
хлопо|та́ть, чу́, ~чешь *impf.* (*of* **по~**) **1.** (*impf. only*) to busy o.s.; to bustle about, toil. **2.** (**о**+*p. or* **+что́бы**) to make efforts; to take trouble, go to pains; to solicit, petition (for); **х., что́бы привести́ кого́-н. в чу́вство** to endeavour to bring s.o. round. **3.** (**за**+*a. or* **о**+*p.*) to plead (for), make efforts on behalf (of).
хлопотли́в|ый (~, ~а) *adj.* **1.** troublesome, bothersome; involving (much) trouble, requiring (great) pains, exacting. **2.** busy, bustling, restless.
хло́пот|ный (~ен, ~на) *adj.* (*coll.*) involving (much) trouble, exacting.
хлопотн|я́, и́ *f.* (*coll.*) efforts, labour, toil.

хлопотýн, á *m.* (*coll.*) busy, restless pers.
хлóпот|ы, хлопóт, ~ам *no sg.* **1.** trouble. **2.** (**о**+*p.*) efforts (on behalf of, for); pains.
хлопýшк|а, и *f.* **1.** fly-swatter. **2.** (Christmas) cracker. **3.** (*cin.*) clapperboard. **4.** (*bot.*) catchfly (*Silene venosa*). **5.** (*tech.*) gate valve.
хлопчáтк|а, и *f.* (*coll.*) cotton (*fabric*).
хлопчáтник, а *m.* cotton(-plant).
хлопчатобумáжный *adj.* cotton; **х. пóрох** gun-cotton.
хлопчáт|ый[1] *adj.*: **~ая бумáга** (*obs.*) (*i*) cotton-plant, (*ii*) cotton (*fabric, thread*).
хлопчáтый[2] *adj.* flaky.
хлóпчик, а *m.* (*coll. or dial.*) boy.
хлопьевид|ный (~ен, ~на) *adj.* flaky, flocculent.
хлóпь|я, ев *no sg.* flakes (*of snow, etc., or as component of name of certain cereal foods*); **кукурýзные х., пшени́чные х.** corn flakes.
хлор, а *m.* (*chem.*) chlorine.
хлори́р|овать, ую *impf. and pf.* to chlorinate.
хлористоводорóдный *adj.* (*chem.*) hydrochloride (of).
хлóристый *adj.* (*chem.*) chlorine; chloride (of); **х. водорóд** hydrogen chloride.
хлори́т, а *m.* (*min.*) chlorite.
хлóрк|а, и *f.* (*coll.*) bleaching powder (*of calcium hypochlorite*).
хлóр|ный *adj. of* ~
хлорóз, а *m.* (*bot. and med.*) chlorosis.
хлорофи́лл, а *m.* (*bot.*) chlorophyll.
хлорофóрм, а *m.* chloroform.
хлороформи́р|овать, ую *impf. and pf.* (*pf. also* **за~**) to chloroform.
хлорпикри́н, а *m.* (*chem. and agric.*) chloropicrin.
хлы́н|уть, у, ешь *pf.* **1.** (*of blood, rain, etc.*) to gush, pour. **2.** (*fig.*) to pour, rush, surge; **на плóщадь ~ула толпá нарóду** a crowd poured into the square.
хлыст[1]**, á** *m.* **1.** whip, switch; **х. и пря́ник** (*fig., coll.*) stick and carrot. **2.** trunk (*of felled tree*).
хлыст[2]**, á** *m.* Khlyst (*member of sect*).
хлыстóвств|о, а *nt.* Khlysts (*Russ. religious sect*).
хлыщ, á *m.* (*coll.*) fop.
хлю́па|ть, ю *impf.* (*coll.*) **1.** to squelch. **2.** to flounder (*through mud, etc.*). **3.** to snivel; **х. нóсом** to sniff.
хлю́пик, а *m.* (*coll.*) sniveller, milksop.
хлю́п|кий (~ок, ~кá, ~ко) *adj.* (*coll.*) **1.** soggy. **2.** rickety. **3.** (*fig.*) frail, feeble.
хлюст[1]**, á** *m.* (*coll.*) smart Alec.
хлюст[2]**, á** *m.* (*coll.*) suit (*in a hand at cards*).
хляб|ь, и *f.* **1.** (*obs. or poet.*) abyss; **~и небéсные развéрзлись** (*joc.*) the heavens opened (*of heavy rain*). **2.** (*coll.*) mud, muddy ground.
хля́стик, а *m.* half-belt (*sewn or buttoned on to back of coat*).
хмелевóд, а *m.* hop-grower.
хмелевóдств|о, а *nt.* hop-growing.
хмел|евóй *adj. of* **~ь**
хмел|ёк, ькá *m. dim. of* **~ь; под ~ькóм** tipsy, tight.
хмелé|ть, ю *impf.* (*of* **за~** *and* **о ~**) to become tipsy, get tight.
хмел|ь, я *m.* **1.** (*bot.*) hop(s); hop-plant. **2.** (**о ~е, во ~ю́**) drunkenness, tipsiness; **под ~ем, во ~ю́,** tipsy, tight.
хмел|ьнóй (~ён, ~ьнá) *adj.* **1.** drunken, tipsy. **2.** intoxicating; *as n.* **~ьнóе, ~ьнóго** *nt.* intoxicating liquor, alcohol.
хмýр|ить, ю, ишь *impf.* (*of* **на~**) **х. лицó** to frown; **х. брóви** to knit one's brows.
хмýр|иться, юсь, ишься *impf.* (*of* **на~**) **1.** to frown. **2.** to become gloomy. **3.** to be overcast, cloudy.
хмýрост|ь, и *f.* **1.** gloom. **2.** cloudiness.
хмýр|ый (~, ~á, ~о) *adj.* **1.** gloomy, sullen. **2.** overcast, cloudy; lowering; **х. день** dull day; **~ое нéбо** lowering sky.
хмы́ка|ть, ю *impf.* (*coll.*) to hem (*expr. surprise, annoyance, doubt, etc.*).
хн|а, ы *f.* henna.
хны́ка|ть, ю (*and* **хны́ч|у, ешь**) *impf.* (*coll.*) to whimper, snivel; (*fig.*) to whine.
хóбби *nt. indecl.* hobby.
хóбот, а *m.* **1.** (*zool.*) trunk, proboscis. **2.** (*tech.*) tool-holder. **3.: х. лафéта** (*mil.*) trail of gun-carriage.
хоботнóй *adj. of* **хóбот 1.**
хóбот|овый *adj. of* ~ **2., 3.**
хобот|óк, кá *m.* proboscis (*of insects*).
ход, а (у), о ~е, в (на) ~е *and* **~ý** *m.* **1.** (**в ~е, на ~ý**) motion, movement, travel, going; speed, pace; **три часá ~у** three hours' going; **зáдний х.** backing, reversing; **мáлый х., ти́хий х.** slow speed; **пóлный х.** full speed; **пóлный х.!** full speed ahead!; **пóлным ~ом** (*fig.*) in full swing; **свобóдный х.** free-wheeling, coasting; **срéдний х.** half-speed; **дать х.** (+*d.*) to set in motion, set going; **дать ~у** (*i*) (*coll.*) to increase pace, go faster, (*ii*) (*coll.*) to take to one's heels; **не дать ~у комý-н.** not to give s.o. a chance, hold s.o. back; **идти́ свои́м ~ом** (*i*) to travel under one's own steam, (*ii*) to take its course; **пойти́ в х.** to come to be widely used, acquire a vogue; **пусти́ть в х.** to start, set in motion, set going (*also fig.*), put into operation, put into service; **быть в ~ý** to be in demand, be in vogue; **на ~ý** (*i*) in transit, on the move, without halting, (*ii*) in motion, in operation; **на пóлном ~ý** at full speed, full blast; **с ~у** (*coll.*) without a pause, straight off. **2.** (*eccl.*) procession. **3.** (**в, на ~е**) (*fig.*) course, progress; **х. мы́слей** train of thought; **х. собы́тий** course of events. **4.** (**в ~е, на ~е** *and* **~ý**) (*tech.*) work, operation, running; **на холостóм ~ý** idling. **5.** (**в, на ~е**; *pl.* **~ы, ~óв**) (*tech.*) stroke (*of piston*), blow (*of press*); cycle; travel; **х. вверх, х. вниз, х. сжáтия** (*of piston*) upstroke, downstroke, compression stroke. **6.** (**на ~е**; *pl.* **~ы́**) (*chess, draughts*) move; (*cards*) lead; **х. бéлых** white's move. **7.** (**в ~е**; *pl.* **~ы**) (*fig.*) move, gambit, manœuvre; **лóвкий х.** shrewd move. **8.** (**в ~е** *and* **~ý**; *pl.* **~ы́**) entrance (*to building*); **знать все ~ы и вы́ходы** to know all the ins and outs. **9.** (**в, на ~е** *and* **~ý**; *pl.* **~ы́, ~óв**) passage, covered way, thoroughfare; **~ы́ сообщéния** (*mil.*) communication trench. **10.** (**в, на ~ý**; *pl.* **~ы́** *and* **~á, ~óв**) (*tech.*) wheel-base; runners (*of sledge*); **гýсеничный х.** caterpillar tracks.
ходáта|й, я *m.* **1.** intercessor, mediator. **2.** (*obs.*) (**по делáм**) solicitor.
ходáтайств|о, а *nt.* **1.** petitioning; entreaty, pleading. **2.** petition; application.
ходáтайств|овать, ую *impf.* (*of* **по~**) **1.** (**о**+*p. or* **за**+*a.*) to petition (for); to apply (for). **2.** (**за**+*a.*) to defend, intercede (for), plead (for).
ходéбщик, а *m.* (*obs.*) hawker, pedlar.
хóдик|и, ов *no sg.* (*coll.*) grandfather clock (*worked by weights*).
хо|ди́ть, жý, ~дишь *impf.* **1.** to (be able to) walk. **2.** (*indet. of* **идти́**) to go (*on foot*); **х. в гóсти** to be invited out, visit (friends); **х. в кинó** to go to the cinema; **х. в атáку** to go into the attack; **х. на парусáх** to go sailing; **х. пó миру** to be a beggar. **3.** (*of trains, etc.*) to run. **4.** to pass, go round; **х. из рук в рýки, по рукáм** to pass from hand to hand; **недóбрые вéсти ~дят** bad news is going round. **5.** (*cards*) to lead, play; (*chess, etc.*) to move; **х. с пик** to lead a spade; **х. ферзём** to move one's queen. **6.** (*indet. only*) (**за**+*i.*) to look after, take care of, tend. **7.** to sway, shake, wobble. **8.** (*coll., obs.*) to cost; to pass, be current. **9.** (**в**+*p.*; *coll.*) to be (= *to occupy the post of, work as*). **10.** (**в**+*p.*) to wear. **11.** (*pf.* **с~**) (*coll.*) to go (= *to excrete*).
хóд|кий (~ок, ~кá, ~ко) *adj.* (*coll.*) **1.** fast, fleet. **2.** saleable, marketable; popular, in great demand, much sought after; **х. товáр** popular line; **~кое выражéние** popular phrase.
ходов|óй *adj.* **1.** (*tech.*) running, working; **~óе врéмя** working time; **х. золотни́к** throttle valve; **~ы́е испытáния** running tests; **х. механи́зм** running gear; **х. рóлик** traveller. **2.** in (good) working order. **3.** (*tech., naut.*) free, running (= *not secured*). **4.** (*coll.*) popular; current; **х. анекдóт** (currently) popular story. **5.** (*coll.*) smart, clever.
ходóк, á *m.* **1.** walker. **2.: быть ~óм (кудá-н.)** (*coll.*) to make regular visits (to). **3.** envoy, petition-bearer. **4.** (**на**+*a.*, **по**+*d.*) (*coll.*) pers. clever (at). **5.** (*tech.*) passage (*in mine*).
ходýл|и, ей *pl.* (*sg.* **~я, ~и** *f.*) stilts.

ходу́л|ьный (~ен, ~ьна) *adj.* stilted; pompous.
ходу́н, а́ *m. now only in phr.* **~о́м ходи́ть** (*coll.*) to shake, rock; (*fig.*) to rush about.
ходун|о́к, ка́ *m.* baby walker.
ходьб|а́, ы́ *f.* walking; **це́рковь нахо́дится в пяти́ мину́тах ~ы́ отсю́да** the church is five minutes' walk from here.
ходя́ч|ий *adj.* **1.** walking; able to walk. **2.** (*fig., coll., iron.*) the personification (of); **~ая доброде́тель** virtue personified. **3.** popular; current; **~ее выраже́ние** current phrase.
хожде́ни|е, я *nt.* **1.** walking; going; **х. по му́кам** (*fig.*) (going through) purgatory. **2.: име́ть х.** to be in circulation, pass current.
хоз... *comb. form, abbr. of* **хозя́йственный**
...хоз *comb. form, abbr. of* **хозя́йство**
хозрасчёт, а *m.* (*econ.*) operation on a self-supporting basis; self-financing.
хозрасчёт|ный *adj. of* **~**
хозя́|ин, ина, *pl.* **~ева, ~ев** *m.* **1.** owner, proprietor. **2.** master; boss. **3.** landlord (*in relation to tenant*). **4.** host; **~ева по́ля** (*sport*) the home team. **5.: хоро́ший, плохо́й х.** good, bad manager. **6.** (*coll.*) husband. **7.** (*biol.*) host.
хозя́йк|а, и, *g. pl.* **хозя́ек** *f.* **1.** owner, proprietress. **2.** mistress. **3.** landlady. **4.** (*coll.*) wife.
хозя́йнича|ть, ю *impf.* **1.** to manage, carry on management. **2.** to keep house. **3.** (*fig., pej.*) to lord it; to throw one's weight about.
хозя́йский *adj.* **1.** *adj. of* **хозя́ин. 2.** solicitous, careful. **3.** (*pej.*) proprietary; imperious.
хозя́йственник, а *m.* economic planner.
хозя́йствен|ный (~, ~на) *adj.* **1.** economic, of the economy; **~ная жизнь страны́** the country's economy. **2.: х. расчёт** *see* **хозрасчёт. 3.** household; home management; **х. инвента́рь** household equipment. **4.** economical, thrifty. **5.** commanding; confident.
хозя́йств|о, а *nt.* **1.** economy; **се́льское х.** agriculture; **дома́шнее х.** housekeeping; **вести́ х.** to manage, carry on management. **2.** equipment. **3.** (*agric.*) farm, holding. **4.** housekeeping; **хлопота́ть по ~у** to be busy about the house.
хозя́йств|овать, ую *impf.* to manage, carry on management.
хозя́йчик, а *m.* (*coll.*) small proprietor.
хокке́ист, а *m.* hockey-player.
хокке́|й, я *m.* hockey; **х. с ша́йбой** ice hockey; **ко́нный х.** polo.
хокке́й|ный *adj. of* **~**; **~ная клю́шка** hockey-stick.
хо́леный *adj.* well-groomed, carefully tended; sleek.
холе́р|а, ы *f.* (*med.*) cholera (*also as expletive*).
холе́рик, а *m.* **1.** choleric pers. **2.** (*coll.*) pers. suffering from cholera.
холери́ческий *adj.* choleric.
холе́р|ный *adj. of* **~а; х. вибрио́н** cholera bacillus.
хо́л|ить, ю, ишь *impf.* to tend, care for.
хо́лк|а, и *f.* withers; **намы́лить ~у кому́-н.** (*coll.*) to give s.o. a dressing-down.
холл, а *m.* hall, vestibule, foyer.
холм, а́ *m.* hill.
холми́ст|ый (~, ~а) *adj.* hilly.
хо́лод, а (у), *pl.* **~а́, ~о́в** *m.* **1.** cold; coldness (*also fig.*); **ди́кий х.** bitter cold. **2.** cold (spell of) weather.
холода́|ть, ю *impf.* **1.** (*pf.* **по~**; *impers.*) to become cold, turn cold. **2.** (*coll.*) to endure cold.
холоде́|ть, ю *impf.* (*of* **по~**) to grow cold; (*impers.*) to turn cold.
холод|е́ц, ца́ *m.* (*coll.*) meat *or* fish in jelly.
холоди́льник, а *m.* **1.** refrigerator; **ваго́н-х.** refrigerator van; **двухсекцио́нный х.** fridge-freezer. **2.** (*tech.*) condenser.
холоди́льн|ый *adj.* refrigeration, refrigeratory; **~ая те́хника** refrigeration engineering; **~ая устано́вка** cold storage plant.
холо|ди́ть, жу́, ди́шь *impf.* **1.** (*pf.* **на~**) (*coll.*) to cool. **2.** to cause a cold sensation (*also impers.*)
хо́лодно[1] *adv.* (*fig.*) coldly.
хо́лодно[2] *as pred.* it is cold; **мне,** *etc.*, **х.** I, *etc.*, am cold, feel cold.
холоднова́т|ый (~, ~а) *adj.* rather cold, chilly.
холоднока́таный *adj.* (*tech.*) cold-rolled.
холоднокро́вный *adj.* (*zool.*) cold-blooded.
холодноло́мкий *adj.* (*tech.*) cold-short.
хо́лодност|ь, и *f.* coldness.
холо́д|ный (хо́лоден, ~на́, хо́лодно) *adj.* **1.** (*in var. senses*) cold; **х. ве́тер** cold wind; **х. отве́т** cold reply; **х. по́яс** (*geog.*) frigid zone; **~ная война́** cold war; **~ное ору́жие** side-arms, cold steel; *as n.* **~ная, ~ной** *f.* (*obs., coll.*) 'the cooler' (= *place of detention*); **~ное, ~ного** *nt.* meat *or* fish in jelly. **2.** inadequate (*of clothing, etc.*; = *not affording protection against cold*).
холод|о́к, ка́ *m.* **1.** coolness, chill (*also fig.*). **2.** cool breeze. **3.** cool place. **4.** cool of the day.
холодосто́|йкий (~ек, ~йка) *adj.* (*agric.*) cold-resistant.
холо́п, а *m.* **1.** (*hist.*) villein, bond slave. **2.** serf. **3.** (*fig., pej.*) lackey.
холо́п|ий *adj. of* **~ 1.**
холо́п|ский *adj.* **1.** *adj. of* **~. 2.** servile.
холо́пств|о, а *nt.* **1.** (*hist.*) villeinage, bond slavery. **2.** servility.
холо́пств|овать, ую *impf.* to display servility.
холостёж|ь, и *f.* (*collect.*) (*coll.*) bachelors.
холо|сти́ть, щу́, сти́шь *impf.* to castrate, geld (*an animal*).
холост|о́й (хо́лост, ~а́) *adj.* **1.** unmarried, single; bachelor. **2.** (*tech.*) idle, free-running; **на ~о́м ходу́** idling. **3.** (*mil.*) blank, dummy; **х. патро́н** blank cartridge.
холостя́к, а́ *m.* bachelor.
холостя́|цкий *adj. of* **~к**
холоще́ни|е, я *nt.* castration, gelding.
холощёный *adj.* castrated, gelded.
холст, а́ *m.* **1.** canvas; sackcloth. **2.** (*art*) canvas.
холсти́н|а, ы *f.* **1.** = **холст. 2.** piece of canvas.
холсти́нк|а, и *f.* (*text.*) gingham.
холу́|й, я́ *m.* (*obs. and fig.*) lackey.
холщо́вый *adj. of* **холст 1.**
хо́л|я, и *f.* (*coll.*) care, attention; **жить в ~е** to be well cared for.
хому́т, а́ *m.* **1.** (*horse's*) collar; (*fig.*) burden. **2.** (*tech.*) clamp, ring.
хомя́к, а́ *m.* hamster.
хонинг|ова́ть, у́ю *impf.* (*tech.*) to hone.
хор, а, *pl.* **~ы́** (*and* **~́ы**) *m.* **1.** choir. **2.** (*mus. and fig.*) chorus; **~́ом** all together.
хора́л, а *m.* chorale.
хорва́т, а *m.* Croat.
Хорва́ти|я, и *f.* Croatia.
хорва́т|ка, ки *f. of* **~**
хорва́тский *adj.* Croatian, Croat.
хо́рд|а, ы *f.* **1.** (*math.*) chord. **2.** (*biol.*) notochord.
хо́рд|овый *adj. of* **~а 2.**; *as n.* **~овые, ~овых** (*zool.*) chordata.
хор|ёвый *adj. of* **~ь**
хоре́йческий *adj.* (*liter.*) trochaic.
хоре́|й, я *m.* (*liter.*) trochee.
хор|ёк, ька́ *m.* polecat, ferret.
хореографи́ческий *adj.* choreographic.
хореогра́фи|я, и *f.* choreography.
хоре́|я, и *f.* (*med.*) chorea, St Vitus' dance.
хори́ст, а *m.* **1.** member of a choir, chorister. **2.** member of a chorus.
хорме́йстер, а *m.* **1.** choirmaster. **2.** chorus master.
хорово́д, а *m.* round dance (*traditional Slavonic folk dance*).
хорово́|диться, жусь, дишься *impf.* (**с**+*i.*) (*coll.*) **1.** to be occupied (with), take up one's time (with). **2.** to carry on (with) (= *to have a sexual liaison*).
хорово́й *adj.* **1.** choral. **2.** (*obs.*) joint, collective.
хоро́м|ы, ~ *no sg.* (*obs.*) mansion.
хорон|и́ть, ю́, ~́ишь *impf.* (*of* **по~**) **1.** (*pf. also* **за~** *and* **с~**) to bury (*also fig.*); to inter. **2.** (*obs. or coll.*) to hide, conceal; **х. концы́** to cover up one's tracks.
хорон|и́ться, ю́сь, ~́ишься *impf.* (*of* **с~**) **1.** (*coll.*) to hide, conceal o.s. **2.** *pass. of* **~и́ть 1.**
хорохо́р|иться, юсь, ишься *impf.* (*coll.*) to swagger; to boast.

хоро́шенький *adj.* pretty, nice (*also iron.*).
хороше́нько *adv.* (*coll.*) properly, thoroughly, well and truly.
хороше́|ть, ю *impf.* (*of* **по~**) to grow prettier.
хоро́ш|ий (~, ~а́, ~о́) *adj.* **1.** (*in var. senses*) good. **2.** nice (*oft. iron.*) **3.** (*short forms*) pretty, good-looking.
хорошо́[1] **1.** *adv.* well; nicely. **2.** *particle, expr. agreement, acceptance* all right!; very well!; (*coll.*) righto! **3.** *n.*; *nt. indecl.* good (*mark*).
хорошо́[2] *as predicate* it is good; it is nice, pleasant; **х., что вы успе́ли прие́хать** it is good that you managed to come; **им х. — ведь у них своя́ маши́на** it is all right for them, they have a car of their own.
хорт, а *m.* (*hunting*) greyhound.
хо́ртый *adj.* smooth-haired (*of a dog*).
хору́гв|ь, и *f.* **1.** (*mil.*; *obs.*) ensign, standard. **2.** (*eccl.*) banner.
хору́нж|ий, его *m.* (*hist.*) **1.** (*mil.*) standard-bearer. **2.** cornet (*junior commissioned rank in Cossack cavalry*).
хо́р|ы, ~ *and* **≁ов** (*musicians'*) gallery.
хор|ь, я́ *m.* polecat.
хор|ько́вый *adj. of* **~ёк**
хоте́ни|е, я *nt.* desire, wish.
хоте́|ть, хочу́, хо́чешь, хо́чет, хоти́м, хоти́те, хотя́т *impf.* (*of* **за~**) (*+g., inf. or* **что́бы**) to want, desire; **я ~л бы** I should like; **х. пить** to be thirsty; **х. сказа́ть** to mean; **е́сли хоти́те** if you like (*also = perhaps*).
хоте́|ться, хо́чется *impf.* (*of* **за~**) (*impers.+d.*) to want; **мне хо́чется** I want; **мне ~лось бы** I should like.
хоти́мчик|и, ~ов *no sg.* (*coll.*) zits, pimples.
хоть *conj. and particle* **1.** *conj.* although. **2.** *conj.* even if (*esp. in set phrr.*); **у него́ де́нег х. отбавля́й** he has money enough and to spare; **х. убе́й, не скажу́** I couldn't tell you to save my life; **х. бы и так** (*coll.*) even so, even at that. **3.** *particle* (*also* **х. бы**) at least, if only; **ты бы посмотре́л х. на мину́точку** you should take a look, if only for a minute. **4.** *particle* (*coll.*) for example, to take only, even; **вот, х. его́ семиле́тняя сестрёнка, ведь, догада́лась** why, even his little seven-year-old sister had guessed it. **5.: х. бы** if only. **6.** *+rel. pron. forms indef. pron.*: **х. кто** anyone; **х. где** anywhere, everywhere; **х. куда́** (*as pred.*; *coll.*) first-rate, terrific. **7.: х. бы что** (*+d.*; *coll.*) it does not affect, does not bother.
хотя́ *conj.* **1.** although, though. **2.: х. бы** even if. **3.** *as particle* **х. бы** if only; **э́то я́вствует х. бы из заключи́тельной фра́зы его́ ре́чи** this is evident if only from the final sentence of his speech.
хохла́т|ый (~, ~а) *adj.* crested, tufted; cristate.
хо́хл|иться, юсь, ишься *impf. of* **на~**
хо́хм|а, ы *f.* joke, quip, gag.
хох|о́л, ла́ *m.* **1.** crest; topknot, tuft of hair. **2.** (*joc.*) Ukrainian (*from custom of shaving head except for single tuft of hair*).
хо́хот, а *m.* guffaw, loud laugh.
хохо|та́ть, чу́, ≁чешь *impf.* to guffaw, laugh loudly.
хохоту́н, а́ *m.* (*coll.*) laugher, joker.
Хошими́н, а *m.* Ho Chi Minh City.
храбре́ц, а́ *m.* brave pers.
храбр|и́ться, ю́сь, и́шься *impf.* (*coll.*) to try not to appear afraid; to make a show of bravery.
хра́брост|ь, и *f.* bravery, courage, valour.
хра́бр|ый (~, ~а́, ~о) *adj.* brave, courageous, valiant.
храм, а *m.* temple, church, place of worship.
храмо́вник, а *m.* (*hist.*) knight Templar.
храм|ово́й *adj. of* **~**; **х. пра́здник** patronal festival.
хране́ни|е, я *nt.* keeping, custody; storage, conservation; **ка́мера ~я** cloakroom, left luggage office; **сдать на х.** to store, deposit, leave in a cloakroom.
храни́лищ|е, а *nt.* storehouse, depository; vault.
храни́тел|ь, я *m.* **1.** keeper, custodian; (*fig.*) repository. **2.** curator.
хран|и́ть, ю́, и́шь *impf.* (*in var. senses*) to keep; to preserve, maintain; to store **х. молча́ние** to keep silence; **х. в та́йне** to keep secret.
храни́т|ься, ~ся *impf.* **1.** to be, be kept. **2.** to be preserved.
храп, а *m.* snore; snoring.
храпан|у́ть, у, ёшь *pf.* (*coll.*) to have a good kip.
храп|е́ть, лю́, и́шь *impf.* **1.** to snore. **2.** (*of an animal*) to snort.
храпови́к, а́ *m.* (*tech.*) ratchet.
храпови́цк|ий: *only in phr.* **зада́ть ~ого** (*coll.*) to fall fast asleep (*and snore*).
храпово́й *adj.* (*tech.*) ratchet; **х. механи́зм** ratchet gear.
хреб|е́т, та́ *m.* **1.** (*anat.*) spine, spinal column; (*fig.*, *coll.*) back. **2.** (mountain) range; ridge; (*fig.*) crest, peak.
хреб|то́вый *adj. of* **~е́т**
хрен, а (у) *m.* horseradish; **говя́дина под ≁ом** roast beef with horseradish sauce; **х. ре́дьки не сла́ще** (*fig.*) it's six of one to half a dozen of the other; **ста́рый х.** (*fig.*, *coll.*) old fogey, old sod; **х. с** (*+i.*) to hell (with).
хрен|о́вый *adj. of* **~**; (*sl.*) rotten, lousy.
хрестомат|и́йный *adj. of* **≁ия**
хрестома́ти|я, и *f.* reader (= *selections of literature, etc. for study*); **х. по дре́вней ру́сской литерату́ре** medieval Russ. literature reader.
хризанте́м|а, ы *f.* chrysanthemum.
хризоли́т, а *m.* (*min.*) chrysolite.
хрип, а *m.* wheeze, wheezing sound.
хрип|е́ть, лю́, и́шь *impf.* to wheeze.
хрипли́в|ый (~, ~а) *adj.* (rather) hoarse.
хри́пл|ый (~, ~а́, ~о) *adj.* hoarse; wheezy.
хри́п|нуть, ну, нешь, *past* **~, ~ла** *impf.* (*of* **о~**) to become hoarse, lose one's voice.
хрипот|а́, ы́ *f.* hoarseness.
христара́дник, а *m.* (*obs.*) beggar, mendicant.
христара́днича|ть, ю *impf.* (*obs.*) to beg; to be a beggar, mendicant.
христианиза́ци|я, и *f.* **1.** conversion to Christianity. **2.** adaptation to Christianity.
христианизи́р|овать, ую *impf. and pf.* to convert to Christianity.
христианизи́р|оваться, уюсь *impf. and pf.* become Christian; to adopt Christianity.
христи|ани́н, ани́на, *pl.* **~а́не, ~а́н** *m.* Christian.
христиа́н|ка, ки *f. of* **~и́н**
христиа́нский *adj.* Christian; **привести́ в х. вид, прида́ть** (*+d.*) **х. вид** (*joc.*) to give an air of respectability.
христиа́нств|о, а *nt.* **1.** Christianity. **2.** (*collect.*) Christendom.
христ|о́в *adj. of* **~о́с**; **Х. день** (*obs. or eccl.*) Easter day; **жить ~о́вым и́менем** (*obs.*) to live by begging, on alms.
Христо́с, Христа́ *m.* Christ; **жить Христа́ ра́ди** (*obs.*, *coll.*) (*i*) to live on alms, (*ii*) **(у кого́-н.)** to live on (s.o.'s) charity; **вот тебе́ (те) Х.** (*obs.*, *coll.*) it's the very truth.
христосла́в|ы, ов *no sg.* carol singers, waits.
христо́с|оваться, уюсь *impf.* (*of* **по~**) to exchange a triple kiss (*as Easter salutation*).
хром[1]**, а** *m.* (*chem.*) chromium, chrome.
хром[2]**, а** *m.* box-calf.
хромати́зм, а *m.* **1.** (*phys.*) chromatism. **2.** (*mus.*) chromatic scale.
хромат|и́ческий *adj. of* **~и́зм; ~и́ческая га́мма** (*mus.*) chromatic scale.
хрома́|ть, ю *impf.* **1.** to limp, be lame; **х. на о́бе ноги** (*fig.*, *coll.*) to be in a poor way. **2.** (*fig.*, *coll.*) to be weak, unsatisfactory; **арифме́тика у тебя́ ~ет** your arithmetic is very shaky.
хроме́|ть, ю *impf.* (*of* **о~**) to go lame.
хроми́р|овать, ую *impf. and pf.* to chromium-plate.
хро́м|истый *adj. of* **~**[1]
хро́мовый[1] *adj.* (*chem.*) chromium, chromic.
хро́м|овый[2] *adj. of* **~**[2]
хром|о́й (~, ~а́, ≁о) *adj.* **1.** lame, limping; **х. на ле́вую но́гу** lame in the left leg; *as n.* **х., ~о́го** *m.*; **~а́я, ~о́й** *f.* lame man, woman. **2.** (*of leg*; *coll.*) lame. **3.** (*of article of furniture*; *coll.*) shaky (*having one leg broken or shorter than others*).
хромоно́г|ий (~, ~а) *adj.* lame, limping.
хромоно́жк|а, и *f.* (*coll.*) lame woman.
хромосо́м|а, ы *f.* (*biol.*) chromosome.
хромот|а́, ы́ *f.* lameness.

хро́ник, а *m.* (*coll.*) chronic invalid.

хро́ник|а, и *f.* **1.** (*hist. and liter.*) chronicle. **2.** (*section of newspaper or radio news service*) chronicle (of events), news items. **3.** (*cin.*) (*i*) newsreel, (*ii*) historical film.

хроника́льный *adj. of* **хро́ника 2., 3.; х. фильм** = **хро́ника 3.**

хроникёр, а *m.* news reporter.

хрони́ческ|ий *adj.* (*med. and fig.*) chronic; **х. больно́й** chronic invalid; **~ая безрабо́тица** chronic unemployment.

хроно́граф[1], **а** *m.* (*hist.*) chronicle.

хроно́граф[2], **а** *m.* stopwatch.

хронологи́ческий *adj.* chronological.

хроноло́ги|я, и *f.* chronology.

хроно́метр, а *m.* chronometer.

хронометра́ж, а *m.* time study, time-keeping.

хрономнетражи́ст, а *m.* time study specialist, timekeeper.

хру́п|кий (~ок, ~ка́, ~ко) *adj.* **1.** fragile, brittle. **2.** (*fig.*) fragile, frail; delicate.

хру́пкост|ь, и *f.* **1.** fragility, brittleness. **2.** (*fig.*) fragility, frailness.

хруст, а *m.* crunch; crackle.

хруста́лик, а *m.* (*anat.*) crystalline lens.

хруста́л|ь, я́ *m.* cut glass, crystal; **го́рный х.** rock crystal.

хруста́льный *adj.* **1.** cut glass, crystal. **2.** (*fig.*) crystal-clear.

хру|сте́ть, щу́, сти́шь *impf.* (*of* **~́стнуть**) to crunch (*of snow, etc.*); to crackle.

хру́ст|нуть, ну, нешь *pf. of* **~е́ть**

хруст|я́щий *pres. part. of* **~е́ть** *and adj.* **х. карто́фель** potato crisps.

хрущ, а́ *m.* cockchafer, may bug.

хрыч, а́ *m.*: **ста́рый х.** (*coll.*) old sod, old fogey.

хрычо́вк|а, и *f.*: **ста́рая х.** (*coll.*) old hag, old bag.

хрю́кань|е, я *nt.* grunting (*of a pig*).

хрю́к|ать, аю *impf.* (*of* **~нуть**) to grunt (*of a pig*).

хрю́к|нуть, ну, нешь *pf.* (*of* **~ать**) to give a grunt (*of a pig*).

хряк, а́ *m.* (*dial.*) hog.

хря́стн|уть, у, ешь *pf.* (*coll.*) **1.** (*dial.*) to snap (off). **2.** to bash.

хрящ[1], **а́** *m.* (*anat.*) cartilage, gristle.

хрящ[2], **а́** *m.* gravel, grit.

хрящева́т|ый[1] **(~, ~а)** *adj.* cartilaginous, gristly.

хрящева́т|ый[2] **(~, ~а)** *adj. of* **хрящ**[2]

хрящ|ево́й[1,2] *adj. of* **~**[1,2]

Хуанхэ́ *f. indecl.* the Yellow River.

худ|е́е *comp. of* **~о́й**[1,3]

худе́|ть, ю *impf.* (*of* **по~**) to grow thin.

ху́д|о[1], **а** *nt.* harm, ill, evil; **нет ~а без добра́** every cloud has a silver lining.

ху́до[2] *adv.* ill, badly.

ху́до[3] *as pred.* (*impers.+d.*) **ему́,** *etc.*, **х.** (*i*) he, *etc.*, feels poorly, unwell, (*ii*) he, *etc.*, is in a bad way; he, *etc.*, is having a bad time.

худоб|а́, ы́ *f.* thinness, leanness.

худо́жественност|ь, и *f.* artistry, artistic merit.

худо́жествен|ный (~, ~на) *adj.* **1.** of art, of the arts; **~ная литерату́ра** belles-lettres, fiction; **~ная само-де́ятельность** amateur art (and dramatic) activities, amateur theatricals; **Х. теа́тр** Arts Theatre (*in Moscow*); **х. фильм** feature film; **~ная шко́ла** art school. **2.** artistic; tasteful; aesthetically satisfying.

худо́жеств|о, а *nt.* **1.** art; *pl.* (*obs.*) the arts; **Акаде́мия ~** Academy of Arts. **2.** (*obs.*) artistry. **3.** (*coll.*) trick, escapade.

худо́жник, а *m.* artist (*practitioner of fine arts; also fig., of writers, craftsmen, etc.*).

худ|о́й[1] **(~, ~а́, ~́о)** *adj.* thin, lean.

худ|о́й[2] **(~, ~а́, ~́о)** *adj.* bad; **на х. коне́ц** if the worst comes to the worst; **не говоря́ ~о́го сло́ва** (*coll.*) without a word, without warning.

худ|о́й[3] **(~, ~а́, ~́о)** *adj.* (*coll.*) in holes, full of holes; worn; tumbledown.

худоро́д|ный (~ен, ~на) *adj.* (*obs.*) of humble birth.

худоро́дств|о, а *nt.* (*obs.*) humble birth.

худоща́вост|ь, и *f.* thinness, leanness.

худоща́в|ый (~, ~а) *adj.* thin, lean.

ху́д|ший *superl. of* **~о́й**[2] *and* **плохо́й**; (the) worst.

хуёвин|а, ы *f.* (*euph.*) = **хуйня́**

ху|ёвый *adj. of* **~й**; (*vulg.*) shitty, crap(py) (= *awful*).

ху́|же *comp. of* **~до́й**[2] *and* **~до**[2], **плохо́й** *and* **пло́хо**; worse.

хуй, ху́я *m.*(*vulg.*) prick, cock (= *penis*); **ни хуя́** (*vulg.*) fuck all.

хуйн|я́, и́ *f.* (*vulg.*) (a load of) bollocks, crap, balls (= *utter nonsense*).

хул|а́, ы́ *f.* abuse, (hostile) criticism.

хулига́н, а *m.* hooligan.

хулига́н|ить, ю, ишь *impf.* to engage in hooliganism; to behave like a hooligan.

хулига́н|ский *adj. of* **~**

хулига́нств|о, а *nt.* hooliganism.

хулига́нствующ|ий *adj.* marauding, rampaging; **~ая молодёжь** young louts.

хули́тел|ьный (~ен, ~ьна) *adj.* abusive.

хул|и́ть, ю́, и́шь *impf.* to abuse, criticize (*from a hostile position*).

ху́нт|а, ы *f.* (*pol.*) junta.

хунти́ст, а *m.* (*pol.*) member of a junta.

хура́л, а *m.* hural (*name of national and local organs of government in Mongolian People's Republic*).

хурм|а́, ы́ *f.* (*bot.*) persimmon (*Diospyros*).

ху́тор, а, *pl.* **~а́** *m.* **1.** farm; farmstead. **2.** small village (*in the Ukraine and areas of Cossack settlement in Southern Russia*).

хуторск|о́й *adj. of* **ху́тор; ~и́е каза́ки** Cossack farmers; **~о́е хозя́йство** individual (*as opp. to collective or State*) farm.

хутор|я́н|ин, ина, *pl.* **~е, ~** *m.* farmer.

Ц

ц. (*abbr. of* **це́нтнер**) q., quintal(s).

ца́нг|и, ~ *no sg.* (*tech.*) pliers, tongs.

ца́нг|овый *adj. of* **~и; ц. патро́н** draw-in attachment.

цап *as pred.* (*coll.*) = **~́нул**

ца́п|ать, аю *impf.* (*of* **~нуть**) **1.** to seize, snatch, grab. **2.** to scratch. **3.** (**за**+*a.*) to snatch, grab.

ца́п|аться, аюсь *impf.* (*of* **~нуться**) (*coll.*) **1.** to scratch one another. **2.** (*pf. also* **по~**) (*fig.*) to bicker, squabble.

ца́пк|а, и *f.* hoe.

ца́п|ля, ли, *g. pl.* **~ель** *f.* heron.

ца́п|нуть(ся), ну(сь), нешь(ся) *pf. of* **~ать(ся)**

ца́пф|а, ы *f.* **1.** (*tech.*) pin, pivot, journal (*of shaft*). **2.** (*mil.*) trunnion.

цап-цара́п *as pred.* (*coll.*) he, *etc.*, grabbed, made a grab.

цара́п|ать, аю *impf.* **1.** (*pf.* **о~** *and* **~нуть**) to scratch. **2.** (*coll.*) to scribble.

цара́па|ться, юсь *impf.* **1.** to scratch (*intrans.*); to scratch one another. **2.** to scramble (along).

цара́пин|а, ы *f.* scratch; abrasion.

цара́п|нуть, ну, нешь *pf. of* **~ать**

царе́вич, а *m.* tsarevich, czarevich (*son of a tsar*).

царе́в|на, ны, *g. pl.* **~ен** *f.* tsarevna, czarevna (*daughter of a tsar*).

царедво́р|ец, ца *m.* (*obs.*) courtier.

цар|ёк, ька́ *m.* princeling, ruler.

цареуби́йств|о, а *nt.* regicide (*action*).

цареуби́йц|а, ы *c.g.* regicide (*agent*).

цари́зм, а *m.* tsarism, czarism.

цари́стский *adj.* tsarist, czarist.

цар|и́ть, ю́, и́шь *impf.* **1.** (*obs.*) to be tsar. **2.** to hold sway.

3. (*fig.*) to reign, prevail; **~и́ла тишина́** silence reigned.
цари́ц|а, ы *f.* **1.** tsarina, czarina (*empress in own right or wife of a tsar*). **2.** (*fig.*) queen.
ца́рск|ий *adj.* **1.** tsar's, of the tsar; royal; **ц. двор** tsar's court; **~ая во́дка** aqua regia; **~ие врата́** (*eccl.*) royal gates (*central doors in iconostasis in Orthodox churches*); **ц. ко́рень** (*bot.*) masterwort. **2.** tsarist, czarist. **3.** (*fig.*) regal, kingly; **~ая ро́скошь** regal splendour.
ца́рствен|ный (~, ~на) *adj.* **1.** (*obs.*) of the tsar. **2.** (*fig.*) regal, kingly.
ца́рств|о, а *nt.* **1.** kingdom, realm. **2.** reign. **3.** (*fig.*) realm, domain; **живо́тное ц.** animal kingdom; **со́нное ц.** land of Nod.
ца́рствовани|е, я *nt.* reign; **в ц.** (+*g.*) during the reign (of).
ца́рств|овать, ую *impf.* to reign (*also fig.*).
цар|ь, я́ *m.* **1.** tsar, czar; **он с ~ём (без ~я́) в голове́** (*coll.*) he is wise (stupid). **2.** (*fig.*) king, ruler.
ца́ц|а, ы *f.* (*coll.*) big-head.
ца́цка|ться, юсь *impf.* (**с кем-н.**; *coll.*) to make a fuss (of s.o.).
цвель, и *f.* (*dial.*) mould (*on foodstuffs or on walls, rocks, pond surfaces, etc.*).
цве|сти́, ту́, тёшь, *past* **~л, ~ла́, ~ло́** *impf.* **1.** to flower, bloom, blossom (*also fig.*); **ц. здоро́вьем** to be radiant with health. **2.** (*fig.*) to prosper, flourish. **3.** to be covered with mould. **4.** (*dial.*) to be covered with spots.
цвет[1], **а,** *pl.* **~а́** *m.* colour; **ц. лица́** complexion.
цвет[2], **а** *m.* **1.** (*pl.* **~ы́**) (*coll.*) flower. **2.** (*fig.*) flower, cream, pick (*best part*). **3.** blossom-time; (*fig.*) prime; **в цвету́** in blossom; **дать ц.** to blossom, flower; **во ~е сил** in one's prime; at the height of one's powers. **4.** blossom.
цвета́ст|ый (~, ~а) *adj.* (*coll.*) gaudy, garish.
цвете́ни|е, я *nt.* (*bot.*) flowering, florescence, blossoming.
цве́т|ень, ня *m.* (*coll.*) pollen.
цвети́ст|ый (~, ~а) *adj.* **1.** multi-coloured, variegated. **2.** (*fig.*) flowery, florid.
цветко́в|ый *adj.*: **~ые расте́ния** (*bot.*) flowering plants, phanerograms.
цветни́к[1], **а́** *m.* **1.** flower-bed. **2.** (*fig.*) array, galaxy.
цветни́к[2], **а́** *m.* (*coll.*) worker in non-ferrous metals industry.
цветн|о́й *adj.* **1.** coloured; colour; **~о́е стекло́** stained glass; **~а́я литогра́фия** chromolithography; **~а́я капу́ста** cauliflower; *as n.* **ц., ~о́го** *m.* coloured pers. **2.** (*tech.*) non-ferrous; **~ы́е мета́ллы** non-ferrous metals.
цветово́д, а *m.* flower-grower.
цветово́дств|о, а *nt.* flower-growing, floriculture.
цветов|о́й *adj. of* **цвет**[1]; **~а́я га́мма** colour spectrum; **~а́я слепота́** colour-blindness.
цвет|о́к, ка́, *pl.* **~ы́, ~о́в** *m.* flower; (*pl. also* **~ки́, ~ко́в**) flower (*opp. other parts of plant*).
цветоло́ж|е, а *nt.* (*bot.*) receptacle.
цветоно́жк|а, и *f.* (*bot.*) peduncle.
цветоно́сный *adj.* flower-bearing.
цвето́ч|ек, ка *m. dim. of* **цвето́к**
цвето́чник, а *m.* florist; flower-seller.
цвето́чниц|а, ы *f.* flower-girl.
цвето́чн|ый *adj. of* **цвето́к; ~ая клу́мба** flower-bed; **ц. магази́н** flower-shop, florist's; **ц. чай** flower tea.
цвету́щий *pres. part. act. of* **цвести́** *and adj.* **1.** flowering, blossoming, blooming (*also fig.*). **2.** (*fig.*) prosperous, flourishing.
це́вк|а, и *f.* (*tech.*) bobbin, spool.
цевни́ц|а, ы *f.* (*obs.*) pipe (*musical instrument*).
цевь|ё, я́ *nt.* **1.** fore-end (*of rifle stock*). **2.** pivot.
цеди́лк|а, и *f.* (*coll.*) strainer (*cul.*), filter.
цеди́льн|ый *adj.* filter, filtering; **~ая бума́га** filter paper; **~ая поду́шка** filter pad.
це|ди́ть, жу́, ~дишь *impf.* **1.** to strain, filter; to percolate. **2.** to decant (*liquids*). **3.** (*coll.*) to say (speaking through set teeth); to mutter (*oft. of a pers. barely containing anger*).
це́др|а, ы *f.* (dried) lemon *or* orange peel.
цежёный *adj.* (*coll.*) strained.
це́зи|й, я *m.* (*chem.*) caesium.
цезу́р|а, ы *f.* (*liter.*) caesura.

Цейло́н, а *m.* Ceylon.
цейло́н|ец, ца *m.* Ceylonese.
цейло́н|ка, ки *f. of* **~ец**
цейло́нский *adj.* of Ceylon, Cingalese, Sinhalese.
цейтно́т, а *m.*: **находи́ться в ~е** to be in time-trouble (*at chess*).
цейхга́уз, а *m.* (*mil.*; *obs*) armoury, stores.
целе́бност|ь, и *f.* curative, healing properties.
целе́б|ный (~ен, ~на) *adj.* curative, healing, medicinal.
цел|ево́й *adj.* **1.** *adj. of* **~ь. 2.** having a special purpose; **~евы́е сбо́ры** funds earmarked for a special purpose.
целенапра́вленност|ь, и *f.* purposefulness, single-mindedness.
целенапра́влен|ный (~, ~на) *adj.* purposeful, single-minded.
целесообра́зност|ь, и *f.* expediency.
целесообра́з|ный (~ен, ~на) *adj.* expedient.
целеустремлённост|ь, и *f.* purposefulness.
целеустремлён|ный (~, ~а́) *adj.* purposeful.
це́лик, а *m.* (*mil.*) sight (*on fire-arm*).
цели́к, а́ *m.* **1.** (*coll.*) virgin land, forest, *etc.* **2.** (*min.*) pillar, block (*of untouched ore*).
целико́м *adv.* **1.** whole; **проглоти́ть ц.** to swallow whole. **2.** wholly, entirely; **ц. и по́лностью** utterly and completely.
целин|а́, ы́ *f.* virgin lands, virgin soil (*esp. of the steppe lands of Kazakhstan and Western Siberia, extensively cultivated since 1954*).
цели́нник, а *m.* worker in the virgin lands (*of Kazakhstan and Western Siberia*).
цели́н|ный *adj. of* **~а́; ~ные зе́мли** virgin lands.
цели́тел|ьный (~ен, ~ьна) *adj.* curative, healing, medicinal.
це́л|ить, ю, ишь *impf.* (*of* **на~**) **1.** to take aim; (**в**+*a.*) to aim (at). **2.** (*obs.*) to mean, intend. **3.** (+*inf.*; *coll.*) to aim (to).
цел|и́ть, ю́, и́шь *impf.* (*obs.*) to heal, cure.
це́л|иться, юсь, ишься *impf.* (*of* **на~**) = **~ить**
целко́в|ый, ого *m.* (*coll.*) one rouble (*obs.*, *silver coin*).
целлофа́н, а *m.* cellophane.
целлуло́ид, а *m.* celluloid.
целлюло́з|а, ы *f.* cellulose.
целова́льник, а *m.* **1.** (*hist.*) tax collector. **2.** (*obs.*) inn-keeper, publican.
цел|ова́ть, у́ю *impf.* (*of* **по~**) to kiss.
цел|ова́ться, у́юсь *impf.* (*of* **по~**) to kiss (one another).
це́л|ое, ого *nt.* **1.** whole. **2.** (*math.*) integer.
целому́дрен|ный (~,~на) *adj.* chaste.
целому́дри|е, я *nt.* chastity.
це́лостност|ь, и *f.* integrity.
це́лост|ный (~ен, ~на) *adj.* integral; entire, complete.
це́лост|ь, и *f.* **1.** safety; **в ~и и сохра́нности** intact. **2.** unity.
це́л|ый *adj.* **1.** whole, entire; **~ое число́** whole number, integer; **в ~ом** as a whole; **по ~ым неде́лям** for weeks on end. **2. (~, ~а́, ~о)** safe, intact; **~ и невреди́м** safe and sound.
цел|ь, и *f.* **1.** target; **бить в ц., попа́сть в ц.** to hit the target; **бить ми́мо ~и** to miss. **2.** aim, object, goal, end, purpose; **с ~ью** (+*inf.*) with the object (of), in order (to); **отвеча́ть ~и** to answer the purpose; **пресле́довать ц.** to pursue an object; **ста́вить себе́ ~ью** (+*inf.*) to set o.s. (to).
цельнометалли́ческий *adj.* all-metal.
це́л|ьный *adj.* **1.** of one piece, solid. **2. (~ен, ~ьна́, ~ьно)** entire, integral; single. **3.** undiluted. **4.** (*coll.*) = **~ый**
це́льност|ь, и *f.* wholeness, entirety, integrity.
Це́льси|й, я *m.* Celsius, centigrade (thermometer); **10° по ~ю** 10° Celsius.
цеме́нт, а *m.* cement.
цемента́ци|я, и *f.* (*tech.*) **1.** cementation. **2.** carbonization (*of wrought iron*), case-hardening.
цементи́р|овать, ую *impf. and pf.* **1.** (*tech.*) to cement; to case-harden. **2.** (*fig.*) to cement.
цеме́нт|ный *adj. of* **~**
цен|а́, ы́, *a.* **~у,** *pl.* **~ы** *f.* **1.** price, cost; **~о́ю** (+*g.*) at the price (of), at the cost (of); **любо́й ~о́й** at any price; **э́тому**

~ы́ **нет** it is invaluable; **э́то в ~е́** it is very costly. **2.** worth, value; **знать ~у** (+*d.*) to know the worth (of); **знать себе́ ~у** to be self-assured, self-possessed.

ценз, а *m.* qualification (*for enjoyment of political rights, etc.*).

це́нз|овый *adj. of* ~

це́нзор, а *m.* censor.

цензу́р|а, ы *f.* censorship.

цензу́р|ный *adj.* **1.** *adj. of* **~а. 2. (~ен, ~на)** decent (*of words or phrr.*).

цензур|ова́ть, у́ю *impf.* (*obs.*) to censor.

цени́тел|ь, я *m.* judge, connoisseur, expert.

цен|и́ть, ю, ~ишь *impf.* **1.** (*coll.*) to fix a price for; (*fig.*) to assess, evaluate. **2.** to value, appreciate; **высоко́ ц.** to rate highly.

це́нник, а *m.* price-list.

це́нност|ь, и *f.* **1.** price, value. **2.** (*fig.*) value, importance. **3.** (*pl.*) valuables; values.

це́н|ный (~ен, ~на) *adj.* **1.** containing valuables; representing a stated value; **~ная бандеро́ль** registered postal packet (*with statement of value of contents*); **~ные бума́ги** (*fin.*) securities. **2.** valuable, costly; **ц. пода́рок** costly present. **3.** (*fig.*) valuable; precious; important; **ц. докуме́нт** important document.

цент, а *m.* cent (*unit of currency*).

це́нтнер, а *m.* quintal (= *100 kilograms*); **англи́йский ц.** Imperial hundredweight (*approx. 50.8 kilograms*); **америка́нский ц.** US hundredweight, cental (*approx. 45.4 kilograms*).

центр, а *m.* (*in var. senses*) centre; **ц. тя́жести** centre of gravity; **мозгово́й ц.** think tank.

центра́л, а *m.* (*hist.*) central prison.

централиза́ци|я, и *f.* centralization.

централи́зм, а *m.* (*pol.*) centralism.

централиз|ова́ть, у́ю *impf. and pf.* to centralize.

центра́л|ь, и *f.* (*tech.*) main (*in electricity transmission network, etc.*).

центра́льн|ый *adj.* (*in var. senses*) central; **~ые газе́ты** national newspapers (*newspapers published in the capital*); **ц. нападáющий** (*sport*) centre forward; **~ая не́рвная систе́ма** central nervous system; **~ое отопле́ние** central heating.

центри́р|овать, ую *impf. and pf.* (*tech.*) to centre.

центрифу́г|а, и *f.* **1.** (*tech.*) centrifuge. **2.** spin drier.

центробе́жный *adj.* centrifugal; **ц. насо́с** rotary pump.

центрово́й *adj.* (*tech.*) central, centre.

центростреми́тельный *adj.* centripetal.

цеп, а́ *m.* (*agric.*) flail.

цепене́|ть, ю *impf.* (*of* **о~**) to become rigid, freeze (up), be rooted to the spot (*from cold or from strong emotion*).

це́п|кий (~ок, ~ка́, ~ко) *adj.* **1.** tenacious, strong (*also fig.*); prehensile. **2.** (*of soil, mud, etc.*) sticky, tacky, loamy. **3.** (*coll.*) obstinate, persistent, strong-willed.

це́пкост|ь, и *f.* **1.** tenacity, strength. **2.** (*coll.*) obstinacy, persistence, strength of will.

цепля́|ть, ю *impf.* (*coll.*) **1. (за**+*a.*) = **~ться. 2.** to clutch (at), try to grasp.

цепля́|ться, юсь *impf.* **1. (за**+*a.*) to clutch (at), try to grasp. **2. (за**+*a.*; *coll.*) to cling (to); to stick (to). **3. (к, за**+*a.*; *coll.*) to pick (on) (= *to carp at, complain of*).

цеп|но́й *adj. of* **~ь; ~на́я соба́ка** watchdog, house-dog; **~но́е колесо́** sprocket wheel; **~на́я ли́ния** (*math.*) catenary; **ц. мост** chain bridge, suspension bridge; **~на́я реа́кция** (*chem., phys.; fig.*) chain reaction; **~на́я тя́га** (*tech.*) chain traction.

цепо́чк|а, и *f.* **1.** (small) chain. **2.** file, series; **идти́ ~ой** to walk in file.

цеп|ь, и, о ~и, на ~и́, *pl.* **~и, ~е́й** *f.* **1.** chain; (*pl.*) chains (= *fetters; also fig.*); **посади́ть на́ ц.** (*or* **на це́пь**) to chain (up), shackle. **2.** row, series; range (*of mountains*). **3.** (*mil.*) line, file. **4.** (*fig.*) series, succession; **ц. катастро́ф** succession of disasters. **5.** (*elec.*) circuit; **ввести́ в ц.** to connect.

Це́рбер, а *m.* (*myth.; fig.*) Cerebrus.

церемониа́л, а *m.* **1.** ceremonial, ritual; order, procedure. **2.: пройти́ ~ом** (*mil.; obs.*) to march past.

церемониа́л|ьный *adj.* **1.** *adj. of* **~. 2.** solemn, ceremonial; **ц. марш** (*mil.*) march-past.

церемонийме́йстер, а *m.* (*obs.*) master of ceremonies.

церемо́н|иться, юсь *impf.* (*of* **по~**) **1.** to stand upon ceremony. **2. (с кем-н.)** to treat excessively considerately.

церемо́ни|я, и *f.* **1.** ceremony. **2.** (*pl.*) ceremony (*pej.*), exaggerated observation of convention, etiquette.

церемо́н|ный (~ен, ~на) *adj.* **1.** ceremonious. **2.** (*pej.*) excessively strict in observing etiquette, protocolaire.

це́ри|й, я *m.* (*chem.*) cerium; **за́кись ~я** cerous oxide; **о́кись ~я** ceric oxide.

церко́вник, а *m.* **1.** churchman, churchgoer. **2.** clergyman, minister of religion.

церковноприхо́дский *adj.* (*eccl.*) parish.

церковнославя́нский *adj.* (*ling.*) Church Slavonic.

церковнослужи́тел|ь, я *m.* church officer (*sexton, etc.*)

церко́вн|ый *adj.* church; **~ое пра́во** ecclesiastical law, canon law; **ц. ста́роста** churchwarden; **ц. сто́рож** sexton.

це́рк|овь, ви, *i.* **~овью,** *pl.* **~ви, ~ве́й, ~ва́м** *f.* church (*building and organization*).

цесаре́вич, а *m.* cesarevitch (*heir to throne in tsarist Russia*).

цеса́рк|а, и *f.* guinea-fowl.

цех, а, в ~е *and* (*coll.*) **в ~у́,** *pl.* **~и** *and* (*coll.*) **~а́** *m.* **1.** shop, section (*in factory*). **2.** (*hist.*) guild, corporation.

цех|ово́й *adj.* **1.** *adj. of* **~. 2.** (*pej.*) limited, parochial.

цеховщи́н|а, ы *f.* (*pej.*) narrow professionalism.

цеце́ *f. indecl.* tsetse (fly).

циа́н, а *m.* (*chem.*) cyanogen.

циа́нистый *adj.* (*chem.*) cyanogen; cyanide (of); **ц. ка́лий** potassium cyanide.

циа́нов|ый *adj.* (*chem.*) cyanic; **~ая кислота́** cyanic acid; **~ая ртуть** mercuric cyanide.

циано́з, а *m.* (*med.*) cyanosis.

ци́бик, а *m.* (*obs.*) tea-chest.

цивилиза́тор, а *m.* (*usu. iron.*) civilizer.

цивилиза́ци|я, и *f.* civilization.

цивилизо́в|анный *p.p.p. of* **~а́ть** *and adj.* civilized.

цивилиз|ова́ть, у́ю *impf. and pf.* to civilize.

цивили́ст, а *m.* (*leg.*) specialist in civil law.

циви́льный *adj.* (*obs.*) civil, civilian; **ц. лист** civil list.

цига́рк|а, и *f.* (*coll.*) home-rolled cigarette.

циге́йк|а, и *f.* beaver lamb.

циге́йковый *adj.* beaver-lamb.

циду́лк|а, и *f.* (*coll., obs*) note; billet-doux.

цика́д|а, ы *f.* cicada.

цикл, а *m.* (*in var. senses*) cycle.

цикламе́н, а *m.* cyclamen.

цикли́ческий *adj.* cyclic(al).

цикли́ч|ный (~ен, ~на) *adj.* = **~еский**

цикло́ид|а, ы *f.* (*math.*) cycloid.

цикло́н, а *m.* (*meteor.*) cyclone.

циклони́ческий *adj.* (*meteor.*) cyclonic.

циклопи́ческий *adj.* (*archit.*) cyclopean.

циклотро́н, а *m.* (*phys.*) cyclotron.

ци́кл|я, и *f.* (*tech.*) scraper.

цико́ри|й, я *m.* chicory.

цико́р|ный *adj. of* **~ий**

цику́т|а, ы *f.* (*bot.*) water hemlock (*Cicuta virosa*).

цили́ндр, а *m.* **1.** (*math.*) cylinder. **2.** (*tech.*) cylinder, drum. **3.** top hat.

цилиндри́ческий *adj.* cylindrical.

цили́ндр|овый *adj. of* **~ 2.**

цимбали́ст, а *m.* cymbalist.

цимба́л|ы, ~ *no sg.* (*mus.*) cymbals.

цинг|а́, и́ *f.* (*med.*) scurvy.

цинг|о́тный *adj. of* **~а́**; scorbutic.

цини́зм, а *m.* cynicism.

ци́ник, а *m.* cynic.

цини́ческий *adj.* cynical.

цини́ч|ный (~ен, ~на) *adj.* cynical.

цинк, а *m.* (*chem.*) zinc.

цинк|ова́ть, у́ю *impf.* (*tech.*) to zinc-plate.

ци́нковый *adj.* zinc.

цино́вк|а, и *f.* mat.

цино́в|очный *adj. of* **~ка**
цирк, а *m.* circus.
цирка́ч, а́ *m.* (*coll.*) circus artiste.
цирка́чес|кий *adj. of* **~тво**
цирка́честв|о, а *nt.* (*fig.*, *pej.*) playing to the gallery, exhibitionism.
цирк|ово́й *adj. of* **~**
цирко́н, а *m.* (*min.*) zircon.
цирко́ни|й, я *m.* (*chem.*) zirconium.
циркора́м|а, ы *f.* (*cin.*) circorama.
циркули́р|овать, ую *impf.* **1.** to circulate (*of liquids, etc.*; *also fig.*); **~овали слу́хи** rumours were circulating. **2.** (*coll.*) to pass, go to and fro.
ци́ркул|ь, я *m.* (pair of) compasses; dividers.
ци́ркуль|ный *adj. of* **~**
циркуля́р, а *m.* (*official*) instruction.
циркуля́рн|ый[1] *adj.* circulated; **~ое письмо́** circular (letter).
циркуля́рный[2] *adj.* circular; circulating; **ц. нож** knife with circular action.
циркуляцио́нный *adj.* (*tech.*) circulating, circulation; **ц. насо́с** circulation pump.
циркуля́ци|я, и *f.* (*in var. senses*) circulation; (*naut.*) gyration.
цирро́з, а *m.* (*med.*) cirrhosis.
цирю́льник, а *m.* (*obs.*) barber.
цирю́л|ьня, ьни, *g. pl.* **~ен** *f.* (*obs.*) barber's shop.
цисте́рн|а, ы *f.* cistern, tank; **ваго́н-ц.** tank-truck (*rail or road transport*).
цитаде́л|ь, и *f.* citadel; (*fig.*) bulwark, stronghold.
цита́т|а, ы *f.* quotation.
цита́тничеств|о, а *nt.* (*pej.*) quotation-mongering (*in political argumentation*).
цитва́рн|ый *adj.* (*bot.*) santonic, wormseed; **~ая полы́нь** santonin; **~ое се́мя** santonin, wormseed (*med.*; *used as anthelmintic*).
цити́р|овать, ую *impf.* (*of* **про~**) to quote.
цитоло́ги|я, и *f.* (*biol.*) cytology.
ци́тр|а, ы *f.* (*mus.*) zither.
ци́трус, а *m.* citrus.
цитрусово́дств|о, а *nt.* citrus-growing.
ци́трус|овый *adj. of* **~**; *as n.* **~овые, ~овых** citrus plants.
цифербла́т, а *m.* dial, face (*of clocks, watches, and measuring instruments*).
цифи́р|ь, и *f.* (*obs.*) **1.** (*collect.*) figures. **2.** counting, calculation; arithmetic.
ци́фр|а, ы *f.* **1.** figure; number, numeral. **2.** (*pl.*) figures (= *statistical data*).
цифр|ова́ть, у́ю *impf.* to number.
цифров|о́й *adj.* **1.** numerical. **2.** digital; **~а́я за́пись** digital recording.
ци́церо *nt. indecl.* (*typ.*) pica.
ЦК *m. indecl.* (*abbr. of* **Центра́льный Комите́т**) Central Committee.
цо́к|ать[1]**, аю** *impf.* (*of* **~нуть**) to clatter (*of the sound of metal against stone*).
цо́к|ать[2]**, аю** *impf.* to pronounce **ч** as **ц** (*as in some North Russ. dialects*).
цо́к|нуть, ну *pf. of* **~ать**[1]
цо́кол|ь, я *m.* **1.** (*archit.*) socle, plinth, pedestal. **2.** (*elec.*) cap (*metal extremity of light bulb which is fitted into socket*).
цо́коль|ный *adj. of* **~**; **ц. эта́ж** ground floor.
цо́кот, а *m.* clatter (*as of horses' hoofs on paving-stones*).
цоко|та́ть, чу́, ~́чешь *impf.* (*coll.*) to clatter.
ЦРУ *nt. indecl.* (*abbr. of* **Центра́льное разве́дывательное управле́ние**) CIA (*Central Intelligence Agency*).
цуг, а *m.* team (*of horses harnessed tandem or in pairs*).
цу́гом *adv.* **1.** (*of horses in harness*) tandem. **2.** (*coll.*) in file.
цука́т, а *m.* candied peel.
ЦУМ, а *m.* (*abbr. of* **центра́льный универса́льный магази́н**) Central Department Store.
цыга́н, а, *pl.* **~е, ~** (*obs.* **~ы, ~ов**) *m.* Gypsy.
цыга́н|ка, ки *f. of* **~**
цыга́нский *adj.* Gypsy.

цы́к|ать, аю *impf.* (*of* **~нуть**) (**на кого́-н.**; *coll.*) to shut up.
цы́к|нуть, ну *pf. of* **~ать**
цы́пк|а, и *f.* (*coll.*) chicken, chick (*also used as affectionate mode of address to women*).
цы́п|ки, ок *pl.* (*sg.* **~ка, ~ки** *f.*) (*coll.*) red spots (*on hands, etc.*).
цыпл|ёнок, ёнка, *pl.* **~я́та, ~я́т** *m.* chick(en).
цыпля́тник, а *m.* chicken-house.
цыпл|я́чий *adj. of* **~ёнок**
цы́почк|и: на ц., на ~ах on tiptoe.
цып-цы́п *int.* chuck! chuck! (*cry made in calling fowl*).
цыц *int.* (*coll.*) (s)hush!
цэрэу́шник, а *m.* (*coll.*) CIA (*Central Intelligence Agency*) agent.
Цю́рих, а *m.* Zurich.

Ч

ч. (*abbr. of* **час**) hour; o'clock.
чаба́н, а́ *m.* shepherd.
чаба́н|ский *adj. of* **~**
ча́б|ер, ра *and* **чаб|ёр, ра́** *m.* (*bot., cul.*) savory.
чабре́ц, а́ *m.* (*bot., cul.*) thyme.
ча́вк|ать, аю *impf.* (*of* **~нуть**) **1.** to champ, smack one's lips (*whilst eating*); to munch noisily. **2.** to tramp, tread noisily; to make a crunching, squelching noise.
ча́вк|нуть, ну, нешь *pf. of* **~ать**
чад, а (у), о ~́е, в ~у́ *m.* **1.** fumes. **2.** (*fig.*) intoxication.
ча|ди́ть, жу́, ди́шь *impf.* (*of* **на~**) to smoke, emit fumes.
ча́д|ный (~ен, ~на, ~но) *adj.* **1.** smoky, smoke-laden; **~но** (*as pred.*) it is smoky, full of smoke. **2.** (*fig.*) doped, drugged, stupefied; stupefying.
ча́д|о, а *nt.* **1.** (*obs. or joc.*) child, offspring, progeny. **2.** (*fig.*) child, product, creature; **ч. двадца́того ве́ка** product of the twentieth century.
чадолюби́в|ый (~, ~а) *adj.* (*obs. or joc.*) fond of one's child(ren).
чадр|а́, ы́ *f.* veil, yashmak (*worn by Moslem women*).
чаёвник, а *m.* (*coll.*) tea-drinker (*pers. partial to tea-drinking*).
чаёвнича|ть, ю *impf.* (*coll.*) to drink tea, indulge in tea-drinking.
чаево́д, а *m.* tea-grower.
чаево́дств|о, а *nt.* tea-growing.
чаево́д|ческий *adj. of* **~ство**
чаев|ы́е, ы́х *no sg.* tip, gratuity.
ча|ёк, ~йка́ (у́) *m.* = **чай**
чаепи́ти|е, я *nt.* tea-drinking.
чаинк|а, и *f.* tea-leaf.
ча|й[1]**, я (ю),** *pl.* **~и́, ~ёв** *m.* **1.** tea; **шипо́вниковый ч.** rose-hip tea. **2.** tea(-drinking); **за ~́ем, за ча́шкой ~́я** over (a cup of) tea; **пригласи́ть на ч., на ча́шку ~́я** to invite to tea. **3.: дать (+*d.*) на ч.** to tip.
чай[2] *as adv.* (*coll.*) **1.** probably, maybe; no doubt; **вам тут, ч., ску́чно** you must find it dull here. **2.** (= **ведь**) after all, for.
ча́йк|а, и, *g. pl.* **ча́ек** *f.* (sea-)gull.
ча́йн|ая, ой *f.* tea-room, tea-shop.
ча́йник, а *m.* teapot; kettle.
ча́йниц|а, ы *f.* tea-caddy.
ча́йнича|ть, ю *impf.* (*coll.*) to drink tea, have tea.
ча́йн|ый *adj.* (*in var. senses*) tea; **~ая колбаса́** bologna sausage; **ч. куст** tea-plant; **~ая ло́жка** tea-spoon; **~ая ро́за** tea-rose; **~ая ча́шка** teacup.

чайхан|а́, ы́ *f.* chaikhana (*tea-drinking establishment in Central Asia*).
чалдо́н, а *m.* native of Siberia (*of Russ. extraction*).
чалдо́н|ский *adj. of* ~
ча́л|ить, ю, ишь *impf.* (*naut.*) to tie up, moor.
ча́лк|а, и *f.* (*naut.*) **1.** tying up, mooring. **2.** tie-rope, mooring rope.
чалм|а́, ы́ *f.* turban.
ча́лый *adj.* (*of colour of horse's coat*) roan.
чан, а, в ∸**е** *or* **в** ~**у́,** *pl.* ~**ы́** *m.* vat, tub, tank.
Чанцзя́н = **Янцзы**
чапы́г|а, и *f.* (*dial.*) plough-handle.
ча́р|а, ы *f.* (*arch. or folk poet.*) cup, goblet.
ча́р|ка, ки *f.* = ~**а**
чар|ова́ть, у́ю *impf.* **1.** (*obs.*) to bewitch. **2.** (*fig.*) to charm, captivate, enchant.
чароде́|й, я *m.* magician, enchanter, wizard (*also fig.*).
чароде́йств|о, а *nt.* magic, charms.
ча́ртерный *adj.*: **ч. рейс** (*aeron.*) charter flight.
ча́р|ы, ~ *no sg.* magic, charms (*also fig.*)
час, а, о ∸**е, в** ~**у́** *and* **в** ∸**е,** *pl.* ~**ы́** *m.* **1.** hour (*also fig.*); **че́тверть** ~**а́** a quarter of an hour; **ч. проби́л** the hour has struck, has come; **ч. в ч.** at the time appointed, on the dot; **ч. о́т** ~**у** with every passing hour; **с** ∸**у на ч.** (*i*) hourly, with every passing hour, (*ii*) any moment; **че́рез ч.** (*i*) in an hour, (*ii*) at hourly intervals; **в до́брый ч.!** good luck! **2.** (*in time measurement*: *g. sg.* ~**а́** *after numerals 2, 3, 4*) o'clock; **час** one o'clock; **два** ~**а́** two o'clock; **во второ́м** ~**у́** between one and two (o'clock); **кото́рый ч.?** what is the time? **3.** (*usu. pl.*) hours, time, period; **ч. пик,** ~**ы́ пик** rush hour; ~**ы́ заня́тий** working hours; **ч. рисова́ния** (*in school, etc.*) drawing period; **«золоты́е** ~**ы́»** prime (*television viewing*) time. **4.** ~**ы́** (*mil.*) guard-duty; **стоя́ть на** ~**а́х** to stand guard. **5.** ~**ы́** (*eccl.*) (canonical) hours.
часа́ми *adv.* for hours.
часо́в|ня, ни, *g. pl.* ~**ен** *f.* chapel.
часов|о́й[1]**, о́го** *m.* sentry, sentinel, guard.
часов|о́й[2] *adj.* (*of* **час**) **1.** of one hour's duration; **ч. переры́в** one hour's interval. **2.** (measured) by the hour; ~**а́я опла́та** payment by the hour; **ч. по́яс** time zone. **3.** one o'clock; **ч. по́езд** one o'clock train.
часов|о́й[3] *adj. of* **часы́; ч. замыка́тель** clockwork fuse; **ч. магази́н** watch shop, watchmaker's, watch repair shop; ~**ы́х дел ма́стер** watchmaker; **ч. механи́зм** clockwork; ~**а́я стре́лка** clock hand, hour hand; **по** ~**о́й стре́лке** clockwise.
часовщи́к, а́ *m.* watchmaker.
ча́сом *adv.* (*coll.*) **1.** sometimes, at times. **2.** by chance, by the way.
часосло́в, а *m.* (*eccl.*) Book of Hours.
часте́нько *adv.* (*coll.*) quite often, fairly often.
части́к, а́ *m.* **1.** thick net. **2.** fish caught in such a net.
ча|сти́ть, щу́, сти́шь *impf.* (*coll.*) **1.** to do sth. *or* speak rapidly, hurriedly. **2.** (**к**) to visit frequently, see much (of).
части́ц|а, ы *f.* **1.** small part, element. **2.** (*phys.*) particle. **3.** (*gram.*) particle.
части́чно *adv.* partly, partially.
части́ч|ный (~**ен,** ~**на)** *adj.* partial.
ча́стник, а *m.* (*coll.*) private trader; private medical practitioner.
частновладе́льческий *adj.* privately-owned.
ча́стн|ое, ого *nt.* (*math.*) quotient.
частносо́бственнический *adj.* private-ownership.
ча́стност|ь, и *f.* detail; **в** ~**и** in particular.
ча́стн|ый *adj.* **1.** private, personal; ~**ым о́бразом** privately; ~**ая пра́ктика** private (*medical*) practice. **2.** (*econ.*) private, privately-owned; ~**ая со́бственность** private property. **3.** particular, individual; *as n.* ~**ое,** ~**ого** *nt.* the particular. **4.** (*mil.*) local; **ч. успе́х** local gain. **5.** (*hist.*) district; **ч. дом** district police station.
ча́сто *adv.* often, frequently.
частоко́л, а *m.* fence, paling; palisade.
частот|а́, ы́, *pl.* ∸**ы** *f.* (*in var. senses*) frequency.
часто́т|ный *adj.* (*tech.*) *of* ~**а́**
часту́шк|а, и *f.* chastushka (*two-line or four-line rhymed poem or ditty on some topical or humorous theme*).
ча́ст|ый (~**, **~**а́, **~**о)** *adj.* **1.** frequent; **он у нас ч. гость** he is a frequent visitor at our house. **2.** close (together); dense, thick; close-woven; **ч. гре́бень** fine-tooth comb; ~**ые дере́вни** villages close together; **ч. дождь** steady rain; ~**ая и́згородь** thick hedge; ~**ое си́то** fine sieve. **3.** quick, rapid; **ч. ого́нь** (*mil.*) rapid fire.
част|ь, и, *pl.* ∸**и,** ~**е́й** *f.* **1.** part; portion; ∸**и ре́чи** (*gram.*) parts of speech; **разобра́ть на** ∸**и** to take to pieces, dismantle; **бо́льшей** ~**ью, по бо́льшей** ∸**и** for the most part, mostly; **рвать кого́-н. на** ∸**и** to give s.o. no peace. **2.** section, department, side; **уче́бная ч.** teaching (*opp. administrative*) side (*in educational institution*). **3.** sphere, field; **э́то не по мое́й** ∸**и** this is not my province; **по** ∸**и** (*+g.*) in connection (with). **4.** (*coll.*) share; **войти́, вступи́ть в ч. с кем-н.** to join forces with s.o. (*usu. in commerce*). **5.** (*mil.*) unit. **6.** (**в** ~**и́**) (*hist.*) administrative region (*of city*); police station (*responsible for such region*); fire brigade. **7.** (*obs.*) fate.
ча́стью *adv.* partly, in part.
час|ы́[1]**, о́в** *no sg.* clock, watch.
часы́[2] *see* **час 4., 5.**
ча́хл|ый (~**, **~**а)** *adj.* **1.** (*of vegetation*) stunted; poor, sorry. **2.** weakly, sickly, puny.
ча́х|нуть, ну, нешь, *past* ~**,** ~**ла** *impf.* (*of* **за**~) **1.** (*of vegetation*) to wither away. **2.** to become weak, (go into a) decline; (*fig.*) to tire o.s. out, become exhausted.
чахо́тк|а, и *f.* (*coll.*) consumption; **карма́нная ч.** (*joc.*) an empty pocket.
чахо́точный *adj.* (*coll.*) **1.** consumptive. **2.** poor, sorry, feeble.
ча-ча-ча́ *nt. indecl.* the cha-cha (*dance*).
ча́ш|а, и *f.* cup, bowl (*also fig.*); (*eccl.*) chalice; **ч. весо́в** scale, pan; **ч. на́шего терпе́ния переполнилась** our patience was exhausted; **сия́ ч. минова́ла его́** he has survived the ordeal.
чашели́стик, а *m.* (*bot.*) sepal.
ча́шечк|а, и *f.* **1.** *dim. of* **ча́шка. 2.** (*bot.*) calyx.
ча́ш|ечный *adj.* **1.** *adj. of* ~**ка. 2.** cup-shaped.
ча́шк|а, и *f.* **1.** cup; bowl, pan. **2.: ч. весо́в** pan (*of scales*). **3.** (**коле́нная**) knee-cap. **4.** (*tech.*) housing.
ча́шник, а *m.* (*hist.*) cellarer.
ча́щ|а, и *f.* thicket.
ча́ще *comp. of* **ча́стый** *and* **ча́сто** more often, more frequently; **ч. всего́** most often, mostly.
ча́яни|е, я *nt.* expectation; aspiration; **па́че** ~**я, сверх** ~**я** unexpectedly, contrary to expectation.
ча́|ять, ю, ешь *impf.* (*obs. or coll.*) **1.** to think, suppose. **2.** (*+g. or inf.*) to hope (for), expect.
чва́н|иться, юсь, ишься *impf.* to boast.
чванли́вост|ь, и *f.* boastfulness, arrogance.
чванли́в|ый (~**, **~**а)** *adj.* boastful, arrogant, conceited.
чва́нный *adj.* conceited, arrogant, proud (*pej.*).
чва́нств|о, а *nt.* conceit, arrogance, pride (*pej.*).
чебота́р|ь, я́ *m.* (*dial.*) cobbler, shoemaker.
чёбот|ы, ов *pl.* (*sg.* ~**,** ~**а** *m.*) (*dial.*) boots, shoes.
чебура́хн|уть, у, ешь *pf.* (*coll.*) to crash down (*trans.*).
чебура́хн|уться, усь, ешься *pf.* (*coll.*) to crash down (*intrans.*)
чебуре́к, а *m.* cheburek (*kind of meat pasty eaten in the Crimea and the Caucasus*).
чебуре́чн|ая, ой *f.* stall selling chebureki.
чего́[1] *interrog. adv.* (*coll.*) why? what for?
чего́[2] *g. of* **что**
чей, чья, чьё *interrog. and rel. pron.* whose.
чей-либо *pron.* anyone's.
чей-нибудь *pron.* anyone's.
че́й-то *pron.* someone's.
чек, а *m.* **1.** cheque; **вы́писать ч.** to draw a cheque. **2.** (*in shops, etc.*) bill, chit (*indicating amount to be paid*); receipt (*for payment, to be presented at counter when claiming purchase*).
чек|а́[1]**, и́** *f.* pin, linchpin, cotter-pin.
Чек|а́[2] *f. indecl. or* (*coll.*) *g.* ~**и́** *f.* (*coll.*) (*hist.*) Cheka (*abbr. of* **Чрезвыча́йная коми́ссия по борьбе́ с контр-**

революцией и саботажем *the Soviet state security organ, 1918–1922*).

чека́н, а *m.* **1.** stamp, die. **2.** caulking-iron. **3.** (*zool.*) chat; **лугово́й ч.** whinchat; **черного́рлый ч.** stonechat.

чека́н|ить, ю, ишь *impf.* **1.** (*pf.* **вы́~, от~**) to mint, coin; to stamp, engrave, emboss, chase. **2.** (*pf.* **от~**) to do, make with precision; **ч. слова́** to enunciate one's words clearly, speak abruptly; **ч. шаг** to measure one's pace, step out. **3.** (*pf.* **рас~**) (*tech.*) to caulk. **4.** (*agric., hort.*) to prune.

чека́нк|а, и *f.* **1.** coinage, coining, minting; stamping, engraving, embossing, chasing. **2.** (*tech.*) caulking. **3.** (*agric., hort.*) pruning. **4.** stamp, engraving, relief work.

чека́нн|ый *adj.* **1.** stamping, engraving, embossing; **~ая рабо́та = чека́нка 4.**. **2.** stamped, engraved, embossed, chased. **3.** (*fig.*) precise, expressive, sharp.

чека́н|очный *adj.* = **~ный 1.**; **ч. пресс** stamping press; **ч. штамп** die.

чека́нщик, а *m.* coiner; stamper, engraver; caulker.

чеки́ст, а *m.* (state) security officer; (*hist.*) Chekist, Cheka agent (*see also* **Чека́**²).

чекма́р|ь, я́ *m.* (*dial.*) rammer, beetle.

чекме́н|ь, я́ *m.* (cloth) jacket.

че́к|овый *adj. of* **~**; **~овая кни́жка** cheque book.

чел́ест|а, ы *f.* (*mus.*) glockenspiel.

чёлк|а, и *f.* fringe (*of hair or as name of hairstyle*); forelock.

чёлн, а́, *pl.* **~ы́**, *or* **~ы** *m.* **1.** dug-out (canoe). **2.** (*obs. or poet.*) boat.

челно́к, а́ *m.* **1.** = **чёлн. 2.** shuttle.

челно́|чный *adj. of* **~к 2.**; **ч. полёт** (*aeron.*) shuttle flight; **~чная диплома́тия** shuttle diplomacy.

чел|о́¹, **а́** *nt.* forehead, brow; **бить ~о́м кому́-н.** (*hist. or iron.*) (*i*) to bow to s.o. (*in greeting*), (*ii*) to petition s.o., (*iii*) to offer s.o. humble thanks.

чел|о́², **а́**, *pl.* **~́а** *nt.* (*tech.*) stoking hole (*in furnace*).

челоби́тн|ая, ой *f.* (*hist.*) petition.

челоби́тчик, а *m.* (*hist.*) petitioner.

челоби́ть|е, я *nt.* (*hist.*) **1.** low bow. **2.** petition.

челове́к, а, *pl.* **лю́ди** (*g. pl., etc.*, **челове́к, ~ам, ~ами, о ~ах** *only in comb. with nums.*) *m.* **1.** man, person, human being. **2.** (*obs.*) servant, man; waiter.

челове́ко-де́нь, ч.-дня́ *m.* (*econ.*) man-day.

человеколюби́в|ый (~, ~а) *adj.* philanthropic.

человеколю́би|е, я *nt.* philanthropy, love of fellow-men.

человеконенави́стник, а *m.* misanthrope.

человеконенави́стнический *adj.* misanthropic.

человеконенави́стничеств|о, а *nt.* misanthropy

человекообра́з|ный (~ен, ~на) *adj.* anthropomorphous; (*zool.*) anthropoid.

человекоподо́б|ный (~ен, ~на) *adj.* resembling a human being.

челове́ко-ча́с, а *m.* (*econ.*) man-hour.

челове́ч|ек, ка *m.* little man.

челове́ческий *adj.* **1.** human. **2.** humane.

челове́честв|о, а *nt.* humanity, mankind.

челове́|чий *adj. of* **~к**

челове́чин|а, ы *c.g. and f.* (*coll.*) **1.** *c.g.* person, human being. **2.** *f.* human flesh (*as meat*).

челове́чност|ь, и *f.* humaneness, humanity.

челове́ч|ный (~ен, ~на) *adj.* humane.

челюстно́й *adj.* jaw; (*anat.*) maxillary

че́люст|ь, и *f.* **1.** jaw, jaw-bone; (*anat.*) maxilla. **2.** dental plate, set of false teeth.

че́ляд|ь, и *f.* (*collect.*; *hist.*) servants, retainers, men.

чем *conj.* **1.** than. **2.** (+*comp.*) **ч...., тем...** the more ..., the more ...; **ч. скоре́е, тем лу́чше** the sooner, the better. **3.** (+*inf.*) rather than, instead of; **чем писа́ть, ты бы лу́чше позвони́л** you'd do better to ring up rather than write. **4.: ч. свет** at daybreak.

чембу́р, а *m.* halter.

чемода́н, а *m.* suitcase.

чемпио́н, а *m.* champion.

чемпиона́т, а *m.* championship.

чемпио́н|ка, ки *f. of* **~**

чемпио́нств|о, а *nt.* champion's title.

чепе́ *nt. indecl.* (*abbr. of* ***чрезвыча́йное происше́ствие***) incident, emergency.

чеп|е́ц, ца́ *m.* (*woman's*) cap.

чепра́к, а́ *m.* saddle-cloth.

чепух|а́, и́ *f.* (*coll.*) **1.** nonsense, rubbish. **2.** a trifle, trifling matter; trivialities.

чепухо́вый *adj.* (*coll.*) **1.** nonsensical. **2.** trifling; trivial; insignificant.

че́пчик, а *m.* **1.** = **чепе́ц. 2.** (*child's*) bonnet.

че́рв|а, ы *f.* (*collect.*) larvae (*of bees*).

червеобра́зный *adj.* vermiform, vermicular; **ч. отро́сток** (*anat.*) appendix.

че́рв|и¹, **е́й** *and* **~ы, ~** *pl.* (*sg.* **~а, ~ы** *f.*) hearts (*card suit*); **коро́ль ~е́й** king of hearts.

че́рв|и² *pl. of* **~ь**

черви́ве|ть, ет *impf.* (*of* **о~**) to become worm-eaten.

черви́в|ый (~, ~а) *adj.* worm-eaten.

червлёный *adj.* (*obs.*) dark red.

черв|о́вый *adj. of* **~́и**¹

черво́н|ец, ца *m.* **1.** (*hist.*) chervonets (*gold coin of 3, 5, or 10 roubles' denomination; or 10 rouble bank-note in circulation 1922–47*). **2.** (*pl.*) (*coll., obs.*) money.

черво́нн|ый¹ *adj.* **1.** (*obs. or dial.*) red, dark red; **~ое зо́лото** pure gold (*as having a reddish tint*). **2.** *adj. of* **черво́нец 1.**

черв|о́нный² *adj. of* **~́и**¹; **ч. туз** ace of hearts.

червото́чин|а, ы *f.* **1.** worm-hole, maggot hole. **2.** (*fig.*) rottenness.

черв|ь, я́, *pl.* **~́и, ~е́й** *m.* **1.** worm; maggot. **2.** (*fig.*) bug, virus, germ; **его́ то́чит ч. сомне́ния** he is nagged by doubts.

червя́к, а́ *m.* **1.** = **червь. 2.** (*tech.*) worm.

червя́чн|ый *adj. of* **червя́к 2.**; **~ое колесо́, ~ая шестерня́** worm wheel; **~ая переда́ча** worm gearing.

червяч|о́к, ка́ *m. dim. of* **червя́к 1.**; **замори́ть ~ка́** (*coll.*) to have a bite to eat.

черда́к, а́ *m.* attic, loft.

черда́|чный *adj. of* **~к**

череви́к|и, ов *pl.* (*sg.* **~, ~а** *m.*) chereviki (*high-heeled leather boots worn by women in the Ukraine*).

черёд, а́, о ~е́, в ~у́ *m.* **1.** turn; **идти́ свои́м ~о́м** to take its course. **2.** (*coll.*) queue.

черед|а́¹, **ы́** *f.* **1.** (*obs.*) = **черёд 1.**. **2.** sequence. **3.** file (*of people*).

черед|а́², **ы́** *f.* (*bot.*) bur-marigold (*Bidens*).

чередова́ни|е, я *nt.* alternation, interchange, rotation; **ч. гла́сных** (*ling.*) vowel interchange.

черед|ова́ть, у́ю *impf.* (**с**+*i.*) to alternate (with).

черед|ова́ться, у́юсь *impf.* to alternate; to take turns.

чередо́м *adv.* (*coll.*) properly.

че́рез *prep.*+*a.* **1.** (*of place*) across; over; through. **2.** via. **3.** through (= *by means of, with the aid of*); **ч. печа́ть** through the press; **ч. перево́дчика** through an interpreter. **4.** (*coll.*) through (= *due to, in consequence of*); **ч. боле́знь** through illness. **5.** (*of time*) in; **ч. полчаса́** in half an hour's time; **я верну́сь ч. год** I shall be back in a year's time. **6.** (*of space*) after; (further) on **ч. три киломе́тра** three kilometres (further) on. **7.** (*i*) *indicates repetition at stated unit of time or space*: **принима́ть ч. час по столо́вой ло́жке** to take one tablespoonful every hour; **ч. ка́ждые три страни́цы** every three pages, (*ii*) *indicates repetition alternating at stated unit of time or space*: **дежу́рить ч. день** to be on duty every other day, on alternate days; **печа́тать ч. строку́** to double-space.

череми́с, а *m.* (*hist.*) Cheremis (*former name of Mari*).

черёмух|а, и *f.* bird cherry (*Padus*).

черёмух|овый *adj. of* **~а**

череш|а́, и́ *f.* (*bot.*) ramson.

черенк|ова́ть, у́ю *impf.* (*of* **от~**) (*hort.*) **1.** to graft. **2.** to take a cutting (of).

черен|о́к, ка́ *m.* **1.** handle, haft (*of implement*). **2.** (*hort.*) graft, cutting, slip.

че́реп, а, *pl.* **~а́** *m.* skull, cranium.

черепа́х|а, и *f.* **1.** tortoise; turtle; **идти́ ~ой** to go at a snail's pace. **2.** tortoise-shell.

черепа́ховый *adj.* tortoise, turtle; tortoise-shell.

черепа́|ший *adj.* **1.** *adj. of* **~ха 1.**. **2.** (*fig.*) very slow.

черепи́ц|а, ы *f.* tile.
черепи́чный *adj.* tile; tiled.
черепн|о́й *adj. of* **че́реп; ~а́я коро́бка** cranium.
череп|о́к, ка́ *m.* broken piece of pottery.
чересполо́сиц|а, ы *f.* strip-farming.
чересседе́льник, а *m.* back-band.
чересчу́р *adv.* too; too much.
чере́шн|евый *adj. of* **~я**
чере́шн|я, и *f.* cherry(-tree) (*Cerasus avium*).
черка́|ть, ю (*and* **чёрка|ть, ю)** *impf.* (*coll.*) to cross out, cross through.
черке́с, а *m.* Circassian.
черке́ск|а, и *f.* Circassian coat (*long, narrow, collar-less coat worn by Caucasian highlanders*).
черке́сский *adj.* Circassian.
черке́шенк|а, и *f. of* **черке́с**
черкн|у́ть, у́, ёшь *pf.* (*coll.*) **1.** to make, leave a line on. **2.** to dash off, scribble.
че́рнет|ь, и *f.* (*zool.*): **морска́я ч.** scaup; **хохла́тая ч.** tufted duck.
черне́|ть, ю *impf.* **1.** (*pf.* **по~**) to turn black, grow black. **2.** to show up black.
черне́ц, а́ *m.* (*hist.*) monk.
черни́к|а, и *f.* bilberry, blaeberry, whortleberry (*Vaccinium myrtillus*).
черни́л|а, ~ *no sg.* ink.
черни́льниц|а, ы *f.* ink-pot, ink-well.
черни́л|ьный *adj.* **1.** *adj. of* **~а; ч. каранда́ш** indelible pencil; **ч. оре́шек** oak-gall, nut-gall. **2.** (*iron.*) paper, verbal.
черн|и́ть, ю́, и́шь *impf.* **1.** (*pf.* **за~** *and* **на~**) to blacken, paint black. **2.** (*pf.* **о~**) (*fig.*) to blacken, slander. **3.** to burnish.
черни́ц|а, ы *f.* (*hist.*) nun.
черни́|чный *adj. of* **~ка**
чернобу́рк|а, и *f.* (*coll.*) silver fox (fur).
чернобы́л, а *m.* (*coll.*) = **чернобы́льник**
чернобы́л|ь, я *m.* (*coll.*) = **чернобы́льник**
чернобы́льник, а *m.* (*bot.*) mugwort.
черови́к, а́ *m.* rough copy, draft.
чернов|о́й *adj.* **1.** rough, draft; preparatory. **2.: ~а́я рабо́та** (*coll.*) heavy, rough, dirty work. **3.** (*tech.*; *of metals*) crude.
черноволо́с|ый (~, ~а) *adj.* black-haired.
черногла́з|ый (~, ~а) *adj.* black-eyed.
черного́р|ец, ца *m.* Montenegrin.
Черного́ри|я, и *f.* Montenegro.
черного́р|ка, ки *f. of* **~ец**
черного́рский *adj.* Montenegrin.
чернозём, а *m.* (*agric.*, *geol.*) chernozem, black earth.
чернозём|ный *adj. of* **~**
чернозо́бик, а *m.* (*zool.*) dunlin.
чернокни́жи|е, я *nt.* (*obs.*) black magic.
чернокни́жник, а *m.* (*obs.*) practitioner of black magic.
черноко́ж|ий (~, ~а) *adj.* black, coloured; *as n.* **ч., ~его** *m.* negro, black (man).
черноле́сь|е, я *nt.* deciduous forest.
черномаз|ый (~, ~а) *adj.* (*coll.*) swarthy.
черномо́р|ец, ца *m.* sailor of Black Sea fleet.
черномо́рский *adj.* Black Sea.
чернорабо́ч|ий, его *m.* unskilled labourer.
чернори́з|ец, ца *m.* (*hist.*) monk.
чернсли́в, а (у) *m.* (*collect.*) prunes.
черносморо́динный *adj.* blackcurrant.
черносо́тен|ец, ца *m.* (*hist. or iron.*) member of 'Black Hundred' (*name of armed anti-revolutionary groups in Russia, active 1905–7*).
черносо́тен|ный *adj. of* **ец**
чернот|а́, ы́ *f.* blackness (*also fig.*); darkness.
черната́л, а *m.* (*bot.*) bay-leaf willow (*Salix pentandra*).
черну́шк|а, и *f.* **1.** (*bot.*) nutmeg flower (*Nigella sativa*). **2.** (*coll.*) swarthy, dark-haired *or* dark-eyed woman.
чёр|ный (~ен, ~на́, ~но́) *adj.* **1.** (*in var. senses*) black; **~ная би́ржа, ч. ры́нок** black market; **ч. глаз** (*coll.*) evil eye; **(отложи́ть на) ч. день** (to put by for) a rainy day; **~ное де́рево** ebony; **~ное духове́нство** regular clergy, monks; **~ное зо́лото** 'black gold' (= *oil*); **ч. лес** deciduous forest; **ч. наро́д** (*hist.*) common people; **ч. пар** bare fallow; **~ное сло́во** (*dial.*) bad language; **держа́ть в ~ном те́ле** to ill-treat; **~ным по бе́лому** in black and white; *as n.* **ч., ~ного** *m.* negro, black (man); (*coll.*) darky. **2.** (*opp.* **пара́дный**) back; **ч. ход** back entrance, back door. **3.** (*of work*) heavy; unskilled. **4.** (*hist.*) State (*opp. privately-owned*). **5.** (*tech.*) ferrous (*opp.* **цветно́й**). **6.** (*fig.*) gloomy, melancholy.
черн|ь[1]**, и** *f.* mob, common people.
черн|ь[2]**, и** *f.* niello; black enamel.
черпа́к, а́ *m.* scoop; bucket; grab.
черпа́лк|а, и *f.* scoop; ladle.
че́рп|ать, аю *impf.* (*of* **~ну́ть**) **1.** to draw (up); to scoop; to ladle. **2.** (*fig.*) to extract, derive, draw.
черп|ну́ть, ну́, нёшь *pf. of* **~ать**
черстве́|ть, ю *impf.* **1.** (*pf.* **за~**) to become stale. **2.** (*pf.* **о~**) to grow hardened, become hard (*fig.*).
чёрств|ый (~, ~а́, ~о) *adj.* **1.** stale. **2.** (*fig.*) hard, callous.
чёрт, а, *pl.* **че́рти, ~е́й** *m.* devil; **ч. (его́) возьми́!** the devil take it!; **ч. его́ зна́ет!** the devil only knows!; **до ~а** devilishly, hellishly; **на кой ч.?** why the hell?; **~а с два** like hell!; **у ~а на рога́х, на кули́чках** at the back of beyond.
черт|а́, ы́ *f.* **1.** line; **провести́ ~у́** to draw a line; **подвести́ ~у́ (под)** (*fig.*) to draw a line (under), put an end (to), dispose (of). **2.** boundary; **ч. осе́длости** (*hist.*) the (Jewish) Pale. **3.** trait, characteristic; **~ы́ лица́** features; **в о́бщих ~а́х** in general outline.
чертёж, а́ *m.* draught, drawing, sketch; blueprint, plan, scheme; **ч. на ка́льке** tracing.
чертёжн|ая, ой *f.* drawing office.
чертёжник, а *m.* draughtsman.
чертёжн|ый *adj.* drawing; **~ая доска́** drawing board; **~ая мастерска́я** drawing office; **~ое перо́** lettering pen.
чертён|ок, ка, *pl.* **~я́та, ~я́т** *m.* (*coll.*) imp.
чер|ти́ть[1]**, чу́, ~тишь** *impf.* (*of* **на~**) to draw; to draw up.
чер|ти́ть[2]**, чу́, ти́шь** *impf.* (*coll.*) to go on a binge, on the booze.
чёртов *adj.* **1.** devil's; **~а дю́жина** baker's dozen. **2.** (*coll.*) devilish, hellish.
черто́вк|а, и *f.* she-devil; (*as term of abuse*) bitch.
черто́вский *adj.* (*coll.*) devilish, damnable.
чертовщи́н|а, ы *f.* **1.** (*collect.*) devils, demons. **2.** (*fig., coll.*) devilry; idiocy.
черто́г, а *m.* (*obs.*) hall, mansion.
чертополо́х, а *m.* thistle.
чёрточк|а, и *f.* **1.** *dim. of* **черта́ 1. 2.** hyphen.
чертых|а́ться, а́юсь *impf.* (*of* **~ну́ться**) (*coll.*) to swear.
чертых|ну́ться, ну́сь, нёшься *pf. of* **~а́ться**
черче́ни|е, я *nt.* drawing; sketching.
чёс, а *m.* (*coll.*) itch(ing); **зада́ть ~у (*i*) кому́-н.** to tick s.o. off, (*ii*) to make off.
чеса́лк|а, и *f.* (*text.*) comb, combing machine.
чеса́льный *adj.* (*text.*) combing, carding.
чеса́льщик, а *m.* (*text*) comber, carder.
чёсаный *adj.* (*text.*) combed, carded.
че|са́ть, шу́, ~шешь *impf.* (*of* **по~**) **1.** to scratch; **ч. заты́лок, в заты́лке** to scratch one's head (*also fig.*); **ч. язы́к** to wag one's tongue. **2.** (*coll.*) to comb (*hair*). **3.** (*text.*) to comb, card. **4.** (*coll.*) *expr. rapid or vigorous action* (*translated in acc. with context*).
че|са́ться, шу́сь, ~шешься *impf.* (*of* **по~**) **1.** to scratch o.s. **2.** (*impf. only*) to itch; **ру́ки у него́** *etc.* **~шутся** (+*inf.*) he is, *etc.*, itching to .... **3.** (*coll.*) to comb one's hair.
чесно́к, а́ (у́) *m.* garlic.
чесно́|чный *adj. of* **~к**
чесо́тк|а, и *f.* **1.** (*med.*) scab; rash; mange. **2.** itch.
чесо́т|очный *adj. of* **~ка; ч. клещ** itch-mite.
че́ствовани|е, я *nt.* **(кого́-н.)** celebration (in honour of s.o.).
че́ств|овать, ую *impf.* to celebrate (*an occasion, etc.*); to honour, arrange a celebration in honour of (*s.o.*).
че|сти́ть, щу́, сти́шь *impf.* **1.** (*coll.*) to abuse. **2.** (*obs.*) to honour.
честн|о́й *adj.* (*obs.*) **1.** (*eccl.*) sanctified, sainted; saintly; **мать ~а́я!** (*coll.*) my sainted aunt! **2.** worthy, honoured; **~а́я компа́ния** (*iron.*) gang, network.
че́стност|ь, и *f.* honesty, integrity.

че́ст|ный (~ен, ~на́, ~но) *adj.* honest, upright; upstanding; **~ное сло́во!** upon my honour!
честолю́б|ец, ца *m.* ambitious pers.
честолюби́в|ый (~, ~а) *adj.* ambitious.
честолю́би|е, я *nt.* ambition.
чест|ь[1], **и** *f.* **1.** honour; **в ч.** (*+g.*) in honour (of); **по ~́и сказа́ть** to say in all honesty; **счита́ть за ч.** to consider (it) an honour; **отда́ть ч.** (*+d.*) (*i*) to salute, (*ii*) (*joc.*) to do honour (to); **проси́ть ~́ью** to urge; **пора́ и ч. знать** (*coll.*) it is time to go (*joc. formula used on taking leave of host, etc.*); **ч. ~́ью** (*coll.*) fittingly, properly; **ч. и ме́сто!** (*coll., obs.*) please be seated! **2.** regard, respect; **быть в ~й** to be in favour.
честь[2], **чту, чтёшь** *impf.* (*obs.*) **1.** to consider. **2.** to read.
чесуч|а́, и́ *f.* tussore.
чесуч|о́вый *adj. of* **~а́**
чёт, а *m.* even number.
чет|а́, ы́ *f.* pair, couple; **счастли́вая ч.** (the) happy couple; **не ч. кому́-н.** no match for s.o. (*as being, by implication, either worse or better*).
четве́рг, а́ *m.* Thursday.
четвере́ньк|и (*coll.*): **на ч., на ~ах** on all fours, on one's hands and knees; **стать на ч.** to go down on all fours.
четвери́к, а́ *m.* chetverik (*old Russ. dry measure, equivalent to 26.239 litres*).
четвёрк|а, и *f.* (*coll.*) **1.** number '4'; No. 4 (*bus, tram, etc.*). **2.** 'four' (*as school mark — out of five, hence* = 'good'). **3.** four (*at cards; team of horses; rowing boat, etc.*).
четверно́й *adj.* fourfold, quadruple.
четверн|я́, и́ *f.* **1.** team of four horses. **2.** quadruplets.
че́твер|о, ы́х *num.* four; **нас бы́ло ч.** there were four of us.
четвероно́г|ий *adj.* four-legged; *as n.* **~ое, ~ого** *nt.* quadruped.
четверости́ши|е, я *nt.* (*liter.*) quatrain.
четверта́к, а́ *m.* (*obs.*) 25 kopecks.
четверти́нк|а, и *f.* (*coll.*) quarter-litre bottle (*of vodka or wine*).
четверти́чный *adj.* (*geol.*) Quaternary.
четвертно́й *adj.* **1.** quarter. **2.** (*obs.*) costing, worth 25 roubles.
четверт|ова́ть, у́ю *impf. and pf.* to quarter (*as means of execution; hist.*)
четвёртый *adj.* fourth.
че́тверт|ь, и, *g. pl.* **~е́й** *f.* **1.** (*in var. senses*) quarter (*as liquid measure, approx. equivalent to 3 litres; as dry measure — to 210 litres*). **2.** quarter (of an hour); **без ~и час** a quarter to one; **ч. деся́того** a quarter past nine. **3.** (*mus.*) fourth. **4.** term.
четвертьфина́л, а *m.* (*sport*) quarter-final.
чёт|ки, ок *no sg.* (*eccl.*) rosary.
чёт|кий (~ок, ~ка́, ~ко) *adj.* **1.** precise; clear-cut; **~кое движе́ние** precise movement. **2.** clear, well-defined; (*of handwriting*) legible; (*of sound*) plain, distinct; (*of speech*) articulate.
чёткост|ь, и *f.* **1.** precision, preciseness. **2.** clarity, clearness, definition; legibility; distinctness.
чётный *adj.* even (*of numbers*).
четы́р|е, ёх, ём, ьмя́, о ~ёх *num.* four.
четы́режды *adv.* four times.
четы́р|еста, ёхсо́т, ёмста́м, ьмяста́ми, о ~ёхста́х *num.* four hundred.
четырёх... *comb. form* four-, quadri-, tetra-.
четырёхгоди́чный *adj.* four-year.
четырёхголо́сный *adj.* (*mus.*) four-part.
четырёхгра́нник, а *m.* (*math.*) tetrahedron.
четырёхгра́нный *adj.* (*math.*) tetrahedral.
четырёхдоро́жечный *adj.* four-track (*of tape recorder*).
четырёхкра́тный *adj.* fourfold.
четырёхле́ти|е, я *nt.* **1.** four-year period. **2.** fourth anniversary.
четырёхле́тний *adj.* **1.** four years', of four years' duration. **2.** four-year-old.
четырёхме́стный *adj.* four-seater.
четырёхме́сячный *adj.* **1.** four-month, four months', of four months' duration. **2.** four-month-old.
четырёхмото́рный *adj.* four-engined
четырёхсотле́ти|е, я *nt.* **1.** four hundred years. **2.** quatercentenary
четырёхсотле́тний *adj.* **1.** four hundred years', of four hundred years' duration **2.** quatercentenary.
четырёхсо́тый *adj.* fourhundredth.
черырёхсто́пный *adj.* (*liter.*) tetrameter.
четырёхсторо́нний *adj.* **1.** quadrilateral. **2.** (*pol., etc.*) quadripartite.
четырёхта́ктный *adj.* **1.** (*tech.*) four-stroke. **2.** (*mus.*) four-beat.
четырёхуго́льник, *adj.* quadrangle.
четырёхуго́льный *adj.* quadrangular.
четырёхчасово́й *adj.* **1.** four hours', of four hours' duration. **2.** four o'clock.
четы́рнадцатый *adj.* fourteenth.
четы́рнадцат|ь, и *num.* fourteen.
чех, а *m.* Czech.
чехард|а́, ы́ *f.* leap-frog (*also fig.; of rapid changes in governmental appointments, etc.*).
Че́хи|я, и *f.* Czech Republic.
чехл|и́ть, ю́, и́шь *impf.* (*of* **за~**) to cover.
чех|о́л, ла́ *m.* **1.** cover, case; **ч. для кре́сла** chair-cover. **2.** underdress.
чехослова́к, а *m.* Czechoslovak.
Чехослова́ки|я, и *f.* Czechoslovakia.
чехослова́цкий *adj.* Czechoslovak.
чехослова́|чка, чки *f. of* **~к**
чечеви́ц|а[1], **ы** *f.* lentil.
чечеви́ц|а[2], **ы** *f.* (*obs.*) lens.
чечеви́|чный *adj. of* **~ца**[1]; **прода́ть за ~чную похлёбку** to sell for a mess of pottage.
чече́н|ец, ца *m.* Chechen.
чечётк|а, и *f.* **1.** (*zool.*) redpoll. **2.** chechotka (*kind of tap-dance*).
че́шк|а, и *f. of* **чех**
че́шский *adj.* Czech.
чешу́йк|а, и *f.* scale (*of fish*).
чешу́йчат|ый *adj.* scaly; squamose, lamellar; **~ые, ~ых** (*zool.*) Squamata.
чешу|я́, и́ *no pl., f.* (*zool.*) scales.
чи́бис, а *m.* (*zool.*) lapwing.
чиж, а́ *m.* (*zool.*) siskin.
чи́жик, а *m.* **1.** = **чиж. 2. ~и** tip-cat (*children's game*).
чи́к|ать, аю *impf.* (*of* **~нуть**) to tick, click.
чи́к|нуть, ну, нешь *pf. of* **~ать**
Чи́ли *nt. indecl.* Chile.
чилибу́х|а, и *f.* (*bot.*) Nux vomica.
чили́|ец, йца *m.* Chilean.
чили́|йка, йки *f. of* **~ец**
чили́йск|ий *adj.* Chilean; **~ая сели́тра** (*chem.*) Chile saltpetre, sodium nitrate.
чили́м, а *m.* (*bot.*) water chestnut (*Trapa natans*).
чин, а, *pl.* **~ы́** *m.* **1.** rank; **быть в ~а́х** to hold, be of high rank. **2.** official. **3.** rite, ceremony, order; **ч. ~́ом** properly, fittingly; **без ~о́в** without ceremony; **держа́ть ч.** (*obs.*) to conduct a ceremony.
чина́р, а *m.* plane (tree).
чина́р|а, ы *f.* = **~**
чинёный *adj.* (*coll.*) old, patched (*of clothing, etc.*).
чин|и́ть[1], **ю́, ~́ишь** *impf.* (*of* **по~**) to repair, mend.
чин|и́ть[2], **ю́, ~́ишь** *impf.* (*of* **о~**) to sharpen.
чин|и́ть[3], **ю́, и́шь** *impf.* to carry out, execute; to cause; **ч. препя́тствия** (*+d.*) to impede; **ч. распра́ву** to carry out reprisals.
чин|и́ться, ю́сь, и́шься *impf.* (*obs.*) to stand on ceremony, hold back, be shy.
чи́нност|ь, и *f.* decorum, propriety, orderliness.
чи́н|ный (~ен, ~на́, ~но) *adj.* decorous, proper, orderly; well-ordered.
чино́вник, а *m.* **1.** (*hist.*) official, functionary. **2.** (*pej.*) bureaucrat.
чино́вни|ческий *adj.* **1.** *adj. of* **~к. 2.** (*pej.*) bureaucratic.
чино́вничеств|о, а *nt.* **1.** (*collect.*) officials, officialdom. **2.**

(*pej.*) red tape.
чино́внич|ий *adj.* = **~еский**
чино́вный *adj.* (*obs.*) **1.** official, holding an official post. **2.** of high rank.
чину́ш|а, и *m.* (*pej.*) bureaucrat.
чи́пс|ы, ов *no sg.* (potato) crisps.
чи́р|ей, ья *m.* (*coll.*) boil.
чири́ка|ть, ю *impf.* to chirp, twitter.
чи́рик|и, ов *or* **чирик|и́, о́в** (*dial.*) shoes.
чири́кн|уть, у, ешь *pf.* to give a chirp.
чи́рк|ать, аю *impf.* (*of* **~нуть**) (**о**+*a.* **по**+*d.*) to strike sharply (against, on); **ч. спи́чкой** to strike a match.
чи́рк|нуть, ну, нешь *pf. of* **~ать**
чир|о́к, ка́ *m.* (*zool.*) teal.
чи́сленност|ь, и *f.* numbers; (*mil.*) strength.
чи́сленный *adj.* numerical.
числи́тел|ь, я *m.* (*math.*) numerator.
числи́тельн|ое, ого *nt.* (*gram.*) numeral.
числи́тельн|ый *adj.*: **и́мя ~ое** (*gram.*) numeral.
чи́сл|ить, ю, ишь *impf.* to count, reckon.
чи́сл|иться, юсь, ишься *impf.* **1.** to be (*in context of calculation or official records*); **в на́шей дере́вне ~ится три́ста жи́телей** there are three hundred inhabitants in our village; **ч. в отпуску́** to be (recorded as) on leave; **он ~ится в ко́нкурсе** his name is down for the competition. **2.** (+*i.*) to be reckoned, be on paper; **он ещё ~ился заве́дующим отде́лом, а все обя́занности исполня́ли его́ замести́тели** he was still head of the department on paper, but all the duties were being performed by his deputies. **3.** (**за**+*i.*) to be attributed (to), have; **за ним ~ится мно́го недоста́тков** he has many failings.
чис|ло́, ла́, *pl.* **~́ла, ~́ел** *nt.* **1.** number; **тео́рия ~́ел** theory of number; **~ло́м** in number; **нет им ~ла́** they are innumerable; **без ~ла́** without number, in great numbers; **в ~ле́** (+*g.*) among; **в том ~ле́** including. **2.** date, day (*of month*); **како́е сего́дня ч.?** what is the date today?; **како́го ~ла́ вы уезжа́ете?** what is the date of your departure, which day are you leaving?; **без ~ла́** undated; **поме́тить (за́дним) ~ло́м** to date (antedate). **3.** (*gram.*) number; **еди́нственное, мно́жественное ч.** singular, plural.
числово́й *adj.* numerical.
чисти́лищ|е, а *nt.* (*relig.*) purgatory.
чи́стильщик, а *m.* cleaner; **ч. сапо́г** shoeblack, bootblack.
чи́|стить, щу, стишь *impf.* **1.** (*pf.* **по~, вы́~**) to clean; **(щёткой)** to brush; to scour; **ч. посу́ду** to wash dishes, wash up; **ч. трубу́** to sweep a chimney. **2.** (*pf.* **по~, вы́~**) to clear; to dredge. **3.** (*pf.* **о~**) to peel (*vegetables, fruit*); to shell (*nuts*); to clean (*fish*). **4.** (*pf.* **по~**) (*pol.*) to purge. **5.** (*coll.*) to clean out (= *to rob*). **6.** (*coll.*) to swear at; to beat up.
чи́|ститься, щусь, стишься *impf.* **1.** (*pf.* **по~, вы́~**) to clean o.s. (up). **2.** *pass. of* **~стить**
чи́стк|а, и *f.* **1.** cleaning; **отда́ть в ~у** to have cleaned, send to be cleaned. **2.** (*pol.*) purge; **этни́ческая ч.** ethnic cleansing.
чи́сто[1] *as pred.* it is clean.
чи́ст|о[2] *adv.* **1.** *adv. of* **~ый; ч.-на́чисто** spotlessly clean. **2.** purely, merely; completely; **я ч. случа́йно его́ нашёл** it was by mere chance that I found it. **3.** *as conj.* (*coll.*) just like, just as if.
чистови́к, а́ *m.* (*coll.*) fair copy.
чистово́й *adj.* **1.** fair, clean; **ч. экземпля́р** fair copy. **2.** (*tech.*) finishing, planishing.
чистога́н, а *m.* (*coll.*) cash, ready money.
чистокро́вный *adj.* thorough-bred, pure-blooded.
чистописа́ни|е, я *nt.* calligraphy.
чистопло́т|ный (~ен, ~на) *adj.* **1.** clean, cleanly; neat, tidy. **2.** (*fig.*) clean, decent, upright.
чистоплю́|й, я *m.* (*coll.*) sissy; fastidious pers.
чистопо́ль|е, я *nt.* (*coll.*) open country.
чистопоро́д|ный (~ен, ~на) *adj.* thoroughbred.
чистопро́бный *adj.* pure (*of gold or silver*).
чистосерде́ч|ие, ия *nt.* = **~ность**
чистосерде́чност|ь, и *f.* frankness, sincerity, candour.
чистосерде́ч|ный (~ен, ~на) *adj.* frank, sincere, candid.
чистот|а́, ы́ *f.* **1.** cleanness, cleanliness; neatness, tidiness. **2.** (*in var. senses*) purity.
чистоте́л, а *m.* (*bot.*) celandine.
чи́ст|ый (~, ~а́, ~о) *adj.* **1.** clean; neat, tidy; (*of speech, voice, etc.*) pure; **экологи́чески ч.** eco-friendly. **2.** (*fig.*) pure, upright, unsullied; **ч. понеде́льник** (*eccl.*) first Monday in Lent; **от ~ого се́рдца, с ~ой со́вестью** with a clear conscience. **3.** pure; undiluted, neat; **~ое зо́лото, ~ая шерсть** pure gold, wool; **~ое иску́сство** art for art's sake; **ч. спирт** pure, neat alcohol; **~ой воды́** (*min.*) of the first water; (*fig.*) pure, first-class; **вы́вести на ~ую во́ду** to expose, unmask; **за ~ые де́ньги** for cash; **приня́ть что-н. за ~ую моне́ту** to take sth. at its face value. **4.** clear; open; **~ое не́бо** clear sky; **на ~ом во́здухе** in the open air; **ч. лист** blank sheet; **ч. пар** clean fallow; **~ое по́ле** open field. **5.** (*fin., etc.*) net, clear; **~ая при́быль** clear profit. **6.** (*obs.*) main; special, ceremonial, show; **ч. вход** front entrance. **7.** (*of work or product of work*) skilled; finished; **~ая рабо́та** craftsmanship. **8.** (*obs.; as social criterion*) better-class, 'best'. **9.** (*coll.*) pure, utter; mere, sheer; complete, absolute; **ч. вздор** utter nonsense; **~ая беста́ктность** sheer tactlessness; **~ая случа́йность** pure chance; **~ая отста́вка** (*obs.*) final retirement; **по ~ой** (*coll.*) finally, once and for all.
чистю́л|я, и *c.g.* (*coll.*) pers. with passion for cleanliness *or* tidiness.
чита́емост|ь, и *f.* popularity, wide circulation (*of literature*).
чита́|емый 1. *pres. part. pass. of* **~ть** *and adj.* widely-read, popular.
чита́льн|ый *adj.*: **ч. зал** = **~я**
чита́л|ьня, ьни, *g. pl.* **~ен** *f.* reading-room.
чита́тел|ь, я *m.* reader.
чита́тель|ский *adj. of* **~**
чита́|ть, ю *impf.* (*of* **про~, проче́сть**) **1.** to read; **ч. с губ** to lip-read. **2.: ч. ле́кции** to lecture, give lectures; **ч. стихи́** to recite poetry; **ч. кому́-н. наставле́ния, нравоуче́ния** to lecture s.o.
чита́|ться, ется *impf.* **1.** *pass. of* **~ть. 2.** to be legible. **3.** (*fig.*) to be visible, be discernible. **4.** (*impers.*): **мне, etc., не ~ется** I, *etc.*, don't feel like reading.
чи́тк|а, и *f.* **1.** reading (*usu. of documents, etc., by a group*). **2.** (*theatr.*) (first) reading, reading through.
чи́тывать *pres. tense not used, impf., freq. of* **чита́ть**
чих, а *m.* (*coll.*) sneeze; *as int., onomat. of sound of sneezing.*
чиха́нь|е, я *nt.* sneezing; **на вся́кое ч. не наздра́вствуешься** you can't please everyone.
чиха́тельный *adj.* causing sneezing, sternutatory; **ч. газ** sneezing gas.
чих|а́ть, а́ю *impf.* (*of* **~ну́ть**) **1.** to sneeze. **2.** (**на**+*a.*; *coll.*) to scorn; **ч. мне на него́!** I don't give a damn for him!
чих|ну́ть, ну́, нёшь *pf. of* **~а́ть**
чихо́т|а, ы *f.* (*coll.*) sneezing (fit).
чи́ще *comp. of* **чи́стый, чи́сто**
член, а *m.* **1.** (*in var. senses*) member; Fellow (*of learned body*); **ч.-корреспонде́нт** corresponding member (*of an Academy*); Associate (*of learned body*); **ч. Короле́вского о́бщества** Fellow of the Royal Society; FRS. **2.** (*math.*) term; (*gram.*) part (*of sentence*). **3.** limb, member. **4.** (*gram.*) article.
члене́ни|е, я *nt.* articulation.
чле́ник, а *m.* (*zool.*) segment.
членистоно́г|ие, их (*zool.*) arthropoda.
чле́нистый *adj.* (*zool.*) articulated, segmented.
член|и́ть, ю́, и́шь *impf.* (*of* **рас~**) to divide into parts, articulate.
членовреди́тельств|о, а *nt.* maiming, mutilation; self-mutilation.
членоразде́л|ьный (~ен, ~ьна) *adj.* articulate.
чле́н|ский *adj. of* **~; ~ские взно́сы** membership fees, dues.
чле́нств|о, а *nt.* membership.
чмо́к|ать, аю *impf.* (*of* **~нуть**) **1.** to make a smacking sound with one's lips. **2.** (*coll.*) to give a smacking kiss. **3.** to squelch, make a squelching sound.
чмо́к|нуть, ну, нешь *pf. of* **~ать**

чóглок, а *m.* hobby (*bird of falcon family*).
чóкань|е, я *nt.* clinking of glasses.
чóк|аться, аюсь *impf.* (*of* **~нуться**) to clink glasses (*when drinking toasts*).
чóкнутый *adj.* odd, rum.
чóк|нуться, нусь, нешься *pf. of* **~аться**
чóпорност|ь, и *f.* primness; standoffishness, stiffness.
чóпор|ный (~ен, ~на) *adj.* prim; stuck-up; standoffish, stiff.
чóхом *adv.* (*coll.*) wholesale.
ЧП = **чепé**
чревáт|ый (~, ~а) *adj.* **1.** (*+i.*) fraught (with). **2.** **~ая** (*obs.*) pregnant.
чрéв|о, а *nt.* (*obs. or rhet., fig.*) belly; womb.
чревовещáни|е, я *nt.* ventriloquy.
чревовещáтел|ь, я *m.* ventriloquist.
чревоугóди|е, я *nt.* gluttony.
чревоугóдник, а *m.* glutton, gourmand.
черед|á, ы *f.* (*obs.*) **1.** (*poet.*) turn, succession. **2.** sphere (*of activity*).
чрез = **чéрез**
чрезвычáйно *adv.* extremely, extraordinarily, exceedingly.
чрезвычá|йный (~ен, ~йна) *adj.* **1.** extraordinary (= *exceptional, unusual*). **2.** special, extreme, extraordinary; **~йные мéры** emergency measures; **~йное положéние** state of emergency; **ч. и полномóчный посóл** ambassador extraordinary and plenipotentiary.
чрезмéрно *adv.* excessively, to excess.
чрезмéр|ный (~ен, ~на) *adj.* excessive, inordinate, extreme.
чрéсл|а, ~ *no sg.* (*arch. or poet.*) hips, loins.
ЧССР *f. indecl.* (*abbr. of* **Чехословáцкая Социалистúческая Респýблика**) Czechoslovak Socialist Republic.
чтéни|е, я *nt.* **1.** reading; **ч. карт** map-reading; **ч. лéкций** lecturing; **худóжественное ч.** dramatic reading; **ч. с губ** lip-reading. **2.** reading-matter.
чтец, á *m.* reader; (*professional*) reciter.
чтúв|о, а *nt.* (*coll., pej.*) reading-matter.
чтить, чту, чтишь, чтят (*and* **чтут**) *impf.* to honour.
чтúц|а, ы *f. of* **чтец**
что[1]**, чегó, чемý, о чём** *interrog. pron.* **1.** what?; **что с тобóй?** what's the matter (with you)?; **что дéлать, что подéлаешь?** it can't be helped; **для чегó?** why?, what ... for?; **к чемý?** why?; **с чегó?** whence?; on what grounds?; **что ты (вы)!** (*expr. surprise, fear, etc.*) you don't mean to say so!; **что емý** *etc.* **до...?** what does it matter to him, *etc.*? **2.** how?; **что сегóдня Нáдя?** how is Nadya today? **3.** why?; **что вы не пьёте?** why aren't you drinking? **4.** (*coll.*) how much?; **что стóит?** how much does it cost?; **что тóлку?** what is the sense?
что[2] (*sometimes printed* **чтó**) *rel. pron.* which, that; (*coll.*) who; **я знáю, что вы имéете в видý** I know what you mean; **пáрень, что стоя́л ря́дом со мной** the fellow (who was) standing next to me; **он всё молчáл, что для негó не характéрно** he said nothing the whole time, which is unlike him.
что[3] (*coll.*) = **чтó-нибудь; éсли что слýчится** if anything happens.
что[4] as far as; **что есть мóчи** with all one's might; **что до, что касáется** (*+g.*) as for, with regard (to), as far as ... is concerned.
что[5] *conj.* that; **то, что...** the fact that ....
чтоб = **чтóбы**
чтóбы *conj.* **1.** (*expr. purpose*) in order to, in order that; **ч.... не** lest. **2.** (*after neg.*) (that); **я никогдá не видáл, ч. он яви́лся пья́ным на рабóту** I have never seen him turn up drunk for work; **сомневáюсь, ч. вам э́то понрáвилось** I doubt whether you will like it. **3.** (*as particle*) *expr. wish*: **ч. я тебя́ бóльше не ви́дел!** may I never see your face again!
что ж (*coll.*) *expr. admission, acceptance of argument*: yes; all right; right you are.
что за (*coll.*) **1.** (*interrog.*) what? what sort of ... ?; **что э́то за пти́ца?** what sort of bird is that? **2.** (*int.*): **что за день!** what a (marvellous) day!; **что за ерундá!** what (utter) nonsense!
что ли (*coll.*) *expr. uncertainty or hesitation*: **порá нам идти́, что ли?** perhaps we should be going?; **позвони́ть тебé, что ли?** do you want me to ring you, then?
чтó-либо, чегó-либо *indef. pron.* anything.
что ни *indef. pron.*: **что ни день** every day, not a day passes but ...; **что ни говори́** no matter what you may say, say what you like; **во что бы то ни стáло** at whatever cost.
чтó-нибудь, чегó-нибудь *indef. pron.* anything
чтó-то[1]**, чегó-то** *indef. pron.* sth.
чтó-то[2] *adv.* (*coll.*) **1.** somewhat, slightly; **на слýшателей егó выступлéние произвелó чтó-то не óчень прия́тное впечатлéние** his speech made a somewhat disagreeable impression on the audience. **2.** somehow, for no obvious reason; **чтó-то мне не хóчется идти́** I don't feel like going for some reason.
чу *int.* hark!
чуб, а, *pl.* **~ы́** *m.* forelock (*hist.*; *single lock on otherwise shaven head, as worn formerly by Ukrainian Cossacks*).
чубáрый *adj.* (*of a horse's coat*) dappled.
чубýк, á *m.* **1.** stem (*of smoking pipe*); chibouk. **2.** grape stalk.
чувáл, а *m.* (*dial.*) pannier, basket.
чувáш, а (*and* **á**), *pl.* **~и, ~ей** (*and* **~и́, ~éй**) *m.* Chuvash.
чувáш|ка, ки *f. of* **~**
чувáшский *adj.* Chuvash.
чуви́х|а, и *f.* (*sl.*) bird (= *girl*).
чýвственност|ь, и *f.* sensuality.
чýвствен|ный *adj.* **1.** (**~, ~на**) sensual. **2.** (*phil.*) perceptible, sensible; **~ное восприя́тие** perception.
чувстви́тельност|ь, и *f.* **1.** (*in var. senses*) sensitivity, sensitiveness; (*of photog. film*) speed. **2.** perceptibility, sensibility. **3.** sentimentality. **4.** tenderness; (deep) feeling.
чувстви́тел|ьный (~ен, ~ьна) *adj.* **1.** (*in var. senses*) sensitive. **2.** perceptible, sensible. **3.** sentimental. **4.** tender; (*of feelings*) deep.
чýвств|о, а *nt.* **1.** (*physiol.*) sense **ч. вкýса** sense of taste; **óрганы ~** senses, organs of sense; **обмáн ~** delusion. **2.** (*sg. or pl.*) senses (= *consciousness*); **без ~** unconscious; **лиши́ться ~, упáсть без ~** to faint, lose consciousness; **привести́ в ч.** to bring round; **прийти́ в ч.** to come round, regain consciousness, come to one's senses. **3.** (*in var. senses*) feeling; sense; **ч. лóктя** feeling of comradeship, of solidarity; **ч. ю́мора** sense of humour; **питáть к комý-н. нéжные ~а** to have a soft spot for s.o.
чýвств|овать, ую *impf.* (*of* **по~**) **1.** to feel, sense; **ч. себя́** to feel (*intrans.*); **ч. гóлод** to feel hungry; **давáть себя́ ч.** to make itself felt; **как вы себя́ ~уете?** how do you feel? **2.** to appreciate, have a feeling (for) (*music, etc.*).
чýвств|оваться, уется *impf.* **1.** to be perceptible; to make itself felt. **2.** *pass. of* **~овать**
чувя́к|и, ов *pl.* (*sg.* **~, ~а** *m.*) slippers (*worn mainly in the Caucasus and Crimea*).
чугýн, á *m.* **1.** cast iron; **ч. в болвáнках** pig-iron. **2.** cast-iron pot, vessel.
чугýнк|а, и *f.* (*coll.*) **1.** (cast-iron) stove. **2.** (*obs.*) railway.
чугýнный *adj.* cast-iron (*also fig.*).
чугунолитéйный *adj.*: **ч. завóд** iron foundry.
чудáк, á *m.* eccentric, crank.
чудáческий *adj.* eccentric.
чудáчеств|о, а *nt.* eccentricity, crankiness.
чудáч|ить, у, ишь *impf.* (*coll.*) = **чуди́ть**
чудáчк|а, и *f. of* **чудáк**
чудéс|ный (~ен, ~на) *adj.* **1.** miraculous; **~ное исцелéние** miraculous healing. **2.** marvellous, wonderful.
чуд|и́ть, *1st pers. not used,* **и́шь** *impf.* (*coll.*) **1.** to behave eccentrically, oddly. **2.** to clown, act the fool.
чýд|иться, ится *impf.* (*of* **по~** *and* **при~**) (*coll.*) to seem.
чуд|нóй (~ён, ~нá, ~нó) *adj.* strange, odd; **~нó** (*as pred.*) it is strange, it is odd.
чýд|ный (~ен, ~на) *adj.* **1.** magic. **2.** (*fig.*) magical; marvellous, wonderful, lovely; **~но** *as pred.* it is marvellous, wonderful, lovely.
чýд|о, а, *pl.* **~есá, ~éс** *nt.* **1.** miracle. **2.** wonder, marvel;

∼еса́ те́хники wonders of technology; **∼еса́ в решете́** (*coll.*) *said of sth. unusual or absurd*; **ч. как** *as adv.* marvellously; **ч., что...** *as pred.* it is a marvel that ....
чу́до-богаты́р|ь, я́ *m.* hero.
чудо́вищ|е, а *nt.* monster; **лохне́сское ч.** Loch Ness monster.
чудо́вищ|ный (∼ен, ∼на) *adj.* **1.** monstrous (*also fig., pej.*). **2.** enormous.
чудоде́|й, я *m.* **1.** (*obs.*) miracle-worker. **2.** (*coll.*) crank.
чудоде́йствен|ный (∼, ∼на) *adj.* miracle-working; miraculous; **∼ное лека́рство** wonder drug.
чу́дом *adv.* miraculously; **ч. спасти́сь** to be saved by a miracle.
чудотво́р|ец, ца *m.* miracle-worker.
чудотво́рный *adj.* miracle-working; (*fig.*) marvellous.
чу́до-ю́до *nt. indecl.* (*folk poet.*) monster.
чужа́к, а́ *m.* (*coll.*) stranger; (*pej.*) alien, interloper.
чужан|и́н, и́на, *pl.* **∼́е, ∼́** *m.* (*folk poet. or coll.*) stranger.
чужби́н|а, ы *f.* foreign land, country.
чужда́|ться, юсь *impf.* (*+g.*) to shun, avoid; to stand aloof (from), remain unaffected (by).
чу́жд|ый (∼, ∼а́, ∼о) *adj.* **1.** (*+d.*) alien (to); extraneous. **2.** (*+g.*) free (from), devoid (of); **он ∼ зло́бы** he is devoid of malice.
чужезе́м|ец, ца *m.* (*obs.*) foreigner, stranger.
чужезе́мный *adj.* (*obs.*) foreign.
чужеро́д|ный (∼ен, ∼на) *adj.* alien, foreign.
чужестра́н|ец, ца *m.* (*obs.*) = **чужезе́мец**
чужестра́нный *adj.* (*obs.*) = **чужезе́мный**
чужея́дный *adj.* (*bot.*) parasitic.
чуж|о́й *adj.* **1.** s.o. else's, another's, others'; **на ч. счёт** at s.o. else's expense; **с ∼и́х слов** at second-hand; *as n.* **∼о́е, ∼о́го** *nt.* s.o. else's belongings, what belongs to others. **2.** strange, alien; foreign; **∼и́е края́ = ∼би́на; попа́сть в ∼и́е ру́ки** to fall into strange hands; *as n.* **ч., ∼о́го** *m.* stranger.
чу́йк|а, и *f.* (*obs.*) **1.** chuyka (*knee-length cloth jacket formerly worn by men as outer garment*). **2.** (*coll.*) nouveau-riche pers.
чуко́тский *adj.* Chukchi.
чу́кч|а, и *m.* Chukchi (man).
чук|ча́нка, ча́нки *f. of* **∼ча**
чула́н, а *m.* **1.** store-room, lumber-room. **2.** larder.
чул|о́к, ка́, *g. pl.* **ч.** *m.* stocking.
чуло́чник, а *m.* stocking-maker.
чуло́чно-носо́чн|ый *adj.* **∼ые изде́лия** hosiery.
чуло́чный *adj. of* **чуло́к**
чум|а́, ы́ *f.* plague (*also as form of abuse*).
чума́з|ый (∼, ∼а) *adj.* (*coll.*) grubby, dirty; *as n.* (*obs., pej.*) **ч., ∼ого** *m.* upstart, parvenu, kulak.
чума́к, а́ *m.* (*obs.*) chumak (*in Ukraine, ox-cart driver transporting fish, salt, and grain*).
чума́|цкий *adj. of* **∼к**
чуми́чк|а, и *f.* **1.** (*dial.*) ladle. **2.** (*coll., obs.*) servant-girl. **3.** (*coll.*) slut, slattern.
чум|но́й *adj. of* **∼а́**; plague-stricken; **∼на́я па́лочка** plague bacillus.
чумово́й *adj.* (*sl.*) crazy, half-witted.
чу́н|и, ей *pl.* (*sg.* **∼я, ∼и** *f.*) (*dial.*) **1.** rope shoes. **2.** galoshes.
чупри́н|а, ы *f.* (*dial.*) = **чуб**
чур *int.* (*coll.*) keep away!; mind!; **ч. меня́** (*in children's games, etc.*) keep away from me!
чура́|ться, юсь *impf.* (*+g.*; *coll.*) to shun, avoid, steer clear (of).
чурба́н, а *m.* **1.** block, log. **2.** (*coll.*) blockhead.
чу́рк|а, и *f.* block, lump, chock.
чу́т|кий (∼ок, ∼ка́, ∼ко) *adj.* **1.** (*of senses of hearing and smell*) keen, sharp, quick; **ч. нюх** keen sense of smell; **∼кая соба́ка** keen-nosed dog; **ч. сон** light sleep. **2.** (*fig.*) sensitive; sympathetic; tactful.
чу́ткост|ь, и *f.* **1.** keenness, sharpness, quickness. **2.** sensitivity; sympathetic attitude; tactfulness.
чуто́к *adv.* (*coll.*) a little.
чу́точк|а, и *f.*: **ни ∼и** (*coll.*) not in the least.
чу́точку *adv.* (*coll.*) a little, a wee bit.
чу́точный *adj.* (*coll.*) tiny, wee.
чу́т|че *comp. of* **∼кий**
чуть (*coll.*) **1.** *adv.* hardly, scarcely; just; **ч. (бы́ло) не, ч. ли не** almost, nearly, all but. **2.** *adv.* (just) a little, very slightly. **3.** *conj.* as soon as; **ч. свет** at daybreak, at first light; **ч. что** at the slightest provocation.
чуть|ё, я́ *nt.* **1.** (*of animals*) scent. **2.** (*fig.*) flair, feeling (for).
чуть-чу́ть *adv.* (*coll.*) a tiny bit; **ч.-ч. не = чуть не.**
чухо́н|ец, ца *m.* (*obs., pej.*) Finn.
чухо́н|ка, ки *f. of* **∼ец**
чухо́нск|ий *adj.* (*obs., pej.*) Finnish; **∼ое ма́сло** butter.
чу́чел|о, а *nt.* **1.** stuffed animal. **2.** scarecrow (*also fig.*).
чу́шк|а, и *f.* **1.** (*coll.*) piglet. **2.** (*tech.*) pig, ingot, bar.
чуш|ь, и *f.* (*coll.*) nonsense, rubbish.
чу́|ять, ю, ешь *impf.* to scent, smell; (*fig.*) to sense, feel.
чу́|яться, ется *impf.* (*impers.*) to make itself felt.

Ш

ша́баш, а *m.* (*relig.*) sabbath; **ш. ведьм** witches' sabbath; (*fig.*) orgy.
шаба́ш, а *m.* **1.** (*obs., coll.*) end of work, knocking-off time. **2.** *as pred.* that's enough!; that'll do!; (*naut.*) ship oars!
шаба́ш|ить, у, ишь *impf.* (*coll.*) (*trans. and intrans.*) to stop (work); to knock off, down tools.
шаба́шник, а *m.* (*coll., pej.*) moonlighter.
шаба́шнича|ть, ю *impf.* (*coll., pej.*) to moonlight.
ша́бер, а *m.* (*tech.*) scraper.
шаб|ёр, ра́ *m.* (*dial.*) neighbour; **жить в ∼ра́х** to live next door.
шабло́н, а *m.* **1.** (*tech.*) template, pattern; mould, form; stencil. **2.** (*fig., pej.*) cliché; (fixed) pattern; routine; **рабо́тать по ∼у** to work by rote, work mechanically.
шабло́нност|ь, и *f.* triteness, banality.
шабло́н|ный *adj.* **1.** *adj. of* **∼. 2. (∼ен, ∼на)** trite, banal; stereotyped; routine.
ша́вк|а, и *f.* (*coll.*) (small) dog.
шаг, а (у) (*after numerals 2, 3, 4* **∼а́**) **о ∼́е, в (на) ∼у́,** *pl.* **∼и́, ∼о́в** *m.* **1.** step (*also fig.*); pace; stride; **ш. на ме́сте** marking time; **ни ∼́у да́льше!** not a step further!, stay where you are!; **идти́ бы́стрыми ∼а́ми** make rapid strides; **∼́у ступи́ть нельзя́ (не даю́т)** one can't do anything; **заме́длить ш.** to slow down; **приба́вить ∼́у** to quicken one's pace; **ши́ре ш.!** (*i*) step out, take bigger strides!, (*ii*) (*fig.*) get a move on!; **в двух ∼а́х, в не́скольких ∼а́х** a stone's throw away; **у́зки в ∼у́** (*of cut of trousers*) tight in the seat; **на ка́ждом ∼у́** everywhere, at every turn, continually; **с пе́рвого ∼́у** (*obs.*) from the outset. **2.** (*tech.*) pitch, spacing.
шаг|а́ть, а́ю *impf.* (*of* **∼ну́ть**) **1.** to step; to walk, stride; to pace. **2.** (*coll.*) to go, come.
шага́|ющий *pres. part. act. of* **∼ть; ш. экскава́тор** self-propelled excavator.
шаги́стик|а, и *f.* (*pej.*) square-bashing (*as part of mil. training*).
шаг|ну́ть, ну́, нёшь *pf.* (*of* **∼а́ть**) to take a step; (*fig.*) to make progress; **ш. нельзя́ (не даю́т)** one can't do anything, there's no scope for action.
ша́гом *adv.* at a walk, at a walking pace; slowly; **ш. марш!** (*mil. word of command*) quick march!
шагоме́р, а *m.* pedometer.
шагре́н|евый *adj. of* **∼ь**

шагре́н|ь, и *f.* shagreen leather.
шажко́м *adv.* (*coll.*) taking short steps.
шаж|о́к, ка́ *m., dim. of* **шаг**
ша́йб|а, ы *f.* **1.** (*tech.*) washer. **2.** (*sport*) puck; **хокке́й с ~ой** ice hockey.
ша́йк|а[1], **и,** *g. pl.* **ша́ек** *f.* tub (*two-handled, of wood or metal*).
ша́йк|а[2], **и,** *g. pl.* **ша́ек** *f.* gang, band.
шайта́н, а *m.* (*in Muslim theology*) evil spirit; (*coll.*; *as term of abuse*) devil.
шака́л, а *m.* jackal.
шала́нд|а, ы *f.* (*flat-bottomed*) barge, lighter.
шала́ш, а́ *m.* (*hunter's or fisherman's*) cabin (*made of branches and straw, etc.*).
шалашо́вк|а, и *f.* (*sl.*) tart, whore.
шале́|ть, ю *impf.* (*of* **о~**) (*coll.*) to go crazy.
шал|и́ть, ю́, и́шь *impf.* **1.** to be naughty (*of children*); to play up, play tricks (*also of inanimate objects*); **~и́шь!** (*as rebuke*) don't try that on!, don't come that with me! **2.** (*obs., coll.*) to carry out robberies.
шаловли́в|ый (~, ~а) *adj.* **1.** (*of children*) naughty, apt to get into mischief. **2.** mischievous; flirtatious.
шалопа́|й, я *m.* (*coll.*) good-for-nothing idler, skiver.
ша́лост|ь, и *f.* **1.** (*childish*) prank, game; (*pl.*) mischief, naughtiness. **2.** (*obs., coll.*) robbery.
шалу́н, а́ *m.* naughty child.
шалу́н|ья, ьи *f. of* **~**
шалфе́|й, я *m.* (*bot.*) sage.
ша́лый *adj.* (*coll.*) mad, crazy.
шал|ь, и *f.* shawl.
шальн|о́й *adj.* mad, crazy; wild; **~ы́е де́ньги** easy money; **~а́я пу́ля** stray bullet.
шама́н, а *m.* (*relig.*) shaman.
шама́н|ский *adj. of* **~**
шама́нств|о, а *nt.* (*relig.*) shamanism.
ша́ма|ть, ю *impf.* (*sl.*) to eat.
ша́мка|ть, ю *impf.* to mumble.
шамо́вк|а, и *f.* (*sl.*) grub (*food*).
шамо́т, а *m.* (*tech.*) fire-clay.
шамо́т|ный *adj. of* **~; ш. кирпи́ч** fire-brick, refractory brick.
шампа́нск|ое, ого *nt.* champagne.
шампиньо́н, а *m.* field mushroom (*Agaricus campestris* or *Psalliota campestris*).
шампу́н|ь, я *m.* shampoo.
шанда́л, а *m.* (*obs.*) candlestick.
ша́н|ец, ца *m.* (*hist.*) field-work; entrenchment.
шанкр, а *m.* (*med.*) chancre.
шанс, а *m.* chance; **име́ть много ~ов, больши́е ~ы (на**+*a.*) to have a good chance (of).
шансо́н, а *m.* ballad.
шансоне́тк|а, и *f.* **1.** (music-hall) song. **2.** singer (*in music-hall or café chantant*).
шансонье́ *m. indecl.* balladeer; singer-songwriter.
шанта́ж, а́ *m.* blackmail.
шантажи́р|овать, ую *impf.* to blackmail.
шантажи́ст, а *m.* blackmailer.
шантрап|а́, ы́ *c.g.* (*coll.*) worthless individual; scum, riff-raff.
Шанха́|й, я *m.* Shanghai.
ша́н|цевый *adj. of* **~ец; ш. инструме́нт** entrenching tool.
ша́пк|а, и *f.* **1.** cap; **академи́ческая ш.** mortarboard; **заломи́ть ~у** to wear one's cap at a rakish angle; **лома́ть ~у (пе́ред;** *obs., coll.*) to touch one's forelock (to); **дать по ~е** (+*d.*; *coll.*) (*i*) to hit, strike, (*ii*) to sack, fire (= *dismiss*); **получи́ть по ~е** (*coll.*) (*i*) to receive a blow, (*ii*) to be sacked, fired; **~ами закида́ем** it's in the bag (= *we expect to win without difficulty*); **на во́ре ш. гори́т** he's given the game away; **по Се́ньке ш.** he's got his deserts. **2.** banner headline(s). **3.** (*fig.*; *of sth. covering or crowning other objects*) cap, crown, head, cupola; **ш. ды́ма** wreath of smoke, smoke-haze.
шапова́л, а *m.* (*obs.*) fuller.
шапокля́к, а *m.* opera-hat.
ша́почк|а, и *f. dim. of* **ша́пка**
ша́почн|ый *adj. of* **ша́пка; ~ое знако́мство** nodding acquaintance; **прийти́ к ~ому разбо́ру** (*fig., coll.*) to miss the bus.

шар, а (*after numerals 2, 3, 4* **~а́**), *pl.* **~ы́** *m.* **1.** (*math.*) sphere; **земно́й ш.** the Earth, globe. **2.** spherical object, ball; **возду́шный ш.** balloon; **хоть ~о́м покати́** completely empty. **3.** (*obs.*) ballot; vote. **4.** (*pl.*) (*sl.*) eyes.
шара́х|ать, аю *impf.* (*of* **~нуть**) (*coll.*) to strike; to hit, shoot.
шара́х|аться, аюсь *impf.* (*of* **~нуться**) (*coll.*) **1.** to shy (*of a horse*); to start (up); to rush, dash. **2.** (**о**+*a.*) to hit, strike.
шара́х|нуть(ся), ну(сь), нешь(ся) *pf. of* **~ать(ся)**
шарж, а *m.* caricature, cartoon; **дру́жеский ш.** harmless, well-meant caricature.
шаржи́р|овать, ую *impf.* to caricature.
ша́рик, а *m. dim. of* **шар; (кровяно́й) ш.** (blood) corpuscle; biro (*propr.*), ball-point (pen).
ша́рик|овый *adj. of* **~; ~овая (авто)ру́чка** ball-point pen; **ш. подши́пник** (*tech.*) ball-bearing.
шарикоподши́пник, а *m.* (*tech.*) ball-bearing.
шарикоподши́пник|овый *adj. of* **~**
ша́р|ить, ю, ишь *impf.* (**в**+*p.* **по**+*d.*) to grope about, feel, fumble (in, through); (*of machine-gun fire, searchlight beams, etc.*) to sweep (*in order to locate a target*).
ша́ркань|е, я *nt.* shuffling (*of the feet or footwear*).
ша́рк|ать, аю *impf.* (*of* **~нуть**) **1.** (+*i.*) to shuffle. **2.** (**ного́й**; *obs.*) to click one's heels. **3.** (*coll.*) to hit, strike.
ша́рк|нуть, ну, нешь *pf. of* **~ать**
шарлата́н, а *m.* charlatan, fraud; quack.
шарлата́н|ить, ю, ишь *impf.* to be a charlatan.
шарлата́н|ский *adj. of* **~**
шарлата́нств|о, а *nt.* charlatanism.
шарло́тк|а, и *f.* (*cul.*) charlotte.
шарма́нк|а, и *f.* barrel-organ, street organ.
шарма́нщик, а *m.* organ-grinder.
шарни́р, а *m.* (*tech.*) hinge, joint; **на ~ах** hinged; **быть как на ~ах** (*fig.*) to be on edge, be restless, fidget.
шарни́р|ный *adj. of* **~; ш. болт** link bolt; **ш. кла́пан** flap valve; **~ная опо́ра** rocker bearing, tip bearing; **~ное соедине́ние** hinge joint, ball and socket joint, toggle joint.
шарова́р|ы, ~ *no sg.* wide trousers (*as worn by certain Eastern peoples, or for certain sports*).
шарови́д|ный (~ен, ~на) *adj.* spherical, globe-shaped.
шар|ово́й *adj. of* **~**; globular; **ш. кла́пан** ball-cock; **ш. шарни́р, ~ово́е шарни́рное соедине́ние** ball and socket joint.
шаромы́г|а, и *c.g.* (*coll.*) parasite; rogue, scoundrel.
шаромы́жник, а *m.* = **шаромы́га**
шарообра́з|ный (~ен, ~на) *adj.* spherical, ball-shaped.
шартрёз, а *m.* Chartreuse (*liqueur*).
шарф, а *m.* scarf.
шасси́ *nt. indecl.* **1.** chassis. **2.** (*aeron.*) undercarriage.
ша́ста|ть, ю *impf.* (*coll.*) to roam, hang about.
шата́ни|е, я *nt.* **1.** swaying, reeling. **2.** roaming, wandering. **3.** (*fig.*) vacillation; instability.
шата́|ть, ю *impf.* to rock, shake, cause to reel.
шата́|ться, юсь *impf.* **1.** (*intrans.*) to rock, sway, reel. **2.** to be, come loose; to be unsteady. **3.** (*coll.*) to roam; to loaf, lounge about.
шата́|ющийся *pres. part of* **~ться** *and adj.* loose (*of a screw, tooth, etc.*).
шате́н, а *m.* pers. with auburn, brown hair.
шате́н|ка, ки *f. of* **~**
шат|ёр, ра́ *m.* **1.** tent, marquee. **2.** (*archit.*) hipped roof.
ша́ти|я, и *f.* (*coll., pej.*) gang, crowd, 'mob'.
ша́т|кий (~ок, ~ка) *adj.* **1.** unsteady; shaky; loose. **2.** (*fig.*) unstable, insecure, shaky; unreliable; vacillating; **ш. в убежде́ниях** lacking the courage of one's convictions.
ша́ткост|ь, и *f.* **1.** unsteadiness; shakiness. **2.** (*fig.*) instability; vacillation.
шатро́в|ый *adj. of* **шатёр; ~ая кры́ша** hipped roof.
шату́н[1], **а́** *m.* (*tech.*) connecting rod.
шату́н[2], **а́** *m.* (*coll.*) loafer, idler.
ша́фер, а, *pl.* **~а́** *m.* best man (*at wedding*).
шафра́н, а *m.* (*bot.*) saffron.
шафра́н|ный *adj. of* **~**
шах[1], **а** *m.* Shah.

шах², **а** *m.* (*chess*) check; **ш. и мат** checkmate; **объяви́ть ш.** (+*d.*) to put in check; **под ~ом** in check.
ша́хер-ма́хер, а *m.* (*coll.*) shady deal.
шахмати́ст, а *m.* chess-player.
ша́хматн|ый *adj.* **1.** chess; **ш. дебю́т** chess opening, opening gambit; **~ая доска́** chess-board; **~ая па́ртия** game of chess. **2.** chess-board, chequered; staggered; **~ая ска́терть** check table-cloth; **ш. флажо́к** chequered flag; **в ~ом поря́дке** staggered.
ша́хмат|ы, ~ *no sg.* **1.** chess. **2.** chessmen.
ша́хт|а, ы *f.* **1.** mine, pit. **2.** (*tech.*) shaft.
шахтёр, а *m.* miner.
шахтёр|ский *adj. of* **~**
ша́хт|ный *adj. of* **~а; ш. ствол** pit-shaft.
ша́хт|овый *adj. of* **~а**
ша́шечниц|а, ы *f.* draught-board, chess-board.
ша́шк|а¹, и *f.* **1.** block (*of stone or wood plank, for paving*). **2.** charge (*of explosive*).
ша́шк|а², и *f.* **1.** draught, draughtsman (*piece in game of draughts*). **2.** (*pl.*) draughts (*game*).
ша́шк|а³, и *f.* sabre, cavalry sword.
шашлы́к, а́ *m.* (*cul.*) shashlik, kebab.
шашлы́чн|ая, ой *f.* shashlik-house.
ша́шн|и, ей *no sg.* (*coll., pej.*) **1.** tricks. **2.** amorous intrigues; affair; **завести́ ш. с** (+*i.*) to take up with.
шва *g. sg. of* **шов**
шва́бр|а, ы *f.* mop, swab.
шваль, и *f.* (*coll.*) **1.** (*collect.*) rubbish, worthless stuff. **2.** good-for-nothing.
шва́льн|я, и *f.* (*obs.*) tailor's shop.
шва́ркн|уть, у, ешь *pf.* (*coll.*) to hurl.
шварто́в, а *m.* (*naut.*) hawser, mooring line; **отда́ть ~ы** to cast off.
шварт|ова́ть, у́ю *impf.* (*of* **при~**) (*naut.*) to moor.
шварт|ова́ться, у́юсь *impf.* (*of* **при́~**) (*naut.*) to moor, make fast.
Шва́рцвальд, а *m.* the Black Forest.
швах *as pred.* (*coll.*) poor, bad; in a bad way.
швед, а *m.* Swede.
шве́д|ка, ки *f. of* **~**
шве́дский *adj.* Swedish.
шве́йник, а *m.* sewer, sewing industry worker.
шве́йн|ый *adj.* sewing; **~ые изде́лия** ready-made garments; **~ая маши́на** sewing-machine; **~ая фа́брика** garment factory.
швейца́р, а *m.* porter, door-keeper, commissionaire.
швейца́р|ец, ца *m.* Swiss.
Швейца́ри|я, и *f.* Switzerland.
швейца́р|ка, ки *f. of* **~ец**
швейца́рск|ая, ой *f.* porter's lodge.
швейца́рский¹ *adj.* Swiss.
швейца́р|ский² *adj. of* **~**
шве́рмер, а *m.* squib (*firework*).
швец, а́ *m.* **1.** (*obs.*) tailor; **и ш., и жнец, и в ду́ду игре́ц** (*fig.*) jack of all trades. **2.** (*dial.*) cobbler.
Шве́ци|я, и *f.* Sweden.
шве|я́, и́ *f.* seamstress; **ш.-мотори́стка** electric sewing-machine operator; **ш.-ру́чница** (*coll.*) hand finisher.
шво́р|ень, ня *m.* = **шкво́рень**
швырко́в|ый *adj.*: **~ые дрова́** logs, firewood.
швыр|ну́ть, ну́, нёшь *pf. of* **~я́ть**
швыр|о́к, ка́ *m.* **1.** throw. **2.** (*collect.*) logs, firewood. **3.** (*moving*) practice target.
швыр|я́ть, я́ю *impf.* (*of* **~ну́ть**) (+*a. or i.*; *coll.*) to throw, fling, chuck, hurl; **ш. де́ньги (деньга́ми)** to fling one's money about.
швыря́|ться, юсь *impf.* (*coll.*) (+*i.*) **1.** to throw, fling, hurl (at one another). **2.** to make light (of), trifle (with).
шевел|и́ть, ю́, и́шь *impf.* (*of* **~ьну́ть** *and* **по~**) **1.** to turn over. **2.** (+*i.*) to move, stir, budge; **ш. мозга́ми** (*coll., joc.*) to use one's wits, use one's loaf.
шевел|и́ться, ю́сь, и́шься *impf.* (*of* **~ьну́ться** *and* **по~**) **1.** to move, stir, budge; **у него́ ~я́тся де́ньги** (*coll.*) he has a tidy bank balance. **2.** (*fig.*) to stir (*of hopes, fears, etc.*). **3. ~и́сь; ~и́тесь!** (*coll.*) get a move on!; get cracking!
шевел|ьну́ть, ьну́, ьнёшь *pf.* (*of* **~и́ть**); **бро́вью не ш.** not to bat an eyelid; **па́льцем не ш.** not to lift a finger.
шевел|ьну́ться, ьну́сь, ьнёшься *pf. of* **~и́ться**
шевелю́р|а, ы *f.* (head of) hair.
шевио́т, а *m.* (*text.*) cheviot (*cloth*).
шевио́т|овый *adj. of* **~**
шевро́ *nt. indecl.* kid (*leather*).
шевро́|вый *adj. of* **~**
шевро́н, а *m.* (*mil.*) long-service stripe.
шеде́вр, а *m.* masterpiece, chef d'œuvre.
шезло́нг, а *m.* deck-chair; lounger.
ше́йк|а, и, *g. pl.* **ше́ек** *f.* **1.** *dim. of* **ше́я**. **2.** (*narrow part of var. objects*) neck; (*tech.*) pin, journal; **ш. ги́льзы** cartridge neck; **ш. ре́льса** web (*of rail*). **3.** (*anat.*) cervix.
ше́йный *adj. of* **ше́я**; (*anat.*) jugular, cervical.
шейх, а *m.* sheikh.
шёл *see* **идти́**
ше́лест, а *m.* rustle, rustling.
шелест|е́ть *1st pers. not used*, **и́шь** *impf.* to rustle.
шёлк, а (у), о ~е, на (в) ~у́, *pl.* **~а́** *m.* silk (*also fig. of an object resembling silk in softness, etc., or of a gentle-natured pers.*); **ш.-сыре́ц** raw silk; **ходи́ть в ~а́х** to wear silks; **в долгу́ как в ~у́** up to the eyes in debt.
шелкови́нк|а, и *f.* silk thread.
шелкови́ст|ый (~, ~а) *adj.* silky.
шелкови́ц|а, ы *f.* mulberry (tree).
шелкови́|чный *adj. of* **~ца; ш. червь** silk-worm.
шелково́д, а *m.* silkworm breeder.
шелково́дств|о, а *nt.* silkworm breeding, seri(ci)culture.
шелково́д|ческий *adj. of* **~ство**
шёлковый *adj.* **1.** silk. **2.** (*fig., coll.*) meek, good (= *tractable*).
шёлкогра́фи|я, и *f.* silk-screen printing.
шелкопря́д, а *m.* silkworm.
шёлкопряде́ни|е, я *nt.* silk-spinning.
шёлкопряд|и́льный *adj. of* **~е́ние**
шёлкотка́цкий *adj.* silk-weaving.
шело́м, а *m.* (*arch. or poet.*) = **шлем**
шелохн|у́ть, у́, ёшь *pf.* to stir, agitate.
шелохн|у́ться, у́сь, ёшься *pf.* to stir, move.
шелуди́в|ый (~, ~а) *adj.* (*coll.*) mangy.
шелух|а́, и́ *f.* skin (*of vegetables or fruit*); peel; pod; scale (*of fish*).
шелуше́ни|е, я *nt.* **1.** peeling, shelling (*action*). **2.** peeling (*of human skin*).
шелуш|и́ть, у́, и́шь *impf.* to peel; to shell.
шелуш|и́ться, и́тся *impf.* **1.** (*of skin*) to peel. **2.** (*of paint, etc.*) to come off, peel off.
ше́льм|а, ы *c.g.* (*coll.*) rascal, scoundrel.
шельмова́т|ый (~, ~а) *adj.* (*coll.*) rascally, sly, wily.
шельм|ова́ть, у́ю *impf.* (*of* **о~**) **1.** (*hist.*) to punish publicly. **2.** (*coll.*) to blacken (*fig.*); to defame.
шельф, а *m.* (*geog.*) shelf.
шемя́кин *adj., only in phr.* **ш. суд** unjust trial.
ше́нкел|ь, я, *pl.* **~я́, ~е́й** *m.* (*horsemanship*) leg (*of rider*).
шепеля́в|ить, лю, ишь *impf.* to lisp, hiss (*pronounce 's', 'z' as 'sh', 'zh'*).
шепеля́в|ый (~, ~а) *adj.* lisping, hissing.
шеп|ну́ть, ну́, нёшь *pf. of* **~та́ть**
шёпот, а *m.* whisper (*also fig.* = *rumour*).
шёпотом *adv.* in a whisper.
шептал|а́, ы́ *f.* (*collect.*) dried apricots *or* peaches.
шеп|та́ть, чу́, ~чешь *impf.* (*of* **~ну́ть**) to whisper.
шеп|та́ться, чу́сь, ~чешься *impf.* to whisper, converse in whispers.
шепту́н, а́ *m.* (*coll.*) **1.** one who speaks in a whisper. **2.** (*fig.*) whisperer, tell-tale, informer.
шербе́т, а *m.* sherbet.
шере́нг|а, и *f.* rank (= *row*); file, column.
шери́ф, а *m.* sheriff.
шерохова́тост|ь, и *f.* roughness (*also fig.*); unevenness.
шерохова́т|ый (~, ~а) *adj.* rough (*also fig.*); uneven; rugged.
шерсте... *comb. form* wool-.
шерсти́нк|а, и *f.* strand of wool.
шерсти́ст|ый (~, ~а) *adj.* woolly, fleecy.

шерст|и́ть, и́т *impf.* **1.** to irritate, tickle (*of a woollen garment*). **2.** (*fig., coll.*) to blow up, tear a strip off.
шерсто... *comb. form* wool-.
шерстоби́т, а *m.* wool-beater.
шерстобо́йн|я, и *f.* wool-beating mill.
шерстопряде́ни|е, я *nt.* wool-spinning.
шерстопряд|и́льный *adj. of* **~е́ние**
шерсточеса́льный *adj.* wool-carding.
шерст|ь, и, *pl.* **~и, ~е́й** *f.* **1.** hair (*of animals*); **гла́дить кого́-н. про́тив ~и** (*fig.*) to rub s.o. up the wrong way. **2.** wool. **3.** woollen material; worsted.
шерстян|о́й *adj.* wool, woollen; **ш. пот** suint; **~а́я пря́жа** wool yarn.
шерхе́бел|ь, я *m.* (*tech.*) rough plane.
шерша́ве|ть, ет *impf.* to become rough.
шерша́в|ый (~, ~а) *adj.* rough; **~ые ру́ки** horny hands.
ше́рш|ень, ня *m.* hornet.
шест, а́ *m.* pole; staff.
ше́стви|е, я *nt.* procession.
ше́ств|овать, ую *impf.* to walk (*as in procession*).
шестерёнк|а, и *f. dim. of* **шестерня́**[2]
шестерён|очный *adj. of* **~ка; ~очная коро́бка** gear-box.
шестёрк|а, и *f.* **1.** figure '6'; six, group of six. **2.** (*cards*) six. **3.** six-in-hand. **4.** six-oar (boat).
шестерно́й *adj.* sixfold, sextuple.
шестерн|я́[1]**, и́,** *g. pl.* **~е́й** *f.* (*obs.*) six-in-hand.
шестер|ня́[2]**, ни́,** *g. pl.* **~ён** *f.* (*tech.*) gear (wheel), cogwheel, pinion.
ше́стер|о, ы́х *collect. num.* six.
шести... *comb. form* six-.
шестигра́нник, а *m.* (*math.*) hexahedron.
шестидесятиле́ти|е, я *nt.* **1.** sixty years, sixty-year period. **2.** sixtieth anniversary.
шестидесятиле́тний *adj.* **1.** of sixty years, sixty-year. **2.** sixty-year-old.
шестидеся́тник, а *m.* (*hist.*) 'man of the sixties' (*of Russ. public figures and social thinkers who flourished in the 1860's — e.g., Chernyshevsky and Dobrolyubov*).
шестидеся́тый *adj.* sixtieth.
шестикла́ссник, а *m.* sixth-former.
шестисотле́ти|е, я *nt.* **1.** six hundred years. **2.** six hundredth anniversary, sexcentenary.
шестисо́тый *adj.* six-hundredth.
шестисто́пный *adj.*: **ш. ямб** (*liter.*) alexandrine.
шестиуго́льник, а *m.* (*math.*) hexagon.
шестиуго́льный *adj.* hexagonal.
шестичасово́й *adj.* **1.** lasting six hours. **2.** (*coll.*) occurring at, timed for six o'clock.
шестнадцати... *comb. form* sixteen-.
шестнадцатиле́тний *adj.* **1.** of sixteen years, sixteen-year. **2.** sixteen-year-old.
шестна́дцатый *adj.* sixteenth.
шестна́дцат|ь, и *num.* sixteen.
шестови́к, а́ *m.* (*sport*) pole-vaulter.
шест|о́й *adj.* sixth; **одна́ ~а́я** one sixth.
шест|о́к, ка́ *m.* **1.** hearth (*in Russ. stove*). **2.** roost.
шест|ь, и́, ью *num.* six.
шестьдеся́т, шести́десяти, шестью́десятью, о шести́десяти *num.* sixty.
шест|ьсо́т, ~исо́т, ~иста́м, ~ьюста́ми, о ~иста́х *num.* six hundred.
ше́стью *adv.* six times.
Шетла́ндск|ие остров|а́, ~их ~о́в *no sg.* the Shetland Islands; the Shetlands.
шеф, а *m.* **1.** (*coll.*) boss, chief. **2.** (*of an organization*) patron, sponsor.
шеф-по́вар, а, *pl.* **~а́, ~о́в** *m.* chef.
ше́ф|ский *adj. of* **~ство**
ше́фств|о, а *nt.* patronage, sponsorship (*in the former USSR, relationship between two organizations — e.g. a factory and a collective farm — in which one 'adopts' the other, or arrangement by which an organization takes a special interest in a priority construction project*); **взять ш. (над)** to take under one's patronage.
ше́фств|овать, ую *impf.* **(над)** to act as patron, sponsor (to).
ше́|я, и *f.* neck; **броса́ться на ~ю кому́-н.** to throw one's arms around s.o.'s neck; **на свою́ ~ю** (*coll.*) to one's own detriment; **бить по ~я́м** (*coll.*) to beat up, knock the daylight out of; **ве́шаться на ~ю кому́-н.** (*fig., coll.*) to hang round s.o.'s neck; **прогна́ть, вытолкать кого́-н. в ~ю, в три ~и** (*coll.*) to throw s.o. out on his ear; **сиде́ть на ~е у кого́-н.** (*coll.*) to live off s.o.; **слома́ть, сверну́ть (себе́) ~ю на чём-н.** (*coll.*) to come a cropper over sth.
шиба́|ть, ю *impf.* (*coll.*) **1.** (*+a. or i.*) to throw, chuck. **2.** to hit (*also, impers., of smells, etc.*).
ши́бер, а *m.* (*tech.*) damper; gate (valve), slide (valve).
ши́б|кий (~ок, ~ка́, ~ко) *adj.* (*coll.*) fast, quick.
ши́бк|о *adv.* (*coll.*) **1.** *adv. of* **~ий. 2.** hard; much, very; **ш. испуга́ться** to be scared stiff.
ши́б|че *comp. of* **~кий** *and* **~ко**
ши́ворот, а *m.* (*coll.*): **за ш.** by the collar, by the scruff of the neck; **ш.-навы́ворот** (*adv.*) topsy-turvy, upside down, haywire.
ши́зик, а *m.* (*sl.*) crackpot, freak.
шизофре́ник, а *m.* (*med.*) schizophrenic.
шизофрени́|я, и *f.* (*med.*) schizophrenia; **вялотеку́щая ш.** creeping schizophrenia.
шии́т, а *m.* Shiite; **мусульма́нин-ш.** Shiite Muslim.
шии́тский *adj.* Shiite.
шик, а (у) *m.* ostentatious smartness, stylishness; style.
шика́рно *as pred.* it is splendid, magnificent.
шика́р|ный (~ен, ~на) *adj.* **1.** chic, smart, stylish. **2.** ostentatious, done for effect. **3.** (*coll.*) splendid, magnificent.
ши́к|ать, аю *impf.* (*of* **~нуть**) (*coll.*) **1.** **(на+a.)** to hush (*by crying 'sh'*). **2.** (*+d.*) to hiss (at), boo, catcall.
ши́к|нуть, ну, нешь *pf. of* **~ать**
шик|ну́ть, ну, нёшь *pf. of* **~ова́ть**
шик|ова́ть, у́ю *impf.* (*of* **~ну́ть**) (*+i. or intrans.; coll.*) to parade; to show off.
ши́л|о, а, *pl.* **~ья, ~ьев** *nt.* awl.
шилохво́ст|ь, и *f.* (*zool.*) pintail.
шимпанзе́ *m. indecl.* chimpanzee.
ши́н|а, ы *f.* **1.** tyre. **2.** (*med.*) splint. **3.** (*electr.*) bus-bar.
шине́л|ь, и *f.* (*mil. or uniform*) greatcoat.
шине́ль|ный *adj. of* **~**
шинка́р|ка, ки *f. of* **~ь**
шинка́рств|о, а *nt.* (*obs.*) bootlegging.
шинка́р|ь, я́ *m.* (*obs.*) **1.** tavern-keeper, publican. **2.** bootlegger.
шинко́в|анный *p.p.p. of* **~а́ть** *and adj.* (*cul.*) shredded, chopped.
шинк|ова́ть, у́ю *impf.* (*cul.*) to shred, chop.
ши́н|ный *adj. of* **~а; ~ное желе́зо** band iron, hoop-iron; **ш. заво́д** tyre factory.
шин|о́к, ка́ *m.* (*obs.*) **1.** tavern. **2.** (*coll.*) bootlegging establishment.
шинши́лл|а, ы *f.* chinchilla.
шип[1]**, а́** *m.* **1.** (*bot.*) thorn, spine. **2.** spike, crampon, nail (*on running shoes, mountaineering boots, etc., to prevent slipping*). **3.** (*tech.*) pin, tenon; lug; **ш. и гнездо́** mortise and tenon.
шип[2]**, а** *m.* (*coll.*) hissing (sound).
шипе́ни|е, я *nt.* hissing; sizzling; sputtering.
шип|е́ть, лю́, и́шь *impf.* **1.** to hiss; to sizzle; to fizz; to sputter. **2.** to make the sound 'sh' (*to comfort a child, etc., or to enjoin silence*).
шипо́вник, а *m.* (*bot.*) dogrose.
шипу́чий *adj.* (*of drinks*) sparkling; fizzy.
шипу́чк|а, и *f.* (*coll.*) fizzy drink.
шип|я́щий *pres. part. act. of* **~е́ть** *and adj.* (*ling.*) sibilant.
ши́р|е *comp. of* **~о́кий** *and* **~око́; ш. шаг,** *see* **шаг**
ширин|а́, ы́ *f.* width, breadth; gauge (*of rail. track*); **ш. фро́нта** (*mil.*) frontage.
ши́ринк|а, и *f.* **1.** (*coll.*) fly (*of trousers*). **2.** (*dial.*) (piece of) cloth.
шир|ить, ю, ишь *impf.* to extend, expand.
шир|иться, ится *impf.* to spread, expand (*intrans.*).
ши́рм|а, ы *f.* screen (*also fig.*).
широ́к|ий (~, ~а́, ~о́, *pl.* **~и́)** *adj.* **1.** wide, broad (*also fig.*);

~ая колея́ (*rail.*) broad gauge; **ш. экра́н** (*cinema*) wide screen; **в ~ом смы́сле** in a broad sense. **2.** (*fig.*) big, extensive, large-scale, general; **~ие пла́ны** big plans; **~ие ма́ссы** the general public; **ш. чита́тель** the average reader, the general reading public; **това́ры ~ого потребле́ния** (*econ.*) consumer goods; **жить на ~ую но́гу** to live in grand style; **у него́ ~ая нату́ра** he likes to do things in a big way (*not pej.*).

широко́ *adv.* **1.** wide, widely, broadly (*also fig.*); **ш. раскры́ть глаза́** to open one's eyes wide; **ш. толкова́ть** to interpret loosely. **2.** extensively, on a large scale.

широко... *comb. form* wide-, broad-.

широковеща́ни|е, я *nt.* (*radio*) broadcasting.

широковеща́тельный *adj.* **1.** broadcasting. **2.** (*pej.*) loud, loud-mouthed; containing large promises.

ширококоле́йный *adj.* (*rail.*) broad-gauge.

ширококо́стный *adj.* big-boned.

широкопле́ч|ий (~, ~а) *adj.* broad-shouldered.

широкопо́лый *adj.* wide-brimmed (*of hats*); full-skirted (*of clothes*).

широкоэкра́нный *adj.* wide-screen.

широт|а́, ы́, *pl.* **~́ы, ~́** *f.* **1.** width, breadth; **ш. взгля́дов** broad-mindedness. **2.** (*geog.*) latitude.

широ́тный *adj.* (*geog.*) latitudinal, of latitude.

широча́йший *superl. of* **широ́кий**

широче́нный *adj.* (*coll.*) very wide, broad.

ширпотре́б, а *m.* (*econ.*; *coll.*) consumption; (*collect.*) consumer goods.

шир|ь, и *f.* (*wide*) expanse; **во всю ш.** to full width; (*fig.*) to the full extent.

ши́то-кры́то *adv.* (*coll.*): **всё ш.-к.** it's all being kept dark.

ши́т|ый *p.p.p. of* **~ь** *and adj.* embroidered.

шить, шью, шьёшь *impf.* (*of* **с~**) **1.** to sew. **2.** make (*by sewing*); **ш. себе́ что-н.** to have sth. made. **3.** (*impf. only*) to embroider.

шить|ё, я́ *nt.* **1.** sewing, needlework; **лоску́тное ш.** patchwork. **2.** embroidery.

ши́фер, а *m.* slate.

ши́фер|ный *adj. of* **~**; **~ное ма́сло** shale oil.

шифо́н, а *m.* (*text.*) chiffon.

шифонье́рк|а, и *f.* chest of drawers.

шифр, а *m.* **1.** cipher; code. **2.** pressmark. **3.** (*obs.*) monogram.

шифрова́льщик, а *m.* cypher clerk.

шифро́в|анный *p.p.p. of* **~а́ть** *and adj.* (in) cypher.

шифр|ова́ть, у́ю *impf.* (*of* **за~**) to encipher.

шифро́вк|а, и *f.* **1.** enciphering. **2.** (*coll.*) cipher communication.

ши́хт|а, ы *f.* (*tech.*) (*furnace*) charge, batch, burden.

шиш, а́ *m.* (*coll.*) **1.** (*vulg.*) fig; **показа́ть ш.** to pull a long nose. **2.** nothing; **ни ~а́** damn all. **3.** (*hist.*) ruffian, brigand.

шиша́к, а́ *m.* (*hist.*) spiked helmet.

ши́шк|а, и *f.* **1.** (*bot.*) cone. **2.** bump; lump. **3.** (*tech.*) (mould) core. **4.** (*coll., joc.*) big-wig, big wheel.

шишкова́т|ый (~, ~а) *adj.* knobby, knobbly; bumpy.

шишкови́д|ный (~ен, ~на) *adj.* cone-shaped.

шишконо́сный *adj.* (*bot.*) coniferous.

шкал|а́, ы́, *pl.* **~́ы** *f.* scale; dial.

шка́лик, а *m.* (*obs.*) **1.** shkalik (*old Russ. unit of liquid volume, equivalent to 0.06 litres*). **2.** bottle *or* glass (*containing above measure*).

шка́н|ечный *adj. of* **~цы́**; **ш. журна́л** log (book).

шка́нц|ы, ев *no sg.* (*naut.*) quarterdeck.

шкап, а *m.* (*arch. or dial.*) = **шкаф**

шкату́лк|а, и *f.* box, casket, case.

шкаф, а, о ~́е, в ~у́, *pl.* **~ы́** *m.* cupboard, wardrobe; dresser; **апте́чный ш.** medicine cabinet; **духово́й ш.** oven; **кни́жный ш.** bookcase (*with doors*); **несгора́емый ш.** safe.

шкафу́т, а *m.* (*naut.*) waist (*of ship*).

шка́фчик, а *m.* closet, locker.

шквал, а *nt.* squall (*also fig., of artillery fire*); **ш. вопро́сов** barrage of questions.

шква́листый *adj.* squally.

шква́льный *adj.*: **ш. ого́нь** (*mil.*) heavy fire, mass barrage.

шква́р|ки, ок *pl.* (*sg.* **~ка, ~ки** *f.*) (*cul.*) crackling.

шкво́р|ень, ня *m.* (*tech.*) pintle, kingpin, kingbolt, draw-bolt.

шкет, а *m.* (*sl.*) boy, lad.

шкив, а, *pl.* **~ы́** *m.* (*tech.*) pulley; sheave.

шки́пер, а, *pl.* **~ы** *and* **~а́** *m.* (*naut.*) skipper, master.

шко́д|а, ы *f.* (*coll.*) **1.** harm, damage. **2.** trick, mischief.

шкодли́в|ый (~, ~а) *adj.* (*coll.*) **1.** harmful. **2.** mischievous.

шко́л|а, ы *f.* **1.** (*in var. senses*) school; **ходи́ть в ~у** to go to school; **око́нчить ~у** to leave school; **ш.-интерна́т** boarding school; **вы́сшая ш.** university, college; (*in abstract sense*) higher education. **2.** schooling, training.

шко́л|ить, ю, ишь *impf.* (*of* **вы́~**) (*coll.*) to train, discipline.

шко́льник, а *m.* schoolboy.

шко́льниц|а, ы *f.* schoolgirl.

шко́льнический *adj.* schoolboy(ish).

шко́льничеств|о, а *nt.* schoolboyish behaviour, schoolboy tricks.

шко́льн|ый *adj.* school; **ш. во́зраст** school age; **со ~ой скамьи́** since one's schooldays; **ш. учи́тель** school-teacher, schoolmaster.

школя́р, а́ *m.* (*obs.*) schoolboy.

школя́рств|о, а *nt.* scholasticism, pedantry.

шкот, а *m.* (*naut.*) sheet.

шко́т|овый *adj. of* **~**; **ш. у́зел** sheet bend.

шку́р|а, ы *f.* **1.** skin (*also fig.*), hide, pelt; **волк в ове́чьей ~е** wolf in sheep's clothing; **быть в чьей-н. ~е** to be in s.o.'s shoes; **драть ~у (с кого́-н.)** to fleece s.o.; **дрожа́ть за свою́ ~у** to be concerned for one's own skin; **чу́вствовать что-н. на свое́й ~е** to know what sth. feels like. **2.** (*coll., pej.*) = **~ник**

шку́рк|а, и *f.* **1.** skin. **2.** (*coll.*) rind. **3.** emery paper, sandpaper.

шку́рник, а *m.* (*coll., pej.*) pers. concerned only with self-advantage.

шку́рный *adj.* (*pej.*) selfish, self-seeking.

шла *see* **идти́**

шлагба́ум, а *m.* barrier (*of swing-beam type, at road or rail crossing*).

шлак, а *m.* slag; dross; cinder; clinker.

шлакобето́н, а *m.* slag concrete (*made of slag, cement, and sand*).

шлакобло́к, а *m.* breeze block (*building material made of cinder with addition of cement*)

шла́к|овый *adj. of* **~**

шланг, а *m.* hose.

шла́ф|ор, а *m.* = **~ро́к**

шлафро́к, а *m.* (*obs.*) housecoat, dressing-gown.

шлейф, а *m.* train (*of dress*).

шлем[1]**, а** *m.* helmet; **вя́заный ш.** balaclava; **защи́тный ш.** (*on building site, etc.*) hard hat.

шлем[2]**, а** *m.* (*cards*) slam; **большо́й, ма́лый ш.** grand, little slam.

шлемофо́н, а *m.* (*mil.*) helmet with earphones, intercom head-set.

шлёпан|цы, цев *pl.* (*sg.* **~ец, ~ца** *m.*) bedroom slippers.

шлёп|ать, аю *impf.* (*of* **~нуть**) **1.** to smack, spank. **2.** (*coll.*) to shuffle; to tramp.

шлёп|аться, аюсь *impf.* (*of* **~нуться**) (*coll.*) to fall with a plop, thud.

шлёп|нуть(ся), ну(сь), нешь(ся) *pf. of* **~ать(ся)**

шлеп|о́к, ка́ *m.* smack, slap.

шле|я́, и́ *f.* breech-band, breast-band (*part of harness*).

шли[1] *see* **идти́**

шли[2] *see* **слать**

шлифова́льный *adj.* (*tech.*) polishing, burnishing; grinding; **ш. материа́л** abrasive(s); **ш. стано́к** grinding-machine.

шлифова́ни|е, я *nt.* (*tech.*) polishing, burnishing; grinding.

шлиф|ова́ть, у́ю *impf.* (*of* **от~**) **1.** (*tech.*) to polish, burnish; to grind. **2.** (*fig.*) to polish, perfect.

шлифо́вк|а, и *f.* (*tech.*) **1.** polishing, burnishing; grinding. **2.** polish (*result of action*).

шли́хт|а, ы *f.* (*tech.*) size.

шлихт|ова́ть, у́ю *impf.* (*tech.*) to smooth, finish; to size, dress.

шло *see* **идти́**

шлюз, а *m.* lock, sluice, floodgate.
шлюз|ова́ть, у́ю *impf. and pf.* **1.** to construct locks (on). **2.** to lock through, convey through a lock.
шлюз|ово́й *adj. of* ~; **~ова́я ка́мера** lock chamber.
шлюпба́лк|а, и *f.* (*naut.*) davit.
шлю́пк|а, и *f.* launch, boat; **спаса́тельная ш.** lifeboat.
шлю́х|а, и *f.* (*vulg.*) streetwalker, tart.
шля́п|а, ы *f. and c.g.* **1.** *f.* hat; **де́ло в ~е** (*coll.*) it's in the bag; all is well. **2.** *c.g.* (*coll., pej.*) duffer.
шля́пк|а, и *f.* **1.** (*woman's*) hat. **2.** head (*of nail, etc.*); cap (*of mushroom*).
шля́пник, а *m.* milliner, hatter.
шля́п|ный *adj. of* **~а**
шля́|ться, юсь *impf.* (*coll.*) to loaf about.
шлях, а, о ~е, на ~у́ *m.* highway, high road (*in the Ukraine and Southern Russia*).
шляхе́т|ский *adj. of* **~ство** *and* **шля́хта**
шляхе́тств|о, а *nt.* **1.** = **шля́хта. 2.** (*hist.*) (Russian) nobility, gentry (*designation used in early 18th century* = **дворя́нство**).
шля́хт|а, ы *f.* (*hist.*) szlachta (*Polish gentry*).
шляхта́нк|а, и *f. of* **шля́хтич**
шля́хтич, а *m.* (*hist.*) member of szlachta.
шмат, а *m.* (*coll.*) sound bite.
шмат|о́к, ка́ *m.* (*coll.*) bit, piece.
шмел|ь, я́ *m.* bumble-bee.
шмона́|ть, ю *impf.* (*sl.*) to frisk.
шмо́т|ки, ок *no sg.* (*coll.*) clothes.
шмуцти́тул, а *m.* (*typ.*) bastard-title.
шмы́г|ать, аю *impf.* (*of* **~ну́ть**) (*coll.*) **1.** (*+i.*) to rub, brush; **ш. но́сом** to sniff. **2.** to rush up and down.
шмыг|ну́ть, ну́, нёшь *pf.* (*coll.*) **1.** *inst. pf. of* **~ать. 2.** to dart, nip, sneak (= *to move rapidly, in order to escape notice*).
шмя́к|ать, аю *impf.* (*of* **~нуть**) (*coll.*) to drop with a thud.
шмя́к|нуть, ну, нешь *pf. of* **~ать**
шнит(т)-лу́к, а *m.* chive.
шни́цел|ь, я *m.* (*cul.*) schnitzel.
шнур, а́ *m.* **1.** cord; lace. **2.** (*electr.*) flex, cable.
шнур|ова́ть, у́ю *impf.* **1.** (*pf.* **за~**) to lace up. **2.** (*pf.* **про~**) to tie (*leaves of a document, etc.*).
шнур|ова́ться, у́юсь *impf.* (*of* **за~**) **1.** to lace o.s. up. **2.** *pass. of* **~ова́ть**
шнуро́вк|а, и *f.* **1.** lacing, tying. **2.** (*obs.*) corset.
шнур|ово́й *adj. of* ~
шнур|о́к, ка́ *m.* lace.
шныр|ну́ть, ну́, нёшь *pf. of* **~я́ть**
шныр|я́ть, я́ю *impf.* (*of* **~ну́ть**) (*coll.*) to dart about, dart in and out.
шов, шва *m.* **1.** seam; **без шва** seamless; **держа́ть ру́ки по швам** to stand to attention; **треща́ть по всем швам** (*fig.*) to burst at the seams, fall to pieces, crack up, collapse. **2.** stitch (*in embroidery*). **3.** (*med.*) stitch, suture; **наложи́ть, снять швы** to put in, remove stitches. **4.** (*tech.*) joint, junction.
шовини́зм, а *m.* chauvinism.
шовини́ст, а *m.* chauvinist.
шовинисти́ческий *adj.* chauvinistic.
шок, а *m.* (*med.*) shock.
шоки́р|овать, ую *impf.* to shock.
шо́ков|ый *adj.*: **~ая терапи́я** shock therapy.
шокола́д, а *m.* chocolate.
шокола́дк|а, и *f.* (*coll.*) bar of chocolate, a chocolate (sweet).
шокола́д|ный *adj.* **1.** *adj. of* **~. 2.** chocolate-coloured.
шо́мпол, а, *pl.* **~а́** *m.* (*mil.*) **1.** cleaning rod. **2.** (*obs.*) ramrod.
шо́мпол|ьный *adj. of* **~; ~ьное ружьё** muzzle-loading gun.
шо́рник, а *m.* saddler, harness-maker.
шо́рн|ый *adj.* harness; **~ая мастерска́я** = **~я**
шо́рн|я, и *f.* saddler's shop, saddler-maker's, harness-maker's.
шо́рох, а *m.* rustle.
шо́рт|ы, ~ *no sg.* shorts.
шо́р|ы, ~ *no sg.* **1.** blinkers (*also fig.*); **держа́ть кого́-н. в ~ах** (*fig.*) to keep s.o. in blinkers. **2.** harness (*with breech-band, but without collar*).
шоссе́ *nt. indecl.* highway; surfaced road.
шоссе́|йный *adj. of* **~; ~йная доро́га** = **~**
шосси́р|овать, ую *impf. and pf.* to metal, surface (*a road*).
шотла́нд|ец, ца *m.* Scotsman, Scot.
Шотла́нди|я, и *f.* Scotland; **Но́вая Ш.** Nova Scotia.
шотла́нд|ка[1], ки *f. of* **~ец**
шотла́нд|ка[2], ки *f.* (*text.*) tartan, plaid.
шотла́ндский *adj.* Scottish, Scots.
шофёр, а *m.* driver (*of a motor vehicle*), chauffeur.
шофёр|ский *adj. of* **~; ~ское свиде́тельство, ~ские права́** driver's, driving licence.
шпа́г|а, и *f.* sword; (*sport*) épée; **обнажи́ть ~у** to draw one's sword; **скрести́ть ~и** to cross swords (*also fig.*); **взять на ~у** (*obs.*) to gain by the sword; **отда́ть ~у** (*obs.*) to surrender.
шпага́т, а *m.* **1.** string, cord; (*agric.*) binder twine. **2.** (*gymnastics*) the splits.
шпагоглота́тел|ь, я *m.* sword-swallower.
шпажи́ст, а *m.* épéeist.
шпа́жк|а, и *f.* (*cul.*) skewer.
шпа́жник, а *m.* (*bot.*) gladiolus.
шпак, а *m.* (*obs., pej.*) civilian.
шпакл|ева́ть, ю́ю, ю́ешь *impf.* (*of* **за~**) to fill, putty, stop (*holes*); (*naut.*) to caulk.
шпаклёвк|а, и *f.* **1.** filling, puttying, stopping up. **2.** putty.
шпа́л|а, ы *f.* (*rail.*) sleeper.
шпале́р|а, ы *f.* **1.** trellis, lattice-work. **2.** hedge, line of trees (*lining road*). **3.** (*mil.*) line (*of soldiers along ceremonial route*); **стоя́ть ~ами** to line the route. **4.** *pl.* (*obs.*) wall-paper.
шпан|а́, ы́ *f.* (*coll.*) hooligan, ruffian; (*also collect.*) rabble.
шпанго́ут, а *m.* (*tech.*) frame (*of aircraft*); ribs (*of ship*).
шпа́н|ка, ки *f.* **1.** black cherry. **2.** = **~ская му́шка**
шпа́нск|ий *adj.*: **~ая ви́шня** black cherry; **~ая му́шка** (*zool., med.*) Spanish fly, cantharides.
шпарга́лк|а, и *f.* (*coll.*) crib (*in school*).
шпа́р|ить, ю, ишь *impf.* (*of* **о~**) (*coll.*) **1.** to scald, pour boiling water on. **2.** to go, speak, read, *etc.*, in a rush.
шпат, а *m.* (*min.*) spar; **полево́й ш.** feldspar.
шпа́тел|ь, я *m.* **1.** (*tech., art*) palette-knife. **2.** (*med.*) spatula.
шпа́ци|я, и *f.* (*typ.*) space.
шпен|ёк, ька́ *m.* pin, peg, prong.
шпига́т, а *m.* (*naut.*) scupper.
шпиг|ова́ть, у́ю *impf.* (*of* **на~**) **1.** (*cul.*) to lard. **2.** (*coll.*): **ш. кого́-н.** to suggest to s.o., work upon s.o., put it into s.o.'s head.
шпик[1], а (у) *m.* (*cul.*) lard.
шпик[2], а́ *m.* (*coll.*) secret agent; plain-clothes detective.
шпил|ь, я *m.* **1.** spire, steeple. **2.** (*naut.*) capstan, windlass.
шпи́льк|а, и *f.* **1.** hairpin; hat-pin. **2.** (*tech.*) peg, dowel, cotter pin; tack, brad. **3.** (*fig.*) caustic remark; **подпусти́ть ~и (кому́-н.)** to get at, have a dig at (s.o.).
шпина́т, а *m.* spinach.
шпингале́т, а *m.* **1.** catch, latch (*of door or window*). **2.** (*coll.*) urchin, boy.
шпио́н, а *m.* spy.
шпиона́ж, а *m.* espionage.
шпио́н|ить, ю, ишь *impf.* (**за**+*i.*) to spy (on), engage in espionage.
шпио́н|ский *adj. of* ~
шпиц[1], а *m.* (*obs.*) spire, steeple.
шпиц[2], а *m.* Pomeranian (*dog*).
Шпицбе́рген, а *m.* Spitsbergen.
шплинт, а *m.* (*tech.*) split pin, cotter-pin.
шпон, а *m.* **1.** (*typ.*) lead. **2.** veneer sheet (*of wood*).
шпо́н|а, ы *f.* = ~
шпо́нк|а, и *f.* (*tech.*) bushing key, dowel.
шпо́р|а, ы *f.* spur; **дать ~ы** (*+d.*) to spur on.
шприц, а *m.* (*med.*) syringe.
шпро́т|ы, ~ *pl.* (*sg.* **~а, ~ы** *f. and* **~, ~а** *m.*) sprats.
шпу́льк|а, и *f.* spool, bobbin.
шпунт, а́ *m.* (*tech.*) groove, tongue, rabbet.

шпур, а *m.* (*min.*) blast-hole, bore-hole.
шпыня́|ть, ю *impf.* (*coll.*) to needle, nag.
шрам, а *m.* scar.
шрапне́л|ь, и *f.* shrapnel.
Шри-Ла́нк|а, и *f.* Sri Lanka.
шрифт, а, *pl.* **~ы́** *m.* **1.** type, type face; **курси́вный ш.** cursive; **прямо́й ш.** upright. **2.** script.
шрифт|ово́й *adj. of* ~
штаб, а, *pl.* **~ы́** *m.* (*mil.*) staff; headquarters.
шта́бел|ь, я, *pl.* **~я́, ~е́й** *m.* stack, pile.
штаби́ст, а *m.* (*coll.*) staff officer.
штаб-кварти́р|а, ы *f.* (*mil.*) headquarters.
штабни́к, а́ *m.* (*coll.*) staff officer.
штаб|но́й *adj. of* ~; **~на́я рабо́та** staff work; **~но́е подразделе́ние** headquarters unit.
штаб-офице́р, а *m.* (*mil., hist.*) officer of field rank.
штабс-капита́н, а *m.* (*hist.*; *in tsarist army*) staff-captain (*officer of rank intermediate between lieutenant and captain*).
штаг, а *m.* (*naut.*) stay.
штади́в, а *m.* (*abbr. of* **штаб диви́зий**) (*mil.*) divisional HQ.
штаке́тник, а *m.* fence, fencing.
шталме́йстер, а *m.* (*hist.*) equerry.
штамб, а *m.* (*bot.*) stem, trunk (*of tree*).
штамм, а *m.* (*biol.*) strain, breed.
штамп, а *m.* **1.** (*tech.*) die, punch. **2.** stamp, impress; letter-head. **3.** (*fig., pej.*) cliché, stock phrase.
штампова́льный *adj.* (*tech.*) punching, stamping, pressing.
штампо́в|анный *p.p.p. of* **~а́ть** *and adj.* **1.** (*tech.*) punched, stamped, pressed. **2.** (*fig.*) trite, hackneyed; stock, standard.
штамп|ова́ть, у́ю *impf.* **1.** (*tech.*) to punch, press. **2.** to stamp, die. **3.** (*fig.*) to carry out, go through mechanically; to rubber-stamp.
штампо́вк|а, и *f.* **1.** (*tech.*) punching, pressing; **горя́чая ш.** drop forging. **2.** (die-)stamping.
штампо́вщик, а *m.* puncher; stamp operator.
штамп-час|ы́, о́в *no sg.* time-clock.
шта́нг|а, и *f.* **1.** (*tech.*) bar, rod, beam. **2.** (*sport*) weight. **3.** (*sport*) post (*of goal*).
штангенци́ркул|ь, я *m.* (*tech.*) sliding callipers, slide gauge.
штанги́ст, а *m.* (*sport*) weight-lifter.
штанда́рт, а *m.* (*obs.*) standard.
штани́н|а, ы *f.* (*coll.*) trouser-leg.
штани́ш|ки, ек *no sg., dim. of* **штаны́**
штан|ы́, о́в *no sg.* trousers, breeches.
шта́пел|ь, я *m.* (*text.*) staple.
шта́пельный *adj.* (*text.*) staple.
штат[1]**, а** *m.* state (*administrative unit*); **Соединённые ~ы Аме́рики** United States of America.
штат[2]**, а** *m.* (*sg. or pl.*) staff, establishment; **~ы ми́рного вре́мени** peace-time establishment; **сокраще́ние ~ов** reduction of staff; **зачи́слить в ш.** to take on the staff, establish; **оста́ться за ~ом** (*i*) (*obs.*) to be disestablished, declared supernumerary, (*ii*) (*fig.*) to be superfluous.
штати́в, а *m.* tripod, base, support, stand.
шта́т|ный *adj. of* ~[2]; **~ная до́лжность** established post; **ш. рабо́тник** permanent member of staff; **~ное расписа́ние** list of members of staff.
шта́тск|ий *adj.* civilian; **~ое (пла́тье)** civilian clothes, civvies, mufti; *as n.* **ш., ~ого** *m.* civilian.
штафи́рк|а, и *m.* (*coll., pej.*) civilian, civvy.
ште́в|ень, ня *m.* (*naut.*) stem- or stern-post.
ште́йгер, а *m.* foreman miner.
штемпел|ева́ть, ю́ю, ю́ешь *impf.* (*of* **за~**) to stamp; to frank, postmark.
ште́мпел|ь, я, *pl.* **~я́** *m.* stamp; **почто́вый ш.** postmark.
ште́мпель|ный *adj. of* ~
ште́псел|ь, я, *pl.* **~я́** *m.* (*electr.*) plug, socket.
ште́псель|ный *adj. of* ~; **~ная ви́лка** plug; **~ная розе́тка** socket.
штибле́т|ы, ~ *pl.* (*sg.* **~а, ~ы** *f.*) **1.** (*lace-up*) boots, shoes. **2.** (*obs.*) gaiters.
штил|ево́й *adj. of* **~ь**
штил|ь, я *m.* (*naut.*) calm.
штифт, а́ *m.* (*tech.*) (joint-)pin, dowel, sprig.
шток, а *m.* **1.** (*tech.*) (coupling) rod; **ш. по́ршня** piston rod. **2.** (*geol.*) stock, shoot.
штокро́з|а, ы *f.* (*bot.*) hollyhock.
што́льн|я, и, *g. pl.* **што́лен** *f.* (*mining*) gallery.
што́пальный *adj.* darning.
што́па|ть, ю *impf.* (*of* **за~**) to darn.
што́пк|а, и *f.* **1.** darning; **худо́жественная ш.** invisible mending. **2.** darning thread, wool. **3.** (*coll.*) darn (*darned place*).
што́пор, а *m.* **1.** corkscrew. **2.** (*aeron.*) spin; **~ом** (*as adv.*) in a spin.
што́пор|ить, ю, ишь *impf.* (*aeron.*) to descend in a spin.
што́р|а, ы *f.* blind.
шторм, а *m.* (*naut.*) strong gale (*wind force 9*); **си́льный ш.** whole gale (*wind force 10*); **жесто́кий ш.** storm (*wind force 11*).
шторм|ова́ть, у́ет *impf.* (*naut.*) to ride out a storm.
штормо́вк|а, и *f.* anorak; parka.
шторм|ово́й *adj. of* ~; **ве́тер ~ово́й си́лы** gale-force wind; **ш. костю́м** weatherproof clothing.
штормтра́п, а *m.* (*naut.*) Jacob's ladder.
што́р|ный *adj. of* **~а**
штоф[1]**, а** *m.* shtof (*old Russ. unit of liquid measure, equivalent to 1.23 litres, or bottle of this measure*).
штоф[2]**, а** *m.* (*text.*) damask, brocade.
што́ф|ный[1] *adj. of* ~[1]; **~ная ла́вка** drinking-shop.
што́ф|ный[2] *adj. of* ~[2]
штраф, а *m.* fine; **взима́ть ш. (с+***g.***)** to fine; **наложи́ть ш.** to impose a fine.
штрафба́т, а *m.* (*abbr. of* **штрафно́й батальо́н**) (*mil.*) penal battalion.
штрафни́к, а́ *m.* (*coll.*) soldier in the 'glasshouse'.
штраф|но́й *adj.* **1.** *adj. of* **~. 2.** penal, penalty; **ш. батальо́н** (*mil.*) penal battalion; **ш. журна́л** (*obs.*) penalties book; **~на́я пло́щадка** (*sport*) penalty area; **ш. уда́р** (*sport*) penalty kick.
штраф|ова́ть, у́ю *impf.* (*of* **о~**) to fine.
штрейкбре́хер, а *m.* strike-breaker, blackleg.
штрейкбре́херств|о, а *nt.* strike-breaking, blacklegging.
штрек, а *m.* (*mining*) drift.
штрих, а́ *m.* **1.** stroke (*in drawing*); hachure (*on map*). **2.** (*fig.*) feature, trait.
штрих|ова́ть, у́ю *impf.* (*of* **за~**) to shade, hatch.
штрих|ово́й *adj. of* ~; **ш. рису́нок** line drawing; **ш. пункти́р** dash line.
штуди́р|овать, ую *impf.* (*of* **про~**) to study.
шту́к|а, и *f.* **1.** item, one of a kind (*oft. not translated*); **по рублю́ ш.** one rouble each; **пять ~ яиц** five eggs; **я возьму́ шесть ~** I'll have six (*of item in question*). **2.** piece (*of cloth, fabric*). **3.** (*coll.*) thing; **вот так ш.!** well I'll be damned! **4.** (*coll.*) trick; **сыгра́ть ~у** to play a trick; **не ш.** it's not too hard; it doesn't take much. **5.** (*sl.*) grand, thou.
штука́р|ь, я́ *m.* (*coll.*) joker; rogue.
штукату́р, а *m.* plasterer.
штукату́р|ить, ю, ишь *impf.* (*of* **о~** *and* **от~**) to plaster.
штукату́рк|а, и *f.* **1.** plastering. **2.** plaster. **3.** stucco.
штукату́р|ный *adj. of* **~ка**
штук|ова́ть, у́ю *impf.* **1.** to mend invisibly. **2.** (*sl.*) to chain-smoke.
штуко́вин|а, ы *f.* (*coll.*) thingumajig, thingummy; gizmo.
штурва́л, а *m.* steering-wheel; controls; **стоя́ть за ~ом** to be at the wheel, helm, controls.
штурва́л|ьный *adj. of* ~; *as n.* **ш., ~ьного** *m.* helmsman, pilot.
штурм, а *m.* (*mil.*) storm, assault.
шту́рман, а, *pl.* **~ы** *and* **~а́** *m.* (*naut., aeron.*) navigator.
шту́рман|ский *adj. of* ~; **~ская ру́бка** (*naut.*) chart house.
штурм|ова́ть, у́ю *impf.* to storm, assault.
штурмови́к, а́ *m.* low-flying attack aircraft.
штурмо́вк|а, и *f.* low-flying air attack.
штурм|ово́й *adj. of* ~ *and* **~о́вка; ~ова́я авиа́ция** ground support aircraft; **~овы́е де́йствия** ground support action; **~ова́я ле́стница** (*hist.*) scaling ladder; **~ова́я ло́дка** assault craft; **~ова́я полоса́** assault course; **ш. самолёт = ~ови́к**

штурмовщи́н|а, ы *f.* (*pej.*) rushed work, production spurt, sporadic effort.
штуф, а *m.* (*min.*) piece of ore.
шту́цер, а, *pl.* **~а́** *m.* **1.** carbine. **2.** (*tech.*) connecting pipe.
шту́чн|ый *adj.* (by the) piece; **ш. пол** parquet floor; **~ая рабо́та** piece-work; **ш. това́р** goods sold by the piece (*and not by weight*); **ш. хлеб** bread rolls.
штык, а́ *m.* **1.** bayonet; **идти́ в ~и́** to fight at bayonet point; **встре́тить, приня́ть в ~и́** (*fig.*) to give a hostile reception (to), oppose adamantly. **2.** (*mil.*) man, soldier. **3.** (*naut.*) bend. **4.** spade's depth. **5.** (*min.*) bar, ingot.
штык|ово́й *adj. of* **~; ш. уда́р** bayonet thrust.
штыр|ь, я́ *m.* (*tech.*) pin, dowel, pintle.
шу́б|а, ы *f.* fur coat.
шу́б|ный *adj.* **1.** *adj. of* **~а. 2.** fur-bearing. **3.: ш. клей** (*obs.*) carpenter's glue.
шуг|а́, и́ *f.* sludge ice.
шуг|а́ть, а́ю *impf.* (*of* **~ну́ть**) (*coll.*) to scare off.
шуг|ну́ть, ну́, нёшь *pf. of* **~а́ть**
шу́йц|а, ы *f.* (*arch.*) left hand.
шу́лер, а, *pl.* **~а́** *m.* card-sharper, cheat.
шу́лер|ский *adj. of* **~**
шу́лерств|о, а *nt.* card-sharping, sharp practice.
шум, а (у) *m.* **1.** noise. **2.** din, uproar, racket; **подня́ть ш.** to kick up a racket. **3.** (*fig.*) sensation, stir. **4.** (*med.*) murmur; **ш. се́рдца** cardiac murmur.
шум|е́ть, лю́, и́шь *impf.* **1.** to make a noise. **2.** (*coll.*) to row, wrangle. **3.** (*coll.*) to make a stir, fuss, to cause a sensation, stir.
шуми́х|а, и *f.* (*coll.*) sensation, stir.
шумли́в|ый (~, ~а) *adj.* noisy.
шу́м|ный (~ен, ~на́, ~но) *adj.* **1.** noisy; loud. **2.** sensational.
шумови́к, а́ *m.* (*theatr.*) sound effects man.
шумо́вк|а, и *f.* (*cul.*) perforated spoon, straining ladle.
шум|ово́й *adj. of* **~; ш. орке́стр** percussion band; **ш. фон** (*radio*) background noise; **~овы́е эффе́кты** sound effects.
шум|о́к, ка́ *m.* (*coll.*) noise; **под ш.** on the quiet.
шу́р|ин, ина, *pl.* **~ья́, ~ьёв** *m.* brother-in-law (*wife's brother*).
шур|ова́ть, у́ю *impf.* to stoke, poke (*a furnace*).
шуру́п, а *m.* (*tech.*) screw.
шурф, а *m.* (*mining*) prospecting shaft.
шурф|ова́ть, у́ю *impf.* (*mining*) to excavate, make a prospecting dig.
шурш|а́ть, у́, и́шь *impf.* to rustle (*also* +*i.*, *trans.*), crackle.
шу́ры-му́ры *pl. indecl.* (*coll.*) love affair(s).
шу́ст|рый (~ёр, ~ра́, ~ро) *adj.* (*coll.*) smart, bright, sharp.
шут, а́ *m.* **1.** (*hist.*) fool, jester. **2.** fool, buffoon, clown; **разыгра́ть ~а́** to play the fool. **3.** (*coll.*) *in certain phrr.* devil; **на кой ш.?, како́го ~а?** why the devil?
шу|ти́ть, чу́, ~тишь *impf.* (*of* **по~**) **1.** to joke, jest; **я же не ~чу́** but I'm not joking; **чем чёрт не ~тит!** (*coll.*) we can but see (what will happen)! **2. (с**+*i.*) to play (with), trifle (with); **ш. с огнём** to play with fire. **3. (над)** to laugh (at), make fun (of).
шути́х|а, и *f.* **1.** *f. of* **шут. 2.** firecracker, rocket.
шу́тк|а, и *f.* **1.** joke, jest; **не ш.** it's no joke; **ш. (ли)** +*inf.* it's not so easy, it's no laughing matter (to); **с ней ~и пло́хи** she is not to be trifled with; **~и в сто́рону, ~и прочь** let's get down to business; **без шу́ток** joking apart; **сказа́ть в ~у** to say as a joke; **не на ~у** in earnest. **2.** trick; **сыгра́ть ~у (с**+*i.*) to play a trick (on). **3.** (*theatr.*) farce.
шутли́в|ый (~, ~а) *adj.* **1.** humorous. **2.** joking, light-hearted.
шутни́к, а́ *m.* joker, wag.
шут|овско́й *adj. of* **шут; ш. колпа́к** fool's cap; **~овски́е вы́ходки** clowning, buffoonery.
шутовств|о́, а́ *nt.* buffoonery.
шу́точ|ный (~ен, ~на) *adj.* comic; joking; **де́ло не ~ное** it's no joke, no laughing matter.
шут|я́ *pres. ger. of* **~и́ть** *and adv.* **1.** easily, lightly; **ш. отде́латься** to get off lightly. **2.** for fun, in jest; **не ш.** in earnest.
шу́шер|а, ы *f.* (*coll.*) rubbish; riff-raff.
шушу́ка|ться, юсь *impf.* (*coll.*) to whisper; (*fig.*) to gossip.
шхе́р|ный *adj. of* **~ы**
шхе́р|ы, ~ *no sg.* (*geog.*) skerries.
шху́н|а, ы *f.* schooner.
ш-ш *int.* ssh!; (s)hush!

Щ

щаве́л|евый *adj.* **1.** *adj. of* **~ь. 2.** (*chem.*) oxalic; **соль ~евой кислоты́** oxalate.
щаве́л|ь, я́ *m.* (*bot.*) sorrel (*Rumex*).
щаве́льник, а *m.* (*coll.*) sorrel soup.
ща|ди́ть, жу́, ди́шь *impf.* (*of* **по~**) to spare; to have mercy (on); **щ. чьи-н. чу́вства** to spare s.o.'s feelings; **не щ. враго́в** to give one's enemies no quarter.
щебёнк|а, и *f.* = **щё́бень**
щё́б|ень, ня *m.* **1.** crushed stone, ballast (*as road surfacing*). **2.** (*geol.*) detritus.
щё́бет, а *m.* twitter, chirp.
щебета́ни|е, я *nt.* twittering, chirping.
щебе|та́ть, чу́, ~чешь *impf.* to twitter, chirp.
щегл|ёнок, ёнка, *pl.* **~я́та, ~я́т** *m.* **1.** young goldfinch. **2.** = **щего́л**
щег|о́л, ла́ *m.* goldfinch.
щеголева́т|ый (~, ~а) *adj.* foppish, dandified.
щёгол|ь, я *m.* fop, dandy.
щегол|ьну́ть, ьну́, ьнёшь *pf. of* **~я́ть 2.**
щегольско́й *adj.* foppish, dandified.
щегольств|о́, а́ *nt.* foppishness, dandyism.
щегол|я́ть, я́ю *impf.* **1.** to dress ultra-fashionably, foppishly; to strut around. **2.** (*pf.* **~ьну́ть**) (+*i.*; *coll.*) to show off, parade, flaunt.
ще́дрост|ь, и *f.* generosity.
щедро́т|ы, ~ *pl.* (*sg.* **~а, ~ы** *f.*) (*obs.*) munificence; **подари́ть от свои́х ~** (*iron.*) to donate generously.
ще́др|ый (~, ~а́, ~о) *adj.* **1.** generous. **2.** lavish, liberal; **щ. на похвалы́** lavish in praises.
щек|а́, и́, *a.* **~у,** *pl.* **~и, ~, ~а́м** *f.* **1.** cheek; **уда́рить кого́-н. по ~е́** to slap s.o.'s face; **упи́сывать, уплета́ть за о́бе ~и́** (*coll.*) to eat ravenously, guzzle. **2.** (*tech.*) side, sidepiece, stock.
щеко́лд|а, ы *f.* latch; catch, pawl.
щеко|та́ть, чу́, ~чешь *impf.* (*of* **по~**) **1.** to tickle (*also fig.*). **2.** (*impers.*): **у меня́ в го́рле,** *etc.*, **~чет** I have a tickle in my throat, *etc.*
щеко́тк|а, и *f.* tickling; **боя́ться ~и** to be ticklish.
щекотли́в|ый (~, ~а) *adj.* **1.** ticklish, delicate; **~ая те́ма** delicate topic. **2.** (*obs.*) = **щепети́льный**
щеко́тно *as pred.* (*impers.*; +*i.*) it tickles.
щел|ево́й *adj.* **1.** *adj. of* **~ь. 2.** = **~и́нный**
щели́нный *adj.* (*ling.*) fricative.
щели́ст|ый (~, ~а) *adj.* (*coll.*) full of chinks.
щёлк, а *m.* snap, crack.
щёлк|а, и *f.* chink.
щёлкань|е, я *nt.* **1.** flicking. **2.** clicking, snapping, cracking, popping. **3.** trilling (*of some birds*).
щёлк|ать, аю *impf.* (*of* **~нуть**) **1.** to flick. **2.** (+*i.*) to click, snap, crack, pop; **щ. затво́ром** to click the shutter (*of a camera*); **щ. па́льцами** to snap one's fingers; **щ. кнуто́м** to crack a whip. **3.** (*impf. only*) to crack (*nuts*). **4.** (*impf. only*) to trill (*of some birds*).
щёлк|нуть, ну, нешь *pf. of* **~ать**
щелкопёр, а *m.* (*obs.*, *pej.*) scribbler, hack.
щелку́нчик, а *nt.* nutcracker.

щёлок, а *m.* alkaline solution, lye.
щелочно́й *adj.* (*chem.*) alkaline.
щёлочност|ь, и *f.* (*chem.*) alkalinity.
щёлоч|ь, и, *pl.* **~и, ~е́й** *f.* (*chem.*) alkali.
щелч|о́к, ка́ *m.* **1.** flick (of the fingers). **2.** (*fig., coll.*) insult, slight, blow.
щел|ь, и, *pl.* **∠и, ~е́й** *f.* **1.** crack; chink; slit; fissure, crevice. **2.** (*mil.*) slit trench. **3.: голосова́я щ.** (*anat.*) glottis.
щем|и́ть, и́т *impf.* **1.** (*coll.*) to press, pinch. **2.** to oppress, grieve (*also impers*).
щем|я́щий *pres. part. act. of* **~и́ть** *and adj.* **1.** aching, nagging; **~я́щая боль** ache. **2.** (*fig.*) painful, melancholy, oppressive.
щен|и́ться, и́тся *impf.* (*of* **о~**) to whelp, cub.
щен|о́к, ка́, *pl.* **~ки́, ~ко́в** *and* **~я́та, ~я́т** *m.* puppy, pup (*also fig.*); whelp, cub.
щеп|а́, ы́, *pl.* **∠ы, ~, ~а́м** *f.* (*wood*) splinter, chip; (*collect.*) kindling.
щеп|а́ть, лю́, ∠лешь *impf.* to chip, chop (*wood*).
щепети́л|ьный (~ен, ~ьна) *adj.* punctilious, correct; (over-)scrupulous, fussy, finicky.
ще́пк|а, и *f.* = **щепа́; худо́й как щ.** thin as a rake; **лес ру́бят — ~и летя́т** (*prov.*) you can't make omelettes without breaking eggs.
щепо́т|ка, ки *f.* = **ще́по́ть**
ще́по́т|ь, и *f.* pinch (*of salt, snuff, etc.*).
щерба́т|ый (~, ~а) *adj.* **1.** dented; chipped. **2.** (*coll.*) pock-marked. **3.** (*coll.*) gap-toothed.
щерби́н|а, ы *f.* **1.** indentation; gap, hole. **2.** pock-mark.
щети́н|а, ы *f.* bristle; (*coll.*) stubble (*of beard*).
щети́нист|ый (~, ~а) *adj.* bristly, bristling; (*coll.*) stubble-covered.
щети́н|иться, ится *impf.* (*of* **о~**) to bristle (*also fig.*).
щётк|а, и *f.* **1.** brush (*also electr.*); **зубна́я щ.** toothbrush; **щ. для воло́с** hairbrush. **2.** fetlock.
щёт|очный *adj. of* **~ка; щ. па́лец** (*elec.*) brush-holder arm.
щёчный *adj. of* **щека́**
щи, щей (*coll.* **щец**), **щам, ща́ми, о щах** *no sg.* shchi (*cabbage soup*); **попа́сть как кур во́ щи** to get into hot water.
щи́колотк|а, и *f.* ankle.
щип|а́ть, лю́, ∠лешь *impf.* **1.** (*pf.* **~ну́ть**) to pinch, nip, tweak. **2.** (*impf. only*) to sting, bite (*of frost, etc.*); to burn (*of condiments, hot liquids, etc.*). **3.** (*impf. only*) to nibble, munch, browse (on). **4.** (*pf.* **об~** *and* **о~**) to pluck.
щип|а́ться, лю́сь, ∠лешься *impf.* (*coll.*) **1.** to pinch (each other). **2.** *pass. of* **~а́ть**
щип|е́ц, ца́ *m.* **1.** (*archit.*) gable. **2.** (*hunting*) muzzle (*of dog*).
щипко́в|ый *adj.*: **~ые музыка́льные инструме́нты** (*mus.*) stringed instruments played by plucking.
щипко́м *adv.* (*mus.*) pizzicato.
щип|ну́ть, ну́, нёшь *pf. of* **~а́ть 1.**
щип|о́к, ка́ *m.* pinch, nip, tweak.
щипц|ы́, о́в *no sg.* tongs, pincers, pliers; forceps; **щ. для зави́вки воло́с** curling-irons; **щ. для са́хара** sugar-tongs.
щи́пчик|и, ов *no sg.* tweezers.
щит, а́ *m.* **1.** (*in var. senses*) shield; **подня́ть на щ.** to extol, eulogize, boost; **верну́ться на ~е́** to suffer defeat; **верну́ться со ~о́м** to be triumphant, victorious. **2.** (*tech.*) shield, screen. **3.** sluice-gate. **4.** (*zool.*) (tortoise-)shell; scutum. **5.** (display) board. **6.** (*tech.*) panel; **распредели́тельный щ.** switchboard.
щитови́дный *adj.* (*anat.*) thyroid.
щит|о́к, ка́ *m.* **1.** *dim. of* **~ 2.–6.**; dashboard (*of motor vehicle*). **2.** (*zool.*) thorax. **3.** (*bot.*) cyme, corymb. **4.** (*sport*) shin-pad.
щу́к|а, и *f.* pike (*fish*).
щуп, а *m.* (*tech.*) **1.** probe, sounding borer. **2.** (*mil.*) probing rod (*in mine detection*). **3.** clearance gauge. **4.** (*coll.*) dipstick.
щу́пальц|е, а, *g. pl.* **щу́палец** *nt.* (*zool.*) tentacle; antenna.
щу́па|ть, ю *impf.* (*of* **по~**) to feel (for), touch; to probe; **щ. глаза́ми** to scan; **щ. пульс** (*med.*) to feel the pulse.
щу́пл|ый (~, ~а́, ~о) *adj.* weak, puny, frail.
щур[1]**, а** *m.* (*ethnol.*) ancestor.
щур[2]**, а́** *m.* (*zool.*) pine grosbeak.
щу́р|ить, ю, ишь *impf.* (*of* **со~**); **щ. глаза́ = ~иться**
щу́р|иться, юсь, ишься *impf.* (*of* **со~**) **1.** to screw up one's eyes. **2.** (*of the eyes*) to narrow.
щу́рк|а, и *f.* (*zool.*) bee-eater.
щу́|чий *adj. of* **~ка; как по ~чьему веле́нью** as if of its own volition; as if by magic.

Э

эбе́новый *adj.* ebony.
э́ва[1] *particle* (*coll. or dial.*) there is, here is.
э́ва[2] *int.* (*coll.*) **1.** (*expr. surprise, incredulity, etc.*) what's that!; you don't mean to say so! **2.** (*expr. disagreement*) nonsense!
эвако... *comb. form, abbr. of* **эвакуацио́нный**
эвакуацио́нный *adj. of* **эвакуа́ция; э. пункт** evacuation centre; **э. райо́н** evacuation area.
эвакуа́ци|я, и *f.* evacuation.
эвакуи́ров|анный *p.p.p. of* **~ать**; *as n.* **э., ~анного** *m.*, **~анная, ~анной** *f.* evacuee.
эвакуи́р|овать, ую *impf. and pf.* to evacuate (*trans.*).
эвакуи́р|оваться, уюсь *impf. and pf.* **1.** to evacuate (*intrans.*). **2.** *pass. of* **~овать**
эвентуа́л|ьный (~ен, ~ьна) *adj.* possible.
Эвере́ст, а *m.* (Mt.) Everest.
эвкали́пт, а *m.* (*bot.*) eucalyptus.
эвкали́пт|овый *adj. of* **~; ~овое ма́сло** eucalyptus oil.
ЭВМ *f. indecl.* (*abbr. of* ***электро́нно-вычисли́тельная маши́на***) computer; **больша́я Э.** mainframe computer; **сверхбольша́я Э., су́пер-ЭВМ** supercomputer; **персона́льная Э.** personal computer.
эволюциони́р|овать, ую *impf. and pf.* to evolve.
эволюциони́ст, а *m.* evolutionist.
эволюцио́нн|ый *adj.* evolutionary; **~ое уче́ние** (*biol.*) doctrine of evolution.
эволю́ци|я, и *f.* **1.** evolution. **2.** (*mil.*) manœuvre.
эвфеми́зм, а *m.* euphemism.
эвфемисти́ческий *adj.* euphemistic.
эвфони́ческий *adj.* euphonious.
эвфони́|я, и *f.* euphony.
Эге́йск|ое мо́р|е, ~ого ~я *nt.* the Aegean Sea; the Aegean.
эги́д|а, ы *f.* aegis; **под ~ой** (+*g.*) under the aegis (of).
эгои́зм, а *m.* egoism, selfishness.
эгои́ст, а *m.* egoist.
эгоисти́ческий *adj.* egoistic, selfish.
эгоисти́ч|ный (~ен, ~на) *adj.* = **~еский**
эготи́зм, а *m.* egotism.
эгре́т, а *m.* egret-plume.
э́дак(ий) = э́так(ий)
эдельве́йс, а *m.* (*bot.*) edelweiss.
Эде́м, а *m.* (*bibl.*) Eden.
эде́мский *adj.* (*bibl.*): **сад Эде́мский** the Garden of Eden.
Э́динбург, а *m.* Edinburgh.
эдинбу́ргский *adj.* Edinburgh.
эди́пов *adj.*: **э. ко́мплекс** (*psych.*) Oedipus complex.
эзо́пов = ~ский
эзо́повский *adj.* Aesopian; **э. язы́к** 'Aesopian language' (*esp. of allegorical language used by Russ. non-conformist publicists to conceal anti-régime sentiments*).
эй *int.* heigh!; hi!
Э́йре *nt. indecl.* Eire.

эйтана́зи|я, и *f.* euthanasia.
Э́йфелев|а ба́шн|я, ~ой ~и *f.* the Eiffel Tower.
эйфори́|я, и *f.* euphoria.
эк (*and* **э́ко, э́ка**) *particle* (*coll.*) *expr. surprise, indignation, etc.*, my goodness!
Эквадо́р, а *m.* Ecuador.
эквадо́р|ец, ца *m.* Ecuadorian.
эквадо́р|ка, ки *f. of* **~ец**
эквадо́рский *adj.* Ecuadorian.
эква́тор, а *m.* equator.
экваториа́льный *adj.* equatorial.
эквивале́нт, а *m.* equivalent.
эквивале́нт|ный (~ен, ~на) *adj.* equivalent.
эквилибри́ст, а *m.* tightrope-walker.
эквилибри́стик|а, и *f.* tightrope-walking (*also fig.*).
экз. (*abbr. of* **экземпля́р**) copy.
экзальта́ци|я, и *f.* exaltation; excitement.
экзальтиро́ван|ный (~, ~на) *adj.* in a state of exaltation, exalté, excited.
экза́мен, а *m.* examination; **держа́ть, сдава́ть э.** to take, sit an examination; **вы́держать, сдать э.** to pass an examination; **провали́ться на ~е** to fail an examination; **э. на вожде́ние** driving test.
экзамена́тор, а *m.* examiner.
экзамен|ацио́нный *adj. of* **экза́мен; э. биле́т** examination question(-paper); **~ацио́нная се́ссия** examination period, exams.
экзамен|ова́ть, у́ю *impf.* (*of* **про~**) to examine.
экзамен|ова́ться, у́юсь *impf.* (*of* **про~**) **1.** to go in for an examination. **2.** *pass. of* **~ова́ть**
экзамен|у́ющийся *pres. part. of* **~ова́ться**; *as n.* **э., ~у́ющегося** *m.* examinee.
экза́рх, а *m.* (*eccl.*) exarch.
экзарха́т, а *m.* (*eccl.*) exarchate.
экзеку́тор, а *m.* (*obs.*) administrator.
экзеку́ци|я, и *f.* (*obs.*) **1.** corporal punishment. **2.** (*leg.*) execution.
экзе́м|а, ы *f.* (*med.*) eczema.
экземпля́р, а *m.* **1.** copy; **в двух, трёх ~ах** in duplicate, in triplicate; **переписа́ть в двух ~ах** to make two copies; **резе́рвный э.** (*comput.*) backup (copy). **2.** specimen, example.
экзистенциали́зм, а *m.* existentialism.
экзистенциали́ст, а *m.* existentialist.
экзо... *comb. form* exo-.
экзо́тик|а, и *f.* exotica, exotic objects.
экзоти́ческий *adj.* exotic.
экиво́к|и, ов *pl.* (*sg.* **~, ~а** *m.*) **1.** double entendre. **2.** quibbling, evasion, hedging; **говори́ть без ~ов** to call a spade a spade. **3.** subtleties, intricacies.
э́кий *pron.* (*coll.*) what (a).
экипа́ж[1], **а** *m.* carriage.
экипа́ж[2], **а** *m.* crew (*of ship, aircraft, tank*); ship's company.
экипир|ова́ть, у́ю *impf. and pf.* to equip.
экипиро́вк|а, и *f.* **1.** equipping. **2.** equipment.
э́ккер, а *m.* (*geod.*) cross-staff (*instrument for erecting a perpendicular*).
эклекти́зм, а *m.* eclecticism.
экле́ктик, а *m.* eclectic.
эклекти́ч|ный (~ен, ~на) *adj.* eclectic.
экли́птик|а, и *f.* (*astron.*) ecliptic.
эклóг|а, и *f.* (*liter.*) eclogue.
э́ко *see* **эк**[2]
эко... *comb. form* eco-.
экологи́ческий *adj.* ecological.
эколо́ги|я, и *f.* ecology.
эконо́м, а *m.* (*obs.*) **1.** steward, housekeeper. **2.** economist.
эконома́йзер, а *m.* (*tech.*) economiser, waste gas heater.
экономи́зм, а *m.* (*hist., pol.*) economism.
эконо́мик|а, и *f.* **1.** economics. **2.** economy (*of a country, etc.*).
экономи́ст, а *m.* economist.
эконо́м|ить, лю, ишь *impf.* (*of* **с~**) **1.** to use sparingly, husband; to save. **2.** (**на**+*p.*) to economise (on), save (on).
экономи́ческ|ий *adj.* economic; **э. райо́н** economic region; **э. журна́л** economics journal; **~ая горе́лка** pilot burner; **~ая ско́рость** cruising speed.
экономи́ч|ный (~ен, ~на) *adj.* economical.
эконо́ми|я, и *f.* **1.** economy, saving; **режи́м ~и** economy effort; **соблюда́ть ~ю** to economize. **2.: полити́ческая э.** political economy. **3.** (*obs.*) estate.
эконо́мк|а, и *f.* housekeeper.
эконо́мнича|ть, ю *impf.* (*coll.*) to be (excessively) economical.
эконо́м|ный (~ен, ~на) *adj.* economical; careful, thrifty.
экосисте́м|а, ы *f.* ecosystem.
ЭКОСО́С *m. indecl.* (*abbr. of* ***Экономи́ческий и Социа́льный Сове́т ООН***) ECOSOC (*Economic and Social Council*).
экра́н, а *m.* **1.** (*cinema*) screen. **2.** (*fig.*) screen (= *cinema industry, cinema art*). **3.** (*phys., tech.*) screen, shield, shade.
экраниза́ци|я, и *f.* (*cinema.*) filming, screening; film version (*of novel, etc.*).
экранизи́р|овать, ую *impf. and pf.* (*cinema*) to film, screen.
экрани́р|овать, ую *impf. and pf.* (*tech.*) to screen, shield.
экра́нн|ый *adj.* (*comput.*) on-screen; **~ая гра́фика** on-screen graphics.
экс-... *pref.* ex-.
экскава́тор, а *m.* (*tech.*) excavator, earth-moving machine.
экскава́торщик, а *m.* excavator operator.
экскреме́нт|ы, ов *no sg.* excrement.
э́кскурс, а *m.* excursus, digression.
экскурса́нт, а *m.* tourist; participant in (conducted) tour *or* excursion.
экскурс|ио́нный *adj. of* **~ия**
экску́рси|я, и *f.* **1.** excursion, (conducted) tour, trip; outing. **2.** tourist group, excursion party.
экскурсово́д, а *m.* guide.
экслибрис, а *m.* book-plate.
экспанси́в|ный (~ен, ~на) *adj.* effusive.
экспансиони́зм, а *m.* (*pol.*) expansionism.
экспа́нси|я, и *f.* (*pol.*) expansion.
экспеди́р|овать, ую *impf. and pf.* to dispatch.
экспеди́тор, а *m.* **1.** forwarding agent, shipping clerk. **2.** (*obs.*) head clerk (*head of a section in a large office*).
экспедицио́нный *adj.* **1.** dispatch, forwarding. **2.** expeditionary.
экспеди́ци|я, и *f.* **1.** dispatch, forwarding. **2.** dispatch office. **3.** (*obs.*) section, department (*of an office*). **4.** expedition.
экспериме́нт, а *m.* experiment.
эксперимента́льный *adj.* experimental.
эксперимента́тор, а *m.* experimenter.
эксперименти́р|овать, ую *impf.* (**над, с**+*i.*) to experiment (on, with).
экспе́рт, а *m.* expert.
эксперти́з|а, ы *f.* (*leg., med.*) **1.** (*expert*) examination, expert opinion; **э. на СПИД** AIDS test; **произвести́ ~у** to make an examination. **2.** commission of experts.
экспе́рт|ный *adj. of* **~; ~ная коми́ссия** commission of experts.
эксплози́вный *adj.* (*ling.*) plosive.
эксплуата́тор, а *m.* exploiter.
эксплуатац|ио́нный *adj. of* **~ия 2.; ~ио́нные ка́чества** operating characteristics; **~ио́нные расхо́ды** running costs; **~ио́нные усло́вия** working conditions.
эксплуата́ци|я, и *f.* **1.** (*pol.*; *pej.*) exploitation. **2.** exploitation (*econ.*); utilization; operation, running; **сдать в ~ю** to commission, put into operation.
эксплуати́р|овать, ую *impf.* **1.** (*pol.*; *pej.*) to exploit. **2.** to exploit (*econ.*); to operate, run, work.
экспози́ци|я, и *f.* **1.** layout (*of an exhibition, etc.*). **2.** (*liter.*) exposition. **3.** (*phot.*) exposure.
экспона́т, а *m.* exhibit.
экспоне́нт, а *m.* **1.** exhibitor. **2.** (*math.*) exponent, index.
экспони́р|овать, ую *impf. and pf.* **1.** to exhibit. **2.** (*phot.*) to expose.
экспоно́метр, а *m.* (*phot.*) exposure meter.
э́кспорт, а *m.* export.
экспортёр, а *m.* exporter.
экспорти́р|овать, ую *impf. and pf.* to export.
э́кспорт|ный *adj. of* **~**
экспре́сс, а *m.* express (*train, motor coach, etc.*).
экспресси́в|ный (~ен, ~на) *adj.* expressive.

экспрессиони́зм, а *m.* (*art*) expressionism.
экспре́сси|я, и *f.* expression.
экспре́сс|ный *adj.* *of* ~
экспро́мт, а *m.* impromptu, improvisation, extemporisation.
экспро́мтом *adv.* **1.** impromptu; **петь, игра́ть,** *etc.*, **э.** to extemporize, improvise. **2.** suddenly, without warning.
экспроприа́тор, а *m.* expropriator.
экспроприа́ци|я, и *f.* expropriation.
экспроприи́р|овать, ую *impf.* *and* *pf.* to expropriate, dispossess.
экста́з, а *m.* ecstasy.
экстенси́в|ный (~ен, ~на) *adj.* extensive.
экстéрн, а *m.* **1.** external student; **око́нчить университе́т ~ом** to take an external degree. **2.** (*obs.*) externe (*unpaid hospital doctor*).
экстерна́т, а *m.* external studies.
экстерриториа́льност|ь, и *f.* extraterritoriality, exterritoriality.
экстерриториа́л|ьный (~ен, ~ьна) *adj.* extraterritorial, exterritorial.
экстерье́р, а *m.* form, figure (*of an animal*).
экстирпа́ци|я, и *f.*: **э. ма́тки** hysterectomy.
экстравага́нт|ный (~ен, ~на) *adj.* eccentric, bizarre, preposterous.
экстраги́р|овать, ую *impf.* *and* *pf.* (*chem.*, *med.*) to extract.
экстради́ци|я, и *f.* (*leg.*) extradition.
экстра́кт, а *m.* **1.** (*cul.*) extract. **2.** résumé, précis.
экстра́кци|я, и *f.* (*chem.*, *med.*) extraction.
экстраордина́р|ный (~ен, ~на) *adj.* extraordinary; **э. профе́ссор** (*obs.*) professor extraordinary.
экстрасе́нс, а *m.* psychic.
э́кстрен|ный (~, ~на) *adj.* **1.** urgent; emergency; **э. вы́зов** urgent summons; **в ~ном слу́чае** in case of emergency. **2.** extra, special; **~ное заседа́ние** extraordinary session; **~ное изда́ние** special edition.
эксце́нтрик[1]**, а** *m.* **1.** clown. **2.** (*obs.*) eccentric (*pers.*).
эксце́нтрик[2] *m.* (*tech.*) cam, eccentric.
эксце́нтрик|а, и *f.* clowning.
эксцентрисите́т, а *m.* (*tech.*) eccentricity.
эксцентри́ческий *adj.* (*tech.*) eccentric, off-centre.
эксцентри́чност|ь, и *f.* eccentricity.
эксцентри́ч|ный (~ен, ~на) *adj.* eccentric.
эксце́сс, а *m.* excess.
экумени́ческий *adj.* ecumenical, oecumenical.
экю́ *m.* *and* *nt.* *indecl.* écu.
эласти́ч|ный (~ен, ~на) *adj.* **1.** elastic (*also fig.*); **~ные брю́ки** stretch pants. **2.** (*fig.*) springy, resilient.
элева́тор, а *m.* **1.** (*agric.*) elevator. **2.** (*tech.*) hoist.
элега́нтност|ь, и *f.* elegance.
элега́нт|ный (~ен, ~на) *adj.* elegant, smart.
элеги́ческий *adj.* (*liter.*, *mus.*) elegiac.
элеги́ч|ный (~ен, ~на) *adj.* melancholy.
эле́ги|я, и *f.* (*liter.*, *mus.*) elegy.
электриза́ци|я, и *f.* (*phys.*, *med.*) electrification; treatment by electric charge(s).
электриз|ова́ть, у́ю *impf.* **1.** (*phys.*, *med.*) to electrify, subject to electric charge(s). **2.** (*fig.*) to electrify.
эле́ктрик, а *m.* electrician.
электри́к *adj.* *indecl.* electric blue.
электрифика́ци|я, и *f.* electrification.
электрифици́р|овать, ую *impf.* *and* *pf.* (*tech.*) to electrify.
электри́ческий *adj.* electric(al).
электри́честв|о, а *nt.* **1.** electricity. **2.** electric light; **заже́чь э.** to turn on the light.
электри́чк|а, и *f.* (*coll.*) (suburban) electric train.
электро... *comb. form* electro-, electric.
электробытов|о́й *adj.* electrical; **~ы́е прибо́ры** (electrical) household appliances.
электрово́з, а *m.* electric locomotive.
электро́д, а *m.* (*phys.*) electrode.
электродви́гател|ь, я *m.* electric motor.
электродви́жущий *adj.* (*phys.*) electromotive.
электродина́мик|а, и *f.* electrodynamics.
электродо́йльный *adj.* electric milking.
электродо́йк|а, и *f.* **1.** electric milking. **2.** electric milking machine.
электродугов|о́й *adj.*: **~а́я сва́рка** electric arc welding.
электроё́мкост|ь, и *f.* (*phys.*) capacity.
электрока́р, а *m.* electric trolley, float.
электрокардиостимуля́тор, а *m.* (*med.*) pacemaker (*device*).
электрола́мп|а, ы *f.* electric light bulb.
электролече́ни|е, я *nt.* (*med.*) electrical treatment.
электро́лиз, а *m.* (*phys.*) electrolysis.
электромагни́т, а *m.* electromagnet.
электромагни́тный *adj.* electromagnetic.
электромеха́ник|а, и *f.* electromechanics.
электромонтё́р, а *m.* electrician.
электро́н, а *m.* (*phys.*) electron.
электро́ник|а, и *f.* electronics.
электро́нно... *comb. form* electronic-.
электро́н|ный *adj.* **1.** *adj.* *of* ~; **~ная ла́мпа** electron tube, thermionic valve; **э. микроско́п** electron microscope. **2.** electronic; **~ная вычисли́тельная маши́на** electronic computer.
электропереда́ч|а, и *f.* electricity transmission.
электропе́ч|ь, и *f.* electric furnace.
электропли́тк|а, и *f.* (electric) hotplate.
электропо́езд, а *m.* electric train.
электрополоте́нц|е, а *nt.* hand-drier.
электроприбо́р, а *m.* electrical appliance.
электропро́вод, а *m.* electricity cable.
электропрово́дк|а, и *f.* electric wiring.
электропромы́шленност|ь, и *f.* electrical industry.
электросва́рк|а, и *f.* electric welding.
электросилов|о́й *adj.* electric power.
электроста́л|ь, и *f.* electric steel.
электроста́нци|я, и *f.* electric power station.
электроте́хник, а *m.* electrical engineer.
электроте́хник|а, и *f.* electrical engineering.
электротех|ни́ческий *adj.* *of* **~ника**
электротя́г|а, и *f.* electric traction.
электрохими́ческий *adj.* electrochemical.
электрохи́ми|я, и *f.* electrochemistry.
электроцентра́л|ь, и *f.* electric power plant.
электроча́йник, а *m.* electric kettle.
электроэне́рги|я, и *f.* electric power.
элеме́нт, а *m.* **1.** (*in var. senses*) element; **э. изображе́ния** (*comput.*) pixel. **2.** (*coll.*) type, character; **подозри́тельный э.** suspicious type. **3.** (*electr.*) cell, battery; **сух́ой э.** dry cell; **рабо́тать от ~ов** to be battery-operated.
элемента́р|ный (~ен, ~на) *adj.* (*in var. senses*) elementary.
элеро́н, а *m.* (*aeron.*) aileron.
эли́т|а, ы *f.* **1.** (*collect.*; *agric.*) best specimens; **э. карто́феля** highest-quality potatoes. **2.** élite.
эли́т|ный *adj.* *of* **~а**
э́ллин, а *m.* ancient Greek, Hellene.
э́ллинг, а *m.* **1.** (*naut.*) slipway. **2.** (*aeron.*) shed, hangar (*for airships or balloons*).
эллини́зм, а *m.* **1.** Hellenism. **2.** (*hist.*) the Hellenistic period.
эллини́ст, а *m.* Hellenist.
эллинисти́ческий *adj.* (*hist.*) Hellenistic.
э́ллин|ка, ки *f.* *of* ~
э́ллинский *adj.* ancient Greek, Hellenic.
э́ллипс, а *m.* (*math.*, *liter.*) ellipse.
э́ллипс|ис, а *m.* = ~
эллипти́ческий *adj.* elliptic(al).
эл|ь, я *m.* ale.
Э́льб|а, ы *f.* **1.** Elba (*island*). **2.** the Elbe (*river*).
Эльза́с, а *m.* Alsace.
эльза́с|ец, ца *m.* Alsatian.
эльза́с|ка, ки *f.* *of* **~ец**
эльза́сский *adj.* Alsatian.
эльф, а *m.* elf.
элю́ви|й, я *m.* (*geol.*) eluvium.
эма́левый *adj.* enamel.
эмалиро́в|анный *p.p.p.* *of* **~а́ть** *and* *adj.* enamelled; **~анная посу́да** enamel ware.
эмалир|ова́ть, у́ю *impf.* to enamel.
эмалиро́вк|а, и *f.* **1.** enamelling. **2.** enamel.
эма́л|ь, и *f.* enamel.

эмана́ци|я, и *f.* emanation.
эмансипа́ци|я, и *f.* emancipation; **боре́ц за ~ю же́нщин** women's liberationist; women's libber.
эмансипи́р|овать, ую *impf. and pf.* to emancipate.
эмба́рго *nt. indecl.* (*econ.*) embargo; **наложи́ть э.** (**на**+*a.*) to embargo, place an embargo (on).
эмбле́м|а, ы *f.* **1.** emblem. **2.** (*mil.*) insignia.
эмболи́|я, и *f.* (*med.*) embolism.
эмбриоло́ги|я, и *f.* embryology.
эмбрио́н, а *m.* (*biol.*) embryo.
эмерита́льн|ый *adj.*: **~ая ка́сса** old age insurance scheme.
эмериту́р|а, ы *f.* (*obs.*) old age benefit (*secured by voluntary contributions*).
эмигра́нт, а *m.* emigré, emigrant.
эмигра́нт|ский *adj. of* ~
эмигра|цио́нный *adj. of* **~ция**
эмигра́ци|я, и *f.* **1.** emigration. **2.** (*collect.*) emigration, emigrés.
эмигри́р|овать, ую *impf. and pf.* to emigrate.
эмисса́р, а *m.* emissary.
эмисс|ио́нный *adj. of* **~ия**
эми́сси|я, и *f.* (*fin., phys.*) emission.
эмоциона́л|ьный (~ен, ~ьна) *adj.* emotional.
эмо́ци|я, и *f.* emotion.
эмпире́|й, я *m.* empyrean; **вита́ть в ~ях** to have one's head in the clouds.
эмпири́зм, а *m.* empiricism.
эмпи́рик, а *m.* empiricist.
эмпириокритици́зм, а *m.* (*phil.*) empirio-criticism.
эмпири́ческий *adj.* **1.** (*phil.*) empiricist. **2.** empirical.
эмпири́ч|ный (~ен, ~на) *adj.* = **~еский 2.**
э́му *m. indecl.* emu.
эму́льси|я, и *f.* emulsion.
эмфа́з|а, ы *f.* (*ling.*) emphasis.
эмфати́ческий *adj.* (*ling.*) emphatic.
эндокри́нн|ый *adj.* (*physiol.*) endocrine; **~ые же́лезы** endocrine glands, ductless glands.
эндокриноло́ги|я, и *f.* endocrinology.
э́ндшпил|ь, я *m.* (*chess*) end-game.
энерге́тик, а *m.* power engineering specialist.
энерге́тик|а, и *f.* power engineering.
энергет|и́ческий *adj. of* **~ика; ~и́ческая ба́за** (*econ.*) power supply sources, power base.
энерги́ч|ный (~ен, ~на) *adj.* energetic, vigorous, forceful.
эне́рги|я, и *f.* **1.** (*phys.*) energy; power; **затра́та ~и** energy consumption; **растра́та ~и** energy loss; **э. ве́тра** wind power. **2.** (*fig.*) energy; vigour, effort.
энерго... *comb. form* power-.
энергоёмкий *adj.* power-consuming.
энергосисте́м|а, ы *f.* power (supply) system.
энкли́тик|а, и *f.* (*llng.*) enclitic.
энклити́ческий *adj.* (*ling.*) enclitic.
э́нн|ый *adj.* (*expr. indefinite quantity, size, duration of time, etc.*): **в ~ой сте́пени** to the *n*th degree; **~ое коли́чество вре́мени** any number of hours.
э́нск|ий *adj.* (*used to designate sth. that cannot be identified for reasons of security*) ... 'X'; a certain ... (that shall remain nameless); **э. заво́д** factory 'X'.
энтомо́лог, а *m.* entomologist.
энтомологи́ческий *adj.* entomological.
энтомоло́ги|я, и *f.* entomology.
энтропи́|я, и *f.* (*phys.*) entropy.
энтузиа́зм, а *m.* enthusiasm.
энтузиа́ст, а *m.* (+*g.*) enthusiast (about, for), devotee (of); **э. футбо́ла** football enthusiast.
энцефали́т, а *m.* (*med.*) encephalitis.
энцефалопати́|я, и *f.* (*med.*): **бы́чья губкови́дная э.** bovine spongiform encephalopathy (*abbr.* BSE).
энци́клик|а, и *f.* (*eccl.*) encyclical.
энциклопеди́зм, а *m.* encyclopaedic learning.
энциклопеди́ст, а *m.* **1.** (*hist.*) Encyclopaedist. **2.** pers. of encyclopaedic learning.
энциклопеди́ческий *adj.* encyclopaedic; **э. слова́рь** encyclopaedia; **э. ум** encyclopaedic brain.
энциклопе́ди|я, и *f.* encyclopaedia; **ходя́чая э.** (*joc.*) walking encyclopaedia.
эоли́т, а *m.* (*archaeol.*) eolithic period.
эо́лов *adj.*: **~а а́рфа** Aeolian harp.
эоце́н, а *m.* (*geol.*) Eocene period.
эпати́р|овать, ую *impf. and pf.* to shock.
эпиго́н, а *m.* (*pej.*) imitator, unoriginal follower.
эпиго́н|ский *adj. of* ~
эпиго́нств|о, а *nt.* (*pej.*) imitation, unoriginal following (*of another's work*).
эпигра́мм|а, ы *f.* epigram.
эпи́граф, а *m.* epigraph.
эпигра́фик|а, и *f.* epigraphy.
эпиде́ми|я, и *f.* epidemic.
эпиде́рм|а, ы *f.* (*obs.*) = **~ис**
эпиде́рмис, а *m.* (*biol.*) epidermis.
эпизо́д, а *m.* episode.
эпизоди́ческий *adj.* episodic; occasional, sporadic.
эпизоо́ти|я, и *f.* epizootic (*of cattle diseases*).
э́пик, а *m.* epic poet.
э́пик|а, и *f.* epic poetry.
эпикуре́|ец, йца *m.* epicurean.
эпикуре́йский *adj.* epicurean.
эпикуре́йств|о, а *nt.* epicureanism.
эпиле́пси|я, и *f.* (*med.*) epilepsy.
эпиле́птик, а *m.* epileptic (*pers.*).
эпилепти́ческий *adj.* epileptic.
эпило́г, а *m.* epilogue.
эпистоля́рный *adj.* epistolary.
эпита́фи|я, и *f.* epitaph.
эпи́тет, а *m.* epithet.
эпице́нтр, а *m.* (*geol.*) epicentre.
эпици́кл, а *m.* (*math.*) epicycle.
эпи́ческий *adj.* epic.
эполе́т|ы, ~ *pl.* (*sg.* **~а, ~ы** *f.*) epaulettes.
эпопе́|я, и *f.* (*liter. or fig.*) epic.
э́пос, а *m.* epos, epic literature.
эпо́х|а, и *f.* epoch, age, era.
эпоха́льный *adj.* epoch-making.
эпю́р, а *m.* diagram, drawing.
э́р|а, ы *f.* era; **до на́шей ~ы** BC (*before Christ*); **на́шей ~ы** AD (*Anno Domini*).
эрг, а *m.* erg (*unit of work*).
э́ре *nt. indecl.* öre, øre (*Scandinavian unit of currency*).
эре́кци|я, и *f.* (*physiol.*) erection.
эрза́ц, а *m.* ersatz.
Эритре́|я, и *f.* Eritrea.
эритроци́т, а *m.* (*physiol.*) erythrocyte, red corpuscle.
э́ркер, а *m.* (*archit.*) oriel (window).
эроге́нн|ый *adj.* erogenous; **~ые зо́ны** erogenous zones.
эроди́р|овать, ую *impf.* to erode.
эро́зи|я, и *f.* erosion.
эроти́зм, а *m.* eroticism.
эро́тик|а, и *f.* sensuality.
эроти́ческий *adj.* erotic, sensual.
эроти́ч|ный (~ен, ~на) *adj.* = **~еский**
эрото́ма́н, а *m.* erotomaniac, sex maniac.
эротома́ни|я, и *f.* erotomania.
Эр-Рия́д, а *m.* Riyadh.
эрсте́д, а *m.* oersted (*unit of magnetism*).
эруди́рован|ный (~, ~на) *adj.* erudite.
эруди́т, а *m.* **1.** polymath. **2. «э.»** 'Polymath' (*Scrabble (propr.)-like board game*).
эруди́ци|я, и *f.* erudition.
эрцге́рцог, а *m.* archduke.
эрцгерцоги́н|я, и *f.* archduchess.
эрцге́рцогств|о, а *nt.* archduchy, archdukedom.
эсде́к, а *m.* (*hist.*) S.D. (*member of Social Democratic Party*).
эсе́р, а *m.* (*hist.*) S.R. (*member of Socialist Revolutionary Party*).
эсе́ровский *adj.* (*hist.*) S.R. (*Socialist Revolutionary*).
эска́др|а, ы *f.* (*naut.*) squadron.
эска́др|енный *adj. of* **~а; э. бронено́сец** (*obs.*) battleship; **э. миноно́сец** destroyer.
эскадри́л|ьный *adj. of* **~ья**
эскадри́л|ья, ьи, *g. pl.* **~ий** *f.* (*aeron.*) squadron.
эскадро́н, а *m.* (*mil.*) (*cavalry*) squadron, troop.
эскадро́н|ный *adj. of* ~

эскала́тор, а *m.* escalator.
эскала́ци|я, и *f.* (*mil.*) escalation.
эскало́п, а *m.* (*cul.*) cutlet(s).
эска́рп, а *m.* (*mil.*) scarp, escarpment.
эски́з, а *m.* sketch, study; draft, outline.
эски́з|ный *adj. of* ~; **э. чертёж** draft, outline sketch.
эскимо́ *nt. indecl.* choc(olate) ice.
эскимо́с, а *m.* Eskimo, Inuit.
эскимо́с|ка, ки *f. of* ~
эскимо́сский *adj.* Eskimo, Inuit.
эско́рт, а *m.* (*mil.*) escort.
эскорти́р|овать, ую *impf. and pf.* (*mil.*) to escort.
эсми́н|ец, ца *m.* (*abbr. of* **эска́дренный миноно́сец**) (*naut.*) destroyer.
эспадро́н, а *m.* (*fencing*) cutting-sword, back-sword.
эспаньо́лк|а, и *f.* imperial (*beard*).
эспарце́т, а *m.* (*bot.*) sainfoin.
эссе́ *nt. indecl.* essay.
эссе́нци|я, и *f.* (*in var. senses*) essence.
эстака́д|а, ы *f.* **1.** viaduct, platform (*carrying elevated rail.*); gantry. **2.** flyover. **3.** (*naut.*) pier. **4.** (*naut.*) boom (*of harbour*).
эстака́д|ный *adj. of* **~а; ~ная желе́зная доро́га** elevated railway; **э. кран** gantry crane.
эста́мп, а *m.* (*art*) print, engraving, plate.
эстафе́т|а, ы *f.* **1.** (*sport*) relay race. **2.** baton (*in relay race*); **приня́ть у кого́-н. ~у** (*fig.*) to carry on s.o.'s work, maintain s.o.'s tradition. **3.** (*obs.*) mail (*carried by relays of horsemen*).
эсте́т, а *m.* aesthete.
эстети́зм, а *m.* aestheticism.
эсте́тик|а, *f.* **1.** aesthetics. **2.** design; **промы́шленная э.** industrial design.
эстети́ческий *adj.* aesthetic.
эсте́т|ский *adj. of* ~
эсте́тств|о, а *nt.* aestheticism.
эсто́н|ец, ца *m.* Estonian.
Эсто́ни|я, и *f.* Estonia.
эсто́н|ка, ки *f. of* **~ец**
эсто́нский *adj.* Estonian.
эстраго́н, а *m.* (*bot.*) tarragon.
эстра́д|а, ы *f.* **1.** stage, platform; **вы́йти на ~у** to come on stage. **2.** variety (*art*); **арти́ст ~ы** variety performer, artiste.
эстра́д|ный *adj. of* **~а; э. конце́рт** variety show; **~ная му́зыка** popular music.
эстуа́ри|й, я *m.* estuary.
эсэнго́вский *adj.* (*coll.*) CIS (*Commonwealth of Independent States*).
эсэ́сов|ец, ца *m.* (*hist.*) SS (*Schutz-Staffel*) man.
эсэ́совский *adj.* (*hist.*) SS (*Schutz-Staffel*).
эта́ж, а́ *m.* storey, floor; **пе́рвый, второ́й,** *etc.*, **э.** ground floor, first floor, *etc.*
этаже́рк|а, и *f.* bookcase, shelves.
эта́жност|ь, и *f.* number of storeys.
э́так *adv.* (*coll.*) **1.** so, thus; **мо́жно э́то сде́лать и так и э.** you can do it like this or like that. **2.** about, approximately.
э́такий *pron.* (*coll.*) such (a), what (a).
этало́н, а *m.* standard (*of weights and measures*).
эта́н, а *m.* (*chem.*) ethane.
эта́п, а *m.* **1.** stage, phase. **2.** (*sport*) lap. **3.** halting-place, stage (*for troops; formerly, for groups of deported convicts in transit*); **отпра́вить по ~у, ~ом** to transport, deport (*under guard*).
эта́пник, а *m.* (*hist.*) convict in transit.
эта́п|ный *adj. of* ~; **~ное собы́тие** (*fig.*) landmark, turning-point; **отпра́вить ~ным поря́дком** (*hist.*) to transport, deport (*under guard*).
э́тик|а, и *f.* ethics.
этике́т, а *m.* etiquette.
этике́тк|а, и *f.* label.
эти́л, а *m.* (*chem.*) ethyl.
этиле́н, а *m.* (*chem.*) ethylene.
эти́л|овый *adj. of* ~; **э. спирт** ethyl alcohol.
этимо́лог, а *m.* etymologist.
этимологи́ческий *adj.* etymological.
этимоло́ги|я, и *f.* etymology; **наро́дная э.** popular etymology.
эти́ческий *adj. of* **э́тика**
эти́ч|ный (~ен, ~на) *adj.* ethical.
этни́ческий *adj.* ethnic.
этно́граф, а *m.* ethnographer, social anthropologist.
этнографи́ческий *adj.* ethnographic(al).
этногра́фи|я, и *f.* ethnography, social anthropology.
э́то[1] *see* **э́тот**
э́то[2] *emph. particle* (*coll.*); **куда́ э. он де́лся?** wherever has he got to?; **что э. ты не гото́в?** why on earth aren't you ready?; **э. вы спра́шивали?** was it *you* who was asking?
э́то[3] *pron.* (*as n.*) this (is), that (is); **э. наш дом** this is our house; **э. вам помо́жет** this will help you; **э. ве́рно** that is true; **не в э́том де́ло** that's not the point; **об э́том я вам пото́м расскажу́** I will tell you about it later; **э. я ви́жу** so I can see.
э́тот, э́та, э́то, *pl.* **э́ти** *pron.* this (these); *as n.* (*i*) this one, (*ii*) the latter.
этру́ск, а *m.* Etruscan.
этру́сский *adj.* Etruscan.
этю́д, а *m.* **1.** (*art, liter.*) study, sketch. **2.** (*mus.*) étude. **3.** (*mus.*) exercise; (*chess*) problem.
эфемери́д|ы, ~ *pl.* (*sg.* **~а, ~ы** *f.*) **1.** (*zool.*) ephemeridae. **2.** (*astron.*) ephemerides.
эфеме́р|ный (~ен, ~на) *adj.* ephemeral.
эфе́с, а *m.* hilt, handle (*of sword, sabre, etc.*).
эфио́п, а *m.* Ethiopian.
Эфио́пи|я, и *f.* Ethiopia.
эфио́п|ка, ки *f. of* ~
эфио́пский *adj.* Ethiopian.
эфи́р, а *m.* **1.** ether; (*fig.*) air; **вре́мя в ~е** air time; **передава́ть в э.** to put on the air, broadcast. **2.** (*chem.*) ether; **просто́й э.** ether; **сло́жный э.** ester.
эфи́р|ный (~ен, ~на) *adj.* **1.** ethereal. **2.** (*chem.*) ether, ester; **~ное ма́сло** essential oil, volatile oil.
эфироно́с, а *m.* volatile-oil-bearing plant.
эфироно́сный *adj.* volatile-oil-bearing.
эффе́кт, а *m.* **1.** effect, impact; **произвести́ э. (на+*a.*)** to have an effect (on), make an impression (on); **парнико́вый** *or* **тепли́чный э.** greenhouse effect. **2.** (*econ.*) result, consequences. **3.** (*pl.*) (*theatr.*) effects; **шумовы́е ~ы** sound effects.
эффекти́в|ный (~ен, ~на) *adj.* effective, efficacious.
эффе́кт|ный (~ен, ~на) *adj.* **1.** effective (= *making an impact*), striking; eye-catching; snazzy. **2.** done for effect.
эх *int. expr. regret, reproval, amazement, etc.*; eh!; oh!
эхма́ *int.* = **эх**
э́х|о, а *nt.* echo.
эхоло́т, а *m.* (*naut.*) sonic depth finder, echo sounder.
эшафо́т, а *m.* scaffold; **взойти́ на э.** to mount the scaffold.
эшело́н, а *m.* **1.** (*mil.*) échelon. **2.** special train.
эшелони́р|овать, ую *impf. and pf.* (*mil.*) to échelon; **э. оборо́ну** to dispose defence in depth.

Ю

Ю (*abbr. of* **юг**) S, South.
юа́н|ь, я *m.* yuan (*Chinese currency unit*).
ЮАР *f. indecl.* (*abbr. of* **Ю́жно-Африка́нская Респу́блика**) Republic of South Africa.
юа́ров|ец, ца *m.* South African.
юа́ровский *adj.* South African.
юбиле́|й, я *m.* **1.** anniversary; jubilee. **2.** anniversary celebrations.
юбиле́й|ный *adj. of* ~

юбиля́р, а *m.* pers. (*or* institution) whose anniversary is celebrated.

ю́бк|а, и *f.* skirt; **ю.-брю́ки** split skirt, culottes; **держа́ться за чью-н. ~у** to cling to s.o.'s apron-strings.

ю́бочк|а, и *f.* short skirt.

ю́бочник, а *m.* (*coll.*) womanizer.

ю́б|очный *adj. of* **~ка**

ювели́р, а *m.* jeweller.

ювели́р|ный *adj.* **1.** *adj. of* **~**; **~ные изде́лия** gold and silver ware, jewellery; **ю. магази́н** jeweller's. **2.** (*fig.*) fine, intricate.

юг, а *m.* south; the South (*of Russia, etc.*); **на ю́ге** in the south; **к ю́гу от** to the south of.

ю́го-восто́к, а *m.* south-east.

ю́го-восто́чный *adj.* south-east(ern).

ю́го-за́пад, а *m.* south-west.

ю́го-за́падный *adj.* south-west(ern).

югосла́в, а *m.* Yugoslav.

Югосла́ви|я, и *f.* Yugoslavia.

югосла́в|ка, ки *f. of* **~**

югосла́вский *adj.* Yugoslav.

юдо́л|ь, и *f.* (*arch.*) valley; **ю. пла́ча, ю. печа́ли, земна́я ю.** 'vale of tears'.

юдофо́б, а *m.* anti-Semite.

юдофо́бств|о, а *nt.* anti-Semitism.

южа́н|ин, ина, *pl.* **~е, ~** *m.* southerner.

южн|е́е, *comp. of* **~́ый; ю. Ло́ндона** to the south of London.

Ю́жно-Африка́нск|ая Респу́блик|а, ~ой ~и *f.* Republic of South Africa.

ю́жный *adj.* south, southern; **Ю. по́люс** South Pole; **Ю. поля́рный круг** antarctic circle; **ю. темпера́мент** (*fig.*) southern temperament.

Ю́жн|ый океа́н, ~ого ~а *m.* the Antarctic Ocean.

ю́зом, *adv.* skidding, in a skid.

ю́кк|а, и *f.* (*bot.*) yucca.

юл|а́, ы́ *f.* **1.** top (*child's toy*). **2.** (*coll.*) fidget. **3.** (*zool.*) woodlark.

юл|и́ть, ю́, и́шь *impf.* (*coll.*) **1.** to fuss, fidget. **2. (пе́ред)** to play up (to).

ю́мор, а *m.* humour; **чу́вство ~а** a sense of humour.

юморе́ск|а, и *f.* (*mus., liter.*) humoresque.

юмори́ст, а *m.* humorist.

юмори́стик|а, и *f.* **1.** (*collect.*) humour. **2.** (*coll.*) sth. funny.

юмористи́ческий *adj.* humorous, comic, funny.

ю́нг|а, и *m.* ship's boy; sea cadet.

ЮНЕСКО *f. indecl.* UNESCO (*abbr. of* United Nations Educational, Scientific and Cultural Organization — *Организа́ция Объединённых На́ций по вопро́сам образова́ния, нау́ки и культу́ры*).

юн|е́ц, ца́ *m.* (*coll.*) youth.

ЮНИСЕФ *m. indecl.* UNICEF (*abbr. of* United Nations International Children's Emergency Fund — *Де́тский фонд Организа́ции Объединённых На́ций*).

ю́нкер, а *m.* (*hist.*) **1.** (*pl.* **~а́, ~о́в**) cadet. **2.** (*pl.* **~ы, ~ов**) Junker (*Prussian landowner*).

ю́нкер|ский *adj. of* **~**

юнко́р, а *m.* (*abbr. of* **ю́ный корреспонде́нт**) young correspondent.

юнна́т, а *m.* (*abbr. of* **ю́ный натурали́ст**) young naturalist.

ю́ност|ь, и *f.* youth (*age*).

ю́нош|а, и *m.* youth (*pers.*).

ю́ношеский *adj.* youthful.

ю́ношеств|о, а *nt.* **1.** youth (*age*). **2.** (*collect.*) youth, young people.

ю́н|ый (~, ~а́, ~о) *adj.* **1.** young; **теа́тр ~ого зри́теля** young people's theatre; **ю. натурали́ст** member of junior natural history study group. **2.** youthful.

юпи́тер, а *m.* floodlight.

юр, а *m. only in phr.* **на ~у́** (*i*) in a high, exposed place, (*ii*) (*fig.*) in the limelight, in the forefront.

ю́р|а, ы *f.* (*geol.*) Jurassic period.

юр|а́, ы́ *f.* (*dial.*) large shoal (*of fish*); school (*of marine animals*).

юриди́ческ|ий *adj.* legal, juridical; **~ая консульта́ция** legal advice office; **~ое лицо́** juridical pers.; **~ие нау́ки** jurisprudence, law; **ю. факульте́т** faculty of law.

юрисди́кци|я, и *f.* jurisdiction.

юриско́нсульт, а *m.* legal adviser.

юриспруде́нци|я, и *f.* jurisprudence, law (*as academic discipline*).

юри́ст, а *m.* legal expert, lawyer.

ю́р|кий (~ок, ~ка́, ~ко) *adj.* **1.** quick-moving, brisk. **2.** (*fig., coll.*) clever, sharp, smart.

юркн|у́ть, у́, ёшь *pf.* to scamper away, dart away, plunge.

юро́див|ый *adj.* **1.** crazy, simple, touched. **2.** *as n.* **ю., ~ого** *m.* 'God's fool' (*idiot believed to possess divine gift of prophecy*).

юро́дств|о, а *nt.* **1.** craziness, idiocy. **2.** idiotic action.

юро́дств|овать, ую *impf.* to behave like an idiot.

ю́рский *adj.* (*geol.*) Jurassic.

ю́рт|а, ы *f.* yurt, yurta (*nomad's tent in Central Asia*).

Ю́рьев *adj.*: **Ю. день** St George's Day; **вот тебе́ и Ю. день!** here's a fine how d'ye do!

юс, а, *pl.* **~ы́** *m.* (*ling.*) yus (*name of two letters originally representing nasal vowels in Old Church Slavonic*); **юс большо́й** large 'yus'; **юс ма́лый** little 'yus'.

юстир|ова́ть, у́ю *impf. and pf.* to adjust, regulate (*instruments*).

юсти́ци|я, и *f.* justice.

ют[1]**, а** *m.* (*hist.*) Jute.

ют[2]**, а** *m.* (*naut.*) quarter-deck.

ю|ти́ться, чу́сь, ти́шься *impf.* to huddle (together); to take shelter.

ю́фт|евый *adj. of* **~ь**

юфт|ь, и *f.* yuft, Russia leather.

юфт|яно́й = **~́евый**

Я

я, меня́, мне, мной (мно́ю), обо мне 1. *pers. pron.* I (me); **я не я** (*coll.*) it's nothing to do with me; **(я) не я бу́ду, е́сли не добью́сь от него́ извине́ния** I'll damn well see that I get an apology from him. **2.** *n.*; *nt. indecl.* the self, the ego; **второ́е я** alter ego.

я́бед|а, ы *f. and c.g.* **1.** *f.* (*obs.*) information, slander. **2.** *c.g.* = **~ник**

я́бедник, а *m.* (*coll.*) informer, sneak.

я́беднича|ть, ю *impf.* (*of* **на~**) **(на**+*a.*; *coll.*) to inform (on), tell tales (about).

я́блок|о, а, *pl.* **~и, ~** *nt.* apple; **глазно́е я.** eyeball; **в ~ах** (*of a horse's coat*) dappled; **я. раздо́ра** bone of contention; **~у не́где упа́сть** there isn't room to swing a cat.

я́блон|евый *adj. of* **~я**

я́блон|ный = **~евый**

я́блон|я, и *f.* apple-tree.

я́блочк|о, а *dim. of* **я́блоко**

я́бло|чный *adj. of* **~ко**

Я́в|а, ы *f.* Java.

ява́н|ец, ца *m.* Javan(ese).

ява́н|ка, ки *f. of* **~ец**

ява́нский *adj.* Javan; Javanese.

яв|и́ть, лю́, ~́ишь *pf.* (*of* **~ля́ть**) to show, display; **я. (собо́й) приме́р** (+*g.*) to give an example (of), display.

яв|и́ться, лю́сь, ~́ишься *pf.* (*of* **~ля́ться**) **1.** to appear, present o.s.; to report; **я. в суд** to appear before the court; **я. на слу́жбу** to report for duty; **я. с пови́нной** to give o.s. up. **2.** to turn up, arrive, show up. **3.** to arise, occur; **у меня́ ~и́лась блестя́щая мысль** I had a brilliant idea;

~йлся удо́бный слу́чай a suitable opportunity presented itself.

я́вк|а, и *f.* **1.** appearance, attendance; **я. в суд** appearance in court. **2.** secret rendezvous; signal for secret rendezvous. **3.** (*obs.*) information.

явле́ни|е, я *nt.* **1.** phenomenon; occurrence, happening; **стихи́йное я.** natural calamity. **2.** (*theatr.*) scene.

явле́нный *adj.* (*relig.*) appearing miraculously (*esp. of icons*)

явля́|ть, ю *impf. of* **яви́ть**

явля́|ться, юсь *impf.* **1.** *impf. of* **яви́ться. 2.** (*impf. only*) (+*i.*) to be; to serve (as); **э́то ~ется кощу́нством** this is blasphemy.

я́вно[1] *adv.* manifestly, patently; obviously.

я́вно[2] *as pred.* it is manifest, patent; it is obvious.

я́в|ный (~ен, ~на) *adj.* **1.** manifest, patent; overt, explicit. **2.** obvious.

я́вор, а *m.* sycamore (*tree*).

я́вор|овый *adj. of* **~**

я́вочн|ый *adj.* **1.** *adj. of* **я́вка 2.; ~ая кварти́ра** secret rendezvous. **2.** (*mil.*) reporting, recruiting; **я. пункт** reporting point (*for conscripts*); **я. уча́сток** recruiting office. **3.: ~ым поря́дком** on the spur of the moment, without prior arrangement.

я́вствен|ный (~, ~на) *adj.* clear, distinct.

я́вств|овать, ует *impf.* to appear; to be clear, apparent, obvious; to follow (*logically*).

яв|ь, и *f.* reality.

ягдта́ш, а *m.* game-bag.

я́гел|ь, я *m.* (*bot.*) Iceland moss, reindeer moss.

ягн|ёнок, ёнка, *pl.* **~я́та, ~я́т** *m.* lamb.

ягн|и́ться, и́тся *impf.* (*of* **о~**) to lamb.

ягня́тник, а *m.* (*zool.*) lammergeyer.

я́год|а, ы *f.* berry; (*collect.*) soft fruit (*strawberries, blackcurrants, etc.*); **ви́нная я.** dried fig; **пойти́ по ~ы** to go berry-picking; **одного́ по́ля я.** soul-mate.

я́годиц|а, ы *f.* buttock(s).

я́годи|чный *adj. of* **~ца**

я́годник, а *m.* **1.** berry plantation. **2.** berry bush. **3.** (*coll.*) berry-picker.

я́год|ный *adj. of* **~а**

ягуа́р, а *m.* jaguar.

яд, а (у) *m.* poison; venom (*also fig.*).

я́дерн|ый *adj.* **1.** (*phys.*) nuclear; **~ое расщепле́ние** nuclear fission; **я. реа́ктор** nuclear reactor; **~ая фи́зика** nuclear physics. **2.** *adj. of* **ядро́**

я́дерщик, а *m.* (*coll.*) nuclear scientist.

ядови́т|ый (~, ~а) *adj.* **1.** poisonous; toxic; **я. газ** poison gas; **~ая змея́** poisonous snake. **2.** (*fig.*) venomous, malicious.

ядохимика́т, а *m.* (*agric.*) (chemical) pesticide.

ядрён|ый (~, ~а) *adj.* (*coll.*) **1.** having a large kernel (*of nuts*); juicy (*of fruit*); hearty (*of cabbages*). **2.** (*fig.*) healthy, vigorous. **3.** (*fig.*) fresh, bracing.

ядр|о́, а́, *pl.* **~а, я́дер, ~ам** *nt.* **1.** kernel; core. **2.** (*phys.*) nucleus. **3.** (*mil., etc.*) main body (*of a unit, group*). **4.** (*hist., mil.*) ball, shot. **5.** (*sport*) shot; **толка́ние ~а́** putting the shot.

ядро́|вый *adj. of* **~ 1.; ~вое мы́ло** high-grade soap.

я́дрышк|о, а, *pl.* **~и** *nt.* **1.** *dim. of* **ядро́. 2.** (*biol.*) nucleolus.

я́зв|а, ы *f.* **1.** ulcer, sore; **я. желу́дка** stomach ulcer; **морова́я я.** plague; **сиби́рская я.** malignant anthrax. **2.** (*fig.*) harm; plague, curse. **3.** (*fig., coll.*) malicious pers.; (*as term of abuse*) scum.

я́звенн|ый *adj.* ulcerous; **~ая боле́знь** stomach ulcer.

я́звин|а, ы *f.* **1.** indentation, pit. **2.** (*coll.*) large ulcer.

язви́тел|ьный (~ен, ~ьна) *adj.* caustic, biting, sarcastic.

язв|и́ть, лю́, и́шь *impf.* (*of* **съ~**) **1.** (*obs.*) to wound; to sting. **2.** to say sarcastically; to mock; **я. на чей-н. счёт** to be sarcastic at s.o.'s expense.

язы́к[1]**, а́,** *pl.* **~и́** *m.* **1.** tongue; **у него́ я. без косте́й** he is too fond of talking; **у него́ что на уме́, то и на ~е́** (*coll.*) he cannot keep his thoughts to himself; **держа́ть я. за зуба́ми, придержа́ть я.** to hold one's tongue; **прикуси́ть я.** (*coll.*) to shut up; **я. у него́ хорошо́ подве́шен** (*coll.*) he has a glib tongue; **распусти́ть я.** (*coll.*) to talk too glibly; **дёргать, тяну́ть кого́-н. за я.** (*coll.*) to make s.o. talk; **сорвало́сь с ~а́** (*fig.*) it slipped out; **лиши́ться ~а́** (*fig.*) to lose one's tongue; **я. у меня́ не поверну́лся э́то сказа́ть** (*coll.*) I could not bring myself to say it; **чеса́ть, болта́ть ~о́м** (*coll.*) to natter, blather; **я. у меня́ чеса́лся** (*coll.*) I was itching to speak; **я. проглоти́шь** (*coll.*) it makes one's mouth water. **2.** (*cul.*) tongue; **копчёный я.** smoked tongue. **3.** clapper (*of a bell*). **4.** (*mil.; coll.*) prisoner who will talk (*will provide information when interrogated*). **5.: морско́й я.** (*zool.*) sole.

язы́к[2]**, а́,** *pl.* **~и́,** *m.* **1.** language (*also fig.*); **владе́ть мно́гими ~а́ми** to know many languages; **говори́ть на ло́маном ру́сском ~е́** to talk in broken Russian; **найти́ о́бщий я.** (*fig.*) to find a common language. **2.** (*pl.* **~и**) (*obs.*) people, nationality, nation.

языка́ст|ый (~, ~а) *adj.* (*coll.*) sharp-tongued.

языкове́д, а *m.* linguist, specialist on linguistics.

языкове́дени|е, я *nt.* linguistics.

языкове́д|ческий *adj. of* **~ение**

языково́й *adj.* linguistic.

языко́вый *adj.* **1.** (*anat.*) tongue, lingual. **2.** (*cul.*) tongue.

языкозна́ни|е, я *nt.* linguistics, science of language.

язы́ческий *adj.* heathen, pagan.

язы́честв|о, а *nt.* heathenism, paganism.

языч|ко́вый *adj. of* **~о́к; я. инструме́нт** (*mus.*) reed instrument.

язы́чник, а *m.* heathen, pagan.

язы́|чный *adj. of* **~к**[1] **1.**

языч|о́к, ка́ *m.* **1.** (*anat.*) uvula. **2.** (*mus.*) reed. **3.** (*tech.*) catch. lug. **4.** *dim. of* **язы́к**

яз|ь, я́ *m.* ide (*fish of carp family*).

яи́чк|о, а *pl.* **~и** *nt.* **1.** (*anat.*) testicle. **2.** *dim. of* **яйцо́**

яи́чник, а *m.* (*anat.*) ovary.

яи́чниц|а, ы *f.* (*cul.*) fried eggs (*also* **я.-глазу́нья**); **я.-болту́нья** scrambled eggs.

яи́чн|ый *adj. of* **яйцо́; я. бело́к** white of eggs; **я. желто́к** yolk of egg; **я. порошо́к** dried egg(s); **~ая скорлупа́** egg-shell.

яйл|а́, ы́ *f.* (*dial.*) mountain pasture (*in Crimea*).

яйцеви́д|ный (~ен, ~на) *adj.* egg-shaped, oval, oviform, ovoid.

яйцево́д, а *m.* (*anat.*) oviduct.

яйцекла́д, а *m.* (*zool*) ovipositor.

яйцекле́тк|а, и *f.* (*biol.*) ovule.

яйцено́ск|ий *adj.* (*agric.*): **~ие ку́ры** good laying hens.

яйцено́скост|ь, и *f.* (*agric.*) egg-laying qualities.

яйцеро́дный *adj.* (*zool.*) oviparous.

яйц|о́, а́, *pl.* **~а, яи́ц, ~ам** *nt.* **1.** egg; (*biol.*) ovum; **нести́ ~а** to lay eggs; **я. всмя́тку** lightly-boiled egg; **я. вкруту́ю** hard-boiled egg; **я. в мешо́чек** medium-boiled egg. **2.** (*pl. coll.*) balls, nuts (= *testicles*).

як, а *m.* yak.

якоби́н|ец, ца *m.* (*hist., pol.*) Jacobin.

якоби́н|ский *adj. of* **~ец**

я́кобы 1. *conj.* (*expr. doubt about validity of another's statement*) that; **говоря́т, я. он у́мер** they say (= *they claim*) that he has died. **2.** *conj.* as if, as though; **он вообрази́л, я. его́ произвели́ в генера́лы** he imagined he had been made a general. **3.** *particle* supposedly, ostensibly, allegedly, purportedly; **мы посмотре́ли э́ту я. стра́шную карти́ну** we have seen this supposedly dreadful film.

я́кор|ный *adj. of* **~ь; ~ная лебёдка** capstan; **~ное ме́сто, ~ная стоя́нка** anchorage.

я́кор|ь, я, *pl.* **~я́, ~е́й** *m.* **1.** (*naut.*) anchor; **я. спасе́ния** (*fig.*) sheet-anchor; **стать на я.** to anchor; **бро́сить я.** to cast, drop anchor; **стоя́ть на ~е** to ride at anchor; **сня́ться с ~я** to weigh anchor. **2.** (*electr.*) armature; rotor.

яку́т, а *m.* Yakut.

яку́т|ка, ки *f. of* **~**

яку́тский *adj.* Yakut.

якша́|ться, юсь *impf.* (**с**+*i.*; *coll.*) to consort (with), hobnob (with).

ял, а *m.* whaler, pinnace; yawl.

я́лик, а *m.* skiff, dinghy; yawl.
я́личник, а *m.* ferryman.
я́ли|чный *adj. of* **~к**
я́лове|ть, ет *impf.* to be barren, dry (*of cows*).
я́ловк|а, и *f.* barren cow, dry cow.
я́ловост|ь, и *f.* barrenness, dryness (*in cows*).
я́ловый *adj.* barren, dry (*of cows*).
Я́лт|а, ы *f.* Yalta.
ям, а *m.* (*hist.*) mail staging-post.
я́м|а, ы *f.* **1.** pit, hole; **возду́шная я.** air pocket; **выгребна́я я.** cesspit; **у́гольная я.** coal bunker; **рыть кому́-н. ~у** (*fig.*) to lay a trap for s.o. **2.** (*geog.*; *coll.*) depression, hollow. **3.** (*obs.*) prison.
яма́|ец, йца *m.* Jamaican.
Яма́йк|а, и *f.* Jamaica.
яма́йский *adj.* Jamaican; **я. ром** Jamaica rum.
ямб, а *m.* (*liter.*) iambus, iambic verse.
ямби́ческий *adj.* iambic.
я́мк|а, и *f. dim. of* **я́ма; я. на щека́х** dimple.
ямщи́к, а́ *m.* coachman.
янва́р|ский *adj. of* **~ь**
янва́р|ь, я́ *m.* January.
я́нки *m.* Yankee.
янта́рн|ый *adj.* **1.** amber; **~ая кислота́** succine acid. **2.** amber-coloured.
янта́р|ь, я́ *m.* amber.
Янцзы́ *f. indecl.* the Yangtze (*river*).
янычáр, а *m.* (*hist.*) janissary.
япо́н|ец, ца *m.* Japanese.
Япо́ни|я, и *f.* Japan.
япо́н|ка, ки *f. of* **~ец**
япо́нский *adj.* Japanese; **я. лак** Japan lacquer, japan.
яр[1], **а, о ~е, на ~у́** *m.* **1.** steep bank (*of river, lake, etc.*); slope (*of ravine*). **2.** ravine.
яр[2], **а** *m.* (*physiol.*) heat.
ярд, а *m.* yard (*measure*).
яре́мн|ый *adj. of* **ярмо́; ~ая ве́на** (*anat.*) jugular vein.
яр|и́ться, ю́сь, и́шься *impf.* **1.** (*obs.*) to rage, be in a fury. **2.** (*physiol.*) to be in heat.
я́рк|а, и *f.* young ewe (*up to first lambing*).
я́р|кий (~ок, ~ка́, ~ко) *adj.* **1.** bright (*of light, colours, etc.*). **2.** (*fig.*) colourful, striking; vivid, graphic; **~кая карти́на** graphic picture; **я. приме́р** striking, glaring example. **3.** (*fig.*) brilliant, outstanding; impressive; **~кая речь** brilliant speech; **я. тала́нт** outstanding gifts.
я́ркост|ь, и *f.* **1.** brightness. **2.** (*fig.*) brilliance.
ярлы́к, а́ *m.* **1.** (*hist.*) yarlyk, edict (*of khans of Golden Horde*). **2.** label, tag. **3.** (*fig.*) label; **приклеи́ть я. кому́-н.** to pin a label on s.o.
я́рмарк|а, и *f.* (trade) fair.
я́рмар|очный *adj. of* **~ка**
ярм|о́, а́, *pl.* **~а** *nt.* yoke (*also fig.*); **сбро́сить с себя́ я.** (*fig.*) to cast off the yoke.
яровиза́ци|я, и *f.* (*agric.*) vernalization.
яровизи́р|овать, ую *impf. and pf.* (*agric.*) to vernalize.
яров|о́й *adj.* (*agric.*) spring; **~а́я пшени́ца** spring wheat; *as n.* **~о́е, ~о́го** *nt.* spring crop.
я́рост|ный (~ен, ~на) *adj.* furious, fierce, savage, frenzied.
я́рост|ь, и *f.* fury, rage, frenzy.
я́рус, а *m.* **1.** (*theatr.*) circle. **2.** tier. **3.** (*geol.*) stage, layer.
я́рус|ный *adj.* **1.** *adj. of* **~**. **2.** tiered; stepped; graduated.
ярча́йший *superl. of* **я́ркий**
я́р|че *comp. of* **~кий**
яры́г|а, и *m.* **1.** (*hist.*) constable. **2.** (*obs.*) drunkard.
я́р|ый[1] **(~, ~а)** *adj.* **1.** furious, raging; violent. **2.** vehement, fervent.
я́рый[2] *adj.* (*obs.*) light; bright.
я́рь-медя́нка, я́ри-медя́нки *f.* (*chem.*) verdigris.
я́с|ельный *adj. of* **~ли**
я́сен|евый *adj. of* **~ь**
я́сен|ь, я *m.* ash-tree.
я́сл|и, ей *no sg.* **1.** manger, crib (*for cattle*). **2.** crèche, day nursery.
ясне́|ть, ет *impf.* to become clear(er).
я́сн|о[1] *adv. of* **~ый**
я́сно[2] *as pred.* **1.** (*of weather*) it is fine. **2.** (*fig.*) it is clear. **3.** (*as affirmative particle*) yes, of course.
ясновиде́ни|е, я *nt.* clairvoyance.
ясновид|ец, ца *m.* clairvoyant.
ясновидящий *adj.* (*also as n.*) clairvoyant.
я́сност|ь, и *f.* clearness, clarity; lucidity; **внести́ я. во что-н.** to clarify sth.
я́с|ный (~ен, ~на́, ~но) *adj.* **1.** clear; bright; (*of weather*) fine; **~ное не́бо** clear sky; **гром средь ~ного не́ба** a bolt from the blue. **2.** distinct. **3.** serene. **4.** (*fig.*) clear, plain; **сде́лать ~ным** to make it clear; **~ное де́ло** of course. **5.** lucid; precise, logical; **я. ум** precise mind.
я́ств|а, ~ *pl.* (*sg.* **~о, ~а** *nt.*) viands, victuals.
я́стреб, а, *pl.* **~а́** *and* **~ы** *m.* hawk.
ястреби́н|ый *adj. of* **я́стреб; ~ая охо́та** falconry; **с ~ым взгля́дом** hawk-eyed; **я. нос** hawk nose.
ястреб|о́к, ка́ *m.* **1.** *dim. of* **я́стреб. 2.** (*coll.*) fighter (*plane*).
ятага́н, а *m.* yataghan.
ятроге́нный *adj.* iatrogenic.
ятры́шник, а *m.* (*bot.*) orchis.
ят|ь, я *m.* yat´ (*name of old Russ. letter* **'Ѣ'**, *replaced by* **'е'** *in 1918*); **на я.** (*coll.*) first-class; splendid(ly).
яфети́ческий *adj.* (*ling.*) Japhetic.
я́хонт, а *m.* **(кра́сный)** ruby; **(си́ний)** sapphire.
я́хонт|овый *adj. of* **~**
я́хт|а, ы *f.* yacht.
яхт-клу́б, а *m.* yacht club.
яхтсме́н, а *m.* yachtsman.
яче́ист|ый (~, ~а) *adj.* cellular, porous.
яче́йк|а, и, *g. pl.* **яче́ек** *f.* **1.** (*biol., pol.*) cell. **2.** (*mil.*) foxhole; slit trench.
яче́йк|овый *adj. of* **~а**
я́честв|о, а *nt.* (*pej.*) individualism, egocentrism.
яче|я́, и́ *f.* (*biol.*) cell.
я́чий *adj. of* **як**
ячме́н|ный *adj. of* **~ь**[1]; **~ное зерно́** barley-corn; **я. отва́р** barley-water; **я. са́хар** barley-sugar, malt-sugar.
ячме́н|ь[1], **я́** *m.* barley.
ячме́н|ь[2], **я́** *m.* sty (*in the eye*).
я́чневый *adj.* of crushed, coarse barley.
я́шм|а, ы *f.* (*min.*) jasper.
я́шм|овый *adj. of* **~а**
я́щериц|а, ы *f.* lizard.
я́щик, а *m.* **1.** box, chest, case; cabinet; (*coll., joc.*) the (goggle- *or* idiot) box (= *television*); **му́сорный я.** dustbin; **почто́вый я.** letter-box; pillar-box; **откла́дывать в до́лгий я.** (*fig.*) to shelve, put off. **2.** drawer. **3.** (*fig.*) hush-hush institution (*designated by post-office box number*).
я́щи|чный *adj. of* **~к**
я́щур, а *m.* foot-and-mouth disease.
я́щур|ный *adj.* **1.** *adj. of* **~**. **2.** infected with foot-and-mouth disease.

ENGLISH–RUSSIAN

A

A [eɪ] *letter*: **from ~ to Z** от нача́ла до конца́; **he knows the subject from ~ to Z** он зна́ет э́тот предме́т как свои́ пять па́льцев; **~ road** гла́вная *or* магистра́льная доро́га; **A1** *adj.* (*coll.*) первокла́ссный; **A-bomb** а́томная бо́мба.

A [eɪ] *n.* **1.** (*mus.*) ля (*nt. indecl.*); **she reached top ~** она́ взяла́ ве́рхнее ля. **2.** (*acad. mark*) «отли́чно», «пятёрка»; **he got an ~ in physics** он получи́л «отли́чно» *or* «пятёрку» по фи́зике.

a [ə, eɪ], **an** [æn, ən] *indef. art.* **1.** *not usu. translated*: **it's an elephant** э́то слон. **2.** (**~** *certain*): **~ Mr. Smith rang** звони́л не́кий господи́н Смит; **in ~ sense** в како́м-то смы́сле; **an old friend of mine** оди́н мой ста́рый знако́мый; **she married ~ Forsyte** она́ вы́шла за́муж за одного́ из (семьи́) Форса́йтов. **3.** (*one*; *the same*): **all of ~ size** все одного́ разме́ра; все одина́ковой величины́. **4.** (*distributive*, *in each*) в+*a.*; **twice ~ week** два ра́за в неде́лю; **10 miles an hour** де́сять миль в час; (*for each*) за+*a.*; **10p ~ pound** 10 пе́нсов за фунт; (*to each*): **he gave out £5 ~ person** он вы́дал ка́ждому по пять фу́нтов; (*from each*) с+*g.*; **they charged £1 ~ head** они́ взя́ли по фу́нту с челове́ка.

AA (*abbr. of* ***Automobile Association***) Ассоциа́ция автомобили́стов.

aardvark [ˈɑːdvɑːk] *n.* трубкозу́б.

aback [əˈbæk] *adv.*: **we were taken ~ by the news** но́вость нас порази́ла; **I was taken ~ by his audacity** я растеря́лся от его́ на́глости.

abacus [ˈæbəkəs] *n.* (*counting aid*) счё|ты (*pl.*, *g.* -ов); (*archit.*) аба́ка.

abandon [əˈbænd(ə)n] *n.* несде́ржанность, самозабве́ние; **with ~** не сде́рживаясь; самозабве́нно.

v.t. **1.** (*forsake*, *desert*) пок|ида́ть, -и́нуть; **he ~ed his wife** он оста́вил (*coll.* бро́сил) свою́ жену́; **~ ship!** поки́нуть кора́бль! **2.** (*renounce*) отка́з|ываться, -а́ться от+*g.*; **we must ~ the idea** мы должны́ отказа́ться от э́той иде́и; **they had ~ed all hope** они́ потеря́ли вся́кую наде́жду. **3.** (*discontinue*) прекра|ща́ть, -ти́ть; **the search was ~ed** по́иски бы́ли прекращены́. **4.** (*surrender*): **the town was ~ed to the enemy** го́род был оста́влен врагу́; **she ~ed herself to grief** она́ предала́сь своему́ го́рю.

abandoned [əˈbænd(ə)nd] *adj.* **1.** (*forsaken*, *deserted*) оста́вленный, забро́шенный; **an ~ child** бро́шенный ребёнок. **2.** (*profligate*) распу́тный.

abandonment [əˈbændənmənt] *n.* **1.** (*forsaking*) оставле́ние. **2.** (*being forsaken*) забро́шенность. **3.** (*renunciation*) отка́з (*от чего*). **4.** (*termination*) прекраще́ние. **5.** (*impulsiveness*) бесшаба́шность.

abase [əˈbeɪs] *v.t.* ун|ижа́ть, -и́зить.

abasement [əˈbeɪsmənt] *n.* униже́ние.

abash [əˈbæʃ] *v.t.* сму|ща́ть, -ти́ть; **she felt ~ed** она́ была́ смущена́.

abate [əˈbeɪt] *v.t.* **1.** (*diminish*) ум|еньша́ть, -е́ньшить; (*mitigate*) ум|еря́ть, -е́рить; (*weaken*) осл|абля́ть, -а́бить; (*lower*, *e.g. price*) сн|ижа́ть, -и́зить. **2.** (*deduct*) сб|авля́ть, -а́вить; **he agreed to ~ sth. from the price** он согласи́лся не́сколько сба́вить це́ну. **3.** (*leg.*, *quash*) отмен|я́ть, -и́ть.

v.i. (*diminish*) ум|еньша́ться, -е́ньшиться; (*weaken*) ослаб|ева́ть, -е́ть; (*of storm*, *epidemic etc.*) ут|иха́ть, -и́хнуть.

abatement [əˈbeɪtmənt] *n.* **1.** (*reduction*) уменьше́ние; (*mitigation*) смягче́ние; (*weakening*) ослабле́ние; (*lowering*) сниже́ние; **noise ~** сниже́ние у́ровня шу́ма; (*of storm etc.*) затиха́ние. **2.** (*deduction*) ски́дка. **3.** (*leg.*) аннули́рование, отме́на.

abattoir [ˈæbəˌtwɑː(r)] *n.* скотобо́йня.

abbess [ˈæbɪs] *n.* аббати́са; настоя́тельница (монастыря́).

abbey [ˈæbɪ] *n.* абба́тство.

abbot [ˈæbət] *n.* абба́т; настоя́тель (*m.*) (монастыря́).

abbreviate [əˈbriːvɪˌeɪt] *v.t.* сокра|ща́ть, -ти́ть; **'ampere' is ~d to A** «ампе́р» сокращённо обознача́ется че́рез «А»; **~d** сокращённый, непо́лный; **he gave me an ~d version of what had happened** он вкра́тце переска́зал мне случи́вшееся.

abbreviation [əˌbriːvɪˈeɪʃ(ə)n] *n.* сокраще́ние.

ABC [ˌeɪbiːˈsiː] *n.* (*alphabet*) а́збука, алфави́т; **it's as easy as ~** э́то (про́сто) как два́жды два — четы́ре; (*reading primer*) буква́рь (*m.*); а́збука; (*fig.*, *rudiments*) а́збука; осно́вы (*f. pl.*).

abdicate [ˈæbdɪˌkeɪt] *v.t.* отка́з|ываться, -а́ться от+*g.*; **~ the throne** (*also* **~** *v.i.*) отр|ека́ться, -е́чься от престо́ла.

abdication [ˌæbdɪˈkeɪʃ(ə)n] *n.* отка́з (*от чего*); отрече́ние (от престо́ла).

abdomen [ˈæbdəmən] *n.* брюшна́я по́лость; живо́т.

abdominal [æbˈdɒmɪn(ə)l] *adj.* брюшно́й; **~ belt** набрю́шник; **~ pain** боль в животе́; **~ wound** ране́ние в живо́т.

abduct [əbˈdʌkt] *v.t.* пох|ища́ть, -и́тить; (наси́льно) ув|ози́ть, -езти́.

abduction [əbˈdʌkʃ(ə)n] *n.* похище́ние, уво́з.

abductor [əbˈdʌktə(r)] *n.* похити́тель (*m.*).

aberrant [əˈberənt] *adj.* заблужда́ющийся; (*biol.*) аберра́нтный.

aberration [ˌæbəˈreɪʃ(ə)n] *n.* **1.** (*error of judgement or conduct*) заблужде́ние; **mental ~** помраче́ние созна́ния. **2.** (*deviation*) отклоне́ние от но́рмы. **3.** (*astron.*, *opt.*) аберра́ция.

abet [əˈbet] *v.t.* подстрека́ть (*impf.*) к+*d.*; **he was ~ted by X** его́ посо́бником был X; **~ s.o. in a crime** соде́йствовать (*impf.*) кому́-н. в соверше́нии преступле́ния; **~ a crime** соде́йствовать (*impf.*) преступле́нию.

abettor [əˈbetə(r)] *n.* посо́бник.

abeyance [əˈbeɪəns] *n.* **1.** (*suspension*) вре́менная отме́на. **2. in ~: the matter is in ~** де́ло вре́менно прекращено́; **the rule has been in ~ since 1935** пра́вило не применя́лось с 1935 го́да.

abhor [əbˈhɔː(r)] *v.t.* пита́ть (*impf.*) (*or* испы́т|ывать, -а́ть) отвраще́ние к+*d.*; **nature ~s a vacuum** приро́да не те́рпит пустоты́.

abhorrence [əbˈhɒrəns] *n.* отвраще́ние; **hold in ~; have an ~ of** пита́ть (*impf.*) отвраще́ние к+*d.*

abhorrent [əbˈhɒrənt] *adj.* отврати́тельный; **the very idea is ~ to me** мне проти́вно да́же ду́мать об э́том.

abidance [əˈbaɪdəns] *n.*: **~ by the rules** соблюде́ние пра́вил.

abide [əˈbaɪd] *v.t.* **1.** (*endure*) терпе́ть (*impf.*); выноси́ть (*impf.*); **I cannot ~ him** я его́ терпе́ть не могу́. **2.** (*submit to*) подв|ерга́ться, -е́ргнуться +*d.*

v.i. **1.** (*remain*) пребыва́ть (*impf.*). **2.: ~ by** (*comply with*) приде́рживаться (*impf.*) +*g.*; **~ by the law** соблюда́ть (*impf.*) зако́н; **~ by one's promise** ост|ава́ться, -а́ться ве́рным своему́ обеща́нию.

abiding [ə'baɪdɪŋ] *adj.* постоя́нный, неизме́нный.

ability [ə'bɪlɪtɪ] *n.* **1.** (*capacity in general*) спосо́бность; **to the best of one's ~** по ме́ре спосо́бностей; **he shows an ~ for music** он проявля́ет музыка́льные спосо́бности; (*knowing how*) уме́ние; (*mental competence*) спосо́бность; **a man of ~** спосо́бный челове́к. **2.** (*pl.*, *gifts*) дарова́ния (*nt. pl.*), спосо́бности (*f. pl.*); **natural ~** врождённые спосо́бности.

abject ['æbdʒekt] *adj.* (*humble*) уни́женный; **an ~ apology** уни́женная мольба́ о проще́нии; (*craven*): **~ fear** малоду́шный страх; (*despicable*) презре́нный; (*pitiful, wretched*) жа́лкий; **in ~ poverty** в кра́йней нищете́.

abject|ion [əb'dʒekʃ(ə)n], **-ness** ['æbdʒektnɪs] *n.* униже́ние; уни́женность.

abjuration [ˌæbdʒʊ'reɪʃ(ə)n] *n.* (кля́твенное) отрече́ние; отка́з (*от чего*).

abjure [əb'dʒʊə(r)] *v.t.* (*renounce on oath*) кля́твенно отр|ека́ться, -е́чься от+*g.*; (*forswear*) отр|ека́ться, -е́чься от+*g.*; отка́з|ываться, -а́ться от+*g.*

ablative ['æblətɪv] *n.* абляти́в, отложи́тельный/твори́тельный паде́ж; **~ absolute** абляти́в абсолю́тный.

adj. абляти́вный.

ablaut ['æblaʊt] *n.* абла́ут.

ablaze [ə'bleɪz] *pred. adj.*: **the fire was soon ~** ого́нь бы́стро разгоре́лся; **the buildings were ~** зда́ния бы́ли охва́чены огнём; **her cheeks were ~ with anger** её щёки пыла́ли гне́вом; **streets ~ with light** за́литые све́том у́лицы.

adv.: **set a house ~** подж|ига́ть, -е́чь дом.

able ['eɪb(ə)l] *adj.* **1.**: **be ~ to** мочь, с-; быть в состоя́нии; **will you be ~ to come?** вы смо́жете прийти́?; (*have the strength or power to*): **he was not ~ to walk any farther** он был не в си́лах идти́ да́льше; **~ to pay** платёжеспосо́бный; **as far as one is ~** по ме́ре сил; (*know how to*) уме́ть (*impf.*): **he is ~ to swim** он уме́ет пла́вать. **2.** (*skilful*) уме́лый; (*capable*) спосо́бный; **~ seaman** матро́с пе́рвого кла́сса.

cpd. **~-bodied** *adj.* здоро́вый, кре́пкий; (*mil.*) го́дный к вое́нной слу́жбе.

ablution [ə'blu:ʃ(ə)n] *n.* (*ceremonial*) омове́ние; (*usu. pl., act of washing o.s.*) умыва́ние; **perform one's ~s** мы́ться, вы́-; ум|ыва́ться, -ы́ться.

abnegate ['æbnɪˌgeɪt] *v.t.* (*renounce*) отр|ека́ться, -е́чься от+*g.*; (*deny o.s.*) отка́з|ывать, -а́ть себе́ в+*p.*

abnegation [ˌæbnɪ'geɪʃ(ə)n] *n.* (*renunciation*) отка́з, отрече́ние (*от чего*); (*self-sacrifice*) самоотрече́ние.

abnormal [æb'nɔ:m(ə)l] *adj.* ненорма́льный; (*deviating from type*) анома́льный; **~ psychology** психопатоло́гия; (*exceptional*) необыкнове́нный.

abnormality [ˌæbnɔ:'mælɪtɪ] *n.* ненорма́льность; анома́лия.

aboard [ə'bɔ:d] *adv.* **1.** (*on a ship*) на корабле́; (*ship or aircraft*) на борту́; (*train*) в по́езде. **2.** (*on to a ship etc.*) на кора́бль; на́ борт; в по́езд; **all ~!** поса́дка зака́нчивается!; (*rail.*) по ваго́нам!; **go ~** сади́ться, сесть на су́дно *и т.п.*; **take ~** взять (*pf.*) на́ борт.

prep.: **~ ship** на борт(у́) корабля́; **~ the bus** в авто́бус(е); **~ the train** на по́езд(е).

abode [ə'bəʊd] *n.* (*dwelling-place*) жили́ще; (*domicile*) местожи́тельство; **take up one's ~** посел|я́ться, -и́ться; **of no fixed ~** без постоя́нного местожи́тельства.

abolish [ə'bɒlɪʃ] *v.t.* уничт|ожа́ть, -о́жить; (*laws, taxes etc.*) отмен|я́ть, -и́ть; (*customs etc.*) упраздн|я́ть, -и́ть.

abolition [ˌæbə'lɪʃ(ə)n] *n.* уничтоже́ние; отме́на; упраздне́ние.

abolitionism [ˌæbə'lɪʃənɪz(ə)m] *n.* аболициони́зм.

abolitionist [ˌæbə'lɪʃənɪst] *n.* аболициони́ст.

abominable [ə'bɒmɪnəb(ə)l] *adj.* отврати́тельный; **the food was ~** корми́ли отврати́тельно; **the A~ Snowman** сне́жный челове́к, йе́ти (*m. indecl.*).

abominate [ə'bɒmɪˌneɪt] *v.t.* пита́ть (*impf.*) отвраще́ние к+*d.*

abomination [əˌbɒmɪ'neɪʃ(ə)n] *n.* (*detestation*) отвраще́ние; **he was held in ~** он вызыва́л всео́бщее отвраще́ние; (*detestable thg.*): **this building is an ~** э́то зда́ние про́сто у́жас; **that is my pet ~** э́то вызыва́ет у меня́ лю́тую не́нависть.

aboriginal [ˌæbə'rɪdʒɪn(ə)l] *n.* = **aborigine**

adj. тузе́мный, коренно́й; (*primitive*) первобы́тный.

aborigine [ˌæbə'rɪdʒɪnɪ] *n.* тузе́м|ец (*fem.* -ка); абориге́н; коренно́й жи́тель.

abort [ə'bɔ:t] *v.t.* **1.** (*terminate pregnancy of*) де́лать, с-або́рт +*d.* **2.** (*fig., terminate or cancel prematurely*) приостан|а́вливать, -ови́ть.

v.i. **1.** (*of a pers.*) выки́дывать, вы́кинуть. **2.** (*fig., come to nothing*) срыва́ться, сорва́ться.

abortion [ə'bɔ:ʃ(ə)n] *n.* **1.** (*miscarriage*) або́рт, вы́кидыш; **backstreet ~** подпо́льный або́рт; **procure an ~** сде́лать (*pf.*) або́рт; **she had an ~** (*by surgery*) она́ сде́лала або́рт. **2.** (*misshapen creature*) уро́дец. **3.** (*hideous object*) уро́дливая вещь. **4.** (*cancellation*) прекраще́ние.

abortionist [ə'bɔ:ʃənɪst] *n.* подпо́льный акуше́р, (*coll.*) абортма́хер.

abortive [ə'bɔ:tɪv] *adj.* (*of a birth*) преждевре́менный; (*fig.*) мертворождённый, неуда́вшийся.

abound [ə'baʊnd] *v.i.* **1.** (*exist in large numbers or quantities*) быть в изоби́лии; находи́ться/име́ться в большо́м коли́честве. **2.**: **~ in** (*be rich in*) изоби́ловать (*impf.*) +*i.*; **the country ~s in oil** страна́ бога́та не́фтью; **~** (*teem*) **with** кише́ть (*impf.*) +*i.*; (*have plenty of*): **a man ~ing in common sense** челове́к, испо́лненный здра́вого смы́сла.

about [ə'baʊt] *adv.* **1.** (*here and there*): **don't leave your clothes ~** не оставля́йте свое́й оде́жды, где попа́ло. **2.** (*in the vicinity; in circulation*) вокру́г, круго́м; **there is a bug of some sort ~** хо́дит како́й-то ви́рус; **there are a lot of soldiers ~** круго́м мно́го солда́т; **is he anywhere ~?** нет его́ где́-нибудь побли́зости?; **there are rumours ~** хо́дят слу́хи; **up and ~** на нога́х; **she is too ill to get ~** она́ так больна́, что не мо́жет выходи́ть. **3.** (*to face the other way*): **~ turn!** (*mil.*) круго́м!; **the wrong way ~** наоборо́т; (*alternately*) **turn and turn ~** по о́череди. **4.** (*almost*) почти́; **that's ~ right** приме́рно так; **dinner is ~ ready** обе́д почти́ гото́в; **it's ~ time we went** пора́ бы нам идти́; **and ~ time too!** давно́ пора́! **5.** (*approximately*) о́коло+*g.*; приблизи́тельно; **~ 3 o'clock** о́коло трёх часо́в; **he is ~ your height** он приблизи́тельно ва́шего ро́ста; **~ twice** ра́за два; **it costs ~ 100 roubles** э́то сто́ит рубле́й сто; **~ a kilogram in weight** ве́сом о́коло килогра́мма; **in ~ half an hour** че́рез каки́е-нибудь полчаса́. **6.** **~ to** (*ready to, just going to*): **he was ~ to leave when I arrived** он собира́лся уходи́ть, когда́ я пришёл; **I was ~ to say** я собира́лся сказа́ть; **the train is ~ to leave** по́езд сейча́с тро́нется; **I was just ~ to do so** я как раз собира́лся э́то сде́лать. **7.** *For phrasal vv. with ~, see relevant v. entries.*

prep. **1.** (*around; near*) вокру́г+*g.*; **the people ~ him** лю́ди, его́ окружа́ющие; **somewhere ~ here** где́-то здесь; **he looked ~ him** он огляде́лся вокру́г; **I have no money ~ me** у меня́ нет при себе́ де́нег. **2.** (*at or to var. places, in*) по+*d.*; **walk ~ the streets** ходи́ть (*indet.*) по у́лицам; **books lay ~ the room** кни́ги лежа́ли по всей ко́мнате. **3.** (*fig., in*) в+*p.*; **there was no vanity ~ him** в нём не́ было тщесла́вия. **4.** (*concerning*) о+*p.*; насчёт+*g.*; по по́воду+*g.*; относи́тельно+*g.*; **what are you talking ~?** о чём вы говори́те?; **what ~ dinner?** как насчёт обе́да?; **how ~ a game of cards?** не сыгра́ть ли нам в ка́рты?; **what is it all ~?** в чём де́ло?; **he has called ~ the rent** он зашёл насчёт квартпла́ты; **a quarrel arose ~ her** из-за неё произошла́ ссо́ра; **she is mad ~ him** она́ без ума́ от него́; **much ado ~ nothing** мно́го шу́ма из ничего́; **there is no doubt ~ it** в э́том нет сомне́ния. **5.** (*engaged in*): **be ~ one's business** занима́ться (*impf.*) свои́ми дела́ми; **he was a long time ~ it** у него́ ушло́ на э́то мно́го вре́мени; **why not ask for £100 while you're ~ it?** почему́ бы не попроси́ть заодно́ сто фу́нтов?

cpds. **~-face, ~-turn** *nn.* (*lit.*) поворо́т круго́м; (*fig.*) ре́зкое измене́ние.

above [ə'bʌv] *n.*: **the ~** вышеупомя́нутое; вышеизло́женное.

adj. (*~-mentioned*) вышеупомя́нутый; (*foregoing*) предыду́щий.

adv. **1.** (*overhead; upstairs*) наверху́; **we live in the flat ~** мы живём в кварти́ре этажо́м вы́ше; (*expr. motion*) наве́рх; **from ~** све́рху. **2.** (*higher up*) вы́ше. **3.** (*relig.*): **the powers ~** си́лы (*f. pl.*) небе́сные. **4.** (*in text, speech etc.*) вы́ше; ра́ньше.

prep. **1.** (*over*; *higher than*) над+*i.*; вы́ше+*g.*; **his voice was heard ~ the noise** его́ го́лос доноси́лся сквозь шум. **2.** (*beyond*; *upstream of*): **3 miles ~ Oxford** в трёх ми́лях вы́ше О́ксфорда по тече́нию. **3.** (*more than*) свы́ше+*g.*; **~ 30 tons** свы́ше 30 тонн. **4.** (*fig.*): **~ me in rank** вы́ше меня́ чи́ном; **~ all praise** вы́ше вся́ких похва́л; **he is ~ such base actions** он не спосо́бен на таки́е по́длости; **~ suspicion** вне подозре́ния; **he is getting ~ himself** он начина́ет зазнава́ться; **he is not ~ cheating at cards** он позволя́ет себе́ жу́льничать в ка́ртах; **he is living ~ his means** он живёт не по сре́дствам; **~ all** пре́жде/бо́льше всего́; са́мое гла́вное; **over and ~** вдоба́вок к+*d.*; **this is ~ my head** э́то вы́ше моего́ понима́ния; **he kept his head ~ water** (*fig.*) он ко́е-как перебива́лся.

cpds. **~-board** *adj.* (*honourable*) че́стный; (*open*, *frank*) откры́тый; **~-mentioned** *adj.* вышеупомя́нутый; **~-named** *adj.* вышена́званный.

abracadabra [ˌæbrəkəˈdæbrə] *n.* абракада́бра.

abrade [əˈbreɪd] *v.t.* (*skin etc.*) сдира́ть, содра́ть; (*bark*) об|дира́ть, -одра́ть.

abrasion [əˈbreɪʒ(ə)n] *n.* (*rubbing off*) истира́ние; (*wounded area of skin*) сса́дина.

abrasive [əˈbreɪsɪv] *n.* абрази́вный материа́л.

adj. сдира́ющий, обдира́ющий; **~ wheel** шлифова́льный круг; (*fig.*) колю́чий; **an ~ personality** ре́зкий хара́ктер; **an ~ tongue** беспоща́дный язы́к; **an ~ voice** ре́зкий/скрипу́чий го́лос.

abreast [əˈbrest] *adv.* в ряд, на одно́й ли́нии; **three ~** по́ трое в ряд; (*naut.*) на тра́верзе; (*fig.*): **we keep ~ of the times** мы идём в но́гу со вре́менем; **~ of events** в ку́рсе собы́тий.

abridge [əˈbrɪdʒ] *v.t.* **1.** сокра|ща́ть, -ти́ть; **an ~d version** сокращённый вариа́нт. **2.** (*rights etc.*) ограни́чи|вать, -ть.

abridgement [əˈbrɪdʒmənt] *n.* сокраще́ние; ограниче́ние; (*summary*) конспе́кт.

abroad [əˈbrɔːd] *adv.* за грани́цей/рубежо́м; (*motion*) за грани́цу; **from ~** из-за грани́цы; **our correspondents ~** на́ши иностра́нные корреспонде́нты; (*fig.*, *in circulation*): **there are rumours ~** хо́дят слу́хи.

abrogate [ˈæbrəˌgeɪt] *v.t.* отмен|я́ть, -и́ть.

abrogation [ˌæbrəˈgeɪʃ(ə)n] *n.* отме́на.

abrupt [əˈbrʌpt] *adj.* **1.** (*disconnected*) отры́вистый. **2.** (*brusque*) ре́зкий. **3.** (*sudden*) внеза́пный. **4.** (*steep*, *precipitous*) круто́й, обры́вистый.

abruptness [əˈbrʌptnɪs] *n.* отры́вистость; ре́зкость; внеза́пность; крутизна́.

abscess [ˈæbsɪs] *n.* абсце́сс.

abscond [əbˈskɒnd] *v.i.* скр|ыва́ться, -ы́ться; укр|ыва́ться, -ы́ться; **he ~ed with the takings** он обчи́стил (*coll.*) ка́ссу и скры́лся.

abseil [ˈæbseɪl, -ziːl] *n.* спуск на верёвке.

v.i. спус|ка́ться, -ти́ться на верёвке.

absence [ˈæbs(ə)ns] *n.* отсу́тствие; **in his ~** в его́ отсу́тствие; **leave of ~** о́тпуск; **~ without leave** самово́льная отлу́чка; **~ of mind** рассе́янность; (*lack*): **in the ~ of evidence** за недоста́точностью ули́к.

absent[1] [ˈæbs(ə)nt] *adj.* **1.** (*not present*) отсу́тствующий; **~ without leave** в самово́льной отлу́чке; **be ~** отсу́тствовать (*impf.*); **he was ~ from school** его́ не́ было в шко́ле. **2.** (*abstracted*) рассе́янный.

cpds. **~-minded** *adj.* рассе́янный; **~-mindedness** *n.* рассе́янность.

absent[2] [əbˈsent] *v.t.*: **~ o.s.** отлуч|а́ться, -и́ться; уклон|я́ться, -и́ться (от+*g.*).

absentee [ˌæbsənˈtiː] *n.* отсу́тствующий; уклоня́ющийся; **there were six ~s** отсу́тствовало шесть челове́к; **~ landlord** владе́лец, сдаю́щий своё име́ние и живу́щий в друго́м ме́сте.

absenteeism [ˌæbsənˈtiːɪz(ə)m] *n.* абсентеи́зм; прогу́л.

absinth(e) [ˈæbsɪnθ] *n.* (*liqueur*) полы́нная во́дка, абсе́нт.

absolute [ˈæbsəˌluːt, -ˌljuːt] *n.* (*phil.*: **the A~**) абсолю́т.

adj. (*perfect*): **~ beauty** соверше́нная красота́; (*pure*): **~ alcohol** чи́стый спирт; (*unconditional*): **an ~ promise** твёрдое обеща́ние; **~ monarchy** абсолю́тная мона́рхия; (*consummate*): **an ~ ruffian** зако́нченный негодя́й; (*indubitable*): **~ proof** несомне́нное доказа́тельство; (*gram.*): **~ construction** абсолю́тная констру́кция.

absolutely [ˈæbsəˌluːtlɪ, -ˌljuːtlɪ] *adv.* **1.** (*completely*) вполне́, абсолю́тно; соверше́нно; (*unquestionably*) безусло́вно. **2.** **~!** (*expr. agreement*) безусло́вно/коне́чно!; абсолю́тно с ва́ми согла́сен.

absolution [ˌæbsəˈluːʃ(ə)n, -ˈljuːʃ(ə)n] *n.* (*forgiveness*) проще́ние; (*eccl.*) отпуще́ние грехо́в; (*leg.*) оправда́ние; **his ~ from blame** призна́ние его́ невино́вным.

absolutism [ˈæbsəluːˌtɪz(ə)m, -ljuːˌtɪz(ə)m] *n.* абсолюти́зм.

absolutist [ˈæbsəˌluːtɪst, -ˌljuːtɪst] *n.* абсолюти́ст.

adj. абсолюти́стский.

absolve [əbˈzɒlv] *v.t.* (*of blame*) призн|ава́ть, -а́ть невино́вным; **he was ~d of all blame** он был при́знан по́лностью невино́вным; (*of sins*) отпус|ка́ть, -ти́ть грехи́ +*d.*; **his sins were ~d** он получи́л отпуще́ние грехо́в; (*of obligation*) освобо|жда́ть, -ди́ть; **he was ~d of obligation** он был освобождён от обяза́тельства.

absorb [əbˈsɔːb, -ˈzɔːb] *v.t.* **1.** (*soak up*) вс|а́сывать, -оса́ть. **2.** (*fig.*): **~ knowledge** впи́т|ывать, -а́ть зна́ния. **3.** (*engross*) погло|ща́ть, -ти́ть; **his business ~s him** он поглощён свои́ми дела́ми; **he listened with ~ed interest** он слу́шал со всепоглоща́ющим интере́сом; **he was ~ed in reading** он был погружён в чте́ние. **4.** (*tech.*) абсорби́ровать (*impf.*, *pf.*); (*of shock*, *vibration etc.*) амортизи́ровать (*impf.*, *pf.*).

absorbability [əbˌsɔːbəˈbɪlɪtɪ, -ˌzɔːbəˈbɪlɪtɪ] *n.* поглоща́емость.

absorbable [əbˈsɔːbəb(ə)l, -ˈzɔːbəb(ə)l] *adj.* поглоща́емый.

absorbency [əbˈsɔːbənsɪ, -ˈzɔːbənsɪ] *n.* впи́тывающая спосо́бность.

absorbent [əbˈsɔːbənt, -ˈzɔːbənt] *adj.* вса́сывающий, поглоща́ющий; **~ cotton** (*US*) (гигроскопи́ческая) ва́та.

absorbing [əbˈsɔːbɪŋ, -ˈzɔːbɪŋ] *adj.* (*engrossing*) захва́тывающий.

absorption [əbˈsɔːpʃ(ə)n, -ˈzɔːpʃ(ə)n] *n.* **1.** (*soaking up*) вса́сывание; впи́тывание. **2.** (*engrossment*): **his ~ in his studies** его́ погружённость в заня́тия. **3.** (*tech.*) абсо́рбция.

abstain [əbˈsteɪn] *v.i.* возде́рж|иваться, -а́ться; **he ~ed (from drinking) on principle** он возде́рживался от спиртны́х напи́тков из при́нципа; **the Opposition decided to ~ (from voting)** оппози́ция реши́ла воздержа́ться (от голосова́ния).

abstainer [əbˈsteɪnə(r)] *n.* (*from drinking*) тре́звенник, непью́щий; (*from voting*) воздержа́вшийся.

abstemious [æbˈstiːmɪəs] *adj.* (*of pers.*) возде́ржанный; (*of a meal etc.*) уме́ренный.

abstemiousness [æbˈstiːmɪəsnɪs] *n.* возде́ржанность.

abstention [əbˈstenʃ(ə)n] *n.* воздержа́ние (*от чего*): **the resolution was passed with three ~s** резолю́ция была́ при́нята при трёх воздержа́вшихся.

abstinence [ˈæbstɪnəns] *n.* воздержа́ние (*от чего*); (*moderation*) уме́ренность; **total ~** по́лный отка́з от употребле́ния спиртны́х напи́тков.

abstinent [ˈæbstɪnənt] *adj.* (*of pers.*) возде́ржанный; (*moderate*) уме́ренный; (*not taking alcohol*) непью́щий.

abstract[1] [ˈæbstrækt] *n.* (*summary*) резюме́ (*indecl.*); (*of dissertation*) рефера́т; **in the ~** в абстра́кции; отвлечённо.

adj. отвлечённый, абстра́ктный; **~ noun** отвлечённое и́мя/существи́тельное; **~ art** абстра́ктное иску́сство; **~ artist** абстракциони́ст.

abstract[2] [əbˈstrækt] *v.t.* **1.** (*remove*, *separate*) отдел|я́ть, -и́ть; (*coll.*, *make away with*) утащи́ть (*pf.*). **2.** (*divert*, *e.g. attention*) отвл|ека́ть, -е́чь. **3.** (*summarize*) резюми́ровать (*impf.*, *pf.*). **4.** (*consider ~ly*) абстраги́ровать (*impf.*, *pf.*).

abstracted [əbˈstræktɪd] *adj.* заду́мавшийся, рассе́янный.

abstraction [əbˈstrækʃ(ə)n] *n.* **1.** (*withdrawal*, *removal*) отделе́ние. **2.** (*process of thought or idea*) отвлече́ние, абстра́кция. **3.** (*absence of mind*) рассе́янность.

abstruse [əbˈstruːs] *adj.* замыслова́тый, мудрёный.

abstruseness [əbˈstruːsnɪs] *n.* замыслова́тость.

absurd [əbˈsɜːd] *adj.* неле́пый, абсу́рдный; **the theatre of the A~** теа́тр абсу́рда; **don't be ~!** како́й вздор!; не смеши́те люде́й!; **you look ~ in that hat** в э́той шля́пе у вас неле́пый вид; **he was ~ly generous** он был до абсу́рда ще́др.

absurdity [əb'sɜ:dɪtɪ] *n.* нелéпость, абсýрдность; **reduce to ~** дов|оди́ть, -ести́ до абсýрда.

abundance [ə'bʌnd(ə)ns] *n.* (*plenty*) изоби́лие; **there was food in ~** еды́ бы́ло вдо́воль; (*affluence*) богáтство, довóльство; **live in ~** жить в достáтке; (*superfluity*) избы́ток.

abundant [ə'bʌnd(ə)nt] *adj.* (из)оби́льный (*чем*); **there is ~ proof** доказáтельств бо́льше чем достáточно; **be ~** изоби́ловать (*impf.*); **~ly clear** предéльно я́сно.

abuse[1] [ə'bju:s] *n.* **1.** (*misuse*) злоупотреблéние; **~ of confidence** злоупотреблéние довéрием. **2.** (*unjust or corrupt practice*): **a crying ~** вопию́щее злоупотреблéние. **3.** (*reviling*) рýгань, брань; ругáтельства (*nt. pl.*); **term of ~** оскорблéние; **he heaped/showered ~ on me** он осыпáл меня́ брáнью.

abuse[2] [ə'bju:z] *v.t.* **1.** (*misuse*) злоупотреб|ля́ть, -и́ть +*i.* **2.** (*revile*) ругáть (*impf.*); оскорб|ля́ть, -и́ть; поноси́ть (*impf.*).

abusive [ə'bju:sɪv] *adj.* (*insulting*) оскорби́тельный; (*using curses*) брáнный, ругáтельный; **~ language** брань, рýгань.

abusiveness [ə'bju:sɪvnɪs] *n.* оскорби́тельность, брань, рýгань.

abut [ə'bʌt] *v.i.*: **~ on** (*border on*) прилегáть (*impf.*) к+*d.*; примыкáть (*impf.*) к+*d.*; грани́чить (*impf.*) с+*i.*; (*lean against*) уп|ирáться, -ерéться в+*a.*

abutment [ə'bʌtmənt] *n.* **1.** (*junction*) стык. **2.** (*part of structure*) пятá; контрфо́рс.

abysmal [ə'bɪzm(ə)l] *adj.* бездо́нный; (*fig.*) безграни́чный; ужасáющий; **~ ignorance** ди́кое невéжество.

abyss [ə'bɪs] *n.* бéздна, про́пасть.

Abyssinia [ˌæbɪ'sɪnɪə] *n.* Абисси́ния.

Abyssinian [ˌæbɪ'sɪnɪən] *n.* абисси́н|ец (*fem.* -ка).
adj. абисси́нский.

AC (*abbr. of* **alternating current**) переме́нный ток.

a/c [ə'kaʊnt] *n.* (*abbr. of* **account**) текýщий счёт.

acacia [ə'keɪʃə] *n.* акáция; **false ~** бéлая акáция.

academia [ˌækə'di:mɪə] *n.* академи́ческий мир; учёные круги́.

academic [ˌækə'demɪk] *n.* учёный.
adj. академи́ческий, наýчный; (*unpractical*) академи́чный; нереáльный, неактуáльный, кабинéтный.

academicals [ˌækə'demɪk(ə)lz] *n.* университéтское облачéние.

academician [əˌkædə'mɪʃ(ə)n] *n.* акадéмик.

academicism [ˌækə'demɪˌsɪz(ə)m] *n.* академи́чность.

academy [ə'kædəmɪ] *n.* акадéмия, учи́лище; (*in Scotland*) срéдняя шкóла; **~ of fine arts** акадéмия изя́щных искýсств; **military ~** воéнное учи́лище.

acanthus [ə'kænθəs] *n.* акáнт.

accede [æk'si:d] *v.i.* **1.** (*agree, assent*) согла|шáться, -си́ться (с+*i.*). **2.**: **~ to** (*grant*): **~ to a request** удовлетвор|я́ть, -и́ть про́сьбу; (*take up, enter upon*) вступ|áть, -и́ть в+*a.*; **~ to the throne** взойти́ (*pf.*) на престо́л; (*join*) присоедин|я́ться, -и́ться к+*d.*

accelerate [ək'seləˌreɪt] *v.t. & i.* уск|оря́ть(ся), -о́рить(ся); (*motoring*) да|вáть, -ть газ.

acceleration [əkˌselə'reɪʃ(ə)n] *n.* ускорéние; **the car has good ~** у автомоби́ля хоро́ший разго́н.

accelerator [ək'seləˌreɪtə(r)] *n.* (*of car*) акселерáтор; (*phys., etc.*) ускори́тель (*m.*); (*chem.*) катализáтор.

accent[1] ['æks(ə)nt, -sent] *n.* **1.** (*orthographical sign; emphasis*) ударéние; акцéнт; **put the ~ on** (*fig.*) дéлать, с- акцéнт на+*p.* **2.** (*mode of speech*) акцéнт; **he speaks with a slight ~** он говори́т с лёгким акцéнтом.

accent[2] [æk'sent] *v.t.* **1.** (*emphasize in speech or fig.*) дéлать, с- ударéние/акцéнт на+*p.*; акценти́ровать (*impf.*). **2.** (*put written ~s on*) стáвить, по- ударéние на+*a.*

accentual [ək'sentjʊəl] *adj.*: **~ prosody** тони́ческое стихосложéние.

accentuate [æk'sentjʊˌeɪt] *v.t.* (*lit.*) = **accent**[2]; (*fig.*) акценти́ровать (*impf.*); подч|ёркивать, -еркнýть; **the difference was ~d** рáзница былá подчёркнута.

accentuation [ækˌsentjʊ'eɪʃ(ə)n] *n.* ударéние; акцентуáция; (*fig.*) акценти́рование; подчёркивание.

accept [ək'sept] *v.t.* **1.** (*agree to receive*) прин|имáть, -я́ть; **he refused to ~ a tip** он отказáлся взять чаевы́е; **she ~ed him** (*as fiancé*) онá приняла́ его́ предложéние; **he was ~ed as one of the group** его́ при́няли в свой круг. **2.** (*recognize, admit*) призн|авáть, -áть; **you must ~ this fact** вы должны́ смири́ться с э́тим фáктом; **I ~ that it may take time** не спо́рю, что для э́того потрéбуется врéмя; **it is an ~ed fact** э́то общепри́знанный факт; **he ~ed defeat gracefully** он при́нял поражéние с досто́инством. **3.** (*comm.*) акцептовáть (*impf., pf.*).

acceptability [əkˌseptə'bɪlɪtɪ] *n.* приéмлемость.

acceptable [ək'septəb(ə)l] *adj.* приéмлемый.

acceptance [ək'sept(ə)ns] *n.* (*willing receipt*) приня́тие; (*approval*) одобрéние; **his words found ~** его́ словá вы́звали одобрéние; (*comm.*) акцéпт.

acceptation [ˌæksep'teɪʃ(ə)n] *n.*: **~ of a word** (при́нятое) значéние слóва.

access ['ækses] *n.* **1.** (*possibility of reaching, using, etc.*) до́ступ; **he gained ~ to the house** он прони́к в дом; **you may have ~ to my library** вы мо́жете по́льзоваться моéй библиотéкой; **easy of ~** (*of places or persons*) достýпный; (*means of approach; way in*) подхо́д; **~ road** подъездно́й путь. **2.** (*attack of illness etc.*) при́ступ, вспы́шка.

accessary [ək'sesərɪ] = **accessory** *n.* **1.**

accessibility [əkˌsesɪ'bɪlɪtɪ] *n.* достýпность; удо́бство подхо́да.

accessible [ək'sesɪb(ə)l] *adj.* достýпный; **he is ~ to argument** он прислýшивается к чужи́м до́водам; **~ to bribery** продáжный; (*open to influence*) поддаю́щийся влия́нию.

accession [ək'seʃ(ə)n] *n.* **1.** (*attaining*) вступлéние; **~ to an office** вступлéние в до́лжность; **~ to power** прихо́д к влáсти; **~ to the throne** вступлéние на престо́л; **~ to manhood** достижéние зрéлости; возмужáние; (*committal*): **~ to a treaty** присоединéние к договóру. **2.** (*addition, growth*) приро́ст. **3.** (*of book into library etc.*) поступлéние; **~ catalogue** катало́г но́вых поступлéний.
v.t. вн|оси́ть, -ести́ в катало́г.

accessory [ək'sesərɪ] *n.* **1.** (*leg., also* **accessary**) соучáстник; **~ to the murder** соучáстник уби́йства; **~ before/after the fact** соучáстник до/по́сле собы́тия преступлéния. **2.** (*pl., ancillary parts of machine etc.*) принадлéжности (*f. pl.*), приспособлéния (*nt. pl.*); (*of clothing*) аксессуáры (*m. pl.*).
adj. вспомогáтельный; дополни́тельный.

accidence ['æksɪd(ə)ns] *n.* (*gram.*) словоизменéние; морфоло́гия.

accident ['æksɪd(ə)nt] *n.* **1.** (*chance*) слýчай, случáйность; **by ~** случáйно; **by the merest ~** чи́сто случáйно; **it was no ~ that he was present** его́ присýтствие нé было случáйным. **2.** (*unintentional action*): **I'm sorry, it was an ~** прости́те, я нечáянно. **3.** (*mishap*) несчáстный слýчай; (*rail.*) крушéние; **road ~** автомоби́льная катастро́фа; **~s in the home** бытовы́е трáвмы; **~ insurance** страховáние от несчáстных слýчаев; **his car met with an ~** его́ автомоби́ль попáл в авáрию; **~s will happen** ≃ чемý быть, того́ не миновáть; вся́кое бывáет; **we arrived without ~** мы доéхали благополýчно. **4.** (*phil.*) акцидéнция.
cpd. **~-prone** *adj.* невезýчий; **~-prone person** бедолáга (*coll., c.g.*); три́дцать три несчáстья.

accidental [ˌæksɪ'dent(ə)l] *n.* (*mus.*) знак альтерáции.
adj. **1.** (*happening by chance*) случáйный; **~ death** смерть в результáте несчáстного слýчая. **2.** (*incidental*) побо́чный.

acclaim [ə'kleɪm] *n.* (*welcome*) привéтствие; (*applause*) овáция.
v.t. (*welcome*) привéтствовать (*impf.*); (*hail*) провозгла|шáть, -си́ть; **he was ~ed king** его́ провозгласи́ли королём; (*applaud*) бýрно аплоди́ровать (*impf.*) +*d.*

acclamation [ˌæklə'meɪʃ(ə)n] *n.* (*loud approval*) шýмное одобрéние; (*enthusiasm*) энтузиáзм; (*pl., shouts of welcome or applause*) привéтственные во́згласы (*m. pl.*); **his books won the ~ of critics** его́ кни́ги вы́звали шýмное одобрéние кри́тиков.

acclimatization [əˌklaɪmətaɪ'zeɪʃ(ə)n] *n.* акклиматизáция.

acclimatize [ə'klaɪməˌtaɪz] *v.t. & i.* акклиматизи́ровать(ся) (*impf., pf.*).

acclivity [ə'klɪvɪtɪ] *n.* поло́гий подъём.

accolade ['ækə,leɪd, -'leɪd] *n.* знак посвяще́ния в ры́цари; **he received the ~** он был посвящён в ры́цари; (*fig.*) похвала́; награ́да; (*mus.*) аккола́да.

accommodat|e [ə'kɒmə,deɪt] *v.t.* **1.** (*find lodging for*) разме|ща́ть, -сти́ть; (*single pers.*) поме|ща́ть, -сти́ть; предост|авля́ть, -а́вить жильё +*d.* (*mil.*) расквартиро́в|ывать, -а́ть. **2.** (*hold, seat*) вме|ща́ть, -сти́ть; **the car will ~e 6 persons** маши́на вмеща́ет шесть челове́к; **a hall ~ing 500** зал на 500 челове́к. **3.** (*oblige*) ока́з|ывать, -а́ть услу́гу +*d.*; **~e s.o. with a loan** предоста́вить (*pf.*) кому́-н. де́ньги взаймы́. **4.** (*equip*) снаб|жа́ть, -ди́ть (*кого чем*). **5.** (*adapt*) приспос|обля́ть, -о́бить; примен|я́ть, -и́ть; **she ~ed herself to circumstances** она примени́лась/приспосо́билась к обстоя́тельствам. **6.** (*reconcile*) примир|я́ть, -и́ть.

accommodating [ə'kɒmə,deɪtɪŋ] *adj.* (*willing to oblige*) покла́дистый, сгово́рчивый, услу́жливый; (*easy to live with*) ужи́вчивый.

accommodation [ə,kɒmə'deɪʃ(ə)n] *n.* **1.** (*lodgings*) жильё; **can you provide a night's ~?** мо́жно останови́ться у вас на́ ночь?; **hotel ~ is scarce** гости́ничных мест не хвата́ет. **2.** (*loan*) ссу́да, креди́т. **3.** (*adaptation*) приспособле́ние. **4.** (*settlement*) соглаше́ние. **5.** (*convenience*) удо́бство; **~ ladder** забо́ртный трап.

accompaniment [ə'kʌmpənɪmənt] *n.* **1.** (*accompanying*) сопровожде́ние. **2.** (*concomitant*): **disease is an ~ of famine** боле́знь — спу́тник го́лода. **3.** (*mus.*) аккомпанеме́нт; (*fig.*): **he spoke to the ~ of laughter** его́ речь то и де́ло прерыва́л смех.

accompanist [ə'kʌmpənɪst] *n.* (*mus.*) аккомпаниа́тор.

accompan|y [ə'kʌmpənɪ] *v.t.* **1.** (*lit., go or be with; fig., occur with*) сопровожда́ть (*impf.*); **~ied by friends** в сопровожде́нии друзе́й; (*lit. and fig., attend*) сопу́тствовать (*impf.*) +*d.*; **many illnesses are ~ied by fever** жар характе́рен для мно́гих боле́зней; (*escort*): **may I ~y you home?** разреши́те проводи́ть вас домо́й? **2.** (*fig., supplement*) сопрово|жда́ть, -ди́ть (*что чем*); **he ~ied his remarks with gestures** он сопровожда́л свои́ замеча́ния же́стами; **your offer must be ~ied by a letter** ва́ше предложе́ние необходи́мо сопроводи́ть письмо́м. **3.** (*mus.*) аккомпани́ровать (*impf.*) +*d.*

accomplice [ə'kʌmplɪs, -'kɒm-] *n.* соуча́стник, соо́бщник.

accomplish [ə'kʌmplɪʃ, ə'kɒm-] *v.t.* (*complete*) заверш|а́ть, -и́ть; (*fulfil, perform*) выполня́ть, вы́полнить; соверш|а́ть, -и́ть.

accomplished [ə'kʌmplɪʃd, ə'kɒm-] *adj.* **1.** (*completed*) завершённый, совершённый; **an ~ fact** соверши́вшийся факт. **2.** (*skilled, experienced*) соверше́нный, иску́сный, зако́нченный. **3.** (*cultivated*) культу́рный, разносторо́нний. **4.** (*egregious*): **an ~ liar** зако́нченный лгун.

accomplishment [ə'kʌmplɪʃmənt, ə'kɒm-] *n.* заверше́ние; выполне́ние; (*achievement*) достиже́ние; **difficult of ~** трудноисполни́мый; (*skill*) уме́ние, соверше́нство; **a man of many ~s** разносторо́нний челове́к.

accord [ə'kɔːd] *n.* **1.** (*agreement*) согла́сие, соглаше́ние; **with one ~** единоду́шно; **be in ~ with** быть согла́сным с+*i.*; быть в согла́сии с+*i.*; согласо́вываться (*impf.*) с+*i.* **2.** (*volition*): **of one's own ~** по со́бственному почи́ну/жела́нию; сам по себе́; **the door opened of is own ~** дверь откры́лась сама́.

v.t. предост|авля́ть, -а́вить (*что кому*); **he was ~ed the necesssary facilities** ему́ предоста́вили всё необходи́мое; **~ permission** да|ва́ть, -ть разреше́ние; **he was ~ed a hero's welcome** его́ встре́тили как геро́я.

v.i.: **~ with** быть в согла́сии с+*i.*; согласо́в|ываться, -а́ться с+*i.*

accordance [ə'kɔːd(ə)ns] *n.* (*agreement*) согла́сие; (*conformity*) соотве́тствие; **in ~ with** в соотве́тствии с+*i.*, согла́сно+*d.*

according [ə'kɔːdɪŋ] *adv.*: **~ as** соотве́тственно +*d.*, в зави́симости от+*g.*; **~ as your work is good or bad** в зави́симости от ка́чества ва́шей рабо́ты; **you may go or stay ~ as you decide** са́ми реша́йте — идти́ и́ли остава́ться; **~ to** (*in keeping or conformity with*) согла́сно+*d.*; **~ to the laws** согла́сно зако́нам; (*in a manner or degree consistent with; corresponding to*) в соотве́тствии с+*i.*, по+*d.*; **books arranged ~ to authors** кни́ги, размещённые по а́вторам; (*depending on*): **~ to circumstances** в зави́симости от обстоя́тельств; (*on the authority or information of*) по+*d.*, согла́сно +*d.*; по мне́нию/слова́м/сообще́нию +*g.*; **the Gospel ~ to St. Mark** ева́нгелие от Ма́рка.

accordingly [ə'kɔːdɪŋlɪ] *adv.* **1.** (*as circumstances suggest*) соотве́тственно. **2.** (*therefore*) поэ́тому; таки́м о́бразом.

accordion [ə'kɔːdɪən] *n.* аккордео́н; **~-pleated skirt** плиссиро́ванная ю́бка.

accordionist [ə'kɔːdɪənɪst] *n.* аккордеони́ст.

accost [ə'kɒst] *v.t.* прист|ава́ть, -а́ть к+*d.* (с разгово́ром).

account [ə'kaʊnt] *n.* **1.** (*comm.*) счёт (*pl.* -а́); **current, credit ~** теку́щий счёт; **deposit ~** депози́тный счёт; **joint ~** о́бщий счёт; **statement of ~** вы́писка из счёта; **~ book** счётная/бухга́лтерская кни́га; **keep ~s** вести́ (*det.*) счета́; **open an ~** откр|ыва́ть, -ы́ть счёт; **settle an ~** опла́|чивать, -ти́ть счёт; распла́|чиваться, -ти́ться по счёту; **render an ~** предст|авля́ть, -а́вить счёт; **put these goods down to my ~** запиши́те э́ти това́ры на мой счёт; **can you give me a little on ~?** мо́жете ли вы мне дать небольшо́й зада́ток?; **£5 on ~ of salary** 5 фу́нтов в счёт жа́лованья; **balance, square ~s** св|оди́ть, -ести́ счета́; подв|оди́ть, -ести́ бала́нс; (*fig.*): **settle ~s with s.o.** (*take revenge*) свести́ (*pf.*) счёты с кем-н.; **he has gone to his ~** (*died*) он поко́нчил счёты с жи́знью. **2.** (*calculation*) расчёт; **money of ~** расчётная едини́ца; **he is quick at ~s** он бы́стро/хорошо́ счита́ет. **3.** (*purpose; benefit*) по́льза; вы́года; **turn sth. to (good) ~** изվл|ека́ть, -е́чь по́льзу из чего́-н.; **he is in business on his own ~** у него́ со́бственное де́ло. **4.** (*statement, report*) отчёт; **by his own ~** по его́ со́бственным слова́м; **by all ~s** су́дя по всему́; **call to ~** приз|ыва́ть, -ва́ть (*кого*) к отве́ту; **give a good ~ of o.s.** (*defend o.s.*) постоя́ть (*pf.*) за себя́; (*perform well*) хорошо́ показа́ть (*pf.*)/зарекомендова́ть (*pf.*) себя́. **5.** (*estimation, consideration*) расчёт, значе́ние; **take into ~, take ~ of** уч|и́тывать, -е́сть; прин|има́ть, -я́ть в расчёт; **leave out of ~, take no ~ of** не уч|и́тывать, -е́сть; не прин|има́ть, -я́ть в расчёт; **a man of no ~** незначи́тельный/ничто́жный челове́к. **6.** (*reason, cause*): **on ~ of** (*for the sake of*) ра́ди+*g.*; (*because of*) из-за+*g.*; (*in consequence of*) по причи́не +*g.*; (*as a result of*) всле́дствие+*g.*; **on no ~** ни в ко́ем слу́чае.

v.t. (*consider*) сч|ита́ть, -есть: **he was ~ed a hero** его́ счита́ли геро́ем.

v.i. **~ for:** (*lit., fig., give a reckoning of*) отчи́т|ываться, -а́ться в+*p.*; да|ва́ть, -ть отчёт в+*p.*; **he had to ~ for his expenses** ему́ пришло́сь отчита́ться в свои́х расхо́дах; (*fig., answer for*) отв|еча́ть, -е́тить за+*a.*; **is everyone ~ed for?** никого́ не забы́ли?; (*explain*) объясн|я́ть, -и́ть; **how do you ~ for being late?** как вы объясня́ете своё опозда́ние?; **there's no ~ing for tastes** о вку́сах не спо́рят; (*be reason for*) явля́ться (*impf.*) причи́ной +*g.*; (*comprise*) сост|авля́ть, -а́вить; **women ~ for about 60% of our audiences** же́нщины составля́ют о́коло 60% на́ших слу́шателей; (*be responsible for; dispose of*): **our company ~ed for 60 of the enemy** на́ша ро́та вы́вела из стро́я 60 неприя́тельских солда́т; **he accounted for all the goals** все мячи́ заби́л он.

accountability [ə,kaʊntə'bɪlɪtɪ] *n.* отве́тственность; (*for money*) подотчётность.

accountable [ə'kaʊntəb(ə)l] *adj.* отве́тственный; **I shall hold you ~** я возложу́ отве́тственность на вас; **he is ~ to me** он отчи́тывается пе́редо мной; **he is not ~ for his actions** он не отвеча́ет за свои́ посту́пки.

accountancy [ə'kaʊntənsɪ] *n.* счетово́дство, бухгалте́рия.

accountant [ə'kaʊnt(ə)nt] *n.* счетово́д, бухга́лтер.

accounting [ə'kaʊntɪŋ] *n.* (*profession*) бухга́лтерское де́ло.

accoutrements [ə'kuːtrəmənt, -təmənt] *n.* (*mil.*) ли́чное снаряже́ние.

accredit [ə'kredɪt] *v.t.* **1.** (*appoint as ambassador*) аккредитова́ть (*impf., pf.*). **2.** (*credit*) выдава́ть, вы́дать креди́т +*d.*

accreditation [ə,kredɪ'teɪʃ(ə)n] *n.* аккредитова́ние.

accredited [ə'kredɪtɪd] *adj.* (*officially recognized*) аккредито́ванный; (*generally accepted*) общепри́нятый.

accrete [ə'kri:t] *v.t.* (*attract*; *recruit*) привл|ека́ть, -е́чь.

v.i. (*grow together*) срас|та́ться, -ти́сь; (*grow around*) обрас|та́ть, -ти́.

accretion [ə'kri:ʃ(ə)n] *n.* приращéние, приро́ст; **~ of strength** возраста́ние сил; **~ of followers** увеличе́ние числа́ сторо́нников.

accrue [ə'kru:] *v.i.* **1.** (*accumulate*) нарас|та́ть, -ти́; **~d interest** наро́сшие проце́нты (*m. pl.*); **~d liabilities** сро́чные обяза́тельства. **2.** (*come about*): **certain advantages will ~ from this** э́то даст определённые преиму́щества. **3.**: **~ to** (*fall to the lot of*) дост|ава́ться, -а́ться +*d.*

accumulate [ə'kju:mjʊ,leɪt] *v.t.* нак|а́пливать, -опи́ть; соб|ира́ть, -ра́ть; аккумули́ровать (*impf.*); **~d experience** нако́пленный о́пыт; **he ~d a fine library** он собра́л хоро́шую библиоте́ку.

v.i. накоп|ля́ться, -и́ться; скоп|ля́ться, -и́ться; **~d dividend** нако́пленные дивиде́нды; **dust ~s** пыль ска́пливается.

accumulation [ə,kju:mjʊ'leɪʃ(ə)n] *n.* **1.** (*piling up*, *amassing*) накопле́ние; (*gathering together*) собра́ние. **2.** (*mass*): **an ~ of dust** скопле́ние пы́ли; **an ~ of snow** сне́жный зано́с.

accumulative [ə'kju:mjʊlətɪv] *adj.* (*acquisitive*) стяжа́тельский; (*growing by addition*) нараста́ющий; **~ evidence** совоку́пность ули́к.

accumulator [ə'kju:mjʊ,leɪtə(r)] *n.* (*amasser*) стяжа́тель (*m.*); (*elec.*) аккумуля́тор.

accuracy ['ækjʊrəsɪ] *n.* то́чность; (*of aim or shot*) ме́ткость.

accurate ['ækjʊrət] *adj.* (*of persons*, *statements*, *instruments etc.*) то́чный; **~ to 6 places of decimals** с то́чностью до одно́й миллио́нной; (*of aim or shot*) ме́ткий.

accurs|ed [ə'kɜ:sɪd, ə'kɜ:st], **-t** [ə'kɜ:st] *adj.* **1.** (*under a curse*) про́клятый. **2.** (*detestable*) прокля́тый.

accusation [,ækju:'zeɪʃ(ə)n] *n.* обвине́ние; **bring an ~ against** выдвига́ть, вы́двинуть обвине́ние про́тив+*g.*

accusative [ə'kju:zətɪv] *n.* вини́тельный паде́ж.

adj. вини́тельный.

accusator|ial [ə,kju:zə'tɔ:rɪəl], **-y** [ə'kju:zətərɪ] *adj.* обвини́тельный.

accuse [ə'kju:z] *v.t.* обвин|я́ть, -и́ть; **he was ~d of stealing** его́ обвини́ли в кра́же.

accused [ə'kju:zd] *n.*: **the ~** обвиня́емый, подсуди́мый.

accuser [ə'kju:zə(r)] *n.* обвини́тель (*m.*).

accusing [ə'kju:zɪŋ] *adj.* укори́зненный, обвиня́ющий.

accustom [ə'kʌstəm] *v.t.* приуч|а́ть, -и́ть (**to**: к+*d.*): **~ o.s.**, **become ~ed** прив|ыка́ть, -ы́кнуть (**to**: к+*d.*); **I am not ~ed to such language** я не привы́к к таки́м выраже́ниям; **he was ~ed to ride every morning** он име́л привы́чку/обыкнове́ние е́здить верхо́м ка́ждое у́тро.

accustomed [ə'kʌstəmd] *adj.* (*usual*) обы́чный, привы́чный.

ace [eɪs] *n.* **1.** (*single pip on dice*, *cards*, *dominoes*) очко́. **2.** (*card*) туз; **he has an ~ up his sleeve** у него́ есть ко́зырь про запа́с. **3.** (*pilot*, *champion sportsman etc.*) ас. **4.**: **within an ~ of** на волосо́к от+*g.*

adj. (*coll.*) первокла́ссный; обалде́нный, клёвый.

acerbic [ə'sɜ:bɪk] *adj.* (*astringent*) те́рпкий; (*of speech*, *manner etc.*) ре́зкий.

acerbity [ə'sɜ:bɪtɪ] *n.* те́рпкость; ре́зкость.

acetate ['æsɪ,teɪt] *n.* ацета́т; уксуснокисл́ая соль; **~ silk** ацета́тный шёлк.

acetic [ə'si:tɪk] *adj.* у́ксусный; **~ acid** у́ксусная кислота́.

acetone ['æsɪ,təʊn] *n.* ацето́н.

acetylene [ə'setɪ,li:n] *n.* ацетиле́н; **~ burner** ацетиле́новая горе́лка.

ach|e [eɪk] *n.* боль.

v.i. боле́ть (*impf.*); ныть (*impf.*); **my head ~es** у меня́ боли́т голова́; **an ~ing tooth** больно́й зуб; **my bones ~e** у меня́ но́ют ко́сти; **my heart ~es** у меня́ се́рдце но́ет; **my heart ~es for him** у меня́ душа́ боли́т за него́; **I ~e to see him** я жа́жду уви́деть его́; **she ~es in every limb** у неё ло́мит всё те́ло; **his death left an ~ing void in her life** его́ смерть оста́вила зия́ющую пустоту́ в её жи́зни.

achievable [ə'tʃi:vəb(ə)l] *adj.* достижи́мый.

achieve [ə'tʃi:v] *v.t.* **1.** (*attain*) дост|ига́ть, -и́чь +*g.*; доби́ться (*pf.*) +*g.*; **he will never ~ greatness** он никогда́ не дости́гнет вели́чия. **2.** (*carry out*) выполня́ть, вы́полнить.

achievement [ə'tʃi:vmənt] *n.* (*attainment*) достиже́ние; (*carrying out*) выполне́ние; (*sth. achieved*; *success*) успе́х, завоева́ние.

Achilles [ə'kɪli:z] *n.* Ахилле́с; **~' heel** ахилле́сова пята́; **~ tendon** ахи́ллово сухожи́лие.

acid ['æsɪd] *n.* кислота́; **~ stomach/indigestion** изжо́га; **~ rain** кисло́тные дожди́; **~ test** (*fig.*) про́бный ка́мень.

adj. (*lit. and fig.*) ки́слый; **~ drop** ки́слый леденец.

cpds. **~-proof**, **~-resistant** *adjs.* кислотоупо́рный.

acidify [ə'sɪdɪ,faɪ] *v.t.* & *i.* (*chem.*) подкисл|я́ть(ся), -и́ть(ся); (*make*, *become sour*) окисл|я́ть(ся), -и́ть(ся).

acidity [ə'sɪdɪtɪ] *n.* кисло́тность.

acidulated [ə'sɪdjʊ,leɪtɪd] *adj.* подки́сленный; (*fig.*) е́дкий.

ack-ack [æ'kæk] *n.* (*mil. sl.*) **1.** (*gun*) зени́тка. **2.** (*gunfire*) зени́тный ого́нь. **3.** (*attr.*): **~ battalion** зени́тный дивизио́н.

acknowledge [ək'nɒlɪdʒ] *v.t.* **1.** (*recognize*; *admit*) призн|ава́ть, -а́ть; созн|ава́ть, -а́ть; **it must be ~d that** ну́жно призна́ть, что; **he refused to ~ defeat** он отказа́лся призна́ть пораже́ние; **he was ~d as (*or* to be) the champion** его́ призна́ли чемпио́ном. **2.** (*confirm receipt of*; *reply to*): **~ a letter** подтвер|жда́ть, -ди́ть получе́ние письма́; **~ a greeting** отве́тить (*pf.*) на приве́тствие. **3.** (*indicate recognition of*): **he did not even ~ me as we passed** он прошёл ми́мо и да́же не поздоро́вался. **4.** (*reward*; *express thanks for*) вознагра|жда́ть, -ди́ть; выража́ть, вы́разить благода́рность за+*a.*

acknowledg(e)ment [ək'nɒlɪdʒmənt] *n.* **1.** (*recognition*, *admission*) призна́ние. **2.** (*confirmation*) подтвержде́ние. **3.** (*reward*): **this is in ~ of your kindness** э́то в благода́рность за ва́шу доброту́.

acme ['ækmɪ] *n.* верх, верши́на; **the ~ of perfection** верх соверше́нства.

acmeism ['ækmɪ,ɪz(ə)m] *n.* (*liter.*) акмеи́зм.

acmeist ['ækmɪ,ɪst] *n.* (*liter.*) акмеи́ст (*fem.* -ка).

acne ['æknɪ] *n.* угри́ (*m.pl.*).

acolyte ['ækə,laɪt] *n.* церко́вный слу́жка; (*fig.*) помо́щник; (*pej.*) приспе́шник.

aconite ['ækə,naɪt] *n.* (*bot.*) акони́т, боре́ц; (*drug*) акони́т.

acorn ['eɪkɔ:n] *n.* жёлудь (*m.*).

acoustic [ə'ku:stɪk] *adj.* акусти́ческий; звуково́й; **an ~ guitar** проста́я гита́ра.

acoustics [ə'ku:stɪks] *n.* (*science*; *acoustic properties*) аку́стика.

acquaint [ə'kweɪnt] *v.t.* знако́мить, по-; **I ~ed him with the facts** я ознако́мил его́ с фа́ктами; **he soon got ~ed with the situation** он бы́стро ознако́мился с положе́нием дел; **be ~ed with s.o.** быть знако́мым с кем-н.; **we have been ~ed for several years** мы знако́мы не́сколько лет.

acquaintance [ə'kweɪnt(ə)ns] *n.* знако́мство; **nodding ~** ша́почное знако́мство; **make the ~ of** познако́миться (*pf.*) с+*i.*; **strike up an ~** зав|оди́ть, -ести́ знако́мство; **for old ~' sake** по ста́рой па́мяти; (*pers.*) знако́мый; **an ~ of mine** оди́н мой знако́мый.

acquaintanceship [ə'kweɪnt(ə)nsʃɪp] *n.* знако́мство; **he has a wide ~** у него́ широ́кий круг знако́мых.

acquiesce [,ækwɪ'es] *v.i.* (*agree tacitly*) согла|ша́ться, -си́ться; **~ in** (*accept*) примир|я́ться, -и́ться с+*i.*

acquiescence [,ækwɪ'esəns] *n.* согла́сие; усту́пчивость, пода́тливость.

acquiescent [,ækwɪ'esənt] *adj.* усту́пчивый, пода́тливый.

acquire [ə'kwaɪə(r)] *v.t.* приобре|та́ть, -сти́; **~ a habit** усв|а́ивать, -о́ить привы́чку; **~ a language** овлад|ева́ть, -е́ть языко́м; **~ a reputation** приобре|та́ть, -сти́ репута́цию; **asparagus is an ~d taste** к спа́рже на́до привы́кнуть.

acquisition [,ækwɪ'zɪʃ(ə)n] *n.* приобрете́ние; поступле́ние; **the ~ of knowledge** приобрете́ние зна́ний; **the ~ of language** овладе́ние языко́м; **he is quite an ~ to our staff** он настоя́щая нахо́дка для на́шего коллекти́ва; **the library's new ~s** но́вые библиоте́чные поступле́ния.

acquisitive [ə'kwɪzɪtɪv] *adj.* стяжа́тельский.

acquisitiveness [ə'kwɪzɪtɪvnɪs] *n.* стяжа́тельство.

acquit [ə'kwɪt] *v.t.* **1.** (*declare not guilty*) опра́вд|ывать, -а́ть; **he was ~ted of murder** его́ призна́ли невино́вным в уби́йстве. **2.: ~ o.s. well** хорошо́ прояви́ть (*pf.*) себя́. **3.: ~ o.s. of** (*discharge*) **a duty** выполня́ть, вы́полнить долг. **4.** (*pay*): **~ a debt** распл|а́чиваться, -ати́ться (по счёту).

acquittal [ə'kwɪt(ə)l] *n.* (*in court of law*) оправда́ние; (*of duty etc.*) выполне́ние; (*of debt etc.*) освобожде́ние.

acquittance [ə'kwɪt(ə)ns] *n.* (*payment of debt*) упла́та/погаше́ние до́лга; (*release from debt*) освобожде́ние от до́лга; (*receipt*) распи́ска.

acre ['eɪkə(r)] *n.* акр; **broad ~s** обши́рные зе́мли (*f. pl.*).

acreage ['eɪkərɪdʒ] *n.* пло́щадь земли́ в а́крах.

acrid ['ækrɪd] *adj.* е́дкий (*lit., fig.*): (*of temper, etc.*) язви́тельный, ехи́дный.

acrimonious [ˌækrɪ'məʊnɪəs] *adj.* язви́тельный, е́дкий.

acrimon|iousness [ˌækrɪ'məʊnɪəsnɪs], **-y** ['ækrɪmənɪ] *nn.* язви́тельность, е́дкость.

acrobat ['ækrəˌbæt] *n.* акроба́т.

acrobatic [ˌækrə'bætɪk] *adj.* акробати́ческий.

acrobatics [ˌækrə'bætɪks] *n.* акроба́тика.

acronym ['ækrənɪm] *n.* аббревиату́ра, акро́ним; сложносокращённое сло́во.

acropolis [ə'krɒpəlɪs] *n.* акро́поль (*m.*).

across [ə'krɒs] *adv.* **1.** (*athwart, crosswise*) попере́к; (*in crosswords*) по горизонта́ли. **2.** (*on the other side*): **he must be ~ by now** он, должно́ быть, уже́ на той стороне́. **3.** (*to the other side*) на ту сто́рону. **4.** (*in width*): **the river here is more than six miles ~** ширина́ реки́ здесь бо́льше шести́ миль; **a beam 2 feet ~** бревно́ толщино́й в два фу́та.

prep. **1.** (*from one side of to the other*) че́рез+*a.*, *sometimes omitted with vv. compounded with* пере…; **he went ~ the street** он перешёл у́лицу; **they were talking ~ the table** они́ говори́ли че́рез стол; **they were talking ~ me** они́ перегова́ривались че́рез мою́ го́лову. **2.** (*over the surface of*) по+*d.*; **he drew a line ~ the page** он провёл черту́ на страни́це; **clouds travelled ~ the sky** облака́ плы́ли по не́бу; **he hit me ~ the face** он уда́рил меня́ по лицу́; **put the rug ~ your knees** положи́те плед на коле́ни; **~ country** напрями́к; **~ the board** (*fig.*) для всех; во всех слу́чаях. **3.** (*athwart*) попере́к+*g.*; **she lay ~ the bed** она́ лежа́ла попере́к крова́ти; **with his arms ~ his breast** скрести́в ру́ки на груди́. **4.** (*on the other side of*) на той стороне́ +*g.*, по ту сто́рону +*g.*; **he is ~ the Channel by now** он уже́ на контине́нте; **he lives ~ (the street) from the park** он живёт напро́тив па́рка; **our friends ~ the ocean** на́ши друзья́ за океа́ном; **a voice from ~ the room** го́лос с друго́го конца́ ко́мнаты; **~ the table from him** про́тив него́ за столо́м.

cpd. **~-the-board** *adj.* всеобщий, поголо́вный, по всем катего́риям; **an ~ pay increase** поголо́вное увеличе́ние зарпла́ты; **an ~ agreement** всеобъе́млющее соглаше́ние.

acrostic [ə'krɒstɪk] *n.* акрости́х.

acrylic [ə'krɪlɪk] *n.* акри́л.

adj. акри́ловый.

act [ækt] *n.* **1.** (*action*) посту́пок; (*feat*) по́двиг; **A~s of the Apostles** Дея́ния (*nt. pl.*) Святы́х Апо́столов; **~ of God** стихи́йное бе́дствие; **catch in the ~** пойма́ть (*pf.*) на ме́сте преступле́ния; **he was in the ~ of putting on his hat** он как раз надева́л шля́пу; **an ~ of kindness** до́брое де́ло. **2.** (*document*) акт, докуме́нт; **~ of sale** акт о прода́же; (*proof*): **~ of confidence** зало́г/проявле́ние дове́рия. **3.** (*law*) акт, зако́н, постановле́ние; **~ of Parliament** акт парла́мента, парла́ментский акт; **he was prosecuted under the ~** его́ привлекли́ к суду́ в соотве́тствии с э́тим зако́ном. **4.** (*of drama*) де́йствие; **a 3-~ play** пье́са в трёх де́йствиях. **5.** (*performance*) но́мер; **circus ~** цирково́й но́мер; (*fig., coll.*): **put on an ~** притвор|я́ться, -и́ться; **they did the hospitality ~** (*coll.*) они́ исполня́ли роль гостеприи́мных хозя́ев.

v.t. игра́ть (*impf.*); **~ a part** (*lit., fig.*) игра́ть роль; **~ Hamlet** игра́ть Га́млета; **~ the fool** валя́ть (*impf.*) дурака́; **~ outraged virtue** разыгра́ть (*pf.*) возмущённую доброде́тель; **~ a play** игра́ть, разыгра́ть (*or* да|ва́ть, -ть) пье́су.

v.i. **1.** (*behave*) поступ|а́ть, -и́ть; вести́ (*det.*) себя́; (*take action, intervene*) прин|има́ть, -я́ть ме́ры; **~ on advice** сле́довать, по- сове́ту; **~ (up)on an order** де́йствовать (*impf.*) по прика́зу; **he ~ed up to his principles** он поступа́л согла́сно свои́м при́нципам; **it is time to ~** пора́ де́йствовать; **he ~s rich** (*coll.*) он разы́грывает из себя́ богача́; (*fig.*) **she is ~ing to get sympathy** она́ де́лает всё, что́бы вы́звать к себе́ симпа́тию. **2.** (*serve, function*) де́йствовать (*impf.*): **~ for s.o.** де́йствовать от и́мени кого́-л.; **~ against s.o.** выступа́ть, вы́ступить про́тив кого́-н.; **she ~ed as secretary** она́ рабо́тала за секретаря́; **he is ~ing as interpreter** он слу́жит перево́дчиком. **3.** (*have or take effect*) де́йствовать, по- (**on:** на+*a*); **the medicine will ~ immediately** лека́рство поде́йствует сра́зу; **the brake refused to ~** то́рмоз отказа́л. **4.** (*theatr.*) игра́ть; **he wants to ~** он хо́чет игра́ть на сце́не; **the play ~s well** э́та пье́са — о́чень сцени́чна.

with advs. **~ out** *v.t.* разы́гр|ывать, -а́ть; **~ up** *v.i.* (*coll., misbehave*) шали́ть (*impf.*), поша́ливать (*impf.*); (*give trouble*); **my car has been ~ing up** моя́ маши́на поша́ливает *or* барахли́т.

acting ['æktɪŋ] *n.* (*theatr.*) игра́; (*as skill*) актёрское мастерство́; **the ~ profession** актёрская профе́ссия; **~ copy of a play** режиссёрский текст пье́сы.

adj. (*doing duty temporarily*): **~ manager** исполня́ющий обя́занности (*abbr.* и.о.) заве́дующего.

action ['ækʃ(ə)n] *n.* **1.** (*acting; activity; effect*) де́йствие; **in ~** в де́йствии; **come into ~** вступ|а́ть, -и́ть в де́йствие; **bring into ~** вв|оди́ть, -ести́ в де́йствие; **put out of ~** выводи́ть, вы́вести из стро́я; **out of ~** него́дный к употребле́нию; **take ~** прин|има́ть, -я́ть ме́ры; **what we need is some ~** ну́жно де́йствовать; **~ group** инициати́вная гру́ппа. **2.** (*deed*) де́ло; **a man of ~** челове́к де́ла; **~s speak louder than words** дела́ говоря́т са́ми за себя́; **he suited the ~ to the word** он подкрепи́л слова́ де́лом. **3.** (*conduct*) поведе́ние; **line of ~** ли́ния поведе́ния. **4.** (*functioning*): **the ~ of the heart** де́ятельность се́рдца; (*of a gun, piano etc.*) де́йствие. **5.** (*physical movement*) движе́ние. **6.** (*theatr.*): **unity of ~** еди́нство де́йствия; **the ~ takes place in London** де́йствие происхо́дит в Ло́ндоне. **7.** (*leg.*) иск, де́ло; **~ for damages** иск об убы́тках; **bring an ~ against** предъявл|я́ть, -и́ть иск к+*d.*; **dismiss an ~** отклон|я́ть, -и́ть иск. **8.** (*mil.*) бой, де́йствие; **killed in ~** уби́тый в бою́; **go into ~** вступ|а́ть, -и́ть в бой; **break off an ~** выходи́ть, вы́йти из бо́я; **he is out of ~** он вы́был/вы́веден из стро́я; **theatre of ~** теа́тр вое́нных де́йствий; **~ stations** боевы́е посты́.

actionable ['ækʃənəb(ə)l] *adj.*: **his words are ~** его́ слова́ даю́т основа́ния для суде́бного пресле́дования.

activate ['æktɪˌveɪt] *v.t.* (*chem., biol.*) активи́ровать (*impf., pf.*); (*phys.*) де́лать, с- радиоакти́вным; (*fig., expedite*) активизи́ровать (*impf., pf.*).

activation [ˌæktɪ'veɪʃ(ə)n] *n.* актива́ция; активиза́ция.

active ['æktɪv] *adj.* **1.** (*lively; energetic; displaying activity*) де́ятельный, акти́вный; **he is old but still ~** несмотря́ на во́зраст, он всё ещё акти́вен/бодр; **an ~ member of the party** акти́вный член па́ртии; **take an ~ interest in** прояв|ля́ть, -и́ть живо́й интере́с к+*d.*; **an ~ brain** живо́й/де́ятельный ум; **an ~ volcano** де́йствующий вулка́н. **2.** (*gram.*) действи́тельный. **3.** (*phys., chem.*) акти́вный. **4.** (*mil.*): **~ defence** акти́вная оборо́на; **on ~ service** на действи́тельной слу́жбе; **~ division** боева́я диви́зия; **on the ~ list** в спи́ске ка́дрового соста́ва.

activist ['æktɪvɪst] *n.* активи́ст (*fem.* -ка).

activit|y [æk'tɪvɪtɪ] *n.* **1.** (*being active; exertion of energy*) акти́вность; (*comm.*): **~y in the market** оживле́ние на ры́нке. **2.** (*usu. pl., pursuit, sphere of action; doings*) де́ятельность; **he indulged in various ~ies** он занима́лся са́мой разли́чной де́ятельностью.

actor ['æktə(r)] *n.* актёр; **the ~'s art** актёрское мастерство́.

actress ['æktrɪs] *n.* актри́са.

actual ['æktʃʊəl, 'æktjʊəl] *adj.* (*real*) действи́тельный; факти́ческий; (*genuine*) по́длинный; (*existing*) существу́ющий; (*current*) теку́щий, настоя́щий; **in ~ fact** в действи́тельности; **those were his ~ words** э́то его́

по́длинные слова́; ~ **time of arrival** факти́ческое вре́мя прибы́тия; **the ~ state of affairs** действи́тельное положе́ние дел; ~ **strength** (*mil.*) нали́чный соста́в.
actuality [,æktʃʊ'ælɪtɪ, ,æktjʊ-] *n.* действи́тельность; **in ~** в действи́тельности; (*reality*) реа́льность; (*topical interest*) актуа́льность.
actualize ['æktʃʊəlaɪz, 'æktjʊəlaɪz] *v.t.* реализова́ть (*impf., pf.*).
actually ['æktʃʊəlɪ] *adv.* **1.** (*really; in fact*) действи́тельно; в су́щности; (*in expansion or correction of former statement*) в/на са́мом де́ле; (*in sense 'to tell the truth'*) вообще́-то (говоря́); со́бственно (говоря́). **2.** (*even*) да́же.
actuarial [,æktʃʊ'eərɪəl] *adj.* актуа́рный.
actuary ['æktʃʊərɪ] *n.* актуа́рий.
actuate ['æktʃʊ,eɪt] *v.t.* **1.** (*bring into action*) прив|оди́ть, -ести́ в де́йствие; (*elec.*) возбу|жда́ть, -ди́ть. **2.** (*motivate*) побу|жда́ть, -ди́ть.
acuity [ə'kju:ɪtɪ] *n.* (*lit., fig.*) острота́.
acumen ['ækjʊmən, ə'kju:mən] *n.* (*judgement*) сообрази́тельность; (*penetration*) проница́тельность.
acupressure ['ækju:,preʃə(r)] *n.* то́чечный масса́ж.
acupuncture ['ækju:,pʌŋktʃə(r)] *n.* акупункту́ра, иглоука́лывание.
acupuncturist ['ækju:,pʌŋktʃərɪst] *n.* иглотерапе́вт.
acute [ə'kju:t] *adj.* (*in var. senses*) о́стрый; ~ **angle** о́стрый у́гол; ~ **shortage** о́страя нехва́тка; ~ **mind** о́стрый ум; ~ **sense of smell** то́нкое обоня́ние; ~ **accent** аку́т.
cpd. **~-angled** *adj.* остроуго́льный.
acuteness [ə'kju:tnɪs] *n.* острота́; (*of intellect*) острота́, проница́тельность.
ACV (*abbr. of* ***air-cushion vehicle***) аппара́т на возду́шной поду́шке.
AD (*abbr. of* **Anno Domini**) н.э., (на́шей э́ры).
ad [æd] (*coll.*) = **advertisement**
adage ['ædɪdʒ] *n.* погово́рка.
adagio [ə'dɑ:ʒɪəʊ] *n., adj. & adv.* ада́жио (*indecl.*).
Adam ['ædəm] *n.* Ада́м; **~'s apple** ада́мово я́блоко, кады́к; **the old ~** ве́тхий Ада́м; **I don't know him from ~** я его́ никогда́ в глаза́ не вида́л.
adamant ['ædəmənt] *adj.* (*fig.*) непрекло́нный.
adapt [ə'dæpt] *v.t.* **1.** приспос|обля́ть, -о́бить; **he soon ~ed himself to the new situation** он бы́стро приспосо́бился к но́вой ситуа́ции; (*apply*) примен|я́ть, -и́ть (*что к чему*). **2.** (*modify*) адапти́ровать (*impf., pf.*; ~ **for the stage** инсцени́ровать (*impf., pf.*).
adaptability [ə,dæptə'bɪlɪtɪ] *n.* приспособля́емость; (*of pers.*): **he showed ~** он прояви́л уме́ние приспособля́ться.
adaptable [ə'dæptəb(ə)l] *adj.* приспособля́емый; (*of pers.*) легко́ приспоса́бливающийся.
adaptation [,ædæp'teɪʃ(ə)n] *n.* приспособле́ние; (*of book etc.*) адапта́ция, инсцениро́вка.
adapt|er, -or [ə'dæptə(r)] *n.* **1.** (*of book etc.*) тот, кто адапти́рует. **2.** (*tech.*) ада́птер; перехо́дная му́фта.
add [æd] *v.t.* **1.** (*make an addition of*) приб|авля́ть, -а́вить; **she ~ed a foot of material to the dress** она́ приба́вила фут мате́рии к пла́тью; **he ~ed** (*contributed*) **£1** он доба́вил оди́н фунт; ~ **sugar to tea** положи́ть (*pf.*) са́хар в чай; подсласти́ть (*pf.*) чай; ~ **salt to** подс|а́ливать, -оли́ть; ~ **fuel to the fire, flames** подл|ива́ть, -и́ть ма́сла в ого́нь; (*join*) присоедин|я́ть, -и́ть; **Alsace was ~ed to France** Эльза́с был присоединён к Фра́нции; **~ed to this is the fact that ...** к э́тому ну́жно приба́вить тот факт, что...; (*build on*) пристр|а́ивать, -о́ить; **a garage was ~ed to the house** к до́му пристро́или гара́ж; (*impart*): ~ **lustre to** прид|ава́ть, -а́ть блеск *+d.* **2.** (*say in addition*) доб|авля́ть, -а́вить; **I have nothing to ~** мне не́чего доба́вить; **what can I ~?** что я могу́ ещё сказа́ть? **3.** (*math.*) скла́дывать, сложи́ть; ~ **two and** (**or to**) **three!** сложи́те два и три!; приба́вьте два к трём!
v.i. **1.** ~ **to** (*increase, enlarge*) увели́чи|вать, -ть; уси́ли|вать, -ть; (*knowledge etc.*) углуб|ля́ть, -и́ть; **this will ~ to the expense** э́то увели́чит расхо́ды; **to ~ to our difficulties it was getting dark** в доверше́ние ко всему́ начина́ло темне́ть; ~ **to one's experience** обога|ща́ть, -ти́ть свой о́пыт; ~ **to a house** пристр|а́ивать, -о́ить к до́му. **2.** (*perform addition*) *see* ~ **up** *v.i.* **3.** ~ **to** (*total*) *see* ~ **up** *v.i.*
with advs. ~ **in** *v.t.* включ|а́ть, -и́ть; ~ **on** *v.t.* приб|авля́ть, -а́вить; **the tip was ~ed on to the bill** чаевы́е бы́ли включены́ в счёт; (*build on*): **the porch was ~ed on later** крыльцо́ пристро́или по́зже; ~ **together** *v.t.* скла́дывать, сложи́ть; ~ **up** *v.t.* (*find sum of*) подсч|и́тывать, -ита́ть; подыто́жи|вать, -ть; *v.i.* (*perform addition*): **you can't ~ up!** вы не уме́ете счита́ть!; (*total*): **it ~s up to 50** э́то составля́ет в су́мме 50; (*coll.*): **it ~s up to this, that ...** э́то сво́дится к тому́, что...; **it doesn't ~ up** (*make sense*) концы́ не схо́дятся.
cpds. **~ing-machine** *n.* счётная маши́на; арифмо́метр; **~-ons** *n. pl.* (*comput.*) вспомога́тельное обору́дование.
addendum [ə'dendəm] *n.* приложе́ние, дополне́ние.
adder ['ædə(r)] *n.* (*snake*) гадю́ка; (*US*) уж.
addict[1] ['ædɪkt] *n.* (**drug ~**) наркома́н; **smoking ~** стра́стный кури́льщик; **opium ~** кури́льщик о́пиума; **theatre ~** завзя́тый театра́л.
addict[2] [ə'dɪkt] *v.t.*: **be, become ~ed to** пристрасти́ться (*pf.*) к*+d.*; **he became ~ed to drugs** он пристрасти́лся к нарко́тикам; **he is ~ed to reading** он чита́ет запо́ем.
addiction [ə'dɪkʃ(ə)n] *n.* пристра́стие (*к чему*); ~ **to drugs** наркома́ния; ~ **to morphine** морфини́зм.
addictive [ə'dɪktɪv] *adj.* выраба́тывающий привыка́ние.
Addis Ababa ['ædɪs 'æbəbə] *n.* Адди́с-Абе́ба.
addition [ə'dɪʃ(ə)n] *n.* **1.** (*adding; supplement*) прибавле́ние; добавле́ние; **an ~ to the family** прибавле́ние семе́йства; **we are making an ~ to our house** мы де́лаем пристро́йку к до́му; **a useful ~ to the staff** поле́зное пополне́ние к шта́ту; **in ~ to** в дополне́ние к*+d.*; **in ~** (*as well*) вдоба́вок; (*moreover*) к тому́ же. **2.** (*math.*) сложе́ние.
additional [ə'dɪʃən(ə)l] *adj.* доба́вочный, дополни́тельный; ~ **charge** допла́та.
additive ['ædɪtɪv] *n.* доба́вка, добавле́ние.
addle ['æd(ə)l] *adj.*: **an ~(d) egg** ту́хлое яйцо́.
v.t. (*confuse*) пу́тать, за-.
v.i. (*of an egg*) ту́хнуть, про-.
cpds. **~-brained, ~-pated** *adjs.* пу́таный; **~-head** *n.* пу́таник, растя́па (*c.g.*).
address [ə'dres] *n.* **1.** (*of letter etc.; place of residence*) а́дрес; **the parcel was sent to the wrong ~** посы́лку напра́вили не по тому́ а́дресу; ~ **book** записна́я кни́жка; а́дресная кни́га; **what is your ~?** (мо́жно записа́ть) ваш а́дрес? **2.** (*discourse*) речь; **make** (**or deliver**) **an ~** выступа́ть, вы́ступить с ре́чью; **public ~ system** громкоговори́тели (*m. pl.*). **3.** (*dexterity*) ло́вкость. **4.** (*manner*) обхожде́ние. **5.** (*pl., courtship*) уха́живание; **pay one's ~es to** уха́живать (*impf.*) за*+i.* **6.: form of ~** фо́рма обраще́ния.
v.t. **1.** (*a letter*) адресова́ть (*impf., pf.*). **2.** (*speak to*) обра|ща́ться, -ти́ться к*+d.*; **he ~ed the meeting** он обрати́лся с ре́чью к собра́вшимся. **3.** (*direct*): ~ **one's remarks to** адресова́ть свои́ замеча́ния *+d.*; ~ **o.s. to business** прин|има́ться, -я́ться за де́ло; ~ **the ball** (*at golf*) наце́ли|ваться, -ться для то́чной пода́чи мяча́.
addressee [,ædre'si:] *n.* адреса́т.
adduce [ə'dju:s] *v.t.* прив|оди́ть, -ести́ (как доказа́тельство).
adenoidal [,ædɪ'nɔɪd(ə)l] *adj.* адено́идный; **he has an ~ voice** он говори́т в нос; он гнуса́вит.
adenoids ['ædɪ,nɔɪdz] *n.* адено́иды (*m. pl.*); **he had his ~ out** ему́ удали́ли адено́иды.
adept ['ædept, ə'dept] *n.* (*expert*) экспе́рт; ма́стер; (*devotee*) аде́пт; приве́рженец.
adj. уме́лый; све́дущий (**at, in:** в*+p.*); **he is ~ at finding excuses** он ма́стер находи́ть оправда́ния.
adeptness ['ædeptnɪs, ə'deptnɪs] *n.* уме́ние; осведомлённость.
adequacy ['ædɪkwəsɪ] *n.* доста́точность; соотве́тствие, адеква́тность; компете́нтность.
adequate ['ædɪkwət] *adj.* **1.** (*sufficient*) доста́точный; **a salary ~ to support a family** зарпла́та, доста́точная для содержа́ния семьи́. **2.** (*suitable*) соотве́тствующий, адеква́тный; ~ **to our requirements** соотве́тствующий на́шим тре́бованиям; **he is ~ to his post** он справля́ется с рабо́той; **his thoughts could not find ~ expression** он не мог как сле́дует вы́разить свои́ мы́сли. **3.** (*of pers., capable*) компете́нтный.

adhere [əd'hɪə(r)] *v.i.* (*lit.*) прил|ипа́ть, -и́пнуть (к+*d.*); (*fig.*): ~ **to an opinion** приде́рживаться (*impf.*) мне́ния (*g. sg.*); ~ **to a promise** сдержа́ть (*pf.*) обеща́ние; ~ **to a programme** сле́довать (*impf.*) програ́мме; ~ (*remain faithful*) **to a party** твёрдо сле́довать (*impf.*) ли́нии па́ртии.

adherence [əd'hɪərəns] *n.* (*lit.*) прилипа́ние; (*fig.*) приве́рженность; **give one's ~ to a plan** оказа́ть (*pf.*) подде́ржку пла́ну.

adherent [əd'hɪərənt] *n.* приве́рженец.

adhesion [əd'hi:ʒ(ə)n] *n.* (*lit.*) прилипа́ние; скле́ивание; (*fig.*) пре́данность.

adhesive [əd'hi:sɪv] *n.* кле́й; кле́йкое вещество́.

adj. ли́пкий; (*sticky*) кле́йкий; ~ **tape** кле́йкая ле́нта, липу́чка (*coll.*), скотч; (*US*) лейкопла́стырь, ли́пкий пла́стырь.

ad hoc [æd 'hɒk] *adv.* для да́нного слу́чая; (*attr.*) специа́льный; ~ **committee** вре́менный комите́т.

adieu [ə'dju:] *n.* проща́ние; **bid ~ to** про|ща́ться, -сти́ться с+*i.*; (*fig.*) распро|ща́ться, -сти́ться с+*i.*; **make one's ~s** про|ща́ться, -сти́ться.

int. проща́й(те).

ad infinitum [æd ˌɪnfɪ'naɪtəm] *adv.* до бесконе́чности.

adipose ['ædɪˌpəʊz] *n.* живо́тный жир.

adj.: ~ **gland** са́льная железа́; ~ **tissue** жирова́я ткань; (*containing fat*) жи́рный.

adiposity [ˌædɪ'pɒsɪtɪ] *n.* ожире́ние, ту́чность.

adjacent [ə'dʒeɪs(ə)nt] *adj.* (*geom.*): ~ **angles** сме́жные углы́; (*neighbouring*) сосе́дний; сме́жный; ~ **villages** близлежа́щие дере́вни; ~ **to** примыка́ющий/прилежа́щий к+*d.*; **our house is ~ to the school** наш дом примыка́ет к шко́ле.

adjectival [ˌædʒɪk'taɪv(ə)l] *adj.* адъекти́вный.

adjective ['ædʒɪktɪv] *n.* (и́мя) прилага́тельное.

adjoin [ə'dʒɔɪn] *v.t.* (*be contiguous with, next to*) примыка́ть (*impf.*) к+*d.*; прилега́ть (*impf.*) к+*d.*

v.i. примыка́ть (*impf.*), прилега́ть (*impf.*); **the two houses ~** э́ти два до́ма примыка́ют друг к дру́гу; **in the ~ing house** в сосе́днем до́ме.

adjourn [ə'dʒɜ:n] *v.t.* (*postpone*) от|кла́дывать, -ложи́ть; **the meeting was ~ed till Monday** заседа́ние бы́ло отло́жено до понеде́льника; (*break off*): **they ~ed the meeting till 2 o'clock** они́ объяви́ли переры́в в заседа́нии до двух часо́в.

v.i. **1.** (*suspend proceedings*) закр|ыва́ть, -ы́ть заседа́ние; (*disperse*) ра|сходи́ться, -зойти́сь; **Parliament has ~ed for the summer** парла́мент распу́щен на ле́то. **2.** (*coll., move*): **shall we ~ to the dining-room?** перейдём в столо́вую?

adjournment [ə'dʒɜ:nmənt] *n.* (*postponement*) отсро́чка; (*dispersal*) ро́спуск; (*break in proceedings*) переры́в; **a week's ~** отсро́чка на неде́лю; неде́льный переры́в.

adjudge [ə'dʒʌdʒ] *v.t.* **1.** (*pronounce*): ~ **s.o. guilty** призн|ава́ть, -а́ть кого́-н. вино́вным; ~ **s.o. bankrupt** объяв|ля́ть, -и́ть кого́-н банкро́том. **2.** (*award judicially*) прису|жда́ть, -ди́ть (*что кому*).

adjudg(e)ment [ə'dʒʌdʒmənt] *n.* (*decision*) суде́бное реше́ние; (*award*) присужде́ние.

adjudicate [ə'dʒu:dɪˌkeɪt] *v.t.* (*decide upon*) выноси́ть, вы́нести реше́ние по+*d.*

v.i. рассуди́ть (*pf.*).

adjudication [əˌdʒu:dɪ'keɪʃ(ə)n] *n.* (*judgement*) суде́бное/арбитра́жное реше́ние; ~ **in bankruptcy** призна́ние несостоя́тельности; (*award*) присужде́ние.

adjudicator [ə'dʒu:dɪˌkeɪtə(r)] *n.* арби́тр; (*judge*) судья́ (*m.*).

adjunct ['ædʒʌŋkt] *n.* (*appendage*) приложе́ние; (*addition*) дополне́ние; (*gram.*) определе́ние, обстоя́тельство.

adjuration [ˌædʒʊə'reɪʃ(ə)n] *n.* заклина́ние; мольба́.

adjure [ə'dʒʊə(r)] *v.t.* заклина́ть (*impf.*); умоля́ть (*impf.*); **he ~d me to tell the truth** он заклина́л меня́ сказа́ть пра́вду.

adjust [ə'dʒʌst] *v.t.* **1.** (*arrange; put right or straight*) прив|оди́ть, -ести́ в поря́док; попр|авля́ть, -а́вить; регули́ровать, от-; ула́|живать, -дить; **he ~ed his tie** он попра́вил га́лстук; ~ **one's dress** застёг|иваться, -ну́ться; (*of mechanism*) регули́ровать, от-; нала́|живать, -дить; **self-~ing watch** часы́ с автомати́ческой регулиро́вкой; (*of a musical instrument*) настр|а́ивать, -о́ить. **2.** (*fit, adapt*) приг|оня́ть, -на́ть; под|гоня́ть, -огна́ть; **you must ~ your expenditure to your income** вы должны́ соразмеря́ть свои́ расхо́ды с дохо́дами; ~ **(o.s.) to** приспос|обля́ться, -о́биться к+*d.*; **well-~ed** (*of pers.*) уравнове́шенный. **3.** (*insurance*): ~ **an average** сост|авля́ть, -а́вить диспа́шу́.

adjustable [ə'dʒʌstəb(ə)l] *adj.* регули́руемый; подвижно́й; ~ **spanner** разводно́й (га́ечный) ключ; **the shelves of the bookcase are ~** по́лки в э́том кни́жном шкафу́ переставля́ются; (*adaptable*) приспособля́емый.

adjuster [ə'dʒʌstə(r)] *n.* (*insurance*) диспаше́р.

adjustment [ə'dʒʌstmənt] *n.* (*regulation*) регул|и́рование, -иро́вка; (*correction*) исправле́ние, попра́вка; (*fitting*) приго́нка; (*adaptation*) приспособле́ние; (*settlement*) ула́живание; (*insurance*) составле́ние диспа́ши.

adjutant ['ædʒʊt(ə)nt] *n.* **1.** (*mil.*) адъюта́нт; ≃ нача́льник шта́ба ча́сти. **2.** (*also* ~ **bird**) инди́йский марабу́ (*m. indecl.*).

cpd. **~-general** *n.* генера́л-адъюта́нт.

ad lib [æd 'lɪb] *adv.* ско́лько уго́дно.

ad-lib [æd 'lɪb] (*coll.*) *n.* экспро́мт, отсебя́тина; **his speech was full of ~s** в свое́й ре́чи он мно́го импровизи́ровал.

v.i. говори́ть (*impf.*) экспро́мтом; нести́ (*impf.*) отсебя́тину.

adman ['ædmæn] *n.* (*coll.*) рекла́мный аге́нт.

administer [əd'mɪnɪstə(r)] *v.t.* **1.** (*manage, govern*) управля́ть (*impf.*) +*i.*; заве́довать (*impf.*) +*i.* **2.**: ~ **a blow** нанести́ (*pf.*) уда́р (*кому*); ~ **a beating to** поро́ть, вы́-; ~ **medicine** да|ва́ть, -ть лека́рство; ~ **an oath to s.o.** прив|оди́ть, -ести́ кого́-н. к прися́ге; ~ **relief to a patient** принести́ (*pf.*) облегче́ние пацие́нту; **the priest ~ed the sacrament of marriage** свяще́нник соверши́л обря́д венча́ния.

administration [ədˌmɪnɪ'streɪʃ(ə)n] *n.* **1.** (*management*) управле́ние, организа́ция; **letters of ~** пра́во на распоряже́ние иму́ществом. **2.** (*of public affairs*) администра́ция; **the A~** прави́тельство; **during the Kennedy ~** при администра́ции Ке́ннеди. **3.**: ~ **of justice** отправле́ние правосу́дия. **4.** (*putting into effect*): ~ **of punishment** примене́ние наказа́ния. **5.**: ~ **of an oath** приведе́ние к прися́ге. **6.**: ~ **of a sacrament** соверше́ние обря́да; отправле́ние та́инства.

administrative [əd'mɪnɪstrətɪv] *adj.* (*pert. to management*) администрати́вный, организацио́нный; ~ **ability** администрати́вные спосо́бности; (*executive*) исполни́тельный.

administrator [əd'mɪnɪˌstreɪtə(r)] *n.* администра́тор, управля́ющий; (*of an estate*) распоряди́тель (*m.*).

admirabl|e ['ædmərəb(ə)l] *adj.* замеча́тельный, прекра́сный, досто́йный восхище́ния; **~y clear** преде́льно я́сно.

admiral ['ædmər(ə)l] *n.* адмира́л.

admiralty ['ædmərəltɪ] *n.* адмиралте́йство; морско́е министе́рство; **Court of A~** адмиралте́йский суд.

admiration [ˌædmɪ'reɪʃ(ə)n] *n.* восхище́ние; **be, win the ~ of all** вызыва́ть, вы́звать у всех восхище́ние; **fill with ~** восхи|ща́ть, -ти́ть; прив|оди́ть, -ести́ в восхище́ние; **my ~ for him is great** я не перестаю́ им восхища́ться; **I am lost in ~** я вне себя́ от восто́рга.

admir|e [əd'maɪə(r)] *v.t.* (*obtain pleasure from looking at*) любова́ться (*impf.*) +*i.* (*or* на+*a.*); **she was ~ing the sunrise** она́ любова́лась восхо́дом со́лнца; **he ~ed himself in the mirror** он любова́лся на себя́ в зе́ркало; (*be delighted with*) восхи|ща́ться, -ти́ться +*i.*; восторга́ться (*impf.*) +*i.*; (*speak or think highly of*): **I forgot to ~e her dress** я забы́л похвали́ть её пла́тье; **~ing glances** восхищённые взгля́ды.

admirer [əd'maɪərə(r)] *n.* покло́нник; **I am an ~ of Picasso** я (большо́й) покло́нник Пика́ссо.

admissibility [ədˌmɪsɪ'bɪlɪtɪ] *n.* прие́млемость, допусти́мость.

admissible [əd'mɪsɪb(ə)l] *adj.* прие́млемый, допусти́мый.

admission [əd'mɪʃ(ə)n] *n.* **1.** (*permitted entry or access*) вход; до́ступ; ~ **by ticket** вход по биле́там; ~ **free** вход свобо́дный; **no ~** вход воспреща́ется; нет вхо́да; **he was refused ~** его́ не впусти́ли; **gain ~ to a society** проби́ться (*pf.*) в о́бщество; ~ **fee** входна́я пла́та; ~ **ticket** входно́й биле́т. **2.** (*acknowledgement*) призна́ние; **he made an ~ of guilt** он призна́л свою́ вину́; **on his own ~** по его́ со́бственному призна́нию.

admit [əd'mɪt] *v.t. & i.* **1.** (*allow, accept*) допус|ка́ть, -ти́ть; **he was ~ted to the examination** его́ допусти́ли к экза́мену; **I ~ that this is true** допуска́ю, что э́то ве́рно; **the matter ~s of no delay** де́ло не те́рпит отлага́тельства; **you must ~ he is right** вы должны́ призна́ть, что он прав; **his conduct ~s of this explanation** его́ поведе́ние допуска́ет подо́бное объясне́ние. **2.** (*let in*) впус|ка́ть, -ти́ть; прин|има́ть, -я́ть; **the public are not ~ted to the gardens** э́тот парк закры́т для широ́кой пу́блики; **he was ~ted to the Party** его́ при́няли в па́ртию; **this ticket ~s one (person)** э́то биле́т на одно́ лицо́; **children are not ~ted** де́тям вход воспрещён. **3.** (*have room for*) вме|ща́ть, -сти́ть; **the harbour ~s large ships** э́та га́вань принима́ет больши́е корабли́. **4.** (*confess*) призн|ава́ть, -а́ть; **he ~s his guilt** он признаёт свою́ вину́; ~ **to feeling ashamed** призн|ава́ться, -а́ться, что сты́дно; ~ **to a crime** созн|ава́ться, -а́ться в преступле́нии; **I don't mind ~ting** гото́в призна́ть(ся).

admittance [əd'mɪt(ə)ns] *n.* (*entry*) вход; **no ~!** вход запрещён!; **gain ~** получи́ть (*pf.*) разреше́ние на вход; (*access*) до́ступ.

admittedly [əd'mɪtɪdlɪ] *adv.* **1.** (*by general admission*) как при́нято счита́ть; по о́бщему призна́нию. **2.** (*in parenthesis: true!; I must agree*) пра́вда; коне́чно; спо́ру нет; призна́ться.

admixture [æd'mɪkstʃə(r)] *n.* (*mixing*) сме́шивание; приме́шивание; (*addition*) при́месь.

admonish [əd'mɒnɪʃ] *v.t.* **1.** (*reprove*) де́лать, с- внуше́ние/замеча́ние +*d.*; **the boys were ~ed for being late** ма́льчикам сде́лали замеча́ние за опозда́ние. **2.** (*exhort*) увещева́ть (*impf.*); наст|авля́ть, -а́вить.

admoni|shment [əd'mɒnɪʃmənt], **-tion** [ˌædmə'nɪʃ(ə)n] *n.* (*reproof*) внуше́ние; (*exhortation*) увещева́ние, наставле́ние.

admonitory [əd'mɒnɪtərɪ] *adj.* увещева́тельный.

ad nauseam [æd 'nɔːzɪˌæm, 'nɔːsɪˌæm] *adv.* до отвраще́ния/тошноты́.

ado [ə'duː] *n.* (*fuss*) суета́, хло́пот|ы (*pl., g.* —); (*difficulty*) затрудне́ние; **without further ~** без дальне́йших церемо́ний; **much ~ about nothing** мно́го шу́ма из ничего́.

adobe [ə'dəʊbɪ, ə'dəʊb] *n.* кирпи́ч-сыре́ц; кирпи́ч возду́шной су́шки; **an ~ hut** глиноби́тная хи́жина.

adolescence [ˌædə'lesəns] *n.* о́трочество.

adolescent [ˌædə'les(ə)nt] *n.* подро́сток; о́трок.
adj. подро́стко́вый, о́троческий.

Adonis [ə'dəʊnɪs] *n.* (*myth., fig.*) Адо́нис.

adopt [ə'dɒpt] *v.t.* **1.** (*a son*) усынов|ля́ть, -и́ть; (*a daughter*) удочер|я́ть, -и́ть; **~ed child** приёмный ребёнок, приёмыш. **2.** (*acquire*) усв|а́ивать, -о́ить; **he is ~ing bad habits** он подхва́тывает дурны́е привы́чки. **3.** (*accept*) прин|има́ть, -я́ть; **they ~ed Christianity** они́ при́няли христиа́нство; **the resolution was ~ed** резолю́ция была́ принята́; (*take over*) перен|има́ть, -я́ть; **his methods should be ~ed** сле́дует переня́ть его́ ме́тоды; (*take up*) зан|има́ть, -я́ть; **he ~ed a condescending attitude** он стал держа́ться снисходи́тельно. **4.** (*ling., borrow*) заи́мствовать (*impf., pf.*); **words ~ed from the French** слова́, заи́мствованные из францу́зского языка́. **5.** (*choose*) выбира́ть, вы́брать; **he was ~ed as candidate** его́ кандидату́ру при́няли.

adoption [ə'dɒpʃ(ə)n] *n.* **1.** усыновле́ние; удочере́ние. **2.** усвое́ние. **3.** приня́тие. **4.** заи́мствование. **5.** вы́бор; **the country of his ~** его́ второ́е оте́чество.

adoptive [ə'dɒptɪv] *adj.* приёмный; ~ **parent** усынови́тель (*fem.* -ница).

adorable [ə'dɔːrəb(ə)l] *adj.* обожа́емый; (*delightful*) преле́стный, восхити́тельный.

adoration [ˌædə'reɪʃ(ə)n] *n.* обожа́ние.

ador|e [ə'dɔː(r)] *v.t.* (*worship*) обожа́ть; поклоня́ться (*impf.*) +*d.*; **her ~ing husband** обожа́ющий её муж; (*coll., love*): **the baby ~es being tickled** ребёнок ужа́сно лю́бит, что́бы его́ щекота́ли.

adorer [ə'dɔːrə(r)] *n.* обожа́тель (*m.*); (*ardent admirer*) покло́нник.

adorn [ə'dɔːn] *v.t.* (*lit., fig.*) укр|аша́ть, -а́сить.

adornment [ə'dɔːnmənt] *n.* украше́ние.

adrenal [ə'driːn(ə)l] *adj.* надпо́чечный; ~ **glands** надпо́чечные же́лезы (*f. pl.*).

adrenalin [ə'drenəlɪn] *n.* адренали́н.

Adriatic [ˌeɪdrɪ'ætɪk] *n.*: **the ~ (Sea)** Адриати́ческое мо́ре.

adrift [ə'drɪft] *pred. adj. & adv.* (*of a boat or its crew*): **go ~** дрейфова́ть (*impf.*); **cut ~** (*v.t.*) пус|ка́ть, -ти́ть; **they were ~ on the open sea** они́ дрейфова́ли в откры́том мо́ре; (*fig.*) **he was all ~** он был сбит с то́лку; **he was turned ~** его́ бро́сили на произво́л судьбы́; **cut (o.s.) ~ from s.o.** пор|ыва́ть, -ва́ть с кем-н.

adroit [ə'drɔɪt] *adj.* (*dexterous*) ло́вкий; (*skilful*) уме́лый, иску́сный; (*resourceful*) нахо́дчивый.

adroitness [ə'drɔɪtnɪs] *n.* ло́вкость; уме́ние, иску́сность; нахо́дчивость.

adulation [ˌædjʊ'leɪʃ(ə)n] *n.* низкопокло́нство, лесть.

adult [ə'dʌlt, 'ædʌlt] *n. & adj.* **1.** взро́слый; ~ **education** обуче́ние взро́слых; ~ **suffrage** всео́бщее избира́тельное пра́во. **2.** (*mature*) зре́лый.

adulterate [ə'dʌltəˌreɪt] *v.t.* (*debase*) по́ртить, ис-; (*dilute*) разб|авля́ть, -а́вить.

adulteration [əˌdʌltə'reɪʃ(ə)n] *n.* по́рча; разбавле́ние.

adulterer [ə'dʌltərə(r)] *n.* неве́рный супру́г.

adulteress [ə'dʌltərɪs] *n.* неве́рная супру́га.

adulterous [ə'dʌltərəs] *adj.* неве́рный.

adultery [ə'dʌltərɪ] *n.* адюльте́р, прелюбоде́яние; **to commit ~** соверш|а́ть, -и́ть прелюбоде́яние.

adulthood ['ædʌlthʊd, ə'dʌlthʊd] *n.* взро́слое состоя́ние; зре́лость, возмужа́лость.

adumbrate ['ædʌmˌbreɪt] *v.t.* **1.** (*sketch out*) набр|а́сывать, -оса́ть. **2.** (*foreshadow*) предвеща́ть (*impf.*); предзнаменова́ть.

adumbration [ˌædʌm'breɪʃ(ə)n] *n.* **1.** набро́сок. **2.** предзнаменова́ние.

advance [əd'vɑːns] *n.* **1.** (*forward move*) продвиже́ние; (*mil.: also*) наступле́ние; ~ **in force** продвиже́ние кру́пными си́лами; **cover an ~** прикр|ыва́ть, -ы́ть наступле́ние; **press an ~** разв|ива́ть, -и́ть наступле́ние; **we made an ~ of 10 miles** мы продви́нулись на 10 миль; (*approach, onset*): **the ~ of old age** наступле́ние ста́рости; (*pl., overtures to a pers.*): **make ~s to** заи́грывать (*impf.*) с+*i.* **2.** (*progress*) прогре́сс; (*in rank, social position etc.*) продвиже́ние; **~s of science** прогре́сс нау́ки; **~s of civilization** достиже́ния (*nt. pl.*) цивилиза́ции; **the country has made great ~s** страна́ доби́лась больши́х успе́хов. **3.** (*increase*) повыше́ние; **an ~ on his original offer** надба́вка к первонача́льному предложе́нию; **any ~ on £5?** 5 фу́нтов — кто бо́льше? **4.** (*loan*) ссу́да; (*payment beforehand*) ава́нс; **an ~ on salary** ава́нс под зарпла́ту; **the bank made me an ~** банк вы́дал мне ава́нс. **5.**: **in ~** (*in front*) вперёд; (*beforehand*) зара́нее; **in ~ of** впереди́+*g.*; **be in ~ of one's time** опереди́ть (*pf.*) своё вре́мя; **he expects to be paid in ~** он ожида́ет, что ему́ запла́тят вперёд. **6.** (*attr.*): ~ **copy** (*of book*) сигна́льный экземпля́р; ~ **copy of a speech** предвари́тельный текст ре́чи; ~ **guard, party** аванга́рд; **I had ~ knowledge of this** я зара́нее знал об э́том; ~ **payment** ава́нсовый платёж; ~ **sale** предвари́тельная прода́жа.

v.t. **1.** (*move forward*) продв|ига́ть, -и́нуть; **he ~d his troops to the frontier** он передви́нул войска́ к грани́це; **the clock had been ~d by an hour** часы́ бы́ли переведены́ на час вперёд; ~ **a pawn** пойти́ (*pf.*) пе́шкой; (*promote*) пов|ыша́ть, -ы́сить в до́лжности; **he was ~d to the rank of general** его́ произвели́ в генера́лы. **2.** (*fig., put forward*): ~ **an opinion** вы́сказать (*pf.*) мне́ние; ~ **a proposal** выдвига́ть, вы́двинуть предложе́ние. **3.** (*fig., further*): ~ **s.o.'s interests** соде́йствовать (*impf.*) чьим-н. интере́сам; послужи́ть (*pf.*) на по́льзу кому́-н.; **he did this to ~ his own interests** он сде́лал э́то ра́ди со́бственной вы́годы. **4.** (*of payment*) плати́ть, за- ава́нсом; (*lend*) ссу|жа́ть, -ди́ть. **5.** (*raise, e.g. prices*) пов|ыша́ть, -ы́сить. **6.** (*bring forward; make earlier*): ~

the date of перенести́ (*pf.*) на бо́лее ра́нний срок.

v.i. **1.** (*move forward*) продв|ига́ться, -и́нуться; **~ on** наступа́ть (*impf.*) на+*a.* **2.** (*progress*) разв|ива́ться, -и́ться; де́лать, с- успе́хи; **~ in knowledge** углуб|ля́ть, -и́ть зна́ния. **3.** (*increase*) пов|ыша́ться, -ы́ситься.

advanced [əd'vɑːnsd] *adj.* **1.** (*far on*): **~ age, years** преклóнный во́зраст; **in an ~ state of decomposition** в кра́йней ста́дии разложе́ния; **he is very ~ for his years** он о́чень ра́звит для свои́х лет. **2.** (*opp. elementary*): **an ~ course** курс для продви́нутого эта́па (обуче́ния); **~ algebra** вы́сшая а́лгебра. **3.** (*progressive*) передово́й. **4.** (*mil.*) передово́й.

advancement [əd'vɑːnsmənt] *n.* (*moving forward*) продвиже́ние; (*promotion*) продвиже́ние по слу́жбе; (*progress*) прогре́сс.

advantage [əd'vɑːntɪdʒ] *n.* **1.** (*superiority; more favourable or superior position*) преиму́щество, досто́инство; **this method has the ~ that ...** преиму́щество э́того ме́тода состои́т в том, что...; **have an ~ over, have the ~ of** иметь (*impf.*) преиму́щество пе́ред+*i.*; **my height gave me an ~ over him** бо́лее высо́кий рост дал мне преиму́щество пе́ред ним; **gain, win an ~ over** брать, взять верх над+*i.* **2.** (*profit, benefit*) вы́года, по́льза; **it is to your ~ to sell** вам бу́дет вы́годно прода́ть; **gain ~ from** извл|ека́ть, -е́чь вы́году из+*g.*; **turn sth. to ~** обра|ща́ть, -ти́ть что-н. себе́ на по́льзу; **take ~ of sth.** воспо́льзоваться (*pf.*) чем-н.; **take ~ of s.o.** провести́ (*pf.*)/перехитри́ть (*pf.*) кого́-н.; **use to ~** вы́годно испо́льзовать (*pf.*); **you should lay out your money to ~** вы должны́ потра́тить де́ньги с то́лком; **you may learn sth. to your ~** вы мо́жете узна́ть/почерпну́ть для себя́ что́-то поле́зное; **the picture can be seen to better ~ from here** отсю́да карти́на лу́чше смо́трится. **3.** (*tennis*): **~ in/out** «бо́льше»/«ме́ньше».

v.t. (*favour*) благоприя́тствовать (*impf.*) +*d.*; (*give ~ to*) да|ва́ть, -ть преиму́щество +*d.*; (*further*) продв|ига́ть, -и́нуть.

advantageous [,ædvən'teɪdʒəs] *adj.* (*favourable*) благоприя́тный; (*profitable*) вы́годный; (*useful*) поле́зный.

advent ['ædvent] *n.* **1.** (*arrival*) прибы́тие. **2.** (*appearance; occurrence*) появле́ние. **3.** (**A~**: *eccl.*) рожде́ственский пост; **Second A~** второ́е прише́ствие.

Adventist ['ædventɪst] *n.* адвенти́ст (*fem.* -ка); **Seventh-day A~** адвенти́ст седьмо́го дня.

adventitious [,ædven'tɪʃəs] *adj.* (*accidental*) случа́йный.

adventure [əd'ventʃə(r)] *n.* (*exciting incident or episode*) приключе́ние; **~s** похожде́ния (*nt. pl.*); **a life of ~** жизнь, по́лная приключе́ний; (*risky or irresponsible activity*) риско́ванная зате́я; авантю́ра; **~ story** приключе́нческий рома́н.

adventurer [əd'ventʃərə(r)] *n.* (*seeker of adventure*) иска́тель (*m.*) приключе́ний; (*speculator*) авантюри́ст; (*one who lives by his wits*) афери́ст, проходи́мец.

adventuress [əd'ventʃərɪs] *n.* авантюри́стка.

adventurism [əd'ventʃə,rɪz(ə)m] *n.* авантюри́зм.

adventurist [əd'ventʃərɪst] *n.* авантюри́ст.

adventurous [əd'ventʃərəs] *adj.* **1.** (*of pers.*) сме́лый; (*enterprising*) предприи́мчивый. **2.** (*of actions*) риско́ванный, авантю́рный; (*dangerous*) опа́сный.

adventurousness [əd'ventʃərəsnɪs] *n.* сме́лость; предприи́мчивость.

adverb ['ædvɜːb] *n.* наре́чие.

adverbial [əd'vɜːbɪəl] *adj.* наре́чный, адвербиа́льный.

adversary ['ædvəsərɪ] *n.* (*antagonist*) проти́вник; (*enemy*) враг; (*rival*) сопе́рник.

adverse ['ædvɜːs] *adj.* (*unfavourable*) неблагоприя́тный; **it is ~ to our interests** э́то противоре́чит на́шим интере́сам; (*harmful*) вре́дный; (*inimical*) вражде́бный; (*contrary*) проти́вный; **~ winds** проти́вные ве́тры (*m.pl.*).

adversity [əd'vɜːsɪtɪ] *n.* бе́дствия (*nt. pl.*), несча́стья (*nt. pl.*); **show courage in, under ~** прояви́ть (*pf.*) му́жество в беде́; **companions in ~** това́рищи по несча́стью; (*particular misfortune*) несча́стье, бе́дствие.

advert ['ædvɜːt] (*coll.*) = **advertisement**

advertise ['ædvə,taɪz] *v.t.* (*boost, publicize*) реклами́ровать (*impf., pf.*); (*in newspaper*) да|ва́ть, -ть (*or* поме|ща́ть, -сти́ть) объявле́ние о+*p.*; **I shall ~ my house for sale in the Times** я дам объявле́ние в «Таймс» о прода́же до́ма; **even if you don't like him you needn't ~ the fact** да́же е́сли он вам неприя́тен, не сле́дует э́то афиши́ровать.

v.i.: **she ~d for a maid** она́ дала́ объявле́ние «тре́буется домрабо́тница».

advertisement [əd'vɜːtɪsmənt, -tɪzmənt] *n.* рекла́ма; объявле́ние; **the ~ page** страни́ца объявле́ний; **his behaviour is a poor ~ for the school** его́ поведе́ние — плоха́я рекла́ма для шко́лы.

advertiser ['ædvə,taɪzə(r)] *n.* рекламода́тель (*m.*).

advertising ['ædvə,taɪzɪŋ] *n.* реклами́рование; **~ agent** рекла́мный аге́нт; **Smith is in the ~ business** Смит рабо́тает в рекла́ме.

advice [əd'vaɪs] *n.* **1.** сове́т; **give s.o. a piece, word of ~** посове́товать кому́-н.; **seek s.o.'s ~** сове́товаться, по- с кем-н.; **take legal ~** обра|ща́ться, -ти́ться за сове́том к юри́сту; консульти́роваться, про- с юри́стом; **take, follow s.o.'s ~** сле́довать, по- чьему́-н. сове́ту; (*of doctor, lawyer etc.*) сове́т, консульта́ция. **2.** (*information*) сообще́ние. **3.** (*comm.: notification*) извеще́ние; **shipping ~** извеще́ние об отгру́зке; **letter of ~** ави́зо (*indecl.*).

advisability [əd,vaɪzə'bɪlɪtɪ] *n.* целесообра́зность.

advisable [əd'vaɪzəb(ə)l] *adj.* целесообра́зный; **it may be ~ to wait** сто́ит, наве́рное, подожда́ть.

advise [əd'vaɪz] *v.t.* **1.** (*counsel*) сове́товать, по- +*d.*; **what do you ~ (me to do)?** что вы мне сове́туете де́лать?; **the doctor ~d complete rest** до́ктор прописа́л по́лный о́тдых; **I have been ~d not to smoke** мне посове́товали не кури́ть; **you would be well ~d to go** вам сто́ило бы пойти́; **you would be better ~d to stay at home** разу́мнее бы́ло бы оста́ться до́ма; **be ~d by me** послу́шайтесь моего́ сове́та; **I ~d him against going** я посове́товал ему́ не ходи́ть туда́; **an ill-~d move** необду́манный шаг; (*give professional advice to*) консульти́ровать (*impf.*). **2.** (*comm.: notify*) изве|ща́ть, -сти́ть (*кого о чём*); **please ~ me of receipt** уве́домите меня́ о получе́нии.

v.i.: **he ~d against marriage** он не сове́товал вступа́ть в брак.

advisedly [əd'vaɪzɪdlɪ] *adv.* наме́ренно.

advis|er, -or [əd'vaɪzə(r)] *n.* сове́тник; (*professional*) консульта́нт; **legal ~** юриско́нсульт; **medical ~** врач.

advisory [əd'vaɪzərɪ] *adj.* совеща́тельный, консультати́вный; **in an ~ capacity** в ка́честве сове́тника; **~ committee** совеща́тельный комите́т; **~ opinion** консультати́вное мне́ние.

advocacy ['ædvəkəsɪ] *n.* (*defence*) защи́та, отста́ивание; (*pleading a cause*) пропага́нда; **he was well known for his ~ of penal reform** он был хорошо́ изве́стен, как боре́ц за рефо́рму пенитенциа́рной систе́мы; (*function of an advocate*) адвокату́ра.

advocate[1] ['ædvəkət] *n.* **1.** (*defender*) защи́тник; (*supporter*) сторо́нник. **2.** (*lawyer*) адвока́т; **Lord A~** (*Sc.*) генера́льный прокуро́р; **devil's ~** (*fig.*) «адвока́т дья́вола».

advocate[2] ['ædvə,keɪt] *v.t.* (*defend*) отст|а́ивать, -оя́ть; подде́рж|ивать, -а́ть; (*speak in favour of*) выступа́ть, вы́ступить за+*a.*; (*advise, recommend*) сове́товать, по-; рекомендова́ть (*impf., pf.*).

adze [ædʒ] *n.* тесло́.

Aegean [iː'dʒiːən] *n.*: **the ~** Эге́йское мо́ре.

aegis ['iːdʒɪs] *n.*: **under the ~ of** под эги́дой +*g.*

aeolian [iː'əʊlɪən] *adj.* **1.: A~ mode** (*mus.*) эоли́йский лад. **2.: ~ harp** Э́олова а́рфа.

aeon ['iːɒn] *n.* (*geol.*) э́ра; (*fig.*) (це́лая) ве́чность.

aerate ['eəreɪt] *v.t.* **1.** (*ventilate*) прове́три|вать, -ить; (*expose to air*) прод|ува́ть, -у́ть. **2.** (*charge with gas*) гази́ровать (*impf.*); (*charge with carbon dioxide*) нас|ыща́ть, -ы́тить углеки́слым га́зом.

aeration [,eə'reɪʃ(ə)n] *n.* **1.** прове́тривание; продува́ние во́здухом; (*of the soil*) аэра́ция. **2.** гази́рование; насыще́ние углеки́слым га́зом.

aerial ['eərɪəl] *n.* анте́нна.

adj. **1.** (*lit., fig.*) возду́шный. **2.** (*performed by aircraft*): **~ advertising** возду́шная рекла́ма; **~ photography** аэрофотосъёмка. **3.:** ~ **railway, ropeway** подвесна́я кана́тная доро́га; ~ **torpedo** авиацио́нная торпе́да.

aero- [ˈeərəʊ] *comb. form*: ~**club** аэроклу́б; ~**engine** авиамото́р, авиацио́нный дви́гатель.

aerobatics [ˌeərəˈbætɪks] *n.* вы́сший/фигу́рный пилота́ж.

aerobic [eəˈrəʊbɪk] *adj.* аэро́бный, аэроби́ческий.

aerobicist [eəˈrəʊbɪsɪst] *n.* аэроби́ст (*fem.* -ка).

aerobics [eəˈrəʊbɪks] *n.* аэро́бика, аэро́бная гимна́стика.

aerodrome [ˈeərəˌdrəʊm] *n.* аэродро́м.

aerodynamic [ˌeərəʊdaɪˈnæmɪk] *adj.* аэродинами́ческий.

aerodynamics [ˌeərəʊdaɪˈnæmɪks] *n.* аэродина́мика.

aerofoil [ˈeərəˌfɔɪl] *n.* (*wing*) крыло́; (*wing shape or design*) про́филь (*m.*) крыла́.

aerogram(me) [ˈeərəˌgræm] *n.* (*message*) радиогра́мма; (*US, air letter*) авиаписьмо́.

aerolite [ˈeərəˌlaɪt] *n.* аэроли́т.

aeronaut [ˌeərəʊˈnɔːt] *n.* аэрона́вт; воздухопла́ватель (*m.*).

aeronautic(al) [ˌeərəʊˈnɔːtɪk(ə)l] *adj.* аэронавигацио́нный, авиацио́нный.

aeronautics [ˌeərəʊˈnɔːtɪks] *n.* аэрона́втика.

aeroplane [ˈeərəˌpleɪn] *n.* самолёт, аэропла́н.

aerosol [ˈeərəˌsɒl] *n.* аэрозо́ль (*m.*).

aerospace [ˈeərəʊˌspeɪs] *n.* возду́шно-косми́ческое простра́нство.

adj. авиацио́нно-косми́ческий; **the** ~ **industry** авиацио́нно-косми́ческая промы́шленность.

aesthete [ˈiːsθiːt] *n.* эсте́т.

aesthetic [iːsˈθetɪk] *adj.* эстети́ческий.

aestheticism [iːsˈθetɪˌsɪz(ə)m] *n.* эстети́зм.

aesthetics [iːsˈθetɪks] *n.* эсте́тика.

aetiology [ˌiːtɪˈɒlədʒɪ] *n.* этиоло́гия.

afar [əˈfɑː(r)] *adv.* (*also* ~ **off**) вдалеке́; **from** ~ и́здали, издалека́.

affability [ˌæfəˈbɪlɪtɪ] *n.* приве́тливость; любе́зность; учти́вость.

affable [ˈæfəb(ə)l] *adj.* приве́тливый; любе́зный; ми́лый.

affair [əˈfeə(r)] *n.* **1.** (*business, matter*) де́ло; **that's my** ~ э́то моё де́ло; **what** ~ **is it of yours?** како́е вам до э́того де́ло?; **he asked me to look after his** ~**s** он попроси́л меня́ проследи́ть за его́ дела́ми; ~ **of honour** де́ло че́сти; дуэ́ль; ~**s of state** госуда́рственные дела́; ~**s of the heart** серде́чные дела́; **Ministry of Foreign A**~**s** министе́рство иностра́нных дел; **man of** ~**s** делово́й челове́к. **2.** (*also* **love** ~) любо́вная связь; рома́н; **they are having an** ~ у них рома́н. **3.** (*social event*): **there's an** ~ **at the town hall tonight** в ра́туше сего́дня приём/ве́чер. **4.** (*coll.*): **this building is a poor** ~ э́то зда́ние о́чень неказисто; **his boat is quite an** ~ да, его́ ло́дка — э́то ве́щь!; **what an** ~! вот так исто́рия/шту́ка!

affect[1] [əˈfekt] *v.t.* **1.** (*act on*) де́йствовать, по- на+*a.*; влия́ть, по- на+*a.*; **the climate** ~**ed his health** э́тот кли́мат повлия́л на его́ здоро́вье. **2.** (*concern*) каса́ться, косну́ться +*g.*; **everyone is** ~**ed by the rise in prices** повыше́ние цен затра́гивает всех. **3.** (*touch emotionally*) тро́|гать, -нуть; волнова́ть, вз-; **he was** ~**ed by the news** э́то изве́стие на него́ о́чень поде́йствовало; **an** ~**ing sight** волну́ющее зре́лище. **4.** (*of disease*): **the lung is** ~**ed** лёгкое пораженó; **several hundred cattle were** ~**ed** пострада́ло не́сколько сот голо́в скота́. **5.: well** ~**ed towards** располо́жен к+*d.*

affect[2] [əˈfekt] *v.t.* (*show preference for*): **she** ~**s bright colours** она́ лю́бит я́ркие цвета́; (*pretend*): ~ **the freethinker** стро́ить (*impf.*) из себя́ вольноду́мца; ~ **indifference** прики́|дываться, -нуться равноду́шным; ~ **to despise** разы́грывать презре́ние к+*d.*; **he** ~**ed not to hear me** он притвори́лся, что не слы́шит меня́.

affectation [ˌæfekˈteɪʃ(ə)n] *n.* **1.** (*pretence*) притво́рство; ~ **of disdain** напускно́е притво́рство. **2.** (*unnatural behaviour*) аффекта́ция. **3.** (*of language or style*) иску́сственность.

affected [əˈfektɪd] *adj.* (*pretended*) притво́рный; (*not natural*) аффекти́рованный.

affection [əˈfekʃ(ə)n] *n.* **1.** (*kindly feeling*) привя́занность (**for:** к+*d*); любо́вь; **I feel** ~ **for him** я к нему́ привя́зан; **gain, win s.o.'s** ~ сниска́ть (*pf.*) чьё-н. расположе́ние; **he is held in great** ~ его́ о́чень лю́бят. **2.** (*med.*) заболева́ние.

affectionate [əˈfekʃənət] *adj.* (*of pers.*) лю́бящий; (*of pers. or things*) не́жный; **yours** ~**ly** лю́бящий Вас.

affective [əˈfektɪv] *adj.* эмоциона́льный; (*pert. to feelings*) относя́щийся к чу́вствам.

affiance [əˈfaɪəns] *v.t.* (*arch.*): **they were** ~**d** они́ бы́ли обручены́.

affidavit [ˌæfɪˈdeɪvɪt] *n.* пи́сьменное показа́ние; **make, swear an** ~ да|ва́ть, -ть показа́ние под прися́гой.

affiliate [əˈfɪlɪˌeɪt] *v.t.* **1.** (*join, attach*) присоедин|я́ть, -и́ть (**to:** к+*d.*); ~**d company** подконтро́льная/доче́рняя компа́ния. **2.** (*adopt as member*) прин|има́ть, -я́ть в чле́ны.

v.i. присоедин|я́ться, -и́ться (**with:** к+*d.*).

affiliation [əˌfɪlɪˈeɪʃ(ə)n] *n.* **1.** присоедине́ние. **2.** приня́тие в чле́ны. **3.** установле́ние отцо́вства, усыновле́ние.

affinity [əˈfɪnɪtɪ] *n.* **1.** (*resemblance*) схо́дство; (*relationship*) родство́; (*connection*) связь; (*closeness*) бли́зость; **there is a close** ~ **between these languages** э́ти языки́ о́чень близки́. **2.** (*blood relationship*) родство́; (*by marriage*) свойство́. **3.** (*liking, attraction*) влече́ние, скло́нность. **4.** (*chem.*) сродство́.

affirm [əˈfɜːm] *v.t.* (*assert*) утвер|жда́ть, -ди́ть; (*leg.*: *make an* ~*ation*) торже́ственно заяв|ля́ть, -и́ть (вме́сто прися́ги).

affirmation [ˌæfəˈmeɪʃ(ə)n] *n.* утвержде́ние; (*leg.*) торже́ственное заявле́ние; (*confirmation*) подтвержде́ние.

affirmative [əˈfɜːmətɪv] *n.*: **he answered in the** ~ он отве́тил утверди́тельно.

adj. утверди́тельный.

affix[1] [ˈæfɪks] *n.* (*gram.*) а́ффикс.

affix[2] [əˈfɪks] *v.t.* прикреп|ля́ть, -и́ть (*что к чему*); ~ **one's signature** ста́вить, по- по́дпись; ~ **a seal/stamp** при|кла́дывать, -ложи́ть печа́ть/ште́мпель (*m.*); ~ **a postage stamp** приклеи́|вать, -ть ма́рку.

afflatus [əˈfleɪtəs] *n.* вдохнове́ние.

afflict [əˈflɪkt] *v.t.* **1.** (*distress*: *of misfortune etc.*) пост|ига́ть, -и́чь (*or* -и́гнуть); **he was** ~**ed by a great misfortune** его́ пости́гло большо́е несча́стье; (*grieve*) огорч|а́ть -и́ть. **2.** (*pass.*: *suffer from*): **be** ~**ed with** страда́ть (*impf.*) +*i.*; **he is** ~**ed with rheumatism** он страда́ет ревмати́змом; **the** ~**ed** стра́ждущие (*pl.*).

affliction [əˈflɪkʃ(ə)n] *n.* (*grief*; *distress*) го́ре, скорбь; (*misfortune*; *calamity*) несча́стье; бе́дствие; (*ordeal*) мыта́рство; (*illness, disease*) боле́знь; неду́г; **the** ~**s of old age** ста́рческие не́мощи (*f.pl.*).

affluence [ˈæflʊəns] *n.* (*wealth*) бога́тство; (*plenty*) изоби́лие.

affluent[1] [ˈæflʊənt] *n.* (*river*) прито́к.

affluent[2] [ˈæflʊənt] *adj.* (*wealthy*) бога́тый; (*abounding*) изоби́льный.

afford [əˈfɔːd] *v.t.* **1.** (*with* **can**, *expr. possibility*): **I can't** ~ **all these books** я не в состоя́нии купи́ть все э́ти кни́ги; **he can** ~ **to laugh** ему́ хорошо́ смея́ться; **they can** ~ **a new car** они́ мо́гут позво́лить себе́ но́вую маши́ну; **I can't** ~ **it** э́то мне не по карма́ну; **I can't** ~ **the time** мне не́когда; **he can't** ~ **to lose the race** он до́лжен прийти́ пе́рвым во что бы то ни ста́ло. **2.** (*yield*; *supply*; *give*) предост|авля́ть, -а́вить; да|ва́ть, -ть; **it will** ~ **me an opportunity to speak to her** э́то даст мне возмо́жность поговори́ть с ней; **it** ~**s me great pleasure** э́то доставля́ет мне большо́е удово́льствие; **if it** ~**s you any consolation** е́сли э́то мо́жет служи́ть вам утеше́нием; **the hill** ~**ed a fine view** с холма́ открыва́лся прекра́сный вид; ~ **a basis for** служи́ть (*impf.*) осно́вой для+*g.*; ~ **cover** (*mil.*) служи́ть укры́тием; ~ **protection** (*mil.*) обеспе́чи|вать, -ть прикры́тие.

afforest [əˈfɒrɪst, æ-] *v.t.* облеси́ть (*pf.*).

afforestation [əˌfɒrɪˈsteɪʃ(ə)n] *n.* лесонасажде́ние, облесе́ние.

affray [əˈfreɪ] *n.* дра́ка, сты́чка; сканда́л; **they were charged with causing, making an** ~ их обвини́ли в том, что они́ затея́ли дра́ку.

affront [əˈfrʌnt] *n.* оскорбле́ние; **it was an** ~ **to his pride** э́то оскорбля́ло его́ го́рдость.

v.t. **1.** (*insult*) оскорб|ля́ть, -и́ть. **2.** (*confront*) смотре́ть (*impf.*) в лицо́ +*d.*

Afghan [ˈæfgæn] *n.* афга́н|ец (*fem.* -ка); (~ *hound*) афга́нская борза́я.

adj. афга́нский.

Afghanistan [æfˈgænɪˌstɑːn, -stæn] *n.* Афганиста́н.

aficionado [əˌfɪsjəˈnɑːdəʊ] *n.* люби́тель. (*m.*)

afield [əˈfiːld] *adv.* **1.** (*lit.*) в по́ле; (*mil.*) на по́ле. **2.** (*fig.*): **far** ~ далеко́, вдалеке́, вдали́; (*expr. motion*) вдаль.

afire [əˈfaɪə(r)] *pred. adj. & adv.*: **the house was** ~ дом был охва́чен огнём; **set sth.** ~ подж|ига́ть, -е́чь что-н.; (*fig.*): **he was** ~ **with enthusiasm** он горе́л энтузиа́змом.

aflame [əˈfleɪm] *pred. adj. & adv.*: **his clothes were** ~ его́ оде́жда загоре́лась; (*fig.*): ~ **with passion** пыла́я стра́стью; **the woods were** ~ **with colour** леса́ горе́ли ра́зными кра́сками.

afloat [əˈfləʊt] *pred. adj. & adv.* **1.** (*floating on water*) на воде́; (*in sailing order*) на плаву́; **get a ship** ~ (*after grounding*) сн|има́ть, -я́ть кора́бль с ме́ли; **they had been** ~ **for several days** они́ плы́ли не́сколько дней. **2.** (*at sea*) в мо́ре; **life** ~ жизнь на воде́/мо́ре; (*in naval service*) в вое́нном фло́те; **officer serving** ~ офице́р плавсоста́ва. **3.** (*awash, flooded*): **after the storm the ground-floor rooms were** ~ по́сле грозы́ пе́рвый эта́ж затопи́ло. **4.** (*fig., in circulation*): **various rumours were** ~ по́лзали ра́зные слу́хи; (*comm.*) в обраще́нии. **5. keep** ~ (*fig., solvent*) *v.t.*: **they kept the newspaper** ~ они́ подде́рживали существова́ние газе́ты; *v.i.* быть свобо́дным от долго́в; не залеза́ть в долги́.

aflutter [əˈflʌtə(r)] *pred. adj. & adv.* трепе́щущий; (*fig.*) взволно́ванный; **he was** ~ **with anticipation** он дрожа́л от нетерпе́ния; **the news set her heart** ~ от э́того изве́стия у неё затрепета́ло се́рдце.

afoot [əˈfʊt] *pred. adj. & adv.* **1.** (*arch., on foot; on one's feet*) пешко́м; **she was early** ~ она́ ра́но вста́ла. **2.** (*in progress or preparation*): **there is a plan** ~ гото́вится план; **there is sth.** ~ что́-то затева́ется; **the game's** ~ пого́ня начала́сь.

afore- [əˈfɔː(r)] *comb. form*: ~**mentioned** *adj.* выше-упомя́нутый; ~**named** *adj.* вышена́званный; ~**said** *adj.* вышеска́занный; **malice** ~**thought** злой у́мысел.

a fortiori [ˌeɪ fɔːtɪˈɔːraɪ] *adv.* тем бо́лее.

afraid [əˈfreɪd] *pred. adj.* испу́ганный; **be** ~ **of** боя́ться (*impf.*) +*g.*; **don't be** ~ не бо́йтесь!; **make s.o.** ~ пуга́ть, ис- кого́-н.; **I'm** ~ **he will die** бою́сь, что он умрёт; **I'm** ~ **of waking him** (*that I may wake him*) я бою́сь его́ разбуди́ть; бою́сь, как бы его́ не разбуди́ть; (*of the consequences*) я бою́сь его́ буди́ть; **I'm** ~ **he is out** к сожале́нию, его́ нет.

afresh [əˈfreʃ] *adv.* сно́ва.

Africa [ˈæfrɪkə] *n.* А́фрика.

African [ˈæfrɪkən] *n.* африка́н|ец (*fem.* -ка).

adj. африка́нский.

Africanize [ˈæfrɪkəˌnaɪz] *v.t.* африканизи́ровать (*impf., pf.*).

Afrikaans [ˌæfrɪˈkɑːns] *n.* (язы́к) африка́анс.

Afrikaner [ˌæfrɪˈkɑːnə(r)] *n.* африка́нер; **she's an Afrikaner** она́ из африка́неров.

Afro[1] [ˈæfrəʊ] *n.* (*hairstyle*) приче́ска «а́фро».

adj.: **an** ~ **hair-do** приче́ска «а́фро»; ~ **clothes** оде́жда в сти́ле «а́фро».

Afro-[2] [ˈæfrəʊ] *comb. form* а́фро-…

Afro-American [ˌæfrəʊəˈmerɪkən] *n.* америка́нск|ий негр (*fem.* -ая негритя́нка).

adj. а́фро-америка́нский.

Afro-Asian [ˌæfrəʊˈeɪʃ(ə)n] *n.* жи́тель а́фро-азиа́тской страны́.

adj. а́фро-азиа́тский.

aft [ɑːft] *adv.* (*naut.*) на корме́; **fore and** ~ от но́са к корме́.

after [ˈɑːftə(r)] *adj.* **1.** (*subsequent*) после́дующий; **in** ~ **years** в после́дующие го́ды. **2.** (*rear*) за́дний; (*naut.*) кормово́й; ~ **deck** ют.

adv. **1.** (*subsequently; then*) пото́м, зате́м; **soon** ~ вско́ре по́сле э́того. **2.** (*later*) поздне́е, по́зже; **3 days** ~ спустя́ три дня; **3.** (*in consequence*) впосле́дствии. **4.** (*coll., as n. in pl.*) сла́дкое; **what's for** ~**s?** что у нас на десе́рт?

prep. **1.** (*in expressions of time*) по́сле+*g.*; за+*i.*; че́рез+*a.*; спустя́+*a.*; ~ **dinner** по́сле обе́да; ~ **you!** за ва́ми!; ~ **that** пото́м, зате́м; **the day** ~ **tomorrow** послеза́втра; **the day** ~ **the invitation** на сле́дующий день по́сле приглаше́ния; **I am tired** ~ **my journey** я уста́л с доро́ги; **the week** ~ **next** неде́ля по́сле сле́дующей; (*in adv. sense*) че́рез две неде́ли; **they met** ~ **10 years** они́ встре́тились че́рез де́сять лет; ~ **passing his exams, he …** сдав экза́мены, он…; **he wrote that** ~ **receiving my letter** он написа́л э́то, уже́ получи́в моё письмо́; ~ **midday** за́ полдень, по́сле полу́дня; ~ **midnight** за́ полночь, по́сле полу́ночи; **it's** ~ **6 (o'clock)** уже́ седьмо́й час; (*in sequence*) **day** ~ **day** день за днём; **one** ~ **another** оди́н за други́м; **we tried shop** ~ **shop without success** мы ходи́ли из магази́на в магази́н, но без успе́ха; ~ **what he has done I shall never trust him again** по́сле того́, что он сде́лал, я никогда́ бо́льше не бу́ду ему́ ве́рить; (*in spite of*) несмотря́ на+*a.*; ~ **all my care** в отве́т на все мои́ забо́ты; ~ **all** (*in the end*) в коне́чном счёте; в конце́ концо́в; (*nevertheless*) всё-таки; **he's your brother,** ~ **all** ведь он ваш брат; **not so bad** ~ **all** не так уж пло́хо. **2.** (*in expressions of place*) за+*i.*; **shut the door** ~ **you** закро́йте за собо́й дверь; **run** ~ **s.o.** бежа́ть за кем-н.; **he ran** ~ **the bus** он бежа́л за авто́бусом; **he climbed up** ~ **Ivan** он влез (вслед) за Ива́ном; **we shouted** ~ **him** мы крича́ли ему́ вслед/вдого́нку; (*fig.*): ~ **Tolstoy, Turgenev is the best Russian writer** по́сле Толсто́го лу́чший ру́сский писа́тель — Турге́нев; **he ranks** ~ **me** он ни́же меня́ чи́ном (*or* по положе́нию). **3.** (*in search of; trying to get*): **the police are** ~ **him** его́ разы́скивает поли́ция; **he likes going** ~ **the girls** он бе́гает за де́вушками; **what is he** ~**?** на что он ме́тит?; что он замышля́ет?; **he is** ~ **your money** он ме́тит на ва́ши де́ньги. **4.** (*in accordance with*) по+*d.*, согла́сно+*d.*; **a man** ~ **my own heart** челове́к мне по ду́ше; **each** ~ **his kind** ка́ждый по своему́; ~ **this fashion** подо́бно э́тому; ~ **a fashion** как-нибу́дь; **he paints** ~ **a fashion** он в своём ро́де худо́жник; **named** ~ на́званный по+*d.* (*or* в честь +*g.*); **the child was christened Cyril** ~ **its father** ребёнка нарекли́ Кири́ллом в честь отца́; **he takes** ~ **his father** он похо́ж на отца́; **a portrait** ~ **Van Dyck** портре́т в мане́ре Ван-Де́йка.

conj. по́сле того́, как.

cpds. ~**birth** *n.* после́д; ~**burner** *n.* дожига́тель (*m.*); ~**-care** *n.* ухо́д (за+*i.*); забо́та (о+*p.*); ~**-dinner** *adj.* послеобе́денный; ~**-effect** *n.* после́дствие; (*tech.*) последе́йствие; ~**glow** *n.* вече́рняя заря́; ~**life** *n.* загро́бная жизнь; ~**math** *n.* ота́ва; (*fig.*) после́дствия (*nt. pl.*); ~**most** *adj.* са́мый за́дний; кра́йний к корме́; ~**noon** *n.* послеполу́денное вре́мя; **in the** ~**noon** днём; по́сле обе́да; пополу́дни; во второ́й полови́не дня; **at 3 in the** ~**noon** в три часа́ дня; **it is a beautiful** ~**noon** како́й прекра́сный день!; **good** ~**noon!** (*in greeting*) до́брый день!; (*in leave-taking*) до свида́ния; (*fig.*): **in the** ~**noon of life** на скло́не лет; (*attr.*): ~**noon nap** послеобе́денный сон; ~**shock** *n.* повто́рные толчки́; ~**taste** *n.* при́вкус; ~**thought** *n.* запозда́лая мысль.

afterwards [ˈɑːftəwədz] *adv.* (*then*) пото́м; (*subsequently*) впосле́дствии; (*later*) по́зже; **(a) long (time)** ~ гора́здо по́зже; **I only heard of it** ~ я то́лько пото́м услы́шал об э́том.

again [əˈgeɪn, əˈgen] *adv.* **1.** (*expr. repetition*) опя́ть; (*afresh, anew*) сно́ва, вновь; (*once more*) ещё раз; (*with certain vv.*) *by use of pref.* пере…; **read** ~ перечи́т|ывать, -а́ть; **open** ~ вновь откр|ыва́ть, -ы́ть; **say** ~ повтор|я́ть, -и́ть; **start** ~ (*v.t.*) возобнов|ля́ть, -и́ть; (*v.i.*) нач|ина́ть, -а́ть сно́ва; **she married** ~ она́ сно́ва вы́шла за́муж; **what's his name** ~**?** как, вы сказа́ли, его́ фами́лия?; ~ **and** ~ сно́ва и сно́ва; **time and (time)** ~**, over and over** ~ то и де́ло; **now and** ~ вре́мя от вре́мени; **once** ~ ещё раз; **same** ~**, please!** ещё стака́нчик!; **he did his work over** ~ он переде́лал рабо́ту. **2.** (*with neg.*: *any more*) бо́льше; **never** ~ никогда́ бо́льше; **don't do it** ~**!** бо́льше э́того не де́лайте!; ≃ пе́рвый раз проща́ется. **3.** (*in addition*): **as far** ~ вдвое́ да́льше; **as much** ~ ещё сто́лько же; **half as much** ~ (в) полтора́ ра́за бо́льше. **4.** (*expr. return to original state or position*): **back** ~ обра́тно; **get sth. back**

~ получ|áть, -и́ть что-н. обрáтно; **you'll soon be well** ~ вы скóро попрáвитесь; **he is himself** ~ он пришёл в себя́. **5.** (*moreover; besides*) к томý же; крóме тогó; (*on the other hand*) с другóй стороны́.

against [ə'geɪnst, ə'genst] *prep.* **1.** (*in opposition to*) прóтив+*g.*; **I have nothing** ~ **it** я ничегó не имéю прóтив э́того; **I was** ~ **his going** я был прóтив тогó, чтóбы он шёл тудá; **is there a law** ~ **spitting?** есть ли закóн, запрещáющий плевáться?; **they did it** ~ **my wishes** они́ сдéлали э́то прóтив моегó желáния; **I acted** ~ **my will** я дéйствовал не по своéй вóле; **swim** ~ **the current** (*lit., fig.*) плыть (*impf.*) прóтив течéния; **they were working** ~ **time** они́ рабóтали наперегóнки́ со врéменем; **act** ~ **the law** поступ|áть, -и́ть противозакóнно; ~ **the rules** не по прáвилам; **fight, struggle** ~ boróться (*impf., pf.*) прóтив+*g.* (*or* c+*i.*); **the battle** ~ **drunkenness** бóрьба с пья́нством; **speak** ~ (*oppose*) выступáть, вы́ступить прóтив+*g.*; (*slander*) нагов|áривать, -ори́ть на+*a.* **2.** (*in spite of*) вопреки́+*d.*; ~ **reason** вопреки́ рассýдку; ~ **my better judgement** вопреки́ гóлосу рассýдка. **3.** (*to the disfavour of*): **his manner is** ~ **him** он вреди́т себé своéй манéрой держáться; **her age is** ~ **her** вóзраст её подвóдит. **4.** (*to oppose or combat*) на+*a.*; **march** ~ **the enemy** наступáть (*impf.*) на врагá. **5.** (*to withstand*) от+*g.*; **a shelter** ~ **the storm** убéжище от бýри; **defend o.s.** ~ **the enemy** защищáться (*impf.*) от врагá. **6.** (*in readiness for, anticipation of*): **make preparations** ~ **his coming** приготóвиться (*pf.*) к егó приéзду; ~ **a rainy day** на чёрный день; **we took measures** ~ **a shortage of water** мы при́няли мéры на слýчай нехвáтки воды́; **they bought provisions** ~ **the winter** они́ купи́ли прови́зии нá зиму. **7.** (*compared with*): **3 deaths this year** ~ **20 last year** три смéрти в э́том годý прóтив двадцати́ в прóшлом. **8.** (*in contrast with*): **it shows up** ~ **a dark background** э́то выделя́ется на тёмном фóне. **9.** (*in collision with*) о+*a.*; **knock** ~ **sth.** удáриться (*pf.*) о что-н.; **he banged his head** ~ **a stone** он удáрился головóй о кáмень; **the ship ran** ~ **a rock** корáбль наскочи́л на скалý. **10.** (*into contact with*) к+*d.*; **he moved the chair** ~ **the wall** он придви́нул стул к стенé; **he stood leaning** ~ **the wall** он стоя́л, прислони́вшись к стенé; **he built a garage** ~ **the house** он пристрóил гарáж к дóму. **11.** (*by; in the vicinity of*) у+*g.*; **she sat** ~ **the window** онá сидéла у окнá. **12.** (*facing*): **over** ~ **the church** напрóтив цéркви; **he held the photograph** ~ **the light** он поднёс фотогрáфию к свéту; **we are up** ~ **strong competition** у нас си́льная конкурéнция; **he is up** ~ **it** емý прихóдится тя́жко; ≃ он прижáт к стенé.

agape [ə'geɪp] *pred. adj. & adv.* рази́нув рот.

agaric ['ægərɪk] *n.* пласти́нчатый гриб.

agate ['ægət] *n.* агáт; (*attr.*) агáтовый.

agave [ə'geɪvɪ] *n.* столéтник, агáва.

age [eɪdʒ] *n.* **1.** (*time of life*) вóзраст; **what** ~ **is he?** какóго он вóзраста?; (*expecting exact answer*) скóлько емý лет?; **he is 40 years of** ~ емý сóрок лет; **he and I are the same** ~ мы с ним ровéсники; **when I was your** ~ когдá я был в вáшем вóзрасте; **a man (of) your** ~ человéк вáшего вóзраста; **at his** ~ **he should be more careful** в егó гóды нáдо быть бóлее осторóжным; **he is at an** ~ (*or* **has reached an** ~) **when ...** он дости́г вóзраста, когдá...; **she looks her** ~ онá не вы́глядит molóже свои́х лет; **I am feeling my** ~ вóзраст берёт своё; **at an early** ~ в дéтском/рáннем вóзрасте; **a man in middle** ~ мужчи́на срéдних лет; **he took up tennis in middle** ~ он заня́лся тéннисом в соли́дном вóзрасте; **be your** ~! (*coll.*) веди́те себя́ как взрóслый человéк!; **over** ~ стáрше полóженного вóзраста; ~ **of consent** брáчный вóзраст; ~ **of discretion** отвéтственный вóзраст; ~ **of reason** сознáтельный вóзраст; (*of inanimate objects*): **the wine lacks** ~ винó недостáточно вы́держано; **what is the** ~ **of this house?** когдá пострóен э́тот дом? **2.** (*majority*): **be of** ~ быть совершеннолéтним; **come of** ~ дост|игáть, -и́чь совершеннолéтия; **he is under** ~ он несовершеннолéтний. **3.** (*old* ~) стáрость; **his back was bent with** ~ он согнýлся от стáрости; **he lived to a ripe (old)** ~ он дóжил до преклóнных лет. **4.** (*period*) пери́од; (*century*) век; **Ice A**~ ледникóвый пери́од; **Stone A**~ кáменный век; **golden** ~ золотóй век; **the Middle A~s** срéдние векá; **the present** ~ ны́нешний век; **the** ~ **we live in** наш век; (*coll., often pl., long time*): **it took an** ~ **to get there** мы добирáлись тудá цéлую вéчность; **the bus left** ~**s ago** автóбус ушёл давны́м-давнó; **we have not seen each other for** ~**s** мы не видáлись цéлую вéчность.

v.t. стáрить, со-; **worries have** ~**d him** забóты егó состáрили; (*of wine*) выдéрживать, вы́держать.

v.i. (*of pers.*) старéть, по-; (*of thg.*) старéть.

cpds. ~**-bracket,** ~**-group** *nn.* возрастнáя грýппа; ~**-limit** *n.* предéльный вóзраст; ~**-long** *adj.* вéчный, векове́чный; ~**-old** *adj.* векóвóй, (старо)дáвний.

aged[1] [eɪdʒd] *adj.* (*of the age of*): ~ **six** шести́ лет.

aged[2] ['eɪdʒɪd] *adj.* (*very old*) престарéлый.

adj. **the** ~ пожилы́е лю́ди, престарéлые.

ag(e)ing ['eɪdʒɪŋ] *n.* старéние; (*of wine*) вы́держка.

adj. старéющий.

ageism ['eɪdʒɪz(ə)m] *n.* дискримини́ция по вóзрасту.

ageist ['eɪdʒɪst] *n.* сторóнник дискримини́ции по вóзрасту.

adj. дискримини́рующий по вóзрасту.

ageless ['eɪdʒlɪs] *adj.* (*always young*) нестарéющий; (*eternal*) вéчный.

agency ['eɪdʒənsɪ] *n.* **1.** (*action*) дéйствие; (*instrumentality*) посрéдство; **by the** ~ **of** посрéдством+*g.*; чéрез+*a.*; при посрéдничестве +*g.* **2.** (*force*): **an invisible** ~ незри́мая си́ла. **3.** (*comm.*) агéнтство; **employment** ~ агéнтство по наймý; **travel** ~ тури́стское агéнтство, бюрó (*indecl.*) путешéствий. **4.** (*organization*): **government** ~ прави́тельственное учреждéние; прави́тельственная организáция. **5.** (*representation*): **sole** ~ еди́нственное представи́тельство.

agenda [ə'dʒendə] *n.* повéстка дня; **it is on the** ~ э́то стои́т на повéстке дня; **put on the** ~ стáвить, по- на повéстку дня.

agent ['eɪdʒ(ə)nt] *n.* **1.** (*pers. acting for others*) агéнт; (*representative*) представи́тель (*m.*); **commission** ~ комиссионéр; **forwarding** ~ экспеди́тор. **2.** (*chem.*) агéнт; срéдство; **chemical** ~ реакти́в, реагéнт; **oxidizing** ~ окисли́тель (*m.*). **3.** (*gram.*) дéятель (*m.*).

agent provocateur [ˌɑːʒɑ̃ prəˌvɒkə'tɜː(r)] *n.* провокáтор.

agglomerate[1] [ə'glɒmərət] *n.* (*geol.*) агломерáт, скоплéние.

agglomerate[2] [ə'glɒməˌreɪt] *v.t. & i.* (*gather*) соб|ирáть(ся), -рáть(ся); (*mass*) ск|áпливать(ся), -опи́ть(ся).

agglomeration [əˌglɒmə'reɪʃ(ə)n] *n.* скоплéние.

agglutinate [ə'gluːtɪˌneɪt] *v.t.* (*ling.*) агглютини́ровать (*impf., pf.*).

agglutination [əˌgluːtɪ'neɪʃ(ə)n] *n.* (*ling.*) агглютинáция.

agglutinative [ə'gluːtɪnətɪv] *adj.* (*ling.*) агглютинати́вный, агглютини́рующий.

aggrandize [ə'grændaɪz] *v.t.* увели́чи|вать, -ть; расш|иря́ть, -и́рить.

aggrandizement [ə'grændɪzmənt] *n.* увеличéние; расширéние.

aggravat|e ['ægrəˌveɪt] *v.t.* **1.** (*make worse*) ух|удшáть, -ýдшить; ~**ing circumstances** отягчáющие винý обстоя́тельства; (*of pain*) обостр|я́ть, -и́ть; уси́ли|вать, -ть. **2.** (*coll., exasperate*) раздраж|áть, -и́ть.

aggravation [ˌægrə'veɪʃ(ə)n] *n.* **1.** ухудшéние; обострéние, усилéние. **2.** раздражéние.

aggregate[1] ['ægrɪgət] *n.* **1.** (*total, mass*) совокýпность; **in the** ~ в совокýпности. **2.** (*phys.*) скоплéние. **3.** (*ingredient of concrete*) заполни́тель (*m.*) (бетóна).

adj. **1.** (*total*) óбщий; ~ **membership** óбщее числó члéнов; **for an** ~ **period of 3 years** в óбщей слóжности нá три гóда. **2.** (*collected together*) сóбранный вмéсте; (*tech.*): ~ **capacity** пóлная мóщность.

aggregate[2] ['ægrɪˌgeɪt] *v.t.* **1.** (*collect into a mass*) соб|ирáть, -рáть в цéлое. **2.** (*amount to*) сост|авля́ть, -áвить; состоя́ть (*impf.*) (в óбщей слóжности) из+*g.*; **these armies** ~**d 500,000 men** э́ти áрмии насчи́тывали 500 000 человéк.

v.i. (*collect or come together*) соб|ирáться, -рáться.

aggregation [ˌægrɪ'geɪʃ(ə)n] *n.* **1.** (*collecting together*) собирáние; (*collection of persons or things*) скоплéние,

конгломера́т. **2.** (*phys.*) скопле́ние; (*mass*) ма́сса.
aggress [ə'gres] *v.t. & i.* нап|ада́ть, -а́сть (на+*a.*).
aggression [ə'greʃ(ə)n] *n.* агре́ссия; (*attack*) нападе́ние; **war of ~** агресси́вная война́.
aggressive [ə'gresɪv] *adj.* агресси́вный; (*attacking*) напада́ющий; **~ defence** акти́вная оборо́на; **~ attack** стреми́тельное нападе́ние; **~ weapons** ору́жие агре́ссии; **an ~ salesman** напо́ристый коммерса́нт.
aggressiveness [ə'gresɪvnɪs] *n.* агресси́вность.
aggressor [ə'gresə(r)] *n.* агре́ссор; **~ nation** страна́-агре́ссор.
aggrieve [ə'gri:v] *v.t.* огор|ча́ть, -чи́ть; **be ~d; feel (o.s.) ~d** быть огорчённым; огорч|а́ться, -и́ться.
aghast [ə'gɑ:st] *pred. adj.* (*terrified*) в у́жасе (*от чего*); (*amazed*) потрясённый; **he stood ~** он оцепене́л от у́жаса.
agile ['ædʒaɪl] *adj.* прово́рный, ло́вкий; **an ~ mind** живо́й ум.
agility [ə'dʒɪlɪtɪ] *n.* прово́рство, ло́вкость; **~ of movement** ло́вкость движе́ний; **~ of mind** жи́вость ума́.
aging ['eɪdʒɪŋ] = **ag(e)ing**
agitate ['ædʒɪˌteɪt] *v.t.* **1.** (*excite*) волнова́ть, вз-; **be ~d about sth.** волнова́ться (*impf.*) из-за чего́-н.; **in an ~d voice** взволно́ванным го́лосом; (*arouse*) возбу|жда́ть, -ди́ть. **2.** (*shake*) трясти́ (*impf.*); (*liquids*) взб|а́лтывать, -олта́ть.
v.i. агити́ровать (*impf.*) (*for, against*: за+*a.*, про́тив+*g.*).
agitation [ˌædʒɪ'teɪʃ(ə)n] *n.* **1.** (*disturbance*) волне́ние; **in a state of ~** взволно́ванный. **2.** (*shaking*) взба́лтывание; (*chem.*) переме́шивание. **3.** (*pol.*) агита́ция.
agitator ['ædʒɪˌteɪtə(r)] *n.* **1.** (*pol.*) агита́тор. **2.** (*apparatus*) меша́лка.
aglow [ə'gləʊ] *pred. adj.* (*lit.*): **be ~** пыла́ть (*impf.*); (*red-hot*) раскалённый до́красна́; (*fig.*) **his face was ~** он раскрасне́лся; **~ with pleasure** раскрасне́вшийся от удово́льствия.
agnail ['ægneɪl] *n.* заусе́ница.
agnostic [æg'nɒstɪk] *n.* агно́стик.
adj. агности́ческий.
agnosticism [æg'nɒstˌɪsɪz(ə)m] *n.* агностици́зм.
ago [ə'gəʊ] *adv.* тому́ наза́д; **long ~** давно́; **not long ~** неда́вно; **it was longer ~ than I thought** э́то бы́ло (ещё) ра́ньше, чем я ду́мал.
agog [ə'gɒg] *pred. adj.*: **she was ~ with excitement** она́ была́ вне себя́ от волне́ния.
adv.: **he listened ~** он слу́шал, затаи́в дыха́ние; **the rumours set the village ~** слу́хи взбудора́жили дере́вню.
agoniz|e ['ægəˌnaɪz] *v.t.* му́чить (*impf.*); **~ed, ~ing shrieks** отча́янные во́пли (*m. pl.*).
v.i. **1.** (*suffer agony*) терза́ться (*impf.*); му́читься (*impf.*); быть в аго́нии. **2.** (*fig.*): **he ~ed over his speech** он му́чился над свое́й ре́чью.
agon|y ['ægənɪ] *n.* (*torment*) муче́ние; (*suffering*) страда́ние; (*pains of death*) аго́ния; **in his last ~y** в предсме́ртной аго́нии; **suffer ~ies** терза́ться (*impf.*); **I was in ~y** я о́чень страда́л; **in an ~y of remorse** терза́ясь раска́янием; **an ~y of joy** взрыв весе́лья; **pile on the ~y** (*coll.*) нагроможда́ть (*impf.*) у́жасы; сгу|ща́ть, -сти́ть кра́ски; **~y column** отде́л ли́чных объявле́ний.
agora ['ægərə] *n.* (*hist.*) агора́.
agoraphobia [ˌægərə'fəʊbɪə] *n.* агорафо́бия.
agrarian [ə'greərɪən] *adj.* агра́рный.
agree [ə'gri:] *v.t.* **1.** (*reach agreement on*) согласо́в|ывать, -а́ть (*что с кем*). **2.** (*accept as correct*) утвер|жда́ть, -ди́ть; прин|има́ть, -я́ть.
v.i. **1.** (*concur; be of like opinion*): **I quite ~ with you** я соверше́нно с ва́ми согла́сен; **we are ~d on this** мы в э́том согла́сны; **make two people ~** прив|оди́ть, -ести́ двух люде́й к согла́сию; **those two will never ~** э́ти дво́е никогда́ не договоря́тся. **2.** (*reach agreement; make common decision*): **we ~d to go together** мы договори́лись е́хать вме́сте; **~ on a price** договори́ться о цене́; **let us ~ to differ** оста́немся ка́ждый при своём мне́нии. **3.** (*consent*) согла|ша́ться, -си́ться (*на что*). **4.** (*accept*): **I ~ that it was wrong** согла́сен, что э́то бы́ло непра́вильно; **~ with** (*accept as correct or right*): **I don't ~ with his policy** я не согла́сен с его́ поли́тикой; **I don't ~ with keeping children up late** я про́тив того́, что́бы по́здно укла́дывать дете́й спать. **5.:** **~ with** (*suit*) под|ходи́ть, -ойти́ +*d.*; годи́ться (*impf.*) +*d.*; **oysters don't ~ with me** от у́стриц мне быва́ет пло́хо. **6.** (*conform; tally*): **the adjective ~s with the noun** прилага́тельное согласу́ется с существи́тельным; **his story ~s with mine** его́ расска́з схо́дится с мои́м.
agreeabl|e [ə'gri:əb(ə)l] *adj.* **1.** (*pleasant*) прия́тный; **~y surprised** прия́тно удивлён; **make o.s. ~e to** стара́ться (*impf.*) угоди́ть +*d.* **2.** (*acceptable*): **if that is ~e to you** е́сли вас э́то устра́ивает; е́сли вам бу́дет уго́дно. **3.** (*prepared to agree*): **be ~e to sth.** согла|ша́ться, -си́ться на что-н. **4.:** **~e to** (*in conformity with*): **this theory is ~e to experience** э́та тео́рия подтвержда́ется пра́ктикой.
agreement [ə'gri:mənt] *n.* **1.** (*consent*) согла́сие; **by mutual ~** по взаи́мному согла́сию; **be in ~ with** согла|ша́ться, -си́ться с+*i.* **2.** (*treaty*) соглаше́ние, догово́р; **come to an ~** при|ходи́ть, -йти́ к соглаше́нию; **enter into, conclude an ~ with** заключ|а́ть, -и́ть соглаше́ние/догово́р с+*i.*; **gentleman's ~** джентльме́нское соглаше́ние; **standstill ~** морато́рий. **3.** (*gram.*) согласова́ние.
agricultural [ˌægrɪ'kʌltʃər(ə)l] *adj.* сельскохозя́йственный; **~ engineering** агроте́хника.
agricultur(al)ist [ˌægrɪ'kʌltʃər(əl)ɪst] *n.* земледе́лец.
agriculture ['ægrɪˌkʌltʃə(r)] *n.* се́льское хозя́йство.
agrimony ['ægrɪmənɪ] *n.* репе́йник, репешо́к.
agrochemical [ˌægrəʊ'kemɪk(ə)l] *n.* агрохимика́т.
adj. агрохими́ческий.
agronomist [ə'grɒnəmɪst] *n.* агроно́м.
agronomy [ə'grɒnəmɪ] *n.* агроно́мия; се́льское хозя́йство, земледе́лие.
aground [ə'graʊnd] *pred. adj. & adv.*: **the ship was ~** кора́бль сиде́л на мели́; **run ~** (*v.i.*) сесть (*pf.*) на мель.
ague ['eɪgju:] *n.* озно́б, лихора́дка.
ah [ɑ:] *int.* ах!; а!
aha [ɑ:'hɑ:, ə'hɑ:] *int.* ага́!
ahead [ə'hed] *adv.* впереди́; (*expr. motion*) вперёд; **he rode ~ of his troops** он е́хал впереди́ свои́х во́йск; **he was ten yards ~ of us** он был на де́сять я́рдов впереди́ нас; **be, get ~ of** опере|жа́ть, -ди́ть; **move ~** продви́нуться (*pf.*) вперёд; **go ~!** продолжа́йте! ну дава́йте!; пожа́луйста!; начина́йте!; **things are going ~** дела́ иду́т; **~ of time** досро́чно, ра́ньше сро́ка; **look ~** (*fig.*) смотре́ть (*impf.*) вперёд; **in the days ~** в бу́дущем; **in line ~** (*naut.*) кильва́терным стро́ем.
ahem [ə'həm, ə'hem] *int.* гм!
ahoy [ə'hɔɪ] *int.*: **~ there!** эй, на корабле́/су́дне!; **ship ~!** вон идёт кора́бль!
aid [eɪd] *n.* **1.** (*help, assistance*) по́мощь; (*support*) подде́ржка; **first ~** пе́рвая по́мощь; **~ agency** организа́ция по оказа́нию по́мощи; **~ worker** рабо́тн|ик (*fem.* -ица) организа́ции по оказа́нию по́мощи; **with, by the ~ of** при по́мощи +*g.*; **call on s.o.'s ~** приб|ега́ть, -е́гнуть к чье́й-н. по́мощи; **lend, give ~ to** ока́з|ывать, -а́ть по́мощь +*d.*; **go to s.o.'s ~** при|ходи́ть, -йти́ кому́-н. на по́мощь; **mutual ~** взаимопо́мощь; **in ~ of** в по́мощь +*d.*; **what is the collection in ~ of?** на что собира́ют де́ньги?; **what is this in ~ of?** (*coll.*) к чему́ э́то?; **an ~ to digestion** сре́дство, спосо́бствующее пищеваре́нию. **2.** (*appliance*) посо́бие; **visual ~s** нагля́дные посо́бия.
v.t. (*help*) пом|ога́ть, -о́чь +*d.*; (*promote*) спосо́бствовать (*impf.*) +*d.*; **~ed school** шко́ла на госуда́рственной дота́ции; **~ing and abetting** посо́бничество и подстрека́тельство.
aide [eɪd] *n.* помо́щни|к (*fem.* -ца).
cpds. **~-de-camp** *n.* адъюта́нт; **~-memoire** *n.* па́мятная запи́ска.
AIDS [eɪdz] *n.* (*abbr. of* ***acquired immune deficiency syndrome***) СПИД, (синдро́м приобретённого имму́нного дефици́та); **an ~ sufferer** страда́ющ|ий (*fem.* -ая) СПИДом; **an ~ vaccine** вакци́на про́тив СПИДа.
aigret(te) ['eɪgret, eɪ'gret] *n.* (*plume*) эгре́т(ка), султа́н, плюма́ж.
aiguillette [ˌeɪgwɪ'let] *n.* аксельба́нт.

aikido ['aɪkɪdəʊ] *n.* айкидó.

ail [eɪl] *v.t.*: **what ~s him?** (*arch.*) о чём он горю́ет? что с ним?

v.i.: **he is always ~ing** он постоя́нно хвора́ет.

aileron ['eɪlə,rɒn] *n.* элерóн.

ailment ['eɪlmənt] *n.* болéзнь; нездорóвье.

aim [eɪm] *n.* **1.** (*purpose*) цель; **with the ~ of** с цéлью +*g.*; **fall short of one's ~s** не дост|ига́ть, -и́чь своéй цéли; **what is the ~ of these questions?** к чему́ э́ти вопрóсы? **2.** (*of a gun, etc.*) прицéл; **take ~ at** прицéл|иваться, -иться в+*a.*; **miss one's ~** не попа́сть (*pf.*) в цель; **is your ~ good?** у вас хорóший глаз?

v.t. нав|оди́ть, -ести́; **~ a rifle at** напр|авля́ть, -а́вить винтóвку на+*a.*; **~ a stone at** цéлиться (*impf.*) ка́мнем в+*a.*; **~ a blow at** зама́х|иваться, -ну́ться на+*a.*; (*fig.*): **~ one's remarks at** предназн|ача́ть, -а́чить свои́ замеча́ния +*d.*

v.i. цéлить (*impf.*); **~ at** (*with rifle*) прицéл|иваться, -иться в+*a.*; (*fig.*): **~ at** (*aspire to*) стреми́ться (*impf.*) к+*d.*; **he ~ed at becoming** (*or* **to become**) **a doctor** он поста́вил себе цéлью стать врачóм; **~ high** мéтить (*impf.*) высокó; **what are you ~ing at?** что вы имéете в виду́? **~ for** напр|авля́ться, -а́виться в/на+*a.*; **he ~ed for the south** он взял направлéние на юг.

aimless ['eɪmlɪs] *adj.* бесцéльный.

aimlessness ['eɪmlɪsnɪs] *n.* бесцéльность.

air [eə(r)] *n.* **1.** (*lit.*) вóздух; **stale ~** спёртый вóздух; **get some fresh ~** подыша́ть (*pf.*) свéжим вóздухом; **liquid ~** жи́дкий вóздух; **in the open ~** на откры́том вóздухе; **let some ~ into a room** провéтри|вать, -ть кóмнату; **let the ~ out of** (*balloon, tyre*) выпуска́ть, вы́пустить вóздух из+*g.*; **take the ~** прогу́л|иваться, -я́ться; **take more fresh ~!** гуля́йте бóльше!; **take to the ~** взлет|а́ть, -éть; **into the ~** вверх; **travel by ~** лета́ть (*impf.*) (самолётом); **a change of ~** перемéна обстанóвки; **birds of the ~** пти́цы небéсные; **mastery of the ~**; **~ supremacy** госпóдство/превосхóдство в вóздухе; **~ current** возду́шное течéние; **~ pollution** загрязнéние вóздуха. **2.** (*in fig. phrr.*): **a plan is in the ~** готóвится план; **the question was left in the ~** вопрóс пови́с в вóздухе; **leave a sentence in the ~** оборва́ть (*pf.*) предложéние; **clear the ~** разря|жа́ть, -ди́ть атмосфéру; **hot ~** (*coll.*) хвастовствó, пустозвóнство; **beat the ~** толóчь вóду в сту́пе; **he vanished into thin ~** егó и след просты́л; **go up in the ~** (*coll.*) вы́йти (*pf.*) из себя́; **live on ~** пита́ться (*impf.*) вóздухом; **castles in the ~** возду́шные за́мки; **he was walking on ~** он ног под собóй не чу́ял; **with his, her head in the ~** задра́в нос. **3.** (*appearance, manner*) вид; **there was a general ~ of desolation** во всём чу́вствовалось запустéние; **with a triumphant ~** с торжеству́ющим ви́дом; **~s and graces** манéрность; **put on** (*or* **give o.s.**) **~s** задава́ться (*impf.*); **he did it with an ~** он сдéлал э́то с ши́ком. **4.** (*mus., song*) пéсня; (*tune*) моти́в. **5.** (*radio*): **the programme is on the ~** програ́мма в эфи́ре; **go on the ~** выходи́ть, вы́йти в эфи́р; (*of pers.*) выступа́ть, вы́ступить по ра́дио; **go off the ~** (*of station*) зак|а́нчивать, -óнчить радиопереда́чу. **6.** (*attr., pert. to aviation*) возду́шный; авиациóнный, авиа...; (*mil.*) воéнно-возду́шный; **~ arm, force** воéнно-возду́шные си́лы; **~ attaché** воéнно-возду́шный атташé (*m. indecl.*); **~ corridor** возду́шный коридóр; **~ cover, umbrella** авиациóнное прикры́тие; **~ defence** противовозду́шная оборóна; **~ base** авиаба́за; **~ crash** авиакатастрóфа; **~ display** возду́шный пара́д; **~ hostess** бортпроводни́ца; **A~ Ministry** министéрство авиа́ции; **A~ Marshal** ма́ршал авиа́ции; **~ mechanic** авиа(циóнный) меха́ник, (*member of aircrew*) бортмеха́ник; **~ passage** полёт; перелёт; **~ piracy** *n.* возду́шное пира́тство; **~ pirate** *n.* возду́шный пира́т; **~ show** авиасалóн; **~ terminal** (городскóй) аэровокза́л; **~ time** *n.* врéмя переда́чи; **~ trial** испыта́тельный полёт; (*pl.*) лётные испыта́ния; **~ waves** *n.* радиовóлны.

v.t. **1.** (*ventilate*) провéтри|вать, -ть; (*dry*) суши́ть, вы-. **2.** (*fig.*): **~ one's knowledge** выставля́ть (*impf.*) напока́з свои́ зна́ния; **~ one's grievances** выска́зывать, вы́сказать своё недовóльство.

v.i.: **she hung the clothes out to ~** онá развéсила вéщи для просу́шки.

cpds. **~-bed** *n.* надувнóй матра́ц; **~borne** *adj.* (*landed by ~*) возду́шно-деса́нтный; (*in the air*): **we were ~borne at 9 o'clock** мы бы́ли в вóздухе в 9 ч.; **~-brake** *n.* возду́шный тóрмоз; **~-brick** *n.* кирпи́ч-сырéц; **~bus** *n.* аэрóбус; **~-conditioned** *adj.* с кондициони́рованным вóздухом; **~-conditioner** *n.* кондиционéр (вóздуха); **~-conditioning** *n.* кондициони́рование вóздуха; **~-cooled** *adj.* охлажда́емый вóздухом; **~craft** *n.* самолёт, (*collect.*) самолёты, авиа́ция; **fighter ~craft** истреби́тельная авиа́ция; **~craft-carrier** *n.* авианóсец; **~craftman** *n.* рядовóй авиа́ции; **~crew** *n.* лётный соста́в; **~-cushion** *n.* надувна́я поду́шка; **~-dried** *adj.* воздушносухóй, возду́шной су́шки; **~-drill** *n.* пневмати́ческий перфора́тор; **~drome** *n.* = **aerodrome; ~-drop** *n.* десанти́рование с вóздуха; сбра́сывание гру́за с самолёта; **~-duct** *n.* воздухопрово́д; **~field** *n.* аэродрóм; **~flow** *n.* ток вóздуха; возду́шная струя́; **~foil** *n.* = **aerofoil; ~-frame** *n.* остóв/карка́с самолёта; **~-freighter** *n.* грузовóй самолёт; **~-gauge** *n.* возду́шный манóметр; **~gun** *n.* духовóе ружьё; **~-gunner** *n.* возду́шный стрелóк; **~-jacket** *n.* надувнóй спаса́тельный нагру́дник/жилéт; **~lane** *n.* возду́шный коридóр; **~-letter** *n.* авиаписьмó; **~lift** *n.* возду́шная перевóзка; *v.t.* перев|ози́ть, -езти́ (*or* перебр|а́сывать, -óсить) по вóздуху; **~line** *n.* авиали́ния; **~-liner** *n.* рéйсовый/пассажи́рский самолёт, возду́шный ла́йнер; **~-lock** *n.* (*compartment*) та́мбур; (*stoppage*) возду́шная прóбка; **~mail** *n.* авиапóчта; **~mail edition** специа́льное изда́ние для пересы́лки авиапóчтой; **~man** *n.* лётчик; **~-operated** *adj.* пневмати́ческий; **~-pillow** *n.* = **~-cushion; ~plane** *n.* = **aeroplane; ~-pocket** *n.* (*aeron.*) возду́шная я́ма; (*tech.*) возду́шный мешóк, га́зовый пузы́рь; **~port** *n.* аэропóрт; **~-power** *n.* возду́шная мощь; **~-pump** *n.* возду́шный насóс; **~-raid** *n.* возду́шный налёт; **~-raid alert, warning** возду́шная тревóга; **~-raid precautions** мéры противовозду́шной оборóны; **~-raid shelter** бомбоубéжище; **~-raid warden** уполномóченный по противовозду́шной оборóне; **~-rifle** *n.* пневмати́ческая винтóвка; **~screw** *n.* (возду́шный) винт; пропéллер; **~-sea rescue** *n.* спаса́тельные операции (*f. pl.*), проводи́мые самолётами на мóре; **~ship** *n.* возду́шный кора́бль; дирижа́бль (*m.*); **~sick** *adj.*: **I was ~sick** меня́ укача́ло в самолёте; **~sickness** *n.* возду́шная болéзнь; **~space** *n.* возду́шное простра́нство; **~speed** *n.* скóрость полёта; возду́шная скóрость; **~stream** *n.* возду́шный потóк; **~strip** *n.* взлётно-поса́дочная полоса́; поса́дочная площа́дка; **~tight** *adj.* воздухонепроница́емый, гермети́ческий; **~tightness** *n.* воздухонепроница́емость, гермети́чность; **~-to-air** *adj.*: **~-to-air missile** реакти́вный снаря́д «вóздух — вóздух»; **~-to-ground** *adj.*: **~-to-ground missile** реакти́вный снаря́д «вóздух — земля́»; **~-torpedo** *n.* авиациóнная торпéда; **~-traffic controller** *n.* авиадиспéтчер; **~way** *n.* (*route*) возду́шная тра́сса; **~woman** *n.* лётчица; **~worthiness** *n.* приго́дность к полёту; **~worthy** *adj.* гóдный к полёту.

Airedale ['eədeɪl] *n.* эрдельтерьéр.

airer ['eərə(r)] *n.* суши́лка.

airily ['eərɪlɪ] *adv.* за́просто; с лёгкостью, небрéжно.

airiness ['eərɪnɪs] *n.* (*freshness*) возду́шность; (*lightness*) лёгкость; (*fig., of manner*) беспéчность.

airing ['eərɪŋ] *n.* **1.** (*admission of air*) провéтривание; **~ cupboard** суши́льный шкаф. **2.** (*excursion*) прогу́лка. **3.** (*fig.*): **give one's views an ~** вы́сказать/обнарóдовать (*pf.*) свои́ взгля́ды.

airless ['eəlɪs] *adj.* (*stuffy*) ду́шный; (*still*) безвéтренный.

airlessness ['eəlɪsnɪs] *n.* духота́, безвéтрие.

airy ['eərɪ] *adj.* **1.** (*well-ventilated*) простóрный, провéтриваемый. **2.** (*light in movement etc.*) возду́шный; **an ~ dress** возду́шное пла́тье. **3.**: **~ phantom** бесплóтный дух. **4.** (*superficial; light-hearted*) вéтреный, беспéчный.

cpd. **~-fairy** *adj.* (*coll., pej.*) вы́чурный, затéйливый.

aisle [aɪl] *n.* боковóй неф; (*in theatre etc.*) прохóд; **to have**

an audience rolling in the ~s уморить (*pf.*) публику со смеху.
aitchbone ['eɪtʃbəʊn] *n.* (*cut of beef*) огузок.
ajar [ə'dʒɑː(r)] *pred. adj.* приоткрытый.
akimbo [ə'kɪmbəʊ] *adj.* подбоченясь; **stand with arms ~** подбочениться (*pf.*).
akin [ə'kɪn] *pred. adj. & adv.* (*related*) родственный; **~ to** сродни *+d.*; **pity is ~ to love** жалость сродни любви; (*similar*) сродный, похожий.
alabaster ['æləˌbɑːstə(r), -ˌbæstə(r), ˌælə'b-] *n.* алебастр; (*attr.*) алебастровый.
à la carte [ˌɑː lɑː 'kɑːt] *adv.* порционно, на заказ, по заказу.
alack [ə'læk] *int.* (*arch.*) увы!
alacrity [ə'lækrɪtɪ] *n.* (*liveliness*) живость; (*zeal*) рвение.
à la mode [ˌɑː lɑː 'məʊd] *adj. & adv.* модный; «а ля мод».
alarm [ə'lɑːm] *n.* **1.** (*warning; warning signal*) тревога; **false ~** ложная тревога; **give, raise, sound the ~** подн|имать, -ять тревогу; **fire ~** пожарная тревога; **~s and excursions** общая суматоха. **2.** (*~-clock*) будильник; **I set the ~ for 6** я поставил будильник на 6 часов. **3.** (*fright*): **he ran away in ~** он убежал в смятении; **take ~ at** быть встревоженным *+i.*; испугаться *+g.*
v.t. тревожить; **don't be ~ed** не тревожьтесь; **~ing news** тревожные новости (*f. pl.*); **there's nothing to be ~ed about** ничего страшного.
alarming [ə'lɑːmɪŋ] *adj.* тревожный.
alarmist [ə'lɑːmɪst] *n.* паникёр (*fem.* -ша).
alas [ə'læs, ə'lɑːs] *int.* увы!
Alaska [ə'læskə] *n.* Аляска; **in ~** на Аляске.
Alaskan [ə'læskən] *n.* аляскин|ец (*fem.* -ка).
adj. аляскинский.
alb [ælb] *n.* стихарь (*m.*).
Albania [æl'beɪnɪə] *n.* Албания.
Albanian [æl'beɪnɪən] *n.* **1.** (*pers.*) албан|ец (*fem.* -ка). **2.** (*language*) албанский язык.
adj. албанский.
albatross ['ælbəˌtrɒs] *n.* альбатрос.
albeit [ɔːl'biːɪt] *conj.* хотя и.
albinism ['ælbɪˌnɪz(ə)m] *n.* альбинизм.
albino [æl'biːnəʊ] *n.* альбинос (*fem.* -ка); **an ~ rabbit** кролик-альбинос.
album ['ælbəm] *n.* альбом.
albumen ['ælbjʊmɪn] *n.* (*white of egg*) яичный белок; (*chem.*) альбумин; (*biol.*) белок.
albuminous [æl'bjuːmɪnəs] *adj.* белковый; (*chem.*) альбуминный.
alcaic [æl'keɪɪk] *adj.* (*pros.*): **~ stanza** алкеева строфа.
alchemist ['ælkəmɪst] *n.* алхимик.
alchemy ['ælkəmɪ] *n.* алхимия.
alcohol ['ælkəˌhɒl] *n.* (*chem.*) алкоголь (*m.*); (*spirit*) спирт; **wood ~** древесный спирт; **he does not touch ~** он спиртного в рот не берёт.
alcoholic [ˌælkə'hɒlɪk] *n.* алкоголик.
adj. алкогольный; **~ beverages** спиртное; спиртные напитки (*m. pl.*); **~ acid** спирткислота.
alcoholism ['ælkəhɒˌlɪz(ə)m] *n.* алкоголизм.
alcove ['ælkəʊv] *n.* (*recess, niche*) альков, ниша; (*summer-house*) беседка.
alder ['ɔːldə(r)] *n.* ольха (чёрная).
ale [eɪl] *n.* эль (*m.*); (*beer*) пиво.
cpd. **~-house** *n.* пивная.
alee [ə'liː] *adv.* под ветром; в подветренную сторону.
alembic [ə'lembɪk] *n.* перегонный куб.
alert [ə'lɜːt] *n.* **1.** (*alarm*) тревога; **give the ~** поднять (*pf.*) тревогу. **2.**: **on the ~** наготове; **keep s.o. on the ~** держать (*impf.*) кого-н. в постоянной готовности.
adj. (*vigilant*) настороженный; (*lively*) живой.
v.t. прив|одить, -ести в состояние готовности; **~ s.o. to a situation** предупредить (*pf.*) кого-н. о создавшейся обстановке.
alertness [ə'lɜːtnɪs] *n.* настороженность; живость.
Aleutians [ə'luːʃənz] *n.*: **the ~** Алеутские острова (*m. pl.*).
A level ['eɪ levəl] *n.* (*Br.*) экзамен по программе средней школы на повышенном уровне; **he has three ~-levels** он сдал три предмета на повышенном уровне.
Alexandria [ˌælɪg'zɑːndrɪə, -'zændrɪə] *n.* Александрия.
Alexandrine [ˌælɪg'zændraɪn] *n.* александрийский стих.
ALF (*abbr. of* ***Animal Liberation Front***) Фронт эмансипации животных.
alfalfa [æl'fælfə] *n.* люцерна.
alfresco [æl'freskəʊ] *adv.* на открытом воздухе.
alga ['ælgə] *n.* морская водоросль.
algebra ['ældʒɪbrə] *n.* алгебра.
algebraic [ˌældʒɪ'breɪɪk] *adj.* алгебраический.
Algeria [æl'dʒɪərɪə] *n.* Алжир.
Algerian [æl'dʒɪərɪən] *n.* алжир|ец (*fem.* -ка).
adj. алжирский.
Algiers [æl'dʒɪəz] *n.* Алжир.
algorithm ['ælgəˌrɪð(ə)m] *n.* алгоритм.
alias ['eɪlɪəs] *n.* кличка, прозвище; **the thief had several ~es** у вора было несколько кличек; **his ~ was ...** он называл себя...; **he travelled under an ~** он путешествовал под вымышленным именем.
adv. иначе называемый; **Jones, ~ Robinson** Джонс, он же Робинсон.
alibi ['ælɪˌbaɪ] *n.* **1.** (*plea or proof of being elsewhere*) алиби (*nt. indecl.*); **establish an ~** устан|авливать, -овить алиби; **plead an ~** ссылаться, сослаться на алиби; **produce an ~** предст|авлять, -авить алиби. **2.** (*coll., excuse*) отговорка.
alien ['eɪlɪən] *n.* чужестран|ец (*fem.* -ка), иностран|ец (*fem.* -ка); **enemy ~s** подданные (*pl*) враждебной державы.
adj. **1.** (*foreign*) иностранный; (*extra-terrestrial*) внеземной. **2.**: **~ to** чуждый *+d.*
alienable ['eɪlɪənəb(ə)l] *adj.* отчуждаемый.
alienate ['eɪlɪəˌneɪt] *v.t.* **1.** (*estrange, antagonize*) отдал|ять, -ить; отвра|щать, -тить. **2.** (*leg.*) отчуждать (*impf.*).
alienation [ˌeɪlɪə'neɪʃ(ə)n] *n.* (*alienating*) отчуждение; (*being alienated*) отчуждённость.
alienist ['eɪlɪənɪst] *n.* психиатр.
alight[1] [ə'laɪt] *pred. adj. & adv.* **1.** (*on fire*) в огне; **catch ~** загор|аться, -еться; **set ~** заж|игать, -ечь; **is your cigarette ~?** у вас сигарета горит? **2.** (*illuminated*) освещённый. **3.** (*fig.*): **eyes ~ with happiness** глаза, сияющие счастьем.
alight[2] [ə'laɪt] *v.i.* **1.** (*dismount from horse or vehicle*) сходить, сойти (с+*g.*); высаживаться, высадиться (из+*g.*). **2.** (*come to earth: of birds etc.*) садиться, сесть; (*of an aircraft*) приземл|яться, -иться.
align [ə'laɪn] *v.t.* выравнивать, выровнять; устан|авливать, -овить в ряд/линию; **~ o.s. with s.o.** стать (*pf.*) на чью-н. сторону; прим|ыкать, -кнуть к кому-н.
alignment [ə'laɪnmənt] *n.* выравнивание; **out of ~** неровно, не в ряд; (*arrangement*) расстановка; **~ with** (*adherence to*) присоединение к *+d.*
alike [ə'laɪk] *pred. adj.* (*similar*) похожий, подобный; **they are very much ~** они очень похожи друг на друга; (*as one*) одинаковый; **all things are ~ to him** ему всё одно.
adv. подобно, одинаково; **treat everyone ~** обращаться (*impf.*) одинаково со всеми; **winter and summer ~** как зимой, так и летом.
aliment ['ælɪmənt] *n.* пища; (*fig.*) поддержка.
alimentary [ˌælɪ'mentərɪ] *adj.* (*of food*): **~ products** пищевые продукты; (*digestive*): **~ canal, tract** пищеварительный тракт.
alimentation [ˌælɪmen'teɪʃ(ə)n] *n.* (*nourishment*) питание; (*maintenance*) содержание.
alimony ['ælɪmənɪ] *n.* (*leg.*) алимент|ы (*pl., g.* -ов).
alive [ə'laɪv] *pred. adj. & adv.* **1.** (*living*) живой; в живых; **who is the greatest man ~?** кто самый великий из живущих людей?; **buried ~** заживо похороненный; **~ and kicking** жив-здоров (*coll.*); **more dead than ~** еле живой; **he was kept ~ with drugs** его поддерживали лекарствами; (*fig., in force*): **keep a claim ~** поддерживать (*impf.*) претензию. **2.** (*alert*): **be ~ to the danger** сознавать (*impf.*) опасность; быть начеку; **look ~!** живее! **3.** (*elec.*) под напряжением. **4.** (*infested*): **the bed was ~ with fleas** кровать кишела блохами.
alkali ['ælkəˌlaɪ] *n.* щёлочь; (*attr.*) щелочной.
alkaline ['ælkəˌlaɪn] *adj.* щелочной.
alkaloid ['ælkəˌlɔɪd] *n.* алкалоид.

all [ɔ:l] *n.*: **he lost his** ~ он потеря́л всё, что име́л; **he staked his** ~ он поста́вил на ка́рту всё.

pron. (*everybody*) все; (*everything*) всё; ~ **of us** мы все; **it cost** ~ **of £10** э́то сто́ило це́лых 10 фу́нтов; **the score is 2** ~ счёт 2:2; **it was** ~ **I could do not to ...** я едва́ сдержа́лся, что́бы не...; **there will be** ~ **the more for us** нам же бо́льше доста́нется; ~ **and sundry** ка́ждый и вся́кий; ~ **but** (*almost*) почти́, едва́ не, чуть не; **he** ~ **but died** он чуть бы́ло не у́мер; ~ **but a few died** почти́ все у́мерли; ма́ло кто оста́лся в живы́х; ~ **in the day's work** де́ло привы́чное; в поря́дке веще́й; ~ **in good time** всё в своё вре́мя; всему́ своё вре́мя; ~ **in** ~ (*in general*) в о́бщем и це́лом; **it's** ~ **one to me** мне всё равно́/едино́; ~ **together now!** а тепе́рь все вме́сте!; **that's** ~ **very well, but ...** всё э́то прекра́сно, но...; *see also* **well**[2]; **above** ~ пре́жде всего́; **after** ~ в конце́ концо́в; в коне́чном счёте; **after** ~**, I did warn you!** я ведь предупреди́л вас; **he came after** ~ он всё же пришёл; **the ship was lost, cargo and** ~ кора́бль затону́л вме́сте с гру́зом и всем, что там бы́ло; **any card at** ~ люба́я ка́рта; **not at** ~ совсе́м/во́все/ соверше́нно не; нисколько, ничу́ть; **'Thank you.' — 'Not at** ~**!'** «Спаси́бо.» — «Не́ за что!»; **they did not know what to do at** ~ они́ не зна́ли, что и де́лать; **he has no money at** ~ у него́ совсе́м нет де́нег; **you have eaten nothing at** ~ вы ничего́ не е́ли; **for** ~ **I care, he may drown** по мне пусть хоть уто́нет; **for** ~ **I know he may be dead** отку́да/почём я зна́ю, мо́жет он и у́мер; **for good and** ~; **once and for** ~ раз навсегда́; **in** ~; ~ **told** в це́лом; всего́.

adj. весь; (*every*) вся́кий; ~ **his life** всю свою́ жизнь; ~ **day long** весь день; ~ **the time** всё вре́мя; **at** ~ **times** в любо́е вре́мя; всегда́; **at** ~ **costs** любо́й цено́й; во что бы то ни ста́ло; **beyond** ~ **doubt** без/вне вся́кого сомне́ния; **by** ~ **accounts** су́дя по всему́; **for** ~ **his wealth** несмотря́ на всё его́ бога́тство; **for** ~ **that** всё-таки; **for** ~ **time** навсегда́; **in** ~ **fairness** со всей справедли́востью; положа́ ру́ку на́ сердце; **of** ~ **the cheek!** кака́я на́глость!; **you of** ~ **people** кто́-кто, а уж вы́-то; **on** ~ **fours** на четвере́ньках; **with** ~ **respect** при всём уваже́нии; **... and** ~ **that** и так да́лее; и про́чее; **it's not** ~ **that hard** (*coll.*), **not as hard as** ~ **that** э́то не так уж тру́дно; **he's very clever and** ~ **that, but ...** он о́чень умён и всё тако́е, но...

adv. (*quite*) совсе́м, соверше́нно; целико́м, всеце́ло; ~ **dressed up** наряди́вшись; разряди́вшись в пух и прах; **she was (dressed)** ~ **in black** она́ была́ оде́та во всё чёрное; **I got** ~ **excited** я разволнова́лся; **he was** ~ **ready to go** он был гото́в идти́; **I'm** ~ **fingers and thumbs** у меня́ всё из рук ва́лится; ~ **along the road** всю доро́гу; на всём пути́; **I knew it** ~ **along** я всегда́ э́то знал; ~ **around** повсю́ду, круго́м; ~ **at once** соверше́нно внеза́пно; и вдруг; ни с того́ ни с сего́; **she lived** ~ **by herself** она́ жила́ одна́-одинёшенька; **she did it** ~ **by herself** она́ сде́лала э́то сама́; **I am** ~ **ears** я весь слух; **I'm** ~ **for it** я целико́м и по́лностью «за»; ~ **in** (*exhausted*) вы́бившийся из сил; (*inclusive of everything*) включа́я всё; **he went** ~ **out to win** он сде́лал всё для побе́ды; ~ **over the room** по всей ко́мнате; ~ **the world over** по всему́ ми́ру; **your hands are** ~ **over tar** у вас все ру́ки в смоле́; **it's** ~ **over now** тепе́рь всё ко́нчено; с э́тим поко́нчено; **it's** ~ **over, up with him** с ним поко́нчено; ему́ кры́шка; ~ **over again** (всё) сно́ва; **he was** ~ **over her** (*coll.*) он ей проходу не дава́л; **that's him** ~ **over** как э́то на него́ похо́же; ~ **the rage** после́дний крик мо́ды; ~ **right** (*satisfactory*) ла́дно; идёт; хорошо́; **is the coffee** ~ **right?** ну, как ко́фе, ничего́?; (*safe*): **we got back** ~ **right** мы верну́лись благополу́чно; (*in good order*) в поря́дке; (*in replies*) хорошо́; (*implying threat*): ~ **right, you wait!** ну хорошо́ же, погоди́те!; **he gave them 10p** ~ **round** он дал им всем по де́сять пе́нсов; ~ **the better** тем лу́чше; **you'll be** ~ **the better for a rest** вам не меша́ло бы отдохну́ть; ~ **the same** (*however*) всё-таки; **if it's** ~ **the same to you** е́сли вам всё равно́; **he was** ~ **set to win** он наце́лился на побе́ду; **he's not** ~ **there** у него́ не все до́ма; **it's** ~ **to the good** э́то всё к лу́чшему; ~ **too soon** сли́шком ско́ро; **you're** ~ **wrong** вы соверше́нно не пра́вы.

cpds. ~**-American** *adj.* чи́сто америка́нский; ~**-clear** *n.* отбо́й (трево́ги); **sound the** ~**-clear** дать (*pf.*) отбо́й; ~**-embracing** *adj.* всеобъе́млющий; ~**-important** *adj.* чрезвыча́йно ва́жный; ~**-in** *adj.*: ~**-in price** цена́, включа́ющая всё; ~**-in wrestling** во́льная борьба́; ~**-night** *adj.*: ~**-night session** заседа́ние, продолжа́ющееся всю ночь; ~**-out** *adj.*: **an** ~**-out effort** максима́льное уси́лие; ~**-party** *adj.* общепарти́йный; ~**-powerful** *adj.* всеси́льный; ~**-purpose** *adj.* универса́льный; ~**-round** *adj.*: **an** ~**-round view** всесторо́нний подхо́д; ~**-round sportsman,** ~**-rounder** разносторо́нний спортсме́н; ~**-Russian** *adj.* всеросси́йский; ~**-seeing** *adj.* всеви́дящий; ~**spice** *n.* души́стый/яма́йский пе́рец; ~**-star** *adj.*: **with an** ~**-star cast** с уча́стием звёзд; ~**-sufficient** *adj.* вполне́/ соверше́нно доста́точный; ~**-time** *adj.*: **at an** ~**-time low** на небыва́ло ни́зком у́ровне; ~**-time record** непревзойдённый реко́рд; ~**-up** *adj.*: ~**-up weight** (*aeron.*) по́лный полётный вес; ~**-wave** *adj.*: ~**-wave receiver** всево́лновый приёмник; ~**-weather** *adj.* на любу́ю пого́ду; всепого́дный; ~**-white** *adj.*: ~**-white government** прави́тельство, состоя́щее то́лько из бе́лых.

Allah ['ælə] *n.* Алла́х.

allay [ə'leɪ] *v.t.* успок|а́ивать, -о́ить; смягч|а́ть, -и́ть; ~ **suspicions** усып|ля́ть, -и́ть подозре́ния; ~ **pain** ун|има́ть, -я́ть боль; ~ **thirst/hunger** утол|я́ть, -и́ть жа́жду/го́лод.

allegation [,ælɪ'geɪʃ(ə)n] *n.* заявле́ние, утвержде́ние; ~**s of corruption were brought against him** его́ обвини́ли в корру́пции.

allege [ə'ledʒ] *v.t.* утвержда́ть (*impf.*); **he** ~**d ill health** он сосла́лся на нездоро́вье; **words** ~**d to have been spoken by him** слова́, припи́сываемые ему́; **he is** ~**d to have died** его́ счита́ют уме́ршим; **an** ~**d murderer** подозрева́емый в убийстве.

allegedly [ə'ledʒɪdlɪ] *adv.* бу́дто бы, я́кобы.

allegiance [ə'li:dʒ(ə)ns] *n.* (*loyalty*) ве́рность; (*devotion*) пре́данность; **owe** ~ **to the queen** быть по́дданным короле́вы.

allegorical [,ælɪ'gɒrɪk(ə)l] *adj.* аллегори́ческий.

allegorize ['ælɪgə,raɪz] *v.t.* толкова́ть (*impf.*) аллегори́чески.

allegory ['ælɪgərɪ] *n.* аллего́рия.

allegretto [,ælɪ'gretəʊ] *n., adj. & adv.* аллегре́тто (*indecl.*).

allegro [ə'leɪgrəʊ, ə'leg-] *n., adj. & adv.* алле́гро (*indecl.*).

alleluia [,ælɪ'lu:jə] *n. & int.* аллилу́йя.

allemande ['ælmɑ̃nd] *n.* аллема́нда.

allergen ['ælədʒ(ə)n] *n.* аллерге́н.

allergic [ə'lɜ:dʒɪk] *adj.* аллерги́ческий; **I'm** ~ **to strawberries** у меня́ аллерги́я к клубни́ке.

allergy ['ælədʒɪ] *n.* аллерги́я.

alleviate [ə'li:vɪ,eɪt] *v.t.* (*relieve, lighten*) облегч|а́ть, -и́ть; (*mitigate, soften*) смягч|а́ть, -и́ть.

alleviation [ə,li:vɪ'eɪʃ(ə)n] *n.* облегче́ние; смягче́ние.

alley ['ælɪ] *n.* **1.** (*narrow street*) переу́лок; **blind** ~ тупи́к; ~ **cat** бездо́мная ко́шка; **that's right up my** ~ (*coll.*) э́то как раз по мое́й ча́сти. **2.** (*walk, avenue*) алле́я.

alliance [ə'laɪəns] *n.* сою́з; **marriage** ~ бра́чный сою́з; брак; **Holy A**~ (*hist.*) Свяще́нный Сою́з.

allied ['ælaɪd] *adj.* (*joined by alliance*) сою́зный; (*related*) ро́дственный; ~ **sciences** сме́жные нау́ки; **a bird** ~ **to the ostrich** пти́ца из отря́да стра́усов; (*closely connected*) схо́дный.

alligator ['ælɪ,geɪtə(r)] *n.* аллига́тор; ~ **pear** аллига́торова гру́ша, авока́до (*indecl.*).

alliteration [ə,lɪtə'reɪʃ(ə)n] *n.* аллитера́ция.

alliterative [ə'lɪtərətɪv] *adj.* аллитери́рующий.

allocate ['ælə,keɪt] *v.t.* (*fin.*: *allot, earmark*) выделя́ть, вы́делить; ассигнова́ть (*impf., pf.*); (*distribute*) распредел|я́ть, -и́ть; (*assign*) назн|ача́ть, -а́чить.

allocation [,ælə'keɪʃ(ə)n] *n.* (*allocating*) выделе́ние; ассигнова́ние; распределе́ние; назначе́ние; (*award*) присужде́ние; (*sum allocated*) ассигнова́ние.

allocution [,ælə'kju:ʃ(ə)n] *n.* обраще́ние.

allot [ə'lɒt] *v.t.* (*distribute*) распредел|я́ть, -и́ть; (*assign*) назн|ача́ть, -а́чить; (*award*) прису|жда́ть, -ди́ть; ~ **a task** да|ва́ть, -ть зада́ние.

allotment [ə'lɒtmənt] *n.* **1.** (*in vbl. senses*) распределе́ние;

назначе́ние; присужде́ние. **2.** (*plot of land*) (земе́льный) уча́сток.

allow [ə'laʊ] *v.t.* **1.** (*permit*) позв|оля́ть, -о́лить; разреш|а́ть, -и́ть; **~ me!** разреши́те!; **as far as circumstances ~** наско́лько позволя́ют обстоя́тельства; **he was ~ed to smoke** ему́ позво́лили кури́ть; **I will not ~ you to be deceived** я не допущу́, что́бы вас обману́ли; **~ no discussion** запре|ща́ть, -ти́ть вся́кое обсужде́ние; **smoking is not ~ed** кури́ть воспреща́ется; **no dogs ~ed** вход с соба́ками воспрещён. **2.** (*grant, provide*) да|ва́ть, -ть; предост|авля́ть, -а́вить; допус|ка́ть, -ти́ть; **he ~s his son £500 a year** он даёт сы́ну 500 фу́нтов в год; **I ~ed him a free hand** я предоста́вил ему́ свобо́ду де́йствий; **at the end of the 6 months ~ed** в конце́ предоста́вленных шести́ ме́сяцев; **~ discount** предост|авля́ть, -а́вить ски́дку; **~ 10p in the pound** де́лать, с- ски́дку в де́сять пе́нсов с ка́ждого фу́нта. **3.** (*admit*) допус|ка́ть, -ти́ть; (*recognize*) призн|ава́ть, -а́ть; **his claim was allowed** его́ тре́бование бы́ло при́нято; **~ an appeal** (*leg.*) удовлетвор|я́ть, -и́ть апелля́цию.

v.i. **1. ~ for** (*take into account*) уч|и́тывать, -е́сть; **~ing for casualties** учи́тывая возмо́жные поте́ри; **not ~ing for expenses** не принима́я в расчёт изде́ржек; **~ £50 for emergencies** выделя́ть, вы́делить 50 фу́нтов на чрезвыча́йный слу́чай; **~ for his being ill** приня́ть (*pf.*) во внима́ние то, что он бо́лен; **~ for wind** брать, взять попра́вку на ве́тер; **~ for shrinkage** де́лать, с- до́пуск на уса́дку. **2. ~ of: his tone ~ed of no reply** его́ тон не допуска́л возраже́ний.

allowable [ə'laʊəb(ə)l] *adj.* допусти́мый, допуска́емый.

allowance [ə'laʊəns] *n.* **1.** (*amount provided*): **monthly ~** ме́сячное содержа́ние; **family ~** посо́бие на семью́; **make s.o. an ~** назна́чить (*pf.*) содержа́ние кому́-н.; (*mil.*) дово́льствие; **~ of ammunition** боево́й компле́кт. **2.** (*discount*) ски́дка; **~ for cash** ски́дка за платёж нали́чными. **3.** (*concession*): **we will make an ~ in your case** мы сде́лаем для вас исключе́ние; **make ~(s) for** уч|и́тывать, -е́сть; прин|има́ть, -я́ть во внима́ние. **4.** (*tech.*) до́пуск; **shrinkage ~** до́пуск на уса́дку; (*correction*): **~ for wind** попра́вка на ве́тер.

alloy ['ælɔɪ, ə'lɔɪ] *n.* (*of metals*) сплав; (*additive*) при́месь; **~ steel** леги́рованная сталь; (*fig.*): **happiness without ~** безо́блачное сча́стье.

v.t. спл|авля́ть, -а́вить; (*of steel*) леги́ровать (*impf., pf.*); (*fig., becloud*) омрач|а́ть, -и́ть.

allud|e [ə'lu:d, ə'lju:d] *v.i.*: **~ to** ссыла́ться, сосла́ться на+*a.*; упом|ина́ть, -яну́ть; (*mean*): **what are you ~ing to?** на что вы намека́ете?

allure [ə'ljʊə(r)] *n.* привлека́тельность, пре́лесть.

v.t. (*entice, attract*) зама́н|ивать, -и́ть; вовл|ека́ть, -е́чь; (*charm*) завл|ека́ть, -е́чь; очаро́в|ывать, -а́ть.

allurement [ə'ljʊəmənt] *n.* (*enticement*) привлече́ние; (*bait*) прима́нка; (*charm*) привлека́тельность, пре́лесть.

alluring [ə'ljʊərɪŋ] *adj.* зама́нчивый; соблазни́тельный; очарова́тельный.

allusion [ə'lu:ʒ(ə)n, ə'lju:-] *n.* намёк; ссы́лка; **make an ~ to** ссыла́ться, сосла́ться на+*a.*

allusive [ə'lu:sɪv, ə'lju:-] *adj.* по́лный намёков.

alluvial [ə'lu:vɪəl] *adj.* аллювиа́льный; **~ deposit** ро́ссыпь.

alluvium [ə'lu:vɪəm] *n.* аллю́вий.

ally[1] ['ælaɪ] *n.* сою́зник.

all|y[2] [ə'laɪ] *v.t.* (*connect*) соедин|я́ть, -и́ть; **~ied to** (*of things*) соединённый с+*i.*, свя́занный с+*i.*, бли́зкий к+*d.*; **to be ~ied to, with** (*of nations*) быть в сою́зе с+*i.*; **~y o.s. with** вступ|а́ть, -и́ть в сою́з с+*i.*

Alma Mater [ˌælmə 'mɑ:tə(r), 'meɪtə(r)] *n.* а́льма-ма́тер (*f. indecl.*).

almanac ['ɔ:lməˌnæk, 'ɒl-] *n.* альмана́х.

almighty [ɔ:l'maɪtɪ] *n.* **the A~** Всемогу́щий, Всевы́шний.

adj. всемогу́щий; (*coll., great*): **an ~ blow** мо́щный уда́р; **we had an ~ row** у нас был ужа́сный сканда́л.

almond ['ɑ:mənd] *n.* минда́ль (*m.*); **a smell of ~s** за́пах миндаля́.

cpds. **~-eyed** *adj.* с миндалеви́дными глаза́ми; **~-tree** *n.* минда́льное де́рево.

almoner ['ɑ:mənə(r)] *n.* (*in hospital*) медици́нский рабо́тник сфе́ры социа́льных пробле́м.

almost ['ɔ:lməʊst] *adv.* почти́; (*with vv.*) почти́, чуть не, едва́ не.

alms [ɑ:mz] *n.* ми́лостыня; **give ~** подава́ть ми́лостыню; **ask, beg ~ of** проси́ть (*impf.*) ми́лостыню у+*g.*

cpds. **~-box** *n.* я́щик для поже́ртвований; **~giving** *n.* разда́ча ми́лостыни; **~house** *n.* богаде́льня.

aloe ['æləʊ] *n.* ало́э (*nt. indecl.*); **(bitter) ~s** ало́э, сабу́р.

aloft [ə'lɒft] *adv.* наверху́; (*of motion*) наве́рх; (*naut.*) на ма́рсе; (*aeron.*) в во́здухе.

alone [ə'ləʊn] *adj.* **1.** (*by o.s., itself*) оди́н; еди́нственный; **he came ~** он пришёл оди́н; **you can't move the piano ~** вы оди́н не смо́жете сдви́нуть роя́ль; **not by bread ~** не хле́бом еди́ным; **she is quite ~** она́ одна́-одинёшенька. **2.** (*... and no other(s)*): **in the month of June ~** то́лько в ию́не ме́сяце; **with that charm which is hers ~** с то́лько ей прису́щим очарова́нием; **she and I are ~ (together)** мы с ней вдвоём/одни́; (*pred.: the only one(s)*): **he was ~ opposing the suggestion** он оди́н был про́тив предложе́ния; **we are not ~ in thinking so** не то́лько мы так ду́маем. **3.: let, leave ~: his parents left him ~ all day** роди́тели оста́вили его́ на це́лый день одного́; **can't you let your work ~ for a while?** вы не мо́жете оста́вить рабо́ту на вре́мя?; **I should leave the dog ~** я бы оста́вил соба́ку в поко́е; **let well ~!** от добра́ добра́ не и́щут; **let ~** (*coll.*) не говоря́ уже́ о+*p.*; **he can't support his family, let ~ save money** у него́ не хвата́ет де́нег на содержа́ние семьи́, что уж тут говори́ть о сбереже́ниях.

along [ə'lɒŋ] *adv.* **1.** (*on; forward*): **move ~** продв|ига́ться, -и́нуться; **move ~, please!** проходи́те/продвига́йтесь, пожа́луйста!; **come ~!** пошли́!; **a few doors ~ from the station** в не́скольких шага́х от вокза́ла; **get ~ with** уж|ива́ться, -и́ться с+*i.*; **they do not get ~** они́ не ла́дят; **get ~ with you!** (*go away*) проходи́те!; (*expr. disbelief*) бро́сьте; **how far ~ are you with the work?** как ва́ши успе́хи в рабо́те? **2.** (*denoting accompaniment*): **come ~ with me** пойдёмте/иди́те со мной; **he brought a book ~** он принёс с собо́й кни́гу. **3.** (*over there; over here*): **he went ~ to the exhibition** он пошёл на вы́ставку; **he'll be ~ in 10 minutes** он бу́дет че́рез де́сять мину́т. **4.: all ~** (*the whole time*) всё вре́мя; **I said so all ~** я э́то всегда́ говори́л; **I knew it all ~** я э́то знал с са́мого нача́ла.

prep. вдоль+*g.*; по+*d.*; вдоль по; **she was walking ~ the river** она́ шла вдоль реки́; **they sailed ~ the river** они́ плы́ли по реке́; **the pilot was flying ~ the frontier** лётчик лете́л вдоль грани́цы; **pink ~ the edges** ро́зовый по края́м.

cpd. **~shore** *adv.* вдоль бе́рега.

alongside [əlɒŋ'saɪd] *adv.* (*naut.*) борт о́ борт; **deliver goods ~** дост|авля́ть, -а́вить това́р к бо́рту су́дна; (*in general*) ря́дом, сбо́ку; **we stopped and the police car drew up ~** мы останови́лись и подъе́хавшая полице́йская маши́на вста́ла ря́дом.

prep. (*also* **~ of**) ря́дом с+*i.*; бок о́ бок +*i.*; у+*g.*; **they were walking ~ us** они́ шли ря́дом с на́ми; **~ the quay** у при́стани; **come ~ a ship/wharf** прист|ава́ть, -а́ть к кораблю́/ве́рфи; (*compared with*) в сравне́нии с+*i.*

aloof [ə'lu:f] *adj.* сде́ржанный, суховáтый.

adv.: **keep, hold ~** держа́ться (*impf.*) в стороне́ (*or* особняко́м); возде́рживаться (*impf.*) (*от кого/чего*).

aloofness [ə'lu:fnɪs] *n.* сде́ржанность, отчуждённость; (*indifference*) равноду́шие, хо́лодность.

aloud [ə'laʊd] *adv.* вслух; **read ~** чита́ть вслух; **she wept ~** она́ (за)пла́кала навзры́д; **cry ~ for vengeance** (*fig.*) взыва́ть (*impf.*) о мще́нии.

alp [ælp] *n.*: **the A~s** А́льп|ы (*pl., g.* —).

alpaca [æl'pækə] *n.* (*animal*) альпака́ (*c.g. indecl.*); (*fabric*) альпака́, альпага́ (*nt. indecl.*).

alpenstock ['ælpənˌstɒk] *n.* альпешто́к.

alpha ['ælfə] *n.* а́льфа; **~ particle** а́льфа-части́ца; **~ plus** (*examination mark*) «отли́чно».

alphabet ['ælfəˌbet] *n.* а́збука, алфави́т.

alphabetical [ˌælfə'betɪk(ə)l] *adj.* а́збучный, алфави́тный; **in ~ order** в алфави́тном поря́дке.

alphanumeric [ˌælfənju:ˈmerɪk] *adj.* алфави́тно-цифрово́й.
alpine [ˈælpaɪn] *adj.* альпи́йский.
alpinist [ˈælpɪnɪst] *n.* альпини́ст.
already [ɔ:lˈredɪ] *adv.* уже́.
Alsace [ælˈsæs] *n.* Эльза́с.
Alsatian [ælˈseɪʃ(ə)n] *n.* **1.** (*pers.*) эльза́с|ец (*fem.* -ка). **2.** (*dog*) неме́цкая овча́рка.
adj. эльза́сский.
also [ˈɔ:lsəʊ] *adv.* то́же; та́кже; (*moreover*) к тому́ же; **not only ... but ~ ...** не то́лько... но и...
cpd. **~-ran** *n.* неуда́чник.
altar [ˈɔ:ltə(r), ˈɒl-] *n.* престо́л; (*in fig. uses*) алта́рь (*m.*); **high ~** гла́вный престо́л; **lead to the ~** вести́ (*det.*) под вене́ц; (*pagan*) алта́рь, же́ртвенник.
cpds. **~-cloth** *n.* напресто́льная пелена́; **~-piece** *n.* запресто́льный о́браз; **~-rail** *n.* огра́да алтаря́; **~-screen** *n.* (*in Russian church*) иконоста́с.
alter [ˈɔ:ltə(r), ˈɒl-] *v.t.* & *i.* меня́ть(ся) (*impf.*); измен|я́ть(ся), -и́ть(ся); **~ for the worse** измени́ться к ху́дшему; **I have not ~ed my convictions** я не измени́л свои́х убежде́ний; **the wind ~ed** ве́тер перемени́лся; **he has ~ed towards her** он перемени́лся к ней; **~ one's mind** переду́мать (*pf.*); (*re-make*) переде́л|ывать, -ать; **the dress needs ~ing** э́то пла́тье на́до переде́лать.
alterable [ˈɔ:ltərəb(ə)l, ˈɒl-] *adj.* изменя́емый.
alteration [ˌɔ:ltəˈreɪʃ(ə)n, ˈɒl-] *n.* (*change*) измене́ние; (*replacement*) переме́на; (*re-making e.g. of clothes*) переде́лка; (*re-building*) перестро́йка; **the theatre is under ~** теа́тр реконструи́руется.
altercate [ˈɔ:ltəˌkeɪt, ˈɒl-] *v.i.* ссо́риться (*impf.*); препира́ться (*impf.*).
altercation [ˌɔ:ltəˈkeɪʃ(ə)n, ˌɒl-] *n.* ссо́ра, перебра́нка, препира́тельство.
alter ego [ˌæltər ˈi:gəʊ, ˈegəʊ] *n.* «а́льтер э́го» (*indecl.*), второ́е «я».
alternate[1] [ɔ:lˈtɜ:nət, ɒl-] *n.* (*US*) замести́тель (*m.*).
alternate[2] [ɔ:lˈtɜ:nət, ɒl-] *adj.* **1.** (*changing*) переме́нный; (*intermittent*) перемежа́ющийся; (*taking turns*) чередую́щийся; **on ~ Saturdays** че́рез суббо́ту; **~ly** попереме́нно. **2.** (*held in reserve*) запасно́й. **3.** (*math.*): **~ angles** противолежа́щие углы́.
alternat|e[3] [ˈɔ:ltəˌneɪt, ˈɒl-] *v.t.* & *i.* чередова́ть(ся) (*impf.*); перемежа́ть(ся) (*impf.*); **~e work and rest** чередова́ть труд с о́тдыхом; **~ing current** переме́нный ток.
alternation [ˌɔ:ltəˈneɪʃ(ə)n, ˌɒl-] *n.* чередова́ние; **the ~ of day and night** сме́на дня и но́чи; (*elec.*) переме́на, полови́на ци́кла.
alternative [ɔ:lˈtɜ:nətɪv, ɒl-] *n.* альтернати́ва; **there is no ~** друго́го вы́бора нет.
adj. альтернати́вный; **~ medicine** паралле́льная медици́на; **an ~ proposal** встре́чное предложе́ние; **~ technology** альтернати́вная техноло́гия; (*held in reserve*) запасно́й.
alternatively [ɔ:lˈtɜ:nətɪvlɪ, ɒl-] *adv.* **1.** (*in turn*) поочерёдно. **2.** (*indicating choice*): **a £5 fine, ~ one month's imprisonment** штраф 5 фу́нтов и́ли оди́н ме́сяц тюре́много заключе́ния.
alternator [ˈɔ:ltəˌneɪtə(r), ˈɒl-] *n.* (*elec.*) генера́тор переме́нного то́ка.
although [ɔ:lˈðəʊ] *conj.* хотя́; (*despite the fact that*) несмотря́ на то, что; **~ ill, he came** несмотря́ на боле́знь, он пришёл; **~ young, he is experienced** он хоть и молодо́й, но о́пытный.
altimeter [ˈæltɪˌmi:tə(r)] *n.* альтиме́тр; высотоме́р.
altitude [ˈæltɪˌtju:d] *n.* высота́; **they flew at an ~ of 10,000 metres** они́ лете́ли на высоте́ 10 000 ме́тров; **~ sickness** го́рная боле́знь.
alto [ˈæltəʊ] *n.* альт; (*attr.*) альто́вый.
altocumulus [ˌæltəʊˈkju:mjʊləs] *n.* высококучевы́е облака́.
altogether [ˌɔ:ltəˈgeðə(r)] *n.*: **in the ~** (*coll.*) в чём мать родила́.
adv. **1.** (*entirely*) вполне́; соверше́нно; **he is not ~ pleased with the result** он не о́чень-то дово́лен результа́том; **it is ~ out of the question** э́то соверше́нно исключено́; (*completely*) совсе́м. **2.** (*in all, in general; as a whole*) в це́лом, в о́бщем, вообще́; всего́; **taking things ~** учи́тывая всё вме́сте; **how much is that ~?** ско́лько всего́?
altostratus [ˌæltəʊˈstreɪtəs, -ˈstrɑ:təs] *n.* высокослои́стые облака́.
altruism [ˈæltru:ˌɪz(ə)m] *n.* альтруи́зм.
altruist [ˈæltru:ɪst] *n.* альтруи́ст.
altruistic [ˌæltru:ˈɪstɪk] *adj.* альтруисти́ческий.
alum [ˈæləm] *n.* квасц|ы́ (*pl., g.* -о́в).
alumin|ium (*US* **-um**) [ˌæljʊˈmɪnɪəm; əˈlu:mɪnəm] *n.* алюми́ний.
alumna [əˈlʌmnə] *n.* (бы́вшая) учени́ца; (*of a university*) (бы́вшая) студе́нтка.
alumnus [əˈlʌmnəs] *n.* (бы́вший) учени́к; (*of a university*) (бы́вший) студе́нт.
always [ˈɔ:lweɪz] *adv.* всегда́; (*constantly*) постоя́нно, всё вре́мя; **he is ~ after money** он то́лько и ду́мает, что о деньга́х; **~ the same old thing** всё одно́ и то же; **this child is ~ crying** э́тот ребёнок всё пла́чет; **there is ~ Mr Smith** на худо́й конец (*or* кро́ме того́) всегда́ есть ми́стер Смит.
Alzheimer's disease [ˈæltsˌhaɪməz] *n.* боле́знь Альцге́ймера.
a.m. (*abbr. of* ***ante meridiem***) утра́; у́тром; **6 ~** шесть часо́в утра́.
amalgam [əˈmælgəm] *n.* амальга́ма; (*fig.*) смесь.
amalgamate [əˈmælgəˌmeɪt] *v.t.* & *i.* (*of metals*) амальгами́ровать(ся) (*impf., pf.*); (*fig., unite*) объедин|я́ть(ся), -и́ть(ся); соедин|я́ть(ся), -и́ть(ся).
amalgamation [əˌmælgəˈmeɪʃ(ə)n] *n.* амальгами́рование; объедине́ние; (*merging*) слия́ние.
amanuensis [əˌmænju:ˈensɪs] *n.* ли́чный секрета́рь.
amass [əˈmæs] *v.t.* накоп|ля́ть, -и́ть.
amateur [ˈæmətə(r)] *n.* люби́тель (*m.*); (*pej.*) дилета́нт; (*attr.*) люби́тельский; **~ theatricals** театра́льная самоде́ятельность; **~ sport** люби́тельский спорт.
amateurish [ˈæmətərɪʃ] *adj.* дилета́нтский; самоде́ятельный; неуме́лый.
amatory [ˈæmətərɪ] *adj.* любо́вный.
amaz|e [əˈmeɪz] *v.t.* изум|ля́ть, -и́ть; **be ~ed at** изум|ля́ться, -и́ться +*d.*; **~ing** изуми́тельный, удиви́тельный.
amazement [əˈmeɪzmənt] *n.* изумле́ние; **I was speechless with ~** я онеме́л от удивле́ния; **he looked at me in ~** он посмотре́л на меня́ с изумле́нием; **to everyone's ~** ко всео́бщему изумле́нию.
Amazon [ˈæməz(ə)n] *n.* (*myth., fig.*) амазо́нка; (*river*) Амазо́нка.
ambassador [æmˈbæsədə(r)] *n.* посо́л; **~ extraordinary and plenipotentiary** чрезвыча́йный и полномо́чный посо́л; (*representative*) представи́тель (*m.*).
ambassadorial [ˌæmbæsəˈdɔ:rɪəl] *adj.* посо́льский.
ambassadress [æmˈbæsədrɪs] *n.* жена́ посла́.
amber [ˈæmbə(r)] *n.* **1.** (*resin*) янта́рь (*m.*). **2.** (*colour*) янта́рный цвет, цвет янтаря́; **he crossed on the ~ (traffic light)** он прое́хал на жёлтый свет.
ambergris [ˈæmbəgrɪs, -ˌgri:s] *n.* се́рая а́мбра.
ambidexterity [ˌæmbɪdekˈsterɪtɪ] *n.* одина́ковое владе́ние обе́ими рука́ми.
ambidext(e)rous [ˌæmbɪˈdekstrəs] *adj.* одина́ково владе́ющий обе́ими рука́ми.
ambience [ˈæmbɪəns] *n.* окруже́ние, среда́; атмосфе́ра.
ambient [ˈæmbɪənt] *adj.* окружа́ющий; **~ temperature** температу́ра окружа́ющего во́здуха.
ambiguity [ˌæmbɪˈgju:ɪtɪ] *n.* двусмы́сленность; тума́нность, нея́сность.
ambiguous [æmˈbɪgjʊəs] *adj.* двусмы́сленный; тума́нный, нея́сный.
ambit [ˈæmbɪt] *n.* **1.** (*surroundings*) окруже́ние; (*sphere*) сфе́ра. **2.** (*bounds, limits*) грани́цы (*f. pl.*); **within the ~ of** в преде́лах +*g.*
ambition [æmˈbɪʃ(ə)n] *n.* (*desire for distinction*) честолю́бие, амби́ция; (*aspiration*) стремле́ние; **he gratified a lifelong ~** он осуществи́л мечту́ свое́й жи́зни; **her great ~ is to be a dancer** её заве́тная мечта́ — стать танцо́вщицей.
ambitious [æmˈbɪʃəs] *adj.* честолюби́вый; амбицио́зный; **he is too ~** он сли́шком мно́гого хо́чет; **he was ~ to**

succeed он добивался успеха во что бы то ни стало; ~ **of wealth** стремящийся к богатству; ~ **of power** властолюбивый; **an ~ attempt** смелая попытка; **an ~ plan** грандиозный план.

ambivalence [æm'bɪvələns] *n.* двойственность.

ambivalent [æm'bɪvələnt] *adj.* двойственный.

amble ['æmb(ə)l] *n.* (*horse's pace*) иноходь; (*easy gait*) лёгкая походка.

v.i. (*of horse*) идти (*det.*) иноходью; (*of pers.*) идти (*det.*) лёгкой походкой.

ambrosia [æm'brəʊzɪə, -ʒjə] *n.* амброзия.

ambrosial [æm'brəʊzɪəl] *adj.* амброзиальный.

ambulance ['æmbjʊləns] *n.* машина скорой помощи; (*mil.*): **field ~** полевой госпиталь; (*attr.*) санитарный; **~ station** медицинский пункт, медпункт; **call an ~!** вызовите скорую помощь!

ambulant ['æmbjʊlənt] *adj.*: ~ **treatment** амбулаторное лечение; ~ **patient** ходячий больной.

ambus|h ['æmbʊʃ], **-cade** [ˌæmbə'skeɪd] *nn.* засада; **lay an ~** устр|аивать, -оить засаду; **lie in ~** сидеть (*impf.*) в засаде; **run into an ~** поп|адать, -асть в засаду.

v.t. нап|адать, -асть на (*кого*) из засады.

ameliorate [ə'mi:lɪəˌreɪt] *v.t. & i.* ул|учшать(ся), -учшить(ся).

amelioration [əˌmi:lɪə'reɪʃ(ə)n] *n.* улучшение.

amen [ɑ:'men, eɪ-] *int.* аминь; **say ~ to** од|обрять, -обрить.

amenability [əˌmi:nə'bɪlɪtɪ] *n.* податливость; (*leg.*) ответственность, подсудность.

amenable [ə'mi:nəb(ə)l] *adj.* (*tractable*) податливый, послушный; (*responsive*) поддающийся (*чему*); ~ **to reason** доступный голосу разума; ~ **to flattery** падкий на лесть; (*leg., of persons*) ответственный; (*of things*) подсудный; **the case is not ~ to ordinary rules** этот случай не подпадает под общие правила.

amend [ə'mend] *v.t.* **1.** (*correct*) испр|авлять, -авить; (*improve*) ул|учшать, -учшить. **2.** (*make changes to*) вн|осить, -ести поправки/добавления в+*a.*; **an ~ed law** закон с (принятыми к нему) поправками.

v.i. испр|авляться, -авиться.

amendment [ə'mendmənt] *n.* **1.** (*reform*) исправление. **2.** (*of document etc.*) поправка, добавление; **make an ~ to** вн|осить, -ести поправку в+*a.* (*or* добавление к+*d.*).

amends [ə'mendz] *n.* возмещение; исправление; **make ~ to s.o.** компенсировать (*impf., pf.*) кому-н. (*за что*).

amenit|y [ə'mi:nɪtɪ, ə'menɪtɪ] *n.* **1.** (*pleasantness*) приятность; (*of persons*) любезность; **exchange ~ies** обмен|иваться, -яться любезностями. **2.** (*pl., pleasant features, attractions*): **it will spoil the ~ies of the village** это испортит всю прелесть села. **3.** (*pl., comforts, pleasures*) удобства, удовольствия (*both nt. pl.*); благоустройство, комфорт; (*public facilities*) удобства; красоты, прелести (*both f. pl.*).

America [ə'merɪkə] *n.* Америка.

American [ə'merɪkən] *n.* американ|ец (*fem.* -ка).

adj. американский; ~ **English** американский вариант английского языка.

Americanism [ə'merɪkəˌnɪz(ə)m] *n.* американизм.

Americanize [ə'merɪkəˌnaɪz] *v.t.* американизировать (*impf., pf.*).

Amerindian [ˌæmə'rɪndɪən] *n.* американск|ий индеец (*fem.* -ая индианка).

adj. относящийся к американским индейцам.

amethyst ['æmɪθɪst] *n.* аметист; (*attr.*) аметистовый.

Amharic [æm'hærɪk] *n.* амхарский язык.

adj. амхарский.

amiability [ˌeɪmɪə'bɪlɪtɪ] *n.* добродушие; приветливость.

amiable ['eɪmɪəb(ə)l] *adj.* добродушный; приветливый.

amicability [ˌæmɪkə'bɪlɪtɪ] *n.* дружелюбие.

amicable ['æmɪkəb(ə)l] *adj.* дружелюбный; **they reached an ~ arrangement** они пришли к дружескому соглашению.

amid(st) [ə'mɪd(st)] *prep.* среди+*g.*

cpd. **~ships** *adv.* по середине корабля; **the torpedo hit us ~** торпеда попала в самый центр нашего корабля; (*naval command*) прямо руль!

amiss [ə'mɪs] *pred. adj.* неправильный; **something is ~** что-то неладно; **what's ~?** в чём дело?

adv. **1.** (*wrongly*) неправильно; **take ~** (*misinterpret*) толковать (*impf.*) превратно; (*take offence at*) об|ижаться, -идеться на+*a.* **2.** (*out of place*) некстати; **it may not be ~ to explain** было бы кстати объяснить; **nothing comes ~ to him** ему всё впрок.

amity ['æmɪtɪ] *n.* дружба; дружеские отношения.

ammeter ['æmɪtə(r)] *n.* амперметр.

ammonia [ə'məʊnɪə] *n.* (*gas*) аммиак; (*attr.*) аммиачный; (*solution; spirit of ~*) аммиачная вода; нашатырный спирт.

ammoniac [ə'məʊnɪˌæk] *adj.* аммиачный; **sal ~** нашатырь (*m.*).

ammonium [ə'məʊnɪəm] *n.* аммоний; **~ chloride** хлористый аммоний; **~ nitrate** азотнокислый аммоний; аммонийная селитра.

ammunition [ˌæmjʊ'nɪʃ(ə)n] *n.* боевые припасы, боеприпасы (*m. pl.*); (*nav.*) боезапас; **draw ~** получ|ать, -ить боеприпасы; **~ belt** патронная лента, патронташ; **~ dump, store** склад боеприпасов; (*fig.*): **this article will provide the ~ I need** эта статья даст мне в руки необходимое оружие.

amnesia [æm'ni:zɪə] *n.* амнезия.

amnesiac [æm'ni:zɪˌæk] *adj.* страдающий амнезией; потерявший память.

amnesty ['æmnɪstɪ] *n.* амнистия; **'A~ International'** «Международная амнистия».

v.t. амнистировать (*impf., pf.*); да|вать, -ть амнистию +*d.*

amoeba [ə'mi:bə] *n.* амёба.

amok [ə'mɒk] = **amuck**

among(st) [ə'mʌŋst] *prep.* **1.** (*between*) между+*i.*; **conversation ~ friends** разговор между друзьями; **they shared the booty ~ themselves** они разделили добычу между собой; **they hadn't £5 ~ them** у них не было и пяти фунтов на всех. **2.** (*in the midst of*) среди+*g.*; между+*g.*; **~ the trees** среди деревьев; **~ those present** в числе присутствующих; (*into the midst of*): **he fell ~ thieves** он попался разбойникам; (*in the opinion of*): **~ the Romans he was considered a great man** у римлян он считался великим человеком; (*shared by*): **there was a legend ~ the Greeks** у греков существовала легенда; (*from the midst of*): **a great leader rose ~ them** из их среды выдвинулся крупный руководитель. **3.** (*expr. one of a number*) из+*g.*; **only one ~ his friends** только один из его друзей; **Leeds is ~ the biggest towns in England** Лидс — один из самых больших городов Англии; **blessed art thou ~ women** благословенна ты меж/среди жён; **he was numbered ~ the dead** его считали погибшим.

amoral [eɪ'mɒr(ə)l] *adj.* аморальный; внеэтический, нейтральный в отношении морали.

amorist ['æmərɪst] *n.* кавалер; дамский угодник.

amorous ['æmərəs] *adj.* (*inclined to love*) влюбчивый; (*in love*) влюблённый; **he gave her an ~ look** он бросил на неё влюблённый взгляд; (*pert. to love*) любовный.

amorousness ['æmərəsnɪs] *n.* влюбчивость; влюблённость.

amorphous [ə'mɔ:fəs] *adj.* (*shapeless*) бесформенный; (*chem. etc.*) аморфный.

amortization [əˌmɔ:taɪ'zeɪʃ(ə)n] *n.* (*of debt*) погашение долга в рассрочку.

amortize [ə'mɔ:taɪz] *v.t.* пога|шать, -сить в рассрочку.

amount [ə'maʊnt] *n.* **1.** (*sum*) сумма; **to the ~ of** на сумму в+*a.* **2.** (*quantity*) количество; **he spent any ~ of money** он истратил кучу денег; **he has any ~ of pride** гордости у него хоть отбавляй; **we have any ~ of books** у нас полно книг.

v.i.: **~ to** (*add up to*) сост|авлять, -авить +*g.*; дост|игать, -ичь +*g.*; **his income does not ~ to £500 a year** его доход не достигает пятисот фунтов в год; **the expenses ~ to £600** расходы составляют шестьсот фунтов; **an invoice ~ing to £100** счёт на сумму в сто фунтов; (*be equivalent to*) быть равным/равносильным +*d.*; **these conditions ~ to a refusal** эти условия равносильны отказу; **it ~s to the same thing** это сводится всё к тому же; **it ~s to saying that ...** это всё равно, что сказать...; **~ to very little, not ~ to much** быть незначительным; **the difference does not ~ to much** разница невелика; **he will never ~ to**

much из него́ никогда́ ничего́ пу́тного не вы́йдет; (*signify*): **what does it ~ to?** к чему́ э́то сво́дится?
amour [ə'mʊə(r)] *n.* любо́вная интри́га.
amour-propre [æ,mʊə 'prɒpr] *n.* самолю́бие.
amp[1] [æmp] *n.* (*abbr. of* **ampere**) А, (ампе́р).
amp[2] [æmp] *n.* (*abbr. of* **amplifier**) (*coll.*) усили́тель (*m.*).
ampere ['æmpeə(r)] *n.* ампе́р.
ampersand ['æmpə,sænd] *n.* знак «&».
amphibia [æm'fɪbɪə] *n.* земново́дные (*nt. pl.*); амфи́бии (*f. pl.*).
amphibian [æm'fɪbɪən] *n.* **1.** (*animal*) земново́дное; амфи́бия. **2.** (*mil.*) (*aircraft*) самолёт-амфи́бия; (*tank*) танк-амфи́бия; (*car*) пла́вающий автомоби́ль.
adj. = **amphibious**
amphibi|ous [æm'fɪbɪəs], **-an** [æm'fɪbɪən] *adj.* земново́дный; (*mil.*) пла́вающий; -амфи́бия (*as suff.*); **~ assault** морско́й деса́нт.
amphibrach ['æmfɪ,bræk] *n.* амфибра́хий.
amphitheatre ['æmfɪ,θɪətə(r)] *n.* амфитеа́тр.
amphora ['æmfərə] *n.* а́мфора.
ample ['æmp(ə)l] *adj.* (*sufficient*) доста́точный; предоста́точно (+*g.*); **we have ~ time** у нас доста́точно вре́мени; **he had ~ opportunity to discover the truth** у него́ была́ по́лная возмо́жность установи́ть пра́вду; (*spacious*) просто́рный; широ́кий; (*extensive*) простра́нный; **a man of ~ proportions** ту́чный челове́к; (*abundant*) оби́льный; **he has ~ means** он челове́к доста́точный.
ampleness ['æmpəlnɪs] *n.* (*sufficiency*) доста́точность; (*of clothes etc.*) ширина́; просто́рность; (*abundance*) оби́лие.
amplification [,æmplɪfɪ'keɪʃ(ə)n] *n.* (*expansion, extension*) расшире́ние; **this article is an ~ of his speech** э́та статья — развёрнутый вариа́нт его́ ре́чи; (*enlargement*) увеличе́ние; (*of sound, radio signal etc.*) усиле́ние.
amplifier ['æmplɪ,faɪə(r)] *n.* усили́тель (*m.*).
amplify ['æmplɪ,faɪ] *v.t.* (*expand, extend*) расш|иря́ть, -и́рить; (*enlarge*) увели́чи|вать, -ть; **~ a theme** разв|ива́ть, -и́ть те́му; (*of sound, radio signal etc.*) уси́ли|вать, -ть.
amplitude ['æmplɪ,tju:d] *n.* (*abundance*) оби́лие; полнота́; (*width*) широта́, разма́х; (*spaciousness*) просто́р; (*phys., elec.*) амплиту́да.
amply ['æmplɪ] *adv.* (*sufficiently*) доста́точно; (*fully*) вполне́; оби́льно; **her innocence was ~ demonstrated** её невино́вность была́ по́лностью устано́влена.
ampoule ['æmpu:l] *n.* а́мпула.
amputate ['æmpjʊ,teɪt] *v.t.* ампути́ровать (*impf., pf.*); отн|има́ть, -я́ть; **his left leg was ~d** ему́ о́тняли ле́вую но́гу.
amputation [,æmpjʊ'teɪʃ(ə)n] *n.* ампута́ция.
Amsterdam [,æmstə'dæm] *n.* Амстерда́м.
am|uck [ə'mʌk], **-ok** [ə'mɒk] *adv.*: **run ~** (*go mad*) обезу́меть (*pf.*): (*behave wildly*) безу́мствовать (*impf.*); бу́йствовать (*impf.*); беси́ться (*impf.*).
amulet ['æmjʊlɪt] *n.* амуле́т.
amus|e [ə'mju:z] *v.t.* (*entertain, divert*) развл|ека́ть, -е́чь; забавля́ть (*impf.*); (*make laugh*) смеши́ть (*impf.*); позаба́вить (*pf.*); **an ~ing little hat** заба́вная шля́пка; **I don't find that ~ing** я не ви́жу в э́том ничего́ смешно́го.
amusement [ə'mju:zmənt] *n.* **1.** (*diversion*) развлече́ние, заба́ва; **they went hunting for ~** они́ ходи́ли на охо́ту для заба́вы (*or* что́бы развле́чься); **I play the piano for my own ~** я игра́ю на фортепья́но для со́бственного удово́льствия; **the town has few ~s** в э́том го́роде ма́ло развлече́ний; **~ arcade, park** аттракцио́ны (*m. pl.*), павильо́н, парк аттракцио́нов. **2.** (*tendency to laughter*): **to everyone's ~ the clown fell over** ко всео́бщему удово́льствию, клоун упа́л; **it afforded me great ~** э́то меня́ о́чень позаба́вило.
anachronism [ə'nækrə,nɪz(ə)m] *n.* анахрони́зм.
anachronistic [ə,nækrə'nɪstɪk] *adj.* анахрони́ческий.
anacoluthon [,ænəkə'lu:θɒn] *n.* анаколу́ф.
anaconda [,ænə'kɒndə] *n.* анако́нда.
anaemia [ə'ni:mɪə] *n.* малокро́вие, анеми́я.
anaemic [ə'ni:mɪk] *adj.* малокро́вный, анеми́чный.
anaesthesia [,ænɪs'θi:zɪə] *n.* анестези́я; обезбо́ливание.
anaesthetic [,ænɪs'θetɪk] *n.* анестези́рующее сре́дство; анесте́тик; **general/local ~** о́бщий/ме́стный нарко́з.
adj. анестези́рующий; обезбо́ливающий.
anaesthetist [ə'ni:sθətɪst] *n.* анестезио́лог.
anaesthetize [ə'ni:sθə,taɪz] *v.t.* анестези́ровать (*impf., pf.*).
anagram ['ænə,græm] *n.* анагра́мма.
anal ['eɪn(ə)l] *adj.* заднепрохо́дный, ана́льный.
analects ['ænə,lekts] *n.* анале́кты (*m. pl.*).
analgesia [,ænæl'dʒi:zɪə, -sɪə] *n.* аналгези́я.
analgesic [,ænæl'dʒi:sɪk, -zɪk] *adj.* болеутоля́ющий.
analogical [,ænə'lɒdʒɪk(ə)l] *adj.* аналоги́ческий.
analogous [ə'næləgəs] *adj.* аналоги́чный.
analogue ['ænə,lɒg] *n.* ана́лог; **~ computer** ана́логовая (вычисли́тельная) маши́на.
analogy [ə'nælədʒɪ] *n.* анало́гия; схо́дство; **by ~ with** по анало́гии с+*i.*
analysable ['ænə,laɪzəb(ə)l] *adj.* поддаю́щийся ана́лизу.
analyse ['ænə,laɪz] *v.t.* анализи́ровать (*impf., pf.*); (*gram.*) раз|бира́ть, -обра́ть; (*psych.*) подв|ерга́ть, -е́ргнуть психоана́лизу.
analysis [ə'nælɪsɪs] *n.* ана́лиз; (*gram.*) разбо́р; **in the last ~** в коне́чном счёте; (*psycho ~*) психоана́лиз.
analyst ['ænəlɪst] *n.* (*chem.*) лабора́нт-хи́мик; (*psych.*) психоанали́тик.
analytic(al) [,ænə'lɪtɪk(ə)l] *adj.* аналити́ческий.
anapaest ['ænə,pi:st] *n.* ана́пест.
anapaestic [,ænə'pi:stɪk] *adj.* анапести́ческий.
anaphrodisiac [æn,æfrə'dɪzɪ,æk] *n.* & *adj.* (сре́дство,) понижа́ющее полово́е возбужде́ние.
anarchic(al) [ə'nɑ:kɪk, ə'nɑ:kɪk(ə)l] *adj.* анархи́ческий.
anarchism ['ænə,kɪz(ə)m] *n.* анархи́зм.
anarchist ['ænəkɪst] *n.* анархи́ст (*fem.* -ка).
adj. анархи́стский.
anarcho-syndicalism [æ'nɑ:kəʊ'sɪndɪkəlɪz(ə)m] *n.* ана́рхо-синдикали́зм.
anarchy ['ænəkɪ] *n.* ана́рхия.
anathema [ə'næθəmə] *n.* ана́фема; (*excommunication*) отлуче́ние от це́ркви; **his name is ~ here** его́ и́мя здесь про́клято.
anathematize [ə'næθəmə,taɪz] *v.t.* пред|ава́ть, -а́ть ана́феме; (*curse*) прокл|ина́ть, -я́сть.
anatomical [,ænə'tɒmɪk(ə)l] *adj.* анатоми́ческий.
anatomist [ə'nætəmɪst] *n.* ана́том.
anatomize [ə'nætə,maɪz] *v.t.* **1.** (*dissect*) анатоми́ровать (*impf., pf.*). **2.** (*analyse*) подв|ерга́ть, -е́ргнуть разбо́ру.
anatomy [ə'nætəmɪ] *n.* **1.** (*science*) анато́мия. **2.** (*dissection*) анатоми́рование. **3.** (*analysis*) разбо́р; ана́лиз. **4.** (*body*) те́ло; **I ache in every part of my ~** у меня́ боли́т всё те́ло.
ANC (*abbr. of* ***African National Congress***) АНК, (Африка́нский национа́льный конгре́сс).
ancestor ['ænsestə(r)] *n.* пре́док, прароди́тель (*m.*); родонача́льник; **~ worship** культ пре́дков.
ancestral [æn'sestr(ə)l] *adj.* родово́й; насле́дственный; **~ home** о́тчий дом.
ancestress ['ænsestrɪs] *n.* прароди́тельница.
ancestry ['ænsestrɪ] *n.* (*ancestors*) пре́дки (*m. pl.*); (*lineage*) происхожде́ние; **he comes of distinguished ~** он благоро́дного происхожде́ния.
anchor ['æŋkə(r)] *n.* (*of a vessel*) я́корь (*m.*); **~ buoy** томбу́й, я́корный буй; **~ chain** я́корная цепь; **cast, drop ~** бр|оса́ть, -о́сить я́корь; **come to ~** ста|нови́ться, -ть на я́корь; **lie, ride at ~** стоя́ть на я́коре; **weigh ~** сн|има́ться, -я́ться с я́коря.
v.t. ста́вить, по- на я́корь; (*fig., secure*) закреп|ля́ть, -и́ть; **his gaze was ~ed on the stage** его́ взгляд был прико́ван к сце́не; **our hopes were ~ed on the captain** мы возлага́ли все наде́жды на капита́на.
v.i. (*of vessel*) ста|нови́ться, -ть на я́корь; (*of crew: cast ~*) бр|оса́ть, -о́сить я́корь.
anchorage ['æŋkərɪdʒ] *n.* (*anchoring-place*) я́корная стоя́нка; (*dues*) порто́вый сбор.
anchorite ['æŋkə,raɪt] *n.* отше́льник; анахоре́т.
anchorman ['æŋkəmən] *n.* (*TV, radio*) веду́щий.
anchovy ['æntʃəvɪ, æn'tʃəʊvɪ] *n.* анчо́ус.
ancient ['eɪnʃ(ə)nt] *n.* **the ~s** дре́вние наро́ды (*m. pl.*): (*writers*) анти́чные писа́тели (*m. pl.*); **the A~ of Days** Предве́чный.

adj. дре́вний; анти́чный; (*very old*) стари́нный; вековой; ~ **history** дре́вняя исто́рия; **that's ~ history!** э́то ста́рая исто́рия; ~ **monument** па́мятник старины́; **an ~ castle** стари́нный за́мок; **an ~ oak** вековой дуб; **an ~** (*-looking*) **hat** ве́тхая/допото́пная шля́па.

ancillary [æn'sɪlərɪ] *adj.* (*auxiliary*) вспомога́тельный; (*subordinate*) подчинённый; **this operation is ~ to the main project** в основно́м прое́кте э́та опера́ция явля́ется подсо́бной/вспомога́тельной.

and [ænd, ənd] *conj.* **1.** (*connecting words or clauses*) и; (*in addition*) и, да; (*with certain closely linked pairs, esp. of persons*) с+*i.*; **bread ~ butter** хлеб с ма́слом; **the doctor ~ his wife came** пришли́ до́ктор с жено́й; **you ~ I** мы с ва́ми; (*with nums. denoting addition*) и; плюс; **2 ~ 2 are 4** два и два — четы́ре; **they walked two ~ two** они́ шли па́рами; (*to form cpd. num.*) *omitted*: **260** две́сти шестьдеся́т; (*with following fraction*) с+*i.*; **4½** четы́ре с полови́ной. **2.** (*intensive*): **he ran ~ ran** он всё бежа́л и бежа́л; **better ~ better** всё лу́чше (и лу́чше); **they talked for hours ~ hours** они́ разгова́ривали часа́ми; **the plain stretched for miles ~ miles** равни́на простира́лась на мно́го миль. **3.** (*in order to*) *omitted before inf.*: **try ~ find out** постара́йтесь узна́ть; **wait ~ see!** погоди́те — ещё уви́дите! **4.** (*expr. consequence*): **move, ~ I shoot!** одно́ движе́ние, и я стреля́ю. **5.** (*adversative*) а; **I shall go, ~ you stay here** я пойду́, а вы остава́йтесь здесь. **6.** (*emph.*) и то; к тому́ же; и прито́м; **he was found, ~ by chance** его нашли́, и то случа́йно; **he speaks English, ~ very well too** он говори́т по-англи́йски, и прито́м о́чень хорошо́.

Andalusia [ˌændə'lu:zɪə] *n.* Андалу́сия.

Andalusian [ˌændə'lu:zɪən] *n.* андалу́з|ец (*fem.* -ка).

adj. андалу́зский; (*geog.*) андалу́сский.

andante [æn'dæntɪ] *n., adj. & adv.* анда́нте (*indecl.*).

Andes ['ændɪ:z] *n.* А́нды (*pl., g.* —).

androgynous [æn'drɒdʒɪnəs] *adj.* двупо́лый; (*bot.*) обоепо́лый.

anecdotal [ˌænɪk'dəʊt(ə)l] *adj.* анекдоти́ческий.

anecdote ['ænɪkˌdəʊt] *n.* исто́рия, расска́з; (*joke*) анекдо́т.

anemometer [ˌænɪ'mɒmɪtə(r)] *n.* анемо́метр.

anemone [ə'nemənɪ] *n.* анемо́н; (*windflower, wood-~*) ве́треница; **sea ~** морско́й анемо́н; акти́ния.

aneroid ['ænəˌrɔɪd] *n. & adj.* (**~ barometer**) (баро́метр-) анеро́ид.

anew [ə'nju:] *adj.* (*again*) сно́ва; (*in a different way*) за́ново; по-но́вому.

anfractuosity [ˌænfræktjʊ'ɒsɪtɪ] *n.* изви́лина.

angel ['eɪndʒ(ə)l] *n.* (*lit., fig.*) а́нгел; **fallen ~** па́дший а́нгел; **guardian ~** а́нгел-храни́тель; **~ of darkness** а́нгел тьмы; **good/bad ~** до́брый/злой ге́ний.

cpd. **~-fish** *n.* морско́й а́нгел.

angelic [æn'dʒelɪk] *adj.* а́нгельский.

angelica [æn'dʒelɪkə] *n.* дя́гиль (*m.*).

anger ['æŋgə(r)] *n.* гнев; **I said it in ~** я сказа́л э́то сгоряча́.

v.t. серди́ть, рас-; разгне́вать (*pf.*); вызыва́ть, вы́звать гнев +*g.*

Angevin ['ændʒɪvɪn] *adj.* (*hist.*) анжу́йский.

angina [æn'dʒaɪnə] *n.* анги́на; **~ (pectoris)** стенокарди́я, грудна́я жа́ба.

angle[1] ['æŋg(ə)l] *n.* у́гол; **acute ~** о́стрый у́гол; **obtuse ~** тупо́й у́гол; **right ~** прямо́й у́гол; **at an ~ of 30°** под угло́м в три́дцать гра́дусов; **the house stands at an ~ to the street** дом стои́т под угло́м к у́лице; **at right ~s** под прямы́м угло́м; **set one's hat at an ~** наде́ть (*pf.*) шля́пу набекре́нь; **~ of elevation** у́гол подъёма; (*artillery*) у́гол прице́ла; **~ of incidence** у́гол паде́ния; (*fig., viewpoint*) то́чка зре́ния, подхо́д; **one must consider all ~s of a question** на́до уче́сть все аспе́кты вопро́са; **we examined the matter from every ~** мы всесторо́нне рассмотре́ли вопро́с.

v.t. ста́вить, по- под угло́м; **he ~d the lamp to shine on his book** он поста́вил ла́мпу так, что́бы свет па́дал на кни́гу; **an ~d deck** накло́нная па́луба; (*fig.*): **an ~d question** тенденцио́зно поста́вленный вопро́с; **the news was ~d** но́вости бы́ли подо́браны/по́даны тенденцио́зно.

cpds. **~-iron** *n.* углово́е желе́зо; **~-parking** *n.* автомоби́льная стоя́нка (располо́женная) под угло́м к тротуа́ру.

angl|e[2] ['æŋg(ə)l] *v.i.* (*fish*) уди́ть (*impf.*) ры́бу; **~e for trout** лови́ть форе́ль; **yesterday we went ~ing** вчера́ мы е́здили на рыба́лку; (*fig.*): **~e for compliments** напра́шиваться (*impf.*) на комплиме́нты; **~e for votes** охо́титься (*impf.*) за голоса́ми.

Angle[3] ['æŋg(ə)l] *n.* (*hist.*): **the ~s** а́нглы (*m. pl.*).

angler ['æŋglə(r)] *n.* рыболо́в.

Anglican ['æŋglɪkən] *n.* англика́нец.

adj. англика́нский.

Anglicanism ['æŋglɪkənɪz(ə)m] *n.* англика́нство.

Anglicism ['æŋglɪˌsɪz(ə)m] *n.* англици́зм.

Anglicize ['æŋglɪˌsaɪz] *v.t.* англизи́ровать (*impf., pf.*).

angling ['æŋglɪŋ] *n.* (спорти́вное) рыболо́вство.

Anglo- ['æŋgləʊ] *comb. form* англо…; англо-…

Anglomania [ˌæŋgləʊ'meɪnɪə] *n.* англома́ния.

Anglomaniac [ˌæŋgləʊ'meɪnɪˌæk] *n.* англома́н (*fem.* -ка).

adj. англома́нский.

Anglophile ['æŋgləʊˌfaɪl] *n.* англофи́л.

adj. англофи́льский.

Anglophobe ['æŋgləʊˌfəʊb] *n.* англофо́б.

Anglophobia [ˌæŋgləʊ'fəʊbɪə] *n.* англофо́бство, англофо́бия.

anglophone ['æŋgləʊˌfəʊn] *adj.* англоязы́чный, англо-говоря́щий.

Anglo-Saxon [ˌæŋgləʊ'sæks(ə)n] *n.* **1.** (*racial type*) англоса́кс; чистокро́вный англича́нин. **2.** (*language*) англосаксо́нский/древнеангли́йский язы́к.

adj. англосаксо́нский, древнеангли́йский.

Angola [æŋ'gəʊlə] *n.* Анго́ла.

Angolan [æŋ'gəʊlən] *n.* анго́л|ец (*fem.* -ка).

adj. анго́льский.

angora [æŋ'gɔ:rə] *n.* (*cloth*) анго́рская шерсть.

adj. анго́рский.

angry ['æŋgrɪ] *adj.* серди́тый, разгне́ванный; **be ~ with** серди́ться/гне́ваться (*both impf.*) на+*a.* (**over, about sth.:** за что-н.); **get ~ with** рассерди́ться/разгне́ваться (*both pf.*) на+*a.*; **make ~** серди́ть, рас-; **I was ~ with him for going** я рассерди́лся на него́ за то, что он пошёл; (*annoyed*): **he is ~ about the delay** он раздражён опозда́нием; **she got extremely ~** она́ вы́шла из себя́; (*fig., of wounds etc.: inflamed*) воспалённый; **she flushed an ~ red** она́ вспы́хнула от гне́ва.

angst [æŋst] *n.* страх; трево́жное состоя́ние.

anguish ['æŋgwɪʃ] *n.* муче́ние; му́ка; страда́ние; (*pain*) боль; **a look of ~, an ~ed look** му́ченический/страда́льческий взгляд; **an ~ed cry** душераздира́ющий крик.

angular ['æŋgjʊlə(r)] *adj.* **1.** (*forming or pert. to an angle*) углово́й; **~ velocity** углова́я ско́рость. **2.** (*having angles*) углова́тый; **an ~ face** лицо́ с ре́зкими черта́ми. **3.** (*of pers., thin, bony*) худо́й, костля́вый; (*fig., awkward*) углова́тый.

angularity [ˌæŋgjʊ'lærɪtɪ] *n.* углова́тость; худоба́; костля́вость.

anile ['eɪnaɪl] *adj.* (*old-womanish*) стару́шечий.

aniline ['ænɪˌli:n, -lɪn, -ˌlaɪn] *n.* анили́н.

adj. анили́новый.

animadversion [ˌænɪmæd'vɜ:ʃ(ə)n] *n.* (*censure*) порица́ние; (*observation*) замеча́ние.

animadvert [ˌænɪmæd'vɜ:t] *v.i.* **~ on** (*censure*) порица́ть (*impf.*); (*comment on*) де́лать, с- замеча́ние по по́воду +*g.*

animal ['ænɪm(ə)l] *n.* живо́тное; **domestic ~s** дома́шние живо́тные; **farm ~s** живо́тные, кото́рых разво́дят на фе́рме; **wild ~** зверь (*m.*), ди́кое живо́тное; **~ painter** анимали́ст; **he eats like an ~** у него́ во́лчий аппети́т.

adj. живо́тный; **the ~ kingdom** живо́тное ца́рство; **~ husbandry** животново́дство; **~ needs** есте́ственные потре́бности; **~ desires** пло́тские жела́ния; **~ spirits** жизнера́достность.

animalcule [ˌænɪ'mælkju:l] *n.* микроскопи́ческое живо́тное.

animate[1] ['ænɪmət] *adj.* (*living*) живо́й; **an ~ noun** одушевлённое и́мя существи́тельное; (*lively*) оживлённый, воодушевлённый.

animate[2] ['ænɪˌmeɪt] *v.t.* (*enliven*) ожив|ля́ть, -и́ть; (*give life to*) вдохну́ть (*pf.*) жизнь в+*a.*; (*inspire, actuate*) вдохнов|ля́ть, -и́ть; (во)одушев|ля́ть, -и́ть; **~d by love of country** воодушевлённый любо́вью к ро́дине; **he is ~d by the best motives** он дви́жим са́мыми лу́чшими побужде́ниями; **become ~d** оживл|я́ться, -и́ться; **~d cartoon** мультипликацио́нный фильм.

animation [ˌænɪˈmeɪʃ(ə)n] *n.* (*liveliness*) оживле́ние; (*enthusiasm*) воодушевле́ние.

animator [ˈænɪˌmeɪtə(r)] *n.* (*cin.*) (худо́жник-)мультиплика́тор.

animism [ˈænɪˌmɪz(ə)m] *n.* аними́зм.

animist [ˈænɪmɪst] *n.* аними́ст.

animosity [ˌænɪˈmɒsɪtɪ] *n.* (*hostility*) вражде́бность; (*bitterness*) озлобле́ние; **feel ~ against** пита́ть (*impf.*) вражду́ к+*d*.

animus [ˈænɪməs] *n.* **1.** (*spirit: atmosphere*) дух; атмосфе́ра. **2.** (*animosity*) вражде́бность.

aniseed [ˈænɪˌsiːd] *n.* ани́с; ани́совое се́мя.

anisette [ˌænɪˈzet] *n.* ани́совый ликёр.

Ankara [ˈæŋkərə] *n.* Анкара́ (*m.*).

ankle [ˈæŋk(ə)l] *n.* лоды́жка, щи́колотка.

cpds. **~-boot** *n.* боти́нок; **~-deep** *adj.*: **~-deep in mud** по щи́колотку в грязи́; **~-length** *adj.*: **~-length dress** пла́тье по щи́колотку; **~-socks** *n. pl.* носки́ (*m. pl.*).

anklet [ˈæŋklɪt] *n.* **1.** (*ornament*) ножно́й брасле́т. **2.** (*pl.*, *fetters*) ножны́е кандалы́ (*m. pl.*).

annalist [ˈænəlɪst] *n.* летопи́сец.

annals [ˈæn(ə)lz] *n.* анна́л|ы (*pl.*, *g.* -ов); ле́топись.

anneal [əˈniːl] *v.t.* отж|ига́ть, -е́чь; (*fig.*) закал|я́ть, -и́ть.

annealing [əˈniːlɪŋ] *n.* о́тжиг; **~ furnace** печь для о́тжига.

annex(e)[1] [ˈæneks] *n.* (*to document*) приложе́ние; (*to a building*) пристро́йка, фли́гель (*m.*); (*separate building*) отде́льный ко́рпус.

annex[2] [æˈneks, əˈn-] *v.t.* присоедин|я́ть, -и́ть; прил|ага́ть, -ожи́ть; (*territory etc.*) аннекси́ровать (*impf.*, *pf.*).

annexation [ˌænekˈseɪʃ(ə)n, ˌən-] *n.* присоедине́ние; анне́ксия, аннекси́рование.

annexationist [ˌænekˈseɪʃ(ə)nɪst, ˌən-] *adj.* захва́тнический.

annihilat|e [əˈnaɪəˌleɪt, əˈnaɪl-] *v.t.* (*destroy*) уничт|ожа́ть, -о́жить; (*extirpate*) истреб|ля́ть, -и́ть; (*fig.*): **an ~ing look** уничтожа́ющий взгляд.

annihilation [əˌnaɪəˈleɪʃ(ə)n, əˌnaɪl-] *n.* уничтоже́ние; истребле́ние.

anniversary [ˌænɪˈvɜːsərɪ] *n.* годовщи́на; **on his fifth wedding ~** в пя́тую годовщи́ну его́ сва́дьбы; **40th ~** сорокова́я годовщи́на, сорокале́тие; **celebrate an ~** пра́здновать, от- годовщи́ну (*чего*).

adj.: **~ edition** юбиле́йное изда́ние.

Anno Domini [ˌænəʊ ˈdɒmɪˌnaɪ] *adv.* на́шей э́ры (*abbr.* н.э.); **400 AD** 400 г. на́шей э́ры; (*as n.*: *age*) го́ды (*m. pl.*), ста́рость, во́зраст.

annotate [ˈænəʊˌteɪt, ˈænəˌteɪt] *v.t.* снаб|жа́ть, -ди́ть примеча́ниями (*impf.*, *pf.*); **~d text** текст с примеча́ниями.

annotation [ˌænəʊˈteɪʃ(ə)n, ˌænəˈteɪʃ(ə)n] *n.* (*annotating*) анноти́рование; (*added note*) примеча́ние; аннота́ция.

annotator [ˈænəʊˌteɪtə(r), ˈænəˌteɪtə(r)] *n.* коммента́тор.

announce [əˈnaʊns] *v.t.* (*state; declare*) объяв|ля́ть, -и́ть (*что or о чём*); заяв|ля́ть, -и́ть (*что or о чём or relative clause*); **he ~d his intention to be present** он объяви́л о своём наме́рении прису́тствовать; он заяви́л, что бу́дет прису́тствовать; **the verdict was ~d yesterday** пригово́р был объя́влен вчера́; **their engagement was ~d in the paper** об их помо́лвке объя́влено в газе́те; (*notify, tell*) да|ва́ть, -ть знать (*о чём кому*); **he ~d the results of his researches** он сообщи́л о результа́тах свои́х иссле́дований; **the footman ~d the guests as they arrived** лаке́й докла́дывал о прибы́тии госте́й; **the chairman ~d the next speaker** председа́тель объяви́л сле́дующего ора́тора.

announcement [əˈnaʊnsmənt] *n.* объявле́ние, заявле́ние; **put an ~ in the newspaper** поме|ща́ть, -сти́ть объявле́ние в газе́те; (*written notification*) извеще́ние; (*on radio etc.*) сообще́ние; **the ~ of his death was made at 4 o'clock** о его́ сме́рти сообщи́ли в 4 часа́.

announcer [əˈnaʊnsə(r)] *n.* (*on radio etc.*) ди́ктор; (*of stage entertainment*) конферансье́ (*m. indecl.*).

annoy [əˈnɔɪ] *v.t.* (*vex*) доса|жда́ть, -ди́ть +*d.*; (*irritate*) раздража́ть (*impf.*); де́йствовать (*impf.*) на не́рвы +*d.*; (*pester*) докуча́ть (*impf.*) +*d.*; **I was ~ed with him** я был на него́ серди́т; **we were ~ed by the dog's barking** соба́ка досажда́ла нам свои́м ла́ем.

annoyance [əˈnɔɪəns] *n.* раздраже́ние; (*cause of ~*) доса́да, неприя́тность.

annoying [əˈnɔɪɪŋ] *adj.* доса́дный; **how ~!** кака́я доса́да!; **an ~ person** невозмо́жный челове́к.

annual [ˈænjʊəl] *n.* **1.** (*publication*) ежего́дник. **2.** (*plant*) одноле́тнее расте́ние, одноле́тник.

adj. **1.** (*happening once a year*): **~ meeting** ежего́дное собра́ние. **2.** (*pert. to whole year*): **~ income** годово́й дохо́д; **~ report** годово́й отчёт; **~ rings** годи́чные ко́льца. **3.** (*bot., lasting for one year*) одноле́тний.

annually [ˈænjʊəlɪ] *adv.* ежего́дно.

annuitant [əˈnjuːɪt(ə)nt] *n.* получа́ющий ежего́дную ре́нту.

annuity [əˈnjuːɪtɪ] *n.* ежего́дная ре́нта; аннуите́т; **life ~** пожи́зненная ре́нта.

annul [əˈnʌl] *v.t.* отмен|я́ть, -и́ть (*impf.*, *pf.*); **the marriage was ~led** брак был при́знан недействи́тельным.

annular [ˈænjʊlə(r)] *adj.* кольцеобра́зный, кольцево́й.

annulment [əˈnʌlmənt] *n.* отме́на, аннули́рование.

annunciation [əˌnʌnsɪˈeɪʃ(ə)n] *n.* возвеще́ние; объявле́ние; (*relig.*) благове́щение.

anode [ˈænəʊd] *n.* ано́д; (*attr.*) ано́дный.

anodyne [ˈænəˌdaɪn] *n.* (*pain-killer*) болеутоля́ющее сре́дство; (*sedative*) успока́ивающее сре́дство.

adj. болеутоля́ющий; успока́ивающий; (*fig.*) ничего́ не зна́чащий.

anoint [əˈnɔɪnt] *v.t.* пома́з|ывать, -ать; **he was ~ed king** его́ пома́зали на ца́рство; **the Lord's A~ed** пома́занник бо́жий.

anomalous [əˈnɒmələs] *adj.* анома́льный.

anomaly [əˈnɒməlɪ] *n.* анома́лия.

anon [əˈnɒn] *adv.* ско́ро, вско́ре; **ever and ~** вре́мя от вре́мени; **see you ~!** пока́!

anonymity [ˌænəˈnɪmɪtɪ] *n.* анони́мность.

anonymous [əˈnɒnɪməs] *adj.* анони́мный; безымя́нный; **~ letter, ~ telephone call** анони́мка.

anopheles [əˈnɒfɪˌliːz] *n.* ано́фелес, маляри́йный кома́р.

anorak [ˈænəˌræk] *n.* анора́к, ку́ртка с капюшо́ном.

anorexia [ˌænəˈreksɪə] *n.* отсу́тствие аппети́та; **~ nervosa** не́рвная анорекси́я.

anorexic [ænəˈreksɪk] *n.* больн|о́й (*fem.* -а́я) анорекси́ей.

adj. страда́ющий анорекси́ей.

another [əˈnʌðə(r)] *pron. & adj.* **1.** (*additional*) ещё; **~ cup of tea?** ещё ча́шку ча́ю?; **will you have ~ (drink)?** хоти́те ещё вы́пить?; **have ~ go!** попыта́йтесь ещё раз!; **in ~ 10 years** ещё че́рез де́сять лет; **and ~ thing** и вот ещё что; **he and ~** он сам-дру́г; **not ~ word!** ни сло́ва бо́льше!; **without ~ word** не говоря́ ни сло́ва; **tell us ~!** (*coll., in disbelief*) расскажи́те кому́-нибудь друго́му!; **ask me ~!** (*coll.*) почём я зна́ю? **2.** (*similar*): **such ~ as I** подо́бный мне; **~ Tolstoy** второ́й Толсто́й; **you're ~!** (*coll.*) сам тако́й!; от тако́го слы́шу!; **taken one with ~** (*together*) вме́сте взя́тые; (*on average*) в сре́днем. **3.** (*different*) друго́й; **I don't want this paper, bring me ~** я не хочу́ э́ту газе́ту, принеси́те мне другу́ю; **~ time** в друго́й раз; **that's ~ matter altogether** э́то совсе́м друго́е де́ло; **one way or ~** так и́ли ина́че. **4.: one ~** (*refl.*) *see* **one**

anschluss [ˈænʃlʊs] *n.* (*hist.*) а́ншлюс(с).

answer [ˈɑːnsə(r)] *n.* **1.** (*reply*) отве́т; **he gave, made an evasive ~** он дал укло́нчивый отве́т; **what was his ~?** что он отве́тил?; **in ~ to your letter** в отве́т на ва́ше письмо́; **he laughed by way of ~** в отве́т он рассмея́лся; (*retort*) возраже́ние; (*defence*): **he has a complete ~ to the charges** он мо́жет отвести́ все обвине́ния. **2.** (*solution*) отве́т; реше́ние; **there is no simple ~ to the problem** пробле́му реши́ть нелегко́; **for some countries democracy is not the ~** для не́которых стран демокра́тия — не то, что ну́жно; **he thinks he knows all the ~s** он ду́мает, что он уже́ всё пости́г.

v.t. **1.** (*reply to*) отв|еча́ть, -е́тить (*кому, на что*); **the question was not ~ed** вопро́с оста́лся без отве́та; **~ the**

door откр|ывáть, -ы́ть дверь; ~ **the door-bell (*or* a knock at the door)** откр|ывáть, -ы́ть (дверь) на звонóк (*or* на стук); ~ **the telephone** под|ходи́ть, -ойти́ к телефóну; отвечáть (*impf.*) на телефóнные звонки́. **2.** (*fulfil*): ~ **requirements** отвечáть (*impf.*) трéбованиям; ~ **the purpose** соответствовать (*impf.*) цéли. **3.** (*correspond to*): **he ~s the description exactly** он тóчно соотвéтствует описáнию. **4.** (*refute*): ~ **a charge** опров|ергáть, -éргнуть обвинéние. **5.** (*solve*) реш|áть, -и́ть. **6.** (*satisfy, grant*): **his claim was ~ed** егó трéбование удовлетвори́ли; **our prayers were ~ed** нáши моли́твы бы́ли услы́шаны; **it ~ed all my hopes** э́то оправдáло все мои́ надéжды.

v.i. **1.** (*reply*) отв|ечáть, -éтить. **2.** (*respond; react*): **the dog ~s to the name of Rex** собáка отзывáется на кли́чку Рекс; **the wound ~ed to treatment** рáна поддавáлась лечéнию; **the horse ~s to the whip** лóшадь слу́шается кнутá; **the ship ~ed (to) the helm** корáбль слу́шался руля́. **3.** ~ **for** (*vouch, accept responsibility for*) ручáться, поручи́ться за+*a.*; **I will ~ for his honesty** я ручáюсь за егó чéстность; (*suffer, bear responsibility for*): **you will ~ for your words** вы отвéтите за э́ти словá; **he has much to ~ for** он за мнóгое в отвéте; с негó мнóгое спрóсится. **4.** (*give an account*): **I ~ to no one** я никомý не обя́зан отчётом. **5.** (*prove satisfactory*): **the plan has not ~ed** план не удáлся. **6.** ~ **back** дерзи́ть, на-.

cpd. **~phone** ['ɑ:nsə,fəʊn] *n.* автоотвéтчик, телефóн-отвéтчик.

answerable ['ɑ:nsərəb(ə)l] *adj.* **1.** (*responsible*) отвéтственный (*перед кем за что*); **you are ~ to me for your conduct** вы несёте передо мнóй отвéтственность за свои́ поступки. **2.** (*capable of being answered*): **the charges are ~** на э́ти обвинéния мóжно возрази́ть; (*capable of solution*) разреши́мый.

ant [ænt] *n.* муравéй; **white ~** терми́т; (*attr.*) муравьи́ный; ~ **eggs** муравьи́ные я́йца.

cpds. **~-bear** *n.* трубкозу́б; гигáнтский муравьéд; **~-eater** *n.* муравьéд; **~-hill, ~-heap** *nn.* муравéйник.

antacid [ænt'æsɪd] *n.* срéдство, нейтрализу́ющее кислоту́.

antagonism [æn'tægə,nɪz(ə)m] *n.* антагони́зм.

antagonist [æn'tægənɪst] *n.* антагони́ст; (*adversary*) проти́вник.

antagonistic [æn,tægə'nɪstɪk] *adj.* антагонисти́ческий.

antagonize [æn'tægə,naɪz] *v.t.* раздражáть (*impf.*); нерви́ровать (*impf.*).

Antarctic [ænt'ɑ:ktɪk] *n.*: **the A~** Антáрктика.

adj. антаркти́ческий; **A~ Circle** Ю́жный поля́рный круг; **A~ Ocean** Ю́жный океáн.

Antarctica [ænt'ɑ:ktɪkə] *n.* Антаркти́да.

ante ['æntɪ] *n.* (*stake*) стáвка; **raise the ~** пов|ышáть, -ы́сить стáвку.

antecedent [,æntɪ'si:d(ə)nt] *n.* **1.** (*preceding thg. or circumstance*) предшéствующее, предыду́щее. **2.** (*gram.*) слóво, к котóрому относи́тся местоимéние. **3.** (*pl., the past*) прóшлое; (*past life*) прóшлая жизнь.

adj. предшéствующий, предыду́щий; (*logically previous*) предваря́ющий.

antechamber ['æntɪ,tʃeɪmbə(r)] *n.* прихóжая, перéдняя, вестибю́ль (*m.*).

antedate [,æntɪ'deɪt] *v.t.* **1.** (*put earlier date on*) пом|ечáть, -éтить зáдним числóм. **2.** (*precede*) предшéствовать (*impf.*) +*d.*

antediluvian [,æntɪdɪ'lu:vɪən, -'lju:vɪən] *adj.* (*lit., fig.*) допотóпный.

antelope ['æntɪ,ləʊp] *n.* антилóпа.

antenatal [,æntɪ'neɪt(ə)l] *adj.* утрóбный; дородовóй; ~ **clinic** жéнская консультáция.

antenna [æn'tenə] *n.* (*radio*) антéнна; (*of insect*) щу́пальце, у́сик.

antenuptial [,æntɪ'nʌpʃ(ə)l] *adj.* добрáчный.

antepenultimate [,æntɪpɪ'nʌltɪmət] *adj.* трéтий с концá.

anterior [æn'tɪərɪə(r)] *adj.* (*of place*) перéдний; (*of time*) предшéствующий.

ante-room ['æntɪ,ru:m, -,rʊm] *n.* перéдняя, прихóжая.

anthem ['ænθəm] *n.* песнопéние, хорáл; **national ~** госудáрственный гимн.

anther ['ænθə(r)] *n.* пы́льник.

anthologist [æn'θɒlədʒɪst] *n.* состави́тель (*m.*) антолóгии.

anthology [æn'θɒlədʒɪ] *n.* антолóгия.

anthracite ['ænθrə,saɪt] *n.* антраци́т.

anthrax ['ænθræks] *n.* сиби́рская я́зва.

anthropocentric [,ænθrəpəʊ'sentrɪk] *adj.* антропоцентри́ческий.

anthropoid ['ænθrə,pɔɪd] *n.* антропóид.

adj. человекообрáзный, антропóидный.

anthropological [,ænθrəpə'lɒdʒɪk(ə)l] *adj.* антропологи́ческий.

anthropologist [,ænθrə'pɒlədʒɪst] *n.* (*biological*) антропóлог; **social ~** этнóграф.

anthropology [,ænθrə'pɒlədʒɪ] *n.* (*biological*) антроплóгия; **social ~** этногрáфия.

anthropomorphic [,ænθrəpə'mɔ:fɪk] *adj.* антропоморфи́ческий.

anthropomorphism [,ænθrəpə'mɔ:fɪz(ə)m] *n.* антропоморфи́зм.

anti- ['æntɪ] *pref.* анти..., противо...

anti-aircraft [,æntɪ'eəkrɑ:ft] *adj.* зени́тный, противовозду́шный; ~ **artillery** зени́тная артиллéрия; ~ **defence** противовозду́шная оборóна (*abbr.* ПВО).

antibiotic [,æntɪbaɪ'ɒtɪk] *n.* антибиóтик.

adj. антибиоти́ческий.

antibody ['æntɪ,bɒdɪ] *n.* антитéло.

Antichrist ['æntɪ,kraɪst] *n.* анти́христ.

antichristian [,æntɪ'krɪstjən, -tɪən] *n.* антихристиáнский.

anticipate [æn'tɪsɪ,peɪt] *v.t.* **1.** (*do, use in advance*) дéлать, с- рáньше срóка; испóльзовать (*impf., pf.*) рáньше врéмени; ~ **payment** уплá|чивать, -ти́ть рáньше срóка; ~ **marriage** сожи́тельствовать (*impf.*) до свáдьбы. **2.** (*accelerate*) уск|оря́ть, -óрить. **3.** (*precede*) опере|жáть, -ди́ть. **4.** (*foresee*) предви́деть (*impf.*); предчу́вствовать (*impf.*); (*expect*) ожидáть (*impf.*); (*with pleasure*) предвку|шáть, -си́ть (*impf.*). **5.** (*forestall*) предвосх|ищáть, -и́тить; предупре|ждáть, -ди́ть; **he ~d my wishes** он предупреди́л мои́ желáния; **the general ~d the enemy's attack** генерáл предупреди́л неприя́тельское наступлéние.

anticipation [æn,tɪsɪ'peɪʃ(ə)n] *n.* **1.** (*looking forward to*) ожидáние; **in ~ of your early reply** в ожидáнии вáшего скóрого отвéта; **thanking you in ~** (*as formula in letter*) зарáнее благодáрный. **2.** (*foreseeing*) предви́дение, предвосхищéние; **in ~ of a cold winter** в предви́дении холóдной зимы́; ~ **of events** предвосхищéние собы́тий. **3.** (*foretasting*) предвкушéние; **half the pleasure lies in the ~** предвкушéние — э́то ужé полови́на удовóльствия.

anticipatory [æn'tɪsɪ,peɪtərɪ] *adj.* предвари́тельный, преждеврéменный.

anticlerical [,æntɪ'klerɪk(ə)l] *adj.* антиклерикáльный.

anticlericalism [,æntɪ'klerɪk(ə)lɪz(ə)m] *n.* антиклерикали́зм.

anticlimactic [,æntɪklaɪ'mæktɪk] *adj.* не опрáвдывающий ожидáний.

anticlimax [,æntɪ'klaɪmæks] *n.* (рéзкий) спад (интерéса *и т.п.*); банáльная развя́зка; разочаровáние.

anticlockwise [,æntɪ'klɒkwaɪz] *adj. & adv.* прóтив часовóй стрéлки.

anti-Communist [,æntɪ'kɒmjʊnɪst] *n.* проти́вник коммуни́зма.

adj. антикоммунисти́ческий.

antics ['æntɪks] *n. pl.* (*physical*) кривля́нье, ужи́мки (*f. pl.*); (*behaviour*) продéлки (*f. pl.*), прокáзы (*f. pl.*).

anticyclone [,æntɪ'saɪkləʊn] *n.* антициклóн.

anti-dazzle [,æntɪ'dæz(ə)l] *adj.*: ~ **spectacles, glasses** защи́тные очки́.

antidepressant [,æntɪdɪ'pres(ə)nt] *n.* антидепрессáнт.

antidote ['æntɪ,dəʊt] *n.* противоя́дие; (*fig.*): **the government sought an ~ to inflation** прави́тельство пытáлось борóться с инфля́цией.

antifreeze ['æntɪ,fri:z] *n.* антифри́з.

anti-gas [,æntɪ'gæs] *adj.* противохими́ческий.

anti-hero ['æntɪ,hɪərəʊ] *n.* антигерóй.

antiknock ['æntɪ,nɒk] *n.* антидетонáтор.

anti-litter [,æntɪ'lɪtə(r)] *adj.*: ~ **campaign** кампáния прóтив заму́соривания (гóрода).

Antilles [æn'tɪli:z] *n.*: **the ~** Анти́льские островá (*m. pl.*).

antilogarithm [,æntɪ'lɒgə,rɪð(ə)m] *n.* антилогари́фм.

antimacassar [,æntɪmə'kæsə(r)] *n.* наки́дка, салфéточка.

anti-missile [,æntɪ'mɪsaɪl] *adj.* противоракéтный; ~ **missile** противоракéтный снаря́д, противоракéта.

antimony ['æntɪmənɪ] *n.* сурьма́; (*attr.*) сурьмя́ный.
antinomy [æn'tɪnəmɪ] *n.* антино́мия, противоре́чие.
antipathetic [ˌæntɪpə'θetɪk] *adj.* антипати́чный.
antipathy [æn'tɪpəθɪ] *n.* антипа́тия; **have, feel an ~ to, against, for** пита́ть (*impf.*) антипа́тию к+*d.*
anti-personnel [ˌæntɪˌpɜːsə'nel] *adj.* противопехо́тный; **~ weapon** ору́жие для пораже́ния ли́чного соста́ва; **~** (*fragmentation*) **bomb** оско́лочная бо́мба.
antiperspirant [ˌæntɪ'pɜːspɪrənt] *n.* антиперспира́нт, сре́дство от поте́ния.
antiphon ['æntɪf(ə)n] *n.* антифо́н.
antiphonal [æn'tɪfən(ə)l] *adj.* антифо́нный.
antipodean [æn'tɪpə'diːən] *adj.* (*geog.*) относя́щийся к антипо́дам; (*fig., opposite*) диаметра́льно противополо́жный.
antipodes [æn'tɪpəˌdiːz] *n.* антипо́ды (*m. pl.*).
antipope ['æntɪˌpəʊp] *n.* антипа́па (*m.*).
antipyretic [ˌæntɪpaɪ'retɪk] *n.* жаропонижа́ющее сре́дство.
adj. жаропонижа́ющий.
antipyrin [ˌæntɪ'paɪrɪn] *n.* антипири́н.
antiquarian [ˌæntɪ'kweərɪən] *n.* антиква́р, антиква́рий.
adj. антиква́рный.
antiquary ['æntɪkwərɪ] *n.* антиква́р, антиква́рий.
antiquated ['æntɪˌkweɪtɪd] *adj.* (*obsolete*) устаре́лый; (*old-fashioned*) старомо́дный.
antique [æn'tiːk] *n.* антиква́рная вещь; **the ~** (*art*) анти́чное иску́сство; **~ shop** антиква́рный магази́н.
adj. (*ancient*) дре́вний, стари́нный; (*pert. to ancient, esp. classical times*) анти́чный; (*old-fashioned*) старомо́дный; **~ type** анти́ква.
antiquit|y [æn'tɪkwɪtɪ] *n.* (*great age*) дре́вность; (*olden times*) дре́вность, глубо́кая/седа́я старина́; (*classical times*) анти́чность; (*pl., ancient objects*) рели́квии (*f. pl.*); **Greek ~ies** древнегре́ческие нахо́дки/рели́квии (*f. pl.*).
antirrhinum [ˌæntɪ'raɪnəm] *n.* льви́ный зев.
antiscorbutic [ˌæntɪskɔː'bjuːtɪk] *adj.* противоцинго́тный.
anti-Semite [ˌæntɪ'siːmaɪt] *n.* антисеми́т (*fem.* -ка), юдофо́б (*fem.* -ка).
anti-Semitic [ˌæntɪsɪ'mɪtɪk] *adj.* антисеми́тский, юдофо́бский.
anti-Semitism [ˌæntɪ'semɪˌtɪz(ə)m] *n.* антисемити́зм, юдофо́бство.
antisepsis [ˌæntɪ'sepsɪs] *n.* антисе́птика.
antiseptic [ˌæntɪ'septɪk] *n.* антисепти́ческое сре́дство.
adj. антисепти́ческий.
anti-skid [ˌæntɪ'skɪd] *adj.* нескользя́щий; препя́тствующий скольже́нию.
anti-social [ˌæntɪ'səʊʃ(ə)l] *adj.* антиобще́ственный.
anti-Soviet [ˌæntɪ'səʊvɪət] *adj.* антисове́тский; **~ propagandist** антисове́тчик; **~ propaganda** антисове́тчина.
antistrophe [æn'tɪstrəfɪ] *n.* антистрофа́.
anti-submarine [ˌæntɪsʌbmə'riːn] *adj.* противоло́дочный; **~ bomb** глуби́нная бо́мба.
anti-tank [ˌæntɪ'tæŋk] *adj.* противота́нковый.
anti-tetanus [ˌæntɪ'tetənəs] *adj.*: **~ injection** противостолбня́чный уко́л.
anti-theft [ˌæntɪ'θeft] *adj.*: **~ device** (*on car*) противоуго́нное устро́йство.
antithesis [æn'tɪθɪsɪs] *n.* (*contrast of opposite ideas*) антите́за; противопоставле́ние; (*contrast*) контра́ст; (*opposite*) противополо́жность; **he is the ~ of his brother** он по́лная противоположность своему́ бра́ту.
antithetic(al) [ˌæntɪ'θetɪk(ə)l] *adj.* антитети́ческий; пря́мо противополо́жный.
antitoxin [ˌæntɪ'tɒksɪn] *n.* антитокси́н.
anti-trade [ˌæntɪ'treɪd, 'æntɪ-] *n.* (*meteor.*) антипасса́т.
anti-typhoid [ˌæntɪ'taɪfɔɪd] *adj.* противотифо́зный.
anti-vivisectionist [ˌæntɪˌvɪvɪ'sekʃəˌnɪst] *n.* проти́вник вивисе́кции.
antler ['æntlə(r)] *n.* оле́ний рог.
antonym ['æntənɪm] *n.* анто́ним.
antrum ['æntrəm] *n.* по́лость.
Antwerp ['æntwɜːp] *n.* Антве́рпен.
anus ['eɪnəs] *n.* за́дний прохо́д, а́нус.
anvil ['ænvɪl] *n.* накова́льня.
anxiety [æŋ'zaɪətɪ] *n.* **1.** (*uneasiness*) беспоко́йство; (*alarm*) трево́га; **cause ~ to** трево́жить, вс-; **relieve s.o.'s ~** рассе́|ивать, -ять чью-н. трево́гу; **be full of ~** волнова́ться (*impf.*), нервнича́ть (*impf.*); **feel ~ for, over** беспоко́иться (*impf.*) о+*p.*; трево́житься (*impf.*) о+*p.* **2.** (*desire; keenness*) жела́ние/стремле́ние +*inf.* **3.** (*pl., cares, worries*) забо́ты (*f. pl.*).
anxious ['æŋkʃəs] *adj.* **1.** (*worried, uneasy*) озабо́ченный; беспоко́ящийся; волну́ющийся; **be ~ about, for, over** беспоко́иться (*impf.*) о+*p.*; трево́житься (*impf.*) о+*p.*; **I am ~ for his safety** я беспоко́юсь, как бы с ним чего́ не случи́лось. **2.** (*causing anxiety*) трево́жный, беспоко́йный; **he gave me some ~ moments** он доста́вил мне не́сколько трево́жных мину́т. **3.** (*keen, desirous*): **I am ~ to see him** мне о́чень хо́чется его́ ви́деть.
any ['enɪ] *pron.* **1.** (*in interrog. or conditional sentences*) кто́-нибудь; что́-нибудь; **if ~ of them should see him** е́сли его́ кто́-нибудь из них уви́дит. **2.** (*in neg. sentences*) никто́; ничто́; ни оди́н; **I don't like ~ of these actors** мне не нра́вится ни оди́н из э́тих арти́стов; **he never spoke to ~ of our friends** он не говори́л ни с кем из на́ших друзе́й; **I looked for the books but couldn't find ~** я иска́л кни́ги, но не нашёл ни одно́й; **neither on that day nor on ~ of the following** ни в тот день, ни в оди́н из после́дующих; **I offered him food but he didn't want ~** я предложи́л ему́ пое́сть, но он ничего́ не хоте́л. **3.** (*in affirmative sentences*) любо́й; **take ~ of these books** возьми́те люб́ую/любы́е из э́тих книг. **4.: he has little money, if ~** у него де́нег ма́ло, а то и во́все нет.
adj. **1.** (*in interrog. or conditional sentences*) *untranslated*: **have you ~ children?** у вас есть де́ти?; **have you ~ matches?** (*request*) нет ли у вас спи́чек?; **were there ~ Russians there?** бы́ли там ру́сские?; **is there ~ news?** есть каки́е-нибудь но́вости?; (*no matter what*) любо́й, како́й уго́дно. **2.** (*in neg. sentences*): **we haven't ~ milk** у нас нет молока́; **haven't you ~ cigarettes?** ра́зве у вас нет сигаре́т?; (*not ~ at all, not a single*) никако́й, ни оди́н; **there wasn't ~ hope** никако́й наде́жды не́ было; **neither in this shop, nor in ~ other** ни в э́том магази́не, ни в како́м друго́м; **there isn't ~ man who would ...** нет тако́го челове́ка, кото́рый бы...; (*with* **hardly**, *vv. of prevention etc.*): **there is hardly ~ doubt** нет почти́ никако́го сомне́ния; **without ~ doubt** без вся́кого сомне́ния; **he tried to prevent ~ loss** он стара́лся предотврати́ть каки́е бы то ни́ было поте́ри; **they stopped us from scoring ~ goals** они́ не да́ли нам заби́ть ни одного́ гола́. **3.** (*no matter which*) любо́й; **at ~ time** в любо́е вре́мя; **at ~ hour of the day** в любо́е вре́мя дня; **~ excuse will do** любо́й предло́г сгоди́тся; (*every*) вся́кий; **in ~ case** во вся́ком слу́чае; **~ father would do the same** вся́кий оте́ц сде́лал бы то же са́мое; **~ student knows this** э́то зна́ет ка́ждый/любо́й студе́нт; **~ amount** *see* **amount**; **~ man, ~ person = ~body, ~one**
adv. **1.** (*in interrog. or conditional sentences*) *untranslated or* ско́лько-нибудь; **do you want ~ more tea?** хоти́те ещё ча́ю?; **will he be ~ better for it?** ра́зве от э́того ему́ бу́дет лу́чше?; **if you stay here ~ longer** е́сли вы здесь ещё хоть немно́го заде́ржитесь. **2.** (*in neg. sentences*) *untranslated or* нисколько; ничу́ть; отню́дь; **I can't go ~ farther** я не могу́ идти́ да́льше; **he doesn't live here ~ more, longer** он здесь бо́льше не живёт; **I am not ~ better** мне ничу́ть не лу́чше; **he did not get ~ nearer** он ниско́лько не прибли́зился; **they have not behaved ~ too well** они́ вели́ себя́ не сли́шком хорошо́. **3.** (*US, at all*): **it didn't snow ~ yesterday** вчера́ сне́га во́все не́ было; **that didn't help us ~** э́то нам ниско́лько не помогло́.
anybody ['enɪˌbɒdɪ], **anyone** ['enɪˌwʌn] *n. & pron.* **1.** (*in interrog. or conditional sentences*) кто́-нибудь; кто́-либо; кто; **did you meet ~?** вы кого́-нибудь встре́тили?; **if ~ rings, don't answer** е́сли кто позвони́т, не отвеча́йте; **is this ~'s seat?** э́то ме́сто за́нято?; **is ~ hurt?** никто́ не ра́нен? **2.** (*in neg. sentences*) никто́; **I didn't speak to ~** я ни с кем не говори́л. **3.** (*~ at all; no matter who*) вся́кий, ка́ждый; любо́й; **~ will tell you** вся́кий вам ска́жет; **~ who says that is a liar** кто бы э́то ни сказа́л, он лжёц; **ask ~ you meet** спроси́те у пе́рвого встре́чного; **that's ~'s guess** ка́ждый во́лен гада́ть по-сво́ему; **~ but you**

кто уго́дно, то́лько не вы; ~ **else** кто́-нибудь друго́й/ещё; **he speaks better than** ~ он говори́т лу́чше всех; **there was hardly** ~ **there** там почти́ никого́ не́ было; **he loved her more than** ~ он люби́л её бо́льше всех; **he's a scholar if** ~ **is** е́сли кто учёный, так э́то он. **4.** (*pers. of note*) знамени́тый челове́к; ва́жное лицо́; **everyone who was** ~ **was invited** пригласи́ли всех, кто что́-то из себя́ представля́л.

anyhow ['enɪ,haʊ] *adv.* **1.** (*in one manner or another*) так и́ли ина́че; ка́к-нибудь; (*neg.*): **we couldn't get into the building** ~ мы ника́к не могли́ попа́сть в зда́ние. **2.** (*haphazardly; carelessly*) ко́е-как; ка́к-нибудь; **the work was done** ~ рабо́та была́ сде́лана ко́е-как. **3.** (*anyway, in any case*) во вся́ком слу́чае; так или ина́че; (*nevertheless*) всё же; **I shall go** ~ я всё равно́ пойду́.

anyone ['enɪ,wʌn] = **anybody**

anything ['enɪθɪŋ] *n. & pron.* **1.** (*in interrog. or conditional sentences*) что́-нибудь; что́-либо; что; **is there** ~ **I can get for you?** вам что́-нибудь ну́жно? я принесу́; **can I do** ~ **to help?** чем я могу́ помо́чь?; **have you** ~ **to say?** у вас (*or* вам) есть что сказа́ть?; **did you see** ~ **of him in London?** вы ви́делись с ним в Ло́ндоне?; **she asked if** ~ **unpleasant had happened** она́ спроси́ла, не случи́лось ли чего́-нибудь (*coll.* чего́) неприя́тного; **better, if** ~ вро́де бы лу́чше. **2.** (*in neg. sentences*) ничто́; **I haven't** ~ **to say to that** мне не́чего сказа́ть на э́то. **3.** (*everything*) всё; **I'd give** ~ **to see him again** я о́тдал бы всё, что́бы уви́деть его́ опя́ть; **we were left without** ~ мы оста́лись без ничего́/всего́; **more, better than** ~ бо́льше всего́; **I like it better than** ~ я э́то люблю́ бо́льше всего́. **4.** (~ *at all*, ~ *you please*) всё что уго́дно: **I will do** ~ **within reason** я сде́лаю всё в преде́лах разу́много; **it's as simple as** ~ э́то про́ще просто́го. **5.** (*whatever*): **I will do** ~ **you suggest** я сде́лаю всё, что вы ска́жете. **6.:** ~ **but: he is** ~ **but a genius** он совсе́м не ге́ний; **it is** ~ **but** (*far from*) **clear** э́то далеко́ не я́сно. **7.:** **like** ~ да ещё как; **he worked like** ~ он рабо́тал изо всех сил; **it's raining like** ~ идёт дождь, да ещё како́й; льёт как из ведра́.

anyway ['enɪ,weɪ] = **anyhow 3.**

anywhere ['enɪ,weə(r)] *adv.* **1.** (*in interrog. and conditional sentences*) где́-нибудь; где́-либо; (*of motion*) куда́-нибудь; куда́-либо; **is there a chemist's** ~? здесь есть апте́ка?; **have you** ~ **to stay?** у вас есть где останови́ться? **2.** (*in neg. sentences*) нигде́; (*of motion*) никуда́; **we haven't been** ~ **for ages** мы уже́ це́лую ве́чность нигде́ не́ были. **3.** (*in any place at all; everywhere*) где уго́дно; везде́; (по)всю́ду; **it is miles from** ~ э́то у чёрта на кули́чках; **he earns** ~ **from 200 to 300 roubles a month** он зараба́тывает не ме́ньше двухсо́т-трёхсот рубле́й в ме́сяц; **it isn't** ~ **near finished** э́то ещё далеко́ не зако́нчено.

a.o.b. (*abbr. of* ***any other business***) ра́зное.

aorist ['eərɪst] *n.* ао́рист.

adj. (*also* **aoristic**) аористи́ческий.

aorta [eɪ'ɔ:tə] *n.* ао́рта.

apace [ə'peɪs] *adv.* (*arch.*) бы́стро.

apache [ə'pætʃɪ] *n.* (**A**~: *Indian*) апа́ч; (*hooligan*) банди́т.

apanage, appanage ['æpənɪdʒ] *n.* **1.** (*hist.*) уде́л; апана́ж; (*property*) достоя́ние. **2.** (*attribute*) атрибу́т.

apart [ə'pɑ:t] *adv.* **1.** (*on, to one side*) в стороне́; в сто́рону; **he held himself** ~ он держа́лся в стороне́; **a room was set** ~ **for them** им отвели́ отде́льную ко́мнату; **his height set him** ~ он выделя́лся свои́м ро́стом; **joking** ~ шу́тки в сто́рону; **style** ~, **the book has its merits** е́сли оста́вить стиль в стороне́, кни́га не лишена́ досто́инств; ~ **from** (*with the exception of*) за исключе́нием +*g.*; кро́ме+*g.*; (*other than; besides*) кро́ме/поми́мо +*g.* **2.** (*separate(ly); asunder*) отде́льно; **the dish came** ~ **in her hands** таре́лка слома́лась у неё в рука́х; **he keeps business and pleasure quite** ~ он чётко разграни́чивает де́ло и удово́льствие; **they lived** ~ **for 2 years** они́ жи́ли два го́да врозь; **the baby pulled its rattle** ~ ребёнок разлома́л погрему́шку на ча́сти; **the tutor pulled his essay** ~ учи́тель разругал его́ сочине́ние; **they took the machine** ~ они́ разобра́ли маши́ну на ча́сти; **I could not tell them** ~ я не мог их различи́ть/отличи́ть; **with one's feet wide** ~ расста́вив но́ги. **3.** (*distant*): **the houses are a mile** ~ дома́ нахо́дятся в ми́ле друг от дру́га.

apartheid [ə'pɑ:teɪt] *n.* апарте́йд.

apartment [ə'pɑ:tmənt] *n.* **1.** (*room*) ко́мната. **2.:** **the royal** ~**s** короле́вские апартаме́нты (*m. pl.*). **3.** (*US*) кварти́ра; ~ **house** многокварти́рный дом.

apathetic [,æpə'θetɪk] *adj.* апати́чный.

apathy ['æpəθɪ] *n.* апа́тия.

ape [eɪp] *n.* (*lit., fig.*) обезья́на; **the higher** ~**s** человекообра́зные обезья́ны, прима́ты (*m. pl.*); **play the** ~ обезья́нничать (*impf.*); **play the** ~ **to** подража́ть (*impf.*) +*d.*

v.t. **1.** (*imitate*) подража́ть (*impf.*) +*d.* **2.** (*mock*) передра́зн|ивать, -и́ть.

cpds. ~**-house** *n.* обезья́нник; ~**-like** *adj.* обезьяноподо́бный.

Apennines ['æpə,naɪnz] *n.* Аппени́н|ы (*pl., g.* -).

aperient [ə'pɪərɪənt] *n.* слаби́тельное.

adj. слаби́тельный, послабля́ющий.

aperitif [ə,perɪ'ti:f, ə'pe-] *n.* аперити́в.

aperture ['æpə,tjʊə(r)] *n.* отве́рстие; (*slit; crack*) прое́м; щель; (*opt.*) аперту́ра.

apex ['eɪpeks] *n.* (*lit., fig.*) верши́на, верх.

aphaeresis [ə'fɪərɪsɪs] *n.* афере́зис.

aphasia [ə'feɪzɪə] *n.* афа́зия.

aphelion [æp'hi:lɪən, ə'fi:lɪən] *n.* афе́лий.

aphid ['eɪfɪd], **aphis** ['eɪfɪs] *nn.* тля.

aphorism ['æfə,rɪz(ə)m] *n.* афори́зм.

aphoristic [,æfə'rɪstɪk] *adj.* афористи́ческий.

aphrodisiac [,æfrə'dɪzɪ,æk] *n.* сре́дство, уси́ливающее полово́е влече́ние.

adj. уси́ливающий полово́е влече́ние; возбужда́ющий.

Aphrodite [,æfrə'daɪtɪ] *n.* Афроди́та.

apiarist ['eɪpɪərɪst] *n.* пчелово́д.

apiary ['eɪpɪərɪ] *n.* пче́льник, па́сека.

apiculture ['eɪpɪ,kʌltʃə(r)] *n.* пчелово́дство.

apiece [ə'pi:s] *adv.* **1.** (*of thg.*): **I sell books for a rouble** ~ я продаю́ кни́ги по рублю́ (за ка́ждую). **2.** (*of pers.*): **we had £10** ~ у ка́ждого из нас бы́ло по де́сять фу́нтов; у нас бы́ло по де́сять фу́нтов на челове́ка; **he gave them 5 roubles** ~ он дал им по пять рубле́й (ка́ждому); **the dinner cost £3** ~ обе́д сто́ил по три фу́нта с ка́ждого; **they scored two goals** ~ ка́ждый из них заби́л по два го́ла.

apish ['eɪpɪʃ] *adj.* (*in appearance or nature*) обезья́ний; (*in manner; imitative*) обезья́нничающий.

aplenty [ə'plentɪ] *adv.* (*arch.*) в изоби́лии.

aplomb [ə'plɒm] *n.* апло́мб.

apocalypse [ə'pɒkəlɪps] *n.* апока́липсис.

apocalyptic [ə,pɒkə'lɪptɪk] *adj.* апокалипти́ческий.

Apocrypha [ə'pɒkrɪfə] *n.* апо́крифы (*m. pl.*).

apocryphal [ə'pɒkrɪf(ə)l] *adj.* **1.** (*bibl.*) апокрифи́ческий. **2.** (*of doubtful authenticity*) недостове́рный.

apodosis [ə'pɒdəsɪs] *n.* апо́дозис.

apogee ['æpə,dʒi:] *n.* (*lit., fig.*) апоге́й.

apolitical [,eɪpə'lɪtɪk(ə)l] *adj.* аполити́чный.

Apollo [ə'pɒləʊ] *n.* Аполло́н.

apologetic [ə,pɒlə'dʒetɪk] *adj.* **1.** извиня́ющийся; **he was very** ~ он о́чень извиня́лся; **an** ~ **smile** винова́тая улы́бка. **2.** (*tract etc.*) защити́тельный, апологети́ческий.

apologetics [ə,pɒlə'dʒetɪks] *n.* апологе́тика.

apologia [,æpə'ləʊdʒɪə] *n.* (*defence*) аполо́гия; (*justification*) оправда́ние.

apologist [ə'pɒlədʒɪst] *n.* апологе́т, защи́тник.

apologize [ə'pɒlə,dʒaɪz] *v.i.* извин|я́ться, -и́ться (*перед кем за что*).

apologue ['æpə,lɒg] *n.* ба́сня.

apolog|y [ə'pɒlədʒɪ] *n.* **1.** (*expression of regret*) извине́ние; **make, offer an** ~**y to s.o. for sth.** прин|оси́ть, -ести́ извине́ние кому́-н. за что-н.; **please accept my** ~**ies** прими́те мои́ извине́ния; **they sent their** ~**ies** они́ переда́ли свои́ извине́ния; **by way of** ~**y** в ка́честве извине́ния. **2.** (*vindication*) оправда́ние. **3.** (*poor substitute*): **this** ~**y for a dinner** э́тот, с позволе́ния сказа́ть, обе́д; э́тот го́ре-обе́д.

apo(ph)thegm ['æpə,θem, 'æpəf,θem] *n.* апофтéгма.

apoplectic [,æpə'plektɪk] *adj.* (*pert. to apoplexy*): **an ~ fit** апоплекси́ческий удáр; (*irascible*) раздражи́тельный, нервóзный.

apoplexy ['æpə,pleksɪ] *n.* апоплéксия; (*stroke*) удáр.

apostasy [ə'pɒstəsɪ] *n.* (*abandonment or loss of faith, principles etc.*) отстýпничество, апостáзия; (*desertion of cause or party*) ренегáтство; (*betrayal*) измéна.

apostate [ə'pɒsteɪt] *n.* отстýпник; ренегáт.
adj. отстýпнический.

apostatize [ə'pɒstə,taɪz] *v.i.* отступ|áться, -и́ться (*от чего*).

a posteriori [,eɪ pɒ,sterɪ'ɔːraɪ] *adj.* апостериóрный; оснóванный на óпыте.
adv. апостериóри; по óпыту.

apostle [ə'pɒs(ə)l] *n.* **1.** (*bibl.*) апóстол; **Acts of the A~s** деяния апóстолов; **A~s' Creed** апóстольский си́мвол. **2.** (*fig.*) побóрник, апóстол.

apostolate [ə'pɒstələt] *n.* апóстольство.

apostolic [,æpə'stɒlɪk] *adj.*: **~ succession** апóстольское наслéдование; **A~ See** пáпский престóл.

apostrophe [ə'pɒstrəfɪ] *n.* (*rhetoric*) апострóфа; (*gram.*) апострóф.

apostrophize [ə'pɒstrəfaɪz] *v.t.* обра|щáться, -ти́ться к+*d.*

apothecary [ə'pɒθəkərɪ] *n.* (*arch.*) аптéкарь (*m.*); **~'s weight** аптéкарский вес.

apothegm ['æpə,θem, 'æpəf,θem] = **apo(ph)thegm**

apotheosis [ə,pɒθɪ'əʊsɪs] *n.* (*lit., fig.*) апофеóз; прославлéние; обожествлéние.

appal [ə'pɔːl] *v.t.* ужас|áть, -нýть; устраш|áть, -и́ть; **we were ~led at the sight** мы ужаснýлись (*or* пришли́ в ýжас) при ви́де э́того; **I was ~led at the cost** ценá меня́ ужаснýла.

Appalachians [,æpə'leɪtʃɪənz] *n.* Аппалáч|и (*pl., g.* -ей).

appalling [ə'pɔːlɪŋ] *adj.* ужáсный, жýткий.

appanage ['æpənɪdʒ] = **apanage**

apparatus [,æpə'reɪtəs, 'æp-] *n.* **1.** (*instrument; appliance*) прибóр, инструмéнт. **2.** (*in laboratory*) аппаратýра; оборýдование. **3.** (*gymnastic*) снаря́ды (*m. pl.*). **4.** (*physiol.*) óрганы (*m. pl.*); **digestive ~** óрганы пищеварéния. **5.** (*set of institutions*) аппарáт; **~ of government** прави́тельственный аппарáт. **6.: critical ~** спрáвочный крити́ческий материáл.

apparel [ə'pær(ə)l] *n.* одея́ние, наря́д, облачéние.
v.t. наря|жáть, -ди́ть; облач|áть, -и́ть; **~led in white** облачённый в бéлое.

apparent [ə'pærənt] *adj.* **1.** (*visible*) ви́димый. **2.** (*plain, obvious*) очеви́дный; я́вный; **heir ~** закóнный/прямóй наслéдник; **be, become ~** обнарýжи|ваться, -ться; выявля́ться, вы́явиться. **3.** (*seeming*) кáжущийся, мни́мый.

apparently [ə'pærəntlɪ] *adv.* **1.** (*clearly*) очеви́дно, я́вно. **2.** (*opp.* really) по (внéшнему) ви́ду. **3.** (*seemingly*) по-ви́димому; (как) бýдто; **~ he's the local doctor** он как бýдто здéшний врач; **~ he was here yesterday** похóже, что он был здесь вчерá.

apparition [,æpə'rɪʃ(ə)n] *n.* **1.** (*manifestation, esp. of ghost*) (по)явлéние. **2.** (*ghost*) привидéние, видéние, при́зрак.

appeal [ə'piːl] *n.* **1.** (*earnest request, plea*) обращéние (с прóсьбой); (*official*) воззвáние; (*call*) призы́в; **an ~ to public opinion** обращéние к общéственному мнéнию; **an ~ on behalf of the Red Cross** обращéние/призы́в от и́мени Крáсного Крестá; **an ~ for sympathy** прóсьба отнести́сь сочýвственно; **an ~ for silence** призы́в к тишинé; **he made an ~ for justice** он призвáл к справедли́вости; (*supplication*) мольбá; **with a look of ~ on her face** с умоля́ющим выражéнием лицá. **2.** (*reference to higher authority*) апелля́ция, обжáлование; **court of ~** апелляциóнный суд; **supreme court of ~** кассациóнный суд; **the judge allowed the ~ which he had lodged** судья́ удовлетвори́л пóданную им апелля́цию; **an ~ to the referee** обращéние к судьé. **3.** (*attraction*) привлекáтельность; **this life has little ~ for me** э́та жизнь меня́ мáло привлекáет.
v.i. **1.** (*make earnest request*) обра|щáться, -ти́ться с прóсьбой; **she ~ed to him for mercy** онá моли́ла егó о милосéрдии; **I ~ to you to support them** я призывáю вас поддержáть их. **2.** (*resort*): **~ to arms** приб|егáть, -éгнуть к орýжию; **~ to history/experience** ссылáться, сослáться на истóрию/óпыт. **3.** (*leg.*) апелли́ровать (*impf., pf.*); под|авáть, -áть апелля́цию; обжáловать (*pf.*) приговóр. **4.: ~ to** (*attract*) привлекáть (*impf.*); нрáвиться (*impf.*) +*d.*; импони́ровать (*impf.*) +*d.*; **his courage ~ed to her** ей импони́ровала егó хрáбрость.

appealing [ə'piːlɪŋ] *adj.* (*imploring*) умоля́ющий; (*attractive*) привлекáтельный.

appear [ə'pɪə(r)] *v.i.* **1.** (*become visible*) покáз|ываться, áться; появ|ля́ться, -и́ться; (*of qualities etc.*) проявля́ться, -и́ться. **2.** (*present o.s.*) выступáть, вы́ступить; **~ in court** яв|ля́ться, -и́ться в суд; предст|авáть, -áть пéред судóм; **~ for the claimant/defendant** выступáть (*impf.*) в кáчестве адвокáта истцá/ответчика; **I don't want to ~ in this affair** я не хочý быть замéшанным в э́том дéле; (*of actor*) игрáть (*impf.*) на сцéне; снимáться (*impf.*) в кинó; (*make an entrance on stage*) выходи́ть, вы́йти на сцéну; (*of book*) выходи́ть, вы́йти (в свет); издавáться (*impf.*); быть и́зданным. **3.** (*seem*) казáться, по-; (*follow as inference*) слéдовать (*impf.*), вытекáть (*impf.*); (*be manifest*) я́вствовать (*impf.*); **it ~s strange to me** мне э́то кáжется стрáнным; **strange as it may ~** как бы стрáнно э́то ни показáлось; **he ~s to have left** он, кáжется, уéхал; **it ~s you are right** выхóдит, что вы прáвы; **if you are angry, don't let it ~ (so)** éсли вы и серди́ты, то не покáзывайте ви́ду. **4.** (*turn out*) окáз|ываться, -áться; **if it ~s that this is so** éсли окáжется, что э́то так; **it ~s his wife is a Swede** окáзывается, егó женá швéдка.

appearance [ə'pɪərəns] *n.* **1.** (*act of appearing*) появлéние; (*in public*) выступлéние; **make (*or* put in) an ~** покáз|ываться, -áться; появ|ля́ться, -и́ться; **his ~ as Hamlet** егó выступлéние в рóли Гáмлета; **make one's first ~** дебюти́ровать (*impf., pf.*); впервы́е выступáть, вы́ступить; **~ in court** я́вка в суд; (*of a book*) опубликовáние; вы́ход в свет; появлéние. **2.** (*phenomenon*) явлéние. **3.** (*look, aspect*) вид; óблик; нарýжность; внéшность; **a pleasing ~** прия́тный вид; **~s are deceptive** нарýжность обмáнчива; **the ~ of the streets** óблик ýлиц; **judge by ~(s)** суди́ть (*impf.*) по внéшнему ви́ду; **in ~** на вид; по ви́ду; **to, by all ~s** по всем при́знакам; сýдя по всемý. **4.** (*semblance*) вид, ви́димость; **keep up ~s** соблюдáть (*impf.*) ви́димость/прили́чия (*nt. pl.*); **keep up the ~ of victors** держáться (*impf.*) с ви́дом победи́теля; **for ~'s sake** для ви́димости; напокáз.

appease [ə'piːz] *v.t.* (*pacify; quieten*) успок|áивать, -óить; (*pol., buy off*) умиротвор|я́ть, -и́ть; (*appetites, passions, demands*) утол|я́ть, -и́ть.

appeasement [ə'piːzmənt] *n.* **1.** успокоéние; (*esp. pol.*) умиротворéние. **2.** (*of hunger, desire etc.*) утолéние.

appeaser [ə'piːzə(r)] *n.* умиротвори́тель (*m.*); успокóитель (*m.*).

appellant [ə'pelənt] *n.* апелля́нт.

appellate [ə'pelət] *adj.* апелляциóнный.

appellati|on [,æpə'leɪʃ(ə)n], **-ve** [ə'pelətɪv] *nn.* назвáние.

append [ə'pend] *v.t.* **1.** (*join*) присоедин|я́ть, -и́ть; (*fasten*) прикреп|ля́ть, -и́ть; **a label was ~ed to the parcel** к посы́лке был прикреплён ярлы́к; (*hang on*) подвé|шивать, -сить. **2.** (*add, in writing etc.*) прил|агáть, -ожи́ть; приб|авля́ть, -áвить; **he ~d a seal to the document** он приложи́л печáть к докумéнту; **notes ~ed to the chapter** примечáния к главé; **they wish to ~ a clause to the treaty** они́ хотя́т добáвить статью́ к договóру.

appendage [ə'pendɪdʒ] *n.* (*lit.*) придáток; (*fig.*) придáток, привéсок.

appendectomy [,æpen'dektəmɪ] *n.* оперáция аппендици́та.

appendicitis [ə,pendɪ'saɪtɪs] *n.* аппендици́т.

appendix [ə'pendɪks] *n.* **1.** (*anat.*) аппéндикс, червеобрáзный отрóсток. **2.** (*addition*) добавлéние; (*of a book, document etc.*) приложéние.

apperception [,æpə'sepʃ(ə)n] *n.* апперцéпция; самосознáние.

appertain [,æpə'teɪn] *v.i.* (*belong*) принадлежáть (*impf.*); (*relate*) относи́ться (*impf.*); **the chapters ~ing to his childhood** глáвы, относя́щиеся к егó дéтству; (*be appropriate*) соотве́тствовать (*impf.*); **the duties ~ing to his office** обя́занности, соотве́тствующие его́ до́лжности.

appetite ['æpɪˌtaɪt] *n.* **1.** (*for food*) аппети́т; **fresh air gives one an ~** све́жий во́здух возбужда́ет аппети́т; **you will spoil your ~** вы испо́ртите себе́ аппети́т; **I have lost my ~** у меня́ пропа́л аппети́т. **2.** (*natural desire*) потре́бность; **sexual ~** полово́е влече́ние; (*thirst*) жа́жда; **~ for revenge** жа́жда ме́сти; (*inclination*) скло́нность (к+*d.*); **he had no ~ for the task** у него́ се́рдце не лежа́ло к э́той рабо́те.

appetizer ['æpɪˌtaɪzə(r)] *n.* (*aperitif*) аперити́в; (*hors d'oeuvre*) заку́ска.

appetizing ['æpɪˌtaɪzɪŋ] *adj.* аппети́тный; (*attractive*) привлека́тельный.

applaud [ə'plɔ:d] *v.t.* (*also v.i., clap*) аплоди́ровать (*impf.*) +*d.*; (*approve*) од|обря́ть, -о́брить; выража́ть, вы́разить одобре́ние +*d*.

applause [ə'plɔ:z] *n.* аплодисме́нты (*m. pl.*); рукоплеска́ния (*nt. pl.*); **a roar of ~** гром аплодисме́нтов; **loud ~** бу́рные аплодисме́нты; (*fig., approval*): **he won the ~ of all** он завоева́л всео́бщее одобре́ние.

apple ['æp(ə)l] *n.* я́блоко; **~ of discord** я́блоко раздо́ра; **she was the ~ of her father's eye** оте́ц души́ в ней не ча́ял.

cpds. **~-blossom** *n.* я́блоневый цвет; **~-cart** *n.*: **upset the ~-cart** (*fig.*) спу́тать (*pf.*) ка́рты; **~-core** *n.* сердцеви́на я́блока; **~-jack** *n.* (*US*) я́блочная во́дка; **~-juice** *n.* я́блочный сок; **~-orchard** *n.* я́блоневый сад; **~-pie** *n.* я́блочный пиро́г; **in ~-pie order** в по́лном поря́дке; **~-sauce** *n.* (*lit.*) я́блочное пюре́ (*indecl.*); **~-tree** *n.* я́блоня.

appliance [ə'plaɪəns] *n.* **1.** (*act of applying*) примене́ние. **2.** (*instrument*) прибо́р, приспособле́ние; **dental ~** проте́з; **domestic ~** бытово́й прибо́р; **electric ~** электроприбо́р; **medical ~** медици́нский прибо́р; **safety ~** предохрани́тельное устро́йство.

applicable ['æplɪkəb(ə)l, ə'plɪkəb(ə)l] *adj.* примени́мый; (*appropriate*) подходя́щий, соотве́тствующий; **the rule is not ~ to this case** пра́вило неприменимо к э́тому слу́чаю.

applicant ['æplɪkənt] *n.* кандида́т; претенде́нт (*for a situation*: на до́лжность).

application [ˌæplɪ'keɪʃ(ə)n] *n.* **1.** (*applying; putting on to a surface*) прикла́дывание; наложе́ние; **~ of paint** наложе́ние кра́ски; **hot and cold ~s** горя́чие и холо́дные примо́чки (*f. pl.*). **2.** (*employment*) примене́ние; приложе́ние. **3.** (*diligence*) прилежа́ние; (*concentration*) сосредото́ченность. **4.** (*request*) заявле́ние; проше́ние; **~ form** бланк, фо́рма; **~ for payment** тре́бование упла́ты; **~ (for permission) to hold a meeting** зая́вка на проведе́ние собра́ния; **prices are sent on ~** расце́нки высыла́ются по тре́бованию; **there were twenty ~s for the job** на э́то ме́сто бы́ло по́дано два́дцать заявле́ний; **make (*or* put in) an ~** под|ава́ть, -а́ть заявле́ние.

applied [ə'plaɪd] *adj.*: **~ sciences** прикладны́е нау́ки.

appliqué [æ'pli:keɪ] *n.* апплика́ция.

appl|y [ə'plaɪ] *v.t.* **1.** (*lay, put on*) при|кла́дывать, -ложи́ть; **the doctor ~ied a plaster to his chest** врач наложи́л ему́ пла́стырь на грудь; **the bandage has been ~ied too tightly** повя́зка сли́шком туга́я; **~y the liniment twice a day** сма́зывать (*impf.*) два́жды в день. **2.** (*bring into action*) прил|ага́ть, -ожи́ть; **he ~ied all his strength** он приложи́л все си́лы; **~y the brakes** тормози́ть, за-. **3.** (*make use of*) примен|я́ть, -и́ть; **he ~ied his knowledge well** он хорошо́ примени́л свои́ зна́ния. **4.: ~y o.s. to** зан|има́ться, -я́ться +*i.*; **it is easy if you ~y your mind to it** э́то легко́, е́сли хороше́нько поду́мать.

v.i.: **~y to** (*concern; relate to*) относи́ться (*impf.*) к+*d.*; (*approach, request*) обра|ща́ться, -ти́ться к+*d.*; **I ~ied to him for permission** я обрати́лся к нему́ за разреше́нием; **have you ~ied for a pass?** вы заказа́ли про́пуск?

appoint [ə'pɔɪnt] *v.t.* **1.** (*fix*) назн|ача́ть, -а́чить; определ|я́ть, -и́ть; **at the ~ed time** в назна́ченное вре́мя. **2.** (*nominate*) назн|ача́ть, -а́чить; **he was ~ed ambassador** он был назна́чен посло́м; **they ~ed him to the post** они́ назна́чили его́ на э́ту до́лжность. **3.** (*equip*): **well ~ed** хорошо́ обору́дованный.

appointee [əˌpɔɪn'ti:] *n.* получи́вший назначе́ние; назна́ченный.

appointment [ə'pɔɪntmənt] *n.* **1.** (*act of appointing*) назначе́ние; **by ~ to Her Majesty the Queen** поставщи́к Её Вели́чества. **2.** (*office*) до́лжность; **permanent ~** шта́тная до́лжность; **hold an ~** состоя́ть (*impf.*) в до́лжности; занима́ть (*impf.*) до́лжность. **3.** (*arrangement to meet*): **I have an ~ with my dentist for 4 o'clock** я запи́сан на приём к зубно́му врачу́ в четы́ре часа́; **they met by ~** их встре́ча была́ зара́нее оговорена́; они встре́тились по договорённости; **she was late for the ~** она́ опозда́ла на свида́ние; **make an ~ to meet s.o.** назна́чить (*pf.*) встре́чу с кем-н.; **he could not keep his ~** он не смог прийти́ на встре́чу. **4.** (*pl., fittings*) обстано́вка; обору́дование.

apportion [ə'pɔ:ʃ(ə)n] *v.t.* распредел|я́ть, -и́ть; раздел|я́ть, -и́ть.

apportionment [ə'pɔ:ʃənmənt] *n.* распределе́ние, разделе́ние.

apposite ['æpəzɪt] *adj.* (*suitable*) подходя́щий; (*appropriate*) соотве́тствующий; (*to the point*) уме́стный; уда́чный.

appositeness ['æpəzɪtnɪs] *n.* уме́стность.

apposition [ˌæpə'zɪʃ(ə)n] *n.* **1.** (*placing side by side*) прикла́дывание. **2.** (*of a seal*) приложе́ние. **3.** (*gram.*) приложе́ние; аппози́ция; **noun in ~** приложе́ние.

appraisal [ə'preɪz(ə)l] *n.* оце́нка.

appraise [ə'preɪz] *v.t.* оце́н|ивать, -и́ть.

appraiser [ə'preɪzə(r)] *n.* оце́нщик, такса́тор.

appreciable [ə'pri:ʃəb(ə)l] *adj.* (*perceptible*) заме́тный; (*considerable*) значи́тельный.

appreciate [ə'pri:ʃɪˌeɪt, -sɪˌeɪt] *v.t.* **1.** (*value*) оц|е́нивать, -ени́ть; (высоко́) цени́ть (*impf.*); **he does not ~ the value of what you are doing** он не це́нит по досто́инству то, что вы де́лаете; **it makes one ~ one's own country** по́сле э́того бо́льше це́нишь свою́ страну́; **we ~ your help** мы це́ним ва́шу по́мощь. **2.** (*understand*) пон|има́ть, -я́ть; (*take into account*) прин|има́ть, -я́ть во внима́ние; **I don't think you ~ my difficulties** вы, ка́жется, не понима́ете мои́х затрудне́ний. **3.** (*enjoy*): **he doesn't ~ French cooking** он не признаёт францу́зскую ку́хню; (*through understanding*): **he has learnt to ~ music** он научи́лся понима́ть и цени́ть му́зыку.

v.i. (*rise in value*) пов|ыша́ться, -ы́ситься; **furniture has ~d in value** це́ны на ме́бель повы́сились.

appreciation [əˌpri:ʃɪ'eɪʃ(ə)n, əˌpri:s-] *n.* **1.** (*estimation, judgement*) оце́нка. **2.** (*critique*) реце́нзия. **3.** (*understanding*) понима́ние, призна́ние досто́инств. **4.** (*rise in value*) повыше́ние в цене́, удорожа́ние; **~ of capital** повыше́ние сто́имости капита́ла. **5.** (*gratitude*) призна́тельность; **in ~ of your kindness** в знак призна́тельности за ва́шу любе́зность.

appreciative [ə'pri:ʃətɪv] *adj.* **1.** (*perceptive of merit*): **an ~ audience** понима́ющая аудито́рия. **2.** (*grateful*) благода́рный, призна́тельный (за+*a*).

apprehend [ˌæprɪ'hend] *v.t.* **1.** (*understand*) пон|има́ть, -я́ть. **2.** (*fear*) опаса́ться (*impf.*) +*g*. **3.** (*foresee, expect*) предчу́вствовать (*impf.*); ожида́ть (*impf.*) +*g*. **4.** (*arrest*) аресто́в|ывать, -а́ть; заде́рж|ивать, -а́ть.

apprehension [ˌæprɪ'henʃ(ə)n] *n.* **1.** понима́ние. **2.** опасе́ние. **3.** предчу́вствие. **4.** аре́ст, задержа́ние.

apprehensive [ˌæprɪ'hensɪv] *adj.* опаса́ющийся, встрево́женный, по́лный трево́ги; предчу́вствующий; **he was ~ of danger** он предчу́вствовал опа́сность; **I am ~ for you** я опаса́юсь за вас.

apprentice [ə'prentɪs] *n.* учени́к, подмасте́рье (*m.*).

v.t. отд|ава́ть, -а́ть в уче́ние (*or* учи́ться) ремеслу́; **he was ~d to a tailor** его́ о́тдали в ученики́ к портно́му.

apprenticeship [ə'prentɪsʃɪp] *n.* учени́чество; (*period*) срок уче́ния; **serve one's ~** про|ходи́ть, -йти́ обуче́ние; (*fig.*) овладе́ть (*pf.*) ремесло́м/мастерство́м.

apprise [ə'praɪz] *v.t.* изве|ща́ть, -сти́ть.

appro ['æprəʊ] *n.* (*coll.*): **on ~** на про́бу.

approach [ə'prəʊtʃ] *n.* **1.** (*drawing near; advance*) приближе́ние; наступле́ние; **at our ~** при на́шем приближе́нии; как/когда́ мы подошли́. **2.** (*fig.*) подхо́д; **his ~ to the subject** его́ подхо́д к предме́ту; **the subject calls for an entirely different ~** вопро́с тре́бует соверше́нно ино́го подхо́да. **3.** (*way, passage*) подхо́д;

the ~ to the river подхóд к рекé; **all the ~es to the palace were blocked by traffic** все пóдступы к дворцý бы́ли запрýжены маши́нами. **4.** (*access*) пóдступ; **the ~es to the town** пóдступы к гóроду; **easy of ~** (*lit., fig.*) (легко)достýпный. **5.** (*fig., overture*) предложéние; **they made unofficial ~es** они́ дéлали неофициáльные авáнсы. **6.** (*approximation*) приближéние; **there was some ~ to the truth in their statements** их заявлéния бы́ли в какóй-то мéре справедли́вы.

v.t. **1.** (*come near to*) прибл|ижáться, -и́зиться к+*d.*; (*come up to — on foot*) под|ходи́ть, -ойти́ к+*d.*; (*come up to — by riding*) подъ|езжáть, -éхать к+*d.*; (*fig.*): **he ~ed the subject in a light-hearted way** он подошёл к вопрóсу несерьёзно/легкомы́сленно; **he is difficult to ~** к немý трýдно подступи́ться. **2.** (*make overtures to*) обра|щáться, -ти́ться к+*d.*; **the beggar ~ed him for money** ни́щий попроси́л у негó дéнег. **3.** (*approximate to*) прибл|ижáться, -и́зиться к+*d.*; **no one can ~ him for style** по сти́лю никтó не мóжет с ним сравни́ться.

v.i. прибл|ижáться, -и́зиться; под|ходи́ть, -ойти́; подъ|езжáть, -éхать.

approachable [ə'prəʊtʃəb(ə)l] *adj.* **1.** (*physically*) достýпный; достижи́мый. **2.** (*fig., of pers.*) достýпный.

approaching [ə'prəʊtʃɪŋ] *adj.* приближáющийся; **the ~ storm** надвигáющаяся бýря.

approbation [ˌæprə'beɪʃ(ə)n] *n.* (*approval*) одобрéние; (*sanction*) сáнкция, апробáция.

approbatory ['æprəˌbeɪtərɪ] *adj.* одобри́тельный.

appropriate[1] [ə'prəʊprɪət] *adj.* соответствующий; **remarks ~ to the occasion** соотвéтствующие слýчаю замечáния; (*suitable*) подходя́щий; **clothing ~ for hot weather** одéжда, подходя́щая для жáркой погóды; (*to the point*) умéстный.

appropriate[2] [ə'prəʊprɪˌeɪt] *v.t.* **1.** (*devote to special purpose*) предназн|ачáть, -áчить; выделя́ть, вы́делить; (*funds*) ассигновáть (*impf., pf.*). **2.** (*take possession of*) присв|áивать, -óить.

appropriation [əˌprəʊprɪ'eɪʃ(ə)n] *n.* **1.** назначéние, выделéние; ассигновáние; **defence ~s** воéнные ассигновáния. **2.** присвоéние.

approval [ə'pruːv(ə)l] *n.* одобрéние; (*confirmation*) утверждéние; (*consent*) соглáсие; (*sanction*) апробáция; **give one's ~ to** од|обря́ть, -óбрить; **meet with ~** получ|áть, -и́ть одобрéние; **submit for ~** предст|авля́ть, -áвить на утверждéние; **on ~** на прóбу.

approv|e [ə'pruːv] *v.t.* од|обря́ть, -óбрить; (*confirm*) утвер|ждáть, -ди́ть; **the report was ~ed** отчёт был утверждён.

v.i. **~e of** од|обря́ть, -óбрить; **an ~ing glance** одобри́тельный взгляд.

approximate[1] [ə'prɒksɪmət] *adj.* приблизи́тельный, приближённый, ориентирóвочный.

approximate[2] [ə'prɒksɪˌmeɪt] *v.t.* **1.** (*bring near*) прибл|ижáть, -и́зить (*что к чему*). **2.** (*come near to*) прибл|ижáться, -и́зиться к+*d.*

v.i.: **~ to** прибл|ижáться, -и́зиться к+*d.*

approximation [əˌprɒksɪ'meɪʃ(ə)n] *n.* приближéние; **this is an ~ to the truth** э́то бли́зко к и́стине.

appurtenance [ə'pɜːtɪnəns] *n.* (*accessory*) принадлéжность; (*appendage*) придáток.

apricot ['eɪprɪˌkɒt] *n.* (*fruit or tree*) абрикóс; **~ jam** абрикóсовый джем.

April ['eɪprɪl, 'eɪpr(ə)l] *n.* апрéль (*m.*); **this ~** в апрéле э́того гóда; **~ fool** первоапрéльский дурачóк; **~ Fool!** с пéрвым апрéля! **~ fool's day** пéрвое апрéля.

adj. апрéльский; **~ shower** внезáпный дождь.

a priori [ˌeɪ praɪ'ɔːraɪ] *adj.* априóрный.

adv. априóри.

apron ['eɪprən] *n.* **1.** (*garment*) перéдник; фáртук. **2.** (*theatr.*) авансцéна. **3.** (*aeron.*) площáдка пéред ангáром.

cpd. **~-strings** *n. pl.*: **he is tied to his mother's ~-strings** он мáменькин сынóк.

apropos ['æprəˌpəʊ, -'pəʊ] *adj. & adv.* (*appropriate*) умéстн|ый, -о; (*timely*) своеврéменн|ый, -о; (*by the way*) кстáти, мéжду прóчим; **~ of** по пóводу +*g.*

apse [æps] *n.* апси́да.

apt [æpt] *adj.* **1.** (*suitable*) подходя́щий; (*apposite*) умéстный, удáчный. **2.** (*intelligent*) спосóбный. **3.**: **~ to** склóнный к+*d.*; **he is ~ to fall asleep** он всё врéмя засыпáет; **~ to break** лóмкий.

apteryx ['æptərɪks] *n.* ки́ви (*m. indecl.*), аптéрикс.

aptitude ['æptɪˌtjuːd] *n.* (*capacity*) спосóбность; **~ for work** работоспосóбность; **~ test** провéрка спосóбностей; квалификациóнный тест; (*propensity*): **~ for** склóнность к+*d.*

aptness [æptnɪs] *n.* спосóбность; склóнность.

aqualung ['ækwəˌlʌŋ] *n.* аквалáнг.

aquamarine [ˌækwəmə'riːn] *n.* (*min.*) аквамари́н; (*colour*) зеленовáто-голубóй цвет.

adj. аквамари́новый; зеленовáто-голубóй.

aquaplane ['ækwəˌpleɪn] *n.* акваплáн.

v.i. катáться (*indet.*) на акваплáне.

aqua regia [ˌækwə 'riːdʒɪə] *n.* цáрская вóдка.

aquarelle [ˌækwə'rel] *n.* акварéль.

aquarellist [ˌækwə'relɪst] *n.* акварели́ст.

aquarist ['ækwərɪst] *n.* аквариуми́ст.

aquarium [ə'kweərɪəm] *n.* аквáриум.

Aquarius [ə'kweərɪəs] *n.* Водолéй.

aquatic [ə'kwætɪk] *adj.* (*of plant or animal*) водянóй; (*of bird*) водоплáвающий; (*of sport*) вóдный.

aquatics [ə'kwætɪks] *n.* вóдный спорт.

aquatint ['ækwətɪnt] *n.* аквати́нта.

aqua vitae [ˌækwə 'viːtaɪ] *n.* спирт, алкогóль (*m.*).

aqueduct ['ækwɪˌdʌkt] *n.* акведýк.

aqueous ['eɪkwɪəs] *adj.* вóдный; водянóй; **~ humour** водяни́стая влáга (глáза).

aquiline ['ækwɪˌlaɪn] *adj.* орли́ный.

aquiver [ə'kwɪfə(r)] *pred. adj.* дрожá; **her hands were ~ with excitement** от волнéния у неё дрожáли рýки.

Arab ['ærəb] *n.* **1.** (*pers.*) арáб (*fem.* -ка); **street a~** беспризóрник. **2.** (*horse*) арáбская лóшадь.

adj. арáбский; **the ~ League** Ли́га арáбских стран.

arabesque [ˌærə'besk] *n.* (*archit., liter., mus.*) арабéск(а).

Arabia [ə'reɪbɪə] *n.* Арáвия.

Arabian [ə'reɪbɪən] *n.* жи́тель Арави́йского полуóстрова.

adj. арави́йский; **~ camel** одногóрбый верблю́д, дромадéр; **the ~ Nights** Ты́сяча и однá ночь.

Arabic ['ærəbɪk] *n.* арáбский язы́к; **in ~** по-арáбски.

adj. арáбский; **a~ numerals** арáбские ци́фры; **gum a~** гуммиарáбик.

Arabist ['ærəbɪst] *n.* араби́ст.

arable ['ærəb(ə)l] *n.* пáхотная земля́.

adj. пáхотный; **~ farming** земледéлие.

arachnid [ə'ræknɪd] *n.* арахни́д, паукообрáзное.

Aramaic [ˌærə'meɪɪk] *n.* арамéйский язы́к.

adj. арамéйский.

arbiter ['ɑːbɪtə(r)] *n.* **1.** (*judge*) арби́тр; **~ of elegance** законодáтель (*m.*) мод. **2.** (*third party*) третéйский судья́; посрéдник. **3.** (*ruler*) власти́тель (*m.*); **he is the ~ of our fate** нáша судьбá в егó рукáх.

arbitrage ['ɑːbɪˌtrɑːʒ, -trɪdʒ] *n.* арбитрáж.

arbitral ['ɑːbɪtr(ə)l] *adj.* арбитрáжный, третéйский.

arbitrament [ɑː'bɪtrəmənt] *n.* (*decision*) (арбитрáжное) решéние; **the ~ of war** решéние конфли́кта путём войны́; (*arbitration*) арбитрáж.

arbitrariness ['ɑːbɪtrərɪnɪs] *n.* произвóл; произвóльность.

arbitrary ['ɑːbɪtrərɪ] *adj.* (*random, capricious*) произвóльный; (*dictatorial*) деспоти́ческий; (*conventional*): **~ symbols** услóвные знáки.

arbitrate ['ɑːbɪˌtreɪt] *v.t.* (*decide*) реш|áть, -и́ть третéйским судóм; (*refer to arbitration*) перед|авáть, -áть в арбитрáж.

v.i. (*act as arbiter*) быть арби́тром; быть третéйским судьёй.

arbitration [ˌɑːbɪ'treɪʃ(ə)n] *n.* арбитрáж; третéйский суд; **refer, submit to ~** перед|авáть, -áть в арбитрáж; (*attr.*) арбитрáжный, третéйский; **~ clause** арбитрáжная оговóрка.

arbitrator ['ɑːbɪˌtreɪtə(r)] *n.* третéйский судья́; арби́тр.

arboreal [ɑː'bɔːrɪəl] *adj.* древéсный.

arboretum [ˌɑːbə'riːtəm] *n.* древéсный питóмник.

arboriculture ['ɑːbərɪˌkʌltʃə(r)] *n.* лесовóдство.

arbour [ˈɑːbə(r)] *n.* бесе́дка.
arbutus [ɑːˈbjuːtəs] *n.* землянй́чное де́рево.
arc [ɑːk] *n.* дуга́.
cpds. **~-lamp** *n.* дугова́я ла́мпа; **~-light** *n.* дугово́й свет; **~-welder** *n.* электросва́рщик; **~-welding** *n.* электродугова́я сва́рка.
arcade [ɑːˈkeɪd] *n.* (*covered passage*) арка́да; (*with shops*) пасса́ж.
Arcadian [ɑːˈkeɪdɪən] *adj.* арка́дский; (*idyllic*) идилли́ческий.
arcana [ɑːˈkeɪnə] *n.* та́йны (*f. pl.*), таи́нственность.
arcane [ɑːˈkeɪn] *adj.* таи́нственный, скры́тый, та́йный.
arch[1] [ɑːtʃ] *n.* (*~way*) а́рка; (*~ed roof*, *vault*) свод; **~es of a bridge** сво́ды моста́; **~ of the foot** свод стопы́; **he suffers from fallen ~es** у него́ плоскосто́пие.
v.t. **1.** (*furnish with ~*) перекр|ыва́ть, -ы́ть сво́дом. **2.** (*form into ~*) прид|ава́ть, -а́ть фо́рму а́рки +*d.*; **the cat ~ed its back** ко́шка вы́гнула спи́ну; **she ~d her eyebrows** она́ подняла́/вски́нула бро́ви.
v.i. (*form an ~*) выгиба́ться, вы́гнуться; из|гиба́ться, -огну́ться.
cpd. **~way** *n.* сво́дчатый прохо́д; прохо́д под а́ркой.
arch[2] [ɑːtʃ] *adj.* лука́вый, игри́вый.
arch-[3] [ɑːtʃ] *comb. form* архи…; гла́вный.
archaeological [ˌɑːkɪəˈlɒdʒɪk(ə)l] *adj.* археологи́ческий.
archaeologist [ˌɑːkɪˈɒlədʒɪst] *n.* архео́лог.
archaeology [ˌɑːkɪˈɒlədʒɪ] *n.* археоло́гия.
archaic [ɑːˈkeɪɪk] *adj.* архаи́ческий, архаи́чный; устаре́вший.
archaism [ˈɑːkeɪˌɪz(ə)m] *n.* архаи́зм.
archangel [ˈɑːkˌeɪndʒ(ə)l] *n.* арха́нгел.
archbishop [ɑːtʃˈbɪʃəp] *n.* архиепи́скоп.
archbishopric [ɑːtʃˈbɪʃəprɪk] *n.* архиепи́скопство, епа́рхия архиепи́скопа.
archdeacon [ɑːtʃˈdiːkən] *n.* архидья́кон.
archdiocese [ɑːtʃˈdaɪəsɪs] = **archbishopric**
archducal [ˈɑːtʃˈdjuːk(ə)l] *adj.* эрцге́рцогский.
archduchess [ɑːtʃˈdʌtʃɪs] *n.* эрцгерцоги́ня.
archduchy [ɑːtʃˈdʌtʃɪ] *n.* эрцге́рцогство.
archduke [ɑːtʃˈdjuːk] *n.* эрцге́рцог.
arched [ɑːtʃd] *adj.* **1.** (*furnished with*, *consisting of*, *arches*) сво́дчатый, а́рочный; **an ~ bridge** а́рочный мост; **an ~ ceiling** сво́дчатый потоло́к. **2.** (*bent*, *curved*) изо́гнутый.
arch-enemy [ɑːtʃˈenəmɪ] *n.* закля́тый враг.
archer [ˈɑːtʃə(r)] *n.* лу́чни|к (*fem.* -ца); стрело́к из лу́ка.
archery [ˈɑːtʃərɪ] *n.* стрельба́ из лу́ка; **~ range** лукодро́м.
archetypal [ˌɑːkɪˈtaɪp(ə)l] *adj.* (*typical*) типи́чный.
archetype [ˈɑːkɪˌtaɪp] *n.* прототи́п.
arch-fiend [ɑːtʃˈfiːnd] *n.* сатана́.
archiepiscopal [ˌɑːkɪɪˈpɪskəp(ə)l] *adj.* архиепи́скопский.
archimandrite [ˌɑːkɪˈmændraɪt] *n.* архимандри́т.
Archimedean [ˌɑːkɪˈmiːdɪən] *adj.*: **~ principle** зако́н Архиме́да.
Archimedes [ˌɑːkɪˈmiːdiːz] *n.* Архиме́д; **~' screw** архиме́дов винт.
archipelago [ˌɑːkɪˈpeləˌgəʊ] *n.* архипела́г.
architect [ˈɑːkɪˌtekt] *n.* архите́ктор; **naval ~** корабе́льный инжене́р, инжене́р-кораблестрои́тель (*m.*); (*fig.*) а́втор, творе́ц, созда́тель.
architectonic [ˌɑːkɪtekˈtɒnɪk] *adj.* архитектони́ческий.
architectonics [ˌɑːkɪtekˈtɒnɪks] *n.* архитекто́ника.
architectural [ˌɑːkɪˈtektʃər(ə)l] *adj.* архитекту́рный; строи́тельный.
architecture [ˈɑːkɪˌtektʃə(r)] *n.* (*science*) архитекту́ра, зо́дчество; (*style*) архитекту́ра; архитекту́рный стиль; (*fig.*, *structure*, *construction*) построе́ние, структу́ра.
architrave [ˈɑːkɪˌtreɪv] *n.* архитра́в.
archival [ɑːˈkaɪv(ə)l] *adj.* архи́вный.
archive [ˈɑːkaɪv] *n.* (*also pl.*) архи́в.
archivist [ˈɑːkɪvɪst] *n.* архива́риус.
archness [ˈɑːtʃnɪs] *n.* лука́вство.
arch-priest [ɑːtʃˈpriːst] *n.* протоиере́й.
arctic [ˈɑːktɪk] *n.*: **the A~** А́рктика.
adj. аркти́ческий; **A~ Circle** Се́верный поля́рный круг; **A~ Ocean** Се́верный Ледови́тый океа́н; **~ region** А́рктика; **~ weather conditions** ≃ креще́нские моро́зы.
Arcturus [ɑːkˈtjʊərəs] *n.* Аркту́р.
ardency [ˈɑːd(ə)nsɪ] *n.* жар, пы́лкость.
ardent [ˈɑːd(ə)nt] *adj.* (*fervent*) горя́чий, пы́лкий; (*passionate*) стра́стный; (*zealous*) ре́вностный.
ardour [ˈɑːdə(r)] *n.* жар, пы́лкость, пыл, рве́ние; **damp s.o.'s ~** ум|еря́ть, -е́рить чей-н. пыл.
arduous [ˈɑːdjuːəs] *adj.* (*difficult*) тру́дный; тя́жкий; (*needing much energy*; *strenuous*; *laborious*) трудоёмкий; **an ~ ascent** тру́дный подъём; **an ~ road** тяжёлая доро́га.
arduousness [ˈɑːdjuːəsnɪs] *n.* тру́дность, трудоёмкость.
area [ˈeərɪə] *n.* **1.** (*measurement*) пло́щадь; **what is the ~ of this triangle?** какова́ пло́щадь э́того треуго́льника?; **a room 12 square metres in ~** ко́мната пло́щадью в 12 $м^2$. **2.** (*defined or designated space*): **the ~ under cultivation** посевна́я пло́щадь; **~ bombing** бомбомета́ние по пло́щади; **landing ~** поса́дочная площа́дка; **training ~** полиго́н; (*expanse*) простра́нство; **vast ~s of forest** огро́мные лесны́е масси́вы/простра́нства; (*portion*) уча́сток; **a small ~ of skin was affected** был поражён небольшо́й уча́сток ко́жи; (*field*): **~ of vision** по́ле зре́ния. **3.** (*region*, *tract*, *zone*) райо́н, край, зо́на; **residential ~** жило́й райо́н; **depressed ~** райо́н экономи́ческой депре́ссии; **wheat-growing ~** пло́щадь под пшени́цей; **sterling ~** сте́рлинговая зо́на; **~** (*regional*) **studies** странове́дение. **4.** (*scope*, *range*) разма́х; (*sphere*) о́бласть, сфе́ра; **in the ~ of research** в сфе́ре иссле́дования; **broad ~s of agreement** соглаше́ние по широ́кому кру́гу вопро́сов. **5.** (*basement courtyard*) вну́тренний двор.
arena [əˈriːnə] *n.* (*lit.*, *fig.*) аре́на; **he entered the ~ of politics** он вступи́л на полити́ческую сце́ну/аре́ну.
arête [æˈret] *n.* о́стрый гре́бень горы́.
argent [ˈɑːdʒ(ə)nt] *adj.* серебри́стый.
argentiferous [ˌɑːdʒənˈtɪfərəs] *adj.* сереброно́сный; содержа́щий серебро́.
Argentina [ˌɑːdʒənˈtɪnə] *n.* (*also* **the Argentine**) Аргенти́на.
Argentin|e[1] [ˈɑːdʒənˌtaɪn, -ˌtiːn], **-ian** [ˌɑːdʒənˈtɪnɪən] *n.* аргенти́н|ец (*fem.* -ка).
adj. аргенти́нский.
argentine[2] [ˈɑːdʒənˌtaɪn, -ˌtiːn] *adj.* (*silvery*) серебри́стый; (*of silver*) сере́бряный.
argillaceous [ˌɑːdʒɪˈleɪʃəs] *adj.* гли́нистый.
argon [ˈɑːgɒn] *n.* арго́н.
Argonaut [ˈɑːgəˌnɔːt] *n.* аргона́вт.
argosy [ˈɑːgəsɪ] *n.* (*hist.*) большо́е торго́вое су́дно; (*poet.*) кора́бль (*m.*).
argot [ˈɑːgəʊ] *n.* арго́ (*indecl.*), жарго́н.
arguable [ˈɑːgjʊəb(ə)l] *adj.* **1.** (*open to argument*) спо́рный. **2.** (*demonstrable by argument*) доказу́емый; **it is ~ that …** допусти́мо, что…; есть основа́ния полага́ть, что…; мо́жно утвержда́ть, что…
argue [ˈɑːgjuː] *v.t.* **1.** (*discuss*, *debate*) обсу|жда́ть, -ди́ть; **let's not ~ the point** дава́йте об э́том не спо́рить. **2.** (*contend*) дока́зывать (*impf.*); **he ~d that the money should be shared** он дока́зывал, что де́ньги сле́дует раздели́ть; **it was ~d that …** утвержда́лось, что… **3.** (*speak in support of*) дока́зывать (*impf.*), отста́ивать (*impf.*); убежда́ть (*impf.*) (*кого в чём*); **he ~d his case eloquently** он красноречи́во отста́ивал свою́ то́чку зре́ния. **4.**: **~ s.o. out of a belief in sth.** разубе|жда́ть, -ди́ть кого́-н. в чём-н.; **~ s.o. out of doing sth.** отгов|а́ривать, -ори́ть кого́-н. от чего́-н.; **~ s.o. into doing sth.** убе|жда́ть, -ди́ть кого́-н. +*inf.* **5.** (*indicate*) дока́зывать (*impf.*); **his action ~s him to be a man of low intellect** его́ посту́пок дока́зывает, что он недалёкий челове́к. **6.**: **he can ~ the hind leg off a donkey** (*coll.*) он заговори́т зу́бы кому́ хоти́те/уго́дно.
v.i. **1.** (*debate*; *disagree*; *quarrel*) спо́рить (*impf.*); препира́ться (*impf.*); (*object*) возража́ть (*impf.*); **get dressed and don't ~!** одева́йся — и никаки́х разгово́ров!; **they ~d over who should drive** они́ спо́рили, кому́ вести́. **2.** (*give reasons*) выступа́ть, вы́ступить (**against:** про́тив+*g.*; *for*, *in favour of*: в по́льзу +*g.*); прив|оди́ть, -ести́ до́воды; вести́ (*impf.*) спор; полемизи́ровать.
with advs.: **~ away: one cannot ~ away the fact that …** невозмо́жно затушева́ть тот факт, что…; **~ out: let's ~ the matter out** дава́йте обсу́дим вопро́с доскона́льно.

arguer [ˈɑːgjʊə(r)] *n.* спо́рщи|к (*fem.* -ца).

argument [ˈɑːgjʊmənt] *n.* **1.** (*reason*) аргуме́нт; до́вод; **advance ~s for** прив|оди́ть, -ести́ до́воды в по́льзу +*g.*; **it's an ~ for staying at home** э́то до́вод в по́льзу того́, что́бы оста́ться до́ма. **2.** (*process of reasoning*) аргумента́ция; **the ~ ran as follows** аргумента́ция была́ такова́. **3.** (*discussion, debate*) спор; **a heated ~ took place** разгоре́лся жа́ркий спор; **he gets the better of me in ~** он побежда́ет меня́ в спо́ре; **who won the ~?** кто победи́л в спо́ре?; **a matter of ~** спо́рный вопро́с; **have an ~ over, about** спо́рить (*impf.*) о+*p*.

argumentation [ˌɑːgjʊmenˈteɪʃ(ə)n] *n.* (*reasoning*) аргумента́ция; (*debate*) спор.

argumentative [ˌɑːgjʊˈmentətɪv] *adj.* лю́бящий спо́рить; спо́рный.

Argus-eyed [ˈɑːgəsˌaɪd] *adj.* (*fig.*) бди́тельный, недре́млющий.

argy-bargy [ˌɑːdʒɪˈbɑːdʒɪ] *n.* (*coll.*) перебра́нка, перепа́лка.

aria [ˈɑːrɪə] *n.* а́рия.

arid [ˈærɪd] *adj.* (*of soil etc.*) сухо́й, пересо́хший; засу́шливый; (*of climate; lit., fig.*) (*dry*) сухо́й; (*barren*) беспло́дный.

aridity [əˈrɪdɪtɪ] *n.* (*lit.*) засу́шливость; (*lit., fig.*) су́хость; беспло́дность.

Aries [ˈeəriːz] *n.* Ове́н.

aright [əˈraɪt] *adv.* пра́вильно.

arise [əˈraɪz] *v.i.* **1.** (*lit., get up; stand up*) вст|ава́ть, -а́ть; (*lit., fig., rise*) восст|ава́ть, -а́ть; (*from the dead*) воскр|еса́ть, -е́снуть. **2.** (*fig., come into being*) возн|ика́ть, -и́кнуть; **if the need should ~** е́сли возни́кнет необходи́мость; **the problem may never ~** пробле́ма мо́жет так и не возни́кнуть; **the question arose** встал вопро́с; **a shout arose from the crowd** из толпы́ разда́лся крик; (*appear*) появ|ля́ться, -и́ться; (*result*) проист|ека́ть, -е́чь; **a misunderstanding may ~ from his statement** его́ слова́ мо́гут дать по́вод к недоразуме́нию.

aristocracy [ˌærɪˈstɒkrəsɪ] *n.* аристокра́тия.

aristocrat [ˈærɪstəˌkræt] *n.* аристокра́т.

aristocratic [ˌærɪstəˈkrætɪk] *adj.* аристократи́ческий.

Aristotelian [ˌærɪstəˈtiːlɪən] *adj.* аристо́телев(ский).

arithmetic [əˈrɪθmətɪk] *n.* арифме́тика.

arithmetical [əˌrɪθˈmetɪk(ə)l] *adj.* арифмети́ческий.

arithmetician [əˌrɪθməˈtɪʃ(ə)n] *n.* матема́тик, специали́ст по арифме́тике.

ark [ɑːk] *n.* ковче́г; **Noah's ~** Но́ев ковче́г; **A~ of the Covenant** ковче́г заве́та.

arm[1] [ɑːm] *n.* **1.** (*of pers.*) рука́; **with a book under his ~** с кни́гой под мы́шкой; **she had a basket on her ~** на руке́ у неё висе́ла корзи́на; **he offered her his ~** он предложи́л ей ру́ку; **within ~'s reach** под руко́й; **he broke his ~** он слома́л себе́ ру́ку; **at ~'s length** (*lit.*) на расстоя́нии вы́тянутой руки́; (*fig.*) на почти́тельном расстоя́нии; **he kept me at ~'s length** он меня́ бли́зко не подпуска́л; **~ in ~** по́д руку; **twist s.o.'s ~** (*lit.*) скру́чивать (*impf.*) (*or* выкру́чивать (*impf.*)) кому́-н. ру́ку; (*fig., coerce*) брать кого́-н. (*impf.*) за го́рло; **chance one's ~** попыта́ться (*pf.*); **with open ~s** (*lit., fig.*) с распростёртыми объя́тиями; **fold one's ~s** сложи́ть (*pf.*) ру́ки; **infant in ~s** младе́нец; **take s.o.'s in one's ~s** заключ|а́ть, -и́ть кого́-н. в объя́тия; **he gathered the books (up) in his ~s** он собра́л кни́ги в оха́пку. **2.** (*of object*): **~ of a garment** рука́в; **~ of a chair** ру́чка кре́сла; **~ of the sea** зали́в; **~ of the river** рука́в реки́; **~ of a lever** плечо́ рычага́; **~ of a balance** коромы́сло весо́в; **~ of a crane** стрела́. **3.** (*fig., authority*): **the secular ~** гражда́нская власть. **4.** (*fig., reach*): **the (long) ~ of the law** (кара́ющая) рука́ зако́на.

cpds. **~band** *n.* нарука́вная повя́зка; **~chair** *n.* кре́сло; **~-hole** *n.* про́йма; **~pit** *n.* подмы́шка; **under one's ~pit** под мы́шкой; **~-rest** *n.* подлоко́тник.

arm[2] [ɑːm] *n.* **1.** (*mil., force*): **air ~** вое́нно-возду́шные си́лы (*f. pl.*). **2.** (*pl., weapons*) ору́жие; **small ~s** стрелко́вое ору́жие; **~s race** го́нка вооруже́ний; **under ~s** под ружьём; **take up ~s** бра́ться, взя́ться за ору́жие; **bear ~s** носи́ть (*impf.*) ору́жие; **lay down one's ~s** (*lit., fig.*) сложи́ть (*pf.*) ору́жие; **by force of ~s** си́лой ору́жия; **passage of ~s** (*lit.*) перестре́лка; (*fig.*) сты́чка; **they were up in ~s** (*lit.*) они́ подняли́сь с ору́жием в рука́х; (*fig.*) они́ взбунтова́лись. **3.** (*her.*) **(coat of) ~s** герб.

v.t. вооруж|а́ть, -и́ть; (*equip*) снаб|жа́ть, -ди́ть; **~ o.s.** (*lit., fig.*) вооруж|а́ться, -и́ться; **~ed forces** вооружённые си́лы; **he was ~ed with an umbrella** он вооружи́лся зо́нтиком; **~ o.s. with patience** набра́ться (*pf.*) терпе́ния.

v.i. вооруж|а́ться, -и́ться.

armada [ɑːˈmɑːdə] *n.* арма́да.

armadillo [ˌɑːməˈdɪləʊ] *n.* армади́лл; броне́но́сец.

Armageddon [ˌɑːməˈged(ə)n] *n.* (*fig.*) реша́ющее сраже́ние; вели́кое побо́ище.

armament [ˈɑːməmənt] *n.* **1.** (*also pl., weapons; military equipment*) вооруже́ние; **~ factory** вое́нный заво́д. **2.** (*armed forces*) вооружённые си́лы (*f. pl.*).

armature [ˈɑːməˌtjʊə(r)] *n.* (*elec.*) я́корь (*m.*), броня́ (ка́беля).

Armenia [ɑːˈmiːnɪə] *n.* Арме́ния.

Armenian [ɑːˈmiːnɪən] *n.* **1.** (*pers.*) арм|яни́н (*fem.* -я́нка). **2.** (*language*) армя́нский язы́к.

adj. армя́нский.

armful [ˈɑːmfʊl] *n.* оха́пка; **he took up an ~ of books** он взял оха́пку книг.

armistice [ˈɑːmɪstɪs] *n.* переми́рие.

armless [ˈɑːmlɪs] *adj.* безру́кий.

armlet [ˈɑːmlɪt] *n.* (*band*) нарука́вная повя́зка; нарука́вник.

armorial [ɑːˈmɔːrɪəl] *adj.* геральди́ческий, ге́рбовый; **~ bearings** герб.

armour [ˈɑːmə(r)] *n.* (*for body*) доспе́хи (*m. pl.*); **he wore (a suit of) ~** он был в доспе́хах; (*fig.*): **his ~ against the world was silence** он отгороди́лся от окружа́ющего ми́ра молча́нием; **the chink in his ~** брешь в окружа́ющей его́ броне́; его́ уязви́мое ме́сто; (*of plant or animal*) па́нцирь (*m.*); (*of vehicle, ship etc.*) броня́; (*coll., armoured vehicles*) бронета́нковые си́лы (*f. pl.*).

v.t. покр|ыва́ть, -ы́ть бронёй; брони́ровать (*impf., pf.*).

cpds. **~-bearer** *n.* оруженосец; **~-clad, ~-plated** *adjs.* брони́рованный; **~-plate** *n.* бронева́я плита́.

armoured [ˈɑːmərd] *adj.* брони́рованный, бронено́сный; **~ car** бронеавтомоби́ль (*m.*), броневи́к; **~ column** бронета́нковая коло́нна; **~ concrete** железобето́н; **~ corps** та́нковый ко́рпус; **~ cruiser** бронено́сный кре́йсер; **~ division** та́нковая диви́зия; **~ glass** арми́рованное стекло́; **~ train** бронепо́езд.

armourer [ˈɑːmərə(r)] *n.* оруже́йный ма́стер; оруже́йник.

armoury [ˈɑːmərɪ] *n.* арсена́л.

army [ˈɑːmɪ] *n.* а́рмия; **he served in the regular ~** он служи́л в регуля́рных частя́х; **join the ~** вступ|а́ть, -и́ть в а́рмию; **~ command** кома́ндование а́рмии; **Salvation A~** А́рмия спасе́ния; (*fig., large number*) а́рмия; мно́жество; (*attr.*) арме́йский; **~ chaplain** арме́йский свяще́нник; **~ contractor** вое́нный поставщи́к; **~ corps** арме́йский ко́рпус; **~ general** генера́л а́рмии; **~ list** спи́сок офице́рского соста́ва.

arnica [ˈɑːnɪkə] *n.* а́рника.

aroma [əˈrəʊmə] *n.* арома́т.

aromatic [ˌærəˈmætɪk] *adj.* арома́тный; благово́нный, аромати́ческий.

around [əˈraʊnd] (*see also* **round**) *adv.* вокру́г; круго́м; **all ~** повсю́ду; **from all ~** отовсю́ду; **for miles ~** на ми́ли вокру́г; **they were standing ~** они́ стоя́ли побли́зости; **hang ~** болта́ться (*impf.*); **he looked ~ for the book** он иска́л кни́гу (повсю́ду); **he stood there and looked ~** (*sc. in all directions*) он осма́тривался; **he's been ~** (*coll.*) он вида́л ви́ды; он челове́к быва́лый; **he travels ~** он мно́го путеше́ствует.

prep. **1.** (*encircling*) вокру́г+*g.*; круго́м+*g.*; **they stood ~ the table** они́ стоя́ли вокру́г стола́; **the path goes ~ the garden** доро́жка огиба́ет сад; **his arm was ~ her waist** он обнима́л её за та́лию; **he took his arm from ~ her waist** он убра́л ру́ку с её та́лии. **2.** (*over*): **he walked ~ the town** он броди́л по го́роду; **he looked ~ the house** он осмотре́л дом. **3.** (*in the vicinity of*) о́коло+*g.* **4.** (*in var. parts of*): **the child played ~ the house** ребёнок игра́л по всему́ до́му; **he stayed ~ the house** он не выходи́л из до́му. **5.** (*approximately*) о́коло+*g.*; приблизи́тельно.

arousal [ə'raʊz(ə)l] *n.* пробужде́ние.

arouse [ə'raʊz] *v.t.* (*awaken from sleep*) буди́ть, раз-; (*fig.*) пробу|жда́ть, -ди́ть; возбу|жда́ть, -ди́ть; **his interest was ~d** у него́ пробуди́лся интере́с; **my suspicions were ~d** у меня́ возни́кли подозре́ния; **she ~d everyone's sympathy** все ей сочу́вствовали; (*stimulate sexually*) возбу|жда́ть, -ди́ть.

arpeggio [ɑː'pedʒɪəʊ] *n.* арпе́джио (*indecl.*).

arrack ['ærək] *n.* ри́совая во́дка.

arraign [ə'reɪn] *v.t.* (*bring to trial*) привл|ека́ть, -е́чь к суду́; (*accuse*) обвин|я́ть, -и́ть.

arraignment [ə'reɪnmənt] *n.* привлече́ние к суду́; обвине́ние.

arrang|e [ə'reɪndʒ] *v.t.* **1.** (*put in order*) прив|оди́ть, -ести́ в поря́док; устр|а́ивать, -о́ить; **she was ~ing flowers** она расставля́ла цветы; **I must ~e my hair** мне на́до сде́лать причёску. **2.** (*put in a certain order*; *group*) распол|ага́ть, -ожи́ть; расст|авля́ть, -а́вить; **~ed in alphabetical order** располо́женный в алфави́тном поря́дке; **he ~ed books on the shelves** он расста́вил кни́ги по по́лкам; (*draw up in line*) выстра́ивать, вы́строить. **3.** (*settle*) ула́|живать, -дить. **4.** (*organize*) устр|а́ивать, -о́ить; организо́в|ывать, -а́ть; (*prepare*; *plan in advance*) подгот|а́вливать, -о́вить; организо́в|ывать, -а́ть; нала́|живать, -дить; **it was an ~ed marriage** их сосва́тали. **5.** (*mus.*) аранжи́ровать (*impf.*, *pf.*). **6.** (*adapt*) приспос|обля́ть, -о́бить; **a novel ~ed for the stage** инсцениро́вка рома́на.

v.i. догов|а́риваться, -ори́ться; усл|а́вливаться, -о́виться; **I ~ed with my friend to go to the theatre** мы с дру́гом договори́лись пойти́ в теа́тр; **I have ~ed for somebody to meet him at the station** я распоряди́лся, что́бы его́ встре́тили на ста́нции.

arrangement [ə'reɪndʒmənt] *n.* **1.** (*setting in order*) приведе́ние в поря́док; **the art of flower ~** иску́сство составле́ния буке́тов. **2.** (*specific order*) расположе́ние. **3.** (*planning*, *preparation*) подгото́вка; (*pl.*) приготовле́ния (*nt. pl.*); **make ~s for** организо́в|ывать, -а́ть; устр|а́ивать, -о́ить; **he made the ~s for the concert** он устро́ил/организова́л э́тот конце́рт. **4.** (*agreement*, *understanding*) соглаше́ние; **they came to an ~** они́ пришли́ к соглаше́нию/договорённости; **we made ~s to meet** мы договори́лись встре́титься. **5.** (*mus.*) аранжиро́вка. **6.** (*adaptation*) приспособле́ние.

arranger [ə'reɪndʒə(r)] *n.* **1.** (*organizer*) устро́итель (*m.*), организа́тор. **2.** (*mus.*) аранжиро́вщик.

arrant ['ærənt] *adj.* (*liter.*) отъя́вленный; су́щий; **~ nonsense** су́щий вздор; **an ~ rogue** отъя́вленный моше́нник; **an ~ fool** кру́глый/наби́тый дура́к.

array [ə'reɪ] *n.* **1.** (*order*): **in battle ~** в боево́м поря́дке. **2.** (*troops*) войска́ (*nt. pl.*). **3.** (*assemblage*) мно́жество; (*display*) собра́ние, колле́кция. **4.** (*dress*, *apparel*) наря́д, одея́ние.

v.t. **1.** (*place in order or line*) выстра́ивать, вы́строить; **the troops were ~ed for battle** войска́ бы́ли вы́строены в боево́м поря́дке. **2.** (*set out*, *display*) выставля́ть, вы́ставить. **3.** (*adorn*) укр|аша́ть, -а́сить; **she was ~ed in all her finery** она́ разоде́лась в пух и прах; (*deck out*, *dress*) од|ева́ть, -е́ть; **~ o.s.** наряди́ться (*pf.*); разоде́ться (*pf.*).

arrears [ə'rɪəz] *n.* **1.** (*state of being behindhand*) отстава́ние; **his work is in ~** у него́ зава́л рабо́ты; (*uncompleted work etc.*): **~ of correspondence** неразо́бранная корреспонде́нция. **2.** (*of payment*) задо́лженность; просро́чка; **~ of rent** задо́лженность по квартпла́те; **fall into ~** (*of pers.*) просро́чи|вать, -ть платёж.

arrest [ə'rest] *n.* **1.** (*seizure*; *leg. apprehension*) аре́ст; **place under ~** сажа́ть, посади́ть под аре́ст; **be under ~** сиде́ть (*impf.*) под аре́стом; **you are under ~!** вы аресто́ваны; **he was put under ~** его́ арестова́ли; **the police made several ~s** поли́ция произвела́ не́сколько аре́стов. **2.** (*stoppage*): **~ of judgement** (*leg.*) приостановле́ние исполне́ния/реше́ния; **cardiac ~** (*med.*) остано́вка се́рдца.

v.t. **1.** (*apprehend*) аресто́в|ывать, -а́ть; (*fig.*, *seize*): **~ s.o.'s attention** прико́в|ывать, -а́ть чьё-н. внима́ние. **2.** (*check*) заде́рж|ивать, -а́ть; **~ed development** заме́дленное разви́тие; (*stop*) приостан|а́вливать, -ови́ть; **inflation has been ~ed** инфля́ция приостано́влена.

arresting [ə'restɪŋ] *adj.* **1.** (*striking*) захва́тывающий; прико́вывающий внима́ние. **2.** (*designed to check or stop*) заде́рживающий; **~ device** остана́вливающий механи́зм.

arrière-pensée [ˌærjerpɑ̃'seɪ] *n.* за́дняя мысль.

arrival [ə'raɪv(ə)l] *n.* **1.** (*act or moment of arriving*) прибы́тие; **on his ~** по его́ прибы́тии; **'to await ~'** «оста́вить до прибы́тия адреса́та»; (*of pers. etc. on foot*; *of vehicles*) прихо́д; (*of pers. by vehicle*) прие́зд; (*by air*) прилёт. **2.** (*pers. or thg.*): **new ~** вновь прибы́вший; (*baby*) новорождённый; **new ~s of iron ore** но́вые па́ртии желе́зной руды́.

arrive [ə'raɪv] *v.i.* **1.** (*reach destination*) приб|ыва́ть, -ы́ть; (*of persons on foot*; *of vehicles*; *also fig.*) при|ходи́ть, -йти́; (*by land transport*) при|езжа́ть, -е́хать; (*by air*) прилет|а́ть, -е́ть. **2.**: **~ at a decision/conclusion** прийти́ (*pf.*) к реше́нию/заключе́нию. **3.** (*of time*) наступ|а́ть, -и́ть. **4.** (*fig.*, *establish one's reputation*) дост|ига́ть, -и́гнуть призна́ния.

arrogance ['ærəgəns] *n.* высокоме́рие, надме́нность.

arrogant ['ærəgənt] *adj.* высокоме́рный, надме́нный.

arrogate ['ærəˌgeɪt] *v.t.* (*claim*) присв|а́ивать, -о́ить себе́; **he ~d himself the right** он присво́ил себе́ пра́во; он претендова́л на пра́во; **he ~d privileges to his staff** он пыта́лся вы́рвать привиле́гии для свои́х сотру́дников.

arrogation [ˌærə'geɪʃ(ə)n] *n.* необосно́ванная прете́нзия, присвое́ние.

arrow ['ærəʊ] *n.* стрела́; (*as symbol or indicator*) стре́лка.

cpds. **~-head** *n.* наконе́чник/остриё стрелы́; **~-headed** *adj.* клинообра́зный; **~root** *n.* арроу́т; **~-shaped** *adj.* стрелови́дный.

arse [ɑːs] (**US ass**) *n.* жо́па (*vulg.*), за́дница.

cpds. **~-hole** *n.* (*pers.*) засра́н|ец (*fem.* -ка); **~-licker** *n.* жополи́з.

arsenal ['ɑːsən(ə)l] *n.* (*lit.*, *fig.*) арсена́л.

arsenic ['ɑːsənɪk] *n.* мышья́к.

adj. (*also* **~al**) мышьяко́вый.

arson ['ɑːs(ə)n] *n.* поджо́г.

arsonist ['ɑːsənɪst] *n.* поджига́тель (*m.*).

art [ɑːt] *n.* **1.** (*skill*, *craft*) иску́сство; **~ is long, life is short** жизнь коротка́, иску́сство ве́чно; **the ~ of war** вое́нное иску́сство; **a work of ~** произведе́ние иску́сства; **mechanical, useful ~s** ремёсла (*nt. pl.*); **black ~** чёрная ма́гия. **2.** (*esp. pl.*) (*device*, *trick*) уло́вки (*f. pl.*); про́иски (*m. pl.*); **female ~s** же́нские ко́зни (*f. pl.*); **there's an ~ to making an omelette** пригото́вить омле́т — то́же иску́сство. **3.** (*decorative*) иску́сство; **fine ~s** изя́щные/изобрази́тельные иску́сства; **applied ~s** прикладны́е иску́сства; **~ deco** ар деко́; **~ nouveau** ар нуво́; **he prefers ~ to music** он предпочита́ет изобрази́тельное иску́сство му́зыке; **~ school** худо́жественное учи́лище; **~ gallery** худо́жественная галере́я; **~ critic** искусствове́д. **4.** (*pl.*, *humanities*) гуманита́рные нау́ки (*f. pl.*); **Bachelor of Arts** бакала́вр гуманита́рных нау́к. **5.** (*attr.*, *artistic*) худо́жественный; (*artificial*) иску́сственный.

artefact, artifact ['ɑːtɪˌfækt] *n.* худо́жественное изде́лие; поде́лка.

artel [ɑː'tel] *n.* арте́ль.

Artemis ['ɑːtɪmɪs] *n.* Артеми́да.

arterial [ɑː'tɪərɪəl] *adj.* **1.** (*anat.*) артериа́льный. **2.**: **~ road** магистра́льная доро́га; магистра́ль; **~ traffic** движе́ние по гла́вным доро́гам.

arteriosclerosis [ɑːˌtɪərɪəʊsklɪə'rəʊsɪs] *n.* артериосклеро́з.

artery ['ɑːtərɪ] *n.* (*anat.*) арте́рия; (*road*) магистра́ль.

artesian [ɑː'tiːzɪən, -ʒ(ə)n] *adj.* артезиа́нский.

artful ['ɑːtfʊl] *adj.* хи́трый, хитроу́мный.

artfulness ['ɑːtfʊlnɪs] *n.* хи́трость, хитроу́мие.

arthritic [ɑː'θrɪtɪk] *n.* больн|о́й (*fem.* -а́я) артри́том.

adj. артри́тный; **an ~ old woman** стару́ха, страда́ющая артри́том.

arthritis [ɑː'θraɪtɪs] *n.* артри́т.

Arthurian [ɑː'θjʊrɪən] *adj.*: **~ romances** рома́ны Арту́рова ци́кла.

artichoke ['ɑːtɪˌtʃəʊk] *n.* артишо́к; **Jerusalem ~** земляна́я гру́ша.

article ['ɑ:tɪk(ə)l] *n.* **1.** (*item*) предме́т; изде́лие; ~ **of clothing** предме́т оде́жды; ~ **of food** пищево́й проду́кт; (*of trade*) **consumer ~s** потреби́тельские това́ры (*m. pl.*). **2.** (*clause etc. of document*) статья́; пункт, пара́граф; **~s of apprenticeship** догово́р учени́чества; **~s of association** уста́в о́бщества; ~ **of faith** догма́т ве́ры. **3.** (*piece of writing*) статья́; **leading** ~ передова́я статья́. **4.** (*gram.*): **(in)definite** ~ (не)определённый арти́кль.

articulate[1] [ɑ:'tɪkjʊlət] *adj.* **1.** (*of speech*) членоразде́льный; (*of thoughts*) отчётливый; (*of pers.*) чётко выража́ющий свои́ мы́сли. **2.** (*zool.*) суста́вчатый.

articulate[2] [ɑ:'tɪkjʊ,leɪt] *v.t.* **1.** (*speech*) отчётливо произн|оси́ть, -ести́. **2.** (*connect by joints*) свя́з|ывать, -а́ть; соедин|я́ть, -и́ть; **~d lorry** автопо́езд.

v.i.: **he ~s well** у него́ хоро́шая артикуля́ция.

articulation [ɑ:,tɪkjʊ'leɪʃ(ə)n] *n.* (*of speech*) артикуля́ция; произноше́ние; (*jointing*) сочлене́ние.

artifact ['ɑ:tɪ,fækt] = **artefact**

artifice ['ɑ:tɪfɪs] *n.* (*device, contrivance*) изобрете́ние, вы́думка; (*cunning*) хи́трость.

artificer [ɑ:'tɪfɪsə(r)] *n.* (*craftsman*) реме́сленник; (*inventor*) изобрета́тель (*m.*); (*mil.*) те́хник; меха́ник.

artificial [,ɑ:tɪ'fɪʃ(ə)l] *adj.* (*not natural*) иску́сственный; ~ **respiration** иску́сственное дыха́ние; (*feigned*) притво́рный.

artificiality [,ɑ:tɪfɪʃɪ'ælɪtɪ] *n.* иску́сственность; притво́рность, притво́рство.

artillery [ɑ:'tɪlərɪ] *n.* артилле́рия; (*attr.*) артиллери́йский.

cpd. **~man** *n.* артиллери́ст.

artiness ['ɑ:tɪnɪs] *n.* (*coll.*) прете́нзия на худо́жественность.

artisan [,ɑ:tɪ'zæn, 'ɑ:-] *n.* реме́сленник; мастерово́й.

artist ['ɑ:tɪst] *n.* **1.** (*practiser of art*) худо́жник; **~'s materials** худо́жественные принадле́жности. **2.** (*skilled performer*) арти́ст; ~ **in words** худо́жник/ма́стер сло́ва; ~ **at cooking** настоя́щий худо́жник в поварско́м де́ле.

artiste [ɑ:'ti:st] *n.* (эстра́дный) арти́ст; (*fem.*) (эстра́дная) арти́стка.

artistic [ɑ:'tɪstɪk] *adj.* худо́жественный; артисти́ческий.

artistry ['ɑ:tɪstrɪ] *n.* артисти́чность, мастерство́.

artless ['ɑ:tlɪs] *adj.* (*unskilled*) неиску́сный; (*ingenuous*) простоду́шный; (*natural*) безыску́сственный, безыску́сный.

artlessness ['ɑ:tlɪsnɪs] *n.* неиску́сность; простоду́шие; безыску́сственность.

arty ['ɑ:tɪ], **~-crafty** *adjs.* (*coll.*) вы́чурный; претенцио́зно-боге́мный; с выкрута́сами; **~-farty** *adj.* боге́мистый.

arum ['eərəm] *n.* а́рум, аро́нник.

Aryan ['eərɪən] *n.* ари́|ец (*fem.* -ка).

adj. ари́йский.

as [æz, əz] *pron.*: **such men ~ knew him** те, кото́рые зна́ли его́; **such ~ need our help** те, кто нужда́ется в на́шей по́мощи.

adv. & conj. **1.** (*expr. comparison or conformity*) как; ~ **I was saying** как я говори́л; ~ **follows** сле́дующим о́бразом; **such countries ~ Spain** таки́е стра́ны, как Испа́ния; **the same ~ ...** то же са́мое, что...; ~ **heavy ~ lead** тяжёлый, как свине́ц; **he is ~ clever ~ she** он так же умён, как она́; **he is ~ kind ~ he is rich** он и добр и бога́т; **I am ~ tall ~ he** я одного́ с ним ро́ста; **walk ~ fast ~ you can** иди́те как мо́жно быстре́е; ~ **quickly ~ possible** как мо́жно скоре́е; **just ~** так же, как; ~ **usual** как всегда́; **we are late ~ it is** мы и так опа́здываем; ~ **things are, you cannot go** положе́ние дел таково́, что вы не мо́жете идти́; **he is tall, ~ are his brothers** как и его́ бра́тья, он высо́кого ро́ста; **he pictured the room ~ it would be** он представля́л себе́ ко́мнату, како́й она́ бу́дет; **he was hungry, ~ they soon saw** он был го́лоден, в чём они́ вско́ре убеди́лись; ~ **it were** так сказа́ть; как бы; ~ **you were!** (*mil.*) отста́вить!; **he arranged matters so ~ to suit everyone** он устро́ил всё так, что́бы все бы́ли дово́льны; ~ **a man sows, so shall he reap** что посе́ешь, то и пожнёшь; **so frank ~ to be insulting** оскорби́тельно-открове́нный; **he was not so foolish ~ to say ...** он был не так глуп, что́бы сказа́ть...; ~ **who should say** как бы говоря́; **so ~ to** (*expr. purpose*) что́бы; (*expr. manner*) так, что́бы; **that's ~ may be** ну, поло́жим; мо́жет быть и так; ~ **well ~ may be** как мо́жно лу́чше. **2.** (*expr. capacity or category*) как; **I regard him ~ a fool** я счита́ю его́ дурако́м; **his appointment ~ colonel** присвое́ние ему́ зва́ния полко́вника; ~ **your guardian, I ...** как ваш опеку́н, я...; **he appeared ~ Hamlet** он вы́ступил в ро́ли Га́млета; ~ **a rule** как пра́вило; **I said it ~ a joke** я сказа́л э́то в шу́тку; **I recognized him ~ the new tenant** я узна́л в нём но́вого жильца́. **3.** (*concessive*): **young** (*US* ~ **young**) ~ **I am** хоть я и мо́лод; **much ~ I should like to** хотя́ мне и о́чень хоте́лось бы; **try ~ he would** как он ни стара́лся. **4.** (*temporal*) когда́; в то вре́мя как; **(just) ~ I reached the door** когда́ (*or* как то́лько) я подошёл к две́ри; ~ **he was still taking off his coat, he heard ...** ещё не сняв пальто́, он услы́шал... **5.** (*causative*) е́сли; раз; ~ **you are ready, let us begin** поско́льку вы уже́ гото́вы, дава́йте начнём. **6.** (*in proportion* ~) по ме́ре того́, как. **7.** (*var.*): ~ **far ~ I know** наско́лько мне изве́стно; **he walked ~ far ~ the station** он дошёл до ста́нции; ~ **far back ~ 1920** ещё/уже́ в 1920 году́; ~ **for you** что каса́ется вас; ~ **from January** начина́я с пе́рвого января́; **the work is ~ good ~ done** рабо́та всё равно́, что сде́лана; **he was ~ good ~ his word** он сдержа́л своё сло́во; **be so good ~ to tell me** бу́дьте добры́, скажи́те мне; ~ **if** бу́дто (бы); как бу́дто (бы); **he made ~ if to go** он дви́нулся бы́ло уходи́ть; **it is not ~ if I was poor** не то, что́бы я был бе́ден; **I will stay ~ long ~ you want me** я пробу́ду сто́лько, ско́лько вы захоти́те; **keep it ~ long ~ you like** держи́те э́то, ско́лько вам уго́дно; ~ **much ~ ...** сто́лько, ско́лько...; ~ **much ~ to say** как бы говоря́; **I thought ~ much!** так я и ду́мал!; **I did not so much ~ hear him** я да́же и не слы́шал его́; **no one so much ~ looked at us** на нас никто́ и не смотре́л; ~ **of this moment** в да́нный моме́нт; ~ **often ~** (*whenever*) **he comes** вся́кий раз, когда́ он прихо́дит; ~ **regards** что каса́ется +*g.*; относи́тельно+*g.*; ~ **soon ~** как то́лько; **I would just ~ soon go** я предпочёл бы пойти́; **the drawings ~ such** рису́нки как таковы́е; ~ **though** бу́дто (бы); как бу́дто (бы); ~ **to** (*regarding*) что каса́ется +*g.*; **he enquired ~ to the date** он спра́вился/осве́домился о да́те; **he said nothing ~ to when he would come** он ничего́ не сказа́л насчёт того́, когда́ он придёт; ~ **well** (*in addition*) та́кже, то́же; **he came ~ well ~ John** и он и Джон пришли́; **you might ~ well help me** вы могли́ бы мне помо́чь; **it is just ~ well you came** хорошо́, что вы пришли́; ~ **yet** ещё; до сих пор.

a.s.a.p. (*abbr. of* **as soon as possible**) как мо́жно скоре́е.

asbestos [æz'bestɒs, æs-] *n.* асбе́ст; (*attr.*) асбе́стовый; **~ply** асбофане́ра.

ascend [ə'send] *v.t.* подн|има́ться, -я́ться по+*d.* (*or* на+*a.*); **he ~ed the stairs** он подня́лся по ле́стнице; ~ **the throne** взойти́ (*pf.*) на престо́л.

v.i. подн|има́ться, -я́ться; восходи́ть (*impf.*); **in ~ing order of magnitude** по возраста́ющей сте́пени ва́жности/зна́чимости.

ascend|ancy, -ency [ə'send(ə)nsɪ] *n.* власть, госпо́дство, dominiрующее влия́ние; **gain, obtain ~ over** брать, взять власть над+*i.*; доби́ться (*pf.*) влия́ния на+*a.*

ascendant [ə'send(ə)nt] *n.*: **his star is in the ~** его́ звезда́ восхо́дит.

adj. (*rising*) восходя́щий; (*predominant*) госпо́дствующий.

ascension [ə'senʃ(ə)n] *n.* (*act of ascending*) восхожде́ние; (*relig.*) **the A~** Вознесе́ние; **A~ Island** о́стров Вознесе́ния.

ascent [ə'sent] *n.* **1.** (*rise in ground; slope*) подъём; **the road has an ~ of 5°** доро́га поднима́ется под угло́м в пять гра́дусов. **2.** (*act of climbing or rising*) восхожде́ние, подъём; ~ **of a mountain** восхожде́ние на́ гору; **they made the ~ in 5 hours** они́ подняли́сь за пять часо́в.

ascertain [,æsə'teɪn] *v.t.* устан|а́вливать, -ови́ть; выясня́ть, вы́яснить.

ascertainable [,æsə'teɪnəb(ə)l] *adj.* устана́вливаемый.

ascetic [ə'setɪk] *n.* аскет.

adj. аскети́ческий.

asceticism [ə'setɪ,sɪz(ə)m] *n.* аскети́зм.

ascorbic [ə'skɔ:bɪk] *adj.* аскорби́новый.

ascribable [ə'skraɪbəb(ə)l] *adj.* припи́сываемый.

ascribe [ə'skraɪb] *v.t.* припи́с|ывать, -а́ть.

ascription [ə'skrɪpʃ(ə)n] *n.* припи́сывание, припи́ска.
Asdic ['æzdɪk] *n.* гидролока́тор.
asepsis [eɪ'sepsɪs, ə-] *n.* асе́птика.
aseptic [eɪ'septɪk] *adj.* асепти́ческий.
asexual [eɪ'seksjʊəl, æ-] *adj.* беспо́лый.
ash[1] [æʃ] *n.* (*bot.*) я́сень (*m.*); **mountain ~** ряби́на; (*attr.*) я́сеневый.
ash[2] [æʃ] *n.* **1.** (*also pl.*) зола́; пе́пел; **he took the ~es out of the stove** он вы́греб золу́ из пе́чки; **this coal makes a lot of ~** от э́того у́гля мно́го золы́; **cigarette ~** пе́пел; **they burnt the town to ~es** они́ сожгли́ го́род дотла́; **A~ Wednesday** пе́рвый день Вели́кого поста́. **2.** (*pl., human remains*) прах; (*fig.*) **his hopes turned to ~es** его́ наде́жды ру́хнули.
cpds. **~-bin** *n.* зо́льник; **~-blond** *n.* пе́пельная блонди́нка; **~-box, ~-pan** *nn.* зо́льник; я́щик для золы́; **~-can** *n.* (*US*) му́сорный я́щик; **~-grey** *adj.* пе́пельно-се́рый; **~tray** *n.* пе́пельница.
ashamed [ə'ʃeɪmd] *adj.* пристыжённый; **I am, feel ~** мне сты́дно; **be ~ of** стыди́ться (*impf.*) +*g.*; **be, feel ~ for s.o.** стыди́ться за кого́-н.; **you make me feel ~** вы заставля́ете меня́ красне́ть; **there's nothing to be ~ of in that** в э́том нет ничего́ зазо́рного/посты́дного; **you ought to be ~ of yourself** как вам не сты́дно!
ash|en ['æʃ(ə)n], **-y** ['æʃɪ] *adjs.* (*ash-coloured*) пе́пельного цве́та; (*pale*) ме́ртвенно-бле́дный.
ashlar ['æʃlə(r)] *n.* тёсаный ка́мень.
ashore [ə'ʃɔ:(r)] *adv.* (*position*) на берегу́; (*motion*) на бе́рег; **go ~** сойти́ на бе́рег; **put ~** выса́живать, вы́садить на бе́рег.
ashy ['æʃɪ] = **ashen**
Asia ['eɪʃə, -ʒə] *n.* А́зия; **~ Minor** Ма́лая А́зия.
Asia|n ['eɪʃ(ə)n, -ʒ(ə)n], **-tic** [ˌeɪʃɪ'ætɪk, ˌeɪz-] *nn.* азиа́т (*fem.* -ка).
adjs. азиа́тский.
aside [ə'saɪd] *n.* ре́плика в сто́рону.
adv. (*place*) в стороне́; (*motion*) в сто́рону; (*in reserve*) отде́льно, в резе́рве; **joking ~** кро́ме шу́ток; **~ from** (*US*) за исключе́нием +*g.*; кро́ме+*g.*; **take s.o. ~** отв|оди́ть, -ести́ кого́-н. в сто́рону; **set ~** (*quash*) отмен|я́ть, -и́ть; **set, put ~** (*reserve*) от|кла́дывать, -ложи́ть; (*of money*) от|кла́дывать, -ложи́ть.
asinine ['æsɪˌnaɪn] *adj.* (*lit., fig.*) осли́ный.
asininity [ˌæsɪ'nɪnɪtɪ] *n.* глу́пость.
ask [ɑ:sk] *v.t.* **1.** (*enquire*) спр|а́шивать, -оси́ть (*что у кого or кого о чём*); рассп|ра́шивать, -оси́ть (*кого о чём*); **he was ~ed his name** у него́ спроси́ли фами́лию; **he ~ed me the time** он спроси́л меня́, кото́рый час; **~ him the way!** спроси́те его́, как пройти́!; **if you ~ me ...** я бы сказа́л...; е́сли хоти́те знать моё мне́ние, то...; **one might ~** спра́шивается; **I ~ you!** скажи́те пожа́луйста! **2.** (*pose*): **~ a question** зад|ава́ть, -а́ть вопро́с. **3.** (*request permission*): **he ~ed to leave the room** он попроси́л разреше́ния вы́йти из ко́мнаты; **he went off without ~ing** он ушёл не спрося́сь. **4.** (*request*) проси́ть, по- (*что у кого or кого о чём*); **may I ~ you a favour?** мо́жно попроси́ть вас об одолже́нии?; **I ~ed him to do it** я попроси́л его́ сде́лать э́то; (*require*) тре́бовать, по- +*g.*; **the society ~s obedience of its members** о́бщество тре́бует от свои́х чле́нов подчине́ния; **if it's not too much to ~** е́сли э́то вас не затрудни́т; *see also* **asking. 5.** (*charge*) проси́ть, за-; **he ~ed a high price** он запроси́л высо́кую це́ну; **what is he ~ing for his car?** ско́лько он про́сит за свою́ маши́ну?; **~ing price** запра́шиваемая цена́. **6.** (*invite*) звать, по-; пригла|ша́ть, -си́ть; **have you been ~ed?** вас (по)зва́ли?; **why don't you ~ him in?** почему́ вы не пригласи́те его́ войти́?; **~ a girl out** пригла|ша́ть, -си́ть де́вушку на свида́ние; **we have been ~ed out to dinner** нас позва́ли на у́жин.
v.i. **1.** (*make enquiries*): **I am going to the station to ~ about the trains** я иду́ на вокза́л узна́ть расписа́ние поездо́в; **she ~ed after your health** она́ осве́домилась/справля́лась о ва́шем здоро́вье; (**~** *to see*): **I ~ed for Mr. Smith** я спроси́л г-на Сми́та; **come to our house and ~ for me** приди́те к нам и спро́сите меня́. **2.** (*make a request*) проси́ть, по-; **~ for help** проси́ть (*impf.*) о по́мощи; **he ~ed him for a pencil** он попроси́л у него́ каранда́ш; **she ~ed for a visa** она́ попроси́ла ви́зу; **he ~ed for advice** он спра́шивал сове́та; **~ for trouble** (*coll.*) напра́шиваться на неприя́тности; лезть (*impf.*) на рожо́н.
askance [ə'skæns, -'skɑ:ns] *adv.* (*lit., fig.*) ко́со, и́скоса; **he looked at me ~** он посмотре́л на меня́ и́скоса.
askew [ə'skju:] *adv.* кри́во, ко́со; **you have hung the picture ~** вы пове́сили карти́ну ко́со; **your hat is ~** у вас шля́па набекре́нь.
asking ['ɑ:skɪŋ] *n.*: **it is yours for the ~** сто́ит то́лько попроси́ть; **food was there for the ~** еды́ там бы́ло ско́лько уго́дно.
aslant [ə'slɑ:nt] *adv.* на́искось, ко́со.
prep. поперёк+*g.*
asleep [ə'sli:p] *pred. adj.* спя́щий; **he was sound, fast ~** он спал кре́пким сном; **fall ~** зас|ыпа́ть, -ну́ть; **he fell ~** (*died*) он усну́л ве́чным сном; (*fig., of limbs*) затёкший; **my leg is ~** я отсиде́л но́гу; (*fig., mentally*) тупо́й, со́нный.
asp [æsp] *n.* а́спид.
asparagus [ə'spærəgəs] *n.* спа́ржа; **~ bed** гря́дка со спа́ржей; **~ tips** спа́ржевые голо́вки.
aspect ['æspekt] *n.* **1.** (*look, appearance; expression*) вид, выраже́ние. **2.** (*fig., facet; mode of presentation*) аспе́кт, сторона́; (*point of view*) то́чка зре́ния; **have you considered the question in all its ~s?** вы рассмотре́ли вопро́с со всех то́чек зре́ния? **3.** (*outlook*) вид; (*side facing a certain direction*) сторона́; **my house has a north ~** мой дом смо́трит на се́вер. **4.** (*gram.*) вид.
aspen ['æspən] *n.* оси́на; (*attr.*) оси́новый.
asperity [ə'sperɪtɪ] *n.* (*roughness*) неро́вность; шерохова́тость; (*severity*) суро́вость; (*sharpness*) ре́зкость; **he spoke with ~** он говори́л ре́зко.
asperse [ə'spɜ:s] *v.t.* **1.** (*eccl., sprinkle*) кропи́ть (*impf.*). **2.** (*fig., slander*) черни́ть, о-; клевета́ть на+*a.*, оклевета́ть.
aspersion [ə'spɜ:ʃ(ə)n] *n.* **1.** (*eccl.*) кропле́ние. **2.** (*slur*) клевета́; **cast ~s** клевета́ть (*impf.*) на+*a.*
asphalt ['æsfælt] *n.* асфа́льт; (*attr.*) асфа́льтовый.
v.t. асфальти́ровать (*impf., pf.*).
asphodel ['æsfəˌdel] *n.* асфоде́ль (*m.*).
asphyxia [æs'fɪksɪə] *n.* уду́шье; асфи́ксия.
asphyxiate [æs'fɪksɪˌeɪt] *v.t.* вызыва́ть, вы́звать уду́шье у+*g.*; (*suffocate*) души́ть, за-; **I was almost ~d by the fumes** я чуть бы́ло не задохну́лся в дыму́.
asphyxiation [æsˌfɪksɪ'eɪʃ(ə)n] *n.* уду́шье, удуше́ние.
aspic ['æspɪk] *n.* заливно́е; **veal in ~** заливна́я теля́тина; заливно́е из теля́тины.
aspidistra [ˌæspɪ'dɪstrə] *n.* аспиди́стра.
aspirant ['æspɪrənt, ə'spaɪərənt] *n.* претенде́нт; **an ~ to high office** претенде́нт/кандида́т на высо́кую до́лжность.
aspirate[1] ['æspərət] *n.* аспира́т; придыха́тельный согла́сный звук.
aspirate[2] ['æspəˌreɪt] *v.t.* произн|оси́ть, -ести́ с придыха́нием.
aspiration [ˌæspɪ'reɪʃ(ə)n] *n.* **1.** (*desire*) стремле́ние; **his ~s to, for, after fame** его́ стремле́ние к сла́ве. **2.** (*phon.*) придыха́ние.
aspirator ['æspɪˌreɪtə(r)] *n.* аспира́тор.
aspir|e [ə'spaɪə(r)] *v.i.* стреми́ться (*impf.*); **he ~es to be a leader** он наде́ется стать ли́дером; **an ~ing politician** гото́вящийся в полити́ческие де́ятели.
aspirin ['æsprɪn] *n.* аспири́н; (*tablet*) табле́тка аспири́на.
ass[1] [æs] (*donkey, lit., fig.*) осёл; **~'s** *or* **~es'** (*as adj.*) осли́ный; **he made an ~ of himself** он сваля́л дурака́; он опростоволо́сился/оплоша́л; **he was made an ~ of** он оста́лся в дурака́х.
ass[2] [æs] (*US vulg.*) = **arse**
assagai ['æsəˌgaɪ] = **assegai**
assail [ə'seɪl] *v.t.* (*lit., fig.*) нап|ада́ть, -а́сть на+*a.*; атакова́ть (*impf., pf.*); **I was ~ed by doubts** меня́ одолева́ли сомне́ния; **~ with criticism** обру́шиться (*pf.*) с кри́тикой на+*a.*; **~ with questions** зас|ыпа́ть, -ы́пать вопро́сами; (*tackle resolutely*) реши́тельно бра́ться, взя́ться за+*a.*
assailable [ə'seɪləb(ə)l] *adj.* откры́тый для нападе́ния; (*vulnerable*) уязви́мый.
assailant [ə'seɪlənt] *n.* напада́ющая/атаку́ющая сторона́.

assassin [ə'sæsɪn] *n.* уби́йца (*c.g.*), террори́ст.

assassinate [ə'sæsɪˌneɪt] *v.t.* уб|ива́ть, -и́ть (по полити́ческим моти́вам).

assassination [əˌsæsɪ'neɪʃ(ə)n] *n.* (преда́тельское) уби́йство; (*fig.*) **character** ~ подры́в репута́ции; (*coll.*) оха́ивание.

assault [ə'sɔːlt, ə'sɒlt] *n.* (*in general*) нападе́ние; (*mil.*) ата́ка, штурм, при́ступ; **carry, take by** ~ брать (*impf.*) шту́рмом/при́ступом; **go into the** ~ идти́ (*det.*) в ата́ку; **mount an** ~ предприн|има́ть, -я́ть ата́ку; **airborne** ~ вы́садка возду́шного деса́нта; ~ **troops** штурмовы́е ча́сти; ~ **boat, craft** деса́нтный ка́тер; штурмова́я ло́дка; (*leg.*): ~ **and battery** оскорбле́ние де́йствием; **indecent** ~ изнаси́лование; попы́тка изнаси́лования.

v.t. нап|ада́ть, -а́сть на+*a.*; (*mil.*) атакова́ть (*impf.*, *pf.*); (*storm*) штурмова́ть (*impf.*); (*sexually*) наси́ловать, из-.

assay [ə'seɪ, 'æseɪ] *n.* (*test*) испыта́ние; (*sampling*) опро́бование; (*analysis*) ана́лиз.

v.t. (*test*) испы́т|ывать, -а́ть; (*analyze*) анализи́ровать (*impf.*, *pl.*).

ass|egai ['æsɪˌgaɪ], **-agai** *n.* дро́тик.

assemblage [ə'semblɪdʒ] *n.* **1.** (*also* **assembly:** *bringing or coming together*) собира́ние, сбор. **2.** (*collection*) собра́ние, скопле́ние. **3.** (*putting together*) сбо́рка.

assemble [ə'semb(ə)l] *v.t.* (*gather together*) соб|ира́ть, -ра́ть; (*call together*) соз|ыва́ть, -ва́ть; (*tech.*, *fit together*) монти́ровать, с-.

v.i. соб|ира́ться, -ра́ться.

assembly [ə'semblɪ] *n.* **1.** (*assembling*): = **assemblage** *n.* **1.**. **2.** (*company of persons*) собра́ние; (*school*) ~ **hall** а́ктовый зал; **unlawful** ~ незако́нное сбо́рище. **3.** (*pol.*) собра́ние; ассамбле́я. **4.** (*mil.*) сбор; ~ **area** райо́н сбо́ра; (*signal*) сигна́л сбо́ра. **5.** (*of machine parts*) сбо́рка; ~ **line** сбо́рочный конве́йер; ~ **shop** сбо́рочный цех; ~ **worker** сбо́рщик.

assent [ə'sent] *n.* согла́сие; **the Royal** ~ короле́вская са́нкция.

v.i. согла|ша́ться, -си́ться (*с чем or на что*).

assert [ə'sɜːt] *v.t.* **1.** (*declare*; *affirm*) утвер|жда́ть, -ди́ть; заяв|ля́ть, -и́ть. **2.** (*stand up for*) отст|а́ивать, -оя́ть; защи|ща́ть, -ти́ть; ~ **one's rights** отст|а́ивать, -оя́ть свои́ права́; ~ **o.s.** самоутвер|жда́ться, -ди́ться.

assertion [ə'sɜːʃ(ə)n] *n.* **1.** (*statement*) утвержде́ние; **a mere, bare** ~ голосло́вное утвержде́ние. **2.** (*defence*) отста́ивание.

assertive [ə'sɜːtɪv] *adj.* утверди́тельный; (*dogmatic*) догмати́ческий; (*insistent*) насто́йчивый.

assess [ə'ses] *v.t.* **1.** (*estimate value of*; *appraise*; *also fig.*) оце́н|ивать, -и́ть; **his work was** ~**ed at its true worth** его́ рабо́та была́ оценена́ по досто́инству. **2.** (*determine amount of*) определ|я́ть, -и́ть су́мму/разме́р +*g.*; **damages were** ~**ed at £10,000** убы́тки占 оцени́ли в 10 000 фу́нтов.

assessable [ə'sesəb(ə)l] *adj.* подлежа́щий обложе́нию/оце́нке.

assessment [ə'sesmənt] *n.* (*valuation*) оце́нка; (*for taxation*) обложе́ние; (*sum to be levied*) су́мма обложе́ния.

assessor [ə'sesə(r)] *n.* **1.** (*of taxes, property etc.*) нало́говый чино́вник. **2.** (*leg.*, *adviser*) экспе́рт(-консульта́нт).

asset ['æset] *n.* **1.** (*advantage*; *useful quality*) це́нность; **knowledge of French is an** ~ **in this job** зна́ние францу́зского языка́ осо́бенно ва́жно для э́той рабо́ты. **2.** (*pl.*, *fin.*: *possessions with money value*) акти́в; **available** ~**s** легко́ реализу́емые акти́вы; **current** ~**s** оборо́тные сре́дства; **fixed** ~**s** основны́е сре́дства; (*item on balance sheet*) статья́ акти́ва; (*property*) иму́щество; **personal** ~**s** дви́жимое иму́щество.

asseverate [ə'sevəˌreɪt] *v.t.* торже́ственно заяв|ля́ть, -и́ть.

asseveration [əˌsevə'reɪʃ(ə)n] *n.* торже́ственное заявле́ние.

assiduity [ˌæsɪ'djuːɪtɪ] *n.* прилежа́ние; усе́рдие.

assiduous [ə'sɪdjʊəs] *adj.* приле́жный; усе́рдный.

assign [ə'saɪn] *n.* (*also* **-ee**) (*leg.*) правопрее́мник.

v.t. **1.** (*leg.*, *transfer*) перед|ава́ть, -а́ть. **2.** (*appoint*; *allot*) переуступ|а́ть, -и́ть; **the task was** ~**ed to me** на меня́ была́ возло́жена зада́ча; **have you had any homework** ~**ed to you?** тебе́ за́дали уро́ки на́ дом? **3.** (*determine*) определ|я́ть, -и́ть; устан|а́вливать, -ови́ть; **a limit must be** ~**ed** на́до установи́ть како́й-то преде́л. **4.** (*ascribe*) припи́с|ывать, -а́ть; **they could** ~ **no cause to the fire** они́ не могли́ установи́ть причи́ну пожа́ра.

assignable [ə'saɪnəb(ə)l] *adj.* припи́сываемый.

assignation [ˌæsɪg'neɪʃ(ə)n] *n.* **1.** (*appointment*) назначе́ние. **2.** (*illicit meeting*) та́йное свида́ние. **3.** (*leg.*, *transfer*) переда́ча, переусту́пка.

assignee [ˌæsaɪ'niː] *n.* **1.** = **assign** *n.* **2.** (*pers. empowered to act for another*) уполномо́ченный.

assignment [ə'saɪnmənt] *n.* **1.** (*allotment*) распределе́ние; (пред)назначе́ние. **2.** (*task, duty*) поруче́ние; зада́ние; рабо́та; (*involving journey*) командиро́вка; (*schoolwork*) зада́ние. **3.** (*fin.*, *transfer*) переда́ча, переусту́пка. **4.** (*ascription*) припи́сывание.

assimilable [ə'sɪmɪˌləb(ə)l] *adj.* уподобля́емый; усвоя́емый, ассимили́руемый.

assimilate [ə'sɪmɪˌleɪt] *v.t.* **1.** (*liken*) упод|обля́ть, -о́бить (*кого/что кому/чему*). **2.** (*absorb by digestion etc., and fig.*) ассимили́ровать (*impf.*, *pf.*); усв|а́ивать, -о́ить; **the immigrants were quickly** ~**d** иммигра́нты бы́стро ассимили́ровались; **new ideas take time to** ~ но́вые иде́и прививáются не сра́зу.

v.i. ассимили́роваться (*impf.*, *pf.*).

assimilation [əˌsɪmɪ'leɪʃ(ə)n] *n.* (*likening*) уподобле́ние; (*physiol.*, *ling.*) ассимиля́ция; (*of knowledge etc.*) усвое́ние, освое́ние.

assist [ə'sɪst] *v.t.* (*help*) пом|ога́ть, -о́чь +*d.*; (*cooperate with*) соде́йствовать (*impf.*, *pf.*) +*d.*; **he was** ~**ed in the task by his wife** в э́том де́ле ему́ помога́ла жена́; **she was** ~**ed to her feet by a passer-by** прохо́жий помо́г ей подня́ться на́ ноги; ~**ed take-off** взлёт с ускори́телем.

v.i. (*take part*) прин|има́ть, -я́ть уча́стие; (*be present*) прису́тствовать (*impf.*); **she** ~**ed at her sister's wedding** она́ была́/прису́тствовала на сва́дьбе свое́й сестры́.

assistance [ə'sɪstəns] *n.* по́мощь; соде́йствие; **he rendered valuable** ~ он оказа́л це́нную по́мощь; **can you come to my** ~**?** вы мо́жете мне помо́чь?; **may I be of** ~**?** могу́ я че́м-нибудь помо́чь?

assistant [ə'sɪst(ə)nt] *n.* помо́щник; ассисте́нт; ~ **manager** помо́щник заве́дующего; ~ **professor** ≃ доце́нт; (*in shop*) продав|е́ц (*fem.* -щи́ца).

assize [ə'saɪz] *n.* (*usu. pl.*) суде́бное заседа́ние; выездна́я се́ссия суда присяжных.

associate[1] [ə'səʊʃɪət, -sɪət] *n.* **1.** (*colleague*) колле́га (*c.g.*), това́рищ, партнёр; (*in business*) компаньо́н; (*at work*) сослужи́вец; (*confederate*) соуча́стник; **his** ~**s in crime** его́ соо́бщники в преступле́нии. **2.** (*commerce*) член о́бщества.

adj. (*closely connected*) свя́занный; соединённый; (*united*) объединённый; ~ **member** непо́лный член; член-корреспонде́нт; ~ **editor** помо́щник реда́ктора.

associate[2] [ə'səʊʃɪˌeɪt, -sɪˌeɪt] *v.t.* соедин|я́ть, -и́ть; свя́з|ывать, -а́ть; (*esp. psych.*) ассоции́ровать (*impf.*, *pf.*); **everyone** ~**s Handel and Bach** Ге́ндель ассоции́руется у всех с Ба́хом; **his name was** ~**d with the cause of reform** его́ и́мя ассоции́ровалось с реформа́торской де́ятельностью; ~ **o.s. with** присоедин|я́ться, -и́ться к+*d.*

v.i. води́ться (*impf.*), обща́ться (*impf.*).

association [əˌsəʊsɪ'eɪʃ(ə)n] *n.* **1.** (*uniting*; *joining*) объедине́ние; соедине́ние. **2.** (*consorting*) обще́ние. **3.** (*connection*; *bond*) связь; ассоциа́ция; ~ **of ideas** мы́сленная ассоциа́ция. **4.** (*group*) ассоциа́ция, о́бщество; (*union*) сою́з; **deed of** ~ уста́в; ~ **football** футбо́л.

associative [ə'səʊʃɪətɪv, ə'səʊs-] *adj.* ассоциати́вный.

assonance ['æsənəns] *n.* ассона́нс; непо́лная ри́фма.

assorted [ə'sɔːtɪd] *adj.* (*sorted, classified*) сортиро́ванный; (*selected*) подо́бранный; ~ **chocolates** шокола́дный набо́р; (шокола́дное) ассорти́ (*indecl.*); (*matched*): **an ill-**~ **couple** неподходя́щая па́ра; (*varied*) разнообра́зный.

assortment [ə'sɔːtmənt] *n.* ассортиме́нт; набо́р; **an** ~ **of books** вы́бор книг.

assuage [ə'sweɪdʒ] *v.t.* (*soothe*) успок|а́ивать, -о́ить; (*alleviate*) смягч|а́ть, -и́ть; (*appetite etc.*) утол|я́ть, -и́ть.

assum|e [ə'sjuːm] *v.t.* **1.** (*put on, e.g. garment*) над|ева́ть, -е́ть. **2.** (*take on*) прин|има́ть, -я́ть; **he** ~**ed command** он при́нял кома́ндование; **I** ~**e full responsibility** я принима́ю на себя́ по́лную отве́тственность; ~**e control of** брать, взять на себя́ управле́ние/руково́дство +*i*.; **her illness ~ed a grave character** её боле́знь приняла́ серьёзный хара́ктер. **3.** (*feign*) напус|ка́ть, -ти́ть на себя́; **he ~ed a new name** он взял себе́ но́вое и́мя; **he went under an ~ed name** он был изве́стен под вы́мышленным и́менем; **she ~ed an air of indifference** она́ напусти́ла на себя́ равноду́шный вид; она́ притвори́лась равноду́шной; **his ~ed indifference** его́ притво́рное равноду́шие. **4.** (*suppose*) предпол|ага́ть, -ожи́ть; допус|ка́ть, -ти́ть; **let us ~e that ...** допу́стим, что...; **always ~ing that ...** при усло́вии, коне́чно, что...

assumption [ə'sʌmpʃ(ə)n] *n.* **1.** (*taking on*) приня́тие (на себя́); **his ~ of power** его́ прихо́д к вла́сти. **2.** (*pretence*): **~ of indifference** притво́рное/напускно́е равноду́шие. **3.** (*supposition*) предположе́ние; допуще́ние; исхо́дное положе́ние; **on the ~ that ...** исходя́ из того́, что...; е́сли допусти́ть, что...; **you are making a dangerous ~** вы де́лаете опа́сное предположе́ние. **4.** (*eccl.*): **the A~** Успе́ние.

assurance [ə'ʃʊərəns] *n.* **1.** (*act of assuring; promise; guarantee*) завере́ние, увере́ние; **have I your ~ of this?** вы мо́жете за э́то поручи́ться?; **I give you my ~ that you will get the money** могу́ вас заве́рить, что вы полу́чите де́ньги. **2.** (*confidence*) уве́ренность (в себе́); **to make ~ doubly sure** для вя́щей ве́рности. **3.** (*presumption*) самоуве́ренность. **4.** (*insurance*) страхова́ние; **life ~ company** о́бщество по страхова́нию жи́зни.

assure [ə'ʃʊə(r)] *v.t.* **1.** (*ensure*) обеспе́чи|вать, -ть; **~ o.s. of sth.** обеспе́чить (*pf.*) себе́ что-н.; **he is ~d of a steady income** ему́ обеспе́чен постоя́нный дохо́д. **2.** (*assert confidently*) ув|еря́ть, -е́рить; зав|еря́ть, -е́рить; **I can ~ you of this** (я) могу́ вас в э́том уве́рить; **you may rest ~d that ...** мо́жете быть уве́рены, что... **3.** (*insure*) страхова́ть, за-.

assuredly [ə'ʃʊərɪdlɪ] *adv.* несомне́нно.

Assyria [ə'sɪrɪə] *n.* Асси́рия.

Assyrian [ə'sɪrɪən] *n.* **1.** (*pers.*) ассири́|ец (*fem.* -ка); айсо́р (*fem.* -ка). **2.** (*language*) ассири́йский язы́к.

adj. ассири́йский.

Assyriologist [ə,sɪrɪ'ɒlədʒɪst] *n.* ассирио́лог.

Assyriology [ə,sɪrɪ'ɒlədʒɪ] *n.* ассириоло́гия.

aster ['æstə(r)] *n.* а́стра.

asterisk ['æstərɪsk] *n.* звёздочка.

v.t. отм|еча́ть, -е́тить звёздочкой.

astern [ə'stɜ:n] *adv.* за кормо́й; на корме́; (*of motion*) наза́д; **full speed ~** по́лный ход наза́д; **pass ~ of** про|ходи́ть, -йти́ позади́+*g.* (*or* за кормо́й +*g.*); **drop ~** отст|ава́ть, -а́ть.

asteroid ['æstə,rɔɪd] *n.* астеро́ид.

asthma ['æsmə] *n.* а́стма.

asthmatic [æs'mætɪk] *n.* астма́тик.

adj. (*pertaining to asthma*) астмати́ческий; (*suffering from asthma*) страда́ющий а́стмой.

astigmatic [,æstɪg'mætɪk] *adj.* астигмати́ческий.

astigmatism [ə'stɪgmə,tɪz(ə)m] *n.* астигмати́зм.

astir [ə'stɜ:(r)] *pred. adj.* (*out of bed*) на нога́х; (*agog*) взбудора́женный.

astonish [ə'stɒnɪʃ] *v.t.* удив|ля́ть, -и́ть; изум|ля́ть, -и́ть; **be ~ed at** удив|ля́ться, -и́ться +*d.*; изум|ля́ться, -и́ться +*d.*; **I was ~ed to learn ...** я порази́лся, узна́в...; **his success was ~ing** он име́л порази́тельный успе́х.

astonishment [ə'stɒnɪʃmənt] *n.* удивле́ние, изумле́ние; **he cried out in ~** он вскри́кнул от удивле́ния; **to my ~** к моему́ изумле́нию.

astound [ə'staʊnd] *v.t.* изум|ля́ть, -и́ть; пора|жа́ть, -зи́ть; **he had an ~ing memory** у него́ была́ порази́тельная па́мять; **I was ~ed at the difference** меня́ порази́ла ра́зница.

astraddle [ə'stræd(ə)l] *adv.* широко́ расста́вив но́ги.

astrakhan [,æstrə'kæn] *n.* (*lambskin*) кара́куль (*m.*); (*attr.*) кара́кулевый.

astral ['æstr(ə)l] *adj.* звёздный; астра́льный; **~ body** астра́льное те́ло.

astray [ə'streɪ] *pred. adj. & adv.*: **you are ~ in your calculations** вы сби́лись/запу́тались в расчётах; **go ~** (*lit., miss one's way*) заблуди́ться (*pf.*); (*fig.*) сб|ива́ться, -и́ться с пути́; **lead ~** (*fig.*) сб|ива́ть, -ить с пути́ (и́стинного).

astride [ə'straɪd] *adv.* (*on animal*) верхо́м; (*with legs apart*) расста́вив но́ги.

prep.: **~ his father's knee** на коле́нях у отца́; **~ the road** попере́к доро́ги.

astringency [ə'strɪndʒ(ə)nsɪ] *n.* вя́жущее сво́йство; (*fig.*) суро́вость.

astringent [ə'strɪndʒ(ə)nt] *n.* вя́жущее сре́дство.

adj. вя́жущий; (*fig.*) суро́вый.

astrolabe ['æstrə,leɪb] *n.* астроля́бия.

astrologer [ə'strɒlədʒə(r)] *n.* астро́лог, звездочёт.

astrological [,æstrə'lɒdʒɪk(ə)l] *adj.* астрологи́ческий.

astrology [ə'strɒlədʒɪ] *n.* астроло́гия.

astronaut ['æstrə,nɔ:t] *n.* астрона́вт, космона́вт.

astronautics [,æstrə'nɔ:tɪks] *n.* астрона́втика, космона́втика.

astronomer [ə'strɒnəmə(r)] *n.* астроно́м.

astronomical [,æstrə'nɒmɪk(ə)l] *adj.* (*lit., fig.*) астрономи́ческий.

astronomy [ə'strɒnəmɪ] *n.* астроно́мия.

astrophysicist [,æstrəʊ'fɪzɪsɪst] *n.* астрофи́зик.

astrophysics [,æstrəʊ'fɪzɪks] *n.* астрофи́зика.

astute [ə'stju:t] *adj.* **1.** (*shrewd*) проницательный. **2.** (*crafty*) хи́трый; ло́вкий.

astuteness [ə'stju:tnɪs] *n.* **1.** проница́тельность. **2.** хи́трость; ло́вкость.

asunder [ə'sʌndə(r)] *adv.* **1.** (*separated from one another*) по́рознь, врозь; (*separately*) отде́льно; (*far apart*) далеко́ друг от дру́га. **2.** (*into pieces*) на куски́, на ча́сти; **tear ~** (*lit.*) разорва́ть (*pf.*) на ча́сти; (*fig., of persons*) разлуч|а́ть, -и́ть.

asylum [ə'saɪləm] *n.* **1.** (*sanctuary*) прию́т; (*place of refuge*) убе́жище. **2.** (*mental home*) сумасше́дший дом.

asymmetrical [,eɪsɪ'metrɪk(ə)l, ,æsɪ'metrɪk(ə)l] *adj.* ассиметри́ческий.

asymmetry [eɪ'sɪmɪtrɪ, æ'sɪmɪtrɪ] *n.* ассиме́трия.

asymptote ['æsɪmp,təʊt, 'æsɪm,təʊt] *n.* ассимпто́та.

at [æt, *unstressed* ət] *prep.* **1.** (*denoting place*) в/на+*p.*; (*near, by*) у+*g.*, при+*p.*; **~ the university** в университе́те; **~ № 10** в до́ме (но́мер) де́сять; **~ home** до́ма; **~ sea** (*lit.*) в мо́ре; **~ the battle** в би́тве; **~ church** в це́ркви; **~ school** в шко́ле; **~ the station** на вокза́ле/ста́нции; **~ the corner** на углу́; **~ the fork in the road** у разви́лки доро́ги; **~ the concert** на конце́рте; **~ that distance** на э́том расстоя́нии; **the thermometer is ~ 90°F.** термо́метр пока́зывает девяно́сто гра́дусов по Фаренге́йту; **~ hand** под руко́й; **~ the piano** у роя́ля; за роя́лем; **~ the helm** у руля́; **~ my aunt's** у мое́й тётки; **~ table** за столо́м; **~ my right** спра́ва от меня́; **~ his feet** у его́ ног; **~ the gates** у воро́т; **~ Court** при дворе́; **a translator ~ the UN** перево́дчик при ООН; **~ death's door** при́ смерти; на поро́ге сме́рти; **he was present ~ this scene** он был при э́той сце́не. **2.** (*denoting motion or direction; lit., fig.*): **he tapped ~ the window** он постуча́л в окно́; **he sat down ~ the table** он сел за стол; **she fell ~ his feet** она́ упа́ла к его́ нога́м; **he arrived ~ the station** он при́был на ста́нцию; **he went in ~ this door** он вошёл в/че́рез э́ту дверь; **he came out ~ this door** он вы́шел из э́той две́ри; **throw a stone ~** бро́сить (*pf.*) ка́мень/ка́мнем в+*a.*; **she is always ~ me to do it** (*coll.*) она ве́чно тре́бует, что́бы я э́то де́лал. **3.** (*denoting time or order*): **~ night** но́чью; **~ present** в настоя́щее вре́мя; **~ 2 o'clock** в два часа́; **~ half-past 2** в полови́не тре́тьего; **~ any moment** в любо́й моме́нт; **~ (the age of) 15** (в во́зрасте) пятна́дцати лет; **~ his death** в моме́нт его́ сме́рти; **~ the first attempt** с пе́рвой попы́тки; **~ intervals** с переры́вами; **~ the third stroke it will be 6 o'clock** при тре́тьем уда́ре/гудке́ бу́дет шесть часо́в; тре́тий уда́р/гудо́к даётся в шесть часо́в; **~ his signal** по его́ сигна́лу; **~ Easter** на Па́сху; **~ dawn** на заре́; на рассве́те; **~ twilight** в су́мерках; **~ midday** в по́лдень; **~ that time** в э́то вре́мя; **~ what hour?** в кото́ром часу́?; **~ the beginning** в нача́ле; **~ first** снача́ла; **he began ~ the beginning** он на́чал снача́ла; **~ parting** при расстава́нии. **4.** (*of activity, state, manner, rate etc.*): **~ work** на рабо́те; за рабо́той; **good ~ languages** спосо́бный к языка́м; **~ war** в состоя́нии войны́; **~ peace** в ми́ре; **~ a gallop** гало́пом; **~ one blow** одни́м уда́ром;

~ **a sitting** в оди́н присе́ст; ~ **60 m.p.h.** со ско́ростью шестьдеся́т миль в час; ~ **full speed** на по́лной ско́рости; ~ **a week's notice** предупреди́в за неде́лю; ~ **my expense** за мой счёт; **estimate** ~ оце́нивать (*impf.*) в+*a.*; ~ **best** в лу́чшем слу́чае; ~ **least** по кра́йней ме́ре; ~ **most** са́мое бо́льшее; ~ **your own risk** на ваш/свой страх и риск; ~ **all** вообще́; (*with neg.*) совсе́м; ~ **your service** к ва́шим услу́гам; ~ **my request** по мое́й про́сьбе; ~ **his dictation** под его́ дикто́вку; ~ **that** (*moreover*) к тому́ же; ~ **first sight** с пе́рвого взгля́да; ~ **a reduced price** по сни́женной цене́; ~ **fivepence a pound** по пяти́ пе́нсов за фунт; ~ **a high rate of interest** под больши́е проце́нты; ~ **a high remuneration** за большо́е вознагражде́ние; ~ **your discretion** по ва́шему усмотре́нию. **5.** (*of cause*): **be impatient** ~ **the delay** волнова́ться (*impf.*) из-за заде́ржки; **delighted** ~ в восто́рге от+*g.*; **he was amazed** ~ **what he heard** он был поражён услы́шанным; **he was angry** ~ **this suggestion** э́то предложе́ние его́ рассерди́ло.

cpd. ~**-home** *n.* приём госте́й, журфи́кс; зва́ный ве́чер.

atavism ['ætə,vɪz(ə)m] *n.* атави́зм.

atavistic [,ætə'vɪstɪk] *adj.* атависти́ческий.

ataxia [ə'tæksɪə] *n.* атакси́я; **locomotor** ~ дви́гательная атакси́я.

atelier [ə'telɪ,eɪ, 'ætə,ljeɪ] *n.* ателье́ (*indecl.*).

atheism ['eɪθɪ,ɪz(ə)m] *n.* атеи́зм, безбо́жие.

atheist ['eɪθɪɪst] *n.* атеи́ст, безбо́жник.

atheistic [,eɪθɪ'ɪstɪk] *adj.* атеисти́ческий.

Athen|a [ə'θi:nə], **-e** [ə'θi:nɪ] *n.* Афи́на.

Athenian [ə'θi:nɪən] *n.* афи́нян|ин (*fem.* -ка).

adj. афи́нский.

Athens ['æθɪnz] *n.* Афи́н|ы (*pl.*, *g.* —).

athirst [ə'θɜ:st] *pred. adj.* (*fig.*): **be** ~ **for** жа́ждать (*impf.*) +*g.*

athlete ['æθli:t] *n.* спортсме́н (*fem.* -ка); атле́т; ~**'s foot** грибко́вое заболева́ние ног.

athletic [æθ'letɪk] *adj.* атлети́ческий.

athletics [æθ'letɪks] *n.* атле́тика.

athwart [ə'θwɔ:t] *adv.* ко́со, попёрек.

prep. попёрек+*g.*; че́рез+*a.*; (*fig.*, *in opposition to*) вопреки́+*d.*

atishoo [ə'tɪʃu:] *int.* (*coll.*) апчхи́.

Atlantic [ət'læntɪk] *n.* Атланти́ческий океа́н; **North** ~ **Treaty Organization (NATO)** Североатланти́ческий сою́з (НАТО).

adj. атланти́ческий.

Atlanticism [ət'læntɪsɪz(ə)m] *n.* атланти́зм.

Atlantis [ət'læntɪs] *n.* Атланти́да.

Atlas[1] ['ætləs] *n.*: ~ **mountains** Атла́сские го́ры (*f. pl.*).

atlas[2] ['ætləs] *n.* а́тлас.

atmosphere ['ætməs,fɪə(r)] *n.* (*lit.*, *fig.*) атмосфе́ра; (*fig.*) колори́т, обстано́вка.

atmospheric [,ætməs'ferɪk] *adj.* атмосфе́рный; ~ **pressure** атмосфе́рное давле́ние; ~ **temperature** температу́ра во́здуха.

atmospherics [,ætməs'ferɪks] *n.* атмосфе́рные поме́хи (*f. pl.*).

atoll ['ætɒl] *n.* ато́лл.

atom ['ætəm] *n.* а́том; **split the** ~ расщеп|ля́ть, -и́ть а́том; ~ **bomb** а́томная бо́мба; (*fig.*) **not an** ~ **of evidence** ни те́ни доказа́тельства; **not an** ~ **of strength** ни ка́пли си́лы.

atomic [ə'tɒmɪk] *adj.* а́томный; **the** ~ **age** а́томный век; ~ **bomb** а́томная бо́мба; ~ **energy, power** а́томная эне́ргия; ~ **number** а́томное число́; ~ **pile/reactor** а́томный котёл/реа́ктор; ~ **warfare** а́томная война́; ~ **weight** а́томный вес.

cpd. ~**-powered** *adj.* с а́томными дви́гателями.

atomization [,ætəmaɪ'zeɪʃ(ə)n] *n.* (*of liquid*) распыле́ние; (*of solid*) измельче́ние.

atomize [,ætə'maɪz] *v.t.* распыл|я́ть, -и́ть; измельч|а́ть, -и́ть.

atomizer ['ætə,maɪzə(r)] *n.* атомиза́тор; (*spray*) пульвериза́тор, распыли́тель (*m.*).

atonal [eɪ'təʊn(ə)l, ə-] *adj.* атона́льный.

atonality [eɪ,təʊ'nælɪtɪ, ə-] *n.* атона́льность.

atone [ə'təʊn] *v.i.*: ~ **for** загла́|живать, -дить; искуп|а́ть, -и́ть; **he** ~**d for his crimes** он искупи́л свои́ преступле́ния.

atonement [ə'təʊnmənt] *n.* искупле́ние; **Day of A**~ Су́дный день.

atonic [ə'tɒnɪk] *adj.* (*ling.*) безуда́рный; глухо́й; (*med.*) атони́ческий, рассла́бленный.

atop [ə'tɒp] *adv.* & *prep.* на верши́не (+*g.*); наверху́.

atrabilious [,ætrə'bɪljəs] *adj.* (*fig.*) жёлчный.

atremble [ə'tremb(ə)l] *adv.* дрожа́.

atrium ['eɪtrɪəm] *n.* а́трий, а́триум.

atrocious [ə'trəʊʃəs] *adj.* зве́рский, жесто́кий; (*very bad*) ужа́сный.

atrociousness [ə'trəʊʃəsnɪs] *n.* жесто́кость, гну́сность.

atrocit|y [ə'trɒsɪtɪ] *n.* жесто́кость, зве́рство; **many** ~**ies were committed** бы́ло совершено́ мно́го зверств; (*hideous object*) уро́дство, у́жас.

atroph|y ['ætrəfɪ] *n.* атрофи́я.

v.t. & *i.* атрофи́ровать(ся) (*impf.*, *pf.*); ~**ied muscles** атрофи́рованные му́скулы.

atropine ['ætrə,pi:n, -pɪn] *n.* атропи́н.

attaboy ['ætə,bɔɪ] *int.* (*US coll.*) молоде́ц!; молодчи́на! (*m.*).

attach [ə'tætʃ] *v.t.* **1.** (*fasten*) прикреп|ля́ть, -и́ть; (*by tying*) привя́з|ывать, -а́ть; (*by sticking*) прикле́и|вать, -ить; ~ **a seal** приложи́ть (*pf.*) печа́ть; **the** ~**ed document** прилага́емый докуме́нт. **2.** (*fig.*, *of pers.*) присоедин|я́ть, -и́ть; (*appoint*) назн|ача́ть, -а́чить; прикомандирова́ть (*pf.*). **3.**: ~ **o.s. to** присоедин|я́ться, -и́ться к+*d.* **4.** (*assign*) прид|ава́ть, -а́ть; (*ascribe*) припи́с|ывать, -а́ть; **he** ~**es much importance to this visit** он придаёт большо́е значе́ние э́тому визи́ту; ~ **blame to** возл|ага́ть, -ожи́ть вину́ на+*a.* **5.** (*of affection*): **she is very** ~**ed to her brother** она́ о́чень привя́зана к своему́ бра́ту. **I am** ~**ed to this necklace** э́то ожере́лье мне о́чень до́рого. **6.** (*leg.*, *seize*) заде́рж|ивать, -а́ть; на|кла́дывать, -ложи́ть аре́ст на+*a.*

v.i. ~ **to** (*inhere in*): **the responsibility that** ~**es to this position** отве́тственность, свя́занная с э́той до́лжностью; **no blame/suspicion** ~**es to him** на него́ не падёт вина́/подозре́ние.

attaché [ə'tæʃeɪ] *n.* атташе́ (*m. indecl.*); ~ **case** портфе́ль (*m.*).

attachment [ə'tætʃmənt] *n.* **1.** (*part attached to a larger unit*) прикрепле́ние, привя́зывание, прикле́ивание. **2.** (*appointment*) прикомандирова́ние. **3.** (*affection*) привя́занность; **form an** ~ **for** привяза́ться (*pf.*) к+*d.*; (*devotion*) пре́данность. **4.** (*leg.*): ~ **of property** наложе́ние аре́ста на иму́щество.

attack [ə'tæk] *n.* **1.** нападе́ние; (*mil.*) ата́ка, наступле́ние, нападе́ние, при́ступ; **make an** ~ **on** атакова́ть (*impf.*, *pf.*); **we went into the** ~ мы пошли́ в ата́ку; **our troops were under** ~ на́ши войска́ бы́ли атако́ваны. **2.** (*fig.*, *criticism*) напа́д|ки (*pl.*, *g.* -ок); **you will be open to** ~ **on all sides** вы ока́жетесь под огнём со всех сторо́н. **3.** (*of illness*) при́ступ; припа́док; **he had a heart** ~ с ним случи́лся серде́чный при́ступ. **4.** (*mus.*) ата́ка.

v.t. **1.** (*lit.*, *fig.*) нап|ада́ть, -а́сть на+*a*; атакова́ть (*impf.*, *pf.*); обру́ши|ваться, -ться на+*a.*; **he was** ~**ed by a lion** на него́ напа́л лев; **he was** ~**ed in the press** его́ атакова́ли в печа́ти; **our troops** ~**ed the enemy** на́ши войска уда́рили по врагу́. **2.** (*of illness*) пора|жа́ть, -зи́ть. **3.** (*harm*) повре|жда́ть, -ди́ть +*d.*; (*of chemical action*) разъ|еда́ть, -е́сть. **4.** (*a task etc.*) набр|а́сываться, -о́ситься на+*a.*

v.i.: **the enemy** ~**ed** враг бро́сился/пошёл в ата́ку.

attacker [ə'tækə(r)] *n.* напада́ющий; (*mil.*) атаку́ющий.

attain [ə'teɪn] *v.t.* (*also* ~ **to**) (*reach*; *gain*; *accomplish*) дост|ига́ть, -и́гнуть (*or* -и́чь) +*g.*; доб|ива́ться, -и́ться +*g.*; **our ends were** ~**ed** мы доби́лись своего́; **he** ~**ed his majority** он дости́г совершенноле́тия; **I shall never** ~ **this ambition** мои́ стремле́ния никогда́ не осуществя́тся.

attainable [ə'teɪnəb(ə)l] *adj.* достижи́мый.

attainder [ə'teɪndə(r)] *n.* гражда́нская казнь.

attainment [ə'teɪnmənt] *n.* (*attaining*) достиже́ние; (*acquisition*) приобрете́ние, завоева́ние; (*accomplishment*): **linguistic** ~**s** лингвисти́ческие позна́ния; **easy/difficult of** ~ легко́/тру́дно досту́пный.

attaint [ə'teɪnt] *v.t.* подв|ерга́ть, -е́ргнуть гражда́нской ка́зни.

attar ['ætɑ:(r)] *n.*: ~ **of roses** ро́зовое ма́сло.

attempt [ə'tempt] *n.* **1.** (*endeavour*) попы́тка; о́пыт; **they made no** ~ **to escape** они́ не пыта́лись убежа́ть; **he**

succeeded at the first ~ у него́ получи́лось с пе́рвой попы́тки; **they failed in all their ~s to persuade him** все их попы́тки убеди́ть его́ потерпе́ли неуда́чу. **2.** (*assault*) покуше́ние; **an ~ was made on his life** покуша́лись на его́ жизнь; **an ~ will be made on Everest this summer** э́тим ле́том бу́дет сде́лана попы́тка подня́ться на Эвере́ст. **3.: ~ at: her ~ at producing a meal** плод её кулина́рных поту́г.

v.t. **1.** (*try; try to do*) пыта́ться, по-; **~ed theft** попы́тка воровства́; **he was charged with ~ed murder** его́ обвини́ли в покуше́нии на жизнь. **2.** (*arch.*) **~ s.o.'s life** поку|ша́ться, -си́ться на чью-н. жизнь.

attend [əˈtend] *v.t.* **1.** (*be present at*) прису́тствовать (*impf.*) на+*p.*; **the concert was well ~ed** на конце́рте бы́ло мно́го пу́блики; **~ school** посеща́ть (*impf.*) шко́лу. **2.** (*lit., fig.; accompany*) сопровожда́ть (*impf.*); **the venture was ~ed with risk** предприя́тие бы́ло сопряжено́ с ри́ском; **may good luck ~ you** пусть вам сопу́тствует уда́ча. **3.** (*serve professionally*) уха́живать (*impf.*) за+*i.*; **three nurses ~ed him** три медсестры́ уха́живали за ним; **he was ~ed by Dr. Smith** его́ лечи́л до́ктор Смит.

v.i. **1.** (*be present*) прису́тствовать (*impf.*). **2.** (*direct one's mind*) удел|я́ть, -и́ть внима́ние +*d.*; обра|ща́ть, -ти́ть внима́ние на+*a.*; (*listen carefully*): **~ to what I am saying** слу́шайте меня́ внима́тельно; **you are not ~ing** вы не слу́шаете. **3.: ~ to** (*take care of, look after*) следи́ть (*impf.*) за+*i.*; забо́титься, по- о+*p.*; **he ~s to the education of his own children** он сам занима́ется воспита́нием свои́х дете́й; **she ~ed to the children** она́ присма́тривала за детьми́; **please ~ to the flowers** пожа́луйста, присмотри́те за цвета́ми; **~ to one's duties** исполня́ть (*impf.*) свои обя́занности; **~ to one's correspondence** занима́ться (*impf.*) свое́й перепи́ской; **~ to s.o.'s needs** забо́титься, по- о чьих-н. ну́ждах; **are you being ~ed to?** (*in shop*) вас (уже́) обслу́живают?; **I have things to ~ to** у меня́ есть дела́. **4.: ~ upon** (*serve*) прислу́живать (*impf.*), обслу́живать (*impf.*); **he ~ed upon the queen** он сопровожда́л короле́ву; (*fig.: accompany*) сопу́тствовать (*impf.*) +*d.*; **the consequences ~ing upon this action** после́дствия, кото́рые повлёк за собо́й э́тот посту́пок.

attendance [əˈtend(ə)ns] *n.* **1.** (*presence*) прису́тствие; (*number of visits or of those present*) посеща́емость; **there was a high, large ~ at church today** сего́дня в це́ркви бы́ло мно́го наро́ду; (*body of persons present*) аудито́рия; пу́блика. **2.** (*looking after s.o.*) ухо́д; **medical ~** враче́бный ухо́д; **the doctor is in ~ from 3 to 5** врач принима́ет с трёх до пяти́ (часо́в). **3.** (*service to, accompaniment of s.o.*) обслу́живание; **he dances ~ on her** он хо́дит перед не́ю на за́дних ла́пках; **I won't dance ~ on him all morning** я не собира́юсь убива́ть на него́ всё у́тро.

attendant [əˈtend(ə)nt] *n.* (*servant*) слуга́ (*m.*), служи́тель (m.); (*one who waits upon or accompanies another*) обслу́живающее/сопровожда́ющее лицо́; **medical ~** врач.

adj. (*accompanying*) сопу́тствующий; сопровожда́ющий; (*present*) прису́тствующий; обслу́живающий.

attender [əˈtendə(r)] *n.*: **he is a regular ~ at church** он регуля́рно хо́дит в це́рковь.

attention [əˈtenʃ(ə)n] *n.* **1.** (*heed*) внима́ние; **pay, give ~ to** обра|ща́ть, -ти́ть внима́ние на+*a.*; **pay, devote much/little ~ to** удел|я́ть, -и́ть мно́го/ма́ло внима́ния +*d.*; **pay ~!** бу́дьте внима́тельны!; **direct, draw ~ to** привл|ека́ть, -е́чь внима́ние к+*d.*; **call s.o.'s ~ to** обра|ща́ть, -ти́ть чьё-н. внима́ние на+*a.*; **compel ~** прико́в|ывать, -а́ть внима́ние; **it slipped my ~** э́то ускользну́ло от моего́ внима́ния; **I am all ~** я весь внима́ние; **(for the) ~ (of)** (*on letters etc.*) на рассмотре́ние +*g.* **2.** (*mil. command*) сми́рно!; (*posture*) **stand to ~** стоя́ть (*impf.*) сми́рно; **he came to ~** он при́нял сто́йку сми́рно (*or* строеву́ю сто́йку). **3.** (*care*) ухо́д; **he was given immediate medical ~** ему́ была́ ока́зана неме́дленная медици́нская по́мощь. **4.** (*politeness; courtesy*) забо́тливость; внима́ние, внима́тельность; **pay one's ~s to** (*court*) уха́живать (*impf.*) за+*i.*

attentive [əˈtentɪv] *adj.* **1.** (*heedful*) внима́тельный; **~ to detail** внима́тельный к ча́стностям; (*careful*) предупреди́тельный. **2.** (*solicitous*) забо́тливый.

attentiveness [əˈtentɪvnɪs] *n.* внима́тельность; предупреди́тельность; забо́тливость.

attenuat|e [əˈtenjʊˌeɪt] *v.t.* (*make slender*) истощ|а́ть, -и́ть; (*fig., reduce gravity of*) смягч|а́ть, -и́ть; **~ing circumstances** смягча́ющие обстоя́тельства.

attenuation [əˌtenjʊˈeɪʃ(ə)n] *n.* истоще́ние; смягче́ние.

attest [əˈtest] *v.t.* (*certify*) удостов|еря́ть, -е́рить; (*bear witness to*) свиде́тельствовать, за-; **~ed copy** заве́ренная ко́пия; **~ed cattle** скот, проше́дший ветнадзо́р; (*confirm*) подтвер|жда́ть, -ди́ть.

v.i. **~ to** свиде́тельствовать (*impf.*) о+*p.*

attestation [ˌæteˈsteɪʃ(ə)n] *n.* засвиде́тельствование, удостовере́ние, подтвержде́ние.

attic[1] [ˈætɪk] *n.* манса́рда, черда́к.

Attic[2] [ˈætɪk] *adj.* атти́ческий.

Attila [əˈtɪlə] *n.* Атти́ла (*m.*).

attire [əˈtaɪə(r)] *n.* наря́д, одея́ние; **in night ~** в ночно́м облаче́нии.

v.t. (*dress*) наря|жа́ть, -ди́ть; од|ева́ть, -е́ть; **she was ~d in white** она́ была́ вся в бе́лом.

attitude [ˈætɪˌtjuːd] *n.* **1.** (*pose*) по́за; **strike an ~** прин|има́ть, -я́ть по́зу. **2.** (*fig., disposition*) отноше́ние; **~ of mind** склад ума́; **what is your ~ to this book?** как вы отно́ситесь к э́той кни́ге?; **that is an odd ~ to take up** э́то стра́нный подхо́д.

attitudinize [ˌætɪˈtjuːdɪˌnaɪz] *v.i.* аффекти́рованно вести́ (*det.*) себя́.

attn. [əˈtenʃ(ə)n] *n.* (*abbr. of* **for the attention of**) вним., (внима́нию) (+*g.*).

attorney [əˈtɜːnɪ] *n.* уполномо́ченный, дове́ренный; **~ at law** пове́ренный в суде́, адвока́т; **by ~** по дове́ренности; **power of ~** дове́ренность.

attract [əˈtrækt] *v.t.* **1.** (*of physical forces*) притя́|гивать, -ну́ть; (*fig.*) привл|ека́ть, -е́чь (к себе́); **can you ~ the waiter's attention?** вы мо́жете привле́чь внима́ние официа́нта?; **bright lights ~ moths** мотыльки́ летя́т на я́ркий свет; **the mystery ~ed him** его́ влекла́/мани́ла та́йна; **his manner ~ed a good deal of criticism** его́ мане́ра держа́ть себя́ вызыва́ла нема́ло нарека́ний. **2.** (*captivate*) плен|я́ть, -и́ть; **he found himself ~ed to her** он почу́вствовал, что увлечён е́ю; **I am not ~ed by the idea** меня́ э́та иде́я не привлека́ет.

attraction [əˈtrækʃ(ə)n] *n.* **1.** (*phys.*) притяже́ние, тяготе́ние. **2.** (*charm, allure*) прима́нка, привлека́тельность; **the ~s of a big city** собла́зны большо́го го́рода. **3.** (*in theatre etc.*) аттракцио́н.

attractive [əˈtræktɪv] *adj.* **1.** (*phys.*): **~ force** си́ла притяже́ния. **2.** (*fig.*) притяга́тельный; привлека́тельный; **an ~ dress** ми́лое/симпати́чное пла́тье.

attractiveness [əˈtræktɪvnɪs] *n.* привлека́тельность.

attributable [əˈtrɪbjʊtəb(ə)l] *adj.* припи́сываемый; **his illness is ~ to drink** его́ боле́знь объясня́ется пья́нством.

attribute[1] [ˈætrɪˌbjuːt] *n.* **1.** (*quality*) сво́йство; (*characteristic*) характе́рная черта́. **2.** (*accompanying feature, emblem*) атрибу́т. **3.** (*gram.*) атрибу́т; определе́ние.

attribute[2] [əˈtrɪbjuːt] *v.t.*: **~ sth to** припи́с|ывать, -а́ть что-н. +*d.*; отн|оси́ть, -ести́ что-н. к+*d.* (*or* за счёт +*g.*).

attribution [ˌætrɪˈbjuːʃ(ə)n] *n.* (*ascription*) припи́сывание, отнесе́ние.

attributive [əˈtrɪbjʊtɪv] *adj.* атрибути́вный; определи́тельный.

attrition [əˈtrɪʃ(ə)n] *n.* тре́ние; истира́ние; (*fig.*) истоще́ние; измо́р; **war of ~** война́ на истоще́ние.

attune [əˈtjuːn] *v.t.* (*lit., fig.*) настр|а́ивать, -о́ить.

atypical [eɪˈtɪpɪk(ə)l] *adj.* нетипи́чный, атипи́ческий.

aubergine [ˈəʊbəʒiːn] *n.* баклажа́н.

auburn [ˈɔːbən] *adj.* тёмно-ры́жий.

au courant [ˌəʊ kuːˈrɑ̃] *pred. adj.* в ку́рсе (*чего*).

auction [ˈɔːkʃ(ə)n] *n.* аукцио́н; **put up for ~** выставля́ть, вы́ставить на аукцио́не; продава́ть (*impf.*) с молотка́; **the house is for sale by ~** дом продаётся с аукцио́на.

v.t. (*also* **~ off**) прод|ава́ть, -а́ть с аукцио́на.

auctioneer [ˌɔːkʃəˈnɪə(r)] *n.* аукциони́ст.

audacious [ɔːˈdeɪʃəs] *adj.* (*daring*) отва́жный; дерзнове́нный; (*impudent*) де́рзкий.

audacity [ɔːˈdæsɪtɪ] *n.* отва́га, сме́лость; дерза́ние; де́рзость.

audibility [ˌɔːdɪˈbɪlɪtɪ] *n.* слы́шимость; вня́тность.

audible [ˈɔːdɪb(ə)l] *adj.* слы́шимый, слы́шный; (*distinct*) вня́тный.

audience [ˈɔːdɪəns] *n.* **1.** (*listeners*) аудито́рия; слу́шатели (*m. pl.*); (*spectators*) зри́тели (*m. pl.*); пу́блика; **a captive ~** зри́тели/слу́шатели понево́ле; **~ participation** уча́стие аудито́рии; **~ research** изуче́ние аудито́рии. **2.** (*hearing; interview*) аудие́нция; **he requested an ~ of the queen** он попроси́л аудие́нцию у короле́вы.

audio-lingual [ˌɔːdɪəʊ ˈlɪŋgw(ə)l] *adj.* аудиоречево́й.

audiotape [ˈɔːdɪəʊˌteɪp] *n.* плёнка звукоза́писи.

audiotypist [ˌɔːdɪəʊˈtaɪpɪst] *n.* фономашини́стка.

audio-visual [ˌɔːdɪəʊˈvɪʒjʊəl] *adj.* а́удио-визуа́льный.

audit [ˈɔːdɪt] *n.* прове́рка, реви́зия.

v.t. пров|еря́ть, -е́рить отчётность +*g.*; ревизова́ть (*impf., pf.*).

audition [ɔːˈdɪʃ(ə)n] *n.* (*listening*) слу́шание, прослу́шивание (*m.*); (*trial hearing*) про́ба.

v.t. прослу́ш|ивать, -ать.

auditor [ˈɔːdɪtə(r)] *n.* **1.** (*hearer*) слу́шатель (*m.*); **2.** (*checker*) бухга́лтер-ревизо́р; фина́нсовый инспе́ктор.

auditorium [ˌɔːdɪˈtɔːrɪəm] *n.* (*where audience sits*) зри́тельный зал; (*public building*) аудито́рия, зал.

auditory [ˈɔːdɪtərɪ] *adj.* слухово́й.

au fait [əʊ ˈfeɪ] *pred. adj.* в ку́рсе; осведомлённый; **can you put me ~ with the situation?** могли́ бы вы ввести́ меня́ в курс де́ла?

Augean [ɔːˈdʒiːən] *adj.*: **~ stables** А́вгиевы коню́шни (*f. pl.*).

auger [ˈɔːgə(r)] *n.* сверло́; (*woodworking tool*) бура́в; (*for boring coal etc.*) бур.

aught [ɔːt] *pron.* (*arch.*) что́-нибудь; **for ~ I know** ≃ отку́да мне знать?; кто его́ зна́ет.

augment [ɔːgˈment] *v.t.* увели́чи|вать, -ть; приб|авля́ть, -а́вить +*g.*; **~ed interval** (*mus.*) увели́ченный интерва́л.

v.i. увели́чи|ваться, -ться; уси́ли|ваться, -ться.

augmentation [ˌɔːgmenˈteɪʃ(ə)n] *n.* увеличе́ние; прираще́ние.

augmentative [ɔːgˈmentətɪv] *adj.* (*gram.*) увеличи́тельный.

augur [ˈɔːgə(r)] *n.* (*hist.*) авгу́р; (*soothsayer*) прорица́тель (*m.*).

v.t. (*portend*) предвеща́ть (*impf.*); (*of pers.: predict*) предска́з|ывать, -а́ть.

v.i. (*of things*) служи́ть (*impf.*) предзнаменова́нием; **the exam results ~ well for his future** результа́ты его́ экза́менов — хоро́шая зая́вка на бу́дущее; (*of pers.*) предви́деть (*impf.*).

augury [ˈɔːgjərɪ] *n.* (*divination*) предсказа́ние; (*omen; sign*) предзнаменова́ние.

August[1] [ˈɔːgəst] *n.* а́вгуст; (*attr.*) а́вгустовский.

august[2] [ɔːˈgʌst] *adj.* вели́чественный.

Augustan [ɔːˈgʌst(ə)n] *adj.*: **the ~ age** (*hist.*) век А́вгуста; век классици́зма в литерату́ре и иску́сстве.

augustness [ɔːˈgʌstnɪs] *n.* вели́чественность.

Augustus [ɔːˈgʌstəs] *n.* А́вгуст.

auk [ɔːk] *n.* гага́рка.

aunt [ɑːnt] *n.* тётя, тётка; **A~ Sally** (*fig.*) предме́т напа́док/оскорбле́ний.

aunt|ie, -y [ˈɑːntɪ] *n.* тётушка, тётенька.

au pair [əʊ ˈpeə(r)] *n.* ≃ ня́ня-иностра́нка; помо́щница по хозя́йству из иностра́нок.

aura [ˈɔːrə] *n.* арома́т; (*atmosphere*) атмосфе́ра; **there is an ~ of tranquillity about him** от него́ ве́ет споко́йствием.

aural [ˈɔːr(ə)l] *adj.* (*pert. to hearing*) слухово́й; **~ly** на слух; (*pert. to the ear*) ушно́й.

aureate [ˈɔːrɪət] *adj.* золоти́стый; позоло́ченный.

aureole [ˈɔːrɪˌəʊl] *n.* (*halo*) орео́л; (*crown*) ве́нчик.

aureomycin [ˌɔːrɪəʊˈmaɪsɪn] *n.* ауреомици́н.

au revoir [əʊ rəˈvwɑː(r)] *int.* до свида́нья.

auricle [ˈɔːrɪk(ə)l] *n.* (*of ear*) нару́жное у́хо; (*of heart*) предсе́рдие.

auricular [ɔːˈrɪkjʊlə(r)] *adj.* **1.** ушно́й, слухово́й; **~ confession** и́споведь на́ ухо свяще́ннику; та́йная и́споведь. **2.** (*pert. to heart*) относя́щийся к предсе́рдию.

auriferous [ɔːˈrɪfərəs] *adj.* золотоно́сный, золотосодержа́щий.

Auriga [ɔːˈraɪgə] *n.* Возни́чий.

aurist [ˈɔːrɪst] *n.* отиа́тр.

aurochs [ˈɔːrɒks, ˈaʊrɒks] *n.* зубр.

aurora [ɔːˈrɔːrə] *n.* **1.** (**A~**: *myth*) Авро́ра; (*poet., dawn*) авро́ра, у́тренняя заря́. **2.** (*atmospheric phenomenon*): **~ borealis/australis** се́верное/ю́жное сия́ние.

Auschwitz [ˈaʊʃvɪts] *n.* Осве́нцим.

auscultation [ˌɔːskəlˈteɪʃ(ə)n] *n.* выслу́шивание, аускульта́ция.

auspices [ˈɔːspɪsɪz] *n.* **1.** (*omens*) предзнаменова́ния (*nt. pl.*); **under favourable ~** при благоприя́тных усло́виях. **2.** (*patronage*) покрови́тельство; эги́да.

auspicious [ɔːˈspɪʃəs] *adj.* (*favourable*) благоприя́тный; (*of good omen*) благоприя́тствующий; **on this ~ day** в э́тот знамена́тельный день.

Aussie [ˈɒzɪ, ˈɒsɪ] (*coll.*) = **Australian**

austere [ɒˈstɪə(r), ɔːˈstɪə(r)] *adj.* (*lit., fig.*) стро́гий, суро́вый.

austerity [ɒˈsterɪtɪ, ɔːˈsterɪtɪ] *n.* стро́гость, суро́вость; (*economy*) стро́гая эконо́мия.

austral [ˈɔːstr(ə)l, ˈɒstr(ə)l] *adj.* ю́жный.

Australasia [ˌɒstrəˈleɪʒə, -ʃə] *n.* Австра́лия и Океа́ния; Австра́лия и Но́вая Зела́ндия.

Australia [ɒˈstreɪlɪə] *n.* Австра́лия; **Commonwealth of ~** Австрали́йский Сою́з.

Australian [ɒˈstreɪlɪən] *n.* австрали́|ец (*fem.* -йка).

adj. австрали́йский.

Austria [ˈɒstrɪə] *n.* А́встрия.

Austria-Hungary [ˈɒstrɪəˈhʌŋgərɪ] *n.* А́встро-Ве́нгрия.

Austrian [ˈɒstrɪən] *n.* австри́|ец (*fem.* -йка).

adj. австри́йский.

Austro-Hungarian [ˌɒstrəʊhʌŋˈgeərɪən] *adj.* а́встро-венге́рский.

autarchy [ˈɔːtɑːkɪ] *n.* автокра́тия, самодержа́вие.

autarkic [ɔːˈtɑːkɪk] *adj.* автаркі́стский.

autarky [ˈɔːtɑːkɪ] *n.* автарки́я.

authentic [ɔːˈθentɪk] *adj.* (*genuine*) по́длинный, аутенти́чный; (*reliable*) достове́рный.

authenticate [ɔːˈθentɪˌkeɪt] *v.t.* удостов|еря́ть, -е́рить по́длинность +*g.*

authentication [ɔːˌθentɪˈkeɪʃ(ə)n] *n.* установле́ние/удостовере́ние по́длинности (*чего*).

authenticity [ˌɔːθenˈtɪsɪtɪ] *n.* по́длинность; аутенти́чность; достове́рность.

author[1] [ˈɔːθə(r)] *n.* **1.** (*of specific work*) а́втор; (*writer in general*) писа́тель (*m.*); а́втор. **2.** (*originator, creator*) творе́ц; созда́тель (*m.*); (*perpetrator*) инициа́тор, зачи́нщик.

author[2] [ˈɔːθə(r)] *v.t.* писа́ть, на-.

authoress [ˈɔːθrɪs, ˌɔːθəˈres] *n.* писа́тельница; **the ~ of the book** а́втор кни́ги.

authoritarian [ɔːˌθɒrɪˈteərɪən] *adj.* авторита́рный, деспоти́ческий.

authoritative [ɔːˈθɒrɪtətɪv] *adj.* авторите́тный.

authority [ɔːˈθɒrɪtɪ] *n.* **1.** (*power; right*) власть; (*legal*) полномо́чие; **~ to sign** пра́во по́дписи; **person in ~** власть иму́щий; челове́к, облечённый вла́стью; **who is in ~ here?** кто здесь гла́вный/нача́льник?; **published by ~ of parliament** опублико́ванный по ука́зу парла́мента; **on one's own ~** на свою́ отве́тственность; по со́бственному почи́ну; **I did it on his ~** я э́то сде́лал по его́ поруче́нию; **who gave you ~ over me?** кто вам дал пра́во мне прика́зывать? **2.** (*usu. pl.: public bodies*) вла́сти (*f. pl.*); о́рганы (*m. pl.*) вла́сти; **the Atomic Energy A~** Управле́ние по а́томной эне́ргии; **he is always getting into trouble with ~** у него́ всё вре́мя неприя́тности с властя́ми. **3.** (*influence, weight*) авторите́т; **carry, have ~** по́льзоваться (*impf.*) авторите́том; **he speaks with ~** он говори́т авторите́тно/внуши́тельно (*or* со зна́нием де́ла). **4.** (*source*) достове́рный исто́чник; **I have it on good ~** я э́то зна́ю из достове́рного исто́чника; **to have sth. on good ~** знать (*impf.*) что-н. из ве́рных рук; **what is your ~ for saying so?** на основа́нии чего́ вы э́то говори́те?; **I said it on his ~** я сказа́л э́то, сосла́вшись на него́. **5.** (*expert*): **he is an ~ on Greek** он кру́пный специали́ст по гре́ческому языку́.

authorization [ˌɔːθəraɪˈzeɪʃ(ə)n] *n.* (*authorizing*) уполномо́чивание; (*sanction*) разреше́ние; са́нкция.

authorize [ˈɔːθəˌraɪz] *v.t.* **1.** (*give authority to*) уполномо́чи|вать,

-ть. **2.** (*permit*; *sanction*) разреш|а́ть, -и́ть; дозв|оля́ть, -о́лить; санкциони́ровать (*impf.*, *pf.*); ~**d expenditure** утверждённые расхо́ды. **3.** (*justify*) опра́вд|ывать, -а́ть.

authorship ['ɔ:θəʃɪp] *n.* а́вторство; **a manuscript of doubtful ~** ру́копись, а́втор кото́рой то́чно не устано́влен; (*profession of writing*) писа́тельство.

autism ['ɔ:tɪz(ə)m] *n.* аути́зм.

autistic [ɔ:'tɪstɪk] *adj.* аутисти́ческий.

autobahn ['ɔ:təʊ,bɑ:n] *n.* автостра́да.

autobiographer [,ɔ:təʊbaɪ'ɒgrəfə(r)] *n.* автобио́граф.

autobiographical [,ɔ:təʊbaɪə'græfɪk(ə)l] *adj.* автобиографи́ческий, автобиографи́чный.

autobiography [,ɔ:təʊbaɪ'ɒgrəfɪ] *n.* автобиогра́фия.

autocephalous [,ɔ:təʊ'sefələs] *adj.* автокефа́льный, самоуправля́емый.

autochthonous [ɔ:'tɒkθ(ə)nəs] *adj.* автохто́нный; ме́стный, первонача́льный.

autocracy [ɔ:'tɒkrəsɪ] *n.* самодержа́вие, автокра́тия.

autocrat ['ɔ:tə,kræt] *n.* самоде́ржец.

autocratic [,ɔ:tə'krætɪk] *adj.* самодержа́вный; (*dictatorial*) деспоти́ческий.

autocross ['ɔ:təʊ,krɒs] *n.* автокро́сс.

autocue ['ɔ:təʊ,kju:] *n.* (*propr.*) телесуфлёр; автосуфлёр.

auto-da-fé [,ɔ:təʊdɑ:'feɪ] *n.* аутодафе́ (*indecl.*).

autodidact ['ɔ:təʊ,daɪdækt] *n.* автодида́кт; само́учка.

autog|iro, -yro [,ɔ:təʊ'dʒaɪərəʊ] *n.* автожи́р.

autograph ['ɔ:tə,grɑ:f] *n.* авто́граф.

v.t. надпи́с|ывать, -а́ть; ~**ed copy** экземпля́р с авто́графом.

autointoxication [,ɔ:təʊɪn,tɒksɪ'keɪʃ(ə)n] *n.* автоинтоксика́ция, самоотравле́ние.

automat ['ɔ:tə,mæt] *n.* автома́т; (*cafeteria*) заку́сочная-автома́т.

automated ['ɔ:tə,meɪtɪd] *adj.* автоматизи́рованный.

automatic [,ɔ:tə'mætɪk] *n.* (*firearm*) автомати́ческое ору́жие.

adj. **1.** (*self-acting*) автомати́ческий; ~ **pilot** автопило́т; ~ **pistol** самозаря́дный пистоле́т; ~ **machine** автома́т. **2.** (*of actions etc.*, *mechanical*) машина́льный, автомати́ческий.

automation [,ɔ:tə'meɪʃ(ə)n] *n.* автоматиза́ция.

automatism [ɔ:'tɒmə,tɪz(ə)m] *n.* автомати́зм.

automaton [ɔ:'tɒmət(ə)n] *n.* автома́т.

automobile ['ɔ:təmə,bi:l] *n.* автомоби́ль (*m.*); (*attr.*) автомоби́льный.

autonomous [ɔ:'tɒnəməs] *adj.* автоно́мный.

autonomy [ɔ:'tɒnəmɪ] *n.* автоно́мия, самоуправле́ние.

autopilot ['ɔ:təʊ,paɪlət] *n.* автопило́т.

autopsy ['ɔ:tɒpsɪ, ɔ:'tɒpsɪ] *n.* вскры́тие тру́па, ауто́псия.

auto-suggestion [,ɔ:təʊsə'dʒestʃ(ə)n] *n.* самовнуше́ние.

autumn ['ɔ:təm] *n.* о́сень; **in ~** о́сенью; (*attr.*) осе́нний; ~ **crocus** лугово́й шафра́н.

autumnal [ɔ:'tʌmn(ə)l] *adj.* осе́нний.

auxiliary [ɔ:g'zɪljərɪ] *n.* (*assistant*) помо́щник; (*gram.*, ~ **verb**) вспомога́тельный глаго́л; (*mil.*) солда́т вспомога́тельных войск; (*pl.*) вспомога́тельные войска́.

adj. (*helpful*; *supporting*) вспомога́тельный; (*additional*) доба́вочный; (*in reserve*) запасно́й.

avail [ə'veɪl] *n.* (*use*) по́льза; (*profit*) вы́года; **his entreaties were of no ~** его́ мольбы́ бы́ли безуспе́шны; **his intervention was of little ~** от его вмеша́тельства бы́ло ма́ло по́льзы.

v.t. **1.** (*benefit*) быть поле́зным/вы́годным +*d.*; **our efforts ~ed us nothing** на́ши уси́лия ни к чему́ не привели́. **2.:** ~**o.s. of** воспо́льзоваться (*pf.*) +*i.*

availability [ə,veɪlə'bɪlɪtɪ] *n.* (*presence*) нали́чие; (*accessibility*) досту́пность.

available [ə'veɪləb(ə)l] *adj.* **1.** (*present, to hand*) нали́чный; (*pred.*) в нали́чии, в распоряже́нии; **if there is money ~** е́сли есть де́ньги (в нали́чии); **he used every ~ argument** он испо́льзовал все досту́пные аргуме́нты; **make ~** предост|авля́ть, -а́вить. **2.** (*accessible*) досту́пный. **3.** (*valid*): **tickets ~ till 31 May** биле́ты, действи́тельные по три́дцать пе́рвое ма́я.

avalanche ['ævə,lɑ:nʃ] *n.* (*lit.*, *fig.*) лави́на.

avant-garde [,ævɑ̃'gɑ:d] *n.* авангарди́сты; (*attr.*) авангарди́стский.

avarice ['ævərɪs] *n.* ску́пость, ска́редность.

avaricious [,ævə'rɪʃəs] *adj.* скупо́й, ска́редный.

avast [ə'vɑ:st] *int.* (*naut.*) стой!; стоп!

avatar ['ævə,tɑ:(r)] *n.* воплоще́ние божества́; авата́ра; (*fig.*) ипоста́сь.

avaunt [ə'vɔ:nt] *int.* (*arch.*) прочь!

Av(e). ['ævə,nju:] *n.* (*abbr. of* **avenue**) пр., (проспе́кт); авеню́.

avenge [ə'vendʒ] *v.t.* мстить, ото- за+*a.*; **he ~d his father's death on the murderer** он отомсти́л уби́йце за смерть своего́ отца́.

avenger [ə'vendʒə(r)] *n.* мсти́тель (*m.*).

avenue ['ævə,nju:] *n.* **1.** (*tree-lined road*) алле́я; (*wide street*) проспе́кт. **2.** (*fig.*, *approach*, *way*) путь (*m.*); **an ~ of escape** путь к спасе́нию; ~ **to fame** путь к сла́ве; **explore every ~** испо́льзовать (*impf.*, *pf.*) все пути́/кана́лы.

aver [ə'vɜ:(r)] *v.t.* утвер|жда́ть, -ди́ть.

average ['ævərɪdʒ] *n.* **1.** (*mean*) сре́днее число́; **strike an ~** выводи́ть, вы́вести сре́днее число́; (*norm*) сре́днее; **above/below ~** вы́ше/ни́же сре́днего; **on an, the ~** в сре́днем. **2.** (*comm.*) ава́рия; **general/particular ~** о́бщая/ча́стная ава́рия; **make up the ~** сост|авля́ть, -а́вить отчёт по ава́рии.

adj. сре́дний; **the ~ age of the class is 12** сре́дний во́зраст кла́сса — двена́дцать лет; **the ~ man** сре́дний челове́к.

v.t. & *i.* **1.** (*find the ~ of*) выводи́ть, вы́вести сре́днее число́ +*g.*; **his salary, when ~d, was £200 a month** его́ сре́дняя зарпла́та соста́вила 200 фу́нтов в ме́сяц. **2.** (*amount to on ~*): **my expenses ~ £10 a day** мои́ расхо́ды составля́ют в сре́днем де́сять фу́нтов в день; (*do on ~*): **he ~s 6 hours' work a day** он рабо́тает в сре́днем шесть часо́в в день; **we ~d sixty on the motorway** мы де́лали на автостра́де в сре́днем шестьдеся́т миль в час; **it ~s out in the end** к концу́ э́то всё ура́внивается/нивели́руется.

averse [ə'vɜ:s] *pred. adj.*: ~ **to** нерасполо́женный к+*d.*; **he is ~ to coming** ему́ не хо́чется приходи́ть; **I am not ~ to a good dinner** я не прочь хорошо́ пообе́дать.

aversion [ə'vɜ:ʃ(ə)n] *n.* (*dislike*) отвраще́ние, антипа́тия; **have an ~ to** пита́ть (*impf.*) отвраще́ние к+*d.*; **take an ~ to** возненави́деть (*pf.*); (*object of dislike*) предме́т антипа́тии; **cats are my (pet) ~** я терпе́ть не могу́ ко́шек.

avert [ə'vɜ:t] *v.t.* **1.** (*turn aside*): ~ **one's glance, eyes** отв|оди́ть, -ести́ взгляд; ~ **one's thoughts** отвл|ека́ть, -е́чь мы́сли. **2.** (*ward off*) предотвра|ща́ть, -ти́ть; **the danger has been ~ed** опа́сность предотврати́ли.

Avesta [ə'vestə] *n.* Аве́ста.

avian ['eɪvɪən] *adj.* пти́чий.

aviary ['eɪvɪərɪ] *n.* пти́чник.

aviation [,eɪvɪ'eɪʃ(ə)n] *n.* авиа́ция; (*attr.*) авиацио́нный; ~ **spirit** авиабензи́н.

aviator ['eɪvɪ,eɪtə(r)] *n.* авиа́тор.

aviculture ['eɪvɪ,kʌltʃə(r)] *n.* птицево́дство.

avid ['ævɪd] *adj.* жа́дный, а́лчный; **he was ~ to hear the results** он жа́ждал узна́ть результа́ты.

avidity [ə'vɪdɪtɪ] *n.* жа́дность, а́лчность.

avionics [,eɪvɪ'ɒnɪks] *n.* авиацио́нная электро́ника.

avocado [,ævə'kɑ:dəʊ] *n.* (~ *pear*) авока́до (*indecl.*).

avocation [,ævə'keɪʃ(ə)n] *n.* побо́чное заня́тие.

avocet ['ævə,set] *n.* шилоклю́вка.

avoid [ə'vɔɪd] *v.t.* **1.** объе́хать (*pf.*); **the car ~ed a pedestrian** маши́на объе́хала пешехо́да; (*escape*, *evade*) избе|га́ть, -жа́ть +*g.*; **I could not ~ meeting him** я не мог избежа́ть встре́чи с ним; (*shun*) сторони́ться (*impf.*) +*g.*; **he ~s all his old friends** он сторони́тся всех свои́х ста́рых друзе́й; (*refrain from*) уклон|я́ться, -и́ться от+*g.*; **she ~ed a direct answer** она уклони́лась от прямо́го отве́та. **2.** (*leg.*) аннули́ровать (*impf.*, *pf.*).

avoidable [ə'vɔɪdəb(ə)l] *adj.* **1.** тако́й, кото́рого мо́жно избежа́ть; **without ~ delay** без нену́жных/изли́шних проволо́чек. **2.** (*leg.*) аннули́руемый.

avoidance [ə'vɔɪd(ə)ns] *n.* **1.** избежа́ние; уклоне́ние; ~ **of strong drink** воздержа́ние от употребле́ния спиртно́го. **2.** (*leg.*) аннули́рование.

avoirdupois [,ævədə'pɔɪz] *n.* (*fig.*, *corpulence*) ту́чность.

avouch [ə'vaʊtʃ] *v.t.* (*arch.*) (*affirm*) утвер|жда́ть, -ди́ть;

(*confess*) призн|ава́ться- а́ться в+*p*.; (*guarantee*) руча́ться, поручи́ться за+*a*.

avow [ə'vaʊ] *v.t.* призн|ава́ть, -а́ть; **he ~s himself an atheist** он называ́ет себя́ атеи́стом; **he is an ~ed racist** он открове́нный/нераска́янный раси́ст; **it was his ~ed intent to emigrate** он откры́то выража́л наме́рение эмигри́ровать; **~edly** по со́бственному призна́нию.

avowal [ə'vaʊ(ə)l] *n.* призна́ние; **make an ~ of** призн|ава́ться, -а́ться в+*p*.

avulsion [ə'vʌlʃ(ə)n] *n.* отры́в.

avuncular [ə'vʌŋkjʊlə(r)] *adj.* дя́дин; **~ manner** оте́ческое обраще́ние.

await [ə'weɪt] *v.t.* ожида́ть (*impf.*) +*g*.; **~ing your reply** в ожида́нии ва́шего отве́та.

awake [ə'weɪk] *pred. adj.*: **1. are you ~ or asleep?** вы спи́те и́ли нет?; **is he ~ yet?** он просну́лся?; **I've been ~ all night** я не сомкну́л глаз всю ночь; **he lay ~ thinking** он лежа́л без сна и ду́мал; **she stayed ~ till her husband came home** она́ не засыпа́ла, пока́ муж не верну́лся домо́й; **the baby was wide ~** у ребёнка сна не́ было ни в одно́м глазу́. **2.** (*fig., vigilant, alert*) бди́тельный; начеку́; **he is not ~ to his opportunity** он упуска́ет слу́чай; **we must be ~ to the possibility of defeat** пораже́ние возмо́жно, и мы не должны́ закрыва́ть на э́то глаза́.

v.t. **1.** (*rouse from sleep*) буди́ть, раз-; **I was awoken by the song of birds** меня́ разбуди́ло пе́ние птиц. **2.** (*fig., inspire*): = **awaken 2.**

v.i. **1.** (*wake from sleep*) прос|ыпа́ться, -ну́ться; **he awoke to find himself famous** нау́тро он просну́лся знамени́тым. **2.: ~ to** (*fig., realize*) осозн|ава́ть, -а́ть; **he awoke to his surroundings** он осозна́л, где нахо́дится.

awaken [ə'weɪkən] *v.t.* **1.** (*lit.*) = **awake** *v.t.* **2.** (*fig., arouse, inspire*) пробуди́ть (*pf.*); **his father's death ~ed him to** (*or* **~ed in him) a sense of responsibility** смерть отца́ пробуди́ла в нём чу́вство отве́тственности.

awakening [ə'weɪkənɪŋ] *n.* пробужде́ние; **a rude ~** (*fig.*) го́рькое разочарова́ние.

award [ə'wɔːd] *n.* (*act of ~ing*) присужде́ние; (*decision*) реше́ние; (*prize*) награ́да, приз.

v.t. прису|жда́ть, -ди́ть (*что кому*); **he was ~ed a medal** его награди́ли меда́лью.

aware [ə'weə(r)] *pred. adj.*: **be ~ of** сознава́ть (*impf.*); (*realise*) знать (*impf.*); **I am well ~ of the dangers** я вполне́ представля́ю себе́ все опа́сности; **he became ~ of someone following him** он почу́вствовал, что за ним следя́т; **I was not ~ of that** я э́того не знал; **you are probably ~ that ...** вам, вероя́тно, изве́стно, что...; **I passed him without being ~ of it** я прошёл ми́мо, не заме́тив его́.

awareness [ə'weərnɪs] *n.* созна́ние.

awash [ə'wɒʃ] *pred. adj.* омы́тый водо́й; **the place was ~ with champagne** шампа́нское лило́сь реко́й.

away [ə'weɪ] *adv.* **1.** (*at a distance*): **the shops are ten minutes' walk ~** магази́ны нахо́дятся в десяти́ мину́тах ходьбы́ отсю́да; **the sea is only 5 miles ~ from our villa** мо́ре всего́ в пяти́ ми́лях от на́шей ви́ллы; **her mother lived half an hour ~ by bus** её мать жила́ в получа́се езды́ на авто́бусе. **2.** (*not present or near*): **he is ~** он в отъе́зде; **he was ~ on leave** он был в о́тпуске; **how long have you been ~?** ско́лько же (вре́мени) вас не́ было?; **we shall be ~ in July** в ию́ле нас не бу́дет; **our team are playing ~ (from home)** на́ша кома́нда игра́ет на чужо́м по́ле; **hold it ~ from the light** не держи́те э́то на свету́. **3.** (*fig., of time or degree*): **~ back in 1930** ещё в тридца́том году́; **out and ~** (*or* **far and ~**) **the best** наилу́чший. **4.** (*expr. continuance*): **he works ~** он знай себе́ рабо́тает; **he was talking ~ to himself** он всё вре́мя сам с собо́й разгова́ривал; **all the time the clock was ticking ~** всё э́то вре́мя часы́ ти́кали не перестава́я. **5.** (*with imper.*): **You have some questions? Ask ~, then!** У вас есть вопро́сы? Ну, валя́йте! **6.: right, straight ~** сейча́с; неме́дленно. **7.: ~ with him!** доло́й его́! чтоб его́ здесь не́ было!; **~ with you!** убира́йтесь; **~ with care!** не́чего уныва́ть!; доло́й забо́ты!

awe [ɔː] *n.* благогове́йный страх; свяще́нный тре́пет; **he stands in ~ of his teacher** он испы́тывает благогове́йный страх пе́ред учи́телем; **his voice struck ~ into the audience** его́ го́лос вы́звал оцепене́ние в за́ле.

v.t. внуш|а́ть, -и́ть (*кому*) благогове́йный страх/тре́пет.

cpds. **~-inspiring** *adj.* внуша́ющий благогове́йный стра́х; **~-struck** *adj.* благогове́йный; прони́кнутый свяще́нным тре́петом.

aweigh [ə'weɪ] *adv.*: **the anchor is ~** я́корь встал.

awesome ['ɔːsəm] *adj.* внуша́ющий страх.

awful ['ɔːfʊl] *adj.* **1.** (*terrible; also coll.: very bad, great etc.*) ужа́сный, стра́шный; **it's an ~ shame** ужа́сно доса́дно; **he has an ~ lot of money** у него́ у́йма де́нег. **2.** (*inspiring awe*) внуша́ющий страх/благогове́ние.

awfully ['ɔːfəlɪ, -flɪ] *adv.* ужа́сно; **~ nice** стра́шно ми́лый; **thanks ~** огро́мное вам спаси́бо; **I'm ~ sorry** прости́те, ра́ди Бо́га.

awheel [ə'wiːl] *adv.* на колёсах.

awhile [ə'waɪl] *adv.* на не́которое вре́мя; **I shan't be ready to leave yet ~** я не смогу́ пое́хать сра́зу.

awkward ['ɔːkwəd] *adj.* **1.** (*clumsy*) неуклю́жий, нело́вкий; **she is at the ~ age** она́ в перехо́дном во́зрасте. **2.** (*inconvenient, uncomfortable*) неудо́бный. **3.** (*difficult*): **an ~ problem** ка́верзная пробле́ма; **an ~ turning** тру́дный поворо́т. **4.** (*embarrassing*): **an ~ silence** нело́вкое молча́ние. **5.** (*of pers., hard to manage*) тру́дный; **he's being ~ (about it)** он чини́т препя́тствия.

awkwardness ['ɔːkwədnɪs] *n.* неуклю́жесть, нело́вкость; неудо́бство.

awl [ɔːl] *n.* ши́ло.

awning ['ɔːnɪŋ] *n.* наве́с; тент; **~ deck** те́нтовая па́луба.

AWOL ['eɪwɒl] *pred. adj.* (*abbr. of* **absent without leave**) в самово́льной отлу́чке.

awry [ə'raɪ] *pred. adj.* криво́й; (*distorted*) искажённый.

adv. ко́со; (*on, to one side*) на́бок; **your tie is all ~** ваш га́лстук съе́хал на́бок; (*fig.*): **things went ~** дела́ пошли́ скве́рно.

axe (*US* **ax**) [æks] *n.* **1.** (*tool*) топо́р; (*large*) колу́н; **I have no ~ to grind** (*fig.*) у меня́ нет коры́стных побужде́ний. **2.** (*fig., execution*) казнь; отсече́ние головы́; **he died by the ~** ему́ отруби́ли го́лову. **3.** (*coll.: reduction of expenditure*) уре́зывание.

v.t. (*fig.*) (*terminate*) отмен|я́ть, -и́ть; **the government intends to ~ public expenditure** прави́тельство наме́рено уре́зать расхо́ды на обще́ственные ну́жды; **many workers have been ~d** уво́лено мно́го рабо́чих.

axial ['æksɪəl] *adj.* осево́й.

axillary [æk'sɪlərɪ] *adj.* подмы́шечный.

axiom ['æksɪəm] *n.* аксио́ма.

axiomatic [ˌæksɪə'mætɪk] *adj.* аксиомати́чный.

axis ['æksɪs] *n.* ось, вал; **the A~ (powers)** (*hist.*) держа́вы (*f. pl.*) Оси́.

axle ['æks(ə)l] *n.* ось.

cpds. **~-box** *n.* подши́пниковая коро́бка, бу́кса; **~-grease** *n.* таво́т; колёсная мазь; **~-pin** *n.* чека́.

ayatollah [ˌaɪə'tɒlə] *n.* аятолла́ (*m.*).

ay(e)[1] [aɪ] *n.* (*affirmative vote*) го́лос «за»; **the ~s have it** большинство́ за.

int. да; есть; **~, ~, Sir!** есть!

aye[2] [eɪ] *adv.* (*poet., ever*) всегда́; **for ~** навсегда́; наве́ки.

aye-aye ['aɪaɪ] *n.* (*zool.*) а́йе-а́йе (*m. indecl.*).

azalea [ə'zeɪlɪə] *n.* аза́лия.

Azerbaijan [ˌæzəbaɪ'dʒɑːn] *n.* Азербайджа́н.

Azerbaijani [ˌæzəbaɪ'dʒɑːnɪ] *n.* (*pers.*) азербайджа́н|ец (*fem.* -ка); (*language*) азербайджа́нский язы́к.

adj. азербайджа́нский.

azimuth ['æzɪməθ] *n.* а́зимут; **~ circle** угломе́рный круг.

Azores [ə'zɔːz] *n.*: **the ~** Азо́рские острова́ (*m. pl.*).

Azov ['ɑːzɒv] *n.*: **Sea of ~** Азо́вское мо́ре.

Aztec ['æztek] *n.* ацте́к.

adj. ацте́кский.

azure ['æʒə(r), -zjə(r), 'eɪ-] *n.* лазу́рь.

adj. лазу́рный, голубо́й.

B

B [bi:] *n.* **1.** (*mus.*) си (*nt. indecl.*). **2.** (*acad. mark*) 4, четвёрка; **she got a ~ in arithmetic** она́ получи́ла четвёрку по арифме́тике.

BA (*abbr. of* ***Bachelor of Arts***) бакала́вр гуманита́рных нау́к; **he has a ~ in Russian** он име́ет сте́пень бакала́вра по ру́сскому языку́.

baa [bɑ:] *n.* бле́яние.

v.i. бле́ять (*impf.*).

cpd. **~-lamb** *n.* бара́шек.

babble ['bæb(ə)l] *n.* (*imperfect speech*) ле́пет; (*idle talk*) болтовня́; (*of water etc.*) журча́ние.

v.t. & i. (*speak inarticulately*) болта́ть (*impf.*); лепета́ть (*impf.*); (*utter trivialities*) болта́ть (*impf.*); моло́ть (*impf.*) вздор; (*let out secrets*) выба́лтывать, вы́болтать; проб|а́лтываться, -олта́ться.

babbler ['bæbl(ə)r] *n.* болту́н (*fem.* -нья), болту́шка (*c.g.*).

babe [beɪb] *n.* (*lit., fig.*) младе́нец; (*US sl.*) де́вушка.

babel ['beɪb(ə)l] *n.* **1.: the tower of B~** вавило́нская ба́шня. **2.** (*fig.*) вавило́нское столпотворе́ние, галдёж.

baboon [bə'bu:n] *n.* бабуи́н, павиа́н.

baby ['beɪbɪ] *n.* **1.** младе́нец; **what is their ~** (*i.e. a boy or a girl*)? кто у них роди́лся?; **the ~ of the family** мла́дший в семье́; **empty out the baby with the bathwater** (*fig.*) вме́сте с водо́й вы́плеснуть (*pf.*) и ребёнка; **they left me holding the ~** (*fig.*) мне пришло́сь за них отдува́ться. **2.** (*of animals etc.*) детёныш. **3.** (*coll., sweetheart*) де́тка. **4.** (*attr.*): **~ elephant** слонёнок; **~ car** малолитра́жный автомоби́ль; **~ grand (piano)** кабине́тный роя́ль.

v.t. обраща́ться (*impf.*) (*с кем*) как с младе́нцем.

cpds. **~-carriage** *n.* де́тская коля́ска; **~-farmer** *n.* челове́к, за пла́ту беру́щий дете́й на воспита́ние; **~-sit** *v.i.* присма́тривать (*impf.*) за детьми́ в отсу́тствие роди́телей; **~-sitter** *n.* приходя́щая ня́ня; **~-sitting** *n.* присмо́тр за детьми́; **~-snatcher** *n.* похити́тель(ница) дете́й; (*joc.*) ≃ жени́ла на себе́ младе́нца; **~-talk** *n.* де́тский язы́к, де́тский ле́пет; (*by adults*) сюсю́кание; **~-word** *n.* де́тское сло́во.

babyhood ['beɪbɪhʊd] *n.* младе́нчество.

babyish ['beɪbɪɪʃ] *adj.* де́тский, ребя́ческий.

Babylon ['bæbɪlən] *n.* Вавило́н.

Babylonian [ˌbæbɪ'ləʊnɪən] *adj.* вавило́нский.

baccalaureate [ˌbækə'lɔ:rɪət] *n.* бакала́врство.

baccarat ['bækəˌrɑ:] *n.* баккара́ (*nt. indecl.*).

Bacchanal ['bækən(ə)l] *n.* (*hist.*) жрец Ва́кха; (*female*) вакха́нка.

adj. вакхана́льный.

Bacchanalia [ˌbækə'neɪlɪə] *n.* вакхана́лия.

Bacchanalian [ˌbækə'neɪlɪən] *adj.* вакхи́ческий, вакхана́льный.

Bacchante [bə'kæntɪ] *n.* вакха́нка.

Bacchic ['bækɪk] *adj.* вакхи́ческий.

Bacchus ['bækəs] *n.* Вакх, Ба́хус.

baccy ['bækɪ] *n.* табачо́к (*coll.*).

bachelor ['bætʃələ(r)] *n.* **1.** холостя́к; **~ girl** холостя́чка. **2.** (*acad.*) бакала́вр.

bachelorhood ['bætʃələ(r)hʊd] *n.* холостя́цкая жизнь; (*acad.*) сте́пень бакала́вра.

bacillus [bə'sɪləs] *n.* баци́лла.

back [bæk] *n.* **1.** (*part of body*) спина́; **~ to ~** спино́й к спине́; **break one's ~** переломи́ть (*pf.*) спинно́й хребе́т; **he fell on his ~** он упа́л на́ спину; **make a ~** (*leap-frog*) подста́вить (*pf.*) спи́ну; **turn one's ~ on** (*lit.*) отв|ора́чиваться, -ерну́ться от+*g.*; (*fig.*) пок|ида́ть, -и́нуть; **as soon as my ~ was turned** не успе́л я отверну́ться. **2.** (*fig. uses*): **at s.o.'s ~** (*giving support*) за чьей-н. спино́й; **behind my ~** за мое́й спино́й; **on one's ~** (*as burden*) на ше́е; **put s.o.'s ~ up** рассерди́ть (*pf.*) кого́-н.; **break the ~ of a task** одоле́ть (*pf.*) трудне́йшую часть зада́ния; **see the ~ of** (*get rid of*) отде́латься (*pf.*) от+*g.*; **with one's ~ against the wall** припёртый к сте́нке; **put one's ~ into sth.** вложи́ть (*pf.*) все си́лы во что-н.; **(you) scratch my ~ and I'll scratch yours** ≃ рука́ ру́ку мо́ет. **3.** (*of chair, dress*) спи́нка; (*of playing card*) руба́шка. **4.** (*other side, rear*): **~ of a brush** обра́тная сторона́ щётки; **~ of a knife** тупо́й край ножа́; **~ of an envelope** обра́тная сторона́ конве́рта; **~ of one's head** заты́лок; **~ of one's hand** ты́льная сторона́ руки́; **know sth. like the ~ of one's hand** знать (*impf.*) что-н. как свои́ пять па́льцев; **~** (*spine*) **of a book** корешо́к кни́ги; **~ of one's leg** нога́ сза́ди; икра́; **at the ~ of the house** в за́дней ча́сти до́ма; (*behind it*) позади́ до́ма; **at the ~ of one's mind** подсозна́тельно; в глубине́ души́; **at the ~ of the book** в конце́ кни́ги; **at the ~ of beyond** на краю́ све́та; **the ~ of a car** за́дняя ча́сть автомоби́ля. **5.** (*sport*): **full ~** защи́тник, бек. **6.** (*attr.*; *see also cpds. as separate headwords*): **~ door** чёрный ход; **~ freight** обра́тный фрахт; **~ seat** за́днее сиде́нье; **~ somersault** за́днее са́льто-морта́ле; **~ stairs** чёрная ле́стница; **~ street** глуха́я у́лица.

adv. **1.** (*to or at the rear*) наза́д, сза́ди; **~ and forth** взад и вперёд; **hold the crowd ~** сде́рживать (*impf.*) толпу́; **sit ~ in one's chair** отки́нуться (*pf.*) на спи́нку сту́ла; усе́сться (*pf.*) глу́бже; **keep ~ the truth** скрыва́ть (*impf.*) пра́вду; **(in) ~ of** (*US*) позади́+*g.*; **~ from the road** в стороне́ от доро́ги. **2.** (*returning to former position etc.*) обра́тно; **he is ~ again** он сно́ва здесь; **we shall be ~ before dark** мы вернёмся за́светло; **take ~ a statement** отказа́ться (*pf.*) от своего́ заявле́ния; **pay s.o. ~** отпла́|чивать, -ти́ть кому́-н.; **hit ~** уд|аря́ть, -а́рить в отве́т; (*coll.*) дать (*pf.*) сда́чи (*кому*); **answer ~** возра|жа́ть, -зи́ть; спо́рить (*impf.*); дерзи́ть, на- (*кому*); **get one's own ~** отплати́ть (*pf.*) (*кому*). **3.** (*ago*) тому́ наза́д; **~ in 1930** ещё в 1930 году́.

v.t. **1.** (*move backwards*) дви|гать, -нуть наза́д (*or* в обра́тном направле́нии); **~ water** таба́нить (*impf.*). **2.** (*support*; *also* **~ up**) подде́рж|ивать, -а́ть; **~** (*bet on*) **a horse** ста́вить, по- на ло́шадь; **~ a bill** индосси́ровать (*impf., pf.*) ве́ксель. **3.** (*line*) покр|ыва́ть, -ы́ть; **~ed with sheet-iron** кры́тый листовы́м желе́зом. **4.** (*form ~ of*) примыка́ть (*impf.*) сза́ди; быть фо́ном (*чего*); **the lake is ~ed by mountains** сза́ди к о́зеру примыка́ют го́ры.

v.i. **1.** (*move backwards*) пя́титься, по-; (*of motor car*) идти́ (*det.*) за́дним хо́дом; **~ and fill** лави́ровать (*impf.*); **the wind ~ed** ве́тер меня́л направле́ние про́тив часово́й стре́лки. **2. ~ down (from)** отступ|а́ться, -и́ться (*от чего*); **~ out (of)** уклон|я́ться, и́ться (*от чего*).

backache ['bækeɪk] *n.* боль в спине́/поясни́це.

backbencher ['bæk'bentʃə(r)] *n.* заднескаме́ечник, рядово́й член парла́мента.

backbite ['bækbaɪt] *v.t. & i.* злосло́вить (*impf.*) (*о ком*).

backbiter ['bækˌbaɪtə(r)] *n.* зло́бный спле́тник.

backbiting ['bækˌbaɪtɪŋ] *n.* злосло́вие.

backblocks ['bækblɒks] *n.* захолу́стье, глушь.

backbone ['bækbəʊn] *n.* **1.** спинно́й хребе́т, позвоно́чник; **British to the ~** брита́нец до мо́зга косте́й. **2.** (*basis*) осно́ва; (*substance*) суть; (*support*) опо́ра; (*strength of character*) твёрдость хара́ктера.

back-chat ['bæktʃæt] *n.* де́рзкий отве́т, де́рзость.

back|cloth ['bækklɒθ], **-drop** *nn.* за́дник.

back-date [bæk'deɪt] *v.t.* пом|еча́ть, -е́тить за́дним число́м.

backdoor ['bækdɔ:(r)] *adj.* (*fig.*) закули́сный, та́йный.

backdrop ['bækdrɒp] *n.* **1.: against the ~ of crisis** на фо́не кри́зиса. **2.** = **backcloth**

back-end ['bækend] *n.* за́дний коне́ц.

backer ['bækə(r)] *n.* оказывающий подде́ржку; субсиди́рующий.

backfall ['bækfɔ:l] *n.* паде́ние на́ спину.

backfire ['bækfaɪə(r)] *n.* (*of a car*) обра́тная вспы́шка.

v.t. да|ва́ть, -ть обра́тную вспы́шку; (*fig.*) прив|оди́ть,

-ести́ к обра́тным результа́там.

back-formation [ˈbækfɔːˌmeɪʃ(ə)n] *n.* обра́тное словообразова́ние.

backgammon [ˈbækˌgæmən, bækˈgæmən] *n.* трикта́к.

background [ˈbækgraʊnd] *n.* **1.** за́дний план, фон; **in the ~ of the picture** на за́днем пла́не карти́ны; **on a dark ~** на тёмном фо́не; **keep in the ~** (*fig.*) держа́ть(ся) (*impf.*) в тени́. **2.** (*of pers.*) ≃ происхожде́ние; образова́ние; о́пыт. **3.** (*to a situation*) предысто́рия. **4.: ~ music** музыка́льное сопровожде́ние/оформле́ние. **5.** (*radio*) посторо́нние шумы́ (*m. pl.*), фон.

backhand [ˈbækhænd] *n.* (*handwriting*) по́черк с накло́ном вле́во; (*sport*: ~ *stroke*) уда́р сле́ва.

backhanded [bækˈhændɪd] *adj.* с накло́ном вле́во; сде́ланный ты́льной стороно́й руки́; (*fig.*) сомни́тельный, двусмы́сленный.

backhander [ˈbækˌhændə(r)] (*bribe*) *n.* взя́тка, бакши́ш.

backing [ˈbækɪŋ] *n.* **1.** (*assistance*) подде́ржка; (*subsidy*) субсиди́рование. **2.** (*motion*) за́дний ход. **3.** (*of cloth*) подкла́дка; (*covering*) покры́тие.

backlash [ˈbæklæʃ] *n.* (*fig.*) реа́кция.

backlog [ˈbæklɒg] *n.* за́лежи (*f. pl.*) накопи́вшейся рабо́ты.

backpack [ˈbækpæk] *n.* рюкза́к.

backpacker [ˈbækpækə(r)] *n.* рюкза́чник.

back-pedal [ˈbækped(ə)l] *v.i.* крути́ть (*impf.*) педа́ли наза́д; (*fig.*) пойти́ (*pf.*) на попя́тный/попя́тную.

backside [bækˈsaɪd, ˈbæk-] *n.* (*coll.*, *buttocks*) зад, за́дница.

backsight [ˈbæksaɪt] *n.* прице́л, це́лик.

back-slapper [ˈbækˌslæpə(r)] *n.* руба́ха-па́рень (*m.*).

back-slapping [ˈbækˌslæpɪŋ] *n.* похло́пывание по спине́; панибра́тство, амикошо́нство.

adj. панибра́тский.

backslide [ˈbækslaɪd] *v.t.* вновь подда́ться (*pf.*) искуше́нию; вновь впасть (*pf.*) в грех.

backslider [ˈbækˌslaɪdə(r)] *n.* ≃ отсту́пник; верну́вшийся к дурны́м привы́чкам.

back-spacer [ˈbækˌspeɪsə(r)] *n.* (*on typewriter*) обра́тный реги́стр; кла́виша «обра́тный ход».

backstage [ˈbæksteɪdʒ] *adj.* (*also fig.*) закули́сный.

adv. за кули́сами.

backstairs [ˈbæksteəz] *adj.* (*fig.*) та́йный, закули́сный.

backstay [ˈbæksteɪ] *n.* форду́н, ба́кштаг.

backstreet [ˈbækstriːt] *adj.* (*illicit*) подпо́льный.

backstroke [ˈbækstrəʊk] *n.* пла́вание на спине́.

back-track [ˈbæktræk] *v.i.* идти́ (*det.*) за́дним хо́дом; пя́титься, по-; (*fig.*) идти́ (*det.*) на попя́тный/попя́тную.

back-up [ˈbækʌp] (*comput.*) резе́рвная ко́пия.

adj. запасно́й; (*comput.*) резе́рвный.

backward [ˈbækwəd] *adj.* **1.** (*towards the back*) обра́тный; **a ~ glance** взгля́д наза́д. **2.** (*lagging*) отста́лый; (*retarded*) слабора́звитый, недора́звитый; **~ children** у́мственно отста́лые де́ти. **3.** (*late*) запозда́лый; (*reluctant*) ме́длящий, нереши́тельный.

adv.: *see next entry.*

backward(s) [ˈbækwədz] *adv.* (*in backward direction*) наза́д; (*in opposite direction*) в обра́тном направле́нии; (*in reverse order*) в обра́тном поря́дке; **sit ~ on a horse** сиде́ть (*impf.*) на ло́шади за́дом наперёд; **walk ~** пя́титься, по-; **~ and forwards** взад и вперёд; туда́ и обра́тно; туда́-сюда́; **know sth. ~** знать (*impf.*) что-н. от ко́рки до ко́рки; **lean over ~ to do sth.** (*fig.*) из ко́жи вон лезть (*pf.*), что́бы сде́лать что-н.

backward-looking [ˈbækwədˈlʊkɪŋ] *adj.* (*fig.*) отста́лый, ретрогра́дный.

backwardness [ˈbækwədnɪs] *n.* отста́лость; (*disinclination*) неохо́та.

backwash [ˈbækwɒʃ] *n.* обра́тный пото́к; (*fig.*) о́тзвук, след.

backwater [ˈbækˌwɔːtə(r)] *n.* за́водь; (*fig.*) ти́хая за́водь.

backwoods [ˈbækwʊdz] *n.* (лесна́я) глушь.

backwoodsman [ˈbækˌwʊdzmən] *n.* обита́тель (*m.*) лесно́й глуши́; дереве́нщина (*c.g.*).

bacon [ˈbeɪkən] *n.* бекóн; **~ and eggs** яи́чница с беко́ном; (*fig.*): **save one's ~** спа|са́ть, -сти́ свою́ шку́ру.

bacterial [bækˈtɪərɪəl] *adj.* бактери́йный.

bacteriological [ˌbæktɪəˈlɒdʒɪk(ə)l] *adj.* бактериологи́ческий; **~ warfare** бактериологи́ческая война́.

bacteriology [ˌbæktɪərɪˈɒlədʒɪ] *n.* бактериоло́гия.

bacteriolysis [bækˌtɪərɪˈɒlɪsɪs] *n.* бактерио́лиз.

bacterium [bækˈtɪərɪəm] *n.* бакте́рия.

Bactrian [ˈbæktrɪən] *adj.*: **~ camel** бактриа́н.

bad [bæd] *n.* **1.** (*evil*) дурно́е, плохо́е; ху́до; **go to the ~** разор|я́ться, -и́ться; сби́ться (*pf.*) с пути́ и́стинного. **2.** (*loss*): **I was £5 to the ~** я понёс убы́ток в пять фу́нтов.

adj. **1.** плохо́й, дурно́й, скве́рный; **not ~!** непло́хо!; **things went from ~ to worse** дела́ шли всё ху́же и ху́же; **too ~!** о́чень жаль!; **it is too ~ of him** э́то о́чень некраси́во с его́ стороны́; **a ~ light** (*to read in*) сла́бый свет. **2.** (*morally bad*) плохо́й, дурно́й; **it is ~ to steal** ворова́ть (*impf.*) ду́рно/пло́хо; **lead a ~ life** вести́ (*det.*) непутёвую/беспу́тную жизнь; **a ~ name** дурна́я репута́ция. **3.** (*spoilt*) испо́рченный; **go ~** по́ртиться, ис-; **a ~ egg** (*lit.*) ту́хлое яйцо́; (*fig.*) непутёвый челове́к. **4.** (*severe*) си́льный; **I caught a ~ cold** я си́льно простуди́лся; **a ~ wound** тяжёлая ра́на. **5.** (*harmful*) вре́дный; **coffee is ~ for him** ко́фе ему́ вре́ден; **smoking is ~ for one** куре́ние вре́дно для здоро́вья. **6.** (*of health*) больно́й; **I feel ~** я чу́вствую себя́ пло́хо; **be taken ~** (*coll.*) заболе́ть (*pf.*). **7.** (*counterfeit*) фальши́вый. **8.** (*var.*): **a ~ mistake** гру́бая оши́бка; **a ~ debt** безнадёжный долг; **a ~ lot, hat** (*coll.*) дрянь-челове́к; **~ language** ру́гань; **he was in ~ with us** (*coll.*) он был у нас на плохо́м счету́.

cpds. **~-mannered** *adj.* невоспи́танный; **~-tempered** *adj.* раздражи́тельный.

baddie [ˈbædɪ] *n.* (*coll.*) злоде́й; плохо́й дя́дя, бя́ка (*m.*).

badge [bædʒ] *n.* значо́к; (*fig.*) си́мвол.

badger [ˈbædʒə(r)] *n.* барсу́к.

v.t. (*coll.*) трави́ть (*impf.*), изводи́ть (*impf.*); **~ s.o. for sth.** пристава́ть (*impf.*) к кому́-н. с про́сьбой о чём-н.

badinage [ˈbædɪˌnɑːʒ] *n.* подшу́чивание.

badly [ˈbædlɪ] *adv.* **1.** (*not well*) пло́хо. **2.** (*very much*) о́чень; си́льно; (*urgently*) сро́чно. **3.: ~ off** в нужде́.

badminton [ˈbædmɪnt(ə)n] *n.* бадминто́н.

badness [ˈbædnɪs] *n.* (*poor quality*) плохо́е ка́чество, недоброка́чественность; него́дность; (*depravity*) поро́чность, безнра́вственность; **the ~ of the weather** плоха́я пого́да, нена́стье, непого́да.

baffle[1] [ˈbæf(ə)l] *n.* (*tech.*) экра́н, щит, дро́ссельная заслóнка.

cpds. **~-board** *n.* отража́тельная доска́; **~-plate** *n.* отража́тельная плита́.

baffle[2] [ˈbæf(ə)l] *v.t.* (*perplex*) сби|ва́ть, -ть с то́лку; **the police are ~d** поли́ция не зна́ет, что де́лать; (*foil*, *hinder*) препя́тствовать (*impf.*) +*d.*; (*disappoint*, *delude*) обма́н|ывать, -у́ть; **it ~s description** э́то не поддаётся описа́нию.

baffling [ˈbæf(ə)lɪŋ] *adj.* сбива́ющий с то́лку; ста́вящий в тупи́к; зага́дочный.

bag [bæg] *n.* **1.** су́мка; (*small ~*, *hand ~*) су́мочка; **shopping ~** хозя́йственная су́мка. **2.** (*large ~*, *sack*) мешо́к. **3.** (*luggage*) чемода́н; **pack one's ~s** упакова́ться (*pf.*); **~ and baggage** со все́ми пожи́тками. **4.** (*game shot by sportsman*) добы́ча. **5.: by diplomatic ~** дипломати́ческой по́чтой. **6.** (*pl.*, *coll.*, *trousers*) штан|ы́ (*pl.*, *g.* -о́в). **7.** (*pl.*, *coll.*, *plenty*): **~s of room** полно́ ме́ста; **~ of money** мешки́ (*m. pl.*) де́нег. **8.** (*var.*): **in the ~** (*coll.*, *assured*) ≃ уже́ в карма́не; **~s under the eyes** мешки́ под глаза́ми; **a ~ of bones** (*fig.*) ко́жа да ко́сти; **the whole ~ of tricks** (*coll.*) всё без оста́тка; **old ~** (*sl.*, *pej.*, *woman*) ста́рая хрычо́вка; **What's your ~?** (*sl.*) что вас интересу́ет *or* колы́шет?; **classical music isn't my ~** класси́ческая му́зыка меня́ не колы́шет.

v.t. **1.** (*put in bag*) класть, положи́ть в мешо́к. **2.** (*shoot down*): **~ game** бить (*impf.*) дичь; **~ an aircraft** сбить (*pf.*) самолёт. **3.: who has ~ged my matches?** кто сти́брил (*coll.*) мои́ спи́чки? **~s I first place!** чур я пе́рвый! (*coll.*).

v.i.: **his trousers ~ at the knees** его́ брю́ки пузы́рятся на коле́нях.

cpds. **~man** *n.* коммивояжёр; **~pipe(s)** *n.* волы́нка; **~piper** *n.* волы́нщик.

bagatelle [ˌbægəˈtel] *n.* пустя́к.
baggage [ˈbægɪdʒ] *n.* **1.** бага́ж. **2.** (*mil.*) вози́мое иму́щество. **3.** (*saucy girl*) наха́лка; озорни́ца. **4.** (*attr.*) бага́жный; (*mil.*) вещево́й; **~ room** ка́мера хране́ния; **~ train** вещево́й обо́з.
bagginess [ˈbægɪnɪs] *n.* мешкова́тость.
baggy [ˈbægɪ] *adj.* мешкова́тый.
Baghdad [bægˈdæd] *n.* Багда́д; (*attr.*) багда́дский.
bagnio [ˈbɑːnjəʊ] *n.* (*brothel*) публи́чный дом.
bah [bɑː] *int.* ба!
Bahamas [bəˈhɑːməz] *n.*: **the ~** Бага́мские острова́ (*m. pl.*).
Bahrain [bɑːˈreɪn] *n.* Бахре́йн.
bail[1] [beɪl] *n.* **1.** (*pledge*) зало́г; поручи́тельство; **release on ~** отпус|ка́ть, -ти́ть на пору́ки. **2.** (*pers.*) поручи́тель (*m.*); **be, stand, go ~ for s.o.** поручи́ться (*pf.*) за кого́-н.
v.t.: **~ s.o. out** брать, взять кого́-н. на пору́ки.
cpd. **~sman** *n.* поручи́тель (*m.*).
bail[2], **bale** [beɪl] *v.t.* (*also* **~ out**) вычёрпывать, вы́черпать (*воду из лодки*).
v.i.: **~ out** (*aeron.*) выбра́сываться, вы́броситься с парашю́том.
bailiff [ˈbeɪlɪf] *n.* **1.** (*leg.*) суде́бный при́став; бе́йлиф. **2.** (*steward*) управля́ющий.
bairn [beən] *n.* (*Sc.*) дитя́ (*nt.*), ребёнок.
bait [beɪt] *n.* прима́нка; (*fishing*) наса́дка, нажи́вка; **ground ~** прива́да, нажи́вка; **live ~** живе́ц; (*fig.*) искуше́ние, прима́нка; **rise to the ~** (*lit.*, *fig.*) попа́сться (*pf.*) на у́дочку.
v.t. **1.** (*attach ~ to*) наса́|живать, -ди́ть нажи́вку на+*a*. **2.** (*entice*) прима́н|ивать, -и́ть. **3.** (*tease*) пресле́довать (*impf.*), изводи́ть (*impf.*); **~ a bear with dogs** трави́ть (*impf.*) медве́дя соба́ками.
baize [beɪz] *n.* ба́йка; **green ~** зелёное сукно́.
bake [beɪk] *v.t.* печь, с-; (*of bricks*) обж|ига́ть, -е́чь.
v.i. пе́чься; **we were baking in the sun** мы жа́рились на со́лнце; **baking-powder** пека́рный порошо́к.
cpd. **~house** *n.* пека́рня.
bakelite [ˈbeɪkəˌlaɪt] *n.* бакели́т.
baker [ˈbeɪkə(r)] *n.* пе́карь (*m.*); (*in charge of ~'s shop*) бу́лочник; **~'s dozen** чёртова дю́жина.
bakery [ˈbeɪkərɪ] *n.* пека́рня; (*shop*) бу́лочная.
bakeware [ˈbeːkweə(r)] *n.* жаропро́чная посу́да.
baksheesh [ˈbækʃiːʃ] *n.* бакши́ш.
Balaam [ˈbeɪlæm] *n.* Валаа́м.
Balaclava [ˌbæləˈklɑːvə] *n.*: **~ helmet** вя́заный шлем.
balalaika [ˌbæləˈlaɪkə] *n.* балала́йка.
balance [ˈbæləns] *n.* **1.** (*machine*) вес|ы́ (*pl.*, *g.* -о́в); **spring ~** пружи́нные весы́. **2.** (*equilibrium*) равнове́сие; **lose one's ~** (*fig.*) теря́ть, по- душе́вное равнове́сие; **hang in the ~** висе́ть (*impf.*) на волоске́; **hold the ~** осуществля́ть (*impf.*) контро́ль; **catch s.o. off ~** засти́гнуть (*pf.*) кого́-н. врасплóх. **3.** (*counterbalance*) противове́с. **4.** (*bookkeeping*) бала́нс; са́льдо (*indecl.*); **~ of account**; **~ in hand** са́льдо в ба́нке; оста́ток счёта в ба́нке; **adverse ~** пасси́вный бала́нс; **~ sheet** бухга́лтерский бала́нс; **~ of payments** платёжный бала́нс; **~ of trade** торго́вый бала́нс; **on ~** в ито́ге, в коне́чном счёте.
v.t. **1.** (*lit.*): **he ~d a pole on his chin** он баланси́ровал шест на подборо́дке. **2.** (*make equal*) уравнове́|шивать, -сить. **3.** (*weigh one thg. against another*) взве́|шивать, -сить; сопо|ставля́ть, -а́вить (*что с чем*). **4.** (*comm.*) баланси́ровать, с/за-; **~ the books** забаланси́ровать (*pf.*) бухга́лтерские кни́ги; **~ foreign trade** сбаланси́ровать (*pf.*) вне́шнюю торго́влю; **the expenses ~ the receipts** расхо́ды уравнове́шиваются дохо́дами.
v.i. (*of accounts*) сходи́ться (*impf.*); (*be in equilibrium*) баланси́ровать (*impf.*).
cpd. **~-wheel** *n.* ма́ятник.
balanced [ˈbælənsd] *adj.* (*of pers.*) уравнове́шенный; **~ judgement** проду́манное сужде́ние; **~ diet** сбаланси́рованная/рациона́льная дие́та.
balcony [ˈbælkənɪ] *n.* балко́н; (*theatr.*) балко́н (пе́рвого я́руса).
bald [bɔːld] *adj.* **1.** лы́сый, плеши́вый; **as ~ as a coot** (*coll.*) го́лый, как коле́но; **~ patch** лы́сина, плешь. **2.** (*bare*) го́лый. **3.** (*unadorned*) неприкра́шенный, прямо́й; (*pej.*) убо́гий.
cpds. **~-head, ~-pate** *nn.* лы́сый (челове́к); **~-headed** *adj.* лы́сый, плеши́вый; **go at sth. ~-headed** (*coll.*) бро́ситься (*pf.*) во что-н. очертя́ го́лову.
baldachin [ˈbɔːldəkɪn] *n.* балдахи́н.
balderdash [ˈbɔːldəˌdæʃ] *n.* галиматья́.
balding [ˈbɔːldɪŋ] *adj.* лысе́ющий.
baldness [ˈbɔːldnɪs] *n.* **1.** плеши́вость. **2.** (*bareness*) оголённость. **3.** (*scantiness*) ску́дость.
baldric [ˈbɔːldrɪk] *n.* пе́ревязь.
bale[1] [beɪl] *n.* ки́па.
v.t. упако́в|ывать, -а́ть в ки́пы; тюкова́ть (*impf.*).
bale[2] [beɪl] *v.i.*: = **bail**[2]
baleen [bəˈliːn] *n.* кито́вый ус.
baleful [ˈbeɪlfʊl] *adj.* злове́щий; серди́тый.
balk, baulk[1] [bɔːk] *n.* (*beam*) оканто́ванное бревно́.
balk, baulk[2] [bɔːlk] *v.t.* (*hinder*) меша́ть, по- (*кому, чему, в чём*); (*frustrate*) расстр|а́ивать, -о́ить; **~ s.o. of his prey** лиши́ть (*pf.*) кого́-н. добы́чи; **he was ~ed of his desires** его́ жела́ния не осуществи́лись.
v.i. **1.** (*of horses*) арта́читься, за- (*при чём*). **2.**: **~ at food** отка́з|ываться, -а́ться от пи́щи; **he ~ed at the expense** таки́е расхо́ды его́ испуга́ли.
Balkan [ˈbɔːlkən] *n.*: **the ~s** Балка́н|ы (*pl.*, *g.* —); Балка́нский полуо́стров.
adj. балка́нский.
Balkanization [ˌbɔːlkənaɪˈzeɪʃ(ə)n] *n.* балканиза́ция.
Balkanize [ˈbɔːlkəˌnaɪz] *v.t.* балканизи́ровать (*impf.*, *pf.*).
balky [ˈbɔːlkɪ] *adj.* стропти́вый.
ball[1] [bɔːl] *n.* (*dance*) бал; **open the ~** откр|ыва́ть, -ы́ть бал; **give a ~** устр|а́ивать, -о́ить бал; **fancy-dress ~** маскара́д.
cpds. **~-dress** *n.* ба́льное пла́тье; **~room** *n.* танцева́льный зал.
ball[2] [bɔːl] *n.* **1.** (*sphere*) шар; **billiard ~** билья́рдный шар. **2.** (*in outdoor games*) мяч; **play ~** игра́ть (*impf.*) в мяч. **3.** (*of wool*) клубо́к. **4.** (*bullet*) пу́ля; (*for cannon*) ядро́; **load with ~** заряди́ть (*pf.*) боевы́ми патро́нами. **5.** (*of thumb*, *foot*) поду́шечка. **6.** (*for voting*) баллотиро́вочный шар. **7.** (*pl.*, *sl.*: *testicles*) я́йца (*nt. pl.*) (*vulg.*); (*nonsense*) чепуха́; **make a ~s of** напорта́чить (*pf.*). **8.** (*tech.*): **~ and socket** шарово́й шарни́р. **9.** (*var. fig. uses*): **on the ~** сметли́вый, (*coll.*) расторо́пный; **get on the ~** смекну́ть (*pf.*); **~ of fire** (*pers.*) сгу́сток эне́ргии; **have, keep one's eye on the ~** (*pursue objective single-mindedly*) идти́ (*det.*) пря́мо к це́ли; быть целеустремлённым; **keep the ~ rolling** (*in conversation*) подде́рж|ивать, -а́ть разгово́р; **set the ~ rolling** (*start sth.*) пус|ка́ть, -ти́ть что-н. в ход.
cpds. **~-bearing** *n.* шарикоподши́пник; **~-cock** *n.* шарово́й кла́пан; **~-park** *adj.*: **a ~-park figure** приме́рная ци́фра; **~-point** (*pen*) *n.* ша́риковая ру́чка, ша́рик.
ballad [ˈbæləd] *n.* балла́да, наро́дная пе́сня, шансо́н.
cpd. **~-monger** *n.* (*hist.*) продаве́ц балла́д.
ballade [bæˈlɑːd] *n.* балла́да.
balladeer [ˌbæləˈdɪə(r)] *n.* шансонье́ (*m. indecl.*).
balladry [ˈbælədrɪ] *n.* балла́ды (*f. pl.*).
ballast [ˈbæləst] *n.* **1.** (*naut.*, *rail*) балла́ст; **in ~** в балла́сте. **2.** (*fig.*) уравнове́шенность, усто́йчивость; **he has no ~** он неуравнове́шенный/неусто́йчивый челове́к. **3.** (*attr.*) балла́стный.
v.t. **1.** грузи́ть, на- балла́стом; (*rail*) зас|ыпа́ть, -ы́пать балла́стом. **2.** (*fig.*) прид|ава́ть, -а́ть усто́йчивость +*d*.
ballerina [ˌbæləˈriːnə] *n.* балери́на.
ballet [ˈbæleɪ] *n.* бале́т.
cpds. **~-dancer** *n.* арти́ст (*fem.* -ка) бале́та; **~-master** *n.* балетме́йстер.
balletomane [ˈbælɪtəʊˌmeɪn] *n.* балетома́н.
balletomania [ˈbælɪtəʊˈmeɪnɪə] *n.* балетома́ния.
ballistic [bəˈlɪstɪk] *adj.* баллисти́ческий; **~ missile** баллисти́ческий снаря́д.
ballistics [bəˈlɪstɪks] *n.* балли́стика.
ballon d'essai [bæˌlɔ̃ deˈseɪ] *n.* про́бный шар.
balloon [bəˈluːn] *n.* аэроста́т; (*also child's*) возду́шный шар;

(*in comic strip, etc.*) овáл; **barrage** ~ аэростáт заграждéния; **captive** ~ привязнóй аэростáт; ~ **glass** (*for brandy*) коньячная рюмка; ~ **tyre** кáмерная шина.

v.i. (*fly in* ~) летáть (*indet.*) на воздушном шаре.

balloonist [bə'lu:nɪst] *n.* воздухоплáватель (*m.*), аэронáвт.

ballot ['bælət] *n.* (*ball*) баллотирóвочный шар; (~-*paper*) избирáтельный бюллетéнь; (*vote*) баллотирóвка; **put a question to the** ~, **take a** ~ стáвить, по- вопрóс на голосовáние; (*number of votes*) колúчество пóданных голосóв; (*drawing lots*) жеребьёвка.

v.i. (*vote*) голосовáть (*impf.*); (*draw, cast lots*) тянуть (*impf.*) жрéбий; метáть/бросáть (*both impf.*) жрéбий; ~ **for precedence** устан|áвливать, -ови́ть порядок очерёдности по жрéбию.

cpd. ~-**box** *n.* избирáтельная урна; ящик для бюллетéней.

ballyhoo [ˌbælɪ'hu:] *n.* (*coll.*) шумиха.

balm [bɑ:m] *n.* (*exudation, fragrance; also fig.*) бальзáм; (*ointment*) бальзáм, болеутоляющее срéдство.

balmy ['bɑ:mɪ] *adj.* **1.** (*fragrant*) аромáтный. **2.** (*soft*) мягкий; (*of wind*) нéжный. **3.** (*soothing*) успокои́тельный, цели́тельный. **4.** (*yielding balm*) бальзами́ческий, бальзáмовый. **5.** (*coll.*) = **barmy 2.**

baloney [bə'ləʊnɪ] *n.* (*sl.*) ерундá.

balsa ['bɒlsə, 'bɔ:l-] *n.* бáльза.

balsam ['bɒlsəm, 'bɔ:l-] *n.* (*resinous product*) бальзáм; (*plant*) бальзами́н, недотрóга; ~ **fir** бальзами́ческая пи́хта.

Balt ['bɔ:lt] *n.* прибáлт (*fem.* -ка).

Baltic ['bɔ:ltɪk, 'bɒl-] *n.*: **the** ~ Балти́йское мóре.

adj. балти́йский; прибалти́йский; ~ **states** прибалти́йские государства, Прибáлтика.

Balto-Slavic ['bɔ:ltəʊ'slɑ:vɪk] *adj.* бáлто-славянский.

baluster ['bæləstə(r)] *n.* балясина.

balustrade [ˌbælə'streɪd] *n.* балюстрáда.

bamboo [bæm'bu:] *n.* бамбук; (*attr.*) бамбуковый.

bamboozle [bæm'bu:z(ə)l] *v.t.* (*coll.*) околпáчи|вать, -ть; одурáчи|вать, -ть; над|увáть, -уть.

ban [bæn] *n.* (*eccl.*) анáфема, проклятие; (*sentence of outlawry*) объявлéние (*кого*) вне закóна; (*banishment*) изгнáние; (*prohibition*) запрещéние, запрéт.

v.t. запре|щáть, -ти́ть.

banal [bə'nɑ:l] *adj.* банáльный.

banality [bə'nælɪtɪ] *n.* банáльность; (*remark*) банáльное замечáние.

banana [bə'nɑ:nə] *n.* банáн; (*pl. coll.: mad*) **he's** ~**s** у негó кры́ша поéхала; **to go** ~**s** чóкнуться (*pf.*), сдви́нуться (*pf.*); **to drive** ~**s** дов|оди́ть, -ести́ до сумасшéствия.

band¹ [bænd] *n.* **1.** (*braid*) тесьмá; (*for decoration*) лéнта; (*on barrel*) óбруч, обод; **rubber** ~ рези́нка. **2.** (*strip*) полосá; **a plate with a blue** ~ **round it** тарéлка с голубы́м ободкóм. **3.** (*radio*): **frequency** ~ полосá частóт. **4.** (*attr.*): ~ **conveyor** лéнточный транспортёр.

cpds. ~**box** *n.* картóнка для шляп; ~-**saw** *n.* лéнточная пилá.

band² [bænd] *n.* (*company*) грýппа; (*detachment*) отряд; (*gang*) бáнда, шáйка; (*mus.*) оркéстр; **jazz** ~ джаз-бáнд, джаз-оркéстр.

v.t. & i. ~ **together** соб|ирáть(ся), -рáть(ся).

cpds. ~**master** *n.* капельмéйстер; ~**sman** *n.* оркестрáнт; ~**stand** *n.* эстрáда для оркéстра.

bandage ['bændɪdʒ] *n.* бинт; (*blindfold*) повязка.

v.t. бинтовáть, за-; перевяз|ывать, -áть.

bandan(n)a [bæn'dænə] *n.* цветнóй платóк.

bandeau ['bændəʊ, -'dəʊ] *n.* (*hair-ribbon*) лéнта для волóс.

banderole [ˌbændə'rəʊl] *n.* вы́мпел.

bandicoot ['bændɪˌku:t] *n.* бандикýт.

bandit ['bændɪt] *n.* разбóйник, банди́т.

banditry ['bændɪtrɪ] *n.* бандити́зм.

bandol|eer, -ier [ˌbændə'lɪə(r)] *n.* нагрýдный патронтáш.

bandy¹ ['bændɪ] *adj.* кривóй.

cpd. ~-**legged** *adj.* кривонóгий.

band|y² ['bændɪ] *v.t.*: **have one's name** ~**ied about** быть предмéтом тóлков; ~**y words** перебрáсываться (*impf.*) словáми.

bane [beɪn] *n.* напáсть, проклятие; **it is the** ~ **of my life** э́то отравляет мне жизнь.

baneful ['beɪnfʊl] *adj.* пáгубный, губи́тельный.

bang¹ [bæŋ] *n.* (*of hair*) чёлка.

bang² [bæŋ] *n.* **1.** (*blow*) удáр. **2.** (*crash*) грóхот; стук. **3.** (*sound of a gun*) вы́стрел; (*of explosion*) взрыв. **4.** (*coll.*): **go with a** ~ (*succeed*) про|ходи́ть, -йти́ блестяще.

v.t. (*strike, thump*) уд|арять, -áрить; (*at the door etc.*) ст|учáть, -ýкнуть +*a.*; ~ **a drum** удáрить (*pf.*) в барабáн; ~ **the piano-keys** удáрить (*pf.*) по клáвишам; ~ **one's fist on the table** стýкнуть (*pf.*) кулакóм по столý; ~ **the door** хлóпнуть (*pf.*) двéрью; ~ **the lid down** захлóпнуть (*pf.*) кры́шку; ~ **the box down on the floor** грóхнуть (*pf.*) ящик нá пол; ~ **out a tune** оттарабáнить (*pf.*) моти́в.

v.i. (*of door, window etc.; also* ~ **to**) захлóпнуться (*pf.*); **the door is** ~**ing** дверь хлóпает; (*of pers.*): ~ **at the door** стучáть/колоти́ть (*impf.*) в дверь; **stop** ~**ing about!** довóльно тарабáнить!; **he** ~**ed away at the ducks** он пали́л по ýткам.

adv. **1.: go** ~ (*of gun*) бáхнуть (*pf.*); ~ **went £100** раз! — и ста фýнтов как не бывáло. **2.** (*suddenly*) вдруг; (*just, exactly*) прямо; как раз; ~ **on** (*coll.*) в аккурáт.

int. бац!; бах!

cpd. ~-**up** *adj.* (*coll.*) первоклáссный.

banger ['bæŋə(r)] *n.* (*coll.*) (*sausage*) соси́ска; (*car*) драндулéт.

Bangladesh [ˌbæŋglə'deʃ, ˌbʌŋg-] *n.* Бангладéш.

Bangladeshi [ˌbæŋglə'deʃɪ, ˌbʌŋg-] *n.* бангладéш|ец (*fem.* -ка).

adj. бангладéшский.

bangle ['bæŋg(ə)l] *n.* браслéт.

banish ['bænɪʃ] *v.t.* (*exile*) высылáть, вы́слать; (*dismiss*) прог|оня́ть, -нáть; изг|оня́ть, -нáть; (*from one's mind*) от|гоня́ть, -огнáть.

banishment ['bænɪʃmənt] *n.* вы́сылка, ссы́лка; изгнáние.

banisters ['bænɪstəz] *n.* пери́л|а (*pl., g.*—).

banjo ['bændʒəʊ] *n.* бáнджо (*indecl.*).

banjoist ['bændʒəʊɪst] *n.* игрóк на бáнджо.

bank¹ [bæŋk] *n.* **1.** (*of river*) бéрег. **2.** (*under-water shelf*) бáнка. **3.:** ~ **of clouds** грядá облакóв; ~ **of fog** полосá тумáна; (*of snow*) занóс, сугрóб; (*sand*-~) óтмель; ~**s of earth between fields** земляны́е валы́ мéжду поля́ми. **4.** (*embankment*) нáсыпь. **5.** (*min.*) зáлежь. **6.** (*of aeroplane etc.*) крен.

v.t. **1.:** ~ **a river** обваловáть (*pf.*) берегá реки́; соору|жáть, -ди́ть дáмбу вдоль реки́. **2.:** ~ **(up) a fire** поддéрж|ивать, -áть огóнь. **3.: the road is** ~**ed** дорóга имéет наклóн. **4.** (*aeron.*) крени́ть, на-.

v.i. **1.** (*also* ~ **up,** *of snow etc.*) образóв|ывать, -áть занóсы. **2.** (*aeron.*) накрен|я́ться, -и́ться.

bank² [bæŋk] *n.* (*tier of oars*) ряд вёсел; (*row of keys*) ряд клавиатýры.

bank³ [bæŋk] *n.* **1.** (*fin.*) банк; ~ **account** счёт в бáнке; **B**~ **of England** Англи́йский банк; ~ **rate** учётная стáвка; **clearing** ~ кли́ринговый банк; **savings** ~ сберегáтельная кáсса, сберкáсса; ~ **of issue** эмиссиóнный банк. **2.** (*at cards etc.*) банк; **break the** ~ сорвáть (*pf.*) банк. **3.: blood** ~ дóнорский пункт. **4.** (*attr.*) бáнковый, бáнковский; ~ **book** бáнковская кни́жка; ~ **card** бáнковская креди́тная кáрта; ~ **clerk** бáнковский слýжащий; ~ **holiday** ≃ прáздничный день.

v.t. (*put into* ~) класть, положи́ть в банк.

v.i. (*keep money in* ~) держáть (*impf.*) дéньги в бáнке; (*at cards*) метáть (*impf.*) банк; ~ **on** (*fig., rely on*) пол|агáться, -ожи́ться на+*a.*; дéлать, с- стáвку на+*a.*

cpd. ~-**note** *n.* креди́тный билéт; банкнóт.

banker ['bæŋkə(r)] *n.* банки́р; (*at cards*) банкомёт.

banking ['bæŋkɪŋ] *n.* (*aeron.*) крен; (*fin.*) бáнковое дéло.

bankrupt ['bæŋkrʌpt] *n.* банкрóт, несостоятельный должни́к; **fraudulent** ~ злóстный банкрóт; **an adjudged** ~ лицó, объявленное по судý банкрóтом.

adj. (*also fig.*) обанкрóтившийся; несостоятельный; **go** ~ обанкрóтиться (*pf.*).

v.t. дéлать, с- несостоятельным; дов|оди́ть, -ести́ до банкрóтства.

bankruptcy ['bæŋkˌrʌptsɪ] *n.* банкрóтство, несостоятельность;

file a declaration of ~ официа́льно объяв|ля́ть, -и́ть себя́ несостоя́тельным; **B~ Court** суд по дела́м несостоя́тельных должнико́в.
banner ['bænə(r)] *n.* (*lit., fig.*) зна́мя (*nt. pl.*); (*flag*) флаг; (*poet.*) стяг; (*with slogan*) плака́т; ~ **headlines** кру́пные заголо́вки.
cpd. **~-bearer** *n.* знамено́сец.
banns [bænz] *n.* оглаше́ние (предстоя́щего бра́ка); **ask, call, read the** ~ огла|ша́ть, -си́ть имена́ жениха́ и неве́сты; **forbid the** ~ заяв|ля́ть, -и́ть проте́ст про́тив заключе́ния бра́ка.
banquet ['bæŋkwɪt] *n.* пир; (*formal*) банке́т.
v.i. пирова́ть (*impf.*).
banquette [bæŋ'ket] *n.* (*seat*) банке́тка.
banshee ['bænʃiː, -'ʃiː] *n.* дух, предвеща́ющий смерть в до́ме.
bantam ['bæntəm] *n.* (*fowl*) бента́мка; (*fig.*) петушо́к.
cpd. **~-weight** *n.* боксёр легча́йшего ве́са.
banter ['bæntə(r)] *n.* подшу́чивание, подтру́нивание.
v.t. подтру́н|ивать, -и́ть над+*i.*; подшу́|чивать, -ти́ть над+*i.*
Bantu [bæn'tuː] *n.* ба́нту (*m. indecl.*).
adj. ба́нту (*indecl.*).
banyan ['bænɪən, -jən] *n.* баньян.
baobab ['beɪəʊ,bæb] *n.* баоба́б.
baptism ['bæptɪz(ə)m] *n.* креще́ние; крести́н|ы (*pl., g.* —); ~ **of fire** боево́е креще́ние.
baptismal [bæp'tɪzm(ə)l] *adj.* крести́льный.
Baptist ['bæptɪst] *n.* **1.: St John the B~** Иоа́нн Крести́тель (*m.*). **2.** (*member of sect*) бапти́ст.
baptist(e)ry ['bæptɪstərɪ] *n.* баптисте́рий.
baptize [bæp'taɪz] *v.t.* крести́ть, о́-; нар|ека́ть, -е́чь; **he was ~d Peter** он был наречён Петро́м.
bar[1] [bɑː(r)] *n.* **1.** (*strip, flat piece*) полоса́; (*ingot*) сли́ток; (*lever*) ва́га; (*fire-, grate-*) колосни́к; **parallel ~s** паралле́льные бру́сья (*m. pl.*); **horizontal** ~ перекла́дина; (*rod, pole*) шта́нга; (*of chocolate*) пли́тка; (*of soap*) кусо́к. **2.** (*bolt*) затво́р, засо́в. **3.** (*obstacle*) прегра́да; препя́тствие; **colour** ~ цветно́й барье́р; ~ **to marriage** препя́тствие к вступле́нию в брак. **4.** (*usu. pl.*) решётка; **behind ~s** за решёткой. **5.** (*naut.*) бар, о́тмель. **6.** (*mus.*) та́ктовая черта́, такт. **7.:** ~ **sinister** (*fig.*) незаконнорождённость.
v.t. (*bolt, lock*) зап|ира́ть, -ере́ть на засо́в; (*obstruct*) прегра|жда́ть, -ди́ть; (*close*) закр|ыва́ть, -ы́ть; загор|а́живать, -оди́ть; (*exclude*) исключ|а́ть, -и́ть; (*prohibit*) запре|ща́ть, -ти́ть; ~ **o.s. in** зап|ира́ться, -ере́ться; ~ **s.o. out** не впус|ка́ть, -ти́ть кого́-н.; **soldiers ~red the way** солда́ты загороди́ли доро́гу.
cpd. **~-code** *n.* бар-ко́д.
bar[2] [bɑː(r)] *n.* (*legal profession*) адвокату́ра; **read for the** ~ гото́виться (*impf.*) к адвокату́ре; **he was called to the** ~ он получи́л пра́во адвока́тской пра́ктики; **be at the** ~ быть адвока́том; **prisoner at the** ~ обвиня́емый (на скамье́ подсуди́мых); (*fig.*): **the** ~ **of public opinion** суд обще́ственного мне́ния.
bar[3] [bɑː(r)] *n.* (*room*) бар, буфе́т; (*counter*) прила́вок; **milk** ~ кафе́-моло́чная; моло́чный бар; **snack** ~ заку́сочная.
cpds. **~fly** *n.* выпиво́ха (*c.g., coll.*); **~maid** *n.* буфе́тчица, официа́нтка в пивно́й, ба́рменша; **~man, ~-tender** *nn.* буфе́тчик, ба́рмен.
bar[4] [bɑː(r)] *n.* (*unit of pressure*) бар.
bar[5] [bɑː(r)] *prep.* (*coll., excluding*) исключа́я, не счита́я; ~ **none** без исключе́ния; **it's all over** ~ **the shouting** (*fig.*) ко́нчен бал.
barathea [,bærə'θiə] *n.* бараtéя.
barb[1] [bɑːb] *n.* **1.** (*fish's feeler*) у́сик. **2.** (*sting, spike*) колю́чка. **3.** (*of arrow, fish-hook etc.*) боро́дка, зубе́ц. **4.** (*cutting remark*) ко́лкость.
v.t. наса́|живать, -ди́ть шип/остриё *и т.п.* на+*a.*; (*see also* **barbed**).
barb[2] [bɑːb] *n.* (*horse*) берберийский конь.
Barbadian [bɑː'beɪdɪən] *n.* барбадо́с|ец (*fem.* -ка).
adj. барбадо́сский.
Barbados [bɑː'beɪdɒs] *n.* Барба́дос.
barbarian [bɑː'beərɪən] *n.* ва́рвар.
adj. ва́рварский.
barbaric [bɑː'bærɪk] *adj.* ва́рварский.
barbarism ['bɑːbə,rɪz(ə)m] *n.* ва́рварство; (*ling.*) варвари́зм.
barbarity [bɑː'bærɪtɪ] *n.* ва́рварство.
barbarize ['bɑːbə,raɪz] *v.t.* (*people*) пов|ерга́ть, -е́ргнуть в состоя́ние ва́рварства; (*language*) засор|я́ть, -и́ть варвари́змами.
barbarous ['bɑːbərəs] *adj.* ва́рварский; (*cruel*) бесчелове́чный.
Barbary ape ['bɑːbərɪ] *n.* маго́т.
barbate ['bɑːbeɪt] *adj.* (*zool.*) уса́тый, борода́тый; (*bot.*) ости́стый.
barbecue ['bɑːbɪ,kjuː] *n.* (*party*) пи́кник, где подаю́т мя́со, зажа́ренное на ве́ртеле.
v.t. жа́рить, за- на ве́ртеле.
barbed [bɑːbd] *adj.* **1.** колю́чий; име́ющий колю́чки/шипы́; ~ **wire** колю́чая про́волока; ~ **wire entanglement** про́волочное загражде́ние. **2.: a** ~ **remark** ко́лкое замеча́ние.
barbel ['bɑːb(ə)l] *n.* (*fish*) уса́ч; (*filament*) у́сик.
barber ['bɑːbə(r)] *n.* парикма́хер; **~'s shop** парикма́херская; **~'s itch, rash** (*med.*) паразита́рный сико́з; **the B~ of Seville** Севи́льский цирю́льник.
barberry ['bɑːbərɪ] *n.* барбари́с.
barbican ['bɑːbɪkən] *n.* барбика́н; навесна́я ба́шня.
barbiturate [bɑː'bɪtjʊrət, -,reɪt] *n.* барбитура́т.
barbituric [,bɑːbɪ'tjʊərɪk] *adj.* барбиту́ровый.
barcarol(l)e ['bɑːkə,rəʊl] *n.* баркаро́ла.
bard [bɑːd] *n.* бард, менестре́ль (*m.*), певе́ц.
bardic ['bɑːdɪk] *adj.*: ~ **poetry** поэ́зия ба́рдов.
bare [beə(r)] *adj.* **1.** (*naked, not covered*) го́лый, наго́й; обнажённый, непокры́тый; **with one's** ~ **hands** го́лыми рука́ми; ~ **feet** босы́е но́ги; **in one's** ~ **skin** голышо́м, нагишо́м; ~ **shoulders** обнажённые пле́чи; **with** ~ **head** с непокры́той голово́й; ~ **trees** го́лые дере́вья; **lay** ~ (*fig.*) вскры|ва́ть, -ть; раскр|ыва́ть, -ы́ть. **2.** (*threadbare*) поно́шенный. **3.** (*empty*) пусто́й; **the room was** ~ **of furniture** в ко́мнате не́ было ме́бели. **4.** (*unadorned*) просто́й, неприкра́шенный. **5.** (*slight, mere*) мале́йший; **a** ~ **majority** о́чень незначи́тельное большинство́; ~ **necessities of life** насу́щные потре́бности жи́зни; **earn a** ~ **living** едва́ зараба́тывать (*impf.*) на жизнь; **believe s.o.'s** ~ **word** ве́рить кому́-н. на́ слово; **they made a** ~ **£100** они́ едва́ набра́ли сто фу́нтов; ~ **profit** ничто́жная при́быль; **at the** ~ **mention of** при одно́м упомина́нии о+*p.* **6.** (*elec.*) го́лый, неизоли́рованный.
v.t. обнаж|а́ть, -и́ть; огол|я́ть, -и́ть; ~ **one's head** обнаж|а́ть, -и́ть го́лову; ~ **one's teeth** ска́лить, о- зу́бы; ~ **one's heart** изли́ть (*pf.*) ду́шу.
cpds. **~back** *adv.* без седла́; **~faced** *adj.* (*fig.*) на́глый, бессты́дный; **~facedness** *n.* на́глость, бессты́дство; **~foot** *adj.* босо́й; *adv.* босико́м; **~footed** *adj.* босо́й, босоно́гий; **~headed** *adj.* простоволо́сый, с непокры́той голово́й; **~legged** *adj.* с го́лыми нога́ми; **~necked** *adj.* с откры́той ше́ей.
barely ['beəlɪ] *adv.* (*simply*) то́лько, про́сто; (*scarcely*) едва́; **I have** ~ **enough money** мне едва́ хва́тит де́нег.
bareness [beə(r)nɪs] *n.* (*lack of covering*) нагота́, неприкры́тость; (*unadorned state*) простота́, неприкра́шенность; (*poorness*) бе́дность, ску́дость.
Barents Sea ['bærənts] *n.* Ба́ренцево мо́ре.
bargain ['bɑːgɪn] *n.* **1.** (*deal*) сде́лка, соглаше́ние; **good/bad** ~ вы́годная/невы́годная сде́лка; **make, strike, drive a** ~ заключ|а́ть, -и́ть сде́лку; **he drives a hard** ~ он неусту́пчив; **it's a** ~! по рука́м!; **a ~'s a** ~ угово́р доро́же де́нег; **into the** ~ в прида́чу. **2.** (*thg. cheaply acquired*) вы́годная поку́пка; ~ **sale** (дешёвая) распрода́жа; ~ **price** распрода́жная цена́.
v.t.: ~ **away** променя́ть (*pf.*) (*что на что*).
v.i. торгова́ться, с-; (*agree*) догов|а́риваться, -ори́ться; ~ **for** (*expect*) ожида́ть (*impf.*); **it was more than I ~ed for** на э́то я не рассчи́тывал.
cpd. **~-hunter** *n.* охо́тник за дешеви́зной.

bargainer ['bɑːgɪnə(r)] *n.* торгу́ющийся; **he is a hard ~** он упо́рно торгу́ется.
bargaining ['bɑːgɪnɪŋ] *n.*: **pay ~** перегово́ры о зарпла́те.
barge [bɑːdʒ] *n.* (*small boat*) ба́рка; (*for transport*) ба́ржа.
v.i. (*coll.*): **~ about** носи́ться (*impf.*), мета́ться (*impf.*); **~ into, against** налет|а́ть, -е́ть на+*a.*; наск|а́кивать, -очи́ть на+*a.*; **~ in** (*intrude*) вва́л|иваться, -и́ться.
cpd. **~-pole** *n.* ба́ржевый баго́р; **I wouldn't touch it with a ~-pole** (*coll.*) я не подойду́ к э́тому и на вы́стрел.
bargee [bɑː'dʒiː] *n.* ба́рочник; **swear like a ~** руга́ться как изво́зчик.
baritone ['bærɪˌtəʊn] *n.* (*voice, singer*) барито́н.
adj. баритона́льный.
barium ['beərɪəm] *n.* ба́рий.
bark[1] [bɑːk] *n.* (*of tree etc.*) кора́; **Peruvian, Jesuits' ~** хи́нная ко́рка.
v.t. (*strip of ~*) окор|я́ть, -и́ть; сдира́ть, содра́ть кору́ +*g.*; **~ one's shins** об|дира́ть, -одра́ть себе́ но́ги.
bark[2], **barque** [bɑːk] *n.* (*vessel*) барк.
bark[3] [bɑːk] *n.* (*of dog*) лай; **his ~ is worse than his bite** ≃ он гро́зен лишь на слова́х; (*of gunfire*) гро́хот; (*cough*) ла́ющий, ре́зкий ка́шель.
v.t.: **~ out** (*e.g. an order*) ря́вк|ать, -нуть.
v.t. (*of dog etc.*) ла́ять (*impf.*) (**at:** на+*a.*); **~ up the wrong tree** (*fig.*) обра|ща́ться, -ти́ться не по а́дресу; (*cough*) отры́висто ка́шлять (*impf.*).
barkentine ['bɑːkənˌtiːn] = **barquentine**
barker ['bɑːkə(r)] *n.* (*tout*) зазыва́ла (*c.g.*).
barley ['bɑːlɪ] *n.* ячме́нь (*m.*); **hulled ~** я́чневая крупа́; **pearl ~** перло́вая ка́ша.
cpds. **~corn** *n.* ячме́нное зерно́; **~-mow** *n.* скирда́ ячменя́; **~-sugar** *n.* леденцы́ (*m. pl.*); **~-water** *n.* ячме́нный отва́р.
barm [bɑːm] *n.* (*yeast*) (пивны́е) дро́жжи (*pl., g.* -е́й); (*leaven*) заква́ска; (*froth*) пе́на.
bar mitzvah [bɑː 'mɪtzvə] *n.* бар-ми́цва.
barmy ['bɑːmɪ] *adj.* **1.** (*full of barm*) заброди́вший, заки́сший; (*frothy*) пе́нистый. **2.** (*coll., silly; also* **balmy**) чо́кнутый, тро́нутый; **go ~** тро́нуться (*pf.*); спя́тить (*pf.*) (с ума́).
barn [bɑːn] *n.* амба́р, сара́й; (*threshing-floor*) гумно́; (*fig., comfortless building*) сара́й.
cpds. **~-door** *n.* воро́т|а (*pl., g.* —); **~fowl** *n.* дома́шняя пти́ца; **~-owl** *n.* сипу́ха; **~stormer** *n.* (*coll.*) бродя́чий актёр.
barnacle ['bɑːnək(ə)l] *n.* **1.** (*on ship's bottom*) морска́я у́точка; (*fig., of pers.*) прилипа́ла (*c.g.*). **2.: ~ goose** белощёкая каза́рка.
barney ['bɑːnɪ] *n.* (*sl.*) перебра́нка.
barograph ['bærəˌgrɑːf] *n.* баро́граф.
barometer [bə'rɒmɪtə(r)] *n.* баро́метр.
barometric [ˌbærəʊ'metrɪk] *adj.* барометри́ческий.
baron ['bærən] *n.* баро́н; (*industrial leader*) магна́т; **~ of beef** то́лстый филе́й.
baroness ['bærənɪs] *n.* барone´сса.
baronet ['bærənɪt] *n.* барoне́т.
baronetcy ['bærənɪtsɪ] *n.* ти́тул баронe´та.
baronial [bə'rəʊnɪəl] *adj.* баро́нский; (*fig.*) ба́рский.
barony ['bærənɪ] *n.* (*title*) баро́нство; (*domain*) владе́ния (*nt. pl.*) баро́на.
baroque [bə'rɒk] *n.* баро́кко (*indecl.*).
adj. баро́чный.
barouche [bə'ruːʃ] *n.* ландо́ (*indecl.*).
barque [bɑːk] = **bark**[2]
barquentine, barkentine ['bɑːkənˌtiːn] *n.* бриганти́на.
barrack[1] ['bærək] *n.* (*usu. pl.*) каза́рма; **confinement to ~s** каза́рменный аре́ст; (*temporary structure*) бара́к; (*austere building*) каза́рма, мра́чное зда́ние.
v.t. (*lodge in ~s*) разме|ща́ть, -сти́ть в каза́рмах.
cpd. **~-square** *n.* каза́рменный плац.
barrack[2] ['bærək] *v.i.* (*coll.*) (*jeer at*) гро́мко высме́ивать (*impf.*); **~ for** подба́дривать (*impf.*) кри́ками.
barracuda [ˌbærə'kuːdə] *n.* баррaку́да.
barrage ['bærɑːʒ] *n.* **1.** (*in watercourse*) запру́да; (*dam*) плоти́на. **2.** (*mil.*) загражде́ние; (*gunfire*) огнево́й вал; **creeping ~** ползу́щий огнево́й вал; **balloon ~** противосамолётное загражде́ние из аэроста́тов; (*fig.*): **a ~ of questions** град/шквал вопро́сов.
barratry ['bærətrɪ] *n.* (*naut.*) бара́трия; (*leg.*) сутя́жничество, кля́узничество.
barrel ['bær(ə)l] *n.* **1.** бо́чка. **2.** (*of firearm*) ствол, (*muzzle*) ду́ло; (*of fountain pen*) резервуа́р. **3.** (*of animal*) ту́ловище.
v.t. (*put in ~s*) разл|ива́ть, -и́ть по бо́чкам; **~led beer** бо́чечное пи́во.
cpds. **~-head** *n.* дно бо́чки; **~-organ** *n.* шарма́нка; **~-roll** *n.* (*aeron.*) бо́чка.
barren ['bærən] *adj.* (*of woman*) беспло́дная; (*of plants, trees etc.*) беспло́дный, неплодоно́сный; **~ land** то́щая/неплодоро́дная/беспло́дная земля́; **a ~ cow** я́ловая коро́ва; (*fig.*) беспло́дный; **a ~ subject** неинтере́сный предме́т; **~ of results** не принёсший (*or* не да́вший) результа́тов.
barrenness ['bærənnɪs] *n.* (*of woman*) беспло́дие; (*of trees, plants*) неплодоно́сность; (*of land*) беспло́дность; неплодоро́дность; (*fig.*) беспло́дность.
barricade [ˌbærɪ'keɪd] *n.* баррика́да.
v.t. баррикади́ровать, за-; **~ o.s. in** забаррикади́роваться (*pf.*).
barrier ['bærɪə(r)] *n.* барье́р; **Great B~ Reef** Большо́й Барье́рный риф; **sound ~** звуково́й барье́р; (*dividing-line*) прегра́да; (*obstacle*) поме́ха, прегра́да.
v.t.: **~ in** загра|жда́ть, -ди́ть; огра|жда́ть, -ди́ть; **~ off** прегра|жда́ть, -ди́ть.
barring ['bɑːrɪŋ] *prep.* за исключе́нием +*g.*
barrister ['bærɪstə(r)] *n.* адвока́т, барри́стер.
barrow[1] ['bærəʊ] *n.* (*archaeol.*) курга́н, моги́льный холм.
barrow[2] ['bærəʊ] *n.* (*hand-~*) ручна́я теле́жка; (*wheel~*) та́чка.
cpd. **~-boy** *n.* лото́чник.
barter ['bɑːtə(r)] *n.* обме́н, ме́на, менова́я торго́вля, товарообме́н.
v.t. обме́н|ивать, -я́ть (*что на что*); **~ away** променя́ть (*pf.*); **the B~ed Bride** (*opera*) Про́данная неве́ста.
v.i. обме́н|иваться, -я́ться +*i.*; меня́ться (*impf.*) +*i.*
barterer ['bɑːtərə(r)] *n.* производя́щий товарообме́н.
basal ['beɪs(ə)l] *adj.* основно́й, лежа́щий в осно́ве.
basalt ['bæsɔːlt] *n.* база́льт; (*attr.*) база́льтовый.
bascule ['bæskjuːl] *n.*: **~ bridge** подъёмный мост.
base[1] [beɪs] *n.* **1.** (*of wall, column etc.*) фунда́мент, пьедеста́л, основа́ние, ба́зис. **2.** (*fig., basis; also math.*) основа́ние. **3.** (*chem.*) основа́ние. **4.** (*gram.*) осно́ва. **5.** (*mil. etc.*) ба́за; **advanced ~** гла́вная передова́я ба́за; **~ camp** ба́за; **~ hospital** ба́зовый го́спиталь; **~ of operations** операцио́нная ба́за, плацда́рм; **supply ~** ба́за снабже́ния. **6.: get to first ~** (*fig.*) доби́ться (*pf.*) пе́рвого успе́ха.
v.t. осно́в|ывать, -а́ть; **~ one's hopes on** возл|ага́ть, -ожи́ть наде́жды на+*a*; **the legend is ~d on fact** в осно́ве э́той леге́нды лежа́т действи́тельные собы́тия; **~ o.s. on** полага́ться (*impf.*) на+*a.*; исходи́ть (*impf.*) из+*g.*
cpds. **~ball** *n.* бейсбо́л; **~line** *n.* исхо́дная ли́ния.
base[2] [beɪs] *adj.* ни́зкий, ни́зменный, по́длый; **~ metal** неблагоро́дный мета́лл.
cpd. **~-born** *adj.* (*of humble origin*) ни́зкого происхожде́ния; (*illegitimate*) незаконнорождённый.
baseless ['beɪslɪs] *adj.* необосно́ванный.
basement ['beɪsmənt] *n.* подва́л; (*attr.*) подва́льный.
baseness ['beɪsnɪs] *n.* ни́зость, ни́зменность.
bash [bæʃ] (*coll.*) *n.* (*attempt*) попы́тка; **have a ~** попыта́ться, попро́бовать; (*party*) гуля́нка, выпиво́н.
v.t. тра́хнуть (*pf.*); **~ s.o.'s head against a wall** тра́хнуть (*pf.*) кого́-н. башко́й об сте́ну (*coll.*); **give s.o. a ~ on the head** тра́хнуть (*pf.*) кого́-н. по башке́ (*coll.*); **~ s.o.'s head in** прошиби́ть (*pf.*) кому́-н. башку́ (*coll.*); **have a ~ at it!** попро́буйте!
bashful ['bæʃfʊl] *adj.* засте́нчивый.
bashfulness ['bæʃfʊlnɪs] *n.* засте́нчивость.
bashi-bazouk [ˌbæʃɪ bə'zuːk] *n.* (*hist.*) башибузу́к.
-bashing[1] ['bæʃɪŋ] *comb. form n.* **Paki-~** избие́ние пакиста́нцев; **queer-~** избие́ние гомосексуали́стов; **union-~** ущемле́ние профсою́зов.

adj. анти…; **union-~ legislation** антипрофсою́зные зако́ны.

bashing² [ˈbæʃɪŋ] *n.* (*thrashing*) взбу́чка, лупцо́вка (*coll.*).

Bashkir [bæʃˈkɪə(r)] *n.* башки́р (*fem.* -ка).

adj. башки́рский.

basic [ˈbeɪsɪk] *adj.* основно́й; **this is ~ to my argument** на э́том осно́вывается моя́ аргумента́ция.

basically [ˈbeɪsɪkəlɪ] *adv.* в основно́м.

basil [ˈbæz(ə)l] *n.* бази́лик.

basilica [bəˈzɪlɪkə] *n.* бази́лика.

basilisk [ˈbæzɪlɪsk] *n.* васили́ск.

basin [ˈbeɪs(ə)n] *n.* **1.** таз, ми́ска. **2.** (*of fountain*) ча́ша. **3.** (*of dock, river*) бассе́йн; **tidal ~** прили́вный бассе́йн. **4.** (*bay*) бу́хта.

basinful [ˈbeɪs(ə)nfʊl] *n.* ми́ска (*чего*); (*coll.*) бо́льше чем доста́точно.

basis [ˈbeɪsɪs] *n.* осно́ва, ба́зис; **~ of negotiations** осно́ва для перегово́ров; **on the ~ of** на осно́ве *+g.*; **on this ~** на э́том основа́нии; исходя́ из э́того; **lay the ~ for** заложи́ть (*pf.*) осно́ву *+g.*

bask [bɑːsk] *v.i.* гре́ться (*impf.*) (**in the sun:** на со́лнце); (*fig.*): **~ in glory** купа́ться (*impf.*) в луча́х сла́вы; **~ in s.o.'s favour** по́льзоваться (*impf.*) чьей-н. по́лной благосклонностью.

basket [ˈbɑːskɪt] *n.* корзи́на, корзи́нка; **clothes, laundry ~** корзи́на для гря́зного белья́; **luncheon ~** корзи́нка для за́втрака; **shopping ~** корзи́на/корзи́нка для поку́пок; (*fig.*) **pick of the ~** сли́в|ки (*pl.*, *g.* -ок) (*чего*).

cpds. **~-ball** *n.* баскетбо́л; **~-chair** *n.* плетёное кре́сло; **~-work** *n.* = **basketry**

basketful [ˈbɑːskɪtfʊl] *n.* корзи́на (*чего*).

basket|ry [ˈbɑːskɪtrɪ], **-work** [ˈbɑːskɪt,wɜːk] *nn.* плете́ние; (*product*) плетёные изде́лия (*nt. pl.*).

Basle [bɑːl] *n.* Ба́зель (*m.*).

Basque [bæsk] *n.* баск (*fem.* баско́нка).

adj. ба́скский.

bas-relief [ˌbɑː rɪˈliːf] *n.* баре́льеф.

bass¹ [bæs] *n.* (*zool.*) ка́менный о́кунь.

bass² [beɪs] *n.* (*mus.*) бас.

adj. басо́вый; **he has a ~ voice** у него́ бас; **~-baritone** бас-барито́н; **~ drum** туре́цкий бараба́н; **~ horn** ту́ба-бас; **~ viol** контраба́совая вио́ла.

basset [ˈbæsɪt] *n.* (**~-hound**) ба́с(с)ет.

basset-horn [ˈbæsɪt,hɔːn] *n.* бассетго́рн.

bassinet [ˌbæsɪˈnet] *n.* плетёная колыбе́ль/коля́ска.

bassoon [bəˈsuːn] *n.* фаго́т; **double ~** контрафаго́т.

bassoonist [bəˈsuːnɪst] *n.* фаготи́ст.

basso profundo [ˈbæsəʊ] *n.* ни́зкий бас.

bast [bæst] *n.* луб, лы́ко, моча́ло; (*strip of ~*) лубо́к; (*attr.*) лубяно́й, лы́ковый, лубо́чный; **~ mat** моча́льная цино́вка; рого́жка; **~ shoe** ла́поть (*m.*).

bastard [ˈbɑːstəd, ˈbæ-] *n.* **1.** (*child*) внебра́чный ребёнок. **2.** (*hybrid*) по́месь. **3.** (*as term of abuse etc.*) мерза́вец; **poor ~** несча́стный ублю́док; **lucky ~** везу́чий дья́вол. **4.** (*attr.*) (*spurious, inferior*) ху́дшего ка́чества; **~ French** испо́рченный францу́зский язы́к.

bastardize [ˈbɑːstə,daɪz] *v.t.* (*declare illegitimate*) объявл|я́ть, -и́ть незаконнорождённым; (*debase*) по́ртить, ис-; иска|жа́ть, -зи́ть.

bastardy [ˈbɑːstədɪ] *n.* незаконнорождённость; **~ order** суде́бное реше́ние о содержа́нии внебра́чного ребёнка.

baste¹ [beɪst] *v.t.* (*stitch*) смёт|ывать, -а́ть; сши|ва́ть, -ть на живу́ю ни́тку.

baste² [beɪst] *v.t.* (*cul.*) пол|ива́ть, -и́ть (*жаркое*).

baste³ [beɪst] *v.t.* (*thrash*) лупи́ть, от-.

bastinado [ˌbæstɪˈneɪdəʊ] *n.* бастона́да.

v.t. бить (*impf.*) па́лками по пя́ткам.

bastion [ˈbæstɪən] *n.* бастио́н; (*fig.*) опло́т.

bat¹ [bæt] *n.* (*zool.*) лету́чая мышь; **he has ~s in the belfry** у него́ ви́нтика не хвата́ет; **blind as a ~** соверше́нно слепо́й; **like a ~ out of hell** о́чень бы́стро, внеза́пно.

bat² [bæt] *n.* (*at games*) бита́, лапта́; (*fig.*): **off one's own ~** по со́бственному почи́ну; самостоя́тельно; **right off the ~** с ме́ста в карье́р.

v.t. бить (*impf.*) (*or* уд|аря́ть, -а́рить) бито́й/лапто́й.

bat³ [bæt] *v.t.*: **he did not ~ an eyelid** (*did not sleep*) он не сомкну́л глаз; (*paid no attention*) он и гла́зом не моргну́л.

bat⁴ [bæt] (*coll.*) *n.*: **he went off at a rare ~** он пусти́лся со всех ног.

v.i.: **~ along** нести́сь (*impf.*), мча́ться (*impf.*).

batch [bætʃ] *n.* **1.** (*of bread*) вы́печка. **2.** (*of pottery etc.*) па́ртия. **3.** (*consignment, collection*) ку́чка, па́чка; гру́ппа; **~ of letters** па́чка пи́сем.

bate [beɪt] *v.t.* (*reduce, restrain*) ум|еньша́ть, -е́ньшить; ум|еря́ть, е́рить; **with ~d breath** зата́ив дыха́ние.

bath [bɑːθ] *n.* ва́нна; (*steam ~*) ба́ня; **mud ~** грязева́я ва́нна; **Turkish ~** туре́цкая ба́ня; **take, have a ~** прин|има́ть, -я́ть ва́нну; купа́ться, вы́-/ис-; **run me a ~!** напусти́те мне ва́нну!; **swimming ~(s)** пла́вательный бассе́йн; **Order of the B~** о́рден Ба́ни; **~chair** инвали́дное кре́сло.

v.t. & i. купа́ть(ся), вы́/ис-.

cpds. **~-attendant** *n.* ба́нщик; **~-house** *n.* купа́льня, ба́ня; **~-mat** *n.* ко́врик для ва́нной; **~robe** *n.* купа́льный хала́т; **~room** *n.* ва́нная (ко́мната); **~-salts** *n.* экстра́кт для ва́нны; **~-towel** *n.* купа́льное полоте́нце; **~-tub** *n.* ва́нна.

bathe [beɪð] *n.* купа́ние; **go for a ~** искупа́ться (*pf.*).

v.t. **1.** (*one's face etc.*) мыть, по-; обм|ыва́ть, -ы́ть; **~ one's eyes, a wound** пром|ыва́ть, -ы́ть глаза́/ра́ну. **2.: he was ~d in sweat** он облива́лся по́том; **a face ~d in tears** лицо́, за́литое слеза́ми. **3.: the seas that ~ England** моря́, омыва́ющие А́нглию. **4.** (*of light, warmth*) зал|ива́ть, -и́ть.

v.i. купа́ться, вы́-/ис-.

bather [ˈbeɪðə(r)] *n.* купа́льщи|к (*fem.* -ца).

bathetic [bəˈθetɪk] *adj.* переходя́щий от высо́кого к коми́ческому.

bathing [ˈbeɪðɪŋ] *n.* купа́ние.

cpds. **~-cabin** *n.* каби́на для переодева́ния; **~-cap** *n.* купа́льная ша́почка; **~-costume, ~-dress, ~-suit** *nn.* купа́льный костю́м; **~-trunks** *n. pl.* пла́в|ки (*pl.*, *g.* -ок).

bathometer [bəˈθɒmɪtə(r)] *n.* бато́метр.

bathos [ˈbeɪθɒs] *n.* перехо́д от высо́кого к коми́ческому.

bathysphere [ˈbæθɪ,sfɪə(r)] *n.* батисфе́ра.

batik [bəˈtiːk, ˈbætɪk] *n.* бати́к; (*attr.*) бати́ковый.

batiste [bæˈtiːst] *n.* бати́ст; (*attr.*) бати́стовый.

batman [ˈbætmən] *n.* денщи́к, ордина́рец.

baton [ˈbæt(ə)n] *n.* **1.** (*staff of office*) жезл. **2.** (*mus.*) дирижёрская па́лочка. **3.** (*sport*) эстафе́тная па́лочка. **4.** (*policeman's*) дуби́нка.

batrachian [bəˈtreɪkɪən] *n.* бесхво́стая амфи́бия; (*pl.*) земново́дные (*nt. pl.*).

bats [bæts] *adj.* (*coll., crazy*) чо́кнутый.

batsman [ˈbætsmən] *n.* игро́к с би́той; отбива́ющий мяч.

battalion [bəˈtælɪən] *n.* батальо́н; **labour ~** строи́тельный батальо́н.

batten¹ [ˈbæt(ə)n] *n.* ре́йка, пла́нка.

v.t.: **~ down** (*naut.*) задра́и|вать, -ть.

batten² [ˈbæt(ə)n] *v.t.*: **~ on** отк|а́рмливаться, -орми́ться на*+p.*; **~ on one's friends** наж|ива́ться, -и́ться за счёт друзе́й.

batter¹ [ˈbætə(r)] *n.* (*cul.*) взби́тое те́сто.

batter² [ˈbætə(r)] *n.* (*US*) = **batsman**

batter³ [ˈbætə(r)] *v.t. & i.* **1.** (*beat*) колоти́ть, по-; дуба́сить, от-; громи́ть, раз-; **~ a wall down** разру́шить (*pf.*) сте́ну; **~ing-ram** тара́н. **2.** (*knock about*): **a ~ed old car/hat** потрёпанная ста́рая маши́на/шля́па.

battery [ˈbætərɪ] *n.* **1.** (*beating*): **assault and ~** (*leg.*) побо́|и (*pl.*, *g.* -ев); оскорбле́ние де́йствием. **2.** (*group of guns*) батаре́я; (*artillery unit*) дивизио́н. **3.** (*elec.*) батаре́я; (*in torch*) батаре́йка. **4.: ~ farming** выра́щивание живо́тных в (кле́точных) батаре́ях; **~ hens** бро́йлерные ку́ры.

cpds. **~-operated** *adj.* на батаре́ях; с батаре́йным пита́нием; **~-farmed** *adj.* вы́ращенный в батаре́е.

batting [ˈbætɪŋ] *n.* (*cotton fibre*) вати́н.

battle [ˈbæt(ə)l] *n.* би́тва, сраже́ние, бой; (*struggle*) борьба́; **drawn ~** безрезульта́тный бой; **pitched ~** сраже́ние; **~ royal** побо́ище; **join ~** вступи́ть (*pf.*) в бой; **give ~** дать (*pf.*) бой; **do ~** сража́ться (*impf.*); **order of ~** боево́й поря́док; **~ of Britain** би́тва за А́нглию; **~ of Waterloo**

сраже́ние при Ватерло́о; ~ **of the Marne** Ма́рнское сраже́ние; ~ **of Stalingrad** би́тва под Сталингра́дом; ~ **of Thermopylae** би́тва при Фермопи́лах; ~ **of Borodino/Tsushima** Бороди́нское/Цуси́мское сраже́ние; ~ **of Jutland** Ютла́ндское морско́е сраже́ние; ~ **casualties** поте́ри в бою́; ~ **fatigue** психи́ческая тра́вма, полу́ченная в хо́де боевы́х де́йствий; **the ~ is ours** побе́да за на́ми; **above the ~** (*fig.*) над схва́ткой; **the ~ of life** би́тва жи́зни; **fight a losing ~** вести́ (*det.*) безнадёжную борьбу́; **fight s.o.'s ~s for him** лезть (*det.*) в дра́ку за кого́-н.; **fight one's own ~s** постоя́ть (*pf.*) за себя́; **half the ~** (*fig.*) зало́г успе́ха, полде́ла.

v.i. боро́ться (*impf.*); сража́ться (*impf.*).

cpds. **~-array** *n.* боево́й поря́док; **~-axe** *n.* алеба́рда; (*fig.*, *termagant*) бой-ба́ба; **~-cruiser** *n.* лине́йный кре́йсер; **~-cry** *n.* боево́й клич; (*fig.*) ло́зунг; **~-dress** *n.* похо́дная фо́рма; **~field** *n.* по́ле сраже́ния/бо́я; **~-fleet** *n.* лине́йный флот; **~-ground** *n.* по́ле сраже́ния/бо́я; **~-piece** *n.* (*picture*) бата́льная карти́на; **~-scarred** *adj.* изра́ненный в боя́х; **~ship** *n.* лине́йный кора́бль, линко́р; **pocket ~ship** (*hist.*) карма́нный линко́р.

battledore [ˈbæt(ə)lˌdɔ:(r)] *n.* (*racket*) раке́тка; **~ and shuttlecock** игра́ в вола́н.

battlement [ˈbæt(ə)lmənt] *n.* зубча́тая стена́; парапе́тная сте́нка с бойни́цами.

battue [bæˈtju:, bæˈtu:] *n.* обла́ва; (*slaughter*) бо́йня.

batty [ˈbætɪ] *adj.* чо́кнутый, тро́нутый (*coll.*).

bauble [ˈbɔ:b(ə)l] *n.* (*trifle*) безделу́шка; (*jester's*) шутовско́й жезл.

baud [bəʊd, bɔ:d] *n.* (*comput.*) бод.

baulk [bɔ:lk, bɔ:k] = **balk**

bauxite [ˈbɔ:ksaɪt] *n.* бокси́т.

Bavaria [bəˈveərɪə] *n.* Бава́рия.

Bavarian [bəˈveərɪən] *n.* (*pers.*) бава́р|ец (*fem.* -ка).

adj. бава́рский.

bawd [ˈbɔ:d] *n.* сво́дница, (*coll.*) сво́дня.

bawd|iness [ˈbɔ:dɪnɪs], **-ry** [ˈbɔ:drɪ] *nn.* непристо́йность, поха́бщина.

bawdy [ˈbɔ:dɪ] *adj.* непристо́йный, поха́бный.

cpd. **~-house** *n.* публи́чный дом.

bawl [bɔ:l] *v.t. & i.* ора́ть (*impf.*); выкри́кивать, вы́крикнуть; **~ at s.o.** ора́ть на кого́-н.; **~ s.o. out** (*coll.*) наора́ть (*pf.*) на кого́-н.

bay[1] [beɪ] *n.* (*bot.*) лавр; (*pl.*, *poet.*) ла́вры (*m. pl.*); (*attr.*) лавро́вый; **~ rum** лавровишнёвая вода́.

cpd. **~-tree** *n.* лавр, ла́вровое де́рево.

bay[2] [beɪ] *n.* (*geog.*) зали́в, бу́хта; **B~ of Biscay** Биска́йский зали́в.

bay[3] [beɪ] *n.* **1.** (*of wall*) пролёт, пане́ль. **2.** (*window recess*) ни́ша; **~ window** э́ркер, фона́рь (*m.*). **3.: sick ~** (*naut.*) судово́й лазаре́т. **4.** (*aeron.*): **bomb ~** бо́мбовый отсе́к.

bay[4] [beɪ] *n.* **1.** (*bark*) лай. **2.** (*fig. uses*): **keep s.o. at ~** держа́ть (*impf.*) кого́-н. на расстоя́нии; не подпуска́ть (*impf.*) кого́-н.; **keep the enemy at ~** сде́рживать (*impf.*) неприя́теля; **stand, be at ~** (*fig.*) быть припёртым к стене́; **bring to ~** загна́ть (*pf.*), затрави́ть (*pf.*); (*fig.*) припере́ть (*pf.*) к стене́.

v.t. & i. ла́ять (*impf.*); залива́ться (*impf.*) ла́ем; выть (*impf.*); **~ (at) the moon** выть на луну́.

bay[5] [beɪ] *n.* (*horse*) гнеда́я (ло́шадь).

adj. гнедо́й.

bayonet [ˈbeɪəˌnet] *n.* штык; **hold s.o. at ~ point** держа́ть кого́-н. на штыка́х; **fix ~s!** примкну́ть штыки́; (*attr.*) штыково́й.

v.t. коло́ть, за- штыко́м.

bazaar [bəˈzɑ:(r)] *n.* (*oriental*) база́р; (*shop*) торго́вые ряды́ (*m. pl.*); ларьки́ (*m. pl.*); **charity ~** благотвори́тельный база́р.

bazooka [bəˈzu:kə] *n.* противота́нковый гранатомёт.

BBC (*abbr. of* ***British Broadcasting Corporation***) Би-Би-Си́ (*nt. indecl.*); **~ English** нормати́вный англи́йский язы́к.

BC (*abbr. of* ***before Christ***) до н.э., (до на́шей э́ры).

be [bi:, bɪ] *v.i.* **1.** быть (*impf.*); (*exist*) существова́ть (*impf.*); (*as copula in the present tense, usu. omitted or expr. by dash*): **the world is round** земля́ кру́глая; **that is a dog** э́то соба́ка. **2.** (*more emphatic uses*): **an order is an order** прика́з есть прика́з; **there is a God** Бог есть; **we should love people as they are** ну́жно люби́ть люде́й таки́ми, каки́е они́ есть; **there are books on all subjects** име́ются кни́ги по всем те́мам. **3.** (*expr. frequency*) быва́ть (*impf.*); **he is in London every Tuesday** он быва́ет в Ло́ндоне по вто́рникам; **there is no smoke without fire** нет ды́ма без огня́. **4.** (*more formally, with complement*) явля́ться (*impf.*) +*i.*; представля́ть (*impf.*) собо́й; (*of membership etc.*) состоя́ть (*impf.*) +*i.* **5.** (*expr. present continuous*): **she is crying** она́ пла́чет. **6.** (*of place, time, cost etc.*): **it is a mile away** э́то в ми́ле отсю́да; **where is the office?** где нахо́дится бюро́?; **he is 21 today** ему́ сего́дня исполня́ется два́дцать оди́н год; **it is 25 pence a yard** э́то сто́ит два́дцать пять пе́нсов в ярд; (*of pers. or obj. in a certain position*) стоя́ть, лежа́ть, сиде́ть (*acc. to sense*; *all impf.*); **the books are on the floor** кни́ги лежа́т на полу́; **the books are on the shelf** кни́ги стоя́т на по́лке; **the ship is at anchor** кора́бль стои́т на я́коре; **there are four matters on the agenda** на пове́стке дня стоя́т четы́ре вопро́са; **Paris is on the Seine** Пари́ж стои́т на Се́не; **he is in hospital** он лежи́т в больни́це; **he is in prison** он (сиди́т) в тюрьме́; **I was at home all day** я сиде́л до́ма весь день; **the elephant is in its cage** слон (нахо́дится) в свое́й кле́тке; (*of continuing states*): **the weather was settled** пого́да стоя́ла хоро́шая; **the heat was unbearable** жара́ стоя́ла невыноси́мая; **prices are high** це́ны сохраня́ются высо́кие. **7.** (*become*): **what are you going to ~ when you grow up?** кем ты ста́нешь/бу́дешь, когда́ вы́растешь? **8.** (*behave, act a part*): **you are ~ing silly** вы ведёте себя́ глу́по; **am I ~ing a bore?** я вам надое́л?; **the child is '~ing' a train** ребёнок игра́ет в по́езд; **you ~ French and I'll ~ German** ты бу́дешь францу́з, а я — не́мец. **9.** (*take place, happen*): **there is a party next door** в сосе́днем до́ме идёт вечери́нка; **the meeting is** (*will be*) **on Friday** заседа́ние состои́тся в пя́тницу. **10.** (*exist, live*): **he is no more** его́ бо́льше нет; **the government that was** тогда́шнее прави́тельство; **'as was'** (*coll.*, *joc.*) не́когда; (*née*) урождённая; **the greatest man that ever was** велича́йший из когда́-либо жи́вших люде́й. **11.** (*remain*): **let him ~!** оста́вьте его́!; **don't ~ too long!** не заде́рживайтесь! **12.** (*expr. motion*): **he is off to London** он уезжа́ет в Ло́ндон; **the dog was after him** за ним гнала́сь соба́ка; **has the postman been?** по́чта уже́ была́? **13.** (*coll.*, *intensive*): **look what you've been and done!** смотри́те, что вы натвори́ли! **14.** (*expr. pass.*): **the house is ~ing built** дом стро́ится; **I am told** мне сказа́ли. **15.** (*uses of pres. part. and gerund*): **~ing a doctor, he knew what to do** бу́дучи врачо́м, он знал, что де́лать; **for the time ~ing** пока́ что, на вре́мя; в да́нное вре́мя; **he is far from ~ing an expert** он далеко́ не специали́ст. **16.** (*with* **at**): **what are you at?** что вы хоти́те?; что вы де́лаете? **17.** (*with* **for**): **I am for tariff reform** я за тари́фную рефо́рму. **18.** (*with* **to**): **I am to inform you** я до́лжен сообщи́ть вам; **he is to ~ married today** он сего́дня же́нится; **you are not to do that** вам нельзя́ (*or* не сле́дует) э́то де́лать; **how was I to know?** как же я мог знать?; **the book is not to ~ found** э́той кни́ги нигде́ не найти́; **when am I to ~ there?** когда́ мне на́до быть там?; **what is the prize to ~?** како́й бу́дет приз?; **it is to ~ hoped that ...** на́до наде́яться, что...; **if I am to die** е́сли мне суждено́ умере́ть; **if I were to die** умри́ я; **he met the woman he was to marry** (*i.e. later married*) он встре́тил же́нщину, на кото́рой впосле́дствии жени́лся; **it is not to ~** э́тому не суждено́ соверши́ться (*or* не быва́ть); **his wife to ~** его́ бу́дущая жена́. **19.** (*var.*): **~ it so! so ~ it!** быть по сему́!; **how are you?** как пожива́ете?; **~ that as it may** как бы то ни́ бы́ло; **as well as can ~** как мо́жно лу́чше; **how is it that ...?** как э́то так, что...?; **what is that to me?** что мне до э́того?; **he was of our company** он был из на́шей компа́нии; **as you were!** (*mil.*) отста́вить!

cpd. **~-all** *n.* (*also* **~-all and end-all**) суть; коне́ц и нача́ло всего́.

See also **being**

beach [bi:tʃ] *n.* пляж; (*seashore*) взмо́рье.

v.t. (*run ashore*) посади́ть (*pf.*) на мель; (*haul up*) выта́скивать, вы́тащить на бе́рег.

cpds. **~-head** *n.* (*mil.*) примо́рский/берегово́й плацда́рм; **~-master** *n.* (*mil.*) команда́нт пу́нкта вы́садки деса́нта; **~-wear** *n.* пля́жная оде́жда.

beacon ['bi:kən] *n.* (*signal light, fire*) сигна́льный ого́нь; (*lighthouse*) мая́к; (*buoy*) ба́кен; (*signal tower*) сигна́льная ба́шня; (*at crossing*) знак пешехо́дного перехо́да.

bead [bi:d] *n.* **1.** бу́син(к)а, би́серина; **glass ~s** би́сер; **pearl ~s** жемчу́жины (*f. pl.*); **string of ~s** бу́сы (*pl. g.* —); **tell one's ~s** перебира́ть (*impf.*) чётки (*pl., g.* -ок). **2.** (*of gun*) му́шка; **draw a ~ on s.o.** прице́ли|ваться, -ться в кого́-н. **3.** (*drop of liquid*) ка́пля. **4.** (*archit.*) ка́пельки (*f. pl.*).

beading ['bi:dɪŋ] *n.* **1.** (*wooden strip*) ва́лик. **2.** (*archit.*) орна́мент в ви́де бус.

beadle ['bi:d(ə)l] *n.* (*univ.*) пе́дель (*m.*).

beady ['bi:dɪ] *adj.*: **~ eyes** глаза́-бу́синки; **a ~ look** испыту́ющий взгляд.

beagle ['bi:g(ə)l] *n.* бигль (*m.*), англи́йская го́нчая.

v.i. охо́титься (*impf.*) с би́глями.

beak[1] [bi:k] *n.* (*of bird etc.*) клюв; (*nose*) нос крючко́м; (*spout*) но́сик.

beak[2] [bi:k] (*coll.*) судья́ (*m.*); учи́тель (*m.*).

beaker ['bi:k(ə)r] *n.* (*for drinking*) ку́бок, ча́ша; (*in laboratory*) мензу́рка.

beaky ['bi:kɪ] *adj.* крючкова́тый.

beam[1] [bi:m] *n.* **1.** (*of timber etc.*) брус, ба́лка, перекла́дина; **the ~ in one's own eye** (*bibl.*) бревно́ в своём глазу́. **2.** (*naut.*) бимс; **broad in the ~** (*lit.*) с широ́кими би́мсами; (*fig., coll.*) толстоза́дый; **the ship was on her ~ ends** кора́бль лежа́л на боку́; **he was on his ~ ends** (*fig.*) он был в тяжёлом положе́нии. **3.** (*of scales*) коромы́сло.

beam[2] [bi:m] *n.* **1.** (*ray*) луч; (*of particles etc.*) пучо́к луче́й; (*as radio signal*) радиосигна́л; **on the ~** (*fig., coll.*) на пра́вильном пути́. **2.** (*smile*) сия́ющая улы́бка.

v.t. напр|авля́ть, -а́вить (сигна́л); **a programme ~ed to women** програ́мма, рассчи́танная на же́нщин.

v.i. (*shine*) свети́ть (*impf.*), сия́ть (*impf.*); (*smile broadly*) сия́ть улы́бкой; оскл|абля́ться, -а́биться; **she ~ed with delight** она́ сия́ла от ра́дости.

beaming ['bi:mɪŋ] *adj.* сия́ющий.

bean [bi:n] *n.* **1.** боб; **broad ~s** бобы́ (*m. pl.*); **French ~s** фасо́ль; **string ~s** зелёная фасо́ль; лопа́точки (*f. pl.*); **he knows how many ~s make five** (*coll.*) он зна́ет, что к чему́. **2.** (*coll., coin*) грош; **I haven't a ~** у меня́ нет ни гроша́. **3.** (*sl., head*) башка́. **4.** (*coll. uses*): **old ~** старина́ (*m.*); **spill the ~s** проболта́ться (*pf.*); **full of ~s** по́лный задо́ра; **give s.o. ~s** взду́ть/взгре́ть (*pf.*) кого́-н. (*coll.*).

v.t. (*US sl.*) сту́кнуть (*pf.*), тре́снуть (*pf.*).

cpds. **~-feast** *n.* пиру́шка, пир горо́й; **~-pod** *n.* бобо́вый стручо́к; **~-stalk** *n.* сте́бель (*m.*) бобо́вого расте́ния.

beano ['bi:nəʊ] *n.* пиру́шка.

bear[1] [beə(r)] *n.* **1.** (*zool., also fig.*) медве́дь (*m.*); **she-~** медве́дица; **~ cub** медвежо́нок; **Teddy ~** ми́шка; **cross as a ~ with a sore head** зол как чёрт. **2.** (*astron.*) **Great/Little B~** Больша́я/Ма́лая Медве́дица. **3.** (*econ.*) спекуля́нт, игра́ющий на пониже́ние.

cpds. **~-baiting** *n.* медве́жья тра́вля; **~-garden** *n.* (*fig.*) (шу́мное) сбо́рище, база́р; **~-leader** *n.* (*fig.*) дя́дька (*m.*), ня́нька; **~-meat** *n.* медвежа́тина; **~-skin** *n.* (*lit.*) медве́жья шку́ра; (*headgear*) мехово́й ки́вер.

bear[2] [beə(r)] *v.t.* **1.** (*carry*) носи́ть (*indet.*), нести́, по- (*det.*); **~ arms** носи́ть ору́жие; **~ one's head high** высоко́ нести́/держа́ть (*impf.*) го́лову; **the ship bore him to Italy** кора́бль доста́вил его́ в Ита́лию; **~ in mind** име́ть (*impf.*) в виду́; **~ tales** разноси́ть (*impf.*) спле́тни. **2.: ~ o.s.** (*behave*) держа́ться (*impf.*). **3.** (*show, have*): **the document ~s your signature** на докуме́нте есть ва́ша по́дпись; **a monument ~ing an inscription** па́мятник с на́дписью; **~ a resemblance to** име́ть (*impf.*) схо́дство с+*i.*; **~ a part in sth.** уча́ствовать (*impf.*) (*or* принима́ть (*impf.*) уча́стие) в чём-н.; **~ the marks of ill-treatment** нести́ (*det.*) на себе́ следы́ дурно́го обраще́ния. **4.** (*harbour*): **~ ill-will** пита́ть (*impf.*) дурны́е чу́вства. **5.** (*provide*): **~ a hand** пода́ть (*pf.*) ру́ку по́мощи; **~ false witness** лжесвиде́тельствовать (*impf.*); **~ s.o. company** соста́вить (*pf.*) компа́нию кому́-н. **6.** (*sustain, support*): **the ice will ~ his weight** лёд вы́держит его́; **~ responsibility/expense/a loss** нести́ (*det.*) отве́тственность/расхо́ды/убы́тки. **7.** (*endure, tolerate*) терпе́ть, с-; выноси́ть, вы́нести; сн|оси́ть, -ести́; **I cannot ~ him** я его́ не выношу́; **grin and ~ it** (*coll.*) му́жественно переноси́ть (*impf.*) страда́ния/неприя́тности. **8.** (*be fit for, capable of*): **the joke ~s repeating** э́тот анекдо́т мо́жно повтори́ть ещё раз; **~ comparison** выде́рживать (*impf.*) сравне́ние. **9.** (*press, push*): **he was borne backwards by the crowd** он был отти́снут толпо́й наза́д; **~ all before one** всё покор|я́ть, -и́ть. **10.** (*give birth to*): **she bore him a son** она родила́ ему́ сы́на; **be born** роди́ться (*impf., pf.*); **a man born in 1919** челове́к 1919 го́да рожде́ния; **he was born with a talent for music** у него́ от рожде́ния (был) тала́нт к му́зыке. **11.** (*yield*): **trees/efforts ~ fruit** дере́вья/уси́лия прино́сят плоды́; **the bonds ~ 5% interest** облига́ции прино́сят пять проце́нтов дохо́да.

v.i. **1.** (*carry*): **the ice does not ~ yet** лёд ещё не окре́п. **2.** (*of direction*): **the cape ~s north of here** мыс располо́жен к се́веру отсю́да; **the road ~s to the right** доро́га идёт впра́во; **the guns ~ on the trench** ору́дия напра́влены на око́п. **3.** (*exert pressure, affect*): **he bore heavily on a stick** он тяжело́ опира́лся на па́лку; **~ hard on** (*oppress*) подавля́ть (*impf.*); **bring one's energy to ~ on** напра́вить (*pf.*) эне́ргию на+*a.*; **taxation ~s on all classes** налогообложе́ние распространя́ется на все́ кла́ссы; **this ~s on our problem** э́то отно́сится к на́шей пробле́ме; **~ with** терпе́ть (*impf.*), переноси́ть (*impf.*); относи́ться (*impf.*) терпи́мо к+*d.*

with advs.: **~ away** *v.t.* ун|оси́ть, -ести́; **~ away the prize** вы́играть (*pf.*) приз; вы́йти (*pf.*) победи́телем; **he was borne away (by his feelings)** он был увлечён; **~ down** *v.t.* (*overcome*) преодол|ева́ть, -е́ть; *v.i.*: **~ down upon s.o.** (*swoop etc.*) устрем|ля́ться, -и́ться на кого́-н.; **~ in** *v.t.*: **it was borne in on me** мне ста́ло я́сно; **~ out** *v.t.* (*carry out*) выноси́ть, вы́нести; (*confirm*) подтвер|жда́ть, -ди́ть; подкреп|ля́ть, -и́ть; **~ up** *v.i.* (*endure*) держа́ться (*impf.*).

bearable ['beərəb(ə)l] *adj.* терпи́мый, сно́сный.

beard [bɪəd] *n.* **1.** борода́; **grow a ~** расти́ть, от- бо́роду; **he had three days' ~** у него́ была́ трёхдне́вная щети́на. **2.** (*of oyster*) жа́бры (*f. pl.*); (*of animal*) боро́дка. **3.** (*bot.*) ость; **old man's ~** ломоно́с.

v.t. бр|оса́ть, -о́сить вы́зов +*d.*; **~ the lion in his den** (*fig.*) лезть (*impf.*) в ло́гово зве́ря.

bearded ['bɪədɪd] *adj.* борода́тый; (*bot.*) ости́стый.

beardless ['bɪədlɪs] *adj.* безборо́дый; (*youthful*) безу́сый.

bearer ['beərə(r)] *n.* **1.** (*one who carries*) несу́щий, нося́щий; **~ of good news** до́брый ве́стник; (*of letter*) пода́тель (*m.*); (*of a cheque*) предъяви́тель (*m.*); **~ bond** облига́ция на предъяви́теля; **~ company** (*mil.*) санита́рная ро́та. **2.** (*porter*) носи́льщик. **3.** (*of tree etc.*) плодонося́щее (де́рево); **this tree is a good/poor ~** э́то де́рево хорошо́/пло́хо плодоно́сит.

bearing ['beərɪŋ] *n.* **1.** (*carrying*) ноше́ние. **2.** (*behaviour*) поведе́ние; (*deportment*) мане́ра держа́ться. **3.** (*relevance*) отноше́ние (к+*d.*); **consider a matter in all its ~s** рассмотре́ть (*pf.*) вопро́с со всех сторо́н. **4.** (*direction*) пе́ленг, румб, а́зимут; **take a compass ~** определ|я́ть, -и́ть магни́тный а́зимут (*or* ко́мпасный пе́ленг); **find, get, take one's ~s** определ|я́ть, -и́ть своё местонахожде́ние/положе́ние; ориенти́роваться (*impf., pf.*); **lose one's ~s** потеря́ть (*pf.*) ориентиро́вку. **5.** (*endurance*) терпе́ние; **it is past all ~** э́то нестерпи́мо/невыноси́мо/несно́сно. **6.** (*tech.*) опо́ра; **roller ~** ро́ликовый подши́пник. **7.** (*pl., her.*) деви́з. **8.** (*bot.*) плодоноше́ние; плодоно́сность; **the trees are in full ~** дере́вья уве́шаны плода́ми.

cpd. **~-rein** *n.* по́вод.

bearish ['beərɪʃ] *adj.* **1.** (*rough*) медве́жий, гру́бый. **2.** (*on stock exchange*) понижи́тельный.

beast [bi:st] *n.* **1.** (*animal*) живо́тное; (*wild animal*) зверь (*m.*); (*pl., cattle*) рога́тый скот; **~ of burden** вью́чное живо́тное; ~ **of prey** хи́щный зверь. **2.** (*savage pers.*) зверь; (*nasty pers.*) скот, скоти́на (*c.g.*); **make a ~ of o.s.** вести́ (*det.*) себя́ по-ско́тски; **it brings out the ~ in man** э́то пробужда́ет в челове́ке зве́ря. **3.: a ~ of a day** отврати́тельный день; **a ~ of a job** дья́вольская рабо́та.

beastings ['bi:stɪŋz] *n.* (*US*) = **beestings**

beastliness ['bi:stlɪnɪs] *n.* ско́тство; сви́нство; отврати́тельность.

beastly ['bi:stlɪ] *adj.* (*like a beast*) живо́тный, звери́ный; (*coarse*) ско́тский; (*unpleasant*) отврати́тельный; ~ **weather** ужа́сная пого́да; **a ~ headache** ме́рзкая/гну́сная головна́я боль.

adv. стра́шно.

beat[1] [bi:t] *n.* **1.** (*of drum*) бой; (*of heart*) бие́ние; (*rhythm*) ритм; (*mus.*) такт; (*of baton*) отбива́ние та́кта. **2.** (*policeman's*) райо́н обхо́да; **be on the ~** соверша́ть (*impf.*) обхо́д; **that is off my ~** (*fig.*) э́то не по мое́й ча́сти.

v.t. **1.** (*strike*) бить, по-; уд|аря́ть, -а́рить; колоти́ть, по-; ~ **s.o. black and blue** исколоти́ть (*pf.*) кого́-н.; изби́ть (*pf.*) кого́-н. до синяко́в (*or* до полусме́рти); ~ **the air** (*fig.*) толо́чь (*impf.*) во́ду в сту́пе; ~ **one's breast** бить (*impf.*) себя́ в грудь; ~ **a carpet** выкола́чивать, вы́колотить (*or* выбива́ть, вы́бить) ковёр; ~ **a drum** бить (*impf.*) в бараба́н; ~ **eggs** взби|ва́ть, -ть я́йца; ~ **one's head against a wall** (*lit., fig.*) би́ться (*impf.*) голово́й о сте́нку; ~ **a path through the forest** протори́ть (*pf.*) тропи́нку че́рез лес; ~ **a retreat** (*lit., fig.*) бить (*impf.*) отбо́й; (*fig.*) идти́ (*det.*) на попя́тную; ~ **a steak** отб|ива́ть, -и́ть бифште́кс; **he ~ the table with his fists** он колоти́л кулака́ми по столу́; ~ **time** отбива́ть (*impf.*) такт; **the bird ~s its wings** пти́ца бьёт кры́льями; ~ **it!** (*sl.*) кати́сь!; ~ **sth. flat** расплю́щ|ивать, -ить что-н.; ~ **the dust out of sth.** выбива́ть, вы́бить пыль из чего́-н.; ~ **one's brains over sth.** лома́ть (*impf.*) го́лову над чем-н.; ~ **a stick into the ground** вбить (*pf.*) па́лку в зе́млю; ~ **sth. into s.o.'s head** вкол|а́чивать, -оти́ть (*or* вби|ва́ть, -ть) что-н. кому́-н. в го́лову; ~ **a forest for game** обры́скать (*pf.*) лес в по́исках ди́чи. **2.** (*defeat, surpass*) поб|ива́ть, -и́ть; разб|ива́ть, -и́ть; побе|жда́ть, -ди́ть; одерж|ивать, -а́ть побе́ду над+*i.*; **he ~ me at chess** он обыгра́л меня́ в ша́хматы; **he always ~s me at golf** он всегда́ выи́грывает, когда́ мы игра́ем в гольф; **these armies have never been ~en** э́ти а́рмии не зна́ли пораже́ния; **he ~ the record** он поби́л реко́рд; **that ~s all (*or* the band)** (*coll.*) э́то превосхо́дит всё; **it ~s me how he does it** (*coll.*) убе́й Бог, е́сли я понима́ю, как ему́ э́то удаётся; **can you ~ it?** (*coll.*) как вам э́то нра́вится?; **I'll ~ you to the top of the hill** я быстре́е вас доберу́сь до верши́ны холма́.

v.i.: **his heart is ~ing** его́ се́рдце бьётся; **he heard drums ~ing** он слы́шал бараба́нный бой; **the rain ~ against the windows** дождь стуча́л в о́кна; ~ **about the bush** (*fig.*) ходи́ть (*indet.*) вокру́г да о́коло; ~ **at, on a door** колоти́ть (*impf.*) в дверь.

with advs.: ~ **about** *v.i.* (*naut.*) лави́ровать (*impf.*); ~ **back** *v.t.* отб|ива́ть, -и́ть; ~ **down** *v.t.*: **the rain ~ down the corn** дождь поби́л хлеба́; **he ~ down the price** он сбил це́ну; он доби́лся ски́дки; **he ~ me down** он заста́вил меня́ уступи́ть в цене́; **he ~ down all opposition** он подави́л вся́кое сопротивле́ние; *v.i.*: **the sun ~ down on us** со́лнце неща́дно пали́ло нас; ~ **in** *v.t.*: ~ **a door in** вы́ломать (*pf.*) дверь; ~ **off** *v.t.*: ~ **off an attack** отб|ива́ть, -и́ть ата́ку; ~ **out** *v.t.*: ~ **out a fire** зат|а́птывать, -опта́ть ого́нь; ~ **out gold** кова́ть, вы- зо́лото; ~ **out a path** проб|ива́ть, -и́ть; (*or* протор|я́ть, -и́ть) тропи́нку; ~ **out a rhythm** отбива́ть (*impf.*) ритм; ~ **s.o.'s brains out** вышиба́ть, вы́шибить мозги́ кому́-н.; ~ **up** *v.t.*: ~ **up eggs/cream** взби|ва́ть, -ть я́йца/сли́вки; ~ **s.o. up** изб|ива́ть, -и́ть кого́-н.; *v.i.* (*naut.*) продвига́ться (*impf.*) про́тив ве́тра.

See also **beaten**

beat[2] [bi:t] *adj.* (*coll., tired*): **dead ~** смерте́льно уста́лый.

beat[3] [bi:t] (*coll.*) *n.* (*beatnik*) би́тник; **the ~ generation** поколе́ние би́тников.

beaten ['bi:t(ə)n] *adj.* би́тый, поби́тый, изби́тый; (*conquered*) разби́тый; ~ **gold** чека́нное/ко́ваное зо́лото; **off the ~ track** не по проторённой доро́жке.

beater ['bi:tə(r)] *n.* (*huntsman*) заго́нщик; (*implement*) пест, колоту́шка, колоти́лка.

beatific [ˌbi:ə'tɪfɪk] *adj.* **1.** (*making blessed*) благослове́нный; **the B~ Vision** виде́ние ра́йского блаже́нства. **2.: a ~ smile** блаже́нная улы́бка.

beatification [bi:ˌætɪfɪ'keɪʃ(ə)n] *n.* беатифика́ция, причисле́ние к ли́ку блаже́нных.

beatify [bi:'ætɪˌfaɪ] *v.t.* (*eccl.*) ≃ канонизи́ровать (*impf. pf.*).

beating ['bi:tɪŋ] *n.* **1.** (*of heart*) бие́ние. **2.** (*thrashing*) битьё, по́рка; **give s.o. a good ~** отлупи́ть (*pf.*) кого́-н.; **the boy deserves a ~** ма́льчик заслу́живает по́рки. **3.** (*defeat*) разгро́м, пораже́ние; **they gave the enemy a thorough ~** врагу́ от них здо́рово доста́лось.

beatitude [bi:'ætɪˌtju:d] *n.* **1.** (*blessedness*) блаже́нство. **2.** (*title*): **His B~** Его́ Блаже́нство. **3.** (*bibl.*): **the B~s** за́поведи (*f. pl.*) блаже́нства.

beat(nik) ['bi:tnɪk] *n.* (*sl.*) би́тник.

beau [bəʊ] *n.* (*fop*) щёголь (*m.*); (*admirer*) ухажёр, покло́нник.

Beaufort scale ['bəʊfət] *n.* бофо́ртова шкала́.

beau ideal [ˌbəʊ i:deɪ'æl] *n.* образе́ц соверше́нства.

beau monde [bəʊ 'mɒnd] *n.* бомо́нд, вы́сший свет.

beauteous ['bju:tɪəs] *adj.* прекра́сный.

beautician [bju:'tɪʃ(ə)n] *n.* космето́лог, космети́чка.

beautiful ['bju:tɪˌfʊl] *adj.* краси́вый; (*excellent*) прекра́сный; **~ly warm** необыкнове́нно тепло́.

beautify ['bju:tɪˌfaɪ] *v.t.* укр|аша́ть, -а́сить.

beauty ['bju:tɪ] *n.* **1.** (*quality*) красота́; ~ **is skin-deep** красота́ недолгове́чна; ~ **parlour** институ́т красоты́; ~ **queen** короле́ва красоты́; ~ **sleep** сон до полу́ночи; ~ **spot** живопи́сная ме́стность; (*on face*) му́шка. **2.** (*woman*) краса́вица; **B~ and the Beast** краса́вица и чудо́вище; **she's no ~** она́ совсе́м не краса́вица. **3.** (*excellence, fine specimen*): **that's the ~ of it** в э́том-то вся пре́лесть; **his car is a ~** у него́ прекра́сная маши́на; **you're a ~!** (*iron.*) хоро́ш (же) ты!

beaver ['bi:və(r)] *n.* **1.** (*zool.*) бобр; **eager ~** (*coll.*) хлопоту́н. **2.** (*fur*) бобёр; (*hat*) бобро́вая ша́пка; касто́ровая шля́па. **3.** (*sl.*) (*beard*) борода́; (*bearded man*) борода́ч.

v.i. (*coll., toil*) вка́лывать (*impf.*).

cpd. **~-rat** *n.* онда́тра.

bebop ['bi:bɒp] *n.* бибо́п.

becalm [bɪ'kɑ:m] *v.t.*: **be ~ed** (*naut.*) штилева́ть (*impf.*); заштил|ева́ть, -е́ть; **a ~ed ship** заштиле́вший кора́бль.

because [bɪ'kɒz] *conj.* потому́ что; (*since*) так как; **all the more ~** тем бо́лее, что; ~ **of** из-за+*g.*, (*thanks to*) благодаря́+*d.*

bechamel ['beʃəˌmel] *n.* бешаме́ль.

beck [bek] *n.*: **be at s.o.'s ~ and call** быть у кого́-н. на побегу́шках.

beckon ['bekən] *v.t. & i.* мани́ть, по-; заз|ыва́ть, -ва́ть; **I ~ed (to) him to approach** я помани́л его́ к себе́; **he ~ed them in** он зазва́л их внутрь.

becloud [bɪ'klaʊd] *v.t.* завол|а́кивать, -о́чь; **tears ~ed his eyes** его́ глаза́ заволокло́ слеза́ми; (*of the mind*) затума́ни|вать, -ть.

become [bɪ'kʌm] *v.t.* (*befit*) годи́ться, подоба́ть, прили́чествовать (*кому*); **it doesn't ~ you to complain** вам не к лицу́ жа́ловаться; (*look well on*) идти́ (*det.*); **the dress ~s you** э́то пла́тье вам идёт; *see also* **becoming**

v.i. (*come to be*) ста|нови́ться, -ть +*i.*; *often expr. by v. in* ...еть; ~ **pale** побледне́ть; ~ **rich** разбогате́ть; ~ **smaller** уме́ньшиться (*all pf.*); **what became of him?** что с ним ста́лось?; **he became a waiter** он поступи́л в официа́нты; **the weather became worse** пого́да испо́ртилась.

becoming [bɪ'kʌmɪŋ] *adj.* (*proper*) подоба́ющий, прили́чествующий; **a fine sense of the ~** то́нкое чу́вство прили́чия; (*of dress etc.*) (иду́щий) к лицу́; **she is ~ly dressed** она́ оде́та к лицу́; **she wore a ~ hat** шля́пка ей о́чень шла.

bed [bed] *n.* **1.** (*esp. bedstead*) крова́ть; (*esp. bedding*) посте́ль; (*in hospital*) ко́йка; (*dog's etc. bedding*) подсти́лка; **single/**

double ~ односпа́льная/двуспа́льная крова́ть; **twin ~s** па́рные крова́ти; **spring** ~ пружи́нный матра́с; **go to** ~ ложи́ться, лечь спать; (*in sexual sense*) переспа́ть (*pf.*) (*с кем*); **put to** ~ укла́дывать, уложи́ть спать; **send to** ~ отпр|авля́ть, -а́вить (*or* от|сыла́ть, -осла́ть) спать; **get into** ~ ложи́ться, лечь в посте́ль/крова́ть; **get out of** ~ вста|ва́ть, -ть с посте́ли/крова́ти; **get out of ~ on the wrong side** (*fig.*) встать (*pf.*) с ле́вой ноги́; **make a** ~ (*arrange for sleep*) стлать, по- (*or* стели́ть, по-) посте́ль; (*tidy after sleep*) заст|ила́ть, -ла́ть (*or* уб|ира́ть, -ра́ть) посте́ль; **as you make your ~, so you must lie on it** что посе́ешь, то и пожнёшь; **take to one's** ~ слечь (*pf.*); **die in one's** ~ умере́ть (*pf.*) свое́й сме́ртью; **keep to one's** ~ не встава́ть (*impf.*) с посте́ли; **~ of thorns** терни́стый путь; **early to ~ and early to rise** (*prov.*) кто ра́но встаёт, тому́ Бог подаёт; **out of** ~ (*up, recovered*) на нога́х; **~ of sickness** одр боле́зни; **~ of Procrustes** прокру́стово ло́же. **2.** (*base, bottom*): (*of concrete etc.*) основа́ние, фунда́мент; (*of rock, clay etc.*) пласт, слой, залега́ние; (*of a road*) полотно́; (*of the sea*) морско́е дно; (*of a river*) речно́е ру́сло, ло́же реки́. **3.** (*place of cultivation*): **~ of flowers** клу́мба; **~ of nettles** за́росль крапи́вы; **~ of potatoes** карто́фельная гря́дка.

v.t. **1.** (*of flowers; also* ~ **out**) сажа́ть, посади́ть; выса́живать, вы́садить. **2.** ~ **a horse** стлать, по- подсти́лку для ло́шади.

v.i. ~ **down** распол|ага́ться, -ожи́ться на ночле́г; (*cohabit*) сожи́тельствовать (*impf.*).

cpds. **~bug** *n.* клоп; **~clothes** *n. pl.* посте́ль; посте́льные принадле́жности (*f. pl.*); **~-cover** *n.* покрыва́ло; **~fellow** *n.* сожи́тель (*fem.* -ница); **misfortune makes strange ~fellows** в нужде́ с кем не поведёшься; **~-head** *n.* изголо́вье; **~-jacket** *n.* ночна́я ко́фта; **~-linen** *n.* посте́льное бельё; **~-pan** *n.* подкладно́е су́дно; **~-plate** *n.* (*tech.*) стани́на; фунда́ментная плита́; **~post** *n.* сто́лбик крова́ти; **between you and me and the ~post** (*coll.*) стро́го ме́жду на́ми; **~ridden** *adj.* прико́ванный к посте́ли; **~rock** *n.* коренна́я поро́да; посте́ль за́лежи; **get down to ~rock** (*fig.*) докопа́ться (*pf.*) до су́ти де́ла; **~room** *n.* спа́льня; **~room farce** алько́вный фарс; **~room slippers** дома́шние ту́фли (*f. pl.*); **~side** *n.*: **keep books at one's ~side** держа́ть (*impf.*) кни́ги на ночно́м сто́лике; **watch at s.o.'s ~side** уха́живать (*impf.*) за больны́м; сиде́ть (*impf.*) у посте́ли больно́го; **a good ~side manner** уме́лый подхо́д к больно́му, враче́бный такт; **~side table** ту́мбочка, ночно́й сто́лик; **~side rug** ко́врик у крова́ти; **~-sitter, ~-sitting-room** *nn.* однокомнатная кварти́ра; **~sore** *n.* про́лежень (*m.*); **~spread** *n.* покрыва́ло; **~stead** *n.* крова́ть; о́стов, стано́к крова́ти; **~time** *n.* вре́мя ложи́ться/идти́ спать; **my ~time is at 11** я ложу́сь спать в оди́ннадцать часо́в; **~time story** ска́зка, расска́з на сон гряду́щий.

B.Ed. (*abbr. of* **Bachelor of Education**) бакала́вр педагоги́ческих нау́к.

bedaub [bɪˈdɔ:b] *v.t.* ма́зать, за-.

bedding [ˈbedɪŋ] *n.* **1.** (*bedclothes*) посте́ль; посте́льные принадле́жности (*f. pl.*). **2.** (*of plants*) выса́живание.

bedeck [bɪˈdek] *v.t.* укр|аша́ть, -а́сить; уб|ира́ть, -ра́ть.

bedevil [bɪˈdev(ə)l] *v.t.* (*confuse*) спу́т|ывать, -ать; вн|оси́ть, -ести́ неразбери́ху в+*a.*

bedevilment [bɪˈdev(ə)lmənt] *n.* (*confusion*) неразбери́ха, пу́таница.

bedew [bɪˈdju:] *v.t.* оро|ша́ть, -си́ть; обры́зг|ивать, -ать.

bedim [bɪˈdɪm] *v.t.* (*of eyes*) затума́ни|вать, -ть; (*of mind*) затемн|я́ть, -и́ть; помрач|а́ть, -и́ть.

bedizen [bɪˈdaɪz(ə)n, -ˈdɪz(ə)n] *v.t.* разря|жа́ть, -ди́ть.

bedlam [ˈbedləm] *n.* (*fig.*) бедла́м, (вавило́нское) столпотворе́ние.

Bed(o)uin [ˈbedoɪn] *n.* бедуи́н (*fem.* -ка).

adj. бедуи́нский.

bedraggled [bɪˈdræg(ə)ld] *adj.* забры́зганный, задры́зганный.

bee [bi:] *n.* **1.** пчела́; **as busy as a** ~ работя́щий, трудолюби́вый; (*fig., busy worker*) работя́га (*c.g.*); **have a ~ in one's bonnet** быть поме́шанным (*на чём*). **2.** (*gathering*) совме́стная рабо́та.

cpds. **~-eater** *n.* щу́рка; **~hive** *n.* у́лей; **~-keeper** *n.* пчелово́д; (*of wild bees*) бо́ртник; **~-keeping** *n.* пчелово́дство; **~-line** *n.* пряма́я; **make a ~-line for** стрело́й помча́ться (*pf.*) к+*d.*; **~swax** *n.* пчели́ный воск.

beech [bi:tʃ] *n.* бук.

cpd. **~mast** *n.* бу́ковый оре́шек.

beechen [bi:tʃən] *adj.* бу́ковый.

beef[1] [bi:f] *n.* **1.** (*meat*) говя́дина; (*fig., energy*) си́ла, эне́ргия. **2.** (*pl. beeves*) говя́жьи ту́ши (*f. pl.*).

v.t.: ~ **up** (*coll., strengthen, increase*) укреп|ля́ть, -и́ть.

cpds. **~burger** *n.* ру́бленый бифште́кс; **~eater** *n.* солда́т охра́ны ло́ндонского Та́уэра; **~steak** *n.* бифште́кс; **~-tea** *n.* кре́пкий бульо́н.

beef[2] [bi:f] *v.i.* (*sl., complain*) стона́ть (*impf.*).

beefy [ˈbi:fɪ] *adj.* (*like beef*) мяси́стый; (*muscular*) мускули́стый.

Beelzebub [bi:ˈelzɪˌbʌb] *n.* Вельзеву́л.

beep [bi:p] *n.* гудо́к.

v.i. гуде́ть, про-.

beer [bɪə(r)] *n.* пи́во; **small** ~ сла́бое пи́во; **he thinks no small ~ of himself** он мно́го о себе́ понима́ет (*coll.*); **life is not all ~ and skittles** не всё коту́ ма́сленица.

beery [ˈbɪərɪ] *adj.* (*smelling of beer*) отдаю́щий пи́вом; **he has ~ breath** от него́ несёт/рази́т пи́вом; (*tipsy*) подвы́пивший.

beestings [ˈbi:stɪŋz] *n.* моло́зиво.

beet [bi:t] *n.* свёкла; (*sugar* ~) са́харная свёкла, свеклови́ца.

cpd. **~root** *n.* свёкла, бура́к; **he blushed as red as a ~root** он покрасне́л как рак.

beetle[1] [ˈbi:t(ə)l] *n.* (*zool.*) жук; **Colorado** ~ колора́дский жук.

cpd. **~-crusher** *n.* (*sl., boot*) сапожи́ще (*m.*).

beetle[2] [ˈbi:t(ə)l] *n.* (*tool*) кува́лда, трамбо́вка.

beetle[3] [ˈbi:t(ə)l] *adj.*: ~ **brows** нави́сшие бро́ви (*f. pl.*).

v.i. нав|иса́ть, -и́снуть.

cpd. **~-browed** *adj.* с нави́сшими бровя́ми.

beetle[4] [ˈbi:t(ə)l] *v.i.*: ~ **off!** кати́сь! (*sl.*).

befall [bɪˈfɔ:l] *v.t. & i.* (*liter.*) приключ|а́ться, -и́ться (с+*i.*); пост|ига́ть, -и́гнуть (*кого/что*); **what has ~en him?** что с ним ста́ло?

befit [bɪˈfɪt] *v.t.* под|ходи́ть, -ойти́ +*d.*; прили́чествовать (*impf.*) +*d.*

befog [bɪˈfɒg] *v.t.* (*lit., fig.*) затума́ни|вать, -ть.

befool [bɪˈfu:l] *v.t.* одура́чи|вать, -ть.

before [bɪˈfɔ:(r)] *adv.* **1.** (*sooner, previously*) ра́ньше; **six weeks** ~ шестью неде́лями ра́ньше; **18 years** ~ 18 лет наза́д. **2.** (*of place*) впереди́.

prep. **1.** (*of time*) пе́ред+*i.*; ~ **leaving** пе́ред отъе́здом; (*earlier than*) до+*g.*; ~ **the war** до войны́; **since ~ the war** с довое́нного вре́мени; **long ~ that** задо́лго до э́того; ~ **now** пре́жде; **the week ~ last** позапро́шлая неде́ля; **don't come ~ I call you** не приходи́те, пока́ я вас не позову́. **2.** (*rather than*) скоре́е чем; **he would die ~ lying** он скоре́е умрёт, чем солжёт. **3.** (*of place*) пе́ред+*i.*; впереди́+*g.*; **your whole life is ~ you** у вас вся жизнь впереди́; ~ **the court** пе́ред судо́м; ~ **witnesses** при свиде́телях; ~ **my eyes** на мои́х глаза́х; ~ **God** пе́ред Бо́гом. **4.** (*fig., ahead of*): **he is ~ me in class** он впереди́ меня́ в кла́ссе. **5.** (*naut.*): ~ **the wind** по ве́тру.

conj. (*earlier than*) ра́ньше чем; (*immediately* ~) пре́жде/пе́ред тем, как; (*at a previous time*) до того́ как; **do it ~ you forget** сде́лайте э́то, пока́ не забы́ли; **it will be years ~ we meet** пройду́т го́ды, пока́ мы встре́тимся; **just ~ you arrived** пе́ред са́мым ва́шим прихо́дом.

cpds. **~hand** *adv.* зара́нее, заблаговре́менно; **be ~hand with s.o.** (*liter.*) предупре|жда́ть, -ди́ть кого́-н.; **~-mentioned** *adj.* вышеупомя́нутый; **~-tax** *adj.* начи́сленный до упла́ты нало́гов.

befoul [bɪˈfaʊl] *v.t.* па́чкать, за-.

befriend [bɪˈfrend] *v.t.* дру́жески отн|оси́ться, -ести́сь к+*d.*; помога́ть (*impf.*) +*d.*

befuddle [bɪˈfʌd(ə)l] *v.t.* одурма́ни|вать, -ть.

beg [beg] *v.t.* проси́ть, по-; умол|я́ть (*impf.*); ~ **money of s.o.** проси́ть (*impf.*) у кого́-н. де́нег; ~ **one's bread**

ни́щенствовать, попроша́йничать, (*coll.*) побира́ться (*all impf.*); ~ **s.o. to do sth.** умоля́ть (*impf.*) кого́-н. сде́лать что-н.; ~ **a favour of s.o.** проси́ть, по- кого́-н. о любе́зности; **they ~ged to come with us** они́ умоля́ли нас взять их с собо́й; **I ~ to state** я позво́лю себе́ утвержда́ть.

v.i. **1.** (*ask for charity*) проси́ть подая́ния, ни́щенствовать, (*coll.*) побира́ться (*all impf.*); ~ **from door to door** побира́ться по двора́м; **~ging letter** проси́тельное письмо́. **2.:** ~ **for sth.** выпра́шивать, вы́просить что-н.; **I ~ of you not to go** я умоля́ю вас не ходи́ть; ~ **off** (*excuse o.s.*) отпр|а́шиваться, -оси́ться. **3.** (*of a dog*) служи́ть (*impf.*). **4.: the cakes are going ~ging** пирожки́ зря пропада́ют.

begad [bɪˈgæd] *int.* (*arch.*) ей-Бо́гу!

beget [bɪˈget] *v.t.* (*lit.*, *fig.*) поро|жда́ть, -ди́ть.

begetter [bɪˈgetə(r)] *n.* роди́тель (*m.*); (*fig.*) вдохнови́тель (*m.*).

beggar [ˈbegə(r)] *n.* **1.** ни́щий; ~ **woman** ни́щенка; **~s cannot be choosers** ≃ голо́дному Федо́ту и щи в охо́ту; **a ~ on horseback** (*fig.*) ≃ из гря́зи в кня́зи. **2.** (*fellow*) па́рень (*m.*), ма́лый; **poor ~** бедня́га (*m.*), бе́дный ма́лый; **little ~s** малыши́ (*m. pl.*).

v.t. (*reduce to beggary*) дов|оди́ть, -ести́ до нищеты́; разор|я́ть, -и́ть; **it ~s description** э́то не поддаётся описа́нию.

beggarly [ˈbegəlɪ] *adj.* ни́щенский, жа́лкий.

beggary [ˈbegərɪ] *n.* нищета́, ни́щенство.

begin [bɪˈgɪn] *v.t.* нач|ина́ть, -а́ть; **he began English** он на́чал изуча́ть англи́йский язы́к; **he began the meeting** он откры́л собра́ние; **he began (on) another bottle** он поча́л но́вую буты́лку; **I began to think she would not come** я поду́мал бы́ло, что она́ не придёт; (*often translated by* за-): ~ **to sing** запе́ть (*pf.*); **he began to cry** он запла́кал.

v.i. нач|ина́ть(ся), -а́ть(ся); **he began at the beginning** он на́чал с са́мого нача́ла; **the meeting began** собра́ние начало́сь; **before winter ~s** до нача́ла зимы́; до того́ как начнётся зима́; **he began as a reporter** он на́чал свою́ карье́ру с рабо́ты репортёра; **well begun is half done** лиха́ беда́ нача́ло; хоро́шее нача́ло полде́ла откача́ло; **to ~ with** во-пе́рвых.

beginner [bɪˈgɪnə(r)] *n.* начина́ющий.

beginning [bɪˈgɪnɪŋ] *n.* нача́ло; (*source*) исто́чник; **at the ~ of April** в нача́ле (*or* в пе́рвых чи́слах) апре́ля; **make a ~** нача́ть (*pf.*); **the ~s of English poetry** ра́нняя англи́йская поэ́зия.

begone [bɪˈgɒn] *v.i.*: (*arch.*) **~!** прочь!

begonia [bɪˈgəʊnjə] *n.* бего́ния.

begrime [bɪˈgraɪm] *v.t.* па́чкать, вы́-; грязни́ть, за-.

begrudge [bɪˈgrʌdʒ] *v.t.* зави́довать, по- (*кому чему*); **I ~ the time** мне жаль вре́мени; **they ~d him his food** они́ укоря́ли/попрека́ли его́ куско́м хле́ба.

beguile [bɪˈgaɪl] *v.t.* **1.** (*charm*) очаро́в|ывать, -а́ть. **2.** (*delude*) завл|ека́ть, -е́чь; **they ~d him into giving them his money** они́ (обма́ном) вы́удили у него́ де́ньги. **3.: ~ one's hunger** обману́ть (*pf.*) го́лод; (*time, journey etc.*) корота́ть, с-.

begum [ˈbeɪgəm] *n.* бегу́ма.

behalf [bɪˈhɑːf] *n.*: **on/in my ~** от моего́ и́мени/лица́; ра́ди меня́; в мои́х интере́сах, в мою́ по́льзу; **he is going on our ~** он идёт за нас; **plead on s.o.'s ~** выступа́ть (*impf.*) в защи́ту кого́-н.

behave [bɪˈheɪv] *v.i.* **1.** (*of pers.*) вести́ (*det.*) себя́, держа́ться (*impf.*); ~ **well, ~ o.s.** вести́ себя́ хорошо́; ~ **badly** пло́хо поступ|а́ть, -и́ть; ~ **(well *etc.*) towards s.o.** (хорошо́) относи́ться (*impf.*) к кому́-н. **2.** (*of thg.*): **my bicycle ~s well** мой велосипе́д хорошо́ слу́жит; **how does this metal ~ under stress?** как ведёт себя́ э́тот мета́лл под давле́нием?

behaviour [bɪˈheɪvjə(r)] *n.* **1.** (*conduct*) поведе́ние; отноше́ние (*к кому*), обраще́ние (*с кем*); **be on one's best ~** вести́ (*det.*) себя́ безупре́чно; **hold office during good ~** занима́ть (*impf.*) до́лжность при усло́вии хоро́шего поведе́ния. **2.: the ~ of glands** рабо́та желёз; **the ~ of steel under stress** поведе́ние ста́ли под давле́нием.

behavioural [bɪˈheɪvjər(ə)l] *adj.* поведе́нческий.

behaviourism [bɪˈheɪvjəˌrɪz(ə)m] *n.* бихевиори́зм.

behead [bɪˈhed] *v.t.* обезгла́в|ливать, -ить.

behemoth [bɪˈhiːmɒθ] *n.* чу́дище; (*bibl.*) бегемо́т.

behest [bɪˈhest] *n.* (*liter.*) повеле́ние.

behind [bɪˈhaɪnd] *n.* (*coll.*) зад, за́дница.

adv. сза́ди, позади́; **a long way ~** далеко́ позади́; **from ~** сза́ди; **he is ~ in his studies** он отста́л в учёбе; **he is ~ with his payments** он запа́здывает с упла́той; **there is more evidence ~** (*still to come*) есть ещё нема́ло доказа́тельств.

prep. (*expr. place*) за+*i.*; (*expr. motion*) за+*a.*; (*more emphatic*) сза́ди, позади́+*g.*; (*after*) по́сле+*g.*; **from ~** из-за+*g.*; **he walked (just) ~ me** он шёл сле́дом за мной; **what is ~ it all?** что стои́т за всем э́тим?; **he has the army ~ him** его́ подде́рживает а́рмия; **he left debts ~ him** он оста́вил по́сле себя́ долги́; **he put the idea ~ him** он бро́сил э́ту мысль; **the country is ~ its neighbours** страна́ отста́ла от свои́х сосе́дей.

cpd. **~hand** *adj.* & *adv.*: **he is ~hand in his work** он запусти́л рабо́ту; **I am ~hand with the rent** я задолжа́л за кварти́ру.

behold [bɪˈhəʊld] *v.t.* (*arch.*) узре́ть (*pf.*); **lo and ~!** о чу́до!

beholden [bɪˈhəʊld(ə)n] *pred. adj.* обя́зан, призна́телен.

beholder [bɪˈhəʊldə(r)] *n.* очеви́дец; **her beauty charmed all ~s** её красота́ очаро́вывала всех, кто её ви́дел.

behoof [bɪˈhuːf] *n.* (*US & arch.*) = **behalf**

behove [bɪˈhəʊv] (*US* **behoove**) [bɪˈhuːv] *v.t.* (*liter.*): **it ~s you to work** вам надлежи́т рабо́тать; **it ill ~s him to complain** ему́ не к лицу́ жа́ловаться.

beige [beɪʒ] *n.* (*material*) мате́рия из некра́шеной ше́рсти.

adj. беж (*indecl.*), бе́жевый.

being [ˈbiːɪŋ] *n.* **1.** (*existence*) бытие́, существова́ние; **fleet in ~** существу́ющий флот; **the firm is still in ~** фи́рма всё ещё существу́ет; **come into ~** возн|ика́ть, -и́кнуть; **call, bring into ~** вы́звать (*pf.*) к жи́зни. **2.** (*creature, pers.*) существо́; **human ~** челове́к; **the Supreme B~** Всевы́шний. **3.** (*nature*) существо́.

Beirut [beɪˈruːt] *n.* Бейру́т; (*attr.*) бейру́тский.

bejewel [bɪˈdʒuːəl] *v.t.* разукра́|шивать, -сить драгоце́нностями.

belabour [bɪˈleɪbə(r)] *v.t.* (*thrash*) вздуть (*pf.*); изб|ива́ть, -и́ть; (*over-emphasize*): ~ **the obvious** дока́зывать (*impf.*) очеви́дное.

Belarus [beləˈrʌs] *n.* Белару́сь.

belated [bɪˈleɪtɪd] *adj.* запозда́лый.

belay [bɪˈleɪ] *v.t.* (*naut.*) завёр|тывать, -ну́ть; **~!** заверну́ть!; (*fig.*) стоп!; **~ing-pin** ко́фель-на́гель (*m.*).

belch [beltʃ] *n.* отры́жка; **give a ~** рыгну́ть (*pf.*); (*of smoke etc.*) столб.

v.t. (*smoke etc.*; *also* ~ **forth, out**) выбра́сывать, вы́бросить; (*lava*) изв|ерга́ть, -е́ргнуть; (*oaths etc.*) изв|ерга́ть, -е́ргнуть; изрыг|а́ть, -ну́ть.

v.i. рыг|а́ть, -ну́ть.

beleaguer [bɪˈliːgə(r)] *v.t.* оса|жда́ть, -ди́ть.

belfry [ˈbelfrɪ] *n.* колоко́льня; *see also* **bat**[1]

Belgian [ˈbeldʒ(ə)n] *n.* бельги́|ец (*fem.* -йка).

adj. бельги́йский.

Belgium [ˈbeldʒəm] *n.* Бе́льгия.

Belgrade [bəlˈgreɪd] *n.* Белгра́д.

Belial [ˈbiːlɪəl] *n.* Велиа́р, Сатана́ (*m.*); **son of ~** нечести́вец.

belie [bɪˈlaɪ] *v.t.* (*contradict*) противоре́чить (*impf.*) +*d.*; (*disappoint*): **our hopes were ~d** на́ши наде́жды не оправда́лись.

belief [bɪˈliːf] *n.* **1.** (*trust*) ве́ра (в+*a.*); дове́рие (к+*d.*). **2.** (*acceptance as true*; *thg. believed*) ве́ра, ве́рование; **entertain the ~ that** пита́ть (*impf.*) уве́ренность в том, что; **to the best of my ~** по моему́ убежде́нию; **he has a strong ~ in education** он глубоко́ убеждён в необходи́мости образова́ния; **beyond ~** невероя́тно, непостижи́мо; **the ~s of the Christian church** ве́рования/вероуче́ния (*nt. pl.*) христиа́нской це́ркви; **strange ~s** стра́нные пове́рья (*nt. pl.*).

believable [bɪˈliːvəb(ə)l] *adj.* правдоподо́бный.

believe [bɪˈliːv] *v.t.* ве́рить, по- (*кому, во что*); ду́мать (*impf.*); **I ~ so** ду́маю, что э́то так; мне так ка́жется; **~ one's eyes** ве́рить, по- свои́м глаза́м; **~ it or not; would you ~ it?** хоти́те ве́рьте, хоти́те — нет; **~ me** мо́жете мне пове́рить; **I ~ him to be honest** я счита́ю его́ че́стным челове́ком; **he deserves to be ~d** он заслу́живает дове́рия; **make ~** де́лать вид, притворя́ться (*impf.*).

v.i. ве́рить (*impf.*); (*esp. relig.*) ве́ровать (*impf.*); **~ in God** ве́рить (*impf.*) в Бо́га; **~ in a remedy** ве́рить (*impf.*) в како́е-н. лека́рство; **~ in s.o.** ве́рить (*impf.*) в кого́-н.; име́ть (*impf.*) дове́рие к кому́-н.; **I ~ in taking exercise** я ве́рю в по́льзу заря́дки.

believer [bɪ'li:və(r)] *n.* **1.** (*relig.*) ве́рующий. **2.** (*advocate*) сторо́нник +*g.*; **~ in discipline** сторо́нник дисципли́ны.

belittle [bɪ'lɪt(ə)l] *v.t.* преум|еньша́ть, -е́ньшить; умал|я́ть, -и́ть; **~ o.s.** уничижа́ться (*impf.*).

bell [bel] *n.* **1.** ко́локол; (*smaller*) колоко́льчик; (*of door, telephone, bicycle etc.*) звоно́к; **cap and ~s** колпа́к с бубенца́ми; **ring the ~** звони́ть (*impf.*) в звоно́к/ко́локол; **that rings a ~** (*fig., coll.*) да, я что́-то припомина́ю; **answer the ~** откры́ть (*pf.*) дверь; яви́ться (*pf.*) на зов; **clear as a ~** чи́стый как звон колоко́льчика; **sound as a ~** в полне́йшем поря́дке. **2.** (*naut.*) ко́локол; **ring the ~s** бить (*impf.*) скля́нки. **3.** (*of flower*) ча́шечка; (*of vase*) растру́б.

v.t.: **~ the cat** (*fig.*) ≃ поста́вить (*pf.*) себя́ под уда́р.

cpds. **~-bottomed** *adj.*: **~-bottomed trousers** брю́ки-клёш, брю́ки с растру́бом; **~boy** *n.* коридо́рный; **~-buoy** *n.* буй с ко́локолом; **~-captain** *n.* (*US*) ста́рший коридо́рный; **~-founder** *n.* колоко́льник, колоко́льный ма́стер; **~-foundry** *n.* колоко́льная мастерска́я; **~-glass** *n.* стекля́нный колпа́к; **~-jar** *n.* стекля́нный колпа́к; **~-metal** *n.* колоко́льная бро́нза; **~-push** *n.* кно́пка звонка́; **~ringer** *n.* звона́рь (*m.*); **~-tent** *n.* кру́глая пала́тка; **~-wether** *n.* бара́н-вожа́к.

belladonna [,belə'dɒnə] *n.* (*plant, drug*) белладо́нна.

belle [bel] *n.* краса́вица; **the ~ of the ball** цари́ца ба́ла.

belles-lettres [bel 'letr] *n.* беллетри́стика.

belletristic [,belə'trɪstɪk] *adj.* беллетристи́ческий.

bellicose ['belɪ,kəʊz] *adj.* во́инственный.

bellicosity ['belɪ'kɒsɪtɪ] *n.* во́инственность.

belligerency [bɪ'lɪdʒərənsɪ] *n.* состоя́ние войны́; ста́тус/положе́ние вою́ющей стороны́; (*aggressiveness*) во́инственность, агресси́вность.

belligerent [bɪ'lɪdʒərənt] *n.* вою́ющая сторона́.

adj. (*waging war*) вою́ющий; **~ rights** права́ вою́ющих сторо́н; (*aggressive*) во́инственный, задири́стый.

bellow ['beləʊ] *n.* (*of animal*) мыча́ние; (*of sea, storm*) рёв.

v.t. (*also* **~ forth, out**) ора́ть (*impf.*).

v.i. **1.** (*of animal*) мыча́ть, про-; реве́ть (*impf.*). **2.** (*shout*) ора́ть (*impf.*); (*roar with pain*) реве́ть (*impf.*), ора́ть (*impf.*); (*of thunder, cannon etc.*) греме́ть (*impf.*), грохот|а́ть, -ну́ть.

bellows ['beləʊz] *n.* (*of furnace, organ*) мехи́ (*m. pl.*); (*domestic*) (ручны́е раздува́льные) мехи́; (*phot.*) мехи́.

belly ['belɪ] *n.* **1.** живо́т, (*coll.*) брю́хо; **pot ~** то́лстое брю́хо; пу́зо; **~ dancer** исполни́тельница та́нца живота́; **his eyes are bigger than his ~** глаза́ у него́ завиду́щие; **he has fire in his ~** он по́лон огня́. **2.** (*of ship etc.*) дни́ще; (*of sail*) пу́зо; (*of violin etc.*) де́ка.

v.t. (*of wind*): **~ (out) a sail** над|ува́ть, -у́ть па́рус.

v.i. (*of sail*) нап|олня́ться, -о́лниться.

cpds. **~-ache** *n.* боль в животе́; *v.i.* (*sl.*) стона́ть, хны́кать, ныть (*all impf.*); **~-band** *n.* подпру́га; **~-flop** *n.* (*coll.*) уда́р живото́м (*при прыжке в воду*); **~-landing** *n.* (*aeron.*) поса́дка на «брю́хо» (*coll.*).

bellyful ['belɪfʊl] *n.*: **he has had his ~ of it** он сыт по го́рло э́тим.

belong [bɪ'lɒŋ] *v.i.* **1.: ~ to** (*be the property of*) принадле́жать (*impf.*) +*d.*; (*be a member of*) состоя́ть (*impf.*) в+*p.*; (*befit, appertain*): **it ~s to me to decide** мне реша́ть; **such amusements ~ to your age** таки́е развлече́ния подхо́дят для люде́й ва́шего во́зраста; **that ~s to my duties** э́то вхо́дит в мои́ обя́занности. **2.** (*match*): **these gloves do not ~** э́ти перча́тки не подхо́дят. **3.** (*of place*): **these books ~ here** э́ти кни́ги стоя́т здесь; э́ти кни́ги отсю́да; **I ~ here** (*was born here*) я ро́дом отсю́да; (*live here*) я отсю́да; я зде́шний; (*am rightly placed here*) я здесь на ме́сте; **this ~s under 'Science'** э́то отно́сится к разде́лу «Нау́ка».

belongings [bɪ'lɒŋɪŋz] *n.* ве́щи (*f. pl.*), пожи́тк|и (*pl., g.* -ов).

Belorussia [,beləʊ'rʌʃə], **-n** [,beləʊ'rʌʃ(ə)n] = **Byelorussia, -n**

beloved [bɪ'lʌvɪd, *pred. also* -lʌvd] *n.* возлю́бленн|ый (*fem.* -ая); **dearly ~!** (*to congregation*) возлю́бленные ча́да!

adj. возлю́бленный, люби́мый.

below [bɪ'ləʊ] *adv.* (*of place*) внизу́; (*of motion*) вниз; (*in text etc.*) ни́же; **from ~** сни́зу; **go ~** (*naut.*) спусти́ться (*pf.*) вниз; **the court ~** (*leg.*) суд ни́жней инста́нции.

prep. (*of place*) под+*i.*; (*of motion*) под+*a.*; (*lower, downstream*) ни́же +*g.*; **on the Volga ~ Saratov** на Во́лге ни́же Сара́това; **he ranks ~ me** он ни́же меня́ чи́ном; **~ 60** моло́же шести́десяти; **~ £10** деше́вле/ме́ньше десяти́ фу́нтов; **he is ~ average height** он ни́же сре́днего ро́ста.

belt [belt] *n.* **1.** (*of leather*) реме́нь (*m.*); (*of linen etc.*) по́яс (*pl.* -а́); (*part of overcoat*) хля́стик; (*mil.*) патро́нная ле́нта; **hit below the ~** уда́рить (*pf.*) под вздох; **tighten one's ~** (*fig.*) затяну́ть (*pf.*) поту́же реме́нь; **seat ~** привязно́й реме́нь, реме́нь безопа́сности. **2.** (*zone*) по́яс, полоса́; **cotton ~** хло́пковый по́яс; **~ of fire** (*mil.*) огнева́я заве́са. **3.** (*tech.*) (приводно́й) реме́нь.

v.t. **1.** (*furnish with ~*) подпоя́с|ывать, -ать; опоя́с|ывать, -ать. **2.** (*fasten*): **~ on a sword** опоя́с|ываться, -аться мечо́м. **3.** (*coll., thrash*) поро́ть, вы́-. **4.: ~ out a song** горла́нить (*impf.*) пе́сню.

belting ['beltɪŋ] *n.* (*tech.*) ремённая переда́ча; бе́льтинг; (*coll., thrashing*) по́рка.

beluga [bə'lu:gə] *n.* белу́га.

belvedere ['belvɪ,dɪə(r)] *n.* бельведе́р.

bemoan [bɪ'məʊn] *v.t.* опла́к|ива́ть, -ать.

bemuse [bɪ'mju:z] *v.t.* пора|жа́ть, -зи́ть; ошелом|ля́ть, -и́ть.

bench [bentʃ] *n.* **1.** (*seat*) скамья́, ла́вка. **2.** (*work-table*) верста́к, стано́к. **3.** (*leg.*): **he was raised to the ~** он стал судьёй; (*judges*) су́дьи (*m. pl.*); суде́йское сосло́вие. **4.** (*theatr.*): **play to empty ~es** игра́ть (*impf.*) пе́ред пусты́м за́лом.

cpd. **~-mark** *n.* репе́р.

bend [bend] *n.* **1.** (*curve*) изги́б; (*in river*) излу́чина; **~ of the arm** локтево́й сгиб руки́; **round the ~** (*coll.*) свихну́вшийся. **2.: the ~s** (*disease*) кессо́нная боле́знь. **3.: ~ sinister** (*fig.*) незаконнорождённость. **4.** (*naut.*) у́зел; **fisherman's ~** рыба́цкий штык.

v.t. **1.** (*twist, incline*): **~ a branch** гнуть, при- ве́тку; **~ an iron bar** из|гиба́ть, -огну́ть желе́зный брус; **the storm bent the tree to the ground** бу́ря пригну́ла де́рево к земле́; **a bent pin** со́гнутая була́вка; **the axle is bent** ось погну́лась; **~ a bow** сгиба́ть, согну́ть лук; **on ~ed knee** преклони́в коле́на; **knees ~!** коле́ни согну́ть!; **~ one's head over a book** склон|я́ться, -и́ться над кни́гой; **~ s.o. to one's will** подчин|я́ть, -и́ть кого́-н. свое́й во́ле. **2.** (*direct*): **~ one's steps homewards** напра́вить (*pf.*) стопы́ к до́му; **all eyes were bent on him** все взо́ры бы́ли напра́влены на него́; **he is bent on learning English** он твёрдо реши́л изучи́ть англи́йский язы́к; **he is bent on mischief** он то́лько и ду́мает, как бы набедоку́рить.

v.i.: **the river ~s here** река́ здесь изгиба́ется; **the trees bent in the wind** дере́вья гну́лись на ветру́; **~ at the knees** сгиба́ться, согну́ться в коле́нях; **~ over one's desk** сгиба́ться, согну́ться над столо́м; **~ before s.o.'s will** склон|я́ться, -и́ться пе́ред чьей-н. во́лей; **~ forward** наклон|я́ться, -и́ться (вперёд); **~ over backwards** (*fig.*) ≃ из ко́жи вон лезть, де́лать (*impf.*) бо́льше, чем мо́жешь.

with advs.: **~ back** *v.t.* (*e.g. a finger*) оття́|гивать, -ну́ть наза́д; **~ down** *v.t.* наг|иба́ть, -ну́ть; сгиба́ть, согну́ть; переклон|я́ть, -и́ть; *v.i.* (*also* **~ over**) наг|иба́ться, -ну́ться; перег|иба́ться, -ну́ться.

bender ['bendə(r)] *n.* (*sl.*) кутёж; **go on a ~** загуля́ть (*pf.*).

beneath [bɪ'ni:θ] *adv.* внизу́.

prep. (*of place*) под+*i.*; (*of motion*) под+*a.*; (*lower than*) ни́же+*g.*; **~ criticism** ни́же вся́кой кри́тики; **marry ~ one** соверши́ть (*pf.*) мезалья́нс; заключи́ть (*pf.*) нера́вный брак; **it is ~ you to complain** жа́ловаться — недосто́йно вас; **it is ~ contempt** э́то не заслу́живает ничего́, кро́ме презре́ния.

Benedictine [ˌbenɪˈdɪktɪn, *in sense* **2.** -ˌtiːn] *n.* **1.** (*monk*) бенедикти́нец; (*nun*) бенедикти́нка. **2.** (*liqueur*) бенедикти́н.

adj. бенедикти́нский.

benediction [ˌbenɪˈdɪkʃ(ə)n] *n.* благослове́ние.

benefaction [ˌbenɪˈfækʃ(ə)n] *n.* (*kind act*) благодея́ние; (*donation*) поже́ртвование.

benefactor [ˈbenɪˌfæktə(r)] *n.* (*one who confers benefit*) благоде́тель (*m.*); (*donor*) благотвори́тель (*m.*).

benefactress [ˈbenɪˌfæktrɪs] *n.* благоде́тельница; благотвори́тельница.

benefice [ˈbenɪfɪs] *n.* бенефи́ций.

beneficence [bɪˈnefɪsəns] *n.* благодея́ние; благотвори́тельность.

beneficent [bɪˈnefɪs(ə)nt] *adj.* благотвори́тельный.

beneficial [ˌbenɪˈfɪʃ(ə)l] *adj.* **1.** благотво́рный, поле́зный, вы́годный; **mutually ~** взаимовы́годный. **2.** (*leg.*) бенефициа́рный.

beneficiary [ˌbenɪˈfɪʃərɪ] *n.* (*leg.*) бенефициа́рий.

benefit [ˈbenɪfɪt] *n.* **1.** (*advantage*) по́льза, вы́года, преиму́щество; **for the ~ of the poor** в по́льзу бе́дных; **for the ~ of mankind** на бла́го челове́чества; **give s.o. the ~ of one's advice** помо́чь (*pf.*) кому́-н. сове́том; (*iron.*) осчастли́вить (*pf.*) кого́-н. сове́том; **I gave him the ~ of the doubt** я ему́ пове́рил (на э́тот раз); **reap the ~ of** пожина́ть (*impf.*) плоды́ +*g.*; **he said that for my ~** (*for me to hear*) он сказа́л э́то специа́льно для меня́; **she wore a new dress for his ~** она́ наде́ла но́вое пла́тье ра́ди него́. **2.** (*favour*) благодея́ние; **confer ~s on** ока́зывать (*impf.*) благодея́ния +*d.* **3.** (*grant*) посо́бие; **maternity ~** посо́бие по бере́менности и ро́дам. **4.: ~ concert** благотвори́тельный конце́рт; **~ society** о́бщество взаимопо́мощи.

v.t. прин|оси́ть, -ести́ по́льзу +*d.*, идти́ (*det.*) на по́льзу +*d.*; (*of health*) прин|оси́ть, -ести́ по́льзу +*d.*

v.i. извл|ека́ть, -е́чь по́льзу (из+*g.*); **you will ~ by a holiday** о́тдых пойдёт вам на по́льзу.

Benelux [ˈbenɪˌlʌks] *n.* Бенилю́кс.

benevolence [bɪˈnevələns] *n.* благожела́тельность, доброжела́тельность; ще́дрость; благотвори́тельность.

benevolent [bɪˈnevələnt] *adj.* благожела́тельный, доброжела́тельный; **~ neutrality** благожела́тельный нейтралите́т; (*munificent*) ще́дрый; (*charitable*) благотвори́тельный.

Bengal [beŋˈgɔːl] *n.* Бенга́лия; (*attr.*) бенга́льский.

Bengali [beŋˈgɔːlɪ] *n.* (*pers.*) бенга́л|ец (*fem.* -ка); (*language*) бенга́льский язы́к.

adj. бенга́льский.

benighted [bɪˈnaɪtɪd] *adj.* засти́гнутый но́чью; (*fig.*) тёмный; обскура́нтский.

benign [bɪˈnaɪn] *adj.* (*of pers.*) добросерде́чный; (*of climate*) благотво́рный; (*of soil*) плодоно́сный; (*med.*) доброка́чественный.

benignity [bɪˈnɪgnɪtɪ] *n.* добросерде́чие, великоду́шие.

Benjamin [ˈbendʒəmɪn] *n.* (*bibl.*, *also fig.*) Вениами́н.

bent[1] [bent] *n.* (*inclination*) скло́нность; (*aptitude*) накло́нность; **to the top of one's ~** в по́лное своё удово́льствие.

adj. (*coll.*, *corrupt*) нече́стный, извращённый, прода́жный; (*homosexual*) гомосексуа́льный.

also p.p. of **bend,** *q.v.*

bent[2] [bent] *n.* (*grass*) полеви́ца.

benzedrine [ˈbenzɪˌdriːn] *n.* бензедри́н.

benz|ene [ˈbenziːn], **-ol** [ˈbenzɒl] *nn.* бензо́л.

benzine [ˈbenziːn] *n.* бензи́н.

benzol [ˈbenzɒl] = **benzene**

bequeath [bɪˈkwiːð] *v.t.* завеща́ть (*impf.*, *pf.*); (*fig.*) оста́вить (*pf.*).

bequest [bɪˈkwest] *n.* (*object*) вещь, оста́вленная в насле́дство; (*as part of museum collection*) фонд, посме́ртный дар; (*act*) завеща́тельный отка́з иму́щества; **make a ~ of** завеща́ть (*impf.*, *pf.*).

berate [bɪˈreɪt] *v.t.* брани́ть (*impf.*), (*coll.*) расп|ека́ть, -е́чь.

Berber [ˈbɜːbə(r)] *n.* бербе́р (*fem.* -ка).

adj. бербе́рский.

bereave [bɪˈriːv] *v.t.*: **a ~d husband** неда́вно овдове́вший муж; **an accident bereft him of his children** несча́стный слу́чай о́тнял у него́ дете́й; **bereft of hope** лишённый наде́жды.

bereavement [bɪˈriːvmənt] *n.* тяжёлая утра́та/потéря.

beret [ˈbereɪ] *n.* бере́т.

bergamot [ˈbɜːgəˌmɒt] *n.* бергамо́т.

beriberi [ˌberɪˈberɪ] *n.* бе́ри-бе́ри (*f. indecl.*).

Bering Sea [ˈberɪŋ] *n.* Бе́рингово мо́ре.

berk [bɜːk] *n.* (*sl.*) болва́н.

Berlin [bɜːˈlɪn] *n.* Берли́н; (*attr.*) берли́нский.

Berliner [bɜːˈlɪnə(r)] *n.* берли́н|ец (*fem.* -ка).

Bermuda [bəˈmjuːdə] *n.*: (*also* **the ~s**) Берму́дские острова́ (*m. pl.*); **~ shorts** шо́рты-берму́ды.

Berne [bɜːn] *n.* Берн.

Bernese [ˈbɜːniːz] *adj.* бе́рнский.

berry [ˈberɪ] *n.* я́года; (*coffee bean*) зерно́; (*of caviar*) икри́нка.

v.i.: **they have gone ~ing** они́ ушли́ по я́годы.

berserk [bəˈsɜːk, -ˈzɜːk] *n.*: **go ~** разъяри́ться (*pf.*), обезу́меть (*pf.*).

berth [bɜːθ] *n.* **1.** (*place at wharf*) при́стань, прича́л; **loading ~** грузово́й прича́л; **covered ~** э́ллинг. **2.: give a ship a wide ~** держа́ться на доста́точном расстоя́нии от корабля́; **give s.o. a wide ~** (*fig.*) обходи́ть (*impf.*) кого́-н. стороно́й (*or* за версту́). **3.** (*sleeping-place on ship*) ко́йка; (*on train*) спа́льное ме́сто. **4.** (*job*) ме́сто, месте́чко.

v.t. **1.** (*moor*) ста́вить (*impf.*) к прича́лу; **~ing-place** ме́сто стоя́нки. **2.** (*give sleeping-room to*) предост|авля́ть, -а́вить спа́льное ме́сто +*d.*

v.i. (*of ship*) прича́ли|вать, -ть; (*of crew*) разме|ща́ться, -сти́ться.

cpd. **~-deck** *n.* жила́я па́луба.

beryl [ˈberɪl] *n.* бери́лл; (*attr.*) бери́лловый.

beryllium [bəˈrɪlɪəm] *n.* бери́ллий.

beseech [bɪˈsiːtʃ] *v.t.* умол|я́ть, -и́ть; моли́ть (*impf.*).

beseem [bɪˈsiːm] *v.t.* (*arch.*) подоба́ть (*impf.*) +*d.*; **it ill ~s you** вам не подоба́ет.

beset [bɪˈset] *v.t.* окруж|а́ть, -и́ть; оса|жда́ть, -ди́ть; **~ting sin** преоблада́ющий поро́к.

beside [bɪˈsaɪd] *prep.* **1.** (*alongside*) ря́дом с+*i.*; (*near*) о́коло+*g.*, у+*g.* **2.** (*compared with*) по сравне́нию с+*i.*; пе́ред+*i.*; **~ him all novelists are insignificant** по сравне́нию с ним все романи́сты ничего́ не сто́ят; **set ~** поста́вить (*pf.*) ря́дом с+*i.* **3.** (*wide of*) ми́мо+*g.*; **that is ~ the point** э́то к де́лу не отно́сится. **4.: ~ o.s.** вне себя́. **5.** (*as well as*) кро́ме+*g.*

besides [bɪˈsaɪdz] *adv.* сверх того́; кро́ме того́.

prep. кро́ме+*g.*

besiege [bɪˈsiːdʒ] *v.t.* (*lit.*, *fig.*) оса|жда́ть, -ди́ть.

besieger [bɪˈsiːdʒə(r)] *n.* осажда́ющий.

besmear [bɪˈsmɪə(r)] *v.t.* заса́ли|вать, -ть; выма́зывать, вы́мазать.

besmirch [bɪˈsmɜːtʃ] *v.t.* па́чкать, вы́-; (*fig.*) запа́чкать, опоро́чить (*both pf.*).

besom [ˈbiːz(ə)m] *n.* метла́, ве́ник.

besotted [bɪˈsɒtɪd] *adj.* одурма́ненный.

bespangle [bɪˈspæŋg(ə)l] *v.t.* ос|ыпа́ть, -ы́пать блёстками; **a ~d sky** усе́янное звёздами не́бо.

bespatter [bɪˈspætə(r)] *v.t.* забры́зг|ивать, -ать.

bespeak [bɪˈspiːk] *v.t.* (*order*) зака́з|ывать, -а́ть; (*reveal*) свиде́тельствовать, говори́ть (*both impf.*) о.

bespoke [bɪˈspəʊk] *adj.* сде́ланный на зака́з; **~ tailor** портно́й, рабо́тающий на зака́з.

bespoken [bɪˈspəʊkən] *adj.* за́нятый.

besprinkle [bɪˈsprɪŋk(ə)l] *v.t.* (*with liquid*) обры́зг|ивать, -ать; (*with powder etc.*) обс|ыпа́ть, -ы́пать.

Bessarabia [ˌbesəˈreɪbɪə] *n.* Бессара́бия.

Bessemer [ˈbesɪmə(r)] *n.*: **~ process** бессеме́ровский проце́сс.

best [best] *n.* (*~ performance*) лу́чший результа́т; *see also adj.*

adj. лу́чший; **the ~ way to the station** са́мый лу́чший путь к ста́нции; **he is the ~ of men** лу́чше его́ никого́ нет; **we are the ~ of friends** мы бли́зкие друзья́; **at ~** в лу́чшем слу́чае; **I did it for the ~** я де́лал э́то с лу́чшими наме́рениями; **dressed in one's ~** оде́т во всё са́мое лу́чшее; **get the ~ of it** взять (*pf.*) верх; **do one's ~** сде́лать (*pf.*) всё возмо́жное; **I know what is ~ for him** я лу́чше зна́ю, что ему́ ну́жно; **to the ~ of one's ability** в ме́ру свои́х сил/спосо́бностей; **to the ~ of my knowledge** наско́лько мне изве́стно; **in the ~ of health** в до́бром здра́вии; **he can drink with the ~** он перепьёт кого́ уго́дно; **give s.o. ~** призна́ть (*pf.*) чьё-н. превосхо́дство; **all the ~!** всего́ наилу́чшего!; **hope for the ~** наде́яться (*impf.*) на лу́чшее; **turn out for the ~** оберну́ться (*pf.*) к лу́чшему; **may the ~ man win** пусть победи́т сильне́йший; **have the ~ of the bargain** оказа́ться (*pf.*) в вы́игрыше; **~ pupil** пе́рвый учени́к; **~ quality** вы́сший сорт; (*greater*): **the ~ part of a week** бо́льшая часть неде́ли; **I waited for the ~ part of an hour** я ждал почти́ це́лый час; **~ man** (*at wedding*) ша́фер; **~ girl** ми́лая, люби́мая.

adv. лу́чше всего́; **he works ~** (*better than others*) он рабо́тает лу́чше всех; **I work ~ in the evening** мне лу́чше всего́ рабо́тается по вечера́м; **you know ~** вам лу́чше знать; **I had ~ tell him** мне бы сле́довало сказа́ть ему́; **do as you think ~** де́лайте, как вам ка́жется лу́чше; **which town did you like ~?** како́й го́род вам бо́льше всего́ понра́вился?; **I liked her ~ (of all)** она́ мне понра́вилась бо́льше всех; **it is ~ forgotten** лу́чше всего́ забы́ть об э́том.

v.t. брать, взять верх над+*i.*

cpds. **~-dressed** *adj.* са́мый элега́нтный; **~-hated** *adj.* са́мый ненави́стный; **~-looking** *adj.* са́мый краси́вый; **~-seller** *n.* (*book*) бестсе́ллер; (*author*) а́втор бестсе́ллера; **~-selling** *adj.* хо́дкий.

bestial [ˈbestiəl] *adj.* звери́ный; (*brutish*) звéрский, звероподо́бный; (*depraved*) ско́тский, живо́тный.

bestiality [ˌbestɪˈælɪtɪ] *n.* зве́рство; (*depravity*) ско́тство; (*leg.*) скотоло́жество.

bestir [bɪˈstɜː(r)] *v.t.*: **~ o.s.** встряхну́ться (*pf.*).

bestow [bɪˈstəʊ] *v.t.* **1.** (*store*) поме|ща́ть, -сти́ть. **2.** (*confer*): **~ gifts on s.o.** ода́р|ивать, -и́ть кого́-н.; **he ~ed a fortune on his nephew** он переда́л племя́ннику це́лое состоя́ние; **~ a title on s.o.** присв|а́ивать, -о́ить кому́-н. ти́тул; **~ honours** возд|ава́ть, -а́ть по́чести. **3.** (*use*): **time well ~ed** хорошо́ испо́льзованное вре́мя.

bestowal [bɪˈstəʊəl] *n.* **1.** (*donation*) дар. **2.: ~ of a title** присвое́ние ти́тула; **~ of honours** воздая́ние/оказа́ние по́честей; награжде́ние по́честями.

bestrew [bɪˈstruː] *v.t.* ус|ыпа́ть, -ы́пать.

bestride [bɪˈstraɪd] *v.t.* (*a chair, fence etc.*) осе́дл|ывать, -а́ть; **~ a horse** сиде́ть (*impf.*) верхо́м.

bet [bet] *n.* пари́ (*nt. indecl.*), ста́вка; **make, lay a ~** держа́ть (*impf.*) пари́; **accept a ~** идти́ (*det.*) на пари́; **an even ~** пари́ с ра́вными ша́нсами; **the grey is the best ~ to win** се́рый/се́рко име́ет бо́льше всех ша́нсов на вы́игрыш; **your best ~ is to go there** вам лу́чше всего́ пойти́ туда́.

v.t. & i. держа́ть (*impf.*) пари́; би́ться, по- об закла́д; **he ~ £5 on a horse** он поста́вил 5 фу́нтов на ло́шадь; **he ~ me £10 I wouldn't do it** он поспо́рил со мной на 10 фу́нтов, что я не сде́лаю э́того; **I ~ he doesn't turn up** держу́ пари́, что он не придёт; **you ~ (your life)!** (*coll.*) ещё вы!; ещё как!

beta [ˈbiːtə] *n.*: **~ particle** бе́та-части́ца; **~ rays** бе́та-лучи́.

betake [bɪˈteɪk] *v.t.*: **~ o.s. to** (*a place*) отпр|авля́ться, -а́виться к+*d.*; **~ o.s. to reading** обра|ща́ться, -ти́ться к чте́нию.

betel [ˈbiːt(ə)l] *n.* бе́тель (*m.*).

cpd. **~-nut** *n.* аре́ковое се́мя.

bête noire [beɪt ˈnwɑː(r)] *n.*: **he is my ~** он мне ненави́стен.

bethink [bɪˈθɪŋk] *v.t.*: **~ o.s.** (*recollect*) всп|омина́ть, -о́мнить; **~ o.s. of** (*devise*) заду́м|ывать, -ать.

Bethlehem [ˈbeθlɪˌhem] *n.* Вифлее́м.

betide [bɪˈtaɪd] (*arch.*) *v.t.*: **woe ~ you** го́ре вам!

v.i.: **whate'er ~** что бы ни приключи́лось.

betimes [bɪˈtaɪmz] *adv.* (*in good time*) своевре́менно; (*early*) ра́но.

betoken [bɪˈtəʊkən] *v.t.* (*indicate*) ука́з|ывать, -а́ть на+*a.*; (*signify*) означа́ть (*impf.*); (*auger*) предвеща́ть (*impf.*); **his complexion ~s bad health** цвет его́ лица́ говори́т о плохо́м здоро́вье.

betony [ˈbetənɪ] *n.* бу́квица.

betray [bɪˈtreɪ] *v.t.* **1.** (*abandon treacherously*) измен|я́ть, -и́ть +*d.*; пред|ава́ть, -а́ть. **2.** (*lead astray*): **the text ~ed him into error** текст ввёл его́ в заблужде́ние; (*seduce*) обма́н|ывать, -у́ть. **3.: ~ s.o.'s hopes** обману́ть (*pf.*) чьи-н. наде́жды; **~ s.o.'s trust** обману́ть чьё-н. дове́рие; не оправда́ть (*pf.*) чьего́-н. дове́рия. **4.** (*disclose, evince*) выдава́ть, вы́дать; **his accent ~ed him** его́ вы́дало произноше́ние; **~ official secrets** выдава́ть, вы́дать госуда́рственные та́йны; **~ surprise** выража́ть, вы́разить удивле́ние.

betrayal [bɪˈtreɪəl] *n.* (*treachery*) преда́тельство, изме́на; (*disclosure*) вы́дача; (*seduction, disappointment*) обма́н; **the ~ of his hopes** круше́ние его́ наде́жд.

betrayer [bɪˈtreɪə(r)] *n.* преда́тель (*m.*); изме́нник.

betroth [bɪˈtrəʊð] *v.t.* (*liter.*) обруч|а́ть, -и́ть; помо́лвить (*pf.*); **she is ~ed to him** она́ с ним обручена́/помо́лвлена.

betrothal [bɪˈtrəʊðəl] *n.* обруче́ние, помо́лвка.

bett|er¹, -or [ˈbetə(r)] *n.* (*one who bets*) держа́щий пари́, понтёр.

better² [ˈbetə(r)] *adj.* лу́чший, лу́чше; **~ still** ещё лу́чше; **all the ~** тем лу́чше; **I hoped for ~ things** я наде́ялся на лу́чшее; **it is ~ that you go** вам бы лу́чше уйти́; **(one's) ~ half** дража́йшая полови́на; **get ~** ул|учша́ться, -у́чшиться; (*in health*) попр|авля́ться, -а́виться; **things are getting ~** дела́ иду́т лу́чше; **go one ~ than s.o.** превзойти́ (*pf.*) кого́-н.; **he was ~ than his word** он сдержа́л своё сло́во с лихво́й; **get the ~ of s.o.** взять (*pf.*) верх над кем-н.; превзойти́ (*pf.*) кого́-н.; **he got the ~ of his anger** он превозмо́г/преодоле́л свой гнев; **a change for the ~** переме́на к лу́чшему; **for ~, for worse** на го́ре и ра́дость; **you will be the ~ for a holiday** о́тдых пойдёт вам на по́льзу; **he is no ~ than a fool** он по́просту дура́к; **she is no ~ than she should be** она́ не отлича́ется стро́гостью поведе́ния; **appeal to s.o.'s ~ feelings** взыва́ть (*impf.*) к чьим-н. лу́чшим чу́вствам; **the ~ part of a day** бо́льшая часть дня; **one's ~s** вышестоя́щие ли́ца; бо́лее о́пытные лю́ди (*m. pl.*).

adv. лу́чше; (*more*) бо́льше; **~ and ~** всё лу́чше и лу́чше; **the more the ~** чем бо́льше, тем лу́чше; **you had ~ stay here** вам бы лу́чше оста́ться здесь; **I thought ~ of it** я разду́мал/переду́мал; **I thought ~ of him** я был лу́чшего мне́ния о нём; **~ off** бо́лее состоя́тельный.

v.t. **1.** (*improve*) ул|учша́ть, -у́чшить; **he ~ed himself** он продви́нулся. **2.** (*improve on*) превзойти́ (pf.).

betterment [ˈbetəmənt] *n.* улучше́ние, соверше́нствование.

betting [ˈbetɪŋ] *n.*: **what's the ~ he marries her?** на ско́лько спо́рим, что он на ней же́нится?

adj.: **he is not a ~ man** он челове́к не аза́ртный.

bettor [ˈbetə(r)] = **better¹**

between [bɪˈtwiːn] *adv.*: **I attended the two lectures and had lunch in ~** я посети́л две ле́кции и пообе́дал в переры́ве; **his appearances are few and far ~** он появля́ется отню́дь не ча́сто.

prep. ме́жду+*g. or i.*; **~ you and me** ме́жду на́ми; **(in) ~ times** вре́мя от вре́мени; **~ two and three months** от двух до трёх ме́сяцев; **choose ~ the two** выбира́ть, вы́брать одно́ из двух; **~ now and then** к тому́ вре́мени; **they scored 150 ~ them** они́ набра́ли сто пятьдеся́т очко́в вме́сте; **we have only a pound ~ us** у нас на двои́х всего́ оди́н фунт; **we bought a car ~ us** мы сообща́ купи́ли маши́ну; мы купи́ли маши́ну вскла́дчину.

betwixt [bɪˈtwɪkst] *adv.*: **~ and between** ни то ни сё, не́что сре́днее.

bevel [ˈbev(ə)l] *n.* (*tool*) ма́лка; (*surface*) скос; **~ edge** фацёт; **~ gear** кони́ческая зу́бчатая переда́ча.

v.t. ск|а́шивать, -оси́ть.

beverage [ˈbevərɪdʒ] *n.* напи́ток.

bevy [ˈbevi] *n.* ста́я, ста́до; (*fig.*) ста́йка.

bewail [bɪˈweɪl] *v.t.* опла́к|ивать, -ать; скорбе́ть (*impf.*) по+*p.*

beware [bɪ'weə(r)] *v.t. & i.* остер|ега́ться, -е́чься (*impf.*) +*g.*; ~ **lest you fall** осторо́жно, а то упадёте; ~ **of the dog** осторо́жно, зла́я соба́ка.

bewilder [bɪ'wɪldə(r)] *v.t.* сби|ва́ть, -ть с то́лку; прив|оди́ть, -ести́ в замеша́тельство; ~**ed** смущённый, озада́ченный.

bewilderment [bɪ'wɪldəmənt] *n.* замеша́тельство, озада́ченность.

bewitch [bɪ'wɪtʃ] *v.t.* (*put spell on*) околдо́в|ывать, -а́ть; (*delight*) очаро́в|ывать, -а́ть.

bewitching [bɪ'wɪtʃɪŋ] *adj.* чару́ющий.

bey [beɪ] *n.* бей.

beyond [bɪ'jɒnd] *n.*: **the** ~ потусторо́нний мир; **he lives at the back of** ~ он живёт на краю́ све́та.

adv. вдали́; вдаль.

prep. (*of place*) за+*i.*; (*of motion*) за+*a.*; (*later than*) по́сле+*g.*; ~ **doubt** вне сомне́ния; ~ **dispute** бесспо́рно; ~ **my comprehension** вы́ше моего́ понима́ния; ~ **my powers** не в мои́х си́лах; ~ **belief** невероя́тно; ~ **expression** невырази́мо; ~ **my expectations** сверх мои́х ожида́ний; **succeed** ~ **one's hopes** да́же не ожида́ть (*impf.*) тако́го успе́ха; **this is** ~ **a joke** здесь уже́ не до шу́ток; **live** ~ **one's income** жить (*impf.*) не по сре́дствам; **nothing** ~ **his pension** ничего́ кро́ме его́ пе́нсии; ~ **measure** сверх ме́ры, чрезме́рно; ~ **hope** безнадёжно; ~ **cure** неизлечи́мый; **beautiful** ~ **all others** краси́вее всех остальны́х; **go** ~ **one's duty** сде́лать (*pf.*) бо́льше, чем обя́зан.

bezant ['bez(ə)nt, bɪ'zænt] *n.* византи́н.

bezique [bɪ'zi:k] *n.* бе́зик, бези́г.

bhang [bæŋ] *n.* гаши́ш.

biannual [baɪ'ænjʊəl] *adj.* выходя́щий два́жды в год; полугодово́й.

bias ['baɪəs] *n.* **1.** предрассу́док, предвзя́тое отноше́ние (*к чему*); (*favourable prejudice*) пристра́стие (к+*d.*); (*adverse*) предубежде́ние (про́тив+*g.*). **2.** (*of material*): **cut on the** ~ крои́ть, с- по косо́й ли́нии (*or* по диагона́ли). **3.** (*of a ball*) нето́чность фо́рмы ша́ра.

v.t. **1.** (*influence*) склон|я́ть, -и́ть; (*prejudice*) предубе|жда́ть, -ди́ть; ~ **s.o. against an idea** настр|а́ивать, -о́ить кого́-н. про́тив како́й-н. иде́и; **a** ~**(s)ed opinion** предвзя́тое мне́ние. **2.** (*deflect*) отклон|я́ть, -и́ть; (*of shape*) **a** ~**ed ball** шар со сре́занным сегме́нтом.

biathlete [baɪ'æθli:t] *n.* биатлони́ст (*fem.* -ка).

biathlon [baɪ'æθlən] *n.* биатло́н.

bib [bɪb] *n.* нагру́дник; **best** ~ **and tucker** (*joc.*) лу́чший наря́д, лу́чшее одея́ние.

bibelot ['bi:bləʊ] *n.* безделу́шка.

Bible ['baɪb(ə)l] *n.* Би́блия; (*fig.*) би́блия.

biblical ['bɪblɪk(ə)l] *adj.* библе́йский.

bibliographer [,bɪblɪ'ɒgrəfə(r)] *n.* библио́граф.

bibliographic(al) [,bɪblɪə'græfɪk(ə)l] *adj.* библиографи́ческий.

bibliography [,bɪblɪ'ɒgrəfɪ] *n.* библиогра́фия.

bibliomania [,bɪblɪəʊ'meɪnɪə] *n.* библиома́ния.

bibliomaniac [,bɪblɪəʊ'meɪnɪ,æk] *n.* библиома́н.

bibliophile ['bɪblɪəʊ,faɪl] *n.* библиофи́л.

bibulous ['bɪbjʊləs] *adj.* пья́нствующий, выпива́ющий.

bicameral [baɪ'kæmər(ə)l] *adj.* двухпала́тный.

bicarbonate [baɪ'kɑ:bənɪt] *n.* двууглеки́слая соль; ~ **of soda** двууглеки́слый на́трий, питьева́я со́да.

bicentenary [,baɪsen'ti:nərɪ] *n.* двухсотле́тие.

adj. двухсотле́тний.

bicentennial [,baɪsen'tenɪəl] *n.* двухсотле́тие.

adj. (*occurring every 200 years*) повторя́ющийся ка́ждые две́сти лет.

bicephalous [baɪ'sefələs] *adj.* двугла́вый.

biceps ['baɪseps] *n.* би́цепс.

bicker ['bɪkə(r)] *v.t.* (*squabble*) перебра́ниваться (*impf.*), препира́ться (*impf.*); (*of a stream*) журча́ть (*impf.*).

bi-coloured ['baɪ,kʌləd] *adj.* двуцве́тный.

biconcave [baɪ'kɒnkeɪv] *adj.* двояковво́гнутый.

biconvex [baɪ'kɒnveks] *adj.* двояковы́пуклый.

bicuspid [baɪ'kʌspɪd] *n.* ма́лый коренно́й зуб.

adj. двузу́бчатый.

bicycle ['baɪsɪk(ə)l] *n.* велосипе́д.

v.i. е́здить (*indet.*), е́хать, по- (*det.*) на велосипе́де.

bicyclist ['baɪsɪklɪst] *n.* велосипеди́ст.

bid [bɪd] *n.* **1.** (*at auction*) зая́вка; предложе́ние цены́; **make a higher** ~ сде́лать (*pf.*) надба́вку. **2.** (*tender*) зая́вка. **3.** (*claim, demand*) зая́вка (на+*a.*); прете́нзия. **4.** (*attempt*) ста́вка; попы́тка; **make a** ~ **for power** сде́лать (*pf.*) ста́вку на захва́т вла́сти. **5.** (*at cards*) зая́вка.

v.t. & i. **1.** (*at auction*) предл|ага́ть, -ожи́ть це́ну (*за что*); ~ **against s.o.** наб|авля́ть, -а́вить це́ну про́тив кого́-н. **2.** (*at cards*) объяв|ля́ть, -и́ть. **3.** (*offer, promise*): ~ **fair to succeed** сули́ть (*impf.*) успе́х; ~ **defiance to** бр|оса́ть, -о́сить вы́зов +*d.* **4.** (*tender*): ~ **for a contract** де́лать, с- зая́вку на контра́кт. **5.** (*liter., order*): ~ **him come in!** вели́те ему́ войти́!; **do as you are** ~**(den)!** де́лай как ска́зано! **6.** (*liter., say*): ~ **s.o. farewell** про|ща́ться, -сти́ться с кем-н.; ~ **s.o. welcome** приве́тствовать (*impf.*) кого́-н.; ~ **s.o. goodnight** пожела́ть (*pf.*) поко́йной но́чи кому́-н. **7.** (*liter., invite*): ~ **s.o. to dinner** проси́ть (*impf.*) кого́-н. к обе́ду; ~**den guest** зва́ный гость.

biddable ['bɪdəb(ə)l] *adj.* послу́шный.

bidder ['bɪdə(r)] *n.* покупщи́к; (*at auction*) аукционе́р; **the highest** ~ предложи́вший наивы́сшую це́ну.

bidding ['bɪdɪŋ] *n.* **1.** (*at auction*) предложе́ние цены́; **the** ~ **was brisk** надба́вки сле́довали одна́ за друго́й. **2.** (*command*): **do s.o.'s** ~ исп|олня́ть, -о́лнить чьи-н. приказа́ния. **3.** (*at cards*) объявле́ние.

bide [baɪd] *v.t.*: ~ **one's time** ждать (*impf.*) благоприя́тного слу́чая.

v.t. (*arch.*) ост|ава́ться, -а́ться.

bidet ['bi:deɪ] *n.* биде́ (*indecl.*).

biennial [baɪ'enɪəl] *n.* (*bot.*) двуле́тник.

adj. двухле́тний.

bier [bɪə(r)] *n.* катафа́лк.

biff [bɪf] (*coll.*) *n.*: **a** ~ **on the nose** уда́р по́ носу.

v.t.: ~ **s.o. in the eye** дать (*pf.*) кому́-н. в глаз.

bifocal [baɪ'fəʊk(ə)l] *adj.* двухфо́кусный, бифока́льный; ~ **spectacles** (*also* ~**s**) бифока́льные очки́.

bifurcate ['baɪfə,keɪt] *v.t. & i.* разветв|ля́ть(ся), -и́ть(ся); (*of road, river: also*) раздв|а́иваться, -о́иться; **a** ~**d tail** раздвоённый хвост.

bifurcation [,baɪfə'keɪʃ(ə)n] *n.* (*division*) раздвое́ние, бифурка́ция; (*point of division*) разви́лина, разветвле́ние.

big [bɪg] *adj.* (*in size*) большо́й, кру́пный; (*great*) кру́пный, вели́кий; (*extensive*) обши́рный; (*intense*) си́льный; (*tall*) высо́кий; (*adult*) взро́слый; (*magnanimous*) великоду́шный; (*important*) ва́жный; **a** ~ **man** (*in stature*) кру́пный мужчи́на; (*in importance*) кру́пная фигу́ра; **a** ~ **voice** си́льный го́лос; **a** ~ **landowner** кру́пный землевладе́лец; **these boots are too** ~ **for me** э́ти сапоги́ мне велики́; ~ (*capital*) **letters** прописны́е бу́квы; **a** ~ **fire** си́льный/большо́й пожа́р; ~ **and small** от ма́ла до вели́ка; **as** ~ **as** величино́й в+*a.*; **too** ~ **for his boots** чересчу́р возомни́вший о себе́; ~ **words** гро́мкие слова́; **talk** ~ хва́статься (*impf.*); **think** ~ мы́слить (*impf.*) сме́ло/ де́рзко; **a** ~ **noise** (*pers.*) ши́шка (*coll.*); **my** ~ **brother** мой ста́рший брат; **Big Dipper** америка́нские го́ры; **in a** ~ **way** с широ́ким разма́хом; **a** ~ **name** (*celebrity*) знамени́тость.

cpds. ~ **end** *n.* (*tech.*) больша́я (кривоши́пная) голо́вка (шатуна́); ~**-headed** *adj.* (*conceited*) зазна́вшийся; возомни́вший о себе́; ~**-hearted** *adj.* великоду́шный; ~**wig** *n.* ши́шка (*coll.*).

bigamist ['bɪgəmɪst] *n.* двоеже́нец, (*fem.*) двуму́жница.

bigamous ['bɪgəməs] *adj.* бигами́ческий, двубра́чный; име́ющий/име́ющая двух жён/муже́й.

bigamy ['bɪgəmɪ] *n.* бига́мия; (*of man*) двоежёнство; (*of woman*) двоему́жие, двуму́жие.

Big Apple [bɪg 'æp(ə)l] *n.* (*coll.*): **the** ~ Нью-Йо́рк.

bight [baɪt] *n.* (*bay*) бу́хта; (*in rope*) шлаг.

bigness ['bɪgnɪs] *n.* величина́.

bigot ['bɪgət] *n.* фана́тик; мракобе́с.

bigoted ['bɪgətɪd] *adj.* фанати́ческий, фанати́чный.

bigotry ['bɪgətrɪ] *n.* фанати́зм; мракобе́сие.

bijou ['bi:ʒu:] *n.*: **a** ~ **villa** ви́лла-игру́шка.

bike [baɪk] *n.* **1.** (*coll.*) = **bicycle.** **2.** (*motorcycle*) мотоци́кл.

v.i. е́здить (*indet.*) на мотоци́кле.

biker ['baɪkə(r)] *n.* мотоцикли́ст (*fem.* -ка).
bikeway ['baɪkweɪ] *n.* велосипе́дная доро́жка.
bikini [bɪ'ki:nɪ] *n.* бики́ни (*nt. indecl.*).
bilabial [baɪ'leɪbɪəl] *adj.* билабиа́льный.
bilateral [baɪ'lætər(ə)l] *adj.* двусторо́нний.
bilberry ['bɪlbərɪ] *n.* черни́ка (*collect.*); я́года черни́ки.
bile [baɪl] *n.* жёлчь; (*fig.*) жёлчность.
cpd. **~-duct** *n.* жёлчный прото́к.
bilge [bɪldʒ] *n.* **1.** (*of ship*) дни́ще; дно трю́ма. **2.** (*coll.*) чепуха́.
cpd. **~-water** *n.* трю́мная вода́.
biliary ['bɪlɪərɪ] *adj.* жёлчный.
bilingual [baɪ'lɪŋgw(ə)l] *adj.* двуязы́чный.
bilingualism [baɪ'lɪŋgw(ə)lɪz(ə)m] *n.* двуязы́чие.
bilious ['bɪljəs] *adj.* **1.** жёлчный; **a ~ headache** мигре́нь. **2.** (*fig.*) жёлчный, раздражи́тельный.
biliousness ['bɪljəsnɪs] *n.* жёлчность, раздражи́тельность.
bilk [bɪlk] *v.t.*: **~ s.o. of sth.** наду́ть (*pf.*) (*coll.*) кого́-н. на что-н.
bill[1] [bɪl] *n.* **1.** (*beak*) клюв. **2.** (*promontory*) мыс.
v.i.: **~ and coo** милова́ться (*impf.*), воркова́ть (*impf.*).
bill[2] [bɪl] *n.* (*also* **~hook**) сека́тор, топо́рик.
bill[3] [bɪl] *n.* **1.** (*parl.*) законопрое́кт, билль (*m.*). **2.** (*certificate*): **clean ~ of health** каранти́нное свиде́тельство. **3.** (*comm.*) счёт (*pl.* -а́); **~ of exchange** ве́ксель (*m.*); **~ of lading** накладна́я, коносаме́нт; **~ of sale** ку́пчая; закладна́я; **pay a ~, foot the ~** заплати́ть (*pf.*) по счёту; опла́|чивать, -ти́ть счёт; **run up a ~** набра́ть (*pf.*) мно́го в долг, мно́го задолжа́ть (*pf.*). **4.** (*advertisement*): **~ of fare** меню́ (*nt. indecl.*); **theatre ~** театра́льная афи́ша; **stick no ~s** (*as notice*) накле́ивать объявле́ния воспреща́ется; **fill the ~** (*satisfy requirements*) отвеча́ть (*impf.*) всем тре́бованиям. **5.** (*US, banknote*) банкно́та; **dollar ~** до́лларовый биле́т.
v.t. **1.** (*announce*) объяв|ля́ть, -и́ть; **he was ~ed to appear in 'Hamlet'** объяви́ли, что он бу́дет игра́ть в «Га́млете»; **get top ~ing** быть помещённым в афи́ше на пе́рвом ме́сте. **2.** (*charge*): **~ me for the goods** пришли́те мне счёт за това́ры.
cpds. **~board** *n.* доска́ объявле́ний; **~fold** *n.* (*US*) бума́жник; **~-poster, ~-sticker** *nn.* раскле́йщик афи́ш.
billet[1] ['bɪlɪt] *n.* (*log*) поле́но.
billet[2] ['bɪlɪt] *n.* **1.** (*order for ~ing*) о́рдер на посто́й. **2.** (*place of lodging*) помеще́ние для посто́я; **be in ~s** быть на посто́е; **every bullet has its ~** (*prov.*) пу́ля вино́вного сы́щет. **3.** (*job*) ме́сто.
v.t. (*assign to ~*) расквартиро́в|ывать, -а́ть; назн|ача́ть, -а́чить (*or* ста́вить, по-) на посто́й (**on s.o.:** к кому́-н.); (*provide ~*) предост|авля́ть, -а́вить посто́й +*d.*
billet-doux [ˌbɪlɪ'du:] *n.* бильеду́ (*nt. decl.*) любо́вное письмо́.
billiard|s ['bɪljədz] *n.* билья́рд.
cpds. **~-ball** *n.* бильа́рдный шар; **~-cue** *n.* кий; **~-marker** *n.* маркёр; **~-room** *n.* бильа́рдная; **~-table** *n.* бильа́рд.
billingsgate ['bɪlɪŋzˌgeɪt] *n.* база́рная ру́гань.
billion ['bɪljən] *n.* (*million millions*) биллио́н; (*thousand millions*) миллиа́рд.
billionaire [ˌbɪljə'neə(r)] *n.* миллиарде́р.
billow ['bɪləʊ] *n.* вал; (*poet., sea*) во́лны (*f. pl.*).
v.i. (*of sea*) вздыма́ться (*impf.*); (*of crowd*) волнова́ться (*impf.*); (*of flames etc.*) трепета́ть (*impf.*), колыха́ться (*impf.*).
billy ['bɪlɪ] *n.* (*also* **~can**) жестяно́й (похо́дный) котело́к.
billy-goat ['bɪlɪˌgəʊt] *n.* козёл.
biltong ['bɪltɒŋ] *n.* вя́леное мя́со.
bimbo ['bɪmbəʊ] *n.* фиф(очк)а.
bimetallic [ˌbaɪmɪ'tælɪk] *adj.* биметалли́ческий.
bimetallism [baɪ'metəˌlɪz(ə)m] *n.* биметалли́зм.
bimonthly [baɪ'mʌnθlɪ] *adj.* **1.** (*fortnightly*) выходя́щий (*и т.п.*) два ра́за в ме́сяц. **2.** (*two-monthly*) выходя́щий (*и т.п.*) раз в два ме́сяца.
adv. **1.** два ра́за в ме́сяц. **2.** раз в два ме́сяца.
bin [bɪn] *n.* (*for coal*) бу́нкер; (*for corn*) закро́м, ларь (*m.*); (*for ashes, dust*) му́сорное ведро́.
binary ['baɪnərɪ] *adj.* (*math.*) двои́чный.
bind [baɪnd] *n.* (*coll., nuisance*) ску́ка, доку́ка.
v.t. **1.** (*tie, fasten*) свя́з|ывать, -а́ть; **~ on one's skis** привя́з|ывать, -а́ть лы́жи; **~ up one's hair** подвя́з|ывать, -а́ть во́лосы; **~ up a wound** перевя́з|ывать, -а́ть ра́ну; **~ s.o. to a stake** привя́з|ывать, -а́ть кого́-н. к столбу́ (для сожже́ния); **~ a belt about o.s.** опоя́с|ываться, -аться ремнём; подвя́з|ываться, -а́ться по́ясом; **~ together** свя́з|ывать, -а́ть. **2.** (*secure*): **~ the edge of a carpet** закреп|ля́ть, -и́ть край ковра́. **3.** (*books etc.*) перепле|та́ть, -сти́; **~ two volumes into one** переплести́ (*pf.*) вме́сте два то́ма; **bound in cloth** в мате́рчатом переплёте. **4.** (*hold firmly*): **frost ~s the soil** моро́з ско́вывает зе́млю; **~ gravel with tar** скреп|ля́ть, -и́ть щё́бень дёгтем; **~ the bowels** закреп|ля́ть, -и́ть желу́док; **this food is ~ing** э́та еда́ крепи́т. **5.** (*oblige, exact promise*) обя́з|ывать, -а́ть; **~ s.o. to secrecy** обя́з|ывать, -а́ть кого́-н. храни́ть та́йну; **I am bound to say** я до́лжен сказа́ть; **I'll be bound** уве́рен; вот уви́дишь; **~ o.s.** обяза́ться (*pf.*); **~ over** (*leg.*) обя́з|ывать, -а́ть; **~ s.o. (as an) apprentice** отд|ава́ть, -а́ть кого́-н. учи́ться ремеслу́. *See also* **binding, bound**[3]
v.i.: **a sauce ~s** (*coheres*) со́ус густе́ет; **cement ~s** (*hardens*) цеме́нт затвердева́ет.
cpd. **~weed** *n.* вьюно́к.
binder ['baɪndə(r)] *n.* **1.** (*book ~*) переплётчик. **2.** (*substance*) свя́зывающее вещество́. **3.** (*machine*) свя́зывающее приспособле́ние. **4.** (*cover for magazines etc.*) па́пка.
binding ['baɪndɪŋ] *n.* (*of book*) переплёт; (*braid etc.*) обши́вка.
adj. обяза́тельный; обя́зывающий; име́ющий обяза́тельную си́лу; **make it ~ on s.o. to do sth.** обя́з|ывать, -а́ть кого́-н. сде́лать что-н.
binge [bɪndʒ] *n.* (*sl.*) кутёж; пья́нка; **go on the ~** закути́ть, запи́ть (*both pf.*).
bingo ['bɪŋgəʊ] *n.* лото́ (*indecl.*).
binnacle ['bɪnək(ə)l] *n.* накто́уз.
binoculars [bɪ'nɒkjʊləz] *n.* бино́кль (*m.*).
binomial [baɪ'nəʊmɪəl] *adj.* двучле́нный, биномиа́льный; **the ~ theorem** бино́м Нью́тона.
biochemical [ˌbaɪəʊ'kemɪk(ə)l] *adj.* биохими́ческий.
biochemist [ˌbaɪəʊ'kemɪst] *n.* биохи́мик.
biochemistry [ˌbaɪəʊ'kemɪstrɪ] *n.* биохи́мия.
biocide ['baɪəʊsaɪd] *n.* биоци́д.
biodegradable [ˌbaɪəʊdɪ'greɪdəb(ə)l] *adj.* подве́рженный биологи́ческому разложе́нию.
bioengineering [ˌbaɪəʊˌendʒɪ'nɪərɪŋ] *n.* биоинжене́рия.
bioenvironmental [ˌbaɪəʊenvaɪərən'məntəl] *adj.* биоэкологи́ческий.
biographer [baɪ'ɒgrəfə(r)] *n.* био́граф.
biographic(al) [ˌbaɪə'græfɪk(ə)l] *adj.* биографи́ческий.
biography [baɪ'ɒgrəfɪ] *n.* биогра́фия.
biological [ˌbaɪə'lɒdʒɪk(ə)l] *adj.* биологи́ческий; **~ warfare** бактериологи́ческая война́.
biologist [baɪ'ɒlədʒɪst] *n.* био́лог.
biology [baɪ'ɒlədʒɪ] *n.* биоло́гия.
biomedical [ˌbaɪəʊ'medɪk(ə)l] *adj.*: **~ research** биомедици́нские иссле́дования.
bionic [baɪ'ɒnɪk] *adj.* биони́ческий.
biophysical [ˌbaɪəʊ'fɪzɪkəl] *adj.* биофизи́ческий.
biophysicist [ˌbaɪəʊ'fɪzɪsɪst] *n.* биофи́зик.
biophysics [ˌbaɪəʊ'fɪzɪks] *n.* биофи́зика.
biopsy ['baɪɒpsɪ] *n.* биопси́я.
bioresources ['baɪɒrɪˌsɔ:sɪs] *n.* биоресу́рс|ы, (*pl., g.* -ов).
biorhythm ['baɪəʊrɪð(ə)m] *n.* биори́тм.
bioscience ['baɪəʊˌsaɪəns] *n.* бионау́ки.
biosphere ['baɪəʊˌsfɪə(r)] *n.* биосфе́ра.
biotechnology [ˌbaɪəʊtek'nɒlədʒɪ] *n.* биотехноло́гия.
bipartisan [ˌbaɪpɑ:tɪ'zæn, baɪ'pɑ:tɪz(ə)n] *adj.* двухпарти́йный.
bipartite [baɪ'pɑ:taɪt] *adj.* (*divided into two parts*) состоя́щий из двух часте́й; (*shared by two parties*) двусторо́нний.
biped ['baɪped] *n.* двуно́гое.
biplane ['baɪpleɪn] *n.* биплА́н.
bipolar [baɪ'pəʊlə(r)] *adj.*: **a ~ world** мир, разделённый на два ла́геря.

bipolarity [ˈbaɪpəʊˈlærɪtɪ] *n.* (*of world politics*) разделе́ние ми́ра на два ла́геря.

birch [bɜːtʃ] *n.* **1.** (*tree*) берёза; (*attr.*) берёзовый. **2.** (*rod*) ро́зга.

v.t. сечь, вы́-.

bird [bɜːd] *n.* **1.** пти́ца; **~ of prey** хи́щная пти́ца; **~ of passage** перелётная пти́ца; **game ~** дичь; **hen ~** са́мка; **~ life** пти́чий мир; **~ of paradise** ра́йская пти́ца; **~ dog** (*US*) соба́ка для охо́ты на птиц; **~'s eye view** вид с (высоты́) пти́чьего полёта; о́бщая перспекти́ва; **the ~ has flown** улете́ла пти́чка; **a ~ in the hand is worth two in the bush** лу́чше сини́ца в руки́, чем жура́вль в не́бе; **~s of a feather flock together** рыба́к рыбака́ ви́дит издалека́; **kill two ~s with one stone** уби́ть (*pf.*) двух за́йцев одни́м уда́ром; **the early ~ catches the worm** кто ра́но встаёт, тому́ Бог подаёт; **a little ~ told me** ≃ слу́хом земля́ по́лнится; **he is too old a ~ to be caught with chaff** ≃ стре́ляного воробья́ на мяки́не не проведёшь; **it's an ill ~ that fouls its own nest** то́лько дурна́я пти́ца га́дит в со́бственном гнезде́; **an early ~** ра́нняя пта́шка; **night ~** (*fig.*) ночно́й гуля́ка; **give an actor the ~** (*sl.*) освиста́ть (*pf.*) актёра. **2.** (*of pers.*): **he's a queer ~** он стра́нный тип; он чуда́к; **he's a wise old ~** он стре́ляный воробе́й; он тёртый кала́ч. **3.** (*sl., girl*) де́вка.

cpds. **~-brain** *n.* (*fig.*) кури́ные мо́зги (*m. pl.*); **~-cage** *n.* кле́тка для птиц; **~-call** *n.* пти́чий крик; **~-fancier** *n.* люби́тель (*m.*) птиц; **~-lime** *n.* пти́чий клей; **~-seed** *n.* пти́чий корм; **~'s nest** *n.* пти́чье гнездо́; **~'s nest soup** суп из ла́сточкиных гнёзд; **go ~'s nesting** охо́титься (*impf.*) за пти́чьими гнёздами; **~-table** *n.* корму́шка для птиц; **~-watcher** *n.* орнито́лог-люби́тель (*m.*).

Biro [ˈbaɪərəʊ] *n.* (*propr.*) ша́риковая ру́чка, ша́рик.

birth [bɜːθ] *n.* **1.** рожде́ние; **he weighed 7lbs. at ~** он ве́сил 7 фу́нтов при рожде́нии; **give ~ to** роди́ть (*impf., pf.*), рожа́ть (*impf.*); (*fig.*) произвести́ (*pf.*) на свет; породи́ть (*pf.*); **premature ~** преждевре́менные ро́ды (*pl., g.* -ов); **since ~** с рожде́ния; о́т роду; **six kittens at a ~** шесть котя́т в око́те; **an Englishman by ~** англича́нин по происхожде́нию; **still ~** рожде́ние мёртвого ребёнка; **there are more ~s than deaths** рожда́емость превыша́ет сме́ртность; **~ certificate** свиде́тельство о рожде́нии; **~ control** регули́рование рожда́емости; (*contraception*) противозача́точные ме́ры (*f. pl.*). **2.** (*descent*): **of noble ~** благоро́дного происхожде́ния. **3.** (*fig.*): **~ of an idea** зарожде́ние мы́сли/иде́и; **new ~** второ́е рожде́ние; **the revolt was crushed at ~** восста́ние бы́ло заду́шено в заро́дыше.

cpds. **~day** *n.* день рожде́ния; рожде́ние; **~day present** пода́рок ко дню рожде́ния; **~day cake** ≃ имени́нный пиро́г; **in one's ~day suit** (*joc.*) в чём мать родила́; **~mark** *n.* роди́мое пятно́; **~place** *n.* ме́сто рожде́ния; ро́дина; **~rate** *n.* рожда́емость; **a fall in the ~rate** паде́ние рожда́емости; **~right** *n.* пра́во первоостро́дства; пра́во по рожде́нию.

Biscay [ˈbɪskeɪ] *n.*: **Bay of ~** Биска́йский зали́в.

biscuit [ˈbɪskɪt] *n.* **1.** пече́нье; **ship's ~** гале́та; **take the ~** (*coll.*) превосходи́ть (*impf.*) всё. **2.** (*porcelain*) бискви́т. **3.** (*attr., of colour*) све́тло-кори́чневый.

bisect [baɪˈsekt] *v.t.* дели́ть, раз- попола́м.

bisection [baɪˈsekʃ(ə)n] *n.* деле́ние попола́м.

bisector [baɪˈsektə(r)] *n.* биссектри́са.

bisexual [baɪˈseksjʊəl] *adj.* (*having organs of both sexes*) двупо́лый, гермафроди́тный; (*attracted by both sexes*) бисексуа́льный.

bishop [ˈbɪʃəp] *n.* (*eccl.*) епи́скоп; (*chess*) слон, (*coll.*) офице́р.

bishopric [ˈbɪʃəprɪk] *n.* (*office*) епи́скопство; (*diocese*) епа́рхия.

bismuth [ˈbɪzməθ] *n.* ви́смут.

bison [ˈbaɪs(ə)n] *n.* бизо́н.

bisque [bɪsk] *n.* (*cul.*) ра́ковый суп.

bissextile [bɪˈsekstaɪl] *adj.* високо́сный.

bistoury [ˈbɪstərɪ] *n.* бистури́ (*nt. indecl.*).

bistre [ˈbɪstə(r)] *n.* бистр; (*attr., of colour*) тёмно-кори́чневый.

bistro [ˈbiːstrəʊ] *n.* бистро́ (*indecl.*).

bit[1] [bɪt] *n.* **1.** кусо́к, кусо́чек; **a ~ of paper** листо́к бума́ги; **a nice ~ of furniture** краси́вый предме́т ме́бели; **come to ~s** развали́ться (*pf.*) на куски́; **eat up every ~** съесть (*pf.*) всё подчисту́ю (*or* без оста́тка); **that's only a ~ of what he spends** э́то лишь ма́лая то́лика того́, что он тра́тит. **2.** (*abstr. uses*): **a ~ of news** но́вость; **a ~ of advice** сове́т; **I am a ~ late** я немно́го опозда́л; **not a ~ of it!** ниско́лько!; ничу́ть!; ничу́ть не быва́ло!; **wait a ~!** подожди́те чуть-чуть!; **a good ~ older** значи́тельно ста́рше; **~ by ~** ма́ло-пома́лу; **not a ~ of use** никако́й по́льзы, никако́го про́ку; **every ~ as good** так же хоро́ш; ниско́лько не ху́же; **a ~ of a coward** трусова́тый; **a nasty ~ of work** (*pers.*) проти́вная осо́ба; **do one's ~** внести́ (*pf.*) свою́ ле́пту; **it will take a ~ of doing** э́то бу́дет нелегко́ сде́лать; **~ part** (*theatr.*) ма́ленькая роль; **~ player** (*theatr.*) актёр на эпизоди́ческих роля́х.

bit[2] [bɪt] *n.* (*comput.*) бит.

cpd. **~-mapped** *adj.* (*comput.*) би́товый.

bit[3] [bɪt] *n.* **1.** (*of drill*) коро́нка; сверло́, бур; (*of plane*) ле́звие. **2.** (*of bridle*) уд|ила́ (*pl., g.* -и́л); мундшту́к; **champ the ~** (*of horse*) грызть (*impf.*) удила́; **take the ~ between one's teeth** (*fig.*) закуси́ть (*pf.*) удила́.

bitch [bɪtʃ] *n.* **1.** (*of dog*) су́ка; (*of fox*) лиси́ца; (*of wolf*) волчи́ца. **2.** (*coll., spiteful woman*) сте́рва; (*promiscuous woman*) су́ка.

v.t. (*also* **~ up**) па́костить, ис- (*coll.*).

v.i. (*sl.*) стона́ть, ныть (*both impf.*).

bitchiness [ˈbɪtʃɪnɪs] *n.* (*coll.*) стерво́зность.

bitchy [ˈbɪtʃɪ] *adj.* (*coll.*) стерво́зный.

bite [baɪt] *n.* **1.** (*act of biting*) куса́ние; **eat sth. at one ~** съесть (*pf.*) что-н. зара́з. **2.** (*mouthful*): **I haven't had a ~ to eat** у меня́ куска́ во рту́ не́ было; **have a ~ of food** перекуси́ть (*pf.*), закуси́ть (*pf.*). **3.** (*wound caused by biting*) уку́с; **snake ~** змеи́ный уку́с. **4.** (*of fish*) клёв; **I have been fishing all day and haven't had a ~** весь день сижу́, а ры́ба не клюёт. **5.** (*grip, hold*) захва́тывание, зажа́тие; **this screw has a good ~** э́тот болт кре́пит надёжно. **6.** (*sharpness, pungency*): **there is a ~ in the air** моро́з пощи́пывает. **7.** (*sl., blackmail*): **put the ~ on s.o.** взять (*pf.*) кого́-н. за гло́тку.

v.t. **1.** куса́ть, укуси́ть; **he bit the apple** он откуси́л я́блоко; **the dog bit him in the leg** соба́ка укуси́ла его́ за́ ногу; **a piece was bitten from the apple** я́блоко бы́ло надку́сано; **he was bitten by midges** его́ искуса́ли комары́; **mustard ~s the tongue** горчи́ца куса́ется (*or* жжёт язы́к); **the sword bit him to the bone** меч прошёл до са́мой ко́сти. **2.** (*fig.*): **what's biting him?** что его́ гло́жет?; **~ off more than one can chew** ≃ де́ло не по плечу́; **~ s.o.'s head off** откуси́ть (*pf.*) кому́-н. го́лову; **~ back a remark** прикуси́ть (*pf.*) язы́к; **he was bitten by this craze** он зарази́лся э́тим увлече́нием; **we have sth. to ~ on** есть за что уцепи́ться; **~ the dust** быть пове́рженным; **once bitten, twice shy** пу́ганая воро́на куста́ бои́тся; обжёгшись на молоке́, бу́дешь дуть на́ воду.

v.i.: **does your dog ~?** ва́ша соба́ка куса́ется?; **the fish won't ~** ры́ба не клюёт; **the wheels won't ~ on this surface** сцепле́ние колёс с э́той пове́рхностью недоста́точно; **I offered him £50 but he wouldn't ~** я предложи́л ему́ 50 фу́нтов, но он на э́то не клю́нул; **~ into sth.** вгр|ыза́ться, -ы́зться во что-н.; **acid ~s into metal** кислота́ разъеда́ет мета́лл.

biter [ˈbaɪtə(r)] *n.* (*pers.*) куса́ющий; (*animal*) куса́ка (*c.g.*); **the ~ bit** попа́лся, кото́рый куса́лся.

biting [ˈbaɪtɪŋ] *adj.* куса́ющий; (*of cold*) ре́зкий; (*of wind*) ре́зкий, прони́зывающий; (*of satire*) е́дкий, язви́тельный.

bitter [ˈbɪtə(r)] *n.* **1.** го́речь; **we must take the ~ with the sweet** ≃ в жи́зни вся́кое быва́ет. **2.** (*pl., drink*) го́рькая насто́йка.

adj. (*lit., fig.*) го́рький; **a ~ wind** ре́зкий ве́тер; **~ conflict** о́стрый конфли́кт; **~ enemy** зле́йший/закля́тый враг; **to the ~ end** до са́мого конца́.

adv.: **~ cold** ужа́сно хо́лодно.

cpd. **~-sweet** *adj.* горькова́то-сла́дкий, сла́достно-го́рький.

bittern [ˈbɪt(ə)n] *n.* выпь.

bitty [ˈbɪtɪ] *adj.* (*coll.*) разбро́санный, раздро́бленный, нецéльный.
bitumen [ˈbɪtjʊmɪn] *n.* биту́м; асфа́льт.
bituminous [bɪˈtju:mɪnəs] *adj.* биту́мный, асфа́льтовый.
bivalve [ˈbaɪvælv] *n.* двуство́рчатый моллю́ск.
bivouac [ˈbɪvʊˌæk] *n.* бива́к.
v.i. распол|ага́ться, -ожи́ться бивако́м.
bi-weekly [baɪˈwi:klɪ] *adj.* **1.** (*fortnightly*) двухнеде́льный; выходя́щий (*и т.п.*) ра́з в две неде́ли. **2.** (*twice a week*) выходя́щий (*и т.п.*) два ра́за в неде́лю.
adv. **1.** раз в две неде́ли. **2.** два ра́за в неде́лю.
bi-yearly [baɪˈjɪəlɪ] *adj.* **1.** (*every two years*) выходя́щий (*и т.п.*) раз в два го́да. **2.** (*every six months*) выходя́щий (*и т.п.*) два ра́за в год.
adv. **1.** раз в два го́да. **2.** два ра́за в год.
biz [bɪz] (*sl.*) = **business**
bizarre [bɪˈzɑ:(r)] *adj.* чудно́й, дико́винный.
bizarrerie [bɪˈzɑ:rərɪ] *n.* необы́чность, стра́нность.
blab [blæb] *v.t.* (*also* ~ **out**) выба́лтывать, вы́болтать; разб|а́лтывать, -олта́ть.
v.i. болта́ть (*impf.*)
blabber [ˈblæbə(r)] *n.* болту́н; пустоме́ля (*c.g.*).
black [blæk] *n.* **1.** (*colour*) чернота́, чёрное; **dress in** ~ одева́ться (*impf.*) в чёрное; **wear** ~ **for s.o.** носи́ть (*indet.*) тра́ур по кому́-н.; **be in the** ~ вести́ де́ло с при́былью. **2.** (*paint*): **give the door a coat of** ~ покры́ть (*pf.*) дверь чёрной кра́ской. **3.** (*soot etc.*): **you have some** ~ **on your sleeve** у вас что-то чёрное на рукаве́. **4.** (*negro*) чёрный, чернoко́жий; негр, (*fem.*) -итя́нка. **5.** (*horse*) ворона́я. **6.** (*fig.*): **two** ~**s don't make a white** злом зла не попра́вишь; **put up a** ~ (*sl.*) опозо́риться (*pf.*); **swear** ~ **is white** называ́ть (*impf.*) чёрное бе́лым.
adj. **1.** (*colour*) чёрный; **as** ~ **as ink** (*etc.*) чёрный как смоль; **a** ~ **eye** подби́тый глаз. **2.** (*fig.*): **a** ~ **deed** чёрное де́ло; ~ **ingratitude** чёрная неблагода́рность; **he is not so** ~ **as he is painted** он не так плох, как его́ изобража́ют; **a** ~ **heart** чёрная душа́; ~ **despair** безысхо́дное отча́яние; ~ **tidings** мра́чные ве́сти. **3.** (*negro*) чёрный; ~ **man** чёрный, чернoко́жий; **B**~ **Power** «Власть чёрным». **4.** (*var.*): ~ **and tan** чёрно-ры́жий; ~ **and white** чёрно-бе́лый; **in** ~ **and white** (*in writing*) чёрным по бе́лому; **he beat him** ~ **and blue** он изби́л его́ до полусме́рти; ~ **art** чёрная ма́гия; **I am in his** ~ **books** я у него́ на плохо́м счету́; ~ **bread** чёрный/ржано́й хлеб; ~ **coffee** чёрный ко́фе; ~ **earth** чернозём; **B**~ **Forest** Шва́рцвальд; ~ **frost** моро́з без и́нея; треску́чий моро́з; ~ **hole** (*astron.*) чёрная дыра́; ~ **ice** гололе́дица; ~ **Maria** чёрный во́рон (*coll.*); **it is a** ~ **mark against him** э́то его́ поро́чит; ~ **economy** тенева́я эконо́мика; ~ **market** чёрный ры́нок; **B**~ **Sea** Чёрное мо́ре.
v.t. **1.** (*paint black*) кра́сить (*impf.*) в чёрное; (*boots etc.*) ва́ксить, на-; ~ **one's face** кра́сить, вы́- лицо́ чёрным; ~ **s.o.'s eye** подб|ива́ть, -и́ть кому́-н. глаз. **2.** (*boycott*) бойкоти́ровать (*impf., pf.*), внести́ в чёрный спи́сок. **3.:** ~ **out** (*texi*) выма́рывать, вы́марать; (*light*) затемн|я́ть, -и́ть.
v.i.: ~ **out** (*lose consciousness*) теря́ть, по- созна́ние; **he** ~**ed out** на него́ нашло́ затме́ние.
cpds. ~**ball** *v.t.* забаллоти́ровать (*pf.*); ~**-beetle** *n.* чёрный тарака́н; ~**berry** *n.* ежеви́ка (*collect*); я́года ежеви́ки; ~**bird** *n.* чёрный дрозд; ~**board** *n.* кла́ссная доска́; ~**cap** *n.* черноголо́вка; ~**cock** *n.* те́терев; ~**currant** *n.* чёрная сморо́дина; ~**-eyed** *adj.* черногла́зый; (*poet.*) черно́окий; ~**-faced** *adj.* черноли́цый; ~**fellow** *n.* австрали́йский абориге́н; ~**guard** *n.* негодя́й; *v.t.* об|зыва́ть, -озва́ть негодя́ем; оскорб|ля́ть, -и́ть; ~**guardly** *adj.* по́длый; ~**head** *n.* у́горь (*m.*); ~**-hearted** *adj.* зло́бный; ~**jack** *n.* (*US, bludgeon*) дуби́нка; ~**-lead** *n.* графи́т; ~**leg** *n.* штрейкбре́хер; ~**-letter** *n.* готи́ческий шрифт; ~**-list** *v.t.* вн|оси́ть, -ести́ в чёрный спи́сок; ~**mail** *n.* шанта́ж, вымога́тельство; *v.t.* шантажи́ровать (*impf.*); ~**mailer** *n.* шантажи́ст, вымога́тель (*m.*); ~**-marketeer** *n.* спекуля́нт, фарцо́вщик; ~**out** *n.* (*in wartime*) затемне́ние; (*electricity failure*) вре́менное отсу́тствие электри́ческого освеще́ния; (*loss of memory*) прова́л па́мяти; затме́ние; (*loss of consciousness or awareness*) поте́ря созна́ния; *v.t.* затемн|я́ть, -и́ть; ~**shirt** *n.* чернoруба́шечник; ~**smith** *n.* кузне́ц; ~**thorn** *n.* (*plant*) тёрн.
blackamoor [ˈblækəˌmʊə(r), -ˌmɔ:(r)] *n.* (*arch.*) ара́п.
blacken [ˈblækən] *v.t.* **1.** (*paint black*) кра́сить, по- в чёрное; (*boots etc.*) ва́ксить, на. **2.** (*soil, dirty*) грязни́ть, за-. **3.** (*reputation*) черни́ть, о-.
v.i. черне́ть, по-.
blacking [ˈblækɪŋ] *n.* (*for boots etc.*) ва́кса, чёрный крем для о́буви.
blackish [ˈblækɪʃ] *adj.* темнова́тый.
blackness [ˈblæknɪs] *n.* чернота́; (*darkness*) темнота́; (*gloominess*) мра́чность.
bladder [ˈblædə(r)] *n.* (*anat., bot.*) пузы́рь (*m.*); (*in ball etc.*) ка́мера; (*in seaweed*) пузырёк.
cpd. ~**wort** *n.* пузырча́тка.
blade [bleɪd] *n.* **1.** (*of knife etc.*) ле́звие. **2.** (*of oar etc.*) ло́пасть, лопа́тка; (*of fan*) крыло́. **3.** (*of grass etc.*) были́нка, стебелёк; **the grass is in the** ~ трава́ зеленéет. **4.** (*fig., sword*) клино́к.
blah [blɑ:] *n.* (*sl.*) пустозво́нство, разглаго́льствование.
blamable [ˈbleɪməb(ə)l] *adj.* предосуди́тельный.
blame [bleɪm] *n.* (*censure*) порица́ние; осужде́ние; (*fault*) вина́; **his conduct was free from** ~ его́ поведе́ние бы́ло безупре́чным; **the** ~ **is mine** я винова́т; **lay, put the** ~ **on s.o.** возложи́ть (*pf.*) вину́ на кого́-н.; **bear, take the** ~ приня́ть (*pf.*) на себя́ вину́/отве́тственность; **shift the** ~ **to s.o. else** свали́ть (*pf.*) вину́ на друго́го; **where does the** ~ **lie?** кто винова́т?
v.t. порица́ть (*impf.*); вини́ть (*impf.*); осу|жда́ть, -ди́ть (*кого за что*); **he was** ~**d for the mistake** вину́ за оши́бку возложи́ли на него́; **he cannot be** ~**d for it** он не винова́т в э́том; **he** ~**d himself for his stupidity** он вини́л/упрека́л себя́ за глу́пость; **he has only himself to** ~ он мо́жет вини́ть то́лько себя́; **I am in no way to** ~ мне не́ в чем упрекну́ть себя́; **he is entirely to** ~ э́то по́лностью его́ вина́; ~ **sth. on s.o.** взва́л|ивать, -и́ть вину́ за что-н. на кого́-н.
cpds. ~**worthiness** *n.* предосуди́тельность; ~**worthy** *adj.* предосуди́тельный; заслу́живающий порица́ния/осужде́ния.
blameless [ˈbleɪmlɪs] *adj.* безупре́чный; неви́нный.
blanch [blɑ:ntʃ] *v.t.* бели́ть, вы́-; ~**ed almonds** бланширо́ванный минда́ль.
v.i. (*of hair etc.*) обесцве́|чиваться, -титься; (*of pers., go pale*) беле́ть, по-.
blancmange [bləˈmɒndʒ] *n.* бланманже́ (*indecl.*).
bland [blænd] *adj.* мя́гкий; (*of manner: soothing*) обходи́тельный; (*nonchalant*) невозмути́мый.
blandish [ˈblændɪʃ] *v.t.* обха́живать (*impf.*); уле|ща́ть, -сти́ть.
blandishment [ˈblændɪʃmənt] *n.* (*usu. pl.*) обха́живание, лесть.
blank [blæŋk] *n.* **1.** (*empty space*) про́пуск; (*fig.*) **fill in the** ~**s in one's education** воспо́лнить (*pf.*) пробе́лы в своём образова́нии; **his death leaves a** ~ по́сле его́ сме́рти жизнь опусте́ла; **my mind is a** ~ **on this subject** у меня́ э́то вы́летело из головы́. **2.** (*in lottery*): **draw a** ~ вы́тянуть (*pf.*) пусто́й биле́т; (*fig.*) иска́ть (*impf.*) беспло́дно/напра́сно. **3.** (*unprinted sheet etc.*) незапеча́танная страни́ца. **4.** (*unstamped disk*) болва́нка. **5.** (*US, form*) бланк.
adj. **1.** (*empty*): **a** ~ **sheet of paper** пусто́й лист бума́ги; **a** ~ **cheque** незапо́лненный чек; (*fig.*) карт-бла́нш; **a** ~ **space** про́пуск; пусто́е ме́сто; ~ **cartridge** холосто́й патро́н. **2.** (*bare, plain*): **a** ~ **wall** глуха́я стена́; **we are up against a** ~ **wall** (*fig.*) мы упёрлись в глуху́ю сте́ну; **a** ~ **key** болва́нка ключа́; ~ **verse** бе́лый стих. **3.** (*fig.*): **my memory is** ~ ничего́ не по́мню; ~ **despair** по́лное отча́яние; **look** ~ (*of pers.*) вы́глядеть (*impf.*) растéрянным; **the future looks** ~ бу́дущее ничего́ не сули́т.
blanket [ˈblæŋkɪt] *n.* одея́ло; (*horse-cloth*) попо́на; ~ **of fog** пелена́ тума́на; ~ **of smoke** пелена́ ды́ма; **the hills lay under a** ~ **of snow** холмы́ бы́ли покры́ты сло́ем сне́га (*or* бы́ли под снегoвы́м покрыва́лом); **wet** ~ (*fig., of*

pers.) кисля́й; **born on the wrong side of the ~** (*coll.*) рождённый вне бра́ка, незаконнорождённый; **~ instructions** о́бщие указа́ния; **~ insurance policy** блок-по́лис.

v.t. (*cover*) оку́т|ывать, -ать; (*stifle, hush up*) зам|ина́ть, -я́ть.

blankety(-blank) [ˈblæŋkətɪˌblæŋk] *adj.* (*joc. expletive*) тако́й-сяко́й.

blankly [ˈblæŋklɪ] *adv.* (*without expression*) бессмы́сленно, ту́по; (*flatly*) реши́тельно, наотре́з.

blankness [ˈblæŋknɪs] *n.* пустота́, пробе́л; **the ~ of his countenance** отсу́тствие како́го бы то ни́ было выраже́ния на его́ лице́.

blare [bleə(r)] *n.* рёв.

v.t.: **~ out** труби́ть, про-; **the band ~d out a waltz** орке́стр гря́нул вальс.

v.i. труби́ть, про-; реве́ть (*impf.*); **the fanfare ~d forth** гря́нули фанфа́ры.

blarney [ˈblɑːnɪ] *n.* загова́ривание зубо́в; **he has kissed the B~ stone** он здо́рово уме́ет зу́бы загова́ривать.

v.t. & i. загов|а́ривать, -ори́ть зу́бы (*кому*).

blasé [ˈblɑːzeɪ] *adj.* пресы́щенный (жи́знью).

blaspheme [blæsˈfiːm] *v.t.* (*revile*) поноси́ть (*impf.*), хули́ть (*impf.*).

v.i. богоху́льствовать (*impf.*), богоху́льничать (*impf.*).

blasphemer [blæsˈfiːmə(r)] *n.* богоху́льник.

blasphemous [ˈblæsfiməs] *adj.* богоху́льный.

blasphemy [ˈblæsfəmɪ] *n.* богоху́льство.

blast [blɑːst] *n.* **1.**: **~ of wind** поры́в ве́тра; **~ of hot air** волна́ горя́чего во́здуха. **2.** (*from explosion*) взрыв; **~ wave** взрывна́я волна́. **3.**: **at full ~** (*fig.*) в по́лном разга́ре; по́лным хо́дом. **4.** (*of an instrument*): **~ on a whistle** свисто́к; **give three ~s on the horn** три́жды протруби́ть (*pf.*) в рог. **5.** (*reprimand*) нахлобу́чка, нагоня́й (*coll.*).

v.t. **1.** (*explode rocks etc.*) вз|рыва́ть, -орва́ть; **~ out a new course for the stream** взры́вом проложи́ть (*pf.*) но́вое ру́сло для пото́ка. **2.** (*shrivel*): **frost ~ed the plants** моро́з поби́л расте́ния; (*hopes*) разру́шить (*pf.*). **3.** (*defeat*) разби́ть (*pf.*). **4.** (*curse*): **~ it!** прокля́тие!; пропади́ всё про́падом; **~ you!** чтоб тебя́ разорва́ло!; чтоб ты ло́пнул!

v.i.: **he ~ed away at the system** он проклина́л/поноси́л систе́му; **~ off** (*rocketry*) взлет|а́ть, -е́ть; стартова́ть (*impf., pf.*).

cpds. **~-furnace** *n.* до́мна, до́менная печь; **~-off** *n.* взлёт; моме́нт ста́рта; отры́в от пусково́й устано́вки.

blasted [ˈblɑːstɪd] *adj.* **1.**: **~ heath** го́лая пу́стошь. **2.** (*cursed*) прокля́тый, окая́нный.

blasting [ˈblɑːstɪŋ] *n.* (*of rocks etc.*) подрывны́е рабо́ты (*f. pl.*).

blastoderm [ˈblæstəʊˌdɜːm] *n.* заро́дышевая оболо́чка.

blatancy [ˈbleɪt(ə)nsɪ] *n.* крикли́вость; беззасте́нчивость, бессты́дство.

blatant [ˈbleɪt(ə)nt] *adj.* крикли́вый; вульга́рный; бессты́дный; (*flagrant*) я́вный, вопию́щий.

blather [ˈblæðə(r)] = **blether**

blatherskite [ˈblæðəˌskaɪt] *n.* хвасту́н.

blaz|e[1] [bleɪz] *n.* **1.** (*of fire*) пла́мя (*nt.*); **burst into a ~e** запыла́ть (*pf.*). **2.** (*of colour, light*) я́ркость; **the garden was a ~e of colour** сад пыла́л я́ркими кра́сками. **3.** (*conflagration*) пожа́р. **4.** (*fig.*): **~e of publicity** шу́мная рекла́ма; **~e of anger** вспы́шка гне́ва. **5.** (*expletive*): **go to ~es** иди́/убира́йся к чёрту/дья́волу!; **what the ~es do you want?** како́го чёрта вам на́до?; **run like ~es** нести́сь, по- (*det.*) сломя́ го́лову.

v.t.: **~e the news abroad** раструби́ть (*impf.*) но́вость.

v.i.: **a fire was ~ing in the hearth** в ками́не пыла́л ого́нь; **the building was ~ing** зда́ние полыха́ло; **he was ~ing with anger** он пыла́л гне́вом; **he was ~ing with decorations** он сверка́л награ́дами.

with advs.: **~e away** *v.i.* (*with rifle etc.*) вести́ (*det.*) ого́нь, (*coll.*) пали́ть (*impf.*); (*work vigorously*) рабо́тать (*impf.*) вовсю́, (*coll.*) жа́рить (*impf.*); **~e up** *v.i.* (*lit., fig.*) всп|ы́хивать, -ы́хнуть; **he ~ed up at her suggestion** он так и взорва́лся от её предложе́ния.

blaze[2] [bleɪz] *n.* (*mark on horse*) звёздочка; (*on tree*) ме́тка.

v.t.: **~ a trail** про|кла́дывать, -ложи́ть путь.

blazer [ˈbleɪzə(r)] *n.* ≃ ку́ртка, пиджа́к, бле́йзер.

blazing [ˈbleɪzɪŋ] *adj.* **1.** (*of fire*) пыла́ющий. **2.** (*of light*) сверка́ющий, сия́ющий. **3.** (*hunting*): **~ scent** горя́чий след. **4.**: **a ~ indiscretion** вопию́щая беста́ктность; **he was in a ~ fury** он пыла́л я́ростью. **5.** (*coll., expletive*): **what's the ~ hurry?** како́го чёрта торопи́ться?; что за спе́шка, чёрт побери́?

blazon [ˈbleɪz(ə)n] *n.* (*her.*) герб; описа́ние ге́рба.

v.t. (*her., inscribe with arms*) укр|аша́ть, -а́сить геральди́ческими зна́ками; (*praise*) просл|авля́ть, -а́вить; восхвал|я́ть, -и́ть.

blazonry [ˈbleɪzənrɪ] *n.* (*her.*) гера́льдика; геральди́ческие зна́ки (*m. pl.*); гербы́ (*m. pl.*); (*fig.*) украше́ния (*nt. pl.*).

bleach [bliːtʃ] *n.* (*~ing agent*) отбе́льное/отбе́ливающее вещество́; (*chloride of lime*) хло́рная и́звесть.

v.t. бели́ть (*impf.*); отбе́л|ивать, -и́ть; **~ing powder** бели́льная и́звесть; (*of hair*) обесцве́|чивать, -тить; **the sun ~ed the curtains** занаве́ски вы́горели на со́лнце.

v.i. беле́ть (*impf.*).

bleacher [ˈbliːtʃə(r)] *n.* отбе́льщ|ик (*fem.* -ица); (*machine*) бели́льный чан.

bleak[1] [bliːk] *n.* (*zool.*) укле́йка.

bleak[2] [bliːk] *adj.* уны́лый, безра́достный, тосkли́вый; (*gloomy*) мра́чный; **a ~ hillside** откры́тый ветра́м склон холма́.

bleakness [ˈbliːknɪs] *n.* уны́лость, тоскли́вость, мра́чность.

bleary [ˈblɪərɪ] *adj.* (*of eyes*) затума́ненный, му́тный; (*of outline*) сму́тный.

bleary-eyed [blɪərɪ] *adj.* с затума́ненными/му́тными глаза́ми.

bleat [bliːt] *n.* бле́яние, мыча́ние; (*coll., complaint*) нытьё.

v.t. & i. мыча́ть (*impf.*), бле́ять (*impf.*); **~ (out) a protest** промыча́ть (*pf.*) возраже́ние.

bleed [bliːd] *v.t.* пус|ка́ть, -ти́ть кровь +*d.*; **~ s.o. in the arm** пус|ка́ть, -ти́ть кому́-н. кровь из руки́; **~ s.o.** (*for money*) выка́чивать, вы́качать де́ньги из кого́-н.; об|ира́ть, -обра́ть кого́-н.; **~ s.o. white** (*fig.*) обескро́в|ливать -ить кого́-н.; **~ a tree** подта́чивать (*impf.*) де́рево.

v.i. (*of pers.*) ист|ека́ть, -е́чь кро́вью; (*of wound*) кровоточи́ть (*impf.*); **his nose is ~ing** у него́ кровь идёт но́сом; **he bled to death** он у́мер от поте́ри кро́ви; **my heart ~s for him** у меня́ се́рдце кро́вью облива́ется при мы́сли о нём.

bleeder [ˈbliːdə(r)] *n.* (*haemophiliac*) гемофи́лик; (*vulg., blighter*) тип, ти́пчик.

bleeding [ˈbliːdɪŋ] *n.* кровотече́ние (*from the nose*: и́з носу); (*blood-letting*) кровопуска́ние.

adj. кровото́чащий; истека́ющий кро́вью; (*fig.*): **with a ~ heart** с чу́вством жа́лости и скo̓рби; (*vulg., blasted*) прокля́тый, чёртов.

bleep [bliːp] *n.* блип.

blemish [ˈblemɪʃ] *n.* (*defect*) недоста́ток, изъя́н; (*stain*) пятно́; **his name is without ~** у него́ незапя́тнанная репута́ция.

v.t. пятна́ть, за; **~ a good piece of work** подпо́ртить (*pf.*) хоро́шую рабо́ту.

blench [blentʃ] *v.i.* уклон|я́ться, -и́ться (*от чего*); отступ|а́ть, -и́ть (*перед чем*).

blend [blend] *n.* смесь; (*of colours*) сочета́ние.

v.t. сме́ш|ивать, -а́ть; (*colours, ideas*) сочета́ть (*impf.*); **the two rivers ~ their waters** э́ти две реки́ слива́ются.

v.i. сме́ш|иваться, -а́ться; (*of colours, ideas*) сочета́ться (*impf.*); гармони́ровать (*impf.*); (*of sounds, waters*) слива́ться, -и́ться; **these teas do not ~ well** из э́тих двух сорто́в ча́я хоро́шей сме́си не получа́ется.

blender [ˈblendə(r)] *n.* (*cul.*) смеси́тель (*m.*), ми́ксер.

bless [bles] *v.t.* **1.** (*relig.*) благослов|ля́ть, -и́ть; **~ me!, ~ my soul!** Го́споди, поми́луй!; **he hasn't a penny to ~ himself with** у него́ нет ни гроша́ за душо́й; **(God) ~ you!** дай вам Бог здоро́вья; (*after sneeze*) бу́дьте здоро́вы!; **well I'm ~ed!** Бо́же мой!; Го́споди, поми́луй!; **I'm ~ed, blest if I know** ей-Бо́гу, не зна́ю; **~ o.s.** (*cross o.s.*) перекрести́ться (*pf.*); осен|я́ть, -и́ть себя́ кре́стным зна́мением. **2.** (*prosper, favour*): **he was ~ed with good health** Бог награди́л его́ здоро́вьем; **~ed are the poor in**

spirit блаже́нны ни́щие ду́хом; **Islands, Isles of the Blest** острова́ блаже́нных. **3.** (*praise, be thankful for*) благослов|ля́ть, -и́ть; **I ~ my (lucky) stars that ...** я благословля́ю судьбу́ за то, что...

blessed ['blesɪd, blest] *adj.* **1.** (*holy*) благослове́нный; **the B~ Virgin** Пресвята́я Де́ва, Богоро́дица; **of ~ memory** блаже́нной па́мяти. **2.** (*happy*) блаже́нный, благослове́нный. **3.** (*coll.*): **not a ~ drop of rain** ни еди́ной ка́пли дождя́.

blessedness ['blesɪdnɪs] *n.* блаже́нство; **single ~** (*joc.*) холоста́я жизнь.

blessing ['blesɪŋ] *n.* **1.** благослове́ние; **give, pronounce a ~ upon** благослов|ля́ть, -и́ть; **ask, say a ~** (*at meal*) произн|оси́ть, -ести́ засто́льную моли́тву; **with ~ of God** с Бо́жьего благослове́ния; **with official ~** с благослове́ния нача́льства. **2.: the ~s of civilization** блага́ цивилиза́ции; **it is a ~ in disguise** ≃ не́ было бы сча́стья, да несча́стье помогло́!; **what a ~ that he came!** како́е сча́стье, что он пришёл!

blether ['bleðə(r)] *n.* болтовня́, трепотня́, пустосло́вие.

v.i. (*also* **blather**) болта́ть (*impf.*), трепа́ться (*impf.*).

bletherer ['bleðərə(r)] *n.* трепа́ч, пустоме́ля (*c.g.*).

blight [blaɪt] *n.* **1.** (*disease*) головня́; ржа. **2.: it cast a ~ on her youth** э́то омрачи́ло её ю́ность; **what a ~ she is!** (*coll.*) кака́я она́ зану́да!

v.t. **1.** пора|жа́ть, -зи́ть ржой. **2.: ~ s.o.'s hopes** разр|уша́ть, -у́шить чьи-н. наде́жды; (*career, plans*) погуби́ть (*pf.*); (*enjoyment*) испо́ртить (*pf.*).

blighted ['blaɪtəd] *adj.* (*of plants*) поги́бший; поражённый ржой; (*of plans etc.*) поги́бший, погу́бленный; **~ affection** растóптанные чу́вства.

blighter ['blaɪtə(r)] *n.* (*coll., fellow*) па́рень (*m.*), тип.

blimey ['blaɪmɪ] *int.* (*vulg.*) чтоб мне провали́ться!; а чтоб тебя!

blind [blaɪnd] *n.* **1.** (*screen*) што́ра, ста́вень (*m.*); **Venetian ~** жалюзи́ (*nt. indecl.*); **shop ~** (*over pavement*) марки́за, тент. **2.** (*mil.*) дымова́я заве́са. **3.** (*pretext*) предло́г, отгово́рка; **his generosity is only a ~** его́ ще́дрость — то́лько ши́рма. **4.** (*coll., spree*) пья́нка.

adj. **1.** слепо́й; **the ~** (*as n.*) слепы́е, слепцы́ (*m. pl.*); **as ~ as a bat** слепа́я ку́рица; **~ in one eye** слепо́й на оди́н глаз; криво́й; **go ~, be struck ~** осле́пнуть (*pf.*); **~ spot** слепо́е пятно́; (*fig.*) пробе́л; **~ flying** слепо́й полёт; **~ man's buff** жму́р|ки (*pl., g.* -ок); **he is ~ to his opportunities** он не ви́дит свои́х возмо́жностей; **turn a ~ eye to sth.** закр|ыва́ть, -ы́ть глаза́ на что-н.; **get on s.o.'s ~ side** (*fig.*) нащу́п|ывать, -ать чью-н. слаби́нку. **2.** (*concealed*): **a ~ corner** непросма́тривающийся поворо́т; **a ~ date** (*US, coll.*) свида́ние с незнако́мым/незнако́мой. **3.** (*closed up*): **a ~ alley** (*lit., fig.*) тупи́к; **a ~-alley job** бесперспекти́вная рабо́та; **a ~ door** (*theatr.*) фальши́вая дверь. **4.: he didn't take a ~ bit of notice** (*coll.*) он э́то абсолю́тно проигнори́ровал.

adv.: **fly ~** лета́ть (*indet.*) по прибо́рам; **~ drunk** мертве́цки пья́ный; **sign a document ~** подпи́с|ывать, -а́ть докуме́нт не чита́я; **go it ~** де́йствовать (*impf.*) втёмную/вслепу́ю.

v.t. **1.** ослеп|ля́ть, -и́ть (*also fig.*); (*temporarily*) слепи́ть (*impf.*); **he was ~ed, went ~ in the left eye** он осле́п на ле́вый глаз. **2.** (*blindfold*) завя́з|ывать, -а́ть глаза́ +*d.* **3.** (*block, obstruct*) затемн|я́ть, -и́ть.

cpds. **~fold** *adj.* с завя́занными глаза́ми; *adv.* (*recklessly*) вслепу́ю; *v.t.* завя́з|ывать, -а́ть глаза́ +*d.*; **~worm** *n.* верете́ница, слепу́н.

blindly ['blaɪndlɪ] *adv.* (*gropingly*) о́щупью; (*recklessly*) сле́по.

blindness ['blaɪndnɪs] *n.* слепота́; (*fig.*) слепота́, ослепле́ние.

blink [blɪŋk] *n.* (*of eye*) морга́ние, мига́ние; (*of light*) мерца́ние; про́блеск.

v.t. & i. (*of pers.*) миг|а́ть, -ну́ть; морг|а́ть, -ну́ть; (*of light*) мерца́ть (*impf.*); **~ at** (*fig., ignore*) закр|ыва́ть, -ы́ть глаза́ на+*a.*

blinkers ['blɪŋkəz] *n.* шо́р|ы (*pl., g.* —) (*also fig.*); нагла́зники (*m. pl.*).

blip [blɪp] *n.* (*on screen*) отражённый и́мпульс.

bliss [blɪs] *n.* блаже́нство.

blissful ['blɪsfʊl] *adj.* блаже́нный.

blister ['blɪstə(r)] *n.* (*on skin*) волды́рь (*m.*); **~ gas** ко́жно-нары́вное отравля́ющее вещество́; (*on paint*) пузы́рь (*m.*); (*in metal*) ра́ковина.

v.t. вызыва́ть, вы́звать волдыри́/пузыри́ на+*p.*

v.i. покр|ыва́ться, -ы́ться волдыря́ми/пузыря́ми.

blithering ['blɪðərɪŋ] *adj.* (*coll.*): **a ~ idiot** зако́нченный идио́т.

blithe(some) ['blaɪð(səm)] *adj.* жизнера́достный, беспе́чный.

B. Litt. (*abbr. of* ***Bachelor of Letters***) бакала́вр литерату́ры.

blitz [blɪts] *n.* бомбёжка.

v.t. разбомби́ть (*pf.*).

blitzkrieg ['blɪtskri:g] *n.* блицкри́г; молниено́сная война́.

blizzard ['blɪzəd] *n.* бура́н, выо́га.

bloated ['bləʊtɪd] *adj.* (*swollen*) разду́тый, разду́вшийся; **he is ~ with pride** его́ распира́ет от го́рдости.

bloater ['bləʊtə(r)] *n.* копчёная сельдь.

blob [blɒb] *n.* (*small mass*) ка́пля; ша́рик; (*spot of colour*) кля́кса; (*coll., zero*) нуль (*m.*).

bloc [blɒk] *n.* блок.

block [blɒk] *n.* **1.** (*of wood*) чурба́н, коло́да; (*of stone, marble*) глы́ба; **~ of soap** бруcо́к мы́ла; **children's ~s** ку́бики (*m. pl.*). **2.** (*for execution*) пла́ха. **3.** (*of houses*) кварта́л; (*of shares, tickets etc.*) па́чка; **~ of flats** многокварти́рный дом. **4.** (*for hats*) болва́нка, болва́н. **5.** (*for lifting*: *also* **~ and tackle**) блок, лебёдка, полиспа́ст. **6.** (*typ.*) клише́ (*indecl.*) печа́тная фо́рма; **~ letters** печа́тные бу́квы. **7.: writing ~** блокно́т. **8.** (*obstruction*): **~ in a pipe** заку́порка/засоре́ние трубы́; **traffic ~** зато́р в движе́нии; про́бка; (*fig.*): **mental ~** у́мственное торможе́ние. **9.** (*stolid pers.*) бревно́. **10.: ~ voting** представи́тельное голосова́ние; **in ~** целико́м; в це́лом.

v.t. **1.** (*obstruct physically*): **roads ~ed by snow** доро́ги, занесённые сне́гом; **~ (up) an entrance** загор|а́живать, -оди́ть вход; **mud ~ed the pipe** грязь заби́ла трубу́; **the sink is ~ed** ра́ковина засори́лась; **~ s.o.'s way** прегра|жда́ть, -ди́ть кому́-н. путь; **~ a wheel** подкли́ни|вать, -ть колесо́. **2.** (*fig.*): **~ the enemy's plan** срыва́ть, сорва́ть пла́ны неприя́теля; **a ~ed account** блоки́рованный счёт. **3.** (*shape, e.g. a hat*) натя́|гивать, -ну́ть на болва́н. **4.: ~ in, out** (*sketch*) набр|а́сывать, -оса́ть.

cpds. **~buster** *n.* (*coll.*) бо́мба большо́го кали́бра; **~head** *n.* болва́н, тупи́ца (*c.g.*), о́лух; **~house** *n.* блокга́уз; **~-ship** *n.* кора́бль, блоки́рующий вход в порт.

blockade [blɒ'keɪd] *n.* блока́да; **raise a ~** снять (*pf.*) блока́ду; **run a ~** прорва́ть (*pf.*) блока́ду.

v.t. блоки́ровать (*impf., pf.*); подв|ерга́ть, -е́ргнуть блока́де.

cpd. **~-runner** *n.* блокадопрорыва́тель (*m.*).

blockish ['blɒkɪʃ] *adj.* тупо́й, тупоголо́вый.

bloke [bləʊk] *n.* (*coll.*) тип; па́рень (*m.*).

blond(e) [blɒnd] *n.* блонди́н (*fem.* -ка).

adj. белоку́рый, све́тлый.

blood [blʌd] *n.* **1.** кровь; **the ~ rushed to his head** кровь бро́силась/уда́рила ему́ в го́лову; **hands covered with ~** ру́ки в крови́; **sweat ~** рабо́тать (*impf.*) до крова́вого по́та; **taste ~** вку|ша́ть, -си́ть кро́ви; **drown a revolt in ~** топи́ть, по- восста́ние в крови́; **welter in one's ~** пла́вать (*indet.*) в лу́же кро́ви; **you cannot get ~ out of a stone** ≃ ка́менное се́рдце не разжа́лобишь. **2.** (*attr.*): **~ bank** до́норский пункт; **~ clot** сгу́сток кро́ви; тромб; **~ donor** до́нор; **~ feud** кро́вная месть; **~ group** гру́ппа кро́ви; **~ horse** чистокро́вная ло́шадь; **~ orange** королёк; **~ plasma** пла́зма; **~ pudding, ~ sausage** кровяна́я колбаса́; **~ sports** охо́та; **~ test** ана́лиз кро́ви; (*for paternity*) иссле́дование кро́ви; **~ transfusion** перелива́ние кро́ви; *see also cpds.* **3.** (*var. fig. uses*): **it made my ~ boil** э́то меня́ взбеси́ло; **his ~ ran cold** кровь сты́ла/леде́нела у него́ в жи́лах; **in cold ~** хладнокро́вно; **his ~ is up** он взбешён; **we need new ~** нам нужны́ но́вые си́лы; **there is bad ~ between them** они́ вражду́ют; **make bad ~ between people** поссо́рить (*pf.*) люде́й. **4.** (*lineage, kinship*): **they are of the same ~** они́ кро́вные ро́дственники; **blue ~** голуба́я кровь; **~ is thicker than water** кровь не води́ца; **prince of the ~** принц кро́ви;

allied by ~ свя́занные у́зами кро́ви. **5.** (*dandy*): **a young** ~ (*coll.*) молодо́й щёголь.

v.t. (*a hound*) приуч|а́ть -и́ть к кро́ви; (*a huntsman*) да|ва́ть, -ть (*кому*) вкуси́ть кро́ви.

cpds. **~-and-thunder** *adj.* (*story etc.*) по́лный у́жасов; **~-bath** *n.* крова́вая ба́ня; **~-brother** *n.* (*natural*) брат; (*by ceremony*) кро́вный брат, побрати́м; (*fig.*) собра́т, това́рищ; **~-brotherhood** *n.* кро́вное бра́тство; **~-count** *n.* ана́лиз кро́ви; **~curdling** *adj.* леденя́щий кровь; **a ~curdling sight** зре́лище, от кото́рого сты́нет кровь в жи́лах; **~-guilty** *adj.* пови́нный в уби́йстве (*or* в проли́тии кро́ви); **~-heat** *n.* температу́ра челове́ческого те́ла; **~hound** *n.* ище́йка; **~-letting** *n.* (*med.*) кровопуска́ние; (*bloodshed*) кровопроли́тие; **~-lust** *n.* жа́жда кро́ви; **~-poisoning** *n.* зараже́ние кро́ви; **~-pressure** *n.* кровяно́е давле́ние; **~-red** *adj.* кровавокра́сный; **~-relation** *n.* кро́вный ро́дственник; **~-relationship** *n.* кро́вное родство́; **~shed** *n.* кровопроли́тие; **~shot** *adj.* на́литый кро́вью; **~stain** *n.* крова́вое пятно́; **~stained** *adj.* запа́чканный кро́вью; **~stained hands** ру́ки в крови́; ру́ки, обагрённые кро́вью; **~stock** *n.* чистокро́вные ло́шади (*f. pl.*); **~stone** *n.* гелиотро́п, крова́вик; **~stream** *n.* ток кро́ви; **~sucker** *n.* (*insect*) пия́вка; (*fig.*) кровопи́йца (*c.g.*), кровосо́с; **~thirstiness** *n.* кровожа́дность; **~thirsty** *adj.* кровожа́дный; **~-vessel** *n.* кровено́сный сосу́д; **he burst a ~vessel** у него́ ло́пнул кровено́сный сосу́д; **~worm** *n.* кра́сный червь.

bloodily [ˈblʌdɪlɪ] *adv.* с проли́тием кро́ви.

bloodless [ˈblʌdlɪs] *adj.* бескро́вный; (*insipid*) безжи́зненный.

bloodlessness [ˈblʌdlɪsnɪs] *n.* (*insipidity*) безжи́зненность.

bloody [ˈblʌdɪ] *adj.* **1.** крова́вый; (*smeared with blood*) окрова́вленный; (*bloodthirsty*) кровожа́дный; (*of meat*) кровяни́стый; **give s.o. a ~ nose** разби́ть (*pf.*) кому́-н. нос в кровь. **2.** (*expletive*): **a ~ liar** отча́янный/отъя́вленный лгун; **stop that ~ row!** прекрати́те э́тот чёртов сканда́л!; **not a ~ thing** ни черта́/хрена́; **no ~ fear!; not ~ likely!** чёрта с два!; фиг-то!

adv. (*sl.*): **~ awful** черто́вский; скве́рный, дрянно́й.

v.t. окрова́вить (*pf.*).

cpds. **~-minded** *adj.* (*coll.*, *obstructive*) зловре́дный, неуслу́жливый, нелюбе́зный; **~-mindedness** *n.* зловре́дность.

bloom[1] [blu:m] *n.* **1.** (*flower*) цвет; цветы́ (*m. pl.*); цвете́ние; (*single flower*) цвето́к; **in ~** в цвету́; **burst into ~** расцве|та́ть, -сти́. **2.** (*prime*) расцве́т; **in the ~ of youth** в расцве́те ю́ности. **3.** (*on cheeks*) румя́нец. **4.** (*down*) пушо́к. **5.** (*of wine*) буке́т. **6.** (*freshness*) све́жесть; **take the ~ off** лиши́ть (*pf.*) све́жести.

v.i. **1.** цвести́ (*impf.*); (*come into ~*) расцве|та́ть, -сти́; зацве|та́ть, -сти́; **finish ~ing** отцве|та́ть, -сти́. **2.** (*fig.*): **~ into sth.** расцвести́ (*pf.*) и преврати́ться (*pf.*) во что-н.

bloom[2] [blu:m] *n.* (*metall.*) блюм; кри́ца.

bloomer [ˈblu:mə(r)] *n.* **1.** (*coll.*, *mistake*) про́мах; (*in speech*) огово́рка; **make a ~** де́лать, с- про́мах; огов|а́риваться, -ори́ться. **2.** (*pl.*) (*undergarment*) пантало́н|ы (*pl.*, *g.* —).

blooming[1] [ˈblu:mɪŋ] *n.* (*metall.*) блю́минг; **~ mill** обжимно́й стан, блю́минг.

blooming[2] [ˈblu:mɪŋ] *adj.* (*flowering*, *flourishing*) цвету́щий; (*expletive*): **a ~ fool** наби́тый дура́к.

blossom [ˈblɒsəm] *n.* цвет, цвете́ние; **in ~** в цвету́; **come into ~** расцве|та́ть, -сти́.

v.i. цвести́ (*impf.*); **finish ~ing** отцве|та́ть, -сти́; (*fig.*): **he ~ed into a statesman** он вы́рос в госуда́рственного де́ятеля.

blot [blɒt] *n.* (*on paper*) кля́кса; (*blemish*) пятно́; **it is a ~ on the landscape** э́то по́ртит вид/пейза́ж; (*fig.*): **without a ~ on one's character** с незапя́тнанной репута́цией.

v.t. & i. **1.** (*smudge*) па́чкать, за-; ста́вить, по- кля́ксу. **2.** (*dry*) промок|а́ть, -ну́ть; **~ting-pad** бюва́р; **~ting-paper** промока́тельная бума́га, (*coll.*) промока́шка. **3.** (*sully*) пятна́ть, за-; **~ one's copybook** (*fig.*) пятна́ть, за- свою́ репута́цию.

with adv.: **~ out** *v.t.* выма́рывать, вы́марать; (*from one's memory*) изгла́|живать, -дить (*or* ст|ира́ть, -ере́ть) из па́мяти; (*a view*) закр|ыва́ть, -ы́ть; заслон|я́ть, -и́ть; (*a nation*) ст|ира́ть, -ере́ть с лица́ земли́.

blotch [blɒtʃ] *n.* пятно́; (*of ink*) кля́кса.

blotchy [ˈblɒtʃɪ] *adj.* в пя́тнах.

blotter [ˈblɒtə(r)] *n.* бюва́р; (*roller-~*) пресс-папье́ (*indecl.*).

blotto [ˈblɒtəʊ] *adj.* (*sl.*) пья́ный в сте́льку.

blouse [blaʊz] *n.* (*workman's*) блу́за; (*woman's*) ко́фточка, блу́зка.

blow[1] [bləʊ] *n.* (*of air, wind*) дунове́ние, поры́в; **give your nose a good ~!** вы́сморкайся хороше́нько (*or* как сле́дует); **let's go out for a ~** (*of fresh air*) пойдём подыша́ть све́жим во́здухом.

v.t. **1.** дуть, ду́нуть; **~ a horn** дуть, ду́нуть в рог; труби́ть (*impf.*); **~ a whistle** свисте́ть, за- в свисто́к; дать (*pf.*) свисто́к; **~ one's nose** сморк|а́ться, -ну́ться; **he blew the pipe clean** он проду́л тру́бку; **~ the dust off a book** сду|ва́ть, -ть пыль с кни́ги; **~ s.o. a kiss** пос|ыла́ть, -ла́ть кому́-н. возду́шный поцелу́й; **~ glass** выдува́ть (*impf.*) стекло́; **~ bubbles** пуска́ть (*impf.*) пузыри́; **~ one's own trumpet** (*fig.*) хвали́ться, похваля́ться (*both impf.*); **~ the gaff** (*fig.*) пробб|а́лтываться, -олта́ться. **2.** (*of wind*): **the wind ~s the rain against the windows** ве́тер с дождём бьёт по о́кнам; **the ship was ~n off course** кора́бль снесло́ с ку́рса; **the wind blew the papers out of my hand** ве́тер вы́рвал бума́ги у меня́ из рук; **he was ~n ashore** его́ вы́несло на бе́рег; **we were ~n out to sea** нас унесло́ в мо́ре. **3.** (*with bellows*): **he blew the fire** он разду́л ого́нь; **~ an organ** разд|ува́ть, -у́ть мехи́ орга́на. **4.** (*elec.*): **~ a fuse** переж|ига́ть, -е́чь про́бку. **5.**: **~ £15 on a dinner** прос|а́живать, -ди́ть (*coll.*) 15 фу́нтов на обе́д. **6.** (*coll.*, *curse*): **I'm ~ed if I know** ей-Бо́гу, не зна́ю; **well, I'm ~ed!** так та́к!; во́т-те ра́з!

v.i. **1.** (*of wind or pers*) дуть, по-, ду́нуть; **it is ~ing hard** си́льно ду́ет; о́чень ве́трено; **puff and ~** пыхте́ть и отдува́ться (*both impf.*); **~ hot and cold** (*fig.*) помину́тно меня́ть (*impf.*) мне́ние. **2.** (*of thg.*): **the door blew open** дверь распахну́лась; **dust blew into the room** пыль налете́ла в ко́мнату; **the whistle blew** разда́лся свисто́к; гудо́к загуде́л; **the fuse blew** про́бка перегоре́ла/сгоре́ла; запа́л срабо́тал. **3.** (*of whale*) пус|ка́ть, -ти́ть струю́ воды́.

with advs.: **~ about** *v.t.*: **the wind blew her hair about** ве́тер развева́л её во́лосы; *v.i.*: **the leaves blew about** носи́лись ли́стья; **~ away** *v.t. & i.* ун|оси́ть(ся), -ести́(сь); **~ down** *v.t.* вали́ть, по-; **he was blown down from the roof** его́ снесло́ с кры́ши; *v.i.*: **the tree blew down** бу́ря повали́ла де́рево; **~ in** *v.t.*: **the gale blew the windows in** урага́ном разби́ло о́кна; *v.i.*: **the wind blows in through the door** ве́тер ду́ет в дверь; **George blew in** (*coll.*) неожи́данно примча́лся Гео́ргий; **~ off** *v.t.*: **the wind blew his hat off** ве́тер сорва́л с него́ шля́пу; **~ off steam** (*lit.*) вы́пустить (*pf.*) пар; (*fig.*) разряди́ться (*pf.*); *v.i.*: **his hat blew off** у него́ слете́ла шля́па; **~ out** *v.t.*: **he blew the candle out** он заду́л свечу́; **~ out one's cheeks** над|ува́ть, -у́ть щёки; **~ out** (*unblock*) **a pipe** прод|ува́ть, -у́ть тру́бку; **~ one's brains out** пусти́ть (*pf.*) себе́ пу́лю в лоб; **the bomb blew out the doors** от взры́ва бо́мбы вы́летели две́ри; *v.i.*: **the candle blew out** свеча́ пога́сла; **the tyre blew out** ши́на ло́пнула; **~ over** *v.t.*: **he was blown over by the wind** его́ свали́ло с ног ве́тром; *v.i.*: **the storm blew over** бу́ря ути́хла; **the scandal blew over** сканда́л улёгся/зати́х; **~ up** *v.t.*: **~ up a bridge** взрыва́ть, взорва́ть мост; **~ up a fire** разд|ува́ть, -у́ть ого́нь; **~ up a tyre** над|ува́ть, -у́ть ши́ну; **~ up a photograph** увели́чи|вать, -ть фотогра́фию; **blown up by pride** разду́тый го́рдостью; **his reputation has been blown up** (*inflated*) у него́ (раз)ду́тая репута́ция; **the boss blew him up** (*coll.*) нача́льник сде́лал ему́ разно́с; *v.i.*: **the mine blew up** ми́на взорва́лась; **it is blowing up for rain** ве́тер нагоня́ет дождь.

cpds. **~-ball** *n.* одува́нчик; **~-fly** *n.* мясна́я му́ха; **~-hole** *n.* (*of whale*) ды́хало; (*opening in ice*) отве́рстие; (*in tunnel*) вентиляцио́нное отве́рстие; **~-job** *n.* (*sl.*) мине́т, отсо́с; **~-lamp** *n.* пая́льная ла́мпа; **~-out** *n.* (*of tyre*) разры́в; (*oil*) фонта́н (не́фти); (*coll.*, *feast*) кутёж, пиру́шка; **~pipe** *n.* (*tool*) пая́льная тру́бка; стеклоду́вная трýбка; (*weapon*) трýбка для выдувáния отрáвленных стрел; **~-torch** *n.* паяльная лáмпа; **~-up** *n.* (*explosion, outburst*) взрыв, вспы́шка; (*phot.*) увеличéние.

blow[2] [bləʊ] *n.* (*lit., fig.: stroke*) удáр; **deliver, deal, strike a ~** нан|оси́ть, -ести́ удáр; **at a ~** одни́м удáром; **strike a ~ at s.o.** нанести́ (*pf.*) удáр комý-н.; **strike a ~ for** (*fig.*) вступи́ться (*pf.*) за+*a.*; **they came to ~s** они́ подрáлись; дéло дошлó до рукопáшной; **get one's ~ in** нанести́ (*pf.*) удáр; удáрить (*pf.*); **without striking a ~** без дрáки; **her death was a ~ to us** её смерть былá удáром для нас; **it was a ~ to our hopes** э́то разби́ло нáши надéжды.

blow[3] [bləʊ] *v.i.* (*be in flower*) цвести́ (*impf.*); (*come into flower*) зацве|тáть, -сти́; расцве|тáть, -сти́; распус|кáться, -ти́ться; **~n roses** распусти́вшиеся рóзы.

blowing-up [ˌbləʊɪŋ'ʌp] *n.* (*explosion*) взрыв; (*coll., reprimand*) разнóс.

blown [bləʊn] *adj.* (*breathless*) запыхáвшийся; (*blooming*) цветýщий, расцвéтший, распусти́вшийся.

blowy ['bləʊɪ] *adj.* вéтреный.

blowzy ['blaʊzɪ] *adj.*: **a ~ woman** растрёпанная жéнщина, (*coll.*) распустёха.

blub [blʌb] *v.i.* (*coll.*) ревéть (*impf.*).

blubber[1] ['blʌbə(r)] *n.* (*whale-fat*) вóрвань.

blubber[2] ['blʌbə(r)] *v.t. & i.* ревéть (*impf.*), рыдáть (*impf.*).

blubber-lipped ['blʌbə(r)] *adj.* толстогýбый.

bludgeon ['blʌdʒ(ə)n] *n.* дуби́нка.

v.t. бить (*impf.*) дуби́нкой; (*fig.*) принуждáть (*impf.*).

blue [blu:] *n.* **1.** (*colour*) синевá, голубизнá; **navy ~** тёмно-си́ний цвет. **2.** (*sky*): **out of the ~** (*fig.*) ни с тогó ни с сегó; **he arrived out of the ~** он нагря́нул неожи́данно; **like a bolt from the ~** (*fig.*) как гром среди́ я́сного нéба. **3.** (*sea*) (си́нее) мóре. **4.: the ~s** (*coll.*) тоскá, уны́ние, хандрá; **have the ~s** хандри́ть (*impf.*); **give s.o. the ~s** нав|оди́ть, -ести́ тоскý на когó-н. **5.: ~s** (*mus.*) блюз.

adj. **1.** (*colour*) (*dark*) си́ний; (*light*) голубóй; **her hands were ~ with cold** её рýки посинéли от хóлода; **his arms are ~ (with bruises)** у негó все рýки в синякáх; **he shouted till he was ~ in the face** он кричáл до изнеможéния; **once in a ~ moon** раз в сто лет; **scream ~ murder** кричáть (*impf.*) во всю глóтку/(*coll.*) ивáновскую; **~ baby** (*med.*) синю́шный младéнец; **~ blood** голубáя кровь; **~ book** «си́няя кни́га» (*сборник официальных документов*); **~funk** (*coll.*) пани́ческий страх; **~ mould** голубáя плéсень; **B~ Peter** флаг отплы́тия; **~ water** откры́тое мóре. **2.** (*coll., sad*): **feel ~** хандри́ть (*impf.*); **look ~** (*of pers.*) вы́глядеть (*impf.*) уны́лым; **things look ~** делá обстоя́т сквéрно. **3.** (*coll., obscene*) скабрёзный.

v.t. (*of laundry*) сини́ть (*impf.*); подси́н|ивать, -и́ть; (*coll., squander*) мотáть, про-.

cpds. **B~beard** *n.* Си́няя Борóдá; **~bell** *n.* колокóльчик; **~bird** *n.* синешéйка; **~-black** *adj.* иссиня-чёрный; **~-blooded** *adj.* голубóй крóви; **~bottle** *n.* мяснáя мýха; **~-eyed** *adj.* синеглáзый, голубоглáзый; **~-eyed boy** (*iron.*) люби́мчик, люби́мец; **~-grey** *adj.* си́зый, си́зо-голубóй; **~-pencil** *v.t.* (*abridge*) сокра|щáть, -ти́ть; (*erase*) вычёркивать, вы́черкнуть; **~print** *n.* (*phot.*) светокóпия, си́нька; (*fig.*) намётка; **~stocking** *n.* (*fig.*) си́ний чулóк, учёная жéнщина.

blueness ['blu:nɪs] *n.* синевá; голубизнá.

bluff[1] [blʌf] *n.* (*headland*) утёс.

adj. (*of cliffs etc.*) обры́вистый, отвéсный; (*of pers.*) грубовáто-добродýшный; прямодýшный.

bluff[2] [blʌf] *n.* блеф; **call s.o.'s ~** застáвить когó-н. раскры́ть кáрты.

v.t. & i. блефовáть (*impf.*); втирáть (*impf.*) очки́ +*d.*; пускáть (*impf.*) пыль в глазá +*d.*

bluish ['blu:ɪʃ] *adj.* синевáтый; голубовáтый.

blunder ['blʌndə(r)] *n.* оши́бка, оплóшность.

v.t. напóртить (*pf.*), напýтать (*pf.*); **~ away** (*forfeit*) прозевáть (*pf.*).

v.i. блуждáть (*impf.*); (*grope*) óщупью пробирáться/ дви́гаться (*impf.*); **~ in one's answers** спотыкáться (*impf.*) в отвéтах; **~ into a table** наткнýться/натолкнýться (*pf.*) на стол; **~ upon the facts** наткнýться (*pf.*) на фáкты; **~ through one's work** дéлать (*impf.*) рабóту кóе-как.

blunderbuss ['blʌndəˌbʌs] *n.* мушкетóн.

blundering ['blʌndəɪŋ] *adj.* (*groping*) идýщий óщупью; (*clumsy*) нескла́дный; (*tactless*) бестáктный.

blunt [blʌnt] *adj.* (*not sharp*) тупóй; **a ~ pencil** неоттóченный карандáш; (*plain-spoken*) прямóй; **the ~ fact is that ...** жестóкая и́стина состои́т в том, что...

v.t. тупи́ть (*impf.*); **~ a needle** притуп|ля́ть, -и́ть иглý; **~ a knife/scissors** затуп|ля́ть, -и́ть нож/нóжницы; (*feelings etc.*) притуп|ля́ть, -и́ть; **~ s.o.'s intelligence** притуп|ля́ть, -и́ть чьё-н.восприя́тие; **~ s.o.'s anger** ум|еря́ть, -éрить чей-н. гнев.

bluntness ['blʌntnɪs] *n.* (*lit.*) тýпость; (*frankness*) прямотá.

blur [blɜ:(r)] *n.* (*smear*) кля́кса, пятнó; (*confused effect*) ды́мка; **she saw him through a ~ of tears** онá ви́дела егó сквозь ды́мку слёз; **the village is now only a ~ in my mind** об э́той дерéвне у меня́ остáлись лишь смýтные воспоминáния.

v.t. (*make indistinct*) смáз|ывать, -ать; **rain ~s the windows** дождь затумáнивает óкна; (*fig.*) затумáни|вать, -ть; затемн|я́ть, -и́ть.

blurb [blɜ:b] *n.* (*coll.*) (издáтельская) аннотáция.

blurry ['blɜ:rɪ] *adj.* затумáненный.

blurt [blɜ:t] *v.t.*: **~ out** выпáливать, вы́палить; выбáлтывать, вы́болтать.

blush [blʌʃ] *n.* **1.** крáска; **put s.o. to the ~** вгоня́ть, вогнáть когó-н. в крáску; **spare s.o.'s ~es** пощади́ть (*pf.*) чью-н. стыдли́вость; **a ~ rose to her cheeks** крáска залилá её щёки. **2.** (*glow*) румя́нец; (*of rose*) рóзовый цвет. **3.: at first ~** с пéрвого рáза.

v.i. краснéть, по-; зардéться (*pf.*); **~ to the roots of one's hair** краснéть, по- до корнéй волóс; **~ crimson** зардéться (*pf.*): **I ~ to suggest** мне сóвестно предположи́ть; **I ~ for you** я краснéю за вас; вы заставля́ете меня́ краснéть.

blusher ['blʌʃə(r)] *n.* (*cosmetic*) румя́на.

blushing ['blʌʃɪŋ] *adj.* (*modest*) застéнчивый, стыдли́вый; **a ~ bride** стыдли́вая невéста.

bluster ['blʌstə(r)] *n.* (*of storm*) рёв; (*of pers.*) грóмкие словá, угрóзы (*f. pl.*).

v.i. (*of storm*) ревéть (*impf.*); (*of pers.*) расшумéться (*pf.*), разбушевáться (*pf.*).

blusterer ['blʌstərə(r)] *n.* забия́ка (*c.g.*).

B.M. (*abbr. of* ***British Museum***) Бритáнский музéй.

B. Mus. (*abbr. of* ***Bachelor of Music***) бакалáвр мýзыки.

BO (*abbr. of* ***body odour***) дурнóй зáпах (тéла).

bo [bəʊ] = **boo** *int.* **2.**

boa ['bəʊə] *n.* (*zool.*) боá (*m. indecl.*); **~ constrictor** удáв; (*wrap*) боá (*nt. indecl.*).

boar [bɔ:(r)] *n.* кабáн.

board [bɔ:d] *n.* **1.** (*piece of wood*) доскá (*also for chess etc.*); **bed of ~s** нáр|ы (*pl., g.* —); **~ game** настóльная игрá. **2.** (*pl., theatr.*) подмóстк|и (*pl., g.* -ов); **go on the ~s** пойти́ (*pf.*) на сцéну; **tread the ~s** игрáть (*impf.*) в сцéне. **3.** (*pl., cover of book*) переплёт; **cloth ~s** коленкóровый переплёт. **4.** (*food*) стол; **~ and lodging; bed and ~** кварти́ра и стол; **full ~** пóлный пансиóн. **5.** (*table*): **groaning ~** (*liter.*) оби́льный (*or* богáто устáвленный) стол; **above ~** (*fig.*) в откры́тую, чéстно; **sweep the ~** (*at cards*) заб|ирáть, -рáть все стáвки. **6.** (*council*) правлéние; **~ of enquiry** коми́ссия по расслéдованию; **~ of directors** правлéние директорóв. **7.** (*naut. etc.*): **on ~** на бортý; **come, go on ~ a ship/aircraft** сади́ться, сесть на корáбль/самолёт; (*comm.*): **free on ~** (f.o.b.) фрáнко борт (фоб); **go by the ~** (*fig.*) быть вы́брошенным зá борт.

v.t. **1.** (*cover with ~s; also ~ up*) обш|ивáть, -и́ть (*or* покр|ывáть, -ы́ть) дóсками. **2.: ~ a ship** (*go on ~*) сади́ться, сесть на корáбль; (*attack*) брать, взять корáбль на абордáж. **3.** (*supply with meals*) предост|авля́ть, -áвить питáние +*d.* **4.: ~ s.o. out** (*find quarters for*) пом|ещáть, -сти́ть когó-н. на пóлный пансиóн.

v.i. (*take meals*) столовáться (*impf.*); (*reside*) жить (*impf.*) на пóлном пансиóне; (*at school*) быть пансионéром.

cpds. **~-room** *n.* помеще́ние правле́ния дире́кторов; **~walk** *n.* доща́тый насти́л.

boarder ['bɔːdə(r)] *n.* пансионе́р (*also at school*) (*fem.* -ка); жиле́ц; **take in ~s** брать (*impf.*) жильцо́в/постоя́льцев.

boarding ['bɔːdɪŋ] *n.* **1.** (*boards*) обши́вка до́сками. **2.** (*naut.*) абορда́ж; (*aeron.*) поса́дка.

cpds. **~-card** *n.* поса́дочный биле́т; **~-house** *n.* пансио́н; **~-school** *n.* шко́ла-интерна́т.

boast [bəʊst] *n.* хвастовство́; (*coll.*) похвальба́; **an empty ~** пусто́е хвастовство́; **make a ~ of** хва́стать, по- +*i.*; **their ~ is that ...** они́ похваля́ются тем, что...; (*pers. or thg. ~ed of*) го́рдость, предме́т го́рдости.

v.t. & i. **1.** (**~** *of*) хва́стать(ся), по- +*i.*; хвали́ться (*or* похваля́ться), по- +*i.*; **it is nothing to ~ of** похва́статься не́чем. **2.** (*possess*) горди́ться (*impf.*) +*i.*

boaster ['bəʊstə(r)] *n.* хвасту́н (*fem.* -ья).

boastful ['bəʊstfʊl] *adj.* хвастли́вый.

boastfulness ['bəʊstfʊlnɪs] *n.* хвастли́вость.

boat [bəʊt] *n.* (*small, rowing* **~**) ло́дка, шлю́пка; (*vessel*) су́дно; (*large* **~**) кора́бль (*m.*), парохо́д; **in the same ~** (*fig.*) в одина́ковом положе́нии; **burn one's ~s** (*fig.*) сжечь (*pf.*) (свой) корабли́; **miss the ~** (*fig.*) прозева́ть (*pf.*) слу́чай; оказа́ться (*pf.*) неуда́чником.

v.i. (*go* **~ing**) ката́ться (*indet.*) на ло́дке; **we ~ed as far as Oxford** мы проплы́ли на ло́дке до (са́мого) О́ксфорда.

cpds. **~-deck** *n.* шлю́почная па́луба; **~-drill** *n.* обуче́ние на спаса́тельных шлю́пках; **~-hook** *n.* баго́р; **~house** *n.* э́ллинг; **~man** *n.* ло́дочник; **~-race** *n.* состяза́ния (*nt. pl.*) по гре́бле; **~swain** *n.* бо́цман; **~-train** *n.* по́езд, согласо́ванный с парохо́дным расписа́нием.

boater ['bəʊtə(r)] *n.* соло́менная шля́па.

bob[1] [bɒb] *n.* **1.** (*weight*) подве́сок; (*on fishing-line*) поплаво́к; (*on pendulum*) ги́ря. **2.** (*hair-style*) коро́ткая стри́жка; (*horse's tail*) подстри́женный хвост.

v.t. (*of hair*) ко́ротко стричь (*impf.*); остр|ига́ть, -и́чь.

cpd. **~tail** *n.* (*tail*) обре́занный хвост; ку́цый хвост; (*horse*) ку́цая ло́шадь; (*dog*) ку́цая соба́ка; **rag-tag and ~tail** сброд; *adj.* (*also* **~-tailed**) с обре́занным/ку́цым хвосто́м.

bob[2] [bɒb] *n.* (*jerk, e.g. of the head*) киво́к; (*curtsey*) приседа́ние,ревера́нс.

v.i. **1.** (*move up and down*) подпры́г|ивать, -нуть; подск|а́кивать, -очи́ть; **~ up** выска́кивать, вы́скочить. **2.** (*curtsey*) прис|еда́ть, -е́сть; **she ~bed him a curtsey** она́ присе́ла в реверáнсе пе́ред ним.

bob[3] [bɒb] *n.* (*coll., shilling*) ши́ллинг.

bob[4] [bɒb] *n.*: **~'s your uncle** (*coll.*) всё в поря́дке.

bobbin ['bɒbɪn] *n.* (*reel, spool*) кату́шка, шпу́лька; (*for raising latch*) рычажо́к.

bobbinet ['bɒbɪˌnet] *n.* маши́нное кру́жево.

bobble ['bɒb(ə)l] *n.* помпо́н(чик).

bobby ['bɒbɪ] *n.* (*coll.*) полисме́н.

bobby-socks ['bɒbɪ ˌsɒks] *n.* коро́ткие носки́ (*m. pl.*).

bobby-soxer ['bɒbɪˌsɒksə(r)] *n.* де́вочка-подро́сток.

bobolink ['bɒbəlɪŋk] *n.* ри́совый тупиа́л.

bob-sled ['bɒbsled], **bob-sleigh** ['bɒbsleɪ] *nn.* бо́бслей.

bobstay ['bɒbsteɪ] *n.* ватершта́г.

Boche [bɒʃ] *n.* (*sl.*) бош.

bod [bɒd] *n.* (*coll.*) тип.

bode [bəʊd] *v.t. & i.* **1.** (*portend*): **~ ill/well** предвеща́ть/сули́ть (*impf.*) недо́брое/хоро́шее; **it ~s no good** э́то не предвеща́ет ничего́ хоро́шего. **2.** (*foresee*) предви́деть (*impf.*), предчу́вствовать (*impf.*).

bodeful ['bəʊdfʊl] *adj.* злове́щий.

bodega [bəʊ'diːgə] *n.* ви́нный погребо́к.

bodice ['bɒdɪs] *n.* корса́ж, лиф.

bodiless ['bɒdɪlɪs] *adj.* бестеле́сный.

bodily ['bɒdɪlɪ] *adj.* теле́сный, физи́ческий; **~ harm** физи́ческое уве́чье/поврежде́ние; **be in ~ fear of s.o.** испы́тывать (*impf.*) физи́ческий страх пе́ред кем-н.

adv.: **he was carried ~ to the doors** его́ на рука́х вы́несли к дверя́м; **the house was moved ~** дом был передви́нут целико́м; **they resigned ~** они́ в по́лном соста́ве по́дали в отста́вку.

bodkin ['bɒdkɪn] *n.* дли́нная тупа́я игла́; ши́ло.

body ['bɒdɪ] *n.* **1.** (*of pers. or animal*) те́ло; (*dim., e.g. baby's*) те́льце; (*build*) телосложе́ние; **~ count** поте́ри уби́тыми; **~ odour** за́пах по́та; **~ scanner** ска́нер; **strong in ~** физи́чески си́льный; **keep ~ and soul together** своди́ть (*impf.*) концы́ с конца́ми; **he is ours ~ and soul** он пре́дан нам душо́й и те́лом. **2.** (*trunk*) ту́ловище, торс; **run s.o. through the ~** пронзи́ть (*pf.*) кого́-н. насквозь; **he was wounded in the ~** его́ ра́нили в ко́рпус. **3.** (*dead pers.*) мёртвое те́ло; уби́т|ый (*fem.* -ая). **4.** (*main portion*): **the ~ of a hall/building** гла́вная часть за́ла/зда́ния; (*of ship*) ко́рпус; (*of car*) ку́зов; (*of aircraft*) фюзеля́ж; **the ~ of his supporters** все его́ сторо́нники; (*of letter, book*) основна́я часть. **5.** (*quantity, aggregate*) ма́сса, гру́ппа; **a large ~ of facts** ма́сса фа́ктов; **a ~ of cold air** ма́сса холо́дного во́здуха; **~ of evidence** совоку́пность доказа́тельств. **6.** (*group, institution, system*): **governing ~** о́рган управле́ния; **legislative ~** законода́тельный о́рган; **learned ~** учёное о́бщество; **public ~** обще́ственная организа́ция; **the ~ politic** госуда́рство; **in a ~** в по́лном соста́ве; **main ~** (*mil.*) гла́вные си́лы (*f. pl.*); **~ of cavalry** отря́д кавале́рии. **7.** (*coll., woman*): **a nice old ~** симпати́чная тётка. **8.** (*object*) те́ло; **the heavenly bodies** небе́сные тела́; **foreign ~** иноро́дное те́ло. **9.** (*strength, consistency*) консисте́нция, вя́зкость.

v.t.: **~ forth** (*give shape to*) вопло|ща́ть, -ти́ть; прид|ава́ть, -а́ть фо́рму +*d.*

cpds. **~-blow** *n.* (*lit.*) уда́р в ко́рпус; (*fig.*) сокруши́тельный уда́р; **~-builder** *n.* (*pers.*) культури́ст; (*apparatus*) экспанде́р; **~-building** *n.* культури́зм; *adj.* пита́тельный; **~guard** *n.* (*group*) ли́чная охра́на; (*individual*) телохрани́тель (*m.*); **~-snatcher** *n.* похити́тель (*m.*) тру́пов; **~-stocking** *n.* трико́ (*indecl.*); **~warmer** *n.* телогре́йка; **~work** *n.* (*of vehicle*) ку́зов.

Boer ['bəʊə(r), bʊə(r)] *n.* бур.

adj. бу́рский; **~ War** а́нгло-бу́рская война́.

boffin ['bɒfɪn] *n.* (*coll.*) техни́ческий экспе́рт, (*coll.*) до́ка (*m.*).

bog [bɒg] *n.* **1.** боло́то, тряси́на; **~ oak** морёный дуб; **~ orchis** мя́котница. **2.** (*sl., latrine*) отхо́жее ме́сто.

v.t.: **get ~ged down** (*fig.*) увя́знуть, завя́знуть (*both pf.*).

bogey ['bəʊgɪ] = **bogy**

boggle ['bɒg(ə)l] *v.i.* отша́т|ываться, -ну́ться; отпря́нуть (*pf.*); **the mind ~s** уму́ непостижи́мо; **he will not ~ at £5** он не бу́дет препира́ться из-за пяти́ фу́нтов.

boggy ['bɒgɪ] *adj.* боло́тистый.

bogie ['bəʊgɪ] *n.* (*rail.*) двухо́сная теле́жка.

bogus ['bəʊgəs] *adj.* мни́мый, фикти́вный, притво́рный.

bogusness ['bəʊgəsnɪs] *n.* фикти́вность, притво́рность.

bog|y, -ey ['bəʊgɪ] *n.* (*bugbear*) бу́ка, пу́гало.

Bohemia [bəʊ'hiːmɪə] *n.* (*geog.*) Боге́мия; (*fig.*) боге́ма.

Bohemian [bəʊ'hiːmɪən] *n.* (*native of Bohemia*) боге́м|ец (*fem.* -ка); чех (*fem.* че́шка); (*raffish artist etc.*) представи́тель (*fem.* -ница) боге́мы.

adj. (*geog.*) боге́мский; (*fig.*) боге́мный.

boil[1] [bɔɪl] *n.* (*tumour*) навы́в, чире́й.

boil[2] [bɔɪl] *n.* (*state of* **~ing**) кипе́ние; **come to the ~** вскипе́ть (*pf.*), закипе́ть (*pf.*); **bring to the ~** довести́ (*pf.*) до кипе́ния; вскипяти́ть (*pf.*); **be on, at the ~** кипе́ть (*impf.*); **go off the ~** переста́ть (*pf.*) кипе́ть.

v.t.: **~ water** кипяти́ть, вс- во́ду; **~ fish/an egg** вари́ть, с- ры́бу/яйцо́; **~ laundry** кипяти́ть (*impf.*) бельё; **~ed shirt** (*coll.*) крахма́льная руба́шка.

v.i.: **the water is ~ing** вода́ кипи́т; **the egg has ~ed** яйцо́ свари́лось; **the kettle has ~ed dry** ча́йник совсе́м вы́кипел; **~ with indignation** кипе́ть (*impf.*) от негодова́ния (*or* негодова́нием).

with advs.: **~ away** *v.i.*: **the kettle was ~ing away** ча́йник кипе́л вовсю́; **the water ~ed away** вода́ вы́кипела; **~ down** *v.t.* (*lit.*) выпа́ривать; вы́парить; (*abridge*) сж|има́ть, -а́ть; *v.i.*: **it ~s down to this, that ...** э́то сво́дится к тому́, что...; **~ over** *v.i.* (*lit.*) уходи́ть, уйти́ (*or* убе|га́ть, -жа́ть) че́рез край; **the milk ~ed over** молоко́ убежа́ло; (*fig., with rage*) вскипе́ть (*pf.*); **he was ~ing over** всё в нём кипе́ло; **~ up** *v.t.* вскипяти́ть (*pf.*); *v.i.* вскип|а́ть, -е́ть.

boiler ['bɔɪlə(r)] *n.* **1.** (*vessel*) кипяти́льник, тита́н; кипяти́льный котёл, бо́йлер; (*of steam engine*) парово́й котёл; (*for domestic heating*) котёл отопле́ния; бо́йлер; (*for laundry*) бак. **2.** (*chicken*) ку́рица для ва́рки.

cpds. **~-house** *n.* коте́льная; **~-maker** *n.* коте́льник, коте́льщик; **~-suit** *n.* комбинезо́н.

boiling ['bɔɪlɪŋ] *n.* **1.** кипе́ние, кипяче́ние, ва́рка. **2.: a ~** (*quantity*) **of potatoes** ва́рево карто́шки; **the whole ~** вся гоп-компа́ния (*coll.*).

adj. (*also of waves etc.*) кипя́щий; **~ water** кипято́к; **~ hot** горя́чий, как кипято́к; **a ~ hot day** зно́йный день.

cpd. **~-point** *n.* то́чка кипе́ния.

boisterous ['bɔɪstərəs] *adj.* (*of pers.*) бу́йный, шумли́вый; (*of sea, weather*) бу́рный; (*of wind*) ре́зкий, бу́йный.

boisterousness ['bɔɪstərəsnɪs] *n.* бу́йность, шумли́вость, бу́рность.

bold [bəʊld] *n.* (*typ.*) жи́рный шрифт.

adj. **1.** сме́лый, отва́жный; **grow ~** осмеле́ть (*pf.*); **he put a ~ face on the matter** в э́той ситуа́ции он и бро́вью не повёл; **make ~ to, make so ~ as to** осме́ли|ваться, -ться; **make ~ with sth.** во́льно обраща́ться (*impf.*) с чем-н.; (*impudent*) наха́льный; **as ~ as brass** бессты́жий. **2.** (*prominent*): **~ features** ре́зкие черты́ лица́; **a ~ headland** ре́зко оче́рченный мыс. **3.** (*clear*) чёткий, отчётливый. **4.: ~ strokes** (*in painting*) широ́кие мазки́; **in ~ relief** вы́пукло.

cpds. **~-face** *n.* (*typ.*) жи́рный шрифт; **~-faced** *adj.* (*impudent*) на́глый, бессты́жий; (*of type*) жи́рный.

boldness ['bəʊldnɪs] *n.* сме́лость, отва́жность, отва́га; (*impudence*) на́глость.

bole [bəʊl] *n.* ствол.

bolero [bəʊ'leərəʊ, 'bɒlərəʊ] *n.* (*dance, jacket*) болеро́ (*indecl.*).

boletus [bəʊ'li:təs] *n.* мохови́к; **edible ~** бе́лый гриб, борови́к.

bolide ['bəʊlaɪd] *n.* боли́д.

Bolivia [bə'lɪvɪə] *n.* Боли́вия.

Bolivian [bə'lɪvɪən] *n.* боливи́|ец (*fem.* -йка).

adj. боливи́йский.

boll [bəʊl] *n.* семенна́я коро́бочка.

cpd. **~-weevil** *n.* долгоно́сик.

bollard ['bɒlɑ:d] *n.* (*on ship or quay*) пал; (*on traffic island*) ту́мба.

bollock ['bɒlək] *n.* (*vulg.*) (*testicle*) яйцо́; *pl.* (*nonsense*) херня́, бредя́тина; **to talk ~s** мудню́ поро́ть (*pf.*) *or* нести́ (*det.*); **~s!** чёрта с два!

bollocking ['bɒləkɪŋ] *n.* (*vulg.*) взъёбка; **give s.o. a ~** дать (*pf.*) взъёбку.

boloney [bə'ləʊnɪ] *n.* (*sl.*) чепуха́, ерунда́.

Bolshevi|k ['bɒlʃəvɪk], **-st** ['bɒlʃəvɪst] *nn.* большеви́|к (*fem.* -чка).

adj. большеви́стский.

Bolshevism ['bɒlʃə,vɪz(ə)m] *n.* большеви́зм.

bolsh|ie, -y ['bɒlʃɪ] *adj.* (*sl.*) кра́сный; (*mutinous*) стропти́вый.

bolster ['bəʊlstə(r)] *n.* ва́лик; (*fig.*) опо́ра.

v.t. (*prop; also fig.*) подп|ира́ть, -ере́ть.

bolt[1] [bəʊlt] *n.* **1.** (*on door etc.*) засо́в, задви́жка. **2.** (*screw*) болт. **3.** (*arrow*): **he has shot his ~** (*fig.*) он исчерпа́л все свои́ возмо́жности; **a fool's ~ is soon shot** с дурако́м мо́жно бы́стро сла́дить. **4.** (*thunderbolt*) уда́р гро́ма. **5.** (*measure of cloth*) руло́н, шту́ка.

adv.: **~ upright** пря́мо; вы́тянувшись.

v.t.: **~ the door** зап|ира́ть, -ере́ть дверь на засо́в/задви́жку.

v.i.: **the door ~s on the inside** дверь запира́ется изнутри́.

bolt[2] [bəʊlt] *n.* (*escape*): **make a ~ for it** удра́ть (*pf.*); дать (*pf.*) стрекача́.

v.t. (*gulp down*) глота́ть, проглоти́ть.

v.i. (*of horse*) понести́ (*pf.*); (*of pers.*) ри́нуться (*pf*), помча́ться (*pf.*), удра́ть (*pf.*).

cpd. **~-hole** *n.* заго́н; (*fig.*) прибе́жище.

bolt[3] [bəʊlt] *v.t.* (*sift*) просе́|ивать, -ять; отсе́|ивать, -ять.

bolter ['bəʊltə(r)] *n.* (*horse*) норови́стая ло́шадь; (*sieve*) решето́, сито, гро́хот.

bolus ['bəʊləs] *n.* пилю́ля.

bomb [bɒm] *n.* бо́мба; (*mortar ~*) ми́на; (*shell*) снаря́д; **incendiary ~** зажига́тельная бо́мба; **high-explosive ~** фуга́сная бо́мба; **flying ~** самолёт-снаря́д; **neutron ~** нейтро́нная бо́мба; **drop a ~** сбро́сить (*pf.*) бо́мбу; **~ disposal** обезвре́живание неразорва́вшихся бомб; (*fig.*) **to cost a ~** сто́ить бе́шеных де́нег.

v.t. & i. бомби́ть, раз-.

with advs.: **~ out** *v.t.* (*a building*) разбомби́ть (*pf.*); **~ up** *v.i.* (*load aircraft*) грузи́ть, на- бо́мбами; прин|има́ть, -я́ть боезапа́с бомб.

cpds. **~-bay** *n.* бо́мбовый отсе́к; **~-carrier** *n.* бомбодержа́тель (*m.*); **~-crater** *n.* воро́нка от бо́мбы; **~-proof** *adj.* бомбосто́йкий; **~shell** *n.* артиллери́йский снаря́д; **the news came as a ~shell to them** весть их как гро́мом порази́ла; **~-shelter** *n.* бомбоубе́жище; **~-sight** *n.* бомбардиро́вочный прице́л, авиаприце́л; **~-site** *n.* разбомблённый уча́сток.

bombard [bɒm'bɑ:d] *v.t.* **1.** бомби́ть, раз-; бомбардирова́ть (*impf.*); обстре́л|ивать, -я́ть. **2.** (*fig.*): **~ s.o. with rotten eggs** забр|а́сывать, -оса́ть кого́-н. ту́хлыми я́йцами; **~ s.o. with abuse** ос|ы́пать, -ыпа́ть кого́-н. оскорбле́ниями; **~ s.o. with questions** бомбардирова́ть (*impf.*) кого́-н. вопро́сами. **3.** (*phys.*) бомбардирова́ть (*impf.*); **~ sth. with particles** облуч|а́ть, -и́ть что-н. части́цами.

bombardier [,bɒmbə'dɪə(r)] *n.* (*artillery rank*) бомбарди́р; у́нтер-офице́р артилле́рии; (*aeron.*) бомбарди́р-наво́дчик.

bombardment [bɒm'bɑ:dmənt] *n.* бомбардиро́вка, бомбёжка; (*with shells*) артиллери́йский обстре́л.

bombardon [bɒm'bɑ:d(ə)n, 'bɒmbəd(ə)n] *n.* бомбардо́н.

bombast ['bɒmbæst] *n.* высокопа́рность, напы́щенность.

bombastic [bɒm'bæstɪk] *adj.* высокопа́рный, напы́щенный.

bombazine ['bɒmbə,zi:n, -'zi:n] *n.* бомбази́н.

bombe [bɔ̃mb] *n.* ба́бка.

bomber ['bɒmə(r)] *n.* (*aircraft*) бомбардиро́вщик; (*pers.*) бомбомета́тель (*m.*), гранатомётчик.

bombinate ['bɒmbɪ,neɪt] *v.i.* (*buzz*) жужжа́ть (*impf.*); **~ (in a vacuum)** (*fig.*) шуме́ть по́пусту.

bombing ['bɒmɪŋ] *n.* бомбомета́ние, бомбардиро́вка; **precision ~** прице́льное бомбомета́ние.

bona fide [,bəʊnə 'faɪdɪ] *adj.* добросо́вестный, че́стный, неподде́льный.

adv. че́стно; без обма́на.

bona fides [,bəʊnə 'faɪdi:z] *n.* че́стное наме́рение; че́стность.

bonanza [bə'nænzə] *n.* (*coll.*) золото́е дно; **strike a ~** напа́сть (*pf.*) на золоту́ю жи́лу; (*attr.*) золотоно́сный.

Bonapartism ['bəʊnə,pɑ:,tɪzəm] *n.* бонапарти́зм.

Bonapartist ['bəʊnə,pɑ:tɪst] *n.* бонапарти́ст (*fem.* -ка).

adj. бонапарти́стский.

bonbon ['bɒnbɒn] *n.* конфе́та.

bond [bɒnd] *n.* **1.** (*link*) связь; **love of music was a ~ between us** нас свя́зывала любо́вь к му́зыке. **2.** (*shackle*): **in ~s** в око́вах; в заключе́нии; **burst one's ~s** разорва́ть (*pf.*) око́вы. **3.** (*obligation*) гара́нтия; **his word is as good as his ~** на его́ сло́во мо́жно положи́ться. **4.** (*fin.*) облига́ция; (*pl.*) бо́ны (*f. pl.*); **interest-bearing ~s** проце́нтные облига́ции; **premium ~s** вы́игрышные облига́ции. **5.** (*comm.*): **goods in ~** това́ры, не опла́ченные по́шлиной.

v.t. **1.** (*of bricks*) сцеп|ля́ть, -и́ть; свя́з|ывать, -а́ть. **2.** (*fin.*): **~ed debt** облигацио́нный заём; консолиди́рованный долг. **3.** (*comm.*): **~ed warehouse** приписно́й тамо́женный склад.

cpds. **~holder** *n.* держа́тель (*m.*) облига́ций/бон; **~servant, ~slave** *nn.* крепостно́й, раб; **~service** *n.* крепостна́я зави́симость; **~sman** *n.* крепостно́й; (*guarantor*) поручи́тель (*m.*); **~swoman** *n.* крепостна́я.

bondage ['bɒndɪdʒ] *n.* нево́ля; закрепоще́ние; **the ~ of sin** пу́т|ы (*pl., g.* —) греха́; **be in ~ to s.o.** быть в кабале́ у кого́-н.

bone [bəʊn] *n.* **1.** кость; **drenched to the ~** промо́кший до косте́й; **he is all skin and ~** он ко́жа да ко́сти; **I feel in my ~s that ...** чу́ет моё се́рдце, что...; **he won't make old ~s** он не доживёт до ста́рости; **hard words break no ~s** брань на воро́ту не ви́снет; **near the ~** (*coll.*) риско́ванный; **cut costs to the ~** сокра|ща́ть, -ти́ть расхо́ды до преде́ла; **the bare ~s** (*of a subject*) элемента́рные поня́тия/зна́ния; **make no ~s about sth.**

не церемо́ниться (*impf.*) с чем-н.; **he made no ~s about telling me ...** он не постесня́лся сказа́ть мне...; **~ of contention** я́блоко раздо́ра; **I have a ~ to pick with you** у меня́ к вам прете́нзия; **take a fish off the ~** отдел|я́ть, -и́ть ры́бу от косте́й. **2.** (*substance*) кость; **buttons made of ~** костяны́е пу́говицы; **~ china** твёрдый англи́йский фарфо́р. **3.** (*cul.*): **broiled ~s** тушёное мя́со. **4.** (*pl.*, *castanets*) кастанье́ты, трещо́тки (*both f. pl.*); (*dice*) игра́льные ко́сти (*f. pl.*).

v.t. **1.: ~ fish/meat** отдел|я́ть, -и́ть ры́бу/мя́со от косте́й. **2.** (*steal*) утяну́ть (*pf.*) (*sl.*).

v.i.: **~ up on** (*coll.*) зубри́ть, вы́-.

cpds. **~-ash** *n.* костяна́я зола́; **~-dry** *adj.* соверше́нно сухо́й; сухо́й-пресухо́й; **~head** *n.* (*sl.*) ду́рень (*m.*), балда́ (*c.g.*); **~headed** *adj.* (*sl.*) тупоголо́вый; **~-idle, ~-lazy** *adjs.* ужа́сно лени́вый; **he is ~idle** он безде́льник/лентя́й/(*coll.*) лоботря́с; **~meal** *n.* костяна́я мука́; **~-setter** *n.* костопра́в.

boneless [bəʊnlɪs] *adj.* беско́стный; (*fig.*, *weak*) бесхребе́тный; **~ wonder** (*contortionist*) челове́к-зме́я.

boner [ˈbəʊnə(r)] *n.* (*sl.*) про́мах, опло́шность; **pull a ~** дать (*pf.*) ма́ху (*coll.*).

bonfire [ˈbɒnˌfaɪə(r)] *n.* костёр; **make a ~ of** (*also fig.*) пред|ава́ть, -а́ть огню́.

bonhomie [ˌbɒnɒˈmiː] *n.* доброду́шие, простоду́шие.

bonhomous [ˈbɒnəməs] *adj.* (*coll.*) доброду́шный, простоду́шный.

boniness [bəʊnɪnɪs] *n.* кости́стость, костля́вость.

bon mot [bɔ̃ ˈməʊ, bɒn-] *n.* остро́та, ме́ткое слове́чко.

bonk [bɒnk] *v.t.* (*coll.*) бара́ть, вы́-; тра́х|ать, -нуть.

v.i. бара́ться, вы́-; тра́х|аться, -нуться.

bonkers [ˈbɒŋkəz] *adj.* (*coll.*): **he's ~** он чо́кнутый; он с приве́том.

bonne bouche [bɒn ˈbuːʃ] *n.* ла́комый кусо́чек.

bonnet [ˈbɒnɪt] *n.* **1.** (*man's*) шотла́ндская ша́почка; (*woman's*) ка́пор; чепе́ц, че́пчик. **2.** (*of car*) капо́т.

bonny [ˈbɒnɪ] *adj.* (*comely*) хоро́шенький; (*fine*): **a ~ fighter** сла́вный воя́ка; (*healthy*): **a ~ baby** кре́пкий ребёнок.

bonus [ˈbəʊnəs] *n.* пре́мия, премиа́льные (*pl.*), бо́нус; **a ~ job** рабо́та с премиа́льным вознагражде́нием.

bony [ˈbəʊnɪ] *adj.* **1.** (*of, like bone*) костяно́й. **2.** (*of pers.*) костяно́й, кости́стый; **~ fingers** костля́вые па́льцы. **3.** (*having many bones*): **~ fish** костля́вая/кости́стая ры́ба; **~ meat** кости́стое мя́со.

bonze [bɒnz] *n.* бо́нза (*m.*).

boo [buː] *n.* шика́нье.

v.t. осви́ст|ывать, -а́ть; шика́ть (*impf.*) +*d.*; оши́кать (*pf.*); **~ an actor off the stage** шика́ньем прогна́ть (*pf.*) актёра со сце́ны.

v.i. улюлю́кать (*impf.*).

int. **1.** (*expr. disapproval*) шш!; у-у! **2.** (*used to startle*) у-у!

boob [buːb] *n.* **1.** (*coll.*, *simpleton*) простофи́ля (*c.g.*), дурачи́на (*c.g.*), дурале́й. **2.** (*coll.*, *mistake*) прома́шка. **3.** (*pl.*, *breasts*) буфера́ (*m. pl.*) (*sl.*).

v.i. (*coll.*) опростоволо́ситься (*pf.*), оплоша́ть (*pf.*); дать (*pf.*) прома́шку.

booby [ˈbuːbɪ] *n.* дурачо́к, дурале́й.

cpds. **~-hatch** *n.* (*sl.*) дом умалишённых; **~-trap** *n.* (*mil.*) ми́на-лову́шка; *v.t.* устан|а́вливать, -ови́ть ми́ны-лову́шки в/на+*p.*

boobyish [ˈbuːbɪɪʃ] *adj.* придуркова́тый.

boodle [ˈbuːd(ə)l] *n.* (*sl.*) де́н|ьги (*pl. g.* -ег).

boogie-woogie [ˌbuːgɪˈwuːgɪ] *n.* бу́ги-ву́ги (*nt. indecl.*).

boohoo [ˌbuːˈhuː] *v.i.* реве́ть (*impf.*).

int. у-у-у!

book [bʊk] *n.* **1.** кни́га; (*small*) кни́жка; **the B~** (*Bible*) Би́блия; **the B~ of Genesis** Кни́га Бытия́; **ship's ~** судово́й журна́л; **talk like a ~** говори́ть как по пи́саному; **it is a closed, sealed ~ to me** э́то для меня́ кни́га за семью́ печа́тями; **read s.o. like a ~** ви́деть (*impf.*) кого́-н. наскво́зь; **he is an open ~** он весь как на ладо́ни; **~ of words** (*instructions*) инстру́кции (*f. pl.*); пра́вила (*nt. pl.*) по́льзования; **go by the ~** сле́довать (*impf.*) предписа́нию/пра́вилам; **the ~ trade** книготорго́вля, кни́жная торго́вля. **2.** (*set*): **~ of tickets/needles** па́чка биле́тов/иго́лок; **~ of matches/stamps** кни́жечка спи́чек/ма́рок. **3.** (*libretto*) либре́тто (*indecl.*). **4.** (*account*): **he is on the firm's ~s** (*an employee*) он в шта́те э́той фи́рмы; **keep the ~s** вести́ (*det.*) бухга́лтерские/счётные кни́ги; **~ value** сто́имость по торго́вым кни́гам; **in s.o.'s good/bad ~s** на хоро́шем/плохо́м счету́ у кого́-н.; **bring s.o. to ~** призва́ть (*pf.*) кого́-н. к отве́ту; посчита́ться (*pf.*) с кем-н.; **that suits my ~** э́то меня́ устра́ивает.

v.t. **1.** (*enter in ~ or list*) зан|оси́ть, -ести в кни́гу; регистри́ровать, за-. **2.** (*reserve, engage*) зака́з|ывать, -а́ть; зан|има́ть, -я́ть; **~ seats at a theatre** заброни́ровать (*pf.*) биле́ты в теа́тре; **~ one's passage** купи́ть (*pf.*) биле́т на парохо́д; **speculators ~ed up all the seats** спекуля́нты скупи́ли все биле́ты; **I am ~ed (up) on Wednesday** я (по́лностью) за́нят в сре́ду; **~ s.o. in at a hotel** брони́ровать, за- для кого́-н. но́мер в гости́нице.

v.i.: **he ~ed in/out last night** он въе́хал/вы́ехал вчера́ ве́чером.

cpds. **~binder** *n.* переплётчик; **~bindery** *n.* переплётная; **~binding** *n.* переплётное де́ло; **~case** *n.* кни́жный шкаф; (*open-fronted*) кни́жные по́лки (*f. pl.*); **~-club** *n.* клуб книголю́бов; **~-ends** *n. pl.* подста́вки (*f. pl.*) для книг; **~-jacket** *n.* супероблo̓жка; **~keeper** *n.* бухга́лтер, счетово́д; **~keeping** *n.* бухгалте́рия, счетово́дство; **~-learned** *adj.* кни́жный; **~-learning** *n.* кни́жность; кни́жные зна́ния; **~-lover** *n.* кни́жник, книголю́б; **~maker** *n.* (*betting*) букме́кер; (*compiler*) компиля́тор; **~man** *n.* литера́тор; **~mark(er)** *n.* (кни́жная) закла́дка; **~plate** *n.* эксли́брис; **~-post** *n.* бандеро́ль; **by ~-post** бандеро́лью; **~-rack** *n.* по́лка для книг; **~-rest** *n.* (насто́льная) подста́вка для книг; **~seller** *n.* торго́вец кни́гами; **second-hand ~seller** букини́ст; **~selling** *n.* книготорго́вля; **~shelf** *n.* кни́жная по́лка; **~shop, ~store** *nn.* кни́жный магази́н; **~stall** *n.* кни́жный кио́ск; **~stand** *n.* (*rack*) стелла́ж; **~work** *n.* (*study*) рабо́та с кни́гами; **~worm** *n.* (*lit.*, *fig.*) кни́жный червь.

bookie [ˈbʊkɪ] (*coll.*) = **bookmaker**

booking [ˈbʊkɪŋ] *n.* зака́з; **advance ~** предвари́тельный зака́з; **return ~** зака́з на обра́тный биле́т; **the ~ for this play is heavy** тру́дно доста́ть биле́ты на э́ту пье́су.

cpds. **~-clerk** *n.* касси́р; **~-office** *n.* биле́тная ка́сса.

bookish [ˈbʊkɪʃ] *adj.* (*literary*, *studious*) кни́жный; (*pedantic*) педанти́чный.

bookishness [ˈbʊkɪʃnɪs] *n.* кни́жность; педанти́чность.

booklet [ˈbʊklɪt] *n.* брошю́ра, букле́т.

boom[1] [buːm] *n.* (*naut.*, *spar*) утле́гарь (*m.*); (*barrier*) плаву́чий бон.

boom[2] [buːm] *n.* (*of gun*, *thunder*, *waves*) гул, ро́кот; (*of voice*) гул; (*of bittern*) вой, у́хание; **supersonic ~** сверхзвуково́й хлопо́к.

v.t. & i. (*of gun*) бу́хать (*impf.*), грохота́ть (*impf*); (*of thunder*) глу́хо грохота́ть (*impf.*), рокота́ть (*impf.*); (*of waves*) рокота́ть (*impf.*); (*of bittern*) выть (*impf.*), у́хать (*impf.*); **the clock ~ed out the hour** часы́ гу́лко про́били час.

int. бум!; бух!

boom[3] [buːm] *n.* (*comm.*) бум, оживле́ние; **~ town** бы́стро расту́щий го́род.

v.t. (*boost*) реклами́ровать (*impf.*, *pf.*).

v.i.: **business is ~ing** де́ло процвета́ет; **Jones is ~ing as a novelist** Джонс процвета́ющий романи́ст.

boomer [ˈbuːmə(r)] *n.* (*Austral.*) саме́ц кенгуру́.

boomerang [ˈbuːməˌræŋ] *n.* бумера́нг.

v.i. (*fig.*): **his plan ~ed** его́ зате́я обрати́лась про́тив него́.

boon[1] [buːn] *n.* (*favour*) дар, благоде́яние; (*advantage*) бла́го, благода́ть.

boon[2] [buːn] *adj.*: **~ companion** до́брый прия́тель.

boor [ˈbʊə(r)] *n.* (*peasant*) мужи́к, дереве́нщина (*c.g.*); (*coarse pers.*) хам, мужи́к.

boorish [ˈbʊərɪʃ] *adj.* ха́мский, мужи́цкий, мужи́чий, мужикова́тый.

boorishness [ˈbʊərɪʃnɪs] *n.* ха́мство, мужикова́тость.

boost [buːst] *n.* **1.** (*advertisement*) реклами́рование, рекла́ма. **2.: give a ~ to the economy** стимули́ровать (*impf.*, *pf.*) эконо́мику.

v.t. (*advertise*) реклами́ровать (*impf., pf.*); (*increase*) пов|ыша́ть, -ы́сить; ~ **a battery** пов|ыша́ть, -ы́сить напряже́ние в батаре́е; ~ **s.o.'s reputation** создава́ть (*impf.*) кому́-н. репута́цию.

booster ['bu:stə(r)] *n.* **1.** (*elec.*) побуди́тель (*m.*), усили́тель (*m.*). **2.:** ~ **rocket** раке́тный ускори́тель; ~ **injection** (*med.*) повто́рная приви́вка.

boot[1] [bu:t] *n.* **1.** (*footwear*) боти́нок, башма́к; (*knee-length*) сапо́г; **riding** ~ (высо́кий) сапо́г; **fur** ~**s** у́нты (*f. pl.*); **football** ~**s** бу́тсы (*f. pl.*); **seven-league** ~**s** семими́льные сапоги́; **die in one's** ~**s** умере́ть (*pf.*) на посту́; **he is not fit to black your** ~**s** он вам и в подмётки не годи́тся; **he is too big for his** ~**s** он зазна́лся; **the** ~ **is now on the other foot** тепе́рь уж всё наоборо́т; де́ло поверну́лось по-друго́му; **put the** ~ **in** прибе́гнуть (*pf.*) к жёстким ме́рам; **like old** ~**s** (*coll.*) си́льно, здо́рово; **my heart was in my** ~**s** у меня́ душа́ в пя́тки ушла́; **you bet your** ~**s!** (*coll.*) бу́дьте уве́рены! **2.** (*pl. as sg. n., hotel servant*) коридо́рный. **3.** (*instrument of torture*) испа́нский сапо́г. **4.** (*dismissal*): **give s.o. the** ~ вы́турить (*pf.*) (*coll.*) кого́-н. (с рабо́ты); **get the** ~ вы́лететь (*pf.*) (*coll.*) (с рабо́ты). **5.** (*of a car*) бага́жник.

v.t.: ~ **s.o. in the face** съе́здить (*pf.*) (*coll.*) кому́-н. по физионо́мии; ~ **s.o. out of his job** вы́турить (*pf.*) (*coll.*) кого́-н.

cpds. ~**black** *n.* чи́стильщик сапо́г; ~**jack** *n.* приспособле́ние для снима́ния сапо́г; ~**lace** *n.* шнуро́к для боти́нок; ~**leg** *n.* (*fig.*): ~**leg whisky** контраба́ндное ви́ски; *v.t. & i.* (*distil*) занима́ться (*impf.*) самогоноку́ре́нием; (*trade*) торгова́ть (*impf.*) самого́ном; ~**legger** *n.* самого́нщик; ~**licker** *n.* (*coll.*) лизоблю́д, подхали́м; ~**maker** *n.* сапо́жник; ~**-polish** *n.* ва́кса; ~**strap** *n.* ушко́; **pull o.s. up by one's own** ~**straps** (*fig.*) спасти́ (*pf.*) себя́ со́бственными рука́ми; ~**-top** *n.* голени́ще; ~**-tree** *n.* сапо́жная коло́дка.

boot[2] [bu:t] *n.*: **to** ~ в прида́чу.

booted ['bu:tɪd] *adj.*: ~ **and spurred** (*fig.*) в по́лной гото́вности.

bootee [bu:'ti:] *n.* (*woman's*) да́мский боти́нок; (*child's*) пине́тка; вя́заный башмачо́к.

Boötes [bəʊ'əʊti:z] (*astron.*) *n.* Волопа́с.

booth [bu:ð, bu:θ] *n.* бу́дка; (*stall in market*) пала́тка; (*tent at fair*) балага́н; (*polling-*~) каби́на для голосова́ния.

bootless ['bu:tlɪs] *adj.* (*unavailing*) бесполе́зный.

booty ['bu:tɪ] *n.* добы́ча.

booze [bu:z] *n.* вы́пивка; попо́йка; **go on the** ~ запи́ть (*pf.*); **be on the** ~ пья́нствовать (*impf.*).

v.i. пья́нствовать (*impf.*), выпива́ть (*impf.*).

cpd. ~**-up** *n.* попо́йка.

boozer ['bu:zə(r)] *n.* (*pers.*) выпиво́ха (*c.g.*); (*pub*) забега́ловка.

boozy ['bu:zɪ] *adj.* (*fuddled*) пья́ный; (*fond of drinking*) выпива́ющий, пью́щий; **a** ~ **type** люби́тель (*m.*) подда́ть (*coll.*).

bo-peep [ˌbəʊ'pi:p] *n.* пря́т|ки (*pl., g.* -ок); **play** ~ игра́ть в пря́тки.

boracic [bə'ræsɪk] *adj.* бо́рный.

borage ['bɒrɪdʒ] *n.* огуре́чник, бура́чник.

borax ['bɔ:ræks] *n.* бура́; (*attr.*) бо́рный.

bordello [bɔ:'deləʊ] *n.* борде́ль (*m.*).

border ['bɔ:də(r)] *n.* **1.** (*side, edging*): ~ **of a lake** бе́рег о́зера; (*of a sheet of paper*) кайма́; (*of a handkerchief*) каёмка; **a** ~ **of tulips** бордю́р из тюльпа́нов; **herbaceous** ~ бордю́р из многоле́тних цвето́в. **2.** (*frontier*) грани́ца; (*fig.*) грань; ~ **incidents** пограни́чные инциде́нты.

v.t.: **the garden is** ~**ed by a stream** сад ограни́чен ручьём; вокру́г са́да протека́ет руче́й; **our garden** ~**s his field** наш сад грани́чит с его́ по́лем.

v.i.: **these countries** ~ **on one another** э́ти стра́ны грани́чат друг с дру́гом; **he is** ~**ing on sixty** ему́ под шестьдеся́т; **this** ~**s on fanaticism** э́то грани́чит с фанати́змом.

cpds. ~**land** *n.* пограни́чная о́бласть; (*fig.*) грань; ~**line** *n.* грани́ца; (*fig.*) грань; (*demarcation line*) демаркацио́нная ли́ния; **a** ~**line case** промежу́точный слу́чай.

borderer ['bɔ:dərə(r)] *n.* жи́тель (*m.*) пограни́чного райо́на.

bore[1] [bɔ:(r)] *n.* (*of tube, pipe*) расто́ченное отве́рстие; (*calibre*) кали́бр, кана́л ствола́; (*hole in earth etc.*) сква́жина.

v.t. сверли́ть, про-; бура́вить, про-; бури́ть, про-; ~ **a tube** раст|а́чивать, -очи́ть трубу́; ~ **a hole** сверли́ть, продыру́.

v.i. бури́ть (*impf.*); ~ **for oil** бури́ть (*impf.*) в по́исках не́фти; ~ **through a crowd** проб|ива́ться, -и́ться через толпу́.

cpd. ~**-hole** *n.* бурова́я сква́жина.

bore[2] [bɔ:(r)] *n.* (*pers.*) ску́чный челове́к; зану́да (*c.g.*); (*thg.*) (что-н.) надое́дливое; **what a** ~**!** кака́я тоска́!; кака́я доку́ка!

v.t. надо|еда́ть, -е́сть +*d.*; нав|оди́ть, -ести́ ску́ку на+*a.*; ~ **s.o. to death, tears** надо|еда́ть, -е́сть кому́-н. до́ смерти. *See also* **bored**

bore[3] [bɔ:(r)] *n.* (*tidal wave*) бор; напо́р волн в у́стье реки́.

boreal ['bɔ:rɪəl] *adj.* се́верный, боре́альный.

Boreas ['bɔ:rɪəs] *n.* Боре́й.

bored ['bɔ:d] *adj.* скуча́ющий; **I am** ~ мне ску́чно; **in a** ~ **voice** ску́чным/скуча́ющим го́лосом; **I am** ~ **with him** он мне надое́л.

boredom ['bɔ:dəm] *n.* ску́ка, тоска́.

borer ['bɔ:rə(r)] *n.* (*pers.*) бури́льщик, сверли́льщик; (*machine*) бур, бура́в, сверло́; (*insect*) древото́чец.

boric ['bɔ:rɪk] *adj.* бо́рный.

boring ['bɔ:rɪŋ] *adj.* (*tedious*) ску́чный, надое́дливый.

born [bɔ:n] *adj.* **1.:** **a** ~ **poet/fool** прирождённый поэ́т/дура́к. **2.:** **be** ~ роди́ться (*pf.*); **he was** ~ **to be hanged** таки́е, как он, конча́ют на ви́селице; **he was** ~ **with a silver spoon in his mouth** он роди́лся в соро́чке; **I wasn't** ~ **yesterday** я не вчера́ роди́лся. **3.:** **in all my** ~ **days** за всю мою́ жизнь.

Borneo ['bɔ:nɪˌəʊ] *n.* Борне́о (*indecl.*).

boron ['bɔ:rɒn] *n.* бор.

borough ['bʌrə] *n.* (*town*) го́род; (*section of town*) райо́н; **parliamentary** ~ го́род, предста́вленный в парла́менте.

borrow ['bɒrəʊ] *v.t. & i.* **1.** (*take for a time*) брать, взять на вре́мя; заи́мствовать, по-; зан|има́ть, -я́ть (*also math.*); (*money*) брать, взять взаймы́; **he is always** ~**ing** он постоя́нно берёт взаймы́ (*or* в долг); ~ **an idea from s.o.** заи́мствовать (*impf., pf.*) у кого́-н. иде́ю; **wear** ~**ed clothes** носи́ть (*impf.*) что-н. с чужо́го плеча́. **2.** (*ling.*) заи́мствовать (*impf.*).

borrowing ['bɒrəʊɪŋ] *n.* **1.** ода́лживание; ~ **is a bad habit** брать взаймы́ — плоха́я привы́чка. **2.** (*ling.*) заи́мствование.

bor(t)sch [bɔ:ʃ] *n.* борщ.

borzoi ['bɔ:zɔɪ] *n.* ру́сская борза́я.

bosh [bɒʃ] *n.* (*coll.*) вздор, чепуха́.

Bosnia and Herzegovina ['bɒznɪə ˌhɜ:tsɪgə'vi:nə] *n.* Бо́сния и Герцегови́на.

bosom ['bʊz(ə)m] *n.* **1.** (*breast*) грудь; (*of clothing*) лиф, мани́шка; (*shirt-front*) грудь; мани́шка. **2.** (*fig.*) се́рдце, душа́; ~ **friend** закады́чный друг; **in one's (own)** ~ в глубине́ души́; **in the** ~ **of one's family** в ло́не семьи́; **the** ~ **of the church** ло́но це́ркви.

v.t.: **a house** ~**ed in trees** дом, утопа́ющий в зе́лени.

bosomy ['bʊzəmɪ] *adj.* (*of woman*) груда́стая.

Bosp(h)orus ['bɒspərəs] *n.* Босфо́р.

boss[1] [bɒs] *n.* (*protuberance*) ши́шка; (*of shield*) умбо́н; (*archit.*) орна́мент в места́х пересече́ний ба́лок.

boss[2] [bɒs] *n.* (*master*) босс, хозя́ин; **industrial** ~**es** промы́шленные запра́вилы/тузы́.

v.t.: ~ **the show** (*coll.*) хозя́йничать (*impf.*); ~ **s.o. about** кома́ндовать (*impf.*) кем-н.; (*coll.*) помыка́ть (*impf.*) кем-н.

boss-eyed ['bɒsaɪd] *adj.* криво́й, косо́й, косогла́зый.

bossy ['bɒsɪ] *adj.* (*overbearing*) команди́рский.

bot [bɒt] *n.* (*also* **bott**): **the** ~**s** (*vet.*) гельминто́з.

cpd. ~**-fly** *n.* о́вод.

botanical [bə'tænɪk(ə)l] *adj.* ботани́ческий.

botanist ['bɒtənɪst] *n.* бота́ник.

botanize ['bɒtəˌnaɪz] *v.i.* ботанизи́ровать (*impf., pf.*).

botany ['bɒtənɪ] *n.* бота́ника.

botch [bɒtʃ] *n.*: **make a ~** напорта́чить (*pf.*).

v.t. (*bungle*) зава́л|ивать, -и́ть; по́ртить, ис-; (*patch roughly*) зала́т|ывать, -а́ть; **~ up an essay** состря́пать (*pf.*) статéечку.

botcher ['bɒtʃə(r)] *n.* (*bungler*) портáч, «сапóжник».

both [bəʊθ] *pron. & adj.* óба (*m.*, *nt.*), óбе (*f.*); и тот и другóй; **~ sledges** óбе пáры санéй; **~ of us** мы óба; **of ~ sexes** обóего пóла; **you cannot have it ~ ways** выбирáйте однó из двух.

adv.: **~ ... and ...** и... и...; **he is ~ tired and hungry** он и устáл и к томý же гóлоден; **I am fond of music, ~ ancient and modern** я люблю́ мýзыку, как стáрую, так и совремéнную; **my sister and I ~ helped him** мы óба помоглú емý, и я и сестрá; мы (вдвоём) с сестрóй емý помоглú.

bother ['bɒðə(r)] *n.* беспокóйство; хлóп|оты (*pl.*, *g.* -óт); возня́; **I had no ~ finding the book** я нашёл кнúгу без трудá.

v.t. (*disturb*) беспокóить, по-; тревóжить, по-; (*importune*) надоедáть (*impf.*) +*d.*; **~ one's head** тревóжиться (*impf.*); **~ (it)!** чёрт возьмú!; **he is always ~ing me to lend him money** он вéчно пристаёт ко мне с прóсьбой одолжúть емý дéнег; **I can't be ~ed** мне нéкогда/лень.

v.i. беспокóиться, по-; **don't ~ to make tea** не возúтесь с чáем.

bothersome ['bɒðəsəm] *adj.* досáдный, надоéдливый.

Bothnia ['bɒθnɪə] *n.*: **Gulf of ~** Ботнúческий залúв.

bott [bɒt] = **bot**

bottle[1] ['bɒt(ə)l] *n.* **1.** бутьíлка; бутьíль; (*for infants*) рожóк; **over a ~ of wine** за бутьíлкой винá; **bring up a child on the ~** вскáрмливать (*impf.*) ребёнка искýсственно; **hot-water ~** грéлка. **2.** (*fig.*): **he is fond of the ~** он приклáдывается к бутьíлке; **take to the ~** пристрастúться (*pf.*) к бутьíлке; **keep s.o. from the ~** удéрж|ивать, -áть когó-н. от пья́нства.

v.t. (*put in ~s*) разл|ивáть, -úть по бутьíлкам; **~d in Moscow** москóвского разлúва; (*keep in ~s*) хранúть (*impf.*) в бутьíлках; **~ fruit** консервúровать (*impf.*, *pf.*) фрýкты; **~ up** (*conceal*) скрьí|вáть, -ть; (*restrain*) сдéрж|ивать, -áть; **~ up one's feelings** скры|вáть, -ть свои чýвства; **~ up the enemy fleet** зап|ирáть, -ерéть неприя́тельский флот.

cpds. **~-baby** *n.* ребёнок, вскóрмленный из рожкá; искýсственник; **~-brush** *n.* ёрш(ик); **~-fed** *adj.* искýсственно вскóрмленный; **~-glass** *n.* бутьíлочное стеклó; **~-green** *n.* бутьíлочный цвет; *adj.* бутьíлочного цвéта; бутьíлочно-зелёный; **~neck** *n.* гóрлышко бутьíлки; (*fig.*) затóр; прóбка; ýзкое мéсто; **~-nose** *n.* нос картóшкой; **~-nosed** *adj.* толстонóсый; **~-nosed whale** бутылконóс; **~-party** *n.* ≃ пирýшка в склáдчину; **~-top** *n.* колпачóк на бутьíлку; **~-washer** *n.* (*pers.*) посýдник, мóйщик бутьíлок; (*machine*) бутыломóйка.

bottle[2] ['bɒt(ə)l] *n.* (*of hay*) сноп; (*of straw*) охáпка.

bottled ['bɒt(ə)ld] *adj.*: **~ beer** бутьíлочное пúво.

bottom ['bɒtəm] *n.* **1.** (*lowest part*) дно; (*of mountain*) поднóжие, подóшва; (*of page*) низ, конéц; (*of stairs*) низ, основáние; **~ shelf** нúжняя пóлка; (*of coat*) подóл; **false ~** двойнóе дно; **~ up(wards)** вверх дном; **~s up!** пей до днá!; **at the ~ of the class** отстающий в клáссе. **2.** (*further end*): **at the ~ of the bed** в ногáх кровáти; **~ (end) of the table** нúжний конéц столá; **~ of the garden** зáдняя часть сáда; **~ of the street** конéц ýлицы. **3.** (*of sea*) дно; **send to the ~** пус|кáть, -тúть на дно; топúть, по-. **4.** (*of a chair*) сидéнье. **5.** (*anat.*) зад; зáдняя часть; зáднее мéсто. **6.** (*of ship*) днúще; **ship goods in British ~s** перев|озúть, -езтú товáры на англúйских судáх. **7.** (*fig.*): **from the ~ of my heart** из глубиньí душú; от всегó сéрдца; **get to the ~ of sth.** доб|ирáться, -рáться до сýти чегó-н.; **he was at the ~ of it** за э́тим стоя́л он; **a good fellow at ~** по существý дóбрый мáлый; **knock the ~ out of a scheme** сорвáть (*pf.*) план; **~ price** сáмая нúзкая ценá; крáйняя ценá; **prices touched ~** цéны достúгли сáмого нúзкого ýровня; **he came ~ in algebra** он был послéдним по áлгебре.

v.t.: **~ a chair** придéл|ывать, -ать сидéнье к стýлу.

bottomless ['bɒtəmlɪs] *adj.* **1.** бездóнный; **~ pit** бездóнная я́ма; (*hell*) ад, преиспóдняя; (*immeasurable*) безгранúчный, беспредéльный. **2.** (*of chair*) без сидéнья.

bottommost ['bɒtəm,məʊst] *adj.* сáмый нúжний.

bottomry ['bɒtəmrɪ] *n.* бодмерéя.

botulism ['bɒtjʊ,lɪz(ə)m] *n.* ботулúзм.

boudoir ['bu:dwɑ:(r)] *n.* будуáр.

bougainvillaea [,bu:gən'vɪlɪə] *n.* бугенвúлия.

bough [baʊ] *n.* сук.

bouillon [bu:'jɔ̃, 'bu:jɒn] *n.* бульóн.

boulder ['bəʊldə(r)] *n.* валýн.

boule ['bu:l] = **buhl**

boulevard ['bu:lə,vɑ:d, 'bu:lvɑ:(r)] *n.* бульвáр.

bounce [baʊns] *n.* (*of ball*) подпрьíгивание, подскóк, отскóк; (*push*, *arrogance*) хвастовствó.

v.t. (*eject*) вышúдывать, вьíкинуть; **~ a ball** бить (*impf.*) мячóм об пол (о зéмлю, об стéнку *и т.п.*); **~ s.o. into a decision** подт|áлкивать, -олкнýть когó-н. приня́ть решéние.

v.i. (*of ball etc.*) отск|áкивать, -очúть; подпрьíг|ивать, -нуть; (*coll.*, *of cheque*) вернýться (*pf.*); (*of pers.*): **~ into a room** влетéть (*pf.*) в кóмнату; **~ out of a room** вьíскочить (*pf.*) из кóмнаты; **~ about** суетúться (*impf.*); **~ back** (*fig.*) бьíстро опрáвиться.

bouncer ['baʊnsə(r)] *n.* (*chucker-out*) вышибáла (*m.*).

bouncing ['baʊnsɪŋ] *adj.* **1.** (*of ball*) прьíгающий, подпрьíгивающий. **2.** (*healthy*) здорóвый; (*lusty*) здоровéнный.

bouncy ['baʊnsɪ] *adj.* (*lit.*, *resilient*) упрýгий; (*in manner*) рéзвый, живóй.

bound[1] [baʊnd] *n.* (*usu. pl.*, *limit*) гранúца, предéл; **set ~s to sth.** стáвить, по- предéл чемý-н.; огранúчи|вать, -ть что-н.; **know no ~s** не знать (*impf.*) гранúц; **beyond the ~s of reason** за предéлами разýмного; **keep sth. within ~s** держáть (*impf.*) что-н. в определённых гранúцах; **within the ~s of possibility** в предéлах возмóжного; **the town is out of ~s to troops** вход в гóрод солдáтам воспрещён.

v.t. (*limit*) огранúчи|вать, -ть; **England is ~ed by Scotland on the north** Áнглия гранúчит на сéвере с Шотлáндией.

bound[2] [baʊnd] *n.* (*jump*) прыжóк; скачóк; **by leaps and ~s** галóпом, стремúтельно; не по дням, а по часáм; **at a ~** однúм прыжкóм; (*bounce*) отскóк.

v.i. прьíг|ать, -нуть; скак|áть, -нýть; **~ over a ditch** переск|áкивать, -очúть чéрез канáву; **he ~ed off to fetch the book** он подпрьíгнул, чтóбы достáть кнúгу; **her heart ~ed with joy** её сéрдце (за)бúлось от рáдости.

bound[3] [baʊnd] *adj.* **1.** (*connected*) свя́занный; **this is ~ up with politics** э́то свя́зано с полúтикой. **2.** (*absorbed*): **he is ~ up in his work** он поглощён рабóтой; **she is ~ up in her son** онá пóлностью занятá сьíном. **3.** (*certain*): **he is ~ to win** он непремéнно вьíиграет; **I'll be ~** я увéрен; гóлову положý, что... **4.** (*obliged*): **you are not ~ to go** вам не обязáтельно идтú. **5.** (*of book*) переплетённый; в переплёте. **6.** (*constipated*) страдáющий запóром. **7.** (*en route*): **the ship is ~ for New York** пароxóд направля́ется в Нью-Йóрк; **where are you ~ for?** кудá вы направля́етесь?; **homeward ~** направля́ющийся на рóдину.

boundary ['baʊndərɪ, -drɪ] *n.* (*of a field etc.*) гранúца, рубéж; (*fig.*) предéл; (*attr.*) пограничный.

bounder ['baʊndə(r)] *n.* хам (*coll.*).

boundless ['baʊndlɪs] *adj.* безгранúчный, беспредéльный.

boundlessness ['baʊndlɪsnɪs] *n.* безгранúчность, беспредéльность.

bounteous ['baʊntɪəs] *adj.* (*generous*) щéдрый; (*plentiful*) обúльный.

bountiful ['baʊntɪ,fʊl] *adj.* щéдрый; обúльный; **lady ~** дáма-патронéсса.

bounty ['baʊntɪ] *n.* **1.** (*generosity*) щéдрость, щедрóты (*f. pl.*). **2.** (*mil.*, *naut.*) поощрúтельная прéмия. **3.** (*comm.*) (экспортная) прéмия.

bouquet [bu:'keɪ, bəʊ-] *n.* (*of flowers*, *wine*) букéт; (*compliment*) одобрéние, хвалá.

bourbon ['bɜːbən, 'bʊə-] *n.* (*whisky*) бе́рбон.
bourdon ['bʊəd(ə)n] *n.* (*of organ*) басо́вый реги́стр; (*of bagpipes*) басо́вая тру́бка.
bourgeois[1] ['bʊəʒwɑː] *n.* буржуа́ (*m. indecl.*); **she is a ~** она́ меща́нка.
adj. буржуа́зный.
bourgeois[2] ['bʊəʒwɑː] *n.* (*typ.*) бо́ргес.
bourgeoisie [ˌbʊəʒwɑː'ziː] *n.* буржуази́я.
bourrée ['bʊreɪ] *n.* бурре́ (*nt. indecl.*).
bourse [bʊəs] *n.* фо́ндовая би́ржа.
bout [baʊt] *n.* **1.** (*at games*) бой, встре́ча, схва́тка; **fencing ~** бой в фехтова́нии; **wrestling ~** схва́тка в борьбе́; **have a ~ with** схва́т|ываться, -и́ться с+*i.* **2.** (*of illness*) при́ступ. **3.** (*drinking-~*) запо́й.
boutique [buː'tiːk] *n.* (небольшо́й) мо́дный магази́н.
bovine ['bəʊvaɪn] *adj.* (*zool.*) быча́чий, бы́чий; (*fig.*) тупо́й.
bow[1] [bəʊ] *n.* **1.** (*weapon*) лук; **draw a ~** натя́|гивать, -ну́ть тетиву́ лу́ка; **draw the long ~** (*fig.*) преувели́чи|вать, -ть; **two strings to one's ~** (*fig.*) ≃ сре́дство, оста́вленное про запа́с; **draw a ~ at a venture** (*fig.*) де́лать, с- что-н. науга́д. **2.** (*rainbow*) ра́дуга. **3.** (*of violin etc.*) смычо́к. **4.** (*of saddle*) лука́. **5.** (*knot*) бант; **tie a ~** завя́з|ывать, -а́ть бант; **tie sth. in a ~** завя́з|ывать, -а́ть что-н. ба́нтиком.
v.i. (*of violinist*) владе́ть (*impf.*) смычко́м.
cpds. **~-head** *n.* гренла́ндский/поля́рный кит; **~-legged** *adj.* кривоно́гий; **~-legs** *n. pl.* кривы́е но́ги (*f. pl.*); **~-line** *n.* (*rope*) були́нь (*m.*); (*knot*) бесе́дочный у́зел; **~man** *n.* (*archer*) лу́чник; **~-saw** *n.* лучко́вая пила́; **~shot** *n.*: **within a ~shot of** на расстоя́нии полёта стрелы́ от+*g.*; **~string** *n.* тетива́; **~-tie** *n.* (га́лстук-)ба́бочка; **~-window** *n.* э́ркер; (*coll.*, *paunch*) пу́зо, брю́хо.
bow[2] [baʊ] *n.* (*salutation*) покло́н; **make a deep/low ~** ни́зко кла́няться, поклони́ться; отве́|шивать, -сить ни́зкий покло́н; **make one's ~** (*début*) дебюти́ровать (*impf.*, *pf.*).
v.t. **1.** (*bend*): **~ the knee** преклон|я́ть, -и́ть коле́на; **~ one's head** склон|я́ть, -и́ть го́лову; **the wind ~ed the trees** ве́тер гнул/клони́л дере́вья; **~ed down by grief** сло́мленный го́рем. **2.** (*usher*, *express by ~ing*): **~ s.o. in/out** ввести́/проводи́ть (*pf.*) кого́-н. с покло́ном; **~ one's thanks** благодари́ть покло́ном.
v.i. **1.** (*salute*) кла́няться, поклони́ться; **~ and scrape** расша́ркиваться (*перед кем-н.*); **I have a ~ing acquaintance with him** у меня́ с ним ша́почное знако́мство; **~ down** (*worship*) преклон|я́ться, -и́ться (пе́ред+*i.*); **~ out** (= *retire*): **~ out of politics** распрости́ться (*pf.*) с поли́тикой. **2.** (*defer*) склон|я́ться, -и́ться (**to, before:** перед+*i.*); **~ to fate** смир|я́ться, -и́ться с судьбо́й.
bow[3] [baʊ] *n.* **1.** (*naut.*) нос; **on the ~** на носовы́х курсовы́х угла́х; **cross s.o.'s ~s** (*fig.*) перебе|га́ть, -жа́ть кому́-н. доро́гу. **2.** (*rower*) ба́ковый гребе́ц.
cpds. **~-compass(es)** *n.* кронци́ркуль (*m.*); **~-oar** *n.* ба́ковое весло́.
bowdlerization [ˌbaʊdləraɪ'zeɪʃ(ə)n] *n.* выхола́щивание; изъя́тие нежела́тельных мест (*в книге*).
bowdlerize ['baʊdləˌraɪz] *v.t.* выхола́щивать, вы́холостить.
bowel ['baʊəl] *n.* **1.** кишка́; **have a ~ movement** име́ть (*impf.*) стул; испражня́ться; **keep one's ~s open** подде́рживать (*impf.*) де́йствие кише́чника; **are your ~s regular?** регуля́рно ли де́йствует у вас кише́чник?; **castor oil is good for moving your ~s** касто́рка хорошо́ сла́бит. **2.: ~s of the earth** не́дра (*pl.*, *g.* —) земли́; **~s of mercy** (*arch.*) сострада́ние, се́рдце.
bower ['baʊə(r)] *n.* (*arbour*) бесе́дка.
cpd. **~-bird** *n.* бесе́дочница, шала́шник.
bowie-knife ['bəʊɪ] *n.* дли́нный охо́тничий нож.
bowing ['bəʊɪŋ] *n.* (*mus.*) владе́ние смычко́м.
bowl[1] [bəʊl] *n.* **1.** (*vessel*) ча́ша, ва́за, ми́ска; **crystal ~** хруста́льная ва́за; **wooden ~** деревя́нная ми́ска. **2.** (*of pipe*) ча́шечка; (*of spoon*) углубле́ние. **3.: the flowing ~** (*fig.*) спиртны́е напи́тки (*m. pl.*).
bowl[2] [bəʊl] *n.* (*ball*) ке́гельный шар; **play ~s** игра́ть (*impf.*) в ке́гли/шары́.
v.t. (*roll*) ката́ть (*indet.*), кати́ть, по-; **~ a hoop** гоня́ть (*indet.*), гнать о́бруч; **~ over** (*lit.*) сшиб|а́ть, -и́ть; (*fig.*); **he was ~ed over by her** она́ срази́ла его́; **he was ~ed over by the news** он был ошара́шен/ошеломлён э́тим изве́стием.
v.i. **1.: ~ along** бы́стро кати́ться. **2.** (*play bowls*) игра́ть (*impf.*) в ке́гли/шары́; **~ing-alley** кегельба́н; **~ing-green** лужа́йка для игры́ в шары́.
bowler[1] ['bəʊlə(r)] *n.* (*at games*) подаю́щий/броса́ющий мяч.
bowler[2] ['bəʊlə(r)] *n.* (**~ hat**) котело́к.
bowlful ['bəʊlfʊl] *n.* ми́ска (*чего*).
bowser ['baʊzə(r)] *n.* бензозапра́вщик.
bowsprit ['bəʊsprɪt] *n.* бушпри́т.
bow-wow ['baʊwaʊ, -'waʊ] *n.* (*bark*) гав-га́в; (*coll.*, *dog*) соба́чка.
int. гав-га́в!
box[1] [bɒks] *n.* (*bot.*) (*also* **~wood**) самши́т.
box[2] [bɒks] *n.* **1.** (*receptacle*) коро́бка, я́щик; **letter-~** почто́вый я́щик; **P.O.** (*abbr. of **post office***) **box** почто́вый я́щик; **~ number** но́мер почто́вого я́щика; **cardboard ~** карто́нка; (*pej.*) **a ~ of a place** коро́бка; **in the same ~** (*fig.*) в одина́ковом затрудни́тельном положе́нии; **play B~ and Cox** ≃ игра́ть (*impf.*) в пря́тки; **~ barrage** (*mil.*) окаймля́ющий загради́тельный ого́нь. **2.: Christmas ~** рожде́ственский пода́рок. **3.** (*driver's seat*) ко́з|лы (*pl.*, *g.* -ел). **4.** (*theatr.*) ло́жа. **5.** (*television*) я́щик, те́лик. **6.** (*for horse*) сто́йло; **loose ~** широ́кое сто́йло. **7.** (*witness-~*) ме́сто для свиде́телей; **be in the ~** свиде́тельствовать (*impf.*); **put s.o. in the ~** вы́звать (*pf.*) кого́-н. в ка́честве свиде́теля. **8.** (*typ.*) ра́мка.
v.t. **1.** класть, положи́ть в коро́бку/я́щик; **~ a horse** ста́вить, по- ло́шадь в тре́йлер. **2.: ~ the compass** (*name points*) наз|ыва́ть, -ва́ть все ру́мбы ко́мпаса; (*fig.*) де́лать, с- по́лный круг (*or* поворо́т на 360°). **3. ~ in, up** (*confine*) сти́с|кивать, -нуть; вти́с|кивать, -нуть; запи́х|ивать, -а́ть; **~ed in** сти́снутый, зажа́тый. **4. ~ up** (*bungle*) порта́чить, на-.
cpds. **~-board** *n.* коро́бочный карто́н; **~-calf** *n.* бокс; хро́мовая теля́чья ко́жа; **~-camera** *n.* я́щичный фотоаппара́т; **~-car** *n.* (*rail*) това́рный ваго́н; **~-kite** *n.* коро́бчатый возду́шный змей; **~-office** *n.* (театра́льная) ка́сса; **~-pleat** *n.* бантова́я скла́дка; **~-pleated** *adj.* в бантову́ю скла́дку; **~room** *n.* кладова́я; **~-seat** *n.* (*theatr.*) ме́сто в ло́же; **~-spring** *n.* дива́нная пружи́на; **~-up** *n.* (*coll.*) пу́таница.
box[3] [bɒks] *n.*: **~ on the ear** оплеу́ха.
v.t.: **~ s.o.'s ears** да|ва́ть, -ть кому́-н. оплеу́ху (*or* по́ уху).
v.i. (*sport*) бокси́ровать (*impf.*).
boxer ['bɒksə(r)] *n.* (*sportsman*; *dog*) боксёр; **~ shorts** боксёрские трусы́; **B~ rebellion** (*hist.*) Ихэтуа́ньское/боксёрское восста́ние.
boxful ['bɒksfʊl] *n.* я́щик, коро́бка (*чего*).
boxing ['bɒksɪŋ] *n.* (*sport*) бокс.
cpd. **~-glove** *n.* боксёрская перча́тка.
Boxing Day ['bɒksɪŋ] *n.* второ́й день Рождества́, день рожде́ственских пода́рков.
boy [bɔɪ] *n.* **1.** (*child*) ма́льчик; **I knew him as** (*when I was*) **a ~** я знал его́, когда́ я был ребёнком; (*when he was*) я знал его́ ма́льчиком; **~ scout** бойска́ут; **~ wonder** вундерки́нд. **2.** (*son*) сын. **3.: grocer's** (*etc.*) **~** ма́льчик в бакале́йной (*и т.п.*) ла́вке. **4.: old ~** стари́на́ (*m.*), стари́к, дружи́ще (*m.*); **~s!** ребя́та (*m. pl.*); **oh ~!** (*coll.*) здо́рово; вот э́то да́!
cpd. **~-friend** *n.* ≃ (*её*) па́рень (*m.*), молодо́й челове́к.
boyar ['bɔɪə] *n.* боя́рин; (*attr.*) боя́рский.
boycott ['bɔɪkɒt] *n.* бойко́т.
v.t. бойкоти́ровать (*impf.*, *pf.*).
boyhood ['bɔɪhʊd] *n.* о́трочество.
boyish ['bɔɪɪʃ] *adj.* мальчи́шеский.
boyishness ['bɔɪɪʃnɪs] *n.* мальчи́шество.
Boyle's law [bɔɪlz] *n.* зако́н Бо́йля-Марио́та.
bra [brɑː] *n.* (*coll.*) ли́фчик, бюстга́льтер.
brace [breɪs] *n.* **1.** (*support*) подпо́рка, распо́рка; (*clasp*) скре́па; (*stay*) оття́жка; (*tie*) связь; (*in building*) связь, подко́с, скоба́. **2.** (*naut.*) брас. **3.** (*strap*) сво́ра; **~s** (*to wear*) подтя́ж|ки (*pl. g.* -ек), по́моч|и (*pl.*, *g.* -ей). **4.** (*typ.*, *bracket*) фигу́рная ско́бка. **5.** (*pair*) па́ра; **in a ~ of shakes**

(*coll.*) ми́гом. **6.**: ~ **and bit** коловоро́т, пёрка. **7.** (*dentistry etc.*) ши́на.

v.t. **1.** (*tie*) свя́з|ывать, -а́ть; (*make fast*) скреп|ля́ть, -и́ть; подкреп|ля́ть, -и́ть; (*support*) подп|ира́ть, -ере́ть; **he ~d himself against the wall** он опёрся о сте́ну. **2.** (*of nerves*) укреп|ля́ть, -и́ть; ~ **s.o. (up)** подбод|ря́ть, -и́ть кого́-н.; **he ~d himself to do it** он собра́лся с ду́хом сде́лать э́то.

bracelet [ˈbreɪslɪt] *n.* брасле́т; (*pl., sl., handcuffs*) нару́чники (*m. pl.*).

bracer [ˈbreɪsə(r)] *n.* (*pick-me-up*) рю́мка для бо́дрости.

brachycephalic [ˌbrækɪsɪˈfælɪk] *adj.* брахикефа́льный, брахицефали́ческий.

bracing [ˈbreɪsɪŋ] *adj.* бодря́щий, укрепля́ющий.

bracken [ˈbrækən] *n.* орля́к; (*collect.*) па́поротник.

bracket [ˈbrækɪt] *n.* **1.** (*support*) кронште́йн; **angular** ~ углово́й кронште́йн; (*lamp-~*) ла́мповый кронште́йн; бра (*nt. indecl.*); **gas** ~ га́зовый рожо́к; **headlamp** ~ кронште́йн фа́ры. **2.** (*shelf*) по́лочка на кронште́йнах. **3.** (*typ.*) ско́бка; **square/round** ~ квадра́тная/кру́глая ско́бка; **open/close ~s** откры́ть/закры́ть (*pf.*) ско́бки. **4.** (*fig.*): **the higher income ~s** гру́ппа населе́ния с бо́лее высо́кими дохо́дами. **5.** (*mil.*) ви́лка.

v.t. **1.** (*enclose in ~s*) заключ|а́ть, -и́ть в ско́бки. **2.** (*link with a ~*) соедин|я́ть, -и́ть ско́бкой; (*fig.*): **do not ~ me with him** не ста́вьте меня́ с ним на одну́ до́ску; **A and B were ~ed for first prize** пе́рвую пре́мию раздели́ли ме́жду А и Б. **3.** (*mil.*) захва́т|ывать, -и́ть в ви́лку.

cpd. **~-lamp** *n.* ла́мпа на кронште́йне.

brackish [ˈbrækɪʃ] *adj.* солонова́тый.

bradawl [ˈbrædɔːl] *n.* ши́ло.

brae [breɪ] *n.* (*Sc.*) склон, отко́с.

brag [bræg] *n.* хвастовство́, бахва́льство.

v.i. хва́стать(ся), по- (*чем*); (*coll.*) бахва́литься (*impf.*).

braggadocio [ˌbrægəˈdəʊtʃɪəʊ, -ˈdəʊʃɪəʊ] *n.* бахва́льство.

braggart [ˈbrægət] *n.* хвасту́н.

bragging [ˈbrægɪŋ] *n.* хвастовство́, бахва́льство.

Brahma [ˈbrɑːmə] *n.* Бра́хма (*m.*).

Brahmin [ˈbrɑːmɪn] *n.* брами́н, брахма́н.

Brahminism [ˈbrɑːmɪnɪz(ə)m] *n.* брахмани́зм.

braid [breɪd] *n.* (*of hair*) коса́; (*band, ribbon*) тесьма́; (*cord-like fabric*) галу́н; **gold** ~ золото́й галу́н.

v.t. (*interweave*) плести́, с-; (*arrange in braids*) запле|та́ть, -сти́; (*confine with ribbon*) стя́|гивать, -ну́ть ле́нтой; (*edge with braid*) обш|ива́ть, -и́ть тесьмо́й.

Braille [breɪl] *n.* шрифт Бра́йля; **read** ~ чита́ть (*impf.*) по Бра́йлю.

brain [breɪn] *n.* **1.** (*anat.*) мозг; (*pl., cul.*) мозги́; ~ **death** *n.* сме́рть (головно́го) мо́зга; **blow one's ~s out** пусти́ть (*pf.*) себе́ пу́лю в лоб. **2.** (*intellect*): **overtax one's ~** перенапряга́ть (*impf.*) свои́ мозги́; **turn s.o.'s ~** вскружи́ть (*pf.*) кому́-н. го́лову; **rack, cudgel, puzzle one's ~s** лома́ть (*impf.*) го́лову (над+*i.*); **pick people's ~s** испо́льзовать (*impf., pf.*) чужи́е мы́сли; присва́ивать (*impf.*) чужи́е иде́и; **use one's ~s** шевели́ть (*impf.*) мозга́ми; **he has that tune on the ~** э́тот моти́в нейдёт у него́ из головы́; **~s trust** мозгово́й трест; **the best ~s in the country** лу́чшие го́ловы в стране́; **he's the ~s of the family** он са́мый башкови́тый/мозгови́тый в семье́; **a great ~** (*pers.*) све́тлая голова́.

v.t. вы́шибить (*pf.*) мозги́ +*d.*; размозжи́ть (*pf.*) го́лову +*d.*

cpds. **~-child** *n.* де́тище/плод ра́зума/воображе́ния; **~ drain** *n.* «уте́чка мозго́в»; **~-fag** *n.* (*coll.*) не́рвное переутомле́ние; **~-fever** *n.* воспале́ние мо́зга; **~-pan** *n.* черепна́я коро́бка; **~-sick** *adj.* поме́шанный, свихну́вшийся; **~storm** *n.* припа́док безу́мия; **~-wash** *v.t.* пром|ыва́ть, -ы́ть мозги́ +*d.*; **~-washing** *n.* промыва́ние мозго́в; **~wave** *n.*: **he had a ~wave** ему́ пришла́ счастли́вая мысль; его́ осени́ла иде́я; **~-work** *n.* у́мственная де́ятельность/рабо́та; **~-worker** *n.* рабо́тник у́мственного труда́.

brainless [ˈbreɪnlɪs] *adj.* безмо́зглый, пустоголо́вый.

brainlessness [ˈbreɪnlɪsnɪs] *n.* безмо́зглость, пустоголо́вость.

brainy [ˈbreɪnɪ] *adj.* (*coll.*) башкови́тый, мозгови́тый.

braise [breɪz] *v.t.* туши́ть (*impf.*).

brake[1] [breɪk] *n.* (*thicket*) ча́ща, за́росль.

brake[2] [breɪk] *n.* (*on vehicle*) то́рмоз (*pl.* -а́); **put on the ~** затормози́ть (*pf.*); (*fig.*) **put a ~ on s.o.'s enthusiasm** уме́рить (*pf.*) чей-н. пыл.

v.t. & i. тормози́ть, за-; **braking distance** тормозно́й путь; **braking power** мо́щность торможе́ния.

cpds. **~-drum** *n.* тормозно́й бараба́н; **~-light** *n.* фона́рь (*m.*) сигна́ла торможе́ния (*or* стоп-сигна́ла); **~-shoe** *n.* тормозно́й башма́к; **~-van** *n.* тормозно́й ваго́н.

brake[3]**, break** [breɪk] *n.* (*vehicle*) фурго́нчик.

bramble [ˈbræmb(ə)l] *n.* ежеви́ка.

brambly [ˈbræmblɪ] *adj.* ежеви́чный.

bran [bræn] *n.* о́труб|и (*pl., g.* -ей); вы́сев|ки (*pl., g.* -ок).

branch [brɑːntʃ] *n.* (*of tree*) ветвь; ве́тка; (*of mountain-range*) отро́г; (*of river*) рука́в; (*of road*) ответвле́ние; ~ **road** бокова́я доро́га; (*of family, genus*) ли́ния, ветвь; (*of railway line*) ве́тка; (*comm.*) филиа́л, отделе́ние; ~ **office** филиа́льное отделе́ние, филиа́л; (*of knowledge, subject, industry*) о́трасль; **the Slavonic ~ of the Indo-European languages** славя́нская ветвь индоевропе́йских языко́в.

v.i. (*of plants*): ~ **forth, out** разветв|ля́ться, -и́ться; раски́|дывать, -нуть ве́тви; (*of organization*): ~ **out** разветв|ля́ться, -и́ться; (*of pers.*): ~ **out in a new direction** расш|иря́ть, -и́рить де́ятельность в но́вом направле́нии; (*of road or rail., also ~* **off**) разветв|ля́ться, -и́ться; ответв|ля́ться, -и́ться; (*of river*) разветв|ля́ться, -и́ться; раздел|я́ться, -и́ться на рукава́.

branchiae [ˈbræŋkɪˌiː] *n.* жа́бры (*f. pl.*).

branchi|al [ˈbræŋkɪəl]**, -ate** [ˈbræŋkɪˌeɪt] *adjs.* жа́берный; жаброви́дный.

brand [brænd] *n.* **1.** (*piece of burning wood*) головня́, голове́шка; **a ~ from the burning** (*fig.*) спасённый. **2.** (*implement*) раскалённое желе́зо; клеймо́. **3.** (*mark of ~ing, also fig.*) клеймо́, тавро́, печа́ть; **the ~ of Cain** Ка́инова печа́ть. **4.** (*trade-mark*) фабри́чная ма́рка; фабри́чное клеймо́. **5.** (*species of goods*) сорт, ма́рка; ~ **name** фи́рменное назва́ние. **6.** (*poet., torch*) све́точ. **7.** (*poet., sword*) меч.

v.t. **1.** (*cattle etc.*) таври́ть, за-; клейми́ть, за-; выжига́ть, вы́жечь клеймо́ на+*p.*; **~ing-iron** клеймо́. **2.** (*fig., imprint*): ~ **sth. on s.o.'s memory** запечатле́ть (*pf.*) что-н. в чьей-н. па́мяти. **3.** (*stigmatize*) клейми́ть, за-. **4.** (*comm.*): **~ed goods** това́ры с фабри́чным клеймо́м.

cpd. **~-new** *adj.* новёхонький; соверше́нно но́вый, с иго́лочки.

brandish [ˈbrændɪʃ] *v.t.* разма́хивать (*impf.*) +*i.*; ~ **threats** угрожа́ть (*impf.*).

brandy [ˈbrændɪ] *n.* конья́к; бре́нди (*nt. indecl.*).

brant [ˈbrænt] = **brent**

brash [bræʃ] *adj.* наха́льный, наглова́тый, дё́рзкий.

brashness [bræʃnɪs] *n.* наха́льство, де́рзость.

Brasilia [brəˈzɪljə] *n.* Бразилия.

brass [brɑːs] *n.* **1.** (*metal*) лату́нь, жёлтая медь; ~ **plate** ме́дная доще́чка (на две́ри); ~ **hat** (*mil. sl.*) ста́рший офице́р; **the top ~** (*sl.*) вы́сшее нача́льство; **get down to ~ tacks** дойти́ (*pf.*) до су́ти де́ла; **it is not worth a ~ farthing** э́то ло́маного гроша́ не сто́ит; **part ~ rags with s.o.** расплева́ться (*pf.*) с кем-н. (*sl.*). **2.** (*also ~-ware*) лату́нные/ме́дные изде́лия; **clean the ~** чи́стить, вы́-ме́дную посу́ду. **3.** (*mus.*): **the ~es** духовы́е инструме́нты (*m. pl.*); медь; ~ **band** духово́й орке́стр. **4.** (*sl., money*) деньга́ (*coll.*). **5.** (*sl., impudence*) наха́льство.

brassard [ˈbræsɑːd] *n.* нарука́вная повя́зка.

brasserie [ˈbræsərɪ] *n.* пивна́я.

brassière [ˈbræzɪə(r), -sɪˌeə(r)] *n.* ли́фчик, бюстга́льтер.

brassy [ˈbrɑːsɪ] *adj.* (*of colour*) ме́дный; (*of sound*) металли́ческий; (*coarse, impudent*) наха́льный.

brat [bræt] *n.* щено́к, (*coll.*) сопля́к.

bravado [brəˈvɑːdəʊ] *n.* брава́да; **out of ~** из жела́ния порисова́ться.

brave [breɪv] *n.* (*American Indian warrior*) инде́йский во́ин.

adj. (*courageous*) хра́брый, сме́лый; (*bold*) де́рзкий; (*fearless, intrepid*) бесстра́шный, му́жественный, отва́жный; **none but the ~ deserves the fair** ≃ сме́лость

горо́да берёт; (*splendid*) превосхо́дный, великоле́пный.
v.t. (*danger etc.*) бр|оса́ть, -о́сить вы́зов +*d.*; ~ **the storm** боро́ться (*impf.*) с бу́рей; ~ **publicity** не боя́ться (*impf.*) гла́сности.

bravery ['breɪvərɪ] *n.* (*courage*) хра́брость, сме́лость; (*splendour*) великоле́пие.

bravo [brɑː'vəʊ] *n.* **1.** (*pl., applause*): **the ~s of the multitude** ова́ция толпы́. **2.** (*desperado*) головоре́з.
int. бра́во!

bravura [brə'vʊərə, -'vjʊərə] *n.* (*mus.*) браву́рность; (*attr.*) браву́рный.

brawl [brɔːl] *n.* сканда́л.
v.i. сканда́лить (*impf.*).

brawler ['brɔːlə(r)] *n.* скандали́ст.

brawn [brɔːn] *n.* (*meat*) зельц; (*fig.*) му́скулы (*m. pl.*).

brawny ['brɔːnɪ] *adj.* мускули́стый.

bray [breɪ] *n.* (*of ass, trumpet etc.*) рёв.
v.i. (*of animal*) реве́ть (*impf.*); (*of trumpet*) труби́ть (*impf.*).

braze [breɪz] *v.t.* (*solder*) пая́ть (*impf.*) твёрдым припо́ем.

brazen ['breɪz(ə)n] *adj.* ме́дный, бро́нзовый; (*of sound*) металли́ческий; (*fig., shameless*) на́глый, бессты́дный.
v.t.: ~ **sth. out** на́гло выкру́чиваться, вы́крутиться из чего́-н.
cpd. ~**-faced** *adj.* на́глый, бессты́дный, бессты́жий.

brazier ['breɪzɪə(r), -ʒə(r)] *n.* (*worker*) ме́дник; (*pan*) жаро́вня.

Brazil [brə'zɪl] *n.* Брази́лия; ~ **nut** америка́нский оре́х; ~ **wood** цезальпи́ния, фернамбу́к.

Brazilian [brə'zɪljən] *n.* брази́л|ец (*fem.* -ьянка).
adj. брази́льский.

breach [briːtʃ] *n.* **1.** (*violation, interruption*) наруше́ние; ~ **of duty** невыполне́ние/несоблюде́ние обя́зательств; ~ **of trust** злоупотребле́ние дове́рием; ~ **of good manners** наруше́ние пра́вил поведе́ния. **2.** (*gap*) проло́м, брешь; **step into the ~** (*fig.*) прийти́ (*pf.*) на по́мощь. **3.** (*quarrel*) ссо́ра, разры́в; **heal the ~** класть, положи́ть коне́ц ссо́ре; помири́ться (*pf.*).
v.t. прор|ыва́ть, -ва́ть.
v.i. (*of whale*) выска́кивать, вы́скочить из воды́.

bread [bred] *n.* хлеб; (*sl., money*) деньга́; **brown ~** се́рый хлеб; **loaf of ~** бато́н, буха́нка; ~ **and butter** (*fig.*) хлеб с ма́слом; **quarrel with one's ~ and butter** (*fig.*) ссо́риться, по- со свои́м хлебода́телем; **daily ~** (*lit., fig.*) хлеб насу́щный; **take the ~ out of s.o.'s mouth** лиш|а́ть, -и́ть кого́-н. куска́ хле́ба; **be on ~ and water** сиде́ть (*impf.*) на хле́бе и воде́; **he knows which side his ~ is buttered on** он зна́ет свою́ вы́году; **half a loaf is better than no ~** лу́чше немно́го, чем ничего́; на безры́бье и рак ры́ба; ~ **and circuses** хлеб и зре́лища; **break ~ with s.o.** раздели́ть (*pf.*) тра́пезу с кем-н.; **eat the ~ of affliction** хлебну́ть (*pf.*) го́ря.
cpds. ~**-and-butter** *adj.* насу́щный; ~**-and-butter issues** насу́щные пробле́мы; ~**-basket** *n.* (*sl.*) брю́хо; ~**-bin** *n.* хле́бница; ~**-board** *n.* хле́бная доска́; ~**-crumb** *n.* кро́шка; (*pl., cul.*) толчёные сухари́ (*m. pl.*); ~**-fruit** *n.* плод хле́бного де́рева; ~**-fruit tree** хле́бное де́рево; ~**-knife** *n.* хле́бный нож; ~**line** *n.*: **on the ~line** в тяжёлом материа́льном положе́нии; ~**-sauce** *n.* хле́бный со́ус; ~**stuffs** *n. pl.* зерно́, хлеб (*m. pl.*); ~**winner** *n.* корми́лец.

breadth [bredθ] *n.* **1.** (*width*) ширина́; **to a hair's ~** (*fig.*) в то́чности; **he missed by a hair's ~** он был на воло́сок от це́ли. **2.** (*fig.*): ~ **of mind** широта́ ума́. **3.** (*boldness of effort*) разма́х.

breadth|ways ['bredθweɪz], **-wise** ['bredθwaɪz] *advs.* в ширину́.

break[1] [breɪk] *n.* **1.** (*broken place, gap*) тре́щина, разры́в; ~ **in the clouds** (*fig.*) луч наде́жды. **2.:** ~ **of day** рассве́т. **3.** (*interval*) переры́в, па́уза; (*rest*) переды́шка. **4.** (*change*) переме́на; **the trip made a pleasant ~** пое́здка внесла́ прия́тное разнообра́зие; (*in voice at puberty*) ло́мка. **5.** (*of bouncing ball*) отско́к в сто́рону. **6.** (*coll., opportunity*): **give him a ~!** да́йте ему́ то́лько возмо́жность!; (*piece of luck*) уда́ча. **7.** (*escape*): **prison ~** побе́г из тюрьмы́.
v.t. (*see also* **broken**) **1.** (*fracture, divide, destroy*) лома́ть, с-; **he broke his leg** он слома́л но́гу; **she broke the plate in two** таре́лка у неё слома́лась попола́м; ~ **sth. in pieces** разл|а́мывать, -ома́ть что-н. на куски́; ~ **a piece off sth.** отл|а́мывать, -ома́ть (*or* -оми́ть) кусо́к от чего́-н.; **he broke the seal** он слома́л печа́ть; ~ **the ice** (*lit., fig.*) лома́ть, с- лёд; ~ **ground** (*lit.*) вск|а́пывать, -опа́ть (*or* взр|ыва́ть, -ыть) зе́млю; ~ **the skin** прор|ыва́ть, -ва́ть ко́жу; ~ **s.o.'s head (open)** прол|а́мывать, -оми́ть кому́-н. че́реп; ~ **s.o.'s nose** разби́ть (*pf.*) кому́-н. нос. **2.** (*fig.*): ~ **new ground** про|кла́дывать, -ложи́ть но́вые пути́; ~ **cover** выходи́ть, вы́йти из укры́тия; ~ **camp** сн|има́ться, -я́ться с ла́геря; ~ **a bottle with s.o.** раздави́ть (*pf.*) буты́лочку с кем-н.; ~ **the bank** (*gambling*) срыва́ть, сорва́ть банк; ~ **prison** бежа́ть (*det.*) из тюрьмы́; ~ **a record** поби́ть (*pf.*) реко́рд; ~ (*defeat*) **a strike** срыва́ть, сорва́ть забасто́вку; ~ **wind** (*fart*) перде́ть, пёрнуть; по́ртить, ис- во́здух; ~ (*into*) **a five-pound note** разме́н|ивать, -я́ть пятифунто́вую бума́жку; ~ **s.o.'s heart** разб|ива́ть, -и́ть кому́-н. се́рдце; ~ **s.o.'s spirit** сломи́ть (*pf.*) кого́-н.; ~ **s.o.'s health** под|рыва́ть, -орва́ть чьё-н. здоро́вье; ~ **a rebellion** подав|ля́ть, -и́ть восста́ние; ~ **a spell** разр|уша́ть, -у́шить ча́ры; ~ **the back of a task** одол|ева́ть, -е́ть трудне́йшую часть зада́ния; **he was broken by the failure of his business** его́ сломи́ла неуда́ча в де́ле. **3.** (*tame*): ~ **a horse to harness** приуч|а́ть, -и́ть ло́шадь к у́пряжи. **4.** (*disaccustom*): ~ **s.o. of a habit** отуч|а́ть, -и́ть кого́-н. от привы́чки. **5.** (*cashier*) ув|ольня́ть, -о́лить со слу́жбы, разжа́ловать (*pf.*). **6.** (*reduce, soften*): ~ **the news** смягч|а́ть, -и́ть дурны́е ве́сти; осторо́жно сообщи́ть (*pf.*) (неприя́тные) но́вости; ~ **a blow** смягч|а́ть, -и́ть уда́р; ~ **a fall** осл|абля́ть, -а́бить си́лу паде́ния; ~ **the force of the wind** осл|абля́ть, -а́бить си́лу ве́тра. **7.** (*violate, e.g. the law, a promise*) нар|уша́ть, -у́шить; ~ **a secret** разгл|аша́ть, -аси́ть та́йну; ~ **a cypher** расшифро́в|ывать, -а́ть (*pf.*) код. **8.** (*interrupt, put an end to*): ~ **silence** нар|уша́ть, -у́шить молча́ние; ~ **one's journey** прер|ыва́ть, -ва́ть путеше́ствие; ~ **a fast** прекра|ща́ть, -ти́ть пост; ~ **s.o.'s rest** прер|ыва́ть, -ва́ть чей-н. о́тдых; ~ **a circuit** (*elec.*) прер|ыва́ть, -ва́ть ток. **9.** (*destroy uniformity or completeness of*): ~ **a set of books** разро́зни|ва́ть, -ть компле́кт книг; ~ **step** лома́ть, с- шаг; ~ **ranks** выходи́ть, вы́йти из стро́я; ~ (*refuse to join*) **a strike** быть штре́йкбре́хером.
v.i. **1.** (*fracture, divide, disperse*) лома́ться, с-; обл|а́мываться, -ома́ться; об|рыва́ться, -рва́ться; (*of glass, china*) би́ться (*or* разбива́ться), раз-; (*of rope etc.*) ло́паться, ло́пнуть; (*of ice*) треща́ть, тре́снуть; ~ **in two** лома́ться, с- попола́м; ~ **in pieces** разл|а́мываться, -ома́ться на куски́; **the door broke open** дверь подда́лась; **the waves ~ on the beach** во́лны бью́тся о бе́рег; **the clouds broke** ту́чи рассе́ялись; **the bank broke** банк ло́пнул; **the troops broke and ran** войска́ дро́гнули и побежа́ли. **2.** (*fig.*): **his heart broke** он был (соверше́нно) уби́т; **their spirit broke** они́ па́ли ду́хом; ~**ing-point** преде́л. **3.** (*burst, dawn*): **the blister/bubble broke** волды́рь/пузы́рь ло́пнул; **day broke** забре́зжил день; рассвело́; **the storm broke** разрази́лась гроза́; **the news broke at 5 o'clock** об э́том ста́ло изве́стно в 5 часо́в; **a cry broke from his lips** крик сорва́лся с его́ уст. **4.** (*change*): **his voice broke** (*puberty*) у него́ слома́лся го́лос; (*emotion*) его́ го́лос дро́гнул/сорва́лся; **the weather broke** пого́да испо́ртилась. **5.** (*var.*): **the ball broke** мяч отлете́л в сто́рону; ~ **even** ост|ава́ться, -а́ться при свои́х; **we broke for lunch** мы сде́лали переры́в на обе́д; **oil ~s when heated** при нагрева́нии нефть расщепля́ется.
with preps.: **burglars broke into the house** граби́тели ворва́лись в дом; **the house was broken into** в до́ме произошёл грабёж со взло́мом; ~ **into song** затя́|гивать, -ну́ть пе́сню; запе́ть (*pf.*); ~ **into a trot** пусти́ться (*pf.*) ры́сью; ~ **into laughter** рассмея́ться (*pf.*); ~ **into s.o.'s time** отн|има́ть, -я́ть у кого́-н. вре́мя; ~ **into a £5 note** разме́н|ивать, -я́ть пятифунто́вую бума́жку; ~ **into the publishing world** проб|ива́ться, -и́ться в изда́тельский мир; **cattle broke through the fence** скот прорва́лся че́рез забо́р; ~ **through s.o.'s reserve** поборо́ть (*pf.*) чью-н. засте́нчивость; **the sun broke through the cloud** со́лнце

пробилось сквозь тучи; **he broke with her** он порвал с ней; ~ **with old habits** покончить (*pf.*) со старыми привычками.

with advs.: ~ **away** *v.i.*: ~ **away from one's gaolers** вырваться (*pf.*) из рук тюремщиков; ~ **away from old habits** отказ|ываться, -аться от старых привычек; покончить (*pf.*) со старыми привычками; ~ **away from a group** отк|алываться, -олоться от группы; ~ **down** *v.t.*: ~ **down a door** выламывать, выломать дверь; ~ **down resistance** сломить (*pf.*) сопротивление; ~ **down expenditure** разб|ивать, -ить расходы по статьям; *v.i.*: **the bridge broke down** мост рухнул; **negotiations broke down** переговоры сорвались; **the car broke down** машина сломалась; **he broke down** он не выдержал; **his health broke down** его здоровье пошатнулось; **the argument ~s down** довод оказывается несостоятельным; ~ **forth** *v.i.* вырываться, вырваться вперёд; ~ **in** *v.t.*: ~ **in a door** вл|амываться, -омиться в дверь; ~ **in a horse** выезжать, выездить лошадь; ~ **in a new employee** приуч|ать, -ить нового служащего к работе; ~ **in a new pair of shoes** разн|ашивать, -осить новые туфли; *v.i.*: ~ **in on a conversation** вмеш|иваться, -аться в разговор; ~ **off** *v.t.*: ~ **off a twig** отл|амывать, -омить веточку; ~ **off relations** пор|ывать, -вать отношения (с+*i.*); ~ **off an engagement** раст|оргать, -оргнуть помолвку; ~ **off a battle** выходить, выйти из боя; *v.i.*: **the nib broke off** кончик пера отломился; **he broke off** (*speaking*) он замолчал; ~ **open** *v.t.*: ~ **open a chest** взл|амывать, -омать сундук; ~ **out** *v.t.*: ~ **out a flag** развёр|тывать, -нуть знамя; *v.i.*: **the prisoner broke out** заключённый сбежал; **fire broke out** вспыхнул пожар; **war broke out** разразилась/вспыхнула война; **his face broke out in pimples** на его лице высыпали прыщи; **she broke out into abuse** она разразилась руганью; ~ **up** *v.t.*: ~ **up furniture** переломать (*pf.*) мебель; ~ **up a meeting** прекра|щать, -тить собрание; ~ **it up!** (*coll.*, *desist*) кончайте; ~ **up a family** (*separate*) разб|ивать, -ить семью; (*cause to quarrel*) вн|осить, -ести разлад в семью; *v.i.* **school ~s up tomorrow** учащихся завтра распускают на каникулы; **he is rapidly ~ing up** он быстро сдаёт; **the crowd broke up** толпа разошлась; **the fine weather is ~ing up** погода портится.

cpds. **~away** *n.* **1.** (*secession*) откол, отделение; **a ~away faction** отколовшаяся фракция. **2.** (*boxing*) брек. **3.** (*premature start to race*) отрыв; **~down** *n.* (*mechanical*) поломка; **~down gang** аварийная команда; **~down van** аварийный грузовик; машина технической помощи; (*of health*) расстройство; упадок сил; **nervous ~down** нервное расстройство; (*of negotiations etc.*) срыв; (*analysis*) подразделение, разбивка; **~-in** *n.* (*raid*) взлом; **~neck** *adj.*: **~neck speed** головокружительная скорость; **~-out** *n.* (*escape*) побег; **~through** *n.* (*mil.*) прорыв; (*fig.*, *e.g. in science*) скачок, перелом; **~-up** *n.* развал, распад; (*of school, assembly*) роспуск; (*of friendship*) разрыв; **~water** *n.* волнолом, волнорез.

break[2] [breɪk] *n.* (*vehicle*) = **brake**[3]

breakable [ˈbreɪkəb(ə)l] *adj.* ломкий.

breakage [ˈbreɪkɪdʒ] *n.* (*break*) поломка; (*pl.*, *broken articles*) бой, поломка, поломанное.

break-dancer [ˈbreɪkdɑːnsə(r)] *n.* брейкер.

break-dancing [ˈbreɪkdɑːnsɪŋ] *n.* брейк.

breaker [ˈbreɪkə(r)] *n.* (*wave*) вал, бурун; **~s ahead!** (*fig.*) берегись!

breakfast [ˈbrekfəst] *n.* завтрак; **have** ~ завтракать, по-; ~ **food** (*cereal*) корнфлекс.

v.i. завтракать, по-.

bream [briːm] *n.* лещ.

breast [brest] *n.* **1.** грудь; **give a child the** ~ да|вать, -ть ребёнку грудь; **child at the** ~ грудной ребёнок. **2.** (*fig.*) грудь, душа; ~ **beating** показное раскаяние; **make a clean ~ of sth.** чистосердечно созн|аваться, -аться в чём-н. **3.:** ~ **of a hill** склон холма. **4.** (*cul.*): ~ **of lamb** баранья грудинка.

v.t.: ~ **the waves** расс|екать, -ечь волны.

cpds. **~bone** *n.* грудная кость, грудина; **~-deep** *adj.* по грудь; **~-fed** *adj.* вскормленный грудью; **~-feeding** *n.* кормление грудью; **~-high** *adj.* доходящий до груди; **~-pin** *n.* булавка для галстука; **~plate** *n.* (*armour*) нагрудник; **~-pocket** *n.* верхний карман; **~-stroke** *n.* брасс; **do the ~-stroke** плавать (*indet.*), плыть (*det.*) брассом; **~work** *n.* бруствер.

breath [breθ] *n.* дыхание; (*single* ~) вздох; **draw** ~ дышать (*impf.*); **he drew a deep** ~ он сделал глубокий вздох; **he drew his last** ~ он испустил последний вздох; **lose one's** ~ зад|ыхаться, -охнуться; **take** ~ перев|одить, -ести дух; отд|ыхать, -охнуть; **take a deep** ~ сделать (*pf.*) глубокий вздох; **out of** ~ задыхаясь; **recover one's** ~ отдышаться (*pf.*); перев|одить, -ести дух; **bad** ~ дурной запах изо рта; **waste one's** ~ говорить (*impf.*) на ветер; попусту тратить (*impf.*) слова; **catch, hold one's** ~ зата|ивать, -ить дыхание; **take s.o.'s** ~ **away** захват|ывать, -ить дух у кого-н.; **with bated** ~ затаив дыхание; **under one's** ~ очень тихо; **music is the** ~ **of life to him** музыка нужна ему как воздух; **in the same** ~ единым/одним духом; **there is not a** ~ **of air** нечем дышать; ни ветерка; **get a** ~ **of air** подышать (*pf.*) свежим воздухом; **it was so cold we could see our** ~ было так холодно, что у нас пар шёл изо рта.

cpd. **~-taking** *adj.* захватывающий.

breathalyse [ˈbreθəlaɪz] *v.t.* проверить (*pf.*) на алкоголь.

Breathalyser [ˈbreθəˌlaɪzə(r)] *n.* (*propr.*) алкометр, алкогольно-респираторная трубка.

breathe [briːð] *v.t.* **1.:** ~ **fresh air** дышать (*impf.*) свежим воздухом; ~ **one's last** испустить (*pf.*) дух (*or* последний вздох). **2.** (*exercise*): ~ **a horse** выва́живать, выводить лошадь. **3.** (*allow to rest*) да|вать, -ть (*кому*) передохнуть. **4.:** ~ **a spirit of tolerance** быть исполненным терпимости; ~ **fragrance** сточать (*impf.*) аромат. **5.:** ~ **new life into** вд|ыхать, -охнуть новую жизнь в+*a.* **6.** (*utter softly*): **he ~d these words** он произнёс эти слова полушёпотом; ~ **a sigh** изд|авать, -ать вздох; **don't** ~ **a word!** ни слова больше!; не пророните ни слова!

v.i. дышать (*impf.*); (*fig.*): ~ **again, freely** вздохнуть (*pf.*) с облегчением (*or* свободно); **give me a chance to** ~ дайте мне вздохнуть; ~ **upon s.o.'s reputation** набр|асывать, -осить тень на чью-н. репутацию.

breather [ˈbriːðə(r)] *n.* (*spell of exercise*) прогулка; (*pause for rest*) передышка; **it's time for a** ~ пора сделать передышку (*or* передохнуть).

breathing [ˈbriːðɪŋ] *n.* **1.** дыхание; **his** ~ **is heavy** он тяжело дышит. **2.** (*gram.*): **smooth** ~ тонкое/лёгкое придыхание; **rough** ~ густое/звонкое придыхание.

adj. (*lifelike*) словно живой.

cpd. **~-space** *n.* передышка.

breathless [ˈbreθlɪs] *adj.* **1.** (*panting*) задыхающийся, запыхавшийся; ~ **speed** захватывающая дух скорость; ~ **attention** напряжённое внимание. **2.** (*lifeless*) бездыханный.

breathy [ˈbreθɪ] *adj.* с придыханием.

breech [briːtʃ] *n.* **1.** (*pl.*, *knee-~es*) панталон|ы (*pl.*, *g.* —); (*riding-~es*) бридж|и (*pl.*, *g.* -ей); **wear the ~es** (*fig.*) верховодить (*impf.*) в доме. **2.** (*of a gun*) казённая часть. **3.:** ~ **delivery, presentation** (*med.*) ягодичное предлежание плода.

cpds. **~-block** *n.* (*mil.*) затвор; **~-loader** *n.* (*mil.*) оружие, заряжающееся с казённой части; **~-loading** *adj.* заряжающийся с казённой части.

breed [briːd] *n.* порода; **he comes of a good** ~ он происходит из хорошего рода; **men of the same** ~ люди одного толка.

v.t. **1.** (*engender, cause*) поро|ждать, -дить. **2.: he was bred a soldier** его с детства готовили в солдаты. **3.** (*animals*) раз|водить, -вести.

v.i. размножаться (*impf.*), плодиться (*impf.*); ~ **true** да|вать, -ть породистый приплод.

breeder [ˈbriːdə(r)] *n.* **1.** (*animal*) производитель (*m.*); **elephants are slow ~s** слоны размножаются медленно. **2.** (*stock-~*) животновод, скотовод; **he is a** ~ **of horses** он разводит лошадей. **3.:** ~ **reactor** (*phys.*) реактор-размножитель (*m.*).

breeding [ˈbriːdɪŋ] *n.* **1.** (*by animals*) размножение; ~ **season**

период размножения; случный сезон; ~ **stock** племенной скот. **2.** (*by stock-breeders*) разведение, выведение. **3.** (*training, education*) воспитание, образование. **4.** (*manners etc.*) воспитанность.

cpd. **~-ground** *n.* (*fig.*) рассадник, очаг.

breeks [bri:ks] *n.* (*Sc.*) штан|ы (*pl., g.* -ов).

breeze [bri:z] *n.* **1.** (*wind*) ветерок; бриз; **moderate/strong** ~ умеренный/сильный ветер; **sea/land** ~ морской/береговой бриз. **2.** (*quarrel*) перебранка, свара. **3.: put the ~ up** (*coll.*) вспугнуть (*pf.*).

v.i.: ~ **in/out** (*coll.*) влететь/вылететь (*pf.*).

breeze-block [bri:z] *n.* шлакобетонный блок.

breeziness ['bri:zɪnɪs] *n.* (*of manner*) живость, беззаботность.

breezy ['bri:zɪ] *adj.* (*of weather*) свежий; (*of locality*) обдуваемый ветрами; (*fig., of pers.*) живой, беззаботный.

Bren [bren] *n.* (~ *gun*) ручной пулемёт Брена; ~ **carrier** транспортёр с пулемётом Брена.

brent [brent], (*US*) **brant** [brænt] *nn.* (*zool.*; *also* **~-goose**) чёрная казарка.

brethren ['breðrɪn] *n.* собратья (*m. pl.*); братия (*f. sg.*).

Breton ['bret(ə)n, brə'tɔ̃] *n.* (*pers.*) бретон|ец (*fem.* -ка); (*language*) бретонский язык.

adj. бретонский.

brevet ['brevɪt] *n.* (*mil.*) патент на следующий чин без изменения оклада.

breviary ['bri:vɪərɪ] *n.* требник.

brevier [brə'vɪə(r)] *n.* петит.

brevity ['brevɪtɪ] *n.* краткость.

brew [bru:] *n.* (*amount brewed*: *of beer*) варка; (*of tea*) заварка; (*beverage*) сваренный напиток, (*pej.*) варево.

v.t. **1.** (*beer*) варить, с-; (*tea*) завар|ивать, -ить. **2.** (*fig.*): ~ **trouble** устр|аивать, -оить беду; ~ **mischief** зам|ышлять, -ыслить недоброе.

v.i. **1.** (*of tea etc.*) завар|иваться, -иться. **2.: a storm is ~ing** (*lit.*) собирается гроза; (*fig.*) гроза надвигается; **there's trouble ~ing** быть беде.

brewer ['bru:ə(r)] *n.* пивовар.

brewery ['bru:ərɪ] *n.* пивоваренный завод; пивоварня.

briar ['braɪə(r)] = **brier**[1,2]

bribe [braɪb] *n.* взятка, подкуп.

v.t. да|вать, -ть взятку +*d.*; подкуп|ать, -ить; ~ **s.o. to silence** взяткой заст|авлять, -авить кого-н. молчать; ~ **s.o. to do sth.** подкупом доб|иваться, -иться чего-н. от кого-н.

brib(e)able ['braɪbəb(ə)l] *adj.* подкупной, продажный.

bribery ['braɪbərɪ] *n.* взяточничество.

bric-à-brac ['brɪkə,bræk] *n.* старьё; безделушки (*f. pl.*).

brick [brɪk] *n.* **1.** кирпич; **~s** (*collect.*) кирпич; (*attr.*) кирпичный; **like a ton of ~s** изо всей силы; **drop a ~** ляпнуть (*pf.*) (*coll.*); **like a cat on hot ~s** как на горячих углях; как карась на сковородке; **make ~s without straw** биться (*impf.*) над чем-н. попусту; **see through a ~ wall** насквозь видеть (*impf.*); **drop sth. like a hot ~** бежать (*det.*) от чего-н. как от чумы; **you're a ~!** (*coll.*) вы молодчина! **2.** (*toy*): **~s** кубики (*m. pl.*). **3.** (*of soap*) брусок; (*of ice-cream*) брикет; (*of tea*) кирпич.

v.t.: ~ **up** за|кладывать, -ложить кирпичами.

cpds. **~bat** *n.* обломок кирпича; (*fig.*) нелестный отзыв; **~-dust** *n.* кирпичная мука; **~-kiln** *n.* печь для обжига кирпича; **~layer** *n.* каменщик; **~-red** *adj.* кирпично-красный; **~work** *n.* кирпичная кладка.

bridal ['braɪd(ə)l] *n.* (*feast*) свадебный пир.

adj. свадебный.

bride [braɪd] *n.* невеста; (*after wedding*) молодая, новобрачная.

cpds. **~groom** *n.* жених; (*after wedding*) новобрачный; **~smaid** *n.* подружка невесты.

bridge[1] [brɪdʒ] *n.* **1.** мост (*also in dentistry*); ~ **of boats** понтонный мост; **suspension** ~ висячий мост; **throw a ~ over a river** навести/перебросить (*pf.*) мост через реку; **we'll cross that ~ when we come to it** нечего заранее волноваться/тревожиться. **2.** (*naut.*) капитанский мостик. **3.** (*of nose*) переносица. **4.** (*of violin*) кобылка. **5.** (*elec.*) шунт; электроизмерительный мост; **Wheatstone's ~** мостик сопротивления.

v.t.: ~ **a river** нав|одить, -ести мост через реку; (*join by bridging*) соедин|ять, -ить мостом; (*fig.*): ~ **a gap** зап|олнять, -олнить пробел; ~ **(over) the difficulties** преодол|евать, -еть трудности.

cpds. **~head** *n.* плацдарм (*also fig.*); предмостное укрепление; предмостная позиция; **establish a ~head** захват|ывать, -ить плацдарм; **~work** *n.* постройка/наводка моста; (*dentistry*) мост, мостик.

bridge[2] [brɪdʒ] *n.* (*game*) бридж.

bridle ['braɪd(ə)l] *n.* узда, уздечка; **give a horse the ~** отдать/ослабить (*pf.*) повод.

v.t. (*of horse, also* ~ **in**) взнузд|ывать, -ать; (*fig.*) обузд|ывать, -ать.

v.i. (*fig.*) зад|ирать, -рать нос.

cpds. **~-path** *n.* верховая тропа; **~-rein** *n.* повод.

brief [bri:f] *n.* **1.** (*papal letter*) папское бреве (*indecl.*). **2.** (*lawyer's*) изложение дела; **hold a ~ for s.o.** вести (*det.*) чьё-н. дело в суде; **he has plenty of ~s** он имеет большую практику; **he threw down his ~** он отказался от ведения дела; (*fig.*): **I hold no ~ for smoking** я отнюдь не сторонник курения. **3.** (*mil. etc., instructions*) инструкция. **4.** (*pl., coll., underpants*) трус|ы (*pl., g.* -ов).

adj. (*of duration*) короткий, недолгий; (*concise*) краткий, сжатый; **in ~** вкратце.

v.t. **1.: ~ a lawyer** поруч|ать, -ить адвокату ведение дела. **2.** (*mil. etc.*) инструктировать (*impf., pf.*).

cpd. **~-case** *n.* портфель (*m.*).

briefing ['bri:fɪŋ] *n.* (*also* ~ **meeting**) инструктаж; (*press*) брифинг.

briefless ['bri:flɪs] *adj.* (*of lawyer*) не имеющий практики.

briefly ['bri:flɪ] *adv.* кратко, сжато; **the point is ~ that ...** говоря вкратце, дело в том, что...

briefness ['bri:fnɪs] *n.* краткость; (*conciseness*) сжатость.

brier[1], **briar**[1] ['braɪə(r)] *n.* (*prickly bush*; *also* **sweet** ~) шиповник.

cpd. **~-rose** *n.* шиповник.

brier[2], **briar**[2] ['braɪə(r)] *n.* (*heather*) вереск, эрика; (~ **pipe**) трубка из корня эрики.

Brig.[1] [,brɪgə'dɪə(r)] *n.* (*abbr. of* **Brigadier**) бригадный генерал.

brig[2] [brɪg] *n.* бриг.

brigade [brɪ'geɪd] *n.* бригада; **fire** ~ пожарная команда; ~ **major** начальник оперативно-разведывательного отделения штаба бригады.

brigadier [,brɪgə'dɪə(r)] *n.* (*also* **~-general**) бригадный генерал.

brigand ['brɪgənd] *n.* разбойник.

brigandage ['brɪgəndɪdʒ] *n.* разбой.

brigantine ['brɪgən,ti:n] *n.* бригантина.

bright [braɪt] *adj.* **1.** (*clear, shining*) яркий, светлый; **a ~ day** ясный день; ~ **red** ярко-красный; **the sun shines ~** солнце светит ярко; **a ~ room** светлая комната. **2.** (*cheerful*): ~ **faces** весёлые лица; **look on the ~ side** смотреть (*impf.*) на вещи оптимистически; **he came ~ and early** он ранёхонько явился. **3.** (*clever*): **a ~ girl** толковая девочка; **a ~ idea** блестящая мысль.

brighten ['braɪt(ə)n] *v.t.* (*also* ~ **up**): (*polish*) полировать, от-; (*enliven*) оживл|ять, -ить; подб|адривать (*or* -одрять), -одрить; скра|шивать, -сить.

v.i. (*also* ~ **up**): **the weather ~ed** погода прояснилась; **his face ~ed** его лицо просветлело; **things are ~ing up** дела улучшаются.

brightness ['braɪtnɪs] *n.* (*lustre*) яркость; (*cheer*) весёлость; (*cleverness*) блеск, смышлёность.

Bright's disease [braɪts] *n.* нефрит, брайтова болезнь.

brill[1] ['brɪl] *n.* камбала, ромб.

brill[2] ['brɪl] *adj.* (*abbr. of* **brilliant**) (*coll.*) балдёжный, потрясный; **~!** Блеск!; Балдёж! **the film is ~** фильм — блеск!

brilliance ['brɪlɪəns] *n.* (*brightness*) яркость; (*magnificence*) великолепие, блеск; (*intelligence*) блеск (ума); блестящие способности (*f. pl.*).

brilliant ['brɪlɪənt] *n.* (*diamond*) бриллиант.

adj. (*lit., fig.*) сверкающий, блестящий; **he is ~ly witty** он блещет остроумием.

brilliantine ['brɪljən,ti:n] *n.* бриллиантин.

brim [brɪm] *n.* край; **fill a glass to the ~** нап|олнять, -олнить стака́н до краёв; (*of hat*) поля́ (*nt. pl.*).

v.i. (*of vessel*) нап|олня́ться, -о́лниться до краёв; **a ~ming cup** напо́лненная до краёв ча́ша; **~ over** перел|ива́ться, -и́ться че́рез край; (*fig.*): **she was ~ming over with the news** её распира́ло жела́ние рассказа́ть но́вости.

cpd. **~-full** *adj.* по́лный до краёв.

brimstone ['brɪmstəʊn] *n.* саморо́дная се́ра.

brindle(d) ['brɪnd(ə)ld] *adj.* кори́чневый с полоса́ми/пя́тнами.

brine [braɪn] *n.* рассо́л.

bring [brɪŋ] *v.t.* **1.** (*cause to come, deliver*): (*a thg.*) прин|оси́ть, -ести́; (*a pers.*) прив|оди́ть, -ести́; (*thg. or pers., by vehicle*) прив|ози́ть, -езти́; **he brought an umbrella** он захвати́л с собо́й зо́нтик; **~ s.o. into the world** произвести́ (*pf.*) кого́-н. на свет; **it brought tears to my eyes** э́то вы́звало у меня́ слёзы; **spring ~s warm weather** с весно́й прихо́дит тепло́; **crime ~s punishment** преступле́ние влечёт за собо́й наказа́ние; **~ sth. into fashion** вв|оди́ть, -ести́ что-н. в мо́ду; **~ a ship into harbour** вв|оди́ть, -ести́ кора́бль в га́вань; **~ into action, effect, play** прив|оди́ть, -ести́ в де́йствие; **~ to light** выявля́ть, вы́явить; **~ to pass** осуществ|ля́ть, -и́ть; **~ to mind** прив|оди́ть, -ести́ на ум; нап|омина́ть, -о́мнить; **~ s.o. to book** приз|ыва́ть, -ва́ть кого́-н. к отве́ту; **~ s.o. low** прин|ижа́ть, -и́зить кого́-н.; **~ to perfection** дов|оди́ть, -ести́ до соверше́нства; **~ to an end** зак|а́нчивать, -о́нчить; заверш|а́ть, -и́ть; **~ pressure to bear on** ока́з|ывать, -а́ть давле́ние на+*a.*; **~ s.o. to his senses** (*lit.*) прив|оди́ть, -ести́ кого́-н. в созна́ние; (*fig.*) образу́м|ливать, -ить кого́-н.; **~ to terms** прив|оди́ть, -ести́ к соглаше́нию; **~ a misfortune upon o.s.** навл|ека́ть, -е́чь на себя́ беду́. **2.** (*yield*): **this ~s me (in) £500 a year** э́то прино́сит мне 500 фу́нтов в год; **the harvest will not ~ much** урожа́й не бу́дет больши́м. **3.** (*induce*): **I could not ~ him to agree** я не мог убеди́ть его́ дать согла́сие; **I cannot ~ myself to do it** я не могу́ заста́вить себя́ сде́лать э́то. **4.** (*leg.*): **~ an action against s.o.** возбу|жда́ть, -ди́ть де́ло про́тив кого́-н.; **~ a charge** выдвига́ть, вы́двинуть обвине́ние.

with advs.: **~ about** *v.t.* (*cause*) вызыва́ть, вы́звать; произв|оди́ть, -ести́; **~ a ship about** пов|ора́чивать, -ерну́ть кора́бль; **~ back** *v.t.* прин|оси́ть, -ести́ (*or* прив|оди́ть, -ести́) наза́д; **they brought back the news that ...** они́ верну́лись с но́востью, бу́дто...; **it ~s back the past** э́то напомина́ет (*or* приво́дит на па́мять) было́е; **~ s.o. back to health** возвраща́ть, верну́ть кому́-н. здоро́вье; **~ down** *v.t.* (*a tree*) сруб|а́ть, -и́ть; вали́ть, по-; (*an aircraft*) сби|ва́ть, -ть; (*a bird*) подстре́л|ивать, -и́ть; **~ down the house** (*fig.*) вызыва́ть, вы́звать гром аплодисме́нтов; **drink has brought him down** пья́нство погуби́ло его́; **~ prices down** сн|ижа́ть, -и́зить це́ны; **he brought his fist down on the table** он сту́кнул кулако́м по́ столу; **~ down s.o.'s wrath on s.o.** навл|ека́ть, -е́чь на кого́-н. чей-н. гнев; **~ forth** *v.t.* (*give birth to*) произв|оди́ть, -ести́; **what will the future ~ forth?** что́-то принесёт бу́дущее?; **his speech brought forth protests** его́ речь вы́звала проте́сты; **~ forward** *v.t.*: **~ a chair forward** выдвига́ть, вы́двинуть стул; **~ forward a proposal** выдвига́ть, вы́двинуть предложе́ние; (*advance date of*) перен|оси́ть, -ести́ на бо́лее ра́нний срок; (*bookkeeping*) де́лать, с- перено́с счёта на сле́дующую страни́цу; **~ in** *v.t.* вн|оси́ть, -ести́; вв|оди́ть, -ести́; **~ in a verdict** выноси́ть, вы́нести верди́кт; **they brought him in not guilty** его́ призна́ли невино́вным; **~ off** *v.t.*: **~ off a manoeuvre** успе́шно заверш|а́ть, -и́ть опера́цию; **the lifeboat brought six men off** спаса́тельная ло́дка доста́вила на бе́рег шесть челове́к; **~ on** *v.t.*: **this brought on a bad cold** э́то вы́звало си́льный на́сморк; **the sun is ~ing on the plants** со́лнце спосо́бствует разви́тию расте́ний; **~ out** *v.t.* выноси́ть, вы́нести; выводи́ть, вы́вести; (*clarify*) выявля́ть, вы́явить, выясня́ть, вы́яснить; (*publish*) выпуска́ть, вы́пустить; (*launch into society*) вывози́ть, вы́везти в свет; **the curtains ~ out the green in the carpet** занаве́ски оттеня́ют зе́лень ковра́; **the sun ~s out the roses** ро́зы распуска́ются под со́лнечными луча́ми; **~ over** *v.t.* (*convert, convince*) переубе|жда́ть, -ди́ть; заста́вить (*pf.*) измени́ть мне́ние; **~ round** *v.t.* (*deliver*) прив|ози́ть, -езти́; дост|авля́ть, -а́вить; (*restore to consciousness*) прив|оди́ть, -ести в себя́; (*persuade*) убе|жда́ть, -ди́ть; **he brought the conversation round to politics** он перевёл разгово́р на поли́тику; **~ through** *v.t.*: **the doctors brought him through** доктора́ вы́тянули его́; **~ to** *v.t.* (*restore to consciousness*) прив|оди́ть, -ести́ в созна́ние/себя́; (*a ship*) остан|а́вливать, -ови́ть; **~ together** *v.t.* (*assemble*) соб|ира́ть, -ра́ть; св|оди́ть, -ести́ вме́сте; (*reconcile*) примир|я́ть, -и́ть; **~ under** *v.t.* (*subdue*) подчин|я́ть, -и́ть; **~ up** *v.t.* (*carry up*) прин|оси́ть, -ести́ наве́рх; (*educate*) воспи́т|ывать, -а́ть; **I was brought up to believe that ...** мне с де́тства внуша́ли, что...; (*stop*) остан|а́вливать, -ови́ть; (*vomit*): **he brought up his dinner** его́ вы́рвало по́сле обе́да; **~ up a subject** подн|има́ть, -я́ть (*pf.*) вопро́с; зав|оди́ть, -ести́ разгово́р о чём-н.; **~ up the rear** замыка́ть (*impf.*) коло́нну/ше́ствие.

brink [brɪŋk] *n.* край (*also fig.*); **on the ~ of despair** на гра́ни отча́яния; **he was on the ~ of tears** он едва́ сде́рживал слёзы; **we were on the ~ of a great discovery** мы вплотну́ю подошли́ к вели́кому откры́тию.

cpd. **~manship** *n.* баланси́рование на гра́ни войны́.

briny ['braɪnɪ] *adj.* солёный; **the ~** (*coll.*) мо́ре.

brio ['bri:əʊ] *n.* жи́вость.

briquette [brɪ'ket] *n.* брике́т.

brisk [brɪsk] *adj.* (*of movement*) ско́рый; (*of air, wind*) све́жий; **~ demand** большо́й спрос; **~ trade** оживлённая торго́вля.

brisket ['brɪskɪt] *n.* груди́нка.

bris|ling ['brɪzlɪŋ, 'brɪs-], **-tling** ['brɪslɪŋ] *n.* шпро́т.

bristle ['brɪs(ə)l] *n.* щети́на.

v.i. (*of hair*) стоя́ть (*impf.*) ды́бом; вста́ть (*pf.*) ды́бом; (*of animal, also fig., of pers.*) ощети́ни|ваться, -ться; **the cat ~d** шерсть у ко́шки поднляла́сь ды́бом; **~ with bayonets** ощети́ниваться (*impf.*) штыка́ми; **the matter ~s with difficulties** де́ло полно́ тру́дностей.

bristling ['brɪslɪŋ] = **brisling**

bristly ['brɪslɪ] *adj.* щети́нистый.

Brit [brɪt] *n.* (*coll.*) = **Briton 1.**

Britain ['brɪt(ə)n] *n.* А́нглия, Брита́ния; (*also* **Great ~**) Великобрита́ния.

Britannia [brɪ'tænjə] *n.* (*poet.*) Великобрита́ния; **~ metal** брита́нский мета́лл.

Britannic [brɪ'tænɪk] *adj.*: **Her ~ Majesty** Её Брита́нское Вели́чество.

Briticism ['brɪtɪˌsɪz(ə)m] *n.* англици́зм.

British ['brɪtɪʃ] *n.*: **the ~** англича́не, брита́нцы (*both m. pl.*).

adj. брита́нский (*also of ancient Britons*); велико-брита́нский, англи́йский; **~ Empire** Брита́нская импе́рия; **~ Commonwealth of Nations** Брита́нское Содру́жество На́ций; **~ Isles** Брита́нские острова́; **~ English** брита́нский вариа́нт англи́йского языка́; **~ warm** коро́ткая шине́ль.

Britisher ['brɪtɪʃə(r)] *n.* брита́н|ец (*fem.* -ка); англича́н|ин (*fem.* -ка).

Briton ['brɪt(ə)n] *n.* **1.** (*native or inhabitant of Great Britain*) брита́н|ец (*fem.* -ка); англича́н|ин (*fem.* -ка). **2.** (*ancient*) бритт.

Brittany ['brɪtənɪ] *n.* Брета́нь.

brittle ['brɪt(ə)l] *adj.* ло́мкий, хру́пкий.

brittleness ['brɪt(ə)lnɪs] *n.* ло́мкость, хру́пкость.

broach[1] [brəʊtʃ] *v.t.* (*pierce*) прот|ыка́ть, -кну́ть; (*start consuming*) поча́ть, откры́ть (*both pf.*); (*discussion*) откр|ыва́ть, -ы́ть; **~ a subject** подн|има́ть, -я́ть вопро́с.

broach[2] [brəʊtʃ] (*also* **~ to**) *v.t.* выводи́ть, вы́вести (*кора́бль*) из ве́тра.

broad [brɔ:d] *n.* (*of the back*) широ́кая часть (спины́).

adj. **1.** (*wide*) широ́кий; **the river is 50 feet ~** ширина́ реки́ 50 фу́тов; **it's as ~ as it's long** то же на́ то же выхо́дит. **2.** (*extensive*): **~ lands** обши́рные зе́мли. **3.: in ~ daylight** средь бе́ла дня. **4.** (*decided*): **a ~ hint** то́лстый намёк; **a ~ accent** ре́зкий/заме́тный/си́льный акце́нт. **5.** (*approximate*): **a ~ definition** о́бщее определе́ние; **in ~**

outline в óбщих чертáх. **6.** (*tolerant*): **he takes a ~ view** у негó ширóкий взгляд на вéщи. **7.** (*coarse*): **a ~ joke** грýбая шýтка.

adv.: **~ awake** вполнé проснýвшийся.

cpds. **~cast** *n.* радиопередáча, радиовещáние, трансля́ция; (*attr.*) радиовещáтельный; *adv.* (*agric.*, *fig.*) вразбрóс; *v.t.* (*agric.*) сéять, по- вразбрóс; (*radio*) перед|авáть, -áть по рáдио; (*spread*, *of news etc.*) распростран|я́ть, -и́ть; *v.i.* вести́ (*det.*) радиопередáчу; выступáть, вы́ступить по рáдио; **~caster** *n.* радиожурнали́ст; **~casting** *n.* радиовещáние, трансля́ция; **~cloth** *n.* тóнкое чёрное сукнó; **~-gauge** *adj.* ширококолéйный; **~-minded** *adj.* ширóких взгля́дов; **~-mindedness** *n.* широтá взгля́дов; **~sheet** *n.* листовóе издáние; **~side** *n.* (*side of ship*) (надвóдный) борт; **be ~side on to sth.** стоя́ть (*impf.*) бóртом к чемý-н.; **fire a ~side** дать (*pf.*) бортовóй залп; (*fig.*, *vbl. onslaught*) обрýшиться (*pf.*) с рéзкими напáдками; **~sword** *n.* палáш; **~tail** *n.* каракульчá; **~ways**, **~wise** *advs.* вширь; в ширинý; поперёк.

broaden [ˈbrɔ:d(ə)n] *v.t.* & *i.* (*lit.*, *fig.*) расш|иря́ть(ся), -и́рить(ся).

broadly [ˈbrɔ:dlɪ] *adv.* (*in the main*) в основнóм; **~ speaking** вообщé говоря́.

broadness [ˈbrɔ:dnɪs] *n.* (*coarseness*) грýбость.

brocade [brəˈkeɪd, brəʊ-] *n.* парчá.

v.t.: **a ~d gown** парчóвый наря́д.

v.i. вырабáтывать (*impf.*) парчý.

broccoli [ˈbrɒkəlɪ] *n.* брóкколи (*nt. indecl.*); капýста спáржевая.

brochure [ˈbrəʊʃə(r), brəʊˈʃʊə(r)] *n.* брошю́ра.

brogue [brəʊg] *n.* (*shoe*) башмáк; (*accent*) ирлáндский акцéнт.

broil[1] [brɔɪl] *n.* (*quarrel*) ссóра, свáра.

broil[2] [brɔɪl] *v.t.* (*cul.*) жáрить, за- на вéртеле (*or* на откры́том огнé).

v.i. (*cul.*) жáриться, за- *etc. as above*; (*fig.*, *be roasted*) жáриться (*impf.*); **a ~ing hot day** знóйный день.

broiler [ˈbrɔɪlə(r)] *n.* (*chicken*) брóйлер.

broke [brəʊk] *adj.* (*coll.*) разори́вшийся, бездéнежный; **stony ~** без грошá.

broken [ˈbrəʊkən] *adj.* **1.**: **a ~ leg** слóманная ногá; **~ English** лóманый англи́йский язы́к. **2.** (**~-*down***): **a ~ marriage** расстрóенный брак; **a ~ home** разби́тая семья́. **3.** (*crushed*): **a ~ man** слóмленный человéк; **~ spirits** подáвленное настроéние, уны́ние. **4.** (*rough*): **~ ground** пересечённая мéстность; **~ water** зыбь, буруны́ (*m. pl.*). **5.** (*interrupted*): **~ sleep** прéрванный сон; **a ~ week** разби́тая недéля; **~ weather** перемéнчивая/неустóйчивая погóда; **~ly** отры́висто, поры́вами. **6.** (**~ in**, *of a horse*) вы́езженный, объéзженный.

cpds. **~-down** *adj.* (*of health*) подóрванный; (*of pers.*) надлóмленный; (*morally*) слóмленный; (*of machine*) слóманный; **a ~-down horse** вы́дохшаяся кля́ча; **~-hearted** *adj.* с разби́тым сéрдцем; **~-winded** *adj.* (*of horse*) с запáлом.

broker [ˈbrəʊkə(r)] *n.* (*of shares etc.*) мáклер, брóкер; (*of distrained goods*) комиссионéр; (*go-between*) посрéдник; **marriage ~** сват.

brokerage [ˈbrəʊkərɪdʒ] *n.* (*business*) мáклерство; (*commission*) куртáж; комиссиóнное вознаграждéние.

broking [ˈbrəʊkɪŋ] *n.* мáклерство, посрéдничество.

brolly [ˈbrɒlɪ] (*coll.*) = **umbrella** *n.* **1.**

bromide [ˈbrəʊmaɪd] *n.* (*chem.*) броми́д; (*fig.*, *coll.*) банáльность.

bromine [ˈbrəʊmi:n] *n.* бром.

bronch|i [ˈbrɒŋkaɪ], **-ia** [ˈbrɒŋkɪə] *nn.* (*anat.*) брóнхи (*m. pl.*).

bronchial [ˈbrɒŋkɪəl] *adj.* бронхиáльный.

bronchitic [brɒŋˈkɪtɪk] *adj.* страдáющий бронхи́том.

bronchitis [brɒŋˈkaɪtɪs] *n.* бронхи́т.

bronco [ˈbrɒŋkəʊ] *n.* полуди́кая лóшадь.

cpd. **~-buster** *n.* (*coll.*) объéздчик полуди́ких лошадéй.

brontosaurus [ˌbrɒntəˈsɔ:rəs] *n.* бронтозáвр.

bronze [brɒnz] *n.* брóнза; (*article*) брóнза, издéлие из брóнзы; (*attr.*) брóнзовый.

v.t. бронзи́ровать (*impf.*, *pf.*); (*tan*) покр|ывáть, -ы́ть загáром; **~d cheeks** загорéлые щёки.

brooch [brəʊtʃ] *n.* брошь.

brood [bru:d] *n.* вы́водок; (*of children*, *also*) потóмство.

v.i. **1.** (*of bird*) сидéть (*impf.*) на яйцáх. **2.**: **~ over one's plans** вынáшивать (*impf.*) плáны; **~ over an insult** копи́ть (*impf.*) в себé оби́ду. **3.** (*of night*, *clouds etc.*) нав|исáть, -и́снуть.

cpds. **~-hen** *n.* насéдка; **~-mare** *n.* племенная кобы́ла.

broody [ˈbru:dɪ] *adj.*: **a ~ hen** (хорóшая) насéдка.

brook[1] [brʊk] *n.* (*stream*) ручéй.

brook[2] [brʊk] *v.t.* (*liter.*): **this ~s no delay** э́то не тéрпит отлагáтельства.

brooklet [brʊklɪt] *n.* ручеёк.

broom [bru:m] *n.* **1.** (*bot.*) раки́тник. **2.** (*implement*) метлá; (*besom*) вéник; **a new ~ sweeps clean** нóвая метлá чи́сто метёт.

cpd. **~stick** *n.* метлови́ще; (*witch's*) помелó.

Bros. [ˈbrʌðəz] *n.* (*abbr. of* **Brother(s)**) Брáтья (*в названии фирмы*).

broth [brɒθ] *n.* мяснóй бульóн; **Scotch ~** перлóвый суп; **a ~ of a boy** (*coll.*) молодéц.

brothel [ˈbrɒθ(ə)l] *n.* публи́чный дом, дом терпи́мости.

brother [ˈbrʌðə(r)] *n.* **1.** (*also relig.*) брат; **own, full ~** роднóй брат; **half ~** свóдный брат; **the Ivanov ~s** брáтья Ивanóвы. **2.** (*fig.*): **~ in arms** собрáт по орýжию; **~ doctor** коллéга-дóктор. **3.** (*eccl.*): **lay ~** пóслушник.

cpd. **~-in-law** *n.* (*sister's husband*) зять (*m.*); (*wife's ~*) шýрин; (*husband's ~*) дéверь (*m.*); (*wife's sister's husband*) своя́к.

brotherhood [ˈbrʌðəˌhʊd] *n.* (*kinship*) брáтство; (*comradeship*) брáтские отношéния; (*association*, *community*) содрýжество, брáтство.

brotherliness [ˈbrʌðəlɪnɪs] *n.* брáтское отношéние.

brotherly [ˈbrʌðəlɪ] *adj.* брáтский.

brouhaha [ˈbru:hɑ:ˌhɑ:] *n.* шуми́ха (*coll.*).

brow [braʊ] *n.* (*eye ~*) бровь; **knit one's ~s** хмýрить, на- брóви; (*forehead*) лоб, челó; (*of cliff*) крóмка, край, вы́ступ; (*of hill*) грéбень (*m.*); **over the ~ of the hill** за грéбнем холмá.

cpd. **~beat** *v.t.* наг|оня́ть, -нáть страх на+*a.*; запýг|ивать, -áть.

brown [braʊn] *n.* (*colour*) кори́чневый цвет; **he was dressed in ~** он был одéт в кори́чневое; (*horse*) карáковая.

adj. **1.** кори́чневый; (*grey-~*) бýрый; **light-~** свéтло-кори́чневый; **~ shoes** жёлтые тýфли; **~ eyes** кáрие глазá; **~ hair** каштáновые вóлосы; **~ bear** бýрый медвéдь; **~ bread** сéрый хлеб; **~ sugar** кори́чневый сáхар; **~ paper** обёрточная бумáга; **~ coal** бýрый ýголь. **2.** (*fig.*): **in a ~ study** в глубóком раздýмье; **do s.o. ~** (*sl.*) надýть/облапóшить (*both pf.*) когó-н. **3.** (*toasted*) поджáренный, подрумя́ненный; **I would like my toast a little ~er** дáйте, пожáлуйста, моемý сухарю́ ещё подрумя́ниться. **4.** (*tanned*) загорéлый; **as ~ as a berry** чёрный, как гáлка; **he returned from his holidays quite ~** он вернýлся из óтпуска тёмным от загáра. **5.** (*dark-skinned*) смýглый.

v.t. (*roast*, *toast*) поджáри|вать, -ть; (*tan*) опал|я́ть, -и́ть; **he is ~ed off** емý всё осточертéло (*sl.*).

cpds. **~-eyed** *adj.* с кáрими глазáми; **~-haired** *adj.* с тёмно-рýсыми волосáми; **B~shirt** *n.* (*hist.*) коричнево-рубáшечник, фаши́ст.

brownie [ˈbraʊnɪ] *n.* (*goblin*) домовóй.

Browning [ˈbraʊnɪŋ] *n.* (*pistol*) брáунинг.

brownish [ˈbraʊnɪʃ] *adj.* коричневáтый.

browse [braʊz] *v.i.* щипáть (*impf.*) травý; пасти́сь (*impf.*); (*fig.*): **~ through a book** просм|áтривать, -отрéть кни́гу; **~ in a bookshop** ры́ться (*impf.*) в кни́гах в кни́жном магази́не.

brr [bɜ:] *int.* бр-р-ру!

Brueghel [ˈbrɔɪg(ə)l] *n.* Брéйгель (*m.*).

Bruges [ˈbru:ʒ] *n.* Брю́гге (*m. indecl.*).

bruin [ˈbru:ɪn] *n.* ми́шка (*m.*), топты́гин.

bruise [bru:z] *n.* синя́к, кровоподтёк; (*of fruit*) помя́тость.

v.t. подст|авля́ть, -áвить синя́к +*d.*; (*fruit*) помя́ть, поби́ть (*both pf.*); **I ~d my shoulder** я уши́б плечó; **this**

apple is ~d э́то я́блоко поби́то; **~ s.o.'s feelings** ра́нить (*impf., pf.*) чьи-н. чу́вства.

v.i. ушиб|а́ться, -и́ться; **she ~s easily** её чуть тронь — и она́ покрыва́ется синяка́ми.

bruiser ['bru:zə(r)] *n.* (*prizefighter*) боре́ц; боксёр; (*thug*) хулига́н.

bruit [bru:t] *v.t.* (*liter.*): **~ sth. about** разн|оси́ть, -ести́ молву́ о чём-н.

Brunei [bru:'naɪ] *n.* Бруне́й.

brunette [bru:'net] *n.* брюне́тка.

adj. тёмный, темноволо́сый.

brunt [brʌnt] *n.* гла́вный уда́р; **bear the ~ of the work** вы́нести (*pf.*) всю тя́жесть рабо́ты.

brush [brʌʃ] *n.* **1.** (*brushwood*) куста́рник, хво́рост, хворости́нник. **2.** (*for sweeping*) щётка; (*painter's*) кисть. **3.** (*fox's tail*) труба́. **4.** (*skirmish, tiff*) сты́чка. **5.** (*abrasion*) сса́дина. **6.** (*brushing*) чи́стка; **give sth. a good ~** хорошо́ почи́стить (*pf.*) что-н.

v.t. (*clean*) чи́стить, по-; **~ mud off a coat** счи́стить (*pf.*) грязь с пальто́; (*touch slightly*): **the twigs ~ed my cheek** ве́тки легко́ косну́лись моéй щеки́.

v.i.: **~ against sth.** слегка́ каса́ться, косну́ться чего́-н.; **~ past s.o.** прон|оси́ться, -ести́сь ми́мо кого́-н.

with advs.: **~ aside** *v.t.*: **~ aside a plea** отмахну́ться (*pf.*) от жа́лобы; **~ aside difficulties** отме|та́ть, -сти́ тру́дности; **~ away** *v.t.*: **~ away a fly** смахну́ть (*pf.*) му́ху; **~ off** *v.i.*: **the mud will ~ off** грязь счи́стится/отчи́стится; **~ out** *v.t.*: **~ out a room** подме|та́ть, -сти́ ко́мнату; **~ out one's hair** причеса́ть (*pf.*) щёткой во́лосы; **~ out** (*obliterate*) **part of a picture** зама́зать (*pf.*) часть карти́ны; **~ up** *v.t.*: **~ up crumbs** сме|та́ть, -сти́ кро́шки; **~ up one's French** восстан|а́вливать, -ови́ть свои́ зна́ния во францу́зском языке́; *v.i.*: **~ up on a subject** освеж|а́ть, -и́ть (*or* подч|ищáть, -и́стить) зна́ния по како́му-н. предме́ту.

cpds. **~-down** *n.*: **give s.o. a ~-down** почи́стить (*pf.*) кого́-н.; **give a horse a ~-down** вы́чистить (*pf.*) коня́; **have a ~-down** почи́ститься (*pf.*); **~-off** *n.*: **give s.o. the ~-off** (*coll.*) отряхну́ть (*pf.*) кого́-н.; **~-up** *n.*: **have a wash and ~-up** привести́ (*pf.*) себя́ в поря́док; **~wood** *n.* хво́рост, вале́жник; **~work** *n.* живопи́сная мане́ра, мане́ра письма́.

brushless ['brʌʃlɪs] *adj.*: **~ shaving-cream** крем для бритья́, употребля́емый без ки́сточки.

brusque [brʊsk, bru:sk, brʌsk] *adj.* ре́зкий.

brusqueness ['brʊsknɪs, bru:sknɪs, brʌsknɪs] *n.* ре́зкость.

Brussels ['brʌs(ə)lz] *n.* Брюссе́ль (*m.*); **~ sprouts** брюссе́льская капу́ста.

brutal ['bru:t(ə)l] *adj.* (*rough*) гру́бый; (*cruel*) жесто́кий.

brutality [bru:'tælɪtɪ] *n.* гру́бость; жесто́кость; (*cruel act*) зве́рство.

brutalization [,bru:təlaɪ'zeɪʃ(ə)n] *n.* огрубле́ние, ожесточе́ние.

brutalize ['bru:tə,laɪz] *v.t.* ожесточ|а́ть, -и́ть; огруб|ля́ть, -и́ть.

brute [bru:t] *n.* (*animal*) живо́тное, зверь (*m.*); (*pers.*) скоти́на (*c.g.*).

adj.: **a ~ beast** гру́бое/бесчу́вственное живо́тное; **~ strength, force** физи́ческая си́ла.

brutish ['bru:tɪʃ] *adj.* гру́бый, бесчу́вственный; (*coarse*) ско́тский, живо́тный; (*stupid*) тупо́й.

bryony ['braɪənɪ] *n.* пересту́пень (*m.*), брио́ния.

B.Sc. (*abbr. of* ***Bachelor of Science***) бакала́вр (есте́ственных) нау́к; **he has a ~ in physics** он име́ет бакала́вр нау́к по фи́зике.

BSE (*abbr. of* ***bovine spongiform encephalopathy***) бы́чья губкови́дная энцефалопа́тия.

BST (*abbr. of* ***British Summer Time***) Брита́нское ле́тнее вре́мя.

bubble ['bʌb(ə)l] *n.* **1.** пузы́рь (*m.*); (*of air, gas in liquid*) пузырёк; (*in glass*) пузырёк во́здуха; **~ and squeak** жарко́е из мя́са, капу́сты и карто́феля; **blow ~s** пус|ка́ть, -ти́ть пузыри́; **prick a, the ~** (*lit.*) проткну́ть (*pf.*) пузы́рь; (*fig.*) доказа́ть (*pf.*) пустоту́/никчёмность чего́-н. **2.** (*gurgle*) бу́лькaнье.

v.t.: **~ a gas through a liquid** пропус|ка́ть, -ти́ть газ че́рез жи́дкость.

v.i. (*of water*) пузыри́ться (*impf.*), кипе́ть (*impf.*); (*of a fountain*) кипе́ть (*impf.*); **~ up** бить (*impf.*) ключо́м; бу́лькать (*impf.*); **~ (over) with laughter** залива́ться (*impf.*) сме́хом; **he ~s (over) with high spirits** из него́ так и бры́зжет весе́лье.

bubbly ['bʌblɪ] *n.* (*coll., champagne*) шипу́чка, шампа́нское.

adj. (*of wine*) шипу́чий, пе́нящийся; (*of glass*) пузыри́стый.

bubonic [bju:'bɒnɪk] *adj.* бубо́нный; **~ plague** бубо́нная чума́.

buccal ['bʌk(ə)l] *adj.* щёчный.

buccaneer [,bʌkə'nɪə(r)] *n.* пира́т.

v.i. занима́ться (*impf.*) пира́тством.

Bucharest [,bu:kə'rest] *n.* Бухаре́ст.

buck[1] [bʌk] *n.* **1.** (*male deer*) оле́нь (*m.*). **2.** (*male animal*) саме́ц; **~ rabbit** саме́ц кро́лика. **3.** (*dandy*) щёголь (*m.*), фат. **4.** (*coll., dollar*) до́ллар; **big ~s** ку́ча де́нег. **5.: pass the ~** (*coll.*) снять (*pf.*) с себя́ отве́тственность.

cpds. **~horn** *n.* оле́ний рог; **~-saw** *n.* лучко́вая пила́; **~shot** *n.* кру́пная дробь; **~skin** *n.* оле́нья (*or* лоси́ная) ко́жа; (*pl.*) ко́жаные штан|ы́ (*pl.*, *g.* -о́в); лоси́ны (*f. pl.*); **~thorn** *n.* круши́на; **~-tooth** *n.* выступа́ющий зуб.

buck[2] [bʌk] *v.t.* **1.: the horse ~ed him off** ло́шадь сбро́сила его́. **2.: we were ~ed by the news** (*coll.*) но́вость ободри́ла нас; **~ s.o. up** (*cheer*) подбодри́ть/встряхну́ть (*pf.*) кого́-н.; **~ things up** (*hasten*) подтолкну́ть (*pf.*) де́ло.

v.i. **1.** (*of horse*) вста|ва́ть, -ть на дыбы́; (*of engine*) трясти́сь (*impf.*). **2.: ~ against fate** проти́виться (*impf.*) судьбе́. **3. ~ up** (*coll.*) (*cheer up*) встряхну́ться, подбодри́ться, оживи́ться (*all pf.*); (*get a move on*) пошеве́ливаться (*impf.*).

bucket ['bʌkɪt] *n.* **1.** ведро́; бадья́; **the rain came down in ~s** дождь лил как из ведра́; **kick the ~** загну́ться (*pf.*) (*coll.*); сыгра́ть (*pf.*) в я́щик (*sl.*). **2.** (*of dredger*) черпа́к, ковш; (*of water-wheel*) ло́пасть. **3.: ~ seat** чашеобра́зное сиде́нье.

v.i. (*gallop*) скака́ть (*impf.*) во всю прыть; (*ride jerkily*) дви́гаться (*impf.*) рывка́ми; (*rain*) **it's ~ing down** льёт, как из ведра́.

bucketful ['bʌkɪtfʊl] *n.* ведро́.

buckle ['bʌk(ə)l] *n.* пря́жка.

v.t. **1.** (*fasten*) застёг|ивать, -ну́ть; **~ on one's sword** пристёг|ивать, -ну́ть меч. **2.** (*crumple*) из|гиба́ть, -огну́ть; сгиба́ть, согну́ть; прог|иба́ть, -ну́ть.

v.i. **1.** (*fasten*) застёг|иваться, -ну́ться. **2.: ~ down to a task, ~ to** прин|има́ться, -я́ться за де́ло. **3.** (*also* **~ up,** *of metal etc.*) сгиба́ться, согну́ться; (*of wheel*) погну́ться (*pf.*).

buckler ['bʌklə(r)] *n.* кру́глый щит; (*fig.*) щит.

buckram ['bʌkrəm] *n.* клеёнка; (*attr.*) клеёнчатый.

buckwheat ['bʌkwi:t] *n.* греча́ха; (*attr.*) гречи́шный, (*cooked*) гре́чневый.

bucolic [bju:'kɒlɪk] *n.*: **B~s** (*poems*) Буко́лики (*f. pl.*).

adj. буколи́ческий.

bud [bʌd] *n.* по́чка; (*flower not fully opened*) буто́н; **the trees are in ~** на дере́вьях появи́лись по́чки; **nip sth. in the ~** уничт|ожа́ть, -о́жить что-н. в заро́дыше.

v.t. (*graft*) прив|ива́ть, -и́ть глазко́м.

v.i. (*of plant*) покр|ыва́ться, -ы́ться по́чками; да|ва́ть, -ть ростки́; (*fig.*) распус|ка́ться, -ти́ться; расцве|та́ть, -сти́.

Budapest [,bju:də'pest] *n.* Будапе́шт.

Buddha ['bʊdə] *n.* Бу́дда (*m.*).

Buddhism ['bʊdɪz(ə)m] *n.* будди́зм.

Buddhist ['bʊdɪst] *n.* будди́ст.

adj. (*also* **~ic**) будди́йский.

buddleia ['bʌdlɪə] *n.* будле́йя.

buddy ['bʌdɪ] *n.* (*US coll.*) дружи́ще (*m.*), прия́тель (*m.*), брато́к.

budge [bʌdʒ] *v.t.*: **I cannot ~ this rock** я не могу́ сдви́нуть э́тот ка́мень; **nothing can ~ him from his position** ничто́ не сдви́нет его́ с ме́ста.

v.i.: **he never ~d the whole time** за всё вре́мя он не пошевельну́лся; **the bookcase won't ~ an inch** кни́жный шкаф невозмо́жно с ме́ста сдви́нуть.

budgerigar ['bʌdʒərɪ,gɑ:(r)] *n.* волни́стый попуга́йчик.

budget [ˈbʌdʒɪt] *n.* бюдже́т; ~ **of news** ку́ча/гру́да новосте́й.

v.t. & *i.*: ~ **(funds) for a project** ассигнова́ть (*impf.*, *pf.*) определённую су́мму на прое́кт.

budgetary [ˈbʌdʒɪtərɪ] *adj.* бюдже́тный.

budgie [ˈbʌdʒɪ] (*coll.*) = **budgerigar**

Buenos Aires [ˈbweɪnɒs ˈaɪrɪz] *n.* Буэ́нос-А́йрес.

buff [bʌf] *n.* (*ox-hide*) быча́чья ко́жа; (*buffalo-hide*) бу́йволовая ко́жа; (*coll.*, *human skin*): **in the** ~ нагишо́м; **strip to the** ~ разде́ть(ся) (*pf.*) догола́; (*colour*) тёмно-жёлтый цвет.

adj. тёмно-жёлтый.

v.t. (*metal*) полирова́ть, от- ко́жей; (*leather*) размягч|а́ть, -и́ть.

cpd. ~**-stick** *n.* полирова́льный брусо́к.

buffalo [ˈbʌfəˌləʊ] *n.* бу́йвол, бизо́н.

buffer [ˈbʌfə(r)] *n.* **1.** (*rail.*) бу́фер; (*fig.*): ~ **state** бу́ферное госуда́рство; ~ **stocks** бу́ферные запа́сы (*m. pl.*). **2.: old** ~ ста́рый хрыч (*coll.*).

buffet[1] [bʌfɪt] *n.* (*blow*) уда́р, шлепо́к.

v.t. уд|аря́ть, -а́рить в+*a.*; **they were** ~**ed by waves** их швыря́ло по волна́м; **they were** ~**ed by the crowd** их затолка́ла толпа́.

buffet[2] [ˈbʊfeɪ, ˈbʌfeɪ] *n.* (*sideboard*) буфе́т, серва́нт; (*refreshment bar*) буфе́т; (*supper*, *reception*) а-ля фурше́т.

buffeting [ˈbʌfɪtɪŋ] *n.* битьё.

buffoon [bəˈfu:n] *n.* шут, фигля́р.

buffoonery [bəˈfu:nərɪ] *n.* шутовство́, фигля́рство.

bug [bʌg] *n.* (*bedbug*) клоп; (*any small insect*) бука́шка, жучо́к; **big** ~ (*coll.*) ши́шка; (*coll.*, *germ*) зара́за; (*concealed microphone*) подслу́шка; (*craze*) пове́трие; **he's got the travelling** ~ он поме́шан на путеше́ствиях.

v.t.: **the room was** ~**ged** (*coll.*) в ко́мнате бы́ли устано́влены подслу́шивающие устро́йства; **the conversation was** ~**ged** разгово́р подслу́шивали.

cpds. ~**-eyed** *adj.* с вы́пученными глаза́ми; ~**-hunter** *n.* (*coll.*) энтомо́лог; ~**-hunting** *n.* (*coll.*) энтомоло́гия.

bugaboo [ˈbʌgəˌbu:] *n.* бу́ка, пу́гало.

bugbear [ˈbʌgbeə(r)] *n.* (*bogy*) бу́ка, пу́гало; (*object of aversion*) жу́пел.

bugger [ˈbʌgə(r)] *n.* (*sodomite*) содоми́т; (*vulg.*, *as term of abuse*) тип; **poor** ~ несча́стный.

v.t. **1.** (*commit sodomy with*) занима́ться (*impf.*) содоми́ей с+*i.* **2.** (*vulg. uses*): ~ **s.o. about** трави́ть, за- кого́-н.; ~ **sth. up** исковерка́ть/запоро́ть (*pf.*, *sl.*) что-н.; **I'm** ~**ed if I know** чёрта с два, е́сли я зна́ю; ~ **all** ни шиша́; ни хрена́; ~ **(it)!** чёрт возьми́! ~ **them!** да хрен с ни́ми!

v.i.: ~ **off!** (*vulg.*) прова́ливай!; убира́йся!

buggery [ˈbʌgərɪ] *n.* содоми́я.

buggy [ˈbʌgɪ] *n.* (*horse-drawn*) кабриоле́т; (*beach*, *dune etc.*) ба́гги.

cpd. ~**-driver** *n.* багги́ст.

bugle[1] [ˈbju:g(ə)l] *n.* горн.

cpd. ~**-call** *n.* сигна́л го́рна.

bugle[2] [ˈbju:g(ə)l] *n.* (*bead*) стекля́рус.

bugler [ˈbju:glə(r)] *n.* горни́ст.

bugloss [ˈbju:glɒs] *n.* волови́к.

buhl, boule [bu:l] *n.* ме́бель сти́ля «буль».

build [bɪld] *n.* (*structure*) констру́кция; фо́рма; (*of human body*) телосложе́ние; **a man of powerful** ~ челове́к могу́чего сложе́ния.

v.t. **1.** стро́ить, по-; выстра́ивать, вы́строить; ~ **a nest** вить, с- гнездо́; ~ **a fire** (*in the open*) разв|оди́ть, -ести́ костёр. **2.: a well-built man** хорошо́ сложённый челове́к. **3.** (*fig.*): ~ **a new world** созд|ава́ть, -а́ть но́вый мир; **he is not built that way** он сде́лан из друго́го те́ста. **4.** (*base*): ~ **one's hopes on sth.** стро́ить, по- наде́жды на чём-н. **5.** (*place*): ~ **beams into a wall** заде́л|ывать, -ать ба́лки в сте́ну.

v.i.: **I shan't** ~ **if I can find a suitable house** я не бу́ду стро́иться, е́сли найду́ подходя́щий дом; **I would not** ~ (*rely*) **on that if I were you** на ва́шем ме́сте я бы не полага́лся на э́то.

with advs.: ~ **in** *v.t.*: (*block up*): ~ **in a window** за|кла́дывать, -ложи́ть окно́; (*surround*): ~ **in a garden with a wall** обн|оси́ть, -ести́ сад стено́й; (*insert into structure*) вмонти́ровать (*pf.*); *see also* **built-in;** ~ **on** *v.t.*: ~ **a wing on to a house** пристр|а́ивать, -о́ить крыло́ к до́му; ~ **up** *v.t.*: ~ **s.o. up** (*in health*) укреп|ля́ть, -и́ть кому́-н. здоро́вье; (*in prestige*) популяризи́ровать (*impf.*, *pf.*) кого́-н.; созд|ава́ть, -а́ть и́мя кому́-н.; ~ **up a theory** стро́ить, по- тео́рию; ~ **up a business** созд|ава́ть, -а́ть де́ло; *v.i.*: **work has built up over the past year** накопи́лось мно́го рабо́ты за после́дний год; **our forces are** ~**ing up** на́ши си́лы расту́т (*see also* **built-up**).

cpds. ~**-down** *n.* (*mil.*) сокраще́ние (вооруже́ний); ~**-up** *n.* (*accumulation*) скопле́ние; рост, разви́тие, развёртывание; (*coll.*, *boosting*) популяриза́ция, созда́ние и́мени; **arms** ~**-up** нара́щивание вооруже́ний; **publicity** ~**-up** рекла́мная кампа́ния.

builder [ˈbɪldə(r)] *n.* строи́тель (*m.*); (*housing contractor*) подря́дчик.

building [ˈbɪldɪŋ] *n.* **1.** (*structure*) зда́ние, постро́йка, строе́ние; (*large edifice*) сооруже́ние; (*premises*) помеще́ние. **2.** (*activity*) (по)стро́йка; (*esp. large-scale*) строи́тельство; ~ **of socialism** построе́ние/строи́тельство социали́зма; ~ **of schools/houses** шко́льное/жили́щное строи́тельство; ~ **estate** жило́й ко́мплекс; микрорайо́н; ~ **materials** строи́тельные материа́лы, стройматериа́лы; ~ **land** земля́ под постро́йку; ~ **society** жили́щно-строи́тельное о́бщество.

built-in [bɪlt] *adj.*: **a** ~ **cupboard** встро́енный/стенно́й шкаф; **he has a** ~ **resistance to this argument** он органи́чески не мо́жет согласи́ться с э́тим аргуме́нтом.

built-up [bɪlt] *adj.*: ~ **area** застро́енный райо́н.

bulb [bʌlb] *n.* (*bot.*, *anat.*) лу́ковица; (*of lamp*) ла́мпочка; (*of thermometer*) ша́рик.

bulbous [ˈbʌlbəs] *adj.* лу́ковичный; луковицеобра́зный; **a** ~ **nose** нос карто́шкой.

Bulgar [ˈbʌlgɑ:(r)] *n.* болга́р|ин (*fem.* -ка).

Bulgaria [bʌlˈgeərɪə] *n.* Болга́рия.

Bulgarian [bʌlˈgeərɪən] *n.* (*pers.*) болга́р|ин (*fem.* -ка); (*language*) болга́рский язы́к; **Old** ~ старославя́нский язы́к.

adj. болга́рский.

bulg|e [bʌldʒ] *n.* (*swelling*) вы́пуклость; ~**e of a curve** горб криво́й; (*temporary increase*) разду́тие, взду́тие; (*mil.*, *salient*) вы́ступ, клин.

v.i. (*swell*) выпя́чиваться, вы́пятиться; (*of wall*) выступа́ть (*impf.*); выдава́ться (*impf.*); (*of bag etc.*) над|ува́ться, -у́ться; разд|ува́ться, -у́ться; **his pockets were** ~**ing with apples** его карма́ны оттопы́ривались от я́блок.

bulgy [bʌldʒɪ] *adj.* вы́пученный, разду́тый, наду́тый, оттопы́ренный.

bulimia [bju:ˈlɪmɪə] *n.* булими́я, ненорма́льно повы́шенное чу́вство го́лода.

bulk [bʌlk] *n.* **1.** (*size*, *mass*, *volume*) величина́, ма́сса, объём; **in** ~ (*not packaged*) нава́лом, (*of liquids*) нали́вом, (*of pourable solids*) на́сыпью. **2.** (*in large quantities*): ~ **purchase** поку́пка гурто́м; ма́ссовая заку́пка; ~ **buying** о́птовые заку́пки. **3.: break** ~ нач|ина́ть, -а́ть разгру́зку. **4.** (*greater part*) основна́я ма́сса/часть.

v.t. (*ascertain weight of*) устан|а́вливать, -ови́ть вес +*g.*; ~ **out** (*enlarge*) увели́чи|вать, -ть.

v.i.: ~ **large** каза́ться (*impf.*) бо́льше; представля́ться (*impf.*) бо́льшим.

cpd. ~**head** *n.* перебо́рка, перегоро́дка.

bulky [ˈbʌlkɪ] *adj.* (*large*) объёмистый; (*unwieldy*) громо́здкий.

bull[1] [bʊl] *n.* **1.** (*ox*) бык; (*buffalo*) бу́йвол; (*elephant*, *whale etc.*) саме́ц; (*fig.*): ~ **in a china shop** слон в посу́дной ла́вке; **take the** ~ **by the horns** взять (*pf.*) быка́ за рога́; **go at sth. like a** ~ **at a gate** лезть/пере́ть (*impf.*) напроло́м. **2.** (*astron.*) Теле́ц. **3.** (~**'s eye**) я́блоко мише́ни. **4.** (*comm.*) спекуля́нт, игра́ющий на повыше́ние. **5.** ('*spit and polish*') надра́йка (*coll.*). **6.** (*sl.*, *nonsense*) неле́пость.

v.t. (*comm.*): ~ **the market** пов|ыша́ть, -ы́сить цены на ры́нке; спекули́ровать (*impf.*) на повыше́ние.

cpds. ~**-baiting** *n.* тра́вля привя́занного быка́ соба́ками; ~**-calf** *n.* бычо́к; (*simpleton*) телёнок; ~**dog** *n.* бульдо́г;

~dog tenacity бульдóжья хвáтка; **~doze** *v.t.* (*clear with ~dozer*) расч|ищáть, -íстить бульдóзером; **~doze s.o. into doing sth.** прин|уждáть, -ýдить когó-н. сдéлать что-н.; **~dozer** *n.* бульдóзер; **driver of a ~dozer** бульдозерист; **~fight, ~fighting** *nn.* бой быкóв; **~fighter** *n.* тореадóр; **~finch** *n.* снегирь (*m.*); **~frog** *n.* лягýшка-бык; **~-headed** *adj.* (*obstinate*) упрямый; **~-necked** *adj.* с бычьей шéей; **~-nosed** *adj.* толстонóсый; **~point** *n.* очкó в чью-н. пóльзу; **~-pup** *n.* щенóк бульдóга; **~-ring** *n.* арéна для бóя быкóв; **~'s-eye** *n.* (*of target*) яблоко; **hit the ~'s-eye** (*fig.*) поп|адáть, -áсть в цель; (*sweetmeat*) ≃ дражé (*indecl.*); **~-terrier** *n.* бультерьéр.

bull[2] [bʊl] *n.* (*edict*) бýлла.

bull[3] [bʊl] *n.*: **Irish ~** нелéпость, нелéпица.

bullace ['bʊlɪs] *n.* тернослíва.

bullet ['bʊlɪt] *n.* пýля; **put a ~ through s.o.** всадíть (*pf.*) в когó-н. пýлю.

cpds. **~-headed** *adj.* круглоголóвый; твердолóбый; **~-hole** *n.* пулевóе отвéрстие; **~-proof** *adj.* пуленепробивáемый; **~-proof vest** бронежилéт.

bulletin ['bʊlɪtɪn] *n.* (*periodical; official statement*) бюллетéнь (*m.*); (*news report*) бюллетéнь (*m.*), вьіпуск, сообщéние.

bullion ['bʊljən] *n.*: **gold ~** зóлото в слíтках.

bullish ['bʊlɪʃ] *adj.* (*comm.*): **a ~ market** повышáющийся рынок; **~ speculators** спекулянты на повышéние цен.

bullock ['bʊlək] *n.* вол.

bullshit ['bʊlʃɪt] *n.* (*vulg.*) брехня, бредятина, херня; **don't give me that ~!** не порí херню!

v.i. (*vulg.*) брехáть (*impf.*).

bullshitter ['bʊlʃɪtə(r)] *n.* (*vulg.*) брехлó, брехýн.

bully[1] ['bʊlɪ] *n.* громíла (*m.*), задíра (*m.*), обíдчик, хулигáн; (*hired ruffian*) наёмный громíла; (*ponce*) сутенёр.

v.t. запýг|ивать, -áть; издевáться/измывáться (*both impf.*) над+*i.*; помыкáть (*impf.*) +*i.*; **~ s.o. into doing sth.** запýгиванием заст|авлять, -áвить когó-н. сдéлать что-н.; **~ s.o. out of sth.** отпýг|ивать, -нýть когó-н. от чегó-н.

v.i.: **~ off** (*at hockey*) скрé|щивать, -стíть клюшки.

bully[2] ['bʊlɪ] *adj.* (*coll.*): **~ for you!** молодéц!

bully[3] ['bʊlɪ] *n.* (*also* **~ beef**) мясныe консéрв|ы (*pl., g.* -ов).

bullyboy ['bʊlɪbɔɪ] *n.* громíла (*m.*), задíра (*m.*).

bulrush ['bʊlrʌʃ] *n.* камыш.

bulwark ['bʊlwək] *n.* (*rampart*) бастиóн, бóльверк; (*mole, breakwater*) мол; (*naut.*) фальшбóрт; (*fig.*): **~ of freedom** оплóт свобóды.

bum [bʌm] *n.* (*coll.*) **1.** (*buttocks*) зад, зáдница; **~ bag** поясная сýмка. **2.** (*loafer*) лóдырь (*m.*), лоботряс; (*US, vagrant*) бродяга (*m.*); **go on the ~** стать (*pf.*) бродягой; **give s.o. the ~'s rush** выгонять, выгнать когó-н. взашéй.

adj. дряннóй.

v.t. (*sl., cadge, scrounge*) клянчить, вы-.

v.i.: **~ around** шатáться (*impf.*).

cpds. **~-bailiff** *n.* (*hist.*) судéбный прíстав; **~boat** *n.* лóдка, доставляющая провíзию на судá.

bumble ['bʌmb(ə)l] *v.i.*: **~ about** идтí (*det.*) неувéренно/спотыкáясь.

bumble-bee ['bʌmb(ə)l,bi:] *n.* шмель (*m.*).

bum|f, -ph [bʌmf] *n.* (*papers*) бумáжки (*f. pl.*).

bump [bʌmp] *n.* **1.** (*thump*) глухóй удáр; **he landed with a ~ on the floor** он шлёпнулся/грóхнулся нá пол; (*collision*) толчóк; **2.** (*swelling, protuberance*) шíшка; **~ of locality** (*fig.*) дар ориентирóвки на мéстности. **3.** (*air pocket*) воздýшная яма; (*in a road*) ухáб, бугóр.

adv.: **he went ~ into the door** он так и врéзался в дверь.

v.t. уд|арять, -áрить; ушиб|áть, -íть; **I ~ed my knee as I fell** я ушиб колéно при падéнии; **the car ~ed the one in front** машíна стýкнулась о другýю, стоявшую/шéдшую впередí; **I ~ed the table and spilt the ink** я толкнýл стол и пролíл чернíла; **~ off** (*kill*) пустíть (*pf.*) в расхóд (*sl.*).

v.i.: **~ against a tree** удáриться (*pf.*) о дéрево; наскочíть/наткнýться (*pf.*) на дéрево; **my head ~ed against the beam** я удáрился головóй о бáлку; **~ along** (*in cart etc.*) трястись (*impf.*); **he ~ed into a lamp-post** он наткнýлся на фонáрный столб; **his car ~ed into ours** егó машíна врéзалась в нáшу; **I ~ed into him in London** я наткнýлся на негó в Лóндоне.

bumper ['bʌmpə(r)] *n.* **1.** (*of car*) бýфер. **2.** (*full glass*) бокáл, пóлный до краёв; **~ crop** небывáлый/невíданный урожáй.

bumph [bʌmf] = **bumf**

bumpkin ['bʌmpkɪn] *n.* мужлáн.

bumptious ['bʌmpʃəs] *adj.* самоувéренный, зазнáвшийся.

bumptiousness ['bʌmpʃəsnɪs] *n.* самоувéренность, зазнáйство.

bumpy ['bʌmpɪ] *adj.* (*of road*) ухáбистый, тряский; **we had a ~ journey** нас тряслó всю дорóгу; **a ~ flight** ≃ болтáнка.

bun [bʌn] *n.* **1.** (*cul.*) бýлочка, плюшка; **take the ~** (*fig.*) превзойтí (*pf.*) всё. **2.** (*of hair*) пучóк.

cpd. **~-fight** *n.* (*coll.*) чаепíтие.

bunch [bʌntʃ] *n.* **1.** (*of flowers*) букéт; (*of grapes*) кисть, гроздь; (*of bananas*) гроздь; **~ of keys** связка ключéй. **2.** (*coll., group*) компáния, грýппа; **the best of the ~** лýчший средí них.

v.t. (*e.g. flowers*) соб|ирáть, -рáть в букéт; **~ up** (*dress etc.*) соб|ирáть, -рáть (плáтье) в сбóрки.

v.i.: **~ together** ск|áпливаться, -опíться; (*of people*) сб|ивáться, -íться в кýчу; **~ up** (*of dress etc.*) собрáться (*impf.*) в сбóрки.

bundle ['bʌnd(ə)l] *n.* **1.** (*of clothes etc.*) ýзел; **~ of rags** узелóк тряпья; (*of sticks*) вязáнка; (*of hay*) охáпка. **2.** (*packet*) пакéт. **3.**: **she is a ~ of nerves** онá комóк нéрвов.

v.t. **1.** **~ up** связ|ывать, -áть в ýзел/вязáнку; **~ up one's hair** соб|ирáть, -рáть вóлосы в пучóк. **2.** (*shove*) запих|ивать, -áть; **~ s.o. into a room** втолкнýть (*pf.*) когó-н. в кóмнату; **~ off** спровá|живать, -дить; выпровáживать, выпроводить; спл|авлять, -áвить (*coll.*).

bung [bʌŋ] *n.* затычка, втýлка.

v.t. **1.** (*cask etc.*) зат|ыкáть, -кнýть; закупóри|вать, -ть; **the sink is ~ed up** рáковина засорíлась; **my nose is ~ed up** у меня залóжен нос. **2.** (*sl., throw*) швыр|ять, -нýть.

cpd. **~hole** *n.* отвéрстие для налíва бóчки.

bungalow ['bʌŋgə,ləʊ] *n.* бýнгало (*indecl.*); одноэтáжная дáча.

bungle ['bʌŋg(ə)l] *v.t.* пóртить, на-; пýтать, с-; (*coll.*) завалíть (*pf.*).

bungler ['bʌŋglə(r)] *n.* портáч, «сапóжник».

bunion ['bʌnjən] *n.* óпухоль/шíшка на ногé.

bunk[1] [bʌŋk] *n.* (*sleeping-berth*) кóйка; **~ bed** двухъярусная кровáть.

v.i. спать (*impf.*) на кóйке.

bunk[2] [bʌŋk] *n.*: **do a ~** (за)д|авáть, -áть дрáла/тягу (*coll.*).

v.i. см|ывáться, -ыться; дрáпа|ть, -нýть (*coll.*); **~ off** (*coll.*): **to ~ off lessons/school** прогýливать (*impf.*) урóки, сачковáть (*impf.*).

bunk[3] [bʌŋk] *n.* (*sl., nonsense*) чепухá, чушь.

bunker ['bʌŋkə(r)] *n.* (*ship's*) бýнкер; (*underground shelter*) блиндáж; (*golf*) яма.

v.t. (*stow in a ~*) бункеровáть (*impf., pf.*).

bunkum ['bʌŋkəm] *n.* (*coll.*) чушь, пустослóвие.

bunny ['bʌnɪ] *n.* (*coll.*) крóлик, зáйчик.

Bunsen burner ['bʌns(ə)n] *n.* бýнзеновская горéлка.

bunting[1] ['bʌntɪŋ] *n.* (*zool.*) овсянка; **snow ~** пýночка.

bunting[2] ['bʌntɪŋ] *n.* (*cloth*) флáжная матéрия; (*naut.*) флагдýк; (*fig., flags*) флáги (*m. pl.*).

buoy [bɔɪ] *n.* буй, бáкен; **mooring-~** швартóвная бóчка; (*life-~*) спасáтельный буй/круг.

v.t. (*mark with ~*) отм|ечáть, -éтить буями; (*of a wreck, channel*) обст|авлять, -áвить буями; **~ up** (*lit.*) поддéрж|ивать, -áть на повéрхности; (*fig.*) поддéрж|ивать, -áть.

buoyancy ['bɔɪənsɪ] *n.* плавýчесть; (*fig.*) жизнерáдостность; оживлéние.

buoyant ['bɔɪənt] *adj.* плавýчий; (*of pers.*) жизнерáдостный; (*of hopes, market*) оживлённый; (*of prices*) повышáтельный.

bur, burr [bɜ:(r)] *n.* репéй, репéйник; **he sticks like a ~** он цепляется как репéй.

burble [ˈbɜːb(ə)l] *v.i.* клокота́ть, болта́ть (*both impf.*); ~ **with laughter** е́ле сде́рживать (*impf.*) смех; зад|ыха́ться, -охну́ться (*impf.*) от сме́ха.

burden [ˈbɜːd(ə)n] *n.* **1.** (*load*) но́ша, груз; (*fig.*) бре́мя (*nt.*); обу́за; **beast of** ~ вью́чное живо́тное; ~ **of taxation** бре́мя нало́гов; ~ **of proof** бре́мя доказывания/доказа́тельства; **become a** ~ **on s.o.** стать (*pf.*) в тя́гость (*or* обу́зой) кому́-н.; **bear the** ~ **and heat of the day** переноси́ть (*impf.*) тя́гость дня и зной. **2.** (*tonnage*) тонна́ж. **3.** (*refrain*) рефре́н, припе́в; (*theme*) основна́я те́ма.

v.t. (*load*) нагру|жа́ть, -зи́ть; (*fig.*) обремен|я́ть, -и́ть; ~ **s.o. with expenses** взва́л|ивать, -и́ть на кого́-н. расхо́ды.

burdensome [ˈbɜːd(ə)nsəm] *adj.* обремени́тельный, тя́гостный.

burdock [ˈbɜːdɒk] *n.* лопу́х.

bureau [ˈbjʊərəʊ, -ˈrəʊ] *n.* (*desk*) бюро́ (*indecl.*), конто́рка; (*chest*) комо́д; (*office*) бюро́; **information** ~ спра́вочное бюро́; **employment** ~ бюро́ по на́йму; **marriage** ~ бра́чное бюро́; ~ **de change** разме́нная конто́ра.

bureaucracy [bjʊəˈrɒkrəsɪ] *n.* бюрокра́тия.

bureaucrat [ˈbjʊərəˌkræt, -rəʊˌkræt] *n.* бюрокра́т, чино́вник.

bureaucratic [bjʊərəˈkrætɪk, -rəʊˈkrætɪk] *adj.* бюрократи́ческий.

burette [bjʊəˈret] *n.* бюре́тка.

burgeon [ˈbɜːdʒ(ə)n] *v.i.* да|ва́ть, -ть по́чки; распус|ка́ться, -ти́ться.

burger [ˈbɜːgə(r)] *n.* котле́та; ~ **bar** га́мбургерная, котле́тная.

burgess [ˈbɜːdʒɪs] *n.* граждани́н/жи́тель го́рода, име́ющего самоуправле́ние.

burgher [ˈbɜːgə(r)] *n.* бю́ргер, горожа́нин.

burglar [ˈbɜːglə(r)] *n.* граби́тель (*m.*), взло́мщик; **cat** ~ граби́тель, проника́ющий в до́м че́рез окно́.

burglarious [bɜːˈgleərɪəs] *adj.* воровско́й.

burglarize [ˈbɜːgləˌraɪz] = **burgle** *v.t.*

burglary [ˈbɜːglərɪ] *n.* грабёж; кра́жа со взло́мом.

burgle [ˈbɜːg(ə)l] (*also* **burglarize**) *v.t.*: гра́бить, о-.

v.i. соверш|а́ть, -и́ть кра́жу со взло́мом.

burgomaster [ˈbɜːgəˌmɑːstə(r)] *n.* бургоми́стр.

burgundy [ˈbɜːgəndɪ] *n.* (*wine*) бурéу́ндское (вино́).

burial [ˈberɪəl] *n.* (*interment*) погребе́ние, захороне́ние; (*funeral*) по́хор|оны (*pl.*, *g.* -он); ~ **service** заупоко́йная слу́жба.

cpds. ~**-ground** *n.* кла́дбище, пого́ст; (*archaeol.*) моги́льник; ~**-mound** *n.* курга́н; ~**-place** *n.* ме́сто погребе́ния.

burin [ˈbjʊərɪn] *n.* грабшти́хель (*m.*).

burke [bɜːk] *v.t.* зам|ина́ть, -я́ть.

burlap [ˈbɜːlæp] *n.* дерю́га.

burlesque [bɜːˈlesk] *n.* (*parody*) бурле́ск.

adj. бурле́скный, фа́рсовый, пароди́йный.

v.t. пароди́ровать (*impf.*, *pf.*).

burly [ˈbɜːlɪ] *adj.* здорове́нный, дю́жий.

Burma [ˈbɜːmə] *n.* Би́рма.

Burm|an [ˈbɜːmən], **-ese** [bɜːˈmiːz] *nn.* (*pers.*) бирма́н|ец (*fem.* -ка); (*language*) бирма́нский язы́к.

adj. бирма́нский.

burn[1] [bɜːn] *n.* (*injury*) ожо́г; **first-degree** ~**s** ожо́ги пе́рвой сте́пени.

v.t. **1.** (*sting*) жечь, с-; (*destroy by fire*) сж|ига́ть, -ечь; ~ **o.s.** обж|ига́ться, -е́чься; ~ **one's fingers** (*lit.*) обже́чь (*pf.*) себе́ па́льцы; (*fig.*) обже́чься (*pf.*) (*на чём*); ~ **a hole in sth.** проже́чь (*pf.*) дыру́ в чём-н.; **the meat is** ~**t** мя́со сгоре́ло/подгоре́ло; **a** ~**t taste/smell** вкус/за́пах горе́лого; ~**t almond** жа́реный минда́ль; ~**t offering** всесожже́ние; **he was** ~**t all over** на нём живо́го ме́ста не оста́лось от ожо́гов; **she was** ~**t at the stake** её сожгли́ на костре́; **he** ~**t himself to death** (*on purpose*) он поко́нчил с собо́й самосожже́нием; **the ship** ~**s oil** кора́бль рабо́тает на не́фти; **acid** ~**s the carpet** кислота́ прожига́ет ковёр; **pepper** ~**s one's mouth** от пе́рца жжёт во рту; **he was** ~**t out of house and home** он погоре́л; у него́ всё сгоре́ло; ~ **paint off a wall** сжечь (*pf.*) кра́ску со стены́. **2.** (*bricks, charcoal etc.*) обж|ига́ть, -е́чь. **3.** (*tan*) опал|я́ть, -и́ть; обж|ига́ть, -е́чь. **4.** (*fig.*): ~ **one's boats** сже́чь (*pf.*) свои́ корабли́; ~ **the candle at both ends** безрассу́дно расхо́довать (*impf.*) си́лы; ~ **the midnight oil** заси́|живаться, -де́ться за рабо́той за́ полночь; **he has money to** ~ у него́ де́нег ку́ры не клюю́т; **money** ~**s a hole in his pocket** де́ньги у него́ не де́ржатся; **a** ~**t child dreads the fire** ≃ обжёгшись на молоке́, бу́дешь дуть и на́ воду; **the fact was** ~**t into his memory** факт вре́зался ему́ в па́мять.

v.i. **1.** горе́ть (*impf.*) (*also fig.*): **the house is** ~**ing** дом гори́т; в до́ме пожа́р; **the lamp is** ~**ing low** ла́мпа догора́ет; **this substance** ~**s blue** э́то вещество́ гори́т си́ним пла́менем; **acid** ~**s into metal** кислота́ разъеда́ет мета́лл; **the spectacle** ~**t into his soul** зре́лище запечатле́лось в его́ душе́; **he** ~**t with fever** он был в жару́; он горе́л в лихора́дке; **he** ~**t with shame/curiosity** он сгора́л от стыда́/любопы́тства; **he** ~**t with passion** он пыла́л стра́стью; **he** ~**t with anger** он кипе́л от зло́сти.

with advs.: ~ **down** *v.t.* сж|ига́ть, -ечь; *v.i.*: **the house** ~**t down** дом сгоре́л дотла́; **the fire** ~**t down** костёр догоре́л; ~ **out** *v.t.*: **the house was** ~**t out** дом сгоре́л дотла́; **the fire** ~**t itself out** пожа́р/костёр догоре́л и загло́х; ~ **o.s. out** (*fig.*) сгоре́ть (*pf.*); ~ **out a fuse** (*elec.*) пережéчь (*pf.*) про́бку; *v.i.*: **the fire** ~**t out** ого́нь поту́х; костёр загло́х; ~ **up** *v.i.*: **make the fire** ~ **up** разж|ига́ть, -е́чь пе́чку/ками́н.

burn[2] [bɜːn] *n.* (*Sc.*, *stream*) руче́й, пото́к.

burner [ˈbɜːnə(r)] *n.* (*of stove etc.*) горе́лка; **to put on the back burner** отодви́нуть (*pf.*) на за́дний план.

burning [ˈbɜːnɪŋ] *n.* горе́ние; обжига́ние, о́бжиг.

adj. (*of fever*) сжига́ющий; (*of shame*) жгу́чий; (*of thirst*) нестерпи́мый; (*of zeal*) неи́стовый.

adv.: ~ **hot** раскалённый.

cpd. ~**-glass** *n.* зажига́тельное стекло́.

burnish [ˈbɜːnɪʃ] *v.t.* полирова́ть, от-.

burnisher [ˈbɜːnɪʃə(r)] *n.* (*pers.*) полиро́вщик; (*instrument*) глади́лка.

burnous [bɜːˈnuːs] *n.* бурну́с.

Burns [bɜːnz] *n.* Бёрнс.

burp [bɜːp] (*coll.*) *n.* отры́жка, рыга́нье.

v.t.: ~ **a baby** да|ва́ть, -ть ребёнку отрыгну́ть.

v.i. рыг|а́ть, -ну́ть.

burr[1] [bɜː(r)] *n.* (*in speech*) карта́вость; грасси́рование; **speak with a** ~ карта́вить (*impf.*), грасси́ровать (*impf.*).

v.t.: ~ **one's R's** карта́во выгова́ривать (*impf.*) «р».

burr[2] [bɜː(r)] *n.* (*on metal*) заусе́нец, грат.

cpd. ~**-drill** *n.* бормаши́на.

burr[3] [bɜː(r)] *n.* (*bot.*) = **bur**

burrow [ˈbʌrəʊ] *n.* нора́.

v.t.: ~ **a hole** рыть, вы- но́ру.

v.i. (*of rabbit/mole*) рыть, вы- но́ру/ходы́; ~ **among archives** ры́ться (*impf.*) в архи́вах; ~ **into a mystery** прон|ика́ть, -и́кнуть в та́йну.

bursar [ˈbɜːsə] *n.* (*treasurer*) казначе́й; (*scholarship-holder*) стипендиа́т.

bursary [ˈbɜːsərɪ] *n.* (*office*) канцеля́рия казначе́я; (*grant*) стипе́ндия.

burst [bɜːst] *n.* взрыв; разры́в; **the** ~ **of a shell** разры́в снаря́да; **a** ~ **of energy** вспы́шка/взрыв эне́ргии; **work in sudden** ~**s** рабо́тать (*impf.*) рывка́ми; ~ **of applause** взрыв аплодисме́нтов; ~ **of anger** вспы́шка гне́ва; взрыв негодова́ния; ~ **of tears** внеза́пный пото́к слёз; ~ **of machine-gun fire** пулемётная о́чередь.

v.t. (*e.g. a shell, tyre, balloon, blood-vessel*) раз|рыва́ть, -орва́ть; **the river** ~ **its banks** река́ вы́шла из берего́в; ~ **one's bonds** разорва́ть (*pf.*) свои́ око́вы; **the boy** ~ **his buttons** у ма́льчика отлете́ли все пу́говицы; ~ **one's sides with laughing** надорва́ть (*pf.*) живо́т от сме́ха; ~ **a door open** распахну́ть (*pf.*) дверь.

v.i.: **the shell** ~ снаря́д разорва́лся; **the balloon** ~ возду́шный шар ло́пнул; **the bubble** ~ пузы́рь ло́пнул; **the granaries are** ~**ing** закрома́ ло́мятся; **the dam** ~ плоти́ну прорва́ло; **full to** ~**ing** по́лный до отка́за; **he is** ~**ing with health** он пы́шет здоро́вьем; ~ **with laughter** расхохота́ться (*pf.*); **he was** ~**ing with pride** его́ распира́ло от го́рдости; **I was** ~**ing to tell her** мне не терпе́лось сказа́ть ей; **the door** ~ **open** дверь распахну́лась.

with preps.: ~ **into bloom** распусти́ться (*pf.*), расцвести́ (*pf.*): ~ **into song** запе́ть (*pf.*); ~ **into tears** разрыда́ться (*pf.*); ~ **into a room** ворва́ться (*pf.*) в ко́мнату; ~ **into flame** вспы́хнуть (*pf.*); **oil** ~ **out of the ground** из земли́ заби́ла нефть; **the sun** ~ **through the clouds** со́лнце прорва́лось сквозь ту́чи; **shouts** ~ **upon our ears** внеза́пно нас оглуши́ли кри́ки; **the truth** ~ **upon him** его́ вдруг осени́ло; **the news** ~ **upon the world** э́та но́вость потрясла́ мир; **the view** ~ **upon our sight** пе́ред на́ми внеза́пно откры́лся вид.

with advs.: ~ **in** *v.i.* (*interrupt*) вме́ш|иваться, -а́ться; **he** ~ **in upon us** он ворва́лся к нам; ~ **out** *v.i.* (*exclaim*) вы́палить (*pf.*); ~ **out laughing** расхохота́ться (*pf.*); ~ **out into threats** разрази́ться (*pf.*) угро́зами.

bur|y [ˈberɪ] *v.t.* **1.** (*inter*) хорони́ть, по-; погре|ба́ть, -сти́; **he is dead and** ~**ied** его́ нет в живы́х; **he** ~**ied** (*lost by death*) **all his relatives** он похорони́л всех свои́х родны́х. **2.** (*hide in earth*) зар|ыва́ть, -ы́ть; зак|а́пывать, -опа́ть. **3.** (*remove from view*): ~**y one's face in one's hands** закры́ть (*pf.*) лицо́ рука́ми; ~**y o.s. in one's books** зары́ться (*pf.*) в кни́ги; ~**y o.s. in the country** похорони́ть (*pf.*) себя́ в дере́вне; ~**ying-ground** = **burial-ground**

Buryat [bʊəˈjɑːt] *n.* (*pers.*) буря́т (*fem.* -ка).

adj. буря́тский.

bus [bʌs] *n.* авто́бус; **miss the** ~ (*fig.*) упусти́ть (*pf.*) слу́чай; (*coll.*: *car*) маши́на.

v.i. (*also* ~ **it**) е́хать (*det.*) авто́бусом.

cpds. ~**-conductor** *n.* конду́ктор авто́буса; ~**-conductress** *n.* же́нщина-конду́ктор; ~**-driver** *n.* води́тель (*m.*)/шофёр авто́буса; ~**man** *n.*: ~**man's holiday** пра́здник, похо́жий на бу́дни; ~**-shelter** *n.* автопавильо́н; ~**-stop** *n.* авто́бусная остано́вка; ~**-ticket** *n.* авто́бусный биле́т.

busby [ˈbʌzbɪ] *n.* гуса́рский ки́вер.

bush [bʊʃ] *n.* (*shrub*) куст; **good wine needs no** ~ хоро́ший това́р сам себя́ хва́лит; **burning** ~ (*bibl.*) неопали́мая купина́; (*thicket*) куста́рник; (*wild land*) некультиви́рованная земля́; ~ **telegraph** бы́строе распростране́ние слу́хов; ≃ молва́.

cpds. **B**~**man** *n.* бушме́н; ~**-ranger** *n.* (*hist.*) разбо́йник (в Австра́лии).

bushel [ˈbʊʃ(ə)l] *n.* бу́шель (*m.*); **hide one's light under a** ~ быть изли́шне скро́мным.

bushing [ˈbʊʃɪŋ] *n.* вту́лка, вкла́дыш.

bushy [ˈbʊʃɪ] *adj.* (*covered with bush*) покры́тый куста́рником; (*of beard etc.*) густо́й.

busily [ˈbɪzɪlɪ] *adv.* делови́то; энерги́чно.

business [ˈbɪznɪs] *n.* **1.** (*task, affair*) де́ло; **he made it his** ~ **to find out ...** он счёл свои́м до́лгом узна́ть...; **what is your** ~ **here?** что вам здесь на́до?; **it is none of your** ~ э́то не ва́ше де́ло; э́то вас не каса́ется; **mind your own** ~ не вме́шивайтесь/су́йтесь не в своё де́ло; **send s.o. about his** ~ прогна́ть (*pf.*) кого́-н.; **it is his** ~ **to keep a record** его́ обя́занность — вести́ за́писи; **you have no** ~ **to say that** не вам э́то говори́ть; **funny, monkey** ~ нечи́стое де́ло; штý́чки (*f. pl.*); **everybody's** ~ **is nobody's** ~ у семи́ ня́нек дитя́ без гла́зу; **I am sick of the whole** ~ мне вся э́та исто́рия надое́ла; **'any other** ~**'** (*on agenda*) «Ра́зное». **2.** (*trouble*): **what a** ~ **it is!** кака́я возня́/исто́рия!; **make a great** ~ **of sth.** преувели́чивать (*impf.*) значе́ние чего́-н. **3.** (*serious purpose, work*): **he means** ~ он име́ет серьёзные наме́рения; **get down to** ~ бра́ться, взя́ться за де́ло; ~ **end** (*coll.*) рабо́чая часть; (*muzzle*) ду́ло. **4.** (*comm. etc.*): **man of** ~ (*agent*) аге́нт; пове́ренный; ~ **of the day, meeting** пове́стка дня; ~ **hours, hours of** ~ (*of an office*) часы́ приёма/заня́тий/рабо́ты; ~ **year** хозя́йственный год; ~ **card** визи́тка, визи́тная ка́рточка; ~ **before pleasure** де́лу вре́мя, поте́хе час; сде́лал де́ло — гуля́й сме́ло; **he is in the wool** ~ он занима́ется торго́влей ше́рстью; он торгу́ет ше́рстью; **big** ~ большо́й би́знес; ~ **as usual** фи́рма рабо́тает как обы́чно; **set up in** ~ нач|ина́ть, -а́ть торго́вое де́ло; **go into** ~ заня́ться (*pf.*) комме́рцией; ~ **is** ~ де́ло есть де́ло; **on** ~ по де́лу; **put s.o. out of** ~ разор|я́ть, -и́ть кого́-н.; **do** ~ **with s.o.** вести́ (*det.*) дела́ с кем-н.; **lose** ~ теря́ть, по- клие́нтов; **talk** ~ говори́ть (*impf.*) по де́лу/существу́; ~ **is slow/brisk** дела́ иду́т вя́ло/хорошо́; ~ **deal, piece of** ~ сде́лка; **a (good) stroke of** ~ уда́ча в де́ле. **5.** (*establishment*) фи́рма, предприя́тие; про́мысел; (*office*) конто́ра. **6.** (*theatr.*) игра́, ми́мика.

cpds. ~**-like** *adj.* делово́й, практи́чный; ~**man** *n.* коммерса́нт, бизнесме́н, деле́ц; ~**woman** *n.* бизнесме́нка.

busker [bʌskə(r)] *n.* у́личный музыка́нт.

buskin [ˈbʌskɪn] *n.* коту́рн.

bust[1] [bʌst] *n.* (*sculpture; bosom*) бюст; (*upper part of body*) грудь, ве́рхняя часть те́ла.

bust[2] [bʌst] (*coll.*) *v.t.* раскол|а́чивать, -оти́ть; ~ **up** разб|ива́ть, -и́ть.

v.i. (*also* **go** ~) раскол|а́чиваться, -оти́ться; ~ **up** разб|ива́ться, -и́ться; **the business went** ~ де́ло ло́пнуло.

cpd. ~**-up** *n.* (*quarrel*) раздо́р, разла́д.

bust[3] [bʌst] *n.* (*coll., spree*) кутёж; **go on the** ~ загуля́ть (*pf.*), закути́ть (*pf.*).

bustard [ˈbʌstəd] *n.* дрофа́.

bustle[1] [ˈbʌs(ə)l] *n.* (*on skirt*) турню́р.

bustle[2] [ˈbʌs(ə)l] *n.* (*activity*) сумато́ха, суета́.

v.i. (*also* ~ **about**) суети́ться, тормоши́ться (*both impf.*).

bustling [ˈbʌslɪŋ] *n.* суета́; суетли́вость.

adj. суетли́вый, суетя́щийся; **a** ~ **city** оживлённый го́род.

busy [ˈbɪzɪ] *adj.* **1.** (*occupied*) за́нятый; **I had a** ~ **day** мой день был о́чень загру́жен; я был за́нят весь день; **he was** ~ **packing** он был за́нят упако́вкой; **keep s.o.** ~ зан|има́ть (*impf.*) кого́-н. (*чем-н.*); **get** ~ **on sth.** заня́ться (*pf.*) чем-н. **2.** (*unresting*) занято́й. **3.**: **a** ~ **street** шу́мная/оживлённая у́лица. **4.** (*meddlesome*) суетли́вый, надое́дливый. **5.**: **a** ~ **pattern** сли́шком подро́бный узо́р.

v.t.: ~ **o.s.** зан|има́ться, -я́ться.

cpd. ~**body** *n.* доку́чливый/назо́йливый челове́к.

busyness [ˈbɪzɪnɪs] *n.* за́нятость.

but [bʌt] *n.*: (~ **me) no** ~**s** никаки́х «но»; без вся́ких «но».

adv. (*liter.*): (*only*) всего́ (лишь); **we can** ~ **try** попы́тка — не пы́тка.

prep. & conj. (*except*): **no one** ~ **me** никто́, кро́ме меня́; **never** ~ **once** оди́н еди́нственный раз; **she is anything** ~ **beautiful** она́ далеко́ не краса́вица; **he all** ~ **failed** он то́лько что не провали́лся; **nothing remains** ~ **to thank her** остаётся то́лько поблагодари́ть её; **he had no choice** ~ **to go there** ему́ не остава́лось ничего́ друго́го, кро́ме как пойти́ туда́; **not a day passes** ~ **there is some trouble** не прохо́дит и дня без неприя́тностей; **next door** ~ **one** че́рез одну́ дверь; **the last** ~ **one** предпосле́дний; ~ **for me he would have stayed** е́сли бы не я, он бы оста́лся; **there is no one** ~ **knows it** нет никого́, кто бы не знал э́того; **she would have fallen** ~ **that I caught her** она́ бы упа́ла, е́сли бы я не подхвати́л её; **he cannot** ~ **agree** ему́ остаётся то́лько согласи́ться; **not** ~ **what I pity her** коне́чно, мне её жаль; (*redundant*): **ten to one** ~ **it was you** де́сять про́тив одного́, что э́то бы́ли вы; **I do not doubt** ~ **that he is honest** я не сомнева́юсь в его́ че́стности; **I cannot help** ~ **think ...** я не могу́ не ду́мать, что...

conj. (*adversative*) но; (*less emphatic*) а; ~ **yet, then, again** но всё же; но опя́ть-таки.

butane [ˈbjuːteɪn, bjuːˈteɪn] *n.* бута́н.

butch [bʊtʃ] *adj.* мужи́цкая, мужеподо́бная (*о же́нщине*).

butcher [ˈbʊtʃə(r)] *n.* **1.** (*tradesman*) мясни́к; ~**'s meat** мя́со; ~**'s (shop)** мясна́я ла́вка, мясно́й магази́н. **2.** (*murderer*) пала́ч.

v.t. (*cattle*) забива́ть (*impf.*); (*people*) истреб|ля́ть, -и́ть; выреза́ть, вы́резать.

cpd. ~**-bird** *n.* сорокопу́т.

butchery [ˈbʊtʃərɪ] *n.* (*trade*) торго́вля мя́сом; (*massacre*) резня́.

butler [ˈbʌtlə(r)] *n.* дворе́цкий.

butt[1] [bʌt] *n.* (*cask*) бо́чка.

butt[2] [bʌt] **1.** (*pl., shooting-range*) тир. **2.** (*fig., target*): **a** ~ **for ridicule** мише́нь для насме́шек; **the** ~ **of the school** посме́шище для всей шко́лы.

butt[3] [bʌt] *n.* (*of rifle*) прикла́д; (*of tree*) ко́мель (*m.*); (*of cigarette*) оку́рок.

v.i.: ~ **out** (*project*) выступа́ть (*impf.*); выдава́ться, вы́даться.

cpd. **~-end** *n.* (*remainder*) оста́ток; (*thick end*) утолщённый коне́ц.

butt[4] [bʌt] *n.* (*blow with the head*) уда́р голово́й.

v.t. бода́ть, за-; ~ **s.o. in the stomach** уда́рить (*pf.*) кого́-н. голово́й в живо́т.

v.i.: ~ **in** (*interrupt*) встр|ева́ть, -я́ть; вмеш|иваться, -а́ться; ~ **into conversation** встрять/вмеша́ться/влезть (*pf.*) в разгово́р; ~ **into** (*run into*) **s.o.** нат|ыка́ться, -кну́ться на кого́-н.

butt[5] [bʌt] *n.* (*US, vulg.*) жо́па.

butter [ˈbʌtə(r)] *n.* **1.** ма́сло; **melted** ~ топлёное ма́сло; **fry sth. in** ~ жа́рить, под- что-н. на ма́сле; **she looks as if** ~ **wouldn't melt in her mouth** на вид она́ ти́ше воды́. **2.** (*fig., flattery*) лесть, ума́сливание.

v.t. нама́з|ывать, -ать ма́слом; (*a dish*) сма́з|ывать, -ать ма́слом; ~ **up** (*fig.*) льсти́ть, по- +*d.*; ума́сл|ивать, -ить.

cpds. **~-bean** *n.* боб (кароли́нский); **~-cooler** *n.* маслёнка с охлажде́нием; **~cup** *n.* лю́тик; **~-dish** *n.* маслёнка; **~-fingered** *adj.* растя́пистый; **~-fingers** *n.* размазня́ (*c.g.*), растя́па (*c.g.*); **~-knife** *n.* нож для ма́сла; **~milk** *n.* па́хта, па́хтанье; **~scotch** *n.* ири́с; **~wort** *n.* жиря́нка.

butterfly [ˈbʌtəˌflaɪ] *n.* **1.** ба́бочка; (*fig.*): **break a** ~ **on a wheel** стреля́ть (*impf.*) из пу́шки по воробья́м; **I have butterflies in my stomach** у меня́ се́рдце ёкает; меня́ мути́т от стра́ха. **2.** (*fig., flighty pers.*) мотылёк. **3.:** ~ **nut** (*tech.*) бара́шек; ~ **stroke** (*swimming*) баттерфля́й.

buttery [ˈbʌtərɪ] *n.* кладова́я.

adj. ма́сленый; масляни́стый, в ма́сле.

buttocks [ˈbʌtəks] *n.* я́годицы (*f. pl.*).

button [ˈbʌt(ə)n] *n.* **1.** пу́говица; **not care a** ~ **about sth.** плева́ть (*impf.*) на что-н. **2.** (*pl., page*) коридо́рный. **3.** (*knob*) кно́пка; **press a** ~ наж|има́ть, -а́ть кно́пку. **4.** (*bud*) буто́н. **5.** (*on foil*) ши́шечка. **6.:** ~ **mushroom** ме́лкий гриб.

v.t. (*also* ~ **up**) застёг|ивать, -ну́ть; ~ **up a child** застёг|ивать, -ну́ть оде́жду на ребёнке; ~ **one's lip** (*sl.*) держа́ть (*impf.*) язы́к за зуба́ми; **the job is ~ed up** (*fig.*) рабо́та з ажу́ре (*coll.*); **~ed up** (*reserved, of pers.*) скры́тный, сде́ржанный, за́мкнутый.

v.i. застёг|иваться, -ну́ться; **the dress ~s up the back** пла́тье застёгивается на спине́.

cpds. **~hole** *n.* петля́, петли́ца; (*flower*) бутонье́рка; *v.t.* (*fig.*) заде́рж|ивать, -а́ть разгово́ром; **~hook** *n.* крючо́к для застёгивания пу́говиц.

buttress [ˈbʌtrɪs] *n.* (*archit.*) контрфо́рс; (*fig.*) опо́ра, подде́ржка; **flying** ~ аркбута́н.

v.t. (*archit.*) подп|ира́ть, -е́ть контрфо́рсом; (*fig.*) укреп|ля́ть, -и́ть; подкреп|ля́ть, -и́ть; служи́ть (*impf.*) опо́рой +*d.*

buxom [ˈbʌksəm] *adj.* (*of woman*) пы́шная, полногру́дая.

buy [baɪ] *n.*: **a good** ~ вы́годная поку́пка.

v.t. **1.** покупа́ть, купи́ть; **money cannot** ~ **happiness** сча́стья не ку́пишь; **the victory was dearly bought** побе́да доста́лась дорого́й ценó́й; ~ **fame at the cost of one's life** приобре|та́ть, -сти́ сла́ву ценó́й жи́зни; ~ **s.o. a drink** ста́вить, по- кому́-н. вы́пивку. **2.** (*bribe*) подкуп|а́ть, -и́ть.

with advs.: ~ **back** *v.t.* сно́ва купи́ть (*pf.*) (*про́данное*); ~ **in** *v.t.* (*stock up*) закуп|а́ть, -и́ть; (*at auction*) выкупа́ть, вы́купить; ~ **off** *v.t.* откуп|а́ться, -и́ться (*от кого*); ~ **out** *v.t.*: ~ **o.s. out of the army** откупи́ться (*pf.*) от вое́нной слу́жбы; ~ **up** *v.t.* скуп|а́ть, -и́ть.

cpd. **~-out** *n.* (*comm.*) вы́куп.

buyer [ˈbaɪə(r)] *n.* **1.** покупа́тель (*m.*); **~'s market** ры́ночная конъюнкту́ра, вы́годная для покупа́телей. **2.** (*firm's agent*) заку́пщи|к (*fem.* -ца).

buzz [bʌz] *n.* **1.** (*of bee etc.*) жужжа́ние; (*of talk*) гул, жужжа́ние. **2.:** **give s.o. a** ~ (*ring*) звя́кнуть (*pf.*) кому́-н. (*coll.*).

v.t.: ~ **an aircraft** пролете́ть (*pf.*) на о́чень бли́зком расстоя́нии ми́мо самолёта; ~ **it abroad** (*spread rumour*) трезво́нить, рас- всем и ка́ждому (*о чём*).

v.i. **1.** (*of insect, projectile*) жужжа́ть (*impf.*); (*of place, people*) гуде́ть (*impf.*); **my ears were ~ing** у меня́ гуде́ло в уша́х. **2.:** ~ **off!** (*sl.*) убира́йся!; прова́ливай!

cpds. **~-bomb** *n.* самолёт-снаря́д; **~-saw** *n.* циркуля́рная пила́; **~-word** *n.* мо́дное слове́чко.

buzzard [ˈbʌzəd] *n.* сары́ч; каню́к.

buzzer [ˈbʌzə(r)] *n.* (*elec.*) зу́ммер.

by [baɪ] *adv.* (*near*) побли́зости; (*alongside*) ря́дом; (*past*) ми́мо; **the days went** ~ дни шли за дня́ми; ~ **and large** в це́лом.

prep. **1.** (*near, close to*): **sit** ~ **the fire(side)** сиде́ть (*impf.*) у ками́на; **I was going** ~ **the house** я шёл ми́мо до́ма; **she sat** ~ **the sick man** она́ сиде́ла у посте́ли больно́го; ~ **o.s.** (*alone*) (соверше́нно) оди́н/одна́; (*unaided*) сам/сама́, самостоя́тельно; **he played billiards** ~ **himself** он игра́л в билья́рд сам с собо́й; **I have no money** ~ **me** у меня́ нет при себе́ де́нег; ~ **and** ~ вско́ре; сейча́с; **side** ~ **side** ря́дом; **pass** ~ **s.o.** про|ходи́ть, -йти́ ми́мо кого́-н.; **a path** ~ **the river** доро́жка у/вдоль реки́; ~ **the** ~; ~ **the way** кста́ти. **2.** (*along, via*): ~ **land and sea** по су́ше и по мо́рю; ~ **the nearest road** ближа́йшей доро́гой; **we travelled** ~ **(way of) Paris** мы е́хали че́рез Пари́ж; ~ **water** по воде́; во́дным путём. **3.** (*during*): ~ **day/night** днём/но́чью; ~ **daylight** при дневно́м све́те. **4.** (*of time-limit*): ~ **Thursday** к четвергу́; ~ **then** к тому́ вре́мени; ~ **now** тепе́рь; **he should know** ~ **now** пора́ бы уж ему́ зна́ть. **5.** (*manner, means or agency*) *often expr. by i. case*; (~ *means of*) при по́мощи +*g.*; **divide** ~ **two** дели́ть, раз- на́ два; **lead** ~ **the hand** вести́ (*det.*) за́ руку; ~ **the name of George** по и́мени Гео́ргий; **have children** ~ **s.o.** име́ть (*impf.*) дете́й от кого́-н.; **a Frenchman** ~ **blood** францу́з по происхожде́нию; **pull up** ~ **the roots** выта́скивать, вы́тащить с ко́рнем; **a book** ~ **Tolstoy** кни́га Толсто́го; **know** ~ **experience** знать (*impf.*) по о́пыту; **perish** ~ **starvation** ги́бнуть, по- от го́лода; ~ **Article 5 of the treaty** согла́сно 5 (пя́той) статье́ догово́ра; ~ **my watch** по мои́м часа́м, на мои́х часа́х; ~ **rail** по желе́зной доро́ге; ~ **the one o'clock train** (с) часовы́м по́ездом; ~ **taxi** на/в такси́; **die** ~ **drowning** утону́ть (*pf.*); **work** ~ **electric light** рабо́тать при электри́ческом све́те; ~ **law** по зако́ну; ~ **radio** по ра́дио; ~ **no means** ни в ко́ем слу́чае; **hang** ~ **a thread** висе́ть (*impf.*) на волоске́; ~ **post** по́чтой, по по́чте; ~ **the morning post** (с) у́тренней по́чтой; ~ **telephone** по телефо́ну; ~ **nature/profession/invitation** по приро́де/профе́ссии/приглаше́нию; **cautious** ~ **nature** осторо́жный от приро́ды; **sold** ~ **auction** про́дан с торго́в/молотка́; ~ **(means of) physical exercises** путём/посре́дством физи́ческих упражне́ний; **a letter written** ~ **hand** письмо́, напи́санное от руки́; ~ **means of** при по́мощи +*g.*; **I knew** ~ **his eyes that he was afraid** я по́нял по его́ глаза́м, что он бои́тся; **he led her** ~ **the hand** он вёл её за́ руку; **he held the horse** ~ **the bridle** он держа́л ло́шадь под уздцы́; **what is meant** ~ **this word?** что означа́ет э́то сло́во? **6.** (*of rate or measurement*): **pay** ~ **the day** плати́ть (*impf.*) подённо; ~ **degrees** постепе́нно; **little** ~ **little** ма́ло-пома́лу; **bread came down in price** ~ **5 copecks** хлеб подешеве́л на пять копе́ек; **he missed** ~ **a foot** он промахну́лся на (це́лый) фут; ~ **what amount do expenses exceed income?** на каку́ю су́мму расхо́ды превыша́ют дохо́ды?; **better** ~ **far** намно́го лу́чше; **sell sth.** ~ **the yard** прод|ава́ть, -а́ть что-н. на я́рды; **tomatoes are sold** ~ **weight,** ~ **the pound** помидо́ры продаю́тся на вес/фу́нты; ~ **the dozen** дю́жинами; **one** ~ **one** оди́н за други́м; по одному́, поодино́чке; **day** ~ **day** день за днём; **we divide thirty** ~ **five** де́лим 30 на 5; **a room 13 feet** ~ **12** ко́мната трина́дцать фу́тов на двена́дцать; **copeck** ~ **copeck** по копе́йке; **they discussed the report paragraph** ~ **paragraph** они́ обсуди́ли докла́д пункт за пу́нктом. **7.:** ~ **God!** кляну́сь Бо́гом; ~ **Jove!** Бо́же мой!; вот те на́!

by-blow [ˈbaɪbləʊ] *n.* (*side-blow*) случа́йный уда́р; (*bastard*) побо́чный ребёнок.

bye [baɪ] *n.*: **draw a** ~ (*sport*) быть свобо́дным от игры́.

bye-bye[1] [ˈbaɪbaɪ, bəˈbaɪ] *n.* (*coll.*): **go to ~(s)** (*sleep*) идти́ (*det.*) ба́иньки/бай-ба́й; (*go to bed*) ложи́ться, лечь ба́иньки.

bye-bye[2] [ˈbaɪbaɪ, bəˈbaɪ] *int.* (*good-bye*) пока́!; всего́ хоро́шего!

bye-law ['baɪlɔː] = **by-law**
by-election ['baɪɪ,lekʃ(ə)n] *n.* дополни́тельные вы́боры (*m. pl.*).
Byelorussia [,bjeləʊ'rʌʃə] *n.* Белору́ссия.
Byelorussian [,bjeləʊ'rʌʃ(ə)n] *n.* (*pers.*) белору́с (*fem.* -ка); (*language*) белору́сский язы́к.
adj. белору́сский.
bygone ['baɪgɒn] *n.* (*usu. pl.*): **let ~s be ~s** что бы́ло, то прошло́; кто ста́рое помя́нет, тому́ глаз вон.
adj. про́шлый, проше́дший, мину́вший; **in ~ days** в давно́ мину́вшие времена́.
by-law, bye-law ['baɪlɔː] *n.* распоряже́ние, постановле́ние (ме́стной вла́сти).
by-line ['baɪlaɪn] *n.* (*journ.*) по́дпись а́втора.
by-pass ['baɪpɑːs] *n.* объе́зд, обхо́д; обхо́дный путь.
v.t. об|ходи́ть, -ойти́ (*also fig.*).
bypath ['baɪpɑːθ] *n.* бокова́я тропа́; око́льный путь (*also fig.*).
byplay ['baɪpleɪ] *n.* побо́чная сце́на, эпизо́д.
by-product ['baɪ,prɒdʌkt] *n.* побо́чный проду́кт.
byre ['baɪə(r)] *n.* хлев, коро́вник.
by-road ['baɪrəʊd] *n.* бокова́я доро́га.
Byron ['baɪrɒn] *n.* Ба́йрон.
Byronic [baɪ'rɒnɪk] *adj.* байрони́ческий.
Byronicism [baɪ'rɒnɪsɪz(ə)m] *n.* байрони́зм.
bystander ['baɪ,stændə(r)] *n.* зри́тель (*m.*); прохо́жий.
by-street ['baɪstriːt] *n.* бокова́я у́лица, переу́лок.
byte [baɪt] *n.* (*comput.*) байт.
byway ['baɪweɪ] *n.* бокова́я доро́га, боково́й путь; (*fig.*): **~s of learning** забро́шенные уголки́ (*m. pl.*) нау́ки/зна́ния.
byword ['baɪwɜːd] *n.*: **a ~ for iniquity** олицетворе́ние несправедли́вости; **become a ~** стать (*pf.*) при́тчей во язы́цех.
by-your-leave [,baɪjɔː'liːv] *n.*: **without (so much as) a ~** не спроси́сь.
Byzantine [bɪ'zæntaɪn, baɪ-, 'bɪzən,tiːn, 'bɪzən,taɪn] *n.* (*pers.*) византи́|ец (*fem.* -йка).
adj. (*lit.*, *fig.*) византи́йский; **~ Empire** Византи́я.
Byzantinologist [bɪ,zæntaɪn'ɒlədʒɪst] *n.* византино́лог.
Byzantium [bɪ'zæntɪəm] *n.* (*city*) Виза́нтий.

C

C¹ [siː] *n.* **1.** (*mus.*) до (*indecl.*). **2.** (*acad. mark*) 3, тро́йка; **she got a ~ in maths** она получи́ла тро́йку по матема́тике.
C² (*abbr. of* ***Celsius*** ['selsɪəs] *or* **centigrade** ['sentɪ,greɪd]) (шкала́) Це́льсия; **20°C** 20°Ц (гра́дусов Це́льсия (*or* по Це́льсию)).
c. *abbr. of* **1. century** ['sentʃərɪ, -tjʊrɪ] в., (век); ст., (столе́тие). **2. circa** ['sɜːkə] ок., (о́коло). **3. cent(s)** [sent(s)] це́нт.
CAB (*abbr. of* ***Citizens Advice Bureau***) Бюро́ консульта́ции населе́ния.
cab [kæb] *n.* **1.** (*hired car or carriage*) изво́зчик (*hist.*), такси́ (*nt. indecl.*); **go by ~** е́хать (*det.*) на такси́. **2.** (*rail.*) бу́дка. **3.** (*of lorry etc.*) каби́на води́теля.
cpds. **~-driver, ~man** *nn.* изво́зчик (*hist.*), шофёр такси́, такси́ст; **~-rank, ~-stand** *nn.* стоя́нка такси́.
cabal [kə'bæl] *n.* полити́ческая кли́ка.
v.i. сост|авля́ть, -а́вить за́говор.
cabaret ['kæbə,reɪ] *n.* (*place*) кабаре́ (*indecl.*); (*entertainment*) кабаре́, эстра́дное представле́ние.
cabbage ['kæbɪdʒ] *n.* капу́ста; **~ butterfly** капу́стница; **~-head** коча́н капу́сты; **~ rose** махро́вая ро́за.
cab(b)alistic [,kæbə'lɪstɪk] *adj.* каб(б)алисти́ческий.
cabby ['kæbɪ] *n.* (*coll.*) изво́зчик (*hist.*); такси́ст.
caber ['keɪbə(r)] *n.*: (*sport*) **tossing the ~** мета́ние ствола́.
cabin ['kæbɪn] *n.* каби́на; (*dwelling*) хи́жина; (*in ship etc.*) каю́та; **~ class** каю́тный класс; (*of aeroplane*) каби́на; **~ boy** каю́т-ю́нга (*m.*).
cabinet ['kæbɪnɪt] *n.* **1.** (*piece of furniture*) го́рка, шкаф; **filing ~** картоте́чный шкаф; **medicine ~** апте́чка. **2.** (*of radio set etc.*) ко́рпус, футля́р. **3.** (*pol.*) кабине́т; **~ crisis** прави́тельственный кри́зис; **~ minister** член кабине́та; **shadow ~** «тенево́й кабине́т».
cpd. **~-maker** *n.* краснодере́вец.
cable ['keɪb(ə)l] *n.* **1.** (*rope*) кана́т, трос. **2.** (*wire*) ка́бель (*m.*); **~ car** ваго́н подвесно́й доро́ги; фуникулёр; **~ railway** кана́тная/подвесна́я доро́га; фуникулёр; **~ TV** ка́бельное телеви́дение. **3.** (*telegram*) телегра́мма.
v.t.: **he cabled his congratulations** он посла́л поздрави́тельную телегра́мму.
v.i. телеграфи́ровать (*impf.*, *pf.*).
cablegram ['keɪb(ə)l,græm] *n.* каблогра́мма, телегра́мма.
cabochon ['kæbə,ʃɒn] *n.* кабошо́н.
caboodle [kə'buːd(ə)l] *n.* (*sl.*): **the whole ~** (*of people*) вся ора́ва/компа́ния; (*of things*) всё хозя́йство.
caboose [kə'buːs] *n.* (*on ship*) ка́мбуз; (*US, on train*) служе́бный ваго́н.
cabotage ['kæbə,tɑːʒ, -tɪdʒ] *n.* кабота́ж.
cabriolet [,kæbrɪəʊ'leɪ] *n.* (*carriage*) кабриоле́т; (*motor-car*) автомоби́ль (*m.*) с откидны́м ве́рхом.
ca'canny [kɑː'kænɪ] *adj.*: **~ strike** италья́нская забасто́вка.
cacao [kə'kɑːəʊ, -'keɪəʊ] *n.* (*tree*) кака́о (*indecl.*), кака́овое де́рево; (*drink*, *seed*) кака́о.
cachalot ['kæʃə,lɒt, -,ləʊt] *n.* кашало́т.
cache [kæʃ] *n.* тайни́к, та́йный склад.
v.t. пря́тать, с- в тайнике́.
cachet ['kæʃeɪ] *n.* **1.** (*mark of distinction*) печа́ть. **2.** (*med.*) ка́псула.
cachinnation [,kækɪ'neɪʃ(ə)n] *n.* хо́хот.
cacique [kə'siːk] *n.* ка́цик; (*fig.*) заправи́ла (*m.*).
cackle ['kæk(ə)l] *n.* куда́хтанье; (*fig.*, *chatter*) трескотня́, болтовня́; **cut the ~!** дово́льно треща́ть!; (*laugh*) хихи́канье.
v.t. & i. куда́хтать (*impf.*); хихи́к|ать, -нуть.
cackler ['kæklə(r)] *n.* болту́н (*fem.* -ья).
cacophonous [kə'kɒfənəs] *adj.* какофони́ческий, какофони́чный.
cacophony [kə'kɒfənɪ] *n.* какофо́ния.
cactaceous [,kæk'teɪʃəs] *adj.* ка́ктусовый.
cactus ['kæktəs] *n.* ка́ктус.
cacuminal [kæ'kjuːmɪn(ə)l] *adj.* (*phon.*) какумина́льный.
CAD (*abbr. of* ***computer-aided design***) автоматизи́рованное проекти́рование.
cad [kæd] *n.* хам.
cadastral [kə'dæstr(ə)l] *adj.* када́стровый.
cadastre [kə'dæstə(r)] *n.* када́стр.
cadaver [kə'deɪvə(r), -'dɑːvə(r)] *n.* труп.
cadaverous [kə'dævərəs] *adj.* мёртвенно-бле́дный.
caddie ['kædɪ] *n.* клюшконо́с.
caddis ['kædɪs] *n.* личи́нка весня́нки; **~ fly** весня́нка.
caddish ['kædɪʃ] *adj.* ни́зкий, ха́мский.
caddishness ['kædɪʃnɪs] *n.* ни́зость, ха́мство.
caddy ['kædɪ] *n.* ча́йница.
cadence ['keɪd(ə)ns] *n.* каде́нция; (*rhythm*) ритм; (*rise and fall of voice*) модуля́ция.
cadenza [kə'denzə] *n.* каде́нция.
cadet [kə'det] *n.* (*younger son*) мла́дший сын; **~ branch of a family** мла́дшая ветвь семьи́; (*mil.*) каде́т, курса́нт; **~ corps** каде́тский ко́рпус.
cadge [kædʒ] *v.t. & i.* попроша́йничать (*impf.*); жить, по- на чужо́й счёт; (*get by sponging*) выкля́нчивать, вы́клянчить; (*coll.*) стрел|я́ть, -ьну́ть (*что у кого*).
cadger ['kædʒə(r)] *n.* попроша́йка (*c.g.*), прихлеба́тель (*m.*).
cadi ['kɑːdɪ, 'keɪdɪ] *n.* ка́ди(й).
Cadiz [kə'dɪz] *n.* Ка́дис.

cadmium [ˈkædmɪəm] *n.* ка́дмий.

cadre [ˈkɑːdə(r), ˈkɑːdrə] *n.* (*mil. etc.*) ка́дровый соста́в; (*pl.*, *key personnel*) ка́дры (*m. pl.*).

caduceus [kəˈdjuːsɪəs] *n.* кадуце́й.

caecum [ˈsiːkəm] *n.* слепа́я кишка́.

Caesar [ˈsiːzə(r)] *n.* Це́зарь; **render unto ~ the things that are ~'s** возд|ава́ть, -а́ть ке́сарю ке́сарево.

Caesarean [sɪˈzeərɪən] *adj.* це́зарев, ке́сарев; **~ birth, operation** ке́сарево сече́ние.

Caesarism [ˈsiːzəˌrɪz(ə)m] *n.* цезари́зм.

caesium [ˈsiːzɪəm] *n.* це́зий.

caesura [sɪˈzjʊərə] *n.* цезу́ра.

café [ˈkæfeɪ, ˈkæfɪ] *n.* кафе́ (*indecl.*).

cafeteria [ˌkæfɪˈtɪərɪə] *n.* кафете́рий.

caffeine [ˈkæfiːn] *n.* кофеи́н.

c|aftan, k- [ˈkæftæn] *n.* кафта́н; же́нское пла́тье в «восто́чном сти́ле».

cage [keɪdʒ] *n.* (*for animals etc.*) кле́тка; (*of lift etc.*) каби́на; (*of staircase*) ле́стничная кле́тка.

v.t. сажа́ть, посади́ть в кле́тку; **a ~d lion** лев в кле́тке.

cag(e)y [ˈkeɪdʒɪ] *adj.* (*coll.*) скры́тный.

caginess [ˈkeɪdʒɪnɪs] *n.* скры́тность.

cagoule [kəˈguːl] *n.* кагу́ль (*m.*), водонепроница́емая ку́ртка.

cagy [ˈkeɪdʒɪ] = **cag(e)y**

cahoots [kəˈhuːts] *n.* (*sl.*): **in ~ with s.o.** в сго́воре с кем-н.

Cain [keɪn] *n.* (*bibl.*) Ка́ин; **raise ~** (*coll.*) подн|има́ть, -я́ть сканда́л.

Cainozoic [ˌkaɪnəʊˈzəʊɪk] *adj.* кайнозо́йский.

caique [kaɪˈiːk] *n.* каи́к.

cairn [keən] *n.* пирами́да из гру́бого ка́мня.

cairngorm [ˈkeəngɔːm] *n.* ды́мчатый топа́з.

Cairo [ˈkaɪrəʊ] *n.* Каи́р.

caisson [ˈkeɪs(ə)n, kəˈsuːn] *n.* (*ammunition chest*) заря́дный я́щик; (*underwater chamber*) кессо́н; **~ disease** кессо́нная боле́знь.

caitiff [ˈkeɪtɪf] *n.* (*poet.*) трус.

cajole [kəˈdʒəʊl] *v.t.* обха́живать (*impf.*); ума́сл|ивать, -ить; уле|ща́ть, -сти́ть.

cajolery [kəˈdʒəʊlərɪ] *n.* лесть; обха́живание.

cake [keɪk] *n.* **1.** (*food*) кекс, торт; (*fancy ~*) пиро́жное. **2.** (*flat piece*) бруsóк, пли́тка; **~ of soap** кусо́к мы́ла. **3.** (*fig.*): **~s and ale** весе́лье; весёлая жизнь; **a piece of ~** (*coll.*) пустяко́вое/(*coll.*)плёвое де́ло; э́то — одно́ удово́льствие; **they sell like hot ~s** э́то раскупа́ется нарасхва́т; **that takes the ~!** (*coll.*) да́льше е́хать не́куда!; **you can't have your ~ and eat it** оди́н пиро́г два ра́за не съешь.

v.t.: **his shoes were ~d with mud** его́ боти́нки бы́ли обле́плены гря́зью.

v.i. сп|ека́ться, -е́чься.

cpds. **~-mix** *n.* порошо́к (*or* брике́т) для ке́кса, пу́динга *и т.п.*; **~-mixer** *n.* ми́ксер; **~-walk** *n.* кеку́ок.

calabash [ˈkæləˌbæʃ] *n.* (*plant*) горля́нка; (*vessel*) буты́лка из горля́нки.

calaboose [ˌkæləˈbuːs] *n.* (*US*) куту́зка, катала́жка (*coll.*).

calabrese [ˌkæləˈbriːz] *n.* спа́ржевая капу́ста.

calamitous [kəˈlæmɪtəs] *adj.* бе́дственный, па́губный.

calamity [kəˈlæmɪtɪ] *n.* бе́дствие.

calcareous [kælˈkeərɪəs] *adj.* известко́вый.

calceolaria [ˌkælsɪəˈleərɪə] *n.* кошелько́ (*m. pl.*).

calcification [ˌkælsɪfɪˈkeɪʃ(ə)n] *n.* обызвествле́ние.

calcify [ˈkælsɪˌfaɪ] *v.t. & i.* обызвеств|ля́ть(ся), -и́ть(ся).

calcination [ˌkælsɪˈneɪʃ(ə)n] *n.* кальцина́ция, о́бжиг, прока́ливание.

calcine [ˈkælsɪn, -saɪn] *v.t. & i.* кальцини́ровать(ся) (*impf.*, *pf.*); обж|ига́ть(ся), -е́чь(ся); прока́л|ивать(ся), -и́ть(ся).

calcium [ˈkælsɪəm] *n.* ка́льций; **~ chloride** хло́ристый ка́льций.

calculability [ˌkælkjʊləˈbɪlɪtɪ] *n.* исчисли́мость.

calculable [ˈkælkjʊləb(ə)l] *adj.* исчисли́мый.

calculat|e [ˈkælkjʊˌleɪt] *v.t.* **1.** (*compute*) вычисля́ть, вы́числить; рассчи́т|ывать, -а́ть; высчи́тывать, вы́считать; **he ~ed the date of the eclipse** он вы́числил день затме́ния; **a ~ing machine** счётная маши́на, арифмо́метр. **2.** (*estimate*) рассчи́т|ывать, -а́ть; калькули́ровать, с-; **I ~ed that he would act in this way** я рассчи́тывал, что он посту́пит таки́м о́бразом. **3.** (*plan*): **a ~ed insult** наме́ренное оскорбле́ние; **a ~ risk** обду́манный риск. **4.** (*past part.*: *fit*, *likely*): **that is ~ed to offend him** весьма́ возмо́жно, что э́то его́ оби́дит.

v.i. (*rely*) рассчи́тывать (*impf.*) (на+*a.*); **we cannot ~e upon fine weather** мы не мо́жем рассчи́тывать на хоро́шую пого́ду.

calculating [ˈkælkjʊˌleɪtɪŋ] *adj.* (*of pers.*) расчётливый, себе́ на уме́.

calculation [ˌkælkjʊˈleɪʃ(ə)n] *n.* **1.** (*mathematical*) вычисле́ние. **2.** (*planning*, *forecast*) расчёт; **my ~s were at fault** мои́ расчёты оказа́лись оши́бочными. **3.** (*estimate*) калькуля́ция.

calculator [ˈkælkjʊˌleɪtə(r)] *n.* **1.** (*pers.*) вычисли́тель (*m.*), калькуля́тор. **2.** (*set of tables*) вычисли́тельные табли́цы (*f. pl.*); (*machine*) счётная маши́на; арифмо́метр.

calculus [ˈkælkjʊləs] *n.* (*math.*) исчисле́ние; (*med.*) ка́мень (*m.*).

Calcutta [kælˈkʌtə] *n.* Кальку́тта.

calèche [kəˈleʃ] *n.* коля́ска.

calendar [ˈkælɪndə(r)] *n.* **1.** (*system*, *table of dates*) календа́рь (*m.*); **Gregorian ~** григориа́нский календа́рь; **Julian ~** юлиа́нский календа́рь; (*relig.*) свя́тц|ы (*pl.*, *g.* -ев). **2.** (*list*) о́пись, рее́стр; (*of cases for trial*) спи́сок де́л, назна́ченных к слу́шанию. **3.**: **~ clock** часы́ с календарём; **~ month** календа́рный ме́сяц.

v.t. регистри́ровать (*impf.*); вн|оси́ть, -ести́ в о́пись; сост|авля́ть, -а́вить и́ндекс +*g.*

calender [ˈkælɪndə(r)] *n.* (*machine*) кала́ндр; лощи́льный пресс.

v.t. (*press cloth*) каландри́ровать (*impf.*); лощи́ть, на-.

calends [ˈkælendz] (*also* **kalends**) *n.* кале́нд|ы (*pl.*, *g.* —); **postpone to the Greek ~** от|кла́дывать, -ложи́ть до гре́ческих кале́нд.

calf[1] [kɑːf] *n.* **1.** (*of cattle*) телёнок; **a cow in ~** сте́льная коро́ва; (*of seal*, *whale etc.*) детёныш. **2.** (*leather*) теля́чья ко́жа; опо́ек; **bound in ~** переплетённый в теля́чью ко́жу. **3.** (*fig.*): **the golden ~** золото́й теле́ц; **kill the fatted ~** закла́ть (*pf.*) упи́танного тельца́.

cpds. **~-love** *n.* ю́ношеское увлече́ние; **~'s foot jelly** *n.* сту́день (*m.*) из теля́чьих но́жек; **~skin** *n.* опо́ек; теля́чья ко́жа.

calf[2] [kɑːf] *n.* (*of leg*) икра́.

calibrate [ˈkælɪˌbreɪt] *v.t.* калиброва́ть (*impf.*), градуи́ровать (*impf.*, *pf.*).

calibration [ˌkælɪˈbreɪʃ(ə)n] *n.* калибро́вка.

calibre [ˈkælɪbə(r)] *n.* (*lit.*, *fig.*) кали́бр.

calico [ˈkælɪˌkəʊ] *n.* коленко́р, митка́ль (*m.*).

cpds. **~-printer** *n.* набо́йщик; **~-printing** *n.* ситценаби́вное де́ло.

California [ˌkælɪˈfɔːnɪə] *n.* Калифо́рния.

Californian [ˌkælɪˈfɔːnɪən] *n.* калифорни́|ец (*fem.* -йка).

adj. калифорни́йский.

calipers [ˈkælɪpəz] = **callipers**

caliph [ˈkeɪlɪf, ˈkæl-] *n.* кали́ф, хали́ф.

caliphate [ˈkeɪlɪˌfeɪt] *n.* халифа́т.

calisthenics [ˌkælɪsˈθenɪks] = **callisthenics**

calk [kɔːk] = **ca(u)lk**

call [kɔːl] *n.* **1.** (*cry*, *shout*) зов, о́клик; **I heard a ~ for help** я услы́шал крик о по́мощи; **they came at my ~** они́ пришли́ на мой зов; **remain within ~** остава́ться (*impf.*) неподалёку (*or* в преде́лах слы́шимости). **2.** (*of bird*) крик; (*of bugle*) зов, сигна́л. **3.** (*message*): **telephone ~** вы́зов по телефо́ну; телефо́нный звоно́к; **he took the ~ in his study** он подошёл к телефо́ну в своём кабине́те. **4.** (*visit*): **pay a ~** нан|оси́ть, -ести́ визи́т; **he returned my ~** он нанёс мне отве́тный визи́т; **port of ~** порт захо́да. **5.** (*invitation*, *summons*, *demand*) зов, клич, призы́в; **the ~ of the sea** зов мо́ря; **the doctor is on ~** врач на вы́зове; **he answered his country's ~** он откли́кнулся на призы́в свое́й ро́дины; **I have many ~s on my time** у меня́ почти́ нет свобо́дного вре́мени. **6.** (*need*): **there is no ~ for him to worry** ему́ не́чего волнова́ться. **7.** (*at cards*) объявле́ние игры́. **8.**: **it was a close ~** е́ле-е́ле/чу́дом спасли́сь.

v.t. **1.** (*name, designate*): наз|ыва́ть, -ва́ть; **he is ~ed John** его́ зову́т Джон; **he ~s himself a colonel** он называ́ет себя́ полко́вником; **~ s.o. names** об|зыва́ть, -озва́ть кого́-н.; **we have nothing we can ~ our own** у нас нет ничего́, что мы могли́ бы счита́ть свои́м; **I ~ that a shame** я счита́ю э́то посты́дным; **let's ~ it £5** сойдёмся на пяти́ фу́нтах; **~ a halt** объяв|ля́ть, -и́ть переры́в/остано́вку; **~ the roll** де́лать, с- перекли́чку; **~ a strike** приз|ыва́ть, -ва́ть к забасто́вке. **2.** (*summon, arouse attention of*): **~ a doctor/taxi!** вы́зовите врача́/такси́!; **duty ~s** долг вели́т; **~ me at 6** разбуди́те меня́ в 6 часо́в; **(this is) London ~ing** говори́т Ло́ндон; *for US sense 'telephone' see* **~ up. 3.** (*announce*): **the case is ~ed for Tuesday** слу́шание де́ла назна́чено на вто́рник; **~ a meeting** соз|ыва́ть, -ва́ть собра́ние; **~ banns of marriage** огла|ша́ть, -си́ть имена́ лиц, вступа́ющих в брак. **4.** (*var. idioms*): **~ in question** ста́вить, по- под сомне́ние; **~ to mind** вызыва́ть, вы́звать в па́мяти; **~ into being** вызыва́ть, вы́звать к жи́зни; **~ attention to** обра|ща́ть, -ти́ть (*чьё-н.*) внима́ние на+*a.*; **~ into play** прив|оди́ть, -ести́ в де́йствие; **~ to witness** приз|ыва́ть, -ва́ть в свиде́тели; **~ to order** приз|ыва́ть, -ва́ть к поря́дку.

v.i. **1.** (*cry, shout*) звать, по-; окл|ика́ть, -и́кнуть; **I heard someone ~** я слы́шал, как кто́-то позва́л; **I ~ed to him** я окли́кнул его́. **2.** (*pay a visit*) за|ходи́ть, -йти́; **I ~ed on him** я зашёл к нему́; **the ship ~ed at Naples** парохо́д зашёл в Неа́поль; **the train ~s at every station** по́езд остана́вливается на ка́ждой ста́нции; **the butcher ~ed** мясни́к заходи́л; **has the laundry ~ed yet?** из пра́чечной уже́ приезжа́ли? **3. ~ for** (*pick up*): **I ~ed for him at 6** я зашёл за ним в 6 часо́в; **to be ~ed for** до востре́бования; (*demand*): **the situation ~s for courage** обстоя́тельства тре́буют му́жества; **they ~ed for his resignation** они́ тре́бовали его́ отста́вки. **4. ~ on, upon** (*require*): **I ~ on you to keep your promise** я призыва́ю вас сдержа́ть своё обеща́ние; (*appeal to*): **I ~ed on him for help** я призва́л его́ на по́мощь; (*invite*) предл|ага́ть, -ожи́ть (*что кому*); **I ~ on Mr. Grey to speak** я предоставля́ю сло́во г-ну Гре́ю; **I feel ~ed on to reply** я чу́вствую, что до́лжен отве́тить.

with advs.: **~ away** *v.t.* от|зыва́ть, -озва́ть; **~ back** *v.t. & i.* (*answer*) откл|ика́ться, -и́кнуться (на+*a.*); (*on telephone*) позвони́ть (*pf.*) сно́ва (+*d.*); перезвони́ть (*pf.*); **~ down** *v.t.*: **~ down curses on s.o.'s head** приз|ыва́ть, -ва́ть прокля́тия на чью-н. го́лову; **~ forth** *v.t.* (*lit., fig.*) вызыва́ть, вы́звать; **~ in** *v.t.* (*books*) тре́бовать, за- наза́д; (*currency*) из|ыма́ть, -ъя́ть из обраще́ния; (*a specialist*) вызыва́ть, вы́звать; **~ off** *v.t.* (*e.g. a dog*) от|зыва́ть, -озва́ть; (*cancel*) отмен|я́ть, -и́ть; **~ out** *v.t.* (*announce*) выклика́ть, вы́кликнуть; (*summon away*) от|зыва́ть, -озва́ть; (*workers, on strike*) приз|ыва́ть, -ва́ть (к+*d.*); вызыва́ть, вы́звать (на+*a.*); (*to a duel*) вызыва́ть, вы́звать; *v.i.* выклика́ть, вы́кликнуть; выкри́кивать, вы́крикнуть; **~ over** *v.t.* (*e.g. names*) де́лать перекли́чку +*g.*; **I ~ ed him over** (*i.e. to come over*) я подозва́л его́; **~ up** *v.t.* (*telephone*) звони́ть, по- (*кому*) по телефо́ну; (*evoke*) вызыва́ть, вы́звать; (*for mil. service*) приз|ыва́ть, -ва́ть.

cpds. **~-box** *n.* телефо́нная бу́дка; **~-boy** *n.* ма́льчик, вызыва́ющий актёров на сце́ну; **~-girl** *n.* проститу́тка, приходя́щая по вы́зову; **~-over** *n.* (*roll-call*) перекли́чка; **~-sign** *n.* (*radio*) позывно́й (сигна́л); **~up** *n.* (*mil.*) призы́в.

caller ['kɔ:lə(r)] *n.* (*visitor*) посети́тель (*fem.* -ница); (*telephone*) позвони́вший (по телефо́ну).

calligrapher [kə'lɪgrəfə(r)] *n.* каллигра́ф.

calligraphic [,kælɪ'græfɪk] *adj.* каллиграфи́ческий.

calligraphy [kə'lɪgrəfɪ] *n.* каллигра́фия.

calling ['kɔ:lɪŋ] *n.* (*summoning*) созы́в; (*profession, occupation*) призва́ние, заня́тие.

cpd. **~-in** *n.* (*withdrawal*) изъя́тие из обраще́ния (*or* употребле́ния).

callipers ['kælɪpəz] *n.* кронци́ркуль.

callisthenics [,kælɪs'θenɪks] *n.* ритми́ческая гимна́стика, ри́тмика; пласти́ческая гимна́стика.

callosity [kə'lɒsɪtɪ] *n.* мозо́ль; огрубе́ние, затверде́ние.

callous ['kæləs] *n.* = **callus**

adj. (*of skin*) огрубе́лый, мозо́листый; (*fig.*) чёрствый.

callousness ['kæləsnɪs] *n.* чёрствость.

callow ['kæləʊ] *adj.* (*unfledged; also fig.*) неопери́вшийся.

callus ['kæləs] *n.* ко́стная мозо́ль.

calm [kɑ:m] *n.* споко́йствие, тишина́; **a dead ~** мёртвая тишина́; (*at sea*) штиль (*m.*), безве́трие.

adj. споко́йный.

v.t. & i. успок|а́ивать(ся), -о́ить(ся).

calmative ['kælmətɪv, 'kɑ:m-] *n.* успока́ивающее сре́дство.

adj. успокои́тельный

calmness ['kɑ:mnɪs] *n.* споко́йствие, тишина́, поко́й

calomel ['kælə,mel] *n.* ка́ломель.

caloric ['kælərɪk] *adj.* теплово́й, терми́ческий.

calorie ['kælərɪ] *n.* кало́рия.

calorific [,kælə'rɪfɪk] *adj.* теплово́й, теплотво́рный; калори́йный; **~ value** теплотво́рная спосо́бность; калори́йность.

calorimeter [,kælə'rɪmɪtə(r)] *n.* калори́метр.

calque [kælk] *n.* (*ling.*) ка́лька.

calumet ['kælјʊ,met] *n.* тру́бка ми́ра.

calumniate [kə'lʌmnɪ,eɪt] *v.t.* клевета́ть, о-; нагов|а́ривать, -ори́ть на+*a.*; огов|а́ривать, -ори́ть; я́бедничать, на- на+*a.*

calumniator [kə'lʌmnɪ,eɪtə(r)] *n.* клеветни́к, наговóрщик, кля́узник.

calumnious [kə'lʌmnɪəs] *adj.* клеветни́ческий, кля́узнический.

calumny ['kæləmnɪ] *n.* клевета́, нагово́р, огово́р.

Calvary ['kælvərɪ] *n.* (*place*) Голго́фа; (*fig., torment*) му́ки (*f. pl.*); кре́стный путь.

calve [kɑ:v] *v.i.* тели́ться, о-.

Calvinism ['kælvɪ,nɪz(ə)m] *n.* кальвини́зм.

Calvinist ['kælvɪ,nɪst] *n.* кальвини́ст.

Calvinistic [,kælvɪ'nɪstɪk] *adj.* кальвини́стский.

calypso [kə'lɪpsəʊ] *n.* кали́псо (*indecl.*).

calyx ['keɪlɪks, 'kæl-] *n.* (*bot.*) ча́шечка; (*anat.*) чашеви́дная по́лость.

cam [kæm] *n.* кулачо́к, копи́р, па́лец.

cpd. **~shaft** *n.* кулачко́вый вал.

camaraderie [,kæmə'rɑ:dərɪ] *n.* това́рищеские отноше́ния.

camarilla [,kæmə'rɪlə] *n.* камари́лья.

camber ['kæmbə(r)] *n.* вы́пуклость, кривизна́, изо́гнутость; (*of road*) попере́чный укло́н.

v.t. & i. выгиба́ть(ся), вы́гнуть(ся).

Cambodia [kæm'bəʊdɪə] *n.* Камбо́джа.

Cambodian [kæm'bəʊdɪən] *n.* (*pers.*) камбоджи́|ец (*fem.* -ка).

adj. камбоджи́йский.

Cambrian ['kæmbrɪən] *adj.* кембри́йский.

cambric ['kæmbrɪk] *n.* бати́ст.

Cambridge ['keɪmbrɪdʒ] *n.* Ке́мбридж; (*attr.*) ке́мбриджский.

camcorder ['kæm,kɔ:də(r)] *n.* камко́рдер.

camel ['kæm(ə)l] *n.* верблю́д; **Arabian ~** дромаде́р, одного́рбый верблю́д; **Bactrian ~** бактриа́н, двуго́рбый верблю́д; **~ corps** кавале́рия на верблю́дах; **the last straw breaks the ~'s back** после́дняя ка́пля переполня́ет ча́шу.

cpds. **~-driver** *n.* пого́нщик верблю́дов; **~-hair** *adj.*: **~-hair coat** пальто́ из верблю́жьей ше́рсти.

camel(l)ia [kə'mi:lɪə] *n.* каме́лия.

cameo ['kæmɪ,əʊ] *n.* каме́я (*fig.*) скетч, эссе́ (*indecl.*), винье́тка; **~ role** эпизоди́ческая роль.

camera ['kæmrə, -ərə] *n.* **1.** (*phot.*) фотоаппара́т. **2. in ~** при закры́тых дверя́х.

cpd. **~man** *n.* (*photographer*) фото́граф, фоторепортёр; (*cin.*) (кино)опера́тор.

camiknickers ['kæmɪ,nɪkəz] *n.* комбина́ция.

camomile ['kæmə,maɪl] *n.* рома́шка.

camouflage ['kæmə,flɑ:ʒ] *n.* камуфля́ж; (*also fig.*) маскиро́вка.

v.t. (*lit., fig.*) маскирова́ть, за-.

camp[1] [kæmp] *n.* ла́герь (*m.*; *pl. in mil. etc. sense* лагеря́, *in pol. sense* ла́гери); бива́к; **pitch ~** расположи́ться/стать (*both pf.*) ла́герем; **break, strike ~** сн|има́ться, -я́ться с ла́геря; **he has a foot in both ~s** ≃ он слу́жит и на́шим и ва́шим.

v.i. разб|ивать, -и́ть ла́герь; распол|ага́ться, -ожи́ться ла́герем; **go ~ing** отпр|авля́ться, -а́виться в (туристи́ческий) похо́д; жить в пала́тках; **~ down** поста́вить (*pf.*) пала́тки; **~ out** спать (*impf.*) на откры́том во́здухе; **~ing site** ке́мпинг, турба́за.

cpds. **~-bed** *n.* похо́дная крова́ть; **~-chair, ~-stool** *nn.* складно́й стул; **~craft** *n.* уме́ние жить на приро́де; **~-fire** *n.* бива́чный костёр.

camp[2] [kæmp] *n.* (*coll.*, *affected behaviour*) аффекта́ция, мане́рность, кэмп.

adj. аффекти́рованный, мане́рный.

v.t. **~ up** перейгр|ывать, -а́ть.

v.i. (*behave affectedly*) лома́ться, выпе́ндриваться (*both impf.*).

campaign [kæmˈpeɪn] *n.* похо́д; (*lit., fig.*) кампа́ния.

v.i. уча́ствовать (*impf.*) в похо́де; (*fig.*) вести́ (*det.*) кампа́нию.

campaigner [kæmˈpeɪnə(r)] *n.* уча́стник кампа́нии; боре́ц; **old ~** ста́рый вояка́; **peace ~** боре́ц за мир.

campanile [ˌkæmpəˈniːlɪ] *n.* колоко́льня.

campanologist [ˌkæmpəˈnɒlədʒɪst] *n.* колоко́льный ма́стер, звона́рь (*m.*).

campanula [kæmˈpænjʊlə] *n.* колоко́льчик.

campeachy [kæmˈpiːtʃɪ] *n.* кампе́шевое/санда́ловое де́рево.

camper [ˈkæmpə(r)] *n.* (*pers.*) ночу́ющий на откры́том во́здухе; тури́ст, живу́щий в пала́тке; (*vehicle*) жило́й/тури́стский автоприце́п.

camphor [ˈkæmfə(r)] *n.* камфара́.

camphorate [ˈkæmfəˌreɪt] *v.t.*: **~d oil** камфа́рное ма́сло.

camping [ˈkæmpɪŋ] *n.* ке́мпинг.

cpd. **~-ground** *n.* террито́рия ке́мпинга.

Campuchea [ˌkæmpʊˈtʃɪə] *n.* Кампучи́я.

campus [ˈkæmpəs] *n.* (*US*, *university and buildings*) университе́тский городо́к; (*attr.*) университе́тский, студе́нческий.

can[1] [kæn] *n.* **1.** (*for liquids*) бидо́н; **milk-~** моло́чный бидо́н. **2.** (*for food etc.*) (консе́рвная) ба́нка; **a ~ of beer/peaches** ба́нка пи́ва/пе́рсиков. **3.: carry the ~** (*sl.*) отдува́ться (*impf.*) (*за кого/что*); **to open a ~ of worms** навле́чь (*pf.*) на себя́ ку́чу неприя́тностей.

v.t. консерви́ровать (*impf.*, *pf.*); **~ned food** консе́рв|ы (*pl.*, *g.* -ов); **~ned vegetables** овощны́е консе́рвы; **~ned music** му́зыка в за́писи; **~ned** (*drunk*) нализа́вшийся, назюзю́кавшийся (*sl.*); **~ it!** (*sl.*, *desist*) заткни́сь!

cpd. **~-opener** *n.* консе́рвный ключ/нож.

can[2] [kæn] *v.i.* (*expr. ability or permission*) мочь (*impf.*); (*expr. capability*) уме́ть (*impf.*); **I ~ speak French** я уме́ю говори́ть по-францу́зски; **I ~ see him** я ви́жу его́; **I ~ understand that** я понима́ю (*or* могу́ поня́ть) э́то; **I could have laughed for joy** я гото́в был смея́ться от ра́дости; **I ~not but feel that ...** я не могу́ не чу́вствовать, что...; **one ~ hardly blame him** едва́ ли мо́жно вини́ть его́ в э́том; **~ it be true?** неуже́ли э́то пра́вда?; **he is as happy as ~ be** он абсолю́тно сча́стлив; **as soon as you ~** как то́лько смо́жете; как мо́жно скоре́е; **we ~ but try** мо́жно всё-таки попыта́ться; **he ~ be very trying** он мо́жет доня́ть кого́ уго́дно.

Canaan [ˈkeɪnən] *n.* (*bibl.*) Ханаа́н.

Canaanite [ˈkeɪnəˌnaɪt] *n.* (*pl.*) ханаане́и (*c.g. pl.*).

adj. ханаа́нский, ханаане́йский.

Canada [ˈkænədə] *n.* Кана́да.

Canadian [kəˈneɪdɪən] *n.* (*pers.*) кана́д|ец (*fem.* -ка).

adj. кана́дский.

canaille [kəˈnɑːɪ] *n.* сброд, чернь.

canal [kəˈnæl] *n.* **1.** (*channel through land*) кана́л; **~ boat** су́дно для кана́лов. **2.** (*anat.*) кана́л, прохо́д; **alimentary ~** пищевари́тельный тракт. **3.** (*Panama*) **C~ Zone** Зо́на Пана́мского кана́ла.

canalization [ˈkænəlaɪˈzeɪʃ(ə)n] *n.* сооруже́ние кана́лов.

canalize [ˈkænəˌlaɪz] *v.t.* напр|авля́ть, -а́вить (*реку*) в кана́лы; (*fig.*) напр|авля́ть, -а́вить по определённому ру́слу.

canapé [ˈkænəpɪ, -ˌpeɪ] *n.* ло́мтик поджа́ренного хле́ба с холо́дным мя́сом *и т.д.*; заку́ска.

canard [kəˈnɑːd, ˈkænɑːd] *n.* ло́жный слух, (газе́тная) у́тка.

canary [kəˈneərɪ] *n.* канаре́йка; **C~ Islands** Кана́рские острова́.

cpds. **~-seed** *n.* канаре́ечное се́мя; **~-yellow** *n.* канаре́ечный цвет.

canasta [kəˈnæstə] *n.* кана́ста.

Canberra [ˈkænbərə] *n.* Канбе́рра.

cancan [ˈkænkæn] *n.* канка́н.

cancel [ˈkæns(ə)l] *n.* (*cancelling*) отме́на; (*on postage stamps*) погаше́ние.

v.t. **1.** (*cross out*) вычёркивать, вы́черкнуть. **2.** (*countermand*) отмен|я́ть, -и́ть; аннули́ровать (*impf.*, *pf.*). **3.** (*nullify*) св|оди́ть, -ести́ на нет.

v.i.: **these items ~ out** э́ти пу́нкты сво́дят друг дру́га на нет.

cancellation [ˌkænsəˈleɪʃ(ə)n] *n.* отме́на, аннули́рование; погаше́ние; вычёркивание.

cancer [ˈkænsə(r)] *n.* **1.** (*astron.*) Рак; **Tropic of C~** тро́пик Ра́ка. **2.** (*med.*) рак. **3.** (*fig.*) я́зва.

cancerous [ˈkænsərəs] *adj.* (*med.*) ра́ковый; (*fig.*) разъеда́ющий.

candelabr|a [ˌkændɪˈlɑːbrə] (*also* **-um**) [ˌkændɪˈlɑːbrəm] *n.* канделя́бр.

candid [ˈkændɪd] *adj.* (*frank*) и́скренний, чистосерде́чный, открове́нный; (*unbiased*) беспристра́стный, прямо́й.

candidacy [ˈkændɪdəsɪ] *n.* кандидату́ра.

candidate [ˈkændɪdət, -ˌdeɪt] *n.* кандида́т.

candidature [ˈkændɪdətjə(r)] *n.* кандидату́ра.

candle [ˈkænd(ə)l] *n.* свеча́; **the game is not worth the ~** игра́ не сто́ит свеч; **burn the ~ at both ends** прожига́ть (*impf.*) жизнь; **she is not fit to hold a ~ to him** она́ ему́ в подмётки не годи́тся.

cpds. **~-end** *n.* ога́рок; **~-light** *n.* свет свечи́/свече́й; свечно́е освеще́ние; **~-power** *n.* (*elec.*) си́ла све́та в свеча́х; **~stick** *n.* подсве́чник.

Candlemas [ˈkænd(ə)lməs, -ˌmæs] *n.* Сре́тение (Госпо́дне).

candour [ˈkændə(r)] *n.* открове́нность, чистосерде́чие, и́скренность, беспристра́стность, прямоду́шие.

candy [ˈkændɪ] *n.* леденцы́ (*m. pl.*) караме́ль; (*US*) конфе́та, сла́сти (*f. pl.*).

v.t.: **candied fruit(s)** заса́харенные фру́кты.

candyfloss [ˈkændɪˌflɒs] *n.* са́харная ва́та.

cane [keɪn] *n.* **1.** (*bot.*) камы́ш, тростни́к; **~ chair** плетёное кре́сло. **2.** (*walking-stick*) трость, па́лка. **3.** (*for punishment*) па́лка; **the boy got the ~** ма́льчика отлупи́ли.

v.t. **1.: ~ a chair** плести́, с- кре́сло из камыша́. **2.: ~ a pupil** нака́з|ывать, -а́ть ученика́ па́лкой.

cpds. **~-brake** *n.* за́росли (*f. pl.*) са́харного тростника́; **~-sugar** *n.* тростнико́вый са́хар.

canicular [kəˈnɪkjʊlə(r)] *adj.* зно́йный.

canine [ˈkeɪnaɪn, ˈkæn-] *adj.* соба́чий; **~ tooth** клык.

caning [ˈkeɪnɪŋ] *n.* (*punishment*) наказа́ние па́лкой.

canister [ˈkænɪstə(r)] *n.* ба́нка, коро́бка.

cpd. **~-shot** *n.* карте́чь.

canker [ˈkæŋkə(r)] *n.* (*med.*) (я́звенный) стомати́т, моло́чница; (*agr.*) рак расте́ний; некро́з плодо́вых дере́вьев.

v.t. разъ|еда́ть, -е́сть.

cpd. **~-worm** *n.* плодо́вый червь; (*fig.*) я́зва, червото́чина.

cankerous [ˈkæŋkərəs] *adj.* разъеда́ющий.

cannabis [ˈkænəbɪs] *n.* гаши́ш; **~ indica** инди́йская конопля́.

cannery [ˈkænərɪ] *n.* консе́рвный заво́д.

cannibal [ˈkænɪb(ə)l] *n.* канниба́л, людое́д.

adj. канниба́льский, людое́дский.

cannibalism [ˈkænɪbəˌlɪz(ə)m] *n.* каннибали́зм, людое́дство.

cannibalistic [ˌkænɪbəˈlɪstɪk] *adj.* канниба́льский, людое́дский.

cannibalize [ˈkænɪbəˌlaɪz] *v.t.* (*mil. etc.*): **~ a machine** сн|има́ть, -ять го́дные дета́ли с неиспра́вной маши́ны; «разде́ть»/«раскула́чить» (*pf.*) маши́ну.

cannikin [ˈkænɪkɪn] *n.* жестя́нка, ба́ночка, кру́жка.

canniness [ˈkænɪnɪs] *n.* хи́трость, осторо́жность; смека́лка.

canning [ˈkænɪŋ] *n.* консерви́рование.

cpd. **~-factory** *n.* консéрвный завóд.
cannon ['kænən] *n.* **1.** (*gun*) пýшка, орýдие. **2.** (*artillery*) артиллéрия. **3.** (*at billiards: also US* **carom**) карамбóль (*m.*).
v.i. (*collide*) ст|áлкиваться, -олкнýться; (*at billiards*) сдéлать (*pf.*) карамбóль.
cpds. **~-ball** *n.* пýшечное ядрó; **~-fodder** *n.* пýшечное мя́со; **~-shot** *n.* (*projectiles*) орýди́йный снаря́д; (*distance*) дáльность вы́стрела; **within ~-shot of** на расстоя́нии пýшечного вы́стрела *+g.*
cannonade [,kænə'neɪd] *n.* канонáда, орудийный огóнь.
v.t. & i. вести́ (*det.*) орудийный огóнь; обстрéл|ивать, -я́ть артиллерийским огнём.
canny ['kænɪ] *adj.* (*shrewd, cautious*) хи́трый, осторóжный; смекáлистый, себé на умé.
canoe [kə'nu:] *n.* канóэ (*nt. indecl.*), челнóк, чёлн, байдáрка; **paddle one's own ~** (*fig.*) идти́ (*det.*) своим путём; дéйствовать (*impf.*) свои́ми си́лами.
v.i. плыть (*det.*) в челнокé (*or* на байдáрке).
canoeist [kə'nu:ɪst] *n.* байдáрочник.
canon ['kænən] *n.* **1.** (*church decree*) канóн; **~ law** канони́ческое прáво. **2.** (*criterion*) прáвило. **3.** (*body of writings*) канóн. **4.** (*list of saints*) святц|ы (*pl., g.* -ев). **5.** (*priest*) канóник. **6.** (*mus.*) канóн.
cañon ['kænjən] = **canyon**
canonical [kə'nɒnɪk(ə)l] *adj.* **1.** (*approved by church law*) канони́ческий; **~s** (*as n.*) церкóвное облачéние. **2.** (*of books*) канони́ческий, канони́чный. **3.** (*mus.*) в фóрме канóна.
canonicity [,kænə'nɪsɪtɪ] *n.* канони́чность.
canonist ['kænənɪst] *n.* канони́ст.
canonization [kænə,naɪ'zeɪʃ(ə)n] *n.* канонизáция.
canonize ['kænə,naɪz] *v.t.* (*recognise as a saint*) канонизи́ровать (*impf., pf.*).
canonry ['kænənrɪ] *n.* дóлжность канóника.
canoodle [kə'nu:d(ə)l] *v.t.* (*coll.*) нéжничать, обнимáться (*both impf.*).
canopy ['kænəpɪ] *n.* **1.** (*covering over bed etc.*) балдахи́н, пóлог. **2.** (*of parachute*) кýпол. **3.** (*fig.*) пóлог, покрóв.
v.t. покр|ывáть, -ы́ть пóлогом.
Canossa [kə'nɒsə] *n.*: **go to ~** (*fig.*) идти́ (*det.*) в Канóссу; уни́женно проси́ть прощéния.
cant[1] [kænt] *n.* (*insincere talk*) ханжество; (*jargon*): **thieves' ~** воровскóй жаргóн, блатнáя мýзыка.
v.i. лицемéрить (*impf.*), ханжи́ть (*impf.*); **a ~ing hypocrite** лицемéр и ханжá.
cant[2] [kænt] *v.t.* (*incline, tilt*) наклон|я́ть, -и́ть; перевёр|тывать, -нýть.
Cantab ['kæntæb] *n.* (*coll.*) = **Cantabrigian**
cantabile [kæn'tɑ:bɪlɪ] *adv.* кантáбиле.
Cantabrigian [,kæntə'brɪdʒɪən] *n.* студéнт Кéмбриджского университéта.
cantaloup(e) ['kæntə,lu:p] *n.* канталýпа; (мýскусная) ды́ня.
cantankerous [kæn'tæŋkərəs] *adj.* сварли́вый.
cantankerousness [kæn'tæŋkərəsnɪs] *n.* сварли́вость.
cantata [kæn'tɑ:tə] *n.* кантáта.
cantatrice ['kæntə,tri:s, ,kæntə'tri:tʃeɪ] *n.* певи́ца.
canteen [kæn'ti:n] *n.* **1.** (*shop*) войсковáя лáвка, воéнный магази́н. **2.** (*eating-place*) столóвая. **3.** (*water-container*) фля́га. **4.** (*case of cutlery*) (похóдный) я́щик со столóвыми принадлéжностями.
canter ['kæntə(r)] *n.* лёгкий галóп; **preliminary ~** (*fig.*) вступлéние, прелю́дия, пристрéлка; **win in a ~** (*fig.*) выи́грывать, вы́играть с лёгкостью.
v.i. éхать (*impf.*) лёгким галóпом.
Canterbury ['kæntəbərɪ] *n.* Кéнтербери (*m. indecl.*); (*attr.*) кентербери́йский.
cantharides [kæn'θærɪ,di:z] *n. pl.* шпáнские мýшки (*f. pl.*).
canticle ['kæntɪk(ə)l] *n.* песнь, гимн, кант.
cantilever ['kæntɪ,li:və(r)] *n.* консóль, кронштéйн, укóсина; **~ bridge** консóльный мост.
canto ['kæntəʊ] *n.* песнь.
canton[1] ['kæntɒn] *n.* **1.** (*Swiss etc.*) кантóн. **2.** (*in shield or flag*) прáвый вéрхний ýгол.
v.t. **1.** (*divide into cantons*) дели́ть, раз- на кантóны. **2.** (*quarter soldiers*) расквартирóв|ывать, -áть.
Canton[2] [kæn'tɒn] *n.* (*geog.*) Кантóн, Гуанчжóу (*m. indecl.*).
cantonal ['kæntən(ə)l, kæn'tɒn(ə)l] *adj.* кантонáльный.
Cantonese [,kæntə'ni:z] *n.* (*pers.*) кантóн|ец (*fem.* -ка); (*dialect*) кантóнский диалéкт (китáйского языкá).
cantonment [kæn'tu:nmənt] *n.* (*mil., station*) лáгерь (*m.*), воéнный городóк.
cantor ['kæntɔ:(r)] *n.* (*choir-leader*) рéгент хóра; (*in synagogue*) кáнтор.
cantrip ['kæntrɪp] *n.* (*Sc., magic spell*) колдовствó, чáр|ы (*pl., g.* —).
Canuck [kə'nʌk] *n.* (*US coll., Canadian*) канáд|ец (*fem.* -ка).
adj. канáдский.
Canute [kə'nju:t] *n.* Кнуд.
canvas ['kænvəs] *n.* **1.** (*cloth*) холст; паруси́на, брезéнт; **under ~** (*in camp*) в палáтках; (*with sails spread*) под парусáми. **2.** (*for painting*) холст. **3.** (*fig., picture*) полотнó, холст. **4.** (*attr.*) холщóвый; брезéнтовый, паруси́новый; **a ~ bag** холщóвый мешóк.
canvass ['kænvəs] *n.* (*for votes*) предвы́борная агитáция.
v.t. & i.: **~ a constituency** вести́ (*det.*) предвы́борную агитáцию в избирáтельном óкруге; **~ opinions** соб|ирáть, -рáть мнéния; **~ a subject** обсу|ждáть, -ди́ть вопрóс; **~ orders** соб|ирáть, -рáть закáзы.
canvasser ['kænvəsə(r)] *n.* агитáтор.
canyon, cañon ['kænjən] *n.* каньóн; глубóкое ущéлье.
caoutchouc ['kaʊtʃʊk] *n.* каучýк.
CAP (*abbr. of* ***Common Agricultural Policy***) Óбщая сельскохозя́йственная поли́тика.
cap [kæp] *n.* **1.** (*worker's*) кéпка; (*of uniform, incl. school*) фурáжка; (*without peak*) шáпка; **dunce's ~** дурáцкий колпáк; **fool's ~** шутовскóй колпáк; **~ and bells** колпáк с бубéнчиками; **~ of liberty, Phrygian ~** фриги́йский колпáк; (*lady's, servant's or nurse's*) чепéц; (*baby's*) чéпчик. **2.** (*of mountain*) верхýшка, верши́на. **3.** (*e.g. of pen or bottle*) кры́шка; **percussion ~** пистóн, кáпсюль (*m.*). **4.** (*fig.*): **he came to us ~ in hand** он яви́лся к нам со смирéнным ви́дом; **if the ~ fits, wear it** вольнó же вам э́то на свой счёт приня́ть; ≃ на вóре шáпка гори́т; **she set her ~ at him** онá реши́ла поймáть/окрути́ть егó; **he put on his thinking ~** он задýмался.
v.t. **1.** (*put a ~ on, cover*) над|евáть, -éть шáпку на+*a.* **2.** (*excel*) прев|осходи́ть, -зойти́; (*a joke etc.*) перещеголя́ть (*pf.*); **to ~ our misfortunes** в довершéние нáших злоключéний. **3.** (*confer degree on*) прису|ждáть, -ди́ть учёную стéпень +*d.* **4.** (*sport*) прин|имáть, -я́ть в состáв комáнды.
cpd. **~-band** *n.* окóлыш.
capability [,keɪpə'bɪlɪtɪ] *n.* спосóбность, возмóжность.
capable ['keɪpəb(ə)l] *adj.* **1.** (*gifted*) спосóбный. **2.** (*~ of*) спосóбный на+*a.*; **he is ~ of telling lies** он спосóбен солгáть. **3.** (*susceptible*) поддаю́щийся; **the situation is ~ of improvement** положéние мóжно испрáвить.
capacious [kə'peɪʃəs] *adj.* простóрный.
capaciousness [kə'peɪʃəsnɪs] *n.* простóрность.
capacity [kə'pæsɪtɪ] *n.* **1.** (*ability to hold*) вмести́мость; **measure of ~** мéра объёма; **the hall's seating ~ is 500** вмести́мость зáла — пятьсóт мест; **the room was filled to ~** кóмната былá запóлнена до откáза; **play to ~** (*theatr.*) дéлать (*impf.*) пóлные сбóры. **2.** (*of engine*) (наибóльшая) мóщность, нагрýзка; (*of ship*) вмести́мость; **to work at, to ~** рабóтать (*impf.*) в пóлную си́лу. **3.** (*fig.*): **a mind of great ~** мóщный ум; **he has little ~ for happiness** он не сóздан для счáстья. **4.** (*position, character*): **in my ~ as critic** как кри́тик; в рóли/кáчестве кри́тика; **I have come in the ~ of a friend** я пришёл как друг; **legal ~** правоспосóбность. **5.** (*elec.*) электри́ческая ёмкость.
cap-à-pie [,kæpə'pi:] *adv.* с головы́ до ног.
caparison [kə'pærɪs(ə)n] *n.* попóна, чепрáк; (*fig.*) убóр.
v.t. покр|ывáть, -ы́ть попóной/чепракóм; (*fig.*) разубрáть (*pf.*).
cape[1] [keɪp] *n.* (*garment*) наки́дка с капюшóном; (*part of garment*) капюшóн.
cape[2] [keɪp] (*geog.*) мыс; **the C~ (of Good Hope)** мыс Дóброй Надéжды; **C~ Coloured** *n.* южноафрикáнский

метис; **C~ Dutch** (*language*) африкаанс; (*attr.*) бурский; **C~ gooseberry** физалис; вишня перувианская; **C~ Province** Капская провинция; **C~ Town, C~town** Кейптаун; ~ **Verde** Зелёный Мыс.

caper[1] ['keɪpə(r)] *n.* (*shrub*) каперсник; (*pl., cul.*) каперсы (*m. pl.*).

caper[2] ['keɪpə(r)] *n.* (*leap*) прыжок.

v.i. (*also* **cut ~s**) скакать (*impf.*); выделывать (*impf.*) антраша.

capercail|lie [,kæpə'keɪlɪ], **-zie** [,kæpə'keɪlzɪ] *n.* глухарь (*m.*).

capful ['kæpfʊl] *n.* полная шапка; **a ~ of wind** лёгкий порыв ветра.

capillary [kə'pɪlərɪ] *adj.* капиллярный; ~ **attraction** капиллярное притяжение.

capital ['kæpɪt(ə)l] *n.* **1.** (*principal city*) столица; (*attr.*) столичный. **2.** (*upper-case letter*) прописная/заглавная буква; **block ~s** прописные печатные буквы; **small ~s** капитель. **3.** (*wealth*) капитал; **circulating ~** оборотный капитал; **fixed ~** основной капитал; **loan ~** ссудный капитал; **paid-up ~** оплаченный акционерный капитал; ~ **and interest** основная сумма и наросшие проценты. **4.** (*fig., advantage*) выигрыш, капитал; **he made ~ out of our mistakes** он ловко воспользовался нашими ошибками. **5.** (*employers*) капитал; ~ **and labour** труд и капитал. **6.** (*archit.*) капитель.

adj. **1.** (*major*) главный, основной. **2.** (*excellent*) капитальный, превосходный. **3.** (*involving death penalty*): **a ~ offence** преступление, караемое смертью; ~ **punishment** смертная казнь. **4.** (*nav.*): ~ **ship** линейный корабль; крейсер. **5.** (*econ.*): ~ **goods** средства производства; ~ **expenditure** капитальные затраты; ~ **assets** основные средства; ~ **levy** налог на капитал. **6.** (*upper-case*) прописная/заглавная буква.

capitalism ['kæpɪtə,lɪz(ə)m] *n.* капитализм.

capitalist ['kæpɪtəlɪst] *n.* капиталист.

capitalistic [,kæpɪtə'lɪstɪk] *adj.* капиталистический.

capitalization [,kæpɪtəlaɪ'zeɪʃ(ə)n] *n.* **1.** (*writing with capital letter*) письмо прописными буквами; замена строчных букв прописными. **2.** (*econ.*) капитализация.

capitalize ['kæpɪtə,laɪz] *v.t. & i.* **1.** (*write with capital letter*) писать, на- прописными буквами. **2.** (*econ.*) капитализировать (*impf., pf.*). **3.** (*fig.*) наж|иваться, -иться; ~ **on s.o.'s misfortune** извл|екать, -ечь выгоду из чьего-н. несчастья.

capitation [,kæpɪ'teɪʃ(ə)n] *n.* исчисление с головы; ~ **tax** подушная подать.

Capitol ['kæpɪt(ə)l] *n.*: ~ **Hill** Капитолийский холм.

capitular [kə'pɪtjʊlə(r)] *adj.* относящийся к капитулу.

capitulate [kə'pɪtjʊ,leɪt] *v.t.* капитулировать (*impf., pf.*).

capitulation [kə,pɪtjʊ'leɪʃ(ə)n] *n.* (*surrender*) капитуляция.

capon ['keɪpən] *n.* каплун.

cappuccino [,kæpʊ'tʃi:nəʊ] *n.* кофе (*m. indecl.*) «капуцин».

capriccio [kə'prɪtʃɪəʊ] *n.* каприч(ч)о (*indecl.*).

caprice [kə'pri:s] *n.* прихоть, каприз, причуда.

capricious [kə'prɪʃəs] *adj.* прихотливый, капризный.

capriciousness [kə'prɪʃəsnɪs] *n.* непостоянство; капризность.

Capricorn ['kæprɪ,kɔ:n] *n.* Козерог; **Tropic of ~** тропик Козерога.

caprine ['kæpraɪn] *adj.* козлиный.

capriole ['kæprɪ,əʊl] *n.* прыжок на месте.

capsicum ['kæpsɪkəm] *n.* стручковый перец.

capsize [kæp'saɪz] *v.t. & i.* опроки|дывать(ся), -нуть(ся).

capstan ['kæpst(ə)n] *n.* кабестан.

capsule ['kæpsju:l] *n.* **1.** (*bot.*) семенная коробочка. **2.** (*med.*) капсула. **3.** (*metal cap*) крышка, колпачок. **4.** (*for space travel*) капсула, отсек. **5.** (*fig.*): ~ **biography** краткая биография.

Capt. ['kæptɪn] *n.* (*abbr. of* **Captain**) кап., (капитан).

captain ['kæptɪn] *n.* **1.** (*leader*) руководитель (*m.*); ~ **of industry** промышленный магнат; (*head of team*) капитан команды. **2.** (*army rank*) капитан. **3.** (*naval rank*) капитан первого ранга; командир корабля.

v.i. руководить (*impf.*); вести (*det.*); быть капитаном +*g.*

captain|cy ['kæptɪnsɪ], **-ship** ['kæptɪnʃɪp] *nn.* звание/должность капитана.

caption ['kæpʃ(ə)n] *n.* (*title, words accompanying picture*) подпись к картинке; (*film subtitle*) титр.

captious ['kæpʃəs] *adj.* придирчивый.

captiousness ['kæpʃəsnɪs] *n.* придирчивость.

captivate ['kæptɪ,veɪt] *v.t.* плен|ять, -ить; очаров|ывать, -ать.

captivating ['kæptɪ,veɪtɪŋ] *adj.* пленительный, чарующий.

captive ['kæptɪv] *n.* пленник, пленный; **take ~** брать, взять в плен; **hold ~** держать (*impf.*) в плену.

adj. пленный; ~ **audience** слушатели (*m. pl.*) поневоле; ~ **balloon** привязной аэростат.

captivity [kæp'tɪvɪtɪ] *n.* плен, пленение.

captor ['kæptə(r), -tɔ:(r)] *n.* захвативший в плен; взявший приз.

capture ['kæptʃə(r)] *n.* (*action*) поимка, захват; (*thg.* **~d**) добыча.

v.t. брать, взять в плен; захват|ывать, -ить; ~ **s.o.'s attention** приков|ывать, -ать чьё-н. внимание.

Capuchin ['kæpju:tʃɪn] *n.* (*friar; monkey*) капуцин.

capybara [,kæpɪ'bɑ:rə] *n.* водосвинка.

car [kɑ:(r)] *n.* **1.** (*motor vehicle*) (легковой) автомобиль, машина; ~ **coat** пальто «три четверти»; ~ **boot sale** продажа (прямо) из багажника; ~ **pool** автобаза предприятия (*or* учреждения). **2.** (*rail vehicle*) вагон; **dining-~** вагон-ресторан; **sleeping-~** спальный вагон; **Pullman ~** пульмановский вагон. **3.** (*hist., poet.*) колесница.

cpds. **~-driver** *n.* шофёр; **~-ferry** *n.* автопаром; **~-hire** *n.* прокат автомобиля; **~-park** *n.* паркинг, автостоянка; **~phone** *n.* автотелефон; **~-port** *n.* навес для автомобиля; **~-race** *n.* автогонка; **~-sick** *adj.*: **he was ~-sick** его укачало в машине.

carabineer [,kærəbɪ'nɪə(r)] *n.* карабинёр.

Caracas [kə'rækəs] *n.* Каракас.

caracole ['kærə,kəʊl] *n.* караколь (*m.*).

v.i. делать, с- караколь.

caracul, karakul ['kærə,kʊl] *n.* каракуль (*m.*).

carafe [kə'ræf, -rɑ:f] *n.* графин.

caramel ['kærə,mel] *n.* (*burnt sugar*) карамель; (*sweetmeat*) карамель, карамелька.

adj. (*~-coloured*) светло-коричневый.

carapace ['kærə,peɪs] *n.* щиток (*черепахи и т.п.*).

carat ['kærət] (*also US* **karat**) *n.* карат.

caravan ['kærə,væn] *n.* караван; (*Gypsy's*) фургон, крытая телега; (*trailer*) дом-автоприцеп.

v.i.: **go ~ing** путешествовать в доме-автоприцепе.

caravanner ['kærəvænə(r)] *n.* путешествующий с автоприцепом.

caravanserai [,kærə'vænsərɪ, -,raɪ] *n.* караван-сарай.

caravel ['kærə,vel] *n.* каравелла.

caraway ['kærə,weɪ] *n.* тмин; ~ **seed** тминное семя.

carbide ['kɑ:baɪd] *n.* карбид; **calcium ~** карбид кальция.

carbine ['kɑ:baɪn] *n.* карабин.

carbohydrate [,kɑ:bə'haɪdreɪt] *n.* углевод.

carbolic [kɑ:'bɒlɪk] *adj.* карболовый.

carbon ['kɑ:bən] *n.* **1.** (*element*) углерод; ~ **monoxide** угарный газ; ~ **dioxide** углекислота, углекислый газ; ~ **dating** датировка/датирование по (радио)углероду. **2.** (*elec.*) уголь (*m.*); угольный электрод. **3.** (*~-paper*) копировальная бумага, копирка; ~ **copy** (*lit.*) копия под копирку; (*fig.*) (точная) копия.

carbonaceous [,kɑ:bə'neɪʃəs] *adj.* углеродистый, углеродный, карбонатный.

carbonic [kɑ:'bɒnɪk] *adj.* угольный, углеродный, углеродистый; ~ **acid** углекислота.

carboniferous [,kɑ:bə'nɪfərəs] *adj.* угленосный; каменноугольный.

carbonization [,kɑ:bənaɪ'zeɪʃ(ə)n] *n.* обугливание, карбонизация.

carbonize ['kɑ:bə,naɪz] *v.t.* **1.** (*convert into carbon*) карбонизировать (*impf., pf.*). **2.** (*apply carbon black to*) покр|ывать, -ыть углём. **3.** (*char*) обугли|вать, -ть; коксовать (*impf.*).

carborundum [,kɑ:bə'rʌndəm] *n.* карборунд.

carboy ['kɑ:bɔɪ] *n.* оплетённая бутыль.

carbuncle ['kɑ:bʌŋk(ə)l] *n.* (*jewel; med.*) карбункул.

carburettor [ˌkɑːbjʊˈretə(r), ˌkɑːbə-] *n.* карбюра́тор.

carcajou [ˈkɑːkəˌdʒuː, -kəˌʒuː] *n.* росома́ха.

carcas|e [ˈkɑːkəs], **-s** [ˈkɑːkəs] *n.* **1.** (*of animal*) ту́ша; ~ **meat** парно́е мя́со; (*fig.*): **save one's** ~ спаса́|ть, -сти́ свою́ шку́ру. **2.** (*of building, ship etc.*) карка́с, осто́в, ко́рпус.

carcinogen [kɑːˈsɪnədʒ(ə)n] *n.* канцероге́нное вещество́.

carcinogenic [ˌkɑːsɪnəˈdʒenɪk] *adj.* канцероге́нный.

carcinoma [ˌkɑːsɪˈnəʊmə] *n.* карцино́ма, ра́ковое новообразова́ние.

card[1] [kɑːd] *n.* **1.** (*piece of pasteboard*) ка́рточка; (*postcard*) откры́тка; **calling ~, visiting** ~ визи́тная ка́рточка; **Party** ~ парти́йный биле́т; **invitation** ~ пригласи́тельный биле́т; **Christmas** ~ рожде́ственская откры́тка; **birthday** ~ поздрави́тельная ка́рточка/откры́тка ко дню рожде́ния; **identity** ~ удостовере́ние ли́чности. **2.** (*playing-~*) игра́льная ка́рта; **play ~s** игра́ть, сыгра́ть в ка́рты; **play a** ~ пойти́ (*pf.*) с (како́й-н.) ка́рты; **house of ~s** (*lit., fig.*) ка́рточный до́мик; **I won £5 at ~s** я вы́играл в ка́рты 5 фу́нтов. **3.** (*in libraries etc.*) катало́жная ка́рточка; **~s** (*documents of employment*) учётная ка́рточка; **give s.o. his ~s** (*dismiss him*) уво́лить (*pf.*) кого́-н. **4.** (*of compass*) карту́шка. **5.** (*coll., queer or comic pers.*) тип. **6.** (*fig.*): **he put his ~s on the table** он раскры́л свои́ ка́рты; **I have a ~ up my sleeve** у меня́ есть в запа́се ко́зырь; **do not show your ~s** не раскрыва́йте свои́х карт; **he holds all the ~s** у него́ все ко́зыри на рука́х; **he plays his ~s well** он уме́ло испо́льзует обстоя́тельства; **it is on the ~s that we shall go** возмо́жно, что мы пойдём.

cpds. **~-carrying** *adj.* зарегистри́рованный, состоя́щий в организа́ции; **~-index** *n.* картоте́ка; *v.t.* (*enter on ~s*) зан|оси́ть, -ести́ на ка́рточки; каталогизи́ровать (*impf., pf.*); **~-party** *n.* ве́чер за ка́ртами; **~-player** *n.* игро́к в ка́рты; картёжник; **~-playing** *n.* игра́ в ка́рты; **~-sharper** *n.* шу́лер; **~-table** *n.* ло́мберный стол.

card[2] [kɑːd] *n.* (*for wool*) ка́рда, чеса́лка.

v.t. чеса́ть, по-; прочёс|ывать, -а́ть; кардова́ть (*impf.*); **~ing-machine** кардочеса́льная маши́на.

cardam|om, -um [ˈkɑːdəməm] *n.* кардамо́н.

cardan [ˈkɑːd(ə)n] *n.* карда́н; ~ **joint** карда́нный шарни́р; ~ **shaft** карда́нный вал.

cardboard [ˈkɑːdbɔːd] *n.* карто́н; ~ **box** карто́нная коро́бка; (*fig.*): ~ **characters** (*in a novel*) ходу́льные персона́жи.

carder [ˈkɑːdə(r)] *n.* (*pers.*) чеса́льщи|к (*fem.* -ца); ворси́льщи|к (*fem.* -ца); (*machine*) ка́рдная маши́на.

cardiac [ˈkɑːdɪˌæk] *adj.* серде́чный; ~ **murmur** шум се́рдца.

cardigan [ˈkɑːdɪgən] *n.* шерстяна́я ко́фта; кардига́н, фуфа́йка; (*man's*) вя́заная ку́ртка.

cardinal [ˈkɑːdɪn(ə)l] *n.* (*eccl., zool.*) кардина́л; **~'s hat** кардина́льская ша́пка.

adj. (*principal*) кардина́льный; ~ **number** коли́чественное числи́тельное; ~ **point** страна́ све́та; ~ **vowel** кардина́льный гла́сный; **a matter of ~ importance** де́ло чрезвыча́йной ва́жности; важне́йшее де́ло; (*scarlet*) яркокра́сный.

cardinalate [ˈkɑːdɪn(ə),leɪt] *n.* сан кардина́ла.

cardiogram [ˈkɑːdɪəʊ,græm] *n.* кардиогра́мма.

cardiology [ˌkɑːdɪˈɒlədʒɪ] *n.* кардиоло́гия.

cardoon [kɑːˈduːn] *n.* ка́рда.

care [keə(r)] *n.* **1.** (*serious attention, caution*) осторо́жность; **he works with** ~ он стара́тельно рабо́тает; **handle this with** ~ обраща́йтесь с э́тим осторо́жно; **glass with** ~ осторо́жно! — стекло́; **take ~ you don't fall** смотри́те, не упади́те; **have a ~!** береги́тесь! **2.** (*charge, responsibility*) забо́та, попече́ние; **he is under the doctor's** ~ он нахо́дится под наблюде́нием врача́; **the child is in my** ~ ребёнок на моём попече́нии; **take a child into** ~ взять (*pf.*) ребёнка в систе́му госуда́рственного призре́ния; **Mr. Smith, ~ of Mr. Jones** г-ну Джо́нсу для г-на Сми́та (*or* для переда́чи г-ну Сми́ту); **that shall be my** ~ я об э́том позабо́чусь; **that will take ~ of** (*meet*) **our needs** э́то обеспе́чит нас необходи́мым; э́того нам хва́тит. **3.** (*anxiety*): **free from** ~ свобо́дный от забо́т; не зна́ющий забо́т, беззабо́тный.

v.i. **1.** (*feel concern or anxiety*): **I don't ~ what they say** мне всё равно́, что они́ ска́жут; **he doesn't ~ a bit** ему́ наплева́ть (*coll.*); **who ~s?** не всё ли равно́?; **I couldn't ~ less** (*coll.*) мне-то что?; мне наплева́ть; **he can go for all I** ~ по мне он мо́жет идти; **not that I** ~ не то, что́бы меня́ э́то волнова́ло/трево́жило/беспоко́ило; **that's all he ~s about** он бо́льше ниче́м не интересу́ется. **2.** (*feel inclination*): **would you ~ for a walk?** не хоти́те ли пойти́ погуля́ть?; **I don't ~ for asparagus** я не люблю́ спа́ржу; **I knew she ~d for him** я знал, что он ей нра́вится (*or* что она́ неравноду́шна к нему́); **you might ~ to look at this letter** вам, мо́жет быть, бу́дет интере́сно взгляну́ть на э́то письмо́. **3.** (*look after*): **he is well ~d for** за ним хоро́ший ухо́д; он окружён забо́той.

cpds. **~free** *adj.* беззабо́тный; **~-laden** *adj.* обременённый забо́тами; **~taker** *n.* сто́рож, смотри́тель (*m.*) зда́ния; **~taker government** вре́менное прави́тельство; **~worn** *adj.* изму́ченный забо́тами.

careen [kəˈriːn] *v.t.* кренгова́ть (*impf.*), килева́ть (*impf.*).

v.i. (*heel over*) крени́ться (*impf.*); (*US, career*) нести́сь, по- (*det.*).

career [kəˈrɪə(r)] *n.* **1.** (*life story*) жи́зненный путь. **2.** (*profession*) карье́ра, де́ятельность, профе́ссия; **~s open to women** профе́ссии, досту́пные же́нщинам; ~ **diplomat(ist)** профессиона́льный диплома́т; **~s master** (*at school*) консульта́нт по профессиона́льной ориента́ции. **3.** (*motion*): **in full** ~ во весь опо́р.

v.i. нести́сь, по- (*det.*); мча́ться (*impf.*).

careerism [kəˈrɪər,ɪz(ə)m] *n.* карьери́зм.

careerist [kəˈrɪərɪst] *n.* карьери́ст.

careful [ˈkeəfʊl] *adj.* **1.** (*attentive*) осторо́жный; забо́тливый, внима́тельный; **be ~ not to fall** бу́дьте осторо́жны, не упади́те; **be ~ where you go** смотри́те по́д ноги; **be ~ of your health** береги́те своё здоро́вье; **he is ~ with his money** он не тра́тит де́нег зря. **2.** (*of work etc.*) тща́тельный, аккура́тный.

carefulness [ˈkeəfʊlnɪs] *n.* осторо́жность; забо́тливость, внима́тельность; тща́тельность, аккура́тность.

careless [ˈkeəlɪs] *adj.* (*thoughtless*) неосторо́жный, неосмотри́тельный; **a ~ driver** неосторо́жный води́тель; **a ~ mistake** оши́бка по невнима́тельности; (*negligent*) небре́жный; (*carefree, unconcerned*) беззабо́тный, беспе́чный; ~ **of danger** не ду́мающий об опа́сности.

carelessness [ˈkeəlɪsnɪs] *n.* небре́жность, хала́тность, неосторо́жность; беззабо́тность, беспе́чность; (*negligence*) неосмотри́тельность.

caress [kəˈres] *n.* ла́ска.

v.t. ласка́ть (*impf.*).

caressing [kəˈresɪŋ] *adj.* ласка́ющий, ла́сковый.

caret [ˈkærət] *n.* знак вста́вки.

cargo [ˈkɑːgəʊ] *n.* груз; ~ **ship, boat** торго́вое/грузово́е су́дно.

Caribbean [ˌkærɪˈbiːən, kəˈrɪbɪən] *adj.* кар(а)и́бский; (*as n.*) **the ~ (sea)** Кар(а)и́бское мо́ре; (*region*) стра́ны (*fem. pl.*) бассе́йна Кар(а)и́бского мо́ря.

caribou [ˈkærɪˌbuː] *n.* кари́бу (*m. indecl.*), кана́дский оле́нь.

caricature [ˈkærɪkətjʊə(r)] *n.* карикату́ра; (*fig., also*) искаже́ние.

v.t. изобра|жа́ть, -зи́ть в карикату́рном ви́де.

caricaturist [ˈkærɪkəˌtjʊərɪst] *n.* карикатури́ст.

caries [ˈkeəriːz, -rɪˌiːz] *n.* костое́да, ка́риес.

carillon [kəˈrɪljən, ˈkærɪljən] *n.* подбо́р колоколо́в; перезво́н.

caring [ˈkeərɪŋ] *adj.* забо́тливый.

carioca [ˌkærɪˈəʊkə] *n.* (*dance, tune*) карио́ка.

carious [ˈkeərɪəs] *adj.* карио́зный.

carking [ˈkɑːkɪŋ] *adj.*: ~ **care** снеда́ющая забо́та.

Carmelite [ˈkɑːmɪˌlaɪt] *n.* кармели́т (*fem.* -ка).

adj. кармели́тский.

carminative [ˈkɑːmɪnətɪv] *adj.* ветрого́нный.

carmine [ˈkɑːmaɪn] *n.* карми́н.

adj. карми́нный.

carnage [ˈkɑːnɪdʒ] *n.* бо́йня.

carnal [ˈkɑːn(ə)l] *adj.* (*sensual*) пло́тский, теле́сный; (*sexual*) полово́й; **have ~ knowledge of** име́ть (*impf.*) половы́е снoше́ния c+*i.*; (*worldly*) земно́й, мирско́й.

carnality [kɑːˈnælɪtɪ] *n.* чу́вственность, по́хоть.

carnation [kɑːˈneɪʃ(ə)n] *n.* (*colour*) а́лый цвет; (*flower*) гвозди́ка.

carnival ['kɑ:nɪv(ə)l] *n.* (*merrymaking*) карнава́л; (*Shrovetide*) ма́сленица.
carnivore ['kɑ:nɪ,vɔ:(r)] *n.* плотоя́дное/хи́щное живо́тное.
carnivorous [kɑ:'nɪvərəs] *adj.* плотоя́дный.
carob ['kærəb] *n.* (*tree*) рожко́вое де́рево; (*bean*) сла́дкий рожо́к.
carol ['kær(ə)l] *n.* (*song*) пе́сня; (*Xmas song*) рожде́ственский гимн.
v.t. & i. восп|ева́ть, -е́ть.
Caroline ['kærə,laɪn] *adj.* относя́щийся к эпо́хе Ка́рла I/II.
Carolingian [,kærə'lɪndʒɪən] *n.* кароли́нг.
adj. кароли́нгский.
carom ['kærəm] = **cannon** *n.* **3.** & *v.i.*
carotid [kə'rɒtɪd] *adj.*: ~ **artery** со́нная арте́рия.
carousal [kə'raʊzəl] *n.* пиру́шка, попо́йка, гуля́нка.
carouse [kə'raʊz] *v.i.* пирова́ть (*impf.*), бра́жничать (*impf.*).
carousel [,kærə'sel, -'zel] *n.* (*roundabout*) карусе́ль.
carouser [kə'raʊzə(r)] *n.* гуля́ка (*c.g.*), кути́ла (*m.*).
carp[1] [kɑ:p] *n.* (*zool.*) карп.
carp[2] [kɑ:p] *v.i.* придира́ться (*impf.*) (**at:** к+*d.*); ~**ing criticism** приди́рчивая кри́тика.
Carpathians [kɑ:'peɪθɪəns] *n.* Карпа́т|ы (*pl.*, *g.* —).
carpenter ['kɑ:pɪntə(r)] *n.* пло́тник.
v.t. изгот|овля́ть, -о́вить (*or* де́лать, с-) из де́рева.
v.i. пло́тничать (*impf.*).
carpentry ['kɑ:pɪntrɪ] *n.* (*occupation*) пло́тничество, пло́тничье де́ло; (*product*) пло́тничьи рабо́ты (*f. pl.*).
carpet ['kɑ:pɪt] *n.* ковёр; **be on the** ~ (*reprimanded*) получ|а́ть, -и́ть нагоня́й/взбу́чку (*coll.*); ~ **bombing** бомбомета́ние по пло́щади; ~ **knight** да́мский уго́дник, сало́нный шарку́н; ~ **slippers** тёплые та́почки.
v.t. покр|ыва́ть, -ы́ть ковро́м; уст|ила́ть, -ла́ть ковра́ми; (*reprimand*) да|ва́ть, -ть нагоня́й/взбу́чку +*d.*; вызыва́ть, вы́звать на ковёр (*coll.*).
cpds. ~**-bag** *n.* саквоя́ж; ~**-beater** *n.* выбива́лка для ковра́; ~**-sweeper** *n.* щётка для ковра́.
carpeting ['kɑ:pɪtɪŋ] *n.* **1.** (*carpet material*) ковро́вая ткань; **felt** ~ полово́й насти́л на во́йлочной подкла́дке; (*covering with carpets*) устила́ние/покрыва́ние ковра́ми. **2.** (*reprimand*) разно́с, нагоня́й.
carpus ['kɑ:pəs] *n.* запя́стье.
carrel ['kær(ə)l] *n.* отсе́к (*в библиотеке*).
carriage ['kærɪdʒ] *n.* **1.** (*road vehicle*) экипа́ж, каре́та, коля́ска; ~ **and pair/four** экипа́ж, запряжённый па́рой/четвёркой лошаде́й. **2.** (*rail car*) пассажи́рский ваго́н. **3.** (*transport of goods*) перево́зка, доста́вка; ~ **forward** сто́имость перево́зки за счёт покупа́теля. **4.** (*manner of standing or walking*) оса́нка; мане́ра держа́ться. **5.** (*gun-*~) лафе́т. **6.** (*of typewriter etc.*) каре́тка.
cpd. ~**way** *n.* прое́зжая часть доро́ги.
carrier ['kærɪə(r)] *n.* **1.** (*transport agent*) транспортёр. **2.** (*receptacle or support for luggage etc.*) бага́жник; ~ **bag** су́мка для поку́пок. **3.** (*of disease*) бациллоноси́тель (*m.*), вирусоноси́тель (*m.*). **4.** (*vehicle, ship etc.*) тра́нспортное сре́дство. **5.** (*aircraft-*~) авиано́сец. **6.:** ~ **pigeon** почто́вый го́лубь.
carriole ['kærɪ,əʊl] *n.* коля́ска.
carrion ['kærɪən] *n.* па́даль, мертвечи́на; ~ **beetle** жук-моги́льщик; ~ **crow** воро́на чёрная.
carrot ['kærət] *n.* **1.** морко́вка; (*pl.*, *collect.*) морко́вь. **2.** (*pl.*, *sl.*, *red hair*) ры́жие во́лосы (*m. pl.*); (*of pers.*) ры́жий.
carroty ['kærətɪ] *adj.* рыжева́тый, рыжеволо́сый.
carry ['kærɪ] *v.t.* **1.** (*bear, transport*) носи́ть, нести́; (*of or by vehicle*) вози́ть (*indet.*), везти́ (*det.*); пере|вози́ть, -везти́; **ships** ~ **goods** корабли́ перево́зят това́ры; **this bicycle has carried me 500 miles** на э́том велосипе́де я прое́хал 500 миль; **pipes** ~ **water** вода́ идёт по тру́бам; **wires** ~ **sound** звук передаётся по провода́м; **pillars** ~ **an arch** коло́нны подде́рживают а́рку; **what weight will the bridge** ~**?** на како́й вес рассчи́тан э́тот мост?; **he carries himself well** он хорошо́ де́ржится; **he carries his liquor well** он уме́ет пить; **the police carried him off to prison** поли́ция увезла́ его́ в тюрьму́; ~**ing trade** тра́нспортное де́ло. **2.** (*have on or about one*): **I always** ~ **an umbrella (money) with me** у меня́ всегда́ с собо́й зо́нтик (всегда́ де́ньги при себе́); **the police** ~ **arms** поли́ция вооружена́; ~ **figures in one's head** держа́ть (*impf.*) ци́фры в голове́; **this crime carries a heavy penalty** э́то преступле́ние влечёт за собо́й тяжёлое наказа́ние. **3.** (*fig.*): ~ **into effect** осуществ|ля́ть, -и́ть; **his voice carries weight** с его́ мне́нием счита́ются; **the argument carries conviction** э́тот аргуме́нт убеди́телен; **he carries modesty too far** он изли́шне скро́мен; ~ **the day** одерж|ивать, -а́ть побе́ду; ~ **all before one** сме|та́ть, -сти́ всё на своём пути́; ~ **one's point** успе́шно отстоя́ть (*pf.*) свою́ то́чку зре́ния; **he carried his hearers with him** он увлёк свои́х слу́шателей; **the bill was carried** законопрое́кт был при́нят. **4.** (*include*): **the book carries many tables** кни́га соде́ржит мно́го табли́ц; **the newspaper carried this report** газе́та помести́ла э́то сообще́ние. **5.** (*fin., comm.*): **the loan carries interest** заём прино́сит проце́нты/дохо́д; **the shop carries hardware** э́тот магази́н торгу́ет скобяны́ми това́рами. **6.** (*math.*): **put down 6 and** ~ **1** записа́ть (*pf.*) 6 и держа́ть (*impf.*) в уме́ оди́н; **'**~ **1'** «оди́н в уме́». **7.** (*extend*): ~ **a wall down to the river** протя́|гивать, -ну́ть сте́ну до са́мой реки́; ~ **a division to 7 places** (*math.*) произв|оди́ть, -ести́ деле́ние до седьмо́го зна́ка.
v.i.: **the shot carried 200 yards** снаря́д пролете́л 200 я́рдов; **his voice carries well** у него́ зву́чный го́лос.
with advs.: ~ **away** *v.t.* (*lit.*) ун|оси́ть, -ести́; **the masts were carried away by the storm** бу́рей унесло́ ма́чты; (*fig.*): **he was carried away by his feelings** он оказа́лся во вла́сти чувств; он увлёкся; ~ **back** *v.t.* (*lit.*) прин|оси́ть, -ести́ обра́тно; (*fig.*): **the incident carried me back to my schooldays** э́тот слу́чай перенёс меня́ обра́тно в мои́ шко́льные го́ды; ~ **forward, over** *vv.t.* (*transfer*) перен|оси́ть, -ести́; ~ **off** *v.t.* (*remove*) ун|оси́ть, -ести́; **death carried off several of them** не́которых из них унесла́ смерть; **he carried the situation off well** он хорошо́ вы́шел из положе́ния; ~ **on** *v.t.* (*conduct, perform*): ~ **on a conversation/business** вести́ (*det.*) разгово́р/де́ло; *v.i.* (*continue*) прод|олжа́ть, -о́лжить; ~ **on with your work** продолжа́йте рабо́ту; (*talk, behave excitedly*) волнова́ться (*impf.*); проявля́ть (*impf.*) несде́ржанность; **don't** ~ **on so!** не распаля́йтесь так!; ~ **out** *v.t.* (*lit.*) выноси́ть, вы́нести; (*execute*) выполня́ть, вы́полнить; ~ **through** *v.t.* (*bring out of difficulties*) выводи́ть, вы́вести из затрудне́ний.
cpds. ~**-all** *n.* вещево́й мешо́к; ~**-cot** *n.* перено́сная де́тская крова́тка.
carrying(s)-on ['kærɪŋ(s)'ɒn] *n.* (*to-do*) сумато́ха, суета́; (*coll., flirtation*) ша́шн|и (*pl.*, *g.* -ей); шу́ры-му́ры (*pl. indecl.*).
cart [kɑ:t] *n.* двуко́лка, теле́жка; **put the** ~ **before the horse** (*fig.*) ста́вить (*impf.*) теле́гу пе́ред ло́шадью; де́лать, с- ши́ворот-навы́ворот; **in the** ~ (*sl.*) в тру́дном положе́нии.
v.t. (*carry in* ~) вози́ть (*indet.*) в теле́жке; ~ **away** отв|ози́ть, -езти́; ув|ози́ть, -езти́; (*coll., carry*) тащи́ть (*impf.*).
cpds. ~**-horse** *n.* ломова́я ло́шадь; ~**-load** *n.* воз, теле́га (*чего*); ~**-road,** ~**-track** *nn.* просёлочная доро́га; ~**wheel** *n.* колесо́ теле́ги; **turn** ~**wheels** кувырк|а́ться, -ну́ться колесо́м; ~**wright** *n.* теле́жный ма́стер.
cartage ['kɑ:tɪdʒ] *n.* (*transport*) (гужево́й) тра́нспорт; (гужева́я) перево́зка; (*charge*) сто́имость (гужево́й) перево́зки.
carte blanche [kɑ:t 'blɑ̃ʃ] *n.* карт-бла́нш.
cartel [kɑ:'tel] *n.* (*comm.*) карте́ль (*m.*).
cartelize ['kɑ:tə,laɪz] *v.t.* (*e.g. an industry*) объедин|я́ть, -и́ть в карте́ли.
carter ['kɑ:tə(r)] *n.* во́зчик.
Cartesian [kɑ:'ti:zjən, -ʒ(ə)n] *adj.* картезиа́нский.
cartful ['kɑ:tfʊl] *n.* теле́га (*чего*).
Carthage ['kɑ:θɪdʒ] *n.* Карфаге́н.
Carthaginian [,kɑ:θə'dʒɪnɪən] *n.* карфагеня́н|ин (*fem.* -ка).
adj. карфаге́нский, пуни́ческий.
Carthusian [kɑ:'θju:zjən] *n.* картезиа́нец, картузиа́нец.
adj. картезиа́нский, картузиа́нский.

cartilage ['kɑːtɪlɪdʒ] *n.* хрящ.
cartilaginous [ˌkɑːtɪ'lædʒɪnəs] *adj.* хрящевой.
cartographer [kɑː'tɒgrəfə(r)] *n.* картограф.
cartographic(al) [kɑːtə'græfɪk(ə)l] *adj.* картографический.
cartography [kɑː'tɒgrəfɪ] *n.* картография.
cartomancy ['kɑːtəˌmænsɪ] *n.* гадание на картах.
carton ['kɑːt(ə)n] *n.* (*container*) картонка; блок.
cartoon [kɑː'tuːn] *n.* (*in fine arts*) картон; (*in newspaper*) карикатура; (*film*) мультипликация, мультфильм.
cartoonist [kɑː'tuːnɪst] *n.* карикатурист; (*film*) мультипликатор.
cartouche [kɑː'tuːʃ] *n.* (*archit.*, *archaeol.*) картуш; (*gun cartridge*) лядунка; патронная сумка.
cartridge ['kɑːtrɪdʒ] *n.* патрон, заряд; **blank ~** холостой патрон.
cpds. **~-belt** *n.* патронташ; патронная лента; **~-case** *n.* патронная гильза; **~-paper** *n.* плотная бумага (*для рисования и т.п.*).
carv|e [kɑːv] *v.t.* (*cut*) резать (*impf.*); вырезать, вырезать; (*shape by cutting*): **~e a statue out of wood** вырезать, вырезать статую из дерева; **he ~ed his initials** он вырезал свои инициалы; **he ~ed out a career for himself** он сделал карьеру; **~e meat** резать, на- мясо; **~ing-fork/knife** вилка/нож для нарезания мяса.
with adv.: **~e up** *v.t.* (*fig.*, *of wealth etc.*) раздел|ять, -ить.
cpd. **~e-up** *n.* (*fig.*) делёж.
carver ['kɑːvə(r)] *n.* (*pers.*) резчик; (*knife*) нож для нарезания мяса.
carving ['kɑːvɪŋ] *n.* (*object*) резная работа, резьба.
caryatid [ˌkærɪ'ætɪd] *n.* кариатида.
cascade [kæs'keɪd] *n.* каскад; водопад.
v.i. падать/ниспадать (*both impf.*) каскадом.
cascara [kæs'kɑːrə] *n.* (*bot.*, *med.*) каскара.
case[1] [keɪs] *n.* **1.** (*instance*, *circumstances*) случай, обстоятельство, дело; **it is (not) the ~ that ...** дело обстоит (не) так, что...; (не) верно, что...; **such being the ~** поскольку это так; поскольку дело обстоит таким образом; **that alters the ~** это меняет дело; **a ~ in point** пример; **a hard ~** (*difficult point to decide*) трудный случай/вопрос; (*hardened criminal*) закоренелый преступник; **meet the ~** под|ходить, -ойти +*d.*; **in that ~** в таком/этом случае; **in any ~** во всяком случае; **as the ~ may be** как получится; в зависимости от обстоятельств; соответственно с обстоятельствами; **in ~ of fire** (*if fire breaks out*) в случае пожара; **in the ~ of Mr. Smith** что касается г-на Смита; в отношении г-на Смита. **2.** (*med.*) случай, заболевание; больной, раненый; **there were five ~s of influenza** было пять случаев гриппа; **the worst ~s were taken to hospital** наиболее тяжело раненых отвезли в больницу; **stretcher ~** носилочный больной (*or* раненый); **mental ~** душевнобольной. **3.** (*hypothesis*): **put the ~ that ...** предположим, что...; **take an umbrella in ~ it rains** (*or* **in ~ of rain**) возьмите зонтик на случай дождя; **just in ~** на всякий случай. **4.** (*leg.*) судебное дело; **try a ~** раз|бирать, -обрать дело в суде; **leading ~** судебный прецедент; **~ law** прецедентное право. **5.** (*sum of arguments*): **he makes out a good ~ for the change** его доводы в защиту изменения убедительны. **6.** (*condition*): **he was in no ~ to answer** он был не в состоянии отвечать. **7.** (*gram.*) падеж.
case[2] [keɪs] *n.* **1.** (*container*) ящик, ларец, коробка; (*for spectacles etc.*) футляр; **glass ~** витрина. **2.** (*typ.*) наборная касса; **lower ~** касса строчных литер; строчные буквы (*f. pl.*).
v.t. класть, положить в ящик; вст|авлять, -авить в оправу.
cpds. **~-harden** *v.t.* (*lit.*) цементировать (*impf.*, *pf.*); **~-hardened** *adj.* (*fig.*) зачерствевший, загрубелый; **~-knife** *n.* нож в футляре; **~-shot** *n.* картечь.
casein ['keɪsɪɪn, 'keɪsiːn] *n.* казеин.
casemate ['keɪsmeɪt] *n.* эскарповая галерея; каземат.
casement ['keɪsmənt] *n.* (*frame*) створный оконный переплёт; (*window*) окно.
caseous ['keɪsɪəs] *adj.* творожистый.
cash [kæʃ] *n.* (*ready money*; *also hard ~*) наличные (ден|ьги, *pl.*, *g.* -ег); **on a ~ basis** за наличные; за наличный расчёт; **~ on delivery** наложенным платежом; **discount for ~** (*payment*) скидка за наличный расчёт; **out of ~** не при деньгах; **petty ~** мелкие суммы (*f. pl.*); касса для мелких расходов; **~ dispenser** денежный автомат; **~ register** кассовый аппарат, касса.
v.t.: **~ a cheque** получ|ать, -ить деньги по чеку.
v.i.: **~ in on** (*fig.*) воспользоваться (*pf.*) +*i.*
cashcard ['kæʃkɑːd] *n.* карточка для денежного автомата.
cashew ['kæʃuː, kæ'ʃuː] *n.* анакард, орех кешью (*indecl.*).
cashier[1] [kæ'ʃɪə(r)] *n.* кассир.
cashier[2] [kæ'ʃɪə(r)] *v.t.* ув|ольнять, -олить со службы.
cashmere ['kæʃmɪə(r)] *n.* кашемир; (*attr.*) кашемировый.
casino [kə'siːnəʊ] *n.* казино (*indecl.*).
cask [kɑːsk] *n.* бочка, бочонок.
casket ['kɑːskɪt] *n.* шкатулка; (*US*, *coffin*) гроб.
Caspian ['kæspɪən] *n.* (**the ~ Sea**) Каспийское море.
casque [kæsk] *n.* (*poet.*) шлем, каска.
cassation [kə'seɪʃ(ə)n] *n.* кассация; **court of ~** кассационный суд.
cassava [kə'sɑːvə] *n.* маниок(а).
casserole ['kæsəˌrəʊl] *n.* кастрюлечка; блюдо, приготовленное в кастрюлечке.
cassette [kæ'set, kə-] *n.* кассета; **~ recorder** кассетный магнитофон.
cassia ['kæsɪə, 'kæʃə] *n.* кассия.
cassock ['kæsək] *n.* ряса, сутана.
cassowary ['kæsəˌweərɪ] *n.* казуар.
cast [kɑːst] *n.* **1.** (*act of throwing*) бросание, метание, бросок. **2.** (*mould*) форма для отливки; (*moulded object*): **plaster ~** гипсовый слепок. **3.** (*theatr.*) состав актёров; список исполнителей. **4.**: **~ of features** черты (*f. pl.*) лица; **~ of mind** склад ума/мыслей. **5.** (*squint*) косоглазие.
v.t. **1.** (*throw*) бр|осать, -осить; кидать, кинуть; **the snake ~s its skin** змея меняет кожу; **his horse ~ a shoe** его лошадь потеряла подкову; **the cow ~ its calf** корова выкинула/скинула телёнка. **2.** (*fig.*): **~ a vote** проголосовать (*pf.*); отдать (*pf.*) голос; **~ lots** тянуть/бросать/кидать (*all impf.*) жребий; **~ doubt on** подв|ергать, -ергнуть сомнению; **~ a gloom on the proceedings** омрач|ать, -ить происходящее; **~ an eye on, over** бросить (*pf.*) взгляд на+*a.*; окинуть (*pf.*) взглядом; **~ in one's lot with** связ|ывать, -ать свою судьбу с+*i.*; **~ a spell (up)on** околдов|ывать, -ать; **~ing vote** решающий голос. **3.** (*pour*, *form in a mould*) отл|ивать, -ить; **~ iron** чугун. **4.** (*calculate*) подсчит|ывать, -ать; **~ (up) a column of figures** сложить (*pf.*) числа столбиком; **~ a horoscope** составить (*pf.*) гороскоп. **5.** (*theatr.*): **~ a play** распредел|ять, -ить роли в пьесе; **he was ~ for the part of Hamlet** ему была поручена роль Гамлета.
with advs.: **~ about** *v.i.*: **~ about for** разыскивать, отыскивать (*both impf.*); **~ away** *v.t.* (*reject*) отбр|асывать, -осить; **he was ~ away on a desert island** он был выброшен на необитаемый остров; **~ down** *v.t.* (*depress*) угнетать (*impf.*); подав|лять, -ить; **~ off** *v.t.* (*abandon*) бр|осать, -осить; сбр|асывать, -осить; *v.i.* (*naut.*) отвал|ивать, -ить; **~ out** *v.t.* выгонять, выгнать; изг|онять, -нать.
cpds. **~away** *n. & adj.* потерпевший кораблекрушение; **~-iron** *adj.* чугунный; (*fig.*) стальной, железный; несгибаемый, непреклонный; **~-off** *n. & adj.*: **~-off clothing** обноск|и (*pl.*, *g.* -ов), старьё.
castanets [ˌkæstə'nets] *n.* кастаньеты (*f. pl.*).
caste [kɑːst] *n.* каста; **lose ~** (*fig.*) утра|чивать, -тить положение в обществе.
castellan ['kæstələn] *n.* кастелян.
castellated ['kæstəˌleɪtɪd] *adj.* (*battlemented*) зубчатый; зазубренный.
caster ['kɑːstə(r)] = **castor**[1]
castigate ['kæstɪˌgeɪt] *v.t.* наказ|ывать, -ать; бичевать (*impf.*).
castigation [ˌkæstɪ'geɪʃ(ə)n] *n.* наказание; бичевание.
castigator ['kæstɪˌgeɪtə(r)] *n.* бичеватель (*m.*), обличитель (*m.*).
Castilian [kə'stɪlɪən] *n.* (*language*) кастильский язык; литературный язык Испании.
adj. кастильский.

casting [ˈkɑːstɪŋ] *n.* **1.** (*tech.*): (*process*) литьё, отли́вка; (*product*) отли́вка. **2.** (*theatr.*) распределе́ние роле́й.

castle [ˈkɑːs(ə)l] *n.* за́мок; **~s in Spain** возду́шные за́мки; (*at chess*) ладья́, тура́.

v.i. (*at chess*) рокирова́ться (*impf., pf.*); **castling on king's/queen's side** коро́ткая/дли́нная рокиро́вка.

cast|or¹, -er [ˈkɑːstə(r)] *n.* **1.** (*wheel on furniture*) ро́лик. **2.:** **~ sugar** са́харный песо́к.

castor² [ˈkɑːstə(r)] *n.:* **~ oil** касто́ровое ма́сло, касто́рка.

castrate [kæˈstreɪt] *v.t.* кастри́ровать (*impf., pf.*).

castration [kæˈstreɪʃ(ə)n] *n.* кастра́ция.

castrato [kæˈstrɑːtəʊ] *n.* кастра́т.

casual [ˈkæʒʊəl, -zjʊəl] *adj.* **1.** (*chance, occasional*) случа́йный; **a ~ meeting** случа́йная встре́ча; **~ labourer** рабо́чий, живу́щий на случа́йные за́работки. **2.** (*careless*) небре́жный, беспе́чный; (*familiar*) развя́зный; **clothes for ~ wear** простая́/бу́дничная оде́жда. **3.** (*freelance*) внешта́тный.

casualness [ˈkæʒʊəlnɪs, -zjʊəlnɪs] *n.* случа́йность; небре́жность, беспе́чность, развя́зность.

casualty [ˈkæʒʊəltɪ, ˈkæzjʊ-] *n.* **1.** (*accident*) несча́стный слу́чай. **2.** (*pers.*) пострада́вший от несча́стного слу́чая; (*mil.*) ра́неный, уби́тый; **the tank became a ~** танк был вы́веден из стро́я; **~ clearing station** эвакуацио́нная ста́нция; **~ list** спи́сок уби́тых и ра́неных; **~ ward** пала́та ско́рой по́мощи.

casuarina [ˌkæsjʊˈriːnə] *n.* казуари́на.

casuist [ˈkæʒjuːɪst, ˈkæʒʊɪst] *n.* казуи́ст.

casuistic(al) [kæʒjuːˈɪstɪk(ə)l, kæʒʊˈɪstɪk(ə)l] *adj.* казуисти́ческий.

casuistry [ˈkæzjʊɪstrɪ] *n.* казуи́стика.

casus belli [ˌkɑːzəs ˈbelɪ, ˌkeɪsəs] *n.* ка́зус бе́лли, по́вод к войне́.

cat [kæt] *n.* **1.** ко́шка; **tom ~** кот; **wild ~** ди́кая ко́шка; (*pl., felines*) коша́чьи (*pl., g.* -х), ко́шки (*f. pl.*). **2.** (*fig., spiteful woman*) ехи́дная же́нщина. **3.:** **~ o'nine tails** ко́шка. **4.** (*idioms and provs.*): **let the ~ out of the bag** проб|а́лтываться, -олта́ться; выба́лтывать, вы́болтать секре́т; **lead a ~-and-dog life** жить (*impf.*) как ко́шка с соба́кой; **see which way the ~ jumps** выжида́ть (*impf.*), куда́ ве́тер поду́ет; **bell the ~** поста́вить (*pf.*) себя́ под уда́р; **there's not room to swing a ~** поверну́ться не́где; **it's raining ~s and dogs** дождь льёт как из ведра́; **a ~ may look at a king** смотре́ть ни на кого́ не возбраня́ется; за просмо́тр де́нег не беру́т; **like a ~ on hot bricks** как на у́гольях/иго́лках; **there are more ways than one to kill a ~** свет не кли́ном сошёлся; **it's enough to make a ~ laugh** э́то ку́рам на́ смех; **when the ~'s away the mice will play** без кота́ мыша́м раздо́лье; **grin like a Cheshire ~** ухмыл|я́ться, -ьну́ться во весь рот; **curiosity killed the ~** любопы́тство до добра́ не дово́дит; **~'s pyjamas, whiskers** (*sl.*) что на́до; пе́рвый сорт.

cpds. **~call** *n.* осви́стывание; **~-fancier** *n.* коша́тник, люби́тель ко́шек; **~fish** *n.* со́мик; **~-like** *adj.* коша́чий; **with ~-like tread** неслы́шной по́ступью; **~mint, ~nip** *nn.* кото́вник; коша́чья мя́та; **~-nap** *v.i.* вздремну́ть (*pf.*); **~'s-eye** *n.* (*gem*) коша́чий глаз; (*reflector*) катафо́т; **~'s-paw** *n.* (*dupe*) ору́дие в чужи́х рука́х; (*breeze*) лёгкий бриз; **~-suit** *n.* «ко́шечка» (комбинезо́н в обтя́жку); **~walk** *n.* рабо́чие мостки́ (*pl., g.* -о́в); (*in fashion-house*) помо́ст, «язы́к».

catachresis [ˌkætəˈkriːsɪs] *n.* катахре́за.

cataclysm [ˈkætəˌklɪz(ə)m] *n.* катакли́зм.

cataclysmic [ˌkætəˈklɪzmɪk] *adj.* катастрофи́ческий.

catacomb [ˈkætəˌkuːm, -ˌkəʊm] *n.* катако́мба.

catafalque [ˈkætəˌfælk] *n.* катафа́лк.

Catalan [ˈkætəlæn] *n.* (*pers.*) катало́н|ец (*fem.* -ка); (*language*) катала́нский язы́к.

adj. катало́нский; (*of language*) катала́нский.

catalepsy [ˈkætəˌlepsɪ] *n.* катале́псия.

cataleptic [ˌkætəˈleptɪk] *adj.* каталепти́ческий.

catalogue [ˈkætəˌlɒg] (*US* **catalog**) *n.* катало́г.

v.t. каталогизи́ровать (*impf., pf.*); включ|а́ть, -и́ть в катало́г.

cataloguer [ˈkætəˌlɒgə(r)] *n.* каталогиза́тор, составит́ель (*fem.* -ница) катало́га.

Catalonia [ˌkætəˈləʊnɪə] *n.* Катало́ния.

catalpa [kəˈtælpə] *n.* ката́льпа.

catalysis [kəˈtælɪsɪs] *n.* ката́лиз.

catalyst [ˈkætəlɪst] *n.* катализа́тор.

catalytic [ˌkætəˈlɪtɪk] *adj.* каталити́ческий; **~ converter** каталити́ческий нейтрализа́тор.

catamaran [ˌkætəməˈræn] *n.* катамара́н.

catamite [ˈkætəˌmaɪt] *n.* ма́льчик-педера́ст.

cataplasm [ˈkætəˌplæz(ə)m] *n.* припа́рка.

catapult [ˈkætəˌpʌlt] *n.* (*toy*) рога́тка; (*hist., aeron.*) катапу́льта; **~ take-off** взлёт/старт с по́мощью катапу́льты; **~ seat** катапульти́руемое сиде́нье.

v.t. выбра́сывать, вы́бросить катапу́льтой; катапульти́ровать (*impf., pf.*).

cataract [ˈkætəˌrækt] *n.* (*waterfall*) водопа́д; (*downpour*) ли́вень (*m.*); (*med.*) катара́кта.

catarrh [kəˈtɑː(r)] *n.* ката́р.

catastrophe [kəˈtæstrəfɪ] *n.* катастро́фа; **natural ~** стихи́йное бе́дствие.

catastrophic [ˌkætəˈstrɒfɪk] *adj.* катастрофи́ческий.

catch [kætʃ] *n.* **1.** (*act of catching*) пои́мка, захва́т; **play ~** игра́ть (*impf.*) в са́лки. **2.** (*amount caught*) уло́в, добы́ча. **3.** (*prize*): **she is a good ~ for somebody** она́ зама́нчивая па́ртия для кого́-то; **no ~** (*coll.*) не велика́ пожи́ва. **4.** (*trap*) уло́вка, лову́шка; **there must be a ~ in it** здесь, должно́ быть, кро́ется подво́х; **a ~ question** ка́верзный вопро́с. **5.** (*device for fastening etc.*) щеко́лда, защёлка, шпингале́т. **6.** (*mus.*) ро́ндо.

v.t. & i. **1.** (*seize*) лови́ть, пойма́ть; хвата́ть, схвати́ть; **he caught the ball** он пойма́л мяч; **~ a fish** пойма́ть (*pf.*) ры́бу; **~ a fly** пойма́ть (*pf.*) му́ху; **~ a fugitive** пойма́ть (*pf.*) беглеца́; **she caught hold of him** она́ схвати́ла его́; **~ at** хвата́ться, схвати́ться за+*a.*; **a dying man will ~ at a straw** умира́ющий за соло́минку хвата́ется. **2.** (*of entanglement, fastening etc.*): **her dress caught on a nail; the nail caught her dress** она́ зацепи́лась пла́тьем за гвоздь; **I caught my finger in the door** я прищеми́л себе́ па́лец две́рью; **the door doesn't ~** дверь не запира́ется; **the car was caught between two trams** автомоби́ль оказа́лся зажа́тым ме́жду двумя́ трамва́ями; **he caught his foot** у него́ застря́ла нога́. **3.** (*intercept, detect*): **I caught him stealing** я заста́л его́, когда́ он крал; **I caught him as he was leaving the house** я заста́л/захвати́л его́ как раз, когда́ он выходи́л и́з дому; **I was caught by the rain** меня́ захвати́ло дождём; **~ me trying to help you again!** ду́дки! бо́льше не бу́ду вам помога́ть; **we were caught in the storm** нас засти́гла бу́ря. **4.** (*be in time for*): **~ a train** поспе́ть (*pf.*) к по́езду; **he caught the post** он успе́л отпра́вить письмо́ с э́той по́чтой. **5.** (*fig.*) пойма́ть, улови́ть, схвати́ть (*all pf.*); **~ s.o.'s words** рассль́ышать (*pf.*) чьи-н. слова́; **I didn't ~ what you said** я прослу́шал, что вы сказа́ли; **~ s.o.'s meaning** улови́ть (*pf.*) чью-н. мысль; **~ a likeness** улови́ть (*pf.*) схо́дство; **~ one's breath** затаи́ть (*pf.*) дыха́ние; **~ s.o.'s eye** привле́чь (*pf.*) чьё-н. внима́ние; **~ fire, alight** загоре́ться (*pf.*); **~ a glimpse of** уви́деть (*pf.*) ме́льком; **~ hold of** схвати́ть, улови́ть (*both pf.*). **6.** (*be hit by*): **he caught it on the forehead** он получи́л уда́р в лоб (*or* по лбу); **this side of the house ~es the east wind** восто́чный ве́тер ду́ет в дом пря́мо с э́то стороны́; (*of punishment*): **you'll ~ it!** тебе́ доста́нется/попадёт. **7.** (*be infected by; lit., fig.*) схвати́ть, получи́ть (*both pf.*); **he caught a fever** он схвати́л лихора́дку; **~ cold** простуди́ться (*pf.*); **he was caught with the general enthusiasm** его́ захвати́л/увлёк о́бщий энтузиа́зм.

with advs.: **~ on** *v.i.*: **the fashion did not ~ on** э́та мо́да не приви́лась; **I don't ~ on** (*coll.*) я не понима́ю; я не схва́тываю; **~ out** *v.t.*: **he was caught out in a mistake** его́ пойма́ли на оши́бке; **~ up** *v.t. & i.* (*pick up quickly*) подхва́т|ывать, -и́ть; **he caught the others up; he caught up with the others** он догна́л остальны́х; **I must ~ up on my work** я запусти́л рабо́ту — тепе́рь на́до нагоня́ть; **this paper got caught up with the others** э́та бума́га затеря́лась среди́ остальны́х; **the police caught up with, on him** поли́ция насти́гла его́.

cpds. **~-all** *n.* вмести́лище; **a ~-all expression** всеобъе́млющая формулиро́вка; **~penny** *adj.* показно́й; рассчи́танный на дешёвый успе́х; **~-phrase, ~word** *nn.* мо́дное слове́чко.

catching [ˈkætʃɪŋ] *adj.* (*of disease*) зара́зный, зарази́тельный, прили́пчивый.

catchment [ˈkætʃmənt] *n.*: **~ area, basin** бассе́йн реки́; водосбо́рная пло́щадь; микрорайо́н, обслу́живаемый шко́лой *и т.п.*

catchy [ˈkætʃɪ] *adj.* привлека́тельный, притяга́тельный; (*of tune etc.*) легко́ запомина́ющийся, прили́пчивый.

catechetic(al) [ˌkætɪˈketɪk(ə)l] *adj.* катехизи́ческий.

catechism [ˈkætɪˌkɪz(ə)m] *n.* катехи́зис.

catechist [ˈkætɪkɪst] *n.* законоучи́тель (*m.*).

catechize [ˈkætɪˌkaɪz] *v.t.* (*teach catechism to*) обуча́ть (*impf.*) катехи́зису; (*fig.*) допра́шивать (*impf.*).

catechumen [ˌkætɪˈkjuːmən] *n.* оглашённый.

categorical [ˌkætɪˈgɒrɪk(ə)l] *adj.* категори́ческий.

categorize [ˈkætɪgəˌraɪz] *v.t.* распредел|я́ть, -и́ть по катего́риям.

category [ˈkætɪgərɪ] *n.* катего́рия.

catenary [kəˈtiːnərɪ] *adj.* цепно́й.

cater [ˈkeɪtə(r)] *v.i.*: **~ for** пост|авля́ть, -а́вить прови́зию для+*g.*; (*fig.*) удовлетвор|я́ть, -и́ть (*кого* or *чьи-н. вкусы*); уго|жда́ть, -ди́ть (*кому*); **the ~ing trade** рестора́нное де́ло.

cater-cornered [ˈkætəˌkɔːnəd] (*US*) *adj.* диагона́льный.

caterer [ˈkeɪtərə(r)] *n.* поставщи́к прови́зии.

caterpillar [ˈkætəˌpɪlə(r)] *n.* (*zool., tech.*) гу́сеница; (*attr.*) гу́сеничный.

caterwaul [ˈkætəˌwɔːl] *n.* коша́чий конце́рт.

v.i. задава́ть (*impf.*) коша́чий конце́рт.

catgut [ˈkætgʌt] *n.* кетгу́т, кише́чная струна́.

catharsis [kəˈθɑːsɪs] *n.* (*med.*) очище́ние желу́дка; (*fig.*) ка́тарсис.

cathartic [kəˈθɑːtɪk] *adj.* (*med.*) слаби́тельный; (*fig.*) очища́ющий.

cathedral [kəˈθiːdr(ə)l] *n.* (кафедра́льный) собо́р.

Catherine [ˈkæθrɪn] *n.* (*hist.*) Екатери́на; **~ de' Medici** Екатери́на Ме́дичи.

Catherine wheel [ˈkæθrɪn] *n.* (*firework*) о́гненное колесо́; (*somersault*) кувырка́нье колесо́м; **turn ~s** кувырка́ться (*impf.*) колесо́м.

catheter [ˈkæθɪtə(r)] *n.* катéтер.

cathode [ˈkæθəʊd] *n.* като́д; **~ rays** като́дные лучи́; като́дное излуче́ние.

catholic [ˈkæθəlɪk, ˈkæθlɪk] *n.* като́л|ик (*fem.* -и́чка); **~ priest** католи́ческий свяще́нник; (*Polish*) ксёндз.

adj. (*relig.*) католи́ческий; **Roman ~** ри́мско-католи́ческий; (*liberal*): **a man of ~ tastes** челове́к широ́ких вку́сов.

Catholicism [kəˈθɒlɪˌsɪz(ə)m] *n.* католици́зм, католи́чество.

catholicity [ˌkæθəˈlɪsɪtɪ] *n.* (*liberality*) широта́ интере́сов.

Catholicize [kəˈθɒlɪˌsaɪz] *v.t.* обра|ща́ть, -ти́ть в католи́чество.

catkin [ˈkætkɪn] *n.* серёжка.

Cato [ˈkeɪtəʊ] *n.* Като́н.

catoptric [kəˈtɒptrɪk] *adj.* катоптри́ческий, отража́тельный.

catoptrics [kəˈtɒptrɪks] *n.* като́птрика.

cattiness [ˈkætɪnɪs] *n.* ехи́дность.

cattle [ˈkæt(ə)l] *n.* (*livestock*) скот, скоти́на; (*bovines*) кру́пный рога́тый скот; (*fig., pej.*) скот, скоти́на; **kittle ~** (*joc.*) капри́зные существа́.

cpds. **~-dealer** *n.* скотопромы́шленник; **~-pen** *n.* заго́н для скота́; **~-plague** *n.* чума́ рога́того скота́; **~-truck** *n.* ваго́н для перево́зки скота́.

cattleya [ˈkætlɪə] *n.* каттле́я.

catty [ˈkætɪ] *adj.* ехи́дный.

Caucasian [kɔːˈkeɪʒ(ə)n, -ˈkeɪzɪən] *n.* (*of Caucasus*) кавка́з|ец (*fem.* -ка); (*of white race*) челове́к бе́лой ра́сы.

adj. кавка́зский.

Caucasus [ˈkɔːkəsəs] *n.* Кавка́з.

caucus [ˈkɔːkəs] *n.* фракцио́нное совеща́ние.

caudal [ˈkɔːd(ə)l] *adj.* хвостови́дный, кауда́льный, хвостово́й.

caul [kɔːl] *n.* (*membrane*) во́дная оболо́чка плода́; соро́чка.

cauldron [ˈkɔːldrən] *n.* котёл.

cauliflower [ˈkɒlɪˌflaʊə(r)] *n.* цветна́я капу́ста; **~ ear** изуро́дованная ушна́я ра́ковина.

ca(u)lk [kɔːk] *v.t.* конопа́тить, за-.

causal [ˈkɔːz(ə)l] *adj.* казуа́льный, причи́нный.

causality [kɔːˈzælɪtɪ] *n.* казуа́льность, причи́нность; причи́нная связь.

causation [kɔːˈzeɪʃ(ə)n] *n.* причине́ние; причи́нность; причи́нная связь.

causative [ˈkɔːzətɪv] *adj.* (*gram.*) каузати́вный.

cause [kɔːz] *n.* **1.** (*that which ~s*) причи́на, по́вод. **2.** (*need*) причи́на, основа́ние; **there is no ~ for alarm** нет основа́ний/причи́н для беспоко́йства. **3.** (*purpose, objective*): **the workers' ~** де́ло трудя́щихся; рабо́чее де́ло; **make common ~ with s.o.** объедин|я́ться, -и́ться с кем-н. ра́ди о́бщего де́ла; **he pleaded his ~** он защища́л своё де́ло; **a lost ~** прои́гранное де́ло.

v.t. вызыва́ть, вы́звать; **~ a disturbance** произв|оди́ть, -ести́ беспоря́дки; **~ s.o. trouble** (*or* **a loss**) причин|я́ть, и́ть кому́-н. беспоко́йство/убы́тки; **what ~d the accident?** от чего́ произошёл несча́стный слу́чай?; **he ~d them to be put to death** он повеле́л уби́ть их.

cpd. **~-list** *n.* (*leg.*) спи́сок дел к слу́шанию.

cause célèbre [ˌkɔːz seˈlebr] *n.* гро́мкий/сканда́льный проце́сс.

causeless [ˈkɔːzlɪs] *adj.* беспричи́нный, необосно́ванный.

causerie [ˈkəʊzərɪ] *n.* непринуждённая бесе́да; (*article*) фельето́н.

causeway [ˈkɔːzweɪ] *n.* да́мба; гать; мощёная доро́га.

caustic [ˈkɔːstɪk] *adj.* каусти́ческий; **~ soda** е́дкий натр; (*fig.*) е́дкий, ко́лкий, язви́тельный.

cauter|ization [ˌkɔːtəraɪˈzeɪʃ(ə)n], **-y** [ˈkɔːtərɪ] *n.* прижига́ние.

cauterize [ˈkɔːtəˌraɪz] *v.t.* (*med.*) приж|ига́ть, -е́чь; (*fig.*) очерств|ля́ть, -и́ть.

caution [ˈkɔːʃ(ə)n] *n.* **1.** (*prudence*) осторо́жность; **with ~** осторо́жно, с осторо́жностью. **2.** (*warning*) предостереже́ние, предосторо́жность; **C~!** (*as notice*) Внима́ние!; Осторо́жно!; **he was let off with a ~** его́ отпусти́ли с предостереже́нием. **3.**: **~ money** зало́г.

v.t. предостер|ега́ть, -е́чь.

cautionary [ˈkɔːʃənərɪ] *adj.* предостерега́ющий; (*deterrent*) предупрежда́ющий.

cautious [ˈkɔːʃəs] *adj.* осторо́жный, осмотри́тельный.

cautiousness [ˈkɔːʃəsnɪs] *n.* осторо́жность, осмотри́тельность, предосторо́жность.

cavalcade [ˌkævəlˈkeɪd] *n.* кавалька́да.

cavalier [ˌkævəˈlɪə(r)] *n.* (*gallant; royalist*) кавале́р.

adj. бесцеремо́нный, надме́нный.

cavalry [ˈkævəlrɪ] *n.* кавале́рия, ко́нница; **two hundred ~** две́сти ко́нников; **a ~ charge** кавалери́йская ата́ка.

cpd. **~man** *n.* кавалери́ст.

cavatina [ˌkævəˈtiːnə] *n.* каватина.

cave[1] [keɪv] *n.* пеще́ра.

cpds. **~-dweller, ~-man** *nn.* (*lit., fig.*) пеще́рный челове́к, троглоди́т; **~-painting** *n.* пеще́рная жи́вопись.

cave[2] [keɪv] *v.i.*: **~ in** (*lit.*) прова́л|иваться, -и́ться; прода́в|ливаться, -и́ться; (*fig.*) сд|ава́ться, -а́ться.

cave[3] [ˈkeɪvɪ] *int.* чур!; (*look out!*) береги́сь!

caveat [ˈkævɪˌæt] *n.* предостереже́ние.

caver [ˈkeɪvə(r)] *n.* спелео́лог.

cavern [ˈkæv(ə)n] *n.* грот, пеще́ра.

cavernous [ˈkæv(ə)nəs] *adj.* пеще́ристый; (*of voice*) глубо́кий.

caviar(e) [ˈkævɪˌɑː(r), ˌkævɪˈɑː(r)] *n.* икра́.

cavil [ˈkævɪl] *n.* приди́рка.

v.i.: **~ at** прид|ира́ться, -ра́ться к+*d.*

caviller [ˈkævɪlə(r)] *n.* приди́ра (*c.g.*).

cavity [ˈkævɪtɪ] *n.* по́лость, впа́дина; (*in tooth*) дупло́.

cavort [kəˈvɔːt] *v.i.* скака́ть (*impf.*).

caw [kɔː] *n.* ка́рканье.

v.t. & i. ка́рк|ать -нуть.

cayenne [keɪˈen] *n.*: **~ pepper** кайе́нский пе́рец.

cayman [ˈkeɪmən] *n.* кайма́н.

CBE (*abbr. of* **Commander of the Order of the British Empire**) кавале́р о́рдена Брита́нской импе́рии.

CD (*abbr. of* **compact disk**) компа́кт-ди́ск; **~-player** прои́грыватель (*m.*) компа́кт-ди́сков.

CD-ROM (*abbr. of* ***compact disk — read-only memory***) компа́кт-ди́ск ПЗУ; ~ **player** проигрыва́тель компа́кт-ди́сков ПЗУ.

cease [si:s] *n.*: **without** ~ непреста́нно, не перестава́я.
v.t. прекра|ща́ть, -ти́ть; перест|ава́ть, -а́ть; ~ **talking** прекрати́ть (*pf.*) разгово́р; замолча́ть (*pf.*); ~ **fire/payment** прекрати́ть (*pf.*) ого́нь/платежи́.
v.i. прекра|ща́ться, -ти́ться.
cpd. ~**-fire** *n.* прекраще́ние огня́.

ceaseless ['si:slɪs] *adj.* непреста́нный, непреры́вный.

cedar ['si:də(r)] *n.* кедр; (*attr.*) кедро́вый; ~ **forest** кедро́вник.

cede [si:d] *v.t.* сда|ва́ть, -ать; уступ|а́ть, -и́ть.

cedilla [sɪ'dɪlə] *n.* седи́ль (*m.*).

ceiling ['si:lɪŋ] *n.* (*lit., fig.*) потоло́к; (*aeron.*) потоло́к, преде́льная высота́; (*fig.*) максима́льный у́ровень; ~ **price** максима́льная цена́; **hit the** ~ (*fig., fly into a rage*) рассвирепе́ть (*pf.*); на́ стену лезть (*impf.*); **he has reached his** ~ он дости́г своего́ потолка́.

celadon ['selə,dɒn] *n.* (*ware*) селадо́н.

celandine ['selən,daɪn] *n.* чистоте́л.

celebrant ['selɪbrənt] *n.* свяще́нник, отправля́ющий церко́вную слу́жбу.

celebrate ['selɪ,breɪt] *v.t. & i.* **1.** (*mark an occasion*) пра́здновать, от-. **2.** (*praise*) просл|авля́ть, -а́вить. **3.** (*relig.*) отпр|авля́ть, -а́вить (церко́вную слу́жбу). **4.** ~ **a marriage** соверш|а́ть, -и́ть обря́д бракосочета́ния.

celebrated ['selɪ,breɪtɪd] *adj.* просла́вленный, знамени́тый.

celebration [selɪ'breɪʃ(ə)n] *n.* пра́зднование, торжества́ (*nt. pl.*), прославле́ние; **this calls for a** ~ э́то сле́дует отпра́здновать/отме́тить; (*of marriage*) соверше́ние.

celebratory [selɪ'breɪtərɪ] *adj.* пра́здничный, торже́ственный.

celebrity [sɪ'lebrɪtɪ] *n.* (*fame*) знамени́тость, изве́стность; (*pers.*) знамени́тость.

celeriac [sɪ'lerɪ,æk] *n.* (корнево́й) сельдере́й.

celerity [sɪ'lerɪtɪ] *n.* быстрота́.

celery ['selərɪ] *n.* (листово́й) сельдере́й.

celestial [sɪ'lestɪəl] *adj.* (*astron., fig.*) небе́сный; ~ **globe** гло́бус звёздного не́ба.

celibacy ['selɪbəsɪ] *n.* целиба́т, безбра́чие.

celibate ['selɪbət] *n. & adj.* холостя́к, холосто́й; да́вший обе́т безбра́чия.

cell [sel] *n.* **1.** (*in prison*) ка́мера; **condemned** ~ ка́мера сме́ртников; **padded** ~ пала́та, оби́тая во́йлоком. **2.** (*in monastery*) ке́лья. **3.** (*of honeycomb*) ячея́, яче́йка. **4.** (*elec.*) элеме́нт. **5.** (*biol.*) кле́тка. **6.** (*pol.*) яче́йка.
cpd. ~**-mate** *n.* сока́мерник.

cellar ['selə(r)] *n.* по́греб, подва́л; **he keeps a good** ~ у него́ хоро́ший запа́с вин.

cellarage ['selərɪdʒ] *n.* (*space*) подва́лы (*m. pl.*); погреба́ (*m. pl.*); (*charge*) пла́та за хране́ние в подва́лах.

cellarer ['selərə(r)] *n.* ке́ларь (*m.*).

cellist ['tʃelɪst] *n.* виолончели́ст.

cello ['tʃeləʊ] *n.* виолонче́ль.

cellophane ['selə,feɪn] *n.* целлофа́н; (*attr.*) целлофа́новый.

cellular ['seljʊlə(r)] *adj.* кле́точный, яче́истый; ~ **tissue** (*anat.*) клетча́тка.

cellule ['selju:l] *n.* кле́точка.

celluloid ['seljʊ,lɔɪd] *n.* целлуло́ид; (*attr.*) целлуло́идный.

cellulose ['seljʊ,ləʊz, -,ləʊs] *n.* (*chem.*) целлюло́за; клетча́тка; (~ **nitrate**) нитра́т целлюло́зы, ни́троцеллюло́за.

C|elt (*also* **K-**) [kelt, selt] *n.* кельт.

C|eltic (*also* **K-**) ['keltɪk, 'seltɪk] *adj.* ке́льтский.

Celticist ['keltɪsɪst] *n.* кельто́лог, специали́ст по ке́льтской культу́ре.

cement [sɪ'ment] *n.* цеме́нт; (*attr.*) цеме́нтный.
v.t. цементи́ровать (*impf., pf.*); (*fig.*): ~ **relations** упро́ч|ивать, -ить отноше́ния; укреп|ля́ть, -и́ть свя́зи.
cpd. ~**-mixer** *n.* меша́лка для цеме́нтного раство́ра.

cemetery ['semɪtərɪ] *n.* кла́дбище.

cenotaph ['senə,tɑ:f] *n.* кенота́ф.

cense [sens] *v.t.* кади́ть (*impf.*) ла́даном.

censer ['sensə(r)] *n.* кади́ло, кури́льница.

censor ['sensə(r)] *n.* це́нзор.
v.t. цензурова́ть (*impf.*); подв|ерга́ть, -е́ргнуть цензу́ре.

censorial [sen'sɔ:rɪəl] *adj.* це́нзорский, цензу́рный.

censorious [sen'sɔ:rɪəs] *adj.* сверхкрити́ческий, приди́рчивый.

censoriousness [sen'sɔ:rɪəsnɪs] *n.* крити́чность, приди́рчивость.

censorship ['sensərʃɪp] *n.* цензу́ра.

censurable ['sensjərəb(ə)l] *adj.* предосуди́тельный, досто́йный порица́ния.

censure ['sensjə(r)] *n.* кри́тика, осужде́ние, порица́ние; **pass a vote of** ~ вы́нести (*pf.*) во́тум недове́рия.
v.t. критикова́ть (*impf.*); осу|жда́ть, -ди́ть; порица́ть (*impf.*).

census ['sensəs] *n.* пе́репись (населе́ния); **take a** ~ произв|оди́ть, -ести́ пе́репись (населе́ния); ~ **paper** бланк для пе́реписи.

cent [sent] *n.* **1.** (*coin*) цент; (*fig.*): **it is not worth a** ~ э́то гроша́ ло́маного не сто́ит. **2.**: **per** ~ проце́нт, на со́тню.

centaur ['sentɔ:(r)] *n.* кента́вр.

centenarian [,sentɪ'neərɪən] *n.* челове́к, дости́гший столе́тнего во́зраста.
adj. столе́тний.

centen|ary [sen'ti:nərɪ], **-nial** [sen'tenɪəl] *n.* (*100th anniversary*) столе́тие.
adj. (*100 years old; pert. to 100th anniversary*) столе́тний; (*happening every 100 years*) происходя́щий раз в сто лет.

centigrade ['sentɪ,greɪd] *adj.*: ~ **thermometer** термо́метр Це́льсия; **20°** ~ 20 гра́дусов Це́льсия (*or* по Це́льсию).

centigram(me) ['sentɪ,græm] *n.* сантигра́мм.

centilitre ['sentɪ,li:tə(r)] *n.* сантили́тр.

centime ['sɑ̃ti:m] *n.* санти́м.

centimetre ['sentɪ,mi:tə(r)] *n.* сантиме́тр.

centipede ['sentɪ,pi:d] *n.* многоно́жка.

cento ['sentəʊ] *n.* компиля́ция.

central ['sentr(ə)l] *adj.* **1.** (*pert. to a centre*) центра́льный; **C~ African Republic** Центральноафрика́нская респу́блика; **C~ America** Центра́льная Аме́рика; ~ **Asia** Сре́дняя А́зия; ~ **European** среднеевропе́йский; ~ **bank** центра́льный банк; **the house is very** ~ дом нахо́дится в са́мом це́нтре го́рода. **2.** (*principal*) центра́льный, гла́вный; ~ **catalogue** сво́дный катало́г; **the** ~ **figure in the story** гла́вный персона́ж расска́за.

centralism ['sentrə,lɪz(ə)m] *n.* централи́зм.

centralist ['sentrəlɪst] *n.* сторо́нник централи́зма.

centralization [,sentrəlaɪ'zeɪʃ(ə)n] *n.* централиза́ция.

centralize ['sentrə,laɪz] *v.t.* централизова́ть (*impf., pf.*).

centre ['sentə(r)] *n.* **1.** (*middle point or section*) центр; (*of a chocolate*) начи́нка; ~ **of gravity** центр тя́жести; **dead** ~ мёртвая то́чка. **2.** (*fig., key-point*): ~ **of attraction** центр внима́ния; ~ **of commerce** комме́рческий центр; **shopping** ~ торго́вый центр; **gardening** ~ (*shop*) «всё для садо́вника»; **cultural** ~ культу́рный центр. **3.** (*pol.*) центр. **4.** (*attr.*) центра́льный.
v.t. **1.** (*fix in central position*) поме|ща́ть, -сти́ть в це́нтре. **2.** (*fig.*) сосредото́чи|вать, -ть; концентри́ровать, с-; ~ **one's thoughts on** сосредото́чить (*pf.*) мы́сли на+*p.*
v.i. сосредото́чи|ваться, -ться; концентри́роваться, с-; **our thoughts** ~ **on** на́ши мы́сли сосредото́чены на (*чём*); **the discussion** ~**d round this point** диску́ссия сосредото́чилась вокру́г э́того вопро́са.
cpds. ~**-bit** *n.* центрово́е сверло́; ~**board** *n.* (*naut.*) выдвижно́й киль; ~**-forward** *n.* (*sport*) центр нападе́ния, центр-фо́рвард; ~**piece** *n.* орнамента́льная ва́за в середи́не стола́; (*fig.*) украше́ние (*коллекции*); ~**-right** *adj.* (*pol.*) правоцентри́стский.

centrifugal [,sentrɪ'fju:g(ə)l, sen'trɪfjʊg(ə)l] *adj.* центробе́жный.

centrifuge ['sentrɪ,fju:dʒ] *n.* центрифу́га.

centripetal [sen'trɪpɪt(ə)l] *adj.* центростреми́тельный.

centrism ['sentrɪz(ə)m] *n.* центри́зм.

centrist ['sentrɪst] *n.* центри́ст.

centuple ['sentjʊp(ə)l] *n.* стокра́тный разме́р.
adj. стокра́тный.

centurion [sen'tjʊərɪən] *n.* центурио́н.

century ['sentʃərɪ, -tjʊrɪ] *n.* (*100 years*) столе́тие, век; ~ **plant** столе́тник; (*set of 100*) со́тня.

cephalic [sɪ'fælɪk, ke-] *adj.* головно́й.

cephalopod ['sefələ,pɒd] *n.* головоно́гий моллю́ск.
ceramic [sɪ'ræmɪk, kɪ-] *adj.* керами́ческий, гонча́рный.
ceramics [sɪ'ræmɪks, kɪ-] *n.* кера́мика; гонча́рное произво́дство.
cereal ['sɪərɪəl] *n.* хле́бный злак; (*breakfast*) ~ корнфле́кс, геркуле́с *и т.п.*
adj. хле́бный, зерново́й.
cerebellum [,serɪ'beləm] *n.* мозжечо́к.
cerebral ['serɪbr(ə)l] *adj.* **1.** (*of the brain*) мозгово́й, церебра́льный; ~ **haemorrhage** кровоизлия́ние в мозг. **2.** (*intellectual*) умозри́тельный, интеллектуа́льный; **he is a ~ person** он живёт рассу́дком. **3.** (*phon.*) церебра́льный.
cerebration [,serɪ'breɪʃ(ə)n] *n.* мозгова́я де́ятельность; **unconscious ~** подсозна́тельная рабо́та мо́зга.
cerebro-spinal [,serɪbrəʊ'spaɪn(ə)l] *adj.* цереброспина́льный.
cerebrum ['serɪbrəm] *n.* головно́й мозг.
cerecloth ['sɪəklɒθ] *n.* са́ван.
ceremonial [,serɪ'məʊnɪəl] *n.* (*relig. rites*) церемониа́л, обря́д, ритуа́л.
adj. церемониа́льный, обря́довый; ~ **dress** пара́дная фо́рма оде́жды.
ceremonious [,serɪ'məʊnɪəs] *adj.* церемо́нный.
ceremoniousness [,serɪ'məʊnɪəsnɪs] *n.* церемо́нность.
ceremony ['serɪmənɪ] *n.* (*rite*) обря́д, церемо́ния; **wedding ~** венча́ние; обря́д венча́ния; (*formal behaviour*) церемо́нность, церемо́ния; **stand (up)on ~** церемо́ниться (*impf.*); наст|а́ивать, -оя́ть на соблюде́нии форма́льностей; **without ~** без церемо́ний.
Ceres ['sɪəri:z] *n.* Цере́ра.
cerise [sə'ri:z, -'ri:s] *adj.* све́тло-кра́сный.
cert [sɜ:t] *n.* (*sl.*): **a (dead) ~** де́ло ве́рное.
certain ['sɜ:t(ə)n, -tɪn] *adj.* **1.** (*undoubted*) несомне́нный; **I cannot say for ~** я не могу́ сказа́ть наверняка́; **make ~ of** (*ascertain*) удостов|еря́ться, -е́риться в чём-н.; (*ensure possession of*) обеспе́чи|вать, -ть; **he faced ~ death** ему́ угрожа́ла ве́рная смерть; **he has no ~ abode** у него́ нет определённого приста́нища; **he is ~ to succeed** он наверняка́/несомне́нно преуспе́ет. **2.** (*confident*) уве́ренный; **he is ~ of success** он уве́рен в успе́хе; **I am ~ he will come** я уве́рен, что он придёт. **3.** (*definite but unspecified*) изве́стный, не́который; оди́н; **a ~ person** не́кто, не́кое лицо́; **in a ~ town** в одно́м го́роде; **a ~ Mr. Jones** не́кий г. Джо́унс; **a ~ type of people** лю́ди изве́стного ро́да; **under ~ conditions** при изве́стных усло́виях; **a lady of a ~ age** да́ма не пе́рвой мо́лодости; **a ~** (*some*) **pleasure** не́которое удово́льствие.
certainly ['sɜ:tənlɪ, -tɪnlɪ] *adv.* (*without doubt*) несомне́нно, наверняка́, наве́рно; (*expr. obedience or consent*) коне́чно, безусло́вно; **'May we go?' — '~ not!'** «Мо́жно нам идти́?» — «Ни в ко́ем слу́чае!».
certainty ['sɜ:təntɪ, -tɪntɪ] *n.* **1.** (*being certainly true*) несомне́нность. **2.** (*certain fact*) несомне́нный факт; **for a ~** наверняка́. **3.** (*confidence*) уве́ренность. **4.** (*accuracy*): **I cannot say with ~** не могу́ определённо сказа́ть; **scientific ~** нау́чная достове́рность.
certifiable [,sɜ:tɪ'faɪəb(ə)l, 'sɜ:t-] *adj.* (*lunatic*) душевнобольно́й.
certificate [sə'tɪfɪkət] *n.* удостовере́ние, свиде́тельство, сертифика́т; ~ **of health** медици́нское свиде́тельство; **birth ~** свиде́тельство о рожде́нии, ме́трика; **marriage ~** свиде́тельство о бра́ке.
v.t.: **a ~d teacher** учи́тель (*m.*) с дипло́мом.
certification [,sɜ:tɪfɪ'keɪʃ(ə)n] *n.* удостовере́ние; вы́дача свиде́тельства.
certify ['sɜ:tɪ,faɪ] *v.t.* **1.** (*attest*) удостов|еря́ть, -е́рить; зав|еря́ть, -е́рить; **this is to ~ that ...** настоя́щим удостоверя́ется, что... **2.** (*of lunatic*) свиде́тельствовать, за- душе́вное заболева́ние +*g.*
certitude ['sɜ:tɪ,tju:d] *n.* уве́ренность; несомне́нность.
cerulean [sə'ru:lɪən] *adj.* небе́сно-голубо́й.
cerumen [sə'ru:men] *n.* ушна́я се́ра.
ceruse ['sɪəru:s, sɪ'ru:s] *n.* бели́л|а (*pl., g.* —).
Cervantes [sə'vænti:z] *n.* Серва́нтес.
cervical [sɜ:'vaɪk(ə)l, 'sɜ:vɪk(ə)l] *adj.* ше́йный; ~ **smear** мазо́к ше́йки ма́тки.
cervix ['sɜ:vɪks] *n.* ше́я; (*of womb*) ше́йка (ма́тки).
Cesarean [sɪ'zeərɪən] (*US*) = **Caesarean**
cess [ses] *n.* (*dial.*): **bad ~ to him!** чтоб ему́ пу́сто бы́ло!
cessation [se'seɪʃ(ə)n] *n.* прекраще́ние, остано́вка; ~ **of hostilities** прекраще́ние вое́нных де́йствий.
cession ['seʃ(ə)n] *n.* усту́пка, переда́ча.
cess|pit ['sespɪt], **-pool** ['sespu:l] *nn.* выгребна́я/помо́йная/ сто́чная я́ма; (*fig.*) помо́йная я́ма, клоа́ка.
cetacean [sɪ'teɪʃ(ə)n] *n.* живо́тное из семе́йства кито́вых.
ceteris paribus [,setərɪs 'pærɪ,bʊs] *adv.* при про́чих ра́вных усло́виях.
Ceylon [sɪ'lɒn] *n.* Цейло́н.
Ceylonese [,selə'ni:z] *n.* (*pers.*) цейло́н|ец (*fem.* -ка).
adj. цейло́нский.
CFCs (*abbr. of* ***chloro-fluorocarbons***) хлори́рованные фторуглеро́ды.
cha-cha ['tʃɑ:tʃɑ:] *n.* ча-ча-ча́ (*nt. indecl.*).
chafe [tʃeɪf] *n.* (*~d place*) сса́дина, раздраже́ние; (*fig., irritation*) раздраже́ние.
v.t. (*rub*) тере́ть (*impf.*); (*make sore*) нат|ира́ть, -ере́ть; **the collar ~d his neck** воротни́к натёр ему́ ше́ю.
v.i. нат|ира́ться, -ере́ться; **her skin ~s easily** у неё ко́жа легко́ воспаля́ется; **he ~d at the delay** отсро́чка раздража́ла его́.
chaff [tʃɑ:f] *n.* **1.** (*husks*) мяки́на; (*fig.*): **an old bird is not caught with ~** ста́рого воробья́ на мяки́не не проведёшь. **2.** (*banter*) подшу́чивание.
v.t. подшу́|чивать, -ти́ть над+*i.*; подтру́н|ивать, -и́ть над+*i.*
cpd. **~-cutter** *n.* соломоре́зка.
chaffer ['tʃæfə(r)] *v.t.* торгова́ться (*impf.*).
chaffinch ['tʃæfɪntʃ] *n.* зя́блик.
chafing-dish ['tʃeɪfɪŋ] *n.* жаро́вня.
chagrin ['ʃægrɪn, ʃə'gri:n] *n.* огорче́ние, доса́да.
v.t. огорч|а́ть, -и́ть.
chain [tʃeɪn] *n.* цепь; цепо́чка; (*surveyor's*) межева́я/ ме́рная цепь; **mountain ~** го́рная цепь; (*pl., fetters*) це́пи (*f. pl.*), око́в|ы (*pl., g.* —); (*fig.*): **~ of events, consequences** цепь собы́тий/после́дствий; **a ~ is as strong as its weakest link** (*prov.*) где то́нок, там и рвётся; **~ reaction** цепна́я реа́кция.
v.t. прико́в|ывать, -а́ть це́пью; скреп|ля́ть, -и́ть це́пью; **the dog is ~ed up** соба́ка поса́жена на цепь.
cpds. **~-armour, ~-mail** *nn.* кольчу́га; **~-bridge** *n.* цепно́й мост; **~-gang** *n.* гру́ппа каторжа́н, ско́ванных о́бщей це́пью; **~-letter** *n.* письмо́, рассыла́емое по цепо́чке; **~-mail** *n.* = **~-armour**; **~-shot** *n.* цепны́е я́дра; **~-smoke** *v.t.* (непреры́вно) заку́ривать (*impf.*) одну́ папиро́су от друго́й; **~-smoker** *n.* зая́длый кури́льщик, табакома́н; **~-stitch** *n.* та́мбурная стро́чка; **~-store** *n.* однοти́пный фи́рменный магази́н.
chair [tʃeə(r)] *n.* **1.** стул; **take a ~!** сади́тесь! **2.** (*~manship*) председа́тельство; **Mr. X took/left the ~** г-н X за́нял/ поки́нул председа́тельское ме́сто. **3.** (*~man*) председа́тель (*m.*); **Madam C~man!** госпожа́ председа́тель! **4.** (*professorship*) ка́федра; **he holds the ~ of physics** он заве́дует ка́федрой фи́зики.
v.t. **1.** (*preside over*) председа́тельствовать (*impf.*) на+*p.* **2.** (*carry triumphantly*) торже́ственно нести́ (*det.*) (победи́теля *и т.п.*).
cpds. **~lift** *n.* подвесно́й подъёмник; **~man, ~-person** *nn.* = **chair 3.**; **~manship** *n.* председа́тельство; обя́занности (*f. pl.*) председа́теля.
chaise longue [ʃeɪz 'lɒŋg] *n.* шезло́нг.
chalcedony [kæl'sedənɪ] *n.* халцедо́н.
Chaldean [kæl'di:ən] *adj.* халде́йский.
chalet ['ʃæleɪ] *n.* шале́ (*indecl.*).
chalice ['tʃælɪs] *n.* (*goblet*) ку́бок, ча́ша; (*eccl.*) поти́р; (*bot.*) ча́шечка.
chalk [tʃɔ:k] *n.* **1.** (*material*) мел; (*attr.*) мелово́й. **2.** (*piece of ~*) мел, мело́к. **3.** (*fig.*): **not by a long ~** отню́дь нет; далеко́ не; **as different as ~ from cheese** похо́же, как гвоздь на панихи́ду.
v.t. (*write or mark with ~*) писа́ть, на- (*or* отм|еча́ть, -е́тить) ме́лом; (*whiten with ~*) бели́ть, по-; **~ out** (*sketch*)

набр|áсывать, -осáть; ~ **up** (*register*) отм|ечáть, -éтить.
cpds. **~-pit, ~-quarry** *nn.* меловóй карьéр.

chalky ['tʃɔ:kɪ] *adj.* (*like chalk*) меловóй; (*containing chalk*) известкóвый.

challenge ['tʃælɪndʒ] *n.* (*to a race etc.*) вы́зов; ~ **cup** переходя́щий кýбок; (*sentry's*) óклик; (*fig.*): **this task was a ~ to his ingenuity** э́та задáча потрéбовала от негó большóй изобретáтельности.
v.t. вызывáть, вы́звать; (*dispute*) оспáривать (*impf.*); ~ **a juryman** отв|оди́ть, -ести́ присяжного; ~ **s.o. to a race/duel** вызывáть, вы́звать когó-н. на состязáние/дуэ́ль; **I ~ you to deny it** попрóбуйте опровéргнуть э́то; **he ~d my right to attend** он возражáл прóтив моегó присýтствия.

challenger ['tʃælɪndʒə(r)] *n.* посылáющий вы́зов; претендéнт.

challenging ['tʃælɪndʒɪŋ] *adv.* (*of opportunity etc.*) трýдный, но интерéсный.

chalybeate [kə'lɪbɪət] *adj.* желéзистый.

chamber ['tʃeɪmbə(r)] *n.* **1.** (*room*) кóмната; (*pl., apartment*) квартúра; (*office*) адвокáтская контóра; кáмера, кабинéт судьи́; ~ **of horrors** зал ýжасов; **bridal** ~ спáльня новобрáчных; ~ **music** кáмерная мýзыка. **2.** (*hall, e.g. of parliament*) зал, зáла. **3.** (*official body*) палáта; **C~ of Commerce** торгóвая палáта; ~ **of deputies** палáта депутáтов. **4.** (*of revolver*) патрóнник. **5.** (~-*pot*) ночнóй горшóк.
cpd. **~maid** *n.* гóрничная.

chamberlain ['tʃeɪmbəlɪn] *n.* мажордóм, камергéр.

chameleon [kə'mi:lɪən] *n.* (*lit., fig.*) хамелеóн.

chamfer ['tʃæmfə(r)] *n.* жёлоб, вы́емка.
v.t. стёс|ывать, -áть óстрые углы́; вынимáть, вы́нуть пазы́.

chammy ['ʃæmɪ] (*US*) = **shammy**

chamois ['ʃæmwɑ:, *sense* **2.** 'ʃæmɪ] *n.* **1.** (*zool.*) сéрна. **2.** (~-*leather*) зáмша.

champ[1] [tʃæmp] *n.* (*chewing action or noise*) чáвканье.
v.t. & i. (*chew noisily*) чáвкать (*impf.*); (*bite on*): ~ **the bit** грызть (*impf.*) удилá; (*fig.*): **he was ~ing to start** он рвáлся в путь.

champ[2] [tʃæmp] (*coll.*) = **champion 2.**

champagne [ʃæm'peɪn] *n.* шампáнское.

champion ['tʃæmpɪən] *n.* **1.** (*defender*) побóрни|к, защи́тни|к (*fem.* -ца); борéц; **a ~ of women's rights** побóрник жéнского равноправия. **2.** (*prize-winning pers. or thg.*) чемпиóн (*fem., coll.* -ка); **a ~ chess-player** чемпиóн по шáхматам.

championship ['tʃæmpɪənʃɪp] *n.* (*advocacy*) защи́та; (*sport*) чемпиóнство, чемпионáт, пéрвенство.

champlevé [,ʃɑ̃lə'veɪ] *n.*: ~ **enamel** вы́емчатая эмáль.

chance [tʃɑ:ns] *n.* **1.** (*casual occurrence*) слýчай, случáйность; **by ~** случáйно; **he left it to ~** он остáвил э́то на вóлю слýчая; **game of ~** азáртная игрá. **2.** (*possibility, likelihood, opportunity*) шанс, возмóжность; **I went there on the ~ of seeing him** я пошёл тудá, надéясь уви́деть егó; **I will take my ~ of going to prison** я готóв (рáди э́того) пойти́ в тюрьмý; **the ~s are that he will come** все шáнсы за то, что он придёт; **I had no ~ of winning** у меня́ нé было никаки́х шáнсов на успéх; **he stands a good ~ of winning** он имéет все шáнсы на успéх; **now is your ~** вот ваш шанс; дéло за вáми; **the ~ of a lifetime** раз в жи́зни представи́вшийся слýчай; **he has an eye to the main ~** он стреми́тся к нажи́ве/обогащéнию; **a fat ~ he has!** кудá уж емý (*coll.*); **he hasn't a dog's ~** у негó нет никаки́х шáнсов; **a ~ companion** случáйный попýтчик/спýтник; **a ~ comer** случáйный посети́тель.
v.t.: **let's ~ it** рискнём!; ~ **one's arm** (*coll.*) пытáть, по-счáстья.
v.i. (*happen*) случ|áться, -и́ться; **I ~d to see him** мне довелóсь уви́деть егó; **he ~d upon the book** емý попáлась э́та кни́га.

chancel ['tʃɑ:ns(ə)l] *n.* алтáрь (*m.*).

chancellery ['tʃɑ:nsələrɪ] *n.* канцеля́рия.

chancellor ['tʃɑ:nsələ(r)] *n.* кáнцлер; **C~ of the Exchequer** кáнцлер казначéйства, министр финáнсов; (*of university*) рéктор, кáнцлер.

chancellorship ['tʃɑ:nsələr,ʃɪp] *n.* звáние кáнцлера, кáнцлерство.

chancery ['tʃɑ:nsərɪ] *n.* **1.** (*leg.*) кáнцлерский суд; **in ~** (*fig.*) в тискáх. **2.** (*of embassy*) канцеля́рия.

chancre ['ʃæŋkə(r)] *n.* твёрдый шанкр.

chancy ['tʃɑ:nsɪ] *adj.* (*coll.*) рискóванный.

chandelier [,ʃændɪ'lɪə(r)] *n.* канделя́бр, люстра.

chandler ['tʃɑ:ndlə(r)] *n.* москатéльщик.

change [tʃeɪndʒ] *n.* **1.** (*alteration*) изменéние; (*substitution*) перемéна; ~ **of air, scene** перемéна обстанóвки; ~ **of life** (*med.*) климактéрий; **for a ~** для разнообрáзия; ~ **of heart** изменéние намéрений; **a ~ for the better** перемéна к лýчшему. **2.** (*spare set*) смéна; **he took a ~ of linen with him** он взял с собóй смéну белья́. **3.** (*money*) мéлкие дéн|ьги (*pl., g.* -ег); мéлочь; (*returned as balance*) сдáча; **have you ~ for a pound?** мóжете ли вы разменя́ть фунт?; **I got no ~ out of him** (*fig.*) я от негó ничегó не добился; **you'll get no ~ out him** с негó взя́тки глáдки (*coll.*). **4.** (*of trains etc.*) пересáдка; **no ~ for Oxford** в Óксфорд без пересáдки. **5.** (*stock exchange*) би́ржа. **6.** (*of bells*) перезвóн, трезвóн; **ring (the) ~s** (*lit.*) вызвáнивать (*impf.*) на колоколáх; (*fig.*) тверди́ть (*impf.*) на все лады́ однó и то же.
v.t. **1.** (*alter, replace*) меня́ть, по-; **she ~d her address** онá переéхала на другóе мéсто; ~ **(one's) clothes** переод|евáться, -éться; смен|я́ть, -и́ть одéжду; ~ **one's shoes** переоб|увáться, -ýться; **the snake ~s its skin** змея́ меня́ет кóжу; ~ **colour** (*turn pale*) бледнéть, по-; измени́ться (*pf.*) в лицé; (*blush*) краснéть, по-; ~ **one's mind** раздýм|ывать, -ать; отдýм|ывать, -ать; передýм|ывать, -ать; ~ **one's tune** (*fig.*) запéть (*pf.*) на другóй лад (*or* по-другóму); ~ **hands** (*of a property*) пере|ходи́ть, -йти́ из рук в рýки; ~ **sides** пере|ходи́ть, -йти́ на другýю стóрону (*or* в другóй лáгерь); ~ **trains** перес|áживаться, -éсть на другóй пóезд; ~ **gear** меня́ть (*impf.*) скóрость; переключи́ть (*pf.*) передáчу; ~ **the subject** смени́ть/перемени́ть (*pf.*) тéму разговóра. **2.** (*re-clothe etc.*): ~ **a child** переод|евáть, -éть ребёнка; (*of baby*) переверну́ть (*pf.*); перепеленáть (*pf.*); ~ **a bed** меня́ть (*impf.*) постéльное бельё. **3.** (*money*): ~ **a pound note** разменя́ть (*pf.*) фýнтовую бумáжку; ~ **francs into pounds** обменя́ть (*pf.*) фрáнки на фýнты стéрлингов. **4.** (*exchange*): ~ **a book** обменя́ть (*pf.*) кни́гу; ~ **places with s.o.** (*lit.*) поменя́ться (*pf.*) местáми с кем-н.; **~ing of the guard** смéна караýла. **5.** (*shift*): **he ~d his weight from one foot to the other** он переступи́л с ноги́ нá ногу.
v.i.: **he has ~d a lot** он си́льно измени́лся/перемени́лся; **caterpillars ~ into butterflies** гýсеницы превращáются в бáбочек; **we ~d to central heating** мы перешли́ на центрáльное отоплéние; **his expression ~d** он измени́лся/перемени́лся в лицé; **the weather ~d to rain** погóда перемени́лась и пошёл дождь; **the wind ~d** вéтер перемени́лся; (*rail.*) перес|áживаться, -éсть; **all ~!** конéчная останóвка!; пересáдка, пóезд дáльше не пойдёт!; (*clothing*): ~ **for dinner** переодéться (*pf.*) к ýжину.
with advs.: ~ **down** *v.i.* (*motoring*) перейти́ (*pf.*) на бóлее ни́зкую скóрость; ~ **over** *v.i.*: **the railways ~d over to electricity** желéзные дорóги перешли́ на электри́чество/электроэнéргию; ~ **up** *v.i.* (*motoring*) перейти́ (*pf.*) на бóлее высóкую скóрость.
cpd. **~-over** *n.*: **~-over to electricity** перехóд на электроэнéргию; (*of leader etc.*) смéна.

changeab|ility [,tʃeɪndʒə'bɪlɪtɪ], **-leness** ['tʃeɪndʒəb(ə)lnɪs] *nn.* перемéнчивость, неустóйчивость; измéнчивость, непостоя́нство.

changeable ['tʃeɪndʒəb(ə)l] *adj.*: ~ **weather** измéнчивая/неустóйчивая погóда; (*of pers.*) измéнчивый, непостоя́нный.

changeful ['tʃeɪndʒfʊl] *n.* пóлный перемéн; измéнчивый, перемéнный.

changeless ['tʃeɪndʒlɪs] *adj.* неизмéнный.

changeling ['tʃeɪndʒlɪŋ] *n.* подменённое дитя́.

changing-room ['tʃeɪndʒɪŋ,ru:m] *n.* раздевáлка; примéрочная.

channel ['tʃæn(ə)l] *n.* **1.** (*strait*) проли́в, канáл; **the English C~** Ла-Мáнш; **the C~ Islands** Нормáндские островá; **C~**

tunnel тоннéль под Ла-Мáншем; (*branch, arm of waterway*) рукáв. **2.** (*bed of a stream*) рýсло. **3.** (*deeper part of a waterway*) фарвáтер. **4.** (*fig.*): **through the usual ~s** обы́чным путём; **~ of information** истóчник информáции. **5.** (*television*) канáл.

v.t. (*make a ~ in*) пров|одúть, -естú канáл в+*p.*; (*cause to flow*): **the river ~led its way through the rocks** рекá проложúла себé путь чéрез скáлы; (*fig.*): **we ~led the information to him** мы передáли емý э́ти свéдения; **his energies are ~led into sport** вся егó энéргия ухóдит на спорт.

with adv.: **~ off** *v.t.* отв|одúть, -естú.

chant [tʃɑːnt] *n.* песнь; (*eccl.*) пéние.

v.t. восп|евáть, -éть.

v.i. петь (*impf.*).

chanterelle [ˌtʃæntə'rel] *n.* лисúчка.

chanteuse [ʃɑː'ntɜːz] *n.* эстрáдная певúца.

chantry ['tʃɑːntrɪ] *n.* (*chapel*) часóвня.

chaos ['keɪɒs] *n.* (*myth.*) хáос; (*disorder*) хаóс.

chaotic [keɪ'ɒtɪk] *adj.* хаотúческий, хаотúчный.

chap[1] [tʃæp] *n.* (*crack*) трéщина; (*on hands*) цы́п|ки (*pl., g.* -ок).

v.t. произв|одúть, -естú трéщину в+*p.*; **~ped hands** потрéскавшиеся рýки.

chap[2] (*also* **chappie**) [tʃæp] *n.* (*coll., fellow*) пáрень (*m.*), мáлый; **a good ~** слáвный мáлый; **old ~** старинá (*m.*), дружúще (*m.*).

chapel ['tʃæp(ə)l] *n.* **1.** (*small church*) часóвня, молéльня; (*Catholic*) капéлла; **~ folk** нонконформúсты (*m. pl.*). **2.** (*part of church*) придéл с алтарём. **3.** (*trade union branch*) отделéние профсоюза (печáтников).

chaperon(e) ['ʃæpəˌrəʊn] *n.* компаньóнка.

v.t. сопрово|ждáть, -дúть.

chaplain ['tʃæplɪn] *n.* капеллáн, свящéнник.

chaplaincy ['tʃæplɪnsɪ] *n.* дóлжность капеллáна.

chaplet ['tʃæplɪt] *n.* (*wreath*) венóк; (*necklace*) ожерéлье; (*rosary*) чёт|ки (*pl., g.* -ок).

chappie ['tʃæpɪ] = **chap**[2]

chapter ['tʃæptə(r)] *n.* **1.** (*of book*) главá; **~ and verse** (*fig.*) тóчная ссы́лка; **to the end of the ~** (*fig.*) до сáмого концá; **~ of accidents** стечéние несчáстий. **2.** (*of clergy*) собрáние канóников (*or* члéнов монáшеского óрдена).

cpd. **~-house** *n.* дом капúтула.

char[1] [tʃɑː(r)] *v.t.* (*burn*) обж|игáть, -éчь; обýгли|вать, -ть.

v.i. обýгли|ваться, -ться.

char[2] [tʃɑː(r)] *n.* (*coll.*) = **~woman**

v.t. (*coll., perform housework*) уб|ирáть, -рáть помещéние подённо.

cpds. **~lady, ~woman** *nn.* приходя́щая рабóтница; (подённая) убóрщица.

char[3] [tʃɑː(r)] *n.* (*tea*) чай; **fancy a cup o' ~?** не хотúте ли чáшку чáю?

character ['kærɪktə(r)] *n.* **1.** (*nature*) свóйство, кáчество; **a book of that ~** кнúга такóго рóда. **2.** (*personal qualities*) харáктер; **a man of ~** человéк с сúльным харáктером; **he lacks ~** он бесхарáктерный человéк; **an interesting ~** интерéсный человéк; **his remark was in (*or* out of) ~** э́то замечáние бы́ло вполнé (*or* не) в егó дýхе/стúле; **a bad ~** тёмная лúчность; **a queer ~** чудáк. **3.** (*well-known pers.*): **a public ~** общéственный дéятель. **4.** (*eccentric or distinctive pers.*): **she is quite a ~** онá оригинáльная лúчность; **a weird ~** стрáнный субъéкт; **a ~ actor** характéрный актёр. **5.** (*fictional*) герóй, тип, óбраз, персонáж; **in the ~ of Hamlet** в óбразе Гáмлета. **6.** (*capacity*) дóлжность, кáчество; **in his ~ of ambassador** в кáчестве послá. **7.** (*reputation*) репутáция; **~ assassination** подры́в репутáции. **8.** (*testimonial*) характерúстика, аттестáция. **9.** (*letter, graphic symbol*) бýква, лúтера; **Chinese ~s** китáйские иерóглифы (*m. pl.*); **Runic ~s** рунúческое письмó.

characteristic [ˌkærɪktə'rɪstɪk] *n.* характéрная чертá, свóйство, осóбенность; (*math.*) характерúстика.

adj. характéрный, типúчный; **it is ~ of him** э́то характéрно для негó.

characterization [ˌkærɪktəraɪ'zeɪʃ(ə)n] *n.* **1.** (*description*) характерúстика. **2.** (*by author or actor*) создáние óбраза; трактóвка.

characterize ['kærɪktəˌraɪz] *v.t.* **1.** (*describe*) (о)характеризовáть (*impf., pf.*); **~ s.o. as a liar** охарактеризовáть когó-н. как лгунá. **2.** (*distinguish*) отлич|áть, -úть; **he is ~d by honesty** он отличáется своéй чéстностью.

characterless ['kærɪktəlɪs] *adj.* (*undistinguished*) бесхарáктерный, заурядный.

charade [ʃə'rɑːd] *n.* шарáда.

charcoal ['tʃɑːkəʊl] *n.* древéсный ýголь; **a ~ drawing** рисýнок углём.

cpds. **~-burner** *n.* ýгольщик; **~-grey** *n. & adj.* тёмно-сéрый (цвет).

charcuterie [ʃɑː'kuːtərɪ] *n.* магазúн мяснóй кулинáрии.

charge [tʃɑːdʒ] *n.* **1.** (*load*) нагрýзка, загрýзка, груз. **2.** (*for gun etc.*) заря́д. **3.** (*elec.*) заря́д, заряжáние; **the battery is on ~ (*or* being ~d)** батарéя заряжáется. **4.** (*her.*) эмблéма, девúз. **5.** (*expense*) ценá, расхóды (*m. pl.*); **what is the ~?** скóлько э́то стóит?; **his ~s are reasonable** у негó цéны вполнé умéренные; **there is a ~ on the bottle** трéбуется залóг за буты́лку; **a ~ account** счёт в магазúне; **~s forward** достáвка за счёт покупáтеля; **at his own ~** на егó/свой сóбственный счёт; **free of ~** бесплáтно. **6.** (*burden*) брéмя (*nt.*); **he became a ~ on the community** он стал брéменем для всей óбщины. **7.** (*duty, care*): **the child is in my ~** э́тот ребёнок на моём попечéнии; **I am in ~ here** я здесь завéдую; я здесь за стáршего; **take ~ of a business** взять (*pf.*) на себя руковóдство дéлом; **his emotions took ~** он оказáлся во влáсти чувств; **give s.o. in ~** перед|авáть, -áть когó-н. в рýки полúции. **8.** (*pers. entrusted*): **the nurse took her ~s for a walk** ня́ня повелá своúх питóмцев на прогýлку. **9.** (*instructions*) напýтствие, наставлéние, предписáние. **10.** (*accusation*) обвинéние; **bring a ~ against s.o.** выдвигáть, вы́двинуть обвинéние прóтив когó-н.; **lay sth. to s.o.'s ~** обвин|я́ть, -úть когó-н. в чём-н.; **he pleaded guilty to the ~ of speeding** он признáл себя винóвным в превышéнии скóрости. **11.** (*attack*) нападéние, атáка; **return to the ~** (*fig.*) возобновúть (*pf.*) атáку.

v.t. **1.** (*load, fill*) нагру|жáть, -зúть; **~ your glasses!** напóлните свой стакáны!; (*elec.*) заря|жáть, -дúть; (*fig.*): **~ one's memory with facts** перегружáть (*impf.*) свою пáмять фáктами. **2.** (*make responsible*): **he was ~d with an important mission** емý бы́ло порýчено вáжное задáние; **I cannot ~ myself with this** я не могý взять на себя ответственность за э́то. **3.** (*instruct*): **I ~ you to obey him** я трéбую, чтóбы вы повиновáлись емý; **the judge ~d the jury** судья́ напýтствовал прися́жных. **4.** (*accuse*) обвин|я́ть, -úть; **he is ~d with murder** егó обвиня́ют в убúйстве. **5.** (*debit*): **~ the amount/goods to me** запишúте сýмму/товáры на мой счёт; **his estate was ~d with the debt; the debt was ~d to his estate** за егó имéнием чúслился долг; **tax is ~d on the proceeds of the sale** дохóды с продáжи подлежáт обложéнию налóгом. **6.** (*ask price*): **he ~d £5 for the book** он запросúл 5 фýнтов за э́ту кнúгу. **7.** (*also v.i.; attack*): **the troops ~d the enemy** войскá атаковáли неприя́теля; **he ~d at me** он набрóсился на меня́.

cpds. **~-nurse** *n.* стáршая медсестрá отделéния; **~-sheet** *n.* полицéйский протокóл.

chargeable ['tʃɑːdʒəb(ə)l] *adj.* **1. ~** (*to be debited*) **to** относúмый за счёт +*g.*; **the expense is ~ to him** э́тот расхóд слéдует отнестú на егó счёт. **2.** (*liable to be accused*): **he is ~ with theft** он мóжет быть обвинён в крáже.

chargé d'affaires [ˌʃɑːʒeɪ dæ'feə(r)] *n.* повéренный в делáх.

charger ['tʃɑːdʒə(r)] *n.* (*horse*) строевáя лóшадь; боевóй конь.

chariness ['tʃerɪnəs] *n.* осторóжность; сдéржанность.

chariot ['tʃærɪət] *n.* колеснúца.

charioteer [ˌtʃærɪə'tɪə(r)] *n.* вознúца (*m.*).

charisma [kə'rɪzmə] *n.* харúзма, обая́ние.

charismatic [ˌkærɪz'mætɪk] *adj.* харизматúческий.

charitable ['tʃærɪtəb(ə)l] *adj.* (*in judgement etc.*) мúлостивый, снисходúтельный; **it would be ~ to suppose that he was drunk** в лýчшем слýчае мóжно предположúть, что он был пьян; (*in almsgiving*) благотворúтельный.

charity [ˈtʃærɪtɪ] *n.* **1.** (*kindness*) любо́вь к бли́жнему; ~ **begins at home** своя́ руба́шка бли́же к те́лу; **he lives on** ~ он живёт ми́лостыней. **2.** (*indulgence*) милосе́рдие; снисхожде́ние; **judge others with** ~ не суди́ть (*impf.*) други́х стро́го. **3.** (*almsgiving*) благотвори́тельность; ми́лостыня; **give, dispense** ~ под|ава́ть, -а́ть ми́лостыню; **cold as** ~ хо́лодно, как в по́гребе. **4.** (*institution*) благотвори́тельные учрежде́ния.

charivari [ˌʃɑːrɪˈvɑːrɪ] *n.* гам, шум.

charlatan [ˈʃɑːlət(ə)n] *n.* шарлата́н, зна́харь (*m.*).

charlatan|ism [ˈʃɑːlətənˌɪz(ə)m], **-ry** [ˈʃɑːlətənrɪ] *nn.* шарлата́нство, зна́харство.

Charlemagne [ˈʃɑːləˌmeɪn] *n.* Карл Вели́кий.

Charles [ˈtʃɑːlz] *n.* (*hist.*) Карл; **~'s Wain** Больша́я Медве́дица.

charlock [ˈtʃɑːlɒk] *n.* горчи́ца полева́я.

charlotte [ˈʃɑːlɒt] *n.* шарло́тка.

charm [tʃɑːm] *n.* **1.** (*attraction*) обая́ние, очарова́ние, очарова́тельность; ~ **of manner** прия́тная мане́ра держа́ться; **her ~s** её пре́лести (*f. pl.*). **2.** (*spell*) ча́ры (*pl.*, *g.* —); **under a** ~ заколдо́ванный; очаро́ванный, околдо́ванный; **it worked like a** ~ э́то оказа́ло маги́ческое де́йствие. **3.** (*talisman*) амуле́т.

v.t. **1.** (*attract, delight*) очаро́в|ывать, -а́ть; **she ~ed away his sorrow** она́ разве́яла его́ печа́ль; **I shall be ~ed to visit you** я бу́ду сча́стлив посети́ть вас. **2.** (*use magic on*) чарова́ть (*impf.*); зачаро́в|ывать, -а́ть; **he bears a ~ed life** он как бы неуязви́м; его́ Бог храни́т.

charmer [ˈtʃɑːmə(r)] *n.* **1.** (*beauty*) чаровни́ца, чаро́дейка. **2.** (*charming pers.*) обая́тельный/очарова́тельный челове́к.

charming [ˈtʃɑːmɪŋ] *adj.* очарова́тельный, обая́тельный, чару́ющий.

charnel-house [ˈtʃɑːn(ə)lˌhaʊs] *n.* склеп.

Charon [ˈkeərən] *n.* Харо́н.

chart [tʃɑːt] *n.* (*nautical map*) морска́я ка́рта; (*record*) табли́ца, гра́фик; **weather** ~ синопти́ческая ка́рта; **temperature** ~ температу́рный гра́фик.

v.t. черти́ть, на- ка́рту +*g.*; нан|оси́ть, -ести́ на ка́рту; ~ **an ocean** начерти́ть (*pf.*) ка́рту океа́на; ~ **s.o.'s progress** сде́лать (*pf.*) диагра́мму чьего́-н. продвиже́ния; ~ **a course of action** наме́тить (*pf.*) план де́йствий.

cpds. **~-house, ~-room** *nn.* шту́рманская ру́бка.

charter [ˈtʃɑːtə(r)] *n.* **1.** (*grant of rights*) ха́ртия, гра́мота. **2.** (*of society*): **C~ of the United Nations** Уста́в ООН; ~ **member** член-основа́тель (*m.*) организа́ции. **3.** (*hire*) фрахто́вка, наём; ~ **flight** зафрахто́ванный полёт.

v.t. **1.** (*grant diploma etc. to*) дарова́ть (*impf.*, *pf.*) ха́ртию/привиле́гию +*d.*; **~ed accountant** бухга́лтер-экспе́рт, ауди́тор. **2.** (*provide on hire*) сд|ава́ть, -ать внаём по ча́ртеру. **3.** (*procure on hire*) фрахтова́ть, за-.

cpd. **~-party** *n.* фрахто́вый контра́кт, ча́ртер-па́ртия.

charterer [ˈtʃɑːtərə(r)] *n.* (*pers. providing on hire*) фрахто́вщик; (*pers. receiving*) фрахтова́тель (*m.*).

Chartism [ˈtʃɑːtɪz(ə)m] *n.* charти́зм.

Chartist [ˈtʃɑːtɪst] *n.* charти́ст; (*attr.*) charти́стский.

chartreuse [ʃɑːˈtrɜːz] *n.* (*liqueur*) шартре́з; (*colour*) желтова́то-зелёный.

chary [ˈtʃeərɪ] *adj.* осторо́жный, сде́ржанный; **he is ~ of praise** он скуп на похвалу́; **I shall be ~ of going there** я два́жды поду́маю, пре́жде чем пойти́ туда́.

chase[1] [tʃeɪs] *n.* **1.** (*act of chasing*) пого́ня; **give ~ to** погна́ться (*pf.*) за+*i.*; пусти́ться (*pf.*) вдого́нку за+*i.*; **in ~ of** в пого́не за+*i.*; **wild goose** ~ напра́сная пого́ня. **2.: the** ~ (*hunting*) охо́та.

v.t. гоня́ться (*indet.*), гна́ться (*det.*) за+*i.*; **the letter has been chasing me for weeks** э́то письмо́ догоня́ло меня́ не́сколько неде́ль; **he owes us a reply — please ~ him up** (*coll.*) мы ждём его́ отве́та — потороп́ите-ка его́!

v.i.: ~ **after** гна́ться, по- за+*i.*; охо́титься (*impf.*) за+*i.*; ~ **off** помча́ться (*pf.*).

chase[2] [tʃeɪs] *v.t.* (*engrave*) гравирова́ть, вы́-.

chaser [ˈtʃeɪsə(r)] *n.* **1.** (*pursuer*) пресле́дователь (*m.*). **2.** (*gun at bow or stern*) судово́е ору́дие. **3.** (*drink*) стака́н пи́ва по́сле спиртно́го *и т.п.*

chasm [ˈkæz(ə)m] *n.* бе́здна, про́пасть (*also fig.*).

chassé [ˈʃæseɪ] *n.* шассе́ (*indecl.*).

chassis [ˈʃæsɪ] *n.* шасси́ (*nt. indecl.*).

chaste [tʃeɪst] *adj.* целому́дренный; (*of style etc.*) стро́гий.

chasten [ˈtʃeɪs(ə)n] *v.t.* (*punish, subdue*) смир|я́ть, -и́ть; **the rebuke had a ~ing effect** упрёк поде́йствовал отрезвля́юще; (*refine, of style etc.*) оч|ища́ть, -и́стить.

chastise [tʃæsˈtaɪz] *v.t.* нака́з|ывать, -а́ть; кара́ть, по-.

chastisement [tʃæsˈtaɪzmənt] *n.* наказа́ние.

chastity [ˈtʃæstɪtɪ] *n.* **1.** целому́дрие, целому́дренность; ~ **belt** по́яс целому́дрия. **2.** (*of style etc.*) стро́гость, чистота́.

chasuble [ˈtʃæzjʊb(ə)l] *n.* ри́за.

chat [tʃæt] *n.* болтовня́, бесе́да; ~ **show** бесе́да/интервью (*nt. indecl.*) со знамени́тостью.

v.t.: ~ **s.o. up** (*coll.*) заи́грывать (*impf.*) с кем-н.

v.i. болта́ть, по-; бесе́довать, по-.

château [ˈʃætəʊ] *n.* за́мок.

chatelaine [ˈʃætəˌleɪn] *n.* (*mistress of house*) хозя́йка до́ма.

chattel [ˈtʃæt(ə)l] *n.* дви́жимое иму́щество; **goods and ~s** всё иму́щество; **he treated his wife like a** ~ он обраща́лся с жено́й, как с принадлежа́щей ему́ ве́щью.

chatter [ˈtʃætə(r)] *n.* **1.** (*talk*) болтовня́, трескотня́. **2.** (*of birds*) щебета́ние; (*of monkeys etc.*) вереща́ние; стре́кот, стрекота́ние. **3.** (*rattle*) треск, дребезжа́ние.

v.i. **1.** болта́ть, таратóрить (*both impf.*). **2.** щебета́ть, треща́ть, вереща́ть, стрекота́ть (*all impf.*); ~ **like a magpie** треща́ть как соро́ка. **3.: his teeth are ~ing** у него́ стуча́т зу́бы.

cpd. **~box** *n.* болту́н (*fem.* -ья); тарато́рка, трещо́тка, пустоме́ля (*all c.g.*).

chatterer [ˈtʃætərə(r)] *n.* болту́н (*fem.* -ья).

chattiness [ˈtʃætɪnɪs] *n.* болтли́вость.

chatty [ˈtʃætɪ] *adj.* болтли́вый, говорли́вый.

chauffeur [ˈʃəʊfə(r), -ˈfɜː(r)] *n.* (наёмный) шофёр.

chauffeuse [ʃəʊˈfɜːz] *n.* же́нщина-шофёр.

chauvinism [ˈʃəʊvɪˌnɪz(ə)m] *n.* шовини́зм.

chauvinist [ˈʃəʊvɪnɪst] *n.* шовини́ст (*fem.* -ка); **male** ~ сторо́нник дискримина́ции же́нщин.

chauvinistic [ʃəʊvɪˈnɪstɪk] *adj.* шовинисти́ческий.

cheap [tʃiːp] *adj.* **1.** (*low in price*) дешёвый; **I bought it** ~ я дёшево э́то купи́л; ~ **and nasty** дёшево да гни́ло; ~ **at the price** вполне́ прили́чно за таку́ю це́ну; **dirt** ~ деше́вле па́реной ре́пы; грошо́вый; **on the** ~ по дешёвке; **he got off** ~ он дёшево отде́лался. **2.** (*facile, tawdry, petty, vulgar*): ~ **flattery** дешёвая лесть; **a** ~ **remark** по́шлое замеча́ние. **3.: I feel** ~ (*out of sorts*) мне не по себе́; (*ashamed*) мне сты́дно; **make o.s.** ~ не уважа́ть (*impf.*) себя́; роня́ть (*impf.*) своё досто́инство.

cpd. **~jack** *n.* разно́счик дешёвых това́ров.

cheapen [ˈtʃiːpən] *v.t.* (*make cheap*) удешев|ля́ть, -и́ть; де́лать, с- деше́вле; ~ **o.s.** (*fig.*) роня́ть (*impf.*) себя́.

v.i. дешеве́ть, по-.

cheapness [ˈtʃiːpnɪs] *n.* дешеви́зна.

cheat [tʃiːt] *n.* (*pers.*) обма́нщик, плут, жу́лик; (*thg., action*) обма́н, плутовство́, жу́льничество.

v.t. & *i.* обма́н|ывать, -у́ть; плутова́ть, на-/с-; пров|оди́ть, -ести́; ~ **s.o. out of sth.** обма́ном лиши́ть кого́-н. чего́-н.; ~ **at cards** жу́льничать, с- в ка́ртах; плутова́ть, на-/с- в ка́ртах; ~ **o.s.** (*e.g. by giving too much change*) обсчита́ть (*pf.*) самого́ себя́; **he ~ed me into believing that ...** он уве́рил меня́ обма́ном, что...; ~ **one's fatigue** отвле́чься от своего́ утомле́ния; ~ **the gallows** избежа́ть (*pf.*) ви́селицы.

check[1] [tʃek] *n.* **1.** (*restraint*) заде́ржка; **wind acts as a ~ upon speed** ве́тер замедля́ет ско́рость; **keep a ~ on your temper** сде́рживайте свой нрав. **2.** (*stoppage*) остано́вка; **they held the enemy in** ~ они́ сде́рживали проти́вника. **3.** (*verification*) контро́ль (*m.*); прове́рка; **keep a ~ on his expenses** держа́ть под контро́лем его́ расхо́ды. **4.** (*for hat, luggage etc.*) номеро́к; квита́нция. **5.** (*at chess*) шах. **6.** (*US, at cards etc.*) фи́шка, ма́рка; **hand in one's ~s** (*coll.*) расквита́ться (*pf.*) с жи́знью. **7.** (*US*) = **cheque. 8.** (*US*) = **bill. 9.** (*US, tick*) га́лочка.

v.t. **1.** (*restrain*) сде́рж|ивать, -а́ть; **he ~ed himself from speaking** он сдержа́лся и промолча́л; **the car ~ed its**

speed автомобиль замедлил скорость. **2.** (*stop*) остан|авливать, -овить; задерж|ивать, -ать. **3.** (*rebuke*) проб|ирать, -рать. **4.** (*verify*) контролировать (*impf.*); пров|ерять, -ерить. **5.** (*deposit, of luggage etc.*) сд|авать, -ать под квитанцию. **6.** (*at chess*) объяв|лять, -ить шах +*d.*; шаховать (*impf.*). **7.** (*US, tick*) отм|ечать, -етить галочкой.

v.i. **1.** (*pause*) остан|авливаться, -овиться. **2.** ~ **on** = ~ **up. 3.:** ~ (*accord*) **with** совп|адать, -асть с+*i.*

with advs.: ~ **in** *v.i.* (*at hotel*) регистрироваться, за-; ~ **out** *v.i.* (*from hotel*) выписываться, выписаться; ~ **up** *v.i.*: ~ **up on sth.** пров|ерять, -ерить что-н.

cpds. ~**-list** *n.* контрольный список, перечень (*m.*); ~**out** *n.* касса; ~**-point,** ~**-post** *nn.* контрольный пункт; ~**-rein** *n.* повод; ~**room** *n.* гардеробная; ~**-up** *n.* проверка; (технический/медицинский) осмотр; (*of motor vehicle*) техосмотр.

int. ~! (*US, coll.*) точно!; (*at chess*) шах!

check[2] [tʃek] *n.* (*pattern*) клетка; (*attr., also* ~**ed**) клетчатый.

checkers ['tʃekəz] *n.* шаш|ки (*pl., g.* -ек).

checkmate ['tʃekmeɪt] *n.* шах и мат; (*fig.*) мат.

v.t. делать, с- мат +*d.*; (*fig.*) нанести (*pf.*) полное поражение +*d.*

cheek [tʃi:k] *n.* **1.** (*part of face*) щека; (*dim., e.g. baby's*) щёчка; ~ **by jowl** бок о бок; **turn the other** ~ подст|авлять, -авить другую щёку. **2.** (*buttock*) половинка (зада). **3.** (*impudence*) наглость; **he had the** ~ **to say ...** у него хватило наглости сказать...

v.t. (*coll.*) дерзить, на- +*d.*

cpd. ~**-bone** *n.* скула.

cheekiness ['tʃi:kɪnɪs] *n.* наглость, нахальство.

cheeky ['tʃi:kɪ] *adj.* нахальный; **a** ~ **little hat** задорная шляпка.

cheep [tʃi:p] *n.* писк. *v.t. & i.* пищать, пискнуть.

cheer ['tʃɪə(r)] *n.* **1.** (*comfort*): **words of** ~ ободряющие/подбадривающие слова; **be of good** ~! не унывайте! **2.** (*food*) угощение; **good** ~ пир горой. **3.** (*shout*): **a round of** ~**s** круговое ура; **three** ~**s for our visitors!** троекратное ура нашим гостям!; ~**s!** (*as toast*) (за) ваше здоровье! **4.** *pl., as int.* (*coll.*) спасибо.

v.t. **1.** (*comfort, encourage*) подбодр|ять, -ить; ободр|ять, -ить; **his visit** ~**ed (up) the patient** его посещение подбодрило больного; ~**ing news** приятная новость. **2.** (*acclaim*) приветствовать (*impf.*); **the spectators** ~**ed the team** зрители криками подбадривали команду.

v.i. подбодр|яться, -иться; ободр|яться, -иться; (*utter* ~*s*) изд|авать, -ать восторженные крики.

with adv.: ~ **up** *v.t. & i.* ободр|ять(ся), -ить(ся); *v.i.* повеселеть (*pf.*); ~ **up!** не унывайте!

cpd. ~**-leader** *n.* заводила (*c.g.*).

cheerful ['tʃɪəfʊl] *adj.* весёлый, радостный, жизнерадостный; **a** ~ **room** весёлая/светлая комната; ~ **workers** люди, работающие с охотой.

cheer|fulness ['tʃɪəfʊlnɪs], **-iness** ['tʃɪərɪnɪs] *nn.* весёлость, радостность, жизнерадостность.

cheerio [,tʃɪrɪ'əʊ] *int.* (*coll.*) всего хорошего!; всего!

cheerless ['tʃɪəlɪs] *adj.* унылый.

cheerlessness ['tʃɪəlɪsnɪs] *n.* унылость.

cheery ['tʃɪərɪ] *adj.* весёлый, радостный, живой.

cheese[1] [tʃi:z] *n.* сыр; **green** ~ молодой сыр; **ripe** ~ выдержанный сыр; ~ **straw** (*cul.*) соломка с сыром.

cpds. ~**burger** *n.* чизбургер; ~**cake** *n.* (*lit.*) ватрушка; (*sl.*) ≃ полураздетая красотка; ~**cloth** *n.* марля; ~**monger** *n.* торговец молочными продуктами; ~**-paring** *n.* крохоборство; *adj.* крохоборский, крохоборческий.

cheese[2] [tʃi:z] *v.t.* (*sl.*): ~ **it!** кончайте!; бросьте!; **he is** ~**d off** (*fed up*) ему всё осточертело.

cheesy ['tʃi:zɪ] *adj.* **1.** (*like cheese*) сырный. **2.** (*sl., shabby, scruffy*) дешёвый.

cheetah ['tʃi:tə] *n.* гепард.

chef [ʃef] *n.* шеф-повар.

chemical ['kemɪk(ə)l] *n.* химический продукт; (*pl.*) химикали|и (*pl., g.* -й); химикаты (*m. pl.*); **fine/heavy** ~**s** продукты (*m. pl.*) тонкой/основной химической промышленности.

adj. химический; ~ **warfare** химическая война.

chemise [ʃə'mi:z] *n.* женская сорочка/рубашка.

chemist ['kemɪst] *n.* **1.** (*scientist*) химик. **2.** (*pharmacist*) аптекарь (*m.*); ~**'s shop** аптека.

chemistry ['kemɪstrɪ] *n.* химия; **agricultural** ~ агрохимия.

chemotherapy [,ki:mə'θerəpɪ] *n.* химиотерапия.

chenille [ʃə'ni:l] *n.* (*yarn*) синель; (*fabric*) шенилъ.

che|que [tʃek] (*US* **-ck**) *n.* чек; **he made the** ~ **out to me** он выписал чек на моё имя; **blank** ~ незаполненный чек; (*fig.*) карт-бланш; **crossed** ~ кроссированный чек; **traveller's** ~ туристский чек; **draw a** ~ **on a bank for £100** выписать (*pf.*) чек на банк на сумму в 100 фунтов.

cpds. ~**-book** *n.* чековая книжка; ~**-stub** *n.* корешок чековой книжки.

chequer ['tʃekə(r)] *n.* (*pl., check or mixed pattern*) клетчатая/пёстрая материя в клетку/шашку.

v.t. (*mark in* ~*s*) графить, раз- в клетку; ~**ed flag** шахматный флажок; ~**ed career** (*fig.*) бурная жизнь; жизнь, полная превратностей.

cherish ['tʃerɪʃ] *v.t.* **1.** (*love, care for*) нежно любить (*impf.*); лелеять (*impf.*). **2.** (*of hopes etc.*) лелеять (*impf.*); дорожить (*impf.*) +*i.*

Cherokee ['tʃerəkɪ] *n.* черок|ез(ец) (*fem.* -езка).

adj. черокезский.

cheroot [ʃə'ru:t] *n.* сигара с обрезанными концами.

cherry ['tʃerɪ] *n.* (*fruit*) вишня; черешня; (*tree*) вишня, вишнёвое дерево; ~ **brandy** черри-бренди (*indecl.*), вишнёвый ликёр; ~ **lips** алые губы; ~ **orchard** вишнёвый сад.

cpds. ~**-blossom** *n.* вишнёвый цвет; ~**-pie** *n.* (*cul.*) пирог с вишнями; ~**-stone** *n.* вишнёвая косточка; ~**wood** *n.* древесина вишнёвого дерева.

cherub ['tʃerəb] *n.* (*relig., art*) херувим; (*fig., child*) херувимчик, ангел.

cherubic [tʃɪ'ru:bɪk] *adj.* херувимский, ангелоподобный, ангельский.

chervil ['tʃɜ:vɪl] *n.* купырь (*m.*).

chess [tʃes] *n.* шахмат|ы (*pl., g.* —); ~ **problem** шахматная задача.

cpds. ~**-board** *n.* шахматная доска; ~**-man** *n.* шахматная фигура; ~**-player** *n.* шахматист (*fem.* -ка).

chest [tʃest] *n.* **1.** (*furniture*) сундук; ~ **of drawers** комод; **medicine** ~ аптечка. **2.** (*treasury, funds*) казна. **3.** (*anat.*) грудная клетка; грудь; **get sth. off one's** ~ облегчить (*pf.*) душу; ~ **cold; cold in the** ~ простуда; **broad-/narrow-**~**ed** широкогрудый/узкогрудый.

cpds. ~**-note** *n.* грудная/низкая нота; ~**-protector** *n.* душегрейка; ~**-voice** *n.* грудной голос.

chesterfield ['tʃestəfi:ld] *n.* (*overcoat*) пальто в талию; (*couch*) большой диван.

chestnut ['tʃesnʌt] *n.* **1.** (*tree, fruit*) каштан; **pull s.o.'s** ~**s out of the fire** таскать (*impf.*) для кого-н. каштаны из огня. **2.** (*stale anecdote*) анекдот с бородой. **3.** (*horse*) гнедая лошадь. **4.** (*attr., of colour*) каштановый.

chesty ['tʃestɪ] *adj.* (*of cold*) грудной.

chetnik ['tʃetnɪk] *n.* четник.

cheval-glass [ʃə'væl] *n.* псише (*indecl.*).

chevalier [ʃevə'lɪə(r)] *n.* рыцарь (*m.*), кавалер.

chevaux de frise [ʃə,vəʊ də 'fri:z] *n.* (*mil.*) рогатки (*f. pl.*); (*on wall-top*) битое стекло (*or* гвозди) на стене.

chevron ['ʃevrən] *n.* шеврон.

chevy ['tʃevɪ] = **chivvy**

chew [tʃu:] *v.t. & i.* жевать (*impf.*); ~ **the cud** жевать жвачку; ~ **upon,** ~ **over** (*fig.*) пережёвывать (*impf.*); ~ **the rag, fat** (*coll.*) чесать (*impf.*) языки; перемывать (*impf.*) косточки; ~**ing-gum** жевательная резинка.

chewy ['tʃu:ɪ] *adj.* (*coll.*) тягучий.

chiaroscuro [kɪ,ɑ:rə'skʊərəʊ] *n.* светотень.

chiasmus [kaɪ'æzməs] *n.* хиазм.

chic [ʃi:k] *n.* элегантность, шик.

adj. элегантный, шикарный.

chicane(ry) [ʃɪ'keɪnərɪ] *n.* крючкотворство.

chichi ['ʃi:ʃi:] *n.* (*affectation*) манерность, жеманство.

adj. (*affected*) манерный, жеманный.

chick [tʃɪk] *n.* птенец; цыплёнок; (*child*) дитя (*nt.*); (*sl., girl*) цыпочка.

cpds. **~pea** *n.* (*bot.*) туре́цкий горо́х; **~weed** *n.* (*bot.*) алзи́на.

chicken ['tʃɪkɪn] *n.* цыплёнок; (*as food*) куря́тина, цыплёнок, ку́рица; (*fig., child*) дитя́ (*nt.*); **she is no ~** она́ не ма́ленькая; **don't count your ~s before they are hatched** цыпля́т по о́сени счита́ют; (*fig., coward*) трус.

v.i. (*behave as coward*) тру́сить, с-.

cpds. **~breasted** *adj.* (*med.*) с кури́ной гру́дью; **~-broth** *n.* кури́ный бульо́н; **~-feed** *n.* (*fig.*) пустяки́ (*m. pl.*); **~-hearted, ~-livered** *adjs.* трусли́вый, малоду́шный; **~-pox** *n.* ветряна́я о́спа; **~-run** *n.* заго́н для кур.

chicory ['tʃɪkərɪ] *n.* цико́рий (полево́й).

chide [tʃaɪd] *v.t.* попрек|а́ть, -ну́ть; брани́ть, вы́-.

chief [tʃi:f] *n.* **1.** (*leader, ruler*) вождь (*m.*), глава́ (*m.*); **Red Indian ~** вождь краснoко́жих; **~ of state** глава́ госуда́рства. **2.** (*boss, senior official*) шеф, нача́льник; **C~ of Staff** нача́льник шта́ба.

adj. **1.** (*most important*) гла́вный, основно́й, важне́йший. **2.** (*senior*) гла́вный, ста́рший; **C~ Justice** верхо́вный судья́; председа́тель (*m.*) верхо́вного суда́; **~ constable** нача́льник поли́ции.

chief|dom ['tʃi:fdəm], **-ship** ['tʃi:fʃɪp] *nn.* главе́нство, старшинство́.

chiefly ['tʃi:flɪ] *adv.* гла́вным о́бразом; в пе́рвую о́чередь.

chieftain ['tʃi:ft(ə)n] *n.* вождь (*m.*); ата́ман, глава́рь (*m.*).

chieftain|cy ['tʃi:ftənsɪ], **-ship** ['tʃi:ftənʃɪp] *nn.* положе́ние вождя́/атама́на/главаря́.

chiffon ['ʃɪfɒn] *n.* шифо́н.

chiffonier [ˌʃɪfə'nɪə(r)] *n.* шифонье́рка.

chignon ['ʃi:njɔ̃] *n.* шиньо́н.

chihuahua [tʃɪ'wɑ:wə] *n.* чихуа́хуа (*indecl.*).

chilblain ['tʃɪlbleɪn] *n.* обморо́женное ме́сто.

child [tʃaɪld] *n.* дитя́ (*nt.*), ребёнок; **his ~** (*sl., myself*) аз гре́шный; (*fig.*): **~ of the devil** исча́дие а́да; **~ren of Israel** (*bibl.*) израильтя́не (*m. pl.*); сыны́ (*m. pl.*) Изра́илевы; **~ of nature** дитя́ приро́ды; **~'s play** (*fig.*) де́тские игру́шки; **with ~** бере́менная, в положе́нии; **he got her with ~** он сде́лал ей ребёнка; **six months gone with ~** на шесто́м ме́сяце бере́менности; **I am a ~ in these matters** я ма́ло смы́слю в э́том; **~'s guide** руково́дство для новичко́в; **from a ~** с де́тства; **~ molester** растли́тель *m.* малоле́тних дете́й; **~ wife** ю́ная жена́; **~ labour** де́тский труд; **~ welfare** охра́на младе́нчества; **a burnt ~ dreads the fire** пу́ганая воро́на куста́ бои́тся; обжёгшись на молоке́, бу́дешь дуть на́ воду.

cpds. **~-bearing** *n.* деторожде́ние; **of ~-bearing age** детoро́дного во́зраста; **~bed, ~birth** *nn.* ро́ды (*pl., g.* -ов); **natural ~birth** ро́ды в есте́ственных усло́виях; **she died in ~bed** она́ умерла́ от ро́дов; **~-minder** *n.* приходя́щая ня́ня; **~-minding** *n.* присмо́тр за детьми́.

childhood ['tʃaɪldhʊd] *n.* де́тство; **second ~** второ́е де́тство.

childish ['tʃaɪldɪʃ] *adj.* де́тский, ребя́ческий.

childishness ['tʃaɪldɪʃnɪs] *n.* де́тскость, ребя́чество.

childless ['tʃaɪldlɪs] *adj.* безде́тный.

childlike ['tʃaɪldlaɪk] *adj.* де́тский, младе́нческий.

Chile ['tʃɪlɪ] *n.* Чи́ли (*nt. indecl.*).

Chilean ['tʃɪlɪən] *n.* чили́|ец (*fem.* -йка).

adj. чили́йский.

chili ['tʃɪlɪ] = **chil(l)i**

chiliastic [ˌkɪlɪ'æstɪk] *adj.* хилиасти́ческий.

chill [tʃɪl] *n.* **1.** (*physical*) хо́лод; **there is a ~ in the air** прохла́дно; холода́ет; **take the ~ off wine** подогре́ть (*pf.*) вино́. **2.** (*fig.*) хо́лод; расхола́живание; **this cast a ~ over the proceedings** э́то поде́йствовало расхола́живающе. **3.** (*med.*) просту́да; **catch a ~** просту|жа́ться, -ди́ться.

adj. холо́дный; расхола́живающий.

v.t. (*lit.*) охлажда́ть, -ди́ть; студи́ть (*impf.*); осту|жа́ть, -ди́ть; **~ed meat** охлаждённое мя́со; (*fig.*) осту|жа́ть, -ди́ть.

chil(l)i ['tʃɪlɪ] *n.* кра́сный стручко́вый пе́рец.

chilliness ['tʃɪlɪnɪs] *n.* (*lit.*) хо́лод; (*fig.*) хо́лодность, су́хость; зя́бкость.

chilly ['tʃɪlɪ] *adj.* холо́дный; (*fig.*) холо́дный, сухо́й; (*sensitive to cold*) зя́бкий.

chime [tʃaɪm] *n.* (*set of bells*) подбо́р колоколо́в; (*sound*) перезво́н.

v.t.: **the clock ~d midnight** часы́ про́би́ли по́лночь; **the clock ~s the quarters** часы́ отбива́ют ка́ждую че́тверть ча́са.

v.i. трезво́нить (*impf.*); (*fig., harmonize*) гармонизи́ровать (*impf., pf.*) (c+*i.*); **~ in** подпева́ть (*impf.*) (*кому*).

chimera [kaɪ'mɪərə, kɪ-] *n.* химе́ра.

chimerical [tʃɪ'merɪk(ə)l] *adj.* химери́ческий.

chimney ['tʃɪmnɪ] *n.* **1.** труба́, дымохо́д; **the letter flew up the ~** письмо́ улете́ло в трубу́; **he smokes like a ~** он дыми́т, как труба́. **2.** (*for lamp*) ла́мповое стекло́. **3.** (*mountaineering*) расще́лина для подъёма на отве́сную скалу́.

cpds. **~-corner** *n.* ме́сто у ками́на; **~-piece** *n.* ками́нная доска́/по́лочка; **~-pot** *n.* колпа́к дымово́й трубы́; **~-pot hat** цили́ндр; **~-stack** *n.* дымова́я труба́; **~-sweep** *n.* трубочи́ст.

chimpanzee [ˌtʃɪmpən'zi:] *n.* шимпанзе́ (*m. indecl.*).

chin [tʃɪn] *n.* подборо́док; **double ~** двойно́й подборо́док; **receding ~** сре́занный подборо́док; **(keep your) ~ up!** (*fig.*) не унывáй(те)!; не́чего нос ве́шать! **take it on the ~** (*fig.*) вы́нести (*pf.*) уда́р.

cpds. **~-strap** *n.* подборо́дочный реме́нь; **~-wag** *n.* (*sl.*) трепотня́; *v.i.* трепа́ться (*impf.*); чеса́ть, по- язы́ки́.

China[1] ['tʃaɪnə] *n.* Кита́й; **~ ink** (кита́йская) тушь; **from ~ to Peru** (*fig.*) с одного́ конца́ све́та на друго́й.

cpds. **~man** *n.* кита́ец; **he hasn't got a ~man's chance** у него́ нет никаки́х ви́дов на успе́х; **~town** *n.* кита́йский кварта́л.

china[2] ['tʃaɪnə] *n.* фарфо́р.

cpds. **~-clay** *n.* каоли́н, фарфо́ровая гли́на; **~-closet, ~-cupboard** *nn.* буфе́т, серва́нт; **~ware** *n.* фарфо́р, фарфо́ровые изде́лия.

chinchilla [tʃɪn'tʃɪlə] *n.* шинши́лла; (*fur*) шинши́лловый мех.

chine [tʃaɪn] *n.* (*anat.*) спинно́й хребе́т; (*mountain ridge*) го́рная гряда́; (*ravine*) уще́лье.

Chinese [tʃaɪ'ni:z] *n.* (*pers.*) кит|а́ец (*fem.* -ая́нка); (*language*) кита́йский язы́к.

adj. кита́йский; **~ lantern** лампио́н; **~ puzzle** (*fig.*) кита́йский фона́рик; **~ white** кита́йские бели́ла.

chink[1] [tʃɪŋk] *n.* (*crevice*) щель.

chink[2] [tʃɪŋk] *n.* (*sound*) звя́канье.

v.i. звя́к|ать, -нуть.

chinoiserie [ʃi:n'wɑ:zərɪ] *n.* (*art*) кита́йский стиль; кита́йские ве́щи (*f. pl.*).

chintz [tʃɪnts] *n.* си́тец; (*attr.*) си́тцевый.

chintzy ['tʃɪntsɪ] *adj.* меща́нский, по́шлый.

chip [tʃɪp] *n.* **1.** (*of wood*) щепа́, ще́пка, лучи́на; стру́жка; (*of stone*) обло́мок; (*of china*) оско́лок. **2.** (*fig.*): **he is a ~ off the old block** он вы́литый оте́ц; он весь в отца́; **he has a ~ on his shoulder** он боле́зненно оби́дчив; он мни́телен. **3.**: **the cup has a ~** на ча́шке щерби́на. **4.** (*food*): **fish and ~s** жа́реная ры́ба с чи́псами. **5.** (*at games*) фи́шка, ма́рка; **bargaining ~** (*fig.*) ко́зырь (*m.*) (в запа́се); **he's in the ~s** (*sl., well-off*) он при деньга́х; у него́ завела́сь моне́та. **6.** (*in microelectronics*) чип.

v.t. **1.** струга́ть, вы́стругать; отк|а́лывать, -оло́ть; отб|ива́ть, -и́ть; обб|ива́ть, -и́ть; **~ paint off a ship** соск|а́бливать, -обли́ть кра́ску с корабля́; **the plates have ~ped edges** у таре́лок отби́тые/щерба́тые края́; **~ potatoes** то́нко наре́з|а́ть, -е́зать карто́фель. **2.** (*coll., banter*) поддра́знивать (*impf.*); подтру́н|ивать, -и́ть над+*i.*

v.i. **1.** отк|а́лываться, -оло́ться; отб|ива́ться, -и́ться; обб|ива́ться, -и́ться. **2.** **~ in** (*coll.*) вме́ш|иваться, -а́ться; влез|а́ть, -ть (в разгово́р).

cpd. **~board** *n.* макулату́рный карто́н; фиброли́т; (*attr.*) фиброли́товый.

chipmunk ['tʃɪpmʌŋk] *n.* бурунду́к.

chipper ['tʃɪpə(r)] *adj.* (*coll.*) бо́дрый.

chiromancer ['kaɪərəʊˌmænsə(r)] *n.* хирома́нт (*fem.* -ка).

chiromancy ['kaɪərəʊˌmænsɪ] *n.* хирома́нтия.

chiropodist [kɪ'rɒpədɪst] *n.* мозо́льный опера́тор, (*fem.*) педикю́рша.

chiropody [kɪ'rɒpədɪ] *n.* педикю́р.

chiropractor ['kaɪərəʊˌpræktə(r)] *n.* хиропра́ктик.

chirp [tʃɜ:p] *n.* чири́канье, щебета́ние.
v.t. & i. чири́кать (*impf.*); щебета́ть (*impf.*).
chirpiness [ˈtʃɜ:pɪnɪs] *n.* (*coll.*) бо́дрость.
chirpy [ˈtʃɜpɪ] *adj.* (*coll.*) бо́дрый, неуныва́ющий.
chirr [tʃɜ:(r)] *n.* стрекота́ние; трескотня́, треск.
v.i. стрекота́ть (*impf.*); треща́ть (*impf.*).
chirrup [ˈtʃɪrəp] *n.* щебе́т, щебета́ние.
v.i. щебета́ть (*impf.*).
chisel [ˈtʃɪz(ə)l] *n.* (*sculptor's*) резе́ц; (*carpenter's*) долото́, стаме́ска, зуби́ло.
v.t. **1.** вая́ть, из-; высека́ть, вы́сечь; **finely ~led features** точёные черты́ лица́. **2.** (*sl., cheat*) над|ува́ть, -у́ть.
chiseller [ˈtʃɪzlə(r)] *n.* (*sl., cheat*) жу́лик, моше́нник, пройдо́ха (*c.g.*).
chit[1] [tʃɪt] *n.* (*girl*) девчо́нка.
chit[2] [tʃɪt] *n.* (*note*) запи́ска.
chit-chat [ˈtʃɪttʃæt] *n.* болтовня́, пересу́д|ы (*pl., g.* -ов).
v.i. болта́ть (*impf.*); суда́чить (*impf.*).
chitterlings [ˈtʃɪtəlɪŋs] *n.* требуха́.
chivalr|ic [ˈʃɪvəlrɪk], **-ous** [ˈʃɪvəlrəs] *adjs.* ры́царский, ры́царственный.
chivalry [ˈʃɪvəlrɪ] *n.* ры́царство; ры́царское поведе́ние.
chive [tʃaɪv] *n.* лук-ре́занец.
chivvy (*also* **chevy**) [ˈtʃɪvɪ] *v.t.* (*coll.*) гоня́ть (*impf.*).
chloric [ˈklɔ:rɪk] *adj.*: **~ acid** хлорнова́тая кислота́.
chloride [ˈklɔ:raɪd] *n.* хлори́д; **~ of lime** хло́рная и́звесть; **~ of potash** хло́ристый ка́лий; **sodium ~** хло́ристый на́трий; пова́ренная соль.
chlorinate [ˈklɔ:rɪˌneɪt] *v.t.* (*impf., pf.*) хлори́ровать.
chlorination [ˌklɔ:rɪˈneɪʃ(ə)n] *n.* хлори́рование.
chlorine [ˈklɔ:ri:n] *n.* хлор.
chloroform [ˈklɒrəˌfɔ:m, ˈklɔ:rə-] *n.* хлорофо́рм.
v.t. хлороформи́ровать (*impf., pf.*); **a ~ed handkerchief** пропи́танный хлорофо́рмом плато́к.
chlorophyll [ˈklɒrəfɪl] *n.* хлорофи́л.
chlorosis [kləˈrəʊsɪs, klɔ:-] *n.* (*med.*) хлоро́з; бле́дная не́мочь; (*bot.*) хлоро́з.
chlorotic [klɔ:ˈrɒtɪk] *adj.* хлоро́зный.
choc-ice [tʃɒk] *n.* моро́женое в шокола́де.
chock [tʃɒk] *n.* клин; подпо́рка, распо́рка; тормозна́я коло́дка; чека́.
v.t. подп|ира́ть, -ере́ть; под|кла́дывать, -ложи́ть клин под+*a.*; **~ up** (*fig.*) загромозди́ть (*pf.*); заста́вить (*pf.*).
cpds. **~-a-block** *adj.* загромождённый; **~-full** *adj.* битко́м наби́тый.
chocolate [ˈtʃɒkələt, ˈtʃɒklət] *n.* **1.** шокола́д (*also drink*); (*~-coated sweet*) шокола́дная конфе́та; **~ biscuit** шокола́дное пече́нье; **~ cream** шокола́дная конфе́та с кре́мовой начи́нкой. **2.** (*attr., colour*) шокола́дный.
choice [tʃɔɪs] *n.* **1.** (*act or power of choosing*) вы́бор, отбо́р; **Hobson's ~** вы́бор поневоле́; ≃ не́ из чего вы́брать; **I have no ~ but to ...** у меня́ нет друго́го вы́бора, кро́ме как (*+inf.*); **the girl of his ~** его́ избра́нница; **for ~** предпочти́тельно; **take your ~!** выбира́йте! **2.** (*thg. chosen*) вы́бор; **this is my ~** я выбира́ю э́то; вот мой вы́бор. **3.** (*variety*) вы́бор; **the shop has a large ~ of hats** в магази́не широ́кий ассортиме́нт головны́х убо́ров.
adj. отбо́рный.
choiceness [ˈtʃɔɪsnɪs] *n.* отбо́рность.
choir [ˈkwaɪə(r)] *n.* (*singers*) хор; (*part of church*) хо́ры (*m. pl.*), кли́рос.
cpds. **~boy** *n.* пе́вчий, ма́льчик-хори́ст; **~master** *n.* хорме́йстер.
choke [tʃəʊk] *n.* (*in car*) возду́шная засло́нка; заглу́шка, дро́ссель (*m.*).
v.t. **1.** (*throttle*) души́ть, за-; **~ the life out of s.o.** вы́шибить (*pf.*) дух из кого́-н.; **anger ~d him** его́ удуши́л гнев. **2.** (*block*) заку́пор|ивать, -ить; засор|я́ть, -и́ть; **the drain is ~d** сток засори́лся; **the garden is ~d with weeds** сорняки́ заглуши́ли сад. **3.: he ~d back his anger** он сдержа́л свой гнев; **he ~d off enquiries** он отде́лался от расспро́сов; **he ~d down his food** он поспе́шно проглоти́л еду́; **she ~d down her rage** она́ сдержа́ла свою́ я́рость.
v.i. зад|ыха́ться, -охну́ться; **he ~d on a plum-stone** он подави́лся сли́вовой ко́сточкой; **he spoke with a choking voice** он говори́л прерыва́ющимся го́лосом.
cpd. **~-damp** *n.* уду́шливый газ.
choker [ˈtʃəʊkə(r)] *n.* коро́ткое ожере́лье, колье́ (*indecl.*).
choky [ˈtʃəʊkɪ] *adj.*: **I felt ~ with emotion** я задыха́лся от волне́ния.
choler [ˈkɒlə(r)] *n.* (*arch., anger*) гнев.
cholera [ˈkɒlərə] *n.* холе́ра; **summer ~** холери́на; ле́тний поно́с.
choleric [ˈkɒlərɪk] *adj.* холери́ческий.
cholesterol [kəˈlestəˌrɒl] *n.* холестери́н.
choose [tʃu:z] *v.t.* выбира́ть, вы́брать; изб|ира́ть, -ра́ть; **there are five to ~ from** мо́жно выбира́ть из пяти́; **there is little to ~ between them** оди́н друго́го сто́ит; одного́ по́ля я́года; два сапога́ па́ра; **the chosen people, race** и́збранный наро́д; **I cannot ~ but obey** я вы́нужден повинова́ться; **he was chosen king** его́ вы́брали/избра́ли королём; **I chose to remain** я предпочёл оста́ться.
v.i. **pick and ~** (*fig.*) быть разбо́рчивым, привере́дничать (*impf.*).
choos(e)y [ˈtʃu:zɪ] *adj.* разбо́рчивый.
chop[1] [tʃɒp] *n.* **1.** (*cut*) рубя́щий уда́р. **2.** (*of meat*) отбивна́я котле́та. **3.: get the ~** (*be dismissed*) вы́лететь (*pf.*) (с рабо́ты) (*coll.*).
v.t. руби́ть (*impf.*); (*cut*) нар|еза́ть, -е́зать; кроши́ть (*impf.*); **~ up** нар|еза́ть, -е́зать; **~ a branch off a tree** сруби́ть (*pf.*) ве́тку с де́рева; **~ a way through the bushes** прорубл|а́ть, -и́ть доро́гу че́рез кусты́; **~ a tree down** сруби́ть (*pf.*) де́рево.
cpd. **~-house** *n.* тракти́р, рестора́н.
chop[2] [tʃɒp] *n.* (*jaw*): **lick one's ~s** обли́з|ываться, -а́ться.
chop[3] [tʃɒp] *v.i.* (*change; also* **~ about**) меня́ться (*impf.*); **~ and change** постоя́нно меня́ть свои́ взгля́ды.
chopper [ˈtʃɒpə(r)] *n.* (*implement*) нож, коса́рь (*m.*); (*sl., helicopter*) вертолёт.
choppy [ˈtʃɒpɪ] *adj.* (*of sea*) неспоко́йный; (*of wind, changeable*) поры́вистый, с меня́ющимся направле́нием.
chopstick [ˈtʃɒpstɪk] *n.* па́лочка для еды́.
chop-suey [tʃɒpˈsu:ɪ] *n.* кита́йское рагу́ (*indecl*).
choral [ˈkɔ:r(ə)l] *adj.* хорово́й.
chorale [kɔ:ˈrɑ:l] *n.* хора́л.
chord [kɔ:d] *n.* **1.** (*string of harp etc.*) струна́; **strike a ~** (*fig., remind of sth.*) вы́звать (*pf.*) о́тклик. **2.** (*anat.*): **vocal ~s** голосовы́е свя́зки (*f. pl.*); **spinal ~** спинно́й мозг. **3.** (*combination of notes*) акко́рд; **common ~** акко́рд терцо́вого строе́ния. **4.** (*geom.*) хо́рда.
chore [tʃɔ:(r)] *n.* (*odd job*) случа́йная рабо́та; (*heavy task*) бре́мя (*nt.*); **household ~s** дома́шняя рабо́та.
choreographer [ˌkɒrɪˈɒgrəfə(r)] *n.* балетме́йстер, хореограф.
choreographic [ˌkɒrɪəgˈræfɪk] *adj.* хореографи́ческий.
choreography [ˌkɒrɪˈɒgrəfɪ] *n.* хореогра́фия.
choriambic [ˌkɒrɪˈæmbɪk] *adj.* хориямби́ческий.
choric [ˈkɔ:rɪk] *adj.* хорово́й.
chorister [ˈkɒrɪstə(r)] *n.* хори́ст, пе́вчий.
chortle [ˈtʃɔ:t(ə)l] *v.i.* фы́ркать (*impf.*); дави́ться (*impf.*) от сме́ха.
chorus [ˈkɔ:rəs] *n.* **1.** (*singers; also in anc. drama*) хор; **in ~** (*lit., fig.*) хо́ром; **~ of approval** хвале́бный хор. **2.** (*refrain*) припе́в, рефре́н.
v.t. & i. петь, с- (*or* произн|оси́ть, -ести́) хо́ром.
cpd. **~-girl** *n.* хори́стка.
chough [tʃʌf] *n.* клуши́ца.
chow [tʃaʊ] *n.* **1.** (*dog*) ча́у-ча́у (*f. indecl.*). **2.** (*sl., food*) жратва́.
chowder [ˈtʃaʊdə(r)] *n.* ≃ тушёная ры́ба; тушёные моллю́ски (*m. pl.*).
chrestomathy [kresˈtɒməθɪ] *n.* хрестома́тия.
chrism [ˈkrɪz(ə)m] *n.* (*oil*) еле́й.
Christ [kraɪst] *n.* **1.** Христо́с; **the ~ child** младе́нец Иису́с; **before ~** до на́шей э́ры (*abbr.* до н.э.). **2.** *as int.* Бо́же (мой)!; Го́споди!
christen [ˈkrɪs(ə)n] *v.t.* **1.** крести́ть (*impf., pf.*); **he was ~ed John** ему́ при креще́нии да́ли и́мя Джон; его́ нарекли́ Джо́ном. **2.** (*fig.*) окрести́ть (*pf.*); да|ва́ть, -ть и́мя *+d.*
Christendom [ˈkrɪsəndəm] *n.* христиа́нский мир.

christening [ˈkrɪs(ə)nɪŋ] *n.* крести́н|ы (*pl., g.* —); креще́ние.
Christian [ˈkrɪstɪən, ˈkrɪstʃ(ə)n] *n.* христи|ани́н (*fem.* -а́нка).
adj. христиа́нский; (*fig., decent*) бо́жеский, уме́ренный; ~ **burial** по́хороны по церко́вному обря́ду; ~ **era** христиа́нская э́ра; ~ **name** и́мя (*nt.*) (*в противоположность фамилии*); ~ **Science** «христиа́нская нау́ка».
Christiania [ˌkrɪstɪˈɑːnɪə] *n.* (*in skiing*) христиа́ния.
Christianity [ˌkrɪstɪˈænɪtɪ] *n.* христиа́нство.
Christianization [ˌkrɪstɪənaɪˈzeɪʃ(ə)n] *n.* обраще́ние в христиа́нство; христианиза́ция.
Christianize [ˈkrɪstɪəˌnaɪz] *v.t.* обра|ща́ть, -ти́ть в христиа́нство; христианизи́ровать (*impf. pf.*).
Christmas [ˈkrɪsməs] *n.* Рождество́; ~ **box, present** рожде́ственский пода́рок; ~ **card** рожде́ственская откры́тка; ~ **day** пе́рвый день Рождества́; ~ **eve** соче́льник; **Father** ~ дед-моро́з; **at** ~ на Рождество́; ~ **rose** моро́зник чёрный; ~ **tree** рожде́ственская ёлка.
cpds. **~-time, ~-tide** *nn.* свя́т|ки (*pl., g.* -ок).
chromatic [krəˈmætɪk] *adj.* **1.** (*pert. to colour*) цветно́й. **2.** (*colourful*) многокра́сочный. **3.** (*mus.*) хромати́ческий.
chromatics [krəˈmætɪks] *n.* нау́ка о цвета́х/кра́сках.
chrome [krəʊm] *n.* **1.** (*chem.*) хром. **2.** (*pigment, also* ~ **yellow**) хром; жёлтый цвет.
chromium [ˈkrəʊmɪəm] *n.* хром.
cpds. **~-plated** *adj.* хроми́рованный; **~-plating** *n.* хроми́рование, хромиро́вка.
chromolithograph [ˌkrəʊməʊˈlɪθəˌgrɑːf] *n.* хромолитогра́фия.
chromolithography [ˌkrəʊməʊlɪˈθɒgrəfɪ] *n.* хромолитогра́фия.
chromosome [ˈkrəʊməˌsəʊm] *n.* хромосо́ма.
chronic [ˈkrɒnɪk] *adj.* **1.** (*med.*) хрони́ческий. **2.** (*fig., incessant*) ве́чный, постоя́нный. **3.** (*coll., very bad*) ужа́сный.
chronicle [ˈkrɒnɪk(ə)l] *n.* хро́ника, ле́топись; **C~s** (*book of Bible*) Паралипомено́н.
v.t. вести́ (*det.*) хро́нику +*g.*; (*hist.*) зан|оси́ть, -ести́ в ле́топись.
chronicler [ˈkrɒnɪklə(r)] *n.* летопи́сец, исто́рик.
chronograph [ˈkrɒnəˌgrɑːf, ˈkrəʊnə-, -ˌgræf] *n.* хроно́граф.
chronographic [krɒnəˈgræfɪk] *adj.* хронографи́ческий.
chronologer [ˌkrəˈnɒlədʒə(r)] *n.* хроно́лог.
chronological [ˌkrɒnəˈlɒdʒɪk(ə)l] *adj.* хронологи́ческий.
chronology [krəˈnɒlədʒɪ] *n.* хроноло́гия; (*table*) хронологи́ческая табли́ца.
chronometer [krəˈnɒmɪtə(r)] *n.* хроно́метр.
chronometric(al) [ˌkrɒnəˈmetrɪk(ə)l] *adj.* хронометри́ческий.
chronometry [krəˈnɒmɪtrɪ] *n.* хронометра́ж.
chrysalis [ˈkrɪsəlɪs] *n.* ку́колка.
chrysanthemum [krɪˈsænθəməm] *n.* хризанте́ма.
chrysoberyl [ˈkrɪsəˌberɪl] *n.* хризобери́лл.
chrysolite [ˈkrɪsəˌlaɪt] *n.* хризоли́т.
chrysoprase [ˈkrɪsəˌpreɪz] *n.* хризопра́з.
chub [tʃʌb] *n.* голa'вль (*m.*).
chubby [ˈtʃʌbɪ] *adj.* круглоли́цый; то́лстенький, пу́хленький.
chuck[1] [tʃʌk] *n.*: **give s.o. the** ~ вы́турить (*pf.*) кого́-н. с рабо́ты (*coll.*).
v.t. **1.:** ~ **s.o. under the chin** потрепа́ть (*pf.*) кого́-н. по подборо́дку. **2.** (*coll., throw*) швыр|я́ть, -ну́ть. **3.** (*coll., give up*) бр|оса́ть, -о́сить; ~ **it!** бро́сьте!
with advs.: (*coll.*): ~ **away** *v.t.* (*lit.*) выбра́сывать, вы́бросить; (*fig.*): ~ **away a chance** упусти́ть (*pf.*) слу́чай; ~ **out** *v.t.* (*thg. or pers.*) вы́кинуть (*pf.*); вы́швырнуть (*pf.*); ~ **up** *v.t.* (*give up*) бр|оса́ть, -о́сить.
chuck[2] [tʃʌk] *int.* (*to fowls*) цып-цып!
chucker-out [ˈtʃʌkə(r)] *n.* вышиба́ла (*m.*).
chuckle [ˈtʃʌk(ə)l] *n.* сда́вленный смешо́к, смех.
v.i. фы́ркать (*impf.*) от сме́ха, посме́иваться (*impf.*).
chuckle-headed [ˈtʃʌkəlˌheded] *adj.* пустоголо́вый.
chuffed [tʃʌft] *adj.* (*coll.*) дово́льный; недово́льный.
chug [tʃʌg] *v.i.*: **the boat ~ged past** ло́дка пропыхте́ла ми́мо.
chum [tʃʌm] *n.* прия́тель (*m.*), дружо́к, ко́реш; **new** ~ (*fig.*) но́вый поселе́нец; новичо́к.
v.i. дружи́ть (*impf.*) (с+*i.*); якша́ться (*impf.*) (с+*i.*); ~ **up with s.o.** сдружи́ться (*pf.*) с кем-н.
chumminess [ˈtʃʌmɪnɪs] *n.* дружелю́бие, общи́тельность.
chummy [ˈtʃʌmɪ] *adj.* дружелю́бный, общи́тельный.
chump [tʃʌmp] *n.* (*log; blockhead*) чурба́н; (*head*) башка́; **he is off his** ~ он рехну́лся/спя́тил (*coll.*); ~ **chop** филе́йный кусо́к.
chunk [tʃʌŋk] *n.* то́лстый кусо́к/ломо́ть (*m.*); куси́ще (*m.*).
chunky [ˈtʃʌŋkɪ] *adj.* корена́стый, пло́тный.
church [tʃɜːtʃ] *n.* **1.** (*institution*) це́рковь; (*building*) це́рковь (*esp. Orthodox*), храм; (*Polish*) костёл; **go to** ~ (*regularly*) ходи́ть (*indet.*) в це́рковь; (*attend a service*) пойти́ (*pf.*) в це́рковь; **poor as a ~ mouse** бе́ден, как церко́вная мышь; **C~ of England/Scotland** англика́нская/пресвитериа́нская це́рковь; **C~ of Rome** ри́мско-католи́ческая це́рковь; ~ **parade** построе́ние на моли́тву; **C~ Slavonic** церковнославя́нский (язы́к). **2.** (*holy orders*): **he entered the** ~ он при́нял духо́вный сан.
cpds. **~goer** *n.*: **he is a regular ~goer** он регуля́рно хо́дит в це́рковь; **~going** *n.* посеще́ние це́ркви; **~man** *n.* церко́вник, ве́рующий; **~warden** *n.* кти́тор, церко́вный ста́роста; **~woman** *n.* ве́рующая; **~yard** *n.* пого́ст, кла́дбище при це́ркви.
churl [tʃɜːl] *n.* хам, мужи́к.
churlish [ˈtʃɜːlɪʃ] *adj.* неотёсанный; ха́мский, хамова́тый, гру́бый.
churlishness [ˈtʃɜːlɪʃnɪs] *n.* неотёсанность, ха́мство, гру́бость.
churn [tʃɜːn] *n.* (*tub*) маслобо́йка; (*can*) бидо́н.
v.t.: ~ **butter** сби|ва́ть, -ть ма́сло; (*fig.*): **he ~s out novels** он печёт рома́ны (как блины́); **the propeller ~ed up the waves** винт взвихри́л во́лны.
churr [tʃɜː(r)] *n.* стрекота́ние, трескотня́.
v.i. стрекота́ть, треща́ть (*both impf.*).
chute [ʃuːt] *n.* (*slide, slope*) жёлоб, спуск; (*for amusement*) гора́, го́рка; (*for rubbish*) мусоросбро́с, мусоропрово́д.
chutney [ˈtʃʌtnɪ] *n.* ча́тни (*nt. indecl.*).
CIA (*abbr. of* **Central Intelligence Agency**) ЦРУ, (Центра́льное разве́дывательное управле́ние).
cica|da [sɪˈkɑːdə, -ˈkeɪdə], **-la** [sɪˈkɑːlə] *nn.* цика́да.
cicatrice [ˈsɪkətrɪs] *n.* шрам, рубе́ц.
cicatrize [ˈsɪkəˌtraɪz] *v.t.* зажив|ля́ть, -и́ть.
v.i. зарубц|о́вываться, -ева́ться.
cicely [ˈsɪsəlɪ] *n.* ке́рвель (*m.*).
Cicero [ˈsɪsəˌrəʊ] *n.* Цицеро́н.
cicerone [ˌtʃɪtʃəˈrəʊnɪ, sɪsəˈrəʊnɪ] *n.* гид, чичеро́не (*m. indecl.*).
CID (*abbr. of* **Criminal Investigation Department**) отде́л/департа́мент уголо́вного ро́зыска.
ci|der [ˈsaɪdə(r)], **cy-** *n.* сидр.
cpd. **~-press** *n.* я́блочный пресс.
ci-devant [ˌsiːdəˈvɑ̃] *adj.* бы́вший.
c.i.f. (*abbr. of* **cost, insurance and freight**) сиф.
cigar [sɪˈgɑː(r)] *n.* сига́ра.
cpds. **~-case** *n.* сига́рочница; **~-holder** *n.* мундшту́к; **~-store** *n.* (*US*) таба́чная ла́вка, таба́чный магази́н.
cigarette [ˌsɪgəˈret] *n.* сигаре́та; (*of Russ. type*) папиро́са.
cpds. **~-case** *n.* портсига́р; **~-end, ~-stub** *nn.* оку́рок; **~-holder** *n.* мундшту́к; **~-lighter** *n.* зажига́лка; **~-paper** *n.* папиро́сная бума́га.
Cimmerian [sɪˈmɪərɪən] *adj.* (*fig.*): ~ **darkness** тьма кроме́шная.
C.-in-C. (*abbr. of* **Commander-in-Chief**) главко́м, (главнокома́ндующий).
cinch [sɪntʃ] *n.* (*sl.*) де́ло ве́рное.
cinchona [sɪŋˈkəʊnə] *n.* хи́нное де́рево.
cincture [ˈsɪŋktʃə(r)] *n.* по́яс; (*archit.*) поясо́к.
v.t. опоя́с|ывать, -ать.
cinder [ˈsɪndə(r)] *n.*: (*pl.*) шлак, зола́, пе́пел; **burn sth. to a** ~ сжечь (*pf.*) что-н. дотла́; ~ **path, track** (бегова́я) га́ревая доро́жка.
Cinderella [ˌsɪndəˈrelə] *n.* Зо́лушка; **education is the ~ of our system** образова́ние — са́мая забро́шенная о́бласть на́шего о́бщества.
cineast(e) [ˈsɪnɪˌæst] *n.* кинолюби́тель (*m.*).
cine-camera [ˈsɪnɪ-] *n.* киноаппара́т.
cine-film [ˈsɪnɪ-] *n.* киноплёнка.
cinema [ˈsɪnɪˌmɑː, -mə] *n.* (*art*) кино́ (*indecl.*), кинематогра́фия; (*place*) кино́ (*indecl.*), кинотеа́тр.

Cinemascope ['sɪnəmə,skəʊp] *n.* (*propr.*) систе́ма широкоэкра́нного кино́.
cinematic [,sɪnɪ'mætɪk] *adj.* кинематографи́ческий.
cinematograph [,sɪnɪ'mætə,grɑ:f] *n.* киноаппара́т.
cinematographic [sɪnɪ,mætə'græfɪk] *adj.* кинематографи́ческий.
cinematography [,sɪnɪmə'tɒgrəfɪ] *n.* кинематогра́фия.
cine-projector ['sɪnɪ] *n.* кинопроекцио́нный аппара́т.
Cinerama [,sɪnə'rɑ:mə] *n.* (*propr.*) синера́ма, систе́ма панора́много кино́.
cineraria [,sɪnə'reərɪə] *n.* цинера́рия.
cinerary ['sɪnərərɪ] *adj.*: ~ **urn** у́рна с пра́хом.
cinnabar ['sɪnə,bɑ:(r)] *n.* (*min., chem.*) ки́новарь.
cinnamon ['sɪnəmən] *n.* кори́ца; (*colour*) све́тло-кори́чневый цвет.
cinquefoil ['sɪŋkfɔɪl] *n.* (*bot.*) лапча́тка; (*archit.*) пятили́стник.
ci|pher ['saɪfə(r)], **cy-** *n.* **1.** (*figure 0*) нуль, ноль (*both m.*). **2.** (*fig., nonentity*) ничто́жество, нуль. **3.** (*monogram*) моногра́мма, ве́нзель (*m.*). **4.** (*secret writing*) шифр, код; **message in** ~, ~ **message** (за)шифро́ванное сообще́ние; ~ **officer** шифрова́льщик; ~ **room** шифрова́льная.
v.t. шифрова́ть, за-.
circa ['sɜ:kə] *prep.* приблизи́тельно; о́коло+*g.*
circadian [sɜ:'keɪdɪən] *adj.*: ~ **rhythm** су́точный ритм.
Circassian [sɜ:'kæsɪən] *n.* черке́|с (*fem.* -шенка).
adj. черке́сский.
Circe ['sɜ:sɪ] *n.* (*myth., fig.*) Цирце́я.
circle ['sɜ:k(ə)l] *n.* **1.** (*math., fig.*) круг, окру́жность; **a** ~ **of trees** кольцо́ дере́вьев; **they stood in a** ~ они́ ста́ли в кру́г; они́ стоя́ли кольцо́м; **square the** ~ найти́ (*pf.*) квадрату́ру кру́га; **great** ~ ортодро́мия; **great** ~ **sailing** пла́вание по дуге́ большо́го кру́га; **Arctic/Antarctic** ~ Се́верный/Ю́жный поля́рный круг; **vicious** ~ поро́чный круг; **go round in a** ~ (*fig., e.g. argument*) возвраща́ться (*impf.*) к исхо́дной то́чке; **run round in** ~**s** (*fig.*) верте́ться (*impf.*), как бе́лка в колесе́. **2.** (*theatr.*): **dress** ~ бельэта́ж; **upper** ~ балко́н. **3.** (*of seasons etc.*) цикл; по́лный оборо́т; **come full** ~ описа́ть (*pf.*) по́лный круг; заверши́ть (*pf.*) цикл.
v.t.: **the earth** ~**s the sun** земля́ враща́ется вокру́г со́лнца; **he** ~**d the misspelt words** он обвёл кружка́ми непра́вильно напи́санные слова́.
v.i.: **the hawk** ~**d** я́стреб кружи́лся (*or* опи́сывал круги́); **the news** ~**d round** но́вость распространи́лась повсю́ду.
circlet ['sɜ:klɪt] *n.* (*ring*) кольцо́; (*headband*) вене́ц; (*bracelet*) брасле́т.
circuit ['sɜ:kɪt] *n.* **1.** (*distance, journey round*): **the** ~ **of the walls is 3 miles** окру́жность стен 3 ми́ли; **he made a** ~ **of the camp** он обошёл ла́герь; (*detour*) окружно́й путь, объе́зд. **2.** (*itinerary*) маршру́т. **3.** (*leg.*) суде́бный круг. **4.** (*elec.*) цепь; схе́ма; **integrated** ~ интегра́льная схе́ма; **short** ~ коро́ткое замыка́ние; ~ **breaker** автомати́ческий выключа́тель; **closed-**~ **television** ка́бельное телеви́дение (по за́мкнутому кана́лу).
v.t. & i. об|ходи́ть, -ойти́ (*or* враща́ться) (вокру́г+*g.*).
circuitous [sɜ:'kju:ɪtəs] *adj.* кру́жный, око́льный.
circular ['sɜ:kjʊlə(r)] *n.* (*letter etc.*) циркуля́р; (*commercial*) проспе́кт.
adj. кругово́й; (*round in shape*) кру́глый, кругообра́зный; ~ **saw** кру́глая/циркуля́рная пила́; ~ **road** (*round a town*) окружна́я доро́га; ~ **letter** циркуля́рное письмо́.
circularize ['sɜ:kjʊlə,raɪz] *v.t.* ра|ссыла́ть, -зосла́ть циркуля́ры +*d.*
circulate ['sɜ:kjʊ,leɪt] *v.t.* (*put about, e.g. rumour*) распростран|я́ть, -и́ть; перед|ава́ть, -а́ть; (*pass round, e.g. port*) передава́ть (*impf.*) по кру́гу.
v.i. циркули́ровать (*impf., pf.*); **blood** ~**s through the body** кровь циркули́рует в те́ле; **she** ~**d among the guests** она́ переходи́ла от одного́ го́стя к друго́му.
circulation [,sɜ:kjʊ'leɪʃ(ə)n] *n.* **1.** (*of blood*) кровообраще́ние; (*of air*) циркуля́ция. **2.** (*of banknotes etc.*) обраще́ние. **3. Smith is back in** ~ Смит сно́ва появи́лся на горизо́нте. **4.** (*of newspaper etc.*) тира́ж; **this paper has a** ~ **of 5,000** у э́той газе́ты тира́ж 5 000.
circumambient [,sɜ:kəm'æmbɪənt] *adj.* окружа́ющий.
circumambulate [,sɜ:kəm'æmbjʊ,leɪt] *v.t.* об|ходи́ть, -ойти́.
circumcise ['sɜ:kəm,saɪz] *v.t.* соверш|а́ть, -и́ть обреза́ние +*d.*
circumcision [,sɜ:kəm'sɪʒ(ə)n] *n.* обреза́ние.
circumference [sɜ:'kʌmfərəns] *n.* окру́жность.
circumflex ['sɜ:kəm,fleks] *n.* (~ *accent*) циркумфле́кс, знак облегчённого ударе́ния.
circumfluent [sə'kʌmflʊənt] *adj.* омыва́ющий, обтека́ющий.
circumjacent [,sɜ:kəm'dʒeɪs(ə)nt] *adj.* окружа́ющий.
circumlocution [,sɜ:kəmlə'kju:ʃ(ə)n] *n.* многосло́вие, околи́чности (*f. pl.*).
circumnavigate [,sɜ:kəm'nævɪ,geɪt] *v.t.* пла́вать (*indet.*) вокру́г+*g.*; **Drake** ~**d the globe** Дрейк соверши́л кругосве́тное путеше́ствие.
circumnavigation [,sɜ:kəmnævɪ'geɪʃ(ə)n] *n.* навига́ция по кру́гу.
circumpolar [,sɜ:kəm'pəʊlə(r)] *adj.* (*geog.*) околопо́люсный; (*astron.*) околополя́рный.
circumscribe ['sɜ:kəm,skraɪb] *v.t.* (*draw line round*) опи́с|ывать, -а́ть; (*fig., restrict*) ста́вить, по- преде́л +*d.*; ограни́чи|вать, -ть.
circumscription [,sɜ:kəm'skrɪpʃ(ə)n] *n.* (*restriction*) ограниче́ние, преде́л; (*inscription*) на́дпись.
circumspect ['sɜ:kəm,spekt] *adj.* осмотри́тельный.
circumspection [,sɜ:kəm'spekʃ(ə)n] *n.* осмотри́тельность.
circumstance ['sɜ:kəmst(ə)ns] *n.* **1.** (*fact, detail*) обстоя́тельство, усло́вие; **in, under the** ~**s** в да́нных усло́виях/обстоя́тельствах; **in, under no** ~**s** ни при каки́х усло́виях/обстоя́тельствах; **extenuating** ~**s** смягча́ющие обстоя́тельства. **2.** (*condition of life*) материа́льное положе́ние; **in easy** ~**s** в хоро́шем материа́льном положе́нии. **3.** (*ceremony*) церемо́ния, торже́ственность.
circumstanced ['sɜ:kəmst(ə)nsd] *adj.*: (*with advs.*) поста́вленный в (определённые) усло́вия; **comfortably** ~ обеспе́ченный.
circumstantial [,sɜ:kəm'stænʃ(ə)l] *adj.*: ~ **evidence** ко́свенные ули́ки (*f. pl.*); **a** ~ **story** обстоя́тельный расска́з.
circumvent [,sɜ:kəm'vent] *v.t.* об|ходи́ть, -ойти́; (*outwit, cheat*) перехитри́ть (*pf.*); пров|оди́ть, -ести́.
circumvention [,sɜ:kəm'venʃ(ə)n] *n.* (*deception*) обма́н.
circus ['sɜ:kəs] *n.* **1.** (*also hist.*) цирк; (*fig.*) балага́н; ~ **rider** (*fem.*) цирковая́ нае́здница. **2.** (intersection of *streets*) (кру́глая) пло́щадь.
cirrhosis [sɪ'rəʊsɪs] *n.* цирро́з.
cirro-cumulus [,sɪrəʊ'kju:mjʊləs] *n.* пе́ристо-кучевы́е облака́.
cirrous ['sɪrəs] *adj.* (*of cloud*) пе́ристый.
cirrus ['sɪrəs] *n.* (*clouds*) пе́ристые облака́.
CIS (*abbr. of* ***Commonwealth of Independent States***) СНГ, (Содру́жество незави́симых госуда́рств); (*attr., coll.*) эсэнго́вский.
cisalpine [sɪs'ælpaɪn] *adj.* цизальпи́нский.
cissy ['sɪsɪ] = **sissy**
Cistercian [sɪ'stɜ:ʃ(ə)n] *n.* цистерциа́нец.
adj. цистерциа́нский.
cistern ['sɪst(ə)n] *n.* цисте́рна, бак.
citadel ['sɪtəd(ə)l, -,del] *n.* (*lit., fig.*) цитаде́ль, тверды́ня.
citation [saɪ'teɪʃ(ə)n] *n.* **1.** (*summons*) вы́зов. **2.** (*quotation*) цита́ция, цити́рование. **3.** (*for bravery*) упомина́ние в прика́зе.
cite [saɪt] *v.t.* **1.** (*summon*) вызыва́ть, вы́звать. **2.** (*quote*) цити́ровать, про-. **3.** (*for bravery*) отм|еча́ть, -е́тить в прика́зе.
cither(n) ['sɪθə(n)] *n.* ци́тра, кифа́ра.
citizen ['sɪtɪz(ə)n] *n.* гражд|ани́н (*fem.* -а́нка); **French** ~ францу́ский граждани́н; (*of city*) жи́тель (*fem.* -ница); **private** ~ ча́стное лицо́.
citizenry ['sɪtɪzənrɪ] *n.* гра́ждане (*m. pl.*), населе́ние.
citizenship ['sɪtɪzənʃɪp] *n.* (*nationality*) гражда́нство, по́дданство.
citric ['sɪtrɪk] *adj.* лимо́нный.
citron ['sɪtrən] *n.* (*tree, fruit*) цитро́н.
citrus ['sɪtrəs] *n.* ци́трус; ~ **fruit** ци́трусовые (*m. pl.*).
city ['sɪtɪ] *n.* го́род; (*of London*) Си́ти (*nt. indecl.*); **the Eternal C**~ Ве́чный го́род; ~ **centre** центр го́рода; ~

council городско́й сове́т; ~ **fathers** отцы́ го́рода; ~ **hall** ра́туша; ~ **state** (*hist.*) го́род-госуда́рство, по́лис.

civet ['sɪvɪt] *n.* **1.** (*also* ~**-cat**) виве́рра. **2.** (*perfume*) цибети́н.

civic ['sɪvɪk] *adj.* гражда́нский; ~ **activity** обще́ственная де́ятельность; ~ **virtues** гражда́нские до́блести.

civics ['sɪvɪks] *n.* осно́вы (*f. pl.*) гражда́нственности.

civil ['sɪv(ə)l, -ɪl] *adj.* **1.** (*pert. to a community*): ~ **war** гражда́нская война́; ~ **rights** гражда́нские права́; ~ **marriage** гражда́нский брак; ~ **servant** госуда́рственный слу́жащий, чино́вник; ~ **service** госуда́рственная слу́жба; ~ **law** гражда́нское пра́во; ~ **engineer** инжене́р-строи́тель (*m.*). **2.** (*civilian*) гражда́нский, шта́тский; ~ **defence** гражда́нская оборо́на. **3.** (*polite*) ве́жливый, учти́вый, любе́зный; **keep a ~ tongue in your head!** бу́дьте повежливей!

civilian [sɪ'vɪlɪən] *n.* & *adj.* шта́тский; ~ **population** ми́рные жи́тели; **what did you do in ~ life?** чем вы занима́лись до а́рмии?

civility [sɪ'vɪlɪtɪ] *n.* ве́жливость, любе́зность, учти́вость; (*pl.*) любе́зности (*f. pl.*).

civilization [ˌsɪvɪlaɪ'zeɪʃ(ə)n] *n.* цивилиза́ция; **deeds that horrified ~** дея́ния, ужасну́вшие цивилизо́ванный мир.

civilize ['sɪvɪˌlaɪz] *v.t.* цивилизова́ть (*impf., pf.*).

civvies ['sɪvɪz] *n.* (*coll.*) шта́тская оде́жда; **in ~** в шта́тском.

clack [klæk] *n.* (*sharp sound*) треск, щёлканье, стук; (*talk*) трескотня́.

v.i. (*lit., fig.*) треща́ть, щёлкать, стуча́ть (*all impf.*); **tongues were ~ing** языки́ болта́ли.

claim [kleɪm] *n.* **1.** (*assertion of right*) притяза́ние; **lay ~ to sth.** предъяви́ть (*pf.*) прете́нзии на что-н.; претендова́ть (*impf.*) на что-н.; **file** (*or* **put in**) **a ~ for damages** предъяви́ть (*pf.*) иск о возмеще́нии убы́тков; **stake out a ~** (*fig.*) закрепля́ть (*impf.*) своё пра́во (*на что*). **2.** (*assertion*) утвержде́ние, заявле́ние. **3.** (*demand*) тре́бование; (*just demand*): **you have no ~ on my sympathies** вы не заслу́живаете моего́ сочу́вствия.

v.t. **1.** (*demand*) тре́бовать (*impf.*) +*g.*; **where do I ~ my baggage?** где здесь выдаю́т бага́ж?; **does anyone ~ this umbrella?** есть ли владе́лец у э́того зо́нтика?; **I ~ the protection of the law** я взыва́ю к зако́ну; **I ~ the right of free speech** я тре́бую осуществле́ния своего́ пра́ва на свобо́ду сло́ва. **2.** (*assert as fact*) утвер|жда́ть, -ди́ть; **he ~s to own the land** он заявля́ет, что э́та земля́ принадлежи́т ему́; **he ~s to have done the work alone** он утвержда́ет, что сде́лал рабо́ту сам; ~ **default** предъяви́ть (*pf.*) тре́бование за неисполне́ние догово́ра. **3.** (*of things*) тре́бовать, по- +*g.*; **this matter ~s attention** э́тот вопро́с заслу́живает внима́ния.

claimant ['kleɪmənt] *n.* претенде́нт (*на что*); (*leg.*) исте́ц.

claimer ['kleɪmə(r)] *n.*: **the ~ of the umbrella** челове́к, заяви́вший, что (на́йденный) зо́нтик принадлежи́т ему́.

clairvoyance [kleə'vɔɪəns] *n.* ясновиде́ние.

clairvoyant [kleə'vɔɪənt] *n.* ясновид|ец (*fem.* -ица).

clam [klæm] *n.* (*shellfish*) двуство́рчатый морско́й моллю́ск; **he shut up like a ~** (*fig.*) он храни́л упо́рное молча́ние.

v.i. (*gather ~s*) собира́ть (*impf.*) моллю́сков.

clamber ['klæmbə(r)] *v.i.* кара́бкаться, вс- (*на что*).

clamminess ['klæmɪnɪs] *n.* ли́пкость.

clammy ['klæmɪ] *adj.* холо́дный и ли́пкий.

clamorous ['klæmərəs] *adj.* шу́мный, шумли́вый.

clamour ['klæmə(r)] *n.* шум, кри́ки (*m. pl.*).

v.i. шуме́ть (*impf.*), крича́ть (*impf.*).

clamp [klæmp] *n.* (*implement*) зажи́м, скоба́, струбци́на.

v.t. заж|има́ть, -а́ть; скреп|ля́ть, -и́ть; (*fig.*): **the police ~ed down a curfew** поли́ция ввела́ коменда́нтский час.

v.i.: ~ **down on** (*fig., suppress*) зажа́ть (*pf.*); прижа́ть (*pf.*).

cpd. ~**down** *n.* стро́гий запре́т, стро́гие ме́ры (*против чего*).

clan [klæn] *n.* клан, род; (*clique*) кли́ка, гру́ппа; (*large family*) семья́, пле́мя (*nt.*).

clandestine [klæn'destɪn] *adj.* та́йный, подпо́льный.

clandestinity [klænˌdes'tɪnɪtɪ] *n.* потаённость, секре́тность.

clang ['klæŋ] *n.* лязг, звон.

v.t. & *i.* ля́зг|ать, -нуть; звене́ть (*impf.*); **the tram-driver ~ed his bell** вагоновожа́тый гро́мко звони́л в звоно́к.

clanger ['klæŋə(r)] *n.*: **he dropped a ~** (*sl.*) он сде́лал ля́псус; он дал ма́ху (*coll.*).

clangorous ['klæŋgərəs] *adj.* ля́згающий.

clangour ['klæŋgə(r)] *n.* звон, ля́зганье.

clank [klæŋk] *n.* звон, лязг, бряца́ние.

v.t. & *i.* ля́зг|ать, -нуть; бряца́ть (*impf.*); греме́ть (*impf.*); **the ghost ~ed its chains** привиде́ние ля́згало/греме́ло цепя́ми.

clannish ['klænɪʃ] *adj.* держа́щийся своего́ кла́на (*or* свое́й гру́ппы).

clansman ['klænzmən] *n.* член кла́на/ро́да.

clap[1] [klæp] *n.* (*of thunder*) уда́р; (*of applause*) хлопо́к, хло́панье; **let's give him a ~!** похло́паем ему́!; (*slap*) хлопо́к; **a ~ on the back** хлопо́к по спине́.

v.t. **1.** (*strike, slap*) хло́п|ать, -нуть; **he ~ped me on the back** он хло́пнул меня́ по спине́; ~ **the lid of a box to** захло́пнуть (*pf.*) кры́шку я́щика; ~ **one's hands** хло́п|ать, -нуть в ладо́ши. **2.** (*put*): ~ **s.o. in prison** упе́чь (*pf.*) кого́-н. в тюрьму́; ~ **duties on goods** взять (*pf.*) да обложи́ть това́ры по́шлиной; ~ **a hat on one's head** нахлобу́чить (*pf.*) шля́пу на го́лову; ~ **handcuffs on s.o.** наде́ть (*pf.*) нару́чники на кого́-н.; **I have not ~ped eyes on him since then** с тех пор я ни ра́зу его́ не ви́дел. **3.** (*applaud*) аплоди́ровать (*impf.*) +*d.*; рукоплеска́ть (*impf.*) +*d.*

v.i. хло́пать (*impf.*); аплоди́ровать (*impf.*); рукоплеска́ть (*impf.*).

cpds. ~**board** *n.* клёпка; дра́нка, гонт; ~**trap** *n.* трееску́чая фра́за, болтовня́.

clap[2] [klæp] *n.* (*vulg., gonorrhoea*) три́ппер.

clapper ['klæpə(r)] *n.* (*of bell*) язы́к; (*rattle*) трещо́тка; *pl.* **go like the ~s** мча́ться как угоре́лый.

claque [klæk, klɑːk] *n.* кла́ка.

claret ['klærət] *n.* кларе́т; бордо́ (*indecl.*); **tap s.o.'s ~** (*joc.*) раскваси́ть кому́-н. нос; ~ **cup** ≃ крюшо́н из кра́сного вина́.

cpd. ~**-coloured** *adj.* цве́та бордо́; бордо́вый.

clarification [ˌklærɪfɪ'keɪʃ(ə)n] *n.* проясне́ние, разъясне́ние; (*of liquid*) очище́ние.

clarify ['klærɪˌfaɪ] *v.t.* вн|оси́ть, -ести́ я́сность в+*a.*; разъясн|я́ть, -и́ть; ~ **one's mind about sth.** уясни́ть (*pf.*) себе́ что-н.; (*butter etc.*) оч|ища́ть, -и́стить; де́лать, с- прозра́чным.

clarinet [ˌklærɪ'net] *n.* кларне́т.

clarinettist [ˌklærɪ'netɪst] *n.* кларнети́ст (*fem.* -ка).

clarion ['klærɪən] *n.* рог, рожо́к; ~ **call** (*fig.*) призы́вный звук; боево́й клич.

clarity ['klærɪtɪ] *n.* я́сность.

clash [klæʃ] *n.* **1.** (*sound*) гул, лязг, звон. **2.** (*conflict*): **I had a ~ with him** у меня́ бы́ло с ним столкнове́ние; ~ **of views** расхожде́ние во взгля́дах; ~ **of colours** дисгармо́ния цвето́в; (*of dates*) совпаде́ние по вре́мени.

v.t.: **he ~ed the cymbals** он уда́рил в цимба́лы.

v.i. **1.** (*sound*): **the cymbals ~ed** зазвене́ли цимба́лы. **2.** (*conflict*): **the armies ~ed** а́рмии столкну́лись; **my interests ~ with his** у нас с ним ста́лкиваются интере́сы; **the two concerts ~** о́ба конце́рта совпада́ют по вре́мени; **the colours ~** э́ти цвета́ не гармони́руют друг с дру́гом.

clasp [klɑːsp] *n.* **1.** (*fastener*) пря́жка, застёжка. **2.** (*grip, handshake*) пожа́тие, сжа́тие, объя́тие.

v.t.: ~ **a bracelet round one's wrist** застёг|ивать, -ну́ть на руке́ брасле́т; ~ **one's hands** сплести́ (*pf.*) па́льцы рук; ~ **s.o. by the hand** сж|има́ть, -ать кому́-н. ру́ку; **they were ~ed in each other's arms** они́ заключи́ли друг дру́га в объя́тия; ~ **hands with s.o.** (*fig.*) пожа́ть (*pf.*) ру́ку кому́-н.

v.i.: **the necklace won't ~** ожере́лье не застёгивается.

cpd. ~**-knife** *n.* складно́й нож.

class [klɑːs] *n.* **1.** (*group, category*) класс, разря́д; (*railway etc.*): **he went first ~** он е́хал пе́рвым кла́ссом; (*fig.*): **he is not in the same ~ as X** ему́ о́чень далеко́ до X; (*biol.*) класс. **2.** (*social*) класс; **lower ~(es)** ни́зшие кла́ссы; **middle ~** буржуази́я; сре́дние слои́ о́бщества; **upper ~(es)**

вы́сшие кла́ссы, аристокра́тия; ~ **conflict** кла́ссовые конфли́кты/противоре́чия; ~ **hatred** кла́ссовая вражда́; ~ **war** кла́ссовая борьба́. **3.** (*scholastic*) класс; **he is top of the** ~ он пе́рвый учени́к в кла́ссе; (*period of instruction*): **a mathematics** ~ уро́к матема́тики; **Mr. X is taking the** ~ г-н X ведёт заня́тия; **he attended** ~**es in French** он посеща́л заня́тия по францу́зскому языку́; (*US*): **the** ~ **of 1955** вы́пуск 1955 го́да. **4.** (*mil.*): **the** ~ **of 1960** набо́р 1960 го́да. **5.** (*distinction*) класс, шик.

v.t. классифици́ровать (*impf.*, *pf.*); **the ship is** ~**ed A1** су́дну присво́ен пе́рвый класс; **you cannot** ~ **him with the Romantics** его́ нельзя́ отнести́ к рома́нтикам.

v.i.: **those who** ~ **as believers** те, кото́рые счита́ются ве́рующими.

cpds. ~**-conscious** *adj.* кла́ссово-созна́тельный; ~**-consciousness** *n.* кла́ссовое созна́ние; ~**fellow,** ~**mate** *nn.* однокла́ссни|к (*fem.* -ца); ~**room** *n.* кла́ссная ко́мната, класс.

classic ['klæsɪk] *n.* **1.** (*writer etc.*) кла́ссик. **2.** (*book etc.*) класси́ческое произведе́ние. **3.** (*ancient writer*) кла́ссик, анти́чный а́втор; **the** ~**s** кла́ссика, класси́ческая литерату́ра. **4.** (*pl.*, *studies*): **he studied** ~**s** он изуча́л класси́ческую филоло́гию. **5.** (*specialist in* ~*s*) кла́ссик, специали́ст по анти́чной филоло́гии.

adj. класси́ческий.

classical ['klæsɪk(ə)l] *adj.* класси́ческий; ~ **scholar** кла́ссик.

classicism ['klæsɪˌsɪz(ə)m] *n.* классици́зм; (*classical scholarship*) изуче́ние класси́ческой филоло́гии.

classicist ['klæsɪˌsɪst] *n.* классици́ст; специали́ст по класси́ческой филоло́гии; сторо́нник класси́ческого образова́ния.

classifiable ['klæsɪˌfaɪəb(ə)l] *adj.* поддаю́щийся классифика́ции.

classification [ˌklæsɪfɪ'keɪʃ(ə)n] *n.* классифика́ция.

classifier ['klæsɪˌfaɪə(r)] *n.* классифика́тор; (*gram.*) показа́тель (*m.*) кла́сса.

classif|y ['klæsɪˌfaɪ] *v.t.* классифици́ровать (*impf.*, *pf.*); ~**ied** (*secret*) засекре́ченный.

classless ['klɑːslɪs] *adj.* бескла́ссовый.

classlessness ['klɑːslɪsnɪs] *n.* бескла́ссовость.

classy ['klɑːsɪ] *adj.* кла́ссный (*coll.*).

clatter ['klætə(r)] *n.* **1.** (*of metal*) гро́хот; (*of hoofs*, *plates*, *cutlery etc.*) стук, звон, звя́канье. **2.** (*chatter*, *noise*) трескотня́.

v.t. стуча́ть, греме́ть, звя́кать (*all impf.*).

v.i. греме́ть; грохота́ть (*both impf.*); **the plates came** ~**ing down** таре́лки с гро́хотом полете́ли на́ пол.

clause [klɔːz] *n.* **1.** (*gram.*) предложе́ние; **principal** ~ гла́вное предложе́ние; **subordinate** ~ прида́точное предложе́ние. **2.** (*provision*) кла́узула, огово́рка; **escape** ~ пункт, предусма́тривающий отка́з от взя́того обяза́тельства; ~**-by-**~ **voting** постате́йное голосова́ние.

claustrophobia [ˌklɔːstrə'fəʊbɪə] *n.* боя́знь за́мкнутого простра́нства; клаустрофо́бия.

claustrophobic [ˌklɔːstrə'fəʊbɪk] *adj.* клаустрофоби́чный; вызыва́ющий клаустрофо́бию.

clavichord ['klævɪˌkɔːd] *n.* клавико́рд|ы (*pl.*, *g.* -ов).

clavicle ['klævɪk(ə)l] *n.* ключи́ца.

claw [klɔː] *n.* (*of animal*, *bird*) ко́готь (*m.*); (*of crustacean*) клешня́; (*bony hand*) костля́вая рука́; **get one's** ~**s into sth.** вцеп|ля́ться, -и́ться когтя́ми во что-н.; (*of machinery*) кула́к, ла́па, клёщ|и (*pl.*, *g.* -ей).

v.t. & i. цара́пать(ся); рвать когтя́ми; когти́ть (*all impf.*); ~ **hold of sth.** вцепи́ться (*pf.*) во что-н.; **the cat** ~**ed at the door** ко́шка цара́палась в дверь; ~ **one's way to the top** (*fig.*) вскара́бкаться (*pf.*) наве́рх.

cpd. ~**-hammer** *n.* молото́к с гвоздодёром.

clay [kleɪ] *n.* гли́на; ~ **soil** гли́нистая по́чва; ~ **pigeon** таре́лочка для стрельбы́ (*в тире*); ~ **pipe** гли́няная тру́бка; **an idol with feet of** ~ куми́р на гли́няных нога́х; (*fig.*): **they are men of a different** ~ они́ (сде́ланы) из ра́зного те́ста.

clayey ['kleɪɪ] *adj.* гли́нистый.

claymore ['kleɪmɔː(r)] *n.* пала́ш.

clean [kliːn] *n.* чи́стка, убо́рка; **he gave the table a good** ~ он хороше́нько вы́тер стол.

adj. **1.** (*not dirty*) чи́стый; **wash sth.** ~ до́чиста вы́мыть (*pf.*) что-н.; **keep a room** ~ содержа́ть (*impf.*) ко́мнату в чистоте́. **2.** (*fresh*): **a** ~ **sheet of paper** чи́стый лист бума́ги; **a** ~ **copy** (*of draft*) чистови́к, белови́к. **3.** (*pure*, *unblemished*) чи́стый, незапя́тнанный. **4.** (*neat*, *smooth*): **the ship has** ~ **lines** у корабля́ пла́вные обво́ды; **a** ~ **cut** ро́вный разре́з; **a** ~ **set of fingerprints** я́сные отпеча́тки па́льцев; **the knife has a** ~ **edge** у ножа́ отто́ченное ле́звие. **5.** (*fig.*): **my hands are** ~ я невино́вен; **make a** ~ **sweep of** подчи́стить под метёлку; **he showed a** ~ **pair of heels** у него́ пя́тки засверка́ли; **come** ~ (*coll.*, *confess or vouchsafe the truth*) созна́ться (*pf.*).

adv.: **I** ~ **forgot** я на́чисто забы́л; **the bullet went** ~ **through his shoulder** пу́ля прошла́ у него́ (навы́лет) сквозь плечо́; ~ **wrong** соверше́нно непра́вильно.

v.t. чи́стить (*impf.*; *for forms of pf. see examples*); ~ **one's nails** почи́стить (*pf.*) но́гти; ~ **a suit** чи́стить, вы́-/по- костю́м; ~ **streets** уб|ира́ть, -ра́ть у́лицы; ~ **a car** мыть, вы́- маши́ну; ~ **a window** прот|ира́ть, -ере́ть окно́; ~ **a rifle** проч|ища́ть, -и́стить ружьё; ~ (*empty*) **one's plate** умя́ть (*pf.*) всю таре́лку; ~**ing fluid** жи́дкость для выведе́ния пя́тен; **he had his suit** ~**ed** он отда́л костю́м в чи́стку.

v.i. чи́ститься (*impf.*); **the sink** ~**s easily** ра́ковина хорошо́ мо́ется; ~**ing day** (*in hostels, shops etc.*) санита́рный день.

with advs.: ~ **down** *v.t.* сч|ища́ть, -и́стить; сме|та́ть, -сти́; ~ **out** *v.t.*: ~ **out a room** убра́ть (*pf.*) ко́мнату; **he was** ~**ed out** (*fig.*) он оста́лся без копе́йки; ~ **up** *v.t.*: ~ **o.s. up** почи́ститься (*pf.*); ~ **up a city** (*fig.*) почи́стить (*pf.*) го́род; ~ **up** (*settle*) **pending cases** разобра́ть (*pf.*) залежа́вшиеся дела́; **he** ~**ed up £1,000** он сорва́л 1000 фу́нтов (*coll.*); *v.i.*: **they** ~**ed up after the picnic** они́ всё убра́ли за собо́й по́сле пикника́.

cpds. ~**-cut** *adj.* ре́зко оче́рченный; ~**-cut features** пра́вильные черты́ лица́; (*fig.*) я́сный, я́вный, отчётливый; ~**-handed** *adj.* (*fig.*) че́стный; ~**-handedness** *n.* че́стность; ~**-limbed** *adj.* стро́йный; ~**-living** *adj.* целому́дренный, чи́стый; ~**-out** *n.* чи́стка, убо́рка; ~**-shaven** *adj.* бри́тый; ~**-up** *n.* (*lit.*) чи́стка; (*fig.*) чи́стка, очи́стка; приведе́ние в поря́док.

cleaner ['kliːnə(r)] *n.* (*pers.*) убо́рщи|к (*fem.* -ца); чи́стильщик (*fem.* -ца); **he sent the suit to the** ~**'s** он отда́л костю́м в чи́стку; (*tool*, *machine*, *substance*) очисти́тель (*m.*).

cleanliness ['klenlɪnɪs] *n.* чистота́; чистопло́тность, опря́тность.

cleanly ['kliːnlɪ] *adj.* чистопло́тный, опря́тный.

cleanness ['kliːnnɪs] *n.* чистота́.

cleans|e [klenz] *v.t.* оч|ища́ть, -и́стить; ~**ing cream** очища́ющий крем; ~**ing department** санита́рное управле́ние; **ethnic** ~**ing** этни́ческая чи́стка.

cleanser ['klenzə(r)] *n.* сре́дство для очи́стки ко́жи.

clear [klɪə(r)] *adj.* **1.** (*easy to see*) я́сный, отчётливый; (*evident*) я́вный, очеви́дный. **2.** (*bright*, *unclouded*) я́ркий, я́сный; **a** ~ **fire** я́ркий ого́нь; **a** ~ **sky** я́сное не́бо; **on a** ~ **day** в пого́жий день. **3.** (*transparent*) прозра́чный. **4.** (*of sound*) чи́стый, отчётливый. **5.** (*intelligible*, *certain*): **make sth.** ~ **to s.o.** объясн|я́ть, -и́ть что-н. кому́-н.; **make o.s.** ~ объясн|я́ться, -и́ться; **I am not** ~ **what he wants** мне нея́сно, чего́ он хо́чет; **as** ~ **as day, crystal** ~ я́сно как день; преде́льно я́сно; ~ **as mud** (*coll.*) соверше́нно нея́сно. **6.** (*safe*, *free*, *unencumbered*) свобо́дный; **the field is** ~ **of trees** на поля́нке нет дере́вьев; **the river is** ~ **of ice** река́ освободи́лась ото льда́; **the 'all** ~**'** отбо́й (*воздушной тревоги*); ~ **of debt** свобо́дный от долго́в; ~ **of suspicion** вне подозре́ний; **my conscience is** ~ моя́ со́весть чиста́; ~ **profit** чи́стая при́быль; **three** ~ **days** це́лых три дня; **keep a** ~ **head** сохраня́ть (*impf.*) я́сный ум. **7.**: **the** ~ (*absolute*) **contrary** по́лная противополо́жность; **in** ~ (*not in cipher*) откры́тым те́кстом, клё́ром; **in the** ~ (*solvent*) платёжеспосо́бный; (*free from suspicion*, *out of trouble*) чи́стый.

adv.: **he spoke loud and** ~ он говори́л гро́мко и я́сно; **stand** ~ **of the gates** стоя́ть (*impf.*) в стороне́ от воро́т;

get ~ of отойти́ (*pf.*) в сто́рону от+*g.*; **keep ~ of** держа́ться (*impf.*) в стороне́ от+*g.*; остерега́ться (*impf.*) +*g.*; избега́ть (*impf.*) +*g.*

v.t. **1.** (*make ~, empty*) оч|ища́ть, -и́стить; **the streets were ~ed of snow** у́лицы очи́стили от сне́га; **~ land** расч|ища́ть, -и́стить зе́млю; **he ~ed his desk** он убра́л свой стол; **she ~ed the table** она́ убрала́ со стола́; **our talk ~ed the air** наш разгово́р разряди́л атмосфе́ру; **he ~ed the country of bandits** он очи́стил страну́ от банди́тов; **~ o.s. (of a charge)** оправда́ться (*pf.*); опрове́ргнуть (*pf.*) обвине́ние; **he was ~ed for security** его́ засекре́тили; **~ s.o.'s mind of doubt** рассе́|ивать, -ять чьи-н. сомне́ния; **to ~ one's conscience** для очи́стки со́вести; **he ~ed his throat** он отка́шлялся; **~ the decks for action** (*lit.*) изгот|а́вливать, -о́вить кора́бль к бо́ю; (*fig.*) пригото́виться (*pf.*) к бо́ю; **~ sth. out of the way** уб|ира́ть, -ра́ть что-н. с доро́ги; отодв|ига́ть, -и́нуть что-н.; **he ~ed the things out of the drawer** он освободи́л я́щик; **he ~ed the children out of the garden** он вы́гнал дете́й из са́да. **2.** (*jump over, get past*): **the horse ~ed the hedge** ло́шадь взяла́ барье́р; **the car ~ed the gate** автомоби́ль прошёл в воро́та. **3.** (*make profit of*): **we ~ed £50** мы получи́ли 50 фу́нтов при́были; **we just ~ed expenses** нам удало́сь лишь покры́ть расхо́ды. **4.: ~** (*ship, cargo etc.*) **(of duty)** оч|ища́ть, -и́стить от по́шлин. **5.: ~ an account** опла́|чивать, -ти́ть счёт.

v.i.: *cf.* **~ up; his brow ~ed** его́ лицо́ проясни́лось.

with advs.: **~ away** *v.t.* уб|ира́ть, -ра́ть; *v.i.* (*disperse*) рассе́|иваться, -яться; **~ off** *v.t.*: **~ off a debt** погаси́ть (*pf.*) долг; **~ off arrears of work** ликвиди́ровать/подчи́стить (*both pf.*) за́лежи рабо́ты; *v.i.* (*coll., go away*) убра́ться (*pf.*); **~ out** *v.t.*: **she ~ed out the cupboard** она́ очи́стила шкаф; (*fig., make destitute*) обчи́стить (*pf.*); *v.i.* (*coll., go away*) убра́ться (*pf.*); **~ up** *v.t.* (*tidy, remove*) убра́ть (*pf.*); **~ up a mystery** распу́тать (*pf.*) та́йну; *v.i.*: **the weather ~ed up** пого́да проясни́лась; **please ~ up after you** бу́дьте добры́, убери́те за собо́й.

cpds. **~-cut** *adj.* (*lit.*) я́сно оче́рченный; (*fig.*) чёткий; **~-eyed** *adj.* ясногла́зый; (*fig.*) проница́тельный; **~-headed** *adj.* толко́вый, у́мный; **~-headedness** *n.* толко́вость; **~-sighted** *adj.* проница́тельный, дальнови́дный; **~-sightedness** *n.* проница́тельность, дальнови́дность; **~way** *n.* скоростна́я автостра́да.

clearance ['klɪərəns] *n.* **1.** (*removal of obstruction etc.*) очи́стка, расчи́стка; **~ sale** распрода́жа. **2.** (*free space*) зазо́р; промежу́ток; **the barge had a ~ of 2 feet** кана́л был на 2 фу́та ши́ре ба́ржи. **3.** (*customs*) очи́стка от тамо́женных по́шлин. **4.: security ~** до́пуск к секре́тной рабо́те; **medical ~** свиде́тельство о го́дности по здоро́вью.

clearing ['klɪərɪŋ] *n.* **1.** (*glade*) про́сека, поля́на, прога́лина. **2.** (*evacuation*): **~ hospital** эвакуацио́нный го́спиталь. **3.** (*fin.*) кли́ринг; **~ agreement** кли́ринговое соглаше́ние; **~ house** расчётная пала́та.

clearly ['klɪəlɪ] *adv.* (*distinctly*) я́сно; (*evidently*) очеви́дно, коне́чно; **it is too dark to see ~** сли́шком темно́, что́бы разгляде́ть; **~ he is wrong** я́сно, что он непра́в.

clearness ['klɪənɪs] *n.* я́сность, очеви́дность.

cleat [kli:t] *n.* **1.** (*strip of wood on gangway etc.*) пла́нка, ре́йка. **2.** (*fitting for attachment of rope*) крепи́тельная у́тка/пла́нка. **3.** (*on sole or heel of shoe*) ско́бка, гвоздь (*m.*).

cleavage ['kli:vɪdʒ] *n.* **1.** (*splitting*) расщепле́ние, раска́лывание. **2.** (*fig., discord*) расхожде́ние, раско́л. **3.** (*of bosom*) «ручеёк», ложби́нка бю́ста.

cleave[1] [kli:v] *v.t.* **1.** (*split*) раск|а́лывать, -оло́ть; расс|ека́ть, -е́чь. **2.** (*fig.*): **he ~d his way through the crowd** он проти́снулся че́рез толпу́. **3.: cleft palate** (*med.*) во́лчья пасть; **cloven hoof** раздво́енное копы́то; **cloven-footed, -hooved** парнокопы́тный; **show the cloven hoof** (*fig.*) обнару́жить свою́ кова́рную приро́ду; **he is in a cleft stick** он зажа́т в тиски́; он в тупике́.

v.i. раск|а́лываться, -оло́ться; **the wood ~s easily** э́то де́рево легко́ ко́лется.

cleave[2] [kli:v] *v.i.* (*adhere*) прил|ипа́ть, -и́пнуть; **his tongue clove to the roof of his mouth** у него́ язы́к к горта́ни прили́п; **he ~s to his friends** он пре́дан свои́м друзья́м.

cleaver ['kli:və(r)] *n.* нож мясника́.

clef [klef] *n.* ключ; **treble ~** скрипи́чный ключ; **bass ~** басо́вый ключ.

cleft[1] [kleft] *n.* тре́щина, рассе́лина.

cleft[2] [kleft] *adj.* = **cleave**[1] **3.**

clematis ['klemətɪs, klə'meɪtɪs] *n.* ломоно́с.

clemency ['klemənsɪ] *n.* (*of pers.*) милосе́рдие; **the defence lawyer appealed for ~** защи́тник призва́л к снисхожде́нию; (*of weather*) мя́гкость.

clement ['klemənt] *adj.* (*of pers.*) милосе́рдный, ми́лостивый; (*of weather*) мя́гкий.

clench [klentʃ] *v.t.*: **~ one's teeth** сти́с|кивать, -нуть зу́бы; **~ one's fist** сж|има́ть, -ать кулаки́; **~ sth. in one's hands** сж|има́ть, -ать что-н. в рука́х.

clepsydra ['klepsɪdrə, -'sɪdrə] *n.* клепси́дра, водяны́е часы́.

clergy ['klɜ:dʒɪ] *n.* духове́нство, клир.

cpd. **~man** *n.* духо́вное лицо́; (*Protestant*) па́стор.

cleric ['klerɪk] *n.* церко́вник, духо́вное лицо́.

clerical ['klerɪk(ə)l] *adj.* **1.** (*of clergy*) клерика́льный; **~ collar** па́сторский воротни́к. **2.** (*of clerks*) канцеля́рский, househoконто́рский; **~ error** канцеля́рская оши́бка.

clericalism ['klerɪk(ə),lɪz(ə)m] *n.* клерикали́зм.

clerk [klɑ:k] *n.* **1.** (*pers. in charge of correspondence*) секрета́рь (*m.*), письмоводи́тель (*m.*); **bank ~** ба́нковский слу́жащий. **2.** (*official*) слу́жащий, чино́вник; **town ~** секрета́рь (*m.*) городско́го сове́та; (*of court*) регистра́тор. **3.** (*US, shop assistant*) продаве́ц, прика́зчик; (*hotel receptionist*) (дежу́рный) администра́тор. **4.: ~ of the works** производи́тель (*m.*) рабо́т; проpа́б.

v.i. (*work as ~*) выполня́ть (*impf.*) конто́рскую рабо́ту.

clerkly ['klɑ:klɪ] *adj.* чино́вничий, канцеля́рский.

clerkship ['klɑ:kʃɪp] *n.* до́лжность секретаря́.

clever ['klevə(r)] *adj.* у́мный, сообрази́тельный; (*skilful*) ло́вкий; **he is ~ at arithmetic** он спосо́бен к арифме́тике; **he is ~ with his fingers** у него́ уме́лые ру́ки; **he was too ~ for us** он перехитри́л нас; **~ clogs/Dick** у́мник.

cpd. **~-~** *adj.* (*coll.*) у́мничающий.

cleverness ['klevənɪs] *n.* сметли́вость; (*skill*) ло́вкость, уме́ние.

clew [klu:] *n.* (*see also* **clue**); (*ball of yarn*) клубо́к, мото́к.

v.t.: **~ up** (*lit.*) см|а́тывать, -ота́ть в клубо́к; (*fig., finish off*) сверну́ть (*pf.*).

cliché ['kli:ʃeɪ] *n.* (*fig.*) клише́ (*indecl.*), штамп, шабло́н.

cpd. **~-ridden** *adj.* по́лный клише́/шта́мпов; шабло́нный.

click [klɪk] *n.* щёлканье, щёлк, щелчо́к; (*phon.*) щёлкающий звук.

v.t. щёлк|ать, -нуть +*i.*; прищёлк|ивать, -нуть +*i.*; **he ~ed his tongue** он (при)щёлкнул языко́м; **he ~ed his heels** он щёлкнул каблука́ми.

v.i. щёлк|ать, -нуть; **the door ~ed shut** дверь защёлкнулась; (*fig., work smoothly*) идти́ (*det.*) гла́дко; (*coll., hit it off*) пола́дить (*pf.*), сойти́сь (*pf.*) (*с кем*).

client ['klaɪənt] *n.* **1.** клие́нт; **~ state** госуда́рство-клие́нт. **2.** (*customer*) клие́нт, зака́зчик.

clientele [,kli:ɒn'tel] *n.* клиенту́ра.

cliff [klɪf] *n.* утёс, скала́.

cpd. **~hanger** *n.* (*coll.*) захва́тывающий расска́з/рома́н/фильм.

climacteric [klaɪ'mæktərɪk, ,klaɪmæk'terɪk] *n.* климакте́рий; (*age*) климактери́ческий во́зраст.

adj. климактери́ческий, крити́ческий.

climate ['klaɪmɪt] *n.* кли́мат; (*fig.*) атмосфе́ра; **~ of opinion** состоя́ние обще́ственного мне́ния.

climatic [,klaɪ'mætɪk] *adj.* климати́ческий.

climax ['klaɪmæks] *n.* кульмина́ция; (*orgasm*) орга́зм.

v.t. (*top off, crown*) довести́ (*pf.*) до кульмина́ции.

v.i. (*culminate*) кульмини́ровать (*impf., pf.*); дойти́ (*pf.*) до кульмина́ции.

climb [klaɪm] *n.* подъём, восхожде́ние; **it was a long ~ to the top** подъём на верши́ну был до́лгим; **rate of ~** (*aeron.*) ско́рость подъёма.

v.t. вл|еза́ть, -езть на+*a.*

v.i. ла́зить (*indet.*), лезть (*det.*); подн|има́ться, -я́ться; **~ up a tree** влезть (*pf.*) на де́рево; **~ over a wall** переле́зть (*pf.*) чéрез стéну; ~ **down a ladder** слезть (*pf.*) с лéстницы; ~ **on to a table** зал|езáть, -éзть на стол; **the sun/aircraft ~ed slowly** сóлнце/самолёт мéдленно поднимáлось/поднимáлся; ~ **to power** подн|имáться, -я́ться к вершúнам влáсти; ~ **down** (*lit.*) слез|áть, -ть; (*fig.*) отступ|áть, -úть.

cpd. **~-down** *n.* (*fig.*) отступлéние, устýпка.

climbable ['klaɪməb(ə)l] *adj.* достýпный для подъёма/восхождéния.

climber ['klaɪmə(r)] *n.* (*pers.*) альпинúст (*fem.* -ка); (*fig.*) карьерúст (*fem.* -ка); (*plant*) вьющееся растéние.

climbing ['klaɪmɪŋ] *n.* (*mountaineering*) альпинúзм.

cpd. **~-irons** *n. pl.* шипы́ (*m. pl.*) на альпинúстской óбуви; трúкони (*pl.*, *indecl*).

clime [klaɪm] *n.* (*poet.*, *region*) край, сторонá.

clinch [klɪntʃ] *n.* захвáт, схвáтывание; (*in boxing*) клинч, захвáт.

v.t. (*make fast*) заклёп|ывать, -áть; (*fig.*): ~ **an argument** завершúть (*pf.*) спор; ~ **a bargain** закрепúть (*pf.*) сдéлку.

clincher ['klɪntʃ(ə)r] *n.* (*coll.*, *decisive remark etc.*) решáющий дóвод.

cling [klɪŋ] *v.i.* (*adhere*) цепля́ться (*impf.*) (за+*a.*); льнýть (*impf.*) (к+*d.*); (*fig.*): **he clung to his possessions** он цепля́лся за своё имýщество; **they clung together** онú держáлись вмéсте (*or* друг за дрýга); **the child clung to its mother** ребёнок льнýл к мáтери; **a ~ing dress** облегáющее плáтье; **a ~ing person** привя́зчивый человéк.

clinic ['klɪnɪk] *n.* клúника, диспансéр.

clinical ['klɪnɪk(ə)l] *adj.* **1.** клинúческий; ~ **record** истóрия болéзни; ~ **thermometer** медицúнский термóметр. **2.** (*fig.*) бесстрáстный.

clinician [klɪ'nɪʃ(ə)n] *n.* клиницúст.

clink[1] [klɪŋk] *n.* звон.

v.t. звенéть (*impf.*) +*i.*; ~ **glasses with s.o.** чóк|аться, -нуться с кем-н.

v.i. звенéть (*impf.*); чóк|аться, -нуться.

clink[2] [klɪŋk] *n.* (*prison*) кутýзка, каталáжка (*sl.*).

clinker ['klɪŋkə(r)] *n.* (*brick*) клúнкер; (*pl.*, *slag*) шлак.

clinker-built ['klɪŋkə,bɪlt] *adj.* обшúтый внакрóй.

clinometer [klaɪ'nɒmɪtə(r)] *n.* клинóметр.

Clio ['klaɪəʊ] *n.* Клúо (*f. indecl.*).

clip[1] [klɪp] *n.* **1.** (*slide-on* ~) скрéпка; (*grip*-~) зажúм, зажúмка. **2.** (*ornament*) клипс. **3.** (*of cartridges*) обóйма.

v.t. заж|имáть, -áть; скреп|ля́ть, -úть; ~ **a paper to a board** прикреп|ля́ть, -úть бумáгу к доскé.

cpds. **~board** *n.* доскá с зажúмом для бумáги; **~-on** *adj.* пристёгивающийся, прикрепля́ющийся.

clip[2] [klɪp] *n.* **1.** (*shearing*) стрúжка; (*amount shorn*) настрúг. **2.** (*coll.*, *blow*): **a ~ on the jaw** удáр по скулé. **3.** (*coll.*, *speed*): **at a fast ~** бы́стрым хóдом. **4.** (*cin.*) отры́вок из фúльма.

v.t. **1.** (*cut*): ~ **a hedge** подстр|игáть, -úчь живýю úзгородь; ~ **a bird's wings** подрéзать (*pf.*) птúце кры́лья; ~ **s.o.'s wings** (*fig.*) подрéзать (*pf.*) комý-н. кры́лышки; ~ **an article out of a newspaper** вырезáть, вы́резать статью́ из газéты; ~ **a coin** обр|езáть, -éзать края́ монéты; ~ **one's words** говорúть (*impf.*) оты́висто; ~ **tickets** пробивáть (*impf.*) (*or* компостúровать) билéты. **2.** (*hit*): ~ **s.o. on the jaw** съéздить (*pf.*) комý-н. по физионóмии (*coll.*).

cpd. **~-joint** *n.* (*coll.*) обирáловка, притóн.

clipper ['klɪpə(r)] *n.* **1.** (*pl.*, *for hair*) машúнка для стрúжки волóс; (*pl.*, *for nails*) кусáч|ки (*pl.*, *g.* -ек). **2.** (*naut.*) клúпер. **3.** (*aeron.*) тяжёлая летáющая лóдка.

clipping ['klɪpɪŋ] *n.* (*from newspaper*) вы́резка; (*pl.*, *nail-~s*) настрúженные нóгти (*m. pl.*).

clique [kli:k] *n.* клúка.

clitoris ['klɪtərɪs, 'klaɪ-] *n.* клúтор, похотнúк.

cloaca [kləʊ'eɪkə] *n.* (*also zool.*) клоáка.

cloak [kləʊk] *n.* (*garment*) плащ, мáнтия; ~ **and dagger stories** расскáзы о шпиóнах; (*covering*): **a ~ of snow** снéжный покрóв; **under the ~ of darkness** под покрóвом темноты́; (*fig.*, *pretext*) мáска.

v.t. (*fig.*) прикр|ывáть, -ы́ть; скр|ывáть, -ы́ть.

cpd. **~room** *n.* (*for clothes*) гардерóб, раздевáльня; (*for luggage*) кáмера хранéния; (*lavatory*) убóрная.

clobber ['klɒbə(r)] *n.* (*sl.*, *gear*) барахлó.

v.t. (*sl.*, *beat*) лупúть, от-; лупцевáть, от- (*both coll.*).

cloche [klɒʃ, kləʊʃ] *n.* **1.** (*for plants*) стеклянный колпáк. **2.** (~ *hat*) шля́пка.

clock[1] [klɒk] *n.* час|ы́ (*pl.*, *g.* -óв); (*in factory*) контрóльные часы́; (*taximeter*) таксóметр; **5 ~s 5** (пар) часóв; **he works round the ~** он рабóтает крýглые сýтки; **he slept the ~ round** (*24 hours*) он проспáл цéлые сýтки (*12 hours*: цéлый день, цéлую ночь); **put the ~ forward** постáвить (*pf.*) часы́ вперёд; **put the ~ back** (*lit.*) отвестú (*pf.*) часы́ назáд; (*fig.*) повернýть (*pf.*) врéмя вспять.

v.t. (*time*) хронометрúровать (*impf.*, *pf.*); (*register*): **she ~ed 11 seconds in this race** онá показáла врéмя 11 секýнд в э́том забéге.

v.i.: ~ **in, on** отм|ечáться, -éтиться по прихóде на рабóту; ~ **out, off** отм|ечáться, -éтиться при ухóде с рабóты.

cpds. **~-face** *n.* циферблáт; **~-maker** *n.* часовщúк; **~-watch** *v.i.* старáться (*impf.*) не перерабóтать; **~watcher** *n.* нерадúвый рабóтник, лóдырь; **~work** *n.* часовóй механúзм; **~work toy** заводня́я игрýшка; **the ceremony went like ~work** церемóния шла без сучкá, без задóринки.

clock[2] [klɒk] *n.* (*on stocking*) стрéлка.

clockwise ['klɒkwaɪz] *adj.* & *adv.* (движущийся) по часовóй стрéлке.

clod [klɒd] *n.* ком, глы́ба.

cpd. **~-hopper** *n.* болвáн, деревéнщина (*c.g.*).

cloddish ['klɒdɪʃ] *adj.* неотёсанный, неуклю́жий.

cloddishness ['klɒdɪʃnɪs] *n.* неотёсанность, неуклю́жесть.

clog[1] [klɒg] *n.* (*shoe*) башмáк на деревя́нной подóшве.

clog[2] [klɒg] *v.t.* (*lit.*, *fig.*) засор|я́ть, -úть; **the sink is ~ged** рáковина засорúлась.

cloisonné ['klwɑ:zɒ,neɪ] *n.*: ~ **enamel** клуазо(н)нé (*indecl.*); перегорóдчатая эмáль.

cloister ['klɔɪstə(r)] *n.* монасты́рь (*m.*), обúтель; (*monastic life*) монасты́рская жизнь; (*covered walk*) аркáда.

v.t. (*fig.*): **he led a ~ed life** он вёл уединённую жизнь.

cloistral ['klɔɪstrəl] *adj.* монасты́рский; монáшеский.

clone [kləʊn] *n.* клон.

v.t. размн|ожáть, -óжить вегетатúвным путём; клонúровать (*impf.*, *pf.*).

clop [klɒp] *n.* (*of hoofs*) цóканье, цóкот.

close[1] [kləʊs] *n.* (*enclosure*, *precinct*) двор.

adj. **1.** (*near*) блúзкий; **he fired at ~ range** он стреля́л с блúзкого расстоя́ния; ~ **combat** блúжний бой; рукопáшный бой; ~ **contact** тéсное общéние; **at ~ quarters** на блúзком расстоя́нии; **in ~ proximity** в непосрéдственной блúзости; ~ **competition** óстрая конкурéнция; **he had a ~ shave, call** он был на волосóк от гúбели; ~ **resemblance** большóе схóдство. **2.** (*intimate*) блúзкий; **a ~ friend** блúзкий друг; **his sister was very ~ to him** онú с сестрóй бы́ли óчень близкú. **3.** (*serried*, *compact*): ~ **writing** убóристый пóчерк; ~ **texture** плóтная ткань; **in ~ order** (*mil.*) сóмкнутым стрóем; ~ **column** (*mil.*) сóмкнутая колóнна; ~ **reasoning** безукорúзненная аргументáция. **4.** (*strict*, *attentive*): **keep a ~ watch on s.o.** тщáтельно следúть (*impf.*) за кем-н.; ~ **examination** тщáтельное обслéдование; ~ **attention** прúстальное внимáние; ~ **confinement** стрóгая изоля́ция; **the suit is a ~ fit** э́тот костю́м хорошó сидúт; **a ~ translation** тóчный перевóд; ~ **blockade** плóтное кольцó блокáды; **a ~ observer** внимáтельный наблюдáтель. **5.** (*restricted*) закры́тый; ~ **season** врéмя, когдá охóта запрещенá. **6.** (*of games etc.*): **a ~ contest** упóрная борьбá, состязáние с почтú рáвными шáнсами. **7.** (*stingy*) скупóй, прижúмистый. **8.** (*reticent*, *secret*) скры́тный; **he is ~ about his affairs** он дéржит свой делá в секрéте; **he lay ~ for a while** он нéкоторое врéмя скрывáлся. **9.** (*stuffy*): (*of air*) дýшный, спёртый; (*of weather*) дýшный, тяжёлый. **10.** (*phon.*): **a ~ vowel** ýзкий/закры́тый глáсный.

adv.: **he lives ~ to, by the church** он живёт поблúзости от цéркви; **keep ~ to me** не отходúте от меня́; **it was ~**

upon midnight бли́зилась по́лночь; ~ **upon 500 boys** почти́ 500 ма́льчиков; **follow ~ behind s.o.** сле́довать (*impf.*) непосре́дственно за кем-н.; **stand ~ against the wall** стоя́ть (*impf.*) вплотну́ю к стене́; **cut one's hair ~** ко́ротко подстри́чься (*pf.*); **come ~r together** (*fig.*) сбли́зиться (*pf.*); подойти́ (*pf.*) вплотну́ю друг к дру́гу; ~ **shut** пло́тно закры́тый; **sail ~ to the wind** (*lit.*) идти́ (*det.*) кру́то к ве́тру; (*fig.*) ходи́ть (*indet.*) по острию́ (ножа́).

cpds. **~-cropped** *adj.* ко́ротко остри́женный; **~-fisted** *adj.* прижи́мистый, скупо́й; **~-fistedness** *n.* прижи́мистость, ску́пость; **~-fitting** *adj.* облега́ющий; **~-grained** *adj.* (*of wood*) мелковолокни́стый; **~-mouthed** *adj.* сде́ржанный, скры́тный; **~-set** *adj.* бли́зко поста́вленный; **~-up** *n.* (*cin.*) кру́пный план.

close² [kləʊz] *n.* (*end*) коне́ц; **at ~ of day** в конце́ дня; на исхо́де дня; ~ **of play** коне́ц игры́; **at the ~ of the nineteenth century** в конце́ девятна́дцатого столе́тия; **bring to a ~** довести́ (*pf.*) до конца́; **the day reached its ~** день ко́нчился; **the meeting drew to a ~** собра́ние подошло́ к концу́.

v.t. **1.** (*shut*) закр|ыва́ть, -ы́ть; **~ a gap** зап|олня́ть, -о́лнить пробе́л; ~ **a knife** скла́дывать, сложи́ть нож; ~ **one's hand** сжать (*pf.*) ру́ку в кула́к; ~ **one's lips** сомкну́ть (*pf.*) гу́бы; ~ **the door on a proposal** отве́ргнуть (*pf.*) предложе́ние; прегради́ть (*pf.*) путь предложе́нию; **~d shop** предприя́тие, нанима́ющее то́лько чле́нов профсою́за; **'road ~d'** «прое́зд закры́т»; **the museum is ~d** музе́й не рабо́тает. **2.** (*end, complete, settle*): ~ **a meeting** закр|ыва́ть, -ы́ть собра́ние; ~ **a deal** заключи́ть (*pf.*) сде́лку; **the closing scene of the play** заключи́тельная сце́на пье́сы; **the closing date is December 1** после́дний срок — пе́рвое декабря́. **3.:** ~ **the ranks** сомкну́ть (*pf.*) ряды́. **4.** (*phon.*): **~d syllable** закры́тый слог.

v.i. **1.** (*shut*) закр|ыва́ться, -ы́ться; **the door ~d** дверь закры́лась; **flowers ~ at night** но́чью цветы́ закрыва́ются; **the theatres ~d** теа́тры закры́лись; **closing day** выходно́й день. **2.** (*cease*): **the performance ~d last night** вчера́ пье́са шла в после́дний раз; **he ~d with this remark** он зако́нчил э́тим замеча́нием. **3.** (*come closer*) сбл|ижа́ться, -и́зиться; прибл|ижа́ться, -и́зиться; **the soldiers ~d up** солда́ты сомкну́ли ряды́; (*mil.*): **left ~!** сомкни́сь нале́во!; **they ~d** (*came to grips*) **with the enemy** они́ схвати́лись с неприя́телем; **I ~d with his offer** я при́нял его́ предложе́ние.

with advs.: ~ **down** *v.t.* закр|ыва́ть, -ы́ть; *v.i.* (*e.g. of a factory*) закр|ыва́ться, -ы́ться; (*broadcasting*) зак|а́нчивать, -о́нчить переда́чу; ~ **in** *v.i.*: **the days are closing in** дни укора́чиваются (*or* стано́вятся коро́че); **the darkness ~d in on us** нас оку́тала темнота́; **the enemy ~d in upon us** неприя́тель подступи́л вплотну́ю; ~ **up** *v.t. & i.* закр|ыва́ть(ся), -ы́ть(ся).

cpd. **~-down** *n.* (*broadcasting*) оконча́ние.

closely ['kləʊslɪ] *adv.*: **it ~ resembles pork** э́то о́чень напомина́ет свини́ну; (*attentively*) внима́тельно; **watch ~** при́стально следи́ть (*impf.*) за+*i.*; ~ **printed** убо́ристо напеча́танный; ~ **connected** те́сно/про́чно свя́занный; **we worked ~ together** мы рабо́тали в те́сном сотру́дничестве; **they questioned him ~** его́ подро́бно расспра́шивали.

closeness ['kləʊsnɪs] *n.* (*proximity, resemblance; intimacy*) бли́зость; (*of texture etc.*) пло́тность; (*of reasoning etc.*) безукори́зненность; тща́тельность; (*attentiveness*) при́стальность; (*reticence*) скры́тность; (*parsimony*) прижи́мистость, ску́пость; (*of air etc.*) духота́, спёртость.

closet ['klɒzɪt] *n.* **1.** (*cupboard*) шкаф; **china ~** буфе́т. **2.** (*arch., study*) кабине́т.

v.t. зап|ира́ть, -ере́ть; **he was ~ed with his solicitor** он совеща́лся со свои́м адвока́том наедине́.

closure ['kləʊʒə(r)] *n.* **1.** (*closing, e.g. of eyelids*) смыка́ние; (*of a wound*) затя́гивание. **2.** (*parl., also* (*US*) **cloture**) прекраще́ние пре́ний.

clot [klɒt] *n.* (*of blood etc.*) сгу́сток, комо́к; (*sl., stupid pers.*) болва́н, тупи́ца (*c.g.*).

v.i. свёр|тываться, -ну́ться; сгу|ща́ться, -сти́ться; **~ted blood** запёкшаяся кровь; **~ted cream** густы́е топлёные сли́вки.

cloth [klɒθ] *n.* **1.** (*material*) ткань, мате́рия; ~ **of gold** золота́я парча́; **bound in ~** в матерча́том переплёте. **2.** (*pl., kinds of material*) сорта́ (*m. pl.*) су́кон. **3.** (*piece of ~*) тря́пка; (*table ~*) ска́терть. **4.** (*fig., clerical status*) духо́вный сан. **5. a ~ cap** (матерча́тая) ке́пка.

clothe [kləʊð] *v.t.* од|ева́ть, -еть; ~ **o.s.** (*acquire clothing*) приоде́ться (*pf.*); (*fig.*): ~ **one's thoughts in words** обле́чь (*pf.*) свои́ мы́сли в слова́; **his face was ~d in smiles** его́ лицо́ расплыло́сь в улы́бке.

clothes [kləʊðz] *n.* пла́тье, оде́жда; **evening ~** вече́рнее пла́тье; (*bed ~*) посте́льное бельё; **old ~ man** старьёвщик; **in plain ~** (*out of uniform*) в шта́тском (пла́тье).

cpds. **~-basket** *n.* корзи́на для белья́; **~-brush** *n.* платяна́я щётка; **~-horse** *n.* напо́льная суши́лка; **~-line** *n.* верёвка для белья́; **~-moth** *n.* моль; **~-peg, ~-pin** *nn.* зажи́мка для белья́.

clothier ['kləʊðɪə(r)] *n.* торго́вец мужско́й оде́ждой.

clothing ['kləʊðɪŋ] *n.* оде́жда.

cloture ['kləʊtʃə(r), -tjʊə(r)] = **closure 2.**

clou [klu:] *n.* (*chief attraction*) гвоздь (*m.*) програ́ммы.

cloud [klaʊd] *n.* **1.** (*in the sky*) о́блако; ту́ча; **every ~ has a silver lining** нет ху́да без добра́; **he is in the ~s** он вита́ет в облака́х; ~ **cuckoo land** мир фанта́зий/грёз. **2.** (*of smoke*) клубы́ (*m. pl.*); (*of dust*) о́блако. **3.** (*fig., mass*) тьма, ту́ча; **a ~ of arrows** ту́ча стрел; **a ~ of words** слове́сная заве́са. **4.** (*in liquid etc.*) помутне́ние. **5.** (*of unhappiness etc.*): **this cast a ~ over our meeting** э́то омрачи́ло на́шу встре́чу; **under a ~** (*fig.*) в неми́лости.

v.t. покр|ыва́ть, -ы́ть облака́ми; (*fig.*) омрач|а́ть, -и́ть; **eyes ~ed with tears** глаза́, затума́ненные слеза́ми; **his troubles ~ed his mind** несча́стья помути́ли его́ рассу́док.

v.i. омрач|а́ться, -и́ться; покр|ыва́ться, -ы́ться облака́ми/ту́чами; нахму́ри|ваться, -ться; **the sky ~ed over** не́бо затяну́ло облака́ми/ту́чами; **his brow ~ed** он нахму́рил лоб.

cpds. **~berry** *n.* моро́шка; **~burst** *n.* ли́вень (*m.*); **~-rack** *n.* несу́щиеся облака́.

cloudiness ['klaʊdɪnɪs] *n.* о́блачность; (*fig.*) тума́нность, нея́сность.

cloudless ['klaʊdlɪs] *adj.* безо́блачный.

cloudlessness ['klaʊdlɪsnɪs] *n.* безо́блачность.

cloudlet ['klaʊdlɪt, -lət] *n.* о́блачко, ту́чка.

cloudy ['klaʊdɪ] *adj.* о́блачный; (*of liquid etc.*) му́тный; (*fig., of ideas*) тума́нный.

clout [klaʊt] *n.* (*coll., blow*) затре́щина, оплеу́ха; (*coll., influence*) влия́ние.

v.t. (*coll., hit*) тре́снуть (*pf.*).

clove¹ [kləʊv] *n.* (*section of bulb*) зубо́к; **a ~ of garlic** зубо́к чеснока́.

clove² [kləʊv] *n.* (*aromatic*) гвозди́ка; **oil of ~s** гвозди́чное ма́сло.

cpds. **~-gillyflower, ~-pink** *nn.* гвозди́ка садо́вая.

clove³ [kləʊv] *n.* (*naut.*): ~ **hitch** вы́бленочный у́зел.

cloven ['kləʊv(ə)n] = **cleave¹ 3.**

clover ['kləʊvə(r)] *n.* кле́вер; **we are in ~** у нас не жизнь, а ма́сленица; мы живём припева́ючи; **four-leaved ~** четырёхли́стный кле́вер.

clown [klaʊn] *n.* (*at circus*) кло́ун; (*ludicrous pers.*) шут; (*boor*) неве́жа (*m.*).

v.i. стро́ить (*impf.*) из себя́ шута́.

clowning ['klaʊnɪŋ] *n.* шутовство́, пая́сничание.

clownish ['klaʊnɪʃ] *adj.* кло́унский, шутовско́й; (*boorish*) гру́бый.

clownishness ['klaʊnɪʃnɪs] *n.* шутовство́, дура́чество; гру́бость.

cloy [klɔɪ] *v.t.* прес|ыща́ть, -ы́тить; **too much honey ~s the palate** сли́шком мно́го мёда притупля́ет вкус; **~ed with pleasure** пресы́тившийся удово́льствиями; **these sweets have a ~ing taste** э́ти сла́дости при́торны до отвраще́ния.

club¹ [klʌb] *n.* (*weapon*) дуби́нка; (*at golf*) клю́шка; (*pl., at cards*) тре́фы (*f. pl.*); **Indian ~** булава́.

v.t. бить (*impf.*) дуби́нкой; **he was ~bed to death** его́ на́смерть заби́ли дуби́нками.

cpds. **~-foot** *n.* изуро́дованная ступня́; **~-footed** *adj.* с изуро́дованной ступнёй; косола́пый.

club² [klʌb] *n.* (*society, building*) клуб.

v.i. скла́дываться, сложи́ться; устр|а́ивать, -о́ить скла́дчину; **they ~bed together to pay the fine** они́ сложи́лись и уплати́ли штраф.

cpds. **~-house** *n.* клуб, помеще́ние клу́ба; **~man** *n.* ≃ све́тский челове́к.

clubbable ['klʌbəb(ə)l] *adj.* общи́тельный, (*coll.*) компане́йский.

cluck [klʌk] *n.* куда́хтанье, клохта́нье.

v.i. куда́хтать, клохта́ть (*both impf.*).

clue (*US* **clew**) [klu:] *n.* ключ, нить; **the police found a ~** поли́ция нашла́ ули́ку; **the ~ to this mystery** ключ к разга́дке э́той та́йны; **I haven't a ~** (*coll.*) поня́тия не име́ю.

clueful ['klu:fʊl] *adj.* (*coll.*) в ку́рсе.

clueless ['klu:lɪs] *adj.* (*coll.*) бестолко́вый; не в ку́рсе.

clump¹ [klʌmp] *n.* (*cluster*) гру́ппа, ку́па; (*of bushes*) куста́рник.

v.t. сажа́ть, посади́ть гру́ппами; соб|ира́ть, -ра́ть в ку́чу; **they are ~ed together** они́ сва́лены в ку́чу.

clump² [klʌmp] *n.* (*heavy tread*) то́пот; тяжёлая по́ступь.

v.i. (*tread heavily*) то́пать (*impf.*); тяжело́ ступа́ть (*impf.*).

clumsiness ['klʌmzɪnɪs] *n.* неуклю́жесть, нело́вкость.

clumsy ['klʌmzɪ] *adj.* неуклю́жий, нескла́дный, нело́вкий; **a ~ joke** неуме́стная/неуклю́жая шу́тка; **a ~ excuse** неуклю́жий предло́г; **a ~ sentence** громо́здкое предложе́ние.

cluster ['klʌstə(r)] *n.* (*of grapes*) гроздь, кисть; (*of flowers*) кисть; (*of bees*) рой; (*of trees*) ку́па; **consonant ~s** скопле́ния (*nt. pl.*) согла́сных.

v.t.: **~ed column** (*archit.*) пучко́вая коло́нна.

v.i. расти́ (*impf.*) пучка́ми; собира́ться (*impf.*) гру́ппами; **roses ~ed round the window** ро́зы разросли́сь под окно́м; **the children ~ed round the teacher** де́ти столпи́лись вокру́г учи́теля; **the village ~s round the church** дома́ дере́вни тесня́тся вокру́г це́ркви.

clutch¹ [klʌtʃ] *n.* **1.** (*act of ~ing*) сжа́тие, захва́т, схва́тывание; **make a ~ at sth.** схвати́ть/захвати́ть (*pf.*) что-н.; **a last ~ at popularity** отча́янная попы́тка завоева́ть популя́рность. **2.** (*pl., grasp*) ла́пы (*f. pl.*), ко́гти (*m. pl.*); **they fell into his ~es** (*fig.*) они́ попа́ли к нему́ в ла́пы. **3.** (*of car*) сцепле́ние; **let in the ~** отпусти́ть сцепле́ние; **the ~ is out** сцепле́ние вы́ключено; **the ~ slips** сцепле́ние проска́льзывает/пробуксо́вывает; **~ pedal** педа́ль сцепле́ния.

v.t. & i. хвата́ться, (с)хвати́ться (за+*a.*); сж|има́ть, -ать; **he ~ed (at) the rope** он ухвати́лся за верёвку; **he ~ed the toy to his chest** он прижа́л игру́шку к груди́.

clutch² [klʌtʃ] *n.* (*of eggs*) я́йца (*nt. pl.*) под насе́дкой; (*brood*) вы́водок.

clutter ['klʌtə(r)] *n.* (*confused mess*) сумато́ха, суета́; (*untidiness*) хао́с, беспоря́док; **the room is in a ~** в ко́мнате хао́с.

v.t. (*also* **~ up**) загромо|жда́ть, -зди́ть.

clyster ['klɪstə(r)] *n.* клисти́р, кли́зма.

cm. ['sentɪˌmi:tə(r)(z)] *n.* (*abbr. of* **centimetre(s)**) см., (сантиме́тр).

CMEA (*abbr.*) = **Comecon**

CND (*abbr. of* ***Campaign for Nuclear Disarmament***) Кампа́ния за я́дерное разоруже́ние.

CO (*abbr. of* ***Commanding Officer***) команди́р.

Co. [kəʊ] *n.* (*abbr. of* **company**) К°, (компа́ния).

coach¹ [kəʊtʃ] *n.* **1.** (*horse-drawn*) каре́та, экипа́ж; **~ and four** каре́та, запряжённая четвёркой. **2.** (*railway*) пассажи́рский ваго́н. **3.** (*motor-bus*) (тури́стский междугоро́дный) авто́бус.

v.i.: **in the old ~ing days** в ста́рое вре́мя, когда́ ещё е́здили в каре́тах.

cpds. **~-box** *n.* ко́з|лы (*pl., g.* -ел); **~-house** *n.* каре́тный сара́й; **~man** *n.* ку́чер; **~-party** *n.* экскурса́нты (*m. pl.*); **~-tour** *n.* экску́рсия.

coach² [kəʊtʃ] *n.* (*tutor*) репети́тор; (*trainer*) тре́нер.

v.t. репети́ровать (*impf.*); (*train*) тренирова́ть, на-; (*prepare for questioning, e.g. a witness*)ната́скивать (*impf.*).

coachful ['kəʊtʃfʊl] *n.*: **a ~ of trippers** це́лый авто́бус экскурса́нтов.

coadjutor [kəʊ'ædʒʊtə(r)] *n.* коадъю́тор, помо́щник.

coagulant [kəʊ'ægjʊlənt] *n.* коагуля́нт.

coagulate [kəʊ'ægjʊˌleɪt] *v.t.* сгу|ща́ть, -сти́ть; коагули́ровать (*impf., pf.*); свёрт|ывать, -ну́ть.

v.i. коагули́роваться (*impf., pf.*); свёр|тываться, -ну́ться.

coagulation [ˌkəʊægjʊ'leɪʃ(ə)n] *n.* коагуля́ция, свёртывание.

coal [kəʊl] *n.* (*mineral*) ка́менный у́голь; **hard ~** (*anthracite*) антраци́т; (*piece of ~*) у́голь (*m.*); уголёк; **~s** у́гли (*m. pl.*); **a live ~** горя́щий уголёк; (*fig.*): **carry ~s to Newcastle** е́хать (*det.*) в Ту́лу со свои́м самова́ром; **heap ~s of fire on s.o.'s head** возд|ава́ть, -а́ть добро́м за зло (что́бы вы́звать угрызе́ния со́вести); **haul s.o. over the ~s** да|ва́ть, -ть нагоня́й кому́-н.

v.i. (*take on ~*) грузи́ться (*impf.*) углём; **~ing-station** у́гольная ста́нция/ба́за.

cpds. **~bed, ~-seam** *nn.* у́гольный пласт; **~-black** *adj.* (*e.g. hair*) чёрный как смоль; **~-burner** *n.* (*ship*) кора́бль на угле́; **~-cellar** *n.* подва́л для хране́ния угля́; **~-dust** *n.* у́гольная пыль; **~-face** *n.* забо́й; грудь забо́я; **~-field** *n.* каменноу́гольный бассе́йн; **~-gas** *n.* каменноу́гольный/свети́льный газ; **~-heaver** *n.* во́зчик угля́; у́гольщик; **~-mine, ~-pit** *nn.* у́гольная ша́хта; **~-miner** *n.* шахтёр; **~-pit** *n.* = **~-mine; ~-scuttle** *n.* ведёрко для угля́; **~-seam** *n.* = **~-bed; ~-tar** *n.* каменноу́гольная смола́; дёготь (*m.*).

coalesce [ˌkəʊə'les] *v.i.* соедин|я́ться, -и́ться; объедин|я́ться, -и́ться.

coalescence [ˌkəʊə'lesəns] *n.* соедине́ние, объедине́ние.

coalition [ˌkəʊə'lɪʃ(ə)n] *n.* (*pol.*) коали́ция; (*attr.*) коалицио́нный.

coarse [kɔ:s] *adj.* (*of material*) гру́бый; (*of sand, sugar*) кру́пный; **~ fish** ры́ба просты́х сорто́в; **~ manners** гру́бые/вульга́рные мане́ры; **a ~ skin** гру́бая ко́жа.

cpds. **~-fibred, ~-grained** *adjs.* (*lit.*) крупноволокни́стый; (*fig.*) гру́бый, неотёсанный.

coarsen ['kɔ:s(ə)n] *v.t.* де́лать, с- гру́бым.

v.i. грубе́ть, о-.

coarseness ['kɔ:snɪs] *n.* (*lit.*) гру́бость; (*fig.*) гру́бость, вульга́рность, неотёсанность.

coast [kəʊst] *n.* (*sea-~*) морско́й бе́рег; побере́жье; **the ~ is clear** (*fig.*) путь свобо́ден.

v.i. (*sail along ~*) пла́вать (*indet.*) вдоль побере́жья; **~ing trade** кабота́жная торго́вля; (*bicycle downhill*) кати́ться (*impf.*) на велосипе́де с горы́.

cpds. **~guard** *n.* (*officer*) член (тамо́женной) берегово́й стра́жи; (*collect.*) берегова́я стра́жа; **~line** *n.* берегова́я ли́ния.

coastal ['kəʊstəl] *adj.* берегово́й, прибре́жный; **~ traffic** кабота́жное пла́вание; **~ command** берегова́я охра́на; **~ waters** прибре́жные во́ды (*f. pl.*); взмо́рье.

coaster ['kəʊstə(r)] *n.* (*ship*) кабота́жное су́дно; (*stand for decanter or glass*) подно́с, подста́вка.

coastwise ['kəʊstwaɪz] *adj.* кабота́жный.

adv. вдоль побере́жья.

coat [kəʊt] *n.* **1.** (*overcoat*) пальто́ (*indecl.*); (*man's jacket*) пиджа́к; (*woman's jacket*) жаке́т; **~ of arms** герб; **~ of mail** кольчу́га; (*fig.*): **trail one's ~** держа́ться (*impf.*) вызыва́юще; **you must cut your ~ according to your cloth** по одёжке протя́гивай но́жки. **2.** (*of animal*) шерсть, мех. **3.** (*of paint etc.*) слой; **this wall needs a ~ of paint** э́ту стену́ на́до покра́сить.

v.t. покр|ыва́ть, -ы́ть; облиц|о́вывать, -ева́ть; **the pill is ~ed with sugar** пилю́ля в са́харной оболо́чке; **he ~ed the wall with whitewash** он побели́л сте́ну; **his tongue is ~ed** у него́ обло́жен язы́к.

cpds. **~-hanger** *n.* ве́шалка; **~-style** *adj.*: **~-style shirt** руба́шка на пу́говицах до́низу; **~-tails** *n. pl.* фа́лды (*f. pl.*) фра́ка; **hang on to s.o.'s ~-tails** (*fig., for protection or help*) держа́ться (*impf.*) за кого́-н.

coatee [kəʊ'ti:] *n.* ку́ртка.
coati [kəʊ'ɑ:tɪ] *n.* носу́ха, коа́ти (*m. indecl.*).
coating ['kəʊtɪŋ] *n.* (*layer*) слой.
co-author [,kəʊ'ɔ:θə(r)] *n.* соа́втор.
v.t. писа́ть, на- в соа́вторстве.
coax [kəʊks] *v.t.* угов|а́ривать, -ори́ть; зад|а́бривать, -о́брить; **he ~ed the child to take its medicine** он уговори́л ребёнка приня́ть лека́рство; **he ~ed the fire to burn** он до́лго вози́лся, пока́ не разжёг ого́нь.
coaxial [kəʊ'æksɪəl] *adj.* (*tech.*): ~ **cable** коаксиа́льный ка́бель.
cob [kɒb] *n.* **1.** (*swan*) ле́бедь-саме́ц. **2.** (*horse*) невысо́кая корена́стая ло́шадь. **3.** (*nut*) оре́х. **4.** (*of maize*) поча́ток; **corn on the ~** поча́ток кукуру́зы.
cobalt ['kəʊbɔ:lt, -bɒlt] *n.* (*chem.*) ко́бальт; (*pigment*) ко́бальтовая синь.
cobber ['kɒbə(r)] *n.* (*Austral.*) ко́реш (*coll.*).
cobble[1] ['kɒb(ə)l] *n.* (*also* **~-stone**) булы́жник.
v.t. (*pave*) мости́ть, за-/вы- булы́жником.
cobble[2] ['kɒb(ə)l] *v.t.* (*mend*) лата́ть, за-.
cobbler ['kɒblə(r)] *n.* (*shoemaker*) сапо́жник; **the ~ should stick to his last** всяк сверчо́к знай свой шесто́к.
co-belligerency [,kəʊbɪ'lɪdʒərənsɪ] *n.* совме́стное веде́ние войны́.
co-belligerent [,kəʊbɪ'lɪdʒərənt] *adj.* совме́стно вою́ющий.
COBOL ['kəʊbɒl] *n.* (*comput.*) КОБОЛ.
cobra ['kəʊbrə, 'kɒbrə] *n.* очко́вая змея́.
cobweb ['kɒbweb] *n.* паути́на; нить паути́ны.
cobwebby ['kɒbwebɪ] *adj.* затя́нутый паути́ной.
coca ['kəʊkə] *n.* ко́ка
Coca-Cola [,kəʊkə'kəʊlə] *n.* (*propr.*) ко́ка-ко́ла.
cocaine [kə'keɪn, kəʊ-] *n.* кокаи́н.
coccyx ['kɒksɪks] *n.* ко́пчик.
cochin ['kəʊtʃɪn] *n.* (**~-china fowl**) кохинхи́нка.
cochineal ['kɒtʃɪ,ni:l, -'ni:l] *n.* кошени́ль.
cochlea ['kɒklɪə] *n.* ули́тка.
cock[1] [kɒk] *n.* **1.** (*male domestic fowl*) пету́х. **2.** (*male bird*) пету́х, саме́ц. **3.: old ~** (*sl., old chap*) старина́ (*m.*), дружи́ще (*m.*); **~ of the walk** верхово́д, заводи́ла (*c.g.*); пе́рвый па́рень на селе́; **that ~ won't fight** э́тот но́мер не пройдёт; **live like a fighting ~** жить (*impf.*) припева́ючи.
v.t. **~ up** (*sl.*) пу́тать, на-; порта́чить, на-.
cpds. **~-a-doodle-doo** *n.* кукареку́ (*nt. indecl.*); **~-and-bull** *adj.*: **~-and-bull story** вздор, небыли́ца (в ли́цах); **~chafer** *n.* ма́йский жук, хрущ; **~-crow** *n.* рассве́т; **before ~-crow** до петухо́в; **~-fighting** *n.* петуши́ные бои́ (*m. pl.*); **this beats ~-fighting** лу́чше не быва́ет; **~-horse** *n.* (*stick with horse's head*) па́лочка-лоша́дка; **~-loft** *n.* черда́к, манса́рда; **~pit** *n.* аре́на для петуши́ного бо́я; (*aeron.*) каби́на; (*fig.*) аре́на борьбы́; **~roach** *n.* тарака́н; **~scomb** *n.* (*crest of* ~) петуши́ный гре́бень; *see also* **coxcomb; ~sure** *adj.* самоуве́ренный; **~sureness** *n.* самоуве́ренность; **~tail** *n.* (*drink*) кокте́йль (*m.*); **~tail dress** коро́ткое выходно́е пла́тье; **~tail party** кокте́йль (*m.*); **~-up** *n.* (*sl.*) неразбери́ха, пу́таница; **make a ~-up of sth.** пу́тать, на-; порта́чить, на-.
cock[2] [kɒk] *n.* **1.** (*tap*) кран. **2.** (*lever in gun*) куро́к; **at half ~** (*lit.*) на пе́рвом взво́де; (*fig.*): **the scheme went off at half ~** план сорва́лся; **at full ~** со взведённым курко́м. **3.** (*vulg., penis*) хер, хуй. **4.** (*sl., nonsense*) вздор.
cock[3] [kɒk] *v.t.* **1.** (*stick up etc.*): **~ one's hat** заломи́ть (*pf.*) ша́пку набекре́нь; **the horse ~ed (up) its ears** ло́шадь насторожи́ла у́ши; **he ~ed an eye at me** он подмигну́л мне; **~ one's nose (*or* a snook) at s.o.** показа́ть (*pf.*) нос кому́-н.; **~ed hat** треуго́лка; **knock s.o. into a ~ed hat** вы́сыпать кому́-н. по пе́рвое число́. **2.** (*of gun*) взв|оди́ть, -ести́ куро́к +*g.*
cpd. **~-eyed** *adj.* (*squinting*) косогла́зый, косо́й; (*askew*) косо́й; (*drunk*) осолове́лый, осове́лый; (*absurd*) дура́цкий.
cock[4] [kɒk] *n.* (*haycock*) стог.
v.t. скла́дывать, сложи́ть (*сено*) в стога́.
cockade [kɒ'keɪd] *n.* кока́рда.
cock-a-hoop [,kɒkə'hu:p] *adj.* хвастли́вый и самодово́льный.
Cockaigne [kɒ'keɪn] *n.* (*fig.*) рай земно́й.
cockatoo [,kɒkə'tu:] *n.* какаду́ (*m. indecl.*).
cockatrice ['kɒkətrɪs, -,traɪs] *n.* васили́ск.
cockboat ['kɒkbəʊt] *n.* небольша́я шлю́пка, я́лик.
cocker[1] ['kɒkə(r)] *n.* (**~ spaniel**) ко́кер-спаниэ́ль (*m.*).
cocker[2] ['kɒkə(r)] *v.t.* (*pamper*) балова́ть, из-; потво́рствовать (*impf.*) +*d.*
cockerel ['kɒkər(ə)l] *n.* петушо́к.
cockiness ['kɒkɪnɪs] *n.* бо́йкость, наха́льство.
cockle[1] ['kɒk(ə)l] *n.* (*plant*) ку́коль (*m.*), плеве́л; (*disease of wheat*) головня́.
cockle[2] ['kɒk(ə)l] *n.* **1.** (*shellfish*) сердцеви́дка. **2.: it warms the ~s of one's heart** э́то согрева́ет ду́шу.
cpds. **~-boat** *n.* плоскодо́нная ло́дка; **~-shell** *n.* ра́ковина сердцеви́дки; (*frail boat*) у́тлое судёнышко; скорлу́пка.
cockney ['kɒknɪ] *n.* & *adj.* ко́кни (*c.g. indecl.*); **~ accent** акце́нт ко́кни.
cocky ['kɒkɪ] *adj.* наха́льный; разбитно́й.
coco ['kəʊkəʊ] *n.* (**~ palm**) коко́совая па́льма.
cpd. **~nut** *n.* коко́с, коко́совый оре́х; (*sl., head*) башка́; **~nut butter, oil** коко́совое ма́сло; **~nut fibre** коко́совое волокно́; **~nut matting** цино́вка из коко́сового волокна́.
cocoa ['kəʊkəʊ] *n.* (*powder or drink*) кака́о (*indecl.*); (*attr.*) кака́овый; **~ bean** боб кака́о.
cocoon [kə'ku:n] *n.* ко́кон.
v.t. (*fig., e.g. aircraft*) ста́вить, по- на консерва́цию; покр|ыва́ть, -ы́ть чехло́м.
cocotte [kə'kɒt] *n.* (*woman*) коко́тка; (*dish*) порцио́нная кастрю́лечка.
COD *abbr. of* **1.** ***cash on delivery*** упла́та при доста́вке. **2.** ***Concise Oxford Dictionary*** Кра́ткий оксфо́рдский слова́рь (англи́йского языка́).
cod[1] [kɒd] *n.* (**~fish**) треска́.
cpds. **~-bank** *n.* тресков́ая о́тмель; **~-fisher** *n.* лове́ц трески́; **~-fishing** *n.* ло́вля трески́; **~-liver oil** *n.* ры́бий жир.
cod[2] [kɒd] *v.t.* (*coll., fool*) одура́чи|вать, -ть; над|ува́ть, -у́ть.
coda ['kəʊdə] *n.* ко́да.
coddle ['kɒd(ə)l] *v.t.* не́жить (*or* изне́живать), из-.
code [kəʊd] *n.* (*of laws*) ко́декс; свод зако́нов; **building ~** положе́ние о застро́йке; (*of conduct*) ко́декс; но́рмы (*f. pl.*); (*set of symbols, cipher*) код; **Morse ~** код/а́збука Мо́рзе.
v.t. (*encode*) коди́ровать (*impf., pf.*); шифрова́ть, за- по ко́ду.
co-defendant [,kəʊdɪ'fendənt] *n.* (*leg.*) соотве́тчик.
codeine ['kəʊdi:n] *n.* кодеи́н.
coder ['kəʊdə(r)] *n.* шифрова́льщик.
codex ['kəʊdeks] *n.* ко́декс; стари́нная ру́копись.
codger ['kɒdʒə(r)] *n.* (*coll.*) чуда́к.
codicil ['kəʊdɪsɪl, 'kɒd-] *n.* дополни́тельное распоряже́ние к завеща́нию.
codification [,kəʊdɪfɪ'keɪʃ(ə)n] *n.* кодифика́ция.
codify ['kəʊdɪ,faɪ, 'kɒd-] *v.t.* кодифици́ровать (*impf., pf*).
codpiece ['kɒdpi:s] *n.* гу́льфик.
codswallop ['kɒdz,wɒləp] *n.* (*coll.*) ерунда́ (на по́стном ма́сле).
co-ed ['kəʊed, kəʊ'ed] *n.* (*US, coll.*) учени́ца сме́шанной шко́лы; студе́нтка (*учебного заведения для лиц обоего пола*).
co-education [,kəʊedju:'keɪʃ(ə)n] *n.* совме́стное обуче́ние.
co-educational [,kəʊedju:'keɪʃ(ə)nəl] *adj.* совме́стного обуче́ния; **this college is ~** в э́том ко́лледже совме́стное обуче́ние.
coefficient [,kəʊɪ'fɪʃ(ə)nt] *n.* коэффицие́нт.
coelacanth ['si:lə,kænθ] *n.* цела́кант.
coenobite ['si:nə,baɪt] *n.* мона́х, и́нок.
coenobitic [,si:nə'bɪtɪk] *adj.* мона́шеский, и́ноческий.
coequal [kəʊ'i:kw(ə)l] *adj.* ра́вный (*по чину, значению и т.п.*).
coerce [kəʊ'ɜ:s] *v.t.* прин|ужда́ть, -у́дить; **~ into silence** заста́вить (*pf.*) молча́ть.
coercion [kəʊ'ɜ:ʃ(ə)n] *n.* принужде́ние; **he paid under ~** он

заплати́л под давле́нием; его́ прину́дили заплати́ть.
coercive [kəʊ'ɜːsɪv] *adj.* принуди́тельный.
coeval [kəʊ'iːv(ə)l] *n.* све́рстни|к; совреме́нни|к (*fem.* -ца). *adj.* одного́ во́зраста (с+*i.*); совреме́нный (+*d.*).
coexist [ˌkəʊɪg'zɪst] *v.i.* сосуществова́ть (*impf*).
coexistence [ˌkəʊɪg'zɪstəns] *n.* сосуществова́ние.
coexistent [ˌkəʊɪg'zɪstənt] *adj.* сосуществу́ющий.
coextensive [ˌkəʊɪk'stensɪv] *adj.* одина́ковой протяжённости во вре́мени (*or* в простра́нстве).
C. of E. (*abbr. of* **Church of England**) Англика́нская це́рковь.
coffee ['kɒfɪ] *n.* ко́фе (*m. indecl.*); **two ~s** две по́рции ко́фе; два ра́за ко́фе; **black ~** чёрный ко́фе; **white ~** ко́фе с молоко́м; **ground ~** мо́лотый ко́фе; **roasted ~** жа́реный ко́фе; **Turkish ~** ко́фе по-туре́цки; **~ ice cream** кофе́йное моро́женое; **instant ~** раствори́мый ко́фе.
cpds. **~-bar** *n.* буфе́т; **~-bean** *n.* кофе́йный боб; (*pl.*) ко́фе в зёрнах; **~-berry** *n.* плод кофе́йного де́рева; **~-break** *n.* переры́в на ко́фе; **~-cup** *n.* кофе́йная ча́шка; **~-grinder, ~-mill** *nn.* кофе́йница, кофе́йная ме́льница, кофемо́лка; **~-grounds** *n. pl.* кофе́йная гу́ща; **~-house** *n.* кафе́ (*indecl.*); **~-mill** *n.* = **~-grinder; ~-maker** *n.* кофева́рка; **~-pot** *n.* кофе́йник; **~-table** *n.* ни́зенький сто́лик.
coffer ['kɒfə(r)] *n.* **1.** (*chest*) сунду́к; (*pl., fig., funds*) казна́. **2.** (*in ceiling*) кессо́н.
coffin ['kɒfɪn] *n.* гроб; **drive a nail into s.o.'s ~** вбить гвоздь в чей-н. гроб.
cog [kɒg] *n.* зуб (*pl.* -ья); зубе́ц; вы́ступ; **a ~ in the machine** (*fig.*) ви́нтик, ме́лкая со́шка; **~ railway** зу́бчатая желе́зная доро́га, фуникулёр.
cpd. **~-wheel** *n.* зу́бчатое колесо́.
cogency ['kəʊdʒənsɪ] *n.* убеди́тельность.
cogent ['kəʊdʒ(ə)nt] *adj.* убеди́тельный.
cogitate ['kɒdʒɪˌteɪt] *v.i.* размышля́ть (*impf.*) (*о чём or над чем*).
cogitation [ˌkɒdʒɪ'teɪʃ(ə)n] *n.* размышле́ние, обду́мывание.
cognac ['kɒnjæk] *n.* конья́к.
cognate ['kɒgneɪt] *adj.* **1.** (*akin*) ро́дственный. **2.** (*ling.*) ро́дственный, однокорнево́й, о́бщего происхожде́ния.
cognition [kɒg'nɪʃ(ə)n] *n.* позна́ние; зна́ние.
cognitive ['kɒgnɪtɪv] *adj.* познава́тельный.
cognizance ['kɒgnɪz(ə)ns, 'kɒn-] *n.* зна́ние, узнава́ние; **take ~ of** приня́ть (*pf.*) во внима́ние.
cognizant ['kɒgnɪz(ə)nt, 'kɒn-] *adj.* зна́ющий, осведомлённый.
cognoscente [ˌkɒnjə'ʃentɪ] *n.* знато́к, цени́тель (*m.*).
cohabit [kəʊ'hæbɪt] *v.t.* сожи́тельствовать (*impf.*).
cohabitation [ˌkəʊhæbɪ'teɪʃ(ə)n] *n.* (внебра́чное) сожи́тельство.
coheir [kəʊ'eə(r)] *n.* сонасле́дник.
coheiress [kəʊ'eə(r)ɪs] *n.* сонасле́дница.
cohere [kəʊ'hɪə(r)] *v.t.* (*stick, together*) сцеп|ля́ться, -и́ться; быть соединённым/объединённым; (*fig., be consistent*) быть свя́зным.
coherenc|e [kəʊ'hɪərəns], **-y** [kəʊ'hɪərənsɪ] *nn.* свя́зность, после́довательность, членоразде́льность.
coherent [kəʊ'hɪərənt] *adj.* свя́зный, после́довательный; членоразде́льный.
cohesion [kəʊ'hiːʒ(ə)n] *n.* сцепле́ние; си́ла сцепле́ния; сплочённость.
cohesive [kəʊ'hiːsɪv] *adj.* спосо́бный к сцепле́нию; связу́ющий; (*united*) сплочённый.
cohesiveness [kəʊ'hiːsɪvnɪs] *n.* спосо́бность к сцепле́нию; сплочённость.
cohort ['kəʊhɔːt] *n.* (*hist.*) кого́рта; (*pl., troops*) во́йско.
coiffure [kwɑː'fjʊə(r)] *n.* приче́ска.
coign [kɔɪn] *n.*: **~ of vantage** удо́бный наблюда́тельный пункт.
coil[1] [kɔɪl] *n.* **1.** (*of rope, snake etc.*) вито́к; кольцо́. **2.** (*elec.*) кату́шка; **~ antenna** (*radio*) ра́мочная анте́нна.
v.t. & i. (*also* **~ up**) свёр|тывать(ся), -ну́ть(ся) кольцо́м (*or* в кольцо́).
coil[2] [kɔɪl] *n.* (*arch., trouble, fuss*) суета́.
coin [kɔɪn] *n.* моне́та; **spin, toss a ~** игра́ть (*impf.*) в орля́нку; подки́|дывать, -нуть моне́тку; **pay s.o. back in his own ~** отплати́ть (*pf.*) кому́-н. той же моне́той; **current ~** ходя́чая моне́та.
v.t. чека́нить (*impf.*) (*моне́ты*); **~ a phrase** созд|ава́ть, -а́ть выраже́ние; **he is ~ing money** (*fig.*) мо́жно поду́мать, что он де́ньги печа́тает.
cpds. **~-box** *n.* моне́тник (*автома́та*); телефо́н-автома́т; **~-operated** *adj.* моне́тный.
coinage ['kɔɪnɪdʒ] *n.* **1.** (*monetary system*) моне́тная систе́ма; **decimal ~** десяти́чная де́нежная систе́ма. **2.** (*inventing*) созда́ние (слов); **a word of his own ~** со́зданное/пу́щенное им сло́во. **3.** (*coined word*) неологи́зм.
coincide [ˌkəʊɪn'saɪd] *v.i.* (*also math.*) совп|ада́ть, -а́сть.
coincidence [kəʊ'ɪnsɪd(ə)ns] *n.* **1.** (*fact of coinciding*) совпаде́ние. **2.** (*curious chance*) совпаде́ние, стече́ние обстоя́тельств.
coincident [kəʊ'ɪnsɪd(ə)nt] *adj.* совпада́ющий.
coincidental [kəʊˌɪnsɪ'dent(ə)l] *adj.* случа́йный.
coiner ['kɔɪnə(r)] *n.* **1.** (*stamper of money*) чека́нщик моне́т, моне́тчик. **2.** (*counterfeiter*) фальшивомоне́тчик. **3.** (*inventor*) вы́думщик, сочини́тель (*m.*).
coir ['kɔɪə(r)] *n.* койр, коко́совое волокно́.
coital ['kəʊɪtəl] *adj.* относя́щийся к ко́итусу.
coit|ion [kəʊ'ɪʃ(ə)n], **-us** ['kəʊɪtəs] *nn.* совокупле́ние, ко́итус.
Coke[1] [kəʊk] *n.* (*propr.*) «Ко́ка-ко́ла», «Кок».
coke[2] [kəʊk] *n.* кокс; **~ oven** ко́ксовая/коксова́льная печь.
v.t. коксова́ть (*impf.*); **coking coal** коксу́ющийся у́голь.
coke[3] [kəʊk] *n.* (= *cocaine*) (*sl.*) марафе́т.
Col. ['kɜːn(ə)l] *n.* (*abbr. of* **Colonel**) полк., (полко́вник).
col [kɒl] *n.* перева́л.
colander ['kʌləndə(r)] *n.* дуршла́г.
colchicum ['kɒltʃɪkəm, 'kɒlkɪ-] *n.* безвреме́нник.
cold [kəʊld] *n.* **1.** хо́лод; **he was left out in the ~** (*fig.*) его́ поки́нули; он оста́лся ни при чём. **2.** (*illness*) просту́да; **catch (a) ~** просту|жа́ться, -ди́ться; схвати́ть (*pf.*) на́сморк/гри́пп; **~ in the head** на́сморк; **~ in the chest** просту́да.
adj. **1.** (*at low temperature*) холо́дный; **I am, feel ~** мне хо́лодно. **2.** (*fig.*): **throw ~ water on s.o.'s plan** окати́ть уша́том холо́дной воды́ кого́-н.; охлади́ть чей-н. пыл; **in ~ blood** хладнокро́вно; **~ steel** холо́дное ору́жие; **~ war** холо́дная война́; **get ~ feet** (*fig., coll.*) стру́сить (*pf.*); **it makes one's blood run ~** от э́того кровь сты́нет/ледене́ет в жи́лах. **3.** (*unemotional, unfeeling*): **a ~ person** холо́дный челове́к; **~ facts** го́лые фа́кты; **~ comfort** сла́бое утеше́ние; **the idea leaves me ~** э́та мысль не волну́ет меня́. **4.** (*of scent*) осты́вший. **5.** (*of colours*) холо́дный.
cpds. **~-blooded** *adj.* (*of animal*) холоднокро́вный; (*fig.*) бесчу́вственный, безжа́лостный; **~-bloodedness** *n.* бесчу́вственность, безжа́лостность; **~-hearted** *adj.* бессерде́чный; **~-heartedness** *n.* бессерде́чие; **~-shoulder** *v.t.* ока́з|ывать, -а́ть кому́-н. холо́дный приём.
coldish ['kəʊldɪʃ] *adj.* холоднова́тый.
coldness ['kəʊldnɪs] *n.* (*of temperature*) хо́лод; (*of character etc.*) холо́дность.
coleoptera [ˌkɒlɪ'ɒptərə] *n.* жесткокры́лые (*nt. pl.*).
coleslaw ['kəʊlslɔː] *n.* капу́стный сала́т.
colic ['kɒlɪk] *n.* ко́лик|и (*pl., g.* —).
colicky ['kɒlɪkɪ] *adj.* страда́ющий ко́ликами.
colitis [kə'laɪtɪs] *n.* коли́т.
collaborate [kə'læbəˌreɪt] *v.i.* сотру́дничать (*impf.*).
collaboration [kəˌlæbə'reɪʃ(ə)n] *n.* сотру́дничество.
collaborator [kə'læbəˌreɪtə(r)] *n.* сотру́дник; (*hist.*) коллаборациони́ст.
collage ['kɒlɑːʒ, kə'lɑːʒ] *n.* колла́ж.
collapse [kə'læps] *n.* (*of a building etc.*) обва́л, паде́ние, обру́шение; (*of hopes etc.*) круше́ние; (*of resistance etc.*) разва́л, крах; (*med.*) колла́пс, упа́док сил, изнеможе́ние; **nervous ~** не́рвное истоще́ние.
v.t. (*e.g. a telescope*) скла́дывать, сложи́ть.
v.i. (*of a building etc.*) обва́л|иваться, -и́ться; ру́хнуть (*pf.*); (*of pers.*) свали́ться (*pf.*); **the house ~d** дом ру́хнул/обвали́лся; **this table ~s** (*folds up*) э́тот стол скла́дывается; **the plan ~d** план ру́хнул.
collapsible [kə'læpsɪb(ə)l] *adj.* складно́й, разбо́рный.
collar ['kɒlə(r)] *n.* **1.** (*part of a garment*) воротни́к;

(*detachable*) воротничо́к; **hot under the ~** (*fig.*, *excited*, *vexed*) рассе́рженный, рассвирипе́вший. **2.** (*necklace etc.*) ожере́лье, колье́. **3.** (*of dog*) оше́йник; (*of horse*) хому́т.

v.t. (*seize*) схва́т|ывать, -и́ть за во́рот/ши́ворот; (*coll.*, *appropriate*) стяну́ть (*pf.*).

cpds. **~-bone** *n.* (*anat.*) ключи́ца; **~-stud** *n.* за́понка (для воротника́).

collate [kə'leɪt] *v.t.* (*e.g. texts*) слич|а́ть, -и́ть; сопост|авля́ть, -а́вить.

collateral [kə'lætər(ə)l] *adj.* побо́чный, дополни́тельный; **~ security** дополни́тельное обеспе́чение.

collation [kə'leɪʃ(ə)n] *n.* (*collating*) сличе́ние, сопоставле́ние; (*meal*) заку́ска.

colleague ['kɒli:g] *n.* колле́га (*c.g.*); сослужи́в|ец (*fem.* -ица).

collect[1] [kə'lekt] *n.* (*prayer*) кра́ткая моли́тва.

collect[2] [kə'lekt] *v.t.* **1.** (*gather together*) соб|ира́ть, -ра́ть; **~ed works** (по́лное) собра́ние сочине́ний. **2.** (*of debts*, *taxes*) соб|ира́ть, -ра́ть; получ|а́ть, -и́ть; **the telegram was sent ~** (*US*) телегра́мма была́ вы́слана «для опла́ты получа́телем». **3.** (*of stamps etc.*) коллекциони́ровать (*impf.*). **4.** (*fetch*) заб|ира́ть, -ра́ть; за|ходи́ть, -йти́ за *+i.*; **he ~ed the children from school** он забра́л дете́й из шко́лы. **5.** (*keep in hand*): **~ o.s.** брать, взять себя́ в ру́ки; **~ one's thoughts** собра́ться (*pf.*) с мы́слями.

v.i. соб|ира́ться, -ра́ться; **a crowd ~ed** собрала́сь толпа́; **dust ~s** пыль ска́пливается.

collected [kə'lektɪd] *adj.* (*calm*) со́бранный; споко́йный.

collectedness [kə'lektɪdnɪs] *n.* со́бранность; споко́йствие.

collection [kə'lekʃ(ə)n] *n.* (*of valuables etc.*) колле́кция; (*accumulation*) скопле́ние; (*church etc.*) сбор, собира́ние; (*of mail*) вы́емка.

collective [kə'lektɪv] *n.* (*co-operative unit*) коллекти́в.

adj. коллекти́вный; **~ farm** колхо́з; **~ farmer** колхо́зни|к (*fem.* -ца); (*gram.*): **~ noun** собира́тельное существи́тельное.

collectivism [kə'lektɪ,vɪz(ə)m] *n.* коллективи́зм.

collectivist [kə'lektɪvɪst] *n.* коллективи́ст.

collectivity [kə,lek'tɪvɪtɪ] *n.* коллекти́вность.

collectivization [kə,lektɪvaɪ'zeɪʃ(ə)n] *n.* коллективиза́ция.

collectivize [kə'lektɪ,vaɪz] *v.t.* коллективизи́ровать (*impf.*, *pf.*).

collector [kə'lektə(r)] *n.* (*of stamps etc.*) коллекционе́р; **a ~'s piece** ре́дкий/уника́льный экземпля́р; (*of taxes*, *debts*) сбо́рщик; (*of tickets*) контролёр.

colleen [kɒ'li:n] *n.* (ирла́ндская) де́вушка.

college ['kɒlɪdʒ] *n.* **1.** (*school*) колле́дж. **2.** (*university*) университе́т; институ́т; вы́сшее уче́бное заведе́ние (*abbr.* вуз); **a ~ education** университе́тское образова́ние. **3.** (*within university*) университе́тский колле́дж. **4.** (*body of colleagues*) колле́гия; **~ of cardinals** колле́гия кардина́лов; **~ of arms** геральди́ческая пала́та.

collegial [kə'li:dʒ(ə)l] *adj.* **1.** (*of college*) университе́тский. **2.** (*of collegium*) коллегиа́льный.

collegian [kə'li:dʒ(ə)n] (*also* (*US*) **colleger**) *nn.* (*member of college*) член колле́джа.

collegiate [kə'li:dʒət] *adj.* **1.** (*of college*) университе́тский. **2.** (*of collegium*) коллегиа́льный. **3.** (*of students*) студе́нческий.

collegium [kə'li:dʒɪəm] *n.* колле́гия.

collide [kə'laɪd] *v.i.* ст|а́лкиваться, -олкну́ться.

collie ['kɒlɪ] *n.* ко́лли (*m. indecl.*), шотла́ндская овча́рка.

collier ['kɒlɪə(r)] *n.* (*miner*) углеко́п; (*ship*; *dealer*) у́гольщик.

colliery ['kɒlɪərɪ] *n.* каменноуго́льная ша́хта.

collision [kə'lɪʒ(ə)n] *n.* столкнове́ние; (*fig.*) колли́зия, столкнове́ние; **come into ~ with** столкну́ться (*pf.*) с*+i.*; **~ course** пу́ть, на кото́ром неизбе́жно столкнове́ние.

collocate ['kɒlə,keɪt] *v.t.* распол|ага́ть, -ожи́ть; расстан|а́вливать, -ови́ть.

collocation [,kɒlə'keɪʃ(ə)n] *n.* расположе́ние, расстано́вка.

collodion [kə'ləʊdɪən] *n.* колло́дий.

colloquial [kə'ləʊkwɪəl] *adj.* разгово́рный.

colloquialism [kə'ləʊkwɪə,lɪz(ə)m] *n.* разгово́рное выраже́ние/сло́во.

colloquy ['kɒləkwɪ] *n.* собесе́дование.

collusion [kə'lu:ʒ(ə)n, -'lju:ʒ(ə)n] *n.* сго́вор; **act in ~** де́йствовать (*impf.*) по сго́вору.

collusive [kə'lu:sɪv] *adj.* совершённый по сго́вору.

collyrium [kə'lɪrɪəm] *n.* глазна́я мазь.

collywobbles ['kɒlɪ,wɒb(ə)lz] *n.* (*coll.*) урча́ние в животе́.

colocynth ['kɒləsɪnθ] *n.* колокви́нт.

Cologne [kə'ləʊn] *n.* Кёльн.

Colombia [kə'lɒmbɪə] *n.* Колу́мбия.

Colombian [kə'lɒmbɪən] *n.* колумби́|ец (*fem.* -йка).

adj. колумби́йский.

Colombo [kə'lʌmbəʊ] *n.* Коло́мбо (*m. indecl.*).

colon[1] ['kəʊlən, -lɒn] *n.* (*anat.*) ободо́чная кишка́.

colon[2] ['kəʊlən, -lɒn] *n.* (*gram.*) двоето́чие.

colonel ['kɜ:n(ə)l] *n.* полко́вник.

cpds. **~-general** *n.* генера́л-полко́вник; **~-in-chief** *n.* шеф полка́.

colonelcy ['kɜ:n(ə)lsɪ] *n.* чин полко́вника.

colonial [kə'ləʊnɪəl] *n.* жи́тель (*fem.* -ница) коло́нии.

adj. колониа́льный; **C~ Office** министе́рство коло́ний; **~ architecture** (*US*) колониа́льный стиль; **~ produce** колониа́льные това́ры.

colonialism [kə'ləʊnɪə,lɪz(ə)m] *n.* колониали́зм.

colonialist [kə'ləʊnɪəlɪst] *n.* колониали́ст.

adj. колониали́стский.

colonic [kə'lɒnɪk] *adj.* (*anat.*) относя́щийся к ободо́чной кишке́.

colonist ['kɒlənɪst] *n.* колони́ст (*fem.* -ка); (*settler*) поселе́нец.

colonization ['kɒlə,naɪ'zeɪʃ(ə)n] *n.* колониза́ция.

colonize ['kɒlə,naɪz] *v.t.* колонизова́ть, колонизи́ровать (*both impf.*, *pf.*); (*settle in*) засел|я́ть, -и́ть.

colonizer ['kɒlə,naɪzə(r)] *n.* колониза́тор.

colonnade [,kɒlə'neɪd] *n.* колонна́да.

colony ['kɒlənɪ] *n.* коло́ния; **~ of ants** коло́ния муравьёв; **the American ~ in Paris** америка́нская коло́ния в Пари́же; **summer ~** ле́тняя коло́ния; да́чный посёлок.

colophon ['kɒlə,fɒn, -fən] *n.* колофо́н.

Colorado beetle [,kɒlə'rɑ:dəʊ] *n.* колора́дский/карто́фельный жук.

coloration [,kʌlə'reɪʃ(ə)n] *n.* (*putting on colour*) окра́шивание; (*varied colour*) окра́ска, раскра́ска, расцве́тка.

coloratura [,kɒlərə'tʊərə] *n.* колорату́ра; **~ soprano** колорату́рное сопра́но.

colorimeter [,kɒlə'rɪmɪtə(r), ,kʌl-] *n.* колори́метр, цветоме́р.

colossal [kə'lɒs(ə)l] *adj.* колосса́льный, грома́дный.

Colosseum [,kɒlə'si:əm] *n.* Колизе́й.

Colossian [kə'lɒʃən] *n.* колосся́нин.

colossus [kə'lɒsəs] *n.* коло́сс.

colour ['kʌlə(r)] *n.* **1.** (*lit.*) цвет; (*of horses*) масть; **primary ~s** основны́е цвета́; **secondary ~s** составны́е цвета́; **complementary ~s** дополни́тельные цвета́; **change ~** (*lit.*) меня́ть (*impf.*) цвет; (*fig.*) побледне́ть/покрасне́ть (*both pf.*); **the film is in ~** э́то цветно́й фильм; **what ~ are his eyes?** како́го цве́та у него́ глаза́?; **see the ~ of s.o.'s money** (*fig.*) получи́ть (*pf.*) от кого́-н. де́ньги; **~ code** цветово́й код; **~ scheme** подбо́р цвето́в; **~ television** цветно́е телеви́дение; (*pl.*, *of team*) фо́рма; **what are their ~s?** в како́й фо́рме они́ игра́ют? **2.** (*of face*) цвет лица́; румя́нец; **she has very little ~** у неё бле́дное лицо́; **lose ~** побледне́ть (*pf.*); **he has a high ~** он о́чень румя́ный; **off ~** (*out of sorts*) не в фо́рме. **3.** (*pl.*, *paints*) кра́ски; **water ~s** акваре́ль; **oil ~s** ма́сляные кра́ски; ма́сло; **paint sth. in bright ~s** (*fig.*) рисова́ть, на- что-н. я́ркими кра́сками; **see sth. in its true ~s** (*fig.*) ви́деть (*impf.*) что-н. в и́стинном све́те. **4.** (*semblance*, *probability*): **the story has some ~ of truth** э́тот расска́з похо́ж на пра́вду; **this fact lent ~ to his tale** э́тот факт прида́л не́которое правдоподо́бие его́ расска́зу; **under ~ of** под ви́дом/предло́гом *+g.*; **he gave a false ~ to the news** он предста́вил но́вость в ло́жном све́те. **5.** (*liveliness*): **his style lacks ~** его́ сти́лю недостаёт кра́сочности; **local ~** ме́стный колори́т. **6.** (*pl.*, *flag*; *also fig.*): **he spent 5 years with the ~s** он прослужи́л 5 лет в а́рмии; **sail under false ~s** плыть (*det.*) под чужи́м фла́гом; выступа́ть (*impf.*) под чужи́м и́менем; выдава́ть (*impf.*) себя́ за друго́го; **pass an examination with flying ~s** сдать (*pf.*) экза́мен с бле́ском; **nail one's ~s to the mast** не отступа́ться (*impf.*)

от своих убеждений; **show one's true ~s** предстать (*pf.*) в истинном свете; **strike one's ~s** капитулировать (*impf.*, *pf.*). **7.** (*of race*): **a person of ~** представитель (*m.*) небелой расы.

v.t. **1.** (*paint, endow with ~*) красить (*impf.*); окра|шивать, -сить; **she wants the walls ~ed green** она хочет покрасить стены в зелёный цвет. **2.** (*embellish*) приукра|шивать, -сить; **a highly ~ed story** сильно приукрашенный рассказ. **3.** (*imbue*): **his action was ~ed by vengefulness** его поступок был отчасти продиктован мстительностью. *See also* **coloured**

v.i. **1.** (*take on ~*): **the leaves ~ in autumn** осенью листья меняют свой цвет. **2.** (*blush*) краснеть, по-.

cpds. **~-bar** *n.* цветной барьер; **~-bearer** *n.* (*mil.*) знаменосец; **~-blind** *adj.* страдающий дальтонизмом; **~-blind person** не различающий цветов, дальтоник; **~-blindness** *n.* неспособность различать цвета, дальтонизм; **~-box** *n.* (*paint-box*) ящик с красками; **~ code** *v.t.* кодировать (*impf.*, *pf.*) по цвету; **~-fast** *adj.* цветостойкий; **~-fastness** *n.* цветостойкость; **~-man** *n.* (*dealer in paints*) торговец красками; **~-printing** *n.* хромотипия, многокрасочная печать; **~-sergeant** *n.* сержант-знамёнщик; **~-wash** *n.* клеевая краска; *v.t.* красить (*impf.*) клеевой краской.

colourable ['kʌlərəb(ə)l] *adj.* (*plausible*) правдоподобный.

coloured ['kʌləd] *adj.* цветной; **~ pencil** цветной карандаш; **~ plate** (*illustration*) цветная иллюстрация; **~ print** цветная гравюра; (*of race*): **~ people** цветные (*pl.*).

colourful ['kʌlə,fʊl] *adj.* красочный, яркий; **a ~ personality** яркая/колоритная личность.

colouring ['kʌlərɪŋ] *n.* окраска; **protective ~** защитная окраска; (*complexion*) цвет лица; (*of a picture*) краски (*f. pl.*); **~ book** (*for children*) альбом для раскрашивания.

adj. красящий; **~ matter** красящее вещество.

colourist ['kʌlərɪst] *n.* колорист.

colourless ['kʌləlɪs] *adj.* (*lit.*, *fig.*) бесцветный.

colt[1] [kəʊlt] *n.* (*young horse*) жеребёнок; (*fig.*, *young man*) сосунок, птенец.

Colt[2] [kəʊlt] *n.* (*~ revolver*) кольт; **~ machine-gun** станковый пулемёт Кольта.

coltish ['kəʊltɪʃ] *adj.* (*lively*) живой, бойкий, игривый.

colubrine ['kɒljʊ,braɪn] *adj.* змеиный.

columbarium [,kɒləm'beərɪəm] *n.* (*in crematorium*) колумбарий.

Columbia [kə'lʌmbɪə] *n.*: **District of ~** округ Колумбия.

columbine ['kɒləm,baɪn] *n.* водосбор.

Columbus [kə'lʌmbəs] *n.* Колумб.

column ['kɒləm] *n.* **1.** (*pillar*) колонна. **2.** (*vertical object or mass*) столб; **~ of smoke** столб дыма; **spinal ~** позвоночный столб; **mercury ~** ртутный столбик. **3.** (*in book etc.*) столбец; **in the ~s of the Times** на страницах «Таймса». **4.** (*regular feature in newspaper*): **weekly ~** еженедельная колонка. **5.** (*of figures*) столбик, столбец, колонка. **6.** (*mil. etc.*) колонна; **~ of ships** колонна кораблей; **close ~** сомкнутая колонна; **in ~** в колонне; **fifth ~** (*fig.*) пятая колонна; **dodge the ~** (*fig.*) уклоняться (*impf.*) от обязанностей.

columnist ['kɒləmnɪst, -mɪst] *n.* обозреватель (*fem.* -ница).

colza ['kɒlzə] *n.* рапс; **~ oil** сурепное/рапсовое масло.

coma ['kəʊmə] *n.* кома.

comatose ['kəʊmə,təʊz] *adj.* коматозный; **he is ~** он в коме.

comb [kəʊm] *n.* **1.** (*for ~ing hair*) расчёска, гребёнка, гребешок; (*as adornment*) гребень (*m.*). **2.** (*part of machine*) бёрдо, чесалка, гребёнка. **3.** (*honey-~*) сот|ы (*pl.*, *g.* -ов). **4.** (*of bird*) гребешок, гребень (*m.*). **5.** (*of wave*) гребень (*m.*).

v.t. **1.** (*hair etc.*) чесать (*impf.*); расчёс|ывать, -ать; причёс|ывать, -ать; (*horse*) чистить (*impf.*) скребницей; (*wool, flax etc.*) чесать (*impf.*); трепать (*impf.*). **2.** (*fig.*, *search*) причёс|ывать, -ать; **the police ~ed the city** полиция прочесала весь город.

cpd. **~-out** *n.* (*mil.*) переосвидетельствование для военной службы.

combat ['kɒmbæt, 'kʌm-] *n.* бой; **single ~** единоборство, поединок; **mortal ~** смертный бой; (*mil.*): **~ fatigue** боевая психическая травма; **~ zone** зона боевых действий.

v.t. бороться (*impf.*) с+*i.* (*or* против+*g.*).

v.i. бороться; сражаться (*both impf.*).

combatant ['kɒmbət(ə)nt, 'kʌm-] *n.* боец; воюющая сторона.

adj. борющийся; сражающийся.

combative ['kɒmbɪnətɪv, 'kʌm-] *adj.* боевой, задиристый.

combativeness ['kɒmbətɪvnɪs, 'kʌm-] *n.* задиристость.

combe [ku:m] = **coomb**

comber ['kəʊmə(r)] *n.* (*machine*) гребнечесальная машина; (*wave*) вал, большая волна.

combination [,kɒmbɪ'neɪʃ(ə)n] *n.* **1.** (*combining*) сочетание, комбинация; **in ~ with** в сочетании с+*i.* **2. motor-cycle ~** мотоцикл с прицепной коляской. **3.** (*pl.*, *garment*) бельё типа купальника. **4.** (*of a safe*) кодовая комбинация; **~ lock** секретный замок.

combine[1] ['kɒmbaɪn] *n.* **1.** (*group of persons*) объединение; (*group of concerns*) комбинат, синдикат. **2.** (**~ harvester**) комбайн.

combine[2] [kəm'baɪn] *v.t.* сочетать (*impf.*); объедин|ять, -ить; комбинировать, с-; **~ forces** объедин|ять, -ить (*or* соедин|ять, -ить) силы; **he ~s business with pleasure** он сочетает приятное с полезным; **~d operations** (*mil.*) общевойсковая операция.

combings ['kəʊmɪŋz] *n.* (*tech.*) гребенные очистки (*f. pl.*).

combo ['kɒmbəʊ] *n.* (*coll.*) небольшой ансамбль; **jazz-combo** джаз-ансамбль (*m.*).

combust [kəm'bʌst] *v.t.* сж|игать, -ечь.

combustible [kəm'bʌstɪb(ə)l] *adj.* горючий, топливный воспламеняемый.

combustion [kəm'bʌstʃ(ə)n] *n.* воспламенение; сгорание, горение; **spontaneous ~** самовоспламенение; **internal ~ engine** двигатель внутреннего сгорания.

come [kʌm] *v.i.* **1.** (*move near, arrive*) при|ходить, -йти; приб|ывать, -ыть; при|езжать, -ехать; **~ and see us!** приходите/заходите к нам!; **he came running** он прибежал; **he has ~ a hundred miles** он приехал за сто миль; **he was long in coming** он долго не появлялся; **he came near to falling** он чуть не упал; **~ along!** пойдёмте!; **~ into the house!** заходите/зайдите в дом! **2.** (*of inanimate things*; *lit.*, *fig.*): **the dress ~s to her knees** платье доходит ей до колен; **the sunshine came streaming into the room** лучи солнца лились в комнату; **dinner came** подали обед; **a parcel has ~** получена посылка; **the ball came on his head** мяч попал ему в голову; **the feeling ~s and goes** это чувство то появляется, то исчезает; **easy ~, easy go** легко нажито, легко прожито; **no work has ~ his way** никакая работа ему не попадалась; **these shirts ~ in three sizes** эти рубашки бывают трёх размеров; **it came as a shock to me** это было для меня ударом; **it came into my head** это пришло мне в голову; **the water came to the boil** вода закипела; **the solution came to me** я (вдруг) нашёл решение; **what are we coming to?** до чего мы дожили?; **when it came to 6 o'clock** когда время подошло к 6 часам; **she takes things as they ~** она спокойно относится ко всему, что бы ни случилось. **3.** (*fig. uses with 'to': see also relevant nn.*): **~ to a decision** прийти (*pf.*) к решению; **~ to blows** дойти (*pf.*) до рукопашной; **~ to terms** прийти (*pf.*) к соглашению; **~ to light** обнаружиться (*pf.*); стать (*pf.*) очевидным; **~ to one's senses** образумиться (*pf.*). **4.** (*fig. uses with 'into': see also relevant nn.*): **the trees have ~ into leaf** на деревьях распустились листья; **he has ~ into a fortune** он получил большое наследство; **he came into his own** он добился признания/своего; **they came into sight** они появились; **the party came into power** партия пришла к власти. **5.** (*occur, happen*) случаться, бывать (*both impf.*); **Christmas ~s once a year** Рождество бывает раз в году; **who ~s next?** кто следующий; **it ~s on page 20** это на двадцатой странице; **no harm will ~ to you** с вами ничего не случится; **he had it coming to him** ему следовало этого ожидать; (*coll.*) он достукался; **how ~ he was late?** как это получилось, что он опоздал?; **how did you ~ to meet**

him? как случи́лось, что вы с ним встре́тились?; **that ~s of grumbling** всё э́то из-за ворча́ния; **no good will ~ of it** ничего́ хоро́шего из э́того не вы́йдет; **books to ~** кни́ги, кото́рые бу́дут вы́пущены; **in years to ~** в после́дующие го́ды; в бу́дущем; **~ what may** будь что бу́дет; **when we ~ to die** когда́ нам придётся умира́ть; **how ~?** (*US*, *sl.*) э́то почему́ же?; как так? **6.** (*amount*, *result*): **the bill ~s to £5** счёт составля́ет 5 фу́нтов; **it ~s to this, that ...** де́ло сво́дится к тому́, что…; **it ~s to the same thing** получа́ется то же са́мое; **if it ~s to that** е́сли уж на то пошло́; **his plans came to nothing** из его́ пла́нов ничего́ не вы́шло; **he is no good when it ~s to talking** когда́ ну́жно говори́ть, он теря́ется. **7.** (*become*, *prove to be*): **his dreams came true** его́ мечты́ осуществи́лись/сбыли́сь; **it ~s cheaper this way** так э́то выхо́дит деше́вле; **it ~s naturally to him** ему́ э́то легко́ даётся; у него́ э́то получа́ется есте́ственно (*or* само́ собо́й); **his shoelace came undone** у него́ развяза́лся шнуро́к боти́нка; **it all came right in the end** в конце́ концо́в всё обошло́сь; всё ко́нчилось благополу́чно; **~ clean** (*sl.*, *confess*) вы́ложить (*pf.*) всё. **8.** (*fig.*, *find o.s. in a position*): **I have ~ to see that he is right** я убеди́лся, что он прав; **how did you ~ to do that?** как вас угора́здило так поступи́ть? **9.** (*of pers.*, *originate*) прои|сходи́ть, -зойти́; **he ~s from Scotland** он уроже́нец Шотла́ндии; **she ~s of a noble family** она́ происхо́дит из зна́тной семьи́. **10.** (*coll. uses*): **don't ~ the bully over me** не кома́ндуйте мной!; **it will be 5 years ago ~ Christmas that ...** на Рождество́ бу́дет пять лет с тех пор, как…; **~ off it** (*desist*)! отста́нь!; конча́й!; переста́нь! **11.** (*imper.*, *fig.*): **~, ~!** (*expostulatory*) ну! ну!; ну, что вы!; **~, tell me what you know** ну́-ка, расскажи́те мне, что вы зна́ете. **12.** (*take form*): **the butter will not ~** ма́сло не сбива́ется. **13.** (*coll.*, *have orgasm*) конча́ть, ко́нчить.

with preps. (*see also* **3.** *and* **4.** *above*): **~ across** (*traverse*) пере|ходи́ть, -йти́ че́рез+*a.*; (*encounter*) нат|а́лкиваться, -олкну́ться на+*a.*; нат|ыка́ться, -кну́ться на+*a.*; **~ after** (*follow*) сле́довать (*impf.*) за+*i.*; **~ at** (*reach*): **the truth is hard to ~ at** до пра́вды тру́дно добра́ться; (*attack*): **the dog came at me** соба́ка набро́силась на меня́; **~ before** (*precede*): **dukes ~ before earls** ге́рцоги стоя́т вы́ше гра́фов; (*appear before*): **he came before the court** он предста́л пе́ред судо́м; **~ by** (*obtain*) дост|ава́ть, -а́ть; **how did he ~ by his death?** от чего́ он у́мер; **~ for** (*attack*): **he came for us with a stick** он набро́сился на нас с па́лкой; **~ from: wine ~s from grapes** вино́ получа́ется из виногра́да; **a sob came from her throat** из её груди́ вы́рвалось рыда́ние; **~ into: he came into a large estate** ему́ доста́лось большо́е име́ние; **~ off** (*lit.*): **~ off the grass!** сойди́те с травы́; (*become detached from*): **a button came off my coat** от моего́ пальто́ оторвала́сь пу́говица; (*fall off*): **she came off her bicycle** она́ упа́ла с велосипе́да; (*fig.*): **Britain came off the gold standard** А́нглия отошла́ от золото́го станда́рта; **~ on: he came on to me for £5** (*coll.*) он потре́бовал от меня́ 5 фу́нтов; **~ out of** (*lit.*): **he came out of the house** он вы́шел и́з дому; (*fig.*): **she came out of mourning** она́ сняла́ тра́ур; **~ over** (*lit.*): **a cloud came over the sky** о́блако набежа́ло на не́бо; (*fig.*): **what came over you?** что на вас нашло́?; **~ round: he came round the corner** он поверну́л за́ угол; **~ through: he came through both wars** он прошёл о́бе войны́; **~ under: what heading does this ~ under?** к како́й ру́брике э́то отно́сится; **he came under her influence** он попа́л под её влия́ние; **~ upon** (*find*) напа́сть (*pf.*) на+*a.*; натолкну́ться (*pf.*) на+*a.*; **fear came upon us** на нас напа́л страх.

with advs.: **~ about** *v.i.* (*happen*) прои|сходи́ть, -зойти́; **~ across** *v.i.* (*coll.*, *pay up*) распла́|чиваться, -ти́ться; (*confess*) выкла́дывать, вы́ложить (*coll.*); **~ again** *v.i.*: **~ again?** (*coll.*, *what did you say?*) ну́-ка повтори́!; скажи́ сно́ва!; **~ apart** *v.i.* (*unfastened*) ра|сходи́ться, -зойти́сь; разва́л|иваться, -и́ться на ча́сти; **~ away** *v.i.* (*become detached*) отл|а́мываться, -ома́ться *or* -оми́ться (*om*+*g.*); **~ back** *v.i.* (*return*) возвра|ща́ться, -ти́ться; верну́ться (*pf.*); **his name came back to me** я вспо́мнил его́ и́мя; (*retort*) возра|жа́ть, -зи́ть; **~ by** *v.i.* (*pass by*) минова́ть (*impf.*, *pf.*); про|ходи́ть, -йти́ ми́мо; **~ down** *v.i.*: **he came down off the ladder** он сошёл с ле́стницы; **her hair ~s down to her waist** у неё во́лосы дохо́дят до по́яса; (*of prices*) па́дать, упа́сть; (*fig.*): **he has ~ down in the world** он опусти́лся; **the story has ~ down to us** до нас дошла́ э́та исто́рия; (*coll.*): **he came down with £100** он вы́ложил 100 фу́нтов; **he came down on me for £50** он потре́бовал с меня́ 50 фу́нтов; **the master came down on the boy for cheating** учи́тель напусти́лся на ма́льчика за спи́сывание; **he came down with influenza** он слёг с гри́ппом; **~ forward** *v.i.* (*present o.s. as candidate*) выдвига́ть, вы́двинуть свою́ кандидату́ру; (*offer one's services*) предл|ага́ть, -ожи́ть свои́ услу́ги; (*become available*) поступ|а́ть, -и́ть; **~ in** *v.i.* (*lit.*) входи́ть, войти́; **~ in!** (*to s.o. knocking*) войди́те; **the tide came in** наступи́л прили́в; **when do oysters ~ in?** когда́ насту́пит сезо́н у́стриц?; **short skirts came in** коро́ткие ю́бки вошли́ в мо́ду; **his horse came in first** его́ ло́шадь пришла́ пе́рвой; **the Conservatives came in** консерва́торы победи́ли на вы́борах; **information came in** поступи́ли све́дения; **the money is ~ing in well** де́ньги поступа́ют хорошо́; **~ in, please!** (*radio etc.*) пожа́луйста, начина́йте!; **where do I ~ in?** како́е э́то име́ет ко мне отноше́ние?; что я получу́ с э́того?; **where does the joke ~ in?** что тут смешно́го?; **it came in handy** э́то пригоди́лось; э́то пришло́сь кста́ти; **he came in for a thrashing** ему́ всы́пали; **~ off** *v.i.* (*become detached*) отва́л|иваться, -и́ться; **the table-leg came off** у стола́ отвали́лась но́жка; **lipstick ~s off on glasses** губна́я пома́да остаётся на стака́нах; (*happen*, *succeed*): **the marriage came off** брак состоя́лся; **the experiment came off** о́пыт уда́лся; **he came off best** он вы́шел победи́телем; (*~ off duty*): **he ~s off at 10** он ухо́дит со слу́жбы в 10; **~ on** *v.i.* (*follow*) сле́довать (*impf.*); **he came on later** он появи́лся поздне́е; **~ on!** (*impatient*) ну!; ну-же; **~ on! I'll race you** дава́йте побежи́м наперегонки́!; (*progress*) де́лать (*impf.*) успе́хи; **the garden is coming on well** всё в саду́ хорошо́ растёт; (*start*, *set in*): **it came on to rain** начался́ дождь; **I have a cold coming on** у меня́ начина́ется просту́да; (*be dealt with*): **when does the case ~ on?** когда́ рассма́тривается э́то де́ло?; (*of actor*; *appear*) появ|ля́ться, -и́ться; выходи́ть, вы́йти на сце́ну; (*of play*; *be performed*): **the play ~s on next week** пье́са бу́дет предста́влена на сле́дующей неде́ле; **~ out** *v.i.* (*lit.*) выходи́ть, вы́йти; **the sun came out** со́лнце появи́лось/вы́глянуло; **the flowers came out** цветы́ распусти́лись; (*become known*, *appear*): **the news came out** но́вость ста́ла изве́стной; **the book came out** кни́га вы́шла; **the paper ~s out on Thursday** э́та газе́та выхо́дит по четверга́м; **he came out well in the photograph** он хорошо́ вы́шел на фотогра́фии; **all his arrogance came out** вся его́ спесь вы́шла нару́жу; (*disappear*): **the stains came out** пя́тна сошли́; **the colour came out** (*faded*) кра́ска вы́цвела/полиня́ла/поблёкла; (*of results*): **the sum came out** зада́ча получи́лась; отве́т зада́чи вы́шел пра́вильным; **he came out first in the exam** он был лу́чшим на э́том экза́мене; (*declare o.s.*): **he came out against the plan** он вы́ступил про́тив пла́на; **the total came out at 700** о́бщий ито́г оказа́лся ра́вным 700; (*make début in society*) дебюти́ровать (*impf.*, *pf*); (*publicly acknowledge one's homosexuality*) откры́то призна́ть (*pf.*) свою́ гомосексуа́льность; (*go on strike*) забастова́ть (*pf.*); выходи́ть, вы́йти на забасто́вку; **he came out with the truth** он рассказа́л всю́ пра́вду; **he came out with an oath** он вы́ругался; **she came out in a rash** она́ покры́лась сы́пью; **~ over** *v.i.*: **they came over to England** они́ прие́хали в А́нглию; **he came over to our side** он перешёл на на́шу сто́рону; **he came over dizzy** (*coll.*) у него́ закружи́лась голова́; у него́ начало́сь головокруже́ние; **~ round** *v.i.* (*make detour*): **we came round by the fields** мы пришли́ кру́жным путём че́рез поля́; (*make trip*): **~ round and see us!** заходи́те к нам!; (*recur*): **Christmas will soon ~ round** ско́ро (насту́пит) Рождество́; (*change mind*): **he came round to my view** он пришёл-таки к моей то́чке зре́ния; (*yield*): **she'll ~ round** она́ усту́пит/

соглаcи́тся; (*recover consciousness*) прийти́ (*pf.*) в себя́; очну́ться (*pf.*); ~ **through** *v.i.* (*survive experience*) пережи́ть (*pf.*); **he came through without a scratch** он вы́шел из э́той исто́рии без еди́ной цара́пины; (*teleph.*): **the call came through at 3 o'clock** разгово́р состоя́лся в 3 часа́; ~ **to** *v.i.* (*recover one's senses*) прийти́ (*pf.*) в себя́; очну́ться (*pf.*); ~ **up** *v.i.*: **the sun came up** со́лнце взошло́; **the seeds came up** семена́ взошли́; **he came up to London** он прие́хал в Ло́ндон; **he came up to me** он подошёл ко мне; **the water came up to my waist** вода́ доходи́ла мне до по́яса; **the question came up** встал вопро́с; **the case ~s up tomorrow** э́то де́ло разбира́ется за́втра; **the book came up to my expectations** кни́га оправда́ла мои́ ожида́ния; **he came up against a difficulty** он натолкну́лся на тру́дности; **they came up with us** они́ нагна́ли нас; **he came up with a suggestion** он внёс предложе́ние.

cpds. **~-and-go** *n.* движе́ние взад-вперёд; **~-at-able** *adj.* (*coll.*) досту́пный; **~back** *n.* (*retort*) возраже́ние; (*return*) возвраще́ние; **~-down** *n.* униже́ние; **~-hither** *adj.* (*coll.*): **a ~-hither look** завлека́ющий взгляд; **~-uppance** *n.* (*coll.*): **he got his ~-uppance** он получи́л по заслу́гам.

Comecon ['kɒmɪˌkɒn] *n.* (*abbr. of* ***Council for Mutual Economic Assistance***) СЭВ, (Сове́т экономи́ческой взаимопо́мощи).

comedian [kə'mi:dɪən] *n.* ко́мик; **low ~** ко́мик-буфф.

comedienne [kəˌmi:dɪ'en] *n.* коми́ческая актри́са.

comedy ['kɒmɪdɪ] *n.* коме́дия; **musical ~** музыка́льная коме́дия.

comeliness ['kʌmlɪnɪs] *n.* милови́дность.

comely ['kʌmlɪ] *adj.* милови́дный.

comer ['kʌmə(r)] *n.*: **the first ~** прише́дший пе́рвым; **he will fight all ~s** гото́в дра́ться с кем уго́дно.

comestible [kə'mestɪb(ə)l] *n.* (*usu. pl.*) съестны́е припа́сы (*pl.*, *g.* -ов).

adj. съестно́й.

comet ['kɒmɪt] *n.* коме́та.

comfit ['kʌmfɪt] *n.* конфе́та, заса́харенный фрукт; (*pl.*) цука́ты (*m. pl.*).

comfort ['kʌmfət] *n.* **1.** (*physical ease*) комфо́рт; удо́бства (*nt. pl.*); **he lives in ~** он живёт, не ве́дая нужды́. **2.** (*relief of suffering*) утеше́ние, отра́да; **cold ~** сла́бое утеше́ние. **3.** (*thg. that brings ~*) утеше́ние, успокое́ние; **his letters are a ~** его́ пи́сьма — большо́е утеше́ние.

v.t. утеша́ть, -е́шить; успок|а́ивать, -о́ить.

comfortabl|e ['kʌmftəb(ə)l, -fətəb(ə)l] *adj.* удо́бный, ую́тный, комфорта́бельный; **I am ~e here** мне здесь удо́бно; **the car holds six people ~y** э́та маши́на свобо́дно вмеща́ет шесть челове́к; **he makes a ~e living** он прили́чно зараба́тывает; **he is ~y off** он живёт в доста́тке.

comforter ['kʌmfətə(r)] *n.* **1.** (*pers.*) утеши́тель; **Job's ~** плохо́й утеши́тель; го́ре-утеши́тель. **2.** (*teat*) со́ска, пусты́шка.

comforting ['kʌmfətɪŋ] *adj.* утеши́тельный, успокои́тельный, отра́дный; **it is ~ to know that ...** утеши́тельно знать, что...

comfortless ['kʌmfətlɪs] *adj.* неую́тный; безра́достный; **a ~ room** неую́тная ко́мната.

comic ['kɒmɪk] *n.* **1.** (*coll.*, *comedian*) ко́мик, юмори́ст. **2.** (*pl.*, *~ papers*) ко́миксы (*m. pl.*).

adj. коми́ческий, юмористи́ческий; **~ book** кни́жка ко́миксов; **~ strip** ко́микс; **the Greek ~ writers** древнегре́ческие комедио́графы.

comical ['kɒmɪk(ə)l] *adj.* коми́чный, смешно́й.

comicality [ˌkɒmɪ'kælɪtɪ] *n.* коми́чность.

Cominform ['kɒmɪnˌfɔ:m] *n.* (*hist.*, *abbr. of* ***Communist Information Bureau**, 1947–56*) Коминфо́рм, (Информацио́нное бюро́ коммунисти́ческих и рабо́чих па́ртий).

coming ['kʌmɪŋ] *n.* прие́зд, прихо́д; **the Second C~** второ́е прише́ствие (Христа́).

adj. бу́дущий, наступа́ющий; **the ~ week** бу́дущая неде́ля; **a ~ man** челове́к с бу́дущим.

Comintern ['kɒmɪnˌtɜ:n] *n.* (*hist.*, *abbr. of* ***Communist International**, 1914–43*) Коминте́рн.

comity ['kɒmɪtɪ] *n.* ве́жливость; **~ of nations** взаи́мное призна́ние зако́нов и обы́чаев ра́зными стра́нами.

comma ['kɒmə] *n.* запята́я; **inverted ~s** кавы́ч|ки (*pl.*, *g.* -ек); **~ bacillus** (холе́рный) вибрио́н.

command [kə'mɑ:nd] *n.* **1.** (*order*) кома́нда; **at the word of ~** по кома́нде. **2.** (*authority*) кома́ндование; **he is in ~ of the army** он кома́ндует а́рмией; **he took ~** он при́нял кома́ндование. **3.** (*control*) контро́ль (*m.*); **~ of the air** госпо́дство в во́здухе; **~ of one's emotions** владе́ние свои́ми чу́вствами. **4.** (*knowledge, ability to use*): **she has a good ~ of French** она́ хорошо́ владе́ет францу́зским языко́м; **she has a great ~ of language** она́ прекра́сно владе́ет сло́вом. **5.** (*mil.*) кома́ндование; **Bomber C~** бомбардиро́вочное авиацио́нное кома́ндование; **High C~** верхо́вное кома́ндование; (*attr.*) кома́ндный; **~ post** кома́ндный пункт, КП.

v.t. & *i.* **1.** (*give orders to*) прика́з|ывать, -а́ть +*d.*; **he ~ed his men to fire** он приказа́л свои́м солда́там откры́ть ого́нь. **2.** (*have authority over*) кома́ндовать (*impf.*) +*i.* **3.** (*restrain*) владе́ть (*impf.*) +*i.*; **~ o.s.** владе́ть (*impf.*) собо́й. **4.** (*be able to use or enjoy*) располага́ть (*impf.*) +*i.*; **he ~s great sums of money** в его́ распоряже́нии кру́пные де́нежные сре́дства; **he ~s respect** он внуша́ет к себе́ уваже́ние. **5.** (*of things*): **the fort ~s the valley** кре́пость госпо́дствует над доли́ной; **this article ~s a high price** э́тот това́р продаётся по высо́кой цене́; **the window ~s a fine view** из окна́ открыва́ется прекра́сный вид.

commandant [ˌkɒmən'dænt, -'dɑ:nt, 'kɒm-] *n.* коменда́нт.

commandantship [ˌkɒmən'dæntʃɪp, -'dɑ:ntʃɪp] *n.* коменда́нтство.

commandeer [ˌkɒmən'dɪə(r)] *v.t.* реквизи́ровать (*impf.*, *pf.*).

commander [kə'mɑ:ndə(r)] *n.* команди́р, кома́ндующий; **C~-in-Chief** главнокома́ндующий; (*naval rank*) капита́н тре́тьего ра́нга; **C~ of the Faithful** (*hist.*) повели́тель (*m.*) правове́рных.

commanding [kə'mɑ:ndɪŋ] *adj.* (*in command*) кома́ндующий; **~ officer** команди́р; **a ~ tone** повели́тельный тон; **~ heights** кома́ндные высо́ты; **a ~ presence** внуши́тельная оса́нка.

commandment [kə'mɑ:ndmənt] *n.*: **the Ten C~s** де́сять за́поведей.

commando [kə'mɑ:ndəʊ] *n.* (*force*) деса́нтно-диверсио́нный отря́д; (*pers.*) солда́т деса́нтно-диверсио́нного отря́да.

comme il faut [ˌkɒm i:l 'fəʊ] *pred. adj.* & *adv.* комильфо́ (*indecl.*).

commemorate [kə'meməˌreɪt] *v.t.* (*celebrate memory of*) отм|еча́ть, -е́тить па́мять +*g.*; ознаменова́ть (*pf.*); (*be in memory of*): **this monument ~s the victory** э́тот па́мятник воздви́гнут в честь побе́ды.

commemoration [kəˌmemə'reɪʃ(ə)n] *n.* ознаменова́ние па́мяти (*кого/чего*).

commemorative [kə'memərətɪv] *adj.* па́мятный, мемориа́льный.

commence [kə'mens] *v.t.* & *i.* нач|ина́ть(ся), -а́ть(ся).

commencement [kə'mensmənt] *n.* нача́ло; (*acad.*) а́ктовый день; торже́ственное вруче́ние дипло́мов.

commend [kə'mend] *v.t.* **1.** (*entrust*) вв|еря́ть, -е́рить; поруч|а́ть, -и́ть; **he ~ed his soul to God** он о́тдал ду́шу Бо́гу. **2.** (*praise*) хвали́ть, по-. **3.** (*recommend*) рекомендова́ть (*impf.*, *pf.*): **the book does not ~ itself to me** э́та кни́га меня́ не привлека́ет.

commendable [kə'mendəb(ə)l] *adj.* похва́льный, досто́йный похвалы́.

commendation [ˌkɒmen'deɪʃ(ə)n] *n.* похвала́, рекоменда́ция.

commendatory [kə'mendətərɪ] *adj.* (*of a trust*) довери́тельный; (*of praise*) похва́льный.

commensura|ble [kə'menʃərəb(ə)l, -sjərəb(ə)l], **-te** [kə'menʃərət, -sjərət] *adjs.* соизмери́мый.

comment ['kɒment] *n.* замеча́ние, коммента́рий; о́тзыв, о́тклик; **her behaviour aroused ~** её поведе́ние вы́звало то́лки.

v.t. & *i.* комменти́ровать (*impf.*, *pf.*); толкова́ть (*impf.*); де́лать, с- замеча́ния; **he ~ed on the book** он вы́сказал своё мне́ние об э́той кни́ге.

commentary ['kɒməntərɪ] *n.* (*also radio ~*) коммента́рий.

commentator ['kɒmənˌteɪtə(r)] *n.* (*textual*) коммента́тор, толкова́тель (*m.*); (*radio etc.*) коммента́тор, обозрева́тель (*m.*).

commerce [ˈkɒmɜːs] *n.* комме́рция, торго́вля; **Chamber of C~** Торго́вая пала́та.

commercial [kəˈmɜːʃ(ə)l] *n.* (*coll.*, *TV advertisement*) рекла́мная переда́ча.

adj. комме́рческий, торго́вый; **~ attaché** торго́вый атташе́ (*indecl.*); **~ traveller** коммивояжёр; **~ television** комме́рческое телеви́дение; **~ vehicle** грузова́я маши́на.

commercialese [kəˈmɜːʃ(ə)liːz] *n.* стиль (*m.*) комме́рческих пи́сем.

commercialism [kəˈmɜːʃ(ə),lɪz(ə)m] *n.* стремле́ние к при́были; торга́шество; (*of style*) делово́й оборо́т ре́чи.

commercialize [kəˈmɜːʃə,laɪz] *n.* ста́вить, по- на комме́рческую но́гу; вн|оси́ть, -ести́ комме́рческий дух в+*a*.

commination [,kɒmɪˈneɪʃ(ə)n] *n.* угро́за ка́рами небе́сными.

commingle [kəˈmɪŋg(ə)l] *v.t. & i.* сме́ш|ивать(ся), -а́ть(ся).

comminute [ˈkɒmɪ,njuːt] *v.t.*: **~d fracture** (*med.*) оско́лочный перело́м.

commiserate [kəˈmɪzə,reɪt] *v.i.* (*feel sympathy*) сочу́вствовать (*impf.*) (*кому*); (*express sympathy*) выража́ть, вы́разить соболе́знование (*кому*).

commiseration [kə,mɪzəˈreɪʃ(ə)n] *n.* сочу́вствие, соболе́знование.

commissar [ˈkɒmɪ,sɑː(r)] *n.* комисса́р.

commissariat [,kɒmɪˈseərɪət, -ˈsærɪ,æt] *n.* **1.** (*office of commissar*) комиссариа́т. **2.** (*mil.*) интенда́нтство.

commissary [ˈkɒmɪsərɪ, kəˈmɪs-] *n.* **1.** (*deputy*) уполномо́ченный. **2.** (*mil.*, *officer*) интенда́нт. **3.** (*US*, *mil. store*) вое́нный магази́н; (*coll.*) каптёрка.

commission [kəˈmɪʃ(ə)n] *n.* **1.** (*authorization*) полномо́чие; **he went beyond his ~** он превы́сил свои́ полномо́чия. **2.** (*errand*) поруче́ние; **I carried out some ~s for him** я вы́полнил не́сколько его́ поруче́ний. **3.** (*action*) соверше́ние; **the ~ of a crime** соверше́ние преступле́ния; **sin of ~** грех дея́нием. **4.** (*reward*) комиссио́нн|ые (*pl.*, *g.* -ых); **he sells goods on ~** он продаёт това́ры за комиссио́нное вознагражде́ние. **5.** (*officer's*) пате́нт на офице́рский чин. **6.** (*official body*) комиссариа́т; **high ~** верхо́вный комиссариа́т. **7.: in ~** (*fit for action*) в испра́вности; в гото́вности; **a ship in ~** кора́бль, гото́вый к пла́ванию; **out of ~** (*out of active service*) в резе́рве; не в строю́; (*out of working order*) в неиспра́вности.

v.t. пору́ч|а́ть, -и́ть (*что кому*); **he ~ed me to buy this** он поручи́л мне купи́ть э́то; **he ~ed a portrait from the artist** он заказа́л худо́жнику портре́т; **the ship was ~ed** кора́бль был введён в строй; **a ~ed officer** офице́р; **he was ~ed from the ranks** он был произведён в офице́ры из рядовы́х.

commissionaire [kə,mɪʃəˈneə(r)] *n.* швейца́р.

commissioner [kəˈmɪʃənə(r)] *n.* комисса́р; член коми́ссии; **high ~** верхо́вный комисса́р.

commit [kəˈmɪt] *v.t.* **1.** (*perform*) соверш|а́ть, -и́ть. **2.** (*entrust*, *consign*): **~ s.o. for trial** пред|ава́ть, -а́ть кого́-н. суду́; **~ to paper** изл|ага́ть, -ожи́ть на бума́ге; **~ to memory** зау́ч|ивать, -и́ть; **~ to the flames** преда́ть (*pf.*) огню́. **3.** (*engage*): **he ~ted himself to helping her** он взя́лся помо́чь ей; **he would not ~ himself** он уклони́лся от чёткого отве́та; он не хоте́л связа́ть себя́ конкре́тными обяза́тельствами. **4.: ~ troops to battle** вв|оди́ть, -ести́ (*or* бр|оса́ть, -о́сить) войска́ в бой. **5.: a ~ted writer** иде́йный писа́тель.

commitment [kəˈmɪtmənt] *n.* (*obligation*) обяза́тельство; **~ to a cause** пре́данность де́лу.

committal [kəˈmɪt(ə)l] *n.*: **~ for trial** преда́ние суду́.

committee[1] [kəˈmɪtɪ] *n.* (*body of persons*) комите́т, коми́ссия; **steering ~** организацио́нный/руководя́щий комите́т.

cpd. **~man** *n.* член комите́та/коми́ссии.

committee[2] [,kɒmɪˈtiː] (*leg.*, *guardian*) опеку́н.

commode [kəˈməʊd] *n.* (*chest of drawers*) комо́д; (*for chamber-pot*) стульча́к для ночно́го горшка́.

commodious [kəˈməʊdɪəs] *adj.* просто́рный, удо́бный.

commodity [kəˈmɒdɪtɪ] *n.* това́р, предме́т потребле́ния; (*attr.*) това́рный.

commodore [ˈkɒmə,dɔː(r)] *n.* (*in navy or merchant marine*) коммодо́р, капита́н пе́рвого ра́нга; (*of yacht club*) командо́р.

common [ˈkɒmən] *n.* **1.** (*land*) пусты́рь (*m.*), вы́гон. **2.** (*sth. usual or shared*): **out of the ~** из ря́да вон выходя́щий; **they have some tastes in ~** у них есть о́бщие вку́сы; **in ~ with most Englishmen, he is fond of sport** как и большинство́ англича́н, он лю́бит спорт.

adj. **1.** (*belonging to more than one*, *general*) о́бщий; **it is ~ ground between us that …** мы согла́сны в том, что…; **it is ~ knowledge that …** общеизве́стно, что… **2.** (*belonging to the public or a specific group*): **~ law** о́бщее/обы́чное/некодифици́рованное пра́во; **he has the ~ touch** он уме́ет находи́ть о́бщий язы́к со вся́ким. **3.** (*ordinary*, *usual*) обы́чный, обы́денный, обыкнове́нный; **~ honesty** простя́/элемента́рная че́стность; **the ~ man** обыкнове́нный/просто́й челове́к; **the ~ people** (просто́й) наро́д; **~ sense** здра́вый смысл; **~ salt** пова́ренная соль; **~ or garden** (*coll.*) обыкнове́нный; **a ~ (or garden) impostor** обма́нщик, каки́х мно́го. **4.** (*vulgar*) вульга́рный, по́шлый. **5.** (*math.*): **~ logarithm** десяти́чный логари́фм. **6.** (*gram.*): **~ gender** о́бщий род; **~ noun** и́мя нарица́тельное. **7.** (*mus.*): **~ time** просто́й такт.

cpds. **~-law** *adj.*: **~-law marriage** незарегистри́рованный брак; **~-law wife** сожи́тельница; **~place** *n.* о́бщее ме́сто, бана́льность; прописна́я и́стина; *adj.* бана́льный; **~-room** *n.* (*senior*) учи́тельская, профе́ссорская; (*junior*) студе́нческая ко́мната о́тдыха; **~-sense** *adj.* здра́вый, разу́мный.

commonalty [ˈkɒmənəltɪ] *n.* (*the common people*) простонаро́дье; (просто́й) наро́д; (*corporate body*) соо́бщество.

commoner [ˈkɒmənə(r)] *n.* недворяни́н, челове́к незна́тного происхожде́ния.

commonly [ˈkɒmənlɪ] *adv.* (*usually*) обы́чно, обыкнове́нно; (*to a normal degree*) про́сто; **if he is ~ honest** е́сли он элемента́рно че́стен.

commonness [ˈkɒmənnɪs] *n.* (*frequency*) обы́чность, обы́денность; (*vulgarity*) вульга́рность, по́шлость.

commons[1] [ˈkɒmənz] *n.* (*common people*) простонаро́дье; **(House of) C~** пала́та о́бщин.

commons[2] [ˈkɒmənz] *n.* (*victuals*) рацио́н; **short ~** ску́дный рацио́н.

commonsensical [,kɒmənˈsensɪk(ə)l] *adj.* здра́вый, разу́мный.

commonwealth [ˈkɒmən,welθ] *n.* (*body politic*) госуда́рство; (*Eng. hist.*) Англи́йская респу́блика; **the British C~** брита́нское Содру́жество (на́ций); **C~ of Australia** Австрали́йский Сою́з; **C~ of Independent States** Содру́жество незави́симых госуда́рств.

commotion [kəˈməʊʃ(ə)n] *n.* волне́ние, возня́; **civil ~** беспоря́дки (*m. pl.*).

communal [ˈkɒmjʊn(ə)l] *adj.* **1.** (*for common use*) обще́ственный, коммуна́льный; **~ flat** коммуна́льная кварти́ра. **2. ~ disturbances** столкнове́ния ме́жду общи́нами.

Communard [ˈkɒmjʊ,nɑːd] *n.* коммуна́р.

commune[1] [ˈkɒmjuːn] *n.* (*administrative unit*) общи́на, комму́на; (*Russ. hist.*, *peasant ~*) мир; **the Paris C~** Пари́жская Комму́на.

commune[2] [kəˈmjuːn] *v.i.* обща́ться (*impf.*) (с+*i.*); быть в те́сном обще́нии (с+*i.*); **~ with nature** обща́ться с приро́дой.

communicable [kəˈmjuːnɪkəb(ə)l] *adj.* передаю́щийся, сообща́емый; **a ~ disease** зара́зная боле́знь.

communicant [kəˈmjuːnɪkənt] *n.* (*relig.*) прича́стни|к (*fem.* -ца).

communicate [kəˈmjuːnɪ,keɪt] *v.t.* сообщ|а́ть, -и́ть; (*a disease*, *also*) перед|ава́ть, -а́ть; (*relig.*) прича|ща́ть, -сти́ть.

v.i. свя́з|ываться, -а́ться; сообщ|а́ть, -и́ть (*кому о чём*); **~ with s.o.** сн|оси́ться, -ести́сь с кем-н.; **the rooms ~** э́ти ко́мнаты сообща́ются; (*relig.*) прича|ща́ться, -сти́ться.

communication [kə,mjuːnɪˈkeɪʃ(ə)n] *n.* **1.** (*act of communicating*) обще́ние; связь, сообще́ние, коммуника́ция; **language is a means of ~** язы́к — сре́дство обще́ния; **get**

into ~ with s.o. установи́ть (*pf.*) связь с кем-н.; **lack of ~** (*understanding*) отсу́тствие взаимопонима́ния. **2.** (*message*) сообще́ние. **3.** (*means of ~*) сре́дства свя́зи/сообще́ния; (*pl.*: *roads, railways etc.*) пути́ (*m. pl.*) сообще́ния; **cut (off) s.o.'s ~s** прерва́ть (*pf.*) связь с кем-н. **4.** (*mil.*): **lines of ~** коммуника́ции; **~ trench** ход сообще́ния.

communicative [kəˈmju:nɪkətɪv] *adj.* общи́тельный, разгово́рчивый.

communicator [kəˈmju:nɪˌkeɪtə(r)] *n.* (*pers.*) сообща́ющий; (*mechanism*) коммуника́тор; переда́точный механи́зм.

communion [kəˈmju:nɪən] *n.* **1.** (*intercourse*) обще́ние; **~ with nature** обще́ние с приро́дой. **2.** (*religious group*): **the Anglican ~** англика́нская це́рковь. **3.** (*sacrament*) прича́стие.

communiqué [kəˈmju:nɪˌkeɪ] *n.* (*indecl.*) коммюнике́.

communism [ˈkɒmjʊˌnɪz(ə)m] *n.* коммуни́зм.

communist [ˈkɒmjʊnɪst] *n.* коммуни́ст (*fem.* -ка).

adj. (*also* **-ic**) коммунисти́ческий.

community [kəˈmju:nɪtɪ] *n.* **1.** (*commonness; joint ownership*): **~ of interest** о́бщность интере́сов; **~ of goods** о́бщность владе́ния (*or* совме́стное владе́ние) иму́ществом. **2.** (*society*) о́бщество. **3.** (*pol., social etc. group*) общи́на, гру́ппа населе́ния.

communization [kɒmjʊˌnaɪˈzeɪʃ(ə)n] *n.* коммуниза́ция.

communize [ˈkɒmjʊˌnaɪz] *v.t.* (*subject to communism*) коммунизи́ровать (*impf., pf.*).

commutation [ˌkɒmju:ˈteɪʃ(ə)n] *n.* **1.** (*commuting*) заме́на (одного́ ви́да платежа́ други́м). **2.** (*payment*) де́ньги, вы́плаченные взаме́н вы́платы нату́рой. **3.** (*leg., of sentence*) смягче́ние (пригово́ра).

commutator [ˈkɒmju:ˌteɪtə(r)] *n.* (*elec.*) колле́ктор, переключа́тель (*m.*), коммута́тор.

commute [kəˈmju:t] *v.t.* замен|я́ть, -и́ть; (*leg.*) смягч|а́ть, -и́ть (*приговор*).

v.i. (*travel to and fro*) соверша́ть (*impf.*) регуля́рные пое́здки из при́города в го́род.

commuter [kəˈmju:tə(r)] *n.* (*traveller*) регуля́рный пассажи́р (*человек, живущий за городом, который регулярно ездит в город на работу*).

compact[1] [ˈkɒmpækt] *n.* (*pact*) соглаше́ние, догово́р.

compact[2] [ˈkɒmpækt] *n.* (*cosmetic case*) пу́дреница.

compact[3] [kəmˈpækt] *adj.* (*closely packed*) компа́ктный; (*tense, concise*) сжа́тый, компа́ктный; **~ disk** компа́кт-ди́ск; **~ disk player** прои́грыватель компа́кт-ди́сков.

v.t. (*press together*) сж|има́ть, -ать; сти́с|кивать, -нуть; уплотн|я́ть, -и́ть.

v.i. (*agree*) заключ|а́ть, -и́ть соглаше́ние/догово́р.

compactness [kəmˈpæktnɪs] *n.* компа́ктность, сжа́тость.

companion[1] [kəmˈpænjən] *n.* **1.** (*pers. who accompanies*): **my ~ on the journey** мой попу́тчик; **~ in adversity** това́рищ по несча́стью; **~ in crime** соуча́стник преступле́ния; **he is an excellent ~** с ним мо́жно отли́чно провести́ вре́мя. **2.** (*object matching another*) па́ра; (*attr.*) па́рный; **~ volume** сопроводи́тельный том. **3.** (*woman paid to keep another company*) компаньо́нка. **4.** (*member of order*); **C~ of the Bath** кавале́р о́рдена Ба́ни. **5.** (*handbook*) спра́вочник, спу́тник; **the Gardener's C~** спра́вочник садо́вника.

companion[2] [kəmˈpænjən] *n.* (*naut.*: *also* **~-way, ~-ladder**) сходно́й трап/люк.

cpd. **~-hatch** *n.* кры́шка лю́ка с па́лубы; **~-ladder, ~-way** *nn., see above.*

companionable [kəmˈpænjənəb(ə)l] *adj.* общи́тельный, (*coll.*) компане́йский.

companionship [kəmˈpænjənʃɪp] *n.* дру́жеское обще́ние; дру́жеские отноше́ния; (*of an order of chivalry*) зва́ние кавале́ра.

company [ˈkʌmpənɪ] *n.* **1.** (*companionship*): **I was glad of his ~** я был рад его́ о́бществу; **keep, bear s.o. ~** сост|авля́ть, -а́вить кому́-н. компа́нию; **part ~** расста́ться (*pf.*); **we parted ~** на́ши пути́ разошли́сь; **keep ~ with** (*as in courting*) уха́живать (*impf.*) за+*i.*; **in ~ with** совме́стно с+*i.*; **he is good ~** с ним хорошо́; с ним не соску́чишься. **2.** (*associates, guests*): **a man is known by the ~ he keeps** скажи́ мне, кто твой друг, и я скажу́, кто ты; **we have ~ this evening** у нас сего́дня бу́дут го́сти; **~ manners** показна́я ве́жливость; **present ~ excepted** не упомина́я прису́тствующих; о прису́тствующих не говоря́т; **two's ~ (but three is none)** где дво́е, там тре́тий ли́шний. **3.** (*commercial firm*) това́рищество, компа́ния; **Jones and Company** (*abbr.* **Co.**) Джо́унз и компа́ния (*abbr.* К°). **4.** (*theatr.*) тру́ппа. **5.** (*naut.*) кома́нда, экипа́ж; **ship's ~** экипа́ж су́дна. **6.** (*mil.*) ро́та; **~ officer** мла́дший офице́р; **~ sergeant major** старшина́ ро́ты.

comparable [ˈkɒmpərəb(ə)l] *adj.* сравни́мый.

comparative [kəmˈpærətɪv] *adj.* **1.** (*proceeding by comparison*) сравни́тельный. **2.** (*relative*) относи́тельный; **he is a ~ newcomer** он сравни́тельно неда́вно при́был сюда́. **3.** (*gram.*) сравни́тельный; (*as n.*): **'better' is the ~ of 'good'** «лу́чший» — сравни́тельная сте́пень от прилага́тельного «хоро́ший».

compare [kəmˈpeə(r)] *n.* (*liter.*): **beyond ~** вне вся́кого сравне́ния.

v.t. **1.** (*assess degree of similarity*) сра́вн|ивать, -и́ть; слич|а́ть, -и́ть; **~ notes with s.o.** обме́н|иваться, -я́ться впечатле́ниями с кем-н. **2.** (*assert similarity of*) сра́вн|ивать, -и́ть; **he is not to be ~d with his father** ему́ далеко́ до отца́. **3.** (*gram., form degrees of comparison*) образо́в|ывать, -а́ть сте́пени сравне́ния.

v.i. сра́вн|иваться, -и́ться; **he ~s favourably with his predecessor** он вы́годно отлича́ется от своего́ предше́ственника; **he cannot ~ with her** его́ нельзя́ и сравни́ть с ней.

comparison [kəmˈpærɪs(ə)n] *n.* сравне́ние; **make a ~** пров|оди́ть, -ести́ сравне́ние; **there is no ~ between them** их нельзя́ сра́внивать; **in, by ~ with** по сравне́нию с+*i.*; (*gram.*): **degrees of ~** сте́пени сравне́ния.

compartment [kəmˈpɑ:tmənt] *n.* (*railway*) купе́ (*indecl.*); (*of ship*) отсе́к; **they live in watertight ~s** (*fig.*) они́ живу́т в по́лной изоля́ции друг от дру́га.

compartmentalize [ˌkɒmpɑ:tˈmentəˌlaɪz] *v.t.* раздроб|ля́ть, -и́ть.

compass [ˈkʌmpəs] *n.* **1.** (*mariner's*) ко́мпас; (*surveying ~*) буссо́ль; **points of the ~** стра́ны све́та; **~ card** карту́шка ко́мпаса; **box the ~** (*lit.*) наз|ыва́ть, -ва́ть все ру́мбы ко́мпаса; (*fig.*) сде́лать (*pf.*) поворо́т на 360° (*or* по́лный круг). **2.** (*geom., also* **pair of ~es**) ци́ркуль (*m.*); **~ window** (*archit.*) полукру́глый э́ркер. **3.** (*extent, range*): **~ of a voice** диапазо́н го́лоса; **within the ~ of a lifetime** в преде́лах одно́й жи́зни; **beyond my ~** вне моего́ понима́ния; вне мои́х возмо́жностей. **4.** (*detour*) кру́жный путь; **fetch a ~** сде́лать (*pf.*) крюк.

v.t. **1.** (*go round*) об|ходи́ть, -ойти́. **2.** (*hem in*) окруж|а́ть, -и́ть. **3.** (*grasp mentally*) схва́т|ывать, -и́ть. **4.** (*contrive*) зам|ышля́ть, -ы́слить.

compassion [kəmˈpæʃ(ə)n] *n.* сострада́ние, сочу́вствие; **show ~ to s.o.** прояви́ть (*pf.*) сострада́ние к кому́-н.

compassionate [kəmˈpæʃənət] *adj.* сострада́тельный, сочу́вствующий; **~ allowance** благотвори́тельное посо́бие; **~ leave** о́тпуск по семе́йным обстоя́тельствам.

compatibility [kəmˌpætəˈbɪlɪtɪ] *n.* совмести́мость.

compatible [kəmˈpætəb(ə)l] *adj.* совмести́мый.

compatriot [kəmˈpætrɪət] *n.* соотե́чественник.

compeer [ˈkɒmpɪə(r), -ˈpɪə(r)] *n.* ро́вня (*c.g.*); това́рищ.

compel [kəmˈpel] *v.t.* заст|авля́ть, -а́вить; прин|ужда́ть, -уди́ть; **~ attention** прико́в|ывать, -а́ть внима́ние; **~ obedience from s.o.** прин|ужда́ть, -у́дить кого́-н. к повинове́нию.

compelling [kəmˈpelɪŋ] *adj.* непреодоли́мый, неотрази́мый; (*fascinating*) захва́тывающий.

compendious [kəmˈpendɪəs] *adj.* конспекти́вный.

compendiousness [kəmˈpendɪəsnɪs] *n.* конспекти́вность.

compendium [kəmˈpendɪəm] *n.* компе́ндиум, конспе́кт.

compensate [ˈkɒmpenˌseɪt] *v.t. & i.* компенси́ровать (*impf., pf.*) (*кому что*); (*tech.*) компенси́ровать (*impf., pf.*); баланси́ровать (*impf., pf.*).

compensation [ˌkɒmpenˈseɪʃ(ə)n] *n.* компенса́ция (*also psych.*); **pay ~** вы́платить (*pf.*) компенса́цию; **in ~ for the loss** в компенса́цию за понесённые убы́тки; (*tech.*)

компенса́ция, вырáвнивание.
compensator [ˈkɒmpen,seɪtə(r)] *n.* (*opt.*) компенса́тор; (*elec.*) автотрансформа́тор.
compensatory [-ˈpensətərɪ, -ˈseɪtərɪ] *adj.* компенси́рующий (*also psych.*); компенсацио́нный.
compère [ˈkɒmpeə(r)] *n.* конферансье́ (*m. indecl.*).
v.t. & i. конфери́ровать (*impf., pf.*).
compete [kəmˈpiːt] *v.i.* (*vie*) конкури́ровать (*impf.*); сопе́рничать (*impf.*); ~ **with, against s.o. for sth.** конкури́ровать (*impf.*) с кем-н. из-за чего́-н.; (*in sport*) состяза́ться (*impf.*).
competenc|e [ˈkɒmpɪt(ə)ns], **-y** [ˈkɒmpɪtənsɪ] *nn.* (*ability, authority*) уме́ние, компете́нтность; (*sufficient income*) доста́ток.
competent [ˈkɒmpɪt(ə)nt] *adj.* **1.** (*qualified*) компете́нтный. **2.** (*adequate*) доста́точный. **3.: it is ~ for him to refuse** в его́ вла́сти отказа́ться.
competition [,kɒmpəˈtɪʃ(ə)n] *n.* **1.** (*rivalry*) сопе́рничество, конкуре́нция; **they are in ~ with us** они́ конкури́руют с на́ми. **2.** (*contest*) состяза́ние, соревнова́ние. **3.** (*examination*) ко́нкурс; ко́нкурсный экза́мен.
competitive [kəmˈpetɪtɪv] *adj.* (*competing*) конкури́рующий; ~ **examination** ко́нкурсный экза́мен; ~ **prices** конкурентоспосо́бные це́ны.
competitor [kəmˈpetɪtə(r)] *n.* конкуре́нт.
compilation [,kɒmpɪˈleɪʃ(ə)n] *n.* (*act*) собира́ние, компили́рование; (*result*) сбо́рник, собра́ние, компиля́ция.
compile [kəmˈpaɪl] *v.t.* соб|ира́ть, -ра́ть; сост|авля́ть, -а́вить; компили́ровать (*impf., pf.*); ~ **materials** соб|ира́ть, -ра́ть материа́лы; ~ **a volume** сост|авля́ть, -а́вить том.
compiler [kəmˈpaɪlə(r)] *n.* составитель (*m.*); собира́тель (*m.*); компиля́тор.
complacenc|e [kəmˈpleɪsəns], **-y** [kəmˈpleɪsənsɪ] *nn.* самодово́льство.
complacent [kəmˈpleɪs(ə)nt] *adj.* самодово́льный.
complain [kəmˈpleɪn] *v.i.* **1.** (*express dissatisfaction*) жа́ловаться (*impf.*). **2.** (*to an authority*) под|ава́ть, -а́ть жа́лобу (на+*a.*); жа́ловаться, по- (на+*a.*). **3.: he ~s of frequent headaches** он жа́луется на ча́стые головны́е бо́ли. **4.** (*poet., lament*) се́товать (*на что*).
complainant [kəmˈpleɪnənt] *n.* (*leg.*) жа́лобщик, исте́ц.
complainer [kəmˈpleɪnə(r)] *n.* ны́тик (*c.g.*).
complainingly [kəmˈpleɪnɪŋlɪ] *adv.* жа́лобно, жа́луясь.
complaint [kəmˈpleɪnt] *n.* жа́лоба; причи́на недово́льства; **lodge, make a ~** под|ава́ть, -а́ть жа́лобу; (*ailment*) неду́г, боле́знь.
complaisance [kəmˈpleɪzəns] *n.* обходи́тельность, услу́жливость.
complaisant [kəmˈpleɪz(ə)nt] *adj.* обходи́тельный, услу́жливый; **a ~ husband** снисходи́тельный муж.
complement [ˈkɒmplɪmənt] *n.* **1.** (*that which completes*) дополне́ние. **2.** (*muster*) ли́чный соста́в, по́лный компле́кт; **ship's ~** ли́чный соста́в корабля́. **3.** (*gram.*) дополне́ние. **4.** (*math.*): **~ of an angle** дополни́тельный у́гол.
v.t. доп|олня́ть, -о́лнить; служи́ть (*impf.*) дополне́нием +*d.*
complementary [,kɒmplɪˈmentərɪ] *adj.* дополни́тельный; **~ medicine** паралле́льная медици́на.
complete [kəmˈpliːt] *adj.* **1.** (*whole*) по́лный; **~ edition** по́лное изда́ние; **car ~ with tyres** автомоби́ль, снабжённый ши́нами. **2.** (*finished*) зако́нченный, завершённый; **when will the work be ~?** когда́ бу́дет завершён э́тот труд? **3.** (*thorough*) соверше́нный; **he is a ~ stranger to me** он мне соверше́нно не знако́м; **a ~ surprise** по́лная/соверше́нная неожи́данность.
v.t. зак|а́нчивать, -о́нчить; заверш|а́ть, -и́ть; (*fill in*) зап|олня́ть, -о́лнить.
completely [kəmˈpliːtlɪ] *adv.* соверше́нно, по́лностью.
completeness [kəmˈpliːtnɪs] *n.* полнота́; зако́нченность, завершённость.
completion [kəmˈpliːʃ(ə)n] *n.* заверше́ние, оконча́ние; (*of a form*) заполне́ние.
complex [ˈkɒmpleks] *n.* (*abstr. or physical whole, also psych.*) ко́мплекс.
adj. сло́жный, ко́мплексный; (*gram.*): **~ sentence** сложноподчинённое предложе́ние.
complexion [kəmˈplekʃ(ə)n] *n.* **1.** (*of face*) цвет лица́. **2.** (*character, aspect*) вид, аспе́кт; **that puts a different ~ on the matter** э́то представля́ет де́ло в ино́м све́те.
complexity [kəmˈpleksɪtɪ] *n.* сло́жность.
compliance [kəmˈplaɪəns] *n.* усту́пчивость, пода́тливость, послуша́ние; **in ~ with his orders** согла́сно его́ прика́зам; во исполне́ние его́ прика́зов; (*pej.*) уго́дливость.
compliant [kəmˈplaɪənt] *adj.* усту́пчивый, пода́тливый, послу́шный; (*pej.*) уго́дливый.
complicate [ˈkɒmplɪ,keɪt] *v.t.* осложн|я́ть, -и́ть; усложн|я́ть, -и́ть.
complicated [ˈkɒmplɪ,keɪtɪd] *adj.* сло́жный, запу́танный, осложнённый.
complication [,kɒmplɪˈkeɪʃ(ə)n] *n.* (*complexity*) сло́жность, запу́танность; (*complicating circumstance*) осложне́ние; (*med.*): **~s set in** после́довали осложне́ния.
complicity [kəmˈplɪsɪtɪ] *n.* соуча́стие.
compliment [ˈkɒmplɪmənt] *n.* **1.** (*praise*) комплиме́нт; похвала́; **a back-handed ~** сомни́тельный комплиме́нт. **2.** (*greeting*) приве́т, поздравле́ние; **~s of the season** новогóдние (*и т.п.*) поздравле́ния; **with the author's ~s** с уваже́нием от а́втора.
v.t. говори́ть (*impf.*) комплиме́нты +*d.* (*по поводу чего*); хвали́ть, по- (за+*a.*); поздр|авля́ть, -а́вить (*с чем*).
complimentary [,kɒmplɪˈmentərɪ] *adj.* **1.** (*laudatory*) похва́льный, ле́стный. **2. ~ copy** (*of book*) да́рственный/беспла́тный экземпля́р; **~ ticket** контрама́рка, пригласи́тельный биле́т.
compline [ˈkɒmplɪn, -plaɪn] *n.* повече́рие.
comply [kəmˈplaɪ] *v.i.*: **~ with** уступ|а́ть, -и́ть (+*d.*); слу́шаться, по- (+*g.*); подчин|я́ться, -и́ться (+*d.*).
compo [ˈkɒmpəʊ] *n.* **1.** (*material*) цеме́нтный раство́р. **2. ~ rations** авари́йный паёк.
component [kəmˈpəʊnənt] *n.* компоне́нт; составна́я часть; дета́ль.
adj. составно́й, составля́ющий.
comport [kəmˈpɔːt] *v.t. & i.*: **~ o.s.** держа́ться (*impf.*); вести́ (*det.*) себя́.
comportment [kəmˈpɔːtmənt] *n.* мане́ра держа́ться; поведе́ние.
compos|e [kəmˈpəʊz] *v.t. & i.* **1.** (*make up, constitute*) сост|авля́ть, -а́вить; компонова́ть, с-; **the party was ~ed of teachers** гру́ппа состоя́ла из учителе́й. **2.** (*liter., mus.*) сочин|я́ть, -и́ть; **~e a picture** сост|авля́ть, -а́вить компози́цию карти́ны. **3.** (*control, assuage*): **~e o.s.** успок|а́иваться, -о́иться; **~e one's features** (*fig.*) прин|има́ть, -я́ть споко́йный вид; **~e a quarrel** ула́|живать, -дить ссо́ру; **a ~ed manner** сде́ржанная мане́ра. **4.** (*typ.*) наб|ира́ть, -ра́ть; **~ing-room** набо́рный цех.
composedly [kəmˈpəʊzɪdlɪ] *adv.* сде́ржанно, споко́йно.
composer [kəmˈpəʊzə(r)] *n.* (*mus.*) компози́тор.
composite [ˈkɒmpəzɪt, -,zaɪt] *n.* составно́й предме́т.
adj. составно́й; **~ carriage** (*rail.*) комбини́рованный ваго́н; **~ photograph** фотомонта́ж.
composition [,kɒmpəˈzɪʃ(ə)n] *n.* **1.** (*act or art of composing*) сочине́ние, составле́ние; **a work of his own ~** произведе́ние его́ со́бственного сочине́ния. **2.** (*liter. or mus. work*) произведе́ние, сочине́ние. **3.** (*school exercise*) сочине́ние. **4.** (*arrangement*) компози́ция, расстано́вка. **5.** (*make-up*) соста́в; **~ of the soil** соста́в по́чвы; **he has a touch of madness in his ~** он с сумасше́дшинкой. **6.** (*artificial substance*) смесь, соедине́ние, спла́в. **7.** (*compromise*): **he made a ~ with his creditors** он дости́г соглаше́ния с кредито́рами. **8.** (*typ.*) набо́р.
compositor [kəmˈpɒzɪtə(r)] *n.* набо́рщик.
compos mentis [,kɒmpɒs ˈmentɪs] *adj.* в здра́вом уме́.
compost [ˈkɒmpɒst] *n.* компо́ст.
v.t. (*make into ~*) гото́вить (*impf.*) компо́ст из+*g.*; (*treat with ~*) уд|обря́ть, -о́брить компо́стом.
composure [kəmˈpəʊʒə(r)] *n.* споко́йствие.
compote [ˈkɒmpəʊt, -pɒt] *n.* компо́т.
compound[1] [ˈkɒmpaʊnd] *n.* (*enclosure*) огоро́женное ме́сто.
compound[2] [ˈkɒmpaʊnd] *n.* (*mixture*) смесь; (*gram.*) сло́жное сло́во; (*chem.*) соедине́ние.

adj. составно́й, сло́жный; ~ **interest** сло́жные проце́нты; ~ **fracture** осложнённый перело́м.
compound[3] [kəm'paʊnd] *v.t.* **1.** (*mix, combine*) сме́ш|ивать, -а́ть; соедин|я́ть, -и́ть; **a dish ~ed of many ingredients** блю́до, пригото́вленное из мно́гих составны́х часте́й. **2.** (*settle by arrangement*) ула́|живать, -дить. **3.** (*aggravate*) отягча́ть (*impf.*).
v.i. (*come to terms*) при|ходи́ть, -йти́ к компроми́ссному соглаше́нию.
comprehend [ˌkɒmprɪ'hend] *v.t.* (*understand*) пон|има́ть, -я́ть; пост|ига́ть, -и́гнуть; восприн|има́ть, -я́ть; (*include*) включ|а́ть, -и́ть; охва́т|ывать, -и́ть.
comprehensible [ˌkɒmprɪ'hensɪb(ə)l] *adj.* поня́тный, постижи́мый.
comprehension [ˌkɒmprɪ'henʃ(ə)n] *n.* (*understanding*) понима́ние, постиже́ние, восприя́тие; (*inclusion, scope*) охва́т, включе́ние.
comprehensive [ˌkɒmprɪ'hensɪv] *adj.* (*pert. to understanding*) поня́тливый, схва́тывающий, восприи́мчивый; (*of wide scope*) всеобъе́млющий, исче́рпывающий; ~ **school** еди́ная сре́дняя шко́ла.
comprehensiveness [ˌkɒmprɪ'hensɪvnɪs] *n.* всеобъе́млемость; широта́ охва́та.
compress[1] ['kɒmpres] *n.* (*to relieve inflammation*) компре́сс; (*to ~ artery etc.*) давя́щая повя́зка.
compress[2] [kəm'pres] *v.t.* (*physically*) сж|има́ть, -ать; сда́в|ливать, -и́ть; **~ed air** сжа́тый во́здух; (*make more concise*) сж|има́ть, -ать; сокра|ща́ть, -ти́ть.
compressible [kəm'presɪb(ə)l] *adj.* сжима́ющийся.
compression [kəm'preʃ(ə)n] *n.* (*lit.*) сжа́тие, сда́вливание; (*fig.*) сжа́тие, сокраще́ние; (*tech.*) компре́ссия, уплотне́ние.
compressor [kəm'presə(r)] *n.* компре́ссор.
comprise [kəm'praɪz] *v.t.* включ|а́ть, -и́ть в себя́; состоя́ть (*impf.*) из+*g.*
compromise ['kɒmprəˌmaɪz] *n.* компроми́сс.
v.t. (*expose to discredit*) компромети́ровать; (*endanger*) ста́вить, по- под угро́зу.
v.i. пойти́ (*pf.*) на компроми́сс; (*reach ~*) при|ходи́ть, -йти́ к компроми́ссу.
comptroller [kən'trəʊlə(r)] = **controller**
compulsion [kəm'pʌlʃ(ə)n] *n.* принужде́ние; **on, under** ~ по принужде́нию.
compulsive [kəm'pʌlsɪv] *adj.* принуди́тельный; **a ~ liar** паталоги́ческий враль.
compulsoriness [kəm'pʌlsərɪnɪs] *n.* обяза́тельность.
compulsory [kəm'pʌlsərɪ] *adj.* обяза́тельный, принуди́тельный; ~ **measures** принуди́тельные ме́ры; ~ **military service** во́инская пови́нность.
compunction [kəm'pʌŋkʃ(ə)n] *n.* угрызе́ния (*nt. pl.*) со́вести; раска́яние.
computable [ˌkɒm'pju:təb(ə)l, 'kɒm-] *adj.* исчисли́мый.
computation [ˌkɒmpju:'teɪʃ(ə)n] *n.* вычисле́ние, вы́кладка.
compute [kəm'pju:t] *v.t.* & *i.* вычисля́ть, вы́числить; де́лать, с- вы́кладки.
computer [kəm'pju:tə(r)] *n.* (*pers.*) счётчик; (*machine*) электро́нно-вычисли́тельная маши́на (*abbr.* ЭВМ); компью́тер; **IBM-compatible** ~ ИБМ-совмести́мый компью́тер; **laptop** ~ наколе́нный компью́тер; ~ **dating** подбо́р супру́гов с по́мощью ЭВМ; (*coll.*) «электро́нная сва́ха»; ~ **graphics** маши́нная гра́фика; ~ **programming** программи́рование; ~ **programmer** программи́ст; ~ **science** вычисли́тельная те́хника.
cpds. **~-aided design** *n.* автоматизи́рованное проекти́рование; **~-aided learning** *n.* маши́нное обуче́ние; **~-assisted** *adj.* автоматизи́рованный.
computerize [kəm'pju:təˌraɪz] *v.t.* осна|ща́ть, -сти́ть ЭВМ.
comrade ['kɒmreɪd, -rɪd] *n.* това́рищ; **~-in-arms** сора́тник; **~-in-exile** това́рищ по ссы́лке.
comradely ['kɒmreɪdlɪ, -rɪdlɪ] *adj.* това́рищеский.
comradeship ['kɒmreɪdʃɪp, -rɪdʃɪp] *n.* това́рищество.
con[1] [kɒn] *see* **pro**[1]
con[2] [kɒn] *v.t.* (*arch., study*) зау́ч|ивать, -и́ть.
con[3] [kɒn] *v.t.* (*sl., dupe*) над|ува́ть, -у́ть; ~ **man** моше́нник, жу́лик, афери́ст.
conative ['kɒnətɪv, 'kəʊ-] *adj.* волево́й.
concatenation [kɒnˌkætɪ'neɪʃ(ə)n] *n.* сцепле́ние, связь; ~ **of circumstances** стече́ние обстоя́тельств.
concave ['kɒnkeɪv] *adj.* во́гнутый.
concavity [kɒn'kævɪtɪ] *n.* (*condition*) во́гнутость; (*surface*) во́гнутость, во́гнутая пове́рхность.
concavo-concave [kɒnˌkeɪvəʊ'kɒnkeɪv] *adj.* двояково́гнутый.
concavo-convex [kɒnˌkeɪvəʊ'kɒnveks] *adj.* во́гнуто-вы́гнутый.
conceal [kən'si:l] *v.t.* скр|ыва́ть, -ы́ть; (*keep secret*) ута́|ивать, -и́ть.
concealment [kən'si:lmənt] *n.* укрыва́тельство, сокры́тие, ута́ивание; **he remained in ~** он продолжа́л скрыва́ться.
concede [kən'si:d] *v.t.* уступ|а́ть, -и́ть; ~ **a point** уступ|а́ть, -и́ть по одному́ пу́нкту; **the candidate ~d the election** кандида́т призна́л себя́ побеждённым на вы́борах; (*sport*): **he ~d ten points to his opponent** он дал своему́ проти́внику фо́ру в де́сять очко́в.
conceit [kən'si:t] *n.* (*vanity*) самомне́ние, самонаде́янность, тщесла́вие, зазна́йство; (*liter. fancy*) причу́дливый о́браз.
conceited [kən'si:tɪd] *adj.* самонаде́янный, зазна́вшийся.
conceivabl|e [kən'si:vəb(ə)l] *adj.* мы́слимый, постижи́мый; **he may ~y be right** не исключено́, что он пра́в.
conceive [kən'si:v] *v.t.* **1.** (*form in the mind, imagine*) заду́м|ывать, -ать; ~ **a dislike for** невзлюби́ть (*pf.*); **I ~ that there may be difficulties** я допуска́ю, что мо́гут встре́титься тру́дности. **2.** (*formulate*) выража́ть, вы́разить; **a letter ~d in simple language** письмо́, напи́санное просты́м языко́м. **3.** (*become pregnant with*) зача́ть (*pf.*); **she ~d a child** она́ зачала́ ребёнка.
v.i. зача́ть, забере́менеть (*both pf.*).
concentrate ['kɒnsənˌtreɪt] *n.* (*of product*) концентра́т.
v.t. **1.** (*bring together, focus*) сосредото́чи|вать, -ть; концентри́ровать, с-; **~d fire** (*mil.*) сосредото́ченный/масси́рованный ого́нь; **~d hate** жгу́чая не́нависть. **2.** (*increase strength of*) концентри́ровать, с-; **a ~d solution** концентри́рованный раство́р; **~d food** концентра́ты (*m. pl.*).
v.i. сосредото́чи|ваться, -ться; концентри́роваться, с-; **he ~d on his work** он сосредото́чился на свое́й рабо́те.
concentration [ˌkɒnsən'treɪʃ(ə)n] *n.* **1.** (*chem.*) концентра́ция, кре́пость. **2.** (*of troops etc.*) сосредото́чение, концентра́ция; ~ **camp** концентрацио́нный ла́герь, концла́герь (*m.*). **3.** (*of attention etc.*) сосредото́ченность.
concentric [kən'sentrɪk] *adj.* концентри́ческий.
concept ['kɒnsept] *n.* поня́тие, конце́пция.
conception [kən'sepʃ(ə)n] *n.* **1.** (*notion*) конце́пция, поня́тие; **I have no ~ of what he means** поня́тия не име́ю, что он хо́чет э́тим сказа́ть. **2.** (*physiol.*) зача́тие; **Immaculate C~** непоро́чное зача́тие.
conceptual [kən'septjʊəl] *adj.* концептуа́льный.
concern [kən'sɜ:n] *n.* **1.** (*affair*) отноше́ние, каса́тельство; **it is no ~ of mine** э́то меня́ не каса́ется; э́то не име́ет ко мне́ никако́го отноше́ния. **2.** (*business*) конце́рн, предприя́тие; **a going ~** де́йствующее предприя́тие. **3.** (*share*) уча́стие, интере́с; **he has a ~ in the enterprise** он уча́ствует в э́том предприя́тии. **4.** (*importance*) ва́жность; значи́тельность; **it is a matter of ~ to us all** э́то де́ло большо́й ва́жности для нас всех. **5.** (*anxiety*) беспоко́йство.
v.t. **1.** (*have to do with*) каса́ться (*impf.*) +*g.*; **~ed** (*involved*) заинтересо́ванный; **I am not ~ed** э́то меня́ не каса́ется; **as far as that is ~ed** что каса́ется э́того; **the parties ~ed** заинтересо́ванные сто́роны. **2.** (*cause anxiety to*) беспоко́ить (*impf.*): **~ed** (*anxious*) озабо́ченный, обеспоко́енный; **I am ~ed about the future** меня́ беспоко́ит бу́дущее; **I am ~ed that he should be heard** я заинтересо́ван в том, что́бы его́ вы́слушали.
concerning [kən'sɜ:nɪŋ] *prep.* относи́тельно+*g.*; каса́тельно+*g.*; к вопро́су о +*p.*
concert[1] ['kɒnsət] *n.* **1.** (*agreement*) согла́сие, соглаше́ние; **he acted in ~ with his colleague** он де́йствовал сообща́ со свои́м колле́гой; **C~ of Europe** (*hist.*) Европе́йский конце́рт. **2.** (*entertainment*) конце́рт; (*fig.*): **they were trained to ~ pitch** их натренирова́ли на сла́ву.
cpds. **~-goer** *n.* посети́тель (*m.*) конце́ртов; **~-hall** *n.* конце́ртный зал.
concert[2] [kən'sɜ:t] *v.t.* **1.** (*arrange*) согласо́в|ывать, -а́ть;

take ~ed action дéйствовать (*impf.*) соглась́ованно; **~ed attack** одновремéнная атáка. **2.** (*mus.*) инструментовáть (*impf., pf.*).

concertina [ˌkɒnsəˈti:nə] *n.* концерти́но, гармóника.

concerto [kənˈtʃeətəʊ, -ˈtʃɜ:təʊ] *n.* концéрт; **piano ~** концéрт для фортепиáно; **~ grosso** кончéрто грóссо (*indecl.*).

concession [kənˈseʃ(ə)n] *n.* **1.** (*yielding; thg. yielded*) устýпка; **I did it as a ~ to his feelings** я сдéлал э́то, щадя́ егó чýвства. **2.** (*mining etc.*) концéссия.

concessionaire [kənˌseʃəˈneə(r)] *n.* концессионéр.

concessionary [kənˈseʃ(ə)nərɪ] *adj.* концессиóнный.

concessive [kənˈsesɪv] *adj.* (*gram.*) уступи́тельный.

conch [kɒŋk, kɒntʃ] *n.* **1.** (*shellfish*) моллю́ск. **2.** (*shell; also poet., trumpet*) рáковина. **3.** (*archit.*) апси́да.

conchology [kɒŋˈkɒlədʒɪ] *n.* конхи(ли)олóгия.

concierge [ˌkɔ̃sɪˈeəʒ, ˌkɒn-] *n.* консьéрж (*fem.* -ка).

conciliar [kənˈsɪlɪə(r)] *adj.* собóрный.

conciliate [kənˈsɪlɪˌeɪt] *v.t.* (*win over*) распол|агáть, -ожи́ть к себé; (*reconcile*) примир|я́ть, -и́ть; (*gain, of affection etc.*) завоёв|ывать, -áть; снискáть (*pf.*).

conciliation [kənˌsɪlɪˈeɪʃ(ə)n] *n.* примирéние.

conciliator [kənˈsɪlɪˌeɪtə(r)] *n.* миротвóрец, посрéдник.

conciliatory [kənˈsɪlɪətərɪ] *adj.* примири́тельный.

concise [kənˈsaɪs] *adj.* крáткий, сжáтый.

concis|eness [kənˈsaɪsnɪs], **-ion** [kənˈsɪʒ(ə)n] *nn.* крáткость, сжáтость.

conclave [ˈkɒnkleɪv] *n.* конклáв; (*fig.*) тáйное совещáние.

conclud|e [kənˈklu:d] *v.t.* **1.** (*terminate*) зак|áнчивать, -óнчить; заверш|áть, -и́ть; **to ~e** в заключéние; **~ing** заключи́тельный, завершáющий; (*session etc.*) закр|ывáть, -ы́ть. **2.** (*agreement etc.*) заключ|áть, -и́ть. **3.** (*infer*) дéлать, с- вы́вод, что...; при|ходи́ть, -йти́ к вы́воду, что...

v.i. (*end*) зак|áнчиваться, -óнчиться; **he ~ed by saying** в заключéние он сказáл.

conclusion [kənˈklu:ʒ(ə)n] *n.* **1.** (*end*) окончáние, заключéние, заверш́ение; **bring to a ~** заверш|áть, -и́ть; дов|оди́ть, -ести́ до концá; **in ~** в заключéние. **2.** (*of agreement etc.*) заключéние. **3.** (*inference*) вы́вод, заключéние; **he jumps to ~s** он дéлает поспéшные вы́воды. **4.: try ~s with s.o.** мéриться, по- си́лами с кем-н.; **it was a foregone ~ that he would win** бы́ло предрешенó, что он победи́т.

conclusive [kənˈklu:sɪv] *adj.* решáющий, окончáтельный, убеди́тельный.

conclusiveness [kənˈklu:sɪvnɪs] *n.* окончáтельность, убеди́тельность.

concoct [kənˈkɒkt] *v.t.* (*of drink etc.*) стря́пать, со-; готóвить, при-/с-; (*of story etc.*) стря́пать, со-; сочин|я́ть, -и́ть.

concoction [kənˈkɒkʃ(ə)n] *n.* (*drink etc.*) смéшивание, смесь; (*invention of story*) сочинéние, придýмывание; (*story invented*) вы́думка, бáсня, небыли́ца.

concomitant [kənˈkɒmɪt(ə)nt] *adj.* сопýтствующий.

concord [ˈkɒnkɔ:d, ˈkɒŋ-] *n.* соглáсие, соглашéние; (*gram.*) согласовáние.

concordance [kənˈkɔ:d(ə)ns, kəŋ-] *n.* (*agreement*) соглáсие; (*vocabulary*) указáтель (*библейских изречений и т.п.*).

concordant [kənˈkɔ:d(ə)nt] *adj.* соглáсный, согласýющийся (*both* с+*i.*); (*mus.*) гармони́чный.

concordat [kənˈkɔ:dæt] *n.* конкордáт.

concourse [ˈkɒnkɔ:s, ˈkɒŋ-] *n.* (*coming together*) стечéние; (*of railway station*) вестибю́ль (*m.*) вокзáла.

concrete[1] [ˈkɒnkri:t, ˈkɒŋ-] *n.* (*building material*) бетóн; **reinforced ~** железобетóн.

v.t. бетони́ровать (*impf.*).

cpd. **~-mixer** *n.* бетономешáлка.

concrete[2] [ˈkɒnkri:t, ˈkɒŋ-] *adj.* конкрéтный; **in the ~** конкрéтно.

concretion [kənˈkri:ʃ(ə)n] *n.* сращéние, срóсшаяся мáсса; (*med.*) кáмни (*m. pl.*), конкремéнты (*m. pl.*).

concretize [ˈkɒnkrɪˌtaɪz, ˈkɒŋ-] *v.t.* конкретизи́ровать (*impf., pf.*).

concubinage [kənˈkju:bɪnɪdʒ] *n.* конкубинáт, внебрáчное сожи́тельство.

concubine [ˈkɒŋkjʊˌbaɪn] *n.* налóжница.

concupiscence [kənˈkju:pɪs(ə)ns] *n.* похотли́вость.

concupiscent [kənˈkju:pɪsənt] *adj.* похотли́вый.

concur [kənˈkɜ:(r)] *v.i.* **1.** (*of circumstance etc.*) совп|адáть, -áсть; сходи́ться, сойти́сь. **2.** (*agree, consent*) согла|шáться, -си́ться (с+*i.*); присоедин|я́ться, -и́ться (к+*d.*); **~ring votes** совпадáющие голосá.

concurrence [kənˈkʌr(ə)ns] *n.* (*of things*) совпадéние, стечéние; (*agreement, consent*) соглáсие.

concurrent [kənˈkʌrənt] *adj.* (*simultaneous, agreeing*) совпадáющий; (*math.*) сходя́щийся, встречáющийся; **~ly** одновремéнно.

concuss [kənˈkʌs] *v.t.* (*med.*) вызывáть, вы́звать сотрясéние мóзга у+*g*.

concussion [kənˈkʌʃ(ə)n] *n.* (*med.*) сотрясéние мóзга.

condemn [kənˈdem] *v.t.* осу|ждáть, -ди́ть; пригов|áривать, -ори́ть; (*blame*) порицáть (*impf.*); **he was ~ed to life imprisonment** он был приговорён к пожи́зненному заключéнию; **~ed cell** кáмера смéртника; (*declare forfeit*) конфисковáть (*impf., pf*); (*declare unfit for use*) призн|авáть, -áть непригóдным; **the building was ~ed** здáние бы́ло при́знано непригóдным для жилья́; **his looks ~ed him** лицó вы́дало егó.

condemnation [ˌkɒndemˈneɪʃ(ə)n] *n.* осуждéние; порицáние; (*of building*) признáние негóдным.

condemnatory [ˌkɒndemˈneɪtərɪ] *adj.* осуждáющий.

condensation [ˌkɒndenˈseɪʃ(ə)n] *n.* (*phys.*) конденсáция, сгущéние, уплотнéние; (*liquefaction*) сжижéние; (*abridgement*) сокращéние.

condense [kənˈdens] *v.t.* **1.** (*phys.*) конденси́ровать (*impf., pf.*); сгу|щáть, -сти́ть; сжи|жáть, -ди́ть; **~d milk** сгущённое молокó. **2.** (*fig.*): **a ~d account of events** сжáтый отчёт о собы́тиях.

condenser [kənˈdensə(r)] *n.* (*tech.*) конденсáтор, газоохлади́тель (*m.*); (*opt*) кондéнсор.

condescend [ˌkɒndɪˈsend] *v.i.* сни|сходи́ть, -зойти́.

condescending [ˌkɒndɪˈsendɪŋ] *adj.* снисходи́тельный.

condescension [ˌkɒndɪˈsenʃ(ə)n] *n.* снисхождéние, снисходи́тельность.

condign [kənˈdaɪn] *adj.* (*liter.*) заслýженный.

condiment [ˈkɒndɪmənt] *n.* припрáва.

condition [kənˈdɪʃ(ə)n] *n.* **1.** (*state*) состоя́ние, положéние; **he is in no ~ to travel** он не в состоя́нии путешéствовать; он не вы́несет поéздки/дорóги. **2.** (*fitness*): **the athlete is out of ~** спортсмéн не в фóрме. **3.** (*pl., circumstances*) услóвия; обстоя́тельства (*both nt. pl.*). **4.** (*requisite, stipulation*) услóвие; **on ~ that ...** при услóвии, что...; **on no ~** ни при каки́х услóвиях. **5.** (*status in life*) положéние.

v.t. **1.** (*determine, govern*) обуслóв|ливать, -ить; **~ed reflex** услóвный рефлéкс. **2.** (*of athletes*) тренировáть, на-. **3.: well-~ed cattle** кондициóнный скот. **4.** (*indoctrinate*) приуч|áть, -и́ть; **he was ~ed to obey unquestioningly** егó приучи́ли беспрекослóвно подчиня́ться.

conditional [kənˈdɪʃən(ə)l] *adj.* услóвный, обуслóвленный; **my agreement is ~ on his coming** я соглáсен при услóвии, что он придёт; (*gram.*): **the ~ (mood)** услóвное наклонéние.

condole [kənˈdəʊl] *v.i.* соболéзновать (*impf.*) (+*d.*); выражáть, вы́разить соболéзнование.

condolence [kənˈdəʊləns] *n.* (*also pl.*) соболéзнование.

condom [ˈkɒndɒm] *n.* презервати́в, кондóм.

condominium [ˌkɒndəˈmɪnɪəm] *n.* кондоми́ниум.

condonation [ˌkɒndəˈneɪʃ(ə)n] *n.* прощéние.

condone [kənˈdəʊn] *v.t.* про|щáть, -сти́ть; попусти́тельствовать (*impf.*) +*d.*; смотрéть (*impf.*) сквозь пáльцы +*a.*

condor [ˈkɒndɔ:(r)] *n.* кóндор.

condottiere [ˌkɒndɒtɪˈjeərɪ] *n.* кондотьéр.

conduce [kənˈdju:s] *v.i.* спосóбствовать (*impf.*) (+*d.*).

conducive [kənˈdju:sɪv] *adj.* спосóбствующий; **health is ~ to happiness** здорóвье — помóщник счáстью.

conduct[1] [ˈkɒndʌkt] *n.* **1.** (*behaviour*) поведéние. **2.** (*manner of ~ing*) ведéние. **3.: safe ~** гарáнтия неприкосновéнности, охрáнная грáмота.

conduct[2] [kənˈdʌkt] *v.t.* **1.** (*lead, guide*) води́ть (*indet*), вести́ (*det.*); руководи́ть (*impf.*) +*i.*; **a ~ed tour** экску́рсия/осмо́тр с ги́дом. **2.** (*manage*) вести́ (*det.*); **he ~s his affairs well** он хорошо́ ведёт свои́ дела́; **~ an experiment** ста́вить, по- о́пыт; **~ o.s.** вести́ себя́, держа́ться (*impf.*). **3.** (*mus.*, *also v.i.*) дирижи́ровать (*impf.*) (+*i.*). **4.** (*phys.*) проводи́ть (*impf.*).

conductance [kən'dʌkt(ə)ns] *n.* (*tech.*) электропрово́дность, проводи́мость.

conduction [kən'dʌkʃ(ə)n] *n.* (*tech.*) проводи́мость, конду́кция; **~ of heat** теплопрово́дность.

conductive [kən'dʌktɪv] *adj.* (*tech.*) проводя́щий.

conductivity [ˌkɒndʌk'tɪvɪtɪ] *n.* (*tech.*) (уде́льная) проводи́мость; электропрово́дность.

conductor [kən'dʌktə(r)] *n.* **1.** (*leader*) руководи́тель (*m.*). **2.** (*mus.*) дирижёр. **3.** (*of bus or tram*) конду́ктор. **4.** (*phys.*) проводни́к.

conductorship [kən'dʌktəʃɪp] *n.* (*mus.*) дирижёрство.

conductress [kən'dʌktrɪs] *n.* (*on bus*) же́нщина-конду́ктор.

conduit ['kɒndɪt, -djʊɪt] *n.* трубопрово́д; водопрово́дная труба́; (*elec.*) изоляцио́нная тру́бка.

Condy's fluid ['kɒndɪz] *n.* марганцо́вка.

cone [kəʊn] *n.* **1.** (*geom.*) ко́нус. **2.** (*bot.*) ши́шка. **3.** (*storm signal*) штормово́й сигна́л. **4.** (*for ice-cream*) ва́фельный стака́нчик.

cpd. **~-shaped** *adj.* конусообра́зный.

coney ['kəʊnɪ] = **cony**

confabulate [kən'fæbjʊˌleɪt] *v.i.* бесе́довать (*impf.*).

confabulation [kənˌfæbjʊ'leɪʃ(ə)n] *n.* обсужде́ние, собесе́дование.

confection [kən'fekʃ(ə)n] *n.* **1.** (*making*) произво́дство. **2.** (*sweetmeat*) сла́ст|и (*pl.*, *g.* -ей), конфе́т|ы (*pl.*, *g.* —). **3.** (*article of dress*) моде́льное пла́тье.

confectioner [kən'fekʃənə(r)] *n.* конди́тер.

confectionery [kən'fekʃənərɪ] *n.* (*wares*) конди́терские изде́лия; (*shop*) конди́терский магази́н, конди́терская.

Confederacy [kən'fedərəsɪ] *n.* (*hist.*) Конфедера́ция.

confederate [kən'fedərət] *n.* сообщник, сою́зник; (*conjurer's*) посо́бник.

adj. сою́зный; (*US hist.*) конфедерати́вный.

confederation [kənˌfedə'reɪʃ(ə)n] *n.* сою́з; федера́ция.

confer[1] [kən'fɜ:(r)] *v.t.* присв|а́ивать, -о́ить; прису|жда́ть, -ди́ть; дарова́ть (*impf.*); (*all что кому*); **~ a degree** (*acad.*) прису|жда́ть, -ди́ть учёную сте́пень; **~ a title** присв|а́ивать, -о́ить ти́тул; **~ a favour** оказа́ть (*pf.*) услу́гу.

confer[2] [kən'fɜ:(r)] *v.i.* (*consult*) совеща́ться; сове́товаться (*both impf.*) (c+*i.*).

conferee [ˌkɒnfə'ri:] *n.* (*member of conference*) уча́стник конфере́нции; (*grantee*) удосто́енный ти́тулом.

conference ['kɒnfərəns] *n.* конфере́нция, совеща́ние; **he is in ~** он на совеща́нии.

cpd. **~-table** *n.* стол для заседа́ний; стол перегово́ров.

conferment [kən'fɜ:mənt] *n.* присвое́ние, присужде́ние.

confess [kən'fes] *v.t.* & *i.* **1.** призн|ава́ть, -а́ть; призн|ава́ться, -а́ться (*or* созн|ава́ться, -а́ться) (в чём); **I ~ I haven't read it** призна́юсь, я э́того не чита́л; **he ~ed to the crime** он призна́лся в преступле́нии; **a ~ed murderer** созна́вшийся уби́йца. **2.** (*eccl.*) (*hear confession of*) испове́д|овать, -ать; (*~ one's sins*) испове́д|оваться, -аться.

confessedly [kən'fesɪdlɪ] *adv.* по со́бственному призна́нию.

confession [kən'feʃ(ə)n] *n.* **1.** (*avowal*) призна́ние, созна́ние. **2.** (*profession of faith*) испове́дание. **3.** (*denomination*) вероиспове́дание. **4.** (*to a priest*) и́споведь.

confessional [kən'feʃən(ə)l] *n.* исповеда́льня.

adj. (*denominational*) вероиспове́дный.

confessor [kən'fesə(r)] *n.* признаю́щийся, сознаю́щийся; **Edward the C~** Эдуа́рд Испове́дник; (*priest*) испове́дник, духовни́к.

confetti [kən'fetɪ] *n.* конфетти́ (*nt. indecl.*).

confidant, -e [ˌkɒnfɪ'dænt, 'kɒn-] *nn.* напе́рсни|к (*fem.* -ца); дове́ренное лицо́.

confide [kən'faɪd] *v.t.* **1.** (*entrust*) поруч|а́ть, -и́ть; вв|еря́ть, -е́рить. **2.** (*impart*) сообщ|а́ть, -и́ть; пов|еря́ть, -е́рить; вв|еря́ть, -е́рить; **he ~d his secret to me** он дове́рил мне свою́ та́йну.

v.i. **~ in** (*liter.*, *rely on*) дов|еря́ться, -е́риться +*d.*; пол|ага́ться, -ожи́ться на+*a.*; (*impart secrets to*) дели́ться, по- (*своими планами и т.п.*) +*i.*

confidence ['kɒnfɪd(ə)ns] *n.* **1.** (*confiding of secrets*) дове́рие; **I tell you this in ~** я говорю́ вам э́то конфиденциа́льно (*or* по секре́ту); **take s.o. into one's ~** дов|еря́ть, -е́рить кому́-н. свои́ та́йны. **2.** (*secret*) та́йна; конфиденциа́льное сообще́ние. **3.** (*trust*): **I have ~ in him** я уве́рен в нём; я ве́рю в него́; **he enjoys her ~** он по́льзуется её дове́рием; **he gained her ~** он завоева́л её дове́рие. **4.** (*certainty*, *assurance*) уве́ренность; самоуве́ренность; **he spoke with ~** он говори́л с уве́ренностью. **5.**: **~ trick** моше́нничество; **~ man, trickster** моше́нник, афери́ст.

confident ['kɒnfɪd(ə)nt] *adj.* уве́ренный, самоуве́ренный; **I am ~ of success** я уве́рен в успе́хе.

confidential [ˌkɒnfɪ'denʃ(ə)l] *adj.* конфиденциа́льный, секре́тный; **a ~ tone** довери́тельный тон.

confiding [kən'faɪdɪŋ] *adj.* дове́рчивый, доверя́ющий.

configuration [kənˌfɪgjʊ'reɪʃ(ə)n, -gə'reɪʃ(ə)n] *n.* конфигура́ция.

confine[1] ['kɒnfaɪn] *n.* (*usu. pl.*) грани́цы (*f. pl.*), преде́лы (*m. pl.*).

confine[2] [kən'faɪn] *v.t.* ограни́чи|вать, -ть; заключ|а́ть, -и́ть; **a bird ~d in a cage** пти́ца, поса́женная в кле́тку; **~ yourself to the subject** приде́рживайтесь те́мы; **be ~d** (*of childbirth*) разреши́ться (*pf.*) от бре́мени, роди́ть (*pf.*).

confinement [kən'faɪnmənt] *n.* **1.** (*restriction*) ограниче́ние. **2.** (*imprisonment*) заключе́ние; **solitary ~** одино́чное заключе́ние. **3.** (*childbirth*) ро́д|ы (*pl.*, *g.* -ов); **she had a difficult ~** у неё бы́ли тяжёлые ро́ды.

confirm [kən'fɜ:m] *v.t.* **1.** (*strengthen*, *e.g. power*) подтвер|жда́ть, -ди́ть; подкреп|ля́ть, -и́ть. **2.** (*establish as certain*) утвер|жда́ть, -ди́ть; подтвер|жда́ть, -ди́ть; **the report is ~ed** сообще́ние подтвержда́ется; **his appointment was ~ed** его́ назначе́ние бы́ло утверждено́. **3.** (*of pers.*): **I was ~ed in this belief by the fact that ...** меня́ укрепи́л в э́том убежде́нии тот факт, что...; **a ~ed drunkard** закорене́лый пья́ница; **a ~ed bachelor** убеждённый холостя́к. **4.** (*relig.*) конфирмова́ть (*impf.*, *pf.*).

confirmation [ˌkɒnfə'meɪʃ(ə)n] *n.* **1.** (*of report etc.*) подтвержде́ние, утвержде́ние, подкрепле́ние. **2.** (*relig.*) конфирма́ция.

confirmatory [kən'fɜ:mətərɪ] *adj.* подверждáющий, утвержда́ющий, подкрепля́ющий.

confiscate ['kɒnfɪˌskeɪt] *v.t.* конфискова́ть (*impf. pf.*).

confiscation [ˌkɒnfɪ'skeɪʃ(ə)n] *n.* конфиска́ция.

conflagration [ˌkɒnflə'greɪʃ(ə)n] *n.* большо́й пожа́р.

conflate [kən'fleɪt] *v.t.* объедин|я́ть, -и́ть (*разные варианты текста и т.п.*).

conflation [kən'fleɪʃ(ə)n] *n.* соедине́ние/объедине́ние ра́зных вариа́нтов те́кста.

conflict[1] ['kɒnflɪkt] *n.* конфли́кт, противоре́чие; **~ of jurisdiction** колли́зия прав.

conflict[2] [kən'flɪkt] *v.i.* быть в конфли́кте (c+*i.*); противоре́чить (*impf.*) (+*d.*).

confluence ['kɒnflʊəns] *n.* слия́ние; **at the ~ of two rivers** при слия́нии двух рек; (*crowd*) стече́ние.

confluent ['kɒnflʊənt] *n.* прито́к.

adj. слива́ющийся.

conform [kən'fɔ:m] *v.t.* приспос|а́бливать, -о́бить; сообразо́в|ывать, -а́ть.

v.i. приспос|а́бливаться, -о́биться (к+*d.*); сообразо́в|ываться, -а́ться (c+*i.*).

conformable [kən'fɔ:məb(ə)l] *adj.* соотве́тствующий, пода́тливый.

conformation [ˌkɒnfɔ:'meɪʃ(ə)n] *n.* структу́ра, устро́йство.

conformism [kən'fɔ:mɪz(ə)m] *n.* конформи́зм.

comformist [kən'fɔ:mɪst] *n.* конформи́ст.

conformity [kən'fɔ:mɪtɪ] *n.* соотве́тствие.

confound [kən'faʊnd] *v.t.* **1.** (*amaze*) пора|жа́ть, -зи́ть; потряс|а́ть, -ти́. **2.** (*confuse*) сме́ш|ивать, -а́ть; спу́т|ывать, -ать. **3.** (*overthrow*) сокруш|а́ть, -и́ть; разр|уша́ть, -у́шить. **4.** (*as expletive*): **~ it!** чёрт возьми́!; **he is a ~ed nuisance** он ужа́сно доку́члив.

confraternity [ˌkɒnfrəˈtɜ:nɪtɪ] *n.* бра́тство.
confrère [ˈkɒnfreə(r)] *n.* собра́т.
confront [kənˈfrʌnt] *v.t.* **1.** (*bring face to face*) ста́вить, по- лицо́м к лицу́ (с+*i.*); (*leg.*) да|ва́ть, -ть о́чную ста́вку (*кому с кем*). **2.** (*face*) смотре́ть (*impf.*) в лицо́ +*d.*; встр|еча́ть, -е́тить; **many difficulties ~ed us** мы столкну́лись со мно́гими тру́дностями. **3.** (*be opposite to*) стоя́ть (*impf.*) напро́тив+*g.*; **my house ~s his** мой дом стои́т пря́мо напро́тив его́ (до́ма).
confrontation [ˌkɒnfrʌnˈteɪʃ(ə)n] *n.* о́чная ста́вка; конфронта́ция (*also pol.*).
Confucian [kənˈfju:ʃ(ə)n] *n.* конфуциа́нец.
adj. конфуциа́нский.
Confucius [kənˈfju:ʃəs] *n.* Конфу́ций.
confuse [kənˈfju:z] *v.t.* **1.** (*throw into confusion*) сму|ща́ть, -ти́ть; прив|оди́ть, -ести́ в замеша́тельство; **his question ~d me** его́ вопро́с смути́л меня́; **the situation is ~d** положе́ние запу́танное. **2.** (*mistake*) спу́т|ывать, -ать; сме́ш|ивать, -а́ть; **he ~d Austria with Australia** он спу́тал А́встрию с Австра́лией.
confusion [kənˈfju:ʒ(ə)n] *n.* смуще́ние, замеша́тельство; (*mix-up*) пу́таница, беспоря́док, неразбери́ха; (*destruction*) поги́бель; **he drank ~ to the King's enemies** он пил за поги́бель всех враго́в короля́.
confutation [ˌkɒnfju:ˈteɪʃ(ə)n] *n.* опроверже́ние.
confute [kənˈfju:t] *v.t.* опров|ерга́ть, -е́ргнуть.
congeal [kənˈdʒi:l] *v.t.* замор|а́живать, -о́зить; сгу|ща́ть, -сти́ть.
v.i. свёр|тываться, -ну́ться; сгу|ща́ться, -сти́ться; заст|ыва́ть, -ы́ть.
congelation [ˌkɒndʒɪˈleɪʃ(ə)n] *n.* замора́живание, застыва́ние.
congener [kənˈdʒi:nə(r)] *n.* соро́дич.
congenial [kənˈdʒi:nɪəl] *adj.* бли́зкий по ду́ху; **a ~ companion** прия́тный спу́тник; **a ~ climate** благоприя́тный кли́мат; **~ employment** рабо́та по душе́.
congeniality [kənˌdʒi:nɪˈælɪtɪ] *n.* конгениа́льность; духо́вная бли́зость.
congenital [kənˈdʒenɪt(ə)l] *adj.*: **~ defect** врождённый дефе́кт; **~ idiot** идио́т от рожде́ния.
conger [ˈkɒŋgə(r)] (*also* **~eel**) морско́й у́горь.
congeries [kənˈdʒɪəri:z, -ˈdʒerɪˌi:z] *n.* ку́ча, гру́да.
congested [kənˈdʒestɪd] *adj.* перенаселённый; перегру́женный; (*of street*) запру́женный; (*med.*) перепо́лненный кро́вью, засто́йный.
congestion [kənˈdʒestʃ(ə)n] *n.* перенаселённость; перегру́женность; (*med.*) гиперемия́, засто́й.
conglomerate[1] [kənˈglɒmərət] *n.* конгломера́т (*also geol.*).
adj. конгломера́тный.
conglomerate[2] [kənˈglɒməˌreɪt] *v.t.* & *i.* соб|ира́ть(ся), -ра́ть(ся); ск|а́пливать(ся), -опи́ться.
conglomeration [kənˌglɒməˈreɪʃ(ə)n] *n.* конгломера́т.
Congo [ˈkɒngəʊ] *n.* (река́, Респу́блика) Ко́нго (*indecl.*).
Congolese [ˌkɒŋgəˈli:z] *n.* (*pers.*) конголе́з|ец (*fem.* -ка).
adj. конголе́зский.
congratulate [kənˈgrætjʊˌleɪt] *v.t.* поздр|авля́ть, -а́вить (*кого с чем*).
congratulation [kənˌgrætjʊˈleɪʃ(ə)n] *n.* поздравле́ние; **~s!** поздравля́ю!; **letter of ~** поздрави́тельное письмо́.
congratulatory [kənˈgrætjʊlətərɪ] *adj.* поздрави́тельный.
congregate [ˈkɒŋgrɪˌgeɪt] *v.t.* соб|ира́ть, -ра́ть.
v.i. соб|ира́ться, -ра́ться; сходи́ться, сойти́сь.
congregation [ˌkɒŋgrɪˈgeɪʃ(ə)n] *n.* (*assembly*) собра́ние; (*in church*) прихожа́не (*m. pl.*), па́ства; (*eccl. brotherhood etc.*) конграга́ция, бра́тство.
congress [ˈkɒŋgres] *n.* **1.** (*organized meeting*) конгре́сс, съезд; **medical ~** конгре́сс/съезд враче́й/хиру́ргов. **2.** (*pol., hist.*) конгре́сс; **C~ of Vienna** Ве́нский конгре́сс. **3.: sexual ~** сои́тие.
cpds. **~man** *n.* член конгре́сса, конгрессме́н; **~woman** *n.* же́нщина-член конгре́сса.
congruence [ˈkɒŋgrʊəns] *n.* согласо́ванность, соотве́тствие.
congruent [ˈkɒŋgrʊənt] *adj.* соотве́тствующий, подходя́щий; (*geom.*) конгруэ́нтный.
congruity [ˌkɒŋˈgru:ɪtɪ] *n.* соотве́тствие.
congruous [ˈkɒŋgrʊəs] *adj.* соотве́тствующий, подходя́щий.
conic [ˈkɒnɪk] *adj.* кони́ческий, ко́нусный; **~ section** кони́ческое сече́ние.
conical [ˈkɒnɪk(ə)l] *adj.* кони́ческий, ко́нусный.
conics [ˈkɒnɪks] *n.* тео́рия кони́ческих сече́ний.
conifer [ˈkɒnɪfə(r), ˈkəʊn-] *n.* хво́йное де́рево.
coniferous [kəˈnɪfərəs] *adj.* хво́йный, шишконо́сный.
conjectural [kənˈdʒektʃər(ə)l] *adj.* предположи́тельный.
conjecture [kənˈdʒektʃə(r)] *n.* предположе́ние, дога́дка.
v.t. & *i.* предпол|ага́ть, -ожи́ть; гада́ть (*impf.*).
conjoin [kənˈdʒɔɪn] *v.t.* & *i.* соедин|я́ть(ся), -и́ть(ся); сочета́ть(ся) (*impf.*).
conjoint [kənˈdʒɔɪnt] *adj.* соединённый, объединённый.
conjugal [ˈkɒndʒʊg(ə)l] *adj.* супру́жеский, бра́чный; **~ rights** супру́жеские права́.
conjugate [ˈkɒndʒʊˌgeɪt] *v.t.* спряга́ть, про-.
conjugation [ˌkɒndʒʊˈgeɪʃ(ə)n] *n.* спряже́ние.
conjunction [kənˈdʒʌŋkʃ(ə)n] *n.* **1.** (*union*) соедине́ние, связь; **in ~ with** совме́стно/сообща́ с+*i.*; **~ of circumstances** стече́ние обстоя́тельств. **2.** (*gram.*) сою́з. **3.** (*astron.*) совпаде́ние.
conjunctive [kənˈdʒʌŋktɪv] *adj.* **1.** (*connective*) соединя́ющий, свя́зывающий. **2.** (*gram.*): **~ pronoun** соедини́тельное местоиме́ние.
conjunctivitis [kənˌdʒʌŋktɪˈvaɪtɪs] *n.* конъюнктиви́т.
conjuncture [kənˈdʒʌŋktʃə(r)] *n.* конъюнкту́ра; стече́ние обстоя́тельств.
conjuration [ˌkɒndʒʊˈreɪʃ(ə)n] *n.* (*appeal; spell*) заклина́ние.
conjure[1] [kənˈdʒʊə(r)] *v.t.* (*urge*) заклина́ть (*impf.*).
conjur|e[2] [ˈkʌndʒə(r)] *v.t.* & *i.* **1.** (*evoke by magic spell*) вызыва́ть, вы́звать. **2.** (*fig.*): **~e up** вызыва́ть, вы́звать в воображе́нии; **his is a name to ~e with** он влия́тельное лицо́; его́ и́мя име́ет волше́бную си́лу. **3.** (*perform tricks*) пока́з|ывать, -а́ть фо́кусы; **he ~ed a rabbit out of a hat** он извлёк из шля́пы за́йца; **~ing trick** фо́кус.
conjur|er, or [ˈkʌndʒərə(r)] *n.* фо́кусник, заклина́тель (*m.*).
conk [kɒŋk] *v.i.* (*usu.* **~ out**) (*break down*) загло́хнуть (*pf.*); (*die*) загну́ться (*pf.*) (*sl.*).
connatural [kəˈnætʃər(ə)l] *adj.* (*innate*) врождённый; (*of like nature*) одноро́дный.
connect [kəˈnekt] *v.t.* (*join*) соедин|я́ть, -и́ть; свя́з|ывать, -а́ть; **the towns are ~ed by railway** э́ти города́ соединены́ желе́зной доро́гой; **please ~ me with the hospital** пожа́луйста, соедини́те меня́ с больни́цей; **what firm are you ~ed with?** с како́й фи́рмой вы свя́заны?; **he is well ~ed** у него́ хоро́шие свя́зи; **they are ~ed by marriage** они́ в свойстве́; они́ породни́лись че́рез брак; (*associate*) связ|ывать, -а́ть; ассоции́ровать (*impf., pf.*); **I ~ him with music** его́ и́мя ассоции́руется у меня́ с му́зыкой.
v.i. соедин|я́ться, -и́ться; свя́з|ываться, -а́ться; **the train ~s with the one from London** э́тот по́езд согласо́ван по расписа́нию с ло́ндонским по́ездом.
connecting-rod [kəˈnektɪŋ] *n.* шату́н, тя́га.
conne|ction, -xion [kəˈnekʃ(ə)n] *n.* **1.** (*joining up, installation*) соедине́ние, связь. **2.** (*fig., link*) связь; **in this ~** в э́той свя́зи. **3.** (*of transport*) согласо́ванность расписа́ния; **the train runs in ~ with the ferry** расписа́ние поездо́в и паро́мов согласо́вано; **I missed my ~** я не успе́л сде́лать переса́дку. **4.** (*of kinship*) родство́; (*by marriage*) свойство́; **he is a ~ of mine** мы с ним в родстве́/свойстве́. **5.** (*clientèle*) клиенту́ра; покупа́тели (*m. pl.*); зака́зчики (*m. pl.*). **6.** (*association*) связь; **he formed a ~ with her** он вступи́л с ней в связь. **7.** (*teleph.*): **the ~ was bad** телефо́н пло́хо рабо́тал. **8.** (*tech.*): **a loose ~ in the engine** сла́бый конта́кт в электросисте́ме дви́гателя.
connective [kəˈnektɪv] *adj.* соедини́тельный, связу́ющий.
connexion [kəˈnekʃ(ə)n] = **connection**
conning-tower [ˈkɒnɪŋ] *n.* (*naut.*) боева́я ру́бка.
connivance [kəˈnaɪv(ə)ns] *n.* потво́рство, попусти́тельство.
connive [kəˈnaɪv] *v.i.*: **~ at** потво́рствовать (*impf.*) +*d.*; попусти́тельствовать (*impf.*) +*d.*
connoisseur [ˌkɒnəˈsɜ:(r)] *n.* знато́к, цени́тель (*m.*).
connotation [ˌkɒnəˈteɪʃ(ə)n] *n.* побо́чное значе́ние; ассоциа́ция, коннота́ция.
connote [kəˈnəʊt] *v.t.* означа́ть (*impf.*).
connubial [kəˈnju:bɪəl] *adj.* супру́жеский, бра́чный.

conquer [ˈkɒŋkə(r)] *v.t. & i.* (*overcome*; *obtain by conquest*) завоёв|ывать, -áть; покор|я́ть, -и́ть; ~ **one's feelings** совладáть (*pf.*) со свои́ми чу́вствами.
conqueror [ˈkɒŋkərə(r)] *n.* завоевáтель (*m.*); **(William) the C~** (*hist.*) Вильгéльм Завоевáтель.
conquest [ˈkɒŋkwest] *n.* завоевáние, побéда; **he made a ~ of her** он покори́л её.
conquistador [kɒnˈkwɪstəˌdɔː(r)] *n.* конкистадóр.
consanguineous [ˌkɒnsæŋˈgwɪnɪəs] *adj.* единокрóвный, рóдственный.
consanguinity [ˌkɒnsæŋˈgwɪnɪtɪ] *n.* единокрóвность, родствó.
conscience [ˈkɒnʃ(ə)ns] *n.* сóвесть; **good, clear ~** чи́стая сóвесть; **bad, guilty ~** нечи́стая сóвесть; **for ~ sake** для успокоéния/очи́стки сóвести; **he has many sins on his ~** у негó на сóвести мнóго грехóв; **have you no ~?** как тóлько у вас сóвести хватáет?; **in all ~** по сóвести говоря́; безусловно, бесспóрно.
cpds. **~-smitten, ~-stricken** *adjs.* испы́тывающий угрызéния сóвести.
conscienceless [ˈkɒnʃ(ə)nslɪs] *adj.* бессóвестный.
conscientious [ˌkɒnʃɪˈenʃəs] *adj.* сознáтельный, добросóвестный, сóвестливый; **~ work** добросóвестная рабóта; **~ objector** откáзывающийся от воéнной слу́жбы по убеждéнию.
conscientiousness [ˌkɒnʃɪˈenʃəsnɪs] *n.* сознáтельность, добросóвестность, сóвестливость.
conscious [ˈkɒnʃəs] *adj.* **1.** (*physically aware*) сознаю́щий, ощущáющий; **he was ~ to the last** он был в сознáнии до послéдней мину́ты; **~ of pain** чу́вствующий боль; **I was ~ of what I was doing** я дéйствовал сознáтельно. **2.** (*mentally aware*) сознаю́щий, понимáющий; **I was ~ of having offended him** я сознавáл, что оскорби́л егó. **3.** (*realized*) сознаю́щий, сознáтельный; **with ~ superiority** с сознáнием своегó превосхóдства; **a ~ effort** сознáтельное уси́лие. **4.** (*self-~*) стеснённый. **5.** (*as suff.*): **class-~** клáссово сознáтельный; **security-~** бди́тельный.
consciousness [ˈkɒnʃəsnɪs] *n.* **1.** (*physical*) сознáние; **he lost ~** он потеря́л сознáние; **she regained ~** онá пришлá в себя́/сознáние. **2.** (*mental*) сознáтельность. **3.** (*self-~*) стесни́тельность, смущéние.
conscript[1] [ˈkɒnskrɪpt] *n.* новобрáнец, призывни́к.
adj. при́званный на воéнную слу́жбу; **~ soldiers** солдáты-призывники́.
conscript[2] [kənˈskrɪpt] *v.t.* приз|ывáть, -вáть на воéнную слу́жбу.
conscription [kənˈskrɪpʃ(ə)n] *n.* вóинская пови́нность; (*call-up*) призы́в на воéнную слу́жбу.
consecrate [ˈkɒnsɪˌkreɪt] *adj.* освящённый, посвящённый.
v.t. освя|щáть, -ти́ть; посвя|щáть, -ти́ть.
consecration [ˌkɒnsɪˈkreɪʃ(ə)n] *n.* освящéние, посвящéние.
consecutive [kənˈsekjʊtɪv] *adj.* послéдовательный; **(on) five ~ days** пять дней подря́д; (*gram.*): **~ clause** придáточное предложéние слéдствия.
consensus [kənˈsensəs] *n.* соглáсие, единоду́шие.
consent [kənˈsent] *n.* соглáсие; **with one ~** единоду́шно, с óбщего соглáсия; **age of ~** брáчный вóзраст.
v.i. согла|шáться, -си́ться; да|вáть, -ть соглáсие.
consentient [kənˈsenʃ(ə)nt] *adj.* соглашáющийся, соглáсный.
consequence [ˈkɒnsɪkwəns] *n.* **1.** (*result*) слéдствие, послéдствие; **you must take the ~s of your acts** вам придётся отвечáть за послéдствия вáших посту́пков; **in ~ of** вслéдствие+*g.*; в результáте +*g.* **2.** (*importance*) вáжность, значéние; **a man of ~** влия́тельный/большóй человéк; **it is of no ~** э́то не имéет значéния.
consequent [ˈkɒnsɪkwənt] *adj.* явля́ющийся результáтом (*чего*); слéдующий/вытекáющий (*из чего*).
consequential [ˌkɒnsɪˈkwenʃ(ə)l] *adj.* **1.** (*consequent*) слéдующий/вытекáющий (*из чего*). **2.** (*self-important*) самодовóльный; пóлный самомнéния.
consequently [ˈkɒnsɪˌkwentlɪ] *adv.* слéдовательно, знáчит, (*coll.*) стáло быть.
conservancy [kənˈsɜːvənsɪ] *n.* (*preservation*) охрáна (прирóды).
conservation [ˌkɒnsəˈveɪʃ(ə)n] *n.* сохранéние, охрáна; **~ area** заповéдник; **~ of energy** (*phys.*) сохранéние энéргии.
conservationist [ˌkɒnsəˈveɪʃənɪst] *n.* борéц за охрáну прирóды.
conservatism [kənˈsɜːvətɪz(ə)m] *n.* консервати́зм, консервати́вность.
conservative [kənˈsɜːvətɪv] *n.* консервáтор.
adj. консервати́вный; **a ~ estimate** скрóмный/умéренный подсчёт.
conservatoire [kənˈsɜːvəˌtwɑː(r)] *n.* консерватóрия.
conservatory [kənˈsɜːvətərɪ] *n.* **1.** (*greenhouse*) оранжерéя. **2.** (*US, mus.*) консерватóрия.
conserve [kənˈsɜːv; *n. only also* ˈkɒnsɜːv] *n.* (*preserved fruit*) консерви́рованные/засáхаренные фру́кты (*m. pl.*).
v.t. консерви́ровать, за-; сохран|я́ть, -и́ть; сбер|егáть, -éчь; **~ one's strength** берéчь (*impf.*) свой си́лы.
consider [kənˈsɪdə(r)] *v.t. & i.* рассм|áтривать, -отрéть; считáть (*impf.*); **we are ~ing going to Canada** мы поду́мываем о поéздке в Канáду; **~ yourself under arrest** считáйте, что вы арестóваны; **he is ~ed clever** егó считáют у́мным; он считáется у́мным; (*make allowance for*) считáться (*impf.*) с+*i.*; прин|имáть, -я́ть во внимáние; **we must ~ his feelings** мы должны́ считáться с егó чу́вствами; **all things ~ed** приня́в всё во внимáние.
considerable [kənˈsɪdərəb(ə)l] *adj.* значи́тельный.
considerate [kənˈsɪdərət] *adj.* внимáтельный, чу́ткий, забóтливый.
considerateness [kənˈsɪdərətnɪs] *n.* внимáние, внимáтельность, чу́ткость, забóтливость.
consideration [kənˌsɪdəˈreɪʃ(ə)n] *n.* **1.** (*reflection*) рассмотрéние; **take into ~** прин|имáть, -я́ть во внимáние; **leave out of ~** упус|кáть, -ти́ть из ви́ду; не прин|имáть, -я́ть во внимáние; **the matter is under ~** дéло рассмáтривается. **2.** (*making allowance*): **in ~ of his youth** принимáя во внимáние егó мóлодость; **he showed ~ for my feelings** он считáлся с мои́ми чу́вствами; он щади́л мои́ чу́вства. **3.** (*reason, factor*) соображéние; **time is an important ~** врéмя — вáжный фáктор; **money is no ~** дéньги не имéют значéния; **on no ~** ни под каки́м ви́дом; ни при каки́х услóвиях. **4.** (*requital*) вознаграждéние; (*leg.*) встрéчное удовлетворéние.
considering [kənˈsɪdərɪŋ] *adv. & prep.* учи́тывая; принимáя во внимáние; **that is not so bad, ~** (*coll.*) в óбщем э́то не так уж плóхо.
consign [kənˈsaɪn] *v.t.* (*forward*) перес|ылáть, -лáть; пос|ылáть, -лáть; (*condemn*) обр|екáть, -éчь; (*entrust*) поруч|áть, -и́ть; вруч|áть, -и́ть; **his body was ~ed to the earth** егó тéло бы́ло прéдано землé.
consignee [ˌkɒnsaɪˈniː] *n.* гру́зополучáтель (*m.*).
consignment [kənˈsaɪnmənt] *n.* (*act of consigning*) отпрáвка; (*goods*) груз, пáртия товáра.
consignor [kənˈsaɪnə(r)] *n.* грузоотправи́тель (*m.*).
consist [kənˈsɪst] *v.i.* **1. ~ of** состоя́ть (*impf.*) из+*g.*; заключáться (*impf.*) в+*p.*; **the committee ~s of nine members** комитéт состои́т из девяти́ человéк; **~ in: his task ~s in defining work norms** егó рабóта состои́т в определéнии норм вы́работки. **2. the doctrine ~s with reason** э́та доктри́на вполнé разу́мна.
consistency [kənˈsɪstənsɪ] *n.* **1.** (*of mixture etc.*; *also* **consistence**) консистéнция. **2.** (*adherence to logic or principle*) послéдовательность.
consistent [kənˈsɪst(ə)nt] *adj.* (*of argument etc.*) послéдовательный; **this fact is ~ with his having written the book** э́тот факт не противорéчит тому́, что он явля́ется áвтором э́той кни́ги; (*of pers.*) послéдовательный.
consistory [kənˈsɪstərɪ] *n.* консистóрия.
consolable [kənˈsəʊləb(ə)l] *adj.* утеши́мый.
consolation [ˌkɒnsəˈleɪʃ(ə)n] *n.* утешéние, отрáда; **it is a ~ that he is here** утеши́тельно знать, что он здесь; **~ prize** утеши́тельный приз.
consolatory [kənˈsɒlətərɪ] *adj.* утеши́тельный.
console[1] [ˈkɒnsəʊl] *n.* **1.** (*bracket*) консóль, кроншттéйн; **~ table** пристéнный стол/стóлик. **2.** (*panel*) пульт управлéния. **3.** (*cabinet*) кóрпус, шкáфчик (*радиоприёмника и т.п.*).
console[2] [kənˈsəʊl] *v.t.* ут|ешáть, -éшить.
consoler [kənˈsəʊlə(r)] *n.* утеши́тель (*m.*).

consolidate [kən'sɒlɪ,deɪt] *v.t.* укреп|ля́ть, -и́ть; консолиди́ровать (*impf.*, *pf.*); **C~d Fund** консолиди́рованный фонд.
v.i. укреп|ля́ться, -и́ться; консолиди́роваться (*impf.*, *pf.*).
consolidation [kən,sɒlɪ'deɪʃ(ə)n] *n.* консолида́ция; укрепле́ние.
consols ['kɒnsɒlz] *n.* консолиди́рованная ре́нта.
consommé [kən'sɒmeɪ] *n.* консоме́ (*indecl.*), бульо́н.
consonance ['kɒnsənəns] *n.* (*agreement*) согла́сие; (*mus.*) консона́нс.
consonant ['kɒnsənənt] *n.* (*phon.*) согла́сный (звук), консона́нт.
adj. (*in accord*) согла́сный, созву́чный.
consonantal [,kɒnsə'nænt(ə)l] *adj.* (*phon.*) консона́нтный; ~ **shift** передвиже́ние/перебо́й согла́сных.
consort[1] ['kɒnsɔ:t] *n.* **1.** (*spouse*) консо́рт, супру́г (*fem.* -а); **Prince C~** принц-консо́рт. **2.** (*ship*) сопровожда́ющий кора́бль.
consort[2] [kən'sɔ:t] *v.t.* **1.** (*associate*) обща́ться (*impf.*). **2.** (*harmonize*) согласо́в|ываться, -а́ться; соотве́тствовать (*impf.*) (+*d.*).
consortium [kən'sɔ:tɪəm] *n.* консо́рциум.
conspectus [kən'spektəs] *n.* конспе́кт, обзо́р.
conspicuous [kən'spɪkjʊəs] *adj.* заме́тный; броса́ющийся в глаза́; выдаю́щийся; **he was ~ by his absence** его́ отсу́тствие броса́лось в глаза́.
conspiracy [kən'spɪrəsɪ] *n.* за́говор; конспира́ция.
conspirator [kən'spɪrətə(r)] *n.* загово́рщик; конспира́тор.
conspiratorial [kən,spɪrə'tɔ:rɪəl] *adj.* загово́рщический, конспира́торский.
conspire [kən'spaɪə(r)] *v.t.* & *i.* устр|а́ивать, -о́ить за́говор; сгов|а́риваться, -ори́ться; **events ~d against him** собы́тия скла́дывались про́тив него́; **they ~d his ruin** они́ сговори́лись погуби́ть/разори́ть его́.
constable ['kʌnstəb(ə)l] *n.* **1.** (*policeman*) полице́йский; **Chief C~** нача́льник поли́ции. **2.** (*hist.*) коннета́бль (*m.*).
constabulary [kən'stæbjʊlərɪ] *n.* поли́ция.
adj. полице́йский.
Constance ['kɒnstəns] *n.*: **Lake ~** Бо́денское/Конста́нцкое о́зеро.
constancy ['kɒnstənsɪ] *n.* постоя́нство; неизме́нность, ве́рность.
constant ['kɒnst(ə)nt] *n.* (*math.*, *phys.*) конста́нта.
adj. постоя́нный; (*faithful*) неизме́нный, ве́рный.
Constantine ['kɒnstən,taɪn] *n.* Константи́н.
Constantinople [,kɒnstæntɪ'nəʊp(ə)l] *n.* (*hist.*) Константино́поль (*m.*).
constantly ['kɒnst(ə)ntlɪ] *adj.* (*continuously*) постоя́нно; (*frequently*) то и де́ло.
constellation [,kɒnstə'leɪʃ(ə)n] *n.* созве́здие, констелля́ция.
consternation [,kɒnstə'neɪʃ(ə)n] *n.* смяте́ние, у́жас; оцепене́ние.
constipate ['kɒnstɪ,peɪt] *v.t.* (*med.*) вызыва́ть, вы́звать запо́р у+*g.*; **he is ~d** у него́ запо́р.
constipation [,kɒnstɪ'peɪʃ(ə)n] *n.* запо́р.
constituency [kən'stɪtjʊənsɪ] *n.* избира́тельный о́круг; **nurse one's ~** забо́титься (*impf.*) об избира́телях своего́ о́круга.
constituent [kən'stɪtjʊənt] *n.* (*elector*) избира́тель (*fem.* -ница); (*element*) составна́я часть.
adj. составля́ющий часть це́лого; (*pol.*) избира́ющий; ~ **assembly** учреди́тельное собра́ние.
constitute ['kɒnstɪ,tju:t] *v.t.* (*make up*) сост|авля́ть, -а́вить; (*set up*) учре|жда́ть, -ди́ть; устан|а́вливать, -ови́ть.
constitution [,kɒnstɪ'tju:ʃ(ə)n] *n.* **1.** (*make-up*) строе́ние, структу́ра; **the ~ of one's mind** склад ума́. **2.** (*of body*) (тело)сложе́ние. **3.** (*pol.*) конститу́ция.
constitutional [,kɒnstɪ'tju:ʃən(ə)l] *n.* (*walk*) моцио́н, прогу́лка.
adj. (*of body*) органи́ческий, конституциона́льный; (*pol.*) конституцио́нный.
constitutionalism [,kɒnstɪ'tju:ʃənə,lɪz(ə)m] *n.* конституционали́зм.
constitutionalist [,kɒnstɪ'tju:ʃənəlɪst] *n.* конституционали́ст; (*expert*) специали́ст по конституцио́нному пра́ву.
constitutive ['kɒnstɪ,tju:tɪv] *adj.* учреди́тельный, суще́ственный.
constrain [kən'streɪn] *v.t.* прин|ужда́ть, -у́дить; заст|авля́ть, -а́вить; вынужда́ть, вы́нудить; **~ed** (*embarrassed*) стеснённый.
constraint [kən'streɪnt] *n.* (*compulsion*) принужде́ние, давле́ние; (*repression of feelings*) ско́ванность.
constrict [kən'strɪkt] *v.t.* сж|има́ть, -ать; сужа́ть, су́зить; **a ~ed outlook** ограни́ченный кругозо́р.
constriction [kən'strɪkʃ(ə)n] *n.* сжа́тие, суже́ние; **I feel a ~ in the chest** я чу́вствую стесне́ние в груди́.
constrictive [kən'strɪktɪv] *adj.* сжима́ющий, сужа́ющий.
construct [kən'strʌkt] *v.t.* конструи́ровать (*impf.*, *pf.*); (*also gram.*, *geom.*) стро́ить, по-.
construction [kən'strʌkʃ(ə)n] *n.* **1.** (*building*, *structure*) построе́ние, строи́тельство, стро́йка; **the road is under ~** доро́га стро́ится; **a car of solid ~** маши́на про́чной констру́кции. **2.** (*interpretation*) истолкова́ние; **he put a wrong ~ on my words** он непра́вильно истолкова́л мои́ слова́. **3.** (*gram.*) констру́кция; (*regimen*) управле́ние; (*geom.*) построе́ние.
constructional [kən'strʌkʃ(ə)nəl] *adj.* структу́рный; (*pert. to building*) строи́тельный.
constructive [kən'strʌktɪv] *adj.* (*pert. to construction*; *helpful*) конструкти́вный; (*implicit*) подразумева́емый; **a ~ denial** ко́свенный отка́з.
constructor [kən'strʌktə(r)] *n.* констру́ктор; строи́тель (*m.*).
construe [kən'stru:] *v.t.* **1.** (*combine grammatically*): **the word is ~d with 'upon'** э́то сло́во тре́бует предло́га «upon». **2.** (*translate*) досло́вно перев|оди́ть, -ести́. **3.** (*interpret*) истолко́в|ывать, -а́ть.
v.i.: **the sentence won't ~** э́то предложе́ние не поддаётся разбо́ру.
consuetude ['kɒnswɪ,tju:d] *n.* (*custom*) обы́чай; непи́санный зако́н.
consul ['kɒns(ə)l] *n.* ко́нсул.
cpd. **~-general** *n.* генера́льный ко́нсул.
consular ['kɒnsjʊlə(r)] *adj.* ко́нсульский.
consulate ['kɒnsjʊlət] *n.* (*also hist.*) ко́нсульство.
consulship ['kɒns(ə)lʃɪp] *n.* до́лжность ко́нсула.
consult [kən'sʌlt] *v.t.* **1.** (*refer to*): **~ a book** спр|авля́ться, -а́виться в кни́ге; **~ one's watch** посмотре́ть (*pf.*) на часы́; **~ a lawyer** сове́товаться, по- с юри́стом. **2.** (*take account of*): **~ s.o.'s interests** прин|има́ть, -я́ть во внима́ние чьи-н. интере́сы.
v.i. сове́товаться, по- (с+*i.*); **~ with s.o.** консульти́роваться (*impf.*, *pf.*) с кем-н.; совеща́ться (*impf.*) с кем-н.; **~ing physician** (врач-)консульта́нт; **~ing hours** приёмные часы́; **~ing room** кабине́т (врача́).
consultant [kən'sʌlt(ə)nt] *n.* консульта́нт.
consultation [,kɒnsəl'teɪʃ(ə)n] *n.* консульта́ция; **he acted in ~ with me** он де́йствовал, сове́туясь со мно́й.
consultative [,kən'sʌltətɪv] *adj.* консультати́вный, совеща́тельный.
consumable [kən'sju:məb(ə)l] *adj.* (*edible*) съедо́бный.
consume [kən'sju:m] *v.t.* **1.** (*eat or drink*) съ|еда́ть, -есть; погло|ща́ть, -ти́ть. **2.** (*use up*) потреб|ля́ть, -и́ть; расхо́доваться, из-. **3.** (*destroy*) истреб|ля́ть, -и́ть; **the fire ~d the huts** пожа́р уничто́жил лачу́ги. **4.**: **he was ~d with envy/curiosity** его́ снеда́ла за́висть; его́ снеда́ло любопы́тство.
consumer [kən'sju:mə(r)] *n.* потреби́тель (*m.*); **~ goods** потреби́тельские това́ры.
consumerism [kən'sju:mə,rɪz(ə)m] *n.* потреби́тельство.
consummate[1] [kən'sʌmɪt, 'kɒnsəmɪt] *adj.* соверше́нный, зако́нченный; **a ~ artist** блестя́щий худо́жник; **a ~ ass** соверше́нный осёл.
consummate[2] ['kɒnsə,meɪt] *v.t.* (*e.g. happiness*) заверш|а́ть, -и́ть; уве́нч|ивать, -а́ть; (*marriage*) осуществ|ля́ть, -и́ть (*брачные отношения*).
consummation [,kɒnsə'meɪʃ(ə)n] *n.* (*completion*, *achievement*) заверше́ние, увенча́ние, осуществле́ние; (*of marriage*) осуществле́ние.
consumption [kən'sʌmpʃ(ə)n] *n.* **1.** (*eating etc.*) потребле́ние, поглоще́ние; **the ~ of beer has gone up** потребле́ние пи́ва подняло́сь. **2.** (*using up*) потребле́ние. **3.** (*destruction*) истребле́ние, изничтоже́ние. **4.** (*med.*) чахо́тка, туберкулёз;

galloping ~ скоротéчная чахóтка.

consumptive [kən'sʌmptɪv] *n.* & *adj.* (*med.*) чахóточный, туберкулёзный (больнóй).

contact ['kɒntækt] *n.* **1.** (*lit., fig.*) контáкт, соприкосновéние; **bring, come into ~ with** установи́ть (*pf.*) контáкт с+*i.*; прийти́ (*pf.*) в соприкосновéние с+*i.*; войти́ (*pf.*) в контáкт с+*i.*; **keep in ~ with** поддéрживать (*impf.*) связь с+*i.*; **our troops are in ~ with the enemy** нáши войскá вошли́ в соприкосновéние с проти́вником; **make/break ~** (*elec.*) включи́ть/вы́ключить (*both pf.*) ток; **~ lenses** контáктные ли́нзы. **2.** (*of pers.*): **he made useful ~s** он завязáл полéзные знакóмства/свя́зи; **who is your ~ in that office?** к комý вы обы́чно обращáетесь в э́том учреждéнии?; **~ man** агéнт. **3.** (*disease carrier*) бациллоноси́тель (*m.*).

v.t. (*coll.*) связáться (*pf.*) с+*i.*

cpds. **~-breaker** *n.* (*elec.*) руби́льник; **~-maker** *n.* (*elec.*) замыкáтель (*m.*), контáктор.

contagion [kən'teɪdʒ(ə)n] *n.* зарáза, инфéкция.

contagious [kən'teɪdʒəs] *adj.* зарáзный, инфекциóнный; **laughter is ~** смех заразúтелен.

contain [kən'teɪn] *v.t.* **1.** (*hold within itself*) содержáть (*impf.*) в себé; **the newspaper ~s interesting reports** в газéте есть/имéются интерéсные сообщéния. **2.** (*comprise*) содержáть (*impf.*); состоя́ть (*impf.*) из+*g.*; **a gallon ~s eight pints** в галлóне вóсемь пинт. **3.** (*be capable of holding*) вмещáть (*impf.*); **how much does this bottle ~?** скóлько вмещáет э́та бути́лка?; каковá ёмкость э́той бути́лки? **4.** (*control*) сдéрж|ивать, -áть; **he could not ~ his enthusiasm** он не мог сдержáть своегó востóрга; **~ yourself!** возьми́те себя́ в рýки!; владéйте собóй! **5.** (*hold in check*) сдéрж|ивать, -áть; **our forces ~ed the enemy** нáши войскá сдéрживали проти́вника. **6.: the angle ~ed by these two lines** ýгол, образóванный э́тими двумя́ ли́ниями.

container [kən'teɪnə(r)] *n.* **1.** (*receptacle*) сосýд. **2.** контéйнер, тáра; **~ ship** контéйнерное сýдно.

containment [kən'teɪnmənt] *n.* (*of enemy forces etc.*) сдéрживание; сдéрживающие дéйствия.

contaminate [kən'tæmɪˌneɪt] *v.t.* зара|жáть, -зи́ть; загрязн|я́ть, -и́ть.

contamination [kənˌtæmɪ'neɪʃ(ə)n] *v.t.* заражéние, загрязнéние.

contemn [kən'tem] *v.t.* (*liter.*) презирáть (*impf.*).

contemplate ['kɒntəmˌpleɪt] *v.t.* **1.** (*gaze at*) созерцáть (*impf.*); при́стально рассмáтривать (*impf.*). **2.** (*view mentally*) рассмáтривать (*impf.*); созерцáть (*impf*). **3.** (*envisage, plan*) обдýм|ывать, -ать; задýм|ывать, -ать; зам|ышля́ть, -ы́слить.

contemplation [ˌkɒntəm'pleɪʃ(ə)n] *n.* созерцáние, размышлéние, обдýмывание; **the work is in ~** э́та рабóта в стáдии зáмысла.

contemplative [kən'templətɪv] *adj.* созерцáтельный, умозри́тельный.

contemporaneity [kənˌtempərə'niːɪtɪ] *n.* совремéнность, одноврéмéнность.

contemporaneous [kənˌtempə'reɪnɪəs] *adj.* совремéнный, одноврéмéнный.

contemporary [kən'tempərərɪ] *n.* совремéнни|к, свéрстни|к (*fem.* -ца).

adj. совремéнный; **~ history** новéйшая истóрия.

contempt [kən'tempt] *n.* презрéние; **fall into ~** заслýж|ивать, -и́ть (*or* вызывáть, вы́звать к себé) презрéние; **bring into ~** вызывáть, вы́звать презрéние +*d.*; **have ~ for** презирáть (*impf.*); **in ~ of rules** невзирáя на прáвила; **~ of court** неуважéние к судý; оскорблéние судá.

contemptible [kən'temptɪb(ə)l] *adj.* презрéнный.

contemptuous [kən'temptjʊəs] *adj.* презри́тельный.

contend [kən'tend] *v.t.* утверждáть (*impf.*).

v.i. (*fight*) борóться (*impf.*) (**with:** с+*i.*; *for:* за+*a.*); (*compete*) состязáться (*impf.*); сопéрничать (*impf.*); **~ for a prize** борóться (*impf.*) за приз; оспáривать (*impf.*) приз; **~ing interests** противополóжные интерéсы.

contender [kən'tendə(r)] *n.* сопéрник, претендéнт.

content[1] ['kɒntent] *n.* (*lit., fig.*) содержáние; **the sugar ~ of beet** содержáние сáхара в свёкле; (*pl.*) содержи́мое; **(table of) ~s** оглавлéние.

content[2] [kən'tent] *n.* (*satisfaction*) довóльство; удовлетворéние; **to one's heart's ~** в своё удовóльствие, вдóволю, всласть.

adj. довóльный.

v.t. удовлетвор|я́ть, -и́ть; **~ o.s.** довóльствоваться; **a ~ed look** довóльный вид.

contention [kən'tenʃ(ə)n] *n.* (*strife*) спор, раздóр; (*assertion*) утверждéние.

contentious [kən'tenʃəs] *adj.* вздóрный, задири́стый.

contentment [kən'tentmənt] *n.* удовлетворённость, довóльство.

contest ['kɒntest; *v. only* kən'test] *n.* кóнкурс, состязáние; **beauty ~** кóнкурс красоты́.

v.t. & *i.* **1.** (*dispute*) осп|áривать, -óрить. **2.** (*contend for*) отст|áивать, -оя́ть; борóться (*impf.*) за+*a.*; **the enemy ~ed every inch of ground** враг отстáивал кáждую пядь земли́; **he ~ed the election** он борóлся на вы́борах.

contestable [kən'testəb(ə)l] *adj.* спóрный, оспáриваемый.

contestant [kən'test(ə)nt] *n.* конкурéнт, учáстник состязáния.

context ['kɒntekst] *n.* (*textual*) контéкст; (*connection*) связь; **in the ~ of today's America** в услóвиях совремéнной Амéрики.

contiguity [ˌkɒntɪ'gjuːɪtɪ] *n.* смéжность, соприкосновéние.

contiguous [kən'tɪgjʊəs] *adj.* смéжный, соприкасáющийся, прилегáющий.

continence ['kɒntɪnəns] *n.* сдéржанность; воздержáние.

continent[1] ['kɒntɪnənt] *n.* континéнт, матери́к; **the C~** (*Europe*) (континентáльная) Еврóпа; **the five ~s** пять континéнтов.

continent[2] ['kɒntɪnənt] *adj.* сдéржанный, воздéржанный.

continental [ˌkɒntɪ'nent(ə)l] *n.* (*inhabitant of Europe*) жи́тель (*m.*) европéйского континéнта; европé|ец (*fem.* -йка).

adj. континентáльный; **~ shelf** материкóвая óтмель; **C~ breakfast** лёгкий ýтренний зáвтрак.

contingency [kən'tɪndʒənsɪ] *n.* **1.** (*uncertainty*) случáйность, слýчай. **2.** (*possible event*) возмóжное обстоя́тельство; **~ plan** вариáнт плáна; **~ planning** плани́рование дéйствий при разли́чных вариáнтах обстанóвки.

contingent [kən'tɪndʒ(ə)nt] *n.* (*mil.*) контингéнт.

adj. случáйный; возмóжный.

continual [kən'tɪnjʊəl] *adj.* постоя́нный, беспреры́вный, беспрестáнный.

continuance [kən'tɪnjʊəns] *n.* продолжи́тельность, продолжéние; (*e.g. in office*) пребывáние.

continuation [kənˌtɪnjʊ'eɪʃ(ə)n] *n.* продолжéние; возобновлéние.

continue [kən'tɪnjuː] *v.t.* прод|олжáть, -óлжить; **'to be ~d'** (*of story etc.*) продолжéние слéдует; **~d on p. 15** (смотри́) продолжéние на стр. 15; **~d from p. 2** (смотри́) начáло на стр. 2; **he was ~d in office** он был остáвлен в (той же) дóлжности.

v.i. прод|олжáться, -óлжиться; **the wet weather ~s** сыря́я погóда дéржится; **if you ~ (to be) obstinate** éсли вы бýдете по-прéжнему упóрствовать.

continuer [kən'tɪnjuːə(r)] *n.* продолжáтель (*m.*).

continuity [ˌkɒntɪ'njuːɪtɪ] *n.* непреры́вность, неразры́вность, беспреры́вность; **~ girl** (*cin.*) монтáжница.

continuous [kən'tɪnjʊəs] *adj.* непреры́вный, неразры́вный, беспреры́вный; (*gram.*) дли́тельный.

continuum [kən'tɪnjʊəm] *n.* конти́нуум.

contort [kən'tɔːt] *v.t.* иска|жáть, -зи́ть; искрив|ля́ть, -и́ть.

contortion [kən'tɔːʃ(ə)n] *n.* искажéние; искривлéние.

contortionist [kən'tɔːʃənɪst] *n.* человéк-змея́.

contour ['kɒntʊə(r)] *n.* кóнтур; **~ line** горизонтáль; **~ map** гипсометри́ческая кáрта.

v.t. (*a map*) вычéрчивать, вы́чертить в горизонтáлях; (*a road*) нан|оси́ть, -ести́ кóнтур +*g.*

contraband ['kɒntrəˌbænd] *n.* контрабáнда; **~ of war** воéнная контрабáнда; **~ goods** контрабáндные товáры.

contrabandist ['kɒntrəˌbændɪst] *n.* контрабанди́ст.

contraception [ˌkɒntrəˈsepʃ(ə)n] *n.* предупрежде́ние бере́менности; примене́ние противозача́точных средств.

contraceptive [ˌkɒntrəˈseptɪv] *n.* противозача́точное сре́дство.
adj. противозача́точный.

contract[1] [ˈkɒntrækt] *n.* (*agreement*) контра́кт, догово́р; **marriage ~** бра́чный контра́кт; **breach of ~** наруше́ние догово́ра/контра́кта; **~ price** догово́рная цена́; **~ (bridge)** бридж-контра́кт.

contract[2] [kənˈtrækt] *v.t.* (*conclude*) заключ|а́ть, -и́ть (*договор/контракт*); **~ a marriage** вступи́ть в брак; (*incur*): **~ an illness** заболе́ть (*pf.*); **~ bad habits** усво́ить (*pf.*) дурны́е привы́чки; **~ debts** влезть (*pf.*) в долги́; наде́лать (*pf.*) долго́в.
v.i. (*agree*) прин|има́ть, -я́ть на себя́ обяза́тельство; **he ~ed to build a bridge** он подряди́лся вы́строить мост; **~ing parties** (*dipl.*) догова́ривающиеся сто́роны (*f. pl.*); **~ out** отказа́ться (*pf.*) от уча́стия в (*чём*); вы́йти (*pf.*) из де́ла.

contract[3] [kənˈtrækt] *v.t.* (*shorten*) сокра|ща́ть, -ти́ть; (*gram.*) стя́|гивать, -ну́ть; (*tighten*) сж|има́ть, -ать; **~ one's brow** нахму́рить/намо́рщить (*pf.*) лоб; (*reduce*) сокра|ща́ть, -ти́ть.
v.i. (*shorten*) сокра|ща́ться, -ти́ться; **metal ~s** мета́лл сжима́ется; (*gram.*) стя́|гиваться, -ну́ться; (*tighten*) сж|има́ться, -а́ться; (*grow smaller*) сокра|ща́ться, -ти́ться.

contracti|ble [kənˈtræktɪb(ə)l], **-le** [kənˈtræktaɪl] *adjs.* сжима́ющий(ся), сокраща́ющий(ся); **~ muscles** сокраща́ющиеся мы́шцы.

contraction [kənˈtrækʃ(ə)n] *n.* **1.** (*shortening*) сокраще́ние, укороче́ние, стя́гивание, суже́ние; (*short form*) стяжённая фо́рма, контракту́ра. **2.** (*of metal*) сжа́тие; (*of muscle etc.*) сокраще́ние, уса́дка. **3.** (*of habit*) приобрете́ние; (*of marriage*) заключе́ние; (*of illness*) заболева́ние (*чем*).

contractor [kənˈtræktə(r)] *n.* (*pers.*) подря́дчик; (*muscle*) стя́гивающая мы́шца.

contractual [kənˈtræktjʊəl] *adj.* догово́рный.

contradict [ˌkɒntrəˈdɪkt] *v.t.* противоре́чить (*impf.*) +*d.*; (*rumours etc.*) опров|ерга́ть, -е́ргнуть.

contradiction [ˌkɒntrəˈdɪkʃ(ə)n] *n.* противоре́чие, опроверже́ние; **~ in terms** логи́ческая несообра́зность; **spirit of ~** дух противоре́чия.

contradictory [ˌkɒntrəˈdɪktərɪ] *adj.* противоречи́вый, противоре́чащий.

contradistinction [ˌkɒntrədɪˈstɪŋkʃ(ə)n] *n.* противопоставле́ние, противополо́жность; **in ~ to** в отли́чие от+*g.*

contra-indicated [ˌkɒntrəˈɪndɪˌkeɪtɪd] *adj.* (*med.*) противопока́занный.

contra-indication [ˌkɒntrəˌɪndɪˈkeɪʃ(ə)n] *n.* (*med.*) противопоказа́ние.

contralto [kənˈtræltəʊ] *n.* (*voice, singer*) контра́льто (*nt. & f., indecl.*).

contraption [kənˈtræpʃ(ə)n] *n.* (*coll.*) приспособле́ние, штуко́вина.

contrapuntal [ˌkɒntrəˈpʌnt(ə)l] *adj.* (*mus.*) контрапункти́ческий, контрапу́нктный.

contrapuntist [ˌkɒntrəˈpʌntɪst] *n.* (*mus.*) контрапункти́ст.

contrariety [ˌkɒntrəˈraɪɪtɪ] *n.* противоре́чие, противоречи́вость.

contrariness [ˈkɒntrərɪnɪs] *n.* (*coll., perversity*) своево́лие, своенра́вность, своенра́вие.

contrariwise [kənˈtreərɪˌwaɪz] *adj.* с друго́й стороны́; наоборо́т.

contrary[1] [ˈkɒntrərɪ] *n.* противополо́жность; противополо́жное, обра́тное; **'wet' and 'dry' are contraries** «мо́крый» и «сухо́й» — анто́нимы; **on, quite the ~** (как раз) наоборо́т; **to the ~** в обра́тном смы́сле; **I have heard nothing to the ~** у меня́ нет основа́ния сомнева́ться в э́том; **unless I hear to the ~** е́сли я не услы́шу чего́-нибудь ино́го/противополо́жного; **there is no evidence to the ~** нет доказа́тельств проти́вного/обра́тного.
adj. противополо́жный, проти́вный, обра́тный; **~ winds** проти́вные ве́тры; **~ information** противополо́жные сообще́ния.
adv.: **he acted ~ to the rules** он поступи́л про́тив пра́вил; **~ to my expectations** вопреки́ мои́м ожида́ниям.

contrary[2] [kənˈtreərɪ] *adj.* (*coll.*) своево́льный, своенра́вный.

contrast [ˈkɒntrɑːst] *n.* контра́ст; противополо́жность; **in ~ to** в противополо́жность +*d.*; **by ~ with** по сравне́нию с+*i.*
v.t. противопост|авля́ть, -а́вить; сопост|авля́ть, -а́вить.
v.i. контрасти́ровать (*impf., pf.*); **the colours ~ well** э́ти цвета́ даю́т хоро́ший контра́ст; **his words ~ with his behaviour** его́ слова́ противоре́чат его́ поведе́нию.

contravene [ˌkɒntrəˈviːn] *v.t.* противоре́чить (*impf.*) +*d.*; **he ~d the law** он нару́шил зако́н.

contravention [ˌkɒntrəˈvenʃ(ə)n] *n.* наруше́ние; **in ~ of** в наруше́ние +*g.*

contretemps [ˈkɔːntrəˌtɑ̃] *n.* неприя́тность; непредви́денное препя́тствие.

contribute [kənˈtrɪbjuːt] *v.t.* (*money etc.*) же́ртвовать, по-; **he ~d £5** он внёс 5 фу́нтов; **he ~d new information** он сообщи́л но́вые све́дения.
v.i. соде́йствовать (*impf.*) +*d.*; спосо́бствовать (*impf.*) +*d.*; **it ~d to his ruin** э́то яви́лось одно́й из причи́н его́ разоре́ния; **he ~s to our magazine** он пи́шет для на́шего журна́ла.

contribution [ˌkɒntrɪˈbjuːʃ(ə)n] *n.*: **a ~ of £5** поже́ртвование/взнос в пять фу́нтов; **his ~ to our success** его́ вклад в наш успе́х; (*to a periodical etc.*) статья́, заме́тка.

contributor [kənˈtrɪbjʊtə(r)] *n.* (*writer*) (постоя́нный) сотру́дник; (*of funds*) же́ртвователь (*m.*).

contributory [kənˈtrɪbjʊtərɪ] *adj.* соде́йствующий, спосо́бствующий; **~ negligence** встре́чная вина́, вина́ потерпе́вшего; **a ~ pension scheme** пенсио́нная систе́ма, осно́ванная на отчисле́ниях из за́работка рабо́тающих.

contrite [ˈkɒntraɪt, kənˈtraɪt] *adj.* сокруша́ющийся, ка́ющийся.

contrition [kənˈtrɪʃ(ə)n] *n.* сокруше́ние, раска́яние, покая́ние.

contrivance [kənˈtraɪv(ə)ns] *n.* (*skill*) изобрета́тельность; (*device*) приспособле́ние, изобрете́ние.

contrive [kənˈtraɪv] *v.t.* (*devise*) заду́м|ывать, -ать; изобре|та́ть, -сти; (*succeed*) наловчи́ться (*pf.*); **he ~d to offend everybody** он ухитри́лся всех оби́деть; **~d** (*artificial*) иску́сственный.

control [kənˈtrəʊl] *n.* **1.** (*power to direct etc.*) управле́ние, регули́рование; **he lost ~ of the car** он потеря́л управле́ние автомоби́лем; **he is in ~ of the situation** он хозя́ин положе́ния; **the situation is under ~** наведён поря́док; **the children are out of ~** де́ти не слу́шаются; **traffic ~** регули́рование у́личного движе́ния; **remote ~** дистанцио́нное управле́ние. **2.** (*means of regulating*) контро́ль (*m.*); **government ~s** госуда́рственный контро́ль; **birth ~** регули́рование рожда́емости. **3.** (*pl., of a machine etc.*) рычаги́ (*m. pl.*) управле́ния; **volume ~** регуля́тор гро́мкости/усиле́ния. **4.: ~ experiment** контро́льный о́пыт; **~ panel** прибо́рная доска́; пульт управле́ния; **~ room** пункт управле́ния; **~ tower** (*aeron.*) контро́льно-диспе́тчерский пункт.
v.t. **1.** (*master, regulate*) регули́ровать (*impf., pf.*); держа́ть (*impf.*) в повинове́нии; **~ children** держа́ть (*impf.*) дете́й в послуша́нии; **~ one's temper** владе́ть (*impf.*) собо́й; **~ prices** регули́ровать це́ны. **2.** (*verify*) контроли́ровать (*impf., pf.*).

controllable [kənˈtrəʊləb(ə)l] *adj.* регули́руемый, контроли́руемый, управля́емый.

con|troller, comp- [kənˈtrəʊlə(r)] *nn.* контролёр, инспе́ктор.

controversial [ˌkɒntrəˈvɜːʃ(ə)l] *adj.* спо́рный, полеми́ческий; **a ~ subject** предме́т, вызыва́ющий поле́мику/спо́ры.

controversialist [ˌkɒntrəˈvɜːʃ(ə)lɪst] *n.* полеми́ст, спо́рщик.

controversy [ˈkɒntrəˌvɜːsɪ, *disp.* kənˈtrɒvəsɪ] *n.* поле́мика, спор.

controvert [ˈkɒntrəˌvɜːt, -ˈvɜːt] *v.t.* противоре́чить (*impf.*) +*d.*

contumacious [ˌkɒntjuːˈmeɪʃəs] *adj.* непоко́рный; (*leg.*) не подчиня́ющийся постановле́нию суда́.

contumacy [ˈkɒntjʊməsɪ] *n.* непоко́рность; (*leg.*) неподчине́ние постановле́нию суда́.

contumely [ˈkɒntjuːmlɪ] *n.* де́рзость, оскорбле́ние, позо́р.

contuse [kənˈtjuːz] *v.t.* конту́зить (*pf.*).

contusion [kən'tjuːʃ(ə)n, -ʒ(ə)n] *n.* контýзия, ушѝб.
conundrum [kə'nʌndrəm] *n.* загáдка, головолóмка.
conurbation [ˌkɒnɜː'beɪʃ(ə)n] *n.* конурбáция, городскáя агломерáция.
convalesce [ˌkɒnvə'les] *v.i.* выздорáвливать (*impf.*).
convalescence [ˌkɒnvə'lesəns] *n.* выздоровлéние, выздорáвливание.
convalescent [ˌkɒnvə'les(ə)nt] *n.* выздорáвливающий.
adj. (*of patient*) выздорáвливающий, поправля́ющийся; ~ **home** санатóрий для выздорáвливающих.
convection [kən'vekʃ(ə)n] *n.* конвéкция.
convector [kən'vektə(r)] *n.* конвéктор.
convene [kən'viːn] *v.t.* (*people*) соб|ирáть, -рáть; (*meeting*) соз|ывáть, -вáть.
v.i. соб|ирáться, -рáться.
conven|er, -or [kən'viːnə(r)] *nn.* организáтор/инициáтор собрáния.
convenience [kən'viːnɪəns] *n.* **1.** удóбство; **marriage of** ~ брак по расчёту; **at your** ~ когдá вам бýдет удóбно; **having the railway close by is a** ~ удóбно жить вблизѝ от желéзной дорóги; **make a** ~ **of s.o.** испóльзовать (*impf.*, *pf.*) когó-н. в своѝх интерéсах; ~ **foods** пищевы́е полуфабрикáты. **2.** (*appliance*) удóбства (*nt. pl.*); **all modern** ~**s** все удóбства. **3.: public** ~ общéственная убóрная.
convenient [kən'viːnɪənt] *adj.* удóбный, подходя́щий; **if it is** ~ **for you** éсли вам удóбно; **the station is** ~**ly near** до стáнции — рукóй подáть.
convenor [kən'viːnə(r)] = **convener**
convent ['kɒnv(ə)nt, -vent] *n.* (жéнский) монасты́рь; **she entered a** ~ онá пострѝглась в монáхини.
convention [kən'venʃ(ə)n] *n.* **1.** (*act of convening*) созы́в. **2.** (*congress*) съезд; **C**~ (*Fr. hist.*) конвéнт. **3.** (*treaty*) конвéнция. **4.** (*custom*) обы́чай, услóвность. **5.** (*at cards*) конвéнция.
conventional [kən'venʃən(ə)l] *adj.* обы́чный, традициóнный; **a** ~ **greeting** (обще)прѝнятое привéтствие; ~ **sign** услóвный знак; ~ **armaments** вооружéние обы́чного тѝпа; **a** ~ **person** человéк, котóрый придéрживается услóвностей; (*banal*) стандáртный; **he has a** ~ **mind** он мы́слит трафарéтно; ~ **war** войнá с применéнием обы́чных вооружéний.
conventionalist [kən'venʃən(ə)lɪst] *n.* сторóнник услóвностей.
conventionality [kənˌvenʃə'nælɪtɪ] *n.* услóвность; благопристóйность.
conventual [kən'ventjʊəl] *adj.* монасты́рский.
converge [kən'vɜːdʒ] *v.i.* сходѝться, сойтѝсь; (*math.*) стремѝться (*impf.*) к предéлу; **the armies** ~**d on the city** áрмии приблѝзились к гóроду.
convergence [kən'vɜːdʒəns] *n.* сходѝмость, конвергéнция.
convergent [kən'vɜːdʒ(ə)nt] *adj.* сходя́щийся в однóй тóчке.
conversable [kən'vɜːsəb(ə)l] *adj.* общѝтельный, разговóрчивый.
conversanc|e [kən'vɜːsəns], **-y** [kən'vɜːsənsɪ] *nn.* знакóмство, осведомлённость.
conversant [kən'vɜːs(ə)nt, 'kɒnvəs(ə)nt] *adj.* знакóмый (с+*i.*), осведомлённый (в+*p.*).
conversation [ˌkɒnvə'seɪʃ(ə)n] *n.* разговóр, бесéда, речь; ~**s** (*e.g. dipl.*) переговóры (*pl.*, *g.* -ов); **make** ~ вестѝ/поддéрживать (*impf.*) пустóй разговóр; ~ **piece** жáнровая картѝна.
conversational [ˌkɒnvə'seɪʃən(ə)l] *adj.* (*pert. to conversation*) разговóрный; (*talkative*) разговóрчивый.
conversationalist [ˌkɒnvə'seɪʃənəlɪst] *n.* (интерéсный) собесéдник.
converse[1] ['kɒnvɜːs] *n.* (*logic, math.*) обрáтное положéние; обрáтная теорéма.
converse[2] [kən'vɜːs] *v.i.* (*talk*) бесéдовать (*impf.*), разговáривать (*impf.*).
conversely ['kɒnvɜːslɪ, kən'vɜːslɪ] *adv.* наоборóт.
conversion [kən'vɜːʃ(ə)n] *n.* **1.** (*transformation*) превращéние, перехóд; ~ **of cream into butter** сбивáние слѝвок в мáсло. **2.** (*relig. etc.*) обращéние (в+*a.*); **there were many** ~**s to Islam** мнóгие перешлѝ в ислáм. **3.** (*math.*) преобразовáние, перевóд; ~ **of pounds into dollars** перевóд фýнтов в дóллары; обмéн фýнтов на дóллары. **4.** (*appropriation*) обращéние в свою́ пóльзу; ~ **of funds to one's own use** присвоéние фóндов. **5.** (*fin.*, *of stocks etc.*) конвéрсия.
convert[1] ['kɒnvɜːt] *n.* (ново)обращённый; **he is a** ~ **to Buddhism** он перешёл в буддѝзм.
convert[2] [kən'vɜːt] *v.t.* **1.** (*change*) превра|щáть, -тѝть; **the house was** ~**ed into flats** дом был разбѝт на кварти́ры. **2.** (*relig. etc.*) обра|щáть, -тѝть; ~**ed natives** крещёные тузéмцы; **I** ~**ed him to my view** я убедѝл егó принять мою́ тóчку зрéния. **3.** (*math.*) пере|водѝть, -вестѝ; ~ **pounds into francs** перевестѝ (*pf.*) фýнты стéрлингов во фрáнки. **4.** (*appropriate*) обра|щáть, -тѝть в свою́ пóльзу.
v.i.: **he** ~**ed to Buddhism** он обратѝлся в буддѝзм; он прѝнял буддѝйскую вéру.
convertibility [kənˌvɜːtɪ'bɪlɪtɪ] *n.* (*fin.*) обратѝмость.
convertible [kən'vɜːtɪb(ə)l] *n.* (*car*) автомобѝль (*m.*) с откидны́м/открывáющимся вéрхом.
adj. обратѝмый, конвертѝруемый; ~ **currency** конвертѝруемая валю́та.
convex ['kɒnveks] *adj.* вы́пуклый, вы́гнутый.
convexity [ˌkɒn'veksɪtɪ] *n.* вы́пуклость, вы́гнутость.
convey [kən'veɪ] *v.t.* **1.** (*carry, transmit*) перев|озѝть, -езтѝ; перепр|авлять, -áвить; **pipes** ~ **water** водá доставля́ется по трýбам. **2.** (*impart*) перед|авáть, -áть; **the words** ~ **nothing to me** э́ти словá мне ничегó не говоря́т; ~ **my greetings to him** передáйте емý привéт от меня́. **3.** (*leg.*) перед|авáть, -áть (*имýщество, прáва*).
conveyance [kən'veɪəns] *n.* (*transmission*) перевóзка, передáча; (*vehicle*) трáнспортное срéдство.
conveyancer [kən'veɪənsə(r)] *n.* (*leg.*) нотáриус, ведýщий делá по передáче имýщества.
conveyancing [kən'veɪənsɪŋ] *n.* (*leg.*) составлéние нотариáльных áктов о передáче имýщества.
conveyer [kən'veɪə(r)] *n.* конвéйер, транспортёр; ~ **belt** конвéйерная/транспортёрная лéнта; лéнточный транспортёр.
convict[1] ['kɒnvɪkt] *n.* осуждённый, кáторжник.
convict[2] [kən'vɪkt] *v.t.* (*leg.*) **1.** осу|ждáть, -дѝть (*в чём*). **2.: he was** ~**ed of error** егó оши́бка былá изобличенá.
conviction [kən'vɪkʃ(ə)n] *n.* **1.** (*leg.*) осуждéние; признáние когó-н. винóвным. **2.** (*settled opinion*) убеждéние, убеждённость. **3.** (*persuasive force*) убеждéние; **these arguments carry** ~ э́ти аргумéнты убедѝтельны; **he spoke without** ~ он говорѝл неувéренно; **I am open to** ~ у меня́ нет твёрдо установѝвшегося мнéния; я готóв вы́слушать вáши дóводы.
convince [kən'vɪns] *v.t.* убе|ждáть, -дѝть.
convincing [kən'vɪnsɪŋ] *adj.* убедѝтельный.
convivial [kən'vɪvɪəl] *adj.* (*of pers.*) компанéйский, весёлый; (*of evening etc.*) весёлый.
conviviality [kənˌvɪvɪ'ælɪtɪ] *n.* весёлость, весéлье.
convocation [ˌkɒnvə'keɪʃ(ə)n] *n.* созы́в, собрáние.
convoke [kən'vəʊk] *v.t.* соз|ывáть, -вáть.
convoluted ['kɒnvəˌluːtɪd] *adj.* завѝтый, изóгнутый; (*fig.*) запýтанный.
convolution [ˌkɒnvə'luːʃ(ə)n] *n.* изóгнутость; **the** ~**s of his argument** запýтанность егó аргумéнтов.
convolvulus [kən'vɒlvjʊləs] *n.* вьюнóк.
convoy ['kɒnvɔɪ] *n.* конвóй; трáнспортная колóнна с конвóем; **the ships sailed under** ~ кораблѝ шли под охрáной конвóя.
v.t. конвоѝровать (*impf.*).
convulse [kən'vʌls] *v.t.* сотряс|áть, -тѝ; потряс|áть, -тѝ; **country** ~**d by war** странá, потрясённая войнóй; **he was** ~**d with laughter** он кóрчился от смéха.
convulsion [kən'vʌlʃ(ə)n] *n.* сотрясéние; (*fig.*) потрясéние; (*pl.*, *med.*) конвýльсия, сýдорога; (*of laughter*) сýдорожный смех.
convulsive [kən'vʌlsɪv] *adj.* конвульсѝвный, сýдорожный.
con|y, -ey ['kəʊnɪ] *n.* (*fur*) крóлик; крóличий мех.
coo[1] [kuː] *n.* воркова́нье.
v.t. & i. воркова́ть (*impf.*).
coo[2] [kuː] *int.* (*vulg. or joc.*) ух ты!; да ну!

cooee ['ku:i:] *int.* аý!

cook [kʊk] *n.* (*male*) пóвар; (*on shipboard*) кок; (*fem.*) кухáрка; **too many ∼s spoil the broth** ≃ у семи́ ня́нек дитя́ без глáзу.

v.t. вари́ть, с-; стря́пать, со-; готóвить, с-/при-; **∼ one's own meals** готóвить самомý; **∼ accounts** (*coll.*) поддéл|ывать, -ать счетá; **∼ up a story** (*coll.*) состря́пать (*pf.*) истóрию; **∼ s.o.'s goose** угрóбить (*pf.*) когó-н. (*coll.*).

v.i. вари́ться, с-; готóвиться, при-; **these apples ∼ well** э́ти я́блоки хорошó пекýтся; **what's ∼ing?** (*coll.*) что тут затевáется?

cpds. **∼-book** *n.* = **cookery-book; ∼-house** *n.* похóдная кýхня; (*on ship*) кáмбуз; **∼-shop** *n.* столóвая, харчéвня.

cooker ['kʊkə(r)] *n.* плитá; печь; (*apple*) я́блоко для вáрки.

cookery ['kʊkərɪ] *n.* кулинáрия, стряпня́.

cpd. **∼-book** (*also* **cook-book**) *n.*повáренная кни́га.

cookie ['kʊkɪ] *n.* **1.** (*coll., cook*) пóвар; (*on ship*) кок. **2.** (*US, small cake*) печéнье. **3.: smart ∼** (*coll.*) ловкáч (*fem.* -ка).

cooking ['kʊkɪŋ] *n.* (*cuisine*) кýхня.

adj. столóвый, кýхонный; **∼ apple** я́блоко для вáрки.

cool [ku:l] *n.* **1.** прохлáда; **in the ∼ of the evening** в вечéрней прохлáде. **2.: lose one's ∼** (*coll.*) вы́йти (*pf.*) из себя́, потеря́ть (*pf.*) самооблададáние.

adj. **1.** (*lit.*) прохлáдный, свéжий. **2.** (*unexcited*) хладнокрóвный, невозмути́мый. **3.** (*impudent*) нáглый, беззастéнчивый. **4.** (*unenthusiastic*) прохлáдный, холóдный; **they gave him a ∼ reception** они́ егó встрéтили с холодкóм. **5.: it cost me a ∼ thousand** (*coll.*) э́то стóило мне дóбрую ты́сячу.

v.t. охла|ждáть, -ди́ть; осту|жáть, -ди́ть; освеж|áть, -и́ть; **rain ∼ed the air** пóсле дождя́ стáло прохлáдно.

v.i. охла|ждáться, -ди́ться; освеж|áться, -и́ться; ост|ывáть, -ы́ть; **his anger ∼ed** егó гнев осты́л; **∼ down, off** ост|ывáть, -ы́ть; **∼ing-off period** пери́од обдýмывания и переговóров.

cpds. **∼-headed** *adj.* уравновéшенный, хладнокрóвный, спокóйный; **∼-headedness** *n.* уравновéшенность, хладнокрóвие, спокóйствие.

coolant ['ku:lənt] *n.* смáзочно-охлаждáющая эмýльсия.

cooler ['ku:lə(r)] *n.* (*vessel*) ведёрко для охлаждéния; (*sl., prison cell*) кáмера, кáрцер.

coolie ['ku:lɪ] *n.* кýли (*m. indecl.*).

coolness ['ku:lnɪs] *n.* прохлáда, хóлод; (*of manner*) холодóк, хóлодность; (*estrangement*) охлаждéние; (*impudence*) беззастéнчивость.

coomb, combe [ku:m] *n.* ложби́на, оврáг.

coop [ku:p] *n.* (*cage*) куря́тник; (*for fish*) вéрша.

v.t. сажáть, посади́ть в клéтку; **∼ up, in** (*fig.*) держáть (*impf.*) взаперти́.

co-op ['kəʊɒp] *n.* (*coll.*) кооперати́вный магази́н.

cooper ['ku:pə(r)] *n.* бондáрь (*m.*), бочáр.

cooperage ['ku:pərɪdʒ] *n.* бондáрное/бочáрное ремеслó; бóндáрство.

co-operate [kəʊ'ɒpə,reɪt] *v.i.* сотрýдничать (*impf.*); коопери́роваться (*impf., pf.*)

co-operation [kəʊ,ɒpə'reɪʃ(ə)n] *n.* сотрýдничество, кооперáция.

co-operative [kəʊ'ɒpərətɪv] *n.* кооперати́в; (*pl., collect.*) кооперáция.

adj. кооперати́вный; (*helpful*) готóвый к сотрýдничеству.

co-operator [kəʊ'ɒpə,reɪtə(r)] *n.* кооперáтор, сотрýдник.

co-opt [kəʊ'ɒpt] *v.t.* коопти́ровать (*impf., pf.*).

co-option [kəʊ'ɒpʃ(ə)n] *n.* кооптáция.

co-ordinate [kəʊ'ɔ:dɪnət; *v. only* kəʊ'ɔ:dɪ,neɪt] *n.* (*math.*) координáта; (*pl.*) óси (*f. pl.*) координáт.

adj. координи́рованный; рáвный по значéнию.

v.t. координи́ровать (*impf., pf.*).

co-ordination [kəʊ,ɔ:dɪ'neɪʃ(ə)n] *n.* координáция.

coot [ku:t] *n.* лысýха; **he is as bald as a ∼** у негó головá гóлая, как колéнка.

cop [kɒp] *n.* **1.** (*sl., policeman*) полицéйский; (*sl.*) мильтóн; **∼s and robbers** (*game*) сы́щики и вóры (*m. pl.*). **2.** (*catch*): **a fair ∼** (*sl.*) пóимка на мéсте преступлéния; **not much ∼** (*sl.*) не фонтáн.

v.t. (*catch, hit*): **you'll ∼ it** ты полýчишь; **I ∼ped him one over the head** я трáхнул егó разóк по башкé (*sl.*).

copal ['kəʊp(ə)l] *n.* копáл.

copartner [kəʊ'pɑ:tnə(r)] *n.* компаньóн, учáстник в при́былях.

copartnership [kəʊ'pɑ:tnəʃɪp] *n.* товáрищество, учáстие в при́былях.

cope[1] [kəʊp] *n.* (*vestment*) ри́за; (*fig., canopy*) свод.

cope[2] [kəʊp] *v.i.* спр|авля́ться, -áвиться (с+*i.*).

copeck (*also* **kope(c)k**) ['kəʊpek, 'kɒpek] *n.* копéйка; **∼ piece** копéйка; **3-∼piece** трёхкопéечная монéта; *see also* **five, ten, twenty, fifty**

Copenhagen [,kəʊpən'heɪgən] *n.* Копенгáген.

Copernican [kə'pɜ:nɪkən] *adj.*: **∼ system** систéма Копéрника.

copier ['kɒpɪə(r)] *n.* (*pers.*) переписчик; (*imitator*) подражáтель (*fem.* -ница); (*machine*) мнóжительный аппарáт, ротáтор.

co-pilot ['kəʊ,paɪlət] *n.* вторóй пилóт.

coping ['kəʊpɪŋ] *n.* парапéтная плитá.

cpd. **∼-stone** *n.* карни́зный/парапéтный кáмень; (*fig.*) завершéние.

copious ['kəʊpɪəs] *adj.* оби́льный.

copiousness ['kəʊpɪəsnɪs] *n.* оби́лие.

copper[1] ['kɒpə(r)] *n.* **1.** (*metal*) медь; **∼ wire** мéдная прóволока; (**∼** *coin*) мéдная монéта. **2.** (*vessel*) мéдный котёл.

v.t. покр|ывáть, -ы́ть мéдью.

cpds. **∼-bottom** *v.t.* обш|ивáть, -и́ть мéдью; **∼-bottomed** *adj.* обши́тый мéдью; (*fig., coll.*) надёжный, вéрный; **a ∼-bottomed excuse** желéзный предлóг; **∼head** *n.* щитомóрдник; **∼plate** *n.* мéдная гравировáльная доскá; (*engraving*) óттиск с мéдной гравировáльной доски́; **∼plate handwriting** каллиграфи́ческий пóчерк; **∼-smith** *n.* мéдник, котéльщик.

copper[2] ['kɒpə(r)] *n.* (*sl., policeman*) полицéйский, (*sl.*) мильтóн.

copperas ['kɒpərəs] *n.* желéзный купорóс.

coppery ['kɒpərɪ] *adj.* цвéта мéди.

coppice ['kɒpɪs], **copse** [kɒps] *nn.* подлéсок, рóщица.

copra ['kɒprə] *n.* кóпра.

coprophagous [kɒ'prɒfəgəs] *adj.* питáющийся экскремéнтами; **∼ beetle** жук-навóзник.

coprophilia [,kɒprə'fɪlɪə] *n.* копрофи́лия.

copse [kɒps] = **coppice**

Copt [kɒpt] *n.* копт (*fem.* -ка).

Coptic ['kɒptɪk] *n.* (*language*) кóптский язы́к.

adj. кóптский.

copula ['kɒpjʊlə] *n.* свя́зка.

copulate ['kɒpjʊ,leɪt] *v.i.* совокуп|ля́ться, -и́ться; спáри|ваться, -ться.

copulation [,kɒpjʊ'leɪʃ(ə)n] *n.* совокуплéние, спáривание, слýчка.

copulative ['kɒpjʊlətɪv] *adj.* (*gram.*) соедини́тельный.

copy ['kɒpɪ] *n.* **1.** (*imitation, version*) кóпия, рýкопись; **fair, clean ∼** чистовáя рýкопись; **rough ∼** чернови́к, черновáя рýкопись. **2.** (*of book etc.*) экземпля́р. **3.** (*for printer*) текст, материáл; **advertising ∼** текст реклáмного объявлéния.

v.t. & i. перепи́с|ывать, -áть; копи́ровать, с-; (*imitate*) подражáть (*impf.*) +*d.*; **∼ out a letter** переписáть (*pf.*) письмó; **he copied in the examination** он спи́сывал на экзáмене.

cpds. **∼-book** *n.* тетрáдь; **blot one's ∼-book** (*fig.*) замарáть (*pf.*) свою́ репутáцию; **∼ book maxims** прописны́е и́стины (*f. pl.*); **∼-cat** *n.* (*coll.*) подражáтель (*fem.* -ница); обезья́на; **∼-editor** *n.* техни́ческий редáктор (*abbr.* техрéд); **∼-reader** *n.* коррéктор; **∼right** *n.* áвторское прáво; *adj.* охраня́емый áвторским прáвом; **this book is (in) ∼right** на э́ту кни́гу распространя́ется áвторское прáво; *v.t.* обеспéчи|вать, -ть áвторское прáво на+*a.*; **∼-typist** *n.* машини́стка-переписчица.

copyist ['kɒpɪɪst] *n.* переписчик, копирóвщик.

coquet [kɒ'ket, kəʊ-] *v.i.* кокéтничать (*impf.*).
coquetry ['kɒkɪtrɪ, 'kəʊk-] *n.* кокéтство.
coquette [kɒ'ket, kə'ket] *n.* кокéтка.
coquettish [kɒ'ketɪʃ, kə'ketɪʃ] *adj.* кокéтливый.
cor [kɔ:(r)] *int.* (*vulg. or joc.*) Гóсподи!; Бóже мой!
coral ['kɒr(ə)l] *n.* корáлл; (*attr., also fig.*) корáлловый.
cor anglais [kɔ:r 'ɒŋgleɪ, ɑ̃'gleɪ] *n.* англи́йский рожóк.
corbel ['kɔ:b(ə)l] *n.* поясóк, вы́ступ; ни́ша.
corbie ['kɔ:bɪ] *n.* (*Sc.*) вóрон.
cord [kɔ:d] *n.* (*rope, string*) верёвка, бечёвка; (*flex*) шнур; **spinal ~** спиннóй мозг; **vocal ~s** голосовы́е свя́зки (*f. pl.*).
v.t. свя́з|ывать, -áть верёвкой; **~ed** (*ribbed*) в рýбчик; рýбчатый.
cordage ['kɔ:dɪdʒ] *n.* (*naut.*) такелáж; снáсти (*pl., g.* -éй).
cordial ['kɔ:dɪəl] *n.* стимули́рующее сердéчное срéдство; подслащённый напи́ток.
adj. (*friendly*) сердéчный, радýшный; (*stimulating*) стимули́рующий; **I took a ~ dislike to him** я всей душóй невзлюби́л егó.
cordiality [,kɔ:dɪ'ælɪtɪ] *n.* сердéчность, радýшие.
cordillera [,kɔ:dɪ'ljeərə] *n.* Кордилье́ры (*f. pl.*).
cordite ['kɔ:daɪt] *n.* корди́т.
cordless ['kɔ:dlɪs] *adj.* беспроводнóй, бесшнуровóй; **~ telephone** беспроводнóй телефóн.
cordon ['kɔ:d(ə)n] *n.* **1.** (*of police etc.*) кордóн. **2.** (*ribbon*) (óрденская) лéнта.
v.t. (*also* **~ off**) оцеп|ля́ть, -и́ть.
cordon bleu [,kɔ:dɒn 'blɜ:, ,kɔ:dɔ̃] *n.* первоклáссный пóвар.
cordovan ['kɔ:dəv(ə)n] *n.* кордóвская кóжа.
corduroy ['kɔ:dərɔɪ, -djʊ,rɔɪ] *n.* вельвéт; рýбчатый плис; (*pl., ~ trousers*) вельвéтовые брю́к|и (*pl., g.* —).
core [kɔ:(r)] *n.* **1.** (*of fruit*) сердцеви́на; (*fig.*) центр, ядрó, суть; **rotten at the ~** гнилóй изнутри́; **English to the ~** англичáнин до мóзга костéй; **this is the ~ of his argument** э́то — суть егó аргумéнта; **hard ~ of a problem** суть проблéмы; **hard ~** (*attr.*) закоренéлый, отчáянный. **2.** (*elec.*) жи́ла кáбеля; (*of nuclear reactor*) акти́вная зóна.
v.t. вырезáть, вы́резать сердцеви́ну *+g.*
co-religionist [,kəʊrɪ'lɪdʒənɪst] *n.* единовéр|ец (*fem.* -ка).
corer ['kɔ:(r)ə(r)] *n.* (*cul.*) нож для вырезáния сердцеви́ны из плодóв.
co-respondent [,kəʊrɪ'spɒnd(ə)nt] *n.* (*leg.*) соответчик (в бракоразвóдном процéссе).
Corfu [kɔ:'fu:] *n.* Кóрфу (*m. indecl.*).
corgi ['kɔ:gɪ] *n.* кóрги (*m. indecl.*).
coriaceous [,kɒrɪ'eɪʃəs] *adj.* кóжистый.
coriander [,kɒrɪ'ændə(r)] *n.* (*bot., also* **~ seed**) кориáндр; (*cul.*) fresh (leaves) кинзá.
Corinthian [kə'rɪnθɪən] *n.* кори́нфян|ин (*fem.* -ка).
adj. кори́нфский.
cork [kɔ:k] *n.* (*material, stopper*) прóбка; (*attr.*) прóбковый; (*float*) поплавóк.
v.t. (*stop up*) зат|ыкáть, -кнýть прóбкой; **~ up one's feelings** сдéрживать (*impf.*) свои́ чýвства; (*blacken, e.g. face*) мáзать (*impf.*) жжёной прóбкой; **the wine is ~ed** винó отдаёт прóбкой.
cpd. **~screw** *n.* штóпор; *v.i.* дви́гаться (*impf.*) по спирáли.
corker ['kɔ:kə(r)] *n.* (*sl., excellent or astonishing thg. or pers.*) (нéчто) шикáрное/потрясáющее; блеск.
corking ['kɔ:kɪŋ] *adj.* (*sl., excellent*) шикáрный.
corky ['kɔ:kɪ] *adj.* (*of taste*) отдаю́щий прóбкой.
cormorant ['kɔ:mərənt] *n.* большóй баклáн.
corn¹ [kɔ:n] *n.* **1.** (*grain, seed*) зернó. **2.** (*cereals in general*) зерновы́е (*pl.*), хлеб; **~ exchange** хлéбная би́ржа. **3.** (*wheat*) пшени́ца; **a field of ~** пшени́чное пóле. **4.** (*US, maize*) кукурýза.
cpds. **~-chandler** *n.* рóзничный торгóвец зернóм; **~-cob** *n.* стéржень (*m.*) кукурýзного почáтка; **~crake** *n.* коростéль (*m.*); **~-factor** *n.* торгóвец зернóм; **~flakes** *n. pl.* корнфлéкс; **~flour** *n.* кукурýзная/ри́совая мукá; **~flower** *n.* васи́лёк.
corn² [kɔ:n] *n.* (*on foot*) мозóль; **tread on s.o.'s ~s** (*fig.*) наступи́ть (*pf.*) комý-н. на люби́мую мозóль.
cpd. **~-plaster** *n.* мозóльный плáстырь.
corn³ [kɔ:n] *v.t.*: **~ed beef** солони́на.
cornea ['kɔ:nɪə] *n.* рогови́ца; роговáя оболóчка.
cornel ['kɔ:n(ə)l] *n.* кизи́л.
cornelian [kɔ:'ni:lɪən] *n.* сердоли́к.
corner ['kɔ:nə(r)] *n.* **1.** (*place where lines etc. meet*) ýгол; **at, on the ~** на углý; **round the ~** (*lit.*) за углóм; (*fig., near*) ря́дом, поблизости; **cut a ~** (*of car*) срéзать (*pf.*) поворóт; **he was driven into a ~** (*fig.*) он был зáгнан в ýгол (*or* припёрт к стенé); **in a tight ~** в затруднéнии; **turn the ~** (*of illness*) благополýчно перенести́ (*pf.*) кри́зис (болéзни); **~ of one's eye** крáешек глáза; **he looked out of the ~ of his eye** он следи́л уголкóм глáза; он наблюдáл укрáдкой. **2.** (*hidden place etc.*) уголóк, закоýлок; **money hidden in odd ~s** дéньги, припря́танные по уголкáм и закоýлкам. **3.** (*region*) край; **all the ~s of the earth** все уголки́ земли́. **4.** (*comm.*) кóрнер; спекуляти́вная скýпка; **he made a ~ in wheat** он сдéлал кóрнер на пшени́це. **5.** (*football*) угловóй удáр, кóрнер.
v.t. заг|оня́ть, -нáть в ýгол; **the fugitive was ~ed** беглецá загнáли в ýгол; **that question ~ed me** э́тим вопрóсом меня́ припёрли к стенé; **he ~ed the market** он завладéл ры́нком, скупи́в весь товáр.
v.i. (*of car*) брать, взять углы́.
cpds. **~-boy** *n.* ýличный зевáка (*m.*); **~-kick** *n.* угловóй удáр; **~-stone** *n.* угловóй кáмень; (*fig.*) краеугóльный кáмень.
cornet ['kɔ:nɪt] *n.* **1.** (*mus. instrument*) корнéт; корнéт-а-пистóн. **2.** (*officer*) корнéт. **3.** (*headdress*) чепéц. **4.** (*for ice-cream*) вáфельный рожóк.
cornettist [kɔ:'netɪst, 'kɔ:nɪtɪst] *n.* корнети́ст.
cornice ['kɔ:nɪs] *n.* **1.** (*archit.*) карни́з, свес. **2.** (*of snow*) нави́сшая глы́ба.
Cornish ['kɔ:nɪʃ] *n.* (*language*) корнуэ́льский язы́к.
adj. кóрнуóллский; (*of language*) корни́йский, кóрнский, корнуэ́льский.
cornucopia [,kɔ:njʊ'kəʊpɪə] *n.* рог изоби́лия.
corny ['kɔ:nɪ] *adj.* (*coll., hackneyed*) плóский, изби́тый.
corolla [kə'rɒlə] *n.* вéнчик.
corollary [kə'rɒlərɪ] *n.* слéдствие, вы́вод; сопýтствующее явлéние.
corona [kə'rəʊnə] *n.* (*astron.*) корóна; (*bot.*) корóна, венéц.
coronach ['kɒrənək, -nəx] *n.* похорóнная пéснь; похорóнный плач.
coronal¹ [kə'rəʊn(ə)l, 'kɒrən(ə)l] *n.* (*wreath, garland*) венóк.
coronal² [kə'rəʊn(ə)l, 'kɒrən(ə)l] *adj.*: **~ suture** (*anat.*) венéчный шов.
coronary ['kɒrənərɪ] *n.* коронаротромбóз.
adj. (*anat.*) коронáрный, венéчный; **~ artery** венéчная артéрия; **~ (thrombosis)** тромбóз венéчных артéрий, коронаротромбóз, инфáркт.
coronation [,kɒrə'neɪʃ(ə)n] *n.* коронáция.
coroner ['kɒrənə(r)] *n.* слéдователь (*m.*), ведýщий делá о наси́льственной или скоропости́жной смéрти.
coronet ['kɒrənɪt, -,net] *n.* (*small crown*) корóна, диадéма; (*garland*) венóк, венéц; (*of horse*) волосéнь.
Corp. [,kɔ:pə'reɪʃ(ə)n] *n.* (*abbr. of* **Corporation**) корпорáция.
corporal¹ ['kɔ:pr(ə)l] *n.* (*officer*) капрáл; **ship's ~** капрáл корабéльной поли́ции.
corporal² ['kɔ:pr(ə)l] *adj.* тéлесный; **~ punishment** тéлесное наказáние.
corporalcy ['kɔ:pr(ə)lsɪ] *n.* капрáльство.
corporate ['kɔ:pərət] *adj.* **1.** (*collective*) óбщий, коллекти́вный; **~ responsibility** коллекти́вная отвéтственность, кругoвáя порýка. **2.** (*of, forming a corporation*) корпорати́вный; **body ~** корпорáция, юриди́ческое лицó. **3.: ~ state** корпорати́вное госудáрство.
corporation [,kɔ:pə'reɪʃ(ə)n] *n.* (*public body*) корпорáция; (*US, company*) акционéрное óбщество; (*coll., paunch*) пýзо, брю́хо.
corporeal [kɔ:'pɔ:rɪəl] *adj.* телéсный, материáльный.
corps [kɔ:(r)] *n.* (*mil., dipl.*) кóрпус; **~ *de ballet*** кордебалéт.
corpse [kɔ:ps] *n.* труп.
corpulenc|e ['kɔ:pjʊləns], **-y** ['kɔ:pjʊlənsɪ] *nn.* полнотá, тýчность, дорóдность.
corpulent ['kɔ:pjʊlənt] *adj.* пóлный, тýчный, дорóдный.

corpus [ˈkɔːpəs] *n.* (*body of writings etc.*) свод, ко́декс; ~ **delicti** соста́в преступле́ния; **C~ Christi** пра́здник те́ла Христо́ва.

corpuscle [ˈkɔːpʌs(ə)l] *n.* корпу́скула, те́льце, части́ца.

corpuscular [kɔːˈpʌskjʊlə(r)] *adj.* корпускуля́рный.

corral [kɒˈrɑːl] *n.* (*enclosure*) заго́н.
v.t. (*drive together*) заг|оня́ть, -на́ть в заго́н.

correct [kəˈrekt] *adj.* **1.** (*right, true*) пра́вильный, ве́рный, то́чный; **an answer ~ to three places of decimals** отве́т с то́чностью до тре́тьего десяти́чного зна́ка. **2.** (*of behaviour*) корре́ктный.
v.t. **1.** (*make right*) испр|авля́ть, -а́вить; попр|авля́ть, -а́вить; **I ~ed my watch by the time signal** я вы́верил свои́ часы́ по сигна́лу вре́мени; ~ **proofs** пра́вить/держа́ть (*impf.*) корректу́ру/гра́нки. **2.** (*admonish, punish*) нака́з|ывать, -а́ть; де́лать, с- замеча́ние +*d*.

correction [kəˈrekʃ(ə)n] *n.* **1.** (*act of correcting*) исправле́ние, поправле́ние, пра́вка; **these figures are subject to** ~ э́ти ци́фры подлежа́т исправле́нию; **under** ~ е́сли я не ошиба́юсь. **2.** (*thg. substituted for what is wrong*) попра́вка, исправле́ние. **3.** (*punishment*) наказа́ние; **house of** ~ исправи́тельный дом.

correctional [kəˈrekʃ(ə)nəl] *adj.* исправи́тельный.

correctitude [kəˈrektɪˌtjuːd] *n.* корре́ктность.

corrective [kəˈrektɪv] *n.* корректи́в, попра́вка.
adj. исправи́тельный.

correctness [kəˈrektnɪs] *n.* пра́вильность, ве́рность, то́чность; (*of behaviour*) корре́ктность.

corrector [kəˈrektə(r)] *n.* корре́ктор.

correlate [ˈkɒrəˌleɪt, ˈkɒrɪ-] *v.t.* прив|оди́ть, -ести́ в соотноше́ние.

correlation [ˌkɒrəˈleɪʃ(ə)n, ˌkɒrɪ-] *n.* соотноше́ние, корреля́ция.

correlative [kɒˈrelətɪv, kə-] *n.* корреля́т.
adj. соотноси́тельный, корреляти́вный.

correspond [ˌkɒrɪˈspɒnd] *v.i.* **1.** (*match, harmonize*) соотве́тствовать (*impf.*) (+*d.*). **2.** (*exchange letters*) перепи́сываться (*impf.*) (с+*i.*).

correspondence [ˌkɒrɪˈspɒnd(ə)ns] *n.* **1.** (*analogy, agreement*) соотве́тствие. **2.** (*letter-writing*) корреспонде́нция, перепи́ска; **I am in ~ with him** я с ним перепи́сываюсь; **he dealt with his ~** он разобра́л свою́ корреспонде́нцию; ~ **column** ру́брика пи́сем (в газе́те); ~ **course** курс зао́чного обуче́ния.

correspondent [ˌkɒrɪˈspɒnd(ə)nt] *n.* (*writer of letters; reporter*) корреспонде́нт; **he is a good ~** он добросо́вестный корреспонде́нт.

corresponding [ˌkɒrɪˈspɒndɪŋ] *adj.* **1.** (*matching*) соотве́тственный, соотве́тствующий. **2.:** ~ **member** (*of a society*) член-корреспонде́нт.

corridor [ˈkɒrɪˌdɔː(r)] *n.* коридо́р.

corrigend|um [ˌkɒrɪˈgendəm, -ˈdʒendəm] *n.* опеча́тка; (*pl., list of ~a*) спи́сок опеча́ток.

corrigible [ˈkɒrɪdʒɪb(ə)l] *adj.* поправи́мый; (*of pers.*) исправи́мый.

corroborate [kəˈrɒbəˌreɪt] *v.t.* подтвер|жда́ть, -ди́ть; подкреп|ля́ть, -и́ть.

corroboration [kəˌrɒbəˈreɪʃ(ə)n] *n.* подтвержде́ние; **in ~** в подтвержде́ние (*чего*).

corroborat|ive [kəˈrɒbərətɪv], **-ory** [kəˈrɒbərətərɪ] *adj.* подтвержда́ющий, подкрепля́ющий.

corroborator [kəˈrɒbərəɪtə(r)] *n.* подтвержда́ющий, подкрепля́ющий.

corrode [kəˈrəʊd] *v.t.* разъ|еда́ть, -е́сть.
v.i. ржаве́ть, за-.

corrosion [kəˈrəʊʒ(ə)n] *n.* корро́зия, разъеда́ние, ржа́вчина.

corrosive [kəˈrəʊsɪv] *adj.* коррози́йный, разъеда́ющий, е́дкий; (*fig.*) разъеда́ющий.

corrosiveness [kəˈrəʊsɪvnɪs] *n.* коррози́йное сво́йство.

corrugate [ˈkɒrʊˌgeɪt] *v.t.* гофрирова́ть (*impf., pf.*); **~d iron** волни́стое/рифлёное желе́зо.

corrugation [ˌkɒrʊˈgeɪʃ(ə)n] *n.* гофриро́вка, рифле́ние.

corrupt [kəˈrʌpt] *adj.* **1.** (*decomposed*) разложи́вшийся. **2.** (*depraved*) развращённый, испо́рченный. **3.** (*venal*) прода́жный, (*coll.*) подкупно́й; ~ **practices** корру́пция, подку́пность и прода́жность. **4.** (*impure*) нечи́стый, испо́рченный; ~ **air** загрязнённый во́здух; ~ **Latin** испо́рченная латы́нь.
v.t. **1.** (*rot*) гнои́ть, с-. **2.** (*deprave*) развра|ща́ть, -ти́ть; разл|ага́ть, -ожи́ть. **3.** (*bribe*) подкуп|а́ть, -и́ть.
v.i. гнить, с-; по́ртиться, ис-; (*of body*) разл|ага́ться, -ожи́ться.

corruptibility [kəˈrʌptəˌbɪlɪtɪ] *n.* (*liability to decay*) подве́рженность по́рче/гние́нию; (*moral*) развраща́емость; (*accessibility to bribes*) подку́пность, прода́жность.

corruptible [kəˈrʌptəbəl] *adj.* **1.** (*liable to decay*) по́ртящийся. **2.** (*morally*) легко́ развраща́емый; (*bribable*) подкупно́й, прода́жный.

corruption [kəˈrʌpʃ(ə)n] *n.* **1.** (*physical*) по́рча, гние́ние, разложе́ние. **2.** (*depravity*) разложе́ние; развраще́ние. **3.** (*bribery*) корру́пция, взя́точничество. **4.** (*deformation*) по́рча, искаже́ние; **this word is a ~ of that** э́то сло́во — испо́рченный вариа́нт того́ сло́ва.

corsage [kɔːˈsɑːʒ] *n.* (*bodice*) корса́ж; (*US, flower adornment*) цвето́к, прико́лотый к корса́жу.

corsair [ˈkɔːseə(r)] *n.* (*pirate*) корса́р, пира́т; (*ship*) ка́пер.

corset [ˈkɔːsɪt] *n.* корсе́т.

corseted [ˈkɔːsɪtɪd] *adj.* затя́нутый в корсе́т.

Corsica [ˈkɔːsɪkə] *n.* Ко́рсика.

Corsican [ˈkɔːsɪkən] *n.* корсика́н|ец (*fem.* -ка).
adj. корсика́нский.

corslet [ˈkɔːslɪt] *n.* (*armour*) ла́т|ы (*pl., g.* —).

cortège [kɔːˈteɪʒ] *n.* корте́ж.

Cortes [ˈkɔːtes, -tez] *n.* корте́сы (*m. pl.*).

cortex [ˈkɔːteks] *n.* (*bark*) кора́; (*anat.*) кора́ больши́х полуша́рий головно́го мо́зга.

cortical [ˈkɔːtɪk(ə)l] *adj.* (*bot., anat.*) ко́рковый.

cortisone [ˈkɔːtɪˌzəʊn] *n.* кортизо́н.

corundum [kəˈrʌndəm] *n.* кору́нд.

coruscat|e [ˈkɒrəˌskeɪt] *v.i.* (*lit., fig.*) сверк|а́ть, -ну́ть; **~ing wit** сверка́ющее остоу́мие.

coruscation [ˌkɒrəˈskeɪʃ(ə)n] *n.* сверка́ние.

corvée [kɔːˈveɪ] *n.* (*hist.*) ба́рщина.

corvette [kɔːˈvet] *n.* корве́т.

corvine [ˈkɔːvaɪn] *adj.* воро́ний.

cos [kɒs] *n.* (*also* ~ **lettuce**) сала́т роме́н.

cosecant [kəʊˈsiːkənt] *n.* (*math.*) косе́канс.

co-seismal [kəʊˈsaɪzm(ə)l] *adj.*: ~ **line** косейсми́ческая крива́я.

cosh [kɒʃ] *n.* дуби́нка; (*sl.*) дрючо́к.
v.t. тра́хнуть (*pf.*) по голове́.

co-signatory [kəʊˈsɪgnətərɪ] *n.* лицо́/госуда́рство, подпи́сывающее (*что*) совме́стно с други́ми ли́цами/госуда́рствами.

cosine [ˈkəʊsaɪn] *n.* ко́синус.

cosiness [ˈkəʊzɪnɪs] *n.* ую́т.

cosmetic [kɒzˈmetɪk] *n.* косме́тика.
adj. космети́ческий.

cosmetician [ˌkɒzmeˈtɪʃ(ə)n] *n.* специали́ст по косме́тике; космети́чка.

cosmic [ˈkɒzmɪk] *adj.* косми́ческий.

cosmogony [kɒzˈmɒgənɪ] *n.* космого́ния.

cosmographer [kɒzˈmɒgrəfə(r)] *n.* космо́граф.

cosmography [kɒzˈmɒgrəfɪ] *n.* космогра́фия.

cosmologist [kɒzˈmɒlədʒɪst] *n.* космо́лог.

cosmology [kɒzˈmɒlədʒɪ] *n.* космоло́гия.

cosmonaut [ˈkɒzməˌnɔːt] *n.* космона́вт.

cosmopolit|an, -e [ˌkɒzməˈpɒlɪt(ə)n] *nn.* космополи́т.
adj. космополити́ческий.

cosmopolitanism [kɒzməˈpɒlɪtənˌɪz(ə)m] *n.* космополити́зм.

cosmos [ˈkɒzmɒs] *n.* (*universe*) ко́смос, вселе́нная.

Cossack [ˈkɒsæk] *n.* каза́|к (*fem.* -чка); (*pl., collect.*) каза́чество; (*attr.*) каза́цкий, каза́чий; ~ **hat** папа́ха.

cosset [ˈkɒsɪt] *v.t.* балова́ть (*impf.*); не́жить (*impf.*).

cost [kɒst] *n.* **1.** (*monetary*) цена́, сто́имость; ~ **price** себесто́имость; **he sold it at ~** он про́дал э́то по себесто́имости; ~ **accounting** хозрасчёт; **~, insurance and freight** (*abbr.* **c.i.f.**) сто́имость това́ра, страхова́ние и фрахт (*abbr.* сиф); ~ **of living** прожи́точный ми́нимум;

~ **of production** издéржки (*f. pl.*) произвóдства. **2.** (*expense, loss*) ценá; **at all ~s** любóй ценóй; **at the ~ of his life** ценóй жи́зни; **count the ~** (*fig.*) взвéсить (*pf.*) возмóжные послéдствия. **3.** (*pl., leg.*) судéбные издéржки (*f. pl.*); **he was awarded ~s** емý присуди́ли судéбные издéржки.

v.t. & i. **1.** (*involve expense*) стóить (*impf.*); об|ходи́ться, -ойти́сь (*кому во что*); **this ~ me £5** э́то стóило мне 5 фýнтов; э́то обошлóсь мне в 5 фýнтов; **it ~ me much trouble** э́то стóило мне значи́тельных хлопóт; **it will ~ you dear** э́то вам дóрого обойдётся. **2.** (*assess ~ of*) оцéн|ивать, -и́ть издéржки (*предприятия и т.п.*).

cpds. **~-effective** *adj.* рентáбельный; **~-effectiveness** *n.* рентáбельность.

costal ['kɒst(ə)l] *adj.* рёберный.

co-star ['kəʊstɑ:(r)] *n.* партнёр (*fem.* -ша) (в другóй глáвной рóли).

v.t.: **a picture ~ring X and Y** фильм с учáстием двух звёзд — X и Y.

v.i.: **they ~red in that picture** они́ снимáлись в э́том фи́льме в глáвных ролях.

Costa Rica ['kɒstə 'ri:kə] *n.* Кóста-Ри́ка.

Costa Rican ['kɒstə 'ri:kən] *n.* костарикáнец (*fem.* -ка).

adj. костарикáнский.

coster(monger) ['kɒstə,mʌŋgə(r)] *n.* ýличный торгóвец фрýктами и овощáми.

costing ['kɒstɪŋ] *n.* калькуля́ция издéржек произвóдства (*чего*).

costive ['kɒstɪv] *adj.* страдáющий запóром.

costiveness ['kɒstɪvnɪs] *n.* запóр.

costliness ['kɒstlɪnɪs] *n.* дороговизнá; высóкая ценá.

costly ['kɒstlɪ] *adj.* дорогóй, дорогостóящий.

costume ['kɒstju:m] *n.* костю́м, плáтье, одéжда; (*coat and skirt; fancy or period dress*) костю́м; (*attr.*): **~ ball** костюми́рованный бал; бал-маскарáд; **~ jewellery** ювели́рные украшéния к плáтью; **~ play** истори́ческая пьéса.

v.t. (*a pers.*) од|евáть, -éть; **~ a play** (*design ~s*) дéлать, с- эски́зы костю́мов к пьéсе.

costum(i)er [kɒ'stju:mɪə(r)] *n.* (*theatr.*) костюмéр; (*maker or seller of costumes*) торгóвец театрáльными и маскарáдными костю́мами.

cosy (*US* **cozy**) ['kəʊzɪ] *adj.* ую́тный.

cot[1] [kɒt] *n.* (*small bed*) дéтская кровáтка; (*cradle*) лю́лька, колыбéль; **~ death** внезáпная смéрть (ребёнка груднóго вóзраста).

cpd. **~-case** *n.* лежáчий больнóй.

cot[2] [kɒt] *n.* (*cottage*) хи́жина.

cotangent [kəʊ'tændʒ(ə)nt] *n.* котáнгенс.

co-tenancy [kəʊ'tenənsɪ] *n.* соарéнда.

co-tenant [kəʊ'tenənt] *n.* соарендáтор.

coterie ['kəʊtərɪ] *n.* кружóк; (*pej.*) клика.

coterminous [kəʊ'tɜ:mɪnəs] *adj.* смéжный, грани́чащий; (*in meaning*) синоними́чный.

cotill(i)on [kə'tɪljən] *n.* котильóн.

cottage ['kɒtɪdʒ] *n.* коттéдж; зáгородный дом, дóмик, дáча; **~ cheese** (прессóванный) твóрóг; **~ industry** надóмное произвóдство; кустáрная промы́шленность; **~ pie** картóфельная запекáнка с мя́сом.

cottager ['kɒtɪdʒə(r)] *n.* живýщий в коттéдже; (*home worker*) кустáрь (*m.*).

cotton[1] ['kɒt(ə)n] *n.* **1.** (*plant*) хлóпок, хлопчáтник. **2.** (*fabric*) хлопчáтая бумáга; (хлопчáто)бумáжная ткань; **~ print** си́тец. **3.** (*thread*) ни́тки (*f. pl.*); (*piece of thread*) ни́тка; **a needle and ~** игóлка с ни́ткой. **4.** (*attr.*) хлóпковый, хлопчáтый, хлопчáтобумáжный. **5.** (*US*) = **~-wool**

cpds. **~-cake** *n.* хлóпковый жмых; **~-gin** *n.* хлопкоочисти́тельная маши́на; **~-grass** *n.* пуши́ца; **~-mill** *n.* хлопкопряди́льная/хлопкоткáцкая фáбрика; **~-picker** *n.* (*pers.*) хлопкорóб; (*machine*) хлопкоубóрочная маши́на; **~-plant** *n.* хлопчáтник; **~-planter** *n.* хлопковóд; **~-seed** *n.* хлóпковое сéмя; семенá (*nt. pl.*) хлопчáтника; **~-spinner** *n.* хлопкопряди́льщик; **~tail** *n.* америкáнский крóлик; **~-waste** *n.* хлóпковые отбрóсы (*m. pl.*); угáр; **~-wool** *n.* вáта; хлóпок-сырéц; **wrap in ~-wool** (*fig.*) оберегáть (*impf.*); трясти́сь (*impf.*) над+*i.*

cotton[2] ['kɒt(ə)n] *v.i.* (*coll.*): **she ~ed** (*took a liking*) **to him** он пришёлся ей по душé; **~ on to** поня́ть (*pf.*), (*coll.*) усéчь (*pf.*).

cotyledon [,kɒtɪ'li:d(ə)n] *n.* семядóля.

couch[1] [kaʊtʃ] *n.* (*sofa*) кушéтка, дивáн; (*bed*) кровáть.

v.t. **1.**: **~** (*lower*) **a spear** взять (*pf.*) копьё наперевéс (*or* нá руку). **2.** (*express*): **he ~ed his reply in friendly terms** он облёк свой отвéт в дрýжескую фóрму.

v.i. (*of animal: crouch*) притаи́ться (*pf.*).

couch[2] [ku:tʃ, kaʊtʃ] *n.* (*also* **~-grass**) пырéй ползýчий.

couchette [ku:'ʃet] *n.* спáльное мéсто.

cougar ['ku:gə(r)] *n.* пýма, кугуáр.

cough [kɒf] *n.* кáшель (*m.*); **he has a bad ~** у негó си́льный кáшель; **he gave a warning ~** он предупреждáюще кашлянýл.

v.t. & i. кáшлять (*impf.*); **~ up** (*lit.*) откáшл|ивать, -янýть; (*fig., coll.*) выклáдывать, вы́ложить.

cpds. **~-drop, ~-lozenge** *nn.* пасти́лка/таблéтка от кáшля; **~-medicine, ~-mixture** *nn.* микстýра от кáшля.

could [kʊd] *v. aux., see* **can**[2]

coulisse [ku:'li:s] *n.* (*pl., theatr.*) кули́сы (*f. pl.*).

coulomb ['ku:lɒm] *n.* кулóн.

coulter ['kəʊltə(r)] *n.* нож плýга; резáк, резéц.

council ['kaʊns(ə)l] *n.* совéт; **town ~** городскóй совéт; муниципалитéт; **~ of war** воéнный совéт; **~ of physicians** консилиум врачéй; **Church ~** церкóвный собóр.

cpds. **~-chamber** *n.* зал заседáний совéта; **~-house** *n.* (*dwelling*) муниципáльный дом; жилóй дом, принадлежáщий муниципáльному совéту.

councillor ['kaʊnsələ(r)] *n.* член совéта; совéтник.

counsel ['kaʊns(ə)l] *n.* **1.** (*advice, consultation*) совéт, совещáние; **take ~ with s.o.** совещáться (*impf.*) с кем-н.; **keep one's (own) ~** помáлкивать (*impf.*); **a ~ of perfection** (*fig.*) превосхóдный, но невыполни́мый совéт; **darken ~** (*obscure the issue*) запýтать (*pf.*) дéло. **2.** (*barrister(s)*) адвокáт; **~ for the defence** защи́тник; **~ for the plaintiff** адвокáт истцá; **~'s opinion** пи́сьменное заключéние адвокáта.

counsellor ['kaʊnsələ(r)] *n.* совéтник.

counsellorship ['kaʊnsələ(r),ʃɪp] *n.* дóлжность совéтника.

count[1] [kaʊnt] *n.* (*nobleman*) граф.

count[2] [kaʊnt] *n.* **1.** (*reckoning*) счёт, подсчёт; **keep ~** считáть (*impf.*); вести́ (*det.*) счёт; **lose ~** потеря́ть (*pf.*) счёт. **2.** (*total*) итóг; **the ~ was 200** итóг равня́лся 200 (двумстáм). **3.** (*leg.*) пункт обвини́тельного заключéния; **he was found guilty on all ~s** егó признáли винóвным по всем пýнктам обвини́тельного заключéния. **4.** (*boxing*): **he took** (*or* **went down for**) **the ~** он был нокаути́рован.

v.t. (*number, reckon*) считáть, со-; подсчи́т|ывать, -áть; пересчи́т|ывать, -áть; **he ~ed (up) the men** он пересчитáл солдáт; **~ your change!** провéрьте сдáчу!; **~ ten!** сосчитáйте до десяти́!; **50 people, not ~ing the children** 50 человéк, не считáя детéй; **I ~ him among my friends** я считáю егó моим дрýгом; **~ me in/out!** включи́те/исключи́те меня́; **he ~s himself our friend** он считáет себя нáшим дрýгом; **I ~ myself fortunate to be here** я счáстлив, что нахожýсь здесь; **I shall ~ it an honour to serve you** я почтý за чéсть служи́ть вам; **do not ~ that against him** не стáвьте емý э́того в винý; **the boxer was ~ed out** боксёр был объя́влен нокаути́рованным; **the meeting was ~ed out** заседáние бы́ло распýщено из-за отсýтствия квóрума.

v.i. **1.** (*reckon, number*) считáть (*impf.*); **~ up to 10!** считáйте до десяти́!; **~ down from 10 to 0!** считáйте в обрáтном поря́дке от десяти́ до нуля́!; **~ing-frame** (*abacus*) счёт|ы (*pl., g.* -ов); **~ing-house** бухгалтéрия; **~ing-out rhyme** (*at games*) считáлка. **2.** (*be reckoned*) считáться (*impf.*); **that doesn't ~** э́то не в счёт (*or* не считáется); **~ for much** имéть большóе значéние; **~ for little** не имéть (*impf.*) большóго значéния; немнóго стóить (*impf.*); **~ for nothing** не имéть никакóго значéния; не идти́ в счёт; ничегó не стóить; **he ~s among our friends** он считáется нáшим дрýгом. **3.** (*rely*) рассчи́тывать (*impf.*) (на+*a.*); **I ~ (up)on you to help** я рассчи́тываю на ва́шу по́мощь.

cpds. **~-down** *n.* обра́тный счёт; отсчёт вре́мени; **~-out** *n.* ро́спуск заседа́ния из-за отсу́тствия кво́рума.

countable ['kaʊntəb(ə)l] *adj.* (*gram.*) исчисля́емый.

countenance ['kaʊntɪnəns] *n.* **1.** (*face*) лицо́, о́блик; выраже́ние лица́. **2.** (*composure*) споко́йствие; **keep one's ~** сохраня́ть (*impf.*) невозмути́мое выраже́ние лица́; **put s.o. out of ~** привести́ (*pf.*) кого́-н. в замеша́тельство. **3.** (*sanction*) подде́ржка.

v.t. подде́рж|ивать, -а́ть.

counter[1] ['kaʊntɪnəns] *n.* **1.** (*at games*) фи́шка, ма́рка; **bargaining ~** (*fig.*) ко́зырь (*m.*) (в запа́се). **2.** (*in shop*) прила́вок; **under the ~** (*fig.*) из-под полы́/прила́вка. **3.** (*device for counting*) счётчик; **Geiger ~** счётчик Ге́йгера.

cpd. **~-jumper** *n.* (*pej.*) прика́зчик.

counter[2] ['kaʊntɪnəns] *n.* (*rejoinder, counterstroke*) встре́чный уда́р; противоде́йствие.

adj. & *adv.* (*contrary*) противополо́жный; напро́тив; **this runs ~ to my wishes** э́то идёт вразре́з с мои́ми жела́ниями.

v.t. & *i.* (*oppose, parry*) противоде́йствовать (*impf.*) +*d.*; отра|жа́ть, -зи́ть.

counteract [ˌkaʊntə'rækt] *v.t.* противоде́йствовать (*impf.*) +*d.*

counteraction [ˌkaʊntər'ækʃ(ə)n] *n.* противоде́йствие.

counter-agent ['kaʊntər'eɪdʒ(ə)nt] *n.* контраге́нт.

counter-attack ['kaʊntərəˌtæk] *n.* контрата́ка, контрнаступле́ние.

v.t. & *i.* контратакова́ть (*impf., pf.*).

counter-attraction ['kaʊntərəˌtrækʃ(ə)n] *n.* зама́нчивая альтернати́ва.

counterbalance ['kaʊntəˌbæləns] *n.* противове́с.

v.t. уравнове́|шивать, -сить.

counterblast ['kaʊntəˌblɑ:st] *n.* отве́тный уда́р/вы́пад.

counterblow ['kaʊntərˌbləʊ] *n.* контруда́р; встре́чный уда́р.

countercharge ['kaʊntəˌtʃɑ:dʒ] *n.* встре́чное обвине́ние.

v.t. предъяв|ля́ть, -и́ть встре́чное обвине́ние +*p.*

counter-claim ['kaʊntəˌkleɪm] *n.* встре́чный иск; контробвине́ние.

v.t. предъяв|ля́ть, -и́ть встре́чный иск (*кому*) на+*a.*

counter-clockwise [ˌkaʊntə'klɒkwaɪz] *adj.* & *adv.* (дви́жущийся) про́тив часово́й стре́лки.

counter-demonstration ['kaʊntərˌdemən'streɪʃən] *n.* ко́нтрдемонстра́ция; встре́чная демонстра́ция.

counter-espionage [ˌkaʊntər'espɪəˌnɑ:ʒ, -ɪdʒ] *n.* контрразве́дка.

counterfeit ['kaʊntəfɪt, -ˌfi:t] *n.* подде́лка, подло́г.

adj. подде́льный, подло́жный.

v.t. & *i.* подде́л|ывать, -ать; (*fig., simulate*) подража́ть (*impf.*) +*d.*; притвор|я́ться, -и́ться.

counterfeiter ['kaʊntəfɪtə(r), -ˌfi:tə(r)] *n.* фальшивомоне́тчик.

counterfoil ['kaʊntəˌfɔɪl] *n.* корешо́к (че́ка, квита́нции *и т.п.*).

counter-intelligence [ˌkaʊntərɪn'telɪdʒ(ə)ns] *n.* контрразве́дка.

counter-irritant [ˌkaʊntər'ɪrɪt(ə)nt] *n.* отвлека́ющее/ ревульси́вное сре́дство.

countermand [ˌkaʊntə'mɑ:nd] *v.t.* отмен|я́ть, -и́ть.

countermarch ['kaʊntəˌmɑ:tʃ] *n.* контрма́рш.

v.i. марширова́ть (*impf.*) в обра́тном направле́нии.

counter-measure ['kaʊntəˌmeʒə(r)] *n.* встре́чная ме́ра, контрме́ра.

countermine ['kaʊntəˌmaɪn] *n.* контрми́на.

v.t. контрмини́ровать (*impf., pf.*); (*fig.*) расстр|а́ивать, -о́ить про́иски.

counter-move ['kaʊntəˌmu:v] *n.* контруда́р.

counter-offensive ['kaʊntərəˌfensɪv] *n.* контрнаступле́ние.

counter-order ['kaʊntərˌɔ:də(r)] *n.* контрприка́з; отменя́ющий прика́з.

counterpane ['kaʊntəˌpeɪn] *n.* покрыва́ло.

counterpart ['kaʊntəˌpɑ:t] *n.* па́ра (*к чему*), дополне́ние; (*pers.*) двойни́к, колле́га (*c.g.*).

counterplot ['kaʊntəˌplɒt] *n.* контрза́говор.

counterpoint ['kaʊntəˌpɔɪnt] *n.* контрапу́нкт.

counterpoise ['kaʊntəˌpɔɪz] *n.* противове́с, равнове́сие.

v.t. уравнове́|шивать, -сить.

counter-pressure ['kaʊntərˌpreʃə(r)] *n.* противодавле́ние.

counter-productive [ˌkaʊntəprə'dʌktɪv] *adj.* приводя́щий к обра́тным результа́там; нецелесообра́зный.

counter-propaganda ['kaʊntərˌprɒpə'gændə)] *n.* контрпропага́нда.

counter-proposal ['kaʊntəprəˌpəʊz(ə)l] *n.* встре́чное предложе́ние; контрпредложе́ние.

counter-reformation [ˌkaʊntəˌrefə'meɪʃ(ə)n] *n.* контрреформа́ция.

counter-revolution [ˌkaʊntəˌrevə'lu:ʃ(ə)n] *n.* контрреволю́ция.

counter-revolutionary [ˌkaʊntəˌrevə'lu:ʃənərɪ] *n.* контрреволюционе́р.

adj. контрреволюцио́нный.

counterscarp ['kaʊntəˌskɑ:p] *n.* контрэска́рп.

countersign ['kaʊntəˌsaɪn] *n.* (*watchword*) паро́ль (*m.*), о́тзыв.

v.t. (*add signature to*) ста́вить, по- втору́ю по́дпись на+*p.*; скреп|ля́ть, -и́ть по́дписью.

countersignature ['kaʊntəˌsɪgnətʃə(r)] *n.* втора́я по́дпись.

counter-spy ['kaʊntəˌspaɪ] *n.* контрразве́дчик.

counterstroke ['kaʊntəˌstrəʊk] *n.* контруда́р; отве́тный уда́р.

countertenor ['kaʊntəˌtenə(r)] *n.* те́нор-альт.

countervail [ˌkaʊntə'veɪl, 'kaʊntə-] *v.t.* & *i.* компенси́ровать (*impf., pf.*); **~ing duty** (*fin.*) компенсацио́нная по́шлина.

counterweight ['kaʊntəˌweɪt] *n.* противове́с, контргру́з.

countess ['kaʊntɪs] *n.* графи́ня.

countless ['kaʊntlɪs] *adj.* бесчи́сленный, несчётный, неисчисли́мый.

countrified ['kʌntrɪˌfaɪd] *adj.* име́ющий дереве́нский вид; **~ person** дереве́нщина (*c.g.*).

country ['kʌntrɪ] *n.* **1.** (*geog., pol.*) страна́; **~ of birth** ро́дина. **2.** (*motherland*) ро́дина, оте́чество; (*liter.*) отчи́зна. **3.** (*opp. town*) дере́вня; **in the ~** за́ городом, на да́че; (**~***side*) приро́да, се́льская ме́стность; **~ life** се́льская/ дереве́нская жизнь; **~ cousin** провинциа́л (*fem.* -ка), (*coll.*) дереве́нщина (*c.g.*); **~ dance** контрда́нс; **~ gentleman** землевладе́лец, поме́щик; **~ house, seat** поме́стье; **~ club** за́городный клуб. **4.** (*terrain*) ме́стность; **difficult ~** труднопроходи́мая ме́стность; **wooded ~** леси́стая ме́стность. **5.** (*fig., domain*) о́бласть, сфе́ра; **the subject is unknown ~ to me** э́то неизве́стная для меня́ о́бласть. **6.: go to the ~** (*pol.*) распусти́ть (*pf.*) парла́мент и назна́чить (*pf.*) но́вые вы́боры.

cpds. **~-bred** *adj.* вы́росший в дере́вне; **~folk** *n.* се́льские жи́тели (*m. pl.*); **~man** *n.* дереве́нский/ се́льский жи́тель (*m.*); (*fellow-~man*) соотечественник, земля́к; **~side** *n.* се́льская ме́стность; ландша́фт; **~-wide** *adj.* распространя́ющийся на всю страну́; *adv.* по всей стране́; **~woman** *n.* дереве́нская/се́льская жи́тельница; (*fellow-~woman*) соотечественница, земля́чка.

county ['kaʊntɪ] *n.* гра́фство; **~ town** гла́вный го́род гра́фства; **~ families** се́мьи (*f. pl.*) дже́нтри.

coup [ku:] *n.* уда́чный ход; *see also* **~ d'état**

cpds. **~ de grâce** *n.* заверша́ющий уда́р; **~ d'état** *n.* госуда́рственный переворо́т.

coupé ['ku:peɪ] *n.* двухме́стный закры́тый автомоби́ль.

couple ['kʌp(ə)l] *n.* **1.** (*objects or people*) па́ра; **married ~** супру́жеская па́ра; **engaged ~** жени́х и неве́ста. **2.** (*leash*) сво́ра.

v.t. **1.** (*rail*) сцеп|ля́ть, -и́ть. **2.** (*associate, assemble*) соедин|я́ть, -и́ть; свя́з|ывать, -а́ть; **the two symphonies are ~d on one record** обе симфо́нии запи́саны на одну́ пласти́нку; **the name of Oxford is ~d with the idea of learning** О́ксфорд ассоцийруется с нау́чными заня́тиями. **3.** (*cause to breed*) спа́р|ивать, -ить; случ|а́ть, -и́ть.

v.i. (*unite sexually*) совокуп|ля́ться, -и́ться; (*of animals*) спа́ри|ваться, -ться.

coupler ['kʌplə(r)] *n.* (*tech.*) сце́пщик.

couplet ['kʌplɪt] *n.* рифмо́ванное двусти́шие.

coupling ['kʌplɪŋ] *n.* (*rail.*) сцепле́ние, сце́пка; (*tech.*) связь, му́фта; (*copulation*) совокупле́ние, спа́ривание, слу́чка.

coupon ['ku:pɒn] *n.* купо́н, тало́н.

courage ['kʌrɪdʒ] *n.* хра́брость, сме́лость, му́жество; **take, pluck up ~** мужа́ться (*impf.*); соб|ира́ться, -ра́ться с ду́хом; **lose ~** пасть (*pf.*) ду́хом; **take one's ~ in both hands** мобилизова́ть (*impf.*, *pf.*) всё своё му́жество; **Dutch ~** хра́брость во хмелю́; **he has the ~ of his convictions** он де́йствует согла́сно свои́м убежде́ниям; **I had not the ~ to refuse** у меня́ не хвати́ло ду́ху отказа́ться; **~!** (*as int.*) мужа́йтесь!

courageous [kə'reɪdʒəs] *adj.* хра́брый, сме́лый, му́жественный.

courgette [kʊə'ʒet] *n.* кабачо́к.

courier ['kʊrɪə(r)] *n.* (*messenger*) курье́р, на́рочный; (*travel guide*) экскурсово́д, сопровожда́ющий.

course [kɔːs] *n.* **1.** (*movement, process*) ход, тече́ние; **~ of events** ход собы́тий; **in ~ of time** с тече́нием вре́мени; **in the ordinary ~** (*of events*) при норма́льном разви́тии собы́тий; **in due ~** в до́лжное/своё вре́мя; до́лжным о́бразом; **of ~** коне́чно; **as a matter of ~** обы́чным поря́дком; **he takes my help as a matter of ~** он принима́ет мою́ по́мощь как не́что само́ собо́й разуме́ющееся; **the disease must run its ~** боле́знь должна́ пройти́ все ста́дии; **I let matters take their ~** я пусти́л дела́ на самотёк; **the law took its ~** де́ло пошло́ зако́нным хо́дом. **2.** (*direction*) курс, направле́ние; (*of a river*) тече́ние; (*naut.*) курс; **our ~ is, lies due north** мы де́ржим курс (*or* направле́ние) на се́вер; **set ~** лечь (*pf.*) на курс; **we are on ~** мы идём по ку́рсу; **we are off ~** мы сби́лись с ку́рса. **3.** (*line of conduct*): **this is the only ~ open to us** э́то — еди́нственная ли́ния поведе́ния, досту́пная нам; **evil ~s** дурны́е привы́чки (*f. pl.*). **4.** (*race-~*) скаково́й круг, доро́жка; **stay the ~** (*fig.*) держа́ться (*impf.*) до конца́. **5.** (*series*) курс; **a ~ of lectures** курс ле́кций; **a ~ of treatment** курс лече́ния. **6.** (*cul.*) блю́до; **main ~** второ́е блю́до; **sweet ~** сла́дкое, десе́рт. **7.** (*masonry*) горизонта́льный ряд кла́дки.

v.t. & i. (*hunt*): **~ a hare** охо́титься (*impf.*) на за́йца с го́нчими.

v.i. (*run about*) бе́гать (*indet.*); (*of water*) бежа́ть (*det.*); (*of blood*) течь (*impf.*).

courser ['kɔːsə(r)] *n.* (*huntsman*) охо́тник с го́нчими.

coursing ['kɔːsɪŋ] *n.* охо́та с го́нчими.

court [kɔːt] *n.* **1.** (*yard*) двор. **2.** (*space for playing games*) площа́дка для игр; (*tennis*) корт; **hard ~** бетони́рованный корт; **grass ~** земляно́й корт. **3.** (*sovereign's etc.*) двор; **hold ~** (*maintain a ~*) содержа́ть (*impf.*) двор; **she was presented at ~** её предста́вили ко двору́; **a friend at ~** (*fig.*) проте́кция; **~ dress** придво́рный костю́м; **~ plaster** ли́пкий пла́стырь. **4.** (*leg.*) суд; **~ of law, justice** суд; **~ of inquiry** сле́дственная коми́ссия; **they settled (the case) out of ~** они́ пришли́ к (полюбо́вному) соглаше́нию; **put o.s. out of ~** потеря́ть (*pf.*) пра́во на иск; **he was brought to ~** (*for trial*) он предста́л пе́ред судо́м; **the judge had the ~ cleared** судья́ очи́стил зал от пу́блики. **5.: pay ~ to s.o.** уха́живать (*impf.*) за кем-н.

v.t. **1.** (*a woman*) уха́живать (*impf.*) за+*i.* **2.** (*seek*): **she ~ed his approval** она́ добива́лась его́ одобре́ния. **3.** (*risk*): **he is ~ing disaster** он игра́ет с огнём.

cpds. **~-card** *n.* фигу́рная ка́рта; **~-house** *n.* зда́ние суда́; **~-martial** *n.* вое́нный суд; *v.t.* суди́ть (*impf.*) вое́нным судо́м; **~-room** *n.* зал суда́; **~yard** *n.* двор.

courteous ['kɜːtɪəs] *adj.* ве́жливый, учти́вый.

courtesan [,kɔːtɪ'zæn, 'kɔːt-] *n.* куртиза́нка.

courtesy ['kɜːtɪsɪ] *n.* (*politeness*) ве́жливость, учти́вость; (*polite act*) любе́зность; **he is accorded the title by ~** ему́ присво́ен э́тот ти́тул по обы́чаю; **by ~ of Mr. X** с любе́зного разреше́ния г-на X.

courtier ['kɔːtɪə(r)] *n.* придво́рный.

courtliness ['kɔːtlɪnɪs] *n.* обходи́тельность.

courtly ['kɔːtlɪ] *adj.* обходи́тельный; **~ love** ры́царская любо́вь.

courtship ['kɔːtʃɪp] *n.* уха́живание.

cousin ['kʌz(ə)n] *n.* (*also* **first ~, ~ german**) (*male*) кузе́н; двою́родный брат; (*fem.*) кузи́на; двою́родная сестра́; **second ~** трою́родный брат (*fem.* трою́родная сестра́); **first ~ once removed** (*son or daughter of first ~*) двою́родный племя́нник (*fem.* двою́родная племя́нница); (*first ~ of parent*) двою́родный дя́дя (*fem.* двою́родная тётя); **our American ~s** на́ши америка́нские ро́дственники.

cpd. **~-in-law** *n.* (*wife's, husband's ~*) своя́|к (*fem.* -ченица).

cousinly ['kʌzənlɪ] *adj.* ро́дственный.

cousinship ['kʌzənʃɪp] *n.* родство́, свойство́.

couturier [kuː'tjʊərɪ,eɪ] *n.* модалье́р.

couvade [kuː'vɑːd] *n.* кува́да, паналуа́ (*indecl.*)

cove[1] [kəʊv] *n.* (*bay*) бу́хточка.

cove[2] [kəʊv] *n.* (*sl., fellow*) па́рень (*m.*), ма́лый.

coven ['kʌv(ə)n] *n.* шаба́ш ведьм.

covenant ['kʌvənənt] *n.* соглаше́ние, догово́р; **C~ of the League of Nations** уста́в Ли́ги На́ций; (*relig.*) заве́т.

v.t. & i. заключ|а́ть, -и́ть соглаше́ние; догов|а́риваться, -ори́ться (*с кем о чём*).

Coventry ['kɒvəntrɪ] *n.*: **send to ~** подв|ерга́ть, -е́ргнуть остраки́зму/бойко́ту.

cover ['kʌvə(r)] *n.* **1.** (*lid*) кры́шка, покры́шка. **2.** (*loose ~ing of chair etc.*) чехо́л; (*pl., bedclothes*) посте́ль. **3.** (*of book etc.*) переплёт, обло́жка; **I read the book from ~ to ~** я прочёл кни́гу от ко́рки до ко́рки; (*dust-~*) суперобло́жка. **4.** (*wrapper, envelope*) обёртка, конве́рт; **under separate ~** в отде́льном конве́рте. **5.** (*shelter, protection*) укры́тие, прикры́тие; **take ~** укр|ыва́ться, -ы́ться; **the ground provided no ~** укры́тия на ме́стности не́ было; **under ~ of darkness** под покро́вом темноты́; **remain ~ed** (*keep hat on*) не снима́ть (*impf.*) шля́пы. **6.** (*concealment*): **the fox broke ~** лиса́ вы́шла из укры́тия. **7.** (*pretence, pretext*) личи́на, ма́ска, ши́рма; **under ~ of friendship** под личи́ной дру́жбы; (*ostensible business, e.g. spy's*) кры́ша, вы́веска; **~ address** подставно́й а́дрес. **8.** (*mil., protective force*) прикры́тие; **fighter ~** прикры́тие истреби́телями. **9.** (*at table*) прибо́р; **~ charge** пла́та «за куве́рт». **10.** (*insurance*) страхова́ние. **11.** (*comm., fin.*) гаранти́йный фонд.

v.t. **1.** (*overspread etc.; also* **~ up, ~ over**) покр|ыва́ть, -ы́ть; закр|ыва́ть, -ы́ть; прикр|ыва́ть, -ы́ть; накр|ыва́ть, -ы́ть; **~ a chair** об|ива́ть, -и́ть стул; **cats are ~ed with hair** ко́шки покры́ты ше́рстью; **she ~ed her face in, with her hands** она́ закры́ла лицо́ рука́ми; **her face is ~ed with freckles** у неё всё лицо́ в весну́шках (*or* усе́яно весну́шками); **the hills are ~ed with pine-trees** холмы́ поросли́ со́снами; **the roads are ~ed with snow** доро́ги занесены́ сне́гом; **trees ~ed with blossom** дере́вья в цвету́; **well ~ed** (*with clothes*) тепло́ оде́тый; (*with flesh*) в те́ле; **the taxi ~ed us with mud** такси́ окати́ло нас гря́зью; **the city ~ed ten square miles** го́род раски́нулся на 10 квадра́тных миль; **~ed** (*indoor*) **court** (*for tennis*) закры́тый корт; **~ed way** кры́тая галере́я; **~ in a grave** зас|ыпа́ть, -ы́пать моги́лу. **2.** (*fig.*) покр|ыва́ть, -ы́ть; скр|ыва́ть, -ы́ть; **he laughed to ~ (up) his nervousness** он засмея́лся, что́бы скрыть своё волне́ние; **he ~ed himself with glory** он покры́л себя́ сла́вой. **3.** (*protect*) закр|ыва́ть, -ы́ть; прикр|ыва́ть, -ы́ть; **warships ~ed the landing** вое́нные корабли́ прикрыва́ли вы́садку войск; **are you ~ed against theft?** вы застрахо́ваны от кра́жи?; **these words ~ you against a libel charge** э́ти слова́ оградя́т вас от обвине́ния в клевете́. **4.** (*aim weapon at*) це́литься (*impf.*) в+*a.*; **he ~ed him** (*with his revolver*) он це́лился в него́ (из револьве́ра); он держа́л его́ под прице́лом; **our guns ~ed the road** на́ши ору́дия прикрыва́ли доро́гу (от неприя́теля). **5.** (*travel*) покр|ыва́ть, -ы́ть; **we ~ed 5 miles by nightfall** мы прошли́ расстоя́ние в 5 миль до наступле́ния темноты́. **6.** (*meet, satisfy*) покр|ыва́ть, -ы́ть; **£10 will ~ my needs** 10 фу́нтов хва́тит на мои́ ну́жды; **we only just ~ed expenses** мы едва́ покры́ли свои́ расхо́ды. **7.** (*embrace, deal with*): **the lectures ~ a wide field** ле́кции охва́тывают широ́кий круг вопро́сов; **the rules ~ every possible case** э́ти пра́вила предусма́тривают все возмо́жные слу́чаи; **the reporter ~ed the conference** корреспонде́нт дава́л репорта́жи о хо́де конфере́нции; **this salesman ~s Essex** э́тот торго́вый аге́нт обслу́живает Э́ссекс. **8.** (*of correspondence*): **~ing letter** сопроводи́тельное письмо́. **9.** (*of male animal*) покр|ыва́ть, -ы́ть.

cpd. **~-up** *n.* (*pretext*) предло́г, ши́рма.

coverage ['kʌvərɪdʒ] *n.* **1.** (*extent or amount dealt with*) охва́т; **news** ~ освеще́ние в печа́ти (*or* по ра́дио). **2.** (*fin.*) покры́тие; гаранти́йный фонд. **3.** (*insurance*) страхова́ние.

coverlet ['kʌvəlɪt] *n.* покрыва́ло.

covert[1] ['kʌvət] *n.* (*thicket*) ча́ща.

covert[2] ['kʌvət] *adj.* скры́тый, завуали́рованный.

covertness ['kʌvətnɪs] *n.* завуали́рованность.

covet ['kʌvɪt] *v.t.* вожделе́ть (*impf.*) к+*d.*; жа́ждать (*impf.*) +*g.*; (*coll.*) за́риться (*impf.*) на+*a.*

covetous ['kʌvɪtəs] *adj.* а́лчный, жа́дный; скупо́й.

covetousness ['kʌvɪtəsnɪs] *n.* а́лчность, жа́дность; ску́пость.

covey ['kʌvɪ] *n.* (*of birds*) вы́водок; (*fig.*) ста́йка.

cow[1] [kaʊ] *n.* **1.** (*bovine*) коро́ва; **till the ~s come home** (*coll.*) до второ́го прише́ствия; (*of other mammals*) са́мка, коро́ва; *expr. by suff., e.g.* ~ **elephant** слони́ха; **sacred** ~ (*fig.*) неприкоснове́нное; «и́стина в после́дней инста́нции». **2.** (*pej., woman*) коро́ва; **silly** ~ дурёха.

cpds. **~bell** *n.* колоко́льчик на ше́е коро́вы; **~boy** *n.* ковбо́й; **~catcher** *n.* скотосбра́сыватель (*m.*); **~herd** *n.* пасту́х; **~hide** *n.* (*leather*) воло́вья ко́жа; **~-house, ~-shed** *nn.* хлев, коро́вник; **~-lick** *n.* чуб, вихо́р; **~-pat** *n.* коровя́к; **~pox** *n.* коро́вья о́спа; **~shed** *n.* = **~-house**

cow[2] [kaʊ] *v.t.* запу́г|ивать, -а́ть.

coward ['kaʊəd] *n.* трус (*fem.* -и́ха); **a moral** ~ малоду́шный челове́к.

cowardice ['kaʊədɪs] *n.* тру́сость, малоду́шие.

cowardly ['kaʊədlɪ] *adj.* трусли́вый, малоду́шный.

cower ['kaʊə(r)] *v.i.* съёжи|ваться, -ться; сж|има́ться, -а́ться.

cowl [kaʊl] *n.* (*hood*) капюшо́н; (*hooded garment*) ря́са, сута́на с капюшо́ном; (*chimney-~*) зонт над домово́й трубо́й.

cowling ['kaʊlɪŋ] *n.* (*tech.*) капо́т дви́гателя; обтека́тель (*m.*).

cowr|ie, -y ['kaʊrɪ] *n.* ка́ури (*nt. indecl.*).

cowslip ['kaʊslɪp] *n.* первоцве́т.

cox [kɒks] *n.* рулево́й.

v.t.: ~ **a boat** управля́ть (*impf.*) рулём ло́дки; сиде́ть (*impf.*) на руле́.

coxcomb ['kɒkskəʊm] *n.* фанфаро́н, фат, хлыщ.

coxcombry ['kɒkskəmrɪ] *n.* фанфаро́нство, фатовство́.

coxswain ['kɒksweɪn, -s(ə)n] *n.* старшина́ шлю́пки; (*helmsman*) рулево́й.

coy [kɔɪ] *adj.* (*bashful*) стыдли́вый; (*affectedly*) жема́нный, коке́тливый; (*secretive*) скры́тный.

coyness ['kɔɪnɪs] *n.* стыдли́вость; скры́тность.

coyote [kɔɪ'əʊtɪ, 'kɔɪəʊt] *n.* койо́т.

coypu ['kɔɪpu:] *n.* койпу (*m. indecl.*).

cozen ['kʌz(ə)n] *v.t.* обма́н|ывать, -у́ть.

cozy ['kəʊzɪ] = **cosy**

Cpl. ['kɔ:pər(ə)l] *n.* (*abbr. of* **Corporal**) капра́л.

CPSU (*abbr. of* ***Communist Party of the Soviet Union***) КПСС, (Коммунисти́ческая па́ртия Сове́тского Сою́за).

CPU (*abbr. of* ***central processing unit***) (*comput.*) ЦП, (центра́льный проце́ссор).

crab[1] [kræb] *n.* краб; **catch a** ~ (*fig.*) «пойма́ть (*pf.*) леща́»; (*astron.*): **the C~** Рак; (*fig., crossgrained pers.*) брюзга́ (*c.g.*).

v.t. (*coll., disparage*) придира́ться (*impf.*) к+*d.*; разноси́ть (*impf.*).

v.i. (*fish for ~s*) лови́ть (*impf.*) кра́бов; (*grumble*) брюзжа́ть (*impf.*).

cpds. **~-like** *adj.* (*sidelong*) дви́жущийся бо́ком; **~-louse** *n.* лобко́вая вошь; площи́ца; (*sl.*) мандаво́шка; **~-pot** *n.* се́тка для ло́вли кра́бов.

crab[2] [kræb] *n.* (*also* **~-apple**) ди́кое я́блоко.

crabbed ['kræbɪd] *adj.* (*sour, irritable*) брюзжа́щий; (*illegible, obscure*) неразбо́рчивый.

crabbedness ['kræbɪdnɪs] *n.* брюзгли́вость; неразбо́рчивость.

crabby ['kræbɪ] *adj.* брюзгли́вый.

crack [kræk] *n.* **1.** (*in a cup, ice etc.*) тре́щина; (*in the ground*) рассе́лина; (*in wall, floor etc.*) щель. **2.** (*sudden noise*) треск, щёлканье; (*of thunder*) треск, уда́р; ~ **of doom** тру́бный глас. **3.: at ~ of dawn** с (пе́рвой) заре́й. **4.** (*blow*) затре́щина; **he got a ~ on the head** он получи́л затре́щину. **5.** (*coll., facetious remark*) остро́та. **6.** (*coll., attempt*) попы́тка; **have a ~ at sth.** попыта́ть (*pf.*) свои́ си́лы в чём-н. **7.: a ~ regiment** отбо́рный полк; **a ~ shot** первокла́ссный стрело́к. **8.** (*drug*) крэк.

v.t. **1.** (*make a ~ in, break open*) проб|ива́ть, -и́ть щель в (чём); взл|а́мывать, -ома́ть; **he fell and ~ed his skull** он упа́л и проломи́л себе́ го́лову; ~ **a nut** расколо́ть (*pf.*) оре́х; ~ (*broach*) **a bottle** раздави́ть (*pf.*) буты́лочку; ~ **a code** разгада́ть (*pf.*) шифр; ~ **a safe** взлома́ть (*pf.*) сейф. **2.** (*of petroleum*) подв|ерга́ть, -е́ргнуть кре́кингу; креки́ровать (*impf., pf.*). **3.: ~ a whip** щёлк|ать, -нуть бичо́м; ~ **a joke** отпусти́ть (*pf.*) шу́тку. **4. ~ed** (*crazy*) чо́кнутый.

v.i. **1.** (*get broken or fissured*) да|ва́ть, -ть тре́щину; тре́снуть (*pf.*); **the glass ~ed** стекло́ тре́снуло; (*fig., give way*): **he did not ~ under torture** пы́тки его́ не сломи́ли. **2.** (*of sound*) щёлк|ать, -нуть; **a rifle ~ed (out)** разда́лся винто́вочный вы́стрел. **3.: the boy's voice ~ed** у ма́льчика слома́лся го́лос; **she sang in a ~ed voice** она́ пе́ла надтре́снутым го́лосом. **4.** *see* **cracking**

with advs.: ~ **down** *v.i.* ~ **down on** распр|авля́ться, -а́виться с+*i.*; прин|има́ть, -я́ть круты́е ме́ры про́тив+*g.*; ~ **up** *v.t.* (*praise*) захва́л|ивать, -и́ть; **the book is not all it's ~ed up to be** э́та кни́га не та́к хороша́, как её расписывают; (*smash up, e.g. a car*) разб|ива́ть, -и́ть вдре́безги; *v.i.*: **the plane ~ed up on landing** самолёт разби́лся при поса́дке; (*of pers.: suffer collapse*) надломи́ться (*pf.*); разв|а́ливаться, -и́ться.

cpds. **~-brained, ~-pot** *adjs.* поме́шанный; **~-down** *n.* распра́ва; **~-jaw** *adj.* (*coll.*) (сло́во —) язы́к слома́ешь; **~-up** *n.* (*breakdown*) упа́док сил.

cracker ['krækə(r)] *n.* **1.** (*firework*) хлопу́шка, шути́ха. **2.** (*biscuit*) кре́кер. **3.** (*pl., nut-~s*) щипц|ы́ (*pl., g.* -о́в) для оре́хов.

crackerjack ['krækə,dʒæk] *adj.* (*coll.*) первокла́ссный; вы́сшего кла́сса.

crackers ['krækəz] *adj.* (*sl., mad*) рехну́вшийся.

cracking ['krækɪŋ] *n.* (*pyrolysis*) кре́кинг; ~ **plant** заво́д креки́рования.

adj. & adv.: **at a ~ pace** стреми́тельно; бо́дрым ша́гом; **we had a ~ good time** мы здо́рово провели́ вре́мя; **get ~!** пошеве́ливайся!; за рабо́ту!

crackle ['kræk(ə)l] *n.* **1.** (*sound*) треск, потре́скивание. **2.** (*on china etc.*) паути́нчатый рису́нок.

v.i. (*of sound*) потре́скивать (*impf.*); (*fig., sparkle*) сверка́ть (*impf.*); (*show marks*) тре́скаться (*or* растре́скиваться), рас-.

crackling ['kræklɪŋ] *n.* **1.** (*sound*) треск, хруст. **2.** (*marks*) сеть тре́щинок; паути́нчатый рису́нок. **3.** (*cul.*) шква́рки (*f. pl.*).

cracknel ['krækn(ə)l] *n.* сухо́е пече́нье.

cracksman ['kræksmən] *n.* взло́мщик.

Cracow ['krækaʊ] *n.* Кра́ков.

cradle ['kreɪd(ə)l] *n.* **1.** (*lit., fig.*) колыбе́ль; лю́лька; **I have known that from my** ~ я зна́ю э́то с колыбе́ли; **from ~ to grave** всю жизнь; **Greece is the ~ of Western civilization** Гре́ция — колыбе́ль за́падной цивилиза́ции. **2.** (*shipbuilding*) спусковы́е сала́з|ки (*pl., g.* -ок); (*basket pulled along lifeline*) лю́лька; (*teleph.*) рыча́г.

v.t.: ~ **a child in one's arms** держа́ть (*impf.*) ребёнка на рука́х; ~ (*put down*) **the receiver** класть, положи́ть тру́бку на рыча́г.

cpd. **~-song** *n.* колыбе́льная (пе́сня).

craft [krɑ:ft] *n.* **1.** (*guile*) хи́трость, хитроу́мие. **2.** (*skill*) ло́вкость, уме́ние. **3.** (*occupation*) ремесло́; **arts and ~s** иску́сства и ремёсла (*nt. pl.*) **4.** (*boat*) су́дно.

cpds. **~sman** *n.* реме́сленник, ма́стер; **~smanship** *n.* мастерство́.

craftiness ['krɑ:ftɪnɪs] *n.* хи́трость, проны́рливость.

crafty ['krɑ:ftɪ] *adj.* хи́трый, проны́рливый.

crag [kræg] *n.* скала́, утёс.

cragginess ['krægɪnɪs] *n.* скали́стость.

craggy ['krægɪ] *adj.* скали́стый.

cram [kræm] *v.t.* **1.** (*insert forcefully*) запи́х|ивать, -а́ть/-ну́ть;

впи́х|ивать, -ну́ть; (*fill*): **an essay ~med with quotations** сочине́ние, напи́чканное цита́тами; **the shelves are ~med with books** по́лки ло́мятся от книг. **2.** (*v.t. & i.*) (*teach, study intensively*) репети́ровать (*impf.*); (*coll.*)ната́ск|ивать, -а́ть; зубри́ть (*impf.*); **~ pupils** репети́ровать/ната́скивать (*impf.*) ученико́в; **~ up a subject** зубри́ть (*impf.*) предме́т.

cpd. **~-full** *adj.* по́лный до отка́за; битко́м наби́тый.

crammer ['kræmə(r)] *n.* (*tutor*) репети́тор.

cramp [kræmp] *n.* **1.** (*of muscles*) су́дорога, спазм, спа́зма; **writer's ~** су́дорога в па́льцах; **the swimmer was seized with ~** пловца́ схвати́ла су́дорога. **2.** (*also* **~-iron**) (*pl.*) клёщ|и (*pl.*, *g.* -е́й).

v.t. (*hamper*) стесн|я́ть, -и́ть; **we are ~ed for room** у нас здесь поверну́ться не́где; **~ s.o.'s style** (*fig.*) не дава́ть (*impf.*) кому́-н. разверну́ться; **a ~ed handwriting** ме́лкий (и) неразбо́рчивый по́черк.

crampon ['kræmpən] *n.* (*pl.*, *hooked levers*) грузовы́е клёщ|и (*pl.*, *g.* -е́й); схва́ты (m. pl.); (*plate with spikes*) подо́шва с шипа́ми; (*pl.*) ко́шки (*f. pl.*).

cranberry ['krænbəri] *n.* клю́ква (*collect.*); я́года клю́квы.

crane [kreɪn] *n.* (*bird*) жура́вль (*m.*); (*machine*) (грузо)подъёмный кран.

v.t.: **~ one's neck** вытя́гивать, вы́тянуть ше́ю.

cpd. **~-fly** *n.* долгоно́жка.

cranial ['kreɪnɪəl] *adj.* черепно́й.

craniometry [,kreɪnɪ'ɒmɪtrɪ] *n.* краниоме́трия.

cranium ['kreɪnɪəm] *n.* че́реп.

crank[1] [kræŋk] *n.* (*handle*) кривоши́п; коле́нчатый рыча́г; рукоя́тка; заводна́я ру́чка.

v.t.: **~ up a car** зав|оди́ть, -ести́ мото́р вручну́ю; **~ a film camera** крути́ть (*impf.*) киноаппара́т.

cpds. **~case** *n.* (*tech.*) ка́ртер (дви́гателя); **~shaft** *n.* (*tech.*) коле́нчатый вал.

crank[2] [kræŋk] *n.* (*pers.*) чуда́|к (*fem.* -чка); челове́к с причу́дами.

crankiness ['kræŋkɪnɪs] *n.* скло́нность к причу́дам, чуда́чество; расша́танность; раздражи́тельность.

cranky ['kræŋkɪ] *adj.* (*eccentric*) с причу́дами/приве́том; (*unsteady*) расша́танный; (*peevish*) раздражи́тельный.

crannied ['krænɪd] *adj.* потре́скавшийся, растре́скавшийся.

cranny ['krænɪ] *n.* тре́щина.

crap[1] [kræp] (*vulg.*) *n.* (*shit*) говно́; (*nonsense*) вздо́р, чепуха́.

v.i. (*shit*) срать (*impf.*).

crap[2] [kræp] *n.* (*pl.*, *game*; *also* **~-*shooting***) игра́ в ко́сти; **shoot ~s** броса́ть (*impf.*) ко́сти.

cpd. **~shooter** *n.* игро́к в ко́сти.

crape [kreɪp] *n.* креп.

cpd. **~-cloth** *n.* шерстяна́я кре́повая ткань.

crappy ['kræpɪ] *adj.* (*vulg.*) дрянно́й, дерьмо́вый.

crapul|ent ['kræpjʊlənt], **-ous** ['kræpjʊləs] *adjs.* находя́щийся в состоя́нии похме́лья.

crash [kræʃ] *n.* **1.** (*noise*) гро́хот, гром, грохота́нье. **2.** (*fall, smash*) ава́рия, круше́ние; **he was killed in a car/plane ~** он поги́б в автомоби́льной/авиацио́нной катастро́фе; (*fig.*, *disaster*) катастро́фа, крах. **3.: a ~** (*intensive*) **programme** ускоре́нная програ́мма.

v.t. разб|ива́ть, -и́ть; гро́хнуть (*pf.*); **he ~ed his fist down on the table** он гро́хнул кулако́м по́ столу; **he ~ed the aircraft** он разби́л самолёт; **~ (*gate-~*) a party** ворва́ться (*pf.*) на ве́чер без приглаше́ния.

v.i.: **the music ~ed out** загреме́ла му́зыка; **the plane ~ed** самолёт потерпе́л ава́рию (*or* разби́лся); **the cars ~ed together** автомоби́ли столкну́лись; **he ~ed into the room** он ворва́лся/вломи́лся в ко́мнату; **he is a ~ing bore** (*coll.*) он невыноси́мый зану́да.

cpds. **~-dive** *n.* (*of submarine*) сро́чное погруже́ние; **~-helmet** *n.* шлем автого́нщика/мотоцикли́ста; мотошле́м; **~-land** *v.t. & i.* соверш|а́ть, -и́ть авари́йную поса́дку; **~-landing** *n.* авари́йная поса́дка.

crass [kræs] *adj.* гру́бый; тупо́й; **~ darkness** кроме́шная тьма; **~ stupidity** непроходи́мая ту́пость.

crassness ['kræsnɪs] *n.* гру́бость; ту́пость.

crate [kreɪt] *n.* я́щик, конте́йнер; (*car etc.*) колыма́га, драндуле́т (*coll.*).

v.t. пакова́ть, у- в я́щик(и).

crater ['kreɪtə(r)] *n.* кра́тер; (*bomb-~*) воро́нка.

cravat [krə'væt] *n.* широ́кий га́лстук; ше́йный плато́к.

crave [kreɪv] *v.t. & i.* **1.** (*beg for*) моли́ть (*impf.*) (*о чём*); умоля́ть (*impf.*) (*кого о чём*). **2.** (*desire*) жа́ждать (*impf.*) +*g.*; **he ~d for a drink** ему́ до́ смерти хоте́лось вы́пить.

craven ['kreɪv(ə)n] *n.* трус.

adj. трусли́вый, малоду́шный.

craving ['kreɪvɪŋ] *n.* стра́стное жела́ние.

craw [krɔ:] *n.* зоб.

crawfish ['krɔ:fɪʃ] = **crayfish**

crawl [krɔ:l] *n.* **1.** (*~ing motion*) по́лзание; **traffic was reduced to a ~** тра́нспорт тащи́лся е́ле-е́ле. **2.** (*swimming stroke*) кроль (*m.*).

v.i. **1.** (*e.g. of reptile*) по́лзать (*indet.*), ползти́ (*det.*); **he ~ed on his hands and knees** он полз на четвере́ньках. **2.** (*go very slowly*) ползти́ (*det.*); **the train ~ed over the damaged bridge** по́езд ме́дленно тащи́лся по повреждённому мосту́. **3.** (*kowtow*) по́лзать (*indet.*) (*перед кем*); пресмыка́ться (*impf.*) (*перед кем*); **he ~s to the boss** он пресмыка́ется перед нача́льником. **4.: the ground is ~ing with ants** земля́ кишмя́ киши́т муравья́ми. **5.** (*tickle*): **my skin is ~ing** у меня́ мура́шки по те́лу бе́гают.

crawler ['krɔ:lə(r)] *n.* **1.** (*obsequious pers.*) низкопокло́нник, подхали́м. **2.** (*pl.*, *baby's garment*) ползунк|и́ (*pl.*, *g.* -о́в).

cray|fish ['kreɪfɪʃ], **craw-** ['krɔ:fɪʃ] *nn.* речно́й рак; лангу́ст(а).

crayon ['kreɪən, -ɒn] *n.* цветно́й каранда́ш; пасте́ль; (*~ drawing*) рису́нок цветны́м карандашо́м (*or* пасте́лью).

v.t. & i. рисова́ть (*impf.*) цветны́м карандашо́м (*or* пасте́лью).

craze [kreɪz] *n.* ма́ния, помеша́тельство; пова́льная мо́да.

v.t. св|оди́ть, -ести́ с ума́.

craziness ['kreɪzɪnɪs] *n.* (*madness*) безу́мие, сумасше́ствие, помеша́тельство; (*rickety state*) ша́ткость.

crazy ['kreɪzɪ] *adj.* **1.** (*mad*) безу́мный, сумасше́дший; **~ about sth.** поме́шанный на чём-н.; **a ~ scheme** безу́мный план; **he is ~ about her** он схо́дит по ней с ума́. **2.** (*rickety*) ша́ткий. **3.** (*motley*): **~ quilt** лоску́тное одея́ло; **~ pavement** мостова́я из камне́й разли́чной фо́рмы.

creak [kri:k] *n.* скрип.

v.i. скрипе́ть (*impf.*).

cream [kri:m] *n.* **1.** (*top part of milk*) сли́в|ки (*pl.*, *g.* -ок); **whipped ~** взби́тые сли́вки; **~ cheese** сли́вочный сыро́к. **2.** (*dish or sweet*) крем; **~ cake** торт с кре́мом; кре́мовое пиро́жное; **~ puff** сло́йка с кре́мом; **chocolate ~s** шокола́дные конфе́ты (*f. pl.*); **salad ~** майоне́з; **~ of celery (soup)** суп-пюре́ из сельдере́я. **3.** (*polish, cosmetic etc.*) крем, мазь; **furniture ~** мазь для полиро́вки ме́бели; **shoe ~** крем для о́буви; **face ~** крем для лица́; **cold ~** кольдкре́м. **4.** (*of other liquid*) пе́на; **~ of tartar** ви́нный ка́мень. **5.** (*best part*): **the ~ of society** сли́вки о́бщества; **the ~ of the joke** соль шу́тки. **6.** (*attr.*, **~-*coloured***) кре́мового цве́та.

v.t. (*take ~ off*) сн|има́ть, -ять сли́вки с+*g*; (*apply ~ to*) на|кла́дывать, -ложи́ть крем на+*a*; нама́з|ывать, -ать кре́мом; **she ~ed her face** она́ наложи́ла на лицо́ крем.

v.i. (*of milk, form ~*) отст|а́иваться, -оя́ться; (*foam, froth*) пе́ниться (*impf.*).

cpds. **~-coloured** *adj.* кре́мового цве́та; кре́мовый; **~-jug** *n.* сли́вочник; **~-laid, ~-wove** *adjs.* (*paper*) верже́ (*indecl.*); веле́невая бума́га кре́мового цве́та; **~-separator** *n.* моло́чный сепара́тор.

creamer ['kri:mə(r)] *n.* (*machine*) сливкоотдели́тель (*m.*), сепара́тор; (*milk, cream substitute*) осветли́тель (*m.*); (*US*) = **cream-jug**

creamery ['kri:mərɪ] *n.* (*place of sale*) моло́чная; (*factory*) маслобо́йный заво́д, маслобо́йня.

creaminess ['kri:mɪnɪs] *n.* жи́рность (молока́).

creamy ['kri:mɪ] *adj.* сли́вочный, кре́мовый.

crease [kri:s] *n.* скла́дка, сгиб, морщи́на; (*in trousers*) скла́дка.

v.t. (*wrinkle*) мять (*or* смина́ть), с-; **~ trousers** (*with iron*) утю́жить, вы- скла́дки брюк.

v.i. (*form* ~*s*) мя́ться (*or* смина́ться), с-.

cpd. **~-resisting** *adj.* немну́щийся.

create [kri:'eɪt] *v.t.* созд|ава́ть, -а́ть; твори́ть, со-; произв|оди́ть, -ести́; **God ~d the world** Бог сотвори́л мир; **Dickens ~d many characters** Ди́ккенс со́здал мно́го о́бразов; **he ~d the role of Higgins** он со́здал о́браз Хи́ггинса; **it ~d a bad impression** э́то произвело́ дурно́е впечатле́ние; **he was ~d a peer** он был произведён в пэ́ры.

creation [kri:'eɪʃ(ə)n] *n.* **1.** (*act, process*) созда́ние, созида́ние; **~ of the world** сотворе́ние ми́ра; **~ of social unrest** возбужде́ние обще́ственного недово́льства. **2.** (*the universe*) мирозда́ние; **the animal ~** живо́тное ца́рство. **3.** (*product of imagination*) творе́ние, произведе́ние. **4.** (*dress*) моде́ль.

creative [kri:'eɪtɪv] *adj.* тво́рческий.

creativeness [kri:'eɪtɪvnɪs] *n.* тво́рческий дар.

creator [kri:'eɪtə(r)] *n.* созда́тель (*m.*), творе́ц.

creature ['kri:tʃə(r)] *n.* **1.** (*living being*) созда́ние, тварь, существо́; **dumb ~s** бесслове́сные тва́ри; **she is a lovely ~** она́ — очарова́тельное созда́ние/существо́; **poor ~** несча́стное созда́ние; бедня́жка (*c.g.*); **a good ~** хоро́ший/добросерде́чный челове́к. **2.** (*of pers., tool*) креату́ра, ста́вленник. **3.: ~ comforts** земны́е блага́.

crèche [kreʃ, kreɪʃ] *n.* (де́тские) ясл|и (*pl., g.* -е́й).

credence ['kri:d(ə)ns] *n.* ве́ра, дове́рие; **give ~ to** пове́рить (*pf.*) +*d.*

credential [krɪ'denʃ(ə)l] *n.* (*usu. pl.*) **1.** (*testimonial*) удостовере́ние; манда́т; **~s committee** комите́т по прове́рке полномо́чий; манда́тная коми́ссия. **2.** (*ambassador's*) вери́тельная гра́мота.

credibility [,kredɪ'bɪlɪtɪ] *n.* (*of pers.*) спосо́бность вы́звать дове́рие; (*of thg.*) правдоподо́бие, достове́рность; (*plausibility*) убеди́тельность.

credible ['kredɪb(ə)l] *adj.* (*of pers.*) заслу́живающий дове́рия; (*of thg.*) правдоподо́бный, вероя́тный, достове́рный.

credit ['kredɪt] *n.* **1.** (*belief, trust, confidence*) ве́ра, дове́рие; **give ~ to, place ~ in** (*a report etc.*) пове́рить (*pf.*) +*d.*; доверя́ть (*impf.*) +*d.*; **this lends ~ to the story** э́то де́лает расска́з правдоподо́бным. **2.** (*honour, reputation*): **a man of the highest ~** челове́к с прекра́сной репута́цией; **the work does you ~** э́та рабо́та де́лает вам честь; **he is cleverer than I gave him ~ for** он умне́е, чем я счита́л; **this is to his ~** э́то говори́т в его́ по́льзу; **he took ~ for the success** он приписа́л успе́х себе́; **give ~ where ~ is due** возда́ть (*pf.*) до́лжное кому́ сле́дует; **~ titles** (*cin., also* ~*s*) вступи́тельные ти́тры (*m. pl.*). **3.** (*book-keeping*) кре́дит; (*fin.*) креди́т; **buy on ~** покупа́ть (*pf.*) в креди́т; **~ balance** кре́дитовый бала́нс, са́льдо (*indecl.*); **~ card** креди́тная ка́рточка; **letter of ~** аккредити́в; **this shop gives no ~** э́тот магази́н не отпуска́ет/продаёт това́ры в креди́т; **his ~ is good for £50** он име́ет креди́т на 50 фу́нтов; **place the sum to my credit** внеси́те э́ту су́мму на мой счёт; **~ squeeze** стеснённый креди́т; (*fig.*): **there is this to be said on the ~ side** вот что мо́жно сказа́ть в защи́ту.

v.t. **1.** (*believe sth.*) ве́рить, по- +*d.*; доверя́ть (*impf.*) +*d.* **2.: I ~ed him with more sense** я счита́л его́ бо́лее благоразу́мным; **the relics are ~ed with miraculous powers** моща́м припи́сывается чудоде́йственная си́ла. **3.** (*fin.*): **I ~ed him with £10 (*or* £10 to him)** я внёс 10 фу́нтов на его́ счёт.

cpds. **~-worthiness** *n.* кредитоспосо́бность; **~-worthy** *adj.* заслу́живающий креди́та, кредитоспосо́бный.

creditable ['kredɪtəb(ə)l] *adj.* (*praiseworthy*) де́лающий честь (+*d.*); (*believable*) правдоподо́бный, вероя́тный.

creditor ['kredɪtə(r)] *n.* кредито́р.

credo ['kreɪdəʊ, 'kri:-] *n.* си́мвол ве́ры; (*fig.*) кре́до (*indecl.*).

credulity [krɪ'dju:lɪtɪ] *n.* легкове́рие, дове́рчивость.

credulous ['kredjʊləs] *adj.* легкове́рный, дове́рчивый.

creed [kri:d] *n.* вероуче́ние; (*fig.*) убежде́ния (*nt. pl.*), кре́до (*indecl.*).

creek [kri:k] *n.* (*inlet*) зали́в, бу́хта; (*small river*) ре́чка; **up the ~** (*coll.*) в беде́.

creel [kri:l] *n.* корзи́на для ры́бы.

creep [kri:p] *n.* **1.** (*act of* ~*ing*) по́лзание. **2.** (*of metal*) пласти́ческая деформа́ция, крип. **3.: it gives me the ~s** (*coll.*) от э́того у меня́ моро́з по ко́же. **4.** (*sl., obnoxious pers.*) несно́сный/отврати́тельный тип, подо́нок.

v.i. **1.** (*crawl, move stealthily*) по́лзать (*indet.*), ползти́ (*det.*); кра́сться (*impf.*). **2.** (*fig.*): **old age ~s upon me** ста́рость подкра́дывается ко мне. **3.** (*of plants*) стла́ться (*impf.*); ви́ться (*impf.*).

creeper ['kri:pə(r)] *n.* (*plant*) ползу́чее/вью́щееся расте́ние; (*pers.*) подхали́м.

creepiness ['kri:pɪnɪs] *n.* жуть.

creeping ['kri:pɪŋ] *adj.* ползу́щий, краду́щийся; **~ barrage** (*mil.*) ползу́щий огнево́й вал; **~ paralysis** (*med.*) прогресси́вная мы́шечная атрофи́я.

creepy ['kri:pɪ] *adj.* **1.** (*producing horror*) броса́ющий в дрожь; наводя́щий жуть; (*coll., obnoxious*) отврати́тельный, несно́сный. **2.** (*of flesh*) в мура́шках.

cpd. **~-crawly** *n.* бука́шка; *adj.* ползу́чий, по́лзающий.

cremate [krɪ'meɪt] *v.t.* креми́ровать (*impf., pf.*).

cremation [krɪ'meɪʃ(ə)n] *n.* крема́ция.

cremator [krɪ'meɪtə(r)] *n.* (*furnace*) кремацио́нная печь.

cremator|ium [,kremə'tɔ:rɪəm], **-y** ['kremətərɪ] *nn.* кремато́рий.

crème de la crème [,krem də lɑ: 'krem] *n.* сли́в|ки (*pl., g.* -ок) о́бщества, эли́та.

crème de menthe [,krem də 'mɑ̃t, 'mɒnt] *n.* мя́тный ликёр.

crenellate ['krenə,leɪt] *v.t.*: **~d walls** зу́бчатые сте́ны.

Creole ['kri:əʊl] *n.* (*of European descent*) крео́л (*fem.* -ка); (*of part-Negro descent, also*) мула́т (*fem.* -ка).

adj. крео́льский.

creosote ['kri:ə,səʊt] *n.* креозо́т.

crêpe [kreɪp] *n.* креп; **~ paper** гофриро́ванная бума́га; **~ soles** каучу́ковые подо́швы; **~ de Chine** крепдеши́н.

crepitate ['krepɪ,teɪt] *v.i.* (*crackle*) хрусте́ть (*impf.*).

crepitation [,krepɪ'teɪʃ(ə)n] *n.* хруст, потре́скивание.

crepuscular [krɪ'pʌskjʊlə(r)] *adj.* су́меречный; **~ insects** ночны́е насеко́мые.

crescendo [krɪ'ʃendəʊ] *n.* креще́ндо (*indecl.*).

adj. креще́ндо.

crescent ['krez(ə)nt, 'kres-] *n.* **1.** (*moon*) лу́нный серп. **2.** (*symbol of Islam*) полуме́сяц. **3.** (*street, row of houses*) ряд домо́в, располо́женных полукру́гом.

adj. (*growing*) расту́щий, возраста́ющий; (*of moon*) увели́чивающийся, возраста́ющий.

cpd. **~-shaped** *adj.* серпови́дный, серпообра́зный.

cress [kres] *n.* кресс(-сала́т).

cresset ['kresɪt] *n.* фа́кел.

crest [krest] *n.* **1.** (*tuft of feathers*) гре́бень (*m.*), хохоло́к. **2.** (*helmet*) шлем; (*top of helmet*) гре́бень (*m.*) шле́ма. **3.** (*her. device*) герб. **4.** (*of wave*) гре́бень (*m.*); **he is on the ~ of a wave** (*fig.*) он на верши́не сла́вы.

v.t.: **~ed notepaper** пи́счая бума́га с ге́рбом; **a golden ~ed bird** пти́ца с золоты́м хохолко́м.

cpd. **~fallen** *adj.* упа́вший ду́хом; удручённый.

cretaceous [krɪ'teɪʃəs] *adj.* мелово́й.

Cretan ['kri:t(ə)n] *n.* жи́тель (*fem.* -ница) Кри́та.

adj. кри́тский.

Crete [kri:t] *n.* Крит.

cretin ['kretɪn] *n.* (*lit., fig.*) крети́н.

cretinism ['kretɪ,nɪzəm] *n.* кретини́зм.

cretinous ['kretɪnəs] *adj.* слабоу́мный (*also fig.*); страда́ющий кретини́змом.

cretonne [kre'tɒn, 'kre-] *n.* крето́н.

crevasse [krə'væs] *n.* рассе́лина в леднике́.

crevice ['krevɪs] *n.* щель, расще́лина.

crew [kru:] *n.* **1.** (*of vessel*) кома́нда, экипа́ж; (*of aircraft*) экипа́ж; (*of train*) брига́да; (*aeron.*): **ground ~** назе́мный обслу́живающий персона́л. **2.** (*team*) брига́да, арте́ль; (*lot, gang*) ба́нда. **3.: ~ cut** стри́жка ёжиком.

v.t. обслу́живать (*impf.*) (*корабль*).

crib [krɪb] *n.* **1.** (*cot*) де́тская крова́тка с се́ткой. **2.** (*hut, shack*) хи́жина, лачу́га. **3.** (*manger*) я́с|ли (*pl., g.* -ей), корму́шка. **4.** (*plagiarism*) плагиа́т. **5.** (*literal translation*) подстро́чник; (*for cheating*) шпарга́лка (*coll.*).

v.t. (*confine*) втис|кивать, -нуть; (*plagiarize*) спис|ывать, -ать (*что у кого*).

v.i. (*of schoolboy*) шпаргалить (*impf.*); сду|вать, -ть (*both sl.*).

cpd. ~ **death** (*US*) = **cot death**

cribbage [ˈkrɪbɪdʒ] *n.* криббидж.

cribber [ˈkrɪbə(r)] *n.* плагиатор; (*at school*) сдувала (*c.g.*) (*sl.*).

crick [krɪk] *n.* растяжение мышц.

v.t. растянуть (*pf.*) мышцу.

cricket[1] [ˈkrɪkɪt] *n.* (*insect*) сверчок.

cricket[2] [ˈkrɪkɪt] *n.* (*game*) крикет; **it isn't** ~ (*fig.*) это нечестно; это не по правилам.

cricketer [ˈkrɪkɪtə(r)] *n.* игрок в крикет.

cri du coeur [ˌkri: də ˈkɜ:(r)] *n.* крик души.

crier [ˈkraɪə(r)] *n.* (*official*) глашатай; (*child etc.*) крикун (*fem.* -ья).

crikey [ˈkraɪkɪ] *int.* (*sl.*) мать честная!; ну и ну!

crime [kraɪm] *n.* **1.** (*act*) преступление; ~ **of violence** преступление с применением насилия. **2.** (~*s in general*) преступность; ~ **fiction** детективный роман. **3.** (*mil.*) проступок.

cpd. ~**-sheet** *n.* обвинительное заключение.

Crimea [kraɪˈmɪə] *n.* Крым; **native of** ~ крымча|к (*fem.* -чка).

Crimean [kraɪˈmɪən] *adj.* крымский.

crime passionnel [ˌkri:m pæsjɒˈnel] *n.* убийство из ревности.

criminal [ˈkrɪmɪn(ə)l] *n.* преступни|к (*fem.* -ца); **war** ~ военный преступник.

adj. **1.** (*guilty*) преступный; **he has a** ~ **history** у него преступное прошлое. **2.** (*pert. to crime*) уголовный, криминальный; ~ **action** (*prosecution*) уголовное дело; ~ **code** уголовный кодекс; ~ **court** суд по уголовным делам; ~ **law** уголовное право.

criminality [ˌkrɪmɪˈnælɪtɪ] *n.* преступность, криминальность.

criminologist [ˌkrɪmɪˈnɒlədʒɪst] *n.* криминолог.

criminology [ˌkrɪmɪˈnɒlədʒɪ] *n.* криминология.

crimp[1] [krɪmp] *n.* (*hist., enticer of recruits*) вербующий обманным путём.

v.t. обманом вербовать, за-.

crimp[2] [krɪmp] *n.* (*fold, curl*) гофрировка, гофр|ы (*pl., g.* —).

v.t. гофрировать (*impf., pf.*); ~**ing-iron** щипцы для завивки волос.

crimson [ˈkrɪmz(ə)n] *n.* малиновый цвет; тёмно-красный цвет.

adj. малиновый; тёмно-красный.

v.t. окра|шивать, -сить в малиновый цвет; **the lake was** ~**ed by the setting sun** заходящее солнце окрасило озеро в багряный цвет.

v.i. краснеть, по-; **she** ~**ed with shame** она залилась краской от стыда.

cringe [krɪndʒ] *v.i.* (*shrink*) съёжи|ваться, -ться (*от чего*); (*behave servilely*) раболепствовать (*impf.*).

crinkle [ˈkrɪŋk(ə)l] *n.* морщина.

v.t. & i. морщить(ся), на-/с-.

crinkly [ˈkrɪŋklɪ] *adj.* сморщенный.

crinoline [ˈkrɪnəlɪn] *n.* кринолин.

crippl|e [ˈkrɪp(ə)l] *n.* калека (*c.g.*).

v.t. калечить, ис-; уродовать, из-; (*fig.*); **the ship was** ~**ed by the storm** буря покалечила корабль; **strikes are** ~**ing industry** забастовки расшатывают промышленность; ~**ing expenses** разорительные расходы.

crisis [ˈkraɪsɪs] *n.* кризис, перелом; поворотный пункт; (*economic etc.*) кризис.

cpd. ~**-ridden** *adj.* подверженный хроническим кризисам.

crisp [krɪsp] *n.* (*potato* ~) жареная картофельная стружка; (*pl.*) хрустящий картофель.

adj. (*of substance*) хрустящий; **a** ~ **biscuit** рассыпчатое печенье; **a** ~ **lettuce** свежий салат; (*of style, orders etc.*) отрывистый, чеканный, отчётливый; (*of air*) бодрящий, свежий.

cpd. ~**bread** *n.* сухари (*m. pl.*); хрустящие хлебцы (*m. pl.*).

crispness [ˈkrɪspnɪs] *n.* свежесть; отрывистость, отчётливость, чеканность.

crispy [ˈkrɪspɪ] *adj.* хрустящий.

criss-cross [ˈkrɪskrɒs] *n.* перекрещивание.

adj. перекрещивающийся, перекрёстный.

adv. крест-накрест; (*fig.*) вкривь и вкось.

v.t. расчер|чивать, -тить крест-накрест.

criterion [kraɪˈtɪərɪən] *n.* критерий.

critic [ˈkrɪtɪk] *n.* (*also* **adverse** ~) критик.

critical [ˈkrɪtɪk(ə)l] *adj.* **1.** (*decisive; judicious*) критический; **the patient's condition is** ~ больной в критическом состоянии. **2.** (*fault-finding*) критический, критичный.

criticaster [ˌkrɪtɪˈkæstə(r), ˈkrɪt-] *n.* критикан.

criticism [ˈkrɪtɪˌsɪz(ə)m] *n.* критика; **textual** ~ критический разбор текста; **beneath** ~ ниже всякой критики; **I have only one** ~ **to make** у меня только одно замечание.

criticize [ˈkrɪtɪˌsaɪz] *v.t.* подв|ергать, -ергнуть критическому разбору; (*adversely*) критиковать (*impf*).

critique [krɪˈti:k] *n.* критика; (*review*) рецензия, критическая статья.

croak [krəʊk] *n.* карканье, кваканье.

v.t. & i. каркать (*impf.*); квакать (*impf.*); (*express dismal views*) каркать; (*die*) загнуться (*pf.*) (*sl.*).

croaker [ˈkrəʊkə(r)] *n.* (*prophet of evil*) прорицатель (*m.*) дурного/худого.

Croat [ˈkrəʊæt] *n.* хорват (*fem.* -ка).

Croatia [krəʊˈeɪʃə] *n.* Хорватия.

Croatian [krəʊˈeɪʃ(ə)n] *adj.* хорватский.

crochet [ˈkrəʊʃeɪ, -ʃɪ] *n.* вязание крючком.

v.t. & i. вязать (*impf.*) крючком.

cpd. ~**-hook** *n.* вязальный крючок.

crock[1] [krɒk] *n.* (*pot*) глиняный кувшин/горшок; (*pl., broken bits of pottery*) черепки (*m. pl.*); бой.

crock[2] [krɒk] *n.* (*worn-out pers., horse*) кляча; (*car*) рыдван.

v.t. (*also* ~ **up**) заездить (*pf.*).

v.i.: ~ **up** вымотаться (*pf.*).

crockery [ˈkrɒkərɪ] *n.* глиняная/фаянсовая посуда.

crocket [ˈkrɒkɪt] *n.* лиственный орнамент.

crocodile [ˈkrɒkəˌdaɪl] *n.* крокодил; ~ **bird** крокодилов сторож; ~ **tears** крокодиловы слёзы; (*of schoolchildren etc.*) прогулка в строю парами.

crocus [ˈkrəʊkəs] *n.* крокус, шафран; **autumn** ~ осенний крокус.

croft [krɒft] *n.* хутор.

crofter [ˈkrɒftə(r)] *n.* хуторянин.

croissant [ˈkrwʌsɑ̃] *n.* рогалик.

Cro-Magnon [krəʊˈmænjɒn, -ˈmægnən] *n.*: ~ **man** кроманьонец.

cromlech [ˈkrɒmlek] *n.* кромлех.

crone [krəʊn] *n.* сгорбленная старуха.

crony [ˈkrəʊnɪ] *n.* дружок, закадычный друг.

cronyism [ˈkrəʊnɪˌɪz(ə)m] *n.* панибратство.

crook [krʊk] *n.* **1.** (*shepherd's*) посох. **2.** (*bend*) поворот, изгиб. **3.** (*coll., criminal*) мошенник, жулик, проходимец.

v.t. сгибать, согнуть; из|гибать, -огнуть; ~ **one's finger** согнуть (*pf.*) палец.

crooked [ˈkrʊkɪd] *adj.* **1.** (*bent*) согнутый, изогнутый; (*with age*) согбенный, сгорбленный. **2.**: **you have got your hat on** ~ у вас шляпа косо/криво надета. **3.** (*coll., dishonest*) бесчестный, мошеннический.

crookedness [ˈkrʊkɪdnɪs] *n.* согнутость, изогнутость; (*dishonesty*) бесчестность, мошенничество.

croon [kru:n] *n.* тихое пение.

v.t. & i. напевать (*impf.*) вполголоса.

crooner [ˈkru:nə(r)] *n.* эстрадный певец, шансонье (*m. indecl.*)

crop [krɒp] *n.* **1.** (*craw*) зоб. **2.** (*of whip*) кнутовище; (*hunting-*~) охотничий хлыст. **3.** (*haircut*) короткая стрижка. **4.** (*produce*) урожай, жатва; **potato** ~ урожай картофеля; (*pl.*) посевы (*m. pl.*), (*grain*) хлеба (*m. pl.*); **land in, under** ~ засеянная земля; **land out of** ~ незасеянная земля; земля под паром. **5.** (*fig.*): **a** ~ **of questions** куча вопросов.

v.t. **1.** (*bite off*) щипать (*impf.*); объ|едать, -есть; **the sheep** ~**ped the grass short** овцы общипали траву. **2.** (*cut short*): (*hair, hedge*) подстр|игать, -ичь; (*tail, ears*) обр|езать, -езать; (*hedge, tail*) подр|езать, -езать. **3.** (*sow*, *plant*) зас|ева́ть, -е́ять; **he ~ped ten acres with wheat** он засе́ял пшени́цей де́сять а́кров.

v.i. **1.** (*yield a ~*) да|ва́ть, -ть (*or* прин|оси́ть, -ести́) урожа́й; **the beans ~ped well** бобы́ да́ли хоро́ший урожа́й; бобы́ хорошо́ уроди́лись. **2. ~ up, out** (*of rock etc.*) обнаж|а́ться, -и́ться. **3.** (*fig.*): **difficulties ~ped up** появи́лись/возни́кли тру́дности.

cpds. **~-dusting** *n.* опы́ливание посе́вов; **~-eared** *adj.* (*with ears cut off*) с обре́занными/подре́занными уша́ми; (*with short hair*) ко́ротко стри́женный.

cropper ['krɒpə(r)] *n.* **1.** (*harvester*) косе́ц, жнец. **2.: he came a ~** (*coll.*) (*lit.*) он шлёпнулся; (*fig.*) он провали́лся.

croquet ['krəʊkeɪ, -kɪ] *n.* кроке́т.

v.t. крокирова́ть (*impf., pf.*).

croquette [krə'ket] *n.* кроке́т.

cro|sier, -zier ['krəʊzɪə(r), -ʒə(r)] *n.* епи́скопский по́сох.

cross [krɒs] *n.* **1.** крест; **he made a ~ on the document** он поста́вил кре́стик на докуме́нте; **St Andrew's ~** крест св. Андре́я; **Red C~** Кра́сный Крест; **Southern ~** Ю́жный Крест. **2.** (*~-stroke, e.g. of a T*) черта́, перекре́щивающая «t». **3.** (*of crucifixion*) крест; **he made the sign of the ~** он перекрести́лся; он осени́л себя́ кресто́м (*or* кре́стным зна́мением). **4.** (*fig., Christianity*) христиа́нство. **5.** (*fig.*): **take up one's ~** нести́ (*pf.*) свой крест; **he is a ~ I have to bear** он крест, кото́рый мне суждено́ нести́. **6.** (*emblem of knighthood, decoration*) крест. **7.: cut on the ~** (*diagonally*) разре́занный на́искось (*or* по диагона́ли). **8.** (*mixing of breeds*) по́месь, гибри́д; **a mule is a ~ between a horse and an ass** мул — по́месь ло́шади с осло́м; **this is a ~ between a sermon and a fable** э́то смесь про́поведи с ба́сней.

adj. (*see also cpds.*) **1.** (*transverse*) попере́чный, перекрёстный; **~ ventilation** попере́чная/сквозна́я вентиля́ция; **~ traffic** пересека́ющиеся пото́ки движе́ния; **~ wind** (*sidewind*) бокови́й/косо́й ве́тер. **2.** (*contrary, unfavourable*) проти́вный, противополо́жный. **3.** (*angry*) серди́тый; злой (на+*a.*); раздражённый; **he is as ~ as two sticks** (*coll.*) он зол/серди́т как чёрт.

v.t. **1.** (*go across, traverse; also ~ over*): **~ a road/bridge** пере|ходи́ть, -йти́ че́рез доро́гу/мост; **~ the Channel** перепл|ыва́ть, -ы́ть Ла-Манш; **~ s.o.'s path** перебежа́ть (*pf.*) кому́-н. доро́гу; (*fig.*) повстреча́ться (*impf.*) с кем-н.; **the idea never ~ed my mind** э́та мысль никогда́ не приходи́ла мне в го́лову; **the ship ~ed our bows** кора́бль пересёк наш путь. **2.** (*draw lines across*): **~ a cheque** перечёрк|ивать, -ну́ть чек; **~ one's T's** (*lit.*) перечёрк|ивать, -ну́ть «t»; **~ one's T's and dot one's I's** (*fig.*) ста́вить, пото́чки над «i». **3.** (*place across*) скре́|щивать, -сти́ть; **~ one's legs** скрести́ть (*pf.*) но́ги; заки́нуть (*pf.*) но́гу за́ ногу; **~ one's arms** скрести́ть (*pf.*) ру́ки; **~ swords with s.o.** (*fig.*) скрести́ть (*pf.*) мечи́/шпа́ги с кем-н.; **keep one's fingers ~ed** (*fig., expr. hope*) ≃ как бы не сгла́зить; **~ s.o.'s palm with silver** позолоти́ть (*pf.*) ру́чку кому́-н.; **the wires are ~ed** (*lit.*) провода́ запу́тались; **~ wires** (*fig.*) запу́т|ывать, -ать де́ло; мути́ть (*impf.*) во́ду. **4.: ~ o.s.** перекрести́ться (*pf.*); **~ my heart!** вот те крест! **5.** (*travel in opposite direction to*): **we ~ed each other on the way** мы размину́лись в пути́; **my letter ~ed your telegram** моё письмо́ размину́лось с ва́шей телегра́ммой. **6.** (*thwart*): **he was ~ed in love** он потерпе́л неуда́чу в любви́; **do not ~ me** не станови́тесь на моём пути́; не перебега́йте мне доро́гу. **7.** (*breed*) скре́|щивать, -сти́ть.

v.i. **1.** (*go across*): **he ~ed to where I was sitting** он перешёл к тому́ ме́сту, где я сиде́л; **he ~ed from Dover to Calais** он перепра́вился из Ду́вра в Кале́. **2.: our letters ~ed** на́ши пи́сьма размину́лись.

with advs.: **~ off, out** *vv.t.* вычёркивать, вы́черкнуть; **~ up** *v.t.* (*coll., disrupt*) срыва́ть, сорва́ть.

cpds. **~-action** *n.* (*leg.*) встре́чный иск; **~bar** *n.* попере́чина, тра́верса, ри́гель (*m.*); **~-bearing** *n.* крюйс-пе́ленг; **~-bench** *n.* (*parl.*) скамья́ для незави́симых депута́тов; **~-bencher** *n.* (*parl.*) незави́симый депута́т; **~bill** *n.* клёст; **~bow** *n.* самостре́л, арбале́т; **~bowman** *n.* арбале́тчик; **~-bred** *adj.* скрещённый, гибри́дный; **~-breed** *n.* по́месь, гибри́д; *v.t. & i.* скре́|щивать(ся), -сти́ть(ся); **~-channel** *adj.*: **~-channel steamer** парохо́д, пересека́ющий Ла-Ма́нш; **~-check** *n.* све́рка; *v.t. & i.* св|еря́ть(ся), -е́рить(ся); **~-country** *adj.*: **a ~-country race** бег по пересечённой ме́стности, кросс; **~-country runner** кроссме́н; **~-country vehicle** вездехо́д; **~-current** *n.* пересека́ющий пото́к; (*fig.*) противополо́жное мне́ние; **~-cut** *adj.*: **~-cut saw** попере́чная пила́; **~-examination** *n.* перекрёстный допро́с; **~-examine** *v.t.* подв|ерга́ть, -е́ргнуть перекрёстному допро́су; (*fig.*) допр|а́шивать, -оси́ть; **~-eyed** *adj.* косогла́зый, косо́й; **~-fertilization** *n.* перекрёстное опыле́ние; скре́щивание (*lit., fig.*); **~-fertilize** *v.t.* перекрёстно опыл|я́ть, -и́ть; **~-fire** *n.* (*mil.*) перекрёстный ого́нь; **~-grained** *adj.* (*of temper*) сварли́вый, несгово́рчивый; **~-hatch** *v.t.* гравирова́ть (*impf.*) перекрёстными штриха́ми; **~-head(ing)** *n.* подзаголо́вок; **~-legged** *adj.* (сидя́щий) положи́в но́гу на́ ногу (*or* скрести́в но́ги по-туре́цки); **~-light** *n.* (*sidelight*) перекрёстное освеще́ние; **~-patch** *n.* (*coll.*) брюзга́ (*c.g.*), злю́ка (*c.g.*); **~piece** *n.* попере́чина, крестови́на; **~-pollinate** *v.t.* перекрёстно опыл|я́ть, -и́ть; **~-pollination** *n.* перекрёстное опыле́ние; **~-purposes** *n. pl.* недоразуме́ние; **~-question** *v.t.* допр|а́шивать, -оси́ть; **~-reference** *n.* перекрёстная ссы́лка; **~road** *n.* перекрёсток; пересека́ющая доро́га; **at the ~roads** (*fig.*) на распу́тье; **~-section** *n.* попере́чное сече́ние; попере́чный разре́з; про́филь (*m.*); **~-section of the population** попере́чный разре́з населе́ния; **~-stitch** *n.* вы́шивка кре́стиком; **~-talk** *n.* пререка́ния (*nt. pl.*); **~-tree** *n.* са́линг; **~ways** *adj.* = **crosswise; ~word** *n.* кроссво́рд.

crosse [krɒs] *n.* клю́шка (для игры́ в лакро́сс).

crossing ['krɒsɪŋ] *n.* **1.** (*going across*) перехо́д; перее́зд. **2.** (*of sea*) перепра́ва, перехо́д; **we had a rough ~** нас си́льно кача́ло (во вре́мя перепра́вы). **3.** (*of road and/or rail*) перекрёсток; перехо́д; перее́зд; **level ~** пересече́ние желе́зной доро́ги с шоссе́ (на одно́м у́ровне); **~ sweeper** подмета́льщик; **pedestrian ~** пешехо́дный перехо́д. **4.** (*in church*) средокре́стие. **5.** (*cross-breeding*) скре́щивание.

crossness ['krɒsnɪs] *n.* (*ill-temper*) раздражи́тельность, сварли́вость.

cross|wise ['krɒswaɪz], **-ways** ['krɒsweɪz] *adjs.* кресто-обра́зный.

advs. крест-на́крест.

crotch [krɒtʃ] *n.* (*of a tree*) разветвле́ние, развили́на; (*anat.; also* **crutch**) проме́жность; **the trousers are tight in the ~** брю́ки жмут в шагу́.

crotchet ['krɒtʃɪt] *n.* (*mus.*) четвертна́я но́та; (*whim*) причу́да.

crotchety ['krɒtʃɪtɪ] *adj.* (*peevish*) раздражи́тельный, брюзгли́вый.

crouch [kraʊtʃ] *v.i.* сгиба́ться, согну́ться; наг|иба́ться, -ну́ться.

croup[1] [kru:p] *n.* (*rump*) круп.

croup[2] [kru:p] *n.* (*med.*) круп.

croupier ['kru:pɪə(r), -ɪ,eɪ] *n.* (*at gambling*) крупье́ (*m. indecl.*).

croûton ['kru:tɒn] *n.* (*cul.*) грено́к.

crow[1] [krəʊ] *n.* воро́на; **carrion ~** чёрная воро́на; **they are a mile away as the ~ flies** они́ в ми́ле отсю́да, если счита́ть по прямо́й; **eat ~** (*US, eat humble pie*) прийти́ (*pf.*) с пови́нной (головой́); **~'s nest** (*naut.*) наблюда́тельный пост на ма́чте, «воро́нье гнездо́»; **~'s feet** (*wrinkles*) морщи́нки в уголка́х глаз; гуси́ные ла́пки.

cpd. **~bar** *n.* лом, ва́га, а́ншпуг.

crow[2] [krəʊ] *n.* (*of cock*) кукаре́канье; (*of baby*) ра́достный крик.

v.t. (*of cock*) кукаре́кать (*impf.*); (*of baby*) изд|ава́ть, -а́ть ра́достный крик; **~ over s.o.** восторжествова́ть (*pf.*) над кем-н.

crowd [kraʊd] *n.* **1.** (*throng*) толпа́; **follow (*or* go with) the ~** (*fig.*) плыть (*impf.*) по тече́нию. **2.** (*clique, social set*) компа́ния, о́бщество. **3.** (*mass, medley*) гора́, ку́ча. **4.** (*naut.*): **a ~ of sail** форси́рованные паруса́.

v.t. **1.** (*overfill*) зап|олня́ть, -о́лнить; переп|олня́ть, -о́лнить; **spectators ~ed the stadium** зри́тели запо́лнили стадио́н; **the buses are ~ed** авто́бусы перепо́лнены; **~ed**

street у́лица, запру́женная наро́дом; **the room was ~ed with furniture** ко́мната была́ загромождена́ ме́белью; **a life ~ed with incident** жизнь, бога́тая происше́ствиями. **2.** (*press, hustle*) оса|жда́ть, -ди́ть. **3.: ~ sail** (*naut.*) идти́ (*det.*) на всех паруса́х. **4.: patients are ~ed out of the hospitals** больни́цы перегру́жены; больны́м бо́льше нет ме́ста; **his article was ~ed out of the magazine** его́ статья́ была́ вы́теснена из журна́ла други́м материа́лом.

v.i. (*assemble in a ~*) толпи́ться, с-; наб|ива́ться, -и́ться битко́м; **they ~ed round the teacher** они́ столпи́лись вокру́г учи́теля; **they ~ed into the room** они́ хлы́нули в ко́мнату; **memories ~ed in upon me** на меня́ нахлы́нули воспомина́ния.

crown [kraʊn] *n.* **1.** коро́на, вене́ц. **2.** (*fig., sovereignty or sovereign*) коро́на, престо́л; **he succeeded to the ~** он унасле́довал коро́ну; **this land belongs to the C~** э́та земля́ принадлежи́т коро́не; **witness for the C~** свиде́тель обвине́ния. **3.** (*wreath*) вене́ц, вено́к; **martyr's ~** му́ченический вене́ц. **4.** (*coin*) кро́на. **5.** (*of head*) маку́шка, те́мя (*nt.*), голова́; (*of hat*) тулья́; (*of road*) вы́пуклость доро́ги; (*of tree*) кро́на, верху́шка. **6.** (*dental work*) коро́нка. **7.** (*fig., culmination or reward*) вене́ц, заверше́ние, верши́на; **the ~ of one's achievements** верши́на достиже́ний; **the ~ of one's labours** заверше́ние трудо́в. **8.** (*attr.*): **~ jewels** короле́вские/ца́рские рега́лии (*f. pl.*); **~ lands** зе́мли, принадлежа́щие коро́не; **~ prince** кронпри́нц, насле́дный принц; **~ princess** кронпринце́сса, насле́дная принце́сса.

v.t. **1.: he was ~ed king** его́ коронова́ли (на ца́рство); **~ed heads** корони́рованные осо́бы. **2.: the hill is ~ed with a wood** верши́на холма́ покры́та ле́сом. **3.** (*fig., reward*): **his efforts were ~ed with success** его́ уси́лия увенча́лись успе́хом. **4.** (*put finishing touch to*) заверш|а́ть, -и́ть; **to ~ the feast we drank champagne** в заверше́ние пра́здника мы вы́пили шампа́нского; **to ~ it all, a storm broke out** в доверше́ние всего́ разрази́лась бу́ря; **~ing mercy** вы́сшее (*or* всё превосходя́щее) милосе́рдие. **5.** (*hit on the head*) тре́снуть (*pf.*) по башке́ (*coll.*). **6.** (*at draughts*) пров|оди́ть, -ести́ в да́мки. **7.: ~ a tooth** ста́вить, по- коро́нку на зуб. **8.: a high/low ~ed hat** шля́па с высо́кой/ни́зкой тулье́й.

cpd. **~-piece** *n.* кро́на.

crozier [ˈkrəʊzɪə(r), -ʒə(r)] = **crosier**

CRT (*abbr. of* ***cathode-ray tube***) ЭЛТ, (электро́нно-лучева́я тру́бка).

crucial [ˈkru:ʃ(ə)l] *adj.* (*decisive*) реша́ющий.

crucian [ˈkru:ʃ(ə)n] *n.* (*also* **~ carp**) кара́сь (*m.*).

crucible [ˈkru:sɪb(ə)l] *n.* ти́гель (*m.*), горн; (*fig.*) горни́ло.

crucifix [ˈkru:sɪfɪks] *n.* распя́тие; (*cross*) крест.

crucifixion [ˌkru:sɪˈfɪkʃ(ə)n] *n.* распя́тие (на кресте́).

cruciform [ˈkru:sɪˌfɔ:m] *adj.* крестообра́зный, крестови́дный.

crucify [ˈkru:sɪˌfaɪ] *v.t.* расп|ина́ть, -я́ть; (*fig., of passions etc.*) умерщвля́ть (*impf.*).

crude [kru:d] *adj.* **1.** (*of materials*): **~ oil** сыра́я нефть; **~ ore** сыра́я/необогащённая руда́; **~ sugar** неочи́щенный са́хар. **2.** (*graceless*) гру́бый, неотёсанный. **3.** (*awkward, ill-made*): **~ paintings** аляпова́тые карти́ны; **a ~ log cabin** гру́бо сколо́ченная деревя́нная хи́жина. **4.** (*unripe, undigested*): **~ schemes** неразрабо́танные/незре́лые пла́ны; **~ facts** го́лые фа́кты. **5.** (*undifferentiated*): **~ death rate** гру́бый подсчёт сме́ртности.

crud|eness [ˈkru:dnɪs], **-ity** [ˈkru:dɪtɪ] *nn.* гру́бость, неотёсанность.

cruel [ˈkru:əl] *adj.* жесто́кий; **~ pain** жесто́кая/ужа́сная боль; **a ~ disease** мучи́тельная боле́знь.

cruelty [ˈkru:əltɪ] *n.* жесто́кость; **~ to animals** жесто́кое обраще́ние с живо́тными.

cruet [ˈkru:ɪt] *n.* графи́нчик, сосу́д.

cpd. **~-stand** *n.* судо́к.

cruis|e [kru:z] *n.* (*of ship*) пла́вание, кре́йсерство; (*of aircraft*) полёт; (*pleasure voyage*) морско́е путеше́ствие, круи́з; **~ missile** крыла́тая раке́та.

v.i. крейси́ровать (*impf.*); соверша́ть (*impf.*) ре́йсы; **~ing altitude** (*of aircraft*) кре́йсерская высота́ полёта; **~ing speed** (*of aircraft*) кре́йсерская ско́рость; (*of car*) эксплуатацио́нная ско́рость.

cruiser [ˈkru:zə(r)] *n.* (*warship*) кре́йсер; **cabin ~** прогу́лочный ка́тер с каю́той.

cpd. **~-weight** *n.* (*boxing*) полутяжёлый вес.

crumb [krʌm] *n.* **1.** (*small piece*) кро́шка; (*fig.*): **~s of information** кро́хи (*f. pl.*)/обры́вки (*m. pl.*) сведе́ний; **~ of comfort** сла́бое утеше́ние. **2.** (*inner part of bread*) мя́киш. **3. ~s!** (*coll.*) ну и ну!

cpd. **~-brush** *n.* щётка для смета́ния кро́шек со стола́.

crumble [ˈkrʌmb(ə)l] *n.* (*cul.*) слоёный фрукто́вый пу́динг.

v.t. (*bread etc.*) кроши́ть, рас-.

v.i. кроши́ться (*impf.*); (*of a wall*) обва́л|иваться, -и́ться; обру́ши|ваться, -ться; (*fig., of empires, hopes etc.*) ру́шиться (*impf., pf.*); ру́хнуть (*pf.*).

crumbly [ˈkrʌmblɪ] *adj.* кроша́щийся; (*of bread*) рассы́пчатый.

crumby [ˈkrʌmɪ] *adj.* (*full of crumbs*) весь в кро́шках.

crummy [ˈkrʌmɪ] *adj.* (*inferior*) дрянно́й, жа́лкий.

crump [krʌmp] *n.* (*sound of shell-burst etc.*) разры́в; (*shell, bomb*) фуга́ска (*coll.*); тяжёлый фуга́сный снаря́д.

crumpet [ˈkrʌmpɪt] *n.* ≃ сдо́бная лепёшка.

crumple [ˈkrʌmp(ə)l] *v.t.* мять (*or* смина́ть) с-; **~ one's clothes** смять (*pf.*) свою́ оде́жду; **~ up a sheet of paper** ско́мкать (*pf.*) лист бума́ги; **~ up the enemy army** сломи́ть (*pf.*) сопротивле́ние проти́вника.

v.i. мя́ться (*or* смина́ться), с-; **these sheets ~** э́ти про́стыни мну́тся; **the wings of the aircraft ~d up** кры́лья самолёта помя́лись; **he ~d up when taxed with the crime** он слома́лся, когда́ его́ обвини́ли в преступле́нии.

crunch [krʌntʃ] *n.* (*noise*) хруст, скрип; (*crucial moment*) реша́ющий моме́нт; кри́зисная ситуа́ция.

v.t. & i. грызть (*impf.*) с хру́стом; хрусте́ть (*impf.*); скрипе́ть (*impf.*); **our feet ~ed the gravel** гра́вий хрусте́л у нас под нога́ми.

crupper [ˈkrʌpə(r)] *n.* (*strap*) подхво́стник; (*hindquarters*) круп.

crural [ˈkrʊər(ə)l] *adj.* бе́дренный.

crusade [kru:ˈseɪd] *n.* (*lit., fig.*) кресто́вый похо́д.

v.i. (*fig.*) идти́ (*det.*) в похо́д (*против чего or за что*); объяв|ля́ть, -и́ть войну́ (*чему*).

crusader [kru:ˈseɪdə(r)] *n.* крестоно́сец (*fig.*); боре́ц.

crush [krʌʃ] *n.* **1.** (*crowd*) толчея́, толкотня́, да́вка; (*crowded party*) столпотворе́ние. **2.** (*infatuation*): **she has a ~ on him** она́ от него́ без ума́. **3.** (*fruit drink*) вы́жатый фрукто́вый сок. **4.: ~ hat** шапокля́к.

v.t. **1.** (*press, squash*) разда́в|ливать, -и́ть; **some people were ~ed to death** кое-кого́ задави́ло; **we ~ed our way through the crowd** мы проби́лись/проти́снулись/протолка́лись сквозь толпу́. **2.** (*crumple*) мять, из-/с-; см|ина́ть, -ять; **her dresses were badly ~ed** её пла́тья си́льно помя́лись. **3.** (*defeat, overcome*) сокруш|а́ть, -и́ть; **he ~ed his enemies** он разгроми́л свои́х враго́в; **our hopes were ~ed** на́ши наде́жды ру́хнули; **she ~ed him with a look** она́ уничто́жила/испепели́ла его́ одни́м взгля́дом; **a ~ing defeat** по́лное пораже́ние, разгро́м.

v.i. мя́ться, из-/с-; см|ина́ться, -я́ться; изм|ина́ться, -я́ться; прот|а́лкиваться, -олка́ться; проти́с|киваться, -нуться; **this material does not ~** э́та мате́рия не мнётся; **they ~ed into the front seats** они́ проти́снулись/протолка́лись на места́ пе́рвого ря́да.

with advs.: **~ out** *v.t.* (*extract*): **~ out fruit juice** выжима́ть, вы́жать сок из фру́ктов; (*extinguish*): **~ out a cigarette** погаси́ть (*pf.*) сигаре́ту; **~ up** *v.t.* (*make into powder*) толо́чь, рас-/ис-.

crust [krʌst] *n.* **1.** (*of bread*) ко́рка; (*of pastry*) ко́рочка; **the earth's ~** земна́я кора́; (*of ice*) ко́рка; (*of wine*) оса́док на сте́нках буты́лки. **2.** (*coll., impudence*) наха́льство, на́глость.

v.t.: **~ed over with ice** обледене́вший; **~ed** (*of wine*) с образова́вшимся оса́дком; (*fig.*): **~ed prejudices** закорене́лые предрассу́дки.

v.i.: **the snow ~ed over** на снегу́ образова́лась твёрдая ко́рка.

crustacean [krʌˈsteɪʃ(ə)n] *n.* ракообра́зное.

adj. ракообра́зный.

crustiness [ˈkrʌstɪnɪs] *n.* (*fig.*) ре́зкость, жёлчность.
crusty [ˈkrʌstɪ] *adj.* (*lit.*) покры́тый ко́ркой; с ко́рочкой; (*fig.*) ре́зкий, жёлчный.
crutch [krʌtʃ] *n.* **1.** (*support*) косты́ль (*m.*); (*fig.*) опо́ра. **2.** = **crotch**
crux [krʌks] *n.* (*difficulty*) затрудне́ние, (*coll.*) загво́здка; (*essential point*) суть; коренно́й вопро́с.
cry [kraɪ] *n.* **1.** (*weeping*) плач; **she had a good ~** она́ всла́сть попла́кала. **2.** (*shout*) крик; **within ~** в преде́лах слы́шимости; (*fig.*): **it is a far ~ to the days of the horse-carriage** мы далеко́ ушли́ от э́ры каре́т, запряжённых лошадьми́. **3.** (*of animal*) крик; **in full ~** (*of hounds*) в бе́шеной пого́не; с дру́жным ла́ем; (*fig.*): **the Opposition were in full ~ after the Prime Minister** оппози́ция со всей си́лой обру́шилась на премье́р-мини́стра. **4.** (*calling of information*) крик; **the night watchman's ~** крик/о́клик ночно́го сто́рожа; **street cries of London** кри́ки ло́ндонских разно́счиков. **5.** (*watch-word*) клич, ло́зунг. **6.** (*entreaty, demand*) мольба́; **there was a ~ for reform** подняли́сь голоса́, тре́бующие рефо́рмы. **7.** (*outcry, clamour*) крик, вопль (*m.*); **they raised the ~ of discrimination** они́ по́дняли крик/во́пли о дискримина́ции.
v.t. **1.** (*weep*) пла́кать (*impf.*); **~ bitter tears** пла́кать (*impf.*) го́рькими/горю́чими слеза́ми; **~ one's eyes out** вы́плакать (*pf.*) (все) глаза́; **she cried herself to sleep** она́ усну́ла в слеза́х. **2.** (*shout, exclaim*) крича́ть (*impf.*); вскри́к|ивать, -нуть; **"Enough!" he cried** «Дово́льно!» — закрича́л он. **3.** (*proclaim*): **~ one's wares** выклика́ть (*impf.*) свои́ това́ры; **~ shame upon s.o.** стыди́ть (*impf.*) кого́-н.; **~ stinking fish** (*fig.*) хули́ть (*impf.*) свой това́р; поноси́ть (*impf.*) самого́ себя́.
v.i. **1.** (*weep*) пла́кать (*impf.*); **~ over sth.** опла́кивать (*impf.*) что-н.; **it's no good ~ing over spilt milk** (*fig.*) сде́ланного не воро́тишь; что с во́зу упа́ло, то пропа́ло. **2.** (*shout, exclaim, plead*) крича́ть (*impf.*); вскри́к|ивать, -нуть; **he cried with pain** он вскри́кнул от бо́ли; **they cried for mercy** они́ умоля́ли о милосе́рдии; **~ for the moon** (*fig.*) жела́ть (*impf.*) невозмо́жного/несбы́точного.
with advs.: **~ down** *v.t.* (*disparage*) умал|я́ть, -и́ть; прин|ижа́ть, -и́зить; **~ off** *v.t. & i.* (*an engagement*) отмен|я́ть, -и́ть (свида́ние); **~ out** *v.i.* (*in pain or distress*) вскри́к|ивать, -нуть; **~ up** *v.t.* (*boost*) превозн|оси́ть, -ести́.
cpd. **~-baby** *n.* пла́кса (*c.g.*), рёва (*c.g.*).
crying [ˈkraɪɪŋ] *n.* (*weeping*) плач; (*calling of wares*) крик, выклика́ние.
adj.: **a ~ shame** безобра́зие; **~ need** о́страя нужда́.
cryolite [ˈkraɪəʊˌlaɪt] *n.* криоли́т.
cryology [kraɪˈɒlədʒɪ] *n.* криоло́гия.
crypt [krɪpt] *n.* кри́пта, склеп.
cryptanalysis [ˌkrɪptəˈnælɪsɪs] *n.* дешифро́вка криптогра́мм.
cryptanalyst [ˌkrɪptˈænəlɪst] *n.* дешифро́вщик.
cryptic [ˈkrɪptɪk] *adj.* таи́нственный, зага́дочный.
crypto-Communist [ˌkrɪptəʊˈkɒmjʊnɪst] *n.* та́йный коммуни́ст.
cryptogam [ˈkrɪptəˌgæm] *n.* тайнобра́чное расте́ние.
cryptogram [ˈkrɪptəˌgræm] *n.* криптогра́мма, та́йнопись.
cryptographer [krɪpˈtɒgrəfə(r)] *n.* шифрова́льщик
cryptographic [ˌkrɪptəˈgræfɪk] *adj.* криптографи́ческий, шифрова́льный.
cryptography [krɪpˈtɒgrəfɪ] *n.* криптогра́фия.
cryptomeria [ˌkrɪptəˈmɪərɪə] *n.* криптоме́рия.
cryptonym [ˈkrɪptənɪm] *n.* (та́йная) кли́чка.
crystal [ˈkrɪst(ə)l] *n.* **1.** (*substance*) го́рный хруста́ль; **~ ornaments** хруста́льные украше́ния; **~ set** (*radio*) приёмник на криста́ллах; дете́кторный приёмник. **2.** (*glassware*) хруста́ль (*m.*); **~ ball** маги́ческий криста́лл. **3.** (*aggregation of molecules*) криста́лл. **4.** (*fig.*): **the ~ waters of the lake** прозра́чные во́ды о́зера. **5.** (*US, watch-glass*) стекло́ ручны́х/карма́нных часо́в.
cpds. **~-clear** *adj.* (*fig.*) я́сный как бо́жий день; **~-gazer** *n.* гада́тель (*m.*), гада́льщик; (*fem.*) гада́лка; **~-gazing** *n.* гада́ние.
crystalline [ˈkrɪstəˌlaɪn] *adj.* хруста́льный; (*fig., also*) криста́льный; **~ lens** (*anat.*) хруста́лик.
crystallization [ˌkrɪstəlaɪˈzeɪʃ(ə)n] *n.* (*lit.*) кристаллиза́ция.
crystallize [ˈkrɪstəˌlaɪz] *v.t.* **1.** (*form into crystals*) кристаллизова́ть (*impf., pf.*); за- (*pf.*). **2.** (*clarify*) вопло|ща́ть, -ти́ть в определённую фо́рму. **3.**: **~d fruit** заса́харенные фру́кты.
v.i. **1.** (*form into crystals*) кристаллизова́ться (*impf., pf.*); вы- (*pf.*). **2.**: **his plans ~d** его́ пла́ны ста́ли определёнными.
crystallographer [ˌkrɪstəˈlɒgrəfə(r)] *n.* кристалло́граф.
crystallography [ˌkrɪstəˈlɒgrəfɪ] *n.* кристаллогра́фия.
CSCE (*abbr. of* ***Conference on Security and Co-operation in Europe***) СБСЕ, (Совеща́ние по безопа́сности и сотру́дничеству в Евро́пе).
CSE (*abbr. of* ***Certificate of Secondary Education***) ≃ аттеста́т о сре́днем образова́нии.
cub [kʌb] *n.* **1.** детёныш; (*bear*) медвежо́нок; (*fox*) лисёнок; (*lion*) львёнок; (*tiger*) тигрёнок; (*wolf*) волчо́нок; (*fig.*): **~ reporter** начина́ющий репортёр; **unlicked ~** зелёный юне́ц, щено́к. **2.** (*ill-mannered youth*) де́рзкий щено́к.
v.i. **1.** (*bring forth ~s*) щени́ться, о-. **2.** (*hunt fox-~s*) охо́титься (*impf.*) на лися́т.
cpd. **~hunting** *n.* охо́та на лися́т.
Cuba [ˈkju:bə] *n.* Ку́ба; **in ~** на Ку́бе.
Cuban [ˈkju:bən] *n.* куби́н|ец (*fem.* -ка).
adj. куби́нский.
cubby-hole [ˈkʌbɪ-] *n.* (*small room*) ко́мнатка, камо́рка.
cube [kju:b] *n.* **1.** (*math.: of a number*) куб; **~ root** куби́ческий ко́рень. **2.** (*solid*) ку́бик; **~ sugar** пилёный са́хар; **sugar ~** ку́бик/кусо́к пилёного са́хара.
v.t. **1.** (*calculate ~ of*) возв|оди́ть, -ести́ (*число*) в куб; **4 ~d** 4 в ку́бе; 4 в тре́тьей сте́пени. **2.** (*cut into ~s*) нар|еза́ть, -е́зать ку́биками.
cubic [ˈkju:bɪk] *adj.* куби́ческий; **~ content** кубату́ра, ёмкость, объём.
cubical [ˈkju:bɪk(ə)l] *adj.* куби́ческий.
cubicle [ˈkju:bɪk(ə)l] *n.* каби́на; бокс.
cubiform [ˈkju:bɪˌfɔ:m] *adj.* кубови́дный.
cubism [ˈkju:bɪz(ə)m] *n.* куби́зм.
cubist [ˈkju:bɪst] *n.* куби́ст.
cubit [ˈkju:bɪt] *n.* ло́коть (*m.*) (*мера длины*).
cubital [ˈkju:bɪt(ə)l] *adj.* локтево́й.
cuckold [ˈkʌkəʊld] *n.* рогоно́сец.
v.t. наст|авля́ть, -а́вить рога́ +*d.*
cuckoo [ˈkʊku:] *n.* куку́шка; **~ clock** часы́ (*m. pl.*) с куку́шкой; **~ flower** горицве́т куку́шкин.
adj. (*coll., crazy*) чо́кнутый, тро́нутый.
v.i. (*utter ~'s cry*) кукова́ть (*impf.*).
cucumber [ˈkju:kʌmbə(r)] *n.* огуре́ц; **~ salad** сала́т из огурцо́в; **cool as a ~** хладнокро́вный, невозмути́мый.
cud [kʌd] *n.* жва́чка; **chew the ~** (*lit., fig.*) жева́ть (*impf.*) жва́чку.
cuddle [ˈkʌd(ə)l] *v.t. & i.* обн|има́ть(ся).
v.i.: **~ up (to s.o.)** приж|има́ться, -а́ться (к кому́-н.).
cuddl|esome [ˈkʌd(ə)lsəm], **-y** [ˈkʌdlɪ] *adjs.* располага́ющий к ла́ске; ми́лый, прия́тный; **~ toy** мягконабивна́я игру́шка.
cudgel [ˈkʌdʒ(ə)l] *n.* дуби́нка, па́лка; **take up the ~s for s.o.** (*fig.*) вы́ступить (*pf.*) в защи́ту кого́-н.
v.t. бить (*impf.*) дуби́нкой/па́лкой; **~ one's brains** лома́ть (*impf.*) го́лову (*над чем*).
cue[1] [kju:] *n.* (*theatr.*) ре́плика; (*fig., hint*) намёк; **take one's ~ from** взять (*pf.*) приме́р с (*кого*); поня́ть (*pf.*) (*чей*) намёк.
cue[2] [kju:] *n.* (*billiards*) кий.
cuff[1] [kʌf] *n.* **1.** (*part of sleeve; linen band*) манже́та; **off the ~** (*fig.*) экспро́мтом. **2.** (*US, trouser turnup*) отворо́т.
cpd. **~-links** *n. pl.* за́понки (*f. pl.*).
cuff[2] [kʌf] *n.* (*blow*) шлепо́к.
v.t. шлёп|ать, -нуть.
cuirass [kwɪˈræs] *n.* (*armour*) кира́са.
cuirassier [ˌkwɪrəˈsɪə(r)] *n.* кираси́р.
cuisine [kwɪˈzi:n] *n.* ку́хня.
cul-de-sac [ˈkʌldəˌsæk, ˈkʊl-] *n.* (*also fig.*) тупи́к.
culinary [ˈkʌlɪnərɪ] *adj.* кулина́рный; **~ plants** о́вощи и фру́кты, го́дные для ва́рки.

cull [kʌl] *n.* (*of seals*) отбо́р, брако́вка.
v.t. **1.** (*select*) от|бира́ть, -обра́ть; под|бира́ть, -обра́ть; (*flowers etc.*) соб|ира́ть, -ра́ть. **2.** (*slaughter*) бить (*impf.*).
culminate ['kʌlmɪ,neɪt] *v.i.* дост|ига́ть, -и́гнуть вы́сшей то́чки (*or* апоге́я).
culmination [,kʌlmɪ'neɪʃ(ə)n] *n.* кульмина́ция; кульминацио́нный пункт.
culottes [kju:'lɒts] *n. pl.* ю́бка-брю́ки.
culpability [,kʌlpə'bɪlɪtɪ] *n.* вино́вность, престу́пность.
culpable ['kʌlpəb(ə)l] *adj.* вино́вный, престу́пный.
culprit ['kʌlprɪt] *n.* (*offender*) престу́пник; (*fig.*) вино́вник.
cult [kʌlt] *n.* культ, обожествле́ние.
cultivable ['kultivəb(ə)l] *adj.* (*of soil*) приго́дный для возде́лывания; (*of plants*) культиви́руемый.
cultivate ['kʌltɪ,veɪt] *v.t.* **1.** (*land*) возде́л|ывать, -ать; (*crops*) культиви́ровать (*impf.*); **~d area** посевна́я пло́щадь. **2.:** **~ one's mind** развива́ть (*impf.*) ум; **~ one's style** соверше́нствовать (*impf.*) свой стиль; **a ~d person** культу́рный/интеллиге́нтный челове́к. **3.:** **~ s.o.('s acquaintance)** подде́рживать (*impf.*) знако́мство с кем-н.
cultivation [,kʌltɪ'veɪʃ(ə)n] *n.* **1.** (*agric.*) (*of soil*) обрабо́тка, культива́ция, возде́лывание; (*of plants*) культиви́рование, разведе́ние. **2.** (*culture*) культу́ра. **3.** (*of acquaintance*) подде́рживание (знако́мства).
cultivator ['kʌltɪ,veɪtə(r)] *n.* (*pers.*) земледе́лец; (*implement*) культива́тор.
cultural ['kʌltʃər(ə)l] *adj.* культу́рный; **~ centre** дом/дворе́ц культу́ры; **~ agreement** догово́р о культу́рном обме́не; **~ institution** культу́рно-просвети́тельное учрежде́ние.
culture ['kʌltʃə(r)] *n.* **1.** (*tillage*) возде́лывание, культива́ция. **2.** (*rearing, production*) разведе́ние, возде́лывание; **~ of oysters** разведе́ние у́стриц; **~ of silk** разведе́ние шелкови́чных черве́й. **3.** (*colony of bacteria*) культу́ра, шта́мм. **4.** (*civilization, way of life*) культу́ра, быт; **physical/mental ~** физи́ческое/у́мственное разви́тие; **a man of ~** интеллиге́нтный челове́к; **Greek ~** гре́ческая культу́ра; **beauty ~** ухо́д за ко́жей; косме́тика.
v.t.: **~d pearls** культиви́рованный же́мчуг; **~d viruses** вы́ращенные ви́русы.
cultured ['kʌltʃəd] *adj.* (*of pers.*) интеллиге́нтный, культу́рный.
culverin ['kʌlvərɪn] *n.* (*hist.*) кулеври́на.
culvert ['kʌlvət] *n.* кульве́рт; дрена́жная труба́; (*elec.*) подзе́мный трубопро́вод для ка́беля.
cumber ['kʌmbə(r)] *v.t.* затрудн|я́ть, -и́ть; препя́тствовать (*impf.*) +*d.*
cumb|ersome ['kʌmbəsəm], **-rous** ['kʌmbrəs] *adjs.* громо́здкий, обремени́тельный.
cumbrousness ['kʌmbrəsnɪs] *n.* громо́здкость, обремени́тельность.
cummerbund ['kʌmə,bʌnd] *n.* широ́кий по́яс (под смо́кинг).
cum(m)in ['kʌmɪn] *n.* тмин.
cumquat ['kʌmkwɒt] *n.* кинка́н, кумква́т.
cumulate ['kju:mjʊ,leɪt] *v.t.*: **~ offices** сосредото́чи|вать, -ть не́сколько должносте́й в одни́х рука́х.
v.i. аккумули́роваться (*impf.*); нак|а́пливаться, -опи́ться.
cumulation [,kju:mjʊ'leɪʃ(ə)n] *n.* аккумуля́ция, накопле́ние.
cumulative ['kju:mjʊlətɪv] *adj.* кумуляти́вный, нако́пленный, совоку́пный; **~ evidence** (*leg.*) совоку́пность у́лик; **~ sentence** (*leg.*) совоку́пность пригово́ров.
cumulo-cirrus ['kju:mjʊləʊ-] *n.* пе́ристо-кучевы́е облака́.
cumulo-nimbus ['kju:mjʊləʊ-] *n.* ку́чево-дождевы́е облака́.
cumulo-stratus ['kju:mjʊləʊ-] *n.* слои́сто-кучевы́е облака́.
cumulus ['kju:mjʊləs] *n.* (*cloud*) кучевы́е облака́.
cuneiform ['kju:nɪ,fɔ:m] *n.* (**~** *writing*) кли́нопись.
adj. (*wedge-shaped*) клинообра́зный; (*of writing*) клинопи́сный.
cunning ['kʌnɪŋ] *n.* (*craftiness*) хи́трость; (*skill*) ло́вкость.
adj. (*crafty*) хи́трый.
cunt [kʌnt] *n.* пизда́ (*vulg.*).
cup [kʌp] *n.* **1.** (*for tea etc.*) ча́шка, (*liter.*) ча́ша; **that is my ~ of tea** (*fig.*) э́то по мне́; э́то в моём вку́се; **another ~ of tea** (*fig.*) совсе́м друго́е де́ло. **2.** (*fig.*): **his ~ was full** (*sc. with happiness*) он был на верху́ блаже́нства; (*with misery*) его́ ча́ша страда́ний перепо́лнилась. **3.** (*as prize*) ку́бок; **~ final** фина́л ро́зыгрыша ку́бка. **4.: in one's ~s** (*fig.*) навеселе́; под хмельком. **5.** (*Communion chalice*) ча́ша, поти́р. **6.: claret ~** крюшо́н из кра́сного вина́. **7.** (*calyx*) ча́шечка; (*socket*) углубле́ние. **8.:** **~ and ball** бильбоке́ (*indecl.*).
v.t. **1.:** **~ one's hand** держа́ть (*impf.*) ру́ку го́рстью; **~ one's hands round a glass** обхвати́ть (*pf.*) стака́н обе́ими рука́ми; **~ one's chin in one's hands** подп|ира́ть, -ере́ть подборо́док ладо́нями. **2.** (*bleed*) ста́вить, по- ба́нки +*d.*; **~ping-glass** (*med.*) ба́нка.
cpds. **~bearer** *n.* виноче́рпий; **~-cake** *n.* кру́глый кекс; **~-tie** *n.* футбо́льный матч на ку́бок.
cupboard ['kʌbəd] *n.* шкаф, буфе́т; **~ love** коры́стная/рассчётливая любо́вь.
cupful ['kʌpfʊl] *n.* по́лная ча́шка (*чего*).
Cupid ['kju:pɪd] *n.* **1.** (*myth.*) Купидо́н; **~'s bow** (*of lip*) гу́бы (*f. pl.*) ба́нтиком. **2.** (*putto*) аму́р.
cupidity [kju:'pɪdɪtɪ] *n.* а́лчность, жа́дность.
cupola ['kju:pələ] *n.* ку́пол.
cuppa ['kʌpə] *n.*: **fancy a ~?** не хоти́те ли ча́шку ча́ю?
cupro-nickel [,kju:prəʊ'nɪk(ə)l] *n.* мельхио́р.
cur [kɜ:(r)] *n.* дворня́жка, дворня́га; (*fig., of pers.*) соба́ка.
curable ['kjʊərəb(ə)l] *adj.* излечи́мый, исцели́мый.
curaçao [,kjʊərə'səʊ] *n.* кюрасо́ (*indecl.*).
curacy ['kjʊərəsɪ] *n.* прихо́д.
curare [kjʊə'rɑ:rɪ] *n.* кура́ре (*indecl.*).
curate ['kjʊərət] *n.* вика́рий, мла́дший прихо́дский свяще́нник.
curative ['kjʊərətɪv] *adj.* целе́бный, цели́тельный.
curator [kjʊə'reɪtə(r)] *n.* (*of museum etc.*) храни́тель (*m.*).
curatorship [kjʊə'reɪtə(r)ʃɪp] *n.* до́лжность храни́теля.
curb [kɜ:b] *n.* **1.** (*horse's*) подгу́бник. **2.** (*fig.*) узда́. **3.** = **kerb**
v.t. **1.** (*of horse*) над|ева́ть, -е́ть узду́ на+*a.* **2.** (*fig.*) обу́зд|ывать, -а́ть.
curd [kɜ:d] *n.* творо́г.
curdle ['kɜ:d(ə)l] *v.t.* створ|а́живать, -ожи́ть; **~ the blood** (*fig.*) леден́ить (*impf.*) кровь.
v.i. свёр|тываться, -ну́ться; створ|а́живаться, -о́житься; (*fig.*): **one's blood ~s** кровь леденеет; кровь сты́нет в жи́лах.
cure ['kjʊə(r)] *n.* **1.** (*remedy*) лека́рство, сре́дство; **this is a ~ for idleness** э́то лека́рство от безде́лья; **past ~** неизлечи́мый. **2.** (*treatment*) лече́ние; **he went to Vichy for the ~** он пое́хал на лече́ние в Виши́. **3.:** **~ of souls** бенефи́ций. **4.** (*vulcanization*) вулканиза́ция.
v.t. **1.** (*make healthy*) выле́чивать, вы́лечить; **he was ~d of asthma** он вы́лечился от а́стмы; **he was ~d of gambling** он излечи́лся от стра́сти к аза́ртной игре́. **2.** (*remedy*): (*disease*) выле́чивать, вы́лечить; излеч|ивать, -и́ть; (*poverty*) уничт|ожа́ть, -о́жить; (*drunkenness*) изж|ива́ть, -и́ть. **3.** (*meat*) соли́ть, по-; вя́лить, про-; (*hides*) обраб|а́тывать, -о́тать; (*tobacco*) фермента́ровать; (*impf., pf.*).
v.i.: **the disease ~d of itself** боле́знь прошла́ сама́ по себе́.
cpd. **~-all** *n.* панаце́я.
curettage [kjʊə'retɪdʒ, -rɪ'tɑ:dʒ] *n.* выска́бливание.
curette [kjʊə'ret] *n.* кюре́тка.
v.t. выска́бливать, вы́скоблить кюре́ткой.
curfew ['kɜ:fju:] *n.* коменда́нтский час; (*hist.*) вече́рний звон; **impose a ~** устан|а́вливать, -ови́ть коменда́нтский час; **lift a ~** отмен|я́ть, -и́ть коменда́нтский час.
curia ['kjʊərɪə] *n.* (па́пская) ку́рия.
curie ['kjʊərɪ] *n.* (*unit*) кюри́ (*nt. indecl.*).
curio ['kjʊərɪəʊ] *n.* антиква́рная вещь, ре́дкость.
curiosity [,kjʊərɪ'ɒsɪtɪ] *n.* **1.** (*inquisitiveness*) любопы́тство, любозна́тельность; **~ killed the cat** (*prov.*) любопы́тство до добра́ не доведёт. **2.** (*unusual object*) дико́вин(к)а; ре́дкость; **~ shop** ла́вка дре́вностей; антиква́рный магази́н.
curious ['kjʊərɪəs] *adj.* **1.** (*interested*): **I am ~ to know what he said** я хочу́ зна́ть, что он сказа́л. **2.** (*inquisitive*) любопы́тный, любозна́тельный. **3.** (*odd*) стра́нный, дико́винный; **~ to relate, ~ly enough** как ни стра́нно.

curium ['kjʊərɪəm] *n.* кю́рий.
curl [kɜ:l] *n.* (*of hair*) ло́кон, завито́к; (*pl.*, *~y hair*) вью́щиеся/кудря́вые/курча́вые во́лосы (*m. pl.*); (*of string*) завито́к, спира́ль; (*of smoke*) кольцо́; (*of wave*) изги́б; (*of lip*) презри́тельная усме́шка/улы́бка.
v.t.: ~ **a string around one's finger** закрути́ть (*pf.*) шнуро́к вокру́г па́льца; ~ **one's hair** зав|ива́ть, -и́ть во́лосы; **~ing-irons/-tongs** щипцы́ (*m. pl.*) для зави́вки; ~ **one's lip** презри́тельно скриви́ть (*pf.*) гу́бы.
v.i.: **her hair ~s naturally** у неё вью́щиеся/кудря́вые от приро́ды во́лосы; **the smoke ~ed upwards** клу́бы ды́ма поднима́лись вверх; **the dog ~ed up by the fire** соба́ка сверну́лась клубко́м у ками́на; **he ~ed up (with shame)** он весь съёжился от стыда́; **he ~ed up** (*of physical collapse*) его́ скрути́ло.
cpd. **~-paper** *n.* папильо́тка.
curlers ['kɜ:ləz] *n.* бигуди́ (*nt. pl.*, *indecl.*).
curlew ['kɜ:lju:] *n.* кроншне́п.
curlicue ['kɜ:lɪˌkju:] *n.* завиту́шка.
curliness ['kɜ:lɪnɪs] *n.* кудря́вость, курча́вость.
curly ['kɜ:lɪ] *adj.* кудря́вый, курча́вый, вью́щийся.
cpd. **~-headed** *adj.* кудря́вый.
curmudgeon [kə'mʌdʒ(ə)n] *n.* скваль́ыга (*c.g.*); скря́га (*c.g.*).
curmudgeonly [kə'mʌdʒ(ə)nlɪ] *adj.* скваль́ыжный, ска́редный.
currant ['kʌrənt] *n.* **1.** (*fruit*, *bush*) сморо́дина. **2.** (*in cake etc.*) изю́м, кори́нка; ~ **bun** бу́лочка с изю́мом.
currency ['kʌrənsɪ] *n.* **1.** (*acceptance*, *validity*): **the rumour gained** ~ э́тот слух прони́к всю́ду; **give** ~ **to a rumour** распространи́ть (*pf.*) слух (*о чём*); **give** ~ **to a word** пусти́ть (*pf.*) сло́во в обраще́ние; **during the** ~ **of the contract** в тече́ние сро́ка де́йствия догово́ра. **2.** (*money*) валю́та; де́н|ьги (*pl.*, *g.* -ег); **paper** ~ бума́жные де́ньги; **gold** ~ золота́я валю́та; **hard** ~ конверти́руемая валю́та; **soft** ~ неконверти́руемая валю́та; **the mark is German** ~ ма́рка — де́нежная едини́ца Герма́нии; ~ **reform** де́нежная рефо́рма.
current ['kʌrənt] *n.* **1.** (*of air*, *water*) струя́, пото́к. **2.** (*elec.*) ток; **alternating** ~ переме́нный ток; **direct** ~ постоя́нный ток. **3.** (*course*, *tendency*) тече́ние, ход.
adj. **1.** (*in general use*, *e.g. words*, *opinions*) ходя́чий, распространённый. **2.** (*of present time*) теку́щий; ~ **events** теку́щие собы́тия; **the** ~ **issue of a magazine** теку́щий/очередно́й но́мер журна́ла; **at** ~ **prices** по существу́ющим це́нам. **3.**: ~ **account** (*comm.*) теку́щий счёт.
currently ['kʌrəntlɪ] *adv.* **1.** (*generally*, *commonly*) обы́чно. **2.** (*at present*) тепе́рь, ны́не, в настоя́щее вре́мя.
curricle ['kʌrɪk(ə)l] *n.* па́рный двухколёсный экипа́ж.
curriculum [kə'rɪkjʊləm] *n.* курс обуче́ния; програ́мма; уче́бный план; ~ **vitae** (кра́ткая) биогра́фия.
currier ['kʌrɪə(r)] *n.* коже́вник.
currish ['kɜ:rɪʃ] *adj.* зло́бный, гру́бый.
curry[1] ['kʌrɪ] *n.* (*cul.*) кэ́рри (*nt. indecl.*).
v.t.: **curried lamb** бара́нина, припра́вленная кэ́рри.
cpd. **~-powder** *n.* кэ́рри; порошо́к из курку́мы.
curry[2] ['kʌrɪ] *v.t.* **1.** (*a horse etc.*) чи́стить, вы- скребни́цей. **2.**: ~ **favour with s.o.** подли́з|ываться, -а́ться к кому́-н.
cpd. **~-comb** *n.* скребни́ца.
curse [kɜ:s] *n.* **1.** (*execration*) прокля́тие; **~s come home to roost** ≃ не рой друго́му я́му, сам в неё попадёшь; **he is under a** ~; **there is a** ~ **upon him** над ним тяготе́ет прокля́тие. **2.** (*bane*) прокля́тие, бич; **the** ~ **of drink** бич пья́нства; **the** ~ (*vulg.*, *menses*) го́сти (*m. pl.*). **3.** (*oath*) богоху́льство, руга́тельство; **it is not worth a** ~ э́то вы́еденного яйца́ не сто́ит.
v.t. **1.** (*pronounce* ~ *on*) прокл|ина́ть, -я́сть. **2.** (*abuse*, *scold*) руга́ть (*impf.*); проклина́ть (*impf.*). **3. he is ~d with a violent temper** Госпо́дь его́ награди́л необу́зданным нра́вом.
v.i. (*swear*, *utter ~s*) руга́ться (*impf.*); сы́пать (*impf.*) прокля́тия; ~ **at s.o.** осыпа́ть (*pf.*) кого́-н. прокля́тиями.
cursed ['kɜ:sɪd, kɜ:st] *adj.* прокля́тый, окая́нный.
cursive ['kɜ:sɪv] *n.* (*script*) ско́ропись.
adj. скорописный.
cursor ['kɜ:sə(r)] *n.* стре́лка, указа́тель (*m.*), движо́к.
cursoriness ['kɜ:sərɪnɪs] *n.* пове́рхностность, поспе́шность.
cursory ['kɜ:sərɪ] *adj.* бе́глый, пове́рхностный, поспе́шный.
curt [kɜ:t] *adj.* кра́ткий, сжа́тый, отры́вистый, ре́зкий.
curtail [kɜ:'teɪl] *v.t.* (*shorten*) сокра|ща́ть, -ти́ть; ~ **an allowance** уре́зать (*impf.*) посо́бие.
curtailment [kɜ:'teɪlmənt] *n.* сокраще́ние, уре́зывание.
curtain ['kɜ:t(ə)n] *n.* **1.** (*of window*, *door*) занаве́ска, што́ра; (*of bed*) по́лог; **draw the ~s** (*close*) задёрнуть (*pf.*) занаве́ски; (*open*) отдёрнуть (*pf.*) занаве́ски. **2.** (*fig.*) заве́са; **draw a** ~ **over sth.** покры́ть (*pf.*) что-н. заве́сой та́йны; скрыть (*pf.*) что-н. от взо́ров; **lift the** ~ **of secrecy** приподня́ть (*pf.*) заве́су та́йны; **Iron C~** желе́зный за́навес. **3.** (*theatr.*) за́навес; **ring up the** ~ подня́ть (*pf.*) за́навес; дать (*pf.*) звоно́к к подня́тию за́навеса; **ring down the** ~ опусти́ть (*pf.*) за́навес; **safety** ~ пожа́рный за́навес; ~ **call** вы́зов; **he took six ~s** его́ вызыва́ли шесть раз.
v.t. занаве́|шивать, -сить; ~ **off** отгор|а́живать, -оди́ть занаве́ской.
cpds. **~-fire** *n.* (*mil.*) огнева́я заве́са; **~-lecture** *n.* (*joc.*) нахлобу́чка му́жу от жены́ наедине́; **~-raiser** *n.* одноа́ктная пье́са, исполня́емая пе́ред нача́лом спекта́кля; (*fig.*) прелю́дия.
curtness ['kɜ:tnɪs] *n.* кра́ткость, сжа́тость, отры́вистость, ре́зкость.
curts(e)y ['kɜ:tsɪ] *n.* ревера́нс, приседа́ние.
v.i. (*also* **make, drop a** ~) прис|еда́ть, -е́сть; де́лать, с- ревера́нс.
curvaceous [kɜ:'veɪʃəs] *adj.* (*coll.*) пы́шная, соблазни́тельная.
curvature ['kɜ:vətʃə(r)] *n.* кривизна́, изги́б, крива́я; ~ **of the earth** кривизна́ земли́; ~ **of the spine** искривле́ние позвоно́чника.
curve [kɜ:v] *n.* (*line*) крива́я; (*pl.*, *of female body*) изги́бы (*m. pl.*); (*bend in road*) изги́б.
v.t. сгиба́ть, согну́ть; из|гиба́ть, -огну́ть.
v.i. из|гиба́ться, -огну́ться; **the road ~s** доро́га извива́ется; **the river ~s round the town** река́ огиба́ет го́род.
curvet [kɜ:'vet] *n.* курбе́т.
v.i. де́лать (*impf.*) курбе́т.
curvilinear [ˌkɜ:vɪ'lɪnɪə(r)] *adj.* криволине́йный.
cushion ['kʊʃ(ə)n] *n.* дива́нная поду́шка; (*billiards*) борт; **a** ~ **of moss** покро́в из мо́ха.
v.t.: **~ed** (*padded*) **seats** мя́гкие сиде́нья; ~ **a blow** смягч|а́ть, -и́ть уда́р.
cushy ['kʊʃɪ] *adj.* (*coll.*): ~ **job** тёпленькое месте́чко.
cusp [kʌsp] *n.* (*of moon*) рог; (*of leaf*) о́стрый коне́ц; (*of tooth*) ко́нчик.
cuspidor ['kʌspɪˌdɔ:(r)] *n.* плева́тельница.
cuss [kʌs] *n.* (*coll.*) (*curse*); **it is not worth a tinker's** ~ э́то вы́еденного яйца́ не сто́ит; (*pers.*): **queer** ~ чуда́к.
cussed ['kʌsɪd] *adj.* стропти́вый.
cussedness ['kʌsɪdnɪs] *n.* стропти́вость.
custard ['kʌstəd] *n.* сла́дкий крем/со́ус из яи́ц и молока́.
cpd. **~-apple** *n.* ано́на чешу́йчатая.
custodian [kʌ'stəʊdɪən] *n.* (*guardian*) опеку́н; (*of property etc.*) администра́тор; (*of museum etc.*) храни́тель (*m.*); (*caretaker*) сто́рож.
custody ['kʌstədɪ] *n.* **1.** (*guardianship*) опе́ка, попече́ние. **2.** (*keeping*): **in safe** ~ на (со)хране́нии. **3.** (*arrest*): **take, give into** ~ брать, взять под стра́жу; арестов|ывать, -а́ть.
custom ['kʌstəm] *n.* **1.** (*habit*, *accepted behaviour*) обы́чай. **2.** (*business patronage*, *clientele*) клиенту́ра, зака́зчики (*m. pl.*), покупа́тели (*m. pl.*). **3.** (*pl.*, *import duties*) тамо́женные по́шлины (*f. pl.*); **~s officer** тамо́женник; **~s union** тамо́женный сою́з; **we got through the ~s** мы прошли́ тамо́женный досмо́тр.
cpds. **~-house** *n.* тамо́жня; **~-made** *adj.* сде́ланный/ изгото́вленный на зака́з.
customary ['kʌstəmərɪ] *adj.* обы́чный, привы́чный; **it is** ~ **to tip** при́нято дава́ть на чай; ~ **law** обы́чное пра́во.
customer ['kʌstəmə(r)] *n.* (*purchaser*) покупа́тель (*m.*); (*giving order*) зака́зчик; **regular** ~ постоя́нный покупа́тель; (*of bank etc.*) клие́нт; (*of restaurant*) посети́тель (*m.*); (*coll.*, *fellow*) субъе́кт, тип; **ugly** ~ жу́ткий субъе́кт.

cut [kʌt] *n.* **1.** (*act of* ~*ting*) ре́зка, ре́зание; (*stroke with sword, whip etc.*) ре́зкий уда́р; **he gave his horse a ~ across the flank** он хлестну́л ло́шадь по кру́пу; **~ and thrust** схва́тка; (*result of stroke*) поре́з, разре́з; **he has ~s on his face from shaving** у него́ на лице́ поре́зы от бритья́; **he got a nasty ~** он си́льно поре́зался. **2.** (*reduction*) сниже́ние, пониже́ние; **~ in salary** сниже́ние жа́лованья; **power ~** прекраще́ние пода́чи электроэне́ргии. **3.** (*omission*): **there were ~s in the film** в фи́льме бы́ли сде́ланы купю́ры (*f. pl.*). **4.** (*piece or quantity* ~): **a nice ~ of beef** хоро́ший кусо́к вы́резки/филе́я; **a ~ off the joint** ломо́ть (*m.*)/кусо́к жа́реного мя́са; **cold ~s** мясно́й ассортиме́нт; **this year's ~ of wool** настри́г ше́рсти э́того го́да. **5.** (*of clothes*) покро́й. **6.** (*in tennis etc.*) уда́р. **7.** (*allusion*) ко́лкое замеча́ние; **that remark was a ~ at me** э́то был вы́пад про́тив меня́; э́то был ка́мешек в мой огоро́д. **8.: short ~** кратча́йший путь; **take a short ~** пойти́ (*pf.*) напрями́к. **9.: he is a ~ above you** он на́ голову вы́ше вас. **10.** (*railway* ~*ting*) вы́емка железнодоро́жного пути́. **11.** (*woodcut etc.*) гравю́ра на де́реве. **12.** (*coll., rake-off*) до́ля, часть; **his ~ was 20%** его́ до́ля составля́ла 20%.

v.t. **1.** (*divide, separate, wound, extract by* ~*ting*) ре́зать (*impf.*); разр|еза́ть, -е́зать; отр|еза́ть, -е́зать; **the knife ~ his finger** нож поре́зал ему́ па́лец; **he ~ himself on the tin** он поре́зался/пора́нился о консе́рвную ба́нку; **he ~ the pages (of a book)** он разре́зал кни́гу; **the wheat has been ~** пшени́ца сжа́та; **~ wood** руби́ть (*impf.*) лес; коло́ть (*impf.*) дрова́; **~** (*p.p.*) **flowers** сре́занные цветы́; **~ tobacco** наре́занный таба́к; **~ coal** (*in a mine*) выруба́ть, вы́рубить у́голь; **~ sth. in two** разр|еза́ть, -е́зать что-н. попола́м; **~ to pieces** (*lit.*) разре́зать (*pf.*) на куски́; (*fig., defeat utterly*) изничто́жить (*pf.*); разби́ть (*pf.*) на́голову; **~ short** (*an article*) сокра|ща́ть, -ти́ть; (*s.o.'s life*) оборва́ть (*pf.*); **he ~ the boat loose** он отвяза́л ло́дку; **~ open** (*e.g. an orange*) разр|еза́ть, -е́зать; (*cin.*) **~!** (*stop shooting*) стоп! **2.** (*make by* ~*ting*): **~ me a piece of cake** отре́жьте мне кусо́к то́рта; **~ steps in the ice** проруб|а́ть, -и́ть ступе́ньки во льду; **~ a road up a hillside** проложи́ть (*pf.*) доро́гу на верши́ну холма́; **~ an inscription** высека́ть, вы́сечь на́дпись (на ка́мне); **~ a key** выреза́ть, вы́резать ключ; **~ a statue in marble** вытёсывать, вы́тесать ста́тую из мра́мора; **~ a jewel** грани́ть (*impf.*) драгоце́нный ка́мень; **~ glass** гранёное стекло́; хруста́ль (*m.*). **3.** (*trim*) подстр|ига́ть, -и́чь; **~ one's nails** подстр|ига́ть, -и́чь но́гти; **have one's hair ~** стри́чься, по-; **~ s.o.'s hair** стричь, о- кого́-н.; **he ~ my hair too short** он сли́шком ко́ротко остри́г мне во́лосы. **4.** (*ignore, neglect*): **she ~ me (dead)** она́ не пожела́ла меня́ узна́ть; **~ a lecture** пропус|ка́ть, -ти́ть ле́кцию. **5.** (*intersect*) пересека́ть (*impf.*); **AB ~s CD at E** AB пересека́ет CD в то́чке E. **6.** (*reduce*) сн|ижа́ть, -и́зить; сокра|ща́ть, -ти́ть; **fares were ~** пла́та за прое́зд была́ сни́жена; **the play was ~** пье́су сократи́ли; **~** (*beat*) **the record by 5 minutes** улу́чшить (*pf.*) реко́рд на 5 мину́т. **7.** (*of clothes*) крои́ть, с-. **8.: the baby ~ a tooth** у ребёнка проре́зался зуб. **9.** (*at cards*): **~ the pack** сн|има́ть, -ять коло́ду. **10.** (*fig.*): **he was ~ to the heart** э́то его́ заде́ло за живо́е; э́то уязви́ло его́ в са́мое се́рдце; **~** (*break*) **one's connection with s.o.** пор|ыва́ть, -ва́ть отноше́ния с кем-н.; **~ it fine** (*leave bare margin*) рассчита́ть (*pf.*) что-н. в обре́з; **that ~s no ice with me** (*coll.*) э́то на меня́ не де́йствует; **~ the ground from under s.o.'s feet** вы́бить у кого́-н. по́чву из-под ног. **11.** (*excise, eschew*): **the third act was ~ (out)** тре́тье де́йствие бы́ло вы́резано/опу́щено; **~ the cackle!** (*sl.*) прекрати́те болтовню́! **12.** (*hit sharply*): **he ~ him across the face with his whip** он хлестну́л его́ плётью по лицу́; (*at tennis etc.*) ср|еза́ть, -е́зать (мяч).

v.i. **1.** (*make incision*) ре́зать (*impf.*); **this knife doesn't ~** э́тот нож не ре́жет. **2.** (*in pass. sense*) ре́заться (*impf.*); **sandstone ~s easily** песча́ник легко́ ре́жется. **3.** (*fig.*): **the argument ~s both ways** э́тот до́вод мо́жно испо́льзовать и так, и э́так; **~ loose** (*sever connection*) прерва́ть (*pf.*) отноше́ния; (*behave wildly*) с цепи́ сорва́ться (*pf.*); **he ~ into the conversation** он вмеша́лся в разгово́р; **it ~ into** (*took up*) **his time** э́то о́тняло у него́ вре́мя. **4.** (*aim a blow; thrust*): **he ~ at me with a stick** он замахну́лся на меня́ па́лкой; **that ~s at all my hopes** э́то нано́сит уда́р всем мои́м наде́ждам; **it ~s across our plans** э́то срыва́ет на́ши пла́ны. **5.** (*cards*): **we ~ for partners** сня́тием карт мы определи́ли партнёров. **6.** (*run, take short* ~): **the boy ~ away** ма́льчик удра́л/умча́лся; **he ~ and ran** он драпану́л (*or* дал стрекача́) (*coll.*); **we ~ across the fields** мы прошли́ кратча́йшим путём че́рез поля́.

with advs.: **~ away** *v.t.* (*e.g. dead wood from a tree*) ср|еза́ть, -е́зать; **~ back** *v.t.* (*prune*) подр|еза́ть, -е́зать; (*fig, reduce, limit*) сокра|ща́ть, -ти́ть; *v.i.* (*cin.*) повтори́ть (*pf.*) да́нный ра́нее кадр; **~ down** *v.t.* (*e.g. a tree*) руби́ть, с-; (*an opponent*) сра|жа́ть, -зи́ть; **~ down expenses** сокра|ща́ть, -ти́ть расхо́ды; **~ down trousers** (*for s.o. shorter*) подкор|а́чивать, -оти́ть брю́ки; **~ down** (*abridge*) **an article** сокра|ща́ть, -ти́ть статью́; **~ s.o. down to size** (*coll.*) сбить (*pf.*) спесь с кого́-н.; **~ in** *v.t.*: **~ s.o. in** (*give them a share*) выделя́ть, вы́делить кому́-н. до́лю; *v.i.* (*interrupt a speaker*) вме́ш|иваться, -а́ться; (*at a dance*) отб|ива́ть, -и́ть у кого́-н. да́му; (*at a card-game*) замен|я́ть, -и́ть вы́шедшего из игры́; (*of a driver*) перере́зать (*pf.*) доро́гу кому́-н.; **~ off** *v.t.*: **he ~ the chicken's head off** он отруби́л цыплёнку го́лову; **he ~ off a yard from the roll (of cloth)** он отре́зал ярд мате́рии от куска́; **I was ~ off while talking** меня́ разъедини́ли/прерва́ли во вре́мя разгово́ра; **they ~ off our electricity** у нас отключи́ли/вы́ключили электри́чество; **the army was ~ off from its base** а́рмия была́ отре́зана от ба́зы; **the stragglers were ~ off** отста́вшие солда́ты бы́ли отре́заны; **we were ~ off by the tide** прили́в отре́зал нас от су́ши; **~ off supplies** прекра|ща́ть, -ти́ть подво́з припа́сов; **he ~ himself off from the world** он отгороди́лся от ми́ра; **he ~ his son off (with a shilling)** он лиши́л своего́ сы́на насле́дства; **he was ~ off in his prime** он поги́б в расцве́те лет; **~ (off) a corner** ср|еза́ть, -е́зать у́гол; **~ out** *v.t.*: **he ~ out a picture from the paper** он вы́резал карти́нку из газе́ты; **she ~ out a dress** она́ скрои́ла пла́тье; **he is not ~ out for the work** он не со́здан для э́той рабо́ты; **he has his work ~ out** ему́ предстои́т нелёгкая зада́ча; (*eliminate*): **he ~ out his rival** он вы́теснил своего́ сопе́рника; **~ out the details** (*in talking*) отбр|а́сывать, -о́сить подро́бности; **~ out smoking** бро́сить (*pf.*) кури́ть; **the engine ~ out** (*failed*) мото́р сдал (*or* вы́шел из стро́я); **~ up** *v.t.*: **he ~ up his meat** он наре́зал мя́со; **they ~ up the enemy forces** они́ уничто́жили врага́; они́ разби́ли врага́ на́голову; **he was ~ up by the news** (*coll.*) его́ срази́ло/подкоси́ло э́то изве́стие; **his book was ~ up by the reviewers** рецензе́нты разнесли́ его́ кни́гу; *v.i.*: **the turkey ~s up well** в индю́шке мно́го мя́са; **the cloth ~ up into three suits** из э́того материа́ла вы́шло три костю́ма; **he ~ up rough** (*coll.*) он рассвирепе́л; **he ~ up for £30,000** (*sl.*) он оста́вил по́сле сме́рти 30 000 фу́нтов.

cpds. **~-and-dried** *adj.*: **~-and-dried opinions** гото́вые/загото́вленные мне́ния; **~away** *adj.*: **~away coat** визи́тка; **~away view of an engine** разре́з маши́ны; **~back** *n.* (*reduction*) подре́зка; (*cin., flashback*) повторе́ние ра́нее пока́занного ка́дра; **~-off** *n.* (*device shutting off steam or liquid*) отсе́чка па́ра/жи́дкости; **~-off date** (*terminal date of a narrative etc.*) после́дняя да́та; **~-out** *n.* (*figure*) вы́резанная фигу́ра; (*elec.*) предохрани́тель (*m.*); автомати́ческий выключа́тель; **~-price** *adj.* продава́емый по сни́женной цене́; **~purse** *n.* карма́нник; **~throat** *n.* головоре́з; **~throat razor** опа́сная бри́тва; **~throat competition** ожесточённая/беспоща́дная конкуре́нция; **~water** *n.* (*of ship's prow*) волноре́з; водоре́з; (*of pier*) волноло́м.

cutaneous [kju:'teɪnɪəs] *adj.* ко́жный.

cute [kju:t] *adj.* (*shrewd*) нахо́дчивый, сообрази́тельный; (*appealing*) симпати́чный.

cutesy ['kju:tsɪ] *adj.* вы́чурный, претенцио́зный.

cuticle ['kju:tɪk(ə)l] *n.* кути́кула.

cutie [ˈkju:tɪ] *n.* (*coll.*) красо́тка, ку́колка.
cutis [ˈkju:tɪs] *n.* ку́тис.
cutlass [ˈkʌtləs] *n.* аборда́жная са́бля.
cutler [ˈkʌtlə(r)] *n.* ножо́вщик; торго́вец ножевы́ми изде́лиями.
cutlery [ˈkʌtlərɪ] *n.* ножевы́е изде́лия.
cutlet [ˈkʌtlɪt] *n.* отбивна́я котле́та.
cutter [ˈkʌtə(r)] *n.* (*tailor*) закро́йщик; (*boat*) ка́тер.
cutting [ˈkʌtɪŋ] *n.* **1.** (*road, rail etc.*) вы́емка. **2.** (*press* ~) вы́резка. **3.** (*of plant*) отро́сток. **4.** (*cin.*) монта́ж.
adj.: **a ~ wind** ре́зкий/прони́зывающий ве́тер; **a ~ retort** язви́тельный/ре́зкий отве́т.
cuttle-fish [ˈkʌt(ə)lfɪʃ] *n.* карака́тица, се́пия.
c.v. (*abbr. of* ***curriculum vitae***) (кра́ткая) автобиогра́фия.
c.w.o. (*abbr. of* ***cash with order***) нали́чный расчёт при вы́даче зака́за.
cwt [ˈhʌndrəd,weɪt] *n.* (*abbr. of* **hundredweight**) (*Imperial — approx. 50.8 kilograms*) англи́йский це́нтнер; (*US — approx. 45.4 kilograms*) америка́нский це́нтнер.
cyanide [ˈsaɪə,naɪd] *n.* соль циа́нистой кислоты́; циани́д.
cyanogen [saɪˈænədʒ(ə)n] *n.* циа́н.
cyanosis [,saɪəˈnəʊsɪs] *n.* циано́з, синю́ха.
cybernetic [,saɪbəˈnetɪk] *adj.* кибернети́ческий.
cybernetics [,saɪbəˈnetɪks] *n.* киберне́тика.
cyclamen [ˈsɪkləmən] *n.* цикламе́н.
cycle [ˈsaɪk(ə)l] *n.* **1.** (*series, rotation*) цикл, круг; **the ~ of the seasons** времена́ (*nt. pl.*) го́да; **song ~** цикл пе́сен; **the Arthurian ~** Арту́ров цикл. **2.** (*bicycle*) велосипе́д. **3.** (*elec.*) пери́од переме́нного то́ка.
v.i. **1.** (*revolve*) де́лать (*impf.*) оборо́ты. **2.** (*ride* ~) е́здить (*indet.*) на велосипе́де.
cpds. **~-car** *n.* малолитра́жный автомоби́ль с мотоциклéтным дви́гателем; **~-track** *n.* велосипе́дная доро́жка; (*for race*) велотре́к.
cyclic(al) [ˈsaɪklɪk(ə)l, ˈsɪk-] *adj.* цикли́ческий.
cycling [ˈsaɪklɪŋ] *n.* езда́ на велосипе́де; велоспо́рт.
cyclist [ˈsaɪklɪst] *n.* велосипеди́ст.
cyclo-cross [ˈsaɪkləʊ,krɒs] *n.* велокро́сс.
cyclone [ˈsaɪkləʊn] *n.* цикло́н.
cyclonic [,saɪˈklɒnɪk] *adj.* циклони́ческий.
Cyclopean [,saɪkləˈpi:ən, -ˈkləʊpɪən] *adj.* циклопи́ческий.
cyclopedia [,saɪkləˈpi:dɪə] *n.* энциклопе́дия.
Cyclops [ˈsaɪklɒps] *n.* Цикло́п.
cyclorama [,saɪkləʊˈrɑ:mə] *n.* кругова́я панора́ма, циклора́ма.
cyclostyle [ˈsaɪklə,staɪl] *n.* рота́тор.
v.t. размн|ожа́ть, -о́жить на рота́торе.
cyclotron [ˈsaɪklə,trɒn] *n.* циклотро́н.
cyder [ˈsaɪdə(r)] = **cider**
cygnet [ˈsɪgnɪt] *n.* молодо́й ле́бедь.
cylinder [ˈsɪlɪndə(r)] *n.* **1.** (*geom. & eng.*) цили́ндр; **~ bore** диа́метр цили́ндра в свету́; **~ head** кры́шка цили́ндра; **fire on all ~s** (*lit., fig.*) рабо́тать (*impf.*) в по́лную мо́щность. **2.** (*typ.*) цили́ндр, ва́лик.
cylindrical [,sɪˈlɪndrɪk(ə)l] *adj.* цилиндри́ческий.
cymbal [ˈsɪmb(ə)l] *n.* таре́лка.
cymbalist [ˈsɪmb(ə)lɪst] *n.* уда́рник.
cymbalo [ˈsɪmbə,ləʊ] *n.* цимба́л|ы (*pl., g.* —).
cymograph [ˈsaɪmə,grɑ:f] *n.* кимо́граф.
Cymric [ˈkɪmrɪk] *adj.* уэ́льский, ки́мрский.
cynic [ˈsɪnɪk] *n.* ци́ник.
adj. (*phil.*) цини́ческий.
cynical [ˈsɪnɪk(ə)l] *adj.* цини́чный.
cynicism [ˈsɪnɪ,sɪz(ə)m] *n.* цини́зм.
cynosure [ˈsaɪnə,zjʊə(r), ˈsɪn-] *n.* (*fig.*) центр внима́ния.
cypher [ˈsaɪfə(r)] = **cipher**
cypress [ˈsaɪprəs] *n.* кипари́с; (*attr.*) кипари́совый.
Cypriot [ˈsɪprɪət] *n.* киприо́т (*fem.* -ка).
adj. ки́прский.
Cyprus [ˈsaɪprəs] *n.* Кипр; **in ~** на Ки́пре.
Cyrillic [sɪˈrɪlɪk] *adj.*: **~ alphabet** кири́ллица.
Cyrus [ˈsaɪrəs] *n.* (*hist.*) Кир.
cyst [sɪst] *n.* киста́.
cystitis [sɪˈstaɪtɪs] *n.* цисти́т.
cytology [saɪˈtɒlədʒɪ] *n.* цитоло́гия.
czar [zɑ:(r)] *etc. see* **tsar** *etc.*
Czech [tʃek] *n.* чех (*fem.* че́шка); (*language*) че́шский язы́к.
adj. че́шский; **~ Republic** Че́хия.
Czechoslovak [,tʃekəˈsləʊvæk] *n.* жи́тель (*fem.* -ница) Чехослова́кии.
adj. чехослова́цкий.
Czechoslovakia [,tʃekəsləˈvækɪə] *n.* Чехослова́кия.

D

D [di:] *n.* **1.** (*mus.*) ре (*indecl.*). **2.** (*acad. mark*) 2, дво́йка; **he got a ~ in English** он получи́л дво́йку по англи́йскому языку́.
cpd. **~-day** *n.* день (*m.*) нача́ла вое́нной опера́ции, день «Д».
dab[1] [dæb] *n.* (*small quantity*) мазо́к.
v.t. & i. при|кла́дывать, -ложи́ть; **she ~bed (at) her eyes with a handkerchief** она́ прикла́дывала к глаза́м плато́к; **he ~bed paint on the picture** он нанёс кра́ски на холст/полотно́.
dab[2] [dæb] *n.* (*fish*) ершова́тка.
dab[3] [dæb] *n.* (*adept; also* **~ hand**) спец, до́ка (*c.g.*) (*coll.*).
dabble [ˈdæb(ə)l] *v.i.*: **~ at** (*fig.*) игра́ть (*impf.*) в+*a.*; балова́ться (*impf.*) +*i.*; **he ~s in politics** он игра́ет в поли́тику.
dabbler [ˈdæblə(r)] *n.* дилета́нт, верхогля́д.
dabchick [ˈdæbtʃɪk] *n.* пога́нка ма́лая.
da capo [dɑ: ˈkɑ:pəʊ] *adv.* с нача́ла.
dace [deɪs] *n.* еле́ц.
dacha [ˈdætʃə] *n.* да́ча.
dachshund [ˈdækshʊnd] *n.* та́кса.
dacron [ˈdeɪkrɒn, ˈdæk-] *n.* (*propr.*) дакро́н.
dactyl [ˈdæktɪl] *n.* да́ктиль (*m.*).
dactylic [dækˈtɪlɪk] *adj.* дактили́ческий.
dad [dæd], **-dy** [ˈdædɪ] *nn.* (*coll.*) па́па (*m.*), па́почка (*m.*).
dadaism [ˈdɑ:də,ɪz(ə)m] *n.* дадаи́зм.
dadaist [ˈdɑ:dəɪst] *n.* дадаи́ст.
daddy [ˈdædɪ] = **dad**
cpd. **~-long-legs** *n.* долгоно́жка; пау́к-сеноко́сец.
dado [ˈdeɪdəʊ] *n.* (*of pedestal*) цо́коль (*m.*); (*of wall*) пане́ль.
daemon [ˈdi:mən] *n.* (*myth.*) де́мон.
daemonic [di:ˈmɒnɪk] *adj.* (*inspired*) демони́ческий.
daffodil [ˈdæfədɪl] *n.* нарци́сс жёлтый.
daft [dɑ:ft] *adj.* тро́нутый, дурно́й (*coll.*).
dagger [ˈdægə(r)] *n.* **1.** (*weapon*) кинжа́л; **they are at ~s drawn** они́ на ножа́х; **she looked ~s at him** она́ пронзи́ла его́ взгля́дом. **2.** (*typ.*) ≃ кре́стик.
daguerreotype [dəˈgerəʊ,taɪp] *n.* (*process*) дагерроти́пия; (*portrait*) дагерроти́п.
dahlia [ˈdeɪlɪə] *n.* георги́н.
daily [ˈdeɪlɪ] *n.* **1.** (*newspaper*) ежедне́вная газе́та. **2.** (*charwoman*) приходя́щая домрабо́тница.
adj. ежедне́вный; **one's ~ bread** хлеб насу́щный.
adv. ежедне́вно, ка́ждый день; постоя́нно.
daintiness [ˈdeɪntɪnɪs] *n.* изы́сканность, утончённость; разбо́рчивость, привере́дливость.
dainty [ˈdeɪntɪ] *n.* ла́комство, деликате́с.
adj. **1.** (*refined, delicate*) утончённый, изя́щный, изы́сканный. **2.** (*fastidious*) привере́дливый, разбо́рчивый.
dairy [ˈdeərɪ] *n.* **1.** (*room or building*) маслоде́льня; сыроде́льный заво́д. **2.** (*shop*) моло́чная; (*attr.*) моло́чный.
cpds. **~maid** *n.* рабо́тница на моло́чной фе́рме; доя́рка; **~man** *n.* рабо́тник моло́чной фе́рмы, доя́р; моло́чник.

dais ['deɪɪs] *n.* помóст.
daisy ['deɪzɪ] *n.* **1.** (*flower*) маргарúтка; **Michaelmas ~** дúкая áстра; **fresh as a ~** пы́шущий здорóвьем. **2.** (*coll.*, *fine specimen*) прéлесть.
Dalai Lama [ˌdælaɪ 'lɑːmə] *n.* далáй-лáма (*m.*).
dale [deɪl] *n.* долúна, дол.
dalesman ['deɪlzmən] *n.* жúтель (*m.*) долúн.
dalliance ['dælɪəns] *n.* (*trifling*) баловствó; (*flirtation*) флирт.
dally ['dælɪ] *v.i.* **1.** (*play, toy*) баловáться (*impf.*) (*чем*). **2.** (*flirt*) флиртовáть (*impf.*). **3.** (*waste time*) трáтить (*impf.*) врéмя пóпусту.
Dalmatian [dæl'meɪʃ(ə)n] *n.* (*dog*) далмáтский дог.
dalmatic [dæl'mætɪk] *n.* далмáтик.
daltonism ['dɔːltəˌnɪz(ə)m] *n.* дальтонúзм.
dam[1] [dæm] *n.* **1.** (*barrier*) дáмба, плотúна, запрýда. **2.** (*reservoir*) водохранúлище.
v.t. запрý|живать, -дúть; **~ up a valley** перекр|ывáть, -ы́ть долúну; **~ up one's feelings** сдéрж|ивать, -áть чýвства.
dam[2] [dæm] *n.* (*zool.*) мáтка.
damag|e ['dæmɪdʒ] *n.* **1.** (*harm, injury*) вред, повреждéние; ущéрб; **do ~e to sth.** нан|осúть, -естú ущéрб/вред чемý-н. **2.** (*coll.*, *cost*): **what's the ~e?** скóлько с нас причитáется? **3.** (*pl.*, *leg.*) убы́тк|и (*pl.*, *g.* -ов); **sue s.o. for ~es** возбу|ждáть, -дúть дéло прóтив когó-н. (*or* предъяв|лять, -úть иск комý-н.) за убы́тки.
v.t. (*physically or morally*) повре|ждáть, -дúть +*d.*; **a ~ing admission** признáние себé в ущéрб.
Damascene ['dæməˌsiːn, ˌdæmə'siːn] *adj.* дамáсский.
v.t. (**d~**): нас|екáть, -éчь зóлотом/серебрóм; воронúть (*impf.*).
Damascus [də'mæskəs] *n.* Дамáск.
damask ['dæməsk] *n.* **1.** (*material*) дамáст, штоф; **~ silk** дамáст, камкá; **~ table-cloth** камчáтная скáтерть. **2.** (*steel*) дамáсская сталь; булáт. **3.: ~ rose** дамáсская рóза.
adj. (*poet.*, *rosy*) áлый.
v.t. (*weave*) ткáть (*impf.*) с узóрами; (*ornament*) нас|екáть, -éчь.
dame [deɪm] *n.* **1.** (*arch. or joc.*, *lady*) госпожá, дáма; **D~ Nature** мать-прирóда; **D~ Fortune** госпожá фортýна. **2.** (*fem. equiv. of knight*) дейм, кавалéрственная дáма. **3.** (*US*, *woman*) бабёнка, крáля (*coll.*).
damfool ['dæmfuːl] *adj.* (*coll.*) идиóтский.
damn [dæm] *n.* **1.** (*curse*) проклятие, ругáтельство. **2.** (*negligible amount*): **I don't care a ~** мне наплевáть.
v.t. **1.** (*doom to hell*) осу|ждáть, -дúть на вéчные мýки. **2.** (*condemn*): **the critics ~ed the play** крúтики забраковáли пьéсу; **he was ~ ed by his association with X** он навлёк на себя́ позóр общéнием с X; **~ with faint praise** похвалúть (*pf.*) так, что не поздорóвится. **3.** (*swear*): **he was ~ing and blasting** он сы́пал проклятиями. **4.** (*as expletive*): **~ (it all)!** чёрт возьмú!; тьфу, прóпасть!; **I'm ~ed if I know** ей-Бóгу, не знáю; **well, I'm ~ed!** чёрт бы меня́ побрáл!; ну и ну!; **~ you(r eyes)!** лóпни твой глазá!; **~ your impudence!** чёрт бы побрáл твоё нахáльство!; **~ all** (*coll.*, *nothing*) ни чертá; **I'm ~ed if I'll go** провалúться мне на э́том мéсте, éсли я пойдý; **I'll see him ~ed before I'll do it** я э́того не сдéлаю, хоть он лóпни. *see also* **damned**
damnable ['dæmnəb(ə)l] *adj.* прокля́тый.
damnation [dæm'neɪʃ(ə)n] *n.* **1.** (*condemnation to hell*) проклятие; осуждéние на вéчные мýки. **2.** (*adverse judgment*) осуждéние. **3. ~!** проклятие!
damned [dæmd] *n.*, *adj.* & *adv.* **1.: the ~** осуждённые на вéчные мýки; прóклятые. **2.: a ~ fool** набúтый дурáк; **it's a ~ nuisance** э́то чертóвски досáдно; **he did his ~est** (*coll.*) он лез из кóжи вон.
damnify ['dæmnɪˌfaɪ] *v.t.* (*leg.*) нан|осúть, -естú вред/ущéрб +*d.*
damning ['dæmɪŋ] *adj.* губúтельный; **~ evidence** изобличáющие улúки.
Damocles ['dæməˌkliːs] *n.*: **sword of ~** дамóклов меч.
damp [dæmp] *n.* **1.** (*moisture*) влáжность, сы́рость; **~ rises from the ground** с землú поднимáются испарéния; от землú вéет сы́ростью. **2.** (**~** *atmosphere*) сы́рость, влáжность. **3.** (*fig.*, *depression*) уны́ние; **this cast a ~ over the outing** э́то испóртило прогýлку. **4.** (*firedamp*) рýдничный газ.
adj. влáжный, сырóй; **~ course** гидроизоля́ция.
v.t. (*also* **dampen**) **1.** (*lit.*) см|áчивать, -очúть; увлажн|я́ть, -úть; **~ down a fire** тушúть, по- огóнь. **2.** (*fig.*): **~ s.o.'s ardour** осту|жáть, -дúть чей-н. пыл. **3.** (*mus.*): **~ a string** заглуш|áть, -úть струнý.
cpd. **~-proof** *adj.* влагонепроницáемый; *v.t.* предохран|я́ть, -úть от влáги.
damper ['dæmpə(r)] *n.* **1.** (*plate in stove etc.*) заслóнка; (*shock absorber*) амортизáтор; (*silencer*) глушúтель (*m.*). **2.** (*fig.*): **the news put a ~ on the stock market** нóвости привелú к понижéнию конъюнктýры на бúрже. **3.** (*in piano*) дéмпфер. **4.** (*for stamps*) рóлик для смáчивания мáрок.
dampish ['dæmpɪʃ] *adj.* сыровáтый.
dampness ['dæmpnɪs] *n.* сы́рость.
damsel ['dæmz(ə)l] *n.* (*arch.*) девúца.
damson ['dæmz(ə)n] *n.* (*fruit*) тернослúв; (*tree*) тёрн.
adj. (*colour*) тёмно-крáсный.
dance [dɑːns] *n.* **1.** тáнец; **we joined the ~** мы присоединúлись к танцýющим. **2.** (*party*) танцевáльный вéчер; тáнцы (*m. pl.*); **give a ~** устр|áивать, -óить тáнцы. **3.** (*fig.*): **lead s.o. a (fine, pretty) ~** водúть (*indet.*) когó-н. зá нос; **St Vitus's ~** пля́ска святóго Вúтта; **~ of death** пля́ска смéрти.
v.t. **1.** танцевáть, с-; исп|олня́ть, -óлнить (*танец*). **2.: ~ a baby on one's knee** качáть (*impf.*) ребёнка на колéнях. **3.** (*fig.*): **~ attendance on s.o.** ходúть (*indet.*) пéред кем-н. на зáдних лáпках.
v.i. танцевáть, с-; плясáть, с-; **he ~d for joy** он плясáл от рáдости; **he ~d with fury** он дрожáл от я́рости; **the leaves ~d in the wind** лúстья кружúлись на ветрý; **the boat ~d on the waves** лóдка качáлась на вóлнáх.
cpds. **~-band** *n.* оркéстр (на тáнцах); **~-hall** *n.* танцевáльный зал, дáнсинг.
dancer ['dɑːnsə(r)] *n.* танцóр (*fem.* -ка); (*professional*) танцóвщи|к (*fem.* -ца).
dancing ['dɑːnsɪŋ] *n.* тáнцы (*m. pl.*).
cpds. **~-girl** *n.* танцóвщица; **~-master** *n.* учúтель (*m.*) тáнцев; **~-partner** *n.* партнёр; **~-shoes** *n. pl.* танцевáльные тýфли (*f. pl.*).
dandelion ['dændɪˌlaɪən] *n.* одувáнчик.
dander ['dændə(r)] *n.* (*US coll.*): **get s.o.'s ~ up** вы́вести (*pf.*) когó-н. из себя́.
dandified ['dændɪˌfaɪd] *adj.* щегольскóй.
dandle ['dænd(ə)l] *v.t.* качáть (*impf.*).
dandruff ['dændrʌf] *n.* пéрхоть.
dandy ['dændɪ] *n.* дéнди (*m. indecl.*), щёголь (*m.*), франт.
adj. (*US coll.*) превосхóдный; пéрвый класс (*pred.*).
dandyish ['dændɪɪʃ] *adj.* щеголевáтый.
dandyism ['dændɪˌɪz(ə)m] *n.* дендúзм, франтовствó, щегольствó.
Dane [deɪn] *n.* датчáн|ин (*fem.* -ка); **Great ~** дог.
danegeld ['deɪngeld] *n.* (*fig.*) дань.
danger ['deɪndʒə(r)] *n.* **1.** (*risk of injury*) опáсность; **~!** осторóжно!; берегúсь!; **in ~** в опáсности; **out of ~** вне опáсности; **he is in ~ of falling** он рискýет упáсть; **the signal is at ~** сигнáл покáзывает, что путь закры́т; **~ money** плáта за опáсную рабóту; плáта за страх; **~ zone** опáсная зóна. **2.** (*pers. or thg. presenting risk*) опáсность, угрóза; **the wreck is a ~ to shipping** облóмки представля́ют опáсность/угрóзу для кораблéй; **~ point** опáсная тóчка; опáсный предéл.
dangerous ['deɪndʒərəs] *adj.* опáсный, рискóванный; **the dog looks ~** у собáки грóзный вид.
dangerousness ['deɪndʒərəsnɪs] *n.* опáсность, риск.
dangle ['dæŋg(ə)l] *v.t.* **1.** (*lit.*) качáть (*impf.*); покáчивать (*impf.*). **2.** (*fig.*): **~ hopes before s.o.** обольщáть (*impf.*) когó-н. надéждами.
v.i. **1.** (*lit.*) качáться (*impf.*); болтáться (*impf.*). **2.** (*fig.*): **her admirers ~d after her** поклóнники волочúлись за ней.
Daniel ['dænj(ə)l] *n.* (*fig.*) неподкýпный/прáведный судья́.
Danish ['deɪnɪʃ] *n.* (*language*) дáтский язы́к.
adj. дáтский.

dank [dæŋk] вла́жный, сыро́й, промо́зглый.
dankness ['dæŋknɪs] *n.* вла́жность, сы́рость.
danse macabre [ˌdɑ̃s mə'kɑːbr] *n.* пля́ска сме́рти.
danseuse [dɑ̃'sɜːz] *n.* танцо́вщица.
Danube ['dænjuːb] *n.* Дуна́й.
daphne ['dæfnɪ] *n.* волчея́годник.
dapper ['dæpə(r)] *adj.* щеголева́тый; бы́стрый, ре́звый.
dapple ['dæp(ə)l] *n.* (*dappled effect*) пестрота́.
adj. (*also* **~d**) пёстрый, испещрённый, пятни́стый.
cpd. **~-grey** *n.* & *adj.* (*horse*) се́рый в я́блоках (конь).
Darby and Joan [ˌdɑːbɪ ənd 'dʒəʊn] (*fig.*) ≃ Филимо́н и Бавки́да.
Dardanelles [ˌdɑːdə'nelz] *n.* Дардане́лл|ы (*pl.*, *g.* —).
dare [deə(r)] *n.* (*challenge*) вы́зов; **take a ~** приня́ть (*pf.*) вы́зов.
v.t. (*challenge*) бр|оса́ть, -о́сить вы́зов +*d.*; (*egg on*) подзадо́ри|вать, -ть; **he will ~ any danger** его́ не остано́вит никака́я опа́сность; **I ~ you to jump over the wall!** а ну, перепры́гни че́рез э́ту стену́!
v.i. **1.** (*have courage*) осме́ли|ваться, -ться; сметь, по-; отва́жи|ваться, -ться. **2.** (*have impudence*) сметь, по-; **how ~ you say that!** как вы сме́ете говори́ть тако́е! **3.: I ~ say (that) ...** на́до ду́мать (*or* полага́ю), что...; **I ~ swear** я уве́рен.
cpd. **~-devil** *adj.* отча́янный, бесшаба́шный.
daring ['deərɪŋ] *n.* отва́га.
adj. отва́жный, де́рзкий.
dark [dɑːk] *n.* темнота́, тьма; **before/after ~** до/по́сле наступле́ния темноты́; (*ignorance*) неве́жество, неве́дение; **I am in the ~ as to his plans** я в неве́дении относи́тельно его́ пла́нов; его́ пла́ны мне неве́домы; (*dark colour*) тень; **the lights and ~s of a picture** игра́ све́та и те́ни на карти́не.
adj. **1.** (*lacking light*) тёмный; **pitch ~** темны́м-темно́; тьма кроме́шная; **~ glasses** (*spectacles*) тёмные/со́лнечные очки́; **~ lantern** потайно́й фона́рь; **~ room** (*phot.*) ка́мера-обску́ра. **2.** (*of colour*) тёмный. **3.** (*of complexion*) сму́глый. **4.** (*fig.*) тёмный; **a ~ horse** тёмная лоша́дка; **the D~ Continent** чёрный контине́нт; **keep the news ~** держа́ть (*impf.*) но́вости в секре́те; **the future is ~** бу́дущее неизве́стно; **a ~ saying** нея́сное выска́зывание; **the D~ Ages** ра́ннее средневеко́вье.
darken ['dɑːkən] *v.t.* затемн|я́ть, -и́ть; **~ counsel** запу́т|ывать, -ать вопро́с; **never ~ my door again!** не переступа́йте бо́льше моего́ поро́га!
v.i. темне́ть, по-; ста|нови́ться, -ть тёмным.
darkling ['dɑːklɪŋ] *adv.* (*poet.*) во мра́ке; во тьме.
darkness ['dɑːknɪs] *n.* темнота́; **the Prince of D~** принц тьмы; **cast into outer ~** (*fig.*) отв|ерга́ть, -е́ргнуть.
darky ['dɑːkɪ] *n.* (*coll.*) чернoко́жий, чёрный.
darling ['dɑːlɪŋ] *n.* дорого́й, ми́лый, родно́й, люби́мый; **she's a ~** она́ пре́лесть; (*favourite*) люби́мец; **Fortune's ~** ба́ловень (*m.*) судьбы́; **mother's ~** ма́менькин сыно́к.
adj. (*beloved*) люби́мый, дорого́й; (*delightful*) очарова́тельный.
darn[1] [dɑːn] *n.* што́пка; зашто́панное ме́сто; **his socks have a ~ in them** у него́ носки́ зашто́паны.
v.t. & *i.* (*mend*) што́пать, за-; *see also* **darning**
darn[2] [dɑːn] *n.* (*coll.*): **I don't give a ~** мне наплева́ть.
v.t. (*as expletive*) проклина́ть (*impf.*); **~ (it)!** про́пасть!; чёрт возьми́!; чёрт подери́!
darnel ['dɑːn(ə)l] *n.* пле́вел.
darning ['dɑːnɪŋ] *n.* **1.** (*action*) што́панье, што́пка. **2.** (*things to be darned*) ве́щи (*f. pl.*) для што́пки.
cpds. **~-ball** *n.* грибо́к; **~-needle** *n.* што́пальная игла́; **~-wool** *n.* шерстяна́я ни́тка.
dart[1] [dɑːt] *n.* **1.** (*light javelin*) стрела́, дро́тик. **2.** (*for indoor game*) стрела́, дро́тик.
cpd. **~board** *n.* мише́нь для стрел.
dart[2] [dɑːt] *n.* (*run*) бросо́к, рыво́к; **he made a ~ for the door** он рвану́лся/бро́сился к две́ри.
v.t. мета́ть (*impf.*); **she ~ed an angry look at him** она́ метну́ла на него́ зло́бный взгля́д; **the snake ~ed out its tongue** змея́ вы́пустила жа́ло.
v.i. устреми́ться; помча́ться; бро́ситься (*all pf.*); **she ~ed into the shop** она́ стрело́й влете́ла в магази́н; **swallows were ~ing through the air** ла́сточки носи́лись в во́здухе.
dart[3] [dɑːt] *n.* (*dressmaking*) вы́тачка, шов.
Darwinian [dɑː'wɪnɪən] *adj.* дарвини́стский.
Darwinism ['dɑːwɪnˌɪz(ə)m] *n.* дарвини́зм.
Darwinist ['dɑːwɪnɪst] *n.* дарвини́ст.
dash [dæʃ] *n.* **1.** (*sudden rush, race*) рыво́к, бросо́к; **let's make a ~ for it** побежи́м-ка туда́; **the 100 yards ~** забе́г на 100 я́рдов. **2.** (*impact*) уда́р, взма́х; **the ~ of waves on a rock** уда́ры волн о скалу́; **the ~ of cold water revived him** струя́ холо́дной воды́ привела́ его́ в чу́вство. **3.** (*admixture*): **a ~ of pepper in the soup** щепо́тка пе́рца в су́пе. **4.** (*written stroke; also in Morse*) тире́ (*indecl.*). **5.** (*vigour*) реши́тельность. **6.** (*show*): **cut a ~** (*coll.*) рисова́ться (*impf.*).
v.t. **1.** (*throw violently*) швыр|я́ть, -ну́ть; **the ship was ~ed against the cliff** су́дно швырну́ло о скалу́; **he ~ed the book down** он отшвырну́л кни́гу. **2.** (*perform rapidly*): **he ~ed off a sketch** он наброса́л эски́з. **3.** (*fig., disappoint*) разр|уша́ть, -у́шить; разб|ива́ть, -и́ть; **his hopes were ~ed** его́ наде́жды ру́хнули. **4.** (*as expletive*): **~ it (all)!** к чёрту!; чёрт побери́!; *see also* **dashed**
v.i. **1.** (*move violently*) бро́ситься (*pf.*); ри́нуться (*pf.*); **the waves ~ed over the rocks** во́лны разбива́лись о ска́лы. **2.** (*run*) мча́ться (*impf.*); нести́сь (*det.*); **she ~ed into the shop** она́ ворвала́сь в магази́н; **he ~ed off to town** он умча́лся в го́род.
dashboard ['dæʃbɔːd] *n.* пане́ль прибо́ров; прибо́рная доска́.
dashed [dæʃd] *adj.* черто́вский, проклят́ый.
dashing ['dæʃɪŋ] *adj.* лихо́й, стреми́тельный.
dashlight ['dæʃlaɪt] *n.* ла́мпочка освеще́ния прибо́рной доски́.
dastard ['dæstəd] *n.* трус, подле́ц.
dastardly ['dæstədlɪ] *adj.* трусли́вый, по́длый.
data ['deɪtə] = **datum**
database ['deɪtəˌbeɪs] *n.* ба́за да́нных.
datable ['deɪtəb(ə)l] *adj.* поддаю́щийся датиро́вке.
date[1] [deɪt] *n.* (**~-palm**) фи́никовая па́льма; (*fruit*) фи́ник.
date[2] [deɪt] *n.* **1.** (*indication of time*) да́та, число́; **what's the ~ today?** како́е сего́дня число́?; **(at) what ~ was that?** в каки́х э́то бы́ло чи́слах?; **The Times of today's ~** сего́дняшний но́мер «Та́ймса»; **the ~ of the letter is 6 October** письмо́ дати́ровано шесты́м окрября́; **what were the ~s of your last employment?** с како́го и по како́е число́ вы рабо́тали на после́днем ме́сте? **2.** (*period*) пери́од; **at an early ~** (*soon*) в ближа́йшем бу́дущем; **by the earliest possible ~** в наикратча́йший срок; **out of ~** устаре́лый; **go out of ~** устар|ева́ть, -е́ть; выходи́ть, вы́йти из мо́ды; **up to ~** нове́йший, совреме́нный; **bring s.o. up to ~** вв|оди́ть, -ести́ кого́-н. в курс де́ла; **bring a catalogue up to ~** обнов|ля́ть, -и́ть катало́г; поп|олня́ть, -о́лнить катало́г совреме́нными да́нными; **our receipts to ~ are £5** на́ши поступле́ния на сего́дняшний день равны́ пяти́ фу́нтам. **3.** (*coll., appointment*) свида́ние.
v.t. **1.** (*indicate ~ on*) дати́ровать (*impf., pf.*); **he ~d the letter 24 May** он дати́ровал письмо́ 24-ым ма́я; **he ~d the letter ahead/back** он поме́тил/дати́ровал письмо́ бу́дущим/за́дним число́м; *see also* **dated**. **2.** (*estimate ~ of*): **can you ~ these coins?** к како́му пери́оду, по-ва́шему, отно́сятся э́ти моне́ты? **3.** (*coll., make appointment with*) назн|ача́ть, -а́чить свида́ние +*d. or c+i.*
v.i. **1.** (*count time*): **Christians ~ from the birth of Christ** христиа́не веду́т своё летоисчисле́ние с Рождества́ Христо́ва. **2.** (*originate*): **this church ~s from the 14th century** э́та це́рковь отно́сится к 14-му ве́ку. **3.** (*become obsolete, show signs of age*) старе́ть (*impf.*); устар|ева́ть, -е́ть; **the play ~s terribly** э́та пье́са ужа́сно устаре́ла.
cpds. **~-line** *n.* (*meridian*) демаркацио́нная ли́ния (су́точного) вре́мени; (*journ.*) указа́ние ме́ста и да́ты репорта́жа; *v.t.* дати́ровать (*impf., pf.*); **a story ~-lined from Cairo** сообще́ние, пе́реданное из Каи́ра; **~-stamp** *n.* ште́мпель-календа́рь (*m.*); календа́рный ште́мпель.
dated ['deɪtɪd] *adj.* (*out of date*) устаре́вший, устаре́лый.

dateless ['deɪtlɪs] *adj.* (*undated*) недати́рованный; (*immemorial*) векове́чный.
dative ['deɪtɪv] *n. & adj.* да́тельный (паде́ж).
datum ['deɪtəm, 'dɑ:təm] *n.* **1.** (*thg. known or granted*) исхо́дный факт. **2.** (*assumption, premise*) исхо́дная то́чка. **3.** (*pl.*, **data**) да́нные (*nt. pl.*); материа́л; **personal** ~ биографи́ческие да́нные; ~ **bank** банк да́нных; ~ **input** ввод да́нных; ~ **processing** обрабо́тка информа́ции.
daub [dɔ:b] *n.* **1.** (*material*) штукату́рка. **2.** (*bad painting*) мазня́, пачкотня́.
v.t. & i. **1.** (*smear*) обма́з|ывать, -ать; ма́зать, на-; ~ **paint on a wall;** ~ **a wall with paint** ма́зать сте́ну кра́ской. **2.** (*paint badly*) па́чкать; ма́зать; мазю́кать (*all impf.*).
dauber ['dɔ:bə(r)] *n.* пачку́н, мази́ла, мази́лка (*both c.g.*).
daughter ['dɔ:tə(r)] *n.* **1.** (*child*) дочь. **2.** ~ **language** (*ling.*) язы́к-пото́мок, язы́к-насле́дник.
cpd. **~-in-law** *n.* неве́стка, снохá.
daughterly ['dɔ:tərlɪ] *adj.* доче́рний, подоба́ющий до́чери.
daunt [dɔ:nt] *v.t.* устраш|а́ть, -и́ть; обескура́жи|вать, -ть; **nothing ~ ed, he asked for more** нима́ло не смуща́ясь, он попроси́л доба́вки.
dauntless ['dɔ:ntlɪs] *adj.* бесстра́шный, неустраши́мый.
dauntlessness ['dɔ:ntlɪsnɪs] *n.* бесстра́шие, неустраши́мость.
dauphin ['dɔ:fɪn, 'dəʊfæ̃] *n.* дофи́н.
davenport ['dævən,pɔ:t] *n.* (*writing-desk*) изя́щный пи́сьменный сто́лик; (*US, sofa*) дива́н.
davit ['dævɪt, 'deɪvɪt] *n.* шлюпба́лка.
Davy Jones's locker [,deɪvɪ 'dʒəʊnz] (*fig.*) морска́я пучи́на; **he's gone to** ~ он утону́л.
Davy lamp ['deɪvɪ] *n.* шахтёрская ла́мпа.
daw [dɔ:] *n.* га́лка.
dawdle ['dɔ:d(ə)l] *v.t.:* ~ **away one's time** зря тра́тить (*impf.*) вре́мя.
v.i. безде́льничать (*impf.*), ло́дырничать (*impf.*).
dawdler ['dɔ:d(ə)lə(r)] *n.* ло́дырь (*m.*), безде́льник.
dawn [dɔ:n] *n.* **1.** (*daybreak*) рассве́т, заря́; **at** ~ на рассве́те; на заре́. **2.** (*fig.*): **the** ~ **of love** пробужде́ние любви́; **the** ~ **of civilization** заря́ цивилиза́ции.
v.i. **1.** (*of daybreak*) света́ть (*impf.*); рассве|та́ть, -сти́; **the day is ~ing** света́ет. **2.** (*fig.*): **it** ~ **ed on me that ...** меня́ осени́ло, что...; **the truth ~ed upon him** ему́ всё ста́ло я́сно.
day [deɪ] *n.* **1.** (*time of daylight*) день (*m.*); (*attr.*) дневно́й; **by** ~ днём; **before** ~ до зари́; **twice a** ~ два ра́за в день; **time of** ~ вре́мя дня; **pass the time of** ~ **with s.o.** обменя́ться (*pf.*) приве́тствиями с кем-н.; **break of** ~ рассве́т; **late in the** ~ (*fig.*) сли́шком по́здно; **as happy as the** ~ **is long** неизме́нно весёлый. **2.** (*24 hours*) су́т|ки (*pl., g.* ок); **a** ~ **and a half** по́лтора су́ток; **solar** ~ астрономи́ческие су́тки; **civil** ~ гражда́нские су́тки. **3.** (*as point of time*): **what** ~ **(of the week) is it?** како́й сего́дня день (неде́ли)?; **one** ~ (*past*) одна́жды; (*future*) когда́-нибудь; **the other** ~ на днях; **every other** ~ че́рез день; **one of these (fine) ~s** в оди́н прекра́сный день; на днях; **some** ~ когда́-нибу́дь; **some** ~ **soon** ка́к-нибудь на днях; вско́ре; **this isn't my** ~ (*coll.*) я сего́дня не в уда́ре; мне сего́дня что́-то не везёт; **the last** ~, ~ **of judgement** день стра́шного суда́; **she's thirty if she's a** ~ ей ника́к не ме́ньше тридцати́ лет; **live from** ~ **to** ~ жить (*impf.*) со дня на́ день; **this** ~ **week** ро́вно че́рез неде́лю; ~ **in,** ~ **out;** ~ **after** ~ изо дня в день; **three years ago to a** ~ ро́вно три го́да наза́д; **(on) the** ~ **I met you** в день на́шей встре́чи; **(on) the** ~ **before** накану́не (*чего*); **to this** ~ до сего́дняшнего дня; **creature of a** ~ недолгове́чное существо́; **she named the** ~ она́ назна́чила день сва́дьбы; **I took a** ~ **off** я взял выходно́й; **we had a** ~ **out** мы провели́ день вне до́ма; **the maid's** ~ **out is Friday** у прислу́ги свобо́дный день в пя́тницу; **he's cleverer than you any** ~ он намно́го умне́е вас. **4.** (*as work period*): **he works a 5-hour** ~ у него́ пятичасово́й рабо́чий день; **he is paid by the** ~ ему́ пла́тят подённо; **let's call it a** ~ (*coll.*) на сего́дня хва́тит; **it's all in the ~'s work** э́то в поря́дке веще́й. **5.** (*festival*) пра́здничный день; **May D~** день Пе́рвого ма́я; **Victory D~** День побе́ды. **6.** (*period*) пора́, вре́мя (*nt.*); **the present** ~ сего́дня; теку́щий моме́нт; **these ~s** (*nowadays*) тепе́рь, сейча́с; в на́ши дни; **in those ~s** в те дни; в то вре́мя; **in ~s of old** в былы́е дни; **in ~s to come** в бу́дущем; **in this** ~ **and age** в на́ше вре́мя; **he has known better ~s** он знава́л лу́чшие времена́; **he fell on evil ~s** он впал в нищету́; **his ~s are numbered** его́ дни́ сочтены́; **end one's ~s** сконча́ться (*pf.*); **the great men of the** ~ ви́дные лю́ди эпо́хи; **he has had his** ~ он отслужи́л своё; **she was a beauty in her** ~ в своё вре́мя она́ была́ краса́вицей; **save for a rainy** ~ от|кла́дывать, -ложи́ть на чёрный день; **in all my born ~s** за всю мою́ жизнь; **salad ~s** пора́ ю́ношеской нео́пытности; **this is the** ~ **of air transport** э́то э́ра возду́шного тра́нспорта. **7.** (*denoting contest*): **win, carry the** ~ одерж|ивать, -а́ть побе́ду; **lose the** ~ проигр|ывать, -а́ть сраже́ние; **the** ~ **is ours** мы одержа́ли побе́ду; **his arrival saved the** ~ его́ прие́зд спас положе́ние.
cpds. **~-bed** *n.* куше́тка; **~-boarder** *n.* полупансионе́р; **~-book** *n.* дневни́к, журна́л; **~-boy** *n.* учени́к, не живу́щий при шко́ле; **~-break** *n.* рассве́т; **~-care** *adj.*: **~-care facilities** детса́д; ясл|и (*pl., g.* -ей); гру́ппа продлённого дня; де́тск|ие учрежде́н|ия (*pl., g.* -их -ий); **~-dream** *n.* грёза, мечта́; *v.i.* мечта́ть (*impf.*); гре́зить (*impf.*) (наяву́); **~dreamer** *n.* мечта́тель (*m.*); **~-fly** *n.* подёнка; **~-girl** *n.* учени́ца, не живу́щая при шко́ле; **~-labour** *n.* подённая рабо́та; **~-labourer** *n.* подёнщи|к (*fem.* -ца); **~light** *n.* (*period*): **in broad ~light** средь бе́ла дня; **~light-saving time** ле́тнее вре́мя; (*dawn*) дневно́й свет; рассве́т; (*fig.*): **let in some ~light on the subject** проли́ть (*pf.*) свет на предме́т; **I begin to see ~light** мне уже́ ви́ден просве́т; (*fig.*): **beat the ~lights out of s.o.** вы́бить (*pf.*) ду́шу (*or* вы́шибить (*pf.*) дух) из кого́-н.; **~-long** *n.* для́щийся це́лый день; **~-nursery** *n.* (*crèche*) де́тские ясл|и (*pl., g.* -ей); **~-school** *n.* шко́ла без пансио́на; **~spring** *n.* (*poet.*) заря́; **~-star** *n.* у́тренняя звезда́; **~-ticket** *n.* обра́тный биле́т, действи́тельный в тече́ние одного́ дня; **~time** *n.* день (*m.*); **in the ~time** днём; *adj.* дневно́й; **~-to-~** *adj.* повседне́вный.
daze [deɪz] *n.*: **he was in a** ~ он был как в дурма́не.
v.t. пора|жа́ть, -зи́ть; ошара́ши|вать, -ть.
dazzle ['dæz(ə)l] *n.* ослепле́ние; ослепи́тельный блеск.
v.t. **1.** (*lit.*) ослеп|ля́ть, -и́ть. **2.** (*fig.*) пора|жа́ть, -зи́ть; ослеп|ля́ть, -и́ть; **she was ~d by his wealth** она́ была́ ослеплена́/заворожена́ его́ бога́тством.
dB ['desɪ,bel] *n.* (*abbr. of* **decibel(s)**) дБ., (децибе́л).
DC (*abbr. of* **direct current**) постоя́нный ток.
DDT (*abbr. of* ***dichlorodiphenyltrichloroethane***) ДДТ, (дихлордифенилтрихлорэта́н).
deacon ['di:kən] *n.* дья́кон.
deaconess [,di:kə'nes, 'di:kənɪs] *n.* диакони́са.
dead [ded] *n.*: **at** ~ **of night** глубо́кой но́чью.
adj. **1.** (*no longer living*) мёртвый, уме́рший; (*in accident etc.*) поги́бший, уби́тый; (*of animal*) до́хлый; ~ **body** труп, мёртвое те́ло; ~ **flowers/leaves** увя́дшие цветы́/ли́стья; **he is** ~ он у́мер/уби́т; ~ **men tell no tales** мёртвые не болта́ют; уме́рший никому́ не поме́ха; ~ **and gone** (*fig.*) давно́ проше́дший; **more** ~ **than alive** полумёртвый; **(as)** ~ **as mutton (*or* as a doornail)** бездыха́нный; **the plan is as** ~ **as mutton** э́тому пла́ну капу́т; ~ **man's handle** автомати́ческий то́рмоз в электропоезда́х; ~ **wood** (*lit.*) сухосто́й; (*fig.*) балла́ст; **a** ~ **fence** глухо́й забо́р; **I wouldn't be seen** ~ **there** меня́ туда́ арка́ном не зата́щишь; (*as n.*: **the** ~) уме́ршие, поко́йные; **rise from the** ~ воскре́снуть (*pf.*); восста́ть (*pf.*) из мёртвых; **let the** ~ **bury their** ~ преда́ть (*pf.*) про́шлое забве́нию; похорони́ть (*pf.*) про́шлое. **2.** (*inanimate, sterile*) неодушевлённый; неплодоро́дный; ~ **matter** нежива́я мате́рия. **3.** (*numb, insensitive*) онеме́лый, омертве́лый; **my foot has gone** ~ у меня́ нога́ онеме́ла/затекла́; ~ **to all sense of shame** потеря́вший со́весть; ~ **with cold** промёрзший насквозь́; ~ **with hunger** умира́ющий с го́лоду; ~ **with fatigue** смерте́льно уста́лый; **he is** ~ **to the world** (*drunk*) он мертве́цки пьян; (*asleep*) он спит мёртвым сном; (*insensible*) он в бесчу́вственном состоя́нии. **4.** (*inert, motionless*) споко́йный, неподви́жный; **in the** ~ **hours of the night** глухо́й но́чью; ~ **end** (*lit., fig.*) тупи́к; **a** ~ **end**

job бесперспекти́вная рабо́та; ~ **weight** (*naut.*) дедве́йт; **the D~ Sea** Мёртвое мо́ре; ~ **season** мёртвый сезо́н; **a ~ ball** (*lacking resilience*) неупру́гий мяч; ~ **stock** (*unsaleable goods*) неходовы́е това́ры; ~ **ground** (*mil.*) мёртвое простра́нство. **5.** (*used, spent, uncharged*): ~ **match** испо́льзованная спи́чка; ~ **wire** (*elec.*) отключённый про́вод; ~ **ball** (*out of play*) вы́шедший из игры́ мяч; **the telephone went** ~ телефо́н умо́лк; **the furnace is** ~ то́пка пога́сла; ~ (*undeliverable*) **letter** непра́вильно адресо́ванное письмо́; **the law is a ~ letter** э́тот зако́н утра́тил си́лу; ~ **volcano** поту́хший вулка́н. **6.** (*dull, of sound or colour*) глухо́й, ту́склый. **7.** (*obsolete, no longer valid*): ~ **language** мёртвый язы́к; **that plan is** ~ э́тот план провали́лся. **8.** (*with no outlet*): **a ~ hole** глуха́я нора́. **9.** (*sham*): ~ **window** фальши́вое/ло́жное окно́. **10.** (*abrupt, exact, complete*) внеза́пный; по́лный; соверше́нный; **in ~ earnest** соверше́нно серьёзно; **come to a ~ stop** останови́ться (*pf.*) как вко́панному; ~ **level** соверше́нно ро́вная ме́стность; (*fig., monotony*) однообра́зие; **he's the ~ spit of his father** (*coll.*) он вы́литый оте́ц; ~ **calm** мёртвый штиль; ~ **loss** (*irrecoverable amount*) чи́стый убы́ток; (*fig., failure*) по́лный прова́л; **he's a ~ loss** он неуда́чник, от него́ то́лку не бу́дет; **a ~ faint** глубо́кий о́бморок; **a ~ certainty** по́лная уве́ренность; **he's a ~ shot** он ме́ткий стрело́к; он стреля́ет без про́маха; **he made a ~ set at her** он во что бы то ни ста́ло реши́л покори́ть её; ~ **centre** (*mech.*) мёртвая то́чка.

adv.: **he stopped** ~ он останови́лся как вко́панный; ~ **on time** то́чно во́время; ~ **drunk** мертве́цки пья́ный; ~ **straight** соверше́нно пря́мо; ~ **tired** смерте́льно уста́лый; ~ **against** реши́тельно про́тив; **he is ~ set on going to London** он реши́л во что бы то ни ста́ло пое́хать в Ло́ндон; ~ **slow** о́чень ме́дленно; ~ **certain** соверше́нно уве́ренный.

cpds. **~-and-alive** *adj.* безжи́зненный, мёртвый; **~-beat** *n.* (*coll., loafer*) безде́льник; парази́т; *adj.* (*coll., worn out*) смерте́льно уста́лый, изнурённый, измо́танный; **~-eye** *n.* (*naut.*) ю́ферс; **~head** *n.* (*passenger*) челове́к, име́ющий пра́во на беспла́тный прое́зд; **~light** *n.* (*naut.*) глухо́й иллюмина́тор; **~line** *n.* преде́л; **~lock** *n.* мёртвая то́чка; тупи́к; засто́й; зато́р; **break a ~lock** вы́йти (*pf.*) из тупика́; *v.t.*: **the negotiations are ~locked** перегово́ры зашли́ в тупи́к; **~pan** *adj.* (*coll.*) с невырази́тельным лицо́м; **~-reckoning** *n.* навигацио́нное счисле́ние.

deaden ['ded(ə)n] *v.t.* осл|абля́ть, -а́бить; заглуш|а́ть, -и́ть; **the drug ~s pain** лека́рство притупля́ет боль; **the walls ~ sound** сте́ны заглуша́ют шум; **gloves ~ the force of a blow** перча́тки ослабля́ют си́лу уда́ра.

deadener ['dedənə(r)] *n.* (*tech.*) глуши́тель (*m.*); материа́л для звукоизоля́ции.

deadliness ['dedlınıs] *n.* смерте́льность.

deadly ['dedlı] *adj.* смерте́льный; смертоно́сный; ~ **poison** смерте́льный яд; ~ **enemy** смерте́льный враг; ~ **sin** сме́ртный грех; (*intense*) ужа́сный; ~ **haste** стра́шная спе́шка; ~ **dullness** смерте́льная ску́ка.

deadness ['dednıs] *n.* омертве́лость, омертве́ние.

deaf [def] *adj.* **1.** глухо́й; ~ **in one ear** глухо́й на одно́ у́хо; ~ **as a post** глуха́я тетеря́; ~ **and dumb** глухонемо́й; ~ **and dumb language** язы́к глухонемы́х; ~ **mute** глухонемо́й; (*as n.*: **the** ~) глухи́е. **2.** (*fig.*): **turn a ~ ear to** не слу́шать (*impf.*); не обраща́ть (*impf.*) внима́ния на+*a.*; ~ **to all entreaty** глух ко всем мольба́м; **none so ~ as those that won't hear** са́мый глухо́й тот, кто не жела́ет слу́шать.

cpd. **~-aid** *n.* слухово́й аппара́т.

deafen ['def(ə)n] *v.t.* (*deprive of hearing*) оглуш|а́ть, -и́ть; (*drown, of sound*) заглуш|а́ть, -и́ть; (*soundproof*) де́лать, с- звуконепроница́емым.

deafening ['defənıŋ] *adj.* оглуши́тельный; заглуша́ющий.

deafness ['defnıs] *n.* глухота́.

deal[1] [di:l] *n.* (*wood*) хво́йная древеси́на; (*board*) ело́вая/сосно́вая доска́; дильс; ~ **furniture** ме́бель из сосны́.

deal[2] [di:l] *n.* **1.** (*amount*) коли́чество; **a great, good ~ (of)** мно́го +*g.*; **she's a good ~ better today** ей сего́дня гора́здо лу́чше; **he didn't succeed, not by a good** ~ он далеко́ не преуспе́л (*в чём*). **2.** (*business agreement*) сде́лка; **it's a ~!** договори́лись!; по рука́м!; **give s.o. a raw/square** ~ (*coll.*) несправедли́во/че́стно обойти́сь (*pf.*) с кем-н. **3.** (*at cards*) сда́ча; **it' s my** ~ моя́ о́черель сдава́ть. **4.: New D~** (*hist.*) «но́вый курс».

v.t. **1.** (*cards*) сда|ва́ть, -ть. **2.** (*apportion*) разд|ава́ть, -а́ть; распреде́л|я́ть, -и́ть; **the money was ~t out fairly** де́ньги бы́ли разделены́ че́стно. **3.** (*inflict*): ~ **s.o. a blow** нан|оси́ть, -ести́ кому́-н. уда́р.

v.i. **1.** (*do business*) торгова́ть (*impf.*); **I no longer ~ with that butcher** я бо́льше не покупа́ю у э́того мясника́; **he is a difficult man to ~ with** с ним тру́дно име́ть де́ло; **he ~s in furs** он торгу́ет меха́ми. **2.** (*treat, manage*) относи́ться (к+*d.*); обраща́ться (с+*i.*); поступа́ть (с+*i.*) (*all impf.*); **what is the best way of ~ing with young criminals?** как лу́чше всего́ поступа́ть с молоды́ми престу́пниками?; **he ~t with the problem skilfully** он уме́ло подошёл к э́тому вопро́су. **3.** (*treat of*) занима́ться (*impf.*) +*i.*; **the book ~s with African affairs** э́та кни́га посвящена́ африка́нским пробле́мам (*or* рассма́тривает/освеща́ет африка́нские пробле́мы). **4.** (*conduct o.s.*) обходи́ться (*impf.*); поступа́ть (*impf.*); **he ~s justly with all** он поступа́ет со все́ми справедли́во.

dealer ['di:lə(r)] *n.* **1.** (*at cards*) сдаю́щий ка́рты. **2.** (*trader*) банкомёт; ~ **in stolen goods** торго́вец кра́деным. **3.: plain** ~ прямо́й/открове́нный челове́к.

dealing ['di:lıŋ] *n.* **1.** (*action*) распределе́ние; **plain** ~ прямота́. **2.** (*trade*): ~ **in real estate** торго́вля недвижи́мостью. **3.** (*pl., association*) торго́вые дела́; сде́лки (*f. pl.*); **have ~s with s.o.** вести́ (*det.*) дела́ с кем-н.

dean [di:n] *n.* (*eccl.*) дека́н, настоя́тель (*m.*); (*acad.*) дека́н; (*dipl.*) дуайе́н.

deanery ['di:nərı] *n.* (*function*) дека́нство; (*acad.*) декана́т; (*house*) дом дека́на.

dear [dıə(r)] *n.* ми́лый, возлю́бленный, дорого́й, ду́шка (*c.g.*); **he's a (perfect)** ~ он о́чень мил; **be a ~ and do this for me** бу́дьте так добры́, сде́лайте э́то для меня́; **eat it up, there's a ~!** дое́шь всё, будь у́мницей!

adj. **1.** (*beloved*) люби́мый, дорого́й. **2.** (*lovable*) сла́вный, ми́лый. **3.** (*as polite address*): **my ~ fellow** дорого́й (мой); голу́бчик; (*in formal letters*) уважа́емый. **4.** (*precious*) дорого́й; **for ~ life** (*fig.*) отча́янно, изо всех сил. **5.** (*heartfelt*): **his ~est wish** его́ сокрове́нное жела́ние; **6.** (*costly*) дорого́й; ~ **money** высо́кая сто́имость за́йма.

int.: **oh ~!**; ~ **me!** о, Го́споди!; ой-ой-ой!

dearly ['dıəlı] *adv.* (*fondly*) не́жно; (*at a high price*) до́рого.

dearness ['dıənıs] *n.* (*high cost*) дорогови́зна.

dearth [dɜ:θ] *n.* нехва́тка, недоста́ток.

deary ['dıərı] *n.* (*beloved one*) дорого́й ми́лый.

int.: ~ **me!** о, Го́споди!; ой-ой-ой!

death [deθ] *n.* **I.**(*act or fact of dying*) смерть; **die the** ~ (*liter.*) поги́бнуть (*pf.*); **meet one's** ~ найти́ (*pf.*) свою́ смерть; **natural** ~ есте́ственная смерть; **violent** ~ наси́льственная смерть; ~ **agony** предсме́ртная аго́ния; **civil** ~ гражда́нская смерть; ~ **certificate** свиде́тельство о сме́рти; ~ **duties** нало́г на насле́дство; ~ **penalty** сме́ртная казнь; **be burnt to** ~ сгоре́ть (*pf.*) за́живо; **drink o.s. to** ~ умере́ть (*pf.*) от пья́нства; **work o.s. to** ~ рабо́тать (*impf.*) на изно́с; **bleed to** ~ исте́чь (*pf.*) кро́вью; **at ~'s door**; **at the point of** ~ при́ смерти; на поро́ге сме́рти; **catch one's ~ (of cold)** простуди́ться (*pf.*) на́смерть; **put to** ~ казни́ть (*pf.*); уби́ть (*pf.*); **sentence to** ~ приговори́ть (*pf.*) к сме́рти; **stone to** ~ заби́ть (*pf.*) камня́ми; **fight to the** ~ би́ться (*impf.*) не на жизнь, а на смерть; **it is ~ to steal** за воровство́ полага́ется сме́ртная казнь; **be in at the** ~ прису́тствовать (*impf.*) при том, как убива́ют (*затравленную лисицу*); (*fig.*) прису́тствовать при заверше́нии (*чего*); **sure as** ~ наверняка́; как пить дать; **he held on like grim** ~ он держа́лся изо всех сил; **he looks like ~** (*coll.*) ≃ кра́ше в гроб кладу́т; ~ **in life**; **living** ~ не жизнь, а ка́торга. **2.** (*instance of dying*) коне́ц, ги́бель; **there were many ~s in the accident** в ава́рии поги́бло мно́го люде́й. **3.**

(*destruction*): **the ~ of his hopes** круше́ние его́ наде́жд. **4.** (*utmost limit*): **he was bored to ~** ему́ бы́ло до́ смерти ску́чно; **tired to ~** смерте́льно уста́лый; **tickled to ~** обра́дованный до́ смерти; **I'm sick to ~ of it** мне э́то до́ смерти надое́ло; **laugh o.s. to ~** хохота́ть (*impf.*) до упа́ду. **5.** (*cause of death*): **this work will be the ~ of me** э́та рабо́та сведёт меня́ в моги́лу; **the Black D~** чёрная смерть. **6.** (*death personified*): **~'s head** че́реп; (*kind of moth*) мёртвая голова́; **snatch s.o. from the jaws of ~** вы́рвать (*pf.*) кого́-н. из когте́й сме́рти.

cpds. **~-bed** *n.* сме́ртное ло́же; **~-blow** *n.* смерте́льный уда́р; **~like** *adj.*: **a ~like silence** гробово́е молча́ние; **~-mask** *n.* посме́ртная ма́ска; **~-pale** *adj.* смерте́льно бле́дный; **~-rate** *n.* сме́ртность; **~-rattle** *n.* предсме́ртный хрип; **~-ray** *n.* смертоно́сный луч; **~-roll** *n.* спи́сок/число́ поги́бших; **~-trap** *n.*: **this theatre is a ~-trap in case of fire** в слу́чае пожа́ра э́тот теа́тр су́щая западня́; **~-warrant** *n.* распоряже́ние о приведе́нии в исполне́ние сме́ртного пригово́ра; **~-watch** *adj.*: **~-watch beetle** жук-моги́льщик; **~-wish** *n.* (*psych.*) стремле́ние к сме́рти.

deathless ['deθlɪs] *adj.* бессме́ртный.

deathlessness ['deθlɪsnɪs] *n.* бессме́ртие.

deathly ['deθlɪ] *adj. & adv.* смерте́льный, роково́й; **~ pale** смерте́льно бле́дный.

deb [deb] (*coll.*) = **debutante**

débâcle [deɪ'bɑːk(ə)l] *n.* (*break-up of ice*) ледохо́д; вскры́тие реки́; (*disorderly collapse*) паде́ние, крах, пани́ческое бе́гство.

debag [diː'bæg] *v.t.* (*coll.*) стяну́ть (*pf.*) портки́ с+*g.*

debar [dɪ'bɑː(r)] *v.t.* препя́тствовать, вос- +*d.*; не допус|ка́ть, -ти́ть +*g.*; **~ s.o. from office** лиш|а́ть, -и́ть кого́-н. возмо́жности заня́ть каку́ю-н. до́лжность; **~ s.o. from voting** лиш|а́ть, -и́ть кого́-н. пра́ва го́лоса.

debark [diː'bɑːk, dɪ-] *v.t. & i.* = **disembark**

debarkation [ˌdiːbɑː'keɪʃ(ə)n] *n.* = **disembarkation**

debase [dɪ'beɪs] *v.t.* **1.** (*lower morally*) ун|ижа́ть, -и́зить; прин|ижа́ть, -и́зить. **2.** (*depreciate, e.g. coinage*) пон|ижа́ть, -и́зить ка́чество/це́нность +*g.*; **style ~d by imitators** стиль, (соверше́нно) испо́рченный подража́нием.

debasement [dɪ'beɪsmənt] *n.* униже́ние; сниже́ние це́нности (*чего*).

debatable [dɪ'beɪtəb(ə)l] *adj.* спо́рный, оспа́риваемый.

debat|e [dɪ'beɪt] *n.* диску́ссия; пре́ния (*nt. pl.*); деба́т|ы (*pl., g.* -ов); **the question under ~e** обсужда́емый вопро́с; **beyond ~e** бесспо́рный.

v.t. & i. **1.** (*discuss*) обсу|жда́ть, -ди́ть; дебати́ровать (*impf.*); дискути́ровать (*impf., pf.*); спо́рить (*impf.*) о+*p.*; **~ing society** дискуссио́нный клуб. **2.** (*ponder*) обду́м|ывать, -ать; взве́|шивать, -сить; **I was ~ing whether to go out or not** я размышля́л, сто́ит выходи́ть и́ли нет. **3.** (*contest*): **the victory was ~ed all day** побе́да доста́лась по́сле це́лого дня борьбы́.

debater [dɪ'beɪtə(r)] *n.* уча́стник деба́тов; спо́рщик; **he's a good ~** он уме́ет спо́рить.

debauch [dɪ'bɔːtʃ] *n.* (*sensual orgy*) дебо́ш, о́ргия, кутёж; (*drinking-bout*) попо́йка; **a ~ of reading** запо́йное чте́ние.

v.t. **1.** (*pervert morally*) развра|ща́ть, -ти́ть. **2.** (*seduce*) совра|ща́ть, -ти́ть; оболь|ща́ть, -сти́ть. **3.** (*vitiate*) извра|ща́ть, -ти́ть; иска|жа́ть, -зи́ть.

debauchee [ˌdɪbɔː'tʃiː, ˌdeb-] *n.* развра́тник.

debauchery [dɪ'bɔːtʃərɪ] *n.* развра́т, распу́щенность.

debenture [dɪ'bentʃə(r)] *n.* долгово́е обяза́тельство; облига́ция акционе́рного о́бщества; **~ stock** долговы́е обяза́тельства.

debilitate [dɪ'bɪlɪˌteɪt] *v.t.* осл|абля́ть, -а́бить; рассл|абля́ть, -а́бить.

debility [dɪ'bɪlɪtɪ] *n.* сла́бость, бесси́лие, тщеду́шие, не́мощность.

debit ['debɪt] *n.* де́бет; **~ side of an account** де́бетовая сторона́ счёта.

v.t. дебетова́ть (*impf., pf.*); вн|оси́ть, -ести́ в де́бет.

debonair [ˌdebə'neə(r)] *adj.* (*suave, urbane*) обходи́тельный, учти́вый.

debouch [dɪ'baʊtʃ, -'buːʃ] *v.i.* **1.** (*of stream etc.*) выходи́ть, вы́йти на откры́тую ме́стность; впа|да́ть, -сть (*or* вл|ива́ться, -и́ться) (*в море и т.п.*). **2.** (*mil.*) дебуши́ровать (*impf., pf.*).

debouchment [dɪ'baʊtʃmənt, -'buːʃmənt] *n.* (*river-mouth*) у́стье; (*mil.*) дебуши́рование.

debrief [diː'briːf] *v.t.* расспр|а́шивать, -оси́ть; **~ s.o.** заслу́ш|ивать, -ать чей-н. отчёт.

debriefing [diː'briːfɪŋ] *n.* расспро́с, опро́с.

debris ['debriː, 'deɪ-] *n.* оско́лки (*m. pl.*); обло́мки (*m. pl.*); разва́лины (*f. pl.*).

debt [det] *n.* **1.** (*of money*) долг; **get, run into ~** влез|а́ть, -ть в долги́; **bad ~** безнадёжный долг; **~ of honour** долг че́сти; **National D~** госуда́рственный долг; **funded ~** консолиди́рованный долг; **floating ~** теку́щая задо́лженность. **2.** (*obligation*): **pay the ~ of nature** (*die*) сконча́ться (*pf.*); **I owe him a ~ of gratitude** я пе́ред ним в долгу́; **I am greatly in your ~** я вам чрезвыча́йно обя́зан.

debtor ['detə(r)] *n.* **1.** должни́к; **~'s prison** долгова́я тюрьма́. **2.** (*bookkeeping term*) деби́тор.

debunk [diː'bʌŋk] *v.t.* (*coll.*) разоблач|а́ть, -и́ть; разве́нч|ивать, -а́ть.

debunker [diː'bʌŋkə(r)] *n.* (*coll.*) разоблачи́тель (*m.*).

debus [diː'bʌs] *v.t. & i.* (*coll.*) выса́живать(ся), вы́садить(ся) из авто́буса.

debut ['deɪbjuː, -buː] *n.* (*of girl*) вы́езд в свет, дебю́т; (*of actor*) дебю́т.

debutante ['debjuːˌtɑːnt, 'deɪb-] *n.* дебюта́нтка.

decade ['dekeɪd, *disp.* dɪ'keɪd] *n.* **1.** (*10 years*) десятиле́тие; (*of one's age*) деся́ток. **2.** (*set of 10*) деся́ток.

decadence ['dekəd(ə)ns] *n.* упа́док, декаде́нтство.

decadent ['dekəd(ə)nt] *n.* декаде́нт.

adj. упа́днический, декаде́нтский.

decaffeinated [diː'kæfɪˌneɪtɪd] *adj.* без кофеина; **~ coffee** бескофеи́новый ко́фе.

decagon ['dekəgən] *n.* десятиуго́льник.

decagonal [dɪ'kægən(ə)l] *adj.* десятиуго́льный.

decagram(me) ['dekəˌgræm] *n.* декагра́мм.

decahedral [ˌdekə'hiːdrəl] *adj.* десятигра́нный.

decahedron [ˌdekə'hiːdrən] *n.* десятигра́нник.

decalcify [diː'kælsɪˌfaɪ] *v.t.* декальцини́ровать (*impf., pf.*).

decalitre ['dekəˌliːtə(r)] *n.* декали́тр.

decalogue ['dekəˌlɒg] *n.* де́сять за́поведей.

decamp [dɪ'kæmp] *v.i.* (*leave camp*) сн|има́ться, -я́ться с ла́геря; (*abscond*) сбе|га́ть, -жа́ть; уд|ира́ть, -ра́ть.

decanal [dɪ'keɪn(ə)l, 'dekə-] *adj.* дека́нский.

decant [dɪ'kænt] *v.t.* (*pour wine*) сце́|живать, -ди́ть; перел|ива́ть, -и́ть из буты́лки в графи́н; (*coll., transfer*): **he was ~ed from the car** его́ вы́волокли из маши́ны.

decanter [dɪ'kæntə(r)] *n.* (*vessel*) графи́н.

decapitate [dɪ'kæpɪˌteɪt] *v.t.* обезгла́в|ливать, -ить; **he was ~d in the accident** ему́ оторва́ло го́лову в ава́рии.

decapitation [dɪˌkæpɪ'teɪʃ(ə)n] *n.* обезгла́вливание.

decapod ['dekəˌpɒd] *n.* десятино́гий рак.

decarbonize [diː'kɑːbəˌnaɪz] *v.t.* **1.** (*chem.*) обезуглеро́|живать, -дить. **2.** (*of car engine*) оч|ища́ть, -и́стить от нага́ра.

decartelization [diːˌkɑːtəlaɪ'zeɪʃ(ə)n] *n.* декартелиза́ция.

decasyllabic [ˌdekəsɪ'læbɪk] *adj.* десятисло́жный.

decathlete [dɪ'kæθliːt] *n.* десятибо́рец.

decathlon [dɪ'kæθlən] *n.* десятибо́рье.

decay [dɪ'keɪ] *n.* **1.** (*physical*) гние́ние, разложе́ние; **tooth ~** разруше́ние зубо́в; **the house is in ~** дом разруша́ется. **2.** (*decayed part*) гниль. **3.** (*moral*) упа́док, загнива́ние, разложе́ние; **civilizations fall into ~** цивилиза́ции прихо́дят в упа́док.

v.i. гнить, с-; разл|ага́ться, -ожи́ться; **~ing vegetables** гнию́щие о́вощи; **our powers ~ in old age** на́ши си́лы слабе́ют к ста́рости; **live in ~ed circumstances** жить (*impf.*) в нищете́.

decease [dɪ'siːs] *n.* кончи́на.

deceased [dɪ'siːst] *adj.* поко́йный, сконча́вшийся, уме́рший; (*as n.*: **the ~**) поко́йник, отоше́дший.

decedent [dɪ'siːd(ə)nt] *n.* (*US*) поко́йный.

deceit [dɪ'siːt] *n.* обма́н, лжи́вость.

deceitful [dɪ'siːtfʊl] *adj.* обма́нчивый, лжи́вый.

deceitfulness [dɪ'siːtfʊlnɪs] *n.* обма́нчивость, лжи́вость.

deceivable [dɪ'si:vəb(ə)l] *adj.*: **he is not easily ~** его́ нелегко́ провести́.

deceive [dɪ'si:v] *v.t. & i.* обма́н|ывать, -у́ть; **~ o.s.** обма́н|ываться, -у́ться; **I have been ~d in him** я в нём обману́лся; **his hopes were ~** он обману́лся в свои́х наде́ждах; **we were ~d into believing that ...** нас обма́ном заста́вили пове́рить, что...

deceiver [dɪ'si:və(r)] *n.* лжец, обма́нщи|к (*fem.* -ца).

decelerate [di:'selə,reɪt] *v.t. & i.* зам|едля́ть, -е́длить (ход).

deceleration [di:,selə'reɪʃ(ə)n] *n.* замедле́ние; торможе́ние.

December [dɪ'sembə(r)] *n.* дека́брь (*m.*); (*attr.*) дека́брьский.

Decembrist [dɪ'sembrɪst] *n.* декабри́ст.

adj. декабри́стский.

decenc|y ['di:sənsɪ] *n.* (*seemliness*) прили́чие, благопристо́йность; **offence against ~y** наруше́ние прили́чий; **observe the ~ies** соблюда́ть (*impf.*) прили́чия.

decennary [dɪ'senərɪ], **decennial** [dɪ'senɪ(ə)l] *adjs.* десятиле́тний.

decent ['di:s(ə)nt] *adj.* **1.** (*not obscene*) прили́чный, присто́йный; благопристо́йный. **2.** (*proper, adequate*) прили́чный, подходя́щий; **~ living conditions** прили́чные жили́щные усло́вия; **a ~ dinner** прили́чный у́жин. **3.** (*coll., kind, well-conducted*) поря́дочный; **he was very ~ to me** он вёл себя́ поря́дочно по отноше́нию ко мне.

decentralization [di:,sentrəlaɪ'zeɪʃ(ə)n] *n.* децентрализа́ция.

decentralize [di:'sentrə,laɪz] *v.t.* децентрализова́ть (*impf., pf.*).

deception [dɪ'sepʃ(ə)n] *n.* обма́н, ложь, хи́трость; **practise a ~ on** обма́н|ывать, -у́ть.

deceptive [dɪ'septɪv] *adj.* обма́нчивый.

deceptiveness [dɪ'septɪvnɪs] *n.* обма́нчивость.

dechristianization [dɪ,krɪstɪənaɪ'zeɪʃ(ə)n] *n.* дехристианиза́ция.

dechristianize [dɪ'krɪstɪə,naɪz] *v.t.* дехристианизи́ровать (*impf., pf.*).

decibel ['desɪ,bel] *n.* децибе́л.

decide [dɪ'saɪd] *v.t.* реш|а́ть, -и́ть; прин|има́ть, -я́ть реше́ние +*p.*; **~ a question** реш|а́ть, -и́ть вопро́с; **~ a dispute** разреш|а́ть, -и́ть спор; **that ~s me** тепе́рь всё я́сно, бо́льше не сомнева́юсь; **what ~d you to give up your job?** почему́ вы реши́ли (*or* что вас заста́вило) бро́сить рабо́ту?

v.i. реш|а́ться, -и́ться; прин|има́ть, -я́ть реше́ние; **~ between adversaries** рассуди́ть (*pf.*) проти́вников; **~ between alternatives** сде́лать (*pf.*) вы́бор; **~ for s.o.** реши́ть (*pf.*) в по́льзу кого́-н.; **~ on going** реши́ть (*pf.*) пое́хать; **~ against going** реши́ть (*pf.*) не е́хать; **she ~d on the green hat** она́ вы́брала зелёную шля́пу; **they ~d on the youngest candidate** они́ останови́ли свой вы́бор на са́мом молодо́м кандида́те.

decided [dɪ'saɪdɪd] *adj.* (*clear-cut*) определённый; **a ~ difference** бесспо́рное разли́чие; **a man of ~ opinions** челове́к категори́ческих взгля́дов.

decidedly [dɪ'saɪdɪdlɪ] *adv.* реши́тельно, несомне́нно, я́вно, бесспо́рно.

deciduous [dɪ'sɪdjʊəs] *adj.* ли́ственный, листопа́дный, ле́тне-зелёный.

decigram(me) ['desɪ,græm] *n.* децигра́мм.

decilitre ['desɪ,li:tə(r)] *n.* децили́тр.

decimal ['desɪm(ə)l] *n.* десяти́чная дробь; **correct to six places of ~s** с то́чностью до шесто́го зна́ка по́сле запято́й; **recurring ~** периоди́ческая десяти́чная дробь.

adj. десяти́чный; **~ point** запята́я, отделя́ющая це́лое от дро́би; **~ coinage** десяти́чная моне́тная систе́ма.

decimalization [,desɪməlaɪ'zeɪʃ(ə)n] *n.* превраще́ние в десяти́чную дробь; перехо́д/перево́д на десяти́чную систе́му.

decimalize ['desɪmə,laɪz] *v.t.* превра|ща́ть, -ти́ть в десяти́чную дробь; перев|оди́ть, -ести́ на десяти́чную систе́му.

decimate ['desɪ,meɪt] *v.t.* **l.** (*hist.*) истреб|ля́ть, -и́ть ка́ждого деся́того из+*g.* **2.** (*devastate*) опустош|а́ть, -и́ть.

decimation [,desɪ'meɪʃ(ə)n] *n.* истребле́ние (ка́ждого деся́того); опустоше́ние.

decimetre ['desɪ,mi:tə(r)] *n.* дециме́тр.

decipher, decypher [dɪ'saɪfə(r)] *n.* расшифро́ванный текст.

v.t. **1.** (*lit.*) расшифро́в|ывать, -а́ть. **2.** (*fig., make out*) раз|бира́ть, -обра́ть; разга́д|ывать, -а́ть.

decipherable [dɪ'saɪfərəb(ə)l] *adj.* поддаю́щийся расшифро́вке.

decipherment [dɪ'saɪfəmənt] *n.* расшифро́вка, дешифро́вка.

decision [dɪ'sɪʒ(ə)n] *n.* **1.** (*deciding*) реше́ние; **make, take, come to a ~** приня́ть (*pf.*) реше́ние. **2.** (*decisiveness*) реши́мость, реши́тельность; **a man of ~** реши́тельный челове́к.

decisive [dɪ'saɪsɪv] *adj.* (*conclusive*) реша́ющий; **~ answer** оконча́тельный отве́т; (*resolute*) реши́тельный.

decisiveness [dɪ'saɪsɪvnɪs] *n.* реши́тельность.

decivilize [di:'sɪvɪlaɪz] *v.t.* прив|оди́ть, -ести́ к одича́нию.

deck[1] [dek] *n.* **1.** (*of ship*) па́луба; **~ cargo** па́лубный груз; **~ house** ру́бка; **~ landing** (*aeron.*) поса́дка на па́лубу; **go up on ~** подня́ться (*pf.*) на па́лубу; **below ~(s)** под па́лубой; **clear the ~s** (*for action*) (*nav.*) пригото́виться (*pf.*) к бо́ю; (*fig.*) пригото́виться (*pf.*) к де́йствиям; **all hands on ~!** все наве́рх!; авра́л! **2.** (*of bus*): **top ~** ве́рхний эта́ж. **3.** (*US, of cards*) коло́да.

cpds. **~-chair** *n.* шезло́нг; **~-hand** *n.* матро́с; **~-tennis** *n.* те́ннис на па́лубных ко́ртах.

deck[2] [dek] *v.t.* (*adorn; also* **~ out**) укр|аша́ть, -а́сить.

deckle ['dek(ə)l] *n.*: **~-edged paper** бума́га с необре́занными края́ми.

declaim [dɪ'kleɪm] *v.t. & i.* **1.** (*speak with feeling*) говори́ть (*impf.*) с па́фосом; деклами́ровать (*impf.*); **~ against s.o.** громи́ть (*impf.*) кого́-н.; напада́ть (*impf.*) на кого́-н. **2.** (*recite*) деклами́ровать (*impf.*).

declamation [,deklə'meɪʃ(ə)n] *n.* (*act*) деклами́рование; (*art*) деклама́ция; (*harangue*) стра́стная речь.

declamatory [dɪ'klæmətərɪ] *n.* декламацио́нный; ора́торский; напы́щенный.

declaration [,deklə'reɪʃ(ə)n] *n.* **1.** (*proclamation*) заявле́ние, деклара́ция; **~ of independence** деклара́ция незави́симости; **~ of war** объявле́ние войны́. **2.** (*affirmation*): **~ of one's income** нало́говая деклара́ция; **~ of love** призна́ние в любви́.

declarative [,de'klærətɪv], **-ory** [,de'klærətərɪ] *adjs.* деклара-ти́вный.

declare [dɪ'kleə(r)] *v.t. & i.* **1.** (*proclaim, make known*) объяв|ля́ть, -и́ть; **~ one's love** объясн|я́ться, -и́ться в любви́. **2.** (*say solemnly*) заяв|ля́ть, -и́ть; провозгла|ша́ть, -си́ть; **he ~d that he was innocent** он заяви́л о свое́й невино́вности; **well, I ~!** одна́ко, скажу́ я вам! **3.** (*pronounce*) объяв|ля́ть, -и́ть; **I ~ the meeting open** объявля́ю собра́ние откры́тым; **~ o.s.** (*avow intentions*) де́лать, с- призна́ние; выступа́ть, вы́ступить; (*reveal character*) пока́з|ывать, -а́ть себя́; **~ for/against s.o.** выска́зываться, вы́сказаться за/про́тив кого́-н. **4.** (*at customs*) деклари́ровать (*impf., pf.*); **have you anything to ~?** предъяви́те ве́щи, подлежа́щие обложе́нию по́шлиной.

declarer [dɪ'kleərə(r)] *n.* объявля́ющий.

déclassé [deɪ'klæseɪ] *adj.* декласси́рованный.

declassification [,di:klæsɪfɪ'keɪʃ(ə)n] *n.* рассекре́чивание (*документов*).

declassify [di:'klæsɪ,faɪ] *v.t.* рассекре́|чивать, -тить (*документы*).

declension [dɪ'klenʃ(ə)n] *n.* **1.** (*deviation, decline*) паде́ние, упа́док, ухудше́ние. **2.** (*gram.*) склоне́ние.

declinable [dɪ'klaɪnəb(ə)l] *adj.* (*gram.*) склоня́емый.

declination [,deklɪ'neɪʃ(ə)n] *n.* (*astron.*) магни́тное склоне́ние; отклоне́ние.

decline [dɪ'klaɪn] *n.* **1.** (*fall*) паде́ние; **~ in prices** сниже́ние/пониже́ние цен. **2.** (*decay*) упа́док, зака́т; **~ of the Roman Empire** упа́док ри́мской импе́рии. **3.** (*in health*) ухудше́ние; **fall into a ~** слабе́ть (*impf.*), ча́хнуть (*impf.*).

v.t. **1.** (*refuse*) отклон|я́ть, -и́ть; **he ~d the invitation** он отклони́л приглаше́ние; **he ~d to answer** он уклони́лся от отве́та; **~ battle** отказа́ться/уклони́ться (*pf.*) от бо́я. **2.** (*cause to droop*) наклон|я́ть, -и́ть; склон|я́ть, -и́ть; опус|ка́ть, -ти́ть. **3.** (*gram.*) склоня́ть, про-.

v. i. **1.** (*sink, draw to a close*) клони́ться (*impf.*) (к+*d.*); **his strength ~d** его́ си́ла пошла́ на у́быль; **prices ~** це́ны

па́дают; **his declining years** его́ прекло́нные го́ды. **2.** (*refuse*) отка́з|ываться, -а́ться.
declinometer [ˌdeklɪˈnɒmɪtə(r)] *n.* уклономе́р, деклино́метр, деклина́тор.
declivity [dɪˈklɪvɪtɪ] *n.* пока́тость, спуск, отко́с, склон.
declutch [diːˈklʌtʃ] *v.i.* расцеп|ля́ть, -и́ть сцепле́ние/му́фту.
decoction [dɪˈkɒkʃ(ə)n] *n.* (*boiling down*) выва́ривание; (*liquor*) отва́р, деко́кт, сиро́п.
decode [diːˈkəʊd] *n.* расшифро́ванный текст.
v.t. расшифро́в|ывать, -а́ть; декоди́ровать (*impf.*, *pf.*).
decollation [ˌdiːkɒˈleɪʃ(ə)n] *n.* обезгла́вливание.
décolletage [ˌdeɪkɒlˈtɑːʒ] *n.* декольте́ (*indecl.*), вы́рез.
décolleté [deɪˈkɒlteɪ] *adj.* декольти́ро́ванный.
decolonization [ˌdiːkɒlənaɪˈzeɪʃ(ə)n] *n.* деколониза́ция.
decomposable [ˌdiːkəmˈpəʊzəb(ə)l] *adj.* разложи́мый, раствори́мый.
decompose [ˌdiːkəmˈpəʊz] *v.t.* разл|ага́ть, -ожи́ть; **a prism ~s light** при́зма расщепля́ет свет.
v.i. (*decay*) разл|ага́ться, -ожи́ться.
decomposition [ˌdiːkɒmpəˈzɪʃ(ə)n] *n.* (*analysis*) разложе́ние; (*corruption*) разложе́ние, распа́д.
decompression [ˌdiːkəmˈpreʃ(ə)n] *n.* пониже́ние давле́ния, декомпре́ссия.
decompressor [ˌdiːkəmˈpresə(r)] *n.* декомпре́ссор.
deconsecrate [diːˈkɒnsɪˌkreɪt] *v.t.* секуляризи́ровать (*impf.*, *pf.*).
decontaminate [ˌdiːkənˈtæmɪˌneɪt] *v.t.* обеззара́|живать, -зить; дегази́ровать (*impf.*, *pf.*).
decontamination [ˌdiːkəntæmɪˈneɪʃ(ə)n] *n.* обеззара́живание, дегаза́ция.
decontrol [ˌdiːkənˈtrəʊl] *v.t.* освобо|жда́ть, -ди́ть от контро́ля.
decor [ˈdeɪkɔː(r), ˈde-] *n.* декора́ции (*f. pl.*); убра́нство.
decorate [ˈdekəˌreɪt] *v.t.* **1.** (*adorn*) укр|аша́ть, -а́сить; декори́ровать (*impf.*, *pf.*); **~d style** (*archit.*) англи́йская го́тика XIV ве́ка. **2.** (*paint, furnish etc.*) отде́л|ывать, -ать. **3.** (*confer medal upon*) награ|жда́ть, -ди́ть.
decoration [ˌdekəˈreɪʃ(ə)n] *n.* **1.** (*adornment*) украше́ние, убра́нство. **2.** (*furnishing etc. of house*) отде́лка; обстано́вка. **3.** (*order, medal*) о́рден, знак отли́чия.
decorative [ˈdekərətɪv] *adj.* (*pert. to decoration*) декорати́вный; (*handsome, pretty*), декорати́вный, декорацио́нный.
decorator [ˈdekəˌreɪtə(r)] *n.* **1.** (*manual worker*) маля́р, обо́йщик. **2.: interior ~** худо́жник по интерье́ру.
decorous [ˈdekərəs] *adj.* прили́чный, присто́йный.
decorticate [diːˈkɔːtɪˌkeɪt] *v.t.* сдира́ть, содра́ть кору́ с+*g.*
decorum [dɪˈkɔːrəm] *n.* вне́шнее прили́чие; этике́т, деко́рум.
decoy [ˈdiːkɔɪ, dɪˈkɔɪ] *n.* **1.** (*real or imitation animal*) прима́нка; **~ duck** мано́к для ди́ких у́ток. **2.** (*pers. or thg. used to entice*) прима́нка, собла́зн. **3.** (*fig., trap*) западня́, лову́шка.
v.t. зама́н|ивать, -и́ть; прима́н|ивать, -и́ть.
decrease [ˈdiːkriːs] *n.* уменьше́ние, убыва́ние; **crime is on the ~** престу́пность идёт на у́быль.
v.t. ум|еньша́ть, -е́ньшить.
v.i. ум|еньша́ться, -е́ньшиться; уб|ыва́ть, -ы́ть.
decreasingly [ˌdiːˈkriːsɪŋlɪ] *adv.* всё ме́ньше и ме́ньше.
decree [dɪˈkriː] *n.* **1.** (*pol.*) ука́з, декре́т, постановле́ние. **2.** (*leg.*) реше́ние. **3.: ~ of nature** зако́н приро́ды.
v.t. & i. изд|ава́ть, -а́ть декре́т; декрети́ровать (*impf.*, *pf.*); **fate ~d otherwise** судьба́ реши́ла ина́че.
decrepit [dɪˈkrepɪt] *adj.* дря́хлый, ве́тхий.
decrepitude [dɪˈkrepɪtjuːd] *n.* дря́хлость, ве́тхость.
decrescendo [ˌdiːkreˈʃendəʊ, ˌdeɪkrɪ-] *n.*, *adj. & adv.* диминуэ́ндо (*indecl.*).
decretals [dɪˈkriːt(ə)lz] *n. pl.* декрета́лии (*f. pl.*).
decrier [dɪˈkraɪə(r)] *n.* хули́тель (*m.*).
decry [dɪˈkraɪ] *v.t.* хули́ть (*impf.*).
decypher [dɪˈsaɪfə(r)] *etc.*, *see* **decipher** *etc.*
dedicate [ˈdedɪˌkeɪt] *v.t.* (*devote; also book etc.*) посвя|ща́ть, -ти́ть; (*assign, set apart*) предназн|ача́ть, -а́чить.
dedicated [ˈdedɪˌkeɪtɪd] *adj.* самозабве́нный, беззаве́тный.
dedication [ˌdedɪˈkeɪʃ(ə)n] *n.* (*devotion*) пре́данность, самоотве́рженность; (*inscription*) посвяще́ние.
dedicator [ˈdedɪˌkeɪtə(r)] *n.* посвяща́ющий.
dedicatory [ˈdedɪˌkeɪtərɪ] *adj.* посвяти́тельный.
deduce [dɪˈdjuːs] *v.t.* (*infer*) выводи́ть, вы́вести; заключ|а́ть, -и́ть.
deduct [dɪˈdʌkt] *v.t.* вычита́ть, вы́честь; удерж|ивать, -а́ть.
deduction [dɪˈdʌkʃ(ə)n] *n.* (*subtraction*) вы́чет, удержа́ние; (*amount deducted*) вычита́емое; (*inference*) вы́вод, заключе́ние.
deductive [dɪˈdʌktɪv] *adj.* дедукти́вный.
deed [diːd] *n.* **1.** (*sth. done*) де́йствие, посту́пок. **2.** (*feat*) по́двиг. **3.** (*actual fact*) де́ло, дея́ние; **in word and ~** сло́вом и де́лом. **4.** (*leg.*) акт, докуме́нт; **~ of gift** да́рственная на́дпись; **~ of partnership** догово́р о това́риществе.
cpd. **~-poll** *n.* односторо́ннее обяза́тельство.
deem [diːm] *v.t.* **1.** (*hold, consider*) полага́ть, счита́ть, признава́ть (*all impf.*). **2.** (*elect to regard*) рассма́тривать/квалифици́ровать (*impf.*) (как...).
deep [diːp] *n.*: **the ~** (*poet.*) пучи́на.
adj. **1.** глубо́кий; **a ~ shelf** широ́кая по́лка; **a ~ drinker** го́рький пья́ница; **in ~ water** (*trouble*) в беде́. **2.** (*with measurement*): **a hole 6 feet ~** отве́рстие глубино́й в 6 фу́тов; **ankle ~ in mud** по щи́колотку в грязи́; **the soldiers were drawn up six ~** солда́ты стоя́ли в строю́ по шесть. **3.** (*submerged, lit., fig.*): **a village ~ in the valley** дере́вня, располо́женная в глубине́ доли́ны; **~ in thought** заду́мавшийся; погружённый в разду́мья; **~ in a book** уше́дший с голово́й в кни́гу; **~ in debt** увя́зший в долга́х; **~ in love** по́ уши (*or* без па́мяти) влюблённый. **4.** (*extreme, profound*) глубо́кий; **~ sorrow** глубо́кая печа́ль; **in ~ mourning** в глубо́ком тра́уре; **a ~ reader** серьёзный чита́тель; **take a ~ breath** де́лать, с- глубо́кий вдох; **heave a ~ sigh** глубоко́ взд|ыха́ть, -охну́ть; **that is too ~ for me** (*fig.*) э́то сли́шком умно́ для меня́. **5.** (*of colour*) тёмный, густо́й; **~ red** тёмно-кра́сный; **a ~ sun-tan** си́льный зага́р. **6.** (*low-pitched*) ни́зкий. **7.** (*cunning, hidden*): **~ designs** скры́тые за́мыслы; **he's a ~ one** он себе́ на уме́.
adv. глубоко́; **dig ~** рыть (*impf.*) глубоко́; **drink ~** кре́пко/си́льно выпива́ть (*impf.*); **~ into the night** до глубо́кой но́чи; **still waters run ~** в ти́хом о́муте че́рти во́дятся.
cpds. **~-drawn** *adj.*: **a ~-drawn sigh** глубо́кий вздох; **~-freeze** *n.* морози́льник; *v.t.* глубоко́ замор|а́живать, -о́зить; **~-frozen** *adj.* заморо́женный; **~-fry** *v.t.* зажа́ри|вать, -ть; жа́рить, за- во фритю́ре; **~-laid** *adj.*: **~-laid scheme** проду́манный план; **~-rooted** *adj.*: **~-rooted belief** глубоко́ укорени́вшееся мне́ние; **~-sea** *adj.*: **~-sea fishing** глубоково́дный лов; **~-seated** *adj.*: **~-seated emotion** затаённое чу́вство.
deepen [ˈdiːpən] *v.t. & i.* **1.** (*make, become deeper*) углуб|ля́ть(ся), -и́ть(ся). **2.** (*intensify*) уси́ли|вать(ся), -ть(ся). **3.** (*make, become lower in pitch*) пон|ижа́ть(ся), -и́зить(ся).
deeply [ˈdiːplɪ] *adv.* глубо́ко́; **he is ~ in debt** он по́ уши в долга́х; **he feels ~ about it** э́то его́ глубоко́ волну́ет.
deepness [ˈdiːpnɪs] *n.* (*of water etc.*) глубина́; (*of colour*) со́чность, насы́щенность; (*of voice*) глубина́.
deer [dɪə(r)] *n.* оле́нь (*m.*); **red ~** благоро́дный оле́нь; **roe ~** косу́ля; **fallow ~** лань.
cpds. **~-forest, ~-park** *nn.* оле́ний запове́дник; **~-hound** *n.* шотла́ндская борза́я; **~skin** *n.* лоси́на, за́мша; (*attr.*) лоси́ный, за́мшевый; **~stalker** *n.* (*sportsman*) охо́тник на оле́ней; (*cap*) охо́тничий шлем; **~stalking** *n.* охо́та на оле́ней.
de-escalate [diːˈeskəˌleɪt] *v.t.* прекра|ща́ть, -ти́ть эскала́цию.
de-escalation [diːeskəˈleɪʃ(ə)n] *n.* деэскала́ция.
deface [dɪˈfeɪs] *v.t.* (*spoil appearance of*) иска|жа́ть, -зи́ть; по́ртить, ис-; уро́довать, из-; (*make illegible*) де́лать, с- неразбо́рчивым.
defacement [dɪˈfeɪsmənt] *n.* по́рча, искаже́ние; стира́ние.
de facto [diː ˈfæktəʊ, deɪ] *adj.* факти́ческий.
adv. де-фа́кто; на де́ле.
defalcate [ˈdiːfælˌkeɪt] *v.i.* присв|а́ивать, -о́ить чужу́ю со́бственность; растра́|чивать, -тить чужи́е де́ньги.
defalcation [ˌdiːfælˈkeɪʃ(ə)n] *n.* растра́та; присвое́ние чужо́й со́бственности.

defalcator [ˈdiːfælˌkeɪtə(r)] *n.* растра́тчик.

defamation [ˌdefəˈmeɪʃ(ə)n, ˌdiːf-] *n.* клевета́, диффама́ция; **~ of character** диффама́ция/компромета́ция ли́чности.

defamatory [dɪˈfæmətərɪ] *adj.* бесче́стящий, клеветни́ческий.

defame [dɪˈfeɪm] *v.t.* клевета́ть, о-; поро́чить, о-.

default [dɪˈfɔːlt, -ˈfɒlt] *n.* **1.** (*want, absence*) отсу́тствие, недоста́ток; **in ~ of** за отсу́тствием +*g.* **2.** (*neglect, failure to act or appear*): **he won the match by ~** он вы́играл матч из-за нея́вки проти́вника; **the court gave judgment by ~** за нея́вкой отве́тчика суд реши́л де́ло в по́льзу истца́. **3.** (*failure to pay*) неупла́та.

v.i. **1.** (*fail to perform a duty*) не выполня́ть (*impf*) обяза́тельства. **2.** (*fail to appear in court*) не яв|ля́ться, -и́ться в суд. **3.** (*fail to meet debts*) прекра|ща́ть, -ти́ть платежи́; **~ on a debt** не выпла́чивать (*impf.*) долг.

defaulter [dɪˈfɔːltə(r), -ˈfɒltə(r)] *n.* **1.** (*one who fails to perform duty*) не выполня́ющий свои́х обяза́тельств. **2.** (*esp. mil.*) провини́вшийся солда́т.

defeat [dɪˈfiːt] *n.* пораже́ние; **the ~ of his hopes** крах его́ наде́жд.

v.t. нан|оси́ть, -ести́ пораже́ние +*d.*; разб|ива́ть, -и́ть; одержа́ть (*pf.*) побе́ду над+*i.*; **our hopes were ~ed** на́ши наде́жды ру́хнули; **they were ~ed** они́ потерпе́ли пораже́ние; **~ one's own purpose** вреди́ть (*impf.*) самому́ себе́.

defeatism [dɪˈfiːtɪz(ə)m] *n.* пораже́нчество.

defeatist [dɪˈfiːtɪst] *n.* пораже́нец; (*fig.*) пессими́ст.

adj. пораже́нческий, пессимисти́ческий.

defecate [ˈdefɪˌkeɪt] *v.i.* испражн|я́ться, -и́ться.

defecation [ˌdefɪˈkeɪʃ(ə)n] *n.* испражне́ние.

defect[1] [dɪˈfekt, ˌdiːfekt] *n.* недоста́ток, изъя́н; дефе́кт; поро́к (*also leg.*); **he has the ~s of his qualities** его́ недоста́тки вытека́ют из его́ досто́инств.

defect[2] [diːˈfekt] *v.i.* дезерти́ровать (*impf., pf.*); перебе|га́ть, -жа́ть; **he ~ed to the West** он перебежа́л на За́пад.

defection [dɪˈfekʃ(ə)n] *n.* дезерти́рство; **there were several ~s from the party** не́сколько челове́к вы́шло из па́ртии.

defective [dɪˈfektɪv] *n.* дефекти́вный; **mental ~s** у́мственно отста́лые.

adj. несоверше́нный; дефе́ктный; **~ memory** плоха́я па́мять; **~ translation** нето́чный перево́д; **~ verb** недоста́точный глаго́л.

defectiveness [dɪˈfektɪvnɪs] *n.* неиспра́вность, несоверше́нство.

defector [dɪˈfektə(r)] *n.* перебе́жчик, невозвраще́нец.

defence (*US* **defense**) [dɪˈfens] *n.* **1.** оборо́на, защи́та; **in ~ of** в защи́ту +*g.*; **he died in ~ of his country** он поги́б, защища́я ро́дину; **~ industry** оборо́нная промы́шленность. **2.** (*means or system of defending*) укрепле́ния (*nt. pl.*); оборони́тельные сооруже́ния; **his ~s are down** он беззащи́тен; **~ in depth** (*mil.*) эшелони́рованная оборо́на. **3.** (*leg.*) защи́та; **counsel for the ~** защи́тник; представи́тель (*m.*) защи́ты.

defenceless [dɪˈfenslɪs] *adj.* беззащи́тный; необороня́емый.

defencelessness [dɪˈfenslɪsnɪs] *n.* беззащи́тность.

defend [dɪˈfend] *v.t.* **1.** оборон|я́ть, -и́ть; защи|ща́ть, -ти́ть; **~ o.s.** защи|ща́ться, -ти́ться; **~ one's ideas** защи|ща́ть, -ти́ть (*or* отст|а́ивать, -оя́ть) свои́ иде́и. **2.** (*leg.*) защи|ща́ть, -ти́ть; выступа́ть, вы́ступить защи́тником +*g.*

defendant [dɪˈfend(ə)nt] *n.* отве́тчик, подсуди́мый, обвиня́емый.

defender [dɪˈfendə(r)] *n.* защи́тник; (*sport, also*) чемпио́н, защища́ющий своё зва́ние.

defenestration [ˌdiːfenɪˈstreɪʃ(ə)n] *n.* выбра́сывание из окна́.

defense [dɪˈfens] = **defence**

defensibility [dɪˌfensɪˈbɪlɪtɪ] *n.* **1.** обороноспосо́бность. **2.** правоме́рность.

defensible [dɪˈfensɪb(ə)l] *adj.* **1.** (*e.g. mil.*) защити́мый. **2.** (*e.g. of an argument*) правоме́рный, опра́вданный.

defensive [dɪˈfensɪv] *n.* оборо́на; **on the ~** в оборо́не.

adj. оборони́тельный, оборо́нный; **he has a ~ manner** он как бу́дто опра́вдывается; он вроде бои́тся, как бы его́ не оби́дели.

defer[1] [dɪˈfɜː(r)] *v.t.* (*postpone*) отсро́чи|вать, -ть; **~ one's departure** от|кла́дывать, -ложи́ть отъе́зд; **a ~red (-rate) telegram** телегра́мма, по́сланная по льго́тному тари́фу; **~red payment** отсро́чка платежа́; **payment on ~red terms** платёж в рассро́чку.

defer[2] [dɪˈfɜː(r)] *v.i.*: **~ to** счита́ться (*impf.*) с+*i.*

deference [ˈdefərəns] *n.* уваже́ние, почти́тельность; **show ~ to s.o.** относи́ться (*impf.*) почти́тельно к кому́-н.; **with all (due) ~ to** при всём уваже́нии к+*d.*; **he acted thus in** (*or* **out of**) **~ to …** он де́йствовал так из уваже́ния к…

deferential [ˌdefəˈrenʃ(ə)l] *adj.* почти́тельный.

deferment [dɪˈfɜːmənt] *n.* откла́дывание, отсро́чка.

defiance [dɪˈfaɪəns] *n.* вы́зов; **bid ~ to** пренебр|ега́ть, -е́чь +*i*; бр|оса́ть, -о́сить вы́зов +*d.*; **in ~ of orders** вопреки́ распоряже́ниям.

defiant [dɪˈfaɪənt] *adj.* вызыва́ющий.

deficiency [dɪˈfɪʃənsɪ] *n.* **1.** (*lack*) нехва́тка, отсу́тствие; **~ disease** авитамино́з. **2.** (*sum lacking*) дефици́т. **3.** (*pl., shortcomings*) недоста́тки (*m. pl.*).

deficient [dɪˈfɪʃ(ə)nt] *adj.* недоста́точный, непо́лный; **~ in courage** недоста́точно сме́лый; **mentally ~** слабоу́мный.

deficit [ˈdefɪsɪt] *n.* дефици́т, недочёт; **meet a ~** покр|ыва́ть, -ы́ть дефици́т.

defier [dɪˈfaɪə(r)] *n.* броса́ющий вы́зов (*чему*).

defile[1] [dɪˈfaɪl] *n.* дефиле́ (*indecl.*), уще́лье.

v.i. дефили́ровать, про-.

defile[2] [dɪˈfaɪl] *v.t.* загрязн|я́ть, -и́ть; осквер|ня́ть, -и́ть.

defilement [dɪˈfaɪlmənt] *n.* загрязне́ние, оскверне́ние.

definable [dɪˈfaɪnəb(ə)l] *adj.* определи́мый.

define [dɪˈfaɪn] *v.t.* **1.** (*state meaning of*) определ|я́ть, -и́ть; толкова́ть (*impf.*); да|ва́ть, -ть определе́ние +*d.* **2.** (*state clearly*): **I ~d his duties** я очерти́л/установи́л круг его́ обя́занностей; **he ~d his position** он определи́л/вы́сказал своё отноше́ние. **3.** (*delimit*): **his powers are ~d by law** его́ полномо́чия устана́вливаются/определя́ются зако́ном; **the frontier is not clearly ~ d** нет определённой/чёткой грани́цы. **4.** (*show clearly*): **a well ~d image** чётко очёрченный о́браз; **the tree was ~d against the sky** де́рево вырисо́вывалось на фо́не не́ба.

definite [ˈdefɪnɪt] *adj.* **1.** (*specific*) определённый. **2.** (*clear, exact*) то́чный, чёткий; **past ~** (*gram.*) проше́дшее вре́мя, перфе́кт.

definitely [ˈdefɪnɪtlɪ] *adv.* определённо, то́чно, чётко; **he is ~ coming** он непреме́нно придёт.

definiteness [ˈdefɪnɪtnɪs] *n.* определённость, то́чность, чёткость.

definition [ˌdefɪˈnɪʃ(ə)n] *n.* (*clearness of outline*) я́сность, чёткость; (*statement of meaning*) определе́ние.

definitive [dɪˈfɪnɪtɪv] *adj.* оконча́тельный, реши́тельный.

deflate [dɪˈfleɪt] *v.t.* **1.** выка́чивать, вы́качать во́здух/газ из+*g.*; **~ a balloon/tyre** вы́пустить (*pf.*) во́здух из ша́ра/ши́ны. **2.** (*fig.*): **~ a rumour** опрове́ргнуть (*pf.*) слух; **~ s.o.'s conceit** сбить (*pf.*) с кого́-н. спесь. **3.**: **they ~d the currency** они́ сократи́ли вы́пуск бума́жных де́нег.

deflation [dɪˈfleɪʃ(ə)n] *n.* (*of tyres etc.*) выка́чивание/выпуска́ние во́здуха/га́за; (*fin.*) дефля́ция.

deflationary [dɪˈfleɪʃ(ə)nərɪ] *adj.* (*fin.*) дефляцио́нный.

deflect [dɪˈflekt] *v.t. & i.* отклон|я́ть(ся), -и́ть(ся).

deflection [dɪˈflekʃ(ə)n] *n.* отклоне́ние.

defloration [ˌdiːflɔːˈreɪʃ(ə)n] *n.* лише́ние де́вственности.

deflower [dɪˈflaʊə(r)] *v.t.* лиш|а́ть, -и́ть де́вственности.

defoliant [diːˈfəʊlɪənt] *n.* дефолиа́нт.

defoliate [diːˈfəʊlɪˌeɪt] *v.t.* лиш|а́ть, -и́ть листвы́.

defoliation [diːˌfəʊlɪˈeɪʃ(ə)n] *n.* лише́ние листвы́.

deforest [diːˈfɒrɪst] *v.t.* обезле́сить (*pf.*).

deforestation [diːˌfɒrɪˈsteɪʃ(ə)n] *n.* обезле́сение.

deform [dɪˈfɔːm] *v.t.* уро́довать, из-; иска|жа́ть, -зи́ть; деформи́ровать (*impf, pf.*); **he has a ~ed foot** у него́ деформи́рована стопа́.

deformation [ˌdiːfɔːˈmeɪʃ(ə)n] *n.* уро́дование, искаже́ние, деформа́ция.

deformity [dɪˈfɔːmɪtɪ] *n.* уро́дливость, уро́дство.

defraud [dɪˈfrɔːd] *v.t.* обма́н|ывать, -у́ть; обма́ном лиши́ть (*pf.*) (*кого чего*).

defray [dɪˈfreɪ] *v.t.* опла́|чивать, -ти́ть; **~ expenses** возме|ща́ть, -сти́ть расхо́ды.

defrayal [dɪˈfreɪəl], **-ment** [dɪˈfreɪmənt] *nn.* опла́та; возмеще́ние расхо́дов.

defreeze [diːˈfriːz] *v.t.* размор|а́живать, -о́зить.

defrost [diːˈfrɒst] *v.t.* оттá|ивать, -ять; размор|áживать, -óзить; ~ **a refrigerator** раст|áпливать, -опи́ть лёд в холоди́льнике; ~ **the windscreen** оч|ищáть, -и́стить ото льдá ветровóе стеклó.

defroster [diːˈfrɒstə(r)] *n.* антиобледени́тель (*m.*), дефрóстер.

deft [deft] *adj.* лóвкий, искýсный.

deftness [ˈdeftnɪs] *n.* лóвкость, искýсность.

defunct [dɪˈfʌŋkt] *adj.* умéрший, покóйный; **a ~ newspaper** бóлее не существýющая газéта; (*as n.*: **the ~**) покóйный.

defuse [diːˈfjuːz] *v.t.* сн|имáть, -ять взрывáтель +*g.*; (*fig.*) разряди́ть (*pf.*).

defy [dɪˈfaɪ] *v.t.* **1.** (*challenge*) вызывáть, вы́звать; бр|осáть, -óсить вы́зов +*d.*; **I ~ you to prove it** попрóбуйте, докажи́те э́то!; ручáюсь, что вы э́того не докáжете. **2.** (*disobey*) пренебр|егáть, -éчь +*i.*; ~ **the law** игнори́ровать (*impf.*, *pf.*) закóн. **3.** (*fig.*): **the problem defies solution** проблéму реши́ть невозмóжно.

degauss [diːˈgaʊs] *v.t.* размагни́|чивать, -тить.

degeneracy [dɪˈdʒenərəsɪ] *n.* дегенерати́вность.

degenerate [dɪˈdʒenərət; *v.* dɪˈdʒenəˌreɪt] *n.* дегенерáт, вы́родок.

adj. вы́родившийся, дегенерати́вный.

v.i. вырождáться, вы́родиться; дегенери́ровать (*impf.*, *pf.*).

degeneration [dɪˌdʒenəˈreɪʃ(ə)n] *n.* **1.** вырождéние, дегенерáция. **2.** (*med.*) перерождéние; **fatty ~ of the heart** ожирéние сéрдца.

degradation [ˌdegrəˈdeɪʃ(ə)n] *n.* **1.** (*in rank*) понижéние, разжáлование. **2.** (*moral*) упáдок, деградáция.

degrade [dɪˈgreɪd] *v.t.* (*reduce in rank*) пон|ижáть, -и́зить; разжáловать (*pf.*). **2.** (*lower morally*) прин|ижáть, -и́зить; ун|ижáть, -и́зить.

v.i. деградировать (*impf.*, *pf.*).

degrading [dɪˈgreɪdɪŋ] *adj.* унизи́тельный.

degree [dɪˈgriː] *n.* **1.** (*unit of measurement*) грáдус. **2.** (*step, stage*) ступéнь, стéпень; ýровень (*m.*); **their work shows varying ~s of skill** их рабóта покáзывает разли́чную стéпень мастерствá; **by ~s** постепéнно; **in the highest ~** в наивы́сшей стéпени; **to the last ~** до послéдней стéпени; **to a ~** óчень, значи́тельно; **not in the slightest ~** ничýть, нискóлько, ни в какóй стéпени; **in some ~** в нéкоторой стéпени; **to what ~ is he interested?** в какóй стéпени э́то егó интересýет?; **third ~** допрóс с применéнием пы́ток; **prohibited ~s** стéпени родствá, при котóрых запрещáется брак; **murder in the first ~** предумы́шленное уби́йство. **3.** (*social position*) положéние; **of high ~** высокопостáвленный. **4.** (*acad.*) диплóм; (*higher ~*) стéпень; **take one's ~** получи́ть (*pf.*) стéпень. **5.** (*gram.*) стéпень; **~s of comparison** стéпени сравнéния.

dehumanize [diːˈhjuːməˌnaɪz] *v.t.* дегуманизи́ровать (*impf.*, *pf.*).

dehumidify [ˌdiːhjuːˈmɪdɪˌfaɪ] *v.t.* осуш|áть, -и́ть.

dehydrate [diːˈhaɪdreɪt, ˌdiːhaɪˈdreɪt] *v.t.* обезвó|живать, -дить; **~d eggs** яи́чный порошóк.

dehydration [ˌdiːhaɪˈdreɪʃ(ə)n] *n.* обезвóживание, дегидратáция.

dehypnotize [diːˈhɪpnəˌtaɪz] *v.t.* выводи́ть, вы́вести из гипноти́ческого состоя́ния.

de-ice [diːˈaɪs] *v.t.* устран|я́ть, -и́ть обледенéние +*g.*

de-icer [diːˈaɪsə(r)] *n.* антиобледени́тель (*m.*).

deicide [ˈdiːɪˌsaɪd, ˈdeɪɪs-] *n.* (*act*) богоуби́йство; (*pers.*) богоуби́йца.

deification [ˌdiːɪfɪˈkeɪʃ(ə)n, ˌdeɪɪfɪˈkeɪʃ(ə)n] *n.* обожествлéние, обоготворéние.

deify [ˈdiːɪˌfaɪ, ˈdeɪɪ-] *v.t.* (*make into a god*) обожеств|ля́ть, -и́ть; обоготвор|я́ть, -и́ть; (*worship*) обоготвор|я́ть, -и́ть; боготвори́ть (*impf.*).

deign [deɪn] *v.t.* сни|сходи́ть, -зойти́; соизвóлить (*pf.*); **he did not ~ to answer us** он не удостóил нас отвéтом.

deism [ˈdiːɪz(ə)m, ˈdeɪ-] *n.* деи́зм.

deist [ˈdiːɪst, ˈdeɪɪst] *n.* деи́ст.

deistic(al) [ˌdiːˈɪstɪk(ə)l, ˌdeɪˈɪstɪk(ə)l] *adj.* деисти́ческий.

deity [ˈdiːɪtɪ, ˈdeɪɪ-] *n.* (*divine nature*) божéственность; (*god*) божествó.

dejected [dɪˈdʒektɪd] *adj.* удручённый, подáвленный.

dejection [dɪˈdʒekʃ(ə)n] *n.* подáвленное настроéние; уны́ние.

de jure [diː ˈdʒʊərɪ, deɪ ˈjʊəreɪ] *adj.* юриди́ческий.

adv. де-ю́ре; юриди́чески.

dekko [ˈdekəʊ] *n.* (*sl.*): **have a ~ at** взглянýть (*pf.*) на+*a.*; брóсить (*pf.*) взгляд на+*a.*

delate [dɪˈleɪt] *v.t.* дон|оси́ть, -ести́ на+*a.*

delation [dɪˈleɪʃ(ə)n] *n.* донóс.

delator [dɪˈleɪtə(r)] *n.* донóсчик.

delay [dɪˈleɪ] *n.* задéржка, отсрóчка, промедлéние; **without ~** немéдленно; **after several ~s** пóсле нéскольких отсрóчек.

v.t. от|клáдывать, -ложи́ть; задéрж|ивать, -áть; мéдлить (*impf.*); **I was ~ed by traffic** я задержáлся из-за прóбок; **~ed action mine** ми́на замéдленного дéйствия.

v.i. задéрж|иваться, -áться.

delectable [dɪˈlektəb(ə)l] *adj.* услади́тельный, прелéстный.

delectation [ˌdiːlekˈteɪʃ(ə)n] *n.* наслаждéние, удовóльствие, услаждéние.

delegate [ˈdelɪgət] *n.* делегáт, представи́тель (*m.*).

v.t. ~ **s.o.** делеги́ровать (*impf.*, *pf.*) когó-н.; послáть (*pf.*) когó-н. делегáтом; обл|екáть, -éчь когó-н. влáстью; ~ **authority** перед|авáть, -áть полномóчие; ~ **a task** порyч|áть, -и́ть рабóту (*комý*).

delegation [ˌdelɪˈgeɪʃ(ə)n] *n.* **1.** (*act of delegating*) посы́лка делегáции; делеги́рование; (*of task, authority*) поручéние, передáча. **2.** (*body of delegates*) делегáция, депутáция.

delete [dɪˈliːt] *v.t.* вычёркивать, вы́черкнуть; из|ымáть, -ъя́ть; выпускáть, вы́пустить.

deleterious [ˌdelɪˈtɪərɪəs] *adj.* врéдный.

deletion [dɪˈliːʃ(ə)n] *n.* вычёркивание.

delft [delft] *n.* (*also* **~ware**) дéлфтский фая́нс.

Delhi [ˈdelɪ] *n.* Дéли (*m. indecl.*).

deliberate[1] [dɪˈlɪbərət] *adj.* (*intentional*) преднамéренный, умы́шленный, нарочи́тый; (*slow, prudent*) осторóжный, осмотри́тельный.

deliberate[2] [dɪˈlɪbəˌreɪt] *v.i.* совещáться (*impf.*); ~ **on, upon, over, about a matter** обсу|ждáть, -ди́ть вопрóс.

deliberation [dɪˌlɪbəˈreɪʃ(ə)n] *n.* (*pondering*) обдýмывание, взвéшивание; (*slowness*) медли́тельность, неторопли́вость.

deliberative [dɪˈlɪbərətɪv] *adj.* совещáтельный.

delicacy [ˈdelɪkəsɪ] *n.* (*exquisiteness, subtlety*) утончённость, тóнкость; (*proneness to injury*) хрýпкость, деликáтность; (*critical nature*) щекотли́вость; (*sensitivity*) нéжность, чувстви́тельность; (*tact*) деликáтность, щепети́льность; (*choice food*) деликатéс, лáкомство.

delicate [ˈdelɪkət] *adj.* **1.** (*fine, exquisite*) изя́щный, тóнкий; ~ **complexion** нéжная кóжа; ~ **workmanship** тóнкое мастерствó. **2.** (*subtle, dainty*) тóнкий, утончённый; **a ~ shade of pink** блéдно-рóзовый оттéнок; ~ **flavour** тóнкий аромáт. **3.** (*easily injured*) хрýпкий, слáбый; ~ **health** слáбое здорóвье; **a ~ person** хрýпкий человéк; **a ~ child** болéзненный ребёнок. **4.** (*critical, ticklish*) щекотли́вый, затрудни́тельный; **a ~ operation** тóнкая/слóжная оперáция. **5.** (*sensitive*) тóнкий, óстрый; **a ~ sense of smell** тóнкое обоня́ние; ~ **instruments** чувстви́тельные прибóры; **the pianist has a ~ touch** у пиани́ста мя́гкое тушé. **6.** (*tactful, considerate*) деликáтный, такти́чный; ~ **behaviour** такти́чное поведéние. **7.** (*careful of propriety*) щепети́льный, осторóжный.

delicatessen [ˌdelɪkəˈtes(ə)n] *n.* (*food*) деликатéсы (*m. pl.*); (*shop*) гастрономи́ческий магази́н, гастронóм.

delicious [dɪˈlɪʃəs] *adj.* óчень вкýсный; (*delightful*) восхити́тельный.

delict [dɪˈlɪkt, ˈdiː-] *n.* (*leg.*) правонарушéние.

delight [dɪˈlaɪt] *n.* **1.** (*pleasure*) удовóльствие, наслаждéние; **take ~ in sth.** на|ходи́ть, -йти́ удовóльствие в чём-н.; **the ~s of life** рáдости (*f. pl.*) жи́зни. **2.** (*source of pleasure*): **music is her ~** мýзыка для неё — истóчник наслаждéния.

v.t. дост|авля́ть, -áвить наслаждéние +*d.*; **I am ~ed to accept the invitation** я óчень рад приня́ть приглашéние.

v.i. насла|ждáться, -ди́ться; **he ~s in reading** он óчень лю́бит читáть.

delightful [dɪ'laɪtfʊl] *adj.* восхити́тельный, очарова́тельный.
delimit [dɪ'lɪmɪt] *v.t.* определ|я́ть, -и́ть грани́цы +*g.*; размежёв|ывать, -а́ть.
delimitation [dɪ,lɪmɪ'teɪʃ(ə)n] *n.* размежева́ние; определе́ние, делимита́ция.
delineate [dɪ'lɪnɪ,eɪt] *v.t.* (*e.g. a frontier*) очéр|чивать, -ти́ть; (*e.g. character*) изобра|жа́ть, -зи́ть; очéр|чивать, -ти́ть.
delineation [dɪ,lɪnɪ'eɪʃ(ə)n] *n.* очéрчивание, изображе́ние.
delinquency [dɪ'lɪŋkwənsɪ] *n.* **1.** (*wrongdoing*) престу́пность; **juvenile ~** престу́пность несовершенноле́тних. **2.** (*misdeed*) правонаруше́ние, преступле́ние.
delinquent [dɪ'lɪŋkwənt] *adj.* правонаруши́тель (*fem.* -ница), престу́пни|к (*fem.* -ца); **juvenile ~** малоле́тний престу́пник.
adj. вино́вный.
deliquesce [,delɪ'kwes] *v.i.* раствор|я́ться, -и́ться; распл|ыва́ться, -ы́ться.
deliquescence [,delɪ'kwesəns] *n.* раствори́мость (*fig.*) расплы́вчатость.
deliquescent [,delɪ'kwesənt] *adj.* растворя́ющийся.
delirious [dɪ'lɪrɪəs] *adj.* (*raving*) в бреду́; (*wildly excited*) вне себя́.
delirium [dɪ'lɪrɪəm] *n.* бред; **~ tremens** бéлая горя́чка.
deliver [dɪ'lɪvə(r)] *v.t.* **1.** (*rescue, set free*) освобо|жда́ть, -ди́ть; изб|авля́ть, -а́вить; **God ~ us!** изба́ви Бог!; Го́споди, поми́луй! **2.** (*of birth*): **she was ~ed (of a child)** она́ разреши́лась от бре́мени; **he ~ed her** он при́нял ро́ды у неё; **the child was ~ed by forceps** при ро́дах пришло́сь наложи́ть щипцы́. **3. ~ o.s. of an opinion** вы́сказать (*pf.*) своё мне́ние. **4.** (*give, present*): **~ judgment** выноси́ть, вы́нести реше́ние; **~ a speech** произн|оси́ть, -ести́ речь; **a well ~ed sermon** хорошо́ прочи́танная про́поведь. **5.** (*hand over*) сда|ва́ть, -ть; перед|ава́ть, -а́ть; **~ up stolen goods** сда|ва́ть, -ть укра́денные това́ры; **~ (over) a fortress to the enemy** сда|ва́ть, -ть кре́пость врагу́. **6.** (*aim, launch*) нан|оси́ть, -ести́; **~ a blow** нанести́ (*pf.*) уда́р; **~ battle** дать (*pf.*) бой. **7.** (*send out, convey*) пост|авля́ть, -а́вить; вруч|а́ть, -и́ть; перед|ава́ть, -а́ть; **the shop ~s daily** магази́н доставля́ет това́ры на́ дом ежедне́вно; **the postman ~s letters** почтальо́н разно́сит пи́сьма; **~ the goods** (*fig., coll.*) выполня́ть, вы́полнить обе́щанное.
deliverance [dɪ'lɪvərəns] *n.* освобожде́ние, избавле́ние.
deliverer [dɪ'lɪvərə(r)] *n.* (*conveyor*) разно́счик, рассы́льный, доста́вщик; (*saviour, rescuer*) избави́тель (*m.*), спаси́тель (*m.*).
delivery [dɪ'lɪvərɪ] *n.* **1.** (*childbirth*) ро́ды (*pl., g.* -ов); **~ room** роди́льная пала́та. **2.** (*surrender*) сда́ча, вы́дача. **3.** (*distribution of goods or letters*) доста́вка; **charges payable on ~** опла́та при доста́вке; **~ the letter came by the first ~** письмо́ пришло́ с пе́рвой по́чтой; **~ note** накладна́я; **~ man** доставля́ющий поку́пки; доста́вщик; **~ van** фурго́н для доста́вки поку́пок на́ дом. **4.** (*of missile*) доста́вка к це́ли. **5.** (*of speech etc.*) произнесе́ние (ре́чи); ди́кция; те́хника ре́чи; **his ~ was poor** он говори́л о́чень невня́тно.
dell [del] *n.* леси́стая доли́на; лощи́на.
delouse [di:'laʊs] *v.t.* дезинсекти́ровать (*impf., pf.*); подв|ерга́ть, -е́ргнуть санобрабо́тке/дезинсе́кции.
delousing [di:'laʊsɪŋ] *n.* санобрабо́тка, дезинсе́кция.
Delphic ['delfɪk] *adj.* (*fig.*) двусмы́сленный.
delphinium [del'fɪnɪəm] *n.* дельфи́ниум.
delta ['deltə] *n.* де́льта; **~ ray** де́льта-луч.
cpd. **~-wing(ed)** *adj.*: с дельтообра́зным крыло́м.
deltoid ['deltɔɪd] *adj.* дельтови́дный, треуго́льный.
delude [dɪ'lu:d, -'lju:d] *v.t.* вв|оди́ть, -ести́ в заблужде́ние; **he ~d himself into believing that …** он уве́рил себя́ в то́м, что…
deluge ['delju:dʒ] *n.* **1.** (*lit.*) пото́п; **the D~** (*bibl.*) всеми́рный пото́п. **2.** (*fig.*) пото́к, град, лави́на; **a ~ of protest** пото́к проте́стов.
v.t. затоп|ля́ть, -и́ть; **he was ~d with questions** его́ засы́пали гра́дом вопро́сов.
delusion [dɪ'lu:ʒ(ə)n, -'lju:ʒ(ə)n] *n.* заблужде́ние; **be under a ~** заблужда́ться (*impf.*); **~s of grandeur** ма́ния вели́чия.
delusive [dɪ'lu:sɪv, -'lju:sɪv] *adj.* обма́нчивый.
de luxe [də 'lʌks, 'lʊks] *adj.* роско́шный; **a ~ cabin** каю́та-люкс.
delve [delv] *v.i.* копа́ть (*impf.*); **~ in archives** ры́ться (*impf.*) в архи́вах.
demagnetize [di:'mægnɪ,taɪz] *v.t.* размагни́|чивать, -тить.
demagogic [,demə'gɒgɪk] *adj.* демагоги́ческий.
demagogue ['demə,gɒg] *n.* демаго́г.
demagogy ['demə,gɒgɪ] *n.* демаго́гия.
demand [dɪ'mɑ:nd] *n.* **1.** (*claim*) тре́бование; **payable on ~** подлежа́щий опла́те по предъявле́нии; **there are many ~s on my time** у меня́ мно́го дел/обя́занностей; **there were ~s for the minister to resign** раздава́лись тре́бования об отста́вке мини́стра. **2.** (*desire to obtain*) потре́бность, спро́с; **there is no ~ for this article** на э́тот това́р нет спро́са; **he is in great ~ for parties** все стара́ются залучи́ть его́ к себе́ в го́сти.
v.t. тре́бовать, по- +*g.*; **piety ~s it of us** э́того тре́бует от нас благоче́стие.
demarcate ['di:mɑ:,keɪt] *v.t.* разграни́чи|вать, -ть; устан|а́вливать, -ови́ть.
demarcation [,di:mɑ:'keɪʃ(ə)n] *n.* разграниче́ние, демарка́ция.
démarche [deɪ'mɑ:ʃ] *n.* дема́рш.
demean[1] [dɪ'mi:n] *v.t.* (*conduct*): **~ o.s.** держа́ть (*impf.*) себя́.
demean[2] [dɪ'mi:n] *v.t.* (*abase*) ун|ижа́ть, -и́зить; **~ o.s.** роня́ть (*impf.*) своё досто́инство.
demeanour [dɪ'mi:nə(r)] *n.* поведе́ние; мане́ра вести́ себя́; мане́ры (*f. pl.*).
demented [dɪ'mentɪd] *adj.* сумасше́дший.
démenti [deɪ'mɑ̃tɪ] *n.* официа́льное опроверже́ние.
dementia [dɪ'menʃə] *n.* слабоу́мие; **~ praecox** ра́ннее слабоу́мие.
demerit [di:'merɪt] *n.* недоста́ток; дурна́я черта́.
demesne [dɪ'mi:n, -'meɪn] *n.* (*estate*) владе́ние, поме́стье.
demigod ['demɪ,gɒd] *n.* полубо́г.
demijohn ['demɪ,dʒɒn] *n.* больша́я оплетённая буты́ль.
demilitarization [di:,mɪlɪtəraɪ'zeɪʃ(ə)n] *n.* демилитариза́ция.
demilitarize [di:'mɪlɪtə,raɪz] *v.t.* демилитаризи́ровать (*impf., pf.*).
demi-mondaine ['demɪmɒn,deɪn, -mɔ̃,deɪn] *n.* да́ма полусве́та.
demi-monde ['demɪ,mɒnd, -'mɔ̃d] *n.* полусве́т.
demise [dɪ'maɪz] *n.* кончи́на; **~ of the Crown** перехо́д коро́ны к насле́днику.
demisemiquaver [,demɪ'semɪ,kweɪvə(r), 'demɪ-] *n.* тридцать втора́я (но́та).
demist [di:'mɪst] *v.t.* предохран|я́ть, -и́ть от запотева́ния; обогр|ева́ть, -е́ть (*стекло*).
demister [di:'mɪstə(r)] *n.* деми́стер; обогрева́тель (*m.*) стекла́.
demi-tasse ['demɪ,tæs, dəmɪ'tæs] *n.* (*US*) ча́шечка чёрного ко́фе.
demiurge ['demɪ,ɜ:dʒ] *n.* (*creator*) творе́ц, созда́тель (*m.*), демиу́рг.
demo ['deməʊ] (*coll.*) = **demonstration**
demob [di:'mɒb] (*coll.*) = **demobilize**
demobilization [di:,məʊbɪlaɪ'zeɪʃ(ə)n] *n.* демобилиза́ция.
demobilize [di:'məʊbɪ,laɪz] *v.t.* демобилизова́ть (*pf.*).
democracy [dɪ'mɒkrəsɪ] *n.* демокра́тия; **Britain is a ~** А́нглия — демократи́ческое госуда́рство.
democrat ['demə,kræt] *n.* демокра́т.
democratic [,demə'krætɪk] *adj.* демократи́ческий, демократи́чный; **she is very ~** она́ о́чень демократи́чна.
democratize [dɪ'mɒkrə,taɪz] *v.t.* демократизи́ровать (*impf., pf.*).
demographer [dɪ'mɒgrəfə(r)] *n.* демо́граф.
demographic [,demə'græfɪk] *adj.* демографи́ческий.
demography [dɪ'mɒgrəfɪ] *n.* демогра́фия.
demoiselle [,demwæ'zel] *n.* (**~ crane**) жура́вль-краса́вка.
demolish [dɪ'mɒlɪʃ] *v.t.* (*e.g. house*) сн|оси́ть, -ести́; разр|уша́ть, -у́шить; (*e.g. theory*) опров|ерга́ть, -е́ргнуть; разб|ива́ть, -и́ть.
demolition [,demə'lɪʃ(ə)n] *n.* **1.** (*lit.*) разруше́ние, снос; **~ gang** подрывна́я брига́да; **~ bomb** фуга́сная бо́мба. **2.** (*of argument etc.*) опроверже́ние.

demon ['di:mən] *n.* **1.** (*devil*) де́мон, дья́вол, бес; **the child is a little ~** э́тот ребёнок — су́щий бес; **the ~ drink** зе́лье, вы́пивка. **2.** (*fierce or energetic pers.*): **he's a ~ for work** он рабо́тает как чёрт.

demonetization [di:ˌmʌnɪtaɪ'zeɪʃ(ə)n] *n.* демонетиза́ция.

demonetize [di:'mʌnɪˌtaɪz] *v.t.* из|ыма́ть, -ъя́ть из обраще́ния.

demoniac(al) [ˌdi:mə'naɪək(ə)l] *adj.* демони́ческий; (*frenzied*) одержи́мый.

demonology [ˌdi:mə'nɒlədʒɪ] *n.* демоноло́гия.

demonstrable ['demɒnstrəb(ə)l, dɪ'mɒnstrəb(ə)l] *adj.* доказу́емый.

demonstrate ['demənˌstreɪt] *v.t.* **1.** (*prove*) дока́з|ывать, -а́ть; **~ one's sympathies** проявл|я́ть, -и́ть свои́ симпа́тии. **2.** (*show in operation*) демонстри́ровать, про-.

v.i. устр|а́ивать, -о́ить демонстра́цию; уча́ствовать (*impf.*) в демонстра́ции.

demonstration [ˌdemən'streɪʃ(ə)n] *n.* (*proof*) доказа́тельство; (*exhibition*): **~ of affection** проявле́ние чу́вства; **~ of a machine** демонстри́рование маши́ны; (*public manifestation*) демонстра́ция; (*mil.*) демонстра́ция си́лы.

demonstrative [dɪ'mɒnstrətɪv] *adj.* **1.** (*of proof*) нагля́дный, убеди́тельный. **2.** (*showing feelings*) экспанси́вный, несде́ржанный. **3.** (*gram.*) указа́тельный.

demonstrativeness [dɪ'mɒnstrətɪvnɪs] *n.* экспанси́вность, несде́ржанность.

demonstrator ['demənˌstreɪtə(r)] *n.* **1.** демонстри́рующий, дока́зывающий. **2.** (*one who displays*) демонстра́тор. **3.** (*assistant to professor*) ассисте́нт. **4.** (*pol.*) демонстра́нт.

demoralization [dɪˌmɒrəlaɪ'zeɪʃ(ə)n] *n.* деморализа́ция; (*corruption*) разложе́ние.

demoralize [dɪ'mɒrəˌlaɪz] *v.t.* деморализова́ть (*impf., pf.*); (*corrupt*) разл|ага́ть, -ожи́ть.

Demosthenes [dɪ'mɒsθəˌni:z] *n.* Демосфе́н.

demote [dɪ'məʊt, di:-] *v.t.* пон|ижа́ть, -и́зить в до́лжности.

demotic [dɪ'mɒtɪk] *adj.* (*popular*) (просто)наро́дный; (*ling.*) демоти́ческий.

demotion [dɪ'məʊʃ(ə)n] *n.* пониже́ние в до́лжности.

demur [dɪ'mɜ:(r)] *n.* возраже́ние; **without ~** без возраже́ний.

v.i. возра|жа́ть, -зи́ть (**~ at, to:** про́тив+*g.*).

demure [dɪ'mjʊə(r)] *adj.* скро́мный, серьёзный; наи́гранно-серьёзный.

demureness [dɪ'mjʊənɪs] *n.* скро́мность, серьёзность; напускна́я серьёзность.

demurrage [dɪ'mʌrɪdʒ] *n.* просто́й; (*compensation*) пла́та за просто́й.

demythologize [ˌdi:mɪ'θɒləˌdʒaɪz] *v.t.* разве́|ивать, -ять миф о+*p.*

den [den] *n.* **1.** (*animal's lair*) берло́га, ло́говище, ло́гово. **2.** (*of thieves*) прито́н; **~ of vice** верте́п. **3.** (*hovel*) камо́рка. **4.** (*sanctum*) «убе́жище», рабо́чий кабине́т.

denarius [dɪ'neərɪəs] *n.* (*hist.*) дена́рий.

denationalization [di:ˌnæʃənəlaɪ'zeɪʃ(ə)n] *n.* **1.** лише́ние по́дданства. **2.** денационализа́ция.

denationalize [di:'næʃənəˌlaɪz] *v.t.* **1.** (*deprive of nationality*) лиш|а́ть, -и́ть по́дданства/гражда́нства. **2.** (*return to private hands*) денационализи́ровать (*impf., pf.*).

denaturalize [di:'nætʃərəˌlaɪz] *v.t.* (*deprive of natural qualities*) лиш|а́ть, -и́ть приро́дных свойств; (*deprive of citizenship*) денатурализова́тиь (*impf., pf.*).

denature [di:'neɪtʃə(r)] *v.t.* измен|я́ть, -и́ть есте́ственные сво́йства +*g.*; денатури́ровать (*impf., pf.*); **~d alcohol** денатура́т.

denazification [di:ˌnɑ:tsɪfɪ'keɪʃ(ə)n, diˌnɑ:zɪfɪ'keɪʃ(ə)n] *n.* денацифика́ция.

denazify [di:'nɑ:tsɪˌfaɪ, -'nɑ:zɪˌfaɪ] *v.t.* денацифици́ровать (*impf., pf.*).

denegation [ˌdi:nɪ'geɪʃ(ə)n] *n.* отрица́ние.

dengue ['deŋgɪ] *n.* (**~ fever**) лихора́дка де́нге (*indecl.*).

deniable [dɪ'naɪəb(ə)l] *adj.* опровержи́мый.

denial [dɪ'naɪəl] *n.* **1.** (*denying*) отрица́ние, опроверже́ние; **a flat ~** категори́ческое опроверже́ние/отрица́ние. **2.** (*refusal*) отка́з; **I'll take no ~** я не приму́ отка́за; **~ of justice** отка́з в правосу́дии. **3.** (*disavowal*) отрече́ние (от+*g.*).

denier[1] [dɪ'naɪə(r)] *n.* (*one who denies*) отрица́ющий.

denier[2] ['denjə(r)] *n.* (*unit of fineness*) денье́ (*indecl.*).

denigrate ['denɪˌgreɪt] *v.t.* (*defame*) черни́ть, о-; клевета́ть, о-; поро́чить, о-.

denigration [ˌdenɪ'greɪʃ(ə)n] *n.* клевета́, опоро́чение.

denigrator ['denɪˌgreɪtə(r)] *n.* клеветни́к.

denim ['denɪm] *n.* джинсо́вая ткань.

adj. джинсо́вый.

denitrify [di:'naɪtrɪˌfaɪ] *v.t.* денитри́ровать (*impf., pf.*); денитрифици́ровать (*impf., pf.*).

denizen ['denɪz(ə)n] *n.* **1.** (*inhabitant*) жи́тель (*m.*), обита́тель (*m.*); **~s of the deep** обита́тели глуби́н. **2.** (*alien admitted to rights of citizenship*) натурализова́вшийся иностра́нец. **3.** (*naturalized animal or plant*) акклиматизи́ровавшееся живо́тное; приви́вшееся расте́ние. **4.** (*habitué*) завсегда́тай.

Denmark ['denmɑ:k] *n.* Да́ния.

denominate [dɪ'nɒmɪˌneɪt] *v.t.* обозн|ача́ть, -а́чить.

denomination [dɪˌnɒmɪ'neɪʃ(ə)n] *n.* **1.** (*name, nomenclature*) наименова́ние. **2.** (*relig.*) вероисповеда́ние. **3.: money of small ~s** купю́ры (*f. pl.*) ма́лого досто́инства.

denominational [dɪˌnɒmɪ'neɪʃənəl] *adj.* (*relig.*) конфессиона́льный, вероиспове́дный.

denominator [dɪ'nɒmɪˌneɪtə(r)] *n.* (*math.*) знамена́тель (*m.*); **reduce to a common ~** прив|оди́ть, -ести́ к о́бщему знамена́телю.

denotation [ˌdi:nə'teɪʃ(ə)n] *n.* обозначе́ние.

denote [dɪ'nəʊt] *v.t.* обозн|ача́ть, -а́чить.

dénouement [deɪ'nu:mɑ̃] *n.* развя́зка.

denounce [dɪ'naʊns] *v.t.* **1.** (*inveigh against*) осу|жда́ть, -ди́ть. **2.** (*inform against*) дон|оси́ть, -ести́ на+*a.* **3.** (*treaty etc.*) денонси́ровать (*impf., pf.*).

dense [dens] *adj.* **1.** (*of liquids, vapour*) пло́тный, густо́й. **2.** (*of objects*) густо́й; **the bracken was ~ on the ground** густо́й па́поротник покрыва́л зе́млю. **3.** (*stupid*) тупо́й.

denseness ['densnɪs] *n.* (*stupidity*) ту́пость, тупоу́мие.

density ['densɪtɪ] *n.* пло́тность, густота́; **~ of population** пло́тность населе́ния; населённость.

dent [dent] *n.* вмя́тина, вы́боина.

v.t. ост|авля́ть, -а́вить вмя́тину в/на+*p.*; вдав|ливать, -и́ть; **the car got ~ed in the collision** при столкнове́нии маши́на получи́ла вмя́тину.

v.i. гну́ться, про-; **this metal ~s easily** э́тот мета́лл легко́ гнётся.

dental ['dent(ə)l] *n.* (*phon.*) зубно́й звук.

adj. (*of teeth*) зубно́й; **~ plaque** зубно́й налёт; (*of dentistry*) зубовраче́бный.

dentifrice ['dentɪfrɪs] *n.* зубно́й порошо́к; зубна́я па́ста.

dentist ['dentɪst] *n.* зубно́й врач, данти́ст, стомато́лог.

dentistry ['dentɪstrɪ] *n.* лече́ние зубо́в; профе́ссия зубно́го врача́.

dentition [den'tɪʃ(ə)n] *n.* (*cutting of teeth*) проре́зывание зубо́в; (*arrangement of teeth*) расположе́ние зубо́в.

denture ['dentʃə(r)] *n.* зубно́й проте́з.

denuclearize [di:'nju:klɪəˌraɪz] *v.t.* превра|ща́ть, -ти́ть в безъя́дерную зо́ну.

denudation [ˌdi:nju:'deɪʃ(ə)n] *n.* оголе́ние, обнаже́ние.

denude [dɪ'nju:d] *v.t.* огол|я́ть, -и́ть; обнаж|а́ть, -и́ть; (*fig.*) об|ира́ть, -обра́ть; **he was ~d by his creditors** кредито́ры обобра́ли его́ до ни́тки.

denunciation [dɪˌnʌnsɪ'eɪʃ(ə)n] *n.* осужде́ние; доно́с; (*of treaty*) денонса́ция.

denunciatory [dɪ'nʌnsɪətərɪ, -'nʌnʃɪətərɪ] *adj.* осужда́ющий; содержа́щий доно́с.

den|y [dɪ'naɪ] *v.t.* **1.** (*contest truth of*) отрица́ть (*impf.*). **2.** (*repudiate*) отр|ека́ться, -е́чься от+*g.* **3.** (*refuse*) отка́з|ывать, -а́ть (*кому в чём*); **he was ~ied admittance** его́ не впусти́ли; **~y o.s. sth.** отка́з|ывать, -а́ть себе́ в чём-н.

deodar ['di:əˌdɑ:(r)] *n.* гимала́йский кедр.

deodorant [di:'əʊdərənt] *n.* дезодора́тор.

deodorize [di:'əʊdəˌraɪz] *v.t.* дезодори́ровать (*impf., pf.*).

deontology [ˌdi:ɒn'tɒlədʒɪ] *n.* деонтоло́гия.

depart [dɪ'pɑ:t] *v.t.*: **~ this life** пок|ида́ть, -и́нуть э́тот (бре́нный) мир.

v.i. **1.** (*go away*) отпр|авля́ться, -а́виться; отб|ыва́ть, -ы́ть; удал|я́ться, -и́ться. **2.:** ~ **from** (*custom, plan etc.*) отступ|а́ть, -и́ть от+*g*.

departed [dɪ'pɑ:tɪd] *n.*: **the (dear)** ~ поко́йный, отоше́дший.
adj. (*bygone*) было́й, мину́вший.

department [dɪ'pɑ:tmənt] *n.* **1.** отде́л; ~ **store** универма́г. **2.** (*of government*) департа́мент, ве́домство. **3.** (*Fr. admin.*) департа́мент. **4.** (*of univ.*) ка́федра.

departmental [ˌdi:pɑ:t'ment(ə)l] *adj.* ве́домственный.

departure [dɪ'pɑ:tʃə(r)] *n.* **1.** (*going away*) отъе́зд, отправле́ние; ~ **platform** платфо́рма отправле́ния; **take one's** ~ уходи́ть, уйти́; уезжа́ть, уе́хать. **2.** (*deviation, change*) отклоне́ние; **new** ~ нововведе́ние.

depend [dɪ'pend] *v.i.* **1.** (*be conditional*) зави́сеть (*impf.*) (от+*g*.); **that** ~**s; it all** ~**s** как сказа́ть; посмо́трим; смотря́ (*где, когда, что и т.п.*); смотря́, как полу́чится. **2.** (*rely*) пол|ага́ться, -ожи́ться (на+*a*.); рассчи́тывать (*impf.*) (на+*a*.).

dependable [dɪ'pendəb(ə)l] *adj.* надёжный.

dependant [dɪ'pend(ə)nt] *n.* иждиве́н|ец (*fem.* -ка).

dependence [dɪ'pend(ə)ns] *n.* зави́симость (от+*g*.); (*reliance*) дове́рие (к+*d*.).

dependency [dɪ'pendənsɪ] *n.* (*pol.*) коло́ния.

dependent [dɪ'pend(ə)nt] *adj.* **1.** (*conditional*) зави́симый, зави́сящий. **2.** (*financial*) зави́симый, находя́щийся на иждиве́нии. **3.** (*gram.*) подчинённый.

depersonalize [di:'pɜ:sənəˌlaɪz] *v.t.* обезли́чи|вать, -ть.

depict [dɪ'pɪkt] *v.t.* изобра|жа́ть, -зи́ть.

depiction [dɪ'pɪkʃ(ə)n] *n.* описа́ние, изображе́ние.

depilatory [dɪ'pɪlətərɪ] *n.* сре́дство для удале́ния воло́с.
adj. удаля́ющий во́лосы.

deplane [di:'pleɪn] *v.t. & i.* выса́живать(ся), вы́садить(ся) из самолёта.

deplete [dɪ'pli:t] *v.t.* истощ|а́ть, -и́ть; исчерп|ывать, -а́ть; ~**d strength** (*physical*) уга́сшие си́лы; (*mil.*) поределые си́лы; **a** ~**d gas-bag** испо́льзованный га́зовый балло́н.

depletion [dɪ'pli:ʃ(ə)n] *n.* истоще́ние, исче́рпывание.

deplorable [dɪ'plɔ:rəb(ə)l] *adj.* плаче́вный, приско́рбный; досто́йный сожале́ния; ~ **handwriting** ужа́сный/невозмо́жный по́черк.

deplore [dɪ'plɔ:(r)] *v.t.* сожале́ть (*impf.*) о+*p*.; счита́ть (*impf.*) предосуди́тельным/возмути́тельным.

deploy [dɪ'plɔɪ] *v.t.* развёр|тывать, -ну́ть.

deployment [dɪ'plɔɪmənt] *n.* развёртывание; размеще́ние.

depolarization [di:ˌpəʊləraɪ'zeɪʃ(ə)n] *n.* деполяриза́ция.

depolarize [di:'pəʊləˌraɪz] *v.t.* деполяризова́ть (*impf., pf.*).

deponent [dɪ'pəʊnənt] *n.* (*leg.*) свиде́тель (*m.*), даю́щий показа́ния под прися́гой; *n. & adj.* (*gram.*) отложи́тельный (глаго́л).

depopulate [di:'pɒpjʊˌleɪt] *v.t.* обезлю́дить (*pf.*).

depopulation [di:ˌpɒpjʊ'leɪʃ(ə)n] *n.* сокраще́ние населе́ния.

deport [dɪ'pɔ:t] *v.t.* **1.:** ~ **o.s.** вести́ (*det.*) себя́. **2.** (*remove, banish*) высыла́ть, вы́слать; ссыла́ть, сосла́ть.

deportation [ˌdi:pɔ:'teɪʃ(ə)n] *n.* вы́сылка, ссы́лка, депорта́ция.

deportee [ˌdi:pɔ:'ti:] *n.* высыла́емый, со́сланный.

deportment [dɪ'pɔ:tmənt] *n.* мане́ры (*f. pl.*); мане́ра держа́ться; оса́нка.

depose [dɪ'pəʊz] *v.t.* (*monarch etc.*) св|ерга́ть, -е́ргнуть (с престо́ла); сме|ща́ть, -сти́ть; низл|ага́ть, -ожи́ть.
v.i. (*testify*) свиде́тельствовать (*impf.*).

deposit [dɪ'pɒzɪt] *n.* **1.** (*sum in bank*) вклад. **2.** (*act of placing*) депози́т; ~ **account** депози́тный счёт. **3.** (*advance payment*) зада́ток; (*layer*) отложе́ние. **4.** (*of ore etc.*) за́лежь, ро́ссыпь.
v.t. класть, положи́ть; (*place in bank*) депони́ровать (*impf., pf.*).

depositary [dɪ'pɒzɪtərɪ] *n.* храни́тель (*m.*), дове́ренное лицо́.

deposition [ˌdi:pə'zɪʃ(ə)n, ˌdep-] *n.* (*dethronement*) сверже́ние, смеще́ние; (*evidence*) показа́ние под прися́гой.

depositor [dɪ'pɒzɪtə(r)] *n.* (*fin.*) депози́тор, депоне́нт, вкла́дчик.

depository [dɪ'pɒzɪtərɪ] *n.* **1.** (*storehouse*) храни́лище. **2.** = **depositary**

depot ['depəʊ] *n.* (*place of storage*) склад; (*for motor transport*) автоба́за.

deprave [dɪ'preɪv] *v.t.* развра|ща́ть, -ти́ть.

depravity [dɪ'prævɪtɪ] *n.* развра́т, развращённость.

deprecate ['deprɪˌkeɪt] *v.t.* осу|жда́ть, -ди́ть; выска́зываться, вы́сказаться про́тив+*g*.; возра|жа́ть, -зи́ть про́тив+*g*.

deprecation [ˌdeprɪ'keɪʃ(ə)n] *n.* осужде́ние (*чего*); возраже́ние (про́тив+*g*.).

deprecatory [ˌdeprɪ'keɪtərɪ] *adj.* (*appeasing*) примири́тельный.

depreciate [dɪ'pri:ʃɪˌeɪt, -sɪˌeɪt] *v.t.* обесце́ни|ва́ть, -ть; (*disparage*) умал|я́ть, -и́ть.
v.i. обесце́ни|ваться, -ться.

depreciation [dɪˌpri:ʃɪ'eɪʃ(ə)n, -sɪ'eɪʃ(ə)n] *n.* обесце́нение; (*disparagement*) умале́ние.

depredation [ˌdeprɪ'deɪʃ(ə)n] *n.* грабёж.

depredator ['deprɪˌdeɪtə(r)] *n.* граби́тель (*m.*).

depress [dɪ'pres] *v.t.* **1.** (*push down*) наж|има́ть, -а́ть на+*a*. **2.** (*fig.*) угнета́ть (*impf.*); ~**ed classes** угнетённые кла́ссы; ~**ed area** райо́н, пострада́вший от экономи́ческой депре́ссии. **3.** (*make sad*) удруч|а́ть, -и́ть; угнета́ть (*impf.*); подав|ля́ть, -и́ть. **4.** (*make less active*): **business is** ~**ed** в дела́х засто́й.

depressant [dɪ'pres(ə)nt] *n.* (*med.*) успокои́тельное сре́дство.

depressing [dɪ'presɪŋ] *adj.* удруча́ющий, гнету́щий, тя́гостный; тру́дный, уны́лый.

depression [dɪ'preʃ(ə)n] *n.* **1.** (*pressing down*) давле́ние. **2.** (*hollow, sunken place*) впа́дина, углубле́ние. **3.** (*slump*) депре́ссия, засто́й. **4.** (*low spirits*) депре́ссия, тоска́, удручённость, уны́ние, пода́вленность. **5.** (*meteor.*) депре́ссия.

deprivation [ˌdeprɪ'veɪʃ(ə)n, ˌdi:praɪ-] *n.* (*being deprived*) лише́ние; (*loss*) утра́та.

deprive [dɪ'praɪv] *v.t.* лиш|а́ть, -и́ть (*кого чего*); ~**d** (*underprivileged*) обездо́ленный.

depth [depθ] *n.* **1.** (*deepness*) глубина́; **what is the** ~ **of the well?** какова́ глубина́ коло́дца?; **6 feet in** ~ глубино́й в шесть фу́тов; **at a** ~ **of 6 feet** на глубине́ шести́ фу́тов; **be out of one's** ~ не достава́ть (*impf.*) нога́ми дна; (*fig.*): **I am out of my** ~ **in this job** э́та рабо́та мне не по плечу́; **I am out of my** ~ **in this subject** э́тот предме́т вы́ше моего́ понима́ния; **in** ~ (*fig., thoroughly*) глубоко́; **defence in** ~ (*mil.*) эшелони́рованная оборо́на. **2.** (*profundity*) глубина́. **3.** (*extremity*): ~ **of despair** по́лное отчая́ние; ~ **of winter** разга́р зимы́; **in the** ~**(s) of the country** в глуши́.
cpds. ~**-charge** *n.* глуби́нная бо́мба; ~**-gauge** *n.* водоме́рная ре́йка; глубоме́р.

deputation [ˌdepjʊ'teɪʃ(ə)n] *n.* (*deputing*) делеги́рование; (*representatives*) депута́ция.

depute [dɪ'pju:t] *v.t.* (*a task*) поруч|а́ть, -и́ть; (*a pers.*) делеги́ровать (*impf., pf.*).

deputize ['depjʊˌtaɪz] *v.i.*: ~ **for s.o.** заме|ща́ть (*impf.*) кого́-н.

deputy ['depjʊtɪ] *n.* **1.** (*substitute*) замести́тель (*m.*); ~ **chairman** замести́тель (*m.*) председа́теля; **by** ~ по уполномо́чию. **2.** (*member of parliament*) депута́т.

deputyship ['depjʊtɪʃɪp] *n.* депута́тство, замеще́ние.

deracinate [di:'ræsɪˌneɪt] *v.t.* искорен|я́ть, -и́ть.

derail [dɪ'reɪl, di:-] *v.t.* св|оди́ть, -ести́ с ре́льсов; **the train was** ~ **ed** по́езд сошёл с ре́льсов; **the partisans** ~**ed the train** партиза́ны пусти́ли по́езд под отко́с.

derailment [dɪ'reɪlmənt, di:-] *n.* сход с ре́льсов; круше́ние.

derange [dɪ'reɪndʒ] *v.t.* (*put out of order*) расстр|а́ивать, -о́ить; (*make insane*) св|оди́ть, -ести́ с ума́.

derangement [dɪ'reɪndʒmənt] *n.* (у́мственное) расстро́йство.

deration [di:'ræʃ(ə)n] *v.t.* отмен|я́ть, -и́ть ка́рточную систе́му на+*a*.

derelict ['derəlɪkt, 'derɪ-] *adj.* (*abandoned*) забро́шенный, запу́щенный.

dereliction [ˌderɪ'lɪkʃ(ə)n] *n.* забро́шенность, запу́щенность; ~ **of duty** наруше́ние до́лга.

derequisition [di:ˌrekwɪ'zɪʃ(ə)n] *v.t.* освобо|жда́ть, -ди́ть от реквизи́ции.

derestrict [ˌdi:rɪ'strɪkt] *v.t.* сн|има́ть, -ять ограниче́ние +*g*.

derestriction [ˌdiːrɪˈstrɪkʃ(ə)n] *n.* сня́тие ограниче́ния.
deride [dɪˈraɪd] *v.t.* высме́ивать, вы́смеять; осме́|ивать, -я́ть.
de rigueur [də rɪˈgɜː(r)] *adj.* стро́го обяза́тельный, тре́буемый этике́том.
derision [dɪˈrɪʒ(ə)n] *n.* осмея́ние, высме́ивание; **hold in ~** насмеха́ться (*impf.*) над+*i.*; **bring into** де́лать, с- посме́шищем.
derisive [dɪˈraɪsɪv] *adj.* (*scornful*) насме́шливый; (*absurd*) смехотво́рный.
derisory [dɪˈraɪsərɪ] *adj.* (*ludicrous*) неле́пый, смешно́й, ничто́жный.
derivable [dɪˈraɪvəb(ə)l] *adj.* извлека́емый.
derivation [ˌderɪˈveɪʃ(ə)n] *n.* происхожде́ние.
derivative [dəˈrɪvətɪv, dɪ-] *adj.* (*gram.*) произво́дный; (*fig.*) втори́чный, несамостоя́тельный.
derive [dɪˈraɪv] *v.t.* **1.** (*obtain*) извл|ека́ть, -е́чь; **~ pleasure from** получ|а́ть, -и́ть удово́льствие от+*g.* **2.** (*trace*) выводи́ть, вы́вести; возв|оди́ть, -ести́; **he ~d his origin from Caesar** он вёл свой род от Це́заря. **3.** (*inherit*) насле́довать, у-; **he ~s his character from his father** он унасле́довал хара́ктер своего́ отца́. **4.** (*originate*) происходи́ть (*impf.*); **words ~d from Latin** слова́ лати́нского происхожде́ния.
dermatitis [ˌdɜːməˈtaɪtɪs] *n.* дермати́т.
dermatologist [ˌdɜːməˈtɒlədʒɪst] *n.* дермато́лог.
dermatology [ˌdɜːməˈtɒlədʒɪ] *n.* дерматоло́гия.
derogate [ˈderəˌgeɪt] *v.i.*: **~ from** (*detract from*) умаля́ть, поро́чить (*both impf.*).
derogation [ˌderəˈgeɪʃ(ə)n] *n.* (*impairment*) умале́ние (*чего*).
derogatory [dɪˈrɒgətərɪ] *adj.* пренебрежи́тельный; **~ to s.o.'s dignity** унижа́ющий чьё-н. досто́инство.
derrick [ˈderɪk] *n.* **1.** (*crane*) де́ррик(-кран). **2.** (*over oil-well*) бурова́я вы́шка.
derring-do [ˌderɪŋˈduː] *n.* хра́брость, удальство́.
dervish [ˈdɜːvɪʃ] *n.* де́рвиш.
desalinate [diːˈsælɪˌneɪt] *v.t.* опресн|я́ть, -и́ть.
desalination [diːˌsælɪˈneɪʃ(ə)n] *n.* опресне́ние (воды́).
descant[1] [ˈdeskænt] *n.* (*mus.*) ди́скант.
descant[2] [dɪsˈkænt] *v.i.*: **~ upon** распространя́ться (*impf.*) о+*p.*
descend [dɪˈsend] *v.t.* сходи́ть, сойти́ с+*g.*; **~ a hill** спус|ка́ться, -ти́ться с холма́; **he ~ed the stairs** он спусти́лся/сошёл по ле́стнице.
v.i. **1.** (*go down*) спус|ка́ться, -ти́ться; сходи́ть, сойти́; **in ~ing order (of importance)** в нисходя́щем поря́дке; от бо́лее ва́жного к ме́нее ва́жному; **~ to details** пере|ходи́ть, -йти́ к подро́бностям. **2.** (*originate*) происходи́ть (*impf.*); **he is ~ed from a ducal family** он происхо́дит из ге́рцогской семьи́. **3.** (*pass by inheritance*) перед|ава́ться, -а́ться (по насле́дству). **4.** (*make an attack*) набр|а́сываться, -о́ситься; **the bandits ~ed upon the village** банди́ты нагря́нули на дере́вню. **5.** (*lower o.s. morally*) опус|ка́ться, -ти́ться; пасть (*pf.*); **~ to cheating** не бре́зговать/гнуша́ться (*impf.*) жу́льничеством.
descendant [dɪˈsend(ə)nt] *n.* пото́мок.
descent [dɪˈsent] *n.* **1.** (*downward slope*) скат, склон. **2.** (*act of descending*) спуск, сниже́ние. **3.** (*ancestry*) происхожде́ние. **4.** (*transmission by inheritance*) переда́ча по насле́дству. **5.** (*attack*) нападе́ние.
describable [dɪˈskraɪbəb(ə)l] *adj.* поддаю́щийся описа́нию.
describe [dɪˈskraɪb] *v.t.* опи́с|ывать, -а́ть (*also geom.*); охарактеризова́ть (*pf.*); **~ s.o. as a scoundrel** изобрази́ть/назва́ть (*both pf.*) кого́-н. подлецо́м; **he ~s himself as a doctor** он называ́ет себя́ врачо́м; он выдаёт себя́ за врача́.
description [dɪˈskrɪpʃ(ə)n] *n.* **1.** (*act of describing*) описа́ние; **answer a ~** соотве́тствовать (*impf.*) описа́нию; **by ~** по описа́нию; **beyond ~** неопису́емый; **it beggars ~** э́то не поддаётся описа́нию. **2.** (*kind*) род, тип, сорт.
descriptive [dɪˈskrɪptɪv] *adj.* описа́тельный.
descry [dɪˈskraɪ] *v.t.* зам|еча́ть, -е́тить; различ|а́ть, -и́ть.
desecrate [ˈdesɪˌkreɪt] *v.t.* оскверн|я́ть, -и́ть.
desecration [ˌdesɪˈkreɪʃ(ə)n] *n.* оскверне́ние.
desegregate [diːˈsegrɪˌgeɪt] *v.t.* & *i.* десегреги́ровать (*impf.*, *pf.*)
desegregation [ˌdiːsegrɪˈgeɪʃ(ə)n] *n.* десегрега́ция.
desensitize [diːˈsensɪˌtaɪz] *v.t.* сн|ижа́ть, -и́зить чувстви́тельность +*g.*
desert[1] [dɪˈzɜːt] *n.* (*merit*) заслу́га; **get one's ~s** получ|а́ть, -и́ть по заслу́гам.
desert[2] [ˈdezət] *n.* (*waste land*) пусты́ня.
adj. пусты́нный; **~ island** необита́емый о́стров.
desert[3] [dɪˈzɜːt] *v.t.* **1.** (*go away from*) ост|авля́ть, -а́вить; пок|ида́ть, -и́нуть; **the streets were ~ed** у́лицы бы́ли пусты́нны. **2.** (*abandon*) пок|ида́ть, -и́нуть; **his courage ~ed him** му́жество измени́ло ему́; **he ~ed his wife** он бро́сил свою́ жену́; **he ~ed his post** он поки́нул свой пост.
v.i. дезерти́ровать (*impf.*, *pf.*); **the regiment ~ed to the enemy** полк перешёл на сто́рону проти́вника.
deserter [dɪˈzɜːtə(r)] *n.* дезерти́р.
desertification [dɪˌsɜːtɪfɪˈkeɪʃ(ə)n] *n.* опусты́нивание.
desertion [dɪˈzɜːʃ(ə)n] *n.* дезерти́рство.
deserve [dɪˈzɜːv] *v.t.* & *i.* заслу́ж|ивать, -и́ть; **he ~s to be well treated** он заслу́живает хоро́шего отноше́ния; **he has ~d well of his country** у него́ бо́льшие заслу́ги пе́ред ро́диной.
deserved [dɪˈzɜːvd] *adj.* заслу́женный.
deserving [dɪˈzɜːvɪŋ] *adj.* похва́льный, досто́йный.
desiccate [ˈdesɪˌkeɪt] *v.t.* высу́шивать, вы́сушить.
desiderate [dɪˈzɪdəˌreɪt, -ˈsɪdəˌreɪt] *v.t.* ощуща́ть (*impf.*) отсу́тствие +*g.*
desiderative [dɪˈzɪdərətɪv, -ˈsɪdərətɪv] *adj.* (*gram.*) дезидерати́вный.
desiderat|um [dɪˌzɪdəˈrɑːtəm, dɪˌsɪd-] *n.* жела́емое; **~a** (*pl.*) пожела́ния (*nt. pl.*).
design [dɪˈzaɪn] *n.* **1.** (*drawing*, *plan*) план; (*industrial*) диза́йн; **~ for a dress** эски́з пла́тья; **~ for a garden** план са́да. **2.** (*art of drawing*) рисова́ние; **school of ~** худо́жественное учи́лище. **3.** (*tech.*: *layout*, *system*) констру́кция, прое́кт; **~ of a car** констру́кция автомоби́ля; **~ of a building** прое́кт зда́ния. **4.** (*pattern*) узо́р, рису́нок; **a vase with a ~ of flowers on it** ва́за с цвето́чным рису́нком. **5.** (*purpose*) у́мысел; **by ~** с у́мыслом; **he has ~s on my job** он име́ет ви́ды на мою́ рабо́ту. **6.** (*industrial*) диза́йн, эсте́тика.
v.t. **1.** (*make designs for*) сост|авля́ть, -а́вить план +*g.*; проекти́ровать, с-; (*e.g. a book*) оф|ормля́ть, -о́рмить; **~ a garden** плани́ровать, рас- сад. **2.** (*intend*) зам|ышля́ть, -ы́слить; предназн|ача́ть, -а́чить; **his parents ~ ed him for the army** роди́тели про́чили его́ в а́рмию; **he ~s to go to Paris** он наме́рен пое́хать в Пари́ж.
v.i.: **he ~s for a dressmaker** он де́лает эски́зы для портни́хи.
designate[1] [ˈdezɪgnət] *adj.* назна́ченный.
designate[2] [ˈdezɪgˌneɪt] *v.t.* обозн|ача́ть, -а́чить; назн|ача́ть, -а́чить.
designation [ˌdezɪgˈneɪʃ(ə)n] *n.* (*appointment*) назначе́ние; (*title*) зва́ние; (*definition*) определе́ние.
designedly [dɪˈzaɪnɪdlɪ] *adv.* умы́шленно.
designer [dɪˈzaɪnə(r)] *n.* (*of dresses*, *decorations*) моделье́р; (*tech.*) констру́ктор; (*industrial*) диза́йнер.
designing [dɪˈzaɪnɪŋ] *adj.* (*scheming*) интригу́ющий, хи́трый, кова́рный.
desirability [dɪˌzaɪərəˈbɪlɪtɪ] *n.* жела́тельность.
desirable [dɪˈzaɪərəb(ə)l] *adj.* жела́тельный, жела́нный.
desire [dɪˈzaɪə(r)] *n.* **1.** (*wish*, *longing*) жела́ние, стремле́ние. **2.** (*lust*) вожделе́ние. **3.** (*request*) про́сьба, пожела́ние. **4.** (*thg. desired*) предме́т жела́ния; **he got all his ~s** все его́ жела́ния сбыли́сь/испо́лнились.
v.t. **1.** (*wish*) жела́ть, по-; **it leaves much to he ~ed** э́то оставля́ет жела́ть мно́го лу́чшего. **2.** (*request*) проси́ть, по-.
desirous [dɪˈzaɪərəs] *adj.* жела́ющий, жа́ждущий; **I am ~ of seeing him** я жела́ю его́ ви́деть.
desist [dɪˈzɪst] *v.i.* возде́рж|иваться, -а́ться (от+*g.*); отка́з|ываться, -а́ться (от+*g.*).
desk [desk] *n.* пи́сьменный стол; конто́рка; **(school ~)** па́рта; (*information centre*) пункт; (*attr.*) насто́льный; **~ set** пи́сьменный прибо́р; **~ work** канцеля́рская рабо́та.

desktop ['desktɒp] *adj.* насто́льный; ~ **publishing** насто́льная полигра́фия.

desolate[1] ['desələt] *adj.* (*ruined, neglected*) забро́шенный, запу́щенный; (*wretched, lonely*) забро́шенный, поки́нутый.

desolate[2] ['desə,leɪt] *v.t.* (*lay waste*) разор|я́ть, -и́ть; опустош|а́ть, -и́ть; (*make sad*) прив|оди́ть, -ести́ в отча́яние.

desolation [,desə'leɪʃ(ə)n] *n.* (*waste*) запусте́ние, забро́шенность, разоре́ние, опустоше́ние; (*sorrow*) забро́шенность, опустошённость, скорбь.

despair [dɪ'speə(r)] *n.* отча́яние; **he is the ~ of his teachers** он прево́дит в отча́яние свои́х учителе́й.

v.i. отча́|иваться, -яться; **I ~ of him** я утра́тил ве́ру в него́; **I ~ of convincing him** я отча́ялся убеди́ть его́; **his life is ~ed of** его́ состоя́ние безнадёжно.

despatch [dɪ'spætʃ] = **dispatch**

desperado [,despə'rɑːdəʊ] *n.* сорвиголова́ (*m.*); головоре́з.

desperate ['despərət] *adj.* **1.** (*wretched, hopeless*) отча́янный, беспросве́тный; доведённый до отча́яния. **2.** (*in extreme need*): **he is ~ for money** он отча́янно нужда́ется в деньга́х; **a ~ remedy** кра́йнее сре́дство. **3.: a ~ criminal** неисправи́мый/закорене́лый престу́пник.

desperation [,despə'reɪʃ(ə)n] *n.* отча́яние; **he drives me to ~** он дово́дит меня́ до отча́яния.

despicable ['despɪkəb(ə)l, dɪ'spɪk-] *adj.* презре́нный.

despise [dɪ'spaɪz] *v.t.* презира́ть (*impf.*); пренебр|ега́ть, -е́чь +*i.*; **the salary is not to be ~d** э́то жа́лованье нема́лое.

despite [dɪ'spaɪt] *n.* (*arch.*): **in ~ of** вопреки́+*d.*

prep. несмотря́ на+*a.*

despoil [dɪ'spɔɪl] *v.t.* гра́бить, о-; разор|я́ть, -и́ть.

despond [dɪ'spɒnd] *v.i.* уныва́ть (*impf.*); па́дать, упа́сть ду́хом.

despondency [dɪ'spɒndənsɪ] *n.* уны́ние.

despondent [dɪ'spɒnd(ə)nt] *adj.* уны́лый, упа́вший ду́хом; пода́вленный.

despot ['despɒt] *n.* де́спот.

despotic [,de'spɒtɪk] *adj.* деспоти́ческий, деспоти́чный.

despotism ['despə,tɪz(ə)m] *n.* деспоти́зм.

dessert [dɪ'zɜːt] *n.* (*sweet course*) десе́рт, сла́дкое, тре́тье; (*fruit, nuts etc.*) сла́ст|и (*pl., g.* -е́й).

cpd. **~-spoon** *n.* десе́ртная ло́жка.

destabilize [diː'steɪbɪ,laɪz] *v.t.* расша́т|ывать, -а́ть; лиш|а́ть, -и́ть усто́йчивости/про́чности; дестабилизи́ровать (*impf., pf.*).

destination [,destɪ'neɪʃ(ə)n] *n.* предназначе́ние; ме́сто назначе́ния.

destine ['destɪn] *v.t.* предназн|ача́ть, -а́чить; предопредел|я́ть, -и́ть; **his parents ~d him for the army** роди́тели про́чили его́ в а́рмию; **he was ~ed to become Prime Minister** ему́ суждено́ бы́ло стать премье́р-мини́стром; **the plan was ~ed to fail** э́тот план был обречён на прова́л.

destiny ['destɪnɪ] *n.* (*fate*) судьба́, уде́л; (*personified*) Па́рки (*f. pl.*).

destitute ['destɪ,tjuːt] *adj.* (*in penury*) нужда́ющийся, обездо́ленный; (*devoid*) лишённый (*чего*).

destitution [,destɪ'tjuːʃ(ə)n] *n.* (*poverty*) нищета́; (*deprivation*) лише́ние.

destroy [dɪ'strɔɪ] *v.t.* разр|уша́ть, -у́шить; разб|ива́ть, -и́ть; истреб|ля́ть, -и́ть; уничт|ожа́ть, -о́жить; **his hopes were ~ed** его́ наде́жды ру́хнули; **the horse had to be ~ed** ло́шадь пришло́сь уби́ть.

destroyer [dɪ'strɔɪə(r)] *n.* **1.** (*one who destroys*) разруши́тель (*m.*). **2.** (*nav.*) эсми́нец; эска́дренный миноно́сец.

destruct [dɪ'strʌkt] *v.t.* под|рыва́ть, -орва́ть в полёте.

destructible [dɪ'strʌktɪb(ə)l] *adj.* разруши́мый.

destruction [dɪ'strʌkʃ(ə)n] *n.* (*act of destroying*) уничтоже́ние, разруше́ние; (*cause of ruin*) ги́бель, па́губа; **gambling was his ~** аза́ртные и́гры погуби́ли его́.

destructive [dɪ'strʌktɪv] *adj.* разруши́тельный, ги́бельный; **a ~ storm** бу́ря, причини́вшая больши́е разруше́ния; **~ criticism** уничтожа́ющая кри́тика; **~ to health** па́губный для здоро́вья; **he is a ~ child** э́тот ребёнок всё лома́ет.

destructiveness [dɪ'strʌktɪvnɪs] *n.* разруши́тельность.

destructor [dɪ'strʌktə(r)] *n.* (*furnace*) мусоросжига́тельная печь.

desuetude [dɪ'sjuːɪ,tjuːd, 'deswɪ-] *n.* неупотреби́тельность.

desultory ['dezəltərɪ] *adj.* отры́вочный; **~ reading** бессисте́мное чте́ние; **~ fire** (*mil.*) беспоря́дочная стрельба́.

detach [dɪ'tætʃ] *v.t.* **1.** (*separate*) отдел|я́ть, -и́ть; разъедин|я́ть, -и́ть; **a ~ed house** особня́к. **2.** (*send on separate mission*) отря|жа́ть, -ди́ть; откомандиро́в|ывать, -а́ть.

detached [dɪ'tætʃd] *adj.* беспристра́стный; **a ~ attitude** равноду́шный подхо́д.

detachment [dɪ'tætʃmənt] *n.* (*separation*) отделе́ние, разъедине́ние; (*indifference*) отчуждённость, равноду́шие; (*body of troops etc.*) отря́д.

detail[1] ['diːteɪl] *n.* **1.** подро́бность, дета́ль; **go into ~(s)** вдава́ться (*impf.*) в подро́бности; **in ~** подро́бно, обстоя́тельно. **2.** (*of a picture*) дета́ль. **3.** (*mil., detachment*) наря́д.

detail[2] ['diːteɪl] *v.t.* **1.** (*give particulars of*) входи́ть, вдава́ться (*both impf.*) в подро́бности +*g.* **2.** (*appoint*) откомандиро́в|ывать, -а́ть.

detain [dɪ'teɪn] *v.t.* **1.** (*delay, cause to remain*) заде́рж|ивать, -а́ть; **he was ~ed at the office** его́ задержа́ли на рабо́те; **the question need not ~ us long** э́тот вопро́с не потре́бует мно́го вре́мени; **he was ~ed by the police** он был заде́ржан поли́цией. **2.** (*withhold*) уде́рж|ивать, -а́ть.

detainee [,diːteɪ'niː] *n.* заде́ржанный.

detect [dɪ'tekt] *v.t.* (*track down*) высле́живать, вы́следить; на|ходи́ть, -йти́; (*perceive*) обнару́жи|вать, -ть.

detectable [dɪ'tektəb(ə)l] *adj.* заме́тный, обнару́живаемый.

detection [dɪ'tekʃ(ə)n] *n.* (*of crime*) рассле́дование, раскры́тие, ро́зыск; **he escaped ~** он избежа́л разоблаче́ния; (*perception*) обнаруже́ние.

detective [dɪ'tektɪv] *n.* сы́щик, детекти́в; **private ~** ча́стный сы́щик; **~ novel** детекти́в; полице́йский рома́н.

adj. детекти́вный; **~ ability** да́нные (*nt. pl.*) детекти́ва.

detector [dɪ'tektə(r)] *n.* (*radio*) дете́ктор.

détente [deɪ'tɑ̃t] *n.* (*pol.*) разря́дка.

detention [dɪ'tenʃ(ə)n] *n.* (*holding, delaying*) заде́ржка; (*at school*) оставле́ние по́сле уро́ков; (*arrest, confinement*) заключе́ние, задержа́ние; **~ pending trial** предвари́тельное заключе́ние.

deter [dɪ'tɜː(r)] *v.t.* уде́рж|ивать, -а́ть.

detergent [dɪ'tɜːdʒ(ə)nt] *n.* мо́ющее сре́дство; стира́льный порошо́к.

deteriorate [dɪ'tɪərɪə,reɪt] *v.t.* & *i.* ух|удша́ть(ся), -у́дшить(ся).

deterioration [dɪ,tɪərɪə'reɪʃ(ə)n] *n.* ухудше́ние.

determinable [dɪ'tɜːmɪnəb(ə)l] *adj.* (*ascertainable*) определи́мый; (*leg., terminable*) истека́ющий.

determinant [dɪ'tɜːmɪnənt] *n.* реша́ющий фа́ктор.

adj. реша́ющий.

determinate [dɪ'tɜːmɪnət] *adj.* определённый, устано́вленный.

determination [dɪ,tɜːmɪ'neɪʃ(ə)n] *n.* **1.** (*deciding upon*) реше́ние. **2.** (*calculating*) установле́ние. **3.** (*resoluteness*) реши́мость, реши́тельность.

determine [dɪ'tɜːmɪn] *v.t.* **1.** (*be deciding factor*) определ|я́ть, -и́ть; **this ~d him to accept** э́то убеди́ло его́ согласи́ться. **2.** (*take decision*) реш|а́ть, -и́ть; **he is ~d to go** (*or* **on going**) он твёрдо реши́л е́хать; **~ the date of a meeting** установи́ть (*pf.*) да́ту собра́ния. **3.** (*ascertain*) устан|а́вливать, -ови́ть. **4.** (*leg., bring to an end*) прекра|ща́ть, -ти́ть.

v.i. (*leg., expire*) ист|ека́ть, -е́чь.

determined [dɪ'tɜːmɪnd] *adj.* (*resolute*) реши́тельный.

determinism [dɪ'tɜːmɪ,nɪz(ə)m] *n.* детермини́зм.

determinist [dɪ'tɜːmɪnɪst] *n.* детермини́ст.

deterministic [dɪ,tɜːmɪ'nɪstɪk] *adj.* детерминисти́ческий, детермини́стский.

deterrence [dɪ'terəns] *n.* устраше́ние, отпу́гивание.

deterrent [dɪ'terənt] *n.* сре́дство устраше́ния/сде́рживания; сде́рживающее сре́дство; **nuclear ~** я́дерный арсена́л (сде́рживания).

detest [dɪ'test] *v.t.* ненави́деть (*impf.*).

detestable [dɪ'testəb(ə)l] *adj.* отврати́тельный.
detestation [ˌdi:te'steɪʃ(ə)n] *n.* не́нависть, отвраще́ние; **have, hold in** ~ испы́тывать/пита́ть (*impf.*) отвраще́ние к+*d*.
dethrone [di:'θrəʊn] *v.t.* св|ерга́ть, -е́ргнуть с престо́ла.
dethronement [di:'θrəʊnmənt] *n.* сверже́ние с престо́ла.
detonate ['detəˌneɪt] *v.t.* детони́ровать (*impf.*, *pf.*).
v.i. вз|рыва́ться, -орва́ться.
detonation [ˌdetə'neɪʃ(ə)n] *n.* детона́ция.
detonator ['detəˌneɪtə(r)] *n.* (*part of bomb or shell*) детона́тор; (*fog-signal*) пета́рда.
detour ['di:tʊə(r)] *n.* объе́зд; око́льный путь; **make a** ~ объ|езжа́ть, -е́хать; де́лать, с- крюк.
detoxification ['di:tɒksɪfɪ'keɪʃ(ə)n] *n.*: ~ **centre** вытрезви́тель.
detract [dɪ'trækt] *v.i.*: ~ **from** умал|я́ть, -и́ть.
detraction [dɪ'trækʃ(ə)n] *n.* (*disparagement*) умале́ние; (*slander*) клевета́.
detractor [dɪ'træktə(r)] *n.* клеветни́к.
detrain [di:'treɪn] *v.t.* & *i.* выса́живать(ся), вы́садить(ся) из по́езда.
detribalize [di:'traɪbəˌlaɪz] *v.t.* разр|уша́ть, -у́шить племенну́ю структу́ру +*g*.
detriment ['detrɪmənt] *n.* уще́рб; **I know nothing to his** ~ я не зна́ю о нём ничего́ предосуди́тельного; **he works long hours to the** ~ **of his health** он мно́го рабо́тает в уще́рб своему́ здоро́вью.
detrimental [ˌdetrɪ'ment(ə)l] *adj.* вре́дный.
detrition [dɪ'trɪʃ(ə)n] *n.* стира́ние.
detritus [dɪ'traɪtəs] *n.* детри́т.
de trop [də 'trəʊ] *adj.* изли́шний.
deuce[1] [dju:s] *n.* (*cards or dice*) дво́йка; (*tennis*) ра́вный счёт.
deuce[2] [dju:s] *n.* (*euph.*, *devil*) чёрт, дья́вол; ~ **take it!** чёрт подери́!; **where the** ~ **did I put it?** куда́ к чёрту я э́то дел?
deuced ['dju:sɪd, dju:st] *adj.* черто́вский.
deuterium [dju:'tɪərɪəm] *n.* дейте́рий.
Deuteronomy [ˌdju:tə'rɒnəmɪ] *n.* Второзако́ние.
devaluation [di:ˌvælju:'eɪʃ(ə)n] *n.* обесце́нение; (*fin.*) девальва́ция.
devalue [di:'vælju:] *v.t.* обесце́ни|вать, -ть; (*fin.*) девальви́ровать (*impf.*, *pf.*).
v.i. пров|оди́ть, -ести́ девальва́цию (*чего*).
devastate ['devəˌsteɪt] *v.t.* опустош|а́ть, -и́ть; разор|я́ть, -и́ть; **a** ~**ing remark** уничтожа́ющее замеча́ние.
devastation [ˌdevə'steɪʃ(ə)n] *n.* опустоше́ние, разоре́ние.
develop [dɪ'veləp] *v.t.* **1.** (*cause to unfold*) разв|ива́ть, -и́ть; обраб|а́тывать, -о́тать. **2.** (*phot.*) проявл|я́ть, -и́ть. **3.** (*contract*): **he** ~**ed a cough** у него́ появи́лся ка́шель. **4.** (*open up for residence etc.*) разв|ива́ть, -и́ть; (*resources*) осв|а́ивать, -о́ить; разраб|а́тывать, -о́тать.
v.i. **1.** (*unfold*) разв|ива́ться, -и́ться; разв|ёртываться, -ерну́ться; превра|ща́ться, -ти́ться; **London** ~**ed into a great city** Ло́ндон разро́сся в большо́й го́род. **2.** (*come to light*) выясня́ться, вы́ясниться.
developer [dɪ'veləpə(r)] *n.*: **1.: he was a late** ~ он по́здно разви́лся. **2.** (*phot.*, *substance*) прояви́тель (*m.*). **3.** (*builder*) застро́йщик; **firm of** ~**s** фи́рма-застро́йщик.
development [dɪ'veləpmənt] *n.* **1.** (*unfolding*) разви́тие, рост. **2.** (*event*) собы́тие, обстоя́тельство. **3.** (*of land etc.*) разви́тие (райо́на), мелиора́ция; (*building*) застро́йка.
developmental [dɪˌveləp'ment(ə)l] *adj.* **1.** (*incidental to growth*) свя́занный с ро́стом; ~ **disease** боле́знь ро́ста. **2.** (*evolutionary*) эволюцио́нный.
deviant ['di:vɪənt] *n.* (*e.g. sexual*) извраще́нец.
adj. отклоня́ющийся от но́рмы
deviate ['di:vɪˌeɪt] *v.i.* отклон|я́ться, -и́ться (от+*g.*).
deviation [ˌdi:vɪ'eɪʃ(ə)n] *n.* отклоне́ние, отхо́д; (*of compass*) девиа́ция.
deviationism [ˌdi:vɪ'eɪʃənˌɪz(ə)m] *n.* уклони́зм.
deviationist [ˌdi:vɪ'eɪʃənɪst] *n.* уклони́ст.
device [dɪ'vaɪs] *n.* **1.** (*plan, scheme*) план, схе́ма, зате́я; (*method*) приём; **he was left to his own** ~**s** он был предоста́влен самому́ себе́. **2.** (*instrument, contrivance*) приспособле́ние, прибо́р. **3.** (*sign, symbol*) эмбле́ма.
devil ['dev(ə)l] *n.* **1.** чёрт, дья́вол; **between the** ~ **and the deep (blue) sea** ме́жду двух огне́й; **go to the** ~! иди́ к чёрту!; ~ **take it!** чёрт побери́!; ~ **take the hindmost** к чертя́м неуда́чников; **talk of the** ~! лёгок на поми́не; **you young** ~! ах ты чертёнок!; **he has the** ~**'s own luck** ему черто́вски везёт; **he ran as though the** ~ **were at his heels** он бежа́л как будто сам чёрт гна́лся за ним по пята́м; **he that sups with the** ~ **must have a long spoon** ≃ связа́лся с чёртом, пеня́й на себя́. **2.** (*wretched pers.*): **poor** ~! бедня́га! **3.** (*drudge, junior*): **printer's** ~ ма́льчик на посы́лках в типогра́фии. **4.** (*as expletive*): **what the** ~ **do you mean?** что вы э́тим хоти́те сказа́ть, чёрт возьми́?; **he ran like the** ~ он бежа́л как чёрт; **I had the** ~ **of a time** я черто́вски хорошо́/пло́хо провёл вре́мя; **a** ~ **of a fellow** отча́янный па́рень; **this is the** ~! (*sc. unpleasant, difficult*) чертовщи́на!; дья́вольщина!; **play the** ~ **with** причин|я́ть, -и́ть вред +*d.*; **there'll be the devil to pay** рассчи́тываться за э́то бу́дет нелегко́.
v.t. (*cul.*) гото́вить (*impf.*) с пря́ностями.
v.i. (*perform hack-work*): ~ **for s.o.** иша́чить (*impf.*) на кого́-н. (*coll.*).
cpds. ~**-fish** *n.* морско́й дья́вол; ~**-may-care** *adj.* бѐсшаба́шный, разуда́лый.
devilish ['devəlɪʃ] *adj.* дья́вольский.
adv. (*coll.*) черто́вски.
devilment ['devəlmənt] *n.* прока́зы (*f. pl.*), чертовщи́на.
devil(t)ry ['devɪl(t)rɪ] *n.* (*wickedness, fiendish cruelty*) жесто́кость, зве́рства (*nt. pl.*); (*mischief*) прока́зы (*f. pl.*); проде́лки (*f. pl.*).
devious ['di:vɪəs] *adj.* (*lit.*) изви́листый, око́льный; (*fig.*) лука́вый, неи́скренний.
deviousness ['di:vɪəsnɪs] *n.* (*lit.*) изви́листость; (*fig.*) лука́вство, хи́трость.
devise [dɪ'vaɪz] *v.t.* (*think out*) приду́м|ывать, -ать; изобре|та́ть, -сти́; изм|ышля́ть, -ы́слить; (*bequeath*) завеща́ть (*impf.*, *pf.*).
devitalize [di:'vaɪtəˌlaɪz] *v.t.* лиш|а́ть, -и́ть жи́зненных сил.
devoid [dɪ'vɔɪd] *adj.* лишённый; ~ **of shame** бессты́дный; ~ **of fear** бесстра́шный.
devolution [ˌdi:və'lu:ʃ(ə)n, -'lju:ʃ(ə)n] *n.* (*delegation*) переда́ча/делеги́рование вла́сти.
devolve [dɪ'vɒlv] *v.t.* (*delegate*) перед|ава́ть, -а́ть.
v.i. пере|ходи́ть, -йти́; **the work** ~**d on me** рабо́та свали́лась на меня́; **the estate** ~**d on a distant cousin** име́ние перешло́ к да́льнему ро́дственнику.
Devonian [dɪ'vəʊnɪən] *n.*: (*geol.*) ~ **period** дево́н, дево́нский пери́од.
adj. (*geol.*) дево́нский.
devote [dɪ'vəʊt] *v.t.* посвя|ща́ть, -ти́ть; **he** ~**s his time to study** он посвяща́ет всё своё вре́мя учёбе; **she is** ~**d to her children** она́ пре́дана свои́м де́тям; она́ всю себя́ отдаёт де́тям; **a** ~**d friend** пре́данный друг.
devotee [ˌdevə'ti:] *n.* приве́рженец.
devotion [dɪ'vəʊʃ(ə)n] *n.* **1.** (*being devoted*) пре́данность; ~ **to tennis** увлече́ние те́ннисом. **2.** (*love*) пре́данность, привя́занность. **3.** (*pl.*, *prayers*) моли́твы (*f. pl.*); **he was at his** ~**s** он моли́лся.
devotional [dɪ'vəʊʃənəl] *adj.* моли́твенный, религио́зный.
devour [dɪ'vaʊə(r)] *v.t.* **1.** (*eat greedily*) пож|ира́ть, -ра́ть. **2.** (*fig.*) погло|ща́ть, -ти́ть; **she** ~**ed his story** она́ жа́дно слу́шала его́ расска́з; **he** ~**ed the book** он проглоти́л кни́гу; ~**ed by anxiety** снеда́емый беспоко́йством; **the fire** ~**ed the forest** пожа́р уничто́жил лес; **he** ~**ed his wife's fortune** он промота́л состоя́ние свое́й жены́.
devout [dɪ'vaʊt] *adj.* (*religious*) благочести́вый; (*devoted*) пре́данный.
devoutness [dɪ'vaʊtnɪs] *n.* благоче́стие, набо́жность.
dew [dju:] *n.* роса́; (*freshness*) све́жесть.
cpds. ~**berry** *n.* ежеви́ка (*collect.*); я́года ежеви́ки; ~**drop** *n.* роси́нка.
dewlap ['dju:læp] *n.* подгру́док.
dewy ['dju:ɪ] *adj.* роси́стый.
cpd. ~**-eyed** *adj.* (*fig.*) с неви́нным взгля́дом; простоду́шный.
dexterity [dek'sterɪtɪ] *n.* ло́вкость, прово́рство, сноро́вка.

dext(e)rous ['dekstrəs] *adj.* ло́вкий, прово́рный.
dhow [daʊ] *n.* одномачто́вое ара́бское су́дно.
diabetes [ˌdaɪə'bi:ti:z] *n.* диабе́т; са́харная боле́знь.
diabetic [ˌdaɪə'betɪk] *n.* диабе́тик.
adj. диабети́ческий.
diablerie [daɪ'ɑ:blərɪ] *n.* чертовщи́на.
diabolic(al) [ˌdaɪə'bɒlɪk(l)] *adj.* дья́вольский.
diabolism [daɪ'æbəˌlɪz(ə)m] *n.* (*devil-worship*) сатани́зм.
diabolist [daɪ'æbəlɪst] *n.* покло́нник сатаны́.
diabolo [dɪ'æbələʊ, daɪ-] *n.* диа́боло (*m. indecl.*).
diachronic [ˌdaɪə'krɒnɪk] *adj.* диахрони́ческий.
diaconal [daɪ'ækən(ə)l] *adj.* дья́конский.
diaconate [daɪ'ækəˌneɪt, -nət] *n.* дья́конство.
diacritic [ˌdaɪə'krɪtɪk] *n.* & *adj.* диакрити́ческий (знак).
diadem ['daɪəˌdem] *n.* (*crown*) диаде́ма; (*wreath*) вено́к, вене́ц.
diaeresis [daɪ'ɪərəsɪs] *n.* диере́за.
diagnose ['daɪəgˌnəʊz] *v.t.* ста́вить, по- диа́гноз +*g*; диагности́ровать (*impf., pf.*); **he ~d (the illness as) cancer** он установи́л, что у больно́го рак; (*med.*) он диагности́ровал рак.
diagnosis [ˌdaɪəg'nəʊsɪs] *n.* диа́гноз; **make a ~** ста́вить, по- диа́гноз.
diagnostic [ˌdaɪəg'nɒstɪk] *adj.* диагности́ческий.
diagnostician [ˌdaɪəgnɒ'stɪʃ(ə)n] *n.* диагно́ст.
diagnostics [ˌdaɪəg'nɒstɪks] *n.* диагно́стика.
diagonal [daɪ'ægən(ə)l] *n.* диагона́ль.
adj. диагона́льный; **~ cloth** диагона́ль; **~ly** по диагона́ли.
diagram ['daɪəˌgræm] *n.* диагра́мма, схе́ма.
diagrammatic(al) [ˌdaɪəgrə'mætɪk(ə)l] *adj.* схемати́ческий.
dial ['daɪ(ə)l] *n.* **1.** (*of clock*) цифербла́т. **2.** (*of radio etc.*) шкала́. **3.** (*of telephone*) диск. **4.** (*face*) ро́жа, фи́зия (*sl.*).
v.t. & i.: **~ a number** наб|ира́ть, -ра́ть но́мер; **~ the police-station** позвони́ть (*pf.*) в поли́цию; **~ling tone** сигна́л «ли́ния свобо́дна».
dialect ['daɪəˌlekt] *n.* диале́кт, наре́чие, го́вор.
dialectal [ˌdaɪə'lekt(ə)l] *adj.* диалекта́льный, диале́ктный.
dialectic(s) [ˌdaɪə'lektɪks] *n.* диале́ктика.
adj. (*also* **-al**) диалекти́ческий.
dialectician [ˌdaɪəlek'tɪʃ(ə)n] *n.* диале́ктик.
dialectology [ˌdaɪəlek'tɒlədʒɪ] *n.* диалектоло́гия.
dialogue ['daɪəˌlɒg] *n.* диало́г, разгово́р; **written in ~** напи́сано в фо́рме диало́га.
diamanté [dɪə'mɑ̃teɪ] *n.* усы́панная блёстками мате́рия.
diamantiferous [ˌdaɪəmæn'tɪfərəs] *adj.* алмазоно́сный.
diameter [daɪ'æmɪtə(r)] *n.* диа́метр; **two feet in ~** два фу́та диа́метром; **this lens magnifies 200 ~s** э́та ли́нза увели́чивает в 200 раз.
diametric(al) [ˌdaɪə'metrɪk(ə)l] *adj.* диаметра́льный.
diamond ['daɪəmənd] *n.* **1.** (*precious stone*) алма́з, бриллиа́нт; **~ of the first water** бриллиа́нт чи́стой воды́; **rough ~** (*fig.*) саморо́док; **~ cut ~** нашла́ коса́ на ка́мень. **2.** (*geom.*) ромб. **3.** (*at cards*) бу́б|ны (*pl., g.* -ён); **the queen of ~s** бубно́вая да́ма. **4.** (*baseball*) площа́дка для игры́ в бейсбо́л. **5.** (*attr.*) алма́зный; бриллиа́нтовый; **~ mine** алма́зная копь; **~ ring** бриллиа́нтовое кольцо́; **~ wedding** бриллиа́нтовая сва́дьба.
diapason [ˌdaɪə'peɪz(ə)n, -'peɪs(ə)n] *n.* диапазо́н.
diaper ['daɪəpə(r)] *n.* (*linen fabric*) узо́рчатое полотно́; (*baby's napkin*) пелёнка.
v.t. (*ornament*) укр|аша́ть, -а́сить ромбови́дным узо́ром.
diaphanous [daɪ'æfənəs] *adj.* прозра́чный, просве́чивающий.
diaphragm ['daɪəˌfræm] *n.* **1.** (*anat.*) диафра́гма. **2.** (*of camera lens*) перегоро́дка. 3. (*of telephone receiver*) мембра́на.
diapositive [ˌdaɪə'pɒzɪtɪv] *n.* диапозити́в.
diarchy ['daɪɑ:kɪ] *n.* двоевла́стие.
diarist ['daɪərɪst] *n.* а́втор дневника́.
diarrhoea [ˌdaɪə'rɪə] *n.* поно́с; расстро́йство желу́дка; **he got over his ~** его́ закрепи́ло.
diary ['daɪərɪ] *n.* (*journal*) дневни́к; (*engagement book*) календа́рь (*m.*).
diaspora [daɪ'æspərə] *n.* диа́спора, рассе́яние.
diastole [daɪ'æstəlɪ] *n.* диа́стола.
diathermic [ˌdaɪə'θɜ:mɪk] *adj.* диатерми́ческий.
diatonic [ˌdaɪə'tɒnɪk] *adj.* диатони́ческий.
diatribe ['daɪəˌtraɪb] *n.* диатри́ба.
dibble ['dɪb(ə)l] *n.* сажа́льный кол.
dibs [dɪbz] *n.* (*sl., money*) деньга́, деньжа́т|а (*pl., g.* —).
dice [daɪs] *n.* (*see also* **die**) (*cube*) игра́льные ко́сти (*f. pl.*); (*game of ~*) игра́ в ко́сти; **no ~!** (*sl.*) так де́ло не пойдёт!; **the ~ are loaded against him** судьба́ — про́тив него́.
v.t. & i. **1.** (*play at ~*) игра́ть (*impf.*) в ко́сти; **~ away one's fortune** проигра́ть (*pf.*) состоя́ние. **2.** (*cul.*) нар|еза́ть, -е́зать ку́биками.
cpd. **~-box** *n.* коро́бочка, из кото́рой броса́ют игра́льные ко́сти.
dicey ['daɪsɪ] *adj.* (*sl.*) риско́ванный.
dichotomy [daɪ'kɒtəmɪ] *n.* дихотоми́я, раздво́енность.
dick [dɪk] *n.* **1.** (*sl., detective*) сы́щик, хвост. **2.** (*coll., fellow*): **a clever D~** у́мник, всезна́йка (*c.g.*). **3.** (*vulg.*) член, со́лоп.
dickens ['dɪkɪnz] *n.* (*coll.*) чёрт; **what the ~ are you up to?** что вы замышля́ете, чёрт возьми́?
Dickensian [dɪ'kenzɪən] *n.* (*admirer of Dickens*) покло́нник Ди́ккенса.
adj. (*typical of Dickens*) ди́ккенсовский.
dicker ['dɪkə(r)] *v.i.* (*bargain*) торгова́ться, с-; (*hesitate*) колеба́ться (*impf.*).
dickhead ['dɪkhed] *n.* (*vulg.*) муда́к, долбоёб.
dicky[1] ['dɪkɪ] *n.* (*shirt-front*) мани́шка; (*seat at back of car*) за́днее откидно́е сиде́нье.
dicky[2] ['dɪkɪ] *adj.* (*coll.*) сла́бый; (*unstable*) ша́ткий, нетвёрдый; (*untrustworthy*) ненадёжный.
dicky-bird ['dɪkɪbɜ:d] *n.* пти́чка; пта́шка.
Dictaphone ['dɪktəˌfəʊn] *n.* (*propr.*) диктофо́н.
dictate[1] ['dɪkteɪt] *n.* веле́ние.
dictate[2] [dɪk'teɪt] *v.t. & i.* (*recite, specify, command*) диктова́ть, про-; **I won't be ~d to** я не позво́лю ста́вить мне усло́вия; я не потерплю́ дикта́та.
dictation [dɪk'teɪʃ(ə)n] *n.* **1.** (*to secretary, class etc.*) дикта́нт, дикто́вка; **take ~** писа́ть (*impf.*) под дикто́вку; **I wrote at his ~** я писа́л под его́ дикто́вку. **2.** (*orders*) предписа́ние; **I did it at his ~** я сде́лал э́то по его́ прика́зу; **I am tired of his constant ~** мне надое́ли его́ постоя́нные указа́ния.
dictator [dɪk'teɪtə(r)] *n.* (*giver of dictation*) дикту́ющий; (*ruler*) дикта́тор.
dictatorial [ˌdɪktə'tɔ:rɪəl] *adj.* дикта́торский, повели́тельный, вла́стный.
dictatorship [dɪk'teɪtəʃɪp] *n.* диктату́ра.
diction ['dɪkʃ(ə)n] *n.* (*style*) стиль (*m.*); (*pronunciation*) ди́кция.
dictionary ['dɪkʃənrɪ, -nərɪ] *n.* слова́рь (*m.*); **pronouncing ~** слова́рь произноше́ния; **~ English** педанти́чно пра́вильный англи́йский язы́к; **a walking ~** ходя́чая энциклопе́дия.
dictograph ['dɪktəˌgrɑ:f] *n.* дикто́граф.
dictum ['dɪktəm] *n.* изрече́ние, афори́зм.
didactic [daɪ'dæktɪk, dɪ-] *adj.* поучи́тельный, дидакти́ческий.
didacticism [daɪ'dæktɪˌsɪz(ə)m, dɪ-] *n.* дидакти́зм.
diddle ['dɪd(ə)l] *v.t.* (*coll.*) над|ува́ть, -у́ть.
die[1] [daɪ] *n.* (*cf.* **dice**) игра́льная кость; **the ~ is cast** жре́бий бро́шен; **straight as a ~** (*fig.*) прямо́й, че́стный.
die[2] [daɪ] *n.* (*stamp for coining etc.*) ма́трица, пуансо́н, штамп.
cpds. **~-casting** *n.* литьё под давле́нием; **~-maker, ~-sinker** *nn.* ре́зчик чека́нов/штемпеле́й.
die[3] [daɪ] *n.* (*archit.*) цо́коль (*m.*).
die[4] [daɪ] *v.i.* **1.** (*of pers.*) ум|ира́ть, -ере́ть; сконча́ться (*pf.*); ги́бнуть, по-; (*of animals*) сд|ыха́ть, -о́хнуть; изд|ыха́ть, -о́хнуть; под|ыха́ть, -о́хнуть; (*of plants*) ув|яда́ть, -я́нуть; вя́нуть, за-; **he ~d a beggar** он у́мер ни́щим; **I would ~ in the last ditch for that principle** я бу́ду стоя́ть на́смерть за э́тот при́нцип; **never say ~!** никогда́ не отча́ивайся!; **he is dying by inches** он умира́ет ме́дленной сме́ртью; **he ~d game** он му́жественно встре́тил смерть; **old habits ~ hard** ста́рые привы́чки живу́чи; **he ~d by violence** он у́мер наси́льственной сме́ртью; **he ~d like a dog** он подо́х, как соба́ка; **he ~d by his own hand** он наложи́л на себя́ ру́ки; **he ~d in his**

bed он у́мер свое́й сме́ртью; **he ~d in harness** он у́мер на посту́; **they ~ like flies** они́ умира́ют как му́хи. **2.** (*fig.*): **I'm dying to see him** я ужа́сно хочу́ его́ ви́деть; **we ~d of laughing** мы умира́ли со́ смеху. **3.** (*of things*): **his anger ~d** его́ гнев утих; **the wind ~d** ве́тер затих; **his secret ~d with him** его́ та́йна умерла́ вме́сте с ним; **the engine ~d** мото́р загло́х.

with advs.: **~ away** (*of sound*) зам|ира́ть, -ере́ть; (*of feeling etc.*) ум|ира́ть, -ере́ть; **~ down** (*of fire*) уг|аса́ть, -а́снуть; (*of noise*) ут|иха́ть, -и́хнуть; зам|ира́ть, -ере́ть; (*of feeling*) ум|ира́ть, -ере́ть; **~ off** умира́ть (*impf.*) оди́н за други́м; **the cattle ~d off** весь скот пал; **~ out** вымира́ть, вы́мереть; **the family ~d out** э́та семья́ вы́мерла; **the dinosaur ~d out** диноза́вры вы́мерли; **the belief ~d out** э́то пове́рье о́тмерло.

cpds. **~hard** *n.* догма́тик; *adj.* твердоло́бый, ко́сный; **~hardism** *n.* догмати́зм, ко́сность.

diesel ['di:z(ə)l] *n.* (**~ engine, motor**) ди́зель (*m.*); **~ locomotive** теплово́з; **~ oil** ди́зельное то́пливо, **~ electric** ди́зель-электри́ческий.

dies non [,daii:z 'nɒn] *n.* (*leg.*) непрису́тственный день.

diet[1] ['daiət] *n.* **1.** (*customary food*) пи́ща, стол. **2.** (*medical régime*) дие́та; **he is on a ~** он на дие́те; **put s.o. on a ~** посади́ть (*pf.*) кого́-н. на дие́ту; **crash ~** уско́ренная дие́та; **milk-free ~** безмоло́чная дие́та.

v.t. & i. соблюда́ть (*impf.*) дие́ту; быть (*impf.*) на дие́те; **she had to ~ (herself)** ей пришло́сь соблюда́ть дие́ту.

diet[2] ['daiət] *n.* (*hist.*) (*Polish*) сейм; (*German*) рейхста́г, ландта́г.

diet|ary ['daiətri], **-etic** [,daiə'tetik] *adjs.* диети́ческий.

dietetics [,daiə'tetiks] *n.* диете́тика.

dietitian [,daiə'tiʃ(ə)n] *n.* диетвра́ч.

differ ['difə(r)] *v.i.* **1.** (*be different*) отлича́ться (*impf.*); различа́ться (*impf.*); **we ~ in our tastes** на́ши вку́сы разли́чны; **tastes ~** (*prov.*) о вку́сах не спо́рят; **they ~ in size** они́ различа́ются разме́ром. **2.** (*disagree*) ра|сходи́ться, -зойти́сь во мне́ниях; **I ~ed with him** я с ним не согласи́лся; **I beg to ~** я позво́лю себе́ не согласи́ться; **we agreed to ~** мы реши́ли прекрати́ть бесполе́зный спор.

difference ['difrəns] *n.* **1.** (*state of being unlike*) отли́чие, разли́чие, ра́зница; **that makes all the ~** в э́том вся ра́зница; **it makes no ~ whether you go or not** соверше́нно безразли́чно, идёте вы и́ли нет. **2.** (*extent of inequality*) ра́зница; (*math.*) ра́зность; **let's split the ~** дава́йте поде́лим попола́м ра́зницу; **I will pay the ~** я доплачу́ ра́зницу. **3.** (*dispute*) разногла́сие, размо́лвка, спор; **I had a ~ with him** мы с ним повздо́рили.

different ['difrənt] *adj.* **1.** (*unlike*) друго́й, ра́зный, разли́чный; **that is quite ~** э́то совсе́м друго́е де́ло; **they live in ~ houses** они́ живу́т в ра́зных дома́х; **she wears a ~ hat each day** она́ ка́ждый день надева́ет но́вую шля́пу; на ней ка́ждый день друга́я шля́па; **of ~ kinds** ра́зного ро́да; **he became a ~ person** он стал други́м челове́ком; **~ from** непохо́жий на+*a.*; отли́чный от+*g.*; **everyone gave him a ~ answer** все отвеча́ли ему́ по-ра́зному. **2.** (*unusual*) необы́чный; **this drink has a really ~ flavour** э́тот напи́ток име́ет пои́стине необы́чный арома́т. **3.** (*various*) разли́чный, ра́зный; **we talked of ~ things** мы говори́ли о ра́зных веща́х; **at ~ times** в ра́зное вре́мя.

differential [,difə'renʃ(ə)l] *n.* **1.** (*difference in wage-rates*) дифференци́рованная опла́та труда́. **2.** (*of a car etc.*; *also* **~ gear**) дифференциа́л.

adj. **1.** (*differing according to circumstances*) дифференци́рованный. **2.** (*math.*) дифференциа́льный.

differentiate [,difə'renʃi,eit] *v.t.* **1.** (*constitute difference*) отлич|а́ть, и́ть. **2.** (*perceive difference*) различ|а́ть, -и́ть. **3.** (*make, point out difference*) де́лать, с- разли́чие; **we do not ~ on grounds of sex** при́знак по́ла для нас не име́ет значе́ния.

v.i. (*become different*) различ|а́ться, -и́ться; отлич|а́ться, -и́ться.

differentiation [,difərenʃi'eiʃ(ə)n] *n.* **1.** (*change*) видоизмене́ние. **2.** (*act of distinguishing*) дифференци́рование; различе́ние. **3.** (*discrimination*) дифференциа́ция.

differently ['difrəntli] *adv.* по-ино́му; по-друго́му; ина́че; **I understand this ~ from you** я понима́ю э́то и́наче, чем вы.

difficult ['difikəlt] *adj.* тру́дный (*also of pers.*); **a ~ child** трудновоспиту́емый ребёнок; **he is ~ to please** ему́ тру́дно угоди́ть; **~ of access** недосту́пный.

difficult|y ['difikəlti] *n.* тру́дность, затрудне́ние; **I have ~y in understanding him** я с трудо́м его́ понима́ю; **don't make ~ies** не создава́йте тру́дностей; **we ran into ~ies** мы столкну́лись с тру́дностями; **he is in financial ~ies** он испы́тывает материа́льные затрудне́ния; **he is in ~ with his work** у него́ тру́дности в рабо́те.

diffidence ['difidəns] *n.* неуве́ренность в себе́; засте́нчивость; стесни́тельность.

diffident ['difid(ə)nt] *adj.* неуве́ренный в себе́; ро́бкий, засте́нчивый, стесни́тельный.

diffuse[1] [di'fju:s] *adj.* (*of light etc.*) рассе́янный; (*of style*) расплы́вчатый.

diffuse[2] [di'fju:z] *v.t.* (*light, heat etc.*) рассе́|ивать, -ять; **~d lighting** рассе́янный свет; (*learning etc.*) распростран|я́ть, -и́ть.

v.i. рассе́|иваться, -яться; распростран|я́ться, -и́ться.

diffuseness [di'fju:snis] *n.* расплы́вчатость.

diffusion [di'fju:ʒ(ə)n] *n.* (*phys.*) диффу́зия, рассе́ивание; распростране́ние.

diffusive [di'fju:siv] *adj.* (*phys.*) диффу́зный; распространя́ющийся.

dig [dig] *n.* **1.** (*thrust, poke*) толчо́к; **~ in the ribs** толчо́к в бок. **2.** (*fig.*) шпи́лька, подковы́рка; **that remark was a ~ at me** э́то замеча́ние — ка́мешек в мой огоро́д. **3.** (*archaeol. site, expedition*) раско́пки (*f. pl.*); **we went on a ~** мы вы́ехали на раско́пки. **4.** (*pl., coll., lodgings*) кварти́ра, «берло́га», «нора́».

v.t. & i. **1.** (*excavate ground*) коп|а́ть, -ну́ть; рыть, вы́-; **the ground is hard to ~** э́ту зе́млю тру́дно копа́ть; **they are ~ging potatoes** они́ копа́ют карто́шку; **he dug a hole** он вы́рыл я́му; **~ging for gold** они́ и́щут зо́лото; **he dug his way through the rubble** он с трудо́м пробира́лся че́рез обло́мки камне́й; **they dug through the mountain** они́ проры́ли тонне́ль в горе́. **2.** (*fig.*) отк|а́пывать, -опа́ть; **you will have to ~ for the information** вам ну́жно бу́дет поры́ться, что́бы найти́ ну́жную информа́цию; **he dug into the archives** он зары́лся в архи́вы. **3.** (*thrust*) толк|а́ть, -ну́ть; ткнуть (*pf.*); **he dug me in the ribs** он толкну́л/ткнул меня́ в бок; **he dug his fork into the pie** он вонзи́л ви́лку в пиро́г. **4.** (*understand, appreciate*) ус|ека́ть, -е́чь (*sl.*).

with advs.: **~ in** *v.t.* зак|а́пывать, -опа́ть; **the soldiers dug (themselves) in** солда́ты окопа́лись; **he dug his toes in** (*fig.*) он упёрся на своём; **~ out** *v.t.* выка́пывать, вы́копать; раск|а́пывать, -опа́ть; **victims of the accident were dug out** же́ртвы катастро́фы бы́ли откры́ты; **it is hard to ~ out the truth** тру́дно докопа́ться до и́стины; **~ up** *v.t.* отк|а́пывать, -опа́ть; **they dug up the land** они́ вскопа́ли зе́млю; **the tree was dug up by the roots** де́рево бы́ло вы́копано/вы́рыто из земли́ с корня́ми; **they dug up an ancient statue** они́ вы́рыли дре́внюю ста́тую; **where did you ~ him up?** (*fig.*) где вы его́ откопа́ли?

digamma [dai'gæmə] *n.* дига́мма.

digest[1] ['daidʒest] *n.* компе́ндиум, резюме́ (*indecl.*).

digest[2] [dai'dʒest, di-] *v.t.* (*food*) перева́р|ивать, -и́ть; (*information etc.*) усв|а́ивать, -о́ить.

v.i. перева́р|иваться, -и́ться; **this food ~s easily** э́та пи́ща легко́ усва́ивается.

digestibility [dai,dʒesti'biliti, di-] *n.* удобовари́мость, усвоя́емость.

digestible [dai'dʒestib(ə)l, di-] *adj.* удобовари́мый.

digestion [dai'dʒestʃ(ə)n] *n.* (*of food*) пищеваре́ние; (*of knowledge*) усвое́ние.

digestive [di'dʒestiv, dai-] *adj.* пищевари́тельный; (*aiding digestion*) спосо́бствующий пищеваре́нию.

digger ['digə(r)] *n.* (*one who digs*) копа́тель (*m.*); копа́льщик, землеко́п; (*searcher for gold*) золотоиска́тель (*m.*).

digging ['digiŋ] *n.* (*action*) рытьё, копа́ние.

digit ['didʒit] *n.* (*finger or toe*) па́лец; (*numeral*) ци́фра.

digital [ˈdɪdʒɪt(ə)l] *adj.* цифрово́й; ~ **clock** цифровы́е/электро́нные часы́ (*pl., g.* -о́в).
digitalis [ˌdɪdʒɪˈteɪlɪs] *n.* дигита́лис, наперстя́нка.
digitizer [ˈdɪdʒɪˌtaɪz] *n.* (*comput.*) коди́рующий преобразова́тель.
digitizing [ˈdɪdʒɪˌtaɪzɪŋ] *adj.*: ~ **tablet** (*comput.*) коди́рующий планше́т.
dignified [ˈdɪgnɪˌfaɪd] *adj.* по́лный досто́инства; велича́вый; вели́чественный.
dignify [ˈdɪgnɪˌfaɪ] *v.t.* облагор|а́живать, -о́дить; велича́ть (*impf.*); **he ~ies his books by the name of a library** он велича́ет/имену́ет своё собра́ние книг библиоте́кой.
dignitary [ˈdɪgnɪtərɪ] *n.* сано́вник; высокопоста́вленное лицо́.
dignity [ˈdɪgnɪtɪ] *n.* **1.** (*worth*) досто́инство; **stand on one's ~** тре́бовать (*impf.*) уваже́ния к себе́; **it is beneath my ~ to reply** отвеча́ть на э́то — ни́же моего́ досто́инства. **2.** (*dignified behaviour*): **keep one's ~** сохран|я́ть, -и́ть своё досто́инство. **3.** (*title*) зва́ние, сан, ти́тул; **confer the ~ of a peerage** присв|а́ивать, -о́ить (*pf.*) ти́тул пэ́ра.
digraph [ˈdaɪgrɑːf] *n.* дигра́ф.
digress [daɪˈgres] *v.i.* отвл|ека́ться, -е́чься; отклон|я́ться, -и́ться.
digression [daɪˈgreʃ(ə)n] *n.* отклоне́ние, отступле́ние.
dihedral [daɪˈhiːdr(ə)l] *adj.* дигедра́льный; ~ **angle** (*aeron.*) двугра́нный у́гол.
dike, dyke [daɪk] *n.* (*ditch*) ров, кана́ва; (*embankment*) да́мба, плоти́на.
v.t. (*drain*) осуш|а́ть, -и́ть; (*surround with embankment*) защищ|а́ть, -и́ть да́мбой.
diktat [ˈdɪktæt] *n.* дикта́т.
dilapidated [dɪˈlæpɪˌdeɪtɪd] *adj.* ве́тхий, полуразру́шенный.
dilapidation [dɪˌlæpɪˈdeɪʃ(ə)n] *n.* (об)ветша́ние, изно́с.
dilatable [daɪˈleɪtəb(ə)l] *adj.* растяжи́мый.
dilatation [ˌdaɪləˈteɪʃ(ə)n] = **dilation**
dilate [daɪˈleɪt] *v.t.* расш|иря́ть, -и́рить; **the horse ~d its nostrils** ло́шадь разду́ла но́здри.
v.i. расш|иря́ться, -и́риться; распростран|я́ться, -и́ться; **his eyes ~d** его́ глаза́ расши́рились; **I could ~ upon this subject** я мог бы простра́нно говори́ть на э́ту те́му.
dilat|ion [daɪˈleɪʃ(ə)n], **-ation** [ˌdaɪləˈteɪʃ(ə)n] *nn.* расшире́ние.
dilatoriness [ˈdɪlətərɪnɪs] *n.* замедле́ние, медли́тельность.
dilatory [ˈdɪlətərɪ] *adj.* замедля́ющий, медли́тельный.
dilemma [daɪˈlemə, dɪ-] *n.* диле́мма; **he is on the horns of a ~** он стои́т пе́ред диле́ммой.
dilettante [ˌdɪlɪˈtæntɪ] *n.* дилета́нт.
adj. дилета́нтский.
dilettantism [ˌdɪlɪˈtæntɪz(ə)m] *n.* дилета́нтство.
diligence[1] [ˈdɪlɪdʒ(ə)ns] *n.* (*zeal*) прилежа́ние, усе́рдие, стара́тельность.
diligence[2] [ˈdɪlɪdʒ(ə)ns, ˌdiːliˈʒɑ̃s] *n.* (*hist., coach*) дилижа́нс.
diligent [ˈdɪlɪdʒ(ə)nt] *adj.* приле́жный, усе́рдный, стара́тельный.
dill [dɪl] *n.* укро́п; ~ **pickle** марино́ванный огуре́ц.
dilly-dally [ˌdɪlɪˈdælɪ] *v.i.* (*coll.*) ме́шкать (*impf.*); колеба́ться (*impf.*).
dilute [ˈdaɪljuːt] *adj.* разба́вленный; разведённый.
v.t. разв|оди́ть, -ести́; разб|авля́ть, -а́вить.
dilution [daɪˈljuːʃ(ə)n] *n.* разведе́ние, разбавле́ние.
diluvial [daɪˈluːvɪəl, dɪ-, -ˈljuːvɪəl] *adj.* (*geol.*) делювиа́льный.
dim [dɪm] *adj.* (*of light etc.*) ту́склый; (*of memory etc.*) сму́тный; (*of eyes*) сла́бый, затума́ненный; (*coll., stupid*) тупо́й; **I take a ~ view of it** (*coll.*) я смотрю́ на э́то неодобри́тельно.
v.t. затума́ни|вать, -ть; ~ **out** затемя́ть, -и́ть; ~ **one's headlights** перейти́ (*pf.*) на «ма́лый» свет.
v.i. затума́ни|ваться, -ться; тускне́ть, по-.
cpds. (*coll.*): **~wit** *n.* тупи́ца (*c.g.*); **~-witted** *adj.* тупоу́мный.
dime [daɪm] *n.* десятице́нтовик; ~ **novel** (*US*) грошо́вый рома́н.
dimension [daɪˈmenʃ(ə)n, dɪ-] *n.* **1.** (*extent*) разме́р; **a room of vast ~s** ко́мната огро́много разме́ра; (*capacity*) объём. **2.** (*direction of measurement*) измере́ние; **the fourth ~** четвёртое измере́ние.
dimeter [ˈdɪmɪtə(r)] *n.* двухстопный разме́р.
diminish [dɪˈmɪnɪʃ] *v.t.* ум|еньша́ть, -е́ньшить; уб|авля́ть, -а́вить; **~ed responsibility** (*leg.*) ограни́ченная уголо́вная отве́тственность; **law of ~ing returns** зако́н сокраща́ющихся дохо́дов; **~ed fifth** (*mus.*) уме́ньшенная кви́нта; **~ed arch** (*archit.*) сжа́тая а́рка.
v.i. ум|еньша́ться, -е́ньшиться; уб|авля́ться, -а́виться.
diminuendo [dɪˌmɪnjʊˈendəʊ] *n.* & *adv.* диминуэ́ндо (*indecl.*).
diminution [ˌdɪmɪˈnjuːʃ(ə)n] *n.* уменьше́ние, сокраще́ние, убыва́ние.
diminutive [dɪˈmɪnjʊtɪv] *n.* (*gram.*) уменьши́тельное сло́во.
adj. (*small*) миниатю́рный.
dimness [ˈdɪmnɪs] *n.* (*of light*) ту́склость; (*of wit*) ту́пость.
dimple [ˈdɪmp(ə)l] *n.* я́мочка; (*ripple*) рябь.
din [dɪn] *n.* гам, гро́хот, галдёж.
v.t. вд|а́лбливать, -олби́ть; **he ~ned it into me that I must obey** он вда́лбливал мне в го́лову, что я до́лжен подчини́ться.
v.i.: **their shouts are still ~ning in my ears** их крик у меня́ всё ещё стои́т в уша́х.
dinar [ˈdiːnɑː(r)] *n.* дина́р.
din|e [daɪn] *v.t.*: **he was wined and ~ed** его́ корми́ли-пои́ли; его́ по́тчевали на сла́ву.
v.i. обе́дать, по- (**on, off:** *чем*); у́жинать, по-; **~ing-car** ваго́н-рестора́н; **~ing-hall** обе́денный зал, столо́вая; **~ing-room** столо́вая; **~ing-table** обе́денный стол.
diner [ˈdaɪnə(r)] *n.* (*pers.*) обе́дающий, у́жинающий; (*dining-car*) ваго́н-рестора́н.
cpd. **~-out** *n.* люби́тель (*m.*) у́жинать вне до́ма.
ding-dong [ˈdɪŋdɒŋ] *n.* динь-дон.
adj.: **a ~ battle** би́тва с переме́нным успе́хом.
adv. рья́но, усе́рдно; **they went at it ~** они́ взя́лись за э́то засучи́в рукава́.
dinghy [ˈdɪŋɪ, ˈdɪŋgɪ] *n.* ма́ленькая шлю́пка, ту́зик, я́лик; (*inflatable*) надувна́я ло́дка.
dinginess [ˈdɪndʒɪnɪs] *n.* грязь; темнота́; мра́чность.
dingle [ˈdɪŋg(ə)l] *n.* лощи́на.
dingo [ˈdɪŋgəʊ] *n.* ди́нго (*m. or f., indecl.*).
dingy [ˈdɪndʒɪ] *adj.* гря́зный, тёмный, мра́чный.
dinkum [ˈdɪŋkəm] *adj.* (*Austral. sl.*) и́стинный, настоя́щий.
dinky [ˈdɪŋkɪ] *adj.* (*coll.*) изя́щный, ми́ленький.
dinner [ˈdɪnə(r)] *n.* обе́д; (*evening meal*) у́жин; **at ~** за у́жином; **ask s.o. to ~** пригла|ша́ть, -си́ть кого́-н. на у́жин; **have ~** у́жинать, по-; **what's for ~?** что на у́жин?
cpds. **~-bell** *n.* звоно́к к обе́ду/у́жину; **~-dress** *n.* вече́рнее пла́тье; **~-hour** *n.* час обе́да/у́жина; **~-jacket** *n.* смо́кинг; **~-pail** *n.* судки́ (*m. pl.*); **~-party** *n.* зва́ный обе́д; **~-plate** *n.* ме́лкая таре́лка; **~-service, ~-set** *nn.* обе́денный серви́з; **~-time** *n.* обе́денное вре́мя; вре́мя у́жина; **~-wagon** *n.* сервиро́вочный сто́лик.
dinosaur [ˈdaɪnəˌsɔː(r)] *n.* диноза́вр.
dint [dɪnt] *n.* **1.** (*dent*) след уда́ра; вмя́тина, вы́боина. **2.** **by ~ of** посре́дством+*g.*; при по́мощи +*g.*
v.t. ост|авля́ть, -а́вить след/вмя́тину в/на+*p.*
diocesan [daɪˈɒsɪs(ə)n] *n.* (*bishop*) епи́скоп.
adj. епархиа́льный.
diocese [ˈdaɪəsɪs] *n.* епа́рхия.
diode [ˈdaɪəʊd] *n.* дио́д.
Dionysi|ac [ˌdaɪəˈnɪsɪˌæk], **-an** [ˌdaɪəˈnɪsɪən] *adjs.* вакхи́ческий.
diopter [daɪˈɒptə(r)] *n.* (*unit*) диоптри́я.
dioptrics [daɪˈɒptrɪks] *n.* дио́птрика.
diorama [ˌdaɪəˈrɑːmə] *n.* диора́ма.
dioramic [ˌdaɪəˈræmɪk] *adj.* диора́мный.
dioxide [daɪˈɒksaɪd] *n.* двуо́кись.
dip [dɪp] *n.* **1.** (*immersion*) погруже́ние; **lucky ~** лотере́йный бараба́н. **2.** (*bathe*) ныря́ние; купа́ние; **have, take a ~** пойти́ (*pf.*) вы́купаться/попла́вать. **3.** (*cleansing liquid*) протра́ва. **4.** (*slope*) спуск, укло́н; **a ~ among the hills** низи́на ме́жду холмо́в. **5.** (*state of being lowered*): **the flag is at the ~** флаг приспу́щен. **6.** (*candle*) са́льная свеча́.
v.t. **1.** (*immerse*) окун|а́ть, -у́ть; мак|а́ть, -ну́ть; погру|жа́ть, -зи́ть; **~ one's pen into ink** обмак|ивать, -ну́ть перо́ в черни́ла; (*fig.*): **~ one's pen in gall** писа́ть, на-

жёлчно; ~ **sheep** купа́ть, вы́- ове́ц в дезинфици́рующем раство́ре; ~ **one's hand into a bag** запусти́ть (*pf.*) ру́ку в су́мку. **2.** (*draw out*) выче́рпывать, вы́черпать; че́рп|ать, -ну́ть; ~ **up a pailful of water** заче́рп|ывать, -ну́ть ведро́ воды́; ~ **water out of a boat** выче́рпывать, вы́черпнуть во́ду из ло́дки. **3.** (*lower briefly*) приспус|ка́ть, -ти́ть; ~ **headlights** переключ|а́ть, -и́ть фа́ры на (*or* включ|а́ть, -и́ть) бли́жний свет.

v.i. **1.** (*go below surface*) окун|а́ться, -у́ться; погру|жа́ться, -зи́ться; **the sun ~ped below the horizon** со́лнце скры́лось за горизо́нтом (*or* нырну́ло за горизо́нт). **2.** (*fig.*): ~ **into one's purse** раскоше́ли|ваться, -ться. **3.** (*slope away*): **the (plot of) land ~s to the south** уча́сток име́ет накло́н к ю́гу. **4.** (*scan, peer*) загля́|дывать, -ну́ть; ~ **into the future** загля́|дывать, -ну́ть в бу́дущее; **I ~ped into the book** я загляну́л в э́ту кни́гу. **5.** (*fall slightly or temporarily*) пон|ижа́ться, -и́зиться; **the road ~s here** здесь доро́га идёт под укло́н.

cpds. **~-needle** *n.* магни́тная стре́лка; **~-stick** *n.* уровнеме́р, (*coll.*) щуп.

diphtheria [dɪf'θɪərɪə, *disp.* dɪp-] *n.* дифтери́я, дифтери́т.

diphthong ['dɪfθɒŋ] *n.* дифто́нг.

diphthongal [ˌdɪf'θɒŋg(ə)l] *adj.* дифтонга́льный, дифтонги́ческий.

diplodocus [dɪp'lɒdəkəs, ˌdɪpləʊ'dəʊkəs] *n.* диплодо́к.

diploma [dɪ'pləʊmə] *n.* дипло́м (по+*d.*).

diplomacy [dɪp'ləʊməsɪ] *n.* диплома́тия; (*tact*) дипломати́чность.

diplomat ['dɪpləˌmæt], **-ist** [dɪ'pləʊmətɪst] *nn.* (*lit., fig.*) диплома́т.

diplomatic [ˌdɪplə'mætɪk] *adj.* (*lit., fig.*) дипломати́ческий; ~ **corps, body** дипломати́ческий ко́рпус; ~ **service** дипломати́ческая слу́жба.

dipper ['dɪpə(r)] *n.* **1.** (*ladle*) ковш, черпа́к; **the Big/Little D~** (*astron.*) Больша́я/Ма́лая Медве́дица. **2.** (*bird*) оля́пка. **3.** (*for headlights*) переключа́тель (*m.*) све́та фар. **4.** (*switchback*) америка́нские го́ры (*f. pl.*).

dippy ['dɪpɪ] *adj.* (*sl.*) поме́шанный, чо́кнутый.

dipso ['dɪpsəʊ] *n.* алка́ш (*sl.*).

dipsomania [ˌdɪpsə'meɪnɪə] *n.* алкоголи́зм.

dipsomaniac [ˌdɪpsə'meɪnɪˌæk] *n.* алкого́лик.

adj. алкоголи́ческий.

dipterous ['dɪptərəs] *adj.* двукры́лый.

diptych ['dɪptɪk] *n.* ди́птих.

dire ['daɪə(r)] *adj.* ужа́сный; **he is in ~ need of help** он кра́йне нужда́ется в по́мощи.

direct [daɪ'rekt, dɪ-] *adj.* (*straight; without intermediary*) прямо́й; (*straightforward*) прямо́й, непосре́дственный; **he has a ~ way of speaking** он говори́т всё пря́мо в лицо́; **the ~ opposite** по́лная противополо́жность; ~ **current** постоя́нный ток.

adv. пря́мо.

v.t. **1.** (*indicate the way*): **can you ~ me to the station?** не ука́жете ли вы мне доро́гу к ста́нции?; не ска́жете ли вы, как пройти́ на вокза́л? **2.** (*address*) адресова́ть (*impf., pf.*); напр|авля́ть, -а́вить; **I ~ed the letter to his bank** я адресова́л письмо́ в его́ банк; **my remarks were ~ed to him** мои́ замеча́ния бы́ли адресо́ваны ему́. **3.** (*manage, control*) руководи́ть (*impf.*) +*i.*; **he ~ed the orchestra** он дирижи́ровал орке́стром; **he ~ed the play** он поста́вил пье́су; **the policeman ~s traffic** полице́йский регули́рует движе́ние. **4.** (*command*) предпи́с|ывать, -а́ть; да|ва́ть, -ть указа́ние; **I ~ed him to take no notice** я веле́л ему́ не обраща́ть внима́ния.

direction [daɪ'rekʃ(ə)n, dɪ-] *n.* **1.** (*course, point of compass*) направле́ние; **he went in the ~ of London** он напра́вился к Ло́ндону; **they dispersed in all ~s** они́ разошли́сь по всем направле́ниям; **he has a good sense of ~** он хорошо́ ориенти́руется; **new ~s of research** но́вые о́бласти (*f. pl.*) иссле́дования. **2.** (*pl., instructions*) указа́ния (*nt. pl.*); **I followed the ~s on the label** я сле́довал указа́ниям на ярлыке́. **3.** (*command, control*) руково́дство; ~ **of labour** распределе́ние рабо́чей си́лы. **4.** (*theatr.*): ~ **of a play** постано́вка/режиссу́ра пье́сы; **stage ~** а́вторская рема́рка. **5.** (*to a jury*) напу́тствие прися́жным.

cpds. **~-finder** *n.* радиопеленга́тор; **~-finding** *adj.*: **~-finding equipment** радиопеленга́торное обору́дование.

directional [daɪ'rekʃən(ə)l, dɪ-] *adj.*: ~ **radio** радиопеленга́ция; ~ **transmitter** радиопеленга́торная ста́нция.

directive [daɪ'rektɪv, dɪ-] *n.* директи́ва, указа́ние.

directly [daɪ'rektlɪ, dɪ-] *adv.* **1.** (*in var. senses of direct*) пря́мо. **2.** (*soon*): **I'll be there ~** я вско́ре/сейча́с там бу́ду. **3.** (*at once*) неме́дленно, то́тчас.

conj. как то́лько.

directness [daɪ'rektnɪs, dɪ-] *n.* прямота́, открове́нность.

director [daɪ'rektə(r), dɪ-] *n.* **1.** (*one who directs*) руководи́тель (*m.*). **2.** (*of company etc.*) дире́ктор; **managing ~** управля́ющий; **~-general** гла́вный дире́ктор. **3.** (*theatr.*) режиссёр.

directorate [daɪ'rektərət, dɪ-] *n.* (*office of director*) дире́кция; (*group of directors*) директора́т; (*admin. body*) управле́ние.

directorial [ˌdaɪrek'tɔːrɪəl, ˌdɪ-] *adj.* дире́кторский.

directorship [daɪ'rektəʃɪp, dɪ-] *n.* дире́кторство.

directory [daɪ'rektərɪ, dɪ-] *n.* **1.** (*reference work*) спра́вочник, указа́тель (*m.*); **telephone ~** телефо́нная кни́га. **2.** (*Fr. hist.*) Директо́рия.

direness ['daɪənɪs] *n.* у́жас.

dirge [dɜːdʒ] *n.* погреба́льное пе́ние.

dirigible ['dɪrɪdʒɪb(ə)l, dɪ'rɪdʒ-] *n.* дирижа́бль (*m.*).

dirk [dɜːk] *n.* кинжа́л.

dirt [dɜːt] *n.* **1.** (*unclean matter*) грязь; **this dress shows the ~** э́то пла́тье ма́ркое; **treat s.o. like ~** трети́ровать (*impf.*) кого́-н.; не счита́ться; (*impf.*) с кем-н.; **do s.o. ~** де́лать, с- кому́-н. по́длость/па́кость; **eat ~** (*fig.*) прогл|а́тывать, -оти́ть оби́ду. **2.** (*loose earth or soil*) грунт, земля́; **a ~ road** грунтова́я доро́га; ~ **track** мотоцикле́тный трек. **3.** (*obscenity*) непристо́йность, грязь. **4.**: **the ~** (*coll., inside story*) подного́тная.

cpd. **~-cheap** *adv.* деше́вле па́реной ре́пы; *adj.* малоце́нный; **I bought the radio ~-cheap** я купи́л ра́дио по дешёвке.

dirtiness ['dɜːtɪnɪs] *n.* грязь, га́дость.

dirty [dɜːtɪ] *adj.* **1.** (*not clean*) гря́зный. **2.** (*rough, stormy*) бу́рный. **3.** (*obscene*) поха́бный, гря́зный, па́костный; ~ **story** поха́бный анекдо́т. **4.** (*nasty*) гря́зный, га́дкий; **he played a ~ trick on me** он подложи́л мне свинью́; **he gave me a ~ look** он серди́то посмотре́л на меня́; **do your own ~ work!** я не бу́ду де́лать за вас ва́шу гря́зную рабо́ту.

v.t. & *i.* грязни́ть(ся), за-; па́чкать(ся), за-; загрязн|я́ть(ся), -и́ть(ся).

disability [ˌdɪsə'bɪlɪtɪ] *n.* (*inability to work*) нетрудоспосо́бность; (*physical defect*) инвали́дность; (*leg.*) неправоспосо́бность.

disable [dɪs'eɪb(ə)l] *v.t.* (*physically*) кале́чить, ис-; **~d soldier** инвали́д войны́; **the ship was ~d** кора́бль был вы́веден из стро́я; (*legally*) лиш|а́ть, -и́ть пра́ва.

disablement [dɪs'eɪbəlmənt] *n.* нетрудоспосо́бность; инвали́дность.

disabuse [ˌdɪsə'bjuːz] *v.t.* выводи́ть, вы́вести из заблужде́ния.

disaccredit [ˌdɪsə'kredɪt] *v.t.* лиш|а́ть, -и́ть полномо́чий.

disaccustom [ˌdɪsə'kʌstəm] *v.t.* отуч|а́ть, -и́ть.

disadvantage [ˌdɪsəd'vɑːntɪdʒ] *n.* невы́года; невы́годное положе́ние; **be at a ~** ока́з|ываться, -а́ться в невы́годном положе́нии; **take s.o. at a ~** воспо́льзоваться (*pf.*) чьим-н. невы́годным положе́нием; **put s.o. at a ~** поста́вить (*pf.*) кого́-н. в невы́годное положе́ние; **I know nothing to his ~** я не зна́ю за ним ничего́ худо́го/плохо́го; **he showed himself to ~** он показа́л себя́ с невы́годной стороны́.

v.t. де́йствовать (*impf.*) в уще́рб +*d.*

disadvantageous [dɪsˌædvən'teɪdʒəs] *adj.* невы́годный.

disaffected [ˌdɪsə'fektɪd] *adj.* недово́льный, неблагонаме́ренный.

disaffection [ˌdɪsə'fekʃ(ə)n] *n.* недово́льство, неблагонаме́ренность.

disagree [ˌdɪsə'griː] *v.i.* **1.** (*differ, not correspond*) не соотве́тствовать (*impf.*) (+*d.*). **2.** (*in opinion*) не согла|ша́ться, -си́ться; **I ~ with you** я с ва́ми не согла́сен; **the witnesses ~** свиде́тели расхо́дятся в показа́ниях. **3.** (*have adverse effect*): **oysters ~ with me** я пло́хо переношу́ у́стриц; от у́стриц у меня́ де́лается несваре́ние желу́дка.

disagreeable [ˌdɪsəˈgri:əb(ə)l] *adj.* (*unpleasant*) неприя́тный, непривлека́тельный; (*of pers.*) неприве́тливый.

disagreeableness [ˌdɪsəˈgri:əbəlnɪs] *n.* непривлека́тельность, неприве́тливость.

disagreement [ˌdɪsəˈgri:mənt] *n.* разногла́сие, разла́д, несогла́сие.

disallow [ˌdɪsəˈlaʊ] *v.t.* (*reject*) отклон|я́ть, -и́ть; (*forbid*) запре|ща́ть, -ти́ть.

disappear [ˌdɪsəˈpɪə(r)] *v.i.* исч|еза́ть, -е́знуть; проп|ада́ть, -а́сть.

disappearance [ˌdɪsəˈpɪərəns] *n.* исчезнове́ние.

disappoint [ˌdɪsəˈpɔɪnt] *v.t.* разочаро́в|ывать, -а́ть; **he was ~ed at this** он был э́тим разочаро́ван; **I am ~ed in you** я в вас разочарова́лся; **he was ~ed of the prize** приз ему́ не доста́лся; **I am sorry to ~ your plans** мне жаль наруша́ть ва́ши пла́ны.

disappointing [ˌdɪsəˈpɔɪntɪŋ] *adj.* разочаро́вывающий; **the weather has been ~** пого́да была́ нева́жная.

disappointment [ˌdɪsəˈpɔɪntmənt] *n.* **1.** (*state of being disappointed*) разочарова́ние; **to my ~** к моему́ огорче́нию; **he met with ~** его́ пости́гло разочарова́ние. **2.** (*pers. or thg. that disappoints*): **he turned out a ~** он обману́л возлага́емые на него́ наде́жды.

disappro|bation [dɪsˌæprəˈbeɪʃ(ə)n], **-val** [ˌdɪsəˈpru:vəl] *nn.* неодобре́ние.

disapprove [ˌdɪsəˈpru:v] *v.t. & i.* не од|обря́ть, -о́брить.

disapproving [ˌdɪsəˈpru:vɪŋ] *adj.* неодобри́тельный.

disarm [dɪsˈɑ:m] *v.t.* разоруж|а́ть, -и́ть; (*fig.*) обезору́жи|вать, -ть; **he ~s criticism** он обезору́живает свои́х кри́тиков.

v.i. разоруж|а́ться, -и́ться.

disarmament [dɪsˈɑ:məmənt] *n.* разоруже́ние.

disarrange [ˌdɪsəˈreɪndʒ] *v.t.* прив|оди́ть, -ести́ в беспоря́док.

disarrangement [ˌdɪsəˈreɪndʒmənt] *n.* дезорганиза́ция, беспоря́док.

disarray [ˌdɪsəˈreɪ] *n.* смяте́ние, расстро́йство.

disassemble [ˌdɪsəˈsemb(ə)l] *v.t.* раз|бира́ть, -обра́ть; демонти́ровать (*impf., pf.*).

disassembly [ˌdɪsəˈsemblɪ] *n.* разбо́рка.

disassociate [ˌdɪsəˈsəʊʃɪˌeɪt, -sɪˌeɪt] = **dissociate**

disaster [dɪˈzɑ:stə(r)] *n.* бе́дствие; **he is courting ~** он накли́кает беду́.

disastrous [dɪˈzɑ:strəs] *adj.* ги́бельный, бе́дственный.

disastrousness [dɪˈzɑ:strəsnɪs] *n.* ги́бельность.

disavow [ˌdɪsəˈvaʊ] *v.t.* дезавуи́ровать (*impf., pf.*); отрица́ть (*impf.*).

disavowal [ˌdɪsəˈvaʊəl] *n.* дезавуи́рование; отрица́ние.

disband [dɪsˈbænd] *v.t.* распус|ка́ть, -ти́ть; расформиро́в|ывать, -а́ть.

v.i. разбе|га́ться, -жа́ться; рассе́|иваться, -яться; **the (theatre) company ~ed** тру́ппа распа́лась.

disbandment [dɪsˈbændmənt] *n.* расформирова́ние, ро́спуск.

disbar [dɪsˈbɑ:(r)] *v.t.* лиш|а́ть, -и́ть зва́ния адвока́та.

disbarment [dɪsˈbɑ:mənt] *n.* лише́ние зва́ния адвока́та.

disbelief [ˌdɪsbɪˈli:f] *n.* неве́рие.

disbelieve [ˌdɪsbɪˈli:v] *v.t.* не ве́рить (*impf.*) +*d.* (*or* в+*a.*).

disburden [dɪsˈbɜ:d(ə)n] *v.t.* сн|има́ть, -ять тя́жесть с+*g.*

disburse [dɪsˈbɜ:s] *v.t.* выпла́чивать, вы́платить.

disbursement [dɪsˈbɜ:smənt] *n.* (*act of paying*) опла́та; (*sum paid*) вы́плаченная су́мма.

disc, disk [dɪsk] *n.* **1.** (*round object*) диск; **the sun's ~** со́лнечный диск; **identification ~** ли́чный знак. **2.** (*gramophone record*) пласти́нка. **3.** (*med.*): **slipped ~** смеще́ние межпозвоно́чного ди́ска. **4.** (*comput.*): **floppy ~** ги́бкий диск; **~ drive** дисково́д, накопи́тель на ди́сках.

cpd. **~-jockey** *n.* диск-жоке́й.

discard [ˈdɪskɑ:d] *n.* **1.** (*card*) сбро́шенная ка́рта. **2.** (*object*) нену́жное, него́дное. **3.: throw sth. into the ~** вы́бросить (*pf.*) что-н. как нену́жное.

v.t. выбра́сывать, вы́бросить; **~ winter clothing** сбр|а́сывать, -о́сить зи́мнюю оде́жду; **~ old beliefs** отбр|а́сывать, -о́сить ста́рые убежде́ния.

discern [dɪˈsɜ:n] *v.t.* разгля́д|ывать, -е́ть; рассм|а́тривать, -отре́ть; различ|а́ть, -и́ть.

discernible [dɪˌsɜ:nˈɪb(ə)l] *adj.* различи́мый.

discerning [dɪˈsɜ:nɪŋ] *adj.* проница́тельный.

discernment [dɪˈsɜ:nmənt] *n.* проница́тельность.

discharge [ˈdɪstʃɑ:dʒ, dɪsˈtʃɑ:dʒ] *n.* **1.** (*unloading*) разгру́зка. **2.** (*emission of fluid etc.*) выделе́ния (*pl.*); (*elec.*) разря́д. **3.** (*performance, e.g. of duty*) исполне́ние; (*of a debt*) упла́та. **4.** (*release, dismissal*) увольне́ние, освобожде́ние; (*from the army*) демобилиза́ция, увольне́ние. **5.** (*firing of a gun*) вы́стрел, залп; **a ~ of arrows** град стрел. **6.** (*receipt*) распи́ска.

v.t. **1.** (*unload*) разгру|жа́ть, -зи́ть. **2.** (*emit liquid, current etc.*) спус|ка́ть, -ти́ть; разря|жа́ть, -ди́ть; **the clouds ~ electricity** облака́ разряжа́ются электри́чеством. **3.** (*fire, let fly*) стреля́ть (*impf.*); выстре́ливать, вы́стрелить. **4.** (*release, dismiss*): (*from the army*) демобилизова́ть (*impf., pf.*); (*from hospital*) выпи́сывать, вы́писать; (*from service*) увольня́ть, -о́лить; **a ~d bankrupt** восстано́вленный в права́х банкро́т.

disciple [dɪˈsaɪp(ə)l] *n.* учени́|к (*fem.* -ца).

discipleship [dɪˈsaɪpəlʃɪp] *n.* учени́чество.

disciplinarian [ˌdɪsɪplɪˈneərɪən] *n.* сторо́нник дисципли́ны; **he is a good ~** он уме́ет подде́рживать дисципли́ну.

disciplinary [ˈdɪsɪplɪnərɪ, -ˈplɪnərɪ] *adj.* дисциплина́рный; **take ~ action** приня́ть (*pf.*) дисциплина́рные ме́ры.

discipline [ˈdɪsɪplɪn] *n.* (*good order; branch of studies*) дисципли́на.

v.t. дисциплини́ровать (*impf., pf.*).

disclaim [dɪsˈkleɪm] *v.t.* отр|ека́ться, -е́чься от+*g.*; отка́з|ываться, -а́ться от+*g.*

disclaimer [dɪsˈkleɪmə(r)] *n.* отрече́ние, отка́з.

disclose [dɪsˈkləʊz] *v.t.* откр|ыва́ть, -ы́ть; раскр|ыва́ть, -ы́ть; разоблач|а́ть, -и́ть; обнару́жи|вать, -ть; **his books ~ great learning** его́ кни́ги свиде́тельствуют о большо́й эруди́ции.

disclosure [dɪsˈkləʊʒə(r)] *n.* раскры́тие, откры́тие, разоблаче́ние, обнаруже́ние.

disco [ˈdɪskəʊ] *n.* (*coll.*) = **discotheque**

discoloration [dɪsˌkʌləˈreɪʃ(ə)n] *n.* обесцве́чивание.

discolour [dɪsˈkʌlə(r)] *v.t. & i.* обесцве́|чивать(ся), -тить(ся).

discomfit [dɪsˈkʌmfɪt] *v.t.* (*defeat*) нан|оси́ть, -ести́ пораже́ние +*d.*; (*disconcert*) сму|ща́ть, -ти́ть; прив|оди́ть, -ести́ в замеша́тельство.

discomfiture [dɪsˈkʌmfɪtjə(r)] *n.* пораже́ние, смуще́ние, замеша́тельство.

discomfort [dɪsˈkʌmfət] *n.* неудо́бство.

v.t. причин|я́ть, -и́ть неудо́бство +*d.*; стесн|я́ть, -и́ть.

discommend [ˌdɪskəˈmend] *v.t.* порица́ть (*impf.*); не од|обря́ть, -о́брить.

discommode [ˌdɪskəˈməʊd] *v.t.* причин|я́ть, -и́ть неудо́бство +*d.*

discompose [ˌdɪskəmˈpəʊz] *v.t.* волнова́ть, вз-; трево́жить, вс-; расстр|а́ивать, -о́ить.

discomposure [ˌdɪskəmˈpəʊʒə(r)] *n.* волне́ние, трево́га, расстро́йство.

disconcert [ˌdɪskənˈsɜ:t] *v.t.* (*agitate*) волнова́ть, вз-; (*disturb*) расстр|а́ивать, -о́ить.

disconnect [ˌdɪskəˈnekt] *v.t.* разъедин|я́ть, -и́ть; (*gas etc.*) отключ|а́ть, -и́ть; **we were ~ed** (*telephone*) нас разъедини́ли/прерва́ли.

disconnected [ˌdɪskəˈnektɪd] *adj.* **1.** (*tech.*) разъединённый, вы́ключенный. **2.** (*ideas etc.*) обры́вочный, разбро́санный, бессвя́зный.

disconnection [ˌdɪskəˈnekʃ(ə)n] *n.* разъедине́ние, отключе́ние.

disconsolate [dɪsˈkɒnsələt] *adj.* неуте́шный.

discontent [ˌdɪskənˈtent] *n.* недово́льство.

v.t. возбу|жда́ть, -ди́ть недово́льство у+*g.*

discontinuance [ˌdɪskənˈtɪnju:əns] *n.* прекраще́ние.

discontinue [ˌdɪskənˈtɪnju:] *v.t.* прекра|ща́ть, -ти́ть.

discontinuity [dɪsˌkɒntɪˈnju:ɪtɪ] *n.* отсу́тствие непреры́вности.

discontinuous [ˌdɪskənˈtɪnjʊəs] *adj.* прерыва́ющийся, преры́вистый.
discord [ˈdɪskɔːd] *n.* (*disagreement*) разногла́сие, разноголо́сица; (*disharmony*) разла́д, раздо́р; (*mus.*) диссона́нс.
discordance [dɪˈskɔːdəns] *n.* разногла́сие, разла́д.
discordant [dɪˈskɔːd(ə)nt] *adj.* несогла́сный; разноголо́сый; (*inharmonious*) диссони́рующий; нестро́йный.
discothèque [ˈdɪskəˌtek] *n.* дискоте́ка; та́нцы (*m. pl.*) под магнитофо́н.
discount [ˈdɪskaʊnt] *n.* **1.** (*rebate*) ски́дка. **2.** (*on bill of exchange etc.*) диско́нт. **3.** (*fig.*): **at a ~** не в ходу́/почёте; непопуля́рный.
v.t. (*bill of exchange etc.*) дисконти́ровать (*impf.*, *pf.*); (*fig.*, *treat sceptically*) отн|оси́ться, -ести́сь с недове́рием к+*d.*; **I ~ed his story** я не о́чень пове́рил его́ расска́зу; я усомни́лся в и́стинности его́ расска́за; (*allow for*): **I ~ed his prejudice** я сде́лал ски́дку на его́ предрассу́дки.
discountenance [dɪˈskaʊntɪnəns] *v.t.* (*disapprove*) не од|обря́ть, -о́брить; (*discourage*) обескура́жи|ва́ть, -ть.
discourage [dɪˈskʌrɪdʒ] *v.t.* (*deprive of courage*) расхол|а́живать, -оди́ть; обескура́жи|вать, -ть; лиш|а́ть, -и́ть му́жества; (*dissuade*) отгов|а́ривать, -ори́ть.
discouragement [dɪˈskʌrɪdʒmənt] *n.* расхола́живание, обескура́живание; (*dissuasion*) отгова́ривание.
discourse[1] [ˈdɪskɔːs, -ˈskɔːs] *n.* речь, рассужде́ние.
discourse[2] [dɪˈskɔːs] *v.i.* рассужда́ть (*impf.*).
discourteous [dɪsˈkɜːtɪəs] *adj.* неве́жливый, нелюбе́зный.
discourtesy [dɪsˈkɜːtəsɪ] *n.* неве́жливость, нелюбе́зность.
discover [dɪˈskʌvə(r)] *v.t.* **1.** (*find*) на|ходи́ть, -йти́; откр|ыва́ть, -ы́ть; обнару́жи|вать, -ть; раскр|ыва́ть, -ы́ть; (*find out*) узн|ава́ть, -а́ть; выясня́ть, вы́яснить. **2. he is ~ed as the curtain rises** он нахо́дится на сце́не, когда́ за́навес поднима́ется.
discoverable [dɪˈskʌvərəb(ə)l] *adj.* обнару́живаемый; открыва́емый; мо́гущий быть откры́тым/обнару́женным.
discoverer [dɪˈskʌvərə(r)] *n.* иссле́дователь (*m.*) (но́вых земе́ль); (перво)открыва́тель (*m.*); **she was the ~ of radium** она́ откры́ла ра́дий.
discovery [dɪˈskʌvərɪ] *n.* откры́тие; **the D~ies** (*hist.*) вели́кие географи́ческие откры́тия.
discredit [dɪsˈkredɪt] *n.* (*loss of repute*) дискредита́ция; **bring s.o. into ~** (*or* **bring ~ upon s.o.**) компромети́ровать, с- кого́-н.; дискредити́ровать (*impf.*, *pf.*) кого́-н.; **he is a ~ to the school** он позо́рит шко́лу.
v.t. дискредити́ровать (*impf.*, *pf.*).
discreditable [dɪsˈkredɪtəb(ə)l] *adj.* дискредити́рующий; (*dishonest*) позо́рный.
discreet [dɪˈskriːt] *adj.* осмотри́тельный, сде́ржанный; (*tactful*) такти́чный; **a ~ silence** благоразу́мное молча́ние; **a ~ quantity** уме́ренное коли́чество.
discrepancy [dɪsˈkrepənsɪ] *n.* расхожде́ние, разногла́сие, противоречи́вость.
discrepant [dɪˈskrepənt] *adj.* противоречи́вый.
discrete [dɪˈskriːt] *adj.* разде́льный.
discreteness [dɪˈskriːtnɪs] *n.* разде́льность.
discretion [dɪˈskreʃ(ə)n] *n.* **1.** (*prudence*, *good judgment*) осмотри́тельность, осторо́жность, благоразу́мие; **~ is the better part of valour** благоразу́мие — гла́вное досто́инство хра́брости; **years, age of ~** во́зраст, с кото́рого челове́к несёт отве́тственность за свой посту́пки. **2.** (*freedom to judge*) усмотре́ние; **I leave this to your ~** я оставля́ю э́то на ва́ше усмотре́ние; **at ~** по усмотре́нию; **surrender at ~** сда́ться (*pf.*) на ми́лость победи́теля; **I gave him wide ~** я дал ему́ широ́кие полномо́чия.
discretionary [dɪˈskreʃənərɪ] *adj.* дискрецио́нный.
discriminate [dɪˈskrɪmɪˌneɪt] *v.t.* (*distinguish*) отлич|а́ть, -и́ть; различ|а́ть, -и́ть.
v.i.: **~ against** дискримини́ровать (*impf.*, *pf.*).
discriminating [dɪˈskrɪmɪˌneɪtɪŋ] *adj.* разбо́рчивый; **~ taste** то́нкий/разбо́рчивый вкус; **a ~ tax** дифференциа́льный нало́г.
discrimination [dɪˌskrɪmɪˈneɪʃ(ə)n] *n.* (*judgment*, *taste*) разбо́рчивость; (*bias*) дискримина́ция (**against s.o.** кого́-н.).
discriminatory [dɪˈskrɪmɪnətərɪ] *adj.* пристра́стный, дифференциа́льный.
discrown [dɪˈskraʊn] *v.t.* лиш|а́ть, -и́ть коро́ны; разве́нч|ивать, -а́ть.
disculpate [ˈdɪskʌlˌpeɪt] *v.t.* опра́вд|ывать, -а́ть.
discursive [dɪˈskɜːsɪv] *adj.* (*digressive*) разбро́санный; (*reasoning*) аргументи́рованный.
discursiveness [dɪˈskɜːsɪvnɪs] *n.* разбро́санность.
discus [ˈdɪskəs] *n.* диск.
discuss [dɪˈskʌs] *v.t.* дискути́ровать (*impf.*, *pf.*); обсу|жда́ть, -ди́ть.
discuss|able [dɪˈskʌsəb(ə)l], **-ible** [dɪˌskʌsˈɪb(ə)l] *adj.* поддаю́щийся обсужде́нию.
discussant [dɪˈskʌsənt] *n.* уча́стник диску́ссий.
discussion [dɪˈskʌʃ(ə)n] *n.* обсужде́ние, диску́ссия; **the question is under ~** вопро́с обсужда́ется/рассма́тривается.
disdain [dɪsˈdeɪn] *n.* презре́ние.
v.t. през|ира́ть, -ре́ть; пренебр|ега́ть, -е́чь +*i.*; **he ~ed to reply** он не соизво́лил отве́тить.
disdainful [dɪsˈdeɪnfʊl] *adj.* презри́тельный.
disease [dɪˈziːz] *n.* боле́знь.
diseased [dɪˈziːzd] *adj.* (*lit.*, *fig.*) больно́й.
disembark (*also* **debark**) [ˌdɪsɪmˈbɑːk] *v.t.* & *i.* выса́живать(ся), вы́садить(ся); выгружа́ть(ся), вы́грузить(ся).
disembarkation (*also* **debarkation**) [ˌdɪsɪmbɑːˈkeɪʃ(ə)n] *nn.* вы́садка, вы́грузка.
disembarrass [ˌdɪsɪmˈbærəs] *v.t.* (*disentangle*) распу́т|ывать, -ать; (*relieve*): **~ s.o. of anxiety** изб|авля́ть, -а́вить кого́-н. от трево́г.
disembarrassment [ˌdɪsɪmˈbærəsmənt] *n.* распу́тывание.
disembod|y [ˌdɪsɪmˈbɒdɪ] *v.t.* (*disband*) расформиро́в|ывать, -а́ть; (*set free from the body*) освобо|жда́ть, -ди́ть от теле́сной оболо́чки; **a ~ied spirit** освобождённая душа́.
disembogue [ˌdɪsɪmˈbəʊg] *v.i.* влива́ться, впада́ть, сбра́сывать во́ды (*all impf.*).
disembowel [ˌdɪsɪmˈbaʊəl] *v.t.* потроши́ть, вы́-.
disembowelment [ˌdɪsɪmˈbaʊəlmənt] *n.* потроше́ние.
disembroil [ˌdɪsɪmˈbrɔɪl] *v.t.* распу́т|ывать, -ать.
disenchant [ˌdɪsɪnˈtʃɑːnt] *v.t.* разочаро́в|ывать, -а́ть; освобо|жда́ть, -ди́ть от чар.
disenchantment [ˌdɪsɪnˈtʃɑːntmənt] *n.* разочарова́ние.
disencumber [ˌdɪsɪnˈkʌmbə(r)] *v.t.* освобо|жда́ть, -ди́ть.
disendow [ˌdɪsɪnˈdaʊ] *v.t.* лиш|а́ть, -и́ть поже́ртвований.
disengage [ˌdɪsɪnˈgeɪdʒ] *v.t.* высвобожда́ть, вы́свободить; освобо|жда́ть, -ди́ть.
v.i. высвобожда́ться, вы́свободиться; освобо|жда́ться, -ди́ться; выпу́тываться, вы́путаться; (*mil.*) от|рыва́ться, -орва́ться от проти́вника; выходи́ть, вы́йти из бо́я.
disengaged [ˌdɪsɪnˈgeɪdʒd] *adj.* (*vacant*; *free of engagements*) свобо́дный, неза́нятый.
disengagement [ˌdɪsɪnˈgeɪdʒmənt] *n.* (*disentangling*) освобожде́ние, высвобожде́ние; (*pol.*, *mil.*) вы́ход из бо́я; взаи́мный вы́вод вооружённых сил; (*from betrothal*) расторже́ние помо́лвки.
disentangle [ˌdɪsɪnˈtæŋg(ə)l] *v.t.* & *i.* распу́т|ывать(ся), -ать(ся); выпу́тывать(ся), вы́путать(ся).
disentanglement [ˌdɪsɪnˈtæŋgəlmənt] *n.* распу́тывание, выпу́тывание.
disentitle [ˌdɪsɪnˈtaɪt(ə)l] *v.t.* лиш|а́ть, -и́ть пра́ва (на+*a.*).
disequilibrate [ˌdɪsiːˈkwɪlɪbreɪt] *v.t.* лиш|а́ть, -и́ть равнове́сия.
disequilibrium [ˌdɪsiːkwɪˈlɪbrɪəm] *n.* неусто́йчивость; (*fig.*) неравнове́сие.
disestablish [ˌdɪsɪˈstæblɪʃ] *v.t.* (*eccl.*) отдел|я́ть, -и́ть (*церковь*) от госуда́рства.
disestablishment [ˌdɪsɪˈstæblɪʃmənt] *n.* отделе́ние це́ркви от госуда́рства.
disesteem [ˌdɪsɪˈstiːm] *n.* неуваже́ние (к+*d.*).
diseuse [diːˈzɜːz] *n.* эстра́дная актри́са.
disfavour [dɪsˈfeɪvə(r)] *n.* неми́лость, опа́ла.
v.t. не од|обря́ть, -о́брить.
disfigure [dɪsˈfɪgə(r)] *v.t.* уро́довать, из-; обезобра́|живать, -зить; **she was ~d in the accident** она́ была́ изуро́дована в катастро́фе.

disfigurement [dɪs'fɪgərmənt] *n.* обезобра́живание, уро́дство.
disfranchise [dɪs'fræntʃaɪz] *v.t.* (*pers.*) лиш|а́ть, -и́ть избира́тельного пра́ва; (*place*) лиш|а́ть, -и́ть пра́ва посыла́ть депута́та в вы́борный о́рган.
disfranchisement [dɪs'fræntʃaɪzmənt] *n.* лише́ние избира́тельного пра́ва.
disgorge [dɪs'gɔːdʒ] *v.t.* изв|ерга́ть, -е́ргнуть; **the bird ~d its prey** хи́щник вы́пустил же́ртву; (*fig., booty etc.*) возвраща́ть (*impf.*), верну́ть (*pf.*).
v.i. (*of river etc.*) влива́ться, впада́ть (*both impf.*).
disgrace [dɪs'greɪs] *n.* (*loss of respect*) бесче́стье, позо́р; **bring ~ upon, bring into ~** навл|eка́ть, -е́чь позо́р на+*a*. **2.** (*disfavour*) неми́лость, опа́ла; **he is in ~** он в неми́лости. **3.** (*cause of shame*) позо́р; **he is a ~ to the school** он позо́р для всей шко́лы.
v.t. позо́рить, о-; (*dismiss with ignominy*) разжа́ловать (*pf.*); (*bring shame upon*): **he ~d the family name** он покры́л позо́ром (*or* он опозо́рил) свою́ семью́.
disgraceful [dɪs'greɪsfʊl] *adj.* позо́рный, посты́дный, недосто́йный.
disgruntled [dɪs'grʌnt(ə)ld] *adj.* недово́льный; в дурно́м настрое́нии.
disguise [dɪs'gaɪz] *n.* **1.** (*clothing*) маскиро́вка, переодева́ние; **in the ~ of a beggar** переоде́тый ни́щим; **he gained entry under the ~ of an inspector** ему́ удало́сь пройти́ по ви́дом инспе́ктора. **2.** (*concealment*) маскиро́вка, личи́на; **it is a blessing in ~** не́ было бы сча́стья, да несча́стье помогло́.
v.t. маскирова́ть, за-; переод|ева́ть, -е́ть; **he ~d his voice/handwriting** он измени́л го́лос/по́черк; **a door ~d as a bookcase** потайна́я дверь в ви́де кни́жного шка́фа; (*fig.*): **he ~d his feelings** он скрыл свои́ чу́вства; **there is no disguising the fact that ...** для вся́кого очеви́дно, что...
disgust [dɪs'gʌst] *n.* отвраще́ние; **he resigned in ~** от возмуще́ния он ушёл с поста́.
v.t. внуш|а́ть, -и́ть отвраще́ние +*d.*; **I am ~ed by his behaviour** я возмущён его́ поведе́нием.
disgusting [dɪs'gʌstɪŋ] *adj.* отврати́тельный.
dish [dɪʃ] *n.* **1.** (*vessel*) посу́да, блю́до; **wash, do the ~es** мыть, вы- посу́ду. **2.** (*contents*) блю́до; (*type of food*) блю́до, ку́шанье; **standing ~** дежу́рное блю́до; **not my ~** (*coll.*) не в моём вку́се. **3.** (*sl., girl*) красо́тка; ла́комый кусо́чек.
v.t. **1.** (*serve; also* **~ up**) под|ава́ть, -а́ть к столу́; (*fig.*) под|ава́ть, -а́ть; преподн|оси́ть, -ести́; **~ out** (*food*) ра|скла́дывать, -зложи́ть (*еду*) по таре́лкам; выкла́дывать, вы́ложить (*еду*) на блю́до. **2.** (*coll., discomfit*) перехитри́ть (*pf.*).
cpds. **~-cloth, ~-towel** *nn.* ку́хонное/посу́дное полоте́нце; **~-cover** *n.* кры́шка; **~-washer** *n.* (*fem.*) судомо́йка; (*machine*) посудомо́ечная маши́на; **~-water** *n.* помо́|и (*pl., g.* -ев).
dishabille [ˌdɪsæ'biːl] *n.* дезабилье́ (*indecl.*).
dishabituate [ˌdɪshə'bɪtjʊˌeɪt] *v.t.* отуч|а́ть, -и́ть.
disharmonious [dɪsˌhɑː'məʊnɪəs] *adj.* дисгармони́чный; (*fig.*) в разла́де; **our relations were ~** ме́жду на́ми был разла́д.
disharmony [dɪs'hɑːmənɪ] *n.* дисгармо́ния, разла́д, разногла́сие.
dishearten [dɪs'hɑːt(ə)n] *v.t.* прив|оди́ть, -ести́ в уны́ние; **I was ~ed** я упа́л ду́хом.
dishevelled [dɪ'ʃev(ə)ld] *adj.* взъеро́шенный, всклоко́ченный, растрёпанный.
dishevelment [dɪ'ʃev(ə)lmənt] *n.* взъеро́шенность, всклоко́ченность, растрёпанность.
dishful ['dɪʃfʊl] *n.* (по́лное) блю́до (*чего*).
dishonest [dɪs'ɒnɪst] *adj.* нече́стный, бесче́стный.
dishonesty [dɪs'ɒnɪstɪ] *n.* нече́стность, бесче́стность.
dishonour [dɪs'ɒnə(r)] *n.* бесче́стье, позо́р; **he brought ~ on his family** он навлёк позо́р на свою́ семью́.
v.t. бесче́стить, о-; позо́рить, о-; **~ one's promise** не сдержа́ть (*pf.*) обеща́ния; **~ a woman** обесче́стить (*pf.*) же́нщину; (*comm.*): **~ a bill** отка́з|ывать, -а́ть в акце́пте ве́кселя.
dishonourable [dɪs'ɒnərəb(ə)l] *adj.* бесче́стный.
dishonourableness [dɪs'ɒnərəbəlnɪs] *n.* бесче́стность.
dishy ['dɪʃɪ] *adj.* (*coll.*) аппети́тный.
disillusion [ˌdɪsɪ'luːʒ(ə)n, -'ljuːʒ(ə)n] *v.t.* разочаро́в|ывать, -а́ть; разр|уша́ть, -у́шить иллю́зии +*g.*
disillusionment [ˌdɪsɪ'luːʒənmənt, -'ljuːʒənmənt] *n.* разочарова́ние; утра́та иллю́зий.
disincentive [ˌdɪsɪn'sentɪv] *n.* сде́рживающее сре́дство/обстоя́тельство.
disinclination [ˌdɪsɪnklɪ'neɪʃ(ə)n] *n.* нежела́ние, неохо́та.
disincline [ˌdɪsɪn'klaɪn] *v.t.* отб|ива́ть, -и́ть чью-н. охо́ту к+*d.*; **he was ~d to help me** ему́ не хоте́лось мне помо́чь.
disinfect [ˌdɪsɪn'fekt] *v.t.* дезинфици́ровать (*impf., pf.*); обеззара́|живать, -зить.
disinfectant [ˌdɪsɪn'fekt(ə)nt] *n.* дезинфици́рующее сре́дство.
disinfection [ˌdɪsɪn'fekʃ(ə)n] *n.* дезинфе́кция.
disinfest [ˌdɪsɪn'fest] *v.t.* (*of rats*) дератизи́ровать (*impf., pf.*); (*of insects*) дезинсекти́ровать (*impf., pf.*).
disinfestation [ˌdɪsɪnfe'steɪʃ(ə)n] *n.* дератиза́ция; дезинсе́кция.
disinformation [ˌdɪsɪnfə'meɪʃ(ə)n] *n.* дезинформа́ция.
disingenuous [ˌdɪsɪn'dʒenjʊəs] *adj.* нейскренний.
disingenuousness [ˌdɪsɪn'dʒenjʊəsnɪs] *n.* нейскренность.
disinherit [ˌdɪsɪn'herɪt] *v.t.* лиш|а́ть, -и́ть насле́дства.
disinheritance [ˌdɪsɪn'herɪtəns] *n.* лише́ние насле́дства.
disintegrate [dɪs'ɪntɪˌgreɪt] *v.t.* прив|оди́ть, -ести́ к дезинтегра́ции; дезинтегри́ровать (*impf., pf.*).
v.i. расп|ада́ться, -а́сться.
disintegration [dɪsˌɪntɪ'greɪʃ(ə)n] *n.* дезинтегра́ция, распа́д.
disinter [ˌdɪsɪn'tɜː(r)] *v.t.* эксгуми́ровать (*impf., pf.*).
disinterest [dɪs'ɪntrɪst] *n.* **1.** (*lack of bias*) беспристра́стие. **2.** (*lack of self-interest*) бескоры́стие. 3. (*lack of concern*) незаинтересо́ванность; безуча́стность.
v.t.: **~ o.s. in sth.** стать (*pf.*) безуча́стным к чему́-н.
disinterested [dɪs'ɪntrɪstɪd] *adj.* **1.** (*unprejudiced*) беспристра́стный. **2.** (*not self-seeking*) бескоры́стный. **3.** (*coll.*): **he is ~ in ballet** он не интересу́ется бале́том.
disinterestedness [dɪs'ɪntrɪstɪdnɪs] *n.* беспристра́стие; бескоры́стие; отсу́тствие интере́са.
disinterment [ˌdɪsɪn'tɜːmənt] *n.* эксгума́ция.
disinvestment [ˌdɪsɪn'vestmənt] *n.* (*econ.*) сокраще́ние капиталовложе́ний.
disjoin [dɪs'dʒɔɪn] *v.t.* разъедин|я́ть, -и́ть.
disjointed [dɪs'dʒɔɪntɪd] *adj.* (*fig.*) бессвя́зный, несвя́зный.
disjunction [dɪs'dʒʌŋkʃ(ə)n] *n.* разделе́ние, разъедине́ние.
disjunctive [dɪs'dʒʌŋktɪv] *adj.* (*separating*) разъединя́ющий; (*gram.*) раздели́тельный.
disk [dɪsk] = **disc**
diskette [dɪ'sket] *n.* (*comput.*) диске́т.
dislikable [dɪs'laɪkəb(ə)l] *adj.* неприя́тный, антипати́чный.
dislike [dɪs'laɪk] *n.* неприя́знь, нелюбо́вь, нерасположе́ние, антипа́тия; **I took a ~ to him** я невзлюби́л его́.
v.t. не люби́ть (*impf.*) +*g.*; недолю́бливать (*impf.*) +*a. or g.*; **I ~ having to go** мне неохо́та идти́; **he made himself ~d** он вы́звал к себе́ неприя́знь.
dislocate ['dɪsləˌkeɪt] *v.t.* вы́вихнуть (*pf.*); (*fig.*): **traffic was ~d** движе́ние бы́ло нару́шено.
dislocation [ˌdɪslə'keɪʃ(ə)n] *n.* вы́вих; наруше́ние.
dislodge [dɪs'lɒdʒ] *v.t.* сме|ща́ть, -сти́ть; (*evict*) выбива́ть, вы́бить; вытесня́ть, вы́теснить.
dislodgement [dɪs'lɒdʒmənt] *n.* смеще́ние, вытесне́ние.
disloyal [dɪs'lɔɪəl] *adj.* нелоя́льный, неве́рный.
disloyalty [dɪs'lɔɪəltɪ] *n.* нелоя́льность, неве́рность.
dismal ['dɪzm(ə)l] *adj.* мра́чный, уны́лый, гнету́щий.
dismalness ['dɪzməlnɪs] *n.* мра́чность, уны́лость.
dismantle [dɪs'mænt(ə)l] *v.t.* (*strip of defences etc.*) демонти́ровать (*impf., pf.*); (*ship*) рассна́|щивать, -сти́ть; (*fortress*) сры|ва́ть, -ть; (*take to pieces*) раз|бира́ть, -обра́ть.
dismast [dɪs'mɑːst] *v.t.*: **the ship was ~ed in the storm** бу́рей обломáло ма́чты корабля́.
dismay [dɪs'meɪ] *n.* смяте́ние, потрясе́ние.
v.t. прив|оди́ть, -ести́ в смяте́ние; потрясти́ (*pf.*).
dismember [dɪs'membə(r)] *v.t.* расчлен|я́ть, -и́ть; (*fig.*) раздел|я́ть, -и́ть.

dismemberment [dɪs'membəmənt] *n.* расчлене́ние, разделе́ние.

dismiss [dɪs'mɪs] *n.*: **the ~** (*mil.*) кома́нда «разойди́сь!».

v.t. **1.** (*send away*) распус|ка́ть, -ти́ть; отпус|ка́ть, -ти́ть; **he ~ed her with a nod** он отпусти́л её кивко́м головы́. **2.** (*discharge from service*) ув|ольня́ть, -о́лить; удал|я́ть, -и́ть; прог|оня́ть, -на́ть. **3.** (*put out of consideration, reject*): **he ~ed it from his mind** он вы́бросил э́то из головы́; **the argument is not to be ~ed lightly** нельзя́ от э́того до́вода про́сто отмахну́ться; **I ~ed the idea** я оста́вил э́ту мысль; я отказа́лся от э́той мы́сли; (*defeat adversary*) разб|ива́ть, -и́ть. **4.** (*leg.*): (*a case*) прекра|ща́ть, -ти́ть; (*an appeal*) отклон|я́ть, -и́ть.

dismissal [dɪs'mɪsəl] *n.* ро́спуск, отстране́ние; (*from service*) увольне́ние.

dismissive [dɪs'mɪsɪv] *adj.* (*contemptuous*) презри́тельный.

dismount [dɪs'maʊnt] *v.t.* (*e.g. an opponent*) выбива́ть, вы́бить из седла́; (*e.g. a gun*) сн|има́ть, -ять с лафе́та.

v.i. (*from horse*) спе́ши|ваться, -ться; (*from vehicle etc.*) сходи́ть, сойти́.

disobedience [ˌdɪsə'bi:dɪəns] *n.* неповинове́ние, непослуша́ние, ослуша́ние.

disobedient [ˌdɪsə'bi:dɪənt] *adj.* непослу́шный.

disobey [ˌdɪsə'beɪ] *v.t.* не слу́шаться, по- +*g.*; не повинова́ться (*impf., pf.*) +*d.*; **my orders were ~ed** мои́ приказа́ния не́ были вы́полнены.

disoblige [ˌdɪsə'blaɪdʒ] *v.t.* не счита́ться (*impf.*) с жела́ниями +*g.*; поступ|а́ть, -и́ть нелюбе́зно с+*i.*

disobliging [ˌdɪsə'blaɪdʒɪŋ] *adj.* нелюбе́зный.

disorder [dɪs'ɔ:də(r)] *n.* (*untidiness*) беспоря́док; (*confusion*) расстро́йство, разбро́д, неуря́дица; (*riot*) беспоря́дки (*m. pl.*); (*med.*) расстро́йство; **mental ~** психи́ческое наруше́ние/расстро́йство.

v.t. расстр|а́ивать, -о́ить; прив|оди́ть, -ести́ в беспоря́док.

disorderliness [dɪs'ɔ:dəlɪnɪs] *n.* беспоря́док; бу́йство.

disorderly [dɪs'ɔ:dəlɪ] *adj.* (*untidy*) беспоря́дочный; (*unruly*) бу́йный, беспоко́йный; **~ conduct** хулига́нство; **~ house** дом терпи́мости.

disorganization [dɪsˌɔ:gənaɪ'zeɪʃ(ə)n] *n.* дезорганиза́ция.

disorganize [dɪs'ɔ:gəˌnaɪz] *v.t.* дезорганизова́ть (*impf., pf.*).

disorient(ate) [dɪs'ɔ:rɪənˌteɪt] *v.t.* дезориенти́ровать (*impf., pf.*).

disorientation [dɪsˌɔ:rɪən'teɪʃ(ə)n] *n.* дезориента́ция.

disown [dɪs'əʊn] *v.t.* отка́з|ываться, -а́ться от+*g.*; отр|ека́ться, -е́чься от+*g.*

disownment [dɪs'əʊnmənt] *n.* отка́з, отрече́ние (от+*g.*).

disparage [dɪ'spærɪdʒ] *v.t.* (*belittle*) преум|еньша́ть, -е́ньшить; очерн|я́ть, -и́ть; говори́ть (*impf.*) с пренебреже́нием о+*p.*

disparagement [dɪ'spærɪdʒmənt] *n.* преуменьше́ние, очерне́ние.

disparaging [dɪ'spærɪdʒɪŋ] *adj.* неле́стный, пренебрежи́тельный.

disparate ['dɪspərət] *adj.* разнообра́зный, несоотве́тственный.

disparity [dɪ'spærɪtɪ] *n.* расхожде́ние, несоотве́тствие.

dispassionate [dɪ'spæʃənət] *adj.* бесстра́стный.

dispassionateness [dɪ'spæʃənətnɪs] *n.* бесстра́стность.

dispatch, despatch [dɪ'spætʃ] *n.* **1.** (*sending off*) отпра́вка. **2.** (*message*) депе́ша, донесе́ние; **he was mentioned in ~es** его́ и́мя упомина́лось в донесе́ниях. **3.** (*promptitude*) быстрота́.

v.t. **1.** (*send off*) отпр|авля́ть, -а́вить; экспеди́ровать (*impf., pf.*); пос|ыла́ть, -ла́ть. **2.** (*deal with, e.g. business*) спр|авля́ться, -а́виться с+*i.* **3.** (*of meal etc.*) разде́л|ываться, -аться с+*i.* **4.** (*kill*) поко́нчить (*pf.*) с+*i.*; отпр|авля́ть, -а́вить на тот свет.

cpds. **~-boat, ~-vessel** *nn.* посы́льное су́дно; **~-case** *n.* полева́я су́мка; **~-rider** *n.* мотоцикли́ст свя́зи.

dispatcher [dɪ'spætʃə(r)] *n.* (*sender*) отправи́тель (*m.*); (*of business etc.*) экспеди́тор; (*regulator*) диспе́тчер.

dispel [dɪ'spel] *v.t.* рассе́|ивать, -ять.

dispensable [dɪ'spensəb(ə)l] *adj.* необяза́тельный, несуще́ственный.

dispensary [dɪ'spensərɪ] *n.* апте́ка; (*clinic*) амбулато́рия.

dispensation [ˌdɪspen'seɪʃ(ə)n] *n.* **1.** (*dealing out*) разда́ча. **2.** (*order*): **a ~ of providence** боже́ственный про́мысл; **under the Mosaic ~** по моисе́еву зако́ну. **3.** (*exemption*) освобожде́ние, исключе́ние.

dispens|e [dɪ'spens] *v.t.* **1.** (*deal out*) разд|ава́ть, -а́ть; распредел|я́ть, -и́ть. **2.** (*of prescription*) пригот|овля́ть, -о́вить; **~ing chemist** апте́карь (*m.*), фармаце́вт. **3.** (*release*) освобо|жда́ть, -ди́ть (*от чего*).

v.i. **~ with** (*do without*) об|ходи́ться, -ойти́сь без+*g.*; (*make unnecessary*): **this machine ~es with labour** э́та маши́на высвобожда́ет рабо́чие ру́ки.

dispenser [dɪ'spensə(r)] *n.* **1.** (*one who deals out*) раздаю́щий, распределя́ющий; **~ of justice** отправля́ющий правосу́дие. **2.** (*of medicines*) фармаце́вт; **3.** (*container*) торго́вый автома́т; **razor-blade ~** автома́т с безопа́сными бри́твами; **toilet-paper ~** автома́т с туале́тной бума́гой.

dispers|al [dɪ'spɜ:səl], **-ion** [dɪ'spɜ:ʃ(ə)n] *nn.* рассредото́чение, рассе́ивание; разго́н.

disperse [dɪ'spɜ:s] *v.t.* рассе́|ивать, -ять; раз|гоня́ть, -огна́ть; **the policeman ~d the crowd** полице́йский разогна́л толпу́; **the troops were ~d over a wide front** войска́ бы́ли рассредото́чены по широ́кому фро́нту; **he ~s his energies** он разбра́сывается.

v.i. рассе́|иваться, -яться; ра|сходи́ться, -зойти́сь.

dispersion [dɪ'spɜ:ʃ(ə)n] *n.* **1.** = **dispersal. 2.: Jews of the D~** иуде́йская диа́спора.

dispirit [dɪ'spɪrɪt] *v.t.* удруч|а́ть, -и́ть; прив|оди́ть, -ести́ в уны́ние.

displace [dɪs'pleɪs] *v.t.* **1.** (*put in wrong place*) сме|ща́ть, -сти́ть; **~d persons** перемещённые ли́ца. **2.** (*replace*) заме|ща́ть, -сти́ть; вытесня́ть, вы́теснить; **he ~d his rival in her affections** он вы́теснил своего́ сопе́рника из её се́рдца.

displacement [dɪs'pleɪsmənt] *n.* (*ousting*) смеще́ние, вытесне́ние; (*replacement*) замеще́ние; (*of ship*) водоизмеще́ние; (*geol.*) сдвиг.

display [dɪ'spleɪ] *n.* **1.** (*manifestation*) пока́з, проявле́ние. **2.** (*ostentation*) хвастовство́; **he made a ~ of his wealth** он кичи́лся свои́м бога́тством. **3.** (*of goods etc.*) вы́ставка; **there was a fine ~ of flowers at the show** на вы́ставке бы́ло мно́го изуми́тельных цвето́в. **4.** (*of computer*) диспле́й.

v.t. прояв|ля́ть, -и́ть; обнару́жи|вать, -ть; (*goods etc.*) выставля́ть, вы́ставить (на пока́з); **he ~s his ignorance** он выка́зывает своё неве́жество; **the peacock ~ed its tail** павли́н распусти́л свой хвост.

displease [dɪs'pli:z] *v.t.* не нра́виться (*impf.*) +*d.*; серди́ть, рас-; вызыва́ть, вы́звать недово́льство +*g.*; **he was ~d at this** ему́ э́то не понра́вилось; **I am ~d with you** я недово́лен ва́ми.

displeasing [dɪs'pli:zɪŋ] *adj.* неприя́тный.

displeasure [dɪs'pleʒə(r)] *n.* недово́льство, неудово́льствие; **incur s.o.'s ~** навл|ека́ть, -е́чь на себя́ (*or* вызыва́ть, вы́звать) чьё-н. недово́льство.

disport [dɪ'spɔ:t] *v.t.*: **~ o.s.** резви́ться (*impf.*).

disposable [dɪ'spəʊzəb(ə)l] *adj.* (*available*) име́ющийся в распоряже́нии; (*for use once only*) однора́зового по́льзования; выбра́сываемый.

disposal [dɪ'spəʊz(ə)l] *n.* **1.** (*bestowing*) переда́ча. **2.** (*getting rid of*) избавле́ние, удале́ние, убо́рка; **the ~ of rubbish** удале́ние му́сора; **bomb ~** обезвре́живание бомб. **3.** (*arrangement*) размеще́ние. **4.** (*management, control*) распоряже́ние; **the money is at your ~** де́ньги в ва́шем распоряже́нии.

dispose [dɪ'spəʊz] *v.t.* **1.** (*arrange*) распол|ага́ть, -ожи́ть. **2.** (*determine*) распол|ага́ть, -ожи́ть; **man proposes, God ~s** челове́к предполага́ет, а Госпо́дь располага́ет. **3.** (*incline*) склон|я́ть, -и́ть; **this ~s me to believe that ...** э́то склоня́ет меня́ к тому мне́нию, что...; **I am not ~d to help him** я не скло́нен ему́ помога́ть; **do you feel ~d for a walk?** располо́жены/хоти́те ли вы погуля́ть?; **he is well ~d towards me** он ко мне хорошо́ отно́сится.

v.i. (*with prep.* **of**) **1.** (*get rid of*) отде́л|ываться, -аться от+*g.*; изб|авля́ться, -а́виться от+*g.* **2.** (*make use of*) распоря|жа́ться, -ди́ться +*i.* **3.** (*bestow, sell*) распоря|жа́ться, -ди́ться +*i.*; **~ of one's daughters in marriage** отд|ава́ть,

-ать дочерей замуж. **4.** (*deal with*): **he ~d of his work/dinner** он управился с работой/обедом. **5.** (*account for, overcome*) разделаться (*pf.*) с+*i.*; **that argument is soon ~d of** этот аргумент легко опровергнуть.

disposition [ˌdɪspəˈzɪʃ(ə)n] *n.* **1.** (*arrangement*) расположение; (*of troops*) диспозиция, дислокация; (*of furniture*) размещение; **he made ~s to withstand the attack** он приготовился к отражению атаки/нападения. **2.** (*character*) нрав, характер; **he has a cheerful ~** у него весёлый нрав. **3.** (*inclination*) склонность; **there was a general ~ to leave early** большинство было склонно уйти рано. **4.** (*order, control*) распоряжение; **a ~ of Providence** божественный промысл, провидение. **5.** (*bestowal*) распоряжение; **who has the ~ of this property?** в чьём распоряжении эта собственность?

dispossess [ˌdɪspəˈzes] *v.t.* лиш|ать, -ить (*кого чего*); от|бирать, -обрать (*что у кого*).

dispossession [ˌdɪspəˈzeʃ(ə)n] *n.* лишение (собственности); (*eviction*) выселение.

dispraise [dɪsˈpreɪz] *n.* осуждение, неодобрение.

v.t. осу|ждать, -дить.

disproof [dɪsˈpruːf] *n.* опровержение.

disproportion [ˌdɪsprəˈpɔːʃ(ə)n] *n.* диспропорция.

disproportionate [ˌdɪsprəˈpɔːʃənət] *adj.* непропорциональный, несоответствующий, чрезмерный.

disprove [dɪsˈpruːv] *v.t.* опров|ергать, -ергнуть.

disputable [dɪˈspjuːtəb(ə)l, ˈdɪspjʊ-] *adj.* спорный, недоказанный.

disputant [dɪˈspjuːt(ə)nt] *n.* диспутант, спорщик.

disputation [ˌdɪspjuːˈteɪʃ(ə)n] *n.* диспут, спор.

disputatious [ˌdɪspjuːˈteɪʃ(ə)s] *adj.* любящий спорить.

dispute [dɪˈspjuːt, ˈdɪspjuːt] *n.* **1.** (*debate, argument*) диспут; **the ownership of the house is in ~** право собственности на этот дом оспаривается; **beyond, past ~** бесспорно, вне всяких сомнений. **2.** (*quarrel*) ссора, разногласие.

v.t. **1.** (*call in question, oppose*) осп|аривать, -орить; **I ~ that point** я оспариваю этот пункт; **our team ~d the victory** наша команда добивалась победы; **the will was ~d** завещание было опротестовано.

v.i. (*argue*) спорить, по-; **they ~d whether to wait or not** они спорили, ждать им или нет; **there is no ~ing about tastes** о вкусах не спорят.

disqualification [dɪsˌkwɒlɪfɪˈkeɪʃ(ə)n] *n.* дисквалификация; **age is no ~** возраст — не помеха/препятствие.

disqualify [dɪsˈkwɒlɪˌfaɪ] *v.t.* дисквалифицировать (*impf., pf.*).

disquiet [dɪsˈkwaɪət] *n.* беспокойство.

v.t. беспокоить, о-.

disquieting [dɪsˈkwaɪətɪŋ] *adj.* тревожный, беспокойный; **a ~ly high proportion of mistakes** количество ошибок, вызывающее тревогу.

disquietude [dɪsˈkwaɪəˌtjuːd] *n.* беспокойство.

disquisition [ˌdɪskwɪˈzɪʃ(ə)n] *n.* (*treatise*) трактат; (*discourse*) рассуждение.

disregard [ˌdɪsrɪˈgɑːd] *n.* пренебрежение +*i.*; игнорирование +*g.*; **he showed ~ for his teachers** он проявлял неуважение к учителям.

v.t. пренебр|егать, -ечь +*i.*; игнорировать (*impf., pf.*).

disrelish [dɪsˈrelɪʃ] *n.* нерасположение.

disremember [ˌdɪsrɪˈmembə(r)] *v.t.* (*coll.*) не помнить (*impf.*) +*g.*

disrepair [ˌdɪsrɪˈpeə(r)] *n.* неисправность; **the house is in ~** дом в запущенном состоянии; **fall into ~** при|ходить, -йти в упадок/запустение.

disreputable [dɪsˈrepjʊtəb(ə)l] *adj.* позорный, неприличный; пользующийся дурной славой; **a ~ old hat** изношенная, грязная шляпа.

disrepute [ˌdɪsrɪˈpjuːt] *n.* дурная слава; **fall into ~** приобре|тать, -сти дурную славу.

disrespect [ˌdɪsrɪˈspekt] *n.* неуважение (к+*d.*); непочтение; непочтительность.

disrespectful [ˌdɪsrɪˈspektfʊl] *adj.* непочтительный.

disrobe [dɪsˈrəʊb] *v.t. & i.* (*undress*) разд|евать(ся), -еть(ся); (*take off robes*) разоблач|ать(ся), -ить(ся).

disrupt [dɪsˈrʌpt] *v.t.* под|рывать, -орвать; срывать, сорвать.

disruption [dɪsˈrʌpʃ(ə)n] *n.* подрыв, срыв; (*geol.*) распад.

disruptive [dɪsˈrʌptɪv] *adj.* разрушительный, подрывной.

dissatisfaction [ˌdɪsætɪsˈfækʃ(ə)n] *n.* неудовлетворённость, недовольство, неудовольствие.

dissatisf|y [dɪˈsætɪsˌfaɪ] *v.t.* не удовлетвор|ять, -ить; **he is ~ied with his job** он недоволен своей работой.

dissect [dɪˈsekt] *v.t.* (*anatomize*) препарировать (*impf., pf.*); вскр|ывать, -ыть; (*fig.*) раз|бирать, -обрать.

dissection [dɪˈsekʃ(ə)n] *n.* препарирование, вскрытие; разбор.

dissemble [dɪˈsemb(ə)l] *v.t.* скры|вать, -ть; **he ~s his emotions** он скрывает свои чувства; **~ a fact** ум|алчивать, -олчать о факте.

v.i. притвор|яться, -иться; прикидываться (*impf.*); лицемерить (*impf.*).

dissembler [dɪˈsemblə(r)] *n.* притворщик, лицемер.

dissembling [dɪˈsemblɪŋ] *n.* притворство.

adj. притворный, притворяющийся.

disseminate [dɪˈsemɪˌneɪt] *v.t.* распростран|ять, -ить.

dissemination [dɪˌsemɪˈneɪʃ(ə)n] *n.* распространение.

disseminator [dɪˈsemɪˌneɪtə(r)] *n.* распространитель (*m.*); сеятель (*m.*).

dissension [dɪˈsenʃ(ə)n] *n.* разногласие, разлад, раздор.

dissent [dɪˈsent] *n.* несогласие; (*eccl.*) раскол, сектантство; **~ing opinion** (*leg.*) особое мнение.

dissenter [dɪˈsentə(r)] *n.* диссидент; (*rebel*) бунтарь (*m.*); (*eccl.*) раскольник, сектант.

dissentient [dɪˈsenʃ(ə)nt] *n. & adj.* несогласный; **the motion was passed with one ~ vote** предложение было принято при одном голосе против.

dissertation [ˌdɪsəˈteɪʃ(ə)n] *n.* (*thesis*) диссертация; (*discourse*) рассуждение.

disservice [dɪsˈsɜːvɪs] *n.* плохая услуга, ущерб; **he did me a ~** он оказал мне плохую услугу; он повредил мне; **his words did great ~ to the cause** его слова нанесли большой ущерб делу.

dissever [dɪˈsevə(r)] *v.t.* раздел|ять, -ить; разъедин|ять, -ить.

dissidence [ˈdɪsɪd(ə)ns] *n.* несогласие, инакомыслие.

dissident [ˈdɪsɪd(ə)nt] *n.* несогласный, диссидент, инакомыслящий.

adj. несогласный, диссидентский.

dissimilar [dɪˈsɪmɪlə(r)] *adj.* несходный.

dissimilarity [ˌdɪsɪmɪˈlærɪtɪ] *n.* несходство.

dissimilate [dɪˈsɪmɪˌleɪt] *v.t. & i.* (*ling.*) диссимилировать(ся) (*impf., pf.*).

dissimilation [ˈdɪsɪmɪˈleɪʃ(ə)n] *n.* диссимиляция.

dissimulate [dɪˈsɪmjʊˌleɪt] *v.t.* скры|вать, -ть, таить (*impf.*).

v.i. лицемерить (*impf.*); притворяться (*impf.*).

dissimulation [dɪˌsɪmjʊˈleɪʃ(ə)n] *n.* лицемерие, притворство.

dissimulator [dɪˈsɪmjʊˌleɪtə(r)] *n.* лицемер, притворщик.

dissipate [ˈdɪsɪˌpeɪt] *v.t.* (*lit., fig.*) рассе|ивать, -ять; (*squander*) растра|чивать, -тить; пром|атывать, -отать.

dissipated [ˈdɪsɪˌpeɪtɪd] *adj.* беспутный, разгульный.

dissipation [ˌdɪsɪˈpeɪʃ(ə)n] *n.* беспутство, разгул.

dis|sociate [dɪˈsəʊʃɪˌeɪt, -sɪˌeɪt], **-associate** [ˌdɪsəˈsəʊʃɪˌeɪt, -sɪˌeɪt] *v.t.* (*disunite*) разобщ|ать, -ить; разъедин|ять, -ить; **I ~ myself from what has been said** я отмежёвываюсь от того, что было сказано; (*think of as separate*) диссоциировать (*impf., pf.*).

dissociation [dɪˌsəʊsɪˈeɪʃ(ə)n, -ʃɪˈeɪʃ(ə)n] *n.* разобщение, диссоциация.

dissolubility [dɪˌsɒljʊˈbɪlɪtɪ] *n.* (*phys.*) растворимость; (*of contract*) расторжимость.

dissoluble [dɪˈsɒljʊb(ə)l] *adj.* (*phys.*) растворимый; (*of contract*) расторжимый.

dissolute [ˈdɪsəˌluːt, -ˌljuːt] *adj.* распущенный, беспутный, распутный.

dissoluteness [ˈdɪsəˌluːtnɪs, -ˌljuːtnɪs] *n.* распущенность, беспутство, распутство.

dissolution [ˌdɪsəˈluːʃ(ə)n, -ˈljuːʃ(ə)n] *n.* (*phys.*) растворение; (*death*) кончина; (*of marriage etc.*) расторжение; (*of parliament*) роспуск.

dissolvable [dɪˈzɒlvəb(ə)l] *adj.* разложимый, расторжимый.

dissolve [dɪˈzɒlv] *v.t.* **1.** (*phys.*) раствор|ять, -ить. **2.: the queen ~d parliament** королева распустила парламент.

3. (*marriage*) раст|орга́ть, -о́ргнуть; **the marriage was ~d** брак был расто́ргнут.

v.i. (*phys.*) раствор|я́ться, -и́ться; **she ~d into tears** она́ залила́сь слеза́ми.

dissolvent [dɪˈzɒlv(ə)nt] *n.* раствори́тель (*m.*).

adj. растворя́ющий.

dissonance [ˈdɪsənəns] *n.* диссона́нс; неблагозву́чие.

dissonant [ˈdɪsənənt] *adj.* диссони́рующий, нестро́йный.

dissuade [dɪˈsweɪd] *v.t.* отгов|а́ривать, -ори́ть (*кого от чего*); отсове́товать (*pf.*) (*что кому*).

dissuasion [dɪˈsweɪʒ(ə)n] *n.* отгова́ривание.

dissymmetrical [ˌdɪsɪˈmetrɪk(ə)l] *adj.* несимметри́чный, асимметри́чный.

dissymmetry [dɪˈsɪmɪtrɪ] *n.* несимметри́чность, асимме́трия.

distaff [ˈdɪstɑːf] *n.* пря́лка; **on the ~ side** по же́нской ли́нии.

distance [ˈdɪst(ə)ns] *n.* **1.** (*measure of space*) диста́нция, расстоя́ние; **it can be seen from a ~ of two miles** э́то ви́дно с расстоя́ния двух миль; **it is some ~ to the school** до шко́лы дово́льно далеко́; **no ~ at all** совсе́м недалеко́; **he lives within walking ~ of the office** от его́ до́ма до рабо́ты мо́жно дойти́ пешко́м; **at what ~?** на како́м расстоя́нии?; **in the ~** вдалеке́; **from a ~** и́здали, издалека́; **middle ~** сре́дний план. **2.** (*of time*) промежу́ток вре́мени; **at this ~ of time I cannot remember** я не могу́ э́того по́мнить сто́лько вре́мени спустя́. **3.** (*fig.*): **keep one's ~** держа́ться (*impf.*) в стороне́ (от+*g.*); **keep s.o. at a ~** держа́ть (*impf.*) кого́-н. на (почти́тельном) расстоя́нии.

v.t. (*in race etc.*) опере|жа́ть, -ди́ть.

distant [ˈdɪst(ə)nt] *adj.* **1.** (*in space*) далёкий, да́льний, отдалённый; **the school is three miles ~** шко́ла нахо́дится на расстоя́нии трёх миль; **we had a ~ view of the mountains** вдали́ мы ви́дели го́ры. **2.** (*in time*) далёкий. **3.** (*fig.*, *remote*): **a ~ cousin** да́льний ро́дственник; **a ~ likeness** отдалённое схо́дство. **4.** (*reserved*) сде́ржанный, холо́дный.

distaste [dɪsˈteɪst] *n.* отвраще́ние (к+*d.*).

distasteful [dɪsˈteɪstfʊl] *adj.* проти́вный, неприя́тный.

distemper[1] [dɪˈstempə(r)] *n.* (*ailment*) нездоро́вье; (*of mind*) душе́вное расстро́йство; (*of dogs*) соба́чья чума́.

v.t.: **a ~ed fancy** расстро́енное воображе́ние.

distemper[2] [dɪˈstempə(r)] *n.* (*method of painting*) те́мпера; (*type of paint*) клеева́я кра́ска.

v.t. кра́сить, по- клеево́й кра́ской.

distend [dɪˈstend] *v.t.* & *i.* над|ува́ть(ся), -у́ть(ся); раз|дува́ть(ся), -у́ть(ся).

distensible [dɪˈstensɪb(ə)l] *adj.* растяжи́мый.

distension [dɪˈstenʃ(ə)n] *n.* расшире́ние, растяже́ние.

distich [ˈdɪstɪk] *n.* ди́стих.

distil [dɪˈstɪl] *v.t.* дистилли́ровать (*impf.*, *pf.*); (*e.g. salt water*) опресн|я́ть, -и́ть; **~ whisky** гнать (*det.*) ви́ски; **the flowers ~ nectar** цветы́ выделя́ют некта́р; (*fig.*): **to ~ poison into s.o.'s mind** отрави́ть (*pf.*) чей-н. ум.

v.i. сочи́ться (*impf.*); ос|еда́ть, -е́сть ка́плями.

distillate [ˈdɪstɪˌleɪt] *n.* дистилля́т.

distillation [ˌdɪstɪˈleɪʃ(ə)n] *n.* (*process*) дистилля́ция, перего́нка; винокуре́ние; (*substance*) дистилля́т.

distiller [dɪˈstɪlə(r)] *n.* дистилля́тор, виноку́р.

distillery [dɪˈstɪlərɪ] *n.* виноку́ренный заво́д.

distinct [dɪˈstɪŋkt] *adj.* **1.** (*clear, perceptible*) вня́тный, отчётливый; **a ~ improvement** заме́тное улучше́ние. **2.** (*different*) отли́чный (от+*g.*).

distinction [dɪˈstɪŋkʃ(ə)n] *n.* **1.** (*difference*) отли́чие. **2.** (*discrimination*) разли́чие; **a ~ without a difference** несуще́ственное разли́чие; **without ~ of rank** без разли́чия зва́ний. **3.** (*special or superior quality*) отличи́тельная осо́бенность; **a writer of ~** выдаю́щийся писа́тель; **his style lacks ~** его́ стиль не отлича́ется оригина́льностью. **4.** (*mark of honour*) отли́чие; **he received several ~s** он получи́л не́сколько зна́ков отли́чия.

distinctive [dɪˈstɪŋktɪv] *adj.* отличи́тельный, различи́тельный; характе́рный, осо́бый.

distinctly [dɪˈstɪŋktlɪ] *adv.* отчётливо, определённо; (*perceptibly*) заме́тно; **~ better** значи́тельно лу́чше; **he spoke ~** он говори́л вня́тно/чётко; **I ~ heard** я я́сно слы́шал.

distinctness [dɪˈstɪŋktnɪs] *n.* отчётливость, определённость.

distinguish [dɪˈstɪŋgwɪʃ] *v.t.* 1. (*perceive*) разли́ч|а́ть, -и́ть; разгля́д|ывать, -е́ть. **2.** (*discern or point out difference*) различ|а́ть, -и́ть. **3.** (*characterize*) отлич|а́ть, -и́ть. **4.**: **~** (*do credit to*) **o.s.** отлич|а́ться, -и́ться.

distinguishable [dɪˈstɪŋgwɪʃəb(ə)l] *adj.* (*visible*) различи́мый, заме́тный; (*different*) отличи́мый.

distinguished [dɪˈstɪŋgwɪʃt] *adj.* выдаю́щийся.

distort [dɪˈstɔːt] *v.t.* иска|жа́ть, -зи́ть; искрив|ля́ть, -и́ть; **~ facts** извра|ща́ть, -ти́ть (*or* передёр|гивать, -нуть) фа́кты.

distortion [dɪˈstɔːʃ(ə)n] *n.* искаже́ние, искривле́ние, извраще́ние.

distract [dɪˈstrækt] *v.t.* **1.** (*draw away*; *make inattentive*) отвл|ека́ть, -е́чь; **it ~s me from my work** э́то отвлека́ет меня́ от рабо́ты. **2.** (*fig.*, *tear apart*) раздира́ть (*impf.*); **he was ~ed between love and duty** он разрыва́лся ме́жду любо́вью и до́лгом. **3.** (*derange mentally*) св|оди́ть, -ести́ с ума́; **he drove her ~ed** он довёл её до безу́мия.

distraction [dɪˈstrækʃ(ə)n] *n.* (*act of diverting*) отвлече́ние; (*cause of inattention*) поме́ха; (*amusement*) развлече́ние; (*frenzy, derangement*) безу́мие; **he loves her to ~** он безу́мно (*or* без па́мяти) её лю́бит; **drive s.o. to ~** дов|оди́ть, -ести́ кого́-н. до безу́мия.

distrain [dɪˈstreɪn] *v.i.* (*leg.*) опи́с|ывать, -а́ть иму́щество за долги́; **~ upon s.o.'s goods** на|кла́дывать, ложи́ть аре́ст на чьи́-н. това́ры для обеспече́ния до́лга.

distraint [dɪˈstreɪnt] *n.* (*leg.*) наложе́ние аре́ста на иму́щество в обеспече́ние до́лга.

distrait [dɪˈstreɪ] *adj.* рассе́янный.

distraught [dɪˈstrɔːt] *adj.* обезу́мевший.

distress [dɪˈstres] *n.* **1.** (*physical suffering*) утомле́ние, изнеможе́ние; **the runner showed signs of ~** бегу́н заме́тно утоми́лся. **2.** (*mental suffering*) огорче́ние, го́ре. **3.** (*indigence*) бе́дность, нужда́. **4.** (*danger*) бе́дствие; **a ship in ~** су́дно, те́рпящее бе́дствие.

v.t. **1.** (*grieve*) причин|я́ть, -и́ть огорче́ние/го́ре +*d.*; огорч|а́ть, -и́ть. **2.** (*impoverish*) истощ|а́ть, -и́ть; **~ed area** райо́н бе́дствия.

distressful [dɪˈstresfʊl] *adj.* го́рестный, бе́дственный.

distressing [dɪˈstresɪŋ] *adj.* огорчи́тельный; **his account was ~ly vague** его́ отчёт огорчи́л нас свое́й неопределённостью.

distributable [dɪˈstrɪbjuːtəb(ə)l] *adj.* подлежа́щий распределе́нию.

distribute [dɪˈstrɪbjuːt, ˈdɪ-] *v.t.* **1.** (*deal out*) распредел|я́ть, -и́ть; разд|ава́ть, -а́ть. **2.** (*spread*) ра|скла́дывать, -зложи́ть; **~ manure over a field** разбр|а́сывать, -оса́ть наво́з по́ полю; **wealth is unfairly ~d** бога́тства распределя́ются несправедли́во; **~ a load evenly** равноме́рно распредел|я́ть, -и́ть груз. **3.** (*classify*): **~ books into classes** распредел|я́ть, -и́ть кни́ги по отде́лам.

distribution [ˌdɪstrɪˈbjuːʃ(ə)n] *n.* **1.** (*dealing out, spreading*) распределе́ние, разда́ча; **the ~ of population is uneven** населе́ние распределено́ неравноме́рно; **~ of prizes** разда́ча награ́д. **2.** (*marketing*) распределе́ние, распростране́ние. **3.** (*classification*) распределе́ние.

distributive [dɪˈstrɪbjʊtɪv] *adj.* распредели́тельный; **the ~ trades** ро́зничная торго́вля; (*gram.*) раздели́тельный.

distributor [dɪˈstrɪbjʊtə(r)] *n.* распредели́тель (*m.*); (*tech.*) распредели́тель (*m.*) зажига́ния.

district [ˈdɪstrɪkt] *n.* райо́н, о́круг; (*attr.*) райо́нный, окружно́й; **consular ~** ко́нсульский о́круг; **postal ~** почто́вый райо́н; (*US*, *constituency*) избира́тельный уча́сток; **D~ of Columbia** о́круг Колу́мбия; **~ attorney** окружно́й прокуро́р.

distrust [dɪsˈtrʌst] *n.* недове́рие.

v.t. не доверя́ть (*impf.*) +*d.*

distrustful [dɪsˈtrʌstfʊl] *adj.* недове́рчивый.

disturb [dɪˈstɜːb] *v.t.* беспоко́ить, о-; меша́ть, по- +*d.*; нар|уша́ть, -у́шить; **~ s.o.'s sleep** нар|уша́ть, -у́шить чей-н. сон; **~ the surface of the water** баламу́тить, взво́ду; **do not ~ yourself** не беспоко́йтесь; **he was ~ed by the news** он был обеспоко́ен но́востью; **his mind was ~ed** у него́ помути́лся рассу́док; **~ the peace** вызыва́ть, вы́звать обще́ственные беспоря́дки; **do not ~ these papers** не тро́гайте э́ти бума́ги.

disturbance [dɪ'stɜ:bəns] *n.* (*act of troubling*) наруше́ние; (*cause of trouble*) трево́га; (*riot*) волне́ния (*nt. pl.*); беспоря́дки (*m. pl.*).

disturbing [dɪ'stɜ:bɪŋ] *adj.* трево́жный.

disunion [dɪs'ju:nɪən] *n.* (*separation*) разобще́ние; (*discord*) разла́д.

disunite ['dɪsju:'naɪt] *v.t.* (*separate, estrange*) разобщ|а́ть, -и́ть; разъедин|я́ть, -и́ть.

disuse [dɪs'ju:s] *n.* забро́шенность, неупотребле́ние; **fall into ~** выходи́ть, вы́йти из употребле́ния.

disused [dɪs'ju:sd] *adj.*: **a ~ well** забро́шенный коло́дец.

disyllabic [ˌdɪsɪ'læbɪk, ˌdaɪ-] *adj.* двусло́жный.

disyllable [dɪ'sɪləb(ə)l, 'daɪ-] *n.* двусло́жное сло́во.

ditch [dɪtʃ] *n.* кана́ва; ров; **die in a ~** (*fig.*) ум|ира́ть, -ере́ть под забо́ром (*or* в нищете́); **die in the last ~** (*fig.*) боро́ться (*impf.*) до конца́.

v.t.: **~ a car** завезти́ маши́ну (*pf.*) в кана́ву; **~ one's plane** сажа́ть, посади́ть самолёт на́ воду; **~ s.o.** (*sl.*) отде́л|ываться, -аться от кого́-н.; бр|оса́ть, -о́сить кого́-н.

v.i. (*make or repair ~es*) копа́ть, вы́- (*or* чи́стить, по-) кана́вы.

cpd. **~-water** *n.* стоя́чая вода́; **dull as ~-water** смерте́льно ску́чный.

dither ['dɪðə(r)] *n.* (*coll.*) смяте́ние; **she was in a ~** она́ не́рвничала (*or* колеба́лась).

v.i. (*coll.*) колеба́ться, по-; быть в нереши́тельности; не́рвничать (*impf.*).

dithery ['dɪðərɪ] *adj.* (*coll.*) нереши́тельный, нерво́зный.

dithyramb ['dɪθɪˌræm, -ˌræmb] *n.* дифира́мб.

dithyrambic [ˌdɪθɪ'ræmbɪk] *adj.* дифирамби́ческий.

ditto ['dɪtəʊ] *n.* то же; сто́лько же; **say ~ to s.o.'s remarks** подда́к|ивать, -нуть чьим-н. замеча́ниям.

ditty ['dɪtɪ] *n.* пе́сенка.

diuretic [ˌdaɪjʊ'retɪk] *n.* мочего́нное сре́дство.

adj. мочего́нный.

diurnal [daɪ'ɜ:n(ə)l] *adj.* дневно́й, ежедне́вный.

diva ['di:və] *n.* примадо́нна, ди́ва.

divagate ['daɪvəˌgeɪt] *v.i.* отклон|я́ться, -и́ться от те́мы.

divagation [ˌdaɪvə'geɪʃ(ə)n] *n.* отклоне́ние от те́мы.

divan [dɪ'væn, daɪ-, 'daɪ-] *n.* тахта́, дива́н; **~ bed** дива́н-крова́ть.

dive [daɪv] *n.* **1.** (*act of diving*) ныро́к, ныря́ние; **high ~** прыжо́к в во́ду с вы́шки; **swallow ~** прыжо́к в во́ду ла́сточкой; (*of submarine*) погруже́ние; (*of aircraft*) пики́рование; **the plane went into a ~** самолёт спики́ровал. **2.** (*underground bar etc.*) погребо́к. **3.** (*drinking or gambling den*) прито́н.

v.i. **1.** (*plunge into water*) ныр|я́ть, -ну́ть; (*in diving suit; also of submarine*) погру|жа́ться, -зи́ться. **2.** (*move sharply downwards*): **the animal ~d into its hole** зверёк юркну́л в но́ру; **he ~d into his pocket** он су́нул ру́ку в карма́н; **he ~d to pick up the handkerchief** он бро́сился поднима́ть плато́к. **3.** (*fig., immerse o.s.*) углуб|ля́ться, -и́ться. *See also* **diving**

cpds. **~-bomb** *v.t.* бомби́ть (*impf.*) с пики́рования; **~-bomber** *n.* пики́рующий бомбардиро́вщик, пикиро́вщик.

diver ['daɪvə(r)] *n.* ныря́льщик; водола́з; (*for pearls*) иска́тель (*m.*) же́мчуга; (*for sponges*) лове́ц гу́бок; (*bird*) гага́ра.

diverge [daɪ'vɜ:dʒ] *v.i.* ра|сходи́ться, -зойти́сь; отклон|я́ться, -и́ться; уклон|я́ться, -и́ться; **he ~d from the path** он сверну́л с тропы́.

divergence [daɪ'vɜ:dʒəns] *n.* расхожде́ние, отклоне́ние.

divergent [daɪ'vɜ:dʒ(ə)nt] *adj.* расходя́щийся, отклоня́ющийся.

diverse [daɪ'vɜ:s, 'daɪ-, dɪ-] *adj.* ра́зный, разнообра́зный.

diversification [daɪˌvɜ:sɪfɪ'keɪʃ(ə)n] *n.* расшире́ние ассортиме́нта.

diversify [daɪ'vɜ:sɪˌfaɪ] *v.t.* разнообра́зить (*impf.*), варьи́ровать (*impf.*).

diversion [daɪ'vɜ:ʃ(ə)n, dɪ-] *n.* **1.** (*turning aside*) отклоне́ние, уклоне́ние; **~ of a stream** отво́д ручья́; **traffic ~** объе́зд. **2.** (*mil.*) диве́рсия. **3.** (*amusement*) развлече́ние. **4.: create a ~** отвл|ека́ть, -е́чь внима́ние.

diversionary [daɪ'vɜ:ʃənərɪ, dɪ-] *adj.* диверсио́нный.

diversionist [daɪ'vɜ:ʃənɪst] *n.* диверса́нт.

diversity [daɪ'vɜ:sɪtɪ, dɪ-] *n.* (*differentness*) несхо́дство, разли́чие; (*variety*) разнообра́зие, разнообра́зность.

divert [daɪ'vɜ:t, dɪ-] *v.t.* (*deflect*) отклон|я́ть, -и́ть; отвл|ека́ть, -е́чь; (*entertain*) развл|ека́ть, -е́чь.

divertimento [dɪˌvɜ:tɪ'mentəʊ, dɪˌveə-] *n.* дивертисме́нт.

diverting [daɪ'vɜ:tɪŋ, dɪ-] *adj.* развлека́ющий, развлека́тельный, заба́вный.

divertissement [ˌdi:veə'ti:smɑ̃] *n.* (*ballet*) дивертисме́нт.

divest [daɪ'vest] *v.t.* (*fig.*) лиш|а́ть, -и́ть; **~ o.s. of functions** сложи́ть (*pf.*) с себя́ обя́занности.

divide [dɪ'vaɪd] *n.* (*geog.*) водоразде́л.

v.t. **1.** (*share*) дели́ть, раз-; **they ~d the money equally** они́ раздели́ли де́ньги по́ровну; **he ~s his time between work and play** он де́лит своё вре́мя ме́жду рабо́той и развлече́ниями. **2.** (*math.*) дели́ть, раз-; **~ 27 by 3** дели́ть, раз- 27 на́ 3. **3.** (*separate*) раздел|я́ть, -и́ть; **dividing-line** разграниче́ние; **the river ~s the two estates** река́ разделя́ет э́ти два име́ния; **he ~d the clever pupils from the stupid ones** он отдели́л спосо́бных ученико́в от тупы́х. **4.** (*cause disagreement*) разъедин|я́ть, -и́ть; раздел|я́ть, -и́ть; **such a small matter should not ~ us** не сто́ит нам спо́рить из-за тако́го пустяка́; **we are ~d on this question** мы расхо́димся в э́том вопро́се; **a ~-and-rule policy** поли́тика «разделя́й и вла́ствуй». **5.** (*parl.*): **the Opposition ~d the House** оппози́ция потре́бовала голосова́ния.

v.i. дели́ться, раз-; **the road ~s** доро́га разветвля́ется; **the House ~d** пала́та проголосова́ла; (*math.*): **18 ~s by 3** 18 де́лится на́ 3.

dividend ['dɪvɪˌdend] *n.* (*math.*) дели́мое; (*fin.*) дивиде́нд.

dividers [dɪ'vaɪdəz] *n.* (*compasses*) ци́ркуль (*m.*).

divination [ˌdɪvɪ'neɪʃ(ə)n] *n.* (*foretelling the future*) гада́ние, прорица́ние, проро́чество; (*accurate guess*) ве́рная дога́дка.

divin|e [dɪ'vaɪn] *n.* богосло́в.

adj. боже́ственный; (*coll., superb*) ди́вный, боже́ственный; **~e right of kings** пра́во пома́занника бо́жьего; **~e service** богослуже́ние.

v.t. (*guess, intuit*) уга́д|ывать, -а́ть; **~ing-rod** прут для отыска́ния воды́.

diviner [dɪ'vaɪnə(r)] *n.* (*seer*) гада́тель (*m.*), прорица́тель (*m.*); (*water-~*) лозоиска́тель (*m.*).

diving ['daɪvɪŋ] *n.* ныря́ние.

cpds. **~-bell** *n.* водола́зный ко́локол; **~-board** *n.* трампли́н, вы́шка (для прыжко́в в во́ду); **~-dress, ~-suit** *nn.* скафа́ндр.

divinity [dɪ'vɪnɪtɪ] *n.* (*quality*) боже́ственность; (*divine being*) божество́; (*theology*) богосло́вие.

divinize ['dɪvɪnaɪz] *v.t.* обожеств|ля́ть, -и́ть.

divisibility [dɪˌvɪzɪ'bɪlɪtɪ] *n.* дели́мость.

divisible [dɪ'vɪzɪb(ə)l] *adj.* (раз)дели́мый.

division [dɪ'vɪʒ(ə)n] *n.* **1.** (*math.*) деле́ние. **2.** (*dividing*) разделе́ние, разде́л; **~ of labour** разделе́ние труда́; **a fair ~ of the money** справедли́вое распределе́ние де́нег. **3.** (*separation*) разделе́ние; **class ~s** кла́ссовые разли́чия. **4.** (*interval on a scale*) деле́ние. **5.** (*discord*) расхожде́ние. **6.** (*mil.*) диви́зия. **7.** (*department*) отде́л. **8.** (*electoral district*) избира́тельный о́круг. **9.** (*parl. vote*) голосова́ние. **10.** (*typ., of words at end of line*) перено́с.

divisional [dɪ'vɪʒənəl] *adj.* (*mil.*) дивизио́нный; **~ headquarters** штаб диви́зии.

divisive [dɪ'vaɪsɪv] *adj.* разделя́ющий, разъединя́ющий; вызыва́ющий разногла́сия.

divisor [dɪ'vaɪzə(r)] *n.* (*math.*) дели́тель (*m.*).

divorce [dɪ'vɔ:s] *n.* **1.** (*severance*) разры́в, разъедине́ние. **2.** (*leg.*) разво́д; **~ court** суд по бракоразво́дным дела́м; **~ rate** разводи́мость, проце́нт разво́дов.

v.t. **1.** (*separate*) отдел|я́ть, -и́ть; **~ a word from its context** вырыва́ть, вы́рвать сло́во из конте́кста. **2.** (*leg.*)

разв|оди́ть, -ести́; **he ~d his wife** он развёлся с женой; **she is ~d** она́ разведена́.

v.i. разв|оди́ться, -ести́сь.

divorcee [ˌdɪvɔːˈsiː] *n.* разведённый муж, разведённая жена́.

divulgation [ˌdaɪvʌlˈgeɪʃ(ə)n, dɪ-] *n.* разглаше́ние.

divulge [daɪˈvʌldʒ, dɪ-] *v.t.* разгла|ша́ть, -си́ть.

DIY (*abbr. of* ***do it yourself***): ~ **store** магази́н «уме́лые ру́ки».

DIYer [diːaɪˈwaɪə(r)] *n.* (*coll.*) дома́шний уме́лец.

dizziness [ˈdɪzɪnɪs] *n.* головокруже́ние.

dizzy [ˈdɪzɪ] *adj.* (*feeling giddy*) испы́тывающий головокруже́ние; (*causing giddiness*) головокружи́тельный; **I feel ~** у меня́ кру́жится голова́.

DJ (*abbr. of* ***disc jockey***) диск-жоке́й.

djinn [dʒɪn] = **jinn(ee)**

D. Litt. (*abbr. of* ***Doctor of Letters***) до́ктор литерату́ры.

DM [ˈdɔɪtʃmɑːk] *n.* (*abbr. of* **Deutschmark**) герма́нская ма́рка.

DNA (*abbr. of* ***deoxyribonucleic acid***) ДНК, (дезоксирибонуклеи́новая кислота́).

do[1] [duː, də] *n.* (*coll.*) **1.** (*swindle*) надува́тельство. **2.** (*entertainment*) вечери́нка, гуля́нка. **3.** (*share*): **fair do's!** всем по́ровну! **4.** (*advice*): **~'s and don'ts** сове́ты (*m. pl.*).

v.t. & aux. **1.** (*as aux. or substitute for v. already used: not translated unless emph.*): **I ~ not smoke** я не курю́; **did you not see me?** ра́зве вы меня́ не ви́дели?; **I ~ want to go** я о́чень хочу́ пойти́; **~ tell me** пожа́луйста, расскажи́те мне; **they promised to help, and they did** они́ обеща́ли помо́чь и помогли́; **so ~ I** я то́же; **he went, but I did not** он пошёл, а я нет; **she plays better than she did** она́ игра́ет лу́чше, чем пре́жде; **he ~es not work, nor ~ I** ни он, ни я не рабо́таем. **2.** (*perform, carry out*): **what can I ~ for you?** чем могу́ служи́ть?; **what ~es he ~ (for a living)?** чем он занима́ется?; кем/где он рабо́тает?; **what ~es your father ~?** кто ваш оте́ц?; **the team did well** кома́нда вы́ступила (весьма́) успе́шно; **what's ~ne cannot be undone** сде́ланного не воро́тишь/попра́вишь; **~ one's duty** выполня́ть, вы́полнить свой долг; **easier said than ~ne** легко́ сказа́ть, но тру́дно сде́лать; **well ~ne!** молоде́ц!; **it isn't ~ne!** э́то не при́нято! **3.** (*bestow, render*): **it ~es him credit** э́то де́лает ему́ честь; **he did me a service** он оказа́л мне услу́гу; **it won't ~ any good** э́то бесполе́зно; **~ into English** перев|оди́ть, -ести́ на англи́йский. **4.** (*effect, produce*): **try what kindness will ~!** снача́ла попро́буйте по-хоро́шему!; **that's ~ne it! now you've ~ne it!** (*iron.*) поздравля́ю! **5.** (*finish*): **I have ~ne** я ко́нчил; **I have ~ne with algebra** я поко́нчил с а́лгеброй; **I have ~ne with him** я с ним поко́нчил. **6.** (*work at*): **he's ~ing algebra** он изуча́ет а́лгебру. **7.** (*solve*): **~ a sum** реш|а́ть, -и́ть арифмети́ческую зада́чу. **8.** (*attend to*): **the barber did me first** парикма́хер обслужи́л меня́ пе́рвым; **we did the Prado** (*coll.*) мы осмотре́ли Пра́до; **he ~es book reviews** он рецензи́рует кни́ги; **we did geography today** сего́дня мы проходи́ли геогра́фию. **9.** (*arrange, clean, tidy*): **~ the flowers** соб|ира́ть, -ра́ть цветы́ в буке́ты; **~ one's hair** прич|ёсываться, -еса́ться; **~ a room** уб|ира́ть, -ра́ть ко́мнату; **~ the dishes** мыть, вы́-посу́ду; **~ one's face** прив|оди́ть, -ести́ лицо́ в поря́док. **10.** (*cook*): **~ne to a turn** зажа́рено как раз в ме́ру; **well ~ne** хорошо́ прожа́ренный; **the potatoes are ~ne** карто́шка свари́лась/гото́ва. **11.** (*enact*): **he did Hamlet** он игра́л Га́млета; **~ the polite** (*coll.*) держа́ть (*impf.*) себя́ ве́жливо. **12.** (*undergo*): **he did 6 years for forgery** он отсиде́л 6 лет за подло́г. **13.** (*cater for*): **they ~ you well at the Savoy** в «Саво́е» хоро́шее обслу́живание. **14.** (*coll., swindle*) над|ува́ть, -у́ть. **15.** (*achieve speed etc.*): **we did 70 miles in two hours** мы проде́лали 70 миль за два часа́; **he was ~ing 60 (miles an hour)** он е́хал со ско́ростью 60 миль в час. **16.: ~ne!** (*agreed*) по рука́м! **17.: I can ~** (*sell*) **you this coat at £50** я уступлю́ вам э́то пальто́ за 50 фу́нтов.

v.i. **1.** (*act, behave*): **~ as I tell you** слу́шайся меня́; **~ as you would be ~ne by** поступа́йте так, как бы вы хоте́ли, что́бы с ва́ми поступа́ли; **you would ~ well to go there** вы хорошо́ сде́лаете, е́сли пойдёте туда́; **we must ~ or die** мы должны́ держа́ться до конца́. **2.** (*be satisfactory, fitting or advisable*): **the scraps will ~ for the dog** объе́дки пригодя́тся (*or* бу́дут хороши́) для соба́ки; **this will never ~** э́то никуда́ не годи́тся; э́то не пойдёт; **that will ~!** (*is enough*) хва́тит!; дово́льно!; **it doesn't ~ to be rude** гру́бость плохо́й помо́щник; **tomorrow will ~** за́втрашний день (мне) подхо́дит; мо́жно и за́втра. **3.** (*fare, succeed*): **how ~ you ~?** здра́вствуйте!; как пожива́ете?; **how did he ~ in his exams?** как он сда́л экза́мены?; **my roses are ~ing well** мои́ ро́зы хорошо́ расту́т; **the patient is ~ing well** больно́й поправля́ется. **4.** (*happen*): **is anything ~ing at the club?** что происхо́дит в клу́бе?; **nothing ~ing!** (*refusal*) не вы́йдет!

with preps.: **what shall we ~ about lunch?** как насчёт обе́да?; **nothing can be ~ne about it** с э́тим ничего́ не поде́лаешь; **~ well by s.o.** хорошо́ обраща́ться (*impf.*) с кем-н.; **~ for** (*clean house etc. for*) вести́ (*det.*) чьё-н. хозя́йство; (*defeat, destroy, damage*): **these shoes are ~ne for** э́тим ту́флям коне́ц; **the storm did for my tulips** бу́ря уничто́жила мои́ тюльпа́ны; **if he finds out, I am ~ne for** е́сли он об э́том узна́ет — я пропа́л; **we're ~ne for** нам кры́шка (*coll.*); **what will you ~ for food?** как вы устро́итесь с пита́нием?; **~ s.o. out of sth.** (*cheat, deprive of*) выма́нивать, вы́манить что-н. у кого́-н.; **what have you ~ne to my watch?** что вы сде́лали с мои́ми часа́ми?; **what have you ~ne with the keys?** куда́ вы де́ли ключи́?; **what is he ~ing with a car?** заче́м ему́ маши́на?; **I could ~ with a drink** я охо́тно (*or* с удово́льствием) вы́пил бы; **that coat could ~ with a clean** не помеша́ло бы вы́чистить э́то пальто́; **I can't be ~ing with her** я её не выношу́; **we shall have to make ~ with margarine** нам придётся обойти́сь маргари́ном; **he ~esn't know what to ~ with himself** он не зна́ет, чем заня́ться; **he has to ~ with lots of people** ему́ прихо́диться име́ть де́ло со мно́гими людьми́; **it is nothing to ~ with you** э́то вас не каса́ется; **the letter is, has to ~ with the bazaar** э́то письмо́ относи́тельно благотвори́тельного база́ра; **hard work had a lot to ~ with his success** упо́рный труд сыгра́л большу́ю роль в его́ успе́хе; **these books are ~ne with** э́ти кни́ги бо́льше не нужны́; **we must ~ without luxuries** мы должны́ обойти́сь без ро́скоши; **some of these books can be ~ne without** без не́которых из э́тих книг мо́жно вполне́ обойти́сь; **I can ~ without his silly jokes** мне надое́ли его́ дура́цкие шу́тки.

with advs.: **~ away** *v.i.*: **~ away with** конча́ть, поко́нчить с+*i.*; **~ away with o.s.** поко́нчить (*pf.*) с собо́й; **~ down** *v.t.* (*coll., cheat*) над|ува́ть, -у́ть; **~ in** *v.t.* (*sl., kill*) уб|ира́ть, -ра́ть; (*coll., exhaust*): **I am ~ne in** я измо́тан; **~ out** *v.t.* (*clean, e.g. a room*) уб|ира́ть, -ра́ть; (*clear, e.g. a cupboard*) вы́чистить (*pf.*); **~ over (again)** *v.t.* переде́л|ывать, -ать; **~ up** *v.t.* (*repair, refurnish*): **~ up a room** отде́л|ывать, -ать ко́мнату; (*fasten*): **~ up a parcel** завя́з|ывать, -а́ть паке́т; **~ up a dress** застёг|ивать, -ну́ть пла́тье; (*sl., exhaust*) утом|ля́ть, -и́ть; му́чить, за-/из-.

cpds. **~-all** *n.* ма́стер на все ру́ки; **~-it-yourself** *adj.* самоде́льный; **~-nothing** *n.* ло́дырь (*m.*); *adj.* лени́вый; **~-or-die** *adj.* отча́янный.

do[2] [dəʊ] *n.* = **doh**

doable [ˈduːəb(ə)l] *adj.* (*feasible*) выполни́мый.

dobbin [ˈdɒbɪn] *n.* рабо́чая ло́шадь.

docile [ˈdəʊsaɪl] *adj.* послу́шный, поко́рный.

docility [dəʊˈsɪlɪtɪ] *n.* послуша́ние, поко́рность.

dock[1] [dɒk] *n.* (*bot.*) ко́нский щаве́ль.

dock[2] [dɒk] *n.* (*in court*) скамья́ подсуди́мых.

dock[3] [dɒk] *n.* **1.** (*naut.*) док; **dry ~** сухо́й док; **floating ~** плаву́чий док; **wet ~** мо́крый док. **2.** (*pl., port facilities*) верфь. **3.** (*wharf*) при́стань.

v.t. (*bring into ~*) ста́вить, по- (*судно*) в док.

v.i. (*go into ~*) входи́ть, войти́ в док; (*of space vehicles*) стыкова́ться, со-.

cpd. **~yard** *n.* верфь.

dock[4] [dɒk] *v.t.* **1.** (*shorten tail of*) обруб|а́ть, -и́ть хвост +*g. or d.* **2.** (*fig., reduce*) уре́з|ывать, -ать; **the soldiers were ~ed of their ration** солда́там уре́зали рацио́н.

cpd. **~-tailed** *adj.* ку́цый.

docker [ˈdɒkə(r)] *n.* до́кер; порто́вый рабо́чий.

docket ['dɒkɪt] *n.* **1.** (*summary*) аннота́ция; (*list*) пе́речень (*m.*). **2.** (*US, leg.*) рее́стр суде́бных дел.
v.t. аннoти́ровать (*impf., pf.*).

docking ['dɒkɪŋ] *n.* (*of space vehicles*) стыко́вка.

doctor ['dɒktə(r)] *n.* **1.** (*acad.*) до́ктор; (*fig.*): **~s disagree** мне́ния авторите́тов расхо́дятся. **2.** (*of medicine*) врач, до́ктор; **woman ~** же́нщина-врач; до́кторша, врачи́ха (*coll.*).
v.t. (*coll., castrate*) кастри́ровать (*impf., pf.*); (*falsify*) подде́л|ывать, -ать; (*food*) фальсифици́ровать (*impf., pf.*).

doctor|al ['dɒktər(ə)l], **-ial** [,dɒk'tɔ:rɪəl] *adjs.* до́кторский.

doctorate ['dɒktərət] *n.* сте́пень до́ктора.

doctrinaire [,dɒktrɪ'neə(r)] *n.* доктринёр.
adj. доктринёрский.

doctrinal [dɒk'traɪn(ə)l, 'dɒktrɪn(ə)l] *adj.* теологи́ческий; относя́щийся к доктри́не.

doctrine ['dɒktrɪn] *n.* доктри́на, уче́ние; **Monroe ~** доктри́на Монро́.

docudrama ['dɒkjʊ,drɑ:mə] *n.* полудокумента́льная пье́са.

document ['dɒkjʊmənt] *n.* докуме́нт.
v.t. **1.** (*prove*) документи́ровать (*impf., pf.*). **2.** (*supply with ~s*) снаб|жа́ть, -ди́ть докуме́нтами; **he is well ~ed** он хорошо́ осведомлён о фа́ктах.

documentary [,dɒkjʊ'mentərɪ] *n.* & *adj.* документа́льный (фильм).

documentation [,dɒkjʊmen'teɪʃ(ə)n] *n.* **1.** (*proof*) подтвержде́ние докуме́нтами; документа́ция. **2.** (*set of documents*) докуме́нты (*m. pl.*).

dodder ['dɒdə(r)] *v.i.* трясти́сь (*impf.*); **a ~ing old man** дря́хлый стари́к.

doddery ['dɒdərɪ] *adj.* трясу́щийся от ста́рости; дря́хлый.

doddle ['dɒd(ə)l] *n.* (*coll.*) лёгкое де́ло, па́ра пустяко́в.

dodecagon [dəʊ'dekəgən] *n.* двенадцатиуго́льник.

dodecahedron [,dəʊdekə'hi:drən] *n.* додека́эдр, двенадцатигра́нник.

dodecaphonic [,dəʊdekə'fɒnɪk] *adj.* додекафони́ческий.

dodge [dɒdʒ] *n.* (*evading movement*) увёртка; (*trick*) увёртка, уло́вка; (*device*) приспособле́ние.
v.t. уви́л|ивать, -ьну́ть от+*g.*; **~ a blow** уверну́ться от (*pf.*) уда́ра; **~ a question** уви́л|ивать, -ьну́ть от отве́та; **~ military service** уклоня́ться (*impf.*) от вое́нной пови́нности.
v.i. уклон|я́ться, -и́ться (от+*g.*); уви́л|ивать, -ьну́ть (от+*g.*); **he ~d behind a tree** он (бы́стро) укры́лся за де́ревом.

dodger ['dɒdʒə(r)] *n.* изворо́тливый челове́к; хитре́ц.

dodgy ['dɒdʒɪ] *adj.* (*coll.*) (*artful*) увёртливый, изворо́тливый; (*tricky, difficult*) ка́верзный; (*unsafe*) ненадёжный.

dodo ['dəʊdəʊ] *n.* дронт; (*fig.*) ко́сный челове́к.

doe [dəʊ] *n.* са́мка (*оленя, зайца и т.п.*).
cpd. **~skin** *n.* оле́нья ко́жа; (*natural*) за́мша; (*text.*) шерстяна́я ткань, имити́рующая за́мшу.

doer ['du:ə(r)] *n.* (*performer; man of action*) де́ятель (*m.*), челове́к де́ла.

doff [dɒf] *v.t.* сн|има́ть, -ять.

dog [dɒg] *n.* **1.** соба́ка, пёс (*also fig., pej.*); **lost ~** бездо́мная соба́ка; (*attr.*) соба́чий, пёсий; **~ family** (*zool.*) семе́йство соба́чьих. **2.** (*male*) кобе́ль (*m.*); **~ fox** саме́ц лисы́, кобе́ль (*m.*); **~ wolf** саме́ц во́лка, кобе́ль (*m.*). **3.** (*astron.*): **~ star** Си́риус; **~ days** пе́кло; са́мые жа́ркие ле́тние дни. **4.** (*fire-iron*) подста́вка для ками́нных щипцо́в. **5.** (*coll., fellow*): **lucky ~** счастли́вчик; **lazy ~** лентя́й; **sly ~** хитре́ц; **dirty ~** су́кин сын; **lame ~** неуда́чник; **top ~** хозя́ин положе́ния. **6.** (*other fig. uses*): **throw s.o. to the ~s** выбра́сывать, вы́бросить кого́-н. к чертя́м соба́чьим; **go to the ~s** разори́ться (*pf.*), пойти́ (*pf.*) пра́хом; **die like a ~** подо́хнуть (*pf.*) как соба́ка; **a ~'s life** соба́чья жизнь; **lead s.o. a ~'s life** отрав|ля́ть, -и́ть кому́-н. жизнь; **give a ~ a bad name and hang him** клевета́ сме́ртиподо́бна; от худо́й сла́вы вдруг не отде́лаешься; **let sleeping ~s lie** не тронь ли́ха, пока спит ти́хо; **not a ~'s chance** нет ни мале́йшего ша́нса; **love me, love my ~** лю́бишь меня́, люби́ мою́ соба́чку; **~ in the manger** соба́ка на се́не; **take a hair of the ~** опохме́л|я́ться, -и́ться; **there's life in the old ~ yet** есть ещё по́рох в пороховни́цах; **you can't teach an old ~ new tricks** ≃ нельзя́ переучи́ть кого́-н. на ста́рости лет; **~ does not eat ~** во́рон во́рону глаз не вы́клюет; **~'s dinner** (*sl., mess, hotchpotch*) мешани́на; неразбери́ха; **he has a black ~ on his back** на него́ тоска́ нашла́; **put on ~** (*sl., show off*) ва́жничать (*impf.*); **the ~s of war** у́жасы (*m. pl.*) войны́; **hot ~** (*coll.*) бу́лка с горя́чей соси́ской; **spotted ~** (*pudding*) варёный пу́динг с кори́нкой.
v.t. ходи́ть (*indet.*) по пята́м за+*i.*; (*fig.*) пресле́довать (*impf.*).
cpds. **~-biscuit** *n.* гале́та для соба́к; **~cart** *n.* двуко́лка; **~-collar** *n.* оше́йник; (*coll., clergyman's*) кру́глый стоя́чий воротни́к; **~-ear** (*fig.*) *n.* за́гнутый уголо́к страни́цы; *v.t.* заг|иба́ть, -ну́ть уголки́ страни́ц +*g.*; **~-eat-~** *adj.* **~-eat-~ competition** жесто́кая/беспоща́дная конкуре́нция, конкуре́нция не на жизнь, а на смерть; **~-fancier** *n.* собаково́д; **~fight** *n.* (*lit.*) дра́ка соба́к; (*fig.*) дра́ка, потасо́вка; (*aeron.*) возду́шный бой; **~fish** *n.* аку́ла; **~-food** *n.* корм для соба́к; **~house** *n.* (*US*) конура́; **in the ~house** (*coll.*) в неми́лости; **~-Latin** *n.* ку́хонная латы́нь; **~-leg** *n.* зигза́г; **~like** *adj.*: **~like devotion** соба́чья пре́данность; **~-lover** *n.* (*coll.*) соба́чни|к (*fem.* -ца); **~-paddle** *v.i.* пла́вать (*indet.*) по-соба́чьи; **~-racing** *n.* соба́чьи бега́; **~rose** *n.* шипо́вник; **~sbody** *n.* иша́к, работя́га (*c.g.*); **~-show** *n.* вы́ставка соба́к; **~-sleigh** *n.* на́рт|ы (*pl., g.* —); **~-tired** *adj.* уста́лый как соба́ка; **~-watch** *n.* полува́хта; **~-whip** *n.* ара́пник; **~wood** *n.* кизи́л; свиди́на крова́во-кра́сная.

doge [dəʊdʒ] *n.* дож.

dogged ['dɒgɪd] *adj.* упо́рный, насты́рный; **it's ~ as does it** (*coll.*) терпе́ние и труд всё перетру́т.

doggedness ['dɒgɪdnɪs] *n.* упо́рство, насты́рность.

doggerel ['dɒgər(ə)l] *n.* ви́рш|и (*pl., g.* -ей).
adj. халту́рный.

doggo ['dɒgəʊ] *adv.* притая́сь; **lie ~** прита́иваться (*impf.*).

doggone ['dɒgɒn] *adj.* (*US sl.*) чёртов.

doggy ['dɒgɪ] *n.* собачо́нка, соба́чка, пёсик.
adj. соба́чий; (*of pers.*) лю́бящий соба́к.

dogma ['dɒgmə] *n.* до́гма; (*specific*) догма́т.

dogmatic [dɒg'mætɪk] *adj.* догмати́ческий; (*assertive*) догмати́ческий, догмати́чный.

dogmatism ['dɒgmə,tɪz(ə)m] *n.* догмати́зм.

dogmatist ['dɒgmətɪst] *n.* догма́тик.

dogmatize ['dɒgmə,taɪz] *v.i.* догматизи́ровать (*impf.*).

doh, do [dəʊ] *n.* (*mus.*) до (*indecl.*).

doily, doyley ['dɔɪlɪ] *n.* кружевна́я салфе́точка.

doing ['du:ɪŋ] *n.* **1.** (*achievement*): **this was his ~** э́то де́ло его́ рук; **it will take some ~** э́то потре́бует труда́; э́то не та́к про́сто. **2.** (*pl., activities*) дела́ (*nt. pl.*); посту́пки (*m. pl.*). **3.** (*pl., coll., accessories*) принадле́жности (*f. pl.*).

dolce far niente [,dɒltʃeɪ ,fɑ: nɪ'entɪ] *n.* блаже́нное ничегонеде́лание; кейф.

dolce vita [,dɒltʃeɪ 'vi:tə] *n.* сла́дкая жизнь.

doldrums ['dɒldrəmz] *n.* (*geog.*) экваториа́льная штилева́я полоса́; (*fig.*) уны́ние, хандра́; **be in the ~** быть в уны́нии, хандри́ть (*impf.*).

dole [dəʊl] *n.* подая́ние; посо́бие по безрабо́тице; **he is on the ~** он безрабо́тный, он получа́ет посо́бие.
v.t. **~ out** ску́по выдава́ть, вы́дать (*or* распредел|я́ть, -и́ть).

doleful ['dəʊlfʊl] *adj.* ско́рбный.

dolefulness ['dəʊlfʊlnɪs] *n.* скорбь.

dolichocephalic [,dɒlɪ,kəʊsɪ'fælɪk] *adj.* долихоцефа́льный.

doll ['dɒl] *n.* **1.** (*toy*) ку́кла; **~'s house** ку́кольный до́мик. **2.** (*coll., sweet creature*) ку́колка.
v.t. & *i.*: **~ (o.s) up** разоде́ться (*pf.*).

dollar ['dɒlə(r)] *n.* до́ллар; **~ diplomacy** диплома́тия до́ллара; **~ gap** до́лларовый дефици́т; **(one's) bottom ~** после́дний грош.

dollop ['dɒləp] *n.* соли́дная по́рция, окова́лок.

dolly ['dɒlɪ] *n.* **1.** = **doll. 2.** (*platform for camera*) опера́торская теле́жка.

dolman ['dɒlmən] *n.* доломáн.

dolmen ['dɒlmən] *n.* до́льмен.

dolomite ['dɒlə,maɪt] доломи́т; **the D~s** Доломи́товые А́льпы (*f. pl.*).
dolorous ['dɒlərəs] *adj.* го́рестный, печа́льный.
dolour ['dɒlə(r)] *n.* (*poet.*) го́ре, печа́ль.
dolphin ['dɒlfɪn] *n.* дельфи́н.
dolphinarium [,dɒlfɪ'neərɪəm] *n.* дельфина́рий.
dolt [dəʊlt] *n.* болва́н, тупи́ца.
doltish ['dəʊltɪʃ] *adj.* тупо́й, глупова́тый.
doltishness ['dəʊltɪʃnɪs] *n.* ту́пость, глупова́тость.
domain [də'meɪn] *n.* **1.** (*estate*) владе́ние, име́ние; (*hist.*) доме́н. **2.** (*realm*) сфе́ра. **3.** (*fig.*) о́бласть; **these matters are in his ~** э́ти дела́ вхо́дят в его́ компете́нцию.
dome [dəʊm] *n.* **1.** (*rounded roof*) ку́пол. **2.** (*of sky etc.*) свод, ку́пол.
domed [dəʊmd] *adj.*: **~ forehead** вы́пуклый лоб.
Domesday Book ['du:mzdeɪ] *n.* (*hist.*) када́стровая кни́га.
domestic [də'mestɪk] *n.* (*servant*) слуга́ (*m.*); прислу́га, домрабо́тница; (*pl., collect.*) прислу́га.
adj. **1.** (*of the home or family*) дома́шний; **~ fuel** бытово́е то́пливо; **~ science** домово́дство; **~ troubles** семе́йные неприя́тности. **2.** (*home-loving*) семе́йственный. **3.** (*of animals*) дома́шний. **4.** (*not foreign*) оте́чественный, вну́тренний.
domesticable [də'mestɪkəb(ə)l] *adj.* прируча́емый.
domesticate [də'mestɪ,keɪt] *v.t.* (*tame*) прируч|а́ть, -и́ть; (*interest in household*) приуч|а́ть, -и́ть к веде́нию хозя́йства; **she is not ~d** она́ не домосе́дка.
domestication [də,mestɪ'keɪʃ(ə)n] *n.* прируче́ние; приуче́ние к веде́нию хозя́йства (*or* к дома́шней рабо́те).
domesticity [,dɒmə'stɪsɪtɪ, ,dəʊ-] *n.* семе́йная/дома́шняя жизнь; (*pl.*) дома́шние дела́.
domicile ['dɒmɪ,saɪl, -sɪl] *n.* (*dwelling*) ме́сто жи́тельства; (*leg.*) домици́лий.
v.t.: **~d in England** име́ющий постоя́нное местожи́тельство в А́нглии.
domiciliary [,dɒmɪ'sɪlɪərɪ] *adj.* дома́шний; **~ visit** (*of doctor etc.*) визи́т на дому́; (*of police*) о́быск.
dominance ['dɒmɪnəns] *n.* преоблада́ние; госпо́дство.
dominant ['dɒmɪnənt] *n.* (*mus., biol.*) домина́нта.
adj. **1.** (*prevailing*) домини́рующий, преоблада́ющий. **2.** (*of heights etc.*) госпо́дствующий, домини́рующий. **3.** (*mus.*) домина́нтовый. **4.** (*biol.*) домина́нтный.
dominate ['dɒmɪ,neɪt] *v.t. & i.* **1.** (*prevail*) домини́ровать (*impf.*) (над+*i.*); преоблада́ть (*impf.*) (над+*i.*). **2.** (*influence*) ока́з|ывать, -а́ть давле́ние; **she ~s her daughter** она́ подавля́ет дочь свое́й ли́чностью. **3.** (*of heights, buildings etc.*) домини́ровать (*impf.*) над+*i.*; возвыша́ться (*impf.*) над+*i.*
domination [,dɒmɪ'neɪʃ(ə)n] *n.* домини́рование, госпо́дство.
domineer [,dɒmɪ'nɪə(r)] *v.i.*: **~ over** помыка́ть (*impf.*) (*кем*); кома́ндовать (*impf.*) (*кем*).
domineering [,dɒmɪ'nɪərɪŋ] *adj.* деспоти́ческий, вла́стный.
dominical [də'mɪnɪk(ə)l] *adj.* (*of Sunday*) воскре́сный.
Dominican [də'mɪnɪkən] *n.* (*relig., pol.*) доминика́н|ец (*fem.* -ка).
adj. доминика́нский; **the ~ Republic** Доминика́нская Респу́блика.
dominie ['dɒmɪnɪ] *n.* (*Sc., teacher*) шко́льный учи́тель.
dominion [də'mɪnɪən] *n.* (*lordship*) влады́чество; (*realm*) владе́ние; (*pol. hist.*) доминио́н.
domino ['dɒmɪ,nəʊ] *n.* **1.** кость домино́; (*pl., also name of game*) домино́ (*indecl.*). **2.** (*disguise*) домино́.
don[1] [dɒn] *n.* **1.** (*Spanish title*) дон; **D~ Juan** (*fig.*) донжуа́н; **D~ Quixote** Дон-Кихо́т. **2.** (*Spaniard*) испа́нец. **3.** (*univ.*) преподава́тель (*m.*); профе́ссор.
don[2] [dɒn] *v.t.* (*arch.*) над|ева́ть, -е́ть.
donate [dəʊ'neɪt] *v.t.* дари́ть, по-; же́ртвовать, по-.
donation [dəʊ'neɪʃ(ə)n] *n.* дар; поже́ртвование.
donjon ['dɒndʒ(ə)n, 'dʌn-] *n.* донжо́н.
donkey ['dɒŋkɪ] *n.* осёл (*also fig.*); (*coll.*) иша́к; **for ~'s years** (*coll.*) с незапа́мятных времён.
cpds. **~-engine** *n.* небольшо́й вспомога́тельный дви́гатель; **~-work** *n.* (*coll.*) чёрная/чернова́я рабо́та.
donnish ['dɒnɪʃ] *adj.* педанти́чный, академи́чный.
donor ['dəʊnə(r)] *n.* же́ртвователь (*m.*); дари́тель (*m.*); (*of blood, transplant*) до́нор.
doodle ['du:d(ə)l] *n.* кара́кули (*f. pl.*).
v.t. & i. чи́ркать (*impf.*).
cpd. **~-bug** *n.* (*coll.*) самолёт-снаря́д.
doom [du:m] *n.* (*ruin*) ги́бель, поги́бель; **his ~ is sealed** его́ ги́бель предопределена́; **crack of ~** тру́бный глас; **till the crack of ~** (*fig.*) до второ́го прише́ствия.
v.t. обр|ека́ть, -е́чь на+*a.*
cpds. **~sday** *n.* стра́шный суд; день стра́шного суда́; **till ~sday** (*fig.*) до второ́го прише́ствия; **~watcher** *n.* проро́к злой судьбы́.
door [dɔ:(r)] *n.* **1.** (*of room etc.*) дверь; (*of car etc.*) две́рца; **sliding ~** задвижна́я дверь; **revolving ~** враща́ющаяся дверь; **front ~** пара́дная дверь; **back ~** за́дняя дверь; чёрный ход; **side ~** бокова́я дверь; **answer the ~** откр|ыва́ть, -ы́ть дверь; **he lives next ~** (*or* **two ~s off**) он живёт в сосе́днем до́ме (*or* че́рез два до́ма отсю́да); **the boy next ~** сосе́дский ма́льчик; **the taxi took us from ~ to ~** такси́ довезло́ нас от до́ма до до́ма; **he sells onions from ~ to ~** он продаёт лук вразно́с; **out of ~s** на све́жем/откры́том во́здухе; на дворе́/у́лице; **within ~s** до́ма, в помеще́нии; **show s.o. the ~** (*expel*) выставля́ть, вы́ставить кого́-н. за дверь; пока́з|ывать, -а́ть кому́-н. на дверь; **behind closed ~s** (*in secret*) за закры́тыми дверя́ми. **2.** (*fig., expr. proximity*): **that is next ~ to slander** от э́того оди́н шаг до клеветы́; **he is next ~ to bankruptcy** он на гра́ни банкро́тства; **lay a crime at s.o.'s ~** вали́ть, с- вину́ на кого́-н.; **he shall never darken my ~ again** ноги́ его́ бо́льше не бу́дет в моём до́ме. **3.** (*fig.*): **a ~ to success** путь к успе́ху; **close the ~ against, to, upon** отр|еза́ть, -е́зать путь к+*d.*; **force an open ~** ломи́ться (*impf.*) в откры́тую дверь.
cpds. **~-bell** *n.* дверно́й звоно́к; **~-curtain** *n.* портье́ра; **~-to-~** *adj.*: **~ salesman** разно́счик; **~-frame** *n.* дверна́я коро́бка/ра́ма; **~-handle** *n.* дверна́я ру́чка; **~-keeper, ~man** *nn.* приврáтник; швейца́р; **~knob** *n.* кру́глая дверна́я ру́чка; **~man** *n.* = **~keeper; ~mat** *n.* полови́к; **~-plate** *n.* доще́чка на дверя́х; **~post** *n.* дверно́й кося́к; **deaf as a ~post** глухо́й как пень; **~step** *n.* поро́г; **~stop** *n.* упо́р две́ри; **~way** *n.* дверно́й прое́м.
dope [dəʊp] *n.* **1.** (*drug*) дурма́н, нарко́тик; **~ fiend** наркома́н; **~ merchant, peddler** нелега́льно торгу́ющий нарко́тиками. **2.** (*sl., fool*) ду́рень (*m.*). **3.** (*sl., information*) све́дения (*nt. pl.*).
v.t. **1.** (*make unconscious*) дурма́нить, о-. **2.** (*put narcotic in*) наркотизи́ровать (*impf., pf.*). **3.** (*stimulate with drug*) взб|а́дривать, -одри́ть нарко́тиками. **4.**: **~ out** (*sl.*) разню́х|ивать, -ать.
dopey ['dəʊpɪ] *adj.* (*bemused by drug or sleep*) одурма́ненный; (*sl., foolish*) чо́кнутый.
dopiness ['dəʊpɪnɪs] *n.* (*stupor*) одуре́ние; (*stupidity*) ду́рость.
doppelgänger ['dɒp(ə)l,geŋə(r)] *n.* дух (*живого человека*).
Dori|an ['dɔ:rɪən], **-c** ['dɒrɪk] *adjs.* дори́ческий.
dormant ['dɔ:mənt] *adj.* (*of animals*) в спя́чке; **~ volcano** неде́йствующий вулка́н; **~ faculties** нераскры́вшиеся спосо́бности; **lie ~** безде́йствовать (*impf.*).
dormer(-window) ['dɔ:mə(r)] *n.* слухово́е окно́.
dormitory ['dɔ:mɪtərɪ] *n.* дортуа́р; **~ suburb** ≃ при́городный посёлок.
dormouse ['dɔ:maʊs] *n.* со́ня.
dorsal ['dɔ:s(ə)l] *adj.* дорса́льный, спинно́й; **~ fin** спинно́й плавни́к.
dory ['dɔ:rɪ] *n.* (*fish*) со́лнечник.
dosage ['dəʊsɪdʒ] *n.* (*dosing*) дозиро́вка; (*dose*) до́за.
dose [dəʊs] *n.* до́за; (*fig.*) по́рция; (*sl., venereal disease*) дурна́я боле́знь; **a (regular) ~ of** (*coll., pej.*) соли́дная по́рция +*g.*
v.t. лечи́ть (*impf.*) до́зами лека́рства; **~ o.s. with quinine** приня́ть (*pf.*) до́зу хини́на; **~ out medicine** дози́ровать (*impf., pf.*) лека́рства.
dosh [dɒʃ] *n.* (*sl.*) ба́шли (*pl. g.* -ей), моне́та.
doss [dɒs] *v.i.* (*coll.; also* **~ down**) ночева́ть, пере-.
cpd. **~-house** *n.* ночле́жка.

dossier [ˈdɒsɪə(r), -ɪˌeɪ] *n.* досье́ (*indecl.*), де́ло.

dot [dɒt] *n.* **1.** (*small mark or object*) то́чка; **on the ~** то́чно; **~s and dashes** а́збука Мо́рзе; **in the year ~** (*coll.*) о́чень давно́; в да́вние времена́; **~ matrix printer** (*comput.*) иго́льчатый *or* то́чечный при́нтер. **2.** (*tiny child*) кро́шка.

v.t. **1.** (*place ~ on*): **~ one's i's** (*lit., fig.*) ста́вить, по- то́чки над «i». **2.** (*mark, indicate with ~s*) отм|еча́ть, -е́тить то́чками/пункти́ром; пункти́ровать (*impf., pf.*); **~ted line** пункти́р; пункти́рная ли́ния; **sign on the ~ted line** (*fig.*) безогово́рочно согла|ша́ться, -си́ться; **~ted note** (*mus.*) удлинённая на полови́ну но́та. **3.** (*scatter*) усе́|ивать, -ять; **villages ~ted about** дере́вни, разбро́санные вокру́г; **sea ~ted with ships** мо́ре, усе́янное корабля́ми. **4.** (*coll., hit*) тре́снуть (*pf.*); **I ~ted him one** я дал ему́ затре́щину. **5.: ~ and carry one** (*fig., limp*) прихра́мывать (*impf.*). **6.: ~ down** (*note briefly*) набр|а́сывать, -оса́ть.

dotage [ˈdəʊtɪdʒ] *n.* ста́рческое слабоу́мие; **he is in his ~** он впал в де́тство/мара́зм.

dotard [ˈdəʊtəd] *n.* вы́живший из ума́.

dote [dəʊt] *v.i.*: **~ on** обожа́ть (*impf.*); сходи́ть (*impf.*) с ума́ по+*d.*

doting [ˈdəʊtɪŋ] *adj.* безу́мно лю́бящий.

dottle [ˈdɒt(ə)l] *n.* оста́ток недоку́ренного таба́ка в тру́бке.

dotty [ˈdɒtɪ] *adj.* (*silly*) придуркова́тый, чо́кнутый; (*marked with dots*) усе́янный то́чками.

double [ˈdʌb(ə)l] *n.* **1.** (*twofold quantity or measure*): **ten is the ~ of five** де́сять вдво́е бо́льше пяти́; **~ or quits** вдвойне́ и́ли ничего́. **2.** (*pers. or thg. resembling another*) двойни́к, дублика́т. **3.** (*running pace*) бе́глый шаг; **at the ~** бе́глым ша́гом. **4.** (*tennis*) па́рная игра́; **mixed ~s** сме́шанные па́ры (*f. pl.*). **5.** (*bridge*) дубль (*m.*). **6.** (*sharp turn*) петля́, круто́й поворо́т; (*of river*) изги́б.

adj. (*in two parts; twice as much*) двойно́й; (*happening twice*) двукра́тный; **~ axe** обоюдоо́стрый топо́р; **~ bed** дву(х)спа́льная крова́ть; **~ bend** (*on road*) зигза́г; **~ daffodil** махро́вый нарци́сс; **~ doors** двойны́е две́ри; **~ eagle** двугла́вый орёл; **~ entry** двойна́я бухгалте́рия; **~ feature** (*cin.*) кинопрогра́мма из двух худо́жественных фи́льмов; **~ knock** двукра́тный стук; **~ room** ко́мната на двои́х; **~ saucepan** кастрю́ля с двойны́м дном; **'Anna' is spelt with a ~ 'n'** «А́нна» пи́шется с двумя́ (*or* че́рез два) н; **serve a ~ purpose** служи́ть, по- двум це́лям. **3.** (*ambiguous, deceitful*): **~ dealer** двуру́шник; **~ dealing** двуру́шничество; **~ meaning** двойно́й смысл, двусмы́сленность; (*pej.*) двусмы́сленное значе́ние; **~ standard** двойна́я ме́рка, двоемы́слие. **4.** (*mus.*): **~ bass** контраба́с.

adv. вдво́е; **bend ~** сгиба́ть(ся), согну́ть(ся) вдво́е; **pay ~** плати́ть (*impf.*) вдвойне́; **he sees ~** у него́ двои́тся в глаза́х; **sleep ~** спать (*impf.*) вдвоём на одно́й крова́ти; **it costs ~ what it used to** э́то сто́ит вдво́е доро́же, чем ра́ньше; **I am ~ his age** я вдво́е ста́рше его́.

v.t. **1.** (*make twice as great*) удв|а́ивать, -о́ить. **2.** (*fold, clench*): **~ a shawl** скла́дывать, сложи́ть шаль вдво́е; **~ one's fists** сж|има́ть, -ать кулаки́; **~ up one's legs** под|гиба́ть, -огну́ть но́ги. **3.** (*cause to bend in pain*) скрю́чи|вать, -ть; **the blow ~d him up** он согну́лся попола́м от уда́ра. **4.** (*round*) огиба́ть, обогну́ть; **the ship ~d Cape Horn** кора́бль обогну́л мыс Горн. **5.** (*combine*) совме|ща́ть, -сти́ть; **the actor ~d two parts** актёр исполня́л две ро́ли. **6.** (*at bridge*): **~ one's adversary** удв|а́ивать, -о́ить зая́вку проти́вника; **5 spades, ~d** пять пик, дубль.

v.i. **1.** (*become twice as great*) удв|а́иваться, -о́иться. **2.** (*turn sharply*): **he ~d back on his tracks** он поверну́л обра́тно по своему́ сле́ду. **3.** (*bend*) ско́рчи|ваться, -ться; **he ~d up with the pain** он скрю́чился от бо́ли. **4.** (*share room etc.*): **you will have to ~ up** вам придётся помести́ться вдвоём в одно́й ко́мнате. **5.** (*run at the ~*) дви́гаться (*impf.*) бе́глым ша́гом. **6.** (*combine roles*): **I ~d for him** я дубли́ровал его́; **the porter ~s as waiter** носи́льщик рабо́тает официа́нтом по совмести́тельству.

cpds. **~-bank** *v.i.* дубли́ровать (*impf.*); *see also* **~park; ~-barrelled** *adj.* двуство́льный; **~-breasted** *adj.* двубо́ртный; **~-check** *v.t.* перепров|еря́ть, -е́рить; **~-cross** *n.* вероло́мство; *v.t.* обма́н|ывать, -у́ть; **~-crosser** *n.* вероло́мный челове́к; **~-decker** *n.* (*ship*) двухпа́лубное су́дно; (*bus*) двухэта́жный авто́бус; **~ Dutch** *n.* тараба́рщина, кита́йская гра́мота; **~-dyed** *adj.* закорене́лый; махро́вый (*coll.*); **~-edged** *adj.* (*lit., fig.*) обоюдоо́стрый; **~-faced** *adj.* двули́чный, двоеду́шный; **~-jointed** *adj.* без косте́й; «гуттапе́рчевый»; **~-lock** *v.t.* зап|ира́ть, -ере́ть на два поворо́та ключа́ (*or* двойны́м поворо́том); **~-park, ~-bank** *v.t. & i.* ста́вить, по- (маши́ну) во второ́й ряд; **~-quick** *adv.* о́чень бы́стро; **~-take** *n.* (*fig.*) заме́дленная реа́кция; **~-talk** *n.* уклóнчивые ре́чи (*f. pl.*); **~-tongued** *adj.* лжи́вый.

double entendre [ˌduːb(ə)l ɑːnˈtɑːndrə] *n.* двусмы́сленность, двусмы́слица.

doublet [ˈdʌblɪt] *n.* (*garment*) камзо́л; (*ling.*) дубле́т.

doubloon [dʌbˈluːn, dəb-] *n.* (*hist.*) дубло́н.

doubly [ˈdʌb(ə)lɪ] *adv.* вдвойне́.

doubt [daʊt] *n.* сомне́ние; **I have my ~s** у меня́ есть сомне́ние; **there is no (room for) ~ that ...** нет сомне́ния в том, что...; **the question is in ~** э́тот вопро́с ещё не я́сен; **he is in ~ what to do** он не зна́ет, что ему́ де́лать; **without ~** вне сомне́ния; несомне́нно; **no ~** без сомне́ния; вероя́тно; **cast ~ upon** под|верга́ть, -е́ргнуть сомне́нию; **when in ~, don't!** не уве́рен — не бери́сь!

v.t. & i. сомнева́ться (*impf.*) (в+*p.*); **I ~ that, whether he will come** я не ду́маю, что́бы он пришёл; **~ing Thomas** Фома́ неве́рный/неве́рующий.

doubter [ˈdaʊtə(r)] *n.* ске́птик.

doubtful [ˈdaʊtfʊl] *adj.* **1.** (*feeling doubt*) сомнева́ющийся; **I am ~ about going** я сомнева́юсь, идти́ и́ли нет. **2.** (*causing doubt*) сомни́тельный; **he is a ~ character** он сомни́тельная ли́чность; **~ weather** неопределённая пого́да.

doubtfulness [ˈdaʊtfʊlnɪs] *n.* сомни́тельность.

doubtless [ˈdaʊtlɪs] *adv.* несомне́нно.

douche [duːʃ] *n.* **1.** (*shower*) душ; **throw a cold ~ on s.o.** (*fig.*) вы́лить (*pf.*) уша́т холо́дной воды́ на кого́-н. **2.** (*internal*) промыва́ние.

v.t. обл|ива́ть, -и́ть из ду́ша.

v.i. прин|има́ть, -я́ть душ.

dough [dəʊ] *n.* те́сто; (*sl., money*) моне́та.

cpds. **~boy** *n.* (*sl.*) пехоти́нец америка́нской а́рмии; **~nut** *n.* по́нчик.

doughty [ˈdaʊtɪ] *adj.* до́блестный, бра́вый.

doughy [ˈdəʊɪ] *adj.* (*of or like dough*) тестообра́зный; (*soft, flabby*) ры́хлый, нездоро́вый.

dour [dʊə(r)] *adj.* суро́вый, непрекло́нный.

dourness [ˈdʊənɪs] *n.* суро́вость, непрекло́нность.

douse [daʊs] *v.t.* (*drench*) зал|ива́ть, -и́ть; (*extinguish*) гаси́ть, по-.

dove [dʌv] *n.* го́лубь (*m.*); **my ~** голу́бушка, голу́бчик.

cpds. **~-colour** *n.* си́зый цвет; **~-coloured** *adj.* си́зый; **~cote** *n.* голубя́тня; **flutter the ~cots** (*fig.*) устр|а́ивать, -о́ить переполо́х; **~like** *adj.* голуби́ный; **~tail** *n.* (*tech.*) ла́сточкин хвост; ла́па; *v.t.* соедин|я́ть, -и́ть ла́сточкиным хвосто́м; вяза́ть, с- в ла́пу; под|гоня́ть, -огна́ть; *v.i.* (*fig.*) увя́з|ываться, -а́ться.

Dover [ˈdəʊvə(r)] *n.* Дувр; **Strait of ~** Ду́врский проли́в, Па-де-Кале́ (*m. indecl.*).

dowager [ˈdaʊədʒə(r)] *n.* вдова́; **~ empress** вдо́вствующая императри́ца; (*elderly lady*) матро́на.

dowdy [ˈdaʊdɪ] *adj.* неря́шливо/ду́рно одева́ющийся.

dowel [ˈdaʊəl] *n.* (*tech.*) дю́бель (*m.*), штифт.

dower [ˈdaʊə(r)] *n.* (*widow's share*) вдо́вья часть насле́дства; (*dowry*) прида́ное; (*fig., gift of nature*) приро́дный дар.

v.t. да|ва́ть, -ть прида́ное +*d.*; одар|я́ть, -и́ть.

down[1] [daʊn] *n.* (*open high land*) безле́сная возвы́шенность.

down[2] [daʊn] *n.* (*hair, fluff*) пух, пушо́к.

down[3] [daʊn] *n.* **1.** (*reverse, of fortune etc.*) невзго́да; **ups and ~s** взлёты (*m. pl.*) и паде́ния (*nt. pl.*); превра́тности (*f. pl.*) судьбы́. **2.** (*coll., dislike*): **have a ~ on (or be ~ on) s.o.** име́ть зуб про́тив кого́-н.

adj. напра́вленный вниз/кни́зу; ~ **draught** (*tech.*) ни́жняя тя́га; ~ **grade** спуск, укло́н; упа́док; **on the** ~ **grade** (*fig.*) ухудша́ющийся; ~ **payment** ава́нс.

adv. **1.** (*expr. direction/state*) вниз/внизу́; **he is not** ~ **yet** (*from bedroom*) он ещё не сошёл вниз; **the sun is** ~ со́лнце се́ло; **the blinds are** ~ што́ры спу́щены; **the river is** ~ (*after a flood*) вода́ в реке́ спа́ла; ~ **south** на ю́ге; **the tyres are** ~ ши́ны спу́щены; **prices are** ~ це́ны сни́зились; (*fig.*): **he is** ~ **with fever** он слёг с высо́кой температу́рой; **he is** ~ **and out** он разби́т и уничто́жен; **be** ~ **in the mouth** ве́шать, пове́сить нос (*coll.*); быть удручённым; ~ **under** (*coll.*) в Австра́лии; **he is £15** ~ он в убы́тке на 15 фу́нтов; **the ship is** ~ **by the head** кора́бль погрузи́лся но́сом; **be** ~ **on s.o.**: *see* ~ *n.* **2.**. **2.** (*expr. movement to lower level*): **climb** ~ слез|а́ть, -ть; **come** ~ спус|ка́ться, -ти́ться; ~! (*to a dog*) лежа́ть!; **we have read** ~ **to here** мы дочита́ли до э́того ме́ста. **3.** (*expr. change of position*): **sit** ~ сади́ться, сесть; **lie** ~ ложи́ться, лечь; **fall** ~ па́дать, упа́сть; **knock s.o.** ~ сби|ва́ть, -ть; **he bent** ~ он нагну́лся. **4.** (*movement to less important place*): **we went** ~ **to Brighton for the day** мы съе́здили на́ день в Бра́йтон. **5.** (*reduction*): **the soles have worn** ~ подмётки износи́лись; **the wind died** ~ ве́тер ути́х; **boil the fat** ~ растопи́ть (*pf.*) жир; **the quality of these goods has gone** ~ ка́чество э́тих това́ров уху́дшилось; **the house burnt** ~ дом сгоре́л дотла́. **6.** (*of writing*): **write sth.** ~ запи́с|ывать, -а́ть что-н.; **take** ~ **a letter** писа́ть, на- письмо́ под дикто́вку; **he is to** ~ **to speak** он в спи́ске выступа́ющих. **7.** (*to end of scale*): **everyone from the manager** ~ **to the office-boy** все — от дире́ктора до посы́льного. **8.** (*at once*): **pay cash** ~ плати́ть, за- нали́чными. **9.** (*var.*): **shout s.o.** ~ кри́ком заст|авля́ть, -а́вить кого́-н. замолча́ть; ~ **with tyranny!** доло́й тирани́ю!; **get** ~ **to business** взя́ться (*pf.*) за де́ло; **up and** ~ (*to and fro*) взад и вперёд; *for other phrasal vv. see relevant v. entry.*

v.t. (*coll., overcome*) одол|ева́ть, -е́ть; оси́ли|вать, -ть; (*coll., swallow*) прогл|а́тывать, -оти́ть; ~ **a glass of beer** осуш|а́ть, -и́ть стака́н пи́ва; (*drop*) бр|оса́ть, -о́сить; ~ **tools** (*leave off work*) прекра|ща́ть, -ти́ть рабо́ту; (*strike*) забастова́ть (*pf.*).

prep. **1.** (*expr. downward direction*): **we walked** ~ **the hill** мы шли́ с горы́ (*or* по́д гору); **tears ran** ~ **her face** слёзы текли́/кати́лись у неё по лицу́; **he glanced** ~ **the list** он ме́льком взгляну́л на спи́сок. **2.** (*at, to a lower or further part of*): **further** ~ **the river** да́льше вниз по реке́; **we sailed** ~ **the Volga** мы плы́ли вниз по Во́лге; мы спуска́лись по Во́лге; **he lives** ~ **the street** он живёт да́льше по э́той у́лице. **3.** (*along*): **he walked** ~ **the street** он шёл по у́лице. **4.** (*var.*): ~ **(the) wind** (*expr. place*) под ве́тром; (*expr. motion*) по ве́тру; ~ **the ages** (*since earliest times*) с да́вних пор/времён; ~ **stage** (*theatr.*) на авансце́не.

down-and-out [daʊnə'naʊt] *n.* бродя́га (*m.*); бездо́мный.

downcast ['daʊnkɑːst] *adj.* (*dejected*) удручённый; пода́вленный.

downfall ['daʊnfɔːl] *n.* (*of rain*) ли́вень (*m.*); (*ruin*) паде́ние, ги́бель.

downgrade ['daʊngreɪd] *v.t.* пон|ижа́ть, -и́зить в чи́не.

downhearted [daʊn'hɑːtɪd] *adj.* пода́вленный, угнетённый.

downhill ['daʊnhɪl] *adj.* накло́нный.

adv. по́д гору; вниз; **go** ~ (*fig.*) кати́ться (*det.*) по накло́нной пло́скости.

down-market ['daʊn'mɑːkɪt] *adj.* дешёвый.

downpour ['daʊnpɔː(r)] *n.* ли́вень (*m.*).

downright ['daʊnraɪt] *adj.* (*straightforward, blunt*) прямо́й; (*absolute*) соверше́нный; я́вный.

adv. соверше́нно, я́вно.

downrightness ['daʊnraɪtnɪs] *n.* прямота́.

Down's syndrome [daʊnz] *n.*боле́знь Да́уна.

downstairs ['daʊnsteəz] *adj.*: ~ **rooms** ко́мнаты пе́рвого этажа́.

adv. (*expr. place*) внизу́; (*expr. motion*) вниз.

downstream ['daʊnstriːm] *adv.* вниз по тече́нию.

downstroke ['daʊnstrəʊk] *n.* (*in writing*) черта́ вниз.

down-to-earth ['daʊntəˌɜːθ] *adj.* практи́чный, реалисти́ческий.

downtown ['daʊntaʊn] *adj.* (*US*) располо́женный в делово́й ча́сти го́рода.

downtrodden ['daʊnˌtrɒd(ə)n] *adj.* угнетённый.

downturn ['daʊntɜːn] *n.* (*fall, reduction*) паде́ние, спад.

downward ['daʊnwəd] *adj.* спуска́ющийся, опуска́ющийся.

downwards ['daʊnwədz] *adv.* вниз.

downy ['daʊnɪ] *adj.* (*fluffy*) пуши́стый; (*coll., wily*) себе́ на уме́.

dowry ['daʊərɪ] *n.* прида́ное.

dowser ['daʊzə(r)] *n.* лозоиска́тель (*m.*).

doxology [dɒk'sɒlədʒɪ] *n.* славосло́вие.

doyen ['dɔɪən, 'dwɑːjæ̃] *n.* дуайе́н, старшина́ (*m.*).

doyley ['dɔɪlɪ] = **doily**

doze [dəʊz] *n.* дремо́та.

v.i. дрема́ть (*impf.*); ~ **off** задрема́ть (*pf.*).

dozen ['dʌz(ə)n] *n.* дю́жина; **by the** ~ дю́жинами; **a round** ~ кру́глая дю́жина; **baker's** ~ чёртова дю́жина; **talk nineteen to the** ~ говори́ть (*impf.*) без у́молку; **six of one and half a** ~ **of the other** что в лоб, что по́ лбу; ~**s of times** ты́сячу раз; **daily** ~ заря́дка, ежедне́вный моцио́н.

doziness ['dəʊzɪnɪs] *n.* дремо́та, сонли́вость.

dozy ['dəʊzɪ] *adj.* дремо́тный, сонли́вый.

DPP (*abbr. of* **Director of Public Prosecutions**) Гла́вный прокуро́р.

Dr. ['dɒktə(r)] *n.* (*abbr. of* **Doctor**) д-р, (до́ктор).

drab[1] [dræb] *n.* неря́ха; шлю́ха.

drab[2] [dræb] *adj.* (*in colour*) ту́скло-кори́чневый; (*dull*) се́рый.

drabness ['dræbnɪs] *n.* се́рость.

drachma ['drækmə] *n.* дра́хма.

Draconi|an [drə'kəʊnɪən], **-c** [drə'kɒnɪk] *adjs.* драко́новский.

draft [drɑːft] *n. see also* **draught. 1.** (*outline, rough copy*) набро́сок, чернови́к. **2.** (*order for payment*) чек, тра́тта. **3.** (*detachment of men for duty*) отря́д. **4.** (*US, conscription*) призы́в; ~ **evasion** уклоне́ние от вое́нной слу́жбы.

v.t. **1.** (*detach for duty*) откомандиро́в|ывать, -а́ть. **2.** (*conscript*) приз|ыва́ть, -ва́ть. **3.** (*prepare* ~ *of*) набр|а́сывать, -оса́ть чернови́к +*g.*; редакти́ровать, от-.

drafter ['drɑːftə(r)] *n.* состави́тель (*m.*) (*законопроекта и т.п.*); реда́ктор.

drafting ['drɑːftɪŋ] *n.* реда́кция, формулиро́вка; ~ **committee** редакцио́нный комите́т.

draftsman ['drɑːftsmən] *n.* (*drafter*) реда́ктор; состави́тель (*m.*) (*законопроекта и т.п.*); (*one who draws*) чертёжник.

drag [dræg] *n.* **1.** (*also* ~**-net**) бре́день (*m.*), не́вод. **2.** (*harrow*) борона́. **3.** (*hindrance*) то́рмоз, препя́тствие, задéржка; **she was a** ~ **on his progress** она́ препя́тствовала его́ продвиже́нию по слу́жбе. **4.** (*pull on cigarette etc.*) затя́жка. **5.** (*hard climb*): **what a** ~ **up these stairs!** ну и крут же подъём по э́той ле́стнице! **6.** (*coll.*) же́нское пла́тье (трансвести́та).

v.t. **1.** (*pull*) тяну́ть, волочи́ть, тащи́ть (*all impf.*); **they** ~**ged him out of hiding** они́ вы́волокли его́ из укры́тия; **I had to** ~ **him to the party** мне пришло́сь чуть не си́лой потащи́ть его́ на вечери́нку; **he could hardly** ~ **his feet along** он е́ле волочи́л но́ги; ~ **one's feet** (*fig.*) тяну́ть (*impf.*); ме́длить (*impf.*). **2.** (*search, dredge*) драги́ровать (*impf., pf.*); чи́стить, по- дно +*g.*

v.i. **1.** (*trail*) волочи́ться (*impf.*); тащи́ться (*impf.*). **2.** (*be slow or tedious*) тяну́ться (*impf.*) затя́|гиваться, -ну́ться; **the soloist** ~**ged behind the orchestra** соли́ст отстава́л от орке́стра.

with advs.: ~ **down** *v.t.*: **he** ~**ged the luggage down** он стащи́л чемода́ны вниз; (*fig.*): **he** ~**ged her down with him** он увлёк её за собо́й к ги́бели; ~ **in** *v.t.*: **why** ~ **in Cicero?** при чём тут Цицеро́н?; ~ **on** *v.i.*: **the performance** ~**ged on till 11** представле́ние затяну́лось до оди́ннадцати часо́в; ~ **out** *v.t.* (*protract*) растя́|гивать, -ну́ть; ~ **up** *v.t.* (*coll., a child*) пло́хо воспи́т|ывать, -а́ть.

draggle ['dræg(ə)l] *v.t. & i.* тащи́ть(ся)/волочи́ть(ся) (*impf.*) по гря́зи.

cpd. ~**-tailed** *adj.* измы́зганный, зама́ранный.

dragoman ['drægəmən] *n.* драгома́н.

dragon ['drægən] *n.* (*fabulous beast*) драко́н; (*formidable woman*) гро́зная осо́ба, дуэ́нья; **~'s teeth** (*anti-tank obstacles*) на́долбы (*f. pl.*).

cpd. **~-fly** *n.* стрекоза́.

dragonish ['drægənɪʃ] *adj.* гро́зный.

dragoon [drə'gu:n] *n.* драгу́н.

v.t. прину|жда́ть, -у́дить; **he was ~ed into obeying** его́ заста́вили подчини́ться.

drain [dreɪn] *n.* **1.** (*channel carrying off sewage etc.*) сток, водосто́к; (*pl.*) канализа́ция; **throw money down the ~** (*fig.*) бр|оса́ть, -о́сить де́ньги на ве́тер; тра́тить (*impf.*) де́ньги впусту́ю; **go down the ~** (*fig.*) кати́ться, по- по накло́нной пло́скости. **2.** (*cause of exhaustion*) истоще́ние; **it is a ~ on my energy** э́то истоща́ет мою́ эне́ргию. **3.** (*residue of liquid*) после́дняя ка́пля; (*pl.*) оста́ток; отсто́й.

v.t. **1.** (*water etc.*) отв|оди́ть, -ести́. **2.** (*land etc.*) осуш|а́ть, -и́ть; дрени́ровать (*impf., pf.*); **~ing-board** суши́лка. **3.** (*deplete*) истощ|а́ть, -и́ть; **the country was ~ed of its manpower** из страны́ вы́качали её рабо́чую си́лу. **4.** (*drink contents of*) осуш|а́ть, -и́ть.

v.i. **1.** (*flow away*) ут|ека́ть, -е́чь. **2.** (*lose moisture, become dry*) высыха́ть, вы́сохнуть; **the field ~s into the river** вода́ с по́ля стека́ет в ре́ку. **3.** (*fig.*): **his life was ~ing away** жизнь по ка́плям уходи́ла из него́.

cpd. **~pipe** *n.* дрена́жная труба́; **~pipe trousers** брю́ки ду́дочкой.

drainage ['dreɪnɪdʒ] *n.* **1.** (*draining or being drained*) дрена́ж, осуше́ние; **~ basin** бассе́йн реки́. **2.** (*system of drains*) канализа́ция.

drainer ['dreɪnə(r)] *n.* (*utensil*) дуршла́г.

drake [dreɪk] *n.* се́лезень (*m.*).

dram [dræm] *n.* (*tot of spirits*) глото́к спиртно́го; **he is fond of a ~** он вы́пить не дура́к.

drama ['drɑ:mə] *n.* **1.** (*play; exciting episode*) дра́ма. **2.** (*dramatic art*) дра́ма, драматурги́я. **3.** (*dramatic quality*) драмати́зм.

dramatic [drə'mætɪk] *adj.* (*pert. to drama; exciting*) драмати́ческий, театра́льный; драмати́чный, порази́тельный, сенсацио́нный.

dramatics [drə'mætɪks] *n.* **1.** (*staging plays*) драмати́ческое иску́сство; спекта́кль (*m.*); **amateur ~** люби́тельский/самоде́ятельный спекта́кль. **2.** (*theatrical behaviour*) драмати́зм.

dramatis personae [ˌdræmətɪs pɜ:'səʊnaɪ, -ni:] *n.* (*characters*) де́йствующие ли́ца; (*list*) спи́сок де́йствующих лиц.

dramatist ['dræmətɪst] *n.* драмату́рг.

dramatization [ˌdræmətaɪ'zeɪʃ(ə)n] *n.* инсцениро́вка, драматиза́ция.

dramatize ['dræməˌtaɪz] *v.t.* (*turn into a play*) инсцени́ровать (*impf., pf.*); драматизи́ровать (*impf., pf.*); (*exaggerate*) драматизи́ровать (*impf., pf.*).

drape [dreɪp] *n.* драпиро́вка, портье́ра; (*US, curtain*) занаве́ска.

v.t. драпирова́ть, за-; задрапиро́в|ывать, -а́ть; **~ a cloak over one's shoulders** оку́т|ывать, -ать пле́чи плащо́м; **~ walls with flags** задрапирова́ть (*pf.*) сте́ны фла́гами; **~ o.s.** наря|жа́ться, -ди́ться.

drapery ['dreɪpərɪ] *n.* (*trade*) торго́вля мануфакту́рой/тексти́лем; (*goods*) мануфакту́ра; тексти́льные изде́лия; тка́ни (*f. pl.*); (*clothing arranged in folds*) драпиро́вка, драпри́ (*nt. indecl.*).

drastic ['dræstɪk, 'drɑ:-] *adj.* сильноде́йствующий; реши́тельный, круто́й.

drat [dræt] *v.t.* (*coll.*): **~ him** чтоб его́!

int. чёрт возьми́!

draught [drɑ:ft] *n. see also* **draft. 1.** (*current of air*) тя́га; сквозня́к; **there is a ~ in this room** в э́той ко́мнате сквози́т; **sit in a ~** сиде́ть (*impf.*) на сквозняке́; **feel the ~** (*fig., coll.*) испы́тывать, -а́ть затрудне́ния. **2.** (*catch of fish*) уло́в. **3.** (*of ships*) оса́дка. **4.** (*supply of liquor*): **~ beer, beer on ~** пи́во из бо́чки. **5.** (*amount drunk*) глото́к; **he drank the glassful in one ~** он за́лпом вы́пил це́лый стака́н. **6.** (*traction by animals*) тя́га. **7.** (*pl., game*) ша́шки (*f. pl.*).

cpds. **~-board** *n.* ша́шечная доска́; **~-horse** *n.* ломова́я ло́шадь.

draughtsman ['drɑ:ftsmən] *n.* (*see also* **draftsman**) **1.** (*one who makes drawings etc.*) чертёжник. **2.** (*in game of draughts*) ша́шка.

draughtsmanship ['drɑ:ftsmənʃɪp] *n.* уме́ние черти́ть/рисова́ть; чертёжное иску́сство.

draughtswoman ['drɑ:ftswʊmən] *n.* чертёжница.

draughty ['drɑ:ftɪ] *adj.*: **this is a ~ room** в э́той ко́мнате постоя́нный сквозня́к.

Dravidian [drə'vɪdɪən] *adj.* драви́дский.

draw [drɔ:] *n.* (*in lottery*) ро́зыгрыш; (*attraction*) привлека́тельность, прима́нка; (*provocative remark*) провока́ционное/наводя́щее замеча́ние; (**~n** *game*) ничья́.

v.t. **1.** (*pull, move*) тяну́ть (*or* натя́гивать), на-; таска́ть (*indet.*), тащи́ть, по- (*det.*); **~ one's hand across one's forehead** пров|оди́ть, -ести́ руко́й по лбу; **~ s.o. aside** отв|оди́ть, -ести́ кого́-н. в сто́рону; **~ the curtains** (*close*) задёр|гивать, -нуть занаве́ски; (*open*) отдёр|гивать, -нуть (*or* раздв|ига́ть, -и́нуть) занаве́ски; **the train was ~n by two engines** по́езд шёл двойно́й тя́гой. **2.** (*extract*) выта́скивать, вы́тащить; **he drew a handkerchief out of his pocket** он вы́тащил плато́к из карма́на; **~ a knife** вы́хватить (*pf.*) нож; **~ a cork** вы́тащить (*pf.*) про́бку; **~ blood** ра́нить (*pf.*) кого́-н. до кро́ви; **~ the sword** обнаж|а́ть, -и́ть меч; **have a tooth ~n**; **~ a tooth** вы́дернуть/вы́рвать (*both pf.*) зуб; **~ s.o.'s teeth** (*fig.*) обезвре́дить (*pf.*) кого́-н.; **~ lots** тяну́ть (*impf.*) жре́бий; **~ a blank** (*fig.*) потерпе́ть (*pf.*) неуда́чу; **~ a card from the pack** брать, взять ка́рту из коло́ды; **her story ~s tears** её расска́з вызыва́ет слёзы. **3.** (*obtain from a source*): **~ (off) water from a well** че́рпать (*impf.*) во́ду из коло́дца; **~ one's salary (money from the bank)** получ|а́ть, -и́ть зарпла́ту (де́ньги в ба́нке); **~ a moral from a story** извл|ека́ть, -е́чь мора́ль из расска́за; **~ inspiration from nature** че́рпать (*impf.*) вдохнове́ние в приро́де; **~ it mild!** (*fig., coll.*) не преувели́чивай!; не сгуща́й кра́ски!; **~ on one's savings** тра́тить (*impf.*) из свои́х сбереже́ний; **~ on s.o.'s help** приб|ега́ть, -е́гнуть к чье́й-н. по́мощи. **4.** (*attract*) привл|ека́ть, -е́чь; **the film drew large audiences** фильм привлёк мно́го зри́телей; **I drew him into the conversation** я втяну́л его́ в разгово́р; **she felt ~n towards him** её тяну́ло к нему́; **~ the enemy s fire** вызыва́ть, вы́звать ого́нь проти́вника (для определе́ния его́ сил). **5.** (*stretch*): **he drew the metal into a long wire** он протяну́л мета́лл в дли́нную про́волоку; **his face was ~n with pain** его́ лицо́ осу́нулось от бо́ли. **6.** (*trace, depict*) рисова́ть, на-; черти́ть, на-; **~ a horse** нарисова́ть (*pf.*) коня́; **~ a line** пров|оди́ть, -ести́ ли́нию. **7.** (*of mental operations*): **~ a distinction/comparison** пров|оди́ть, -ести́ разли́чие/сравне́ние; **~ conclusions** при|ходи́ть, -йти́ к вы́водам. **8.** (*of documents*): **~ a cheque** выпи́сывать, вы́писать чек; **~ (up) a contract** сост|авля́ть, -а́вить догово́р. **9.** (*of ship*): **she ~s 20 feet of water** су́дно име́ет оса́дку в 20 фу́тов. **10.** (*of contest*): **the match was ~n** матч был сы́гран (*or* око́нчился) вничью́. **11.** (*disembowel*): **hanged, ~n and quartered** пове́шен и четверто́ван; **~ a chicken** потроши́ть, вы- ку́рицу.

v.i. **1.** (*admit air*) тяну́ть, по-; втя|гивать, -ну́ть; **this pipe ~s well** э́та тру́бка хорошо́ тя́нет. **2.** (*move, come*) придв|ига́ться, -и́нуться; **he drew near** он придви́нулся побли́же; **they drew round the table** они́ собрали́сь вокру́г стола́; **the day drew to a close** день бли́зился к концу́; **the ships drew level** корабли́ поравня́лись. **3.** (*infuse*) наст|а́иваться, -оя́ться; **he let the tea ~** он дал ча́ю настоя́ться. **4.** (*pull*): **~ at a cigarette** затя|гиваться, -ну́ться папиро́сой. *See also* **drawing**

with advs.: **~ back** *v.t.*: **he drew back the curtain** он отдёрнул занаве́ску; *v.i.*: **he drew back in alarm** он в стра́хе отпря́нул; **~ down** *v.t.* (*e.g. blinds*) спус|ка́ть, -ти́ть; **he drew down reproaches on his head** он навлёк на себя́ упрёки; **~ in** *v.t.*: **he drew in the details** он изобрази́л дета́ли; **the cat drew in its claws** ко́шка втяну́ла ко́гти; *v.i.*: **the train drew in** по́езд подошёл к перро́ну; **the car**

drew in to the roadside автомоби́ль подъе́хал к обо́чине; (*shorten*): **the days are ~ing in** дни стано́вятся коро́че; **~ off** *v.t.* (*e.g. water*) че́рп|ать, -ну́ть; *v.i.* (*retire*): **the enemy drew off** враг отступи́л; **~ on** *v.t.*: **~ on one's gloves** натя́|гивать, -ну́ть перча́тки; *v.i.* (*advance*): **autumn ~s on** о́сень приближа́ется; **~ out** *v.t.* (*extract*) выта́скивать, вы́тащить; вытя́гивать, вы́тянуть; (*prolong*) протя́|гивать, -ну́ть; **the battle was long ~n-out** би́тва оказа́лась затяжно́й; (*outline*): **~ out a scheme** набр|а́сывать, -оса́ть план; (*encourage to speak*): **~ s.o. out** вызыва́ть, вы́звать кого́-н. на разгово́р; заста́вить (*pf.*) кого́-н. заговори́ть; *v.i.*: **the train drew out** по́езд вы́шел (со ста́нции); **the car drew out into the road** автомоби́ль вы́ехал на доро́гу; **~ up** *v.t.*: **~ o.s. up** (*to one's full height*) выпрямля́ться, вы́прямиться; **~ one's chair up to the table** пододв|ига́ть, -и́нуть (*or* подта́|скивать, -щи́ть) стул к столу́; **~ up troops** выстра́ивать, вы́строить войска́; (*plan, contract etc.*) сост|авля́ть, -а́вить; оф|ормля́ть, -о́рмить; *v.i.*: **the taxi drew up at the door** такси́ подъе́хало к две́ри; **the troops drew up before the general** войска́ вы́строились пе́ред генера́лом.

cpds. **~back** *n.* (*disadvantage*) недоста́ток, поме́ха, препя́тствие; (*refund of duty*) возвра́тная по́шлина; **~bridge** *n.* подъёмный мост.

drawee [drɔːˈiː] *n.* (*fin.*) трасса́т.

drawer [ˈdrɔːə(r), *senses* **3.** *and* **4.** drɔː(r)] *n.* **1.** (*author of drawing*) рисова́льщик. **2.** (*fin.*) трасса́нт; (*of cheque*) чекода́тель (*m.*). **3.** (*in table etc.*) (выдвижно́й) я́щик; я́щик (пи́сьменного стола́; **chest of ~s** комо́д; **bottom ~** (*fig., trousseau*) прида́ное; **she is out of the top ~** (*fig., well-bred*) она́ прекра́сно воспи́тана. **4.** (*pl., underpants*) кальсо́н|ы (*pl., g.* —).

drawing [ˈdrɔːɪŋ] *n.* **1.** (*technique*) рисова́ние; **out of ~** нарисо́ванный с наруше́нием перспекти́вы. **2.** (*piece of ~*) рису́нок.

cpds. **~-board** *n.* чертёжная доска́; **~-master** *n.* учи́тель (*m.*) рисова́ния; **~-pad** *n.* блокно́т для рисова́ния; **~-paper** *n.* бума́га для рисова́ния; **~-pin** *n.* кно́пка; **~-room** *n.* гости́ная; **~-room comedy** сало́нная коме́дия.

drawl [drɔːl] *n.* протя́жное произноше́ние.

v.t. & i. тяну́ть (*impf.*) (слова́).

dray [dreɪ] *n.* ломова́я теле́га.

cpds. **~-horse** *n.* ломова́я ло́шадь; **~man** *n.* ломово́й изво́зчик.

dread [dred] *n.* у́жас, страх; **stand in ~ of s.o.** боя́ться (*impf.*) кого́-н.; **in ~ of one's life** в стра́хе за свою́ жизнь.

adj. ужа́сный, гро́зный.

v.t. боя́ться (*impf.*) +*g.*; **I ~ to think what may happen** мне стра́шно поду́мать, что мо́жет случи́ться.

cpd. **~nought** *n.* дредно́ут.

dreadful [ˈdredfʊl] *adj.* ужа́сный.

dreadfulness [ˈdredfʊlnɪs] *n.* у́жас.

dream [driːm] *n.* **1.** (*appearance in sleep*) сон, сновиде́ние. **2.** (*fantasy*) мечта́, мечта́ние; (*poet.*) грёза; **land of ~s** ца́рство грёз. **3.** (*bemused state*): **he goes about in a ~** он хо́дит как во сне. **4.** (*delightful object*) мечта́, ска́зка; **she looked a perfect ~** она́ была́ ска́зочно хороша́; **~ house** дом-ска́зка.

v.t. & i. **1.** (*in sleep*) ви́деть (*impf.*) сон; **I ~t that I was in the forest** мне сни́лось, что я в лесу́; **I ~t of you** вы мне сни́лись; я вас ви́дел во сне. **2.** (*imagine*) пом|ышля́ть, -ы́слить о+*p.*; фантази́ровать (*impf.*); **I never ~t of doing so** я и не помышля́л сде́лать э́то; **you must have ~t it** э́то вам помере́щилось/присни́лось; **he ~t up a plan** (*coll.*) он сочини́л план. **3.** (*spend time in reverie*) гре́зить (*impf.*); мечта́ть (*impf.*); **he ~t away his life** он провёл жизнь в мечта́х; он жил в ми́ре грёз.

cpds. **~-land, ~-world** *nn.* ца́рство грёз; **~-like** *adj.* ска́зочный.

dreamer [ˈdriːmə(r)] *n.* (*in sleep*) ви́дящий сны (*dreamy pers.*) мечта́тель (*m.*); (*visionary*) фантазёр.

dreaminess [ˈdriːmɪnɪs] *n.* мечта́тельность.

dreamless [ˈdriːmlɪs] *adj.* без сновиде́ний; **he fell into a ~ sleep** он погрузи́лся в глубо́кий сон.

dreamy [ˈdriːmɪ] *adj.* мечта́тельный; (*coll., lovely*) восхити́тельный.

dreariness [ˈdrɪərɪnɪs] *n.* се́рость.

dreary [ˈdrɪərɪ] *adj.* (*gloomy*) тосикли́вый; (*dull*) тоскли́вый, се́рый.

dredge [dredʒ] *n.* (*net*) дра́га; (*machine*) дра́га, землечерпа́лка.

v.t. & i. драги́ровать (*impf., pf.*); **~ a harbour** оч|ища́ть, -и́стить порт; **~ up** выла́вливать, вы́ловить; **~ for oysters** лови́ть (*impf.*) у́стриц се́тью.

dredger [ˈdredʒə(r)] *n.* землечерпа́лка, землесо́с.

dreg [dreg] *n.* (*usu. pl.*) **1.** (*of liquor*) отсто́й, оса́док; **drain to the ~s** пить, вы- до дна. **2.** (*pl., fig.*) подо́нки (*m. pl.*).

dreggy [dregɪ] *adj.* содержа́щий оса́док.

drench [drentʃ] *n.* (*downpour*) ли́вень (*m.*).

v.t. пром|а́чивать, -очи́ть; **we got a ~ing** мы промо́кли насквόзь; **he was ~ed to the skin** он вы́мок до ни́тки; он промо́к до косте́й.

Dresden [ˈdrezd(ə)n] *n.* Дре́зден; (*attr.*) дре́зденский.

dress [dres] *n.* **1.** (*clothing, costume*) наря́д, туале́т, пла́тье; **she thinks of nothing but ~** она́ ни о чём не ду́мает, кро́ме наря́дов/туале́тов; **full ~** пара́дная фо́рма; **morning ~** (*formal*) визи́тка; **national ~** национа́льный костю́м; **evening ~** фрак; (*woman's*) вече́рнее пла́тье; **~ circle** бельэта́ж; **~ coat** фрак; **~ rehearsal** генера́льная репети́ция; **day ~** обы́чный костю́м, обы́чное пла́тье; **~ suit** фрак; фра́чная па́ра; **~ shirt** фра́чная соро́чка. **2.** (*woman's garment*) пла́тье. **3.** (*guise, covering*) одея́ние; (*plumage*) опере́ние.

v.t. **1.** (*clothe*) од|ева́ть, -е́ть; **the boy can ~ himself** ма́льчик уме́ет сам одева́ться; **she was ~ed in white** она́ была́ оде́та в бе́лое; **~ed up to the nines, ~ed to kill** расфранчённый; разоде́тый в пух и прах; (*theatr.*): **who ~ed the play?** кто сде́лал костю́мы для спекта́кля? **2.** (*prepare*) припр|авля́ть, -а́вить; **~ leather** выде́лывать, вы́делать ко́жу; **~ a salad** запр|авля́ть, -а́вить сала́т; **~** (*clean*) **a chicken** потроши́ть, вы- ку́рицу. **3.** (*brush*) прич|ёсывать, -еса́ть; **~ down a horse** чи́стить, по- ло́шадь; **~ s.o. down** (*fig.*) зад|ава́ть, -а́ть кому́-н. головомо́йку. **4.** (*of a wound*) перевя́з|ывать, -а́ть. **5.** (*adorn*) наря|жа́ть, -ди́ть; **~ a shop window** оф|ормля́ть, -о́рмить витри́ну; **the streets are ~ed with flags** у́лицы укра́шены фла́гами. **6.** (*mil., align*) выра́внивать, вы́ровнять.

v.i. **1.** (*put on one's clothes*) од|ева́ться, -е́ться; **she takes an hour to ~** она́ одева́ется це́лый час; **~ up** (**~** *elaborately*) наря|жа́ться, -ди́ться; разря|жа́ться, -ди́ться; **they ~ed up as pirates** они́ наряди́лись пира́тами. **2.** (*put on evening ~*) перeод|ева́ться, -е́ться в вече́рнее пла́тье; **no-one ~es for dinner** никто́ не переодева́ется к обе́ду. **3.** (*choose clothes*) од|ева́ться, -е́ться; **he ~es well** он хорошо́ одева́ется. **4.** (*of troops*) выра́вниваться, вы́ровняться; **right ~!** равне́ние напра́во!

cpds. **~maker** *n.* портни́ха; **~maker's** *n.* ателье́ (*indecl.*) (мод); **~making** *n.* шитьё/поши́в да́мской оде́жды; **~-preserver, ~-shield** *nn.* подмы́шник.

dressage [ˈdresɑːʒ, -sɑːdʒ] *n.* объе́здка лошаде́й.

dresser[1] [ˈdresə(r)] *n.* **1.** (*chooser of clothes etc.*): **she is a good ~** она́ уме́ет одева́ться. **2.** (*theatr.*) костюме́р (*fem.* -ша). **3.** (*in hospital*) хирурги́ческая сестра́. **4.** (*of leather*) коже́вник.

dresser[2] [ˈdresə(r)] *n.* (*sideboard*) ку́хонный шкаф.

dressiness [ˈdresɪnɪs] *n.* шик, наря́дность.

dressing [ˈdresɪŋ] *n.* **1.** (*art of dress*) одева́ние. **2.** (*for wounds*) перевя́зочный материа́л; повя́зки, перевя́зки (*both f. pl.*). **3.** (*of salad etc.*) запра́вка, припра́ва. **4.** (*manure*) удобре́ние.

cpds. **~-case** *n.* несессе́р; **~down** *n.* (*coll.*) головомо́йка, трёпка; **~-gown** *n.* хала́т; **~-room** *n.* (*theatr., etc.*) грим-убо́рная; **~-station** *n.* (*mil.*) перевя́зочный пункт; **~-table** *n.* туале́т, туале́тный сто́лик.

dressy [ˈdresɪ] *adj.* шика́рный, наря́дный.

dribble [ˈdrɪb(ə)l] *n.* (*trickle*) стру́йка.

v.t.: **~ a ball** вести́ (*det.*) мяч.

v.i. (*of baby*) пуска́ть, распусти́ть слю́ни.

dribbler ['drɪblə(r)] *n.* ведýщий мяч.
driblet ['drɪblɪt] *n.* кáпелька; **in ~s** понемнóжку; по кáпле.
drier ['draɪə(r)] *n.* (*siccative*) сиккати́в; (**hair-~**) суши́лка; (**clothes-~**) суши́льный автомáт.
drift [drɪft] *n.* **1.** (*of tide etc.*) течéние, самотёк. **2.** (*heap of snow, leaves etc.*) нанóс, кýча. **3.** (*meaning*) смысл; **I get his ~** я понимáю, кудá он клóнит. **4.** (*tendency*) направлéние. **5.** (*inactivity*) пасси́вность; **their policy is one of ~** у них всё пýщено на самотёк.
v.t.: **the wind ~ed the snow into high banks** вéтер намёл высóкие сугрóбы.
v.i. дрейфовáть (*impf.*); **the boat ~ed out to sea** лóдку унеслó в мóре; **we ~ed downstream** нас отнеслó вниз по течéнию; **we are ~ing towards disaster** мы дви́жемся к катастрóфе; **they were friends but ~ed apart** они́ бы́ли друзья́ми, но их пути́ постепéнно разошли́сь.
cpds. **~-ice** *n.* дрейфýющая льди́на; **~-net** *n.* дри́фтерная сеть; **~wood** *n.* сплавнóй лес.
drifter ['drɪftə(r)] *n.* (*aimless pers.*) летýн; перекати́-пóле.
drill[1] [drɪl] *n.* (*instrument*) сверлó, бурáв, бур.
v.t. сверли́ть, про-; бури́ть, про-; **~ a hole** (*lit.*) сверли́ть, про- отвéрстие; (*fig.*) продыря́в|ливать, -ить; **~ a tooth** сверли́ть (*impf.*) зуб.
v.i. бури́ть (*impf.*); **~ for oil** бури́ть (*impf.*) нефтянýю сквáжину.
drill[2] [drɪl] *n.* **1.** (*military exercise*) строевáя подготóвка, (*coll.*) муштрá. **2.** (*thorough practice*) трениро́вка. **3.** (*coll., procedure*) процедýра; **what's the ~ for getting tickets?** каковá процедýра получéния билéтов?
v.t. **1.** (*troops*) обуч|áть, -и́ть стрóю; муштровáть, вы-. **2.: ~ s.o. in grammar** натáск|ивать, -áть когó-н. по граммáтике; **I have ~ed him in what he is to say** я вдолби́л емý, что он дóлжен говори́ть.
v.i. упражня́ться (*impf.*); про|ходи́ть, -йти́ строевóе обучéние; **the troops were ~ing all morning** войскá обучáлись стрóю всё ýтро.
cpds. **~-book** *n.* строевóй устáв; **~-hall** *n.* учéбный зал; **~-sergeant** *n.* сержáнт-инстрýктор по стрóю.
drill[3] [drɪl] *n.* (*text.*) тик.
drily, dryly ['draɪlɪ] *adv.* ирони́чно; с лёгким ехи́дством.
drink [drɪŋk] *n.* **1.** (*liquid*) питьё, напи́ток. **2.** (*quantity*) глотóк; **give me a ~ of water** дáйте мне воды́/води́чки. **3.** (*alcoholic*) спиртнóй напи́ток; **take to ~** пристрасти́ться (*pf.*) к винý; **the worse for ~** вы́пивший; **drive s.o. to ~** дов|оди́ть, -ести́ когó-н. до пья́нства; **in ~** в пья́ном ви́де; **who is providing the ~s?** кто стáвит вы́пивку?; **he smells of ~** от негó несёт спиртны́м. **4.: the ~** (*coll., sea*) мóре.
v.t. **1.** (*consume liquid*) пить, вы-; **~ down, off** выпивáть, вы́пить зáлпом; **~ up** доп|ивáть, -и́ть; **~ing-fountain** питьевóй фонтáнчик; **~ing-water** питьевáя водá. **2.** (*of plants, soil etc.*) впи́т|ывать, -áть; **the flowers have drunk all that water** цветы́ впитáли всю вóду. **3.** (*absorb with the mind*) впи́т|ывать, -áть; **she drank the story in** онá жáдно слýшала расскáз. **4.** (*of alcoholic liquor*) пить (*or* выпивáть) вы́-; **he drank himself to death** пья́нство свелó егó в моги́лу; **he ~s half his earnings** он пропивáет полови́ну своегó зáработка; **~ s.o. under the table** перепи́ть (*pf.*) когó-н.; **~ing-bout** попóйка, пья́нка, кутёж; **~ing-horn** рог (для пи́ва); **~ing-song** застóльная пéсня. **5.: ~ a toast** провозгласи́ть (*pf.*) тост; подня́ть (*pf.*) бокáл (за+*a.*); **~ s.o.'s health** пить (*impf.*) за чьё-н. здорóвье; **I ~ to your success** я пью за ваш успéх.
v.i. (*consume liquid*) пить (*impf.*); **~ deep** мнóго пить; (*be a drunkard*) пить запóем, пья́нствовать (*impf.*); **do you ~?** вы пьёте?; **he ~s like a fish** он пьёт как сапóжник.
drinkable ['drɪŋkəb(ə)l] *adj.* (*capable of being drunk*) питьевóй, гóдный для питья́; (*palatable*) вкýсный.
drinker ['drɪŋkə(r)] *n.* (*one who drinks, esp. alcohol*) пью́щий; **he is an occasional ~** он иногдá выпивáет; (*drunkard*) пья́ница.
drip [drɪp] *n.* кáпанье; (*sl., weak or dull pers.*) занýда (*c.g.*).
v.t.: **he was ~ping sweat** с негó кати́лся пот.
v.i. кáпать (*impf.*); пáдать (*impf.*) кáплями; **his shirt ~ped with blood** егó рубáшка промóкла от крóви; **~ping wet** наскво́зь промóкший; **the wall ~s** стенá протекáет.
cpds. **~-drop** *n.* кáпанье; шум кáпель; **~-dry** *adj.* не трéбующий глáжки; *v.t.* суши́ть (*impf.*) на вéшалке, не выжимáя; **~-feed** *n.* кáпельное внутривéнное вливáние; питáтельная кли́зма.
dripping ['drɪpɪŋ] *n.* (*pl., liquid*) кáпли (*f. pl.*); (*cul.*) топлёный жир.
cpd. **~-pan** *n.* прóтивень (*m.*).
drive [draɪv] *n.* **1.** (*ride in vehicle*) ездá; **go for a ~** прокати́ться (*det.*), покатáться (*indet.*) (*both pf.*) на маши́не; **take s.o. for a ~** прокати́ть/покатáть (*pf.*) когó-н. на маши́не; **the station is an hour's ~ away** до стáнции час езды́. **2.** (*private road*) подъезднáя дорóга. **3.** (*hit, stroke, at tennis etc.*) драйв, си́льный удáр. **4.** (*energy*) напóристость, си́ла. **5.** (*organized effort*) кампáния; **a ~ for new members** кампáния по привлечéнию нóвых члéнов. **6.** (*tournament*) состязáние. **7.** (*driving gear*) передáча, привóд; **front-wheel ~** перéдний привóд; **left-hand ~** лéвое рулевóе управлéние.
v.t. **1.** (*force to move*) гоня́ть (*indet.*), гнать (*det.*); выбивáть, вы́бить; **~ away** прог|оня́ть, -нáть; **~ in** заг|оня́ть, -нáть; **~ out** выгоня́ть, вы́гнать; **~ cattle to market** гнать (*det.*) скот на ры́нок; **~ s.o. into a corner** (*fig.*) загнáть (*pf.*) когó-н. в ýгол. **2.** (*operate*) управля́ть (*impf.*) +*i.*; прáвить (*impf.*) +*i.*; **~ a car** води́ть (*indet.*) маши́ну; **the machinery is ~n by steam** маши́на привóдится в дéйствие пáром; маши́на рабóтает на парý. **3.** (*convey*) отв|ози́ть, -езти́; **I was ~n to the station** меня́ отвезли́ на стáнцию. **4.** (*impel, of objects*): **the gale drove the ship on to the rocks** штóрм гнал корáбль на скáлы; **the wind drove the rain against the windows** дождь и вéтер стучáли в óкна, **he drove a nail into the plank** он вбил гвоздь в дóску; **he drove the ball into our court** (*tennis*) он послáл мяч на нáшу полови́ну кóрта; **~n snow** сугрóб; **~ home** (*nail etc.*) загоня́ть, загнáть; вкол|áчивать, -оти́ть; вби|вáть, -ть; **~ sth. home to s.o.** убеди́ть (*pf.*) когó-н. в чём-н.; довести́ (*pf.*) когó-н. до сознáния чегó-н.; **~ one's sword through s.o.'s body** пронз|áть, -и́ть когó-н. мечóм; **this drove the matter out of my head** э́то вы́шибло у меня́ всё из головы́. **5.** (*impel, fig.*): **failure drove him to despair** неудáча довелá егó до отчáяния; **~ s.o. mad** св|оди́ть, -ести́ когó-н. с умá; дов|оди́ть, -ести́ когó-н. до безýмия; **hunger drove him to steal** гóлод застáвил егó воровáть. **6.** (*force to work hard*) гоня́ть, гнáть; **he has been driving his staff too much** он совершéнно загоня́л свои́х подчинённых; **he is hard ~n** егó совсéм загоня́ли. **7.** (*engineering*) про|клáдывать, -ложи́ть; пров|оди́ть, -ести́; **~ a tunnel through a hill** проложи́ть (*pf.*) туннéль чéрез гóру. **8.** (*effect, conclude*): **~ a roaring trade** вести́ (*det.*) оживлённую торгóвлю; **~ a bargain** заключ|áть, -и́ть сдéлку.
v.i. **1.** (*operate vehicle*) води́ть (*indet.*), вести́ (*det.*) маши́ну; **we drove up to the door** мы подъéхали/подкати́ли пря́мо к двéри; **~ yourself car hire** прокáт маши́н без шофёра. **2.** (*be impelled*): **the ship drove on to the rocks** корáбль нёсся на скáлы; **rain drove against the panes** дождь бил в окóнные стёкла; **he let ~ at me with his fist** он стýкнул меня́ кулакóм; **driving rain** проливнóй дождь. **3.** (*be active*): **he drove away at his work** он нажáл во всю; **what is he driving at?** к чемý он клóнит?; кудá он гнёт? **4.** (*of vehicle*): **the car ~s easily** э́ту маши́ну легкó вести́.
drivel ['drɪv(ə)l] *n.* (*nonsense*) чушь.
v.t. & i. порóть (*impf.*) чушь; плести́ (*impf.*) вздор/чепухý; **~ away one's time** разбазáри|вать, -ть своё врéмя; **~ling idiot** закóнченный крети́н.
driver ['draɪvə(r)] *n.* (*of vehicle*) води́тель (*m.*), шофёр; (*of animals*) погóнщик, гуртовщи́к; (*one who overworks his staff*) надсмóтрщик, поги́нщик.
driverless ['draɪvəlɪs] *adj.* без води́теля.
driving ['draɪvɪŋ] *n.* ездá; вождéние автомоби́ля; **~ instructor** преподавáтель (*m.*) автошкóлы.

cpds. **~-belt** *n.* приводно́й реме́нь; **~-licence** *n.* води́тельские права́; **~-mirror** *n.* зе́ркало за́днего обзо́ра; **~-school** *n.* автошко́ла; **~-test** *n.* экза́мен на вожде́ние; **~-wheel** *n.* веду́щее колесо́.

drizzle ['drɪz(ə)l] *n.* и́зморось.
v.i. мороси́ть (*impf.*).

drizzly ['drɪzlɪ] *adj.* морося́щий.

droll [drəʊl] *n.* шутни́к.
adj. чудно́й, заба́вный.

drollery ['drəʊlərɪ] *n.* игри́вость, шу́тки (*f. pl.*).

drollness ['drəʊlnɪs] *n.* заба́вность.

dromedary ['drɒmɪdərɪ, 'drʌm-] *n.* дромаде́р.

drone [drəʊn] *n.* **1.** (*bee*; *also fig.*, *idler*) тру́тень (*m.*). **2.** (*of engine*) гуде́ние; (*of voice*) жужжа́ние.
v.t. & i. (*hum*) жужжа́ть (*impf.*); гуде́ть (*impf.*); (*speak monotonously*) бубни́ть (*impf.*).

drool [dru:l] *v.i.* пус|ка́ть, -ти́ть слю́ни.

droop [dru:p] *n.* (*attitude or position*) опуска́ние, поника́ние.
v.t. (*e.g. head*) опус|ка́ть, -ти́ть; (*e.g. eyes*) потуп|ля́ть, -у́пить.
v.i. (*of flowers etc.*) склон|я́ться, -и́ться; (*fig.*): **his spirits ~ed** он пал ду́хом.

droopy ['dru:pɪ] *adj.* (*lit.*) склоня́ющийся, склонённый; (*fig.*) пони́кший, сни́кший, уны́лый.

drop [drɒp] *n.* **1.** (*small quantity of liquid*) ка́пля; **~ by ~** ка́пля по ка́пле; (*fig.*): **a ~ in the bucket, ocean** ка́пля в мо́ре; **he had a ~ too much** он хвати́л ли́шнего. **2.** (*small round object*): **acid ~** монпансье́ (*indecl.*), ледене́ц; **ear ~** серьга́, подве́ска. **3.** (*fall*) паде́ние; **~ in prices/temperature** паде́ние цен; пониже́ние температу́ры; **at the ~ of a hat** (*fig.*) сра́зу/то́тчас же; **there is a ~ of 30 feet behind this wall** за э́той стено́й обры́в в 30 фу́тов высоты́. **4.** (*trapdoor*) люк, опускна́я дверь.
v.t. **1.** (*allow, cause to fall*) роня́ть, урони́ть; **~ anchor** бр|оса́ть, -о́сить я́корь; **~ a stitch** спус|ка́ть, -ти́ть петлю́; **~ a letter into the box** опус|ка́ть, -ти́ть письмо́ в я́щик; **~ supplies by parachute** сбр|а́сывать, -о́сить припа́сы на парашю́те; **~ a parcel at s.o.'s house** ост|авля́ть, -а́вить паке́т у чьего́-н. до́ма. **2.** (*impel, force down*) сра|жа́ть, -зи́ть; **~ shells into a town** обстре́л|ивать, -я́ть го́род; **he ~ped a bird with every shot** ка́ждым вы́стрелом он подбива́л пти́цу; **he ~ped the ball to the back of the court** он посла́л мяч в коне́ц ко́рта. **3.** (*give birth to young*) (*lamb or kid*) оягни́ться (*pf.*); (*calf etc.*) отели́ться (*pf.*). **4.** (*lower*): **~ one's voice** пон|ижа́ть, -и́зить го́лос; **~ one's eyes** поту́пить (*pf.*) глаза́. **5.** (*send, utter casually*): **~ s.o. a line** черкну́ть (*pf.*) кому́-н. па́ру строк; **~ a hint** оброни́ть (*pf.*) намёк. **6.** (*omit, cease*) опус|ка́ть, -ти́ть; пропус|ка́ть, -ти́ть; **this word can safely he ~ped** э́то сло́во мо́жно споко́йно опусти́ть; **~ it!** переста́ньте!; бро́сьте! **7.** (*allow to descend, disembark*) выса́живать, вы́садить; спус|ка́ть, -ти́ть с бо́рта; **please ~ me at the station** пожа́луйста, вы́садите меня́ у ста́нции; **~ the pilot** спус|ка́ть, -ти́ть ло́цмана. **8.** (*abandon*) бр|оса́ть, -о́сить; **let us ~ the subject** дава́йте оста́вим э́ту те́му; **he ~ped all his friends** он порва́л со все́ми свои́ми друзья́ми; **you should ~ smoking** вы должны́ бро́сить кури́ть. **9.** (*coll., lose*) теря́ть, по-; **he ~ped £100** он потра́тил сто фу́нтов. **10.**: **~ a goal** заб|ива́ть, -и́ть гол.
v.i. **1.** (*fall, descend*) па́дать, упа́сть; опус|ка́ться, -ти́ться; **you could hear a pin ~** (*fig.*) бы́ло слы́шно, как му́ха пролети́т; **~ (down) on s.o.** (*fig.*) набр|а́сываться, -о́ситься (*or* нап|ада́ть, -а́сть) на кого́-н.; **~ into a habit** входи́ть, войти́ в привы́чку; приобре|та́ть, -сти́ привы́чку; **~ into one's club** загля́|дывать, -ну́ть в клу́б. **2.** (*become weaker or lower*) па́дать, упа́сть; пон|ижа́ться, -и́зиться; **the wind ~ped** ве́тер стих/ути́х; **prices ~ped** це́ны упа́ли; **his voice ~ped** он пони́зил го́лос; **the boat ~ped downstream** ло́дка шла вниз по тече́нию. **3.** (*expr. separation etc.*): **~ behind the others** отст|ава́ть, -а́ть от остальны́х; **he ~ped from sight** он исче́з из по́ля зре́ния. **4.** (*sink, collapse*) па́дать, упа́сть; опус|ка́ться, -ти́ться; **he ~ped into a chair** он опусти́лся на стул; **he ~ped (on) to his knees** он упа́л/опусти́лся на коле́ни; **I felt ready to ~** я вали́лся с ног; **his jaw ~ped** его́ че́люсть отви́сла; **he ~ped dead** он внеза́пно у́мер; **~ dead!** (*coll.*) подо́хни!; чтоб ты сдох! **5.** (*cease, be abandoned*): **the correspondence ~ped** перепи́ска прерва́лась; **we let the matter ~** мы бро́сили э́то. **6.** (*meet casually*): **I ~ped across him** я наткну́лся на него́; я столкну́лся с ним. **7.**: **~ on** (*encounter*): **I ~ped on the book I wanted** я нашёл кни́гу, кото́рая мне нужна́; (*pick on*): **why does he ~ on me?** что ему́ от меня́ на́до?
with advs.: **~ in** *v.i.* (*coll.*): **he ~ped in on me** он загляну́л ко мне; **~ off** *v.i.* (*become fewer or less*) ум|еньша́ться, -е́ньшиться; **attendance ~ped off** посеща́емость упа́ла; (*coll., doze off*) засну́ть (*pf.*); **~ out** *v.i.*: **five runners ~ped out** пять бегуно́в вы́были из состяза́ния; **he ~ped out of school** он бро́сил шко́лу.
cpds. **~-curtain** *n.* (*theatr.*) опускно́й/па́дающий за́навес; **~-forging** *n.* горя́чая штампо́вка; **~-hammer** *n.* копёр; **~-head** *n.* автомоби́ль с откидны́м ве́рхом; **~-kick** *n.* уда́р с полулёта; *v.t.* уд|аря́ть, -а́рить с полулёта; **~-leaf** *n.* откидна́я доска́; **~-leaf table** откидно́й сто́лик; **~-out** *n.* челове́к, поста́вивший себя́ вне о́бщества; (*from school*) недоу́чка (*c.g.*); **~-scene** *n.* (*curtain*) опускно́й за́навес; (*final scene*) заключи́тельная сце́на.

droplet ['drɒplət] *n.* ка́пелька.

dropper ['drɒpə(r)] *n.* (*instrument*) пипе́тка; ка́пельница; **eye ~** глазна́я пипе́тка.

dropping ['drɒpɪŋ] *n.* **1.** (*pl., of wax etc.*) ка́пли (*f. pl.*); **the tablecloth was covered with candle ~s** ска́терть была́ зака́пана во́ском от свече́й. **2.** (*pl., of animals and birds*) помёт.
cpds. **~-zone** *n.* зо́на вы́садки деса́нта; зо́на сбра́сывания гру́за.

dropsical ['drɒpsɪk(ə)l] *adj.* водя́ночный, отёчный.

dropsy ['drɒpsɪ] *n.* водя́нка.

droshky ['drɒʃkɪ] *n.* дро́ж|ки (*pl., g.* -ек).

dross [drɒs] *n.* шлак, дросс; (*fig.*) отбро́сы (*m. pl.*); бро́совый това́р.

drought [draʊt] *n.* за́суха.

drove [drəʊv] *n.* (*herd*) ста́до, гурт; (*crowd*) толпа́, гурьба́.

drover ['drəʊvə(r)] *n.* гуртовщи́к.

drown [draʊn] *v.t.* **1.** (*kill by immersion*) топи́ть, у-; **~ one's sorrows in drink** топи́ть, у- го́ре в вине́; **~ o.s.** топи́ться, у-; **be ~ed** утону́ть (*pf.*). **2.** (*of sound*) приглуш|а́ть, -и́ть. **3.** (*bathe, immerse*) погру|жа́ть, -зи́ть; **a face ~ed in tears** лицо́, за́литое слеза́ми; **~ed in sleep** погружённый в глубо́кий сон; **like a ~ed rat** (*fig.*) мо́крый как мышь. **4.**: **they were ~ed out of their home** их дом был зато́плен при наводне́нии.
v.i. тону́ть, у-; утопа́ть (*impf.*); **a ~ing man will catch at a straw** утопа́ющий хвата́ется за соло́минку; **death by ~ing** утопле́ние; **he met his death by ~ing** он утону́л.

drowse [draʊz] *n.* полусо́н, сонли́вость; **in a ~** в дремо́те.
v.t.: **~ away the time** продрема́ть (*pf.*) всё вре́мя.
v.i. дрема́ть (*impf.*); быть в полусне́.

drowsiness ['draʊzɪnɪs] *n.* дремо́та, сонли́вость.

drowsy ['draʊzɪ] *adj.* (*feeling sleepy*) со́нный, дре́млющий; (*soporific*) усыпля́ющий, снотво́рный.

drub [drʌb] *v.t.* колоти́ть, по-; **~ an idea into s.o.'s head** вбить/вдолби́ть (*pf.*) мысль кому́-н. в го́лову.

drubbing ['drʌbɪŋ] *n.* битьё, трёпка, взбу́чка; **give s.o. a ~** над|ава́ть, -а́ть кому́-н. колоту́шек.

drudge [drʌdʒ] *n.* работя́га (*c.g.*), иша́к.
v.i. выполня́ть (*impf.*) изнури́тельную рабо́ту; (*coll.*) иша́чить (*impf.*).

drudgery ['drʌdʒərɪ] *n.* изнури́тельная рабо́та.

drug [drʌg] *n.* **1.** (*medicinal substance*) медикаме́нт, лека́рство. **2.** (*narcotic or stimulant*) нарко́тик; **~ addict** наркома́н; **the ~ habit** наркома́ния; **~ ring** наркосиндика́т; **~ trafficker** *or* **pusher** наркоделе́ц; **~ trafficking** торго́вля нарко́тиками; **~ traffic** контраба́нда нарко́тиками. **3.** (*fig.*): **a ~ on the market** неходово́й това́р.
v.t. (*food etc.*) подме́ш|ивать, -а́ть яд/нарко́тики в (*еду*); (*pers.*) да|ва́ть, -ть нарко́тики +*d.*; одурма́ни|вать, -ть.
v.i. (*take ~s*) прин|има́ть, -я́ть нарко́тики.

cpds. **drug-abuse** *adj.*: **~-abuse clinic** наркологи́ческий диспансе́р; **~store** *n.* (*US*) ≃ апте́ка.
drugget ['drʌgɪt] *n.* (*text.*) ткань для доро́жек, половико́в.
druggist ['drʌgɪst] *n.* апте́карь (*m.*).
Druid ['dru:ɪd] *n.* друи́д.
Druidess ['dru:ɪdɪs] *n.* друи́дка.
Druidic(al) [dru:'ɪdɪk(ə)l] *adj.* друиди́ческий.
Druidism ['dru:ɪd,ɪz(ə)m] *n.* друиди́зм.
drum [drʌm] *n.* **1.** (*instrument*) бараба́н; **beat the big ~** (*fig.*) звони́ть (*impf.*) во все колокола́; **bass ~** большо́й бараба́н. **2.** (*container for oil etc.*) желе́зная бо́чка. **3.** (*cylinder for winding cable etc.*) ка́бельный бараба́н. **4.** (*ear~*) бараба́нная перепо́нка.
v.t. бараба́нить (*impf.*); бить (*impf.*) в бараба́н; **~ s.o. out of the army** с позо́ром выгоня́ть, вы́гнать кого́-н. из а́рмии; **~ up support** соз|ыва́ть, -ва́ть на подмо́гу; **~ sth. into s.o.'s head** вд|а́лбливать, -олби́ть что-н. кому́-н. в го́лову.
v.i. бараба́нить (*impf.*); бить (*impf.*) в бараба́н; **~ with one's fingers on the table** бараба́нить (*impf.*) па́льцами по́ столу; **I have a ~ming in my ears** у меня́ стучи́т в уша́х.
cpds. **~-beat** *n.* бараба́нный бой; **~fire** *n.* урага́нный ого́нь; **~head** *n.* ко́жа на бараба́не; **~head court martial** вое́нно-полево́й суд; **~-major** *n.* тамбурмажо́р; **~-majorette** *n.* тамбурмажоре́тка; **~stick** *n.* бараба́нная па́лочка; (*of fowl*) но́жка.
drummer ['drʌmə(r)] *n.* (*also* **~-boy**) бараба́нщик; (*commercial traveller*) коммивояжёр.
drunk [drʌŋk] *n.* (*pers.* **~**) пья́ный; (*sl., drinking bout*) попо́йка.
adj. пья́ный; **~ driver** автоалкого́лик; **half ~** подвы́пивший; **dead ~** мертве́цки пья́ный; **~ as a lord** пья́ный в сте́льку; **~ with success** опьянённый успе́хом; **get ~ on brandy** нап|ива́ться, -и́ться коньяка́; пьяне́ть, о- от коньяка́.
drunkard ['drʌŋkəd] *n.* пья́ница (*c.g.*), алкого́лик.
drunken ['drʌŋkən] *adj.* пья́ный; **~ brawl** пья́ная ссо́ра.
drunkenness ['drʌŋkənnɪs] *n.* пья́нство.
Druse [dru:z] *n.* друз.
dry [draɪ] *adj.* **1.** (*free from moisture or rain*) сухо́й; пересо́хший, засо́хший; **~ as a bone** сухо́й-пресухо́й; **~ spell** пери́од без оса́дков; **wipe ~** вытира́ть, вы́тереть на́сухо. **2.** (*not supplying water etc.*) вы́сохший, сухо́й; **a ~ well** вы́сохший коло́дец; **the cows are ~** коро́вы не до́ятся; **my pen is ~** черни́ла в мое́й ру́чке вы́сохли. **3.: ~ measure** ме́ра сыпу́чих тел; **~ goods** (*drapery*) мануфакту́рные това́ры. **4.: ~ run** (*trial*) про́бный забе́г. **5.** (*of wine*) сухо́й. **6.** (*causing thirst*): **~ work** рабо́та, от кото́рой в го́рле пересыха́ет. **7.** (*dull, plain*) сухо́й; **~ as dust** (*fig., of pers.*) суха́рь (*m.*). **8.** (*of humour*) сухо́й, сухова́тый; (*of remark etc.*) ирони́ческий; *see also* **drily. 9.: ~ shampoo** сухо́й шампу́нь; **~ battery** суха́я электри́ческая батаре́я. **10.: the country went dry** в стране́ ввели́ сухо́й зако́н.
v.t. суши́ть (*or* высу́шивать), вы́-; **~ o.s.** вытира́ться, вы́тереться; **~ one's tears** ут|ира́ть, -ере́ть слёзы; **~ the dishes** вытира́ть, вы́тереть посу́ду; **~ one's hands** вытира́ть, вы́тереть ру́ки; **dried fruit(s)** сушёные фру́кты; **dried egg** яи́чный порошо́к; **dried milk** сухо́е молоко́; **the drought dried up the wells** за́суха вы́сушила коло́дцы; **the wind dries up one's skin** ве́тер су́шит ко́жу; **a dried-up man** сухо́й челове́к, суха́рь (*m.*).
v.i. со́хнуть (*impf.*); суши́ться (*or* высу́шиваться), вы́-; **our clothes have dried** на́ша оде́жда вы́сохла; **the well dried up** коло́дец вы́сох; **his imagination dried up** его́ фанта́зия исся́кла; **~ up!** заткни́сь! (*coll.*); **he dried up** (*coll., theatr.*) он забы́л роль; **hang sth. up to ~** ве́шать, пове́сить что-н. для просу́шки.
cpds. **~-clean** *v.t.* подв|ерга́ть, -е́ргнуть хими́ческой чи́стке; **~-cleaning** *n.* хими́ческая чи́стка, химчи́стка; **~-eyed** *adj.* без слёз; с сухи́ми глаза́ми; **~-nurse** *n.* ня́ня; *v.t.* ня́нчить, вы-; **~-point** *n.* (*needle*) суха́я игла́; (*engraving*) гравю́ра, испо́лненная сухой игло́й; **~-rot** *n.* суха́я гниль; **~-salter** *n.* москате́льщик; **~-shod** *adv.* не замочи́в ног.
dryad ['draɪæd, 'draɪəd] *n.* дриа́да.
drying ['draɪɪŋ] *n.* су́шка; **spin ~** отжи́м белья́ центрифу́гой.
cpd. **~-cupboard** *n.* шкаф для су́шки белья́.
dryish ['draɪɪʃ] *adj.* сухова́тый.
dryly ['draɪlɪ] = **drily**
dryness ['draɪnɪs] *n.* су́хость, сушь.
DSS (*abbr. of* ***Department of Social Security***) Министе́рство социа́льного обеспе́чения.
DTI (*abbr. of* ***Department of Trade and Industry***) Министе́рство торго́вли и промы́шленности.
DTP (*abbr. of* ***desktop publishing***) насто́льная полигра́фия.
DT's [di:'ti:z] *n.* (*coll.*) бе́лая горя́чка.
dual ['dju:əl] *n.* (*gram.*) дво́йственное число́.
adj. дво́йственный, двойно́й; **~ ownership** совме́стное владе́ние; **the D~ Monarchy** дуалисти́ческая мона́рхия; **~ personality** раздвое́ние ли́чности; **~ control** двойно́е управле́ние; **~ nationality** двойно́е по́дданство.
cpd. **~-purpose** *adj.* двойно́го назначе́ния.
dualism ['dju:ə,lɪz(ə)m] *n.* дуали́зм.
duality [,dju:'ælɪtɪ] *n.* дво́йственность, раздво́енность.
dub [dʌb] *v.t.* **1.** (*a knight*) посвя|ща́ть, -ти́ть в ры́цари; (*fig., call*) проз|ыва́ть, -ва́ть; крести́ть, о-. **2.** (*coll., film*) дубли́ровать (*impf.*); **his voice was ~bed** он дубли́ровал друго́го актёра.
dubbing ['dʌbɪŋ] *n.* (*of film*) дубли́рование.
dubiety [dju:'baɪətɪ] *n.* сомне́ние.
dubious ['dju:bɪəs] *adj.* (*feeling doubt*) сомнева́ющийся; (*inspiring mistrust; ambiguous*) сомни́тельный.
dubiousness ['dju:bɪəsnɪs] *n.* сомни́тельность.
Dublin ['dʌblɪn] *n.* Ду́блин; (*attr.*) ду́блинский.
ducal ['dju:k(ə)l] *adj.* ге́рцогский.
ducat ['dʌkət] *n.* дука́т.
duchess ['dʌtʃɪs] *n.* герцоги́ня; **grand ~** (*wife*) вели́кая княги́ня; (*daughter*) вели́кая княжна́.
duchy ['dʌtʃɪ] *n.* ге́рцогство, кня́жество; **Grand D~ of Muscovy** Вели́кое кня́жество Моско́вское.
duck[1] [dʌk] *n.* (*text.*) паруси́на; (*pl.*) паруси́новые брю́ки (*pl., g.* —).
duck[2] [dʌk] *n.* **1.** (*water-bird*) у́тка; (*as food*) утя́тина; **wild ~** ди́кая у́тка; **take to sth. like a ~ to water** чу́вствовать, по- себя́ в чём-н. как ры́ба в воде́; **sitting ~** (*fig.*) лёгкая же́ртва/добы́ча; **like water off a ~'s back** как с гу́ся вода́; **a fine day for the ~s** дождли́вая пого́да; **like a dying ~** как мо́края ку́рица; **dead ~** (*fig.*) ко́нченый челове́к; ги́блое де́ло; **play ~s and drakes** (*skimming stones*) печь (*impf.*) блины́; (*fig., squander*) пром|а́тывать, -ота́ть; разбаза́ри|вать, -ть; **lame ~** неуда́чник. **2.** (*dear creature*) ду́шка, ду́шенька. **3.** (*also* **~'s egg:** *zero score*) нулево́й счёт; **make a ~** сыгра́ть (*pf.*) с нулевы́м счётом.
cpds. **~-bill (platypus)** *n.* утконо́с; **~-boards** *n. pl.* доща́тый насти́л; **~-pond** *n.* пруд для у́ток; **~('s)-egg blue** *n. & adj.* зеленова́то-голубо́й (цвет); **~-shooting** *n.* охо́та на ди́ких у́ток; **~weed** *n.* ря́ска.
duck[3] [dʌk] *n.* (*landing-craft*) автомоби́ль-амфи́бия.
duck[4] [dʌk] *n.* (*~ing motion, dip*) погруже́ние, ныря́ние, окуна́ние.
v.t. погру|жа́ть, -зи́ть; окун|а́ть, -у́ть; **~ one's head** бы́стро нагну́ть (*pf.*) го́лову; **~ s.o.** окун|а́ть, -у́ть кого́-н.; тол|ка́ть, -ну́ть кого́-н. в во́ду; (*evade*): **~ a question** увёр|тываться, -ну́ться от отве́та.
v.i. окун|а́ться, -у́ться; **~ to avoid a blow** наклон|я́ться, -и́ться, что́бы избежа́ть уда́ра; (*as curtsey*), де́лать, с- релева́нс; прис|еда́ть, -е́сть.
ducking ['dʌkɪŋ] *n.* погруже́ние в во́ду; **give s.o. a ~** опус|ка́ть, -ти́ть чью-н. го́лову в во́ду; **it rained and we got a ~** шёл дождь, и мы промо́кли насквозь.
duckling ['dʌklɪŋ] *n.* утёнок; **ugly ~** га́дкий утёнок.
ducky ['dʌkɪ] *n.* (*coll.*) ду́шечка, голу́бушка.
duct ['dʌkt] *n.* (*anat.*) кана́л, прото́к.
ductile ['dʌktaɪl] *adj.* (*tech.*) тягу́чий, ко́вкий; (*of pers.*) пода́тливый.
ductility [,dʌk'tɪlɪtɪ] *n.* (*tech.*) тягу́честь, ко́вкость.
ductless ['dʌktlɪs] *adj.*: **~ gland** железа́ вну́тренней секре́ции.

dud [dʌd] *n.* (*coll.*) **1.** (*bomb*) неразорва́вшаяся бо́мба; (*shell*) неразорва́вшийся снаря́д; (*cheque etc.*) подде́лка, ли́па; (*pers.*) пусто́е ме́сто. **2.** (*pl., clothes*) тря́пки (*f. pl.*).

adj. неприго́дный, подде́льный.

dude [dju:d, du:d] *n.* пижо́н (*coll.*).

dudgeon ['dʌdʒ(ə)n] *n.* возмуще́ние, оби́да; **in (high)** ~ с глубо́ким возмуще́нием; негоду́я.

due [dju:] *n.* **1.** (~ *credit*) до́лжное; **to give him his ~, he tried hard** на́до отда́ть ему́ до́лжное — он о́чень стара́лся. **2.** (*pl., charges*) сбо́ры (*m. pl.*), взно́сы (*m. pl.*); **membership ~s** чле́нские взно́сы; **harbour ~s** порто́вые сбо́ры.

adj. **1.** (*owing, payable*) причита́ющийся; **debts ~ to us** причита́ющиеся нам долги́; **when is the rent ~?** когда́ на́до плати́ть за кварти́ру?; **the bill falls ~ on October 1** срок платежа́ по ве́кселю наступа́ет пе́рвого октября́. **2.** (*proper*) до́лжный, надлежа́щий; **with ~ attention** с до́лжным внима́нием; **in ~ time** в своё вре́мя; **after ~ consideration** по́сле надлежа́щего рассмотре́ния; **in ~ course** в свою́ о́чередь, свои́м чередо́м; **I am ~ for a haircut** мне пора́ постри́чься. **3.** (*expected*): **he is ~ to speak twice** он до́лжен вы́ступить два́жды; **the mail is ~ tomorrow** по́чта должна́ быть за́втра. **4.:** ~ **to** (*coll., owing to*) благодаря́+*d.*; из-за+*g.*

adv. то́чно, пря́мо; **it lies ~ south** э́то лежи́т пря́мо на юг отсю́да.

duel ['dju:əl] *n.* дуэ́ль, поеди́нок; ~ **of wits** состяза́ние в остроу́мии.

v.i. дра́ться (*impf.*) на дуэ́ли.

duellist ['dju:əlɪst] *n.* дуэля́нт.

duenna [dju:'enə] *n.* дуэ́нья.

duet [dju:'et] *n.* дуэ́т.

duettist [dju:'etɪst] *n.* оди́н из исполни́телей дуэ́та.

duff|el, -le ['dʌf(ə)l] *n.* **1.** (*text.*): ~ **coat** коро́ткое пальто́ из шерстяно́й ба́йки с капюшо́ном. **2.:** ~ **bag** (*kit-bag*) вещево́й мешо́к.

duffer ['dʌfə(r)] *n.* простофи́ля (*c.g.*) болва́н; **he is a ~ at games** в и́грах от него́ нет никако́го то́лку.

dug [dʌg] *n.* (*udder*) вы́мя (*nt.*); (*nipple*) сосо́к.

dugong ['du:gɒŋ] *n.* дюго́нь (*m.*).

dug-out ['dʌgaʊt] *n.* (*shelter*) блинда́ж; (*canoe*) челно́к; (*sl., officer recalled to service*) офице́р, при́званный из запа́са.

duiker ['daɪkə(r)] *n.* ду́кер.

duke [dju:k] *n.* ге́рцог; **grand** ~ вели́кий князь.

dukedom ['dju:kdəm] *n.* ге́рцогство; кня́жество.

dulcet ['dʌlsɪt] adj. сла́дкий; не́жный.

dulcimer ['dʌlsɪmə(r)] *n.* цимба́л|ы (*pl., g.* —).

dull [dʌl] *adj.* **1.** (*not clear or bright*) ту́склый; **a ~ sound** глухо́й звук; **a ~ mirror** ту́склое зе́ркало; ~ **weather** па́смурная пого́да. **2.** (*slow in understanding*) тупо́й. **3.** (*uninteresting*) ску́чный; **as ~ as ditchwater** невыноси́мо ску́чный; ску́ка сме́ртная. **4.** (*not sharp*) тупо́й; **a ~ knife** тупо́й нож; **a ~ pain** тупа́я боль. **5.** (*slack*) вя́лый; **the market was ~** торго́вля на ры́нке шла вя́ло.

v.t. притуп|ля́ть, -и́ть.

cpds. **~-eyed** *adj.* с ту́склыми глаза́ми; **~-witted** *adj.* тупоу́мный, недалёкий.

dullard ['dʌləd] *n.* тупи́ца.

dullish ['dʌlɪʃ] *adj.* тупова́тый; скучнова́тый.

dullness ['dʌlnɪs] *n.* ту́пость; ску́ка.

duly ['dju:lɪ] *adv.* до́лжным о́бразом; в до́лжное вре́мя; своевре́менно; **I ~ went there** как и сле́довало, я пошёл туда́.

dumb [dʌm] *adj.* **1.** (*unable to speak*) немо́й; ~ **animals** бесслове́сные живо́тные. **2.** (*temporarily silent*) онеме́вший, немо́й; **he was struck ~** он онеме́л; **the class remained ~** класс продолжа́л молча́ть; ~ **show** нема́я сце́на. **3.** (*US coll., stupid*) глу́пый.

cpds. **~-bell** *n.* ганте́ль; **~-waiter** *n.* враща́ющийся сто́лик для заку́сок; лифт для пода́чи ку́шаний из ку́хни в столо́вую.

dum(b)found [dʌm'faʊnd] *v.t.* ошара́ш|ивать, -ить; ошелом|ля́ть, -и́ть.

dumbness ['dʌmnɪs] *n.* немота́.

dummy ['dʌmɪ] *n.* **1.** ку́кла; **tailor's ~** манеке́н; **baby's ~** пусты́шка, со́ска; **he stands there like a (stuffed) ~** он стои́т истука́ном. **2.** (*at cards*) «болва́н». **3.** (*stand-in*) марионе́тка, подставно́е лицо́.

adj. (*imitation*) подставно́й; ~ **window** ло́жное окно́; ~ **cartridge** уче́бный патро́н; ~ **run** испыта́тельный рейс.

dump [dʌmp] *n.* **1.** (*heap of refuse*) му́сорная ку́ча. **2.** (*place for tipping refuse*) помо́йная я́ма; сва́лка; помо́йка. **3.** (*ammunition store*) вре́менный полево́й скла́д. **4.** (*seedy place*) дыра́ (*coll.*).

v.t. **1.** (*put in a ~*) выбра́сывать, вы́бросить на сва́лку/помо́йку. **2.** (*deposit carelessly*) сва́л|ивать, -и́ть.

dumping ['dʌmpɪŋ] *n.* сва́лка; (*comm.*) де́мпинг.

dumpling ['dʌmplɪŋ] *n.* клёцка; **a little ~ of a child** карапу́зик.

dumps [dʌmps] *n.* (*coll.*): **the ~** уны́ние.

dumpy ['dʌmpɪ] *adj.* призе́мистый; ма́ленький, коро́тенький.

dun[1] [dʌn] *n.* назо́йливый кредито́р.

v.t. нап|омина́ть, -о́мнить об упла́те до́лга.

dun[2] [dʌn] *adj.* серова́то-кори́чневый; (*of animal*) була́ный, мыша́стый; (*dark*) су́мрачный.

dunce [dʌns] *n.* тупи́ца (*m.*).

dunderhead ['dʌndə,hed] *n.* болва́н.

dunderheaded ['dʌndə,hedɪd] *adj.* тупоголо́вый.

dune [dju:n] *n.* дю́на.

dung [dʌŋ] *n.* наво́з.

v.t. унаво́|живать, -зить.

cpds. **~-beetle** *n.* наво́зный жук; наво́зник; **~-cart** *n.* наво́зная та́чка; **~-fork** *n.* наво́зные ви́лы (*f. pl.*); **~hill** *n.* наво́зная ку́ча.

dungarees [,dʌŋgə'ri:z] *n.* рабо́чий комбинезо́н.

dungeon ['dʌndʒ(ə)n] *n.* темни́ца, казема́т.

dunk [dʌŋk] *v.t.* мак|а́ть, -ну́ть.

duo ['dju:əʊ] *n.* дуэ́т; (*of comedians*) коми́ческая па́ра.

duodecimal [,dju:əʊ'desɪm(ə)l] *adj.* двенадцатери́чный; ~ **notation** двенадцатери́чная систе́ма счисле́ния.

duodecimo [,dju:əʊ'desɪ,məʊ] *n.* форма́т кни́ги в двена́дцатую до́лю листа́.

adj. разме́ром в двена́дцатую до́лю листа́

duodenal [,dju:əʊ'di:nəl] *adj.* дуодена́льный.

duodenary [,dju:əʊ'di:nərɪ] *adj.* двена́дцатери́чный.

duodenum [,dju:əʊ'di:nəm] *n.* двенадцатипе́рстная кишка́.

duologue ['dju:ə,lɒg] *n.* диало́г.

dupe [dju:p] *n.* же́ртва обма́на, простофи́ля (*c.g.*).

v.t. ост|авля́ть, -а́вить в дурака́х; над|ува́ть, -у́ть.

duplex ['dju:pleks] *adj.* двойно́й; ~ **house** двухкварти́рный дом; ~ **apartment** кварти́ра, располо́женная на двух этажа́х.

duplicate[1] ['dju:plɪkət] *n.* дублика́т; (то́чная) ко́пия; **in ~** в двух экземпля́рах; **these keys are ~s (of each other)** э́ти ключи́ одина́ковы.

adj. двойно́й, удво́енный; одина́ковый.

duplicate[2] ['dju:plɪ,keɪt] *v.t.* (*double*) удв|а́ивать, -о́ить; сдв|а́ивать, -о́ить; (*copy*) дубли́ровать (*impf.*); сн|има́ть, -я́ть ко́пию с+*g.*; (*overlap with*) дубли́ровать (*impf.*); повтор|я́ть, -и́ть.

duplication [,dju:plɪ'keɪʃ(ə)n] *n.* удвое́ние; сня́тие ко́пии; размноже́ние; ~ **of effort** нену́жное повторе́ние уси́лий.

duplicator ['dju:plɪ,keɪtə(r)] *n.* (*machine*) копирова́льный аппара́т.

duplicity [dju:'plɪsɪtɪ] *n.* двули́чность.

durability [,djʊərə'bɪlɪtɪ] *n.* про́чность, долгове́чность.

durable ['djʊərəb(ə)l] *n.*: **consumer ~s** това́ры (*m. pl.*) дли́тельного по́льзования.

adj. про́чный; долгове́чный.

duralumin [djʊə'ræljʊmɪn] *n.* дюралюми́ний.

duration [djʊə'reɪʃ(ə)n] *n.* (*fact of continuing*) продолжи́тельность, продолже́ние; (*length of time*) продолжи́тельность; **for the ~ (of the war)** на (всё) вре́мя войны́; **of short ~** непродолжи́тельный, недолгове́чный.

duress [djʊə'res, 'djʊə-] *n.* принужде́ние, нажи́м, давле́ние; **under ~** под нажи́мом/давле́нием.

during ['djʊərɪŋ] *prep.* (*throughout*) в тече́ние+*g.*; (*at some point in*) во вре́мя+*g.*

dusk [dʌsk] *n.* су́мер|ки (*pl., g.* -ек); су́мрак.

duskiness ['dʌskɪnɪs] *n.* су́мрак; (*swarthiness*) сму́глость.

dusky ['dʌskɪ] *adj.* су́меречный; (*of complexion*) темноко́жий, сму́глый.

dust [dʌst] *n.* **1.** (*powdered earth etc.*) пыль; **gold ~** золотоно́сный песо́к; **bite the ~** па́|дать, -сть сражённым; **lick the ~** (*fig.*) пресмыка́ться (*impf.*) (*перед кем*); **shake the ~ off one's feet** отрясти́ (*pf.*) прах с ног свои́х; **throw ~ in s.o.'s eyes** пус|ка́ть, -ти́ть пыль в глаза́ кому́-н.; втира́ть (*impf.*) кому́-н. очки́. **2.** (*human remains*) прах; **~ and ashes** прах и тлен. **3.** (*cloud of ~*) пыль; **make, raise a ~** (*lit.*) подн|има́ть, -я́ть пыль; (*fig.*) подн|има́ть, -я́ть шум/переполо́х.

v.t. **1.** (*remove ~ from*) ст|ира́ть, -ере́ть; (*or* стря́х|ивать, -ну́ть) пыль с+*g.*; **~ furniture** смах|ивать, -ну́ть (*or* ст|ира́ть, -ере́ть) пыль с ме́бели; **~ a room** уб|ира́ть, -ра́ть ко́мнату. **2.** (*sprinkle*) пос|ыпа́ть, -ы́пать; **~ sugar on to a cake** пос|ыпа́ть, -ы́пать торт са́харной пу́дрой.

cpds. **~bin** *n.* му́сорный я́щик; **~-bowl** *n.* (*fig.*) засу́шливый райо́н; **~-cart** *n.* фурго́н для сбо́ра му́сора, мусорово́з; **~-colour** *n. & adj.* серова́то-кори́чневый (цвет); **~-cover** *n.* (*for chair etc.*) чехо́л; (*of book*) супероблóжка; **~-jacket, ~-wrapper** *nn.* (*of book*) супероблóжка; **~man** *n.* му́сорщик; **~pan** *n.* сово́к для му́сора; **~-proof** *adj.* пыленепроница́емый; **~-sheet** *n.* защи́тное покрыва́ло; **~-storm** *n.* пы́льная бу́ря; **~-up** *n.* (*coll.*) ссо́ра, сва́ра; **~-wrapper** *n.* = **~-jacket**

duster ['dʌstə(r)] *n.* пы́льная тря́пка.

dustiness ['dʌstɪnɪs] *n.* запылённость.

dusty ['dʌstɪ] *adj.* пы́льный; **not so ~** (*coll.*) недурно; **~ answer** обескура́живающий отве́т.

Dutch [dʌtʃ] *n.* **1.** (*language*) голла́ндский/нидерла́ндский язы́к; **double ~** кита́йская гра́мота, тараба́рщина. **2.** (*pl., people*) голла́ндцы (*m. pl.*).

adj.: **~ auction** «голла́ндский аукцио́н»; **~ tile** ка́фель (*m.*); изразе́ц; (*fig.*): **~ courage** хра́брость во хмелю́; **~ treat** угоще́ние в скла́дчину; **talk to s.o. like a ~ uncle** чита́ть, про- кому́-н. нота́цию; жури́ть (*impf.*) кого́-н.; **in ~** (*coll.*) не в фаво́ре.

cpds. **~man** *n.* голла́ндец; **that's Smith, or I'm a ~man** я не я бу́ду, е́сли э́то не Смит; **the Flying ~man** летучий голла́ндец; **~woman** *n.* голла́ндка.

dutiable ['dju:tɪəb(ə)l] *adj.* подлежа́щий обложе́нию по́шлиной.

dutiful ['dju:tɪ,fʊl] *adj.* послу́шный, пре́данный.

dutifulness ['dju:tɪfʊlnɪs] *n.* послуша́ние, пре́данность.

duty ['dju:tɪ] *n.* **1.** (*moral obligation*) долг, обя́занность; **he has a strong sense of ~** у него́ си́льно ра́звито чу́вство до́лга; **a ~ call** официа́льный визи́т; визи́т по обя́занности; **bounden ~** свяще́нная обя́занность; **we are in ~ bound** долг повелева́ет нам. **2.** (*official employment*) служе́бные обя́занности; дежу́рство; **on ~** на дежу́рстве; **come on ~** при|ходи́ть, -йти́ на дежу́рство; **off ~** свобо́дный; вне слу́жбы; в свобо́дное/неслужéбное вре́мя; **I am off ~ today** я сего́дня не рабо́таю; **go off ~** уходи́ть, уйти́ с дежу́рства; **take up one's duties** присту́п|ать, -и́ть к исполне́нию свои́х обя́занностей; **~ officer** дежу́рный (офице́р); **~ journey** служе́бная командиро́вка. **3.** (*fig., of things*): **a box did ~ for a table** я́щик служи́л столо́м; **a heavy ~ engine** сверхмо́щный мото́р. **4.** (*fin.*) по́шлина, сбор; **customs ~** тамо́женная по́шлина; **stamp ~** ге́рбовый сбор; **estate ~** иму́щественный нало́г.

cpds. **~-free, ~-paid** *adjs.* беспо́шлинный.

duumvir [dju:'ʌmvə(r), 'dju:əm-] *n.* (*hist.*) дуумви́р.

duumvirate [dju:'ʌmvɪrət, 'dju:əm-] *n.* (*hist.*) дуумвира́т.

duvet ['du:veɪ] *n.* пухова́я пери́на.

dux [dʌks] *n.* отли́чник; пе́рвый учени́к.

dwarf [dwɔ:f] *n.* ка́рлик; **~ plant** ка́рликовое расте́ние.

v.t. (*stunt growth of*) меша́ть, по- ро́сту +*g.*; остан|а́вливать, -ови́ть рост +*g.*; (*fig.*): **our efforts are ~ed by his** его́ уси́лия затмева́ют на́ши.

dwarfish ['dwɔ:fɪʃ] *adj.* ка́рликовый.

dwell [dwel] *v.i.* **1.** (*live*) жить (*impf.*); обита́ть (*impf.*); **her memory ~s with me** па́мять о ней живёт во мне. **2. ~ (up)on** (*expatiate on*) распространя́ться (*impf.*) о+*p.*; **it is unnecessary to ~ on the difficulties** не ну́жно остана́вливаться на тру́дностях; (*in singing*): **he dwelt on that note** он вы́держал/вы́тянул э́ту но́ту.

dweller ['dwelə(r)] *n.* жи́тель, обита́тель (*fem.* -ница).

dwelling ['dwelɪŋ] *n.* жильё, жили́ще.

cpds. **~-house** *n.* жило́й дом; **~-place** *n.* местожи́тельство.

dwindle ['dwɪnd(ə)l] *v.i.* сокра|ща́ться, -ти́ться, ум|еньша́ться, -е́ньшиться.

Dyak ['daɪæk] *n.* дая́к.

adj. дая́кский.

dyarchy ['daɪɑ:kɪ] = **diarchy**

dye [daɪ] *n.* кра́ска; **a scoundrel of the deepest ~** отъя́вленный негодя́й.

v.t. **1.** (*colour artificially*) кра́сить, по-; окра́|шивать, -сить; **~ a dress black** кра́сить, по- пла́тье в чёрный цвет; **~d-in-the-wool** (*fig.*) зако́нченный, по́лный, закорене́лый. **2.** (*fig.*): **blushes ~d her cheeks** она́ зарде́лась.

v.i. кра́ситься, по-; **this material ~s well** э́тот материа́л хорошо́ кра́сится.

cpds. **~stuff** *n.* краси́тель (*m.*); **~-works** *n.* краси́льня.

dyer ['daɪə(r)] *n.* краси́льщик.

dying ['daɪɪŋ] *adj.* умира́ющий, предсме́ртный; **till one's ~ day** до конца́ дней свои́х.

dyke [daɪk] = **dike**

dynamic [daɪ'næmɪk] *n.* (*force*) дви́жущая си́ла; (*pl., science*) дина́мика.

adj. (*pertaining to force*) динами́ческий; (*energetic*), динами́чный.

dynamism ['daɪnə,mɪz(ə)m] *n.* динами́зм.

dynamite ['daɪnə,maɪt] *n.* динами́т (*also fig.*).

v.t. вз|рыва́ть, -орва́ть динами́том.

dynamiter ['daɪnə,maɪtə(r)] *n.* динами́тчик.

dynamo ['daɪnə,məʊ] *n.* дина́мо (*indecl.*); дина́мо-маши́на; **a human ~** энерги́чный/неутоми́мый челове́к.

dynamometer [,daɪnə'mɒmɪtə(r)] *n.* динамо́метр.

dynast ['dɪnæst, 'daɪ-] *n.* представи́тель (*m.*) дина́стии.

dynastic [dɪ'næstɪk] *adj.* династи́ческий.

dynasty ['dɪnəstɪ] *n.* дина́стия.

dyne [daɪn] *n.* ди́на.

dysentery ['dɪsəntərɪ, -trɪ] *n.* дизентери́я.

dysfunction [dɪs'fʌŋkʃ(ə)n] *n.* дисфу́нкция.

dysgenic [dɪs'dʒenɪk] *adj.* спосо́бствующий вырожде́нию.

dyslexia [dɪs'leksɪə] *n.* дисле́ксия.

dyslexic [dɪs'leksɪk] *adj.*: **he is ~** он дисле́ктик.

dyspepsia [dɪs'pepsɪə] *n.* диспепси́я.

dyspeptic [dɪs'peptɪk] *n. & adj.* страда́ющий диспепси́ей.

dystrophy ['dɪstrəfɪ] *n.* дистрофи́я.

E

E [i:] *n.* **1.** (*mus.*) ми (*nt. indecl.*). **2.** (*acad. mark*) 1, едини́ца, «кол»; **he got an ~ in physics** он получи́л едини́цу по фи́зике.

each [i:tʃ] *pron. & adj.* ка́ждый; **he gave ~ (one) of us a book** он ка́ждому из нас дал по кни́ге; **he sat with a child on ~ side of him** он сиде́л ме́жду двух дете́й; **we took a tray ~ from the table** мы взя́ли со сто́лика по подно́су; **the apples cost 5 pence ~** я́блоки сто́ят пять пе́нсов шту́ка (*or* за шту́ку); **~ other** друг дру́га; **~ and every one, ~ and all** все до одного́; все без исключе́ния; **2 ~** два/дво́е; **5 ~** по пяти́, (*coll.*) по пять; **100 ~** по́ сто; **200 ~** по двести; **500 ~** по пятисо́т.

eager ['i:gə(r)] *adj.* стремя́щийся (к+*d.*); жа́ждущий (+*g.*); **he is ~ to go** он рвётся идти́; **~ pursuit** неотсту́пная пого́ня.

eagerness ['i:gənɪs] *n.* рве́ние, стремле́ние.

eagle ['i:g(ə)l] *n.* орёл; **he is not an ~** (*fig.*) невелика́ пти́ца; **~ eye** зо́ркий взгляд; **~ owl** фили́н.

cpd. **~-eyed** *adj.* зо́ркий, проница́тельный.

eaglet ['i:glɪt] *n.* орлёнок.

ear[1] [ɪə(r)] *n.* **1.** (*anat.*) у́хо; (*dim. e.g. baby's*) у́шко; **give s.o. a thick ~** дать (*pf.*) в у́хо кому́-н. **2.** (*of vessel*) ру́чка, ду́жка. **3.: ~ for music** музыка́льный слух; **she plays by ~** она́ игра́ет по слу́ху; **play it by ~** (*fig.*) пол|ага́ться, -ожи́ться на чутьё. **4.** (*var. idioms*): **I am all ~s** я весь обрати́лся в слух; **it went in at one ~ and out at the other** в одно́ у́хо вошло́, в друго́е вы́шло; **up to one's ~s in work/debt** по́ уши в рабо́те/долга́х; **he set the whole village by the ~s** он перессо́рил всю дере́вню; **gain s.o.'s ~** доби́ться (*pf.*) чьего́-н. благоскло́нного внима́ния; **(may I have) a word in your ~** мне ну́жно кое-что вам сказа́ть на у́шко; **prick up one's ~s** навостри́ть (*pf.*) у́ши; **he is over head and ~s in debt** он по́ уши в долга́х; **were your ~s burning last night?** у вас у́ши не горе́ли вчера́?; **he brought a storm about his ~s** он навлёк на себя́ негодова́ние; **I could not believe my ~s** я свои́м уша́м не пове́рил; **lend an ~, give ~ to** прислу́ш|иваться, -аться к+*d.*; **his words fell on deaf ~s** его́ слова́ бы́ли гла́сом вопию́щего в пусты́не; **turn a deaf ~ to** пропусти́ть (*pf.*) ми́мо уше́й; **it came to my ~s that ...** до меня́ дошли́ слу́хи, что...; **he has his ~ to the ground** (*fig.*) он де́ржит у́хо востро́; **on one's ~** (*tipsy*) под му́хой (*coll.*).

cpds. **~ache** *n.* боль в у́хе; **~drop** *n.* (*pendant*) (серьга́-)подве́ска; (*pl., medicinal*) ушны́е ка́пли (*f. pl.*); **~drum** *n.* бараба́нная перепо́нка; **~-flap** *n.* нау́шник ша́пки; **~mark** *v.t.* на|кла́дывать, -ложи́ть тавро́ на+*a.*; (*fig.*) предназн|ача́ть, -а́чить; ассигнова́ть (*impf., pf.*); **~phone, ~piece** *nn.* нау́шник; ра́ковина телефо́нной тру́бки; **~-piercing** *adj.* пронзи́тельный; **~-plug** *n.* заты́чка для уше́й; ушно́й вкла́дыш; **~ring** *n.* серьга́; **~shot** *n.*: **within ~shot** в преде́лах слы́шимости; **out of ~shot** вне преде́лов слы́шимости; **~-splitting** *adj.* оглуши́тельный; **~-trumpet** *n.* слухово́й рожо́к; **~-wax** *n.* ушна́я се́ра.

ear[2] [ɪə(r)] *n.* (*bot.*) ко́лос; **corn in the ~** колося́щаяся пшени́ца.

earl [ɜ:l] *n.* граф.

earldom ['ɜ:ldəm] *n.* гра́фство.

earless ['ɪəlɪs] *adj.* безу́хий.

earl|y ['ɜ:lɪ] *adj.* ра́нний; **he is an ~y riser** он ра́но встаёт; **he keeps ~y hours** он ра́но ложи́тся спать и ра́но встаёт; **in one's ~y days, life** в ю́ности/мо́лодости; **in the ~y part of this century** в нача́ле э́того столе́тия; **we are ~y** мы пришли́ ра́но; **at an ~y date** в ближа́йшие дни; **an ~y reply** незамедли́тельный отве́т; **on Tuesday at (the) ~iest** не ра́ньше вто́рника; **~y man** первобы́тный челове́к; **~ music** стари́нная му́зыка; **~y peaches** ра́нние/скороспе́лые пе́рсики; **~ warning** (*radar*) да́льнее обнару́же́ние.

adv. ра́но; **come as ~y as possible** приходи́те как мо́жно ра́ньше; **~y on** в нача́ле; **~ier on** ра́ньше, ра́нее; **two hours ~ier** на два часа ра́ньше; **as ~y as March** уже́/ещё в ма́рте.

earn [ɜ:n] *v.t. & i.* зараб|а́тывать, -о́тать; (*deserve*) заслу́ж|ивать, -и́ть; **~ one's living** зараба́тывать (*impf.*) на жизнь; **~ed income** трудово́й дохо́д.

earnest[1] ['ɜ:nɪst] *n.* (*advance payment*) зада́ток (*fig.*) зало́г; **in ~ of** в зало́г +*g.*

earnest[2] ['ɜ:nɪst] *n.*: **in ~** серьёзно, всерьёз; **I am in ~** (*not joking*) я не шучу́; я говорю́ серьёзно; **it is raining in real ~** дождь разошёлся не на шу́тку.

adj. серьёзный.

earnestness ['ɜ:nɪstnɪs] *n.* серьёзность.

earnings ['ɜ:nɪŋz] *n.* за́работок.

earth [ɜ:θ] *n.* **1.** (*planet, world*) земля́; **on the face of the ~** на пове́рхности земли́; **to the ends of the ~** на край све́та; **come back to ~** (*fig.*) спусти́ться (*pf.*) с облако́в на зе́млю; **why on ~?** с како́й ста́ти?; заче́м то́лько?; **who on ~?** кто то́лько?; **like nothing on ~** ни на что не похо́жий; **move heaven and ~** пусти́ть (*pf.*) в ход все сре́дства; **down to ~** (*fig.*) практи́чный, трёзвый. **2.** (*dry land*) земля́; **scorched ~** вы́жженная земля́. **3.** (*soil*) земля́, по́чва. **4.** (*animal's hole*) нора́; **stop an ~** заде́л|ывать, -ать но́ру; **go to ~** скр|ыва́ться, -ы́ться в но́ру; притаи́ться (*pf.*); **run s.o. to ~** (*fig.*) высле́живать, вы́следить кого́-н. **5.** (*chem.*) по́чва, грунт. **6.** (*elec.*) земля́, заземле́ние.

v.t. **1.: ~ up the roots of a shrub** оку́чи|вать, -ть куст. **2.: ~ an aerial** заземл|я́ть, -и́ть анте́нну.

cpds. **~-born** *adj.* (*mortal*) сме́ртный; (*myth.*) порождённый землёй; **~-bound** *adj.* земно́й; **~-closet** *n.* засыпна́я убо́рная; **~-light** *n.* (*astron.*) пе́пельный свет (Луны́); **~quake** *n.* землетрясе́ние; **~quake-proof** *adj.* антисейсми́ческий, сейсмосто́йкий; **~-shaking** *adj.* всеми́рного значе́ния; **~works** *n. pl.* земляны́е рабо́ты (*f. pl.*); **~worm** *n.* земляно́й червь.

earthen ['ɜ:θ(ə)n] *adj.* земляно́й.

cpd. **~ware** *n.* гонча́рные изде́лия; гли́няная посу́да.

earthiness ['ɜ:θɪnɪs] *n.* приземлённость, грубова́тость.

earthly ['ɜ:θlɪ] *adj.* земно́й; **there is no ~ reason why ...** нет ни мале́йшей причи́ны, что́бы...; **he hasn't an ~** (*coll.*) у него́ нет ни мале́йшего ша́нса.

cpd. **~-minded** *adj.* земно́й.

earthy ['ɜ:θɪ] *adj.* (*smell etc.*) земляно́й; (*fig.*) земно́й, приземлённый, грубова́тый.

earwig ['ɪəwɪg] *n.* уховёртка.

ease [i:z] *n.* **1.** (*facility*) лёгкость. **2.** (*comfort*) поко́й, о́тдых, досу́г; **take one's ~** отд|ыха́ть, -охну́ть; **a life of ~** лёгкая жизнь; **he was ill at ~** ему́ бы́ло не по себе́; **stand at ~** (*mil.*) стоя́ть (*impf.*) во́льно; **march at ~** (*mil.*) дви́гаться (*impf.*) по кома́нде «во́льно»; **be, feel at ~** чу́вствовать (*impf.*) себя́ непринуждённо; **put s.o. at his ~** приободри́ть (*pf.*) кого́-н.

v.t. **1.** (*loosen*) отпус|ка́ть, -ти́ть; **~ a drawer** испра́вить (*pf.*) я́щик, что́бы он ле́гче выдвига́лся; **~ a coat under the armpits** выпуска́ть, вы́пустить пиджа́к под мы́шками. **2.** (*slow down, reduce pressure on*): **~ down the speed of a boat** зам|едля́ть, -е́длить ход ло́дки; **~ her!** (*naut.*) ма́лый ход!; **~ the helm** (*naut.*) уб|авля́ть, -а́вить руля́. **3.** (*relieve*) облегч|а́ть, -и́ть; **~ s.o.'s anxiety** успок|а́ивать, -о́ить кого́-н.

v.i. (*relax*) облегч|а́ться, -и́ться; слабе́ть, о-, осла́бнуть; **tension ~d (off)** напряже́ние осла́бло; **~ off on drinking** (*coll.*) пить (*impf.*) ме́ньше; **the pressure of work ~d (up)** напряжённость рабо́ты спа́ла.

easel ['i:z(ə)l] *n.* мольбе́рт.

easement ['i:zmənt] *n.* (*leg.*) сервиту́т.

easily ['i:zɪlɪ] *adv.* (*freely*) свобо́дно; (*without difficulty*) легко́, без труда́; **he is ~ the best** он безусло́вно са́мый лу́чший; **he may ~ be late** он вполне́ мо́жет опозда́ть.

easiness ['i:zɪnɪs] *n.* (*facility*) лёгкость; (*comfort*) удо́бство; (*informality*) непринуждённость.

east [i:st] *n. & adv.* восто́к; на восто́к; к восто́ку; **Far E~** Да́льний Восто́к; **Near E~** Бли́жний Восто́к; **Middle E~** Сре́дний/Бли́жний Восто́к; **the wind is in the ~** ве́тер ду́ет с восто́ка; **~ by north** ост-тень-норд; **~ northeast** ост-норд-ост; **(to the) ~ of London** к восто́ку от Ло́ндона; **travel ~** дви́гаться (*impf.*) на восто́к; **sail due ~** плыть (*impf.*) по направле́нию к восто́ку; **face ~** быть обращённым на восто́к.

adj. восто́чный.

cpds. **~about** *adj. & adv.* (*making a circle ~wards*) в обхо́д с восто́ка; **~bound** *adj.* напра́вленный на восто́к.

Easter ['i:stə(r)] *n.* Па́сха; (*attr.*) пасха́льный; **at ~** на Па́сху; **~ Day, Sunday** Све́тлое/Христо́во Воскресе́нье; Па́сха; **~ egg** пасха́льное яйцо́; **~ eve** кану́н Па́схи; Вели́кая Суббо́та; **~ week** пасха́льная неде́ля; свята́я/све́тлая седми́ца; **~ Monday (Tuesday** *etc.*) Све́тлый Понеде́льник (Вто́рник *и т.п.*); **~ Island** о́стров Па́схи.

easterly ['i:stəlɪ] *adj.*: **the wind is ~** ве́тер ду́ет с восто́ка.

eastern ['i:st(ə)n] *adj.* восто́чный; **E~ Empire** Византи́йская импе́рия.

easternmost [ˈiːst(ə)n,məʊst] *adj.* са́мый восто́чный.
easting [ˈiːstɪŋ] *n.* (*naut.*) курс на ост; отше́ствие на восто́к.
eastward [ˈiːstwəd] *n.*: **6 miles to the ~** 6 миль на восто́к.
adj. дви́жущийся на восто́к.
adv. (*also* **~s**) на восто́к; в восто́чном направле́нии.
easy [ˈiːzɪ] *adj.* **1.** (*not difficult*) лёгкий; **~ of access** досту́пный; **the book is ~ to read** кни́га легко́ чита́ется; **~ money** легко́ на́житые де́ньги; **~ come, ~ go** как на́жито, так и про́жито; **he is ~ to get on with** у него́ лёгкий хара́ктер; **woman of ~ virtue** же́нщина лёгкого поведе́ния; **an ~ mark** (*coll.*) проста́к; **easier said than done** легко́ сказа́ть; **as ~ as ABC** (*or* **falling off a log**) ле́гче лёгкого; про́ще просто́го. **2.** (*comfortable, unconstrained*) споко́йный, лёгкий; **he leads an ~ life** у него́ лёгкая жизнь; **~ in one's mind** споко́йный; **~ chair** кре́сло; **~ manners** непринуждённые мане́ры; **in E~ Street** в дово́льстве/доста́тке; **on ~ terms** на лёгких усло́виях; **I am ~** (*coll., have no preference*) мне всё равно́.
adv.: **~ does it!** ти́ше е́дешь — да́льше бу́дешь; **~!** споко́йно!; **take it ~!** (*don't exert yourself*) не усе́рдствуйте!; (*don't worry*) не волну́йтесь!; (*don't hurry*) не спеши́те!; **~ all!** (*stop rowing*) суши́ть вёсла!
cpds. **~-going** *adj.* (*of pers.*) благоду́шный; **~-goingness** *n.* благоду́шие.
eat [iːt] *v.t. & i.* **1.** (*of pers.*) есть, съ-; (*politely, of others*) ку́шать, по-/с-; **~ one's dinner** пообе́дать/поу́жинать (*pf.*); **he ~s well** он хоро́ший едо́к; у него́ хоро́ший аппети́т; (**~s** *good food*) он хорошо́ пита́ется; **~ one's head off** объеда́ться (*impf.*); **~, drink and be merry** есть, пить и весели́ться (*all impf.*); **good to ~** (*edible*) съедо́бный; (*palatable*) вку́сный, прия́тный на вкус. **2.** (*of animal etc.*) есть, съ-; жрать, со-; **the moths ate holes in my coat** моё пальто́ изъе́дено мо́лью; **the horse is ~ing its head off** э́ту ло́шадь прокорми́ть — деше́вле похорони́ть; **what's ~ing you?** (*coll.*) кака́я му́ха вас укуси́ла? **3.** (*of physical substances*) раз|ъеда́ть, -е́сть; **acids ~ (into) metals** кисло́ты разъеда́ют мета́ллы; **the river has ~en away its banks** река́ подмы́ла берега́. **4.** (*idioms*): **~ one s words** брать, взять свои́ слова́ наза́д; **~ one's heart out** исстрада́ться (*pf.*); жесто́ко тоскова́ть (*impf.*); **~ humble pie** прийти́ (*pf.*) с пови́нной голово́й; **~ s.o. out of house and home** объ|еда́ть, -е́сть кого́-н.; **~ out of s.o.'s hand** (*fig.*) ста|нови́ться, -ть ручны́м; **he can't ~ you** он вас не съест; **I'll ~ my hat if …** даю́ го́лову на отсече́ние, е́сли… **5.** (*in passive sense*): **these apples ~ well** э́ти я́блоки вку́сные; **it ~s like pork** э́то напомина́ет свини́ну.
with advs.: **~ away** *v.t.* разъ|еда́ть, -е́сть; **the wood was ~en away by worms** че́рви изгры́зли де́рево; **~ in** *v.i.* (*at home*) пита́ться (*impf.*) до́ма; **~ out** *v.i.* есть (*impf.*) вне до́ма; **~ up** *v.t.* до|еда́ть, -е́сть; (*fig.*): **he is ~en up with pride/curiosity** его́ съеда́ет го́рдость/любопы́тство.
eatable [ˈiːtəb(ə)l] *adj.* съестно́й; съедо́бный; (*as n. pl.*) съестны́е припа́сы (*pl., g.* -ов), съестно́е.
eater [ˈiːtə(r)] *n.* едо́к; **he is a big ~** он мно́го ест; едо́к он о́чень хоро́ший.
eating [ˈiːtɪŋ] *n.* еда́.
adj.: **are these ~ apples?** мо́жно э́ти я́блоки есть сыры́ми?
cpd. **~-house** *n.* столо́вая.
eats [iːts] *n.* харчи́ (*m. pl.*) (*coll.*).
eau-de-Cologne [,əʊdəkəˈləʊn] *n.* одеколо́н.
eau-de-Nil [,əʊdəˈniːl] *adj.* (*colour*) зеленова́тый.
eaves [iːvz] *n.* карни́з.
cpds. **~drop** *v.i.* подслу́ш|ивать, -ать; **~dropper** *n.* подслу́шивающий; **~dropping** *n.* подслу́шивание.
ebb [eb] *n.* (*of tide*) отли́в; **the tide is on the ~** наступи́л отли́в; **~ and flow** отли́в и прили́в; (*fig.*) упа́док; **his strength is at a low ~** его́ си́лы иссяка́ют.
v.i. (*of tide*) уб|ыва́ть, -ы́ть; (*fig.*) ослаб|ева́ть, -е́ть; **daylight is ~ing away** день угаса́ет; **his strength is ~ing** его́ си́лы слабе́ют.
cpd. **~-tide** *n.* отли́в.
ebonite [ˈebə,naɪt] *n.* эбони́т.
ebony [ˈebənɪ] *n.* эбе́новое/чёрное де́рево; (*fig., black*) чёрный как смоль.
ebullience [ɪˈbʌlɪəns] *n.* кипу́честь.
ebullient [ɪˈbʌlɪənt] *adj.* кипу́чий, по́лный энтузиа́зма.
ebullition [e,bʊˈlɪʃ(ə)n] *n.* (*boiling*) кипе́ние, вскипа́ние; (*fig.*) вспы́шка, взрыв.
écarté [eɪˈkɑːteɪ] *n.* (*game*) экарте́ (*indecl.*).
eccentric [ɪkˈsentrɪk, ek-] *n.* **1.** (*pers.*) чуда́к; оригина́л; эксцентри́чный челове́к. **2.** (*tech.*) эксце́нтрик.
adj. **1.** (*of pers.*) эксцентри́чный. **2.** (*math., astron.*) эксцентри́ческий; (*tech.*) эксце́нтриковый.
eccentricity [,ɪksenˈtrɪsɪtɪ, ,ek-] *n.* (*of pers.*) чуда́чество, эксцентри́чность; (*geom., tech.*) эксцентри́чность; эксцентрисите́т.
Ecclesiastes [ɪ,kliːzɪˈæstiːz] *n.* (*bibl.*) Кни́га Екклесиа́ста/Пропове́дника.
ecclesiastic [ɪ,kliːzɪˈæstɪk] *n.* духо́вное лицо́.
ecclesiastical [ɪ,kliːzɪˈæstɪk(ə)l] *adj.* духо́вный, церко́вный.
Ecclesiasticus [ɪ,kliːzɪˈæstɪkəs] *n.* (*bibl.*) Кни́га Прему́дрости Иису́са, сы́на Сира́хова.
echelon [ˈeʃə,lɒn, ˈeɪʃə,lɔ̃] *n.* **1.** (*mil. formation*) эшело́н; **in ~** эшело́нами. **2.** (*grade*) чин, ранг.
v.t. (*mil.*) эшелони́ровать (*impf., pf.*).
echidna [ɪˈkɪdnə] n. ехи́дна.
echo [ˈekəʊ] *n.* э́хо; **he was cheered to the ~** ему́ устро́или бу́рную ова́цию.
v.t. вто́рить (*impf.*) +*d.*; **~ s.o.'s words** вто́рить чьим-н. слова́м.
v.i. отд|ава́ться, -а́ться э́хом; **the thunder ~ed amongst the hills** гром отдава́лся э́хом в гора́х; **the house ~ed to the children's laughter** дом звене́л от де́тского сме́ха.
cpd. **~-sounding** *n.* измере́ние эхоло́том.
echoic [eˈkəʊɪk] *adj.* звукоподража́тельный.
éclair [eɪˈkleə(r), ɪˈkleə(r)] *n.* экле́р.
éclat [eɪˈklɑː, ˈeɪklɑː] *n.* блеск.
eclectic [ɪˈklektɪk] *adj.* эклекти́ческий; эклекти́чный.
eclecticism [ɪˈklektɪ,sɪz(ə)m] *n.* эклекти́зм.
eclipse [ɪˈklɪps] *n.* **1.** (*astron.*) затме́ние; **partial/total ~** части́чное/по́лное затме́ние. **2.** (*fig.*) помраче́ние; **his fame suffered an ~** его́ сла́ва поме́ркла.
v.t. (*lit., fig.*) затм|ева́ть, -и́ть.
ecliptic [ɪˈklɪptɪk] *n.* эклип́тика.
eclogue [ˈeklɒg] *n.* экло́га.
eco-friendly [ˈiːkəʊ,frendlɪ] *adj.* экологи́чески безвре́дный.
ecological [,iːkəˈlɒdʒɪk(ə)l] *adj.* экологи́ческий.
ecology [ɪˈkɒlədʒɪ] *n.* эколо́гия.
econometric [ɪ,kɒnəˈmetrɪk] *adj.* эконометри́ческий.
econometrics [ɪ,kɒnəˈmetrɪks] *n.* экономе́трия, экономе́трика.
economic [,iːkəˈnɒmɪk, ,ek-] *adj.* **1.** экономи́ческий, хозя́йственный; **~ warfare** экономи́ческая война́. **2.** (*paying*) рента́бельный.
economical [,iːkəˈnɒmɪk(ə)l, ,ek-] *adj.* эконо́мный, бережли́вый, хозя́йственный; **~ of time and energy** сохраня́ющий вре́мя и эне́ргию; **he is ~ with words** он скуп на слова́.
economics [,iːkəˈnɒmɪks, ,ek-] *n.* эконо́мика; **the ~ of poultry-farming** эконо́мика птицево́дства.
economist [ɪˈkɒnəmɪst] *n.* экономи́ст; (*thrifty pers.*) бережли́вый челове́к.
economize [ɪˈkɒnə,maɪz] *v.t. & i.* эконо́мить, с-; **~ fuel** эконо́мить, с- то́пливо; **he ~d by drinking less** он эконо́мил на вы́пивке.
economizer [ɪˈkɒnə,maɪzə(r)] *n.* бережли́вый челове́к.
econom|y [ɪˈkɒnəmɪ] *n.* **1.** (*thrift*) эконо́мия, хозя́йственность, бережли́вость; **false ~y** бессмы́сленная эконо́мия; **little ~ies** эконо́мия на мелоча́х; **~y of truth** (*iron.*) зама́лчивание пра́вды; лжи́вость. **2.** (**~ic** *system*) эконо́мика, хозя́йство; **rural ~y** се́льское хозя́йство; **political ~y** полити́ческая эконо́мия.
ECOSOC [ˈiːkəʊ,sɒk] *n.* (*abbr. of* ***Economic and Social Council***) ЭКОСОС, (Экономи́ческий и Социа́льный Сове́т ООН).
ecosystem [ˈiːkəʊ,sɪstəm] *n.* экосисте́ма.
ecru [ˈeɪkruː] *adj.* цве́та небелёного/суро́вого полотна́; серова́то-бе́жевый.
ecstas|y [ˈekstəsɪ] *n.* **1.** (*strong emotion*) экста́з; **she went**

into ~ies over it э́то привело́ её в экста́з; **in an ~y of fear** вне себя́ от стра́ха. **2.** (*trance*) транс, самозабве́ние.
ecstatic [ɪk'stætɪk] *adj.* (*joyful*) экстати́ческий, в экста́зе.
ectopic [ek'tɒpɪk] *adj.* эктопи́ческий; ~ **pregnancy** внема́точная бере́менность.
ectoplasm ['ektəʊ,plæz(ə)m] *n.* эктопла́зма.
ecu ['ekju:] *n.* экю́ (*m. & nt. indecl.*).
Ecuador ['ekwə,dɔ:(r)] *n.* Эквадо́р.
Ecuadorean [,ekwə'dɔ:rɪən] *n.* эквадо́р|ец (*fem.* -ка).
adj. эквадо́рский.
e|cumenical [,i:kju:'menɪk(ə)l, 'ek-], **oe-** *adj.* (*eccles.*) экумени́ческий, вселе́нский; ~ **council** вселе́нский собо́р; ~ **patriarch** вселе́нский патриа́рх.
e|cumenism [i:'kju:mə,nɪz(ə)m], **oe-** *n.* (*eccles.*) экумени́зм, экумени́ческое движе́ние.
eczema ['eksɪmə] *n.* экзе́ма.
eczematous [ek'zi:mətəs, ek'zem-] *adj.* экземато́зный.
eddy ['edɪ] *n.* водоворо́т; вихрь; (*m.*).
v.i. клуби́ться (*impf.*); крути́ться (*impf.*).
edelweiss ['eɪd(ə)l,vaɪs] *n.* эдельве́йс.
Eden ['i:d(ə)n] *n.* Эде́м; **Garden of** ~ эде́мский сад; (*paradise*) рай.
edentate [ɪ'denteɪt] *adj.* неполнозу́бый.
edge [edʒ] *n.* **1.** (*sharpened side*) остриё, ле́звие; **the knife has no** ~ нож затупи́лся; **take the** ~ **off** (*lit.*) притуп|ля́ть, -и́ть; затуп|ля́ть, -и́ть; (*fig., e.g. appetite*) испо́ртить (*pf.*); **put an** ~ **on a razor** точи́ть, на- бри́тву. **2.** (*fig.*): **be on** ~ быть в не́рвном состоя́нии; **set one's teeth on** ~ вызыва́ть, вы́звать ощуще́ние оско́мины; **give s.o. the** ~ **of one's tongue** ре́зко поговори́ть (*pf.*) с кем-н. **3.** (*border*) грань; край; **black-~d notepaper** почто́вая бума́га с тра́урной каймо́й. **4.** (*of book*) обре́з; **gilt ~s** золото́й обре́з. **5.** (*skating*): **inside** ~ дуга́ внутрь; **outside** ~ дуга́ нару́жу. **6.**: **have the** ~ **on s.o.** (*coll.*) име́ть преиму́щество над кем-н.
v.t. & i. **1.** (*border*) окайм|ля́ть, -и́ть; ~ **a handkerchief with lace** окайм|ля́ть, -и́ть носово́й плато́к кру́жевом; ~ **a path with plants** обса́|живать, -ди́ть доро́жку цвета́ми. **2.** (*make sharp*) точи́ть, на-; **~d tool** ре́жущий инструме́нт; **play with ~d tools** (*fig.*) игра́ть (*impf.*) с огнём. **3.** (*move obliquely*): ~ **one's way through a crowd** проб|ира́ться, -ра́ться че́рез толпу́; ~ **a piano through a door** с трудо́м прота́|скивать, -щи́ть пиани́но в дверь; ~ **one's chair towards the fire** пододви́нуть (*pf.*) стул к ками́ну; **he ~d closer to me** он пододви́нулся ко мне.
edge|ways ['edʒweɪz], **-wise** ['edʒwaɪz] *adv.* бо́ком; **I could not get a word in** ~ я не мог сло́ва вста́вить.
edging ['edʒɪŋ] *n.* (*border*) кайма́.
edgy ['edʒɪ] *adj.* (*irritable*) раздражи́тельный.
edibility [,edɪ'bɪlɪtɪ] *n.* съедо́бность.
edible ['edɪb(ə)l] *adj.* съедо́бный.
edict ['i:dɪkt] *n.* эди́кт, ука́з.
edification [,edɪfɪ'keɪʃ(ə)n] *n.* назида́ние, поуче́ние.
edifice ['edɪfɪs] *n.* зда́ние; (*fig.*) структу́ра, систе́ма.
edify ['edɪ,faɪ] *v.t.* наст|авля́ть, -а́вить; поуча́ть (*impf.*).
edifying ['edɪ,faɪɪŋ] *adj.* назида́тельный, поучи́тельный, нравоучи́тельный.
Edinburgh ['edɪnbərə, -brə] *n.* Э́динбург; (*attr.*) эдинбу́ргский.
edit ['edɪt] *v.t.* (*a text, newspaper*) редакти́ровать, от-; **the passage was ~ed out** э́тот отры́вок вы́черкнули; (*film etc.*) монти́ровать, с-.
editing ['edɪtɪŋ] *n.* редакти́рование, реда́кция.
edition [ɪ'dɪʃ(ə)n] *n.* изда́ние; (*e.g. of newspaper*) вы́пуск; **revised** ~ испра́вленное изда́ние; **limited** ~ изда́ние, вы́пущенное ограни́ченным тиражо́м; **an** ~ **of 50,000 copies** изда́ние в 50 000 экземпля́ров; **the book ran into 20 ~s** кни́га вы́держала 20 изда́ний; (*fig.*): **she is a more charming** ~ **of her sister** она́ ко́пия свое́й сестры́, но ещё бо́лее очарова́тельна.
editor ['edɪtə(r)] *n.* реда́ктор; **sports** ~ реда́ктор спорти́вного отде́ла.
editorial [,edɪ'tɔ:rɪəl] *n.* передови́ца, передова́я статья́.
adj. редакцио́нный; реда́кторский; ~ **office** реда́кция; ~ **staff** редакцио́нная колле́гия, редколле́гия; ~ **changes** (*in a text*) реда́кторская пра́вка.
editorship ['edɪtəʃɪp] *n.* реда́кторство.
educa(ta)ble ['edjʊk(eɪt)əb(ə)l] *adj.* обуча́емый, поддаю́щийся обуче́нию.
educate ['edjʊ,keɪt] *v.t.* да|ва́ть, -ть образова́ние +*d.*; воспи́т|ывать, -а́ть; **where were you ~d?** где вы получи́ли образова́ние?; **he was ~d for the law** он получи́л юриди́ческое образова́ние; **a well ~d man** образо́ванный/интеллиге́нтный челове́к; **~d speech** культу́рная речь; ~ **s.o.'s taste** разв|ива́ть, -и́ть чей-н. вкус.
education [,edjʊ'keɪʃ(ə)n] *n.* образова́ние, культу́ра; (*upbringing*) воспита́ние; **universal compulsory** ~ всео́бщее обяза́тельное обуче́ние; **higher** ~ вы́сшее образова́ние; **Ministry of E~** Министе́рство просвеще́ния; **lack of** ~ необразо́ванность; **a liberal** ~ гуманита́рное образова́ние; **it was an** ~ **to work with him** рабо́та с ним мно́го мне дала́; **physical** ~ физи́ческое воспита́ние, физкульту́ра; **public** ~ наро́дное образова́ние.
educational [,edjʊ'keɪʃənəl] *adj.* (*pert. to education*) образова́тельный; (*instructive*) воспита́тельный, уче́бный; ~ **film** уче́бный фильм.
education(al)ist [,edjʊ'keɪʃən(əl)ɪst] *n.* педаго́г(-методи́ст).
educative ['edjʊ,kətɪv] *adj.* поучи́тельный.
educator ['edjʊ,keɪtə(r)] *n.* воспита́тель (*m.*), педаго́г.
Edward ['edwəd] *n.* Эдуа́рд.
EEC (*abbr. of* ***European Economic Community***) ЕЭС, (Европе́йское экономи́ческое соо́бщество).
eel [i:l] *n.* у́горь (*m.*); **he is as slippery as an** ~ (*fig.*) он ско́льзкий как у́горь.
e'en [i:n] (*poet.*) = **even**[1], **even**[2] *adv.*
e'er [eə(r)] (*poet.*) = **ever**
eer|ie (*US* **-y**) ['ɪərɪ] *adj.* жу́ткий.
efface [ɪ'feɪs] *v.t.* ст|ира́ть, -ере́ть; (*fig.*) изгла́|живать, -дить; ~ **o.s.** стушёв|ываться, -а́ться; держа́ться (*impf.*) в тени́.
effaceable [ɪ'feɪsəb(ə)l] *adj.* изгла́живаемый, стира́емый.
effacement [ɪ'feɪsmənt] *n.* стира́ние.
effect [ɪ'fekt] *n.* **1.** (*result*) результа́т; **punishment had no** ~ **on him** наказа́ние на него́ не поде́йствовало; **of no** ~ безрезульта́тный; **to no** ~ безрезульта́тно; **take** ~ (*e.g. medicine*) де́йствовать, по-; **give** ~ **to a decision** осуществ|ля́ть, -и́ть реше́ние; **in** ~ в су́щности, факти́чески. **2.** (*validity*) де́йствие; **come into** ~ вступ|а́ть, -и́ть в си́лу; **put, bring into** ~ вводи́ть (*impf.*) в де́йствие; **with** ~ **from today** начина́я с сего́дняшнего дня; **in** ~ (*operative*) де́йствующий, в си́ле; **of no** ~ (*invalid*) недействи́тельный. **3.** (*sensual etc. impression*) впечатле́ние, эффе́кт; **sound ~s** (*e.g. on radio*) шумовы́е эффе́кты; **he does it all for** ~ он де́лает всё напока́з. **4.** (*meaning*) содержа́ние, смысл; **he spoke to this** ~ смысл его́ слов был сле́дующий; **or words to that** ~ и́ли что́-то в э́том ро́де; верне́е, тако́в был смысл ска́занного. **5.** (*pl., property*) пожи́тк|и (*pl., g.* -ов); иму́щество; **the innkeeper seized his ~s** хозя́ин гости́ницы завладе́л его́ иму́ществом; **"no ~s"** (*on cheque*) нет средств.
v.t.: ~ **one's purpose** осуществ|ля́ть, -и́ть цель; ~ **a cure** излечи́ть (*pf.*) больно́го; ~ **payment** произв|оди́ть, -ести́ платёж; ~ **a compromise** пойти́ (*pf.*) на компроми́сс; прив|оди́ть, -ести́ к компроми́ссу; ~ **an insurance policy** оф|ормля́ть, -о́рмить страхово́й по́лис.
effective [ɪ'fektɪv] *adj.* **1.** (*efficacious*) эффекти́вный. **2.** (*striking*) эффе́ктный. **3.** (*operative*) име́ющий си́лу; де́йствующий; **become** ~ входи́ть, войти́ в си́лу; ~ **range** (*mil.*) да́льность действи́тельного огня́; ~ **strength** (*of an army*) нали́чный соста́в; **~s** (*pl., as n.*) боевы́е подразделе́ния; нали́чный боево́й соста́в. **4.** (*virtual*) действи́тельный.
effectiveness [ɪ'fektɪvnɪs] *n.* (*efficacy*) эффекти́вность, де́йственность; (*of decor etc.*) эффе́ктность.
effectual [ɪ'fektʃʊəl, -tjʊəl] *adj.* де́йственный; действи́тельный.
effectuate [ɪ'fektjʊ,eɪt] *v.t.* прив|оди́ть, -ести́ в исполне́ние.
effeminacy [ɪ'femɪnəsɪ] *n.* изне́женность.

effeminate [ɪ'femɪnət] *adj.* женоподо́бный.
effervesce [,efə'ves] *v.i.* пузыри́ться (*impf.*); (*fig.*) искри́ться (*impf.*).
effervescence [,efə'vesəns] *n.* шипе́ние; (*fig.*) весёлое оживле́ние.
effervescent [,efə'vesənt] *adj.* пузыря́щийся, шипу́чий; (*fig.*) искря́щийся, брызжущий весе́льем.
effete [ɪ'fi:t] *adj.* сла́бый, упа́дочный; (*degenerate*) вы́родившийся.
efficacious [,efɪ'keɪʃəs] *adj.* эффекти́вный, де́йственный.
efficacy ['efɪkəsɪ] *n.* эффекти́вность, де́йственность.
efficiency [ɪ'fɪʃənsɪ] *n.* делови́тость, уме́ние; эффекти́вность, производи́тельность, продукти́вность; ~ **expert** экспе́рт по вопро́сам организа́ции труда́.
efficient [ɪ'fɪʃ(ə)nt] *adj.* делови́тый, исполни́тельный, уме́лый; эффекти́вный, производи́тельный, продукти́вный.
effigy ['efɪdʒɪ] *n.* изображе́ние; **burn s.o. in** ~ сжечь (*pf.*) чьё-н. изображе́ние/чу́чело.
efflorescence [,eflɔ:'resəns] *n.* цвете́ние, расцве́т; (*fig.*) расцве́т.
effluent ['efluənt] *n.* пото́к, вытека́ющий из о́зера/реки́; (*of sewage etc.*) сток.
effluvium [ɪ'flu:vɪəm] *n.* испаре́ние; миа́змы (*f. pl.*)
efflux ['eflʌks] *n.* истече́ние.
effort ['efət] *n.* уси́лие, попы́тка; (*pl.*) рабо́та; **make an** ~ приложи́ть (*pf.*) уси́лие; **spare no** ~ не щади́ть (*impf.*) уси́лий; **his ~s at persuading her failed** его́ уси́лия убеди́ть её оказа́лись тще́тными; (*coll., performance*): **a good** ~ уда́чная попы́тка.
effortless ['efətlɪs] *adj.* непринуждённый; не тре́бующий уси́лий; **with** ~ **skill** с непринуждённой ло́вкостью.
effrontery [ɪ'frʌntərɪ] *n.* на́глость, наха́льство.
effulgence [ɪ'fʌldʒəns] *n.* лучеза́рность, сия́ние.
effulgent [ɪ'fʌldʒ(ə)nt] *adj.* лучеза́рный, сия́ющий.
effusion [ɪ'fju:ʒ(ə)n] *n.* излия́ние (*also fig.*).
effusive [ɪ'fju:sɪv] *adj.* неуме́ренный, экспанси́вный; **he was ~ in his gratitude** он рассыпа́лся в благода́рностях.
effusiveness [ɪ'fju:sɪvnɪs] *n.* экспанси́вность, неуме́ренность.
EFTA ['eftə] *n.* (*abbr. of* **European Free Trade Association**) ЕАСТ, (Европе́йская ассоциа́ция свобо́дной торго́вли).
e.g. (*abbr. of* **exempli gratia**) напр., (наприме́р).
egad [i:'gæd] *int.* (*arch.*) ей-Бо́гу.
egalitarian [ɪ,gælɪ'teərɪən], **equalitarian** [i:,kwɒlɪ'teərɪən] *adjs.* эгалита́рный, уравни́тельный.
egalitarianism [ɪ,gælɪ'teərɪən,ɪz(ə)m], **equalitarianism** [i:,kwɒlɪ'teərɪən,ɪz(ə)m] *nn.* эгалитари́зм, уравни́ловка.
egality [ɪ'gælɪtɪ] *n.* ра́венство.
egg[1] [eg] *n.* **1.** (*lit.*) яйцо́; **lay ~s** нести́сь (*impf.*); нести́, с-яйца; **new-laid** ~ свежеснесённое яйцо́; **boiled** ~ яйцо́ в мешо́чек; **soft-boiled** ~ яйцо́ всмя́тку; **hard-boiled** ~ круто́е яйцо́; **fried** ~ яи́чница-глазу́нья; **scrambled ~s** яи́чница-болту́нья; **poached** ~ яйцо́-пашо́т; **baked** ~ печёное яйцо́; **rotten** ~ ту́хлое яйцо́; **you have got ~ on your chin** у вас оста́тки яйца́ на подборо́дке; ~ **and spoon race** шу́точный бег с ло́жкой, в кото́рой лежи́т сыро́е яйцо́; **in the** ~ (*fig.*) в заро́дыше; **put all one's ~s in one basket** ≃ поста́вить (*pf.*) всё на ка́рту; **as sure as ~s is ~s** (*coll.*) ≃ я́сно как два́жды два четы́ре; **don't teach your grandmother to suck ~s** ≃ я́йца ку́рицу не у́чат. **2.** (*coll., chap*) па́рень (m.); **good** ~ сла́вный ма́лый; **bad** ~ непутёвый ма́лый. **3.** (*coll.*): **good** ~! отли́чно!
cpds. **~-beater, ~-whisk** *nn.* весёлка, муто́вка; **~-cosy** *n.* чехо́льчик для сохране́ния яйца́ горя́чим; **~-cup** *n.* рю́мка для яйца́; **~-flip, ~-nog** *nn.* яи́чный флип; **~head** *n.* (*sl.*) интеллиге́нтик; **~-plant** *n.* баклажа́н; **~-shaped** *adj.* яйцеви́дный; **~-shell** *n.* скорлупа́; **~-shell paint** ма́товая кра́ска; **~-shell china** то́нкий фарфо́р; **~-spoon** *n.* яи́чная ло́жечка; **~-timer** *n.* (песо́чные) часы́ для ва́рки яи́ц; **~-whisk** *n.* = **~-beater**
egg[2] [eg] *v.t.*: ~ **on** подстрек|а́ть, -ну́ть.
eggy ['egɪ] *adj.* (*covered with egg*) вы́мазанный яйцо́м.
eglantine ['eglən,taɪn] *n.* ро́за эглантерия.
ego ['i:gəʊ] *n.* э́го (*indecl.*); я (*nt. indecl.*); субъе́кт; (*amour-propre*) самолю́бие; (*selfishness*) эгои́зм.
egocentric [,i:gəʊ'sentrɪk] *adj.* эгоцентри́ческий, эгоцентри́чный.
egocentrism [i:gəʊ'sentrɪz(ə)m] *n.* эгоцентри́зм.
egoism ['i:gəʊ,ɪz(ə)m] *n.* эгои́зм, эгоисти́чность.
egoist ['i:gəʊɪst, 'eg-] *n.* эгои́ст (*fem.* -ка).
egoistic(al) [,i:gəʊ'ɪstɪk(ə)l, 'eg-] *adj.* эгоисти́ческий, эгоисти́чный.
egomania [,i:gəʊ'meɪnɪə] *n.* эгоцентри́зм.
egomaniac [,i:gəʊ'meɪnɪ,æk, ,eg-] *n.* эгоцентри́ст.
adj. эгоцентри́ческий.
egotism ['i:gə,tɪz(ə)m] *n.* эготи́зм.
egotist ['i:gə,tɪst, 'eg-] *n.* эготи́ст (*fem.* -ка), эгоце́нтрик.
egotistic(al) [,i:gə'tɪstɪk(ə)l, ,eg-] *adj.* эгоцентри́ческий.
egregious [ɪ'gri:dʒəs] *adj.* вопию́щий, отъя́вленный.
egress ['i:gres] *n.* (*exit*) вы́ход.
egret ['i:grɪt] *n.* бе́лая ца́пля.
Egypt ['i:dʒɪpt] *n.* Еги́пет.
Egyptian [ɪ'dʒɪpʃ(ə)n] *n.* египтя́н|ин (*fem.* -ка); **spoil the ~s** (*fig.*) поживи́ться (*pf.*) за счёт врага́.
adj. еги́петский.
Egyptologist [,i:dʒɪp'tɒlədʒɪst] *n.* египто́лог.
Egyptology [,i:dʒɪp'tɒlədʒɪ] *n.* египтоло́гия.
eh [eɪ] *int.* а?; да неуже́ли?; как?
eider ['aɪdə(r)] *n.* (*also* ~ **duck**) га́га.
cpd. **~down** *n.* (*feathers*) гага́чий пух; (*quilt*) пухо́вое одея́ло.
Eiffel Tower ['aɪf(ə)l] *n.* Э́йфелева ба́шня.
eight [eɪt] *n.* (число́/но́мер) во́семь; (~ *people*) во́сьмеро, во́семь челове́к; **we** ~, **the** ~ **of us** мы восьмеро́м; мы, во́семь челове́к; ~ **each** по восьми́; **in ~s**, ~ **at a time** по восьми́, восьмёрками; (*figure*; *thg. numbered 8*; *group or crew of* ~) восьмёрка; **he cut a figure of** ~ он сде́лал восьмёрку; (*with var. nn. expressed or understood*: *cf. examples under* **five**): **piece of** ~ мексика́нский до́ллар; **he had one over the** ~ (*coll.*) он хвати́л ли́шнего; **~s** (*contest*) гребны́е состяза́ния (в О́ксфорде).
adj. во́семь +*g. pl.*; (*for people and pluralia tantum, also*) во́сьмеро +*g. pl.*; ~ **twos are sixteen** во́семью (*or* во́семь на) два — шестна́дцать.
cpds. **~fold** *adj.* восьмикра́тный; *adv.* в во́семь раз (бо́льше); **~some** *n.* (*group of 8*) во́сьмеро.
eighteen [eɪ'ti:n] *n.* восемна́дцать; **in the 1820s** в двадца́тые го́ды (*or* в двадца́тых года́х) XIX (девятна́дцатого) ве́ка.
adj. восемна́дцать +*g. pl.*
eighteenth [eɪ'ti:nθ] *n.* (*date*) восемна́дцатое число́; (*fraction*) одна́ восемна́дцатая; восемна́дцатая часть.
adj. восемна́дцатый.
eighth [eɪtθ] *n.* (*date*) восьмо́е (число́); (*fraction*) одна́ восьма́я; восьма́я часть.
adj. восьмо́й; ~ **note** (*US, mus*) восьма́я но́та.
eightieth ['eɪtɪɪθ] *n.* одна́ восьмидеся́тая; восьмидеся́тая часть.
adj. восьмидеся́тый.
eight|y ['eɪtɪ] *n.* во́семьдесят; **in the ~ies** (*decade*) в восьмидеся́тых года́х; в восьмидеся́тые го́ды; (*temperature*) за во́семьдесят гра́дусов (по Фаренге́йту); **he is in his ~ies** ему́ за во́семьдесят.
Eire ['eərə] *n.* Э́йре (*indecl.*).
eirenic [aɪ'ri:nɪk] = **irenic**
either ['aɪðə(r), 'i:ðə(r)] *pron. & adj.* (*one or other*) любо́й, ка́ждый; тот и́ли друго́й; **do ~ of these roads lead to town?** кака́я-нибу́дь из э́тих доро́г ведёт к го́роду?; ~ **book will do** люба́я из э́тих книг годи́тся; **I do not like ~ (one)** мне не нра́вится ни тот, ни друго́й; ~ **way you will lose** и так и э́так вы проигра́ете; **on ~ side of the window** по обе́им сторона́м окна́; **without ~ good or bad intentions** без каки́х бы то ни́ было, до́брых и́ли дурны́х, наме́рений; ~ **of you may come** любо́й из вас мо́жет прийти́; **has ~ of you seen him?** кто-нибу́дь из вас ви́дел его́?
adv. & conj. **I do not like Smith, or Jones ~** я не люблю́ ни Сми́та, ни Джо́нса; **he did not go, and I did not ~** ни он, ни я не пошли́; (*intensive*): **it was not long ago ~** э́то бы́ло не так уж давно́; ~ ... **or** и́ли... и́ли; ли́бо... ли́бо; то ли... то ли; не то... не то; ~ **I or he will go** оди́н из

нас пойдёт; и́ли он и́ли я пойдём.

ejaculate [ɪ'dʒækjʊ,leɪt] *v.t.* (*utter suddenly*) воскл|ица́ть, -и́кнуть; (*emit*) изв|ерга́ть, -е́ргнуть.

ejaculation [ɪ,dʒækjʊ'leɪʃ(ə)n] *n.* (*exclamation*) восклица́ние; (*emission*) изверже́ние; (*sexual*) семяизверже́ние, эякуля́ция.

ejaculatory [ɪ'dʒækjʊ,leɪtərɪ] *adj.* (*exclamatory*) восклица́тельный.

eject [ɪ'dʒekt] *v.t.* (*lit., fig.*) выбра́сывать, вы́бросить; выселя́ть, вы́селить; (*emit*) изв|ерга́ть, -е́ргнуть.

v.i. (*aeron.*): **the pilot ~ed** лётчик катапульти́ровался.

eject|ion [ɪ'dʒekʃ(ə)n], **-ment** [ɪ'dʒektmənt] *nn.* (*expulsion*) исключе́ние; (*from house*) выселе́ние; (*emission*) изверже́ние.

ejector [ɪ'dʒektə(r)] *n.*: **~ seat** (*aeron.*) катапульти́руемое сиде́нье.

eke[1] [i:k] *adv.* (*arch.*) та́кже, то́же.

eke[2] [i:k] *v.t.*: **~ out** (*supplement*) поп|олня́ть, -о́лнить; восп|олня́ть, -о́лнить; **~ out a livelihood** ко́е-как перебива́ться (*impf.*).

elaborate[1] [ɪ'læbərət] *adj.* иску́сно сде́ланный; отде́ланный; сло́жный; **an ~ pattern** замыслова́тый рису́нок; **an ~ dinner** изы́сканный обе́д.

elaborate[2] [ɪ'læbə,reɪt] *v.t.* разраб|а́тывать, -о́тать; отде́л|ывать, -ать.

elaboration [ɪ,læbə'reɪʃ(ə)n] *n.* (*working out*) разрабо́тка; (*making more elaborate*) отде́лка, усоверше́нствование.

élan [eɪ'lɑ̃] *n.* поры́в, подъём.

eland ['i:lənd] *n.* южноафрика́нская антило́па.

elapse [ɪ'læps] *v.i.* про|ходи́ть, -йти́; прот|ека́ть, -е́чь.

elastic [ɪ'læstɪk, ɪ'lɑ:stɪk] *n.* (*material*) рези́нка.

adj. (*lit.*) эласти́чный; упру́гий; **~ band** рези́нка; (*fig.*) ги́бкий; **~ rules** нестро́гие пра́вила; **an ~ conscience** беспринци́пность.

cpd. **~-sided** *adj.*: **~-sided boots** боти́нки с рези́новыми вста́вками по бока́м.

elasticity [ɪlæs'tɪsɪtɪ] *n.* эласти́чность, упру́гость; (*fig.*) ги́бкость.

elate [ɪ'leɪt] *v.t.* прив|оди́ть, -ести́ в восто́рг; **he was ~d at the news** но́вость окрыли́ла его́.

elation [ɪ'leɪʃ(ə)n] *n.* припо́днятое настрое́ние; ликова́ние, восто́рг.

Elba ['elbə] *n.* Э́льба.

Elbe [elb] *n.* Э́льба.

elbow ['elbəʊ] *n.* **1.** (*lit.*) ло́коть (*m.*); **at one's ~** (*fig.*) под руко́й; **out at ~s** (*of garment*) с про́дранными локтя́ми; поно́шенный; **he is out at ~s** (*fig.*) он впал в нужду́; **lift one's ~** (*fig.*) выпива́ть (*impf.*); **more power to his ~!** (*coll.*) дай Бог ему́ уда́чи!; **rub ~s with** якша́ться (*impf.*) c+*i.* (*coll.*). **2.** (*of pipe etc.*) коле́но.

v.t. пих|а́ть, -ну́ть; толка́ть (*impf.*) локтя́ми; **~ one's way** прот|а́лкиваться, -олкну́ться; **~ s.o. aside** отпихну́ть (*pf.*) кого́-н. в сто́рону.

cpds. **~-grease** *n.* (*joc.*) уси́ленная полиро́вка; **it needs ~-grease** придётся попоте́ть; **~-rest** *n.* подлоко́тник; **~-room** *n.* просто́р.

elder[1] ['eldə(r)] *n.* **1.** (*older pers.*) ста́рец, ста́рший; **we should respect our ~s** мы должны́ уважа́ть ста́рших; **he is my ~ by seven years** он ста́рше меня́ на семь лет. **2.** (*official, senior member of tribe*) старе́йшина (*m.*). **3.** (*eccl.*) свяще́нник, старшина́ (*m.*).

adj. ста́рший; **the ~ Pitt** Питт ста́рший; **which is the ~ of the two?** кто из них двух ста́рше?

elder[2] ['eldə(r)] *n.* (*bot.*) бузина́.

cpd. **~berry** *n.* я́года бузины́.

elderly ['eldəlɪ] *adj.* пожило́й.

eldership ['eldərʃɪp] *n.* старшинство́.

eldest ['eldɪst] *adj.* са́мый ста́рший.

eldritch ['eldrɪtʃ] *adj.* (*Sc.*) жу́ткий, таи́нственный.

elect [ɪ'lekt] *adj.* и́збранный; **president ~** и́збранный президе́нт; (*as n.*) **the ~** (*esp. relig.*) избра́нники (*m. pl.*).

v.t. изб|ира́ть, -ра́ть; выбира́ть, вы́брать; **they ~ed him king** они́ избра́ли его́ королём; **the president is ~ed** президе́нт избира́ется; **he ~ed to go** он предпочёл пойти́.

election [ɪ'lekʃ(ə)n] *n.* **1.** (*pol.*) вы́боры (*m. pl.*); **general ~** всео́бщие вы́боры; **hold an ~** пров|оди́ть, -ести́ вы́боры; **~ campaign** предвы́борная/избира́тельная кампа́ния. **2.** (*choice*) избра́ние.

electioneer [ɪ,lekʃə'nɪə(r)] *v.i.* агити́ровать (*impf.*); **~ing** (*campaign*) предвы́борная кампа́ния.

elective [ɪ'lektɪv] *adj.* **1.** (*filled by election*) избира́тельный; вы́борный; **an ~ office** вы́борная до́лжность. **2.** (*empowered to elect*): **an ~ assembly** избира́тельное собра́ние. **3.** (*optional*) факультати́вный.

elector [ɪ'lektə(r)] *n.* **1.** (*voter*) избира́тель (*m.*). **2.** (*Ger. hist.*) курфю́рст.

electoral [ɪ'lektər(ə)l] *adj.* **1.** избира́тельный; **~ college** колле́гия вы́борщиков; **~ register** спи́сок избира́телей. **2.** (*hist.*) курфю́рстский; **~ Saxony** Саксо́ния под вла́стью курфю́рста.

electorate [ɪ'lektərət] *n.* **1.** (*body of electors*) избира́тели (*m. pl.*). **2.** (*Ger. hist.*) курфю́ршество.

electress [ɪ'lektrɪs] *n.* **1.** (*voter*) избира́тельница. **2.** (*Ger. hist.*) жена́ курфю́рста, курфю́рстина.

electric [ɪ'lektrɪk] *adj.* электри́ческий; **~ blanket** одеяло-гре́лка; **~ blue** (*n. & adj.*) (цвет) электри́к (*indecl.*); **~ field** электри́ческое по́ле; **~ light** электри́ческий свет; **~ locomotive** электрово́з; (*fig.*): **this had an ~ effect on him** э́то наэлектризова́ло его́.

electrical [ɪ'lektrɪk(ə)l] *adj.* электри́ческий; **~ engineer** инжене́р-эле́ктрик; **~ engineering** электроте́хника.

electrician [,ɪlek'trɪʃ(ə)n] *n.* (электро)монтёр.

electricity [,ɪlek'trɪsɪtɪ, ,el-] *n.* электри́чество.

electrification [ɪ,lektrɪfɪ'keɪʃ(ə)n] *n.* (*phys.*) электриза́ция; (*tech.*) электрифика́ция.

electrify [ɪ'lektrɪ,faɪ] *v.t.* **1.** (*charge with electricity; also fig.*) электризова́ть, на-. **2.** (*e.g. a railway*) электрифици́ровать (*impf., pf.*).

electro- [ɪ'lektrəʊ] *pref.* электро…

electrocardiogram [ɪ,lektrəʊ'kɑ:dɪə,græm] *n.* электрокардиогра́мма.

electrocute [ɪ'lektrə,kju:t] *v.t.* (*execute*) казни́ть (*impf., pf.*) на электри́ческом сту́ле; **he was ~d** (*by accident*) его́ уби́ло то́ком.

electrocution [ɪ,lektrə'kju:ʃ(ə)n] *n.* казнь на электри́ческом сту́ле.

electrode [ɪ'lektrəʊd] *n.* электро́д.

electrodynamics [ɪ,lektrəʊdaɪ'næmɪks] *n.* электродина́мика.

electro-encephalogram [ɪ,lektrəʊɪn'sefələ,græm] *n.* электроэнцефалогра́мма.

electrolysis [,ɪlek'trɒlɪsɪs, ,el-] *n.* электро́лиз.

electrolyte [ɪ'lektrə,laɪt] *n.* электроли́т.

electromagnet [ɪ,lektrəʊ'mægnɪt] *n.* электромагни́т.

electromagnetic [ɪ,lektrəʊmæg'netɪk] *adj.* электромагни́тный.

electrometer [,ɪlek'trɒmɪtə(r), ,el-] *n.* электро́метр.

electromotive [ɪ,lektrəʊ'məʊtɪv] *adj.* электродви́жущий.

electron [ɪ'lektrɒn] *n.* электро́н.

electronic [,ɪlek'trɒnɪk, ,el-] *adj.* электро́нный.

electronics [,ɪlek'trɒnɪks, ,el-] *n.* электро́ника.

electroplate [ɪ'lektrə,pleɪt] *n.* посеребрённые предме́ты (*m. pl.*).

v.t. гальванизи́ровать (*impf., pf.*); покр|ыва́ть, -ы́ть мета́ллом с по́мощью электро́лиза.

electroscope [ɪ'lektrə,skəʊp] *n.* электроско́п.

electrotype [ɪ'lektrəʊ,taɪp] *n.* электроти́пия; гальва́но (*indecl.*), гальваностереоти́п.

elegance ['elɪgəns] *n.* элега́нтность, изя́щество.

elegant ['elɪgənt] *adj.* элега́нтный, изя́щный.

elegiac [,elɪ'dʒaɪək] *adj.* элеги́ческий, элеги́чный.

elegiacs [,elɪ'dʒaɪəks] *n.* элеги́ческие стихи́ (*m. pl.*).

elegy ['elɪdʒɪ] *n.* эле́гия.

element ['elɪmənt] *n.* **1.** (*earth, air etc.*) стихи́я; **exposed to the ~s** бро́шенный на произво́л стихи́й; (*fig.*): **in one's ~** в свое́й стихи́и; **out of one's ~** как ры́ба, вы́нутая из воды́. **2.** (*chem.*) элеме́нт. **3.** (*pl., rudiments*) нача́ла (*nt. pl.*); азы́ (*m. pl.*); **~s of politeness** элемента́рные пра́вила ве́жливости. **4.** (*feature, constituent*) элеме́нт; составна́я часть. **5.** (*trace*) след, до́ля. **6.** (*eccles.*): **the E~s** святы́е дары́ (*m. pl.*). **7.** (*elec.*) элеме́нт.

elemental [,elɪ'ment(ə)l] *adj.* стихи́йный.

elementary [ˌelɪ'mentərɪ] *adj.* элемента́рный; ~ **school** нача́льная шко́ла.
elephant ['elɪfənt] *n.* слон; ~ **calf** слонёнок; ~ **cow** слони́ха; ~ **gun** ружьё для охо́ты на слоно́в; **white** ~ (*fig.*) обремени́тельное иму́щество.
elephantiasis [ˌelɪfən'taɪəsɪs] *n.* слоно́вая боле́знь.
elephantine [ˌelɪ'fæntaɪn] *adj.* слоно́вый; **an** ~ **task** непоси́льная зада́ча; ~ **humour** тяжелове́сный ю́мор.
elevate ['elɪˌveɪt] *v.t.* (*lit.*) подн|има́ть, -я́ть; ~**d railway** надзе́мная желе́зная доро́га; (*fig.*) пов|ыша́ть, -ы́сить; (*ennoble*) облагор|а́живать, -о́дить; **he was** ~**d to the peerage** его́ возвели́ в зва́ние пэ́ра.
elevated ['elɪˌveɪtɪd] *adj.* (*lofty*) высо́кий, возвы́шенный; (*coll., tipsy*) подвы́пивший, навеселе́.
elevating ['elɪˌveɪtɪŋ] *adj.* облагора́живающий; подъёмный.
elevation [ˌelɪ'veɪʃ(ə)n] *n.* **1.** (*act of raising*) подня́тие, возвыше́ние. **2.** (*e.g. of a gun*) вертика́льная наво́дка. **3.** (*height*) возвыше́ние, возвы́шенность. **4.** (*drawing*) вертика́льный разре́з; **front** ~ фаса́д; **side** ~ боково́й фаса́д. **5.** (*fig., of style etc.*) возвы́шенность. **6.:** ~ **to the peerage** возведе́ние в зва́ние пэ́ра.
elevator ['elɪˌveɪtə(r)] *n.* **1.** (*machine*) грузоподъёмник, элева́тор. **2.** (*storehouse*) элева́тор. **3.** (*US, lift*) лифт; ~ **operator** лифтёр. **4.** (*aeron.*) руль (*m.*) высоты́.
eleven [ɪ'lev(ə)n] *n.* оди́ннадцать; **chapter** ~ оди́ннадцатая глава́; (*team of* ~ *men*) кома́нда (из оди́ннадцати челове́к); **at** ~ **(o'clock)** в оди́ннадцать (часо́в); **half past** ~ полови́на двена́дцатого.
elevenses [ɪ'levənzɪz] *n.* (*coll.*) лёгкий за́втрак о́коло оди́ннадцати часо́в утра́.
eleventh [ɪ'levənθ] *n.* (*date*) оди́ннадцатое (число́); (*fraction*) одна́ оди́ннадцатая; оди́ннадцатая часть.
adj. оди́ннадцатый; **at the** ~ **hour** (*fig.*) в после́днюю мину́ту.
elf [elf] *n.* эльф.
cpd. ~**-lock** *n.* спу́танные во́лосы (*m. pl.*).
el|fin ['elfɪn], **-fish** ['elfɪʃ], **-vish** ['elvɪʃ] *adjs.* подо́бный фе́е; волше́бный.
elicit [ɪ'lɪsɪt, e'lɪsɪt] *v.t.* извл|ека́ть, -е́чь; допы́т|ываться, -а́ться; ~ **a fact** выявля́ть, вы́явить факт; ~ **a reply** доби́ться (*pf.*) отве́та.
elide [ɪ'laɪd] *v.t.* выпуска́ть, вы́пустить; опус|ка́ть, -ти́ть.
eligibility [ˌelɪdʒɪ'bɪlɪtɪ] *n.* (*pol.*) пра́во на избра́ние.
eligible ['elɪdʒɪb(ə)l] *adj.* мо́гущий быть и́збранным; жела́тельный; **an** ~ **young man** подходя́щий жени́х.
Elijah [ɪ'laɪdʒə] *n.* (*bibl.*) Илия́ (*m.*), Илья́-проро́к.
eliminate [ɪ'lɪmɪˌneɪt] *v.t.* **1.** (*do away with*) устран|я́ть, -и́ть. **2.** (*rule out*) исключ|а́ть, -и́ть. **3.** (*physiol., chem.*) оч|ища́ть, -и́стить. **4.** (*math.*) элимини́ровать (*impf.*); исключ|а́ть, -и́ть. **5.** (*sport*): **he was** ~**d on the first round** он вы́был в пе́рвом ту́ре.
elimination [ɪˌlɪmɪ'neɪʃ(ə)n] *n.* устране́ние, исключе́ние, очище́ние; (*sport*) отбо́рочное соревнова́ние.
elision [ɪ'lɪʒ(ə)n] *n.* (*phon.*) эли́зия.
élite [eɪ'li:t, ɪ-] *n.* эли́та; **an** ~ **regiment** отбо́рный полк.
élitist [eɪ'li:tɪst, ɪ-] *adj.* элита́рный.
elixir [ɪ'lɪksɪə(r)] *n.* эликси́р.
Elizabeth [ɪ'lɪzəbəθ] *n.* (*bibl.*) Елисаве́та; (*hist.*) Елизаве́та.
Elizabethan [ɪˌlɪzə'bi:θ(ə)n] *n.* елизаве́тинец.
adj. елизаве́тинский.
elk [elk] *n.* лось (*m.*).
cpd. ~**-hound** *n.* оленего́нная, ла́йка.
ell [el] *n.*: **give him an inch and he'll take an** ~ дай ему́ па́лец, он всю ру́ку отку́сит.
ellipse [ɪ'lɪps] *n.* э́ллипс, ова́л.
ellipsis [ɪ'lɪpsɪs] *n.* э́ллипсис.
ellipsoid [ɪ'lɪpsɔɪd] *n.* эллипсо́ид.
adj. (*also* ~**al**) эллипсоида́льный, элипсо́идный.
elliptical [ɪ'lɪptɪkəl] *adj.* (*math., gram.*) эллипти́ческий.
elm [elm] *n.* вяз; (*wood*), древеси́на вя́за.
Elmo ['elməʊ] *n.*: **St** ~**'s fire** огни́ (*m. pl.*) свято́го Э́льма
elocution [ˌelə'kju:ʃ(ə)n] *n.* ора́торское иску́сство; те́хника ре́чи.
elocutionary [ˌelə'kju:ʃənərɪ] *adj.* декламацио́нный.
elocutionist [ˌelə'kju:ʃənɪst] *n.* (*teacher*) учи́тель (*fem.* -ница) деклама́ции; (*reciter*) деклама́тор.
elongate ['i:lɒŋˌgeɪt] *adj.* (*also* ~**d**) удлинённый.
v.t. удлин|я́ть, -и́ть.
elongation [ˌi:lɒŋ'geɪʃ(ə)n] *n.* удлине́ние.
elope [ɪ'ləʊp] *v.i.* (та́йно) бежа́ть (*det.*) (с возлю́бленным).
elopement [ɪ'ləʊpmənt] *n.* та́йное бе́гство (с возлю́бленным).
eloquence ['eləkwəns] *n.* красноре́чие.
eloquent ['eləkwənt] *adj.* красноречи́вый.
El Salvador [el 'sælvəˌdɔ:(r)] *n.* Сальвадо́р.
else [els] *adj. & adv.* друго́й; **no-one** ~ никто́ друго́й; бо́льше никто́; **everyone** ~ все остальны́е; **nowhere** ~ ни в како́м друго́м ме́сте; **nowhere** ~ **but ...** нигде́, кро́ме...; **everywhere** ~ везде́, то́лько не зде́сь/там; **someone** ~**'s** не свой, чужо́й; **what** ~ **could I say?** что ещё я мог сказа́ть?; **do you want anything** ~ (*more*)? вы хоти́те ещё что-нибу́дь?; **how** ~ **can I manage?** как (же) ещё я могу́ спра́виться с э́тим?; **or** ~ и́ли же; ина́че; а (не) то; **run, or** ~ **you'll be late** беги́те, а то опозда́ете.
cpd. ~**where** *adv.* где́-нибудь ещё (в друго́м ме́сте); куда́-нибудь ещё (в друго́е ме́сто).
elucidate [ɪ'lu:sɪˌdeɪt, ɪ'lju:s-] *v.t.* разъясн|я́ть, -и́ть, прол|ива́ть, -и́ть свет на+*a.*
elucidation [ɪˌlu:sɪ'deɪʃ(ə)n, ɪˌlju:s-] *n.* разъясне́ние.
elucidatory [ɪ'lu:sɪˌdeɪtərɪ, ɪ'lju:s-] *adj.* поясни́тельный.
elude [ɪ'lu:d, ɪ'lju:d] *v.t.* изб|ега́ть, -е́гнуть *g.*; ускольз|а́ть, -ну́ть от+*g.*
elusion [ɪ'lu:ʒ(ə)n, ɪ'lju:ʒ(ə)n] *n.* уклоне́ние, увёртка.
elusive [ɪ'lu:sɪv, ɪ'lju:sɪv] *adj.* неулови́мый; (*evasive*) укло́нчивый.
elusiveness [ɪ'lu:sɪvnɪs, ɪ'lju:sɪvnɪs] *n.* неулови́мость; укло́нчивость.
elver ['elvə(r)] *n.* молодо́й у́горь.
elvish ['elvɪʃ] = **elfin**
Elysian [ɪ'lɪzɪən] *adj.* елисе́йский; (*fig.*) ра́йский.
emaciate [ɪ'meɪsɪˌeɪt, ɪ'meɪʃɪˌeɪt] *v.t.* изнур|я́ть, -и́ть; (*soil*) истощ|а́ть, -и́ть.
emaciation [ɪˌmeɪsɪ'eɪʃ(ə)n, ɪˌmeɪʃɪ'eɪʃ(ə)n] *n.* изнуре́ние; истоще́ние.
email ['i:meɪl] *n.* (*also* **e-mail**) электро́нная по́чта.
emanate ['eməˌneɪt] *v.i.* излуча́ться (*impf.*); истека́ть (*impf.*); **the suggestion** ~**d from him** предложе́ние исходи́ло от него́.
emanation [ˌemə'neɪʃ(ə)n] *n.* истече́ние, излуче́ние.
emancipate [ɪ'mænsɪˌpeɪt] *v.t.* эмансипи́ровать (*impf., pf.*); свобо|жда́ть, -ди́ть.
emancipation [ɪˌmænsɪ'peɪʃ(ə)n] *n.* эмансипа́ция, освобо-жде́ние.
emancipator [ɪ'mænsɪˌpeɪtə(r)] *n.* эмансипа́тор, освободи́тель (*m.*).
emasculate [ɪ'mæskjʊˌleɪt] *v.t.* (*castrate*) кастри́ровать (*impf., pf.*); (*fig.*) выхола́щивать, вы́холостить; (*e.g. language*) обедн|я́ть, -и́ть.
emasculation [ɪˌmæskjʊ'leɪʃ(ə)n] *n.* кастра́ция; выхола́щивание, обедне́ние.
embalm [ɪm'bɑ:m] *v.t.* бальзами́ровать, на-; (*fig.*): **his memory is** ~**ed in our hearts** па́мять о нём жива́ в на́ших сердца́х; (*make fragrant*) нап|олня́ть, -о́лнить благоуха́нием.
embalmment [ɪm'bɑ:mmənt] *n.* бальзами́рование.
embank [ɪm'bæŋk] *v.t.* обн|оси́ть, -ести́ ва́лом.
embankment [ɪm'bæŋkmənt] *n.* (*wall etc.*) на́сыпь, гать; (*roadway*) на́бережная.
embargo [em'bɑ:gəʊ, ɪm-] *n.* эмба́рго (*indecl.*); **oil is under** ~ торго́вля не́фтью запрещена́; **lay an** ~ **on** нал|ага́ть, -ожи́ть эмба́рго на+*a.*; **lift, raise an** ~ сни|ма́ть, -ять эмба́рго (с+*g.*).
v.t. (*forbid trade in*) нал|ага́ть, -ожи́ть эмба́рго на+*a.*; (*seize*) конфискова́ть (*impf., pf.*); реквизи́ровать (*impf., pf.*).
embark [ɪm'bɑ:k] *v.t.* (*goods*) грузи́ть, на-; (*people*) грузи́ть, по-.
v.i. (*go on board*) грузи́ться, по-; сади́ться, сесть на кора́бль; (*fig.*) пус|ка́ться -ти́ться (в+*a.*); прин|има́ться, -я́ться (за+*a.*); ~ **on an undertaking** предприн|има́ть, -ять де́ло; ~ **on a discussion** пус|ка́ться -ти́ться в диску́ссию.

embarkation [ˌembɑːˈkeɪʃ(ə)n] *n.* (*of goods*) погру́зка; (*of people*) поса́дка.
embarrass [ɪmˈbærəs] *v.t.* (*cause confusion to*) сму|ща́ть, -ти́ть; прив|оди́ть, -ести́ в замеша́тельство; (*cumber*) затрудн|я́ть, -и́ть.
embarrassing [ɪmˈbærəsɪŋ] *adj.* щекотли́вый, вызыва́ющий смуще́ние; затрудни́тельный.
embarrassment [ɪmˈbærəsmənt] *n.* смуще́ние, замеша́тельство.
embassy [ˈembəsɪ] *n.* (*mission, building*) посо́льство; **he was sent on an ~ to Paris** он был по́слан с ми́ссией в Пари́ж.
embattle [ɪmˈbæt(ə)l] *v.t.* (*set in battle array*) стро́ить, по- в боево́й поря́док; (*furnish with battlements*) оснаща́ть (*impf.*) бойни́цами.
embed [ɪmˈbed] *v.t.*: **stones ~ded in rock** ка́мни, вмуро́ванные в скалу́; **facts ~ded in one's memory** фа́кты, вре́завшиеся в па́мять.
embellish [ɪmˈbelɪʃ] *v.t.* укр|аша́ть, -а́сить; (*a tale etc.*) приукра́|шивать, -сить.
embellishment [ɪmˈbelɪʃmənt] *n.* приукра́шивание.
ember-goose [ˈembə(r)] *n.* гага́ра поля́рная.
embers [ˈembəz] *n. pl.* (*coals etc.*) тле́ющие уго́льки́ (*m. pl.*); (*fig.*): **~ of an old love** ещё не забы́тая любо́вь.
embezzle [ɪmˈbez(ə)l] *v.t.* растра́|чивать, -тить; присв|а́ивать, -о́ить.
embezzlement [ɪmˈbezəlmənt] *n.* растра́та, присвое́ние.
embezzler [ɪmˈbezələ(r)] *n.* растра́тчик.
embitter [ɪmˈbɪtə(r)] *v.t.* озл|обля́ть, -о́бить; ожесточ|а́ть, -и́ть; нап|олня́ть, -о́лнить го́речью; **relations between them were ~ed** отноше́ния ме́жду ни́ми обостри́лись.
embitterment [ɪmˈbɪtəmənt] *n.* озло́бленность.
emblazon [ɪmˈbleɪz(ə)n] *v.t.* распи́с|ывать, -а́ть (*герб*); укр|аша́ть, -а́сить геральди́ческими зна́ками; (*fig., extol*) превозн|оси́ть, -ести́.
emblem [ˈembləm] *n.* эмбле́ма.
emblematic [ˌembləˈmætɪk] *adj.* эмблемати́ческий.
emblematize [ɪmˈblemәˌtaɪz] *v.t.* служи́ть (*impf.*) эмбле́мой +*g*.
embodiment [ɪmˈbɒdɪmənt] *n.* воплоще́ние, олицетворе́ние.
embod|y [ɪmˈbɒdɪ] *v.t.* вопло|ща́ть, -ти́ть; олицетвор|я́ть, -и́ть; (*contain*) содержа́ть (*impf.*); **this model ~ies new features** э́та моде́ль включа́ет в себя́ но́вые элеме́нты.
embolden [ɪmˈbəʊld(ə)n] *v.t.* подбодр|я́ть, -и́ть; ободр|я́ть, -и́ть; да|ва́ть, -ть сме́лость +*d*.
embolism [ˈembəˌlɪz(ə)m] *n.* эмболи́я.
embonpoint [ˌɑ̃bɔ̃ˈpwæ̃] *n.* пу́хлость, полнота́, доро́дность.
embosom [ɪmˈbʊz(ə)m] *v.t.* (*liter.*): **a house ~ed in trees** дом, окружённый дере́вьями.
emboss [ɪmˈbɒs] *v.t.* выбива́ть, вы́бить; чека́нить, от-/вы́-; **~ed notepaper** тиснёная бума́га; **a vase ~ed with a design of flowers** ва́за с релье́фным цвето́чным узо́ром.
embrace [ɪmˈbreɪs] *n.* объя́тие.
v.t. **1.** (*clasp in one's arms*) обн|има́ть, -я́ть. **2.** (*an offer, theory etc.*) прин|има́ть, -я́ть. **3.** (*include, comprise*) включ|а́ть, -и́ть. **4.** (*take in with eye or mind*) охва́т|ывать, -и́ть.
v.i. обн|има́ться, -я́ться.
embrasure [ɪmˈbreɪʒə(r)] *n.* (*for gun*) амбразу́ра, бойни́ца; (*of door, window*) проём.
embrocation [ˌembrəʊˈkeɪʃ(ə)n] *n.* примо́чка.
embroider [ɪmˈbrɔɪdə(r)] *v.t.* вышива́ть, вы́шить; (*a story etc.*) приукра́|шивать, -сить.
embroidery [ɪmˈbrɔɪdərɪ] *n.* вышива́ние, вы́шивка; **~ frame** пя́л|ьцы (*pl., g.* ец).
embroil [ɪmˈbrɔɪl] *v.t.* (*confuse*) запу́т|ывать, -ать; (*involve in quarrel*) ссо́рить, по- (*кого с кем*).
embroilment [ɪmˈbrɔɪlmənt] *n.* запу́тывание, запу́танность; (*quarrel*) ссо́ра.
embryo [ˈembrɪəʊ] *n.* (*biol.*) эмбрио́н; (*fig.*) заро́дыш; **in ~** в заро́дыше.
embryology [ˌembrɪˈɒlədʒɪ] *n.* эмбриоло́гия.
embryonic [ˌembrɪˈɒnɪk] *adj.* эмбриона́льный; (*fig.*) недора́звитый; в заро́дыше.
embus [ɪmˈbʌs] (*mil.*) *v.t.* сажа́ть, посади́ть в автомаши́ны.
v.i. грузи́ться, по- в автомаши́ны.
emend [ɪˈmend] *v.t.* испр|авля́ть, -а́вить.
emendation [ˌiːmenˈdeɪʃ(ə)n] *n.* исправле́ние (те́кста).
emerald [ˈemər(ə)ld] *n.* изумру́д; (*attr.*) изумру́дный; **~ green** изумру́дно-зелёный.
emerge [ɪˈmɜːdʒ] *v.i.* всплы|ва́ть, -ть; появ|ля́ться, -и́ться; **the moon ~d from behind clouds** луна́ вы́шла из-за облако́в; **the submarine ~d** подво́дная ло́дка всплыла́; (*fig.*) возн|ика́ть, -и́кнуть; я́вствовать (*impf.*); **no new facts ~d** никаки́х но́вых фа́ктов не всплы́ло.
emergence [ɪˈmɜːdʒəns] *n.* появле́ние, возникнове́ние.
emergency [ɪˈmɜːdʒənsɪ] *n.* кра́йняя необходи́мость; ава́рия; чрезвыча́йное положе́ние; (*attr.*) чрезвыча́йный, э́кстренный; (*for use in ~*) запасно́й, запа́сный, вре́менный; **rise to an ~** оказа́ться (*pf.*) на высоте́ положе́ния; **~ landing** вы́нужденная поса́дка; **~ powers** чрезвыча́йные полномо́чия; **~ ration** неприкоснове́нный запа́с.
emergent [ɪˈmɜːdʒ(ə)nt] *adj.* всплыва́ющий на пове́рхность; (*fig.*) нараста́ющий, развива́ющийся.
emeritus [ɪˈmerɪtəs] *adj.*: **professor ~** заслу́женный профе́ссор в отста́вке.
emery [ˈemərɪ] *n.* нажда́к; **~ cloth** нажда́чное полотно́; шку́рка; **~ paper** нажда́чная бума́га.
emetic [ɪˈmetɪk] *n.* рво́тное сре́дство.
adj. рво́тный; (*fig.*) тошнотво́рный.
emigrant [ˈemɪgrənt] *n.* эмигра́нт (*fem.* -ка).
adj. эмигра́нтский.
emigrate [ˈemɪˌgreɪt] *v.i.* эмигри́ровать (*impf., pf.*).
emigration [ˌemɪˈgreɪʃ(ə)n] *n.* эмигра́ция.
émigré [ˈemɪˌgreɪ] *n.* эмигра́нт (*fem.* -ка).
adj. эмиграцио́нный, эмигра́нтский; **~ government** прави́тельство в изгна́нии.
eminence [ˈemɪnəns] *n.* **1.** (*high ground*) высота́; возвыше́ние. **2.** (*celebrity*) знамени́тость; **reach, win, attain ~** доби́ться (*pf.*) сла́вы/изве́стности. **3.** (*title*): **His E~** Его́ Высокопреосвяще́нство; **grey ~** (*fig.*) се́рое преосвяще́нство, се́рый кардина́л.
eminent [ˈemɪnənt] *adj.* (*of pers.*) выдаю́щийся, знамени́тый; (*of qualities*) замеча́тельный, выдаю́щийся; **~ly suitable** на ре́дкость подходя́щий.
emir [eˈmɪə(r)] *n.* (*ruler*) эми́р.
emirate [ˈemɪərət] *n.* эмира́т; **United Arab E~s** Объединённые Ара́бские Эмира́ты.
emissary [ˈemɪsərɪ] *n.* эмисса́р.
emission [ɪˈmɪʃ(ə)n] *n.* (*of currency*) вы́пуск, эми́ссия; (*of semen*) выделе́ние; (*of light*) излуче́ние; (*of heat*) теплоотда́ча.
emit [ɪˈmɪt] *v.t.* (*e.g. smoke*) испус|ка́ть, -ти́ть; (*light, heat etc.*) излуч|а́ть, -и́ть; (*currency*) выпуска́ть, вы́пустить.
emollient [ɪˈmɒlɪənt] *n.* мягчи́тельное сре́дство.
adj. смягча́ющий; мягчи́тельный.
emolument [ɪˈmɒljʊmənt] *n.* (*usu. pl.*) жа́лованье, дохо́д.
emote [ɪˈməʊt] *v.i.* (*coll.*) выража́ть, вы́разить чу́вства; (*of actor*) игра́ть (*impf.*) с чу́вством.
emotion [ɪˈməʊʃ(ə)n] *n.* (*feeling*) эмо́ция; (*agitation*) волне́ние.
emotional [ɪˈməʊʃən(ə)l] *adj.* эмоциона́льный; **an ~ appeal** волну́ющий призы́в.
emotionalism [ɪˈməʊʃənəlˌɪz(ə)m] *n.* эмоциона́льность.
emotive [ɪˈməʊtɪv] *adj.* эмоциона́льный; эмоциона́льно волну́ющий/укра́шенный.
empanel [ɪmˈpæn(ə)l] *v.t.* вн|оси́ть, -ести́ в спи́сок прися́жных; **~ a jury** сост|авля́ть, -а́вить спи́сок прися́жных.
empathetic [ˌempəˈθetɪk] *adj.* эмпати́ческий.
empathy [ˈempəθɪ] *n.* эмпа́тия.
emperor [ˈempərə(r)] *n.* импера́тор; **~ penguin** импера́торский пингви́н; **purple ~** (*butterfly*) ба́бочка-нимфахи́на.
emphasis [ˈemfəsɪs] *n.* **1.** (*stress, prominence*) ударе́ние, вырази́тельность, эмфа́за; **lay ~ on** подчёрк|ивать, -ну́ть; де́лать, с- ударе́ние на+*a. or p.* **2.** (*phon.*) ударе́ние, акце́нт. **3.** (*typ.*) выделе́ние, выдели́тельный шрифт; **'~ added'** (*in quoting*) разря́дка на́ша; курси́в наш.
emphasize [ˈemfəˌsaɪz] *v.t.* подчёрк|ивать, -ну́ть; де́лать, с- упо́р на+*a*.

emphatic [ɪmˈfætɪk] *adj.* эмфати́ческий, вырази́тельный; **he was ~ on this point** он придава́л осо́бое значе́ние э́тому; **that is my ~ opinion** э́то моё твёрдое убежде́ние.
emphysema [ˌemfɪˈsi:mə] *n.* эмфизе́ма.
empire [ˈempaɪə(r)] *n.* **1.** (*state*) импе́рия; **Lower E~** (*Byzantium*) Восто́чная Ри́мская импе́рия; Византи́я; **Russian E~** Росси́йская импе́рия; **E~ style** стиль ампи́р. **2.** (*rule*) влады́чество; **responsibilities of ~** бре́мя вла́сти.
empiric(al) [ɪmˈpɪrɪk(ə)l] *adj.* эмпири́ческий.
empiricism [ɪmˈpɪrɪˌsɪz(ə)m] *n.* эмпири́зм.
empiricist [ɪmˈpɪrɪsɪst] *n.* эмпи́рик.
emplacement [ɪmˈpleɪsmənt] *n.* **1.** (*location*) местоположе́ние. **2.** (*mil.*) оруди́йный око́п; огнева́я то́чка.
emplane [ɪmˈpleɪn] *v.t.* (*persons*) сажа́ть, посади́ть на самолёт; (*goods*) грузи́ть, по- на самолёт.
v.i. сади́ться, сесть на самолёт; грузи́ться, по- на самолёт.
employ [ɪmˈplɔɪ] *n.* заня́тие, слу́жба; **he is in my ~** он рабо́тает у меня́.
v.t. **1.** (*engage*) нан|има́ть, -я́ть; держа́ть (*impf.*) на слу́жбе; предост|авля́ть, -а́вить рабо́ту *+d.*; **they ~ five servants** они́ де́ржат пять слуг (*or* пять челове́к прислу́ги); **~ o.s.** занима́ться (*impf.*) (*чем*); **be ~ed** (*for hire*) рабо́тать (*impf.*), служи́ть (*impf.*). **2.** (*use*) примен|я́ть, -и́ть; употреб|ля́ть, -и́ть.
employable [ɪmˈplɔɪəb(ə)l] *adj.* трудоспосо́бный.
employee [ˌemplɔɪˈi:, -ˈplɔɪi] *n.* слу́жащий; **he is an ~ of this firm** он рабо́тает в э́той фи́рме; он слу́жащий э́той фи́рмы.
employer [ɪmˈplɔɪə(r)] *n.* работода́тель (*m.*); предпринима́тель (*m.*).
employment [ɪmˈplɔɪmənt] *n.* **1.** (*service for pay*) рабо́та, слу́жба; **in ~** на слу́жбе/рабо́те; **out of ~** без рабо́ты; **full ~** по́лная за́нятость; **~ agency** аге́нтство по на́йму рабо́чей си́лы; бюро́ по трудоустро́йству; **~ exchange** би́ржа труда́. **2.** (*occupation*) заня́тие. **3.** (*use*) примене́ние, испо́льзование.
emporium [emˈpɔ:rɪəm] *n.* (*trading centre*) торго́вый центр; (*shop*) большо́й магази́н, универма́г.
empower [ɪmˈpaʊə(r)] *v.t.* уполномо́чи|вать, -ть.
empress [ˈemprɪs] *n.* императри́ца; (*fig.*) цари́ца; **~ dowager** вдо́вствующая императри́ца.
emptiness [ˈemptɪnɪs] *n.* (*lit., fig.*) пустота́.
empt|y [ˈemptɪ] *adj.* **1.** пусто́й; поро́жний; **the car is ~y of petrol** в маши́не ко́нчился бензи́н; (*fig.*): **~y words** пусты́е слова́; **his mind is ~y of ideas** у него́ нет никаки́х мы́слей; **on an ~y stomach** на пусто́й желу́док; натоща́к; **~y hours** бесце́льно проведённые часы́; **I feel ~y** я го́лоден. **2.** (*pl.*, *~y bottles etc.*) поро́жняя та́ра; буты́лки из-под вина́ и т.п.
v.t. опор|а́жнивать, -ожни́ть; **he ~ied his pockets** он опорожни́л карма́ны; **~y one drawer into another** пере|кла́дывать, -ложи́ть ве́щи из одного́ я́щика в друго́й; **~y water out of a jug** вы́лить (*pf.*) во́ду из кувши́на.
v.i. опорожн|я́ться, -и́ться; **the water ~ies slowly** вода́ ме́дленно вытека́ет; **the Rhine ~ies into the North Sea** Рейн впада́ет в Се́верное мо́ре; **the streets ~ied** у́лицы опусте́ли.
cpds. **~y-handed** *adj.* с пусты́ми рука́ми; **~y-headed** *adj.* пустоголо́вый.
empurple [ɪmˈpɜ:p(ə)l] *v.t.* обагр|я́ть, -и́ть.
empyrean [ˌempaɪˈri:ən, ˌempɪ-] *n.* эмпире́й.
adj. неземно́й, небе́сный.
EMS (*abbr. of* ***European Monetary System***) ЕВС, (Европе́йская валю́тная систе́ма).
emu [ˈi:mju:] *n.* э́му (*m. indecl.*).
emulate [ˈemjʊˌleɪt] *v.t.* соревнова́ться (*impf.*) с+*i.*; сопе́рничать (*impf.*) с+*i.*
emulation [ˌemjʊˈleɪʃ(ə)n] *n.* соревнова́ние, сопе́рничество.
emulator [ˈemjʊˌleɪtə(r)] *n.* соревну́ющийся, сопе́рник.
emulous [ˈemjʊləs] *adj.* соревну́ющийся.
emulsion [ɪˈmʌlʃ(ə)n] *n.* эму́льсия.
enable [ɪˈneɪb(ə)l] *v.t.* (*make able*) да|ва́ть, -ть возмо́жность *+d.*; (*authorize*) уполномо́чи|вать, -ть; (*make possible*) де́лать, с- возмо́жным.
enact [ɪˈnækt] *v.t.* (*ordain*) постанов|ля́ть, -и́ть; предпи́с|ывать, -а́ть; (*act*) игра́ть, сыгра́ть (*роль*); разы́гр|ывать, -а́ть; (*perform*) соверш|а́ть, -и́ть.
enactment [ɪˈnæktmənt] *n.* (*ordaining*) постановле́ние, предписа́ние; (*ordinance*) постановле́ние, ука́з; (*theatr.*) игра́.
enamel [ɪˈnæm(ə)l] *n.* (*also of teeth*) эма́ль; **~ paint** эма́левые кра́ски; **~ware** эмалиро́ванная посу́да.
v.t. эмалирова́ть (*impf.*); (*poet., adorn*) разукра́|шивать, -сить.
enamour [ɪˈnæmə(r)] *v.t.*: **he was ~ed of her** он был е́ю очаро́ван; **~ed of books** влюблённый в кни́ги.
en bloc [ɑ̃ ˈblɒk] *adv.* целико́м; **the government resigned ~** прави́тельство ушло́ в отста́вку в по́лном соста́ве.
encamp [ɪnˈkæmp] *v.t. & i.* распол|ага́ть(ся), -ожи́ть(ся) ла́герем.
encampment [ɪnˈkæmpmənt] *n.* расположе́ние ла́герем; (*camp*) ла́герь (*m.*).
encapsulate [ɪnˈkæpsjʊˌleɪt] *v.t.* (*fig.*) заключ|а́ть, -и́ть в себе́; **an ~d dream** сон во сне.
encase [ɪnˈkeɪs] *v.t.*: **~d in armour** зако́ванный в ла́ты.
encash [ɪnˈkæʃ] *v.t.* реализова́ть (*impf., pf.*); получ|а́ть, -и́ть нали́чными/деньга́ми
encashment [ɪnˈkæʃmənt] *n.* реализа́ция.
encaustic [ɪnˈkɔ:stɪk] *adj.*: **~ brick/tile** разноцве́тный кирпи́ч/изразе́ц.
encephalic [ˌenkɪˈfælɪk, ˌens-] *adj.* мозгово́й.
encephalitis [enˌkefəˈlaɪtɪs, enˌsef-] *n.* энцефали́т.
encephalogram [enˈkefələʊˌgræm, enˈsef-] *n.* энцефалогра́мма.
enchain [ɪnˈtʃeɪn] *v.t.* (*fig.*) прико́в|ывать, -а́ть; ско́в|ывать, -а́ть.
enchant [ɪnˈtʃɑ:nt] *v.t.* (*bewitch*) зачаро́в|ывать, -а́ть; заколдо́в|ывать, -а́ть; околдо́в|ывать, -а́ть; (*delight*) обвор|а́живать, -ожи́ть; очаро́в|ывать, -а́ть; восхи|ща́ть, -ти́ть.
enchanter [ɪnˈtʃɑ:ntə(r)] *n.* (*wizard*) волше́бник, чароде́й.
enchanting [ɪnˈtʃɑ:ntɪŋ] *adj.* волше́бный, чару́ющий, обворожи́тельный.
enchantment [ɪnˈtʃɑ:ntmənt] *n.* (*spell*) волшебство́, ча́р|ы (*pl., g.* —); (*charm*) очарова́ние, обая́ние; (*delight*) восхище́ние.
enchantress [ɪnˈtʃɑ:ntrɪs] *n.* (*witch, charmer*) волше́бница, чароде́йка.
enchase [ɪnˈtʃeɪs] *v.t.* (*set*) обр|амля́ть, -а́мить; (*inlay*) инкрусти́ровать (*impf., pf.*).
encipher, encypher [ɪnˈsaɪfə(r)] *v.t.* зашифро́в|ывать, -а́ть.
encipherment [ɪnˈsaɪfəmənt] *n.* шифро́вка.
encircl|e [ɪnˈsɜ:k(ə)l] *v.t.* окруж|а́ть, -и́ть; **~ing manoeuvre** обхо́дный манёвр; манёвр на окруже́ние.
encirclement [ɪnˈsɜ:kəlmənt] *n.* окруже́ние.
enclasp [ɪnˈklɑ:sp] *v.t.* обхва́т|ывать, -и́ть.
enclave [ˈenkleɪv] *n.* террито́рия, окружённая чужи́ми владе́ниями; анкла́в.
enclitic [enˈklɪtɪk] *n.* энкли́тика.
adj. энклити́ческий.
enclos|e, inclose [ɪnˈkləʊz] *v.t.* **1.** (*surround, fence*) окруж|а́ть, -и́ть; **~e a garden with a wall** обн|оси́ть, -ести́ сад стено́й; **~e in parentheses** заключ|а́ть, -и́ть в ско́бки. **2.** (*in letter etc.*) при|кла́дывать, -ложи́ть; **I ~e herewith** при сём прилага́ю; **a letter ~ing an invoice** письмо́ с приложе́нием счёта.
enclosure [ɪnˈkləʊʒə(r)] *n.* (*act of enclosing*) огора́живание; (*fence*) огражде́ние, огра́да; (*in letter*) приложе́ние.
encode [ɪnˈkəʊd] *v.t.* коди́ровать (*impf., pf.*); шифрова́ть, за-.
encomiastic [enˌkəʊmɪˈæstɪk] *adj.* хвалё́бный, панегири́ческий.
encomium [enˈkəʊmɪəm] *n.* панеги́рик; комплиме́нт.
encompass [ɪnˈkʌmpəs] *v.t.* (*surround*) окруж|а́ть, -и́ть; (*contain, comprise*) заключ|а́ть, -и́ть; (*cope with, accomplish*) осуществ|ля́ть, -и́ть; охва́т|ывать, -и́ть.
encore [ˈɒŋkɔ:(r)] *n. & int.* бис; **he gave six ~s** он биси́ровал шесть раз.
v.t. вызыва́ть, вы́звать (*кого*) на бис.
encounter [ɪnˈkaʊntə(r)] *n.* (*meeting*) встре́ча; (*contest, competition*) состяза́ние.

v.t. встр|еча́ться, -е́титься с+*i.*; ст|а́лкиваться, -олкну́ться с+*i.*

encourage [ɪnˈkʌrɪdʒ] *v.t.* ободр|я́ть, -и́ть; поощр|я́ть, -и́ть; подде́рж|ивать, -а́ть; спосо́бствовать (*impf.*) +*d.*; **I ~d him to go** я угова́ривал его́ идти́; **do not ~ him in his idle ways** не поощря́йте его́ безде́лья; **I was ~d by the result** результа́т меня́ обнадёжил.

encouragement [ɪnˈkʌrɪdʒmənt] *n.* ободре́ние, поощре́ние, подде́ржка; **this acted as an ~ to him** э́то ободри́ло его́; **I gave him no ~** я не поощря́л его́.

encouraging [ɪnˈkʌrɪdʒɪŋ] *adj.* ободря́ющий, ободри́тельный, обнадёживающий.

encroach [ɪnˈkrəʊtʃ] *v.i.* поку|ша́ться, -си́ться (на+*a.*); вт|орга́ться, -о́ргнуться (в+*a.*); **~ on s.o.'s rights** посяг|а́ть, -ну́ть на чьи-н. права́; **the sea is ~ing on the land** мо́ре наступа́ет на су́шу.

encroachment [ɪnˈkrəʊtʃmənt] *n.* посяга́тельство; вторже́ние.

en|crust, in- [ɪnˈkrʌst] *v.t. & i.* (*of ice, rust etc.*) покр|ыва́ть(ся), -ы́ть(ся); **~ a wall with marble** инкрусти́ровать (*impf.*, *pf.*) сте́ну мра́мором; **salt ~ed on the bottom of the kettle** дно ча́йника покры́лось сло́ем со́ли.

encumber [ɪnˈkʌmbə(r)] *v.t.* **1.** (*burden*) обремен|я́ть, -и́ть; **~ o.s. with luggage** взва́л|ивать, -и́ть на себя́ бага́ж. **2.** (*cram*) загромо|жда́ть, -зди́ть.

encumbrance [ɪnˈkʌmbrəns] *n.* обу́за, препя́тствие; (*leg.*) обремене́ние.

encyclical [enˈsɪklɪk(ə)l] *n.* энци́клика.

encyclopedia [enˌsaɪkləˈpiːdɪə, ɪn-] *n.* энциклопе́дия; **walking ~** ходя́чая энциклопе́дия.

encyclopedic [enˌsaɪkləˈpiːdɪk, ɪn-] *adj.* энциклопеди́ческий.

encyclopedist [enˌsaɪkləˈpiːdɪst, ɪn-] *n.* (*Fr. hist.*) энциклопеди́ст.

encypher [ɪnˈsaɪfə(r)] = **encipher**

end [end] *n.* (*extremity; lit., fig.*) коне́ц; **the ~ house** кра́йний дом; **I read the book from ~ to ~** я прочита́л кни́гу от ко́рки до ко́рки; **from ~ to ~ of the country** из кра́я в край страны́; по всей стране́; **two hours on ~** (*in succession*) два часа́ подря́д; **he began at the wrong ~** он на́чал не с того́ конца́; **third from the ~** тре́тий с кра́ю; **is everything all right at your ~?** всё ли благополу́чно у вас?; **to the ~s of the earth** ≃ к чёрту на кули́чки; на край све́та; **at the ~ of the passage** в конце́ коридо́ра; **at the ~ of the world** на краю́ све́та; **at the ~ of August** в конце́ (*or* в после́дних чи́слах) а́вгуста. **2.** (*of elongated object*) коне́ц, край; **he stood the box on (its) ~** он поста́вил я́щик стойма́ (*or* на попа́); **the ships collided ~ on** корабли́ столкну́лись нос к но́су; **he placed the tables ~ to ~** он соста́вил столы́ в длину́ оди́н к друго́му; **turn sth. ~ for ~** поверну́ть (*pf.*) что-н. други́м концо́м; **the business ~ of a gun** (*coll.*) ду́ло пистоле́та; **her hair stood on ~** у неё во́лосы вста́ли ды́бом. **3.** (*var. idioms*): **keep one's ~ up** ≃ не уда́рить (*pf.*) лицо́м в грязь; **I am at the ~ of my tether, rope** я дошёл до то́чки/ру́чки; **this is the ~!** (*coll., last straw, limit*) да́льше е́хать не́куда!; **he got hold of the wrong ~ of the stick** он по́нял всё наоборо́т; **loose ~s** (*unfinished business*) запу́щенные дела́; **I am at a loose ~** я шата́юсь без де́ла; **he went off the deep ~** (*coll.*) он взорва́лся; **make (both) ~s meet** своди́ть (*impf.*) концы́ с конца́ми; **play both ~s against the middle** игра́ть (*impf.*) на противополо́жных интере́сах. **4.** (*remnant, small part*): **candle ~** ога́рок; **cigarette ~** оку́рок; **rope's ~** линёк. **5.** (*conclusion, termination*) оконча́ние; **in the ~** в конце́ концо́в; в коне́чном счёте; **the war is at an ~** войне́ коне́ц; **our stores are at an ~** на́ши запа́сы на исхо́де; **come to an ~** ок|а́нчиваться, -о́нчиться; конча́ться, ко́нчиться; **put an ~ to, make an ~ of** класть, положи́ть коне́ц +*d.*; **there s an ~ (of it)!** вот и всё!; **what will the ~ be?** чем э́то ко́нчится?; **faithful to the ~** ве́рный до конца́; **till the ~ of time** наве́чно; до сконча́ния ве́ка; **dead ~** тупи́к; **he came to a bad ~** он пло́хо ко́нчил; **world without ~** на ве́ки ве́чные; **the ~ of the matter was that ...** де́ло ко́нчилось те́м, что...; **we shall never hear the ~ of it** э́тому конца́-кра́ю не бу́дет; **they fought to the bitter ~** они́ сража́лись до после́дней ка́пли кро́ви; **he stayed till the bitter ~** он остава́лся на ме́сте до са́мого конца́; **~ product** коне́чный проду́кт; **I had no ~ of trouble finding him** мне сто́ило невероя́тного труда́ найти́ его́; **he has no ~ of books** у него́ у́йма книг; **we had no ~ of a time** мы прекра́сно провели́ вре́мя; **he is no ~ of a boaster** он отча́янный хвасту́н; **he was no ~ disappointed** он был соверше́нно разочаро́ван. **6.** (*death*) коне́ц; **he is nearing his ~** он при́ сме́рти; **she came to an untimely ~** она́ безвре́менно сконча́лась. **7.** (*purpose*) цель; **gain, win, achieve one's ~** дост|ига́ть, -и́чь свое́й це́ли; **to this ~, with this ~ in view** с э́той це́лью; **to the ~ that ...** для того́, что́бы; **to no ~** (*in vain*) бесце́льно; **any means to an ~** все сре́дства хороши́.

v.t. конча́ть, ко́нчить; **~ a quarrel** прекра|ща́ть, -ти́ть ссо́ру; **~ one's days** рассчита́ться с жи́знью.

v.i. конча́ться, ко́нчиться; **the road ~s here** доро́га конча́ется здесь; **the story ~s happily** э́то расска́з со счастли́вым концо́м; **~ the meeting ~ed with a vote of thanks** собра́ние око́нчилось выраже́нием благода́рности; **he ~ed as a clerk** он (так и) ко́нчил карье́ру просты́м чино́вником; **he will ~ by marrying her** он в конце́ концо́в на ней же́нится; **all's well that ~s well** всё хорошо́, что хорошо́ конча́ется; **~ in smoke** (*fig.*) око́нчиться (*pf.*) ниче́м; рассе́яться (*pf.*) как дым; улете́учиться (*pf.*).

with advs.: **~ off** *v.t.*: **he ~ed off his speech with a quotation** он зако́нчил свою́ речь цита́той; **~ up** *v.i.*: **he ~ed up in jail** он ко́нчил за решёткой; **he ~ed up at the opera** в конце́ концо́в он попа́л-таки в о́перу.

cpds. **~-game** *n.* (*at chess*) э́ндшпиль (*m.*), оконча́ние; **~long** *adv.* (*lengthwise*) вдоль; (*on end*) стойма́; **~most** *adj.* са́мый да́льний; кра́йний; **~paper** *n.* (*of a book*) форза́ц; **~ways, ~wise** *advs.* (*with end towards spectator*) за́дом напере́д; (*end to end*) в длину́ (оди́н к друго́му); (*upright*) стойма́.

endanger [ɪnˈdeɪndʒə(r)] *v.t.* подв|ерга́ть, -е́ргнуть опа́сности; ста́вить (*impf.*) под угро́зу; угрожа́ть (*impf.*) +*d.*; **~ed species** вымира́ющий вид.

endear [ɪnˈdɪə(r)] *v.t.*: **~ o.s. to s.o.** внуш|а́ть, -и́ть кому́-н. любо́вь к себе́; **this speech ~ed him to me** э́та речь расположи́ла меня́ к нему́; **an ~ing smile** покоря́ющая/подкупа́ющая улы́бка.

endearment [ɪnˈdɪəmənt] *n.* ла́ска; **term of ~** ла́сковое обраще́ние.

endeavour [ɪnˈdevə(r)] *n.* стара́ние.

v.i. стара́ться, по-.

endemic [enˈdemɪk] *adj.* эндеми́ческий.

ending [ˈendɪŋ] *n.* оконча́ние (*also gram.*); **happy ~** счастли́вый коне́ц.

endive [ˈendaɪv, -dɪv] *n.* сала́т энди́вий (зи́мний), цико́рий-энди́вий.

endless [ˈendlɪs] *adj.* бесконе́чный, нескончае́мый; **~ patience** беспреде́льное терпе́ние; **~ attempts** бесконе́чные попы́тки; **she is an ~ talker** она́ болта́ет без у́молку; (*tech.*): **~ chain** цепь приво́да.

endocarditis [ˌendəʊkɑːˈdaɪtɪs] *n.* эндокарди́т.

endocrine [ˈendəʊkraɪn, -ˌkrɪn] *adj.* эндокри́нный; **~ glands** же́лезы вну́тренней секре́ции.

endocrinology [ˌendəʊkrɪˈnɒlədʒɪ] *n.* эндокриноло́гия.

endogamous [enˈdɒgəməs] *adj.* эндога́мный.

endogamy [enˈdɒgəmɪ] *n.* эндога́мия.

en|dorse, in- [ɪnˈdɔːs] *v.t.* **1.** (*sign*) индосси́ровать (*impf.*, *pf.*); распи́с|ываться, -а́ться; **~ a cheque** распи́с|ываться, -а́ться на че́ке. **2.** (*inscribe comment on*) де́лать, с- поме́тку на оборо́те (*документа*). **3.** (*support*) подвер|жда́ть, -ди́ть; подде́рж|ивать, -а́ть; **I ~ your opinion** я подде́рживаю ва́ше мне́ние; **he ~d Blank's pills** он реклами́ровал пилю́ли Бла́нка.

en|dorsement, in- [ɪnˈdɔːsmənt] *n.* **1.** переда́точная на́дпись; индоссаме́нт. **2.** (*inscribed comment*) отме́тка. **3.** (*support, approval*) подтвержде́ние; одобре́ние.

endosmosis [ˌendəzˈməʊsɪs] *n.* эндо́смос.

endosperm [ˈendəʊˌspɜːm] *n.* эндоспе́рм.

endow [ɪnˈdaʊ] *v.t.* одар|я́ть, -и́ть; надел|я́ть, -и́ть; **~ a school** поже́ртвовать (*pf.*) капита́л на содержа́ние шко́лы; **~ a professorial chair** осно́в|ывать, -а́ть ка́федру; **he is ~ed with patience** он наделён терпе́нием.

endowment [ɪn'daʊmənt] *n.* **1.** (*act of endowing*) поже́ртвование. **2.** (*funds*) вклад, дар, поже́ртвование, фонд. **3.** (*talent*) одарённость. **4.:** ~ **insurance** страхова́ние-вклад.
en|due, in- [ɪn'dju:] *v.t.* облач|а́ть, -и́ть; надел|я́ть, -и́ть; одар|я́ть, -и́ть.
endurable [ɪn'djʊərəb(ə)l] *adj.* прие́млемый, сно́сный.
endurance [ɪn'djʊərəns] *n.* (*physical*) про́чность; ~ **test** испыта́ние на про́чность; (*mental*) выно́сливость; **past, beyond** ~ невыноси́мый.
endure [ɪn'djʊə(r)] *v.t.* выноси́ть, вы́нести; терпе́ть, вы-; выде́рживать, вы́держать; перен|оси́ть, -ести́; ~ **toothache** терпе́ть зубну́ю бо́ль; **I cannot** ~ **him** я его́ терпе́ть не могу́; **I cannot** ~ **seeing animals ill-treated** я не переношу́, когда́ му́чают живо́тных; (*admit of*) допус|ка́ть, -ти́ть.
v.i. (*suffer*) терпе́ть (*impf.*); (*last*) прод|олжа́ться, -о́лжиться; дли́ться, про-.
enduring [ɪn'djʊərɪŋ] *adj.* (*lasting*) дли́тельный, продолжи́тельный.
enema ['enɪmə] *n.* (*injection*; *syringe*) кли́зма.
enemy ['enəmɪ] *n.* **1.** враг, не́друг; **make an** ~ **of s.o.** наж|ива́ть, -и́ть себе́ врага́ в ком-н.; **he is his own worst** ~ он сам себе́ злейший враг; **the E~** (*the devil*) дья́вол, сатана́ (*m.*). **2.** (*mil., in collect. sense*) враг, проти́вник, непри́ятель (*m.*); **20 of the** ~ **were killed** проти́вник потеря́л 20 челове́к уби́тыми. **3.** (*attr.*) вра́жеский; неприя́тельский; ~ **alien, national** граждани́н враждебного госуда́рства; ~ **property** иму́щество проти́вника.
energetic [ˌenə'dʒetɪk] *adj.* энерги́чный.
energize ['enəˌdʒaɪz] *v.t.* побужда́ть (*impf.*) к де́йствию; (*tech.*) пита́ть (*impf.*) эне́ргией.
energ|y ['enədʒɪ] *n.* (*phys. or mental*) эне́ргия; **devote all one's ~ies to a task** приложи́ть (*pf.*) все си́лы к выполне́нию зада́чи.
enervate¹ [ɪ'nɜ:vət] *adj.* обесси́ленный; рассла́бленный.
enervat|e² ['enəˌveɪt] *v.t.* обесси́ли|вать, -ть; рассл|абля́ть, -а́бить; ~**ing** обесси́ливающий.
en famille [ɑ̃ fæ'mi:j] *adv.* в семе́йном кругу́.
enfeeble [ɪn'fi:b(ə)l] *v.t.* осл|абля́ть, -а́бить, рассл|абля́ть, -а́бить.
enfeeblement [ɪn'fi:bəlmənt] *n.* ослабле́ние, расслабле́ние.
en fête [ɑ̃ 'feɪt] *adv.* в пра́здничном настрое́нии.
enfilade [ˌenfɪ'leɪd] *n.* (*mil.*) продо́льный ого́нь.
v.t. обстре́л|ивать, -я́ть продо́льным огнём.
en|fold, in- [ɪn'fəʊld] *v.t.* (*contain, envelop*) завёр|тывать, -ну́ть; заку́т|ывать, -ать; (*embrace*) обн|има́ть, -я́ть.
enforce [ɪn'fɔ:s] *v.t.* **1.** (*strengthen*) уси́ли|вать, -ть; ~ **an argument** подкреп|ля́ть, -и́ть аргуме́нт. **2.:** ~ **obedience on s.o.** заст|авля́ть, -а́вить кого́-н. подчини́ться. **3.:** ~ **a judgment** (*leg.*) прив|оди́ть, -ести́ в исполне́ние суде́бное реше́ние; ~ **a law** пров|оди́ть, -ести́ зако́н в жи́знь; следи́ть (*impf.*) за соблюде́нием зако́на; ~ **payment** взыска́ть (*pf.*) платёж.
enforceable [ɪn'fɔ:səb(ə)l] *adj.* осуществи́мый, обеспе́ченный правово́й са́нкцией.
enforcement [ɪn'fɔ:smənt] *n.* осуществле́ние; **law** ~ наблюде́ние за соблюде́нием зако́нов; ~ **action** принуди́тельные де́йствия.
enfranchise [ɪn'fræntʃaɪz] *v.t.* (*set free*) отпус|ка́ть, -ти́ть на во́лю; освобо|жда́ть, -ди́ть; (*give the vote to*) предост|авля́ть, -а́вить избира́тельные права́ +*d*.
enfranchisement [ɪn'fræntʃaɪzmənt] *n.* освобожде́ние; предоставле́ние избира́тельных прав (*кому*).
engage [ɪn'geɪdʒ] *v.t.* **1.** (*hire*) нан|има́ть, -я́ть; ~ **a servant** нан|има́ть, -я́ть прислу́гу; ~ **s.o. as a guide** нан|има́ть, -я́ть кого́-н. ги́дом. **2.** (*introduce*): **he ~d the key in the lock** он вста́вил ключ в замо́к. **3.** (*occupy*) зан|има́ть, -я́ть; **he is ~d in reading** он за́нят чте́нием; **he ~d me in conversation** он вовлёк меня́ в разгово́р; **my time is fully ~d** у меня́ нет ни мину́ты свобо́дной; **the line is ~d** (*teleph.*) но́мер за́нят; **the lavatory is ~d** убо́рная занята́. **4.** (*attract*) привл|ека́ть, -е́чь; **the sight ~d my attention** зре́лище привлекло́ моё внима́ние. **5.** (*pledge to marry*): **Tom and Mary are ~d** Том и Мэ́ри помо́лвлены; **to whom is he ~d?** с кем он помо́лвлен?; **they got ~d** они́ обручи́лись. **6.** (*attack*) вступ|а́ть, -и́ть в бой с+*i.*; **we ~d the enemy** мы откры́ли ого́нь по врагу́. **7.** (*tech.*) зацеп|ля́ть, -и́ть; включ|а́ть, -и́ть. **8.** (*archit.*): **an ~d column** сцеплённая полуколо́нна.
v.i. **1.** (*undertake, promise*) бра́ться, взя́ться; обеща́ть (*impf., pf.*). **2.** (*embark, busy o.s.*) зан|има́ться, -я́ться чем-н.; **he ~d in this venture** он взя́лся за э́то предприя́тие. **3.** (*lock together*) зацеп|ля́ть, -и́ть; **the cogs ~d** зубцы́ шестерён вошли́ в зацепле́ние.
engagé [ɑ̃'gæʒeɪ] *adj.* иде́йный.
engagement [ɪn'geɪdʒmənt] *n.* **1.** (*hiring*) наём. **2.** (*promise, debt*) обяза́тельство; **he cannot meet his ~s** он не мо́жет вы́полнить свои́х обяза́тельств. **3.** (*to marry*) помо́лвка; **she broke off the** ~ она́ расто́ргла помо́лвку; ~ **ring** обруча́льное кольцо́. **4.** (*appointment to meet etc.*) свида́ние, встре́ча; **I have numerous ~s (for) next week** у меня́ о́чень мно́го встреч на сле́дующей неде́ле; ~ **book** календа́рь (*m.*). **5.** (*mil.*) бой; **the enemy broke off the** ~ проти́вник вы́шел из бо́я. **6.** (*of wheels etc.*) зацепле́ние.
engaging [ɪn'geɪdʒɪŋ] *adj.* располага́ющий; привлека́тельный; **an** ~ **smile** располага́ющая улы́бка; **with** ~ **frankness** с подкупа́ющей и́скренностью.
engender [ɪn'dʒendə(r)] *v.t.* (*fig.*) поро|жда́ть, -ди́ть.
engine ['endʒɪn] *n.* дви́гатель (*m.*); мото́р; **we had** ~ **trouble** (*motoring*) у нас бы́ли непола́дки с мото́ром.
cpds. ~**-driver** *n.* машини́ст; ~**-house** *n.* парово́зное депо́ (*indecl.*); ~**-room** *n.* маши́нное отделе́ние.
engineer [ˌendʒɪ'nɪə(r)] *n.* **1.** (*technician*) инжене́р, меха́ник; **civil** ~ инжене́р-строи́тель; **mining** ~ го́рный инжене́р; **mechanical** ~ инжене́р-меха́ник. **2.** (*man in charge of engines*) меха́ник; **chief** ~ (*of a ship*) гла́вный меха́ник; (*US, engine-driver*) машини́ст. **3.** (*mil.*) сапёр.
v.t. (*tech.*) проекти́ровать, с-; конструи́ровать, с-; (*fig.*) зат|ева́ть, -е́ять; осуществ|ля́ть, -и́ть.
engineering [ˌendʒɪ'nɪərɪŋ] *n.* машинострое́ние; **civil** ~ гражда́нское строи́тельство; **chemical** ~ хими́ческая техноло́гия; **genetic** ~ ге́нная инжене́рия; **railway** ~ железнодоро́жное строи́тельство; (*mil.*) вое́нно-инжене́рное де́ло; (*fig., contriving*) махина́ции (*f. pl.*).
engirdle [ɪn'gɜ:d(ə)l] *v.t.* опоя́с|ывать, -ать.
England ['ɪŋglənd] *n.* А́нглия.
English ['ɪŋglɪʃ] *n.* **1.** (*language*) англи́йский язы́к; **he speaks** ~ он говори́т по-англи́йски; **in plain** ~ (*fig.*) без обиняко́в; **Old** ~ древнеангли́йский язы́к; **Middle** ~ среднеангли́йский язы́к; **British/American** ~ брита́нский/америка́нский вариа́нт англи́йского языка́; **the King's, Queen's, standard** ~ нормати́вный/литерату́рный англи́йский язы́к; **what is the** ~ **for 'стол'?** как по-англи́йски «стол»? **2.: he studied, read** ~ **at university** он изуча́л в университе́те англи́йскую филоло́гию. **3.: the** ~ (*people*) англича́не.
adj. англи́йский; ~ **studies** англи́стика; ~ **teacher** учи́тель (*fem.* -ница) англи́йского языка́; **Early** ~ (*archit.*) раннеангли́йский стиль.
cpds. ~**man** *n.* англича́нин; ~**woman** *n.* англича́нка.
engraft [ɪn'grɑ:ft] *v.t.* (*bot.*) прив|ива́ть, -и́ть; (*fig.*) прив|ива́ть, -и́ть; внедр|я́ть, -и́ть.
engrave [ɪn'greɪv] *v.t.* гравирова́ть, вы́-; ~**d with an inscription** с вы́гравированной на́дписью; (*fig.*): ~ **sth. on s.o.'s memory** запечатл|ева́ть, -е́ть что-н. в чьей-н. па́мяти.
engraver [ɪn'greɪvə(r)] *n.* гравёр.
engraving [ɪn'greɪvɪŋ] *n.* (*craft*) гравиро́вка, гравирова́ние; (*product*) гравю́ра.
engross [ɪn'grəʊs] *v.t.* (*absorb*) погло|ща́ть, -ти́ть; **an ~ing conversation** захва́тывающий разгово́р; **he was ~ed in his work** он был поглощён рабо́той.
engulf [ɪn'gʌlf] *v.t.* погло|ща́ть, -ти́ть.
enhance [ɪn'hɑ:ns] *v.t.* уси́ли|вать, -ть; (*of price*) пов|ыша́ть, -ы́сить.
enhancement [ɪn'hɑ:nsmənt] *n.* усиле́ние, повыше́ние.
enharmonic [ˌenhɑ:'mɒnɪk] *adj.* (*mus.*) энгармони́ческий.
enigma [ɪ'nɪgmə] *n.* зага́дка.
enigmatic [ˌenɪg'mætɪk] *adj.* зага́дочный.

enjambment [en'dʒæmmənt] *n.* (*pros.*) анжанбема́н, перено́с.

enjoin [ɪn'dʒɔɪn] *v.t.* **1.** (*order*) предпи́с|ывать, -а́ть; веле́ть (*impf., pf.*); **~ silence upon s.o.** веле́ть кому́-н. молча́ть; **I ~ed that they should be well treated** я потре́бовал, что́бы к ним хорошо́ относи́лись. **2.** (*leg., prohibit*) запре|ща́ть, -ти́ть.

enjoy [ɪn'dʒɔɪ] *v.t.* **1.** (*get pleasure from*) насла|жда́ться, -ди́ться +*i.*; **~ one's food** есть (*impf.*) с удово́льствием; люби́ть (*impf.*) пое́сть; **I ~ed talking to him** мне доставля́ло удово́льствие говори́ть с ним; **he ~s a good laugh** он лю́бит хоро́шую шу́тку; **how did you ~ the play?** как вам понра́вилась пье́са?; **we ~ed our holiday** мы хорошо́ провели́ о́тпуск; **~ o.s.** весели́ться (*impf.*); наслажда́ться (*impf.*); хорошо́ пров|оди́ть, -ести́ вре́мя; **we ~ed ourselves** нам бы́ло ве́село/прия́тно. **2.** (*possess*) располага́ть (*impf.*) +*i.*; облада́ть (*impf.*) +*i.*; **~ good/bad health** облада́ть хоро́шим/плохи́м здоро́вьем; **~ a good income** име́ть хоро́ший дохо́д.

enjoyable [ɪn'dʒɔɪəb(ə)l] *adj.* прия́тный.

enjoyment [ɪn'dʒɔɪmənt] *n.* **1.** (*pleasure*) наслажде́ние, удово́льствие; **~ of music** любо́вь к му́зыке. **2.** (*possession*) облада́ние +*i.*, по́льзование +*i.*

enkindle [ɪn'kɪnd(ə)l] *v.t.* (*fig.*) разж|ига́ть, -е́чь; воспламен|я́ть, -и́ть.

enlace [ɪn'leɪs] *v.t.* (*encircle*) окруж|а́ть, -и́ть; (*enfold*) обёр|тывать, -ну́ть; (*entwine*) обв|ива́ть, -и́ть.

enlarge [ɪn'lɑːdʒ] *v.t.* увели́чи|вать, -ть; **~ one's house** де́лать, с- пристро́йку к до́му; **an ~d meeting** расши́ренное заседа́ние.

v.i. расш|иря́ться, -и́риться; **the photograph will ~ well** фотогра́фия бу́дет чёткой и при увеличе́нии; **he ~d on the point** он подро́бнее останови́лся на э́том.

enlargement [ɪn'lɑːdʒmənt] *n.* увеличе́ние; расшире́ние.

enlarger [ɪn'lɑːdʒə(r)] *n.* (*phot. apparatus*) увеличи́тель (*m.*).

enlighten [ɪn'laɪt(ə)n] *v.t.* просве|ща́ть, -ти́ть.

enlightening [ɪn'laɪt(ə)nɪŋ] *adj.* поучи́тельный.

enlightenment [ɪn'laɪtənmənt] *n.* просвещённость; **the E~** (*hist.*) Просвеще́ние.

enlist [ɪn'lɪst] *v.t.* вербова́ть, за-; **~ a recruit** вербова́ть, за- новобра́нца; **~ed man** (*US*) рядово́й; **~ s.o.'s support** заруч|а́ться, -и́ться чьей-н. подде́ржкой; **~ s.o. in a cause** привлека́ть (*impf.*) кого́-н. к де́лу.

v.i. поступ|а́ть, -и́ть на вое́нную слу́жбу.

enlistment [ɪn'lɪstmənt] *n.* вербо́вка; поступле́ние на вое́нную слу́жбу.

enliven [ɪn'laɪv(ə)n] *v.t.* ожив|ля́ть, -и́ть.

en masse [ɑ̃ 'mæs] *adv.* в ма́ссе; ма́ссовым поря́дком.

enmesh [ɪn'meʃ] *v.t.* опу́т|ывать, -ать; запу́т|ывать, -ать.

enmity ['enmɪtɪ] *n.* вражда́; **be at ~ with** враждова́ть (*impf.*) с+*i.*

ennoble [ɪ'nəʊb(ə)l] *v.t.* (*raise to peerage*) возв|оди́ть, -ести́ в дворя́нство; (*make nobler*) облагор|а́живать, -о́дить.

ennoblement [ɪ'nəʊbəlmənt] *n.* пожа́лование дворя́нством; облагора́живание.

Enoch ['iːnɒk] *n.* (*bibl.*) Ено́х.

enormity [ɪ'nɔːmɪtɪ] *n.* (*grossness*) чудо́вищность; (*crime*) чудо́вищное преступле́ние.

enormous [ɪ'nɔːməs] *adj.* грома́дный, огро́мный; **~ly** чрезвыча́йно; **he enjoyed himself ~ly** он получи́л огро́мное удово́льствие.

enormousness [ɪ'nɔːməsnɪs] *n.* грома́дность, огро́мность.

enough [ɪ'nʌf] *n.* доста́точное коли́чество; дово́льно, доста́точно; **£5 is ~** пяти́ фу́нтов доста́точно; **he has ~ and to spare** у него́ бо́лее чем доста́точно; **~ is as good as a feast** от добра́ добра́ не и́щут; **I had ~ to do to catch the train** я и так едва́ успева́л на по́езд; **it is ~ to make one weep** э́того доста́точно, что́бы распла́каться; **(that's) ~!** доста́точно!; дово́льно!; **~ said!** всё поня́тно; **there is ~ to go round** хва́тит на всех; **I have had ~ of your lies** надое́ла мне ва́ша ложь; **it is not ~ to buy a book, one must also read it** ма́ло купи́ть кни́гу, на́до ещё чита́ть её.

adj. доста́точный; **is there ~ wine for all of us?** хва́тит ли вина́ на всех?; **I have just ~ money** де́нег у меня́ в обре́з (на+*a.*).

adv. доста́точно; **are you warm ~?** вы не замёрзли?; вам тепло́?; **it is boiled just ~** э́то как раз свари́лось; **you know well ~** вы прекра́сно зна́ете; **be kind/good ~ to do this** бу́дьте добры́/любе́зны сде́лать э́то; **I was foolish ~ to believe her** я был насто́лько глуп, что пове́рил ей; (*fairly, rather*) дово́льно; **she sings well ~** она́ непло́хо поёт; **curiously ~** как ни стра́нно; **sure ~, he came** он действи́тельно пришёл.

en passant [ˌɑ̃ pæ'sɑ̃] *adv.* (*by the way*) попу́тно, мимохо́дом; (*chess*) на прохо́де.

enquire (*see also* **inquire**) [ɪn'kwaɪə(r), ɪŋ-] *v.t.* спр|а́шивать, -оси́ть; запр|а́шивать, -оси́ть; **I ~d his name** я спроси́л, как его́ зову́т.

v.i. осв|едомля́ться, -е́домиться; **~ into a matter** рассле́довать (*pf.*) де́ло; **~ after s.o.** спр|а́шивать, -оси́ть о ком-н.; **I ~d after his wife** я спроси́л, как пожива́ет его́ жена́; **~ for s.o.** спр|а́шивать, -оси́ть кого́-н.; **~ for the furnishing department** (*in a shop*) спроси́ть (*pf.*), где нахо́дится ме́бельный отде́л.

enquirer [ɪn'kwaɪərə(r), ɪŋ-] *n.* спра́шивающий, вопроша́ющий.

enquiring [ɪn'kwaɪərɪŋ, ɪŋ-] *adj.*: **an ~ look** вопроси́тельный взгляд; **an ~ mind** пытли́вый ум.

enquir|y [ɪn'kwaɪərɪ, ɪŋ-] *n.* (*see also* **inquiry**) расспро́сы (*m. pl.*); рассле́дование; **make ~ies** нав|оди́ть, -ести́ спра́вки; **there is not much ~y for these goods** на э́ти това́ры нет большо́го спро́са.

enrage [ɪn'reɪdʒ] *v.t.* беси́ть, вз-; **he was ~d at her stupidity** её ту́пость взбеси́ла его.

enrapture [ɪn'ræptʃə(r)] *v.t.* восхи|ща́ть, -ти́ть.

enrich [ɪn'rɪtʃ] *v.t.* обога|ща́ть, -ти́ть; (*soil*) уд|обря́ть, -о́брить; (*a collection*) поп|олня́ть, -о́лнить.

enrichment [ɪn'rɪtʃmənt] *n.* обогаще́ние; (*of soil*) удобре́ние.

enrobe [ɪn'rəʊb] *v.t.* облач|а́ть, -и́ть.

enrol [ɪn'rəʊl] *v.t. & i.* зач|исля́ть(ся), -и́слить(ся); запи́с|ывать(ся), -а́ться; **17,000 students are ~led at the university** в университе́те 17 000 студе́нтов.

enrolment [ɪn'rəʊlmənt] *n.* зачисле́ние, приём.

en route [ɑ̃ 'ruːt] *adv.* по/в пути́.

ensanguined [ɪn'sæŋgwɪnd] *adj.* окрова́вленный.

ensconce [ɪn'skɒns] *v.t.*: **~ o.s.** устро́иться (*pf.*), укры́ться (*pf.*).

ensemble [ɒn'sɒmb(ə)l] *n.* (*dress, music*) анса́мбль (*m.*); (*general effect*) о́бщее впечатле́ние.

enshrine [ɪn'ʃraɪn] *v.t.* поме|ща́ть, -сти́ть в ра́ку; (*fig.*) **memories ~d in her heart** воспомина́ния, храни́мые как святы́ня в её се́рдце.

enshroud [ɪn'ʃraʊd] *v.t.* заку́т|ывать, -ать; оку́т|ывать, -ать.

ensign ['ensaɪn, -s(ə)n] *n.* **1.** (*flag*) (кормово́й) флаг. **2.** (*hist., standard-bearer*) пра́порщик. **3.** (*US nav.*) мла́дший лейтена́нт.

ensilage ['ensɪlɪdʒ] *n.* (*storage*) силосова́ние; (*fodder*) си́лос.

v.t. (*also* **ensile** [ɪn'saɪl]) силосова́ть (*impf., pf.*).

enslave [ɪn'sleɪv] *v.t.* порабо|ща́ть, -ти́ть; **he is ~d to this habit** он раб э́той привы́чки; **she ~d him by her charms** она́ покори́ла его́ свои́м обая́нием.

enslavement [ɪn'sleɪvmənt] *n.* порабоще́ние.

ensnare [ɪn'sneə(r)] *v.t.* (*lit.*) лови́ть, пойма́ть в лову́шку; (*fig.*) зама́н|ивать, -и́ть в западню́.

ensu|e [ɪn'sjuː] *v.i.* (*result*) сле́довать (*impf.*) из+*g.*; (*follow*) сле́довать (*impf.*) за+*i.*; **silence ~ed** после́довало молча́ние; **in ~ing years** в после́дующие го́ды.

ensure (*see also* **insure**) [ɪn'ʃʊə(r)] *v.t.* (*make safe*) гаранти́ровать (*impf.*); (*make certain; secure*) обеспе́чи|вать, -ть.

entablature [ɪn'tæblətʃə(r)] *n.* (*archit.*) антабleме́нт.

entail[1] [ɪn'teɪl, en-] *n.* (*leg.*) запове́дное иму́щество (ограни́ченное в поря́дке насле́дования); майора́т.

v.t. (*~ on eldest son*) закреп|ля́ть, -и́ть по майора́ту.

entail[2] [ɪn'teɪl, en-] *v.t.* (*necessitate*) влечь (*impf.*) за собо́й; **the work ~s expense** э́та рабо́та свя́зана с расхо́дами.

entailment [ɪn'teɪlmənt, en-] *n.* (*leg.*) ограниче́ние пра́ва распоряже́ния со́бственностью.

entangle [ɪn'tæŋg(ə)l] *v.t.* (*lit.*) запу́т|ывать, -ать (*fig.*)

впу́т|ывать, -ать; **he ~d himself with women** он запу́тался в отноше́ниях с же́нщинами.

entanglement [ɪn'tæŋg(ə)lmənt] *n.* запу́танность; затрудне́ние; **barbed-wire ~** загражде́ние из колю́чей про́волоки.

entelechy [ɪn'teləkɪ] *n.* энтеле́хия.

Entente [ɒn'tɒnt] *n.* (*hist.*) Анта́нта; **~ cordiale** серде́чное согла́сие.

enter ['entə(r)] *v.t. & i.* **1.** (*go into*) входи́ть, войти́ в+*a.*; **~ hospital** ложи́ться, лечь в больни́цу; **~ school** поступ|а́ть, -и́ть в шко́лу; **~ the army** вступ|а́ть, -и́ть в а́рмию; **~ the Church** (*be ordained*) прин|има́ть, -я́ть сан свяще́нника; **~ s.o.'s service** поступ|а́ть, -и́ть на слу́жбу к кому́-н.; **~ one's fiftieth year** вступ|а́ть, -и́ть в свой пятидеся́тый год; **France ~ed the war** Фра́нция вступи́ла в войну́; **the idea never ~ed my head** э́та мысль никогда́ не приходи́ла мне в го́лову; **~ Macbeth** (*stage direction*) вхо́дит Ма́кбет. **2.** (*include in record*) запи́с|ывать, -а́ть; **~ one's name in a list** внести́ (*pf.*) своё и́мя в спи́сок; **~ (up) an item in an account-book** де́лать, с- за́пись в расчётной кни́ге; **~ a horse for a race** заяв|ля́ть, -и́ть ло́шадь для ска́чек; **~ a boy at a school** запи́с|ывать, -а́ть ма́льчика в шко́лу; **~ (o.s.) for an examination** пода́ть (*pf.*) на уча́стие в экза́мене; **~** (*make*) **an appearance** появ|ля́ться, -и́ться; **~ a protest** заяв|ля́ть, -и́ть проте́ст.

with preps.: **~ into conversation** вступ|а́ть, -и́ть в разгово́р; **~ into details** входи́ть (*impf.*) в подро́бности; **~ into s.o.'s feelings** пон|има́ть, -я́ть чьи-н. чу́вства; **the fact ~ed into our calculations** э́тот факт входи́л в на́ши расчёты; **he ~ed into the spirit of the game** он прони́кся ду́хом игры́; **~ (up)on a subject** присту́п|а́ть, -и́ть к те́ме; **~ (up)on a career** нач|ина́ть, -а́ть профессиона́льную де́ятельность; **~ (up)on one's inheritance** вступ|а́ть, -и́ть во владе́ние насле́дством.

enteric [en'terɪk] *n.* (*fever*) брюшно́й тиф.

adj. кише́чный, брюшно́й.

enteritis [ˌentə'raɪtɪs] *n.* воспале́ние то́нких кишо́к; энтери́т.

enterprise ['entəˌpraɪz] *n.* **1.** (*undertaking, adventure*) предприя́тие. **2.** (*initiative*) предприи́мчивость; **a man of ~** предприи́мчивый челове́к. **3.** (*econ.*): **private ~** ча́стное предпринима́тельство.

enterprising ['entəˌpraɪzɪŋ] *adj.* предприи́мчивый, инициати́вный.

entertain [ˌentə'teɪn] *v.t.* развл|ека́ть, -е́чь; прин|има́ть, -я́ть; **~ friends** уго|ща́ть, -сти́ть друзе́й; **he ~s a great deal** у него́ ча́сто быва́ют го́сти; (*amuse*) развл|ека́ть, -е́чь; **~ a proposal** разду́мывать (*impf.*) над предложе́нием; **~ ideas** носи́ться (*impf.*) с иде́ями; **~ doubts** пита́ть (*impf.*) сомне́ния.

entertainer [ˌentə'teɪnə(r)] *n.* арти́ст эстра́ды; зате́йник.

entertaining [ˌentə'teɪnɪŋ] *adj.* интере́сный, занима́тельный.

entertainment [ˌentə'teɪnmənt] *n.* **1.** (*social*) приём госте́й; **~ allowance** сре́дства на представи́тельские расхо́ды. **2.** (*amusement*) развлече́ние. **3.** (*spectacle*) представле́ние; **~ tax** нало́г на зре́лища.

enthral [ɪn'θrɔːl] *v.t.* (*fascinate*) увл|ека́ть, -е́чь; **an ~ling play** захва́тывающая пье́са.

enthralment [ɪn'θrɔːlmənt] *n.* увлече́ние.

enthrone [ɪn'θrəʊn] *v.t.* (*a king, bishop*) возв|оди́ть, -ести́ на престо́л; (*fig.*) **he was ~d in their hearts** он овладе́л их сердца́ми.

enthronement [ɪn'θrəʊnmənt] *n.* возведе́ние на престо́л; воцаре́ние.

enthuse [ɪn'θjuːz, -'θuːz] *v.i.* (*coll.*) восторга́ться (*impf.*) (*чем*).

enthusiasm [ɪn'θjuːzɪˌæz(ə)m, -'θuːzɪˌæz(ə)m] *n.* восто́рг, энтузиа́зм.

enthusiast [ɪn'θjuːzɪˌæst, -'θuːzɪˌæst] *n.* энтузиа́ст (*fem.* -ка).

enthusiastic [ɪnˌθjuːzɪ'æstɪk, -ˌθuːzɪ'æstɪk] *adj.* восто́рженный; по́лный энтузиа́зма; **he was ~ about the play** он был в восто́рге от пье́сы.

entice [ɪn'taɪs] *v.t.* соблазн|я́ть, -и́ть; зама́н|ивать, -и́ть; переман|ивать, -и́ть; **~ a man from his duty** заст|авля́ть, -а́вить челове́ка забы́ть о до́лге; **~ a girl away from home** уговори́ть (*pf.*) де́вушку уйти́ из дому.

enticement [ɪn'taɪsmənt] *n.* (*action*) перема́нивание, зама́нивание; (*lure*) прима́нка, собла́зн.

entire [ɪn'taɪə(r)] *adj.* **1.** це́лый, по́лный, це́льный; **that is the ~ cost** по́лная сто́имость; **~ affection** глубо́кая привя́занность; **an ~ delusion** по́лное заблужде́ние; **~ly** всеце́ло, целико́м, соверше́нно; **he is ~ly wrong** он соверше́нно непра́в. **2.** (*not gelded*) некастри́рованный.

entirety [ɪn'taɪərətɪ] *n.* полнота́, це́льность; **in its ~** по́лностью; во всей полноте́.

entitle [ɪn'taɪt(ə)l] *v.t.* **1.** (*a book etc.*) озагла́в|ливать, -ить; **a book ~d 'Progress'** кни́га под загла́вием «Прогре́сс». **2.** (*bestow title on*) жа́ловать, по- ти́тул +*d.* **3.** (*authorize*) да|ва́ть, -ть пра́во на+*a.*; **you are ~d to two books a month** вам полага́ется две кни́ги в ме́сяц.

entitlement [ɪn'taɪt(ə)lmənt] *n.* (*right*) пра́во; (*regular due*) поло́женная но́рма.

entity ['entɪtɪ] *n.* (*object, body*) существо́, органи́зм, организа́ция; **Germany as a single ~** Герма́ния как еди́ное це́лое.

entomb [ɪn'tuːm] *v.t.* (*bury*) погре|ба́ть, -сти́; **the explosion ~ed several miners** взры́вом завали́ло не́сколько шахтёров.

entombment [ɪn'tuːmmənt] *n.* погребе́ние.

entomological [ˌentəmə'lɒdʒɪk(ə)l] *adj.* энтомологи́ческий.

entomologist [ˌentə'mɒlədʒɪst] *n.* энтомо́лог.

entomology [ˌentə'mɒlədʒɪ] *n.* энтомоло́гия.

entourage [ˌɒntʊə'rɑːʒ] *n.* сви́та, окруже́ние.

entr'acte ['ɒntrækt] *n.* антра́кт.

entrails ['entreɪlz] *n.* вну́тренности (*f. pl.*); (*fig.*) не́др|а (*pf., g.* —).

entrain [ɪn'treɪn] *v.t.* сажа́ть, посади́ть в по́езд.

v.i. сади́ться, сесть в по́езд.

entrainment [ɪn'treɪnmənt] *n.* поса́дка в по́езд.

entrance[1] ['entrəns] *n.* **1.** (*door, passage etc.*) вход; **front ~** пара́дный ход; **back ~** чёрный ход. **2.** (*entering*) вход, вступле́ние; **upon his ~** когда́ он вошёл; **~s and exits** (*theatr.*) вы́ходы и вхо́ды (*m. pl.*); **force an ~** вл|а́мываться, -оми́ться; **~ upon one's duties** вступле́ние в до́лжность; **~ examination** вступи́тельный экза́мен; **~ fee, money** вступи́тельный взно́с; **~ hall** прихо́жая, вестибю́ль (*m.*).

entranc|e[2] [ɪn'trɑːns] *v.t.* восторга́ть (*impf.*); **an ~ing sight** восхити́тельный вид.

entrant ['entrənt] *n.* (*pers. entering school, profession etc.*) поступа́ющий, приступа́ющий; (*competitor*) уча́стник.

entrap [ɪn'træp] *v.t.* лови́ть, пойма́ть в лову́шку; **he was ~ped into confessing** обма́нным путём его́ заста́вили призна́ться.

entreat [ɪn'triːt] *v.t.* умол|я́ть, -и́ть; упр|а́шивать, -оси́ть; **~ a favour** умоля́ть (*impf.*) (*кого*) об одолже́нии.

entreaty [ɪn'triːtɪ] *n.* мольба́; **with a look of ~** умоля́ющим взгля́дом.

entrechat [ˌɒntrə'ʃɑː] *n.* антраша́ (*m. indecl.*).

entrecôte ['ɒntrəˌkəʊt] *n.* антреко́т.

entrée ['ɒntreɪ, 'ãtreɪ] *n.* **1.** (*admittance*) до́ступ; **he has the ~ to the Minister** у него́ есть до́ступ к мини́стру. **2.** (*cul.*) блю́до, подава́емое пе́ред жарки́м; (*US, main dish*) гла́вное блю́до.

entrench [ɪn'trentʃ] *v.t.* окруж|а́ть, -и́ть око́пами; **the enemy were ~ed nearby** враг окопа́лся вблизи́; **~ o.s.** ок|а́пываться, -опа́ться; **~ing-tool** (*mil.*) ша́нцевый инструме́нт; (*fig.*) **customs ~ed by tradition** обы́чаи, закреплённые тради́цией.

entrenchment [ɪn'trentʃmənt] *n.* (*mil.*) око́п.

entrepôt ['ɒntrəˌpəʊ] *n.* (*storehouse*) пакга́уз; (*trade centre*) склад; **~ trade** транзи́тная торго́вля.

entrepreneur [ˌɒntrəprə'nɜː(r)] *n.* предпринима́тель (*m.*).

entrepreneurial [ˌɒntrəprə'nɜːrɪəl, -'njʊərɪəl] *adj.* предпринима́тельский.

entresol ['ɒntrəˌsɒl] *n.* антресо́ли (*f. pl.*); полуэта́ж.

entropy ['entrəpɪ] *n.* (*phys.*) энтропи́я.

en|trust, in- [ɪn'trʌst] *v.t.* вв|еря́ть, -е́рить; возл|ага́ть, -ожи́ть; **I ~ed the task to him** (*or* **~ed him with the task**) я дал ему́ (*or* возложи́л на него́) поруче́ние.

entry ['entrɪ] *n.* **1.** (*going in*) вход; **the ~ of the US into the**

war вступле́ние США в войну́; **the Romans' ~ into Britain** вторже́ние ри́млян в Брита́нию; **the ~ of the Nile into the Mediterranean** впаде́ние Ни́ла в Средизе́мное мо́ре; **bullet's point of ~** то́чка попада́ния пу́ли; **the actress made an impressive ~** актри́са сде́лала эффе́ктный вы́ход. **2.** (*access*) до́ступ; **he gained ~ to the house** он пробра́лся в дом. **3.** (*place of ~y*; *~y way*) вход; **the south ~ of a church** ю́жный вход це́ркви. **4.** (*item*) за́пись; **dictionary ~** слова́рная статья́; **~ in a diary** за́пись в дневнике́; **bookkeeping by double ~** двойна́я бухгалте́рия. **5.** (*inscription*; *competitor*): **~ form** вступи́тельная анке́та; **there was a large ~ for the race** на ска́чках записа́лось мно́го уча́стников. **6.** (*immigration*) въезд; **~ permit** разреше́ние на въезд.

entwine [ɪnˈtwaɪn] *v.t.* (*interweave*) впле|та́ть, -сти́; (*wreathe*) обв|ива́ть, -и́ть.

enumerate [ɪˈnjuːməˌreɪt] *v.t.* переч|исля́ть, -и́слить.

enumeration [ɪˌnjuːməˈreɪʃ(ə)n] *n.* перечисле́ние; (*list*) пе́речень (*m.*).

enunciate [ɪˈnʌnsɪˌeɪt] *v.t.* (*set forth*) формули́ровать, с-; (*pronounce*) произн|оси́ть, -ести́.

enunciation [ɪˌnʌnsɪˈeɪʃ(ə)n] *n.* формулиро́вка, произноше́ние.

enuresis [ˌenjʊəˈriːsɪs] *n.* недержа́ние мочи́, энуре́з.

envelop [ɪnˈveləp] *v.t.* обёр|тывать, -ну́ть; оку́т|ывать, -ать; **hills ~ed in mist** холмы́, оку́танные тума́ном; **a baby ~ed in a shawl** младе́нец, завёрнутый в шаль; **~ed in mystery** покры́тый та́йной; (*mil.*) окруж|а́ть, -и́ть; охва́т|ывать, -и́ть.

envelope [ˈenvəˌləʊp, ˈɒn-] *n.* (*of letter*) конве́рт; (*of balloon etc.*) оболо́чка; (*bot., biol.*) обвёртка, плёнка.

envelopment [ɪnˈveləpmənt] *n.* обёртывание; (*mil.*) окруже́ние, охва́т.

envenom [ɪnˈvenəm] *v.t.* отрав|ля́ть, -и́ть; **~ a quarrel** обостр|я́ть, -и́ть ссо́ру.

enviable [ˈenvɪəb(ə)l] *adj.* (*of pers.*) возбужда́ющий за́висть, счастли́вый; (*of thg.*) зави́дный.

envier [ˈenvɪe(r)] *n.* зави́стник.

envious [ˈenvɪəs] *adj.* зави́стливый.

environ [ɪnˈvaɪərən] *v.t.* окруж|а́ть, -и́ть.

environment [ɪnˈvaɪərənmənt] *n.* окруже́ние, среда́; **the ~** окружа́ющая среда́.

cpd. **~-friendly** *adj.* природобезвре́дный, природосберега́ющий.

environmental [ɪnˌvaɪərənˈment(ə)l] *adj.* окружа́ющий; **~ studies** изуче́ние окружа́ющей среды́.

environmentalism [ɪnˌvaɪərənˈmentəlɪz(ə)m] *n.* экологи́зм.

environmentalist [ɪnˌvaɪərənˈmentəlɪst] *n.* сторо́нник защи́ты окружа́ющей среды́.

environs [ɪnˈvaɪərənz, ˈenvɪrənz] *n.* окре́стности (*f. pl.*).

envisage [ɪnˈvɪzɪdʒ] *v.t.* (*face*) смотре́ть (*impf.*) в лицо́ (*or* в глаза́) +*d.*; (*consider*) рассм|а́тривать, -отре́ть; (*visualize*) предви́деть (*impf.*); **I had not ~d seeing him so soon** я не предполага́л, что уви́жу его́ так ско́ро; **we ~ holding a meeting** мы наме́рены устро́ить собра́ние.

envision [ɪnˈvɪʒ(ə)n] *v.t.* предст|авля́ть, -а́вить себе́; вообра|жа́ть, -зи́ть.

envoy[1] [ˈenvɔɪ] *n.* (*to a poem*) заключи́тельная строфа́.

envoy[2] [ˈenvɔɪ] *n.* (*messenger*) посла́нец; (*diplomat*) диплома́т; **~ extraordinary** чрезвыча́йный посла́нник.

envy [ˈenvɪ] *n.* за́висть; **she was green with ~** она́ чуть не ло́пнула от за́висти; **his skill was the ~ of his friends** его́ ло́вкость была́ предме́том за́висти его́ друзе́й.

v.t. зави́довать, по- +*d.*; **I ~ him** я ему́ зави́дую; **I ~ his patience** я зави́дую его́ терпе́нию.

enwrap [ɪnˈræp] *v.t.* зав|ёртывать, -ерну́ть; заку́т|ывать, -ать.

enzyme [ˈenzaɪm] *n.* энзи́м.

Eocene [ˈiːəʊˌsiːn] *n.* эоце́н.

eohippus [ˌiːəʊˈhɪpas] *n.* эоги́ппус.

eolith [ˈiːəlɪθ] *n.* эоли́т.

eolithic [ˌiːəˈlɪθɪk] *adj.* эоли́товый, эолити́ческий.

Eozoic [iːəʊˈzəʊɪk] *adj.* эозо́йский.

epact [ˈiːpækt] *n.* эпа́кта.

eparchy [ˈepɑːkɪ] *n.* епа́рхия.

epaulette [ˈepəlɐt, ˈepɔːˌlet, ˈepəʊˌlet, ˌepəˈlet] *n.* эполе́т.

epée [ˈepeɪ] *n.* шпа́га; **~ fencer** шпажи́ст.

epenthesis [eˈpenθɪsɪs, ɪ-] *n.* эпенте́за.

epenthetic [ˌepenˈθetɪk] *adj.* вставно́й, эпентети́ческий.

ephemera [ɪˈfemərə, ɪˈfiːm-] *n.* (*zool.*) подёнка; (*ephemeral things, esp. writings*) эфемери́ды (*f. pl.*).

ephemeral [ɪˈfemər(ə)l, ɪˈfiːm-] *adj.* однодне́вный, кратковре́менный; (*fig.*) эфеме́рный.

Ephesian [ɪˈfiːʒən] *n.* (*bibl.*) ефеся́нин.

adj. ефе́сский.

Ephesus [ˈefɪsəs] *n.* Эфе́с.

epic [ˈepɪk] *n.* эпи́ческая поэ́ма, эпопе́я.

adj. эпи́ческий; (*on a grand scale*) грандио́зный; **an ~ biography** биогра́фия эпи́ческого масшта́ба.

epicene [ˈepɪˌsiːn] *adj.* **1.** (*bisexual*) гермафроди́тический. **2.** (*effeminate*) женоподо́бный. **3.** (*gram.*) о́бщего ро́да.

epicentre [ˈepɪˌsentə(r)] *n.* эпице́нтр.

epicure [ˈepɪˌkjʊə(r)] *n.* эпикуре́ец; люби́тель (*m.*) вку́сно пое́сть.

epicurean [ˌepɪkjʊəˈriːən] *n.* эпикуре́ец (*also phil.*).

adj. эпикуре́йский.

epicur(ean)ism [ˌepɪkjʊə(ˈriːən)ˈɪz(ə)m] *n.* эпикуре́йство.

Epicurus [ˌepɪˈkjʊərəs] *n.* Эпику́р.

epicycle [ˈepɪˌsaɪk(ə)l] *n.* эпици́кл.

epidemic [ˌepɪˈdemɪk] *n.* эпиде́мия.

adj. эпидеми́ческий.

epidemiology [ˌepɪdiːmɪˈɒlədʒɪ] *n.* эпидемиоло́гия.

epiderm|al [ˌepɪˈdɜːməl], **-ic** [ˌepɪˈdɜːmɪk] *adjs.* эпидерми́ческий.

epidermis [ˌepɪˈdɜːmɪs] *n.* эпиде́рмис, эпиде́рма.

epidiascope [ˌepɪˈdaɪəˌskəʊp] *n.* эпидиа́скоп.

epigastric [ˌepɪˈgæstrɪk] *adj.* надчре́вный, подло́жечный.

epiglottis [ˌepɪˈglɒtɪs] *n.* надгорта́нник.

epigone [ˈepɪˌgəʊn] *n.* эпиго́н.

epigram [ˈepɪˌgræm] *n.* эпигра́мма.

epigrammatic(al) [ˌepɪgrəˈmætɪkəl] *adj.* эпиграммати́ческий.

epigrammatist [ˌepɪˈgræmətɪst] *n.* эпиграммати́ст.

epigraph [ˈepɪˌgrɑːf] *n.* эпи́граф.

epigraphist [eˈpɪgrəfɪst] *n.* эпиграфи́ст.

epigraphy [eˈpɪgrəfɪ] *n.* эпигра́фика.

epilepsy [ˈepɪˌlepsɪ] *n.* эпиле́псия.

epileptic [ˌepɪˈleptɪk] *n.* эпиле́птик.

adj. эпилепти́ческий; **he had an ~ fit** у него́ был эпилепти́ческий припа́док.

epilogue [ˈepɪˌlɒg] *n.* эпило́г.

Epiphany [eˈpɪfənɪ, ɪˈpɪf-] *n.* Богоявле́ние, Креще́ние.

epiphyte [ˈepɪˌfaɪt] *n.* эпифи́т.

episcopal [ɪˈpɪskəp(ə)l] *adj.* (*of bishop*) епи́скопский; (*of system*) епископа́льный.

Episcopalian [ɪˌpɪskəˈpeɪlɪən] *n.* (*Anglican*) член англика́нской це́ркви; (*pl.*) англика́нцы.

episcopate [ɪˈpɪskəpət] *n.* (*office of bishop*) епа́рхия; (*collect., bishops*) епископа́т; епи́скопы (*m. pl.*).

episode [ˈepɪˌsəʊd] *n.* эпизо́д; (*occurrence*) слу́чай, происше́ствие.

episodic [ˌepɪˈsɒdɪk] *adj.* (*composed of episodes*) состоя́щий из отде́льных эпизо́дов; (*incidental, occasional*) эпизоди́ческий.

epistemological [ɪˌpɪstɪməˈlɒdʒɪk(ə)l] *adj.* гносеологи́ческий, эпистемологи́ческий.

epistemology [ɪˌpɪstɪˈmɒlədʒɪ] *n.* гносеоло́гия, эпистемоло́гия.

epistle [ɪˈpɪs(ə)l] *n.* посла́ние.

epistolary [ɪˈpɪstələrɪ] *adj.* эпистоля́рный.

epitaph [ˈepɪˌtɑːf] *n.* эпита́фия, надгро́бная на́дпись.

epithalamium [ˌepɪθəˈleɪmɪəm] *n.* эпитала́ма.

epithelium [ˌepɪˈθiːlɪəm] *n.* эпите́лий.

epithet [ˈepɪˌθet] *n.* эпи́тет.

epitome [ɪˈpɪtəmɪ] *n.* (*summary*) конспе́кт; (*personification*) эпито́м, воплоще́ние.

epitomize [ɪˈpɪtəˌmaɪz] *v.t.* (*summarize*) резюми́ровать (*impf., pf.*); (*personify*) вопло|ща́ть, -ти́ть.

epizootic [ˌepɪzəʊˈɒtɪk] *adj.* эпизооти́ческий.

epoch [ˈiːpɒk] *n.* эпо́ха; **this discovery marks a new ~** э́то откры́тие знамену́ет собо́й но́вую эпо́ху.

cpd. **~-making** *adj.* эпоха́льный.

epode [ˈepəʊd] *n.* эпо́д.

eponym [ˈepənɪm] *n.* эпони́м.

eponymous [ɪ'pɒnɪməs] *adj.* эпони́мный.
epos ['epɒs] *n.* э́пос.
Epsom salts ['epsəm] *n.* англи́йская соль.
equable ['ekwəb(ə)l] *adj.* (*of climate, temper*) ро́вный, уравнове́шенный.
equal ['i:kw(ə)l] *n.* (*pers. or thg.*) ро́вня; **he has no ~** ему́ нет ра́вного; **he was her ~ at tennis** он игра́л в те́ннис не ху́же её; **he only mixes with his ~** он обща́ется то́лько с ра́вными себе́.
adj. **1.** (*same, equivalent*) ра́вный, одина́ковый; **~ in** (*or* **of ~**) **ability** одина́ковых спосо́бностей; **the totals are ~** ито́ги равны́; **other things being ~** при про́чих ра́вных усло́виях; **~ shares** ро́вные до́ли; **two boys of ~ height** два ма́льчика одного́ ро́ста; **he speaks French and German with ~ ease** он одина́ково свобо́дно говори́т по-францу́зски и по-неме́цки. **2.** (*capable, adequate*) спосо́бный; **he is ~ to the task** он вполне́ мо́жет спра́виться с э́той зада́чей; **are you ~ to a whole bottle of wine?** вы одоле́ете це́лую буты́лку вина́? **3.** (*unbiased, evenly balanced, stable*) ро́вный, равнопра́вный, уравнове́шенный; **~ laws** ра́вные права́; **an ~ fight** ра́вный бой.
v.t. & i. **1.** (*math.*) равня́ться (*impf.*) (*чему*); **twice 2 ~s 4** два́жды два равня́ется четырём; **x = y** x ра́вен y; **the ~s sign** знак ра́венства. **2.: he ~s me in strength** он ра́вен мне по си́ле; **I know nothing to ~ it** я не зна́ю ничего́ подо́бного; **it will he hard to ~ his record** бу́дет тру́дно повтори́ть его́ реко́рд.
equalitarian [i:ˌkwɒlɪ'teərɪən], **-ism** [i:ˌkwɒlɪ'teərɪənɪz(ə)m] = **egalitarian, -ism**
equality [ɪ'kwɒlɪtɪ] *n.* ра́венство, равнопра́вие; **on an ~ with** на ра́вных усло́виях/права́х с+*i*.
equalization [ˌi:kwəlaɪ'zeɪʃ(ə)n] *n.* уравне́ние, ура́внивание.
equalize ['i:kwəˌlaɪz] *v.t. & i.* ура́вн|ивать, -я́ть; **~ (the score)** равня́ть (*or* сра́внивать), с- счёт.
equally ['i:kwəlɪ] *adv.* **1.** (*to an equal extent*) одина́ково; **he is ~ to blame** он винова́т в той же сте́пени. **2.** (*also, likewise*) ра́вным о́бразом; наравне́; **~ it can be said that ...** с таки́м же успе́хом мо́жно сказа́ть, что...; **we, ~ with them ...** мы, наравне́ с ни́ми... **3.** (*evenly*): **he divided the money ~** он раздели́л де́ньги по́ровну.
equanimity [ˌekwə'nɪmɪtɪ, ˌi:k-] *n.* душе́вное равнове́сие; споко́йствие; **with ~** споко́йно.
equate [ɪ'kweɪt] *v.t.* (*make equal*) ура́вн|ивать, -я́ть; **they ~d his salary to mine** они́ уравня́ли его́ окла́д с мои́м; (*consider or treat as equal*) отождеств|ля́ть, -и́ть; приравн|ивать, -я́ть; **he ~s wealth with happiness** он отождествля́ет бога́тство со сча́стьем.
v.i.: **~ with** (*be equal, correspond to*) быть ра́вным +*d*.
equation [ɪ'kweɪʒ(ə)n] *n.* **1.** (*making equal, balancing*) выра́внивание; **~ of demand and supply** соотве́тствие спро́са и предложе́ния. **2.** (*math., chem.*) уравне́ние; **quadratic ~** квадра́тное уравне́ние.
equator [ɪ'kweɪtə(r)] *n.* эква́тор; **celestial ~** небе́сный эква́тор.
equatorial [ˌekwə'tɔ:rɪəl, ˌi:k-] *adj.* экваториа́льный.
equerry ['ekwərɪ, ɪ'kwerɪ] *n.* коню́ший, шталме́йстер.
equestrian [ɪ'kwestrɪən] *n.* нае́здник, вса́дник.
adj. ко́нный; **~ statue** ко́нная ста́туя.
equestrianism [ɪ'kwestrɪəˌnɪz(ə)m] *n.* ко́нный спорт.
equestrienne [ɪˌkwestrɪ'en] *n.* вса́дница; (*in circus*) нае́здница.
equidistance [ˌi:kwɪ'dɪstəns] *n.* равноудалённость.
equidistant [ˌi:kwɪ'dɪst(ə)nt] *adj.* равноотстоя́щий; **these towns are ~ from London** э́ти города́ располо́жены на одина́ковом расстоя́нии от Ло́ндона.
equilateral [ˌi:kwɪ'lætər(ə)l] *adj.* равносторо́нний.
equilibrate [ɪ'kwɪlɪˌbreɪt, ˌi:kwɪ'laɪbreɪt] *v.t.* уравнове́|шивать, -сить.
equilibration [ɪˌkwɪlɪ'breɪʃ(ə)n, ˌi:kwɪˌlaɪbreɪʃ(ə)n] *n.* уравнове́шивание.
equilibrist [ɪ'kwɪlɪbrɪst] *n.* эквилибри́ст (*fem.* -ка).
equilibrium [ˌi:kwɪ'lɪbrɪəm] *n.* (*lit., fig.*) равнове́сие; **in stable ~** в усто́йчивом равнове́сии.
equine ['i:kwaɪn, 'ek-] *adj.* лошади́ный, ко́нский.
equinoctial [ˌi:kwɪ'nɒkʃ(ə)l, ˌek-] *adj.* равноде́нственный; **~ gales** што́рмы равноде́нствия.
equinox ['i:kwɪˌnɒks, 'ek-] *n.* равноде́нствие; **autumnal ~** осе́ннее равноде́нствие; **vernal, spring ~** весе́ннее равноде́нствие.
equip [ɪ'kwɪp] *v.t.* снаря|жа́ть, -ди́ть; (*a ship*) осна|ща́ть, -сти́ть; (*soldiers*) снаря|жа́ть, -ди́ть; экипирова́ть (*impf., pf.*); **~ o.s. with sth.** вооруж|а́ться, -и́ться чем-н.; **he is ~ped with sound sense** он наделён здра́вым рассу́дком.
equipage ['ekwɪpɪdʒ] *n.* (*carriage*) экипа́ж; (*attendants*) сви́та.
equipment [ɪ'kwɪpmənt] *n.* снаряже́ние, экипиро́вка; **mental ~** у́мственный бага́ж.
equipoise ['ekwɪˌpɔɪz, 'i:-] *n.* (*balance*) равнове́сие.
equipollent [ˌi:kwɪ'pɒlənt] *adj.* равноси́льный.
equitable ['ekwɪtəb(ə)l] *adj.* справедли́вый.
equitation [ˌekwɪ'teɪʃ(ə)n] *n.* верхова́я езда́.
equity ['ekwɪtɪ] *n.* **1.** (*fairness*) справедли́вость; **in ~** по справедли́вости. **2.** (*pl., fin.*) обыкнове́нные а́кции (*f. pl.*). **3.** (*leg.*) пра́во справедли́вости.
equivalenc|e [ɪ'kwɪvələns], **-y** [ɪ'kwɪvələnsɪ] *nn.* эквивале́нтность.
equivalent [ɪ'kwɪvələnt] *n.* эквивале́нт; **a university degree or the ~** университе́тский дипло́м и́ли ра́вное ему́ удостовере́ние.
adj. эквивале́нтный; **his words were ~ to an insult** его́ слова́ бы́ли равноси́льны оскорбле́нию.
equivocal [ɪ'kwɪvək(ə)l] *adj.* двусмы́сленный, сомни́тельный.
equivocate [ɪ'kwɪvəˌkeɪt] *v.i.* говори́ть (*impf.*) двусмы́сленно; увил|ивать, -ну́ть от прямо́го отве́та.
equivocation [ɪˌkwɪvə'keɪʃ(ə)n] *n.* укло́нчивость, увёртка.
equivocator [ɪ'kwɪvəˌkeɪtə(r)] *n.* говоря́щий двусмы́сленно; нейскренний челове́к.
er [ɜ:(r)] *int.* (*expr. hesitation*) а; э-э.
era ['ɪərə] *n.* э́ра.
eradicable [ɪ'rædɪkəb(ə)l] *adj.* искорени́мый.
eradicate [ɪ'rædɪˌkeɪt] *v.t.* искорен|я́ть, -и́ть.
eradication [ɪˌrædɪ'keɪʃ(ə)n] *n.* искорене́ние.
erasable [ɪ'reɪzəb(ə)l] *adj.* стира́емый.
erase [ɪ'reɪz] *v.t.* ст|ира́ть, -ере́ть; соск|а́бливать, -обли́ть; **~ sth. from one's memory** вычёркивать, вы́черкнуть что-н. из па́мяти.
eraser [ɪ'reɪzə(r)] *n.* рези́нка.
erasure [ɪ'reɪʒə(r)] *n.* стира́ние, подчи́стка.
ere [eə(r)] (*arch., poet.*) = **before**
Erebus ['erɪbəs] *n.* (*myth.*) Эре́б.
erect [ɪ'rekt] *adj.* прямо́й; **with head ~** с по́днятой голово́й; **stand ~** держа́ться пря́мо.
v.t. (*build, set up*) воздв|ига́ть, -и́гнуть; соору|жа́ть, -ди́ть; **~ a monument** воздв|ига́ть, -и́гнуть па́мятник; **~ a tent** ста́вить, по- пала́тку; **~ a staff** водру|жа́ть, -зи́ть ма́чту; (*fig.*): **~ a custom into law** возв|оди́ть, -ести́ обы́чай в зако́н.
erection [ɪ'rekʃ(ə)n] *n.* (*setting up*) сооруже́ние; (*building*) зда́ние; (*physiol.*) эре́кция.
erectness [ɪ'rektnɪs] *n.* прямота́.
erector [ɪ'rektə(r)] *n.* (*builder*) строи́тель (*m.*); **~ muscle** выпрямля́ющая мы́шца.
eremitic(al) [ˌerɪ'mɪtɪk(ə)l] *adj.* отше́льнический.
erethism ['erɪˌθɪz(ə)m] *n.* эрети́зм.
erg [ɜ:g] *n.* (*phys.*) эрг.
ergo ['ɜ:gəʊ] *adv.* сле́довательно.
ergonomic [ˌɜ:gə'nɒmɪk] *adj.* эргономи́ческий.
ergonomics [ˌɜ:gə'nɒmɪks] *n.* эргоно́мика, эргоно́мия.
ergonomist [ɜ:'gɒnəmɪst] *n.* эргономи́ст.
ergot ['ɜ:gət] *n.* (*fungus, drug*) спорынья́.
ergotism ['ɜ:gəˌtɪz(ə)m] *n.* эрготи́зм.
Erin ['erɪn, 'ɪərɪn] *n.* (*poet.*) Ирла́ндия.
Eritrea [ˌerɪ'treɪə] *n.* Эритре́я.
ERM (*abbr. of* **exchange-rate mechanism**) механи́зм обме́на валю́т.
ermine ['ɜ:mɪn] *n.* (*animal, fur*) горноста́й.
erode [ɪ'rəʊd] *v.t.* разъ|еда́ть, -е́сть; (*fig.*) подт|а́чивать, -очи́ть.
erogenous [ɪ'rɒdʒɪnəs] *adj. adj.* эроге́нный; **~ zones** эроге́нные зо́ны.

Eros [ˈɪərɒs] *n.* (*myth.*) Э́рос.
erosion [ɪˈrəʊʒ(ə)n] *n.* разъеда́ние, эро́зия (*fig.*); **the ~ of his hopes** постепе́нное разруше́ние его́ наде́жд.
erosive [ɪˈrəʊsɪv] *adj.* разъеда́ющий; эрози́вный.
erotic [ɪˈrɒtɪk] *adj.* эроти́ческий, любо́вный, чу́вственный.
erotica [ɪˈrɒtɪkə] *n.* (*pl.*) эро́тика.
eroticism [ɪˈrɒtɪˌsɪz(ə)m] *n.* эроти́чность.
erotism [ˈerəˌtɪz(ə)m] *n.* эроти́зм.
erotomania [ɪˌrəʊtəˈmeɪnɪə] *n.* эротома́ния.
err [ɜː(r)] *v.i.* ошиб|а́ться, -и́ться; заблужда́ться (*impf.*); **to ~ is human** челове́ку сво́йственно ошиба́ться.
errancy [ˈerənsɪ] *n.* заблужде́ние.
errand [ˈerənd] *n.* поруче́ние; предприя́тие; **go on ~s for s.o.** исполня́ть (*impf.*) чьи-н. поруче́ния; **a fool's ~** беспло́дная зате́я.
cpd. **~-boy** *n.* ма́льчик на посы́лках/побегу́шках; посы́льный, рассы́льный.
errant [ˈerənt] *adj.* **1.** (*mistaken*) заблужда́ющийся. **2.** (*stray, wandering*) стра́нствующий; **knight ~** стра́нствующий ры́царь. **3.** (*misbehaving*) заблу́дший.
erratic [ɪˈrætɪk] *adj.* **1.** неусто́йчивый; (*of pers.*) беспоря́дочный, сумасбро́дный; **he is an ~ shot** он не о́чень-то ме́ткий стрело́к; **~ally** нерегуля́рно; **the engine fires ~ally** мото́р рабо́тает с перебо́ями. **2.** (*geol.*): **~ blocks** валуны́ (*m. pl.*).
errat|um [ɪˈrɑːtəm] *n.* опеча́тка; **~a** (*pl., list*) спи́сок опеча́ток.
erring [ˈɜːrɪŋ] *adj.* заблу́дший, гре́шный.
erroneous [ɪˈrəʊnɪəs] *adj.* оши́бочный.
erroneousness [ɪˈrəʊnɪəsnɪs] *n.* оши́бочность.
error [ˈerə(r)] *n.* **1.** (*mistake*) оши́бка, заблужде́ние; **make, commit an ~** соверш|а́ть, -и́ть (*or* допус|ка́ть, -ти́ть) оши́бку; **he is in ~** он заблужда́ется; **fall into (an) ~** впа|да́ть, -сть в заблужде́ние; **the letter was sent in ~** письмо́ бы́ло по́слано по оши́бке; **clerical ~** опи́ска; **printer's ~** опеча́тка; **~ of fact** факти́ческая оши́бка; **~ of judgment** неве́рное сужде́ние; оши́бка в расчётах; **~ of observation** оши́бочное наблюде́ние; **he saw the ~ of his ways** он осозна́л свои́ оши́бки; **~s and omissions excepted** не счита́я оши́бки и про́пуски. **2.** (*transgression*) просту́пок; **the ~s of his youth** грехи́ (*m. pl.*) его́ мо́лодости. **3.** (*astron.*) погре́шность; **~ of a planet** отклоне́ние наблюда́емого положе́ния плане́ты от расчётного.
ersatz [ˈɜːzæts, ˈeə-] *n.* эрза́ц, суррога́т; **~ coffee** эрза́ц-ко́фе (*m. indecl.*).
Erse [ɜːs] *n.* (*Sc. Celtic language*) гэ́льский язы́к; (*Irish*) ирла́ндский язы́к.
adj. (*Sc. Celtic*) гэ́льский; (*Irish*) ирла́ндский.
erst [ɜːst] *adv.* (*poet.*) не́когда.
erstwhile [ˈɜːstwaɪl] *adj.* да́вний, давни́шний; **an ~ friend** да́вний/стари́нный друг.
erubescence [ˌeruːˈbesəns] *n.* покрасне́ние.
erubescent [ˌeruːˈbes(ə)nt] *adj.* красне́ющий.
eructation [ˌiːrʌkˈteɪʃ(ə)n] *n.* (*of pers.*) отры́жка; (*of volcano etc.*) изверже́ние.
erudite [ˈeruːˌdaɪt] *adj.* эруди́рованный, учёный.
erudition [ˌeruːˈdɪʃ(ə)n] *n.* эруди́ция.
erupt [ɪˈrʌpt] *v.i.* (*of volcano etc.*) изв|ерга́ться, -е́ргнуться; (*of teeth*) проp|еза́ться, -е́заться.
eruption [ɪˈrʌpʃ(ə)n] *n.* **1.** (*of volcano etc.*) изверже́ние. **2.** (*of teeth*) проре́зывание. **3.** (*on face etc.*) сыпь. **4.** (*fig.*) взрыв.
eruptive [ɪˈrʌptɪv] *adj.* изве́рженный; (*med.*) сопровожда́емый сы́пью.
erysipelas [ˌerɪˈsɪpɪləs] *n.* ро́жа, ро́жистое воспале́ние.
Esau [ˈiːsɔː] *n.* (*bibl.*) Иса́в.
escalade [ˌeskəˈleɪd] *v.t.* штурмова́ть (*impf.*) с по́мощью ле́стниц.
escalate [ˈeskəˌleɪt] *v.t.* эскали́ровать (*impf., pf.*); обостр|я́ть, -и́ть.
v.i. разраста́ться (*impf.*); расш|иря́ться, -и́риться.
escalation [ˌeskəˈleɪʃ(ə)n] *n.* эскала́ция, расшире́ние.
escalator [ˈeskəˌleɪtə(r)] *n.* эскала́тор; **~ clause** усло́вие «скользя́щей шкалы́».
escalope [ˈeskəˌlɒp] *n.* эскало́п.
escapable [ɪˈskeɪpəb(ə)l] *adj.* избега́емый.
escapade [ˈeskəˌpeɪd, ˌeskəˈpeɪd] *n.* эскапа́да; шальна́я вы́ходка.
escape [ɪˈskeɪp] *n.* **1.** (*becoming free*) побе́г, бе́гство; **make one's ~** убежа́ть (*pf.*); **there have been few ~s from this prison** побе́ги из э́той тюрьмы́ весьма́ ре́дки; **~ clause** пункт догово́ра, избавля́ющий сто́рону от отве́тственности; **~ hatch** авари́йный люк; **~ ladder** пожа́рная ле́стница; **~ velocity** (*of rocket*) втора́я косми́ческая ско́рость. **2.** (*avoidance*) спасе́ние, избавле́ние; **he had a narrow ~ from shipwreck** он едва́ спа́сся при кораблекруше́нии; **that was a lucky ~** э́то бы́ло счастли́вым избавле́нием. **3.** (*of gas etc.*) уте́чка. **4.** (*fig., mental relief*) ухо́д/бе́гство от действи́тельности; **~ literature** литерату́ра, уводя́щая от о́стрых пробле́м действи́тельности; эскапи́стская литерату́ра.
v.t. избе|га́ть, -жа́ть +*g.*; **he ~d being laughed at** он избежа́л насме́шек; **he ~d death** он оста́лся в живы́х; **he ~d with a scratch** он отде́лался цара́пиной; **the words ~d his lips** слова́ сорвали́сь у него́ с языка́; **I cannot ~ the feeling that …** я не могу́ отде́латься от чу́вства, что…; **nothing ~s you!** ничто́ не ускольза́ет от вас!; вы всё замеча́ете!; **his name ~s me** не могу́ припо́мнить его́ фами́лии; его́ фами́лия вы́пала у меня́ из па́мяти.
v.i. бежа́ть (*det.*); уходи́ть, уйти́; соверши́ть (*pf.*) побе́г; **the prisoner ~d** заключённый (с)бежа́л; **an ~d prisoner** бе́глый ареста́нт; **the canary ~d from its cage** канаре́йка вы́порхнула из кле́тки; **the lion ~d** лев вы́рвался на во́лю; **gas is escaping** происхо́дит уте́чка га́за.
cpds. **~-pipe** *n.* выпускна́я труба́; **~-seat** *n.* (*aeron.*) катапульти́руемое кре́сло; **~-valve** *n.* выпускно́й кла́пан.
escapee [ɪskeɪˈpiː] *n.* бегле́ц.
escapement [ɪˈskeɪpmənt] *n.* (*of watch etc.*) сторожо́к, спуск, регуля́тор хо́да.
escapism [ɪˈskeɪpɪz(ə)m] *n.* бе́гство от действи́тельности; эскапи́зм.
escapist [ɪˈskeɪpɪst] *n.* челове́к, уходя́щий от действи́тельности; эскапи́ст.
adj. уходя́щий от действи́тельности; эскапи́стский.
escapologist [ˌeskəˈpɒlədʒɪst] *n.* фо́кусник, выполня́ющий трюк самоосвобожде́ния от цепе́й.
escarole [ˈeskərəʊl] (*US*) энди́вий (зи́мний), цико́рий-энди́вий.
escarp(ment) [ɪˈskɑːpmənt] *n.* (*geol.*) вертика́льное обнаже́ние поро́ды.
eschatological [ˌeskətəˈlɒdʒɪk(ə)l] *adj.* эсхатологи́ческий.
eschatology [ˌeskəˈtɒlədʒɪ] *n.* эсхатоло́гия.
escheat [ɪsˈtʃiːt] *v.i.*: **the property ~ed to the Crown** (вы́морочное) иму́щество перешло́ в казну́.
eschew [ɪsˈtʃuː] *v.t.* возде́рж|иваться, -а́ться от+*g.*; сторони́ться (*impf.*) +*g.*
eschscholtzia [ɪsˈkɒlʃə, eˈʃɒltsɪə] *n.* эшо́льция.
escort[1] [ˈeskɔːt] *n.* (*mil., nav.*) конво́й, эско́рт; **~ carrier** эско́ртный авиано́сец; **~ fighter** истреби́тель сопровожде́ния; **~ ship, vessel** сторожево́й/эско́ртный кора́бль; **police ~** (*of criminal*) конво́й; **her ~ to the ball** её кавале́р на балу́.
escort[2] [ɪˈskɔːt] *v.t.* сопрово|жда́ть, -ди́ть; (*mil., nav.*) эскорти́ровать (*impf., pf.*); конвои́ровать (*impf.*); **he ~ed her to the ball** он сопровожда́л её на бал; **I ~ed him to his seat** я провёл его́ на ме́сто; **the heckler was ~ed from the hall** челове́ка, перебива́вшего ора́торов, вы́вели из за́ла.
escritoire [ˌeskrɪˈtwɑː(r)] *n.* секрете́р.
escudo [eˈskjuːdəʊ] *n.* эску́до (*indecl.*).
esculent [ˈeskjʊlənt] *adj.* съедо́бный.
escutcheon [ɪˈskʌtʃ(ə)n] *n.* щит герба́; **a blot on s.o.'s ~** (*fig.*) пятно́ на чье́й-н. репута́ции.
Eskimo [ˈeskɪˌməʊ] *n.* эскимо́с (*fem.* -ка).
adj. эскимо́сский; **~ dog** ла́йка.
esophagus [iːˈsɒfəgəs] = **oesophagus**
esoteric [ˌiːsəʊˈterɪk, ˌe-] *adj.* эзотери́ческий.

ESP (*abbr. of* **extra-sensory perception**) сверхчу́вственное восприя́тие, экстрасенсо́рика.
espagnolette [espanjə'let] *n.* шпингале́т.
espalier [ɪ'spælɪə(r)] *n.* (*lattice*) шпале́ра; (*plant*) шпале́рник.
esparto [e'spɑ:təʊ] *n.* (*also* ~ **grass**) эспа́рто (*indecl.*), трава́ а́льфа.
especial [ɪ'speʃ(ə)l] *adj.* специа́льный; осо́бенный; **for your ~ benefit** специа́льно для вас.
Esperantist [ˌespə'ræntɪst] *n.* эсперанти́ст (*fem.* -ка).
Esperanto [ˌespə'ræntəʊ] *n.* эспера́нто (*m. indecl.*); **in ~** на языке́ эспера́нто.
espionage ['espɪəˌnɑ:ʒ] *n.* шпиона́ж.
esplanade [ˌesplə'neɪd] *n.* (*promenade*) эспланáда.
espousal [ɪ'spaʊz(ə)l] *n.* (*betrothal*) обруче́ние; (*marriage*) сва́дьба.
espouse [ɪ'spaʊz] *v.t.* **1.** (*arch., marry*) (*of man*) жени́ться (*impf., pf.*) на+*p.*; (*of woman*) выходи́ть, вы́йти за́муж за+*a.* **2.** (*fig.*) посвя|ща́ться, -ти́ться +*d.*; отд|ава́ться, -а́ться +*d.*; ~ **a cause** (целико́м) отд|ава́ться, -а́ться де́лу.
espresso [e'spresəʊ] *n.* (*machine*) «эспре́сс».
esprit de corps [e'spri: də 'kɔ:(r), 'espri:] *n.* ≃ чу́вство солида́рности; забо́та о че́сти (*школы, полка и т.п.*).
espy [ɪ'spaɪ] *v.t.* зам|еча́ть, -е́тить; обнару́жи|вать, -ть.
esquire [ɪ'skwaɪə(r)] *n.* **1.** (*hist.*) оруженосец. **2.: W. Jones, E~** (*on envelope*) г-ну В. Джо́нсу.
essay[1] ['eseɪ] *n.* (*attempt*) попы́тка, про́ба; (*literary composition*) о́черк; эссе́ (*indecl.*); этю́д.
essay[2] [e'seɪ] *v.t.* про́бовать, по-.
v.i. пыта́ться, по-.
essayist ['eseɪɪst] *n.* очерки́ст, эссеи́ст.
essence ['es(ə)ns] *n.* **1.** (*philos.*) су́щность, существо́; (*gist*) суть; **speed is of the ~** всё де́ло в ско́рости. **2.** (*extract*) эссе́нция.
Essene ['esi:n, e'si:n] *n.* (*relig.*) ессе́й.
essential [ɪ'senʃ(ə)l] *n.* (~ *feature, element*) су́щность; **~s of mathematics** осно́вы (*f. pl.*) матема́тики.
adj. **1.** (*necessary*) необходи́мый; **is wealth ~ to happiness?** необходи́мо ли бога́тство для сча́стья?; **it is ~ that I should know** о́чень ва́жно, что́бы я знал. **2.** (*fundamental*) суще́ственный; **~ly** суще́ственно; по существу́; в су́щности; **he is ~ly an amateur** он в су́щности дилета́нт. **3.: ~ oils** эфи́рные масла́.
essentialness [ɪ'senʃəlnɪs] *n.* необходи́мость.
establish [ɪ'stæblɪʃ] *v.t.* **1.** (*found, set up*) учре|жда́ть, -ди́ть; устан|а́вливать, -ови́ть; ~ **a republic** провозгл|аша́ть, -си́ть респу́блику; ~ **contact** устан|а́вливать, -ови́ть конта́кт; ~ **o.s. in business** осно́в|ывать, -а́ть де́ло; ~ **one's son in business** помо́чь (*pf.*) сы́ну нача́ть делову́ю карье́ру. **2.** (*settle*) устр|а́ивать, -о́ить; **we are ~ed in our new home** мы обжили́сь в но́вом до́ме. **3.** (*prove, gain acceptance for*) утвер|жда́ть, -ди́ть; ~ **a claim** обосно́в|ывать, -а́ть прете́нзию; ~ **one's reputation** созд|ава́ть, -а́ть себе́ репута́цию; **Newton ~ed the law of gravity** Нью́тон откры́л зако́н тяготе́ния; **it is ~ed that he saw her** устано́влено, что он её ви́дел; **an ~ed custom** укорени́вшийся обы́чай; **~ed church** госуда́рственная це́рковь.
establishment [ɪ'stæblɪʃmənt] *n.* **1.** (*setting up*) учрежде́ние, установле́ние. **2.** (*of a claim, fact etc.*) установле́ние, обоснова́ние. **3.** (*business concern*) заведе́ние, де́ло. **4.** (*household*) дом; **he keeps a large ~** он живёт на широ́кую но́гу; **they maintain two ~s** они́ живу́т на́ два до́ма. **5.** (*institution*) учрежде́ние, заведе́ние; **educational ~** уче́бное заведе́ние. **6.** (*mil. strength*): **peace/war ~** шта́ты (*m. pl.*) ми́рного/вое́нного вре́мени. **7.** (*set of institutions or key persons*): **the ~** «исте́блишмент», пра́вящая эли́та.
estate [ɪ'steɪt] *n.* **1.** (*landed property*) поме́стье, име́ние; ~ **agent** аге́нт по прода́же недви́жимости; ~ **car** автомоби́ль с ку́зовом «универса́л»; **housing ~** жило́й масси́в; **industrial ~** промы́шленный ко́мплекс. **2.** (*property*) иму́щество; **real ~** недви́жимость; **personal ~** дви́жимость; **the deceased's ~ amounted to £15,000** состоя́ние поко́йного составля́ло 15000 фу́нтов. **3.** (~ *of the realm*) сосло́вие; **E~s General** (*hist.*) Генера́льные шта́ты (*m. pl.*). **4.** (*condition*) положе́ние; **man's ~** совершенноле́тие.
esteem [ɪ'sti:m] *n.* уваже́ние; **we have great ~ for you** мы пита́ем к вам большо́е уваже́ние; **he lowered himself in my ~** он упа́л в мои́х глаза́х.
v.t. уважа́ть (*impf.*); **I ~ him highly** я его́ высоко́ ценю́; **I would ~ it a favour if ...** я счёл бы за любе́зность, е́сли...
Esther ['estə(r)] *n.* (*bibl.*) Эсфи́рь.
esthete ['i:sθi:t] *etc., see* **aesthete** *etc.*
estimable ['estɪməb(ə)l] *adj.* досто́йный уваже́ния.
estimate[1] ['estɪmət] *n.* **1.** (*assessment*) оце́нка; **I formed an ~ of his abilities** я соста́вил себе́ представле́ние о его́ спосо́бностях. **2.** (*comm.*) сме́та; **the builder exceeded his ~** строи́тель превы́сил сме́ту.
estimate[2] ['estɪˌmeɪt] *v.t.* оце́н|ивать, -и́ть; **I ~ his income at £20,000** по мои́м подсчётам его́ дохо́д ра́вен двадцати́ ты́сячам фу́нтов.
v.i. сост|авля́ть, -а́вить сме́ту (*чего*); **the builder ~d for the repairs** строи́тель соста́вил сме́ту ремо́нта.
estimation [ˌestɪ'meɪʃ(ə)n] *n.* (*judgment*) оце́нка, сужде́ние.
Estonia [ɪ'stəʊnɪə] *n.* Эсто́ния.
Estonian [ɪ'stəʊnɪən] *n.* эсто́н|ец (*fem.* -ка).
adj. эсто́нский.
estrange [ɪ'streɪndʒ] *v.t.* отдал|я́ть, -и́ть; (*repel*) отт|а́лкивать, -олкну́ть; **Mr X is ~d from his wife** г-н и г-жа X живу́т врозь; **the children were ~d from their mother** ме́жду детьми́ и их ма́терью возни́кло отчужде́ние.
estrangement [ɪ'streɪndʒmənt] *n.* отчужде́ние, разры́в.
estuary ['estjʊərɪ] *n.* эстуа́рий, у́стье.
esurient [ɪ'sjʊərɪənt] *adj.* голо́дный, жа́дный.
ETA (*abbr. of* **estimated time of arrival**) предполага́емое вре́мя прибы́тия.
étagère [ˌeɪtɑ:'ʒe(r)] *n.* этаже́рка.
et al [et 'æl] (*abbr. of* ***et alii***) и други́е.
etatism [eɪ'tɑ:tɪz(ə)m] *n.* этати́зм.
etc. [et 'setərə, 'setrə] *adv.* (*abbr. of* **et cetera**) и т.д., и т.п., (и так да́лее; и тому́ подо́бное).
et cetera [et 'setərə, 'setrə] *adv, & n.* и так да́лее; и тому́ подо́бное; **~s** (*as n., sundries*) вся́кая вся́чина, всё остально́е.
etch [etʃ] *v.t. & i.* трави́ть, вы́-; гравирова́ть, вы́-; (*fig.*): **it is ~ed on my memory** э́то запечатле́лось у меня́ в па́мяти.
etcher ['etʃə(r)] *n.* гравёр, офорти́ст.
etching ['etʃɪŋ] *n.* (*craft*) гравиро́вка; (*product*) офо́рт, гравю́ра.
eternal [ɪ'tɜ:n(ə)l] *adj.* ве́чный (*also fig.*); **the E~** (*God*) Предве́чный; **the E~ City** Ве́чный го́род; **the ~ triangle** любо́вный треуго́льник.
etern(al)ize [ɪ'tɜ:nəlaɪz] *v.t.* увекове́чи|вать, -ть.
eternity [ɪ'tɜ:nɪtɪ] *n.* ве́чность; **for, to all ~** на ве́ки ве́чные; **it seemed an ~ till he came** каза́лось, прошла́ ве́чность, пока́ он (не) пришёл; **send, launch s.o. into ~** отпр|авля́ть, -а́вить кого́-н. на тот свет.
Etesian [ɪ'ti:ʒ(ə)n] *adj.*: ~ **winds** ле́тние се́веро-за́падные пасса́тные ве́тры.
ethane ['eθeɪn, 'i:θ-] *n.* эта́н.
ether ['i:θə(r)] *n.* (*phys., chem.*) эфи́р.
ether|eal, -ial [ɪ'θɪərɪəl] *adj.* эфи́рный, неземно́й; ~ **beauty** неземна́я красота́.
etherization [ˌi:θəraɪ'zeɪʃ(ə)n] *n.* примене́ние эфи́ра для нарко́за.
etherize ['i:θəˌraɪz] *v.t.* усып|ля́ть, -и́ть эфи́ром
ethic ['eθɪk] *n.* (*moral code; also* **~s**) э́тика; мора́ль.
adj. эти́ческий; эти́чный; ~ **dative** (*gram.*) да́тельный эти́ческий.
ethical ['eθɪk(ə)l] *adj.* (*pert. to ethics*) эти́ческий; (*conforming to a code*) эти́чный; **it is not ~ for doctors to advertise** врача́м неэти́чно создава́ть себе́ рекла́му.
Ethiopia [ˌi:θɪ'əʊpɪə] *n.* Эфио́пия.
Ethiopian [ˌi:θɪ'əʊpɪən] *n.* эфио́п (*fem.* -ка).
adj. (*also* **Ethiopic**) эфио́пский.
ethnic ['eθnɪk(ə)l] *adj.* этни́ческий; ~ **group** (*within a state*) национа́льность; ~ **cleansing** этни́ческая чи́стка.

ethnographer [eθ'nɒgrəfə(r)] *n.* этно́граф.
ethnographic(al) [ˌeθnə'græfɪk(ə)l] *adj.* этнографи́ческий.
ethnography [eθ'nɒgrəfɪ] *n.* этногра́фия.
ethnological [ˌeθnə'lɒdʒɪk(ə)l] *adj.* этнологи́ческий.
ethnologist [eθ'nɒlədʒɪst] *n.* этно́лог.
ethnology [eθ'nɒlədʒɪ] *n.* этноло́гия.
ethos ['i:θɒs] *n.* дух.
ethyl ['i:θaɪl, 'eθɪl] *n.* эти́л.
etiolate ['i:tɪəʊˌleɪt] *v.t.* этиоли́ровать (*impf.*, *pf.*); **~d** (*fig.*) обескро́вленный, безжи́зненный.
etiquette ['etɪˌket, -'ket] *n.* этике́т.
Etruscan [ɪ'trʌskən] *n.* этру́ск; (*language*) этру́сский язы́к.
adj. этру́сский.
étude ['eɪtju:d, -'tju:d] *n.* (*mus.*) этю́д.
étui [e'twi:] *n.* иго́льник.
etymological [ˌetɪmə'lɒdʒɪk(ə)l] *adj.* этимологи́ческий.
etymologist [ˌetɪ'mɒlədʒɪst] *n.* этимо́лог.
etymologize [ˌetɪ'mɒləˌdʒaɪz] *v.t.*: **~ a word** определ|я́ть, -и́ть этимоло́гию сло́ва.
etymology [ˌetɪ'mɒlədʒɪ] *n.* этимоло́гия.
eucalyptus [ju:kə'lɪptəs] *n.* эвкали́пт.
Eucharist ['ju:kərɪst] *n.* евхари́стия.
eucharistic [ˌju:kə'rɪstɪk] *adj.* евхаристи́ческий.
Euclid ['ju:klɪd] *n.* Эвкли́д.
Euclidean [ju:'klɪdɪən] *adj.* эвкли́дов.
eudaemonism [ju:'di:məˌnɪz(ə)m] *n.* эвдемони́зм.
eugenic [ju:'dʒenɪk] *adj.* евгени́ческий.
eugeni(ci)st [ju:'dʒenɪsɪst] *n.* евгени́ст.
eugenics [ju:'dʒenɪks] *n.* евге́ника.
Euler ['ɔɪlə(r)] *n.* Э́йлер.
eulogist ['ju:lədʒɪst] *n.* панегири́ст.
eulogistic [ˌju:lə'dʒɪstɪk] *adj.* панегири́ческий.
eulogize ['ju:ləˌdʒaɪz] *v.t.* восхвал|я́ть, -и́ть.
eulogy ['ju:lədʒɪ] *n.* панеги́рик; похвала́.
eunuch ['ju:nək] *n.* е́внух, кастра́т.
eupeptic [ju:'peptɪk] *adj.* име́ющий хоро́шее пищеваре́ние.
euphemism ['ju:fɪˌmɪz(ə)m] *n.* эвфеми́зм.
euphemistic [ˌju:fɪ'mɪstɪk] *adj.* эвфемисти́ческий.
euphonious [ju:'fəʊnɪəs] *adj.* благозву́чный.
euphonium [ju:'fəʊnɪəm] *n.* саксофо́н-бас.
euphony ['ju:fənɪ] *n.* благозву́чность, благозву́чие.
euphorbia [ju:'fɔ:bɪə] *n.* молоча́й.
euphoria [ju:'fɔ:rɪə] *adj.* эйфори́я.
euphoric [ju:'fɒrɪk] *adj.* в припо́днятом настрое́нии.
euphrasy ['ju:frəsɪ] *n.* оча́нка.
Euphrates [ju:'freɪti:z] *n.* Евфра́т.
euphuism ['ju:fju:ˌɪz(ə)m] *n.* эвфуи́зм.
euphuistic [ˌju:fju:'ɪstɪk] *adj.* эвфуисти́ческий.
Eurasia [jʊə'reɪʒɪə] *n.* Евра́зия.
Eurasian [jʊə'reɪʒ(ə)n] *n.* еврази́|ец (*fem.* -йка).
adj. еврази́йский.
Euratom [jʊə'rætəm] *n.* (*abbr. of* ***European Atomic Energy Community***) Евра́том, (Европе́йское соо́бщество по а́томной эне́ргии).
eureka [jʊə'ri:kə] *int.* э́врика.
eurhythmic [jʊə'rɪðmɪk] *adj.* гармони́чный, ритми́чный.
eurhythmics [jʊə'rɪðmɪks] *n.* ри́тмика, худо́жественная гимна́стика.
Euro- ['jʊərəʊ] *comb. form* евро…; **~-MP** депута́т Европарла́мента; **~parliament** Европарла́мент; **~sceptic** евроске́птик.
Europe ['jʊərəp] *n.* Евро́па; **to go into ~** (*pol.*) войти́ (*pf.*) в Евро́пу; вступи́ть (*pf.*) в Европе́йское экономи́ческое соо́бщество.
European [jʊərə'pɪən] *n.* европе́|ец (*fem.* -йка); **a staunch ~** (*pol.*) рья́ный сторо́нник еди́ной Евро́пы.
adj. европе́йский.
Europeanism [jʊərə'pɪənɪz(ə)m] *n.* иде́я еди́ной Евро́пы.
Europeanist [jʊərə'pɪənɪst] *n.* сторо́нник еди́ной Евро́пы.
Europeanization [jʊərəˌpɪənaɪ'zeɪʃ(ə)n] *n.* европеиза́ция.
Europeanize [jʊərə'pɪənaɪz] *v.t.* европеизи́ровать (*impf.*, *pf.*).
Eurovision ['jʊərəʊˌvɪʒ(ə)n] *n.* Еврови́дение.
Eurydice [jʊ'rɪdɪsɪ] *n.* (*myth.*) Эвриди́ка.
Eustachian tube [ju:'steɪʃ(ə)n] *n.* евста́хиева труба́.
euthanasia [ju:θə'neɪzɪə] *n.* умерщвле́ние из милосе́рдия; эйтана́зия.
evacuate [ɪ'vækjʊˌeɪt] *v.t.* **1.** (*pers. or place*) эваку́ировать (*impf.*, *pf.*). **2.** (*physiol.*) оч|ища́ть, -и́стить.
evacuation [ɪˌvækjʊ'eɪʃ(ə)n] *n.* (*removal*) эвакуа́ция; (*physiol.*) очище́ние кише́чника, испражне́ние.
evacuee [ɪˌvækju:'i:] *n.* эваку́ированный.
evade [ɪ'veɪd] *v.t.* избе|га́ть, -жа́ть *+g.*; избе́гнуть (*pf.*) *+g.*; уклон|я́ться, -и́ться от*+g.*; **~ a blow/question** уклон|я́ться, -и́ться от уда́ра/отве́та; **~ paying one's debts** уклон|я́ться, -и́ться от упла́ты долго́в.
evaluate [ɪ'væljʊˌeɪt] *v.t.* оце́н|ивать, -и́ть; **he ~d the damage at £50** он оцени́л уще́рб в 50 фу́нтов; (*math.*) выража́ть, вы́разить в чи́слах.
evaluation [ɪˌvæljʊ'eɪʃ(ə)n] *n.* оце́нка; (*math.*) выраже́ние в чи́слах.
evanesce [ˌi:və'nes, ˌe-] *v.i.* исч|еза́ть, -е́знуть; ст|ира́ться, -ере́ться.
evanescence [ˌi:və'nesəns, ˌe-] *n.* исчезнове́ние.
evanescent [ˌi:və'nes(ə)nt, ˌe-] *adj.* исчеза́ющий, мимолётный.
evangelical [ˌi:væn'dʒelɪk(ə)l] *n.* протеста́нт.
adj. ева́нгельский; (*Protestant*) евангели́ческий.
evangelism [ɪ'vændʒəˌlɪz(ə)m] *n.* про́поведь Ева́нгелия; (*fig.*) пропове́дничество.
evangelist [ɪ'vændʒəlɪst] *n.* (*author of gospel*) евангели́ст; (*preacher*) пропове́дник Ева́нгелия.
evangelize [ɪ'vændʒəˌlaɪz] *v.t.* обра|ща́ть, -ти́ть в христиа́нство.
evaporate [ɪ'væpəˌreɪt] *v.t.* & *i.* испар|я́ть(ся), -и́ть(ся) (*also fig.*); **Jones ~d** (*coll.*) Джонс испари́лся/исче́з; **his anger ~d** его́ гнев рассе́ялся.
evaporation [ɪˌvæpə'reɪʃ(ə)n] *n.* испаре́ние; (*fig.*) исчезнове́ние.
evasion [ɪ'veɪʒ(ə)n] *n.* (*avoidance*) уклоне́ние; (*prevarication*) увёртка.
evasive [ɪ'veɪsɪv] *adj.* (*of answer*) укло́нчивый; (*of pers.*) увёртливый; **the ship took ~ action** кора́бль маневри́ровал переме́нным ку́рсом.
Eve[1] [i:v] *n.* (*bibl.*) Е́ва.
eve[2] [i:v] *n.* **1.** (*arch.*) = **evening. 2.** (*day or evening before*) кану́н (*also fig.*); **on the ~ of** накану́не *+g.*; **Christmas E~** (Рожде́ственский) соче́льник; **New Year's E~** нового́дняя ночь, кану́н Но́вого го́да.
even[1] ['i:v(ə)n] *n.* (*poet.*) = **evening**
cpds. **~song** *n.* вече́рняя моли́тва; **~tide** *n.* вече́рняя пора́.
even[2] ['i:v(ə)n] *adj.* **1.** (*level, smooth*) ро́вный; **fill** (*glass, etc.*) **~ with the brim** напо́лнить (*pf.*) до краёв; **~ with the ground** вро́вень с землёй. **2.** (*uniform*) равноме́рный; **his work is not very ~** он рабо́тает дово́льно неро́вно; **at an ~ speed** с постоя́нной ско́ростью. **3.** (*equal*) ра́вный; **the score is ~** счёт ра́вный; **the horses were ~ in the race** ло́шади на ска́чках шли голова́ к голове́; **an ~ chance** ра́вные ша́нсы; **get ~ with s.o.** расквита́ться (*pf.*) с кем-н.; **now we are ~** тепе́рь мы кви́ты; **break ~** ост|ава́ться, -а́ться при свои́х; **letter of ~ date** письмо́ от сего́дняшнего числа́. **4.** (*divisible by 2*) чётный; **on ~ dates** по чётным чи́слам. **5.** (*calm*) ро́вный, споко́йный; **~ temper** ро́вный хара́ктер. **6.** (*exact*) ро́вный; **an ~ dozen** ро́вно дю́жина.
adv. да́же; и; хотя́ бы; **he disputes ~ the facts** он оспа́ривает да́же фа́кты; **he won't ~ notice** он и не заме́тит; **~ if** е́сли да́же; **~ so** всё равно́; да́же в тако́м слу́чае; **not ~** да́же не; **~ though I don't like him** хотя́ он мне не нра́вится; **does he ~ suspect the danger?** подозрева́ет ли он вообще́ об опа́сности?; **I have only one suit, and ~ it is shabby** у меня́ всего́ оди́н костю́м, да и тот потрёпанный; **this applies ~ more to French** э́то ещё в бо́льшей сте́пени отно́сится к францу́зскому языку́; **~ as I spoke, I realised …** уже́ когда́ я говори́л э́то, я по́нял…; **~ as a child he was …** ещё/уже́ ребёнком он был…
v.t. (*make even or equal*) выра́внивать, вы́ровнять; **that ~s (up) the score** э́то ура́внивает счёт.
v.i. выра́вниваться, вы́ровняться.
cpds. **~-handed** *adj.* беспристра́стный; **~-handedness** *n.* беспристра́стность; **~-tempered** *adj.* уравнове́шенный.
evening ['i:vnɪŋ] *n.* ве́чер; **in the ~** ве́чером; **(on) that ~** в тот ве́чер; **one ~** одна́жды ве́чером; **this ~** сего́дня

ве́чером; **tomorrow ~** за́втра ве́чером; **last, yesterday ~** вчера́ ве́чером; **on the ~ of the 8th** восьмо́го ве́чером; **musical ~** музыка́льный ве́чер; (*attr.*) вече́рний; **~ service** (*relig.*) вече́рня; вече́рняя моли́тва; **~ dress, clothes** (*men's or women's*) вече́рний туале́т; **~ dress, gown** (*woman's*) вече́рнее пла́тье.

evenly [ˈiːvənlɪ] *adv.* ро́вно, равноме́рно; **he spoke ~** он говори́л споко́йно (*or* не повыша́я го́лоса); **spread the butter ~** нама́з|ывать, -ать ма́сло ро́вным сло́ем; **the odds are ~ balanced** ша́нсы — ра́вные.

evenness [ˈiːvənnɪs] *n.* (*physical smoothness*) гла́дкость; (*uniformity*) равноме́рность; (*of temper, tone etc.*) ро́вность, уравнове́шенность; (*of odds, contest etc.*) ра́венство.

event [ɪˈvent] *n.* **1.** (*occurrence*) собы́тие; **current ~s** теку́щие собы́тия; **in the natural course of ~s** при норма́льном разви́тии собы́тий; **it was quite an ~** э́то бы́ло це́лое собы́тие. **2.** (*outcome*) исхо́д; **in the ~ he was unsuccessful** в коне́чном счёте он потерпе́л неуда́чу; **wise after the ~** за́дним умо́м кре́пок. **3.** (*hypothesis*) слу́чай; **in the ~ of his coming** в слу́чае его́ прихо́да; **in any ~** в любо́м слу́чае; **in either ~** так и́ли ина́че; **at all ~s** во вся́ком слу́чае. **4.** (*sports item*) забе́г, зае́зд; вид спо́рта; **combined ~s** многобо́рье.

eventful [ɪˈventfʊl] *adj.* насы́щенный собы́тиями.

eventual [ɪˈventjʊəl] *adj.* (*possible*) возмо́жный, эвентуа́льный; (*final*) коне́чный, оконча́тельный; **~ success** успе́шный коне́ц; **his ~ departure surprised us** то, что он в конце́ концо́в уе́хал, порази́ло нас.

eventuality [ɪˌventjʊˈælɪtɪ] *n.* возмо́жность, слу́чай; **prepared for any ~** гото́вый ко вся́ким случа́йностям.

eventually [ɪˈventjʊəlɪ] *adv.* со вре́менем; в конце́ концо́в; в коне́чном счёте; ра́но и́ли по́здно.

eventuate [ɪˈventjʊˌeɪt] *v.i.* (*turn out*) разреш|а́ться, -и́ться (*чем*); (*happen*) случ|а́ться, -и́ться; возн|ика́ть, -и́кнуть.

ever [ˈevə(r)] *adv.* **1.** (*always*) всегда́; **for ~ (and a day** *or* **and ~)** навсегда́, наве́чно; во все времена́; (*relig.*) во ве́ки веко́в; **~ after, since** с тех (са́мых) пор; **~ since** (*conj.*) с тех пор, как…; **yours ~, ~ yours, as ~** (*in letters*) Ваш/Твой…; пре́данный Вам; **~ and anon** (*arch.*) вре́мя от вре́мени; **with ~ increasing pleasure** со всё возраста́ющим удово́льствием. **2.** (*at any time*): **do you ~ see him?** вы его́ когда́-нибудь ви́дите?; **nothing ~ happens** ничего́ не происхо́дит; **scarcely, hardly ~** почти́ никогда́; о́чень ре́дко; **not then or ~** ни тогда́, ни когда́-либо ещё; **as good as ~** не ху́же, чем ра́ньше; **better than ~** лу́чше, чем когда́-либо; **did you ~!** вида́ли?!; как вам э́то нра́вится? вот э́то да!; **this is the best ~** тако́го ещё не быва́ло. **3.** (*intensive*): **as soon as ~ I can** при пе́рвой возмо́жности; **why ~ did you do it?** заче́м же вы э́то сде́лали?; **how ~ did you manage it?** как то́лько вам э́то удало́сь?; **~ so rich** ужа́сно бога́тый; страсть как бога́тый (*coll.*); **be he ~ so rich** как бы он ни́ был бога́т; **I have not seen him for ~ so long** я его́ о́чень давно́ не ви́дел; **thank you ~ so much** я вам чрезвыча́йно благода́рен; **Sunday as ~ is** (*coll.*) в ближа́йшее воскресе́нье.

cpds. **~-blooming** *adj.* ве́чно цвету́щий; **~green** *n.* (*bot.*) вечнозелёное расте́ние; *adj.* вечнозелёный; (*fig.*) неувяда́емый; **~lasting** *adj.* (*eternal; incessant*) ве́чный; **~lasting flower** имморте́ль (*m.*); бессме́ртник; (*as n.*) **the E~lasting (God)** Всевы́шний, Предве́чный; **from ~lasting** испоко́н веко́в; **~lastingness** *n.* ве́чность; **~-loving** *adj.* всегда́ лю́бящий; **~more** *adv.*: **for ~more** навсегда́, наве́чно; **~-present** *adj.* постоя́нный.

every [ˈevrɪ] *adj.* ка́ждый, вся́кий; **not ~ animal can swim** не все живо́тные пла́вают; **~ man Jack (***or* **mother's son)** все без исключе́ния; все как оди́н; **~ (single) word is a mockery** что ни сло́во, то насме́шка; **you have ~ reason to be satisfied** у вас есть все основа́ния быть дово́льным; **I have ~ confidence in him** я в нём соверше́нно уве́рен; **I wish you ~ success** жела́ю вам вся́ческого/по́лного успе́ха; **~ ten minutes** ка́ждые де́сять мину́т; **~ other car** ка́ждый второ́й автомоби́ль; **(on) ~ other day** че́рез день; **~ one of them** все до одного́; **~ now and again; ~ so often; ~ once in a while** вре́мя от вре́мени; по времена́м; иногда́; **I ate ~ bit of it** я съел всё до после́днего кусо́чка; **this is ~ bit as good** э́то ничу́ть не уступа́ет; **~ bit as much** то́чно сто́лько же; **~ time (that) he comes** вся́кий раз, когда́ он прихо́дит; **in ~ way** во всех отноше́ниях; вся́чески, все́ми возмо́жными спо́собами; **I expect him ~ minute** я жду его́ с мину́ты на мину́ту.

cpds. **~body, ~one** *prons.* ка́ждый; вся́кий; все (*pl.*); **~body knows that!** э́то ка́ждый зна́ет; **~body else** все остальны́е; **~body knows ~body else** все со все́ми знако́мы; **~day** *adj.* каждодне́вный, повседне́вный; обыкнове́нный, бытово́й; **E~man** *n.* (*the common man*) рядово́й/обыкнове́нный челове́к; обыва́тель (*m.*); **~one** *pron.* = **~body; ~thing** *pron.* всё; **speed is ~thing to him** для него́ ско́рость — э́то всё; **money is not ~thing** де́ньги — э́то ещё не всё; **~thing is not clear** не всё я́сно; **~thing comes to him who waits** терпе́нье и тру́д всё перетру́т; **~where** *adv.* везде́, повсю́ду; **~where else** во всех други́х места́х.

evict [ɪˈvɪkt] *v.t.* выселя́ть, вы́селить.

eviction [ɪˈvɪkʃ(ə)n] *n.* выселе́ние.

evidence [ˈevɪd(ə)ns] *n.* **1.** (*clarity, visibility*) очеви́дность; **he was much in ~ at the party** он о́чень выделя́лся на вечери́нке; **flowers were much in ~** цветы́ бы́ли повсю́ду. **2.** (*indication, confirmation*) доказа́тельство, свиде́тельство; **there was ample ~ of foul play** всё свиде́тельствовало о соверше́нном преступле́нии; **the ~ of the charred letter** ули́ка в ви́де полусожжённого письма́; **there is no ~ for this belief** нет основа́ний для э́того убежде́ния; **~s of glacial action** следы́ (*m. pl.*) движе́ния ледника́. **3.** (*leg.*) свиде́тельское показа́ние; да́нные (*nt. pl.*); **give ~** да|ва́ть, -ть свиде́тельское показа́ние; **he turned King's, Queen's, state's ~** он вы́дал соуча́стников и стал свиде́телем обвине́ния; **circumstantial ~** ко́свенные ули́ки (*f. pl.*); **cumulative ~** совоку́пность ули́к; **law of ~** доказа́тельственное пра́во; **presumptive ~** фа́кты, создаю́щие презу́мпцию доказа́тельства; опроверж́имое доказа́тельство.

v.t. служи́ть, по- доказа́тельством (*чего*).

evident [ˈevɪd(ə)nt] *adj.* очеви́дный, я́сный; **it was ~ from his behaviour that ...** бы́ло ви́дно по его́ поведе́нию, что…; **he is ~ly a fool** он я́вно дура́к; **~ly not** (*as reply*) разуме́ется, нет; ока́зывается, что нет.

evidential [ˌevɪˈdenʃ(ə)l] *adj.* доказа́тельный.

evil [ˈiːv(ə)l, -ɪl] *n.* зло; **wish s.o. ~** жела́ть (*impf.*) кому́-н. зла; **speak ~ of s.o** злосло́вить (*impf.*) о ком-н.; **the ~s of civilization** поро́ки (*m. pl.*) цивилиза́ции.

adj. злой, дурно́й; **he was her ~ genius** он был её злым ге́нием; **she has an ~ tongue** у неё злой язы́к; **the E~ One** (*devil*) нечи́стый; **a man of ~ repute** челове́к с плохо́й репута́цией; **fallen on ~ days** впа́вший в нищету́.

cpds. **~-doer** *n.* злоде́й; **~-doing** *n.* злодея́ние; **~-minded** *adj.* злонаме́ренный; **~-mindedness** *n.* злонаме́ренность.

evilness [ˈiːvəlnɪs, -ɪlnɪs] *n.* зло́бность

evince [ɪˈvɪns] *v.t.* прояв|ля́ть, -и́ть.

eviscerate [ɪˈvɪsəˌreɪt] *v.t.* потроши́ть, вы́-; (*fig.*) выхола́щивать, вы́холостить.

evisceration [ɪˌvɪsəˈreɪʃ(ə)n] *n.* потроше́ние; (*fig.*) выхола́щивание.

evocation [ˌevəˈkeɪʃ(ə)n] *n.* вызыва́ние; воскреше́ние в па́мяти.

evocative [ɪˈvɒkətɪv] *adj.* навева́ющий воспомина́ния.

evoke [ɪˈvəʊk] *v.t.* вызыва́ть, вы́звать; пробу|жда́ть, -ди́ть; нап|омина́ть, -о́мнить.

evolution [ˌiːvəˈluːʃ(ə)n, -ˈljuːʃ(ə)n] *n.* **1.** эволю́ция; **theory of ~** эволюцио́нная тео́рия. **2.** (*mil.*) манёвр. **3.** (*of dancers etc.*) фигу́ры (*f. pl.*).

evolutionary [ˌiːvəˈluːʃənərɪ, -ˈljuːʃənərɪ] *adj.* эволюцио́нный.

evolutionism [ˌiːvəˈluːʃənɪz(ə)m, -ˈljuːʃənɪz(ə)m] *n.* эволюциони́зм; эволюцио́нная тео́рия.

evolutionist [ˌiːvəˈluːʃənɪst, -ˈljuːʃənɪst] *n.* эволюциони́ст.

evolve [ɪˈvɒlv] *v.t.* разв|ива́ть, -и́ть; **he ~d a plan** он разрабо́тал план.

v.i. разв|ива́ться, -и́ться; эволюциони́ровать (*impf., pf.*).

ewe [juː] *n.* овца́; **~ lamb** ове́чка; (*fig.*) еди́нственное дитя́/сокро́вище; **~ in lamb** суя́гная овца́.

ewer [ˈjuːə(r)] *n.* кувши́н.

ex[1] [eks] *prep.* (*comm.*): ~ **warehouse** (*from warehouse*) со скла́да; (*free of charges as far as warehouse*) фра́нко склад; **shares** ~ **dividend** а́кции без дивиде́нда; **an** ~**-directory telephone number** но́мер, не внесённый в телефо́нную кни́гу.

ex-[2] [eks] *pref.* (*former*) экс-..., бы́вший; ~**husband/president** бы́вший муж/президе́нт.

exacerbate [ekˈsæsəˌbeɪt, ɪg-] *v.t.* (*pers.*) раздраж|а́ть, -и́ть; (*pain etc.*) обостр|я́ть, -и́ть.

exacerbation [ekˌsæsəˈbeɪʃ(ə)n, ɪg-] *n.* раздраже́ние, обостре́ние.

exact [ɪgˈzækt] *adj.* то́чный; **an** ~ **memory** це́пкая па́мять.

v.t. (*e.g. payment*) взы́ск|ивать, -а́ть; (*e.g. obedience*) тре́бовать, по- +*g*.

exacting [ɪgˈzæktɪŋ] *adj.* взыска́тельный, тре́бовательный.

exaction [ɪgˈzækʃ(ə)n] *n.* (*demand, extortion*) тре́бование, вымога́тельство; (*unjust tax*) чрезме́рный нало́г.

exact|itude [ɪgˈzæktɪˌtjuːd] = **-ness**

exactly [ɪgˈzæktlɪ] *adv.* то́чно; (*of numbers, quantities*) ро́вно; **he measured it** ~ он э́то то́чно изме́рил; ~ **a kilogram** ро́вно килогра́мм; **(in)** ~ **(the same way) as** так то́чно как; ~ **the same** то же са́мое; ~**!** (*as reply*) и́менно!; ~ **how much do you need?** ско́лько и́менно вам ну́жно?; **not** ~ **ugly** не тако́й уж уро́дливый; **he did not** ~ **complain, but he was discontented** он не то что(бы) жа́ловался, но был недово́лен.

exact|ness [ɪgˈzæktnɪs], **-itude** [ɪgˈzækt] *nn.* то́чность.

exaggerate [ɪgˈzædʒəˌreɪt] *v.t.* преувели́чи|вать, -ть.

exaggeration [ɪgˌzædʒəˈreɪʃ(ə)n] *n.* преувеличе́ние.

exalt [ɪgˈzɔːlt] *v.t.* (*make higher in rank etc.*) пов|ыша́ть, -ы́сить; (*praise*) превозн|оси́ть, -ести́.

exaltation [ˌegzɔːlˈteɪʃ(ə)n] *n.* **1.** (*raising in rank etc.*) повыше́ние. **2.** (*worship*) возвели́чение. **3.: E**~ **of the Cross** (*relig.*) воздвиже́ние Креста́. **4.** (*mental or emotional transport*) экзальта́ция.

exam [ɪgˈzæm] (*coll.*) = **examination 3.**

examination [ɪgˌzæmɪˈneɪʃ(ə)n] *n.* **1.** (*inspection*) осмо́тр; **customs** ~ тамо́женный досмо́тр; ~ **of passports** прове́рка паспорто́в. **2.** (*interrogation*) допро́с; **the prisoner is under** ~ заключённого допра́шивают. **3.** (*acad. etc.*; *also* **exam**) экза́мен; ~ **paper** (*written by examinee*) экзаменацио́нная рабо́та; (*questions set*) вопро́сы (*m. pl.*) (для экзаменацио́нной рабо́ты); **competitive** ~ ко́нкурсный экза́мен; **entrance** ~ вступи́тельный экза́мен; **go in for** (*or* **take**) **an** ~ сда|ва́ть, -ть экза́мен; **sit an** ~ экзаменова́ться, про-; **pass an** ~ сдать/вы́держать (*both pf.*) экза́мен; **fail (in) an** ~ провали́ться (*pf.*) на экза́мене.

examine [ɪgˈzæmɪn] *v.t.* **1.** (*inspect*) осм|а́тривать, -отре́ть; ~ **passports** пров|еря́ть, -е́рить паспорта́; ~ **records** изуч|а́ть, -и́ть докуме́нты; ~ **a signature** пров|еря́ть, -е́рить по́длинность по́дписи; ~ **a patient** осм|а́тривать, -отре́ть больно́го; ~ **one's conscience** спр|а́шивать, -оси́ть свою́ со́весть; ~ **claims** рассм|а́тривать, -отре́ть жа́лобы; **he had his eyes** ~**d (by s.o.)** он прове́рил глаза́ (у кого́-н.). **2.** (*interrogate*) допр|а́шивать, -оси́ть. **3.** (*acad.*) экзаменова́ть, про-; ~ **pupils in Latin (***or* **on Homer)** экзаменова́ть, про- ученико́в по латы́ни (*or* по тво́рчеству Гоме́ра).

examinee [ɪgˌzæmɪˈniː] *n.* экзамену́ющийся; **he is a bad** ~ он не уме́ет прояви́ть себя́ на экза́менах.

examiner [ɪgˈzæmɪnə(r)] *n.* (*acad.*) экзамена́тор; (*of a prisoner, witness etc.*) сле́дователь (*m.*).

example [ɪgˈzɑːmp(ə)l] *n.* **1.** (*illustration, model*) приме́р; **for (***or* **by way of)** ~ наприме́р; **follow s.o.'s** брать (*impf.*) с кого́-н. приме́р; **set an** ~ **to s.o.** подава́ть (*impf.*) кому́-н. приме́р. **2.** (*warning*) уро́к; **let this be an** ~ **to you** пусть э́то послу́жит вам уро́ком; **make an** ~ **of s.o.** наказа́ть (*pf.*) кого́-н. в назида́ние други́м. **3.** (*specimen*) образе́ц.

exanthema [ˌeksænˈθiːmə] *n.* сыпь.

exarch [ˈeksɑːk] *n.* (*hist., eccl.*) экза́рх.

exarch|ate [ˈeksɑːkeɪt], **-y** [ˈeksɑːkɪ] *nn.* экзарха́т.

exasperate [ɪgˈzɑːspəˌreɪt] *v.t.* изв|оди́ть, -ести́; раздраж|а́ть, -и́ть.

exasperating [ɪgˈzɑːspəˌreɪtɪŋ] *adj.* раздража́ющий.

exasperation [ɪgˌzɑːspəˈreɪʃ(ə)n] *n.* раздраже́ние.

excavate [ˈekskəˌveɪt] *v.t.* копа́ть (*impf.*); выка́пывать, вы́копать; раск|а́пывать, -опа́ть; ~ **a trench** копа́ть око́п; ~ **a buried city** раскопа́ть (*pf.*) погребённый го́род.

excavation [ˌekskəˈveɪʃ(ə)n] *n.* раско́пки (*f. pl.*); выка́пывание.

excavator [ˈekskəˌveɪtə(r)] *n.* (*pers.*) землеко́п; (*machine*) экскава́тор.

exceed [ɪkˈsiːd] *v.t.* прев|ыша́ть, -ы́сить; ~ **s.o. in height** быть вы́ше кого́-н. ро́стом; ~ **expectations** превзойти́ (*pf.*) ожида́ния.

exceedingly [ɪkˈsiːdɪŋlɪ] *adv.* чрезвыча́йно.

excel [ɪkˈsel] *v.t.* прев|осходи́ть, -зойти́.

v.i. выдава́ться (*impf.*); выделя́ться (*impf.*); **he** ~**s as an orator** он выдаю́щийся ора́тор; **he** ~**s in sport** он превосхо́дный спортсме́н.

excellence [ˈeksələns] *n.* превосхо́дство; превосхо́дное ка́чество; ~ **in French** соверше́нство во францу́зском языке́.

excellency [ˈeksələnsɪ] *n.*: **His E**~ его́ превосходи́тельство.

excellent [ˈeksələnt] *adj.* отли́чный.

excelsior [ɪkˈselsɪˌɔː(r)] *adv., int.* (всё) вы́ше.

except [ɪkˈsept] *v.t.* исключ|а́ть, -и́ть; **we** ~**ed him from the rule** мы сде́лали для него́ исключе́ние; **present company** ~**ed** о прису́тствующих не говоря́т.

prep. (*also* ~**ing**) исключа́я+*a.*; кро́ме+*g.*; за исключе́нием+*g.*; ра́зве лишь/то́лько; **the essay is good** ~ **for the spelling mistakes** сочине́ние хоро́шее, е́сли не счита́ть орфографи́ческих оши́бок; **I knew nothing** ~ **that he was away** я не знал ничего́, кроме того́, что его́ не́ было; **I would go** ~ **that it is too far** я бы пошёл, да то́лько э́то сли́шком далеко́; **take no orders** ~ **from me** не слу́шайте ничьи́х прика́зов, кро́ме мои́х; **the area is well defended** ~ **here** райо́н, кроме э́того уча́стка, укреплён хорошо́; ~ **in Germany** кро́ме как в Герма́нии.

exception [ɪkˈsepʃ(ə)n] *n.* **1.** (*sth. excepted*) исключе́ние; **with the** ~ **of** за исключе́нием+*g.*; **an** ~ **to a rule** исключе́ние из пра́вила; **the** ~ **proves the rule** исключе́ние подтвержда́ет пра́вило. **2.** (*objection*) оби́да; **take** ~ **to** об|ижа́ться, -и́деться на+*a.*

exceptionable [ɪkˈsepʃənəb(ə)l] *adj.* вызыва́ющий возраже́ния; небезупре́чный.

exceptional [ɪkˈsepʃən(ə)l] *adj.* исключи́тельный.

excerpt [ˈeksɜːpt] *n.* вы́держка, цита́та.

v.t.: ~ **a passage from a book** процити́ровать (*pf.*) отры́вок из кни́ги; прив|оди́ть, -ести́ вы́держку из кни́ги.

excess [ɪkˈses, ˈekses] *n.* **1.** (*exceeding*) изли́шек, избы́ток; ~ **of imports over exports** превыше́ние и́мпорта над э́кспортом; **in** ~ **of £20** свы́ше двадцати́ фу́нтов; **expenditure in** ~ **of income** расхо́ды, превыша́ющие дохо́д. **2.** (*exceeding what is proper or normal*) эксце́сс, кра́йность; **he carries grief to** ~ он неуме́ренно предаётся го́рю; **the** ~**es of the military** бесчи́нства вое́нщины; **drink to** ~ злоупотребля́ть (*impf.*) алкого́лем; ~ **fare** допла́та; ~ **postage** почто́вая допла́та; ~ **luggage** изли́шек багажа́; **we had to pay** ~ мы должны́ бы́ли доплати́ть; ~ **profits tax** нало́г на сверхпри́быль.

excessive [ɪkˈsesɪv] *adj.* изли́шний; (*extreme*) чрезме́рный.

excessiveness [ɪkˈsesɪvnɪs] *n.* изли́шество, чрезме́рность.

exchange [ɪksˈtʃeɪndʒ] *n.* **1.** (*act of exchanging*) обме́н +*g./i.*; **in** ~ **for** в обме́н на+*a.*; ~ **of prisoners** обме́н пле́нными; ~ **of shots** перестре́лка; ~ **professor** профе́ссор, преподаю́щий в друго́й стране́ в поря́дке обме́на; ~ **is no robbery** ме́на — не грабёж. **2.** (*fin.*) разме́н, обме́н; ~ **rate/control** валю́тный курс/контро́ль; **lose on the** ~ потеря́ть (*pf.*) на обме́не де́нег. **3.** (*place of business*) би́ржа; **stock** ~ фо́ндовая би́ржа; ~ **broker** биржево́й ма́клер. **4.** (*teleph.*) (центра́льная) телефо́нная ста́нция; (*in building*) коммута́тор. **5.: labour** ~ би́ржа труда́.

v.t. меня́ть, об-/по- (*что на что*); (*reciprocally*) меня́ться, об-/по- +*i.*; обме́ниваться (*impf.*) +*i.*; **we** ~**d places** мы поменя́лись места́ми; **we** ~**d opinions** мы обменя́лись мне́ниями; **he** ~**d a palace for a cell** он променя́л дворе́ц на ке́лью; **he** ~**d one job for another** он перешёл с одно́й рабо́ты на другу́ю.

v.i.: **he ~d with me on the roster** мы с ним поменя́лись дежу́рствами; **a mark ~s for one Swiss franc** ма́рка обме́нивается на оди́н швейца́рский франк.

exchangeable [ɪks'tʃeɪndʒəb(ə)l] *adj.* подлежа́щий обме́ну, го́дный для обме́на; **this coupon is ~ for lunch** э́тот тало́н даёт пра́во на обе́д.

exchequer [ɪks'tʃekə(r)] *n.* казначе́йство, казна́; **Chancellor of the E~** ка́нцлер казначе́йства; (*fig.*, *joc. finances*) фина́нсы (*m. pl.*).

excise[1] ['eksaɪz] *n.* акци́з; **~ officer** акци́зный чино́вник.

excise[2] ['eksaɪz] *v.t.* выреза́ть, вы́резать; отр|еза́ть, -е́зать.

excision [ɪk'sɪʒ(ə)n] *n.* выреза́ние, отреза́ние.

excitability [ɪk,saɪtə'bɪlɪtɪ] *n.* повы́шенная возбуди́мость.

excitable [ɪk'saɪtəb(ə)l] *adj.* легко́ возбуди́мый.

excite [ɪk'saɪt] *v.t.* **1.** (*cause*, *arouse*, *stimulate*) возбу|жда́ть, -ди́ть; вызыва́ть, вы́звать; **~ a riot** подн|има́ть, -я́ть бунт; **the drug ~s the nerves** э́то лека́рство стимули́рует не́рвную систе́му. **2.** (*thrill*, *agitate*) волнова́ть, вз-; **don't ~ yourself** (*or* **get ~d**) не волну́йтесь.

excitement [ɪk'saɪtmənt] *n.* возбужде́ние, волне́ние; **what is all the ~ about?** что за шум?; в чём де́ло?; **the ~s of town life** пре́лести городско́й жи́зни.

exciting [ɪk'saɪtɪŋ] *adj.* захва́тывающий, увлека́тельный; **how ~!** как интере́сно!

exclaim [ɪk'skleɪm] *v.t. & i.* воскл|ица́ть, -и́кнуть; **~ against** протестова́ть (*impf.*) про́тив+*g.*; **~ at** удив|ля́ться, -и́ться +*d.*

exclamation [,eksklə'meɪʃ(ə)n] *n.* восклица́ние; **~ mark** восклица́тельный знак.

exclamatory [ɪk'sklæmətərɪ] *adj.* восклица́тельный.

exclude [ɪk'sklu:d] *v.t.* исключ|а́ть, -и́ть; **~ from membership** лиш|а́ть, -и́ть чле́нства; **~ immigrants** не впус|ка́ть, -ти́ть иммигра́нтов.

exclusion [ɪk'sklu:ʒ(ə)n] *n.* исключе́ние.

exclusive [ɪk'sklu:sɪv] *adj.* **1.** (*sole*) исключи́тельный, еди́нственный; **he is the ~ agent for this product** он еди́нственный аге́нт по сбы́ту э́того това́ра. **2.**: **~ of** (*not counting*) без+*g.*, не счита́я+*g.* **3.** (*reserved*, *restricted*) специа́льный, исключи́тельный; **an ~ interview** интервью́, да́нное то́лько одно́й газе́те; **an ~ club** клуб для и́збранных; **we have ~ rights to his invention** мы владе́ем исключи́тельными права́ми на его́ изобрете́ние.

exclusiveness [ɪk'sklu:sɪvnɪs] *n.* исключи́тельность.

excogitate [eks'kɒdʒɪ,teɪt] *v.t.* приду́м|ывать, -ать; выду́мывать, вы́думать.

excogitation [eks,kɒdʒɪ'teɪʃ(ə)n] *n.* приду́мывание, выду́мывание.

excommunicate [,ekskə'mju:nɪ,keɪt] *v.t.* отлуч|а́ть, -и́ть от це́ркви.

excommunication [ekskə,mju:nɪ'keɪʃ(ə)n] *n.* отлуче́ние от це́ркви.

excoriate [eks'kɔ:rɪ,eɪt] *v.t.* сдира́ть, содра́ть ко́жу с+*g.*; (*fig.*) разн|оси́ть, -ести́.

excoriation [eks,kɔ:rɪ'eɪʃ(ə)n] *n.* сдира́ние ко́жи; (*fig.*) разно́с.

excrement ['ekskrɪmənt] *n.* экскреме́нты (*m. pl.*).

excrescence [ɪk'skres(ə)ns] *n.* наро́ст.

excreta [ek'skri:tə, ɪk-] *n.* (*pl.*, *physiol.*) экскреме́нты (*m. pl.*), выделе́ния (*nt. pl.*).

excrete [ɪk'skri:t] *v.t.* выделя́ть, вы́делить.

excretion [ɪk'skri:ʃ(ə)n] *n.* экскре́ция, выделе́ние.

excret|ive [ɪk'skri:tɪv], **-ory** [ɪk'skri:tərɪ] *adjs.* экскрето́рный, выдели́тельный.

excruciate [ɪk'skru:ʃɪ,eɪt] *v.t.* (*fig.*) терза́ть (*impf.*); му́чить (*impf.*).

excruciating [ɪk'skru:ʃɪ,eɪtɪŋ] *adj.* мучи́тельный.

exculpate ['ekskʌl,peɪt] *v.t.* опра́вд|ывать, -а́ть.

exculpation [,ekskʌl'peɪʃ(ə)n] *n.* оправда́ние.

exculpatory [,eks'kʌlpətərɪ] *adj.* оправда́тельный.

excursion [ɪk'skɜ:ʃ(ə)n] *n.* (*trip*) экску́рсия; **make** (*or* **go on**) **an ~** идти́/пое́хать (*det.*) на экску́рсию; (*digression*, *interlude*) э́кскурс.

excursionist [ɪk'skɜ:ʃənɪst] *n.* экскурса́нт.

excursus [ek'skɜ:səs, ɪk-] *n.* э́кскурс.

excusable [ɪk'skju:zəb(ə)l] *adj.* прости́тельный, извини́тельный.

excusably [ɪk'skju:zəblɪ] *adv.*: **he was ~ annoyed** его́ раздраже́ние мо́жно бы́ло поня́ть.

excuse[1] [ɪk'skju:s, ek-] *n.* извине́ние, оправда́ние, отгово́рка; **he pleaded ignorance in ~ of his conduct** в оправда́ние своего́ поведе́ния он сосла́лся на незна́ние; **ignorance is no ~** незна́ние — не оправда́ние; **a lame, poor ~** сла́бая отгово́рка; **he was absent without ~** он отсу́тствовал без уважи́тельной причи́ны; **please make my ~s to the hostess** пожа́луйста, переда́йте мои́ извине́ния хозя́йке.

excuse[2] [ɪk'skju:z] *v.t.* **1.** (*justify*, *palliate*) опра́вд|ывать, -а́ть; **~ o.s.** прин|оси́ть, -ести́ извине́ния. **2.** (*forgive*) извин|я́ть, -и́ть; про|ща́ть, -сти́ть; **please ~ my coming late** (*or* **me for coming late**) извини́те, что я пришёл по́здно; **~ me, what time is it?** прости́те, кото́рый час?; **~ me, but you are wrong** прости́те, но вы непра́вы. **3.** (*dispense*, *release*): **I ~d him from attending** я позво́лил ему́ не прису́тствовать; **may I be ~d from coming?** могу́ я не приходи́ть?; **we ~d him the fee** мы освободи́ли его́ от упла́ты.

exeat ['eksɪ,æt] *n.* кратковре́менный о́тпуск; отпускно́й биле́т.

execrable ['eksɪkrəb(ə)l] *adj.* отврати́тельный.

execrate ['eksɪ,kreɪt] *v.t.* испы́т|ывать, -а́ть отвраще́ние к+*d.*

execration [,eksɪ'kreɪʃ(ə)n] *n.* омерзе́ние; **hold s.o. up to ~** выставля́ть, вы́ставить кого́-н. на всео́бщее порица́ние.

executable ['eksɪ,kju:təb(ə)l] *adj.* (*feasible*) исполни́мый, выполни́мый.

executant [ɪg'zekjʊt(ə)nt] *n.* исполни́тель (*m.*).

execute ['eksɪ,kju:t] *v.t.* **1.** (*carry out*) выполня́ть, вы́полнить; исп|олня́ть, -о́лнить; **~ a will** исп|олня́ть, -о́лнить завеща́ние. **2.** (*leg.*) оф|ормля́ть, -о́рмить. **3.** (*put to death*) казни́ть (*impf.*, *pf.*). **4.** (*music etc.*) исп|олня́ть, -о́лнить.

execution [,eksɪ'kju:ʃ(ə)n] *n.* **1.** (*carrying out*) исполне́ние, выполне́ние; **carry, put into ~** прив|оди́ть в исполне́ние. **2.** (*of music etc.*) исполне́ние. **3.** (*destructive effect*): **the artillery did great ~** артиллери́йский ого́нь произвёл больши́е разруше́ния. **4.** (*capital punishment*) казнь; **there were five ~s last year** в про́шлом году́ казни́ли пятеры́х.

executioner [,eksɪ'kju:ʃənə(r)] *n.* пала́ч.

executive [ɪg'zekjʊtɪv] *n.* (руководя́щий) рабо́тник; **chief ~** президе́нт (США); **the ~** (*sc. power*) исполни́тельная власть.

adj. **1.** (*executing laws etc.*) исполни́тельный; **the ~ branch of government** исполни́тельная власть. **2.** (*managing*) руководя́щий; **~ ability** администрати́вные спосо́бности; **~ session** (*US*, *closed session*) закры́тое заседа́ние.

executor[1] [ɪg'zekjʊtə(r)] *n.* (*one who carries out*) исполни́тель (*m.*).

executor[2] [ɪg'zekjʊtə(r)] *n.* (*of a will*) душеприка́зчик.

executrix [ɪg'zekjʊtrɪks] *n.* душеприка́зчица.

exegesis [,eksɪ'dʒi:sɪs] *n.* толкова́ние.

exegete ['eksɪ,dʒi:t] *n.* толкова́тель (*m.*).

exegetic [,eksɪ'dʒetɪk] *adj.* объясни́тельный.

exemplar [ɪg'zemplə(r), -plɑ:(r)] *n.* образе́ц, экземпля́р.

exemplary [ɪg'zemplərɪ] *adj.* приме́рный, образцо́вый.

exemplification [ɪg,zemplɪfɪ'keɪʃ(ə)n] *n.* приведе́ние приме́ров; приме́р.

exemplify [ɪg'zemplɪ,faɪ] *v.t.* (*illustrate by example*) прив|оди́ть, -ести́ приме́р +*g.*; (*be an example of*) служи́ть, по- приме́ром +*g.*

exempt [ɪg'zempt] *adj.* освобождённый, свобо́дный (*от чего*).

v.t. освобожда́ть, -ди́ть.

exemption [ɪg'zempʃ(ə)n] *n.* освобожде́ние (*от чего*).

exequatur [,eksɪ'kweɪtə(r)] *n.* (*consul's*) экзеквату́ра.

exequies ['eksɪkwɪz] *n.* (*liter.*) по́хор|оны (*pl.*, *g.* -он).

exercise ['eksə,saɪz] *n.* **1.** (*use*, *exertion*) проявле́ние (*чего*); вы́казывание (*чего*); **the ~ of patience is essential** ва́жно прояви́ть терпе́ние. **2.** (*physical activity*) заря́дка, упражне́ние, моцио́н; **you should take more ~** вам ну́жно де́лать бо́льше физи́ческих упражне́ний. **3.** (*mental or physical training*) упражне́ние, трениро́вка; ~ **bicycle** велотренажёр; **slimming ~s** упражне́ния для сниже́ния ве́са. **4.** (*trial operation*) уче́ние; **military ~s** строево́е уче́ние, вое́нная игра́; (*fig.*): **the object of the ~** цель э́того предприя́тия. **5.** (*US, ceremony*): **graduation ~s** выпускно́й акт.

v.t. **1.** (*exert, use*) выка́зывать, вы́казать; прояв|ля́ть, -и́ть; ~ **authority** примен|я́ть, -и́ть власть; ~ **one's rights** осуществ|ля́ть, -и́ть свои́ права́. **2.** (*physically*) упражня́ть (*impf.*); ~ **a dog** прогу́ливать (*impf.*) соба́ку. **3.** (*worry, perplex*) беспоко́ить (*impf.*), трево́жить (*impf.*); **the problem ~d our minds** пробле́ма заста́вила нас заду́маться.

v.i. упражня́ться (*impf.*).

cpd. **~-book** *n.* (учени́ческая) тетра́дь.

exert [ɪg'zɜːt] *v.t.* осуществ|ля́ть, -и́ть; ока́з|ывать, -а́ть; ~ **influence** ока́з|ывать, -а́ть влия́ние; ~ **o.s.** постара́ться (*pf.*).

exertion [ɪg'zɜːʃ(ə)n] *n.* напряже́ние, уси́лие; **the ~ of patience** проявле́ние терпе́ния; **the ~s of travelling** тя́готы (*f. pl.*) пути́.

exeunt omnes [nd'eksɪʌnt 'ɒmneɪz] (*stage direction*) (все) ухо́дят.

ex gratia [eks 'greɪʃə] *adj.* доброво́льный; **an ~ payment** доброво́льная упла́та.

exhalation [ˌekshə'leɪʃ(ə)n] *n.* (*mist, vapour*) пар; испаре́ние; (*act of exhaling*) выдыха́ние.

exhale [eks'heɪl, ɪgz-] *v.t.* (*give off*) испус|ка́ть, -ти́ть.

v.i. (*breathe out*) выдыха́ть, вы́дохнуть.

exhaust [ɪg'zɔːst] *n.* (*apparatus*) вы́хлоп, вы́пуск; (*expelled gas*) отрабо́танный газ; ~ **pipe** выхлопна́я труба́; **I could smell the ~** я почу́вствовал за́пах выхлопны́х га́зов.

v.t. **1.** (*consume, tire out*) истощ|а́ть, -и́ть; изнур|я́ть, -и́ть; **my patience is ~ed** моё терпе́ние исся́кло; **the climb ~ed us** восхожде́ние изнури́ло нас; **be ~ed** изнем|ога́ть, -о́чь; **I feel ~ed** я соверше́нно без сил. **2.** (*empty*) исче́рп|ывать, -ать; ~ **a well** вы́черпать (*pf.*) коло́дец до дна́; ~ **land** истощ|а́ть, -и́ть зе́млю. **3.** (*explore thoroughly*) исче́рп|ывать, -ать.

exhaustibility [ɪgˌzɔːstɪ'bɪlɪtɪ] *n.* истощи́мость, утомля́емость.

exhaustible [ɪg'zɔːstɪb(ə)l] *adj.* истощи́мый.

exhausting [ɪg'zɔːstɪŋ] *adj.* изнури́тельный, изнуря́ющий, утоми́тельный.

exhaustion [ɪg'zɔːstʃ(ə)n] *n.* изнуре́ние, истоще́ние; (*fatigue*) переутомле́ние, изнеможе́ние.

exhaustive [ɪg'zɔːstɪv] *adj.* исче́рпывающий, всесторо́нний.

exhaustiveness [ɪg'zɔːstɪvnɪs] *n.* всесторо́нность, полнота́.

exhibit [ɪg'zɪbɪt] *n.* (*in museum etc.*) экспона́т; (*leg.*) веще́ственное доказа́тельство.

v.t. **1.** (*e.g. painting*) экспони́ровать (*impf.*, *pf.*); выставля́ть, вы́ставить; (*e.g. film*) демонстри́ровать, про-. **2.** (*fig., display*) прояв|ля́ть, -и́ть.

exhibition [ˌeksɪ'bɪʃ(ə)n] *n.* (*public show*) вы́ставка; (*showing*) пока́з; **be on ~** быть вы́ставленным; **he made an ~ of himself** он сде́лал себя́ посме́шищем; (*scholarship*) стипе́ндия.

exhibitioner [ˌeksɪ'bɪʃənə(r)] *n.* стипендиа́т.

exhibitionism [ˌeksɪ'bɪʃəˌnɪz(ə)m] *n.* (*showing off*) рисо́вка; хвастовство́; (*med.*) эксгибициони́зм.

exhibitionist [eksɪ'bɪʃənɪst] *n.* хвасту́н (*coll.*); вообража́ла (*c.g.*); (*med.*) эксгибициони́ст.

exhibitionistic [eksɪˌbɪʃə'nɪstɪk] *adj.* (*ostentatious*) показно́й.

exhibitor [ɪg'zɪbɪtə(r)] *n.* экспоне́нт.

exhilarat|e [ɪg'zɪləˌreɪt] *v.t.* весели́ть, раз-; ра́довать, об-; **he felt ~ed** он был в припо́днятом настрое́нии; **~ing news** ра́достное изве́стие.

exhilaration [ɪgˌzɪlə'reɪʃ(ə)n] *n.* весе́лье; прия́тное возбужде́ние.

exhort [ɪg'zɔːt] *v.t.* приз|ыва́ть, -ва́ть (*кого к чему*); увещева́ть (*impf.*).

exhortation [ˌegzɔː'teɪʃ(ə)n, ˌeks-] *n.* призы́в, увещева́ние.

exhumation [eksˌhjuː'meɪʃ(ə)n, ɪgˌzjuː'meɪʃ(ə)n] *n.* эксгума́ция, извлече́ние тру́па из земли́; (*fig.*) раска́пывание.

exhume [eks'hjuːm, ɪg'zjuːm] *v.t.* эксгуми́ровать (*impf.*, *pf.*); (*fig.*) раск|а́пывать, -опа́ть.

exigenc|e ['eksɪdʒ(ə)ns], **-y** ['eksɪdʒənsɪ, ɪg'zɪdʒ-] *nn.* нетло́жность, кра́йность; кра́йняя необходи́мость; **the ~ies of the time** веле́ние вре́мени.

exigent ['eksɪdʒ(ə)nt] *adj.* (*urgent*) неотло́жный, сро́чный; (*demanding*) тре́бовательный.

exiguity [egˌzɪ'gjuːɪtɪ, ɪg-] *n.* ску́дость, незначи́тельность.

exiguous [eg'zɪgjʊəs, ɪg-] *adj.* ску́дный, незначи́тельный, ма́лый.

exile ['eksaɪl, 'egz-] *n.* **1.** (*banishment*) изгна́ние; ссы́лка; **send into ~** ссыла́ть, сосла́ть; **place of ~** ме́сто ссы́лки. **2.** (*pers.*) изгна́нник; ссы́льный.

v.t. изг|оня́ть, -на́ть; ссыла́ть, сосла́ть.

exist [ɪg'zɪst] *v.i.* **1.** (*be, live*) существова́ть (*impf.*), жить (*impf.*); **he ~s on £50 per week** он существу́ет на 50 фу́нтов в неде́лю. **2.** (*be found*) име́ться, стреча́ться, находи́ться (*all impf.*); **lime ~s in many soils** и́звесть встреча́ется во мно́гих по́чвах.

existence [ɪg'zɪst(ə)ns] *n.* существова́ние; (*presence*) нали́чие; (*life*) жизнь; **in ~** существу́ющий, нали́чный, име́ющийся; **the largest ship in ~** са́мый большо́й кора́бль из всех существу́ющих.

existent [ɪg'zɪst(ə)nt] *adj.* существу́ющий.

existential [ˌegzɪ'stenʃ(ə)l] *adj.* экзистенциа́льный.

existentialism [ˌegzɪ'stenʃəˌlɪz(ə)m] *n.* экзистенциали́зм.

existentialist [ˌegzɪ'stenʃəlɪst] *n.* экзистенциали́ст.

exit ['eksɪt, 'egzɪt] *n.* вы́ход; **make one's ~** у|ходи́ть, -йти́.

v.i. у|ходи́ть, -йти́; ~ **Macbeth** (*stage direction*) Макбе́т ухо́дит.

ex-libris [eks'liːbrɪs] *n.* экслибрис.

exodus ['eksədəs] *n.* ма́ссовый отъе́зд/ухо́д; **E~** (*bibl.*) Исхо́д, Втора́я кни́га Моисе́ева.

ex officio [ˌeks ə'fɪʃɪəʊ] *adv. & adj.* по до́лжности.

exogamous [ek'sɒgəməs] *adj.* экзога́мный.

exogamy [ek'sɒgəmɪ] *n.* экзога́мия.

exonerate [ɪg'zɒnəˌreɪt] *v.t.* опра́вд|ывать, -а́ть; реабилити́ровать (*impf.*, *pf.*); сн|има́ть, -я́ть обвине́ние с+*g.* (*в чем*).

exoneration [ɪgˌzɒnə'reɪʃ(ə)n] *n.* оправда́ние, реабилита́ция.

exophthalmic [ˌeksɒf'θælmɪk] *adj.*: ~ **goitre** базе́дова боле́знь.

exorbitance [ɪg'zɔːbɪtəns] *n.* непоме́рность, чрезме́рность.

exorbitant [ɪg'zɔːbɪt(ə)nt] *adj.* непоме́рный, чрезме́рный.

exorcism ['eksɔːˌsɪz(ə)m] *n.* изгна́ние злых ду́хов.

exorcist ['eksɔːsɪst] *n.* заклина́тель (*m.*).

exorcize ['eksɔːˌsaɪz] *v.t.* изг|оня́ть, -на́ть злых ду́хов из+*g.*

exordium [ek'sɔːdɪəm] *n.* введе́ние.

exotic [ɪg'zɒtɪk] *adj.* экзоти́ческий.

expand [ɪk'spænd] *v.t.* (*lit., fig.*) расш|иря́ть, -и́рить; **heat ~s metals** при нагрева́нии мета́ллы расширя́ются; **the essay was ~ed into a book** о́черк был развёрнут в кни́гу.

v.i. расш|иря́ться, -и́риться; увели́чи|ваться, -ться в объёме; **trade ~ed** торго́вля расши́рилась; **his face ~ed in a smile** его́ лицо́ расплыло́сь в улы́бке; **he ~ed after a few drinks** он разошёлся по́сле не́скольких рю́мок.

expanse [ɪk'spæns] *n.* протяже́ние; широ́кое простра́нство; расшире́ние; (*of sea, sky etc.*) просто́р; ширь; **a broad ~ of brow** высо́кий лоб.

expansibility [ɪkˌspænsɪ'bɪlɪtɪ] *n.* растяжи́мость.

expansible [ɪk'spænsɪb(ə)l] *adj.* растяжи́мый.

expansion [ɪk'spænʃ(ə)n] *n.* расшире́ние, растяже́ние; (*pol.*) экспа́нсия; (*increase*) подъём; **chest ~** расшире́ние грудно́й клётки; **territorial ~** территориа́льные захва́ты (*m. pl.*).

expansionism [ɪk'spænʃ(ə)ˌnɪz(ə)m] *n.* (*pol.*) экспансиони́зм.

expansionist(ic) [ɪkˌspænʃ(ə)'nɪstɪk] *adj.* (*pol.*) экспансиони́стский.

expansive [ɪk'spænsɪv] *adj.* (*extensive*) обши́рный; (*of pers.*) экспанси́вный; **an ~ smile** широ́кая улы́бка.

expansiveness [ɪk'spænsɪvnɪs] *n.* (*of pers.*) экспанси́вность.

ex parte [eks 'pɑːtɪ] (*leg.*) исходя́щий от одно́й лишь стороны́; ~ **A.B.** от и́мени А.Б.

expatiate [ɪk'speɪʃɪˌeɪt] *v.i.* распространя́ться (*impf.*) (*на какую-н. тему*); (*coll.*) разглаго́льствовать (*impf.*).

expatiation [ɪkˌspeɪʃɪ'eɪʃ(ə)n] *n.* разглаго́льствование; простра́нное рассужде́ние.

expatriate[1] [eks'pætrıət, -'peıtrıət] *n. & adj.* экспатриа́нт (*fem.* -ка), экспатрии́рованный; **an ~ American** америка́нец-экспатриа́нт.

expatriate[2] [eks'pætrı,eıt, -'peıtrı,eıt] *v.t.* (*banish*) экспатрии́ровать (*impf.*, *pf.*); изг|оня́ть, -на́ть из оте́чества; **~ o.s.** (*leave one's country*) эмигри́ровать (*impf.*, *pf.*); (*renounce allegiance*) отка́з|ываться, -а́ться от гражда́нства.

expatriation [eks,pætrı'eıʃ(ə)n, -,peıtrı'eıʃ(ə)n] *n.* (*banishing*) экспатриа́ция; изгна́ние из оте́чества; (*emigration*) эмигра́ция; (*renouncing nationality*) отка́з от гражда́нства.

expect [ık'spekt] *v.t.* **1.** (*of future or probable event*) ждать (*impf.*), ожида́ть (*impf.*) +*g.*; **I ~ to see him** я рассчи́тываю встре́титься с ним; я жду встре́чи с ним; **I ~ him to dinner** я жду его́ к обе́ду; **you would ~ them to have thought of that** каза́лось бы, они́ должны́ бы́ли об э́том поду́мать; **just as I ~ed** так я и ду́мал. **2.** (*require*) ожида́ть (*impf.*) +*g.*; рассчи́тывать (*impf.*) на+*a.*; тре́бовать (*impf.*) +*g.*; **I ~ you to be punctual** я наде́юсь/рассчи́тываю, что вы бу́дете пунктуа́льны. **3.** (*suppose*) полага́ть (*impf.*); предполага́ть (*impf.*); **I ~ you are hungry** я полага́ю, что вы голодны́; вы, наве́рное/вероя́тно, голодны́. **4.: she is ~ ing** (*coll.*, *pregnant*) она́ ожида́ет ребёнка.

expectancy [ık'spektənsı] *n.* ожида́ние; предвкуше́ние.

expectant [ık'spekt(ə)nt] *adj.* выжида́ющий; **an ~ mother** бу́дущая мать.

expectation [,ekspek'teıʃ(ə)n] *n.* **1.** (*anticipation*) ожида́ние; **in ~ of** в ожида́нии +*g.*; **contrary to ~** вопреки́ ожида́ниям; **come up to ~s** оправда́ть (*pf.*) ожида́ния; **fall short of ~s** не оправда́ть (*pf.*) ожида́ний. **2.** (*prospect*) наде́жда; **a young man with ~s** молодо́й челове́к с ви́дами на насле́дство; **~ of life** вероя́тная продолжи́тельность жи́зни.

expectorant [ek'spektərənt] *n.* (*med.*) отха́ркивающее сре́дство.

expectorate [ek'spektə,reıt] *v.t. & i.* (*spit*) отха́рк|ивать(ся), -нуть(ся).

expectoration [ek,spektə'reıʃ(ə)n] *n.* отха́ркивание.

expedienc|e [ık'spi:dıəns], **-y** [ık'spi:dıənsı] *nn.* (*suitability*) целесообра́зность; (*promptness*) быстрота́; (*self interest*) вы́годность; (*pej.*) оппортуни́зм.

expedient [ık'spi:dıənt] *n.* приём, спо́соб.

adj. целесообра́зный; (*advantageous*) вы́годный.

expedite ['ekspı,daıt] *v.t.* уск|оря́ть, -о́рить.

expedition [,ekspı'dıʃ(ə)n] *n.* (*journey*) экспеди́ция; (*promptness*) быстрота́.

expeditionary [,ekspı'dıʃənərı] *adj.* экспедицио́нный; **~ force** экспедицио́нные войска́.

expeditious [,ekspı'dıʃəs] *adj.* бы́стрый, ско́рый.

expeditiousness [,ekspı'dıʃəsnıs] *n.* быстрота́, ско́рость.

expel [ık'spel] *v.t.* (*emit*) пос|ыла́ть, -ла́ть; (*compel to leave*) исключ|а́ть, -и́ть; выгоня́ть, вы́гнать; (*dislodge, e.g. troops*) изг|оня́ть, -на́ть.

expellee [,ıkspe'li:] *n.* (*from school*) исключённый; (*from country*) изгна́нник.

expend [ık'spend] *v.t.* (*capital*) расхо́довать, из-; тра́тить, ис-; (*ammunition*) расхо́довать, из-; (*time, efforts*) тра́тить, ис-/по-.

expendable [ık'spendəb(ə)l] *adj.* (*of acceptable sacrifice*) ≃ спи́санный в расхо́д.

expenditure [ık'spendıtʃə(r)] *n.* расхо́д, тра́та; **~ of energy** затра́та эне́ргии.

expense [ık'spens] *n.* **1.** (*monetary cost*) расхо́д; **at my ~** (*lit.*) за мой счёт; **at public ~** за казённый счёт; **go to ~** нести́ (*det.*) расхо́ды; **put s.o. to ~** ввести́ (*pf.*) кого́-н. в расхо́д; **spare no ~** не жале́ть (*impf.*) расхо́дов; **~ account** отчёт о понесённых расхо́дах; счёт подотчётных сумм; **travelling ~s** доро́жные расхо́ды. **2.** (*detriment*): **he became famous at the ~ of his health** он приобрёл изве́стность цено́й своего́ здоро́вья; **a joke at my ~** шу́тка на мой счёт; **idealism at others' ~** идеали́зм за чужо́й счёт.

expensive [ık'spensıv] *adj.* дорого́й, дорогосто́ящий; **he has ~ tastes** у него́ вкус к дороги́м веща́м; **an ~ education** образова́ние, сто́ившее больши́х де́нег.

expensiveness [ık'spensıvnıs] *n.* дорогови́зна.

experience [ık'spıərıəns] *n.* **1.** (*process of gaining knowledge etc.*) о́пыт; **we learn by ~** мы у́чимся на со́бственном о́пыте; **I know that from ~** я зна́ю э́то по о́пыту. **2.** (*event*) слу́чай; **an unpleasant ~** неприя́тный слу́чай.

v.t. испы́т|ывать, -а́ть; переж|ива́ть, -и́ть.

experienced [ık'spıərıənst] *adj.* о́пытный, све́дущий; квалифици́рованный, со ста́жем.

experiential [ık,spıərı'enʃ(ə)l] *adj.* эмпири́ческий.

experiment [ık'sperımənt, -,ment] *n.* экспериме́нт, о́пыт; **learn sth. by ~** убежда́ться (*impf.*) в чём-н. на основа́нии о́пыта.

v.i. эксперименти́ровать (*impf.*).

experimental [ık,sperı'ment(ə)l] *adj.* эксперимента́льный, про́бный; **at the ~ stage** на ста́дии экспериме́нта.

experimentation [ık,sperımen'teıʃ(ə)n] *n.* эксперименти́рование.

experimenter [ık'sperı,mentə(r)] *n.* эксперимента́тор.

expert ['ekspɜ:t] *n.* económ экспе́рт, знато́к, специали́ст (*по чему*); **a chemical ~** специали́ст-хи́мик; **she is an ~ with her needle** она́ иску́сная швея́.

adj. квалифици́рованный; **an ~ driver** о́пытный шофёр; **~ advice** сове́т специали́ста; **he is ~ at persuading people** он ма́стер угова́ривать.

expertise [,ekspɜ:'ti:z] *n.* (*skill, knowledge*) компете́нтность, квалифика́ция, о́пыт.

expertness ['ekspɜ:tnıs] *n.* высо́кая квалифика́ция.

expiable ['ekspıəb(ə)l] *adj.* искупи́мый.

expiate ['ekspı,eıt] *v.t.* искуп|а́ть, -и́ть.

expiation [,ekspı'eıʃ(ə)n] *n.* искупле́ние.

expiatory ['ekspıətərı, 'ekspı,eıtərı] *adj.* искупи́тельный.

expiration [,ekspı'reıʃ(ə)n] *n.* (*breathing out*) вы́дох; (*expiry*) истече́ние (*срока*).

expiratory [ık'spaıərətərı] *adj.* экспирато́рный, выдыха́тельный.

expire [ık'spaıə(r)] *v.i.* **1.** (*breathe out*) выдыха́ть, вы́дохнуть. **2.** (*of period, truce, licence etc.*) ист|ека́ть, -е́чь. **3.** (*die*) уг|аса́ть, -а́снуть.

expiry [ık'spaıərı] *n.* истече́ние (сро́ка).

explain [ık'spleın] *v.t.* объясн|я́ть, -и́ть; изъясн|я́ть, -и́ть; **~ o.s.** (*make o.s. clear*) разъясни́ть (*pf.*) свою́ то́чку зре́ния; (*account for one's conduct*) опра́вд|ываться, -а́ться; **~ sth. away** на|ходи́ть, -йти́ объясне́ние (*неудобному факту*); отгов|а́риваться, -ори́ться от чего́-н.

explainable [ık'spleınəb(ə)l] *adj.* объясни́мый.

explanation [,eksplə'neıʃ(ə)n] *n.* объясне́ние; **in (by way of) ~** в ка́честве объясне́ния.

explanatory [ık'splænətərı] *adj.* объясни́тельный.

expletive [ık'spli:tıv] *n.* (*oath*) бра́нное выраже́ние; (*fill-in*) вставно́е сло́во.

explicable [ık'splıkəb(ə)l, 'ek-] *adj.* объясни́мый.

explicit [ık'splısıt] *adj.* я́сный, чёткий, то́чный; (*of pers.*) прямо́й.

explicitness [ık'splısıtnıs] *n.* я́сность, чёткость, то́чность; (*of pers.*) прямота́.

explode [ık'spləʊd] *v.t.* вз|рыва́ть, -орва́ть; (*fig.*): **~ a theory** опров|ерга́ть, -е́ргнуть тео́рию.

v.i. вз|рыва́ться, -орва́ться; (*fig.*): **he ~d with rage/laughter** он разрази́лся гне́вом/сме́хом.

exploit[1] ['eksplɔıt] *n.* по́двиг.

exploit[2] [ık'splɔıt] *v.t.* (*use or develop economically*) разраб|а́тывать, -о́тать; эксплуати́ровать (*impf.*). **2.** (*an advantage etc.*) по́льзоваться, вос- +*i.*; испо́льзовать (*impf.*, *pf.*). **3.** (*a pers.*) эксплуати́ровать (*impf.*).

exploitable [ık'splɔıtəb(ə)l] *adj.* го́дный для разрабо́тки.

exploitation [,eksplɔı'teıʃ(ə)n] *n.* разрабо́тка; эксплуата́ция (*also of pers.*).

exploitative [ık'splɔıtətıv] *adj.* эксплуата́торский, эксплуатацио́нный.

exploiter [ık'splɔıtə(r)] *n.* эксплуата́тор.

exploration [,eksplə'reıʃ(ə)n] *n.* (*geog.*) иссле́дование; (*of a wound etc.*) зонда́ж; (*of possibilities etc.*) изуче́ние.

exploratory [ık'splɒrətərı] *adj.* иссле́довательский; **~ talks** предвари́тельные перегово́ры.

explore [ık'splɔ:(r)] *v.t.* **1.** (*geog.*) иссле́довать (*impf.*, *pf.*).

2. (*possibilities etc.*) изуч|а́ть, -и́ть. 3. (*wound etc.*) зонди́ровать (*impf.*).

explorer [ɪk'splɔːrə(r)] *n.* иссле́дователь (*m.*); (*instrument*) зонд; **Polar ~** поля́рник; поля́рный иссле́дователь.

explosion [ɪk'spləʊʒ(ə)n] *n.* (*of bomb etc.*) взрыв; (*of rage etc.*) вспы́шка; (*fig.*): **population ~** бу́рный рост народонаселе́ния, демографи́ческий взрыв.

explosive [ɪk'spləʊsɪv] *n.* взры́вчатое вещество́; **high ~** дробя́щее взры́вчатое вещество́.

adj. взры́вчатый, взрывно́й; **~ bomb** фуга́сная бо́мба; **~ bullet** разрывна́я пу́ля; (*fig.*) вспы́льчивый.

explosiveness [ɪk'spləʊsɪvnɪs] *n.* взрыва́емость.

exponent [ɪk'spəʊnənt] *n.* 1. (*advocate*) сторо́нник; представи́тель (*m.*). 2. (*math.*) показа́тель (*m.*) сте́пени.

exponential [,ekspə'nenʃ(ə)l] *adj.* (*math.*) экспоненциа́льный, показа́тельный.

export[1] ['ekspɔːt] *n.* э́кспорт, вы́воз; **~ duty** э́кспортная по́шлина; **~ drive** э́кспортная кампа́ния; **~s increased in value** це́нность/сто́имость э́кспорта возросла́; **~s amounted to ...** э́кспорт соста́вил...; **sugar is an important ~** са́хар — ва́жная статья́ э́кспорта.

export[2] [ek'spɔːt, 'ek-] *v.t.* экспорти́ровать (*impf., pf.*); вывози́ть, вы́везти.

exportable [ek'spɔːtəb(ə)l] *adj.* экспорти́руемый; го́дный на э́кспорт.

exportation [,ekspɔː'teɪʃ(ə)n] *n.* экспорти́рование.

exporter [ek'spɔːtə(r)] *n.* экспортёр.

expose [ɪk'spəʊz] *v.t.* 1. (*physically*) выставля́ть, вы́ставить; **~ one's body to sunlight** подст|авля́ть, -а́вить те́ло со́лнцу; **~ o.s.** (*indecently*) обнаж|а́ться, -и́ться; **~d to the weather** незащищённый от непого́ды; **~ an infant** (*to die*) подки́|дывать, -нуть ребёнка; бр|оса́ть, -о́сить ребёнка на ве́рную смерть; **an ~d position** (*mil.*) незащищённая пози́ция. 2. (*fig., subject*) подв|ерга́ть, -е́ргнуть; **he was ~d to insult** его́ сде́лали мише́нью для оскорбле́ний. 3. (*display*) выставля́ть, вы́ставить. 4. (*fig., unfold*) раскр|ыва́ть, -ы́ть. 5. (*unmask*) разоблач|а́ть, -и́ть. 6. (*phot.*) экспони́ровать (*impf.*); дава́ть (*impf.*) вы́держку +*d*.

exposé [ek'spəʊzeɪ] *n.* (*exposition*) экспозе́ (*indecl.*).

exposition [,ekspə'zɪʃ(ə)n] *n.* (*setting forth facts etc.*) изложе́ние; (*exhibition*) экспози́ция, вы́ставка.

expository [ɪk'spɒzɪtərɪ] *adj.* объясни́тельный.

ex post facto [,eks pəʊst 'fæktəʊ] *adj. & adv.* пост фа́ктум.

expostulate [ɪk'spɒstjʊ,leɪt] *v.i.*: **~ with s.o.** увещева́ть (*impf.*) кого́-н.; усо́вещивать (*impf.*) кого́-н.

expostulation [ɪk,spɒstjʊ'leɪʃ(ə)n] *n.* увещева́ние.

expostulatory [ɪk'spɒstjʊlətərɪ] *adj.* увещева́тельный.

exposure [ɪk'spəʊʒə(r)] *n.* 1. (*physical*): **~ to light** выставле́ние на свет; **indecent ~** обнаже́ние; **he died of ~** он поги́б от хо́лода; **house with a southern ~** дом о́кнами на юг; (*of infants*) оставле́ние на произво́л судьбы́. 2. (*subjection*): **~ to ridicule** выставле́ние на посме́шище. 3. (*of goods for sale*) вы́ставка. 4. (*unmasking*) разоблаче́ние. 5. (*phot.*) экспози́ция; **~ meter** экспоно́метр.

expound [ɪk'spaʊnd] *v.t.* (*a theory*) изл|ага́ть, -ожи́ть; (*a text*) толкова́ть (*impf.*).

express[1] [ɪk'spres] *n.* (**~** *train*) экспре́сс; курье́рский по́езд.

adj. 1. (*urgent, high-speed*) сро́чный; **~ letter** сро́чное письмо́; **~ mail** э́кстренная по́чта; **~ messenger** на́рочный; **~ rifle** винто́вка с высо́кой нача́льной ско́ростью. 2. (*US, forwarding*): **~ company** ча́стная тра́нспортная конто́ра.

v.t. отпр|авля́ть, -а́вить с на́рочным; отпр|авля́ть, -а́вить че́рез тра́нспортную конто́ру.

adv. сро́чно, спе́шно; с на́рочным; **the goods were sent ~** (*urgently*) това́р был отпра́влен большо́й ско́ростью.

express[2] [ɪk'spres] *adj.* 1. (*clear*) чёткий; **~ orders** чёткие приказа́ния; **~ consent** пря́мо вы́раженное согла́сие. 2. (*exact, specific*) то́чный, осо́бенный; **for the ~ purpose of** со специа́льной це́лью +*g*.

v.t. 1. (*press out*) выжима́ть, вы́жать. 2. (*show in words etc.*) выража́ть, вы́разить; **~ o.s.** выража́ться, вы́разиться; выска́зывать, вы́сказать; **not to be ~ed** (*inexpressible*) невырази́мый. 3.: **a cheque ~ed in francs** чек, вы́писанный во фра́нках.

expressible [ɪk'spresɪb(ə)l] *adj.* вырази́мый.

expression [ɪk'spreʃ(ə)n] *n.* 1. (*act of expressing*) выраже́ние; **past, beyond ~** невырази́мый; **give ~ to** выража́ть, вы́разить; **find ~** выража́ться, вы́разиться. 2. (*mus.*): **he plays with ~** он игра́ет вырази́тельно. 3. (*word, term*) выраже́ние (*also math.*); **a geographical ~** географи́ческое поня́тие.

expressionism [ɪk'spreʃə,nɪz(ə)m] *n.* экспрессиони́зм.

expressionist [ɪk,spreʃə'nɪst] *n.* экспрессиони́ст.

expressionistic [ɪk,spreʃə'nɪstɪk] *adj.* экспрессиони́стский.

expressive [ɪk'spresɪv] *adj.* вырази́тельный; **a look ~ of despair** взгляд, по́лный отча́яния.

expressiveness [ɪk'spresɪvnɪs] *n.* вырази́тельность.

expropriate [eks'prəʊprɪ,eɪt] *v.t.* (*pers.*) лиш|а́ть, -и́ть со́бственности; (*property*) экспроприи́ровать (*impf., pf.*).

expropriation [eks,prəʊprɪ'eɪʃ(ə)n] *n.* экспроприа́ция; лише́ние со́бственности.

expulsion [ɪk'spʌlʃ(ə)n] *n.* изгна́ние; исключе́ние.

expunge [ɪk'spʌndʒ] *v.t.* вычёркивать, вы́черкнуть.

expurgate ['ekspə,geɪt] *v.t.*: **~ a book** исключ|а́ть, -и́ть (*or* изыма́ть, изъя́ть) нежела́тельные места́ из кни́ги.

expurgation [,ekspə'geɪʃ(ə)n] *n.* исключе́ние/изъя́тие нежела́тельных мест из кни́ги.

exquisite ['ekskwɪzɪt, ek'skwɪzɪt] *n.* (*fop*) фат, щёголь (*m.*).

adj. (*perfected*) утончённый; (*delicate*) то́нкий; **~ sensibility** обострённая чувстви́тельность; **~ pain** о́страя боль; **~ torture** изощрённая пы́тка.

exquisiteness [eks'kwɪzɪtnɪs] *n.* утончённость; (*of pain*) острота́.

ex-service [eks'sɜːvɪs] *adj.* демобилизо́ванный, отставно́й.

ex-serviceman [eks'sɜːvɪsmən] *n.* демобилизо́ванный; отставно́й вое́нный.

extant [ek'stænt, ɪk'st-, 'ekst(ə)nt] *adj.* сохрани́вшийся.

extemporaneous [ɪk,stempə'reɪnɪəs] *adj.* импровизи́рованный.

extempore [ɪk'stempərɪ] *adj.* импровизи́рованный.

adv. экспро́мтом.

extemporization [ɪks,tempəraɪ'zeɪʃ(ə)n] *n.* импровиза́ция.

extemporize [ɪk'stempə,raɪz] *v.t. & i.* и|мпровизи́ровать, сы-; **he ~d a speech** он произнёс импровизи́рованную речь.

extend [ɪk'stend] *v.t.* 1. (*stretch out*) протя́|гивать, -ну́ть; **~ a rope between two posts** натя́|гивать, -ну́ть верёвку ме́жду двумя́ столба́ми; **an ~ed battle-line** растя́нутая ли́ния фро́нта; **~ed order** (*mil.*) расчленённый строй. 2. (*offer, accord*) ока́з|ывать, -а́ть; **~ a welcome** выка́зывать, вы́казать раду́шие; раду́шно встр|еча́ть, -е́тить (*кого*). 3. (*make longer, wider or larger*) удлин|я́ть, -и́ть; расш|иря́ть, -и́рить; **~ a railway** продли́ть (*pf.*) железнодоро́жную ли́нию; **~ a table** (*by means of a leaf*) раздв|ига́ть, -и́нуть стол; **~ one's premises** расш|иря́ть, -и́рить помеще́ние. 4. (*prolong*) продл|ева́ть, -и́ть; **~ ones leave/passport** продл|ева́ть, -и́ть о́тпуск/па́спорт; **an ~ed** (*lengthy*) **visit** дли́тельный визи́т. 5. (*fig., enlarge, widen*) увели́чи|вать, -ть; расш|иря́ть, -и́рить; **~ one's influence** распростран|я́ть, -и́ть своё влия́ние; **an ~ed course in mathematics** расши́ренный курс матема́тики. 6. (*exert*): **~ o.s.** напр|яга́ться, -я́чься; стара́ться (*impf.*) изо всех сил; **we are fully ~ed** мы на преде́ле (на́ших) сил.

v.i. простира́ться (*impf.*); **the garden ~s to the river** сад простира́ется до реки́; **my leave ~s till Tuesday** мой о́тпуск продолжа́ется до вто́рника; **this rule ~s to first-year students** э́то пра́вило распространя́ется и на первоку́рсников.

exten|dible [ɪk'stendɪb(ə)l], **-sible** [ɪk'stensɪb(ə)l] *adjs.* (*e.g. table, ladder*) раздвижно́й.

extension [ɪk'stenʃ(ə)n] *n.* 1. (*extent*) протяже́ние. 2. (*stretching out*) вытя́гивание, удлине́ние. 3. (*enlarging in space or time*) расшире́ние, увеличе́ние; **~ of a railway** удлине́ние железнодоро́жной ли́нии; **an ~ railway** железнодоро́жная ве́тка; **~ ladder** раздвижна́я ле́стница; **~ of leave** продле́ние о́тпуска; **~ of time (to pay debt)** дополни́тельный срок (для упла́ты до́лга); **an ~ course in physics** дополни́тельный курс фи́зики. 4. (*additional*

part of building etc.) пристро́йка (к+*d.*). **5.** (*teleph.*) доба́вочный (но́мер); **my number is 5652, ~ 10** мой но́мер 5652, доба́вочный 10.
extensive [ɪk'stensɪv] *adj.* (*wide, far-reaching*) простра́нный; **an ~ park** обши́рный парк; **~ knowledge** обши́рные зна́ния; **~ plans** далеко́ иду́щие пла́ны; (*opp. intensive*) экстенси́вный.
extensiveness [ɪk'stensɪvnɪs] *n.* простра́нность; обши́рность.
extensor [ɪk'stensə(r)] *n.* (*also* **~ muscle**) разгиба́ющая мы́шца.
extent [ɪk'stent] *n.* **1.** (*phys. size, length etc.*) протяже́ние; **a vast ~ of marsh** обши́рное заболо́ченное простра́нство. **2.** (*fig., range*) разме́р; круг; диапазо́н; **~ of s.o.'s knowledge** круг чьих-н. зна́ний; **~ of damage** разме́р поврежде́ний; **he helped to the ~ of his resources** он помо́г в ме́ру свои́х возмо́жностей. **3.** (*degree*) сте́пень; **to some (***or* **a certain) ~** до не́которой/изве́стной сте́пени; **to a large ~** в значи́тельной ме́ре; **to the utmost ~** во всю ширь; **he is in debt to the ~ of £100** у него́ долги́ в разме́ре 100 фу́нтов; **I have never played golf to any ~** я со́бственно почти́ никогда́ не игра́л в гольф; **he went to the ~ of borrowing money** он пошёл да́же на то, что́бы заня́ть де́ньги.
extenuat|e [ɪk'stenjʊ,eɪt] *v.t.* преум|еньша́ть, -е́ньшить; **~e s.o.'s behaviour** опра́вдывать (*impf.*) чьё-н. поведе́ние; **~ing circumstances** смягча́ющие обстоя́тельства.
extenuation [ɪkstenjʊ'eɪʃ(ə)n] *n.* приуменьше́ние; оправда́ние.
exterior [ɪk'stɪərɪə(r)] *n.* (*of object*) вне́шняя сторона́; (*archit.*) экстерье́р; (*of pers.*) вне́шность; нару́жность.
adj. вне́шний.
exteriorize [ɪk'stɪərɪə,raɪz] = **externalize**
exterminate [ɪk'stɜ:mɪ,neɪt] *v.t.* (*disease; ideas*) искоренія́ть, -и́ть; (*people*) уничт|ожа́ть, -о́жить; (*people, vermin*) истреб|ля́ть, -и́ть.
extermination [ɪk,stɜ:mɪ'neɪʃ(ə)n] *n.* искорене́ние; уничтоже́ние; истребле́ние.
exterminator [ɪk'stɜ:mɪ,neɪtə(r)] *n.* (*pers., substance*) истреби́тель (*m.*).
external [ɪk'stɜ:n(ə)l] *n.* вне́шность; **the ~s of religion** вне́шняя сторона́ рели́гии; **judge by ~s** суди́ть (*impf.*) по вне́шнему ви́ду.
adj. вне́шний; **the ~ world** вне́шний мир; **~ affairs** иностра́нные дела́, вне́шние сноше́ния; **an ~ student** экстерн, зао́чни|к (*fem.* -ца); **for ~ use only** то́лько для нару́жного употребле́ния.
externalize [ɪk'stɜ:nə,laɪz] *v.t.* (*manifest*) прояв|ля́ть, -и́ть.
exterritorial [,eksterɪ'tɔ:rɪəl] = **extraterritorial**
extinct [ɪk'stɪŋkt] *adj.* (*of volcano*) поту́хший; (*of species, custom*) вы́мерший; (*of feelings etc.*) уга́сший; (*of title*) исче́знувший.
extinction [ɪk'stɪŋkʃ(ə)n] *n.* угаса́ние; (*of a disease*) ликвида́ция, искорене́ние; **he is bored to ~** он помира́ет/подыха́ет со ску́ки.
extinguish [ɪk'stɪŋgwɪʃ] *v.t.* (*light, fire*) гаси́ть, по-; (*hopes etc.*) уб|ива́ть, -и́ть; (*a debt*) пога|ша́ть, -си́ть.
extinguisher [ɪk'stɪŋgwɪʃə(r)] *n.* (*for candle*) гаси́льник; (*chemical apparatus*) огнетуши́тель (*m.*).
extirpate ['ekstə,peɪt] *v.t.* вырыва́ть, вы́рвать с ко́рнем; искорен|я́ть, -и́ть.
extirpation [,ekstə'peɪʃ(ə)n] *n.* искорене́ние.
extirpator ['ekstə,peɪtə(r)] *n.* экстирпа́тор.
extol [ɪk'stəʊl, ɪk'stɒl] *v.t.* превозн|оси́ть, -ести́.
extort [ɪk'stɔ:t] *v.t.* вымога́ть (*impf.*); выжима́ть, вы́жать.
extortion [ɪk'stɔ:ʃ(ə)n] *n.* вымога́тельство.
extortionate [ɪk'stɔ:ʃənət] *adj.* вымога́тельский.
extortioner [ɪk'stɔ:ʃənə(r)] *n.* вымога́тель (*m.*).
extra ['ekstrə] *n.* **1.** (*additional item*) что-н. дополни́тельное; **music is an ~** му́зыка преподаётся факультати́вно; **no ~s** без вся́ких припла́т; (*edition*) э́кстренный вы́пуск. **2.** (*minor performer*) стати́ст (*fem.* -ка).
adj. **1.** (*additional*) доба́вочный, дополни́тельный; **it costs £1, postage ~** э́то сто́ит 1 фунт без пересы́лки; **I paid an ~ £5** я заплати́л ли́шних 5 фу́нтов; **£5 ~** 5 фу́нтов дополни́тельно; **this sum is ~ to his wages** э́та су́мма выпла́чивается дополни́тельно к его́ за́работку. **2.** (*special*) осо́бый.
adv. сверх-, осо́бо; **~ strong** (*e.g. drink*) осо́бой кре́пости.
extra-atmospheric ['ekstrə-] *adj.* внеатмосфе́рный.
extra-cellular [,ekstrə'seljʊlə(r)] *adj.* внекле́точный.
extract[1] ['ekstrækt] *n.* **1.** (*concentrated substance*) экстра́кт; **beef ~** мясно́й экстра́кт. **2.** (*from book etc.*) вы́держка.
extract[2] [ɪk'strækt] *v.t.* (*cork*) выта́скивать, вы́тащить; (*tooth*) удал|я́ть, -и́ть; (*bullet from wound*) извл|ека́ть, -е́чь; (*information, admission*) вырыва́ть, вы́рвать; (*money*) вымога́ть (*impf.*); (*math.*) извл|ека́ть, -е́чь (*корень*); (*pleasure from a situation*) извл|ека́ть, -е́чь; **~ passages** (*from a book*) де́лать, с- вы́держки; (*juices etc.*) выжима́ть, вы́жать; **~ a book** (*make extracts from it*) выпи́сывать, вы́писать цита́ты из кни́ги.
extractable [ɪk'stræktəb(ə)l] *adj.* извлека́емый.
extraction [ɪk'strækʃ(ə)n] *n.* (*extracting*) извлече́ние; (*of tooth*) удале́ние, экстра́кция; (*descent, origin*) происхожде́ние.
extractive [ɪk'stræktɪv] *adj.*: **~ industries** добыва́ющие о́трасли промы́шленности.
extractor [ɪk'stræktə(r)] *n.* экстра́ктор; (*forceps*) щип|цы́ (*pl., g.* -о́в); **~ fan** вентиля́тор.
extra-curricular [,ekstrəkə'rɪkjʊlə(r)] *adj.* проводи́мый сверх уче́бного пла́на; внеаудито́рный, вне програ́ммы.
extraditable ['ekstrə,daɪtəb(ə)l] *adj.* (*pers.*) подлежа́щий вы́даче; (*crime*) обусло́вливающий вы́дачу.
extradite ['ekstrə,daɪt] *v.t.* (*hand over*) выдава́ть, вы́дать (*обвиняемого преступника*); (*obtain extradition of*) доб|ива́ться, -и́ться вы́дачи +*g*.
extradition [,ekstrə'dɪʃ(ə)n] *n.* вы́дача (престу́пника).
extragalactic [,ekstrəgə'læktɪk] *adj.* внегалакти́ческий
extra-judicial [,ekstrədʒu:'dɪʃ(ə)l] *adj.*: **~ confession** призна́ние, сде́ланное вне заседа́ния суда́.
extra-legal ['ekstrə-] *adj.* не предусмо́тренный зако́ном.
extra-marital [,ekstrə'mærɪt(ə)l] *adj.*: **~ affair** внебра́чная связь.
extramural [,ekstrə'mjʊər(ə)l] *adj.* (*outside city*) за́городный; (*acad.*): **~ student** ≃ вече́рни|к (*fem.* -ца).
extraneous [ɪk'streɪnɪəs] *adj.* посторо́нний, чужо́й.
extraordinariness [ɪkstrə'ɔ:dɪnərɪnɪs] *n.* (*strangeness*) стра́нность, необыча́йность.
extraordinary [ɪk'strɔ:dɪnərɪ, ,ekstrə'ɔ:dɪnərɪ] *adj.* чрезвыча́йный, необыча́йный, выдаю́щийся; **professor ~** экстраордина́рный профе́ссор.
extrapolate [ɪk'stræpə,leɪt] *v.t.* & *i.* (*math., fig.*) экстраполи́ровать (*impf., pf.*).
extrapolation [ɪk,stræpə'leɪʃ(ə)n] *n.* (*math.*) экстраполя́ция.
extrasensory [,ekstrə'sensərɪ] *adj.*: **~ perception** внечу́вственное восприя́тие.
extra-special ['ekstrə-] *adj.* чрезвыча́йный.
extraterrestrial [,ekstrətɪ'restrɪəl] *adj.* внеземно́й.
extraterritorial [,ekstrə,terɪ'tɔ:rɪəl] *adj.* (*also* **exterritorial**) экстерриториа́льный.
extraterritoriality [,ekstrə,terɪ,tɔ:rɪ'ælɪtɪ] *n.* экстерриториа́льность.
extra-uterine [,ekstrə-'ju:təraɪn] *adj.* внема́точный.
extravagance [ɪk'strævəgəns] *n.* изли́шество; экстрава́гантность; расточи́тельность.
extravagant [ɪk'strævəgənt] *adj.* **1.** (*excessive*) изли́шний. **2.** (*fantastic*) экстрава́гантный, сумасбро́дный. **3.** (*over-spending*) расточи́тельный; **he was ~ with the sugar** он расхо́довал сли́шком мно́го са́хара; **this method is ~ of one's time** э́тот ме́тод ведёт к чрезме́рной затра́те вре́мени.
extravaganza [ɪk,strævə'gænzə] *n.* фее́рия; (*fantastic behaviour*) экстрава́гантность.
extravasate [ɪk'strævə,seɪt] *v.i.* вытека́ть, вы́течь из сосу́дов в ткань.
extravasation [ɪk,strævə'seɪʃ(ə)n] *n.* кровоподтёк.
extravert ['ekstrə,vɜ:t] = **extrovert**
extreme [ɪk'stri:m] *n.* **1.** (*high degree*) кра́йность; **wearisome in the ~** в вы́сшей сте́пени ску́чный. **2.** (*of conduct etc.*) кра́йность; **he went to the opposite ~** он впал в другу́ю кра́йность; **he went to ~s to satisfy them** он пошёл на кра́йние ме́ры, что́бы угоди́ть им; **carry things to ~s**

впада́ть (*impf.*) в кра́йность. **3.** (*pl., opposing qualities etc.*): **~s of behaviour** кра́йности поведе́ния; **~s of heat and cold** экстрема́льно/кра́йне высо́кие и ни́зкие температу́ры; **~s meet** кра́йности схо́дятся. **4.** (*pl., math., of ratio or series*) кра́йние чле́ны (*m. pl.*).

adj. **1.** (*furthest, utmost, last*) кра́йний, преде́льный; **the ~ edge of the city** са́мая окра́ина го́рода; **(the one) on the ~ right** кра́йний спра́ва; (*in politics*) кра́йне пра́вый; **~ old age** глубо́кая ста́рость; **the ~ penalty of the law** вы́сшая ме́ра наказа́ния; **~ unction** (*relig.*) собо́рование. **2.** (*very great*) чрезвыча́йный. **3.** (*taking sth. to its highest pitch*) кра́йний, преде́льный; **an ~ fashion** (*in clothes*) экстрава́гантная мо́да.

extremely [ɪk'stri:mlɪ] *adv.* кра́йне.

extremeness [ɪk'stri:mnɪs] *n.* (*of measures etc.*) кра́йность.

extremism [ɪk'stri:mɪz(ə)m] *n.* экстреми́зм.

extremist [ɪk'stri:mɪst] *n.* экстреми́ст.

adj. экстреми́стский.

extremit|y [ɪk'stremɪtɪ] *n.* **1.** (*end, extreme point*) край. **2.** (*pl., hands and feet*) коне́чности (*f. pl.*). **3.** (*extreme quality*) кра́йность; **the ~y of his grief** безме́рность его́ го́ря. **4.** (*hardship*) кра́йность; **reduced to ~y** доведённый до кра́йности. **5.** (*pl., extreme measures*) кра́йние ме́ры (*f. pl.*); **go to ~ies** пойти́ (*pf.*) на кра́йние ме́ры.

extricable ['ekstrɪˌkəb(ə)l] *adj.* распу́тываемый.

extricate ['ekstrɪˌkeɪt] *v.t.* высвобожда́ть, вы́свободить; **~ o.s. from a difficulty** вы́путаться (*pf.*) из затрудне́ния.

extrication [ˌekstrɪ'keɪʃ(ə)n] *n.* высвобожде́ние, выпу́тывание; распу́тывание.

extrinsic [ek'strɪnsɪk] *adj.* посторо́нний; не прису́щий; несво́йственный.

extr|overt, -avert ['ekstrəˌvɜ:t] *n.* челове́к с откры́той нату́рой, экстрове́рт.

extrude [ɪk'stru:d] *v.t.* выта́лкивать, вы́толкнуть; вытесня́ть, вы́теснить.

extrusion [ɪk'stru:ʒ(ə)n] *n.* вытесне́ние, выта́лкивание.

exuberance [ɪg'zju:bərəns] *n.* (*profusion*) изоби́лие; (*of character*) экспанси́вность.

exuberant [ɪg'zju:bərənt] *adj.* (*of foliage etc.*) бу́йный; (*of imagination etc.*) бога́тый, бу́йный; (*of spirits etc.*) экспанси́вный.

exuberate [ɪg'zju:bəˌreɪt] *v.i.* (*fig.*) (*blossom*) процвета́ть (*impf.*); (*exult*) торжествова́ть (*impf.*).

exudation [ˌeksjʊ'deɪʃ(ə)n] *n.* выделе́ние; (*fluid*) экссуда́т.

exude [ɪg'zju:d] *v.i.* проступ|а́ть, -и́ть; выделя́ть, вы́делить; **he ~d cheerfulness** он излуча́л весе́лье.

exult [ɪg'zʌlt] *v.i.* торжествова́ть (*impf.*); ликова́ть (*impf.*).

exultant [ɪg'zʌltənt] *adj.* торжеству́ющий, лику́ющий.

exultation [ɪgˌzʌl'teɪʃ(ə)n] *n.* торжество́, ликова́ние.

eye [aɪ] *n.* **1.** (*organ of vision*) глаз; (*dim.*) глазо́к (*pl.* гла́зки); (*arch., poet.*) о́ко; **glass ~** стекля́нный глаз; **have a cast in one's ~** быть косогла́зым; **I can see well out of this ~** я хорошо́ ви́жу э́тим гла́зом; **I have sth. in my ~** мне что́-то попа́ло в глаз; **blind in one ~** криво́й; **evil ~** дурно́й глаз; **put the evil ~ on** сгла́зить (*pf.*). **2.** (*var. idioms*): **give s.o. a black ~** подби́ть (*pf.*) глаз кому́-н.; **~s right!/left!** (*mil.*) равне́ние напра́во/нале́во!; **have a straight ~** име́ть ве́рный глаз; **with the naked ~** невооружённым гла́зом; **with half an ~** одни́м глазко́м; **mind your ~!** (*look out*) бу́дьте осторо́жны!; **cock an ~** (*glance*) взгляну́ть (*pf.*); (*wink*) подми́г|ивать, -ну́ть; **in the twinkling of an ~** в мгнове́ние о́ка; **make ~s at s.o.; give s.o. the glad ~** (*coll.*) стро́ить (*impf.*) гла́зки кому́-н.; **be all ~s** гляде́ть (*impf.*) во все глаза́; **you can see that with half an ~** э́то ви́дно с пе́рвого взгля́да; **it leaps to the ~** э́то броса́ется в глаза́; **set, lay ~s on** зам|еча́ть, -е́тить; **fix, glue, rivet one's ~s on** не спуска́ть (*impf.*) глаз с+*g.*; уста́виться (*pf.*) на+*a.*; **keep an ~ on** (*e.g. a saucepan*) следи́ть (*impf.*) за+*i.*; (*e.g. children*) следи́ть (*impf.*) за+*i.*; присм|а́тривать, -отре́ть за+*i.*; (*the time*) следи́ть (*impf.*) за+*i.*; **keep one's ~s open, skinned, peeled** (*coll.*) смотре́ть (*impf.*) в о́ба; **take one's ~s off s.o./sth.** отв|оди́ть, -ести́ глаза́ от кого́/чего́-н.; **get one's ~ in** (*at games etc.*) наби́ть (*pf.*) ру́ку на+*p.*; **damn your ~s!** черт тебя́ побра́л/побери́!; **an ~ for an ~** о́ко за о́ко; **pull the wool over s.o.'s ~s** вт|ира́ть, -ере́ть очки́ кому́-н.; **under, before s.o.'s very ~s** на глаза́х у кого́-н.; **I would give my ~s to see it** я отда́л бы мно́гое, что́бы э́то уви́деть; **make s.o. open his ~s** (*with astonishment*) заста́вить (*pf.*) кого́-н. широко́ раскры́ть глаза́; **he has an ~ for colour** он чу́вствует цвет; **he has an ~ for the ladies** он зна́ет толк в же́нщинах; **pipe one's ~** (*coll.*) лить (*impf.*) слёзы; **cry one's ~s out** вы́плакать (*pf.*) все глаза́; **dry one's ~** осуши́ть (*pf.*) слёзы; **his ~s are bigger than his stomach** глаза́ у него́ завиду́щие; **wipe s.o.'s ~** (*at sport etc.*) (*coll.*) утере́ть (*pf.*) нос кому́-н.; **that's all my ~** (*coll.*) всё э́то вздор; **in the mind's ~** мы́сленным взо́ром; **I could not believe my ~s** я не мог пове́рить свои́м глаза́м; **he ran his ~ (or cast an ~) over the paper** он пробежа́л глаза́ми газе́ту; **feast one's ~s on** (*a sight*) наслажда́ться (*impf.*) (зре́лищем); **I caught her ~** я пойма́л её взгляд; **do s.o. in the ~** (*sl.*) наду́ть (*pf.*) кого́-н.; **it offends the ~** э́то ре́жет глаз; **easy on the ~** (*coll.*) прия́тной нару́жности; **~ of day** (*poet., sun*) «небе́сное о́ко»; **have ~s at the back of one's head** всё ви́деть/подмеча́ть (*impf.*); **have one's ~ on the ball** (*fig.*) быть начеку́; **see ~ to ~ with** сходи́ться (*impf.*) во взгля́дах с+*i.*; **up to the ~s in work** по́ уши в рабо́те; **I opened his ~s to the situation** я откры́л ему́ глаза́ на положе́ние веще́й; **he closed his ~s to the danger** он закрыва́л глаза́ на опа́сность; **turn a blind ~ to** смотре́ть (*impf.*) сквозь па́льцы на+*a.*; **in my ~s** (*judgment*) в мои́х глаза́х, на мой взгляд; **he found favour in her ~s** она́ отнесла́сь к нему́ благоскло́нно; **in the public ~** в це́нтре внима́ния; **with an ~ to pleasing her** что́бы понра́виться ей; **he has an ~ to business** у него́ комме́рческий подхо́д к веща́м; **he viewed it with a jealous ~** он смотре́л на э́то ревни́вым взгля́дом; **there is more in this than meets the ~** э́то не так про́сто, как ка́жется на пе́рвый взгляд. **3.** (*special senses*): **~ of a needle** иго́льное ушко́; **in the ~ of the storm** в эпице́нтре бу́ри; **hooks and ~s** крючки́ (*m. pl.*) и пе́тли (*f. pl.*); (*of a potato*) глазо́к (*pl.* глазки́); **~s of a peacock's tail** глазки́ павли́ньего хвоста́; **private ~** (*sl., detective*) ча́стный сы́щик.

v.t. разгля́д|ывать, -е́ть; наблюда́ть (*impf.*); **he ~d me with suspicion** он разгля́дывал меня́ с подозре́нием; **the dog ~d the plate of meat** соба́ка уста́вилась на таре́лку с мя́сом.

cpds. **~ball** *n.* глазно́е я́блоко; **~-bank** *n.* запа́с рогови́цы для переса́дки; **~-bath, ~-cup** *nn.* глазна́я ва́нночка; **~bright** *n.* оча́нка; **~brow** *n.* бровь; **~brow pencil** каранда́ш для брове́й; **up to the ~brows** (*fig.*) по́ уши; **raise one's ~brows** (*fig.*) подня́ть (*pf.*) бро́ви от удивле́ния, неодобре́ния и т.п.; **~-catching** *adj.* эффе́ктный; **~-cup** *n.* = **~-bath; ~ doctor** *n.* глазни́к, глазно́й врач, окули́ст; **~-dropper** *n.* пипе́тка; **~glass** *n.* (*monocle*) моно́кль (*m.*); (*pl., spectacles*) очк|и́ (*pl., g.* -о́в); **~hole** *n.* (*spyhole*) глаз|о́к (*pl.* -ки́); **~ hospital** *n.* глазна́я больни́ца; **~lash** *n.* ресни́ца; **~-level** *n.*: **at ~-level** на у́ровне глаз; **~lid** *n.* ве́ко; **hang on by one's ~lids** (*coll.*) висе́ть (*impf.*) на волоске́; **without batting an ~lid** (*coll.*) гла́зом не моргну́в; **~liner** *n.* каранда́ш для подкра́шивания глаз; **~-lotion** *n.* примо́чка для глаз; **~-opener** *n.* (*coll., revelation*) открове́ние; **~-shadow** *n.* те́ни (*f. pl.*) для век; **~sight** *n.* зре́ние; **he has good ~sight** у него́ хоро́шее зре́ние; **his ~sight failed** его́ зре́ние уху́дшилось; **~-socket** *n.* глазни́ца, глазна́я впа́дина; **~sore** *n.* уро́дство; **~strain** *n.* напряже́ние зре́ния; **~-tooth** *n.* глазно́й зуб; **~wash** *n.* (*lotion*) примо́чка для глаз; (*fig., coll.*) очковтира́тельство; **~witness** *n.* очеви́дец.

eyed[1] [aɪd] *adj.* (*e.g. peacock*) пятни́стый; в пя́тнах.

-eyed[2] [aɪd] *suff.*: **blue-~** голубогла́зый.

eyeful ['aɪfʊl] *n.* (*coll.*) зре́лище; **she is an ~** не же́нщина, а загляде́ние.

eyeless ['aɪlɪs] *adj.* безгла́зый.

eyelet ['aɪlɪt] *n.* ушко́; пете́лька.

eyot [aɪt] *n.* (*arch.*) острово́к.

eyrie ['aɪərɪ, 'ɪərɪ, 'ɜ:rɪ] *n.* орли́ное гнездо́.

Ezekiel [ɪ'zi:kɪəl] *n.* (*bibl.*) Иезеки́иль (*m.*).

Ezra ['ezrə] *n.* (*bibl.*) Е́зд(д)ра.

F

F[1] [ef] *n.* (*mus., also* **fa, fah**) фа (*nt. indecl.*).
F[2] ['færən,haɪt] (*abbr. of* **Fahrenheit**) °Ф, (шкала́ термо́метра Фаренге́йта); **30°F** 30°Ф (гра́дусов по Фаренге́йту).
FA (*abbr. of* ***Football Association***) Футбо́льная ассоциа́ция; ~ **Cup** кубо́к Футбо́льной ассоциа́ции.
fa [fɑː] *n.* = **fah**
Fabian ['feɪbɪən] *n.* (*socialist*) фабиа́нец.
adj. (*of socialism*) фабиа́нский; (*of tactics generally*) выжида́тельный, медли́тельный.
Fabianism ['feɪbɪə,nɪz(ə)m] *n.* фабиа́нство.
fable ['feɪb(ə)l] *n.* (*apologue*) ба́сня; (*invented tale*) небыли́ца, вы́думка.
fabled ['feɪbəld] *adj.* (*celebrated*) легенда́рный; (*fictitious*) легенда́рный, ска́зочный.
fabric ['fæbrɪk] *n.* (*text.*) ткань, мате́рия; ~ **gloves** нитя́ные перча́тки; (*of a building etc.*) констру́кция, структу́ра; (*fig.*) структу́ра.
fabricate ['fæbrɪ,keɪt] *v.t.* (*invent*) сочин|я́ть, -и́ть; (*falsify, forge*) фабрикова́ть, с-; подде́л|ывать, -ать; **a ~d charge** сфабрико́ванное обвине́ние.
fabrication [,fæbrɪ'keɪʃ(ə)n] *n.* (*story etc.*) вы́думка; **complete** ~ сплошна́я вы́думка; (*falsification*) фабрика́ция, подде́лка.
fabulist ['fæbjʊlɪst] *n.* баснопи́сец.
fabulous ['fæbjʊləs] *adj.* (*legendary*) легенда́рный; мифи́ческий; (*coll., marvellous*) роско́шный, басносло́вный.
façade [fə'sɑːd] *n.* (*archit.*) фаса́д; (*fig.*): **his politeness is a** ~ его́ ве́жливость чи́сто показна́я.
face [feɪs] *n.* **1.** (*front part of head*) лицо́; (*dim.*) ли́чико; **he fell on his** ~ он упа́л ничко́м; **he hit him in the** ~ он уда́рил его́ по лицу́; **look s.o. in the** ~ (*lit.*) посмотре́ть (*pf.*) кому́-н. в глаза́; **I came ~ to ~ with him** я столкну́лся с ним лицо́м к лицу́; **I brought them ~ to face** я свёл их друг с дру́гом; **I told him so to his** ~ я сказа́л ему́ э́то в лицо́; **I dare not show my ~ there** я не сме́ю глаз показа́ть там; **the sun was shining in our ~s** со́лнце свети́ло нам пря́мо в лицо́; **she laughed in my** ~ она́ рассмея́лась мне в лицо́; **he shut the door in my** ~ он захло́пнул дверь пе́ред мои́м но́сом; **red in the** ~ (*from anger/effort/embarrassment*) кра́сный/багро́вый (от гне́ва/уси́лия/смуще́ния); **her ~ is her fortune** красота́ — её еди́нственное бога́тство; **it's written all over his** ~ э́то у него́ на лице́/лбу/физионо́мии напи́сано; **you may talk till you are black, blue in the** ~ мо́жете говори́ть, пока́ не охри́пните; **full** ~ (*of a portrait*) анфа́с (*adv.*); **she had her ~ lifted** ей подтяну́ли ко́жу на лице́; **in the ~ of danger** пе́ред лицо́м опа́сности; **in the ~ of difficulties** несмотря́ на тру́дности; **he flew in the ~ of his orders** он де́рзко нару́шил прика́з; **he deserted in the ~ of the enemy** он дезерти́ровал пе́ред лицо́м неприя́теля; **ruin stares us in the** ~ нам грози́т разоре́ние; **he sets his ~ against bribery** он реши́тельно бо́рется со взя́точничеством. **2.** (*facial expression*) лицо́; выраже́ние лица́; **he made a** ~ он ско́рчил/состро́ил ро́жу; **he pulled a long** ~ у него́ вы́тянулось лицо́; **he kept a straight** ~ он храни́л невозмути́мый вид; **he put a bold ~ on the matter** он сде́лал хоро́шую ми́ну при плохо́й игре́; **his ~ fell** он измени́лся в лице́; у него́ вы́тянулось лицо́; **a good judge of ~s** хоро́ший физиономи́ст. **3.** (*composure, effrontery*): **he saved his** ~ он спас свою́ репута́цию; **they saved his** ~ они́ изба́вили его́ от позо́ра; **he had the ~ to tell me ...** у него́ хвати́ло на́глости сказа́ть мне… **4.** (*outward show, aspect*) вне́шний вид; **on the ~ of it** (*apparently*) на вид, на пе́рвый взгляд; **this puts a new ~ on things** э́то представля́ет де́ло в но́вом све́те. **5.** (*physical surface, facade*) лицо́; лицева́я сторона́; (*of clock*) цифербла́т; (*of banknote*) лицева́я сторона́; **they disappeared from the ~ of the earth** они́ исче́зли с лица́ земли́; **he laid the card ~ down** он положи́л ка́рту лицо́м вниз (*or* руба́шкой вверх); **the miner worked at the coal** ~ шахтёр рабо́тал в у́гольном забо́е; ~ **value** (*of currency*) номина́льная сто́имость; **I took his words at ~ value** я при́нял его́ слова́ за чи́стую моне́ту.
v.t. **1.** (*physically*) стоя́ть (*impf.*) лицо́м к+*d.*; смотре́ть (*impf.*) на+*a.*; **turn round and ~ me!** поверни́тесь и смотри́те на меня́; **the man facing us** челове́к, сидя́щий *и т.п.* про́тив нас; **a seat facing the engine** сиде́нье по хо́ду по́езда. **2.** (*confront*) смотре́ть (*impf.*) в лицо́ (*чему*); **we must ~ facts** на́до смотре́ть фа́ктам в лицо́; на́до счита́ться с фа́ктами; **let's ~ it!** (*coll.*) на́до гляде́ть пра́вде в глаза́!; бу́дем открове́нны!; ска́жем пря́мо!; ~ **s.o. down** осади́ть (*pf.*) кого́-н.; **the problem that ~s us** зада́ча, стоя́щая пе́ред на́ми; **we are ~d with bankruptcy** мы стои́м пе́ред банкро́тством. **3.** (*mil., cause to turn*) пов|ора́чивать, -ерну́ть; **he ~d his men about** он поверну́л солда́т круго́м. **4.** (*cover*): **a wall ~d with stone** стена́, облицо́ванная ка́мнем; **a coat ~d with silk** пальто́, отде́ланное шёлком.
v.i.: **the house ~s south** дом обращён фаса́дом на юг; **the house ~s on to a park** о́кна до́ма выхо́дят на парк; дом обращён фаса́дом к па́рку; **their house ~s ours** их дом — напро́тив на́шего; **he ~d up to the difficulties** он не испуга́лся тру́дностей; (*mil.*) **about ~!** круго́м!; **please ~ (towards) the camera** пожа́луйста, смотри́те в объекти́в.
cpds. **~-ache** *n.* невралги́я (лица́); **~-card** *n.* фигу́ра; **~-cloth** *n.* ли́чное полоте́нце; **~-cream** *n.* крем для лица́; **~-lift** *n.* опера́ция подня́тия ко́жи на лице́; (*fig.*) вне́шнее обновле́ние, космети́ческий ремо́нт; **~-pack** *n.* космети́ческая ма́ска; **~-powder** *n.* пу́дра; **~-saving** *adj.* (*fig.*) для спасе́ния репута́ции/прести́жа; **~-worker** *n.* (*miner*) забо́йщик.
faceless ['feɪslɪs] *adj.* (*anonymous*) безли́чный, безли́кий.
facer ['feɪsə(r)] *n.* (*coll., difficulty*) загво́здка.
facet ['fæsɪt] *n.* грань, фаце́т; (*fig.*) аспе́кт.
faceted ['fæsɪtɪd] *adj.* гранёный.
facetious [fə'siːʃəs] *adj.* шутли́вый, шу́точный; (*pej.*) неуме́стно-шутли́вый; **talk ~ly** остри́ть (*impf.*) (некста́ти).
facetiousness [fə'siːʃəsnɪs] *n.* (неуме́стная) шутли́вость.
facia ['feɪʃɪə] *n.* (*over shop-front*) вы́веска; (*dashboard*) щито́к; прибо́рная доска́.
facial ['feɪʃ(ə)l] *n.* масса́ж лица́.
adj. лицево́й; ~ **expression** выраже́ние лица́.
facile ['fæsaɪl] *adj.* (*easy, fluent*) лёгкий, свобо́дный; (*superficial*) пове́рхностный.
facileness ['fæsaɪlnɪs] *n.* лёгкость, свобо́да; пове́рхность.
facilitate [fə'sɪlɪ,teɪt] *v.t.* облегч|а́ть, -и́ть; спосо́бствовать (*impf.*) +*d.*; соде́йствовать (*impf.*) +*d.*
facilitation [fə,sɪlɪ'teɪʃ(ə)n] *n.* облегче́ние (*чего*); соде́йствие (*чему*).
facilit|y [fə'sɪlɪtɪ] *n.* (*ease*) лёгкость; (*skill*) спосо́бность (*к чему*); (*aid, appliance, installation*) сооруже́ние; **~ies for study** усло́вия (*nt. pl.*) для учёбы; **sports ~ies** спорти́вное обору́дование, помеще́ния (*nt. pl.*) для заня́тия спо́ртом; **payment ~ies** льго́ты (*f. pl.*) по платежа́м.
facing ['feɪsɪŋ] *n.* (*of wall etc.*) облицо́вка; (*of coat etc.*) отде́лка.
facsimile [fæk'sɪmɪlɪ] *n.* факсимиле́ (*indecl.*).
fact [fækt] *n.* **1.** (*deed*): **accessory before the** ~ соуча́стник до собы́тия преступле́ния. **2.** (*sth. known or presented as true*) факт; **the ~ that he was there shows that ...** тот факт, что он был там, говори́т о том, что…; **as a matter of** ~ факти́чески; в су́щности; в действи́тельности; на са́мом де́ле; со́бственно (говоря́); по пра́вде сказа́ть; **the ~ is that ...** де́ло в том, что…; **in (point of)** ~ (*actually*)

фактически; в/на самом деле; (*intensifying*): **very much, in ~** очень даже; **I think so, in ~ I'm quite sure** я так думаю, более того, я уверен в этом; (*summing up*): **in ~ the whole thing is most unsatisfactory** в сущности, всё это весьма неудовлетворительно; **a story founded on ~** рассказ, основанный на действительном происшествии.

cpd. **~-finding** *adj.* занимающийся собиранием фактов; **~-finding tour** ознакомительная поездка.

faction ['fækʃ(ə)n] *n.* фракция, клика; (*party strife*) фракционная борьба.

factionalism ['fækʃənəl,ɪz(ə)m] *n.* фракционность.

factionalist ['fækʃənəlɪst] *n.* фракционер.

factious ['fækʃəs] *adj.* фракционный, раскольнический.

factiousness ['fækʃəsnɪs] *n.* фракционность, раскольничество.

factitious [fæk'tɪʃəs] *adj.* искусственный.

factitive ['fæktɪtɪv] *adj.* (*gram.*) казуальный, фактитивный.

factor ['fæktə(r)] *n.* **1.** (*math.*) множитель (*m.*), фактор. **2.** (*contributing cause*) фактор; **this was a ~ in his success** это содействовало его успеху. **3.** (*Sc., steward*) управляющий (имением).

factorial [fæk'tɔːrɪəl] *adj.*: **~ 4** факториал 4.

factorize ['fæktə,raɪz] *v.t.* разложить (*pf.*) на множители.

factory ['fæktərɪ] *n.* **1.** (*place of manufacture*) фабрика, завод; (*attr.*) фабричный, заводской. **2.: ~ ship** (*whaling*) плавучая китобойная база.

factotum [fæk'təʊtəm] *n.* фактотум, доверенный слуга.

factual ['fæktjʊəl] *adj.* фактический.

facult|y ['fækəltɪ] *n.* **1.** (*power, aptitude*) способность; **in possession of one's ~ies** в здравом уме. **2.** (*acad.*) факультет. **3.** (*US, body of teachers*) профессорско-преподавательский состав. **4.: the ~y** (*med. profession*) медики (*m. pl.*).

fad [fæd] *n.* (*craze*) увлечение, поветрие; (*whim*) прихоть, причуда, пунктик.

faddiness ['fædɪnɪs] *n.* капризность.

faddish ['fædɪʃ] *adj.* прихотливый.

faddist ['fædɪst] *n.* привередник, чудак.

faddy ['fædɪ] *adj.* капризный.

fade [feɪd] *v.t.* **1.** (*cause to lose colour*) обесцве|чивать, -тить; **the sunlight ~d the curtains** занавески выгорели на солнце. **2.** (*cin., radio*): **~ one scene into another** плавно перев|одить, -ести одну сцену в другую; **~ out** постепенно ум|еньшать, -еньшить силу звука; **~ in** постепенно увеличи|вать, -ть силу звука.

v.i. **1.** (*lose colour*) обесцве|чиваться, -титься; **the flowers ~d** цветы завяли/поблёкли; (*of sound*) зам|ирать, -ереть; **the sound ~d** звук замер; (*of strength*) уг|асать, -аснуть. **2.** (*fig.*): **his hopes ~d** его надежды испарились; **she is fading away** (*dying*) она тает.

cpds. **~-in** *n.* (*cin., radio*) постепенное появление звука/изображения; **~-out** *n.* (*cin., radio*) постепенное исчезновение звука/изображения.

fading [feɪdɪŋ] *n.* (*radio etc.*) затухание, фединг.

faecal ['fiːk(ə)l] *adj.* фекальный.

faeces ['fiːsiːz] *n.* фекалии (*f. pl.*); испражнения (*nt. pl.*).

Faeroes ['feərəʊz] *n.*: **the ~** (*also* **Faeroe Islands**) Фарерские острова (*m. pl.*).

Faeroese [,feərəʊ'iːz] *n.* (*pers.*) фарер|ец (*fem.* -ка); (*language*) фарерский язык.

adj. фарерский.

fag[1] [fæg] *n.* **1.** (*coll., fatigue*) усталость, утомление. **2.** (*schoolboy*) младший ученик, прислуживающий старшему.

v.t. (*tire*) утом|лять, -ить; выматывать, вымотать; **I am ~ged out** я вконец вымотался.

v.i. (*toil*) корпеть (*impf.*) (*над чем*).

fag[2] [fæg] *n.* (*coll., cigarette*) сигарета, папироска.

cpd. **~-end** *n.* (*butt*) окурок, (*sl.*) чинарик; (*fig.*) конец (*чего*); остаток (*чего*).

fag[3] [fæg] = **faggot** *n.* **2.**

faggot ['fægət] *n.* **1.** (*bundle of sticks*) вязанка, фашина; **~ wood** фашинник. **2.** (*US coll., homosexual*) гомосексуалист, педик.

fa(h) [fɑː] *n.* (*mus.*) фа (*nt. indecl.*).

Fahrenheit ['færən,haɪt] *n.* (*abbr.* **F**) Фаренгейт; **at 30°~** при тридцати градусах по Фаренгейту.

faience ['faɪɑ̃s] *n.* фаянс.

fail [feɪl] *n.*: **without ~** обязательно, непременно.

v.t. **1.** (*reject in exam*) провал|ивать, -ить. **2.** (*disappoint, desert*) подв|одить, -ести; **words ~ me** я не нахожу слов; **his heart ~ed him** у него не хватило духу.

v.i. **1.** (*fall short, decline*) ух|удшаться, -удшиться; недоставать (*impf.*); **the crops ~ed** хлеб не уродился; **the water supply ~ed** водоснабжение прекратилось; **his eyesight is ~ing** его зрение слабеет; **he is in ~ing health** его здоровье ухудшается. **2.** (*not succeed*): **he ~ed in the exam** он провалился на экзамене; **his scheme ~ed** его план провалился; **he ~ed to convince her** ему не удалось (*or* он не сумел) убедить её; **I ~ to see why ...** я не понимаю, почему... **3.** (*omit*) упус|кать, -тить; **he never ~s to write** он никогда не забывает писать; **he ~ed to let us know** он не дал нам знать. **4.** (*go bankrupt*): **the bank ~ed** банк лопнул.

cpd. **~-safe** *adj.* самоотключающийся (при аварии).

failing ['feɪlɪŋ] *n.* (*defect*) недостаток, слабость.

prep. за неимением+*g.*; **~ this** за неимением этого; если этого не случится; **~ an answer** не получив ответа; **~ Smith, we can invite Jones** если Смита нет, мы можем пригласить Джонса.

faille [feɪl] *n.* фай.

failure ['feɪljə(r)] *n.* **1.** (*unsuccess*) неудача, неуспех, провал; **the venture was a ~** затея провалилась. **2.** (*pers.*) неудачник; **he was a ~ as a teacher** как педагог он никуда не годится. **3.** (*of crops etc.*) неурожай. **4.** (*bankruptcy*) банкротство, несостоятельность. **5.** (*non-functioning*) авария; **heart ~** паралич сердца; **engine ~** отказ двигателя. **6.** (*omission, neglect*): **his ~ to answer is a nuisance** очень досадно, что он не отвечает.

fain[1] [feɪn] *adv.* (*poet.*) охотно, с радостью.

fain[2] [feɪn] *v.t.*: **~(s) I!** (*coll.*) чур не я!

faint [feɪnt] *n.* (*loss of consciousness*) обморок; **in a dead ~** в глубоком обмороке.

adj. **1.** (*weak, indistinct*) слабый, неотчётливый; **his strength grew ~** его силы угасали; **he was ~ with hunger** он ослаб от голода; **I haven't the ~est idea** понятия не имею; я не имею ни малейшего понятия. **2.** (*timid*) робкий; **~ heart never won fair lady** смелость города берёт. **3.** (*giddy, likely to swoon*) близкий к обмороку; **I feel ~** мне дурно.

v.i. (*lose consciousness; also* **~ away**) падать, упасть в обморок; (*grow weak*) слабеть (*impf.*); **he was ~ing with hunger** он слабел от голода; **~ fit** обморок.

cpds. **~-hearted** *adj.* трусливый, малодушный; **~-heartedness** *n.* трусость, малодушие.

faintish ['feɪntɪʃ] *adj.* слабоватый; **I feel ~** мне дурно/нехорошо.

faintly ['feɪntlɪ] *adv.* (*feebly*) слабо; (*slightly*) слабо, слегка.

faintness ['feɪntnɪs] *n.* слабость; (*giddiness*), дурнота.

fair[1] [feə(r)] *n.* (*open-air market etc.*) ярмарка; (*exhibition*) выставка; **book ~** книжная ярмарка.

cpd. **~-ground** *n.* ярмарочная площадь.

fair[2] [feə(r)] *adj.* **1.** (*beautiful*) прекрасный, красивый; **the ~ sex** прекрасный пол; **~ maid** (*poet.*) красна девица. **2.** (*specious*) показной; **~ words** красивые слова. **3.** (*of weather*) ясный; **the barometer is at set ~** барометр стоит на «ясно». **4.** (*abundant, favourable*): **he is in a ~ way to succeed** он на пути к успеху; **a ~ wind** попутный ветер; **a ~ amount** (*a lot*) значительное/изрядное количество. **5.** (*average*) сносный, посредственный; **he has a ~ chance of success** у него неплохие шансы на успех; **she has a ~ amount of sense** у неё достаточно здравого смысла; **his performance was only ~** его выступление было всего лишь сносным; '**~**' (*as school mark*) посредственно; **~ to middling** так себе; неважный. **6.** (*equitable*): **~ share** справедливая доля; **~ price** подходящая цена; **~ play** честная игра; справедливость; **by ~ means or foul** любыми средствами; всеми правдами и неправдами; **it is ~ to say that ...** со всей справедливостью можно сказать, что...; **~ and square** открытый, честный; **~**

game зако́нная добы́ча; ~ **comment** непредвзя́тая/беспристра́стная кри́тика. **7.** (*clean, unblemished*): ~ **copy** чистови́к; **spoil s.o.'s** ~ **name** пятна́ть, за- чьё-н. до́брое и́мя. **8.** (*of hair*) све́тлый, (*blond*) белоку́рый; **a** ~ **complexion** све́тлый цвет лица́; **a** ~ **man** блонди́н.

adv.: **I spoke him** ~ (*liter.*) я говори́л с ним любе́зно/ве́жливо; **he fought** ~ он боро́лся че́стно (*or* по пра́вилам); **he bids** ~ **to succeed** у него́ есть ша́нсы на успе́х; **he wrote the letter out** ~ он переписа́л письмо́ на́чисто; **I hit him** ~ **(and square) in the midriff** я уда́рил его́ пря́мо в со́лнечное сплете́ние; **I tell you** ~ **and square that ...** я скажу́ вам напрями́к, что...

cpds. **~-complexioned** *adj.* све́тлой ма́сти; **~-dealing** *n.* че́стность, прямота́; *adj.* че́стный, прямо́й; **~-haired** *adj.* белоку́рый; **~-minded** *adj.* справедли́вый; **~-mindedness** *n.* справедли́вость; **~-spoken** *adj.* ве́жливый, любе́зный, учти́вый; **~way** *n.* (*naut.*) фарва́тер; **~-weather** *adj.* **~-weather friends** ненадёжные друзья́, друзья́ до пе́рвой беды́.

fairish ['feərɪʃ] *adj.* сно́сный; (*coll.*) подходя́щий.

fairly ['feəlɪ] *adv.* **1.** (*handsomely*) краси́во, прекра́сно; **the town is** ~ **situated** го́род краси́во располо́жен. **2.** (*completely, positively*) факти́чески, буква́льно; **we were** ~ **in the trap** мы попа́ли пря́мо в лову́шку; **he** ~ **shook with indignation** он буква́льно дрожа́л от негодова́ния. **3.** (*moderately*) дово́льно, сно́сно, терпи́мо; **he writes** ~ **well** он дово́льно хорошо́ пи́шет. **4.** (*justly*) че́стно, справедли́во; со всей справедли́востью.

fairness ['feənɪs] *n.* (*equity*) справедли́вость, че́стность; **in all** ~ со всей справедли́востью.

fairy ['feərɪ] *n.* **1.** фе́я, волше́бница; **bad** ~ зла́я фе́я; злой дух; (*attr.*) волше́бный, ска́зочный; ~ **voices** волше́бные голоса́; ~ **lamps, lights** цветны́е фона́рики; кита́йские фона́рики. **2.** (*sl., homosexual*) пе́дик.

cpds. **~land** *n.* волше́бное ца́рство; волше́бная/ска́зочная страна́; **~-like** *adj.*подо́бный фе́е; **~-story, ~-tale** *nn.* ска́зка; (*fig.*) ска́зка, небыли́ца.

fait accompli [,feɪt ə'kɒmpli:, ə'kɔ̃pli:] *n.* соверши́вшийся факт.

faith [feɪθ] *n.* **1.** (*trust*) ве́ра, дове́рие; **put one's** ~ **in s.o.** дов|еря́ться, -е́риться кому́-н.; возл|ага́ть, -ожи́ть наде́жды на кого́-н.; **I have no** ~ **in doctors** я не ве́рю доктора́м. **2.** (*relig. conviction*) ве́ра. **3.** (*relig. system*) вероисповеда́ние, ве́ра. **4.** (*promise, warranty*) обеща́ние, руча́тельство; **keep/break** ~ **with s.o.** сдержа́ть/нару́шить (*pf.*) обеща́ние, да́нное кому́-н.; **in** ~ **whereof ...** (*leg.*) в удостовере́ние чего...; **breach of** ~ наруше́ние обеща́ния; **on the** ~ (*basis, authority*) **of** на основа́нии+*g.*; полага́ясь на+*a.* **5.** (*sincerity*) че́стность; **good** ~ добросо́вестность; **in bad** ~ вероло́мно; с нече́стными наме́рениями; **in good** ~ че́стно, добросо́вестно; с чи́стой со́вестью.

cpds. **~-healer** *n.* зна́харь (*fem.* -ка); **~-healing** *n.* зна́харство, лече́ние внуше́нием.

faithful ['feɪθfʊl] *adj.* то́чный, достове́рный; **a** ~ **translation** то́чный перево́д; (*as n.*) **the** ~ (*believers*) правове́рные; **Commander of the F~** повели́тель (*m.*) правове́рных.

faithfully ['feɪθfʊlɪ] *adv.* то́чно, ве́рно; **I promise you** ~ я вам то́чно обеща́ю; **yours** ~ (*letter-ending*) с соверше́нным почте́нием; **deal** ~ **with** (*treat candidly*) добросо́вестно относи́ться к+*d.*

faithfulness ['feɪθfʊlnɪs] *n.* ве́рность.

faithless ['feɪθlɪs] *adj.* вероло́мный.

faithlessness ['feɪθlɪsnɪs] *n.* вероло́мство.

fake [feɪk] *n.* (*sham*) подде́лка, фальши́вка; (*attr.*) подде́льный, фальши́вый; **a** ~ **antique** подде́лка под антиква́рную вещь.

v.t. (*also* ~ **up**) подде́л|ывать, -ать; **a ~d illness** притво́рная боле́знь.

faker ['feɪkə(r)] *n.* (*fabricator*) подде́лыватель (*m.*); (*fraudulent pers.*) обма́нщик.

fakery ['feɪkərɪ] *n.* подде́лка; притво́рство.

fakir ['feɪkɪə(r), fə'kɪə(r)] *n.* факи́р.

Falange [fæ'lændʒ] *n.* (*pol.*) фала́нга.

falcon ['fɔ:lkən, 'fɒlkən] *n.* со́кол.

falconer ['fɔ:lkənə(r), 'fɒl-] *n.* соко́льничий; соколи́ный охо́тник.

falconry ['fɔ:lkənrɪ, 'fɒl-] *n.* соколи́ная охо́та.

Falkland ['fɔ:lklənd] *n.*: **the ~s** (*also* **the** ~ **Islands**) Фолкле́ндские острова́ (*m. pl.*).

fall [fɔ:l] *n.* **1.** (*physical drop, act of ~ing*) паде́ние; **he had a bad** ~ он упа́л и си́льно ушиб́ся; **a heavy** ~ **of rain** ли́вень (*m.*), проливно́й дождь; ~ **of snow** снегопа́д; **he is riding for a** ~ (*fig.*) он сломае́т себе́ ше́ю. **2.** (*moral*) паде́ние; ~ **from grace** нра́вственное паде́ние; паде́ние в чьих-то глаза́х; **the** ~ **of man** (*relig.*) грехопаде́ние. **3.**: **the** ~ **of the Roman Empire (of Paris)** паде́ние Ри́мской импе́рии (Пари́жа). **4.** (*diminution*) пониже́ние; ~ **in prices** паде́ние цен. **5.** (*pl., waterfall*) водопа́д; **Niagara F~s** Ниага́рский водопа́д. **6.** (*US, autumn*) о́сень. **7.** (*wrestling and fig.*): **try a** ~ **with s.o.** поме́риться (*pf.*) си́лами с кем-н.

v.i. **1.** па́дать, упа́сть; **he fell over a chair** он упа́л, споткну́вшись о стул; **he fell full length** он растяну́лся во весь рост; **he fell dead** он у́мер на ме́сте; **rain fell at last** наконе́ц вы́пал дождь; **many trees fell in the storm** бу́рей повали́ло мно́го дере́вьев; **leaves** ~ ли́стья летя́т/опада́ют; **lambs** ~ (*are born*) ягня́та рожда́ются; **the river ~s into the lake** река́ впада́ет в о́зеро; **the arrow fell short** стрела́ не долете́ла до це́ли; **he fell off his horse** он упа́л с ло́шади; **he fell on his feet** (*fig.*) он счастли́во отде́лался; **the joke fell flat** шу́тка не име́ла успе́ха; **his work fell short of expectations** его́ рабо́та не оправда́ла ожида́ний/наде́жд; **he fell into the trap** он попа́л(ся) в лову́шку; ~ **over o.s.** (*coll.*) (*from clumsiness*) споткну́ться и упа́сть (*pf.*); (*from eagerness*) перестара́ться (*pf.*); лезть (*impf.*) из ко́жи вон. **2.** (*drop, sink*) па́дать, пасть (*or* упа́сть); **the river has ~en** вода́ в реке́ спа́ла; **the barometer fell** баро́метр упа́л; **prices fell** це́ны сни́зились/упа́ли; **the temperature fell** температу́ра упа́ла; **my spirits fell** ~ я упа́л ду́хом; **his eyes fell** он опусти́л глаза́; **the wind fell** ве́тер стих; **his voice fell to a whisper** он перешёл на шёпот. **3.** (*of defeat etc.*) па́|дать, -сть; **the city fell** го́род пал; **he fell in battle** он пал в бою́; **the ~en** (*in war*) па́вшие (*m. pl.*) в боя́х; **the government fell** прави́тельство па́ло; **many lions fell to his rifle** он уби́л мно́го льво́в. **4.** (*morally*): **he was tempted and fell** он подда́лся искуше́нию; **~en women** па́дшие же́нщины. **5.** (*hang down*) па́дать (*impf.*); **his beard fell to his chest** борода́ па́дала ему́ на грудь; **her hair fell over her shoulders** во́лосы па́дали ей на пле́чи. **6.** (*pass into a state*): **the horse fell lame** ло́шадь захрома́ла; **he fell silent** он замолча́л; **he fell ill** он заболе́л; **the rent fell due** подошёл срок плати́ть за кварти́ру; **he fell into disgrace** он впал в неми́лость; **the garden fell into neglect** сад пришёл в запусте́ние; **she fell an easy prey to him** она́ оказа́лась для него́ лёгкой добы́чей; **he fell in love with her** он влюби́лся в неё; **they fell into conversation** они́ разговори́лись. **7.** (*come, alight*): **darkness fell** наступи́ла темнота́; **fear fell upon them** на них нашёл/напа́л страх; **I fell to wondering** я заду́мался; **his eye fell on a strange object** его́ взгляд упа́л на стра́нный предме́т; **sounds fell on our ears** до нас долете́ли зву́ки; **suspicion fell on her** подозре́ние па́ло на неё; **stress falls on the first syllable** ударе́ние па́дает на пе́рвый слог; **the subject ~s into four parts** э́тот предме́т распада́ется на четы́ре ча́сти; **most of the fighting fell on this regiment** э́тому полку́ доста́лся са́мый тру́дный уча́сток бо́я; **it fell to his lot** ему́ вы́пало на до́лю; **it fell to me to welcome the speaker** мне на́до бы́ло приве́тствовать ора́тора; **he fell on evil days** для него́ наступи́ли чёрные дни; **Christmas Day ~s on a Tuesday** Рождество́ прихо́дится на вто́рник; **Easter ~s early this year** в э́том году́ ра́нняя Па́сха. **8.** (*be uttered*): **these words fell from his lips** э́то слете́ло у него́ с языка́; **she let** ~ **a few words** она́ oброни́ла не́сколько слов.

with preps. (*further examples*): ~ **for** (~ *in love with*) увл|ека́ться, -е́чься +i.; влюб|ля́ться, -и́ться в+a.; (*be taken in by*): **he fell for her story** он пове́рил её слова́м; он попа́лся ей на у́дочку; ~ **over: he fell over a cliff** он сорва́лся со скалы́; **he fell over a bucket** он споткну́лся о ведро́ и упа́л; ~ **to** (*begin*): **he fell to work** он приня́лся за рабо́ту; ~ **upon** (*attack*) нап|ада́ть, -а́сть; набр|а́сываться, -о́ситься; **they fell upon the enemy** они́ напа́ли на врага́; **he fell upon his dinner** он набро́сился на еду́.

with advs.: ~ **about (with laughter)** (*coll.*) лежа́ть (*impf.*) (от сме́ха); **the audience fell about** пу́блика лежа́ла; ~ **apart** расп|ада́ться, -а́сться; ~ **astern** (*naut.*) стро́иться, по- в кильва́тер; ~ **away: his supporters fell away** сторо́нники поки́нули его́ (*or* отступи́лись от него́); **prejudices fell away** предрассу́дки исче́зли; ~ **back** (*retreat*) приб|ега́ть, -е́гнуть к чему́-н.; ~ **back on sth.** приб|ега́ть, -е́гнуть к чему́-н.; ~ **behind** (*e.g. in walking*) отст|ава́ть, -а́ть; (*with letters*) заде́рж|иваться, -а́ться с отве́том; (*with rent*) зап|а́здывать, -озда́ть с упла́той за кварти́ру; ~ **down** (*lit.*) упа́сть (*pf.*); **he fell down on the task** (*coll.*) он не спра́вился с зада́нием; он завали́л рабо́ту; ~ **in** впасть (*во что*); **the roof fell in** кры́ша ру́хнула/обвали́лась; **the soldiers fell in** солда́ты ста́ли в строй (*or* постро́ились); ~ **in!** (*mil.*) станови́сь!; **the lease fell in** срок аре́нды истёк; **I fell in with him at the station** я столкну́лся с ним на вокза́ле; **he fell in with my views** он согласи́лся со мно́й; (*v.t.*) **he fell the men in** (*mil.*) он постро́ил солда́т; ~ **off** упа́сть (*с чего*); **the enemy fell off** (*withdrew*) неприя́тель отступи́л; **attendance is ~ing off** посеща́емость па́дает; **the quality fell off** ка́чество сни́зилось; **~ing-off** (*deterioration*) паде́ние, упа́док; ~ **out** выпада́ть, вы́пасть; **his hair fell out** у него́ вы́пали во́лосы; (*quarrel*) поссо́риться (*pf.*); **~ing-out** (*quarrel*) размо́лвка, ссо́ра; (*mil.*) выходи́ть, вы́йти из стро́я; разойти́сь (*pf.*); ~ **out!** разойди́сь!; (*v.t.*): **he fell the men out** он приказа́л солда́там разойти́сь; (*happen, result*) случ|а́ться, -и́ться; (*withdraw*): **six competitors fell out** ше́стеро вы́пали из соревнова́ний; ~ **over** (*lit.*) упа́сть; **he fell over backwards to please** он лез из ко́жи вон, что́бы угоди́ть *+d.*; ~ **through** прова́л|иваться, -и́ться; ~ **to** (*start eating or fighting*) набр|а́сываться, -о́ситься (друг на дру́га) (на еду́).

cpds. **~-in** *n.* (*mil.*) построе́ние; **~-out** *n.* (*mil.*) вы́ход из стро́я; (*nuclear*) радиоакти́вные оса́дки (*m. pl.*); выпаде́ние радиоакти́вных оса́дков.

fallacious [fəˈleɪʃəs] *adj.* оши́бочный, ло́жный.

fallaciousness [fəˈleɪʃəsnɪs] *n.* оши́бочность, ло́жность.

fallacy [ˈfæləsɪ] *n.* (*false belief*) заблужде́ние; **popular** ~ распространённое заблужде́ние; (*false reasoning*) оши́бочный/ло́жный вы́вод; **pathetic** ~ олицетворе́ние приро́ды.

fal-lal [fælˈlæl] *n.* (*usu. pl.*) безделу́шка.

fallibility [ˌfælɪˈbɪlɪtɪ] *n.* погреши́мость; подве́рженность оши́бкам/заблужде́ниям.

fallible [ˈfælɪb(ə)l] *adj.* подве́рженный оши́бкам, мо́гущий ошиба́ться.

Fallopian tube [fəˈləʊpɪən] *n.* Фалло́пиева труба́.

fallow [ˈfæləʊ] *adj.* вспа́ханный под пар; ~ **land** пар; **lie** ~ ост|ава́ться, -а́ться под па́ром; (*fig., e.g. of an author*): **he is lying** ~ он набира́ется сил; ≃ он ещё себя́ пока́жет.

v.t. подн|има́ть, -я́ть (*пар*).

fallow-deer [ˈfæləʊ] *n.* лань.

false [fɒls, fɔːls] *adj.* **1.** (*wrong, incorrect*) ло́жный, оши́бочный, фальши́вый; ~ **weight** непра́вильный вес; **a** ~ **note** фальши́вая но́та; **a** ~ **step** ло́жный шаг; **he was in a** ~ **position** он оказа́лся в ло́жном положе́нии; **is this statement true or** ~**?** ве́рно э́то утвержде́ние и́ли нет?; ~ **pride** ло́жная го́рдость; ~ **start** фальста́рт (*races*); срыв в са́мом нача́ле; ~ **alarm** ло́жная трево́га. **2.** (*deceitful, treacherous*) лжи́вый, вероло́мный; **bear** ~ **witness** лжесвиде́тельствовать (*impf.*); **F~ Dmitry** (*hist.*) Лжедми́трий; **he was** ~ **to her** он был ей неве́рен; **sail under** ~ **colours** плыть (*impf.*) под чужи́м фла́гом; (*fig.*) выступа́ть (*impf.*) под ма́ской/личи́ной; ~ **pretences** обма́н, притво́рство; (*adv.*): **he played me** ~ он пре́дал меня́. **3.** (*sham, apparent*) фальши́вый; ~ **hair** фальши́вая коса́; накладны́е во́лосы; ~ **teeth** иску́сственные зу́бы; ~ **bottom** двойно́е дно; ~ **pregnancy** ло́жная бере́менность; ~ **acacia** ло́жная ака́ция, лжеака́ция.

cpds. **~-hearted** *adj.* вероло́мный; **~-heartedness** *n.* вероло́мство.

falsehood [ˈfɒlshʊd, ˈfɔːls-] *n.* ложь, непра́вда; **he told a** ~ он сказа́л непра́вду; **truth and** ~ пра́вда и ложь; **he was found guilty of** ~ он был уличён во лжи.

falseness [ˈfɒlsnɪs, ˈfɔːlsnɪs] *n.* (*wrongness*) ло́жность, оши́бочность; (*insincerity*) нейскренность; (*treachery*) лжи́вость, вероло́мство.

falsetto [fɒlˈsetəʊ, fɔːl-] *n.* фальце́т; **in a** ~ **tone** фальце́том.

falsies [ˈfɒlsɪz, ˈfɔːl-] *n. pl.* (*coll.*) иску́сственный бюст.

falsification [ˌfɒlsɪfɪˈkeɪʃ(ə)n, ˌfɔːls-] *n.* фальсифика́ция.

falsifier [ˈfɒlsɪˌfaɪə(r), ˈfɔːls-] *n.* фальсифика́тор.

falsif|y [ˈfɒlsɪˌfaɪ, ˈfɔːls-] *v.t.* (*e.g. accounts*) подде́л|ывать, -ать; фальсифици́ровать (*impf., pf.*); **my hopes were ~ied** мои́ наде́жды бы́ли напра́сны.

falsity [ˈfɒlsɪtɪ, ˈfɔːlsɪtɪ] *n.* (*falsehood, inaccuracy*) ло́жность, оши́бочность.

faltboat [ˈfæltbəʊt] *n.* складна́я шлю́пка.

falter [ˈfɒltə(r), ˈfɔːl-] *v.t. & i.* (*move, walk or act hesitatingly*) поша́тываться, спотыка́ться, колеба́ться (*all impf.*); **he ~ed out a few words** он, запина́ясь, пробормота́л не́сколько слов.

faltering [ˈfɒltərɪŋ, ˈfɔːl-] *adj.* запина́ющийся, прерыва́ющийся; ~ **gait** неве́рная похо́дка; **a** ~ **voice** дрожа́щий/прерыва́ющийся го́лос; **he spoke ~ly** он говори́л с запи́нкой.

fame [feɪm] *n.* сла́ва; репута́ция; **house of ill** ~ публи́чный дом.

v.t.: **he was ~d for valour** он просла́вился свое́й до́блестью.

familial [fəˈmɪlɪəl] *adj.* семе́йный, фами́льный.

familiar [fəˈmɪlɪə(r)] *n.* (*intimate*) бли́зкий друг.

adj. **1.** (*common, usual*) обы́чный, привы́чный. **2.** (*of acquaintance*) знако́мый; **I am** ~ **with the subject** я знако́м с э́тим предме́том; **the subject is** ~ **to me** э́тот предме́т знако́м/изве́стен мне; **your face is** ~ ва́ше лицо́ мне знако́мо. **3.** (*friendly*) дру́жеский. **4.** (*casual, impudent*) бесцеремо́нный, фамилья́рный.

familiarity [fəˌmɪlɪˈærɪtɪ] *n.* **1.** (*close acquaintance with pers. or thg.*) бли́зкое знако́мство (с+*i.*); ~ **breeds contempt** чем бли́же зна́ешь челове́ка, тем ме́ньше его́ уважа́ешь. **2.** (*of manner*) фамилья́рность; (*pl., caresses etc.*) во́льности (*f. pl.*).

familiarization [fəˌmɪlɪəraɪˈzeɪʃ(ə)n] *n.* ознакомле́ние (*с чем*).

familiarize [fəˈmɪlɪəˌraɪz] *v.t.* ознак|омля́ть, -о́мить (*кого с чем*); ~ **o.s. with sth.** ознако́миться (*pf.*) с чем-н.

family [ˈfæmɪlɪ, ˈfæmlɪ] *n.* **1.** (*parents and children*) семья́; **extended** ~ расши́ренная семья́; **nuclear** ~ нуклеа́рная семья́; **the Holy F~** Свято́е семе́йство. **2.** (*children*) де́т|и (*pl., g.* -е́й); **they have a large** ~ у них мно́го дете́й. **3.** (*descendants of common ancestor*) семья́, род; **a man of good** ~ челове́к из хоро́шей семьи́. **4.** (*of animals etc.*) семе́йство. **5.** (*attr.*) семе́йный; ~ **allowance** семе́йное посо́бие; **a** ~ **man** семе́йный челове́к; ~ **likeness** семе́йное/фами́льное схо́дство; ~ **friend** друг семьи́; ~ **name** (*surname*) фами́лия; ~ **tree** родосло́вное де́рево; ~ **planning** контро́ль (*m.*) над рожда́емостью; **in the** ~ **way** бере́менная, в интере́сном положе́нии.

famine [ˈfæmɪn] *n.* го́лод; **water** ~ о́страя нехва́тка воды́; ~ **prices** це́ны, взви́нченные о́строй нехва́ткой това́ров.

famish [ˈfæmɪʃ] *v.t.* мори́ть (*impf.*) го́лодом; **I'm ~ed** я си́льно проголода́лся; я умира́ю с го́лоду; **the child looks half ~ed** у ребёнка замо́ренный/голо́дный вид.

famous [ˈfeɪməs] *adj.* знамени́тый, просла́вленный; **the road is** ~ **for its views** э́та доро́га изве́стна тем, что о́чень живопи́сна; (*coll.*) **he has a** ~ **appetite** у него́ зави́дный аппети́т.

fan[1] [fæn] *n.* ве́ер; ~ **vaulting** ве́ерный свод; (*ventilator*) вентиля́тор.

v.t.: ~ **o.s.** обма́хиваться (*impf.*) ве́ером; **he ~ned the spark into a blaze** он разжёг из и́скры пла́мя; ~ **the flame** (*fig.*) разжига́ть, -е́чь стра́сти; **the breeze ~ned our faces** ветеро́к обвева́л нам лицо́.

v.i.: ~ **out** (*e.g. roads*) расходи́ться (*impf.*) ве́ером; (*e.g. soldiers*) развёр|тываться, -ну́ться ве́ером.

cpds. **~-belt** *n.* реме́нь (*m.*) вентиля́тора; **~-fold** *adj.*: **~-fold paper** (*comput.*) фальцо́ванная бума́га; **~-light** *n.*

веерообра́зное окно́; **~-tail** *adj.*: **~-tail pigeon** труба́стый го́лубь; **~-vaulting** *n.* ребри́стый свод.

fan[2] [fæn] *n.* (*coll.*, *devotee*) боле́льщик, люби́тель (*m.*).

cpd. **~-mail** *n.* пи́сьма (*nt. pl.*) от покло́нников/почита́телей.

fanatic [fə'nætɪk] *n.* фана́тик.

adj. (*also* **~al**) фанати́чный, фанати́ческий.

fanaticism [fə'nætɪ,sɪz(ə)m] *n.* фанати́зм.

fancier ['fænsɪə(r)] *n.* люби́тель (*m.*), знато́к (*чего*).

fanciful ['fænsɪ,fʊl] *adj.* капри́зный; прихотли́вый, причу́дливый.

fancifulness ['fænsɪ,fʊlnɪs] *n.* прихотли́вость, причу́дливость.

fancy ['fænsɪ] *n.* **1.** (*imagination*) фанта́зия, воображе́ние. **2.** (*thg. imagined*, *supposition*) фанта́зия. **3.** (*liking*) скло́нность; **he took a ~ to her** он е́ю увлёкся; **it caught my ~** э́то мне понра́вилось (*or* пришло́сь по вку́су); **a passing ~** мимолётное увлече́ние. **4.** (*as adj.*): **a ~ portrait** (*based on imagination*) вообража́емый портре́т; **~ cakes** фигу́рные пиро́жные; **~ dress** маскара́дный костю́м; **a ~ price** непоме́рная цена́; **~ goods** безделу́шки (*f. pl.*); мо́дные това́ры (*m. pl.*); галантере́я; **~ man** (*souteneur*) сутенёр; **this dress is too ~ to wear to work** для рабо́ты ну́жно пла́тье поскромне́е.

v.t. **1.** (*imagine*) вообра|жа́ть, -зи́ть; фантази́ровать (*impf.*); **~ (that)!** вообрази́те!; поду́мать то́лько!; **~ his being here!** кто б мог поду́мать, что он здесь! **2.** (*suppose*, *feel*) полага́ть (*impf.*); счита́ть (*impf.*); **she fancied him to be dead** она́ полага́ла, что он у́мер; **I ~ he will come** мне сдаётся, что он придёт. **3.** (*like*, *wish*) хоте́ть (*impf.*) *+g.*; жела́ть (*impf.*); **I don't ~ this place** мне не по душе́ (*or* не нра́вится) э́то ме́сто; **he fancies himself as a speaker** он вообража́ет себя́ ора́тором; **what do you ~ for dinner?** чего́ бы вам хоте́лось на у́жин?

cpds. **~-free** *adj.* свобо́дный от привя́занностей; невлюблённый; **~-work** *n.* вы́шивка, вышива́ние, рукоде́лие.

fandango [fæn'dæŋgəʊ] *n.* фанда́нго (*indecl.*).

fane [feɪn] *n.* (*poet.*) храм.

fanfare ['fænfeə(r)] *n.* фанфа́ра.

fanfaronade [,fænfærə'neɪd] *n.* фанфаро́нство.

fang [fæŋ] *n.* (*of wolf etc.*) клык; (*of snake*) ядови́тый зуб.

fanny ['fænɪ] *n.* (*Br. vulg.*, *female genitals*) пизда́; (*US sl.*, *buttocks*) за́дница, по́пка.

fantasia [fæn'teɪzɪə, ,fæntə'zɪə] *n.* фанта́зия.

fantasize ['fæntə,saɪz] *v.i.* фантази́ровать (*impf.*).

fantastic [fæn'tæstɪk] *adj.* (*wild*, *strange*, *absurd*) фантасти́ческий, фантасти́чный; (*coll.*, *marvellous*) потряса́ющий, изуми́тельный.

f|antasy, ph- ['fæntəsɪ, -zɪ] *n.* фанта́зия.

fanwise ['fænwaɪz] *adv.* веерообра́зно.

FAO (*abbr. of* **Food and Agriculture Organization of the United Nations**) ФА́О, (Продово́льственная и сельскохозя́йственная организа́ция Объединённых На́ций).

f.a.o. (*abbr. of* **for the attention of**) вним. (*+g.*), (внима́нию (*+g.*)).

far [fɑː(r)] *n.* (*of distance or amount*): **have you come from ~?** вы издалека́ прие́хали?; **this is better by ~** э́то намно́го лу́чше.

adj. да́льний, далёкий, отдалённый; **a ~ country** далёкая страна́; **a ~ journey** да́льнее путеше́ствие; **the F~ East** Да́льний Восто́к; **at the ~ end of the street** на друго́м конце́ у́лицы.

adv. далеко́; **~ away, off** о́чень далеко́; **~ and near, wide** повсю́ду; **they came from ~ and wide** они́ съе́хались отовсю́ду (*or* со всех концо́в); **~ into the air** высоко́ в во́здух; **~ into the ground** глубоко́ в зе́млю; **~ into the night** далеко́ за́ полночь; **~ better** (на)мно́го/гора́здо лу́чше; **~ different** соверше́нно друго́й; **~ (and away) the best** несравне́нно/намно́го лу́чше други́х; **it is ~ from true** э́то совсе́м не так; э́то весьма́ далеко́ от и́стины; **~ from satisfactory** весьма́ неудовлетвори́тельный; **not ~ wrong** не так уж далеко́ от и́стины; **~ from it!** ничу́ть!; отню́дь нет!; **~ be it from me to condemn him** я далёк от того́, что́бы осужда́ть его́; **~ from helping, he made things worse** он не то́лько не помо́г де́лу, но про́сто всё испо́ртил; **as ~ back as January** ещё/уже́ в январе́; **so ~** (*until now*) до сих пор; пока́ (что); **so ~, so good** пока́ всё хорошо́; **as, so ~ as** (*of distance*) до (*чего*); (*of extent*) наско́лько; поско́льку; **as ~ as I know** наско́лько мне изве́стно; **as ~ as I am concerned** что каса́ется меня́; **he went so ~ as to say ...** он да́же сказа́л…; **in so ~ as** (*to the extent that*) поско́льку, насто́лько; **how ~** (*of distance*) как далеко́; (*of extent*) наско́лько; **he will go ~** (*succeed*) он далеко́ пойдёт; **£5 will not go ~** на пять фу́нтов далеко́ не уе́дешь; **this will go ~ to pay our expenses** э́то почти́ покро́ет на́ши расхо́ды; **he has gone too ~ this time** на э́то раз он зашёл сли́шком далеко́; **he is ~ gone** (*of illness*) он совсе́м плох; (*of dotage*) он вы́жил из ума́; **few and ~ between** ре́дкие (*pl.*).

cpds. **~-away** *adj.* (*distant*) далёкий, отдалённый; (*absent*): **a ~-away look** отсу́тствующий взгляд; **F~ Eastern** *adj.* дальневосто́чный; **F~ Easterner** *n.* жи́тель (*fem.* -ница) Да́льнего Восто́ка; **~-famed** *adj.* широко́ изве́стный; **~-fetched** *adj.* с натя́жкой; притя́нутый за́ волосы/уши; **~-flung** *adj.* обши́рный; широко́ раски́нувшийся; **~-off** *adj.* отдалённый; **~-reaching** *adj.* име́ющий серьёзные после́дствия; чрева́тый серьёзными после́дствиями; **~-seeing** *adj.* дальнови́дный, прозорли́вый; **~-sighted** *adj.* (*prudent etc.*) дальнови́дный, прозорли́вый, предусмотри́тельный; (*long-sighted*) дальнозо́ркий.

farad ['færəd] *n.* (*electr.*) фара́да.

farce [fɑːs] *n.* (*theatr.*, *fig.*) фарс.

farcical ['fɑːsɪk(ə)l] *adj.* смехотво́рный, нele ́пый.

fare[1] [feə(r)] *n.* **1.** (*cost of journey*) пла́та за прое́зд; **what is the ~?** ско́лько сто́ит прое́зд/биле́т?; **'F~s, please!'** «плати́те за прое́зд». **2.** (*passenger*) пассажи́р.

v.i. **1.** (*travel*) путеше́ствовать (*impf.*); **~ forth** отпра́виться (*pf.*) в путеше́ствие. **2.** (*progress*, *prosper*): **how did you ~ on the journey?** как вы съе́здили?; **it ~d well with him** всё ему́ благоприя́тствовало; **you may go further and ~ worse** дово́льствуйтесь тем, что есть; ≃ от добра́ добра́ не и́щут.

cpd. **~-paying** *adj.* платя́щий за прое́зд.

fare[2] [feə(r)] *n.* (*food*) стол; съестны́е припа́с|ы (*pl.*, *g.* -ов); **bill of ~** меню́ (*nt. indecl.*).

farewell [feə'wel] *n.* проща́ние; **~ dinner** проща́льный у́жин; **make one's ~s, bid ~ (to)** про|ща́ться, -сти́ться (с+*i.*).

int. проща́й(те).

farinaceous [,færɪ'neɪʃəs] *adj.* мучни́стый, мучно́й.

farm [fɑːm] *n.* фе́рма; (*in former USSR*, *collective ~*) колхо́з; **state ~** совхо́з; (*outside former USSR*) госхо́з; **dairy ~** моло́чная фе́рма; **~ worker** рабо́тни|к (*fem.* -ца) на фе́рме; сельскохозя́йственный рабо́чий.

v.t. & i. **1.** (*agric.*) занима́ться (*impf.*) се́льским хозя́йством; быть фе́рмером; **he ~s 200 hectares** он обраба́тывает 200 гекта́ров земли́. **2.**: **~ out** (*taxes*) отд|ава́ть, -а́ть на о́ткуп; **~ out work** отда́ть (*pf.*) часть рабо́ты.

cpds. **~-hand, ~-labourer** *nn.* рабо́тник на фе́рме; сельскохозя́йственный рабо́чий; **~house** *n.* фе́рмерский дом; **~stead** *n.* фе́рма со слу́жбами; хозя́йство; **~yard** *n.* двор фе́рмы.

farmer ['fɑːmə(r)] *n.* фе́рмер.

faro ['feərəʊ] *n.* фарао́н.

farouche [fə'ruːʃ] *adj.* ди́кий, нелюди́мый.

farrago [fə'rɑːgəʊ] *n.* мешани́на; вся́кая вся́чина; (*nonsense*) чепуха́.

farrier ['færɪə(r)] *n.* ко́вочный кузне́ц; (*mil.*) конов́од.

farrow ['færəʊ] *n.* опоро́с; **15 at one ~** 15 порося́т в одно́м опоро́се; **in ~** супоро́с(н)ая.

v.i. пороси́ться, о-.

fart [fɑːt] (*vulg.*) *n.* пердёж.

v.i. перде́ть, пёрнуть.

farther ['fɑːðə(r)] (*see also* **further**) *adj.* бо́лее отдалённый; дальне́йший.

adv. да́льше, да́лее.

farthermost ['fɑːðə,məʊst] *adj.* (*see also* **furthermost**) са́мый да́льний/отдалённый.

farthest ['fɑːðɪst] (*see also* **furthest**) *adj.* са́мый да́льний.
adv. да́льше всего́; **at ~** (*at most*) са́мое бо́льшее.
farthing ['fɑːðɪŋ] *n.* (*hist.*) фа́ртинг; **the uttermost ~** после́дний грош; **I don t care a brass ~!** мне наплева́ть!
farthingale ['fɑːðɪŋˌgeɪl] *n.* (*hist.*) ю́бка с фи́жмами.
fascia ['feɪʃə] *n.* (*archit.*) поясо́к, ва́лик, фа́ска.
fascicle ['fæsɪk(ə)l] *n.* (*bot.*) пучо́к, гро́здь; (*of book*) (отде́льный) вы́пуск.
fascinate ['fæsɪˌneɪt] *v.t.* (*of snake etc.*) гипнотизи́ровать, за- взгля́дом; завор|а́живать, -ожи́ть; (*charm*) очаро́в|ывать, -а́ть; плен|я́ть, -и́ть.
fascinating ['fæsɪˌneɪtɪŋ] *adj.* обворожи́тельный, очарова́тельный, плени́тельный; (*story*) захва́тывающий.
fascination [ˌfæsɪ'neɪʃ(ə)n] *n.* очарова́ние, обая́ние, пре́лесть.
fascinator ['fæsɪˌneɪtə(r)] *n.* (*charmer*) чаро́дей.
Fascism ['fæʃɪz(ə)m] *n.* фаши́зм.
Fascist ['fæʃɪst] *n.* фаши́ст (*fem.* -ка).
adj. фаши́стский.
fash [fæʃ] *v.t.* (*Sc.*): **~ o.s.** беспоко́иться (*impf.*), му́читься (*impf.*).
fashion ['fæʃ(ə)n] *n.* **1.** (*way*) о́браз, мане́ра; **after a ~** (*indifferently*) до не́которой сте́пени; с грехо́м попола́м; **after the ~ of** по образцу́ *+g.*; на мане́р *+g.* **2.** (*prevailing style*) мо́да; **set the ~** зад|ава́ть, -а́ть тон; (*for sth.*) вв|оди́ть, -ести́ (что-н.) в мо́ду; **in the ~** в мо́де; **out of ~** вы́шедший из мо́ды; **man of ~** све́тский челове́к; **woman of ~** све́тская да́ма; **in the height of ~** по после́дней мо́де; после́дний крик мо́ды; **~ designer** моделье́р; **~ house** дом моде́лей; **~ magazine, paper** журна́л мод; **~ parade** пока́з мод.
v.t. (*e.g. an object*) прид|ава́ть, -а́ть фо́рму *+d.*; **fully ~ed** (*stockings*) чулки́ со швом; (*e.g. s.o.'s taste*) формирова́ть, с-.
cpd. **~-plate** *n.* мо́дная карти́нка.
fashionable ['fæʃnəb(ə)l] *adj.* мо́дный.
fashionableness ['fæʃ(ə)nəbəlnɪs] *n.* соотве́тствие мо́де.
fast[1] [fɑːst] *n.* пост; **break one's ~** разгов|ля́ться, -е́ться.
v.i. пости́ться (*impf.*); **the medicine is to be taken ~ing** лека́рство сле́дует принима́ть натоща́к.
cpd. **~-day** *n.* по́стный день.
fast[2] [fɑːst] *adj.* (*firm, secure*) про́чный, кре́пкий; **the post is ~ in the ground** столб про́чно вбит в зе́млю; **he made the boat ~** он привяза́л ло́дку; **the door is ~** дверь пло́тно закры́та (*or* кре́пко заперта́); **~ friends** ве́рные друзья́; **~ colours** сто́йкие цвета́.
adv. про́чно, кре́пко; **the ship was ~ aground** кора́бль про́чно сел на мель; **she was ~ asleep** она́ кре́пко спала́; **he stood ~** он стоя́л твёрдо; (*fig.*) он твёрдо стоя́л на своём; **the car stuck ~** маши́на застря́ла/завя́зла; **he played ~ and loose with her affection** он игра́л её чу́вствами; **~ bind, ~ find** (*prov.*) кре́пче запрёшь — верне́е найдёшь.
fast[3] [fɑːst] *adj.* **1.** (*rapid*) ско́рый, бы́стрый; **he is a ~ worker** он бы́стро рабо́тает; **my watch is ~** мои́ часы́ спеша́т; **a ~ lens** (*phot.*) светоси́льный объекти́в; **pull a ~ one on s.o.** наду́ть (*pf.*) кого́-н.; объегори́ть (*pf.*) кого́-н. (*sl.*). **2.** (*dissipated*) беспу́тный; **a ~ woman** же́нщина лёгкого поведе́ния.
fasten ['fɑːs(ə)n] *v.t.* **1.** (*doors, windows*) зап|ира́ть, -ере́ть; (*dress, glove*) застёг|ивать, -ну́ть; (*shoelaces*) завя́з|ывать, -а́ть; (*with rope etc.*) привя́з|ывать, -а́ть; (*make firmer*) прикреп|ля́ть, -и́ть; **he ~ed the sheets of paper together** он скрепи́л вме́сте листы́ бума́ги. **2.** (*fig.*): **he ~ed his eyes on me** он уста́вился на меня́; **they ~ed the nickname on him** они́ да́ли ему́ э́то про́звище; **they ~ed the crime on him** ему́ приписа́ли э́то преступле́ние.
v.i. **1.** зап|ира́ться, -ере́ться; **the door won't ~** дверь не закрыва́ется/запира́ется; **the dress ~s down the back** пла́тье застёгивается на спине́. **2.**: **he ~ed upon the idea** он ухвати́лся за э́ту мысль; **the bees ~ed upon me** пчёлы налете́ли на меня́.
fasten|er ['fɑːs(ə)nə(r)], **-ing** ['fɑːsnɪŋ] *nn.* запо́р, задви́жка; (*on dress*) застёжка.
fastidious [fæ'stɪdɪəs] *adj.* привере́дливый, щепети́льный; разбо́рчивый; **a ~ critic** тре́бовательный/стро́гий кри́тик.
fastidiousness [fæ'stɪdɪəsnɪs] *n.* привере́дливость, щепети́льность; разбо́рчивость, дото́шность.
fastness[1] ['fɑːstnɪs] *n.* (*of dyes etc.*) про́чность, сто́йкость; (*stronghold*) опло́т, цитаде́ль.
fastness[2] ['fɑːstnɪs] *n.* (*speed*) ско́рость, быстрота́.
fat [fæt] *n.* **1.** (*animal substance*) жир; (*opp. to lean meat*) жир, са́ло; **the ~ is in the fire** (*fig.*) ≃ быть беде́!; **live on one's own ~** (*fig.*) жить (*impf.*) ста́рыми запа́сами. **2.** (*corpulence*) полнота́, жиро́к; **he has run to ~** он растолсте́л/располне́л. **3.** (*fig., richness*): **they live on the ~ of the land** они́ купа́ются в ро́скоши.
adj. **1.** (*of pers. etc.*) то́лстый, жи́рный, ту́чный; **get ~** растолсте́ть (*pf.*); **~ cheeks** пу́хлые щёки; **~ fingers** то́лстые па́льцы; (*of food*) жи́рный. **2.** (*rich, fertile*): **a ~ profit** больша́я при́быль; (*pej.*) жи́рный кусо́к; **~ soil** плодоро́дная/ту́чная земля́; **a ~ part** (*theatr., coll.*) вы́игрышная роль. **3.** (*coll., iron.*): **a ~ lot you care!** а тебе́ наплева́ть!; о́чень тебя́ э́то беспоко́ит!; **that's a ~ lot of use** мно́го с э́того то́лку.
v.t. (*also* **~ up**) отк|а́рмливать, -орми́ть; раск|а́рмливать, -орми́ть.
cpds. **~head** *n.* (*coll.*) болва́н, о́лух, тупи́ца (*c.g.*); **~-headed, ~-witted** *adjs.* тупоголо́вый.
fatal ['feɪt(ə)l] *adj.* **1.** (*causing death*) смерте́льный, ги́бельный, па́губный; **a ~ accident** несча́стный слу́чай со смерте́льным исхо́дом; **this was ~ to our plans** э́то оказа́лось роковы́м для на́ших пла́нов. **2.** (*fateful*) роково́й, фата́льный.
fatalism ['feɪtəˌlɪz(ə)m] *n.* фатали́зм.
fatalist ['feɪtəlɪst] *n.* фатали́ст.
fatalistic [ˌfeɪtə'lɪstɪk] *adj.* фаталисти́ческий, фаталисти́чный.
fatality [fə'tælətɪ] *n.* (*natural calamity*) стихи́йное бе́дствие; (*fatal accident*) смерть от несча́стного слу́чая; (*destiny*) рок, фата́льность.
fata morgana [ˌfɑːtə mɔː'gɑːnə] *n.* фа́та-морга́на, мира́ж.
fate [feɪt] *n.* **1.** (*personified destiny*) судьба́, рок; **as sure as ~** несомне́нно; **the F~s** (*myth.*) Па́рки (*f. pl.*), Мо́йры (*f. pl.*). **2.** (*what is in store for one*) судьба́, у́часть, уде́л, до́ля; **they met their various ~s** ка́ждому из них доста́лся свой уде́л. **3.** (*death*) ги́бель, смерть; **he sent him to his ~** он посла́л его́ на ги́бель.
v.t. предопредел|я́ть, -и́ть; **he was ~d to die** ему́ суждено́ бы́ло поги́бнуть.
fateful ['feɪtfʊl] *adj.* роково́й.
father ['fɑːðə(r)] *n.* **1.** (*male parent, also fig.*) оте́ц, роди́тель (*m.*); **the wish was ~ to the thought** он при́нял жела́емое за действи́тельное; **God the F~** Бог-Оте́ц; **our Heavenly F~** Оте́ц Небе́сный; **Our F~** (*prayer*) О́тче наш. **2.** (*pl., ancestors*) отцы́, де́ды (*m. pl.*). **3.** (*founder, leader*) оте́ц, родонача́льник; **city ~s** отцы́ го́рода; **the Pilgrim F~s** отцы́-пилигри́мы. **4.** (*oldest member*) старе́йшина (*m.*). **5.** (*in personifications*): **F~ Christmas** дед-моро́з; **F~ Thames** ма́тушка Те́мза; **F~ Time** вре́мя; **the F~ of lies** сатана́ (*m.*), лука́вый. **6.** (*priest*) оте́ц, ба́тюшка; **the Holy F~** его́ святе́йшество; (*as title*): **F~ Sergius** оте́ц Се́ргий.
v.t. **1.** (*beget*) поро|жда́ть, -ди́ть; быть (*impf.*)/стать (*pf.*) отцо́м *+g.* **2.** (*fig., originate*) поро|жда́ть, -ди́ть. **3.** (*pass as author of*) быть а́втором/творцо́м (*чего*). **4.** (*fix responsibility*): **do not ~ this scheme on me** не припи́сывайте э́тот пла́н мне.
cpds. **~-figure** *n.* кто-н., заменя́ющий отца́; **~-in-law** *n.* (*husband's ~*) свёкор; (*wife's ~*) тесть (*m.*); **~land** *n.* оте́чество, отчи́зна, ро́дина.
fatherhood ['fɑːðəhʊd] *n.* отцо́вство.
fatherless ['fɑːðəlɪs] *adj.* без отца́.
fatherliness ['fɑːðəlɪnɪs] *n.* оте́ческое отноше́ние.
fatherly ['fɑːðəlɪ] *adj.* оте́ческий.
fathom ['fæð(ə)m] *n.* морска́я саже́нь.
v.t. (*lit.*) изм|еря́ть, -е́рить глубину́ *+g.*; (*fig.*) пост|ига́ть, -и́гнуть; вн|ика́ть, -и́кнуть в*+a.*
fathometer [fə'ðɒmɪtə(r)] *n.* эхоло́т.
fathomless ['fæðəmlɪs] *adj.* (*very deep*) бездо́нный; (*incomprehensible*) непостижи́мый.
fatigue [fə'tiːg] *n.* уста́лость (*also* **metal ~**); (*mil.*) хозя́йственная рабо́та; (*pl. dress*) наря́д на рабо́ту.

v.t. утом|ля́ть, -и́ть.

cpds. **~-dress** *n.* рабо́чая оде́жда; спецоде́жда; **~-duty** *n.* хозя́йственные рабо́ты (*f. pl.*); **~-party** *n.* рабо́чая кома́нда.

fatling [ˈfætlɪŋ] *n.* отко́рмленное на убо́й живо́тное.

fatness [ˈfætnɪs] *n.* полнота́.

fatten [ˈfæt(ə)n] *v.t.* (*animal*) отк|а́рмливать, -орми́ть на убо́й; (*soil*) уд|обря́ть, -о́брить.

v.i. жире́ть (*impf.*); толсте́ть (*impf.*).

fattening [ˈfæt(ə)nɪŋ] *adj.* калори́йный.

fattiness [ˈfætɪnɪs] *n.* (*of meat etc.*) жи́рность.

fattish [ˈfætɪʃ] *adj.* толстова́тый, полнова́тый.

fatty [ˈfætɪ] *n.* (*coll.*) толстя́к.

adj. жи́рный, жирово́й; **~ bacon** жи́рный бeко́н; **~ tissue** жирова́я ткань; **~ degeneration** (*med.*) жирово́е перерожде́ние.

fatuity [fəˈtjuːɪtɪ] *n.* самодово́льная глу́пость.

fatuous [ˈfætjʊəs] *adj.* самодово́льно-глу́пый; бессмы́сленный.

faucet [ˈfɔːsɪt] *n.* ве́нтиль (*m.*), вту́лка, зату́чка; (*US, tap*) кран.

faugh [fɔː] *int.* тьфу!; фу!

fault [fɒlt, fɔːlt] *n.* **1.** (*imperfection*) недоста́ток, дефе́кт; **generous to a ~** чересчу́р ще́дрый; **find ~ with s.o.** на|ходи́ть, -йти́ недоста́тки у кого́-н.; прид|ира́ться, -ра́ться к кому́-н.; **my memory was at ~** па́мять мне измени́ла (*or* подвела́ меня́). **2.** (*physical defect*) дефе́кт; **there was a ~ in the electric connection** в электри́ческой сети́ была́ неиспра́вность. **3.** (*error*) оши́бка; **~s of syntax** синтакси́ческие оши́бки. **4.** (*blame*) вина́; **it's (all) your ~** э́то ва́ша вина́; э́то всё из-за вас; **the ~ lies with him** он винова́т. **5.** (*at tennis etc.*) непра́вильная пода́ча; **double ~** двойна́я оши́бка. **6.** (*hunting*) поте́ря сле́да; **the hounds are at ~** го́нчие потеря́ли след. **7.** (*geol.*) разло́м, сдвиг, сброс.

v.t. на|ходи́ть, -йти́ недоста́тки в+*p.*; прид|ира́ться, -ра́ться к+*d.*; **I could not ~ his argument** я не мог придра́ться к его́ аргумента́ции.

cpds. **~-finder** *n.* приди́ра (*c.g.*); **~-finding** *n.* приди́рчивость; *adj.* приди́рчивый.

faultiness [ˈfɒltɪnɪs, ˈfɔːltɪnɪs] *n.* оши́бочность.

faultless [ˈfɒltlɪs, ˈfɔːlt-] *adj.* (*without blame*) непогреши́мый; безоши́бочный; (*without blemish*): **~ precision** безупре́чная то́чность; **~ evening dress** безукори́зненно сидя́щий вече́рний костю́м.

faulty [ˈfɒltɪ, ˈfɔːltɪ] *adv.* оши́бочный; с изъя́ном; **a ~ memory** сла́бая па́мять; **a ~ connection** (*tech.*) повреждённое соедине́ние.

faun [fɔːn] *n.* фавн.

fauna [ˈfɔːnə] *n.* фа́уна.

faute de mieux [ˌfəʊt də ˈmjɜː] за неиме́нием лу́чшего.

favour [ˈfeɪvə(r)] *n.* **1.** (*goodwill*) благоскло́нность; расположе́ние (к+*d.*); **win s.o.'s ~**; **find ~ in s.o.'s eyes** сниска́ть (*pf.*) чьё-н. расположе́ние (*or* чью-н. благоскло́нность); **look with ~ on** благоскло́нно/доброжела́тельно относи́ться (*impf.*) к+*d.*; **curry ~ with s.o.** зaи́скивать (*impf.*) пе́ред кем-н.; **he is out of ~ with his superiors** он не в чести́ у нача́льства; **I am in ~ of the plan** я — за э́тот план. **2.** (*kindly act*) одолже́ние, любе́зность, услу́га; **he did me a ~** он оказа́л мне любе́зность; он сде́лал мне одолже́ние; **we request the ~ of your company** мы про́сим почти́ть нас свои́м прису́тствием; **he enjoyed her ~s** он по́льзовался её благоскло́нностью. **3.** (*advantage, credit*) по́льза; **this is in his ~** э́то говори́т в его́ по́льзу; **the exchange rate is in our ~** курс обме́на валю́ты вы́годен для нас; **the cheque was drawn in my ~** чек был вы́писан на моё и́мя. **4.** (*privilege*): **I don't ask for any ~s** я не прошу́ одолже́ний/привиле́гий. **5.** (*prejudice*) предвзя́тость, предпочте́ние; **without fear or ~** беспристра́стно. **6.** (*comm.*): **your ~ of yesterday** ва́ше вчера́шнее письмо́. **7.** (*badge, ribbon, etc.*) значо́к, бант, розе́тка.

v.t. **1.** (*approve, support*) благоприя́тствовать (*impf.*) +*d.*; подде́рж|ивать, -а́ть; **fortune ~s the brave** сме́лость города́ берёт; **this ~s my theory** э́то подтвержда́ет мою́ тео́рию; **the weather ~ed our voyage** пого́да благоприя́тствовала на́шему путеше́ствию. **2.** (*choose*) предпоч|ита́ть, -е́сть; **I ~ the grey horse (to win)** по-мо́ему, у се́рой ло́шади бо́льше ша́нсов вы́играть; **she ~ed a pink dress** она́ вы́брала ро́зовое пла́тье. **3.** (*treat with partiality*) ока́з|ывать, -а́ть предпочте́ние +*d.*; быть пристра́стным к +*d.*; **he ~s certain pupils** он ока́зывает предпочте́ние не́которым ученика́м. **4.** (*oblige, treat favourably*): **she ~ed us with a song** она́ оказа́ла нам любе́зность, испо́лнив пе́сню; **most ~ed nation** наибо́лее благоприя́тствуемая на́ция; **most ~ed nation clause** огово́рка о наибо́льшем благоприя́тствовании; **the ~ed few** немно́гие и́збранные. **5.** (*resemble*) походи́ть (*impf.*) на+*a.*; **the child ~s its father** ребёнок похо́ж на своего́ отца́.

favourable [ˈfeɪvərəb(ə)l] *adj.* благоприя́тный, благоскло́нный; **~ weather** благоприя́тная пого́да; **a ~ report** положи́тельный отчёт; **he is ~ to the plan** он благоскло́нно/одобри́тельно отно́сится к э́тому пла́ну.

favourableness [ˈfeɪvərəbəlnɪs] *n.* благоприя́тное/благоскло́нное отноше́ние (к+*d.*).

favourer [ˈfeɪvərə(r)] *n.* люби́тель (*m.*) (*кого, чего*); покрови́тельствующий +*d.*; сторо́нник; приве́рженец.

favourite [ˈfeɪvərɪt] *n.* (*preferred pers.*) люби́мец, фавори́т; (*preferred thg.*) люби́мая вещь; (*horse*) фавори́т.

adj. люби́мый, излю́бленный; **my ~ food** моя́ люби́мая еда́.

favouritism [ˈfeɪvərɪˌtɪz(ə)m] *n.* фаворити́зм.

fawn[1] [fɔːn] *n.* (*deer*) молодо́й оле́нь; **in ~** сте́льная (лань); (*colour*) желтова́то-кори́чневый цвет.

adj. (*also* **~-coloured**) желтова́то-кори́чневый.

v.t. & i. (*of deer*) тели́ться, о-.

fawn[2] [fɔːn] *v.i.* (*of dog*) ласка́ться (*impf.*); виля́ть (*impf.*) хвосто́м; (*of pers.*): **~ on s.o.** подли́з|ываться, -а́ться к кому́-н.; выслу́живаться (*impf.*) пе́ред кем-н.

fax [fæks] *n.* факс; **~ machine** факсими́льный аппара́т, телефа́кс.

v.t. перед|ава́ть, -а́ть по фа́ксу.

fay [feɪ] *n.* (*poet.*) фе́я.

faze [feɪz] *v.t.* сму|ща́ть, -ти́ть; прив|оди́ть, -ести́ в недоуме́ние.

FBI (*abbr. of* ***Federal Bureau of Investigation***) ФБР, (Федера́льное бюро́ рассле́дований).

fealty [ˈfiːəltɪ] *n.* ве́рность васса́ла феода́лу; **swear, do ~ to s.o.** прися́г|а́ть, -ну́ть на ве́рность кому́-н.

fear [fɪə(r)] *n.* **1.** (*terror, anxiety*) страх, боя́знь, опасе́ние; **in ~ and trembling** дрожа́ от стра́ха; **the ~ of God** страх бо́жий; **I put the ~ of God into him** (*coll.*) я нагна́л на него́ стра́ху; **he was in ~ of his life** он боя́лся за свою́ жизнь; **I could not speak for ~** от стра́ха я не мог говори́ть; **your ~s are groundless** ва́ши опасе́ния напра́сны. **2.** (*of precaution, likelihood*): **I was silent for ~ of offending him** я молча́л, боя́сь оби́деть его́; **we tethered the horse for ~ it should escape** мы привяза́ли ло́шадь, что́бы она́ не убежа́ла; **there is no ~ of my losing the money** не бо́йтесь, я не потеря́ю де́ньги; **no ~!** (*coll.*) ни-ни́!; ни за что!

v.t. & i. боя́ться (*impf.*) +*g.*; опаса́ться (*impf.*) +*g.*; **he ~s death** он бои́тся сме́рти; **he ~ed to speak** он боя́лся говори́ть; **I ~ the worst** я опаса́юсь ху́дшего; **I ~ for his life** я опаса́юсь за его́ жизнь; **he will come, never ~!** не бо́йтесь, он придёт; (*expr. regret*): **I ~ you must stay** бою́сь, вам придётся оста́ться.

cpd. **~-monger** *n.* панике́р.

fearful [ˈfɪəfʊl] *adj.* (*terrible*) стра́шный, ужа́сный; (*coll., frightful*) ужа́сный, чудо́вищный, стра́шный; (*timorous*) ро́бкий, боязли́вый; **I was ~ of waking him** я боя́лся разбуди́ть его́.

fearfulness [ˈfɪəfʊlnɪs] *n.* страх, у́жас; (*timidity*) ро́бость, боязли́вость.

fearless [ˈfɪəlɪs] *adj.* бесстра́шный, неустраши́мый; **he was ~ of the consequences** он не боя́лся после́дствий.

fearlessness [ˈfɪəlɪsnɪs] *n.* бесстра́шие, неустраши́мость.

fearsome [ˈfɪəsəm] *adj.* устраша́ющий, гро́зный.

feasibility [ˌfiːzɪˈbɪlɪtɪ] *n.* осуществи́мость, выполни́мость.

feasible [ˈfiːzɪb(ə)l] *adj.* осуществи́мый, выполни́мый.

feast [fi:st] *n.* **1.** (*relig.*) (церко́вный) пра́здник; престо́льный пра́здник; **movable ~** подвижно́й пра́здник. **2.** (*meal*) пир, пи́ршество; **enough is as good as a ~** от добра́ добра́ не и́щут; (*fig.*): **a ~ of reason** интеллектуа́льная бесе́да.

v.t. & i. пирова́ть (*impf.*); пра́здновать (*impf.*); **they ~ed away the night** они́ (про)пирова́ли всю ночь; **he ~ed his friends** он ще́дро угоща́л свои́х друзе́й; **he ~ed his eyes on the scene** он любова́лся э́тим зре́лищем.

cpd. **~-day** *n.* пра́здник, пра́здничный день; **today is my ~-day** сего́дня мои́ имени́н|ы (*pl., g.* —); я сего́дня имени́нни|к (*fem.* -ца).

feaster ['fi:stə(r)] *n.* пиру́ющий, уча́стник пи́ра.

feat [fi:t] *n.* по́двиг; **~ of engineering** выдаю́щееся достиже́ние инжене́рного иску́сства; **~ of valour** до́блестный по́двиг; **it was a ~ to get him to come** бы́ло нелёгким де́лом затащи́ть его́ сюда́.

feather ['feðə(r)] *n.* перо́; **that is a ~ in his cap** он мо́жет э́тим горди́ться; **he showed the white ~** он стру́сил; **in high ~** в припо́днятом настрое́нии; **you could have knocked me down with a ~** ни за что бы не пове́рил (э́тому).

v.t. опер|я́ть, -и́ть; укр|аша́ть, -а́сить пе́рьями; **our ~ed friends** на́ши перна́тые друзья́; **~ one's nest** (*lit.*) выстила́ть, вы́стелить гнездо́ пе́рьями; (*fig.*) наби́ть (*pf.*) себе́ карма́н; **~ an oar** выноси́ть, вы́нести весло́ плашмя́; **~ a propeller blade** устан|а́вливать, -ови́ть ло́пасть во флю́герном положе́нии.

cpds. **~-bed** *n.* пери́на, пухови́к; *v.t.* (*fig.*) балова́ть, из-; изне́жи|вать, -ть; **~-bedding** *n.* (*fig.*) баловство́; (*econ.*) иску́сственное раздува́ние шта́тов; **~-brain, ~-head** *nn.* пуста́я башка́; **~-brained, ~-headed** *adjs.* пустоголо́вый; **he is ~-brained** у него́ ве́тер в голове́; **~-grass** *n.* (*bot.*) ковы́ль (*m.*); **~-head(ed)** *n. & adj.* = **~-brain(ed); ~weight** *n.* вес пера́; *adj.* в ве́се пера́; о́чень лёгкий.

feathery ['feðərɪ] *adj.* пухово́й; лёгкий, как пёрышко.

feature ['fi:tʃə(r)] *n.* **1.** (*part of face*) черта́; **he has strong ~s** у него́ волево́е лицо́. **2.** (*geog.*) черта́/подро́бность релье́фа; **a ~ of the landscape** осо́бенность ландша́фта. **3.** (*aspect*) черта́, осо́бенность; **the main ~s of his programme** основны́е пу́нкты (*m. pl.*) его́ програ́ммы. **4.** (*object of special attention, main item*): **this journal makes a ~ of sport** э́тот журна́л широко́ освеща́ет спорти́вные собы́тия; **~ (article)** темати́ческая статья́; **~ (film)** худо́жественный фильм.

v.t. (*give prominence to*) поме|ща́ть, -сти́ть на ви́дном ме́сте; **the newspaper ~d the murder story** газе́та помести́ла на ви́дном ме́сте сообще́ние об уби́йстве; **the film ~s a new actress** в фи́льме гла́вную роль поручи́ли но́вой актри́се.

v.i. (*figure prominently*) быть характе́рной черто́й.

cpds. **~-length** *adj.* (*film*) полнометра́жный; **~-writer** *n.* очеркист.

featureless ['fi:tʃəlɪs] *n.* невырази́тельный, бесцве́тный, бле́дный; **a ~ existence** бесцве́тное существова́ние.

febrifuge ['febrɪ,fju:dʒ] *n.* жаропонижа́ющее сре́дство.

febrile ['fi:braɪl] *adj.* (*lit., fig.*) лихора́дочный.

February ['febrʊərɪ] *n.* февра́ль (*m.*); (*attr.*) февра́льский.

fec|al ['fi:k(ə)l], **-es** ['fi:si:z] = **faec|al, -es**

feckless ['feklɪs] *adj.* безала́берный.

fecklessness ['feklɪsnɪs] *n.* безала́берность.

fecund ['fi:kənd, 'fek-] *adj.* плодоро́дный, плодови́тый.

fecundate ['fi:kən,deɪt, 'fek-] *v.t.* де́лать, с- плодоро́дным; оплодотвор|я́ть, -и́ть.

fecundation [,fi:kən'deɪʃ(ə)n, ,fek-] *n.* оплодотворе́ние.

fecundity [fɪ'kʌndɪtɪ] *n.* плодоро́дие, плодови́тость.

federal ['fedər(ə)l] *adj.* федера́льный; (*in titles of states*) федерати́вный; **F~ Republic of Germany** Федерати́вная Респу́блика Герма́нии.

federalism ['fedərə,lɪz(ə)m] *n.* федерали́зм.

federalist ['fedərəlɪst] *n.* федерали́ст.

federate[1] ['fedərət] *adj.* федерати́вный.

federate[2] ['fedə,reɪt] *v.t. & i.* объедин|я́ть(ся), -и́ть(ся) на федерати́вных нача́лах.

federation [,fedə'reɪʃ(ə)n] *n.* федера́ция; (*of societies etc.*) объедине́ние.

federative ['fedərətɪv] *adj.* федерати́вный.

fedora [fɪ'dɔ:rə] *n.* мя́гкая шля́па.

fee [fi:] *n.* **1.** (*professional charge*) гонора́р; **school ~s** пла́та за обуче́ние; **club ~s** чле́нские взно́сы (*m. pl.*) в клуб; **(TV, radio) licence ~** абонеме́нтная пла́та; **retaining ~** предвари́тельный гонора́р. **2.** (*estate*) лен; феода́льное поме́стье; **land held in ~ simple** земля́, унасле́дованная без ограниче́ний.

v.t. плати́ть, за-/у- гонора́р *+d.*

feeble ['fi:b(ə)l] *adj.* хи́лый, сла́бый.

cpds. **~-minded** *adj.* слабоу́мный; **~-mindedness** *n.* слабоу́мие.

feebleness ['fi:bəlnɪs] *n.* хи́лость, сла́бость.

feed [fi:d] *n.* **1.** (*animal's*) корм; (*baby's*) еда́, кормле́ние; (*coll.*): **we had a good ~** мы хорошо́ перекуси́ли. **2.** (*fodder*) корм, фура́ж; **the horse is out at ~** ло́шадь на подно́жном корму́. **3.** (*of machine etc.*) пита́ние, пода́ча материа́ла.

v.t. **1.** (*give food to*) корми́ть, на-; пита́ть, на-; да|ва́ть, -ть корм *+d.*; **what do you ~ your dog on?** чем вы ко́рмите свою́ соба́ку?; **the hotel ~s you well** в гости́нице хорошо́ ко́рмят; **the child cannot ~ itself** ребёнок ещё не мо́жет есть сам; **the child needs ~ing up** ребёнка на́до подкорми́ть; **~ing-bottle** (де́тский) рожо́к; (*fig.*): **I am fed up** (*coll.*) я сыт по го́рло; мне надое́ло. **2.** (*give as food*) ск|а́рмливать, -орми́ть; **we ~ oats to horses** мы ко́рмим лошаде́й овсо́м. **3.** (*fig.*): **the moving belt ~s the machine** пита́ние маши́не подаётся транспортёром; **the lake is fed by two rivers** вода́ в о́зеро поступа́ет из двух рек; **he fed information into the computer** он ввёл да́нные в компью́тер; **the news fed his jealousy** э́та но́вость разожгла́ его́ ре́вность.

v.i. (*of animals*) корми́ться (*impf.*); (*graze*) пасти́сь (*impf.*); (*coll., of pers.*) пита́ться (*impf.*); корми́ться, про-.

cpds. **~-back** *n.* (*elec.*) обра́тное пита́ние; (*fig.*) о́тклик, реа́кция; **~-back from readers** о́тклики чита́телей; **~-bag** *n.* (*horse's*) то́рба; **~-pipe** *n.* (*tech.*) пита́тельная/подаю́щая труба́.

feeder ['fi:də(r)] *n.* **1.** едо́к; **he is a big ~** он обжо́ра; он лю́бит пое́сть. **2.** (*feeding-bottle*) (де́тский) рожо́к. **3.** (*bib*) нагру́дник. **4.** (*tributary*) прито́к; **~ line** (*railway*) ве́тка; (*airline*) ме́стная авиали́ния.

feel [fi:l] *n.* (*sensation*) ощуще́ние; (*contact*) осяза́ние; **cold to the ~** холо́дный на о́щупь; **have a ~ of this cloth** пощу́пайте э́ту мате́рию; **it has a soapy ~** на о́щупь э́то похо́же на мы́ло; **there will be frost tonight by the ~ of it** чу́вствуется, что но́чью бу́дет моро́з; **there is money in that envelope by the ~ of it** похо́же, что в э́том конве́рте — де́ньги; **if you practise you'll soon get the ~ of it** е́сли вы бу́дете упражня́ться, то ско́ро осво́ите э́тот приём (*or* набьёте ру́ку); **he has a ~ for language** у него́ есть чу́вство языка́.

v.t. **1.** (*explore by touch*) щу́пать, по-; ощу́п|ывать, -ать; про́бовать, по-; **~ the edge of a knife** потро́гать (*pf.*) ле́звие ножа́; **~ s.o.'s pulse** пощу́пать (*pf.*) кому́-н. пульс; (*fig.*) прощу́п|ывать, -ать кого́-н.; **he felt my muscles** он потро́гал мои́ мы́шцы; **~ the weight of this box!** чу́вствуете, ско́лько ве́сит э́тот я́щик!; **~ whether there are any bones broken** пощу́пайте, не сло́маны ли ко́сти; (*fig.*): **he felt out public opinion** он зонди́ровал обще́ственное мне́ние. **2.** (*grope*) пробира́ться (*impf.*) о́щупью; **he felt his way in the dark** он пробира́лся о́щупью в темноте́; **they are ~ing their way towards an agreement** они́ нащу́пывают по́чву для соглаше́ния. **3.** (*be aware of*) чу́вствовать, по-; ощу|ща́ть, -ти́ть; испы́т|ывать, -а́ть; **I can ~ a nail in my shoe** я чу́вствую, у меня́ в боти́нке гвоздь; **did you ~ the earthquake?** вы почу́вствовали землетрясе́ние?; **a felt want** ощути́мая нужда́. **4.** (*be affected by*) чу́вствовать, по-; ощу|ща́ть, -ти́ть; пережива́ть (*impf.*); **he felt the insult** он почу́вствовал оскорбле́ние; **he ~s (*or* is ~ing) the heat** жара́ на него́ пло́хо де́йствует; он пло́хо перено́сит жару́; **he felt the loss of his mother keenly** он о́стро переживáл смéрть мáтери; **we felt the force of his argument** мы сознавáли сúлу егó дóводов; **the horse is ~ing his oats** лóшадь взыгрáла/разрезвúлась. **5.** (*be of opinion*): **I ~ you should go** по-мóему, вам слéдует пойтú; **I ~ the plan to be unwise** я считáю, что э́тот план неблагоразу́мен.

v.i. **1.** (*experience sensation*): **I ~ cold** мне хóлодно; **I ~ hungry** я гóлоден; **I ~ sure** я увéрен; **I don't ~ quite myself** мне не по себé; **I ~ bound to say ...** я дóлжен сказáть...; **I ~ bad about not inviting him** мне сóвестно, что я не пригласúл егó; **I ~ as if my head were splitting** у меня́ такóе чу́вство, слóвно головá раскáлывается; **I ~ strongly about this** у меня́ твёрдое мнéние на э́то счёт; **I ~ like (going for) a walk** мне хóчется прогуля́ться; **do you ~ like dancing?** хотúте потанцевáть?; **I don't ~ up to going** я не в состоя́нии идтú; **how do you ~ about going there?** как вы относúтесь к тому́, чтóбы пойтú тудá?; **it ~s like rain** похóже, что быть дождю́; **I ~ for you** я вам сочу́вствую. **2.** (*produce sensation*) да|вáть, -ть ощущéние (*чего*); **your hands ~ cold** у вас холóдные ру́ки; **the air ~s chilly** здесь прохлáдно; **how does it ~ to be home?** каковó оказáться дóма? **3.** (*grope*): **he felt in his pocket for a coin** он пошáрил в кармáне, ищá монéту; **he felt along the wall for the door** он пытáлся нащу́пать дверь в стенé.

feeler ['fi:lə(r)] *n.* (*zool.*) щу́пальце, у́сик; (*fig.*): **he put out ~s** он закúнул у́дочку; он пустúл прóбный шар.

feeling ['fi:lɪŋ] *n.* **1.** (*power of sensation*) ощущéние, чу́вство; **sense of ~** ощущéние; **he lost all ~ in his legs** у негó онемéли нóги. **2.** (*sense, sensation*) сознáние, чу́вство; **I had a ~ of safety** я чу́вствовал себя́ в безопáсности. **3.** (*opinion*): **I have a ~ he won't come** у меня́ предчу́вствие, что он не придёт; **the general ~ is that ...** óбщее мнéние таковó, что... **4.** (*emotion*) чу́вство, страсть; **he spoke with ~** он говорúл с чу́вством; **I have mixed ~s** у меня́ э́то вызывáет смéшанные чу́вства; **good ~** доброжелáтельность; **no hard ~s, I hope** надéюсь, никакóй обúды; **~ ran high** стрáсти разгорéлись; **the speech aroused strong ~s** э́та речь разожглá стрáсти; **he appealed to their better ~s** он взывáл к их лу́чшим чу́вствам. **5.** (*sensitivity*) чувствúтельность; **you hurt his ~s** вы егó обúдели. **6.** (*sympathy*) сочу́вствие; **have you no ~ for his troubles?** неужéли егó бéды не вызывáют у вас сочу́вствия? **7.** (*aptitude*) понимáние, чутьё; **he has a ~ for the work** у негó есть дáнные для э́той рабóты.

adj. (*sympathetic*) пóлный сочу́вствия; (*sensitive*) чувствúтельный; **~ly** (*showing emotion*) прочу́вствованно; **he spoke ~ly** он говорúл с чу́вством.

feign [feɪn] *v.t.* (*simulate*) притвор|я́ться, -úться +*i.*; симулúровать (*impf., pf.*); **~ madness** симулúровать безу́мие; (*invent*) придóм|ывать, -ать; изобре|тáть, -стú.

feint[1] [feɪnt] *n.* (*pretence*) притвóрство; (*sham attack*) лóжная атáка, финт, дивéрсия.

v.i. нан|осúть, -естú отвлекáющий удáр.

feint[2] [feɪnt] *adj.* блéдный.

fel(d)spar ['feldspɑ:(r)] *n.* полевóй шпат.

felicitate [fə'lɪsɪ,teɪt] *v.t.* поздр|авля́ть, -áвить; желáть, по- счáстья +*d.*

felicitation [fə,lɪsɪ'teɪʃ(ə)n] *n.* (*usu. pl.*) поздравлéние; пожелáние счáстья.

felicitous [fə'lɪsɪtəs] *adj.* мéткий, умéстный, удáчный.

felicity [fə'lɪsɪtɪ] *n.* (*bliss*) блажéнство; (*aptness*) умéстность; (*apt phrase*) мéткое/удáчное замечáние.

feline ['fi:laɪn] *n.* живóтное из семéйства кошáчьих.

adj. кошáчий; (*fig.*): **a ~ remark** ехúдное замечáние.

fell[1] [fel] *n.* (*hide, hair*) шку́ра.

fell[2] [fel] *n.* (*hill*) горá; (*moorland*) верескóвая пу́стошь; откры́тая холмúстая мéстность.

fell[3] [fel] *adj.* (*poet.*) свирéпый, беспощáдный, лю́тый.

fell[4] [fel] *v.t.* (*pers.*) сби|вáть, -ть с ног; (*tree*) рубúть, с-; валúть, с-/по-.

fellah ['felə] *n.* (*pl.* **-een**) феллáх.

fellatio [fɪ'leɪʃɪəʊ, fe'lɑ:tɪəʊ] *n.* минéт.

feller ['felə(r)] *n.* (*of trees*) дровосéк.

fell|oe ['feləʊ], **-y** ['felɪ] *n.* óбод колесá, кося́к.

fellow ['feləʊ] *n.* **1.** (*chap; also coll.* **feller**) (*man, boy*) пáрень (*m.*); **a good ~** слáвный мáлый; **my dear ~** дорогóй мой!; **old ~!** старинá (*m.*), дружúще (*m.*); **young ~-my-lad!** молодóй человéк!; **a little ~** малы́ш, мальчугáн; **poor ~** бедня́га (*m.*); **what does the ~ want?** что э́тому человéку ну́жно?; **a ~ gets bored sitting here all day** осточертéет сидéть тут цéлый день; **can you spare a ~ the price of a drink?** мóжешь постáвить мне стакáнчик? **2.** (*comrade, companion*) товáрищ, собрáт; **~s in misfortune** товáрищи по несчáстью; **~s in crime** соучáстники преступлéния. **3.** (*equal, contemporary etc.*) рáвный; свéрстник; товáрищ; **he surpassed all his ~s** он превзошёл всех своúх свéрстников. **4.** (*of a pair*) пáра; **where is the ~ to this glove?** где вторáя перчáтка. **5.** (*acad. & professional*) коллéга; сотру́дник, сослужúвец; (*of a college*) член совéта коллéджа.

cpds. **~-being** *n.* блúжний; **~-Christian** *n.* брат/сестрá во Христé; единовéр|ец (*fem.* -ка); **~-citizen** *n.* сограждан|úн (*fem.* -анка); **~-countryman** *n.* соотéчественник; **~-countrywoman** *n.* соотéчественница; **~-creature** *n.* блúжний; **~-Englishman** *n.* соотéчественник-англичáнин; **~-exile** *n.* товáрищ по ссы́лке; **~-feeling** *n.* симпáтия, сочу́вствие; **~-man** *n.* блúжний; **~-soldier** *n.* товáрищ по ору́жию; однополчáнин; **~-student** *n.* товáрищ по университéту; сокýрсник; **~-traveller** *n.* (*lit., fig.*) попу́тчик; **~-travelling** *adj.*: **~-travelling writer** писáтель-попу́тчик.

fellowship ['feləʊʃɪp] *n.* (*companionship*) товáрищество, брáтство; **good ~** товáрищеские взаимоотношéния; (*association*) корпорáция; коллéгия (*адвокатов и т.п.*); (*of a college*) звáние члéна совéта коллéджа.

felly ['felɪ] = **felloe**

felon ['felən] *n.* уголóвный престу́пник.

felonious [fɪ'ləʊnɪəs] *adj.* престу́пный.

felony ['felənɪ] *n.* уголóвное преступлéние.

felspar ['felspɑ:(r)] = **fel(d)spar**

felt [felt] *n.* (*material*) вóйлок, фетр; **~ boots** вáленки (*m. pl.*); **~ hat** фéтровая шля́па; **~ slippers** вóйлочные ту́фли.

v.t. (*cover with ~*) покр|ывáть, -ы́ть вóйлоком.

cpd. **~-tip (pen)** *n.* фломáстер.

felting ['feltɪŋ] *n.* (*process of making felt*) валя́ние, вáлка; (*cloth*) вóйлок.

felucca [fɪ'lʌkə] *n.* фелю́га.

female ['fi:meɪl] *n.* (*woman or girl*) жéнщина; (*pej.*) бáба; (*animal*) сáмка, мáтка; (*plant*) жéнская óсобь.

adj. жéнский; **~ child** дéвочка; **~ slave** рабы́ня, рабá; **~ insect** насекóмое-сáмка; **~ plant** жéнская óсобь; **~ suffrage** избирáтельное прáво для жéнщин; **~ worker** рабóтница; **~ screw** гáйка.

feme [fi:m] *n.* (*leg.*): **~ covert** заму́жняя жéнщина; **~ sole** незаму́жняя жéнщина.

feminine ['femɪnɪn] *adj.* жéнский; (*as n.*): **the eternal ~** вéчная жéнственность; (*gram.*) жéнский; жéнского рóда; (*pros.*): **~ rhyme** жéнская рúфма.

femininity [,femɪ'nɪnɪtɪ] *n.* жéнственность.

feminism ['femɪ,nɪz(ə)m] *n.* феминúзм.

feminist ['femɪnɪst] *n.* феминúст (*fem.* -ка).

feministic [,femɪ'nɪstɪk] *adj.* феминúстский.

femme fatale [,fæm fæ'tɑ:l] *n.* роковáя жéнщина.

femoral ['femər(ə)l] *adj.* бéдренный.

femur ['fi:mə(r)] *n.* бедрó.

fen [fen] *n.* топь, болóто.

fence[1] [fens] *n.* **1.** (*barrier*) забóр, и́згородь, ográда; **put a horse at a ~** подв|одúть, -естú лóшадь к препя́тствию; (*fig.*) **rush one's ~s** бр|осáться, -óситься очертя́ гóлову; **sit on the ~** держáться (*impf.*) нейтрáльной/выжидáтельной позúции; **come down on the right side of the ~** вста|вáть, -ть на стóрону победúтеля; **mend one's ~** укреп|ля́ть, -úть свои позúции. **2.** (*receiver of stolen goods*) бары́га (*m.*).

v.t. (*also* **~ in, off, about, round**) огор|áживать, -одúть.

cpd. **~-mending** *n.* (*fig.*) налáживание отношéний.

fence[2] [fens] *n.* фехтовáние; **master of ~** (*swordsman*)

иску́сный фехтова́льщик; (*debater*) иску́сный спо́рщик.
v.i. фехтова́ть; ~ **with a question(er)** пари́ровать (*impf.*, *pf.*) вопро́с; увил|ивать, -ьну́ть от прямо́го отве́та.
fenceless ['fenslɪs] *adj.* (*unenclosed*) неогоро́женный.
fencer ['fensə(r)] *n.* **1.** (*swordsman*) фехтова́льщик. **2.** (*of horse*): **a good** ~ ло́шадь, хорошо́ беру́щая барье́р.
fencing ['fensɪŋ] *n.* **1.** (*fences*) и́згородь, забо́р, огра́да; (*material*) до́ски (*f. pl.*) для забо́ра; материа́л для и́згороди. **2.** (*swordplay*) фехтова́ние.
cpd. **~-master** *n.* учи́тель (*m.*) фехтова́ния.
fend [fend] *v.t.* отра|жа́ть, -зи́ть; пари́ровать (*impf.*, *pf.*); ~ **off a blow** отра|жа́ть, -зи́ть уда́р.
v.i.: ~ **for o.s.** полага́ться (*impf.*) на себя́.
fender ['fendə(r)] *n.* **1.** (*in front of fire*) ≃ ками́нная решётка. **2.** (*of train*) предохрани́тельная решётка. **3.** (*US*, *of car*) крыло́.
fenestration [,fenɪ'streɪʃ(ə)n] *n.* (*archit.*) распределе́ние о́кон в зда́нии.
Fenian ['fi:nɪən] *n.* (*hist.*) фе́ний.
adj. фениа́нский.
Fenianism ['fi:nɪən,ɪz(ə)m] *n.* фениа́нство.
fennel ['fen(ə)l] *n.* фе́нхель (*m.*), сла́дкий укро́п.
fenugreek ['fenju:,gri:k] *n.* па́житник, шамбала́.
feral ['fɪər(ə)l, 'fer(ə)l] *adj.* ди́кий, одича́вший.
ferial ['fɪərɪəl, 'fer-] *adj.* бу́дничный, бу́дний.
ferment[1] ['fɜ:ment] *n.* заква́ска; ферме́нт; (*fig.*): **in a** ~ в броже́нии.
ferment[2] [fə'ment] *v.t.* (*e.g. beer*) выха́живать, вы́ходить.
v.i. броди́ть (*impf.*).
fermentation [,fɜ:men'teɪʃ(ə)n] *n.* броже́ние (*also fig.*); фермента́ция.
fern [fɜ:n] *n.* па́поротник.
cpd. **~-seed** *n.* спо́ра па́поротника.
fernery ['fɜ:nərɪ] *n.* (*place*) за́росли (*f. pl.*) па́поротника; (*collection*) па́поротники (*m. pl.*).
ferocious [fə'rəʊʃəs] *adj.* свире́пый, лю́тый.
ferocity [fə'rɒsɪtɪ] *n.* свире́пость, лю́тость.
ferret ['ferɪt] *n.* (*zool.*) хорёк.
v.t.: ~ **out** (*fig.*) выи́скивать, вы́искать; разню́х|ивать, -ать (*e.g. a secret*).
v.i. (*hunt with* ~*s*) охо́титься (*impf.*) с хорько́м; ~ **about** (*fig.*) ры́скать (*impf.*); ша́рить (*impf.*).
ferrety ['ferɪtɪ] *adj.* хорько́вый; ~ **eyes** ры́сьи глаза́.
ferriage ['ferɪɪdʒ] *n.* перево́з, перепра́ва; (*charge*) пла́та за перево́з.
ferriferous [fe'rɪfərəs] *adj.* желе́зистый, железосодержа́щий.
Ferris wheel ['ferɪs] *n.* чёртово колесо́; колесо́ обозре́ния.
ferro-alloy ['ferəʊ 'ælɔɪ] *n.* ферроспла́в.
ferroconcrete [,ferəʊ'kɒŋkri:t] *n.* железобето́н.
ferromagnetic [,ferəʊmæg'netɪk] *adj.* ферромагни́тный.
ferrous ['ferəs] *adj.* желе́зистый; ~ **metals** чёрные мета́ллы.
ferruginous [fə'ru:dʒɪnəs] *adj.* желе́зистый, железосодержа́щий; (*in colour*) цве́та ржа́вчины.
ferrule ['feru:l] *n.* (*tip*) металли́ческий наконе́чник; (*strengthening band*) о́бод; му́фта.
ferry ['ferɪ] *n.* (*boat*) паро́м; **Charon's** ~ ладья́ Харо́на; (*plane*) перего́ночный самолёт; (~*ing-place*) перепра́ва, перево́з.
v.t. (*convey to and fro*) перев|ози́ть, -езти́ (*or* перепр|авля́ть, -а́вить) на паро́ме; отв|ози́ть, -езти́.
cpds. **~-boat** *n.* паро́м; **~man** *n.* паро́мщик, перево́зчик; **~-pilot** *n.* пило́т перего́ночной ча́сти.
fertile ['fɜ:taɪl] *adj.* **1.** (*of soil*) плодоро́дный; (*of eggs*) оплодотворённый; (*of humans, animals*) плодови́тый. **2.** (*fig.*): **a** ~ **imagination** бога́тое воображе́ние; **he is** ~ **in expedients** он всегда́ найдёт вы́ход из положе́ния.
fertility [,fɜ:'tɪlɪtɪ] *n.* плодоро́дие; плодови́тость; ~ **drug** препара́т про́тив беспло́дия.
fertilization [,fɜ:tɪlaɪ'zeɪʃ(ə)n] *n.* (*biol.*) оплодотворе́ние; (*of soil*) удобре́ние.
fertilize ['fɜ:tɪ,laɪz] *v.t.* (*biol.*) оплодотвор|я́ть, -и́ть; (*of soil*) уд|обря́ть, -о́брить.
fertilizer ['fɜ:tɪ,laɪzə(r)] *n.* (*biol.*) оплодотвори́тель (*m.*); (*of soil*) удобре́ние.
ferule ['feru:l] *n.* феру́ла, лине́йка, трость.
fervent ['fɜ:v(ə)nt] *adj.* (*fig.*) горя́чий, пы́лкий, пла́менный.
fervid ['fɜ:vɪd] *adj.* пы́лкий, пла́менный.
fervour ['fɜ:və(r)] *n.* жар, пыл, страсть.
festal ['fest(ə)l] *adj.* пра́здничный.
fester ['festə(r)] *v.i.* гнои́ться, за-/на-; нагн|а́иваться, -ои́ться; **the cut** ~**ed** поре́з загнои́лся; **the insult** ~**ed** оскорбле́ние жгло́ (*его и т.п.*).
festival ['festɪv(ə)l] *n.* фестива́ль (*m.*); пра́зднество; **Church** ~ церко́вный пра́здник; ~ **of music** фестива́ль (*m.*) му́зыки.
festive ['festɪv] *adj.* пра́здничный.
festivit|y [fe'stɪvɪtɪ] *n.* пра́зднество, торжество́; **wedding** ~**ies** сва́дебные торжества́.
festoon [fe'stu:n] *n.* гирля́нда; (*archit.*) фесто́н.
v.t укр|аша́ть, -а́сить гирля́ндами/фесто́нами.
Festschrift ['festʃrɪft] *n.* юбиле́йный сбо́рник.
fet|al ['fi:t(ə)], **-us** ['fi:t(ə)s] = **foet|al, -us**
fetch [fetʃ] *v.t.* **1.** (*go and get*) прин|оси́ть, -ести́; прив|оди́ть, -ести́; пойти́ (*pf.*) за+*i.*; ~ **me my hat** принеси́те мою́ шля́пу; **they** ~**ed the doctor** они́ вы́звали врача́; **he expects me to** ~ **and carry all day** он хочет, что́бы я весь день был на побегу́шках. **2.** (*draw forth*) вызыва́ть, вы́звать; **it** ~**ed tears from my eyes** э́то вы́звало у меня́ слёзы. **3.** (*utter*): **he** ~**ed a sigh** он (гро́мко) вздохну́л. **4.: I** ~**ed him a blow** я нанёс ему́ уда́р. **5.** (*of price*): **his house** ~**ed £50,000** он вы́ручил 50 000 фу́нтов за свой дом; **it won't** ~ **more than £20** кра́сная цена́ э́тому — 20 фу́нтов (*coll.*).
v.i.: ~ **up** (*coll., come to rest*) остан|а́вливаться, -ови́ться; **we** ~**ed up at the bar** в конце́ концо́в мы очути́лись в ба́ре; (*coll., vomit*): **he** ~**ed up** его́ вы́рвало.
fetching ['fetʃɪŋ] *adj.* привлека́тельный, соблазни́тельный.
fête [feɪt] *n.* пра́зднество, пра́здник; **village** ~ се́льский пра́здник.
v.t. пра́здновать, от-.
fetid ['fetɪd, 'fi:tɪd] *adj.* воню́чий, зловонный.
fetish ['fetɪʃ] *n.* (*lit.*, *fig.*) фети́ш.
fetishism ['fetɪʃ,ɪz(ə)m] *n.* фетиши́зм (*also psych.*).
fetishist ['fetɪʃɪst] *n.* фетиши́ст.
fetishistic [,fetɪ'ʃɪstɪk] *adj.* фетиши́стский.
fetlock ['fetlɒk] *n.* щётка; ~**-deep in mud** по щи́колотку в грязи́.
fetor ['fi:tə(r)] *n.* вонь, злово́ние.
fetter ['fetə(r)] *n.* (*pl.*) ножны́е кандал|ы́ (*pl.*, *g.* -ов); (*fig.*) око́в|ы (*pl.*, *g.* —)
v.t. зако́в|ывать, -а́ть в кандалы́; (*of horse*) спу́т|ывать, -ать; (*fig.*, *of pers.*) свя́з|ывать, -а́ть по рука́м и нога́м; ~ **s.o.'s discretion** ско́в|ывать, -а́ть кого́-н. в де́йствиях.
fettle ['fet(ə)l] *n.*: **in good** ~ в хоро́шем состоя́нии/настрое́нии.
fetus ['fi:təs] = **foetus**
feud [fju:d] *n.* (*quarrel*) междоусо́бица, вражда́; **blood** ~ кро́вная месть; **be at** ~ **with** враждова́ть (*impf.*) с+*i.*
v.i. (*carry on a* ~) вести́ (*det.*) вражду́ (*с кем*).
feudal ['fju:d(ə)l] *adj.* феода́льный; ~ **lord** феода́л; ~ **system** феода́льный строй.
feudalism ['fju:dəl,ɪz(ə)m] *n.* феодали́зм.
feudatory ['fju:dətərɪ] *n.* васса́л.
adj. васса́льный.
fever ['fi:və(r)] *n.* **1.** (*body temperature*) жар; высо́кая температу́ра; **he has a high** ~ у него́ жар. **2.** (*disease*) лихора́дка; **yellow** ~ жёлтая лихора́дка; **typhoid** ~ брюшно́й тиф; **rheumatic** ~ ревмати́зм; **scarlet** ~ скарлати́на. **3.** (*fig.*): **in a** ~ **of impatience** сгора́я от нетерпе́ния; **at** ~ **heat** в си́льном возбужде́нии; в са́мом разга́ре.
fevered ['fi:vəd] *adj.* лихора́дочный, горя́чечный; **a** ~ **brow** пыла́ющий лоб; ~ **imagination** бу́йное воображе́ние.
feverfew ['fi:və,fju:] *n.* пире́трум.
feverish ['fi:vərɪʃ] *adj.* лихора́дочный; **the child is** ~ у ребёнка повы́шенная температу́ра; **a** ~ **swamp** маляри́йное боло́то.
few [fju:] *n. & adj.* немно́гие (*pl.*); немно́го (+*g.*); ма́ло +*g.*; **the discriminating** ~ немно́гие знатоки́; **a faithful** ~

stayed with him с ним оста́лась ку́чка ве́рных; ~ **(people) know the truth** немно́гие зна́ют пра́вду; **a ~ (people)** немно́гие (лю́ди); не́сколько челове́к; **a, some ~** немно́го, не́сколько (+*g.*); **quite a ~, a good ~** дово́льно мно́го +*g.*; **not a ~** нема́ло +*g.*; **his friends are ~** у него́ ма́ло друзе́й; **the ~ books (that) I have** те не́сколько книг, что у меня́ есть; те немно́гие кни́ги, каки́е у меня́ есть; **~ and far between** ре́дкие; **every ~ minutes** ка́ждые не́сколько мину́т; **a man of ~ words** немногосло́вный челове́к; **the tree's ~ leaves** поре́девшая листва́ де́рева.

fewer [ˈfju:ə(r)] *n. & adj.* ме́нее, ме́ньше; **few know and even ~ will tell** ма́ло кто зна́ет, и ещё ме́ньше тех, кто вы́скажутся; **he wrote no ~ than 60 books** он написа́л ни мно́го ни ма́ло 60 книг.

fewness [ˈfju:nɪs] *n.* немногочи́сленность.

fey [feɪ] *adj.* (*clairvoyant*) ясновидящий; (*whimsical*) шально́й, с чуди́нкой.

fez[1] [fez] *n.* фе́ска.

Fez[2] [fez] *n.* Фес.

fiancé [fɪˈɒnseɪ, fɪˈɑ̃seɪ] *n.* жени́х.

fiancée [fɪˈɒnseɪ, fɪˈɑ̃seɪ] *n.* неве́ста.

fiasco [fɪˈæskəʊ] *n.* фиа́ско (*indecl.*), прова́л.

fiat [ˈfaɪæt, ˈfaɪət] *n.* декре́т, ука́з.

fib [fɪb] *n.* вы́думка, непра́вда.

v.i. выду́мывать, вы́думать; подвира́ть (*impf.*).

fibber [ˈfɪbə(r)] *n.* врун (*fem.* -ья); враль (*m.*).

fibre (*US* **fiber**) [ˈfaɪbə(r)] *n.* **1.** (*filament*) волокно́. **2.** (*substance made of ~s*) фи́бра (*also fig.*); **moral ~** мора́льные усто́и (*m. pl.*); **a man of coarse ~** гру́бый челове́к.

cpds. **~-board** *n.* фи́бровый карто́н; листова́я фи́бра; **~-glass** *n.* стекловолокно́, фибергла́с; стеклопла́стик.

fibrositis [ˌfaɪbrəˈsaɪtɪs] *n.* фибро́зное воспале́ние.

fibrous [ˈfaɪbrəs] *adj.* волокни́стый, фибро́зный.

fibula [ˈfɪbjʊlə] *n.* (*brooch*) фи́була.

fichu [ˈfɪʃu:, ˈfi:ʃu:] *n.* фишю́ (*nt. indecl.*).

fickle [ˈfɪk(ə)l] *adj.* переме́нчивый, непостоя́нный.

fickleness [ˈfɪkəlnɪs] *n.* переме́нчивость, непостоя́нство.

fiction [ˈfɪkʃ(ə)n] *n.* **1.** (*invention, pretence*) вы́мысел, вы́думка, фи́кция; **legal ~** юриди́ческая фи́кция; **polite ~** ве́жливая фи́кция; **truth is stranger than ~** пра́вда поро́й чудне́е вы́мысла. **2.** (*novels etc.*) беллетри́стика; **work of ~** худо́жественное произведе́ние; **~ writer** беллетри́ст, романи́ст.

fictional [ˈfɪkʃənəl] *adj.* вы́мышленный; беллетристи́ческий.

fictionalized [ˈfɪkʃənəlaɪzd] *adj.* беллетризо́ванный.

fictitious [fɪkˈtɪʃəs] *adj.* подло́жный, фикти́вный; **a ~ name** вы́мышленное и́мя.

fictitiousness [fɪkˈtɪʃəsnɪs] *n.* фикти́вность.

fictive [ˈfɪktɪv] *adj.* вы́мышленный, вы́думанный; фикти́вный.

fiddle [ˈfɪd(ə)l] *n.* **1.** (*violin*) скри́пка; (*fig.*): **fit as a ~** в до́бром здра́вии; **play second ~ to s.o.** игра́ть (*impf.*) втору́ю скри́пку у кого́-н. (*or* при ком-н.); поды́грывать (*impf.*) кому́-н.; подпева́ть (*impf.*) кому́-н. **2.** (*naut.*) ≃ се́тка на столе́. **3.** (*sl., piece of cheating or 'graft'*) жу́льничество.

v.t. (*falsify, 'cook'*) подде́л|ывать, -ать; подтасо́в|ывать, -а́ть.

v.i. **1.** (*play ~*) игра́ть (*impf.*) на скри́пке. **2.** (*fidget, meddle, tamper*) верте́ться (*impf.*); крути́ться (*impf.*); вози́ться (*impf.*); **he ~d with his tie** он теребил свой га́лстук; **don't ~ with my papers!** не тро́гайте мои́ бума́ги!

cpds. **~-bow** *n.* смычо́к; **~-faddle** *n.* пустяки́ (*m. pl.*); чепуха́, вздор; **~-stick** *n.* смычо́к; **~-sticks!** *int., see next.*

fiddle-de-dee [ˌfɪdəldɪˈdi:] *n. & int.* чепуха́, ерунда́, вздор.

fiddler [ˈfɪdlə(r)] *n.* (*musician*) скрипа́ч; (*coll., cheat*) моше́нник, жу́лик.

fiddling [ˈfɪdlɪŋ] *adj.* (*trifling*) пустя́чный, пустяко́вый.

fidelity [fɪˈdelɪtɪ] *n.* (*loyalty*) ве́рность; (*accuracy*) то́чность.

fidget [ˈfɪdʒɪt] *n.* **1.** (*~y pers.*) непосе́да (*c.g.*), егоза́ (*c.g.*). **2. he's got the ~s** (*coll.*) ему́ на ме́сте не сиди́тся.

v.t. (*make nervous or uneasy*) нерви́ровать (*impf.*); раздраж|а́ть, -и́ть.

v.i. (*make aimless movements*) ёрзать (*impf.*); суети́ться (*impf.*); (*show impatience*) не́рвничать (*impf.*).

fidgety [ˈfɪdʒɪtɪ] *adj.* суетли́вый, непосе́дливый.

fiduciary [fɪˈdju:ʃərɪ] *n.* попечи́тель (*m.*); опеку́н.

adj. дове́ренный, пору́ченный; **~ issue** (*fin.*) вы́пуск банкно́т, не покры́тых зо́лотом.

fie [faɪ] *int.* фу!; тьфу!; **~ upon you!** (как не) сты́дно!

fief [fi:f] *n.* феод.

field [fi:ld] *n.* **1.** (*piece of ground*) по́ле; **a fine ~ of wheat** прекра́сное пшени́чное по́ле; **~ sports** спорти́вные заня́тия на откры́том во́здухе; **~ events** лёгкая атле́тика. **2.** (*physical range, area*) по́ле; **~ of vision** по́ле зре́ния; **~ of fire** (*mil.*) се́ктор обстре́ла; **gravitational ~** гравитацио́нное по́ле; по́ле (земно́го) тяготе́ния. **3.** (*mil.*): **~ of battle** по́ле би́твы/сраже́ния; **take the ~** нач|ина́ть, -а́ть боевы́е де́йствия/манёвры; **hold the ~** (*fig.*) не сда|ва́ть, -ть пози́ции; **this theory holds the ~** э́та тео́рия име́ет хожде́ние; **~ artillery** полева́я артилле́рия; **~ officer** ста́рший офице́р; **F~ Marshal** фельдма́ршал; **~ hospital** полево́й го́спиталь; **~ telegraph** полево́й телегра́ф. **4.: in the ~** (*away from headquarters*) на места́х/ме́стности. **5.** (*area of activity or study*) о́бласть; по́ле/сфе́ра де́ятельности; **an expert in his ~** специали́ст в свое́й о́бласти; **that is outside my ~** э́то не моя́ о́бласть; **the whole ~ of history** вся исто́рия; **in the international ~** на междунаро́дной аре́не. **6.** (*participants in race etc.*) уча́стники (*m. pl.*) состяза́ния.

v.t.: **~ a ball** прин|има́ть, -я́ть мяч; (*fig.*): **~ a difficult question** спр|авля́ться, -а́виться с тру́дным вопро́сом; **~** (*muster*) **a team** выставля́ть, вы́ставить кома́нду.

v.i. (*at cricket etc.*) находи́ться (*impf.*) в по́ле.

cpds. **~-day** *n.* (*day of outdoor activity*) день, проведённый на откры́том во́здухе; (*athletics*) состяза́ния (*nt. pl.*) на откры́том во́здухе; (*nature study*) уче́бная экску́рсия; (*mil.*) такти́ческие заня́тия в по́ле; (*fig., day of successful exploits*) знамена́тельный/па́мятный день; **~-glasses** *n. pl.* (*binoculars*) полево́й бино́кль; **~-gun** *n.* полева́я пу́шка; **~mouse** *n.* полева́я мышь; **~sman** *n.* принима́ющий/полево́й игро́к (*крикет*); **~-work** *n.* (*agric. work*) полевы́е рабо́ты (*f. pl.*); (*research*) иссле́дование на ме́сте; (*earthwork*) полево́е укрепле́ние; **~-worker** *n.* (*agric. worker*) сельскохозя́йственный рабо́чий; (*researcher*) иссле́дователь (*m.*) на ме́стности.

fieldfare [ˈfi:ldfeə(r)] *n.* дрозд-ряби́нник.

fiend [fi:nd] *n.* (*devil*) дья́вол; (*evil pers.*) злоде́й, и́зверг; (*fig.*): **a bridge ~** зая́длый игро́к в бридж.

fiendish [ˈfi:ndɪʃ] *adj.* дья́вольский, злоде́йский.

fiendishness [ˈfi:ndɪʃnɪs] *n.* злоде́йство.

fierce [fɪəs] *adj.* свире́пый, лю́тый; **~ heat** нестерпи́мая жара́; **~ competition** жесто́кая конкуре́нция; **~ prices** (*coll.*) сумасше́дшие це́ны.

fierceness [ˈfɪəsnɪs] *n.* свире́пость, лю́тость.

fieriness [ˈfaɪərɪnɪs] *n.* вспы́льчивость.

fiery [ˈfaɪərɪ] *adj.* о́гненный, пла́менный; **~ eyes** о́гненный взор; **~ sky** пламене́ющее не́бо; **a ~ temper** вспы́льчивый/горя́чий хара́ктер; **a ~ horse** горя́чая ло́шадь.

fiesta [fɪˈestə] *n.* пра́здник, фие́ста.

FIFA [ˈfi:fə] *n.* (*abbr. of* ***Fédération Internationale de Football Association***) ФИФА, (Междунаро́дная федера́ция футбо́ла).

fife [faɪf] *n.* ду́дка; ма́ленькая фле́йта.

fifer [ˈfaɪfə(r)] *n.* ду́дочник; флейти́ст.

fifteen [fɪfˈti:n, ˈfɪf-] *n.* пятна́дцать; **she is ~** ей пятна́дцать лет; **a girl of ~** пятнадцатиле́тняя де́вушка.

adj. пятна́дцать +*g. pl.*; **~ hundred** ты́сяча пятьсо́т, полторы́ ты́сячи.

fifteenth [fɪfˈti:nθ, ˈfɪf-] *n.* (*date*) пятна́дцатое (число́); (*fraction*) одна́ пятна́дцатая; пятна́дцатая часть.

adj. пятна́дцатый.

fifth [fɪfθ] *n.* (*date*) пя́тое (число́); (*fraction*) одна́ пя́тая; пя́тая часть; (*mus.*) кви́нта.

adj. пя́тый; **~ column** пя́тая коло́нна.

fifthly [ˈfɪfθlɪ] *adv.* в-пя́тых.

fiftieth [ˈfɪftɪɪθ] *n.* (*fraction*) одна́ пятидеся́тая; пятидеся́тая часть.

adj. пятидеся́тый.

fift|y ['fɪftɪ] *n.* пятьдеся́т, полсо́тни; **the ~ies** (*decade*) пятидеся́тые го́ды; (*latitude*) пятидеся́тые широ́ты; **he is in his ~ies** ему́ за пятьдеся́т (лет); ему́ пошёл шесто́й деся́ток; **we shared expenses ~-~** мы раздели́ли расхо́ды попола́м.

adj. пятьдеся́т +*g. pl.*

cpd. **~-fold** *adj. & adv.* в пятьдеся́т раз.

fig[1] [fɪg] *n.* (*fruit*) фи́га, инжи́р, ви́нная я́года; **green ~s** све́жий инжи́р; **I don't care a ~** мне наплева́ть.

cpds. **~-leaf** *n.* фи́говый листо́к; **~-tree** *n.* фи́говое де́рево.

fig[2] [fɪg] *n.* (*dress, get-up*): **in full ~** в по́лном облаче́нии.

fig.[3] [fɪg] *n.* (*abbr. of* **figure 4.**) рис., (рису́нок); **in ~ 6** на рис. 6.

fight [faɪt] *n.* **1.** бой, схва́тка, дра́ка; **stand-up ~** кула́чный бой; **sham ~** уче́бный/показно́й бой; **free ~** всео́бщая потасо́вка; сва́лка; **running ~** (*retreating*) отступле́ние с боя́ми; (*continuous*) продолжи́тельный бой; **he is spoiling for a ~** он и́щет ссо́ры; **~ to a finish** борьба́ до побе́дного конца́; **he put up a (good) ~** он (упо́рно) сопротивля́лся. **2.** (*boxing-match*) боксёрский поеди́нок/бой. **3.** (*~ing spirit*) задо́р; **he has ~ in him yet** в нём ещё оста́лся боево́й задо́р; **he showed ~** он был гото́в к борьбе́; он рва́лся в бой; **the news took all the ~ out of him** от э́той но́вости он совсе́м приуны́л.

v.t. & i. дра́ться, по-; сра|жа́ться, -зи́ться; (*wage war*) воева́ть (*impf.*); **the boys/dogs are ~ing** ма́льчики/соба́ки деру́тся; **Britain fought Germany** Великобрита́ния воева́ла с Герма́нией (*or* выступа́ла про́тив Герма́нии); **~ a battle** вести́ (*det.*) бой; **~ a duel** дра́ться (*impf.*) на дуэ́ли; **~ an election** вести́ (*det.*) предвы́борную борьбу́; **~ a lawsuit** суди́ться (*impf.*); **~ a case** (*leg.*) защища́ть (*impf.*) де́ло в суде́; **the patient is ~ing for breath** больно́й задыха́ется; **he fought shy of the problem** он уклоня́лся от реше́ния э́той зада́чи; **he fought his way forward** он пробива́лся/прота́лкивался вперёд; **he fought like a lion** он сража́лся как лев; **he fought off a cold** он (бы́стро) спра́вился с просту́дой; **I fought off my desire to sleep** я переборо́л сон; **they fought off the enemy** они́ отби́ли врага́; **they fought it out (*or* to a finish)** они́ сража́лись/боро́лись до конца́; **~ back** *v.i.* отб|ива́ться, -и́ться; **~ down** *v.t.* (*repress, e.g. a feeling*) побе|жда́ть, -ди́ть; **you should ~ down that tendency** вам на́до боро́ться с э́той накло́нностью.

fighter ['faɪtə(r)] *n.* **1.** (*one who fights*) бое́ц; (*fig.*) боре́ц. **2.** (*~ aircraft*) истреби́тель (*m.*); **~ cover** прикры́тие истреби́телями; **~ escort** сопровожде́ние истреби́телями; **~ patrol** патрули́рование истреби́телями.

cpds. **~-bomber** *n.* истреби́тель-бомбардиро́вщик; **~-pilot** *n.* лётчик-истреби́тель (*m.*).

fighting ['faɪtɪŋ] *n.* бой, сраже́ние; **hand-to-hand ~** рукопа́шный бой.

adj. боево́й; **we have a ~ chance** сто́ит попыта́ться.

cpds. **~-cock** *n.* бойцо́вый пету́х; **he lived like a ~-cock** он жил как у Христа́ за па́зухой; он жил припева́ючи; **~-mad** *adj.* (*very angry*): **he was ~-mad** он рассвирепе́л.

figment ['fɪgmənt] *n.* вы́мысел; фи́кция; **a ~ of the imagination** плод воображе́ния.

figurative ['fɪgjʊrətɪv, 'fɪgər-] *adj.* фигура́льный; перено́сный, метафори́ческий; (*pictorial*) изобрази́тельный.

figure ['fɪgə(r)] *n.* **1.** (*numerical sign*) ци́фра; **double ~s** двузна́чные чи́сла; **a six-~ number** шестизна́чное число́; **I bought it at a low ~** я э́то дёшево купи́л. **2.** (*geom.*) фигу́ра, те́ло. **3.** (*pl., arithmetic*): **he is good at ~s** он силён в арифме́тике. **4.** (*diagram, illustration*) рису́нок, диагра́мма, иллюстра́ция. **5.** (*image, effigy*) о́браз, изображе́ние, ста́туя, фигу́ра; **lay ~** манеке́н. **6.** (*human form*) фигу́ра; **I saw a ~ approaching** я уви́дел приближа́вшуюся ко мне фигу́ру; **she has a good ~** у неё хоро́шая фигу́ра; **a fine ~ of a man** хорошо́ сложённый мужчи́на; **he is a ~ of fun** он про́сто смешо́н; **landscape with ~s** пейза́ж с фигу́рами люде́й. **7.** (*pers. of importance*) фигу́ра, выдаю́щаяся ли́чность; **he is a great ~ in this town** он изве́стная фигу́ра в э́том го́роде; **he was the greatest ~ of his age** он был са́мой выдаю́щейся ли́чностью своего́ вре́мени. **8.** (*show, appearance*) вид; **he cut a brilliant ~** он блиста́л; **he cut a poor ~** он име́л жа́лкий вид. **9.** (*~ of speech*) ритори́ческая фигу́ра; о́бразное выраже́ние. **10.** (*in dancing*) фигу́ра.

v.t. **1.** (*make patterns etc. in*): **~d silk** узо́рчатый шёлк. **2.** (*picture, imagine*) вообра|жа́ть, -зи́ть; предст|авля́ть, -а́вить себе́. **3.: ~ out** (*calculate*) вычисля́ть, вы́числить; (*understand*) пон|има́ть, -я́ть; пост|ига́ть, -и́гнуть; **I can't ~ him out** я не могу́ его́ поня́ть (*or* раскуси́ть (*coll.*)); **~ out how much we owe you** подсчита́йте, ско́лько мы вам должны́.

v.i. **1.** (*appear*) фигури́ровать (*impf.*); **he ~s in history** он вошёл в исто́рию; **this did not ~ in my plans** э́то не входи́ло в мои́ пла́ны; **~ in a play** (*as actor*) игра́ть (*impf.*) в пье́се; (*as character*) фигури́ровать (*impf.*). **2.** (*US coll.*): **it ~s** (*makes sense, is plausible*) э́то похо́же на пра́вду; **I ~d on seeing him** я рассчи́тывал уви́деться с ним; **I ~ they'll be late** я ду́маю, что они́ опозда́ют.

cpds. **~-head** *n.* носово́е украше́ние, фигу́ра на носу́ корабля́; (*fig.*) номина́льный руководи́тель; **~-of-eight** *n.* восьмёрка; **~-skater** *n.* конькобе́жец-фигури́ст; **~skating** *n.* фигу́рное ката́ние.

figurine [ˌfɪgjʊ'ri:n, 'fɪg-] *n.* фигу́рка, статуэ́тка.

Fiji ['fi:dʒi:] *n.* Фи́джи (*nt. indecl.*).

Fijian [fi:'dʒi:ən] *n.* фиджи́|ец (*fem.* -йка).

adj. фиджи́йский.

filament ['fɪləmənt] *n.* (*animal fibre*) волокно́; (*bot.*) нить; (*elec.*) нить нака́ла; **~ lamp** ла́мпа нака́ливания.

filbert ['fɪlbət] *n.* (*tree*) лещи́на; (*nut*) фунду́к.

filch [fɪltʃ] *v.t.* стяну́ть (*pf.*) (*coll.*).

file[1] [faɪl] *n.* (*tool*) напи́льник; (*nail-~*) пи́лочка для ногте́й.

v.t. подпи́л|ивать, -и́ть; опи́л|ивать, -и́ть; **~ one's nails** подпи́л|ивать, -и́ть но́гти; **he ~d away the roughness** он отшлифова́л гру́бую пове́рхность; **he ~d the rod in two** он распили́л брус на́двое.

file[2] [faɪl] *n.* **1.** (*for papers*) па́пка, регистра́тор для бума́г, скоросшива́тель (*m.*). **2.** (*set of papers etc.*) подши́тые бума́ги (*f. pl.*); де́ло, досье́ (*indecl.*); **a newspaper ~** подши́вка газе́ты; **the correspondence is on our ~s** э́та перепи́ска храни́тся у нас в де́ле; **~ copy** (*of outgoing letter*) ко́пия исходя́щей бума́ги.

v.t. **1.** (*place on ~*) подш|ива́ть, -и́ть; регистри́ровать, за-; **the letters were ~d away** пи́сьма бы́ли подши́ты к де́лу. **2.: ~** (*lodge*) **a complaint** под|ава́ть, -а́ть жа́лобу; **~** (*hand in*) **a message** перед|ава́ть, -а́ть сообще́ние/депе́шу; **~ suit against s.o.** возбу|жда́ть, -ди́ть суде́бное де́ло про́тив кого́-н.

file[3] [faɪl] *n.* **1.** (*rank, row*) ряд, шере́нга; коло́нна; **they marched in double ~** они́ шли коло́нной по́ два; **in single, Indian ~** гусько́м; по одному́; **rank and ~** (*mil.*) рядовы́е (*m. pl.*); (*fig., as adj.*) рядово́й (*работник и т.п.*). **2.** (*chess*) вертика́ль.

v.i. идти́ (*det.*) гусько́м/коло́нной; **the prisoners ~d out** заключённые выходи́ли гусько́м друг за дру́гом.

filet ['fɪlɪt] *n.*: **~ lace** филе́ (*indecl.*), филе́йное кру́жево.

filial ['fɪlɪəl] *adj.* (*pert. to son or daughter*) сыно́вний, доче́рний; (*dutiful*) почти́тельный.

filiation [ˌfɪlɪ'eɪʃ(ə)n] *n.* (*parentage*) отцо́вство, матери́нство; (*descent*) происхожде́ние; (*genealogical relationship*) генеало́гия; (*fig., e.g. of a manuscript*) происхожде́ние; (*determination of paternity*) установле́ние отцо́вства.

filibuster ['fɪlɪˌbʌstə(r)] *n.* (*pirate*) флибустье́р, пира́т; (*fig., obstructionist*) обструкциони́ст; (*obstruction*) обстру́кция.

v.i. занима́ться (*impf.*) морски́м разбо́ем; (*fig.*) тормози́ть (*impf.*) приня́тие зако́на путём обстру́кции.

filigree ['fɪlɪˌgri:] *n.* филигра́нь; (*fig.*) филигра́нная рабо́та; **a ~ brooch** филигра́нная брошь.

filing ['faɪlɪŋ] *n.* (*of papers*) регистра́ция бума́г.

cpds. **~-cabinet** *n.* шкаф, сейф; **~-clerk** *n.* делопроизводи́тель (*m.*), регистра́тор.

filings ['faɪlɪŋz] *n. pl.* металли́ческие опи́л|ки (*pl., g.* -ок).

Filipino [ˌfɪlɪ'pi:nəʊ] *n.* филиппи́н|ец (*fem.* -ка).

adj. филиппи́нский.

fill [fɪl] *n.*: **he ate his ~** он нае́лся до́сыта; **give me a ~ for my pipe** да́йте мне табаку́ на одну́ тру́бку.

v.t. **1.** (*make full*) нап|олня́ть, -о́лнить; зап|олня́ть, -о́лнить; **he ~ed the tank with petrol** он напо́лнил бак бензи́ном; **he ~ed the hole with sand** он запо́лнил я́му песко́м; **smoke ~ed the room** ко́мната напо́лнилась ды́мом; **the sofa ~s that end of the room** дива́н занима́ет э́ту часть ко́мнаты; **I was ~ed with admiration** я был по́лон восхище́ния; **tears ~ed her eyes** её глаза́ напо́лнились слеза́ми. **2.** **~ a tooth** пломбирова́ть, за-. **3.** (*fig., of office etc.*) зан|има́ть, -я́ть; **~ a vacancy** зап|олня́ть, -о́лнить вака́нтную до́лжность; поста́вить (*pf.*) кого́-н. на вака́нтное ме́сто; **~ s.o.'s place** зан|има́ть, -я́ть чьё-н. ме́сто. **4.** (*execute*) выполня́ть, вы́полнить.

v.i. **1.** (*become full*) нап|олня́ться, -о́лниться; **the sails ~ed** (*with wind*) паруса́ наду́лись; **his cheeks ~ed (out)** у него́ округли́лись щёки.

with advs.: **~ in** *v.t.* (*complete*) зап|олня́ть, -о́лнить; **he ~ed in the form** он запо́лнил бланк/анке́ту; **he ~ed in his name** он вписа́л своё и́мя; (*coll., inform*): **I ~ed him in** я ввёл его́ в курс де́ла; *v.i.*: **I am ~ing in while X is away** я замеща́ю X в его́ отсу́тствие; **~ out** *v.t.* (*a form*) зап|олня́ть, -о́лнить; *v.i.* расш|иря́ться, -и́риться; попра́виться (*pf.*); нап|олня́ться, -о́лниться; **~ up** *v.t.* (*make full*) нап|олня́ть, -о́лнить; **we ~ed up** (*the car*) **with petrol** мы запра́вились (бензи́ном); (*a form*) зап|олня́ть, -о́лнить; *v.i.* (*become full*) нап|олня́ться, -о́лниться.

cpd. **~-in** *n.* (*pers. or thg.*) заме́на.

fillet [ˈfɪlɪt] *n.* **1.** (*head-band*) ле́нта, повя́зка. **2.** (*of meat, fish*) филе́ (*indecl.*).

v.t. (*of fish, take off bone*) отдел|я́ть, -и́ть мя́со от косте́й.

filling [ˈfɪlɪŋ] *n.* (*in tooth*) пло́мба; (*in cake*) начи́нка.

adj. наполня́ющий, заполня́ющий; (*of food*) сы́тный.

cpd. **~-station** *n.* автозапра́вочная *or* бензозапра́вочная ста́нция; (бензо)запра́вка.

fillip [ˈfɪlɪp] *n.* щелчо́к, толчо́к; (*fig.*) **give a ~ to** да|ва́ть, -ть толчо́к +*d*; стимули́ровать (*pf.*).

filly [ˈfɪlɪ] *n.* молода́я кобы́ла; (*coll., girl*) (шу́страя) девчо́нка.

film [fɪlm] *n.* **1.** (*thin coating*) плёнка; **a ~ of dust** налёт пы́ли; **a ~ of mist** ды́мка. **2.** (*photographic material*) фотоплёнка; (*cin.*) киноплёнка; **a roll of ~** кату́шка фотоплёнки. **3.** (*motion picture*) фильм; **~ clip** отры́вок из фи́льма; **~ crew** киносъёмочная кома́нда; **~ critic** кинообозрева́тель (*m.*); **~ distributor** кинопрока́тчик; **~ star** кинозвезда́; **~ studies** кинове́дение; **~ studio** киносту́дия; **~ test** кинопро́ба актёра; **do you go to (the) ~s?** вы хо́дите в кино́?; **~ projector** киноустано́вка; **~ rights** права́ на экраниза́цию; **~ set** съёмочная площа́дка.

v.t. сн|има́ть, -я́ть.

v.i. **1.**: **his eyes ~ed (over)** его́ глаза́ затума́нились. **2.**: **she ~s well** она́ фотогени́чна; **the story ~s well** э́тот расска́з/сюже́т хоро́ш для экраниза́ции.

filmy [ˈfɪlmɪ] *adj.* покры́тый плёнкой, тума́нный.

filter [ˈfɪltə(r)] *n.* (*for liquid*) фильтр, цеди́лка; (*for light*) светофи́льтр; **~ light** (*traffic sign*) светофо́р со стре́лкой; **~ tip** (*cigarette*) сигаре́та с фи́льтром.

v.t. (*purify*) фильтрова́ть (*impf.*); проце́|живать, -ди́ть.

v.i. (*fig.*): **the news ~ed out** но́вости просочи́лись.

filth [fɪlθ] *n.* (*dirt*) грязь, отбро́сы (*m. pl.*); (*obscenity*) непристо́йность, грязь.

filthiness [ˈfɪlθɪnɪs] *n.* грязь, загрязне́ние.

filthy [ˈfɪlθɪ] *adj.* гря́зный, непристо́йный; **~ lucre** (*joc.*) презре́нный мета́лл.

fin [fɪn] *n.* плавни́к; (*of aircraft etc.*) стабилиза́тор; киль (*m.*); плавни́к.

finagle [fɪˈneɪg(ə)l] *v.i.* (*coll.*) моше́нничать (*impf.*).

final [ˈfaɪn(ə)l] *n.* **1.** (*examination*) выпускно́й экза́мен; госэкза́мен; **he took his ~s in June** он сдава́л выпускны́е/госуда́рственные экза́мены в ию́не. **2.** (*match*) фина́л; **tennis ~s** фина́л по те́ннису. **3.** (*newspaper edition*) после́дний вы́пуск.

adj. **1.** (*last in order*) после́дний; заверша́ющий, заключи́тельный. **2.** (*decisive*) оконча́тельный, реша́ющий; **I won't come, and that's ~** я не приду́, и э́то моё после́днее сло́во. **3.** (*gram.*): **~ clause** прида́точное предложе́ние це́ли. **4.** (*phil.*): **~ cause** коне́чная цель.

finale [fɪˈnɑːlɪ, -leɪ] *n.* (*mus., fig.*) фина́л; **grand ~** торже́ственный фина́л.

finalist [ˈfaɪnəlɪst] *n.* финали́ст.

finality [faɪˈnælɪtɪ] *n.*: **he spoke with (an air of) ~** он говори́л об э́том, как о де́ле решённом; он вы́сказался категори́чески.

finalization [ˌfaɪnəlaɪˈzeɪʃ(ə)n] *n.* заверше́ние.

finalize [ˈfaɪnəˌlaɪz] *v.t.* (*give final form to*) заверш|а́ть, -и́ть; прид|ава́ть, -а́ть оконча́тельную фо́рму +*d.*; (*settle, e.g. arrangements*) (оконча́тельно) ула́дить (*pf.*).

finance [ˈfaɪnæns, fɪˈnæns, faɪˈnæns] *n.* фина́нсы (*m. pl.*); дохо́ды (*m. pl.*); **Minister of F~** мини́стр фина́нсов; **my ~s are low** у меня́ с фина́нсами ту́го (*coll.*).

v.t. финанси́ровать (*impf., pf.*).

financial [faɪˈnænʃ(ə)l, fɪ-] *adj.* фина́нсовый; **he is in ~ difficulties** у него́ де́нежные затрудне́ния.

financier [faɪˈnænsɪə(r), ˌfɪ-] *n.* финанси́ст.

finch [fɪntʃ] *n.* зя́блик.

find [faɪnd] *n.* (*discovery, esp. valuable*) нахо́дка; **the new cook is a ~** но́вый по́вар — настоя́щая нахо́дка.

v.t. **1.** (*discover, encounter*) на|ходи́ть, -йти́; (*by search*) раз|ыска́ть, от- (*both impf.*); **we found a house** мы присмотре́ли дом; **I could ~ nothing to say** я не нашёлся, что сказа́ть; **he found his tongue** он обрёл дар ре́чи; **a letter was found on him** на нём нашли́ письмо́; **pine-trees are found in several countries** сосна́ растёт/встреча́ется во мно́гих стра́нах; **I found him waiting for me** он уже́ ждал меня́; **the bullet found its mark** пу́ля попа́ла в цель; **water ~s its own level** вода́ устана́вливает свой у́ровень; **we found the beds comfortable** мы нашли́ крова́ти удо́бными; **you must take us as you ~ us** вам придётся приня́ть нас таки́ми, каки́е мы есть; **I found I had forgotten the key** я обнару́жил, что забы́л ключ; **I ~ it hard to understand him** мне тру́дно поня́ть его́; **he found himself in hospital** он оказа́лся/очути́лся в больни́це; **he will ~ himself** (*discover his powers etc.*) **by degrees** со вре́менем он найдёт себя́ (*or* своё призва́ние); **I called, but found her out** я зашёл, но не заста́л её. **2.** (*compute, ascertain, judge*): **I ~ the total to be £20** у меня́ получа́ется, что о́бщая су́мма составля́ет 20 фу́нтов; **the jury found him guilty** прися́жные призна́ли его́ вино́вным; **the judge found for the plaintiff** судья́ реши́л де́ло в по́льзу истца́. **3.** (*provide*) предост|авля́ть, -а́вить; **I will ~ the money for the excursion** я раздобу́ду де́ньги на экску́рсию; **she ~s herself in clothes** ей опла́чивают всё, кро́ме оде́жды. **4.** (*obtain, achieve*) получ|а́ть, -и́ть; **I ~ pleasure in reading** я получа́ю удово́льствие от чте́ния; **he found favour with his employer** он сниска́л благоскло́нность у своего́ нача́льника; **he found time to read** он улуча́л вре́мя для чте́ния; **he found courage to ask her to marry him** он набра́лся хра́брости и сде́лал ей предложе́ние. **5.** **~ out** (*detect*) узн|ава́ть, -а́ть; разузн|ава́ть, -а́ть; **his sins will ~ him out** его́ грехи́ вы́дадут его́; **found out in a lie** уличённый во лжи́; (*ascertain*) выясня́ть, вы́яснить; **I found out the answer** я нашёл отве́т; **have you found out (about) the trains?** вы узна́ли расписа́ние поездо́в?

findable [ˈfaɪndəb(ə)l] *adj.* находи́мый.

finder [ˈfaɪndə(r)] *n.* (*pers. who finds*): **the ~ will be rewarded** наше́дший полу́чит вознагражде́ние; **'~s keepers'** кому́ на́ руку попа́ло...; нашёл — зна́чит моё; (*lens*) (видо)иска́тель (*m.*).

finding [ˈfaɪndɪŋ] *n.* (*discovery*) откры́тие, нахо́дка, нахожде́ние; (*conclusion; also pl.*) вы́вод(ы); (*leg.*) постановле́ние, реше́ние.

fine[1] [faɪn] *n.* (*punishment*) штраф, пе́ня.

v.t. штрафова́ть, о-; **he was ~d £5** его́ оштрафова́ли на 5 фу́нтов.

fine[2] [faɪn] *n.*: **in ~** (*arch.*) в о́бщем, вкра́тце.

fine[3] [faɪn] *adj.* **1.** (*of weather*) я́сный, хоро́ший; **it has turned ~** проясни́лось; **one ~ day, one of these ~ days** в оди́н прекра́сный день. **2.** (*pleasant, handsome, excellent*) прекра́сный, замеча́тельный; **a ~ view** прекра́сный вид;

a ~ girl (*looks or character*) преле́стная/чуде́сная де́вушка; **we had a ~ time** мы прекра́сно/замеча́тельно провели́ вре́мя; **a ~ excuse!** (*iron.*) то́же мне предло́г!; **that is all very ~, but ...** всё э́то о́чень хорошо́, но... **3.** (*noble*, *virtuous*) благоро́дный, возвы́шенный; **a ~ gentleman/lady** ба́рин/ба́рышня. **4.** (*delicate*, *exquisite*) то́нкий; **~ workmanship** то́нкая рабо́та; **~ silk** то́нкий шёлк. **5.** (*of small particles*) ме́лкий; **~ dust** ме́лкая пыль; **~ rain** ме́лкий дождь. **6.** (*slender*, *thin*, *sharp*) то́нкий, о́стрый; **~ thread** то́нкая нить/ни́тка; **a pencil with a ~ point** о́стро отто́ченный каранда́ш. **7.** (*pure*) чи́стый, высокопро́бный; **~ gold** чи́стое зо́лото. **8.** (*refined*, *subtle*) утончённый, то́нкий; **a ~ taste in art** то́нкий худо́жественный вкус; **a ~ distinction** то́нкое разли́чие; **the ~ arts** изобрази́тельные/изя́щные иску́сства. **9.** (*elegant*, *distinguished*) изя́щный.

adv.: **he cut it ~** (*of time*) он оста́вил себе́ вре́мени в обре́з; **that suits me ~** (*coll.*) э́то меня́ вполне́ устра́ивает.

v.t. оч|ища́ть, -и́стить; **~ down** (*e.g. liquid*) оч|ища́ть, -и́стить.

v.i.: **~ down** (*e.g. a girl's figure*) ста|нови́ться, -ть то́ньше.

cpds. **~-drawn** *adj.* (*fig.*) иску́сный; **~-grained** *adj.* мелкозерни́стый; **~-spun** *adj.* (*fig.*) хитросплетённый, запу́танный.

fineness ['faɪnnɪs] *n.* (*delicacy*) то́нкость, утончённость, изя́щество; (*of gold etc.*) чистота́, высо́кое содержа́ние мета́лла.

finery ['faɪnərɪ] *n.* пы́шный наря́д; пы́шное убра́нство; (*of birds*) опере́ние.

finesse [fɪ'nes] *n.* (*delicacy*) делика́тность, утончённость, то́нкость.

v.i. де́йствовать (*impf.*) иску́сно; хитри́ть.

finger ['fɪŋgə(r)] *n.* па́лец (*also of glove*); (*of clock*) стре́лка; **index ~** указа́тельный па́лец; **middle ~** сре́дний па́лец; **ring ~** безымя́нный па́лец; **little ~** мизи́нец; **eat sth. with one's ~s** есть что-н. рука́ми; **I can twist him round my little ~** он всё сде́лает, что я ни захочу́; **lay a ~ on** (*touch*, *molest*) тро́|гать, -нуть па́льцем; **he put his ~ on it** он попа́л в са́мую то́чку; **I will not lift a ~ to help him** я и па́льцем не пошевельну́, что́бы помо́чь ему́; **my ~s itched to strike him** меня́ так и подмыва́ло дать ему́ хороше́нько; **his ~s are all thumbs** у него́ ру́ки — крю́ки; **he has a ~ in the pie** он заме́шан в э́том; он приложи́л ру́ку к э́тому; **she worked her ~s to the bone** она́ рабо́тала не поклада́я рук; **snap one's ~s** (*lit.*) щёлк|ать, -нуть па́льцами; **snap one's ~s at** (*fig.*) ни в грош не ста́вить (*impf.*); **money sticks to his ~s** он на́ руку нечи́ст; **the criminal slipped through our ~s** престу́пник ускользну́л у нас из-под но́са; **he burnt his ~s in that business** он обжёгся на э́том де́ле; **they can be counted on the ~s of one hand** их по па́льцам мо́жно сосчита́ть; **point the ~ of scorn at** обл|ива́ть, -и́ть кого́-н. презре́нием.

v.t.: **~ a piece of cloth** щу́пать, по- мате́рию; **~ an instrument** (*mus.*) перебира́ть (*impf.*) па́льцами кла́виши/стру́ны; **~ a piece of music** ука́з|ывать, -а́ть аппликату́ру/пальцо́вку музыка́льного произведе́ния.

cpds. **~-alphabet** *n.* (*for deaf and dumb*) а́збука глухонемы́х; **~-bowl** *n.* ча́шка для спола́скивания па́льцев; **~-hole** *n.* (*mus.*) кла́пан; **~-mark** *n.* пятно́ от па́льца; ; **~-nail** *n.* но́готь (*m.*); **~-plate** *n.* (*on door*) нали́чник дверно́го замка́; **~-post** *n.* указа́тельный столб; **~-print** *n.* отпеча́ток па́льца; дактилоскопи́ческий отпеча́ток; *v.t.* (*take s.o.'s ~-prints*) сн|има́ть, -ять отпеча́тки па́льцев у+*g.*; **~-stall** *n.* напа́льчник; **~-tip** *n.* ко́нчик па́льца; **he has the subject at his ~-tips** он зна́ет э́тот предме́т как свой пять па́льцев; **he is a musician to his ~-tips** он музыка́нт до мо́зга косте́й.

fingering ['fɪŋgərɪŋ] *n.* (*mus.*) аппликату́ра, пальцо́вка.

finial ['fɪnɪəl] *n.* (*archit.*) шпиль (*m.*); флеро́н.

finic|al ['fɪnɪk(ə)l], **-king** ['fɪnɪkɪŋ], **-ky** ['fɪnɪkɪ] *adjs.* разбо́рчивый, приди́рчивый, привере́дливый; скрупулёзный.

finis ['fɪnɪs, 'fi:nɪs, 'faɪnɪs] *n.* коне́ц.

finish ['fɪnɪʃ] *n.* **1.** (*conclusion*) оконча́ние, коне́ц; **it was a close ~** они́ зако́нчили почти́ одновреме́нно; **they fought to a ~** они́ би́лись до конца́; **he was in at the ~** он прису́тствовал при развя́зке. **2.** (*polish*) отде́лка; **mahogany ~** отде́лка из кра́сного де́рева; **the manufacture lacks ~** изде́лию не хвата́ет отде́лки; **his manners lack ~** у него́ грубова́тые мане́ры; **she was ~ed in Paris** она́ зако́нчила своё образова́ние в Пари́же.

v.t. **1.** (*smooth*, *polish*) отде́л|ывать, -ать; **the work is beautifully ~ed** рабо́та отлича́ется соверше́нством. **2.** (*perfect*) соверше́нствовать (*impf.*); **a ~ed performance** отто́ченное исполне́ние; **~ing touch** после́дний штрих; **~ing-school** пансио́н для де́вушек (*гото́вящий их к све́тской жи́зни*). **3.** (*end*) зак|а́нчивать, -о́нчить; конча́ть, ко́нчить; **I ~ed** (*sc. writing*, *reading*) **the book** я (за)ко́нчил кни́гу; **he ~ed (off, up) the pie** он дое́л весь пиро́г; **we will ~ the job** мы зако́нчим рабо́ту. **4.** (*of manufacture*): **~ed goods** гото́вые изде́лия. **5.** (*coll.*, *exhaust*, *kill*) изнур|я́ть, -и́ть; прик|а́нчивать, -о́нчить; **the climb ~ed me** (*coll.*) э́тот подъём докона́л меня́; **the fever ~ed him off** лихора́дка докона́ла/прико́нчила его́.

v.i. конча́ться, ко́нчиться; зак|а́нчиваться, -о́нчиться; **they ~ed (off, up) by singing a song** в заключе́ние они́ спе́ли пе́сню; **have you ~ed with that book?** вам бо́льше не нужна́ э́та кни́га?; **I am ~ed with him** между на́ми всё ко́нчено; (*in race*) финиши́ровать (*impf.*, *pf.*); **he ~ed fourth** он за́нял четвёртое ме́сто; **~ing-post** фи́ниш.

finisher ['fɪnɪʃə(r)] *n.* (*craftsman*) отде́лочник, аппрету́рщик; (*coll.*, *crushing blow*) сокруша́ющий уда́р.

finite ['faɪnaɪt] *adj.* коне́чный; име́ющий преде́л; (*gram.*): **~ verb** ли́чный глаго́л.

Finland ['fɪnlənd] *n.* Финля́ндия.

Finn [fɪn] *n.* фин|н (*fem.* -ка).

Finnic ['fɪnɪk] *adj.* фи́нский.

Finnish ['fɪnɪʃ] *n.* (*language*) фи́нский язы́к.

adj. фи́нский.

Finno-Ugrian ['fɪnəʊ'u:grɪən], **-Ugric** [ˌfɪnəʊ'u:grɪk, -'ju:grɪk] *adjs.* фи́нно-уго́рский.

fiord, fjord [fjɔ:d] *n.* фьорд, фио́рд.

fir [fɜ:(r)] *n.* (*also* **~-tree**) ель; **Scotch ~** сосна́.

cpds. **~-cone** *n.* ело́вая ши́шка; **~-needle** *n.* ело́вая иго́лка; хвоя́.

fire ['faɪə(r)] *n.* **1.** (*phenomenon of combustion*) ого́нь (*m.*); **the house is on ~** дом загоре́лся/гори́т; **set on ~, set ~ to** подж|ига́ть, -е́чь; **he will never set the Thames on ~** он по́роха не вы́думает; **catch ~** загор|а́ться, -е́ться; **strike ~ from flint** высека́ть, вы́сечь ого́нь уда́ром по кре́мню; **there is no smoke without ~** нет ды́ма без огня́; **I would go through ~ and water for him** я за него́ пойду́ в ого́нь и в во́ду; **St Elmo's ~** огни́ (*m. pl.*) свято́го Э́льма; **play with ~** (*fig.*) игра́ть (*impf.*) с огнём. **2.** (*burning fuel*) ого́нь (*m.*); **camp ~** костёр; **he lit a ~** он разжёг ого́нь/ками́н; **the weather is too warm for ~s** ещё тепло́, ками́н топи́ть ра́но; **lay a ~** раскла́дывать, разложи́ть ого́нь; **make a ~** (*indoors*) зат|а́пливать, -опи́ть ками́н; **light a ~** разж|ига́ть, -е́чь ками́н; топи́ть, за- печь; **there is a ~ in the next room** в сосе́дней ко́мнате то́пится (*or* гори́т ками́н). **3.** (*conflagration*) пожа́р; **~!** пожа́р!; (*excl. by someone in burning building*) гори́м!; **where's the ~?** где гори́т?; **put to ~ and sword** пред|ава́ть, -а́ть огню́ и мечу́. **4.** (*of* **~arms**) ого́нь (*m.*), стрельба́; **open ~** откр|ыва́ть, -ы́ть ого́нь; **cease ~** прекра|ща́ть, -ти́ть ого́нь; **running ~** бе́глый ого́нь; (*fig.*, *e.g. criticism*) град напа́док; **between two ~s** (*fig.*) меж двух огне́й; **miss ~** да|ва́ть, -ть осе́чку; **hang ~** (*of a gun*) произв|оди́ть, -ести́ затяжно́й вы́стрел; (*fig.*): **the scheme hung ~** план засто́порился; **under ~** (*lit.*, *also fig.*, *of criticism etc.*) под огнём; **draw s.o.'s ~** вызыва́ть, вы́звать ого́нь проти́вника; (*fig.*) стать (*pf.*) мише́нью для чьих-н. напа́док; **hold one's ~** приоста́н|авливать, -ови́ть веде́ние огня́; (*fig.*) сде́рж|иваться, -а́ться. **5.** (*ardour*) пыл, ого́нь (*m.*); воодушевле́ние; **a speech full of ~** пла́менная речь.

v.t. **1.** (*set fire to*) подж|ига́ть, -е́чь; заж|ига́ть, -е́чь; (*fig.*): **it ~d her imagination** э́то воспламени́ло её воображе́ние. **2.** (*bake*, *e.g. bricks or pottery*) обж|ига́ть, -е́чь. **3.** (*fuel*): **an oil-~d furnace** то́пка, рабо́тающая на жи́дком то́пливе. **4.** (*of* **~arms**) стреля́ть (*impf.*) из+*g.*; **~ a rifle** стреля́ть (*impf.*) из ружья́; ~ **a shot** произв|оди́ть, -ести́ вы́стрел; вы́стрелить (*pf.*); ~ **a salute** (*of many guns*) произвести́ (*pf.*) артиллери́йский салю́т; **he ~d off his ammunition** он израсхо́довал все патро́ны; (*fig.*): **he ~d off a telegram** он настрочи́л телегра́мму.

v.i. **1.** (*of ~arms*) стреля́ть (*impf.*); вы́стрелить (*pf.*); **the troops ~d at the enemy** войска́ стреля́ли по врагу́; **they ~d at the target** они́ стреля́ли в цель; **the guns ~d** ору́дия стреля́ли; ~ **away!** (*fig., coll.*) валя́й!; выкла́дывай!

cpds. **~-alarm** *n.* (*alert*) пожа́рная трево́га; (*device*) автомати́ческий пожа́рный сигна́л; **~arm** *n.* огнестре́льное ору́жие; **~ball** *n.* (*meteor*) боли́д; (*nucl.*) о́гненный шар; **~-bird** *n.* (*myth.*) жар-пти́ца; **~-bomb** *n.* зажига́тельная бо́мба; **~-box** *n.* то́пка, огнева́я коро́бка; **~brand** *n.* зачи́нщик, подстрека́тель (*m.*); **~-break** *n.* загради́тельная противопожа́рная полоса́; **~-brick** *n.* огнеупо́рный кирпи́ч; **~-brigade** *n.* пожа́рная кома́нда; **~-bug** *n.* (*coll., arsonist*) поджига́тель (*m.*); **~clay** *n.* огнеупо́рная гли́на; **~-cracker** *n.* фейерве́рк; **~damp** *n.* ру́дничный/грему́чий газ; **~dog** *n.* подста́вка для ками́нного прибо́ра; **~-drill** *n.* пожа́рное уче́ние, обуче́ние приёмам противопожа́рной защи́ты; **~-eater** *n.* (*at circus*) пожира́тель (*m.*) огня́; (*fig.*) драчу́н, зади́ра (*c.g.*); **~-engine** *n.* пожа́рная маши́на; **~-escape** *n.* пожа́рная ле́стница; **~-extinguisher** *n.* огнетуши́тель (*m.*); **~-fighter** *n.* пожа́рник, пожа́рный; **~fly** *n.* светля́к; **~-guard** *n.* (*screen*) ками́нная решётка; **~-hose** *n.* пожа́рный шланг; **~-insurance** *n.* страхова́ние от огня́; **~-irons** *n.* ками́нный прибо́р; **~light** *n.* свет от ками́на; **~-lighter** *n.* расто́пка; **~man** *n.* (*stoker*) кочега́р; (*member of ~ brigade*) пожа́рник, пожа́рный; **~place** *n.* ками́н, оча́г; **~-plug** *n.* пожа́рный кран, гидра́нт; **~-policy** *n.* по́лис страхова́ния от огня́; **~-power** *n.* огнева́я мощь; **~proof** *adj.* огнеупо́рный; **a ~proof dish** жа́роупо́рное/огнеупо́рное блю́до; **a ~proof door** несгора́емая дверь; *v.t.* прид|ава́ть, -а́ть огнесто́йкость +*d.*; **~proofing** *n.* огнесто́йкая отде́лка; прида́ние огнесто́йкости; **~-pump** *n.* пожа́рный насо́с; **~-raiser** *n.* поджига́тель (*m.*); **~-raising** *n.* поджо́г; **~-screen** *n.* ками́нный экра́н; **~-ship** *n.* бра́ндер; **~side** *n.* ме́сто о́коло ками́на; (*fig.*) дома́шний оча́г; **~-station** *n.* пожа́рное депо́ (*indecl.*); **~-stone** *n.* огнеупо́рная гли́на; **~-tongs** *n. pl.* ками́нные щипцы́ (*pl., g.* -о́в); **~-trap** *n.* «лову́шка» (*в случае пожара*); **~-watcher** *n.* доброво́лец пожа́рной охра́ны; дежу́рный, следя́щий за зажига́тельными бо́мбами; **~-watching** *n.* охра́на от зажига́тельных бомб; **~-water** *n.* горячи́тельные напи́тки (*m. pl.*); **~wood** *n.* дров|а́ (*pl., g.* —); **~work(s)** *n.* фейерве́рк (*also fig.*); **~work display** фейерве́рк; **~-worship** *n.* огнепокло́нничество; **~-worshipper** *n.* огнепокло́нник.

firing [ˈfaɪərɪŋ] *n.* (*shooting*) стрельба́.

cpds. **~-line** *n.* ли́ния огня́; **~-party, ~-squad** *nn.* (*at funeral etc.*) салю́тная кома́нда; (*for execution*) кома́нда, наря́женная для расстре́ла.

firm[1] [fɜːm] *n.* фи́рма.

firm[2] [fɜːm] *adj.* **1.** (*physical*) кре́пкий, твёрдый; ~ **ground** су́ша; **we are on ~ ground in asserting this** мы с уве́ренностью утвержда́ем э́то. **2.** (*fig.*) усто́йчивый, сто́йкий, непоколеби́мый; **he is ~ in his beliefs** он непоколеби́м в свое́й ве́ре; **you must he ~ with him** вы должны́ быть с ним постро́же; ~ **prices** твёрдые це́ны; **a ~ offer** твёрдое предложе́ние.

adv. твёрдо, усто́йчиво; **stand ~** стоя́ть (*impf.*) твёрдо.

v.t. (*make ~; also ~* **up**) (*e.g. a mixture*) уплотн|я́ть, -и́ть; (*e.g. a project*) укреп|ля́ть, -и́ть.

v.i. (*also ~* **up**) (*become ~*) уплотн|я́ться, -и́ться; укреп|ля́ться, -и́ться.

firmament [ˈfɜːməmənt] *n.* небе́сный свод.

firmness [ˈfɜːmnɪs] *n.* (*physical*) твёрдость; (*moral*) сто́йкость, непоколеби́мость.

firmware [ˈfɜːmweə(r)] *n.* (*comput.*) встро́енные програ́ммы.

adj. (*comput.*) аппара́тно-програ́ммный.

first [fɜːst] *n.* **1.** (*beginning*): **at ~** снача́ла, сперва́; **from ~ to last** с нача́ла до конца́; **from the ~** с са́мого нача́ла. **2.** (*date*) пе́рвое (число́); **on the ~ of May** пе́рвого ма́я. **3.** (*acad.*) вы́сшая оце́нка/отме́тка; **he got a ~ in physics** он получи́л вы́сшую оце́нку по фи́зике. **4.** (*edition*) пе́рвое изда́ние. **5.** (*pl., best quality articles*) това́ры (*m. pl.*) вы́сшего ка́чества.

adj. **1.** (*in time or place*) пе́рвый; ~ **aid** пе́рвая по́мощь; **the ~ comer** пе́рвый встре́чный; **on the ~ floor** на второ́м этаже́; (*US*) на пе́рвом этаже́; ~ **form** пе́рвый класс; **at ~ glance** на пе́рвый взгляд; **hear sth. at ~ hand** узна́ть (*pf.*) что-н. из пе́рвых рук; **at ~ light** как то́лько на́чало/начнёт света́ть; ~ **name** и́мя; ~ **night** (*theatr.*) премье́ра; **I asked the ~ person I saw** я спроси́л пе́рвого встре́чного; ~ **person singular** пе́рвое лицо́ еди́нственного числа́; **in the ~ place** во-пе́рвых, в пе́рвую о́чередь; **I will go there ~ thing tomorrow** за́втра я пе́рвым де́лом зайду́ туда́; **he said the ~ thing that came to mind** он сказа́л пе́рвое, что пришло́ ему́ в го́лову; **the ~ time I saw him** когда́ я в пе́рвый раз уви́дел его́; **he got it right ~ time (off)** у него́ получи́лось э́то с пе́рвого ра́за; **he would be the ~ to admit that ...** он пе́рвый призна́ет, что... **2.** (*in rank or importance*) пе́рвый; **he travels ~ class** он е́здит пе́рвым кла́ссом; **put ~ things ~** де́лать (*impf.*) в пе́рвую о́чередь са́мое гла́вное; ~ **team** (*sport*) основно́й соста́в; ~ **cousin** двою́родный брат, двою́родная сестра́; ~ **violin** пе́рвая скри́пка. **3.** (*basic*) основно́й; ~ **principles** основны́е при́нципы; **he doesn't know the ~ thing about dogs** он ничего́ не понима́ет в соба́ках.

adv. **1.** (*before all; also ~* **and foremost, ~ of all**) пре́жде всего́; в пе́рвую о́чередь; ~ **catch your hare!** ≃ не говори́ «гоп», пока́ не перепры́гнешь; ~ **come, ~ served** кто пе́рвым пришёл, того́ пе́рвым и обслу́жат; **I'll see you damned ~!** так я э́то и сде́лал. **2.** (*initially*) сперва́, снача́ла; (*in the ~ place*) во-пе́рвых; (*for the ~ time*) впервы́е; **I ~ met him last year** я познако́мился с ним в про́шлом году́; **when they were ~ married** в нача́ле их супру́жеской жи́зни; когда́ они́ то́лько пожени́лись.

cpds. **~-aid** *adj.*: **~-aid kit** санита́рная су́мка; **~-aid post** пункт пе́рвой по́мощи; **~-aid room, station** медпу́нкт; **~-born** *n.* пе́рвенец; *adj.* ста́рший, роди́вшийся пе́рвым; **~-class** *adj.* (*excellent*) первокла́ссный; *adv.* (*of travel*) пе́рвым кла́ссом; **~-floor** *adj.* второ́го этажа́, на второ́м этаже́; (*US*) пе́рвого этажа́, на пе́рвом этаже́; **~-form** *adj.*: **~-form pupil** первокла́ссник; **~-fruits** *n. pl.* пе́рвые плоды́ (*m. pl.*); **~-hand** *adj.* из пе́рвых рук; **~-night** *adj.*: **~-night nerves** волне́ние пе́ред премье́рой; **~-nighter** *n.* завсегда́тай премье́р; **~-rate** *adj.* первокла́ссный, превосхо́дный; *int.* прекра́сно!; превосхо́дно!; **~-strike** *adj.*: **~-strike weapons** ору́жие для пе́рвого уда́ра.

firstly [ˈfɜːstlɪ] *adv.* во-пе́рвых.

firth [fɜːθ] *n.* зали́в; лима́н; **the F~ of Forth** зали́в Форт.

fiscal [ˈfɪsk(ə)l] *adj.* фиска́льный, фина́нсовый.

fish [fɪʃ] *n.* **1.** ры́ба; **catch ~** лови́ть, пойма́ть ры́бу; **drink like a ~** пить (*impf.*) запо́ем; **a ~ out of water** челове́к, попа́вший не в свою́ среду́; **neither ~, flesh, nor fowl** ни ры́ба, ни мя́со; **I have other ~ to fry** у меня́ есть дела́ поважне́е; (*fig., creature*): **a cold ~** холо́дный челове́к; **a poor ~** никуды́шный челове́к; **a queer ~** чуда́к, стра́нный тип.

v.t. & i. лови́ть/уди́ть (*impf.*) ры́бу; ~ **a river** лови́ть ры́бу в реке́; (*fig.*): ~ **for compliments** напра́шиваться (*impf.*) на комплиме́нты; ~ **for information** выу́живать, вы́удить све́дения; **he is ~ing in troubled waters** он ло́вит ры́бку в му́тной воде́; **he ~ed through his pockets** он поры́лся у себя́ в карма́нах.

with advs.: ~ **out** *v.t.* выу́живать, вы́удить; ~ **up** *v.t.* выта́скивать, вы́тащить.

cpds. **~bone** *n.* ры́бья кость; **~-cake** *n.* ≃ ры́бная котле́та; **~-eye** *adj.*: **~-eye lens** фотообъекти́в «ры́бий глаз»; ; **~-farm** *n.* рыборазво́дный садо́к; **~-finger** *n.* ры́бная па́лочка; **~-glue** *n.* ры́бий клей; **~-hook** *n.* рыболо́вный крючо́к; **~-knife** *n.* нож для ры́бы; **~-meal** *n.* ры́бная мука́; **~monger** *n.* торго́вец ры́бой; **~net** *n.* рыболо́вная сеть; **~net stockings** ажу́рные чулки́; **~-oil** *n.* ры́бий жир; **~-pond** *n.* пруд для разведе́ния ры́бы; ры́бный садо́к; **~-slice** *n.* нож для разреза́ния ры́бы;

~-spear *n.* острóга; **~tail** *n.* ры́бий хвост; **~wife** *n.* торгóвка ры́бой.

fisher(man) [ˈfɪʃəmən] *n.* рыбáк; (*angler for pleasure*) рыболóв; (*for pearls etc.*) ловéц.

fishery [ˈfɪʃərɪ] *n.* рыболóвство; ры́бный прóмысел; **pearl/coral ~** добы́ча/лóвля жéмчуга/корáллов.

fishing [ˈfɪʃɪŋ] *n.* ры́бная лóвля; рыболóвство; **~ rights** прáво ры́бной лóвли; **the boys have gone ~** мáльчики ушли́ на рыбáлку.

cpds. **~-line** *n.* лесá, лéска; **~-net** *n.* рыболóвная сеть; **~-rod** *n.* уди́лище; **~-tackle** *n.* рыболóвные снáсти (*f. pl.*).

fishy [ˈfɪʃɪ] *adj.* ры́бий, ры́бный; **a ~ taste** ры́бный при́вкус; (*coll., suspect*) нечи́стый, подозри́тельный; не вызывáющий довéрия.

fissile [ˈfɪsaɪl] *adj.* (*phys.*) расщепля́ющийся; (*geol.*) сланцевáтый.

fission [ˈfɪʃ(ə)n] *n.* (*biol.*) размножéние путём делéния клéток; (*phys.*) расщеплéние/делéние (ядрá); **nuclear ~** áтомный распáд.

fissionable [ˈfɪʃənəb(ə)l] *adj.* спосóбный к я́дерному распáду; расщепля́емый.

fissure [ˈfɪʃə(r)] *n.* трéщина, расщéлина.

v.i. трéскаться, по-; трéснуть (*pf.*).

fist [fɪst] *n.* кулáк; (*dim., e.g. baby's*) кулачóк; **shake one's ~ at s.o.** грози́ть, по- комý-н. кулакóм; **with clenched ~s** сжав кулаки́.

fistful [ˈfɪstfʊl] *n.* горсть, при́горшня.

fisticuffs [ˈfɪstɪˌkʌfs] *n.* кулáчный бой.

fistula [ˈfɪstjʊlə] *n.* (*med.*) фи́стула, свищ.

fit[1] [fɪt] *n.* **1.** (*attack of illness*) при́ступ, припáдок; **apoplectic ~** апоплекси́ческий удáр; **he was subject to ~s as a child** ребёнком он был подвéржен припáдкам; (*fig.*): **she would have, throw a ~ if she knew** онá закати́ла бы сцéну/истéрику, éсли бы узнáла. **2.** (*outburst*): **~ of coughing** при́ступ кáшля; **the book sent me into ~s of laughter** э́та кни́га рассмеши́ла меня́ до слёз; **his jokes had us in ~s** от егó шýток мы покáтывались сó смеху; **in a ~ of passion** в поры́ве стрáсти. **3.** (*transitory state*): **by ~s and starts** уры́вками; **he works when the ~ is on him** он рабóтает под настроéние.

fit[2] [fɪt] *n.* (*of a garment etc.*): **this jacket is a tight ~** э́тот пиджáк узковáт; **six people in the car is a tight ~** шесть человéк едвá умещáются в маши́не.

adj. **1.** (*suitable*) гóдный, пригóдный, подходя́щий; **this food is not ~ to eat** э́та пи́ща несъедóбна; **he was passed ~ for military service** егó при́знали гóдным к воéнной слýжбе; **survival of the ~test** естéственный отбóр; **see, think ~** считáть, почéсть нýжным; **a meal ~ for a king** цáрская трáпеза; **you are not ~ to be seen** вам нельзя́ покáзáться в такóм ви́де. **2.** (*ready*) готóвый, спосóбный; **he was ~ to drop** он едвá держáлся на ногáх; **dressed ~ to kill** разодéтый в пух и прах. **3.** (*in good health*) здорóвый; в хорóшей фóрме; **fighting ~** здорóвый как бык; **keep (o.s.) ~** следи́ть (*impf.*) за свои́м здорóвьем.

v.t. **1.** (*equip*: *also* **~ out; ~ up**) снаря|жáть, -ди́ть; снаб|жáть, -ди́ть; э́кипировáть (*impf., pf.*); оборýдовать (*impf., pf.*); **the house is ~ted for electricity** в дóме есть провóдка; **he was ~ted out with a new suit** емý вы́дали нóвый костю́м; **he went to the tailors to be ~ted** он пошёл к портнóму на примéрку; **~ a ship out** снаря|жáть, -ди́ть корáбль. **2.** (*install, fix in place*): **~ted carpet** ковёр во всю кóмнату; **he ~ted a new lock on the door** он встáвил нóвый замóк в дверь; (*fig., accommodate*): **I can ~ you in next week** я могý назнáчить вам встрéчу на слéдующей недéле. **3.** (*make suitable, adapt*) приспос|áбливать, -óбить; **he is not ~ted for heavy work** он не годи́тся для тяжёлых рабóт; **they are well ~ted for each other** они́ подхóдят друг дрýгу; **I had a suit ~ted** я примéрил костю́м; **I ~ted in my holiday with his** я подогнáл врéмя своегó óтпуска к егó; (*correspond to in dimensions*: *also v.i.*) под|ходи́ть, -ойти́ +*d.*; **the dress ~s you** э́то плáтье хорошó на вас сиди́т; **will the letter ~ (into) this envelope?** войдёт письмó в э́тот конвéрт?; **a key to ~ this lock** ключ к э́тому замкý; **that ~s in with my plans** э́то вполнé совпадáет с мои́ми плáнами; **his story ~s in with hers** егó расскáз подтверждáет её словá. **4.** (*insert*: *also v.i.*): **he ~ted the cigarette into the holder** он встáвил сигарéту в мундштýк; **tubes that ~ into one another** трýбки, вставля́ющиеся однá в другýю. **5.** (*suit*) соотвéтствовать (*impf.*) +*d.*; **he made the punishment ~ the crime** он определи́л наказáние, соотвéтствующее преступлéнию.

fitful [ˈfɪtfʊl] *adj.* нерóвный, прерывистый.

fitment [ˈfɪtmənt] *n.* предмéт обстанóвки; часть оборýдования.

fitness [ˈfɪtnɪs] *n.* (*suitability*) соотвéтствие, пригóдность; (*health*) хорóшее здорóвье.

fitter [ˈfɪtə(r)] *n.* (*tailor's assistant*) портнóй, занимáющийся примéркой; (*mechanic*) монтёр, сбóрщик.

fitting [ˈfɪtɪŋ] *n.* **1.** (*of clothes*) примéрка. **2.** (*fixture in building*) оборýдование; **light ~s** освети́тельные прибóры (*m. pl.*). **3.** (*furnishing*) оборýдование, установка.

adj. подходя́щий, гóдный.

cpd. **~-room** *n.* примéрочная.

five [faɪv] *n.* (числó/нóмер) пять; (**~** *people*) пя́теро; пять человéк; **we ~** нас пя́теро; **(the) ~ of us went** мы пошли́ впятерóм; нас пошлó пять человéк; **~ each** по пяти́; **in ~s, ~ at a time** по пяти́, пятёрками; (*figure, thg. numbered 5, group of* **~**) пятёрка; (*of things purchased in* **~s**, *e.g. eggs*) пятóк; (**~**-*copeck piece*) пятáк, пятачóк; (*with var. nn. expr. or understood; cf. also examples under* **two**): **~ (o'clock)** пять (часóв); **chapter ~ (5)** пя́тая (5) главá; **he is ~** емý пять лет; **at ~ (years old)** в пять лет, в пятилéтнем вóзрасте; **~ of spades** пятёрка пик; **~ to 4 (o'clock)** без пяти́ четы́ре; **~ past 6** пять минýт шестóго; **have you got this dress in a ~?** есть у вас пя́тый размéр э́того плáтья; **she takes ~s in shoes** у неё пя́тый размéр óбуви; **let's take five** (*coll.*) пойдём на перекýр.

adj. пять +*g. pl.*; (*for people and pluralia tantum, also*) пя́теро +*g. pl.*; **~ sixes are thirty** пя́тью шесть — три́дцать; **~ eggs** (*as purchase*) пятóк яи́ц; **~ times as good** впя́теро лýчше.

cpds. **~-day** *adj.*: **~-day week** пятиднéвная недéля, пятиднéвка; **~-finger** *adj.*: **~-finger exercise** упражнéние для пяти́ пáльцев; **~fold** *adj.* пятикрáтный; *adv.* впя́теро; в пятикрáтном размéре; **the crop has increased ~fold** урожáй увели́чился в пять раз; **~-pound** *adj.*: **~-pound note** пятифунтóвая бумáжка; **~-sided** *adj.* пятисторóнний; **~-sided figure** пятиугóльник; **~-storey** *adj.* пятиэтáжный; **~-year** *adj.* пятилéтний; **~-year plan** пятилéтний план, пятилéтка; **~-year-old** *n.* пятилéтний ребёнок.

fiver [ˈfaɪvə(r)] *n.* пятёрка (*coll.*).

fix [fɪks] *n.* (*coll., dilemma*) затрудни́тельное положéние; затруднéние; (*determination of position*) определéние мéста; (*coll., injection of drug*) укóл.

v.t. **1.** (*fasten, make firm*) укреп|ля́ть, -и́ть; **~ bayonets!** примкнýть штыки́!; (*fig.*): **I ~ed him with a glance** я при́стально посмотрéл на негó; **the event was ~ed in his mind** э́то собы́тие запечатлéлось у негó в мозгý; **~ the blame on s.o.** взвáл|ивать, -и́ть винý на когó-н. **2.** (*direct steadily*) напр|авля́ть, -áвить; **~ one's eyes (up)on** остан|áвливать, -ови́ть взгляд на+*p.*; **~ one's attention on** сосредотóчи|вать, -ть внимáние на+*p.*; **~ed gaze** при́стальный/засты́вший взгляд. **3.** (*determine, settle*: *also v.i.*) **let us ~ (on) a date** давáйте договори́мся о дáте. **4.** (*chem.*) сгу|щáть, -сти́ть; свя́з|ывать, -áть. **5.** (*phot.*) фикси́ровать (*impf., pf.*). **6.** (*provide*: *also* **~ up**) **can you ~ (up) a room for me?** (*or* **~ me up with a room?**) мóжете ли вы найти́ для меня́ кóмнату? **7.** (*coll., attend to*): **he ~ed the radio in no time** он в два счёта почини́л радиоприёмник; **I will ~ the drinks** я приготóвлю напи́тки. **8.** (*sl., get even with*) расквитáться (*pf.*) с+*i.*

fixation [fɪkˈseɪʃ(ə)n] *n.* (*phot.*) фиксáция, закреплéние; (*psych.*) фиксáция.

fixative [ˈfɪksətɪv] *n.* фиксати́в, фиксáтор.

adj. фикси́рующий, закрепля́ющий.

fixed [ˈfɪksd] *adj.* неподви́жный, закреплённый, постоя́нный; **~ idea** навя́зчивая идéя, идéя фикс; **~ point** (*geom.*) постоя́нная тóчка; **~ rate** устанóвленная/постоя́нная стáвка; **~ star** неподви́жная звездá.

fixedly ['fɪksɪdlɪ] *adv.* при́стально; в упо́р; (*of smile*) де́ланно.
fixer ['fɪksə(r)] *n.* (*phot.*) фикса́ж; (*sl., arranger*) посре́дник, ма́клер, толка́ч.
fixture ['fɪkstʃə(r)] *n.* **1.** (*fitting in building*) приспособле́ние. **2.** (*tech.*) неподви́жная/закреплённая дета́ль. **3.** (*sporting event*) предстоя́щее спорти́вное состяза́ние/мероприя́тие. **4.** (*coll., permanent feature*) обы́чное явле́ние.
fizz [fɪz] *n.* (*sound*) шипе́ние; (*champagne*) игри́стое (*coll.*). *v.i.* шипе́ть (*impf.*); и́скри́ться (*impf.*).
fizzle ['fɪz(ə)l] *v.i.* шипе́ть (*impf.*); ~ **out** выдыха́ться, вы́дохнуться; (*fig.*) око́нчиться (*pf.*) ниче́м.
fizzy ['fɪzɪ] *adj.* шипу́чий.
fjord [fjɔːd] = **fiord**
flabbergast ['flæbə,gɑːst] *v.t.* (*coll.*) ошелом|ля́ть, -и́ть; ошара́ши|вать, -ть.
flabbiness ['flæbɪnɪs] *n.* вя́лость, дря́блость; (*fig.*) сла́бость, слабохара́ктерность, мягкоте́лость.
flabby ['flæbɪ] *adj.* вя́лый, дря́блый; (*fig.*) сла́бый, слабохара́ктерный, мягкоте́лый.
flaccid ['flæksɪd, 'flæsɪd] *adj.* отви́слый, вя́лый; (*fig.*) сла́бый, вя́лый, бесси́льный.
flag[1] [flæg] *n.* (*emblem*) флаг, зна́мя (*nt.*), стяг; **black** ~ пира́тский/чёрный флаг; **the red** ~ кра́сное зна́мя; **show the white** ~ выве́шивать, вы́весить бе́лый флаг; **yellow** ~ каранти́нный флаг; **hoist, raise, run up the** ~ подн|има́ть, -я́ть (*or* водру|жа́ть, -зи́ть) флаг; **lower, strike the** ~ (*naut.*) опус|ка́ть, -ти́ть флаг; (*surrender*) сд|ава́ться, -а́ться; **show the** ~ подн|има́ть, -я́ть флаг; (*fig.*) напо́мнить (*pf.*) о своём существова́нии; ~ **of convenience** удо́бный флаг; **keep the** ~ **flying** (*fig.*) высоко́ держа́ть (*impf.*) зна́мя (*чего*); **put the** ~**s out** (*fig.*) пра́здновать (*impf.*) побе́ду; **F~ Day** (*US*), День установле́ния госуда́рственного фла́га США; ~ **officer** адмира́л, коммодо́р; кома́ндующий.
v.t. **1.** (*deck with* ~*s*) укр|аша́ть, -а́сить фла́гами. **2.** (*signal: also v.i.*) сигнализи́ровать (*impf., pf.*) фла́гом; (*fig.*): ~ **(down) a passing car** останови́ть (*pf.*) проезжа́ющую маши́ну.
cpds. ~**-captain** *n.* команди́р фла́гманского корабля́; ~**-day** *n.* день сбо́ра денег на благотвори́тельные це́ли; ~**-lieutenant** *n.* флаг-адъюта́нт; ~**man** *n.* сигна́льщик; ~**pole** *n.* флагшто́к; ~**ship** *n.* фла́гманский кора́бль, фла́гман; ~**staff** *n.* флагшто́к; ~**-wagging** *n.* (*coll., signalling*) сигнализа́ция флажка́ми; (*coll., demonstrative patriotism*) ура́-патриоти́зм.
flag[2] [flæg] *n.* (*bot.*) каса́тик, и́рис.
flag[3] [flæg] *n.* (~ *stone*) ка́менная плита́, плитня́к.
v.t. выстила́ть, вы́стлать пли́тами.
flag[4] [flæg] v.i. (*hang limp*) пон|ика́ть, -и́кнуть; сн|ика́ть, -и́кнуть; (*grow weary*) ослаб|ева́ть, -е́ть; (*fig.*): **the conversation was** ~**ging** разгово́р не кле́ился.
flagellant ['flædʒələnt, flə'dʒelənt] *n.* флагелла́нт.
flagellate ['flædʒə,leɪt] *v.t.* бичева́ть (*impf.*).
flagellation [,flædʒə'leɪʃ(ə)n] *n.* бичева́ние; (*self-*~) самобичева́ние.
flageolet [,flædʒə'let, 'flædʒ-] *n.* (*mus.*) флажоле́т.
flagon ['flægən] *n.* графи́н/кувши́н для вина́.
flagrancy ['fleɪgrənsɪ] *n.* чудо́вищность, возмути́тельность.
flagrant ['fleɪgrənt] *adj.* вопию́щий, возмути́тельный.
flagrante delicto [flə'græntɪ dɪ'lɪktəʊ] *adv.*: **capture** ~ поимка на ме́сте преступле́ния.
flail [fleɪl] *n.* цеп.
v.t. & i. молоти́ть, с-; (*fig.*) маха́ть (*impf.*); **he charged with his hands** ~**ing** он наступа́л, разма́хивая рука́ми.
flair ['fleə(r)] *n.* нюх, чутьё; **a** ~ **for languages** спосо́бности (*f. pl.*) к языка́м.
flak [flæk] *n.* зени́тный ого́нь; ~ **jacket** защи́тная ку́ртка; (*fig.*) **he took a lot of** ~ **from the critics** ему́ доста́лось от кри́тиков.
flake [fleɪk] *n.* (*pl.*) хло́пья (*pl., g.* -ев); ~**s of snow** снежи́нки (*f. pl.*); **corn** ~**s** корнфле́кс; **soap** ~**s** мы́льная стру́жка.
v.i. (*peel*) шелуши́ться (*impf.*); слои́ться (*impf.*); **the rust** ~**d off** ржа́вчина отслои́лась.
flaky ['fleɪkɪ] *adj.* слои́стый.
flambeau ['flæmbəʊ] *n.* фа́кел.
flamboyanc|e [flæm'bɔɪəns], **-y** [flæm'bɔɪənsɪ] *nn.* цвети́стость; я́ркость; (*fig.*) аффекта́ция; наи́гранность.
flamboyant [flæm'bɔɪənt] *adj.* цвети́стый; я́рко окра́шенный; (*fig.*) бро́ский, показно́й; **F~ architecture** «пламене́ющий» стиль (го́тики).
flame [fleɪm] *n.* **1.** (*burning gas; pl., fire*) ого́нь (*m.*), пла́мя (*nt.*); **burst into** ~**(s)** вспы́х|ивать, -нуть; **the house was in** ~**s** дом был охва́чен пла́менем; **commit to the** ~**s** преда́ть (*pf.*) огню́; **add fuel to the** ~**s** (*fig.*) подли́ть (*pf.*) ма́сла в ого́нь; **fan the** ~**s of passion** (*love*) разд|ува́ть, -у́ть пла́мя стра́сти; (*excitement*) разж|ига́ть, -е́чь стра́сти. **2.** (*blaze of light or colour*) пла́мя (*nt.*), вспы́шка. **3.** (*specific colour: also adj.*) о́гненный (цвет). **4.** (*coll., sweetheart*) предме́т стра́сти; **she is an old** ~ **of mine** она́ моя́ ста́рая па́ссия.
v.i. горе́ть, пыла́ть, пламене́ть (*all impf.*); (*fig.*): ~ **up** (*get angry; blush*) вспы́хнуть (*pf.*).
cpds. ~**-proof** *adj.* огнесто́йкий; ~**-thrower** *n.* огнемёт.
flamenco [flə'meŋkəʊ] *n.* флaméнко (*indecl.*).
flaming ['fleɪmɪŋ] *adj.* **1.** (*ablaze; very hot*) пыла́ющий, горя́щий. **2.** (*brightly coloured*) я́ркий, пламене́ющий. **3.** (*fig., violent*): **they had a** ~ **row** у них произошёл стра́шный сканда́л; **he was in a** ~ **temper** он был в бе́шенстве. **4.** (*sl.*): **it's a** ~ **nuisance** э́то черто́вски доса́дно.
flamingo [flə'mɪŋgəʊ] *n.* флами́нго (*m. indecl.*).
flammable ['flæməb(ə)l] *adj.* горю́чий; легко́ воспламеня́ющийся.
flan [flæn] *n.* ола́дья.
Flanders ['flɑːndəz] *n.* Фла́ндрия.
flâneur [flæ'nɜːr] *n.* фланёр.
flange [flændʒ] *n.* фла́нец, кро́мка.
v.t. фланцева́ть (*impf.*).
flank [flæŋk] *n.* **1.** (*of the body*) бок. **2.** (*of a building*) торцо́вая сторона́. **3.** (*of a hill*) склон. **4.** (*of an army*) фланг; **turn the enemy's** ~ обойти́ (*pf.*) врага́ с фла́нга; ~ **attack** фла́нговая ата́ка.
v.t. **1.** (*be or go alongside*) находи́ться (*impf.*) (*or* идти́) сбо́ку. **2.** (*protect*) прикр|ыва́ть, -ы́ть фланг +*g.* **3.** (*menace or cut off by* ~*ing movement*) угрожа́ть (*impf.*) с фла́нга +*g.*; отр|еза́ть, -еза́ть фланг; **he was** ~**ed by guards** по о́бе его́ стороны́ шла/стоя́ла стра́жа.
flannel ['flæn(ə)l] *n.* **1.** (*kind of cloth*) флане́ль. **2.** (*piece of cloth*) флане́лька; **face** ~ махро́вая рукави́чка для лица́. **3.** (*pl., trousers*) флане́левые брю́ки (*pl. g.* —). **4.** (*coll.*) очковтира́тельство.
adj. флане́левый.
v.t. прот|ира́ть, -ере́ть флане́лью.
flannelette [,flænə'let] *n.* фланеле́т, ба́йка.
flap[1] [flæp] *n.* **1.** (*hinged piece etc.*): **the table has two** ~**s** у стола́ две откидны́е доски́; **a jacket with a** ~ **at the back** пиджа́к с двумя́ разре́зами сза́ди; (*of pocket*) кла́пан; (*tech.*): ~ **valve** пласти́нчатый откидно́й кла́пан; (*aeron.*) закры́лок; **with** ~**s down** с опу́щенными закры́лками. **2.** (*waving motion*) взмах. **3.** (*sound*) хлопо́к. **4.** (*blow with flat object*) шлепо́к.
v.t. & i. взма́х|ивать, -ну́ть +*i.*; мах|а́ть, -ну́ть +*i.*; хло́п|ать, -нуть; шлёп|ать, -нуть; развева́ть(ся) (*impf.*); **the bird** ~**ped its wings** пти́ца взмахну́ла кры́льями; **the flags** ~**ped in the wind** фла́ги развева́лись на ветру́; **he** ~**ped away the flies** он отгоня́л мух (хлопу́шкой).
cpd. ~**-eared** *adj.* длинноу́хий, лопоу́хий.
flap[2] [flæp] *n.* (*coll., state of alarm*) переполо́х; **don't get into a** ~! не паникуйте!
v.i. переполоши́ться (*pf.*).
flapdoodle [flæp'duːd(ə)l, 'flæp-] *n.* (*sl.*) чепуха́, белиберда́.
flapjack ['flæpdʒæk] *n.* **1.** (*biscuit*) овся́ное пече́нье. **2.** (*US*) блин, ола́дья.
flapper ['flæpə(r)] *n.* **1.** (*instrument*) хлопу́шка для мух; колоту́шка для птиц. **2.** (*appendage; fin*) ласт; плавни́к. **3.** (*arch. sl., flighty girl*) верту́шка.
flare[1] [fleə(r)] *n.* **1.** (*effect of flame*) сия́ние, сверка́ние; вспы́шка; (*illuminating device*) сигна́льная раке́та;

освети́тельный патро́н; **the ship sent out ~s** кора́бль посыла́л сигна́льные раке́ты.

v.i. сверк|а́ть, -ну́ть; горе́ть (*impf.*) неро́вным пла́менем; (*fig.*) вспы́х|ивать, -нуть; вспыли́ть (*pf.*); **she ~s up at the least thing** она́ взрыва́ется от ка́ждого пустяка́.

cpds. **~-path** *n.* освещённая взлётно-поса́дочная полоса́; **~-up** *n.* (*lit., fig.*) вспы́шка.

flare² [fleə(r)] *n.* (*widening-out*) расшире́ние.

v.t. & i. расш|иря́ться, -и́риться; **~d skirt** ю́бка-клёш.

flash [flæʃ] *n.* **1.** (*burst of light*) вспы́шка, про́блеск; **a ~ of lightning** вспы́шка мо́лнии; **~ in the pan** (*fig.*) осе́чка; **he had a ~ of inspiration** на него́ нашло́ вдохнове́ние. **2.** (*instant*) мгнове́ние, миг; **he answered in a ~** он мгнове́нно отве́тил. **3.** (*on uniform*) нарука́вная наши́вка; эмбле́ма ча́сти/соедине́ния. **4.**: **news ~** э́кстренное сообще́ние.

adj. (*gaudy*) безвку́сный, крича́щий; (*counterfeit*) фальши́вый.

v.t.: **he ~ed the light in my face** он напра́вил свет мне в лицо́; **they were ~ing signals to the enemy** они́ посыла́ли светов́ые сигна́лы врагу́; (*fig.*): **he ~ed a glance at her** он метну́л на неё взгля́д; **her eyes ~ed fire** её глаза́ мета́ли мо́лнии.

v.i. сверк|а́ть, -ну́ть; вспы́х|ивать, -нуть; мельк|а́ть, -ну́ть; **the light ~ed on and off** свет то вспы́хивал, то гас; **the lightning ~ed** сверкну́ла/блесну́ла мо́лния; **the sword ~ed in his hand** меч сверка́л в его́ руке́; **~ing beacon** про́блесковый мая́к; **~ing eyes** сверка́ющие глаза́; **the thought ~ed across my mind** э́та мысль промелькну́ла у меня́ в голове́; **cars ~ed by** маши́ны мча́лись ми́мо.

cpds. **~back** *n.* (*cin.*) ретроспе́кция, обра́тный кадр; **~-bulb** *n.* (*phot.*) ла́мпа-вспы́шка; **~-gun** *n.* ла́мпа для ма́гниевой вспы́шки, «блиц»; **~light** *n.* (*for signalling*) сигна́льный ого́нь; проже́ктор; (*phot.*) вспы́шка (ма́гния); (*torch*: *also* **~-lamp**) карма́нный/электри́ческий фона́рь; **~-point** *n.* температу́ра вспы́шки; то́чка воспламене́ния.

flashiness ['flæʃɪnɪs] *n.* показу́ха.

flashy ['flæʃɪ] *adj.* крича́щий, показно́й, эффе́ктный.

flask [flɑːsk] *n.* фля́га, фля́жка; ко́лба; оплетённая буты́ль.

flat [flæt] *n.* **1.** (*level object or area*) пло́скость; пло́ская пове́рхность; **the ~ of the hand** ладо́нь; **on the ~** на пло́скости. **2.** (*mus.*) бемо́ль (*m.*); **the key of A ~** тона́льность ля бемо́ль. **3.** (*apartment*) кварти́ра; **block of ~s** многокварти́рный дом. **4.** (*coll., punctured tyre*) спу́щенная ши́на.

adj. & adv. **1.** (*level*) пло́ский, ро́вный; **~ car** ваго́н-платфо́рма; **he has ~ feet** у него́ плоскосто́пие; **~ race, racing** ска́чка без препя́тствий; **~ spin** (*aeron.*) пло́ский што́пор; **get into a ~ spin** (*sl.*) впасть (*pf.*) в па́нику; **~ trajectory fire** насти́льный ого́нь; **~ tyre** спу́щенная ши́на; **the battery is ~** батаре́я се́ла; **he fell ~ on his back** он упа́л на́взничь; **my hair won't lie ~** у меня́ во́лосы не лежа́т. **2.** (*uniform, undifferentiated*) однообра́зный; **~ rate** еди́ная ста́вка. **3.** (*unqualified*) прямо́й, категори́ческий; **~ broke** вконе́ц разори́вшийся; **~ out** (*sl. exhausted*) вы́дохшийся; **drive ~ out** (*coll., at top speed*) гнать (*impf.*) во весь опо́р (*or* во всю мочь); **in ten seconds ~** ро́вно за де́сять секу́нд; **I tell you ~!** я скажу́ вам пря́мо! (*or* без обиняко́в); **I've said no, and that's ~** я сказа́л нет — и то́чка. **4.** (*dull, insipid*) ску́чный, вя́лый, бесцве́тный; **the wine has gone ~** вино́ вы́дохлось; **the story fell ~** расска́з не вы́звал интере́са. **5.** (*expressionless*) безжи́зненный, уны́лый. **6.** (*mus.*): **she sings ~ on the high notes** она́ фальши́вит (*or* не дотя́гивает) на высо́ких но́тах.

cpds. **~-fish** *n.* пло́ская ры́ба; **~-foot** *n.* (*policeman*) мильто́н (*sl.*); **~-footed** *adj.* страда́ющий плоскосто́пием; (*fig., clumsy*) неуклю́жий; **he was caught ~-footed** он был засти́гнут врасплóх; **~-iron** *n.* утю́г.

flatlet ['flætlət] *n.* однокóмнатная/малогабари́тная кварти́ра.

flatly ['flætlɪ] *adv.* (*expressionlessly*) безжи́зненно, уны́ло; (*bluntly*) категори́чески, наотре́з, пря́мо.

flatness ['flætnɪs] *n.* пло́скость; (*fig.*) бана́льность.

flatten ['flæt(ə)n] *v.t.* **1.** (*make smooth*) выра́внивать, вы́ровнять; разгла́|живать, -дить. **2.** (*reduce thickness of*) расплю́щи|вать, -ть; **he ~ed himself against the wall** он прижа́лся к стене́. **3.** (*lay low*) повали́ть, приmя́ть (*both pf.*); **the gale ~ed the corn** бу́рей примя́ло хлеба́; (*fig.*): **he was ~ed by her look of scorn** он был изничто́жен её презри́тельным взгля́дом.

v.i. выра́вниваться, вы́ровняться; **the pilot ~ed out at fifty metres** пило́т вы́ровнял самолёт на высоте́ 50 ме́тров; **the rise in prices will soon ~ out** це́ны ско́ро вы́ровняются.

flatter ['flætə(r)] *v.t.* **1.** (*praise insincerely or unduly*) льсти́ть, по- *+d.* **2.** (*represent too favourably*) приукра́|шивать, -сить; **the picture ~s her** худо́жник ей польсти́л. **3.** (*gratify vanity of*): **~ o.s.** те́шить (*impf.*) себя́; льсти́ть (*impf.*) себя́ наде́ждой; **it ~s his self-esteem** э́то льстит его́ самолю́бию; **I ~ myself I'm a good judge of horses** я сме́ю ду́мать, что разбира́юсь в лошадя́х.

flatterer ['flætərə(r)] *n.* льсте́ц.

flattering ['flætərɪŋ] *adj.* ле́стный, льсти́вый; (*of pers.*) льсти́вый.

flattery ['flætərɪ] *n.* лесть.

flatulence ['flætjʊləns] *n.* скопле́ние га́зов; (*fig.*) напы́щенность, высокопа́рность.

flatulent ['flætjʊlənt] *adj.* вызыва́ющий га́зы; взду́вшийся от га́зов; (*fig.*) напы́щенный, высокопа́рный.

flaunt [flɔːnt] *v.t.* афиши́ровать (*impf.*); щегол|я́ть, -ьну́ть *+i.*; похваля́ться (*impf.*) *+i.*; выставля́ть, вы́ставить напока́з.

flautist ['flɔːtɪst] *n.* флейти́ст.

flavour ['fleɪvə(r)] *n.* арома́т, вкус; (*fig.*) при́вкус.

v.t. припр|авля́ть, -а́вить; (*fig.*) прид|ава́ть, -а́ть при́вкус *+d.*; сд|а́бривать, -о́брить.

flavourful ['fleɪvəfʊl] *adj.* аппети́тный, арома́тный.

flavouring ['fleɪvərɪŋ] *n.* припра́ва; спе́ции (*f. pl.*); эссе́нция.

flavourless ['fleɪvəlɪs] *adj.* безвку́сный.

flaw [flɔː] *n.* (*crack*) тре́щина; (*defect*) изъя́н, недоста́ток; **I detect a ~ in your argument** я ви́жу сла́бое ме́сто в ва́ших доказа́тельствах.

v.t. по́ртить, ис-; **all ~ed articles are reduced** брако́ванные това́ры продаю́тся по сни́женным це́нам.

flawless ['flɔːlɪs] *adj.* безупре́чный.

flax [flæks] *n.* (*plant*) лён; (*fibre*) куде́ль.

flaxen ['flæks(ə)n] *adj.* **1.** (*of flax*) льняно́й. **2.** (*colour*) светло-жёлтый, соло́менный.

cpd. **~-haired** *adj.* с льняны́ми волоса́ми.

flay [fleɪ] *v.t.* свежева́ть, о-; сдира́ть, содра́ть ко́жу с*+g.*; **he will ~ me alive if he finds out** он с меня́ живьём шку́ру сдерёт, е́сли узна́ет; (*fig.*): **the wind ~ed his face** ве́тер обжига́л ему́ лицо́; **~ one's opponents** разн|оси́ть, -ести́ в пух и пра́х.

flea [fliː] *n.* блоха́; **I sent him off with a ~ in his ear** он получи́л от меня́ хоро́ший разно́с; он ушёл как оплёванный; **~ market** бара́хо́лка, толку́чка.

cpds. **~bite** *n.* блоши́ный уку́с; (*coll.*) ме́лочь, була́вочный уко́л; **~-bitten** *adj.* иску́санный бло́хами; **~-pit** *n.* (*sl., cinema*) кино́шка; **~-powder** *n.* порошо́к от блох.

fleck [flek] *n.* кра́пинка, пятно́; (*freckle*) весну́шка; (*of dust*) пыли́нка; (*of sunlight*) со́лнечные бли́ки (*m. pl.*).

v.t. покр|ыва́ть, -ы́ть пя́тками/кра́пинками.

fledge [fledʒ] *v.t.* (*bird, arrow*) опер|я́ть, -и́ть; **fully ~d** (*lit., fig.*) опери́вшийся; (*fig.*) вста́вший на́ ноги.

fledg(e)ling ['fledʒlɪŋ] *n.* то́лько что опери́вшийся птене́ц; (*fig.*) желторо́тый юне́ц.

flee [fliː] *v.t.* избе|га́ть, -жа́ть; **~ the country** бежа́ть из страны́.

v.i. бежа́ть, с-; исч|еза́ть, -е́знуть; **all hope had fled** все наде́жды ру́хнули.

fleece [fliːs] *n.* руно́, ове́чья шерсть.

v.t. (*fig.*) об|ира́ть, -обра́ть.

fleecy ['fliːsɪ] *adj.* шерсти́стый; **~ clouds** кудря́вые облака́; **~ hair** кудря́вые/курча́вые во́лосы; **~ lining** мехова́я подкла́дка.

fleet[1] [fliːt] *n.* **1.** (*collection of vessels*) флоти́лия, флот. **2.** (*naval force*) вое́нно-морско́й флот; **Admiral of the F~** адмира́л фло́та; **the Home F~** флот метропо́лии; **F~ Air Arm** морска́я авиа́ция. **3.** (*of vehicles*) парк.

fleet[2] [fliːt] *adj.* (*liter.*) бы́стрый, прово́рный; **~ of foot** быстроно́гий.

fleeting ['fliːtɪŋ] *adj.* бе́глый, мимолётный; **a ~ glimpse** бе́глый взгляд.

Fleet Street [fliːt] *n.* (*fig.*) ло́ндонская пре́сса.

Fleming ['flemɪŋ] *n.* флама́нд|ец (*fem.* -ка).

Flemish ['flemɪʃ] *n.* (*language*) флама́ндский язы́к; **the ~** (*people*) флама́ндцы (*m. pl.*).

adj. флама́ндский.

flesh [fleʃ] *n.* **1.** (*bodily tissue*) плоть, те́ло; **insist on one's pound of ~** (*fig.*) ≃ безжа́лостно тре́бовать (*impf.*) упла́ты до́лга (*u m.n.*); **lose ~** худе́ть, по-; (*meat*) мя́со; **pig's ~** свини́на; (*surface of body*): **~ tint** теле́сный цвет; **~ wound** пове́рхностное ране́ние; **make s.o.'s ~ creep** (*fig.*) прив|оди́ть, -ести́ кого́-н. в содрога́ние. **2.** (*fig.*): **all ~ is grass** всё живо́е тле́нно; **he went the way of all ~** он раздели́л у́часть всех сме́ртных; **man and wife are one ~** муж и жена́ — оди́н дух, одна́ плоть; **sins of the ~** пло́тские грехи́; **see s.o. in the ~** уви́деть (*pf.*) кого́-н. во плоти́; **appear in ~ and blood** появи́ться (*pf.*) со́бственной персо́ной; **more than ~ and blood can stand** свы́ше сил челове́ческих; **my own ~ and blood** (*children*) моя́ плоть и кровь; (*relatives*) моя́ родня́. **3.** (*of plant or fruit*) мя́со, мя́коть.

v.t. **1.: ~ a hound** приуч|а́ть, -и́ть соба́ку к охо́те вку́сом кро́ви. **2. ~ a sword** обагр|я́ть, -и́ть меч кро́вью; (*fig.*, *initiate*) подве́ргнуть (*pf.*) (*кого*) боево́му креще́нию. **3.** (*fig.*): **his characters are well ~ed out** его́ геро́и о́чень жи́зненны. **4.: ~ing knife** нож мясника́.

cpds. **~-coloured** *adj.* теле́сного цве́та; **~pot** *n.* котёл для ва́рки мя́са; **the ~pots of Egypt** (*fig.*) бога́тство и изоби́лие.

fleshly ['fleʃlɪ] *adj.* (*carnal*) пло́тский, чу́вственный; (*corpulent*) то́лстый, ту́чный; в те́ле.

fleshy ['fleʃɪ] *adj.* (*of persons*) то́лстый, ту́чный; (*of meat, plant, fruit*) мяси́стый.

fleur de lis [ˌflɜːdə'liː] *n.* (*her.*) геральди́ческая ли́лия.

flex[1] [fleks] *n.* (ги́бкий) шнур.

flex[2] [fleks] *v.t.* сгиба́ть, согну́ть; **~ one's muscles** напр|яга́ть, -я́чь му́скулы.

flexibility [ˌfleksɪ'bɪlɪtɪ] *n.* эласти́чность; (*fig.*) ги́бкость.

flexible ['fleksɪb(ə)l] *adj.* эласти́чный, ги́бкий, гну́щийся; (*fig.*) ги́бкий.

flexidisc ['fleksɪˌdɪsk] *n.* ги́бкая пласти́нка.

flexion ['flekʃ(ə)n] *n.* изги́б, изо́гнутость; (*math.*) кривизна́, изги́б; (*gram.*) фле́ксия, оконча́ние.

flexitime ['fleksɪˌtaɪm] *n.* свобо́дный режи́м рабо́чего дня.

flexor ['fleksə(r)] *n.* (**~** *muscle*) сгиба́ющая мы́шца.

flibbertigibbet [ˌflɪbətɪ'dʒɪbɪt, 'flɪb-] *n.* болту́шка (*c.g.*), пустозво́н, вертопра́х.

flick [flɪk] *n.* **1.** (*jerk*) толчо́к; **with a ~ of the wrist** взмахну́в ки́стью руки́; (*light touch*): **a ~ of the whip** лёгкий уда́р хлысто́м. **2.** (*coll., film*) кинофи́льм; (*pl., cinema*) кино́ (*indecl.*).

v.t. (*shake with a jerk*) встряхну́ть (*pf.*); (*propel with finger end*) щёлкнуть (*pf.*); (*touch e.g. with whip*) стегну́ть (*pf.*); хлестну́ть (*pf.*).

cpds. **~-flack** *n.* (*sport*) фляк, переворо́т наза́д; **~-knife** *n.* пружи́нный нож.

flicker ['flɪkə(r)] *n.* (*of light*) мерца́ние; (*movement*) трепета́ние; (*fig.*): **a ~ of hope** про́блеск наде́жды.

v.i. (*flutter*) трепета́ть (*impf.*); колыха́ться (*impf.*); (*burn or shine fitfully*) мерца́ть (*impf.*); (*fig.*) мельк|а́ть, -ну́ть.

flier ['flaɪə(r)] = **flyer**

flight[1] [flaɪt] *n.* **1.** полёт; **shoot birds in ~** стреля́ть (*impf.*) птиц на лету́; (*fig.*) **the ~ of time** бег вре́мени; (*journey by air*): **a non-stop ~** беспоса́дочный полёт; **a round-the-world ~** полёт вокру́г све́та; **the next ~ from London to Paris** сле́дующий рейс по маршру́ту Ло́ндон-Пари́ж; **~ number** но́мер ре́йса; **~ recorder** бортово́й самопи́сец; **~ simulator** лётный тренажёр. **2.** (*fig.*): **~ of fancy** полёт фанта́зии; **~s of rhetoric** взлёты (*m. pl.*) красноре́чия. **3. ~ of steps** ле́стничный марш; (*in front of house*) крыльцо́. **4. a ~ of birds** ста́я птиц; (*fig.*): **in the first ~** в пе́рвых ряда́х. **5. a ~ of aircraft** звено́ самолётов.

cpds. **~-commander** *n.* (*US*) команди́р авиазвена́; **~-deck** *n.* (*of carrier*) полётная па́луба; (*of aircraft*) каби́на экипа́жа; **~-lieutenant** *n.* капита́н авиа́ции; **~-sergeant** *n.* ста́рший сержа́нт авиа́ции.

flight[2] [flaɪt] *n.* бе́гство, побе́г; **put to ~** обра|ща́ть, -ти́ть в бе́гство; **take (to) ~** обра|ща́ться, -ти́ться в бе́гство; **the soldiers took to ~** солда́ты бежа́ли; **the army was in full ~** а́рмия стреми́тельно отступа́ла.

flightiness ['flaɪtɪnɪs] *n.* ве́треность.

flighty ['flaɪtɪ] *adj.* ве́треный, взба́лмошный, капри́зный.

flimsiness ['flɪmzɪnɪs] *n.* то́нкость, хру́пкость, непро́чность; (*fig.*) ша́ткость, непро́чность.

flimsy ['flɪmzɪ] *n.* (*coll., copying paper*) папиро́сная бума́га.

adj. то́нкий, непро́чный; **a ~ dress** о́чень лёгкое пла́тье; **a ~ structure** непро́чная постро́йка; **a ~ excuse** сла́бое оправда́ние, неубеди́тельный предло́г.

flinch [flɪntʃ] *v.i.* (*wince*) вздр|а́гивать, -о́гнуть; (*give way*) уклон|я́ться, -и́ться (*от чего*).

fling [flɪŋ] *n.* **1.** (*throw*) бросо́к. **2.** (*attempt*) попы́тка. **3.** (*jibe*) насме́шка. **4.: Highland ~** шотла́ндский та́нец. **5.: he had his ~** он повесели́лся/нагуля́лся вво́лю.

v.t.: **~ o.s. into a chair** бр|оса́ться, -о́ситься в кре́сло; **~ o.s. into the saddle** вск|а́кивать, -очи́ть в седло́; **he flung himself into the project** он с голово́й окуну́лся в осуществле́ние прое́кта; **he was flung into prison** его́ бро́сили в тюрьму́; **he was flung by his horse** ло́шадь сбро́сила его́; **I ~ myself (up)on your mercy** я взыва́ю к ва́шему милосе́рдию; **she flung her arms around me** она́ обняла́ меня́; **he flung the words in my face** он бро́сил мне в лицо́ э́ти слова́; **~ caution to the winds** отбро́сить (*pf.*) вся́кое благоразу́мие.

v.i.: **~ out of the room** вы́скочить/вы́лететь (*both pf.*) из ко́мнаты.

with advs.: **~ o.s. about** разбра́сываться (*impf.*); **~ one's money around** транжи́рить (*impf.*) де́ньги; сори́ть (*impf.*) деньга́ми; **he flung her aside** он оттолкну́л её в сто́рону; **~ away an advantage** отка́з|ываться, -а́ться от преиму́щества; **~ o.s. down on the ground** бр|оса́ться, -о́ситься на зе́млю; **she flung her clothes off** она́ сбро́сила с себя́ оде́жду; **~ open the window** распа́х|ивать, -ну́ть окно́; **he was flung out** его́ вы́швырнули вон; **he flung a few things together** он на́скоро собра́л свои́ ве́щи; **the horse flung up its heels** ло́шадь взбрыкну́ла; **she flung up her arms in horror** она́ в у́жасе всплесну́ла рука́ми; **I nearly flung up the job** я чуть не отказа́лся от рабо́ты.

flint [flɪnt] *n.* кре́мень (*m.*); **Stone Age ~s** кремнёвые ору́дия ка́менного ве́ка; **he has a heart of ~** у него́ ка́менное се́рдце; (*attr.*) кремнёвый, ка́менный.

cpds. **~-glass** *n.* флинтгла́с, англи́йский хруста́ль; **~-head** *n.* ка́менный наконе́чник; **~lock** *n.* замо́к кремнёвого ружья́; кремнёвое ружьё; **~stone** *n.* кремéнь (*m.*); кремнёвый ка́мень.

flinty ['flɪntɪ] *adj.* кремнёвый, кремни́стый; (*fig.*) ка́менный, суро́вый.

cpd. **~-eyed** *adj.* с суро́вым взгля́дом.

flip [flɪp] *n.* **1.** (*flick*) щелчо́к; **he gave the boy a ~ on the ear** он легóнько уда́рил ма́льчика по́ уху. **2.** (*drink*) флип; **egg ~** яи́чный флип. **3.** (*coll., short flight*) коро́ткий полёт. **4.** (*coll.*): **the ~ side of a record** обра́тная сторона́ пласти́нки.

adj. (*flippant*) де́рзкий.

v.t. щёлк|ать, -нуть.

flip-flop ['flɪpflɒp] *n.* **1.** (*noise*) шлёпанье, хло́панье. **2.** (*backward somersault*) са́льто-морта́ле (*indecl.*). **3.** (*footwear*) вьетна́мка. **4.** (*elec.*) три́ггер.

flippancy ['flɪpənsɪ] *n.* легкомы́слие, ве́треность.

flippant ['flɪpənt] *adj.* легкомы́сленный, ве́треный.

flipper ['flɪpə(r)] *n.* пла́вник, ласт; (*diver's appendage*) ласт; (*direction indicator of car*) стре́лка.

flirt [flɜːt] *n.* коке́тка; люби́тель (*m.*) поуха́живать.

v.i. флиртова́ть (*impf.*) (с+*i.*); коке́тничать (*impf.*)

(c+*i*.); (*fig*.): ~ **with danger** игра́ть (*impf*.) с огнём; ~ **with** (*an idea etc*.) поду́мывать о+*p*.; **they ~ed with the Fascists** они́ зайгрывали с фаши́стами.

flirtation [flз:'teɪʃ(ə)n] *n*. флирт; коке́тство, (*fig*.) игра́.

flirtatious [flз:'teɪʃəs] *adj*. коке́тливый.

flit [flɪt] *n*.: **the tenants did a moonlight** ~ жильцы́ потихо́ньку смы́лись (*coll*.).

v.i. (*fly lightly*) порх|а́ть, -ну́ть; (*fig*.): **the thought ~ted across my mind** э́та мысль пронесла́сь у меня́ в голове́.

flitch [flɪtʃ] *n*. (*of bacon*) засо́ленный и копчёный свино́й бок.

flitter ['flɪtə(r)] *v.i*. порх|а́ть, -ну́ть; маха́ть (*impf*.) кры́льями.

float [fləʊt] *n*. **1.** (*for supporting line or net*) поплаво́к, буй; (*of a seaplane*) поплаво́к. **2.** (*cart*) платфо́рма на колёсах; **milk** ~ электрока́р для заво́зки молока́. **3.** (*pl*., *footlights*) ра́мпа.

v.t. спус|ка́ть, -ти́ть на́ воду; сн|има́ть, -я́ть с мели; (*comm*.): ~ **a company** учре|жда́ть, -ди́ть акционе́рное о́бщество; ~ **a loan** разм|еща́ть, -сти́ть заём; (*fin*.): ~ **the pound** перев|оди́ть, -ести́ фунт сте́рлингов на пла́вающий курс.

v.i. **1.** пла́вать (*indet*.), плыть (*det*.); **oil ~s on water** ма́сло не то́нет в воде́; **the boat ~ed down-river** ло́дку несло́ тече́нием вниз по реке́. **2.** (*in air*) (*aeroplane*) плани́ровать (*impf*.); (*clouds etc*.) плыть (*det*.). **3.** (*fig*.): **his past ~ed before him** его́ про́шлое пронесло́сь пе́ред ним. **4.** (*vacillate*) колеба́ться.

floater ['fləʊtə(r)] *n*. **1.** (*sl*., *blunder*) оплошность. **2.** (*undecided voter*) колеблющийся избира́тель.

floating ['fləʊtɪŋ] *adj*. пла́вающий, плаву́чий; ~ **bridge** понто́нный/наплавно́й мост; ~ **capital** оборо́тный капита́л; ~ **debt** краткосро́чный долг; теку́щая задо́лженность; ~ **dock** плаву́чий док; ~ **kidney** блужда́ющая по́чка; ~ **light** плаву́чий мая́к; ~ **population** теку́чее народонаселе́ние; ~ **vote** избира́тели, на кото́рых нельзя́ твёрдо рассчи́тывать; ~ **voter** колеблющийся избира́тель.

flocculent ['flɒkjʊlənt] *adj*. хлопьеви́дный.

flock[1] [flɒk] *n*. (*of birds*) ста́я; (*of sheep or goats*) ста́до; (*of people*) толпа́; (*relig*.) па́ства.

v.i. стека́ться (*impf*.); дви́гаться (*impf*.) толпо́й; **they ~ed for miles to hear him** они́ стека́лись отовсю́ду, что́бы послу́шать его́.

flock[2] [flɒk] *n*. (*tuft*) пучо́к, клочо́к; (*material*) шерстяны́е/хлопча́тобума́жные очёски (*m. pl*.); ~ **bed** матра́ц, наби́тый очёсками.

floe [fləʊ] *n*. плаву́чая льди́на.

flog [flɒg] *v.t*. **1.** (*beat*) стега́ть, от-; поро́ть, вы́-; сечь, вы́-; **he is ~ging a dead horse** (*fig*.) он пыта́ется возроди́ть то, что безнадёжно устаре́ло. **2.** (*sell*) заг|оня́ть, -на́ть; толк|а́ть, -ну́ть; (*both coll*.).

flogging ['flɒgɪŋ] *n*. по́рка.

flood [flʌd] *n*. **1.** (*tide*) прили́в. **2.** (*inundation*) наводне́ние, полово́дье, разли́в; **the F~** (*bibl*.) пото́п; ~ **relief** по́мощь пострада́вшим от наводне́ния; **the river is in** ~ река́ разлила́сь. **3.** (*torrent of water*) пото́к. **4.** (*fig*.): **she burst into ~s of tears** она́ разрыда́лась; **a ~ of abuse** пото́к оскорбле́ний.

v.t. затоп|ля́ть, -и́ть; наводн|я́ть, -и́ть; **the basement was ~ed** подва́л затопи́ло; **they were ~ed out** их дом по́лностью затопи́ло; из-за наводне́ния им пришло́сь поки́нуть дом; **he was ~ed with replies** о́тклики так и посы́пались на него́.

v.i. разл|ива́ться, -и́ться; выходи́ть, вы́йти из берего́в; **the river ~s every spring** река́ разлива́ется ка́ждую весну́.

cpds. **~-gate** *n*. шлюз; **open the ~-gates** (*fig*.) да|ва́ть, -ть во́лю (*чему*); **~light** *n*. проже́ктор; *v.t*. осве|ща́ть, -ти́ть проже́кторами; **~lighting** *n*. проже́кторное освеще́ние; **~-plain** *n*. заливно́й луг; **~-tide** *n*. прили́в.

flooding ['flʌdɪŋ] *n*. затопле́ние.

floor [flɔ:(r)] *n*. **1.** пол; **it fell to the** ~ э́то упа́ло на́ пол; **the child was playing on the** ~ ребёнок игра́л на полу́; **he could wipe the** ~ **with you** он мог бы смеша́ть вас с грязью. **2.**: **take the** ~ (*in public assembly*) брать, взять сло́во; (*in dance hall*) вы́ступить (*pf*.) в та́нце. **3.**: **ground** ~ пе́рвый эта́ж. **4.**: **shop** ~ цех; **threshing** ~ гумно́, ток. **5.** (*geol*.) посте́ль, подстила́ющая поро́да. **6.** (*minimum level of prices etc*.) минима́льный у́ровень.

v.t. **1.** (*provide floor for*) наст|ила́ть, -ла́ть пол в+*p*. **2.** (*coll*., *knock down*) сби|ва́ть, -ть с ног; (*fig*., *nonplus*) сра|жа́ть, -зи́ть; ошелом|ля́ть, -и́ть; ста́вить, по- в тупи́к; **the question ~ed him** вопро́с срази́л его́.

cpds. **~board** *n*. полови́ца; **~-cloth** *n*. полова́я тря́пка; **~-polish** *n*. масти́ка (для нати́рки поло́в); **~-show** *n*. представле́ние в кабаре́; **~-space** *n*. пло́щадь по́ла; **~-walker** *n*. (*US*) дежу́рный администра́тор в универма́ге.

flooring ['flɔ:rɪŋ] *n*. насти́л, пол; насти́лка поло́в.

floo|sie, -zie ['flu:zɪ] *n*. (*sl*.) шлю́ха.

flop [flɒp] *n*. (*motion*, *sound*) шлепо́к, хлопо́к; (*coll*., *failure*) прова́л.

adv. & *int*. шлёп!; плюх! (*coll*.).

v.i. **1.** (*move limply*): ~ **down in a chair** плю́х|аться, -нуться в кре́сло; ~ **around in slippers** шлёпать (*impf*.) в дома́шних ту́флях. **2.** (*coll*., *fail*) прова́л|иваться, -и́ться.

cpds. **~-eared** *adj*. лопоу́хий; **~-house** *n*. (*US sl*.) ночле́жка.

floppy ['flɒpɪ] *adj*. болта́ющийся, свиса́ющий, мешкова́тый; мя́гкий, обви́слый; ~ **disk** (*comput*.) ги́бкий диск.

flora ['flɔ:rə] *n*. фло́ра.

floral ['flɔ:r(ə)l, 'flɒ-] *adj*. цвето́чный; ~ **tribute** подноше́ние цвето́в.

Florence ['flɒrəns] *n*. Флоре́нция.

Florentine ['flɒrən,taɪn] *n*. флоренти́н|ец (*fem*. -ка).

adj. флоренти́йский.

florescence [flɔ:'res(ə)ns, flɒ-] *n*. цвете́ние; (*fig*.) расцве́т.

florescent [flɔ:'resənt, flɒ-] *adj*. цвету́щий.

floriculture ['flɒrɪ,kʌltʃə(r), 'flɔ:-] *n*. цветово́дство.

florid ['flɒrɪd] *adj*. (*ornate*) цвети́стый, витиева́тый; (*ruddy*) кра́сный, багро́вый.

Florida ['flɒrɪdə] *n*. Флори́да.

florin ['flɒrɪn] *n*. (*hist*) флори́н.

florist ['flɒrɪst] *n*. (*dealer*) продаве́ц цвето́в; (*fem*.) цвето́чница; (*grower*) цветово́д.

floruit ['flɒrʊɪt, 'flɔ:-] *n*. пери́од де́ятельности (*кого*).

floss [flɒs] *n*. шёлк-сыре́ц; **candy** ~ са́харная ва́та; **dental** ~ шёлковая нить для чи́стки ме́жду зуба́ми.

flossy ['flɒsɪ] *adj*. шелкови́стый.

flotation [fləʊ'teɪʃ(ə)n] *n*. основа́ние (*предприятия*).

flotilla [flə'tɪlə] *n*. флоти́лия (ме́лких судо́в).

flotsam ['flɒtsəm] *n*. вы́брошенный и пла́вающий на пове́рхности груз; (*fig*.) обло́мки (*m. pl*.).

flounce[1] [flaʊns] *n*. (*abrupt movement*) рыво́к.

v.i. бр|оса́ться, -о́ситься; ~ **out (of a room)** вылета́ть, вы́лететь из ко́мнаты.

flounce[2] [flaʊns] *n*. (*trimming*) обо́рка.

v.i. отде́л|ывать, -ать обо́рками.

flounder[1] ['flaʊndə(r)] *n*. (*zool*.) ме́лкая ка́мбала.

flounder[2] ['flaʊndə(r)] *v.i*. бара́хтаться (*impf*.); (*fig*.) пу́таться в слова́х.

flour ['flaʊə(r)] *n*. (*from grain*) мука́; ~ **paste** кле́йстер; (*powder*) порошо́к.

cpds. **~-bin** *n*. ба́нка для муки́; **~-mill** *n*. мукомо́льная ме́льница; мукомо́льня.

flourish ['flʌrɪʃ] *n*. **1.** (*wave of hand etc*.) широ́кий жест; разма́хивание. **2.** (*embellishment of literary style*) цвети́стость; цвети́стое выраже́ние; (*fanfare*) фанфа́ры (*f. pl*.); туш; (*of penmanship*) ро́счерк, завиту́шка.

v.t. разма́хивать (*impf*.) +*i*.

v.i. (*grow healthily*) пы́шно расти́ (*impf*.); (*prosper*; *be active*) процвета́ть (*impf*.).

flourishing ['flʌrɪʃɪŋ] *adj*. процвета́ющий, преуспева́ющий; **a ~ business** процвета́ющее де́ло; **'How are you?' — 'Oh, ~!'** «Как пожива́ете?» — «Прекра́сно!»; «Лу́чше всех!»; **I hope you are** ~ наде́юсь, у вас всё благополу́чно.

floury ['flaʊərɪ] *adj*. (*of potato*) рассы́пчатый, мучни́стый.

flout [flaʊt] *v.t*. поп|ира́ть, -ра́ть; (*mock*) насмеха́ться (*impf*.) над+*i*.; глуми́ться (*impf*.) над+*i*.

flow [fləʊ] *n.* тече́ние, пото́к, струя́; **ebb and ~** прили́в и отли́в; **the tide is on the ~** наступа́ет прили́в; (*fig.*) тече́ние; **interrupt the ~ of conversation** прер|ыва́ть, -ва́ть пла́вное тече́ние разгово́ра; **~ of spirits** жизнера́достность; **in full ~** в разга́ре.

v.i. **1.** течь, ли́ться, струи́ться (*all impf.*); **a land ~ing with milk and honey** ≃ моло́чные ре́ки и кисе́льные берега́; **the wine ~ed freely** вино́ лило́сь реко́й; **the Oka ~s into the Volga** Ока́ впада́ет в Во́лгу. **2.** (*fig., proceed, move freely*) ли́ться (*impf.*); течь (*impf.*); (*hang freely*) ниспада́ть (*impf.*).

cpds. **~meter** *n.* расходоме́р; **~-sheet** *n.* технологи́ческая схе́ма.

flower ['flaʊə(r)] *n.* цвето́к; цветко́вое расте́ние; **in ~** в цвету́; **come into ~** расцве|та́ть, -сти́; **~ arrangement** расположе́ние цвето́в; **~ piece** карти́на с изображе́нием цвето́в; **~ show** вы́ставка цвето́в; (*fig.*): **the ~ of the nation's youth** цвет молодёжи страны́; **~s of speech** краси́вые оборо́ты (*m. pl.*) ре́чи; (*pej.*) цвети́стые выраже́ния.

v.t. укр|аша́ть, -а́сить цвето́чным узо́ром.

v.i. (*blossom; flourish*) цвести́ (*impf.*).

cpds. **~-bed** *n.* клу́мба; **~-girl** *n.* цвето́чница; **~-pot** *n.* цвето́чный горшо́к.

flowering ['flaʊərɪŋ] *n.* цвете́ние.

adj. цвету́щий.

flowery ['flaʊərɪ] *adj.* покры́тый цвета́ми; (*fig.*) цвети́стый.

flowing ['fləʊɪŋ] *adj.*: **the ~ bowl** по́лная ча́ша; **~ hair** развева́ющиеся во́лосы; **~ lines** мя́гкие/пла́вные ли́нии; **~ style** гла́дкий стиль.

flu [flu:] *n.* (*coll.*) грипп; **go down with ~** слечь (*pf.*) с гри́ппом.

fluctuate ['flʌktjʊ,eɪt] *v.i.* колеба́ться (*impf.*); колыха́ться (*impf.*).

fluctuation [,flʌktjʊ'eɪʃ(ə)n] *n.* колеба́ние, колыха́ние.

flue [flu:] *n.* дымохо́д.

cpd. **~-pipe** *n.* (*tech.*) жарова́я труба́.

fluency ['flu:ənsɪ] *n.* пла́вность, гла́дкость, бе́глость.

fluent ['flu:ənt] *adj.* пла́вный, гла́дкий, бе́глый; **he speaks Russian ~ly** он свобо́дно говори́т по-ру́сски.

fluff [flʌf] *n.* пух, пушо́к; **bit of ~** (*fig.*) ку́колка, ла́почка (*sl.*).

v.t. **1.** (*make fluffy*) взби|ва́ть, -ть; распуши́ть (*pf.*); **~ up a cushion** взби|ва́ть, -ть поду́шку; **the bird ~ed out its feathers** пти́ца распуши́ла пе́рья. **2.** (*sl., bungle*) пу́тать, с-; **~ one's lines** произн|оси́ть, -ести́ свою́ роль с запи́нкой.

fluffy ['flʌfɪ] *adj.* пуши́стый, взби́тый.

fluid ['flu:ɪd] *n.* жи́дкость; **cleaning ~** жи́дкость для чи́стки; **correction ~** бели́л|а (*pl., g.* —).

adj. жи́дкий, теку́чий; (*fig.*) неопределённый, переме́нчивый, подви́жный.

fluidity [,flu:'ɪdɪtɪ] *n.* теку́честь; жи́дкое состоя́ние; (*fig.*) переме́нчивость, неопределённость, подви́жность.

fluke[1] [flu:k] *n.* (*lucky stroke*) (неожи́данная) уда́ча, случа́йность.

fluke[2] [flu:k] *n.* (*worm*) глист.

fluke[3] [flu:k] *n.* (*of an anchor*) ла́па.

flummery ['flʌmərɪ] *n.* (*humbug*) вздо́р; бре́дн|и (*pl., g.* -ей).

flummox ['flʌməks] *v.t.* (*coll.*) ошелом|ля́ть, -и́ть; огоро́ши|вать, -ть.

flunk [flʌŋk] *v.t.* & *i.* (*US coll.*): **he ~ed his exam** он провали́лся/засы́пался на экза́мене.

flunkey ['flʌŋkɪ] *n.* (*servant*) лаке́й; (*servile pers.*) лаке́й, подхали́м.

fluoresce [flʊə'res] *v.i.* свети́ться, флюоресци́ровать (*both impf.*).

fluorescence [flʊə'res(ə)ns] *n.* свече́ние, флюоресце́нция.

fluorescent [flʊə'res(ə)nt] *adj.* флюоресце́нтный.

fluoride ['flʊəraɪd] *n.* фтори́д.

fluoridize ['flʊərɪdaɪz] *v.t.* фтори́ровать (*impf., pf.*).

fluorine ['flʊəri:n] *n.* фтор.

fluor|ite ['flʊəraɪt], **-spar** ['flʊəspɑ:(r)] *nn.* флюори́т; пла́виковый шпат.

flurry ['flʌrɪ] *n.* (*gust, squall*) шквал; (*agitation*) волне́ние, сумато́ха.

v.t. волнова́ть, вз-; будора́жить, вз-.

flush[1] [flʌʃ] *n.* (*flow of water*) внеза́пный прили́в; пото́к; (*flow of blood; blush*) прили́в кро́ви; румя́нец; кра́ска на лице́; **hot ~** при́ступ лихора́дки; (*fig.*): **in the ~ of youth** в расцве́те ю́ности; **in the first ~ of discovery** упое́нный ра́достью откры́тия.

v.t. **1.** (*swill clean*) пром|ыва́ть, -ы́ть; **~ the lavatory** спус|ка́ть, -ти́ть во́ду в убо́рной. **2.** (*make red*) зал|ива́ть, -и́ть кра́ской. **3.: he is ~ed with pride** его́ распира́ет го́рдость.

v.i. красне́ть, по-; зал|ива́ться, -и́ться кра́ской.

flush[2] [flʌʃ] *n.* (*cards*) ка́рты одно́й ма́сти; **royal ~** флешь-роя́ль, коро́нка; **busted ~** (*sl.*) прова́л, неуда́ча; (*pers.*) неуда́чник.

flush[3] [flʌʃ] *adj.* **1.** (*coll., well supplied with money*): **he is ~** у него́ де́нег ку́ры не клюю́т. **2.** (*on the same level*) заподлицо́ (*adv.*); (находя́щийся) на одно́м у́ровне (*с чем*).

flush[4] [flʌʃ] *v.t.* (*birds etc.*) вспу́г|ивать, -ну́ть.

flushed [flʌʃd] *adj.* охва́ченный (*чем*); упоённый; **~ with victory** упоённый побе́дой.

fluster ['flʌstə(r)] *n.* суета́, волне́ние.

v.t. волнова́ть, вз-; будора́жить, вз-.

flute[1] [flu:t] *n.* (*instrument*) фле́йта.

v.i. (*fig.*) мелоди́чно свисте́ть (*impf.*) (*or* говори́ть (*impf.*) *и т.п.*).

flute[2] [flu:t] *n.* (*groove*) желобо́к; каннелю́ра.

v.t. желоби́ть (*impf.*).

fluted ['flu:tɪd] *adj.* гофриро́ванный, рифлёный.

fluting ['flu:tɪŋ] *n.* (*archit.*) канелю́ры (*f. pl.*); ри́фля.

flutist ['flu:tɪst] (*US*) = **flautist**

flutter ['flʌtə(r)] *n.* **1.** (*of wings, leaves, flags etc.*) трепета́ние, дрожь. **2.** (*agitation*) волне́ние, тре́пет; **to be in a ~ of expectation** с тре́петом ждать (*impf.*). **3.** (*gambling venture*) риск.

v.t. мах|а́ть, -ну́ть +*i.*; (*fig., agitate*) прив|оди́ть, -ести́ в тре́пет; взволнова́ть (*pf.*).

v.i. трепета́ть (*impf.*); (*of birds*) переп|а́рхивать, -орхну́ть.

fluvial ['flu:vɪəl] *adj.* речно́й.

flux [flʌks] *n.* **1.** (*succession of changes*) постоя́нная сме́на; **everything was in a state of ~** всё бы́ло в состоя́нии непреры́вного измене́ния. **2.** (*med.*) *see next.* **3.** (*metall.*) флюс, пла́вень (*m.*).

fluxion ['flʌkʃ(ə)n] *n.* (*med.*) паталоги́ческое оби́льное истече́ние; (*math.*) флю́ксия, дифференциа́л.

fly[1] [flaɪ] *n.* му́ха; (*fig.*): **~ in the ointment** ло́жка дёгтя в бо́чке мёду; **there are no flies on him** к нему́ не подкопа́ешься (*coll.*).

cpds. **~-blown** *adj.* заси́женный му́хами; **~-catcher** *n.* (*bird*) мухоло́вка; **~-fishing** *n.* уже́ние ры́бы на му́ху; **~-paper** *n.* ли́пкая бума́га (*or* ли́пкие ле́нты (*f.pl.*)) от мух; **~-spray** *n.* (*fluid*) жи́дкость от мух; (*instrument*) аэрозо́ль (*m.*) от мух; **~-weight** *n.* вес «му́хи»; наилегча́йший боксёрский вес.

fly[2] [flaɪ] *n.* **1.** (*carriage*) одноко́нный экипа́ж. **2.** (*of flag*) поло́тнище; (*on trousers*) шири́нка; **his ~ is open, undone** у него́ шири́нка расстёгнута. **3.** (*pl., theatr.*) колосники́ (*m. pl.*). **4.** (*speed regulator*) баланси́р.

cpds. **~-button** *n.* пу́говица шири́нки; **~-leaf** *n.* форза́ц; **~-wheel** *n.* махово́е колесо́, махови́к.

fly[3] [flaɪ] *adj.* (*sl.*) себе́ на уме́.

fly[4] [flaɪ] *v.t.* **~ the Atlantic** перелет|а́ть, -е́ть че́рез Атланти́ческий океа́н; **~ an aircraft** управля́ть (*impf.*) самолётом; **~ home the wounded** дост|авля́ть, -а́вить ра́неных в тыл самолётом; **~ a kite** запус|ка́ть, -ти́ть зме́я; пуска́ть (*impf.*) зме́я; (*fig., put out feeler or lure*) пус|ка́ть, -ти́ть про́бный шар; **~ a flag** выве́шивать, вы́весить флаг; (*naut.*) носи́ть, нести́ флаг; **~ the British flag** пла́вать (*indet.*) под брита́нским фла́гом; **~ the country** бежа́ть (*det.*) из страны́.

v.i. **1.** (*move through the air*) лета́ть (*indet.*), лете́ть, по- (*det.*); **as the crow flies** напрями́к; по прямо́й; **he has never flown** он никогда́ не лета́л; **~ in the face of fortune** искуша́ть (*impf.*) судьбу́; **the pieces flew in all directions** куски́ разлете́лись во все сто́роны. **2.** (*move or pass* *swiftly*) пролет|а́ть, -е́ть; **I must ~!** ну, я побежа́л!; **he flew downstairs** он ку́барем скати́лся с ле́стницы; **the dog flew at him** соба́ка бро́силась за ним; **~ into a passion** вспыли́ть (*pf.*); **~ to s.o.'s defence** бро́ситься (*pf.*) на защи́ту кого́-н.; **let ~ (at s.o.)** вы́ругать (*pf.*) кого́-н.; **~ off the handle** (*coll.*) сорва́ться (*pf.*); взорва́ться (*pf.*); при|ходи́ть, -йти́ в я́рость; **make the money ~** промота́ть (*pf.*) де́ньги; **send ~ing** швыр|я́ть, -ну́ть; (*of pers.*) сби|ва́ть, -ть с ног; **time flies** вре́мя лети́т; **the flag is ~ing** флаг развева́ется. **3.** (*flee*) бежа́ть (*det.*); **the bird has flown** (*fig.*) пти́чка улете́ла.

with advs.: **leaves were ~ing about** повсю́ду кружи́лись ли́стья; **~ away** улет|а́ть, -е́ть; **the plane flew in to refuel and flew off again** самолёт прилете́л на запра́вку и вновь/сно́ва улете́л; **~ off at a tangent** сорва́ться (*pf.*); отклон|я́ться, -и́ться; **the door flew open** дверь распахну́лась на́стеж; **she flew out to join her husband** она́ улете́ла к му́жу.

cpds. **~-by-night** *n.* ненадёжный челове́к; **~over** *n.* (*bridge, overpass*) эстака́да; путепрово́д; **~-past** *n.* возду́шный пара́д.

flyer, flier ['flaɪə(r)] *n.* (*aviator*) лётчик; (*pers. of promise*) подаю́щий больши́е наде́жды челове́к; **he is a ~** он далеко́ пойдёт.

flying ['flaɪɪŋ] *n.* полёт; **he likes ~** он лю́бит лета́ть; **~ field** лётное по́ле; **~ instructor** лётчик-инстру́ктор; **~ kit** лётное обмундирова́ние; **~ school** лётная шко́ла; **~ visit** блицвизи́т.

adj.: **~ bomb** самолёт-снаря́д; плани́рующая бо́мба; **~ buttress** а́рочный контрфо́рс, аркбута́н; **pass with ~ colours** пройти́ (*pf.*) с бле́ском; **~ column** лету́чий снаря́д; **~ leap** прыжо́к с разбе́га; **F~ Officer** ста́рший лейтена́нт авиа́ции; **~ saucer** лета́ющее блю́дце; **F~ Squad** специа́льный отря́д полице́йских для бы́строго налёта; **off to a ~ start** с ме́ста в карье́р; **pay a ~ visit** нанести́ (*pf.*) мимолётный визи́т.

cpds. **~-boat** *n.* лета́ющая ло́дка; **~-fish** *n.* лету́чая ры́ба; **~-machine** *n.* лета́тельный аппара́т.

FM *abbr. of* **1.** ***Field Marshal*** фельдма́ршал. **2.** ***frequency modulation*****:** **~ radio** частóтно-модули́рованное ра́дио.

FO (*abbr. of* ***Foreign Office***) Министе́рство иностра́нных дел, Фо́рин О́фис.

foal [fəʊl] *n.* жеребёнок; **the mare is in ~** кобы́ла жерёбая.

v.i. жереби́ться, о-.

foam [fəʊm] *n.* пе́на; **~ extinguisher** огнетуши́тель (*m.*); **~ rubber** по́ристая рези́на; пенопла́ст.

v.i. пе́ниться (*impf.*); **he was ~ing at the mouth** у него́ была́ пе́на на губа́х.

fob[1] [fɒb] *n.* (*watch pocket*) карма́шек для часо́в.

fob[2] [fɒb] *v.t.*: **~ s.o. off with promises** корми́ть (*impf.*) кого́-н. обеща́ниями; **~ off a cheap article on s.o.** всучи́ть (*pf.*) кому́-н. каку́ю-н. дешёвку.

f.o.b. (*abbr. of* ***free on board***) фоб, (фра́нко-борт).

focal ['fəʊk(ə)l] *adj.* фо́кусный; **~ distance, length** фо́кусное расстоя́ние; (*fig.*): **the ~ point in his argument** гла́вный пункт его́ доказа́тельств.

fo'c's'le ['fəʊks(ə)l] *n.* (*naut.*) бак, полуба́к.

focus ['fəʊkəs] *n.* (*math., phys., phot.*) фо́кус; **bring into ~** поме|ща́ть, -сти́ть в фо́кусе; **out of ~** не в фо́кусе; (*fig.*) центр, средото́чие; **he became the ~ of interest** он оказа́лся в це́нтре внима́ния.

v.t. соб|ира́ть, -ра́ть; сосредото́чи|вать, -ть; **he ~(s)ed his attention on the book** он сосредото́чил всё своё внима́ние на кни́ге.

fodder ['fɒdə(r)] *n.* корм для скота́; фура́ж.

v.t. зад|ава́ть, -а́ть корм (*скоту*).

foe [fəʊ] *n.* враг, не́друг.

foeman ['fəʊmən] *n.* неприя́тель (*m.*).

foetal, fetal ['fi:t(ə)l] *adj.* заро́дышевый, эмбриона́льный; **~ position** положе́ние эмбрио́на (в ма́тке).

foetus, fetus ['fi:təs] *n.* плод, заро́дыш.

fog [fɒg] *n.* тума́н; (*phot.*) вуа́ль; (*fig.*): **in a ~** как в тума́не; в расте́рянности.

v.t. оку́т|ывать, -ать тума́ном; затума́ни|вать, -ть; напус|ка́ть, -ти́ть тума́ну на+*a.*; (*fig.*): **I'm a bit ~ged** я озада́чен; **the windows are ~ged up** о́кна запоте́ли.

cpds. **~-bank** *n.* полоса́ тума́на над мо́рем; **~-bound** *adj.* оку́танный тума́ном; **~-horn** *n.* тума́нный горн; **~-lamp** *n.* фа́ра с цветны́ми стёклами; **~-signal** *n.* сигна́л при тума́не.

fog(e)y ['fəʊgɪ] *n.* старомо́дный/отста́лый челове́к.

fogg|y ['fɒgɪ] *adj.* тума́нный; (*fig.*): **I haven't the ~iest idea** я не име́ю ни мале́йшего представле́ния.

foible ['fɔɪb(ə)l] *n.* сла́бость; сла́бая стру́нка.

foil[1] [fɔɪl] *n.* (*thin metal*) фольга́, стани́оль (*m.*); (*fig., contrast*) контра́ст, противопоставле́ние; **her plainness serves as a ~ to the others** её некраси́вая вне́шность оттеня́ет/подчёркивает красоту́ остальны́х.

foil[2] [fɔɪl] *n.* (*fencing sword*) рапи́ра; **~ fencer** рапири́ст (*fem.* -ка).

foil[3] [fɔɪl] *v.t.* сби|ва́ть, -ть со сле́да; расстр|а́ивать, -о́ить (*or* срыва́ть, сорва́ть) пла́ны +*g.*

foist [fɔɪst] *v.t.* навя́з|ывать, -а́ть (*что кому*).

fold[1] [fəʊld] *n.* скла́дка; **the ~s of a dress** скла́дки пла́тья; **a ~ in the hills** лощи́на.

v.t. **1.** (*double over*) скла́дывать, сложи́ть; св|ёртывать (*or* -ора́чивать), -ерну́ть; сгиба́ть, согну́ть; **~ one's arms** скре́|щивать, -сти́ть ру́ки на груди́; **~ back the bedclothes** отки́|дывать, -нуть одея́ло; **~ (up) the newspaper** скла́дывать, сложи́ть газе́ту. **2.** (*embrace*) обн|има́ть, -я́ть; **she ~ed the child in her arms** она́ заключи́ла ребёнка в объя́тия; **the hills were ~ ed in mist** холмы́ бы́ли оку́таны мглой.

v.i. скла́дываться, сложи́ться; (*fig.*): **the attack ~ed (up)** ата́ка захлебну́лась (*coll.*); **the play ~ed after a week** пье́са сошла́ (со сце́ны) че́рез неде́лю.

fold[2] [fəʊld] *n.* (*for sheep*) заго́н; **return to the ~** (*fig.*) верну́ться (*pf.*) в ло́но (*церкви и т.п.*).

folder ['fəʊldə(r)] *n.* (*brochure*) несши́тая брошюра; (*container for papers*) скоросшива́тель (*m.*); па́пка-планше́т.

folding ['fəʊldɪŋ] *adj.* складно́й; **~ doors** складны́е две́ри, две́ри гармо́шкой.

cpds. **~-bed** *n.* раскладу́шка; **~-chair** *n.* складно́й стул.

foliage ['fəʊlɪɪdʒ] *n.* листва́; **~ plant** ли́ственное расте́ние.

folio ['fəʊlɪəʊ] *n.* (*large folded sheet of paper; book size*) ин-фо́лио (*indecl.*); (*book*) фолиа́нт; (*ledger sheet*) лист бухга́лтерской кни́ги.

folk [fəʊk] *n.* **1.** (*sing. or pl., coll., persons*) наро́д, лю́д|и (*pl., g.* -е́й); **some ~ have all the luck!** везёт же лю́дям!; **the old ~s** старики́; роди́тели (*both m. pl.*); **old ~s' home** дом для престаре́лых. **2.** (*pl., coll., relatives*) родня́, родны́е (*pl.*).

cpds. **~lore** *n.* фолькло́р; **~-music** *n.* наро́дная му́зыка; **~-song** *n.* наро́дная пе́сня.

folklorist ['fəʊk,lɔ:rɪst] *n.* фольклори́ст.

folksy ['fəʊksɪ] *adj.* (*coll.*) просте́цкий, фамилья́рный, панибра́тский.

follicle ['fɒlɪk(ə)l] *n.* (*anat.*) фолли́кул; (*bot.*) стручо́к.

follow ['fɒləʊ] *v.t. & i.* **1.** (*proceed or happen after*) сле́довать, по- за+*i.*; **the dog ~s him about** соба́ка хо́дит за ним по пята́м; **he ~ed his wife to the grave** (*attended funeral*) он проводи́л свою́ жену́ в после́дний путь; **he ~ed (in) his father's footsteps** он пошёл по стопа́м отца́; **~ the crowd** (*fig.*) плыть (*det.*) по тече́нию; **~ the hounds** охо́титься (*impf.*) с соба́ками; **~ suit** (*at cards*) ходи́ть (*indet.*) в масть; (*fig.*) сле́довать, по- чьему́-н. приме́ру; **the frost was ~ed by a thaw** моро́з смени́лся о́ттепелью; **he was ~ed on the throne by his son** по́сле него́ на трон взошёл его́ сын; **as ~s** сле́дующим о́бразом; как сле́дует ни́же; **his plan was as ~s** его́ план был тако́в. **2.** (*as inference*) сле́довать (*impf.*) из+*g.*; **it does not ~ that ...** э́то во́все не зна́чит, что... **3.** (*pursue*) следи́ть (*impf.*) за+*i.*; **he ~ed the ball with his eye** он следи́л за мячо́м; **don't look now, we're being ~ed** не огля́дывайтесь, но за на́ми следя́т; (*fig.*): **~ one's bent** сле́довать (*impf.*) свои́м накло́нностям. **4.** (*keep to*) приде́рживаться (*impf.*) +*g.*; **~ this road** сле́дуйте/иди́те по э́той доро́ге; **~ the policy of one's predecessor** продолжа́ть (*impf.*) поли́тику своего́ предше́ственника; (*fig., engage in*): **~ a trade** име́ть (*impf.*) профе́ссию; **~ the sea** (*fig.*) быть моряко́м;

(*fig.*, *be guided by*): ~ **s.o.'s advice/example** сле́довать, по- чьему́-н. сове́ту/приме́ру; **play ~-my-leader** (*fig.*) сле́по подража́ть (*impf.*) кому́-н. **5.** (*fig.*, *keep track of*): ~ **s.o.'s arguments** следи́ть (*impf.*) за хо́дом чьих-н. рассужде́ний; **I don t ~ you** я вас не понима́ю; ~ **the news in the papers** следи́ть (*impf.*) за новостя́ми в газе́тах.

with advs.: ~ **on** *v.t.* & *i.* сле́довать, по- (за+*i.*); ~ **out** *v.t.* осуществ|ля́ть, -и́ть; выполня́ть, вы́полнить; ~ **through** *v.t.* & *i.* сле́довать (*impf.*) (за+*i.*) до конца́; ~ **up** *v.t.* дов|оди́ть, -ести́ до конца́; ~ **up an advantage** (*mil.*) разв|ива́ть, -и́ть успе́х; (*in general*) по́лностью испо́льзовать (*impf.*, *pf.*) вы́годы положе́ния; ~ **up a clue** рассле́довать ули́ку; ~ **up a suggestion** уч|и́тывать, -е́сть чьё-н. предложе́ние.

cpd. **~-up** *n.* продолже́ние; (*med.*) контро́ль (*m.*).

follower ['fɒləʊwə(r)] *n.* после́дователь (*m.*); сторо́нник; (*wooer*, *coll.*) ухажёр, покло́нник.

following ['fɒləʊwɪŋ] *n.* после́дователи (*m. pl.*); приве́рженцы (*m. pl.*); **the preacher gained a large ~** пропове́дник собра́л мно́го приве́рженцев.

adj. **1.** (*ensuing*) сле́дующий; **(on) the ~ day** на сле́дующий день; (*about to be specified*): **we shall need the ~** нам потре́буется сле́дующее. **2.** (*coming behind*) попу́тный; **a ~ tide** попу́тное тече́ние; **a ~ wind** попу́тный ве́тер.

folly ['fɒlɪ] *n.* (*foolishness*) безрассу́дство, глу́пость; (*caprice*) причу́да, капри́з.

foment [fə'ment, fəʊ-] *v.t.* класть, положи́ть припа́рку к+*d.*; (*fig.*) подстрек|а́ть, -ну́ть; разд|ува́ть, -у́ть.

fomentation [,fəʊmen'teɪʃ(ə)n] *n.* припа́рка; (*fig.*) подстрека́тельство, раздува́ние.

fond [fɒnd] *adj.* **1.** (*pred.*, *with* **of**): **he became ~ of her** он привяза́лся к ней; **are you ~ of music?** вы лю́бите му́зыку? **2.** (*loving*) не́жный, лю́бящий. **3.** (*credulous*) дове́рчивый; **I ~ly imagined** я тще́тно воображáл.

fondant ['fɒnd(ə)nt] *n.* ≃ пома́дка.

fondle ['fɒnd(ə)l] *v.t.* ласка́ть (*impf.*); гла́дить, по-.

font[1] [fɒnt] *n.* (*eccl.*) купе́ль.

font[2] [fɒnt] *n.* (*US*, *typ.*) = **fount 2.**

food [fu:d] *n.* пи́ща, пита́ние; еда́, ку́шанье; ~ **supplies** продово́льственные припа́сы (*m. pl.*); провиа́нт; ~ **and drink** еда́ и питьё; **go without ~** голода́ть (*impf.*); **baby ~** де́тское пита́ние; **the government's ~ policy** поли́тика прави́тельства по снабже́нию населе́ния продово́льствием; (*fig.*): ~ **for thought** пи́ща для размышле́ний.

cpds. **~-processor** *n.* ку́хонный комба́йн; **~-store** *n.* продово́льственный магази́н; **~stuff** *n.* пищево́й проду́кт.

fool[1] [fu:l] *n.* (*simpleton*) дура́к, глупе́ц; **any ~ could do that** э́то ка́ждый дура́к мо́жет; **he is nobody's ~** он совсе́м не дура́к; **I was a ~ to accept** дура́к я был, что согласи́лся; **like a ~, I told him** я был так глуп, что сказа́л ему́; **a ~ and his money are soon parted** у дурака́ де́ньги до́лго не де́ржатся; **he was sent on a ~'s errand** его́ посла́ли с бессмы́сленным поруче́нием; **he lived in a ~'s paradise** он жил в вы́думанном ми́ре; **~'s mate** (*at chess*) «де́тский» мат; (*jester*) шут; **~'s cap** шутовско́й колпа́к; **play the ~** дура́читься (*impf.*); валя́ть (*impf.*) дурака́; **April ~** одура́ченный пе́рвого апре́ля; **All F~s' Day** пе́рвое апре́ля; **make a ~ (out) of s.o.** дура́чить, о- кого́-н.; **make a ~ of o.s.** ста́вить, по- себя́ в дура́цкое положе́ние.

adj. (*coll.*) глу́пый, безрассу́дный.

v.t. **1.** (*delude*, *deceive*) одура́чи|ва́ть, -ть; **he was ~ed into going there** обма́ном его́ убеди́ли пойти́ туда́. **2.:** ~ **away one's time** тра́тить (*impf.*) вре́мя по́пусту.

v.i. дура́читься (*impf.*); ~ **about, around** валя́ть (*impf.*) дурака́; **don't ~ about with the watch, you may break it!** поосторо́жней с часа́ми, а то слома́ете их!

cpd. **~proof** *adj.* безотка́зный; несло́жный, безопа́сный.

fool[2] [fu:l] *n.* (*fruit dish*) ≃ кисе́ль (*m.*) со сби́тыми сли́вками.

foolery ['fu:lərɪ] *n.* дура́чество, глу́пость; глу́пое поведе́ние.

foolhardiness ['fu:l,hɑ:dɪnɪs] *n.* безрассу́дная хра́брость.

foolhardy ['fu:l,hɑ:dɪ] *adj.* безрассу́дно хра́брый; отча́янный; лю́бящий риск.

foolish ['fu:lɪʃ] *adj.* глу́пый, безрассу́дный; дура́цкий.

foolishness ['fu:lɪʃnɪs] *n.* глу́пость, безрассу́дство.

foolscap ['fu:lskæp] *n.* (*stationery*) пи́счая бума́га форма́том 330 x 200 мм.

foot [fʊt] *n.* **1.** (*extremity of leg*) ступня́, нога́; стопа́ ноги́; (*dim.*) но́жка; (*of an animal*) ла́па; (*of a garment*) низ, подо́л; (*of a chair*) но́жка; (*lowest part*, *bottom*) ни́жняя часть, ни́жний край; **at the ~ of the hill** у подно́жия холма́; **at the ~ of the page** в конце́ страни́цы; **at the ~ of the stairs** внизу́ ле́стницы; **at the ~ of the bed** в нога́х (*or* у изно́жья) крова́ти; (*tread*): **she is light of ~** у неё лёгкая похо́дка.

phrr.: **we came here on ~** мы пришли́ сюда́ пешко́м; **plans are on ~ to change all this** проекти́руются больши́е измене́ния; **set sth. on ~** (*fig.*) нача́ть/зате́ять (*pf.*) что-н.; **she is on her feet all day** она́ це́лый день на нога́х; **he was on his feet in an instant** он то́тчас вскочи́л на́ ноги; **the patient is on his feet again** больно́й уже́ на нога́х; **the business got off on the wrong ~** де́ло с са́мого нача́ла пошло́ не так; **she was swept off her feet** (*fig.*) она́ потеря́ла го́лову; **he fell on his feet** (*fig.*) он сча́стливо отде́лался; ему́ повезло́; **find one's feet** нащу́п|ывать, -ать по́чву под нога́ми; **get, rise to one's feet** подня́ться, встать (*both pf.*); **have the ball at one's feet** (*fig.*) быть хозя́ином положе́ния; **have one ~ in the grave** стоя́ть (*impf.*) одно́й ного́й в моги́ле; **have both feet on the ground** (*fig.*) кре́пко стоя́ть (*impf.*) на нога́х; **have feet of clay** стоя́ть (*impf.*) на гли́няных нога́х; **keep one's feet** уде́рживаться (*pf.*) на нога́х; **kneel at s.o.'s feet** пасть (*pf.*) на коле́ни пе́ред кем-н.; **put one's ~ down** (*fig.*) заня́ть (*pf.*) твёрдую/реши́тельную пози́цию; (*accelerate*) дать (*pf.*) га́зу; **put one's ~ in it** (*fig.*) дать (*pf.*) ма́ху; **put one's best ~ forward, foremost** приба́вить (*pf.*) ша́гу; **put one's feet up** сиде́ть (*impf.*) с по́днятыми нога́ми; (*fig.*) отдыха́ть (*impf.*); **set ~ in** вступи́ть (*pf.*) в+*a.*; **set s.o. on his feet again** подня́ть (*pf.*) кого́-н. на́ ноги; **stand on one's own (two) feet** стоя́ть (*impf.*) на свои́х нога́х; быть самостоя́тельным; **trample under ~** поп|ира́ть, -ра́ть; **it's wet under ~** на земле́ мо́кро; **wipe one's feet** вытира́ть, вы́тереть но́ги. **2.** (*unit of length*) фут; **six ~ (*or* feet) tall** шести́ фу́тов ро́стом. **3.** (*pros.*) стопа́. **4.** (*infantry*) пехо́та; **unit of ~** подразделе́ние пехо́ты; ~ **guards** гварде́йская пехо́та.

v.t. **1.:** ~ **a stocking** надвя́з|ывать, -а́ть чуло́к. **2.:** ~ **the bill** опла́|чивать, -ти́ть счёт.

cpds. **~-and-mouth** (*disease*) *n.*я́щур; **infected with ~-and-mouth** больно́й я́щуром, я́щурный; **~ball** *n.* футбо́л; **~ball player** футболи́ст; **~baller** *n.* футболи́ст; **~-bath** *n.* ножна́я ва́нна; **~-board** *n.* подно́жка; ступе́нька; запя́т|ки (*pl.*, *g.* -ок); **~-brake** *n.* ножно́й то́рмоз; **~bridge** *n.* пешехо́дный мо́стик; **~dragging** *n.* проволо́чка, затя́гивание; **~-drill** *n.* обуче́ние пе́шему стро́ю; **~fall** *n.* по́ступь; шаги́ (*m. pl.*), звук шаго́в; **~hills** *n. pl.* предго́рье; **~hold** *n.* то́чка опо́ры; (*mil.*) опо́рный пункт; **~lights** *n. pl.* ра́мпа (*sg.*); **~man** *n.* лаке́й; **~mark** *n.* след ноги́; **~note** *n.* сно́ска; **~pad** *n.* разбо́йник с большо́й доро́ги; **~path** *n.* тропа́, тропи́нка; **~plate** *n.* площа́дка машини́ста; **~-pound** *n.* (*tech.*) футофу́нт; **~print** *n.* след ноги́; **~-race** *n.* состяза́ние в бе́ге; **~-rot** *n.* копы́тная гниль; **~-rule** *n.* лине́йка длино́й в оди́н фут; **~-slog** *v.i.* тащи́ться (*impf.*) пешко́м; **~-slogger** *n.* пехоти́нец, пехтура́ (*m.*); **~-soldier** *n.* пехоти́нец; **~sore** *adj.* со стёртыми нога́ми; **~step** *n.* шаг, по́ступь; **~stool** *n.* скаме́ечка для ног; **~sure** *adj.* не спотыка́ющийся; уве́ренно ступа́ющий; (*fig.*) уве́ренно иду́щий к це́ли; **~way** *n.* пешехо́дная доро́жка, тротуа́р; **~wear** *n.* о́бувь; **~work** *n.* рабо́та ног.

footage ['fʊtɪdʒ] *n.* длина́ в фу́тах, метра́ж.

footing ['fʊtɪŋ] *n.* (*foothold*) опо́ра для ног(и́); **lose one's ~** оступи́ться (*pf.*); (*fig.*) потеря́ть (*pf.*) по́чву под нога́ми; **on an equal ~** на ра́вной ноге́; **on a friendly ~** на дру́жеской ноге́; **the army was placed on a war ~** а́рмия была́ введена́ в боеву́ю гото́вность.

footle [ˈfuːt(ə)l] *v.i.* (*coll.*) дури́ть (*impf.*); дура́читься (*impf.*).

footling [ˈfuːtlɪŋ] *adj.* (*coll.*) пустя́чный, ерундо́вый.

fop [fɒp] *n.* фат, хлыщ, щёголь (*m.*).

foppish [ˈfɒpɪʃ] *adj.* фатова́тый, щеголева́тый, щегольско́й.

for [fə(r), fɔː(r)] *prep.* **1.** (*with the object or purpose of*) для+*g.*; ра́ди+*g.*; **~ example** наприме́р; **I did it ~ fun** я сде́лал э́то для сме́ху; **~ a laugh** шу́тки ра́ди; **~ the sake of peace** ра́ди ми́ра; **they have gone ~ a walk** они́ отпра́вились гуля́ть; **who's coming ~ dinner?** кто придёт к у́жину?; **what ~?** заче́м?; **there is no need ~ this** в э́том нет никако́й на́добности; **a house ~ sale** дом на прода́жу; **save up ~ a house** копи́ть (*impf.*) (де́ньги) на поку́пку до́ма; **he sent ~ the doctor** он посла́л за врачо́м; **I've come ~ the rent** я пришёл получи́ть за кварти́ру; **run ~ a train** бежа́ть (*det.*), по- к по́езду; **run ~ it!** беги́те изо всех сил!; **now ~ it!** а тепе́рь — дава́й!; (*destination*) на+*a.*; к+*d.*; **the train ~ Moscow** по́езд на Москву́; **he made ~ the exit** он напра́вился к вы́ходу; **he left ~ home** он отпра́вился домо́й; **where are you ~?** куда́ вы направля́етесь? **you're in ~ a shock** вас ждёт больша́я неприя́тность; (*aspiration*): **who could ask ~ more?** чего́ же ещё жела́ть?; **he begged ~ money** он проси́л де́нег; **a cry ~ help** крик о по́мощи; зов на по́мощь; **oh ~ a drink!** эх, вы́пить бы!; **greed ~ money** жа́дность к деньга́м; **longing ~ home** тоска́ по ро́дине; **demand ~ coal** спрос на у́голь; **prospecting ~ oil** разве́дка на нефть. **2.** (*denoting reason; on account of*) ра́ди+*g.*, для+*g.*; **cry ~ joy** пла́кать (*impf.*) от ра́дости; **~ fear of being found out** из боя́зни разоблаче́ния; **grateful ~ help** благода́рный за по́мощь; **you can't move here ~ books** из-за книг здесь не́где поверну́ться; **he can't see the wood ~ trees** он за дере́вьями не ви́дит ле́са; **~ the love of God** ра́ди Бо́га; **~ shame!** как не сты́дно; **~ pity's sake!** пощади́те!; ра́ди Бо́га!; **my shoes are the worse ~ wear** мои́ боти́нки поизноси́лись; **but (*or* if it had not been) ~ me he would have died** ка́бы не я, он бы у́мер; **he is known ~ his generosity** он изве́стен свое́й ще́дростью; **they married ~ love** они́ жени́лись по любви́; **selected ~ their physique** ото́бранные по физи́ческим да́нным; (*accorded to*): **the penalty ~ treason is death** наказа́ние за изме́ну — сме́ртная казнь; **a prize ~ a novel** пре́мия за рома́н; **a decoration ~ bravery** о́рден за отва́гу; (*on the occasion of*): **I gave him a book ~ his birthday** я подари́л ему́ кни́гу на день рожде́ния; **he went abroad ~ his holidays** он пое́хал за грани́цу в о́тпуск; **she wore black ~ the funeral** она́ наде́ла всё чёрное на по́хороны; **the church was decorated ~ Easter** це́рковь была́ укра́шена к Па́схе; **what are we having ~ dinner?** что у нас на у́жин? **3.** (*representative of*): **A ~ Anna** А как в сло́ве «А́нна»; **the member (of parliament) ~ Oxford** член парла́мента из О́ксфорда; **red is ~ danger** кра́сный цвет знамену́ет опа́сность; **he stands ~ all that is noble** он воплоще́ние благоро́дства; **he signed ~ the government** он поста́вил по́дпись от и́мени прави́тельства; (*in support; in favour of*): **who is not ~ me is against me** кто не за меня́, тот про́тив меня́; **a vote ~ freedom** го́лос за свобо́ду; **I'm all ~ it** я по́лностью за (э́то); **stand up ~ one's rights** отст|а́ивать, -оя́ть свои́ права́; (*denoting purpose*): **they need premises ~ a school** им ну́жно помеще́ние под шко́лу; **a report ~ the director** докладна́я на и́мя дире́ктора; **a candidate ~ the presidium** кандида́т в прези́диум; **the order ~ retreat** прика́з об отступле́нии; **this barrel is meant ~ wine** э́та бо́чка предназна́чена под вино́; **ready ~ departure** гото́в к отъе́зду; (*on behalf of*) за+*a.*, от+*g.*; **speak ~ yourself!** говори́те за себя́!; **see ~ yourself!** смотри́те са́ми!; **pray ~ the sick** моли́ться (*impf.*) за больны́х; **who is he in mourning ~?** по ком он но́сит тра́ур? **4.** (*denoting intended recipient*): **a dinner ~ 10 people** обе́д на де́сять челове́к; **there is a letter ~ you** вам письмо́; **votes ~ women** пра́во го́лоса для же́нщин; **he and she were meant ~ each other** они́ бы́ли со́зданы друг для дру́га. **5.** (*denoting duration or extent*): **~ a time** на вре́мя; **~ a long time** на до́лгое вре́мя; в тече́ние до́лгого вре́мени; **he stayed ~ the night** он оста́лся на́ ночь; **he was away ~ ages** он о́чень до́лго был в отъе́зде; **I haven't seen him ~ (some) days** я не ви́дел его́ не́сколько дней; **the forest stretches ~ miles** лес простира́ется на не́сколько киломе́тров; **there is no house ~ miles** круго́м на мно́го вёрст ни еди́ного до́ма; **a weather report ~ the past week** сво́дка пого́ды за про́шлую неде́лю; (*intended duration*): **~ ever and ever** навсегда́, на ве́ки ве́чные; **I've lost it ~ good** я навсегда́/оконча́тельно потеря́л его́/её; **I shan't stay ~ long** я до́лго не задержу́сь; **~ the future we must be more careful** в бу́дущем мы должны́ быть бо́лее осторо́жными; **they are going away ~ a few days** они́ уезжа́ют на не́сколько дней; **imprisoned ~ life** пожи́зненно заключённый. **6.** (*denoting relationship; in respect of*): **I ~ my part ...** со свое́й стороны́, я…; **~ the rest** в остально́м; что каса́ется остально́го; **as ~ me, myself** что каса́ется меня́; **he is hard up ~ money** у него́ пло́хо/ту́го с деньга́ми; **luckily ~ her** на её сча́стье, к сча́стью для неё; **~ one thing it's too short, and ~ another I don't like it** во-пе́рвых, э́то о́чень ко́ротко, во-вторы́х, мне э́то не нра́вится; (*responsive to*): **an eye ~ a bargain** намётанный глаз на вы́годную поку́пку; **an ear ~ music** музыка́льный слух; **a weakness ~ sweets** сла́бость к сла́дкому; (*in relation to what is normal or suitable*): **warm ~ the time of year** тепло́ для э́того вре́мени го́да; **cold ~ summer** не по ле́тнему холо́дный; **it's cold enough ~ snow** хо́лодно — того́ и гляди́ пойдёт снег; **he is too thoughtful ~ his age** он сли́шком серьёзен для свои́х лет; он заду́мчив не по лета́м; **not bad ~ a beginner** для новичка́ непло́хо; **that's no job ~ a woman** э́то не же́нская рабо́та; **how's that ~ a stroke of luck?** вот э́то уда́ча! **7.** (*in return ~, instead of*): **an eye ~ an eye** о́ко за о́ко; **new lamps ~ old** но́вые ла́мпы вме́сто ста́рых; **get something ~ nothing** получи́ть (*pf.*) что-н. да́ром; **so much ~ your promises!** вот чего́ сто́ят ва́ши обеща́ния; **not ~ the world** ни за что (на све́те); **once (and) ~ all** раз и навсегда́; **thank you ~ nothing!** ну́ уж, удружи́л — не́чего сказа́ть!; **seven ~ a pound** семь штук на фунт; **how many books can I buy ~ that money?** ско́лько книг я смогу́ купи́ть на э́ти де́ньги?; **you'll pay ~ this!** вы мне за э́то запла́тите!; **~ every good apple there were 10 bad ones** на ка́ждое хоро́шее я́блоко бы́ло 10 плохи́х. **8.** (*as being; in the capacity of*): **what do you take me ~?** за кого́ вы меня́ принима́ете?; **take sth. ~ granted** приня́ть (*pf.*) что-н. как само́ собо́й разуме́ющееся. **9.** (*up to; incumbent upon*): **it's ~ you to decide** вам реша́ть; **it's not ~ me to say** не мне́ об э́том говори́ть. **10.** (*despite*): **~ all that, I still love him** несмотря́ на всё э́то, я его́ люблю́. **11.** (*ethic dative*): **there's gratitude ~ you!** и вот вам благода́рность!; **there's a marvellous shot ~ you!** вот замеча́тельный вы́стрел! **12.** (*with certain expressions of time*): **~ the first time** в пе́рвый раз; **~ the last time, will you shut up!** говорю́ тебе́ в после́дний раз — замолчи́!; **~ once I agree with you** на э́тот раз я с ва́ми согла́сен; **the wedding is arranged ~ June the 1st** сва́дьба назна́чена на пе́рвое ию́ня; **I ordered meat ~ Thursday** я заказа́л мя́со к четвергу́. **13.** (*with following inf.*): **it will be better ~ us all to leave** бу́дет лу́чше нам всем уйти́; **~ the experiment to succeed, certain conditions must be fulfilled** что́бы о́пыт уда́лся, должны́ быть вы́полнены определённые усло́вия; **it was absurd ~ him to do that** э́то бы́ло неле́по с его́ стороны́. **14.: ~ all I know, he may he there already** почём я зна́ю, мо́жет быть он уже́ там; **~ all his boasting** при всём его́ хвастовстве́; ка́к бы он ни хва́стался; **you can go away ~ all I care** а по мне — хоть сейча́с уходи́те.

conj. так как, ибо.

forage [ˈfɒrɪdʒ] *n.* фура́ж, корм.

v.i. (*mil.*) фуражи́ровать (*impf.*); (*search*) разы́скивать (*impf.*).

cpd. **~-cap** *n.* фура́жка.

forasmuch as [ˌfɒrəzˈmʌtʃ] *conj.* (*arch.*) ввиду́ того́, что; поско́льку.

foray [ˈfɒreɪ] *n.* набе́г.

v.i. соверш|а́ть, -и́ть набе́г.

forbear[1] [ˈfɔːbeə(r)] *n.* = **forebear**

forbear² [fɔːˈbeə(r)] *v.t. & i.* воздéрж|иваться, -áться (*от чего*); быть терпели́вым.
forbearance [fɔːˈbeərəns] *n.* воздéржанность, терпели́вость, терпéние.
forbid [fəˈbɪd] *v.t.* запре|щáть, -ти́ть (*кому что*); **God ~!** Бóже упаси́!/сохрани́!
forbidden [fəˈbɪd(ə)n] *adj.* запрещённый, запрéтный.
forbidding [fəˈbɪdɪŋ] *adj.* (*repellent*) оттáлкивающий; (*unfriendly*) неприя́зненный; (*threatening*) грóзный; **a ~ air** непристýпный вид.
force [fɔːs] *n.* **1.** (*strength: lit., fig.*) си́ла; **use ~** приб|егáть, -éгнуть к си́ле; **in full ~** в пóлном состáве; **by ~** си́лой, наси́льно; **from ~ of habit** в си́лу привы́чки; **by ~ of circumstance(s)** в си́лу обстоя́тельств; **the ~s of darkness** си́лы тьмы́. **2.** (*body of men, usu. armed*) вооружённый отря́д; **he attacked with a small ~** он атаковáл с небольши́м отря́дом; **Air F~** воéнно-воздýшные си́лы; **(Police) F~** поли́ция; (*pl.*) **the (Armed) F~s** áрмия, вооружённые си́лы. **3.** (*binding power, validity*) дéйственность; **the agreement has the ~ of law** э́то соглашéние имéет си́лу закóна; **in ~** (*of law etc.*) в си́ле; **come into ~** вступ|áть, -и́ть в си́лу; (*significance, cogency*) смысл, значéние; **he explained the ~ of the word** он объясни́л тóчное значéние э́того слóва; **there is ~ in what you say** вы говори́те убеди́тельно; в вáших словáх есть смысл. **4.** (*phys.*) си́ла; **the ~ of gravity** си́ла притяжéния.
v.t. **1.** (*compel, constrain*) заст|авля́ть, -áвить; прин|уждáть, -ýдить; **he was ~ed to sell the house** он был вы́нужден продáть дом; **you are not ~d to answer** вы не обя́заны отвечáть; **~ s.o.'s hand** прин|уждáть, -ýдить когó-н. к дéйствию; форси́ровать (*impf., pf.*) собы́тия; **~d** (*laugh etc.*) принуждённый; **~d labour** принуди́тельный труд; **~d landing** вы́нужденная посáдка. **2.** (*effect by ~*): **~ an entry** вл|áмываться, -оми́ться; врывáться, ворвáться; **~ a quarrel on s.o.** навя́з|ывать, -áть комý-н. ссóру; (*apply ~ to*): **~ (open) the door** вылáмывать, вы́ломать дверь; **~ a lock** взл|áмывать, -омáть замóк; **~ one's voice** напр|ягáть, -я́чь гóлос. **3.** (*increase under stress*): **~ the bidding** пов|ышáть, -ы́сить стáвки; **~ the pace** уск|оря́ть, -óрить шаг; (*produce under stress*): **~ a laugh** смея́ться (*impf.*) чéрез си́лу. **4.** (*cause accelerated growth*): **~ plants** уск|оря́ть, -óрить рост растéний.
cpds. **~-feed** *v.t.* корми́ть (*impf.*) наси́льно; **~-feeding** *n.* наси́льственное кормлéние.
forceful [ˈfɔːsfʊl] *adj.* си́льный, убеди́тельный.
force majeure [ˌfɔːs mæˈʒɜː(r)] *n.* форс-мажóр.
forcemeat [ˈfɔːsmiːt] *n.* фарш.
forceps [ˈfɔːseps] *n.* хирурги́ческие щипц|ы́ (*pl., g.* -óв); (*small*) пинцéт.
forcible [ˈfɔːsɪb(ə)l] *adj.* наси́льственный; (*forceful*) вéский; убеди́тельный; **~ entry** наси́льственное вторжéние.
forclos|e [fɔːˈkləʊz], **-ure** [fɔːˈkləʊzjə(r)] = **for(e)clos|e, -ure**
ford [fɔːd] *n.* брод.
v.t. пере|ходи́ть, -йти́ вброд.
fore [fɔː(r)] *n.* **1.: he finished the race well to the ~** он закóнчил бег, намнóго опереди́в други́х; **this subject has recently come to the ~** в послéднее врéмя э́тот вопрóс оказáлся в цéнтре внимáния. **2.** (*naut.*) нос; носовáя часть.
adj. перéдний; (*naut.*) носовóй; (*as pref.*) пред…
adv. впереди́; **~ and aft** на носý и на кормé; вдоль всегó сýдна.
forearm¹ [ˈfɔːrɑːm] *n.* предплéчье.
forearm² [fɔːrˈɑːm] *v.t.* зарáнее вооружá|ть, -и́ть; **forewarned is ~ed** кто предостережён, тот вооружён.
forebear [ˈfɔːbeə(r)] *n.* прéдок.
forebode [fɔːˈbəʊd] *v.t.* (*portend*) предвещáть (*impf.*) (дурнóе); (*have presentiment of*) предчýвствовать (*impf.*).
foreboding [fɔːˈbəʊdɪŋ] *n.* (*omen*) предзнаменовáние; (*presentiment*) дурнóе предчýвствие.
forecast [ˈfɔːkɑːst] *n.* предсказáние; **weather ~** прогнóз погóды.
v.t. & i. предскáз|ывать, -áть; **weather ~ing** синóптика.
forecaster [ˈfɔːkɑːstə(r)] *n.*: **weather ~** синóптик.
forecastle [ˈfəʊks(ə)l] *n.* (*naut.*) бак, полубáк.
for(e)close [fɔːˈkləʊz] *v.t. & i.* (*preclude*) исключ|áть, -и́ть; (*mortgage*) лишáть (*impf.*) прáва вы́купа залóженного имýщества.
for(e)closure [fɔːˈkləʊzjə(r)] *n.* (*leg.*) лишéние прáва вы́купа залóженного имýщества.
forecourt [ˈfɔːkɔːt] *n.* перéдний двор.
foredge [ˈfɔːredʒ] *n.* перéдний обрéз (кни́ги).
foredoom [fɔːˈduːm] *v.t.* (зарáнее) обр|екáть, -éчь.
forefather [ˈfɔːˌfɑːðə(r)] *n.* прéдок, прáотец.
forefinger [ˈfɔːˌfɪŋgə(r)] *n.* указáтельный пáлец.
forefoot [ˈfɔːfʊt] *n.* перéдняя лáпа/ногá.
forefront [ˈfɔːfrʌnt] *n.*: **in the ~ of the battle** на передовóй (ли́нии).
foregather [fɔːˈgæðə(r)] = **forgather**
forego¹ [fɔːˈgəʊ] *v.i.* (*precede*) предшéствовать (*impf.*) +*d.*; **the ~ing** вышеупомя́нутое; **a ~ne conclusion** предрешённый исхóд.
forego² [fɔːˈgəʊ] = **forgo**
foreground [ˈfɔːgraʊnd] *n.* (*lit., fig.*) перéдний план.
forehand [ˈfɔːhænd] *adj.* (*tennis*): **~ stroke** удáр спрáва.
forehead [ˈfɒrɪd, ˈfɔːhed] *n.* лоб.
foreign [ˈfɒrɪn, ˈfɒrən] *adj.* **1.** (*of or pertaining to another country or countries*) инострáнный, заграни́чный; **~ affairs** междунарóдные делá; **Ministry of F~ Affairs** Министéрство инострáнных дел; **~ passport** заграни́чный пáспорт; **~ policy** внéшняя поли́тика; **~ service** (*service abroad*) слýжба за грани́цей; **F~ Service** (*institution or career*) дипломати́ческая слýжба; **~ trade** внéшняя торгóвля; **in ~ parts** в чужи́х края́х. **2.** (*alien*) чужóй, чýждый; **~ soil** чужáя земля́, чужби́на. **3.** (*med.*) инорóдный; **~ body** (*lit., fig.*) инорóдное тéло.
foreigner [ˈfɒrɪnə(r), ˈfɒrənə(r)] *n.* инострáн|ец (*fem.* -ка).
foreignness [ˈfɒrɪnnɪs, ˈfɒrənnɪs] *n.* инострáнное происхождéние; чýждость.
foreknow [fɔːˈnəʊ] *v.t.* знать (*impf.*) зарáнее.
foreknowledge [fɔːˈnɒlɪdʒ] *n.* предви́дение.
foreland [ˈfɔːlænd] *n.* мыс.
foreleg [ˈfɔːleg] *n.* перéдняя лáпа/ногá.
forelock [ˈfɔːlɒk] *n.* прядь волóс на лбу; чуб; вихóр; **take time by the ~** лови́ть (*impf.*) момéнт; не зевáть (*impf.*).
foreman [ˈfɔːmən] *n.* мáстер, деся́тник; прорáб, (производи́тель рабóт); **~ of the jury** старшинá (*m.*) прися́жных.
foremast [ˈfɔːmɑːst, -məst] *n.* фок-мáчта.
foremost [ˈfɔːməʊst] *adj.* сáмый перéдний.
adv.: **first and ~** прéжде всегó; в пéрвую óчередь.
forename [ˈfɔːneɪm] *n.* и́мя (*nt.*) (*в отличие от фамилии*).
forenoon [ˈfɔːnuːn] *n.* врéмя до полýдня; ýтро.
forensic [fəˈrensɪk] *adj.* судéбный.
foreordain [ˌfɔːrɔːˈdeɪn] *v.t.* предопредел|я́ть, -и́ть.
forerunner [ˈfɔːˌrʌnə(r)] *n.* предшéственник, предтéча (*c.g.*).
foresail [ˈfɔːseɪl, -s(ə)l] *n.* фок.
foresee [fɔːˈsiː] *v.t.* предви́деть (*impf.*).
foreseeable [fɔːˈsiːəb(ə)l] *adj.*: **in the ~ future** в обозри́мом бýдущем.
foreshadow [fɔːˈʃædəʊ] *v.t.* предвещáть (*impf.*).
foreshore [ˈfɔːʃɔː(r)] *n.* береговáя полосá, затопля́емая прили́вом.
foreshorten [fɔːˈʃɔːt(ə)n] *v.t.* черти́ть, на- в перспекти́ве/ рáкурсе.
foresight [ˈfɔːsaɪt] *n.* **1.** (*knowledge of future*) предви́дение. **2.** (*care for future*) предусмотри́тельность. **3.** (*of gun*) мýшка.
foreskin [ˈfɔːskɪn] *n.* крáйняя плоть.
forest [ˈfɒrɪst] *n.* **1.** (*extensive woodland*) лес; **~ fire** леснóй пожáр; **a ~ of masts** лес мачт. **2.** (*hunting preserve*) охóтничий заповéдник; **deer ~** заповéдник для охóты на оленéй.
v.t. засá|живать, -ди́ть лéсом; **heavily ~ed country** леси́стая/леснáя мéстность.
forestall [fɔːˈstɔːl] *v.t.* предвосх|ищáть, -ти́ть; опере|жáть, -ди́ть; предупре|ждáть, -ди́ть.
forester [ˈfɒrɪstə(r)] *n.* (*forest dweller*) обитáтель (*m.*) лéса; (*official*) лесни́к; (*specialist*) лесни́чий.

forestry ['fɒrɪstrɪ] *n.* лесово́дство; **F~ Commission** коми́ссия по охра́не лесо́в.
foretaste ['fɔ:teɪst] *n.* предвкуше́ние.
foretell [fɔ:'tel] *v.t.* предска́з|ывать, -а́ть.
forethought ['fɔ:θɔ:t] *n.* предусмотри́тельность.
forever [fə'revə(r)] *adv.* навсегда́, наве́чно; (*continually*) постоя́нно, ве́чно.
forewarn [fɔ:'wɔ:n] *v.t.* предупре|жда́ть, -ди́ть; предостер|ега́ть, -е́чь; **~ed is forearmed** кто предостережён, тот вооружён.
forewoman ['fɔ:,wʊmən] *n.* (же́нщина-)деся́тник/ма́стер; (*of a jury*) (же́нщина-)старшина́ прися́жных.
foreword ['fɔ:wɜ:d] *n.* предисло́вие.
forfeit ['fɔ:fɪt] *n.* (*penalty*) штраф, конфиска́ция; **his life was ~** ≃ он мог поплати́ться жи́знью (за+*a.*); (*trivial fine, e.g. at games*) фант; **play at ~s** игра́ть в фа́нты.
v.t. теря́ть, по- (пра́во на) +*a.*; **he ~ed his self-respect** он потеря́л уваже́ние к себе́.
forfeiture ['fɔ:fɪtʃə(r)] *n.* конфиска́ция; лише́ние пра́ва (на+*a*).
forfend [fɔ:'fend] *v.t.* предохран|я́ть, -и́ть.
forgather, foregather [fɔ:'gæðə(r)] *v.i.* соб|ира́ться, -ра́ться.
forge [fɔ:dʒ] *n.* (*workshop*) ку́зница; (*hearth or furnace*) кузне́чный горн.
v.t. & i. **1.** (*shape metal*) кова́ть (*impf.*). **2.** (*fabricate*) изобре|та́ть, -сти́; выду́мывать, вы́думать; (*counterfeit*) подде́л|ывать, -ать. **3.: ~ ahead** выры́ваться, вы́рваться вперёд.
forger ['fɔ:dʒə(r)] *n.* подде́лыватель (*m.*); фальсифика́тор.
forgery ['fɔ:dʒərɪ] *n.* (*act*) подде́лка, подло́г; (*object*) подде́лка; подло́жный докуме́нт.
forget [fə'get] *v.t. & i.* заб|ыва́ть, -ы́ть; **I forgot all about the lecture ~** я соверше́нно забы́л о ле́кции; **'What is his name?' — 'I ~'** «Как его́ зову́т?» — «Я забы́л»; **his deeds will never be forgotten** его́ дея́ния не забу́дутся; **it is easy to ~** э́то легко́ забыва́ется; э́то с трудо́м уде́рживается в па́мяти; **he drinks to ~** он пьёт, что́бы забы́ться; **~ it!** (*coll.*) ла́дно!; бро́сьте!; **~ o.s.** (*act unselfishly*) забыва́ть (*impf.*) себя́ ра́ди други́х; (*act without decorum*) заб|ыва́ться, -ы́ться.
cpd. **~-me-not** *n.* (*bot.*) незабу́дка.
forgetful [fə'getfʊl] *adj.* забы́вчивый.
forgetfulness [fə'getfʊlnɪs] *n.* забы́вчивость.
forging ['fɔ:dʒɪŋ] *n.* ко́вка.
forgivable [fə'gɪvəb(ə)l] *adj.* прости́тельный.
forgive [fə'gɪv] *v.t. & i.* про|ща́ть, -сти́ть; **I ~ you for everything** я вам всё проща́ю; **~ me, I didn't hear what you said** прости́те, я не расслы́шал, что вы сказа́ли.
forgiveness [fə'gɪvnɪs] *n.* проще́ние.
forgiving [fɔ:'gɪvɪŋ] *adj.* (все)проща́ющий.
forgo, forego [fɔ:'gəʊ] *v.t.* отка́з|ываться, -а́ться от+*g.*; возде́рж|иваться, -а́ться от+*g.*
fork [fɔ:k] *n.* **1.** (*for cul. or table use*) ви́лка. **2.** (*agric.*) ви́лы (*f. pl.*). **3.** (*bifurcation*) разви́лка, разветвле́ние, распу́тье; (*crotch*) пах.
v.t. **1.** (*dig or turn with ~*): **~ over a rose-bed** разрыхл|я́ть, -и́ть ви́лами гря́дку с ро́зами; **~ out, up** (*lit., dig roots etc.*) выка́пывать, вы́копать.
v.i. (*bifurcate*) раздв|а́иваться, -о́иться; разветв|ля́ться, -и́ться; (*of road-direction*): **you must ~ right at the church** у це́ркви (, где доро́га разветвля́ется,) возьми́те напра́во; **~ out** (*sl., provide money*) раскоше́ли|ваться, -ться.
cpd. **~-lift** *adj.*: **~-lift truck** автопогру́зчик.
forked [fɔ:kt] *adj.* раздво́енный, разветвлённый, вилообра́зный; **~ lightning** зигзагообра́зная мо́лния; **a ~ tail** вилообра́зный хвост.
forlorn [fɔ:'lɔ:n] *adj.* забро́шенный, поки́нутый, жа́лкий, несча́стный; **~ hope** ги́блое де́ло; безнадёжное предприя́тие; **he looked ~** у него́ был потéрянный/жа́лкий вид.
form [fɔ:m] *n.* **1.** (*shape, aspect*) фо́рма, вид; (*figure, body*) фигу́ра. **2.** (*species, kind, variant*) вид, фо́рма; **~ of government** госуда́рственный строй; фо́рма правле́ния; (*gram.*) фо́рма. **3.** (*accepted or expected behaviour*) но́рмы (*f. pl.*) прили́чия/поведе́ния; **that is not good ~** так вести́ себя́ не при́нято; э́то дурны́е мане́ры; **that is common ~** э́то обы́чно; так при́нято. **4.** (*ritual, formality*) тип, вид; **~s of worship** обря́ды (*m. pl.*). **5.** (*of health*) состоя́ние; **in good ~** в хоро́шей фо́рме; (*of spirits*): **he appeared in great ~** он был в отли́чной фо́рме. **6.** (*document*) бланк, анке́та. **7.** (*class*) класс. **8.** (*bench*) скамья́. **9.** (*mould*) фо́рма. **10.** (*body of type*) печа́тная фо́рма. **11.** (*hare's lair*) нора́.
v.t. **1.** (*fashion, shape*) формирова́ть, с-; прид|ава́ть, -а́ть фо́рму +*d.*; **he ~ed the clay into a vase** гли́на под его́ рука́ми преврати́лась в ва́зу; **the rocks are ~ed by wave action** ска́лы формиру́ются под возде́йствием волн; **she ~s her letters well** она́ хорошо́ выво́дит бу́квы; **he can ~ simple sentences** она́ уме́ет составля́ть просты́е предложе́ния; **his style is ~ed on the classics** его́ стиль сложи́лся/образова́лся под влия́нием кла́ссиков; (*by discipline, training etc.*) тренирова́ть, на-; дисциплини́ровать (*impf., pf.*); разв|ива́ть, -и́ть; **his character was ~ed at school** его́ хара́ктер сформирова́лся в шко́ле (*or* был сформиро́ван шко́лой). **2.** (*organize, create*) организ|о́вывать, -ова́ть; образ|о́вывать, -ова́ть; созд|ава́ть, -а́ть; формирова́ть, с-; **they ~ed an alliance** они́ со́здали/образова́ли сою́з; **he was unable to ~ a government** он оказа́лся не в состоя́нии (*or* он не смог) сформирова́ть прави́тельство. **3.** (*conceive*): **they ~ed a plan** они́ вы́работали план; у них возни́к за́мысел; **~ an opinion** соста́вить (*pf.*) мне́ние; **I ~ed the conclusion that ...** я пришёл к заключе́нию, что... **4.** (*develop, acquire*): **habits ~ed in childhood** привы́чки, сложи́вшиеся с де́тства. **5.** (*constitute*) сост|авля́ть, -а́вить; представля́ть собо́й, явля́ться (*both impf.*); **this ~s the basis of our discussion** э́то составля́ет осно́ву на́шей диску́ссии; **the room ~s part of the museum** э́та ко́мната составля́ет часть (*or* явля́ется ча́стью) музе́я. **6.** (*gram.*) образ|о́вывать, -ова́ть; **the plural is ~ed by adding 's'** мно́жественное число́ образо́вывается при по́мощи добавле́ния бу́квы **'s'**. **7.** (*mil. etc.*) стро́ить, по-; **they ~ed a column of march** они́ вы́строились в похо́дную коло́нну; **the troops were ~ed (up) into line** солда́т вы́строили в ряд; **~ a queue** образова́ть (*pf.*) о́чередь.
v.i. (*take shape, appear, come into being*): **mist was ~ing in the valley** в доли́не собира́лся тума́н; **ice ~ed on the window** на окне́ образова́лся/возни́к моро́зный узо́р; **an idea ~ed in his mind** в его́ мозгу́ возни́кла иде́я (*or* возни́кло представле́ние); (*mil. etc.; also* **~ up**) стро́иться, по-; **the children ~ed up in groups** де́ти стро́ились отде́льными гру́ппами/отря́дами.
cpds. **~-filling** *n.* заполне́ние бла́нков; **~-master** *n.* кла́ссный руководи́тель; **~-mistress** *n.* кла́ссная руководи́тельница; **~-room** *n.* кла́ссная ко́мната.
formal ['fɔ:m(ə)l] *adj.* **1.** (*pertaining to form*) к фо́рме. **2.** (*in outward form*) вне́шний; форма́льный. **3.** (*conventional*) общепри́нятый; надлежа́щий; **~ garden** англи́йский сад/парк. **4.** (*official*) официа́льный. **5.** (*done for the sake of form*) для профо́рмы. **6.** (*ceremonious*) церемо́нный.
formaldehyde [fɔ:'mældɪ,haɪd] *n.* формальдеги́д.
formalism ['fɔ:mə,lɪz(ə)m] *n.* формали́зм.
formalist ['fɔ:məlɪst] *n.* формали́ст.
formalistic [,fɔ:mə'lɪstɪk] *adj.* формалисти́ческий.
formality [fɔ:'mælɪtɪ] *n.* форма́льность.
formalization [,fɔ:məlaɪ'zeɪʃ(ə)n] *n.* оформле́ние.
formalize ['fɔ:mə,laɪz] *v.t.* оф|ормля́ть, -о́рмить.
format ['fɔ:mæt] *n.* форма́т.
formation [fɔ:'meɪʃ(ə)n] *n.* **1.** (*creation*) образова́ние, формирова́ние. **2.** (*mil.*) строй, расположе́ние, поря́док; (*aeron.*) боево́й поря́док; строй самолётов в во́здухе; **~ flying** полёт в боево́м поря́дке. **3.** (*geol.*) форма́ция.
formative ['fɔ:mətɪv] *adj.* формиру́ющий, образу́ющий; **he spent his ~ years in France** го́ды, когда́ скла́дывался его́ хара́ктер, он провёл во Фра́нции.
former[1] ['fɔ:mə(r)] *n.* (*maker*) состави́тель (*m.*); созда́тель (*m.*); творе́ц.
former[2] ['fɔ:mə(r)] *adj.* **1.** (*earlier*) предше́ствующий; **in ~ times** в пре́жние времена́; **my ~ husband** мой бы́вший муж. **2.** (*first mentioned of two*) пе́рвый.

formerly [ˈfɔːməlɪ] *adv.* пре́жде, ра́ньше.
formic [ˈfɔːmɪk] *adj.* муравьи́ный; ~ **acid** муравьи́ная кислота́.
formidable [ˈfɔːmɪdəb(ə)l, *disp.* fɔːˈmɪd-] *adj.* устраша́ющий, гро́зный; (*task*) невероя́тно тру́дный.
formless [ˈfɔːmlɪs] *adj.* бесфо́рменный.
formula [ˈfɔːmjʊlə] *n.* (*set form of words*) выраже́ние, формулиро́вка; (*recipe*) реце́пт; (*math., chem.*) фо́рмула.
formulary [ˈfɔːmjʊlərɪ] *n.* спра́вочник; свод пра́вил; (*eccl.*) тре́бник.
formulate [ˈfɔːmjʊˌleɪt] *v.t.* формули́ровать, с-.
formulation [ˌfɔːmjʊˈleɪʃ(ə)n] *n.* формулиро́вка.
fornicate [ˈfɔːnɪˌkeɪt] *v.i.* развра́тничать (*impf.*); вести́ (*det.*) распу́тную жизнь.
fornication [ˌfɔːnɪˈkeɪʃ(ə)n] *n.* развра́т.
fornicator [ˈfɔːnɪˌkeɪtə(r)] *n.* развра́тни|к (*fem.* -ца).
forsake [fəˈseɪk, fɔː-] *v.t.* пок|ида́ть, -и́нуть; ост|авля́ть, -а́вить; бр|оса́ть, -о́сить.
forsooth [fəˈsuːθ, fɔː-] *adv.* (*arch.*) вои́стину, пои́стине; **a doctor,** ~! го́ре-до́ктор!; то́же мне до́ктор!
forswear [fɔːˈsweə(r)] *v.t.* отр|ека́ться, -е́чься от+*g.*; ~ **o.s.** нару́шить (*pf.*) кля́тву.
fort [fɔːt] *n.* форт; **hold the** ~ (*fig.*) держа́ть/уде́рживать (*impf.*) пози́цию.
forte[1] [ˈfɔːteɪ] *n.* (*strong point*) си́льная сторона́.
forte[2] [ˈfɔːteɪ] *n.* & *adv.* (*mus.*) фо́рте (*indecl.*).
forth [fɔːθ] *adv.* вперёд, да́льше; **back and** ~ взад и вперёд; **and so** ~ и так да́лее; **from this day** ~ с э́того дня; впредь; **let** ~ **a yell** изд|ава́ть, -а́ть вопль.
forthcoming [fɔːθˈkʌmɪŋ, *attrib.* ˈfɔːθ-] *adj.* предстоя́щий; (*helpful*) услу́жливый; **the money was not** ~ де́ньги не поступа́ли; **the clerk was not very** ~ **with information** чино́вник не о́чень охо́тно дава́л све́дения.
forthright [ˈfɔːθraɪt] *adj.* прямо́й, прямолине́йный.
forthwith [fɔːθˈwɪθ, -ˈwɪð] *adv.* неме́дленно, то́тчас.
fortieth [ˈfɔːtɪɪθ] *n.* (*fraction*) одна́ сорокова́я; сорокова́я часть.
adj. сороково́й.
fortification [ˌfɔːtɪfɪˈkeɪʃ(ə)n] *n.* укрепле́ние, фортифика́ция.
fortif|y [ˈfɔːtɪˌfaɪ] *v.t.* укреп|ля́ть, -и́ть; ~**ied in his belief** укреплённый в своём убежде́нии; ~**ied wines** креплёные ви́на; (*food*) витаминизи́ровать (*impf. and pf.*).
fortissimo [fɔːˈtɪsɪˌməʊ] *n.* & *adv.* форти́ссимо (*indecl.*); **a** ~ **passage** отры́вок/часть форти́ссимо.
fortitude [ˈfɔːtɪˌtjuːd] *n.* сто́йкость; си́ла ду́ха.
fortnight [ˈfɔːtnaɪt] *n.* две неде́ли; **next Tuesday** ~ че́рез две неде́ли, счита́я со сле́дующего вто́рника; **last Tuesday** ~ за две неде́ли до про́шлого вто́рника.
fortnightly [ˈfɔːtˌnaɪtlɪ] *n.* (*publication*) двухнеде́льное изда́ние.
adj. двухнеде́льный.
adv. раз в две неде́ли.
fortress [ˈfɔːtrɪs] *n.* кре́пость.
fortuitous [fɔːˈtjuːɪtəs] *adj.* случа́йный.
fortuit|ousness [fɔːˈtjuːɪtəsnɪs], **-y** [fɔːˈtjuːɪtɪ] *nn.* случа́йность, слу́чай.
fortunate [ˈfɔːtjʊnət, -tʃənət] *adj.* счастли́вый, уда́чный; **he was** ~ **to escape** ему́ посчастли́вилось убежа́ть; ~**ly** к сча́стью.
fortune [ˈfɔːtjuːn, -tʃuːn] *n.* **1.** (*chance*) уда́ча, сча́стье, форту́на; **by good** ~ по сча́стью; по счастли́вой случа́йности; **he had** ~ **on his side** сча́стье бы́ло на его́ стороне́; **the** ~**s of war** вое́нная форту́на, превра́тности (*f. pl.*) войны́; **try one's** ~ попыта́ть (*pf.*) сча́стья. **2.** (*fate*) судьба́; **the Gypsy (woman) told my** ~ цыга́нка (по/на)гада́ла мне. **3.** (*prosperity, large sum*) состоя́ние, бога́тство; **come into a** ~ унасле́довать (*pf.*) состоя́ние; получи́ть (*pf.*) насле́дство; **make a** ~ разбогате́ть (*pf.*); нажи́ть (*pf.*) состоя́ние; **I spent a small** ~ **today** я истра́тил у́йму де́нег сего́дня.
cpds. ~**-hunter** *n.* охо́тник за бога́тыми неве́стами (*or* за прида́ным); ~**-teller** *n.* гада́лка, ворожея́.
fort|y [ˈfɔːtɪ] *n.* со́рок; **the** ~**ies** (*decade*) сороковы́е го́ды (*m. pl.*); **they are both in their** ~**ies** (*age*) им обо́им за со́рок; **the roaring** ~**ies** (*latitude*) реву́щие сороковы́е.
adj. со́рок +*g. pl.*; **a man of** ~**y** сорокале́тний челове́к; **have** ~**y winks** вздремну́ть (*pf.*).
forum [ˈfɔːrəm] *n.* (*hist.*) фо́рум; (*fig., court*) суд; **the** ~ **of conscience** суд со́вести; (*fig., discussion*) обсужде́ние; (*meeting*) фо́рум, съезд; **the magazine provides a** ~ **for discussion** журна́л предоставля́ет чита́телям возмо́жность вести́ диску́ссии.
forward [ˈfɔːwəd] *n.* (*sport*) напада́ющий.
adj. (*situated to the fore*) пере́дний; (*moving onward*) иду́щий вперёд; (*progressive*) прогресси́вный; (*precocious*) скоспе́лый, преждевре́менный; (*prompt, ready*) гото́вый (*на* что); (*pert*) нагло́ва́тый, назо́йливый, развя́зный; (*comm.*) сро́чный.
adv. (*onward; towards one*) вперёд; ~**, march!** ша́гом марш!; **please come** ~ пожа́луйста, вы́йдите вперёд; **carry** ~ (*on a ledger*) перен|оси́ть, -ести́ на другу́ю страни́цу; **the meeting has been brought** ~ **a day** собра́ние перенесли́ на́ день ра́ньше; **walk back(wards) and** ~**(s)** ходи́ть (*indet.*) взад и вперёд; (*towards the future*): **I look** ~ **to meeting her** я с нетерпе́нием жду встре́чи с ней; **from this time** ~ начина́я с э́того вре́мени; (*into prominence*): **bring** ~ **new evidence** предст|авля́ть, -а́вить но́вые доказа́тельства/ули́ки; (*naut.*) в носово́й ча́сти; в носову́ю часть.
v.t. (*promote, encourage*) продв|ига́ть, -и́нуть; (*send*) пос|ыла́ть, -ла́ть; отпр|авля́ть, -а́вить; (*send on*) перес|ыла́ть, -ла́ть.
cpd. ~**-looking** *adj.* предусмотри́тельный, дальнови́дный.
forwardness [ˈfɔːwədnɪs] *n.* ра́ннее разви́тие; (*impudence*) наха́льство.
fosse [fɒs] *n.* транше́я, ров.
fossil [ˈfɒs(ə)l] *n.* окамене́лость; (*also fig.*) ископа́емое; **he is an old** ~ из него́ песо́к сы́плется.
adj. окамене́лый, ископа́емый.
fossilization [ˌfɒsɪlaɪˈzeɪʃ(ə)n] *n.* окамене́ние.
fossilize [ˈfɒsɪlaɪz] *v.t.* & *i.* превра|ща́ть(ся), -ти́ть(ся) в окамене́лость; (*fig.*) закосне́ть (*pf.*).
foster [ˈfɒstə(r)] *v.t.* (*tend*) ходи́ть (*indet.*) за (*детьми*); (*rear*) воспи́т|ывать, а́ть; (*fig.*): ~ **evil thoughts** вына́шивать (*impf.*) недо́брые мы́сли.
cpds. ~**-brother** *n.* моло́чный брат; ~**-child** *n.* приёмыш, воспи́танник; ~**-father** *n.* приёмный оте́ц; ~**-mother** *n.* приёмная мать.
foul [faʊl] *n.* (*sport*) наруше́ние (пра́вил игры́).
adj. гря́зный, отврати́тельный; **a** ~ **chimney** засорённая/заби́тая са́жей труба́; **a** ~ **smell** злово́ние; ~ **air** загрязнённый во́здух; ~ **language** руга́тельства (*nt. pl.*); сквернросло́вие; ~ **weather** отврати́тельная пого́да; непого́да; **a** ~ **deed** тёмное де́ло; ~ **play** (*sport*) гру́бая игра́; (*violence*) нечи́стое де́ло; **by fair means or** ~ любы́ми сре́дствами; **fall** ~ **of** поссо́риться (*pf.*) с+*i.*
v.t. (*defile*) загрязн|я́ть, -и́ть; па́чкать, за-; засор|я́ть, -и́ть; ~ **one's own nest** (*fig.*) га́дить, на- в своём гнезде́; (*obstruct*) образо́в|ывать, -а́ть зато́р в+*p.*; (*collide with*) ст|а́лкиваться, -олкну́ться с+*i.*
v.i. (*become entangled*) запу́т|ываться, -аться.
cpds. ~**-mouthed** *adj.* сквернросло́вящий; ~**-mouthed person** сквернросло́в; ~**-up** *n.* неразбери́ха, завару́ха.
foulard [fuːˈlɑːd] *n.* фуля́р.
found[1] [faʊnd] *v.t.* осно́в|ывать, -а́ть; за|кла́дывать, ложи́ть; ~ **a city** за|кла́дывать, -ложи́ть го́род; (*endow*) осно́в|ывать, -а́ть; учре|жда́ть, -ди́ть; (*base*) осно́в|ывать, -а́ть; **the story is** ~**ed on fact** в осно́ву расска́за поло́жено действи́тельное происше́ствие.
found[2] [faʊnd] *v.t.* (*melt metal etc.*) пла́вить (*impf.*); лить (*impf.*).
foundation [faʊnˈdeɪʃ(ə)n] *n.* **1.** (*establishing*) основа́ние, учрежде́ние; (*endowment*) учрежде́ние; (*founded institution*) учрежде́ние, существу́ющее на поже́ртвованный фонд; (*fund*) фонд. **2.** (*base of building etc.*) фунда́мент; **lay the** ~ за|кла́дывать, -ложи́ть фунда́мент/осно́ву; (*fig.*) осно́ва; **lay the** ~**s of one's career** класть, положи́ть нача́ло свое́й карье́ре; **the story has no** ~ **in fact** расска́з не име́ет ни мале́йшего основа́ния. **3.:** ~ **cream** крем под пу́дру; ~ **garment** корсе́т, гра́ция.

cpd. **~-stone** *n.* фундаме́нтный ка́мень; (*fig.*) краеуго́льный ка́мень, осно́ва.

founder[1] ['faʊndə(r)] *n.* основа́тель (*m.*); учреди́тель (*m.*); **~'s shares** учреди́тельские а́кции.

cpd. **~-member** *n.* член-основа́тель (*m.*).

founder[2] ['faʊndə(r)] *n.* (*metall.*) лите́йщик, плави́льщик.

founder[3] ['faʊndə(r)] *v.i.* (*collapse*) ос|еда́ть, -е́сть; (*of a horse, go lame*) охроме́ть (*pf.*); (*from fatigue*) вали́ться, с-; (*of a ship*) идти́ (*det.*) ко дну.

foundling ['faʊndlɪŋ] *n.* подки́дыш, найдёныш.

foundress ['faʊndrɪs] *n.* основа́тельница, учреди́тельница.

foundry ['faʊndrɪ] *n.* лите́йная; **~ hand** лите́йщик.

fount[1] [faʊnt] *n.* (*source*) исто́чник, ключ.

fount[2] [faʊnt] (*US* **font**) *n.* (*typ.*) компле́кт шри́фта.

fountain ['faʊntɪn] *n.* фонта́н, исто́чник, ключ; (*fig.*) исто́чник; **drinking ~** фонта́нчик для питья́.

cpds. **~-head** *n.*: **go to the ~-head** обрати́ться (*pf.*) к первоисто́чнику; **~-pen** *n.* авторучка, ве́чное перо́.

four [fɔː(r)] *n.* (число́/но́мер) четы́ре; (**~** *people*) че́тверо; **we ~** нас че́тверо; **(the, all) ~ of us went** мы пошли́ вчетверо́м; нас пошло́ четы́ре челове́ка; **~ each** по четы́ре; **in ~s, ~ at a time** по четы́ре; четвёрками; (*figure*; *thg. numbered 4*; *set, team, crew of* **~**) четвёрка; (*cut, divide*) **in ~** на четы́ре ча́сти; **fold in ~** сложи́ть (*pf.*) вче́тверо; (*with var. nn. expr. or understood*: *cf. also examples under* **two**): **carriage and ~** каре́та, запряжённая четвёркой лошаде́й; **make up a ~ at bridge** соста́вить (*pf.*) па́ртию в бридж; **he got down on all ~s** он опусти́лся на четвере́ньки; **the examples are not on all ~s** э́ти приме́ры не аналоги́чны; **form ~s!** ряды́ вздвой!

adj. четы́ре *+g. sg.*; (*for people and pluralia tantum, also*) че́тверо *+g. pl.* (*cf. examples under* **two**); **he and ~ others** он и ещё че́тверо други́х; **~ fives are twenty** четы́режды (*or* четы́ре на) пять — два́дцать; **~ times as good** вче́тверо (*or* в четы́ре ра́за) лу́чше; **~ times as big** в четы́ре ра́за бо́льше; **from the ~ corners of the earth** со всех концо́в земли́; **~ figures** (*sum*) четырёхзна́чная су́мма.

cpds. **~-course** *adj.*: **~-course meal** обе́д из четырёх блюд; **~fold** *adj.* четырёхкра́тный; *adv.* в четы́ре ра́за (бо́льше); **~-hundredth** *adj.* четырёхсо́тый; **~-lane** *adj.*: **~-lane highway** шоссе́ с движе́нием в четы́ре ря́да; **~-letter** *adj.*: **~-letter word** (*fig.*) руга́тельство; непристо́йное сло́во; **~-poster (bed)** *n.* крова́ть с по́логом на четырёх сто́лбиках; **~-pounder** (*gun*) *n.* ору́дие, стреля́ющее четырёхфунто́выми снаря́дами; **~score** *n.* (*arch.*) во́семьдесят; **~-seater** *n.* (*car*) четырёхме́стная маши́на; **~-square** *adj.* квадра́тный; (*fig.*) твёрдый, прямо́й; **~-stroke** *adj.*: **~-stroke engine** четырёхта́ктный дви́гатель (вну́треннего сгора́ния); **~-wheel** *adj.*: **~-wheel drive** (*attr.*) с приво́дом на четы́ре колеса́; **~-wheeler** *n.* (*hist.*) изво́зчичья каре́та.

foursome ['fɔːsəm] *n.* четвёрка; две па́ры; **we made a ~** мы игра́ли дво́е на́ двое (*or* вчетверо́м).

fourteen [fɔː'tiːn] *n.* & *adj.* четы́рнадцать (*+g. pl.*).

fourteenth [fɔː'tiːnθ] *n.* (*date*) четы́рнадцатое (число́); (*fraction*) одна́ четы́рнадцатая; четы́рнадцатая часть.

adj. четы́рнадцатый.

fourth [fɔːθ] *n.* **1.** (*date*) четвёртое (число́). **2.** (*fraction*) одна́ четвёртая; четвёртая часть; че́тверть. **3.** (*mus.*) ква́рта; четвёртая.

adj. четвёртый; **the ~ dimension** четвёртое измере́ние.

fowl [faʊl] *n.* (*arch., bird*) пти́ца; **the ~s of the air** пти́цы небе́сные; перна́тые; (*domestic*) дома́шняя пти́ца; (*chicken*) ку́рица.

v.i. охо́титься (*impf.*) на дичь.

cpd. **~-pest** *n.* пти́чья холе́ра.

fowler ['faʊlə(r)] *n.* птицело́в, охо́тник.

fox [fɒks] *n.* лиса́, лиси́ца; (*fur*) ли́сий мех; (*wily man*) хитре́ц; лиса́ (*c.g.*).

v.t. (*deceive*) обма́н|ывать, -у́ть; (*puzzle*) ста́вить, по- в тупи́к; озада́чи|вать, -ть.

v.i. (*sham*) хитри́ть (*impf.*); прики́|дываться, -нуться.

cpds. **~glove** *n.* наперстя́нка; **~hole** *n.* ли́сья нора́; (*mil.*) стрелко́вая яче́йка; одино́чный око́п; **~hound** *n.* го́нчая; **~-hunting** *n.* (верхова́я) охо́та на лис; **~-terrier** *n.* фокстерье́р; **~trot** *n.* фокстро́т.

foxy ['fɒksɪ] *adj.* (*crafty*) хи́трый; с хитрецо́й; (*reddish-brown*) ры́жий.

foyer ['fɔɪeɪ] *n.* фойе́ (*indecl.*).

Fr. ['fɑːðə(r)] *n.* (*abbr. of* **Father**) оте́ц.

fr. ['fræŋk(z)] *n.* (*abbr. of* **franc(s)**) фр., (франк).

fracas ['frækɑː] *n.* сканда́л, шу́мная ссо́ра.

fraction ['frækʃ(ə)n] *n.* **1.** (*arith.*) дробь; **decimal ~** десяти́чная дробь; **common, vulgar ~** прост́ая дробь; **improper ~** непра́вильная дробь; **~ of a second** до́ля секу́нды. **2.** (*small piece or amount*) части́ца, крупи́ца; **£5 and not a ~ less** пять фу́нтов — и ни гроша́ ме́ньше. **3.** (*chem.*) фра́кция, части́чный проду́кт перего́нки. **4.** (*small sect or party*) фра́кция.

fractional ['frækʃən(ə)l] *adj.* дро́бный, части́чный; **the difference is ~** ра́зница незначи́тельна; **~ distillation** фракцио́нная/дро́бная перего́нка.

fractionalism ['frækʃənə,lɪz(ə)m] *n.* (*formation of sects*) фракцио́нность, фракционе́рство.

fractious ['frækʃəs] *adj.* капри́зный, раздражи́тельный; неуправля́емый.

fracture ['fræktʃə(r)] *n.* тре́щина, изло́м, разры́в; (*of a bone*) перело́м; **simple/compound ~** закры́тый/откры́тый перело́м.

v.t. & *i.* лома́ть(ся), с-; раск|а́лывать(ся), -оло́ть(ся).

fragile ['frædʒaɪl, -dʒɪl] *adj.* (*brittle*) ло́мкий, хру́пкий; (*frail*) хру́пкий.

fragility [frə'dʒɪlɪtɪ] *n.* ло́мкость, хру́пкость.

fragment ['frægmənt] *n.* обло́мок, оско́лок; (*of writing or music*) фрагме́нт; **~s of conversation** обры́вки (*m. pl.*) разгово́ра.

fragmentary ['frægməntərɪ] *adj.* отры́вочный, фрагмента́рный.

fragmentation [,frægmən'teɪʃ(ə)n] *n.* разры́в на ме́лкие ча́сти; **~ bomb** оско́лочная бо́мба.

fragrance ['freɪgrəns] *n.* арома́т.

fragrant ['freɪgrənt] *adj.* арома́тный.

frail [freɪl] *adj.* хру́пкий, непро́чный; (*in health*) хи́лый, хру́пкий, боле́зненный; (*in moral sense*) сла́бый, неусто́йчивый.

frailty ['freɪltɪ] *n.* хру́пкость, непро́чность; (*of health*) хру́пкость, боле́зненность; (*of morals*) сла́бость, неусто́йчивость.

frame [freɪm] *n.* **1.** (*structural skeleton*) о́стов, скеле́т, костя́к; (*of a ship or aircraft*) ко́рпус, о́стов; (*printing*) подра́мник; (*textiles*) тка́цкий стано́к. **2.** (*wood or metal surround*) ра́ма, ра́мка; **picture ~** ра́ма (для) карти́ны; **window ~** око́нная ра́ма. **3.** (*hort.*) парнико́вая ра́ма. **4.** (*body*): **more than the human ~ can bear** свы́ше сил челове́ческих; **sobs shook her ~** рыда́ния сотряса́ли её (те́ло). **5.**: **~ of mind** настрое́ние; расположе́ние ду́ха. **6.** (*order, system*) структу́ра, систе́ма. **7.** (*cin.*) кадр.

v.t. **1.** (*compose, devise*) сост|авля́ть, -а́вить; созд|ава́ть, -а́ть; **~ a constitution/sentence** сост|авля́ть, -а́вить конститу́цию/предложе́ние; **he ~d his question carefully** он то́чно сформули́ровал свой вопро́с. **2.** (*surround*): **~ a picture** вст|авля́ть, -а́вить карти́ну в ра́м(к)у; обр|амля́ть, -а́мить карти́ну; **he was ~d in the doorway** он стоя́л в прое́ме две́ри. **3.** (*sl., concoct case against*) приши́ть (*pf.*) де́ло *+d.*; сфабрикова́ть (*pf.*) ули́ку про́тив*+g.*

cpds. **~-house** *n.* карка́сный дом; **~-saw** *n.* ра́мная пила́; **~-up** *n.* (*sl.*) сфабрико́ванное обвине́ние; **~work** *n.* карка́с, о́стов; (*fig.*): **the ~work of society** структу́ра о́бщества; **within the ~work of the constitution** в ра́мках конститу́ции.

franc [fræŋk] *n.* франк.

France [frɑːns] *n.* Фра́нция.

franchise ['fræntʃaɪz] *n.* (*right of voting*) пра́во го́лоса; (*comm.*) привиле́гия.

Francis ['frɑːnsɪs] *n.* (*hist.*) **1.** Франци́ск; **St ~ of Assisi** Франци́ск Асси́зский. **2.** **~ Joseph** Франц-Ио́сиф.

Franciscan [fræn'sɪskən] *n.* францискáнец.

adj. франциска́нский.

Francophile ['fræŋkə,faɪl] *n.* франкофи́л.
adj. франкофи́льский.
francophone ['fræŋkə,fəʊn] *n.* and *adj.* франкоязы́чный; говоря́щий на францу́зском языке́.
franc tireur [frɑ̃ tɪə'tɜ:] *n.* франтирёр, партиза́н.
frangipani [,frændʒɪ'pɑ:nɪ] *n.* (*bot.*) кра́сный жасми́н.
Frank[1] [fræŋk] *n.* (*hist.*) франк.
frank[2] [fræŋk] *adj.* открове́нный, и́скренний.
frank[3] [fræŋk] *v.t.* франки́ровать (*impf., pf.*); **~ing machine** франкирова́льная маши́на.
frankfurter ['fræŋk,fɜ:tə(r)] *n.* соси́ска.
frankincense ['fræŋkɪn,sens] *n.* ла́дан.
frankness ['fræŋknɪs] *n.* открове́нность, и́скренность.
frantic ['fræntɪk] *adj.* неи́стовый, безу́мный; **she became ~ with grief** она́ обезу́мела от го́ря; **the noise is driving me ~** шум выво́дит меня́ из себя́; **he was in a ~ hurry** он ужа́сно спеши́л.
fraternal [frə'tɜ:n(ə)l] *adj.* бра́тский.
fraternity [frə'tɜ:nɪtɪ] *n.* бра́тство; (*student association*) студе́нческая общи́на.
fraternization [,frætənaɪ'zeɪʃ(ə)n] *n.* брата́ние.
fraternize ['frætə,naɪz] *v.i.* брата́ться (*impf.*).
fratricidal [,frætrɪ'saɪd(ə)l] *adj.* братоуби́йственный.
fratricide ['frætrɪ,saɪd] *n.* (*crime*) братоуби́йство; (*criminal*) братоуби́йца.
fraud [frɔ:d] *n.* (*fraudulent act*) обма́н, моше́нничество; (*impostor*) обма́нщик, моше́нник; (*thg. that deceives or disappoints*) фальши́вка, подде́лка.
fraudulence ['frɔ:djʊləns] *n.* обма́нчивость, фальши́вость.
fraudulent ['frɔ:djʊlənt] *adj.* обма́нный, фальши́вый, моше́ннический; **~ conversion** присвое́ние иму́щества обма́нным путём.
fraught [frɔ:t] *adj.* по́лный, преиспо́лненный, чрева́тый; **the expedition is ~ with danger** экспеди́ция чрева́та опа́сностями; **his words were ~ with meaning** его́ слова́ бы́ли полны́ значе́ния; (*tense*) напряжённый.
fray[1] [freɪ] *n.* дра́ка; побо́ище; **eager for the ~** рву́щийся в бой.
fray[2] [freɪ] *v.t. & i.* прот|ира́ть(ся), -ере́ть(ся); (*fig.*): **her nerves are ~ed** у неё соверше́нно истрёпаны не́рвы.
frazzle ['fræz(ə)l] *n.*: **worn to a ~** доведённый до изнеможе́ния; **beaten to a ~** весь изби́тый.
freak [fri:k] *n.* (*unusual occurrence*): **a ~ storm** необы́чная бу́ря; (*abnormal pers. or thg.*) уро́д, вы́родок; уро́дство; (*absurd or fanciful idea*) причу́да, заско́к; **~ of nature** оши́бка приро́ды; (*enthusiast*) фана́т; **health ~** поме́шанный на здоро́вье; **film ~** кинома́н.
freakish ['fri:kɪʃ] *adj.* причу́дливый, стра́нный, чудно́й.
freckle ['frek(ə)l] *n.* весну́шка.
v.t. покр|ыва́ть, -ы́ть весну́шками; **a ~d face** весну́шчатое лицо́.
Frederick ['fredrɪk] *n.* Фреде́рик; (*Ger. hist.*) Фри́дрих.
free [fri:] *adj.* **1.** свобо́дный, во́льный; **you are ~ to leave** вы мо́жете уйти́; **they gave us a ~ hand** они́ да́ли нам по́лную свобо́ду де́йствий; **he let the thief go ~** он упусти́л во́ра; (*after capture*) он отпусти́л во́ра (на во́лю); **break ~** вырыва́ться, вы́рваться на во́лю; **set ~** освобо|жда́ть, -ди́ть; **~ of disease** здоро́вый; **~ from blame** неви́нный; **I left one end ~** (*unfastened*) я оста́вил оди́н коне́ц свобо́дным/незакреплённым; **I am not a ~ agent** я не во́лен в свои́х де́йствиях; **~ composition** сочине́ние на свобо́дную те́му; **~ on board** фра́нко-борт; **~ speech** свобо́да сло́ва; **~ translation** во́льный перево́д; **~ verse** во́льный стих; **~ will** свобо́да во́ли; **he left of his own ~ will** он ушёл доброво́льно/сам (*or* по свое́й во́ле). **2.** (*without constraint*) непринуждённый, раско́ванный; **~ and easy** непринуждённый; **make ~ with** свобо́дно распоряжа́ться (*impf.*) +*i.*; **he made ~ with my cigars** он распоряжа́лся мои́ми сига́рами, как свои́ми; **make s.o. ~ of sth.** предост|авля́ть, -а́вить что-н. в чьё-н. распоряже́ние. **3.** (*without payment*) беспла́тный; **the price is £5 post ~** цена́ 5 фу́нтов с беспла́тной доста́вкой по по́чте; **~ of charge** беспла́тный; **~ gift** полу́ченное да́ром; **~ pass** (*on railway etc.*) беспла́тный прое́зд; (*admission*) про́пуск. **4.** (*unoccupied*) свобо́дный, неза́нятый; **my hands are ~** (*fig.*) у меня́ развя́заны ру́ки. **5.** (*liberal*) ще́дрый; **~ with one's money** ще́дрый, расточи́тельный; **~ with advice** всегда́ гото́вый дава́ть сове́ты. **6.** (*chem.*) несвя́занный.
v.t. (*release, e.g. a rope*) высвобожда́ть, вы́свободить; (*liberate*) освобо|жда́ть, -ди́ть.
cpds. **~board** *n.* надво́дный борт; **~booter** *n.* граби́тель (*m.*); пира́т; **~-born** *adj.* свобо́днорождённый; **~-for-all** *n.* (*competition*) откры́тый для всех ко́нкурс; (*fight*) всео́бщая дра́ка/сва́лка; ку́ча мала́ (*indecl.*); **~hand** *adj.*: **~hand drawing** рису́нок, сде́ланный от руки́; **~hold** *n.* неограни́ченное пра́во со́бственности на недви́жимость; **~holder** *n.* свобо́дный со́бственник; **~lance(r)** *n.* лицо́ свобо́дной профе́ссии, рабо́тающий по договора́м; внешта́тник (*coll.*); **F~mason** *n.* масо́н; **F~masonry** *n.* (*lit.*) масо́нство; (*fig.*) кружковщи́на, ка́стовость; **~-range** *adj.* **~-range hens** ку́ры на свобо́дном вы́гуле; **~-spoken** *adj.* открове́нный, прямо́й; **~stone** *n. & adj.* ка́мень несло́истой структу́ры; **~-thinker** *n.* вольноду́м|ец (*fem.* -ка); **~-thinking** *adj.* вольноду́мный; **~-wheel** *v.i.* (*lit.*) дви́гаться (*impf.*) свобо́дным хо́дом; **~-wheeling** *adj.* (*fig.*) во́льный, неско́ванный.
freedom ['fri:dəm] *n.* свобо́да; **~ of speech** свобо́да сло́ва; **~ of worship** свобо́да отправле́ния религио́зных ку́льтов; (*privilege*) привиле́гия, пра́во; (*undue familiarity*) во́льности (*f. pl.*).
freesia ['fri:zjə, -ʒə] *n.* фре́зия.
freez|e [fri:z] *n.* (*period of frost*) замора́живание, застыва́ние; хо́лод, моро́з; (*stabilization*) замора́живание; **wage ~e** замора́живание за́работной пла́ты.
v.t. замор|а́живать, -о́зить; **frozen food** моро́женые проду́кты; **the news froze his blood** от э́того изве́стия его́ охвати́л у́жас; **~e assets/prices** замор|а́живать, -о́зить фо́нды/це́ны; **~e out** (*exclude*) вы́курить (*pf.*) (*sl.*).
v.i. **1.** (*impers.*) моро́зить (*impf.*); **it's ~ing outside** на дворе́ стра́шный моро́з; **will it ~e tonight?** бу́дет сего́дня но́чью моро́з? **2.** (*congeal with cold*): **the lake is frozen up, over, across** о́зеро покры́лось льдом; **the roads are frozen** доро́ги покры́лись льдом; **the pipes are frozen (up)** тру́бы промёрзли; **~e on to s.o.** (*sl.*) вцепи́ться (*pf.*) в кого́-н.; **~ing point** то́чка замерза́ния. **3.** (*fig., become rigid*) заст|ыва́ть, -ы́ть; **he froze where he stood** он засты́л на ме́сте; **his features froze** его́ лицо́ как бу́дто засты́ло; **'~e!'** (*coll., remain motionless*) замри́! **4.** (*become chilled*) зам|ерза́ть, -ёрзнуть; **he froze to death** он продро́г/промёрз до косте́й; он закочене́л; **I'm ~ing** я замёрз.
freezer ['fri:zə(r)] *n.* (*domestic appliance*) морози́льник; **~ compartment** морози́лка.
freight [freɪt] *n.* **1.** (*carriage of goods*) фрахт, груз; **~ charge** сто́имость прово́за. **2.** (*goods carried*) груз.
v.t. (*charter*) фрахтова́ть, за-; (*load*) грузи́ть, на-.
cpd. **~-train** *n.* (*US*) това́рный по́езд.
freightage ['freɪtɪdʒ] *n.* фрахтова́ние; перево́зка гру́зов; (*capacity*) грузосовмести́мость.
freighter ['freɪtə(r)] *n.* (*chartering or loading agent*) фрахто́вщик; (*carrier*) перево́зчик; (*vessel*) грузово́е су́дно; (*aircraft*) грузово́й самолёт.
French [frentʃ] *n.* (*language*) францу́зский язы́к; **the ~** (*people*) францу́зы (*m. pl.*).
adj. францу́зский; **~ bean** фасо́ль; **French Canadian** кана́д|ец-францу́з (*fem.* -ка-францу́женка); **~ chalk** мы́льный ка́мень; портня́жный мел; **~ horn** валто́рна; **take ~ leave** уйти́ (*pf.*), не проща́ясь (*or* «по-англи́йски»); **~ letter** (*contraceptive*) презервати́в; **~ loaf** (дли́нный) бато́н; **~ polish** политу́ра; **~ window** двуство́рчатое окно́ до по́ла.
cpds. **~man** *n.* францу́з; **~woman** *n.* францу́женка.
Frenchified ['frentʃɪ,faɪd] *adj.* офранцу́женный.
frenetic [frə'netɪk] *adj.* неи́стовый; лихора́дочный.
frenzied ['frenzɪd] *adj.* неи́стовый, взбешённый; **~ applause** неи́стовая ова́ция.
frenzy ['frenzɪ] *n.* неи́стовство, бе́шенство.
frequency ['fri:kwənsɪ] *n.* частота́; (*rate*), ча́стность; **high**

~ **transmission** высокочасто́тная переда́ча; ~ **modulation** часто́тная модуля́ция.
frequent[1] ['fri:kwənt] *adj.* ча́стый.
frequent[2] [frɪ'kwent] *v.t.* ча́сто посеща́ть (*impf.*).
frequentative [frɪ'kwentətɪv] *adj.* (*gram.*) многокра́тный; обознача́ющий многокра́тное де́йствие.
frequently ['fri:kwəntlɪ] *adv.* ча́сто.
fresco ['freskəʊ] *n.* фре́ска; фре́сковая жи́вопись.
v.t. распи́с|ывать, -а́ть (фре́сками).
fresh [freʃ] *adj.* **1.** (*new*) све́жий, но́вый; (*more*): **make some ~ tea** завари́ть (*pf.*) све́жего ча́ю. **2.** (*recent in origin*): ~ **bread** све́жий хлеб; ~ **paint** све́жая кра́ска; ~ **from university** пря́мо с университе́тской скамьи́; **it is still ~ in my memory** э́то ещё свежо́ в моe´й па́мяти. **3.** (*not salt*) пре́сный. **4.** (*cool, refreshing*) све́жий, прохла́дный; **a ~ breeze** све́жий ветеро́к. **5.** (*unspoilt, unsullied*) све́жий, незапя́тнанный; ~ **air** све́жий во́здух; **a ~ complexion** све́жий цвет лица́. **6.** (*lively*) бо́дрый, живо́й. **7.** (*US, impudent*) развя́зный, де́рзкий.
cpds. **~-air** *adj.* **~-air system** вентиля́ция; **~man** *n.* новичо́к (в университе́те); первоку́рсник; **~-water** *adj.* пресново́дный.
freshen ['freʃ(ə)n] *v.t.* освеж|а́ть, -и́ть.
v.i. свеже́ть, по-; **the wind is ~ing** ве́тер свеже́ет; **she's gone to ~ up** она́ пошла́ привести́ себя́ в поря́док.
freshly ['freʃlɪ] *adv.* свежо́, бо́дро; (*recently*) неда́вно; то́лько что.
freshness ['freʃnɪs] *n.* (*novelty*) све́жесть, оригина́льность; (*coolness*) све́жесть; (*brightness*) све́жесть, я́ркость; (*US, impudence*) развя́зность, де́рзость.
fret[1] [fret] *n.* (*of a guitar etc.*) лад.
fret[2] [fret] *n.* раздраже́ние, волне́ние.
v.t. (*wear by rubbing etc.*) изн|а́шивать, -оси́ть; разъ|еда́ть, -е́сть; (*worry*) раздража́ть (*impf.*); волнова́ть, вз-.
v.i. раздража́ться; волнова́ться; му́читься (*all impf.*); ~ **and fume** рвать и мета́ть (*impf.*); **babies ~ in hot weather** ма́ленькие де́ти пло́хо перено́сят жа́ркую пого́ду.
fret[3] [fret] *v.t.* (*decorate by cutting*) укр|аша́ть, -а́сить резьбо́й.
cpds. **~saw** *n.* ло́бзик; пи́лка для мета́лла; **~work** *n.* резно́е украше́ние, резьба́.
fretful ['fretfʊl] *adj.* раздражи́тельный, капри́зный.
fretfulness ['fretfʊlnɪs] *n.* раздражи́тельность.
Freudian ['frɔɪdɪən] *n.* фрейди́ст.
adj. фрейди́стский; ~ **slip** огово́рка по Фре́йду.
FRG (*abbr. of* **Federal Republic of Germany**) ФРГ (Федерати́вная Респу́блика Герма́нии).
friable ['fraɪəb(ə)l] *adj.* кроша́щийся, ры́хлый.
friar ['fraɪə(r)] *n.* мона́х (ни́щенствующего о́рдена).
friary ['fraɪərɪ] *n.* мужско́й монасты́рь.
fricassee ['frɪkə,si:, -'si:] *n.* фрикасе́ (*indecl.*).
v.t. гото́вить (*impf.*) фрикасе́ из+*g*.
fricative ['frɪkətɪv] *n.* & *adj.* фрикати́вный (звук).
friction ['frɪkʃ(ə)n] *n.* тре́ние; (*fig.*) тре́ния (*nt. pl.*).
cpd. **~-gear** *n.* фрикцио́нная переда́ча.
Friday ['fraɪdeɪ, -dɪ] *n.* пя́тница; **Good ~** Страстна́я/Вели́кая Пя́тница; **man ~** (*servant*) Пя́тница; **girl ~** ≃ помо́щница.
fridge [frɪdʒ] *n.* (*coll.*) холоди́льник.
cpd. **~-freezer** *n.* двухсекцио́нный холоди́льник, «дву́шка».
friend [frend] *n.* **1.** (*close ~*) друг, прия́тель (*fem.* -ница); (*acquaintance*) знако́м|ый (*fem.* -ая); (*woman's fem.* ~) подру́га; **a ~ in need is a ~ indeed** друзья́ познаю́тся в беде́; **make ~s** подружи́ться (*pf.*) (*с кем*); **he makes ~s easily** он легко́ схо́дится с людьми́; **let's shake hands and be ~s** дава́йте помири́мся; **he is no ~ of mine** он мне не друг. **2.** (*in addressing or referring to persons in public*) колле́га (*c.g.*); **my honourable ~** мой достопочте́нный колле́га/собра́т. **3.** (*benefactor, sympathizer*) доброжела́тель (*m.*), сторо́нник; **I am no ~ to such measures** я не сочу́вствую таки́м ме́рам. **4.** (*Quaker*) ква́кер; **Society of F~s** се́кта ква́керов.
friendless ['frendlɪs] *adj.* не име́ющий друзе́й.
friendliness ['frendlɪnɪs] *n.* дружелю́бие.
friendly ['frendlɪ] *adj.* дру́жеский, това́рищеский; **F~ Society** о́бщество взаимопо́мощи; ~ **to our cause** сочу́вствующий на́шему де́лу.
friendship ['frendʃɪp] *n.* дру́жба.
frieze[1] [fri:z] *n.* (*decorative band*) бордю́р, фриз.
frieze[2] [fri:z] *n.* (*text.*) бо́брик; гру́бая шерстяна́я ткань; ба́йка.
frigate ['frɪgɪt] *n.* (*hist.*) фрега́т; (*small destroyer*) эска́дренный миноно́сец; сторожево́й кора́бль.
cpd. **~-bird** *n.* фрега́т.
fright [fraɪt] *n.* **1.** (*fear; frightening experience*) страх, испу́г; **I almost died of ~** я чуть не у́мер от стра́ха; **give s.o. a ~** испуга́ть (*pf.*) кого́-н.; напуга́ть (*pf.*) кого́-н.; **I got the ~ of my life** я жу́тко испуга́лся. **2.** (*absurd-looking pers.*) пу́гало, страши́лище; **she looks a (perfect) ~** она́ вы́глядит настоя́щим пу́галом.
frighten ['fraɪt(ə)n] *v.t.* пуга́ть, на-/ис-; устраш|а́ть, -и́ть; **she is ~ed of the dark** она́ бои́тся темноты́; **don't ~ the birds away** не спугни́те птиц; **he was ~ed into signing** его́ угро́зами заста́вили подписа́ться; **he was ~ed out of the idea** его́ так запуга́ли, что он отказа́лся от э́той мы́сли; **~ing** *adj.* ужа́сный.
frightful ['fraɪtfʊl] *adj.* (*terrible*) ужа́сный, стра́шный; (*coll., hideous*) безобра́зный; (*coll., very great*) колосса́льный.
frightfulness ['fraɪtfʊlnɪs] *n.* (*as war policy etc.*) запу́гивание, устраше́ние.
frigid ['frɪdʒɪd] *adj.* **1.** (*cold*) холо́дный; ~ **zone** аркти́ческий по́яс. **2.** (*unfeeling*) холо́дный, безразли́чный; (*sexually*) холо́дный, фриги́дный.
frigidity [,frɪ'dʒɪdɪtɪ] *n.* хо́лодность, фриги́дность.
frill [frɪl] *n.* обо́рочка; сбо́рки (*f. pl.*); **~s** (*fig.*) выкрута́с|ы (*pl., g.* -ов); **put on ~s** лома́ться (*impf.*); мане́рничать (*impf.*).
v.t.: **a ~ed skirt** ю́бка с обо́рочками.
frilly ['frɪlɪ] *adj.* с обо́рочками.
fringe [frɪndʒ] *n.* **1.** (*ornamental border*) бахрома́. **2.** (*of hair*) чёлка. **3.** (*fig., edge, margin*) край, кайма́; ~ **benefits** дополни́тельные льго́ты (*f. pl.*).
v.t. окайм|ля́ть, -и́ть.
frippery ['frɪpərɪ] *n.* мишура́, дешёвые украше́ния; безделу́шки (*f. pl.*).
Frisian ['frɪzɪən] *n.* (*pers.*) фриз (*fem.* -ка); (*language*) фри́зский язы́к.
adj. фри́зский.
frisk[1] [frɪsk] *v.t.* (*US coll., search*) обы́ск|ивать, -а́ть.
frisk[2] [frɪsk] *v.i.* резви́ться (*impf.*); пры́гать (*impf.*).
frisky ['frɪskɪ] *adj.* ре́звый, игри́вый.
fritter[1] ['frɪtə(r)] *n.* (*cul.*) ≃ ола́дья.
fritter[2] ['frɪtə(r)] *v.t.*: ~ **away** транжи́рить, рас-; ~ **one's time away** по́пусту тра́тить (*impf.*) вре́мя.
frivol ['frɪv(ə)l] (*coll.*) *v.i.* дура́читься (*impf.*).
frivolity [,frɪ'vɒlɪtɪ] *n.* (*behaviour*) легкомы́слие; (*object*) пустя́к.
frivolous ['frɪvələs] *adj.* (*of object*) пустя́чный; (*of pers.*) легкомы́сленный, пусто́й.
frivolousness ['frɪvələsnɪs] *n.* легкомы́сленность.
frizz [frɪz] *n.* (*of hair*) ку́дри (*f. pl.*).
v.t. зав|ива́ть, -и́ть.
frizzle[1] ['frɪz(ə)l] *n.* (*of hair*) ме́лкая зави́вка.
v.t. & *i.* зав|ива́ть(ся), -и́ть(ся).
frizzle[2] ['frɪz(ə)l] *v.t.* & *i.* (*fry etc.*) жа́рить(ся) (*impf.*) с шипе́нием; **the bacon is all ~d up** беко́н пережа́рен.
frizzy ['frɪzɪ] *adj.* вью́щийся, курча́вый.
fro [frəʊ] *adv.*: **to and ~** взад и вперёд.
frock [frɒk] *n.* пла́тье; **party ~** вече́рнее пла́тье.
cpd. **~-coat** *n.* сюрту́к.
frog[1] [frɒg] *n.* **1.** (*zool.*) лягу́шка; **I've got a ~ in my throat** я охри́п. **2.** (**F~**: *sl., Frenchman*) францу́зик.
cpds. **~man** *n.* легководола́з; **~-march** *v.t.* тащи́ть (*impf.*) за́ руки и за́ ноги лицо́м вниз; **~-spawn** *n.* лягуша́чья икра́.
frog[2] [frɒg] *n.* (*belt attachment for bayonet etc.*) петля́, крючо́к (для холо́дного ору́жия); (*coat fastening*) застёжка из тесьмы́/сутажа́.

frog[3] [frɒg] *n.* (*rail.*) крестови́на стре́лочного перево́да.
Froggy ['frɒgɪ] *n.* (*sl.*) францу́зик.
frolic ['frɒlɪk] *n.* ша́лость; весе́лье, ре́звость.
v.i. шали́ть (*impf.*); резви́ться (*impf.*).
frolicsome ['frɒlɪksəm] *adj.* шаловли́вый, ре́звый.
from [frəm, frɒm] *prep.* **1.** (*denoting origin of movement, measurement or distance*): **the train ~ London to Paris** по́езд из Ло́ндона в Пари́ж; **guests ~ the Ukraine** го́сти с Украи́ны; **where is he ~?** отку́да он? (*родом и т.п.*); **10 miles ~ here** в десяти́ ми́лях отсю́да; **we are 2 hours' journey ~ there** мы в двух часа́х пути́ отту́да; **~ the beginning of the book** с нача́ла кни́ги; **~ cradle to grave** от колыбе́ли до моги́лы; **the lamp hung ~ the ceiling** ла́мпа свиса́ла с потолка́; **she rose ~ the piano** она́ вста́ла из-за роя́ля; **extracts ~ a novel** отры́вки из рома́на; **bark ~ a tree** кора́ с де́рева; **~ end to end** от одного́ конца́ до друго́го; **~ the bottom** со дна; **~ the top** све́рху; **~ my point of view** с мое́й то́чки зре́ния; **far ~ it!** отню́дь!; во́все нет! **2.** (*expr. separation*): **I took the key ~ him** я взял у него́ ключ; **part ~ s.o.** расст|ава́ться, -а́ться с кем-н.; **hide ~** пря́таться, с- от+*g.*; **saved ~ death** спасённый от сме́рти; **released ~ prison** вы́пущенный из тюрьмы́. **3.** (*denoting personal origin*): **a letter ~ my son** письмо́ от моего́ сы́на; **tell him ~ me** переда́йте ему́ от меня́; **she is ~ a good family** она́ из хоро́шей семьи́. **4.** (*expr. material origin*): **wine is made ~ grapes** вино́ де́лается из виногра́да. **5.** (*expr. origin in time*): **~ the very beginning** с са́мого нача́ла; **~ beginning to end** с нача́ла до конца́; **blind ~ birth** слепо́й от приро́ды; **~ childhood** с де́тства; **~ the age of seven** с семиле́тнего во́зраста; **~ now on** с э́того моме́нта; **~ dusk to dawn** от зари́ до зари́; **~ day to day** изо дня в день; со дня на́ день; **~ February to October** с февраля́ по октя́брь; **~ spring to autumn** с весны́ до о́сени; **~ time to time** вре́мя от вре́мени. **6.** (*expr. source or model*): **I see ~ the papers that ...** я зна́ю из газе́т, что...; **he quoted ~ memory** он цити́ровал по па́мяти; **judging ~ appearances** су́дя по вне́шности (*or* вне́шнему ви́ду); **he spoke ~ the heart** он говори́л от души́; **~ mouth to mouth** из уст в уста́; **paint ~ nature** писа́ть (*impf.*) с нату́ры; **change ~ a rouble** сда́ча с рубля́. **7.** (*expr. cause*) от/с+*g.*; **~ grief** с го́ря; **suffer ~ arthritis** страда́ть (*impf.*) артри́том; **die ~ poisoning** ум|ира́ть, -ере́ть от отравле́ния; **~ jealousy** из ре́вности; **~ the best of motives** из лу́чших побужде́ний; **he drinks ~ boredom** он пьёт от/со ску́ки. **8.** (*expr. difference*): **I can't tell him ~ his brother** я не могу́ отличи́ть его́ от его́ бра́та; **they live differently ~ us** они́ живу́т не так как мы. **9.** (*expr. change*): **things went ~ bad to worse** де́ло шло всё ху́же и ху́же; **~ being a nonentity, he became famous** из ничто́жества он преврати́лся в знамени́тость. **10.** (*with numbers*): **~ 1 to 10** от одного́ до десяти́; **it will last ~ 10 to 15 days** э́то продли́тся 10-15 дней; **~ 15 August to 10 September** с пятна́дцатого а́вгуста по деся́тое сентября́; **they cost ~ £5 (upwards)** они́ сто́ят 5 фу́нтов и вы́ше. **11.** (*with advs.*): **~ above** све́рху; **~ below** сни́зу; **~ inside** изнутри́; **~ outside** снару́жи; **~ afar** издалека́; **~ over the sea** из-за мо́ря; **~ under the table** из-под стола́; **~ of old** с да́вних времён; и́здавна.
frond [frɒnd] *n.* ва́йя; ветвь с ли́стьями.
front [frʌnt] *n.* **1.** (*foremost side or part*) перёд; пере́дняя сторона́; **he walked in ~ of the procession** он шёл впереди́ проце́ссии; **in ~ of the house** пе́ред до́мом; **at the ~ of the house** в пере́дней ча́сти до́ма; **in ~ of the children** при де́тях; **she sat at the ~ of the class** она́ сиде́ла на пере́дней па́рте; **back to ~** за́дом наперёд; **in the ~ of the book** в нача́ле кни́ги. **2.** (*archit.*) фаса́д. **3.** (*fighting line*) фронт; **he was sent to the ~** его́ посла́ли на фронт; **on all ~s** на всех фронта́х; **in the ~ line** на передово́й ли́нии; **popular ~** (*pol.*) наро́дный фронт; **present a united ~** вы́ступить (*pf.*) еди́ным фро́нтом. **4.** (*road bordering sea*) на́бережная. **5.** (*meteor.*) фронт. **6.** (*shirt-~*) накрахма́ленная мани́шка. **7.** (*face, in fig. senses*): **put on a bold ~** напус|ка́ть, -ти́ть на себя́ хра́брый вид; **have the ~ to** име́ть (*impf.*) на́глость (*сделать что-н.*). **8.** (*cover*): **~ (organization)** организа́ция, слу́жащая вы́веской (для чего́-н.). **9.** (*attr.*): **~ benches** (*pol.*) скамьи́ для мини́стров и ли́деров оппози́ции в парла́менте; **~ door** пара́дная дверь; **~ garden** сад пе́ред до́мом; палиса́дник; **~ page** пе́рвая страни́ца/полоса́; **~ page news** основны́е но́вости в газе́те; **in the ~ rank** (*fig.*) в пе́рвых ряда́х; **~ vowels** гла́сные пере́днего ря́да; **we had ~ seats** мы сиде́ли в пе́рвых ряда́х.
v.t. **1.** (*face on to*) выходи́ть (*impf.*) на+*a.*; быть обращённым к+*d.* **2.** (*confront*) стоя́ть (*impf.*) лицо́м к+*d.* **3.: ~ed with stone** облицо́ванный ка́мнем. **4.: double-~ed house** дом с двумя́ вхо́дами.
frontage ['frʌntɪdʒ] *n.* (*of building*) пере́дний фаса́д.
frontal ['frʌnt(ə)l] *adj.* лобово́й; (*mil.*) фронта́льный.
frontier ['frʌntɪə(r), -'tɪə(r)] *n.* грани́ца; (*fig.*) грани́ца, преде́л; **~s of knowledge** преде́лы зна́ний.
adj. пограни́чный.
frontiersman ['frʌntɪəzmən, -'tɪəzmən] *n.* жи́тель (*m.*) пограни́чной полосы́.
frontispiece ['frʌntɪsˌpiːs] *n.* фронтиспи́с.
frost [frɒst] *n.* **1.** моро́з; **ten degrees of ~** де́сять гра́дусов моро́за; **black ~** моро́з без и́нея; **hard, sharp ~** си́льный моро́з; **hoar, white ~** моро́з с и́неем; **Jack F~** ≃ Моро́з Кра́сный Нос; **the ~ has got my beans** мои́ бобы́ прихва́чены моро́зом. **2.** (*sl., fiasco*) прова́л.
v.t.: **the windows were ~ed over** о́кна замёрзли; (*fig.*): **~ a cake** покр|ыва́ть, -ы́ть торт глазу́рью; **~ed glass** ма́товое стекло́.
cpds. **~-bite** *n.* отмороже́ние, обмороже́ние; **~-bitten** *adj.* обморо́женный; **~-bound** *adj.* ско́ванный моро́зом.
frosting ['frɒstɪŋ] *n.* (*cul.*) глазу́рь.
frosty ['frɒstɪ] *adj.* моро́зный; (*fig., unfriendly*) холо́дный, ледяно́й.
froth [frɒθ] *n.* пе́на; (*fig.*) чепуха́, болтовня́.
v.t. сби|ва́ть, -ть в пе́ну.
v.i. пе́ниться (*impf.*); **~ at the mouth** бры́згать (*impf.*) слюно́й; **the milk ~ed up** молоко́ подняло́сь.
frothy ['frɒθɪ] *adj.* пе́нистый; (*fig.*) пусто́й.
frou-frou ['fruːfruː] *n.* шурша́ние.
froward ['frəʊəd] *adj.* (*arch.*) вздо́рный, непоко́рный.
frown [fraʊn] *n.* хму́рый взгляд.
v.i. хму́риться, на-; **the authorities ~ on gambling** вла́сти неодобри́тельно отно́сятся к аза́ртным и́грам.
frowst [fraʊst] *n.* (*coll.*) спёртый во́здух.
v.i. (*coll.*) сиде́ть (*impf.*) в духоте́.
frowsty ['fraʊstɪ] *adj.* спёртый, за́тхлый.
frowzy ['fraʊzɪ] *adj.* (*fusty*) спёртый, за́тхлый; (*slatternly*) неря́шливый.
frozen ['frəʊz(ə)n] *adj.* замёрзший, засты́вший; (*icebound*) ско́ванный льдом; (*fig.*): **~ smile** засты́вшая улы́бка.
FRS (*abbr. of* **Fellow of the Royal Society**) член Короле́вского о́бщества.
fructify ['frʌktɪˌfaɪ] *v.i.* прин|оси́ть, -ести́ плоды́; (*of money*) приноси́ть (*impf.*) дохо́д.
frugal ['fruːg(ə)l] *adj.* (*of pers.*) бережли́вый; **a ~ meal** ску́дная еда́.
frugality [ˌfruː'gælɪtɪ] *n.* бережли́вость.
frugivorous [fruː'dʒɪvərəs] *adj.* плодоя́дный.
fruit [fruːt] *n.* **1.** (*class of food*) фрукт; **dried ~** сухофру́кты; **soft ~** плоды́ (*m. pl.*) фрукто́вых дере́вьев; **forbidden ~** (*fig.*) запре́тный плод. **2.** (*bot.*) плод. **3.** (*vegetable products*) плоды́, фру́кты; **the ~s of the earth** плоды́ земли́. **4.** (*offspring*): **the ~ of his loins** (*of her womb*) плод его́ чресл (её чре́ва). **5.** (*fig., result, reward*) плод; **this book is the ~ of long research** э́та кни́га — плод дли́тельных иссле́дований; **enjoy the ~s of one's labours** наслажда́ться (*impf.*) плода́ми свои́х трудо́в.
cpds. **~-cake** *n.* фрукто́вый торт; **~-drop** *n.* ледене́ц; **~-grower** *n.* плодово́д; **~-growing** *n.* плодово́дство; **~-juice** *n.* фрукто́вый сок; **~-knife** *n.* фрукто́вый нож; **~-salad** *n.* сала́т из сыры́х фру́ктов; **~-tree** *n.* фрукто́вое де́рево.
fruitarian [fruː'teərɪən] *n.* челове́к, пита́ющийся исключи́тельно фру́ктами; фрукто́ед.
fruiterer ['fruːtərə(r)] *n.* торго́вец фру́ктами.
fruitful ['fruːtfʊl] *adj.* (*of soil*) плодоро́дный; (*fig.*)

плодотво́рный, тво́рческий.

fruitfulness ['fru:tfʊlnɪs] *n.* плодоро́дие, плодотво́рность.

fruition [fru:'ɪʃ(ə)n] *n.* (*realization*) осуществле́ние; **come to** ~ осуществ|ля́ться, -и́ться; сб|ыва́ться, -ы́ться.

fruitless ['fru:tlɪs] *adj.* (*lit.*, *fig.*) беспло́дный.

fruity ['fru:tɪ] *adj.* фрукто́вый; напомина́ющий фру́кты; (*fig.*) пика́нтный, сканда́льный; (*of voice*) со́чный, зву́чный.

frump [frʌmp] *n.* старомо́дно и пло́хо оде́тая же́нщина.

frump|ish ['frʌmpɪʃ], **-y** ['frʌmpɪ] *adjs.* старомо́дно оде́тый.

frustrate [frʌ'streɪt, 'frʌs-] *v.t.* разочаро́в|ывать, -а́ть; расстр|а́ивать, -о́ить (*планы*); **I feel ~d** я обескура́жен.

frustration [frʌ'streɪʃ(ə)n] *n.* **1.** (*thwarting*) круше́ние (*планов/надежд*). **2.** (*disappointment*) разочарова́ние; **sense of** ~ чу́вство безысхо́дности. **3.** (*psych.*) фрустра́ция.

frustum ['frʌstəm] *n.* усечённая пирами́да; усечённый ко́нус.

fry[1] [fraɪ] *n.* (*fish*) мальк|и́ (*pl.*, *g.* -о́в); **small** ~ (*fig.*) мелюзга́; ме́лкая со́шка.

fry[2] [fraɪ] *n.* (*fried food*) жа́реное мя́со; жа́реная ры́ба.

v.t. жа́рить, за-/из-; **I have other fish to** ~ у меня́ други́е забо́ты; **~ing-pan** сковорода́; **out of the ~ing-pan into the fire** из огня́ да в по́лымя.

v.i. жа́риться (*impf.*).

fuchsia ['fju:ʃə] *n.* фу́ксия.

fuck [fʌk] (*vulg.*) *n.*: **he doesn't give a** ~ ему́ насра́ть.

v.t. & i. еть/ети́, у-; ~ **off!** отъеби́сь (от меня́)!; пошёл на́ хуй!

fucking ['fʌkɪŋ] *n.* ёбля (*vulg.*).

adj. (*expletive*) ёбаный.

fuddle ['fʌd(ə)l] *v.t.* подп|а́ивать, -ои́ть; (*stupefy*) одурма́ни|вать, -ть.

fuddy-duddy ['fʌdɪ,dʌdɪ] *n.* and *adj.* устаре́лый, с устаре́вшими взгля́дами.

fudge[1] [fʌdʒ] *n. & int.* (*nonsense*) чепуха́, вздор.

fudge[2] [fʌdʒ] *n.* (*sweetmeat*) сли́вочная пома́дка.

fudge[3] [fʌdʒ] *v.t. & i.*: ~ **accounts** подде́л|ывать, -ать счета́; ~ **up an excuse** вы́думать (*pf.*) предло́г.

fuel ['fju:əl] *n.* то́пливо, горю́чее; ~ **cock** кран, регули́рующий пода́чу горю́чего; ~ **gauge** бензиноме́р; то́пливный расходоме́р; ~ **oil** мазу́т; ~ **pump** бензопо́мпа; **add ~ to the flames** подл|ива́ть, -и́ть ма́сла в ого́нь; **smokeless ~s** безды́мное то́пливо; **lighter** ~ бензи́н/газ для зажига́лок.

v.t. снаб|жа́ть, -ди́ть то́пливом; запр|авля́ть, -а́вить горю́чим.

v.i. запр|авля́ться, -а́виться горю́чим.

fug [fʌg] *n.* (*coll.*) духота́; спёртый во́здух.

fugal ['fju:g(ə)l] *adj.* фу́говый.

fugato [fjʊ'gɑ:təʊ] *n. & adv.* фуга́то (*indecl.*).

fugitive ['fju:dʒɪtɪv] *n.* бегле́ц; **a ~ from justice** лицо́, скрыва́ющееся от правосу́дия.

adj. (*runaway*) бе́глый; (*fleeting*) бе́глый, мимолётный.

fugue [fju:g] *n.* фу́га.

Führer ['fjʊərə(r)] *n.* фю́рер.

fulcrum ['fʊlkrəm, 'fʌl-] *n.* то́чка опо́ры; то́чка приложе́ния си́лы.

fulfil [fʊl'fɪl] *v.t.* выполня́ть, вы́полнить; исп|олня́ть, -о́лнить; ~ **a task** выполня́ть, вы́полнить зада́чу; ~ **all expectations** опра́вд|ывать, -а́ть все ожида́ния.

fulfilment [fʊl'fɪl mənt] *n.* (*accomplishment*) выполне́ние, исполне́ние; осуществле́ние; (*satisfaction*) удовлетворе́ние.

full [fʊl] *n.* **1.** (*entirety, complete state*) полнота́; **the moon is past the** ~ луна́ пошла́ на у́быль; луна́ на уще́рбе. **2.** (*limit*): **enjoy sth. to the** ~ в по́лной ме́ре наслажда́ться (*impf.*) чем-н.

adj. **1.** (*filled to capacity*) по́лный; ~ **to the brim** (*or* **to overflowing**) по́лный до краёв; **the hotel is ~ (up)** все ко́мнаты в гости́нице за́няты; **he ate till he was ~ (up)** он нае́лся до отва́ла; **my heart is too ~ for words** нет слов, что́бы вы́разить переполня́ющие меня́ чу́вства; ~ **house** (*theatr.*) все биле́ты про́даны; аншла́г; (*having plenty*): ~ **of ideas** по́лон иде́й/за́мыслов; ~ **of life** жизнера́достный; по́лон жи́зни; (*thinking or talking only*): ~ **of o.s.** за́нят одни́м собо́й; **she's very ~ of herself** она́ уж о́чень мно́го о себе́ мнит/вообража́ет. **2.** (*copious*) подро́бный; **he gave ~ details** он сообщи́л все подро́бности. **3.** (*complete; whole; reaching the limit*): **the radio was going ~ blast** ра́дио бы́ло включено́ на по́лную мо́щность; **in ~ bloom** в по́лном цвету́; ~ **brother** родно́й брат; ~ **dress** костю́м для торже́ственных слу́чаев; пара́дная фо́рма; **the ~ effect of the medicine** по́лное де́йствие лека́рства; ~ **face view** вид спе́реди; **at ~ gallop** на по́лном скаку́; **we waited a ~ hour** мы жда́ли це́лый час; **he lay at ~ length** он растяну́лся во весь рост; ~ **moon** полнолу́ние; **on ~ pay** на по́лной ста́вке; ~ **professor** ордина́рный профе́ссор; **at ~ speed** на по́лной ско́рости; ~ **steam ahead!** по́лный вперёд!; ~ **stop** то́чка; **he came to a ~ stop** он останови́лся; **in ~ swing** в по́лном разга́ре; **he ran ~ tilt into me** он так и налете́л на меня́. **4.** (*plump*) по́лный; ~ **in the face** круглоли́цый. **5.** (*amply fitting*) широ́кий; **a ~ skirt** пы́шная ю́бка.

adv. **1.** (*arch., very*): **you know ~ well** вы са́ми прекра́сно зна́ете; вам прекра́сно изве́стно; ~ **many a time** уж мно́го раз. **2.** (*completely*): **she turned the radio on ~** она́ включи́ла ра́дио на по́лную мо́щность; ~ **out** по́лностью. **3.** (*squarely*) пря́мо; **he took the blow ~ in the face** уда́р пришёлся ему́ пря́мо в лицо́.

cpds. **~-back** *n.* защи́тник; **~-blooded** *adj.* полнокро́вный; **~-blown** *adj.* распусти́вшийся; (*fig.*) зре́лый; самостоя́тельный; **~-bodied** *adj.* кре́пкий; **~-bottomed** *adj.*: **~-bottomed wig** дли́нный пари́к; **~-dress** *adj.*: **~-dress uniform** пара́дная фо́рма; (*fig.*) тща́тельно подгото́вленный; обстоя́тельный; по всей фо́рме; **~-face** *adv.* анфа́с; **~-fledged** *adj.* вполне́ опери́вшийся; (*fig.*) зако́нченный; полнопра́вный; **~-grown** *adj.* взро́слый; **~-hearted** *adj.* безоговоро́чный; от всего́ се́рдца; **~-length** *adj.* во всю длину́; **~-length dress** пла́тье до́ полу; **~-length play** многоа́ктная пье́са; **~-page** *adj.* во всю страни́цу; **~-scale** *adj.* в по́лном объёме; **~-time** *adj.* (*of job*) занима́ющий всё (рабо́чее) вре́мя; **~-timer** *n.* рабо́чий, за́нятый по́лную рабо́чую неде́лю.

fuller ['fʊlə(r)] *n.* (*craftsman*) валя́льщик, сукнова́л; **~'s earth** сукнова́льная/валя́льная гли́на.

ful(l)ness ['fʊlnɪs] *n.* **1.** (*full state*) полнота́. **2.** (*sense of repletion*) сы́тость. **3.**: **in the ~ of time** в надлежа́щее вре́мя.

fully ['fʊlɪ] *adv.* вполне́, по́лностью, соверше́нно, до конца́; ~ **satisfied** по́лностью удовлетворённый; **it will take ~ five hours** э́то займёт це́лых пять часо́в.

cpds. **~-clothed** *adj.* по́лностью оде́тый; **~-fashioned** *adj.*: **~-fashioned stockings** чулки́ со швом.

fulmar ['fʊlmə(r)] *n.* глупы́ш (*птица*).

fulminate ['fʌlmɪ,neɪt, 'fʊl-] *n.*: ~ **of mercury** грему́чая ртуть.

v.i. (*flash*) сверк|а́ть, -ну́ть; (*fig., protest vehemently*) громи́ть (*impf.*); мета́ть (*impf.*) гро́мы и мо́лнии.

fulmination [,fʌlmɪ'neɪʃ(ə)n, ,fʊl-] *n.* (*fig.*) я́ростный проте́ст, инвекти́ва.

fulness ['fʊlnɪs] = **ful(l)ness**

fulsome ['fʊlsəm] *adj.* чрезме́рный, при́торный, тошнотво́рный.

fumble ['fʌmb(ə)l] *v.t.* теребить (*impf.*) в рука́х; ~ **a ball** упусти́ть (*pf.*) мяч.

v.i. ры́ться (*impf.*); копа́ться (*impf.*); неуме́ло обраща́ться (*impf.*) (*с чем-н.*); **he ~d in his pockets for a key** он ры́лся в карма́нах, ища́ ключ.

fumbler ['fʌmblə(r)] *n.* растя́па (*c.g.*).

fume [fju:m] *n.* дым, ко́поть; **~s of wine** ви́нные пары́ (*m. pl.*); **he was overcome by ~s** он потеря́л созна́ние от уду́шливых испаре́ний.

v.t. оку́р|ивать, -и́ть; копти́ть, за-; **~d oak** морёный дуб.

v.i. (*fig.*): **fuming with rage** кипя́щий гне́вом.

fumigate ['fju:mɪ,geɪt] *v.t.* оку́р|ивать, -и́ть.

fumigation [,fju:mɪ'geɪʃ(ə)n] *n.* оку́ривание.

fumitory ['fju:mɪtərɪ] *n.* дымя́нка.

fun [fʌn] *n.* шу́тка, весе́лье, заба́ва, (*coll.*) хо́хма; **it was only meant in ~** э́то была́ шу́тка; **just for the ~ of it** про́сто ра́ди удово́льствия; **he never has any ~** он никогда́ не весели́тся/развлека́ется; **make ~ of, poke ~ at** насмеха́ться (*impf.*) над+*i.*; **he is ~ to be with** с ним не соску́чишься; **it's no ~ walking in the rain** что за удово́льствие броди́ть под дождём!; **what ~!** вот здо́рово!; как ве́село!; **when my father finds out there will be ~ and games** когда́ оте́ц узна́ет об э́том, вот бу́дет поте́ха; **figure of ~** предме́т насме́шек; **we had ~ at the party** в гостя́х бы́ло ве́село.

cpds. **~-fair** *n.* увесели́тельный парк; **~-run** *n.* джо́ггинг; **~-runner** *n.* бегу́н-люби́тель.

funambulist [fju:'næmbjʊlɪst] *n.* канатохо́дец.

function ['fʌŋkʃ(ə)n] *n.* **1.** (*proper activity, purpose*) фу́нкция, назначе́ние. **2.** (*social gathering*) ве́чер; приём. **3.** (*math.*) фу́нкция.

v.i. функциони́ровать, де́йствовать (*both impf.*).

functional ['fʌŋkʃən(ə)l] *adj.* функциона́льный.

functionary ['fʌŋkʃənərɪ] *n.* должностно́е лицо́; чино́вник.

fund [fʌnd] *n.* фонд, запа́с, резе́рв; **a ~ of common sense** запа́с здра́вого смы́сла; (*sum of money*) фонд, капита́л; **relief ~** фонд по́мощи; **sinking ~** амортизацио́нный фонд; (*pl., resources*) фо́нды (*m. pl.*); де́нежные сре́дства; **public ~s** госуда́рственные сре́дства; **money in the ~s** де́ньги в госуда́рственных бума́гах; **he is in ~s** он при деньга́х.

v.t. консолиди́ровать (*impf., pf.*); фунди́ровать (*impf., pf.*); финанси́ровать (*impf., pf.*).

cpd. **~-raising** *n.* сбор средств; **a ~-raising appeal** объявле́ние о сбо́ре средств; **a ~-raising dinner** (*for charity*) благотвори́тельный банке́т.

fundament ['fʌndəmənt] *n.* зад, я́годицы (*f. pl.*).

fundamental [,fʌndə'ment(ə)l] *n.* **1.** (*usu. pl., principle*) осно́ва, при́нцип; **the ~s of mathematics** осно́вы матема́тики. **2.** (*mus.*) основно́й тон.

adj. **1.** (*basic*) основно́й, суще́ственный; **~ly** в основно́м; по существу́. **2.** (*mus.*) основно́й.

funeral ['fju:nər(ə)l] *n.* по́хор|оны (*pl., g.* -о́н); **that's your ~!** э́то ва́ша забо́та!; **~ expenses** расхо́ды на по́хороны; **~ march** похоро́нный марш; **~ parlour, home** (*US*) бюро́ похоро́нных проце́ссий; **~ pyre** погреба́льный костёр; **~ rites** похоро́нный обря́д.

funereal [fju:'nɪərɪəl] *adj.* мра́чный, безотра́дный; тра́урный.

fungicide ['fʌndʒɪ,saɪd] *n.* фунгици́д.

fungoid ['fʌŋgɔɪd] *adj.* грибови́дный, грибообра́зный.

fungus ['fʌŋgəs] *n.* грибо́к; ни́зший гриб.

funicular [fju:'nɪkjʊlə(r)] *n.* фуникулёр; кана́тная (желе́зная) доро́га.

adj. кана́тный.

funk [fʌŋk] (*coll.*) *n.* **1.** (*fear*) страх; **in a (blue) ~** в у́жасе. **2.** (*coward*) трус.

v.t.: **he ~ed the contest** он увильну́л от уча́стия в соревнова́ниях.

v.i. тру́сить, с-.

funnel ['fʌn(ə)l] *n.* воро́нка; (*of ship*) дымова́я труба́.

v.t. лить (*impf.*) че́рез воро́нку; (*fig.*): **applications are ~ed through this office** заявле́ния направля́ются че́рез э́ту конто́ру.

funny ['fʌnɪ] *adj.* **1.** (*amusing*) смешно́й, заба́вный, поте́шный; **no ~ business!** без фо́кусов!; **~ man** (*clown*) остря́к. **2.** (*strange*) стра́нный; **I have a ~ feeling you're right!** у меня́ стра́нное чу́вство, что вы пра́вы; **it's a ~ thing, but ...** э́то о́чень стра́нно, но...; **funnily enough I never met him** как э́то ни стра́нно, я никогда́ не встреча́лся с ним; **~ farm** (*mental hospital*) психу́шка.

cpd. **~-bone** *n.* вну́тренний мы́щелок плечево́й кости́, локтево́й суста́в.

fur [fɜ:(r)] *n.* **1.** (*animal hair*) шерсть; **make the ~ fly** подня́ть (*pf.*) бу́чу; **~ and feather** пушно́й зверь и пти́ца. **2.** (*as worn*) мех (*pl.* -а́); **a fox ~** ли́сий мех; **~ coat** мехово́е пальто́; мехова́я шу́ба; **~ farm** зверофе́рма; **~ farmer** зверово́д; **~ farming** зверово́дство. **3.** (*coating of tongue*) налёт. **4.** (*deposit on kettle*) на́кипь.

v.t.: **~red tongue** обло́женный язы́к; **~red kettle** ча́йник, покры́тый на́кипью.

cpd. **~-bearing** *adj.* пушно́й; **~-seal** *n.* ко́тик.

furbelow ['fɜ:bɪ,ləʊ] *n.* обо́рка, фалбала́; **frills and ~s** тря́пки (*f. pl.*).

furbish ['fɜ:bɪʃ] *v.t.* полирова́ть, от-; поднов|ля́ть, -и́ть.

furious ['fjʊərɪəs] *adj.* **1.** (*violent*) бу́йный, неи́стовый; **the fun was fast and ~** весе́лье бы́ло бу́йным; **a ~ struggle** я́ростная схва́тка; **drive at a ~ pace** е́хать (*det.*) на бе́шеной ско́рости. **2.** (*enraged*) взбешённый; **it makes me ~ to hear him abused** меня́ бе́сит, когда́ я слы́шу, как его́ поно́сят; **she was ~ with him** она́ разозли́лась на него́ не на шу́тку.

furl [fɜ:l] *v.t.* (*sails*) свёр|тывать, -ну́ть; (*umbrella*) скла́дывать, сложи́ть.

furlong ['fɜ:lɒŋ] *n.* восьма́я часть ми́ли.

furlough ['fɜ:ləʊ] *n.* о́тпуск; **on ~** в отпуску́, в о́тпуске.

furnace ['fɜ:nɪs] *n.* горн, оча́г, печь, то́пка; **blast ~** до́менная печь; до́мна.

furnish ['fɜ:nɪʃ] *v.t.* **1.** (*provide*) снаб|жа́ть, -ди́ть (*кого чем*); предост|авля́ть, -а́вить (*что кому*). **2.** (*equip with furniture*) обст|авля́ть, -а́вить; **fully ~ed house** по́лностью обста́вленный дом; **~ed apartment** меблиро́ванная кварти́ра.

furnishings ['fɜ:nɪʃɪŋz] *n.* принадле́жности (*f. pl.*); (*furniture*) обстано́вка.

furniture ['fɜ:nɪtʃə(r)] *n.* ме́бель; **~ polish** политу́ра/лак для ме́бели; **~ removers** аге́нтство по перево́зке ме́бели; **~ van** автофурго́н для перево́зки ме́бели; (*fig., trappings*) украше́ния (*nt. pl.*).

furore [fjʊə'rɔ:rɪ] *n.* фуро́р.

furrier ['fʌrɪə(r)] *n.* мехови́к, скорня́к.

furrow ['fʌrəʊ] *n.* **1.** (*in the earth etc.*) борозда́, жёлоб; **plough a lonely ~** (*fig.*) де́йствовать (*impf.*) в одино́чку. **2.** (*wrinkle*) глубо́кая морщи́на.

v.t. борозди́ть, вз-; (*fig.*): **~ed brow** морщи́нистый лоб.

furry ['fɜ:rɪ] *adj.* покры́тый ме́хом; пушно́й.

further ['fɜ:ðə(r)] *adj.* (*see also* **farther**) **1.** дальне́йший; (*additional*) доба́вочный, дополни́тельный; **until ~ notice** до дальне́йшего уведомле́ния; **without ~ ado** без ли́шних хлопо́т; **we need ~ proof** нам необходи́мы дополни́тельные доказа́тельства; **we need a ~ five pounds** нам ну́жно ещё пять фу́нтов. **2.** (*more distant*) да́льний; **on the ~ side** на друго́й стороне́; по ту сто́рону.

adv. **1.** (*additionally*) в дополне́ние; **~ to my last letter** в дополне́ние к моему́ после́днему письму́. **2.** (*to or at a more distant point*) да́лее, да́льше; **I can go no ~** я не могу́ да́льше идти́; **I'll go ~ than that, he's a liar** бо́лее того́, он лгун; **we need look no ~** смотре́ть да́льше не́чего. **3.** (*moreover*) бо́лее того́. **4.** (*euph.*): **I'll see him ~ first** ≃ как бы не та́к!

v.t. продв|ига́ть, -и́нуть; соде́йствовать (*impf.*) +*d.*; спосо́бствовать (*impf.*) +*d.*

furtherance ['fɜ:ðərəns] *n.* продвиже́ние; соде́йствие (*чему*); **in ~ of this plan** для осуществле́ния э́того пла́на.

furthermore [,fɜ:ðə'mɔ:(r)] *adv.* к тому́ же; кро́ме того́.

furthermost ['fɜ:ðə,məʊst] *adj.* са́мый да́льний/отдалённый.

furthest ['fɜ:ðɪst] *adj.* са́мый да́льний.

adv. да́льше всего́; **the ~ I can go is to say that ...** са́мое бо́льшее, что я могу́ сказа́ть, э́то то, что...

furtive ['fɜ:tɪv] *adj.* (*of movements*) краду́щийся; та́йный; скры́тый; (*of a pers.*) скры́тный.

furtiveness ['fɜ:tɪvnɪs] *n.* скры́тность.

fury ['fjʊərɪ] *n.* **1.** (*violence*) неи́стовство, я́рость, бе́шенство; **the ~ of the elements** я́рость стихи́й. **2.** (*fit of anger*) я́рость; **she flew into a ~** она́ пришла́ в я́рость. **3.** (**F~**: *myth.*) фу́рия. **4.** (*fig., termagant*) фу́рия.

furze [fɜ:z] *n.* утёсник.

fuse[1] [fju:z] *n.* (*elec.*) предохрани́тель (*m.*), про́бка.

v. t. & i. **1.** (*make or become liquid*) пла́вить(ся) (*impf.*). **2.** (*join by fusion*) спл|авля́ть(ся), -а́вить(ся); (*fig.*) сли|ва́ть(ся), -ть(ся); (*elec.*): **he ~d the lights** он пережёг про́бки; **the lights ~d** про́бки перегоре́ли.

cpds. **~-box** *n.* коро́бка с про́бками; **~-wire** *n.* про́волока для предохрани́теля.

fuse[2], **fuze** [fju:z] *n.* (*igniting device*) запа́л, затра́вка, фити́ль (*m.*); (*detonating device*) заря́дная тру́бка; взрыва́тель (*m.*).

v.t. вст|авля́ть, -а́вить взрыва́тель в+*a*.
fuselage ['fju:zəˌlɑ:ʒ, -lɪdʒ] *n.* фюзеля́ж.
fusible ['fju:zɪb(ə)l] *adj.* пла́вкий.
fusilier [ˌfju:zɪ'lɪə(r), -zə'lɪə(r)] *n.* фузилёр, стрело́к.
fusillade [ˌfju:zɪ'leɪd] *n.* стрельба́.
v.t. обстре́л|ивать, -я́ть.
fusion ['fju:ʒ(ə)n] *n.* **1.** (*melting together*) сплавле́ние, пла́вка; ~ **bomb** термоя́дерная бо́мба. **2.** (*blending, coalition*) сплав, слия́ние.
fuss [fʌs] *n.* сута́, шум (из-за пустяко́в); **cause a lot of ~ and bother** причин|я́ть, -и́ть ма́ссу хлопо́т и забо́т; **get into a ~** разволнова́ться (*pf.*); **make a ~ about, over sth.** суети́ться (*impf.*) вокру́г чего́-н.; **make a ~ of s.o.** суетли́во опека́ть (*impf.*) кого́-н.
v.i. суети́ться (*impf.*); **she ~es over her children** она́ ве́чно во́зится со свои́ми детьми́.
cpd. **~-pot** *n.* (*coll.*) хлопоту́н (*fem.* -ья); суетли́вый челове́к.
fusser ['fʌsə(r)] *n.* суетли́вый челове́к.
fussiness ['fʌsɪnɪs] *n.* суетли́вость.
fussy ['fʌsɪ] *adj.* **1.** (*worrying over trifles*) суетли́вый, беспоко́йный. **2.** (*coll., fastidious*) разбо́рчивый; **I'm not ~ (about) what I eat ~** я не приве́редлив в еде́. **3.** (*of dress, style etc.*) вы́чурный.
fustian ['fʌstɪən] *n.* (*cloth*) бумазе́я, флане́ль; (*bombast*) напы́щенные высокопа́рные ре́чи (*f. pl.*).
fusty ['fʌstɪ] *adj.* (*stale-smelling*) за́тхлый, спёртый; (*fig., old-fashioned*) старомо́дный.
futile ['fju:taɪl] *adj.* напра́сный, тще́тный.
futility [ˌfju:'tɪlɪtɪ] *n.* тще́тность, бесполе́зность.
future ['fju:tʃə(r)] *n.* **1.** бу́дущее; **in (the) ~** в бу́дущем; **for the ~** на бу́дущее; **he has a great ~ before him** у него́ большо́е бу́дущее; ему́ предстои́т блестя́щая бу́дущность; **there's not much ~ in teaching** преподава́ние не обеща́ет блестя́щей карье́ры. **2.** (*gram.*) бу́дущее вре́мя.
adj. бу́дущий; **belief in a ~ life** ве́ра в загро́бную жизнь; (*gram.*): **~ tense** бу́дущее вре́мя; **~ perfect tense** бу́дущее соверше́нное вре́мя.
futureless ['fju:tʃəlɪs] *adj.* без бу́дущего.
futurism ['fju:tʃəˌrɪz(ə)m] *n.* футури́зм.
futurist ['fju:tʃərɪst] *n.* футури́ст.
futuristic [ˌfju:tʃə'rɪstɪk] *adj.* футуристи́ческий.
futurity [fju:'tjʊərɪtɪ] *n.* бу́дущее, бу́дущность.
fuze [fju:z] = **fuse**[2]
fuzz[1] [fʌz] *n.* (*fluffy mass*) пух; (*blur*) мгла.
v.t. (*blur*) затемн|я́ть, -и́ть.
fuzz[2] [fʌz] *n.* (*sl.*): **the ~** мусор|а́ (*pl. g.* -о́в), менту́ра.
fuzzy ['fʌzɪ] *adj.* (*fluffy*) пуши́стый; (*blurred*) расплы́вчатый.

G

G [dʒi:] *n.* (*mus.*) соль (*nt. indecl.*).
cpds. **~-string** *n.* (*cloth etc.*) набе́дренная повя́зка; **~-suit** *n.* противоперегру́зочный костю́м.
g. [græm] *n.* (*abbr. of* **gram(me)(s)**) гм, (грамм).
gab [gæb] (*coll.*) *n.*: **he has the gift of the ~** у него́ язы́к хорошо́ подве́шен.
v.i. трепа́ться (*impf.*); точи́ть (*impf.*) ля́сы (*coll.*).
cpd. **~-fest** *n.* (*US sl.*) трёп, трепотня́.
gabardine, gaberdine ['gæbəˌdi:n, -'di:n] *n.* (*material*) габарди́н; (*attr.*) габарди́новый.
gabble ['gæb(ə)l] *n.* бормота́ние; (*sl.*) трёп, трепотня́.
v.t. & i. бормота́ть, про-; (*of geese*) гогота́ть (*impf.*).
gabbler ['gæblə(r)] *n.* болту́н.
gabby ['gæbɪ] *adj.* (*coll.*) болтли́вый, трепли́вый.
gaberdine ['gæbəˌdi:n, -'di:n] = **gabardine**
gable ['geɪb(ə)l] *n.* щипе́ц; (*pediment*) фронто́н; **~(d) roof** двуска́тная/щипцо́вая кры́ша.
Gabon [gə'bɒn] *n.* Габо́н.
Gabriel ['geɪbrɪəl] *n.* (*bibl.*) Гаврии́л.
gad[1] [gæd] *v.i.* (*also* **~ about**) шля́ться (*impf.*); шата́ться (*impf.*).
cpd. **~about** *n. & adj.* праздношата́ющийся.
gad[2] [gæd] *int.* (*also* **by ~**) вот-те на́!; ей-Бо́гу!
gadfly ['gædflaɪ] *n.* о́вод, слепе́нь (*m.*).
gadget ['gædʒɪt] *n.* (*coll.*) штучка.
gadgetry ['gædʒɪtrɪ] *n.* (*coll.*) техни́ческие нови́нки (*f. pl.*).
Gael [geɪl] *n.* гэл, кельт.
Gaelic ['geɪlɪk, 'gæ-] *n.* (*language*) гэ́льский язы́к.
adj. гэ́льский.
gaff[1] [gæf] *n.* (*spear, stick*) баго́р, острога́.
v.t. багри́ть (*impf.*).
gaff[2] [gæf] *n.*: **blow the ~** (*coll.*) проболта́ться (*pf.*).
gaffe [gæf] *n.* ло́жный шаг, опло́шность.
gaffer ['gæfə(r)] *n.* стари́к, дед; (*foreman*) ма́стер (це́ха).
gag [gæg] *n.* **1.** (*to prevent speech etc.*) кляп; (*surgery*) роторасшири́тель (*m.*); (*parl.*) прекраще́ние пре́ний; (*fig.*): **a ~ on free speech** подавле́ние свобо́ды сло́ва. **2.** (*interpolation*) отсебя́тина. **3.** (*joke*) шу́тка, хо́хма.
v.t. вст|авля́ть, -а́вить кляп +*d.*; (*fig.*) зат|ыка́ть, -кну́ть рот +*d.*; **the press was ~ged** пре́ссу заста́вили замолча́ть.
v.i. (*of actor*) вст|авля́ть, -а́вить отсебя́тину; (*retch, choke*) дави́ться (*impf.*).
cpds. **~-man, ~-writer** *nn.* (*theatr.*) ко́мик; сочини́тель (*m.*) остро́т и шу́ток (*для эстрады и т.п.*).
gaga ['gɑ:gɑ:] *adj.* (*sl.*) чо́кнутый, слабоу́мный; **go ~** впа|да́ть, -сть в мара́зм.
gage [geɪdʒ] *n.* (*pledge*) зало́г; (*fig.*): **throw down one's ~** бро́сить (*pf.*) вы́зов/перча́тку (*кому*). *See also* **gauge**
gaggle ['gæg(ə)l] *n.* (*of geese*) ста́я, ста́до; (*fig., joc.*) ста́йка, толпа́.
gaiety ['geɪətɪ] *n.* (*cheerfulness*) весёлость; (*usu. pl.: entertainment*) увеселе́ния (*nt. pl.*), весе́лье.
gain [geɪn] *n.* **1.** (*profit*) при́быль; вы́года; вы́игрыш; **love of ~** корыстолю́бие. **2.** (*pl., things ~ed*) дохо́ды (*m. pl.*); нажи́ва; (*achievements*) завоева́ния; **ill-gotten ~s** нече́стно на́житое. **3.** (*increase*) увеличе́ние; **a ~ in weight** приба́вка в ве́се; **a ~ to knowledge** расшире́ние зна́ний.
v.t. **1.** (*reach*) доб|ира́ться, -ра́ться до+*g.*; дост|ига́ть, -и́гнуть +*g.*; **the swimmer ~ed the shore** плове́ц дости́г бе́рега. **2.** (*win, acquire*) овлад|ева́ть, -е́ть; доб|ива́ться, -и́ться +*g.*; доб|ыва́ть, -ы́ть; приобре|та́ть, -сти́; **~ one's living** зараба́тывать (*impf.*) на жизнь; **~ a victory** одержа́ть (*pf.*) побе́ду; **~ the upper hand** взять (*pf.*) верх (над+*i.*); **~ time** вы́игр|ывать, вы́играть вре́мя; **~ s.o.'s ear** доб|ива́ться, -и́ться чьего́-н. внима́ния; **~ a friend** приобрести́ (*pf.*) дру́га; **what ~ed him such a reputation?** что со́здало ему́ таку́ю репута́цию?; **he ~ed 5 pounds in weight** он попра́вился на 5 фу́нтов; **the patient is ~ing strength** пацие́нт набира́ется сил. **3.** (*also* **~ over**; *persuade, bring on to one's side*) перемани́ть (*pf.*) на свою́ сто́рону; переубеди́ть (*pf.*).
v.i. **1.** (*reap profit, benefit, advantage*) извл|ека́ть, -е́чь по́льзу/вы́году; **how do I stand to ~ from it?** кака́я мне от э́того по́льза/вы́года?; **he has ~ed in experience** он приобрёл о́пыт. **2.** (*move ahead*): **my watch ~s (three minutes a day)** мои́ часы́ спеша́т (на три мину́ты в день); **he ~ ed on his rival** он нагоня́л сопе́рника; **the sea is ~ing on the land** мо́ре захва́тывает су́шу.
gainer ['geɪnə(r)] *n.*: **he was a ~ by the transaction** он вы́играл на э́той сде́лке.
gainful ['geɪnfʊl] *adj.* при́быльный; дохо́дный; **~ employment** опла́чиваемая рабо́та.
gainings ['geɪnɪŋz] *n.* (*earnings*) за́работок; (*profit*) дохо́д.
gainsa|y [geɪn'seɪ] *v.t.* (*liter.*) противоре́чить (*impf.*) +*d.*; **the facts cannot be ~id** фа́кты неопровержи́мы.
gait [geɪt] *n.* похо́дка.
gaiter ['geɪtə(r)] *n.* гама́ша; (*pl.*) ге́тр|ы (*pl., g.* —).
gaitered ['geɪtəd] *adj.* в гама́шах.

gal [gæl] *n.* (*joc.*) = **girl**

gala ['gɑːlə] *n.* пра́зднество; ~ **day** пра́здничный день; ~ **dress** пара́дный костю́м/туале́т; ~ **night** (*theatr.*) гала́-представле́ние.

galactic [gə'læktɪk] *adj.* галакти́ческий.

galantine ['gælən,tiːn] *n.* заливно́е.

Galatians [gə'leɪʃənz, -ʃɪənz] *n.* (*bibl.*) гала́ты (*m. pl.*).

galaxy ['gæləksɪ] *n.* гала́ктика; (*fig.*) плея́да.

gale [geɪl] *n.* бу́ря; шторм; **it is blowing a** ~ ду́ет штормово́й ве́тер; (*fig.*): ~**s of laughter** взры́вы (*m. pl.*) хо́хота.

Galicia [gə'lɪʃɪə, -'lɪʃə] *n.* (*in Spain*) Гали́сия; (*in Eastern Europe*) Гали́ция.

Galician [gə'lɪʃɪən, -ʃən] *n.* (*in Spain*) галиси́|ец (*fem.* -йка); (*in Eastern Europe*) галича́н|ин (*fem.* -ка).
adj. **1.** галиси́йский. **2.** галици́йский.

Galilean [,gælɪ'liːən] *n.* (*bibl.*) галиле́янин.
adj. (*of Galilee*) галиле́йский; (*of Galileo*): ~ **telescope** телеско́п Галиле́я.

Galilee ['gælɪ,liː] *n.* Галиле́я; **Sea of** ~ Галиле́йское мо́ре.

Galileo [,gælɪ'leɪəʊ] *n.* Галиле́й.

gall[1] [gɔːl] *n.* **1.** жёлчь; (*fig., bitterness*) жёлчность; ~ **and wormwood** нож о́стрый (*fig.*); (*rancour*): **dip one's pen in** ~ писа́ть (*impf.*) жёлчью. **2.** (*coll., impudence*) на́глость.
cpds. ~**-bladder** *n.* жёлчный пузы́рь; ~**stone** *n.* жёлчный ка́мень.

gall[2] [gɔːl] *n.* (*swelling; sore*) потёртость; сса́дина.
v.t. (*lit.*) ссади́ть (*pf.*); нат|ира́ть, -ере́ть; **when I ride my horse the saddle** ~**s his back** когда́ я е́зжу, седло́ натира́ет ло́шади спи́ну; (*fig.*) злить, разо-.

gall[3] [gɔːl] *n.* (*bot.*) галл.
cpd. ~**-fly** *n.* орехотво́рка.

gallant[1] ['gælənt, gə'lænt] *n.* (*ladies' man*) да́мский уго́дник.
adj. (*attentive to ladies*) гала́нтный; (*amatory*) любо́вный.

gallant[2] ['gælənt] *adj.* (*brave*) до́блестный; (*of ship*) велича́вый; (*of horse*) лихо́й, рети́вый.

gallantry ['gæləntrɪ] *n.* (*bravery*) до́блесть; (*courtliness to women*) гала́нтность; (*amatory adventure*) любо́вное похожде́ние.

galleon ['gælɪən] *n.* галео́н.

gallery ['gælərɪ] *n.* **1.** (*walk, passage*) галере́я; **shooting** ~ тир. **2.** (*picture* ~) карти́нная галере́я. **3.** (*raised floor or platform*) хо́р|ы (*pl., g.* -ов); **minstrels'** ~ хо́ры (*pl.*); **press** ~ места́ для представи́телей печа́ти. **4.** (*theatr.*) галёрка; **play to the** ~ (*fig.*) иска́ть (*impf.*) дешёвой популя́рности. **5.** (*mining*) што́льня.

galley ['gælɪ] *n.* **1.** (*ship*) гале́ра. **2.** (*ship's kitchen*) ка́мбуз; (*in aircraft*) пищебло́к. **3.** (*typ.*) (*tray*) верста́тка; (~*-proof*) гра́нка.
cpd. ~**-slave** *n.* раб на гале́рах.

gallic[1] ['gælɪk] *adj.* (*chem.*) ~ **acid** га́лловая кислота́.

Gallic[2] ['gælɪk] *adj.* (*Gaulish*) га́лльский; (*French*) францу́зский.

Gallican ['gælɪkən] *adj.* (*eccl. hist.*) галлика́нский.

Gallicanism ['gælɪkə,nɪzəm] *n.* галлика́нство.

Gallicism ['gælɪ,sɪzəm] *n.* галлици́зм.

Gallicize ['gælɪ,saɪz] *v.t.* офранцу́зить (*pf.*).

gallimaufry [,gælɪ'mɔːfrɪ] *n.* мешани́на.

galling ['gɔːlɪŋ] *adj.* (*fig.*) раздража́ющий; **it's** ~ **not to be invited** когда́ тебя́ не приглаша́ют, чу́вствуешь себя́ уязвлённым.

gallipot ['gælɪ,pɒt] *n.* апте́чная ба́нка/скля́нка.

gallium ['gælɪəm] *n.* га́ллий.

gallivant ['gælɪ,vænt] *v.i.* (*coll.*) шля́ться (*impf.*); слоня́ться (*impf.*).

Gallomania [,gæləʊ'meɪnɪə] *n.* галлома́ния.

gallon ['gælən] *n.* галло́н.

galloon [gə'luːn] *n.* галу́н.

gallop ['gæləp] *n.* гало́п; **he rode off at a/full** ~ он поскака́л во весь опо́р; **we went for a** ~ мы отпра́вились на верхову́ю прогу́лку.
v.t.: ~ **a horse** пус|ка́ть, -ти́ть ло́шадь гало́пом (*or* в гало́п); (*fig.*): **we** ~**ed through our work** мы бы́стро провернули всю рабо́ту; ~**ing consumption** скороте́чная чахо́тка.

Gallophile ['gæləʊ,faɪl] *n.* галлофи́л, франкофи́л.
adj. франкофи́льский.

Gallophobe [,gæləʊ'fəʊb] *n.* галлофо́б, франкофо́б.
adj. франкофо́бский.

Gallophobia [,gæləʊ'fəʊbɪə] *n.* галлофо́бия, франкофо́бия.

gallows ['gæləʊz] *n.* (*also* ~**-tree**) ви́селица; **he will come to the** ~ ему́ не минова́ть ви́селицы; **send s.o. to the** ~ отпра́вить (*pf.*) кого́-н. на ви́селицу; **cheat the** ~ избежа́ть (*impf.*) ви́селицы; **he has a** ~ **look** у него́ разбо́йничий вид.
cpds. ~**-bird** *n.* ви́сельник; ~**-humour** *n.* ю́мор ви́сельника.

galore [gə'lɔː(r)] *adv.* (*coll.*) в изоби́лии, ско́лько уго́дно.

galosh [gə'lɒʃ] *n.* гало́ша.

galumph [gə'lʌmf] *v.i.* (*coll.*) пры́гать (*impf.*) от ра́дости; (*walk clumsily*) то́пать (*impf.*).

galvanic [gæl'vænɪk] *adj.* (*elec.*) гальвани́ческий, электризу́ющий.

galvanism ['gælvə,nɪz(ə)m] *n.* гальвани́зм; (*med.*) гальваниза́ция.

galvanization [,gælvənaɪ'zeɪʃ(ə)n] *n.* гальваниза́ция.

galvanize ['gælvə,naɪz] *v.t.* гальванизи́ровать (*impf., pf.*); ~**d iron** оцинко́ванное желе́зо; (*fig.*) побу|жда́ть, -ди́ть; возбу|жда́ть, -ди́ть; гальванизи́ровать.

galvanometer [,gælvə'nɒmɪtə(r)] *n.* гальвано́метр.

gambit ['gæmbɪt] *n.* (*chess*) гамби́т; (*trick*) уxва́тка.

gamble ['gæmb(ə)l] *n.* аза́ртная игра́; (*risky undertaking*) риско́ванное предприя́тие; **take a** ~ пойти́ (*pf.*) на риск.
v.t. & i. игра́ть (*impf.*) в аза́ртные и́гры; ~ **away a fortune** проигра́ть (*pf.*) состоя́ние.

gambler ['gæmblə(r)] *n.* игро́к; картёжник.

gambling ['gæmblɪŋ] *n.* аза́ртные и́гры (*f. pl.*).
cpds. ~**-den** *n.* иго́рный прито́н; ~**-game** *n.* аза́ртная игра́.

gamboge [gæm'bəʊʒ, -'buːʒ] *n.* гуммигу́т; жёлтый пигме́нт.

gambol ['gæmb(ə)l] *n.* прыжо́к, скачо́к.
v.i. пры́г|ать, -нуть.

game[1] [geɪm] *n.* **1.** игра́; **we had a** ~ **of golf** мы сыгра́ли па́ртию в гольф; **he plays a good** ~ **of bridge** он хорошо́ игра́ет в бридж; **play the** ~ (*fig.*) игра́ть (*impf.*) по пра́вилам; **I am off my** ~ я не в фо́рме; ~**s** (*at school*) физкульту́ра; **Olympic G**~**s** Олимпи́йские и́гры; **what is the state of the** ~? (*score*) како́й счёт?; **he won two** ~**s in the first set** (*tennis*) в пе́рвом се́те он вы́играл две игры́ (*or* два ге́йма); **we bought the child a** ~ мы купи́ли ребёнку насто́льную игру́; **beat s.o. at his own** ~ поби́ть (*pf.*) кого́-н. его́ же ору́жием. **2.** (*scheme, plan, trick*) игра́; **what's the** ~? что за э́тим кро́ется?; **he is playing a deep** ~ он ведёт сло́жную игру́; **you are playing his** ~ вы игра́ете ему́ на́ руку; **two can play at that** ~ (*fig.*) я могу́ отплати́ть вам (*и т.п.*) той же моне́той; **he gave the** ~ **away** он раскры́л свои́ ка́рты; **the** ~ **is up** ста́вка би́та; ко́нчен бал!; **make** ~ **of s.o.** высме́ивать, вы́смеять кого́-н.; **the** ~ **is not worth the candle** игра́ не сто́ит свеч; **none of your** ~**s!** э́тот но́мер не пройдёт! **3.** (*hunted animal, quarry*) дичь; зверь (*m.*); **big** ~ кру́пный зверь; **fair** ~ (*fig.*) объе́кт тра́вли; **do you like eating** ~? вы лю́бите дичь?; ~ **laws** зако́н об охра́не ди́чи.
adj. боево́й; задо́рный; **he died** ~ он держа́лся до конца́; **are you** ~ **for a ten-mile walk?** у вас есть настрое́ние соверши́ть прогу́лку миль на де́сять?
v.t. & i. игра́ть, сыгра́ть; **he** ~**d away his money** он проигра́л свои́ де́ньги; **gaming-house** иго́рный дом; **gaming-table** иго́рный стол.
cpds. ~**-bag** *n.* ягдта́ш; ~**-bird** *n.* перна́тая дичь; ~**-cock** *n.* бойцо́вый пету́х; ~**keeper** *n.* лесни́к, охраня́ющий дичь; ~**-preserve** *n.* охо́тничий запове́дник; ~**s-master/mistress** *nn.* преподава́тель(ница) физкульту́ры; ~**-warden** *n.* е́герь/лесни́к, охраня́ющий дичь.

game[2] [geɪm] *adj.* (*lame*) хромо́й.

gamesmanship ['geɪmzmənʃɪp] *n.* (*joc.*) ≃ психи́ческое возде́йствие на проти́вника.

gamester ['geɪmstə(r)] *n.* игро́к; картёжник.

gamete ['gæmiːt, gə'miːt] *n.* гаме́та.

gamma ['gæmə] *n.*: ~ **moth** со́вка-га́мма; ~ **rays** га́мма-лучи́ (*m. pl.*).

gammon[1] ['gæmən] *n.* (*ham, bacon*) о́корок.

gammon[2] ['gæmən] *n.* (*humbug*) обма́н; (*nonsense*) чушь.

v.t. обма́н|ывать, -у́ть.

gammy ['gæmɪ] *adj.* (*coll.*) хромо́й.

gamp [gæmp] *n.* (*coll.*) зонт.

gamut ['gæmət] *n.* (*mus.*) га́мма; (*fig.*) диапазо́н, га́мма; **she ran the ~ of the emotions** она́ передала́ всю га́мму чувств.

gamy ['geɪmɪ] *adj.* (*of scent, flavour*) с душко́м.

gander ['gændə(r)] *n.* (*male goose*) гуса́к; (*sl., look*): **take a ~ at** взгля́|дывать, -ну́ть на+*a*.

gang [gæŋ] *n.* (*of workmen*) брига́да; (*of prisoners*) па́ртия (заключённых); (*of criminals*) ша́йка, ба́нда; (*coll. or pej., company*) ша́йка, вата́га.

v.i.: **they ~ together** они́ собира́ются в ба́нду (*or* ба́ндой); **they ~ed up on me** они́ ополчи́лись про́тив/на меня́.

cpds. **~-bang** *n.* & *v.t.* (*sl.*) группово́е изнаси́лование; наси́ловать, из- гру́ппой; **~land** *n.* престу́пный мир; **~-board, ~-plank** *nn.* схо́дни (*f. pl.*); **~way** *n.* (*from ship to shore*) схо́дни (*f. pl.*); (*from aircraft to ground*) трап; (*in theatre etc.*) прохо́д; (*coll. int., clear the way!*) прочь с доро́ги!; сторони́сь!

ganger ['gæŋə(r)] *n.* деся́тник, бригади́р.

Ganges ['gændʒi:z] *n.* Ганг.

gangling ['gæŋglɪŋ] *adj.* долговя́зый.

ganglion ['gæŋglɪən] *n.* га́нглий, не́рвный у́зел.

gangrene ['gæŋgri:n] *n.* гангре́на.

gangrenous ['gæŋgrɪnəs] *adj.* гангрено́зный.

gangster ['gæŋstə(r)] *n.* га́нгстер.

gangsterdom ['gæŋstədəm] *n.* (*community of gangsters*) га́нгстеры (*m. pl.*); (*gangsterism*) бандити́зм, гангстери́зм.

gangue [gæŋ] *n.* ру́дная поро́да.

gannet ['gænɪt] *n.* (*bird*) о́луша; (*fig., glutton*) обжо́ра.

gantry ['gæntrɪ] *n.* помо́ст; ~ **crane** эстака́дный кран.

gaol [dʒeɪl] *n.* тюрьма́; (*imprisonment*) тюре́мное заключе́ние; **break ~** бежа́ть (*pf.*) из тюрьмы́.

v.t. заключ|а́ть, -и́ть в тюрьму́.

cpds. **~-bird** *n.* ареста́нт, рецидиви́ст; **~-break** *n.* побе́г из тюрьмы́; **~-delivery** *n.* отпра́вка из тюрьмы́ на суд.

gaoler ['dʒeɪlə(r)] *n.* тюре́мщик, тюре́мный надзира́тель (*m.*).

gap [gæp] *n.* **1.** (*in a wall etc.*) брешь, проло́м; (*in defences*) проры́в; (*in ranks*) брешь; **fill a ~** (*supply deficiency*) устрани́ть (*pf.*) недоста́тки; **he filled up the ~s in his education** он восполнил пробе́лы в своём образова́нии; **there is a wide ~ between their views** они́ ре́зко расхо́дятся во взгля́дах; **export ~** э́кспортный дефици́т. **2.** (*gorge, pass*) прохо́д; уще́лье.

cpd. **~-toothed** *adj.* с ре́дкими зуба́ми.

gap|e [geɪp] *n.*: **the ~es** (*disease of poultry; yawning fit*) зево́та.

v.i. (*stare*) зева́ть (*impf.*) (на+*a.*); глазе́ть (*impf.*) (на+*a.*); **a ~ing wound** зия́ющая ра́на; **the chasm ~ed before him** пе́ред ним зия́ла про́пасть.

gaper ['geɪpə(r)] *n.* (*pers.*) зева́ка (*c.g.*).

garage ['gærɑ:dʒ, -rɪdʒ] *n.* гара́ж.

v.t. ста́вить, по- в гара́ж.

cpd. **~-hand** *n.* рабо́чий/меха́ник в гараже́; автослеса́рь (*m.*).

garb [gɑ:b] *n.* наря́д.

v.t. наря|жа́ть, -ди́ть; ~ **o.s. as a sailor** наря|жа́ться, -ди́ться в матро́сскую оде́жду.

garbage ['gɑ:bɪdʒ] *n.* отбро́сы (*m. pl.*); му́сор; (*fig.*) му́сор; макулату́ра.

cpds. **~-can** *n.* му́сорный я́щик; **~-collector** *n.* му́сорщик.

garble ['gɑ:b(ə)l] *v.t.* (*distort*) иска|жа́ть, -зи́ть; кове́ркать, ис-.

garboard ['gɑ:bəd] *n.* (*naut., also ~ strake*) шпунтово́й по́яс обши́вки.

garden ['gɑ:d(ə)n] *n.* **1.** (*plot of ground*) сад; **vegetable ~** огоро́д; **we haven't much ~** у нас сад небольшо́й; **lead up the ~ path** (*coll.*) води́ть за́ нос (*indet.*); **everything in the ~'s lovely** (*coll., all is well*) всё в поря́дке. **2.** (*attr.*) садо́вый; огоро́дный; **common or ~** обы́денный; зауря́дный; ~ **flowers/plants** садо́вые цветы́/расте́ния; ~ **city** го́род-сад; ~ **gate** садо́вая кали́тка; ~ **party** приём на откры́том во́здухе; ~ **plot** садо́вый уча́сток; ~ **seat** садо́вая скамья́; ~ **suburb** да́чный посёлок. **3.** (*pl., park*) сад; парк; **Zoological G~s** зоологи́ческий сад; зоопа́рк.

v.i. занима́ться (*impf.*) садово́дством; **he is fond of ~ing** он лю́бит садово́дство; **~ing tools** садо́вые инструме́нты.

gardener ['gɑ:dnə(r)] *n.* садо́вник; (*horticulturist*) садово́д.

gardenia [gɑ:'di:nɪə] *n.* гарде́ния.

garfish ['gɑ:fɪʃ] *n.* па́нцирная ры́ба/щу́ка; сарга́н.

gargantuan [gɑ:'gæntjʊən] *adj.* гига́нтский, колосса́льный.

gargle ['gɑ:g(ə)l] *n.* полоска́ние.

v.i. полоска́ть, про- го́рло.

gargoyle ['gɑ:gɔɪl] *n.* горгу́лья.

garish ['geərɪʃ] *adj.* пёстрый, бро́ский, крича́щий.

garishness ['geərɪʃnɪs] *n.* пестрота́, бро́скость.

garland ['gɑ:lənd] *n.* гирля́нда; вено́к; (*fig., prize etc.*) па́льма пе́рвенства.

v.t. укр|аша́ть, -а́сить гирля́ндами.

garlic ['gɑ:lɪk] *n.* чесно́к; **clove of ~** зубо́к чеснока́.

garment ['gɑ:mənt] *n.* одея́ние; (*pl., clothes*) оде́жда; **nether ~s** (*joc.*) брю́к|и (*pl., g.* —); **the ~ industry** (*dressmaking, tailoring*) шве́йная промы́шленность.

garn [gɑ:n] *int.* (*sl.*) да ну!; иди́ ты!; брось!

garner ['gɑ:nə(r)] *v.t.* (*liter.*) сс|ыпа́ть, -ы́пать в амба́р; (*fig.*): ~ **experience** нак|а́пливать, -опи́ть о́пыт.

garnet ['gɑ:nɪt] *n.* грана́т.

garnish ['gɑ:nɪʃ] *n.* отде́лка, украше́ние; (*cul.*) гарни́р.

v.t. (*furnish*) обст|авля́ть -а́вить; (*decorate*) укр|аша́ть, -а́сить; (*cul.*) гарни́ровать (*impf., pf.*).

garniture ['gɑ:nɪtʃə(r)] *n.* (*accessories*) гарниту́р; (*adornment*) отде́лка; украше́ние; (*cul.*) гарни́р.

garret ['gærɪt] *n.* манса́рда; черда́к.

garrison ['gærɪs(ə)n] *n.* гарнизо́н; (*attr.*) гарнизо́нный; **place on ~ duty** назн|ача́ть, -а́чить на гарнизо́нную слу́жбу.

v.t.: ~ **a town** ста́вить, по- гарнизо́н в го́роде.

gar(r)otte [gə'rɒt] *n.* гарро́та.

v.t. души́ть, у-; дави́ть, у-.

garrulity [gə'ru:lɪtɪ] *n.* болтли́вость, говорли́вость.

garrulous ['gærʊləs] *adj.* болтли́вый, говорли́вый.

garter ['gɑ:tə(r)] *n.* подвя́зка; **Order of the G~** о́рден Подвя́зки.

cpd. **~-snake** *n.* подвя́зковая змея́.

gas [gæs] *n.* **1.** (*aeriform fluid*) газ; **natural ~** приро́дный газ; **put the kettle on the ~** поста́вить ча́йник на газ; **turn the ~ on/off** включи́ть/вы́ключить газ; (*dentist's*) эфи́р; (*poison ~*) ядови́тый газ; отравля́ющее вещество́; (*mining*) гре́му́чий газ; (*flatulence*) га́зы (*m. pl.*). **2.** (*attr.*) га́зовый; ~ **alarm, alert** хими́ческая трево́га; ~ **bomb** хими́ческая бо́мба; ~ **bracket** га́зовый рожо́к; ~ **burner** га́зовая горе́лка; ~ **chamber** (*for lethal purposes*) га́зовая ка́мера; ~ **coal** га́зовый у́голь; ~ **coke** га́зовый кокс; ~ **cooker** га́зовая плита́; ~ **engine** га́зовый дви́гатель; ~ **field** месторожде́ние га́за; ~ **fire** га́зовый ками́н; ~ **fitter** газовщи́к; ~ **helmet** противога́з; ~ **lighter** (*for cigarettes etc.*) га́зовая зажига́лка; ~ **lighting** га́зовое освеще́ние; ~ **main** газопрово́д; ~ **mantle** кали́льная се́тка; ~ **mask** противога́з; ~ **meter** га́зовый счётчик; ~ **motor** га́зовый мото́р; ~ **oven** (*domestic*) га́зовая духо́вка; (*for extermination*) га́зовая печь; ~ **pipe** га́зовая труба́; ~ **producer** газогенера́тор; ~ **ring** га́зовое кольцо́; ~ **shell** хими́ческий снаря́д; ~ **shelter** газоубе́жище; ~ **stove** га́зовая плита́; ~ **torch** га́зовый реза́к; ~ **warfare** хими́ческая война́; *see also cpds.* **3.** (*US, petrol*) бензи́н, горю́чее; **step on the ~** (*coll.*) да|ва́ть, -ть га́зу; ~ **station** бензоколо́нка; ~ **tank** бензоба́к. **4.** (*coll., empty talk*) болтовня́, трепотня́.

v.t. (*poison with ~*) отрав|ля́ть, -и́ть га́зом; (*kill with ~*) умер|щвля́ть, -тви́ть га́зом.

v.i. **1.** (*coll., talk long and emptily*) болта́ть (*impf.*); моло́ть (*impf.*). **2.** ~ **up** (*take in petrol*) запра́виться (*pf.*) горю́чим.

cpds. **~bag** *n.* оболо́чка аэроста́та; (*coll.*, *chatterer*) пустоме́ля (*c.g.*); **~holder** *n.* газго́льдер, газохрани́лище; **~-jet** *n.* га́зовый рожо́к; **~light** *n.* га́зовое освеще́ние; **~-lit** *adj.* освещённый га́зом; **~man** *n.* (*fitter*) (сле́сарь-)газовщи́к; (*inspector*) инспе́ктор-газовщи́к; **~proof** *adj.* газонепроница́емый; **~works** *n.* га́зовый заво́д.

Gascon ['gæskən] *n.* гаско́н|ец (*fem.* -ка).

adj. гаско́нский.

gasconade [,gæskə'neɪd] *n.* бахва́льство.

Gascony ['gæskənɪ] *n.* Гаско́нь.

gaseous ['gæsɪəs] *adj.* га́зовый; газообра́зный.

gash [gæʃ] *n.* разре́з; глубо́кая ра́на.

v.t. разр|еза́ть, -е́зать; полосну́ть (*pf.*).

gasification [,gæsɪfɪ'keɪʃ(ə)n] *n.* газифика́ция.

gasify ['gæsɪ,faɪ] *v.t. & i.* газифици́ровать.

gasket ['gæskɪt] *n.* прокла́дка; тесьма́.

gasohol ['gæsə,hɒl] *n.* бензоспи́рт.

gasol|ine, -ene ['gæsə,li:n] *n.* газоли́н; (*US*, *petrol*) бензи́н.

gasometer [gæ'sɒmɪtə(r)] *n.* газо́метр; газоме́р, га́зовый счётчик.

gasp [gɑ:sp] *n.* глото́к во́здуха; перехва́т дыха́ния; **his breath came in ~s** он преры́висто дыша́л; **at one's last ~** при после́днем издыха́нии.

v.t. & i. зад|ыха́ться, -охну́ться; а́хнуть (*pf.*); **he ~ed out a few words** задыха́ясь, он произнёс не́сколько слов; **he was ~ing for breath** он задыха́лся; **he ~ed with astonishment** он откры́л рот (*or* задохну́лся) от удивле́ния; **the fish was ~ing on the bank** ры́ба, вы́брошенная на берег, лови́ла ртом во́здух.

gasper ['gɑ:spə(r)] *n.* (*sl.*) дешёвая сигаре́та.

gassy ['gæsɪ] *adj.* (*of beer etc.*) газиро́ванный; (*fig.*, *of talk*) пустопоро́жний.

gasteropod ['gæstərə,pɒd] *n.* ули́тка из кла́сса брюхоно́гих.

gastrectomy [gæ'strektəmɪ] *n.* гастрэктоми́я.

gastric ['gæstrɪk] *adj.* желу́дочный; **~ fever** брюшно́й тиф; **~ juice** желу́дочный сок; **~ ulcer** я́зва желу́дка.

gastritis [gæ'straɪtɪs] *n.* гастри́т.

gastro-enteritis [,gæstrəʊ,entə'raɪtɪs] *n.* гастроэнтери́т.

gastronome(r) ['gæstrə,nəʊm, gæs'trɒnəmə(r)] *nn.* гастроно́м.

gastronomic [,gæstrə'nɒmɪk] *adj.* гастрономи́ческий.

gastronomy [gæ'strɒnəmɪ] *n.* гастроно́мия.

gate [geɪt] *n.* **1.** вор|о́та (*pl.*, *g.* -о́т); кали́тка; (*city ~*) городски́е воро́та; (*garden ~*) садо́вая кали́тка; (*water-~*) шлю́зные воро́та; **give s.o. the ~** (*US coll.*) выгоня́ть, вы́гнать кого́-н. **2.** (*fig.*) (*size of audience*) коли́чество зри́телей; (*takings*) сбор, вы́ручка.

v.t. (*confine to college*) запрети́ть (*pf.*) (*кому*) вы́ход за преде́лы колле́джа.

cpds. **~-crash** *v.t. & i.* при|ходи́ть, -йти́ незва́ным; про|ходи́ть, -йти́ без биле́та; **~-crasher** *n.* незва́ный гость; (*spectator*) безбиле́тный зри́тель (*m.*), «за́яц»; **~-fold** *n.* складна́я ка́рта/табли́ца *и т.п.*; **~-house** *n.* сторо́жка; **~-keeper** *n.* привра́тник; **~-leg(ged)** *adj.*: **~-legged table** стол с откидно́й кры́шкой; **~-money** *n.* входна́я пла́та; **~post** *n.* воро́тный столб; **between you and me and the ~post** ме́жду на́ми (говоря́); **~way** *n.* подворо́тня; (*fig.*) подхо́д.

gateau ['gætəʊ] *n.* пиро́жное; торт.

gather ['gæðə(r)] *n.* (*in cloth*) сбо́рки (*f. pl.*).

v.t. **1.** (*pick*, *cull*: *e.g. flowers*, *nuts*, *harvest*; *also ~* **in**) соб|ира́ть, -ра́ть. **2.** (*collect*, *also ~* **up**) соб|ира́ть, -ра́ть; **things ~ dust** ве́щи собира́ют пыль; **he ~ed his papers together** он собра́л свои́ бума́ги; **he was ~ed to his fathers** он отпра́вился к пра́отцам; **~ impressions/experience** нака́пливать (*impf.*) впечатле́ния/о́пыт; **he ~ed up the thread of the story** он подхвати́л нить расска́за. **3.** (*receive addition of*) наб|ира́ть, -ра́ть *+a. or g.*; **the ship ~ed way** кора́бль набра́л ход. **4.** (*understand*, *conclude*) заключ|а́ть, -и́ть; де́лать, с- вы́вод (*pf.*) (*на основании чего-н.*); **I ~ he's abroad** он как бу́дто за грани́цей; **I ~ you don't like him** мне сдаётся, что он вам не нра́вится; **as far as I can ~** наско́лько я могу́ суди́ть. **5.** (*draw*, *pull together*): **he ~ed his cloak about him** он заверну́лся в плащ; **he ~ed her in his arms** он заключи́л её в объя́тия; **he ~ed his brows** он сдви́нул бро́ви; **~ one's thoughts, wits (together)** соб|ира́ться, -ра́ться с мы́слями. **6.** (*sewing*) соб|ира́ть, -ра́ть в скла́дки.

v.i. **1.** (*collect*) соб|ира́ться, -ра́ться; **a crowd ~ed** собрала́сь толпа́; **the clouds are ~ing** собира́ются ту́чи; **the abscess ~ed** нары́в созре́л. **2.** (*increase*) нараст|а́ть, -и́; **the tale ~ed like a snowball** исто́рия разраста́лась как сне́жный ком.

gatherer ['gæðərə(r)] *n.* (*picker-up*, *collector*) сбо́рщи|к (*fem.* -ца).

gathering ['gæðərɪŋ] *n.* (*assembly*) собра́ние; встре́ча; (*swelling*) нагное́ние.

GATT [gæt] *n.* (*abbr. of* ***General Agreement on Tariffs and Trade***) ГАТТ, (Генера́льное соглаше́ние по тари́фам и торго́вле).

gauche [gəʊʃ] *adj.* нело́вкий; неуклю́жий.

gauche|ness ['gəʊʃnɪs], **-rie** ['gəʊʃə,ri:] *nn.* нело́вкость, неуклю́жесть.

gaucho ['gaʊtʃəʊ] *n.* га́учо (*m. indecl.*).

gaud [gɔ:d] *n.* (*liter.*) безделу́шка; мишура́.

gaudiness ['gɔ:dɪnɪs] *n.* безвку́сица; крикли́вость.

gaudy ['gɔ:dɪ] *n.* (*feast*) пра́зднество.

adj. (*of colour*) крича́щий; безвку́сный.

gauge (*US* **gage**) [geɪdʒ] *n.* **1.** (*thickness*, *diameter etc.*) разме́р; (*rail.*): **standard ~** станда́ртная колея́; **broad ~** широ́кая колея́; **narrow ~** у́зкая колея́. **2.** (*instrument*) шабло́н; лека́ло; этало́н.

v.t. **1.** (*measure*) изм|еря́ть, -е́рить. **2.** (*fig.*, *estimate*) оце́н|ивать, -и́ть; взве́сить (*pf.*); **~ the strength of the wind** определ|я́ть, -и́ть си́лу ве́тра.

Gaul [gɔ:l] *n.* (*hist.*, *country*) Га́ллия; (*inhabitant*) галл; (*joc.*, *Frenchman*) францу́з.

Gaulish ['gɔ:lɪʃ] *adj.* га́лльский.

Gaullism ['gəʊlɪz(ə)m] *n.* голли́зм; дего́ллевская поли́тика.

Gaullist ['gəʊlɪst] *n.* голли́ст; после́дователь (*m.*) приве́рженец де Го́лля, (*coll.*) дего́ллевец.

adj. голли́стский.

gaunt [gɔ:nt] *adj.* исхуда́лый; измождённый; (*grim*) угрю́мый.

gauntlet[1] ['gɔ:ntlɪt] *n.* рукави́ца; (*armoured glove*) ла́тная рукави́ца; **throw down the ~** (*fig.*) бро́сить (*pf.*) перча́тку/вы́зов; **pick up the ~** приня́ть (*pf.*) вы́зов.

gauntlet[2] ['gɔ:ntlɪt] *n.*: **run the ~** про|ходи́ть, -йти́ сквозь строй; (*fig.*, *of criticism etc.*) подв|ерга́ться, -е́ргнуться суро́вой кри́тике.

gauntness ['gɔ:ntnɪs] *n.* худоба́.

gauss [gaʊs] *n.* га́усс.

gauze [gɔ:z] *n.* ма́рля, газ.

gavel ['gæv(ə)l] *n.* молото́к.

gavotte [gə'vɒt] *n.* гаво́т.

gawk [gɔ:k] *n.* рази́ня (*c.g.*).

v.i. (*also* **gawp**) глазе́ть (*impf.*); пя́лить (*impf.*) глаза́ (на+*a.*).

gawky ['gɔ:kɪ] *adj.* нело́вкий, неуклю́жий.

gawp [gɔ:p] = **gawk** *v.i.*

gay [geɪ] *adj.* весёлый; **~ colours** я́ркие цвета́; **the street was ~ with flags** у́лица пестре́ла фла́гами; (*licentious*) беспу́тный; (*coll.*, *homosexual*) гомосексуа́льный, голубо́й; (*as n.*) го́мик, педера́ст.

gaz|e [geɪz] *n.* при́стальный взгляд; **a strange sight met his ~e** его́ взо́ру откры́лось стра́нное зре́лище.

v.i. при́стально глядеть; **stop ~ing around!** переста́ньте глазе́ть по сторона́м!

gazebo [gə'zi:bəʊ] *n.* бельведе́р.

gazelle [gə'zel] *n.* газе́ль.

gazer ['geɪzə(r)] *n.* рази́ня (*c.g.*).

gazette [gə'zet] *n.* (*official journal*) официа́льные ве́домости (*f. pl.*); (*newspaper*) газе́та.

v.t.: **he was ~d colonel** он получи́л зва́ние полко́вника.

gazetteer [,gæzɪ'tɪə(r)] *n.* географи́ческий спра́вочник; слова́рь географи́ческих назва́ний.

GB (*abbr. of* ***Great Britain***) Великобрита́ния.

GBH (*abbr. of* ***grievous bodily harm***) (*leg.*) тяжёлые теле́сные поврежде́ния.

GCSE (*abbr. of* ***General Certificate of Secondary Education***) ≃ аттеста́т о сре́днем образова́нии.

GDR (*abbr. of* **German Democratic Republic**) ГДР, (Германская Демократическая Республика).

gear [gɪə(r)] *n.* **1.** (*apparatus, mechanism*) механизм. **2.** (*equipment, utensils, clothing*) принадлежности (*f. pl.*), аксессуары (*m. pl.*); одежда; **hunting ~** охотничье снаряжение; **household ~** хозяйственные принадлежности. **3.** (*of car etc.*) зубчатая передача; **high ~** высокая передача; **top ~** высшая передача; **bottom ~** первая передача; **low ~** низкая передача; **reverse ~** задний ход; **change ~** переключ|ать, -ить передачу; **the car is in ~** машина на передаче; у машины включена передача; **out of ~** (*disconnected*) невключённый; (*out of order*) недействующий; **throw out of ~** (*fig.*) расстр|аивать, -оить.

v.t.: **~ up** уск|орять, -орить; **~ down** зам|едлять, -едлить; (*fig., adjust, correlate*) приспос|облять, -обить; **production is ~ed to demand** производство приспособлено к спросу.

cpds. **~-box, ~-case** *nn.* коробка передач; **~-lever** *n.* рычаг переключения передач/скоростей; **~-ratio** *n.* передаточное число; **~-shift** *n.* переключение передач; **~-wheel** *n.* зубчатое колесо.

gecko ['gekəʊ] *n.* геккон.

gee[1]**(-gee)** [dʒi:] *n.* лошадка; **~ up!** но!

gee[2] [dʒi:] *int.* (*also* **~ whiz!**) вот здорово!; вот так штука!; ух ты!

geezer ['gi:zə(r)] *n.* (*sl.*) старикашка (*m.*).

Gehenna [gɪ'henə] *n.* геенна.

Geiger ['gaɪgə(r)] *n.*: **~ count** определение степени радиоактивности.

cpd. **~-counter** *n.* счётчик Гейгера.

geisha ['geɪʃə] *n.* гейша.

gelatine ['dʒelə,ti:n] *n.* желатин.

gelatinous [dʒɪ'lætɪnəs] *adj.* желатиновый.

geld [geld] *v.t.* кастрировать (*impf., pf.*).

gelding ['geldɪŋ] *n.* мерин.

gelid ['dʒelɪd] *adj.* ледяной; студёный; леденящий.

gelignite ['dʒelɪg,naɪt] *n.* гелигнит.

gem [dʒem] *n.* (*jewel*) драгоценный камень; (*fig., outstanding specimen*) жемчужина, сокровище.

v.t.: **the night was ~med with stars** ночь сияла звёздами.

cpd. **~stone** *n.* драгоценный камень.

Gemini ['dʒemɪ,naɪ, -,ni:] *n.* Близнецы (*m. pl.*).

gemmology [dʒe'mɒlədʒɪ] *n.* наука о драгоценных камнях.

gemsbok ['gemzbʌk] *n.* сернобык.

gen [dʒen] *n.* (*sl.*) данные (*nt. pl.*); информация.

gendarme ['ʒɒndɑ:m] *n.* жандарм.

gendarmerie [ʒɒn'dɑ:mərɪ] *n.* жандармерия.

gender ['dʒendə(r)] *n.* род; (*coll., sex*) пол.

gene [dʒi:n] *n.* ген.

genealogical [,dʒi:nɪə'lɒdʒɪk(ə)l] *adj.* родословный; генеалогический; **~ tree** генеалогическое дерево.

genealogist [,dʒi:nɪ'ælədʒɪst] *n.* специалист по генеалогии.

genealogy [,dʒi:nɪ'ælədʒɪ] *n.* генеалогия.

general ['dʒenər(ə)l] *n.* **1.** генерал; **~ of the Air Force** (*US*) генерал ВВС/авиации; **~ of the Army** (*US*) генерал армии. **2.** (*strategist*) полководец.

adj. **1.** (*universal or nearly so*) общий; генеральный; **~ rule** общее правило; **~ election** всеобщие выборы; **~ strike** всеобщая забастовка; **~ knowledge** общие знания; **~ practitioner** терапевт; **~ hospital** больница общего типа; **~ reader** массовый читатель; **G~ Assembly** (*of UN*) Генеральная Ассамблея; **~ store** сельпо (*indecl.*); **a book of ~ interest** неспециализированная книга. **2.** (*usual, prevalent*) обычный; повсеместный; **~ opinion** общее мнение; **in ~, in a ~ way** вообще; **as a ~ rule** как правило, обыкновенно. **3.** (*approximate; not specific*) общий; **~ resemblance** общее сходство; **~ idea** общее представление; **he spoke in ~ terms** он говорил в общих выражениях. **4.** (*chief*) главный; **~ staff** генеральный штаб; **~ headquarters** главное командование, ставка; **G~ Post Office** главпочтамт.

cpds. **~-in-chief** *n.* главнокомандующий; **~-purpose** *adj.* многоцелевой; универсальный.

generalissimo [,dʒenərə'lɪsɪ,məʊ] *n.* генералиссимус.

generalit|y [,dʒenə'rælɪtɪ] *n.* **1.** (*majority*) большинство. **2.** (*general statement*) общее место, общая фраза; **he spoke in ~ies** он говорил/отделался общими фразами.

generalization [,dʒenərəlaɪ'zeɪʃ(ə)n] *n.* обобщение.

generalize ['dʒenərə,laɪz] *v.t. & i.* обобщ|ать, -ить; (*make general*) распростран|ять, -ить.

generally ['dʒenərəlɪ] *adv.* **1.** (*usually*) обычно. **2.** (*widely*) широко; большей частью; **the plan was ~ welcomed** план получил всеобщее одобрение; **~ received ideas** общепринятые понятия. **3.** (*approximately, summarily*) вообще; **~ speaking** вообще говоря. **4.** (*as a class*): **this is true of Frenchmen ~** это относится к французам вообще.

generalship ['dʒenər(ə)lʃɪp] *n.* (*rank or office*) звание/чин генерала; (*military skill*) стратегическое/полководческое искусство.

generat|e ['dʒenə,reɪt] *v.t.* поро|ждать, -дить; вызывать, вызвать; генерировать (*impf.*); **~e heat** выделять (*impf.*) тепло; **~e hatred** вызывать (*impf.*) ненависть; **~ing station** электростанция.

generation [,dʒenə'reɪʃ(ə)n] *n.* **1.** (*of heat etc.*) генерация. **2.** (*geneal.*) поколение; **from ~ to ~** из поколения в поколение; **the rising ~** подрастающее поколение; **a ~ ago** в прошлом поколении; **I have known them for three ~s** я знал (целых) три поколения этой семьи; **the ~ gap** проблема отцов и детей. **3.** (*fig., of weapons etc.*) этап развития.

generative ['dʒenərətɪv] *adj.* (*productive*) производительный, производящий; (*biol.*) генеративный.

generator ['dʒenə,reɪtə(r)] *n.* производитель (*m.*); (*tech.*) генератор.

generic [dʒɪ'nerɪk] *adj.* (*of a class*) родовой; (*general*) общий; (*of drug*) непатентованный, общего типа.

generosity [,dʒenə'rɒsɪtɪ] *n.* великодушие; щедрость.

generous ['dʒenərəs] *adj.* **1.** (*magnanimous*) великодушный. **2.** (*liberal*) щедрый; **he is ~ with his time** он щедро/расточительно тратит своё время. **3.** (*plentiful*) обильный; **a ~ helping of meat** щедрая/солидная порция мяса; **a ~ harvest** обильный/щедрый урожай. **4.** (*full-flavoured*): **a ~ wine** крепкое/выдержанное вино.

genesis ['dʒenɪsɪs] *n.* генезис; возникновение; **(Book of) G ~** книга Бытия.

genet ['dʒenɪt] *n.* генетта; виверра.

genetic [dʒɪ'netɪk] *adj.* генетический; **~ fingerprinting** генная дактилоскопия.

geneticist [dʒɪ'netɪsɪst] *n.* генетик.

genetics [dʒɪ'netɪks] *n.* генетика.

Geneva [dʒɪ'ni:və] *n.* Женева; **Lake ~** Женевское озеро; **~ Convention** Женевская конвенция.

Genev|an [dʒɪ'ni:v(ə)n], **-ese** [,dʒenɪ'vi:z] *adj.* женевский.

Genghis Khan ['dzengɪs,kɑ:n] *n.* Чингисхан.

genial ['dʒi:nɪəl] *adj.* **1.** (*jovial, kindly*) радушный, сердечный, добродушный. **2.** мягкий; **a ~ climate** мягкий/благотворный климат; **~ sunshine** ласковое солнце; **the ~ influence of good wine** благотворное действие хорошего вина.

geniality [,dʒi:nɪ'ælɪtɪ] *n.* радушие; добродушие.

genie ['dʒi:nɪ] *n.* джинн, дух.

genital ['dʒenɪt(ə)l] *adj.* половой; (*pl.*) половые органы (*m. pl.*), гениталии (*f. pl.*).

genitive ['dʒenɪtɪv] *n. & adj.* родительный (падеж).

genito-urinary [,dʒenɪtəʊ'jʊərɪnərɪ] *adj.* мочеполовой.

genius ['dʒi:nɪəs] *n.* **1.** (*pers.; mental power; attendant spirit*) гений; **a man of ~** гениальный человек; **he has a ~ for languages** у него замечательный талант к языкам; **he was her evil ~** он был её злым гением. **2.** (*distinctive character*): **the French ~** французский дух; дух французского народа.

Genoa ['dʒenəʊə] *n.* Генуя.

genocidal [,dʒenə'saɪd(ə)l] *adj.* геноцидный.

genocide ['dʒenə,saɪd] *n.* геноцид.

Genoese [,dzenəʊ'i:z] *n.* генуэз|ец (*fem.* -ка).

adj. генуэзский.

genre ['ʒɑ̃rə] *n.* жанр; (*attr.*) жанровый, бытовой.

gent [dʒent] *n.* (*coll.*) тип; **~s** (*lavatory*) мужская уборная.

genteel [dʒen'ti:l] *adj.* благовоспитанный; «благородный»; мещански-претенциозный; с аристократическими замашками; **they live in ~ poverty** они живут в гордой нищете́.

genteelism [dʒen'ti:lɪz(ə)m] *n.* благопристо́йное выраже́ние; аристократи́ческая зама́шка.

gentian ['dʒenʃ(ə)n, -ʃɪən] *n.* гореча́вка.

gentile ['dʒentaɪl] *n.* неевре́й; (*bibl.*) язы́чник.

adj. неевре́йский; язы́ческий.

gentility [dʒen'tɪlɪtɪ] *n.* благовоспи́танность; (*pej.*) аристократи́ческие зама́шки (*f. pl.*).

gentle[1] ['dʒent(ə)l] *n.* (*zool.*) личи́нка.

gentle[2] ['dʒent(ə)l] *adj.* **1.: a man of ~ birth** челове́к благоро́дного происхожде́ния; зна́тный челове́к. **2.** (*mild, tender, kind*) мя́гкий, ти́хий, делика́тный; **~ heat** лёгкое тепло́; **a ~ slope** отло́гий скло́н; **a ~ breeze** лёгкий ветеро́к; **a ~ hint** то́нкий намёк; **the ~ sex** сла́бый/прекра́сный пол; **~ reader** (*arch.*) любе́зный чита́тель.

v.t. (*of a horse, break in*) объезжа́ть, объе́здить; (*handle gently*) обраща́ться (*impf.*) мя́гко с+*i.*

cpds. **~folk** *n.* дворя́нство; знать; **~woman** *n.* да́ма; ле́ди (*f. indecl.*); (*hist.*) фре́йлина.

gentleman ['dʒent(ə)lmən] *n.* **1.** (*arch., man of gentle birth*) (нетитуло́ванный) дворяни́н. **2.** (*man of social position and/or refined behaviour*) джентльме́н; **~'s agreement** джентльме́нское соглаше́ние; **a ~ has called to see you** како́й-то господи́н жела́ет вас ви́деть; **gentlemen!** господа́!; **~ farmer** фе́рмер-дже́нтльме́н; **the old ~** (*joc., euph.*) дья́вол.

cpds. **~-at-arms** *n.* лейб-гварде́ец; **~-in-waiting** *n.* камерге́р.

gentleman|like ['dʒent(ə)lmən,laɪk], **-ly** ['dʒent(ə)lmənlɪ] *adjs.* джентльме́нский; по-джентльме́нски.

gentleness ['dʒent(ə)lnɪs] *n.* мя́гкость, не́жность; делика́тность.

gently ['dʒentlɪ] *adv.* мя́гко; делика́тно; **hold it ~!** держи́те осторо́жно!; **the road slopes ~** доро́га идёт слегка́ под укло́н; **~!** (*not so fast*) поле́гче!; осторо́жно!

gentry ['dʒentrɪ] *n.* нетитуло́ванное дворя́нство; дже́нтри (*nt. indecl.*); **these ~** (*pej.*) э́ти господа́.

genuflect ['dʒenjʊ,flekt] *v.i.* преклон|я́ть, -и́ть коле́но.

genuflection [,dʒenjʊ'flekʃ(ə)n] *n.* коленопреклоне́ние.

genuine ['dʒenjʊɪn] *adj.* настоя́щий; по́длинный; **a ~ Rubens** по́длинный Ру́бенс; **~ sorrow** и́скренняя печа́ль; **a ~ person** прямо́й/и́скренний челове́к.

genus ['dʒi:nəs, 'dʒenəs] *n.* род.

geocentric [,dʒi:əʊ'sentrɪk] *adj.* геоцентри́ческий.

geodesy [dʒi:'ɒdɪsɪ] *n.* геоде́зия.

geodetic [,dʒi:əʊ'detɪk] *adj.* геодези́ческий.

geographer [dʒɪ'ɒgrəfə(r)] *n.* гео́граф.

geographic(al) [,dʒi:ə'græfɪk(ə)l] *adj.* географи́ческий.

geography [dʒɪ'ɒgrəfɪ] *n.* геогра́фия.

geological [,dʒi:ə'lɒdʒɪk(ə)l] *adj.* геологи́ческий.

geologist [dʒɪ'ɒlədʒɪst] *n.* гео́лог.

geology [dʒɪ'ɒlədʒɪ] *n.* геоло́гия.

geometric(al) [,dʒɪə'metrɪkəl] *adj.* геометри́ческий.

geometrician [,dʒi:əmɪ'trɪʃ(ə)n] *n.* геоме́тр.

geometry [dʒɪ'ɒmɪtrɪ] *n.* геоме́трия; **plane ~** планиме́трия; **solid ~** стереоме́трия.

geophysical [,dʒi:əʊ'fɪzɪkəl] *adj.* геофизи́ческий.

geophysics [,dʒi:əʊ'fɪzɪks] *n.* геофи́зика.

geopolitical [,dʒi:əʊpə'lɪtɪk(ə)l] *adj.* геополити́ческий.

geopolitics [,dʒi:əʊ'pɒlɪtɪks] *n.* геополи́тика.

geoprobe ['dʒi:əʊ,prəʊb] *n.* геофизи́ческая раке́та.

George [dʒɔ:dʒ] *n.* (*saint*) Гео́ргий; (*king*) Гео́рг; **by ~!** вот те на́!; ей-Бо́гу!

Georgia ['dʒɔ:dʒɪə] *n.* (*USA*) Джо́рджия; (*in Caucasus*) Гру́зия.

Georgian[1] ['dʒɔ:dʒ(ə)n] *n.* (*native of Georgia in the Caucasus*) грузи́н (*fem.* -ка). *adj.* грузи́нский.

Georgian[2] ['dʒɔ:dʒ(ə)n] *adj.* (*Br.*): **~ architecture** георгиа́нский стиль в архитекту́ре.

Georgics ['dʒɔ:dʒɪks] *n.* (*poem*) гео́ргик|и (*pl., g.* —).

geosciences [,dʒi:əʊ'saɪənsɪs] *n. pl.* нау́ки о Земле́.

geostationary [,dʒi:əʊ'steɪʃənərɪ] *adj.* геостациона́рный.

geranium [dʒə'reɪnɪəm] *n.* гера́нь.

gerfalcon ['dʒɜ:,fɔ:lkən, ,fɔ:kən] *n.* кре́чет.

geriatric [,dʒerɪ'ætrɪk] *adj.* гериатри́ческий; **~ ward** гериатри́ческое отделе́ние.

geriatrician [,dʒerɪə'trɪʃ(ə)n] *n.* гериатро́лог.

geriatrics [,dʒerɪ'ætrɪks] *n.* гериатри́я.

germ [dʒɜ:m] *n.* заро́дыш; микро́б; **~ warfare** бактериологи́ческая война́; (*fig.*) зача́тки (*m. pl.*); зерно́; **the ~ of an idea** зарожде́ние иде́и.

cpds. **~-cell** *n.* заро́дышевая кле́тка; **~-plasm** *n.* заро́дышевая пла́зма.

german[1] ['dʒɜ:mən] *adj.*: **cousin ~** двою́родный брат; двою́родная сестра́.

German[2] ['dʒɜ:mən] *n.* **1.** (*pers.*) не́м|ец (*fem.* -ка); **Swiss ~** (*or* **~ Swiss**) швейца́рский не́мец. **2.** (*language*) неме́цкий язы́к.

adj. неме́цкий; (*esp. pol.*) герма́нский; **Old High ~** древневерхненеме́цкий; **High ~** ве́рхненеме́цкий; **Low ~** ни́жненеме́цкий; **~ measles** красну́ха; **~ silver** нейзи́льбер; мельхио́р.

cpd. **~-American** *n.* америка́нец неме́цкого происхожде́ния; *adj.* герма́но-америка́нский.

germane [dʒɜ:'meɪn] *adj.* уме́стный; подходя́щий.

Germanic [dʒɜ:'mænɪk] *adj.* герма́нский; **~ studies** германи́стика.

Germanism ['dʒɜ:mənɪz(ə)m] *n.* (*in language*) германи́зм.

Germanist ['dʒɜ:mənɪst] *n.* германи́ст.

germanium [dʒɜ:'meɪnɪəm] *n.* герма́ний.

Germanization [dʒɜ:mə,naɪ'zeɪʃ(ə)n] *n.* германиза́ция; онеме́чение.

Germanize ['dʒɜ:mə,naɪz] *v.t.* германизи́ровать (*impf., pf.*); онеме́чи|вать, -ть.

Germanophil(e) [dʒɜ:'mænə,faɪl] *n.* германофи́л.

adj. германофи́льский.

Germanophobe [dʒɜ:'mænə,fəʊb] *n.* германофо́б.

Germanophobia [dʒɜ:'mænə,fəʊbɪə] *n.* германофо́бия.

Germanophobic [dʒɜ:'mænə,fəʊbɪk] *adj.* германофо́бский.

Germany ['dʒɜ:mənɪ] *n.* Герма́ния; **Federal Republic of ~ (FRG)** Федерати́вная Респу́блика Герма́ния (*abbr.* ФРГ).

germicidal [,dʒɜ:mɪ'saɪd(ə)l] *adj.* бактерици́дный.

germicide ['dʒɜ:mɪ,saɪd] *n.* гермици́д, бактерици́дный препара́т.

germinal ['dʒɜ:mɪn(ə)l] *adj.* заро́дышевый.

germinate ['dʒɜ:mɪ,neɪt] *v.i.* прораст|а́ть, -и́; (*fig.*) дава́ть (*impf.*) всхо́ды.

germination [,dʒɜ:mɪ'neɪʃ(ə)n] *n.* прораста́ние; (*fig.*) зарожде́ние; разви́тие.

gerontocracy [,dʒerɒn'tɒkrəsɪ] *n.* правле́ние старе́йших.

gerontologist [,dʒerɒn'tɒlədʒɪst] *n.* геронто́лог.

gerontology [,dʒerɒn'tɒlədʒɪ] *n.* геронтоло́гия.

gerrymander(ing) [,dʒerɪ'mændər(ɪŋ)] *n.* предвы́борные махина́ции (*f. pl.*) (*свя́занные с непра́вильной разби́вкой на округа*).

gerund ['dʒerənd] *n.* геру́ндий.

gerundive [dʒe'rʌndɪv] *n.* герунди́в.

gesso ['dʒesəʊ] *n.* гипс.

Gestalt [gə'stɑ:lt] *n.*: (*attr.*) **~ psychology** гештальтпсихоло́гия.

Gestapo [ge'stɑ:pəʊ] *n.* геста́по (*indecl.*); (*attr.*) геста́повский; **~ man** геста́повец.

gestate [dʒe'steɪt] *v.t.* вына́шивать, вы́носить.

gestation [dʒe'steɪʃ(ə)n] *n.* бере́менность; (*fig.*) созрева́ние.

gesticulate [dʒe'stɪkjʊ,leɪt] *v.i.* жестикули́ровать (*impf.*).

gesticulation [dʒe,stɪkjʊ'leɪʃ(ə)n] *n.* жестикуля́ция.

gesture ['dʒestʃə(r)] *n.* жест; телодвиже́ние; (*fig.*) жест.

v.i. жестикули́ровать (*impf.*).

get [get] *v.t.* **1.** (*obtain, receive*) получ|а́ть, -и́ть; **I got your telegram** я получи́л ва́шу телегра́мму; **we got dinner at the hotel** мы поу́жинали в гости́нице; **I got Paris on the radio** я пойма́л по приёмнику Пари́ж; **I've got it!** (*answer to problem etc.*) э́врика!; дошло́!; **I ~ you** (*sl., understand*) по́нял!; **have you got that (down)?** (*e.g. to secretary*) (вы э́то) записа́ли?; гото́во?; **I never ~ time to see him** ника́к не могу́ вы́брать вре́мя повида́ться с ним; **this room ~s a lot of sun** э́та ко́мната о́чень со́лнечная; **he got his own way** он доби́лся своего́; **I ~ 9.5** (*as answer to calculation*) у меня́ получи́лось 9,5; **he got the poem by**

heart он вы́учил стихотворе́ние наизу́сть; **I got** (*bought*) **a new suit** я приобрёл/купи́л но́вый костю́м; **I got a glimpse of him** я его́ уви́дел ме́льком; **how does he ~ his living?** чем он зараба́тывает на жизнь? **2.** (*of suffering etc.*): **he got 2 years** (*sentence*) он получи́л 2 го́да (тюрьмы́); **he got the measles** он заболе́л ко́рью; **he got a blow on the head** он получи́л уда́р по голове́; **she got her feet wet** она́ промочи́ла но́ги; **he got his face slapped** он получи́л пощёчину. **3.** (*procure, fetch, reach, lay hands on*) дост|ава́ть, -а́ть; доб|ыва́ть, -ы́ть; **I got him a chair** я принёс ему́ стул; **the book is not in stock, but we can ~ it for you** э́той кни́ги нет на скла́де, но мы мо́жем её вам доста́ть; **we cannot ~ a plumber** мы не мо́жем найти́/доби́ться водопрово́дчика; **~ me the manager!** мне заве́дующего!; **I got him by telephone** я с ним связа́лся по телефо́ну; **the police got their man** поли́ция задержа́ла разы́скиваемого челове́ка (*or* того́, кого́ иска́ла). **4.** (*bring into a position or state*): **we got him home** мы доста́вили его́ домо́й; **he got the sum right** он пра́вильно реши́л приме́р/зада́чу; **he got her with child** она́ забере́менела от него́; он сде́лал ей ребёнка; **we got the room tidy** мы прибра́ли ко́мнату; мы убра́лись в ко́мнате; **we got the piano through the door** мы пронесли́ пиани́но че́рез дверь; **they got their daughter married** им удало́сь вы́дать дочь за́муж; **I got the clock going** я почини́л часы́; **I've got him where I want him** тепе́рь он у меня́ в рука́х. **5.** (*p.p., expr. possession*): **he has got a book** у него́ есть кни́га. **6.** (*p.p., expr. obligation*): **I have got to go** я до́лжен идти́; (*coll., expr. inference*) **you've got to be joking** вы, коне́чно (*or* должно́ быть), шу́тите. **7.** (*induce, persuade*) заст|авля́ть, -а́вить; **I got him to talk** я заста́вил его́ заговори́ть/разговори́ться; **I could not ~ the tree to grow** я не суме́л вы́растить э́то де́рево; **I got the maid to take the children out** я посла́л/отпра́вил прислу́гу погуля́ть с детьми́; **I got the fire to burn** мне удало́сь разже́чь ого́нь. **8.** (*factitive*): **I got my hair cut** я подстри́гся; **I got the table made by the carpenter** я заказа́л стол у столяра́. **9.** (*conquer, captivate*) завоёв|ывать, -а́ть; **there you have got me** вот тут-то вы меня́ и пойма́ли; **he 'got' his audience** он расшевели́л пу́блику. **10.** (*denoting progress or achievement*): **I got to know him** я его́ узна́л бли́же; **I could not ~ to see him** мне не удало́сь с ним уви́деться; **I got to like travelling** я полюби́л путеше́ствия; **they got to be friends** они́ ста́ли друзья́ми; они́ подружи́лись; **he got to be manager** он стал дире́ктором. **11.** (*see, experience*): **you never ~ working men standing for parliament** вы не встре́тите рабо́чего, кото́рый бы выставля́л свою́ кандидату́ру в парла́мент; **you won't ~ me inviting him again** бу́дьте поко́йны — я его́ никогда́ бо́льше не позову́! **12.** (*sl., kill, 'do for'*) поко́нчить (*pf.*) c+*i*.

v.i. **1.** (*become, be*) ста|нови́ться, -ть; **he got red in the face** он покрасне́л; **he got angry** он разозли́лся; **he got drunk** он напи́лся; **he got married** он жени́лся; **he got busy** (*coll.*) он заня́лся; **he got going** он разошёлся; **he got ready** он пригото́вился; **he got left behind** он отста́л; **he got killed** его́ уби́ли; он поги́б; **we got talking** мы разговори́лись. **2.** (*arrive*) приб|ыва́ть, -ы́ть; **when did you ~ here?** когда́ вы сюда́ при́были?; **I got to bed at 11** я лёг спать в 11 часо́в; **how far have you got in your work?** каку́ю часть рабо́ты (*or* ско́лько) вы сде́лали?; **he did not ~ beyond chapter 5** он не пошёл да́льше пя́той главы́; он не осилил бо́льше пяти́ глав; **where has my book got to?** куда́ де́лась/дева́лась моя́ кни́га?; **we cannot ~ home tonight** мы сего́дня не попадём домо́й. **3.** (*US sl., begone*): **I told him to ~** я веле́л ему́ кати́ться/убира́ться.

with preps.: **he got above himself** он мно́го о себе́ возомни́л; **the officer got his troops across the river** офице́р перепра́вил свои́ войска́ че́рез ре́ку; **he got ahead of his competitors** он обогна́л свои́х сопе́рников; **I cannot ~ at the books** я не могу́ добра́ться до э́тих книг; **the children got at the cake** де́ти добра́лись до пирога́; **we must ~ at the truth** мы должны́ добра́ться до пра́вды; **what is he ~ting at?** (*trying to say*) что он хо́чет сказа́ть?; куда́ он гнёт?; **she is always ~ting at me** (*criticizing, nagging*) она всегда́ ко мне придира́ется; **the witness was got at** на свиде́теля бы́ло ока́зано давле́ние со стороны́; **he got in(to) the taxi** он сел в такси́; **I cannot ~ into these shoes** я не могу́ влезть в э́ти ту́фли; **he got into a rage** он пришёл в я́рость; **what got into him?** что на него́ нашло́?; **he got into bad habits** у него́ завели́сь дурны́е привы́чки; **he got into bad company** он завёл (*or* попа́л в) плоху́ю компа́нию; **he got into the club** его́ при́няли в клуб; **I got into the way of seeing her** я привы́к с ней ви́деться/встреча́ться; **he got into trouble** он попа́л в беду́; **he got it into his head** (*imagined wrongly*) **that ...** он почему́-то реши́л (*or* вбил себе́ в го́лову), что...; **I could not ~ it into his head that ...** я не мог вбить ему́ в го́лову, что...; **~ this into your head** заруби́те себе́ э́то на носу́; **he got off his horse** он соскочи́л с коня́; **~ off the grass!** сойди́те с газо́на!; **she got the ring off her finger** она́ (с трудо́м) сняла́ кольцо́ с па́льца; **he got on his bicycle** он сел на велосипе́д; **he got on his feet** он встал/вскочи́л на́ ноги; **he got on to** (*set about*) **the task** он взя́лся за де́ло; он приступи́л к зада́нию; **I got on to** (*fathomed*) **his game** (*coll.*) я по́нял, к чему́ он кло́нит; **I got on to** (*contacted*) **him by telephone** я связа́лся с ним по телефо́ну; **the lion got out of its cage** лев вы́скочил из кле́тки; **my hat got out of shape** моя́ шля́па потеря́ла фо́рму; **I got out of going to the party** я отверте́лся/уклони́лся от вечери́нки; **he got out of the habit of seeing her** он переста́л с ней ви́деться/встреча́ться; **they got a confession out of him** они́ вы́рвали у него́ призна́ние; **I got £6 out of him** я вы́жал из него́ 6 фу́нтов; **what did you ~ out of his lecture?** что вы вы́несли/почерпну́ли из его́ ле́кции?; **we got over the wall** мы переле́зли че́рез сте́ну; **I cannot ~ over his rudeness** я не могу́ опо́мниться (*or* прийти́ в себя́) от его́ гру́бости; **he could not ~ over the loss** он не мог пережи́ть э́той утра́ты; **she got over her shyness** она́ преодоле́ла свою́ засте́нчивость; **we got round the difficulty** нам удало́сь преодоле́ть э́ту тру́дность; **she got round him** ей удало́сь его́ уговори́ть/провести́; **I got through the work** я проде́лал/проверну́л всю рабо́ту; **he got through all his money** он истра́тил все свои́ де́ньги; **he got through his exam** он вы́держал экза́мен; **he got her through the exam** он помо́г ей сдать экза́мен; **he got the bill through parliament** он провёл законопрое́кт че́рез парла́мент; **how can we ~ through** (*pass*) **the time?** как бы нам скорота́ть вре́мя; **the rescuers got to the drowning man** спаса́тели добра́лись до утопа́ющего; **they got to fighting** де́ло у них дошло́ до дра́ки; **let us ~ to business** дава́йте присту́пим к де́лу; **I cannot ~ to the meeting** я не могу́ яви́ться на собра́ние; **we got to Paris by noon** мы добра́лись до Пари́жа в по́лдень; **when it ~s to 10 o'clock I begin to feel tired** к десяти́ часа́м я начина́ю чу́вствовать уста́лость; *see also v.t.* **10.**; **the children got up to mischief** де́ти расшали́лись; **we got up to 10,000 feet** мы подняли́сь на высоту́ 10 000 (десяти́ ты́сяч) фу́тов; **we got up to chapter 5** мы дошли́ до 5 (пя́той) главы́.

with advs.: **~ about, ~ around** *v.i.*: **he ~s about a great deal** он мно́го разъезжа́ет; **a car makes it easier to ~ about** с маши́ной ле́гче поспева́ть всю́ду; **the news got about** но́вость распространи́лась; **she's been around** (*coll.*) за ней мно́го жи́зненного о́пыта; **~ across** *v.t.*: **the speaker got his point across** выступа́ющий чётко изложи́л свою́ то́чку зре́ния; **~ along** *v.i.*: **we can ~ along without him** мы мо́жем обойти́сь без него́; **they ~ along** (*agree*) **very well** они́ отли́чно ла́дят; **~ along/away with you!** брось!; иди́ ты!; да ну тебя́!; **I must be ~ting along** я до́лжен идти́; **~ around** *v.i.* = **~ about** *or* **~ round; ~ away** *v.t.*: **we got him away to the seaside** мы увезли́ его́ к мо́рю; *v.i.*: **the prisoner got away** заключённый бежа́л; **you cannot ~ away from this fact** от э́того фа́кта не уйдёшь; **the thieves got away with the money** во́ры удра́ли с деньга́ми; **he got away with cheating** ему́ удало́сь сжу́льничать; **~ back** *v.t.*: **he got his books back** он получи́л обра́тно/наза́д свои́ кни́ги; **he got his own back** (*revenge*) он отомсти́л за себя́; **I got him back to London** я привёз его́ обра́тно в Ло́ндон; *v.i.*: **he got back from the country** он верну́лся из дере́вни; **he got back into bed** он сно́ва лёг в крова́ть; **he got back at her** (*paid her out*) он отплати́л ей; ~ **by** *v.i.*: **please let me ~ by** (*pass*) разреши́те мне пройти́, пожа́луйста; **can I ~ by** (*coll.*, *pass muster*) **in a dark suit?** тёмный костю́м сойдёт?; ~ **down** *v.t.*: **he got a book down from the shelf** он снял кни́гу с по́лки; **he got his weight down** он сбро́сил (ли́шний) вес; **the secretary got the conversation down** секрета́рша записа́ла разгово́р; **I could not ~ the medicine down** я не мог проглоти́ть лека́рство; **this weather ~s me down** э́та пого́да де́йствует на меня́ удруча́юще; **things got him down** его заéл быт; *v.i.*: **he got down from his horse** он соскочи́л/слез с коня́; **the child got down (from table)** ребёнок встал из-за стола́; **he got down to his work** он засе́л за рабо́ту; **let us ~ down to the facts** дава́йте займёмся фа́ктами; ~ **in** *v.t.*: **they got the crops in** они́ убра́ли урожа́й; **we got a plumber in** мы позва́ли водопрово́дчика; **he got his blow in first** он пе́рвым нанёс уда́р; **I could not ~ a word in** я не мог вста́вить ни сло́ва; **I got my work in** (*done*) **before dinner** я зако́нчил рабо́ту до у́жина; *v.i.*: **the burglar got in through the window** взло́мщик прони́к в дом че́рез окно́; **the train got in early** по́езд пришёл ра́но; **we didn't ~ in to the concert** мы не попа́ли на конце́рт; **he got in** (*was elected*) **for Chester** он прошёл на вы́борах в Че́стере; **he got in with a bad crowd** он связа́лся с плохо́й компа́нией; ~ **off** *v.t.* (*remove*) сн|има́ть, -ять; (*dispatch*): **we got the letters off** мы отпра́вили пи́сьма; **we got the children off to school** мы отпра́вили дете́й в шко́лу; **we got the baby off to sleep** мы (е́ле-е́ле) уложи́ли ребёнка спать; **his lawyer got him off** (*acquitted*) адвока́т доби́лся его́ оправда́ния; **I got him off** (*had him excused from*) **school** я попроси́л, что́бы ему́ разреши́ли пропусти́ть шко́лу; *v.i.*: **he got off at the next station** он сошёл (с по́езда) на сле́дующей ста́нции; **I got off (to sleep) early** я ра́но засну́л; **we got off** (*started*) **at 9 a.m.** мы вы́шли/вы́ехали/отпра́вились в 9 часо́в; **he got off with a fine** он отде́лался штра́фом; **I told him where he got off** (*coll.*) я поста́вил его́ на ме́сто; **they got off (together) at once** (*coll.*) ме́жду ни́ми сра́зу возни́кла симпа́тия; они́ сра́зу пола́дили; ~ **on** *v.t.*: **I cannot ~ the lid on** я не могу́ наде́ть кры́шку; ~ **your clothes on!** оде́ньтесь!; **the teacher got his pupils on well** учи́тель хорошо́ подгото́вил свои́х ученико́в; *v.i.*: **how are you ~ting on?** как дела́?; **she is ~ting on** (*making progress*) она́ де́лает успе́хи; (*growing old*) она́ старе́ет; **~ting on (in years)** в лета́х; **he is ~ting on for 70** ему́ уже́ к семи́десяти идёт; **~ting on for** (*nearly*) почти́; **it is ~ting on for 4 o'clock** уже́ почти́ 4 часа́; вре́мя идёт к четырём часа́м; ~ **on with your work!** займи́тесь свое́й рабо́той!; **they ~ on (well) together** они́ ла́дят ме́жду собо́й; **he is easy to ~ on with** с ним легко́ ла́дить; ~ **out** *v.t.*: **the chauffeur got the car out** шофёр вы́вел маши́ну; **he got out his spectacles** он вы́нул очки́; **they got the book out** (*published*) они́ изда́ли/вы́пустили кни́гу; **he managed to ~ out** (*utter*) **a few words** ему́ удало́сь вы́молвить не́сколько слов; *v.i.*: ~ **out!** (*begone!*) убира́йтесь!; (*sl, expr. incredulity*) да ну́! иди́ ты!; **the secret got out** секре́т стал изве́стен; ~ **over** *v.t.*: **I got the main point over to him** я внуши́л/растолкова́л ему́ гла́вное/суть; **I shall be glad to ~ the meeting over (with)** скоре́е бы уж состоя́лось э́то собра́ние!; ~ **(a)round** *v.i.*: **I haven't got round to writing to him** я ещё не собра́лся написа́ть ему́; ~ **through** *v.t.* (*an exam*) выде́рживать, вы́держать экза́мен; *v.i.* (*of a bill*) про|ходи́ть, -йти́ в парла́мент; **the message got through to him** поруче́ние/запи́ску ему́ переда́ли; (*fig.*, *coll.*) он по́нял в чём де́ло; ~ **together** *v.t.*: **he got an army together** он собра́л а́рмию; *v.i.*: **we must ~ together and have a talk** мы должны́ встре́титься и поговори́ть; ~ **under** *v.t.* (*subdue*): **the fire was got under** пожа́р потуши́ли; **the revolt was got under** восста́ние бы́ло пода́влено; ~ **up** *v.t.*: **they got me up at 7** они́ по́дняли меня́ в 7 часо́в; **they got up a party** они́ устро́или вечери́нку; **they got up a subscription** они́ организова́ли подпи́ску; **the engine-driver got up steam** машини́ст развёл пары́; **she got herself up beautifully** она́ была́ прекра́сно оде́та; **he got himself up as a pirate** он наряди́лся пира́том; **the book is well got up** кни́га хорошо́ офо́рмлена; **I must ~ up my German** я до́лжен нажа́ть/нале́чь на неме́цкий; *v.i.* (*from bed, chair etc.*) вста|ва́ть, -ть; **she got up behind him** (*on horse*) она́ усе́лась на ло́шадь сза́ди его́; **the wind/sea is ~ting up** поднима́ется ве́тер; мо́ре начина́ет волнова́ться.

cpds. **~-at-able** *adj.* (*coll.*) досту́пный; **~away** *n.* бе́гство; **make one's ~** бежа́ть (*det.*; *impf*, *pf.*); **~-out** *n.* (*escape, subterfuge*) вы́ход; увёртка; **as all ~-out** (*US coll., extremely*) чрезвыча́йно, дья́вольски; **~-together** *n.* (*meeting, gathering*) встре́ча, слёт, сбо́рище; (*entertainment*) вечери́нка; **~-up** *n.* (*of book etc.*) оформле́ние; (*dress*) наря́д; **~-up-and-go** *n.* (*coll., energy*) эне́ргия; предприи́мчивость.

Gethsemane [geθ'semənı] *n.* Гефсима́ния.

gettable ['getəb(ə)l] *adj.* (*coll.*) досту́пный.

gewgaw ['gju:gɔ:] *n.* безделу́шка; мишура́.

geyser ['gaızə(r), 'gi:-] *n.* (*hot spring*) ге́йзер; (*apparatus*) коло́нка для нагре́ва воды́.

Ghana ['gɑ:nə] *n.* Га́на

Ghanaian [gɑ:'neıən] *n.* га́нец.

adj. га́нский.

ghastliness ['gɑ:stlınıs] *n.* у́жас; отврати́тельность.

ghastly ['gɑ:stlı] *adj.* ужа́сный, отврати́тельный, кошма́рный; **a ~ crime** ужа́сное преступле́ние; **a ~ accident** ужа́сная катастро́фа; **you look ~** у вас жу́ткий вид; на вас лица́ нет; **a ~ dinner** отврати́тельный у́жин.

adv. ужа́сно.

Ghent [gent] *n.* Гент.

gherkin ['gɜ:kın] n. корнишо́н.

ghetto ['getəʊ] *n.* ге́тто (*indecl.*); ~ **blaster** (*coll.*) крупногабари́тная магнито́ла.

ghost [gəʊst] *n.* **1.** (*life, spirit*): **give up the ~** испусти́ть (*pf.*) дух; **Holy G~** Свято́й Дух. **2.** (*of dead pers.*) привиде́ние; дух; **do you believe in ~s?** вы ве́рите в привиде́ния?; **lay a ~** заста́вить (*pf.*) привиде́ние исче́знуть; **he looked as if he had seen a ~** у него́ был тако́й вид, сло́вно ему́ яви́лось привиде́ние. **3.** (*vestige*): **he hasn't the ~ of a chance** у него́ нет ни мале́йшего ша́нса; **the ~ of a smile** чуть заме́тная улы́бка. **4.** (**~-writer**) литобрабо́тчик, «невиди́мка». **5.** (*opt. or television: duplicated image*) побо́чное изображе́ние.

v.t. (*also* **~-write**): **the autobiography was ~ed** автобиогра́фию за него́ написа́л друго́й.

cpds. **~buster** *n.* охо́тник за привиде́ниями; **~-like** *adj.* = **ghostly 2.**; **~-story** *n.* расска́з с привиде́ниями; **~-word** *n.* несуществу́ющее сло́во; сло́во-при́зрак.

ghostly ['gəʊstlı] *adj.* **1.** (*arch., spiritual*) духо́вный. **2.** (*ghost-like*) похо́жий на привиде́ние.

ghoul [gu:l] *n.* **1.** (*myth.*) вампи́р. **2.** (*grave-robber*) кладби́щенский вор. **3.** (*pers. delighting in horror*) люби́тель (*m.*) у́жасов.

ghoulish ['gu:lıʃ] *adj.* наслажда́ющийся у́жасами.

GHQ (*abbr. of* ***General Headquarters***) ста́вка, гла́вное кома́ндование.

GI (*abbr. of* ***government issue***; = *US private soldier*) «джи-а́й» (*indecl.*); солда́т.

giant ['dʒaıənt] *n.* **1.** (*fabulous being*) гига́нт. **2.** (*very tall pers. etc.*) велика́н, исполи́н. **3.** (*fig.*): **an intellectual ~** гига́нт мы́сли. **4.** (*attr.*) гига́нтский; исполи́нский; ~ **cactus** исполи́нский ка́ктус; **G~ Panda** бамбу́ковый медве́дь; **he made ~ strides in his work** он сде́лал гига́нтские успе́хи в рабо́те.

giantess ['dʒaıəntıs] *n.* велика́нша.

giantism ['dʒaıənt,ız(ə)m] *n.* гиганти́зм.

giaour ['dʒaʊə(r)] *n.* гяу́р.

gibber ['dʒıbə(r)] *v.i.* тарато́рить (*impf.*); говори́ть (*impf.*) невня́тно; лопота́ть (*impf.*) (*coll.*).

gibberish ['dʒıbərıʃ] *n.* тараба́рщина, лопота́ние.

gibbet ['dʒıbıt] *n.* ви́селица.

v.t. ве́шать, пове́сить; (*fig.*) выставля́ть (*impf.*) на позо́р.

gibbon ['gıbən] *n.* гиббо́н.

gibbous [ˈgɪbəs] *adj.*: ~ **moon** горба́тый ме́сяц.
gibe, jibe [dʒaɪb] *n.* насме́шка.
v.i.: ~ **at** насмеха́ться над+*i.*
giblets [ˈdʒɪblɪts] *n.* гуси́ные потрох|а́ (*pl.*, *g.* -о́в).
Gibraltar [gɪˈbrɔːltə] *n.* Гибралта́р; **Strait of** ~ Гибралта́рский проли́в.
giddap [gɪˈdæp] *int.* (*US*) но!
giddiness [ˈgɪdɪnɪs] *n.* головокруже́ние; ве́треность.
giddy [ˈgɪdɪ] *adj.* **1.** головокружи́тельный; **I feel** ~ у меня́ кру́жится голова́; **a** ~ **height** головокружи́тельная высота́. **2.** (*capricious*): **a** ~ **girl** ве́треная девчо́нка; **play the** ~ **goat** валя́ть (*impf.*) дурака́.
giddy-up [ˌgɪdɪˈʌp] *int.* но!
gift [gɪft] *n.* **1.** (*act of giving*) даре́ние; пожа́лование. **2.** (*right to bestow*): **this office is in his** ~ он во́лен назна́чить на э́то место кого́ хо́чет. **3.** (*thg. given*) пода́рок; дар; **I would not have it as a** ~ я э́то и да́ром не возьму́; ~ **shop** магази́н пода́рков; ~ **voucher/token** пода́рочный тало́н. **4.** (*talent*) дарова́ние; дар; **he has a** ~ **for languages** у него́ спосо́бности (*f. pl.*)/тала́нт к языка́м; **a man of many** ~**s** разносторо́нне одарённый челове́к. **5.** (*coll.*, *easy*): **the exam was a** ~ экза́мен был пустяко́вый.
v.t. **1.** (*bestow*) дари́ть, по-. **2.** (*endow with* ~) надел|я́ть, -и́ть; **he was** ~**ed with rare talents** он был наделён ре́дкими тала́нтами.
cpds. ~**-horse** *n.*: **you must not look a** ~**-horse in the mouth** дарёному коню́ в зу́бы не смо́трят; ~**-wrap** *v.t.* завёр|тывать, -ну́ть в пода́рочную упако́вку.
gifted [ˈgɪftɪd] *adj.* одарённый.
gig [gɪg] *n.* **1.** (*carriage*) двуко́лка. **2.** (*boat*) ги́чка.
cpd. ~**-lamps** *n. pl.* (*coll.*) очк|и́ (*pl.*, *g.* -о́в).
giga- [ˈgɪgə, ˈgaɪgə] *comb. form* гига...; ~**byte** гигаба́йт; ~**watt** гигава́тт.
gigantic [dʒaɪˈgæntɪk] *adj.* гига́нтский.
giggle [ˈgɪg(ə)l] *n.* хихи́канье; **for a** ~ сме́ха/шу́тки ра́ди; (*coll.*) для хо́хмы; **he had a fit of the** ~**s** на него́ смех(у́нчик) напа́л.
v.i. хихи́к|ать, -нуть.
gigolo [ˈʒɪgəˌləʊ, ˈdʒɪg-] *n.* жи́голо (*m. indecl.*); наёмный партнёр в та́нцах.
gigue [ʒiːg] *n.* жи́га, джи́га.
gild [gɪld] *v.t.* **1.** (*cover or tinge with gold*) золоти́ть, по-. **2.** (*fig.*) укр|аша́ть, -а́сить; ~ **the pill** позолоти́ть (*pf.*) пилю́лю; ~ **the lily** переб|а́рщивать, -орщи́ть; ≃ ма́сло ма́сляное; ~**ed youth** золота́я молодёжь.
gilder [ˈgɪldə(r)] *n.* позоло́тчик.
gilding [ˈgɪldɪŋ] *n.* позоло́та.
gill[1] [gɪl] *n.* (*of fish*) жа́бра; **he looks green about the** ~**s** (*fig.*) он вы́глядит больны́м.
gill[2] [dʒɪl] *n.* (*measure*) че́тверть пи́нты.
gillie [ˈgɪlɪ] *n.* ≃ помо́щник охо́тника.
gillyflower [ˈdʒɪlɪˌflaʊə(r)] *n.* левко́й.
gilt[1] [gɪlt] *n.* позоло́та; **take the** ~ **off the gingerbread** лиша́ть (*что*) привлека́тельности.
cpd. ~**-edged** *adj.* (*book etc.*) с золочёным обре́зом; ~**-edged securities** первокла́ссные (*or* осо́бо надёжные) це́нные бума́ги.
gilt[2] [gɪlt] *n.* (*young sow*) подсви́нок.
gimbals [ˈdʒɪmb(ə)lz] *n.* карда́нов подве́с, карда́н.
gimcrack [ˈdʒɪmkræk] *adj.* мишу́рный.
gimlet [ˈgɪmlɪt] *n.* бура́в; бура́вчик.
cpd. ~**-eyed** *adj.* остроглаз́ый; проница́тельный.
gimmick [ˈgɪmɪk] *n.* (*coll.*) трюк; финт, ухищре́ние.
gimmickry [ˈgɪmɪkrɪ] *n.* (*coll.*) трю́ки (*m. pl.*); трюка́чество.
gimmicky [ˈgɪmɪkɪ] *adj.* (*coll.*) трюка́ческий; с выкрута́сами.
gimp [gɪmp] *n.* (*text.*) гипю́р; позуме́нт; кани́тель.
gin[1] [dʒɪn] *n.* (*trap*) западня́, сило́к.
gin[2] [dʒɪn] *n.* (*cotton*-~) джин, волокноотдели́тель (*m.*).
v.t. оч|ища́ть, -и́стить.
gin[3] [dʒɪn] *n.* (*drink*) джин.
ginger [ˈdʒɪndʒə(r)] *n.* **1.** (*bot.*, *cul.*) имби́рь (*m.*); (*attr.*) имби́рный. **2.** (*mettle, dash*) задо́р; ~ **group** активи́сты, инициати́вная гру́ппа; (*zest*) «изю́минка».
adj. (*colour*) ры́жий.
v.t.: ~ **up** подзадо́ри|вать, -ть.
cpds. ~**ale,** ~**-beer,** ~**-pop** *nn.* имби́рное пи́во; ~**bread** *n.* имби́рная коври́жка; ~**-nut,** ~**-snap** *nn.* имби́рный пря́ник.
gingerly [ˈdʒɪndʒəlɪ] *adj.* (кра́йне) осторо́жный.
adv. осторо́жно.
gingery [ˈdʒɪndʒərɪ] *adj.* **1.** (*like ginger in taste etc.*) имби́рный. **2.** (*colour*) рыжева́тый. **3.** (*fig.*, *irascible*) раздражи́тельный.
gingham [ˈgɪŋəm] *n.* пестротка́нный гринсбо́н.
gingival [ˌdʒɪnˈdʒaɪv(ə)l] *adj.* дёсенный.
gingivitis [ˌdʒɪndʒɪˈvaɪtɪs] *n.* воспале́ние дёсен, гингиви́т.
gink [gɪŋk] *n.* (*sl.*) па́рень (*m.*), ма́лый.
ginkgo [ˈgɪŋkgəʊ], **gingko** [ˈgɪŋkəʊ] *n.* ги́нкго (*indecl.*).
ginormous [dʒaɪˈnɔːməs] *adj.* (*coll.*) огрома́дный.
ginseng [ˈdʒɪnseŋ] *n.* женьше́нь (*m.*).
Gipsy, Gypsy [ˈdʒɪpsɪ] *n.* цыга́н (*fem.* -ка); **g**~ **moth** непа́рный шелкопря́д.
adj. цыга́нский.
giraffe [dʒɪˈrɑːf, -ˈræf] *n.* жира́ф(а).
girandole [ˈdʒɪrənˌdəʊl] *n.* канделя́бр.
girasol(e) [ˈdʒɪrəˌsɒl] *n.* о́гненный опа́л.
gird[1] [gɜːd] *v.t.* **1.** (*with belt etc.*) опоя́с|ывать, -ать; ~ **(up) one's loins** (*fig.*) ≃ засучи́ть (*pf.*) рукава́; собра́ться (*pf.*) с си́лами; ~ **on one's sword** прикрепи́ть (*pf.*) са́блю к по́ясу. **2.** (*encircle, e.g. fortress or island*) окруж|а́ть, -и́ть.
gird[2] [gɜːd] *v.i.* (*jeer*) насмеха́ться (*impf.*) (над+*i.*).
girder [ˈgɜːdə(r)] *n.* (*beam*) ба́лка; брус; (*span of bridge etc.*) перекла́дина; фе́рма.
girdle [ˈgɜːd(ə)l] *n.* **1.** (*belt etc.*) по́яс; куша́к. **2.** (*corset*) корсе́т. **3.** (*ring round tree*) кольцо́. **4.** (*fig.*): **a** ~ **of fields round a town** поля́, окружа́ющие го́род.
v.t. **1.** (*encircle*) окруж|а́ть, -и́ть. **2.**: ~ **a tree** кольцева́ть (*impf.*) де́рево.
girl [gɜːl] *n.* (*child*) де́вочка; (*young woman*) де́вушка; (*pej.*) девчо́нка; ~ **guide, scout** де́вочка-скау́т, гёрл-скау́т, гёрл-гайд; (*maid-servant*) служа́нка; (*sweetheart*; *also* **best** ~) возлю́бленная; **old** ~ (*coll.*, *old woman*; *also as affec. term of address*) стару́шка; (*ex-pupil of school*) выпускни́ца (*данной школы*); ~ **Friday** ≃ помо́щница.
cpd. ~**-friend** *n.* (*female friend*) подру́га; (*mistress*) ≃ де́вушка/прия́тельница.
girlhood [ˈgɜːlhʊd] *n.* деви́чество, о́трочество; **in her** ~ в деви́честве; **a type of English** ~ образе́ц англи́йской де́вушки.
girlie [ˈgɜːlɪ] *n.* (*coll.*) де́вочка, девчу́шка; ~ **magazine** журна́л с фотогра́фиями (полу)обнажённых же́нщин.
girlish [ˈgɜːlɪʃ] *adj.* деви́ческий; (*of a boy*) изне́женный, (*coll.*) как девчо́нка.
girlishness [ˈgɜːlɪʃnɪs] *n.* поведе́ние, сво́йственное де́вочке.
girth [gɜːθ] *n.* (*of horse*) подпру́га; (*of tree, pers. etc.*) обхва́т; разме́р.
gist [dʒɪst] *n.* суть.
give [gɪv] *n.* **1.** (*elasticity*) пода́тливость, эласти́чность; **there's no** ~ **in a stone floor** ка́менный пол не прогиба́ется; **there is no** ~ **in this rope** э́та верёвка не растя́гивается; **there is no** ~ **in his attitude** он за́нял непреклóнную пози́цию. **2.**: ~ **and take** взаимоотда́ча, взаимообме́н; взаи́мные усту́пки (*f. pl.*).
v.t. **1.** да|ва́ть, -ть; ~ **lessons** дава́ть уро́ки; **I** ~ **you my word** даю́ вам сло́во; ~ (*play*) **us some Chopin** сыгра́йте нам Шопе́на; **I gave the porter my luggage** ~ я о́тдал свой бага́ж носи́льщику; **you must** ~ **and take in this life** в жи́зни ну́жно не то́лько брать, но и дава́ть что-то взаме́н; **two years,** ~ **or take a month or so** о́коло двух лет — ме́сяцем бо́льше и́ли ме́ньше. **2.** (*imper.*, *expr. preference*): ~ **me the good old days!** где на́ше до́брое ста́рое вре́мя?!; ~ **me Bach every time** я всем и всегда́ предпочита́ю Ба́ха; ~ **me liberty or** ~ **me death!** свобо́да и́ли смерть! **3.** (*present, bestow, surrender*) дари́ть, по-; **he was** ~**n a book** ему́ подари́ли кни́гу; **he gave him his daughter in marriage** он отда́л ему́ свою́ дочь в жёны; **she gave herself to him** она́ ему́ отдала́сь; **the thief was** ~**n in charge** во́ра отда́ли под стра́жу. **4.** (*propose*): **I** ~ **you** (*the toast of*) **the Queen** я предлага́ю тост за

королéву. **5.** (~ *in exchange*): **I gave a good price for it** я за э́то хорошó заплати́л; **what will you ~ me for this coat?** скóлько вы мне дади́те за э́то пальтó?; **I would ~ anything to know where she is** я бы всё отдáл, чтóбы узнáть, где онá; **he gave as good as he got** он заплати́л той же монéтой; **I don't ~ a damn!** а мне наплевáть! **6.** (*provide, furnish, impart, inflict*): **the sun ~s light** сóлнце — истóчник свéта; **he ~s me a lot of trouble** он мне доставля́ет мнóго хлопóт; **he has ~n me his cold** я зарази́лся от негó нáсморком; он награди́л меня́ свои́м нáсморком; **the place gave its name to the battle** би́тва берёт своё назвáние от мéстности; би́тва нáзвана по мéстности, где онá произошлá; **the news was ~n to the world** нóвость былá обнарóдована; **he gave** (*cited*) **an example** он привёл примéр; **he gave me to understand that ...** он дал мне поня́ть, что...; **~ him my regards** передáйте емý от меня́ привéт; **a literal translation is ~n** привóдится буквáльный перевóд; **~ evidence** (*in court*) да|вáть, -ть показáния; **~ pleasure** дост|авля́ть, -áвить удовóльствие; **the court gave him 6 months** суд приговори́л егó к шести́ мéсяцам (тюрьмы́); емý дáли 6 мéсяцев; **I gave him a look** я (*сердито и т.п.*) взглянýл на негó; **the noise ~s me a headache** у меня́ головá боли́т от шýма; **he gave the signal to start** он дал сигнáл начинáть; **he gave no sign of life** он не подавáл при́знаков жи́зни. **7.** (*indicate*): **this book ~s you the answers** отвéты вы найдёте в э́той кни́ге; **he gave no reason for his absence** он не объясни́л своегó отсýтствия. **8.** (*decide*): **the case was ~n against him** дéло реши́ли не в егó пóльзу. **9.** (*devote, sacrifice*) удел|я́ть, -и́ть; посвя|щáть, -ти́ть; **he gave a lot of time to the work** он удели́л э́той рабóте мнóго врéмени; **he gave his life for her** он отдáл за неё жизнь; **he gave thought to the question** он мнóго дýмал над э́тим вопрóсом; **he gave me his attention** он внимáтельно меня́ слýшал. **10.** (*allow, estimate*): **I ~ you an hour to get ready** я даю́ вам час приготóвиться; **I ~ him three months to fail** вот уви́дите — чéрез три мéсяца он провáлится; **to ~ him his due, he tried hard** нáдо отдáть емý дóлжное — он óчень старáлся; **it was ~n me to see her once more** мне довелóсь уви́деть её ещё раз; **I would ~ him** (*estimate his age at*) **50** я бы дал емý лет 50. **11.** (*organize*) устр|áивать, -óить; **they gave a dance** они́ устрóили танцевáльный вéчер. **12.** (*perform action*): **the horse gave a kick** лóшадь (вз)брыкнýла; **he gave a loud laugh** он грóмко рассмея́лся; **the dog gave a bark** собáка залáяла. **13.** (*with pronominal object*): **~ it to him!** (*beating etc.*) дай емý!; **I gave him what for** (*coll.*) я зáдал емý трёпку; **I gave him best** я уступи́л емý; **I gave him one** (*a blow*) **over the head** я стýкнул егó по башкé. **14.** (*special uses of* **~n**): **~n under my hand and seal** за моéй собственнорýчной пóдписью и печáтью; мнóю подпи́сано и скрепленó печáтью; **under the ~n** (*existing*) **conditions** в дáнных обстоя́тельствах/услóвиях; **~n time, it can be done** при нали́чии врéмени э́то мóжно сдéлать; **at a ~n** (*specified, agreed, particular*) **time** в определённое врéмя; **~n name** (*forename*) и́мя (*nt.*); **he is ~n to boasting** он склóнен к хвастовствý; **~ that ...** при том, что...

v.i. **1.: he ~s generously** он óчень щедр; **~ of one's best** вложи́ть (*pf.*) дýшу. **2.** (*yield*) подд|авáться, -áться; под|авáться, -áться; **the branch gave but did not break** вéтка согнýлась, но не сломáлась; **his knees gave** егó колéни подкоси́лись; **the ground gave under our feet** земля́ подалáсь под нáшими ногáми; **the frost is beginning to ~** (*weaken*) морóз начинáет сдавáть; **the rope gave** (*broke*) верёвка оборвалáсь (*or* не вы́держала). **3.** (*face*): **the window ~s on to the yard** окнó выхóдит во двор.

with advs.: **~ away** *v.t.* дари́ть, по-; (*distribute, e.g. prizes*) разд|авáть, -áть; **he gave away the secret** он вы́дал секрéт; **don't ~ me away!** не выдавáйте меня́!; **he gave the game away** (*blew the gaff*) он проболтáлся; он вы́дал секрéт; (*lost on purpose*) он умы́шленно проигрáл; (*by bad play*) он игрáл из рук вон плóхо; **~ back** *v.t.* (*restore*) возвра|щáть, -ти́ть; отд|авáть, -áть; **the wall gave back an echo** стенá отрази́ла звук; **~ forth** *v.t.* (*emit*) изд|авáть, -áть; испус|кáть, -ти́ть; (*publish*) объяв|ля́ть, -и́ть; обнарóдовать (*pf.*); **~ in** *v.t.*: **he gave in his name** он записáлся/зарегестри́ровался; **he gave in his** (*exam*) **paper** он сдал свою́ экзаменациóнную рабóту; *v.i.* (*yield*) подд|авáться, -áться; уступ|áть, -и́ть; **he gave in to my persuasion** он поддáлся мои́м уговóрам; **~ off** *v.t.* (*emit, e.g. smell or smoke*) испус|кáть, -ти́ть; изд|авáть, -áть; **~ out** *v.t.* (*distribute*) распредел|я́ть, -и́ть; (*announce*) объяв|ля́ть, -и́ть; **he gave himself out to be the prince** он выдавáл себя́ за при́нца; *v.i.* кончáться, кóнчиться; **the rations gave out** продовóльствие кóнчилось; **his strength gave out** егó си́лы иссякли; **~ over** *v.t.* (*hand over*) перед|авáть, -áть; (*abandon*) ост|авля́ть, -áвить; **he was ~n over to vice** он предáлся порóку; **~ over!** (*coll., desist!*) брóсьте!; **~ over pushing!** перестáньте толкáться!; (*devote*) **the time was ~n over to discussion** врéмя бы́ло óтдано/посвященó диску́ссии; **~ up** *v.t.* ост|авля́ть, -áвить; (*resign, surrender*) откáз|ываться, -áться *+g.*; **he gave up his seat to her** он уступи́л ей мéсто; **the murderer gave himself up** уби́йца сдáлся; (*desist from*) бр|осáть, -óсить; **he gave up smoking** он брóсил кури́ть; (*abandon hope of*): **the doctors gave him up** врачи́ отказáлись от негó; **they gave him up for lost** они́ реши́ли, что он пропáл; **you were so late that we gave you up** вы пришли́ так пóздно, что мы вас и ждать перестáли; **we gave it up as a bad job** (*desisted from hopeless attempt*) мы махнýли рукóй на э́то дéло; **after the quarrel she gave him up** пóсле ссóры онá с ним порвáла; *v.i.* **the swimmer gave up** пловéц сошёл с дистáнции; **I ~ up!** сдаю́сь!

cpd. **~-away** *n.* (*coll.*) (*betrayal of secret etc.*) (само)разоблачéние; разглашéние; (*free gift*) подáрок.

giver [ˈgɪvə(r)] *n.* даю́щий; **he is a generous ~** он óчень щедр.

gizmo [ˈgɪzməʊ] *n.* (*US*) штукóвина, штукéнция.

gizzard [ˈgɪzəd] *n.* вторóй желýдок (*у птиц*); (*fig., coll.*) желýдок; **it sticks in my ~** (*coll.*) мне э́то поперёк гóрла стáло.

glacé [ˈglæseɪ] *adj.*: **~ kid** гля́нцевое шеврó (*indecl.*); **~ fruits** засáхаренные фрýкты.

glacial [ˈgleɪʃ(ə)l, -sɪəl] *adj.* ледóвый; ледянóй; **the ~ era** ледникóвый перúод; (*fig.*) **a ~ smile** ледянáя/холóдная улы́бка.

glaciation [ˌgleɪsɪˈeɪʃ(ə)n] *n.* оледенéние; замерзáние.

glacier [ˈglæsɪə(r)] *n.* ледни́к; глéтчер.

glacis [ˈglæsɪs, -siː] *n.* (*mil.*) глáсис, перéдний скат брýствера.

glad [glæd] *adj.* **1.** (*pleased*) довóльный; **I am ~ to meet you** рад с вáми познакóмиться; **I shall be ~ if you will send me your bill** бýду рад получи́ть от вас счёт; **I should be ~ of a few pounds** я был бы рад (и) нéскольким фýнтам. **2.** (*happy*) рáдостный; **she gave a ~ cry** онá издалá рáдостный крик; онá рáдостно вскри́кнула; **this is the ~dest day of my life** э́то сáмый счастли́вый день в моéй жи́зни. **3.** (*coll.*): **~ rags** прáздничное плáтье.

gladden [ˈglæd(ə)n] *v.t.* рáдовать, об-; **flowers ~ the scene** цветы́ оживля́ют вид; **wine ~s the heart** винó весели́т дýшу; **a ~ing sight** отрáдное зрéлище.

glade [gleɪd] *n.* поля́на, прогáлина.

gladiator [ˈglædɪˌeɪtə(r)] *n.* гладиáтор.

gladiatorial [ˈglædɪəˈtɔːrɪəl] *adj.* гладиáторский.

gladiolus [ˌglædɪˈəʊləs] *n.* гладиóлус.

gladly [ˈglædlɪ] *adv.* (*joyfully*) рáдостно; (*willingly, with pleasure*) охóтно.

gladness [ˈglædnɪs] *n.* рáдость.

Glagolitic [ˌglægəˈlɪtɪk] *adj.* глаголи́ческий; **the ~ alphabet, script** глагóлица.

glamorous [ˈglæmərəs] *adj.* обольсти́тельный; плени́тельный; (*of job etc.*) замáнчивый.

glamour [ˈglæmə(r)] *n.* волшебствó, очаровáние; шик; **~ boy/girl** шикáрный пáрень, шикáрная деви́ца.

glamo(u)rize [ˈglæməˌraɪz] *v.t.* приукрá|шивать, -сить; прид|авáть, -áть орéол *+d.*

glanc|e [glɑːns] *n.* **1.** (*quick look*) взгляд; **I took a ~e at the newspaper** я заглянýл в газéту; **I recognised him at a ~e** я узнáл егó с пéрвого взгля́да. **2.** (*flash*) блеск, блик.

v.t. & i. **1.** (*look*) взглянýть (*pf.*); брóсить (*pf.*) взгляд; **he ~ed at the clock** он взглянýл на часы́; **he ~ed round the room** он оглядéл кóмнату; **he ~ed over the figures** он скользнýл взгля́дом по ци́фрам; **he ~ed down the page** он пробежáл страни́цу глазáми. **2.** (*allude briefly*): **he ~ed at the subject** он слегкá коснýлся тéмы. **3.: the sword ~ed aside** меч скользнýл (по повéрхности щитá *и т.п.*); **a ~ ing blow** скользя́щий удáр.

gland [glænd] *n.* железá.

glanders ['glændəz] *n.* сап.

glandular ['glændjʊlə(r)] *adj.* желéзистый.

glare [gleə(r)] *n.* (*fierce light*) ослепи́тельный свет/блеск; (*fig.*): **~ of publicity** реклáмная шуми́ха; (*angry look*) свирéпый взгляд.

v.t. & i. ослепи́тельно сверкáть; **the sun ~d down** сóлнце пали́ло; **~ at s.o.** испепел|я́ть, -и́ть когó-н. взгля́дом; **they ~d defiance at each other** они́ с вы́зовом смотрéли друг на дрýга.

glaring ['gleərɪŋ] *adj.* (*e.g. headlights*) слепя́щий, ослепи́тельный; (*of colour*) кричáщий, я́ркий; (*fierce, angry*) свирéпый; (*of mistake etc.*) грýбый.

glasnost ['glæznɒst, 'glɑːs-] *n.* глáсность.

glass [glɑːs] *n.* **1.** (*substance*) стеклó; **~ eye** стекля́нный глаз; **~ case** стекля́нный колпáк; **people who live in ~ houses should not throw stones** тот, кто сам не безупрéчен, не дóлжен осуждáть другúх; ≃ в чужóм глазý уви́дит сори́нку, а в своём бревнá не замечáет. **2.** (*for drinking*) (*tumbler*) стакáн; (*wine-~*) рю́мка, бокáл; **he had a ~ too much** он сли́шком мнóго вы́пил; он вы́пил ли́шнего; **they clinked ~es** они́ чóкнулись. **3.** (*~ware*) стеклянная посýда. **4.: tomatoes under ~** (*in ~houses*) помидóры в тепли́це. **5.** (*mirror*) зéркало. **6.** (*spy ~*) подзóрная трубá. **7.** (*barometer*) барóметр. **8.** (*pl., spectacles*) очк|и́ (*pl., g.* -óв).

v.t.: **a ~ed-in veranda** застеклённая/остеклённая верáнда.

cpds. **~-blower** *n.* стеклодýв; **~-blowing** *n.* стеклодýвное дéло; **~house** *n.* тепли́ца; **~-maker** *n.* стекóльщик; **~-making** *n.* стекóльное дéло; **~-snake** *n.* америкáнский желтопýзик; **~ware** *n.* стеклянная посýда.

glassful ['glɑːsfʊl] *n.* стакáн (*чего*).

glassiness ['glɑːsɪnɪs] *n.* (*e.g. of eyes*) тýсклость, безжи́зненность; (*e.g. of river, lake*) зеркáльность.

glassy ['glɑːsɪ] *adj.*: **a ~ stare** тýсклый/засты́вший взгляд; **a ~ lake** зеркáльная гладь óзера.

glaucoma [glɔː'kəʊmə] *n.* глаукóма.

glaucous ['glɔːkəs] *adj.* тýсклый, серовáто-зелёный; покры́тый налётом.

glaze [gleɪz] *n.* (*substance*) муравá, глазýрь; (*~d surface*) гля́нец; глазýрь.

v.t. **1.** (*pottery, paint etc.*) глазуровáть (*impf., pf.*). **2. his eyes were ~d in death** егó глазá мéртвенно остекленéли.

v.i.: **his eyes ~d over** егó взгляд потускнéл.

glazier ['gleɪzjə(r)] *n.* стекóльщик.

glazing ['gleɪzɪŋ] *n.* (*material*) глазýрь; (*glasswork*) остеклéние; **double ~** двойны́е рáмы (*f. pl.*).

GLC (*hist., abbr. of* ***Greater London Council***) Совéт Большóго Лóндона.

gleam [gliːm] *n.* прóблеск; **a ~ of hope** прóблеск надéжды; **a dangerous ~ in the eye** опáсный блеск в глазáх; **without a ~ of humour** без тéни ю́мора.

v.i. поблёскивать (*impf.*); блестéть (*impf.*).

glean [gliːn] *v.t.* (*lit., also v.i.*) подбирáть (*impf.*) (колоски́); (*fig.*) соб|ирáть, -рáть (по крупи́цам).

gleaner ['gliːnə(r)] *n.* сбóрщи|к (*fem.* -ца) колóсьев.

gleanings ['gliːnɪŋz] *n.* (*fig.*) крупи́цы (*f. pl.*).

glee [gliː] *n.* (*delight*) весéлье; ликовáние; (*song*) пéние «а капéлла»; **~ club** клуб певцóв-люби́телей.

gleeful ['gliːfʊl] *adj.* ликýющий.

glen [glen] *n.* лощи́на.

glib [glɪb] *adj.* бóйкий на язы́к; речи́стый; **a ~ excuse** благови́дный предлóг.

glibness ['glɪbnɪs] *n.* словоохóтливость; краснобáйство.

glide [glaɪd] *n.* (*movement, also phon.*) скольжéние; (*mus.*) хромати́ческая гáмма.

v.i. скольз|и́ть, -нýть; **the time ~d by** врéмя пролетéло; (*in aircraft*) плани́ровать, с-.

cpd. **~-path** *n.* (*aeron.*) глиссáда.

glider ['glaɪdə(r)] *n.* планёр; **~ pilot** планери́ст.

gliding ['glaɪdɪŋ] *n.* (*sport*) планери́зм.

glimmer ['glɪmə(r)] *n.* тýсклый свет; мерцáние; **a ~ of hope/intelligence** прóблеск надéжды/умá.

v.i. мерцáть (*impf.*).

glimpse [glɪmps] *n.* прóблеск; **I caught a ~ of him** он промелькнýл у меня́ пéред глазáми.

v.t. уви́деть (*pf.*) мéльком.

glint [glɪnt] *n.* блеск; (*reflection*) óтблеск.

v.i. блестéть (*impf.*); (*flash*) вспы́х|ивать, -нуть.

glissade [glɪ'sɑːd, -'seɪd] *n.* **1.** (*mountaineering*) соскáльзывание. **2.** (*ballet*) глиссé (*indecl.*).

v.i. **1.** сколь|зи́ть, -нýть. **2.** дéлать, с- глиссé.

glissando [glɪ'sændəʊ] *n.* глиссáндо (*indecl.*).

glisten ['glɪs(ə)n] *v.i.* сверк|áть, -нýть; перели́ваться (*impf.*).

glitch [glɪtʃ] *n.* внезáпная авáрия.

glitter ['glɪtə(r)] *n.* блеск, сверкáние.

v.i. блестéть (*impf.*); сверкáть (*impf.*).

glitz [glɪts] *n.* (показнóй) блеск, шик.

glitzy ['glɪtsɪ] *adj.* мишýрный, показýшный.

gloaming ['gləʊmɪŋ] *n.* сýмер|ки (*pl., g.* -ек).

gloat [gləʊt] *v.i.* смотрéть (*impf.*) с вожделéнием (на+*a.*); (*maliciously*) злорáдствовать (*impf.*).

global ['gləʊb(ə)l] *adj.* (*total*) всеóбщий; (*world-wide*) глобáльный.

globe [gləʊb] *n.* **1.** (*spherical body*) шар; глóбус; **~ of the eye** глазнóе я́блоко; **~ artichoke** артишóк. **2.: terrestrial ~** земнóй шар; **celestial ~** небéсный глóбус.

cpds. **~-fish** *n.* ры́ба-собáка; **~-trotter** *n.* заядлый тури́ст.

globular ['glɒbjʊlə(r)] *adj.* шарови́дный.

globule ['glɒbjuːl] *n.* шáрик; кáпелька.

glockenspiel ['glɒkən,spiːl, -ʃpiːl] *n.* металлофóн.

gloom [gluːm] *n.* (*dark*) тьма; мрак; (*despondency*) мрáчность; уны́ние; **the news cast a ~ over us** нóвость омрачи́ла/испóртила нам настроéние.

v.i. (*coll., behave ~ily*) пред|авáться, -áться уны́нию.

gloominess ['gluːmɪnɪs] *n.* мрáчность.

gloomy ['gluːmɪ] *adj.* (*dark*) мрáчный; (*depressing*) гнетýщий; (*depressed*) хмýрый; уны́лый.

glorification [,glɔːrɪfɪ'keɪʃ(ə)n] *n.* прославлéние, восхвалéние.

glorifier ['glɔːrɪ,faɪə(r)] *n.*: **he is a ~ of old times** он превознóсит всё стáрое.

glorif|y ['glɔːrɪ,faɪ] *v.t.* **1.** (*worship*) восхваля́ть (*impf.*). **2.** (*honour, extol*) просл|авля́ть, -áвить. **3.: a ~ied barn** разукрáшенный сарáй.

gloriole ['glɔːrɪ,əʊl] *n.* нимб, ореóл.

glorious ['glɔːrɪəs] *adj.* слáвный, великолéпный; **a ~ day** (*weather*) изуми́тельный день; (*iron.*) **he made a ~ mess of it** он запýтал делá как нельзя́ лýчше.

glor|y ['glɔːrɪ] *n.* **1.** (*renown, honour*) слáва. **2.** (*splendour*) великолéпие. **3.** (*source of honour*): **the ~ies of Rome** слáва/вели́чие Ри́ма. **4.** (*heavenly bliss*): **go to ~y** умерéть (*pf.*); почи́ть (*pf.*). **5.: Old G~** (*US coll.*) флаг США.

v.i. упивáться (*impf.*) +*i.*; горди́ться (*impf.*) +*i.*; **~y in one's strength** упивáться своéй си́лой.

cpd. **~-hole** *n.* (*coll.*) свáлка.

gloss[1] [glɒs] *n.* (*comment, explanation*) глóсса, пояснéние; замéтка; (*interpretation*) толковáние.

v.t. комменти́ровать, про-; толковáть (*impf.*).

gloss[2] [glɒs] *n.* (*lit., fig.*) лоск.

v.t.: **~ over faults** обойти́ (*pf.*) оши́бки молчáнием; замáз|ывать, -ать недостáтки.

glossary ['glɒsərɪ] *n.* глоссáрий.

glossiness ['glɒsɪnɪs] *n.* лоск.

gloss|y ['glɒsɪ] *adj.* глянцеви́тый; лощёный; **a ~y photograph** гля́нцевая фотогрáфия; **~y magazines** (*also coll.* **~ies**) ≃ дороги́е иллюстри́рованные журнáлы.

glottal ['glɒt(ə)l] *adj.* относя́щийся к голосовóй щéли; **~ stop** гортáнный взрыв.

glottis ['glɒtɪs] *n.* голосовáя щель.

glove [glʌv] *n.* перчáтка; (*fig.*): **fit like a ~** быть впóру (*or* в са́мый раз); **handle s.o. with kid ~s** церемо́ниться (*impf.*) с кем-н.; **with the ~s off** всерьёз; **~ compartment** (*in car*) я́щик для мелоче́й; бардачо́к.

v.t.: **a ~d hand** рука́ в перча́тке.

cpd. **~-stretcher** *n.* болва́нка для растя́жки перча́ток.

glover ['glʌvə(r)] *n.* перча́точник.

glow [gləʊ] *n.* (*of bodily warmth*) жар; (*of fire, sunset etc.*) за́рево; (*of feelings*) пыл.

v.i. (*incandesce*) нака́л|иваться, -и́ться; (*shine*) свети́ться (*impf.*), сверка́ть (*impf.*); **~ing metal** раскалённый мета́лл; **a forest ~ing with autumn tints** лес, пыла́ющий осе́нними кра́сками; **he ~ed with pride** его́ распира́ла го́рдость; **he described the trip in ~ing colours** он расписа́л путеше́ствие в ра́дужных тона́х.

cpds. **~-lamp** *n.* ла́мпа нака́ливания; **~-worm** *n.* светля́к.

glower ['glaʊə(r)] *v.i.* серди́то смотре́ть (*impf.*).

gloxinia [glɒk'sɪnɪə] *n.* глокси́ния.

glucose ['glu:kəʊs, -kəʊz] *n.* глюко́за.

glue [glu:] *n.* клей.

v.t. прикле́и|вать; (*fig.*): **he ~d his eyes to the floor** он уста́вился в пол; **he ~d his ear to the keyhole** он прини́к у́хом к замо́чной сква́жине.

cpds. **~-pot** *n.* клееváрка; **~-sniffer** *n.* токсикома́н; **~-sniffing** *n.* токсикома́ния.

gluey ['glu:ɪ] *adj.* кле́йкий.

glum [glʌm] *adj.* угрю́мый.

glumness ['glʌmnɪs] *n.* угрю́мость.

glut [glʌt] *n.* избы́ток; затова́ривание.

v.t. нас|ыща́ть, -ы́тить; **~ one's appetite** на|еда́ться, -е́сться; **~ o.s.** нас|ыща́ться, -ы́титься; **~ the market** затова́ри|вать, -ть ры́нок; **the animals were ~ted** живо́тные нае́лись до отва́ла.

gluten ['glu:t(ə)n] *n.* клейкови́на.

glutinous ['glu:tɪnəs] *adj.* кле́йкий, ли́пкий, вя́зкий.

glutton ['glʌt(ə)n] *n.* **1.** обжо́ра (*c.g.*); **a ~ for work** жа́дный к рабо́те. **2.** (*zool.*) росома́ха.

gluttonous ['glʌtənəs] *adj.* прожо́рливый.

gluttony ['glʌtənɪ] *n.* обжо́рство.

glycerin(e) ['glɪsə,ri:n] *n.* глицери́н.

GMT = **Greenwich (mean) time**

gnarl|ed [nɑ:ld], **-y** ['nɑ:lɪ] *adjs.* шишкова́тый; сучкова́тый.

gnash [næʃ] *v.t.*: **~ one's teeth** скрежета́ть (*impf.*) зуба́ми.

gnat [næt] *n.* кома́р; **strain at a ~** (*fig.*) придира́ться (*impf.*) к мелоча́м.

gnaw [nɔ:] *v.t. & i.* грызть (*impf.*); **the dog ~ed (at) a bone** соба́ка глода́ла кость; **rats ~ed away the woodwork** кры́сы изгры́зли де́рево; **pain ~ed his vitals** боль терза́ла его́ те́ло; **~ing pangs of hunger** мучи́тельные при́ступы го́лода; **~ing anxiety** грызу́щее беспоко́йство.

gneiss [naɪs] *n.* гнейс.

gnome [nəʊm] *n.* (*goblin etc.*) гном.

gnomic ['nəʊmɪk] *adj.* гноми́ческий; афористи́чный.

gnomon ['nəʊmɒn] *n.* гномо́н, стре́лка/сто́лбик со́лнечных часо́в.

Gnostic ['nɒstɪk] *n.* гно́стик.

adj. гности́ческий.

Gnosticism ['nɒstɪ,sɪz(ə)m] *n.* гностици́зм.

GNP (*abbr. of* ***Gross National Product***) ВНП, (валово́й национа́льный проду́кт).

gnu [nu:, nju:] *n.* гну (*m. indecl.*).

go [gəʊ] *n.* **1.** (*movement, animation*) движе́ние; ход; **she's on the ~ from morning to night** она́ с утра́ до ве́чера на нога́х; **she has no ~ in her** нет в ней изю́минки/огонька́ (*coll.*). **2.** (*turn, attempt, shot*) попы́тка; **now it's my ~** тепе́рь моя́ о́чередь; **why don't you have a ~?** почему́ бы вам не попро́бовать?; **he scored 50 in one ~** он набра́л 50 очко́в в одно́м захо́де. **3.** (*coll., success*) успе́х; **he tried to make a ~ of it** он стара́лся доби́ться успе́ха (в э́том де́ле); **it's no ~** э́то де́ло безнадёжное. **4.** (*fashion*) мо́да; **it's all the ~ just now** э́то сейча́с в большо́й мо́де. **5.** (*business*): **it's a rum ~** (*coll.*) ну и дела́. **6.: let ~ of** отпус|ка́ть, -ти́ть.

v.i. (*see also* **gone**). **1.** (*on foot*) (*det.*) идти́; (*indet.*) ходи́ть; (*ride etc.*) (*det.*) е́хать; (*indet.*) е́здить; (*by train*) е́хать по́ездом; (*by plane*) лете́ть (*det.*) (самолётом); **the clock is ~ing** часы́ иду́т/хо́дят; **this train ~es to London** э́тот по́езд идёт в Ло́ндон; **he went cycling** он пое́хал ката́ться на велосипе́де; **who ~es there?** кто идёт?; **mind how you ~!** осторо́жно! **2.** (*fig., with general idea of motion or direction*): **~!** (*at games*) марш; **from the word ~** (*fig.*) с са́мого нача́ла; **where do we ~ from here?** (*what is next step or development?*) что же да́льше?; **this road ~es to York** э́та доро́га ведёт в Йорк; **he ~es to school** (*is a schoolboy*) он хо́дит в шко́лу; **he went to** (*was educated at*) **Eton** он око́нчил И́тон; **he went sick** (*mil.*) он получи́л освобожде́ние по боле́зни; **let me ~!** отпусти́те меня́!; **there you ~ again!** ну вот, опя́ть!; **there is still an hour to ~** ещё час в запа́се; **where do these forks ~?** куда́ положи́ть э́ти ви́лки?; **if you follow me, you can't ~ wrong** де́лайте как я и вы не оши́бётесь; **his plans went wrong** с его́ за́мыслами не получи́лось; **his arguments went unheeded** к его́ до́водам не прислу́шались; **his daughter went wrong** его́ дочь сби́лась с пути́; **the criminal decided to ~ straight** престу́пник реши́л испра́виться. **3.** (*with cognate etc. object*): **he went a long way** он пошёл/ушёл далеко́; **~ it!** дава́й!; **they went halves** они́ раздели́ли всё попола́м; **can Britain ~ it alone?** спра́вится ли Великобрита́ния в одино́чку?; **he went one better than me** он превзошёл меня́; **the balloon went 'pop'** шар ло́пнул; **the sheep went 'baa'** овца́ забле́яла. **4.** (*idea of progress or outcome*): **how ~es it?** (*health, affairs*); **how's it ~ing?** как дела́?; как пожива́ете?; **everything is ~ing well** всё (идёт) хорошо́; **here ~es!** приступа́ю!; **~ easy!** (*slowly, gently*) осторо́жно!; **~ easy with the sugar!** не клади́те сто́лько са́хару!; не налега́йте на са́хар!; **he is ~ing strong** он по́лон сил; он молоде́ц; **he is ~ing all out to win** он изо всех сил стара́ется вы́играть; **the party/play went well** вечери́нка/пье́са прошла́ хорошо́; **how did the election ~?** (*who won it?*) как прошли́ вы́боры?; **she is 6 months ~ne with child** она́ на седьмо́м ме́сяце (бере́менности). **5.** (*idea of extension or distance*): **the differences ~ deep** разногла́сия захо́дят глубоко́/далеко́; **I will ~** (*offer*) **as high as £100** я гото́в вы́ложить и сто фу́нтов; **his land ~es as far as the river** его́ зе́мли простира́ются до реки́; **£5 will not ~ far** пяти́ фу́нтов надо́лго не хва́тит; **he will ~ far** (*attain distinction*) он далеко́ пойдёт; **you ~ too far** (*impudence, presumption*) вы захо́дите сли́шком далеко́; **he is far ~ne** (*sick in mind or body*) он совсе́м плох; пло́хо его́ де́ло; **I will ~ so far as to say** я бы да́же сказа́л, что…; **this is all right as far as it ~es** пока́ что всё в поря́дке. **6.** (*expr. tenor or tendency*): **how does the poem ~?** как звучи́т э́то стихотворе́ние?; **the story ~es that …** расска́зывают, что…; **it ~es to a cheerful tune** э́то сопровожда́ется весёлой мело́дией; **it ~es against the grain** э́то не по нутру́/душе́/вку́су (*кому*); **this ~es to show that he is wrong** э́то пока́зывает, что он не прав; **promotion ~es by favour** карье́ра стро́ится на проте́кции; **dreams ~ by contraries** сны сле́дует толкова́ть наоборо́т; **qualities that ~ to make a hero** ка́чества, необходи́мые геро́ю. **7.** (*set out, depart*): **the post ~es at 5 p.m.** по́чта ухо́дит в 5 часо́в дня. **8.** (*pass, come to an end, disappear*): **our holiday went in a flash** на́ши кани́кулы пролете́ли мгнове́нно; **as soon as we buy cheese it ~es** не успе́ем мы купи́ть сыр, как его́ уже́ нет; **it's ~ne 4** (*o'clock*) уже́ бо́льше четырёх; пошёл пя́тый час; **the Minister must ~** (*be got rid of*) мини́стр до́лжен уйти́ в отста́вку; **be ~ne!** (*liter.*) прова́ливайте!; **my sight is ~ing** я теря́ю зре́ние; **I wish this pain would ~** хоть бы прошла́ э́та боль!; **my jewels have ~** мои́ драгоце́нности пропа́ли; **all my money is ~ne** все мои́ де́ньги уплы́ли; **his interest in literature has ~ne** у него́ пропа́л интере́с к литерату́ре; **~ing, ~ne!** (*at auction*) кто бо́льше? про́дано!; **the committee is not the same now that George has ~ne** по́сле ухо́да Джо́рджа, комите́т уже́ не тот. **9.** (*be in a certain state*): **he ~es in fear of his life** он живёт под стра́хом сме́рти; **the children ~ barefoot** де́ти хо́дят боси́ком; **I went hungry last night** я не ел вчера́ ве́чером. **10.** (*become*): **the milk went sour** молоко́ прокисло; **she went red in the face** она́ покрасне́ла; **the country went Communist** к влáсти в странé пришли́ коммуни́сты. **11.** (*function, succeed*): **I can't get my watch to ~** у меня́ не заводя́тся часы́; **this machine ~es by electricity** э́та маши́на рабóтает на электри́честве; **his tongue ~es nineteen to the dozen** он говори́т без ýмолку; **he made the party ~** он был душóй óбщества. **12.** (*cease to function, die*): **if the bulb ~es, change it** éсли лáмпочка перегори́т, поменя́йте её; **poor old Smith has ~ne** бéдного Сми́та не стáло. **13.** (*sound*): **come in when the bell ~es** входи́те, когдá зазвони́т звонóк. **14.** (*make specified motion*): **~ like this with your left foot** сдéлайте так лéвой ногóй. **15.** (*be known, accepted, usual*): **what he says ~es** егó слóво — закóн; **anything ~es** всё сойдёт; **I let it ~ at that** я реши́л э́то так остáвить; **it ~es without saying** э́то самó собóй разумéется **he ~es by the name of Smith** он извéстен под и́менем Смит; **she is a good cook as cooks ~** по сравнéнию с други́ми онá неплóхо готóвит; **it is cheap as yachts ~** для я́хты э́то недóрого. **16.** (*be sold, offered for sale*): **the picture went for a song** карти́ну прóдали за бесцéнок; **these cakes are ~ing cheap** э́ти пирóжные стóят дёшево (*or* идýт по дешёвке). **17.** (*expr. impending or predicted action*): **I'm ~ing to sneeze** я сейчáс чихнý; **it's ~ing to rain** собирáется дождь; **the train is just ~ing to start** пóезд вот-вот трóнется; **you are ~ing to do as I tell you** вы сдéлаете то, что я вам скажý; **he's not ~ing to** (*shan't*) **cheat me** меня́ он не проведёт; **he's not ~ing to argue over 25 pence** он не стáнет спóрить из-за двадцати́ пяти́ пéнсов. **18.** (*expr. intention*): **I am ~ing to ask him** я реши́л спроси́ть егó. **19.** (*emph. v.*): **don't ~ telling him the whole story** не взду́майте рассказáть емý всё; **he went and told his mother** он взял и рассказáл мáтери; **what have you ~ne and done?** ну, что вы там натвори́ли?

with preps.: **how shall I ~ about this?** как мне за э́то взя́ться; **he went about his business** он занялся́ свои́ми делáми; **if the price ~es above £50** éсли ценá превы́сит 50 фýнтов; **he went after** (*sought to win*) **the prize** он борóлся за приз; **the dog went after the hare** собáка погнáлась за зáйцем; **the decision went against them** решéние бы́ло не в их пóльзу; **it ~es against my principles** э́то противорéчит мои́м при́нципам; **he went at it like a bull at a gate** он брóсился очертя́ гóлову; **he went before the magistrates** он предстáл пéред судóм; **he went beyond his instructions** он превы́сил полномóчия; **he went** (*passed*) **by the window** он прошёл ми́мо окнá; **his interests went by the board** с егó интерéсами совершéнно не посчитáлись; **I ~ by what I hear** я исхожý из тогó, что слы́шу; **this book is nothing to ~ by** по э́той кни́ге нельзя́ ни о чём суди́ть; **they went down the river** они́ поплы́ли вниз по рекé; **I went for a drink** я отпрáвился вы́пить; **his plans went for six** (*coll.*) егó плáны провали́лись; **the dog went for his legs** собáка хватáла егó зá ноги; **I went for** (*fetched*) **him** я пошёл за ним; (*attacked, verbally or physically*) я обрýшился на негó; **my efforts went for nothing** мои́ уси́лия ни к чемý не привели́; **he will always ~ for the best** он всегдá бýдет стреми́ться к лýчшему; **I ~ for that** (*like it: US coll.*) э́то мне по душé/вкýсу; **that ~es for** (*applies to*) **you too** (*e.g. an order*) э́то вас тóже касáется; **he went into the house** он вошёл в дом; **he went into Parliament** он прошёл в парлáмент; **the car went into a wall** маши́на врéзалась в стéну; **he had to ~ into hospital** емý пришлóсь лечь в больни́цу; **I shall not ~ into details** я не бýду вдавáться в подрóбности; **it won't ~ into the box** (*is too big*) э́то не войдёт в корóбку; **6 into 30 ~es 5 times** шесть содéржится в тридцати́ пять раз; **I will ~ into the matter** я э́то дéло рассмотрю́; **the law ~es into effect** закóн вхóдит в си́лу; **they went into mourning** они́ надéли трáур; **they went into raptures** они́ пришли́ в востóрг; **he went off his food** он перестáл есть; **he went off his head** он сошёл с умá; **I've ~ne off prawns** (*coll.*) я разлюби́л кревéтки; **he went off the deep end** (*coll.*) он разошёлся; **the children wanted to ~ on the swings** дéти хотéли покачáться на качéлях; **I am ~ing on a course** я поступáю на кýрсы; **all his money went on food** все егó дéньги пошли́/уходи́ли на едý; **he is ~ne on** (*obsessed by*) **her** он пó уши влюблён в неё; он помешáлся на ней; **he went on his way** он пошёл свои́м путём; **we have no evidence to ~ on** для э́того у нас нет никаки́х дáнных; **~ out of sight** исч|езáть, -éзнуть и́з виду; **he went out of his mind** он сошёл с умá; **she went out of her way to help** онá вся́чески старáлась помóчь; **we went over the house** мы осмотрéли дом; **she went over the floor with a mop** онá прошлáсь швáброй пó полу; **the shell went over his head** снаря́д пролетéл у негó над головóй; **his words went right over my head** я пропусти́л егó словá ми́мо ушéй; **I went over his work with him** вмéсте с ним я прошёлся по егó рабóте; **we have ~ne over** (*discussed*) **that** мы э́то обсуждáли; **we went round the gallery** мы обошли́ галерéю; **we went round the block** мы обошли́ квартáл; **we have to ~ round the one-way system** здесь прихóдится дéлать объéзд из-за односторóннего движéния; **my trousers won't ~ round me any longer** на мне ужé не схóдятся брю́ки; **~ through the main gate!** проходи́те чéрез глáвные ворóта!; **the ball went through** (*i.e. broke*) **the window** мяч разби́л окнó; **she went through his pockets** онá общáрила у негó все кармáны; **he has ~ne through a lot** емý довелóсь мнóго испытáть; **I went through his papers** я просмотрéл егó бумáги; **he went through the money in a week** он растрáтил дéньги за недéлю; **large sums went through his hands** чéрез егó рýки прошли́ больши́е сýммы дéнег; **they went through the ceremony** они́ прошли́ чéрез (*or* вы́держали) э́ту церемóнию; они́ подвéрглись э́той церемóнии; **the book went through six editions** кни́га вы́держала шесть издáний; **I'll ~ through the main points again** я хочý повтори́ть глáвные пýнкты; **the estate went to her nephew** имýщество перешлó её племя́ннику; **the prize went to him** он вы́играл приз; **our best thanks ~ to Mr X** мы горячó благодари́м г-на X; **he went to great expense** он пошёл на больши́е расхóды; **12 inches ~ to the foot** 12 дю́ймов составля́ют фут; **~ to it!** за дéло!; **the money will ~ towards a new car** дéньги пойдýт на покýпку нóвой маши́ны; **this will ~ a long way towards satisfying him** э́то почти́ пóлностью егó устрóит; **he went under the anaesthetic** он заснýл под наркóзом; **he went under an assumed name** он жил под вы́мышленным/чужи́м и́менем; **~ up the hill** поднимáться (*impf.*)/идти́/éхать (*both det.*) в гóру; **he went up the ladder** он стал поднимáться (*or* пошёл вверх) по лéстнице; **this tie ~es with your suit** э́тот гáлстук подхóдит к вáшему костю́му; **five acres ~ with the house** пять áкров земли́ отхóдят с дóмом; **crime ~es with poverty** престýпность идёт рукá óб руку с бéдностью; **he has been ~ing with her for months** он встречáется с ней ужé нéсколько мéсяцев; **we went without a holiday** мы обошли́сь без óтпуска.

with advs.: **~ about** *v.i.* **he ~es about looking for trouble** он тóлько и дéлает, что лéзет на рожóн; **the story is ~ing about that ...** хóдят слýхи, что...; **they ~ about together** они́ повсю́ду хóдят вмéсте; **~ ahead!** вперёд!; **~ along** *v.i.*: **I went along to see** я пошёл посмотрéть; **they sang as they went along** они́ шли с пéснями; **the play got better as it went along** к концý пьéса смотрéлась лýчше; **will you ~ along to the station with him?** вы пойдёте с ним до стáнции?; вы доведёте егó до стáнции?; **I cannot ~ along with that** я не могý с э́тим согласи́ться; **~ around** *v.i.*: **he went around with a long face** он ходи́л/разгýливал с ки́слым ви́дом; **he is ~ing around with my sister** он встречáется с моéй сестрóй; **~ away** *v.i.* уходи́ть, уйти́; **~ away!** уходи́те!; **~ back** *v.i.* идти́ (*det.*) назáд; возвра|щáться, -ти́ться; **to ~ back to what I was saying** возвращáясь к томý, что я сказáл; **he went back on his word** он не сдержáл своегó слóва; **this custom ~es back to the 15th century** э́тот обы́чай восхóдит к XV (пятнáдцатому) вéку; **~ before** *v.i.* (*die*): **those who have ~ne before** отошéдшие в мир инóй; **~ below** (*deck*) *v.i.*: **when the storm broke they went below** когдá разрази́лся шторм, они́ спусти́лись в каю́ту; **~ by** *v.i.*: **he let the opportunity ~ by** он упусти́л слýчай; **as the years ~ by** с годáми; с течéнием лет; **in days ~ne by** в мину́вшие дни; **he has just ~ne by** он то́лько что прошёл ми́мо; **~ down** *v.i.*: спус|ка́ться, -ти́ться; **he went down on his knees** он опусти́лся на коле́ни; **the sun went down** со́лнце се́ло; **the ship went down** кора́бль затону́л; **she went down with 'flu** она́ слегла́ с гри́ппом; **the undergraduates ~ down in July** студе́нты зака́нчивают заня́тия в ию́ле; **he has ~ne down in the world** он опусти́лся; **prices are ~ing down** це́ны па́дают; **~ing down!** (*of lift*) вниз!; **the pill won't ~ down** табле́тка не прогла́тывается; **his story went down well** его́ расска́з был хорошо́ при́нят; **his fame will ~ down to posterity** его́ сла́ва сохрани́тся в века́х; **this history book ~es down to 1914** э́тот уче́бник исто́рии конча́ется 1914 го́дом; **Rome went down before the barbarians** Рим пал под на́тиском ва́рваров; **the wind has ~ne down** ве́тер ути́х; **~ forth** *v.i.*: **the order went forth** прика́з был опублико́ван; **~ forward** *v.i.*: **the plan went forward** план вступи́л в де́йствие; **~ in** *v.i.* (*enter*) входи́ть, войти́; **the sun went in** со́лнце зашло́; **he ~es in for sport** он занима́ется спо́ртом; **he's ~ing in for medicine** он собира́ется заня́ться медици́ной; **he went in for the competition** он при́нял уча́стие в ко́нкурсе **~ off** *v.i.*: **he went off without a word** он ушёл без еди́ного сло́ва; **Hamlet ~es off** (*exits*) Га́млет ухо́дит; **she went off into a faint** она́ потеря́ла созна́ние; она́ упа́ла в о́бморок; **the servant went off with** (*stole*) **the spoons** слуга́ укра́л ло́жки и скры́лся; **the goods went off** (*sold*) **well** това́р сбы́ли по хоро́шей цене́; **the goods went off** (*were sent*) **today** това́р отпра́вили сего́дня; **the gun went off** ружьё вы́стрелило; **has the baby ~ne off** (*to sleep*)? ребёнок засну́л?; **the alarm clock went off** буди́льник зазвене́л; **the light has ~ne off** свет пога́с; **the fruit has ~ne off** фру́кты погни́ли; **his work has ~ne off lately** в после́днее вре́мя он стал рабо́тать ху́же; **the party went off well** вечери́нка прошла́ хорошо́; **it went off according to plan** всё прошло́ согла́сно пла́ну; **~ on** *v.i.*: **the shoe will not ~ on** э́тот боти́нок не ле́зет; **the lights went on** загоре́лся свет; **I can't ~ on any longer** я так бо́льше не могу́; **~ on from where you left off** продолжа́йте с того́ ме́ста, где останови́лись; **shall we ~ on to the next item?** дава́йте перейдём к сле́дующему пу́нкту?; **~ on playing!** продолжа́йте игра́ть; **~ on!** (*coll., expr. incredulity*) да ну́!; (*urging action*) дава́йте!; валя́йте!; **the work is ~ing on well** рабо́та идёт хорошо́; **that is enough to ~** (*or* **be ~ing**) **on with** э́того пока́ хва́тит; **he went on to say that ...** зате́м он сказа́л, что...; **it is ~ing on for a year since we met** уже́ почти́ год, как мы познако́мились; **what is ~ing on here?** что тут происхо́дит?; **~ on at** (*nag*) пили́ть (*impf.*); набра́сываться (*impf.*) на+*a.*; **he does ~ on so** (*coll.*) он ве́чно ну́дит; **he went on ahead of the others** он опереди́л/обогна́л остальны́х; **he went on** (*stage*) **after the interval** он вы́шел на сце́ну по́сле антра́кта; **the show must ~ on** что бы ни случи́лось, спекта́кль продолжа́ется; **as time ~es on** со вре́менем; **~ out** *v.i.* (*exit*) выходи́ть, вы́йти; **the light went out** свет пога́с; **he went out to Australia** он вы́ехал в Австра́лию; **the tide was ~ing out** шёл отли́в; **the year went out** (*ended*) **gloomily** год ко́нчился пло́хо; **our hearts ~ out to them** мы всей душо́й с ни́ми; **he went all out for success** он рва́лся к успе́ху; **long skirts have ~ne out** дли́нные ю́бки вы́шли из мо́ды; **~ over** *v.i.*: **he went over to the shop** он пошёл в магази́н; **~ over to the enemy** перейти́ (*pf.*) в стан врага́; **he went over to France** он перепра́вился во Фра́нцию; **the country went over to decimal coinage** страна́ перешла́ на десяти́чную моне́тную систе́му; **how did your talk ~ over?** как прошла́ ва́ша ле́кция?; **it went over big** (*coll.*) э́то име́ло огро́мный успе́х; **~ round** *v.i.*: **I went round to see him** я пошёл его́ навести́ть; **we had to ~ round by the park** нам пришло́сь идти́ в обхо́д че́рез парк; **he ~es round collecting money** он обхо́дит всех и собира́ет де́ньги; **is there enough food to ~ round?** хва́тит ли еды́ на всех?; **everything's ~ing round** (*describing dizziness*) всё идёт круго́м; **~ through** *v.i.*: **I cannot ~ through with the plan** я не могу́ осуществи́ть э́тот план; **the deal went through** сде́лка состоя́лась; **has their divorce ~ne through?** они́ уже́ развели́сь?; **the bill went through** (*parl.*) прое́кт был при́нят; **~ together** *v.i.*: **they were ~ing together** (*keeping company*) **for years** они́ встреча́лись мно́гие го́ды; **these colours ~ together** э́ти цвета́ гармони́руют; **poverty and disease ~ together** где бе́дность, там и боле́зни; **~ under** *v.i.*: **it is the poor who ~ under** бе́дному ху́же всех; **the drowning man went under** утопа́ющий пошёл ко дну; **the patient went under** (*the anaesthetic*) пацие́нт усну́л под нарко́зом; **his business went under** его́ де́ло ло́пнуло; **~ up** *v.i.* подн|има́ться, -я́ться; **he went up to bed** он пошёл спать; **I went up to town** я пое́хал в го́род; **prices have ~ne up** це́ны повы́сились; **the lights went up** загоре́лся свет; **houses are ~ing up** (*being built*) дома́ поднима́ются/стро́ятся/расту́т; **the house went up in flames** дом сгоре́л; **his plans went up in smoke** его́ пла́ны разве́ялись как дым; **he ~es up to Oxford next year** он посту́пит в О́ксфордский университе́т на бу́дущий год; **he is ~ing up in the world** он выбива́ется в лю́ди.

cpds. **~-ahead** *n.* разреше́ние, «добро́», «зелёная у́лица»; *adj.* предприи́мчивый; насты́рный; **~-as-you-please** *adj.* свобо́дный от пра́вил; **~-between** *n.* посре́дник; **~-by** *n.*: **give s.o./sth. the ~-by** проигнори́ровать (*pf.*) кого́/что-н.; уклон|я́ться, -и́ться от чего́-н.; **~-cart** *n.* (де́тская) коля́ска; (*for racing, also* **~-kart**) карт; **~-getter** *n.* (*coll.*) проны́ра (*c.g.*); **~-getting** *adj.* (*coll.*) проны́рливый, пробивно́й; **~-off** *n.*: **from the first ~-off** с са́мого нача́ла; **~-slow** *n.* части́чная забасто́вка, «ме́дленная рабо́та»; *adj.* заме́дленный; **~-to-meeting** *adj.*: **~-to-meeting clothes** пра́здничная оде́жда.

goad [gəʊd] *n.* кол; (*fig.*) сти́мул.

v.t. погоня́ть (*impf.*); (*prod*) пришпо́ри|вать, -ть; (*tease, torment*) раздража́ть (*impf.*); дёргать (*impf.*).

goal [gəʊl] *n.* **1.** фи́ниш; (*fig., destination, objective*) цель; **he set himself a difficult ~** он поста́вил себе́ тру́дную зада́чу/цель. **2.** (*sport*) воро́т|а (*pl., g.* —); **Jackson was in ~** в воро́тах стоя́л Дже́ксон; **keep ~** защи|ща́ть, -ти́ть воро́та; (*point scored*) гол; **our team won by three ~s to one** на́ша кома́нда вы́играла со счётом три — оди́н.

cpds. **~-keeper** *n.* врата́рь (*m.*); **~-kick** *n.* уда́р от воро́т; **~-mouth** *n.* ширина́ воро́т; **~-post** *n.* шта́нга.

goalie ['gəʊlɪ] *n.* (*coll.*) врата́рь (*m.*).

goat [gəʊt] *n.* **1.** коза́; (*male*) козёл; **act, play the (giddy) ~** (*coll.*) валя́ть (*impf.*) дурака́; **he gets my ~** (*sl.*) он меня́ раздража́ет; **separate the sheep from the ~s** (*fig.*) отдели́ть (*pf.*) а́гнцев от ко́злищ. **2.** (*fig., lecherous pers.*) кобе́ль (*m.*), (ста́рый) козёл.

cpds. **~-herd** *n.* козопа́с; **~-meat** *n.* козля́тина; **~skin** *n.* ко́зья шу́ба; (*for wine*) бурдю́к.

goatee [gəʊ'ti:] *n.* козли́ная боро́дка.

goatish ['gəʊtɪʃ] *adj.* (*lecherous*) похотли́вый.

gob[1] [gɒb] *n.* (*vulg.*) (*hump*) кусо́к; (*of spittle*) плево́к.

gob[2] [gɒb] *n.* (*vulg.*) (*mouth*) гло́тка; **shut your ~!** заткни́ гло́тку!

gobbet ['gɒbɪt] *n.* (*lit., fig.*) кусо́к.

gobble[1] ['gɒb(ə)l] *v.t.* жрать, по-/со-.

v.i. ло́пать, с-; бы́стро и шу́мно есть (*impf.*).

gobble[2] ['gɒb(ə)l] *v.i.* (*of a turkey*) кулды́кать (*impf.*); (*fig., with rage*) шипе́ть (*impf.*).

gobbledygook ['gɒb(ə)ldɪ,gu:k, -,gʊk] *n.* (*sl.*) воляпю́к.

Gobelin ['gəʊbəlɪn, gɔ'blæ̃] *n.* (*tapestry*) гобеле́н.

goblet ['gɒblɪt] *n.* ку́бок, бока́л.

goblin ['gɒblɪn] *n.* домово́й.

goby ['gəʊbɪ] *n.* бычо́к.

god [gɒd] *n.* **1.** (*deity*) бог; **a feast for the ~s** пир бого́в; **a sight for the ~s** боже́ственное/преле́стное зре́лище; **in the lap of the ~s** у Христа́ за па́зухой; **ye ~s!** (*joc.*) Бо́же мой!; си́лы небе́сные!; (*fig., revered object or pers.*) и́дол, куми́р; (**G~**: *supreme being*) Бог; божество́; **act of G~** стихи́йное бе́дствие; **Almighty G~** всемогу́щий Бог; **he thinks he's G~ Almighty** он счита́ет себя́ всемогу́щим; **G~ bless** (*you*)! благослови́ вас Бог; (*after sneeze*) бу́дьте здоро́вы!; **my G~!** Бо́же мой!; Го́споди!; **G~ damn you!** чёрт вас возьми́!; **G~ help you!** да помо́жет вам Бог!; **on G~'s earth** на бо́жьем/бе́лом свете́; **G~ forbid!** Бо́же сохрани́!; изба́ви Бог!; **so help me G~** Госпо́дь свиде́тель;

G~ knows where he is Бог знáет, где он; **I've suffered enough, G~ knows** вúдит Бог — я страдáл достáточно; **for G~'s sake!** рáди Бóга!; **thank G~ (for that)!** слáва Бóгу!; **G~'s truth** святáя прáвда; **G~ willing** даст Бог; с бóжьей пóмощью; éсли бýдем живы́; **he is with G~** егó Бог прибрáл. **2.** (*pl., theatr.*) галёрка; **a seat in the ~s** мéсто на галёрке.

cpds. **~-almighty** *adj.* (*sl.*) проклятый, дьявольский; **~-awful** *adj.* (*coll.*) жýткий, богомéрзкий; **~child** *n.* крéстни|к (*fem.* -ца); **~dam** *adj.* (*US sl.*) чёртов; **~daughter** *n.* крéстница; **~father** *n.* крёстный (отéц); **~-fearing** *adj.* богобоязненный; **~-forsaken** *adj.* забрóшенный; **~-forsaken place** медвéжий ýгол; **~mother** *n.* крёстная (мать); **~parent** *n.* крёстный (отéц); крёстная (мать); **~send** *n.* нахóдка; ≃ сам Бог послáл; **~son** *n.* крéстник; **~-speed!** *int.* с Бóгом!

goddess [ˈgɒdɪs] *n.* богúня.

godhead [ˈgɒdhed] *n.* божéственность; божествó.

godless [ˈgɒdlɪs] *adj.* безбóжный.

godlike [ˈgɒdlaɪk] *adj.* богоподóбный.

godliness [ˈgɒdlɪnɪs] *n.* нáбожность.

godly [ˈgɒdlɪ] *adj.* нáбожный.

godown [gəʊˈdaʊn] *n.* хранúлище.

goer [ˈgəʊə(r)] *n.* **1.** (*performer*): **this watch is a good ~** э́ти часы́ отлúчно идýт. **2.** (*coll., energetic pers.*) упóрный человéк. **3. comers and ~s** приезжáющие и отъезжáющие.

goffer [ˈgəʊfə(r), ˈgɒf-] *n.* щипц|ы́ (*pl., g.* -óв) для гофрирóвки.

v.t. гофрировáть (*impf., pf.*).

goggle [ˈgɒg(ə)l] *v.i.* тарáщить (*impf.*) глазá; **she ~d at the news** от э́той нóвости у неё глазá на лоб полéзли.

cpds. **~-box** *n.* (*sl.*) тéлик, «я́щик»; **~-eyed** *adj.* пучеглáзый.

goggles [gɒg(ə)lz] *n.pl.* тёмные/защúтные очк|ú (*pl., g.* -óв).

going [ˈgəʊɪŋ] *n.* **1.** (*departure*) отъéзд, ухóд; **there will be no tears at his ~** по нём плáкать не бýдут. **2.** (*state of track*) состоя́ние беговóй дорóжки; **the next mile is rough ~** слéдующая мúля бýдет трýдной. **3.** (*progress, speed*) скóрость; **fifty miles an hour is good ~** 50 миль в час — э́то хорóшая скóрость; **let's get out while the ~ is good** смóемся, пока не пóздно; **this book is heavy ~** э́та кнúга трýдно читáется; **he is heavy ~** он нýдный человéк; **the conversation was heavy ~** разговóр не клéился.

adj. **1.** (*working, flourishing*): **a ~ concern** дéйствующее предприя́тие. **2.** (*to be had*): **one of the best newspapers ~** однá из лýчших ны́нешних газéт; **there are plenty of sandwiches ~** бутербрóдов скóлько угóдно.

cpds. **~-away** *adj.*: **~-away dress** дорóжное плáтье; **~-over** *n.* (*coll., scrutiny*) осмóтр; (*coll., cleaning*) прочúстка; (*sl., beating*) трёпка; **~s-on** *n. pl.* (*coll.*) поведéние; постýпки (*m. pl.*); делá (*nt. pl.*); «делúшки» (*nt. pl.*); **there have been strange ~s-on lately** в послéднее врéмя творя́тся стрáнные вéщи.

goitre [ˈgɔɪtə(r)] *n.* зоб; базéдова болéзнь.

goitrous [ˈgɔɪtrəs] *adj.* зóбный; страдáющий зóбом.

gold [gəʊld] *n. & adj.* **1.** (*metal*) зóлото; **bar ~** зóлото в слúтках; **beaten ~** чекáнное зóлото; **~ braid** сусáльное зóлото; **~ plate** (*tableware*) золотáя посýда; (*gilding*) позолóта; **(made of) solid ~** из чúстого зóлота; **the ~ standard** золотóй стандáрт; **a currency backed by ~** валю́та, обеспéченная зóлотом; **£50 in ~** 50 фýнтов зóлотом; **he's as good as ~** он зóлото, а не ребёнок; **she has a heart of ~** у неё золотóе сéрдце. **2.** (*riches*) богáтство.

cpds. **~-bearing** *adj.* золотонóсный; **~-beater** *n.* золотобóец; **~-digger** *n.* золотоискáтель (*m.*); (*sl.*) вымогáтельница; **~-dust** *n.* золотóй песóк; **~field** *n.* золотóй прúиск; **~finch** *n.* щеглóл; **~fish** *n.* золотáя ры́бка; **~-leaf** *n.* сусáльное зóлото; **~-mine** *n.* золотóй рудни́к; (*fig.*): **the shop is a ~-mine** э́тот магазúн — золотóе дно; **~-rush** *n.* золотáя лихорáдка; **~smith** *n.* золоты́х дел мáстер.

golden [ˈgəʊld(ə)n] *adj.* (*lit., fig.*) золотóй; (*of colour*) золотúстый; **the ~ age** золотóй век; **~ rod** (*bot.*) золотáрник; **~ section** (*geom.*) золотóе сечéние; **~ syrup** свéтлая пáтока; **receive a ~ handshake on retirement** получúть (*pf.*) вознаграждéние при ухóде на пéнсию; **~ hours** золотáя порá; **the ~ mean** золотáя серединá; **miss a ~ opportunity** упустúть (*pf.*) редчáйшую возмóжность; **celebrate one's ~ wedding** прáздновать, от- золотýю свáдьбу.

cpd. **~-haired** *adj.* златокýдрый, золотоволóсый.

Goldilocks [ˈgəʊldɪˌlɒks] *n.* Златовлáска.

golf [gɒlf] *n.* гольф.

v.i. игрáть (*impf.*) в гольф.

cpds. **~-ball** *n.* мяч для игры́ в гольф; **~-club** *n.* (*association*) клуб любúтелей игры в гольф; (*implement*) клю́шка; **~-course, ~-links** *nn.* площáдка/пóле для игры́ в гольф.

golfer [ˈgɒlfə(r)] *n.* игрóк в гольф.

golfing [ˈgɒlfɪŋ] *n.* игрá в гольф.

Golgotha [ˈgɒlgəθə] *n.* Голгóфа.

Goliath [gəˈlaɪəθ] *n.* Голиáф; (*fig.*) великáн.

golliwog [ˈgɒlɪˌwɒg] *n.* чёрная кýкла.

golly [ˈgɒlɪ] *int.* (*coll.*) Бóже мой!; **by ~!** ей-Бóгу!

golosh [gəˈlɒʃ] = **galosh**

gonad [ˈgəʊnæd] *n.* гонáда; половáя железá.

gondola [ˈgɒndələ] *n.* (*boat; airship car*) гондóла.

gondolier [ˌgɒndəˈlɪə(r)] *n.* гондольéр.

gone [gɒn] *adj.* (*see also* **go**). **1.** (*departed, past*) уéхавший; ушéдший. **2.** (*doomed, hopeless*) пропáщий. **3.** (*dead*) умéрший, усóпший.

goner [ˈgɒnə(r)] *n.* (*sl.*) кóнченый человéк.

gong [gɒŋ] *n.* (*instrument*) гонг; (*medal*) бля́ха (*coll.*).

goniometer [ˌgəʊnɪˈɒmɪtə(r)] *n.* гониóметр.

gonorrhoea [ˌgɒnəˈrɪə] *n.* гонорéя.

goo [guː] *n.* (*coll.*) что-н. клéйкое, лúпкое.

good [gʊd] *n.* **1.** (*~ness, ~ action*) добротá, добрó; **there is some ~ in everyone** в кáждом человéке есть чтó-то хорóшее; **he spends his life doing ~** всю жизнь он дéлает/творúт добрó; **he is up to no ~** он задýмал чтó-то недóброе. **2.** (*benefit*) пóльза; **drink it! it will do you ~** вы́пейте э́то — вам полéзно; **it's no ~ complaining** что прóку жáловаться?; **that will do no ~** э́то не принесёт пóльзы; **what's the ~ of making a fuss?** какóй смысл поднимáть шум?; **it's all to the ~** всё к лýчшему; **for the ~ of the cause** для пóльзы дéла; **much ~ may it do you!** (*iron.*) ну и на здорóвье; **I finished up £15 to the ~** в концé концóв я вы́играл 15 фýнтов. **3.: for ~** (*permanently*) навсегдá. **4.** (*pl., property*) добрó; **~s and chattels** пожúтк|и (*pl., g.* -ов). **5.** (*pl., merchandise*) товáр(ы); **are you sure he can deliver the ~s?** (*coll., fig.*) а вы увéрены, что он не подведёт?; **~s train** товáрный пóезд; **~s vehicle** грузовóй автомобúль/фургóн.

adj. **1.** (*in most senses*) хорóший; дóбрый; (*of food*) вкýсный; **my ~ sir!** (*arch.*) любéзнейший!; почтéнный!; **how is your ~ lady?** (*arch.*) как поживáет вáша почтéнная супрýга?; **~ old Dad!** ай да папáша!; **that shows ~ sense** в э́том вúден здрáвый смысл; **~ idea!** прекрáсная мысль!; **very ~** (*expr. acquiescence*) лáдно; хорошó; (*servant's reply*) (*arch.*) слýшаюсь; **~ works** дóбрые делá; **a ~ player** сúльный игрóк; **lead a ~ life** вестú (*det.*) достóйную жизнь; **the G~ Book** бúблия; **G~ Friday** Страстнáя Пя́тница; **~ heavens!** Бóже мой! **2.** (*of health, condition etc.*) хорóший; здорóвый; **I don't feel so ~ today** (*coll.*) я себя́ невáжно чýвствую сегóдня; **these eggs are not very ~** э́ти я́йца не óчень свéжие; **apples are ~ for you** я́блоки полéзны для здорóвья. **3.** (*favourable, fortunate*): **~ luck!** желáю успéха; **a ~ sign** дóбрый знак; **it's a ~ thing we stayed at home** хорошó, что мы остáлись дóма; **he's gone, and a ~ thing too!** он ушёл, и слáва Бóгу!; **~ for you!** (*coll.*) молодчúна (*c.g.*). **4.** (*kind*) любéзный, дóбрый; **be a ~ fellow** бýдьте (так) добры́; **be so ~ as to let me in** бýдьте добры́, впустúте меня́; **that's very ~ of you** э́то óчень мúло с вáшей стороны́. **5.** (*of skill*): **he is ~ at games** он хорóший спортсмéн; **he is ~ at French** он силён во францýзском; **he is no ~ at his job** он взя́лся не за своё дéло. **6.** (*suitable*) подходя́щий. **7.** (*well-behaved*) воспúтанный; послýшный;

be ~! веди́ себя́ прили́чно!; **be a ~ boy!** веди́ себя́ хорошо́!; будь у́мницей!; **as ~ as gold** (*of child*) зо́лотко; **~ dog!** молоде́ц, соба́ка. **8.** (*var.*): **~ morning!** до́брое у́тро!; **I bade him ~ night** я пожела́л ему́ споко́йной но́чи; **it's ~ to see you** прия́тно вас ви́деть; **a ~ joke** хоро́шая/заба́вная шу́тка; **that's a ~ one!** (*iron.*) ну, зна́ете!; како́й вздо́р!; **~ looks** краси́вая вне́шность; **I took ~ care to consult him** я предусмотри́тельно посове́товался с ним; **he's had a ~ few, many drinks already** он уже́ успе́л изря́дно вы́пить; **a ~ deal of noise** мно́го шу́ма; **a ~ way off** дово́льно далеко́; **a ~ while ago** давны́м-давно́; **the jug holds a ~ pint** кувши́н вмеща́ет до́брую пи́нту; **~ and hard** (*coll.*) здо́рово, как сле́дует; **he was as ~ as his word** он сдержа́л своё сло́во; **he as ~ as refused to go** он факти́чески отказа́лся идти́; **the car is ~ for another 5 years** э́тот автомоби́ль прослу́жит ещё лет 5; **his credit is ~ for £5,000** он мо́жет по́льзоваться креди́том в 5000 фу́нтов. **9.: make ~** *v.t.* (*fulfil*) исп|олня́ть, -о́лнить; (*substantiate*) обосно́в|ывать, -а́ть; (*recompense for*) возме|ща́ть, -сти́ть; (*repair*) прив|оди́ть, -ести́ в поря́док; *v.i.* (*coll., succeed*) преусп|ева́ть, -е́ть.

cpds. **~-for-nothing** *n.* негодя́й, безде́льник; *adj.* никуды́шный; никчёмный; **~-humoured** *adj.* доброду́шный; **~-looking** *adj.* краси́вый; хоро́ш/хороша́ собо́й; **~-natured** *adj.* доброду́шный; **~-neighbour** *adj.*: **~-neighbour policy** поли́тика добрососе́дства; **~-neighbourliness** *n.* добрососе́дство; ; **~-night** *n.* проща́ние пе́ред сном; *int.* поко́йной но́чи!; **~-tempered** *adj.* доброду́шный; **~-timer** *n.* гуля́ка (*m.*); весельча́к; **~will** *n.* (*friendship*) доброжела́тельность; (*willingness*) до́брая во́ля; (*of business*) популя́рность; репута́ция; клиенту́ра.

goodbye [gʊd'baɪ] *n.* проща́ние; **a ~ kiss** проща́льный поцелу́й; **wave ~** помаха́ть (*pf.*) руко́й на проща́нье.

int. до свида́ния!; проща́йте.

goodish ['gʊdɪʃ] *adj.* ничего́ (себе́).

goodly ['gʊdlɪ] *adj.* (*large*) кру́пный; (*handsome*) краси́вый, милови́дный.

goodness ['gʊdnɪs] *n.* **1.** (*virtue*) доброта́. **2.** (*kindness*) любе́зность; **please have the ~ to move** бу́дьте любе́зны, подви́ньтесь. **3.** (*quality, nourishment*): **these apples are full of ~** э́ти я́блоки о́чень хороши́. **4.** (*euph., God*): **G~ me!** вот те на́!; **G~ (only) knows** кто его́ зна́ет!; **I wish to ~ (that) ...** как бы мне хоте́лось, что́бы…; **thank ~!** сла́ва Бо́гу!

goody ['gʊdɪ] *n.* (*coll.*) **1.** (*sweetmeat*) конфе́та. **2.** (*character in film etc.*) положи́тельный геро́й. **3.** (*also* **~-~**) па́инька (*c.g.*). **4.** (*int., coll.*) прекра́сно!; замеча́тельно!; отли́чно!

gooey ['gu:ɪ] (*coll.*) *adj.* кле́йкий; ли́пкий.

goof [gu:f] *n.* балбе́с, пе́нтюх (*coll.*).

v.i. (*US sl.*) зава́ливать, -и́ть де́ло.

goon [gu:n] *n.* (*sl.*) (*stupid pers.*) болва́н; (*hired thug*) наёмный банди́т.

goosander [gu:'sændə(r)] *n.* большо́й кроха́ль.

goose [gu:s] *n.* **1.** гусь (*m.*); (*fem., also*) гусы́ня; **his ~ is cooked** (*fig.*) его́ пе́сенка спе́та; **he killed the ~ that laid the golden eggs** (*prov.*) он уби́л ку́рицу, несу́щую золоты́е я́йца; **he couldn't say bo(o) to a ~** (*fig.*) он боязли́в как лань; **wild-~-chase** (*fig.*) сумасбро́дная зате́я; пого́ня за химе́рами. **2.** (*simpleton*) простофи́ля (*c.g.*).

cpds. **~berry** *n.* крыжо́вник (*collect.*); я́года крыжо́вника; **I went with them to play ~berry** (*coll.*) я пошёл с ни́ми как сопровожда́ющий; **~-egg** *n.* гуси́ное яйцо́; **~-flesh** *n.* гуся́тина; гуси́ная ко́жа; **it gives me ~-flesh** у меня́ от э́того мура́шки по те́лу бе́гают; **~-step** *n.* (*coll.*) строево́й шаг.

gopher ['gəʊfə(r)] *n.* го́фер; колумби́йский су́слик.

gore[1] [gɔ:(r)] *n.* (*blood*) проли́тая/запёкшаяся кровь.

gore[2] [gɔ:(r)] *n.* (*gusset*) клин.

gore[3] [gɔ:(r)] *v.t.* бода́ть, за-.

gorge [gɔ:dʒ] *n.* **1.** (*ravine*) уще́лье. **2. the sight made my ~ rise** меня́ затошни́ло от э́того зре́лища.

v.t. & i. объ|еда́ться, -е́сться; **the lion ~ed (itself) on its prey** лев жа́дно поглоща́л свою́ добы́чу.

gorgeous ['gɔ:dʒəs] *adj.* (*magnificent*) великоле́пный; (*richly coloured*) кра́сочный; (*ornate*) витиева́тый; (*coll., enjoyable*) роско́шный; изуми́тельный; **we had a ~ time** мы великоле́пно провели́ вре́мя.

Gorgon ['gɔ:gən] *n.* (*lit.*) Горго́на; Меду́за; (*fig.*) меѓера, ве́дьма.

gorilla [gə'rɪlə] *n.* гори́лла.

gormandize ['gɔ:mən,daɪz] *v.i.* объеда́ться (*impf.*).

gormless ['gɔ:mlɪs] *adj.* (*dial. and coll.*) безду́мный; дура́шливый.

gorse [gɔ:s] *n.* утёсник обыкнове́нный.

gory ['gɔ:rɪ] *adj.* окрова́вленный; кровопроли́тный.

gosh [gɒʃ] *int.* (*coll.*) Бо́же мой!

goshawk ['gɒshɔ:k] *n.* большо́й я́стреб.

gosling ['gɒzlɪŋ] *n.* гусёнок.

gospel ['gɒsp(ə)l] *n.* ева́нгелие; **preach the ~** пропове́довать (*impf.*) Ева́нгелие; **the G~ according to St. John** Ева́нгелие от Иоа́нна; от Иоа́нна свято́е благове́ствование; (*fig.*): **~ truth** и́стинная пра́вда; **she takes everything for ~** она́ всё принима́ет на ве́ру.

gossamer ['gɒsəmə(r)] *n.* **1.** (*spider web*) осе́нняя паути́нка. **2.** (*gauzy material*) газ.

gossip ['gɒsɪp] *n.* **1.** (*talk*) спле́тня; **they met to have a good ~** они́ встре́тились, что́бы хороше́нько посплетни́чать. **2.** (*pers. addicted to ~ing*) спле́тни|к (*fem.* -ца). **3.** (*attr.*): **~ column/writer** коло́нка/репортёр све́тской хро́ники.

v.i. спле́тничать, на-.

gossipy ['gɒsɪpɪ] *adj.* болтли́вый, лю́бящий поспле́тничать.

Goth [gɒθ] *n.* гот.

Gothic ['gɒθɪk] *n.* **1.** (*language*) го́тский язы́к. **2.** (*archit.*) готи́ческий стиль. **3.** (*script*) готи́ческий шрифт.

adj. (*of style or script*) готи́ческий.

gouache [gʊ'ɑ:ʃ, gwɑ:ʃ] *n.* гуа́шь.

gouge [gaʊdʒ] *n.* полукру́глое долото́.

v.t. выда́лбливать, вы́долбить; **~ s.o.'s eyes out** выка́лывать, вы́колоть кому́-н. глаза́.

goulash ['gu:læʃ] *n.* гуля́ш.

gourd [gʊəd] *n.* (*bot.*) горля́нка, ты́ква буты́лочная; (*vessel*) калеба́са, сосу́д из ты́квы.

gourmet ['gʊəmeɪ] *n.* гурма́н; гастроно́м.

gout [gaʊt] *n.* пода́гра.

gouty ['gaʊtɪ] *adj.*: **a ~ person** пода́грик; **~ feet** подагри́ческие но́ги.

govern ['gʌv(ə)n] *v.t.* **1.** (*rule; also v.i.*) пра́вить (*impf.*) +*i.*; **~ing body** (*of hospital, school etc.*) дире́кция, правле́ние; (*control, influence*) руководи́ть (*impf.*) +*i.*; управля́ть (*impf.*) +*i.*; **he finds it hard to ~ his tongue** он несде́ржан на язы́к; **be ~ed by my advice!** сле́дуйте моему́ сове́ту. **2.** (*apply to*): **the same principle ~s both cases** оди́н и тот же при́нцип примени́м в обо́их слу́чаях. **3.** (*gram.*) управля́ть (*impf.*) +*i.*

governance ['gʌvənəns] *n.* управле́ние (*чем*); руково́дство (*чем*).

governess ['gʌvənɪs] *n.* гуверна́нтка.

governessy ['gʌvənɪsɪ] *adj.*: **a ~ tone** наստави́тельный тон.

government ['gʌvənmənt] *n.* (*rule*) правле́ние; (*system*) фо́рма правле́ния; **local ~** ме́стное самоуправле́ние; (*pol.*) прави́тельство; **central ~** центра́льное прави́тельство; **the Prime Minister formed a ~** премье́р-мини́стр сформирова́л прави́тельство; **~ house** резиде́нция губерна́тора; **~ securities** госуда́рственные це́нные бума́ги.

governmental [,gʌvən'ment(ə)l] *adj.* прави́тельственный.

governor ['gʌvənə(r)] *n.* **1.** (*ruling official*) губерна́тор. **2.** (*member of governing body*) член правле́ния. **3.** (*coll., boss*) хозя́ин; шеф; (*coll., as voc.*) господи́н. **4.** (*regulating mechanism*) регуля́тор.

cpd. **~-general** *n.* генера́л-губерна́тор.

governorship ['gʌvənəʃɪp] *n.* губерна́торство.

gowk [gaʊk] *n.* (*coll.*) дура́к; обалду́й.

gown [gaʊn] *n.* (*woman's*) пла́тье; (*academic or official*) ма́нтия.

GP (*abbr. of* ***general practitioner***) врач о́бщей пра́ктики; райо́нный врач; терапе́вт широ́кого про́филя.

GPO (*abbr. of* ***General Post Office***) главпочта́мт.

grab [græb] *n.* **1.** (*snatch*): **he made a ~ for the money** он попыта́лся схвати́ть де́ньги. **2.** (*mechanical device*) экскава́тор; черпа́к.

v.t. & *i.* схва́т|ывать, -и́ть; **he ~bed me by the lapels** он схвати́л меня́ за ла́цканы; **how does that ~ you?** что вы на э́то ска́жете?

grace [greɪs] *n.* **1.** (*elegance*) гра́ция; **airs and ~s** (*iron.*) жема́нство; (*quality*): **his speech had the saving ~ of brevity** его́ речь отлича́лась спаси́тельной кра́ткостью. **2.** (*favour*) благоскло́нность; **act of ~** поми́лование; **by the ~ of God** бо́жьей ми́лостью; **there, but for the ~ of God, go I** то́лько ми́лость госпо́дня уберегла́ меня́ от тако́й же судьбы́; **I am not in his good ~s** я у него́ в неми́лости; (*dispensation*) отсро́чка; **the law allows 3 days' ~** зако́н даёт 3 дня отсро́чки (*or* льго́тных дня); **he fell from ~** он сошёл с пути́ и́стинного; (*fell into disgrace*) он впал в неми́лость; **in the year of ~ 1900** в ле́то госпо́дне 1900; (*sense of the seemly*): **he had the ~ to apologize** он был насто́лько такти́чен, что извини́лся; (*easy or pleasant manner*): **he could lose the game with a good ~** он уме́л прои́грывать с досто́инством; **with an ill** (*or* **a bad**) **~** нелюбе́зно; (*prayer before meal*) моли́тва; **say ~** моли́ться (*impf.*) пе́ред едо́й. **3.** (*myth.*): **the three G~s** три гра́ции. **4.** (*courtesy title*): **his G~** све́тлость/сия́тельство; (*eccl.*) его́ преосвяще́нство.

v.t. удост|а́ивать, -о́ить; награ|жда́ть, -ди́ть; **he ~d the meeting with his presence** он удосто́ил собра́ние свои́м прису́тствием; **she is ~d with good looks** она́ наделена́ прия́тной вне́шностью.

cpd. **~-note** *n.* (*mus.*) фиориту́ра.

graceful ['greɪsfʊl] *adj.* грацио́зный; изя́щный.

gracefulness ['greɪsfʊlnɪs] *n.* грацио́зность; изя́щество.

graceless ['greɪslɪs] *adj.* (*rude*) нетакти́чный; бессты́дный; (*inelegant*) неуклю́жий.

gracious ['greɪʃəs] *adj.* ми́лостивый; любе́зный; **~ living** краси́вая жизнь.

int. **good(ness) ~ (me)!** ба́тюшки!; Бо́же мой!

graciousness ['greɪʃəsnɪs] *n.* ми́лость; любе́зность.

gradation [grə'deɪʃ(ə)n] *n.* града́ция.

grade [greɪd] *n.* **1.** (*assessed category*) сте́пень; (*of quality*) сорт; **low-~ oil** нефть ни́зкого ка́чества; (*of rank*) сте́пень; класс; (*US, class in school*) класс; **~ school** нача́льная шко́ла. **2.** (*US, school rating*) отме́тка; оце́нка; (*fig., coll.*): **he will scarcely make the ~** он едва́ ли с э́тим спра́вится. **3.** (*US*): **~ crossing** пересече́ние железнодоро́жного пути́ с шоссе́ (*и т.п.*) на одно́м у́ровне. **4.** (*fig., coll.*): **on the down ~** на спа́де.

v.t. **1.** (*classify*) сортирова́ть, рас-. **2.** (*reduce slope of*) профили́ровать (*impf.*). **3.** (*cattle etc.*) улучша́ть (*impf.*) поро́ду путём скре́щивания.

grader ['greɪdə(r)] *n.* (*road-building*) гре́йдер.

gradient ['greɪdɪənt] *n.* **1.** (*ratio of slope*) градие́нт; (*up/down*) градие́нт подъёма/укло́на; **a ~ of 1 in 5** укло́н оди́н к пяти́. **2.** (*slope*) подъём; склон.

gradual ['grædjʊəl] *adj.* постепе́нный.

gradualist ['grædjʊəlɪst] *n.* постепе́новец.

graduate[1] ['grædjʊət] *n.* (*of university, school etc.*) выпускни́|к (*fem.* -ца); **he is an Oxford ~** он око́нчил О́ксфордский университе́т; **~ student** аспира́нт (*fem.* -ка); **~ study** аспиранту́ра.

graduate[2] ['grædjʊ,eɪt] *v.t.* **1.** (*mark with degrees*) градуи́ровать, про-. **2.** (*arrange by grade*) распол|ага́ть, -ожи́ть на шкале́. **3.** (*give university degree to*) прису|жда́ть, -ди́ть дипло́м +*d.*; (*coll.*) выпуска́ть, вы́пустить.

v.i. (*from university*) ок|а́нчивать, -о́нчить университе́т/вуз; (*coll.*) получи́ть (*pf.*) дипло́м.

graduation [,grædjʊ'eɪʃ(ə)n] *n.* **1.** (*marking with degrees*) градуиро́вка. **2.** (*pl., degrees so marked*) деле́ния (*nt. pl.*). **3.** (*arrangement in grades*) расположе́ние на шкале́. **4.** (*conferring degree*) присужде́ние дипло́ма (в ву́зе); присужде́ние сте́пени; (*US, school*) вы́дача аттеста́та зре́лости. **5.** (*receiving degree*) получе́ние дипло́ма/сте́пени; (*US*) оконча́ние шко́лы.

graffiti [grə'fi:ti:] *n.* на́дписи (*f. pl.*) (на сте́нах/забо́рах).

graft[1] [grɑ:ft] *n.* **1.** (*scion*) черено́к; (*tissue*) переса́женная ткань; (*process applied to trees*) приви́вка. **2.** (*surgery*) опера́ция переса́дки. **3.** (*coll.*) (*hard work*) вка́лывание.

v.t. (*surg.*) переса́|живать, -ди́ть; (*hort., also fig.*) прив|ива́ть, -и́ть.

graft[2] [grɑ:ft] *n.* (*coll., bribery etc.*) взя́точничество; блат.

grafter[1] ['grɑ:ftə(r)] *n.* (*coll.*) (*hard worker*) трудя́га (*c.g.*).

grafter[2] ['grɑ:ftə(r)] *n.* (*coll.*) жу́лик.

grail [greɪl] *n.*: **the Holy G~** свято́й гра́аль.

grain [greɪn] *n.* **1.** (*collect., seed of cereal plants*) зерно́; хле́бные зла́ки (*m. pl.*); (*single seed*) зерно́, зёрнышко, крупи́нка. **2.** (*small particle*) зёрнышко; крупи́нка; **~ of sand** песчи́нка; **you must take his words with a ~ of salt** его́ слова́ сле́дует принима́ть с огово́ркой; **this affords me some ~s of comfort** э́то даёт мне хоть како́е-то утеше́ние; **there is not a ~ of truth in it** в э́том нет ни крупи́цы/гра́на/ка́пли пра́вды. **3.** (*weight*) гран. **4.** (*texture*) волокно́; узело́к. **5.** (*of wood*) тексту́ра; **it goes against the ~ with me** (*fig.*) э́то мне не по душе́/нутру́.

v.t. (*leather*) зерни́ть (*impf.*), шагрени́ровать (*impf.*); (*wood*) придава́ть тексту́ру +*d.*

gram [græm] = **gram(me)**

grammar ['græmə(r)] *n.* грамма́тика; **this sentence is bad ~** э́то негра́мотная фра́за.

cpds. **~-book** *n.* уче́бник грамма́тики; **~-school** *n.* сре́дняя шко́ла с гуманита́рным укло́ном.

grammarian [grə'meərɪən] *n.* граммати́ст.

grammatical [grə'mætɪk(ə)l] *adj.* граммати́ческий; **a ~ sentence** гра́мотное (*or* пра́вильно соста́вленное) предложе́ние.

gram(me) [græm] *n.* грамм.

gramophone ['græmə,fəʊn] *n.* патефо́н; (*with horn*) граммофо́н; **~ record** грампласти́нка.

grampus ['græmpəs] *n.* дельфи́н-каса́тка.

gran [græn] = **granny**

granary ['grænərɪ] *n.* амба́р; зернохрани́лище.

grand [grænd] *n.* (*piano*) роя́ль (*m.*); (*sl., 1000 dollars, pounds, etc.*) шту́ка, кося́я.

adj. **1.** (*title*) вели́кий; **~ duke** вели́кий князь (*m.*); **~ master** (*chess*) гроссме́йстер. **2.** (*great, important*) вели́кий; грандио́зный; **the G~ Canal** (*Venice*) Большо́й кана́л; **~ opera** больша́я о́пера; **~ piano** роя́ль (*m.*). **3.** (*elevated, imposing*) вели́чественный; **the ~ style** высо́кий стиль; **a ~ air** ва́жный вид. **4.** (*all embracing*): **~ finale** торже́ственный фина́л; **~ total** о́бщая су́мма. **5.** (*coll., very fine*) восхити́тельный; великоле́пный; роско́шный; **we had a ~ time** мы потряса́юще провели́ вре́мя.

cpds. **~child** *n.* внук; вну́чка; **~dad** *n.* (*coll.*) де́душка (*m.*); **~daughter** *n.* вну́чка; **~father** *n.* де́душка (*m.*); **~father clock** высо́кие напо́льные часы́; **~(mam)ma** *n.* (*coll.*) ба́бушка; **~mother** *n.* ба́бушка; **teach one's ~mother to suck eggs** ≃ я́йца ку́рицу не у́чат; **~(pa)pa** *n.* (*coll.*) де́душка (*m.*); **~parent** *n.* де́душка; ба́бушка; **~son** *n.* внук; **~stand** *n.* трибу́на. *For kinship terms see also cpds. of* **great**

grandee [græn'di:] *n.* гранд.

grandeur ['grændjə(r), -ndʒə(r)] *n.* вели́чие; великоле́пие.

grandiloquence [,græn'dɪləkwəns] *n.* высокопа́рность.

grandiloquent [,græn'dɪləkwənt] *adj.* высокопа́рный.

grandiose ['grændɪ,əʊs] *adj.* грандио́зный.

grange [greɪndʒ] *n.* (*farmstead*) уса́дьба.

granite ['grænɪt] *n.* грани́т.

adj. грани́тный.

granny ['grænɪ] *n.* (*coll.*) ба́бушка; **~ knot** «ба́бий» у́зел.

grant [grɑ:nt] *n.* (*conferment*) присвое́ние; дарова́ние; (*sum etc. conferred*) дота́ция; субси́дия; (*to student*) стипе́ндия.

v.t. **1.** (*bestow*) дарова́ть (*impf., pf.*); жа́ловать; **I ~ my consent** я даю́ согла́сие; **~ me this favour!** сде́лайте мне э́то одолже́ние! **2.** (*concede*) призн|ава́ть; -а́ть; **I ~ you that** в э́том вы пра́вы; **~ed, he has done all he could** согла́сен, он сде́лал всё, что мог. **3.: he takes my help for ~ed** он принима́ет мою́ по́мощь как до́лжное.

granular ['grænjʊlə(r)] *adj.* гранули́рованный.

granulate ['grænjʊ,leɪt] *v.t.* & *i.* дроби́ть, раз-; **~d sugar** са́харный песо́к.

granule ['grænju:l] *n.* зерно́.

grape [greɪp] *n.*: **a ~** виногра́дина; **the ~, ~s** виногра́д; **bunch of ~s** гроздь виногра́да; **sour ~s** (*fig.*) зе́лен виногра́д.

cpds. **~fruit** *n.* гре́йпфрут; **~-shot** *n.* кру́пная карте́чь; **~-vine** *n.* виногра́дная лоза́; (*fig.*): **I heard on the ~-vine that ...** молва́ донесла́ до меня́, что...

graph [grɑ:f, græf] *n.* гра́фик.

cpd. **~-paper** *n.* бума́га в кле́тку; миллиметро́вая бума́га.

graphic ['græfɪk] *adj.* **1.** (*pertaining to drawing etc.*) изобрази́тельный; **the ~ arts** изобрази́тельные иску́сства; гра́фика. **2.** (*vivid*) кра́сочный; нагля́дный; **the papers give a ~ account of the events** газе́ты даю́т я́ркое описа́ние собы́тий. **3.** (*using diagrams*) графи́ческий.

graphite ['græfaɪt] *n.* графи́т.

adj. графи́товый.

graphologist [grə'fɒlədʒɪst] *n.* графо́лог.

graphology [grə'fɒlədʒɪ] *n.* графоло́гия.

graphomania [,græfəʊ'meɪnɪə] *n.* графома́ния.

grapnel ['græpn(ə)l] *n.* (*anchor*) шлю́почный я́корь; (*for boarding*) аборда́жный крюк.

grappl|e ['græp(ə)l] *v.t.* схва́т|ывать, -и́ть.

v.i. схва́т|ываться, -и́ться; **~e with the enemy** схвати́ться с враго́м; **~e with a problem** бра́ться, взя́ться за пробле́му; **~ing-iron** крюк.

grasp [grɑ:sp] *n.* **1.** (*grip*) хва́тка; **he took my hand in a firm ~** он кре́пко пожа́л/сжал мне ру́ку; (*fig.*): **victory is within our ~** побе́да уже́ близка́. **2.** (*comprehension*) понима́ние; **he has a good ~ of the subject** он хорошо́ в э́том разбира́ется; **it is beyond my ~** э́то вы́ше моего́ понима́ния.

v.t. (*seize*) схва́т|ывать, -и́ть; **~ the nettle** (*fig.*) взять (*pf.*) быка́ за рога́; (*embrace*) обхва́т|ывать, -и́ть; (*comprehend*) схва́т|ывать, -и́ть смысл +*g.*

v.i.: **~ at, for** (*lit., fig.*) ухвати́ться (*pf.*) за+*a.*; **a ~ing person** стяжа́тель (*fem.* -ница).

grass [grɑ:s] *n.* **1.** трава́; **blade of ~** трави́нка; **he lets the ~ grow under his feet** он сиди́т сложа́ ру́ки; **the land was laid to ~** земля́ была́ отведена́/пу́щена под луг; (*gramineous species*) злак; (*pasture*) па́стбище; **the horse was put (out) to ~** ло́шадь вы́гнали на подно́жный корм; **~ widow** соло́менная вдова́. **2.** (*lawn*) газо́н; **keep off the ~** (*notice*) по траве́ не ходи́ть. **3.** (*sl., marijuana*) марихуа́на, «тра́вка». **4.** (*sl., police informer*) стука́ч.

v.t. зас|ева́ть, -е́ять траво́й; об|кла́дывать, -ложи́ть дёрном; **the ground has been ~ed over** уча́сток засе́ян траво́й.

v.i. (*sl., inform*) стуча́ть, на-.

cpds. **~hopper** *n.* кузне́чик; **~land** *n.* луг; **~-roots** *adj.* (*coll.*) низово́й, из низо́в; **~-roots opinion is against the plan** рядовы́е гра́ждане настро́ены про́тив э́того пла́на; **~-seed** *n.* семена́ (*nt. pl.*) трав; **~-snake** *n.* уж.

grassy ['grɑ:sɪ] *adj.* травяно́й; травяни́стый.

grate[1] [greɪt] *n.* (*fireplace*) ками́нная решётка; ками́н.

grate[2] [greɪt] *v.t.* тере́ть (*impf.*); **~d cheese** тёртый сыр; **~ one's teeth** скрежета́ть (*impf.*) зуба́ми.

v.i. **1.** (*rub*) тере́ться (*impf.*); **~ on** (*fig.*) раздража́ть (*impf.*); нерви́ровать (*impf.*); **it ~s on my ear** э́то мне ре́жет слух. **2.** (*make harsh sound*) скр|ипе́ть, -и́пнуть.

grateful ['greɪtfʊl] *adj.* (*thankful*) благода́рный; (*agreeable*) прия́тный.

gratefulness ['greɪtfʊlnɪs] *n.* благода́рность.

grater ['greɪtə(r)] *n.* тёрка.

gratification [,grætɪfɪ'keɪʃ(ə)n] *n.* удовлетворе́ние.

gratify ['grætɪ,faɪ] *v.t.* **1.** (*give pleasure to*) дост|авля́ть, -а́вить удово́льствие +*d.*; ублаж|а́ть, -и́ть; **the results were most ~ing** результа́ты бы́ли са́мыми обнадёживающими. **2.** (*indulge*) удовлетвор|я́ть, -и́ть.

grating ['greɪtɪŋ] *n.* решётка.

gratis ['grɑ:tɪs, 'greɪ-] *adj.* беспла́тный.

adv. беспла́тно.

gratitude ['grætɪ,tju:d] *n.* благода́рность.

gratuitous [grə'tju:ɪtəs] *adj.* **1.** (*free*) дарово́й; безвозме́здный; **~ advice** беспла́тный (*coll.*) сове́т. **2.** (*unwarranted*) беспричи́нный; **a ~ insult** незаслу́женное оскорбле́ние.

gratuity [grə'tju:ɪtɪ] *n.* (*bounty on retirement etc.*) посо́бие; пре́мия; (*tip*) чаевы́|е (*pl., g.* -х).

gravamen [grə'veɪmen] *n.* (*grievance*) жа́лоба; (*of accusation*) суть, основно́й пункт.

grave[1] [greɪv] *n.* моги́ла; **an old man with one foot in the ~** стари́к, стоя́щий одно́й ного́й в моги́ле; **he would turn in his ~ if he heard you** е́сли бы он вас услы́шал, он переверну́лся бы в гробу́; **someone is walking over my ~** меня́ ни с того́ ни с сего́ дрожь пробира́ет; (*death*) смерть; **he went to his ~** он сошёл в моги́лу; **life beyond the ~** загро́бная жизнь; **the ~ of all his hopes** круше́ние всех его́ наде́жд.

cpds. **~-clothes** *n.* са́ван; **~-digger** *n.* моги́льщик; **~side** *n.*: **at the ~** на краю́ моги́лы; **~stone** *n.* надгро́бный ка́мень; **~yard** *n.* кла́дбище.

grave[2] [greɪv] *adj.* (*of pers.*) серьёзный; (*of events*) серьёзный, тяжёлый; **~ news** трево́жные ве́сти; **a ~ crime** тя́жкое преступле́ние.

grave[3] [grɑ:v] *adj.* (*gram.*): **~ accent** тупо́е ударе́ние.

grave[4] [greɪv] *v.t.* высека́ть, вы́сечь; гравирова́ть (*impf.*); **her face is ~d on my memory** её лицо́ запечатле́лось в мое́й па́мяти; **~n image** и́дол, куми́р.

gravel ['græv(ə)l] *n.* гра́вий; **a ~ path** доро́жка, посы́панная гра́вием; (*geol.*) золотоно́сный песо́к; (*med.*) мочево́й песо́к; ка́мни (*m. pl.*) (в мочево́м пузыре́).

v.t. (*strew with ~*) пос|ыпа́ть, -ы́пать гра́вием; (*coll., perplex*) прив|оди́ть, -ести́ в замеша́тельство.

gravelly ['grævəlɪ] *adj.* грави́йный; (*fig., of the voice*) скрипу́чий.

graver ['greɪvə(r)] *n.* (*pers.*) ре́зчик, гравёр; (*tool*) резе́ц.

gravitate ['grævɪ,teɪt] *v.i.* прит|я́гиваться, -яну́ться; (*fig.*) тяготе́ть (*impf.*) (*к чему*).

gravitation [,grævɪ'teɪʃ(ə)n] *n.* (*sinking*) опуска́ние; (*phys. force*) притяже́ние, тяготе́ние; (*fig.*) тяготе́ние.

gravitational [,grævɪ'teɪʃən(ə)l] *adj.* гравитацио́нный.

gravity ['grævɪtɪ] *n.* **1.** (*force*) си́ла притяже́ния. **2.** (*weight*) тя́жесть; **centre of ~** центр тя́жести; **law of ~** зако́н всеми́рного тяготе́ния; **specific ~** уде́льный вес. **3.** (*seriousness*) серьёзность; опа́сность; тя́жесть. **4.** (*solemnity*) торже́ственность.

gravy ['greɪvɪ] *n.* подли́вка.

cpd. **~-boat** *n.* со́усник.

gray [greɪ] = **grey**

graze[1] [greɪz] *n.* (*abrasion*) цара́пина; сса́дина.

v.t. зад|ева́ть, -е́ть; сса́|живать, -ди́ть; **the bullet ~d his cheek** пу́ля оцара́пала ему́ щёку; **he fell and ~d his knee** он упа́л и ссади́л коле́но.

v.i.: **the bullet ~d past him** пу́ля пролете́ла ми́мо, почти́ не заде́в его́.

graze[2] [greɪz] *v.t.* пасти́; **~ sheep** пасти́ ове́ц; **~** (*feed in*) **a field** пасти́сь на по́ле/лугу́.

v.i.: **he has 40 sheep out to ~** у него́ (в ста́де/ота́ре) пасётся 40 ове́ц.

grazier ['greɪzɪə(r)] *n.* скотово́д.

grazing ['greɪzɪŋ] *n.* па́стбище; **~ land** вы́пас.

grease [gri:s] *n.* (*fat*) жир; (*lubricant*) сма́зка, таво́т.

v.t. сма́з|ывать, -ать; (*fig.*): **~ s.o.'s palm** (*with a bribe*) «подма́зать» кого́-н.; **he ran off like ~d lightning** он помча́лся пу́лей.

cpds. **~-gun** *n.* шприц для сма́зки; таво́т-пресс; **~-monkey** *n.* (авто)меха́ник; авиамеха́ник; **~-paint** *n.* грим; **~proof** *adj.* жиронепроница́емый; **~-spot** *n.* то́чка сма́зки.

greasy ['gri:sɪ, -zɪ] *adj.* жи́рный; (*of a road*) ско́льзкий; (*fig., unctuous*) еле́йный.

great [greɪt] *adj.* **1.** большо́й, вели́кий; (*famous*) знамени́тый; **a ~ nuisance** большо́е неудо́бство; **they are ~ friends** они́ больши́е друзья́; **a ~ (big) boy** ро́слый ма́льчик; **a ~ scoundrel** большо́й негодя́й; **a girl of ~ promise** де́вушка, подаю́щая больши́е наде́жды; **a ~ many people** ма́сса наро́ду; **a ~ deal of courage** незауря́дная хра́брость; **I've a ~ mind to ...** мне бы о́чень хоте́лось...; **a ~ while ago** давны́м-давно́; **he lived to a ~ age** он до́жил до глубо́кой ста́рости; **the ~ majority**

значи́тельное/подавля́ющее большинство́; **take ~ care!** бу́дьте о́чень/преде́льно осторо́жны; **he shows ~ ignorance** он проявля́ет по́лное неве́жество (*в чём*). **2.** (*enthusiastic, assiduous*): **a ~ reader** стра́стный чита́тель; **a ~ walker** завзя́тый ходо́к. **3.** (*coll., splendid, marvellous*) замеча́тельный; **we had a ~ time** мы замеча́тельно провели́ вре́мя; **he thinks he's the ~est** (*US sl.*) он мно́го о себе́ вообража́ет; **he is ~ at repairing a car** он великоле́пно чи́нит/ремонти́рует маши́ну. **4.** (*eminent, distinguished*) вели́кий; **Alexander the G~** Алекса́ндр Македо́нский/Вели́кий; **~ minds think alike** вели́кие умы́ схо́дятся; **the G~ Powers** вели́кие держа́вы; **Peter the G~** Пётр Пе́рвый/Вели́кий; **a ~ occasion** торже́ственное собы́тие. **5.** (*var.*): **the G~ Bear** Больша́я Медве́дица; **G~ Britain** Великобрита́ния; **~ circle** большо́й круг; **~ circle sailing** пла́вание по ортодро́мии.

cpds. **~-aunt** *n.* двою́родная ба́бушка; **~coat** *n.* пальто́ (*indecl.*); **~-granddaughter** *n.* пра́внучка; **~-grandfather** *n.* пра́дед; **~-grandmother** *n.* праба́бушка; **~-grandson** *n.* пра́внук; **~-hearted** *adj.* великоду́шный; **~-nephew** *n.* внуча́тый племя́нник; **~-niece** *n.* внуча́тая племя́нница; **~-uncle** *n.* двою́родный дед.

greatly ['greɪtlɪ] *adv.* о́чень, си́льно, значи́тельно; **I was ~ amused** э́то меня́ си́льно позаба́вило; **~ esteemed** глубокоуважа́емый; **~ daring, I replied ...** набра́вшись ду́ху, я отве́тил.

greatness ['greɪtnɪs] *n.* вели́чие.

greaves [gri:vz] *n.* (*armour*) наголе́нники (*m. pl.*).

grebe [gri:b] *n.* пога́нка (*птица*).

Grecian ['gri:ʃ(ə)n] *adj.* гре́ческий.

Greece [gri:s] *n.* Гре́ция.

greed [gri:d], **-iness** ['gri:dɪnɪs] *nn.* жа́дность; а́лчность; (*for food*) прожо́рливость.

greedy ['gri:dɪ] *adj.* (*for money etc.*) жа́дный; а́лчный; (*for honour etc.*) жа́ждущий +*g.*; а́лчущий +*g.*; (*for food*) прожо́рливый.

cpd. **~-guts** *n.* (*sl.*) жа́дина (*c.g.*).

Greek [gri:k] *n.* **1.** (*pers.*) гре|к (*fem.* -ча́нка). **2.** (*language*) гре́ческий язы́к; **Ancient ~** древнегре́ческий язы́к; **Modern ~** новогре́ческий язы́к; **it's ~ to me** э́то для меня́ кита́йская гра́мота.

adj. гре́ческий.

green [gri:n] *n.* **1.** (*colour*) зелёный цвет; зелёное; **dressed in ~** оде́тый в зелёное. **2.** (*pl., vegetables*) зе́лень; **spring ~s** ра́нние о́вощи (*m. pl.*); (*cut foliage*) ли́стья (*pl.*). **3.** (*grassy area*) лужа́йка; (*on golf course*) площа́дка вокру́г лу́нки.

adj. зелёный; **a ~ belt round the city** зелёный по́яс (вокру́г) го́рода; **he got the ~ light and went ahead** (*fig.*) получи́в «зелёную у́лицу», он нача́л де́йствовать; **she has ~ fingers** она́ уме́лый садово́д; **~ with envy** зелёный от за́висти; (*unripe*) незре́лый; **~ wood** невы́держанная/«зелёная» древеси́на; (*fig., inexperienced, gullible*) «зелёный»; (*lively, flourishing*): **the events are still ~ in my memory** собы́тия всё ещё свежи́ в мое́й па́мяти; **he lived to a ~ old age** он до́жил до преклóнного во́зраста, но был ещё по́лон сил.

cpds. **~back** *n.* (*US*) банкно́та; **~-eyed** *adj.* зеленогла́зый; (*fig.*) ревни́вый; **the ~-eyed monster** ре́вность; **~finch** *n.* зелену́шка; **~fly** *n.* тля; **~gage** *n.* ренкло́д; **~grocer** *n.* зеленщи́к; **~grocery** *n.* зелённая ла́вка; **~horn** *n.* новичо́к; **~house** *n.* тепли́ца; **~house effect** парнико́вый *or* тепли́чный эффе́кт; **~-room** *n.* актёрская убо́рная; **~stuff** *n.* о́вощ|и (*pl. g.* -е́й); **~sward** *n.* (*arch.*) газо́н.

greenery ['gri:nərɪ] *n.* зе́лень.

greenish ['gri:nɪʃ] *adj.* зеленова́тый.

Greenland ['gri:nlənd] *n.* Гренла́ндия.

adj. гренла́ндский.

greenness ['gri:nnɪs] *n.* зе́лень; (*fig.*) нео́пытность.

Greenwich (mean) time ['grenɪtʃ, 'grɪnɪdʒ] *n.* вре́мя по Гри́нвичу.

greet [gri:t] *v.t.* (*socially*) здоро́ваться, по- с+*i.*; кла́няться, рас- с+*i.*; (*welcome*) приве́тствовать (*impf.*); (*e.g. the dawn*) встр|еча́ть, -е́тить; **the soldiers were ~ed by abuse** солда́т встре́тили оскорбле́ниями; **a fine view ~ed us at the summit** с верши́ны нам откры́лся прекра́сный вид.

greeting ['gri:tɪŋ] *n.* (*on meeting*) приве́тствие; **~s** (*in a letter*) приве́т; **~s!** приве́т!; приве́тствую!; (*on a special occasion*): **birthday ~s** поздравле́ние с днём рожде́ния; **~ card** поздрави́тельная откры́тка.

gregarious [grɪ'geərɪəs] *adj.* ста́дный; (*fig., also*) общи́тельный.

gregariousness [grɪ'geərɪəsnɪs] *n.* ста́дность; общи́тельность.

Gregorian [grɪ'gɔ:rɪən] *adj.* григориа́нский.

Gregory ['gregərɪ] *n.* Григо́рий.

gremlin ['gremlɪn] *n.* (*coll.*) злой дух.

grenade [grɪ'neɪd] *n.* грана́та.

grenadier [,grenə'dɪə(r)] *n.* гренаде́р.

grey, gray [greɪ] *n.* се́рый цвет; се́рое; **dressed in ~** оде́тый в се́рое.

adj. се́рый; **~ area** (*fig.*) о́бласть неопределённости; **~ eminence** «се́рый кардина́л»; **~ matter** (*fig.*) «се́рое вещество́»; ум; «мо́зги» (*m. pl.*); **he has gone quite ~** он си́льно поседе́л; **his face turned ~** он побледне́л.

cpds. **~beard** *n.* стари́к; **~-haired, ~-headed** *adjs.* седо́й, седовла́сый; **~hound** *n.* гре́йгаунд, англи́йская борза́я.

greyish ['greɪɪʃ] *adj.* серова́тый.

greyness ['greɪnɪs] *n.* се́рость; (*of hair*) седина́.

grid [grɪd] *n.* **1.** (*grating*) решётка; **luggage ~** бага́жный стелла́ж; бага́жная се́тка. **2.** (*gridiron*) ра́шпер. **3.** (*map reference squares*) координа́тная се́тка; **~ reference** координа́ты (*f. pl.*). **4.** (*elec.*) сеть электропереда́ч. **5.** (*power supply system*) энергосисте́ма.

cpd. **~iron** *n.* ра́шпер; (*US coll.*) футбо́льное по́ле.

griddle ['grɪd(ə)l] *n.* сковоро́дка.

cpd. **~cake** *n.* лепёшка; блин.

grief [gri:f] *n.* (*sorrow*) го́ре, печа́ль, скорбь; (*cause of sorrow*) огорче́ние; (*disaster*): **he will come to ~** он пло́хо ко́нчит.

grievance ['gri:v(ə)ns] *n.* прете́нзия; недово́льство; **he likes airing his ~s** он лю́бит излива́ть своё недово́льство.

grieve [gri:v] *v.t.* огорч|а́ть, -и́ть; печа́лить, о-; **I am ~d to hear of it** мне бо́льно э́то слы́шать.

v.i. печа́литься, о-; горева́ть (*impf.*); **she ~d for her husband** она́ горева́ла о му́же.

grievous ['gri:vəs] *adj.* го́рестный; печа́льный; **~ harm** тяжёлый уще́рб; **~ pain** мучи́тельная боль.

griffin ['grɪfɪn], **griffon** ['grɪf(ə)n], **gryphon** ['grɪf(ə)n] *n.* грифо́н.

grill[1] [grɪl] *n.* (*gridiron*) ра́шпер; (*dish*) жа́реное мя́со; **mixed ~** ассорти́ (*nt. indecl.*) из жа́реного мя́са.

v.t. (*cook*) жа́рить, под-; (*coll. interrogate*) учин|я́ть, -и́ть допро́с +*d.*

v.i. (*of food*) жа́риться, под-; **we lay ~ing in the sun** мы жа́рились на со́лнце.

cpd. **~room** *n.* гриль-ба́р.

grill[2], **-e** [grɪl] *n.* решётка.

grim [grɪm] *adj.* суро́вый, мра́чный, гро́зный; **he held on like ~ death** он вцепи́лся мёртвой хва́ткой; **the prospect is ~** перспекти́вы мра́чные/безра́достные.

grimace ['grɪməs, grɪ'meɪs] *n.* грима́са.

v.i. грима́сничать (*impf.*).

grime [graɪm] *n.* са́жа; грязь.

grimy ['graɪmɪ] *adj.* чума́зый; гря́зный.

grin [grɪn] *n.* усме́шка; оска́л.

v.i. усмех|а́ться, -ну́ться; ухмыл|я́ться, -ну́ться; ска́лить (*impf.*) зу́бы; **you must ~ and bear it** вы должны́ му́жественно перенести́ э́то.

grind [graɪnd] *n.* (*coll.*) изнури́тельный труд; рабо́та на изно́с; **this work is a fearful ~** э́та рабо́та до у́жаса изнуря́ет.

v.t. **1.** (*crush*) моло́ть, с-; **~ corn** моло́ть, пере- зерно́; **ground almonds** минда́льная кро́шка; мо́лотый минда́ль; **ground rice** рис-се́чка; дроблёный рис; (*fig.*) угнета́ть (*impf.*); **he got rich by ~ing the faces of the poor** он разбогате́л, эксплуати́руя бе́дных. **2.** (*wear down*) изн|а́шивать, -оси́ть; **ground glass** ма́товое стекло́; **the valves need ~ing in** кла́паны нужда́ются в прити́рке;

(*sharpen*) точи́ть, на-; **I have no axe to ~** (*fig.*) у меня́ нет своекоры́стных це́лей; (*make smooth*) шлифова́ть, от-. **3. ~ one's teeth** скрежета́ть/скрипе́ть (*impf.*) зуба́ми. **4. ~ one's heel into the earth** вдáв|ливать, -и́ть каблу́к в зе́млю. **5.** (*on barrel-organ*): **~ out a tune** крути́ть шарма́нку.

v.i. **1.** (*abs.*): **the mills of God ~ slowly** ≃ Бог пра́вду ви́дит, да не ско́ро ска́жет. **2.** (*respond to ~ing*) ста́чиваться, сточи́ться. **3.** (*rub, grate*) раст|ира́ть, -ере́ть. **4.** (*coll., work hard*) изм|а́тываться, -ота́ться; **~ away at one's studies** грызть (*impf.*) грани́т нау́ки. **5.: ~ to a halt** остан|а́вливаться, -ови́ться (с ля́згом); засто́пориться (*pf.*).

cpd. **~stone** *n.* точи́ло; **he kept his nose to the ~stone** он труди́лся без о́тдыха; он не дал себе́ переды́шки.

grinder ['graɪndə(r)] *n.* **1.** (*for crushing*) дроби́лка; (*coffee-~*) кофемо́лка, кофе́йная ме́льница. **2.** (*for abrasive work*) точи́льный ка́мень; шлифова́льный стано́к. **3.** (*tooth*) коренно́й зуб.

grip [grɪp] *n.* **1.** (*grasp*) схва́тывание; (*fig.*) понима́ние; **he has a powerful ~** у него́ кре́пкая хва́тка; **he was in the ~ of an illness** боле́знь кре́пко держа́ла его́; **come to ~s with a problem** вплотну́ю заня́ться (*pf.*) пробле́мой; **take a ~ of yourself!** возьми́те себя́ в ру́ки!; **he got a ~ of the facts** он разобра́лся в фа́ктах; **he is losing his ~** хва́тка у него́ уже́ не та. **2.** (*handle; part held*) рукоя́тка; ру́чка. **3.** (*travelling-bag*) саквоя́ж.

v.t. (*hold tightly*) схва́т|ывать, -и́ть; (*of a disease*) не отпуска́ть, кре́пко держа́ть (*both impf.*); (*hold the attention of*) захва́т|ывать, -и́ть; **a ~ ping story** захва́тывающий расска́з.

v.i. схва́т|ываться, -и́ться; **the brakes failed to ~** тормоза́ отказа́ли.

gripe [graɪp] (*coll.*) *n.* **1.** (*pl., colic pains*) ко́лик|и (*pl., g.* —). **2.** (*grumble, complaint*) ворча́ние.

v.i. (*complain*) ворча́ть (*impf.*).

cpd. **~-water** *n.* укро́пная вода́.

grisaille [grɪ'zeɪl, -'zaɪl] *n.* гриза́ль.

grisly ['grɪzlɪ] *adj.* ужаса́ющий.

grist [grɪst] *n.* помо́л; зерно́ для помо́ла; (*fig.*): **it will bring ~ to the mill** э́то принесёт дохо́д; **all is ~ to his mill** он из всего́ извлека́ет вы́году.

gristle ['grɪs(ə)l] *n.* хрящ.

gristly ['grɪslɪ] *adj.* хрящево́й; с хряща́ми.

grit [grɪt] *n.* **1.** (*small bits of stone*) гра́вий; песо́к; **I've a piece of ~ in my eye** мне в гла́з попа́ла сори́нка. **2.** (*coll., courage and endurance*) вы́держка; му́жество. **3.** (*pl., coarse meal*) овся́нка.

v.t. **1.** (*spread ~ on*): **the streets were ~ted at the first sign of frost** при пе́рвых при́знаках моро́за у́лицы посы́пали песко́м. **2.: ~ one's teeth** скрипе́ть (*impf.*) зуба́ми; (*fig.*) сти́снуть (*pf.*) зу́бы.

gritty ['grɪtɪ] *adj.* песча́ный; (*fig., of style*) шерохова́тый.

grizzle ['grɪz(ə)l] *v.i.* (*coll., fret*) капри́зничать (*impf.*); хны́кать (*impf.*).

grizzled ['grɪz(ə)ld] *adj.* седо́й.

grizzly ['grɪzlɪ] *n.* (**~-bear**) гри́зли (*m. indecl.*).

groan [grəʊn] *n.* стон.

v.i. стона́ть, за; **he was ~ing for help** он взыва́л о по́мощи.

groats [grəʊts] *n.* крупа́.

grocer ['grəʊsə(r)] *n.* бакале́йщик.

grocery ['grəʊsərɪ] *n.* (*trade*) бакале́йное де́ло; (*shop*) бакале́йная ла́вка; магази́н бакале́йных това́ров; (*pl., goods*) бакале́я.

grog [grɒg] *n.* грог; пунш.

groggy ['grɒgɪ] *adj.* нетвёрдый на нога́х.

grogram ['grɒgrəm] *n.* фай.

groin [grɔɪn] *n.* (*anat.*) пах; (*archit.*) кресто́вый свод.

groom [gru:m] *n.* (*for horses*) ко́нюх; (*bride~*) жени́х.

v.t. **1. ~ a horse** ходи́ть (*impf.*) за ло́шадью. **2. well-~ed** (*of pers.*) хорошо́ причёсанный и оде́тый; (*coll.*) ухо́женный. **3.** (*prepare, coach*) гото́вить; **he is being ~ed for President** его́ про́чат в президе́нты.

cpd. **~sman** *n.* ша́фер.

groove [gru:v] *n.* желобо́к; (*fig.*) рути́на; **my life runs on in the same ~** моя́ жизнь идёт тем же чередо́м; **it is easy to get into a ~** войти́ в привы́чную колею́ легко́.

v.t. прор|еза́ть, -е́зать кана́вки *+p.*

groovy ['gru:vɪ] *adj.* (*sl., smart in the fashion*) шика́рный; клёвый.

grope [grəʊp] *v.t. & i.* идти́ (*det.*) о́щупью; ощу́п|ывать, -ать; **he ~d his way toward the door** он о́щупью добра́лся до две́ри; (*fig.*): **~ after truth** доиска́ться (*impf.*) пра́вды.

grosgrain ['grəʊgreɪn] *n.* ткань в у́точный ру́бчик.

gross [grəʊs] *n.* (*number*) гросс.

adj. **1.** (*coarse; flagrant*) гру́бый; вульга́рный. **2.** (*luxuriant*) бу́йный, пы́шный. **3.** (*obese*) ту́чный. **4.** (*opp. net*) валово́й; **~ weight** вес бру́тто; **in the ~** (*wholesale*) о́птом, гурто́м.

v.t. (*coll., make a ~ profit*): **we ~ed £1,000** мы получи́ли о́бщую при́быль в 1000 фу́нтов.

grossness ['grəʊsnɪs] *n.* гру́бость; вульга́рность; (*luxuriance*) пы́шность; (*obesity*) ту́чность.

grotesque [grəʊ'tesk] *n.* (*pers., figure etc.*) гроте́ск.

adj. гроте́сковый; гроте́скный.

grotesquerie [grəʊ'teskərɪ] *n.* гроте́скные предме́ты (*m. pl.*), гроте́скность.

grotto ['grɒtəʊ] *n.* грот.

grouch [graʊtʃ] *n.* (*coll.*) прете́нзия; **he has a ~ against me** он на меня́ в оби́де; (*grumbler*) ворчу́н; брюзга́ (*c.g.*).

grouchy ['graʊtʃɪ] *adj.* (*coll.*) ворчли́вый; брюзгли́вый.

ground [graʊnd] *n.* **1.** (*surface of earth*) земля́; грунт; **the building has 6 storeys above ~** в зда́нии шесть (надзе́мных) этаже́й; **he is still above ~** (*alive*) он ещё жив; **don't wait until I'm under the ~** не жди́те моей сме́рти; **the tree fell to the ~** де́рево упа́ло на зе́млю; **he cut the ~ from under my feet** он вы́бил у меня́ по́чву из-под ног; **his plan fell to the ~** его́ план ру́хнул; **the plane was a long while getting off the ~** самолёт де́лал большо́й разбе́г пе́ред взлётом; **the plan will never get off the ~** прое́кт так и оста́нется на бума́ге; **he has both feet on the ~** (*fig.*) он про́чно стои́т на нога́х; **thin on the ~** (*coll., sparse*) ≃ раз, два и обчёлся; **it suits me down to the ~** э́то меня́ вполне́ устра́ивает; **from the ~ up** сни́зу до́верху; **~ crew** назе́мная кома́нда; **~ control** назе́мное управле́ние; **~ floor** пе́рвый эта́ж; **he got in on the ~ floor** (*fig.*) с са́мого нача́ла он был на ра́вных; **~ forces** сухопу́тные войска́; **~ speed** (*aeron.*) путева́я ско́рость; **~ staff** нелётный соста́в; **~ swell** мёртвая зыбь, до́нные во́лны (*f. pl.*). **2.** (*soil, also fig.*) по́чва; **~ frost** за́морозк|и (*pl., g.* -ов); подмёрзшая земля́; **his words fell on stony ~** его́ слова́ бы́ли гла́сом вопию́щего в пусты́не; **this theory breaks fresh ~** э́та тео́рия проклады́вает но́вые пути́; **you are** (*treading*) **on dangerous ~** вы вступи́ли на ско́льзкую по́чву. **3.** (*position*) положе́ние; **our forces gained ~** на́ши ча́сти продвига́лись вперёд; **this opinion is gaining ~** э́та то́чка зре́ния набира́ет си́лу; **he had to give ~** он до́лжен был уступи́ть; **he stood his ~ like a man** он держа́лся как мужчи́на; **they held their ~ well** они́ сто́йко держа́лись; **he has shifted his ~ so many times** он сто́лько раз меня́л свою́ пози́цию; **I prefer to meet him on my own ~** я предпочита́ю встреча́ться с ним на свое́й террито́рии; **there is much common ~ between us** у нас мно́го о́бщего. **4.** (*area, distance*) расстоя́ние; **the car certainly covers the ~** маши́на идёт совсе́м непло́хо; **we covered a lot of ~** (*distance*) мы покры́ли большо́е расстоя́ние; (*fig., work*) мы заме́тно продви́нулись вперёд. **5.** (*defined area of activity*) площа́дка; **fishing ~s** места́, отведённые для ры́бной ло́вли; **football ~** футбо́льная площа́дка; **parade ~** плац; **sports ~** спорти́вная площа́дка; **home ~** своё по́ле. **6.** (*pl., estate*) сад, парк, зе́мли (*f. pl.*); **house and ~s** дом и земе́льный уча́сток. **7.** (*pl. dregs*) гу́ща; **coffee ~s** кофе́йная гу́ща. **8.** (*reason*) основа́ние; **I have no ~s for complaint** у меня́ нет основа́ний жа́ловаться; **he has good ~(s) for saying so** у него́ есть все основа́ния так говори́ть. **9.** (*surface for painting, printing etc.*) фон; **a design on a white ~** рису́нок на бе́лом фо́не. **10.: ~ (bass)** (*mus.*) те́ма.

v.t. **1.** (*run aground*) сажáть, посадúть на мель. **2.** (*prevent from flying*) запре|щáть, -тúть полёты +*g.*; отстран|я́ть, -úть от полётов. **3.** (*base*) обоснóв|ывать, -áть; **his fears were well ~ed** егó опасéния бы́ли пóлностью обоснóваны. **4.** (*give basic instruction to*) подгот|áвливать, -óвить. **5.** (*mil.*): **~ arms!** бросáй орýжие! **6.** (*elec., connect to earth*) заземл|я́ть, -úть.

v.i. (*of a vessel*) садúться, сесть на мель.

cpds. **~-bait** *n.* дóнная блеснá; **~-controlled** *adj.* управля́емый с землú; **~-floor** *adj.* на пéрвом этажé; **~-hog** *n.* сурóк леснóй (америкáнский); **~nut** *n.* землянóй орéх; **~-plan** *n.* план пéрвого этажá здáния; (*fig.*) óбщие намётки (*f. pl.*); **~-rent** *n.* земéльная рéнта; **~-to-air** *adj.*: **~-to-air missile** ракéта клáсса «землá — вóздух»; **~-work** *n.* фундáмент, оснóвы (*f. pl.*).

grounding ['graʊndɪŋ] *n.* (*basic instruction*) подготóвка; оснóвы (*f. pl.*).

groundless ['graʊndlɪs] *adj.* беспричúнный, беспóчвенный, необоснóванный.

groundsel ['graʊns(ə)l] *n.* крестóвник.

group [gru:p] *n.* **1.** (*assemblage*) грýппа; коллектúв; (*for artistic purposes*) грýппа; ансáмбль (*m.*); (*interest ~, e.g. at school*) кружóк; (*political etc. unit*) группирóвка; фрáкция. **2.** (*attr.*) группово́й; **~ practice** (*med.*) грýппа врачéй, ведýщих приём в однóм мéсте.

v.t. & i. группировáть(ся), с-.

cpd. **~-captain** *n.* полкóвник авиáции.

grouping ['gru:pɪŋ] *n.* (*action*) группировáние, классифицúрование; (*group*) группирóвка.

grouse[1] [graʊs] *n.* (*bird*) шотлáндская куропáтка.

grouse[2] [graʊs] (*coll.*) (*complaint*) жáлоба; претéнзия.

v.i. ворчáть (*impf.*).

grout [graʊt] *n.* (*mortar*) цемéнтный раствóр.

v.t. зал|ивáть, -úть цемéнтом.

grove [grəʊv] *n.* рóща.

grovel ['grɒv(ə)l] *v.i.* лежáть (*impf.*) ниц/распростёршись; (*fig.*) пресмыкáться (*impf.*) (*перед кем*); пá|дать, -сть в нóги.

grow [grəʊ] *v.t.* растúть, вы́-; выращивать (*impf.*); разводúть (*impf.*); **cotton is ~n in the South** хлóпок выращивают на юге; **he is ~ing a beard** он отрáщивает бóроду.

v.i. **1.** (*of vegetable habitat*) растú, вы́расти; **ivy ~s on walls** плющ растёт на стéнах; **strawberries ~ wild in the wood** дúкая землянúка растёт в лесý; **money doesn't ~ on trees** дéньги не растýт на дерéвьях. **2.** (*of vegetable or animal development*): **he has ~n tall** он óчень вы́рос/вы́тянулся; **he grew (by) 5 inches** он вы́рос на 5 дю́ймов; **he is ~ing out of his clothes** он вырастáет из своéй одéжды; **she has ~n into a young lady** онá превратúлась в молодýю жéнщину; **she is letting her hair ~** онá отрáщивает вóлосы; **he looks quite ~n up** он вы́глядит совсéм взрóслым; **~n-ups** взрóслые (*pl.*); **I grew to like him** со врéменем он мне стал нрáвиться; **it grew out of nothing** всё началóсь с пустякá; **it's a habit I've never ~n out of** э́то привы́чка, от котóрой я никогдá не мог избáвиться; **he grew out of his clothes** он вы́рос из одéжды; **full(y)- ~n** зрéлый; **a ~n man** взрóслый человéк; **~ing pains** невралгúческие/ревматúческие бóли в дéтском вóзрасте; (*fig.*) болéзнь рóста; **good ~ing weather** погóда, благоприя́тная для урожáя; (*increase*) увелúчи|ваться, -ться; усúли|ваться, -ться; **he grew daily in wisdom** он с кáждым днём набирáлся умá; **his influence is ~ing** егó влия́ние растёт; **he listened with ~ing impatience** он слýшал с растýщим нетерпéнием; **the tune ~s on one** э́тот мотúв начинáет нрáвиться со врéменем. **3.** (*become*) становúться, стать; *also expr. by inchoative pref.*; **it grew suddenly dark** вдруг стáло темнó (*or* стемнéло); **the trees ~ green in spring** веснóй дерéвья зеленéют/распускáются; **as he grew older, he ...** с вóзрастом он...; **she grew pale** онá побледнéла; **he grew rich** он разбогатéл.

grower ['grəʊə(r)] *n.* (*cultivator*) садовóд; **a fast ~** (*plant*) быстрорастýщее растéние.

growl [graʊl] *n.* рычáние; (*of thunder*) грóхот.

v.i. рычáть (*impf.*); гремéть (*impf.*).

growth [grəʊθ] *n.* (*development*) рост; (*increase*) прирóст; **three days' ~ of beard** трёхднéвная щетúна; (*path.*) нарóст.

grub[1] [grʌb] *n.* (*larva*) личúнка; червь (*m.*); (*food*) жратвá (*coll.*).

grub[2] [grʌb] *v.t.* выкáпывать, вы́копать; **a hoe for ~bing out weeds** мотыга для прополки сорнякóв.

v.i. ры́ться (*impf.*); **pigs ~ about for food** свиньи рóются вокрýг/повсю́ду в пóисках пúщи.

grubby ['grʌbɪ] *adj.* (*dirty*) гря́зный, запáчканный.

grudg|e [grʌdʒ] *n.* претéнзия, недоброжелáтельность; **I bear him no ~e** я на негó не в обúде.

v.t. завúдовать, по- +*d.*; жалéть, по- (*чего*); **I do not ~e him his success** я не завúдую егó успéху; **he ~es me the very food I eat** он попрекáет меня́ кускóм хлéба; **I ~e paying so much** мне жаль платúть так мнóго; **~ing praise** скупáя похвалá; **he obeyed ~ingly** он неохóтно вы́полнил приказáние.

gruel ['gru:əl] *n.* (жúдкая) кáшица.

gruelling ['gru:əlɪŋ] *adj.* изматывающий; изнурúтельный.

gruesome ['gru:səm] *adj.* жýткий; вселя́ющий стрáх.

gruff [grʌf] *adj.* (*of demeanour*) неприветливый; рéзкий; (*of voice*) хрúплый.

gruffness ['grʌfnɪs] *n.* неприветливость; рéзкость.

grumble ['grʌmb(ə)l] *n.* (*complaint*) ворчáние; (*rumbling noise*) грóхот.

v.i. (*complain*) ворчáть (*impf.*); жáловаться, по-; (*rumble*) грохотáть (*impf.*).

grumbler ['grʌmblə(r)] *n.* ворчýн.

grumpy ['grʌmpɪ] *adj.* сварлúвый.

grunt [grʌnt] *n.* (*animal*) хрю́канье; (*human*) ворчáние.

v.i. (*of animals*) хрю́к|ать, -нуть; (*of humans*; *also v.t.*) ворчáть, про-.

gryphon ['grɪf(ə)n] = **griffin**

guano ['gwɑ:nəʊ] *n.* гуáно (*indecl.*).

guarantee [,gærən'ti:] *n.* **1.** (*undertaking*) гарáнтия; поручúтельство; **this watch carries a ~** э́ти часы́ с гарáнтией. **2.** (*guarantor*) гарáнт; поручúтель (*m.*); **will you stand ~ for me?** вы за меня́ порýчитесь? **3.** (*security*) гарáнтия (*чего*). **4.** (*determinant*) залóг; **money is no ~ of success** дéньги ещё не гарантúруют успéх.

v.t. **1.** (*stand surety*; *undertake, promise*) гарантúровать (*impf., pf.*). **2.** (*ensure*) обеспéчи|вать, -ть. **3.** (*coll., feel sure, wager*) ручáться, поручúться. **4.** (*insure*) страховáть, за-; **it is ~d to last 10 years** срок гóдности/гарáнтии — 10 лет; **~d against rust** гарантúрованный от ржáвчины.

guarantor [,gærən'tɔ:(r), 'gærəntə(r)] *n.* поручúтель (*m.*); гарáнт.

guaranty ['gærəntɪ] *n.* гарáнтия (по дóлгу), залóг, поручúтельство.

guard [gɑ:d] *n.* **1.** (*state of alertness*) насторожённость; **be on your ~ against pickpockets** остерегáйтесь кармáнников; **he was caught off his ~** егó застáли врасплóх; (*defence*): **on ~!** (*fencing*) к бóю!; **his ~ was down** (*fig.*) егó бдúтельность ослáбла; он ослáбил бдúтельность; (*mil.*): **mount ~** вступ|áть, -úть в караýл; **on ~ duty** на часáх; в караýле; **they kept ~ by day and night** онú стоя́ли на стрáже днём и нóчью; **the soldiers stood ~ over the prisoner** солдáты охраня́ли заключённого. **2.** (*man appointed to keep ~*) охрáнник, караýльный; (*collect.*) охрáна, стрáжа; **advance ~** авангáрд; **a ~ was set on the gates** у ворóт вы́ставили охрáну; **changing of the ~** смéна караýла; **prison ~** тюрéмный надзирáтель; охрáнник в тюрьмé; **~ of honour** почётный караýл; **Home G~** ополчéние; отря́ды (*m. pl.*) мéстной оборóны. **3.** (*pl., collect.*) гвáрдия; **Brigade of G~s** гвардéйская бригáда; **G~s officer** гвардéйский офицéр. **4.** (*of a train*) проводнúк; **~'s van** багáжный вагóн. **5.** (*protective device*) защúтное устрóйство, предохранúтель (*m.*); (*of a sword*) эфéс.

v.t. охраня́ть (*impf.*); берéчь; **the prisoners were closely ~ed** заключённые находúлись под усúленной охрáной; **he will ~ your interests** он бýдет охраня́ть вáши интерéсы; **you must ~ your tongue** вам нýжно быть бóлее сдéржанным на язы́к.

v.i. беречься (*impf.*), остерегаться (*impf.*) (**against:** +*g.*); **everything was done to ~ against infection** были приняты все меры против инфекции.

cpds. **~-house** *n.* караульное помещение; караульня; **~-rail** *n.* перил|а (*pl.*, *g.* —); **~-room** *n.* гауптвахта; **~sman** *n.* гвардеец.

guarded ['gɑːdɪd] *adj.* сдержанный; осторожный.

guardee [gɑː'diː] *n.* (*coll.*, *guardsman*) гвардеец.

guardian ['gɑːdɪən] *n.* **1.** (*protector*) опекун; попечитель (*m.*); **~ angel** ангел-хранитель (*m.*); **~ of the public interest** защитник общественных интересов. **2.** (*leg.*) опекун.

guardianship ['gɑːdɪən,ʃɪp] *n.* опека; опекунство.

Guatemala [,gwɑːtə'mɑːlə] *n.* Гватемала.

Guatemalan [,gwɑːtə'mɑːlən] *n.* гватемал|ец (*fem.* -ка).

adj. гватемальский.

guava ['gwɑːvə] *n.* гуава.

gudgeon ['gʌdʒ(ə)n] *n.* (*zool.*) пескарь (*m.*).

guelder-rose ['geldə(r)] *n.* калина.

guerdon ['gɜːd(ə)n] *n.* награда.

Guernsey ['gɜːnzɪ] *n.* (остров) Гернси (*m. indecl.*); (*attr.*) гернсейский.

guer(r)illa [gə'rɪlə] *n.* партизан; **~ warfare** партизанская война.

guess [ges] *n.* догадка; предположение; **at a rough ~** грубо/ориентировочно; **by ~** наугад; **my ~ is that ...** мне сдаётся, что...; **it's anybody's ~** никому неизвестно.

v.t. **1.** (*estimate*) прики|дывать, -нуть; **I would ~ his age at 40** я дал бы ему лет 40. **2.** **~ a riddle** отгад|ывать, -ать загадку. **3.** (*conjecture*) догад|ываться, -аться (*о чём*); угад|ывать, -ать; **I can't ~ how it happened** ума не приложу, как это случилось. **4.** (*US coll.*, *expect*, *suppose*) полагать (*impf.*); **I ~ you are right** вероятно, вы правы.

v.i. гадать (*impf.*); **she likes to keep him ~ing** ей нравится держать его в неведении; **~ing game** викторина; «угадайка».

cpd. **~work** *n.* догадки (*f. pl.*).

guest [gest] *n.* **1.** (*one privately entertained*) гость (*m.*); **paying ~** ≃ жилец; **~ of honour** почётный гость; **~ artist, star** гастролирующий артист; звезда на гастролях. **2.** (*at a hotel etc.*) постоялец. **3.** (*zool.*, *biol.*) паразит.

cpds. **~-house** *n.* пансион; жильё для гостей; дом приезжих; **~-night** *n.* ≃ званый вечер; **~-room** *n.* комната для гостей.

guff [gʌf] *n.* (*sl.*) трёп; трепотня.

guffaw [gʌ'fɔː] *n.* гогот.

v.i. гоготать (*impf.*).

guggle ['gʌg(ə)l] *n.* бульканье.

v.i. булькать (*impf.*).

guidance ['gaɪd(ə)ns] *n.* руководство.

guide [gaɪd] *n.* **1.** (*leader*) руководитель (*m.*); наставник; (*for travellers*, *tourists etc.*) гид, экскурсовод; (*mil.*) разведчик. **2.** (*directing principle*) руководство. **3.** **(~-book): ~ to Germany** путеводитель (*m.*) по Германии; (*manual*) учебник; **~ to fishing** руководство по рыбной ловле. **4.** **(Girl) G~** девочка-скаут.

v.t. **1.** (*lead*, *take around*) водить (*indet.*), вести, по- (*det.*); руководить (*impf.*) +*i.*; **he ~d them around the city** он поводил их по городу; **be ~d by principles** руководствоваться (*impf.*) принципами; **be ~d by circumstances** действовать (*impf.*) по обстоятельствам. **2.** (*direct*) напр|авлять, -авить; **~d missile** управляемая ракета.

cpds. **~-book** *n.* путеводитель (*m.*); **~-dog** *n.* собака-поводырь; **~line** *n.* директива; **~-post** *n.* указатель (*m.*); **~-rail** *n.* направляющий рельс; **~-rope** *n.* (*aeron.*) гайдроп.

guild [gɪld] *n.* **1.** (*hist.*) гильдия. **2.** ассоциация, союз.

cpd. **~hall** *n.* ратуша.

guilder ['gɪldə(r)] *n.* гульден.

guile [gaɪl] *n.* лукавство, коварство.

guileful ['gaɪlfʊl] *adj.* лукавый, коварный.

guileless ['gaɪllɪs] *adj.* простодушный; бесхитростный.

guillemot ['gɪlɪ,mɒt] *n.* кайра.

guillotine ['gɪlə,tiːn] *n.* **1.** гильотина. **2.** (*for paper*, *metal etc.*) резальная машина. **3.** (*parl.*) гильотинирование прений.

v.t. (*execute*) гильотинировать (*impf.*, *pf.*); (*pages etc.*) обр|езать, -езать.

guilt [gɪlt] *n.* вина; **~ complex** комплекс вины.

guiltiness ['gɪltɪnɪs] *n.* виновность.

guiltless ['gɪltlɪs] *adj.* невиновный (*в чём*).

guilty ['gɪltɪ] *adj.* виновный; **he pleaded ~ to the crime** он признал себя виновным в преступлении; **he was found ~** он был признан виновным; **a verdict of not ~** вердикт невиновности; **~ conscience** нечистая совесть; **a ~ look** виноватый вид.

guinea[1] ['gɪnɪ] *n.* гинея.

Guinea[2] ['gɪnɪ] *n.* Гвинея.

cpds. **g~-fowl, hen** *nn.* цесарка; **g~-pig** *n.* (*lit.*) морская свинка; (*fig.*) «подопытный кролик».

Guinean [gɪn'eɪən] *n.* гвине|ец (*fem.* -йка).

adj. гвинейский.

guise [gaɪz] *n.* (*dress*) наряд; (*pretence*) предлог; **under the ~ of friendship** под видом дружбы.

guitar [gɪ'tɑː(r)] *n.* гитара.

guitarist [gɪ'tɑːrɪst] *n.* гитарист.

gulch [gʌltʃ] *n.* (*US*) узкое ущелье.

gulf [gʌlf] *n.* **1.** (*deep bay*) залив; бухта; **the G~ Stream** Гольфстрим. **2.** (*abyss*) бездна. **3.** (*fig.*) пропасть.

gull[1] [gʌl] *n.* (*bird*) чайка.

gull[2] [gʌl] *n.* (*arch.*, *dupe*) простофиля (*c.g.*).

v.t. дурачить, о-.

gullet ['gʌlɪt] *n.* пищевод; **it sticks in my ~** (*fig.*) это мне поперёк горла.

gullibility [,gʌlɪ'bɪlɪtɪ] *n.* легковерие.

gullible ['gʌlɪb(ə)l] *adj.* легковерный.

gully ['gʌlɪ] *n.* лощина; волосток.

gulp [gʌlp] *n.* большой глоток; **at one ~** залпом; **he took a ~ of tea** он глотнул чаю.

v.t. глот|ать, -нуть; **don't ~ down your food!** не глотай еду/пищу!; **she ~ed back her tears** она глотала слёзы.

v.i.: **he ~ed with astonishment** он поперхнулся от удивления.

gum[1] [gʌm] *n.* (*anat.*) десна.

cpds. **~boil** *n.* флюс; **~shield** *n.* капа, назубник.

gum[2] [gʌm] *n.* (*adhesive*) смола; клей; (*resin*) камедь; (*chewing-~*) жевательная резинка.

v.t. склеи|вать, -ть; **~ up the works** (*sl.*) испортить (*pf.*) всё дело.

cpds. **~-boots** *n. pl.* (*coll.*) резиновые сапоги (*m. pl.*); **~-tree** *n.*: **he was up a ~-tree** (*sl.*) он попал в переделку.

gummy ['gʌmɪ] *adj.* клейкий.

gumption ['gʌmpʃ(ə)n] *n.* (*coll.*) смышлёность; находчивость.

gun [gʌn] *n.* **1.** (*cannon*) пушка; (*pistol*) пистолет; (*rifle*) ружьё; **~ crew** орудийный расчёт; **heavy ~s** тяжёлая артиллерия; **starting ~** стартовый пистолет; **the ~s fired a salute** был произведён орудийный залп; **bring up the big ~s** (*fig.*) пус|кать, -тить в ход тяжёлую артиллерию; **he stuck to his ~s** (*fig.*) он не сдал позиций; **it was blowing great ~s** разыгралась буря; **jump the ~** (*fig.*) соваться, сунуться раньше времени; **son of a ~** (*sl.*) парень (*m.*), малый; **spike s.o.'s ~s** (*fig.*) сорвать (*pf.*) чьи-н. планы. **2.** (*device resembling ~*) пистолет. **3.** (*member of shooting-party*) стрелок; охотник.

v.t. стрелять (*impf.*); **the refugees were ~ned down** беженцев расстреляли.

v.i. охотиться (*impf.*); **he is ~ning for me** (*sl.*) он точит на меня нож.

cpds. **~-barrel** *n.* дуло; **~-battle, ~-fight** *nn.* перестрелка; **~boat** *n.* канонерская лодка, канонерка; **~-carriage** *n.* лафет; **~-cotton** *n.* пироксилин; **~-dog** *n.* охотничья собака; **~-fight** *n.* = **~-battle; ~fire** *n.* орудийный огонь; **~man** *n.* бандит; террорист; **~-metal** *n.* пушечный металл; **~-point** *n.*: **at ~-point** угрожая оружием; под дулом пистолета; **~powder** *n.* порох; **~-room** *n.* (*nav.*) кают-компания; **~-runner** *n.* контрабандист, торгующий оружием; **~-running** *n.* незаконный ввоз оружия; контрабанда оружием; **~-ship** *n.* вооружённый вертолёт; **~shot** *n.* дальность выстрела; **out of ~shot** вне досягаемости орудия; **~-shy** *adj.* пугающийся выстрелов; **~smith** *n.* оружейный мастер.

gung-ho [gʌŋ'həʊ] *adj.* разуха́бистый, у́харский.
gunner ['gʌnə(r)] *n.* канони́р; артиллери́ст; **rear ~** стрело́к хвостово́й устано́вки.
gunnery ['gʌnərɪ] *n.* артиллери́йское де́ло.
gunny ['gʌnɪ] *n.* рого́жка.
gunwale ['gʌn(ə)l] *n.* планши́р.
gurgle ['gɜːg(ə)l] *n.* бу́льканье.
v.i. бу́лькать (*impf.*).
Gurkha ['gɜːkə] *n.* гу́рк(х)а (*m. indecl.*).
adj. гу́рк(х)ский.
guru ['gʊruː, 'guːruː] *n.* гу́ру (*m. indecl.*).
gush [gʌʃ] *n.* пото́к; **a ~ of enthusiasm** вспы́шка энтузиа́зма.
v.i. хлы́нуть (*pf.*); **the water ~ed from the tap** вода́ хлы́нула из кра́на; (*fig., speak effusively*) излива́ться (*impf.*).
gusher ['gʌʃə(r)] *n.* (*of oil*) фонта́н; (*of pers.*) говору́н.
gushing ['gʌʃɪŋ] *adj.*: **she has a ~ manner** она́ вся выкла́дывается; она́ сли́шком суети́тся.
gusset ['gʌsɪt] *n.* (*in a garment*) клин.
gust [gʌst] *n.* (*of wind etc.*) поры́в ве́тра; (*fig.*) взрыв.
gustatory ['gʌstətərɪ] *adj.* вкусово́й.
gusto ['gʌstəʊ] *n.* смак; (*zeal*) жар, рве́ние.
gusty ['gʌstɪ] *adj.* бу́рный; поры́вистый; **a ~ day** ве́треный день.
gut [gʌt] *n.* **1.** (*intestine*) кишка́; **blind ~** слепа́я кишка́; (*for strings of instrument*) струна́. **2.** (*pl.*) (*intestines, stomach*) ки́шки (*f. pl.*); потрох|а́ (*pl., g.* -о́в); (*fig., gist, essential contents*) су́щность; (*fig., courage and determination*) вы́держка; **he is a man with no ~s** он бесхара́ктерный челове́к; у него́ кишка́ тонка́; **he hadn't the ~s to tackle the burglar** у него́ не хвати́ло му́жества задержа́ть взло́мщика; **~ reaction** инстинкти́вная реа́кция; **I hate his ~s** я его́ на́ дух не принима́ю.
v.t. **1.** (*eviscerate*) потроши́ть, вы́-. **2.** (*destroy contents of*) опустош|а́ть, -и́ть; **the house was ~ted by fire** дом сгоре́л дотла́. **3.** (*extract essential from*) выжима́ть, вы́жать суть из+*g*.
cpd. **~s-ache** *n.* (*sl.*) ре́зи (*f. pl.*) в животе́.
gutless ['gʌtlɪs] *adj.* бесхребе́тный, бесхара́ктерный.
gutsy ['gʌtsɪ] *adj.* упо́рный, де́рзкий.
gutta-percha [ˌgʌtə'pɜːtʃə] *n.* гуттапе́рча.
gutter[1] ['gʌtə(r)] *n.* (*under eaves*) водосто́чный жёлоб; (*at roadside*) сто́чная кана́ва; (*fig.*): **his name was dragged into, through the ~** его́ и́мя бы́ло вто́птано в грязь; **the language of the ~** язы́к низо́в; гру́бый/вульга́рный язы́к; **the ~ press** бульва́рная пре́сса.
cpd. **~-snipe** *n.* у́личный мальчи́шка.
gutter[2] ['gʌtə(r)] *v.i.* (*of a candle*) опл|ыва́ть, -ы́ть.
guttural ['gʌtər(ə)l] *n.* веля́рный звук.
adj. горта́нный; горлово́й; (*phon.*) веля́рный, заднеё́бный.
guy[1] [gaɪ] *n.* (**~-rope**) оття́жка.
guy[2] [gaɪ] *n.* (*effigy*) пу́гало; (*grotesquely dressed pers.*) чу́чело, пу́гало (огоро́дное); (*US coll., fellow*) ма́лый; **tough ~** желе́зный ма́лый; **wise ~** у́мник.
v.t. (*hold up to ridicule*) осме́|ивать, -я́ть.
Guyana [gaɪ'ænə] *n.* Гайа́на.
Guyanese [ˌgaɪə'niːz] *n.* гайа́н|ец (*fem.* -ка).
adj. гайа́нский.
guzzle ['gʌz(ə)l] *v.t.* про|еда́ть, -е́сть.
v.i. объ|еда́ться, -е́сться.
guzzler ['gʌzlə(r)] *n.* обжо́ра (*c.g.*).
gym [dʒɪm] *n.* (*coll.*) (*gymnasium*) гимнасти́ческий зал; (*gymnastics*) гимна́стика.
cpds. **~-master, ~-mistress** *nn.* учи́тель (*fem.* -ница) физкульту́ры; **~-shoe** *n.* спорти́вная та́почка; **~-slip, ~-tunic** *nn.* пла́тье-сарафа́н в скла́дку.
gymkhana [dʒɪm'kɑːnə] *n.* конноспорти́вные состяза́ния (*nt. pl.*).
gymnasium [dʒɪm'neɪzɪəm] *n.* гимнасти́ческий зал; (*school*) гимна́зия.
gymnast ['dʒɪmnæst] *n.* гимна́ст.
gymnastic [dʒɪm'næstɪk] *adj.* гимнасти́ческий.
gymnastics [dʒɪm'næstɪks] *n.* гимна́стика.
gynaecological [ˌgaɪnɪkə'lɒdʒɪk(ə)l] *adj.* гинекологи́ческий.
gynaecologist [ˌgaɪnɪ'kɒlədʒɪst] *n.* гинеко́лог.
gynaecology [ˌgaɪnɪ'kɒlədʒɪ] *n.* гинеколо́гия.
gyp [dʒɪp] *n.* (*sl.*): **give s.o. ~** зад|ава́ть, -а́ть кому́-н. трёпку.
gypsum ['dʒɪpsəm] *n.* гипс.
Gypsy ['dʒɪpsɪ] = **Gipsy**
gyrate [ˌdʒaɪə'reɪt] *v.i.* враща́ться (*impf.*).
gyration [ˌdʒaɪ'reɪʃ(ə)n] *n.* враще́ние.
gyratory [ˌdʒaɪrətərɪ, -'reɪtərɪ] *adj.* враща́тельный.
gyro(scope) ['dʒaɪərəˌskəʊp] *n.* гироско́п.
cpds. **~-compass** *n.* гироко́мпас; **~plane** *n.* автожи́р.
gyroscopic [ˌdʒaɪrə'skɒpɪk] *adj.* гироскопи́ческий.
gyve [dʒaɪv] *n.* око́ва, канда́л.

H

H-bomb ['eɪtʃbɒm] *n.* водоро́дная бо́мба.
ha [hɑː] *int.* ага́!; **~, ~** (*expr. laughter*) ха-ха-ха́!
ha. ['hekteə(r), -tɑː(r)] *n.* (*abbr. of* **hectare(s)**) га, (гекта́р).
habanera [ˌhæbə'neərə] *n.* хабане́ра.
habeas corpus [ˌheɪbɪəs 'kɔːpəs] *n.* Ха́беас Ко́рпус (*indecl.*).
haberdasher ['hæbəˌdæʃə(r)] *n.* галантере́йщик.
haberdashery ['hæbəˌdæʃərɪ] *n.* (*shop*) галантере́йный магази́н; (*wares*) галантере́я.
habit ['hæbɪt] *n.* **1.** (*settled practice*) привы́чка; обыкнове́ние; **get into a ~** прив|ыка́ть, -ы́кнуть (+*inf.*); **get out of a ~** отв|ыка́ть, -ы́кнуть (+*inf. or* от+*g.*); **break (o.s.) of a bad ~** отуч|а́ть(ся), -и́ть(ся) от дурно́й привы́чки; **I am in the ~ (or make a ~) of rising early** я обыкнове́нно встаю́ ра́но; **he got into bad ~s** он усво́ил дурны́е привы́чки; **I wish you'd get out of that ~** я хочу́, что́бы вы бро́сили э́ту привы́чку; **from force of ~** в си́лу привы́чки; по привы́чке. **2.** (*arch., condition, constitution*) телосложе́ние; **a cheerful ~ of mind** весёлый нрав; **a man of corpulent ~** ту́чный/доро́дный челове́к. **3.** (*monk's dress*) ря́са. **4.** (*riding-~*) амазо́нка.
cpd. **~-forming** *adj.* создаю́щий привы́чку.
habitable ['hæbɪtəb(ə)l] *adj.* обита́емый.
habitat ['hæbɪˌtæt] *n.* есте́ственная среда́ (*растения, животного*).
habitation [ˌhæbɪ'teɪʃ(ə)n] *n.*: **unfit for ~** неприго́дный для жилья́; (*dwelling-place*) жили́ще.
habitual [hə'bɪtjʊəl] *adj.* привы́чный; обы́чный; **a ~ drunkard** беспробу́дный пья́ница; **a ~ liar** завзя́тый лгун.
habituate [hə'bɪtjʊˌeɪt] *v.t.* приуч|а́ть, -и́ть (*кого к чему*); **he is ~d to hardship** он привы́к к тру́дностям.
habituation [həˌbɪtjʊ'eɪʃ(ə)n] *n.* (*becoming accustomed*) приобрете́ние привы́чки; (*habit*) привы́чка.
habitude ['hæbɪˌtjuːd] *n.* скло́нность; предрасполо́женность; (*habit*) обыкнове́ние.
habitué [hə'bɪtjʊˌeɪ] *n.* завсегда́тай.
hachure [hæ'ʃjʊə(r)] *n.* гашю́ра; штрих.
hacienda [ˌhæsɪ'endə] *n.* гасие́нда.
hack[1] [hæk] *n.* (*chopping blow*) ру́бящий уда́р.
v.t. **1.** разруб|а́ть, -и́ть; руби́ть (*impf.*); (*coll.*) кромса́ть, ис-. **2.** (*football*) «подкова́ть» (*impf.*).
v.i. **1.: ~ at** *see v.t.* **1.. 2.: a ~ing cough** си́льный сухо́й ка́шель.
cpd. **~-saw** *n.* ножо́вка.
hack[2] [hæk] *n.* (*horse*) наёмная ло́шадь; (*writer*) литерату́рный подёнщик; халту́рщик.
v.i. ≃ ката́ться (*impf.*) на ло́шади.
cpd. **~-work** *n.* халту́ра.

hacker ['hækə(r)] *n.* компью́терный взло́мщик.

hackles ['hæk(ə)lz] *n. pl.* пе́рья (*nt. pl.*) на ше́е петуха́; (*fig.*) **it makes my ~ rise** э́то приво́дит меня́ в бе́шенство.

hackney ['hæknɪ] *v.t.*: **a ~ed expression** затёртое/иста́сканное выраже́ние.

cpd. **~-carriage** *n.* наёмный экипа́ж; такси́ (*nt. indecl.*).

haddock ['hædək] *n.* пи́кша.

Hades ['heɪdi:z] *n.* Гаде́с.

h(a)ematite ['hi:məˌtaɪt] *n.* кра́сный железня́к.

h(a)emoglobin [ˌhi:mə'gləʊbɪn] *n.* гемоглоби́н.

h(a)emophilia [ˌhi:mə'fɪlɪə] *n.* гемофи́лия.

h(a)emorrhage ['hemərɪdʒ] *n.* кровотече́ние; кровоизлия́ние.

h(a)emorrhoids ['heməˌrɔɪdz] *n. pl.* геморро́й.

haft [hɑ:ft] *n.* рукоя́тка.

hag [hæg] *n.* карга́.

cpd. **~-ridden** *adj.* изнемога́ющий (*от чего*); измо́танный (*чем*); зада́вленный (*чем*).

haggard ['hægəd] *adj.* измождённый; осу́нувшийся.

haggle ['hæg(ə)l] *v.i.* торгова́ться (*impf.*).

hagiography [ˌhægɪ'ɒgrəfɪ] *n.* описа́ния жити́й святы́х.

Hague [heɪg] *n.*: **The ~** Гаа́га.

hail[1] [heɪl] *n.* (*frozen rain*) град; (*fig.*) **a ~ of blows** град уда́ров.

v.t. (*fig.*): **he ~ed down curses upon us** он осыпа́л нас прокля́тиями.

v.i.: **it is ~ing** идёт град; (*fig.*) сы́паться гра́дом.

cpds. **~stone** *n.* гра́дина; **~storm** *n.* гроза́ с гра́дом.

hail[2] [heɪl] *n.* (*salutation*) приве́тствие; **within ~** на расстоя́нии слы́шимости.

v.t. **1.** (*acclaim*) провозгла|ша́ть, -си́ть; (*praise*) превозноси́ть (*impf.*); приве́тствовать (*impf.*); **he was ~ed by the critics** кри́тики восто́рженно при́няли его́. **2.** (*greet*) приве́тствовать (*impf.*); окл|ика́ть, -и́кнуть; **he ~ed me in the street** он окли́кнул меня́ на у́лице. **3.** (*summon*) под|зыва́ть, -озва́ть; **he ~ed a taxi** он подозва́л такси́.

v.i. происходи́ть (*impf.*); **he ~s from Scotland** он ро́дом из Шотла́ндии.

cpd. **~-fellow-well-met** *adj.* запанибра́тский.

hair [heə(r)] *n.* **1.** (*single strand*) во́лос, волосо́к; **I didn't touch a ~ of his head** я к нему́ и па́льцем не прикосну́лся; **he came within a ~'s breadth of success** он почти́ доби́лся успе́ха; **he never turned a ~** он и бро́вью не повёл; **that is splitting ~s** э́то спор по пустяка́м; **you should take a ~ of the dog that bit you** вам сле́дует опохмели́ться; **you have him by the short ~s** (*sl.*) он у вас в рука́х. **2.** (*dim.*, *e.g. baby's*) воло́сик(и). **3.** (*head of ~*) во́лосы (*m. pl.*); **~ conditioner** опола́скиватель (*m.*) (для воло́с); **have, get one's ~ cut** стри́чься, по-; **lose one's ~** лысе́ть, об-/по-; **keep your ~ on!** (*sl.*) споко́йно!; не горячи́тесь!; **let one's ~ down** (*lit.*) распус|ка́ть, -ти́ть во́лосы; (*fig.*) разоткрове́нничаться (*pf.*); **this will make your ~ stand on end** от э́того у вас во́лосы вста́нут ды́бом; **she put her ~ up** она́ подобрала́ во́лосы. **4.** (*of animals*) шерсть, щети́на.

cpds. **~('s)-breadth** *n.*: **within a ~'s breadth of death** на волосо́к от сме́рти; **they had a ~breadth escape** они́ едва́-едва́ спасли́сь; **~-brush** *n.* щётка для воло́с; **~-clip** *n.* зако́лка для воло́с; **~cut** *n.* стри́жка; **have a ~cut** подстри́чься (*pf.*); **~-do** *n.* (*coll.*) причёска; **~dresser** *n.* парикма́хер; **~dresser's** *n.* (*shop, salon*) парикма́херская; **~dressing** *n.* парикма́херское иску́сство; **~-dryer** *n.* фен; **~-grip** *n.* зако́лка для воло́с; **~-line** *n.* (*edge of ~*) ли́ния воло́с; **~-net** *n.* се́тка для воло́с; **~-oil** *n.* ма́сло для воло́с; **~-piece** *n.* накладны́е во́лосы; **~pin** *n.* шпи́лька; **~pin bend** круто́й поворо́т; **~-raising** *adj.* жу́ткий; **~-restorer** *n.* сре́дство от облысе́ния; **~-shirt** *n.* власяни́ца; **~-splitting** *n.* привере́дливость; *adj.* привере́дливый, ме́лочный; **~spray** *n.* (*substance*) лак для воло́с; (*container*) аэрозо́ль (*m.*) для воло́с; **~-spring** *n.* волоско́вая пружи́на; **~-style** *n.* причёска; **~stylist** *n.* парикма́хер; **~-trigger** *n.* шне́ллер *adj.* (*fig.*) на взво́де.

hairiness ['heərɪnɪs] *n.* волоса́тость.

hairless ['heəlɪs] *adj.* безволо́сый.

hairy ['heərɪ] *adj.* **1.** волоса́тый. **2.** (*sl.*) (*frightening*) стра́шный.

Haiti ['heɪtɪ, hɑ:'i:tɪ] *n.* Гаи́ти (*m. indecl.*).

Haitian ['heɪʃɪən, hɑ:'i:ʃən] *n.* гаитя́н|ин (*fem.* -ка)

adj. гаитя́нский.

hake [heɪk] *n.* хек.

halberd ['hælbəd] *n.* алеба́рда.

halberdier [ˌhælbə'dɪə(r)] *n.* во́ин, вооружённый алеба́рдой.

halcyon ['hælsɪən] *adj.* (*fig.*) ти́хий, безмяте́жный.

hale[1] [heɪl] *adj.* кре́пкий; здоро́вый; **~ and hearty** кре́пкий и бо́дрый.

hale[2] [heɪl] *v.t.* тащи́ть (*impf.*); тяну́ть (*impf.*); **he was ~d before the court** его́ притащи́ли в суд.

half [hɑ:f] *n.* **1.** (*one of two equal parts*) полови́на; пол- (*pref.*: *see examples and cpds.*); **one and a ~** полтора́; **he cut the loaf in ~** он разре́зал хлеб попола́м; **getting there is ~ the battle** добра́ться туда́ — полови́на де́ла; **~ an hour** полчаса́; **~ an hour later** получа́сом по́зже; **~ and ~** попола́м, по́ровну; **~ a loaf is better than no bread** бу́дем дово́льствоваться ма́лым; **I have ~ a mind to go** я не прочь пойти́; **~ a minute!** (одну́) мину́точку!; **~ past two** полови́на тре́тьего; (*coll.*) полтре́тьего; **he is too clever by ~** он чересчу́р уж у́мный; **don't do it by halves** не остана́вливайтесь на полпути́; **they agreed to go halves** они́ согласи́лись подели́ть попола́м; **that's not the ~ of it!** и э́то ещё далеко́ не всё. **2.** (*one of two parts*) часть; **the greater ~ of the audience** бо́льшая часть аудито́рии; **my better ~** моя́ дража́йшая/лу́чшая полови́на; **let's see how the other ~ lives** посмо́трим, как живу́т други́е. **3.** (*of a game*) тайм; (*of academic year*) семе́стр; (*~-back*) полузащи́тник.

adj. (*see also cpds.*): **he's not one for ~ measures** он не сторо́нник полуме́р.

adv.: **~ asleep** со́нный; **I feel ~ dead** я едва́ жив; **the meat is only ~ done** мя́со недова́рено/недожа́рено; **~ as much** вдво́е ме́ньше; **~ as much again** в полтора́ ра́за бо́льше; **a pound is not ~ enough** одного́ фу́нта ника́к не хва́тит; **I ~ expected it** я почти́ ждал э́того; **that's not ~ bad!** (*coll.*) э́то совсе́м непло́хо; **not ~!** (*coll.*) ещё бы!; а как же!; **he wasn't ~ annoyed!** (*coll.*) он был поря́дком раздоса́дован; **it was ~ raining, ~ snowing** шёл не то дождь, не то снег.

cpds. **~-and-~** *adv.* полови́на на полови́ну; (*fig.*) и да и нет; ни то ни сё; **~-arsed** *adj.* (*vulg.*) недоде́ланный; **~-back** *n.* полузащи́тник; **~-baked** *adj.* недопечённый; (*fig.*) недорабо́танный, непроду́манный; (*pers.*) незре́лый; **~-breed** *n.* мети́с (*fem.* -ка); **~-brother** *n.* единокро́вный/единоутро́бный брат; **~-caste** *n.* мети́с; **~-cock** *n.* предохрани́тельный взвод; **the scheme went off at ~-cock** был пу́щен в ход совсе́м ещё сыро́й план; **~-dozen** *n.*, *also* **~ a dozen** полдю́жины; **~-hearted** *adj.* нереши́тельный; без энтузиа́зма; **~-holiday** *n.* непо́лный рабо́чий/уче́бный день; **~-hour** *n.*, *also* **~ an hour** полчаса́; **every ~-hour** ка́ждые полчаса́; **the last ~-hour** после́дние полча́са; **after the first ~-hour** по́сле пе́рвого получа́са; *adj.* получасово́й; **~-hourly** *adj.* получасово́й; *adv.* ка́ждые полчаса́; **~-length** *n.* (*portrait*) поясно́й портре́т; **~-life** *n.* (*phys.*) пери́од полураспа́да; **~-light** *n.* полутьма́; **~-mast** *n.*: **at ~-mast** приспу́щенный; **~-mile** *n.*, *also* **~ a mile** полми́ли; **~-moon** *n.* полуме́сяц; **~-nelson** *n.* полуне́льсон; (*fig.*): **get a ~-nelson on s.o.** положи́ть кого́-н. на лопа́тки; **~-pay** *n.* полови́нный/непо́лный окла́д/жа́лованье; **~penny** *n.* полпе́нни (*indecl.*); **~-pound** *n.*, *also* **~ a pound** полфу́нта; *adj.* полуфунто́вый; **~-price** *adj.* полцены́; **at ~-price** за полцены́; **children under 5 ~-price** за дете́й до пяти́ лет пла́тят полови́ну; **~-seas-over** *pred. adj.* (*sl.*) пьян; навеселе́; **~-sister** *n.* единокро́вная/единоутро́бная сестра́; **~-term** *n.*: **~-term (holiday)** кани́кул|ы (*pl.*, *g.* —) в середи́не триме́стра; **~-timbered** *adj.* фахве́рковый; **~-timbering** *n.* фахве́рк; карка́сная/фахве́рковая констру́кция; **~-time** *n.* коне́ц та́йма; переры́в ме́жду та́ймами; **the teams changed ends at ~-time** кома́нды поменя́лись места́ми по́сле пе́рвого та́йма; (*reduced working hours*): **the men were put on ~-time** рабо́чих перевели́ на непо́лную рабо́чую неде́лю; **~-tone** *n.* (*mus.*) полуто́н; (*typ.*) автоти́пия; **~-track** *n.* полугу́сеничная маши́на; **~-truth** *n.* полупра́вда; **~-turn** *n.* пол-оборо́та; **~-volley** *n.* уда́р с полулёта; **~-way** *adj.* лежа́щий на полпути́; **~-way house** (*fig.*) компроми́сс; полуме́ра; *adv.* на полпути́; **we met ~-way from the station** мы встре́тились на полпути́ от вокза́ла; **we turned back ~-way** мы верну́лись с полпути́; **I'll meet you ~-way** (*fig.*) я гото́в пойти́ вам навстре́чу; **~-wit** *n.* дура́к; **~-witted** *adj.* слабоу́мный, полоу́мный; **~-yearly** *adj.* шестиме́сячный; *adv.* раз в полго́да.

halibut [ˈhælɪbət] *n.* па́лтус.

halitosis [ˌhælɪˈtəʊsɪs] *n.* дурно́й за́пах изо рта́.

hall [hɔːl] *n.* **1.** (*place of assembly*) зал; **servants' ~** помеще́ние для слуг; **town ~** ра́туша; (*college dining-~*) столо́вая. **2.** (*country mansion*) поме́щичий дом. **3.** (*lobby*; *also* **~way**) пере́дняя, прихо́жая, холл; **~ of mirrors** алле́я сме́ха.

cpds. **~mark** *n.* проби́рное клеймо́; про́ба; (*fig.*) отличи́тельный при́знак; печа́ть; *v.t.* ста́вить, по- про́бу на+*p.*; **~-stand** *n.* ве́шалка в прихо́жей.

hallelujah [ˌhælɪˈluːjə] *n.* & *int.* аллилу́йя.

hallo [həˈləʊ] *n.* & *int.* (*greeting*) здра́сте!; приве́т!; (*on telephone*) алло́!; (*expr. surprise*) вот те на́!

halloo [həˈluː] *int.* (*in hunting*) ату́!; эй!

v.t. натра́вливать (*impf.*) соба́к.

v.i. улюлю́кать (*impf.*); **don't ~ till you're out of the wood** (*prov.*) не говори́ гоп, пока́ не перепры́гнешь.

hallow [ˈhæləʊ] *v.t.* освя|ща́ть, -ти́ть; **~ed be thy name** да святи́тся и́мя твоё; **in ~ed memory of** све́тлой па́мяти +*g.*

Hallowe'en [ˌhæləʊˈiːn] *n.* кану́н Дня всех святы́х (*31 октября*).

hallucination [həˌluːsɪˈneɪʃ(ə)n] *n.* галлюцина́ция; **have ~s** галлюцини́ровать (*impf.*), страда́ть (*impf.*) галлюцина́циями.

hallucin|atory [həˈluːsɪnətərɪ], **-ogenic** [həˌluːsɪnəˈdʒenɪk] *adjs.* вызыва́ющий галлюцина́ции.

hallucinogen [həˈluːsɪnədʒen] *n.* галлюциноге́н.

halo [ˈheɪləʊ] *n.* (*astron.*) гало́ (*indecl.*); сия́ние; (*round saint's head*) нимб; (*fig.*) орео́л.

halt[1] [hɒlt, hɔːlt] *n.* (*in march or journey*) остано́вка; **come to a ~** остан|а́вливаться, -ови́ться; **the train came to a ~** по́езд останови́лся; **bring to a ~** остан|а́вливать, -ови́ть; **his work was brought to a ~** он был вы́нужден приостанови́ть рабо́ту; **call a ~** де́лать, с- прива́л; (*fig.*) да|ва́ть, -ть отбо́й; (*stopping-place on railway*) полуста́нок.

v.t. остан|а́вливать, -ови́ть; **he ~ed his men** он останови́л солда́т; **progress was ~ed** прогре́сс был приостано́влен.

v.i. (*stop*) остан|а́вливаться, -ови́ться; **~! who goes there?** стой! кто идёт?

halt[2] [hɒlt, hɔːlt] *adj.* (*arch.*, *crippled*) хромо́й; искале́ченный.

v.i. (*esp. pres. part.*: *limp*, *falter*) хрома́ть (*impf.*); зап|ина́ться, -ну́ться; **a ~ing gait** неве́рная похо́дка; **a ~ing voice** запина́ющийся го́лос.

halter [ˈhɒltə(r), ˈhɔːl-] *n.* (*for a horse*) по́вод; недоу́здок; (*for execution*) верёвка; уда́вка.

halva [ˈhælvɑː] *n.* халва́.

halve [hɑːv] *v.t.* (*divide in two*) дели́ть, раз- попола́м; (*reduce by half*) ум|еньша́ть, -е́ньшить (*or* сокра|ща́ть, -ти́ть) наполови́ну.

halyard [ˈhæljəd] *n.* фал.

ham [hæm] *n.* **1.** (*thigh of pig*) о́корок; (*meat from this*) ветчина́; **~ sandwich** бутербро́д с ветчино́й. **2.** (*human thigh*) ля́жка; **he squatted on his ~s** он присе́л на ко́рточки. **3.** (*sl.*, *poor actor*) безда́рный актёр. **4.** (*sl.*, *amateur radio operator*) радиолюби́тель (*m.*).

v.t. & *i.* (*sl.*) скве́рно игра́ть (*impf.*); **~ it up** перейгр|ывать, -а́ть; преврати́ть (*pf.*) всё в мелодра́му.

cpds. **~-fisted, ~-handed** *adjs.* тяжёлый на́ руку; неуклю́жий; (*fig.*) топо́рный; **~string** *v.t.* подр|еза́ть, -е́зать поджи́лки +*d.*; (*fig.*) подре́зать (*pf.*) кры́лья +*d.*

hamburger [ˈhæmˌbɜːgə(r)] *n.* га́мбургер; ру́бленая котле́та.

Hamitic [həˈmɪtɪk] *adj.* хами́тский.

hamlet [ˈhæmlɪt] *n.* дереву́шка.

hammer [ˈhæmə(r)] *n.* молото́к, мо́лот; **~ and sickle** серп и мо́лот; **throwing the ~** мета́ние мо́лота; **he went at it ~ and tongs** он бро́сил на э́то все си́лы; (*auctioneer's*) молото́к; **the estate came** (*or* **was brought**) **under the ~** име́ние пошло́ с молотка́.

v.t. (*beat*) уд|аря́ть, -а́рить; бить, по-; **~ in** вби|ва́ть, -ть; вкол|а́чивать, -оти́ть; приб|ива́ть, -и́ть; **he ~ed in the nails** он вбил гво́зди; **the smith ~s the metal into shape** кузне́ц куёт мета́лл; **the mechanic ~ed out the dents** меха́ник вы́ровнял зазу́брины молотко́м; **he was ~ing a box together** он скола́чивал я́щик; **the enemy got a good ~ing** неприя́телю кре́пко доста́лось; **the idea was ~ed into his head** э́ту мысль вби́ли ему́ в го́лову; **we ~ed out a plan** мы разрабо́тали план.

v.i. стуча́ть (*impf.*); колоти́ть (*impf.*); **someone was ~ing on the door** кто́-то колоти́л в дверь; **he ~ed away on the piano** он бараба́нил по роя́лю; **he ~ed away at the problem** он упо́рно би́лся над э́той зада́чей.

cpds. **~-blow** *n.* (*fig.*) сокруши́тельный/тяжёлый уда́р; **~-head** *n.* голо́вка молотка́; (*shark*) мо́лот-ры́ба; **~-toe** *n.* молоткообра́зное искривле́ние большо́го па́льца ноги́.

hammock [ˈhæmək] *n.* гама́к.

hammy [ˈhæmɪ] *adj.* перейгрывающий.

hamper[1] [ˈhæmpə(r)] *n.* корзи́на с кры́шкой.

hamper[2] [ˈhæmpə(r)] *v.t.* меша́ть, по- +*d.*; стесня́ть (*impf.*).

hamster [ˈhæmstə(r)] *n.* хомя́к.

hand [hænd] *n.* **1.** (*lit.*, *fig.*) рука́, кисть; **the ~ of God** перст бо́жий; (*dim.*, *e.g. baby's*) ру́чка; (*attr.*) ручно́й; **~ luggage** ручно́й бага́ж; (*of animal or bird*) ла́па, ла́пка; **she waits on him ~ and foot** она́ у него́ в по́лном ра́бстве; **he was bound ~ and foot** его́ связа́ли по рука́м и нога́м; **they won ~s down** они́ с лёгкостью победи́ли; **I shall have my ~s full next week** я бу́ду о́чень за́нят на сле́дующей неде́ле; **he was ~ in glove with the enemy** он был в сго́воре с враго́м; **~ in ~** (*lit.*, *fig.*) рука́ о́б руку; **~s up!** ру́ки вверх!; **~s off!** ру́ки прочь (от+*g.*)!; **he is making money ~ over fist** он загреба́ет де́ньги лопа́той; **they fought ~ to ~** они́ би́лись врукопа́шную; **it's too much for one pair of ~s** одно́й па́ры рук для э́того недоста́точно. **2.** (*vbl. phrr.*): **he asked for her ~** (*in marriage*) он проси́л её руки́; **the money changed ~s** де́ньги перешли́ в други́е ру́ки; **he refuses to do a ~'s turn** он отка́зывается и па́льцем пошевельну́ть; **force s.o.'s ~** заста́вить (*pf.*) кого́-н. раскры́ть свои́ ка́рты; **he gained, got the upper ~** он взял/одержа́л верх; **get one's ~ in** наби́ть (*pf.*) ру́ку (*на чём*); осв|а́иваться, -о́иться с рабо́той; **let me give, lend you a ~!** дава́йте я вам помогу́!; **they gave the singer a big ~** (*coll.*) певцу́ бу́рно аплоди́ровали; **he was given a free ~** ему́ предоста́вили по́лную свобо́ду де́йствий; **she had a ~ in his downfall** в его́ паде́нии она́ сыгра́ла не после́днюю роль; **I'll have no ~ in it!** я не хочу́ име́ть к э́тому никако́го отноше́ния; **they were holding ~s** они́ держа́лись за́ руки; **hold one's ~** (*restrain o.s.*) сдерж|иваться, -а́ться; **keep one's ~ in** подде́рживать (*impf.*) фо́рму; **if only I could lay my ~s on a dictionary** е́сли бы я то́лько мог раздобы́ть слова́рь; **don't dare to lay a ~ on her** не смей прикаса́ться к ней; **he rules with an iron ~** он пра́вит желе́зной руко́й; **he set his ~ to** (*set about*) **the work** он взя́лся за рабо́ту; **let me shake your ~** позво́льте пожа́ть ва́шу/вам ру́ку; **(let's) shake ~s on it!** по рука́м!; **I'm willing to take a ~** я гото́в приня́ть уча́стие; **try one's ~ at sth.** попро́бовать (*pf.*) себя́ в чём-н.; **my ~s are tied** (*fig.*) у меня́ свя́заны ру́ки; **he can turn his ~ to anything** он уме́ет де́лать что уго́дно; **I wash my ~s of it** я умыва́ю ру́ки. **3.** (*prepositional phrr.*): **the hour is at ~** приближа́ется час/вре́мя; **he lives close at ~** он живёт совсе́м ря́дом; **she suffered at his ~s** она́ натерпе́лась с ним; **he started the car by ~** он завёл маши́ну вручну́ю; **the letter was delivered by ~** письмо́ бы́ло доста́влено с на́рочным; **he died by his own ~** он наложи́л на себя́ ру́ки; **the watch passed from ~ to ~** часы́ переходи́ли из рук в ру́ки; **he lives from ~ to mouth** он ко́е-как сво́дит концы́ с конца́ми; **I have enough**

money in ~ у меня́ при себе́ доста́точно де́нег; **he took the matter in** ~ он взял де́ло в свои́ ру́ки; **please attend to the matter in** ~ пожа́луйста, займи́тесь очередны́м де́лом; **you should take that child in** ~ вы должны́ взять э́того ребёнка на́ руки; **we have the situation well in** ~ мы по́лностью хозя́ева положе́ния; **the matter is no longer in my** ~**s** я бо́льше э́тим не занима́юсь; **he fell into the** ~**s of money lenders** он попа́л к ростовщика́м в ла́пы; **don't let this book fall into the wrong** ~**s** смотри́те, что́бы э́та кни́га не попа́ла к кому́ не на́до; **you are playing into his** ~**s** вы игра́ете ему́ на́ руку; **my eldest daughter is off my** ~**s** моя́ ста́ршая дочь уже́ пристро́ена; **on** ~ в нали́чии; в распоряже́нии; **he has a sick father on his** ~**s** у него́ на рука́х больно́й оте́ц; **time hangs heavy on my** ~**s** я не зна́ю, как уби́ть вре́мя; **he refused out of** ~ он тут же отказа́лся; **things are getting out of** ~ собы́тия выхо́дят из-под контро́ля; **she will eat out of his** ~ она́ всеце́ло ему́ пре́дана; **the letters passed through his** ~**s** пи́сьма проходи́ли че́рез его́ ру́ки; **news has come to** ~ дошли́ ве́сти; есть све́дения, что...; **your letter to** ~ (*comm.*) ва́ше письмо́ полу́чено на́ми; **his gun was ready to** ~ ружьё бы́ло у него́ под руко́й. **4.** (*member of crew or team*): **all** ~**s on deck!** все наве́рх; **the ship went down with all** ~**s** кора́бль затону́л со всем экипа́жем (*or* со все́ми, кто был на борту́); **factory** ~ фабри́чный рабо́чий; **farm** ~ рабо́тник на фе́рме. **5.** (*practitioner*): **he is an old** ~ **(at the game)** он тёртый кала́ч; **a picture by the same** ~ карти́на того́ же худо́жника; **I am a poor** ~ **at writing letters** я не ахти́ како́й корреспонде́нт. **6.** (*source*): **I heard it at first/second** ~ я узна́л э́то из пе́рвых/втор́ых рук. **7.** (*side*): **on the right** ~ по пра́вую ру́ку; **at his right** ~ по его́ пра́вую ру́ку; **on the one** ~ **..., on the other** ~ (*fig.*) с одно́й стороны́..., с друго́й стороны́; **they came at him on every** ~ они́ ки́нулись на него́ со всех сторо́н. **8.** (*handwriting*): **he writes a good** ~ у него́ хоро́ший по́черк; **a large/small** ~ кру́пный/ме́лкий по́черк. **9.** (*signature*): **I cannot set my** ~ **to this document** я не могу́ подписа́ться под э́тим докуме́нтом. **10.** (*of a clock*) стре́лка. **11.** (*measure*) ладо́нь (*10 сантиметров*). **12.** (*player at cards*) игро́к; (*set of cards*) ка́рты (*f. pl.*); **show one's** ~ (*fig.*) раскры́ть ка́рты; (*round in a card game*) кон, па́ртия.

v.t. перед|ава́ть, -а́ть; под|ава́ть, -а́ть; ~ **me the paper, please** переда́йте мне газе́ту, пожа́луйста; **he** ~**ed her out of the carriage** он помо́г ей вы́йти из ваго́на; **I** ~ **it to you** (*coll., acknowledge your skill etc.*) я до́лжен призна́ть — вы (по э́той ча́сти) ма́стер.

with advs.: **he** ~**ed back the money** он верну́л де́ньги; ~ **me down that book from the shelf** сними́те мне э́ту кни́гу с по́лки; **the custom was** ~**ed down** э́тот обы́чай переходи́л из поколе́ния в поколе́ние; **will you** ~ **in your resignation?** вы подади́те заявле́ние об ухо́де?; **the estate was** ~**ed on to the heirs** име́ние перешло́ к насле́дникам; **the teacher** ~**ed out books** учи́тель разда́л кни́ги; **the king** ~**ed over his authority** коро́ль переда́л свою́ власть.

cpds. ~**bag** *n.* да́мская су́мка; ~**ball** *n.* ручно́й мяч; (*game*) гандбо́л; ~**bell** *n.* колоко́льчик; ~**bill** *n.* рекла́мный листо́к; афи́ша; ~**book** *n.* посо́бие; спра́вочник; руково́дство; ~**-brake** *n.* ручно́й то́рмоз; ~**cart** *n.* ручна́я теле́жка; ~**-clap** *n.* хлопо́к (рука́ми); **slow** ~**-clap** ме́дленные аплодисме́нты в унисо́н; ~**cuff** *n.* нару́чник; *v.t.* над|ева́ть, -е́ть нару́чники +*d.*; ~**-drier** *n.* электрополоте́нце; ~**-grenade** *n.* (*shell*) ручна́я грана́та; ~**grip** *n.* пожа́тие/сжа́тие руки́; ~**hold** *n.* опо́ра; заце́пка; ~**-made** *adj.* сде́ланный вручну́ю; ручно́й рабо́ты; ~**maid** *n.* служа́нка; ~**-out** *n.* (*gift*) ми́лостыня; подая́ние; (*for press*) заявле́ние для печа́ти; ~**over** *n.* (*e.g. of responsibility*) переда́ча; ~**-picked** *adj.* тща́тельно подо́бранный; ~**rail** *n.* пери́л|а (*pl., g.* —); ~**saw** *n.* ножо́вка; ~**set** *n.* (*telephone*) тру́бка; ~**shake** *n.* рукопожа́тие; **golden** ~**shake** (*coll.*) отста́вка с хоро́шими награ́дными; ~**s-off** *adj.*: ~**s-off policy** поли́тика невмеша́тельства; ~**s-on** *adj.*: ~**s-on experience** практи́ческий о́пыт; ~**spring** *n.* «колесо́», са́льто (*indecl.*); ~**stand** *n.* сто́йка на рука́х; ~**-to-**~ *adj.* рукопа́шный; ~**-to-**~ **fighting** рукопа́шный бой; ~**-to-mouth** *adj.*: **a** ~**-to-mouth existence** жизнь впро́голодь; ~**work** *n.* ручна́я рабо́та; ~**writing** *n.* по́черк; ~**writing expert** графо́лог; ~**written** *adj.* напи́санный от руки́.

handful ['hændfʊl] *n.* горсть; при́горшня; (*coll.*): **this child is a** ~ с э́тим ребёнком хлопо́т не оберёшься; э́тот ребёнок су́щее наказа́ние.

handicap ['hændɪ,kæp] *n.* **1.** (*hindrance*) поме́ха, препя́тствие. **2.** (*sport*) гандика́п.

v.t. **1.** (*put at disadvantage*) чини́ть (*impf.*) препя́тствия (*кому*); ста́вить, по- в невы́годное положе́ние; ~**ped children** де́ти-инвали́ды. **2.** (*sport*) ста́вить (*кого*) в ме́нее вы́годные усло́вия, что́бы уравнове́сить ша́нсы на побе́ду.

handicraft ['hændɪ,krɑ:ft] *n.* ремесло́, ручна́я рабо́та; (*attr.*) реме́сленный; куста́рный.

handiwork ['hændɪ,wɜ:k] *n.* ручна́я рабо́та; **this is his** ~ э́то сде́лано его́ рука́ми; (*fig.*) э́то его́ рук де́ло.

handkerchief ['hæŋkətʃɪf, -,tʃi:f] *n.* носово́й плато́к.

handle ['hænd(ə)l] *n.* ру́чка, рукоя́ть, рукоя́тка; (*fig.*): **don't fly off the** ~! (*coll.*) не кипяти́сь!; не лезь в буты́лку!; **he has a** ~ **to his name** у него́ есть ти́тул; **he gave a** ~ **to his critics** он дал свои́м кри́тикам заце́пку.

v.t. **1.** (*take or hold in the hands*) тро́гать (*impf.*); брать, взять рука́ми. **2.** (*manage, deal with, treat*) обраща́ться (*impf.*) с+*i.*; обходи́ться (*impf.*) с+*i.*; спр|авля́ться, -а́виться с+*i.*; **he can** ~ **a horse with skill** он уме́ет обраща́ться с лошадьми́; **he** ~**d the affair very well** он прекра́сно спра́вился с э́тим де́лом; **he** ~**d himself well** (*US*) он хорошо́ держа́лся; **the officer** ~**d his men well** офице́р уме́ло кома́ндовал свои́ми солда́тами; **he came in for some rough handling** с ним обошли́сь суро́во; ему́ доста́лось. **3.** (*comm., deal in*) торгова́ть (*impf.*) +*i.*

v.i.: **this car** ~**s well** э́та маши́на удо́бна в управле́нии.

cpd. ~**-bars** *n. pl.* (*of a bicycle*) руль (*m.*); ~**-bar moustache** (*joc.*) за́гнутые ко́нчиками вверх усы́ (*m. pl.*).

handler ['hændlə(r)] *n.* тре́нер, дрессиро́вщик.

handsome ['hænsəm] *adj.* (*of appearance*) краси́вый; (*generous*): **a** ~ **present** ще́дрый пода́рок; ~ **is as** ~ **does** су́дят не по слова́м, а по дела́м.

handy ['hændɪ] *adj.* **1.** (*clever with hands*) ло́вкий; ма́стер (на все ру́ки); **he is** ~ у него́ золоты́е ру́ки. **2.** (*easy to handle*) удо́бный для по́льзования. **3.** (*to hand, available*) (име́ющийся) под руко́й. **4.** (*convenient*) удо́бный, (*coll.*) сподру́чный; **it may come in** ~ э́то мо́жет пригоди́ться.

cpd. ~**-man** *n.* рабо́чий для ра́зных поде́лок.

hang [hæŋ] *n.* **1.** (*way in which a thg. hangs*) вид (*висящей вещи*). **2.** (*knack, sense*) смысл; «что к чему́»; **I can't get the** ~ **of this machine (*or* of his argument)** я не могу́ разобра́ться в э́той маши́не (*or* в его́ до́водах)). **3.** (*coll.*) **I don't give, care a** ~ а мне како́е де́ло?; мне (на)плева́ть.

v.t. **1.** (*suspend*) ве́шать, пове́сить; **game must be hung for several days** дичь должна́ повисе́ть не́сколько дней; **this gate has been hung badly** э́ти воро́та пло́хо подве́шены; ~ **the blame on s.o.** взва́л|ивать, -и́ть вину́ на кого́-н. **2.** (*let droop*) пове́сить (*pf.*); **she hung her head in shame** она́ опусти́ла го́лову от стыда́. **3.** (*decorate, furnish*) разве́|шивать, -сить; **the hall was hung with flags** зал был уве́шен фла́гами. **4.** (*execute by* ~*ing*) ве́шать, пове́сить; **Judas** ~**ed himself** Иу́да пове́сился. **5.** (*as imprecation*): ~ **it all!** чёрт возьми́!; пропади́ всё про́падом!; **I'll be** ~**ed if I'll go** (хоть) заре́жьте — не пойду́ туда!

v.i. **1.** (*be suspended*) висе́ть (*impf.*); (*fig.*): **his life** ~**s by a thread** его́ жизнь (виси́т) на волоске́; **the outcome** ~**s in the balance** ещё нея́сно, чем всё э́то ко́нчится (*or* како́й оборо́т при́мет де́ло); **the threat of dismissal hung over him** над ним нави́сла угро́за увольне́ния; **she hung on his lips** она́ лови́ла ка́ждое его́ сло́во; **everything** ~**s on his decision** всё упира́ется в его́ реше́ние. **2.** (*lean*) све́шиваться (*impf.*); **don't** ~ **out of the window** не высо́вывайтесь из окна́. **3.** (*droop*) висе́ть (*impf.*); свиса́ть (*impf.*). **4.** (*be executed*): **he will** ~ **for it** он попадёт за э́то на ви́селицу; (*fig.*) **he let things go** ~ он бро́сил всё к чёрту. **5.** (*loiter, stay close*): **he hung round the door** он задержа́лся у две́ри; **the children hung about their mother** де́ти льну́ли к ма́тери.

with advs.: ~ **about,** ~ **around** *v.i.* болта́ться (*impf.*); шля́ться (*impf.*); шата́ться (*impf.*); ~ **back** *v.i.* упира́ться (*impf.*); ~ **on** *v.i.* (*cling*) держа́ться (*impf.*) (*за что*); цепля́ться (*impf.*); (*persist*) упо́рствовать (*impf.*); не сдава́ться (*impf.*); ~ **on!** (*coll.*) погоди́те!; посто́йте!; мину́точку!; ~ **out** *v.t.* выве́шивать, вы́весить; **she hung out the washing** она́ вы́весила бельё; *v.i.* (*protrude*): **his shirt was ~ing out** у него́ руба́шка вы́лезла из брюк; (*endure*): **the besieged hung out for a month** осаждённые держа́лись ме́сяц; (*coll., live*) обита́ть (*impf.*); ~ **together** *v.i.* (*stand by one another*) держа́ться (*impf.*) вме́сте; (*make sense*): **the story doesn't ~ together** ≃ концы́ с конца́ми не схо́дятся; ~ **up** *v.t.* (*fasten on peg, nail etc.*) пове́сить (*pf.*); (*coll., usu. pass., delay*): **I got hung up in the traffic** я застря́л в у́личной про́бке; *v.i.* (*end telephone conversation*) пове́сить (*pf.*) тру́бку.

cpds. **~dog** *adj.*: **a ~dog expression** затра́вленный вид; **~-glider** *n.* (*craft*) дельтапла́н; (*pers.*) дельтапланери́ст; **~-gliding** *n.* дельтапланёрный спорт; **~man** *n.* пала́ч; **~-nail** *n.* заусе́ница; **~out** *n.* (*sl.*) местожи́тельство, местопребыва́ние; **~over** *n.* (*survival*) пережи́ток, насле́дие; (*from drink*) похме́лье, перепо́й; **I had a ~over** у меня́ разболе́лась голова́ от похме́лья; **~-up** *n.* (*hitch*) зато́р, зами́нка; (*obsession, inhibition*) пу́нктик, бзик (*coll.*); **he has a ~-up about it** он заклини́лся/зацикли́лся на э́том.

hangar ['hæŋə(r)] *n.* анга́р.

hanger ['hæŋə(r)] *n.* (*for clothes*) ве́шалка; (*wood on hillside*) лес на скло́не холма́.

cpd. **~-on** *n.* прихлеба́тель (*m.*), приспе́шник.

hanging ['hæŋıŋ] *n.* **1.** висе́ние; (*execution*) пове́шение; **a ~ judge** суро́вый судья́; ~ **committee** (*of Academy*) жюри́ (*nt. indecl.*) по приёму карти́н на вы́ставку; **it is not a ~ matter** (*fig.*) э́то не тако́е уж стра́шное преступле́ние. **2.** (*pl., tapestry etc.*) портье́ры (*f. pl.*); драпиро́вки (*f. pl.*).

adj. вися́чий.

hank [hæŋk] *n.* мото́к.

hanker ['hæŋkə(r)] *v.i.*: ~ **after** жа́ждать +*g.*

hanky ['hæŋkı] (*coll.*) = **handkerchief**

hanky-panky [ˌhæŋkı'pæŋkı] *n.* (*coll.*) проде́л|ки (*pl., g.* -ок); моше́нничество.

Hanoi [hæ'nɔı] *n.* Хано́й; (*attr.*) хано́йский.

Hanover ['hænəʊvə(r)] *n.* Ганно́вер.

Hanoverian [ˌhænə'vıərıən] *adj.* ганно́верский.

Hanseatic [ˌhænsı'ætık] *adj.* ганзе́йский.

Hansen's disease ['hæns(ə)nz] *n.* прока́за.

hansom ['hænsəm] *n.* (~ **cab**) двухколёсный экипа́ж.

ha'penny ['heıpnı] = **halfpenny**

haphazard [hæp'hæzəd] *adj.* случа́йный.

adv. случа́йно; науда́чу.

hapless ['hæplıs] *adj.* несча́стный; злополу́чный; незада́чливый.

haply ['hæplı] *adv.* (*arch.*) (*by chance*) случа́йно; (*perhaps*) возмо́жно.

happen ['hæpən] *v.i.* **1.** (*occur*) случ|а́ться, -и́ться; прои|сходи́ть, -зойти́; получ|а́ться, -и́ться; **accidents will ~** ≃ вся́кое быва́ет; **I hope nothing has ~ed to him** наде́юсь, с ним ничего́ не случи́лось. **2.** (*chance*): **it (so) ~ed that I was there** случи́лось так, что я был там; **as it ~s I can help you** ~ я в да́нном слу́чае могу́ вам помо́чь; **do you ~ to know her?** вы случа́йно не зна́ете её?; **I ~ed to be out** меня́ не оказа́лось до́ма; **we ~ed to meet** мы неожи́данно/случа́йно встре́тились; **this ~s to be my birthday** сего́дня как раз мой день рожде́ния; **he ~ed to mention it** он ка́к-то упомяну́л об э́том. **3.:** ~ **by, in** (*coll., call in casually*) за|ходи́ть, -йти́ (*к кому*); заск|а́кивать, -очи́ть (*к кому*). **4.:** ~ **on** случа́йно наткну́ться (*pf.*) на+*g.*

happening ['hæpənıŋ, -pnıŋ] *n.* слу́чай; собы́тие; (*improvisation*) «хэ́ппенинг».

happily ['hæpılı] *adv.* **1.** (*contentedly*) сча́стливо; **and they lived ~ ever after** ≃ и ста́ли они́ жить-пожива́ть, да добра́ нажива́ть. **2.** (*fortunately*) к сча́стью.

happiness ['hæpınıs] *n.* сча́стье.

happy ['hæpı] *adj.* **1.** (*contented*) счастли́вый. **2.** (*fortunate, felicitous*) счастли́вый, уда́чливый; уда́чный; **by a ~ coincidence** по счастли́вой случа́йности; **a ~ thought** счастли́вая/уда́чная мысль; ~ **medium** золота́я середи́на; **her death was a ~ release** смерть была́ её счастли́вым избавле́нием; ~ **birthday!** с днём рожде́ния; ~ **Christmas!** с Рождество́м (христо́вым). **3.** (*pleased*) дово́льный (*чем*); **we shall be ~ to come** мы с удово́льствием придём; **I'm not ~ about, with that suggestion** мне э́то предложе́ние не нра́вится; меня́ э́то предложе́ние не совсе́м устра́ивает.

cpd. **~-go-lucky** *adj.* беззабо́тный; беспе́чный.

hara-kiri [ˌhærə'kırı] *n.* хараки́ри (*nt. indecl.*).

harangue [hə'ræŋ] *n.* разглаго́льствование; стра́стная/горя́чая речь.

v.t. увещева́ть (*impf.*).

v.i. разглаго́льствовать (*impf.*).

harass ['hærəs, *disp.* hə'ræs] *v.t.* изводи́ть (*impf.*); трави́ть, за-; ~ **the enemy** изма́тывать (*impf.*) врага́; не дава́ть (*impf.*) врагу́ поко́я.

harassment ['hærəsmənt, hə'ræs-] *n.* тра́вля; изма́тывание.

harbinger ['hɑ:bındʒə(r)] *n.* предве́стник.

harbour ['hɑ:bə(r)] *n.* га́вань, порт; ~ **dues** порто́вые сбо́ры (*m. pl.*); (*fig.*) убе́жище.

v.t. да|ва́ть, -ть убе́жище +*d.*; укр|ыва́ть, -ы́ть; **~ing a criminal** укрыва́тельство/сокры́тие престу́пника; **dirt ~s disease** грязь — расса́дник боле́зней; (*fig.*): **I ~ no grudge against him** я не держу́ на него́ зла.

cpd. **~-master** *n.* нача́льник по́рта.

hard [hɑ:d] *adj.* **1.** (*firm, resistant, solid*) твёрдый; про́чный; ~ **core** (*fig., nucleus of resistance etc.*) ядро́; ~ **and fast rules** жёсткие пра́вила; ~ **bread** чёрствый хлеб; ~ **copy** (*comput.*) печа́тная ко́пия; ~ **hat** защи́тный шлем; ~ **tack** гале́та; суха́рь (*m.*). **2.** (*of money*): ~ **cash** нали́чность; нали́чные (де́ньги); ~ **currency** твёрдая валю́та. **3.** (*difficult*) тру́дный; **do sth. the ~ way** идти́ тру́дным путём; **you're ~ to please** вам тру́дно угоди́ть; **she played ~ to get** она́ разы́грывала из себя́ недотро́гу; она́ набива́ла себе́ це́ну; **it's ~ to say yet** пока́ тру́дно сказа́ть; **bargains are ~ to come by** нелегко́ доста́ть ве́щи по дешёвой цене́. **4.:** ~ **of hearing** глухова́тый; туго́й на́ ухо. **5.** (*unsentimental, relentless*): **he drives a ~ bargain** с ним не сторгу́ешься; **a ~ drinker** го́рький пья́ница; **don't be too ~ on her!** не бу́дьте к ней сли́шком стро́ги; ~ **sell** навя́зывание това́ра; ~ **words** ре́зкие слова́. **6.** (*vigorous, harsh*): ~ **times** тяжёлые времена́; **a ~ climate** суро́вый кли́мат; **it's a ~ life** жизнь трудна́; тру́дно живётся; **take a ~ line** заня́ть (*pf.*) жёсткую пози́цию; **a ~ master** стро́гий хозя́ин; **as ~ as nails** (*fig.*) закалённый; (**~-hearted**) жестокосе́рдный; **a ~ light** ре́зкий свет; ~ **liquor** кре́пкие напи́тки; ~ **drugs** сильноде́йствующие нарко́тики; ~ **carriage** (*rail.*) жёсткий ваго́н; ~ **water** жёсткая вода́; **a ~ consonant** твёрдый согла́сный. **7.** (*intensive*): ~ **work** тяжёлая/тру́дная рабо́та; **a ~ blow** си́льный уда́р; ~ **labour** исправи́тельно-трудовы́е рабо́ты; (*fig.*) ка́торга; **a ~ worker** усе́рдный/приле́жный рабо́тник; **a ~ rider** неутоми́мый ездо́к. **8.** (*coll., unfortunate*): ~ **lines (luck, cheese)!** не везёт!; как вам (*и т.п.*) не повезло́!; **he told a ~-luck story** он пыта́лся разжа́лобить слу́шателей свои́ми го́рестями; **his parents are ~ up** его́ роди́тели — лю́ди небога́тые.

adv. **1.** (*solid*): **the ground froze ~** земля́ промёрзла. **2.** (*with force*): **it is raining ~** дождь льёт вовсю́; **he had to brake ~** ему́ пришло́сь ре́зко затормози́ть; **~ a-starboard!** пра́во на борт!; ~ **hit** (*fig.*) си́льно пострада́вший. **3.** (*unremittingly*) усе́рдно; **he rode ~ all day** он проскака́л на ло́шади весь день, нигде́ не остана́вливаясь; **he was ~ pressed for money** ему́ до заре́зу нужны́ бы́ли де́ньги; **I was ~ put to it to answer** мне нелегко́ бы́ло найти́ отве́т. **4.** (*adversely*): **it will go ~ with him** ему́ ту́го придётся; ~ **done by** обделённый; пострада́вший. **5.** (*persistently*): **he looked ~ in my direction** он при́стально посмотре́л в мою́ сто́рону; **I looked ~ for the book** я до́лго иска́л кни́гу; **look ~!** хороше́нько поищи́те!; **did** you look ~? вы как слéдует искáли?; **work** (*study*) ~ усéрдно занимáться (*impf.*); **we worked** ~ мы мнóго рабóтали; **work ~er** рабóтать (*impf.*) (ещё) бóльше/лýчше; **I tried ~ to make him understand** я изо всех сил старáлся разъяснить емý (*что*). **6.:** ~ **by** (*liter.*) поблизости.

cpds. **~back** *n.* (*book*) книга в жёстком переплёте; **~-bitten** *adj.* стóйкий, несгибáемый; **~board** *n.* древесноволокнистая плитá; **~-boiled** *adj.* (*lit.*) свáренный вкрутýю; **a ~-boiled egg** крутóе яйцó; яйцó вкрутýю; (*fig.*) прожжённый; видáвший виды; **~-core** *adj.* закоренéлый; **~-cover** *adj.* в жёстком переплёте; в твёрдой облóжке; **~-earned** *adj.* заработанный тяжким трудóм; **~-faced** *adj.* с сурóвым видом; **~-fisted** *adj.* прижимистый; **~-headed** *adj.* трéзвый; практичный; **~-hearted** *adj.* жестокосéрдный; неумолимый; **~-hitting** *adj.* (*e.g. speech*) жестóкий; скáзанный напрямик; **~-line** *adj.* неустýпчивый, бескомпромиссный; **~-liner** *n.* (*coll., one who takes a ~ line*) сторóнник жёсткой линии; **~-mouthed** *adj.* тугоýздый; (*fig.*) упрямый; строптивый; **~ware** *n.* скобяные издéлия/товáры; (*mil., coll.*) тéхника, матчáсть; (*comput.*) аппаратýра; аппарáтное обеспечéние; **~-wearing** *adj.* нóский; **~wood** *n.* твёрдая древесина; **~-working** *adj.* работящий, усидчивый.

harden ['hɑ:d(ə)n] *v.t.* укреп|лять, -ить; прид|авáть, -áть твёрдость +*d.*; **~ed steel** закалённая сталь; (*fig.*): **he ~ed his heart** он ожесточил своё сéрдце; **his body was ~ed by exercise** он укрепил свои мышцы, занимáясь спóртом; **a ~ed criminal** закоренéлый престýпник; рецидивист.

v.i. (*fig.*): **opinion ~ed** мнéние укрепилось/укоренилось; **prices are ~ing** (*rising*) цéны растýт.

hardihood ['hɑ:dɪ,hʊd] *n.* дéрзость; дерзáние.

hardiness ['hɑ:dɪnɪs] *n.* выносливость; закáлка.

hardly ['hɑ:dlɪ] *adv.* **1.** (*with difficulty*) едвá (ли). **2.** (*only just*): **I had ~ sat down when the phone rang** тóлько я сел, как зазвонил телефóн; **I ~ know him** я егó почти не знáю. **3.** (*not reasonably*): **he can ~ have arrived yet** вряд ли он ужé приéхал; **you can ~ expect her to agree** вы едвá (*or* вряд) ли мóжете рассчитывать на её соглáсие. **4.** (*almost not*): ~ **ever** почти никогдá; **there's ~ any money left** дéнег почти не остáлось; **I need ~ say** самó собóй разумéется; сáми понимáете. **5.** (*severely*): **he has been ~ treated** с ним грýбо/сурóво обошлись.

hardness ['hɑ:dnɪs] *n.* твёрдость, жёсткость.

hardship ['hɑ:dʃɪp] *n.* невзгóды (*f. pl.*); испытáние.

hardy ['hɑ:dɪ] *adj.* **1.** (*bold*) отвáжный; дéрзкий. **2.** (*robust*) закалённый; выносливый; (*of plants*) морозоустóйчивый; ~ **annual** (*lit.*) морозостóйкое однолéтнее растéние; (*fig., recurrent subject etc.*) надоéвший вопрóс.

hare [heə(r)] *n.* зáяц; ~ **and hounds** (*game*) зáяц и собаки; **run with the ~ and hunt with the hounds** (*fig.*) служить (*impf.*) и нáшим и вáшим; **first catch your ~** цыплят по óсени считáют; **mad as a March ~** одурéвший, ошалéвший; **who started this ~?** (*fig.*) кто заварил кáшу? (*coll.*).

v.i. (*sl.*) уд|ирáть, -рáть.

cpds. **~bell** *n.* колокóльчик круглолистый; **~-brained** *adj.* опромéтчивый; шальнóй; **~lip** *n.* зáячья губá.

Hare Krishna [,hɑ:rɪ 'krɪʃnə] *n.* (*cult member*) кришнаит.

adj. кришнаитский.

harem ['hɑ:ri:m, hɑ:'ri:m] *n.* гарéм.

haricot ['hærɪ,kəʊ] *n.* (**~ bean**) фасóль (*collect.*).

Harijan ['hærɪdz(ə)n] *n.* хариджáн.

hark [hɑ:k] *v.i.* **1.** (*listen*) вн|имáть, -ять +*d.*; **just ~ at him!** вы тóлько егó послýшайте! **2.** ~ **back to** (*recall*) упом|инáть, -янýть; вернýться (*pf.*) к (*теме и т.п.*); (*date back to*) восходить к+*d.*

harlequin ['hɑ:lɪkwɪn] *n.* арлекин.

harlequinade [,hɑ:lɪkwɪ'neɪd] *n.* арлекинáда; (*fig.*) шутовствó, паясничание.

harlot ['hɑ:lət] *n.* (*arch.*) шлюха.

harlotry ['hɑ:lətrɪ] *n.* (*arch.*) блуд, разврáт.

harm [hɑ:m] *n.* вред, ущéрб; **it can do no ~** от э́того вредá не бýдет; **there's no ~ (in) trying** попытка не пытка; **he will come to no ~** с ним ничегó не случится; **I meant no ~** я не хотéл (вас *и т.п.*) обидеть; **out of ~'s way** от грехá подáльше; **there is no ~ done** никтó не пострадáл.

v.t. вредить, по- +*d.*; причин|ять, -ить (*or* нан|осить, -ести) вред +*d.*; об|ижáть, -идеть; **be ~ed** пострадáть (*pf.*).

harmful ['hɑ:mfʊl] *adj.* врéдный.

harmless ['hɑ:mlɪs] *adj.* (*not injurious*) безврéдный; безопáсный; (*innocent*) безобидный.

harmonic [hɑ:'mɒnɪk] *adj.* гармонический.

harmonica [hɑ:'mɒnɪkə] *n.* гармóника.

harmonious [hɑ:'məʊnɪəs] *adj.* (*lit., fig.*) гармоничный; (*amicable*) дрýжный; слáженный; соглáсный.

harmonium [hɑ:'məʊnɪəm] *n.* фисгармóния.

harmonization [,hɑ:mənaɪ'zeɪʃ(ə)n] *n.* (*lit., fig.*) гармонизáция.

harmonize ['hɑ:mə,naɪz] *v.t.* **1.** (*mus., put chords to melody*) гармонизировать (*impf.*). **2.** (*bring into agreement*) согласóв|ывать, -áть; увяз|ывать, -áть.

v.i.: **these colours ~ well** э́ти цветá гармонируют (мéжду собóй).

harmony ['hɑ:mənɪ] *n.* **1.** (*mus., theory*) гармóния. **2.** (*of sounds, colours*) гармоничность. **3.** (*agreement*) гармóния; слáженность; **their thoughts are in ~** их идéи созвýчны.

harness ['hɑ:nɪs] *n.* ýпряжь; (*fig.*): **he died in ~** он ýмер на (трудовóм) постý; **they run in double ~** они рабóтают в пáре.

v.t. запр|ягáть, -ячь; (*fig.*) (*of natural forces*) обуздывать, -áть; покор|ять, -ить; (*of energies etc.*) мобилизóв|ывать, -áть.

harp [hɑ:p] *n.* áрфа.

v.i. (*fig.*): ~ **on sth.** твердить (*impf.*) о чём-н.

harp|er ['hɑ:pə(r)], **-ist** ['hɑ:pɪst] *nn.* арфист (*fem.* -ка).

harpoon [hɑ:'pu:n] *n.* гарпýн.

v.t. бить гарпунóм; гарпýнить, за-.

harpsichord ['hɑ:psɪ,kɔ:d] *n.* клавесин.

harpy ['hɑ:pɪ] *n.* (*myth.*) гáрпия; (*fig., rapacious pers.*) рвач; хищник.

harridan ['hærɪd(ə)n] *n.* стáрая каргá; вéдьма.

harrier ['hærɪə(r)] *n.* (*dog*) гóнчая; (*runner*) учáстник крóсса.

harrow ['hærəʊ] *n.* боронá.

v.t. **1.** (*agric.; also v.i.*) боронить (*impf.*). **2.** (*fig., lacerate*) терзáть, ис-; рáнить (*impf.*) (*чувства*); **a ~ing tale** душераздирáющая истóрия.

harry ['hærɪ] *v.t.* (*ravage*) разор|ять, -ить; опустош|áть, -ить; (*harass*) изв|одить, -ести; мýчить, из-.

harsh [hɑ:ʃ] *adj.* **1.** (*rough*) грýбый, рéзкий; **a ~ taste** рéзкий вкус; ~ **colours** рéзкие (*or* рéжущие глаз) цветá. **2.** (*severe*) сурóвый.

harshness ['hɑ:ʃnɪs] *n.* рéзкость, сурóвость.

hart [hɑ:t] *n.* олéнь-самéц.

hartebeest ['hɑ:tɪ,bi:st] *n.* корóвья антилóпа; бубáл.

harum-scarum [,heərəm'skeərəm] *adj.* беззабóтный, бесшабáшный.

harvest ['hɑ:vɪst] *n.* (*yield*) урожáй; (*~ing*) жáтва, сбор урожáя; (*garnering*) убóрка; **the ~ is ripe** урожáй созрéл; ~ **festival** прáздник урожáя; ~ **home** конéц жáтвы; (*fig.*) плоды (*m. pl.*) трудá; **he reaped a ~ of praise** он прослáвился.

v.t. & i. соб|ирáть, -рáть (урожáй); жать, с-.

harvester ['hɑ:vɪstə(r)] *n.* (*reaper*) жн|ец (*fem.* -ица); (*machine*) убóрочная машина.

has-been ['hæzbi:n] *n.* (*coll.*) человéк, пережи́вший свою слáву; ≃ «из бывших»; **he is a ~** егó врéмя прошлó.

hash[1] [hæʃ] *n.* мéлко нарéзанное мясо; (*fig.*): **he made a ~ of it** он завалил/загубил всё дéло; **I'll settle his ~** я сдéлаю из негó котлéту; я егó проучý.

v.t. (*also* ~ **up**) мéлко рéзать, на- (*мясо*).

hash[2] [hæʃ] *n.* (*coll.*) анашá.

cpd. **~-head** *n.* (*sl.*) анашист.

hash|ish, -eesh ['hæʃi:ʃ] *n.* гашиш.

Hasidic [hæ'sɪdɪk] *adj.* (*relig.*) хаси́дский.
hasp [hɑːsp] *n.* засо́в.
hassle ['hæs(ə)l] *n.* (*coll.*) тру́дность, препя́тствие.
hassock ['hæsək] *n.* поду́шечка для коленопреклоне́ния.
haste [heɪst] *n.* спе́шка, торопли́вость; **he went off in great ~** он поспе́шно ушёл; **make ~!** потора́пливайтесь!; **more ~, less speed** ти́ше е́дешь — да́льше бу́дешь.
hasten ['heɪs(ə)n] *v.t.* торопи́ть, по-; уск|оря́ть, -о́рить; убыстр|я́ть, -и́ть.
v.i. торопи́ться (*impf.*), спеши́ть (*impf.*); **I ~ to add that ...** спешу́ доба́вить, что...
hasty ['heɪstɪ] *adj.* (*hurried*) поспе́шный; торопли́вый; (*rash, ill-considered*) поспе́шный; скоропали́тельный; (*quick-tempered*) вспы́льчивый; горя́чий.
hat [hæt] *n.* шля́па; **a bad ~** (*sl.*) подо́нок; проходи́мец; **my ~!** (*coll.*) на́до же!; ну и ну!; **top ~** цили́ндр; **if he wins I'll eat my ~** (*coll.*) пусть меня́ пове́сят, е́сли он вы́играет; **I refuse to go ~ in hand to him** я не ста́ну пе́ред ним расша́ркиваться; **keep it under your ~** (*coll.*) никому́ об э́том ни сло́ва; **they passed, sent the ~ round** они́ пусти́ли ша́пку по кру́гу; **I take off my ~ to him** я преклоня́юсь пе́ред ним; **he's talking through his ~** он несёт ахине́ю (*coll.*); **at the drop of a ~** (*coll.*) неме́дленно, то́тчас же; по мале́йшему по́воду; **he wears two ~s** (*fig.*) он игра́ет две ро́ли сра́зу; **old ~** (*sl.*) устаре́лый; старо́!
cpds. **~-band** *n.* ле́нта на шля́пе; **~-pin** *n.* зако́лка для шля́пы; **~rack** *n.* ве́шалка для шляп; **~-stand** *n.* стоя́чая ве́шалка для шляп; **~-trick** *n.*: **he scored a ~-trick** (*fig.*) он доби́лся успе́ха три ра́за подря́д.
hatch[1] [hætʃ] *n.* (*opening*) люк; отве́рстие; (*cover*) кры́шка; две́рцы (*f. pl.*); **under ~es** под па́лубой; (*fig.*) в надёжном ме́сте; **down the ~!** (*coll.*) пей до дна!
cpds. **~-back** *n.* пятидве́рная маши́на; **~way** *n.* люк.
hatch[2] [hætʃ] *v.t.* (*produce by incubation; incubate*) вына́шивать, вы́носить; (*fig., plot*): **what are you ~ing?** что вы там замышля́ете?
v.i. (*also* **~ out**) вылу́пливаться, вы́лупиться.
hatchery ['hætʃərɪ] *n.* инкуба́тор.
hatchet ['hætʃɪt] *n.* топо́р, топо́рик; **let's bury the ~!** дава́йте поми́римся!
cpds. **~-faced** *adj.* остроли́цый, с о́стрым лицо́м; **~man** *n.* (ро́бот-)уби́йца, запле́чный ма́стер.
hatching ['hætʃɪŋ] *n.* штрих, штрихо́вка.
hatchment ['hætʃmənt] *n.* мемориа́льная табли́чка с изображе́нием гербá.
hate [heɪt] *n.* не́нависть.
v.t. ненави́деть (*impf.*); (*dislike strongly*) не терпе́ть/выноси́ть, о́чень не люби́ть (*all impf.*); **I ~ getting up early** я ненави́жу ра́но встава́ть; **I ~ to trouble you, but ...** мне о́чень не хо́чется вас беспоко́ить, но...
hateful ['heɪtfʊl] *adj.* ненави́стный.
hater ['heɪtə(r)] *n.*: **he is a ~ of gossip** он ненави́дит спле́тни; **he is a good ~** он уме́ет ненави́деть.
hatless ['hætlɪs] *adj.* с непокры́той голово́й.
hatred ['heɪtrɪd] *n.* не́нависть; **have a ~ of sth.** не терпе́ть/выноси́ть чего́-н.; **feel ~ for** пита́ть не́нависть к+*d.*
hatter ['hætə(r)] *n.* шля́пник; **mad as a ~** сумасше́дший; полоу́мный; ≃ не все до́ма.
haughtiness ['hɔːtɪnɪs] *n.* высокоме́рие; зазна́йство.
haughty ['hɔːtɪ] *adj.* зано́счивый; высокоме́рный.
haul [hɔːl] *n.* **1.** (*act of pulling*) вытя́гивание; тя́га. **2.** (*distance pulled*) рейс, пробе́г; **a long ~** (*fig.*) до́лгое де́ло. **3.**: **a ~ of fish** то́ня; (*fig., booty*) добы́ча; «уло́в».
v.t. & i. тяну́ть (*impf.*); тащи́ть (*impf.*); (*fig.*): **they were ~ed before the magistrate** их привлекли́ к суду́; **~ over the coals** пропесо́чить (*pf.*); устро́ить (*pf.*) разно́с +*d.* (*both coll.*).
with advs.: **~ down,** *v.t.*: **the flag was ~ed down** флаг был спу́щен; **~ in** *v.t.* вт|я́гивать, -яну́ть; **~ out** *v.t.* вытя́гивать, вы́тянуть; **~ up** *v.t.* подн|има́ть, -я́ть; (*coll., summon*) притащи́ть (*pf.*).
haulage ['hɔːlɪdʒ] *n.* транспортиро́вка, перево́зка; **~ contractor** подря́дчик на грузовы́е перево́зки.
haulier ['hɔːlɪə(r)] *n.* перево́зчик.
haunch [hɔːntʃ] *n.* бедро́, ля́жка; **he got down on his ~es** он присе́л на ко́рточки.
haunt [hɔːnt] *n.* излю́бленное (*or* ча́сто посеща́емое) ме́сто; **our childhood ~s** места́, где мы люби́ли быва́ть в де́тстве.
v.t. & i. неотвя́зно пресле́довать (*impf.*); **a ~ed house** дом с привиде́ниями; **a ~ing melody** навя́зчивый моти́в; **she ~s my memory** мысль о ней пресле́дует меня́.
Hausa ['haʊzə] *n. & adj.* ха́уса (*m. indecl.*).
hautboy ['əʊbɔɪ] *n.* гобо́й.
hauteur [əʊ'tɜː(r)] *n.* высокоме́рие; надме́нность.
Havana [hə'vænə] *n.* Гава́на; **(~ cigar)** гава́нская сига́ра.
have [hæv, həv] *n.*: **the ~s and the ~-nots** иму́щие и неиму́щие.
v.t. **1.** име́ть; (*possess*) облада́ть +*i.*; *often expr. by* у+*g.*; **she has blue eyes** у неё голубы́е глаза́; **I ~ no doubt** у меня́ нет сомне́ний; **he has no equal** он не име́ет себе́ (*or* ему́ нет) ра́вных; **~ the goodness to ...** бу́дьте добры́; не откажи́те в любе́зности; **he had the courage to refuse** он име́л му́жество отказа́ться; **I ~ no idea** поня́тия не име́ю; **he has no languages** он не зна́ет иностра́нных языко́в; **they cannot ~ children** они́ не мо́гут име́ть дете́й; **they ~ large reserves of oil** они́ владе́ют больши́ми запа́сами не́фти. **2.** (*contain*): **June has 30 days** в ию́не 30 дней. **3.** (*experience*): **~ a good time!** жела́ю вам хорошо́ провести́ вре́мя; (*suffer from*): **he has a cold** у него́ на́сморк; **do you often ~ toothache?** у вас ча́сто боля́т зу́бы? **4.** (*bear*) роди́ть (*impf., pl.*); рожа́ть (*impf.*); **she is having a baby in May** в ма́е у неё бу́дет ребёнок. **5.** (*receive, obtain*): **we had news of him yesterday** вчера́ мы получи́ли о нём изве́стие; **you always ~ your own way** ты ве́чно наста́иваешь на своём; **there was nothing to be had** там ничего́ не́ было; **the play had a great success** пье́са име́ла большо́й успе́х; (*accept*): **I'm not having any!** (*coll.*) э́то не для меня́; ну уж нет!; (*tolerate*): **I won't ~ it!** э́того я не потерплю́! **6.** (*show, exercise*): **~ pity on** сжа́литься над+*i.*; **~ pity on me** сжа́льтесь на́до мной; **he had no mercy** он был безжа́лостен. **7.** (*undertake, perform*): **~ a game of tennis** сыгра́ть (*pf.*) в те́ннис; **~ a go** (*coll.*) попыта́ться (*pf.*); попро́бовать (*pf.*). **8.** (*partake of, enjoy*): **~ dinner** у́жинать (*impf.*). **9.** (*puzzle, put at a loss*): **you ~ me there** вы меня́ озада́чили. **10.** (*coll., swindle*): **you've been had** вас провели́/околпа́чили. **11.** (*cause, order*): **~ him come here!** приведи́те/пришли́те его́ сюда́; заста́вьте его́ прийти́ сюда́; **I must ~ my shoes mended** мне на́до отда́ть ту́фли в почи́нку; я до́лжен почини́ть ту́фли; **I would ~ you know** да бу́дет вам изве́стно; **what would you ~ me do?** так что, по-ва́шему, я до́лжен де́лать?; (*suffer*): **he had his leg smashed** он слома́л но́гу. **12.** (*with inf., be obliged to*) быть вы́нужденным/обя́занным; **I ~ to** я до́лжен; мне прихо́дится; **it has to be done** э́то необходи́мо сде́лать; **you don't ~ to go** вы не обя́заны идти́; **I didn't want to, but I had to** я не хоте́л, но был вы́нужден. **13.** (*phrr. with it*): **I ~ it!** (*the answer, solution*) нашёл!; **let him ~ it!** (*sl., attack him*) дай ему́ хороше́нько!; покажи́ ему́!; **he's had it!** (*sl.*) (*is too old or old-fashioned*) его́ вре́мя прошло́; (*has missed an offer or opportunity*) ну всё, он прогоре́л/пропа́л; пиши́ пропа́ло; **rumour has it that ...** хо́дят слу́хи, что...; **as he would ~ it** как он утвержда́ет; **you can't ~ it both ways** (*coll.*) и́ли то, и́ли друго́е; ≃ вы хоти́те, что́бы во́лки бы́ли сы́ты и о́вцы це́лы; **he had it coming (to him)** (*coll.*) он сам на э́то нарва́лся; **he has it in for me** (*coll.*) у него́ зуб на меня́; **~ it off** (**~** *sexual intercourse*) пересна́ть (*pf.*), (*sl.*) живану́ть (*pf.*); **~ it out with s.o.** объясн|я́ться, -и́ться с кем-н.; **I had it in mind to go there** у меня́ была́ мысль пойти́ туда́; **~ it your own way!** будь по-ва́шему!; **he has never had it so good** ему́ ещё никогда́ так хорошо́ не жило́сь.
with advs.: **can I ~ my watch back?** могу́ я получи́ть свои́ часы́ обра́тно?; **may we ~ the blinds down?** мо́жно опусти́ть што́ры?; **we had her parents down** (*to stay*) у нас гости́ли её роди́тели; **we are having the painters in next week** на сле́дующей неде́ле приду́т маляры́; **~ we enough food in for the weekend?** у нас доста́точно проду́ктов на суббо́ту и воскресе́нье?; **he had his coat**

off он был без пальто́; **she had his coat off** (*took it off him*) **in a moment** она́ сра́зу же сняла́ с него́ пальто́; **she had a red dress on** на ней бы́ло кра́сное пла́тье; ~ **you anything on tonight?** у вас есть пла́ны на сего́дняшний ве́чер?; **we** ~ **a lot of work on at present** у нас сейча́с мно́го/ма́сса рабо́ты; ~ **s.o. on** разы́гр|ывать, -а́ть кого́-н.; **I must** ~ **this tooth out** мне ну́жно удали́ть э́тот зуб; **they had the road up last week** на про́шлой неде́ле э́ту доро́гу ремонти́ровали; **we'll** ~ **the tent up in no time** мы ми́гом устано́вим пала́тку; **he was had up for speeding** (*coll.*) его́ задержа́ли за превыше́ние ско́рости.

misc. phrr.: ~ **at you!** держи́тесь!; «иду́ на вы!»; **I** ~ **nothing against it** я ничего́ про́тив э́того не име́ю; **you had better, best give the book back** вам лу́чше бы верну́ть кни́гу; ~ **done with sth.** поко́нчить (*pf.*) с чем-н.; ~ **you might as well pay and** ~ **done with it** заплати́те — и де́лу коне́ц; **it has to do with his work** э́то свя́зано с его́ рабо́той; **it has nothing to do with you** вас э́то не каса́ется; **I'll** ~ **nothing to do with it** я не жела́ю име́ть никако́го отноше́ния к э́тому.

haven ['heɪv(ə)n] *n.* га́вань; (*fig.*) прию́т, приста́нище.

haver ['heɪvə(r)] *v.i.* (*dither*) ме́шкать, колеба́ться (*both impf.*); (*talk nonsense*) нести́ (*det.*) чушь.

haversack ['hævəˌsæk] *n.* су́мка/рюкза́к для прови́зии.

havoc ['hævək] *n.* разгро́м; опустоше́ние; (*fig.*) **make** ~ **of, play** ~ **with** вн|оси́ть, -ести́ беспоря́док/хао́с в+*a.*

haw[1] [hɔː] *n.* я́года боя́рышника.

cpd. ~**thorn** *n.* боя́рышник.

haw[2] [hɔː] *v.i. see* **hum** *v.t. & i.* **3.**

Hawaii [hə'waɪi] *n.* Гава́йи (*m. indecl.*).

Hawaiian [hə'waɪən] *n.* гава́|ец (*fem.* -йка).

adj. гава́йский.

hawk[1] [hɔːk] *n.* я́стреб (*also fig., pol.*); со́кол.

v.i. охо́титься (*impf.*) с я́стребом/со́колом.

cpds. ~**-eyed** *adj.* зо́ркий, с орли́ным взгля́дом; ~**-moth** *n.* бра́жник; су́меречная ба́бочка; ~**weed** *n.* ястреби́нка.

hawk[2] [hɔːk] *v.i.* (*clear throat*) отка́шл|иваться, -яться.

hawk[3] [hɔːk] *v.t.* (*for sale*) торгова́ть (*impf.*) вразно́с +*i.*; (*fig.*) быть разно́счиком +g.

hawker ['hɔːkə(r)] *n.* торго́вец-разно́счик; лото́чник.

hawser ['hɔːzə(r)] *n.* (стально́й) трос.

hay [heɪ] *n.* се́но; ~ **fever** сенна́я лихора́дка; **hit the** ~ (*sl., go to bed*) отпр|авля́ться, -а́виться на бокову́ю; **make** ~ (*lit.*) вороши́ть|загота́вливать (*both impf.*) се́но; **make** ~ **while the sun shines** ≃ куй желе́зо, пока горячо́; **make** ~ **of** (*fig., reduce to confusion*) разби́ть в пух и прах.

cpds. ~**cock** *n.* копна́; ~**-fork** *n.* ви́л|ы (*pl. g.* —); ~**maker** *n.* рабо́чий на сенозагото́вках; (*coll., swinging blow*) си́льный уда́р; ~**making** *n.* сеноко́с, загото́вка се́на; ~**rick** *n.* стог се́на; ~**seed** *n.* (*coll., yokel*) мужи́к, дереве́нщина (*c.g.*); ~**stack** *n.* стог се́на; ~**wire** *n.* (*sl.*): **everything went** ~**wire** всё пошло́ наперeко́с.

hazard ['hæzəd] *n.* **1.** (*risk*) риск; **at all** ~**s** чего́ бы э́то ни сто́ило; любо́й цено́й. **2.** (*danger*) опа́сность; **at** ~ в опа́сности; **road** ~**s** опа́сности на доро́гах.

v.t. **1.** (*endanger*) риск|ова́ть, -ну́ть +*i.*; ста́вить, по- под уда́р; **he** ~**ed his life for her** ради неё он рискова́л жи́знью. **2.** (*venture upon*) рискну́ть (*pf.*) +*i.*; отва́ж|иваться, -иться на+*a.*; **he** ~**ed a remark** он отва́жился вы́сказать замеча́ние.

hazardous ['hæzədəs] *adj.* риско́ванный; опа́сный.

haze [heɪz] *n.* ды́мка; (*fig.*) тума́н в голове́.

v.t. затума́н|ивать, -ить; оку́т|ывать, -ать ды́мкой.

v.i.: **the windows** ~**d over** о́кна запоте́ли.

hazel ['heɪz(ə)l] *n.* (*tree*) лесно́й оре́х; (*colour*) оре́ховый цвет; ~ **eyes** ка́рие глаза́.

cpd. ~**-nut** *n.* лесно́й оре́х.

haziness ['heɪzɪnɪs] *n.* (*atmospheric*) тума́нность; ды́мка; (*mental*) расплы́вчатость; тума́нность.

hazy ['heɪzɪ] *adj.* подёрнутый ды́мкой; затума́ненный; (*fig.*) сму́тный, тума́нный.

HDTV (*abbr. of* **high-definition television**) ТВЧ, (телеви́дение высо́кой чёткости).

he[1] [hiː, hɪ] *n.* **1.** (*coll., male human*) мужчи́на; (*child*) ма́льчик; (*animal*) саме́ц. **2.** он; тот; (*in children's game*) тот, кто во́дит; са́лка, горе́лка, вожа́к, водя́щий; (*etc., acc. to game*); **who is '**~**'?** кто во́дит?; чья о́чередь?; кому́ води́ть?; ~ **who believes** тот, кто ве́рит; ~**'s a clever man, our teacher** он у́мный челове́к, наш учи́тель.

cpds. ~**-bear** *n.* медве́дь-саме́ц; ~**-goat** *n.* козёл; ~**-man** *n.* настоя́щий мужчи́на.

he[2] [hiː, hɪ] *int.* ~, ~ (*expr. laughter*) хи-хи!

head [hed] *n.* **1.** голова́; (*dim., e.g. baby's*) голо́вка; **he was hit on the** ~ его́ уда́рили по голове́; ~ **first, foremost** голово́й вперёд; **he was** ~ **over heels in love** он был по́ уши влюблён; **over** ~ **and ears in debt** по́ уши в долга́х; **covered in dust from** ~ **to foot, toe** покры́тый пы́лью с головы́ до ног; **a good** ~ **of hair** густы́е во́лосы; **I could do it standing on my** ~ я могу́ э́то сде́лать одно́й ле́вой; **he goes about with his** ~ **in the air** он задира́ет но́с; он задаётся; **his** ~ **is in the clouds** он вита́ет в облака́х; **he is keeping his** ~ **above water** (*fig.*) он де́ржится на пове́рхности; **he will never hold up his** ~ **again** он бо́льше не смо́жет смотре́ть лю́дям в глаза́; **he hung his** ~ **for shame** он пове́сил го́лову от стыда́; **shake one's** ~ покача́ть (*pf.*) голово́й; **he turned his** ~ он поверну́л го́лову; **I cannot make** ~ **or tail of it** я не могу́ в э́том разобра́ться; я не могу́ взять э́то в толк; **he was promoted over my** ~ ему́ да́ли повыше́ние че́рез мою́ го́лову; **this is all completely over my** ~ э́то всё вы́ше моего́ понима́ния; **keep your** ~ **down** (*lit.*) пригни́тесь; опусти́те го́лову; (*fig.*) не су́йтесь; не ле́зьте на рожо́н; **it's time to get your** ~ **down** (*coll., go to bed*) пора́ на бокову́ю; **he is reading his** ~ **off** он чита́ет до одуре́ния; **he can talk your** ~ **off** он вас заговори́т; **the horse is eating its** ~ **off** (*coll.*) на э́ту ло́шадь ко́рма не напасёшься; **bury one's** ~ **in the sand** (*fig.*) отка́зываться (*impf.*) смотре́ть фа́ктам в лицо́; (*attr.*) головно́й; **a** ~ **cold** на́сморк; **a** ~ **voice** головно́й реги́стр; **a** ~ **wind** встре́чный ве́тер. **2.** (*as measure*): **he gave me a** ~ **start** он дал мне фо́ру; **he is taller by a** ~ он вы́ше на́ голову; **he stands** ~ **and shoulders above the rest** (*fig.*) он на́ голову вы́ше остальны́х. **3.** (*mind, brain*): **two** ~**s are better than one** ум хорошо́, а два лу́чше; **he has a good** ~ **for figures** он хорошо́ счита́ет; **he's a bit weak in the** ~ у него́ ви́нтика не хвата́ет; **he's off his** ~ он спя́тил; **an old** ~ **on young shoulders** из молоды́х, да ра́нний; **you can do the sum in your** ~ вы мо́жете вы́числить э́то в уме́; **it came into my** ~ мне э́то пришло́ в го́лову; **I can't keep it in my** ~ э́то не де́ржится у меня́ в голове́; **they put their** ~**s together** они́ ста́ли ду́мать вме́сте (*or* обсужда́ть совме́стно); **I made it up out of my** ~ я э́то вы́думал; **put it out of your** ~**!** вы́бросьте э́то из головы́!; **what put that into your** ~**?** отку́да вы э́то взя́ли?; с чего́ э́то вам взбрело́ (в го́лову)?; **he took it into his** ~ **to invite them** ему́ взбрело́ в го́лову их пригласи́ть; **it went clean out of my** ~ э́то у меня́ соверше́нно вы́скочило из головы́; я на́чисто забы́л об э́том; **it never entered my** ~ мне э́то никогда́ не приходи́ло в го́лову; (*faculties*): **the wine went to his** ~ вино́ уда́рило ему́ в го́лову; **success went to his** ~ успе́х вскружи́л ему́ го́лову; **the next day I had a thick** ~ на сле́дующий день у меня́ треща́ла/гуде́ла голова́; (*balance, composure*): **he kept his** ~ он сохраня́л прису́тствие ду́ха; он не теря́л го́лову; **he has no** ~ **for heights** у него́ кру́жится голова́ от высоты́; он бои́тся высоты́; (*freedom, scope*): **he gave the horse its** ~ он дал ло́шади по́лную во́лю. **4.** (*on a coin*): ~**s or tails?** орёл и́ли ре́шка?; ~**s I win** е́сли орёл, я вы́играл. **5.** (*personage*): **crowned** ~**s** корона́ванные осо́бы. **6.** (*unit*): **£5 a** ~ пять фу́нтов с ка́ждого; **forty** ~ **of cattle** со́рок голо́в скота́. **7.** (*life*): **it cost him his** ~ он поплати́лся за э́то голово́й; **Charles I lost his** ~ Карл I сложи́л голову на пла́хе; **he had a price on his** ~ его голова́ была оценена́; **on your own** ~ **be it!** на ваш страх и риск!; **their blood is on his** ~ их кровь на его́ со́вести. **8.** (*upper or principal end*): **at the** ~ **of the table** во главе́ стола́; **at the** ~ **of the stairs** на ве́рхней площа́дке ле́стницы; **at the** ~ **of the page** в нача́ле страни́цы; **at the** ~ **of the procession** во главе́ проце́ссии. **9.** (*principal member*) глава́ (*c.g.*), ста́рший; ~ **of state** глава́ госуда́рства; ~ **of the family** глава́ семьи́; (*attr., principal*): ~ **boy** ста́рший учени́к; ста́роста шко́лы; ~ **waiter** метрдоте́ль (*m.*); ~ **office** гла́вная конто́ра, центр. **10.** (*category*): **these all come under one** ~ всё э́то отно́сится к одному́ разря́ду. **11.** (*culmination*): **things come to a** ~ наступи́л перело́мный моме́нт; **the revolt came to a** ~ бунт назре́л; **he brought the issue to a** ~ он поста́вил вопро́с ребро́м. **12.** (*of tool, plant, vegetable, flower*) голо́вка; (*of river*) верхо́вье; (*of water, steam*) напо́р, давле́ние; (*froth*) пе́на; (*promontory*) мыс.

v.t. **1.** (*steer, direct*): **he is ~ed for home** он направля́ется домо́й; **I managed to** ~ **him off** (*fig.*) мне удало́сь переключи́ть его на другу́ю те́му. **2.** (*strike with head*): **he ~ed the ball into the net** он заби́л мяч голово́й в се́тку. **3.** (*be first in*): **he ~ed the team** он возглавля́л кома́нду; **he ~ed the list** он был пе́рвым в спи́ске.

v.i. (*move, steer*) напр|авля́ться, -а́виться; (*fig.*): **he is ~ing for disaster** он пло́хо ко́нчит.

cpds. **~ache** *n.* головна́я боль; **I have a ~ache** у меня́ боли́т голова́; **~-band** *n.* головна́я повя́зка; **~board** *n.* спи́нка/щит в изголо́вье крова́ти; **~dress** *n.* (замыслова́тый/экзоти́ческий) головно́й убо́р; **~gear** *n.* головно́й убо́р; **~-hunter** *n.* канниба́л, собира́ющий го́ловы уби́тых как трофе́и; **~lamp, ~-light** *nn.* фа́ра; (*rail. etc.*) лобово́й фона́рь; **~land** *n.* (*promontory*) мыс; **~light** *n.* = **~lamp; ~line** *n.* заголо́вок; **he hit the ~lines** о нём крича́ли все газе́ты; **~long** *adj.* (*fig.*): **~long flight** стреми́тельное бе́гство; *adv.* голово́й/но́сом вперёд; стремгла́в; очертя́ го́лову; **~man** *n.* гла́вный; ста́рший; **~master, ~mistress** *nn.* дире́ктор шко́лы; **~most** *adj.* головно́й, пере́дний; **~-on** *adj.* лобово́й, встре́чный; **a ~-on collision** столкнове́ние «но́сом к но́су»; *adv.*: **the wind blew ~-on** ве́тер дул нам в лицо́; **~phone** *n.* нау́шник; **~piece** *n.* (*coll., brain*) голова́; мо́зги (*m. pl.*); башка́; **~quarters** *n.* штаб-кварти́ра; (*mil.*) штаб, ста́вка; **~-rest** *n.* подголо́вник; **~-room** *n.* габари́тная высота́; **~-scarf** *n.* косы́нка; **~set** *n.* (*pair of ~-phones*) нау́шники (*m. pl.*); **~-shrinker** *n.* (*coll., joc.*) психиа́тр; **~sman** *n.* пала́ч; **~stone** *n.* (*tombstone*) надгро́бный ка́мень; **~strong** *adj.* своево́льный, упря́мый, упо́рный; **~waters** *n.* исто́ки (*m. pl.*); **~way** *n.* продвиже́ние вперёд; (*fig.*): **we are not making much ~way** мы продвига́емся сли́шком ме́дленно; **~-word** *n.* загла́вное сло́во, вока́була.

header [ˈhedə(r)] *n.* **1.** (*dive, fall*) прыжо́к со вхо́дом в во́ду голово́й; **he took a** ~ он нырну́л; он упа́л голово́й вниз. **2.** (*blow with head*) уда́р голово́й.

heading [ˈhedɪŋ] *n.* (*direction*) направле́ние; курс; (*title*) заголо́вок, загла́вие; ру́брика.

headless [ˈhedlɪs] *adj.* обезгла́вленный.

headship [ˈhedʃɪp] *n.* главе́нство.

heady [ˈhedɪ] *adj.* кре́пкий, хмельно́й; (*fig.*) пьяня́щий.

heal [hiːl] *v.t.* исцел|я́ть, -и́ть; залéч|ивать, -и́ть; **~ing ointment** лече́бная мазь; (*fig.*): **time ~s all wounds** вре́мя всё ле́чит.

v.i. заж|ива́ть, -и́ть; **his wounds ~ed up, over** его́ ра́ны за́жили.

healer [ˈhiːlə(r)] *n.* ле́карь (*m.*); (ис)цели́тель (*m.*); (*fig.*): **time is the great** ~ вре́мя — лу́чший ле́карь.

healing [ˈhiːlɪŋ] *n.* лече́ние; заживле́ние.

health [helθ] *n.* **1.** (*state of body or mind*) здоро́вье; **in good** ~ здоро́вый; **he suffers from poor** ~ у него́ сла́бое здоро́вье; **Ministry of H~** министе́рство здравоохране́ния; **mental** ~ душе́вное здоро́вье; ~ **centre** поликли́ника; ~ **food** натура́льная/све́жая/витаминизи́рованная пи́ща; ~ **resort** куро́рт, санато́рий; ~ **service** здравоохране́ние. **2.** (*toast*): **we drank (to) his** ~ мы вы́пили за его́ здоро́вье; **here's a** ~ **to her Majesty!** за здоро́вье её вели́чества!

healthful [ˈhelθfʊl] *adj.* здоро́вый, целе́бный.

healthy [ˈhelθɪ] *adj.* здоро́вый; **a** ~ **economy** процвета́ющая эконо́мика.

heap [hiːp] *n.* **1.** (*pile*) ку́ча, гру́да; **I was struck all of a** ~ (*coll.*) меня́ как о́бухом по голове́ уда́рили. **2.** (*esp. pl., coll., large quantity*) ма́сса, у́йма; **he has ~s of money** у него́ у́йма/ку́ча де́нег; **I have ~s to tell you** у меня́ у́йма новосте́й для вас.

v.t.: **a ~ed spoonful** ло́жка с ве́рхом; **they ~ed honours on him** его́ осы́пали почестями; **the table was ~ed with food** стол ломи́лся от яств.

hear [hɪə(r)] *v.t.* & *i.* **1.** (*perceive with ear*) слы́шать, у-; **I can't** ~ **a word** я не слы́шу ни сло́ва; **he can't** ~ **as well as he used to** он стал ху́же слы́шать; **I** ~ **someone coming** я слы́шу (чьи́-то) шаги́; **I ~d him shout** я слы́шал, как он закрича́л; **he was ~d to say** слы́шали что/как он говори́л; **I have ~d it said that ...** я слы́шал, бу́дто...; **the shot was ~d a mile away** вы́стрел бы́ло слы́шно за ми́лю. **2.** (*listen to*): ~ **evidence** слу́шать, за- показа́ния свиде́телей; **his prayer was ~d** его́ моли́твы бы́ли услы́шаны; **will you** ~ **me my lines?** прове́рьте, пожа́луйста, как я вы́учил роль; ~ **s.o. out** вы́слушать (*pf.*) кого́-н.; **I won't** ~ **of it!** я и слы́шать об э́том не хочу́! **3.** (*be told; learn*) слы́шать, у-; **have you ~d the news?** вы слы́шали но́вости?; **have you ~d from your brother?** что слы́шно от ва́шего бра́та?; **I** ~ **he has been ill** я слы́шал, что он был бо́лен; **I ~d about it from a friend** я узна́л об э́том от одного́ моего́ дру́га; **I've never ~d of him** я о нём никогда́ не слы́шал; **I never ~d of such a thing** э́то неслы́ханно; **you will** ~ **more of this** вам э́то так не пройдёт; **I never ~d (tell) of it** я об э́том никогда́ не слыха́л. **4. ~!, ~!** пра́вильно!; ве́рно ска́зано!

cpd. **~say** *n.* слу́хи (*m. pl.*); то́лки (*m. pl.*); **~say evidence** показа́ние с чужи́х слов.

hearer [ˈhɪərə(r)] *n.* слу́шатель (*fem.* -ница).

hearing [ˈhɪərɪŋ] *n.* **1.** (*perception*) слух; ~ **aid** слухово́й аппара́т; **he is hard of** ~ он туг на́ ухо. **2.** (*earshot*): **wait till he gets out of** ~ да́йте ему́ сперва́ отойти́ (, а то он мо́жет услы́шать); **don't say that in my** ~ не говори́те э́того при мне. **3.** (*attention*): **give him a fair** ~ вы́слушайте его́; да́йте ему вы́сказаться. **4.** (*leg.*) слу́шание.

hearken [ˈhɑːkən] *v.i.* вн|има́ть, -ять +*d.*; слу́шать (*impf.*).

hearse [hɜːs] *n.* катафа́лк, похоро́нные дро́ги (*pl., g.* —).

heart [hɑːt] *n.* **1.** (*organ*) се́рдце; ~ **attack** серде́чный при́ступ; ~ **disease** боле́знь се́рдца; ~ **failure** разры́в се́рдца; **his** ~ **stopped beating** у него́ се́рдце останови́лось; **my** ~ **was in my mouth** у меня́ душа́ в пя́тки ушла́; **it will break his** ~ он бу́дет в отчая́нии; **his** ~ **sank** у него́ се́рдце упа́ло. **2.** (*soul; seat of emotions*) се́рдце, душа́; **she has a** ~ **of gold** у неё золото́е се́рдце; **at** ~ по приро́де; по су́ти свое́й; в глубине́ души́; **I am sick at** ~ у меня́ тяжело́ на душе́; **he's a man after my own** ~ он мне по душе́/се́рдцу; **his** ~ **is in the right place** в су́щности он неплохо́й челове́к; **in one's** ~ **of ~s** в глубине́ души́; **to one's ~'s content** ско́лько душе́ уго́дно; **she achieved her ~'s desire** её заве́тное жела́ние осуществи́лось; **I agree with you** ~ **and soul** я всей душо́й с ва́ми согла́сен; **bless my** ~! Бо́же мой!; вот те на!; **bless his** ~ дай Бог ему́ здоро́вья; **from the bottom of one's** ~ из глубины́ души́; **he had a change of** ~ он переду́мал/разду́мал; **she cried her** ~ **out** она́ вы́плакала все глаза́; **it did his** ~ **good to see her so happy** у него́ душа́ ра́довалась, гля́дя на её сча́стье; **I cannot find it in my** ~ **to be angry** я не в си́лах серди́ться; **he has your interests at** ~ ему́ до́роги ва́ши интере́сы; **have a** ~! (*coll.*) сжа́льтесь!; поми́луйте!; **how can you have the** ~? как вы мо́жете быть столь бессерде́чным; **lay this to** ~! запо́мните э́то хороше́нько!; **he lost his** ~ **to her** он полюби́л её (всем се́рдцем); **my** ~ **goes out to you** се́рдцем я с ва́ми; **with all my** ~ всем се́рдцем; **he had set his** ~ **on winning** он стра́стно жела́л вы́играть; **he speaks from his** ~ он говори́т от чи́стого се́рдца; **don't take it to** ~ не принима́йте э́то бли́зко к се́рдцу; **he wears his** ~ **on his sleeve** у него́ душа́ нараспа́шку; **he won their ~s** он завоева́л их сердца́; (*enthusiasm*): **he has no** ~ **for the job** у него́ не лежи́т се́рдце к э́той рабо́те; **his** ~ **is not in his work** он не лю́бит свою́ рабо́ту; (*courage*): **he lost** ~ он пал ду́хом; **take** ~! не па́дайте ду́хом!; (*memory*): **I learnt it by** ~ я вы́учил э́то наизу́сть. **3.** (*centre*) середи́на, сердцеви́на; **in the** ~ **of the forest** в глуши́ леса; **this book gets to the ~ of the matter** эта книга затрагивает самую суть дела; (*of a cabbage*) кочерыжка. **4.** (*pl., cards*) черв|и (*pl., g.* -ей); **ace of ~s** червонный туз, туз червей. **6.** (*endearment*): **dear ~** сердце моё.

cpds. **~ache** *n.* боль в сердце; **~-beat** *n.* сердцебиение; **~break** *n.* большое горе; **~-breaking** *adj.* душераздирающий; **~-broken** *adj.* с разбитым сердцем; **~burn** *n.* изжога; **~-burning** *n.* ревность; досада; **~felt** *adj.* душевный, глубоко прочувствованный; **~land** *n.* сердце, центр; **~-rending** *adj.* душераздирающий; **~-searching** *n.* душевные терзания; **~'s-ease** *n.* анютины глазки (*m. pl.*); **~-sick** *adj.* подавленный, удручённый; **~-strings** *n. pl.* душевные струны (*f. pl.*); **he played on her ~-strings** он играл её чувствами; **~-throb** *n.* (*coll.*) любимец; **~-to-~** *adj.*: **a ~-to-~ talk** разговор по душам; **~-warming** *adj.* радостный; тёплый; трогательный; **~-whole** *adj.*: **she is quite ~-whole** сердце у неё свободно; **~wood** *n.* ядровая древесина.

hearten ['hɑ:t(ə)n] *v.t.* ободр|ять, -ить; **a ~ing experience** поднимающее настроение событие.

hearth [hɑ:θ] *n.* очаг; (*fig., home*) домашний очаг.

cpds. **~-rug** *n.* коврик перед камином; **~stone** *n.* каменная плита на дне очага.

heartily ['hɑ:tılı] *adv.* **1.** (*from the heart*) сердечно, искренне; **I am ~ sick of it** мне это до смерти надоело. **2.** (*with relish, enthusiasm*) охотно, усердно; **he agreed with me ~** он всецело со мной согласился; **the boys ate ~** мальчики ели с аппетитом.

heartiness ['hɑ:tınıs] *n.* сердечность, добродушие.

heartless ['hɑ:tlıs] *adj.* бессердечный.

heartlessness ['hɑ:tlısnıs] *n.* бессердечие.

heart|y ['hɑ:tı] *n.* **1.** (*addressing sailors*): **my ~ies!** ребята! **2.** (*athletic type*) здоровяк, крепыш; (*breezily extrovert*) рубаха-парень (*m.*).

adj. **1.** (*cordial, sincere*) сердечный. **2.** (*healthy, vigorous*): **he is still hale and ~y** он всё ещё здоров и бодр; **a ~y appetite** прекрасный аппетит. **3.** (*abundant*): **he ate a ~y breakfast** он плотно позавтракал. **4.** (*cheerful*) весёлый.

heat [hi:t] *n.* **1.** (*hotness*) жара, тепло, теплота; **white ~** белое каление; **latent ~** удельная/скрытая теплота; (*hot weather*) жара; **the ~ of the day** (*lit.*) полдневный зной; **he feels the ~** (*badly*) он плохо переносит жару; **prickly ~** потница; (*heating*): **the ~ was turned on** (*lit.*) отопление было включено; (*fig., pressure was applied*) был оказан нажим; **~ engine** тепловой двигатель; **~ treatment** (*med.*) теплолечение; (*metall.*) теплообработка. **2.** (*warmth of feeling*) теплота, горячность; **he spoke with some ~** он говорил горячо; **in the ~ of the moment** сгоряча; **this took the ~ out of the situation** это разрядило обстановку. **3.** (*in race etc.*) забег, заезд; (*in swimming*) заплыв; **dead ~** мёртвый гит. **4.** (*of animals*) период течки; **be on ~** находиться (*impf.*) в периоде течки.

v.t. **1.** (*raise temperature of*) нагр|евать, -еть; **the potatoes were ~ed up** картошку разогрели. **2.** (*inflame*) накал|ять, -ить; горячить, раз-; **~ed with wine** разгорячённый вином; **a ~ed argument** жаркий спор; **he replied ~edly** он ответил запальчиво.

cpds. **~-proof, ~-resistant** *adjs.* жаростойкий, жаропрочный; **~stroke** *n.* тепловой удар; **~-wave** *n.* полоса/период сильной жары.

heater ['hi:tə(r)] *n.* печка, нагреватель, калорифер; батарея.

heath [hi:θ] *n.* **1.** (*waste land*) пустошь; **he returned to his native ~** (*fig.*) он вернулся в родные пенаты. **2.** (*shrub*) вереск.

heathen ['hi:ð(ə)n] *n.* язычник; **the ~** язычники.

adj. языческий

heathen|dom ['hi:ðəndəm], **-ism** ['hi:ðən'ız(ə)m] *nn.* язычество.

heather ['heðə(r)] *n.* вереск; **~ mixture** пёстрая шерстяная ткань.

heating ['hi:tıŋ] *n.* обогревание; отопление; **central ~** центральное отопление.

heave [hi:v] *n.* (*lifting effort*) подъём; (*throw*) бросок; (*act of retching*) рвота.

v.t. (*lift*) подн|имать, -ять; (*throw*) бр|осать, -осить; **~ a sigh** (тяжело) вздохнуть (*pf.*).

v.i. **1.** (*pull*): **they ~d on the rope** они выбрали канат; **~ ho!** раз-два взяли!; эй, ухнем! **2.** (*retch*) тужиться (*impf.*) (при рвоте). **3.** (*rise and fall*) вздыматься (*impf.*); **her bosom was heaving** её грудь вздымалась; **heaving billows** вздымающиеся волны. **4.:** **~ to** (*naut.*) ложиться в дрейф. **5.:** **~ in sight** показ|ываться, -аться на горизонте.

heaven ['hev(ə)n] *n.* **1.** (*sky, firmament*) небо, небесный свод; **the ~s opened** (*of heavy rain*) небеса разверзлись; **move ~ and earth** приложить все усилия. **2.** (*state of bliss*) блаженство; **in the seventh ~** на седьмом небе. **3.** (*paradise*) рай, царство небесное. **4.** (*God, Providence*) Бог, провидение; **~ knows where he is** Бог знает, где он; **~ forbid!** Боже упаси!; **thank ~ for that** слава Богу; **for ~'s sake** ради Бога; **(good) ~s (above)!** Господи!; Боже мой!

cpd. **~sent** *adj.* благодатный.

heavenly ['hevənlı] *adj.* **1.** (*in or of heaven*) небесный; **~ bodies** небесные тела/светила (*nt. pl.*); **the ~ host** силы небесные (*f. pl.*); небесное воинство; **the ~ Twins** Близнецы (*m. pl.*). **2.** (*coll., excellent, wonderful*) изумительный; дивный; **we had a ~ time** мы чудесно провели время.

heavenward(s) ['hevənwədz] *adv.* ввысь, в небо.

heavily ['hevı] *adv.* (*very, seriously*) значительно, интенсивно; **the rain is falling ~** идёт сильный дождь; **he fell ~** он тяжело рухнул; **they were ~ defeated** они понесли тяжёлое поражение.

heaviness ['hevınıs] *n.* **1.** (*weight*) тяжесть. **2.** (*drowsiness, lethargy*) вялость, апатия. **3.:** **~ of heart** тяжесть на сердце.

Heaviside layer ['hevı,saıd] *n.* слой Хэвисайда.

heavy ['hevı] *adj.* тяжёлый; **~ artillery** тяжёлая артиллерия; **a ~ blow** (*lit., fig.*) тяжёлый удар; **~ breathing** сопение; **a ~ cold** сильный насморк; **there will be a ~ crop this year** в этом году будет обильный урожай; **he had a ~ day** у него был тяжёлый день; **he is a ~ drinker** он человек пьющий; **~ expenses** большие расходы; **he had a ~ fall** он сильно ударился при падении; **~ father** (*theatr.*) амплуа (*nt. indecl.*) сурового родителя; **under ~ fire** под сильным огнём; **~ food** тяжёлая пища; **his book is ~ going** его книга трудно читается; **with a ~ heart** с тяжёлым сердцем; **~ industry** тяжёлая промышленность; **~ losses** большие потери; **~ metal** (*coll., mus.*) металлический рок; **~ metallist** (*coll., mus.*) металлист; **a ~ programme** насыщенная/напряжённая программа; **~ rain** сильный/проливной дождь; **a ~ sea** бурное море; **a ~ silence** тягостное молчание; **a ~ sleep** глубокий/тяжёлый сон; **he is a ~ sleeper** он крепко спит; **a ~ sky** хмурое небо; **~ taxes** большие налоги; **~ tidings** недобрые вести; **~ traffic** интенсивное движение; **~ type** жирный шрифт; **~ water** тяжёлая вода.

cpds. **~-duty** *adj.* сверхпрочный; ноский; **~-eyed** *adj.*: **he is ~-eyed** у него слипаются глаза; **~-fisted, ~-handed** *adjs.* тяжеловесный; неуклюжий; **~-hearted** *adj.* с тяжёлым сердцем; **~-laden** *adj.* тяжело нагруженный (*чем*); (*fig.*) удручённый; **~weight** *n.* & *adj.* (*sport*) (боксёр/борец) тяжёлого веса.

hebdomadal [heb'dɒməd(ə)l] *adj.* еженедельный.

hebetude ['hebı,tju:d] *n.* притуплённость; вялость.

Hebraic [hi:'breıık] *adj.* древнееврейский.

Hebraist ['hi:breııst] *n.* специалист по древнееврейской филологии.

Hebrew ['hi:bru:] *n.* **1.** (*Jew*) еврей. **2.** (*language*) древнееврейский язык; (*modern*) (язык) иврит.

adj. (древне)еврейский.

Hebridean [,hebrı'di:ən] *adj.* гебридский.

Hebrides ['hebrı,di:z] *n.*: **the ~** Гебридские острова (*m. pl.*).

hecatomb ['hekə,tu:m] *n.* гекатомба.

heckle ['hek(ə)l] *v.t.* & *i.* (*fig.*) прерывать (*impf.*) (оратора) каверзными вопросами.

heckler ['heklə(r)] *n.* человек, который пытается сбить оратора каверзными вопросами.

hectare [ˈhekteə(r), -tɑː(r)] *n.* гекта́р.

hectic [ˈhektɪk] *adj.* (*flushed*) чахо́точный; (*exciting*) лихора́дочный, бу́рный.

hectograph [ˈhektəˌgrɑːf] *n.* гекто́граф.

hectolitre [ˈhektəˌliːtə(r)] *n.* гектоли́тр.

Hector[1] [ˈhektə(r)] *n.* (*myth.*) Ге́ктор.

hector[2] [ˈhektə(r)] *v.t.* задира́ть (*impf.*).

hedge [hedʒ] *n.* жива́я и́згородь.

v.t. **1.** (*enclose*) обса́|живать, -ди́ть куста́рником; огор|а́живать, -оди́ть; (*fig.*) **~d in, round with regulations** в тиска́х пра́вил и предписа́ний. **2.: ~ one's bets** (*fig.*) перестрахо́вываться (*impf.*).

v.i. **1.** (*prevaricate*) увил|ивать, -ну́ть. **2.** (*maintain a ~*) уха́живать (*impf.*) за живо́й и́згородью.

cpds. **~hog** *n.* ёж; **~-hopping** *n.* бре́ющий полёт; **~row** *n.* шпале́ра, жива́я и́згородь; **~-sparrow** *n.* завиру́шка лесна́я.

hedonism [ˈhiːdəˌnɪz(ə)m, ˈhe-] *n.* гедони́зм.

hedonist [ˈhiːdəˌnɪst, ˈhe-] *n.* гедони́ст.

hedonistic [ˌhiːdəˈnɪstɪk, ˈhe-] *adj.* гедонисти́ческий.

heed [hiːd] *n.* внима́ние, внима́тельность; **she paid no ~ to his advice** она́ не послу́шалась его́ сове́та; **take ~** (*arch.*)! бу́дьте осторо́жны!

v.t. уч|и́тывать, -е́сть +*d.*

heedful [ˈhiːdfʊl] *adj.* внима́тельный (*к чему*); предусмотри́тельный.

heedfulness [ˈhiːdfʊlnɪs] *n.* внима́тельность, забо́тливость, осмотри́тельность.

heedless [ˈhiːdlɪs] *adj.* беззабо́тный; беспе́чный; **~ of danger** пренебрега́ющий опа́сностями.

heedlessness [ˈhiːdlɪsnɪs] *n.* неосмотри́тельность; неосторо́жность; беззабо́тность.

hee-haw [ˈhiːhɔː] *n.* и-а (*крик осла*); (*laugh*) гру́бый смех.

heel[1] [hiːl] *n.* **1.** (*part of foot*) пя́тка; **he arrived on John's ~s** он пришёл вслед за Джо́ном; **the dog followed at, on his ~s** соба́ка сле́довала за ним по пята́м; **he called the dog to ~** он позва́л соба́ку «к ноге́»; **he fell head over ~s** он полете́л вверх торма́шками; **he kicked up his ~s and ran** он побежа́л — то́лько пя́тки засверка́ли; **they laid him by the ~s** они́ его́ арестова́ли/схвати́ли; **he was left to cool his ~s** ему́ остава́лось то́лько ждать; **he took to his ~s** он бро́сился наутёк; **he showed a clean pair of ~s** то́лько его́ и ви́дели; **he turned on his ~** он кру́то поверну́лся; **they suffered under the ~ of a tyrant** они́ страда́ли под и́гом тира́на. **2.** (*of a shoe*) каблу́к; набо́йка; **these shoes are down at ~** у э́тих ту́фель сби́лись каблуки́. **3.** (*of a stocking*) пя́тка. **4.** (*US sl., cad*) хам, подо́нок.

v.t. **1.: ~ a stocking** вяза́ть, с- пя́тку чулка́. **2.: ~ shoes** ста́вить, по- набо́йки/каблуки́ на ту́фли. **3.: ~ a football** уд|ар́ять, -а́рить мяч пя́ткой.

heel[2] [hiːl] *v.i.* **the ship ~ed over** су́дно накрени́лось.

hefty [ˈheftɪ] *adj.* здорове́нный; ро́слый.

Hegelian [heɪˈgiːlɪən] *adj.* гегелья́нский.

Hegelianism [heɪˈgiːlɪənˌɪz(ə)m] *n.* гегелья́нство.

hegemony [hɪˈdʒemənɪ, -ˈgemənɪ] *n.* гегемо́ния.

heifer [ˈhefə(r)] *n.* тёлка, не́тель.

heigh-ho [ˈheɪˈhəʊ] *int.* эх!; ох-ох-ох!

height [haɪt] *n.* **1.** высота́; (*of pers.*) рост; **he was six feet in ~** он был ро́стом в 6 фу́тов; **a wall six feet in ~** стена́ высото́й в 6 фу́тов; **he drew himself up to his full ~** он встал во весь рост; **the house stands at a ~ of 500 feet** дом нахо́дится на высоте́ 500 фу́тов; **he fell from a great ~** он упа́л с большо́й высоты́; **the plane is losing ~** самолёт теря́ет высоту́. **2.** (*high ground*) верши́на, верху́шка. **3.** (*utmost degree*) вы́сшая сте́пень; **the ~ of folly** верх глу́пости; **the ~ of fashion** после́дний крик мо́ды; **the gale was at its ~** шторм был в разга́ре.

heighten [ˈhaɪt(ə)n] *v.t.* (*make higher*) пов|ыша́ть, -ы́сить; (*increase*) усили|вать, -ть; **~ed colour** (*of face*) румя́нец.

v.i. (*fig.*) уси́ливаться (*impf.*).

heinous [ˈheɪnəs, ˈhiːnəs] *adj.* гну́сный, омерзи́тельный.

heinousness [ˈheɪnəsnɪs, ˈhiːnəsnɪs] *n.* гну́сность, омерзи́тельность.

heir [eə(r)] *n.* насле́дник; **~ apparent** прямо́й/непосре́дственный насле́дник; **~ presumptive** предполага́емый насле́дник; (*fig.*): **the ills that flesh is ~ to** несча́стья, угото́ванные ро́ду челове́ческому.

heiress [ˈeərɪs] *n.* насле́дница.

heirloom [ˈeəluːm] *n.* фами́льная рели́квия.

heist [haɪst] *n.* (*US sl.*) ограбле́ние.

Helen [ˈhelɪn] *n.* Еле́на; **~ of Troy** Еле́на Прекра́сная.

helical [ˈhelɪk(ə)l] *adj.* спира́льный, вито́й.

helicopter [ˈhelɪˌkɒptə(r)] *n.* вертолёт.

v.t. перебр|а́сывать, -о́сить на вертолёте/вертолётах.

heliograph [ˈhiːlɪəˌgrɑːf] *n.* гелио́граф.

heliotrope [ˈhiːlɪəˌtrəʊp, ˈhel-] *n.* гелиотро́п.

adj. (*colour*) лило́вый.

heliport [ˈhelɪˌpɔːt] *n.* вертодро́м, вертолётная ста́нция.

helium [ˈhiːlɪəm] *n.* ге́лий.

helix [ˈhiːlɪks] *n.* спира́ль; завито́к.

hell [hel] *n.* **1.** (*place or state*) ад; **he went through ~** он перенёс му́ки а́да; **he made her life a ~ (on earth)** он преврати́л её жизнь в су́щий ад; **I gave him ~** (*coll.*) я за́дал ему́ жа́ру; **he hasn't a hope in ~** (*coll.*) ни черта́ у него́ не вы́йдет; **he will raise ~** (*coll.*) он подни́мет стра́шный шум. **2.** (*gambling-~*) иго́рный прито́н. **3.** (*coll. or sl., expr. vexation or emphasis*) **oh ~!** чёрт возьми́!; **go to ~!** иди́ к чёрту; **what the ~ do you want?** что вам ну́жно, чёрт возьми́/побери́?; **what the ~!** (*sc. does it matter*) како́го чёрта!; **I wish to ~ I'd never done it!** чёрт меня́ попу́тал!; **'Do you agree?' — 'Like ~ I do!'** (*sc. not at all*) «Вы согла́сны?» — «Чёрта с два!»; **it hurts like ~** черто́вски бо́льно; **to ~ with it!** чёрт с ним/ней!; **they made the ~ of a noise** они́ ужа́сно шуме́ли; **we had the ~ of a time** мы повесели́лись на всю кату́шку; **all ~ broke loose** начала́сь свистопля́ска; **he rode ~ for leather** он мча́лся сломя́ го́лову; **just for the ~ of it** за здо́рово живёшь; **come ~ or high water** будь, что бу́дет.

cpds. **~-bent** *adj.* с дья́вольским упо́рством (добива́ющийся чего́-н.); **~-cat** *n.* ве́дьма; **~-fire** *n.* а́дский ого́нь; **~-hound** *n.* дья́вол, злоде́й; **~-raiser** *n.* бузотёр, скандали́ст.

Hellas [ˈheləs] *n.* Элла́да.

Hellene [ˈheliːn] *n.* э́ллин.

Hellenic [heˈlenɪk, -ˈliːnɪk] *adj.* э́ллинский.

Hellenism [ˈhelɪˌnɪz(ə)m] *n.* эллини́зм.

Hellenist [ˈhelɪnɪst] *n.* эллини́ст.

Hellenistic [ˌhelɪˈnɪstɪk] *adj.* эллинисти́ческий.

Hellenize [ˈhelɪˌnaɪz] *v.t.* подверга́ть (*impf.*) гре́ческому влия́нию.

Hellespont [ˈhelɪˌspɒnt] *n.* Геллеспо́нт.

hellish [ˈhelɪʃ] *adj.* а́дский.

hello [həˈləʊ] *int.* (*greeting*) здра́сте!; приве́т; (*on telephone*) алло́!; (*expr. surprise*) вот те на́!

cpd. **~-girl** *n.* (*coll., operator*) телефони́стка.

helm [helm] *n.* (*tiller*) руль, ру́мпель (*both m.*); **take the ~** (*lit., fig.*) стать (*pf.*) у штурва́ла (*or* у корми́ла правле́ния); (*fig.*) **man at the ~** ко́рмчий.

cpd. **~-sman** *n.* рулево́й.

helmet [ˈhelmɪt] *n.* шлем; (*modern soldier's or fireman's*) ка́ска; **sun ~** тропи́ческий шлем.

helminthology [ˌhelmɪnˈθɒlədʒɪ] *n.* гельминтоло́гия.

helot [ˈhelət] *n.* идо́т, раб.

helotry [ˈhelətrɪ] *n.* ра́бство.

help [help] *n.* **1.** (*assistance*) по́мощь; **he walks with the ~ of a stick** он хо́дит с па́лкой; **she manages without** (*domestic*) **~** она́ обхо́дится без прислу́ги; **can I be of (any) ~?** я могу́ вам че́м-нибудь помо́чь?; **your advice was a great ~ to us** вы о́чень помогли́ нам сове́том; **they were not (of) much ~ to me** они́ мне не осо́бенно помогли́; они́ ма́ло что могли́ сде́лать. **2.** (*remedy*): **there's no ~ for it** ничего́ не поде́лаешь. **3.** (*domestic servant*) прислу́га.

v.t. **1.** (*assist*) пом|ога́ть, -о́чь; **please ~ me up** помоги́те мне, пожа́луйста, подня́ться; **he ~ed her out of the car** он помо́г ей вы́йти из маши́ны; **he ~ed her off with her coat** он помо́г ей снять пальто́. **2.** (*alleviate*) облегч|а́ть, -и́ть. **3.** (*serve with food etc.*) уго|ща́ть, -сти́ть; положи́ть/дать (*pf.*) (*что кому*); **may I ~ you to salad?** могу́ я положи́ть вам немно́го сала́та?; **~ yourself!** угоща́йтесь!; бери́те, пожа́луйста!; **he ~ed himself to the spoons** он стащи́л ло́жки (*coll.*). **4.** (*avoid, prevent; also v.i.*): **I can't ~ it** я не могу́ ничего́ поде́лать; от меня́ э́то не зави́сит; **I can't ~ laughing** я не могу́ удержа́ться от сме́ха; я не могу́ не смея́ться; **I won't go a step farther than I can ~** я не сде́лаю ни одного́ ли́шнего ша́га; **don't stay longer than you can ~** не остава́йтесь до́льше, чем на́до; **it can't be ~ed** ничего́ не поде́лаешь. **5.: so ~ me (God)!** да помо́жет мне Бог!

v.i. (*avail, be of use*) быть поле́зным; **crying won't ~** слеза́ми го́рю не помо́жешь.

cpds. **~-mate, ~-meet** *nn.* подру́га жи́зни.

helper ['helpə(r)] *n.* помо́щник, подру́чный.

helpful ['helpfʊl] *adj.* поле́зный; (*obliging*) услу́жливый.

helpfulness ['helpfʊlnɪs] *n.* поле́зность; услу́жливость.

helping ['helpɪŋ] *n.* по́рция; таре́лка (*чего*).

adj.: **she lent a ~ hand** она́ протяну́ла ру́ку по́мощи.

helpless ['helplɪs] *adj.* беспо́мощный, бесси́льный.

helplessly ['helplɪslɪ] *adv.*: **~ drunk** пьян в сте́льку; **he was laughing ~** он смея́лся до упа́ду.

helplessness ['helplɪsnɪs] *n.* беспо́мощность, бесси́лие.

Helsinki ['helsɪŋkɪ, hel'sɪŋkɪ] *n.* Хе́льсинки (*m. indecl.*); (*attr.*) хе́льсинский.

helter-skelter [,heltə'skeltə(r)] *adv.* беспоря́дочно (и поспе́шно); врассыпну́ю.

helve [helv] *n.*: **throw the ~ after the hatchet** ≃ махну́ть (*pf.*) на всё руко́й.

hem [hem] *n.* край, кайма́.

v.t. **1.** (*sew the edge of*) подш|ива́ть, -и́ть; подруб|а́ть, -и́ть. **2.: ~ in, ~ about, ~ round** окруж|а́ть, -и́ть.

cpds. **~-line** *n.* ≃ длина́ ю́бки; **~-stitch** *n.* подру́бочный шов; *v.t.* подш|ива́ть, -и́ть.

hema-, hemo- ['hi:məʊ] = **h(a)ema-, h(a)emo-**

hemiplegia [,hemɪ'pli:dʒɪə] *n.* гемипле́гия.

hemisphere ['hemɪ,sfɪə(r)] *n.* полуша́рие.

hemispherical [,hemɪ'sferɪk(ə)l] *adj.* полусфери́ческий.

hemistich ['hemɪstɪk] *n.* полусти́шие.

hemlock ['hemlɒk] *n.* болиголо́в, цику́та.

hemp [hemp] *n.* (*plant*) конопля́; (*fibre*) пенька́; **Indian ~** канна́бис.

hempen ['hempən] *adj.* конопля́ный; пенько́вый.

hen [hen] *n.* (*domestic fowl*) ку́рица; (*female of bird species*) пти́ца-са́мка.

cpds. **~-bane** *n.* белена́; **~-blindness** *n.* кури́ная слепота́; **~-coop, ~-house** *nn.* куря́тник; **~-party** *n.* (*coll.*) «деви́чник»; **~pecked** *adj.* под каблуко́м у жены́; **~-roost** *n.* насе́ст.

hence [hens] *adv.* (*from here*) отсю́да; (*liter.*) отсе́ль; (*from now*): **3 years ~** че́рез три го́да; (*consequently*) отсю́да, сле́довательно.

cpds. **~forth, ~forward** *advs.* впредь, с э́того вре́мени.

henchman ['hentʃmən] *n.* приспе́шник.

henna ['henə] *n.* хна.

v.t.: **~ed hair** во́лосы, кра́шенные хной.

Henry ['henrɪ] *n.* Ге́нрих.

hepatitis [,hepə'taɪtɪs] *n.* гепати́т.

heptagon ['heptəgən] *n.* семиуго́льник.

her [hɜ:(r), hə(r)] *poss. adj.* её; (*referring to subj. of sentence*) свой.

herald ['her(ə)ld] *n.* (*official*) член геральди́ческой пала́ты; (*messenger, forerunner*) геро́льд, ве́стник.

v.t. возве|ща́ть, -сти́ть; предвеща́ть (*impf.*).

heraldic [he'rældɪk] *adj.* геральди́ческий.

heraldry ['herəldrɪ] *n.* гера́льдика.

herb [hɜ:b] *n.* трава́, лека́рственное расте́ние; (*pl., cul.*) коре́н|ья (g. -ев); ку́хонные тра́вы.

herbaceous [hɜ:'beɪʃəs] *adj.* травяно́й; **~ border** цвето́чный бордю́р

herbal ['hɜ:b(ə)l] *n.* тра́вник; **~ medicine** траволече́ние.

adj. травяно́й.

herbalist ['hɜ:bəlɪst] *n.* специали́ст по (лека́рственным) тра́вам.

herbarium [hɜ:'beərɪəm] *n.* герба́рий.

herbicide ['hɜ:bɪ,saɪd] *n.* гербици́д.

herbivore ['hɜ:bɪ,vɔ:(r)] *n.* травоя́дное живо́тное.

herbivorous [,hɜ:'bɪvərəs] *adj.* травоя́дный.

Herculean [,hɜ:kjʊ'li:ən, -'kju:lɪən] *adj.* геркуле́сов; (*fig.*): **~ efforts** титани́ческие уси́лия.

Hercules ['hɜ:kjʊ,li:z] *n.* Геркуле́с; **the labours of ~** по́двиги Гера́кла.

herd [hɜ:d] *n.* (*animals*) ста́до; (*people*) толпа́; **the common ~** чернь, плебс; **~ instinct** ста́дное чу́вство.

v.t. сгоня́ть, согна́ть (вме́сте).

v.i. (*fig.*) ходи́ть (*indet.*) ста́дом/ско́пом.

cpd. **~-sman** *n.* пасту́х.

here [hɪə(r)] *n.*: **from ~ to there** отсю́да — туда́/доту́да; **my house is near ~** мой дом ря́дом.

adv. **1.** (*in this place*) здесь; (*coll.*) тут; **the book doesn't belong ~** э́той кни́ге здесь не ме́сто; **~ below** (*on earth*) в э́том ми́ре. **2.** (*to this place, in this direction*): **come ~!** иди́те сюда́!; **look ~!** (*lit.*) посмотри́те сюда́; (*expr. emph., impatience etc.*) послу́шайте! **3.** (*demonstrative*): **~ I am!** вот и я!; я тут!; **~ he comes!** вот и он!; **~ we are at last!** наконе́ц-то (мы) пришли́/прие́хали/при́были; **~ we go (again)!** (*coll., fig.*) ≃ опя́ть два́дцать пять!; **~ goes!** (*coll.*) будь что бу́дет!; **~'s how it happened** вот как э́то случи́лось; **~'s to our victory!** за на́шу побе́ду!; **Mr Smith ~ is a surgeon** вот ми́стер Смит, он хиру́рг. **4.** (*with offers*): **~ you are!** пожа́луйста; **~ is my hand!** вот вам моя́ рука́. **5.** (*at this point*): **~ she began to cry** тут она́ запла́кала. **6.** (*for emph.*): **~, take this** вот, возьми́те э́то. **7.: same ~!** и я то́же! **8.** (*misc. phrr.*): **he looked ~ and there** он поиска́л там и сям; **I've been ~, there and everywhere** я был повсю́ду; **it's neither ~ nor there** э́то здесь ни при чём; э́то ни к селу́ ни к го́роду.

hereabouts [,hɪərə'baʊts] *adv.* побли́зости.

hereafter [hɪər'ɑ:ftə(r)] *n.*: **the ~** загро́бная жизнь.

adv. впосле́дствии.

hereby [hɪə'baɪ] *adv.* сим (*arch.*); э́тим; настоя́щим.

hereditament [,herɪ'dɪtəmənt, hɪ'redɪ-] *n.* иму́щество, мо́гущее быть предме́том насле́дования; насле́дуемое (иму́щество).

hereditary [hɪ'redɪtərɪ] *adj.* насле́дственный.

heredity [hɪ'redɪtɪ] *n.* насле́дственность.

herein [hɪə'rɪn] *adv.*: **I enclose ~ ...** при сём прилага́ю…

hereinafter [,hɪərɪn'ɑ:ftə(r)] *adv.* ни́же, в дальне́йшем.

hereof [hɪər'ɒv] *adj.* сего́; настоя́щего (*документа и т.п.*).

heresy ['herəsɪ] *n.* е́ресь.

heretic ['herətɪk] *n.* ерети́|к (*fem.* -чка).

heretical [hɪ'retɪk(ə)l] *adj.* ерети́ческий.

hereto [hɪə'tu:] *adv.* к сему́ (*arch.*); к э́тому.

heretofore [,hɪətʊ'fɔ:(r)] *adv.* пре́жде; до сих пор.

hereupon [,hɪərə'pɒn] *adv.* вслед за э́тим.

herewith [hɪə'wɪð, -'wɪθ] *adv.* при сём.

heritable ['herɪtəb(ə)l] *adj.* (*capable of being inherited*) насле́дуемый; (*capable of inheriting*) мо́гущий насле́довать.

heritage ['herɪtɪdʒ] *n.* насле́дство; (*fig.*) насле́дие.

herm [hɜ:m] *n.* ге́рма.

hermaphrodite [hɜ:'mæfrə,daɪt] *n.* гермафроди́т.

hermaphroditic [hɜ:,mæfrə'dɪtɪk] *adj.* двупо́лый; (*fig.*) гибри́дный.

hermaphroditism [hɜ:'mæfrədɪt,ɪz(ə)m] *n.* гермафроди́тизм.

Hermes ['hɜ:mi:z] *n.* Герме́с.

hermetic [hɜ:'metɪk] *adj.* гермети́ческий; **~ally sealed** герметизо́ванный.

hermit ['hɜ:mɪt] *n.* отше́льник.

cpd. **~-crab** *n.* рак-отше́льник.

hermitage ['hɜ:mɪtɪdʒ] *n.* оби́тель/прию́т отше́льника; **H~** (*museum*) Эрмита́ж.

hernia ['hɜ:nɪə] *n.* гры́жа.

hero ['hɪərəʊ] *n.* геро́й.

cpd. **~-worship** *n.* преклоне́ние пе́ред геро́ями; (*pej.*) культ ли́чности.

Herod ['herəd] *n.* И́род.

heroic [hɪ'rəʊɪk] *adj.* геро́йский, герои́ческий; **~ couplet** герои́ческий двусти́х.

heroics [hɪ'rəʊɪks] *n.* напы́щенность, ходу́льность; треску́чие фра́зы (*f. pl.*).

heroin ['herəʊɪn] *n.* геро́ин.
heroine ['herəʊɪn] *n.* герои́ня.
heroism ['herəʊˌɪz(ə)m] *n.* герои́зм.
heron ['herən] *n.* ца́пля.
herpes ['hɜːpiːz] *n.* лиша́й.
herpetic [hɜː'petɪk] *adj.* герпети́ческий.
herring ['herɪŋ] *n.* сельдь; (*as food*) селёдка; **red ~** (*fig.*) отвлека́ющий манёвр.
cpds. **~-bone** *n.* & *adj.* (*stitch*) «в ёлочку»; (*archit. pattern*) кла́дка «в ёлку»; **~-fishery** *n.* лов се́льди.
hers [hɜːz] *pron.*: **is this handkerchief ~?** э́то её плато́к?; **your dress is prettier than ~** у вас пла́тье краси́вее, чем у неё; **I don't like that husband of ~** я не люблю́ её му́жа!; **some friends of ~** её друзья́.
herself [hə'self] *pron.* **1.** (*refl.*) себя́, -ся (*suff.*); **she fell down and hurt ~** она́ упа́ла и ушиблась. **2.** (*emph.*): **she said so ~** она́ сама́ э́то сказа́ла; **I saw the Queen ~** я ви́дел саму́ короле́ву. **3.** (*after preps.*): **she lives by ~** она́ живёт одна́; **can she do it by ~?** она́ мо́жет сама́ э́то сде́лать?; **she kept it to ~** она́ не дели́лась э́тим ни с кем; она́ об э́том пома́лкивала. **4.** (*her normal state*): **she is not ~ today** сего́дня она́ сама́ не своя́; **she will soon come to ~** она́ ско́ро придёт в себя́.
hertz [hɜːts] *n.* герц.
hesitanc|e ['hezɪtəns], **-y** ['hezɪtənsɪ] *nn.* колеба́ние, нереши́тельность.
hesitant ['hezɪt(ə)nt] *adj.* колеблющийся, нереши́тельный.
hesitate ['heziˌteɪt] *v.i.* колеба́ться (*imp.*); **don't ~ to ask** проси́те, не смуща́йтесь!; не стесня́йтесь спроси́ть; **I ~ to say this** не зна́ю, сле́дует ли мне об э́том говори́ть; **he who ~s is lost** ≃ промедле́ние сме́рти подо́бно.
hesitation [ˌhezɪ'teɪʃ(ə)n] *n.* колеба́ние, сомне́ние.
Hesperides [he'sperɪˌdiːz] *n.* Гесперид|ы (*pl.*, *g.*—).
Hesperus ['hespərəs] *n.* вече́рняя звезда́, Вене́ра.
Hesse ['hesə] *n.* Ге́ссен.
hessian ['hesɪən] *n.* (*cloth*) мешкови́на; джу́товая ткань.
adj. **(H~)** ге́ссенский; **H~ boots** высо́кие сапоги́; ботфо́рты (*m. pl.*).
het [het] *adj.*: **he got ~ up** он распсихова́лся (*sl.*).
het|aera [hɪ'tɪərə], **-aira** [hɪ'taɪrə] *n.* гете́ра.
heterodox ['hetərəʊˌdɒks] *adj.* неортодокса́льный.
heterodoxy ['hetərəʊˌdɒksɪ] *n.* неортодокса́льность.
heterodyne ['hetərəʊˌdaɪn] *adj.* гетероди́нный.
heterogeneity [ˌhetərəʊdʒɪ'niːɪtɪ] *n.* неодноро́дность, разнохара́ктерность.
heterogeneous [ˌhetərəʊ'dʒiːnɪəs] *adj.* неодноро́дный, разнохара́ктерный.
heterosexual [ˌhetərəʊ'seksjʊəl] *n.* гетеросексуали́ст (*fem.* -ка).
adj. гетеросексуа́льный.
heterosexuality [ˌhetərəʊseksjʊ'ælɪtɪ] *n.* гетеросексуа́льность.
hetman ['hetmən] *n.* ге́тман.
heuristic [hjʊə'rɪstɪk] *adj.* эвристи́ческий.
hew [hjuː] *v.t.* руби́ть (*impf.*); **they ~ed down a tree** они́ сруби́ли де́рево; **a branch had been ~n off** кто́-то сруби́л ве́тку; (*fig.*): **he ~ed his way through** он проложи́л себе́ доро́гу; **he must ~ out his own career** он до́лжен сам проби́ться в жи́зни.
hewer ['hjuːə(r)] *n.*: **~s of wood and drawers of water** (*fig.*) тру́женики (*m. pl.*), работя́ги (*c.g.*, *pl.*).
hexagon ['heksəgən] *n.* шестиуго́льник.
hexagonal [ˌhek'sægən(ə)l] *adj.* шестиуго́льный.
hexameter [hek'sæmɪtə(r)] *n.* гекза́метр.
hey [heɪ] *int.* эй!; **~ presto!** але́-гоп!
heyday ['heɪdeɪ] *n.* расцве́т, зени́т.
hi [haɪ] *int.* **1.** (*to call attention*) эй! **2.** (*US*, *in greeting*, *also* **~ there!**) приве́т!; салю́т!
hiatus [haɪ'eɪtəs] *n.* **1.** (*gap*) про́пуск, пробе́л. **2.** (*between vowels*) зия́ние.
hibernate ['haɪbəˌneɪt] *v.i.* находи́ться (*impf.*) в зи́мней спя́чке; **these animals ~** э́ти живо́тные впада́ют в зи́мнюю спя́чку.
hibernation [ˌhaɪbə'neɪʃ(ə)n] *n.* зи́мняя спя́чка.
Hibernian [haɪ'bɜːnɪən] *n.* (*arch. or joc.*) ирла́нд|ец (*fem.* -ка).
adj. ирла́ндский.
hibiscus [hɪ'bɪskəs] *n.* гиби́скус.
hicc|up, -ough ['hɪkʌp] *n.* ико́та; (*slight delay*) запи́нка.
v.i. ик|а́ть, -ну́ть.
hick [hɪk] *n.* (*US coll.*) дереве́нщина (*c.g.*); **a ~ town** захолу́стный го́род.
hickory ['hɪkərɪ] *n.* пека́н.
hidalgo [hɪ'dælgəʊ] *n.* ида́льго (*m. indecl.*).
hide[1] [haɪd] *n.* ко́жа, шку́ра; **I'll tan his ~ for him** я дам ему́ взбу́чку; **he lied to save his ~** он солга́л, что́бы спасти́ свою́ шку́ру.
cpd. **~-bound** *adj.* ограни́ченный, с у́зким кругозо́ром; закосне́вший, окостене́лый.
hide[2] [haɪd] *v.t.* пря́тать, с-; скры|ва́ть, -ть; **~ one's face** закр|ыва́ть, -ы́ть лицо́ рука́ми; **~ one's feelings** скры|ва́ть, -ть свои́ чу́вства; **the house was hidden from the road** дом не́ был ви́ден с доро́ги; **clouds hid the sun** ту́чи закры́ли со́лнце; **a hidden meaning** скры́тый смысл.
v.i. пря́таться, с-.
cpds. **~-and-seek** *n.* пря́т|ки (*pl.*, *g.* -ок); **~away, ~out** *nn.* укры́тие.
hideous ['hɪdɪəs] *adj.* уро́дливый, безобра́зный.
hideousness ['hɪdɪəsnɪs] *n.* уро́дливость, безобра́зие.
hidey-hole ['haɪdɪˌhəʊl] *n.* (*coll.*) укры́тие.
hiding[1] ['haɪdɪŋ] *n.* (*coll.*, *thrashing*): **she gave him a good ~** она́ его́ вы́порола как сле́дует.
hiding[2] ['haɪdɪŋ] *n.* (*concealment*) укры́тие; **he went into ~** он скры́лся; он ушёл в подпо́лье; **he is in ~** он скрыва́ется.
cpd. **~-place** *n.* укры́тие.
hierarchical [ˌhaɪə'rɑːkɪk(ə)l] *adj.* иерархи́ческий, иерархи́чный.
hierarchy ['haɪəˌrɑːkɪ] *n.* иера́рхия.
hieratic [ˌhaɪə'rætɪk] *adj.* иерати́ческий.
hieroglyph ['haɪərəglɪf] *n.* иеро́глиф.
hieroglyphic [ˌhaɪərə'glɪfɪk] *adj.* иероглифи́ческий.
hieroglyphics [ˌhaɪərə'glɪfɪks] *n.* иеро́глифика; иерати́ческие письм|ена́ (*pl.*, *g.* -ён).
hierophant ['haɪərəˌfænt] *n.* верхо́вный жрец.
hi-fi ['haɪfaɪ] *n.* (*coll.*) прои́грыватель (*m.*) с высо́кой то́чностью воспроизведе́ния зву́ка.
higgledy-piggledy [ˌhɪgəldɪ'pɪgəldɪ] *adj.* беспоря́дочный; сумбу́рный.
adv. впереме́шку; беспоря́дочно.
high [haɪ] *n.* **1.** (*peak*) вы́сшая то́чка; **prices reached a new ~** це́ны дости́гли небыва́ло высо́кого у́ровня. **2.** (*anticyclone*) антицикло́н. **3.: on ~** на небеса́х; **from on ~** свы́ше.
adj. **1.** (*tall*, *elevated*) высо́кий (*also mus.*); **a ~ building** высо́кое/высо́тное зда́ние; **a ~ chair** высо́кий стул; **ten feet ~** высото́й в 10 фу́тов; **~ jump** прыжо́к в высоту́; **he's for the ~ jump** (*sl.*) ему́ попадёт/влети́т; **~ tide, water** больша́я вода́, прили́в; **~ and dry** вы́брошенный на бе́рег; (*fig.*) на мели́; **he acted with a ~ hand** он вёл себя́ вла́стно; **don't get on your ~ horse** (*coll.*) не ва́жничайте; (*geog.*): **~ latitudes** высо́кие широ́ты. **2.** (*chief*, *important*): **~ altar** гла́вный престо́л; **~ command** вы́сшее кома́ндование; **~ days and holidays** выходны́е дни и пра́здники; **~ life** све́тская жизнь; **H~ Mass** торже́ственная ме́сса; **~ and mighty** (*coll.*, *arrogant*) надме́нный, вла́стный; **the Most H~** Всевы́шний; **in ~ places** (*fig.*) в верха́х, в вы́сших сфе́рах; **~ priest** первосвяще́нник; **~ school** сре́дняя шко́ла; **~ society** вы́сшее о́бщество; **the ~ spot of the evening** гвоздь програ́ммы; **~ street** гла́вная у́лица; **~ table** почётный стол; **~ tea** ≃ по́лдник; **~ treason** госуда́рственная изме́на. **3.** (*greater than average*; *extreme*): **~ antiquity** седа́я старина́; **~ blood-pressure** высо́кое (кровяно́е) давле́ние; **a ~ colour** (*complexion*) я́ркий румя́нец; **in the ~est degree** в вы́сшей сте́пени; **in ~ dudgeon** уязвлённый до глубины́ души́; **held in ~ esteem** по́льзующийся больши́м уваже́нием; **~ explosive** дробя́щее (бриза́нтовое) взры́вчатое вещество́; **in ~ favour** в большо́м фаво́ре; **in ~ gear** на большо́й ско́рости; **~ jinks** (*coll.*) шу́мное весе́лье; **they are having a ~ old time** они́ веселя́тся вовсю́; **it is a ~ price to pay** сли́шком уж велика́ цена́; **on the ~ seas** в откры́том

мо́ре; **in ~ spirits** в отли́чном/припо́днятом настрое́нии; **~ tension** си́льное напряже́ние; **H~ Tory** кра́йний консерва́тор; **a ~ wind** си́льный ве́тер. **4.** (*at its peak*): **~ noon** по́лдень; **~ summer** середи́на/разга́р ле́та; **it is ~ time I was gone** мне уже́ давно́ пора́ идти́. **5.** (*noble, lofty*): **a ~ calling** высо́кое призва́ние; **a man of ~ character** челове́к высо́ких мора́льных при́нципов. **6.** (*of food*) (*tainted*) с душко́м. **7.** (*intoxicated*) навеселе́; (*on drugs*) в дурма́не.

adv. **1.** (*aloft; at or to a height*): **~ up** высоко́; (*of direction*) ввысь; **the ball rose ~ into the air** мяч взлете́л высоко́ в во́здух; **you must aim ~** (*fig.*) вы должны́ ме́тить вы́ше; **he held his head ~** (*fig.*) он ходи́л с высоко́ по́днятой голово́й; **I searched ~ and low** я иска́л повсю́ду. **2.** (*at a ~ level*): **the seas were running ~** мо́ре бы́ло неспоко́йно; **feelings ran ~** стра́сти разгора́лись; **he played ~** (*for high stakes*) он игра́л по-кру́пному.

cpds. **~ball** *n.* (*US*) хайбо́л; **~-born** *adj.* зна́тного происхожде́ния; **~brow** *n.* интеллектуа́л; *adj.* интеллектуа́льный, серьёзный; претенцио́зный; **~-calorie** *adj.* калори́йный; **~-class** *adj.* высо́кого кла́сса; **~-falutin(g)** *adj.* (*coll.*) высокопа́рный, велере́чивый; **~-fidelity** *adj.* с высокой то́чностью воспроизведе́ния; **~-flown** *adj.* высокопа́рный; витиева́тый; **~-flyer, ~-flier** *nn.* (*pers. likely to succeed*) подаю́щий больши́е наде́жды (*or* многообеща́ющий) челове́к; **~-frequency** *adj.* коротково́лновый, высокочасто́тный; **~-grade** *adj.* высокока́чественный; **~-handed** *adj.* вла́стный; своево́льный; бесцеремо́нный; **~-hat** *adj.* (*US coll.*) спеси́вый, надму́тый; *v.t.* (*US coll.*) относи́ться (*impf.*) высокоме́рно к+*d.*; **~land** *adj.* го́рский; **H~lander** *n.* го́р|ец (*fem.* -янка); **the H~lands** *n. pl.* се́вер и се́веро-за́пад Шотла́ндии; **~-level** *adj.* на высо́ком у́ровне; **~light** *n.* (*in painting*) блик; (*phot.*) светово́й эффе́кт; (*fig.*) кульминацио́нный моме́нт; *v.t.* (*fig., emphasize*) выделя́ть, вы́делить; заостр|я́ть, -и́ть внима́ние на+*p.*; **~-minded** *adj.* благоро́дный, великоду́шный; **~-necked** *adj.* (*of dress*) закры́тый; **~-pitched** *adj.* (*of a sound*) высо́кий; (*of a roof*) с круты́ми ска́тами; **~-powered** *adj.* (*of an engine*) большо́й мо́щности; (*of a pers.*) динами́чный, операти́вный; **~-pressure** *adj.* (*aggressive*) агресси́вный; **~-pressure work** напряжённная рабо́та; **~-priced** *adj.* дорогосто́ящий; **~-ranking** *adj.* высокопоста́вленный; **~-rise** *adj.*: **~-rise apartment blocks** высо́тные многокварти́рные дома́; **~road** *n.* шоссе́ (*indecl.*); **~-sounding** *adj.* напы́щенный; **~-sounding words** гро́мкие слова́; **~-speed** *adj.* сверхскоростно́й, высокоскоростно́й; **~-spirited** *adj.* ре́звый; разыгра́вшийся; **~-technology** *n.* высокосло́жная техноло́гия; **~-up** *n.* **the ~-ups** верхи́ (*m. pl.*); *adj.* высокопоста́вленный; **~-water line** *n.* ли́ния наибо́льшего прили́ва; **~-water mark** *n.* у́ровень по́лной воды́; (*fig.*) верши́на; **~way** *n.* шоссе́ (*indecl.*): **H~way Code** пра́вила у́личного движе́ния; **~way robbery** (*lit.*) грабёж на большо́й доро́ге; (*fig.*) грабёж, обира́ловка; **~wayman** *n.* разбо́йник (с большо́й доро́ги).

higher ['haɪə(r)] *adj.* (*senior, advanced*) вы́сший; **a ~ card** (*in the pack*) ста́ршая ка́рта.

adv.: **~ up the hill** вы́ше на холме́ (*or* по скло́ну); **~ up the road** да́льше по э́той доро́ге/у́лице.

highly ['haɪlɪ] *adv.* весьма́, о́чень; **~ paid** высокоопла́чиваемый; **~ polished** (*lit.*) хорошо́ отполиро́ванный; тща́тельно отде́ланный; **he speaks ~ of you** он о вас о́чень хорошо́ отзыва́ется; **~ strung** взви́нченный; нерво́зный; **she is ~ thought of** её о́чень це́нят.

highness ['haɪnɪs] *n.* **1.** (*loftiness*) высота́, возвы́шенность. **2.** (*title*) высо́чество; **His Royal H~** Его́ Короле́вское Высо́чество.

hijack ['haɪdʒæk] *n.* уго́н, похище́ние.

v.t. уг|оня́ть, -на́ть; пох|ища́ть, -и́тить.

hijacker ['haɪˌdʒækə(r)] *n.* уго́нщик, похити́тель (*m.*).

hike[1] [haɪk] *n.* (*coll., walk*) экску́рсия пешко́м.

v.i. броди́ть (*impf.*).

hike[2] [haɪk] (*US coll.*) *n.* (*rise*) подъём.

v.t. (*raise*) подн|има́ть, -я́ть.

hiker ['haɪkə(r)] *n.* (*coll.*) путеше́ственник, экскурса́нт.

hilarious [hɪ'leərɪəs] *adj.* весёлый, поте́шный, умори́тельный.

hilarity [hɪ'lærɪtɪ] *n.* весе́лье, потéха.

hill [hɪl] *n.* холм, приго́рок; **down the ~** с горы́, по́д гору; **as old as the ~s** ста́ро как мир; **the village lies just over the ~** дере́вня лежи́т пря́мо за холмо́м; **this car takes the ~s well** э́та маши́на хорошо́ идёт в го́ру; **up the ~** в го́ру; **up ~ and down dale** повсю́ду; **I cursed him up ~ and down dale** я клял его́ на чём свет стои́т.

cpds. **~-fort** *n.* кре́пость на холме́; **~man** *n.* жи́тель (*m.*) холми́стых мест; **~side** *n.* склон холма́; **~top** *n.* верши́на холма́.

hilliness ['hɪlɪnɪs] *n.* холми́стость.

hillock ['hɪlək] *n.* хо́лмик, бугóр.

hilly ['hɪlɪ] *adj.* холми́стый.

hilt [hɪlt] *n.* рукоя́тка, эфе́с; **proved up to the ~** (*fig.*) неопровержи́мо дока́зано.

Himalayan [ˌhɪmə'leɪən] *adj.* гимала́йский.

Himalayas [ˌhɪmə'leɪəz] *n.* Гимала́|и (*pl., g.* -ев).

himself [hɪm'self] *pron.* **1.** (*refl.*) себя́, -ся; **I hope he behaves ~** наде́юсь, что он бу́дет вести́ себя́ прили́чно. **2.** (*emph.*) сам; **he did the job ~** он сам сде́лал э́ту рабо́ту. **3.** (*after preps.*): **he lives by ~** он живёт оди́н; **he did it by ~** он сде́лал э́то сам; **he was talking to ~** он разгова́ривал сам с собо́й. **4.** (*in his normal state*): **he will see you when he is ~ again** он повида́ется с ва́ми, когда́ придёт в себя́.

hind[1] [haɪnd] *n.* (*deer*) са́мка оле́ня.

hind[2] [haɪnd] *adj.* за́дний; **the dog stood on its ~ legs** соба́ка вста́ла на за́дние ла́пы.

cpds. **~most** *adj.* са́мый после́дний/отдалённый; **devil take the ~most** го́ре неуда́чникам; спаса́йся, кто мо́жет!; **~-quarters** *n.* зад; **~sight** *n.* (*of gun*) за́дний прице́л; (*coll., wisdom after the event*): **he spoke with ~sight** он говори́л, зна́я, чем ко́нчилось де́ло.

hinder[1] ['haɪndə(r)] *adj.* за́дний.

hinder[2] ['hɪndə(r)] *v.t.* меша́ть, по-; **he ~ed me from working** он меша́л (*or* не дал) мне рабо́тать.

Hindi ['hɪndɪ] *n.* (*language*) хи́нди (*m. indecl.*).

hindrance ['hɪndrəns] *n.* поме́ха.

Hindu ['hɪndu:, -'du:] *n.* инду́с (*fem.* -ка).

adj. инду́сский.

Hinduism ['hɪndu:ˌɪz(ə)m] *n.* индуи́зм.

Hinduistic [ˌhɪndu:'ɪstɪk] *adj.* инду́сский.

Hindustani [ˌhɪndʊ'stɑ:nɪ] *n.* (*language*) хиндуста́ни (*m. indecl.*).

hinge [hɪndʒ] *n.* петля́, шарни́р; (*fig.*) сте́ржень (*m.*), кардина́льный пункт.

v.t. наве́|шивать, -сить на пе́тли.

v.i. висе́ть (*impf.*); враща́ться (*impf.*) на пе́тлях; (*fig.*) **it all ~d on this event** всё бы́ло свя́зано с э́тим собы́тием.

hinny ['hɪnɪ] *n.* лоша́к.

hint [hɪnt] *n.* (*suggestion*) намёк; **can't you take a ~?** намёка не понима́ете?; **he is always dropping ~s** он говори́т намёками; **a broad/gentle ~** я́сный/то́нкий намёк; **there was a ~ of frost** начина́ло подмора́живать; **~ of garlic** чу́точка чеснока́; (*written advice*) сове́т; **~s for housewives** сове́ты домохозя́йкам.

v.t. & i. намек|а́ть, -ну́ть на+*a.*; **I ~ed that I needed a holiday** я намекну́л, что хоте́л бы взять о́тпуск; **what are you ~ing (at)?** на что вы намека́ете?

hinterland ['hɪntəˌlænd] *n.* (*inland area*) райо́ны (*m. pl.*), удалённые от побере́жья; (*supply area*) прилега́ющие райо́ны снабже́ния.

hip[1] [hɪp] *n.* бедро́; **he stood with his hands on his ~s** он стоя́л подбоче́нясь; **what do you measure round the ~s?** како́й у вас разме́р бёдер?; **I have him on the ~** (*arch., joc.*) ≃ я положи́л его́ на лопа́тки; **he smote them ~ and thigh** (*arch., joc.*) он разби́л их на́голову.

cpds. **~-bath** *n.* сидя́чая ва́нна; **~-flask** *n.* карма́нная фля́жка; **~-joint** *n.* тазобе́дренный суста́в; **~-pocket** *n.* за́дний карма́н.

hip[2] [hɪp] *n.* (*fruit*) я́года шипо́вника.

hip[3] [hɪp] *int.*: **~, ~, hooray!** гип-гип, ура́.

hipp|ie, -y ['hɪpɪ] *n.* (*coll.*) хи́ппи (*c.g., indecl.*).
hippo ['hɪpəʊ] *n.* (*coll.*) гиппопота́м, бегемо́т.
hippodrome ['hɪpə,drəʊm] *n.* (*hist.*) ипподро́м.
hippopotamus [,hɪpə'pɒtəməs] *n.* гиппопота́м, бегемо́т.
hippy ['hɪpɪ] = **hippie**
hire ['haɪə(r)] *n.* **1.** (*payment*) по на́йму; **he worked for ~** он рабо́тал по на́йму; **the labourer is worthy of his ~** (*prov.*) како́в рабо́тник — такова́ и пла́та. **2.** (*engagement of pers.*) наём; (*of thg.*) наём, прока́т; **cars for ~** маши́ны напрока́т; **he let his boat out on ~** он сда(ва́)л свою́ ло́дку напрока́т.
v.t. **1.** (*obtain use of, employ*) нан|има́ть, -я́ть; сн|има́ть, -я́ть; **they ~d the hall for a night** они́ сня́ли зал на ве́чер; **~d help** (*domestic servant*) слуга́ (*m.*); служа́нка, домрабо́тница. **2.** (*let out for hire*) сда|ва́ть, -ть внаём/напрока́т.
cpd. **~-purchase** *n.* поку́пка в рассро́чку.
hireling ['haɪəlɪŋ] *n.* наёмник, найми́т.
hirer ['haɪərə(r)] *n.* беру́щий внаём/напрока́т; (*employer*) работода́тель (*m.*).
hiring ['haɪərɪŋ] *n.* (**~ out**) сда́ча внаём/напрока́т; (*borrowing*) наём, прока́т.
Hiroshima [,hɪrɒ'ʃi:mə, hɪ'rɒʃɪmə] *n.* Хироси́ма.
hirsute ['hɜ:sju:t] *adj.* волоса́тый, косма́тый.
his [hɪz] *pron.*: **what is ~ by right** то, что принадлежи́т ему́ по пра́ву; **my bicycle is newer than ~** у меня́ велосипе́д нове́е, чем у него́.
poss. adj. его́; (*referring to subj. of sentence*) свой.
Hispanic [hɪ'spænɪk] *adj.* испа́нский; латиноамерика́нский; **the ~ world** испа́но- и португалоязы́чный мир; **~ studies** испани́стика.
Hispanist ['hɪspənɪst] *n.* испани́ст.
hiss [hɪs] *n.* шипе́ние, свист.
v.t. (*an actor*) осви́ст|ывать, -а́ть; **he was ~ed off the stage** его́ освиста́ли.
v.i. шипе́ть, за-/про-.
historian [hɪ'stɔ:rɪən] *n.* исто́рик.
historic [hɪ'stɒrɪk] *adj.* истори́ческий; (*significant*) знамена́тельный; (*gram.*): **the ~ present** истори́ческое/повествова́тельное настоя́щее.
historical [hɪ'stɒrɪk(ə)l] *adj.* истори́ческий.
historicity [,hɪstə'rɪsɪtɪ] *n.* истори́чность.
history ['hɪstərɪ] *n.* исто́рия; **make (*or* go down in) ~** войти́ (*pf.*) в исто́рию; **~ is silent on that point** исто́рия об э́том ума́лчивает; **this chair has a ~** э́тот стул име́ет свою́ исто́рию; **that is ancient ~!** (*fig.*) э́то старо́!; **the histories of Shakespeare** истори́ческие хро́ники (*f. pl.*) Шекспи́ра.
cpd. **~-book** *n.* уче́бник исто́рии.
histrionic [,hɪstrɪ'ɒnɪk] *adj.* (*pert. to acting*) актёрский, сцени́ческий; (*stagy*) театра́льный, наи́гранный.
histrionics [,hɪstrɪ'ɒnɪks] *n.* (*performance*) представле́ние; (*behaviour*) театра́льность, наи́гранность.
hit [hɪt] *n.* (*blow*) уда́р, толчо́к; **~ man** наёмный/профессиона́льный уби́йца; (*strike or shot which reaches target*) попада́ние; (*stroke of sarcasm*) вы́пад, ко́лкость; (*coll., success*) успе́х; (*popular song*) популя́рная пе́сенка; шля́гер.
v.t. **1.** (*strike*) уд|аря́ть, -а́рить; бить, по-; сту́к|ать, -нуть; **he fell and ~ his head on a stone** он упа́л и уда́рился голово́й о ка́мень; **he was ~ on the head** его́ уда́рили по голове́; **don't ~ a man when he's down** лежа́чего не бьют; **the car ~ a tree** маши́на вре́залась в де́рево; **he ~ the nail on the head** (*fig.*) он попа́л пря́мо в то́чку; **the bullet ~ him in the shoulder** пу́ля попа́ла ему́ в плечо́; **he was ~ by a falling stone** его́ заде́ло па́дающим ка́мнем. **2.** (*fig. uses*): **you've ~ it!** вы попа́ли в то́чку; **the idea suddenly ~ me** меня́ вдруг осени́ло; **the town was ~ by an earthquake** го́род был поражён землетрясе́нием; **~ the trail, road** (*coll.*) выступа́ть, вы́ступить в похо́д; стартова́ть (*impf., pf.*); **he ~s the bottle now and again** (*coll.*) у него́ быва́ют запо́и. **3.** (*encounter*): **he ~ a bad patch** (*coll.*) он попа́л в плоху́ю полосу́.
v.i.: **he ~ on an idea** ему́ пришла́ в го́лову мысль.
with advs.: **~ back** *v.t.*: **he ~ the ball back** он отби́л мяч; **if he ~s you, ~ him back** е́сли он вас уда́рит, да́йте сда́чи; **~ off** *v.t.* (*describe aptly*) ме́тко описа́ть (*pf.*) (*or* изобрази́ть (*pf.*)); **~ it off** ла́дить (*impf.*); **~ out** *v.i.*: **he ~ out at his opponents** он дал ре́зкий отпо́р свои́м проти́вникам; **~ up** *v.t.*: **he ~ up a good score** он сыгра́л с хоро́шим счётом.
cpd. **~-or-miss** *adj.* сде́ланный как попа́ло (*or* ко́е-как).
hitch [hɪtʃ] *n.* (*jerk*) рыво́к; (*knot*) у́зел; (*temporary stoppage; snag*) заде́ржка, загво́здка; **without a ~** гла́дко, без сучка́ и задо́ринки.
v.t. **1.** (*fasten*) привя́з|ывать, -а́ть; прицеп|ля́ть, -и́ть; **~ one's wagon to a star** (*fig.*) дерза́ть (*impf.*); высоко́ ме́тить (*impf.*). **2.** (*lift*): **~ up one's trousers** подтя́|гивать, -ну́ть брю́ки. **3.** (*coll.*): **~ a lift** подъе́хать (*pf.*) на попу́тной маши́не. **4.** (*sl.*): **get ~ed** жени́ться (*impf., pf.*); вступи́ть (*pf.*) в брак.
v.i. (*coll., travel by getting free rides; also* **~-hike**) е́здить автосто́пом.
cpds. **~-hiker** *n.* (*coll.*) автосто́повец; **~-hiking** *n.* «голосова́ние», езда́ автосто́пом (*or* на попу́тных маши́нах).
hither ['hɪðə(r)] *adv.* сюда́.
cpd. **~to** *adv.* до сих пор.
Hitler|ian [,hɪt'lɪərɪən]**,-ite** ['hɪtlə,raɪt] *adjs.* ги́тлеровский.
Hitlerism ['hɪtlə,rɪz(ə)m] *n.* гитлери́зм.
Hittite ['hɪtaɪt] *n.* хетт; (*language*) хе́ттский язы́к.
adj. хе́ттский.
HIV (*abbr. of med.,* ***human immunodeficiency virus***) ВИЧ, (ви́рус иммунодефици́та челове́ка).
hive [haɪv] *n.* у́лей; (*fig.*): **the office is a ~ of industry** рабо́та в конто́ре кипи́т.
v.t. **1.**: **~ bees** сажа́ть, посади́ть пчёл в у́лей; **~ honey** запас|а́ть, -ти́ мёд в у́лей. **2.** (*fig.*): **they ~d off and formed a new party** они́ отколо́лись/отрои́лись и со́здали но́вую па́ртию; **certain jobs were ~d off to other departments** не́которые ви́ды рабо́т бы́ли пору́чены други́м отде́лам.
hives [haɪvz] *n.* (*med.*) крапи́вница.
hm [hm] *int.* гм!
ho [həʊ] *int.* (*arch., voc.*) эй; **~, ~** (*laughter*) ха-ха; **westward ~!** на за́пад!; **land ~!** земля́!
hoar [hɔ:(r)] *adj.* седо́й.
cpd. **~-frost** *n.* и́ней, и́зморозь.
hoard [hɔ:d] *n.* (та́йный) запа́с, склад.
v.t. припря́тывать (*impf.*); ск|а́пливать, -опи́ть больши́е запа́сы; **~ing food is illegal** зако́н запреща́ет припря́тывать продово́льствие.
hoarding ['hɔ:dɪŋ] *n.* **1.** (*fence round building site*) забо́р вокру́г стройплоща́дки. **2.** (*for poster display*) рекла́мный щит. **3.** (*stocking up*) накопле́ние; (*fin.*) тезаври́рование.
hoarse [hɔ:s] *adj.* хри́плый, си́плый; **he talked himself ~** он договори́лся до хрипоты́.
hoarseness ['hɔ:snɪs] *n.* хрипота́, си́плость.
hoary ['hɔ:rɪ] *adj.* (*grey or white with age*) седо́й, седовла́сый; (*ancient*) дря́хлый, дре́вний; **a ~ joke** ста́рая шу́тка; анекдо́т с бородо́й.
hoax [həʊks] *n.* надува́тельство, ро́зыгрыш.
v.t. над|ува́ть, -у́ть; разыгр|ывать, -а́ть; дура́чить, о-.
hob [hɒb] *n.* по́лка в ками́не/печи́.
hobble ['hɒb(ə)l] *v.t.*: **~ a horse** стрено́жить (*pf.*) ло́шадь.
v.i. ковыля́ть (*impf.*); прихра́мывать (*impf.*).
cpd. **~-skirt** *n.* дли́нная, зау́женная кни́зу ю́бка.
hobbledehoy ['hɒbəldɪ,hɔɪ] *n.* нескла́дный/углова́тый подро́сток; юне́ц.
hobby ['hɒbɪ] *n.* (*leisure pursuit*) хо́бби (*nt. indecl.*).
cpd. **~-horse** *n.* игру́шечная лоша́дка; (*fig.*) конёк.
hobgoblin ['hɒb,gɒblɪn] *n.* чертёнок, бесёнок; прока́зливый дух.
hobnail ['hɒbneɪl] *n.* сапо́жный гвоздь; **~ed boots** подби́тые гвоздя́ми боти́нки.
hobnob ['hɒbnɒb] *v.i.* води́ться (*impf.*), якша́ться (*impf.*) (*с кем*).
hobo ['həʊbəʊ] *n.* (*US sl.*) бродя́га (*m.*).
Hobson's choice ['hɒbs(ə)nz] *n.* вы́бор без вы́бора.
Ho Chi Minh City [həʊ tʃɪ 'mɪn] *n.* Хошими́н.

hock[1] [hɒk], **hough** [hɒk] *nn.* (*leg joint*) колéнное сухожи́лие; (*pl.*) поджи́л|ки (*g.* -ок).

hock[2] [hɒk] *n.* (*wine*) рейнвéйн.

hock[3] [hɒk] *n.* (*sl.*, *pawn*): **in ~** в ломбáрде; в заклáде.
v.t. за|клáдывать, -ложи́ть.

hockey ['hɒkɪ] *n.* (*on field*) травянóй хоккéй; **ice ~** хоккéй (с шáйбой).
cpds. **~-player** *n.* хоккеи́ст (*fem.* -ка); **~-stick** *n.* клю́шка.

hocus-pocus [ˌhəʊkəs'pəʊkəs] *n.* фóкус, махинáция, трюк.

hod [hɒd] *n.* (строи́тельный) лотóк.

hodge-podge ['hɒdʒpɒdʒ] *n.* (*coll.*) мешани́на; «сбóрная соля́нка».

hoe [həʊ] *n.* моты́га, тя́пка.
v.t. & i. моты́жить (*impf.*); выпáлывать, вы́полоть; **he ~d up the weeds** он вы́полол сорняки́.

hog [hɒg] *n.* бóров; (*US*, *also fig.*) свинья́; **go the whole ~** дов|оди́ть, -ести́ дéло до концá; идти́ (*det.*) на всё.
v.t. (*coll.*) (*eat greedily*) жрать, со-; (*monopolize*): **he ~ged the conversation** он не давáл никомý слóва встáвить.
cpds. **~'s-back** *n.* (*ridge*) грéбень (*m.*); хребéт; **~shead** *n.* бóчка; *мера ёмкости* ≃ 240 ли́тров; **~wash** *n.* (*pig-swill*) пóйло; (*coll.*, *rubbish*) чушь, вздор.

hoggish ['hɒgɪʃ] *adj.* сви́нский, свиноподóбный.

hogmanay ['hɒgməˌneɪ, -'neɪ] *n.* (*Sc.*) канýн Нóвого гóда.

hoi(c)k [hɔɪk] *v.t.* (*jerk*, *yank*) рвану́ть (*pf.*).
v.i. (*clear throat noisily*) грóмко откáшливаться (*impf.*).

hoi polloi [ˌhɔɪ pə'lɔɪ] *n.* простонарóдье.

hoist [hɔɪst] *n.* подъёмник.
v.t. подн|имáть, -я́ть; **he was ~ by his own petard** он попáл в сóбственную ловýшку.

hoity-toity [ˌhɔɪtɪ'tɔɪtɪ] *adj.* (*haughty*, *fussy*) кичли́вый, с гóнором.
int. ну и нý!

hokey-pokey [ˌhəʊkɪ'pəʊkɪ] *n.* (*coll.*, *trickery*) надувáтельство, махинáция.

hokum ['həʊkəm] *n.* (*sl.*) вздор, чепухá.

hold [həʊld] *n.* **1.** (*grasp*, *grip*) удéрживание, захвáт; **he caught ~ of the rope** он ухвати́лся за канáт; **he kept ~ of the reins** он не выпускáл повóдья из рук; **he laid, seized, took ~ of my arm** он схвати́л/взял меня́ зá руку; **don't lose ~; don't let go your ~** держи́те, не отпускáйте; (*fig.*); **I got ~ of a plumber** я нашёл/отыскáл водопровóдчика; **where did you get ~ of that idea?** откýда вы э́то взя́ли? **2.** (*in boxing or wrestling*) захвáт; **they fought with no ~s barred** они́ борóлись с применéнием любы́х захвáтов; (*fig.*) они́ прибегáли к всевозмóжным улóвкам; **once the flu gets a ~, it is hard to shake off** грипп такóе дéло: éсли запусти́ть — не скóро поправишься. **3.** (*means of pressure*): **he has a ~ on, over him** он дéржит егó в рукáх. **4.** (*support*): **his feet could find no ~ on the cliff face** егó ногá не моглá найти́ опóры на повéрхности утёса. **5.** (*ship's*) трюм.
v.t. **1.** (*clasp*, *grip*) держáть (*impf.*); **they sat ~ing hands** они́ сидéли, держáсь зá руки. **2.** (*maintain*, *keep in a certain position*): **~ yourself straight!** держи́сь пря́мо!; **~ it!** (*coll.*) (*don't move*) не дви́гайтесь!; не шевели́тесь!; (*fig.*, *keep*): **he held himself in readiness** он был наготóве; **they were held to a draw** их вы́нудили к ничьéй; **they held the enemy at bay** они́ не подпускáли неприя́теля; **I won't ~ you to your promise** я не трéбую, чтóбы вы сдержáли своё слóво; **~ the line!** (*teleph.*) ждите у телефóна!; не клади́те трýбку! **3.** (*detain*): **he was held prisoner** егó держáли в пленý; **they held him for questioning** егó задержáли для допрóса. **4.** (*contain*): **the hall ~s a thousand** зал вмещáет ты́сячу человéк; **~ one's liquor** переноси́ть (*impf.*) спиртнóе; **his theory will not ~ water** (*fig.*) егó тéория несостоя́тельна. **5.** (*consider*, *believe*) полагáть (*impf.*), считáть (*impf.*); **the court held that ...** суд признáл, что...; **~ dear** высокó цени́ть (*impf.*); **he is held in great esteem** он пóльзуется больши́м уважéнием; **he was held responsible** емý пришлóсь отвечáть; **I don't ~ it against him** я не стáвлю емý э́то в винý; **he held the law in contempt** он презирáл закóн. **6.** (*restrain*): **she held her breath** онá затаи́ла дыхáние; **he held his hand** (*fig.*, *took no action*) он сдержáл себя́; **~ everything!** (*coll.*) останови́тесь!; **~ your noise!** не шуми́те!; **~ your tongue!** молчи́те!; помáлкивайте!; **~ your horses** (*coll.*) лéгче на поворóтах!; **there's no ~ing him** на негó (*or* емý) нет ýдержу. **7.** (*have*, *own*): **he ~s the ace** у негó туз; **all this land is held by one man** всей э́той землёй владéет оди́н человéк; **~ the record** быть рекордсмéном; **~ shares** быть держáтелем áкций; **the opinion is widely held** э́то мнéние широкó распространенó; **we ~ the same views** мы придéрживаемся одинáковых взгля́дов. **8.** (*occupy*, *remain in possession of*): **how long has he held office?** как давнó он занимáет э́ту дóлжность; **he held his ground** (*lit.*) он не уступáл; (*fig.*) он не сдавáлся; **I can ~ my own against anyone** я могý потягáться с кем ýгодно; **he ~s the rank of sergeant** он имéет звáние сержáнта; **the sight held his attention** э́то зрéлище приковáло егó внимáние. **9.** (*carry on*, *conduct*, *convene*): **they were ~ing a conversation** они́ бесéдовали; **the meeting was held at noon** собрáние состоя́лось в пóлдень.
v.i. **1.** (*grasp*): **~ tight!** держи́те крéпче/крéпко. **2.** (*adhere*): **he ~s firmly to his beliefs** он твёрдо дéржится свои́х убеждéний; **I ~ by what I said** я придéрживаюсь тогó, что сказáл рáньше. **3.** (*agree*, *approve*): **I don't ~ with that** я так не считáю; я э́того не одобря́ю. **4.** (*remain*): **he held aloof** он держáлся особнякóм; **~ still!** не дви́гайтесь!; **the argument ~s good** дóвод сохраня́ет си́лу. **5.** (*remain unbroken*, *unchanged*, *intact*): **will the rope ~?** вы́держит ли верёвка?; **how long will the weather ~?** дóлго ли продéржится (простои́т) такáя погóда?
with advs.: **~ apart** *v.t.*: **they held the brawlers apart** они́ растащи́ли спóрящих; **~ back** *v.t.* (*restrain*): **I couldn't ~ him back** я не мог егó удержáть; (*withhold*): **he held back part of their wages** он удержáл часть их зарплáты; (*repress*): **I had to ~ back a smile** мне пришлóсь сдержáть улы́бку; *v.i.* (*hesitate*) мéшкать (*impf.*); (*refrain*): воздéрж|иваться, -áться (*от чего*); **~ down** *v.t.* (*lit.*): **~ your head down!** не поднимáйте головы́!; (*fig.*): **do you think you can ~ the job down?** сумéете ли вы удержáться на э́той дóлжности; **we will try to ~ prices down** мы постарáемся не допусти́ть рóста цен; **~ forth** *v.t.* (*offer*) протя́|гивать, -нýть; *v.i.* (*coll.*, *orate*) разглагóльствовать (*impf.*); вещáть (*impf.*); **~ in** *v.t.* (*lit.*): **her waist was held in by a belt** её тáлия былá стя́нута пóясом; (*fig.*): **I could hardly ~ myself in** я едвá сдержáлся; **~ off** *v.t.* (*keep away*, *repel*): **he held his dog off** он придержáл собáку; **they held off the attack** они́ отби́ли атáку; **he held off going to the doctor** он отклáдывал визи́т к врачý; *v.i.* (*stay away*): **the rain held off all morning** дождя́ так и нé было всё ýтро; **~ on** *v.t.* (*keep in position*) прикреп|ля́ть, -и́ть; **the handle was held on with glue** рýчка держáлась на клею́; *v.i.* (*cling*) держáться (*за что*); **she held on to the banisters** онá держáлась за пери́ла; (*fig.*): **you should ~ on to those shares** вам нáдо бы держáться за э́ти áкции; (*coll.*, *wait*): **~ on a minute till I'm ready** подождите — я бýду готóв чéрез минýту; (*on the telephone*): **~ on, please!** не вéшайте трýбку!; **~ out** *v.t.* (*extend*): **he greeted me and held out his hand** он произнёс привéтствие и протянýл мне рýку; (*fig.*, *offer*): **I can't ~ out any hope** я не могý вас ничéм обнадёжить; *v.i.* (*endure*, *refuse to yield*): **the fortress held out for 6 weeks** крéпость продержáлась 6 недéль; **the men are ~ing out for more money** рабóчие не уступáют, трéбуя повышéния зарплáты; **he held out on me** (*coll.*) он утáивал (*что*) от меня́; он скры́тничал; (*last*): **supplies cannot ~ out much longer** запáсов надóлго не хвáтит; **~ over** *v.t.* (*defer*) от|клáдывать, -ложи́ть; **~ together** *v.t.*: **the box was held together with string** корóбка былá перевя́зана бечёвкой (, чтóбы не развали́лась); (*fig.*) **the leader held his party together** ли́дер сплоти́л пáртию; *v.i.* (*fig.*): **his arguments do not ~ together** в его дóводах есть неувя́зка; **~ under** *v.t.* (*fig.*): **this nation has been held under for generations** э́та странá ужé давнó нахóдится под гнётом; **~ up** *v.t.* (*lift*, *hold erect*): **the boy**

held up his hand мáльчик пóднял рýку; (*fig., display, expose*): **he was held up as an example** егó постáвили в примéр; **he was held up to ridicule** егó вы́ставили на посмéшище; (*delay*) задéрж|ивать, -áть; **we were held up on the way** по дорóге нас задержáли; **traffic was held up by fog** движéние остановилось из-за тумáна; **I hope you will not ~ up your decision** надéюсь, вы не бýдете мéдлить с решéнием; **the censor held up the play** цензýра задержáла пьéсу; **work is (*or* has been) held up** рабóта стáла; (*waylay*): **the robbers held them up at pistol point** бандиты ограбили их, угрожáя пистолéтом; *v.i.*: **do you think the table will ~ up under the weight?** вы дýмаете, стол вы́держит такóй вес?; (*fig.*): **if the weather ~s up, we can go out** éсли такáя погóда продéржится, мы мóжем пойти кудá-нибудь.

cpds. **~-all** *n.* вещевóй мешóк; сýмка; **~-up** *n.* (*stoppage, delay*) задéржка; **what's the ~-up?** за чем дéло стáло?; (*robbery*) вооружённый грабёж.

holder ['həʊldə(r)] *n.* **1.** (*possessor, e.g. of a passport*) владéлец, предъявитель (*m.*); обладáтель (*m.*); **~ of an office** занимáющий дóлжность. **2.** (*device for holding*) держáтель (*m.*).

holding ['həʊldɪŋ] *n.* **1.** (*of land*) учáсток (земли́). **2.** (*property*) вклáды (*m. pl.*), авуáры (*m. pl.*). **3.** (*pl.*) (*stock*) запáс; (*of library*) фонд.

adj.: **~ company** компáния-держáтель; **~ operation** оперáция для сохранéния стáтуса кво (*or* для удержáния пози́ций).

hole [həʊl] *n.* **1.** (*cavity*) дырá. **2.** (*opening*) отвéрстие. **3.** (*rent*) щель, прóрезь. **4.** (*burrow*) норá. **5.** (*pej. of a place*) дырá. **6.** (*predicament*) бедá. **7.** (*in golf*) лýнка. **8.** (*phrr.*): **it made a ~ in his savings** плáкали егó сбережéния; **he is always picking ~s** он ко всемý придирáется; **a square peg in a round ~** человéк не на своём мéсте.

v.t. **1.** (*make ~ in*) дéлать отвéрстия в+*p.* **2.** (*make ~ through*) продыря́в|ливать, -ить. **3.** (*golf*) заг|оня́ть, -нáть (мяч) в лýнку.

cpd. **~-and-corner** *adj.* закули́сный.

holiday ['hɒlɪˌdeɪ, -dɪ] *n.* **1.** (*day off*) выходнóй (день); **bank ~** нерабóчий день (, когдá закры́ты бáнки); **church ~** церкóвный прáздник. **2.** (*annual leave*) óтпуск, óтдых; (*school, university vacation*) кани́кул|ы (*pl., g.* —); (*leisure time*) óтдых; **he is on ~** он в отпускý; у негó кани́кулы; **I take my ~s in June** я берý óтпуск в ию́не; **where are you spending your ~?** где вы бýдете отдыхáть?; **~ camp** (лéтний) лáгерь; **~ home** дом óтдыха.

cpd. **~-maker** *n.* отдыхáющий; тури́ст (*fem.* -ка).

holiness ['həʊlɪnɪs] *n.* свя́тость, священность; **His H~ (the Pope)** егó Святéйшество.

Holland[1] ['hɒlənd] *n.* (*country or province*) Голлáндия.

holland[2] ['hɒlənd] *n.* (*fabric*) холст; (*pl., spirit*) можжевéловая вóдка.

Hollander ['hɒləndə(r)] *n.* (*arch.*) голлáндец.

holler ['hɒlə(r)] *v.t. & i.* (*US coll.*) орáть (*impf.*); вопи́ть (*impf.*).

hollo(a) ['hɒləʊ] *v.i.* улюлю́кать (*impf.*).

hollow ['hɒləʊ] *n.* **1.** (*small depression*) вы́емка, впáдина; **hold s.o. in the ~ of one's hand** держáть когó-н. в рукáх. **2.** (*dell*) лощи́на, низи́на.

adj. **1.** (*not solid*) пустóй, пóлый. **2.** (*of sounds*) глухóй. **3.** (*fig., false, insincere*) фальши́вый, лжи́вый; **~ laughter** неестéственный/ирони́ческий смех; **a ~ victory** бесплóдная побéда. **4.** (*sunken*) ввали́вшийся, впáлый; **~ cheeks** ввали́вшиеся щёки.

adv.: **we beat them ~** (*coll.*) мы разби́ли их в пух и прах.

v.t. (*usu.* **~ out**) выдáлбливать, вы́долбить; дéлать, с-углублéние в+*p.*

hollowness ['hɒləʊnɪs] *n.* (*insincerity*) нейскренность.

holly ['hɒlɪ] *n.* остроли́ст.

hollyhock ['hɒlɪˌhɒk] *n.* алтéй рóзовый.

holly-oak ['hɒlɪ], **holm-oak** [həʊm] *nn.* дуб кáменный.

holocaust ['hɒləˌkɔːst] *n.* мáссовое уничтожéние; бóйня; **the H~** холокáуст; **nuclear ~** я́дерная катастрóфа.

hologram ['hɒləˌgræm] *n.* голográмма.

holograph ['hɒləˌgrɑːf] *n.* собственнорýчно напи́санный доку́мéнт.

adj. собственнорýчный.

holster ['həʊlstə(r)] n. кобурá.

holy ['həʊlɪ] *n.*: **the H~ of Holies** (*lit., fig.*) Святáя Святы́х.

adj. свящéнный, святóй; **H~ Communion** Святóе Причáстие; **the H~ Father** егó Святéйшество; **the H~ Ghost, Spirit** Святóй Дух; **the H~ Land** Святáя земля́; **~ orders** духóвный сан; **~ place** святи́лище; **the H~ Places** Святы́е Местá; **H~ Russia** Святáя Русь; **the H~ See** Святéйший Престóл; **a ~ terror** (*coll.*) наказáние госпóдне; **a ~ war** свящéнная войнá; **~ water** святáя водá; **H~ Week** Страстнáя недéля; **H~ Writ** (*arch.*) свящéнное писáние.

cpd. **~stone** *n.* песчáник, пéмза.

homage ['hɒmɪdʒ] *n.* (*feudal*) феодáльная пови́нность; (*fig.*) почтéние, преклонéние; **we pay ~ to his genius** мы преклоня́емся пéред егó гéнием.

home [həʊm] *n.* **1.** (*place where one resides or belongs*) дом; (*attr.*) домáшний; **~ economics** домоводство; **~ help** приходя́щая домработница; **it was a ~ from ~** там бы́ло как дóма; **a ~ of one's own** сóбственный дом; **his ~ is in London** он жи́тель Лóндона; **he made his ~ in Bristol** он посели́лся в Бри́столе; **he made London his second ~** Лóндон стал егó вторы́м дóмом; **he looks on Paris as his spiritual ~** он считáет Пари́ж своéй духóвной рóдиной; **he has gone to his last ~** он отпрáвился в послéдний путь; **she left ~** онá поки́нула (роди́тельский) дом; **at home** (*in one's house*) дóма; (*on one's ~ ground*) у себя́; (*e.g. football*) на своём пóле; **she is not at ~ to anyone** онá никогó не принимáет; **make yourself at ~** бýдьте как дóма; **I feel at ~ here** я чýвствую себя́ здесь как дóма; **I don't feel at ~ in Spanish** я в испáнском не силён; **he is away from ~** он в отъéзде. **2.** (*institution*): **a ~ for the disabled** дом инвали́дов; **he put his parents into a ~** он помести́л свои́х роди́телей в дом для престарéлых. **3.** (*habitat*) рóдина, мéсто распространéния, ареáл. **4.** (*in games*): **the ~ stretch** фи́нишная прямáя. **5.** (*attr., opp. foreign; native, local*): **~ affairs** внýтренние делá; **H~ Counties** грáфства, окружáющие Лóндон; **H~ Guard** отря́ды (*m. pl.*) мéстной оборóны, ополчéние; **of ~ manufacture** отéчественного произвóдства; **the ~ market** внýтренний ры́нок; **H~ Office** министéрство внýтренних дел; **~ team** комáнда хозя́ев пóля; **~ rule** самоуправлéние; **~ town** роднóй гóрод.

adv. **1.** (*at or to one's own house*): **is he ~ yet?** он (ужé) дóма?; **he was on his way ~** он шёл/éхал домóй; **go ~!** убирáйтесь восвоя́си!; **nothing to write ~ about** (*fig.*) ничегó осóбенного (*or* из ря́да вон выходя́щего); **he is ~ and dry** (*fig.*) он благополýчно отдéлался. **2.** (*in or to one's own country*): **things are different back ~** (*coll.*) у нас э́то не так (*or* инáче); **he came ~ from abroad** он вернýлся из-за грани́цы. **3.** (*to the point aimed at*): **the nails were driven ~** гвóзди бы́ли заби́ты; **he drove his argument ~** он растолковáл свои́ дóводы; **bring sth. ~ to s.o.** довести́ (*pf.*) что-н. до чьегó-н. сознáния; **it was brought ~ to him how lucky he was** до негó дошлó, как емý повезлó; **his remarks struck ~** егó замечáния попáли в цель; (*attr.*) **~ truths** нелицеприя́тные и́стины (*f. pl.*); гóрькая прáвда.

v.i.: **~ on to a beacon** настр|áиваться, -óиться на мая́к; **homing instinct** тя́га домóй; **homing pigeon** почтóвый гóлубь.

cpds. **~-baked** *adj.* домáшней вы́печки; **~-bird** *n.* (*fig.*) домосéд (*fem.* -ка); **~-brewed** *adj.* домáшнего изготовлéния; **~coming** *n.* возвращéние домóй; **~-grown** *adj.* доморóщенный; **~land** *n.* рóдина, родная странá; **~-like** *adj.* домáшний, непринуждённый; **~-lover** *n.* домосéд (*fem.* -ка); **~-made** *adj.* домáшнего изготовлéния; **~sick** *adj.* скучáющий/тоскýющий по дóму/рóдине; **~sickness** *n.* ностальги́я; **~spun** *n. & adj.* домоткáный; (*fig.*) сермя́жный, грубовáтый; **~stead** *n.* усáдьба; фéрма; **~work** *n.* домáшнее задáние; зáданный урóк; **what was the ~work?** что бы́ло зáдано нá дом?

homeless ['həʊmlɪs] *adj.* бездо́мный.

homeliness ['həʊmlɪnɪs] *n.* **1.** дома́шний ую́т. **2.** непритяза́тельность, неприхотли́вость. **3.** непригля́дность, невзра́чность.

homely ['həʊmlɪ] *adj.* **1.** (*like home*) дома́шний, ую́тный; **a ~ atmosphere** дома́шняя обстано́вка. **2.** (*unpretentious*): **a ~ old lady** простя́/ми́лая стару́шка; **a ~ meal** неприхотли́вая еда́. **3.** (*US, unattractive*) некраси́вый; **a ~ girl** дурну́шка.

homeopath ['həʊmɪəʊˌpæθ, 'hɒmɪ-] *n.* гомеопа́т.

homeopathic [ˌhəʊmɪəʊ'pæθɪk, 'hɒmɪ-] *adj.* гомеопати́ческий.

homeopathy [ˌhəʊmɪ'ɒpəθɪ, ˌhɒmɪ-] *n.* гомеопа́тия.

Homer[1] ['həʊmə(r)] *n.* Гоме́р.

homer[2] ['həʊmə(r)] *n.* (*pigeon*) почто́вый го́лубь.

Homeric [həʊ'merɪk, hə'm-] *adj.* гоме́ровский; **the ~ poems** поэ́мы Гоме́ра; **~ scholar** гоме́рове́д; **~ laughter** гомери́ческий хо́хот.

homeward ['həʊmwəd] *adj.* иду́щий/веду́щий к до́му; **~ voyage** обра́тный рейс/путь.

adv. (*also* **~s**) домо́й; восвоя́си.

hom(e)y ['həʊmɪ] *adj.* (*US coll.*) дома́шний, ую́тный.

homicidal [ˌhɒmɪ'saɪd(ə)l] *adj.* (*intending murder*) замышля́ющий уби́йство; **~ mania** ма́ния уби́йства.

homicide ['hɒmɪˌsaɪd] *n.* (*crime*) уби́йство; **~ squad** отря́д сыскно́й поли́ции по рассле́дованию уби́йств.

homily ['hɒmɪlɪ] *n.* про́поведь; (*reprimand*) нота́ция.

hominid ['hɒmɪnɪd] *n.* гомини́д.

hominy ['hɒmɪnɪ] *n.* марёная кукуру́за, мамалы́га.

homo ['həʊməʊ] *n.* го́мо (*m. indecl.*), го́мик (*coll.*).

homoeopath ['həʊmɪəʊˌpæθ, 'hɒmɪ-], **-ic** [ˌhəʊmɪəʊ'pæθɪk, 'hɒmɪ-], **-y** [ˌhəʊmɪ'ɒpəθɪ, ˌhɒmɪ-] = **homeopath** *etc.*

homogeneity [ˌhəʊməʊdʒɪ'niːɪtɪ] *n.* одноро́дность.

homogeneous [ˌhəʊməʊ'dʒiːnɪəs, ˌhɒməʊ-] *adj.* одноро́дный.

homogenization [həmɒdʒɪˌnaɪ'zeɪʃ(ə)n] *n.* гомогениза́ция.

homogenize [hə'mɒdʒɪˌnaɪz] *v.t.* гомогенези́ровать (*impf.*).

homograph ['hɒməˌgrɑːf] *n.* омо́граф.

homologous [hə'mɒləgəs] *adj.* соотве́тственный; гомологи́ческий.

homonym ['hɒmənɪm] *n.* омо́ним.

homonym|ic [ˌhɒmə'nɪmɪk], **-ous** [hə'mɒnɪməs] *adjs.* омоними́ческий.

homophone ['hɒməˌfəʊn] *n.* омофо́н.

homo sapiens [ˌhəʊməʊ 'sæpɪenz] *n.* хо́мо са́пиенс (*m. indecl.*).

homosexual [ˌhəʊməʊ'seksjʊəl, ˌhɒm-] *n.* гомосексуали́ст.

adj. гомосексуа́льный.

homosexuality [ˌhəʊməʊˌseksjʊ'ælɪtɪ, ˌhɒm-] *n.* гомосексуали́зм.

homunculus [hə'mʌŋkjʊləs] *n.* гому́нкул(ус); (*dwarf*) ка́рлик, лилипу́т.

homy ['həʊmɪ] = **homey**

Honduran(ean) [hɒn'djʊərən] *n.* гондура́с|ец (*fem.* -ка).

adj. гондура́сский.

Honduras [hɒn'djʊərəs] *n.* Гондура́с.

hone [həʊn] *n.* осело́к; точи́льный ка́мень.

v.t. точи́ть, за-/на-.

honest ['ɒnɪst] *adj.* (*fair, straightforward*) че́стный; (*sincere*): **an ~ attempt** че́стная попы́тка; (*expressive of honesty*): **an ~ face** откры́тое лицо́; (*candid*): **if you want the ~ truth** е́сли вы хоти́те знать всю/чи́стую пра́вду; **to be ~ (with you)** че́стно говоря́; (*legitimate*): **he turns an ~ penny** он зараба́тывает (на жизнь) че́стным путём; (*respectable*): **he made an ~ woman of her** он прикры́л грех зако́нным бра́ком.

cpds. **~-to-god, ~-to-goodness** *adjs.* настоя́щий, взапра́вдашний; *adv.* че́стно!; ей-Бо́гу!

honestly ['ɒnɪstlɪ] *adv.* **1.** (*straightforwardly*) че́стно. **2.** (*candidly*) чистосерде́чно; **~!** че́стное сло́во!; **~, that's all the money I have** э́то все мои де́ньги, пове́рьте. **3.** (*remonstrance*) поми́луйте!; ну, зна́ете!

honesty ['ɒnɪstɪ] *n.* **1.** (*integrity*) че́стность. **2.** (*candour*) чистосерде́чие, прямота́. **3.** (*bot.*) лу́нник.

honey ['hʌnɪ] *n.* мёд; (*US coll., darling*) дорого́й, ми́лый; (*fig.*) **his new car is a ~** его́ но́вая маши́на — конфе́тка.

cpds. **~-bee** *n.* пчела́ медоно́сная; **~comb** *n.* со́т|ы (*pl., g.* -ов); *v.t.* (*fig.*): **the countryside is ~combed with caves** э́тот райо́н усе́ян пеще́рами; **the administration is ~combed with spies** администра́ция киши́т шпио́нами; **~-dew** *n.* медвя́ная роса́; (*melon*) муска́тная ды́ня; **~moon** *n.* медо́вый ме́сяц; *v.i.* пров|оди́ть, -ести́ медо́вый ме́сяц; **~suckle** *n.* жи́молость; **~-sweet** *adj.* сла́дкий как мёд.

hon|eyed, -ied ['hʌnɪd] *adj.*: **~ words** сла́дкие ре́чи.

Hong Kong [hɒŋ'kɒŋ] *n.* Гонко́нг.

honk [hɒŋk] *n.* **1.** (*of goose*) крик (ди́ких гусе́й). **2.** (*of motor horn*) гудо́к.

v.i. **1.** крича́ть (*impf.*). **2.** гуде́ть (*impf.*).

Honolulu [ˌhɒnə'luːluː] *n.* Гонолу́лу (*m. indecl.*).

honorarium [ˌɒnə'reərɪəm] *n.* гонора́р.

honorary ['ɒnərərɪ] *adj.* (*conferred as honour*) почётный; (*unpaid*) неоплачиваемый.

honorific [ˌɒnə'rɪfɪk] *n.* почти́тельное обраще́ние; (*in oriental languages*) фо́рма ве́жливости.

adj. почти́тельный, ве́жливый; **an ~ post** почётный пост.

honour ['ɒnə(r)] *n.* **1.** (*good character, reputation*) честь; **a man of ~** благоро́дный/че́стный челове́к; **affair of ~** дуэ́ль; **code of ~** ко́декс че́сти; **debt of ~** долг че́сти; **he considered himself in ~ bound to obey** он счёл свои́м до́лгом подчини́ться; **his ~ is at stake** на ка́рту поста́влена его́ честь; **(on my) word of ~!** че́стное сло́во; (*chastity*) честь, целому́дрие. **2.** (*dignity, credit*): **it's an ~ to work with him** рабо́тать с ним — больша́я честь; **it does you ~** э́то де́лает вам честь; **guard of ~** почётный карау́л; **maid of ~** фре́йлина; **the reception was held in his ~** приём был устро́ен в его́ честь; **he won ~ in war** он был уве́нчан боево́й сла́вой; (*in polite formulae*): **will you do me the ~ of accepting this gift?** окажи́те мне честь, приня́в э́тот дар; **I have the ~ to inform you** име́ю честь сообщи́ть вам. **3.** (*usu. pl., mark of respect, distinction*): **Birthday H~s** награ́ды (*f. pl.*) по слу́чаю дня рожде́ния мона́рха; **~s list** спи́сок пожа́лованных мона́рхом почётных зва́ний и ти́тулов; **he was buried with military ~s** он был похоро́нен с во́инскими по́честями; **let me do the ~s** я бу́ду за хозя́ина; (*as title*) **your H~** ва́ша честь. **4.** (*pl., academic distinction*): **~s course** курс, даю́щий пра́во на дипло́м с отли́чием; **pass with ~s** сдать (*pf.*) экза́мен с отли́чием. **5.** (*in card games*) онёры (*m. pl.*).

v.t. **1.** (*respect, do ~ to*) ока́з|ывать, -а́ть честь +*d.* **2.** (*confer dignity on*): **he ~ed me with a visit** он удосто́ил меня́ визи́том. **3.** (*fulfil obligation*): **he failed to ~ the agreement** он не вы́полнил соглаше́ния; **will the cheque be ~ed?** бу́дет ли упла́чено по э́тому че́ку?

honourable ['ɒnərəb(ə)l] *adj.* **1.** (*upright*) че́стный, досто́йный. **2.** (*consistent with honour*): **an ~ peace** почётный мир; **are his intentions ~?** честны́ ли его́ наме́рения? **3.** (*title: also* **right ~**) достопочте́нный.

hooch [huːtʃ] *n.* (*sl.*) спиртно́е, вы́пивка.

hood [hʊd] *n.* **1.** (*headgear*) капюшо́н, ка́пор. **2.** (*of car or carriage*) складно́й верх; (откидна́я) кры́ша. **3.** (*US, of car engine*) капо́т. **4.** (*US sl.*) = **hoodlum**

v.t. (*cover with ~*) покр|ыва́ть, -ы́ть капюшо́ном.

hoodlum ['huːdləm] *n.* (*US sl.*) хулига́н, банди́т, громи́ла (*m.*).

hoodoo ['huːduː] *n.* несча́стье, по́рча, сглаз.

v.t. (*also* **put the ~ on**) приноси́ть (*impf.*) несча́стье +*d.*; сгла́зить (*pf.*).

hoodwink ['hʊdwɪŋk] *v.t.* одура́чи|вать, -ть; (*coll.*) провести́ (*pf.*).

hooey ['huːɪ] *n.* (*sl.*) бред, чушь.

hoof [huːf] *n.* копы́то; **on the ~** (*of cattle*) живо́й.

v.t. (*sl.*): **~ out** вы́гнать (*pf.*); вы́ставить (*pf.*); **~ it** идти́ пёхом (*sl.*).

hoo-ha ['huːhɑː] *n.* (*sl.*) сует́а, шуми́ха.

hook [hʊk] *n.* **1.** (*curved, usu. metal, device*) крючо́к (*also for fishing*), крюк; **the receiver was off the ~** тру́бка была́ снята́; **he swallowed the tale ~, line and sinker** (*fig.*) он попа́лся на у́дочку; **let off the ~** (*coll.*) выруча́ть, вы́ручить; вызволя́ть, вы́зволить из беды́; (*dress fastening*): **~ and eye** крючо́к; (*agric. tool*) сека́ч; **by ~ or by crook** все́ми пра́вдами и непра́вдами; **off one's own ~**

по своей инициати́ве. **2.** (*boxing blow*) хук, боково́й уда́р. **3.** (*geog.*): **the H~ of Holland** Хук ван Хо́лланд.

v.t. (*catch*) пойма́ть (*pf.*); **she ~ed a rich husband** (*coll.*) она́ подцепи́ла бога́того му́жа; **he is ~ed on drugs** (*sl.*) он пристрасти́лся к нарко́тикам. **2.** (*usu. with advs., fasten*): **she ~ed up her dress** она́ застегну́ла пла́тье (на крючки́). **3.** (*sl., steal*) стяну́ть (*pf.*); **4.: ~ it** (*sl.*) смы́ться (*pf.*).

v.i. (*fasten*): **the dress ~s (up) at the back** пла́тье застёгивается сза́ди.

cpds. **~-nosed** *adj.* с крючкова́тым но́сом; **~-up** *n.* сцепле́ние; (*radio*) одновреме́нная трансля́ция; **~worm** *n.* немато́да.

hookah ['hʊkə] *n.* кальян.

hooker ['hʊkə(r)] *n.* (*coll., ship*) су́дно, посу́дина; (*sl., prostitute*) проститу́тка.

hookey ['hʊkɪ] *n.*: **play ~** (*US, sl.*) прогу́ливать (*impf.*) (уро́ки).

hooligan ['hu:lɪgən] *n.* хулига́н.

hooliganism ['hu:lɪgənɪz(ə)m] *n.* хулига́нство.

hoop [hu:p] *n.* **1.** (*of barrel etc.; plaything; in circus*) о́бруч; **they put him through the ~s** (*fig.*) они́ подве́ргли его́ тру́дным испыта́ниям. **2.** (*croquet*) воро́т|а (*pl., g.* —).

v.t. (*bind with ~s*) скреп|ля́ть, -и́ть о́бручем.

cpds. **~-la** *n.* (*game*) ко́льца (*nt. pl.*); **~-skirt** *n.* криноли́н.

hoopoe ['hu:pu:] *n.* удо́д.

hooray! [hʊ'reɪ] *int.* ура́.

hoot [hu:t] *n.* **1.** (*derisive noise*) шика́нье, гвалт; **he doesn't give two ~s (or a ~)** ему́ на э́то наплева́ть (*coll.*); (*owl's cry*) у́ханье; (*warning note of vessel, car, siren etc.*) гудо́к, сигна́л.

v.t. оши́к|ивать, -ать; **he was ~ed down; they ~ed him off (the stage)** его́ оши́кали.

v.i. (*in derision or amusement*) улюлю́кать (*impf.*); **we ~ed with laughter** мы пока́тывались со́ смеху; (*of an owl*) у́х|ать, -нуть; (*of a vessel, car etc.*) гуде́ть, про-; сигна́лить, про-; да|ва́ть, -ть гудо́к.

hooter ['hu:tə(r)] *n.* **1.** (*of factory*) гудо́к. **2.** (*sl.*) (*nose*) руби́льник, пая́льник.

Hoover ['hu:və(r)] *n.* (*propr.*) пылесо́с.

v.t. (**h~**) пылесо́сить, про-.

hop[1] [hɒp] *n.* **1.** подско́к, скачо́к (на одно́й ноге́); **~, skip and jump** тройно́й прыжо́к; **I was caught on the ~** (*coll.*) меня́ заста́ли врасплох. **2.** (*dance*) танцу́лька (*coll.*). **3.** (*stage of flight*) перелёт.

v.t.: **~ it!** (*sl.*) кати́сь!

v.i. пры́гать, скака́ть (*both impf.*); **he ~ped over the ditch** он перепры́гнул че́рез кана́ву; **she ~ped over to see me** (*coll.*) она́ забежа́ла ко мне; **where has he ~ped off to?** (*coll.*) куда́ э́то он ускака́л?; **he was ~ping mad** (*coll.*) он рассвирепе́л/остервене́л.

cpds. **~-o'-my-thumb** *n.* ма́льчик с па́льчик; **~scotch** *n.* кла́ссы (*m. pl.*) (*игра*).

hop[2] [hɒp] *n.* (*bot.*) хмель (*m.*).

cpds. **~-field** *n.* хме́льник; **~-picker** *n.* (*pers.*) сбо́рщи|к (*fem.* -ца) хме́ля; (*machine*) хмелеубо́рочная маши́на.

hop|e [həʊp] *n.* наде́жда; **I have high ~es of him** я возлага́ю на него́ больши́е наде́жды; **we live in ~e(s)** мы живём наде́ждой; **don't raise my ~es in vain** не обнадёживайте меня́ понапра́сну; **~e chest** (*US*) сунду́к для прида́ного; **his ~es were dashed** его́ наде́жды ру́хнули; **I can hold out little ~e** я не могу́ вас обнадёжить; **I went in the ~e of finding him** я пошёл в наде́жде найти́ его́; **there's not much ~e of that** на э́то ма́ло наде́жды; **he is the ~e of the side** он наде́жда кома́нды; **things are past all ~e** положе́ние безнадёжно.

v.t. & i.: **I ~e to see you soon** наде́юсь, мы ско́ро уви́димся; **let's ~e so!** бу́дем наде́яться!; **I ~e not** наде́юсь, что нет; **I am ~ing against ~e** я продолжа́ю наде́яться, несмотря́ ни на что.

hopeful ['həʊpfʊl] *n.*: **young ~** (*joc.*) подаю́щий наде́жды ребёнок.

adj. **1.** (*having hope*): **I am ~ of success** я наде́юсь/рассчи́тываю на успе́х. **2.** (*inspiring hope*): **a ~ prospect** обнадёживающая перспекти́ва; **a ~ sign** благоприя́тный при́знак.

hopefully ['həʊpfʊlɪ] *adv.* (*in sense 'it is hoped'*): **~ he will arrive soon** на́до наде́яться, он ско́ро приедет.

hopefulness ['həʊpfʊlnɪs] *n.* наде́жда, оптими́зм.

hopeless ['həʊplɪs] *adj.* **1.** (*feeling no hope*) отча́явшийся. **2.** (*affording no hope*): **a ~ situation** безнадёжное положе́ние; **a ~ illness** неизлечи́мая боле́знь. **3.** (*coll., incapable*): **he's quite ~ at science** то́чные нау́ки ему́ соверше́нно не даю́тся; **he is a ~ ass** он безнадёжно глуп. **4.: he fell ~ly in love** он влюби́лся по́ уши.

hopelessness ['həʊplɪsnɪs] *n.* безнадёжность.

hopper[1] ['hɒpə(r)] *n.* (*for grain*) воро́нка.

hopper[2] ['hɒpə(r)] = **hop-picker**

Horace ['hɒrɪs] *n.* (*poet*) Гора́ций.

Horatian [hə'reɪʃ(ə)n] *adj.* гора́циев.

horde [hɔ:d] *n.* (*of nomads*) орда́; (*fig.*) по́лчище, ту́ча, ку́ча.

horizon [hə'raɪz(ə)n] *n.* (*lit., fig.*) горизо́нт; **over the ~** за горизо́нт(ом).

horizontal [ˌhɒrɪ'zɒnt(ə)l] *n.* горизонта́ль.

adj. горизонта́льный.

hormone ['hɔ:məʊn] *n.* гормо́н; (*attr.*) гормо́нный, гормона́льный.

horn [hɔ:n] *n.* **1.** (*of cattle*) рог; **I took the bull by the ~s** (*fig.*) я взял быка́ за рога́; **he drew in his ~s** (*fig.*) он присмире́л/прити́х. **2.** (*hist., drinking-vessel*) рог, ку́бок; **~ of plenty** рог изоби́лия. **3.** (*mus.*): **French ~** валто́рна; (*hunting-~*) рог. **4.** (*warning device*) гудо́к, свисто́к; (*of a car*) клаксо́н, гудо́к; **he sounded his ~** он дал сигна́л. **5.** (*substance*) рог. **6.: on, between the ~s of a dilemma** в тиска́х диле́ммы. **7.** (*geog.*): **the H~** мыс Горн; **the Golden H~** Золото́й Рог.

v.i.: **he ~ed in on our conversation** (*coll.*) он влез в наш разгово́р.

cpds. **~beam** *n.* граб; **~bill** *n.* пти́ца-носоро́г; **~blende** *n.* амфибо́л; **~pipe** *n.* хо́рнпайп; **~-rimmed** *adj.* в рогово́й опра́ве.

horned [hɔ:nd] *adj.* рога́тый, с рога́ми.

hornet ['hɔ:nɪt] *n.* ше́ршень (*m.*); **his words stirred up a ~'s nest** его́ слова́ потрево́жили оси́ное гнездо́.

horny ['hɔ:nɪ] *adj.* **1.** рогово́й; **~ hands** мозо́листые ру́ки. **2.** (*coll., lustful*) похотли́вый.

cpd. **~-handed** *adj.* с мозо́листыми рука́ми.

horology [hə'rɒlədʒɪ] *n.* (*measuring time*) измере́ние вре́мени; (*making clocks*) часово́е де́ло.

horoscope ['hɒrəˌskəʊp] *n.* гороско́п; **she had her ~ cast** ей соста́вили гороско́п.

horrendous [hə'rendəs] *adj.* ужа́сный, жу́ткий.

horri|ble ['hɒrɪb(ə)l], **-d** ['hɒrɪd] *adjs.* ужа́сный, ужаса́ющий; (*coll., unpleasant*) ужа́сный, отврати́тельный; **you're being ~** ты зло́й!

horrific [hə'rɪfɪk] *adj.* ужаса́ющий.

horrif|y ['hɒrɪˌfaɪ] *v.t.* (*fill with horror*) ужас|а́ть, -ну́ть; (*shock*) потряс|а́ть, -ти́; **I was ~ied at his behaviour** его́ поведе́ние меня́ ужасну́ло.

horror ['hɒrə(r)] *n.* у́жас; **the ~s** (*coll., DT's*) бе́лая горя́чка; **~s!** како́й у́жас!; жуть!; **the ~s of war** у́жасы войны́; **~ film** фильм у́жасов; (*extreme dislike*) **I have a ~ of cats** я терпе́ть не могу́ ко́шек; (*joc., shocking pers.*) жу́ткий тип.

cpd. **~-struck** *adj.* в у́жасе.

hors de combat [ˌɔr də 'kɔ̃ba:] *adv.* вне игры́; вы́шедший из строя.

hors d'oeuvres [ɔ:'dɜ:vr, -'dɜ:v] *n.* заку́ски (*f. pl.*).

horse [hɔ:s] *n.* **1.** (*animal*) ло́шадь, конь (*m.*); **to ~!** по коня́м!; **he backs ~s** он игра́ет на ска́чках; **he lost (money) on the ~s** он проигра́лся на ска́чках; **he backed the wrong ~** (*fig.*) он просчита́лся; он поста́вил не на ту ло́шадь; **he drove a ~ and cart** он е́хал на теле́ге; **he eats like a ~** он ест за семеры́х; **you are flogging a dead ~** зря стара́етесь!; ги́блое де́ло!; не рвись!; **hold your ~s!** (*coll.*) ле́гче на поворо́тах!; **put the cart before the ~** (*fig.*) поста́вить (*pf.*) (всё) с ног на́ голову; **he learnt to ride a ~** он научи́лся е́здить верхо́м; **that's a ~ of another colour**

(*fig.*) э́то совсе́м друго́й коленко́р; **a dark ~** тёмная лоша́дка; **I had it straight from the ~'s mouth** я зна́ю э́то из первоисто́чника (*or* из пе́рвых рук); **he got on his high ~** он стал в по́зу. **2.** (*cavalry*) ко́нница, кавале́рия; **H~ Guards** конногварде́йский полк. **3.** (*in gymnasium*) конь (*m.*).

cpds. **~back** *n.*: **on ~back** верхо́м; **~back riding** (*US*) = **~-riding; ~-block** *n.* подста́вка (для поса́дки); **~-box** *n.* тре́йлер, автофурго́н; **~-breaker** *n.* объе́здчик; **~-chestnut** *n.* кашта́н ко́нский; **~-cloth** *n.* попо́на; **~flesh** *n.* кони́на; **he is a good judge of ~flesh** он большо́й зното́к лошаде́й; **~-fly** *n.* слепе́нь (*m.*); **~hair** *n.* ко́нский во́лос; *adj.* из ко́нского во́лоса; **~-laugh** *n.* хо́хот, ржа́ние; **~man** *n.* нае́здник, вса́дник; **~manship** *n.* иску́сство верхово́й езды́; **~play** *n.* шу́мная игра́/возня́; **~-power** *n.* лошади́ная си́ла; **20 ~-power** 20 лошади́ных сил; **~-race, ~-racing** *nn.* ска́чки (*f. pl.*), бега́ (*m. pl.*); **~-radish** *n.* хрен; **~-riding** *n.* верхова́я езда́; **~-sense** *n.* просто́й здра́вый смысл; **~shoe** *n.* подко́ва; **~-trade** *n.* (*fig.*) сде́лка; **~-trading** *n.* торги́ (*m. pl.*); **~whip** *n.* хлыст; *v.t.* хлеста́ть; **~-woman** *n.* нае́здница, вса́дница.

horsy [ˈhɔːsɪ] *adj.* (*fond of horses*) лю́бящий лошаде́й.

hortat|ive [ˈhɔːtətɪv], **-ory** [ˈhɔːtətərɪ] *adjs.* увещáтельный; наставИ́тельный.

horticultural [ˌhɔːtɪˈkʌltʃər(ə)l] *adj.* садово́дческий.

horticultur(al)ist [ˌhɔːtɪˈkʌltʃər(əl)ɪst] *n.* садово́д.

horticulture [ˈhɔːtɪˌkʌltʃə(r)] *n.* садово́дство.

hosanna [həʊˈzænə] *n. & int.* оса́нна.

hose [həʊz] *n.* **1.** (*stockings*) чуло́чные изде́лия; (*US*) чулки́ (*m. pl.*). **2.** (*tube, also* **~-pipe**) шланг; **fire ~** брандспо́йт, пожа́рный рука́в.

v.t.: **he was hosing down the car** он полива́л маши́ну водо́й из шла́нга.

hosier [ˈhəʊzɪə(r), ˈhəʊʒə(r)] *n.* торго́вец трикота́жными това́рами.

hosiery [ˈhəʊzɪərɪ, ˈhəʊʒərɪ] *n.* (*shop*) магази́н трикота́жных изде́лий; (*wares*) трикота́жные изде́лия (*nt. pl.*).

hospice [ˈhɒspɪs] *n.* гости́ница, прию́т, богаде́льня; (*for terminal patients*) больни́ца для безнадёжных пацие́нтов.

hospitable [ˈhɒspɪtəb(ə)l, hɒˈspɪt-] *adj.* гостеприи́мный.

hospital [ˈhɒspɪt(ə)l] *n.* больни́ца; (*esp. military*) го́спиталь (*m.*); **he went into ~** он лёг в больни́цу; **he is in ~** он лежи́т в больни́це; **~ ship** плаву́чий го́спиталь.

hospitality [ˌhɒspɪˈtælɪtɪ] *n.* гостеприи́мство.

hospitalization [ˌhɒspɪtəlaɪˈzeɪʃ(ə)n] *n.* госпитализа́ция.

hospitalize [ˈhɒspɪtəˌlaɪz] *v.t.* госпитализи́ровать (*impf., pf.*).

hospitaller [ˈhɒspɪtələ(r)] *n.* (*hist.*) госпитальéр.

host[1] [həʊst] *n.* хозя́ин (*also zool.*); **he is a good ~** он гостеприи́мный/раду́шный хозя́ин.

v.t.: **the conference was ~ed by the British** хозя́евами конфере́нции бы́ли брита́нцы.

host[2] [həʊst] *n.* (*army, multitude*) мно́жество, сонм; **the Heavenly H~** си́лы небе́сные (*f. pl.*); **the Lord of ~s** Госпо́дь сил; **a ~ of difficulties** ма́сса тру́дностей.

host[3] [həʊst] *n.* (*sacrament*) го́стия.

hostage [ˈhɒstɪdʒ] *n.* зало́жник; **~s to fortune** (*fig.*) жена́ и де́ти.

hostel [ˈhɒst(ə)l] *n.* общежи́тие; **youth ~** молодёжная тури́стская ба́за.

hostelry [ˈhɒstəlrɪ] *n.* (*arch., joc.*) постоя́лый двор, гости́ница.

hostess [ˈhəʊstɪs] *n.* хозя́йка; (*on aircraft*) стюарде́сса; (*in night-club*) пла́тная партнёрша.

hostile [ˈhɒstaɪl] *adj.* вражде́бный, неприя́зненный; **he is ~ to the idea** он про́тив э́той иде́и.

hostility [hɒˈstɪlɪtɪ] *n.* (*enmity, ill-will*) вражде́бность; (*pl., warlike activity*) вое́нные/вооружённые де́йствия.

hostler [ˈɒslə(r)] = **ostler**

hot [hɒt] *adj.* **1.** горя́чий; жа́ркий; **I am ~** мне жа́рко; **he got ~ playing** ему́ ста́ло жа́рко от игры́; **~ air** (*coll.*) бахва́льство; **these goods are selling like ~cakes** э́тот това́р идёт нарасхва́т; **a ~ day** жа́ркий день; **a ~ flush** прили́в кро́ви; **~ rod** (*sl.*) маши́на с мо́щным мото́ром; **in the ~ seat** (*coll.*) как на иго́лках; **the issue is too ~ to handle** (*fig.*) э́то сли́шком щекотли́вый вопро́с; **they made things too ~ for him** они́ вы́жили его́; **you'll get into ~ water** вы попадёте в беду́; вам не поздоро́вится. **2.** (*spicy*) о́стрый. **3.** (*ardent*) горя́чий, пла́менный; **~ on the scent, trail** по горя́чему сле́ду. **4.** (*angry*) раздражённый. **5.** (*excited*) взволно́ванный, возбуждённый; **~ under the collar** (*coll.*) распалённый, взбешённый. **6.** (*exciting*) отли́чный, шика́рный; **not so ~** (*coll.*) ничего́ осо́бенного; **a ~ number** (*sl.*) шика́рная вещь; (*girl*) шика́рная де́вочка; **~ stuff** (*coll.*) (*pers.*) молодчи́на, гига́нт; (*something new and exciting*) блеск!; шик! **7.** (*fresh*): **~ money** «горя́чие де́ньги»; **~ news** све́жие но́вости; **~ from the press** то́лько что из типогра́фии. **8.** (*racing etc.*): **~ favourite** всео́бщий фавори́т; **a ~ tip** де́льный сове́т. **9.** (*emergency*): **~ line** пряма́я телефо́нная/телета́йпная связь.

adv. (*fig. uses*): **he blows ~ and cold** ≃ у него́ семь пя́тниц; **I gave it him ~ and strong** я отчита́л его как сле́дует.

v.t. (*usu.* **~ up**) нагр|ева́ть, -е́ть; подогр|ева́ть, -е́ть; разогр|ева́ть, -е́ть.

v.i.: **~ up** (*fig.*): **the game ~ted up** игра́ оживи́лась.

cpds. **~bed** *n.* парни́к; (*fig.*) оча́г; **a ~bed of vice** гнездо́ поро́ка; **~-blooded** *adj.* пы́лкий, стра́стный; **~foot** *adv.* стремгла́в, поспе́шно; **~head** *n.* бу́йная/бедо́вая голова́; **~-headed** *adj.* вспы́льчивый, горя́чий; **~house** *n.* оранжере́я, тепли́ца; **~-plate** *n.* электри́ческая/га́зовая пли́тка; **~pot** *n.* туше́ное мя́со с овоща́ми; **~-water-bottle** *n.* гре́лка.

hotch-potch [ˈhɒtʃpɒtʃ] *n.* мешани́на; «сбо́рная соля́нка».

hotel [həʊˈtel] *n.* оте́ль (*m.*), гости́ница.

hotelier [həʊˈtelɪə(r)] *n.* хозя́ин оте́ля.

hotly [ˈhɒtlɪ] *adv.*: **her cheeks flushed ~** её щёки я́рко зарде́лись; **he replied ~** он отве́тил ре́зко (*or* с жа́ром).

hotsy-totsy [ˈhɒtsɪˈtɒtsɪ] *adj.* (*coll.*) в поря́дке, что на́до.

Hottentot [ˈhɒtənˌtɒt] *n.* готтенто́т (*fem.* -ка).

adj. готтенто́тский.

hough [hɒk] = **hock**[1]

hound [haʊnd] *n.* **1.** (*for hunting*) охо́тничья соба́ка; **he rides to ~s** он охо́тится на лиси́ц (с соба́ками); (*coll., any dog*) пёс, соба́ка. **2.** (*despicable man*) соба́ка.

v.t. (*with advs.*): **~ down** вы́ловить (*pf.*); **~ on** натра́в|ливать, -и́ть.

hour [aʊə(r)] *n.* **1.** (*period*) час; **it will take me an ~** мне потре́буется час; **boats for hire by the ~** прока́т ло́док с почасово́й опла́той; **he works an 8-~ day** у него́ восьмичасово́й рабо́чий день; **~ after ~** час за ча́сом. **2.** (*of clock-time*): **the clock strikes the ~s and half-~s** часы́ отбива́ют час и полчаса́; **every ~ on the ~** в нача́ле ка́ждого ча́са; **every ~ on the half-~** ка́ждый час в середи́не ча́са; **at the eleventh ~** (*fig.*) в после́дний моме́нт; под за́навес. **3.** (*time of day or night*): **we are open at all ~s** мы откры́ты круглосу́точно; **at an early ~** ра́но; **they keep late ~s** они́ по́здно ложа́тся (и встаю́т); **in the small ~s** в предрассве́тные часы́; **regardless of the ~** в любо́е вре́мя (дня и но́чи). **4.** (*specific period of time*): **our working ~s are long** у нас до́лгий рабо́чий день; **I had to work after ~s** мне пришло́сь рабо́тать сверхуро́чно; **he worked through his lunch ~** он рабо́тал в обе́денный переры́в; **in office ~s** в рабо́чее вре́мя; **out of ~s** в нерабо́чее вре́мя; **after ~s** по́сле закры́тия. **5.** (*fig., moment*): **the ~ has come** про́бил час; **in the ~ of danger** в мину́ту опа́сности; **in an evil ~** в недо́брый час; **questions of the ~** злободне́вные вопро́сы.

cpds. **~-glass** *n.* песо́чные час|ы́ (*pl., g.* -о́в); **~-hand** *n.* часова́я стре́лка; **~-long** *adj.* одночасово́й; продолжа́ющийся час.

houri [ˈhʊərɪ] *n.* гу́рия.

hourly [ˈaʊəlɪ] *adj.* **1.** (*occurring once an hour*) ежеча́сный. **2.** (*constant*) постоя́нный, непреста́нный. **3.**: **an ~ wage** почасова́я пла́та.

adv. (*once every hour*) ежеча́сно; (*at any hour*) с ча́су на час; в любо́е вре́мя; (*constantly*) непреста́нно.

house[1] [haʊs] *n.* **1.** (*habitation*) дом, зда́ние; **~ arrest** дома́шний аре́ст; **~ guest** гость (живу́щий в до́ме); **~ of**

cards (*lit.*, *fig.*) ка́рточный до́мик; ~ **of God** дом бо́жий, це́рковь; **they get on like a ~ on fire** они́ прекра́сно ла́дят; **keep ~** вести́ (*det.*) хозя́йство; **they kept open ~** у них был откры́тый дом; **put, set one's ~ in order** (*fig.*) прив|оди́ть, -ести́ свои́ дела́ в поря́док; **as safe as ~s** в по́лной безопа́сности; **set up ~ together** зажи́ть (*pf.*) свои́м; **turn s.o. out of ~ and home** вы́гнать (*pf.*) кого́-н. из дому; (*inn*): **public ~** паб, пите́йное заведе́ние; **have a drink on the ~** вы́пить (*pf.*) за счёт хозя́ина; (*of boarding school*) ≃ интерна́т, общежи́тие; (*parl.*): **H~ of Commons** пала́та о́бщин; **H~ of Lords** пала́та ло́рдов; **the H~** парла́мент; (*Stock Exchange*) би́ржа. **2.** (*audience*) зал, аудито́рия; **they played to a full ~** на их выступле́нии зал был по́лон; **she brought down the ~** её выступле́ние произвело́ фуро́р; (*performance*) представле́ние; (*cinema*) сеа́нс. **3.** (*dynasty*) дом, дина́стия. **4.** (*business concern*) учрежде́ние, фи́рма.

cpds. **~-agent** *n.* жили́щный аге́нт; **~boat** *n.* плаву́чий дом; **~bound** *adj.* прико́ванный к до́му; **~-boy** *n.* ма́льчик-слуга́ (*m.*); **~breaker** *n.* граби́тель-взло́мщик; **~breaking** *n.* грабёж со взло́мом; **~coat** *n.* (дома́шний) хала́т; **~-dog** *n.* сторожева́я соба́ка; **~-father, ~-mother** *nn.* заве́дующ|ий, -ая интерна́том/прию́том; **~-fly** *n.* му́ха ко́мнатная; **~hold** *n.* дом; дома́шний круг; (*attr.*): **~hold appliances** бытовы́е прибо́ры; **~hold gods** (*hist.*) пена́т|ы (*pl.*, *g.* -ов); (*fig.*) семе́йные рели́квии; **~hold troops** гва́рдия; **a ~hold word** обихо́дное выраже́ние; **~holder** *n.* домовладе́лец; **~-hunting** *n.* по́иски (*m. pl.*) кварти́ры/до́ма; **~keeper** *n.* эконо́мка; дома́шняя хозя́йка; **~keeping** *n.* дома́шнее хозя́йство; **~keeping expenses** расхо́ды на хозя́йство; **~-maid** *n.* го́рничная; **~-maid's knee** воспале́ние су́мки надколе́нника; **~master** *n.* заве́дующий одни́м из интерна́тов; **~painter** *n.* маля́р; **~-physician** *n.* врач, живу́щий при больни́це; **~-proud** *adj.* лю́бящий занима́ться благоустро́йством и украше́нием до́ма; **~-room** *n.*: **I wouldn't give it ~-room** я не бу́ду захламля́ть э́тим дом; **~-surgeon** *n.* хиру́рг, живу́щий при больни́це; **~-to-~** *adj.*: **a ~-to-~ search** обхо́д всех домо́в подря́д с о́быском; пова́льный о́быск; **~top** *n.* кры́ша, кро́вля; **don't cry it from the ~tops** не кричи́те об э́том на всех перекрёстках; **~-trained** *adj.* приу́ченный жить (*or* не па́чкать) в до́ме; **~-warming** *n.* новосе́лье; **~wife** *n.* домохозя́йка; **~wifely** *adj.* хозя́йственный, домови́тый; **~work** *n.* рабо́та по до́му.

house[2] [haʊz] *v.t.* **1.** (*provide house(s) for*) предост|авля́ть, -а́вить жильё +*d.*; сели́ть, по-. **2.** (*accommodate*) вме|ща́ть, -сти́ть; **this building ~s the city council** в э́том зда́нии размеща́ется муниципалите́т. **3.** (*store*) храни́ть (*impf.*). **4.** (*place securely*) уб|ира́ть, -ра́ть; пря́тать, с-.

housing ['haʊzɪŋ] *n.* **1.** (*provision of houses*) обеспе́чение жильём; **the ~ problem** жили́щная пробле́ма. **2.** (*houses built in quantity*): **~ estate** жило́й микрорайо́н. **3.** (*casing*) ко́рпус, ко́жух.

hovel ['hɒv(ə)l] *n.* лачу́га, шала́ш.

hover ['hɒvə(r)] *v.i.* пари́ть (*impf.*); (*fig.*): **he ~ed around her** он увива́лся за ней; **he ~ed between life and death** он был ме́жду жи́знью и сме́ртью.

cpds. **~craft** *n.* ховеркра́фт; су́дно на возду́шной поду́шке; **~train** *n.* аэропо́езд.

how [haʊ] *n.*: **he wanted to know the ~ and why of it** он хоте́л знать все «заче́м» и «почему́».

adv. **1.** (*in direct and indirect questions*) как; каки́м о́бразом?; **~ come?** (*coll.*) как э́то?; **~ the devil did you find out?** как вы э́то узна́ли, чёрт возьми́?; **~ on earth did it happen?** как же э́то случи́лось?; **~ comes it that you are late?** почему́ э́то вы опа́здываете?; **~ are you?** как пожива́ете?; **~ do I know?** почём я зна́ю?; **~ do you know that?** отку́да вы э́то зна́ете?; **~ do you mean?** что вы хоти́те сказа́ть?; в како́м смы́сле?; **~'s that?** (*enquiring reason*) ка́к это?; (*inviting comment*): **~'s that for a jump!** ничего́ себе́ прыжо́к!; **~ about a drink?** не хоти́те ли вы́пить?; не вы́пить ли нам?; **~ about that!** (*coll.*, *expr. admiration etc.*) ну и ну!; **~ now?** (*arch. & joc.*) как дела́?; **~ so?** почему́ э́то?; то́ есть?; **~ ever does he do it?** как же он э́то де́лает? **2.** (*with adjs. and advs.*): **~ far is it?** как далеко́ э́то нахо́дится?; како́е расстоя́ние (до+*g.*)?; **~ many, much?** ско́лько?; **tell me ~ old she is** скажи́те мне, ско́лько ей лет? **3.** (*in indirect statements or questions*): **I told him ~ I'd been abroad** я рассказа́л ему́, как я съе́здил за грани́цу. **4.** (*in exclamations*): **~ he goes on!** до чего́ он зану́да!; **~ I wish I were there!** как бы мне хоте́лось сейча́с быть там!; **and ~!** (*coll.*) ещё как!; **~ beautifully she plays!** как она́ прекра́сно игра́ет!

howbeit [haʊ'biːɪt] *conj.* (*arch.*) тем не ме́нее.

howdah ['haʊdə] *n.* паланки́н (*на спине слона*).

how-d'ye-do ['haʊ,djə'duː] *n.* (*coll.*) щекотли́вое положе́ние.

how|ever [haʊ'evə(r)] *adv.* (*also* (*arch.*) **-soever**): **~ hard he tried** как он ни стара́лся.

conj. одна́ко; и всё же.

howitzer ['haʊɪtsə(r)] *n.* га́убица.

howl [haʊl] *n.* (*cry of pain or grief*) вопль (*m.*), стон; (*cry of derision*) вой, гул; (*of an animal*) вой, завыва́ние; (*of the wind*) завыва́ние; (*radio interference*) вой, рёв.

v.t. & i. выть (*impf.*); **the baby was ~ing its head off** ребёнок надрыва́лся от кри́ка; **he was ~ed down** его́ го́лос заглуши́ли; его́ перекрича́ли; **listen to the wolves ~ing!** послу́шайте, как во́ют во́лки; **the wind ~s in the chimney** ве́тер завыва́ет в трубе́; **a ~ing gale** завыва́ющий ве́тер; **the show was a ~ing success** (*coll.*) спекта́кль име́л невероя́тный/колосса́льный/бе́шеный успе́х; **a ~ing shame** жу́ткий позо́р; стыд и срам; **a ~ing wilderness** глухома́нь.

howler ['haʊlə(r)] *n.* (*coll.*, *solecism*) грубе́йшая оши́бка, ля́псус.

howsoever [,haʊsəʊ'evə(r)] (*arch.*) = **however** *adv.*

hoy[1] [hɔɪ] *n.* (*boat*) небольшо́е берегово́е су́дно.

hoy[2] [hɔɪ] *int.* эй!

hoyden ['hɔɪd(ə)n] *n.* бой-де́вка.

h.p. (*abbr. of* **horsepower**) л.с., (лошади́ная си́ла).

HQ (*abbr. of* **headquarters**) штаб, ста́вка.

HRH (*abbr. of* ***Her/His Royal Highness***) Её/Его́ Короле́вское Высо́чество.

hub [hʌb] *n.* вту́лка; (*fig.*): **the ~ of the universe** пуп земли́.

hubble-bubble ['hʌb(ə)l,bʌb(ə)l] *n.* (*hookah*) калья́н.

hubbub ['hʌbʌb] *n.* шум, го́вор, го́мон, гвалт.

hubby ['hʌbɪ] *n.* муженёк (*coll.*).

hubris ['hjuːbrɪs] *n.* горды́ня; надме́нность.

hubristic [,hjuː'brɪstɪk] *adj.* высокоме́рный, надме́нный.

huckaback ['hʌkə,bæk] *n.* суро́вое полотно́.

huckleberry ['hʌkəlbərɪ] *n.* черни́ка (*collect.*); я́года черни́ки.

huckster ['hʌkstə(r)] *n.* торго́вец, бары́шник.

huddle ['hʌd(ə)l] *n.* **1.** (*disorderly mass*) ку́ча, гру́да, во́рох. **2.: they went into a ~** (*coll.*) они́ ста́ли та́йно совеща́ться/шушу́каться.

v.t. вали́ть, с- в ку́чу.

v.i. толпи́ться, с-; **he lay ~d up** он лежа́л, сверну́вшись кала́чиком; **they ~d together for warmth** они́ прижа́лись друг к дру́гу, что́бы согре́ться (*or* для тепла́).

hue[1] [hjuː] *n.* (*colour*) отте́нок, тон (*pl.* -а́).

hue[2] [hjuː] *n.*: **~ and cry** кри́ки (*m. pl.*); во́згласы (*m. pl.*); **raise a ~ and cry** подн|има́ть, -я́ть крик.

huff [hʌf] *n.* вспы́шка раздраже́ния/оби́ды; **he walked off in a ~** он ушёл вконе́ц разоби́женный.

v.t. **1.** (*in game of draughts*) взять (*pf.*) фук. **2.: you can ~ and puff but you won't stop me** мо́жете зли́ться, но меня́ э́то не остано́вит.

huffy ['hʌfɪ] *adj.* оби́женный, рассе́рженный.

hug [hʌg] *n.* объя́тие.

v.t. **1.** (*embrace*) обн|има́ть, -я́ть; (*fig.*): **I ~ged myself on my good fortune** я поздра́вил себя́ с уда́чей. **2.** (*fig.*, *cling to*, *keep close to*): **the ship ~ged the shore** кора́бль шёл вдоль са́мого бе́рега; **they still ~ their old beliefs** они́ всё ещё цепля́ются за свои́ ста́рые убежде́ния.

huge [hjuːdʒ] *adj.* огро́мный, грома́дный; **he ate a ~ supper** за у́жином он нае́лся до отва́ла; **a ~ joke** великоле́пный ро́зыгрыш.

hugely ['hjuːdʒlɪ] *adv.* весьма́, чрезвыча́йно, стра́шно.

hugeness ['hjuːdʒnɪs] *n.* грома́дность, грандио́зность.

hugger-mugger ['hʌgə,mʌgə(r)] *n.* (*secrecy*) секре́тность; (*confusion*) сумбу́р, беспоря́док.
adj. секре́тный; сумбу́рный, беспоря́дочный.
adv. секре́тно; сумбу́рно.

Huguenot ['hju:gə,nəʊ, -,nɒt] *n.* гугено́т.
adj. гугено́тский

huh [hə] *int.* (*interrogation*) гм?, а?; (*expr. contempt*) хм!, гм!

hulk [hʌlk] *n.* (*body of dismantled ship*) ко́рпус; (*unwieldy vessel*) неповоро́тливое су́дно, «коры́то»; (*large clumsy pers.*) «медве́дь» (*m.*); у́валень (*m.*).

hulking ['hʌlkɪŋ] *adj.* неуклю́жий, неповоро́тливый.

hull[1] [hʌl] *n.* (*of ship*) ко́рпус; (*of aircraft*) фюзеля́ж.
v.t.: **~ a ship** (*strike in* ~) проби́ть (*pf.*) ко́рпус корабля́.

hull[2] [hʌl] *n.* (*shell, pod*) кожура́; скорлупа́.
v.t. лущи́ть (*impf.*), шелуши́ть (*impf.*).

hullabaloo [,hʌləbə'lu:] *n.* шум, шуми́ха.

hullo [hʌ'ləʊ] *int.* (*greeting*) здра́сте!; приве́т!; (*on telephone*) алло́!; (*expr. surprise*) вот те на́!

hum [hʌm] *n.* жужжа́ние.
v.t. & i. **1.** (*make murmuring sound*): **~ming bird** коли́бри (*m. indecl.*); **~ming-top** волчо́к. **2.** (*sing with closed lips*) напева́ть (*impf.*). **3.: ~and ha(w)** мя́млить (*impf.*). **4.** (*coll., be active*) идти́ (*det.*) по́лным хо́дом; кипе́ть (*impf.*); **he made things ~** у него́ рабо́та кипе́ла. **5.** (*sl., stink*) воня́ть (*impf.*).

human ['hju:mən] *n.* челове́к.
adj. челове́ческий, челове́чий; **~ being** челове́к; **~ error** оши́бка, свойственная челове́ку; **~ kind** челове́чество; **~ nature** челове́ческая приро́да; **the ~ race** род людско́й; **he did all that was ~ly possible** он сде́лал всё, что в челове́ческих си́лах.

humane [hju:'meɪn] *adj.* **1.** (*compassionate*) гума́нный, челове́чный; **~ killer** инструме́нт для безболе́зненного убо́я живо́тных; **H~ Society** о́бщество спаса́ния утопа́ющих. **2.: ~ studies** гуманита́рные нау́ки (*f. pl.*).

humaneness [hju:'meɪnnɪs] *n.* гума́нность, челове́чность.

humanism ['hju:mə,nɪz(ə)m] *n.* (*classical studies*; *non-religious ethics*) гумани́зм.

humanist ['hju:mənɪst] *n.* гумани́ст.

humanistic [,hju:mə'nɪstɪk] *adj.* гуманисти́ческий.

humanitarian [hju:,mænɪ'teərɪən] *n.* гумани́ст.
adj. гума́нный, челове́чный, человеколюби́вый.

humanitarianism [hju:,mænɪ'teərɪə,nɪz(ə)m] *n.* человеколю́бие.

humanity [hju:'mænɪtɪ] *n.* **1.** (*human nature*) челове́чность, челове́ческие ка́чества. **2.** (*the human race*) челове́чество; род людско́й. **3.** (*crowd*) ма́сса люде́й, толпа́, наро́д. **4.** (*humaneness*) гума́нность. **5.: the ~ies** гуманита́рные нау́ки (*f. pl.*).

humanize ['hju:mə,naɪz] *v.t.* (*make human*) очелове́чи|вать, -ть; (*make humane*) де́лать, с- бо́лее челове́чным.

humble ['hʌmb(ə)l] *adj.* **1.** (*lacking self-importance*) поко́рный, смире́нный; **in my ~ opinion** по моему́ непросвещённому мне́нию; **your ~ servant** ваш поко́рный слуга́; **he was made to eat ~ pie** ему́ пришло́сь покори́ться. **2.** (*lowly*) просто́й, скро́мный; **of ~ birth** из простонаро́дья.
v.t. смир|я́ть, -и́ть; ун|ижа́ть, -и́зить; **~ o.s.** уничижа́ться (*impf.*).

humble-bee ['hʌmb(ə)l,bi:] *n.* шмель (*m.*).

humbleness ['hʌmbəlnɪs] *n.* смире́ние, скро́мность.

humbug ['hʌmbʌg] *n.* (*deceit, hypocrisy*) надува́тельство; (*hypocrite, fraud*) обма́нщик, очковтира́тель (*m.*); (*nonsense*) чушь, вздо́р; (*boiled sweet*) ледене́ц.
v.t. над|ува́ть, -у́ть; провести́ (*pf.*).

humdinger ['hʌm,dɪŋə(r)] *n.* (*sl.*) «блеск», чу́до.

humdrum ['hʌmdrʌm] *adj.* однообра́зный, ну́дный.

humerus ['hju:mərəs] *n.* плечева́я кость.

humid ['hju:mɪd] *adj.* вла́жный.

humidifier [hju:'mɪdɪ,faɪ(ə)r] *n.* увлажни́тель (*m.*) во́здуха.

humidity [hju:'mɪdɪtɪ] *n.* вла́жность.

humidor ['hju:mɪ,dɔ:(r)] *n.* увлажни́тель (*m.*).

humiliate [hju:'mɪlɪ,eɪt] *v.t.* ун|ижа́ть, -и́зить.

humiliation [hju:,mɪlɪ'eɪʃ(ə)n] *n.* униже́ние.

humility [hju:'mɪlɪtɪ] *n.* смире́ние; скро́мность.

hummock ['hʌmək] *n.* бугор, приго́рок; **~s of ice** торо́сы (*m. pl.*).

humongous [hju:'mɒŋgəs] *adj.* (*coll.*) огрома́дный.

humoresque [,hju:mə'resk] *n.* юморе́ска.

humorist ['hju:mərɪst] *n.* (*facetious pers.*) остря́к, весельча́к; (*humorous writer etc.*) юмори́ст.

humorous ['hju:mərəs] *adj.* юмористи́ческий; **a ~ author** писа́тель-юмори́ст; **a ~ situation** коми́ческое положе́ние.

humour ['hju:mə(r)] *n.* **1.** (*disposition*) нрав, душе́вный склад; **in an ill ~** не в ду́хе; в плохо́м настрое́нии; **this will put you in a good ~** э́то подни́мет вам настрое́ние; **he is out of ~** он не в ду́хе; **I am in no ~ for argument** у меня́ нет настрое́ния спо́рить; **he will work when the ~ takes him** он рабо́тает по настрое́нию. **2.** (*amusement*) ю́мор; **his speech was full of ~** в его́ ре́чи бы́ло мно́го ю́мора; **he has little sense of ~** у него́ сла́бое чу́вство ю́мора.
v.t. потака́ть (*impf.*) +*d.*; ублаж|а́ть, -и́ть +*d.*

humourless ['hju:məlɪs] *adj.* лишённый чу́вства ю́мора; ску́чный.

hump [hʌmp] *n.* **1.** (*protuberance on back*) горб. **2.** (*rounded hillock*) буго́р, бугоро́к; **we are over the ~ now** (*fig.*) са́мое тру́дное позади́. **3.** (*fit of depression*) пода́вленное состоя́ние, хандра́; **it gives me the ~** э́то наво́дит на меня́ тоску́.
v.t. **1.** (*make ~-shaped*) выгиба́ть, вы́гнуть; го́рбить; **the cat ~ed up its back** ко́шка вы́гнула спи́ну. **2.** (*carry, shoulder*) нести́ (*det.*) (на плеча́х); взва́ливать (*impf.*) на́ спину. **3.** (*engage in sexual intercourse*) тра́х|ать, -нуть.
v.i. (*engage in sexual intercourse*) тра́х|аться, -нуться.
cpd. **~-backed** *adj.* горба́тый.

humph [həmf] *int.* хм!

humus ['hju:məs] *n.* гу́мус, перегно́й.

Hun [hʌn] *n.* гунн; (*pej., German*) немчура́ (*m.*).

hunch [hʌntʃ] *n.* **1.** (*hump*) горб. **2.** (*US coll., intuitive feeling*) чутьё, интуи́ция; **I had a ~ he would come** я предчу́вствовал, что он придёт **he acted on a ~** он де́йствовал интуити́вно.
v.t.: **he ~ed (up) his shoulders** он ссуту́лился/сго́рбился.
cpd. **~-back** *n.* горбу́н.

hundred ['hʌndrəd] *n.* (число́, но́мер) сто; (*collect*) со́тня; **about 100** о́коло ста; **100 each** по́ сто; **up to 100** до ста; **page 100** со́тая страни́ца; **room 100** со́тая ко́мната, со́тый но́мер; **a ~ and fifty** сто пятьдеся́т, полтора́ста; **~s of people** со́тни люде́й; **sell by the ~** прод|ава́ть, -а́ть по сто штук (*or* со́тнями); **~s of thousands** со́тни ты́сяч; **I have a ~ and one things to do** я до́лжен сде́лать ку́чу дел; **~ per cent** (*as adj.*) стопроце́нтный; (*adv.*) на (все) сто проце́нтов; **I'm one ~ per cent behind you** я целико́м и по́лностью на ва́шей стороне́; **a ~ to one** наверняка́; сто про́тив одного́; **it's a ~ to one they will not meet again** руча́юсь, что они́ бо́льше не встре́тятся; **he lived to be a ~** он до́жил до ста лет; **at fourteen ~ hours** (*mil.*) в четы́рнадцать (часо́в) ноль-ноль (мину́т); в 14 ч. ро́вно; **the nineteen ~s** в девятисо́тые го́ды.
adj. сто +*g. pl.*; **two** (*etc. to* **nine**) **~** две́сти, три́ста, четы́реста, пятьсо́т, шестьсо́т, семьсо́т, восемьсо́т, девятьсо́т (*all* +*g. pl.*); **a ~ miles away** (*fig.*) за ты́сячу вёрст; далеко́.
cpds. **~fold** *adj.* стокра́тный; *adv.* во́ сто крат, в сто раз; **~-rouble note** сторублёвая бума́жка, сторублёвка; **~weight** *n.* (*Imperial — approx. 50.8 kilograms*) англи́йский це́нтнер; (*US — approx. 45.4 kilograms*) америка́нский це́нтнер.

hundredth ['hʌndrədθ] *n.* (*fraction*) одна́ со́тая.
adj. со́тый.

Hungarian [hʌŋ'geərɪən] *n.* (*pers.*) венгр, венге́р|ец (*fem.* -ка); (*language*) венге́рский язы́к.
adj. венге́рский.

Hungary ['hʌŋgərɪ] *n.* Ве́нгрия.

hunger ['hʌŋgə(r)] *n.* го́лод; (*fig., strong desire*) жа́жда.
v.i. (*fig.*) жа́ждать (*impf.*); **she ~ed for excitement** она́ жа́ждала развлече́ний.
cpds. **~-march** *n.* голо́дный похо́д; **~-strike** *n.* голодо́вка.

hungover [hʌŋ'əʊvə(r)] *adj.* (*coll.*) страда́ющий с похме́лья/перепо́я.

hungry [ˈhʌŋgrɪ] *adj.* голо́дный; (*fig., avid*) жа́ждущий; (*fig., of soil*) беспло́дный.
hunk [hʌŋk] *n.* большо́й кусо́к; (*of bread*) ломо́ть (*m.*) хле́ба.
hunkers [ˈhʌŋkəz] *n.* (*Sc.*) я́годицы (*f. pl.*); **on one's ~** на ко́рточках.
hunky-dory [ˌhʌŋkɪˈdɔːrɪ] *adj.* (*coll.*): **everything's ~** всё в ажу́ре.
Hunnish [ˈhʌnɪʃ] *adj.* гу́ннский; (*barbarous*) ва́рварский.
hunt [hʌnt] *n.* **1.** (*~ing expedition*) охо́та. **2.** (*~ing association*) охо́тничье о́бщество. **3.** (*search*) охо́та, по́иск|и; (*pl., g.* -ов) (*чего*).
v.t. & i. (*e.g. animals*) охо́титься (*impf.*) (на+*a.*); (*persons or things*) охо́титься (*impf.*) за+*i.*; вести́ (*det.*) по́иски +*g.*; **he had a ~ed look** у него́ был затра́вленный вид.
with advs.: **the criminal was ~ed down** престу́пника пойма́ли; **she ~ed out some old clothes** она́ отыска́ла где́-то ста́рую оде́жду; **will you ~ up the address for me?** мо́жете разыска́ть для меня́ э́тот а́дрес?
hunter [ˈhʌntə(r)] *n.* **1.** (*one who hunts*) охо́тник; **I'm as hungry as a ~** я го́лоден как волк. **2.** (*horse*) гу́нтер; охо́тничья ло́шадь.
hunting [ˈhʌntɪŋ] *n.* охо́та.
cpds. **~-box** *n.* охо́тничий до́мик; **~-crop** *n.* охо́тничий хлыст; **~-ground** *n.* охо́тничье уго́дье; **happy ~-ground(s)** (*fig., heaven*) рай; **~-horn** *n.* охо́тничий рог.
huntress [ˈhʌntrɪs] *n.* же́нщина-охо́тник; (*goddess*) боги́ня охо́ты.
huntsman [ˈhʌntsmən] *n.* охо́тник; е́герь (*m.*).
hurdle [ˈhɜːd(ə)l] *n.* (*fencing*) (перено́сная) загоро́дка; (*in athletics & fig.*) барье́р, препя́тствие.
v.t. (*fence off*) огор|а́живать, -оди́ть.
v.i. (*engage in ~-jumping*) уча́ствовать в бе́ге с барье́рами.
hurdler [ˈhɜːdlə(r)] *n.* (*fence-maker*) рабо́чий, ста́вящий огра́ды; (*athlete*) барьери́ст (*fem.* -ка).
hurdy-gurdy [ˈhɜːdɪˌgɜːdɪ] *n.* шарма́нка.
hurl [hɜːl] *v.t.* бр|оса́ть, -о́сить; швыр|я́ть, -ну́ть; **he ~ed abuse at me** он осыпа́л меня́ оскорбле́ниями.
hurly-burly [ˈhɜːlɪˌbɜːlɪ] *n.* переполо́х, сумя́тица.
hurr|ah [hʊˈrɑː], **-ay** [hʊˈreɪ] *n. & int.* ура́!
v.t. крича́ть (*impf.*) «ура́».
hurricane [ˈhʌrɪkən, -ˌkeɪn] *n.* урага́н; **~ lamp** фона́рь «мо́лния».
hurr|y [ˈhʌrɪ] *n.* спе́шка, поспе́шность; **what's the ~y?** куда́/заче́м спеши́ть?; **there's no ~y!** спеши́ть не́куда; **she is always in a great ~y** она́ ве́чно торо́пится; **he was in no ~y to go** он не спеши́л уходи́ть; **in his ~y, he forgot his brief-case** в спе́шке он забы́л взять портфе́ль; **you won't need that again in a ~y** вам тепе́рь э́то не ско́ро пона́добится; **you won't beat that in a ~ y** попро́буйте переплю́нуть э́то! (*coll.*).
v.t. & i. **1.** (*perform hastily*): **don't ~y the job** рабо́тайте не спеша́; **he ~ied over his breakfast** он поспе́шно проглоти́л свой за́втрак; **he had a ~ied meal** он на́скоро перекуси́л. **2.** (*move or cause to move hastily*): **if you ~y him, he'll make mistakes** е́сли вы бу́дете его́ торопи́ть/подгоня́ть, он наде́лает оши́бок; **he ~ied the book out of sight** он поспе́шно убра́л кни́гу; **she ~ied down the road** она́ торопли́во (за)шага́ла вдоль у́лицы.
with advs.: **~y along there, please!** потора́пливайтесь, пожа́луйста!; **you need not ~y back** не спеши́те возвраща́ться; **he ~ied away, off** он бы́стро удали́лся; **the boy was ~ied off to bed** ма́льчика бы́стро уложи́ли спать; **~y up!** потора́пливайтесь!; **can't you ~ him up?** ра́зве вы не мо́жете его́ поторопи́ть?
hurt [hɜːt] *n.* вред, ущéрб; **she can come to no ~** ничего́ с ней не сде́лается; **it was a ~ to his pride** э́то заде́ло его́ самолю́бие.
v.t. & i. (*inflict pain on*): **I won't ~ you** я вам не причиню́ бо́ли (*or* не сде́лаю бо́льно); **my arm ~s** у меня́ боли́т/но́ет рука́; **these shoes ~ (me)** э́ти ту́фли мне жмут; **it didn't ~ a bit** ниско́лько не́ было бо́льно; **where does it ~?** что/где у вас боли́т?; (*damage, harm*) ушиб|а́ть, -и́ть; **he fell and ~ his back** он упа́л и ушиб спи́ну; **he was more frightened than ~** он не сто́лько ушибся, ско́лько испуга́лся; **~ o.s.** ушиби́ться (*pf.*), уда́риться (*pf.*); **it won't ~ this chair to get wet** от воды́ э́тому сту́лу ничего́ не бу́дет; **it wouldn't ~ to try it** (*coll.*) попы́тка не пы́тка; **it won't ~ to wait** не меша́ло бы подожда́ть; (*offend, pain*): **she was deeply ~ by my remark** моё замеча́ние её о́чень оби́дело/заде́ло; **now you've ~ his feelings** ну вот, вы его́ и оби́дели; **a ~ expression** оби́женное/оскорблённое выраже́ние.
hurtful [ˈhɜːtfʊl] *adj.* **1.** (*detrimental*) вре́дный, па́губный. **2.**: **a ~ remark** оби́дное замеча́ние.
hurtle [ˈhɜːt(ə)l] *v.t. & i.* нести́сь (*impf.*), мча́ться (*impf.*).
husband [ˈhʌzbənd] *n.* муж (*pl.* -ья́).
v.t. бере́чь (*impf.*); **we must ~ our resources** мы должны́ бере́чь/эконо́мить на́ши ресу́рсы.
cpd. **~man** *n.* (*arch.*) земледе́лец.
husbandry [ˈhʌzbəndrɪ] *n.* **1.** (се́льское) хозя́йство; **animal ~** скотово́дство. **2.** (*frugality*) бережли́вость.
hush [hʌʃ] *n.* молча́ние, тишь.
v.t.: **she ~ed the baby to sleep** она́ убаю́кала ребёнка; **the scandal was ~ed up** сканда́л замя́ли.
v.i.: **~!** (*as int.*) ти́ше!; молчи́те!
cpds. **~-~** *adj.* (*coll.*) та́йный, засекре́ченный; **~-money** *n.* взя́тка за молча́ние.
hushaby [ˈhʌʃəˌbaɪ] *int.* ба́ю-бай.
husk [hʌsk] *n.* шелуха́, скорлупа́, плёнка; (*fig.*) вне́шняя оболо́чка, шелуха́.
v.t. очища́ть (*impf.*); лущи́ть (*impf.*).
huskiness [ˈhʌskɪnɪs] *n.* (*hoarseness*) хрипловáтость.
husky[1] [ˈhʌskɪ] *n.* (*Eskimo dog*) эскимо́сская ла́йка.
husky[2] [ˈhʌskɪ] *adj.* **1.** (*with husks*) покры́тый шелухо́й. **2.** (*dry*) сухо́й. **3.** (*hoarse*) сухо́й, хри́плый. **4.** (*coll., brawny*) ро́слый, здоро́вый.
hussar [hʊˈzɑː(r)] *n.* гуса́р.
Hussite [ˈhʌsaɪt] *n.* гуси́т.
adj. гуси́тский.
hussy [ˈhʌsɪ] *n.* (*pert girl*) де́рзкая девчо́нка; (*trollop*) шлю́ха, потаску́шка.
hustings [ˈhʌstɪŋz] *n.* (*fig.*) вы́боры (*m. pl.*) в парла́мент.
hustle [ˈhʌs(ə)l] *n.* су́толока, да́вка.
v.t. **1.** (*jostle*) толка́ть (*impf.*); пиха́ть (*impf.*); **he ~d his way through the crowd** он проти́снулся сквозь толпу́. **2.** (*thrust, impel*): **the police ~d him away** его́ забра́ли полице́йские.
v.i. толка́ться (*impf.*); проти́скиваться (*impf.*); (*act strenuously*) пробива́ться (*impf.*).
hustler [ˈhʌslə(r)] *n.* (*bustler, strenuous pers.*) пробивно́й челове́к; (*coll., prostitute*) проститу́тка.
hut [hʌt] *n.* (*small building*) хи́жина, лачу́га; (*barrack*) бара́к.
hutch [hʌtʃ] *n.* (*for pets*) кле́тка; (*derog., small house*) хиба́рка.
hutment [ˈhʌtmənt] *n.* (*mil.*) вре́менный ла́герь.
hyacinth [ˈhaɪəsɪnθ] *n.* гиаци́нт.
hybrid [ˈhaɪbrɪd] *n.* гибри́д.
adj. гибри́дный; сме́шанный.
hybridization [ˌhaɪbrɪdaɪˈzeɪʃ(ə)n] *n.* гибридиза́ция.
hybridize [ˈhaɪbrɪˌdaɪz] *v.t.* скре́|щивать, -сти́ть; гибридизи́ровать (*impf.*).
hydatid [ˈhaɪdətɪd] *n.* (*cyst*) гидати́да; (*tapeworm*) эхиноко́кк.
hydra [ˈhaɪdrə] *n.* ги́дра.
hydrangea [haɪˈdreɪndʒə] *n.* горте́нзия.
hydrant [ˈhaɪdrənt] *n.* гидра́нт.
hydrate [ˈhaɪdreɪt] *n.* гидра́т, гидроо́кись.
v.t. гидрати́ровать.
hydraulic [haɪˈdrɔːlɪk, -ˈdrɒlɪk] *adj.* гидравли́ческий.
hydraulics [haɪˈdrɔːlɪks, -ˈdrɒlɪks] *n.* гидра́влика.
hydro [ˈhaɪdrəʊ] *n.* (*coll.*) оте́ль-водолече́бница.
hydrocarbon [ˌhaɪdrəˈkɑːbən] *n.* углеводоро́д.
hydrocephaly [ˌhaɪdrəˈsefəlɪ] *n.* водя́нка головно́го мо́зга, гидроцефа́лия.
hydrochloric [ˌhaɪdrəˈklɔːrɪk, -ˈklɒrɪk] *adj.*: **~ acid** соля́ная кислота́.

hydrodynamic [ˌhaɪdrəʊdaɪ'næmɪk] *adj.* гидродинами́ческий.
hydroelectric [ˌhaɪdrəʊɪ'lektrɪk] *adj.* гидроэлектри́ческий; ~ **power station** гидроэлектроста́нция (*abbr.* ГЭС).
hydrofoil ['haɪdrəˌfɔɪl] *n.* су́дно на подво́дных кры́льях (*abbr.* СПК); ракéта.
hydrogen ['haɪdrədʒ(ə)n] *n.* водоро́д; ~ **bomb** водоро́дная бо́мба.
hydrographic [ˌhaɪdrə'græfɪk] *adj.* гидрографи́ческий.
hydrolysis [haɪ'drɒlɪsɪs] *n.* гидро́лиз.
hydrometer [haɪ'drɒmɪtə(r)] *n.* гидро́метр, водоме́р.
hydropathic [ˌhaɪdrə'pæθɪk] *adj.* водолече́бный
hydrophobia [ˌhaɪdrə'fəʊbɪə] *n.* водобоя́знь.
hydroplane ['haɪdrəˌpleɪn] *n.* гидросамолёт.
hydroxide [haɪ'drɒksaɪd] *n.* гидроо́кись, гидра́т о́киси.
hyena [haɪ'iːnə] *n.* гие́на.
hygiene ['haɪdʒiːn] *n.* гигие́на.
hygienic [haɪ'dʒiːnɪk] *adj.* гигиени́ческий.
hymen ['haɪmen] *n.* (*anat.*) де́вственная пле́ва; (**H~**, *myth.*) Гимене́й.
hymeneal [ˌhaɪme'niːəl] *adj.* (*poet.*) сва́дебный.
hymn [hɪm] *n.* (церко́вный) гимн.
v.t.: **he insists on ~ing my praises** он не перестаёт петь мне дифира́мбы.
cpd. **~-book** *n.* (*also* **hymnal**) сбо́рник церко́вных ги́мнов.
hype [haɪp] *n.* крикли́вая рекла́ма.
adj.: **~d-up** ду́тый, ли́повый.
hyperactive [ˌhaɪpə'ræktɪv] *adj.* чрезме́рно акти́вный.
hyperactivity [ˌhaɪpəræk'tɪvɪtɪ] *n.* повы́шенная акти́вность.
hyperbola [haɪ'pɜːbələ] *n.* (*geom.*) гипе́рбола.
hyperbole [haɪ'pɜːbəlɪ] *n.* гипе́рбола, преувеличе́ние.
hyperbolical [ˌhaɪpə'bɒlɪk(ə)l] *adj.* гиперболи́ческий, преувели́ченный.
hypercritical [ˌhaɪpə'krɪtɪk(ə)l] *adj.* въе́дливый, приди́рчивый.
hyperglycaemia [ˌhaɪpəglaɪ'siːmɪə] *n.* (*US* **hyperglycemia**) гипергликеми́я.
hypermarket ['haɪpəˌmɑːkɪt] *n.* кру́пный универса́м (*в пригороде*).
hypersensitive [ˌhaɪpə'sensɪtɪv] *adj.* с повы́шенной чувстви́тельностью.
hypertension [ˌhaɪpə'tenʃ(ə)n] *n.* (*med.*) высо́кое кровяно́е давле́ние.
hypertrophy [haɪ'pɜːtrəfɪ] *n.* гипертрофи́я.
hyphen ['haɪf(ə)n] *n.* дефи́с, чёрточка.
v.t. **a ~ed word** сло́во, кото́рое пи́шется че́рез дефи́с/чёрточку.
hyphenate ['haɪfəˌneɪt] *v.t.* писа́ть, на- че́рез дефи́с/чёрточку.
hypnosis [hɪp'nəʊsɪs] *n.* гипно́з.
hypnotic [hɪp'nɒtɪk] *n.* (*subject*) загипнотизи́рованный; (*drug*) гипноти́ческое сре́дство.
adj. гипноти́ческий, завора́живающий.
hypnotism ['hɪpnəˌtɪz(ə)m] *n.* гипноти́зм.
hypnotist ['hɪpnətɪst] *n.* гипнотизёр.
hypnotize ['hɪpnəˌtaɪz] *v.t.* гипнотизи́ровать, за-.
hypochondria [ˌhaɪpə'kɒndrɪə] *n.* ипохо́ндрия.
hypochondriac [ˌhaɪpə'kɒndrɪˌæk] *n.* ипохо́ндрик.
adj. ипохондри́ческий.
hypocoristic [ˌhaɪpəkɔː'rɪstɪk] *adj.* ласка́тельный; уменьши́тельный.
hypocrisy [hɪ'pɒkrɪsɪ] *n.* лицеме́рие.
hypocrite ['hɪpəkrɪt] *n.* лицеме́р.
hypocritical [ˌhɪpə'krɪtɪk(ə)l] *adj.* лицеме́рный, нейскренний.
hypodermic [ˌhaɪpə'dɜːmɪk] *adj.*: ~ **injection** подко́жное впры́скивание; подко́жная инъе́кция; ~ **syringe/needle** шприц/игла́ для подко́жных инъе́кций.
hypotenuse [haɪ'pɒtəˌnjuːz] *n.* гипотену́за.
hypothecate [haɪ'pɒθɪˌkeɪt] *v.t.* за|кла́дывать, -ложи́ть.
hypothermia [ˌhaɪpəʊ'θɜːmɪə] *n.* гипотерми́я.
hypothesis [haɪ'pɒθɪsɪs] *n.* гипо́теза.
hypothesize [haɪ'pɒθɪˌsaɪz] *v.i.* предпол|ага́ть, -ожи́ть; стро́ить (*impf.*) дога́дки.
hypothetical [ˌhaɪpə'θetɪk(ə)l] *adj.* гипотети́ческий.
hyssop ['hɪsəp] *n.* иссо́п.
hysterectomy [ˌhɪstə'rektəmɪ] *n.* удале́ние ма́тки.
hysteria [hɪ'stɪərɪə] *n.* истери́я.
hysterical [hɪ'sterɪk(ə)l] *adj.* истери́чный; в исте́рике.
hysterics [hɪ'sterɪks] *n.* исте́рика.

I

I [aɪ] *pron.* я; **it is ~** э́то я; **he and ~ were there** мы с ним бы́ли там; **~ too** и я то́же; **he is older than ~** он ста́рше меня́.
iambic [aɪ'æmbɪk] *n.* ямби́ческий стих.
adj. ямби́ческий.
iambus [aɪ'æmbəs] *n.* ямб.
iatrogenic [aɪˌætrə'dʒenɪk] *adj.* ятроге́нный.
Iberia [aɪ'bɪərɪə] *n.* (*peninsula*) Ибе́рия.
Iberian [aɪ'bɪərɪən] *n.* ибе́р (*fem.* -ка).
adj. ибери́йский.
ibex ['aɪbeks] *n.* ка́менный козёл, козеро́г.
ibid(em) ['ɪbɪˌdem] *adj.* там же, в том же ме́сте.
ibis ['aɪbɪs] *n.* и́бис.
ICBM (*abbr. of* ***intercontinental ballistic missile***) МБР, (межконтинента́льная баллисти́ческая раке́та).
ice [aɪs] *n.* **1.** лёд; **black ~** гололе́дица; **he broke the ~** (*lit., fig.*) он слома́л/разби́л лёд; **that cuts no ~ with me** э́то меня́ ниско́лько не впечатля́ет; **he is skating on thin ~** (*fig.*) он игра́ет с огнём; **the proposal was kept on ~** прое́кт заморо́зили; **~ age** леднико́вый пери́од. **2.** (*~-cream*) моро́женое; **do they sell ~s?** продаётся ли моро́женое?
v.t. **1.** (*freeze; of wine, coffee etc., chill*) замор|а́живать, -о́зить. **2.** (*cover with ~*): **the pond was soon ~d over** пруд вско́ре затяну́ло/скова́ло льдом. **3.** (*cul.*) глазирова́ть (*impf., pf.*)
cpds. **~-axe** *n.* ледору́б; **~-blink** *n.* ледяно́й о́тблеск; **~bound** *adj.* затёртый/ско́ванный льда́ми; **~-box** *n.* ле́дник, холоди́льник; **~breaker** *n.* ледоко́л; **~-bucket** *n.* ведёрко со льдом; (*for making ~-cream*) моро́женица; **~-cap** *n.* леднико́вый покро́в, ледни́к; **~-cold** *adj.* ледяно́й; **~-cream** *n.* моро́женое; **~-cream man** моро́женщик; **~-cream maker** (*appliance*) моро́женица; **~-cream parlour** кафе́-моро́женое; **~-drift** *n.* дрейф льда; ледохо́д; **~-field** *n.* ледяно́е по́ле; **~-floe** *n.* плаву́чая льди́на; **~-free** *adj.* свобо́дный ото льда, незамерза́ющий; **~-hockey** *n.* хокке́й (на льду); **~-house** *n.* льдохрани́лище; **~-lolly** *n.* (*coll.*) моро́женое на па́лочке; **~man** *n.* (*US*) разво́зчик/продаве́ц льда; **~-pack** *n.* **1.** (*pack ~*) ледяно́й пак, торо́систый лёд. **2.** пузы́рь со льдом; **~-pick** *n.* кайла́; (*cul.*) пешня́ для льда; **~-rink** *n.* като́к; **~-run** *n.* ледяна́я го́рка; **~-show** *n.* бале́т на льду; **~-skate** *n.* конёк; *v.i.* ката́ться (*impf.*) на конька́х; **~-yacht** *n.* бу́ер.
iceberg ['aɪsbɜːg] *n.* а́йсберг.
Iceland ['aɪslənd] *n.* Исла́ндия.
Icelander ['aɪsləndə(r)] *n.* исла́нд|ец (*fem.* -ка).
Icelandic [aɪs'lændɪk] *n.* исла́ндский язы́к.
adj. исла́ндский.
ichneumon [ɪk'njuːmən] *n.* **1.** (*animal*) ихневмо́н; фарао́нова мышь. **2.** (**~-fly**) нае́здник.
ichor ['aɪkɔː(r)] *n.* (*path.*) су́кровица; (*myth.*) ихо́р.
ichthyology [ˌɪkθɪ'ɒlədʒɪ] *n.* ихтиоло́гия.
ichthyosaurus [ˌɪkθɪə'sɔːrəs] *n.* ихтиоза́вр.
icicle ['aɪsɪk(ə)l] *n.* сосу́лька.
icing ['aɪsɪŋ] *n.* (*on cake*) са́харная глазу́рь; (*of surfaces*) глазиро́вка, обледене́ние.
icon, ikon ['aɪkɒn] *n.* ико́на; о́браз (*pl.* -а́); ~ **lamp** лампа́д(к)а.
iconoclasm [aɪ'kɒnəˌklæz(ə)m] *n.* иконобо́рство.

iconoclast [aɪˈkɒnəˌklæst] *n.* иконобо́рец; (*fig.*) бунта́рь (*m.*).
iconoclastic [aɪˌkɒnəˈklæstɪk] *adj.* (*fig.*) иконобо́рческий.
iconography [ˌaɪkəˈnɒgrəfɪ] *n.* иконогра́фия.
iconostasis [ˌaɪkəˈnɒstəsɪs, aɪˌkɒnəˈstæsɪs] *n.* иконоста́с.
ictus [ˈɪktəs] *n.* икт.
icy [ˈaɪsɪ] *adj.* (*cold, lit., fig.*) ледяно́й; (*covered with ice*) покры́тый льдом.
ID (*abbr. of* **identification)** удостовере́ние ли́чности; **have you got some ~?** у вас есть удостовере́ние ли́чности?
id [ɪd] *n.* ид.
idea [aɪˈdɪə] *n.* **1.** (*mental concept*) иде́я; **fixed ~** навя́зчивая иде́я; **he tried to force his ~s on me** он стара́лся навяза́ть мне свои́ иде́и; **where did you get that ~?** отку́да вы э́то взя́ли? **2.** (*thought*) мысль; **I can't bear the ~ of it** (одна́) мысль об э́том мне проти́вна; **he is disturbed by the ~ of a possible accident** его́ беспоко́ит мысль о возмо́жной беде́; **don't put ~s into his head** не внуша́йте ему́ нену́жных иде́й; **the (very) ~ (of it)!** поду́мать то́лько! **3.** (*notion; understanding*) поня́тие; **I've no ~** я поня́тия не име́ю; **he has little ~ of physics** у него́ сла́бое представле́ние о фи́зике; **I have a good ~ of his abilities** я прекра́сно представля́ю себе́, на что он спосо́бен; **he gave me a general ~ of the story** он в о́бщих черта́х пересказа́л мне расска́з. **4.** (*scheme; plan*) иде́я, за́мысел, наме́рение; **a bright ~** блестя́щая иде́я; **a man (full) of ~s** челове́к, по́лный иде́й; **my ~ is to start afresh** я ду́маю нача́ть всё снача́ла; **what's the big ~?** (*coll.*) в чём смысл всего́ э́того?; э́то ещё заче́м?; **I studied Russian with the ~ of visiting Moscow** я изуча́л ру́сский язы́к с наме́рением съе́здить в Москву́; **I have run out of ~s** у меня́ ко́нчились все иде́и; **that's the ~!** вот и́менно!; э́то то, что ну́жно! **5.** (*way of thinking*): **the young ~** де́тский ум.
ideal [aɪˈdiːəl] *n.* идеа́л.
adj. идеа́льный; соверше́нный; превосхо́дный.
idealism [aɪˈdɪəˌlɪz(ə)m] *n.* идеали́зм.
idealist [aɪˈdɪəlɪst] *n.* идеали́ст.
idealistic [aɪˌdɪəˈlɪstɪk] *adj.* идеалисти́ческий.
idealization [aɪdɪəˌlaɪˈzeɪʃ(ə)n] *n.* идеализа́ция.
idealize [aɪˈdɪəˌlaɪz] *v.t.* идеализи́ровать (*impf., pf.*).
idée fixe [ˌiːdeɪ ˈfiːks] *n.* навя́зчивая иде́я, иде́я фикс.
idem [ˈɪdem] *n.* тот же.
identical [aɪˈdentɪk(ə)l] *adj.* **1.** (*the same*): **the ~ room where he was born** та са́мая ко́мната, в кото́рой он роди́лся. **2.** (*exactly similar*) тожде́ственный, иденти́чный; **the handwriting in the two manuscripts is ~** по́черк обе́их ру́кописей иденти́чен; **~ twins** однояйцевые близнецы́.
identification [aɪˌdentɪfɪˈkeɪʃ(ə)n] *n.* **1.** (*recognition; establishing identity*): **~ of a body** опозна́ние тру́па; **~ of a prisoner** установле́ние ли́чности аресто́ванного; (*attr.*) опознава́тельный; **~/identity disc** ли́чный знак; **~ marks** опознава́тельные зна́ки; **~ papers** докуме́нты, удостоверя́ющие ли́чность; **~ parade** процеду́ра опозна́ния подозрева́емого (свиде́телем и́ли пострада́вшим). **2.** (*treating as identical*) отождествле́ние.
identif|y [aɪˈdentɪˌfaɪ] *v.t.* **1.** (*recognize; establish identity of*) опозн|ава́ть, -а́ть; устан|а́вливать, -ови́ть ли́чность +*g.* **2.** (*treat as identical*) отождеств|ля́ть, -и́ть. **3.** (*associate*), *also v.i.* (*coll.*): **he ~ied (himself) with the movement** он солидаризова́лся с э́тим движе́нием.
identikit [aɪˈdentɪkɪt] *n.*: **an ~ (picture)** фоторо́бот (*подозреваемого преступника, сделанный по описаниям очевидцев*).
identity [aɪˈdentɪtɪ] *n.* **1.** (*sameness*) иденти́чность, тожде́ственность. **2.** (*who one is*) ли́чность; **he proved his ~** он предста́вил удостовере́ние свое́й ли́чности; **a case of mistaken ~** (суде́бная/сле́дственная) оши́бка в установле́нии престу́пника *и т.п.*; **~ card** удостовере́ние ли́чности; **~ disc = identification disc**
ideo|gram [ˈɪdɪəˌgræm], **-graph** [ˈɪdɪəˌgrɑːf] *nn.* идеогра́мма.
ideographic(al) [ˌɪdɪəˈgræfɪk(ə)l] *adj.* идеографи́ческий.
ideological [ˌaɪdɪəˈlɒdʒɪk(ə)l] *adj.* идеологи́ческий, иде́йный.
ideologist [ˌaɪdɪəˈɒlədʒɪst] *n.* идео́лог.
ideology [ˌaɪdɪˈɒlədʒɪ] *n.* идеоло́гия.
Ides [aɪdz] *n.* и́д|ы (*pl., g.* —).
idiocy [ˈɪdɪəsɪ] *n.* (*mental condition*) идиоти́зм; (*med.*) слабоу́мие; (*stupidity; stupid behaviour*) идио́тство, глу́пость.
idiom [ˈɪdɪəm] *n.* (*expression*) идио́ма; (*language; way of speaking*) наре́чие, го́вор, язы́к; (*fig., style of writing etc.*) стиль (*m.*), (чей) тво́рческий по́черк.
idiomatic [ˌɪdɪəˈmætɪk] *adj.* идиомати́ческий; **he speaks ~ Russian** он свобо́дно владе́ет ру́сским языко́м; он говори́т по-ру́сски как ру́сский; **an ~ language** язы́к, бога́тый идио́мами.
idiosyncrasy [ˌɪdɪəʊˈsɪŋkrəsɪ] *n.* своеобра́зие; (*med.*) идиосинкрази́я.
idiosyncratic [ˌɪdɪəʊsɪŋˈkrætɪk] *adj.* своеобра́зный; (*med.*) идиосинкрази́ческий.
idiot [ˈɪdɪət] *n.* идио́т, дура́к; **a drivelling ~** зако́нченный идио́т, кру́глый дура́к; **don't be an ~** (*coll.*) не валя́йте дурака́; не дури́те; (*attr.*): **an ~ child** слабоу́мный ребёнок; **~ box** (*coll.*) те́лик.
idiotic [ɪdɪˈɒtɪk] *adj.* идио́тский, дура́цкий.
idle [ˈaɪd(ə)l] *adj.* **1.** (*not working*) нерабо́тающий, безде́йствующий; (*unemployed*) безрабо́тный; **the strike made thousands ~** из-за забасто́вки ты́сячи люде́й оказа́лись без рабо́ты; (*unoccupied*) неза́нятый, свобо́дный; (*inactive*) безде́ятельный; **he has his hands ~ all day** он весь день безде́льничает; (*doing nothing*) пра́здный; **he stands ~ while others work** он безде́льничает, пока́ други́е рабо́тают; (*of factories etc.*) безде́йствующий; (*of machinery*) проста́ивающий; **the machines stood ~ all week** маши́ны простоя́ли це́лую неде́лю; (*of money*): **~ capital** мёртвый капита́л; (*of time*): **in an ~ moment** в свобо́дную мину́ту. **2.** (*lazy; slothful*) пра́здный, лени́вый; **he leads an ~ existence** он ведёт пра́здную жизнь. **3.** (*purposeless*): **out of ~ curiosity** из пра́здного/пусто́го любопы́тства; **~ talk** пуста́я болтовня́; **~ gossip** пусты́е спле́тни; (*fruitless; vain*): **an ~ attempt** тще́тная попы́тка; напра́сное уси́лие; **~ hopes** пусты́е/тще́тные наде́жды; **~ dreams** пусты́е мечты́; **it is ~ to expect him to help** бесполе́зно рассчи́тывать на его́ по́мощь; (*baseless*): **~ rumours** необосно́ванные/пусты́е слу́хи; **~ fears** напра́сные стра́хи/опасе́ния.
v.t.: **he ~d away his life** он растра́тил свою́ жизнь впусту́ю.
v.i. **1.** (*be ~*) безде́льничать (*impf.*); **stop idling about!** перест́аньте безде́льничать!; (*loiter*): **they ~d about the streets** они́ пра́здно слоня́лись по у́лицам. **2.** (*of an engine*): **the motor ~s well** мото́р хорошо́ рабо́тает на холосто́м ходу́.
idleness [ˈaɪdəlnɪs] *n.* пра́здность; безде́лье; лень; **she lives in ~** она́ живёт в пра́здности; она́ ведёт пра́здную жизнь.
idler [ˈaɪdlə(r)] *n.* безде́льник, лентя́й; (*stroller*) флане́р.
idly [ˈaɪdlɪ] *adv.* лени́во; (*absently*) рассе́янно.
idol [ˈaɪd(ə)l] *n.* и́дол, куми́р; **the ~ of the public** люби́мец пу́блики.
idolater [aɪˈdɒlətə(r)] *n.* идолопокло́нник.
idolatrous [aɪˈdɒlətrəs] *adj.* идолопокло́ннический, обоготворя́ющий; (*fig.*) поклоня́ющийся (*кому-н.*).
idolatry [aɪˈdɒlətrɪ] *n.* идолопокло́нство; (*fig.*) обожа́ние.
idolization [ˌaɪdəlaɪˈzeɪʃ(ə)n] *n.* обоготворе́ние; (*fig.*) обожа́ние.
idolize [ˈaɪdəˌlaɪz] *v.t.* обоготвор|я́ть, -и́ть; (*fig.*) боготвори́ть (*impf.*); обожа́ть (*impf.*).
idyll [ˈɪdɪl] *n.* иди́ллия.
idyllic [ɪˈdɪlɪk] *adj.* идилли́ческий.
i.e. (*abbr. of* **id est**) т.е., (то есть).
if [ɪf] *n.*: **I want no ~s and buts** (я не хочу́ слы́шать) никаки́х отгово́рок; **there are no ~s about it** никаки́х «е́сли»!; **it is a very big ~** э́то ещё большо́й вопро́с; э́то ещё о́чень сомни́тельно.
conj. **1.** (*condition or supposition*) е́сли, е́сли бы; **~ he is reading** е́сли он чита́ет; **~ he were reading** е́сли бы он чита́л; **~ he comes** е́сли он придёт; **~ I were you** на ва́шем ме́сте; **~ necessary** е́сли необходи́мо; **~ so** е́сли/коль так; **the debts, ~ any, were recovered** е́сли и бы́ли каки́е-либо долги́, они́ пога́шены; **~ anything she is more**

stupid than he е́сли уж на то пошло́, она́ глупе́е его́; **hold on, ~ not you'll fall** держи́тесь, а то упадёте; **nobody, ~ not he** е́сли не он, то и никто́; **~ only they arrive in time!** хоть бы они́ прие́хали во́время!; **~ only I had known!** е́сли бы я то́лько знал!; **~ only to please him** хотя́ бы для того́, что́бы доста́вить ему́ удово́льствие; **he talks as ~ he were the boss** он говори́т, как бу́дто он нача́льник; **he stood there as ~ dumb** он стоя́л, бу́дто немо́й; **as ~ by chance** бу́дто бы случа́йно; **as ~ you didn't know!** как бу́дто вы не зна́ли!; **it's not as ~ you had no money** друго́е де́ло, е́сли б у вас не́ было де́нег; **even ~** е́сли да́же. **2.** (*though*) хотя́, пусть; **~ they are poor, they are nevertheless happy** хотя́ они́ и бедны́, они́ всё же сча́стливы; **a pleasant, ~ chilly, day** прия́тный, хотя́ и прохла́дный день. **3.** (*whether*): **do you know ~ he is at home?** вы не зна́ете, он до́ма?; **see ~ the door is locked** посмотри́те, заперта́ ли дверь. **4.** (*in excl.*): **~ I haven't lost my gloves again!** поду́мать то́лько, я опя́ть потеря́л перча́тки!

igloo [ˈɪgluː] *n.* и́глу (*nt. indecl.*).

Ignatius [ɪgˈneɪʃɪəs] *n.* Игна́тий.

igneous [ˈɪgnɪəs] *adj.* (*of rock*) изве́рженный, пироге́нный; вулкани́ческого происхожде́ния.

ignis fatuus [ˌɪgnɪs ˈfætjʊəs] *n.* блужда́ющий огонёк; (*fig.*) обма́нчивая наде́жда.

ignite [ɪgˈnaɪt] *v.t.* & *i.* заж|ига́ть(ся), -е́чь(ся); воспламен|я́ть(ся), -и́ть(ся).

ignition [ɪgˈnɪʃ(ə)n] *n.* (*igniting*) зажига́ние, воспламене́ние; (*~ system in engine*) зажига́ние; **~ coil** кату́шка зажига́ния; **~ key** ключ зажига́ния.

ignoble [ɪgˈnəʊb(ə)l] *adj.* (*base*) по́длый, ни́зкий, ни́зменный, посты́дный; (*of lowly birth*) ни́зкого происхожде́ния.

ignominious [ˌɪgnəˈmɪnɪəs] *adj.* позо́рный, посты́дный; **an ~ death** бесcла́вная смерть.

ignominy [ˈɪgnəmɪnɪ] *n.* (*dishonour*) позо́р, бесче́стье; (*infamous conduct*) ни́зкое/посты́дное поведе́ние.

ignoramus [ˌɪgnəˈreɪməs] *n.* неве́жда.

ignorance [ˈɪgnərəns] *n.* (*in general*) неве́жество, неве́жественность; **he displayed total ~** он обнару́жил по́лное неве́жество; (*of certain facts*) незна́ние, неве́дение; **he did it in ~ of the facts** он сде́лал э́то по незна́нию фа́ктов (*or* по неве́дению); **in a state of blissful ~** в состоя́нии блаже́нного неве́дения.

ignorant [ˈɪgnərənt] *adj.* неве́жественный; **~ of music** несве́дущий в му́зыке; **I was ~ of his intentions** я не знал о его́ наме́рениях; я не́ был посвящён в его́ пла́ны.

ignore [ɪgˈnɔː(r)] *v.t.* игнори́ровать (*impf., pf.*); не обра|ща́ть, -ти́ть внима́ния на+*a.*

iguana [ɪgˈwɑːnə] *n.* игуа́на.

ikon [ˈaɪkɒn] = **icon**

ilex [ˈaɪleks] *n.* па́дуб.

iliac [ˈɪlɪˌæk] *adj.* подвздо́шный.

Iliad [ˈɪlɪˌæd] *n.* илиа́да.

ilk [ɪlk] *n.*: **and others of his ~** (*coll.*) и други́е того́ же ро́да; и ему́ подо́бные; (*liter.*) и и́же с ним.

ill [ɪl] *n.* **1.** (*evil, harm*) зло; **I meant him no ~** я не жела́л ему́ зла. **2.** (*pl., misfortunes*) бе́ды (*f. pl.*), несча́стья (*nt. pl.*).

adj. **1.** (*unwell*) больно́й, нездоро́вый; **he looks ~** он вы́глядит больны́м; **he was taken (*or* fell) ~ of a fever** он заболе́л лихора́дкой; **I feel ~** мне нехорошо́; я пло́хо себя́ чу́вствую; **the mentally ~** психи́чески больны́е. **2.** (*bad*): **~ effects** па́губные после́дствия; **~ fame, repute** дурна́я сла́ва; плоха́я репута́ция; **house of ~ fame** публи́чный дом; **~ feeling** неприя́знь, вражде́бность, оби́да; **I did it to show there was no ~ feeling** я сде́лал э́то, что́бы показа́ть, что я не пита́ю оби́ды; **~ fortune** несча́стье, неуда́ча; **~ health** нездоро́вье, недомога́ние; **~ humour, temper** (*disposition*) дурно́й нрав/хара́ктер; (*mood*) дурно́е настрое́ние; **in an ~ humour** в раздраже́нии; **he had ~ luck** ему́ не повезло́; **as ~ luck would have it** как на зло; как на грех/беду́; по несча́стью; **a run of ~ luck** полоса́ невезе́нья; **~ omen** дурно́е предзнаменова́ние; **bird of ~ omen** (*fig.*) предве́стник беды́/несча́стья; **he met with ~ success** он потерпе́л неуда́чу; **~ treatment** дурно́е обраще́ние; **~ weeds grow apace** дурна́я трава́ в рост идёт; **~ will** зла́я во́ля, зло́ба; *see also* **~ feeling; I bear you no ~ will** я не жела́ю вам зла; **it's an ~ wind (that blows nobody any good)** нет ху́да без добра́.

adv. пло́хо, ду́рно; **~ at ease** не по себе́; **I can ~ afford it** я с трудо́м могу́ себе́ э́то позво́лить; **it ~ becomes you** э́то вам не идёт; **he behaved ~** (*liter.*) он (по)вёл себя́ пло́хо/ду́рно; **he took it ~ that ...** он оби́делся на то, что...; **it went ~ with him** ему́ не повезло́; **I have never spoken ~ of him** я никогда́ не отзыва́лся о нём пло́хо.

cpds. **~-advised** *adj.* не(благо)разу́мный; **~-bred, ~-mannered** *adjs.* невоспи́танный, пло́хо воспи́танный; **~-conditioned** *adj.* (*of pers.*) дурно́го нра́ва, недо́брый; (*of thg.*) в плохо́м состоя́нии; **~-considered, ~-judged** *adjs.* необду́манный; **~-defined** *adj.* неопределённый; **~-disposed** *adj.* (*malicious*) зло́бный, злонра́вный; (*unfavourable*) недоброжела́тельный (*к кому*); не располо́жен (*к кому*); **~-famed** *adj.* по́льзующийся дурно́й сла́вой/репута́цией; **~-fated** *adj.* злосча́стный, рокaво́й; **~-favoured** *adj.* (*in appearance*) непривлека́тельный, некраси́вый; **~-gotten** *adj.* нече́стно на́житый; **~-humoured** *adj.* дурно́го нра́ва, в дурно́м настрое́нии; **~-informed** *adj.* пло́хо осведомлённый; **~-intentioned** *adj.* зловре́дный, злонаме́ренный; **~-judged** *adj.* = **~-considered; ~-mannered** *adj.* = **~-bred; ~-matched** *adj.* неподходя́щий; **~-natured** *adj.* зло́бный, зловре́дный; **~-omened** *adj.* злове́щий; **~-starred** *adj.* злосча́стный; **~-tempered** *adj.* вспы́льчивый, зло́бный; **~-timed** *adj.* несвоевре́менный; **~-treat, ~-use** *v.t.* пло́хо об|ходи́ться, -ойти́сь с+*i.*; пло́хо обраща́ться (*impf.*) с+*i.*; **~-will** *n.* недоброжела́тельность, вражде́бность.

illegal [ɪˈliːg(ə)l] *adj.* незако́нный, нелега́льный.

illegality [ˌɪliːˈgælɪtɪ] *n.* незако́нность, нелега́льность.

illegibility [ɪˌledʒɪˈbɪlɪtɪ] *n.* неразбо́рчивость, неудобочита́емость.

illegible [ɪˈledʒɪb(ə)l] *adj.* неразбо́рчивый, неудобочита́емый.

illegitimacy [ˌɪlɪˈdʒɪtɪməsɪ] *n.* (*of action*) незако́нность; (*of birth*) незаконнорождённость.

illegitimate [ˌɪlɪˈdʒɪtɪmət] *adj.* (*of action*) незако́нный; (*of pers.*) незаконнорождённый; (*of conclusion*) необосно́ванный.

illiberal [ɪˈlɪbər(ə)l] *adj.* (*unenlightened*) непросвещённый; (*narrow-minded*) ограни́ченный, недалёкий; (*intolerant*) нетерпи́мый; (*stingy*) скупо́й.

illiberality [ɪˌlɪbəˈrælɪtɪ] *n.* непросвещённость; ограни́ченность; нетерпи́мость; ску́пость.

illicit [ɪˈlɪsɪt] *adj.* незако́нный, недозво́ленный.

illiteracy [ɪˈlɪtərəsɪ] *n.* негра́мотность, безгра́мотность.

illiterate [ɪˈlɪtərət] *n.* негра́мотный; (*pej.*) не́уч.

adj. (*esp. of pers.*) негра́мотный; (*esp. of writing*) безгра́мотный.

illness [ˈɪlnɪs] *n.* боле́знь; **he caught a serious ~** он зарази́лся тяжёлой боле́знью; **she had a long ~** она́ перенесла́ дли́тельную боле́знь; **he was absent through ~** он отсу́тствовал по боле́зни; **~ of the mind** душе́вная/психи́ческая боле́знь; (*ill-health*) нездоро́вье, сла́бое здоро́вье; (*incidence of ~*) заболева́емость; **has there been much ~ in your family?** страда́ли ли чле́ны ва́шей семьи́ серьёзными заболева́ниями?; (*onset of ~*) заболева́ние; **his ~ began with a chill** заболева́ние начало́сь с озно́ба.

illogical [ɪˈlɒdʒɪk(ə)l] *adj.* нелоги́чный.

illogicality [ɪˌlɒdʒɪˈkælɪtɪ] *n.* нелоги́чность.

illuminat|e [ɪˈluːmɪˌneɪt, ɪˈljuː-] *v.t.* **1.** (*light*) осве|ща́ть, -ти́ть; **an ~ed sign** светя́щаяся рекла́ма. **2.** (*decorate with lights*) иллюмини́ровать (*impf., pf.*); **the town was ~ed for the festival** к пра́зднику в го́роде устро́или иллюмина́цию. **3.** (*of manuscripts etc.*) иллюмини́ровать (*impf., pf.*); **an ~ed manuscript** заста́вочная ру́копись. **4.** (*shed light on; explain*) осве|ща́ть, -ти́ть; прол|ива́ть, -и́ть свет на+*a.*; **an ~ing talk** поучи́тельная бесе́да.

illumination [ɪˌluːmɪˈneɪʃ(ə)n, ɪˈljuː-] *n.* **1.** освеще́ние. **2.** иллюмина́ция; **let's go and see the ~s** пойдёмте посмо́трим иллюмина́цию. **3.** (*of manuscript*) заста́вка.

illumine [ɪ'lju:mɪn, ɪ'lu:-] *v.t.* (*liter.*) **1.** (*light up*) осве|ща́ть, -ти́ть; (*with sunshine, a smile etc.*) озар|я́ть, -и́ть. **2.** (*enlighten*) просве|ща́ть, -ти́ть.

illusion [ɪ'lu:ʒ(ə)n, ɪ'lju:-] *n.* иллю́зия, обма́н; **optical ~** опти́ческая иллю́зия, обма́н зре́ния; **I was under an ~** я был во вла́сти иллю́зии; **I have no ~s about him** относи́тельно его́ у меня́ нет никаки́х иллю́зий.

illusionist [ɪ'lu:ʒənɪst, ɪ'lju:-] *n.* иллюзиони́ст, фо́кусник.

illus|ive [ɪ'lu:sɪv, ɪ'lju:-], **-ory** [ɪ'lu:sərɪ, ɪ'lju:-] *adjs.* иллюзо́рный, при́зрачный.

illustrate ['ɪlə,streɪt] *v.t.* **1.** (*decorate with pictures*) иллюстри́ровать (*impf., pf.*). **2.** (*make clear by examples*) иллюстри́ровать; поясн|я́ть, -и́ть; **this ~s the advantages of cooperation** э́то пока́зывает преиму́щества сотру́дничества.

illustration [,ɪlə'streɪʃ(ə)n] *n.* иллюстри́рование; иллюстра́ция, поясне́ние.

illustrative ['ɪləstrətɪv] *adj.* иллюстрати́вный, поясни́тельный; **a work ~ of his genius** произведе́ние, пока́зывающее его́ гениа́льность.

illustrator ['ɪlə,streɪtə(r)] *n.* иллюстра́тор.

illustrious [ɪ'lʌstrɪəs] *adj.* просла́вленный, знамени́тый.

ILO (*abbr. of* **International Labour Organization**) МОТ, (Междунаро́дная организа́ция труда́).

image ['ɪmɪdʒ] *n.* **1.** (*representation*) изображе́ние. **2.** (*statue*) ста́туя, скульпту́ра; **graven ~** и́дол, куми́р. **3.** (*likeness; counterpart*) ко́пия, портре́т; **he was the ~ of his father** он был то́чной ко́пией (*or* живы́м портре́том) своего́ отца́. **4.** (*idea; conception*) о́браз. **5.** (*simile or metaphor*) о́браз; **he spoke in ~s** он говори́л о́бразно. **6.** (*opt.*) изображе́ние; (*reflection*) отраже́ние. **7.** (*impression made on others*) репута́ция, прести́ж.

v.t. (*represent, portray*) предст|авля́ть, -а́вить; изобра|жа́ть, -зи́ть; (*reflect*) отра|жа́ть, -зи́ть; отобра|жа́ть, -зи́ть.

cpd. **~-worship** *n.* идолопокло́нство.

imagery ['ɪmɪdʒərɪ] *n.* (*in writing*) о́бразность.

imaginable [ɪ'mædʒɪnəb(ə)l] *adj.* вообрази́мый; **we had the greatest trouble ~** у нас бы́ли невообрази́мые хло́поты.

imaginary [ɪ'mædʒɪnərɪ] *adj.* вообража́емый, вы́мышленный; (*also math.*) мни́мый.

imagination [ɪ,mædʒɪ'neɪʃ(ə)n] *n.* воображе́ние; **he let his ~ run riot** он дал во́лю своему́ воображе́нию; **use your ~!** напряги́те своё воображе́ние!

imaginative [ɪ'mædʒɪnətɪv] *adj.* с воображе́нием; одарённый/облада́ющий (больши́м/бога́тым) воображе́нием; **~ writing** худо́жественная литерату́ра, беллетри́стика.

imagin|e [ɪ'mædʒɪn] *v.t.* **1.** (*form mental picture of*) вообра|жа́ть, -зи́ть; **she is always ~ing things** ей ве́чно что́-то мере́щится. **2.** (*conceive*) предст|авля́ть, -а́вить себе́; **I cannot ~e how it happened** я не могу́ предста́вить себе́ как э́то случи́лось; **I ~e Peter to be tall** я представля́ю себе́ Петра́ высо́ким. **3.** (*suppose*) предпол|ага́ть, -ожи́ть; полага́ть (*impf.*); **do you ~e I like it?** неуже́ли вы полага́ете, что мне э́то нра́вится? **4.** (*think*) ду́мать, по-; **I ~ed I heard footsteps** мне показа́лось, что я слы́шал шаги́. **5.** (*fancy*): **~e seeing you here!** кто бы мог поду́мать, что я уви́жу вас здесь? **6.** (*guess*) дога́д|ываться, -а́ться; пон|има́ть, -я́ть; **I cannot ~e what you mean** ума́ не приложу́, что вы име́ете в виду́.

imagism ['ɪmɪ,dʒɪz(ə)m] *n.* имажини́зм.

imago [ɪ'meɪgəʊ] *n.* (*zool.*) има́го (*indecl.*).

imam [ɪ'mɑ:m] *n.* има́м.

imbalance [ɪm'bæləns] *n.* отсу́тствие равнове́сия, неусто́йчивость; несоотве́тствие.

imbecile ['ɪmbɪ,si:l] *n.* (*pers. of weak intellect*) крети́н; слабоу́мный; (*fool*) глупе́ц, дура́к (*coll.*).

adj. слабоу́мный; (*stupid*) глу́пый.

imbecility [,ɪmbɪ'sɪlɪtɪ] *n.* имбеци́льность, кретини́зм; слабоу́мие; (*stupidity*) глу́пость.

imbib|e [ɪm'baɪb] *v.t.* (*drink*) погло|ща́ть, -ти́ть; пить, вы́-; (*fig., assimilate*) усв|а́ивать, -о́ить; впи́т|ывать, -а́ть; **he ~ed new ideas** он впита́л но́вые иде́и.

v.i.: **he has been ~ing** (*coll.*) он вы́пивши.

imbroglio [ɪm'brəʊlɪəʊ] *n.* пу́таница.

imbrue [ɪm'bru:] *v.t.* (*liter.*) обагр|я́ть, -и́ть; **hands ~d with blood** ру́ки, обагрённые кро́вью.

imbue [ɪm'bju:] *v.t.* **1.** (*lit., saturate*) пропи́т|ывать, -а́ть; (*dye*) окра́|шивать, -сить. **2.** (*fig., inspire*) всел|я́ть, -и́ть (*что в кого*); **the war ~d the nation with the spirit of patriotism** война́ всели́ла в наро́д дух патриоти́зма; (*fill*): **~d with hatred** прони́кнутый не́навистью.

IMF (*abbr. of* **International Monetary Fund**) МВФ, (Междунаро́дный валю́тный фонд).

imitate ['ɪmɪ,teɪt] *v.t.* **1.** (*follow example of*) подража́ть (*impf.*) +*d.*; **you should ~ his virtues** вы должны́ подража́ть его́ доброде́телям. **2.** (*copy; mimic*) копи́ровать (*impf.*); имити́ровать (*impf.*); передра́зн|ивать, -и́ть. **3.** (*make sth. similar to*) имити́ровать (*impf.*); подде́л|ывать, -ать; **he ~s diamonds in paste** он изготовля́ет подде́льные бриллиа́нты; **~ oak by graining** кра́сить (*impf.*) под дуб; **fabric made to ~ silk** материа́л, имити́рующий шёлк.

imitation [,ɪmɪ'teɪʃ(ə)n] *n.* **1.** (*imitating; mimicry*) подража́ние; **in ~ of her teacher** в подража́ние своему́ учи́телю; **(built in) ~ Gothic** постро́енный в псевдоготи́ческом сти́ле; **he does bird ~s** он уме́ет подража́ть пти́цам. **2.** (*copy*) имита́ция, подде́лка; **wood painted in ~ of marble** де́рево, окра́шенное под мра́мор; **beware of ~s!** остерега́йтесь подде́лок; (*attr.*) иску́сственный, подде́льный; **~ leather** иску́сственная ко́жа; **~ antiques** подде́льные антиква́рные изде́лия.

imitative ['ɪmɪtətɪv] *adj.*: **~ words** звукоподража́тельные слова́; **the ~ arts** изобрази́тельные иску́сства; **an ~ animal** подража́ющее живо́тное; **~ behaviour** подража́тельное поведе́ние.

imitator ['ɪmɪ,teɪtə(r)] *n.* подража́тель (*fem.* -ница).

immaculate [ɪ'mækjʊlət] *adj.* **1.** (*pure*) незапя́тнанный; **the I~ Conception** непоро́чное зача́тие. **2.** (*faultless*) безупре́чный, безукори́зненный.

immanence ['ɪmənəns] *n.* прису́щность; (*phil.*) иммане́нтность.

immanent ['ɪmənənt] *adj.* (*inherent*) прису́щий; (*pervading*) вездесу́щий; (*phil.*) иммане́нтный.

immaterial [,ɪmə'tɪərɪəl] *adj.* (*not corporeal*) невеще́ственный; бестеле́сный; (*unimportant*) несуще́ственный; **it is quite ~ to me** мне реши́тельно всё равно́.

immature [,ɪmə'tjʊə(r)] *adj.* незре́лый.

immaturity [,ɪmə'tjʊərɪtɪ] *n.* незре́лость.

immeasurable [ɪ'meʒərəb(ə)l] *adj.* неизмери́мый.

immediacy [ɪ'mi:dɪəsɪ] *n.* **1.** (*directness*) непосре́дственность. **2.** (*in time*) незамедли́тельность; (*urgency*) безотлага́тельность.

immediate [ɪ'mi:dɪət] *adj.* **1.** (*direct, closest possible*) непосре́дственный, прямо́й, ближа́йший; (*next in order*) очередно́й; **in the ~ neighbourhood** в непосре́дственной бли́зости; **my ~ neighbours** мои́ ближа́йшие сосе́ди; **on his ~ left** сра́зу нале́во от него́; **the ~ heir** прямо́й насле́дник; **in the ~ future** в ближа́йшем бу́дущем. **2.** (*without delay*) неме́дленный, мгнове́нный; **there was an ~ silence** наступи́ла мгнове́нная тишина́. **3.** (*urgent*) безотлага́тельный.

immediately [ɪ'mi:dɪətlɪ] *adv.* (*directly*) непосре́дственно; (*without delay, at once*) неме́дленно, то́тчас (же), сра́зу, мгнове́нно.

conj.: **~ I heard the news** как то́лько я узна́л но́вости.

immemorial [,ɪmɪ'mɔ:rɪəl] *adj.* незапа́мятный; **from time ~** с незапа́мятных времён.

immense [ɪ'mens] *adj.* (*huge*) огро́мный, грома́дный; (*vast*) безме́рный, необозри́мый, необъя́тный; (*countless*) несме́тный; (*coll., very great*): **it was an ~ disappointment** э́то бы́ло огро́мным разочарова́нием; **he is an ~ eater** он неуме́ренный едо́к; **we enjoyed ourselves ~ly** мы получи́ли огро́мное удово́льствие; **she was ~ly proud of her son** она́ невероя́тно горди́лась свои́м сы́ном.

immensity [ɪ'mensɪtɪ] *n.* безме́рность, необъя́тность, необозри́мость.

immerse [ɪ'mɜ:s] *v.t.* **1.** погр|ужа́ть, -зи́ть; окун|а́ть, -у́ть;

~d in thought погружённый в ду́му; **she ~d herself in a book** она́ погрузи́лась в чте́ние. **2.** (*fig.*, *entangle*) запу́т|ывать, -ать; **he was ~d in debt** он погря́з в долга́х.
immersion [ɪˈmɜːʃ(ə)n] *n.* (*lit.*, *fig.*) погруже́ние; **~ heater** погружа́емый нагрева́тель.
immigrant [ˈɪmɪgrənt] *n.* иммигра́нт (*fem.* -ка).
immigrate [ˈɪmɪˌgreɪt] *v.i.* иммигри́ровать (*impf.*, *pf.*).
immigration [ˌɪmɪˈgreɪʃ(ə)n] *n.* иммигра́ция; **~ officer** сотру́дник иммиграцио́нного ве́домства (*or* иммиграцио́нной слу́жбы).
imminence [ˈɪmɪnəns] *n.* нави́сшая угро́за, опа́сность.
imminent [ˈɪmɪnənt] *adj.* надвига́ющийся; **a storm was ~** надвига́лась гроза́; (*of danger*) непосре́дственный, нави́сший.
immobile [ɪˈməʊbaɪl] *adj.* неподви́жный.
immobility [ˌɪməʊˈbɪlɪtɪ] *n.* неподви́жность.
immobilization [ɪˌməʊbɪlaɪˈzeɪʃ(ə)n] *n.* (*med.*) дли́тельный посте́льный режи́м; (*of limb etc.*) иммобилиза́ция; (*of troops*) ско́вывание.
immobilize [ɪˈməʊbɪˌlaɪz] *v.t.* иммобилизова́ть (*pf.*); (*mil.*) ско́в|ывать, -а́ть; парализова́ть (*impf.*, *pf.*); **our troops were ~d** на́ши войска́ бы́ли парализо́ваны; **I was ~d by a broken leg** я не мог дви́гаться из-за сло́манной ноги́; **he ~d his car** он вы́вел свой автомоби́ль из стро́я; **their funds were ~d** их фо́нды бы́ли заморо́жены.
immoderate [ɪˈmɒdərət] *adj.* неуме́ренный.
immodest [ɪˈmɒdɪst] *adj.* нескро́мный; (*indecent*) неприли́чный.
immodesty [ɪˈmɒdɪstɪ] *n.* нескро́мность; (*indecency*) неприли́чие.
immolate [ˈɪməˌleɪt] *v.t.* (*lit.*, *fig.*) прин|оси́ть, -ести́ в же́ртву.
immolation [ˌɪməˈleɪʃ(ə)n] *n.* жертвоприноше́ние.
immoral [ɪˈmɒr(ə)l] *adj.* безнра́вственный, амора́льный; **~ earnings** сомни́тельные дохо́ды.
immorality [ˌɪməˈrælɪtɪ] *n.* безнра́вственность, амора́льность.
immortal [ɪˈmɔːt(ə)l] *n.* & *adj.* бессме́ртный; **~ fame** неувяда́емая сла́ва.
immortality [ˌɪmɔːˈtælɪtɪ] *n.* бессме́ртие.
immortalization [ɪˌmɔːtəlaɪˈzeɪʃ(ə)n] *n.* увекове́чение.
immortalize [ɪˈmɔːtəˌlaɪz] *v.t.* увекове́чи|вать, -ть; обессме́ртить (*pf.*).
immovability [ɪˌmuːvəˈbɪlɪtɪ] *n.* неподви́жность; (*steadfastness*) непоколеби́мость.
immovable [ɪˈmuːvəb(ə)l] *n.* (*usu. pl.*) недви́жимость.
adj. (*that cannot be moved*; *stationary*; *fixed*, *e.g. of property*) недви́жимый; (*motionless*) неподви́жный; недви́жимый; (*steadfast*) непоколеби́мый; (*emotionless*) невозмути́мый.
immune [ɪˈmjuːn] *adj.*: **~ to, from, against disease** невосприи́мчивый к боле́зни; **~ against poison** иммýнный к я́ду; **~ from criticism** неподвла́стный кри́тике; **~ from taxes** свобо́дный/освобождённый от нало́гов.
immunity [ɪˈmjuːnɪtɪ] *n.* **1.** (*from disease etc.*) невосприи́мчивость, иммуните́т (*к чему*). **2.** (*in law*) неприкоснове́нность, иммуните́т; **diplomatic ~** дипломати́ческий иммуните́т. **3.** (*from tax*) освобожде́ние (от нало́га).
immunization [ˌɪmjuːnaɪˈzeɪʃ(ə)n] *n.* иммуниза́ция.
immunize [ˈɪmjuːˌnaɪz] *v.t.* иммунизи́ровать (*impf.*, *pf.*) (*кого к чему*).
immunology [ˌɪmjuːˈnɒlədʒɪ] *n.* иммуноло́гия.
immunotherapy [ˌɪmjuːnəʊˈθerəpɪ] *n.* иммунотерапи́я.
immure [ɪˈmjʊə(r)] *v.t.* заточ|а́ть, -и́ть; замуро́в|ывать, -а́ть; зап|ира́ть, -ере́ть; **he ~d himself in his study** он заперся́ в кабине́те.
immutability [ɪˌmjuːtəˈbɪlɪtɪ] *n.* неизме́нность, непрело́жность.
immutable [ɪˈmjuːtəb(ə)l] *adj.* неизме́нный, непрело́жный.
imp [ɪmp] *n.* (*lit.*; *fig.*, *mischievous child*) дьяволёнок, чертёнок, бесёнок; (*fig. only*) постре́л.
impact [ˈɪmpækt] *n.* (*collision*) столкнове́ние; (*striking force*) уда́р, толчо́к; (*fig.*, *effect*, *influence*) возде́йствие, влия́ние; **his words made an immediate ~** его́ слова́ возыме́ли неме́дленное де́йствие.
impacted [ɪmˈpæktɪd] *adj.*: **~ fracture** вколо́ченный перело́м; **~ tooth** ретини́рованный зуб.
impair [ɪmˈpeə(r)] *v.t.* (*damage*) повре|жда́ть, -ди́ть; (*spoil*) по́ртить, ис-; (*undermine*) под|рыва́ть, -орва́ть; (*weaken*) осл|абля́ть, -а́бить; (*make worse*) ух|удша́ть, -у́дшить; **smoking will ~ your health** куре́ние подорвёт ва́ше здоро́вье; **the view was ~ed by a chimney** вид был испо́рчен дымово́й трубо́й; **his vision was ~ed** его́ зре́ние пострада́ло; **this ~ed the force of his argument** э́то осла́било си́лу его́ до́вода.
impairment [ɪmˈpeəmənt] *n.* поврежде́ние; по́рча; подры́в; ослабле́ние; ухудше́ние.
impale [ɪmˈpeɪl] *v.t.* прок|а́лывать, -оло́ть; пронз|а́ть, -и́ть; прот|ыка́ть, -кну́ть; (*hist.*) сажа́ть, посади́ть на́ кол; **he ~d himself on his sword** он пронзи́л себя́ мечо́м; **he fell and was ~d on the railings** он свали́лся на огра́ду и проткну́л себе́ живо́т.
impalpable [ɪmˈpælpəb(ə)l] *adj.* (*not felt by touch*) неосяза́емый; (*by senses or mind*) неощути́мый; (*elusive*) неулови́мый.
impanel [ɪmˈpæn(ə)l] *v.t.* включ|а́ть, -и́ть в спи́сок прися́жных.
imparity [ɪmˈpærɪtɪ] *n.* нера́венство.
impart [ɪmˈpɑːt] *v.t.* **1.** (*lend*; *give*) прид|ава́ть, -а́ть; **he ~ed a serious tone to the conversation** он при́дал разгово́ру серьёзный тон. **2.** (*communicate*, *e.g. news*) перед|ава́ть, -а́ть; сообщ|а́ть, -и́ть. **3.** (*pass on*, *e.g. knowledge*) дели́ться, по- *+i.*; **he ~ed his skill to** он подели́лся с на́ми свои́м уме́нием.
impartial [ɪmˈpɑːʃ(ə)l] *adj.* беспристра́стный, непредвзя́тый.
impartiality [ɪmˌpɑːʃɪˈælɪtɪ] *n.* беспристра́стность, непредвзя́тость.
impassable [ɪmˈpɑːsəb(ə)l] *adj.* (*on foot*) непроходи́мый; (*for vehicles*) непрое́зжий.
impasse [ˈæmpæs, ˈɪm-] *n.* (*lit.*, *fig.*) тупи́к; **things reached an ~** дела́ зашли́ в тупи́к.
impassioned [ɪmˈpæʃ(ə)nd] *adj.* стра́стный, пы́лкий.
impassive [ɪmˈpæsɪv] *adj.* (*unmoved*) бесстра́стный; (*serene*) безмяте́жный.
impassivity [ˌɪmpæˈsɪvɪtɪ] *n.* бесстра́стие; безмяте́жность.
impasto [ɪmˈpæstəʊ] *n.* наложе́ние кра́сок густы́м сло́ем.
impatience [ɪmˈpeɪʃəns] *n.* нетерпе́ние, нетерпели́вость; **he was all ~ to begin** ему́ не терпе́лось нача́ть; (*irritation*) раздраже́ние.
impatient [ɪmˈpeɪʃ(ə)nt] *adj.* нетерпели́вый; (*irritable*) раздражи́тельный, раздражённый; **he was growing, getting ~** он теря́л терпе́ние, он раздража́лся; **he is ~ of advice** он не те́рпит сове́тов; **she was ~ for a letter** она́ нетерпели́во ждала́ письма́; **he is ~ to begin** ему́ не те́рпится нача́ть.
impeach [ɪmˈpiːtʃ] *v.t.* **1.** (*accuse*) обвин|я́ть, -и́ть (*кого в чём*); **he was ~ed (for treason)** ему́ предъяви́ли обвине́ние в госуда́рственной изме́не. **2.** (*call in question*) осп|а́ривать, -о́рить; **are you ~ing my honour?** неуже́ли вы ста́вите под сомне́ние мою́ честь?
impeachment [ɪmˈpiːtʃmənt] *n.* **1.** (*accusation*) обвине́ние; (*on charge of treason etc.*) импи́чмент. **2.** (*calling in question*) выраже́ние сомне́ния в+*p.* (*or* недове́рия *+d.*).
impeccability [ɪmˌpekəˈbɪlɪtɪ] *n.* (*rectitude*) непогреши́мость; (*faultlessness*) безупре́чность.
impeccable [ɪmˈpekəb(ə)l] *adj.* (*without sin*) непогреши́мый; (*faultless*) безупре́чный.
impecuniosity [ˌɪmpɪkjuːnɪˈɒsɪtɪ] *n.* безде́нежье.
impecunious [ˌɪmpɪˈkjuːnɪəs] *adj.* безде́нежный.
impedance [ɪmˈpiːd(ə)ns] *n.* (*elec.*) по́лное сопротивле́ние; импеда́нс.
impede [ɪmˈpiːd] *v.t.* (*obstruct*) препя́тствовать (*impf.*) *+d.*; прегра|жда́ть, -ди́ть; (*delay*) заде́рж|ивать, -а́ть; (*hinder*) меша́ть, по- (*кому/чему*); затрудн|я́ть, -и́ть; осложн|я́ть, -и́ть; **the traffic was ~d** у́личное движе́ние бы́ло заде́ржано; **negotiations were ~d** перегово́ры бы́ли затруднены́.
impediment [ɪmˈpedɪmənt] *n.* **1.** (*obstruction*) препя́тствие, прегра́да, поме́ха; (*hindrance*, *delay*) заде́ржка; **an ~ to progress** препя́тствие на пути́ прогре́сса. **2.** (*speech*

defect) заика́ние; **he has an ~ in his speech** он заика́ется.

impedimenta [ɪm,pedɪ'mentə] *n.* (*mil.*) обо́зы (*m. pl.*); (*baggage*) бага́ж.

impel [ɪm'pel] *v.t.* **1.** (*propel*) прив|оди́ть, -ести́ в движе́ние. **2.** (*drive*; *force*) прин|ужда́ть, -у́дить; пон|ужда́ть, -у́дить; заст|авля́ть, -а́вить; побу|жда́ть, -ди́ть; **conscience ~led him to speak the truth** со́весть прину́дила его́ говори́ть пра́вду; **he was ~led to crime by poverty** бе́дность толкну́ла его́ на преступле́ние; **I feel ~led to say** я вы́нужден сказа́ть.

impend [ɪm'pend] *v.i.* **1.** (*be imminent*; *approach*) надв|ига́ться, -и́нуться; прибл|ижа́ться, -и́зиться; **war was ~ing** война́ надвига́лась; **his ~ing arrival** его́ предстоя́щий прие́зд. **2.** (*threaten*) угрожа́ть (*impf.*); нав|иса́ть, -и́снуть; **~ing danger** нави́сшая опа́сность/угро́за.

impenetrability [ɪm,penɪtrə'bɪlɪtɪ] *n.* (*lit., fig.*) непроница́емость.

impenetrable [ɪm'penɪtrəb(ə)l] *adj.* непроница́емый; **an ~ forest** непроходи́мый лес; **an ~ mystery** непостижи́мая та́йна; **~ darkness** непрогля́дная тьма; **a mind ~ by, to new ideas** ко́сный ум.

impenitence [ɪm'penɪtəns] *n.* нераска́янность, закосне́лость.

impenitent [ɪm'penɪt(ə)nt] *adj.* нераска́янный, закосне́лый.

imperative [ɪm'perətɪv] *n.* (*gram.*) повели́тельное наклоне́ние, императи́в.

adj. **1.** (*urgent*; *essential*): **an ~ request** настоя́тельное тре́бование; **it is ~ that you come at once** вам необходи́мо то́тчас яви́ться. **2.** (*imperious*) повели́тельный, вла́стный. **3.** (*gram.*) повели́тельный.

imperceptible [,ɪmpə'septɪb(ə)l] *adj.* (*that cannot be perceived*) незаме́тный; (*very slight, gradual*) незначи́тельный.

imperfect [ɪm'pɜ:fɪkt] *n.* (*gram.*) проше́дшее несоверше́нное вре́мя, имперфе́кт.

adj. (*faulty*) несоверше́нный, дефе́ктный; (*incomplete*) непо́лный; (*unfinished*) незако́нченный; (*gram.*) проше́дший, несовершённый.

imperfection [,ɪmpə'fekʃ(ə)n] *n.* (*incompleteness, faultiness*) несоверше́нство, неполнота́; (*fault*) дефе́кт, изъя́н; недоста́ток.

imperfective [,ɪmpə'fektɪv] *n.* & *adj.* (*gram.*) несоверше́нный (вид).

imperial [ɪm'pɪərɪəl] *n.* (*beard*) эспаньо́лка.

adj. **1.** (*of an empire*) импе́рский; **~ Rome/Russia** Ри́мская/Росси́йская импе́рия. **2.** (*of an emperor*) импера́торский; **the ~ crown** импера́торская коро́на; **His I~ Majesty** его́ импера́торское вели́чество. **3.** (*majestic*) великоле́пный; **with ~ disdain** с ца́рственным презре́нием. **4.** (*of Br. measures*) импе́рский.

imperialism [ɪm'pɪərɪə,lɪz(ə)m] *n.* империали́зм.

imperialist [ɪm'pɪərɪəlɪst] *n.* империали́ст.

imperialist(ic) [ɪm,pɪərɪə'lɪst(ɪk)] *adj.* империалисти́ческий, империали́стский.

imperil [ɪm'perɪl] *v.t.* подв|ерга́ть, -е́ргнуть опа́сности; ста́вить, по- под угро́зу.

imperious [ɪm'pɪərɪəs] *adj.* (*domineering*) повели́тельный, вла́стный; (*urgent, imperative*) настоя́тельный, императи́вный.

imperiousness [ɪm'pɪərɪəsnɪs] *n.* повели́тельность, вла́стность; настоя́тельность, императи́вность.

imperishable [ɪm'perɪʃəb(ə)l] *adj.* (*lit.*) непо́ртящийся; (*fig.*) нетле́нный; **~ fame** ве́чная/неувяда́емая сла́ва.

impermanence [ɪm'pɜ:mənəns] *n.* непостоя́нство, неусто́йчивость.

impermanent [ɪm'pɜ:mənənt] *adj.* непостоя́нный, неусто́йчивый.

impermeability [ɪm,pɜ:mɪə'bɪlɪtɪ] *n.* непроница́емость.

impermeable [ɪm'pɜ:mɪəb(ə)l] *adj.* непроница́емый.

impermissible [,ɪmpə'mɪsɪb(ə)l] *adj.* непозволи́тельный, недозво́ленный.

impersonal [ɪm'pɜ:sən(ə)l] *adj.* безли́кий, безли́чный; **~ forces** объекти́вные си́лы; (*gram.*) безли́чный.

impersonality [ɪm,pɜ:sə'nælɪtɪ] *n.* безли́кость, безли́чность.

impersonate [ɪm'pɜ:sə,neɪt] *v.t.* (*act the part of*) игра́ть (*impf.*) роль +*g.*; изобра|жа́ть, -зи́ть; (*pretend to be*) выдава́ть (*impf.*) себя́ за+*a.*

impersonation [ɪm,pɜ:sə'neɪʃ(ə)n] *n.* изображе́ние; **he gave an ~ of the professor** он изобрази́л профе́ссора; (*leg.*) персона́ция, незако́нная вы́дача себя́ за друго́е лицо́.

impersonator [ɪm'pɜ:sə,neɪtə(r)] *n.*: **female ~** эстра́дный арти́ст, изобража́ющий же́нщину.

impertinence [ɪm'pɜ:tɪnəns] *n.* (*rudeness*) де́рзость, на́глость, наха́льство; (*irrelevance*) неуме́стность.

impertinent [ɪm'pɜ:tɪnənt] *adj.* де́рзкий, на́глый, наха́льный; неуме́стный.

imperturbability [,ɪmpə,tɜ:bə'bɪlɪtɪ] *n.* невозмути́мость.

imperturbable [,ɪmpə'tɜ:bəb(ə)l] *adj.* невозмути́мый.

impervious [ɪm'pɜ:vɪəs] *adj.* непроница́емый; **~ to light** све́тонепроница́емый; (*fig.*): **~ to criticism** глух к кри́тике.

impetigo [,ɪmpɪ'taɪgəʊ] *n.* импети́го (*indecl.*).

impetuosity [ɪm,petjʊ'ɒsɪtɪ] *n.* стреми́тельность, поры́вистость, необду́манность, горя́чность.

impetuous [ɪm'petjʊəs] *adj.* (*moving violently*) стреми́тельный, бу́рный, поры́вистый; (*acting or done with rash energy*) стреми́тельный, поры́вистый; горя́чий; (*impulsive*) импульси́вный; (*unpremeditated*) необду́манный.

impetus ['ɪmpɪtəs] *n.* толчо́к; и́мпульс; **the car travelled for several yards under its own ~** автомоби́ль прое́хал не́сколько ме́тров по ине́рции; (*fig.*) толчо́к, сти́мул; **this will give an ~ to trade** э́то даст торго́вле толчо́к.

impiety [ɪm'paɪətɪ] *n.* не(благо)чести́вость.

impinge [ɪm'pɪndʒ] *v.i.* па́дать (*impf.*) на+*a.*; ударя́ться (*impf.*) о+*a.*; **rays of light ~ on the retina** лучи́ све́та па́дают на сетча́тку.

impious ['ɪmpɪəs] *adj.* не(благо)чести́вый.

impish ['ɪmpɪʃ] *adj.* прока́зливый, озорно́й.

impishness ['ɪmpɪʃnɪs] *n.* прока́зливость, озорство́.

implacability [ɪm,plækə'bɪlɪtɪ] *n.* неумоли́мость.

implacable [ɪm'plækəb(ə)l] *adj.* неумоли́мый, безжа́лостный.

implant [ɪm'plɑ:nt] *v.t.* вв|оди́ть, -ести́; (*fig., instil*) внедр|я́ть, -и́ть; наса|жда́ть, -ди́ть, всел|я́ть, -и́ть; **he ~ed a doubt in her mind** он посе́ял в ней сомне́ние.

implausibility [ɪm,plɔ:zɪ'bɪlɪtɪ] *n.* неправдоподо́бность, невероя́тность.

implausible [ɪm'plɔ:zɪb(ə)l] *adj.* неправдоподо́бный, невероя́тный.

implement[1] ['ɪmplɪmənt] *n.* ору́дие, инструме́нт; **farm ~s** сельскохозя́йственные ору́дия.

implement[2] ['ɪmplɪ,ment] *v.t.* выполня́ть, вы́полнить; осуществ|ля́ть, -и́ть; пров|оди́ть, -ести́ в жизнь; **when the scheme is ~ed** когда́ план бу́дет осуществлён.

implementation [,ɪmplɪmen'teɪʃ(ə)n] *n.* выполне́ние, осуществле́ние.

implicate ['ɪmplɪ,keɪt] *v.t.* вовл|ека́ть, -е́чь; вме́ш|ивать, -а́ть; заме́ш|ивать, -а́ть; впу́т|ывать, -ать; **the evidence ~d him** ули́ки пока́зывали на его́ прича́стность; **I refuse to be ~d** я отка́зываюсь быть заме́шанным.

implication [,ɪmplɪ'keɪʃ(ə)n] *n.* (*involvement*) вовлече́ние; (*implying*; *thg. implied*) скры́тый смысл; намёк; **by ~** ко́свенно; **I do not like your ~** мне не нра́вится ваш намёк; **I wish to avoid any ~ of hostility** я хоте́л бы избежа́ть како́го бы то ни́ было отте́нка вражде́бности; (*significance*) значе́ние.

implicit [ɪm'plɪsɪt] *adj.* **1.** (*implied*) подразумева́емый, недоска́занный; **~ threat** скры́тая угро́за; **~ consent** молчали́вое согла́сие; **~ in his statement was a denial** его́ заявле́ние подразумева́ло отка́з. **2.** (*unquestioning*) безоговоро́чный; **I have ~ belief in him** я безоговоро́чно ве́рю в него́.

implore [ɪm'plɔ:(r)] *v.t.* умол|я́ть, -и́ть; **he ~d my forgiveness** он моли́л меня́ о проще́нии.

imploringly [ɪm'plɔ:rɪŋlɪ] *adv.* умоля́юще.

implosive [ɪm'pləʊsɪv, -zɪv] *adj.* имплози́вный.

impl|y [ɪm'plaɪ] *v.t.* **1.** (*of a pers.: suggest, hint at*) подразумева́ть (*impf.*), намека́ть (*impf.*) на+*a.*; **what are you ~ying by that?** что вы хоти́те э́тим сказа́ть?; **he ~ied that I was wrong** он намека́л на то (*or* дал поня́ть), что я не прав. **2.** (*of a statement, action etc.*) подразумева́ть (*impf.*); (об)означа́ть (*impf.*); **what do his words ~y?** что означа́ют его́ слова́?; **I knew what was**

~ied я знал, что подразумева́лось; **silence ~ies consent** молча́ние — знак согла́сия; **these conclusions were ~ied by the evidence** э́ти вы́воды вытека́ли из ули́к.
impolite [ˌɪmpəˈlaɪt] *adj.* невежливый, неучти́вый.
impoliteness [ˌɪmpəˈlaɪtnɪs] *n.* невежливость, неучти́вость.
impolitic [ɪmˈpɒlɪtɪk] *adj.* не(благо)разу́мный, неполити́чный.
imponderable [ɪmˈpɒndərəb(ə)l] *adj.* (*fig.*) неулови́мый.
import[1] [ˈɪmpɔːt] *n.* **1.** (*bringing from abroad*) и́мпорт, ввоз; (*pl.*, *goods introduced*) и́мпортные/ввози́мые/ввозны́е това́ры (*m. pl.*); (*attr.*) и́мпортный, привозно́й; **~ duty** ввозна́я по́шлина. **2.** (*meaning*) значе́ние.
import[2] [ɪmˈpɔːt, ˈɪm-] *v.t.* **1.** (*bring in*) импорти́ровать (*impf.*, *pf.*); вв|ози́ть, -езти́; **wheat is ~ed from abroad** пшени́ца вво́зится из-за грани́цы. **2.** (*signify*) означа́ть (*impf.*).
importance [ɪmˈpɔːt(ə)ns] *n.* значе́ние, значи́тельность, ва́жность; (*standing*) вес; **attach ~ to sth.** придава́ть (*impf.*) значе́ние чему́-н.; **it is of no ~** э́то не име́ет значе́ния; э́то незначи́тельно; **a person of some ~** ва́жное лицо́; ли́чность, име́ющая вес; **of little ~** малова́жный; **a matter of great ~** де́ло огро́мной ва́жности; **it is of the utmost ~ that ...** кра́йне ва́жно, что́бы...
important [ɪmˈpɔːt(ə)nt] *adj.* значи́тельный, ва́жный; (*weighty*) ве́ский; **he went away on ~ business** он уе́хал по ва́жному де́лу; **~ people** ва́жные/влия́тельные лю́ди; **he likes to look ~** он лю́бит ва́жничать; **it is ~ for you to realize it** ва́жно, что́бы вы по́няли э́то; **more ~ly ...** что ещё бо́лее ва́жно...
importation [ˌɪmpɔːˈteɪʃ(ə)n] *n.* и́мпорт, ввоз.
importer [ɪmˈpɔːtə(r)] *n.* импортёр.
importunate [ɪmˈpɔːtjʊnət] *adj.* назо́йливый, навя́зчивый, доку́чливый; **~ demands** настоя́тельные тре́бования.
importune [ɪmˈpɔːtjuːn, -ˈtjuːn] *v.t.* докуча́ть (*impf.*) +*d.*; **he ~d me for a loan** он докуча́л мне про́сьбами о ссу́де.
importunity [ˌɪmpɔːˈtjuːnɪtɪ] *n.* назо́йливость, навя́зчивость, доку́чливость, домога́тельство.
impose [ɪmˈpəʊz] *v.t.* (*obligation*) возл|ага́ть, -ожи́ть (*что на кого*); (*tax, penalty etc.*) нал|ага́ть, -ожи́ть (*что на кого*); обл|ага́ть, -ожи́ть (*кого чем*); **the judge ~d a fine of 20 roubles** судья́ наложи́л штраф в 20 рубле́й; **the government ~d a tax on wealth** госуда́рство обложи́ло бога́тых нало́гом; **this will ~ a heavy burden on the people** э́то ля́жет тя́жким бре́менем на наро́д; **he ~d himself on our company** он навяза́лся/наби́лся к нам в компа́нию; **he ~s his views on everyone** он навя́зывает всем свои́ взгля́ды.
v.i.: **~ on** (*deceive*) обма́н|ывать, -у́ть; **we have been ~d upon** нас обману́ли; (*take advantage of*): **he ~s on his friends** он испо́льзует свои́х друзе́й.
imposing [ɪmˈpəʊzɪŋ] *adj.* внуши́тельный, импоза́нтный, представи́тельный.
imposition [ˌɪmpəˈzɪʃ(ə)n] *n.* **1.** (*imposing of obligation, burden etc.*) возложе́ние, наложе́ние. **2.** (*thg. imposed; tax etc.*) обложе́ние, нало́г. **3.** (*school punishment*) дополни́тельное зада́ние. **4.** (*fraud*) обма́н, моше́нничество. **5.** (*unreasonable demand*) чрезме́рное тре́бование.
impossibility [ɪmˌpɒsɪˈbɪlɪtɪ] *n.* невозмо́жность.
impossible [ɪmˈpɒsɪb(ə)l] *adj.* невозмо́жный; **don't ask me to do the ~** не тре́буйте от меня́ невозмо́жного; **an ~ person** невозмо́жный/несно́сный челове́к.
impost [ˈɪmpəʊst] *n.* нало́г.
impostor [ɪmˈpɒstə(r)] *n.* обма́нщи|к (*fem.* -ца); самозва́н|ец (*fem.* -ка).
imposture [ɪmˈpɒstʃə(r)] *n.* обма́н; самозва́нство.
impotence [ˈɪmpət(ə)ns] *n.* бесси́лие; (*sexual*) импоте́нция.
impotent [ˈɪmpət(ə)nt] *adj.* бесси́льный; **he is ~** (*sexually*) он импоте́нт.
impound [ɪmˈpaʊnd] *v.t.* (*cattle etc.*) заг|оня́ть, -на́ть; (*property*) конфискова́ть (*impf.*, *pf.*).
impoverish [ɪmˈpɒvərɪʃ] *v.t.* (*reduce to poverty*) обедн|я́ть, -и́ть; дов|оди́ть, -ести́ до бе́дности/обнища́ния; **become ~ed** бедне́ть, о-; нища́ть, об-; **~ed** (*adj.*) бе́дный, обедне́вший; обнища́вший, ни́щий; (*of soil; make barren*) истощ|а́ть, -и́ть; (*of health*) расстр|а́ивать, -о́ить; (*of ideas, style etc.*) обедн|я́ть, -и́ть; **an ~ed mind** убо́гий/ску́дный ум.
impoverishment [ɪmˈpɒvərɪʃmənt] *n.* обедне́ние, обнища́ние; истоще́ние.
impracticability [ɪmˌpræktɪkəˈbɪlɪtɪ] *n.* невыполни́мость, неисполни́мость, неосуществи́мость.
impracticable [ɪmˈpræktɪkəb(ə)l] *adj.*: **an ~ scheme** невыполни́мый/неосуществи́мый план; **~ ideas** неосуществи́мые иде́и; **~ roads** непроходи́мые/непрое́зжие доро́ги.
imprecation [ˌɪmprɪˈkeɪʃ(ə)n] *n.* прокля́тие.
impregnability [ɪmˌpregnəˈbɪlɪtɪ] *n.* непристу́пность.
impregnable [ɪmˈpregnəb(ə)l] *adj.* непристу́пный; (*fig.*): **~ virtue** непоколеби́мая доброде́тель; **an ~ argument** неопровержи́мый до́вод.
impregnate [ˈɪmpregˌneɪt] *v.t.* (*fertilize*) оплодотвор|я́ть, -и́ть; (*saturate*) пропи́т|ывать, -а́ть; нас|ыща́ть, -ы́тить; **~d wood** ипрегни́рованная древеси́на.
impregnation [ˌɪmpregˈneɪʃ(ə)n] *n.* оплодотворе́ние; пропи́тывание, насыще́ние.
impresario [ˌɪmprɪˈsɑːrɪəʊ] *n.* импреса́рио (*m. indecl.*), антрепенёр.
impress[1] [ˈɪmpres] *n.* (*lit., typ.*) о́ттиск; (*also fig.*) отпеча́ток, печа́ть; **his work bears the ~ of genius** его́ рабо́та несёт печа́ть ге́ния.
impress[2] [ɪmˈpres] *v.t.* **1.** (*make by imprinting*) отти́с|кивать, -нуть; вытисня́ть, вы́тиснить; (*fig., on the mind*) запечатл|ева́ть, -е́ть; внуш|а́ть, -и́ть (*кому*); **the words were ~ed on his memory** слова́ запечатле́лись в его́ па́мяти; **we ~ed on them the need for caution** мы внуши́ли им необходи́мость соблюда́ть осторо́жность. **2.** (*make imprint on*) де́лать, с- отпеча́ток на+*p.*; (*fig., have a strong effect on*) произв|оди́ть, -ести́ впечатле́ние на+*a.*; **he did not ~ me at all** он не произвёл на меня́ никако́го впечатле́ния. **3.** (*for mil. service*) наси́льно вербова́ть, за-.
v.i. произв|оди́ть, -ести́ впечатле́ние.
impression [ɪmˈpreʃ(ə)n] *n.* **1.** (*imprint*) отпеча́ток, о́ттиск; **his fingers left an ~** его́ па́льцы оста́вили отпеча́тки; **the dentist took an ~** зубно́й врач сде́лал сле́пок. **2.** (*typ., copies printed*) тира́ж; (*reprint*) печа́тание, перепеча́тка. **3.** (*effect*) эффе́кт, результа́т; впечатле́ние; **make, create an ~** произв|оди́ть, -ести́ впечатле́ние; **she scrubbed the floor but could make no ~ on the dirt** она́ дра́ила пол, но без ощути́мого/вся́кого результа́та. **4.** (*notion*) впечатле́ние, представле́ние; **I have, get an ~ (or my ~ is) that he is not sincere** у меня́ сложи́лось впечатле́ние, что он нейскренен; **I was under the ~ that ...** я полага́л, что...; **I have a strong ~ that ...** я почти́ уве́рен, что...; **one cannot rely on first ~s** нельзя́ доверя́ть пе́рвому впечатле́нию.
impressionable [ɪmˈpreʃənəb(ə)l] *adj.* впечатли́тельный, восприи́мчивый; **she is at an ~ age** она́ о́чень впечатли́тельна — у неё тако́й во́зраст.
impressionism [ɪmˈpreʃəˌnɪz(ə)m] *n.* импрессиони́зм.
impressionist [ɪmˈpreʃənɪst] *n.* **1.** (*art*) импрессиони́ст. **2.** (*mimic*) пароди́ст, имита́тор; (*attr.*) импрессиони́стский.
impressionistic [ɪmˌpreʃəˈnɪstɪk] *adj.* импрессионисти́ческий, импрессиони́стский.
impressive [ɪmˈpresɪv] *adj.* внуши́тельный, впечатля́ющий, си́льный; **an ~ speech** я́ркая речь; **an ~ scene** впечатля́ющая/волну́ющая карти́на.
imprest [ˈɪmprest] *n.* ава́нс, подотчётная су́мма.
imprimatur [ˌɪmprɪˈmeɪtə(r), -ˈmɑːtə(r), -tʊə(r)] *n.* (*eccl.*) разреше́ние (на печа́тание); (*fig., sanction*) са́нкция, одобре́ние.
imprint[1] [ˈɪmprɪnt] *n.* (*lit., fig.*) отпеча́ток; (*fig.*) печа́ть; **publisher's ~** выходны́е да́нные (*nt. pl.*); **her face bore the ~ of sorrow** на её лице́ запечатле́лась грусть.
imprint[2] [ɪmˈprɪnt] *v.t.* отпеча́т|ывать, -ать; вытисня́ть, вы́тиснить; (*fig.*) запечатл|ева́ть, -е́ть; **the words became ~ed on our minds** э́ти слова́ запа́ли нам в ду́шу; **he ~ed a kiss on her cheek** он запечатле́л поцелу́й на её щеке́.
imprison [ɪmˈprɪz(ə)n] *v.t.* заключ|а́ть, -и́ть в тюрьму́; заточ|а́ть, -и́ть; (*fig.*): **feelings ~ed in his breast** его́ потаённые чу́вства.

imprisonment [ɪm'prɪzənmənt] *n.* тюре́мное заключе́ние; заточе́ние; **he was sentenced to life** ~ его́ приговори́ли к пожи́зненному заключе́нию.

improbability [ɪm,prɒbə'bɪlɪtɪ] *n.* неправдоподо́бие, невероя́тность.

improbable [ɪm'prɒbəb(ə)l] *adj.* неправдоподо́бный, невероя́тный.

improbity [ɪm'prəʊbɪtɪ] *n.* бесче́стность.

impromptu [ɪm'prɒmptju:] *n.* (*mus.*) экспро́мт.

adj. импровизи́рованный.

adv. экспро́мтом, без подгото́вки.

improper [ɪm'prɒpə(r)] *adj.* **1.** (*unsuitable*) неподходя́щий, несоотве́тствующий; неуме́стный; **behaviour** ~ **to the occasion** поведе́ние, неподходя́щее к слу́чаю; **an** ~ **question** неуме́стный вопро́с; **an** ~ **friendship** недосто́йное знако́мство. **2.** (*incorrect*) непра́вильный; ~ **fraction** непра́вильная дробь; **put sth. to** ~ **use** испо́льзовать что-н. не по назначе́нию. **3.** (*unseemly, indecent*) неприли́чный, непристо́йный.

impropriety [,ɪmprə'praɪətɪ] *n.* неуме́стность; непра́вильность; непристо́йность, неприли́чие.

improvable [ɪm'pru:vəb(ə)l] *adj.* поддаю́щийся улучше́нию.

improv|e [ɪm'pru:v] *v.t.* **I.** (*make better*) ул|учша́ть, -у́чшить; ~**ing** (*edifying*) **literature** поучи́тельная литерату́ра; **he** ~**ed his French** он сде́лал успе́хи во францу́зском языке́. **2.** (*turn to good account*): ~**e the occasion** воспо́льзоваться (*pf.*) слу́чаем.

v.i. **1.** (*become better*) ул|учша́ться, -у́чшиться; **he has** ~**ed in manners** его́ мане́ры улу́чшились; **her looks have** ~**ed** она́ похороше́ла; **wine** ~**es with age** вино́ улучша́ется с года́ми; **it will** ~**e with use** э́то бу́дет улучша́ться по ме́ре по́льзования; **he is** ~**ing in his studies** он стал лу́чше учи́ться; **things are** ~**ing** дела́ нала́живаются; **his health is** ~**ing** он (*or* его́ здоро́вье) поправля́ется; (*of prices: rise*) подн|има́ться, -я́ться; пов|ыша́ться, -ы́ситься. **2.:** ~**e on** (*produce sth. better than*): **I can** ~**e on that** я могу́ предложи́ть не́что лу́чшее; **he** ~**ed on my ideas** он разви́л да́льше мои́ мы́сли; **the design cannot be** ~**ed upon** моде́ль не поддаётся дальне́йшему улучше́нию.

improvement [ɪm'pru:vmənt] *n.* улучше́ние; **there has been an** ~ **in the weather** пого́да улу́чшилась; **your writing is in need of** ~ вам сле́дует испра́вить ваш по́черк; **there is room for** ~ могло́ бы быть лу́чше; **this is an** ~ **on your first attempt** ва́ша втора́я попы́тка значи́тельно лу́чше пе́рвой; (*rebuilding etc.*) перестро́йка; перестано́вка; **he is carrying out** ~**s on his house** он за́нят усоверше́нствованием своего́ до́ма.

improvidence [ɪm'prɒvɪd(ə)ns] *n.* непредусмотри́тельность; расточи́тельность, небережли́вость.

improvident [ɪm'prɒvɪd(ə)nt] *adj.* (*heedless of the future*) непредусмотри́тельный; (*wasteful*) расточи́тельный, небережли́вый.

improvisation [,ɪmprəvaɪ'zeɪʃ(ə)n] *n.* импровиза́ция.

improvise ['ɪmprə,vaɪz] *v.t. & i.* (*music, speech etc.*) импровизи́ровать (*impf.*); (*arrange as makeshift*) мастери́ть, с-; **she** ~**d a bed on the floor** она́ сооруди́ла посте́ль на полу́; **an** ~ **d dinner** импровизи́рованный у́жин.

imprudence [ɪm'pru:d(ə)ns] *n.* опроме́тчивость, неблагоразу́мие, неосторо́жность.

imprudent [ɪm'pru:d(ə)nt] *adj.* опроме́тчивый, неблагоразу́мный, неосторо́жный.

impudence ['ɪmpjʊd(ə)nt] *n.* де́рзость; бессты́дство; наха́льство; на́глость.

impudent ['ɪmpjʊd(ə)nt] *adj.* (*audacious*) де́рзкий; (*shameless*) бессты́дный; (*insolent*) наха́льный, на́глый: **an** ~ **fellow** наха́л, нагле́ц.

impugn [ɪm'pju:n] *v.t.* осп|а́ривать, -о́рить; **he** ~**ed my honesty** он подве́рг мою́ че́стность сомне́нию.

impulse ['ɪmpʌls] *n.* (*lit., phys.*) толчо́к; (*elec.*) и́мпульс; (*fig., impetus, stimulus*): **the war gave an** ~ **to trade** война́ дала́ толчо́к торго́вле; **he lost all** ~ **to work** он потеря́л вся́кое влече́ние к рабо́те.

impulsion [ɪm'pʌlʃ(ə)n] *n.* толчо́к, побужде́ние, и́мпульс.

impulsive [ɪm'pʌlsɪv] *adj.* импульси́вный.

impunity [ɪm'pju:nɪtɪ] *n.*: **with** ~ безнака́занно.

impure [ɪm'pjʊə(r)] *adj.* нечи́стый, гря́зный; (*indecent*) непристо́йный.

impurity [ɪm'pjʊərɪtɪ] *n.* нечистота́, грязь; (*unchastity*) нечистопло́тность.

imputable [ɪm'pju:təb(ə)l] *adj.* припи́сываемый.

imputation [ɪm,pju:'teɪʃ(ə)n] *n.* **1.** (*imputing, ascription*) вмене́ние в вину́; обвине́ние, припи́сывание; **he could not avoid the** ~ **of dishonesty** он не мог избежа́ть подозре́ния в бесче́стности. **2.** (*aspersion*) тень, пятно́; ~**s were cast on his character** на его́ репута́цию была́ бро́шена тень.

impute [ɪm'pju:t] *v.t.* вмен|я́ть, -и́ть; припи́с|ывать, -а́ть; **the faults** ~**d to him** недоста́тки, припи́сываемые ему́.

in [ɪn] *n.*: **he knew all the** ~**s and outs of the affair** он знал все то́нкости де́ла.

adj. (*coll., fashionable*) популя́рный, мо́дный; **he knows all the '**~**' people** он зна́ет всех ну́жных люде́й.

adv. **1.** (*at home*) до́ма; **tell them I'm not** ~ скажи́те, что меня́ нет до́ма; (~ *one's office etc.*): **the boss is not** ~ **yet** нача́льника (в кабине́те) ещё нет; **he has been** ~ **and out all day** он весь день то приходи́л, то уходи́л. **2.** (*arrived at station, port etc.*): **the train has been** ~ **(for) 10 minutes** по́езд пришёл 10 мину́т тому́ наза́д. **3.** (*inside*) внутри́, внутрь; **he wore a coat with the fur side** ~ он носи́л пальто́ ме́хом вовну́трь. **4.** (*harvested*): **the crops were** ~ урожа́й был со́бран. **5.** (*available for purchase*): **strawberries are** ~ начался́ сезо́н клубни́ки. **6.** (~ *fashion*): **short skirts are** ~ **again** коро́ткие ю́бки опя́ть в мо́де. **7.** (~ *office*): **which party was** ~ **then?** кака́я па́ртия была́ тогда́ у вла́сти? **8.** (*burning*): **is the fire still** ~**?**ками́н ещё гори́т? **9.** (*batting*): **England was** ~ **all day** кома́нда А́нглии отбива́ла мяч весь день. **10.: day** ~**, day out** изо дня в день. **11.** (*involved*): **count me** ~**!** включи́те и меня́!; **he was** ~ **at, from the start** он принима́л уча́стие с са́мого нача́ла. **12.** (*with preps.*): **we are** ~ **for a storm** грозы́ не минова́ть; быть грозе́; **he is** ~ **for a surprise** его́ ожида́ет сюрпри́з; **are you** ~ **for the next race?** вы уча́ствуете в сле́дующем забе́ге?; ~ **for a penny,** ~ **for a pound** семь бед — оди́н отве́т; **he has got it** ~ **for me** (*coll.*) он про́тив меня́ что́-то име́ет; **you'll be** ~ **for it when she finds out** вам доста́нется за э́то, когда́ она́ узна́ет; **are you** ~ **on his plans?** (*coll.*) вы в ку́рсе его́ пла́нов?; ~ **with** (*coll., on good terms with*) вхож в+*a.*, к+*d.*; **he is well** ~ **with the council** у него́ в сове́те свои́ лю́ди.

prep. **1.** (*position*) в/на+*p.*; (*inhabited places*): ~ **Moscow** в Москве́; **he is the best worker** ~ **the village** он пе́рвый рабо́тник на селе́; (*countries and territories*): ~ **France** во Фра́нции; ~ **the Crimea** в Крыму́; ~ **the Ukraine** на Украи́не; ~ **the Western Ukraine** в За́падной Украи́не; (*islands and promontories*): ~ **the British Isles** на Брита́нских острова́х; ~ **Alaska** на Аля́ске; (*mountainous regions within Russia*): ~ **the Caucasus** на Кавка́зе; (*mountainous regions elsewhere*): ~ **the Alps** в А́льпах; (*open spaces and flat areas*): ~ **the street** на у́лице; ~ **the square** на пло́щади; **in the country** в дере́вне; ~ **the garden** в саду́; ~ **the field** в по́ле; ~ **the fields** на поля́х; (*buildings*): ~ **the theatre** в теа́тре; (*places of learning*): ~ **school** в шко́ле; ~ **the university** в университе́те; (*places of work*): ~ **the factory** на заво́де; (*activities*): ~ **the lesson** на уро́ке; ~ **a duel** на дуэ́ли/поеди́нке; ~ **the war** на войне́; во вре́мя войны́; ~ **the Civil War** в гражда́нской войне́; (*groups*): ~ **the crowd** в толпе́; (*points of compass*): ~ **the (Far) East** на (Да́льнем) Восто́ке; (*vehicles*): **let's go** ~ **the car** пое́дем на маши́не; **they were travelling** ~ **his car** они́ е́хали в его́ маши́не; (*parts of body*): **hold this** ~ **your hand** держи́те э́то в руке́; **she had a child** ~ **her arms** у неё на рука́х был ребёнок; **he is lame** ~ **one leg** он хром на одну́ но́гу; (*natural phenomena*): ~ **the sun** на со́лнце; ~ **the fresh air** на све́жем во́здухе; ~ **darkness** в темноте́; ~ **the rain** под дождём; **he went out** ~ **the rain** он вы́шел в дождь; ~ **the sky** в/на не́бе; ~ **a strong wind** при си́льном ве́тре; на си́льном ветру́;

(*books*): ~ **the Bible** в Би́блии; (*authors*): ~ **Shakespeare** у Шекспи́ра; (*close to*): **she was sitting ~ the window** она́ сиде́ла у окна́. **2.** (*motion*) в (*rarely* на) +*a.*: **they arrived ~ the city** они́ при́были в го́род; **look ~ the mirror** посмотри́те в зе́ркало; **he threw the letter ~ the fire** он бро́сил письмо́ в ого́нь; **he whispered ~ my ear** он шепта́л мне на́ ухо. **3.** (*time*) (*i*) (*specific centuries, years and decades*): ~ **the 20th century** в двадца́том ве́ке; ~ **1975** в ты́сяча девятьсо́т се́мьдесят пя́том году́; ~ **May** в Ма́е; ~ **future** в бу́дущем; ~ **childhood** в де́тстве; ~ **old age** на ста́рости лет; **he is ~ his fifties** ему́ за пятьдеся́т; ему́ шесто́й деся́ток; (*ii*) (*ages of history, events, periods*): ~ **the Middle Ages** в сре́дние века́; ~ **the Stone Age** в ка́менном ве́ке; ~ **that period** в тот пери́од; ~ **the sixties** в шестидеся́тые го́ды; ~ **these days** в э́ти дни; ~ **the days of my youth** в дни мое́й мо́лодости; ~ **our day** в на́ши дни; ~ **my time** в моё вре́мя; ~ **my lifetime** на моём веку́; ~ **peacetime** в ми́рное вре́мя; **injured ~ the explosion** ра́неный во вре́мя взры́ва; ~ **the course of** в тече́ние+*g.* (*see also vii*); **3 times ~ one day** три ра́за в оди́н день; (*iii*): ~ **the first minute of the game** на пе́рвой мину́те игры́; (*iv*) (*seasons*): ~ **spring** весно́й; (*times of day*): ~ **the morning** у́тром; ~ **the mornings** по утра́м; ~ **the afternoon** днём; по́сле полу́дня; (*v*) (*with gerund*): ~ **crossing the river** при перехо́де реки́; переходя́ ре́ку; (*of reigns: during*): ~ **Napoleon's time** при Наполео́не; (*vi*) (*at the end of*): **I shall finish this book ~ 3 days' time** я ко́нчу э́ту кни́гу че́рез три дня; ~ **less than 3 weeks** ра́ньше чем че́рез три неде́ли; (*vii*) (*in the course of*): **how many will come ~ one day?** ско́лько приду́т за день?; **I haven't been there ~ the last 3 years** за после́дние три го́да я не́ был там; **I shall write the story ~ (the space of) 3 weeks** я напишу́ э́тот расска́з в три (*or* за три) неде́ли; **he wrote twice ~ one week** он написа́л два́жды за одну́ неде́лю; **he completed it ~ 6 weeks** он зако́нчил э́то в тече́ние шести́ неде́ль. **4.** (*condition, situation*): ~ **his absence** в его́ отсу́тствие; ~ **his presence** в его́ прису́тствии; ~ **these circumstances** при э́тих усло́виях; ~ **custody** под аре́стом; **cry out ~ fear** вскри́кнуть (*pf.*) от стра́ха; ~ **place** на ме́сте; **I am not ~ a position to** я не име́ю возмо́жности (+*inf.*); ~ **power** у вла́сти; ~ **the wake of** вслед за+*i.*; ~ **the way** (*lit.*) попере́к доро́ги; (*fig.*): **these books are ~ my way** э́ти кни́ги мне меша́ют; **he is not ~ it** (*i.e. in the running*) он не чета́ (*кому*). **5.** (*dress*): **she was ~ white** она́ была́ в бе́лом (пла́тье); **he was dressed ~ ...** на нём был...; **she dresses ~ bright colours** она́ одева́ется в я́ркие цвета́. **6.** (*form; mode; arrangement; quantity*): ~ **pairs** па́рами; ~ **folds** скла́дками; **payment ~ silver** опла́та серебро́м; **they died ~ (their) thousands** они́ умира́ли ты́сячами; ~ **writing** в пи́сьменном ви́де (*or* пи́сьменно); ~ **a row** в ряду́; (*successively*) подря́д; ~ **a circle** в кругу́; ~ **short** вкра́тце; в не́скольких слова́х; ~ **dozens** по дю́жинам. **7.** (*manner*): ~ **a whisper** шёпотом; ~ **a businesslike way** деловы́м о́бразом; по-делово́му; ~ **a loud voice** гро́мким го́лосом; ~ **detail** подро́бно; ~ **full** по́лностью; ~ **part** ча́стью, части́чно; ~ **secret** под секре́том, по секре́ту; ~ **succession** подря́д, после́довательно; ~ **turn** по о́череди; ~ **haste** в спе́шке, второпя́х. **8.** (*language*): ~ **Russian** по-ру́сски; ~ **several languages** на не́скольких языка́х. **9.** (*material*): **a statue ~ marble** ста́туя из мра́мора. **10.** (*medium*): **he paints ~ oils** он пи́шет ма́слом. **11.** (*cul.*): ~ **butter** на ма́сле. **12.** (*solvent; diluent*): **take the medicine ~ water** лека́рство принима́ть с водо́й. **13.** (*contained ~; inherent ~*): **there are 7 days ~ a week** в неде́ле семь дней; **there's no sense ~ complaining** жа́ловаться бессмы́сленно; **he has nothing of the hero ~ him** в нём нет ничего́ геро́йского; **he hasn't got it ~ him to succeed** у него́ нет зада́тков к успе́ху; **there's nothing ~ it** (*coll., it is easy*) па́ра пустяко́в; (*coll., there is no difference*) нет никако́й ра́зницы; **there's nothing ~ it** (*coll. no benefit*) **for me** мне э́то ничего́ не даст. **14.** (*consisting ~*): **the enemy lost a thousand ~ killed and wounded** неприя́тель потеря́л ты́сячу челове́к уби́тыми и ра́неными; **we have lost a good friend ~ him** в нём (*or* в его́ лице́) мы потеря́ли хоро́шего дру́га. **15.** (*ratio: out of*): **only 1 ~ every 10 survived** из ка́ждых десяти́ то́лько оди́н вы́жил; **he has 1 chance ~ 5 of success** его́ ша́нсы на успе́х — оди́н к пяти́; **they had to pay 10p ~ the pound** им пришло́сь плати́ть де́сять пе́нсов с фу́нта. **16.** (*division*): **he broke the plate ~ pieces** он разби́л таре́лку на куски́. **17.** (~ *respect of*): **they differ ~ size but not ~ colour** они́ различа́ются по разме́ру, а не по цве́ту; **he was senior ~ rank** он был ста́рший по чи́ну; **a lecture ~ anatomy** ле́кция по анато́мии; **an expert ~ economics** специали́ст по эконо́мике; **strong ~ mathematics** силён (*pred.*) в матема́тике; **weak ~ French** слаб (*pred.*) во францу́зском языке́; **broad ~ the shoulders** широ́к (*pred.*) в плеча́х; (*dimension*): **4 feet ~ length** четы́ре фу́та в длину́; (*of bodily defects*): **blind ~ one eye** слеп (*pred.*) на оди́н глаз; (*of physique or natural characteristics*): **slight ~ build** хру́пкого сложе́ния; **poor ~ quality** плохо́го ка́чества; **he is young ~ appearance** он молодо́й на вид; **a land rich ~ iron** страна́, бога́тая желе́зом; **he was unfortunate ~ his friends** ему́ не везло́ с друзья́ми; **he is advanced ~ years** ему́ уже́ не ма́ло лет; он уже́ не мо́лод; **what's new ~ hats?** каки́е шля́пы тепе́рь мо́дны?; **they were 7 ~ number** их бы́ло се́меро. **18.** (*according to*): ~ **my opinion** по моему́ мне́нию; по-мо́ему; ~ **common decency** из элемента́рной поря́дочности. **19.:** ~ **reply to** в отве́т на+*a.*; ~ **honour of** в честь +*g.*; ~ **memory of** в па́мять +*g.*; ~ **protest** в знак проте́ста. **20.** (*engaged ~*): ~ **business** в де́ле; ~ **battle** в бою́; ~ **search of** в по́исках +*g.*; ~ **self-defence** для самооборо́ны; в поря́дке самозащи́ты. **21.** (*with other parts of speech, forming phrasal conjs.*): ~ **that** тем, что; так как; ~ **between** ме́жду+*i.*; **something ~ between** не́что сре́днее.

inability [ˌɪnəˈbɪlɪtɪ] *n.* неспосо́бность.

in absentia [ˌɪn æbˈsentɪə] *adv.* зао́чно.

inaccessibility [ˌɪnækˌsesɪˈbɪlɪtɪ] *n.* недосту́пность, непристу́пность.

inaccessible [ˌɪnækˈsesɪb(ə)l] *adj.* недосту́пный, непристу́пный.

inaccuracy [ɪnˈækjʊrəsɪ] *n.* нето́чность.

inaccurate [ɪnˈækjʊrət] *adj.* нето́чный.

inaction [ɪnˈækʃ(ə)n] *n.* (*inactive state*) безде́йствие; (*pej., doing nothing*) безде́лье, (*coll.*) ничегонеде́ланье.

inactive [ɪnˈæktɪv] *adj.* **1.** безде́йственный, безде́йствующий; **he leads an ~ life** он ведёт безде́ятельный/пасси́вный о́браз жи́зни; **the machines were ~** маши́ны проста́ивали. **2.** (*of chemicals etc.*) ине́ртный, неде́ятельный.

inactivity [ˌɪnækˈtɪvɪtɪ] *n.* безде́йствие.

inadequacy [ɪnˈædɪkwəsɪ] *n.* недоста́точность, неполноце́нность; (*personal*) неспосо́бность.

inadequate [ɪnˈædɪkwət] *adj.* (*insufficient*) недоста́точный; **words are ~ to express my joy** слов недостаёт (*or* не хвата́ет), что́бы вы́разить мою́ ра́дость; (*less than capable of*) неспосо́бный; **he was ~ to the task** он оказа́лся неспосо́бным к выполне́нию э́той зада́чи.

inadmissible [ˌɪnədˈmɪsɪb(ə)l] *adj.* (*unacceptable*) неприе́млемый; (*impermissible*) недопусти́мый.

inadvertence [ˌɪnədˈvɜːt(ə)ns] *n.* (*inattention*) невнима́тельность; (*oversight*) недосмо́тр; (*false step*) неосторо́жность.

inadvertent [ˌɪnədˈvɜːt(ə)nt] *adj.* неумы́шленный, неча́янный, нево́льный.

inadvisability [ˌɪnədvaɪzəˈbɪlɪtɪ] *n.* нецелесообра́зность, нежела́тельность.

inadvisable [ˌɪnədˈvaɪzəb(ə)l] *adj.* нецелесообра́зный, нежела́тельный.

inalienability [ɪnˈeɪlɪənəˈbɪlɪtɪ] *n.* неотчужда́емость, неотъе́млемость.

inalienable [ɪnˈeɪlɪənəb(ə)l] *adj.* неотчужда́емый, неотъе́млемый.

inalterable [ɪnˈɒltərəb(ə)l] *adj.* неизменя́емый, неизме́нный.

inamorata [ɪnˌæməˈrɑːtə] *n.* возлю́бленная.

inane [ɪˈneɪn] *adj.* бессмы́сленный, глу́пый, пусто́й, неле́пый.

inanimate [ɪnˈænɪmət] *adj.* неодушевлённый, неживо́й; ~

nature нежива́я приро́да; **an ~ noun** неодушевлённое существи́тельное; (*lifeless*; *also fig.*, *without animation*) безжи́зненный.
inanition [ˌɪnəˈnɪʃ(ə)n] *n.* (*med.*) истоще́ние, изнуре́ние.
inanity [ˌɪnˈænɪtɪ] *n.* бессмы́сленность, глу́пость; пустота́, неле́пость; глу́пое замеча́ние.
inapplicability [ɪnˌæplɪkəˈbɪlɪtɪ, ˌɪnəplɪk-] *n.* неприменимость.
inapplicable [ɪnˈæplɪkəb(ə)l, ˌɪnəˈplɪk-] *adj.* неприменимый; (*unsuitable*) неподходя́щий.
inapposite [ɪnˈæpəzɪt] *adj.* неуме́стный.
inappreciable [ˌɪnəˈpriːʃəb(ə)l] *adj.* (*imperceptible*) незаме́тный; (*insignificant*) незначи́тельный.
inappropriate [ˌɪnəˈprəʊprɪət] *adj.* неуме́стный, неподходя́щий; несоотве́тствующий (+*d.*).
inappropriateness [ˌɪnəˈprəʊprɪətnɪs] *n.* неуме́стность, несоотве́тствие.
inapt [ɪnˈæpt] *adj.* (*unskilful*) неиску́сный, неуме́лый, неспосо́бный; (*unsuitable*) неподходя́щий, неуме́стный, несоотве́тствующий.
inaptitude [ɪnˈæptɪˌtjuːd] *n.* (*lack of skill*) неуме́ние, неспосо́бность (к+*d.*).
inarticulate [ˌɪnɑːˈtɪkjʊlət] *adj.* (*of speech*) невня́тный, нечленоразде́льный; (*of pers.*) косноязы́чный; (*taciturn*) молчали́вый; (*dumb*) немо́й.
inarticulateness [ˌɪnɑːˈtɪkjʊlətnɪs] *n.* нечленоразде́льность; косноязы́чие; молчали́вость, немота́.
inartistic [ˌɪnɑːˈtɪstɪk] *adj.* нехудо́жественный.
inasmuch as [ˌɪnəzˈmʌtʃ] *adj.* так как; ввиду́ того́, что; поско́льку.
inattent|ion [ˌɪnəˈtenʃ(ə)n], **-iveness** [ˌɪnəˈtentɪvnɪs] *nn.* невнима́ние, невнима́тельность (к+*d.*).
inattentive [ˌɪnəˈtentɪv] *adj.* невнима́тельный.
inaudibility [ɪnˌɔːdɪˈbɪlɪtɪ] *n.* плоха́я слы́шимость; невня́тность.
inaudible [ɪnˈɔːdɪb(ə)l] *adj.* неслы́шный; (*indistinct*) невня́тный.
inaugural [ɪˈnɔːgjʊr(ə)l] *n.* торже́ственная речь при вступле́нии в до́лжность.
adj. вступи́тельный.
inaugurate [ɪˈnɔːgjʊˌreɪt] *v.t.* (*install with ceremony*) (торже́ственно) вв|оди́ть, -ести́ в до́лжность; **the President was ~d** президе́нт вступи́л в до́лжность. **2.** (*launch*; *officiate at opening of*) откр|ыва́ть, -ы́ть; (*fig.*): **they ~d many reforms** они́ ввели́ мно́го рефо́рм; **he ~d a new policy** он положи́л нача́ло но́вой поли́тике; **a new era was ~d** начала́сь но́вая э́ра.
inauguration [ɪˌnɔːgjʊˈreɪʃ(ə)n] *n.* вступле́ние в до́лжность; инаугура́ция; откры́тие; нача́ло.
inauspicious [ˌɪnɔːˈspɪʃəs] *adj.* (*of ill omen*) злове́щий; (*unlucky*) несчастли́вый.
in-basket [ˈɪnbɑːskɪt] *n.* корзи́нка для входя́щей корреспонде́нции.
inboard [ˈɪnbɔːd] *adj.* располо́женный внутри́ су́дна.
inborn [ˈɪnbɔːn] *adj.* врождённый, прирождённый, насле́дственный.
inbred [ɪnˈbred, ˈɪn-] *adj.* (*innate*) = **inborn**; (*result of inbreeding*) рождённый от роди́телей, состоя́щих в кро́вном родстве́ ме́жду собо́й.
inbreeding [ɪnˈbriːdɪŋ] *n.* (*of animals*) ро́дственное спа́ривание; инбри́динг; (*of people*) узкоро́дственные бра́чные отноше́ния.
Inca [ˈɪŋkə] *n.* И́нка (*c.g.*).
incalculable [ɪnˈkælkjʊləb(ə)l] *adj.* **1.** (*too great for calculation*) неисчисли́мый, бессчётный, бесчи́сленный, несме́тный; **it has done ~ harm** э́то причини́ло неисчисли́мый/огро́мный вред. **2.** (*of pers.*: *unreliable*) ненадёжный; (*unpredictable*) капри́зный, причу́дливый.
in camera [ɪn ˈkæmərə] *adv.*: **the trial will be held ~** проце́сс бу́дет закры́тым (*or* бу́дет идти́ при закры́тых дверя́х).
incandescence [ˌɪnkænˈdes(ə)ns] *n.* нака́л, нака́ливание, кале́ние.
incandescent [ˌɪnkænˈdes(ə)nt] *adj.* накалённый, раскалённый; (*of light*) светя́щийся от нагре́ва; **~ lamp (*or* light bulb)** ла́мпа нака́ливания.
incantation [ˌɪnkænˈteɪʃ(ə)n] *n.* заклина́ние, закля́тие.
incapability [ɪnˌkeɪpəˈbɪlɪtɪ] *n.* неспосо́бность.
incapable [ɪnˈkeɪpəb(ə)l] *adj.* **1.** (*not having a particular capacity*) неспосо́бный; **he is ~ of understanding** он неспосо́бен поня́ть (*что*); он неспосо́бен к понима́нию; **~ of speech** невладе́ющий ре́чью; **~ of pleading** (*leg.*) невменя́емый; **~ of lying** неспосо́бный на ложь; **they are an ~ lot** э́то никчёмные лю́ди. **2.** (*not susceptible*) не поддаю́щийся (*чему*).
incapacitate [ˌɪnkəˈpæsɪˌteɪt] *v.t.*: **~ for, from** (*render incapable of or unfit for*) де́лать, с- неспосо́бным/ неприго́дным к+*d.*; **his illness ~d him for work** из-за боле́зни он стал нетрудоспосо́бным; (*disable*): **he was ~d for 3 weeks** он вы́был из стро́я на три неде́ли; (*mil.*) выводи́ть, вы́вести из стро́я; **the enemy's tanks were ~d** та́нки проти́вника бы́ли вы́ведены из стро́я; (*disqualify*) лиш|а́ть, -и́ть (*кого чего*); **they were ~d from voting** они́ бы́ли лишены́ пра́ва го́лоса.
incapacity [ˌɪnkəˈpæsɪtɪ] *n.* неспосо́бность; (*leg.*) ограниче́ние дееспосо́бности.
incarcerate [ɪnˈkɑːsəˌreɪt] *v.t.* заточ|а́ть, -и́ть (в тюрьму́).
incarceration [ɪnˌkɑːsəˈreɪʃ(ə)n] *n.* заточе́ние (в тюрьму́).
incarnate[1] [ɪnˈkɑːnət] *adj.* (*in bodily form*) воплощённый; **he is the Devil ~** он дья́вол во пло́ти; (*personified*) олицетворённый; **modesty ~** олицетворе́ние скро́мности, сама́ скро́мность.
incarnate[2] [ˈɪnkɑːˌneɪt, -ˈkɑːneɪt] *v.t.* вопло|ща́ть, -ти́ть; олицетвор|я́ть, -и́ть; **she ~d all the virtues** она́ воплоща́ла в себе́ (*or* олицетворя́ла собо́й) все доброде́тели.
incarnation [ˌɪnkɑːˈneɪʃ(ə)n] *n.* **1.** (*taking on bodily form*): **the I~** воплоще́ние (божества́ в Христе́); (*re-birth*) инкарна́ция; **in a future ~** в но́вом рожде́нии. **2.** (*embodiment, personification*) воплоще́ние, олицетворе́ние.
incautious [ɪnˈkɔːʃəs] *adj.* неосторо́жный, опроме́тчивый.
incendiarism [ɪnˈsendɪərˌɪz(ə)m] *n.* поджо́г.
incendiary [ɪnˈsendɪərɪ] *n.* **1.** (*arsonist*) поджига́тель (*m.*); (*fig.*, *firebrand*) подстрека́тель (*m.*). **2.** (**~ bomb**) зажига́тельная бо́мба.
adj. зажига́тельный; (*fig.*) подстрека́ющий.
incense[1] [ˈɪnsens] *n.* ла́дан, фимиа́м (*also fig.*); **they were burning ~** они́ кади́ли ла́даном.
cpd. **~-burner** *n.* (*vessel*) кади́льница.
incense[2] [ˈɪnsens] *v.t.* разгне́вать (*pf.*); прив|оди́ть, -ести́ в я́рость; **she was ~d at, by his behaviour** его́ поведе́ние привело́ её в я́рость.
incentive [ɪnˈsentɪv] *n.* побужде́ние, сти́мул; **he lacks all ~ to work** у него́ нет никако́го сти́мула для рабо́ты; **~ bonus** поощри́тельная пре́мия.
inception [ɪnˈsepʃ(ə)n] *n.* нача́ло, начина́ние.
incertitude [ɪnˈsɜːtɪˌtjuːd] *n.* неуве́ренность.
incessant [ɪnˈses(ə)nt] *adj.* непреста́нный, непреры́вный.
incest [ˈɪnsest] *n.* кровосмеше́ние.
incestuous [ɪnˈsestjʊəs] *adj.* кровосмеси́тельный; (*pers.*) вино́вный в кровосмеше́нии.
inch [ɪntʃ] *n.* дюйм; **he moved forward by ~es** ма́ло-пома́лу он дви́гался вперёд; **the car missed me by ~es** автомоби́ль едва́ меня́ не задави́л; **he was every ~ a sailor** он был моряко́м с головы́ до пят; **he did not yield an ~** он не уступи́л ни на йо́ту; **give him an ~ and he'll take an ell** дай ему́ па́лец, он всю ру́ку отхва́тит; **he was flogged within an ~ of his life** его́ изби́ли до полусме́рти; (*pl.*, *stature*): **a man of your ~es** челове́к ва́шего ро́ста.
v.i. with advs.: **he was ~ing along** он ме́дленно тащи́лся; **the car began to ~ forward** маши́на ме́дленно тро́нулась с ме́ста.
inchoate [ɪnˈkəʊeɪt, ˈɪn-] *adj.* зача́точный.
inchoative [ɪnˈkəʊətɪv] *adj.* (*gram.*) начина́тельный.
incidence [ˈɪnsɪd(ə)ns] *n.* **1.** (*phys.*, *falling*; *contact*) паде́ние, накло́н; **angle of ~** у́гол паде́ния. **2.** (*range or scope of effect*) охва́т, сфе́ра де́йствия; **the ~ of taxation** охва́т налогообложе́нием; **the ~ of a disease** число́ заболе́вших.
incident [ˈɪnsɪd(ə)nt] *n.* слу́чай, собы́тие; происше́ствие, инциде́нт; **frontier ~** пограни́чный инциде́нт; **without ~** без происше́ствий; (*in play, novel etc.*) эпизо́д.
adj. **~ to** (*connected with*) свя́занный с+*i.*; (*characteristic of*) прису́щий +*d.*, сво́йственный +*d.*

incidental [ˌɪnsɪ'dent(ə)l] *adj.* **1.** (*casual*) случа́йный; (*passing*) попу́тный; (*inessential*) несуще́ственный; (*secondary*) побо́чный; ~ **expenses** побо́чные расхо́ды; ~ **music** музыка́льное сопровожде́ние. **2.:** ~ **to** (*accompanying*, *contingent on*) сопряжённый с+*i*.; (*resulting from*) вытека́ющий из+*g*.; **fatigue** ~ **to a journey** уста́лость, сопряжённая с путеше́ствием.

incidentally [ˌɪnsɪ'dentəlɪ] *adv.* (*in passing*) попу́тно; (*parenthetically*) ме́жду про́чим; кста́ти; к сло́ву сказа́ть.

incinerate [ɪn'sɪnəˌreɪt] *v.t.* испепел|я́ть, -и́ть; сж|ига́ть, -ечь дотла́; (*cremate*) креми́ровать (*impf.*, *pf.*).

incineration [ɪnˌsɪnə'reɪʃ(ə)n] *n.* сжига́ние дотла́; (*cremation*) крема́ция.

incinerator [ɪn'sɪnəˌreɪtə(r)] *n.* мусоросжига́тельная печь; кремацио́нная печь.

incipient [ɪn'sɪpɪənt] *adj.* зарожда́ющийся.

incise [ɪn'saɪz] *v.t.* (*make cut in*) надр|еза́ть, -е́зать; (*engrave*) выреза́ть, вы́резать.

incision [ɪn'sɪʒ(ə)n] *n.* надре́з.

incisive [ɪn'saɪsɪv] *adj.* ре́жущий; (*fig.*): **an** ~ **tone** ре́зкий тон; **an** ~ **mind** о́стрый/проница́тельный ум.

incisiveness [ɪn'saɪsɪvnɪs] *n.* ре́зкость; острота́, прони́тельность.

incisor [ɪn'saɪzə(r)] *n.* (*tooth*) резе́ц.

incite [ɪn'saɪt] *v.t.* (*stir up*) возбу|жда́ть, -ди́ть; (*encourage*, *urge*, *impel*) побу|жда́ть, -ди́ть; подстрек|а́ть, -ну́ть; **he** ~**d them to revolt** он подстрека́л их к мятежу́.

incitement [ɪn'saɪtmənt] *n.* (*inciting*) подстрека́тельство; (*spur*, *stimulus*) побужде́ние, сти́мул.

incivility [ˌɪnsɪ'vɪlɪtɪ] *n.* неучти́вость, неве́жливость.

inclemency [ɪn'klemənsɪ] *n.* суро́вость.

inclement [ɪn'klemənt] *adj.* суро́вый.

inclination [ˌɪnklɪ'neɪʃ(ə)n] *n.* **1.** (*bending*; *slanting*) наклоне́ние, накло́н; **an** ~ **of the head** киво́к; накло́н головы́. **2.** (*slope*) накло́н, скат, отко́с; **the** ~ **of a roof** скат кры́ши. **3.** (*tendency*) накло́нность, скло́нность; **an** ~ **to stoutness** скло́нность/предрасполо́женность к полноте́. **4.** (*desire*) охо́та, жела́ние; **he has lost all** ~ **to work** он потеря́л вся́кую охо́ту к рабо́те; **I have no** ~ **to go out** у меня́ нет никако́го жела́ния выходи́ть; **he follows his own** ~**s** он сле́дует свои́м жела́ниям; **I went with him against my** ~ я пошёл с ним вопреки́ со́бственному жела́нию.

incline[1] ['ɪnklaɪn] *n.* накло́нная пло́скость, накло́н, скат.

incline[2] [ɪn'klaɪn] *v.t.* **1.** (*cause to lean or slant*) наклон|я́ть, -и́ть; **his cap was** ~**d at a rakish angle** его́ ке́пка была́ ли́хо сдви́нута на́ ухо; ~**d plane** накло́нная пло́скость; (*bend forward or down*) склон|я́ть, -и́ть. **2.** (*turn*, *direct*) напр|авля́ть, -а́вить; **he** ~**d his ear to their plea** он благоскло́нно вы́слушал их про́сьбу. **3.** (*fig.*, *dispose*) склон|я́ть, -и́ть; **his heart** ~**d him to pity** его́ до́брое се́рдце склоня́ло его́ к жа́лости; **he is** ~**d to grow fat** он скло́нен к полноте́; **I am** ~**d to agree with you** я скло́нен с ва́ми согласи́ться; **if you feel** ~**d (to do so)** е́сли вы располо́жены э́то сде́лать; **favourably** ~**d to** благоскло́нный к+*d*.

v.i. **1.** (*lean*, *slope*) наклон|я́ться, -и́ться; склон|я́ться, -и́ться. **2.: right** ~! (*drill command*) пол-оборо́та напра́во! **3.** (*tend*) склон|я́ться, -и́ться; **he** ~**s to(wards) leniency** он скло́нен к снисходи́тельности; **I** ~ **to think that ...** я скло́нен ду́мать, что...

inclinometer [ˌɪnklɪ'nɒmɪtə(r)] *n.* уклономе́р, угломе́р, креноме́р.

inclose [ɪn'kləʊz] = **enclose**

includ|e [ɪn'klu:d] *v.t.* включ|а́ть, -и́ть; (*place on a list*) вн|оси́ть, -ести́; **I** ~**e you among my friends** я включа́ю вас в число́ свои́х друзе́й; **they were all there, wives** ~**ed** все бы́ли в сбо́ре, включа́я жён; **5 members,** ~**ing the President** пять чле́нов, включа́я президе́нта; **we saw several of them,** ~**ing your brother** мы ви́дели не́которых из них, в том числе́ (и) ва́шего бра́та; **service** ~**ed** включа́я услу́ги; **your work will** ~**e sweeping the floor** в ва́ши обя́занности бу́дет входи́ть подмета́ние поло́в; (*contain*) заключа́ть (*impf.*); содержа́ть (*impf.*) в себе́; **this book** ~**es all his poems** в э́той кни́ге со́браны все его́ стихи́.

inclusion [ɪn'klu:ʒ(ə)n] *n.* включе́ние.

inclusive [ɪn'klu:sɪv] *adj.* & *adv.* **1.:** ~ **of** (*including*) включа́я; включа́ющий в себя́; содержа́щий в себе́. **2.: from Feb. 2nd to 20th** ~ со второ́го февраля́ по двадца́тое включи́тельно. **3.:** ~ **terms** (*at hotel*) цена́ ко́мнаты с по́лным содержа́нием.

incognito [ˌɪnkɒg'ni:təʊ] *n.*, *adj.* & *adv.* инко́гнито (*m.*, *nt.*, *indecl.*).

incoherence [ˌɪnkəʊ'hɪərəns] *n.* несвя́зность, непосле́довательность, бессвя́зность.

incoherent [ˌɪnkəʊ'hɪərənt] *adj.* несвя́зный, непосле́довательный; (*of speech*) бессвя́зный.

incombustible [ˌɪnkəm'bʌstɪb(ə)l] *adj.* негорю́чий, невоспламеня́емый, огнесто́йкий.

income ['ɪnkʌm, 'ɪŋkəm] *n.* дохо́д, прихо́д; **earned** ~ за́работок; **unearned** ~ ре́нта, нетрудовы́е дохо́ды (*m. pl.*); **private** ~ ча́стные дохо́ды; **live on one's** ~ жить на свои́ сре́дства; **live within (or up to) one's** ~ жить по сре́дствам; **exceed, live beyond one's** ~ жить не по сре́дствам.

cpd. ~**-tax** *n.* подохо́дный нало́г.

incoming ['ɪnˌkʌmɪŋ] *n.* (*pl.*, *income*) дохо́ды (*m. pl.*).

adj. входя́щий, поступа́ющий, прибыва́ющий; **the** ~ **year** наступа́ющий год; **the** ~ **tide** прили́в; **the** ~ **president** новои́збранный президе́нт; ~ **mail** входя́щая по́чта; ~ **profit** поступа́ющая при́быль; ~ **tenant** но́вый жиле́ц.

incommensurability [ˌɪnkəˌmenʃərə'bɪlɪtɪ, -sjərə'bɪlɪtɪ] *n.* несоизмери́мость; несоразме́рность.

incommensurable [ˌɪnkə'menʃərəb(ə)l, -sjərəb(ə)l] *adj.* несоизмери́мый; несоразме́рный.

incommensurate [ˌɪnkə'menʃərət, -sjərət] *adj.* (*out of proportion*) несоразме́рный (с+*i*.); (*inadequate*) несоотве́тствующий (+*d*.); (*disproportionate*) несоизмери́мый.

incommode [ˌɪnkə'məʊd] *v.t.* (*disturb*, *put out*) беспоко́ить, о-; (*make difficulties for*) стесн|я́ть, -и́ть; (*hinder*) меша́ть, по- +*d*.

incommunicable [ˌɪnkə'mju:nɪkəb(ə)l] *adj.* (*not to be shared*) непередава́емый; (*not to be told*) невырази́мый.

incom(m)unicado [ˌɪnkəˌmju:nɪ'kɑ:dəʊ] *adj.* & *adv.* лишённый пра́ва перепи́ски и сообще́ния; в изоля́ции.

incomparable [ɪn'kɒmpərəb(ə)l] *adj.* (*not comparable to or with*) несравни́мый (с+*i*.); (*matchless*) несравне́нный, бесподо́бный.

incompatibility [ˌɪnkəmˌpætɪ'bɪlɪtɪ] *n.* несоотве́тствие; несовмести́мость; **a divorce on grounds of** ~ разво́д по причи́не несхо́дства хара́ктеров.

incompatible [ˌɪnkəm'pætɪb(ə)l] *adj.* несовмести́мый; ~ **colours** несочета́емые цвета́.

incompetence [ɪn'kɒmpɪt(ə)ns] *n.* неспосо́бность, некомпете́нтность; неуме́ние.

incompetent [ɪn'kɒmpɪt(ə)nt] *adj.* (*lacking ability*) неспосо́бный (*к чему or inf.*); (*lacking qualifications*) некомпете́нтный (*в чём*); (*inefficient*, *unskilful*) неуме́лый.

incomplete [ˌɪnkəm'pli:t] *adj.* (*not full*) непо́лный; **an** ~ **set** непо́лный компле́кт; (*defective*, *lacking*) несоверше́нный; (*unfinished*) незавершённый, незако́нченный; **the book was** ~ **at his death** ко дню его́ сме́рти кни́га оста́лась незако́нченной.

incompleteness [ˌɪnkəm'pli:tnɪs] *n.* неполнота́; несоверше́нство; незавершённость; незако́нченность.

incomprehensibility [ɪnˌkɒmprɪhensɪ'bɪlɪtɪ] *n.* непоня́тность, непостижи́мость.

incomprehensible [ɪnˌkɒmprɪ'hensɪb(ə)l] *adj.* непоня́тный, непостижи́мый.

incomprehension [ɪnˌkɒmprɪ'henʃ(ə)n] *n.* непонима́ние.

incompressible [ˌɪnkəm'presɪb(ə)l] *adj.* несжима́емый, несжима́ющийся, неуплотня́емый.

incomunicado [ˌɪnkəˌmju:nɪ'kɑ:dəʊ] = **incom(m)unicado**

inconceivable [ˌɪnkən'si:vəb(ə)l] *adj.* (*incomprehensible*) непостижи́мый; (*unimaginable*) невообрази́мый; (*coll.*, *unbelievable*, *most unlikely*) немы́слимый.

inconclusive [ˌɪnkən'klu:sɪv] *adj.* (*of argument etc.*)

неубеди́тельный; (*of action*) нереши́тельный; **the vote was ~** голосова́ние не́ дало определённых результа́тов.
inconclusiveness [ˌɪnkənˈkluːsɪvnɪs] *n.* неубеди́тельность; нереши́тельность, неопределённость.
incongruity [ˈɪnkɒŋˈgruːɪtɪ] *n.* несоотве́тствие; неуме́стность; неле́пость.
incongruous [ɪnˈkɒŋgrʊəs] *adj.* (*out of keeping*) несоотве́тствующий, неподходя́щий, несоотве́тственный; (*out of place, inappropriate*) неуме́стный; (*absurd*) неле́пый.
inconsequence [ɪnˈkɒnsɪkwəns] *n.* непосле́довательность.
inconsequent [ɪnˈkɒnsɪkwənt], **-ial** [ɪnˌkɒnsɪˈkwenʃ(ə)l, ˌɪnkɒn-] *adjs.* (*not following logically*) непосле́довательный; (*disconnected, disjointed*) несвя́зный; (*irrelevant, immaterial*) несуще́ственный.
inconsiderable [ˌɪnkənˈsɪdərəb(ə)l] *adj.* незначи́тельный; **his income was ~** его́ за́работок был ничто́жным.
inconsiderate [ˌɪnkənˈsɪdərət] *adj.* невнима́тельный (к други́м), нечу́ткий; **he is ~ of, to everyone** он невнима́телен ко всем; он ни с кем не счита́ется; (*thoughtless, rash*) необду́манный, опроме́тчивый.
inconsiderateness [ˌɪnkənˈsɪdərətnɪs] *n.* невнима́тельность, нечу́ткость; опроме́тчивость.
inconsistenc|y [ˌɪnkənˈsɪst(ə)nsɪ] *n.* несовмести́мость; непосле́довательность; противоречи́вость, сби́вчивость; **there are ~ies in his argument** его́ до́воды непосле́довательны (*or* полны́ противоре́чий).
inconsistent [ˌɪnkənˈsɪst(ə)nt] *adj.* (*incompatible, not in agreement*) несовмести́мый (*с чем*); (*inconsequent*) непосле́довательный; (*containing contradictions*) противоречи́вый, сби́вчивый.
inconsolable [ˌɪnkənˈsəʊləb(ə)l] *adj.* неуте́шный, безуте́шный.
inconspicuous [ˌɪnkənˈspɪkjʊəs] *adj.* незаме́тный; **he made himself ~** он постара́лся оста́ться незаме́ченным.
inconstancy [ɪnˈkɒnst(ə)nsɪ] *n.* непостоя́нство, изме́нчивость, переме́нчивость; неве́рность.
inconstant [ɪnˈkɒnst(ə)nt] *adj.* непостоя́нный, изме́нчивый, переме́нчивый; (*in love or friendship*) неве́рный.
incontestable [ˌɪnkənˈtestəb(ə)l] *adj.* неоспори́мый.
incontinence [ɪnˈkɒntɪnəns] *n.* невозде́ржанность; несде́ржанность; (*of urine/faeces*) недержа́ние мочи́/ка́ла.
incontinent [ɪnˈkɒntɪnənt] *adj.* невозде́ржанный (*esp. sexually*); несде́ржанный; (*of urine/faeces*): **he was ~** он страда́л недержа́нием (мочи́/ка́ла).
incontrovertible [ˌɪnkɒntrəˈvɜːtɪb(ə)l] *adj.* неоспори́мый.
inconvenience [ˌɪnkənˈviːnɪəns] *n.* неудо́бство, беспоко́йство; **he was put to great ~** ему́ причини́ли большо́е неудо́бство; **at great personal ~** ценой большо́го неудо́бства для себя́.
v.t. причин|я́ть, -и́ть неудо́бство +*d.*; беспоко́ить, о-; стесн|я́ть, -и́ть.
inconvenient [ˌɪnkənˈviːnɪənt] *adj.* неудо́бный; **if it is not ~ to you** е́сли э́то вам удо́бно.
inconvertibility [ˌɪnkənvɜːtɪˈbɪlɪtɪ] *n.* (*fin.*) необрати́мость.
inconvertible [ˌɪnkənˈvɜːtɪb(ə)l] *adj.* (*fin.*) необрати́мый, неконверти́руемый; **~ currency** необрати́мая валю́та.
incorporate[1] [ɪnˈkɔːpərət] *adj.* зарегистри́рованный в ка́честве юриди́ческого лица́.
incorporate[2] [ɪnˈkɔːpəˌreɪt] *v.t.* **1.** (*unite, combine*) объедин|я́ть, -и́ть; соедин|я́ть, -и́ть; **fertilizers should be ~d with the soil** удобре́ния должны́ быть переме́шаны с землёй. **2.** (*include, introduce*) включ|а́ть, -и́ть; содержа́ть (*impf.*); **his suggestions were ~d in the plan** его́ предложе́ния бы́ли включены́ в план; **his survey ~s the latest trends** в его́ обзо́ре рассма́триваются нове́йшие тече́ния; **~ in, into** (*annex to*) присоедин|я́ть, -и́ть; **Austria was ~d into Germany** А́встрия была́ включена́ в Герма́нию (*or* присоединена́ к Герма́нии). **3.** (*form into corporation*) регистри́ровать, за- как корпора́цию.
v.i. соедин|я́ться, -и́ться; **the firm ~d with others** фи́рма слила́сь с други́ми.
incorporation [ɪnˌkɔːpəˈreɪʃ(ə)n] *n.* объедине́ние, соедине́ние; включе́ние (в соста́в); инкорпора́ция, присоедине́ние; регистра́ция/оформле́ние о́бщества в ка́честве юриди́ческого лица́.
incorporeal [ˌɪnkɔːˈpɔːrɪəl] *adj.* (*not material*) невеще́ственный; (*without bodily form*) бестеле́сный, беспло́тный.
incorrect [ˌɪnkəˈrekt] *adj.* (*inaccurate; displaying errors, of style etc.*) непра́вильный; (*untrue; erroneous, of statements etc.*) неве́рный; (*of behaviour or conduct*) некорре́ктный.
incorrectness [ˌɪnkəˈrektnɪs] *n.* непра́вильность; неве́рность; некорре́ктность.
incorrigibility [ɪnˌkɒrɪdʒɪˈbɪlɪtɪ] *n.* неисправи́мость.
incorrigible [ɪnˈkɒrɪdʒɪb(ə)l] *adj.* (*incurable*) неисправи́мый; (*inveterate*) закорене́лый.
incorruptibility [ˌɪnkərʌptɪˈbɪlɪtɪ] *n.* (*honesty*) неподку́пность; (*imperishability*) неподве́рженность по́рче; нетле́нность.
incorruptible [ˌɪnkəˈrʌptɪb(ə)l] *adj.* (*proof against bribery etc.*) неподку́пный; (*proof against decay*) непо́ртящийся, нетле́нный.
increase[1] [ˈɪnkriːs] *n.* (*measurable*) увеличе́ние; **~ of speed** увеличе́ние ско́рости; **~ in value** увеличе́ние сто́имости; (*growth*) рост, возраста́ние; увеличе́ние; **~ in population** рост населе́ния; **unemployment is on the ~** безрабо́тица растёт/увели́чивается; (*amount of ~*) приро́ст; **my shares show an ~ of 5%** мои́ а́кции подняли́сь на пять проце́нтов; **we had an ~ (of pay)** мы получи́ли приба́вку/надба́вку.
increase[2] [ɪnˈkriːs] *v.t.* увели́чи|вать, -ть; **he ~d his wealth** он увели́чил своё состоя́ние; (*extend*): **~ one's influence** расш|иря́ть, -и́рить своё влия́ние; (*raise*): **~ prices** пов|ыша́ть, -ы́сить це́ны; (*quicken*): **~ one's pace** уск|оря́ть, -о́рить шаг; (*multiply*): **~ one's efforts** умн|ожа́ть, -о́жить (*or* удв|а́ивать, -о́ить) уси́лия; (*strengthen*): **this merely ~d his determination** э́то то́лько уси́лило его́ реши́мость.
v.t. увели́чи|ваться, -ться; (*grow*) расти́ (*impf.*); возраст|а́ть, -и́ (с+*g.*, до+*g.*); (*intensify*) уси́ли|ваться, -ться; (*expand*) расш|иря́ться, -и́риться; **the speed ~d** ско́рость увели́чилась; **the pace of life ~s** темп жи́зни ускоря́ется; (*multiply*): **his efforts ~d tenfold** его́ уси́лия возросли́/умно́жились в де́сять раз; (*rise*): **sugar ~d in price** са́хар повы́сился в цене́ (*or* подорожа́л).
increasingly [ɪnˈkriːsɪŋlɪ] *adv.* всё бо́лее; всё бо́льше и бо́льше; **it becomes ~ difficult** стано́вится всё трудне́е.
incredibility [ɪnˌkredɪˈbɪlɪtɪ] *n.* неправдоподо́бность, невероя́тность.
incredibl|e [ɪnˈkredɪb(ə)l] *adj.* (*lit., unbelievable*) неправдоподо́бный, невероя́тный, неимове́рный; (*coll., extraordinary*) невероя́тный, неслы́ханный; **he was ~y stupid** он был невероя́тно глуп.
incredulity [ˌɪnkrɪˈdjuːlɪtɪ] *n.* недове́рчивость.
incredulous [ɪnˈkredjʊləs] *adj.* недове́рчивый.
increment [ˈɪnkrɪmənt] *n.* (*increase*) рост, приро́ст; (*profit*) при́быль; (*amount of regular increase*) приба́вка.
incriminate [ɪnˈkrɪmɪˌneɪt] *v.t.* (*accuse*) обвин|я́ть, -и́ть; (*expose; show to be guilty*) изоблич|а́ть, -и́ть; **his confession ~d his brother in the affair** его́ призна́ние ука́зывало на прича́стность бра́та к де́лу; **he refused to ~ himself** он отказа́лся дава́ть показа́ния про́тив себя́.
incriminatory [ɪnˈkrɪmɪnətərɪ] *adj.* инкримини́рующий.
incrust [ɪnˈkrʌst] = **encrust**
incrustation [ˌɪnkrʌˈsteɪʃ(ə)n] *n.* (*encrusting*) инкруста́ция; (*crust, hard coating*) на́кипь.
incubate [ˈɪŋkjʊbeɪt] *v.t.* (*of a bird: hatch out*) выси́живать, вы́сидеть; выводи́ть, вы́вести; (*hatch by artificial heat*) инкуби́ровать (*impf., pf.*); (*fig.*) вына́шивать, вы́носить; выси́живать, вы́сидеть.
v.i. сиде́ть (*impf.*) на я́йцах.
incubation [ˌɪŋkjʊˈbeɪʃ(ə)n] *n.* (*of eggs*) выси́живание, инкуба́ция; (*stage of disease*) инкуба́ция; **~ period** инкубацио́нный пери́од.
incubator [ˈɪŋkjʊˌbeɪtə(r)] *n.* инкуба́тор.
incubus [ˈɪŋkjʊbəs] *n.* (*fig.*): **his wife was an ~ to him** жена́ была́ ему́ обу́зой.
inculcate [ˈɪnkʌlˌkeɪt] *v.t.* внедр|я́ть, -и́ть; внуш|а́ть, -и́ть.
inculcation [ˌɪnkʌlˈkeɪʃ(ə)n] *n.* внедре́ние, внуше́ние.
inculpate [ˈɪnkʌlˌpeɪt] *v.t.* (*expose*) изоблич|а́ть, -и́ть; (*accuse*) обвин|я́ть, -и́ть.

inculpation [ˌɪnkʌlˈpeɪʃ(ə)n] *n.* изобличе́ние, обвине́ние.
incumbency [ɪnˈkʌmbənsɪ] *n.* (*church*) бенефи́ций; (*tenure*) по́льзование бенефи́цием; пребыва́ние в до́лжности.
incumbent [ɪnˈkʌmbənt] *n.* **1.** (*eccl.*) приходско́й свяще́нник. **2.** занима́ющий (*какую-н.*) до́лжность.
adj.: **the ~ president** ны́нешний президе́нт; **~ upon** возлежа́щий на+*p.*; возло́женный на+*a.*; **it is ~ upon you to warn them** вы обя́заны предупреди́ть их.
incur [ɪnˈkɜː(r)] *v.t.* (*bring on o.s.*) навл|ека́ть, -е́чь на себя́; **she ~red the blame** она́ навлекла́ на себя́ обвине́ния; (*run into*) подв|ерга́ться, -е́ргнуться +*d.*; **I ~red his displeasure** я навлёк на себя́ его́ неудово́льствие; **he ~red heavy expenses** он понёс больши́е расхо́ды.
incurable [ɪnˈkjʊərəb(ə)l] *adj.* (*of sick pers.*) безнадёжный; (*fig.*): **an ~ optimist** неисправи́мый оптими́ст; (*of disease*) неизлечи́мый; (*of habit etc.*) неискорени́мый.
incurious [ɪnˈkjʊərɪəs] *adj.* нелюбопы́тный.
incursion [ɪnˈkɜːʃ(ə)n] *n.* вторже́ние, наше́ствие, налёт, набе́г.
indebted [ɪnˈdetɪd] *adj.* (*owing money*) в долгу́, до́лжный; **he was ~ to the bank** он задолжа́л ба́нку; **how much am I ~ to you?** ско́лько я вам до́лжен (за э́то)?; (*owing gratitude*) обя́занный; **to whom am I ~ for this?** кому́ я обя́зан за э́то.
indebtedness [ɪnˈdetɪdnɪs] *n.* задо́лженность; обя́занность.
indecency [ɪnˈdiːs(ə)nsɪ] *n.* неприли́чие, непристо́йность; **an act of gross ~** непристо́йное де́йствие.
indecent [ɪnˈdiːs(ə)nt] *adj.* **1.** (*unseemly*) неподоба́ющий, неблагови́дный; **she left with ~ haste** она́ ушла́ с неподоба́ющей поспе́шностью. **2.** (*obscene*) неприли́чный, непристо́йный.
indecipherable [ˌɪndɪˈsaɪfərəb(ə)l] *adj.* не поддаю́щийся расшифро́вке; (*of handwriting etc.*) неразбо́рчивый.
indecision [ˌɪndɪˈsɪʒ(ə)n] *n.* нереши́тельность, неуве́ренность.
indecisive [ˌɪndɪˈsaɪsɪv] *adj.* (*irresolute, hesitant*) нереши́тельный; (*not producing a decision or result*) не реша́ющий; **an ~ battle** бой, не име́ющий реша́ющего значе́ния; **an ~ argument** недоста́точно убеди́тельный аргуме́нт.
indeclinable [ˌɪndɪˈklaɪnəb(ə)l] *adj.* несклоня́емый.
indecorous [ɪnˈdekərəs] *adj.* (*improper*) неприли́чный; (*unseemly*) неподоба́ющий.
indecorum [ˌɪndɪˈkɔːrəm] *n.* наруше́ние прили́чий; неблагопристо́йность.
indeed [ɪnˈdiːd] *adv.* **1.** (*really, actually*) действи́тельно; в са́мом де́ле; вот и́менно; **and ~** да и; (*confirmatory, 'to be sure'*) и то́чно; **if ~** е́сли то́лько/вообще́. **2.** (*expr. emphasis*): **yes, ~** ну коне́чно!; ну да!; (а) ка́к же!; **very glad ~** о́чень, о́чень рад; **thanks very much ~** премно́го вам благода́рен; **no, ~** ну уж нет!; как бы не так; куда́!; где там!; **this is generosity ~** вот э́то ще́дрость!; **why ~?** действи́тельно, заче́м?; зачем со́бственно?; **"Will you come?" — "I will ~"** «Вы придёте?» — «Непреме́нно/обяза́тельно»; **"Did you have any trouble?" — "We did ~"** «У вас бы́ли неприя́тности?» — «Ещё каки́е!»; (**"Who is X?" —**) **"Who is he ~?!"** (*sc. nobody knows*) «В са́мом де́ле, кто он тако́й?»; (*sc. you ought to know*) «Что вы спра́шиваете!». **3.** (*expr. intensification*) к тому́ же; ма́ло/бо́лее того́; да́же; **she was worried, ~ desperate** она́ была́ озабо́чена, да́же в отча́янии; **I saw him recently, ~ yesterday** я ви́дел его́ неда́вно, не да́лее как вчера́. **4.** (*admittedly*) пра́вда; хотя́ (и); коне́чно; разуме́ется; **there are ~ exceptions** коне́чно, есть и исключе́ния; **I may ~ be wrong** допуска́ю, что я, мо́жет быть, непра́в; **he is ~ rich, but ...** он разуме́ется, бога́т, но... **5.** (*acknowledging information*) пра́вда?; вот как! **6.** (*iron.*): **charity ~!** ничего́ себе́ благотвори́тельность!; **is it ~!** в са́мом де́ле!; **progress ~!** то́же мне шаг вперёд!; шаг вперёд, не́чего сказа́ть!
indefatigable [ˌɪndɪˈfætɪgəb(ə)l] *adj.* неутоми́мый; (*unremitting*) неосла́бный.
indefeasible [ˌɪndɪˈfiːzɪb(ə)l] *adj.* неотъе́млемый.
indefectible [ˌɪndɪˈfektɪb(ə)l] *adj.* (*unfailing*) неизме́нный.
indefensible [ˌɪndɪˈfensɪb(ə)l] *adj.* (*mil.*) неприго́дный для оборо́ны; (*unjustified*) не име́ющий оправда́ния, непрости́тельный; **an ~ statement** неприе́млемое утвержде́ние.
indefinable [ˌɪndɪˈfaɪnəb(ə)l] *adj.* неопредели́мый.
indefinite [ɪnˈdefɪnɪt] *adj.* **1.** (*not clearly defined*) неопределённый. **2.** (*unlimited*) неограни́ченный; **he was away for an ~ time** он уе́хал на неопределённый срок. **3.** (*gram.*): **~ article** неопределённый арти́кль; **the past ~ (tense)** проше́дшее неопределённое (вре́мя).
indelible [ɪnˈdelɪb(ə)l] *adj.* (*lit., fig.*) несмыва́емый; **~ ink** несмыва́емые черни́ла; (*fig., unforgettable*) неизглади́мый.
indelicacy [ɪnˈdelɪkəsɪ] *n.* неделика́тность; беста́ктность.
indelicate [ɪnˈdelɪkət] *adj.* (*unrefined, immodest*) неделика́тный; (*tactless*) нетакти́чный, беста́ктный.
indemnification [ɪnˌdemnɪfɪˈkeɪʃ(ə)n] *n.* страхова́ние; предоставле́ние индемните́та; возмеще́ние, компенса́ция.
indemnif|y [ɪnˈdemnɪˌfaɪ] *v.t.* **1.** (*insure, protect*) страхова́ть, за-; **~y s.o. against loss** застрахова́ть кого́-н. на слу́чай убы́тков. **2.** (*give legal security to*) предост|авля́ть, -а́вить индемните́т +*d.*; освобо|жда́ть, -ди́ть от отве́тственности. **3.** (*compensate*) возме|ща́ть, -сти́ть (*что кому*); компенси́ровать (*impf., pf.*) (*что кому*); **he was ~ied for all his expenses** ему́ бы́ли возмещены́ все расхо́ды.
indemnity [ɪnˈdemnɪtɪ] *n.* (*security against damage or loss*) гара́нтия возмеще́ния убы́тков; (*legal security*) индемните́т; (*compensation*) возмеще́ние; (*paid to war victor*) контрибу́ция.
indemonstrable [ɪnˈdemənstrəb(ə)l, ˌɪndɪˈmɒn-] *adj.* недоказу́емый; не тре́бующий доказа́тельства.
indent[1] [ˈɪndent] *n.* (*requisition or order for goods*) зая́вка, наря́д.
indent[2] [ɪnˈdent] *v.t.* **1.** (*make notches or recesses in*) зазу́бр|ивать, -и́ть; нас|ека́ть, -е́чь; выреза́ть, вы́резать; изре́з|ывать, -ать; **an ~ed coastline** изви́листая берегова́я ли́ния. **2.** (*make dent in*) выда́лбливать, вы́долбить. **3.** (*draw up in duplicate*) сост|авля́ть, -а́вить (докуме́нт) в двух экземпля́рах. **4.** (*typ.*): **~ed** (напи́санный/напеча́танный) с о́тступом; **the first line of each paragraph is ~ed** ка́ждый абза́ц начина́ется с кра́сной строки́.
v.i. (*make an order or requisition*): **the government ~ed on our factory for its paper supplies** прави́тельство сде́лало на́шей фа́брике зака́з на поста́вку бума́ги.
indentation [ˌɪndenˈteɪʃ(ə)n] *n.* (*notch, cut*) зубе́ц, вы́рез, зазу́брина; (*in coastline etc.*) изви́лина.
indention [ɪnˈdenʃ(ə)n] *n.* (*typ.*) абза́ц, о́тступ.
indenture [ɪnˈdentʃə(r)] *n.* контра́кт, догово́р ме́жду ученико́м и хозя́ином.
v.t. связ|ывать, -а́ть контра́ктом.
independence [ˌɪndɪˈpend(ə)ns] *n.* **1.** незави́симость (от+*g.*), самостоя́тельность; **war of ~** война́ за незави́симость; война́ за (национа́льное) освобожде́ние; **I~ Day** День незави́симости. **2.** (*independent income*) самостоя́тельный дохо́д.
independent [ˌɪndɪˈpend(ə)nt] *n.* (*pol.*) незави́симый.
adj. незави́симый, самостоя́тельный; не зави́сящий (от+*g.*); **~ proof** объекти́вное доказа́тельство; **an ~ witness** непредубеждённый свиде́тель; **an ~ clause** (*gram.*) гла́вное предложе́ние; (*in adv. sense*): **~ of** незави́симо от+*g.*; поми́мо+*g.*; **she is an ~ person** у неё незави́симый хара́ктер; **an ~ state** незави́симое госуда́рство; **an ~ income** незави́симый/самостоя́тельный дохо́д; **we are travelling ~ly** (*separately*) мы путеше́ствуем врозь/отде́льно.
in-depth [ɪnˈdepθ] *adj.* обстоя́тельный, углублённый.
indescribable [ˌɪndɪˈskraɪbəb(ə)l] *adj.* неопису́емый.
indestructibility [ˌɪndɪstrʌktɪˈbɪlɪtɪ] неразруши́мость.
indestructible [ˌɪndɪˈstrʌktɪb(ə)l] *adj.* неразруши́мый.
indeterminable [ˌɪndɪˈtɜːmɪnəb(ə)l] *adj.* (*unascertainable, indefinable*) неопредели́мый.
indeterminacy [ˌɪndɪˈtɜːmɪnəsɪ] *n.* неопределённость, нереши́тельность.
indeterminate [ˌɪndɪˈtɜːmɪnət] *adj.* (*not fixed; indefinite*) неопределённый; **an ~ sentence** неопределённый пригово́р; (*not settled; undecided*) нерешённый; неоко́нча́тельный; **an ~ result** неоконча́тельный

результа́т; (*vague*; *indefinable*) нея́сный, сму́тный.

indeterminateness [ˌɪndɪ'tɜːmɪnətnɪs] = **indeterminacy**

index ['ɪndeks] *n.* **1.** (*indicator, pointer on instrument*) стре́лка. **2.** (*indicative figure or value*) и́ндекс; **retail price ~** и́ндекс ро́зничных цен; (*fig., indication*) показа́тель (*m.*); **his behaviour was an ~ of his true feelings** по его́ поведе́нию мо́жно бы́ло сде́лать вы́вод об его́ и́стинных чу́вствах. **3.** (*alphabetical*) указа́тель (*m.*); **subject ~** предме́тный указа́тель; **card ~** картоте́ка; **~ card** (картоте́чная) ка́рточка. **4.** (*math.*) показа́тель (*m.*) сте́пени. **5.** (*also* **~ finger**) указа́тельный па́лец.

v.t. **1.** (*compile ~ to*) снаб|жа́ть, -ди́ть указа́телем. **2.** (*insert in ~*) зан|оси́ть, -ести́ в указа́тель.

India ['ɪndɪə] *n.* И́ндия; **~ paper** кита́йская бума́га, би́бльдрук.

cpd. **i~ rubber** *n.* рези́нка, ла́стик.

Indian ['ɪndɪən] *n.* **1.** (*native of India*) инди́|ец (*fem.* -а́нка). **2. (American, red ~)** инд|е́ец (*fem.* -иа́нка), краснoко́жий. **3.: West ~** вест-и́нд|ец (*fem.* -ка).

adj. **1.** (*of India*) инди́йский; **~ hemp** кенды́рь (*m.*); **~ ink** тушь; **~ Ocean** Инди́йский океа́н. **2.** (*North American*) инде́йский; **~ club** булава́; **~ corn** кукуру́за, маи́с; **in i~ file** гусько́м; **~ summer** ба́бье ле́то. **3. West ~** вест-и́ндский.

indicate ['ɪndɪˌkeɪt] *v.t.* (*point out*) пока́з|ывать, -а́ть; ука́з|ывать, -а́ть (*кого/что or на кого/что*); **he ~d the way** он указа́л/показа́л путь; (*fig., point to*) ука́з|ывать, -а́ть; **he ~d the need for secrecy** он указа́л на необходи́мость соблюде́ния та́йны; (*show*) обозн|ача́ть, -а́чить; **the frontier is ~d in red** грани́ца обозна́чена кра́сным (цве́том); (*state*) выража́ть, вы́разить; **he ~d his intentions** он вы́разил свои́ наме́рения; (*be a sign of*) свиде́тельствовать (*impf.*) о+*p.*; означа́ть (*impf.*); быть при́знаком +*g.*; **his manner ~d willingness to assist** его́ поведе́ние свиде́тельствовало о жела́нии помо́чь; **rust ~s neglect** ржа́вчина свиде́тельствует о плохо́м ухо́де; (*call for*) тре́бовать (*impf.*) +*g.*; **an operation is ~d** опера́ция необходи́ма/пока́зана; (*measure by indicator*): **~d horsepower** индика́торная мо́щность.

indication [ˌɪndɪ'keɪʃ(ə)n] *n.* (*pointing out*) указа́ние; (*sign*) знак, указа́тель (*m.*); **~ of a right of way** указа́тель пра́ва прое́зда; **all the ~s are that he has left the country** всё свиде́тельствует о том, что он уе́хал из страны́; (*suggestion*; *intimation*) при́знак, намёк; **he gave no ~ of his feelings** он ниче́м не вы́дал свои́х чувств; (*portent*) при́знак; **there are ~s of trouble ahead** есть при́знаки гряду́щих неприя́тностей.

indicative [ɪn'dɪkətɪv] *n.* (*gram.*) изъяви́тельное наклоне́ние.

adj. **1.: ~ of** (*suggesting, showing*) ука́зывающий (*на что*); свиде́тельствующий (*о чём*); **a headache may be ~ of eyestrain** головна́я боль иногда́ свиде́тельствует о перенапряже́нии глаз; **this may be ~ of his intentions** э́то, возмо́жно, ука́зывает на его́ наме́рения. **2.** (*gram.*) изъяви́тельный.

indicator ['ɪndɪˌkeɪtə(r)] *n.* **1.** (*pointer of instrument*) стре́лка; указа́тель (*m.*). **2.** (*other indicating device*) индика́тор; **direction ~s** (*road signs*) доро́жные зна́ки (*m. pl.*); указа́тели направле́ния; **traffic ~s** (*on a vehicle*) указа́тели поворо́тов; **~ board** (*showing train arrivals and departures*) табло́ (*indecl.*); **~ light** (*e.g. on dashboard*) светово́й сигна́л. **3.** (*chem.*) индика́тор; **litmus paper is an ~ of acid** ла́кмусовая бума́га явля́ется индика́тором кислоты́. **4.** (*fig., sign, symptom*) показа́тель (*m.*), при́знак.

indict [ɪn'daɪt] *v.t.* предъявл|я́ть, -и́ть обвине́ние +*d.*; **he was ~ed for theft** он был обвинён в кра́же.

indictable [ɪn'daɪtəb(ə)l] *adj.*: **an ~ offence** преступле́ние, пресле́дуемое по обвини́тельному а́кту.

indictment [ɪn'daɪtmənt] *n.* (*charge*) обвини́тельный акт; (*action*) предъявле́ние обвине́ния; **bring an ~ against s.o.** предъявл|я́ть, -и́ть обвине́ние кому́-н.; (*fig.*): **these figures are an ~ of government policy** э́ти ци́фры слу́жат обвини́тельным докуме́нтом про́тив поли́тики прави́тельства.

Indies ['ɪndɪz] *n. pl.*: **the East ~** Ост-И́ндия; **the West ~** Вест-И́ндия.

indifference [ɪn'dɪfrəns] *n.* **1.** (*absence of interest*) безразли́чие; индифферéнтность; равноду́шие; **he regarded the matter with ~** он отнёсся к э́тому де́лу с равноду́шием. **2.** (*absence of feeling*) безразли́чие; равноду́шие; **he showed complete ~ to their sufferings** он прояви́л по́лное равноду́шие к их страда́ниям. **3.** (*neutrality*) нейтра́льность; **he maintained an attitude of ~** он держа́лся нейтра́льной ли́нии. **4.** (*small importance*) малова́жность; **it is a matter of ~ to me** мне э́то безразли́чно; э́то для меня́ не име́ет значе́ния.

indifferent [ɪn'dɪfrənt] *adj.* (*without interest*) безразли́чный; равноду́шный; индифферéнтный; (*neutral*; *unbiased*) нейтра́льный; (*mediocre*) посре́дственный.

indigence ['ɪndɪdʒ(ə)ns] *n.* нищета́, нужда́.

indigenous [ɪn'dɪdʒɪnəs] *adj.* тузе́мный; ме́стный; **kangaroos are ~ to Australia** кенгуру́ во́дятся в Австра́лии.

indigent ['ɪndɪdʒ(ə)nt] *adj.* бе́дный, ни́щий.

indigestible [ˌɪndɪ'dʒestɪb(ə)l] *adj.* неудобовари́мый; тру́дно перева́риваемый; (*fig.*) тру́дный, неудобовари́мый.

indigestion [ˌɪndɪ'dʒestʃ(ə)n] *n.* несваре́ние, диспепси́я; **the meal has given me ~** э́та еда́ вы́звала у меня́ расстро́йство желу́дка; **he gets ~ after eating** по́сле еды́ у него́ быва́ет изжо́га; **mental ~** неспосо́бность усво́ить всю информа́цию, перегру́зка информа́цией.

indignant [ɪn'dɪgnənt] *adj.* возмущённый; негоду́ющий; **I was ~ at his remark** его́ замеча́ние меня́ возмути́ло; **he became ~ with me** он вознегодова́л на меня́; **an ~ protest** гне́вный проте́ст.

indignation [ˌɪndɪg'neɪʃ(ə)n] *n.* возмуще́ние, негодова́ние, гнев; **the sight aroused his ~** э́то зре́лище вы́звало у него́ возмуще́ние; **he was full of ~ against the police** он был возмущён поведе́нием поли́ции; **an ~ meeting** (ма́ссовый) ми́тинг проте́ста.

indignit|y [ɪn'dɪgnɪtɪ] *n.* униже́ние, оскорбле́ние; **he was treated with ~y** его́ подве́ргли оскорби́тельному обраще́нию; **we were subjected to various ~ies** мы подве́рглись вся́ческим униже́ниям.

indigo ['ɪndɪˌgəʊ] *n.* (*dye*) инди́го (*indecl.*); **~ blue** цвет инди́го; си́не-фиоле́товый цвет.

indirect [ˌɪndaɪ'rekt] *adj.* непрямо́й, ко́свенный; опосре́дствованный; **an ~ route** обходно́й/око́льный путь; **~ lighting** рассе́янный свет; **~ tax** ко́свенный нало́г; **an ~ reference** ко́свенная ссы́лка; (*secondary*) побо́чный, втори́чный; **~ effect** побо́чный/дополни́тельный эффе́кт; (*gram.*): **~ object** ко́свенное дополне́ние; **~ speech** ко́свенная речь.

indiscernible [ˌɪndɪ'sɜːnɪb(ə)l] *adj.* неразличи́мый.

indiscipline [ɪn'dɪsɪplɪn] *n.* недисциплини́рованность.

indiscreet [ˌɪndɪ'skriːt] *adj.* (*incautious*) неосторо́жный; неосмотри́тельный; (*foolish*; *imprudent*) неблагоразу́мный; (*tactless*) беста́ктный; **an ~ question** нескро́мный вопро́с.

indiscretion [ˌɪndɪ'skreʃ(ə)n] *n.* (*indiscreetness*) нескро́мность; (*indiscreet act*) неосторо́жный/неблагоразу́мный посту́пок; (*revelation of secret*) неосторо́жность в выска́зываниях; **he committed an ~** он проговори́лся.

indiscriminate [ˌɪndɪ'skrɪmɪnət] *adj.* **1.** (*undiscriminating*) неразбо́рчивый; **an ~ reader** нетре́бовательный/неразбо́рчивый чита́тель; **to be ~ in one's friendships** води́ться (*impf.*) с любы́м и ка́ждым; быть неразбо́рчивым в друзья́х. **2.** (*random*) де́йствующий без разбо́ра; **he gives ~ praise** он хва́лит без разбо́ра; **he hit out ~ly** он наноси́л уда́ры куда́ попа́ло (*or* напра́во и нале́во). **3.** (*disorderly*; *unselected*) беспоря́дочный; **an ~ mass of data** ку́ча беспоря́дочной информа́ции.

indispensability [ɪndɪˌspensə'bɪlɪtɪ] *n.* необходи́мость; незамени́мость.

indispensable [ˌɪndɪ'spensəb(ə)l] *adj.* (*of thg.*) необходи́мый; **air is ~ to life** во́здух необходи́м для жи́зни; (*of pers.*) незамени́мый.

indisposed [ˌɪndɪ'spəʊzd] *adj.* (*disinclined*): **I am ~ to believe you** я не скло́нен вам ве́рить; (*unwell*) (немно́го) нездоро́вый; **the Queen is ~** короле́ве нездоро́вится.

indisposition [ˌɪndɪspə'zɪʃ(ə)n] *n.* (*disinclination*) нерасположе́ние, нежела́ние; (*feeling unwell*) недомога́ние.

indisputability [ˌɪndɪsˌpjuːtəˈbɪlɪtɪ] *n.* неоспори́мость.

indisputabl|e [ˌɪndɪˈspjuːtəb(ə)l] *adj.* неоспори́мый; **his genius is ~e** он бесспо́рно гениа́льный челове́к; **you are ~y correct** вы бесспо́рно пра́вы.

indissolubility [ˌɪndɪˌsɒljʊˈbɪlɪtɪ] *n.* неруши́мость.

indissoluble [ˌɪndɪˈsɒljʊb(ə)l] *adj.* неразры́вный; неруши́мый; **~ bonds of friendship** неразры́вные у́зы дру́жбы; (*chem.*) нераствори́мый.

indistinct [ˌɪndɪˈstɪŋkt] *adj.* (*of things seen or heard*) нея́сный; невня́тный; **his speech was ~** он говори́л невня́тно; (*vague*; *obscure*) сму́тный, расплы́вчатый; **I have only an ~ memory of him** я по́мню его́ о́чень сму́тно.

indistinctness [ˌɪndɪˈstɪŋktnɪs] *n.* (*of sense objects*) нея́сность, неотчётливость; (*of mental images*) расплы́вчатость, нея́сность.

indistinguishable [ˌɪndɪˈstɪŋgwɪʃəb(ə)l] *adj.* (*not recognizably different*) неразличи́мый, неотличи́мый; **he is ~ from his brother** его́ невозмо́жно отличи́ть от бра́та; **the two are ~** э́ти дво́е неразличи́мы; (*unrecognizable*; *imperceptible*) незаме́тный.

indite [ɪnˈdaɪt] *v.t.* сочин|я́ть, -и́ть; (*write*) писа́ть, на-.

individual [ˌɪndɪˈvɪdjʊəl] *n.* **1.** (*single being*) ли́чность, индиви́дуум, едини́ца, о́собь; **the rights of the ~** права́ ли́чности. **2.** (*type of pers.*) челове́к, тип, субъе́кт; **an unpleasant ~** неприя́тный тип.

adj. **1.** (*single*, *particular*) отде́льный. **2.** (*of or for one pers.*) ли́чный, ча́стный; **the teacher gave each pupil ~ attention** учи́тель уделя́л внима́ние ка́ждому ученику́. **3.** (*distinctive*) характе́рный, осо́бенный; **he has an ~ style of writing** у него́ оригина́льный/осо́бый/своеобра́зный стиль письма́.

individualism [ˌɪndɪˈvɪdjʊəˌlɪz(ə)m] *n.* индивидуали́зм.

individualist [ˌɪndɪˈvɪdjʊəlɪst] *n.* индивидуали́ст.

individualistic [ˌɪndɪvɪdjʊəˈlɪstɪk] *adj.* индивидуалисти́ческий.

individuality [ˌɪndɪvɪdjʊˈælɪtɪ] *n.* (*separate existence*) индивидуа́льность; (*individual character*) индивидуа́льность; ли́чность.

individualization [ˌɪndɪvɪdjʊəlaɪˈzeɪʃ(ə)n] *n.* индивидуализа́ция.

individualize [ˌɪndɪˈvɪdjʊəˌlaɪz] *v.t.* (*give distinct character to*) индивидуализи́ровать (*impf.*, *pf.*); (*specify*) подро́бно определ|я́ть, -и́ть.

indivisibility [ˌɪndɪˌvɪzɪˈbɪlɪtɪ] *n.* недели́мость.

indivisible [ˌɪndɪˈvɪzɪb(ə)l] *adj.* недели́мый.

Indochina [ˈɪndəʊˈtʃaɪnə] *n.* Индокита́й.

indocile [ɪnˈdəʊsaɪl] *adj.* непослу́шный.

indocility [ˌɪnˈdəʊˈsɪlɪtɪ] *n.* непослуша́ние.

indoctrinate [ɪnˈdɒktrɪˌneɪt] *v.t.* внуш|а́ть, -и́ть при́нципы +*d.*; подв|ерга́ть, -е́ргнуть идеологи́ческой обрабо́тке.

indoctrination [ɪnˌdɒktrɪˈneɪʃ(ə)n] *n.* идеологи́ческая обрабо́тка.

Indo-European [ˌɪndəʊjʊərəˈpɪən] *n.* индоевропе́|ец (*fem.* -йка).

adj. индоевропе́йский.

Indo-Germanic [ˌɪndəʊdʒɜːˈmænɪk] *adj.* индогерма́нский.

indolence [ˈɪndələns] *n.* ле́ность, вя́лость, нера́дивость.

indolent [ˈɪndələnt] *adj.* лени́вый, вя́лый, нера́дивый.

indomitability [ɪnˌdɒmɪtəˈbɪlɪtɪ] *n.* неукроти́мость.

indomitable [ɪnˈdɒmɪtəb(ə)l] *adj.* неукроти́мый.

Indonesia [ˌɪndəʊˈniːzɪə] *n.* Индоне́зия.

Indonesian [ˌɪndəˈniːzjən, -ʒ(ə)n, -ʃ(ə)n] *n.* (*pers.*) индонези́|ец (*fem.* -йка); (*language*) индонези́йский язы́к.

adj. индонези́йский.

indoor [ˈɪndɔː(r)] *adj.* ко́мнатный; **~ aerial** вну́тренняя/ко́мнатная анте́нна; **~ games** ко́мнатные и́гры; **~ swimming-pool** закры́тый бассе́йн; **~ work** рабо́та в помеще́нии (*or* по до́му).

indoors [ɪnˈdɔːz] *adv.* (*expr. position*) в до́ме; взаперти́; в четырёх сте́нах; **we stayed ~ all morning** мы просиде́ли до́ма (*or* никуда́ не выходи́ли) всё у́тро; (*expr. motion*) в дом.

indorse [ɪnˈdɔːs], **-ment** [ɪnˈdɔːsmənt] = **endorse, -ment**

indubitable [ɪnˈdjuːbɪtəb(ə)l] *adj.* несомне́нный; бесспо́рный.

induc|e [ɪnˈdjuːs] *v.t.* **1.** (*persuade, prevail on*) убеж|да́ть, -ди́ть; возде́йствовать (*impf.*, *pf.*) на+*a.*; **nothing will ~e him to change his mind** ничто́ не заста́вит его́ измени́ть реше́ние. **2.** (*bring about*) вызыва́ть, вы́звать; **illness ~ed by fatigue** боле́знь, вы́званная переутомле́нием; **sleep-~ing drugs** снотво́рные сре́дства; **~e a birth** стимули́ровать (*impf.*, *pf.*) ро́ды. **3.** (*elec.*) индукти́ровать (*impf.*, *pf.*); **~ed current** индукти́рованный ток. **4.** (*log.*) выводи́ть, вы́вести путём инду́кции.

inducement [ɪnˈdjuːsmənt] *n.* (*motive*, *incentive*) сти́мул; **there is no ~ for me to stay here** ничто́ не уде́рживает меня́ зде́сь; (*lure*) прима́нка; **the ~s of the capital** притяга́тельная си́ла столи́чной жи́зни (*or* столи́цы).

induct [ɪnˈdʌkt] *v.t.* (*install in post*) вв|оди́ть, -ести́; назн|ача́ть, -а́чить на до́лжность; (*initiate*) вв|оди́ть, -ести́; посвя|ща́ть, -ти́ть; (*US*, *into armed forces*) приз|ыва́ть, -ва́ть на вое́нную слу́жбу.

inductance [ɪnˈdʌkt(ə)ns] *n.* индукти́вность.

induction [ɪnˈdʌkʃ(ə)n] *n.* **1.** (*installation in post*) введе́ние в до́лжность; (*introduction*, *initiation*) введе́ние, вступле́ние; (*US*, *into armed forces*) призы́в на вое́нную слу́жбу. **2.** (*log.*) инду́кция. **3.** (*elec.*) инду́кция. **4.** (*med.*, *of a birth*) стимуля́ция ро́дов.

inductive [ɪnˈdʌktɪv] *adj.* (*log.*) индукти́вный; (*elec.*) индукти́вный; индукцио́нный.

indue [ɪnˈdjuː] = **endue**

indulge [ɪnˈdʌldʒ] *v.t.* (*gratify*, *give way to*) потво́рствовать (*impf.*, *pf.*) +*d.*; потака́ть (*impf.*) +*d.*; **she ~d all his wishes** она́ потака́ла всем его́ жела́ниям; **he ~d himself in nothing** он себе́ во всём отка́зывал; (*spoil*) по́ртить (*impf.*); балова́ть, из-; **their children have been over-~d** они́ избалова́ли свои́х дете́й; (*entertain*) пита́ть (*impf.*); леле́ять (*impf.*); **I still ~ the hope that …** я всё ещё леле́ю наде́жду, что…

v.i. (*allow o.s. pleasure*) увлека́ться (*impf.*) (*чем*); не отказа́ть (*pf.*) себе́ в удово́льствии; **he ~s in a cigar** он позволя́ет себе́ вы́курить сига́ру; **she rarely ~s in a new dress** она́ ре́дко позволя́ет себе́ поку́пку но́вого пла́тья; (*coll.*, *partake of drink*) выпива́ть (*impf.*).

indulgence [ɪnˈdʌldʒ(ə)ns] *n.* **1.** (*gratification of others*) потво́рство, потака́ние, побла́жка; (*of o.s.*) потво́рство свои́м при́хотям. **2.** (*tolerance*) снисходи́тельность, терпи́мость. **3.** (*pleasure indulged in*) удово́льствие; **smoking is his only ~** куре́ние — его́ еди́нственная сла́бость. **4.** (*eccl.*) индульге́нция.

indulgent [ɪnˈdʌldʒ(ə)nt] *adj.* (*compliant*) потво́рствующий; (*tolerant*) снисходи́тельный, терпи́мый; **~ criticism** снисходи́тельная кри́тика; **~ parents** не сли́шком стро́гие роди́тели.

Indus [ˈɪndəs] *n.* Инд.

industrial [ɪnˈdʌstrɪəl] *n.* (*one engaged in industry*) промы́шленник; (*pl.*, *shares in joint-stock enterprise*) а́кции (*f. pl.*) промы́шленных предприя́тий.

adj. промы́шленный, индустриа́льный; **~ accident** несча́стный слу́чай на произво́дстве; произво́дственная тра́вма; **~ action** забасто́вочные де́йствия; **~ area** индустриа́льный райо́н; **~ crops** техни́ческие культу́ры; **~ design** промы́шленный диза́йн, промы́шленная эсте́тика; **~ disease** профессиона́льное заболева́ние; **~ dispute** трудово́й конфли́кт; **~ relations** отноше́ния, возника́ющие в проце́ссе произво́дства; **the I~ Revolution** промы́шленный переворо́т; **~ training** произво́дственное обуче́ние.

industrialism [ɪnˈdʌstrɪəˌlɪz(ə)m] *n.* индустриали́зм.

industrialist [ɪnˈdʌstrɪəlɪst] *n.* промы́шленник; фабрика́нт.

industrialization [ɪnˌdʌstrɪəlaɪˈzeɪʃ(ə)n] *n.* индустриализа́ция.

industrialize [ɪnˈdʌstrɪəˌlaɪz] *v.t.* индустриализи́ровать (*impf.*).

industrious [ɪnˈdʌstrɪəs] *adj.* трудолюби́вый, усе́рдный.

industr|y [ˈɪndəstrɪ] *n.* **1.** (*branch of manufacture*) о́трасль; **home ~ies** о́трасли оте́чественной промы́шленности; **cottage ~** надо́мный про́мысел; куста́рная промы́шленность; **a dying ~y** отмира́ющая о́трасль промы́шленности. **2.** (*the world of manufacture*) инду́стрия; промы́шленность; **he intends to go into ~y** он хо́чет заня́ться промы́шленной де́ятельностью. **3.** (*diligence*) трудолю́бие; усе́рдие.

indwelling [ɪnˈdwelɪŋ] *adj.* прису́щий.

inebriate[1] [ɪ'ni:brɪət] *n.* пья́ница (*c.g.*), выпиво́ха (*coll.*, *c.g.*), алкого́лик.
adj. пья́ный; опьянённый.
inebriate[2] [ɪ'ni:brɪ,eɪt] *v.t.* (*usu. in p.p.*) вызыва́ть, вы́звать опьяне́ние у+*g.*; **he became ~d** он опьяне́л.
inebriety [,ini:'braɪətɪ] *n.* алкоголи́зм; опьяне́ние.
inedibility [ɪn,edɪ'bɪlɪtɪ] *n.* несъедо́бность.
inedible [ɪn'edɪb(ə)l] *adj.* несъедо́бный.
ineducable [ɪn'edjʊkəb(ə)l] *adj.* необуча́емый.
ineffable [ɪn'efəb(ə)l] *adj.* неопису́емый, невырази́мый.
ineffaceable [,ɪnɪ'feɪsəb(ə)l] *adj.* неизглади́мый.
ineffective [,ɪnɪ'fektɪv] *adj.* неде́йственный, безрезульта́тный; напра́сный, неэффекти́вный; (*of pers.*, *inefficient*) неуме́лый, неспосо́бный.
ineffectiveness [,ɪnɪ'fektɪvnɪs] *n.* безрезульта́тность, неэффекти́вность; неуме́ние.
ineffectual [ɪnɪ'fektjʊəl, -ʃʊəl] *adj.* безрезульта́тный, неуда́чный; **an ~ person** неуда́чник.
inefficacious [,ɪnefɪ'keɪʃəs] *adj.* неэффекти́вный, бесполе́зный.
inefficacy [ɪn'efɪkəsɪ] *n.* бесполе́зность, неэффекти́вность.
inefficiency [,ɪnɪ'fɪʃ(ə)nsɪ] *n.* неспосо́бность, неэффекти́вность, нерасторо́пность.
inefficient [,ɪnɪ'fɪʃ(ə)nt] *adj.* (*of persons*) неуме́лый, неспосо́бный, нерасторо́пный; (*of organizations, measures etc.*) неэффекти́вный, неде́йственный; малопроизводи́тельный; (*of machines*) непроизводи́тельный.
inelastic [,ɪnɪ'læstɪk] *adj.* неэласти́чный; (*lit.*, *fig.*) неги́бкий; жёсткий.
inelasticity [,ɪnɪlæs'tɪsɪtɪ] *n.* неэласти́чность; (*lit.*, *fig.*) неги́бкость; жёсткость.
inelegance [ɪn'elɪgəns] *n.* неэлега́нтность.
inelegant [ɪn'elɪgənt] *adj.* неэлега́нтный.
ineligibility [ɪn,elɪdʒɪ'bɪlɪtɪ] *n.* неприго́дность, нежела́тельность.
ineligible [ɪn'elɪdʒɪb(ə)l] *adj.* (*for office*) неподходя́щий; (*for military service*) него́дный (к+*d.*).
ineluctable [,ɪnɪ'lʌktəb(ə)l] *adj.* неотврати́мый, неизбе́жный.
inept [ɪ'nept] *adj.* (*out of place*) неуме́стный; (*clumsy*) неуме́лый; (*stupid*; *absurd*) глу́пый, неле́пый.
ineptitude [ɪ'neptɪ,tju:d] *n.* неуме́стность, неуме́ние; глу́пая вы́ходка.
inequalit|y [,ɪnɪ'kwɒlɪtɪ] *n.* **1.** (*lack of equality*) нера́венство; несоотве́тствие; **~y of distribution** неравноме́рность распределе́ния; **~ies in wealth** иму́щественное нера́венство. **2.** (*difference*; *dissimilarity*) несхо́дство. **3.** (*pl.*, *variability*) изме́нчивость; **the ~ies in his work** неро́вность его́ рабо́ты. **4.** (*of surface*: *irregularity*) неро́вность.
inequitable [ɪn'ekwɪtəb(ə)l] *adj.* несправедли́вый.
inequity [ɪn'ekwɪtɪ] *n.* несправедли́вость.
ineradicable [,ɪnɪ'rædɪkəb(ə)l] *adj.* неискорени́мый.
inert [ɪ'nɜ:t] *adj.* (*of substance*) ине́ртный; (*of the body, movements etc.*) тяжёлый, неповоро́тливый; (*fig.*, *of pers.*) вя́лый, безде́ятельный.
inertia [ɪ'nɜ:ʃə, -ʃɪə] *n.* (*phys.*) ине́рция; (*inertness, sloth*) ине́ртность; (*inactivity*) ине́ртность; безде́йствие.
inertial [ɪ'nɜ:ʃ(ə)l] *adj.* инерцио́нный.
inertness [ɪ'nɜ:tnɪs] = **inertia**
inescapable [,ɪnɪ'skeɪpəb(ə)l] *adj.* неизбе́жный.
inessential [,ɪnɪ'senʃ(ə)l] *adj.* незначи́тельный; малова́жный; малозна́чащий; несуще́ственный.
inestimable [ɪn'estɪməb(ə)l] *adj.* неоцени́мый.
inevitability [ɪn,evɪtə'bɪlɪtɪ] *n.* неизбе́жность.
inevitable [ɪn'evɪtəb(ə)l] *adj.* неизбе́жный, немину́емый; (*coll.*, *customary*) неизме́нный.
inexact [,ɪnɪg'zækt] *adj.* нето́чный.
inexactitude [,ɪnɪg'zæktɪtju:d] *n.* нето́чность.
inexcusable [,ɪnɪk'skju:zəb(ə)l] *adj.* непрости́тельный.
inexhaustible [,ɪnɪg'zɔ:stɪb(ə)l] *adj.* (*unfailing*) неистощи́мый, неисчерпа́емый; **~ energy** неистощи́мая эне́ргия; **~ patience** неистощи́мое терпе́ние; **an ~ supply** неисчерпа́емый запа́с; (*untiring*) неутоми́мый.
inexorability [ɪn,eksərə'bɪlɪtɪ] *n.* неумоли́мость, непрекло́нность.
inexorable [ɪn'eksərəb(ə)l] *adj.* (*relentless*, *unyielding*) неумоли́мый, непрекло́нный; безжа́лостный; **~ demands** непрекло́нные/безжа́лостные тре́бования; **~ logic** неумоли́мая ло́гика.
inexpediency [,ɪnɪk'spi:dɪənsɪ] *n.* нецелесообра́зность.
inexpedient [,ɪnɪk'spi:dɪənt] *adj.* нецелесообра́зный.
inexpensive [,ɪnɪk'spensɪv] *adj.* недорого́й.
inexperience [,ɪnɪk'spɪərɪəns] *n.* нео́пытность.
inexperienced [,ɪnɪk'spɪərɪənsd] *adj.* нео́пытный.
inexpert [ɪn'ekspɜ:t] *adj.* неуме́лый.
inexpiable [ɪn'ekspɪəb(ə)l] *adj.* (*of crime or offence*) неискупи́мый; (*of feelings*: *unappeasable*) непримири́мый.
inexplicable [,ɪnɪk'splɪkəb(ə)l, ɪn'eks-] *adj.* необъясни́мый.
inexplicit [,ɪnɪk'splɪsɪt] *adj.* непоня́тный; нея́сный.
inexpressible [,ɪnɪk'spresɪb(ə)l] *adj.* невырази́мый, неизъясни́мый, неопису́емый.
inexpressive [,ɪnɪk'spresɪv] *adj.* невырази́тельный.
inexpugnable [,ɪnɪk'spʌgnəb(ə)l] *adj.* неодоли́мый.
inextinguishable [,ɪnɪk'stɪŋgwɪʃəb(ə)l] *adj.* (*lit.*, *fig.*) неугаси́мый; (*fig.*) неистреби́мый; **~ hatred** неугаси́мая не́нависть.
inextricable [ɪn'ekstrɪkəb(ə)l, ,ɪnɪk'strɪk-] *adj.* запу́танный, сло́жный; **an ~ situation** безвы́ходное положе́ние; **~ difficulties** неразреши́мые тру́дности; **everything was in ~ confusion** всю́ду цари́л невероя́тный хао́с.
infallibility [,ɪnfælɪ'bɪlɪtɪ] *n.* **1.** (*incapability of error*) безоши́бочность; **Papal ~** непогреши́мость Па́пы. **2.** (*dependability*) надёжность.
infallible [ɪn'fælɪb(ə)l] *adj.* (*incapable of error*) безоши́бочный, непогреши́мый; (*unfailing*) надёжный; **an ~ method** надёжный/ве́рный спо́соб; **~ proof** неопровержи́мое доказа́тельство.
infamous ['ɪnfəməs] *adj.* позо́рный, посты́дный.
infamy ['ɪnfəmɪ] *n.* (*evil repute*) дурна́я сла́ва; (*moral depravity*) ни́зость; (*infamous conduct*) позо́рное поведе́ние; (*shame, disgrace*) позо́р.
infancy ['ɪnfənsɪ] *n.* младе́нчество; **the child died in ~** ребёнок у́мер во младе́нчестве; **from his earliest ~** с ра́ннего де́тства; (*leg.*) де́тский во́зраст; (*fig.*) ра́нняя ста́дия разви́тия, младе́нчество.
infant ['ɪnf(ə)nt] *n.* младе́нец; (*leg.*) несовершенноле́тний; **~ mortality** де́тская сме́ртность; **~ prodigy** вундерки́нд; **~ school** шко́ла для малыше́й; (*fig.*): **an ~ nation** молода́я на́ция; **~ industry** зарожда́ющаяся промы́шленность.
infanta [ɪn'fæntə] *n.* инфа́нта.
infante [ɪn'fæntɪ] *n.* инфа́нт.
infanticide [ɪn'fæntɪ,saɪd] *n.* (*pers.*) детоуби́йца (*c.g.*); (*crime*) детоуби́йство.
infantile ['ɪnfən,taɪl] *adj.* **1.** де́тский, младе́нческий; **~ paralysis** де́тский парали́ч. **2.** (*childish*) инфанти́льный.
infantilism [ɪn'fæntɪ,lɪz(ə)m] *n.* инфантили́зм.
infantry ['ɪnfəntrɪ] *n.* пехо́та; **~ regiment** пехо́тный полк.
cpd. **~man** *n.* пехоти́нец.
infatuate [ɪn'fætjʊ,eɪt] *v.t.*: **he is ~d with her** она́ ему́ вскружи́ла го́лову; **he was ~d with the idea** иде́я его́ ослепи́ла.
infatuation [ɪn,fætjʊ'eɪʃ(ə)n] *n.* (*for s.o.*) влюблённость, увлече́ние; (*with sth.*) увлече́ние.
infect [ɪn'fekt] *v.t.* (*lit.*, *fig.*) зара|жа́ть, -зи́ть; **the wound became ~ed** ра́на загнои́лась.
infection [ɪn'fekʃ(ə)n] *n.* (*infecting*) инфе́кция; (*infectious disease*) инфекцио́нное заболева́ние; **he caught the ~ from his brother** (*lit.*, *fig.*) он зарази́лся от бра́та; **the ~ of enthusiasm** зарази́тельность энтузиа́зма.
infectious [ɪn'fekʃəs] *adj.* (*carrying infection, liable to infect*) инфекцио́нный; (*fig.*) зарази́тельный; **his enthusiasm was ~** энтузиа́зм оказа́лся зарази́тельным.
infelicitous [,ɪnfɪ'lɪsɪtəs] *adj.* неуда́чный, неуме́стный.
infelicity [,ɪnfɪ'lɪsɪtɪ] *n.* неуме́стность.
infer [ɪn'fɜ:(r)] *v.t.* **1.** (*deduce*) заключ|а́ть, -и́ть; **am I to ~ that you disagree?** зна́чит ли э́то, что вы несогла́сны?; **he ~red the worst from her expression** по выраже́нию её лица́ он предположи́л са́мое ху́дшее. **2.** (*imply*) подразумева́ть (*impf.*).
inferable [ɪn'fɜ:rəb(ə)l] *adj.* выводи́мый.

inference [ˈɪnfərəns] *n.* (*inferring*) выведе́ние; **by ~** путём выведе́ния; (*conclusion*) вы́вод; заключе́ние; **I drew the obvious ~** я сде́лал есте́ственный вы́вод.
inferential [ˌɪnfəˈrenʃ(ə)l] *adj.* (*inferred*) вы́веденный.
inferior [ɪnˈfɪərɪə(r)] *n.* (*in rank, social status etc.*) подчинённый; (*in skill, mental attributes etc.*): **he is her ~ in horsemanship** он е́здит на ло́шади ху́же, чем она́.
adj. **1.** (*lower in position, rank etc.*) ни́зший; **he held an ~ position** он занима́л (бо́лее) ни́зкое положе́ние; **the rank of captain is ~ to that of major** капита́н ни́же майо́ра по зва́нию. **2.** (*poorer in quality*) ху́дший; **this batch is in no way ~ to the others** э́та па́ртия това́ра ничу́ть не ху́же други́х. **3.** (*of poor quality*) плохо́й, скве́рный, низкосо́ртный, низкопро́бный; **an ~ specimen** плохо́й образе́ц. **4.** (*of less importance*) неполноце́нный; **he makes me feel ~** в его́ прису́тствии у меня́ появля́ется ко́мплекс неполноце́нности.
inferiority [ɪnˌfɪərɪˈɒrɪtɪ] *n.* (*of position*) бо́лее ни́зкое положе́ние; (*of rank*) бо́лее ни́зкое зва́ние; (*of quality*) низкосо́ртность; (*of ability*) неполноце́нность; **~ complex** ко́мплекс неполноце́нности.
infernal [ɪnˈfɜːn(ə)l] *adj.* **1.** (*of hell*) а́дский; **the ~ regions** преиспо́дняя. **2.** (*devilish, abominable*) а́дский, дья́вольский, инферна́льный; **an ~ machine** а́дская маши́на; **~ cruelty** нечелове́ческая жесто́кость. **3.** (*coll., confounded*) черто́вский; **an ~ nuisance** проклятье; **he is ~ly clever** он черто́вски умён.
inferno [ɪnˈfɜːnəʊ] *n.* (*lit., fig.*) ад; **the building became a blazing ~** дом преврати́лся в пыла́ющий/о́гненный ад.
infertile [ɪnˈfɜːtaɪl] *adj.* неплодоро́дный, беспло́дный, стери́льный.
infertility [ˌɪnfɜːˈtɪlɪtɪ] *n.* неплодоро́дность, беспло́дность, стери́льность.
infest [ɪnˈfest] *v.t.* наводня́ть (*impf.*); **the house is ~ed with rats** дом наводнён кры́сами; **his clothes were ~ed with lice** его́ оде́жда кише́ла вша́ми; **pirates ~ed the coast** прибре́жные во́ды кише́ли пира́тами.
infestation [ˌɪnfeˈsteɪʃ(ə)n] *n.* наводне́ние.
infidel [ˈɪnfɪd(ə)l] *n. & adj.* неве́рный.
infidelity [ˌɪnfɪˈdelɪtɪ] *n.* неве́рность, изме́на.
in-fighting [ˈɪnˌfaɪtɪŋ] *n.* (*boxing*) инфа́йтинг; бли́жний бой; бой с бли́жней диста́нции; (*fig.*) междоусо́бная дра́ка; вну́тренняя борьба́; вну́тренний конфли́кт.
infiltrate [ˈɪnfɪlˌtreɪt] *v.t.* (*pass through filter*) фильтрова́ть (*impf.*); (*permeate*) инфильтрова́ть (*impf.*); пропи́т|ывать, -а́ть; (*fig.*) прон|ика́ть, -и́кнуть; **the enemy ~d our lines** враг прони́к к нам в тыл.
v.i. (*lit., fig.*) прос|а́чиваться, -очи́ться; (*fig.*) инфильтрова́ть (*impf.*).
infiltration [ˌɪnfɪlˈtreɪʃ(ə)n] *n.* (*lit.*) инфильтра́ция; (*fig., mil. and pol.*) проникнове́ние, инфильтра́ция.
infinite [ˈɪnfɪnɪt] *n.* бесконе́чность; бесконе́чное простра́нство; **the ~** (**~** *space*) бесконе́чность.
adj. (*boundless*) бесконе́чный; **the ~ goodness of God** беспреде́льная благода́ть бо́жья; (*countless*) несме́тный; **there are ~ possibilities** возмо́жности неисчерпа́емы; (*very great*) огро́мный.
infinitesimal [ˌɪnfɪnɪˈtesɪm(ə)l] *adj.* бесконе́чно ма́лый; стремя́щийся к нулю́; **~ calculus** исчисле́ние бесконе́чно ма́лых.
infinitive [ɪnˈfɪnɪtɪv] *n.* инфинити́в.
infinitude [ɪnˈfɪnɪˌtjuːd] *n.* (*boundlessness*) бесконе́чность; (*boundless extent*) обши́рность; (*boundless number*) бесконе́чно большо́е число́.
infinity [ɪnˈfɪnɪtɪ] *n.* бесконе́чность.
infirm [ɪnˈfɜːm] *adj.* (*physically*) не́мощный, дря́хлый; (*of mind, judgement etc.*) нетвёрдый; **~ of purpose** нереши́тельный.
infirmary [ɪnˈfɜːmərɪ] *n.* (*hospital*) лазаре́т; (*sick quarters*) изоля́тор.
infirmity [ɪnˈfɜːmɪtɪ] *n.* не́мощь; дря́хлость.
inflame [ɪnˈfleɪm] *v.t.* **1.: her eyes were ~d with weeping** от слёз у неё воспали́лись глаза́; **the wound became ~d** ра́на воспали́лась/загнои́лась. **2.** (*arouse*) возбу|жда́ть, -ди́ть; **his speech ~d popular feeling** его́ речь распали́ла стра́сти; **~d with passion** пыла́ющий стра́стью.
inflammable [ɪnˈflæməb(ə)l] *adj.* легко́ воспламеня́ющийся, горю́чий; (*fig.*) вспы́льчивый.
inflammation [ˌɪnfləˈmeɪʃ(ə)n] *n.* (*inflaming, lit., fig.*) воспламене́ние; вспы́шка; (*inflamed state of organ or skin*) воспале́ние.
inflammatory [ɪnˈflæmətərɪ] *adj.* (*lit.*) воспали́тельный; (*fig.*) зажига́тельный; подстрека́тельный.
inflatable [ɪnˈfleɪtəb(ə)l] *n.* надувна́я игру́шка.
adj. надувно́й.
inflate [ɪnˈfleɪt] *v.t.* **1.** (*fill with air, gas etc.*) над|ува́ть, -у́ть; нака́ч|ивать, -а́ть; (*fig.*): **~d with pride** надu̯тый от ва́жности; **~d language** напы́щенный язы́к; **~d importance** разду́тое значе́ние. **2.** (*fin.*): **~d prices** взви́нченные це́ны.
inflation [ɪnˈfleɪʃ(ə)n] *n.* (*of balloon, tyre etc.*) надува́ние; (*econ.*) инфля́ция.
inflationary [ɪnˈfleɪʃənərɪ] *adj.* инфляцио́нный.
inflect [ɪnˈflekt] *v.t.* (*gram.*) склоня́ть, про-; (*modulate*) модули́ровать (*impf.*).
infle|ction, -xion [ɪnˈflekʃ(ə)n] *n.* (*gram.*) фле́ксия, склоне́ние; (*of voice*) интона́ция.
inflexibility [ɪnˌfleksɪˈbɪlɪtɪ] *n.* неги́бкость, жёсткость; (*fig.*) непреклонность, непоколеби́мость.
inflexible [ɪnˈfleksɪb(ə)l] *adj.* неги́бкий, жёсткий; (*fig.*) непрекло́нный, непоколеби́мый.
inflexion [ɪnˈflekʃ(ə)n] = **inflection**
inflict [ɪnˈflɪkt] *v.t.* нан|оси́ть, -ести́ (*удар*); причин|я́ть, -и́ть (*боль*); **he ~ed a mortal blow** он нанёс смерте́льный уда́р; **a self-~ed wound** ра́на, нанесённая самому́ себе́; **the judge ~ed a severe penalty** судья́ вы́нес суро́вый пригово́р; **I don't wish to ~ myself upon you** я не хочу́ навя́зываться вам.
infliction [ɪnˈflɪkʃ(ə)n] *n.* (*of blow, wound etc.*) причине́ние (*боли*); (*of penalty etc.*) назначе́ние (*наказания*); (*painful or troublesome experience*) страда́ние; наказа́ние.
in-flight [ˈɪnflaɪt] *adj.* происходя́щий в полёте, на борту́ самолёта.
inflow [ˈɪnfləʊ] *n.* (*of liquid*) втека́ние; (*of goods, money etc.*) наплы́в, прито́к.
influence [ˈɪnflʊəns] *n.* (*power to affect or change*) влия́ние, возде́йствие; **she is a good ~ on him** она́ на него́ хорошо́ влия́ет; **he is an ~ for good** он хорошо́ возде́йствует на окружа́ющих; он подаёт хоро́ший приме́р; **fall under s.o.'s ~** поп|ада́ть, -а́сть под чьё-н. влия́ние; **under the ~ (of drink)** под возде́йствием (алкого́ля); **he has ~ with the government** прави́тельство с ним счита́ется; (*power due to position or wealth*) влия́ние; авторите́т; **use your ~ on my behalf** не откажи́те замо́лвить за меня́ сло́во/слове́чко; **a man of ~** влия́тельный челове́к.
v.t. влия́ть, по- на+*a.*; ока́з|ывать, -а́ть влия́ние на+*a.*; де́йствовать, по- (*or* возде́йствовать *impf., pf.*) на+*a.*; **nothing will ~ me to change my mind** ничто́ не изме́нит моего́ реше́ния; **he was ~d by what he saw** он оказа́лся под влия́нием уви́денного; **don't be ~d by bad examples** не поддава́йтесь возде́йствию плохи́х приме́ров.
influential [ˌɪnflʊˈenʃ(ə)l] *adj.* влия́тельный.
influenza [ˌɪnflʊˈenzə] *n.* инфлюэ́нца, грипп.
influx [ˈɪnflʌks] *n.* (*fig.*) наплы́в.
infold [ɪnˈfəʊld] = **enfold**
inform [ɪnˈfɔːm] *v.t.* **1.** (*tell; make aware*) информи́ровать (*impf.*); сообщ|а́ть, -и́ть +*d.*; осв|едомля́ть, -е́домить; ста́вить, по- в изве́стность; **I was not ~ed of the facts** мне не сообщи́ли о фа́ктах; я не́ был осведомлён; **keep me ~ed** держи́те меня́ в ку́рсе дел; **according to ~ed opinion** согла́сно осведомлённым круга́м; **he is a well ~ed man** он хорошо́ осведомлён; **an ~ed guess** дога́дка, осно́ванная на зна́ниях. **2.** (*pervade; inspire; fill*) (во)одушев|ля́ть, -и́ть; нап|олня́ть, -о́лнить (*чувствами и т.п.*).
v.i. дон|оси́ть, ести́; **he ~ed against, on his comrades** он доноси́л на свои́х това́рищей.
informal [ɪnˈfɔːm(ə)l] *adj.* неофициа́льный; непринуждённый; **it will be an ~ party** ≃ соберёмся за́просто; **~ dress** повседне́вная оде́жда; **an ~ meeting**

неофициа́льная встре́ча; встре́ча в непринуждённой обстано́вке.
informality [ɪn,fɔː'mælɪtɪ] *n.* непринуждённость.
informant [ɪn'fɔːmənt] *n.* информа́тор; осведоми́тель (*fem.* -ница); исто́чник/носи́тель (*m.*) информа́ции.
information [,ɪnfə'meɪʃ(ə)n] *n.* **1.** (*something told; knowledge*) информа́ция; све́дения (*nt. pl.*); спра́вка; да́нные (*nt. pl.*); **a useful piece of ~** поле́зная информа́ция; **according to my ~** согла́сно мои́м све́дениям; **can you give me any ~ about fares**? не мо́жете ли дать мне спра́вку о сто́имости прое́зда?; **he is a mine of ~** он кла́дезь зна́ний; **for your ~** к ва́шему све́дению; **~ bureau** спра́вочное бюро́; **~ desk** спра́вочный стол; **~ science** информа́тика. **2.** (*leg.*) жа́лоба; **lay, lodge an ~ against s.o.** пода́ть жа́лобу в суд на кого́-н.; донести́ на кого́-н.
informative [ɪn'fɔːmətɪv] *adj.* информацио́нный, информи́рующий; поучи́тельный; **I found him most ~** он снабди́л меня́ о́чень поле́зной информа́цией; **an ~ article** содержа́тельная/поучи́тельная статья́.
informer [ɪn'fɔːmə(r)] *n.* осведоми́тель (*fem.* -ница); (*against s.o.*) доно́счи|к (*fem.* -ца).
infraction [ɪn'frækʃ(ə)n] *n.* наруше́ние.
infra dig [,ɪnfrə 'dɪg] *pred. adj.* (*coll.*) унизи́тельно.
infra-red [,ɪnfrə'red] *adj.* инфракра́сный.
infrastructure ['ɪnfrə,strʌktʃə(r)] *n.* инфраструкту́ра.
infrequency [ɪn'friːkwənsɪ] *n.* ре́дкость.
infrequent [ɪn'friːkwənt] *adj.* ре́дкий.
infringe [ɪn'frɪndʒ] *v.t. & i.* нар|уша́ть, -у́шить; посяга́ть (*impf.*) на+*a.*; ущем|ля́ть, -и́ть; **this does not ~ on your rights** э́то не ущемля́ет ва́ших прав.
infringement [ɪn'frɪndʒmənt] *n.* наруше́ние; посяга́тельство; ущемле́ние.
infuriat|e [ɪn'fjʊərɪ,eɪt] *v.t.* прив|оди́ть, -ести́ в я́рость/бе́шенство; **an ~ing delay** приводя́щая в бе́шенство заде́ржка; **he became ~ed with me** он разозли́лся на меня́.
infuse [ɪn'fjuːz] *v.t.* (*pour in*) вли|ва́ть, -ть; (*steep in liquid*) зава́р|ивать, -и́ть; наста́ивать (*impf.*); (*inspire*) всел|я́ть, -и́ть; внуш|а́ть, -и́ть.
v.i. наста́иваться (*impf.*); **let the tea ~ for 5 minutes** пусть чай наста́ивается пять мину́т.
infusion [ɪn'fjuːʒ(ə)n] *n.* влия́ние; (*fig.*) внуше́ние; (*of tea, herbs etc.*) наста́ивание; (*liquid made by ~*) насто́йка.
ingathering [ɪn'gæðərɪŋ] *n.* (*harvest*) сбор урожа́я.
ingenious [ɪn'dʒiːnɪəs] *adj.* изобрета́тельный; остроу́мный; **an ~ solution** остроу́мное/гениа́льное реше́ние; (*of a device, machine etc.*) иску́сный; замыслова́тый.
ingénue [,æʒeɪ'njuː] *n.* инженю́ (*f. indecl.*).
ingenuity [,ɪndʒɪ'njuːɪtɪ] *n.* изобрета́тельность; оригина́льность.
ingenuous [ɪn'dʒenjʊəs] *adj.* (*sincere; candid*) и́скренний, чистосерде́чный; открове́нный; (*simple, unsophisticated*) просто́й, простоду́шный, безыску́сный; (*naive*) простоду́шный.
ingenuousness [ɪn'dʒenjʊəsnɪs] *n.* и́скренность, чистосерде́чность; простоду́шие.
ingest [ɪn'dʒest] *v.t.* глота́ть (*impf.*); прогл|а́тывать, -оти́ть.
ingestion [ɪn'dʒestʃ(ə)n] *n.* приём (пи́щи).
ingle-nook ['ɪŋg(ə)l,nʊk] *n.* месте́чко у ками́на.
inglorious [ɪn'glɔːrɪəs] *adj.* (*ignominious*) бессла́вный; (*obscure*) незаме́тный.
ingoing ['ɪn,gəʊɪŋ] *adj.* входя́щий; **the ~ tenant** но́вый жиле́ц.
ingot ['ɪŋgɒt, -gət] *n.* сли́ток.
ingrained [ɪn'greɪnd, *attrib.* 'ɪn-] *adj.* **1.** прони́кший; въе́вшийся; **~ dirt** въе́вшаяся грязь. **2.** (*fig.*) закорене́лый, врождённый; **~ prejudice** укорени́вшийся предрассу́док.
ingrate ['ɪngreɪt, -'greɪt] *n.* (*liter.*) неблагода́рный челове́к.
ingratiat|e [ɪn'greɪʃɪ,eɪt] *v.t.*: **he ~ed himself with the new manager** он вошёл в дове́рие к но́вому нача́льнику; **an ~ing smile** заи́скивающая улы́бка.
ingratitude [ɪn'grætɪ,tjuːd] *n.* неблагода́рность.
ingredient [ɪn'griːdɪənt] *n.* составна́я часть, ингредие́нт, компоне́нт; **the ~s of a cake** ингредие́нты пирога́; **hard work is an important ~ of success** упо́рный труд — одно́ из основны́х усло́вий успе́ха.
ingress ['ɪngres] *n.* (*entry*) до́ступ; вхожде́ние; (*right of entry*) пра́во вхо́да.
ingrowing ['ɪn,grəʊɪŋ] *adj.* враста́ющий; **~ toe-nail** враста́ющий но́готь ноги́.
inguinal ['ɪŋgwɪn(ə)l] *adj.* пахово́й.
ingurgitate [ɪn'gɜːdʒɪ,teɪt] *v.t.* жа́дно глота́ть (*impf.*); погло|ща́ть, -ти́ть.
ingurgitation [ɪn,gɜːdʒɪ'teɪʃ(ə)n] *n.* загла́тывание; поглоще́ние.
inhabit [ɪn'hæbɪt] *v.t.* жить (*impf.*) в+*p.*; обита́ть (*impf.*) в+*p.*; населя́ть (*impf.*); **his family ~ed a large estate** его́ семья́ жила́ в большо́м поме́стье; **is the island ~ed?** э́тот о́стров обита́ем; **the house was ~ed by foreigners** дом был населён иностра́нцами; **many birds ~ the forest** в лесу́ во́дится мно́го птиц.
inhabitable [ɪn'hæbɪtəb(ə)l] *adj.* приго́дный для жилья́; жило́й.
inhabitant [ɪn'hæbɪt(ə)nt] *n.* жи́тель (*fem.* -ница); жиле́ц.
inhalant [ɪn'heɪlənt] *n.* ингаля́тор.
inhalation [,ɪnhə'leɪʃ(ə)n] *n.* ингаля́ция.
inhale [ɪn'heɪl] *v.t.* вд|ыха́ть, -охну́ть.
v.i. затя́гиваться (*сигаретой и т.п.*); **it is dangerous to ~** затя́гиваться вре́дно.
inhaler [ɪn'heɪlə(r)] *n.* (*device*) ингаля́тор.
inharmonious [,ɪnhɑː'məʊnɪəs] *adj.* (*of sounds*) негармони́чный; (*fig.*) негармони́рующий.
inhere [ɪn'hɪə(r)] *v.i.* быть прису́щим/сво́йственным; быть неотъе́млемым, принадлежа́ть (+*d.*).
inherent [ɪn'hɪərənt, ɪn'herənt] *adj.* сво́йственный, прису́щий; (*inalienable*) неотъе́млемый.
inherit [ɪn'herɪt] *v.t. & i.* насле́довать (*impf., pf.; pf. also* у-); полу|ча́ть, -и́ть насле́дство.
inheritable [ɪn'herɪtəb(ə)l] *adj.* насле́дуемый.
inheritance [ɪn'herɪt(ə)ns] *n.* (*inheriting*) насле́дование; (*sth. inherited*) насле́дство; (*fig.*): **an ~ of misery** го́рькое насле́дство.
inheritor [ɪn'herɪtə(r)] *n.* насле́дни|к (*fem.* -ца).
inhibit [ɪn'hɪbɪt] *v.t.* (*forbid*) запре|ща́ть, -ти́ть; (*hinder, restrain*) сде́рж|ивать, -а́ть; подав|ля́ть, -и́ть; ско́в|ывать, -а́ть; **fear ~s his actions** страх ско́вывает его́ де́йствия; **an ~ed person** ско́ванный челове́к.
inhibition [,ɪnhɪ'bɪʃ(ə)n] *n.* (*inhibiting*) запреще́ние, запре́т; (*restraint*) сде́рживание/подавле́ние (чувств); (*psych.*) торможе́ние.
inhospitable [,ɪnhɒ'spɪtəb(ə)l, ɪn'hɒsp-] *adj.* негостеприи́мный, неприве́тливый; **an ~ coast** суро́вый бе́рег.
inhospitality [ɪn,hɒspɪ'tælɪtɪ] *n.* негостеприи́мность, неприве́тливость.
inhuman [ɪn'hjuːmən] *adj.* бесчелове́чный; античелове́ческий.
inhumane [,ɪnhjuː'meɪn] *adj.* негума́нный.
inhumanity [,ɪnhjuː'mænɪtɪ] *n.* бесчелове́чность.
inhume [ɪn'hjuːm] *v.t.* погре|ба́ть, -сти́; пред|ава́ть, -а́ть земле́.
inimical [ɪ'nɪmɪk(ə)l] *adj.* (*hostile; conflicting*) вражде́бный; недружелю́бный; (*harmful*) вре́дный, неблагоприя́тный; **factors ~ to success** обстоя́тельства, неблагоприя́тствующие успе́ху; **~ to one's health** вре́дный для здоро́вья.
inimitable [ɪ'nɪmɪtəb(ə)l] *adj.* неподража́емый; несравне́нный.
iniquitous [ɪ'nɪkwɪtəs] *adj.* чудо́вищный; несправедли́вый.
iniquity [ɪ'nɪkwɪtɪ] *n.* несправедли́вость; зло.
initial [ɪ'nɪʃ(ə)l] *n.*: **what are your ~s?** ва́ши инициа́лы?; (*pl., as signature*) пара́ф.
adj. нача́льный; **in the ~ stage** в первонача́льной ста́дии; **~ cost** первонача́льная сто́имость; **~ velocity** нача́льная ско́рость; **~ letter** нача́льная бу́ква.
v.t.: **~ a document** ста́вить, по- инициа́лы под докуме́нтом; парафи́ровать (*impf., pf.*) докуме́нт.
initiate[1] [ɪ'nɪʃɪət] *n.* посвящённый.
initiate[2] [ɪ'nɪʃɪ,eɪt] *v.t.* **1.** (*set in motion*) нач|ина́ть, -а́ть. **2.** (*introduce*) вв|оди́ть, -ести́; посвяти́ть (*pf.*); **they ~d him into society** они́ ввели́ его́ в о́бщество; **he was ~d into the mysteries of science** его́ посвяти́ли в та́йны нау́ки.
initiation [ɪ,nɪʃɪ'eɪʃ(ə)n] *n.* (*beginning*) основа́ние, установле́ние, учрежде́ние; (*admission; introduction*) введе́ние (в

о́бщество); ~ **ceremonies** обря́ды посвяще́ния.

initiative [ɪ'nɪʃətɪv, ɪ'nɪʃɪətɪv] *n.* **1.** (*lead*) инициати́ва, почи́н; **he took the** ~ он взял на себя́ инициати́ву; **he acted on his own** ~ он де́йствовал по со́бственной инициати́ве; **you have the** ~ инициати́ва в ва́ших рука́х. **2.** (*enterprise*) инициати́ва, инициати́вность; **he showed considerable** ~ он прояви́л недю́жинную предприи́мчивость; **a man of** ~ инициати́вный челове́к.

initiator [ɪ'nɪʃɪeɪtə(r)] *n.* инициа́тор.

inject [ɪn'dʒekt] *v.t.* вв|оди́ть, -ести́; впры́с|кивать, -нуть; **the drug was** ~**ed into the blood-stream** лека́рство ввели́ в ве́ну; **the nurse** ~**ed his arm with morphia** сестра́ сде́лала ему́ уко́л мо́рфия в ру́ку; **he learned to** ~ **himself with insulin** он научи́лся де́лать себе́ уко́лы инсули́на; (*fig.*): **he will** ~ **new life into the government** он вдохнёт но́вую жизнь в де́ятельность прави́тельства; **he** ~**ed a remark into the conversation** он вста́вил замеча́ние в разгово́р.

injection [ɪn'dʒekʃ(ə)n] *n.* впры́скивание; инъе́кция; **have you had an** ~ **for cholera?** вы привива́лись про́тив холе́ры?

injudicious [ˌɪndʒuː'dɪʃəs] *adj.* неблагоразу́мный; неразу́мный.

injudiciousness [ˌɪndʒuː'dɪʃəsnɪs] *n.* неблагоразу́мие.

injunction [ɪn'dʒʌŋkʃ(ə)n] *n.* (*command*) прика́з, предписа́ние; (*leg.*) суде́бный запре́т.

injure ['ɪndʒə(r)] *v.t.* (*physically*) ушиб|а́ть, -и́ть; повре|жда́ть, -ди́ть; ра́нить, по-; **he was** ~**d in a fall** он ушиќбся при паде́нии; **he fell and** ~**d himself** он упа́л и ушиќбся; **washing may** ~ **this fabric** э́тот материа́л мо́жет пострада́ть при сти́рке; (*fig.*): **crops** ~**d by storms** поби́тые непого́дой хлеба́ +*d.*; **this may** ~ **his prospects** э́то мо́жет повреди́ть его́ бу́дущему; **he will** ~ **his own reputation** он сам испо́ртит себе́ репута́цию; (*offend*) ра́нить, по-; об|ижа́ть, -и́деть; оскорб|ля́ть, -и́ть; **you have** ~**d his feelings** вы ра́нили/оскорби́ли его́ чу́вства.

injured ['ɪndʒəd] *adj.* (*suffering injury*) ра́неный; **an** ~ **soldier** ра́неный солда́т; **the** ~ **party** пострада́вшая сторона́; (*as n.*): **the dead and** ~ уби́тые и ра́неные; (*showing sense of wrong*) оби́женный, оскорблённый; **in an** ~ **voice** оби́женным то́ном; ~ **innocence** оскорблённая неви́нность.

injurious [ɪn'dʒʊərɪəs] *adj.* вре́дный, губи́тельный; ~ **to health** вре́дный для здоро́вья; **remarks** ~ **to his reputation** замеча́ния, подрыва́ющие его́ репута́цию.

injur|y ['ɪndʒərɪ] *n.* (*to the body*) ра́на, ране́ние, уши́б, тра́вма; **a war** ~**y** боево́е ране́ние; **his** ~**ies were superficial** его́ ра́ны бы́ли несерьёзные; **he sustained multiple** ~**ies** он получи́л мно́жество ране́ний; **he threatened to do me an** ~**y** он грози́лся меня́ поби́ть; (*to property etc.*) ущéрб; **the building suffered** ~**y by fire** зда́ние пострада́ло от пожа́ра; (*wrongful treatment*) оскорбле́ние; **that is adding insult to** ~**y** э́то равноси́льно но́вому оскорбле́нию; (*fig., damage*) вред, уще́рб; **this will do great** ~**y to our cause** э́то нанесёт большо́й вред на́шему де́лу.

injustice [ɪn'dʒʌstɪs] *n.* несправедли́вость; **you do him an** ~ вы к нему́ несправедли́вы; **you are doing yourself an** ~ вы де́лаете себе́ во вред.

ink [ɪŋk] *n.* черни́л|а (*pl., g.* —); **the words were underlined in red** ~ слова́ бы́ли подчёркнуты кра́сными черни́лами; **the sky was as black as** ~ не́бо бы́ло чёрное как смоль; **printer's** ~ типогра́фская кра́ска; **the** ~ **came off on my hands** я изма́зался черни́лами; **an** ~ **drawing** рису́нок ту́шью.

v.t.: ~ **one's fingers** па́чкать, за- па́льцы черни́лами.

with advs.: ~ **in a drawing** покр|ыва́ть, -ы́ть рису́нок ту́шью; ~ **over pencil lines** обв|оди́ть, -ести́ каранда́шные ли́нии черни́лами.

cpds. ~**-blot** *n.* черни́льная кля́кса; ~**-bottle** *n.* пузырёк для черни́л; ~**-jet** *adj.*: ~**-jet printer** (*comput.*) (краско)стру́йный при́нтер; ~**-pad** *n.* штемпельная поду́шечка; ~**-pot** *n.* черни́льница; ~**-slinger** *n.* (*coll.*) писа́ка (*m.*); борзопи́сец; ~**-stand** *n.* черни́льный прибо́р; ~**-well** *n.* черни́льница.

inkling ['ɪŋklɪŋ] *n.* намёк; сла́бое подозре́ние; **I had not the least** ~ **of their intentions** я не име́л ни мале́йшего представле́ния об их наме́рениях.

inky ['ɪŋkɪ] *adj.* (*stained with ink*) запа́чканный черни́лами; (*black*) чёрный как смоль.

inland ['ɪnlənd, 'ɪnlænd] *adj.* располо́женный внутри́ страны́; **an** ~ **sea** вну́треннее мо́ре; ~ **trade** вну́тренняя торго́вля; **the I**~ **Revenue** управле́ние нало́говых сбо́ров.

adv. (*motion*) внутрь/вглубь страны́; (*place*) внутри́ страны́; **they travelled** ~ они́ е́хали вглубь страны́; **storms are more frequent** ~ бу́ри быва́ют ча́ще в райо́нах, удалённых от мо́ря.

in-law ['ɪnlɔː] *n.* сво́йственник, родня́ со стороны́ му́жа/жены́; ~**s** свояки́ (*m. pl.*).

inla|y [ɪn'leɪ] *n.* инкруста́ция; моза́ика; (*dentistry*) пло́мба.

v.t. покр|ыва́ть, -ы́ть моза́икой; инкрусти́ровать (*impf., pf.*); **an** ~**id floor** пол, покры́тый моза́икой; парке́тный пол.

inlet ['ɪnlet, -lɪt] *n.* **1.** (*small arm of water*) у́зкий зали́в. **2.** (*insertion in garment*) вста́вка. **3.:** ~ **valve** впускно́й кла́пан.

inmate ['ɪnmeɪt] *n.* (*of house*) жиле́ц; (*of hospital, mental home etc.*) обита́тель (*m.*); больно́й, пацие́нт; (*of prison*) заключённый.

in medias res [ɪn ˌmiːdɪæs 'reɪz] *adv.* с ме́ста в карье́р.

in memoriam [ɪn mɪ'mɔːrɪˌæm] *prep.* в па́мять +*g*; па́мяти +*g*.

inmost ['ɪnməʊst, -məst], **innermost** ['ɪnərməʊst, -məst] *adjs.* глубоча́йший; (*fig.*) сокрове́ннейший.

inn [ɪn] *n.* гости́ница, тракти́р; постоя́лый двор.

cpds. ~**keeper** *n.* хозя́ин гости́ницы; ~**-sign** *n.* вы́веска придоро́жного тракти́ра.

innards ['ɪnədz] *n.* (*coll.*) вну́тренности (*f. pl.*).

innate [ɪ'neɪt, 'ɪ-] *adj.* врождённый, приро́дный.

inner ['ɪnə(r)] *adj.* (*nearer to centre*) вну́тренний; **an** ~ **room** вну́тренняя ко́мната; ~ **tube** ка́мера ши́ны; (*intimate*) инти́мный, сокрове́нный; **my** ~ **convictions** мои́ вну́тренние убежде́ния; **the** ~ **man** (*joc., stomach*) желу́док.

innermost ['ɪnəməʊst, -məst] = **inmost**

innings ['ɪnɪŋz] *n.* о́чередь уда́ра (*крикет*); (*fig.*): **the Socialists had a long** ~ социали́сты до́лго держа́лись у вла́сти; **he had a good** ~ он про́жил до́лгую и счастли́вую жизнь.

innocence ['ɪnəs(ə)ns] *n.* **1.** (*guiltlessness*) невино́вность; **his** ~ **was established** его́ невино́вность была́ дока́зана. **2.** (*freedom from sin*) неви́нность; (*chastity*) целому́дрие. **3.: I thought in my** ~ **that he would repay me** я по наи́вности наде́ялся, что он вернёт мне долг.

innocent ['ɪnəs(ə)nt] *n.* неви́нный младе́нец; **slaughter of the** ~**s** (*bibl.*) избие́ние младе́нцев.

adj. **1.** (*leg.*) невино́вный. **2.** (*harmless*) неви́нный, безоби́дный; **an** ~ **amusement** неви́нное развлече́ние. **3.** (*without sin*) неви́нный, безгре́шный; ~ **as a babe** неви́нный как дитя́. **4.** (*naive, simple*) наи́вный, простоду́шный.

innocuous [ɪ'nɒkjʊəs] *adj.* безвре́дный, безоби́дный.

innovate ['ɪnəˌveɪt] *v.i.* вв|оди́ть, -ести́ нововведе́ния; произв|оди́ть, -ести́ измене́ния/переме́ны; вв|оди́ть, -ести́ но́вшество.

innovation [ˌɪnə'veɪʃ(ə)n] *n.* нововведе́ние, но́вшество, нова́торство.

innovative ['ɪnəˌveɪtɪv] *adj.* нова́торский.

innovator ['ɪnəˌveɪtə(r)] *n.* нова́тор.

innuendo [ˌɪnjʊ'endəʊ] *n.* ко́свенный намёк; недомо́лвка; инсинуа́ция; **he spoke in** ~**es** он говори́л намёками.

innumerable [ɪ'njuːmərəb(ə)l] *adj.* бесчи́сленный, неисчисли́мый, бессчётный.

innumeracy [ɪ'njuːmərəsɪ] *n.* цифрова́я негра́мотность.

innumerate [ɪ'njuːmərət] *adj.* не уме́ющий счита́ть.

inoculate [ɪ'nɒkjʊˌleɪt] *v.t.* де́лать, с- приви́вку; приви|ва́ть, -ть; **he was** ~**d against smallpox** ему́ приви́ли о́спу.

inoculation [ɪˌnɒkjʊ'leɪʃ(ə)n] *n.* приви́вка; **I have to have an** ~ **for typhoid** мне ну́жно сде́лать приви́вку от ти́фа.

inodorous [ɪn'əʊdərəs] *adj.* непа́хнущий, не име́ющий за́паха.

inoffensive [ˌɪnə'fensɪv] *adj.* (*giving no offence*) необи́дный, неоскорби́тельный; (*harmless*) безоби́дный.

inoffensiveness [ˌɪnəˈfensɪvnɪs] *n.* безоби́дность.

inoperable [ɪnˈɒpərəb(ə)l] *adj.* (*untreatable by surgery*) неопера́бельный; (*unworkable*) неприменимый; **the plan proved to be ~** план оказа́лся невыполни́мым.

inoperative [ɪnˈɒpərətɪv] *adj.* неэффекти́вный, недействи́тельный.

inopportune [ɪnˈɒpəˌtju:n] *adj.* неуме́стный, несвоевре́менный.

inordinate [ɪnˈɔ:dɪnət] *adj.* (*immoderate*; *uncontrolled*) беспоря́дочный; (*excessive*) чрезме́рный; неуме́ренный.

inorganic [ˌɪnɔ:ˈgænɪk] *adj.* неоргани́ческий.

in-patient [ˈɪnˌpeɪʃ(ə)nt] *n.* стациона́рный/ко́ечный больно́й; **~ treatment** стациона́рное лече́ние.

input [ˈɪnpʊt] *n.* (*to computer*) ввод, пода́ча (информа́ции).

inquest [ˈɪnkwest, ˈɪŋ-] *n.* (*official enquiry*) сле́дствие, дозна́ние; (*coroner's ~*) перви́чное рассле́дование причи́н и обстоя́тельств сме́рти; сле́дствие, проводи́мое ко́ронером и его́ жюри́; (*investigation*) рассле́дование, разбира́тельство.

inquir|e [ɪnˈkwaɪə(r), ɪŋ-] (*see also* **enquire**) *v.t.* спр|а́шивать, -оси́ть; узн|ава́ть, -а́ть; **may I ~e your name?** могу́ я узна́ть, как вас зову́т?; **I ~ed of a passer-by how to find your house** я спроси́л прохо́жего, как найти́ ваш дом.

v.i. спр|авля́ться, -а́виться; нав|оди́ть, -ести́ спра́вку; **we ~ed about the train service** мы спра́вились относи́тельно расписа́ния поездо́в; **she ~ed after your health** она́ справля́лась о ва́шем здоро́вье; **has he ~ed for me?** он меня́ спра́шивал?; **we must ~e into the matter** мы должны́ рассле́довать э́то де́ло; **an ~ing mind** пытли́вый ум.

inquirer [ɪnˈkwaɪərə(r), ɪŋ-] *n.* де́лающий запро́с.

inquir|y [ɪnˈkwaɪərɪ, ɪŋ-] (*see also* **enquiry**) *n.* **1.** (*question*) наведе́ние спра́вок; **I made ~ies** я навёл спра́вки; **on ~y** в отве́т на вопро́с. **2.** (*investigation*) рассле́дование; сле́дствие; **court of ~y** сле́дственная коми́ссия; **the police are making ~ies** поли́ция рассле́дует де́ло; **there will be a full ~y** назна́чено по́лное рассле́дование э́того де́ла.

inquisition [ˌɪnkwɪˈzɪʃ(ə)n, ˌɪŋ-] *n.* иссле́дование, изыска́ние; **he was subjected to an ~** он был под сле́дствием; (*hist.*) инквизи́ция.

inquisitive [ɪnˈkwɪzɪtɪv, ɪŋ-] *adj.* любозна́тельный, любопы́тный, пытли́вый.

inquisitiveness [ɪnˈkwɪzɪtɪvnɪs, ɪŋ-] *n.* любозна́тельность, любопы́тство, пытли́вость.

inquisitor [ɪnˈkwɪzɪtə(r), ɪŋ-] *n.* (*hist.*) инквизи́тор.

inquisitorial [ɪnˌkwɪzɪˈtɔ:rɪəl, ɪŋ-] *adj.* иссле́довательский; сле́дственный; инквизи́торский.

inroad [ˈɪnrəʊd] *n.* (*raid*) набе́г; (*encroachment*) посяга́тельство; **the holiday will make a large ~ on my savings** кани́кулы поглотя́т бо́льшую часть мои́х сбереже́ний.

inrush [ˈɪnrʌʃ] *n.* (*of water etc.*) внеза́пный прито́к; (*of people*) внеза́пное вторже́ние.

insalubrious [ˌɪnsəˈlu:brɪəs, -ˈlju:brɪəs] *adj.* нездоро́вый.

insane [ɪnˈseɪn] *adj.* безу́мный, сумасше́дший; невменя́емый; **he went ~** он лиши́лся рассу́дка; он сошёл с ума́; **he was certified ~** врачи́ призна́ли его́ психи́чески больны́м; (*as n.*): **the ~** душевнобольны́е; **home for the ~** сумасше́дший дом; психиатри́ческая больни́ца.

insanitary [ɪnˈsænɪtərɪ] *adj.* антисанита́рный, негигиени́чный.

insanity [ɪnˈsænɪtɪ] *n.* **1.** (*madness*) душе́вная/психи́ческая боле́знь; безу́мие; невменя́емость; **the defendant pleaded ~** обвиня́емый сосла́лся на невменя́емость. **2.** (*folly*) безу́мие; **it would be ~ to proceed** бы́ло бы безу́мием продолжа́ть.

insatiability [ɪnˌseɪʃəˈbɪlɪtɪ] *n.* ненасы́тность.

insatia|ble [ɪnˈseɪʃəb(ə)l], **-te** [ɪnˈseɪʃɪət] *adjs.* ненасы́тный; **his appetite is ~ble** у него́ ненасы́тный аппети́т; **~ble of power** жа́ждущий вла́сти.

inscribe [ɪnˈskraɪb] *v.t.* **1.** (*engrave*) выреза́ть, вы́резать; начерта́ть (*pf.*); **the stone was ~d with their names** их имена́ бы́ли вы́сечены на ка́мне; **a verse is ~d on his tomb** на его́ надгро́бном ка́мне вы́сечена стихотво́рная эпита́фия. **2.** (*write*; *sign*) надпи́с|ывать, -а́ть; **please ~ your name in the book** пожа́луйста, распиши́тесь в кни́ге. **3.** (*dedicate*) посвя|ща́ть, -ти́ть; **the poems were ~d to his wife** стихотворе́ния бы́ли посвящены́ его́ жене́. **4.** (*geom.*) впи́с|ывать, -а́ть. **5.** (*comm.*): **~d stock** зарегистри́рованные це́нные бума́ги.

inscription [ɪnˈskrɪpʃ(ə)n] *n.* на́дпись.

inscrutability [ɪnˌskru:təˈbɪlɪtɪ] *n.* зага́дочность, непроница́емость; непостижи́мость.

inscrutable [ɪnˈskru:təb(ə)l] *adj.* зага́дочный, непроница́емый; (*incomprehensible*) непостижи́мый.

insect [ˈɪnsekt] *n.* насеко́мое; **~ bite** уку́с насеко́мого; **~ powder** порошо́к от насеко́мых.

insecticide [ɪnˈsektɪˌsaɪd] *n.* инсектици́д.

insectivorous [ɪnˌsekˈtɪvərəs] *adj.* насекомоя́дный.

insecure [ˌɪnsɪˈkjʊə(r)] *adj.* **1.** (*unsafe*; *unreliable*) ненадёжный, небезопа́сный; **the ladder was ~** ле́стница была́ неусто́йчива; **the window was ~ly fastened** окно́ бы́ло непло́тно закры́то; **his position in the firm is ~** у него́ ша́ткое положе́ние в фи́рме. **2.** (*lacking confidence*) неуве́ренный (в себе́); **I feel ~ of the future** я не уве́рен в бу́дущем.

insecurity [ˌɪnsɪˈkjʊrɪtɪ] *n.* ненадёжность, небезопа́сность; неуве́ренность.

inseminate [ɪnˈsemɪˌneɪt] *v.t.* оплодотвор|я́ть, -и́ть.

insemination [ɪnˌsemɪˈneɪʃ(ə)n] *n.* оплодотворе́ние; **artificial ~** иску́сственное оплодотворе́ние.

insensate [ɪnˈsenseɪt] *adj.* (*without sensibility*) бесчу́вственный, безду́шный; (*senseless*; *mad*) неразу́мный.

insensibility [ɪnˌsensɪˈbɪlɪtɪ] *n.* нечувстви́тельность; (*unconsciousness*) о́бморочное состоя́ние; (*lack of appreciation*; *indifference*) бесчу́вственность, безразли́чие, равноду́шие.

insensible [ɪnˈsensɪb(ə)l] *adj.* (*without physical sensation*) нечувстви́тельный; **his hands were ~ with cold** от хо́лода его́ ру́ки потеря́ли чувстви́тельность; (*unconscious*) потеря́вший созна́ние; (*unaware*) не сознаю́щий; **he was ~ of his danger** он не сознава́л опа́сности; (*without emotion*; *unsympathetic*) бесчу́вственный; (*imperceptible*) незаме́тный.

insensitive [ɪnˈsensɪtɪv] *adj.* нечувстви́тельный; невосприи́мчивый, равноду́шный; **~ to light** нечувстви́тельный к све́ту; **~ to beauty** равноду́шный к красоте́.

insensitivity [ɪnˌsensɪˈtɪvɪtɪ] *n.* нечувстви́тельность; (*indifference*) невосприи́мчивость, равноду́шие.

insentient [ɪnˈsenʃ(ə)nt] *adj.* неодушевлённый, неживо́й.

inseparable [ɪnˈsepərəb(ə)l] *adj.* неразде́льный, неразры́вный; **~ companions** неразлу́чные прия́тели; **he was ~ from his books** его́ невозмо́жно бы́ло оторва́ть от книг; **an ~ quality** неотъе́млемое ка́чество.

insert[1] [ˈɪnsɜ:t] *n.* вста́вка; (*in book*, *newspaper etc.*) вкла́дыш, вкла́дка.

insert[2] [ɪnˈsɜ:t] *v.t.* вст|авля́ть, -а́вить; поме|ща́ть, -сти́ть; **he ~ed the key in the lock** он вста́вил ключ в замо́к; **have you ~ed a coin?** вы опусти́ли моне́ту?; **I ~ed an advertisement in the paper** я помести́л объявле́ние в газе́те.

insertion [ɪnˈsɜ:ʃ(ə)n] *n.* (*inserting*) вставле́ние, введе́ние; (*sth. inserted*) вста́вка.

inset[1] [ˈɪnset] *n.* (*in book*) вкла́дка, вкле́йка; (*small map*) ка́рта-вре́зка; (*in dress*) вста́вка.

inset[2] [ɪnˈset] *v.t.* (*insert*) вст|авля́ть, -а́вить; вкла́дывать, вложи́ть; (*indent*) печа́тать, на- с о́тступом (**three spaces:** в три зна́ка).

inshore [ɪnˈʃɔ:(r), ˈɪn-] *adj.* прибре́жный.

adv. (*position*) у бе́рега; (*motion*) к бе́регу, на взмо́рье; **the wind was blowing ~** ве́тер дул по направле́нию к бе́регу.

inside [ɪnˈsaɪd] *n.* **1.** (*interior*) вну́треннее простра́нство; вну́тренняя часть; **have you seen the ~ of the house?** вы бы́ли внутри́ до́ма?; **the door was bolted on the ~** дверь была́ заперта́ изнутри́; **~ out** наизна́нку; **the thieves turned everything ~ out** во́ры всё переверну́ли вверх дном; **he knows the subject ~ out** он зна́ет предме́т назубо́к. **2.** (*of a garment*) изна́нка. **3.** (*of road*): **it is forbidden to pass on the ~** обго́н спра́ва запрещён. **4.** (*of circular objects*: *part nearest centre*) вну́тренняя пове́рхность; **the ~ of the bearing was worn** вну́тренняя пове́рхность подши́пника снoси́лась. **5.** (*stomach; intestines*) вну́тренности (*f. pl.*); **he complained of a pain in his ~** он жа́ловался на боль в желу́дке.

adj. вну́тренний; **~ passenger** пассажи́р, сидя́щий внутри́ авто́буса; **~ pocket** вну́тренний карма́н; **~ left/right** (*football*) ле́вый/пра́вый полусре́дний; **he received ~ information** он получи́л секре́тную информа́цию; **it was an ~ job** (*coll.*) э́то сде́лал кто́-то из свои́х.

adv. **1.** (*in or on the inner surface*) внутрь; **she wore her coat with the fur ~** она́ носи́ла шу́бу ме́хом внутрь. **2.** (*in the interior*) внутри́; **I opened the box and there was nothing ~** я откры́л коро́бку — в ней ничего́ не оказа́лось. **3.** (*indoors*) внутри́, в помеще́нии, до́ма; **stay ~ till the rain stops** остава́йтесь до́ма, пока́ дождь не прекрати́тся; **come ~ out of the rain!** заходи́те внутрь, не сто́йте под дождём! **4.** (*in prison*): **he did 6 weeks ~** (*coll.*) он просиде́л 6 неде́ль (за решёткой). **5.** (*of a vehicle*) внутрь; **get ~!** сади́тесь в маши́ну!

prep. **1.** (*of place*) внутрь+*g.*; в+*p.*; **she was just ~ the door** она́ стоя́ла пря́мо в дверя́х; **dogs are not allowed ~ the shop** с соба́ками вход в магази́н запрещён; **have you seen ~ the house?** вы ви́дели дом изнутри́? **2.** (*of time*) в преде́лах+*g.*; **the job can't be done ~ (of) a month** э́ту рабо́ту невозмо́жно сде́лать/зако́нчить в тече́ние ме́сяца; **I shall be back ~ (of) a week** я верну́сь не поздне́е, чем че́рез неде́лю.

insider [ɪn'saɪdə(r)] *n.* свой/непосторо́нний челове́к.

insidious [ɪn'sɪdɪəs] *adj.* (*treacherous; crafty*) преда́тельский, кова́рный; (*making stealthy progress*) подстерега́ющий, кова́рный; **an ~ disease** кова́рная боле́знь.

insidiousness [ɪn'sɪdɪəsnɪs] *n.* преда́тельство, кова́рство.

insight ['ɪnsaɪt] *n.* проница́тельность; понима́ние; **he shows great ~ into human character** он прекра́сно понима́ет люде́й; **gain an ~ into sth.** пости́|гнуть, -чь что-н.; **a man of ~** проница́тельный челове́к; **she had a sudden ~ into the consequences** она́ вдруг предста́вила себе́ все после́дствия.

insignia [ɪn'sɪgnɪə] *n.* (*decorations*) зна́ки (*m. pl.*) отли́чия, ордена́ (*m. pl.*); (*badges of rank etc.*) зна́ки (*m. pl.*) разли́чия, эмбле́мы (*f. pl.*) вла́сти.

insignificance [,ɪnsɪg'nɪfɪkəns] *n.* малова́жность, ничто́жность.

insignificant [,ɪnsɪg'nɪfɪkənt] *adj.* малова́жный, ничто́жный.

insincere [,ɪnsɪn'sɪə(r)] *adj.* нейскренний.

insincerity [,ɪnsɪn'serɪtɪ] *n.* нейскренность.

insinuat|e [ɪn'sɪnjʊ,eɪt] *v.t.* **1.** (*introduce*): **he ~ed himself into their company** он втёрся/прони́к в их о́бщество. **2.** (*hint*) намек|а́ть, -ну́ть на+*a.*; (и́сподволь) внуш|а́ть, -и́ть; нашёпт|ывать, -а́ть; говори́ть (*impf.*) намёками; **what are you ~ing?** на что вы намека́ете?

insinuation [ɪn,sɪnjʊ'eɪʃ(ə)n] *n.* (*hint*) намёк; инсинуа́ция; нашёптывание; **there was an ~ of foul play** ко́е-кто намека́л на возмо́жность нече́стной игры́.

insipid [ɪn'sɪpɪd] *adj.* безвку́сный, пре́сный; (*fig.*) неинтере́сный; вя́лый.

insipidity [,ɪnsɪ'pɪdɪtɪ] *n.* отсу́тствие вку́са; пре́сность; (*fig.*) ску́ка; вя́лость.

insist [ɪn'sɪst] *v.t. & i.* наст|а́ивать, -оя́ть на+*p.*; тре́бовать, по- +*g.*; упо́рствовать (*impf.*); **he ~ed on his rights** он наста́ивал на свои́х права́х; **he ~ed on his innocence** он наста́ивал на свое́й невино́вности; **he ~ed on my accompanying him** он настоя́л на том, что́бы я его́ сопровожда́л; **very well, if you ~!** ну ла́дно, ко́ли вы наста́иваете!

insistence [ɪn'sɪst(ə)ns] *n.* (*quality*) насто́йчивость, упо́рство; (*act*) настоя́ние, насто́йчивое тре́бование.

insistent [ɪn'sɪst(ə)nt] *adj.* (*repeatedly urged*) насто́йчивый, упо́рный; **~ demands** насто́йчивые/настоя́тельные тре́бования; (*determinedly urging*) насто́йчивый/настоя́тельный; **he was ~ that I should go** он наста́ивал на том, что́бы я пошёл.

in situ [ɪn 'sɪtjuː] *adv.* на ме́сте.

insobriety [,ɪnsəʊ'braɪɪtɪ] *n.* нетре́звость, пья́нство.

insofar as [,ɪnsəʊ'fɑː(r)] *conj.* (посто́льку) поско́льку; в той ме́ре/сте́пени, в како́й...; наско́лько.

insolation [,ɪnsəʊ'leɪʃ(ə)n] *n.* инсоля́ция; освеще́ние со́лнечными луча́ми.

insole ['ɪnsəʊl] *n.* сте́лька.

insolence ['ɪnsələns] *n.* (*contempt*) высокоме́рие; (*insulting behaviour*) наха́льство, де́рзость.

insolent ['ɪnsələnt] *adj.* (*contemptuous*) высокоме́рный; (*insulting; disrespectful*) наха́льный, де́рзкий.

insolubility [ɪn,sɒljʊ'bɪlɪtɪ] *n.* нераствори́мость; неразреши́мость.

insoluble [ɪn'sɒljʊb(ə)l] *adj.* (*of substance*) нераствори́мый; (*of problem*) неразреши́мый.

insolvency [ɪn'sɒlv(ə)nsɪ] *n.* неплатёжеспосо́бность; банкро́тство; несостоя́тельность.

insolvent [ɪn'sɒlv(ə)nt] *adj.* неплатёжеспосо́бный; несостоя́тельный.

insomnia [ɪn'sɒmnɪə] *n.* бессо́нница.

insomniac [ɪn'sɒmnɪ,æk] *n.* страда́ющий бессо́нницей.

insouciance [ɪn'suːsɪəns] *n.* небре́жность.

insouciant [ɪn'suːsɪənt, ǣ'sʊsjɑ̃] *adj.* небре́жный.

inspect [ɪn'spekt] *v.t.* осм|а́тривать, -отре́ть; инспекти́ровать (*impf., pf.*); **the Queen ~ed the troops** короле́ва произвела́ смотр войска́м.

inspection [ɪn'spekʃ(ə)n] *n.* (*examination*) осмо́тр, инспе́кция; **on closer ~** при бо́лее внима́тельном рассмотре́нии; **medical ~** медици́нский осмо́тр; **the house is open to ~** дом откры́т для всео́бщего обозре́ния; **these goods will not pass ~** при прове́рке э́ти това́ры бу́дут забрако́ваны; (*review*) пара́д, смотр; **the general held an ~** генера́л произвёл смотр войска́м.

inspector [ɪn'spektə(r)] *n.* (*inspecting official*) инспе́ктор, ревизо́р; (*police officer*) инспе́ктор (поли́ции).

inspectorate [ɪn'spektərət] *n.* инспе́кторство; до́лжность инспе́ктора; (*institution*) инспе́кция.

inspiration [,ɪnspɪ'reɪʃ(ə)n] *n.* **1.** (*source of creative activity; idea*) вдохнове́ние; **he drew his ~ from nature** он че́рпал вдохнове́ние в приро́де; **I had an ~** меня́ осени́ла мысль. **2.** (*divine guidance*) вдохнове́ние, найти́е. **3.** (*pers. or thg. that inspires; stimulus*) вдохнове́ние, вдохнови́тель (*m.*).

inspire [ɪn'spaɪə(r)] *v.t.* **1.** (*influence creatively*) вдохнов|ля́ть, -и́ть; **his friend's death ~d him to write an elegy** смерть дру́га вдохнови́ла его́ на эле́гию; **he is an ~d musician** он вдохнове́нный музыка́нт; **in an ~d moment** в моме́нт вдохнове́ния. **2.** (*instil; imbue*) всел|я́ть, -и́ть; **his actions ~d alarm in the neighbourhood** его́ поведе́ние встрево́жило всю окру́гу; **his work does not ~ me with confidence** его́ рабо́та не вызыва́ет у меня́ дове́рия; **~ s.o. with courage** внуш|а́ть, -и́ть му́жество кому́-н. (*or* в кого́-н.). **3.** (*put about*) инспири́ровать (*impf.*); распростран|я́ть, -и́ть (*слухи и т.п.*).

inspirer [ɪn'spaɪərə(r)] *n.* вдохнови́тель (*fem.* -ница); (*of rumour etc.*) распространи́тель (*fem.* -ница).

inspirit [ɪn'spɪrɪt] *v.t.* воодушев|ля́ть, -и́ть; ободр|я́ть, -и́ть; **~ing words** ободря́ющие слова́.

inst. [ɪnst] *n.* (*comm., abbr. of* **instant** *adj.* **4.**) с.м., (сего́ ме́сяца).

instability [,ɪnstə'bɪlɪtɪ] *n.* неусто́йчивость; (*of character*) неуравнове́шенность.

install [ɪn'stɔːl] *v.t.* **1.** (*place in office; induct*) вв|оди́ть, -ести́ в до́лжность. **2.** (*settle*) устр|а́ивать, -о́ить; поме|ща́ть, -сти́ть; **he ~ed his family in a hotel** он помести́л свою́ семью́ в гости́нице; **we are comfortably ~ed in our new home** мы удо́бно устро́ились в но́вом до́ме; **she ~ed herself in an armchair** она́ устро́илась в кре́сле. **3.** (*fix in position*) устан|а́вливать, -ови́ть; **the workmen came to ~ a new cooker** рабо́чие пришли́ установи́ть но́вую ку́хонную плиту́.

installation [,ɪnstə'leɪʃ(ə)n] *n.* (*of pers.*) введе́ние в до́лжность; (*of thg.*) устано́вка; (*equipment etc. installed*) устано́вка, устро́йство; (*buildings etc. for tech. purposes*) сооруже́ния (*nt. pl.*); **a military ~** вое́нные сооруже́ния; вое́нные устано́вки (*f. pl.*).

instalment [ɪn'stɔːlmənt] *n.* **1.** (*partial payment*) взнос; **we are paying for our carpet by ~s (*or* on the ~ plan)** мы пла́тим за ковёр в рассро́чку. **2.** (*of published work*) отры́вок, вы́пуск; отде́льная часть.

instance [ˈɪnst(ə)ns] *n.* **1.** (*example*) приме́р; **for ~** наприме́р; **let me give you an ~** я вам приведу́ приме́р. **2.** (*particular case*) слу́чай; **in this ~** в э́том/да́нном слу́чае; **in the first ~** в пе́рвую о́чередь. **3.** (*request*) тре́бование, про́сьба; **at the ~ of** по про́сьбе/предложе́нию +*g.*

v.t. прив|оди́ть, -ести́ в ка́честве приме́ра.

instant [ˈɪnst(ə)nt] *n.* **1.** (*precise moment*) мгнове́ние; **come here this ~!** иди́ сюда́ сию́ же мину́ту!; **he left that very ~** он момента́льно (*or* в то́т же моме́нт) удали́лся; **I recognized him the ~ I saw him** я сра́зу же его́ узна́л. **2.** (*momentary duration*) мгнове́ние, миг; **I shall be back in an ~** я — ми́гом; я верну́сь че́рез мину́ту; **I was only away for an ~** я отлучи́лся то́лько на мину́ту.

adj. **1.** (*immediate*) неме́дленный; мгнове́нный; **I felt ~ relief** я то́тчас же почу́вствовал облегче́ние; **the book was an ~ success** кни́га име́ла мгнове́нный успе́х. **2.** (*insistent*) насто́йчивый. **3.** (*of food preparation*): **~ coffee** раствори́мый ко́фе. **4.** (*abbr.* **inst.**) теку́щий; **your letter of the 5th ~** ва́ше письмо́ от пя́того числа́ сего́ ме́сяца (*abbr.* с.м.).

instantaneous [ˌɪnstənˈteɪnɪəs] *adj.* (*done in an instant*) мгнове́нный; **it was an ~ decision** э́то бы́ло решено́ мгнове́нно; (*immediate*) неме́дленный; **death was ~** смерть наступи́ла мгнове́нно.

instead [ɪnˈsted] *adv.* взаме́н (+*g.*); **~ of** вме́сто+*g.*, **let me go ~ (of you)** дава́йте я пойду́ вме́сто вас; **if the steak is off I'll have chicken ~** е́сли бифште́ксов нет, я возьму́ ку́рицу; **why don't you go out ~ of reading?** вме́сто того, что́бы чита́ть, вы лу́чше бы пошли́ погуля́ть; **we are going by train ~ of by car** мы е́дем по́ездом, а не на маши́не.

instep [ˈɪnstep] *n.* подъём (ноги́).

instigate [ˈɪnstɪˌgeɪt] *v.t.* подстрека́ть (*impf.*); **they were ~d to rebel** их подстрека́ли на бунт (*or* к бу́нту); **he ~d the murder** он провоци́ровал уби́йство.

instigation [ˌɪnstɪˈgeɪʃ(ə)n] *n.* подстрека́тельство, науще́ние; **the boy stole at his brother's ~** ма́льчик соверши́л кра́жу по науще́нию бра́та.

instigator [ˈɪnstɪˌgeɪtə(r)] *n.* подстрека́тель (*fem.* -ница).

instil [ɪnˈstɪl] *v.t.* (*lit.*) вл|ива́ть, -и́ть; ка́п|ать, на-; (*fig.*) внуш|а́ть, -и́ть; прив|ива́ть, -и́ть; **he tried to ~ some discipline into his pupils** он пыта́лся приви́ть свои́м ученика́м чу́вство дисципли́ны (*or* приучи́ть свои́х ученико́в к дисципли́не); **his love of science was ~led at an early age** с ма́лых лет ему́ внуша́ли любо́вь к нау́ке.

instinct[1] [ˈɪnstɪŋkt] *n.* инсти́нкт; **herd ~** ста́дное чу́вство; **my ~ told me to turn back** инсти́нкт подсказа́л мне верну́ться обра́тно; **he acted by, on ~** он де́йствовал по интуи́ции (*or* инстинкти́вно); **he is a creature of ~** он челове́к интуити́вный; (*natural liking or propensity*) спосо́бность, чутьё; **he has an ~ for a bargain** у него́ приро́дное чутьё к вы́годным поку́пкам; **he has an uncanny ~ for making mistakes** у него́ необыкнове́нная спосо́бность де́лать оши́бки.

instinct[2] [ɪnˈstɪŋkt] *adj.* (*liter.*) по́лный; **the painting is ~ with life** карти́на испо́лнена жи́зни.

instinctive [ɪnˈstɪŋktɪv] *adj.* инстинкти́вный, безотчётный, подсозна́тельный; **I took an ~ dislike to him** у меня́ возни́кла безотчётная неприя́знь к нему́.

institute [ˈɪnstɪˌtjuːt] *n.* институ́т.

v.t. **1.** (*found; establish*) устан|а́вливать, -ови́ть; учре|жда́ть, -ди́ть; **marriage was ~d for the rearing of children** институ́т бра́ка возни́к для воспита́ния дете́й; **~ a law** вв|оди́ть, -ести́ зако́н. **2.** (*set on foot*) нач|ина́ть, -а́ть; **the police ~d proceedings** поли́ция возбуди́ла де́ло; **they ~d a search** они́ произвели́ о́быск.

institution [ˌɪnstɪˈtjuːʃ(ə)n] *n.* **1.** (*setting up*) установле́ние, учрежде́ние. **2.** (*established custom or practice*) институ́т, учрежде́ние; **the old nurse had become quite an ~ in the family** ста́рая ня́ня ста́ла непреме́нным атрибу́том семьи́. **3.** (*organization with social purpose*) организа́ция, заведе́ние; **charitable ~** благотвори́тельное учрежде́ние; **mental ~** психиатри́ческая лече́бница.

institutional [ˌɪnstɪˈtjuːʃən(ə)l] *adj.* устано́вленный; учреждённый; **~ religion** организо́ванная рели́гия; **she is in need of ~ care** её сле́дует госпитализи́ровать.

instruct [ɪnˈstrʌkt] *v.t.* **1.** (*teach*) учи́ть, на- (*кого чему*); обуч|а́ть, -и́ть (*кого чему*); **he ~s the class in English** он преподаёт англи́йский язы́к. **2.** (*order; direct*) инструкти́ровать (*impf., pf.; pf. also* про-); прика́з|ывать, -а́ть; **I was ~ed to call on you** мне бы́ло ве́лено к вам зайти́; **I shall ~ my solicitor** я поручу́ де́ло своему́ адвока́ту.

instruction [ɪnˈstrʌkʃ(ə)n] *n.* **1.** (*teaching*) обуче́ние; **he received ~ in mathematics** он получи́л математи́ческое образова́ние. **2.** (*direction*) инструкта́ж, инструкти́рование; руково́дство; **follow the ~s on the packet** сле́дуйте указа́ниям на паке́те; **I have my ~s** был дан прика́з; **he had ~s to return** ему́ веле́ли/приказа́ли (*or* ему́ бы́ло ве́лено/прика́зано) верну́ться.

cpd. **~-book** *n.* руково́дство.

instructive [ɪnˈstrʌktɪv] *adj.* поучи́тельный.

instruct|or [ɪnˈstrʌktə(r)], **-ress** [ɪnˈstrʌktrɪs] *nn.* инстру́ктор; учи́тель (*fem.* -ница); преподава́тель (*fem.* -ница).

instrument [ˈɪnstrəmənt] *n.* **1.** (*implement*) инструме́нт; **he was knocked out with a blunt ~** его́ оглуши́ли тупы́м предме́том; (*apparatus*) аппара́т, прибо́р; **~ panel** пульт управле́ния; (*machine or device*) ору́дие; **~ of torture** ору́дие пы́тки. **2.** (*musical ~*) (музыка́льный) инструме́нт. **3.** (*fig., means*) ору́дие; **he was the ~ of another's vengeance** он был ору́дием чужо́й ме́сти. **4.** (*formal document*) докуме́нт; акт.

v.t. инструменти́ровать (*impf., pf.*); оркестрова́ть (*impf., pf.*); **the piece was ~ed for full orchestra** произведе́ние бы́ло инструменто́вано для по́лного соста́ва орке́стра.

instrumental [ˌɪnstrəˈment(ə)l] *n.* (*gram.*) твори́тельный паде́ж.

adj. **1.** (*serving as means*): **~ to our purpose** поле́зный для на́шей це́ли; **he was ~ in obtaining the order** они спосо́бствовал получе́нию (*or* соде́йствовал в получе́нии) зака́за. **2.** (*mus.*) инструмента́льный. **3.** (*gram.*) твори́тельный, инструмента́льный.

instrumentalist [ˌɪnstrəˈmentəlɪst] *n.* инструментали́ст.

instrumentality [ˌɪnstrəmenˈtælɪtɪ] *n.* соде́йствие; **by the ~ of** при соде́йствии +*g.*

instrumentation [ˌɪnstrəmenˈteɪʃ(ə)n] *n.* **1.** (*mus.*) инструменто́вка, оркестро́вка. **2.** (*provision of tools etc.*) оснаще́ние инструме́нтами.

insubordinate [ˌɪnsəˈbɔːdɪnət] *adj.* неподчиня́ющийся; непоко́рный; неповину́ющийся.

insubordination [ˌɪnsəˌbɔːdɪˈneɪʃ(ə)n] *n.* неподчине́ние; непоко́рность; неповинове́ние.

insubstantial [ˌɪnsəbˈstænʃ(ə)l, -ˈstɑːnʃ(ə)l] *adj.* (*not real*) нереа́льный, иллюзо́рный; (*groundless*) неоснова́тельный.

insufferable [ɪnˈsʌfərəb(ə)l] *adj.* несно́сный, невыноси́мый.

insufficiency [ˌɪnsəˈfɪʃənsɪ] *n.* недоста́точность, недоста́ток, нехва́тка.

insufficient [ˌɪnsəˈfɪʃ(ə)nt] *adj.* недоста́точный, ограни́ченный, непо́лный; **our food supply is ~ for a week** нам не хва́тит проду́ктов на неде́лю; **that in itself is ~ excuse** само́ по себе́ э́то недоста́точное оправда́ние.

insular [ˈɪnsjʊlə(r)] *adj.* островно́й; (*fig.*) ограни́ченный, у́зкий.

insularity [ˌɪnsjʊˈlærɪtɪ] *n.* ограни́ченность, у́зость.

insulat|e [ˈɪnsjʊˌleɪt] *v.t.* (*separate; detach*) отдел|я́ть, -и́ть; изоли́ровать (*impf., pf.*); (*protect from escape of heat or electricity*) изоли́ровать (*impf., pf.*); **~ing tape** изоляцио́нная ле́нта; **~e one's roof** утепл|я́ть, -и́ть (*or* теплоизоли́ровать) кры́шу.

insulation [ˌɪnsjʊˈleɪʃ(ə)n] *n.* (*insulating*) (тепло)изоля́ция; (*substance*) изоляцио́нный материа́л.

insulator [ˈɪnsjʊˌleɪtə(r)] *n.* непроводни́к.

insulin [ˈɪnsjʊlɪn] *n.* инсули́н.

insult[1] [ˈɪnsʌlt] *n.* оскорбле́ние; оби́да; **this book is an ~ to the intelligence** э́та кни́га возмуща́ет ра́зум; **he took it as a personal ~** он э́то восприня́л как ли́чное оскорбле́ние; *see also* **injury**

insult[2] [ɪnˈsʌlt] *v.t.* оскорб|ля́ть, -и́ть; **I have never been so**

~ed меня́ в жи́зни никто́ так не оскорбля́л; **~ing language** оскорби́тельные выраже́ния.

insuperable [ɪn'su:pərəb(ə)l, ɪn'sju:-] *adj.* непреодоли́мый.

insupportable [ˌɪnsə'pɔ:təb(ə)l] *adj.* нестерпи́мый, невыноси́мый, несно́сный.

insurable [ɪn'ʃʊərəb(ə)l] *adj.* могу́щий быть застрахо́ванным.

insurance [ɪn'ʃʊərəns] *n.* страхова́ние, страхо́вка; (*sum insured*) су́мма страхова́ния; **~ agent** страхово́й аге́нт; **~ company** страхова́я компа́ния, страхово́е о́бщество; **~ policy** страхово́й по́лис; **~ premium** страхова́я пре́мия; **life ~** страхова́ние жи́зни; **National I~** госуда́рственное страхова́ние; **take out ~** страхова́ться, за-; **he is a bad ~ risk** его́ риско́ванно страхова́ть.

insure [ɪn'ʃʊə(r)] *v.t.* **1.** (*pay for guarantee of*) страхова́ть, за-; **he ~d his house for £20,000** он застрахова́л свой дом на 20 000 фу́нтов; **is your life ~d?** вы застрахова́ли свою́ жизнь?; **the ~d** (*pers.*) застрахо́ванный. **2.** (*guarantee*) гаранти́ровать (*impf.*); страхова́ть; **Lloyd's ~s ships** Ллойд страху́ет корабли́. **3.** = **ensure**

v.i. страхова́ться; **have you ~d against fire?** вы застрахова́лись от пожа́ра?

insurer [ɪn'ʃʊərə(r)] *n.* страховщи́к, страхова́тель (*m.*).

insurgent [ɪn'sɜ:dʒ(ə)nt] *n.* повста́нец.

adj. восста́вший.

insurmountable [ˌɪnsə'maʊntəb(ə)l] *adj.* непреодоли́мый.

insurrection [ˌɪnsə'rekʃ(ə)n] *n.* восста́ние.

intact [ɪn'tækt] *adj.* (*untouched*) нетро́нутый, це́лый; **I hope to keep my savings ~** наде́юсь, что мне уда́стся сохрани́ть свои́ сбереже́ния; **the burglars left his stamp collection ~** граби́тели не тро́нули его́ колле́кцию ма́рок; (*unharmed*) невреди́мый, нетро́нутый; **she kept her honour ~** она́ сберегла́ свою́ честь.

intaglio [ɪn'tælɪəʊ, -'tɑ:lɪəʊ] *n.* (*process*) глубо́кая печа́ть; (*design*) инта́лия; (*gem*) ге́мма с углублённым изображе́нием.

intake ['ɪnteɪk] *n.* (*of recruits etc.*) набо́р; (*consumption*) потребле́ние.

intangible [ɪn'tændʒɪb(ə)l] *adj.* **1.** (*non-material*) неосяза́емый, неулови́мый; **~ assets** нематериа́льные акти́вы, неосяза́емые це́нности. **2.** (*vague, obscure*): **~ ideas** сму́тные/нея́сные представле́ния.

integer ['ɪntɪdʒə(r)] *n.* це́лое число́.

integral ['ɪntɪgr(ə)l] *adj.* **1.** (*essential*) неотъе́млемый, суще́ственный. **2.** (*whole; complete*) по́лный, це́льный. **3.** (*math.*) интегра́льный; **~ calculus** интегра́льное исчисле́ние.

integrate ['ɪntɪˌgreɪt] *v.t.* **1.** (*combine into whole*) объедин|я́ть, -и́ть в еди́ное це́лое; **an ~d personality** це́льная ли́чность. **2.** (*complete by adding parts*) заверш|а́ть, -и́ть; прид|ава́ть, -а́ть зако́нченный вид (*чему*). **3.** (*assimilate*) ассимили́ровать (*impf., pf.*); **racially ~d schools** шко́лы совме́стного обуче́ния для дете́й разли́чных рас. **4.** (math.) интегри́ровать (*impf., pf.*).

v.i. (*join together*) объедин|я́ться, -и́ться.

integrated ['ɪntɪˌgreɪtɪd] *adj.*: **~ circuit** интегра́льная схе́ма.

integration [ˌɪntɪ'greɪʃ(ə)n] *n.* объедине́ние, интегри́рование; (*of armed forces, races etc.*) интегра́ция.

integrity [ɪn'tegrɪtɪ] *n.* **1.** (*uprightness; honesty*) че́стность, це́льность; **a man of ~** че́стный/принципиа́льный/неподку́пный челове́к. **2.** (*complete state*) це́лостность; **territorial ~** территориа́льная це́лостность.

integument [ɪn'tegjʊmənt] *n.* ко́жа, кожура́, скорлупа́.

intellect ['ɪntɪˌlekt] *n.* интелле́кт, ум, рассу́док; **the ~s of the age** вели́кие умы́ эпо́хи.

intellectual [ˌɪntɪ'lektjʊəl] *n.* интеллиге́нт (*fem.* -ка), интеллектуа́л; (*pl., collect.*) интеллиге́нция.

adj. интеллектуа́льный; **~ process** мысли́тельный проце́сс; **~ pursuits** у́мственная рабо́та, заня́тие для ума́.

intellectualism [ˌɪntɪ'lektjʊəˌlɪz(ə)m] *n.* интеллектуали́зм.

intellectuality [ˌɪntɪlektjʊ'ælɪtɪ] *n.* интеллектуа́льность; интеллиге́нтность.

intelligence [ɪn'telɪdʒ(ə)ns] *n.* **1.** (*mental power*) ум, интелле́кт; **~ quotient** коэффицие́нт у́мственного разви́тия; **~ test** испыта́ние у́мственных спосо́бностей; **high/low ~** высо́кий/ни́зкий интелле́кт; **obvious to the meanest ~** вся́кому дураку́ я́сно. **2.** (*quickness of understanding; sagacity*) ум, сообрази́тельность; **he has ~** он сообража́ет; **a person of ~** у́мный/неглу́пый челове́к; **I had the ~ to refuse his offer** у меня́ хвати́ло ума́ не приня́ть его́ предложе́ния. **3.** (*news, information*) изве́стия (*nt. pl.*), све́дения (*nt. pl.*). **4.** (*mil.*) разве́дка; разве́дывательное управле́ние.

intelligent [ɪn'telɪdʒ(ə)nt] *adj.* у́мный, смышлённый, сообрази́тельный.

intelligentsia [ɪnˌtelɪ'dʒentsɪə] *n.* интеллиге́нция.

intelligibility [ɪnˌtelɪdʒɪ'bɪlɪtɪ] *n.* поня́тность, вня́тность, вразуми́тельность.

intelligible [ɪn'telɪdʒɪb(ə)l] *adj.* поня́тный, вня́тный, вразуми́тельный; **his words were barely ~** его́ слова́ едва́ мо́жно бы́ло поня́ть.

intemperance [ɪn'tempərəns] *n.* (*immoderation*) невозде́ржанность; (*lack of self-control*) несде́ржанность; (*immoderate drinking*) невозде́ржанность; пристра́стие к спиртны́м напи́ткам.

intemperate [ɪn'tempərət] *adj.* (*immoderate*) невозде́ржанный; (*lacking self-control*) несде́ржанный; (*addicted to drink*) невозде́ржанный, пью́щий.

intend [ɪn'tend] *v.t.* **1.** (*purpose; have in mind*) хоте́ть, собира́ться, намерева́ться (*all impf.*); **I ~ed him to do it** (*or* **that he should do it**) я хоте́л, что́бы он э́то сде́лал; **was this ~ed?** э́то бы́ло сде́лано преднаме́ренно? **2.** (*design; mean*) предназн|ача́ть, -а́чить; **his son is ~ed for the bar** он гото́вит сы́на в юри́сты; **a book ~ed for advanced students** кни́га, рассчи́танная на продви́нутый эта́п обуче́ния студе́нтов; **a measure ~ed to secure peace** ме́ра, напра́вленная на укрепле́ние ми́ра; **is this sketch ~ed to be me?** э́то я изображён на рису́нке?

intended [ɪn'tendɪd] *n.* (*betrothed*) нарече́нный, жени́х; (*fem.*) нарече́нная, неве́ста.

intense [ɪn'tens] *adj.* **1.** (*extreme*) си́льный, интенси́вный; **~ cold** си́льный хо́лод; **~ red** насы́щенный кра́сный цвет; **~ hatred** о́страя не́нависть; **~ly annoyed** кра́йне рассе́рженный. **2.** (*ardent; emotionally charged*) напряжённый, не́рвный; **an ~ expression** напряжённое выраже́ние.

intenseness [ɪn'tensnɪs] *n.* си́ла, напряжённость, насы́щенность.

intensification [ɪnˌtensɪfɪ'keɪʃ(ə)n] *n.* интенсифика́ция, усиле́ние, увеличе́ние.

intensif|y [ɪn'tensɪˌfaɪ] *v.t.* уси́ли|вать, -ть; увели́чи|вать, -ть; **he ~ied his efforts** он приложи́л ещё бо́льше уси́лий.

intensity [ɪn'tensɪtɪ] *n.* си́ла, интенси́вность, глубина́.

intensive [ɪn'tensɪv] *adj.* интенси́вный, напряжённый; **~ methods of farming** интенси́вное земледе́лие; **~ bombing** уси́ленная бомбардиро́вка; **~ care unit** блок интенси́вной терапи́и.

intent[1] [ɪn'tent] *n.* наме́рение, цель; **I did it with good ~** я сде́лал э́то из до́брых побужде́ний; **to all ~s and purposes** на са́мом де́ле; по существу́.

intent[2] [ɪn'tent] *adj.* **1.** (*earnest, eager*) увлечённый, ре́вностный; **there was an ~ expression on his face** у него́ бы́ло сосредото́ченное выраже́ние лица́. **2.** (*sedulously occupied*) погружённый (*во что*); поглощённый (*чем*); **he was ~ on his work** он был поглощён свое́й рабо́той. **3.** (*resolved*) по́лный реши́мости; **he was ~ on getting a first** он был по́лон реши́мости получи́ть дипло́м с отли́чием.

intention [ɪn'tenʃ(ə)n] *n.* наме́рение; у́мысел; **it was quite without ~** э́то бы́ло сде́лано/ска́зано без у́мысла; **I have no ~ of going to the party** я во́все не намерева́юсь идти́ на вечери́нку; **his ~s are good** у него́ хоро́шие наме́рения; **has he made known his ~s?** он уже́ объяви́л о свои́х наме́рениях?

intentional [ɪn'tenʃən(ə)l] *adj.* умы́шленный, преднаме́ренный; наро́чный, созна́тельный; **my absence was not ~** моё отсу́тствие не́ было преднаме́ренным; **he ignored me ~ly** он умы́шленно меня́ не заме́тил.

inter [ɪn'tɜ:(r)] *v.t.* хорони́ть, по-/за-; погре|ба́ть, -сти́.

inter- ['ɪntə(r)] *comb. form* взаимо…, меж(ду)…

interact [ɪntər'ækt] *v.i.* взаимоде́йствовать (*impf.*).

interaction [ˌɪntərˈækʃ(ə)n] *n.* взаимоде́йствие.
interactive [ˌɪntərˈæktɪv] *adj.* интеракти́вный, диало́говый.
inter alia [ˌɪntər ˈeɪlɪə, ˈælɪə] *adv.* среди́ про́чих.
interbreed [ˌɪntəˈbriːd] *v.t. & i.* скр|е́щивать(ся), -ести́ть(ся).
intercalary [ɪnˈtɜːkələrɪ, -ˈkælərɪ] *adj.* (*day, month*) приба́вленный для согласова́ния календаря́ с со́лнечным го́дом; ~ **year** високо́сный год.
intercede [ˌɪntəˈsiːd] *v.i.* заступ|а́ться, -и́ться (*за кого перед кем*); ходата́йствовать, по- (*о ком/чем перед кем*).
intercept [ˌɪntəˈsept] *v.t.* перехва́т|ывать, -и́ть; (*listen in on*) подслу́ш|ивать, -ать; **a blind to ~ the light** што́ра не пропуска́ющая свет; **the view was ~ed by trees** дере́вья заслоня́ли вид.
interception [ˌɪntəˈsepʃ(ə)n] *n.* перехва́тывание, перехва́т, подслу́шивание.
intercession [ˌɪntəˈseʃ(ə)n] *n.* хода́тайство; засту́пничество.
intercessor [ˌɪntəˈsesə(r)] *n.* хода́тай; засту́пник.
interchange [ˈɪntəˌtʃeɪndʒ] *n.* **1.** (*transposition*) перестано́вка. **2.** (*exchange*) обме́н; ~ **of views** обме́н мне́ниями. **3.** (*alternation*) чередова́ние.
v.t. **1.** (*transpose*) перест|авля́ть, -а́вить. **2.** (*exchange*) обме́н|ивать, -я́ть; обме́н|иваться, -я́ться +*i*. **3.** (*alternate*) чередова́ть (*impf.*); **he ~d work and play** он чередова́л рабо́ту с досу́гом.
interchangeability [ˌɪntəˌtʃeɪndʒəˈbɪlɪtɪ] *n.* (взаимо)заменя́емость; равноце́нность.
interchangeable [ˌɪntəˈtʃeɪndʒəb(ə)l] *adj.* взаимозаменя́емый; (*equivalent*) равноце́нный.
inter-city [ˌɪntəˈsɪtɪ] *adj.* межгородско́й.
intercollegiate [ˌɪntəkəˈliːdʒət] *adj.* (*US*) межуниверсите́тский.
intercom [ˈɪntəˌkɒm] *n.* (*coll.*) (вну́тренняя телефо́нная) связь; переговóрное устро́йство; селе́ктор.
intercommunicat|e [ˌɪntəkəˈmjuːnɪˌkeɪt] *v.i.* обща́ться (*impf.*) друг с дру́гом; **the prisoners are allowed to ~e** заключённым разреша́ется обще́ние друг с дру́гом; **~ing bedrooms** сме́жные спа́льни.
intercommunication [ˌɪntəkəˌmjuːnɪˈkeɪʃ(ə)n] *n.* обще́ние, связь.
intercommunion [ˌɪntəkəˈmjuːnɪən] *n.* (*eccl.*) причаще́ние протеста́нтов в католи́ческой це́ркви *и т.п.*
interconnect [ˌɪntəkəˈnekt] *v.i.* переплета́ться (*impf.*).
interconnected [ˌɪntəkəˈnektɪd] *adj.* взаимосвя́занный.
interconnecting [ˌɪntəkəˈnektɪŋ] *adj.*: ~ **rooms** сме́жные ко́мнаты.
interconnection [ˌɪntəkəˈnekʃ(ə)n] *n.* взаимосвя́зь.
intercontinental [ˌɪntəˌkɒntɪˈnent(ə)l] *adj.* межконтинента́льный.
intercourse [ˈɪntəˌkɔːs] *n.* (*social*) обще́ние; (*diplomatic or commercial*) сноше́ние, связь; (*sexual*) половы́е сноше́ния; **have ~ with s.o.** вступи́ть (*pl.*) в половы́е сноше́ния с кем-н.
interdepartmental [ˌɪntəˌdiːpɑːtˈment(ə)l] *adj.* меж(ду)ве́домственный.
interdependence [ˌɪntədɪˈpendəns] *n.* взаимозави́симость.
interdependent [ˌɪntədɪˈpendənt] *adj.* взаимозави́симый.
interdict [ˈɪntədɪkt] *n.* (*eccl.*) интерди́кт.
interdiction [ˌɪntəˈdɪkʃ(ə)n] *n.* запре́т.
interest [ˈɪntrəst, -trɪst] *n.* **1.** (*attention, curiosity, concern*) интере́с; **feel, show, take a great, keen ~ in sth.** проявл|я́ть, -и́ть большо́й интере́с к чему́-н.; **I have no ~ in games** спорт меня́ не интересу́ет. **2.** (*quality arousing ~*) занима́тельность; **his books lack ~ for me** меня́ его́ кни́ги не занима́ют; **it is of ~ to note that ...** интере́сно заме́тить, что...; **it is of no ~ to me whether we win or lose** меня́ соверше́нно не интересу́ет, вы́играем мы или нет; **matters of ~ to everybody** вопро́сы, ва́жные для всех. **3.** (*pursuit*) интере́с; **my chief ~s are art and history** я интересу́юсь гла́вным о́бразом иску́сством и исто́рией; **a man of wide ~s** челове́к с широ́ким кру́гом интере́сов. **4.** (*oft. pl., advantage, benefit*) по́льза, вы́года; **it is in, to your ~ to listen to his advice** в ва́ших же интере́сах прислу́шаться к его́ сове́там; **I acted in your ~s** я де́йствовал в ва́ших интере́сах; **you must look after your own ~s** вы должны́ блюсти́ свои́ интере́сы; **in the ~ s of truth** в интере́сах и́стины; **I know where my ~s lie** я зна́ю свою́ вы́году. **5.** (*legal or financial right or share*) до́ля, часть; **he has an ~ in that firm** он име́ет до́лю в э́той фи́рме; **American ~s in Europe** америка́нские капиталовложе́ния в Евро́пе. **6.** (*group having common concern*) заинтересо́ванные круги́ (*m. pl.*); **business ~s** торго́вые предпринима́тели (*m. pl.*). **7.** (*charge on loan*) ссу́дный проце́нт; проце́нты (*m. pl.*); проце́нтный дохо́д; **pay ~ on a loan** плати́ть (*impf.*) проце́нты по за́йму; **lend money at 7% ~ p.a.** дать (*impf.*) де́ньги (в рост) под семь проце́нтов годовы́х; **rate of ~** проце́нтная ста́вка; **at a high rate of ~** под больши́е проце́нты; **he lives on the ~ from his investments** он живёт на дохо́д со свои́х капиталовложе́ний; (*fig.*): **he returned the blow with ~** он отве́тил на уда́р с лихво́й; **my kindness was repaid with ~** меня́ ще́дро вознагради́ли за мою́ любе́зность.
v.t. интересова́ть (*impf.*); **this will ~ you** вам э́то бу́дет интере́сно; **can I ~ you in another drink?** могу́ я вам предложи́ть ещё рю́мочку?; **when he mentioned money I was ~ed at once** как то́лько он заговори́л о деньга́х, я то́тчас же заинтересова́лся; **I shall be ~ed to know what happens** держи́те меня́ в изве́стности о дальне́йшем.
cpds. **~-bearing** *adj.* проце́нтный, принося́щий проце́нт; **~-free** *adj.* беспроце́нтный.
interested [ˈɪntrəstɪd, ˈɪntrɪstɪd] *adj.* **1.** (*having or showing interest*) интересу́ющийся; **are you ~ in football?** вы интересу́етесь футбо́лом? **2.** (*not impartial*) коры́стный, заинтересо́ванный; **he acted from ~ motives** он де́йствовал из коры́стных побужде́ний; **an ~ party** заинтересо́ванная сторона́.
interesting [ˈɪntrəstɪŋ, -trɪstɪŋ] *adj.* интере́сный.
interethnic [ˌɪntəˈeθnɪk] *adj.* межнациона́льный.
interface [ˈɪntəˌfeɪs] *n.* стык; (*comput.*) интерфе́йс; (*fig.*) взаимосвя́зь, взаимоде́йствие; координа́ция.
interfer|e [ˌɪntəˈfɪə(r)] *v.i.* **1.** (*meddle; obtrude o.s.*) вме́ш|иваться, -а́ться; **don't ~e in my affairs** не вме́шивайтесь в мои́ дела́; **it is unwise to ~e between husband and wife** неразу́мно вме́шиваться в дела́ ме́жду му́жем и жено́й; **she is an ~ing old lady** она́ назо́йливая стару́ха; **don't ~e with this machine** не тро́гайте э́ту маши́ну; **my papers have been ~ed with** кто́-то тро́гал мои́ бума́ги. **2.** (*come in the way; present an obstacle*) меша́ть, по- +*d.*; **I am going to London tomorrow if nothing ~es** я за́втра пое́ду в Ло́ндон, е́сли ничто́ не помеша́ет. **3.** (*coll., molest sexually*): **the little girl had been ~ed with** де́вочку изнаси́ловали.
interference [ˌɪntəˈfɪərəns] *n.* вмеша́тельство, поме́ха; (*radio*) поме́хи (*f. pl.*).
interferometer [ˌɪntəfəˈrɒmɪt(ə)r] *n.* интерферо́метр.
intergalactic [ˌɪntəgəˈlæktɪk] *adj.* межзвёздный.
interim [ˈɪntərɪm] *n.* промежу́ток вре́мени; **in the ~** тем вре́менем.
adj. вре́менный, предвари́тельный, промежу́точный; **~ report** предвари́тельный докла́д.
interior [ɪnˈtɪərɪə(r)] *n.* **1.** (*inside*) вну́тренность; **the earth's ~** не́дра (*nt. pl.*) земли́. **2.** (*of building*) интерье́р; **~ decorator** худо́жник по интерье́ру; **~ decoration** вну́треннее оформле́ние интерье́ра. **3.** (*painting*) интерье́р. **4.** (*inland areas*) глуби́нные райо́ны (*m. pl.*); **he made a journey into the ~ of Brazil** он соверши́л путеше́ствие вглубь Брази́лии. **5.** (*home affairs*): **Minister of the I~** мини́стр вну́тренних дел.
adj. вну́тренний.
interject [ˌɪntəˈdʒekt] *v.t.* вст|авля́ть, -а́вить; (*coll.*) верну́ть (*pf.*) (*замечание*); **'It's not true,' he ~ed** «Э́то непра́вда», — заме́тил он вскользь.
interjection [ˌɪntəˈdʒekʃ(ə)n] *n.* восклица́ние; (*gram.*) междоме́тие.
interlace [ˌɪntəˈleɪs] *v.t. & i.* перепле|та́ть(ся), -сти́(сь); сплe|та́ть(ся), -сти́(сь).
interlard [ˌɪntəˈlɑːd] *v.t.*: **his prose is ~ ed with foreign words** его́ про́за пересы́пана иностра́нными слова́ми.
interleave [ˌɪntəˈliːv] *v.t.* про|кла́дывать, -ложи́ть чи́стые листы́ ме́жду страни́цами; **an ~ed text** текст с проло́женными чи́стыми листа́ми.

interline [ˌɪntəˈlaɪn] *v.t.* (*insert between lines*) впи́с|ывать, -а́ть ме́жду строк.
interlinear [ˌɪntəˈlɪnɪə(r)] *adj.* междустро́чный; подстро́чный.
interlink [ˌɪntəˈlɪŋk] *v.t. & i.* взаимосвя́з|ывать(ся), -а́ть(ся).
interlock [ˌɪntəˈlɒk] *v.t. & i.* соедин|я́ть(ся), -и́ть(ся); **they ~ed hands** они́ (кре́пко) держа́лись за́ руки.
interlocutor [ˌɪntəˈlɒkjʊtə(r)] *n.* собесе́дник.
interloper [ˈɪntəˌləʊpə(r)] *n.* тре́тий ли́шний; незва́ный гость.
interlude [ˈɪntəˌluːd, -ˌljuːd] *n.* (*interval of play*) антра́кт; (*mus. & fig.*) интерлю́дия.
intermarriage [ˌɪntəˈmærɪdʒ] *n.* брак ме́жду людьми́ ра́зных рас/национа́льностей *и т.п.*
intermarry [ˌɪntəˈmærɪ] *v.i.* сме́ш|иваться, -а́ться; родни́ться, по- путём бра́ка.
intermediary [ˌɪntəˈmiːdɪərɪ] *n.* посре́дник.
adj. (*acting as go-between*) посре́днический; (*intermediate*) промежу́точный, посре́дствующий.
intermediate [ˌɪntəˈmiːdɪət] *adj.* промежу́точный; **at an ~ stage** на перехо́дной ста́дии.
interment [ɪnˈtɜːmənt] *n.* погребе́ние.
intermezzo [ˌɪntəˈmetsəʊ] *n.* интерме́ццо (*indecl.*).
interminable [ɪnˈtɜːmɪnəb(ə)l] *adj.* бесконе́чный, нескончáемый, ве́чный.
intermingle [ˌɪntəˈmɪŋg(ə)l] *v.t. & i.* сме́ш|ивать(ся), -а́ть(ся).
intermission [ˌɪntəˈmɪʃ(ə)n] *n.* переры́в, па́уза; **I work from 8 to 4 without ~** я рабо́таю с восьми́ до четырёх без переры́ва.
intermit [ˌɪntəˈmɪt] *v.t.* прер|ыва́ть, -ва́ть; прек|раща́ть, -ти́ть.
intermittent [ˌɪntəˈmɪt(ə)nt] *adj.* прерыва́ющийся; преры́вистый.
intermix [ˌɪntəˈmɪks] *v.t. & i.* переме́ш|ивать(ся), -а́ть(ся); сме́ш|ивать(ся), -а́ть(ся).
intermixture [ˌɪntəˈmɪkstʃə(r)] *n.* смесь; смеше́ние.
intern[1] [ˈɪntɜːn] *n.* (*US*) студе́нт медици́нского ко́лледжа; молодо́й врач (*работающий в больнице и живущий при ней*).
intern[2] [ɪnˈtɜːn] *v.t.* интерни́ровать (*impf., pf.*).
internal [ɪnˈtɜːn(ə)l] *adj.* вну́тренний; **~ strife** вну́тренние раздо́ры; **~ injuries** пораже́ния вну́тренних о́рганов; **~ combustion engine** дви́гатель (*m.*) вну́треннего сгора́ния; **~ evidence** доказа́тельство, лежа́щее в само́м докуме́нте.
internally [ɪnˈtɜːn(ə)lɪ] *adv.* изнутри́, вну́тренне.
international [ˌɪntəˈnæʃən(ə)l] *n.* (*socialist organization*) Интернациона́л; (*sporting event*) междунаро́дные состяза́ния (*nt. pl.*); (*participant*) уча́стник междунаро́дных состяза́ний.
adj. междунаро́дный, интернациона́льный.
Internationale [ˌɪntəˌnæʃjəˈnɑːl] *n.* Интернациона́л.
internecine [ˌɪntəˈniːsaɪn] *adj.* междоусо́бный; смертоно́сный; разруши́тельный.
internee [ˌɪntɜːˈniː] *n.* интерни́рованный.
internment [ɪnˈtɜːnmənt] *n.* интерни́рование; **~ camp** ла́герь (*m.*) для интерни́рованных (лиц).
interpellation [ɪnˌtɜːpeˈleɪʃ(ə)n] *n.* запро́с, интерпелля́ция.
interpenetrate [ˌɪntəˈpenɪˌtreɪt] *v.t.* взаимопроника́ть (*impf.*).
interpersonal [ˌɪntəˈpɜːsən(ə)l] *adj.* межли́чностный.
interphone [ˈɪntəˌfəʊn] *n.* (*US*) вну́тренний телефо́н.
interplanetary [ˌɪntəˈplænɪtərɪ] *adj.* межплане́тный.
interplay [ˈɪntəˌpleɪ] *n.* взаимоде́йствие, взаимосвя́зь.
interpolate [ɪnˈtɜːpəˌleɪt] *v.t.* интерполи́ровать (*impf., pf.*); вст|авля́ть, -а́вить.
interpolation [ɪnˌtɜːpəˈleɪʃ(ə)n] *n.* интерполя́ция.
interpose [ˌɪntəˈpəʊz] *v.t.* **1.** (*insert; cause to intervene; also v.i.*) вме́ш|иваться, -а́ться; вст|авля́ть, -а́вить; **the fire was so hot that we ~d a screen** ого́нь пыла́л так си́льно, что мы заслони́ли ками́н экра́ном; **he ~d (himself) between the disputants** он разня́л спо́рящих; **~ an objection** выдвига́ть, вы́двинуть возраже́ние. **2.** (*interrupt*) переб|ива́ть, -и́ть.
interposition [ˌɪntəpəˈzɪʃ(ə)n] *n.* (*intervention*) вмеша́тельство.
interpret [ɪnˈtɜːprɪt] *v.t.* **1.** (*expound meaning of*) толкова́ть (*impf.*); истолк|о́вывать, -ова́ть; интерпрети́ровать (*impf.*); **how do you ~ this dream?** как вы объясня́ете э́тот сон?; **this passage has been ~ed in various ways** э́тот отры́вок истолко́вывали по-ра́зному; (*of an actor*) трактова́ть (*impf.*). **2.** (*understand*) истолко́в|ывать, -а́ть; **I ~ed his silence as a refusal** я истолкова́л его́ молча́ние как отка́з.
v.i. перев|оди́ть, -ести́ (у́стно); **he ~ed for the President** он был перево́дчиком (*or* он перевёл слова́) президе́нта.
interpretation [ɪnˌtɜːprɪˈteɪʃ(ə)n] *n.* (*expounding; exposition*) интерпрета́ция, толкова́ние; (*by an actor*) тракто́вка, интерпрета́ция; (*understanding, construction*) толкова́ние; **he puts a different ~ on the facts** он ина́че истолко́вывает э́ти фа́кты; (*oral translation*) (у́стный) перево́д.
interpreter [ɪnˈtɜːprɪtə(r)] *n.* перево́дчи|к (*fem.* -ца).
interracial [ˌɪntəˈreɪʃ(ə)l] *adj.* межра́совый.
interregnum [ˌɪntəˈregnəm] *n.* междуца́рствие.
interrelate [ˌɪntərɪˈleɪt] *v.t.* взаимосвя́зывать (*impf.*).
interrelation(ship) [ˌɪntərɪˈleɪʃ(ə)nʃɪp] *n.* взаимоотноше́ние, соотнесённость, взаи́мная связь.
interrogate [ɪnˈterəˌgeɪt] *v.t.* допр|а́шивать, -оси́ть.
interrogation [ɪnˌterəˈgeɪʃ(ə)n] *n.* допро́с; **mark of ~** вопроси́тельный знак.
interrogative [ˌɪntəˈrɒgətɪv] *adj.* вопроси́тельный.
interrogator [ɪnˈterəˌgeɪtə(r)] *n.* сле́дователь (*m.*).
interrogatory [ˌɪntəˈrɒgətərɪ] *adj.* вопроси́тельный.
interrupt [ˌɪntəˈrʌpt] *v.t.* **1.** (*break in on; also v.i.*) прер|ыва́ть, -ва́ть; переб|ива́ть, -и́ть; **don't ~ when I am speaking** не перебива́йте, когда́ я говорю́; **he ~ed me as I was reading** он прерва́л моё чте́ние. **2.** (*disturb*) нар|уша́ть, -у́шить; меша́ть, по- *+d.*; **my sleep was ~ed by the noise of trains** шум поездо́в то и де́ло меня́ буди́л; **his performance was ~ed by coughing** его́ выступле́ние прерыва́лось ка́шлем в за́ле; **war ~s trade** война́ наруша́ет торго́влю. **3.** (*obstruct*) заслон|я́ть, -и́ть; препя́тствовать (*impf.*) *+d.*; **these trees ~ the view** э́ти дере́вья заслоня́ют вид.
interruption [ˌɪntəˈrʌpʃ(ə)n] *n.* переры́в; поме́ха; наруше́ние; вторже́ние; **he continued to speak despite ~s** он продолжа́л говори́ть, невзира́я на поме́хи; **~ of communications** наруше́ние свя́зи.
intersect [ˌɪntəˈsekt] *v.t. & i.* перес|ека́ть(ся), -е́чь(ся); перекр|е́щивать(ся), -ести́ть(ся).
intersection [ˌɪntəˈsekʃ(ə)n] *n.* (*intersecting*) пересече́ние; (*point of ~*) то́чка пересече́ния; (*crossroads*) перекрёсток.
intersperse [ˌɪntəˈspɜːs] *v.t.* разбр|а́сывать, -оса́ть; расс|ыпа́ть, -ы́пать; **red flowers ~d with yellow ones** кра́сные цветы́ впереме́жку с жёлтыми; **his talk was ~d with anecdotes** он пересыпа́л своё выступле́ние анекдо́тами.
interstate [ˈɪntəˌsteɪt] *adj.* межшта́тный, межгосуда́рственный.
interstellar [ˌɪntəˈstelə(r)] *adj.* межзвёздный.
interstice [ɪnˈtɜːstɪs] *n.* промежу́ток, расще́лина, скважи́на.
intertribal [ˌɪntəˈtraɪb(ə)l] *adj.* межплеменно́й.
intertwine [ˌɪntəˈtwaɪn] *v.t. & i.* спле|та́ть(ся), -сти́(сь); **their arms were ~d** их ру́ки бы́ли сплетены́; **the two subjects are ~d** э́ти два предме́та те́сно свя́заны ме́жду собо́й.
interurban [ˌɪntərˈɜːb(ə)n] *adj.* междугоро́дный.
interval [ˈɪntəv(ə)l] *n.* **1.** (*of time*) промежу́ток, отре́зок вре́мени; **there was an ~ of a week between his two visits** ме́жду двумя́ его́ посеще́ниями прошла́ неде́ля; **we see each other at ~s** вре́мя от вре́мени мы ви́димся; **at ~s of an hour** ка́ждый час. **2.** (*of place*) расстоя́ние; **the posts were set at ~s of 10 feet** столбы́ бы́ли расста́влены на расстоя́нии десяти́ фу́тов. **3.** (*fig.*) разры́в; **there is a wide ~ between the classes** ме́жду кла́ссами существу́ет большо́й разры́в. **4.** (*theatr.*) антра́кт. **5.** (*mus.*) интерва́л.
intervene [ˌɪntəˈviːn] *v.i.* **1.** (*of an event*): **we were to have met, but his death ~d** мы должны́ бы́ли встре́титься, но его́ смерть э́тому помеша́ла; **if nothing ~s** е́сли ничего́ не случи́тся; **some years ~d** с тех пор прошло́ не́сколько лет. **2.** (*interpose one's influence*) вме́ш|иваться, -а́ться; **the government ~d in the dispute** прави́тельство вмеша́лось в конфли́кт.

intervention [ˌɪntəˈvenʃ(ə)n] *n.* вмеша́тельство; интерве́нция.
interventionism [ˌɪntəˈvenʃəˌnɪz(ə)m] *n.* поли́тика вмеша́тельства.
interventionist [ˌɪntəˈvenʃənɪst] *n.* интерве́нт.
interview [ˈɪntəˌvju:] *n.* деловая встре́ча; собесе́дование; интервью́ (*nt. indecl.*); **I am having an ~ for the job** у меня́ собесе́дование в связи́ с но́вой рабо́той; **he gave an ~ to the press** он дал журнали́стам интервью́.
v.t. & i. интервьюи́ровать (*impf., pf.*); взять (*pf.*) интервью́ у+*g.*; **only certain candidates were ~ed** бесе́довали то́лько с не́сколькими кандида́тами; **he ~s well** (*conducts an ~*) он хоро́ший интервьюе́р; (*acquits himself*) он хорошо́ де́ржится во вре́мя интервью́.
interviewee [ˌɪntəvju:ˈi:] *n.* интервьюи́руемый, даю́щий интервью́.
interviewer [ˈɪntəˌvju:ə(r)] *n.* интервьюе́р.
inter-war [ˌɪntəˈwɔ:(r)] *adj.* (име́вший ме́сто) ме́жду двумя́ мировы́ми во́йнами.
interweave [ˌɪntəˈwi:v] *v.t.* вплеǀта́ть, -сти́; (*insert*) вставля́ть, -а́вить; **truth interwoven with fiction** пра́вда, переме́шанная с вы́мыслом.
intestacy [ɪnˈtestəsɪ] *n.* отсу́тствие завеща́ния.
intestate [ɪnˈtestət] *adj.* уме́рший без завеща́ния.
intestinal [ˌɪnteˈstaɪn(ə)l] *adj.* кише́чный.
intestine[1] [ɪnˈtestɪn] *n.* кише́чник.
intestine[2] [ɪnˈtestɪn] *adj.* вну́тренний, междоусо́бный.
intimacy [ˈɪntɪməsɪ] *n.* (*also euph., sexual intercourse*) инти́мность, бли́зость.
intimate[1] [ˈɪntɪmət] *n.* бли́зкий друг.
adj. **1.** (*close, familiar*) закады́чный; **~ friends** закады́чные/задуше́вные друзья́; **they are on ~ terms** они́ в бли́зких отноше́ниях. **2.** (*private, personal*) инти́мный, ли́чный; **the ~ details of his life** подро́бности его́ ли́чной жи́зни; **an ~ diary** инти́мный дневни́к. **3.** (*detailed*) основа́тельный, глубо́кий, доскона́льный; **he has an ~ knowledge of the subject** он доскона́льно зна́ет предме́т.
intimate[2] [ˈɪntɪmeɪt] *v.t.* (*convey*) увǀедомля́ть, -е́домить; (*hint, imply*) намекǀа́ть, -ну́ть на+*a.*; вскользь упомǀина́ть, -яну́ть.
intimation [ˌɪntɪˈmeɪʃ(ə)n] *n.* намёк, уведомле́ние.
intimidate [ɪnˈtɪmɪˌdeɪt] *v.t.* запу́гǀивать, -а́ть; угрожа́ть (*impf.*) +*d.*; терроризи́ровать (*impf., pf.*).
intimidation [ɪnˌtɪmɪˈdeɪʃ(ə)n] *n.* запу́гивание; угро́зы (*f. pl.*).
into [ˈɪntʊ, ˈɪntə] *prep.* **1.** (*expr. motion to a point within*) в+*a.*; **I was going ~ the theatre** я входи́л в теа́тр. **2.** (*expr. extent*) до; **far ~ the night** до по́здней но́чи. **3.** (*expr. change or process*) *usu.* в+*a.*; **the rain turned ~ snow** дождь перешёл в снег; **translate ~ French** перевǀоди́ть, -ести́ на францу́зский; **he thrust a pistol ~ his belt** он заткну́л пистоле́т за по́яс. **4.** (*coll., devotee*): **I'm not ~ Shakespeare** я не увлека́юсь Шекспи́ром; **he's ~ jazz** он увлека́ется джа́зом.
intolerable [ɪnˈtɒlərəb(ə)l] *adj.* невыноси́мый, несно́сный.
intolerance [ɪnˈtɒlərəns] *n.* нетерпи́мость; **his body developed an ~ to antibiotics** у него́ развила́сь аллерги́я к антибио́тикам.
intolerant [ɪnˈtɒlərənt] *n.* нетерпи́мый; **~ of** (*unable to bear*) не выно́ся́щий +*g.*
intonation [ˌɪntəˈneɪʃ(ə)n] *n.* (*intoning*) интона́ция; (*modulation of voice*) модуля́ция.
intone [ɪnˈtəʊn] *v.t.* интони́ровать; модули́ровать; чита́ть нараспе́в (*all impf.*).
in toto [ɪn ˈtəʊtəʊ] *adv.* целико́м, по́лностью, в це́лом.
intoxicatǀe [ɪnˈtɒksɪˌkeɪt] *v.t.* (*lit., fig.*) опьянǀя́ть, -и́ть; **~ing liquor** опьяня́ющий напи́ток; **become ~ed** опьяне́ть (*pf.*).
intoxication [ɪnˌtɒksɪˈkeɪʃ(ə)n] *n.* интоксика́ция, отравле́ние; опьяне́ние.
intra- [ˈɪntrə] *pref.* внутри…
intractability [ɪnˌtræktəˈbɪlɪtɪ] *n.* упря́мство, непоко́рность, несгово́рчивость.
intractable [ɪnˈtræktəb(ə)l] *adj.* упря́мый, непоко́рный, несгово́рчивый; **an ~ temper** упря́мый хара́ктер; **an ~ beast** непоко́рное живо́тное; (*of thgs.*) непода́тливый, трудноуправля́емый; **~ metal** непода́тливый мета́лл; **~ pain** неустрани́мая боль.
intramural [ˌɪntrəˈmjʊər(ə)l] *adj.*: **~ studies** о́чные заня́тия, о́чное обуче́ние.
intransigence [ɪnˈtrænsɪdʒ(ə)ns, -zɪdʒ(ə)ns] *n.* непримири́мость; непреклóнность.
intransigent [ɪnˈtrænsɪdʒ(ə)nt, -zɪdʒ(ə)nt] *adj.* непримири́мый; непрекло́нный.
intransitive [ɪnˈtrænsɪtɪv, ɪnˈtrɑ:n-, -zɪtɪv] *adj.* неперехо́дный.
intra-uterine [ˌɪntrəˈju:təˌraɪn, -rɪn] *adj.*: **~ device** (*abbr.* **IUD**) внутрима́точный контрацепти́в.
intravenous [ˌɪntrəˈvi:nəs] *adj.* внутриве́нный.
intrepid [ɪnˈtrepɪd] *adj.* неустраши́мый, бесстра́шный.
intrepidity [ˌɪntrɪˈpɪdɪtɪ] *n.* неустраши́мость, бесстра́шие.
intricacy [ˈɪntrɪkəsɪ] *n.* запу́танность, сло́жность.
intricate [ˈɪntrɪkət] *adj.* запу́танный, сло́жный.
intriguǀe [ɪnˈtri:g, ˈɪn-] *n.* (*secret plotting*) интри́га; про́иски (*m. pl.*); (*amour*) любо́вная связь, интри́га, интри́жка.
v.t. интригова́ть, за-; интересова́ть, за-; **I was ~ed to learn** мне бы́ло интере́сно узна́ть; **an ~ing prospect** зама́нчивая перспекти́ва; **they ~ed against the king** они́ интригова́ли про́тив короля́.
intrinsic [ɪnˈtrɪnzɪk] *adj.* прису́щий, сво́йственный, по́длинный; **~ value** вну́тренняя це́нность.
intro [ˈɪntrəʊ] *n.* (*coll.*) введе́ние.
introducǀe [ˌɪntrəˈdju:s] *v.t.* **1.** (*insert*): **he ~ed the key into the lock** он вста́вил ключ в замо́к. **2.** (*bring in*) ввǀоди́ть, -ести́; (при)внǀоси́ть, -ести́; **the motor works are ~ing a new model** автозаво́д выпуска́ет но́вую моде́ль; **many improvements have been ~ed** ввели́ мно́го усоверше́нствований; **tobacco was ~ed from America** впервы́е таба́к был завезён из Аме́рики; **a new manager was ~ed into the store** в магази́н назна́чили но́вого заве́дующего; **~e a bill** ввǀоди́ть, -ести́ законопрое́кт; **~e a custom** завести́ (*pf.*) обы́чай. **3.** (*present*) предстǀавля́ть, -а́вить; знако́мить, по- (*кого с кем*); **may I ~e my fiancée?** разреши́те мне предста́вить мою́ неве́сту; **have we been ~ed (to each other)?** мы знако́мы?; **my father ~ed me to chess** мой оте́ц научи́л меня́ игра́ть в ша́хматы. **4.** (*begin*): **he ~ed his speech with a quotation** он на́чал своё выступле́ние с цита́ты.
introduction [ˌɪntrəˈdʌkʃ(ə)n] *n.* **1.** (*inserting*) ввод, введе́ние, включе́ние. **2.** (*bringing in, instituting*) введе́ние, установле́ние. **3.** (*sth. brought in*) но́вшество; **a recent ~ from abroad** заграни́чная нови́нка; нововведе́ние из-за грани́цы. **4.** (*presentation*) представле́ние; **the hostess made ~s all round** хозя́йка всех перезнако́мила; **this wine needs no ~ from me** э́то вино́ в мое́й рекоменда́ции не нужда́ется; **letter of ~** рекоменда́тельное письмо́. **5.** (*title of book*): **An I~ to Nuclear Physics** «Введе́ние в я́дерную фи́зику». **6.** (*preliminary matter in book, speech etc.*) введе́ние, вступле́ние.
introductory [ˌɪntrəˈdʌktərɪ] *adj.* вступи́тельный, вво́дный.
introspect [ˌɪntrəˈspekt] *v.i.* занима́ться (*impf.*) самоана́лизом.
introspection [ˌɪntrəˈspekʃ(ə)n] *n.* интроспе́кция, самоана́лиз.
introspective [ˌɪntrəˈspektɪv] *adj.* интроспекти́вный.
introvert [ˈɪntrəˌvɜ:t] *n.* челове́к, сосредото́ченный на само́м себе́; ро́бкий, засте́нчивый челове́к.
v.t.: **an ~ed nature** за́мкнутая нату́ра.
intrudǀe [ɪnˈtru:d] *v.t.*: **he ~ed his foot into the doorway** он су́нул но́гу в дверь; **he ~ed himself into our company** он навяза́л нам своё о́бщество; **I don't wish to ~e my opinions on you** я не хочу́ вам навя́зывать свои́ мне́ния; **the thought ~ed itself into my mind** э́та мысль засе́ла у меня́ в голове́.
v.i. втǀорга́ться, -о́ргнуться; **I hope I'm not ~ing** наде́юсь, я вам не помеша́ю; **you are ~ing on my time** вы посяга́ете на моё вре́мя.
intruder [ɪnˈtru:də(r)] *n.* (*intrusive pers.*) навя́зчивый челове́к; (*burglar*) граби́тель (*m.*); (*raiding aircraft*) самолёт вторже́ния.
intrusion [ɪnˈtru:ʒ(ə)n] *n.* вторже́ние; **an ~ on my privacy** наруше́ние моего́ уедине́ния/поко́я; вторже́ние в мою́ ли́чную жизнь.
intrusive [ɪnˈtru:sɪv] *adj.* незва́ный; назо́йливый.
intrust [ɪnˈtrʌst] = **entrust**

intuit [ɪn'tju:ɪt] *v.t.* пост|игáть, -и́гнуть интуити́вно.

intuition [,ɪntju:'ɪʃ(ə)n] *n.* интуи́ция; чутьё; **I had an ~ of her death** я почу́вствовал, что онá умерлá.

intuitive [ɪn'tju:ɪtɪv] *adj.* интуити́вный; **women are more ~ than men** жéнщины обладáют бóлее рáзвитой интуи́цией, чем мужчи́ны.

inundate ['ɪnən,deɪt] *v.t.* затоп|ля́ть, -и́ть; наводн|я́ть, -и́ть; **floods ~d the valley** доли́на былá залитá в результáте наводнéний; (*fig.*) нап|олня́ть, -óлнить; наводн|я́ть, -и́ть; **I was ~d with letters** меня́ засы́пали пи́сьмами; **the town was ~d with tourists** гóрод был наводнён тури́стами.

inundation [,ɪnən'deɪʃ(ə)n] *n.* наводнéние; (*fig.*) наплы́в.

inure [ɪ'njʊə(r)] *v.t.* приуч|áть, -и́ть; прив|ивáть, -и́ть нáвык (*к чему*); **working in the fields ~d his body to heat and cold** рабóта в пóле приучи́ла егó органи́зм к жáре и хóлоду.

inutility [,ɪnju:'tɪlɪtɪ] *n.* бесполéзность, непригóдность.

invade [ɪn'veɪd] *v.t.* захвáт|ывать, -и́ть; зан|имáть, -я́ть; **Germany ~d France** Гермáния вто́рглась во (*or* напáла на) Фрáнцию; (*fig.*) охвáт|ывать. -и́ть; наводн|я́ть, -и́ть; овлад|евáть, -éть +*i.*; **doubts ~d her mind** éю овладéли сомнéния; **crowds of tourists ~d the restaurants** тóлпы тури́стов наводни́ли ресторáны; **~ s.o.'s rights** посяг|áть, -нýть на чьи́-н. правá.

invader [ɪn'veɪdə(r)] *n.* захвáтчик.

invalid[1] ['ɪnvə,li:d, -lɪd] *n.* (*sick pers.*) больнóй; **~ chair** крéсло для инвали́дов; **~ diet** диéта для больны́х.

v.t.: **he was ~ed out (of the army)** егó демобилизовáли по состоя́нию здорóвья; егó комиссовáли.

invalid[2] [ɪn'vælɪd] *adj.* (*groundless*) несостоя́тельный, непригóдный; **~ argument** несостоя́тельный дóвод; (*having no legal force*) недействи́тельный, не имéющий закóнной си́лы.

invalidate [ɪn'vælɪ,deɪt] *v.t.* дéлать, с- неполноцéнным; лиш|áть, -и́ть закóнной си́лы; аннули́ровать (*impf., pf.*).

invalidation [ɪn,vælɪ'deɪʃ(ə)n] *n.* лишéние (закóнной) си́лы; аннули́рование.

invalidity [,ɪnvə'lɪdɪtɪ] *n.* недействи́тельность, незакóнность.

invaluable [ɪn'væljʊəb(ə)l] *adj.* неоцени́мый, бесцéнный.

invariable [ɪn'veərɪəb(ə)l] *adj.* неизмéнный, постоя́нный.

invasion [ɪn'veɪʒ(ə)n] *n.* вторжéние, нападéние, нашéствие; **the ~ of Europe** вторжéние в Еврóпу; **~ of privacy** нарушéние покóя/уединéния; вторжéние в (*чью-н.*) ли́чную жизнь.

invective [ɪn'vektɪv] *n.* инвекти́ва, брань.

inveigh [ɪn'veɪ] *v.i.*: **~ against** я́ростно нап|адáть, -áсть на+*a.*; поноси́ть (*impf.*); дéлать, с- вы́пады прóтив+*g.*

inveigle [ɪn'veɪg(ə)l, -'vi:g(ə)l] *v.t.* соблазн|я́ть, -и́ть; оболь|щáть, -сти́ть; **they ~d him into the conspiracy** они́ вовлекли́ егó в зáговор; **he was ~d into signing a cheque** егó обмáном застáвили подписáть чек.

invent [ɪn'vent] *v.t.* (*devise, originate*) изобре|тáть, -сти́; **when was this machine ~ed?** когдá былá изобретенá э́та маши́на?; (*think up*) приду́м|ывать, -ать; вы́дýмывать, вы́думать.

invention [ɪn'venʃ(ə)n] *n.* (*designing; contrivance*) изобретéние; (*inventiveness*) изобретáтельность, нахóдчивость; (*fabrication*) вы́думка; **his story is pure ~** егó расскáз — сплошнáя вы́думка; **a writer of great ~** писáтель с богáтой фантáзией.

inventive [ɪn'ventɪv] *adj.* изобретáтельный, нахóдчивый.

inventor [ɪn'ventə(r)] *n.* изобретáтель (*m.*).

inventory ['ɪnvəntərɪ] *n.* инвентáрь (*m.*).

inverse ['ɪnvɜ:s, -'vɜ:s] *adj.* обрáтный, противополóжный; **in ~ ratio, proportion to** в обрáтной пропорционáльности к+*d.*

inversion [ɪn'vɜ:ʃ(ə)n] *n.* (*turning upside down*) перестанóвка; перевёртывание; (*reversing order or relation*) изменéние поря́дка/послéдовательности; (*gram.*) инвéрсия.

invert[1] ['ɪnvɜ:t] *n.* (*homosexual*) гомосексуали́ст.

invert[2] [ɪn'vɜ:t] *v.t.* (*turn upside down*) перев|opáчивать, -ернýть; **~ed commas** кавы́чки (*f. pl.*); (*reverse order or relation*) перест|авля́ть, -áвить; меня́ть, по- (*or* измен|я́ть, -и́ть) поря́док.

invertebrate [ɪn'vɜ:tɪbrət, -,breɪt] *n.* беспозвонóчное (живóтное).

adj. беспозвонóчный.

invest [ɪn'vest] *v.t.* **1.** (*clothe, usu. fig.*) од|евáть, -éть; облач|áть, -и́ть; **he was ~ed with a robe** егó облачи́ли в мáнтию; **he was ~ed with full authority** егó облекли́ всéми полномóчиями; **the house was ~ed with an air of mystery** дом был окýтан тáйной. **2.** (*lay out as ~ment*) поме|щáть, -сти́ть; вклáдывать, вложи́ть; инвести́ровать (*impf., pf.*). **3.** (*lay siege to*) оса|ждáть, -ди́ть; окруж|áть, -и́ть.

v.i. поме|щáть, -сти́ть дéньги/капитáл; (*coll., spend money usefully*): **I must ~ in a new hat** мне придётся потрáтиться на (*or* приобрести́) нóвую шля́пу.

investigate [ɪn'vestɪ,geɪt] *v.t.* расслéдовать (*impf., pf.*); исслéдовать (*impf., pf.*).

investigation [ɪn,vestɪ'geɪʃ(ə)n] *n.* расслéдование, слéдствие; исслéдование.

investigative [ɪn'vestɪgətɪv] *adj.*: **~ journalism** журнали́стика расслéдований.

investigator [ɪn'vestɪ,geɪtə(r)] *n.* слéдователь (*m.*); исслéдователь (*m.*).

investiture [ɪn'vestɪ,tjʊə(r)] *n.* инвеститýра; формáльное введéние в дóлжность; пожáлование звáния.

investment [ɪn'vestmənt] *n.* **1.** (*investing*) инвести́рование, капиталовложéние, помещéние капитáла; **a wise ~** разýмное испóльзование дéнег; (*sum invested*) инвести́ция; вклад; (*lucrative acquisition*) удáчное приобретéние. **2.** (*siege*) осáда.

investor [ɪn'vestə(r)] *n.* вклáдчик.

inveterate [ɪn'vetərət] *adj.* закоренéлый, зая́длый; **an ~ disease** закоренéлая болéзнь; **~ hatred** глубокó укорени́вшаяся нéнависть; **an ~ smoker** зая́длый кури́льщик.

invidious [ɪn'vɪdɪəs] *adj.* оскорби́тельный; вызывáющий оби́ду/зáвисть; **an ~ comparison** оби́дное/оскорби́тельное сравнéние.

invidiousness [ɪn'vɪdɪəsnɪs] *n.* оскорби́тельность.

invigilate [ɪn'vɪdʒɪ,leɪt] *v.t. & i.* надзирáть (*impf.*) за (*кем*); следи́ть (*impf.*) за экзаменýющимися.

invigilation [ɪn,vɪdʒɪ'leɪʃ(ə)n] *n.* надзóр за экзаменýющимися.

invigilator [ɪn'vɪdʒɪ,leɪtə(r)] *n.* следя́щий/надзирáющий за экзаменýющимися.

invigorat|e [ɪn'vɪgə,reɪt] *v.t.* укреп|ля́ть, -и́ть; прид|авáть, -áть си́лу +*d.*; (*fig.*) воодушев|ля́ть, -и́ть; вдохнов|ля́ть, -и́ть; **his ideas are ~ing** егó идéи вдохновля́ют.

invincibility [ɪn,vɪnsɪ'bɪlɪtɪ] *n.* непобеди́мость.

invincible [ɪn,vɪnsɪb(ə)l] *adj.* непобеди́мый; **~ will** несгибáемая вóля.

inviolability [ɪn,vaɪələ'bɪlɪtɪ] *n.* неруши́мость; неприкосновéнность.

inviolable [ɪn'vaɪələb(ə)l] *adj.* неруши́мый; неприкосновéнный; **~ oath** неруши́мая кля́тва.

inviolate [ɪn'vaɪələt] *adj.* ненарýшенный; нетрóнутый.

invisibility [ɪn,vɪzɪ'bɪlɪtɪ] *n.* неви́димость.

invisible [ɪn'vɪzɪb(ə)l] *adj.* неви́димый, незри́мый; **~ to the naked eye** незамéтный для невооружённого глáза; **when I called he was ~** когдá я пришёл, он никогó не принимáл; **~ exports** неви́димый э́кспорт; **~ ink** симпати́ческие черни́ла; **~ repair** худóжественная штóпка.

invitation [,ɪnvɪ'teɪʃ(ə)n] *n.* приглашéние; **send out ~s** ра|ссылáть, -зослáть приглашéния; **an ~ to lunch** приглашéние на обéд; **I came at your ~** я пришёл по вáшему приглашéнию; **admission by ~ only** вход тóлько по пригласи́тельным билéтам.

invite[1] ['ɪnvaɪt] *n.* (*coll., invitation*) приглашéние.

invit|e[2] [ɪn'vaɪt] *v.t.* **1.** (*request to come*) пригла|шáть, -си́ть; **she ~ed him into her flat** онá пригласи́ла егó к себé на квартиру; **I am seldom ~ed out** меня́ рéдко кудá-либо приглашáют; **I was not ~ed** меня́ не звáли; **~e o.s.** напроси́ться (*pf.*) в гóсти. **2.** (*request*) предл|агáть, -ожи́ть; проси́ть, по-; **I ~ed him to reconsider** я предложи́л емý пересмотрéть своё решéние; **we were ~ed to choose** нам был предостáвлен вы́бор; **the speaker ~ed questions from the audience** лéктор проси́л пýблику задавáть вопрóсы. **3.** (*encourage*) привл|екáть, -éчь; распол|агáть, -ожи́ть; **the soft air ~es one to dream** на свéжем вóздухе хорошó мечтáется; **his manner ~es confidence** егó обращéние вызывáет довéрие; (*tend to provoke*) вызывáть (*impf.*), способствовать (*impf.*) +*d.*; **are you trying to ~e trouble?** вы что, напрáшиваетесь на неприятности? **4.** (*attract*) привл|екáть, -éчь; **her clothes ~ed attention** её одéжда привлекáла внимáние; **the water looks ~ing** водá мáнит.

invocation [ˌɪnvəˈkeɪʃ(ə)n] *n.* взывáние (к Бóгу); молитва.

invoice [ˈɪnvɔɪs] *n.* (счёт-)фактýра.

v.t.: **~ goods to s.o.** выписывать, выписать счёт/фактýру комý-н. на товáры.

invoke [ɪnˈvəʊk] *v.t.* **1.** (*call on*) приз|ывáть, -вáть; **~ the law** взывáть, воззвáть к закóну; **he ~d the dictionary in support of his statement** он сослáлся на словáрь для подкреплéния своегó утверждéния. **2.** (*call for*) взывáть, воззвáть (*о чём*), молить (*impf.*); **~ God's blessing** молить Бóга о благословéнии; **she ~d his aid** онá взывáла к егó пóмощи; **she ~d a curse on his family** онá проклялá егó семью.

involuntary [ɪnˈvɒləntərɪ] *adj.* (*forced*) вынужденный, неохóтный; (*accidental*) случáйный; (*unintentional*) ненамéренный; (*uncontrollable*) невóльный, непроизвóльный.

involve [ɪnˈvɒlv] *v.t.* **1.** (*entangle*; *implicate*) вовл|екáть, -éчь; впýт|ывать, -ать; **I don't want to get ~d in this business** я не хочý впýтываться в это дéло; **he is ~d with stocktaking just now** он сейчáс зáнят инвентаризáцией; **he was ~d in debt** он запýтался в долгáх; **he ~d himself with an actress** он связáлся с актрисой; **it will not ~ you in any expense** это не введёт вас в расхóды. **2.** (*have as consequence*; *entail*) влечь (*impf.*) за собóй; вызывáть, вызвать; **it would ~ my living in London** в такóм слýчае мне бы пришлóсь жить в Лóндоне; **I want to know what is ~d** я хочý знать, с чем это сопряженó.

involved [ɪnˈvɒlvd] *adj.* слóжный, запýтанный.

involvement [ɪnˈvɒlvmənt] *n.* (*participation*) причáстность; (*complicated situation*) слóжное положéние; (*financial*) дéнежное затруднéние; (*personal*) связь, вовлечённость.

invulnerability [ɪnˌvʌlnərəˈbɪlɪtɪ] *n.* неуязвимость.

invulnerable [ɪnˈvʌlnərəb(ə)l] *adj.* неуязвимый.

inward [ˈɪnwəd] *adj.* (*lit.*, *fig.*) внýтренний; **I was ~ly relieved** в душé (*or* про себя) я вздохнýл с облегчéнием.

adv. = **inward(s)**

inwardness [ˈɪnwədnɪs] *n.* истинная прирóда; сýщность, суть.

inward(s) [ˈɪnwədz] *adv.* внýтренне; (*expr. motion*) внутрь.

iodine [ˈaɪəˌdiːn, -ɪn] *n.* йод.

iodoform [aɪˈəʊdəˌfɔːm, -ˈɒdəˌfɔːm] *n.* йодофóрм.

ion [ˈaɪən] *n.* иóн.

Ionic [aɪˈɒnɪk] *adj.* ионический.

ionization [ˌaɪənaɪˈzeɪʃ(ə)n] *n.* ионизáция.

ionize [ˈaɪəˌnaɪz] *v.t.* ионизировать (*impf.*).

ionosphere [aɪˈɒnəˌsfɪə(r)] *n.* ионосфéра.

ionospheric [aɪˌɒnəˈsferɪk] *adj.* ионосфéрный.

iota [aɪˈəʊtə] *n.* (*lit.*, *fig.*) йóта; **we will not yield one ~** мы не отстýпим ни на йóту/пядь; **I don't care one ~** мне решительно всё равнó.

IOU [ˌaɪəʊˈjuː] *n.* (*coll.*) долговáя расписка.

IPA (*abbr. of* ***International Phonetic Alphabet***) Междунарóдный фонетический алфавит.

ipecacuanha [ˌɪpɪˌkækjʊˈɑːnə] *n.* ипекакуáна, рвóтный кóрень.

ipse dixit [ˌɪpsɪ ˈdɪksɪt] *n.* голословное утверждéние.

ipso facto [ˌɪpsəʊ ˈfæktəʊ] *adv.* тем сáмым; по самомý фáкту.

IQ (*abbr. of* ***intelligence quotient***) коэффициéнт ýмственного развития.

IRA (*abbr. of* ***Irish Republican Army***) Ирлáндская республикáнская áрмия.

Iran [ɪˈrɑːn] *n.* Ирáн.

Iranian [ɪˈreɪnɪən] *n.* ирáн|ец (*fem.* -ка).

adj. ирáнский.

Iraq [ɪˈrɑːk] *n.* Ирáк.

Iraqi [ɪˈrɑːkɪ] *n.* ирáкец, житель (*fem.* -ница) Ирáка.

irascibility [ɪˌræsɪˈbɪlɪtɪ] *n.* раздражительность, вспыльчивость.

irascible [ɪˈræsɪb(ə)l] *adj.* раздражительный, вспыльчивый.

irate [aɪˈreɪt] *adj.* сердитый, гнéвный.

irateness [aɪˈreɪtnɪs] *n.* гнев, злóба.

IRBM (*abbr. of* ***intermediate-range ballistic missile***) БРСД (баллистическая ракéта срéдней дáльности).

ire [ˈaɪə(r)] *n.* (*liter.*) гнев, злóба.

Ireland [ˈaɪələnd] *n.* Ирлáндия.

irenic, eirenic [aɪˈriːnɪk] *adj.* примиряющий, миротвóрческий.

iridescence [ˌɪrɪˈdes(ə)ns] *n.* рáдужность; игрá цветóв.

iridescent [ˌɪrɪˈdes(ə)nt] *adj.* рáдужный, переливчатый.

iridium [ɪˈrɪdɪəm] *n.* иридий.

iridologist [ˌɪrɪˈdɒlədʒɪst] *n.* иридóлог.

iridology [ˌɪrɪˈdɒlədʒɪ] *n.* иридодиагнóстика.

iris [ˈaɪərɪs] *n.* **1.** (*plant*) ирис. **2.** (*of eye*) рáдужная оболóчка.

Irish [ˈaɪərɪʃ] *n.* **1.** (*language*) ирлáндский язык. **2.**: **the ~** ирлáндцы (*m. pl.*).

adj. ирлáндский; **it sounds ~ to me** (*coll.*) мне кáжется, это всё нелогично; **~ stew** ≃ тушёная барáнина с картóшкой.

cpds. **~man** *n.* ирлáндец; **~woman** *n.* ирлáндка.

irk [ɜːk] *v.t.* надоедáть (*impf.*) +*d.*; раздражáть (*impf.*).

irksome [ˈɜːksəm] *adj.* раздражительный, надоéдливый, докýчливый.

irksomeness [ˈɜːksəmnɪs] *n.* раздражительность, надоéдливость, докýчливость.

iron [ˈaɪən] *n.* **1.** (*metal*) железо; **the I~ Age** желéзный век; **his muscles are of ~** у негó стальные мýскулы; **the ~ entered into his soul** «в желéзо вошлá душá егó»; он был подáвлен гóрем; **strike while the ~ is hot** (*prov.*) куй желéзо, покá горячó. **2.** (*flat- or smoothing ~*) утюг; **electric ~** электрический утюг; **run the ~ over my trousers, please** поглáдьте мне, пожáлуйста, брюки. **3.** (*pl.*, **fire-~s**) камúнный прибóр; **he has too many ~s in the fire** он берётся за слишком мнóго дел срáзу. **4.** (*pl.*, *fetters*) окóв|ы (*pl.*, *g.* —); (*handcuffs*) нарýчники (*m. pl.*); **the ringleaders were put in ~s** зачинщиков заковáли в кандалы. **5.** (**branding-~**) клеймó. **6.** (*support for leg*) ножнóй протéз.

adj. (*lit.*, *fig.*) желéзный; **the I~ Curtain** желéзный зáнавес; **~ lung** искýсственное лёгкое; **~ rations** неприкосновéнный запáс; **an ~ tonic** тонизирующее срéдство, содержáщее желéзо; **he ruled with an ~ hand** он управлял/прáвил желéзной рукóй; **the ~ hand in the velvet glove** желéзная рукá в бáрхатной перчáтке; **an ~ will** желéзная вóля.

v.t. & i. (*smooth with flat-~*) утюжить, вы-; глáдить, по-/вы-; **she spent the whole evening ~ing** онá глáдила бельё весь вéчер; **~ out** (*fig.*) сглá|живать, -дить; **the difficulties have all been ~ed out** все осложнéния устранены.

cpds. **~-age** *adj.* принадлежáщий желéзному вéку; **~clad** *n.* броненóсец; **~-foundry** *n.* чугунолитéйный цех; **~-grey** *adj.* стальнóго цвéта; **~master** *n.* фабрикáнт; **~monger** *n.* торгóвец скобяным товáром; **~-ware** *n.* скобянóй товáр; **~work** *n.* чугýнные украшéния; **~-works** *n.* чугунолитéйный завóд.

ironic(al) [aɪˈrɒnɪkəl] *adj.* иронический.

ironing [ˈaɪənɪŋ] *n.* **1.** (*action*) утюжка, глáженье; **~-board** гладильная доскá. **2.** (*linen*) бельё для глáженья.

ironist [ˈaɪrənɪst] *n.* насмéшник.

iron|y [ˈaɪrənɪ] *n.* ирóния; **the ~y of fate** ирóния судьбы; **one of life's ~ies** однá из преврáтностей судьбы; **the ~y of it is that ...** ирóния в том, что...

irradiate [ɪˈreɪdɪˌeɪt] *v.t.* (*subject to light rays*) осве|щáть, -тить; бр|осáть, -óсить свет на+*a.*; (*subject to radiation*) излуч|áть, -ить; облуч|áть, -ить; (*fig.*, *light up*) озар|ять, -ить.

irradiation [ɪˌreɪdɪˈeɪʃ(ə)n] *n.* освещéние; (*fig.*) лучезáрность.

irrational [ɪˈræʃən(ə)l] *adj.* (*not endowed with reason*) неразýмный, не обладáющий рáзумом; (*illogical*; *absurd*) иррационáльный, нелогичный, неразýмный; (*math*) иррационáльный.

irrationality [ɪˌræʃəˈnælɪtɪ] *n.* неразýмность, иррационáльность, нелогичность.

irreclaimable [ˌɪrɪˈkleɪməb(ə)l] *adj.* безвозврáтный.

irreconcilability [ɪˌrekənˌsaɪləˈbɪlɪtɪ] *n.* непримиримость; несовместимость.

irreconcilable [ɪ'rekən,saɪləb(ə)l] *adj.* (*of persons*) непримири́мый; (*of ideas etc.*) несовмести́мый, противоречи́вый; **this is ~ with his previous statement** э́то противоре́чит его́ предыду́щему заявле́нию.

irrecoverable [,ɪrɪ'kʌvərəb(ə)l] *adj.* невозмести́мый; (*irremediable*) непоправи́мый.

irredeemable [,ɪrɪ'di:məb(ə)l] *adj.* непоправи́мый; (*of currency*) неразме́нный; (*of an annuity*) не подлежа́щий вы́купу.

irredentist [,ɪrɪ'dentɪst] *n.* (*Ital. hist.*) ирреденти́ст.

irreducible [,ɪrɪ'dju:sɪb(ə)l] *adj.* преде́льный, минима́льный; **the ~ minimum** преде́льный ми́нимум; **~ to order** не поддаю́щийся упоря́дочению.

irrefragable [ɪ'refrəgəb(ə)l] *adj.* неоспори́мый, неопровержи́мый.

irrefutability [ɪ,refjʊtə'bɪlɪtɪ, ɪrɪ,fju:-] *n.* неопровержи́мость.

irrefutable [ɪ'refjʊtəb(ə)l, ,ɪrɪ'fju:-] *adj.* неопровержи́мый.

irregular [ɪ'regjʊlə(r)] *n.* (*usu. pl., mil.*) нерегуля́рные войска́.

adj. **1.** (*contrary to rule or norm*) непра́вильный; необы́чный; непри́нятый; **~ proceeding** де́йствие, наруша́ющее заведённый поря́док; **an ~ marriage** незако́нный брак; **he leads an ~ life** он ведёт беспоря́дочную жизнь. **2.** (*variable in occurrence*) нерегуля́рный; **he keeps ~ hours** он встаёт и ложи́тся когда́ попа́ло; **he is ~ in attending lectures** он посеща́ет ле́кции нерегуля́рно. **3.** (*unsymmetrical*) непра́вильный, несимметри́чный; **an ~ polygon** несимметри́чный многоуго́льник. **4.** (*uneven*) неро́вный; **~ teeth** неро́вные зу́бы; **an ~ surface** неро́вная пове́рхность. **5.** (*unequal*; *heterogeneous*) неравноме́рный, неодина́ковый; **at ~ intervals** с неодина́ковыми интерва́лами. **6.** (*not straight*) неро́вный; **an ~ coastline** изре́занная берегова́я ли́ния. **7.** (*gram.*) непра́вильный.

irregularity [ɪ,regjʊ'lærɪtɪ] *n.* (*of conduct, procedure*) беспоря́док; незако́нность; (*of occurrence*) непра́вильность, нерегуля́рность; (*of form*) несимметри́чность, непра́вильность, неро́вность.

irrelevanc|e [ɪ'relɪv(ə)ns], **-y** [ɪ'relɪv(ə)nsɪ] *nn.* неуме́стность; (*remark*) неуме́стное замеча́ние.

irrelevant [ɪ'relɪv(ə)nt] *adj.* неуме́стный, неподходя́щий; **~ to the matter in hand** не относя́щийся к де́лу.

irreligion [,ɪrɪ'lɪdʒ(ə)n] *n.* неве́рие.

irreligious [,ɪrɪ'lɪdʒəs] *adj.* неве́рующий.

irremediable [,ɪrɪ'mi:dɪəb(ə)l] *adj.* непоправи́мый, неизлечи́мый.

irremovable [,ɪrɪ'mu:vəb(ə)l] *adj.* неустрани́мый; (*from office*) не поддаю́щийся смеще́нию.

irreparable [ɪ'repərəb(ə)l] *adj.*: **an ~ mistake** непоправи́мая оши́бка; **an ~ loss** безвозвра́тная потéря/утра́та; **my watch suffered ~ harm** мои́ часы́ оконча́тельно слома́лись.

irreplaceable [,ɪrɪ'pleɪsəb(ə)l] *adj.* незамени́мый.

irrepressible [,ɪrɪ'presɪb(ə)l] *adj.* неукроти́мый, неугомо́нный, неудержи́мый; **an ~ child** неугомо́нный ребёнок; **~ optimism** нестреби́мый оптими́зм.

irreproachable [,ɪrɪ'prəʊtʃəb(ə)l] *adj.* безукори́зненный, безупре́чный.

irresistible [,ɪrɪ'zɪstɪb(ə)l] *adj.* непреодоли́мый, неотрази́мый; **an ~ impulse** безу́держный поры́в; **an ~ argument** неопровержи́мый до́вод; **her smile was ~** у неё была́ покоря́ющая улы́бка.

irresolute [ɪ'rezə,lu:t, -,lju:t] *adj.* нереши́тельный.

irresolut|ion [ɪ,rezə'lu:ʃ(ə)n, -'lju:ʃ(ə)n], **-eness** [ɪ'rezə,lu:tnɪs, -,lju:tnɪs] *nn.* нереши́тельность.

irrespective [,ɪrɪ'spektɪv] *adj.*: **~ of** невзира́я/несмотря́ на+*a.*

irresponsibility [,ɪr,ɪspɒnsɪ'bɪlɪtɪ] *n.* безотве́тственность.

irresponsible [,ɪrɪ'spɒnsɪb(ə)l] *adj.* безотве́тственный.

irretrievability [,ɪrɪ,tri:və'bɪlɪtɪ] *n.* невозмести́мость, невосполни́мость; безнадёжность, непоправи́мость.

irretrievable [,ɪrɪ'tri:vəb(ə)l] *adj.* (*unrecoverable*) невозмести́мый, невосполни́мый; (*beyond rescue*) безнадёжный; (*irreparable*) непоправи́мый.

irreverence [ɪ'revərəns] *n.* непочти́тельность, неуваже́ние.

irreverent [ɪ'revərənt] *adj.* непочти́тельный, неуважи́тельный.

irreversibility [,ɪrɪ,vɜ:sɪ'bɪlɪtɪ] *n.* необрати́мость.

irreversible [,ɪrɪ'vɜ:sɪb(ə)l] *adj.* (*e.g. process*) необрати́мый; (*e.g. decision*) неотменя́емый.

irrevocability [ɪ,revəkə'bɪlɪtɪ] *n.* бесповоро́тность; (*finality*) оконча́тельность.

irrevocable [ɪ'revəkəb(ə)l] *adj.* (*unalterable*) неотменя́емый; (*gone beyond recall*) бесповоро́тный.

irrigate ['ɪrɪ,geɪt] *v.t.* **1.** (*supply water to*) оро|ша́ть, -си́ть. **2.** (*med.*) пром|ыва́ть, -ы́ть.

irrigation [,ɪrɪ'geɪʃ(ə)n] *n.* **1.** (*supply of water*) ороше́ние, ирригáция; **~ canal** ирригацио́нный кана́л. **2.** (*med*) промыва́ние.

irritability [,ɪrɪtə'bɪlɪtɪ] *n.* раздражи́тельность; чувстви́тельность, раздражи́мость.

irritable ['ɪrɪtəb(ə)l] *adj.* **1.** (*easily annoyed*) раздражи́тельный. **2.** (*of skin etc.*) чувстви́тельный, не́жный, раздражи́мый.

irritant ['ɪrɪt(ə)nt] *n.* раздражи́тель (*m.*).

adj. раздража́ющий.

irritat|e ['ɪrɪ,teɪt] *v.t.* **1.** (*annoy*) раздража́ть (*impf.*); **he was in an ~ing mood** он был соверше́нно невозмо́жен. **2.** (*cause discomfort to*) раздража́ть (*impf.*); **the smoke ~es one's eyes** дым ест глаза́.

v.i. (*coll., itch*): **the scab began to ~e** струп стал зуде́ть/чеса́ться.

irritation [,ɪrɪ'teɪʃ(ə)n] *n.* (*annoyance; discomfort*) раздраже́ние; (*coll., itch*) зуд, чесо́тка.

irruption [ɪ'rʌpʃ(ə)n] n. вторже́ние.

Isaac ['aɪzək] *n.* Исаа́к.

Isaiah [aɪ'zaɪə] *n.* (*bibl.*) Иса́йя (*m.*).

ISBN (*abbr. of* **international standard book number**) междунаро́дный станда́ртный кни́жный но́мер.

Isfahan [,ɪsfə'hɑ:n] *n.* Исфаха́н.

isinglass ['aɪzɪŋ,glɑ:s] *n.* ры́бий желати́н/клей.

Islam ['ɪzlɑ:m, -læm, -'lɑ:m] *n.* исла́м, мусульма́нство.

Islamic [ɪz'læmɪk] *adj.* мусульма́нский, ислами́стский.

island ['aɪlənd] *n.* о́стров; **traffic ~** острово́к безопа́сности.

islander ['aɪləndə(r)] *n.* островитя́н|ин (*fem.* -ка).

isle [aɪl] *n.* о́стров; **the British I~s** Брита́нские острова́.

islet ['aɪlɪt] *n.* острово́к.

ism ['ɪz(ə)m] *n.* (*coll.*) уче́ние, тео́рия, «изм».

isobar ['aɪsəʊ,bɑ:(r)] *n.* изоба́ра.

isogloss ['aɪsəʊ,glɒs] *n.* изогло́сса.

isolate ['aɪsə,leɪt] *v.t.* **1.** изоли́ровать (*impf., pf.*) (*also med.*); разобщ|а́ть, -и́ть; **villages were ~d by the snow** из-за снегопа́да сообще́ние с деревня́ми бы́ло нару́шено; **an ~d village** отдалённая дере́вня; **an ~d occasion** ча́стный/отде́льный слу́чай; **you cannot ~ one aspect of the subject** нельзя́ рассма́тривать э́то де́ло исключи́тельно с одно́й то́чки зре́ния. **2.** (*chem.*) выделя́ть, вы́делить.

isolation [,aɪsə'leɪʃ(ə)n] *n.* (*separation*) изоля́ция, разобще́ние; **a policy of ~** поли́тика изоля́ции; (*detachment*) уедине́ние; **he lives in splendid ~** он живёт в благослове́нном уедине́нии; **a case considered in ~** отде́льно взя́тый слу́чай; (*med.*) изоля́ция; **~ hospital** инфекцио́нная больни́ца.

isolationism [,aɪsə'leɪʃə,nɪz(ə)m] *n.* изоляциони́зм.

isolationist [,aɪsə'leɪʃə,nɪst] *n.* изоляциони́ст.

isometric [,aɪsəʊ'metrɪk] *adj.* изометри́ческий.

isosceles [aɪ'sɒsɪ,li:z] *adj.* равнобе́дренный.

isotherm ['aɪsəʊ,θɜ:m] *n.* изоте́рма.

isotope ['aɪsə,təʊp] *n.* изото́п.

Israel ['ɪzreɪl] *n.* (*bibl., pol.*) Изра́иль (*m.*); **children, sons of ~** сыны́ Изра́илевы.

Israeli [ɪz'reɪlɪ] *n.*, **Israelite** ['ɪzrɪə,laɪt, -rə,laɪt] *n.* (*bibl.*) израильтя́н|ин (*fem.* -ка).

adj. изра́ильский.

issue ['ɪʃu:, 'ɪsju:] *n.* **1.** (*outflowing; emergence*) вытека́ние; (*place of emergence*) вы́ход. **2.** (*putting out, publication, production*) вы́пуск; **an ~ of stamps** вы́пуск ма́рок; **on the day of ~** в день вы́хода/вы́пуска; (*sth. published or produced*) вы́пуск, изда́ние; **recent ~s of a magazine** после́дние номера́ журна́ла; **an ~ of winter clothing**

компле́кт зи́мней оде́жды. **3.** (*question, topic*) вопро́с; предме́т обсужде́ния; **the point at** ~ предме́т спо́ра; **I don't want to make an** ~ **of it** я не хочу́ де́лать из э́того исто́рию; **join, take** ~ **with s.o. on sth.** нач|ина́ть, -а́ть спо́рить с кем-н. о чём-н. **4.** (*outcome*) исхо́д; ито́г; **I await the** ~ я жду результа́та; **the matter was brought to a successful** ~ де́ло зако́нчилось благополу́чно. **5.** (*leg., offspring*) пото́мство.

v.t. **1.** (*utter, publish*) изд|ава́ть, -а́ть; выпуска́ть, вы́пустить; **an order was** ~**d for everyone to remain at home** был и́здан прика́з не выходи́ть на у́лицу; **he** ~**d a solemn warning** он сде́лал серьёзное предупрежде́ние; **a book** ~**d last year** кни́га, и́зданная в про́шлом году́. **2.** (*supply*) выдава́ть, вы́дать; снаб|жа́ть, -ди́ть; **everyone was** ~**d with ration cards** всем вы́дали продово́льственные ка́рточки.

v.i. **1.** (*go, come out*) выходи́ть, вы́йти; вытека́ть (*impf.*); **smoke** ~**d from the chimney** дым шёл/вали́л из трубы́; **water** ~**d from the rock** вода́ точи́лась из скалы́; **no sound** ~**d from his lips** он не пророни́л ни зву́ка; **blood was issuing from his wounds** кровь сочи́лась из его́ ран. **2.** (*proceed, emanate*) проис|ходи́ть, -зойти́; **where do these rumours** ~ **from?** отку́да пошли́ э́ти слу́хи? **3.** (*result*) конча́ться, ко́нчиться; заверш|а́ться, -и́ться; **their dispute** ~**d in bloodshed** их ссо́ра зако́нчилась кровопроли́тием.

Istanbul [ˌɪstænˈbuːl, -ˈbʊl] *n.* Стамбу́л.

isthmus [ˈɪsməs, ˈɪsθ-] *n.* пereше́ек, переми́чка.

it [ɪt] *pron.* **1.** он (она́, оно́); э́то; *often untranslated, see examples*: **he loved his country and died for** ~ он люби́л свою́ страну́ и поги́б за неё; **who is it?** кто э́то?; ~**'s the postman** э́то почтальо́н; **I don't speak Russian but I understand** ~ я не говорю́ по-ру́сски, но понима́ю; **the shed has no roof over** ~ сара́й не име́ет кры́ши; ~ **is unpleasant, of course** э́то, коне́чно, неприя́тно; **that's just** ~ то́-то и оно́; в то́м-то и де́ло; **that's not** ~ э́то не то; не в том де́ло. **2.** (*impersonal or indefinite*): ~ **is winter** (стои́т) зима́; ~ **was in winter** де́ло бы́ло зимо́й; ~ **is cold** хо́лодно; ~ **is 6 o'clock** (сейча́с) шесть часо́в; ~ **is raining** идёт дождь; ~ **is 5 miles to Oxford** до О́ксфорда пять миль; **we had to walk** ~ нам пришло́сь пойти́ пешко́м; **run for** ~! беги́те изо всех сил (*or* что есть мо́чи)!; **he had a bad time of** ~ ему́ здо́рово доста́лось; **if** ~ **were not for him** е́сли бы не он; не будь его́; **how goes** ~? как дела́?; ~ **is said** говоря́т; ~ **is no use going there** не́зачем идти́ туда́. **3.** (*anticipating logical subject*): ~ **is hard to imagine** тру́дно себе́ предста́вить; **I thought** ~ **best to inform you** я почёл за лу́чшее сообщи́ть вам; ~ **appears I was wrong** выхо́дит, что я был непра́в. **4.** (*emph. another word*): ~ **was John who said that** э́то сказа́л Джон; ~ **is to him you must write** э́то ему вы должны́ написа́ть; ~ **is here that the trouble lies** вот в чём беда́; ~ **was a purse that she dropped and not a bag** урони́ла-то она́ кошелёк, а не су́мку; ~ **was here that I met her** здесь-то мы с ней и встре́тились. **5.** (*other emph. uses*): **he thinks he's** ~ (*coll.*) он (поря́дком) зазнаётся; **that's** ~ (*the problem*) вот и́менно; (*right*) (вот) и́менно, ве́рно; (*coll., the end*) вот и всё; и то́чка; **this is** ~ (*expected event*) наконе́ц-то. **6.: '**~**'** (*at children's games*) водя́щий (*etc., depending on game; see also* **he**): **who is** ~? кто во́дит?; чья о́чередь води́ть?

Italian [ɪˈtæljən] *n.* (*pers.*) италья́н|ец (*fem.* -ка); (*language*) италья́нский язы́к.

adj. италья́нский.

italicize [ɪˈtælɪˌsaɪz] *v.t.* выделя́ть, вы́делить курси́вом.

italics [ɪˈtælɪks] *n.* курси́в; **in** ~ курси́вом.

Italy [ˈɪtəlɪ] *n.* Ита́лия.

itch [ɪtʃ] *n.* **1.** (*irritation of skin*) зуд. **2.** (*disease*) чесо́тка. **3.** (*hankering*) стремле́ние; зуд; **he has an** ~ **to travel** он жа́ждет путеше́ствовать.

v.i. **1.** (*irritate*) чеса́ться (*impf.*); **he has an** ~**ing palm** он жа́дный (до де́нег). **2.** (*feel a longing*) испы́тывать (*impf.*) зуд; **I was** ~**ing to strike him** у меня́ рука́ так и зуде́ла/чеса́лась уда́рить его́.

itchy [ˈɪtʃɪ] *adj.* зудя́щий.

item [ˈaɪtəm] *n.* пункт, но́мер; ~**s on the agenda** пу́нкты пове́стки дня; **the first** ~ **on the programme** (*entertainment*) пе́рвый но́мер програ́ммы; ~ **of expenditure** статья́ расхо́да; **the list comprises 11** ~**s** спи́сок включа́ет 11 предме́тов; **news** ~ (коро́ткое) сообще́ние.

itemization [ˌaɪtəmaɪˈzeɪʃ(ə)n] *n.* (*list*) пе́речень (*m.*); спи́сок.

itemize [ˈaɪtəˌmaɪz] *v.t.* переч|исля́ть, -и́слить; сост|авля́ть, -а́вить пе́речень +*g.*; **an** ~**d account** подро́бный счёт.

iterate [ˈɪtəˌreɪt] *v.t.* повтор|я́ть, -и́ть; возобнов|ля́ть, -и́ть.

iteration [ˌɪtəˈreɪʃ(ə)n] *n.* повторе́ние, возобновле́ние.

itinerant [aɪˈtɪnərənt, ɪ-] *adj.* стра́нствующий, скита́ющийся; ~ **musicians** стра́нствующие/бродя́чие музыка́нты; **an** ~ **judge** судья́, объезжа́ющий свой о́круг.

itinerary [aɪˈtɪnərərɪ, ɪ-] *n.* (*route*) маршру́т, путь (*m.*).

its [ɪts] *poss. adj.* его́, её; (*pert. to subject of sentence*) свой; **the horse broke** ~ **leg** ло́шадь слома́ла (себе́) но́гу.

itself [ɪtˈself] *n.* **1.** (*refl.*) себя́; -ся (*suff.*); **the cat was washing** ~ кот мы́лся; **the monkey saw** ~ **in the mirror** обезья́на уви́дела себя́ в зе́ркале. **2.** (*emph.*) сам; **she is kindness** ~ она́ сама́ доброта́; она́ воплоще́ние доброты́; **the house** ~ **is not worth much** дом сам по себе́ мно́гого не сто́ит; **by** ~ (*alone*) оди́н, одино́ко, в отдале́нии; (*automatically*) самостоя́тельно; **the clock stood by** ~ **in the corner** в углу́ стоя́ли то́лько часы́; **in** ~ сам по себе́; **of** ~ сам (по себе́); **the house looked** ~ **again** дом сно́ва приобрёл пре́жний вид.

ITV (*abbr. of* **Independent Television**) незави́симое (комме́рческое) телеви́дение.

IUD (*abbr. of* **intra-uterine device**) ВМК, (внутрима́точный контрацепти́в).

ivied [ˈaɪvɪd] *adj.* уви́тый плющо́м.

ivory [ˈaɪvərɪ] *n.* **1.** (*substance*) слоно́вая кость; **the I**~ **Coast** Бе́рег Слоно́вой Ко́сти. **2.** (*colour*) цвет слоно́вой ко́сти. **3.** (*pl., coll., piano keys*) кла́виши (*m. pl.*).

adj. (*made of* ~) из слоно́вой ко́сти; (*of the colour of* ~) ма́товый, кре́мовый; ~ **skin** ма́товая ко́жа.

ivy [ˈaɪvɪ] *n.* плющ.

J

jab [dʒæb] *n.* **1.** (*sharp blow*) тычо́к; **he gave me a** ~ **in the ribs with his elbow** он ткнул меня́ ло́ктем в бок; (*with foot or knee*) пино́к; (*in boxing*) коро́ткий прямо́й уда́р по ко́рпусу. **2.** (*coll., injection*) уко́л; **they gave him (*or* he got) a** ~ ему́ сде́лали уко́л; **have you had your smallpox** ~? вам уже́ сде́лали приви́вку от о́спы?

v.t. **1.** (*poke*) ты́кать, ткнуть; **don't** ~ **me in the eye with your umbrella!** смотри́те, не проткни́те мне ва́шим зо́нтиком глаз!; (*pierce*) кол|о́ть, -ну́ть; пырну́ть (*pf.*) (ножо́м); **he was** ~**bed with a bayonet** его́ проткну́ли штыко́м. **2.** (*thrust*) втыка́ть, воткну́ть; **he** ~**bed his knee into my stomach** он пнул мне в живо́т коле́ном; **they** ~**bed a needle into his arm** они́ воткну́ли иго́лку ему́ в ру́ку.

v.i.: **he** ~**bed at my chin** он ткнул меня́ в подборо́док; **a** ~**bing pain** ко́лющая боль.

jabber [ˈdʒæbə(r)] *n.* трескотня́, тараба́рщина.

v.t. & i. трещ́ать (*impf.*); тарато́рить, про-.

jabot [ˈʒæbəʊ] *n.* жабо́ (*indecl.*).

jacaranda [ˌdʒækəˈrændə] *n.* джакара́нда.

jacinth [ˈdʒæsɪnθ, ˈdʒeɪ-] *n.* гиаци́нт.

jack [dʒæk] *n.* **1.** (*name*): **J**~ **Frost** Моро́з Кра́сный Нос; **before you could say J**~ **Robinson** момента́льно; в два счёта; в мгнове́ние о́ка; ≃ и а́хнуть не успе́л; **J**~ **Tar**

матро́с; **every man ~** все до еди́ного; **~ of all trades** ма́стер на все ру́ки; **he is ~ of all trades and master of none** он за всё берётся и ничего́ то́лком не уме́ет; **~ rabbit** (*US*) кро́лик-саме́ц. **2.** (*card*) вале́т; **~ of spades** пи́ковый вале́т. **3.** (*flag*) гюйс; **Union J~** госуда́рственный флаг Соединённого Короле́вства. **4.** (*lifting device*) домкра́т.

v.t.: **~ up** (*of car etc.*) подн|има́ть, -я́ть домкра́том; (*fig., of prices etc.*) пов|ыша́ть, -ы́сить.

cpds. **~ass** *n.* осёл; (*fool*) осёл, дура́к; **~boot** *n.* сапо́г; (*hist.*) ботфо́рт; **~daw** *n.* га́лка; **~-in-office** *n.* чину́ша (*c.g.*), бюрокра́т; **~-in-the-box** *n.* я́щик с выска́кивающей фигу́ркой; **~knife** *n.* большо́й складно́й нож; (*fig., dive*) прыжо́к (в во́ду) согну́вшись; *v.i.* (*dive*) пры́гать (*impf.*) в во́ду согну́вшись; **~-plane** *n.* шерхе́бель (*m.*), руба́нок; **~pot** *n.* (*at cards*) банк при «пра́зднике»; **he hit the ~pot** (*fig.*) ему́ кру́пно повезло́.

jackal [ˈdʒæk(ə)l] *n.* шака́л.

jackanapes [ˈdʒækəˌneɪps] *n.* (*coxcomb*) вы́скочка; фат; (*pert child*) де́рзкий ребёнок.

jacket [ˈdʒækɪt] *n.* **1.** ку́ртка; (*part of suit*) пиджа́к; (*woman's*) жаке́т2. **2.** (*tech., insulating cover*) ко́жух; оши́вка. **3.** (*of book*) суперобло́жка. **4.** (*skin of potato*) кожура́; **potatoes in their ~s** (*or* **~ potatoes**) карто́фель в мунди́ре.

Jacob [ˈdʒeɪkəb] *n.* (*bibl.*) Иа́ков.

Jacobin [ˈdʒækəbɪn] *n.* якоби́нец.

adj. якоби́нский.

Jacobinism [ˈdʒækəbɪnˌɪz(ə)m] *n.* якоби́нство.

Jacobite [ˈdʒækəˌbaɪt] *n.* якоби́т.

adj. якоби́тский.

jade[1] [dʒeɪd] *n.* **1.** (*min.*) нефри́т; гага́т; (*attr.*) нефри́товый. **2.** (**~ green**) цвет нефри́та.

jade[2] [dʒeɪd] *n.* (*arch.*) (*horse*) кля́ча; (*pej., woman*) шлю́ха.

v.t. (*esp. p.p.*): **you look ~d** у вас утомлённый вид; **a ~d appetite** вя́лый аппети́т.

Jaeger [ˈjeɪɡə(r)] *n.* (*propr.*) е́геровская ткань, шерстяно́й трикота́ж для белья́.

Jaffa [ˈdʒæfə] *n.* Я́ффа; **~ oranges** изра́ильские апельси́ны.

jag[1] [dʒæɡ] *n.* (*sharp projection*) о́стрый вы́ступ; зубе́ц; (*notch*) зазу́брина; (*tear*) ды́рка.

jag[2] [dʒæɡ] *n.* (*sl.*): **go on a ~** уйти́ (*pf.*) в запо́й.

jagged [ˈdʒæɡɪd] *adj.* (*notched*) зазу́бренный; **~ mountain tops** зубча́тые верши́ны; (*unevenly cut, torn*) неро́вно наре́занный/отóрванный.

jaguar [ˈdʒæɡjʊə(r)] *n.* ягуа́р.

jail [dʒeɪl] = **gaol**

jailer [ˈdʒeɪlə(r)] = **gaoler**

Jain [dʒaɪn] *n.* чле́н се́кты джа́йна.

Jainism [ˈdʒaɪˌnɪz(ə)m] *n.* уче́ние се́кты джа́йна.

jalopy [dʒəˈlɒpɪ] *n.* (*sl.*) (*car*) драндуле́т; (*car or plane*) «консе́рвная ба́нка».

jalousie [ˈʒælʊˌziː] *n.* (*blind*) жалюзи́ (*nt. indecl.*); (*shutter*) ста́вень (*m.*).

jam[1] [dʒæm] *n.* джем; варе́нье; **~ tart** пиро́г с варе́ньем; **it was money for ~** э́то бы́ло одно́ удово́льствие.

cpds. **~-jar, ~-pot** *nn.* ба́нка для дже́ма; (*empty*) ба́нка из-под дже́ма.

jam[2] [dʒæm] *n.* **1.** (*crush*) да́вка; **traffic ~** зато́р, про́бка. **2.** (*stoppage*) остано́вка. **3.** (*dilemma*) нело́вкое положе́ние; **get into a ~** вли́пнуть (*pf.*) (*coll.*).

v.t. **1.** (*cram*) наб|ива́ть, -и́ть; втис|кивать, -нуть; **she ~med everything into the cupboard** она́ всё запихну́ла в шка́ф; **he ~med his foot into the doorway** он просу́нул но́гу в дверь; **he ~med his hat on his head** он нахлобу́чил шля́пу; **they were ~med in like sardines** они́ наби́лись (туда́) как се́льди в бо́чке; (*force*): **a chair was ~med up against the door** дверь была́ забаррикади́рована кре́слом; **he ~med the brakes on** он ре́зко затормози́л. **2.** (*trap*) прищем|ля́ть, -и́ть; **the child ~med its fingers in the door** ребёнок прищеми́л себе́ па́льцы две́рью. **3.** (*cause to stick or stop*): **the machine got ~med** стано́к засто́порило/заклини́ло; (*wedge*): **~ the door open!** закрепи́те дверь откры́той! **4.** (*obstruct; crowd*) заб|ива́ть, -и́ть; **the crowds ~med every exit** толпа́ заби́ла все вы́ходы; **the roads were ~med with cars** доро́ги бы́ли запру́жены маши́нами; **the room was ~med with people** ко́мната была́ битко́м наби́та; **the room was ~med with furniture** ко́мната была́ загромождена́ ме́белью; (*radio*) глуши́ть, за-.

v.i. (*get stuck*) застр|ева́ть, -я́ть; за|еда́ть, -е́сть; **the door ~med** дверь зае́ло.

cpds. **~-packed** *adj.* наби́тый до отка́за; битко́м наби́тый; **~-session** *n.* импровиза́ция джа́зового орке́стра.

Jamaica [dʒəˈmeɪkə] *n.* Яма́йка; **~ rum** яма́йский ром.

Jamaican [dʒəˈmeɪkən] *n.* яма́ец; жи́тель(ница) Яма́йки.

adj. яма́йский.

jamb [dʒæm] *n.* (*of door, window*) кося́к.

jamboree [ˌdʒæmbəˈriː] *n.* **1.** (*of Scouts etc.*) слёт. **2.** (*celebration*) пра́здество; (*spree*) весе́лье.

James [ˈdʒeɪmz] *n.* (*bibl.*) Иа́ков; (*hist.*) Яков.

jamming [ˈdʒæmɪŋ] *n.* (*stoppage*) заеда́ние; (*radio*) заглуше́ние.

jangl|e [ˈdʒæŋɡ(ə)l] *n.* ре́зкий звук.

v.t. & i. издава́ть (*impf.*) ре́зкий звук; бренча́ть (*impf.*); **a ~ing piano** разби́тый роя́ль; **their voices ~ed my nerves** их голоса́ де́йствовали мне на не́рвы.

janitor [ˈdʒænɪtə(r)] *n.* приврáтник, швейца́р, дво́рник.

jani|zary, -ssary [ˈdʒænɪzərɪ] *n.* яныча́р.

January [ˈdʒænjʊərɪ] *n.* янва́рь (*m.*); (*attr.*) янва́рский.

Janus [ˈdzeɪnəs] *n.* (*myth.*) Я́нус.

Jap [dʒæp] *n.* япо́шка (*c.g.*) (*coll.*).

Japan[1] [dʒəˈpæn] *n.* Япо́ния

japan[2] [dʒəˈpæn] *n.* (*varnish*) чёрный лак.

v.t. лакирова́ть, от-.

Japanese [ˌdʒæpəˈniːz] *n.* (*pers.*) япо́н|ец (*fem.* -ка); (*language*) япо́нский язы́к.

adj. япо́нский.

jape [dʒeɪp] *n.* шу́тка.

v.i. шути́ть, по-.

japonica [dʒəˈpɒnɪkə] *n.* айва́ япо́нская.

jar[1] [dʒɑː(r)] *n.* (*vessel*) ба́нка.

jar[2] [dʒɑː(r)] *n.* **1.** (*harsh sound*) неприя́тный звук. **2.** (*shock, vibration*) сотрясе́ние; (*on nerves or feelings*) неприя́тный эффе́кт; **the news gave him a ~** изве́стие неприя́тно порази́ло его́. **3.** (*disagreement*) несогла́сие; (*quarrel*) ссо́ра.

v.t. (*shake*) сотряс|а́ть, -ти́; (*fig., shock*) потряс|а́ть, -ти́.

v.i. **1.** (*emit harsh sound*) изд|ава́ть, -а́ть ре́зкий звук; (*sound discordantly*) дисгармони́ровать (*impf.*). **2.: ~on, against** (*strike with grating sound*) скрежета́ть (*impf.*) по+*d.*; **~ on** (*irritate, annoy*) раздраж|а́ть, -и́ть. **3.** (*disagree*) ст|а́лкиваться, -олкну́ться; (*fig.*): **these colours ~** э́ти цвета́ не сочета́ются.

jardinière [ˌʒɑːdɪˈnjeə(r)] *n.* жардинье́рка.

jargon [ˈdʒɑːɡən] *n.* жарго́н; (*gibberish*) тараба́рщина.

jasmine [ˈdʒæsmɪn, ˈdʒæz-], **jessamine** [ˈdʒesəmɪn] *nn.* жасми́н.

jasper [ˈdʒæspə(r)] *n.* я́шма.

jaundice [ˈdʒɔːndɪs] *n.* желту́ха.

v.t. (*usu. p.p.*): **a ~d complexion** жёлтый цвет лица́; **he took a ~d view of the affair** он ко́со смотре́л на э́то де́ло.

jaunt [dʒɔːnt] *n.* увеселите́льная пое́здка/прогу́лка.

jauntiness [ˈdʒɔːntɪnɪs] *n.* бо́йкость, ли́хость; беспе́чность, небре́жность.

jaunty [ˈdʒɔːntɪ] *adj.* (*sprightly*) бо́йкий, лихо́й; (*carefree*) беспе́чный, небре́жный.

Java [ˈdʒɑːvə] *n.* Я́ва.

Javanese [ˌdʒɑːvəˈniːz] *n.* (*pers.*) ява́н|ец (*fem.* -ка); (*language*) ява́нский язы́к.

adj. ява́нский.

javelin [ˈdʒævəlɪn, -vlɪn] *n.* мета́тельное копьё; **(throwing) the ~** (*contest*) мета́ние копья́.

cpd. **~-thrower** *n.* мета́тель (*fem.* -ница) копья́.

jaw [dʒɔː] *n.* **1.** че́люсть; (*pl., mouth*) рот; (*of animal*) пасть; **the dog held the bird in its ~s** соба́ка держа́ла пти́цу в зуба́х; **in the ~s of a vice** в тиска́х; **in the ~s of death** в ко́гтя́х сме́рти. **2.** (*coll., talk, admonition*): **give s.o. a ~(ing)** дать (*pf.*) кому́-н. вздрю́чку; **they had a good ~**

они́ всласть поболта́ли; **hold your ~!** заткни́сь.

v.t. (*coll., lecture; rebuke*) чита́ть (*impf.*) нота́цию +*d.*; отчи́тывать (*impf.*).

v.i. (*coll., talk at length*) пережёвывать (*impf.*) одно́ и то же; ну́дно говори́ть (*impf.*).

cpds. **~bone** *n.* челюстна́я кость; **~-breaker** *n.* (*coll.*) труднопроизноси́мое сло́во.

jay [dʒeɪ] *n.* со́йка.

cpds. **~-walk** *v.i.* неосторо́жно пере|ходи́ть, -йти́ у́лицу; **~-walker** *n.* неосторо́жный пешехо́д.

jazz [dʒæz] *n.* джаз; **and all that ~** (*sl.*) и всё тако́е про́чее; (*attr.*), джа́зовый.

v.t.: **~ up** (*fig., enliven*) ожив|ля́ть, -и́ть.

cpds. **~-band** *n.* джаз-орке́стр; **~man, ~-player** *nn.* джази́ст; уча́стник джаз-орке́стра.

jazzy ['dʒæzɪ] *adj.* (*like jazz*) джа́зовый; (*showy*) бро́ский, я́ркий.

jealous ['dʒeləs] *adj.* **1.** (*of affection etc.*) ревни́вый; **she was ~ of her husband's secretary** она́ ревнова́ла му́жа к секрета́рше; **a ~ god** бог ревни́тель. **2.** (*vigilant in defence*): **he is ~ of his rights** он ревни́во оберега́ет свои́ права́. **3.** (*envious*) зави́стливый; **I am ~ of his success!** я зави́дую его́ успе́ху.

jealousy ['dʒeləsɪ] *n.* ре́вность, ревни́вость; (*envy*) за́висть.

jean [dʒi:n] *n.* (*text.*) джинсо́вая ткань; (*pl., trousers*) джи́нс|ы (*pl., g.* -ов); (*overalls*) джинсо́вый комбинезо́н.

jeep [dʒi:p] *n.* джип, вездехо́д.

jeer [dʒɪə(r)] *n.* насме́шка, глумле́ние; (*taunt*) издёвка.

v.t. & i. глуми́ться (*impf.*) (над+*i.*); насмеха́ться (*impf.*) (над+*i.*); **the crowd ~ed (at) him** толпа́ глуми́лась над ним; **he was ~ed off the stage** он ушёл со сце́ны под улюлю́канье.

Jehovah [dʒə'həʊvə] *n.* Иегова́ (*m.*).

Jehu ['dʒi:hju:] *n.* (*bibl.*) Ииу́й; (*fig.*): **he drives like ~** он лиха́ч.

jejune [dʒɪ'dʒu:n] *adj.* ску́дный; пусто́й; бессодержа́тельный.

jejuneness [dʒɪ'dʒu:nnɪs] *n.* ску́дность; бессодержа́тельность.

jell [dʒel] *v.i.* (*coll., set into jelly*) заст|ыва́ть, -ы́ть; (*fig.*) формирова́ться, с-.

jellied ['dʒelɪd] *adj.* засты́вший; преврати́вшийся в желе́; **~ eels** заливно́е из угре́й.

jelly ['dʒelɪ] *n.* желе́ (*indecl.*); (*aspic*) сту́день (*m.*); **royal ~** ма́точное молочко́.

cpd. **~fish** *n.* меду́за.

jemmy ['dʒemɪ] (*US* **jimmy**) *n.* «фо́мка», отмы́чка (*coll.*).

jenny ['dʒenɪ] *n.* (*crane*) подвижна́я лебёдка; (*spinning-~*) пряди́льный стано́к периоди́ческого де́йствия.

cpd. **~-wren** *n.* королёк, крапи́вник.

jeopardize ['dʒepə,daɪz] *v.t.* (*endanger*) подв|ерга́ть, -е́ргнуть опа́сности; (*put at risk*) рискова́ть (*impf.*) +*i.*; **he ~d his chances of success** он рискова́л свои́ми ша́нсами на успе́х.

jeopardy ['dʒepədɪ] *n.* (*danger*) опа́сность; (*risk*) риск; **his life was in ~** его́ жизнь была́ в опа́сности.

jerboa [dʒɜ:'bəʊə] *n.* тушка́нчик.

jeremiad [,dʒerɪ'maɪæd] *n.* иереми́да, го́рестная по́весть.

Jeremiah [,dʒerɪ'maɪə] *n.* (*bibl.*) Иереми́я (*m.*).

Jericho ['dʒerɪ,kəʊ] *n.* Иерихо́н.

jerk [dʒɜ:k] *n.* **1.** (*pull*) рыво́к; (*jolt; shock*) уда́р; **the train stopped with a ~** по́езд ре́зко затормози́л; **he gave the handle a ~** он дёрнул за ру́чку. **2.** (*twitch*) су́дорожное вздра́гивание; **with a ~ of his head** дёрнув голово́й. **3.: physical ~s** (*coll.*) гимна́стика, заря́дка. **4.:** (*US sl., despicable pers.*) подо́нок.

v.t. (*push*) ре́зко толк|а́ть, -ну́ть; (*pull, twitch*) дёр|гать, -нуть; (*throw*) швыр|я́ть, -ну́ть; **he ~ed his head back** он вски́нул го́лову.

v.i.: **the train ~ed to a halt** по́езд ре́зко останови́лся.

jerkin ['dʒɜ:kɪn] *n.* ку́ртка-безрука́вка.

jerk|y ['dʒɜ:kɪ] *adj.* (*moving in jerks*) дви́гающийся ре́зкими толчка́ми; **~y movements** су́дорожные движе́ния; **we had a ~y ride** в доро́ге нас си́льно трясло́; **he spoke ~ily** он говори́л отры́висто.

jerry ['dʒerɪ] *n.* **1.** (*sl., chamber pot*) ночно́й горшо́к. **2.** **(J~:** *German*) фриц, немчура́ (*m.*) (*both coll.*).

cpds. **~-builder** *n.* подря́дчик, возводя́щий постро́йки из плохо́го материа́ла; **~-building** *n.* непро́чная постро́йка; **~-built** *adj.* постро́енный ко́е-как; **~can** *n.* кани́стра.

jersey ['dʒɜ:zɪ] *n.* (*fabric, garment*) дже́рси (*nt. indecl.*); **football ~** футбо́лка; **J~ cow** джерсе́йская коро́ва.

Jerusalem [dʒə'ru:sələm] *n.* Иерусали́м; **~ artichoke** земляна́я гру́ша.

jessamine ['dʒesəmɪn] = **jasmine**

jest [dʒest] *n.* шу́тка; **in ~** в шу́тку; **many a true word is spoken in ~** в ка́ждой шу́тке есть до́ля пра́вды; **make a ~ of** шути́ть (*impf.*) над+*i.*; (*object of ridicule*) объе́кт насме́шек/шу́ток, посме́шище.

v.i. шути́ть, по-; (*speak amusingly*) балагу́рить (*impf.*); **~ at** шути́ть над+*i.*

jester ['dʒestə(r)] *n.* (*hist.*) шут; **court ~** придво́рный шут.

jesting ['dʒestɪŋ] *adj.* шутли́вый.

Jesuit ['dʒezjʊɪt] *n.* иезуи́т; (*attr.*) иезуи́тский.

Jesuitical [,dʒezjʊ'ɪtɪk(ə)l] *adj.* иезуи́тский.

Jesuitry ['dʒezjʊɪtrɪ] *n.* иезуи́тство.

Jesus ['dʒi:zəs] *n.* Иису́с.

jet[1] [dʒet] *n.* (*min.*) гага́т.

adj. гага́товый; (*~-black*) чёрный как смоль.

jet[2] [dʒet] *n.* **1.** (*stream of water etc.*) струя́. **2.** (*spout, nozzle*) со́пло. **3.** **(~ engine)** реакти́вный дви́гатель; **(~ aircraft)** реакти́вный самолёт; **~ pilot** пило́т реакти́вного самолёта.

v.i. (*spurt, gush*) бить (*impf.*) струёй; (*coll., fly by ~*) лета́ть (*indet.*) на реакти́вном самолёте.

cpds. **~-fighter** *n.* реакти́вный истреби́тель; **~-lag** *n.* наруше́ние су́точного ри́тма; **~-propelled** *adj.* реакти́вный; **~-set** *n.* у́зкий круг бога́тых путеше́ственников; междунаро́дная элита.

jetsam ['dʒetsəm] *n.* груз, вы́брошенный за́ борт при угро́зе ава́рии.

jettison ['dʒetɪs(ə)n, -z(ə)n] *v.t.* (*lit., fig.*) выбра́сывать, вы́бросить (за́ борт).

jetty ['dʒetɪ] *n.* при́стань, мол.

Jew [dʒu:] *n.* евре́й (*fem.* -ка); иуде́й (*fem.* -ка).

cpds. **~-baiting** *n.* пресле́дование евре́ев; **j~'s-harp** *n.* варга́н.

jewel ['dʒu:əl] *n.* (*precious stone*) драгоце́нный ка́мень; (*in watch*) ка́мень; (*ornament containing ~*) ювели́рное изде́лие; драгоце́нность; (*fig., of pers. or thg.*) сокро́вище.

v.t. (*esp. p.p.*): **a ~led watch** час|ы́ (*pl., g.* -о́в) на камня́х; (*set in ~s*) часы́, укра́шенные бриллиа́нтами; **a ~led sword** меч, укра́шенный драгоце́нными камня́ми.

cpds. **~-box, ~-case** *nn.* футля́р/шкату́лка для ювели́рных изде́лий.

jeweller ['dʒu:ələ(r)] *n.* ювели́р.

jewel|lery, -ry ['dʒu:əlrɪ] *n.* ювели́рные изде́лия; драгоце́нности (*f. pl.*).

Jewess ['dʒu:es] *n.* евре́йка; иуде́йка.

Jewish ['dʒu:ɪʃ] *adj.* евре́йский; иуде́йский.

Jewry ['dʒʊərɪ] *n.* (*collect., Jews*) евре́и (*m. pl.*), евре́йство; (*quarter*) евре́йский кварта́л.

Jezebel ['dʒezə,bel] *n.* (*bibl.*) Иезаве́ль; (*fig.*) распу́тная/на́глая же́нщина.

jib[1] [dʒɪb] *n.* **1.** (*naut.*) кли́вер; **the cut of s.o.'s ~** (*coll., personal appearance*) вне́шний вид, физионо́мия. **2.** (*of crane*) стрела́.

cpd. **~-boom** *n.* утле́гарь (*m.*).

jib[2] [dʒɪb] *v.i.* (*of horse or pers.*) уп|ира́ться, -ере́ться; **~ at sth.** уклоня́ться (*impf.*) от чего́-н.

jibe[1] [dʒaɪb] (*mock*) = **gibe**

jibe[2] [dʒaɪb] (*US, fit, agree*) соотве́тствовать (+*d.*), согласова́ться (с+*i.*) (*both impf.*).

jiffy ['dʒɪfɪ] *n.* (*coll.*) миг; **wait a ~!** подожди́те мину́тку; **in a ~** одни́м ми́гом; **I'll come in a ~** я ми́гом.

jig[1] [dʒɪg] *n.* (*dance*) джи́га.

v.t.: **she was ~ging the baby up and down** она́ подбра́сывала ребёнка.

v.i. (*dance*) танцева́ть (*impf.*) джи́гу; (*move jerkily; fidget*): **~ about** припля́сывать (*impf.*); **~ up and down** пры́гать (*impf.*).

jig[2] [dʒɪg] *n.* (*tech.*) зажи́мное приспособле́ние.
cpd. **~-saw** *n.* (*tool*) ажу́рная пила́; (*puzzle*) (составна́я) карти́нка-зага́дка.
jigger ['dʒɪgə(r)] *v.t.* (*coll.*): **I'll be ~ed!** (*expr. surprise*) ну и ну!; ну и дела́!; не мо́жет быть!
jiggery-pokery [ˌdʒɪgərɪ'pəʊkərɪ] *n.* (*coll.*) ко́зн|и (*pl.*, *g.* -ей); плу́тни (*f. pl.*).
jiggle ['dʒɪg(ə)l] *v.t.* пока́ч|ивать, -а́ть.
jilt [dʒɪlt] *n.* коке́тка.
v.t. бр|оса́ть, -о́сить.
jim-jams ['dʒɪmdʒæmz] *n.* (*sl.*): **it gives me the ~** у меня́ от э́того мандра́ж/мура́шки по ко́же (бе́гают).
jimmy ['dʒɪmɪ] = **jemmy**
jingle ['dʒɪŋg(ə)l] *n.* (*ringing sound*) звя́канье; (*pej.*, *rhyme*) ри́фма; избы́точная аллитера́ция.
v.t. & *i.* звя́к|ать, -нуть (+*i.*); **he ~d the keys** он позвя́кивал/звя́кнул ключа́ми; **the bell ~d** колоко́льчик звя́кнул.
jingo ['dʒɪŋgəʊ] *n.* шовини́ст, джинго́ист; ура́-патрио́т; **by ~!** ёлки-па́лки!; ей-Бо́гу!; чёрт возьми́!
jingoism ['dʒɪŋgəʊˌɪz(ə)m] *n.* шовини́зм, ура́-патриоти́зм.
jingoistic [ˌdʒɪŋgəʊ'ɪstɪk] *adj.* шовинисти́ческий.
jink [dʒɪŋk] *n.* (*coll.*): **high ~s** (шу́мное/бу́рное) весе́лье.
jinn(ee) [dʒɪ'niː] *n.* джин.
jinx [dʒɪŋks] *n.* (*coll.*) злы́е ча́ры (*f. pl.*); **put a ~ on** сгла́зить (*pf.*).
jitter ['dʒɪtə(r)] *n.* (*coll.*): **have the ~s** не́рвничать (*impf.*); **it gave me the ~s** меня́ о́торопь взяла́.
v.i. не́рвничать (*impf.*).
cpd. **~bug** *n.* (*nervous pers.*) псих (*coll.*).
jittery ['dʒɪtərɪ] *adj.* (*coll.*) не́рвный.
jive [dʒaɪv] *n.* (*sl.*) джа́зовая му́зыка.
v.i. танцева́ть (*impf.*) под джа́зовую му́зыку.
Jnr. ['dʒuːnɪə(r)] *n.* (*abbr. of* **Junior**) мл., (мла́дший).
Joan [dʒəʊn] *n.*: **~ of Arc** Жа́нна д'Арк.
Job[1] [dʒəʊb] *n.* (*bibl.*) Ио́в; **it would try the patience of ~** э́то вы́ведет из себя́ да́же а́нгела; **a ~'s comforter** го́ре-утеши́тель (*m.*).
job[2] [dʒɒb] *n.* **1.** (*piece of work*; *task*) рабо́та; зада́ние; **he does a good ~ (of work)** он хорошо́ рабо́тает; **my ~ is to wash the dishes** моя́ обя́занность — мыть посу́ду; **odd ~s** случа́йная рабо́та; **payment by the ~** сде́льная опла́та; **he is on the ~ by 8 o'clock** он прихо́дит на рабо́ту в во́семь часо́в; **fall down on the ~** (*coll.*) прова́л|ивать, -и́ть де́ло; (*difficult task*): **we had a ~ finding them** мы наси́лу их отыска́ли. **2.** (*product of work*): **you've made a good ~ of that** вы сде́лали э́то хорошо́; **this bike is a nice ~** (*coll.*) э́тот велосипе́д недурна́я шту́чка; **just the ~** (*coll.*) то, что на́до. **3.** (*employment*; *position*) рабо́та; ме́сто; **what is your ~?** кака́я у вас рабо́та?; ке́м/где вы рабо́таете?; **he has a good ~** он име́ет хоро́шую рабо́ту; **he is good at his ~** он хоро́ший рабо́тник; **look for a ~** иска́ть (*impf.*) рабо́ту; **get a ~** нах|оди́ть, -йти́ рабо́ту; **lose one's ~** теря́ть, по- рабо́ту/ме́сто; **out of a ~** без рабо́ты; **provide ~s for the boys** разд|ава́ть, -а́ть «тёпленькие» месте́чки по бла́ту (*coll.*). **4.** (*coll.*, *crime*, *esp. theft*) воровство́, «де́ло». **5.** (*transaction*): **a put-up ~** махина́ция; **it's a good ~ you stayed at home** хорошо́, что вы оста́лись до́ма; **it's a good ~ for you the inspector's not here** ва́ше сча́стье, что инспе́ктора здесь нет; **he's gone, and a good ~ too!** он ушёл — и сла́ва Бо́гу!; **make the best of a bad ~** переби́ться (*pf.*), обойти́сь (*pf.*); дово́льствоваться (*impf.*) ма́лым; не унывать́; **give up as a bad ~** махну́ть (*pf.*) руко́й на+*a.*
v.i. (*do ~s*): **~bing gardener** наёмный садо́вник; (*deal in stocks*) быть ма́клером.
jobber ['dʒɒbə(r)] *n.* (*broker*) ма́клер.
jobbery ['dʒɒbərɪ] *n.* спекуля́ция.
jobless ['dʒɒblɪs] *adj.* безрабо́тный.
jockey ['dʒɒkɪ] *n.* жоке́й.
v.t. (*cheat*) обма́н|ывать, -у́ть; обжу́ли|вать, -ть; (*manoeuvre*): **~ s.o. into sth.** обма́ном склон|я́ть, -и́ть кого́-н. к чему́-н.; **he was ~ed out of his job** его́ подсиде́ли (*coll.*).
v.i.: **~ for position** (*fig.*) оттира́ть (*impf.*) друг дру́га (*в борьбе за выгодное положение и т.п.*).
jock-strap ['dʒɒkstræp] *n.* суспензо́рий.
jocose [dʒə'kəʊs] *adj.* игри́вый.
jocos|eness [dʒə'kəʊsnɪs], **-ity** [dʒə'kɒsɪtɪ] *nn.* игри́вость.
jocular ['dʒɒkjʊlə(r)] *adj.* (*merry*) весёлый; (*humorous*) шутли́вый, заба́вный.
jocularity [ˌdʒɒkjʊ'lærɪtɪ] *n.* весёлость, шутли́вость.
jocund ['dʒɒkənd] *adj.* (*cheerful*) весёлый; (*lively*) живо́й.
jodhpurs ['dʒɒdpəz] *n.* брю́к|и (*pl.*, *g.* —); галифе́ (*nt. pl.*, *indecl.*).
jog [dʒɒg] *n.* **1.** (*push*; *nudge*) толчо́к. **2.** (*trot*) рысь; бег трусцо́й; оздорови́тельный бе́г.
v.t.: **~ up and down** подбра́сывать (*impf.*); **~ s.o.'s elbow** толк|а́ть, -ну́ть кого́-н. под ло́коть; **~ s.o.'s memory** освеж|а́ть, -и́ть чью-н. па́мять.
v.i. **1.** (*coll.*, *run slowly*) бе́гать (*indet.*) трусцо́й; **he ~ged along (on horseback)** он труси́л (на ло́шади); **business is ~ging along** дела́ иду́т свои́м чередо́м. **2.**: **~ up and down** подпры́гивать (*impf.*).
cpd. **~-trot** *n.*: **at a ~-trot** ры́сью, рысцо́й.
jogger ['dʒɒgə(r)] *n.* люби́тель (*m.*) оздорови́тельного бе́га, джо́ггер.
jogging ['dʒɒgɪŋ] *n.* (*trot*) бег трусцо́й; (*sport*) оздорови́тельный бе́г; джо́ггинг.
joggle ['dʒɒg(ə)l] *v.t.* & *i.* пока́чиваться (*impf.*).
Johannesburg [dʒəʊ'hænɪsˌbɜːg] *n.* Йоха́ннесбург.
John[1] [dʒɒn] *n.* (*bibl.*, *hist.*) Иоа́нн.
john[2] [dʒɒn] *n.* (*US*, *lavatory*) сорти́р (*coll.*).
johnny-come-lately ['dʒɒnɪ] *n.* (*coll.*) ≃ новичо́к, прише́лец; запозда́лый гость.
joie de vivre [ˌʒwɑː də 'viːvrə] *n.* жизнера́достность.
join [dʒɔɪn] *n.* связь, соедине́ние.
v.t. **1.** (*connect*) соедин|я́ть, -и́ть; **the towns are ~ed by a railway** э́ти города́ соединя́ет желе́зная доро́га; **~ hands** взя́ться (*pf.*) за́ руки; (*fasten*) свя́з|ывать, -а́ть (*что с чем*); (*unite*) объедин|я́ть, -и́ть; **they ~ed forces** они́ объедини́ли уси́лия; **~ in marriage** венча́ть, об-. **2.** (*enter*) вступ|а́ть, -и́ть в+*a.*; **he ~ed the party** (*pol.*) он вступи́л в па́ртию; **he ~ ed their ranks** он примкну́л к их ряда́м; **~ battle** вступ|а́ть, -и́ть в бой; нача́ть (*pf.*) сраже́ние; **~ issue** вступ|а́ть, -и́ть в спор; **~ a club** стать (*pf.*) чле́ном клу́ба; **~ the army** вступи́ть/пойти́ (*pf.*) в а́рмию; **~** (*sc. rejoin*) **one's regiment (*or* ship)** верну́ться (*pf.*) в полк (*or* на кора́бль). **3.** (*enter s.o.'s company*) присоедин|я́ться, -и́ться к+*d.*; (*side with*) прим|ыка́ть, -кну́ть к+*d.*; (*meet*) встр|еча́ться, -е́титься с+*i.*; **may I ~ you?** (*at table*) разреши́те мне присе́сть?; **will you ~ us in a walk?** не хоти́те ли прогуля́ться с на́ми?; **he ~ed us in approving the decision** он присоедини́л свой го́лос к на́шему одобре́нию э́того реше́ния. **4.** (*flow or lead into*) соедин|я́ться, -и́ться с+*i.*; сл|ива́ться, -и́ться с+*i.*; **where the Cherwell ~s the Thames** где река́ Че́рвелл впада́ет в Те́мзу; **there is a restaurant where you ~ the motorway** у въе́зда на автостра́ду есть рестора́н.
v.i. **1.** (*be connected*, *fastened*, *united*; *come or flow together*) соедин|я́ться, -и́ться; свя́з|ываться, -а́ться; объедин|я́ться, -и́ться; сходи́ться, сойти́сь; сл|ива́ться, -и́ться; (*border on each other*) грани́чить (*impf.*) друг с дру́гом. **2.** (*take part*): **may I ~ in the game?** мо́жно мне поигра́ть с ва́ми?; **he ~ed in the applause** он присоедини́лся к аплоди́рующим; **they all ~ed in the chorus** все пе́ли припе́в хо́ром. **3.** (*become a member*) стать (*impf.*) чле́ном (*чего*).
with advs.: **~ in** *v.i.* (*take part*) прин|има́ть, -я́ть уча́стие; (*in conversation*) вступ|а́ть, -и́ть в бесе́ду; **~ on** *v.t.* & *i.* присоедин|я́ть(ся), -и́ть(ся); **~ together** *v.t.* свя́з|ывать, -а́ть; соедин|я́ть, -и́ть; **~ up** *v.t.* & *i.* соедин|я́ть(ся), -и́ть(ся); *v.i.* (*coll.*, *enlist*) поступ|а́ть, -и́ть на вое́нную слу́жбу.
joiner ['dʒɔɪnə(r)] *n.* **1.** (*woodworker*) столя́р; **~'s shop** столя́рная мастерска́я; **be a ~** столя́рничать (*impf.*). **2.** (*coll.*, *one who joins societies etc.*) член мно́гих организа́ций и клу́бов.
joinery ['dʒɔɪnərɪ] *n.* столя́рная рабо́та; **do, practise ~** столя́рничать (*impf.*).
joint [dʒɔɪnt] *n.* **1.** (*place of juncture*; *means of joining*) соедине́ние; стык; **the pipe is leaking at the ~s** труба́

течёт в сты́ке; **ball and socket ~** шарни́р; шарово́е соедине́ние. **2.** (*anat.*) суста́в, сочлене́ние; **out of ~** (*pred.*) вы́вихнут; (*fig.*) не в поря́дке; **my ~s ache** у меня́ ло́мит в суста́вах. **3.: a ~ of meat** кусо́к мя́са (к обе́ду); **a cut off the ~** кусо́к зажа́ренного мя́са. **4.** (*resort*) ха́та (*sl.*). **5.** (*sl., marijuana cigarette*) кося́к, масты́рка.

adj. **1.** (*combined; shared*) совме́стный; **~ action** совме́стное де́йствие; **take ~ action** де́йствовать (*impf.*) сообща́; (*common*) о́бщий; **~ account** о́бщий счёт; **~ efforts** о́бщие/совме́стные уси́лия; **at our ~ expense** за наш о́бщий счёт; (*united*) соединённый; **~ venture** совме́стное предприя́тие. **2.** (*sharing*): **~ owner** совладе́лец; **~ author** соа́втор; **~ heir** сонасле́дник.

v.t. **1.** (*connect by ~s*) соедин|я́ть, -и́ть; **a ~ed doll** ку́кла на шарни́рах. **2.** (*divide into ~s*) расчлен|я́ть, -и́ть.

cpd. **~-stock** *n.* (*attr.*) акционе́рный.

jointure [ˈdʒɔɪntʃə(r)] *n.* иму́щество, заве́щанное жене́.

joist [dʒɔɪst] *n.* ба́лка.

jok|e [dʒəʊk] *n.* шу́тка; (*story*) анекдо́т; (*witticism*) остро́та; (*laughing-stock*) посме́шище; **it's no ~e** э́то не шу́тка!; **crack, make a ~e** шути́ть, по-; **make a ~e of sth.** оберну́ть (*pf.*) что-н. в шу́тку; свести́ (*pf.*) что-н. к шу́тке; **play a ~e on s.o.** сыгра́ть (*pf.*) шу́тку с кем-н.; подшу́|чивать, -ти́ть над кем-н.; **he couldn't see the ~e** он не по́нял шу́тки; **can't you take a ~e?** вы что, шу́ток не понима́ете?; **it was a standing ~e** э́то бы́ло объе́ктом постоя́нных шу́ток; **dirty ~e** непристо́йная/неприли́чная шу́тка; **practical ~e** ро́зыгрыш; **the ~e was on him** э́то он в дурака́х оста́лся.

v.i. шути́ть, по-; **I was only ~ing** я всего́ лишь пошути́л; **~ing apart** шу́тки в сто́рону; кро́ме шу́ток.

joker [ˈdʒəʊkə(r)] *n.* (*one who jokes*) шутни́к; (*coll., fellow*) па́рень (*m.*); (*cards*) джо́кер.

jollification [ˌdʒɒlɪfɪˈkeɪʃ(ə)n] *n.* увеселе́ние.

jollity [ˈdʒɒlɪtɪ] *n.* весе́лье, увеселе́ние.

jolly [ˈdʒɒlɪ] *adj.* (*cheerful*) весёлый; (*festive; entertaining*) пра́здничный; (*slightly drunk*) подвы́пивший; (*pred.*) навеселе́; (*coll., pleasant*) прия́тный.

adv. (*coll., very*) о́чень; **~ well** (*coll., definitely*) впрямь; **you'll ~ well have to do it** всё-таки придётся э́то сде́лать; **she is 40 and ~ well looks it** она́ вы́глядит на все свои́ 40 лет.

v.t.: **~ s.o. along**ума́сл|ивать, -ить кого́-н.

cpd. **~-boat** *n.* четвёрка; судова́я шлю́пка.

jolt [dʒəʊlt, dʒɒlt] *n.* толчо́к; (*fig.*) уда́р, потрясе́ние.

v.t. & i. трясти́(сь) (*impf.*); **we were ~ed about** нас швыря́ло во все сто́роны; **the cart ~ed along** теле́гу подбра́сывало; (*fig.*) потряс|а́ть, -ти́; пора|жа́ть, -зи́ть; **it ~ed him out of his routine** э́то вы́било его́ из коле́й.

Jonah [ˈdʒəʊnə] *n.* Ио́на (*m.*); (*fig.*) челове́к, принося́щий несча́стье.

Jonathan [ˈdʒɒnəθ(ə)n] *n.* Ионафа́н.

jonquil [ˈdʒɒnkwɪl] *n.* жонки́лия.

Jordan [ˈdʒɔːd(ə)n] *n.* (*river*) Иорда́н; (*country*) Иорда́ния.

Jordanian [dʒɔːˈdeɪnɪən] *n.* иорда́н|ец (*fem.* -ка).

adj. иорда́нский.

jorum [ˈdʒɔːrəm] *n.* ча́ша.

Joseph [ˈdʒəʊzɪf] *n.* Ио́сиф.

josh [dʒɒʃ] (*US sl.*) *n.* до́брая шу́тка, мистифика́ция, ро́зыгрыш.

v.t. разы́грывать (*impf.*); подшу́|чивать, -ти́ть над+*i.*

Joshua [ˈdʒɒʃwə] *n.* (*bibl.*) Иису́с (Нави́н).

joss-stick [dʒɒs] *n.* паху́чая па́лочка.

jostle [ˈdʒɒs(ə)l] *v.t.* толк|а́ть, -ну́ть; отт|ира́ть, -ере́ть; **I was ~d from every side** меня́ толка́ли со всех сторо́н.

v.i. толка́ться (*impf.*); **he ~d against me** он оттира́л меня́.

jot[1] [dʒɒt] *n.* (*small amount*) йо́та; **he was not one ~ the worse for it** э́то ему́ ничу́ть не повреди́ло.

jot[2] [dʒɒt] *v.t.*: **~ down** набр|а́сывать, -оса́ть; кра́тко запи́с|ывать, -а́ть.

jotter [ˈdʒɒtə(r)] *n.* (*pad*) блокно́т.

jottings [ˈdʒɒtɪŋz] *n.* за́писи (*f. pl.*).

joule [dʒuːl] *n.* джо́уль (*m.*).

journal [ˈdʒɜːn(ə)l] *n.* (*newspaper*) газе́та; (*periodical*) журна́л; (*ship's log*) (судово́й) журна́л; (*bookkeeping*) журна́л.

journalese [ˌdʒɜːnəˈliːz] *n.* газе́тный штамп.

journalism [ˈdʒɜːnəˌlɪz(ə)m] *n.* журнали́стика.

journalist [ˈdʒɜːnəlɪst] *n.* журнали́ст.

journalistic [ˌdʒɜːnəˈlɪstɪk] *adj.* журнали́стский.

journey [ˈdʒɜːnɪ] *n.* (*expedition; trip*) путеше́ствие, пое́здка; рейс; **(under)take a ~** предприн|има́ть, -я́ть (*or* соверш|а́ть, -и́ть) путеше́ствие; **break one's ~** прер|ыва́ть, -ва́ть пое́здку; **be, go on a ~** путеше́ствовать (*impf.*); **he did the ~ on foot** он соверши́л путеше́ствие пешко́м; **he reached his ~'s end** он дости́г конца́ пути́; он про́жил жизнь; **the bus makes 6 ~s a day** авто́бус соверша́ет шесть ре́йсов в день; (*travel; travelling time*): **on the return ~** на обра́тном пути́; **will there be any refreshments on the ~?** бу́дут ли в пути́ дава́ть лёгкие заку́ски?; **London is 6 hours' ~ from here** отсю́да до Ло́ндона шесть часо́в езды́; **it was a wasted ~** путеше́ствие бы́ло напра́сным.

v.i. путеше́ствовать (*impf.*).

cpd. **~man** *n.* (*hired worker*) наёмный рабо́чий/рабо́тник.

joust [dʒaʊst] *n.* (ры́царский) турни́р.

v.i. состяза́ться (*impf.*) на турни́ре.

Jove [dʒəʊv] *n.* Юпи́тер; **by ~!** вот те на́!; ну и дела́!

jovial [ˈdʒəʊvɪəl] *adj.* (*merry*) весёлый; (*convivial*) общи́тельный.

joviality [ˌdʒəʊvɪˈælɪtɪ] *n.* весёлость; общи́тельность.

jowl [dʒaʊl] *n.* (*jaw*) че́люсть; (*dewlap*) подгру́док; (*chin*): **a heavy ~** тяжёлый подборо́док.

joy [dʒɔɪ] *n.* **1.** (*gladness*) ра́дость; (*pleasure*) удово́льствие; **jump for ~** скака́ть (*impf.*) от ра́дости; **one of the ~s of life** одна́ из ра́достей жи́зни; **life was no ~** жизнь была́ не в ра́дость; **I wish you ~ of it** (*iron.*) с чем и поздравля́ю. **2.** (*coll., success, response*): **I kept 'phoning but got no ~** я звони́л-звони́л, но никако́го то́лку.

cpds. **~-bells** *n. pl.* пра́здничный звон; **~ride** *n.* пое́здка ра́ди заба́вы на чужо́й автомаши́не (без разреше́ния); **~rider** *n.* автово́р-лиха́ч; **~stick** *n.* (*aeron., sl.*) рыча́г/ру́чка управле́ния; (*comput.*) джо́йстик.

joyful [ˈdʒɔɪfʊl] *adj.* ра́достный, счастли́вый.

joyfulness [ˈdʒɔɪfʊlnɪs] *n.* ра́дость.

joyless [ˈdʒɔɪlɪs] *adj.* безра́достный.

joylessness [ˈdʒɔɪlɪsnɪs] *n.* безра́достность.

joyous [ˈdʒɔɪəs] *adj.* ра́достный; (*happy*) весёлый.

JP (*abbr. of* **Justice of the Peace**) мирово́й судья́.

jubilant [ˈdʒuːbɪlənt] *adj.* лику́ющий; **be ~** ликова́ть (*impf.*).

jubilation [ˌdʒuːbɪˈleɪʃ(ə)n] *n.* ликова́ние.

jubilee [ˈdʒuːbɪˌliː] *n.* **1.** (*anniversary*) юбиле́й; **golden/silver ~** пятидесятиле́тний/двадцатипятиле́тний юбиле́й; (*attr.*) юбиле́йный. **2.** (*rejoicing*) пра́зднество.

Judaic [dʒuːˈdeɪɪk] *adj.* иуде́йский.

Judaism [ˈdʒuːdeɪˌɪz(ə)m] *n.* иуда́изм.

Judas [ˈdʒuːdəs] *n.* (*bibl.*) Иу́да (*m.*); (*fig.*) преда́тель (*m.*).

cpd. **~-tree** *n.* багря́нник; иу́дино де́рево.

judder [ˈdʒʌdə(r)] *v.i.* вибри́ровать (*impf.*) с гро́хотом.

judge [dʒʌdʒ] *n.* **1.** (*legal functionary*) судья́ (*m.*); **J~ Advocate** вое́нный прокуро́р; **(book of) J~s** (*bibl.*) Кни́га Суде́й (Изра́илевых). **2.** (*arbiter*) арби́тр; **let me be the ~ of that** оста́вьте мне суди́ть об э́том; **the ~s** (*of a contest*) жюри́ (*nt. indecl.*); **he is one of the ~s** он в соста́ве жюри́; он вхо́дит в соста́в суде́йской колле́гии. **3.** (*expert, connoisseur*) экспе́рт, знато́к; **a ~ of wines** знато́к вин; **a ~ of art** цени́тель (*m.*) иску́сства.

v.t. **1.** (*pass ~ment on*) суди́ть (*impf.*) о+*i.*; **don't ~ him by appearances!** не суди́те о нём по вне́шности!; **who ~d the race?** кто суди́л на э́том состяза́нии?; (*assess*) оце́н|ивать, -и́ть. **2.** (*consider*) счита́ть (*impf.*); **he was ~d to be innocent** его́ сочли́ невино́вным; **I ~d it better to keep quiet** я счёл за лу́чшее промолча́ть; (*suppose*) полага́ть (*impf.*); **I ~d him to be about 50** я полага́л, что ему́ о́коло пятидесяти. **3.** (*hear and try*): **the case was ~d in secret** де́ло слу́шалось в закры́том суде́.

v.i. **1.** (*make an appraisal or decision*) суди́ть (*impf.*); **to ~ from what you say** су́дя по тому́, что вы сказа́ли. **2.**

(*act as* ~; *arbitrate*) быть арби́тром, суди́ть (*impf.*).

judg(e)ment [ˈdʒʌdʒmənt] *n.* **1.** (*sentence*) пригово́р; **pass ~ (on)** выноси́ть, вы́нести пригово́р +*d.*; суди́ть (*impf.*) о+*p.*; **a reserved ~** отсро́ченное реше́ние; **the ~ was in his favour** реше́ние суда́ бы́ло в его́ по́льзу; **it was a ~ on him** э́то бы́ло ему́ наказа́нием; **a ~ on sin** ка́ра за грех; (*act or process of judging*): **sit in ~** (*fig.*) суди́ть (*impf.*) други́х свысока́; **J~ Day** Су́дный день; **the Last J~** Стра́шный суд. **2.** (*opinion*; *estimation*) мне́ние; сужде́ние; **in my ~** по моему́ мне́нию; **private ~** ча́стное мне́ние; **a hasty ~** опроме́тчивое сужде́ние; **against one's better ~** вопреки́ го́лосу ра́зума; **an error of ~** оши́бка в сужде́нии; **I reserve ~ about that** я (пока́) воздержу́сь от сужде́ния по э́тому по́воду. **3.** (*criticism*) осужде́ние. **4.** (*discernment*) рассуди́тельность; **he shows good ~** он здра́во су́дит.

cpd. **~-seat** *n.* суде́йское ме́сто; (*tribunal*) суд.

judgeship [ˈdʒʌdʒʃɪp] *n.* суде́йская до́лжность.

judicature [ˈdʒuːdɪkətʃə(r), -ˈdɪkətʃə(r)] *n.* судоустро́йство; систе́ма суде́йских о́рганов; **Supreme Court of J~** Верхо́вный суд; (*judge's office*) суде́йская до́лжность; (*judge's term of office*) срок пребыва́ния на до́лжности судьи́.

judicial [dʒuːˈdɪʃ(ə)l] *adj.* **1.** суде́бный; **~ proceedings** суде́бный проце́сс; **~ murder** узако́ненное уби́йство. **2.** (*critical*; *impartial*) рассуди́тельный; беспристра́стный.

judiciary [dʒuːˈdɪʃɪərɪ] *n.* су́дьи (*m. pl.*).

judicious [dʒuːˈdɪʃəs] *adj.* здравомы́слящий, рассуди́тельный.

judiciousness [dʒuːˈdɪʃəsnɪs] *n.* рассуди́тельность.

judo [ˈdʒuːdəʊ] *n.* дзюдо́ (*indecl.*).

judoist [ˈdʒuːdəʊɪst] *n.* дзюдои́ст (*fem.* -ка).

jug [dʒʌg] *n.* (vessel) кувши́н; (*prison*) тюря́га (*sl.*); **be in ~** сиде́ть (*impf.*) за решёткой; **put in ~** посади́ть (*pf.*) за решётку.

jugful [ˈdʒʌgfʊl] *n.* по́лный кувши́н (*чего*).

Juggernaut [ˈdʒʌgəˌnɔːt] *n.* (*relig.*) Джагерна́ут; (*fig.*) безжа́лостная неумоли́мая си́ла; (*lorry*) многото́нный грузови́к.

juggins [ˈdʒʌgɪnz] *n.* (*sl.*) проста́к, глупе́ц.

juggle [ˈdʒʌg(ə)l] *n.* (*sleight of hand*) фо́кус, трюк; (*fraud*) обма́н.

v.t. (*lit.*, *fig.*, *manipulate*) жонгли́ровать (*impf.*) +*i.*; (*defraud*): **~ s.o. out of sth.** вы́манить (*pf.*) что-н. у кого́-н.

v.i. (*lit.*, *fig.*) жонгли́ровать (*impf.*).

juggler [ˈdʒʌglə(r)] *n.* жонглёр.

juggl|ery [ˈdʒʌglərɪ], **-ing** [ˈdʒʌglɪŋ] *nn.* жонгли́рование.

Jugoslav [ˈjuːgəˌslɑːv], **-ia** [juːgəˈslɑːvɪə] = **Yugoslav, -ia**

jugular [ˈdʒʌgjʊlə(r)] *n.* (**~ vein**) яре́мная ве́на.

adj. ше́йный.

juice [dʒuːs] *n.* **1.** (*bot.*, *physiol.*) сок; (*fruit ~*) фрукто́вый сок; **stew in one's own ~** (*coll.*) вари́ться (*impf.*) в со́бственном соку́. **2.** (*sl.*, *petrol*) бензи́н. **3.** (*sl.*, *elec. current*) (электри́ческий) ток.

juicer [ˈdʒuːsə(r)] *n.* соковыжима́лка.

juiciness [ˈdʒuːsɪnɪs] *n.* со́чность.

juicy [ˈdʒuːsɪ] *adj.* со́чный; (*coll.*, *racy*, *scandalous*) сма́чный.

ju-jitsu [dʒuːˈdʒɪtsuː] *n.* джи́у-джи́тсу (*nt. indecl.*).

ju-ju [ˈdʒuːdʒuː] *n.* (*fetish*) амуле́т; (*magic*) колдовство́.

jujube [ˈdʒuːdʒuːb] *n.* (*lozenge*) ююба.

juke-box [ˈdʒuːkbɒks] *n.* автома́т-прои́грыватель (*m.*).

julep [ˈdʒuːlep] *n.*: **mint ~** (*US*) мя́тный напи́ток из ви́ски со льдом.

Julian [ˈdʒuːlɪən] *adj.* юлиа́нский.

July [dʒuːˈlaɪ] *n.* ию́ль (*m.*); (*attr.*) ию́льский.

jumble [ˈdʒʌmb(ə)l] *n.* (*untidy heap*) беспоря́дочная ку́ча; (*disorder*, *muddle*) беспоря́док, пу́таница; (*coll.*, *unwanted articles*) хлам; **~ sale** дешёвая распрода́жа (на благотвори́тельном база́ре).

v.t. (*also* **~ up**) переме́ш|ивать, -а́ть.

jumbo [ˈdʒʌmbəʊ] *n.* (*coll.*, *elephant*) слон; (*attr.*, *very large*) гига́нтский; большу́щий; **~ jet** реакти́вный ла́йнер.

jump [dʒʌmp] *n.* прыжо́к, скачо́к; **long/high ~** прыжо́к в длину́/высоту́; **he's for the high ~** (*sc. hanging*) по нему́ ви́селица пла́чет; **take a running ~** (*lit.*) пры́г|ать, -нуть с разбе́га; (*fig.*, *coll.*): **I told him to take a running ~** я веле́л ему́ прова́ливать; (*obstacle in steeplechase*) препя́тствие; **water ~** ров с водо́й; (*fig.*, *abrupt rise*): **there was a big ~ in the temperature** температу́ра си́льно подскочи́ла; (*fig.*, *start*, *shock*) вздра́гивание; **you gave me a ~** вы меня́ напуга́ли.

v.t. **1.** (**~ over, across**) перепры́г|ивать, -нуть че́рез+*a.* **2.** (*cause to ~*): **he ~ed his horse at the fence** он посла́л свою́ ло́шадь че́рез забо́р. **3.** (*var. fig. uses*): **~ bail** нару́шить (*pf.*) усло́вия освобожде́ния под зало́г; **~ the gun** (*coll.*) нача́ть (*pf.*) ска́чки до сигна́ла; нача́ть что-н. до поло́женного вре́мени; **~ the queue** пройти́ (*pf.*) без о́череди; **the train ~ed the rails** по́езд сошёл с ре́льсов; **~ ship** бежа́ть, с- с корабля́ до истече́ния сро́ка слу́жбы; дезерти́ровать (*impf.*, *pf.*) с су́дна; **you've ~ed a few lines** вы пропусти́ли (*or* перескочи́ли че́рез) не́сколько строк.

v.i. **1.** пры́г|ать, -нуть; (*on horseback*) вск|а́кивать, -очи́ть; (*with parachute*) пры́г|ать, -нуть с парашю́том. **2.** (*fig.*): **he ~ed from one topic to another** он переска́кивал с одно́й те́мы на другу́ю. **3.** (*start*): **the noise made me ~** звук заста́вил меня́ вздро́гнуть. **4.** (*make sudden movement*): **shares ~ed to a new level** а́кции подскочи́ли. **5.** (*fig. uses*): **I would ~ at the chance** я бы ухвати́лся за э́ту возмо́жность; **he ~ed at my offer** он ухвати́лся за моё предложе́ние; **~ for joy** пры́гать/скака́ть (*impf.*) от ра́дости; **~ on s.o.** (*attack*) набро́ситься (*pf.*) на кого́-н.; (*rebuke*) ре́зко осади́ть (*pf.*) кого́-н.; **~ to conclusions** де́лать (*impf.*) поспе́шные вы́воды; **~ to it!** потора́пливайтесь!; **he ~ed to his feet** он вскочи́л на́ ноги.

with advs.: **they ~ed about to keep warm** они́ пры́гали, что́бы согре́ться; **he ~ed back in surprise** он отпря́нул в удивле́нии; **she ~ed down from the fence** она́ соскочи́ла с забо́ра; **he took off his clothes and ~ed in** он разде́лся и пры́гнул в во́ду; **if you want a lift, ~ in!** е́сли хоти́те, что́бы я вас подбро́сил, залеза́йте в маши́ну!; **don't ~ off before the bus stops!** не спры́гивайте на ходу́ (*or* до по́лной остано́вки авто́буса); **~ing-off point** (*fig.*) отправна́я то́чка; **as the train began to move I ~ed on** я впры́гнул в по́езд, когда́ он уже́ тро́нулся; **~ up from one's chair** вск|а́кивать, -очи́ть со сту́ла; **~ up and down** пры́гать/подпры́гивать (*impf.*) вверх и вниз; **~ed-up** *adj.* (*coll.*): **a ~ed-up person** вы́скочка (*c.g.*).

cpds. **~-jet** *n.* реакти́вный самолёт вертика́льного взлёта; **~-off** *n.* (*to decide tie*) дополни́тельный круг на бега́х с препя́тствиями (*при одинаковых результатах*); **~-seat** *n.* откидно́е сиде́нье; **~-suit** *n.* комбинезо́н.

jumper [ˈdʒʌmpə(r)] *n.* (*athlete*; *horse*) прыгу́н, скаку́н; (*garment*) дже́мпер; (*US*, *pinafore dress*) сарафа́н; (*sailor's*) фо́рменка.

jumpy [ˈdʒʌmpɪ] *adj.* не́рвный, дёрганый.

junction [ˈdʒʌŋkʃ(ə)n] *n.* **1.** (*joining*) соедине́ние. **2.** (*meeting point*: *of railways*) у́зел; узлово́й пункт; (*of roads*) скреще́ние (доро́г), перекрёсток; (*of rivers*) слия́ние. **3.** (*elec.*): **~ box** соедини́тельная му́фта.

juncture [ˈdʒʌŋktʃə(r)] *n.* (*joining*) соедине́ние; (*concurrence of events*) стече́ние обстоя́тельств; **at a critical ~** в крити́ческий моме́нт; **at this ~** в э́тот моме́нт, сейча́с.

June [dʒuːn] *n.* ию́нь (*m.*); (*attr.*) ию́ньский.

Jungian [ˈjʊŋɪən] *adj.* юнгиа́нский.

jungle [ˈdʒʌŋg(ə)l] *n.* джу́нгл|и (*pl.*, *g.* -ей); **the law of the ~** зако́н джу́нглей; **~ warfare** боевы́е де́йствия в джу́нглях.

junior [ˈdʒuːnɪə(r)] *n.* & *adj.* мла́дший; **John Jones ~** Джон Джонс мла́дший; **he is 6 years my ~** он моло́же меня́ на шесть лет; (*coll.*): **and what will J~ have to drink?** а что бу́дет пить молодо́й челове́к?; **~ partner** мла́дший партнёр; **~ school** нача́льная шко́ла; **~ common-room** студе́нческая ко́мната о́тдыха; **in his ~ year** (*US*) на предпосле́днем ку́рсе.

juniper [ˈdʒuːnɪpə(r)] *n.* можжеве́льник; (*attr.*) можжевёловый.

junk[1] [dʒʌŋk] *n.* (*rubbish*) ру́хлядь, хлам, ути́ль (*m.*); **~ food** неполноце́нная пи́ща.

v.t. (*sl.*, *discard*) вы́бросить (*pl.*) в ути́ль.

cpds. **~-heap** *n.*: **it is only fit for the ~-heap** э́то пора́ сдать в ути́ль; **~-shop** *n.* ла́вка старьёвщика.

junk[2] [dʒʌŋk] *n.* (*sailing vessel*) джóнка.
Junker ['jʊŋkə(r)] *n.* ю́нкер.
junket ['dʒʌŋkɪt] *n.* **1.** (*dish*) сла́дкий творо́г со сли́вками. **2.** (*also* ~**ing**) пиру́шка. **3.** (*US*, *outing*) пикни́к. **4.** (*US*, *free trip*) увесели́тельная пое́здка на казённый счёт *и т.п.*
junk|ie, -y ['dʒʌŋkɪ] *n.* (*sl.*, *drug addict*) наркома́н.
Juno ['dʒu:nəʊ] *n.* Юно́на.
Junoesque [ˌdʒu:nəʊ'esk] *adj.* подо́бный Юно́не.
junta ['dʒʌntə] *n.* (*also* **junto**) ху́нта, кли́ка.
Jupiter ['dʒu:pɪtə(r)] *n.* (*myth.*, *astron.*) Юпи́тер.
Jurassic [dʒʊə'ræsɪk] *n.* **(~ period)** ю́рский пери́од; ю́ра.
adj. ю́рский.
juridical [dʒʊə'rɪdɪk(ə)l] *adj.* юриди́ческий.
jurisconsult [ˌdʒʊərɪskən'sʌlt] *n.* юриско́нсульт.
jurisdiction [ˌdʒʊərɪs'dɪkʃ(ə)n] *n.* (*legal authority*) юрисди́кция; **have ~ over** име́ть (*impf.*) юрисди́кцию над+*i.*; **it does not lie within my ~** э́то не вхо́дит в мою́ компете́нцию.
jurisprudence [ˌdʒʊərɪs'pru:d(ə)ns] *n.* юриспруде́нция.
jurist ['dʒʊərɪst] *n.* юри́ст.
juristic [ˌdʒʊə'rɪstɪk] *adj.* юриди́ческий.
juror ['dʒʊərə(r)] *n.* член жюри́, прися́жный (заседа́тель).
jury ['dʒʊərɪ] *n.* жюри́ (*nt. indecl.*); прися́жные (заседа́тели) (*m. pl.*); **grand ~** (*US hist.*) большо́е жюри́.
cpds. **~-box** *n.* скамья́ прися́жных; **~man** *n.* прися́жный; **~woman** *n.* же́нщина-прися́жный заседа́тель.
jussive ['dʒʌsɪv] *adj.* (*gram.*) повели́тельный.
just [dʒʌst] *adj.* (*equitable*) справедли́вый; **act ~ly to(wards) s.o.** быть справедли́вым по отноше́нию к кому́-н.; (*deserved*) заслу́женный; **receive one's ~ deserts** получи́ть (*pf.*) по заслу́гам; (*well-grounded*) обосно́ванный, справедли́вый; (*proper, correct*) ве́рный; **he gave a ~ account** он дал то́чный отчёт.
adv. то́чно, как раз; **it was ~ 3 o'clock** бы́ло ро́вно три часа́; **~ then** как раз тогда́; в ту мину́ту; **that's ~ the trouble** в то́м-то и беда́; **~ how did you do it?** как (же) и́менно вам удало́сь э́то сде́лать?; **~ like, as** (*expr. comparison*) так же как (и); то́чно как; **that's ~ like him** (*typical*) э́то так похо́же на него́; **that's ~ like me** э́то вы́литый я!; **that's ~ it** вот и́менно; **that's ~ the point** в то́м-то и де́ло; **~ the thing** и́менно то, что на́до; **the hat is ~ my size** шля́па мне в са́мую по́ру; **~ so** то́чно/и́менно так; (*exactly arranged*) тю́телька в тю́тельку; **~ so** (*you are quite right*) так то́чно; **he is ~ as lazy as ever** он всё тако́й же лени́вый; **~ as much** сто́лько же; **I'd ~ as soon stay at home** я предпочёл бы оста́ться до́ма; **it's ~ as well I warned you** хорошо́, что я вас предупреди́л; **thank you ~ the same** спаси́бо и на э́том. **3.: ~ about** (*approximately*): **~ about right** почти́ пра́вильно; (*almost*): **I've ~ about finished** я почти́ ко́нчил. **4.** (*expr. time*) то́лько что; (*very recently*): **I saw him ~ now** я то́лько что ви́дел его́; **as you were ~ saying** как вы то́лько что сказа́ли; **~ as** (*expr. time*) (как) то́лько; **~ as he entered the room** то́лько он вошёл в ко́мнату; (*at this moment*): **I'm ~ off** я ухожу́ сию́ мину́ту; **the show is ~ beginning** представле́ние как раз начина́ется. **5.** (*barely, no more than*) едва́; **I ~ caught the train** я едва́ успе́л на по́езд; **he had ~ come in when the 'phone rang** едва́ он вошёл, (как) зазвони́л телефо́н; **he is (only) ~ beginning to speak Russian** он едва́ (*or* то́лько-то́лько) начина́ет говори́ть по-ру́сски; **I've got ~ enough for my fare** у меня́ де́нег то́лько-то́лько хва́тит на биле́т; **(wait) ~ a minute!** (одну́) мину́т(к)у! **6.** (*merely, simply*) то́лько; **~ listen to this!** вы то́лько послу́шайте!; **I went ~ to hear him** я пошёл, то́лько что́бы послу́шать его́; **it's ~ that I don't like him** де́ло про́сто в том, что он мне неприя́тен; **~ fancy!** поду́мать то́лько!; (то́лько) предста́вьте себе́!; **~ you wait!** ну, погоди́!; **~ for fun** шу́тки ра́ди; **~ in case** на вся́кий слу́чай. **7.** (*positively, absolutely*) так и; про́сто(-на́просто); **the coffee ~ would not boil** ко́фе ника́к не закипа́л; **it's ~ splendid!** э́то про́сто великоле́пно!; **don't I ~!** ещё бы!; **not ~ yet** ещё не/нет.
justice ['dʒʌstɪs] *n.* **1.** (*fairness; equity*) справедли́вость; **do ~ to** отд|ава́ть, -а́ть до́лжное +*d.*; **you are not doing yourself ~** вы не проявля́ете себя́ в по́лную си́лу; **to do him ~** к че́сти его́ сказа́ть; **with ~** со всей справедли́востью. **2.** (*system of institutions*) юсти́ция; (*judicial proceedings*) правосу́дие; **administer ~** отправля́ть (*impf.*) правосу́дие; **bring s.o. to ~** отд|ава́ть, -а́ть кого́-н. под суд; привл|ека́ть, -е́чь кого́-н. к суде́бной отве́тственности; **Court of J~** суд. **3.** (*magistrate; judge*) судья́ (*m.*); **J~ of the Peace** мирово́й судья́.
justiciable [dʒʌ'stɪʃəb(ə)l] *adj.* подлежа́щий юрисди́кции.
justiciary [dʒʌ'stɪʃjərɪ] *n.* суде́йский чино́вник.
adj. суде́йский.
justifiable ['dʒʌstɪˌfaɪəb(ə)l] *adj.* опра́вданный; **~ homicide** уби́йство в це́лях самозащи́ты *и т.п.*
justification [ˌdʒʌstɪfɪ'keɪʃ(ə)n] *n.* **1.** оправда́ние; **he objected, and with ~** он возрази́л и не без основа́ний; **it was said in ~** э́то бы́ло ска́зано в оправда́ние. **2.** (*typ.*) вы́ключка строки́.
justificatory ['dʒʌstɪfɪˌkeɪtərɪ] *adj.* оправда́тельный.
justif|y ['dʒʌstɪˌfaɪ] *v.t.* **1.** (*establish rightness of*) опра́вд|ывать, -а́ть; **I was ~ied in suspecting ...** я име́л все основа́ния подозрева́ть...; **~y o.s. (*or* one's actions, conduct)** опра́вд|ываться, -а́ться. **2.** (*typ.*) выключа́ть, вы́ключить (*строку*).
jut [dʒʌt] *v.i.* (*usu.* **~ out**) выступа́ть (*impf.*); выдава́ться (*impf.*).
jute[1] [dʒu:t] *n.* джут.
Jute[2] [dʒu:t] *n.* ют.
Jutish ['dʒu:tɪʃ] *adj.* ю́тский.
juvenile ['dʒu:vəˌnaɪl] *n.* подро́сток (*fem.* де́вочка-подро́сток).
adj. ю́ный, ю́ношеский; **~ delinquent** малоле́тний престу́пник; **~ delinquency** де́тская престу́пность; **~ books** кни́ги для ю́ношества; **~ court** суд по дела́м несовершеннолетних.
juvenilia [ˌdʒu:və'nɪlɪə] *n.* ю́ношеские произведе́ния.
juxtapose [ˌdʒʌkstə'pəʊz] *v.t.* поме|ща́ть, -сти́ть бок о́ бок; (*for comparison*) сопост|авля́ть, -а́вить (*кого с кем or что с чем*).
juxtaposition [ˌdʒʌkstəpə'zɪʃ(ə)n] *n.* сосе́дство, бли́зость; (*for comparison*) сопоставле́ние.

K

K *abbr. of* **1.** ***Kelvin(s)*** °K, (по Ке́львину). **2. kilobyte** килоба́йт. **3. £1,000** ты́сяча фу́нтов, ко́сая (*sl.*); **he earns 35K a year** он зараба́тывает 35 косы́х в год.
k (*abbr. of* **kilometre(s)**) км, (киломе́тр).
Kabul [kə'bʊl, 'kɑ:bʊl] *n.* Кабу́л.
Kaf(f)ir ['kæfə(r)] *n.* (*pers.*) кафр; (*language*) ка́фрский язы́к; **k~ corn** со́рго ка́фрское.
kaftan ['kæftæn] = **caftan**
Kaiser ['kaɪzə(r)] *n.* ка́йзер.
kale [keɪl] *n.* листова́я капу́ста.
kaleidoscope [kə'laɪdəˌskəʊp] *n.* (*lit.*, *fig.*) калейдоско́п.
kaleidoscopic [kəˌlaɪdə'skɒpɪk] *adj.* калейдоскопи́ческий.
kalends ['kælendz] = **calends**
Kalmuck ['kælmʌk] *n.* (*pers.*) калмы́|к (*fem.* -чка); (*language*) калмы́кский язы́к.
adj. калмы́цкий.
kamikaze [ˌkæmɪ'kɑ:zɪ] *n.* (*pilot*) камика́дзе (*m. indecl.*), лётчик-сме́ртник.
Kampuchea [ˌkæmpʊ'tʃɪə] *n.* Кампучи́я.
Kampuchean [ˌkæmpʊ'tʃɪən] *n.* кампучи́|ец (*fem.* -йка).
adj. кампучи́йский.

kangaroo [ˌkæŋgəˈruː] *n.* кенгуру́ (*m. indecl.*); ~ **court** незако́нное суде́бное разбира́тельство.
Kantian [ˈkæntɪən] *adj.* кантиа́нский.
kaolin [ˈkeɪəlɪn] *n.* каоли́н.
kapellmeister [kəˈpelˌmaɪstə(r)] *n.* капельме́йстер, дирижёр.
kapok [ˈkeɪpɒk] *n.* капо́к.
Karachi [kəˈrɑːtʃɪ] *n.* Кара́чи (*m. indecl.*).
karakul [ˈkærəˌkʊl] = **carakul**
Kara Sea [ˈkɑːrə] *n.* Ка́рское мо́ре.
karat [ˈkærət] (*US*) = **carat**
karate [kəˈrɑːtɪ] *n.* карате́ (*nt. indecl.*).
karateka [kəˈrɑːtɪˌkæ] *n.* карате́ка, карати́ст.
Karelia [kəˈriːlɪə] *n.* Каре́лия.
Karelian [kəˈriːlɪən] *n.* каре́л (*fem.* -ка).
adj. каре́льский.
karst [kɑːst] *n.* карст; (*attr.*) ка́рстовый.
Kashmir [kæʃˈmɪə(r)] *n.* Кашми́р.
Kashmiri [kæʃˈmɪərɪ] *n.* (*pers.*) кашми́р|ец (*fem.* -ка); (*language*) кашми́рский язы́к.
kayak [ˈkaɪæk] *n.* кая́к.
Kazakh [kəˈzɑːk, kɑː-] *n.* (*pers.*) каза́|х (*fem.* -шка); (*language*) каза́хский язы́к.
Kazakhstan [ˌkɑːzɑːkˈstæn, -ˈstɑːn] *n.* Казахста́н.
Kazan [kəˈzæn, -ˈzɑːn] *n.* Каза́нь.
kebab [kɪˈbæb] *n.* кеба́б, шашлы́к; ~ **house** кеба́бная, шашлы́чная.
keel [kiːl] *n.* (*of ship*) киль (*m.*); **false** ~ фальшки́ль (*m.*); **on an even** ~ не кача́ясь; (*fig.*) усто́йчивый, стаби́льный.
v.t. (*impf.*) перев|ора́чивать, -ерну́ть ки́лем вверх; килева́ть (*impf.*, *pf.*).
v.i.: ~ **over** опроки́|дываться, -нуться.
cpds. ~**-block** *n.* кильбло́к; ~**-haul** *v.t.* прота́скивать (*impf.*) под ки́лем; (*fig.*, *reprimand*) пропесо́чи|вать, -ть (*coll.*).
keen[1] [kiːn] *n.* (*lament*) причита́ние/плач по поко́йнику.
v.i. голоси́ть (*impf.*).
keen[2] [kiːn] *adj.* (*lit.*, *fig.*: *sharp*, *acute*) о́стрый; ~ **eyesight** о́строе зре́ние; **a** ~ **intellect** о́стрый/проница́тельный ум; (*piercing*) пронзи́тельный; **a** ~ **glance** пронзи́тельный/о́стрый взгляд; **a** ~ **wind** ре́зкий/прони́зывающий ве́тер; ~ **frost** си́льный моро́з; (*strong*, *intense*) си́льный; ~ **desire** си́льное/о́строе жела́ние; ~ **interest** живо́й интере́с; (*eager*; *energetic*) ре́вностный; энерги́чный; **a** ~ **businessman** энерги́чный деле́ц; **a** ~ **pupil** усе́рдный/приле́жный учени́к; ~ **competition** тру́дное соревнова́ние; ожесточённая конкуре́нция; **a** ~ **demand for sth.** большо́й спрос на что-н.; (*enthusiastic*) стра́стный; **a** ~ **sportsman** стра́стный спортсме́н; энтузиа́ст/люби́тель (*m.*) спо́рта; **be** ~ **on** си́льно/стра́стно увл|ека́ться, -е́чься +*i.*; **I am not** ~ **on chess** я не осо́бенно увлека́юсь ша́хматами; **he is** ~ **on your coming** ему́ о́чень хо́чется, что́бы вы пришли́; **they are** ~ **on getting (***or* **to get) the work done** они́ стремя́тся око́нчить де́ло; им не те́рпится зако́нчить рабо́ту.
keenness [ˈkiːnnɪs] *n.* (*sharpness*) острота́; (*of cold etc.*) си́ла, интенси́вность; (*eagerness*, *enthusiasm*) усе́рдие; энтузиа́зм.
keep[1] [kiːp] *n.* (*tower*) гла́вная ба́шня (за́мка).
keep[2] [kiːp] *n.* **1.** (*maintenance*) содержа́ние. **2.** (*sustenance*) прокóрм, пропита́ние; **earn one's** ~ зараб|а́тывать, -о́тать себе́ на пропита́ние; **he's not worth his** ~ от него́ про́ку ма́ло; (*fodder*) фура́ж, корм. **3.: for** ~**s** насовсе́м (*coll.*).
v.t. **1.** (*retain possession of*) держа́ть (*impf.*), не отдава́ть (*impf.*); ост|авля́ть, -а́вить (себе́ *or* при себе́); ~ **the change!** сда́чи не на́до!; (*preserve*) храни́ть (*impf.*); сохран|я́ть, -и́ть; (*save*, *put by*): **I shall** ~ **this paper to show my mother** я сохраню́ э́ту газе́ту, что́бы показа́ть ма́тери; **I'm** ~**ing this for a rainy day** я берегу́ э́то на чёрный день; **you can't** ~ **milk for more than a day** молоко́ ки́снет в тече́ние су́ток; **he** ~**s all her letters** он храни́т все её пи́сьма; (*hold on to*): **she kept the book a long time** она́ до́лго держа́ла (*or* не возвраща́ла) кни́гу; (*appropriate*) присв|а́ивать, -о́ить себе́; **when I lent you my umbrella I didn't mean you to** ~ **it** одолжи́в вам зо́нтик, я не ду́мал, что вы его́ присво́ите. **2.** (*cause to remain*): **the traffic kept me awake** у́личное движе́ние не дава́ло мне спать; **the garden** ~**s me busy** сад не даёт мне сиде́ть сложа́ ру́ки; **this will** ~ **him quiet for a bit** всё э́то отвлечёт его́ немно́жко; ~ **sth. safe** храни́ть (*impf.*) что-н. в безопа́сности; ~ **it dark!** об э́том никому́ ни сло́ва!; ~ **o.s. alive** подде́рживать (*impf.*) свою́ жизнь (*чем*); ~ **hope alive** подде́рж|ивать, -а́ть наде́жду; ~ **an issue alive** не да|ва́ть, -ть вопро́су заглóхнуть; ~ **the house clean** содержа́ть (*impf.*) дом в чистоте́/поря́дке; ~ **one's hands clean** держа́ть ру́ки чи́стыми; (*fig.*) не мара́ть (*impf.*) рук; ~ **your mouth shut!** держи́те язы́к за зуба́ми!; **I want the door kept open** я хочу́, что́бы дверь остава́лась откры́той; **I'm** ~**ing my ears open** я держу́ у́шки на маку́шке; ~ **s.o. supplied** снабжа́ть (*impf.*) кого́-н.; ~ **the grass cut** регуля́рно стричь (*impf.*) траву́; ~ **s.o. in the dark** держа́ть кого́-н. в неве́дении; ~ **s.o. in suspense** держа́ть кого́-н. в напряжённом ожида́нии; **he kept his hands in his pockets** он держа́л ру́ки в карма́нах; ~ **it to yourself** пома́лкивайте об э́том; ~ **an eye on sth.** пригля́дывать (*impf.*) за чем-н.; ~ **your mind on your work** не отвлека́йтесь от свое́й рабо́ты; ~ **sth. in mind, view** име́ть (*impf.*) что-н. в виду́; ~ **sth. in order** держа́ть что-н. в поря́дке; ~ **s.o. in order** держа́ть кого́-н. в узде́; **where do you** ~ **the salt?** где вы храни́те соль? **3.** (*cause to continue*): **he kept me standing for an hour** он продержа́л меня́ на нога́х це́лый час; **I don't like to be kept waiting** я не люблю́, когда́ меня́ заставля́ют ждать; **they kept him working late** они́ заде́рживали его́ на рабо́те допоздна́; **that will** ~ **you going till lunch-time** тепе́рь вы продержи́тесь до обе́да. **4.** (*remain in*, *on*): ~ **one's seat** (*remain sitting*) не встава́ть (*impf.*); ~ **the saddle** удéрж|иваться, -а́ться в седле́; ~ **one's feet** удержа́ться на нога́х, устоя́ть (*both pf.*); ~ **one's bed** лежа́ть (*impf.*) в посте́ли; (*retain*, *preserve*): ~ **one's balance** сохраня́ть/уде́рживать (*both impf.*) равнове́сие; ~ **one's own counsel** молча́ть (*impf.*); ~ **one's distance** соблю|да́ть, -сти́ расстоя́ние/диста́нцию; **she has kept her figure** она́ сохрани́ла стро́йность; (*for phrr. of the kind* '~ **company**'; '~ **guard**'; '~ **order**'; '~ **time**' *etc. see under nn.*). **5.** (*have charge of*; *manage*, *own*; *rear*, *maintain*) име́ть, держа́ть, содержа́ть (*all impf.*); **who** ~**s the keys?** у кого́ храня́тся ключи́?; **they** ~ **2 cars** у них две маши́ны; **the shop was kept by an Italian** владе́льцем ла́вки был италья́нец; **he wants to** ~ **pigs** он хо́чет держа́ть свине́й; **he** ~**s a mistress in town** он соде́ржит любо́вницу в го́роде; у него́ в го́роде любо́вница; **a kept woman** содержа́нка; **I have a wife and family to** ~ у меня́ на иждиве́нии жена́ и де́ти; **that won't even** ~ **him in cigarettes** э́того ему́ не хва́тит да́же на сигаре́ты; ~ **house** вести́ (*det.*) (дома́шнее) хозя́йство; **he** ~**s open house** у него́ дом откры́т для всех; **a well-kept garden** хорошо́ ухо́женный сад. **6.** (*maintain*, ~ *entries in*) вести́ (*det.*); ~ **books/accounts** вести́ счета́; **do you** ~ **a diary?** ведёте ли вы дневни́к?; **how long have records been kept?** как до́лго вели́сь за́писи?; **are you** ~**ing the score?** вы ведёте счёт? **7.** (*detain*) заде́рж|ивать, -а́ть; **I won't** ~ **you** я вас не задержу́; **there was nothing to** ~ **me there** меня́ там ничто́ не держа́ло; **they kept him in prison** его́ держа́ли в тюрьме́. **8.** (*stock*; *have for sale*): **we don't** ~ **cigarettes** мы не продаём сигаре́ты; **we do not** ~ **such goods** таки́х това́ров мы не де́ржим. **9.** (*defend*, *protect*): ~ **goal** стоя́ть (*impf.*) на воро́тах; защища́ть (*impf.*) воро́та; **God** ~ **you!** да храни́т вас Госпо́дь! **10.** (*observe*; *be faithful to*; *fulfil*) сде́рж|ивать, -а́ть; соблю|да́ть, -сти́; ~ **the law** соблюда́ть зако́н; ~ **one's word** держа́ть, с- сло́во; ~ **faith** сохран|я́ть, -и́ть ве́рность; **he kept the arrangements to the letter** он в то́чности соблюда́л распоряже́ния; **I can't** ~ **the appointment** я не могу́ прийти́ на встре́чу. **11.** (*celebrate*) пра́здновать, от-; отм|еча́ть, -е́тить. **12.** (*guard*, *not divulge*) храни́ть (*impf.*); сохран|я́ть, -и́ть.
v.i. **1.** (*remain*) держа́ться (*impf.*); остава́ться (*impf.*); **the weather kept fine** стоя́ла хоро́шая пого́да; **if it** ~**s fine** е́сли продéржится хоро́шая пого́да; е́сли пого́да не испо́ртится; **I can't** ~ **warm here** я здесь не могу́ согре́ться; ~ **cool** (*fig.*) не теря́ть (*impf.*) головы́: **the**

food will ~ warm in the oven в духо́вке еда́ оста́нется тёплой; **please ~ quiet!** пожа́луйста, не шуми́те!; **how are you ~ing?** как живёте-мо́жете? (*coll.*); **I'm ~ing quite well** (я) на здоро́вье не жа́луюсь; **I exercise to ~ fit** я занима́юсь гимна́стикой/спо́ртом, что́бы быть в фо́рме; **we still ~ in touch** мы всё ещё подде́рживаем отноше́ния/связь; **~ in line** не выходи́ть (*impf.*) из стро́я; **~ in step** шага́ть (*impf.*) в но́гу. **2.** (*continue*) продолжа́ть (*impf.*) +*inf.*; **she ~s giggling** она́ всё хихи́кает; **~ going!** продолжа́йте идти́!; **~ straight on!** иди́те/поезжа́йте пря́мо вперёд! **3.** (*remain fresh*): **the food will ~ in the refrigerator** еда́ в холоди́льнике не испо́ртится; (*fig.*): **my news will ~ till tomorrow** с мои́ми новостя́ми мо́жно подожда́ть до за́втра.

with preps.: (*for phrr. with* **in** *or* **on** *+n. see under v.t.* **2.** *or v.i.* **1.** *or under n.*): **~ after** (*continue to pursue*) продолжа́ть (*impf.*) пого́ню за+*i.*; (*chivvy*) пристава́ть (*impf.*) к+*d.*; **we are ~ing ahead of schedule** мы продолжа́ем опережа́ть гра́фик; **he ~s his pupils at it** он заставля́ет ученико́в труди́ться; **you must ~ at it till it's finished** вы не должны́ отрыва́ться, пока́ не ко́нчите; **I kept at him to start the job** я наста́ивал, что́бы он на́чал рабо́ту; **he kept his hands behind his back** он держа́л ру́ки за спино́й; **he kept behind me all the way** он шёл позади́ меня́ всю доро́гу; **his brothers kept his share from him** его́ бра́тья удержа́ли его́ до́лю; **what are you trying to ~ from me?** что вы скрыва́ете от меня́?; **my umbrella ~s me from getting wet** зо́нтик спаса́ет меня́ от дождя́; **I kept him from hurting himself** я не дал ему́ ушиби́ться; **I could hardly ~ (myself) from laughing** я едва́ удержа́лся от сме́ха; **'~ off the grass!'** «по газо́нам не ходи́ть»; **I have to ~ off sugar** мне на́до избега́ть са́хара; **he can't ~ off (the subject of) politics** он ника́к не мо́жет съе́хать с разгово́ров о поли́тике; **I couldn't ~ my eyes off her ~** я не мог отвести́ от неё глаз; **they tried to ~ me out of the room** они́ пыта́лись не пуска́ть меня́ в ко́мнату; **he kept out of the room** он не входи́л в ко́мнату; **I kept the sweets out of his reach** я держа́л конфе́ты пода́льше от него́; **he kept his gun out of sight** он припря́тал ружьё (с глаз доло́й); **they kept him out of the talks** его́ не допуска́ли к перегово́рам; **~ out of s.o.'s way** (*avoid him*) избега́ть (*impf.*) кого́-н.; (*not hinder him*) не меша́ть (*impf.*) кому́-н.; **I kept out of their quarrel** я не вме́шивался в их ссо́ру; **he cannot ~ out of trouble for long** он ве́чно попада́ет в исто́рии; **I kept him to his promise** я заста́вил его́ вы́полнить обеща́ние; **he kept the news to himself** он ни с кем не дели́лся но́востью; **he ~s his feelings to himself** он скрыва́ет свои́ чу́вства; **he ~s himself to himself** он замыка́ется в себе́; **we must ~ costs to a minimum** мы должны́ свести́ расхо́ды до ми́нимума; **~ to one's bed** остава́ться (*impf.*) в посте́ли; **~ to the path** держа́ться (*impf.*) тропи́нки; **~ to the point** не отклон|я́ться, -и́ться от те́мы; **he ~s to his former opinion** он приде́рживается пре́жнего мне́ния; **he ~s the boys under control** он де́ржит ма́льчиков в узде́; **~ s.o. under observation** следи́ть (*impf.*) за кем-н.

with advs.: **~ away** *v.t.*: **the rain kept people away** дождь отпугну́л наро́д; **she kept her daughter away from school** она́ не пуска́ла дочь в шко́лу; **a spray to ~ flies away** аэрозо́ль (*m.*) для отпу́гивания мух; **we could not ~ him away from books** мы не могли́ удержа́ть его́ от чте́ния; *v.i.*: **he tried to ~ away from them** он стара́лся их избега́ть; **he kept away for fear of ridicule** из стра́ха показа́ться смешны́м он держа́лся в стороне́; **he kept away from spirits** он остерега́лся спиртны́х напи́тков; **~ back** *v.t.* (*restrain*) сде́рж|ивать, -а́ть; **the police could not ~ the crowd back** поли́ция не могла́ сдержа́ть толпу́; (*retain*): **they ~ back £1 from my wages** из моéй зарпла́ты уде́рживают оди́н фунт; (*repress*): **she could hardly ~ back her tears** она́ с трудо́м сде́рживала слёзы; (*conceal*): **he kept back the sad news from her** он скрыва́л от неё печа́льные изве́стия; (*retard*): **illness kept back his development** боле́знь задержа́ла его́ разви́тие; *v.i.* держа́ться (*impf.*) в стороне́; **~ down** *v.t.*: **~ your head down!** не поднима́йте головы́!; (*fig.*, *coll.*) не высо́вывайся!; **~ your voice down!** не повыша́йте го́лоса!; (*limit, control*): **they tried to ~ down expenses** они́ стара́лись ограни́чить расхо́ды; **a mistaken policy was ~ing production down** оши́бочная поли́тика затормáживала произво́дство; **unemployment was kept down** безрабо́тице не дава́ли разраста́ться; **how do you ~ the weeds down?** как вы бо́ретесь с сорняка́ми?; (*oppress*) держа́ть (*impf.*) в подчине́нии; (*suppress*) подав|ля́ть, -и́ть; (*digest*): **he can't ~ anything down** у него́ желу́док ничего́ не принима́ет; *v.i.* (*lie low*) притаи́ться (*pf.*); **~ in** *v.t.* (*confine*): **I ~ the children in when it rains** когда́ идёт дождь, я держу́ дете́й до́ма; **he was kept in after school** его́ оста́вили по́сле уро́ков; (*maintain*): **we ~ the fire in overnight** мы подде́рживаем ого́нь всю ночь; **I practise to ~ my eye, hand in** я трениру́юсь/практику́юсь, что́бы не отвы́кнуть; *v.i.* (*stay indoors*) ост|ава́ться, -а́ться до́ма; **~ in with s.o.** подде́рживать (*impf.*) хоро́шие отноше́ния с кем-н.; **~ off** *v.t.* (*restrain*): **they kept the hounds off till the signal was given** го́нчих не подпуска́ли, пока́ не да́ли сигна́л; (*ward off, repel*): **I kept his blows off with my stick** я отрази́л его́ уда́ры па́лкой; **my hat will ~ the rain off** моя́ шля́па защити́т меня́ от дождя́; *v.i.* (*stay at a distance*): **I hope the rain ~s off** я наде́юсь, что дождь не начнётся; **the crowd kept off till the very end** толпа́ до са́мого конца́ держа́лась в отдале́нии; **~ on** *v.t.* (*continue to wear*): **women ~ their hats on in church** в це́ркви же́нщины не снима́ют шляп; **~ your shirt, hair on!** (*sl.*) споко́йно!; не не́рвничайте!; (*continue to employ, educate*): **they kept the workers on** они́ оста́вили рабо́чих; **they won't ~ you on after 60** они́ уво́лят вас, когда́ вам испо́лнится 60 лет; **I'm ~ing my boy on (at school) for another year** я оставля́ю сы́на в шко́ле ещё на́ год; (*leave in place*): **~ the lid on** не снима́йте кры́шку; *v.i.* (*with pres. part., continue*): **he kept on reading** он продолжа́л чита́ть; **she kept on glancing out of the window** она́ беспреста́нно выгля́дывала из окна́; **he kept on falling** он постоя́нно па́дал; (*continue, persist*): **the rain kept on all day** дождь шёл весь день; **she kept on till the job was finished** она́ рабо́тала, пока́ всё не зако́нчила; (*continue talking*): **he will ~ on about his dogs** он как зала́дит (*coll.*) о соба́ках; (*nag*): **if you ~ on at him, he'll take you to the theatre** е́сли вы не отста́нете от него́, он в конце́ концо́в поведёт вас в теа́тр; **~ out** *v.t.* (*exclude*): **this coat ~s out the cold very well** э́то пальто́ хорошо́ защища́ет от хо́лода; **I drink to ~ out the cold** я пью, что́бы согре́ться; **we put up a fence to ~ out trespassers** мы постро́или/поста́вили забо́р, что́бы посторо́нние не заходи́ли на террито́рию; (*leave in view*): **I kept these papers out to show you** я оста́вил э́ти бума́ги, что́бы показа́ть их вам; *v.i.*: **'Private — ~ out!'** (*notice*) «посторо́нним вход воспрещён/запрещён!»; **~ together** *v.t.*: **this folder will ~ your papers together** в э́ту па́пку вы смо́жете сложи́ть все докуме́нты; **he has hardly enough to ~ body and soul together** он едва́ сво́дит концы́ с конца́ми; **the conductor kept the band together** дирижёр сплоти́л орке́стр; *v.i.*: **the mountaineers kept together for safety** для безопа́сности альпини́сты держа́лись вме́сте; **~ under** *v.t.* держа́ть (*impf.*) в подчине́нии; **~ up** *v.t.* (*prevent from falling or sinking*): **he could not ~ his trousers up** у него́ всё вре́мя сва́ливались брю́ки; **the wall was kept up by a buttress** стена́ держа́лась на подпо́рке; (*fig., sustain, maintain*): **~ up one's spirits** не па́дать (*impf.*) ду́хом; **~ one's strength up** подкрепля́ть (*impf.*) си́лы; **~ one's end up** держа́ть (*impf.*) хвост пистоле́том (*coll.*); не уда́рить (*pf.*) лицо́м в грязь; **~ up appearances** соблюда́ть (*impf.*) прили́чия/ви́димость прили́чий; держа́ть (*impf.*) ма́рку; **the house is expensive to ~ up** э́тот дом до́рого содержа́ть; **~ up the conversation** подде́рживать (*impf.*) разгово́р; (*continue*): **~ up the good work!** продолжа́йте в том же ду́хе!; **he can ~ it up for hours** он в э́том неутоми́м; **he could not ~ up the payments** он не мог регуля́рно плати́ть; **the custom has been kept up for centuries** э́тот обы́чай сохраня́лся столе́тия; **I wish I had kept up my Latin** жаль, что я забро́сил латы́нь; (*prevent from going *to bed*): **the baby kept us up half the night** ребёнок не дава́л нам спать полно́чи; *v.i.* (*stay upright, afloat etc.*): **the tent may not ~ up if the wind gets stronger** пала́тка мо́жет не усто́ять/вы́держать, е́сли ве́тер уси́лится; (*stay high, e.g. a kite*; *temperature*) держа́ться (*impf.*); (*continue*): **if the weather ~s up we will have a picnic** е́сли хоро́шая пого́да продержи́тся, мы устро́им пикни́к; (*stay level*): **we kept up with them the whole way** всю доро́гу мы не отстава́ли от них; **stop! I can't ~ up** подожди́те! я за ва́ми не поспева́ю; **the unions demand that wages should ~ up with prices** профсою́зы тре́буют, что́бы зарпла́та росла́ вме́сте с це́нами; **~ up with the times** не отстава́ть (*impf.*) от собы́тий; шага́ть (*impf.*) в но́гу со вре́менем; **~ up with the Joneses** быть не ху́же други́х/люде́й; (*remain in touch*): **I try to ~ up with the news** я стара́юсь следи́ть за собы́тиями; **I ~ up with several old friends** я подде́рживаю отноше́ния ко́е с кем из ста́рых друзе́й.

cpd. **~-fit** *adj.*: **~-fit exercises** заря́дка.

keeper [ˈki:pə(r)] *n.* **1.** (*guardian*) храни́тель (*m.*), сто́рож; (*in zoo*) служи́тель (*m.*) (зоопа́рка); (*in prison*) надзира́тель (*m.*); (*in asylum*) санита́р; **I am not my brother's ~** я не сто́рож моему́ бра́ту; (*lighthouse-~*, *museum-~*) смотри́тель (*m.*); (*of shop, restaurant etc.*) владе́лец; хозя́ин; (*goal-~*) врата́рь (*m.*). **2.: this apple is a good ~** э́тот сорт я́блок мо́жет до́лго лежа́ть.

keeping [ˈki:pɪŋ] *n.* **1.: in safe ~** в надёжных рука́х; в по́лной сохра́нности. **2.: be in ~ with** соотве́тствовать (*impf.*) +*d.*; **that remark is out of ~ with his character** э́то замеча́ние для него́ не типи́чно.

keepsake [ˈki:pseɪk] *n.* сувени́р; **as a ~** на па́мять.

keg [keg] *n.* бочо́нок.

Kelt [kelt] = **Celt**

ken [ken] *n.*: **beyond my ~** вне мое́й компете́нции; за преде́лами мои́х позна́ний.

v.t. (*Sc.*) знать (*impf.*).

kendo [ˈkɛndəʊ] *n.* ке́ндо.

kennel [ˈken(ə)l] *n.* **1.** конура́. **2.** (*pl., for hounds*) пса́рня. **3.** (*mean dwelling*) хи́жина; хиба́рка, конура́.

v.t. (*keep in ~*) держа́ть (*impf.*) в конуре́; (*drive into ~*) заг|оня́ть, -на́ть в конуру́.

Kenya [ˈkenjə, ˈki:njə] *n.* Ке́ния.

Kenyan [ˈkenjən, ˈki:njən] *n.* кени́|ец (*fem.* -йка).

adj. кени́йский.

kepi [ˈkepɪ, ˈkeɪpɪ] *n.* ке́пи (*nt. indecl.*).

kerb [kɜ:b] *n.* обо́чина.

cpd. **~stone** *n.* бордю́рный ка́мень.

kerchief [ˈkɜ:tʃi:f, -tʃɪf] *n.* плато́к, косы́нка.

kerfuffle [kəˈfʌf(ə)l] *n.* шум, заваруха.

kernel [ˈkɜ:n(ə)l] *n.* (*of nut or fruit-stone*) ядро́; (*of seed, e.g. wheat grain*) зерно́; (*fig., essence*) суть, су́щность.

keros|ene, -ine [ˈkerəˌsi:n] *n.* кероси́н; (*attr.*) кероси́новый.

kestrel [ˈkestr(ə)l] *n.* пустельга́.

ketch [ketʃ] *n.* кеч.

ketchup [ˈketʃʌp] *n.* ке́тчуп.

kettle [ˈket(ə)l] *n.* ча́йник; (*pot for boiling, e.g. fish*) котело́к; **here's a pretty ~ of fish!** вот так но́мер!; хоро́шенькое де́ло!; **that's quite another ~ of fish** э́то совсе́м из друго́й о́перы.

cpds. **~-drum** *n.* лита́вра; **~-drummer** *n.* литаври́ст, лита́врщик.

key [ki:] *n.* **1.** ключ; **~ to the door/clock** ключ от две́ри/часо́в; **~ money** зада́ток при получе́нии ключе́й от кварти́ры. **2.** (*fig., sth. providing access or solution*) ключ; **the ~ to the political situation** ключ к понима́нию полити́ческой ситуа́ции; **the ~ to a mystery** разга́дка та́йны; **the ~ to success is hard work** зало́г успе́ха — упо́рная рабо́та; (*to foreign text*) подстро́чник; (*to map*) леге́нда. **3.** (*attr., important, essential*) ва́жный, важне́йший; веду́щий; **~ position** ключева́я пози́ция; **~ question** стержнево́й вопро́с; **a ~ man** незамени́мый рабо́тник; **~ industries** веду́щие о́трасли промы́шленности. **4.** (*of piano or typewriter*) кла́виш, кла́виша; (*pl.*) клавиату́ра; (*of wind instrument*) кла́пан; **Morse ~** ключ Мо́рзе; **shift ~** смен|я́ть, -и́ть реги́стр. **5.** (*mus.*) ключ, тона́льность; **in a low ~** (*fig.*) сде́ржанно.

v.t.: **~ up** взви́н|чивать, -ти́ть.

cpds. **~board** *n.* клавиату́ра; **~board instrument** кла́вишный инструме́нт; **~hole** *n.* замо́чная сква́жина; **~note** *n.* (*mus.*) основна́я но́та ключа́; (*fig.*) лейтмоти́в; основна́я мысль; **~note address** програ́ммная речь; **~-ring** *n.* кольцо́ для ключе́й; **~stone** *n.* замко́вый ка́мень; (*fig.*) краеуго́льный ка́мень; **~word** *n.* ключево́е сло́во.

KG (*abbr. of* ***Knight of the Order of the Garter***) кавале́р о́рдена Подвя́зки.

kg. [ˈkɪləˌgræm] *n.* (*abbr. of* **kilogram(me)(s)**) кг, (килогра́мм).

KGB (*abbr. of Russ.* ***Komitet gosudarstvennoy bezopasnosti***) КГБ, (*Комитет государственной безопасности*); **~ agent** кагебе́шник, геби́ст.

khaki [ˈkɑ:kɪ] *n.* защи́тный цвет, ха́ки (*nt. indecl.*); **dressed in ~** оде́тый в ха́ки.

adj.: **a ~ shirt** руба́шка цве́та ха́ки.

khan [kɑ:n, kæn] *n.* хан.

khanate [ˈkɑ:neɪt, ˈkæneɪt] *n.* ха́нство.

Kharkov [ˈxarjkəf] *n.* Ха́рьков.

khedive [kɪˈdi:v] *n.* хеди́в.

Khmer [kmeə(r)] *n.* кхмер; **~ Rouge** кра́сные кхме́ры.

adj. кхме́рский.

kibbutz [kɪˈbʊts] *n.* киб(б)у́ц.

kibitzer [ˈkɪbɪtsə(r), kɪˈbɪtsə(r)] *n.* (*coll.*) непро́шенный сове́тчик при игре́ в ка́рты.

kibosh [ˈkaɪbɒʃ] *n.* (*sl.*): **put the ~ on** прихло́пнуть (*pf.*).

kick [kɪk] *n.* **1.** уда́р, пино́к; **give s.o. a ~** уд|аря́ть, -а́рить (*or* ляг|а́ть, -ну́ть) кого́-н. ного́й; **give a ~** (*of horse*) ляг|а́ться, -ну́ться; (*football*) **the referee gave a free ~** судья́ объяви́л штрафно́й уда́р. **2.** (*recoil*) отда́ча. **3.** (*fig., resilience*): **he has no ~ left in him** он вы́дохся. **4.** (*coll., stimulus*): **get a ~ out of sth.** получ|а́ть, -и́ть удово́льствие от чего́-н.; **he does it for ~s** (*sl.*) он де́лает э́то из озорства́; **this vodka has real ~ in it** в э́той во́дке есть гра́дус.

v.t. уд|аря́ть, -а́рить ного́й; **he ~ed me on the shin** он уда́рил меня́ по го́лени; **you mustn't ~ a man when he's down** нельзя́ бить лежа́чего; **I could have ~ed myself** я рвал на себе́ во́лосы; **he ~ed the ball** он уда́рил по мячу́; **he ~ed a goal** он заби́л гол; **~ the bucket** дать (*pf.*) ду́ба (*sl.*); **~ one's heels** ждать (*impf.*) с нетерпе́нием; **he kept me ~ing my heels for 2 hours** он меня́ протоми́л два часа́; **~ the habit** (*sl., give up drug-taking*) бро́сить (*pf.*) нарко́тики.

v.i. (*of animals*) ляга́ться (*impf.*); брыка́ться (*impf.*); (*fig.*): **~ at, against sth.** протестова́ть (*impf.*) про́тив чего́-н.; **~ over the traces** взбунтова́ться (*pf.*); **he is still alive and ~ing** он всё ещё жив-здоро́в.

with advs.: **~ about, around** *v.t.*: **they were ~ing a ball about** они́ гоня́ли мяч; (*discuss informally*): **~ an idea around** обсужда́ть (*impf.*) пробле́му в ча́стном поря́дке; (*treat badly*): **he felt he had been ~ed around too long** он чу́вствовал, что его́ сли́шком уж шпыня́ют; *v.i.* (*coll.*): **is his father still ~ing around?** его́ оте́ц ещё жив?; **I don't want the children ~ing around when I'm working** я не хочу́, что́бы де́ти верте́лись под нога́ми, когда́ я рабо́таю; **there are plenty of jobs ~ing around** круго́м мест ско́лько уго́дно; **don't leave your shoes ~ing around** не разбра́сывай свои́ ту́фли; **~ back** *v.t.*: **the goalie ~ed the ball back into play** врата́рь вбро́сил мяч в игру́; *v.i.* (*retaliate*) соверши́ть (*pf.*) отве́тный уда́р; (*recoil*) отдава́ть (*impf.*); **~ in** *v.t.*: **~ the door in** взл|а́мывать, -ома́ть дверь; **~ s.o.'s teeth in** выбива́ть, вы́бить кому́-н. зу́бы; **~ off** *v.t.* (*e.g. shoes*) сбр|а́сывать, -о́сить; *v.i.* (*football*) нач|ина́ть, -а́ть игру́; (*coll., begin*) нач|ина́ть, -а́ть; **~ out** *v.t.* (*eject, expel*) выгоня́ть, вы́гнать, вы́швырнуть (*pf.*); *v.i.* выбра́сывать, вы́бросить но́ги; ляга́ться (*impf.*); **~ over** *v.t.* опроки́|дывать, -нуть; **~ up** *v.t.*: **the herd ~ed up a cloud of dust** ста́до по́дняло о́блако пы́ли; **the horse ~ed up its heels** ло́шадь взбрыкну́ла; **he ~ed up a stone** он подбро́сил ка́мень ного́й; (*coll., create*): **~ up a row** устр|а́ивать, -о́ить сканда́л; **~ up a din** подн|има́ть, -я́ть шум.

cpds. **~-back** *n.* (*recoil*) отда́ча; (*payment*) магары́ч;

~-**off** *n.* нача́ло (игры́); ~-**start** *v.t.* (*lit. & fig.*): **to ~-start the economy** дать толчо́к эконо́мике; ~-**starter** *n.* ножно́й ста́ртер.

kicker ['kɪkə(r)] *n.* (*horse*) брыкли́вая ло́шадь.

kid[1] [kɪd] *n.* **1.** (*young goat*) козлёнок. **2.** (*leather*) шевро́ (*indecl.*); (*attr.*) шевро́вый; (*for gloves*) ла́йка; ~ **glove** ла́йковая перча́тка; **use, wear ~ gloves** (*fig.*) осторо́жно/мя́гко обраща́ться (*impf.*) (*с кем*). **3.** (*coll., child*) малы́ш; **he's just a ~** он всего́ лишь ребёнок; **my ~ brother** мой мла́дший брат; **that's ~(s') stuff!** ≃ просто́е де́ло; раз плю́нуть.

cpd. ~-**glove** *adj.*: ~-**glove methods** делика́тные/осторо́жные ме́тоды.

kid[2] [kɪd] *v.t.* **1.** (*coll., deceive*) над|ува́ть, -у́ть; **who are you ~ding?** кого́ вы хоти́те обману́ть?; **don't ~ yourself!** не обма́нывайте себя́! **2.** (*tease*) дразни́ть (*impf.*); ~ **s.o. on, along** води́ть (*impf.*) кого́-н. за́ нос.

v.i. (*tease with untruths*): **you're ~ding!** врёшь!

kidd|y, -ie ['kɪdɪ] *n.* (*coll.*) де́тка (*c.g.*).

kidnap ['kɪdnæp] *v.t.* пох|ища́ть, -и́тить.

kidnapper ['kɪdnæpə(r)] *n.* похити́тель (*m.*).

kidney ['kɪdnɪ] *n.* **1.** по́чка; ~ **soup** суп из по́чек; ~ **machine** аппара́т «иску́сственная по́чка»; ~ **transplant** переса́дка по́чек. **2.** (*type, temperament*): **they are of the same ~** они́ одного́ по́ля я́годы; они́ одни́м ми́ром ма́заны.

cpds. ~-**bean** *n.* фасо́ль (*collect.*); ~-**shaped** *adj.* почкови́дный; ~-**stone** *n.* га́лька.

Kiev ['ki:ef] *n.* Ки́ев.

Kievan [ki:'efən] *n.* киевля́н|ин (*fem.* -ка).

adj. ки́евский.

kill [kɪl] *n.* **1.** (*of hunted animal*) отстре́л; (*of enemy aircraft etc.*) уничтоже́ние; **be in at the ~** (*fig.*) прибы́ть (*pf.*) к дележу́ добы́чи. **2.** (*animal(s) ~ed*) добы́ча; **a good ~** бога́тая добы́ча.

v.t. **1.** уб|ива́ть, -и́ть; (*rats etc.*) мори́ть, вы́-; **he was ~ed in an accident** он поги́б при ава́рии; **~ed in action** уби́т в бою́ (*or* на по́ле сраже́ния); ~ **o.s.** (*lit.*) ко́нчить самоуби́йством; (*fig., coll.*) перенапряга́ться (*impf.*); **the villain gets ~ed in the end** злоде́й в конце́ концо́в погиба́ет; ~ **two birds with one stone** уби́ть (*pf.*) двух за́йцев одни́м уда́ром; **the shock ~ed her** потрясе́ние её уби́ло; **my feet are ~ing me** я без за́дних ног; **the frost ~ed my roses** мои́ ро́зы поги́бли от моро́за. **2.** (*animals for food*) ре́зать, за-; зак|а́лывать, -оло́ть; (*esp. in quantity*) заб|ива́ть, -и́ть; **the wolf ~ed the calf** волк заре́зал телёнка. **3.** (*destroy, put an end to*) уничт|ожа́ть, -о́жить; разб|ива́ть, -и́ть; **this drug ~s the pain** э́то лека́рство утоля́ет боль; ~ **a proposal** провали́ть (*pf.*) предложе́ние. **4.** (*neutralize, e.g. colours*) нейтрализова́ть (*impf., pf.*); **the orchestra ~ed the violin** орке́стр заглуши́л скри́пку; **cigarettes ~ the appetite** папиро́сы по́ртят аппети́т; ~ **time** уб|ива́ть, -и́ть вре́мя; корота́ть, с- вре́мя. **5.** (*coll., switch off*) выключа́ть, вы́ключить. **6.** (*coll., finish off*): **shall we ~ the bottle?** разда́вим/прико́нчим буты́лку? **7.** (*sport*): ~ **the ball** (*football*) останови́ть (*pf.*) мяч; (*tennis*) погаси́ть (*pf.*) мяч. **8.** (*overwhelm*): ~ **s.o. with kindness** погуби́ть кого́-н. чрезме́рной добното́й; **your jokes are ~ing me!** ва́ши шу́тки меня́ умори́ли!; **dressed to ~** разоде́тый в пух и прах.

v.i.: **thou shalt not ~!** не убий!; ~ **or cure** ≃ риско́ванное сре́дство.

with advs.: ~ **off** *v.t.* переб|ива́ть, -и́ть.

cpd. ~**joy** *n.* брюзга́ (*c.g.*).

killer ['kɪlə(r)] *n.* (*murderer*) уби́йца (*c.g.*); ~ **whale** коса́тка; (*fatal disease*): **typhus is a ~** тиф — смерте́льная боле́знь; (*poison*): **rat ~** крыси́ный яд.

killing ['kɪlɪŋ] *n.* (*murder*) уби́йство; **mercy ~** уби́йство из гума́нных соображе́ний; (*slaughter of animals*) убо́й, забо́й; (*fig., coll.*): **he made a ~** он сорва́л большо́й куш.

adj. (*exhausting*) уби́йственный; (*amusing*) умори́тельный; ~**ly funny** умопомрачи́тельно смешно́й.

kiln [kɪln] *n.* печь.

cpd. ~-**dry** *v.t.* суши́ть, вы́- в печи́.

kilo ['ki:ləʊ] *n.* кило́ (*indecl.*).

kilobyte ['kɪlə,baɪt] *n.* килоба́йт.

kilocycle ['kɪlə,saɪk(ə)l] *n.* килоци́кл; ~ **per second** килоге́рц.

kilogram(me) ['kɪlə,græm] *n.* килогра́мм.

kilohertz ['kɪlə,hɜ:ts] *n.* килоге́рц.

kilolitre ['kɪlə,li:tə(r)] *n.* килоли́тр.

kilometre ['kɪlə,mi:tə(r), *disp.* kɪ'lɒmɪtə(r)] *n.* киломе́тр.

kilometric [,kɪlə'metrɪk] *adj.* километро́вый.

kiloton ['kɪlə,tʌn] *n.* килото́нна.

kilovolt ['kɪlə,vɒlt] *n.* килово́льт.

kilowatt ['kɪlə,wɒt] *n.* килова́тт.

cpd. ~-**hour** *n.* килова́тт-час.

kilt [kɪlt] *n.* (шотла́ндская) ю́бка.

v.t. под|тыка́ть, -откну́ть (ю́бку).

kilted ['kɪltɪd] *adj.* нося́щий шотла́ндскую ю́бку.

kimono [kɪ'məʊnəʊ] *n.* кимоно́ (*indecl.*).

kin [kɪn] *n.* (*family*) семья́; (*relations*) родня́ (*collect.*); ро́дственники (*m. pl.*); **kith and ~** родны́е и бли́зкие; (*fig.*) бра́тья по кро́ви; **next of ~** ближа́йший ро́дственник, ближа́йшая ро́дственница.

pred. adj. (*arch.*): **he is ~ to me** он мне ро́дственник; **we are ~** мы в родстве́.

kinaesthetic [,kɪnəs'θetɪk] *adj.* кинестети́ческий.

kind [kaɪnd] *n.* **1.** (*race*) род; **human ~** род челове́ческий. **2.** (*class, sort, variety*) род, сорт, разнови́дность; **all ~s of goods** вся́кие това́ры; **something of the ~** что́-то (*or* что́-нибудь) в э́том ро́де; **of a different (*or* another) ~** друго́го ро́да; **nothing of the ~** ничего́ подо́бного; **an actor of a ~** в изве́стном смы́сле актёр; **he is a ~ of actor** он в своём ро́де актёр; **one of a ~** у́никум; уника́льный; **two of a ~** (*at cards*) па́ра; (*fig.*) два сапога́ па́ра; **what ~ of?** что за?; како́й?; **what ~ of a painter is he?** что он за худо́жник?; **what ~ of box do you want?** како́го ро́да коро́бка вам нужна́?; **that ~ of person is never satisfied** тако́й челове́к всегда́ че́м-то недово́лен; **that ~ of thing** таки́е ве́щи/шту́ки; всё в тако́м ро́де; **these ~s of people annoy me** лю́ди тако́го ти́па меня́ раздража́ют. **3.**: ~ **of** (*coll., to some extent*): **I ~ of expected it** я вро́де бы ожида́л э́того; **I felt ~ of sorry for him** мне его́ бы́ло ка́к-то жаль. **4.** (*natural character*) ка́чество; **differ in ~** отлича́ться по ка́честву; различа́ться по свое́й приро́де. **5.**: **in ~** нату́рой; **pay in ~** плати́ть, за- нату́рой; **repay in ~** (*fig.*) отпла́|чивать, -ти́ть то́й же моне́той.

adj. до́брый, любе́зный; **be so ~ as to close the door** бу́дьте любе́зны, закро́йте дверь; **with ~ regards** с серде́чным приве́том.

cpds. ~-**hearted** *adj.* добросерде́чный; ~**heartedness** *n.* доброта́.

kindergarten ['kɪndə,gɑ:t(ə)n] *n.* де́тский сад.

kindle ['kɪnd(ə)l] *v.t.* разж|ига́ть, -е́чь; (*fig., arouse*) возбу|жда́ть, -ди́ть; (*evoke*) вызыва́ть, вы́звать.

v.i. загор|а́ться, -е́ться; (*fig.*) вспы́х|ивать, -нуть.

kindliness ['kaɪndlɪnɪs] *n.* доброта́.

kindling ['kɪndlɪŋ] *n.* (*firewood*) расто́пка; ще́пки (*f. pl.*).

kindly ['kaɪndlɪ] *adj.* до́брый, доброду́шный; (*fig., of climate etc.*) благоприя́тный, мя́гкий.

adv. **1.** (*in a kind manner*) любе́зно, ми́ло. **2.** (*please*): ~ **ring me tomorrow** бу́дьте добры́, позвони́те мне за́втра. **3.**: **the cat took ~ to its new home** ко́шка прижила́сь в но́вом до́ме; **he took ~ to my suggestion** он хорошо́ отнёсся к моему́ предложе́нию; **he does not take ~ to criticism** он не лю́бит кри́тики.

kindness ['kaɪndnɪs] *n.* **1.** (*benevolence, kind nature*) доброта́; **he was ~ itself** он был сама́ доброта́; **he did it out of (the) ~ (of his heart)** он сде́лал э́то по доброте́ (серде́чной); **it would be a mistaken ~ to give him the money** дать ему́ де́ньги бы́ло бы медве́жьей услу́гой. **2.** (*kind act; service*) любе́зность; одолже́ние; **do s.o. a ~** ока́з|ывать, -а́ть кому́-н. любе́зность; де́лать, с- кому́-н. одолже́ние.

kindred ['kɪndrɪd] *n.* **1.** (*blood relationship*) (кро́вное) родство́; **claim ~ with** претендова́ть (*impf.*) на родство́ c+*i.* **2.** (*one's relatives*) родня́ (*collect.*).

adj. (*lit., fig.*) ро́дственный; ~ **ideas** ро́дственные иде́и; **a ~ spirit** родна́я душа́.

kine [kaɪn] *n. pl.* (*arch.*) коро́вы (*f. pl.*).
kinematic [ˌkaɪnɪˈmætɪk] *adj.* кинемати́ческий.
kinematics [ˌkɪnɪˈmætɪks, ˌkaɪ-] *n.* кинема́тика.
kinetic [kɪˈnetɪk, kaɪ-] *adj.* кинети́ческий.
kinetics [kɪˈnetɪks, kaɪ-] *n.* кине́тика.
king [kɪŋ] *n.* **1.** коро́ль (*m.*); (*anc. and bibl.*) царь (*m.*); **Gentlemen, the K~!** (*toast*) господа́, здоро́вье короля́!; **the book of K~s** Кни́га Царе́й; **the K~'s English** пра́вильный англи́йский язы́к; **turn ~'s evidence** изобли́ч|а́ть, -и́ть свои́х соо́бщников; **~'s evil** (*arch.*) золоту́ха; **K~'s messenger** дипломати́ческий курье́р; **K~ of K~s** Царь Царе́й. **2.** (*fig.*): **oil ~** нефтяно́й коро́ль; **~ of beasts/birds** царь звере́й/птиц; (*chess*): **White K~** бе́лый коро́ль; **~'s pawn** короле́вская пе́шка; (*draughts, checkers*) да́мка; (*cards*): **~ of diamonds** бубно́вый коро́ль.
cpds. **~fisher** *n.* (голубо́й) зимоpо́док; **~pin** *n.* (*bolt*) шкво́рень (*m.*); (*in skittles*) центра́льная ке́гля; (*fig.*) гла́вное лицо́; **~-size(d)** *adj.* кру́пный; бо́льшего разме́ра.
kingdom [ˈkɪŋdəm] *n.* короле́вство; **the United K~** Соединённое Короле́вство; **the animal ~** живо́тное ца́рство; **the ~ of heaven** ца́рство небе́сное; **thy ~ come** да прии́дет Ца́рствие Твое́; **send s.o. to ~ come** (*coll.*) отпра́вить (*pf.*) кого́-н. на тот свет (*or* к пра́отцам); **you'll wait from now to ~ come** (*coll.*) ну, тепе́рь бу́дете ждать до второ́го прише́ствия.
king|like [ˈkɪŋlaɪk], **-ly** [ˈkɪŋlɪ] *adjs.* короле́вский, ца́рский; (*fig.*) вели́чественный.
kingship [ˈkɪŋʃɪp] *n.* короле́вский сан.
kink [kɪŋk] *n.* (*in rope etc.*) переги́б; (*in metal*) изги́б; (*fig., in character*) причу́да.
kinkajou [ˈkɪŋkəˌdʒuː] *n.* кинкажу́ (*m. indecl.*).
kinky [ˈkɪŋkɪ] *adj.* (*twisted*) кручёный; (*coll., perverted*) извращённый; со стра́нностями.
kinsfolk [ˈkɪnzfəʊk] *n.* родня́ (*collect.*).
kinship [ˈkɪnʃɪp] *n.* (*relationship*) родство́; (*similarity*) схо́дство.
kinsman [ˈkɪnzmən] *n.* ро́дственник.
kinswoman [ˈkɪnzˌwʊmən] *n.* ро́дственница.
kiosk [ˈkiːɒsk] *n.* кио́ск; **telephone ~** телефо́нная бу́дка, автома́т.
kip [kɪp] *n.* (*coll.*) (*lodging*) ночле́жка; (*bed*) ко́йка; (*sleep*) сон.
v.i. **1.**: **~ down for the night** устро́иться (*pf.*) на ночь. **2.** (*sleep*) кема́рить, по- (*coll.*).
kipper [ˈkɪpə(r)] *n.* копчёная селёдка.
v.t. копти́ть, за-.
Kirghiz [kɪəˈgɪz, ˈkɜːgɪz] *n.* (*pers.*) кирги́з (*fem.* -ка); (*language*) кирги́зский язы́к.
adj. кирги́зский.
Kirghizia [kɜːˈgiːzɪə] *n.* Кирги́зия.
kirk [kɜːk] *n.* шотла́ндская (пресвитериа́нская) це́рковь.
kirsch [kɪəʃ] *n.* вишнёвая во́дка, киршва́ссер.
kirtle [ˈkɜːt(ə)l] *n.* ве́рхняя ю́бка.
kismet [ˈkɪsmet, ˈkɪz-] *n.* рок, судьба́.
kiss [kɪs] *n.* поцелу́й; **give s.o. a ~ on the cheek** поцелова́ть (*pf.*) кого́-н. в щёку; **blow s.o. a ~** посла́ть (*pf.*) кому́-н. возду́шный поцелу́й; **steal a ~** сорва́ть (*pf.*) поцелу́й; **give her a ~ from me!** поцелу́й её за меня́!; **~ of life** иску́сственное дыха́ние; **Judas ~** поцелу́й Иу́ды.
v.t. целова́ть, по-; **he ~ed away her tears** поцелу́ями он осуши́л её слёзы; **~ the book** целова́ть, по- Би́блию (принима́я прися́гу); **~ the dust** (*fig.*) пасть (*pf.*) ниц; покори́ться (*pf.*); **they ~ed each other goodbye** они́ поцелова́лись на проща́нье; **you can ~ goodbye to the inheritance** вы мо́жете распроща́ться с насле́дством; пла́кало ва́ше насле́дство; **he ~ed his hand to me** он посла́л мне возду́шный поцелу́й; **~ the rod** (*fig.*) поко́рно прин|има́ть, -я́ть наказа́ние.
v.i. целова́ться, по-.
cpd. **~-curl** *n.* ло́кон на лбу (*or* у виска́).
kisser [ˈkɪsə(r)] *n.* (*mouth*) ва́режка (*sl.*).
kit [kɪt] *n.* (*personal equipment, esp. clothing*) снаряже́ние; **a soldier's ~** солда́тское снаряже́ние; **~ inspection** прове́рка снаряже́ния; (*workman's tools*) набо́р инструме́нтов; (*for particular sport or activity*) набо́р/компле́кт (спорти́вных) принадле́жностей; **survival ~** набо́р са́мого необходи́мого; (*set of parts for assembly*) констру́ктор.
v.t. & i. (*usu.* **~ out, up**) снаря|жа́ть(ся), -ди́ть(ся).
cpd. **~bag** *n.* вещево́й мешо́к/ра́нец; вещмешо́к.
kitchen [ˈkɪtʃɪn, -tʃ(ə)n] *n.* ку́хня; **~ garden** огоро́д; **~ sink** мо́йка; ра́ковина; **~ unit** ку́хонный комба́йн.
cpds. **~-maid** *n.* судомо́йка; **~-ware** *n.* ку́хонная у́тварь.
kitchenette [ˌkɪtʃɪˈnet, -tʃəˈnet] *n.* ма́ленькая ку́хонька.
kite [kaɪt] *n.* **1.** (*bird*) (кра́сный) ко́ршун. **2.** (*toy*) (возду́шный/бума́жный) змей; **fly a ~** (*lit.*) запус|ка́ть, -ти́ть змея́; (*fig., to test reaction*) пус|ка́ть, -ти́ть про́бный шар; **~ balloon** зме́йковый аэроста́т. **3.** (*sl., aeroplane*) самолёт. **4.** (*comm.*): **fly a ~** получи́ть (*pf.*) де́ньги под фикти́вный ве́ксель.
kith [kɪθ] *see* **kin**
kitsch [kɪtʃ] *n.* китч, дешёвка.
kitten [ˈkɪt(ə)n] *n.* котёнок; **our cat has had ~s** на́ша ко́шка окоти́лась; у на́шей ко́шки котя́та; **she nearly had ~s** она́ на сте́нку ле́зла (*fig., coll.*).
kittenish [ˈkɪtənɪʃ] *adj.* игри́вый.
kittiwake [ˈkɪtɪˌweɪk] *n.* моёвка.
kitty [ˈkɪtɪ] *n.* (*at cards etc.*) пу́лька, банк; (*cat*) ки́ска.
kiwi [ˈkiːwiː] *n.* ки́ви (*f. indecl.*); **K~** (*coll.*) новозела́нд|ец (*fem.* -ка).
KKK [ˌkuːklʌksˈklæn, ˌkjuː-] *n.* (*abbr. of* **Ku Klux Klan**) ККК, (ку-клукс-кла́н).
Klansman [ˈklænzmən] *n.* куклукскла́новец.
klaxon [ˈklæks(ə)n] *n.* кла́ксон.
kleptomania [ˌkleptəʊˈmeɪnɪə] *n.* клептома́ния.
kleptomaniac [ˌkleptəʊˈmeɪnɪˌæk] *n.* клептома́н (*fem.* -ка).
klieg [kliːg] *n.* (*light*) «со́лнце», «со́лнечный» проже́ктор.
km. [ˈkɪləˌmiːtə(r)(z), *disp.* kɪˈlɒmɪtə(r)(z)] *n.* (*abbr. of* **kilometre(s)**) км, (киломе́тр).
knack [næk] *n.* (*skill, faculty*) сноро́вка, уме́ние; **have the ~ of** име́ть (*impf.*) сноро́вку (*в чём*); **there's a ~ to it** де́ло тре́бует сноро́вки.
knacker [ˈnækə(r)] *n.* ску́пщик ста́рых лошаде́й; **~'s yard** живоде́рня.
knapsack [ˈnæpsæk] *n.* ра́нец.
knave [neɪv] *n.* **1.** (*arch., rogue*) плут, моше́нник. **2.** (*cards*) вале́т; **~ of hearts** вале́т черве́й.
knavery [ˈneɪvərɪ] *n.* плутовство́.
knavish [ˈneɪvɪʃ] *adj.* плутовско́й.
knead [niːd] *v.t.* (*e.g. dough or clay*) меси́ть, за-/с-; **~ing-machine** тестомеси́льная маши́на; **~ing-trough** квашня́; (*massage*) масси́ровать (*impf., pf.*).
knee [niː] *n.* коле́н|о (*pl.* и); **he was on his ~s** он стоя́л на коле́нях; **go down on one's ~s (*or* on bended ~)** стать/упа́сть (*pf.*) на коле́ни (*fig.*); **go on one's ~s to s.o.** на коле́нях моли́ть (*impf.*) кого́-н.; **bring s.o. to his ~s** ста́вить, по- кого́-н. на коле́ни; **bend, bow the ~** преклон|я́ть, -и́ть коле́на; **I went weak at the ~s** у меня́ задрожа́ли поджи́лки (*or* подкоси́лись но́ги); **on the ~s of the gods** в руце́ бо́жьей; **I learnt it at my mother's ~** я впита́л э́то с молоко́м ма́тери; **they were up to their ~s in mud** они́ бы́ли по коле́но в грязи́; **the ~s of his trousers were worn** его́ брю́ки протёрлись в коле́нках.
v.t. уд|аря́ть, -а́рить коле́ном.
cpds. **~-bend** *n.* приседа́ние; **~-breeches** *n. pl.* бри́дж|и (*pl., g.* -ей); **~-cap** *n.* коле́нная ча́шка; (*protection*) наколе́нник; **~-capping** *n.* вы́стрел в коле́нную ча́шку; **~-deep** *pred. adj. & adv.*: **he stood ~-deep in water** он стоя́л по коле́но в воде́; **~-high** *pred. adj. & adv.* (*reaching to the ~*): **the grass was ~-high** трава́ была́ по коле́но; **~-jerk** *adj.* автомати́ческий, непроизво́льный; **~joint** *n.* (*anat.*) коле́нный суста́в; (*tech.*) коле́нчатое сочлене́ние; **~-length** *adj.* до коле́н.
kneel [niːl] *v.i.* **1.** (*also* **~ down:** *go down on one's knees*) ста|нови́ться, -ть на коле́ни; **~ to s.o.** преклон|я́ть, -и́ть коле́на пе́ред кем-н. **2.** (*be in ~ing position*) стоя́ть (*impf.*) на коле́нях; **they knelt in prayer** они́ моли́лись на коле́нях.

knell [nel] *n.* погреба́льный/похоро́нный звон; (*fig.*): **his death sounded the ~ of their hopes** его́ смерть означа́ла коне́ц их наде́ждам.
knickerbockers ['nɪkəˌbɒkə(r)z] *n.* бри́дж|и (*pl.*, *g.* -ей).
knickers ['nɪkəz] *n.* (*fem. undergarment*) пантало́н|ы (*pl.*, *g.* —).
(k)nick-(k)nack ['nɪknæk] *n.* безделу́шка.
knife [naɪf] *n.* но́ж; (*pocket* ~) но́жик; **before one could say ~** молента́льно; в мгнове́ние о́ка; **he has his ~ into me** (*fig.*) он име́ет зуб на меня́; **hold a ~ to s.o.'s throat** прист|ава́ть, -а́ть с ножо́м к го́рлу к кому́-н.; **it was war to the ~ between them** ме́жду ни́ми шла война́ не на жизнь, а на смерть; **you could cut the atmosphere with a ~** во́здух был тако́й, что хоть топо́р ве́шай; (*fig.*) атмосфе́ра была́ накалённая; **he had an accent you could cut with a ~** акце́нт выдава́л его́ с голово́й.
v.t. зак|а́лывать, -оло́ть ножо́м.
cpds. **~-edge** *n.* (*blade*) остриё ножа́; **on a ~-edge** (*fig.*) вися́щий на волоске́; **~-fight** *n.* поножо́вщина; **~-grinder** *n.* точи́льщик; **~-point** *n.*: **at ~-point** угрожа́я ножо́м; **~-rest** *n.* подста́вка для ножа́.
knight [naɪt] *n.* **1.** (*hist.*) ры́царь (*m.*); (*in anc. Rome*) вса́дник. **2.** (*mod.*) ≃ ли́чный дворяни́н. **3.** (*member of order*) кавале́р; **K~ of the Garter** кавале́р о́рдена Подвя́зки; **K~ Commander** кавале́р о́рдена второ́й сте́пени; **K~ Grand Cross** кавале́р о́рдена пе́рвой сте́пени. **4.** (*chess*) конь (*m.*); **~'s move** ход конём.
v.t. (*hist.*) возв|оди́ть, -ести́ в ры́царское досто́инство; (*mod.*) ≃ присв|а́ивать, -о́ить (*кому*) ненасле́дственное дворя́нское зва́ние.
cpds. **~-errant** *n.* стра́нствующий ры́царь; **~-errantry** *n.* донкихо́тство.
knighthood ['naɪthʊd] *n.* ры́царство; ры́царское зва́ние; **he was recommended for a ~** его́ предста́вили к ры́царскому зва́нию.
knit [nɪt] *v.t.* **1.**: **~ wool into stockings** (*or* **stockings from wool**) вяза́ть, с- чулки́ из ше́рсти; **~ up** (*repair*) што́пать, за-; **hand-/machine-~ted garments** вя́заная/трикота́жная оде́жда; вя́занки (*f. pl.*). **2.** (*fasten*; *also* **~ together**) скреп|ля́ть, -и́ть; **a well-~ frame** складна́я фигу́ра; **a closely-~ argument** хорошо́ мотиви́рованный до́вод; (*unite*) соедин|я́ть, -и́ть; **families ~ together by marriage** се́мьи, соединённые бра́ком. **3.**: **~ one's brows** хму́рить, на- бро́ви; хму́риться, на-.
v.i. **1.** (*do ~ting*) вяза́ть (*impf.*). **2.** (*of bones*) сраст|а́ться, -и́сь.
cpd. **~wear** *n.* трикота́жные изде́лия.
knitting ['nɪtɪŋ] *n.* (*action*) вяза́ние; (*fig.*) скрепле́ние, соедине́ние; (*material being knitted*) вяза́нье.
cpds. **~-machine** *n.* вяза́льная маши́на; **~-needle** *n.* вяза́льная спи́ца; **~-yarn** *n.* трикота́жная пря́жа.
knob [nɒb] *n.* **1.** (*protuberance*) вы́пуклость; (*on body*) ши́шка. **2.** (*handle*) ру́чка; (*button*) кно́пка. **3.** (*of butter etc.*) кусо́чек. **4.** (*on walking-stick*) набалда́шник.
knobbly ['nɒblɪ] *adj.* шишкова́тый.
knock [nɒk] *n.* **1.** (*rap, rapping sound*) стук; **double ~** двукра́тный стук; **give a ~ on the door** стуча́ть, по- в дверь; **there came a loud ~** разда́лся гро́мкий стук. **2.** (*sound of ~ing in engine*) (детонацио́нный) стук; детона́ция; **anti-~** (*additive*) антидетона́тор. **3.** (*blow*) уда́р; **he got a nasty ~ on the head** он си́льно уда́рился голово́й; его́ си́льно уда́рили по голове́. **4.** (*fig.*): **the pound has taken some ~s lately** в после́днее вре́мя курс фу́нта сте́рлингов си́льно пострада́л.
v.t. **1.** (*hit*) удар|я́ть, -а́рить; **the blow ~ed him flat** уда́р сбил его́ с ног; **he ~ed the ball into the net** он заби́л мяч в се́тку; **he ~ed the table with his hammer** он уда́рил по́ столу молотко́м; **she ~ed her arm against the chair** она́ сту́кнулась руко́й о стул; **~ sth. to bits** разб|ива́ть, -и́ть что-н. вдре́безги; **he ~ed a nail into the wall** он вбил гвоздь в сте́ну; **he ~ed a hole in, through the wall** он проби́л ды́рку в стене́; **he ~ed the glass off the table** он смахну́л стака́н со стола́; **~ s.o. on, over the head** уда́рить/сту́кнуть (*both pf.*) кого́-н. по голове́; **I ~ed the gun out of his hand** я вы́бил из его́ руки́ пистоле́т. **2.** (*fig. uses*): **the idea was ~ed on the head** э́тому предложе́нию не да́ли хо́ду; **I tried to ~ some sense into his head** я пыта́лся впра́вить ему́ мо́зги (*or* образу́мить его́); **~ into shape** прив|оди́ть, -ести́ в поря́док; **he ~ed the ash off his cigarette** он стряхну́л пе́пел с папиро́сы; **I'll ~ a pound off the price** я сбро́шу/ски́ну/сба́влю фунт с цены́; **he ~ed five seconds off the record time** он поби́л реко́рд на пять секу́нд; **you can ~ my name off the list** вы мо́жете меня́ вы́черкнуть из спи́ска; **that ~s the bottom out of his argument** э́то сво́дит на нет его́ до́вод. **3.** (*criticize*) ха́ять (*impf.*) (*sl.*).
v.i. **1.** (*rap*) стуча́ть; **~ at the door** стуча́ть(ся), по- в дверь; **'~ before entering'** «без сту́ка не входи́ть»; **~ on wood** (*US*) тьфу-тьфу́, не сгла́зить! **2.**: **~ against** (*collide with*) нат|ыка́ться, -кну́ться на+*a.*; (*coll., meet*) столкну́ться (*pf.*) с+*i.* **3.** (*of engine*) стуча́ть (*impf.*). **4.** (*coll., travel*): **he spent a year ~ing round Europe** он год болта́лся по Евро́пе.
with advs.: **~ about** *v.t.* (*treat roughly*) помя́ть/намя́ть (*pf.*) бока́ (*кому*); лома́ть, по-/с- (*что*); *v.i. also* **~ (a)round** (*travel, wander*): **he's ~ed about a bit in his time** он в своё вре́мя поброди́л/пое́здил по све́ту; (*coll., keep company*): **she's ~ing around with a married man** она́ связа́лась с жена́тым челове́ком; **~ back** *v.t.* (*lit.*): **the electric shock ~ed him back against the wall** уда́ром то́ка его́ отбро́сило к стене́; (*disconcert*): **the news ~ed me back** изве́стие привело́ меня́ в замеша́тельство; (*coll., consume*): **he can ~ back 5 pints in as many minutes** он за пять мину́т мо́жет опроки́нуть/вы́лакать пять пинт (пи́ва); (*coll., cost*): **that will ~ me back a bit** э́то ста́нет мне в копе́ечку; **~ down** *v.t.* (*strike to ground*) сби|ва́ть, -ть с ног; вали́ть, с-; **he was ~ed down by a car** его́ сби́ла маши́на; **you could have ~ed me down with a feather** я был поражён как мо́лнией; (*demolish*) сн|оси́ть, -ести́; (*dismantle*) раз|бира́ть, -обра́ть; (*at auction*) прису|жда́ть, -ди́ть; **the auctioneer ~ed down the vase to the French bidder** аукциони́ст про́дал ва́зу францу́зскому покупщику́; **the vase was ~ed down for £5** ва́за пошла́ (*or* была́ про́дана́) за пять фу́нтов; (*reduce*) сн|ижа́ть, -и́зить; **~ in** *v.t.*: **~ a nail in** вби|ва́ть, -ть (*or* заб|ива́ть, -и́ть) гвоздь; **~ off** *v.t.* (*lit.*) сби|ва́ть, -ть; сшиб|а́ть, -и́ть; сма́х|ивать, -ну́ть; (*coll. uses*): (*deduct from price*) сб|авля́ть, -а́вить; (*compose or complete rapidly*): **he can ~ off an article in half an hour** он мо́жет состря́пать/сварга́нить (*sl.*) статью́ за полчаса́; (*steal*) сти́брить (*pf.*) (*sl.*); *v.i.* (*stop work*) шаба́шить, по- (*sl.*); **~ out** *v.t.* (*lit.*): **he ~ed a pane out** он вы́бил стекло́ из ра́мы; **he ~ed two of my teeth out** он вы́бил мне два зу́ба; (*empty by ~ing*): **he ~ed out his pipe** он вы́колотил/вы́бил тру́бку; (*make unconscious*) оглуш|а́ть, -и́ть; **the blow on his head ~ed him out** он был оглушён уда́ром по голове́; (*boxing*) нокаути́ровать (*impf., pf.*); (*overwhelm*) потряс|а́ть, -ти́; (*eliminate from contest*): **he was ~ed out in the first round** он вы́был в пе́рвом ту́ре; **~ over** *v.t.* опроки́|дывать, -нуть; **~ together** *v.t.*: **he ~ed together a cupboard** он на́спех сколоти́л шкаф; **~ up** *v.t.* (*lit.*): **I ~ed his arm up** я уда́рил его́ по руке́ сни́зу вверх; **she ~ed up the ball with her racket** она́ подбро́сила мяч раке́ткой; (*prepare*): **I can soon ~ up a meal** я на́скоро/бы́стренько пригото́влю еду́; (*waken*) буди́ть, раз-; (*sl., exhaust*) выма́тывать, вы́мотать; (*sl., make ill*): **after the party he was ~ed up for a week** вечери́нка вы́била его́ из коле́й на неде́лю; (*US, make pregnant*) обрюха́тить (*pf.*) (*sl.*); *v.i.* (*tennis*) разм|ина́ться, -я́ться (*coll.*).
cpds. **~about** *adj.*: **~about humour** гру́бый фарс; **~down** *adj.*: **a ~down blow** сокруши́тельный уда́р; **at a ~down price** по дешёвке (*coll.*); **~down furniture** разбо́рная ме́бель; **~-kneed** *adj.* с вы́вернутыми внутрь коле́нями; **~out** *n.* (*boxing*) нока́ут; (*competition*) соревнова́ния (*nt. pl.*) по олимпи́йской систе́ме; (*fig., sth. striking*) не́что сногсшиба́тельное; (*attr.*): **~out blow** сокруши́тельный уда́р; **~out drops** нарко́тик (*добавляемый в вино, чтобы привести жертву в бессознательное состояние*); **~-up** *n.* (*tennis*) разми́нка.

knocker ['nɒkə(r)] *n.* (*on door*) (дверно́й) молото́к; (*pl.*, *breasts*) буфера́ (*m. pl.*) (*sl.*).

cpd. **~-up** *n.* челове́к, кото́рый хо́дит из до́ма в дом и бу́дит рабо́чих на рабо́ту.

knocking ['nɒkɪŋ] *n.* (*noise*) стук.

knocking-shop ['nɒkɪŋ,ʃɒp] *n.* (*sl.*) публи́чный дом.

knoll [nəʊl] *n.* хо́лмик, буго́р, бугоро́к.

knot [nɒt] *n.* **1.** (*in rope etc.*; *in wood*; *measure of speed*) у́зел; **tie a ~ in a rope** завя́з|ывать, -а́ть у́зел на верёвке; **tie sth. in a ~** завя́з|ывать, -а́ть что-н. узло́м; **tie o.s. (up) in(to) ~s** (*fig.*) запу́таться (*pf.*); **I had him tied up in ~s** я его́ вконе́ц запу́тал; **cut the Gordian ~** разруби́ть (*pf.*) го́рдиев у́зел; **a vessel of 20 ~s** су́дно со ско́ростью два́дцать узло́в; **we are flying at 500 ~s** мы лети́м со ско́ростью 500 узло́в в час. **2.** (*group*, *cluster*) ку́чка.

v.t. & i. завя́з|ывать(ся), -а́ть(ся).

cpd. **~-hole** *n.* дыра́ от сучка́.

knotted ['nɒtɪd] *adj.* **1.** (*also* **knotty:** *gnarled*) узлова́тый, сучкова́тый. **2.: a ~ed rope** верёвка с узла́ми; верёвка, завя́занная узло́м.

knotty ['nɒtɪ] *adj.* **1.** = **knotted 1.**. **2.: a ~ problem** запу́танная/тру́дная пробле́ма.

knout [naʊt, nu:t] *n.* кнут.

know [nəʊ] *n.*: **be in the ~** быть в ку́рсе де́ла.

v.t. **1.** (*be aware*, *have knowledge of*) знать (*impf.*): **I ~ nothing about it** я об э́том ничего́ не зна́ю; **I ~ for a fact that …** я достове́рно зна́ю, что…; **as far as I ~** наско́лько мне изве́стно; **for all I ~** почём (*sl.*) мне знать; кто его́ зна́ет; **don't I ~!** мне да (*or* мне ли э́того) не знать!; **who ~s?** как знать?; **I wouldn't ~** пра́во, не зна́ю; отку́да мне знать?; **he's a fool and I let him ~ it** он дура́к, и я ему́ так и сказа́л; **he let it be ~n that …** он дал поня́ть, что…; **never let it be ~n** никогда́ в э́том не признава́йтесь; **that's all you ~ (about it)** мно́го вы зна́ете; **you (should) ~ best** вам лу́чше знать; **he did all he knew to avoid it** он сде́лал всё возмо́жное, что́бы э́того избежа́ть; **before I knew it we had arrived** я не успе́л огляну́ться, как мы при́были; **before you ~ where you are** не успе́ешь огляну́ться; в два счёта; **I knew it!** (я) так и знал!; **I don't ~ that I like this** я не уве́рен, что мне э́то нра́вится; мне э́то не сли́шком нра́вится; **he ~s what's what** он зна́ет, что к чему́; **he ~s his own mind** он зна́ет, чего́ (он) хо́чет; **he doesn't ~ his own mind** он сам не зна́ет, чего́ хо́чет; он не мо́жет ни на что реши́ться; **he ~s a thing or two** он ко́е в чём разбира́ется; он зна́ет, что к чему́; **he has been ~n to be wrong** у него́ быва́ли оши́бки; **he has been ~n to steal** ворова́ть ему́ не вно́ве; **he is ~n to have been married before** изве́стно, что он уже́ был жена́т; **I ~ what!** вот что!; зна́ете что?; **I ~ what, let's begin again!** Иде́я! Дава́йте начнём снача́ла!; **you ~ what?** (*US* **you ~ something?**) зна́ете что?; **not if I ~ it!** я э́того не допущу́; у меня́ э́тот но́мер не пройдёт; **you ~ what he is** (ну, да) вы его́ зна́ете; вы зна́ете, како́й он; **he ~s what he is about** он своё де́ло зна́ет; **I meant to be early, but you ~ what it is** я собира́лся прийти́ пора́ньше, но зна́ете, как э́то быва́ет. **2.** (*recognize*, *distinguish*) знать, у-; узн|ава́ть, -а́ть; отлич|а́ть, -и́ть; **I ~ him by sight** я зна́ю его́ в лицо́; **I might not ~ him again** я могу́ его́ не узна́ть (при встре́че); **he knew her at once** он её сра́зу узна́л; **I shouldn't ~ him from his brother** я его́ не отличи́л бы от бра́та; **I don't ~ him from Adam** я его́ (в жи́зни) в глаза́ не вида́л; **I knew him for a liar** я знал, что он лжец; **I'd ~ him anywhere** я узна́ю его́ да́же во сне; **he is ~n as a gambler** за ним во́дится сла́ва игрока́; **he is ~n to his friends as Jumbo** друзья́ кли́чут его́ Слоно́м; **this plant is ~n as heartsease** э́то расте́ние но́сит назва́ние «аню́тины гла́зки»; **he ~s a good thing when he sees it** он понима́ет, что хорошо́ и что пло́хо; у него́ губа́ не ду́ра. **3.** (*be acquainted*, *familiar with*) знать (*impf.*); быть знако́мым с+*i.*; **get to ~ s.o.** знако́миться, по- с кем-н.; **I have ~n him since childhood** я с ним знако́м с де́тства; **I ~ him slightly** у меня́ с ним бе́глое знако́мство; **I don't ~ him to speak to** я с ним недоста́точно знако́м, что́бы вступа́ть в разгово́р; **make o.s. ~n to s.o.** предст|авля́ться, -а́виться кому́-н.; **he is ~n to the police** он у поли́ции на заме́тке. **4.** (*be versed in*; *understand*; *have experience in*) знать, понима́ть (*impf.*), разбира́ться (*impf.*) в+*p.*; **he ~s Russian** он зна́ет ру́сский язы́к; он владе́ет ру́сским языко́м; **~ by heart** знать наизу́сть (*coll.*) назубо́к; **~ how to** уме́ть, с-. **5.** (*experience*): **he ~s no peace** он не зна́ет поко́я; **he has ~n many privations** он пережи́л/испыта́л мно́го лише́ний; **I have ~n worse to happen** мне изве́стны слу́чаи и похуже; **I have never ~n him tell a lie** я не по́мню, что́бы он когда́-нибудь солга́л. **6.** (*be subject to*): **he ~s no shame** он не ве́дает стыда́; **her happiness knew no bounds** её сча́стье не зна́ло грани́ц; её сча́стью не́ было преде́ла. *See also* **known**

v.i.: **let s.o. ~** сообщ|а́ть, -и́ть (*or* да|ва́ть, -ть знать) кому́-н.; **will you let me ~?** вы сообщи́те мне?; **(the) Lord only ~s!** Бог его́ зна́ет!; одному́ Бо́гу изве́стно; **how should I ~?** почём я зна́ю?; **what do you ~ (about that)?** поду́майте (то́лько)!; ишь ты!; **you never ~** как знать?; **he doesn't want to ~** (*refuses to take notice*, *interest*) он (и) знать не хо́чет; **you never ~, he may come back** как знать, он мо́жет и верну́ться; **I ~ better than to …** я не так прост, что́бы…; **I should have ~n better than to ask his advice** и дёрнуло же меня́ спроси́ть его́ сове́та!; **(do) you ~** (*in parenthesis*) зна́ете ли; понима́ете; **it's too hot to work, you ~** жа́рко рабо́тать-то; **do you ~ of a good restaurant?** вы зна́ете (*or* вы мо́жете порекомендова́ть) хоро́ший innstора́н?; **'Have you met him?' — 'Not that I ~ of'** «Вы встреча́лись с ним?» — «Наско́лько мне изве́стно, нет»; **I don't ~ him but I ~ of him** ли́чно я с ним незнако́м, но наслы́шал о нём; **did you ~ about the accident?** вы зна́ли об э́том несча́стном слу́чае?; **he ~s about cars** он разбира́ется в маши́нах; **I don't ~ about that** (*expr. doubt*) я не зна́ю, не уве́рен!; сомнева́юсь; ой ли. *See also* **known**

cpds. **~-all** *n.* всезна́йка (*c.g.*); **~-how** *n.* уме́ние; но́у-ха́у; о́пыт; у́ровень (*m.*) зна́ний; секре́ты (*m. pl.*) произво́дства; техноло́гия; **have the ~-how** облада́ть (*impf.*) уме́нием; (*body of experience*): **professional/technical ~-how** профессиона́льные/техни́ческие на́выки (*m. pl.*).

knowable ['nəʊəb(ə)l] *adj.* познава́емый.

knowing ['nəʊɪŋ] *n.*: **there's no ~ what may happen** невозмо́жно предви́деть, что мо́жет случи́ться/произойти́; **I did it without ~** я сде́лал э́то бессозна́тельно.

adj. (*intelligent*) у́мный; (*knowledgeable*) осведомлённый; (*shrewd*) проница́тельный; (*understanding*) понима́ющий; (*bright*): **a ~ child** смышлёный ребёнок; (*significant*): **a ~ look** многозначи́тельный взгляд.

knowingly ['nəʊɪŋlɪ] *adv.* (*significantly*) многозначи́тельно; (*intentionally*, *consciously*) наро́чно, созна́тельно.

knowledge ['nɒlɪdʒ] *n.* зна́ние; **he has a thorough ~ of Russian** у него́ основа́тельные зна́ния по ру́сскому языку́; **field, branch of ~** о́бласть зна́ния; о́трасль нау́ки; (*understanding*): **our ~ of the subject is as yet limited** на́ши позна́ния в э́той о́бласти пока́ ограни́чены; (*experience*) о́пыт; (*information*) изве́стия (*nt. pl.*), све́дения (*nt. pl.*); **our earliest ~ of the Slavs** на́ши пе́рвые све́дения о славя́нах; **I have no ~ of that** я не име́ю об э́том све́дений; (*range of information or experience*): **to the best of my ~** наско́лько мне изве́стно; **it came to my ~ that …** мне ста́ло изве́стно, что…; **to my certain ~** как мне достове́рно изве́стно; **not to my ~** мне э́то неизве́стно; наско́лько я зна́ю — нет; **without s.o.'s ~** без чьего́-н. ве́дома.

knowledgeable ['nɒlɪdʒəb(ə)l] *adj.* хорошо́ осведомлённый.

known [nəʊn] *adj.*: **it is a ~ fact that …** изве́стно, что; **a scene ~ to him from childhood** карти́на, знако́мая ему́ с де́тства; **everything gets ~** всё стано́вится изве́стным. *See also* **know** *v.t.*

knuckle ['nʌk(ə)l] *n.* **1.** (*anat.*) суста́в; **rap s.o. over the ~s** (*fig.*) дать (*pf.*) нагоня́й кому́-н.; **near the ~** (*coll.*) на гра́ни неприли́чного; скабрёзный, риско́ванный. **2.** (*joint of meat*) но́жка, голя́шка.

v.i.: ~ **down to one's work** прин|има́ться, -я́ться за де́ло; ~ **under (to)** уступ|а́ть, -и́ть (+*d.*); покор|я́ться, -и́ться (+*d.*).

cpds. ~**-bone** *n.* ба́бка; ~**-duster** *n.* касте́т.

KO (*abbr. of* **knockout**) нока́ут.

v.t. нокаути́ровать (*impf.*, *pf.*).

koala [kəʊ'ɑːlə] *n.* **(~ bear)** коа́ла (*m.*), су́мчатый медве́дь.

kohlrabi [kəʊl'rɑːbɪ] *n.* кольра́би (*f. indecl.*)

kolinsky [kə'lɪnskɪ] *n.* колоно́к; (*fur*) мех колонка́.

kolkhoz ['kɒlkɒz, kʌlk'hɔːz] *n.* колхо́з.

Komsomol ['kɒmsəˌmɒl] *n.* (*association*) комсомо́л; (*member*) комсомо́л|ец (*fem.* -ка); (*attr.*) комсомо́льский.

kopeck ['kəʊpek, 'kɒpek] = **copeck**

Koran [kɔː'rɑːn, kə-] *n.* кора́н.

Korea [kə'riːə] *n.* Коре́я.

Korean [kə'riːən] *m.* (*pers.*) коре́|ец (*fem.* -я́нка); (*language*) коре́йский язы́к.

adj. коре́йский.

kosher ['kəʊʃə(r), 'kɒʃ-] *adj.* коше́рный.

koumiss ['kuːmɪs] *n.* кумы́с.

ko(w)tow [kaʊ'taʊ] *n.* ни́зкий покло́н.

v.i. де́лать, с- ни́зкий покло́н; (*fig.*) раболе́пствовать (*impf.*), пресмыка́ться (*impf.*) (*перед кем*).

kraal [krɑːl] *n.* кра́аль (*m.*).

kremlin ['kremlɪn] *n.* кремль (*m.*); **the K~** Кремль; (*attr.*) кремлёвский.

cpds. ~**-watcher** *n.* кремлеве́д, кремлено́лог; ~**-watching** *n.* кремлеве́дение, кремлиноло́гия.

Kremlinologist [ˌkremlɪn'ɒlədʒɪst] *n.* кремлеве́д, кремлино́лог.

Kremlinology [ˌkremlɪn'ɒlədʒɪ] *n.* кремлеве́дение, кремлиноло́гия.

krill [krɪl] *n.* криль (*m.*).

kris [kriːs] *n.* мала́йский кинжа́л.

Krishna ['krɪʃnə] *n.* Кри́шна (*m.*).

cpd. ~**-Consciousness** *n.* (*attr.*) кришнаи́тский.

krona ['krəʊnə] *n.* (шве́дская) кро́на.

krone ['krəʊnə] *n.* (да́тская, норве́жская) кро́на.

krypton ['krɪptɒn] *n.* крипто́н.

Kubla(i) ['kuːblə, 'kuːblaɪ] *n.* Хубила́й.

kudos ['kjuːdɒs] *n.* сла́ва.

Ku-Klux-Klan [ˌkuːklʌks'klæn, ˌkjuː-] *n.* ку-клукс-кла́н.

Ku Klux Klaner [ˌkuːklʌks'klænə(r), ˌkjuː-] куклукскла́новец.

kulak ['kuːlæk] *n.* (*hist.*) кула́к.

kummel ['kʊməl] *n.* тми́нная во́дка, кю́ммель (*m.*).

kumquat ['kʌmkwɒt] *n.* кумква́т.

kung fu [kʊŋ 'fuː, kʌŋ] *n.* кун-фу́ (*nt. indecl.*).

Kuomintang [ˌkʊəmɪn'tæŋ] *n.* (*hist.*) гоминда́н.

Kurd [kɜːd] *n.* курд (*fem.* -ка).

Kurdish ['kɜːdɪʃ] *n.* ку́рдский язы́к.

adj. ку́рдский.

Kurdistan [ˌkɜːdɪ'stɑːn] *n.* Курдиста́н.

Kuwait [kʊ'weɪt] *n.* Куве́йт.

Kuwaiti [kʊ'weɪtɪ] *n.* куве́йт|ец (*fem.* -ка).

adj. куве́йтский.

kvass [kvɑːs] *n.* квас.

kW ['kɪləˌwɒt] *n.* (*abbr. of* **kilowatt(s)**) кВт, (килова́тт).

Kymric ['kɪmrɪk] *adj.* = **Cymric**

L

L (*abbr. of* **learner**): ~**-plate** ≃ щито́к с на́дписью «уче́бная» (*на маши́не*).

l. ['liːtə(r)(z)] *n.* (*abbr. of* **litre(s)**) л, (литр).

la [lɑː] *n.* (*mus.*) ля (*nt. indecl.*).

lab [læb] (*coll.*) = **laboratory**

label ['leɪb(ə)l] *n.* ярлы́к, этике́тка; **(stick-on ~)** накле́йка; (*tag*) би́рка; **pin, stick a ~ on** (*lit.*, *fig.*) прикле́и|вать, -ть (*or* прилеп|ля́ть, -и́ть) ярлы́к/этике́тку +*d.*; (*gram. or stylistic ~*, *gloss*) поме́та.

v.t. (*stick ~ on*) накле́и|вать, -ть ярлы́к на+*a.*; (*fasten ~ to*) привя́з|ывать, -а́ть ярлы́к/би́рку к+*d.*; (*fig.*): **he was ~led a fascist** ему́ прикле́или ярлы́к фаши́ста.

labial ['leɪbɪəl] *n.* **(~ consonant)** губно́й/лабиа́льный согла́сный.

adj. (*of the lips*) губно́й; (*phon.*) губно́й, лабиа́льный.

labile ['leɪbaɪl, -bɪl] *adj.* (*phys.*, *chem.*) неусто́йчивый, лаби́льный.

labiodental [ˌleɪbɪəʊ'dent(ə)l] *adj.* гу́бно-зубно́й, ла́био-дента́льный.

laboratory [lə'bɒrətərɪ] *n.* лаборато́рия; (*in school*) кабине́т; **in ~ conditions** в лаборато́рных усло́виях; ~ **assistant** лабора́нт (*fem.* -ка).

laborious [lə'bɔːrɪəs] *adj.* **1.** (*difficult*) тру́дный, тяжёлый, тя́жкий; (*toilsome*) трудоёмкий; (*wearying*) утоми́тельный. **2.** (*of style*, *forced*) вы́мученный; (*involved*) громо́здкий, тяжёлый.

laboriousness [lə'bɔːrɪəsnɪs] *n.* трудоёмкость; (*of style*) громо́здкость.

labour ['leɪbə(r)] *n.* **1.** (*toil*, *work*) труд, рабо́та; **manual ~** физи́ческий труд; **lost ~** напра́сный труд; **a ~ of love** бескоры́стный труд; люби́мое де́ло; ~ **camp** исправи́тельно-трудово́й ла́герь; ~ **colony** трудова́я коло́ния. **2.** (*pol.*, *workers*) трудя́щиеся, рабо́чий класс; **Ministry of L~** министе́рство труда́; **International L~ Organization (ILO)** Междунаро́дная организа́ция труда́ (МОТ); **L~ Day** День (*m.*) труда́. **3.** (*workforce*) рабо́чие (*pl.*), рабо́чая си́ла; **skilled ~** квалифици́рованные рабо́чие; **shortage of ~** нехва́тка рабо́чей си́лы; ~ **dispute** трудово́й конфли́кт; ~ **exchange** би́ржа труда́; ~ **relations** трудовы́е отноше́ния. **4. (L~ Party)** лейбори́стская па́ртия, лейбори́сты (*m. pl.*); **Vote L~!** голосу́йте за лейбори́стскую па́ртию!; **the L~ government** лейбори́стское прави́тельство; **a L~ MP** член парла́мента от лейбори́стской па́ртии. **5.** (*childbirth*) ро́д|ы (*pl.*, *g.* -ов); ~ **pains** родовы́е схва́тки (*f. pl.*); ~ **ward** роди́льная пала́та; **she went into ~** у неё начали́сь ро́ды; **be in ~** рожа́ть (*impf.*).

v.t.: ~ **a point** входи́ть (*impf.*) в изли́шние подро́бности; распространя́ться (*impf.*) о чём-н.

v.i. **1.** (*toil*, *work*) труди́ться (*impf.*), рабо́тать (*impf.*); **a ~ing man** рабо́чий. **2.** (*strive*, *exert o.s.*): **he is ~ing to finish his book** он прилага́ет все уси́лия, что́бы ко́нчить кни́гу; ~ **for peace** боро́ться (*impf.*) за мир. **3.** (*move*, *work etc. with difficulty*): ~ **for breath** задыха́ться (*impf.*); дыша́ть (*impf.*) с трудо́м; **the ship was ~ing** кора́бль боро́лся с волна́ми; **the car ~ed up the hill** маши́на с трудо́м взбира́лась в го́ру **3.**: ~ **under** (*suffer from*): **you are ~ing under a delusion** вы нахо́дитесь в заблужде́нии.

cpds. ~**-intensive** *adj.* трудоёмкий; ~**-saving** *adj.* рационализа́торский; трудосберега́ющий.

laboured ['leɪbəd] *adj.* **1.** (*difficult*): ~ **breathing/movement** затруднённое дыха́ние/движе́ние. **2.** (*forced*): ~ **style/compliment** вы́мученный стиль/комплиме́нт.

labourer ['leɪbərə(r)] *n.* рабо́чий.

labourite ['leɪbəˌraɪt] *n.* лейбори́ст (*fem.* -ка).

adj. лейбори́стский.

Labrador ['læbrəˌdɔː(r)] *n.* Лабрадо́р; (*dog*) лабрадо́р.

laburnum [lə'bɜːnəm] *n.* золото́й дождь.

labyrinth ['læbərɪnθ] *n.* (*lit.*, *fig.*) лабири́нт.

labyrinthine [ˌlæbə'rɪnθaɪn] *adj.* (*lit.*) лабири́нтный; (*fig.*) запу́танный.

lac [læk] *n.* (*resin*, *varnish*) лак; сыро́й шелла́к.

lace [leɪs] *n.* **1.** (*open-work fabric*) кру́жево, кружева́ (*nt. pl.*); ~ **collar** кружевно́й воротни́к; ~ **factory** кружевна́я фа́брика. **2.** (*braid*) позуме́нт; (*mil.*) галу́н. **3.** (*of shoe etc.*) шнуро́к.

v.t. **1.** (*fasten or tighten with ~*) шнурова́ть, за-; зашнуро́в|ывать, -а́ть; **he ~d up his shoes** он зашнурова́л боти́нки; **she ~d in her waist** она́ затя́гивалась в корсе́т.

2. (*interlace*) спле|та́ть, -сти́. **3.** (*trim with* ~) отде́л|ывать, -ать кружева́ми. **4.** (*fortify*): ~ **coffee with rum** подл|ива́ть, -и́ть ром в ко́фе.

v.i.: ~ **into s.o.** намя́ть (*pf.*) бока́ кому́-н. (*coll.*).

cpds. **~-maker** *n.* (*fem.*) кружевни́ца; **~-making** *n.* (*by hand*) плете́ние кру́жев; (*by machine*) произво́дство кру́жев.

lacerate [ˈlæsəˌreɪt] *v.t.* (*lit., fig.*) терза́ть, рас-/ис-; растерз|ывать, -а́ть; (*wound*) ра́нить (*impf., pf.*).

laceration [ˌlæsəˈreɪʃ(ə)n] *n.* (*tearing*) терза́ние, разрыва́ние; (*wound*) рва́ная ра́на.

lachrymal [ˈlækrɪm(ə)l] *adj.* слёзный.

lachrymose [ˈlækrɪˌməʊs] *adj.* слезли́вый, плакси́вый.

lack [læk] *n.* недоста́ток; **for ~ of money** из-за недоста́тка (*or* за неиме́нием) де́нег; **for ~ of evidence** за отсу́тствием ули́к; **there was no ~ of people** в лю́дях не́ было недоста́тка; **there was no ~ of water** воды́ бы́ло вполне́ доста́точно.

v.t. & i.: **he ~s sth.** ему́ чего́-то недостаёт; **he ~s, is ~ing in courage** у него́ не хвата́ет хра́брости; **we ~ money** мы нужда́емся в деньга́х; **a subject on which information is ~ ing** предме́т, о кото́ром ничего́ не изве́стно; **a week ~ing in incident** неде́ля, бе́дная собы́тиями; **he ~s for nothing** у него́ ни в чём нет недоста́тка.

cpd. **~-lustre** *adj.* ту́склый, без бле́ска.

lackadaisical [ˌlækəˈdeɪzɪk(ə)l] *adj.* то́мный, вя́лый, апати́чный; **in a ~ manner** спустя́ рукава́, без воодушевле́ния.

lackey [ˈlækɪ] *n.* (*lit., fig.*) лаке́й; (*fig.*) подхали́м.

laconic [ləˈkɒnɪk] *adj.* (*of pers.*) неразгово́рчивый, немногосло́вный; (*of speech etc.*) лакони́чный, сжа́тый.

lacon(ic)ism [ˈlækəˌnɪz(ə)m, ləˈkɒnɪˌsɪz(ə)m] *n.* лакони́зм; (*saying*) лакони́чное изрече́ние.

lacquer [ˈlækə(r)] *n.* политу́ра (*no pl.*); лак.

v.t. лакирова́ть (*impf.*).

cpd. **~-ware** *n.* лакиро́ванные изде́лия.

lacrosse [ləˈkrɒs] *n.* лакро́сс.

lactate [lækˈteɪt] *v.i.* выделя́ть (*impf.*) молоко́.

lactation [lækˈteɪʃ(ə)n] *n.* лакта́ция, выделе́ние молока́; (*breast-feeding*) кормле́ние гру́дью.

lactic [ˈlæktɪk] *adj.* моло́чный.

lactovegetarian [ˌlæktəʊˌvedʒɪˈteərɪən] *n.* младовегетариа́нец.

lacuna [ləˈkjuːnə] *n.* пробе́л, лаку́на.

lacustrine [ləˈkʌstraɪn] *adj.* озёрный; ~ **dwellings** сва́йные постро́йки (*f. pl.*) (на о́зере).

lad [læd] *n.* (*boy*) ма́льчик; (*fellow, youth*) па́рень (*m.*), ма́лый; (*pl.*) ребя́т|а (*pl., g.* —); **~s and lasses** хло́пцы и девча́т|а (*pl., g.* —); **good ~!** молоде́ц!; молодча́га! (*m.*); молодчи́на (*m.*); **just you wait, my ~!** погоди́, па́рень!; **he's a good ~** он па́рень свойский; **a regular ~** рубаха-па́рень; **a bit of a ~** гуля́ка (*m.*).

ladder [ˈlædə(r)] *n.* **1.** ле́стница; **folding/extending ~** складна́я/выдвижна́я ле́стница; (*fig.*): **~ of success** путь к успе́ху; **climb the social ~** поднима́ться (*impf.*) по обще́ственной ле́стнице; **he has one foot on the ~** он на́чал де́лать карье́ру. **2.** (*on a ship*) трап. **3.** (*in stocking*) спусти́вшаяся петля́; **mend a ~** подн|има́ть, -я́ть пе́тлю.

v.t. & i.: **I have ~ed my stocking; my stocking has ~ed** у меня́ спусти́лась петля́ на чулке́; **you have ~ed my stocking** вы мне порва́ли чуло́к.

cpd. **~-proof** *adj.* неспуска́ющийся.

laddie [ˈlædɪ] = **lad**

lade [leɪd] *v.t.* (*usu. p.p.*) грузи́ть, на-; нагру|жа́ть, -зи́ть; **he returned ~n with books** он верну́лся нагру́женный кни́гами; **the table was ~n with food** стол ломи́лся от еды́/яств; **she was ~n with cares** она́ была́ обременена́ забо́тами.

la-di-da [ˌlɑːdɪˈdɑː] *adj.* (*coll.*) мане́рный, жема́нный.

ladies [ˈleɪdɪs] *n. see* **lady** *n.* **6.**

lading [ˈleɪdɪŋ] *n.* (*process*) погру́зка; (*cargo*) груз; (*on hired ship*) фрахт; **bill of ~** коноса́мент, тра́нспортная накладна́я.

ladle [ˈleɪd(ə)l] *n.* ковш; **soup ~** развива́тельная ло́жка.

v.t. че́рпать (*impf.*); отче́рп|ывать, -а́ть; ~ **out soup** разл|ива́ть, -и́ть суп; (*fig.*): ~ **out compliments** выдава́ть (*impf.*) комплиме́нты (напра́во и нале́во).

lady [ˈleɪdɪ] *n.* **1.** (*woman of social status*) да́ма; **society ~** све́тская да́ма; **first ~** (*US*) супру́га президе́нта; **L~ Bountiful** благотвори́тельница; (*in address*): **my ~** суда́рыня; (*as title*) ле́ди (*f. indecl.*). **2.** (*relig.*): **Our L~** Богоро́дица; **L~ chapel** приде́л Богома́тери; **L~ Day** Благове́щение. **3.** (*courteous or formal for woman*) да́ма, госпожа́; **Ladies and Gentlemen** да́мы и господа́; **ladies first!** доро́гу да́мам; **old ~** пожила́я же́нщина; **young ~** ба́рышня; (*sweetheart*) возлю́бленная; (*fiancée*) неве́ста; **leading ~** (*theatr.*) веду́щая актри́са; **ladies' man** да́мский уго́дник, волоки́та (*m.*). **4.** (*attr.*): ~ **doctor** же́нщина-врач. **5.** (*wife*): **your good ~; your ~ wife** ва́ша супру́га. **6.**: **the ladies'** (*or* **ladies**) (*coll., lavatory*) же́нская убо́рная.

cpds. **~bird,** (*US*) **~bug** *nn.* бо́жья коро́вка; **~-in-waiting** *n.* фре́йлина; **~-killer** *n.* сердцее́д; **~like** *adj.* (*refined, elegant*) изя́щный, делика́тный, благоро́дный; **~-love** *n.* возлю́бленная; да́ма се́рдца; **~'s-maid** *n.* камери́стка.

ladyship [ˈleɪdɪʃɪp] *n.*: **her/your ~** её/ва́ша ми́лость.

lag[1] [læg] *n.* (*delay*) запа́здывание; ~ **of the tide** запа́здывание прили́ва.

v.i. отст|ава́ть, -а́ть; **the children were ~ging (behind)** де́ти тащи́лись сза́ди; **they worked badly and ~ged behind** они́ пло́хо рабо́тали и плели́сь в хвосте́.

lag[2] [læg] *n.* (*coll., convict*) каторжа́нин, ка́торжник; **old ~** рецидиви́ст.

lag[3] [læg] *v.t.* (*wrap in felt etc.*) изоли́ровать/покрыва́ть (*impf.*) (во́йлоком); (*encase with boards*) обш|ива́ть, -и́ть до́сками.

lager [ˈlɑːgə(r)] *n.* све́тлое пи́во.

laggard [ˈlægəd] *n.* ло́дырь (*m.*); отстаю́щий.

lagging [ˈlægɪŋ] *n.* (*for pipes etc.*) терми́ческая изоля́ция, термоизоля́ция, обши́вка.

lagoon [ləˈguːn] *n.* лагу́на.

laicization [ˌleɪɪsaɪˈzeɪʃ(ə)n] *n.* секуляриза́ция.

laicize [ˈleɪɪˌsaɪz] *v.t.* секуляризи́ровать (*impf., pf.*).

laid-back [leɪdˈbæk] *adj.* непринуждённый, споко́йный.

lair [leə(r)] *n.* ло́говище; (*of bear*) берло́га; (*fig.*): **thieves' ~** воровско́й прито́н.

laird [ˈleəd] *n.* поме́щик (в Шотла́ндии).

laissez-faire [ˌleseɪˈfeə(r)] *n.* невмеша́тельство; поли́тика невмеша́тельства прави́тельства в эконо́мику.

laity [ˈleɪɪtɪ] *n.* (*relig.*) миря́не (*m. pl.*); (*those outside a profession*) профа́ны (*m. pl.*); непрофессиона́лы (*m. pl.*); обыва́тели (*m. pl.*).

lake[1] [leɪk] *n.* о́зеро; (*attr.*): **L~ District** Озёрный край; **L~ Superior** Ве́рхнее о́зеро.

cpds. **~-dwelling** *n.* сва́йная постро́йка; **~side** *n.* бе́рег о́зера.

lake[2] [leɪk] *n.* (*pigment*) кра́сочный лак.

Lallans [ˈlælənz] *n.* диале́кт ю́жной ча́сти Шотла́ндии.

lam [læm] (*sl.*) *v.t.* колоти́ть, от-.

v.i.: ~ **into s.o.** набро́ситься (*pf.*) на кого́-н.

lama [ˈlɑːmə] *n.* ла́ма (*m.*).

Lamaism [ˈlɑːməˌɪz(ə)m] *n.* ламаи́зм.

lamasery [ˈlɑːməsərɪ, ləˈmɑːsərɪ] *n.* ламаи́стский монасты́рь.

lamb [læm] *n.* ягнёнок, бара́шек; **L~ of God** А́гнец Бо́жий; **Persian ~** кара́куль (*m.*); **as innocent as a ~** (*fig.*) су́щий младе́нец; наи́вная душа́; **lead like a ~ to the slaughter** повести́ (*pf.*) как а́гнца на закла́ние; **as well be hanged for a sheep as a ~** семь бед — оди́н отве́т; (*fig., of child or mild pers.*) ягнёнок, ове́чка; (*meat*) бара́шек; **leg of ~** бара́нья нога́.

v.i. (*of ewe*) ягни́ться, о(б)-; **the ~ing season** вре́мя ягне́ния.

cpds. **~like** *adj.* кро́ткий, сми́рный; **~skin** *n.* овчи́на; бара́шек; мерлу́шка; **~'s-wool** *n.* поя́рок.

lambast(e) [læmˈbeɪst] *v.t.* дуба́сить, от- (*coll.*).

lambent [ˈlæmbənt] *adj.* (*flickering*) игра́ющий, мерца́ющий; (*glowing*) светя́щийся, сия́ющий.

lambkin [ˈlæmkɪn] *n.* ягнёночек.

lame [leɪm] *adj.* **1.** хромо́й; **be, walk ~** хрома́ть (*impf.*); **he is ~ in one leg** он хрома́ет на одну́ но́гу; **the halt and the**

~ хромы́е и не́мощные (*pl.*). **2.** (*fig., of argument, speech etc.*) сла́бый; **a ~ excuse** сла́бая отгово́рка; (*of metre*) хрома́ющий.

v.t. кале́чить, ис-; (*maim*) уве́чить, из-.

cpds. **~-brain** *n.* тугоду́м, тупи́ца; **~-brained** *adj.* тупо́й, бестолко́вый.

lamé ['lɑ:meɪ] *n.* ламе́ (*indecl.*).

lameness ['leɪmnɪs] *n.* хромота́; (*fig., of excuse etc.*) неубеди́тельность.

lament [lə'ment] *n.* (*expression of grief*) се́тование, причита́ние; (*in music or verse*) плач; эле́гия.

v.t.: **~ one's fate** се́товать, по- (*or* ропта́ть, воз-) на судьбу́; **~ one's youth** опла́к|ивать, -ать свою́ мо́лодость; **late ~ed** поко́йный, незабве́нный.

v.i. се́товать, по-; причита́ть (*impf.*) (по+*p.*); (*complain*) жа́ловаться (*impf.*).

lamentable ['læməntəb(ə)l] *adj.* плаче́вный; приско́рбный, жа́лкий.

lamentation [ˌlæmən'teɪʃ(ə)n] *n.* (*lamenting*) се́тование, причита́ние; (*lament*) плач, жа́лобы (*f. pl.*); **L~s** (*bibl.*) Кни́га Плач Иереми́и; **they raised a cry of ~** они́ по́дняли вопль.

laminate[1] ['læmɪnət] *adj.* (*in plates*) пласти́нчатый; (*in layers*) расслоённый, слои́стый.

laminate[2] ['læmɪˌneɪt] *v.t.* (*roll into plates*) прока́т|ывать, -а́ть в листы́; (*split into layers*) рассл|а́ивать, -ои́ть.

v.i. расщеп|ля́ться, -и́ться.

lamination [ˌlæmɪ'neɪʃ(ə)n] *n.* (*splitting*) расслое́ние; (*rolling*) прока́тка; раска́тывание; (*geol.*) слои́стость.

lamp [læmp] *n.* ла́мпа; **standard ~** торше́р; **table ~** насто́льная ла́мпа; (*on vehicle*) фа́ра; (*lantern*; *street ~*) фона́рь (*m.*); (*electric bulb*) ла́мп(очк)а; (*eccles.*) свети́льник; (*icon-~*) лампа́да.

cpds. **~black** *n.* (ла́мповая) са́жа; ко́поть; **~-chimney, ~-glass** *nn.* ла́мповое стекло́; **~light** *n.* (*indoors*) свет ла́мпы; (*in street*) фона́рный свет; **~lighter** *n.* фона́рщик; **~-oil** *n.* кероси́н; **~-post, ~-standard** *nn.* у́личный фона́рь; **~shade** *n.* абажу́р.

lampoon [læm'pu:n] *n.* па́сквиль (*m.*).

v.t. писа́ть, на- па́сквиль на+*a.*

lampoonist [læm'pu:nɪst] *n.* пасквиля́нт.

lamprey ['læmprɪ] *n.* мино́га.

LAN (*abbr. of* **local area network**) (*comput.*) лока́льная сеть.

lance [lɑ:ns] *n.* (*for throwing*) копьё; (*cavalry weapon*) пи́ка; (*for fishing*) остро́га; (*fig.*): **break a ~ for s.o.** лома́ть (*impf.*) ко́пья за кого́-н.; **break a ~ with s.o.** скре́|щивать, -сти́ть шпа́ги с кем-н.

v.t. (*pierce with ~*) коло́ть, за- пи́кой; (*med.*) вскры|ва́ть, -ть ланце́том.

cpd. **~-corporal** *n.* мла́дший капра́л.

lancer ['lɑ:nsə(r)] *n.* ула́н; (*pl., regiment*) ула́нский полк; (*pl., dance*) лансье́ (*indecl.*).

lancet ['lɑ:nsɪt] *n.* (*surg.*) ланце́т; (*archit.*): **~ arch** ланце́тная/стре́льчатая а́рка; **~ window** стре́льчатое окно́.

land [lænd] *n.* **1.** земля́; **~ mass** земе́льный масси́в; (*dry ~*) су́ша; **they sighted ~** они́ уви́дели су́шу/зе́млю; **travel by ~** е́хать (*det.*) су́шей (*or* по су́ше); **carriage by ~** сухопу́тная перево́зка; **~ forces** (*mil.*) сухопу́тные войска́; **reach, make ~** дост|ига́ть, -и́гнуть бе́рега; **~ breeze** береговой ве́тер; **see how the ~ lies** (*fig.*) пров|еря́ть, -е́рить как обстоя́т дела́. **2.** (*ground, soil*) грунт, по́чва; **he works on the ~** он рабо́тает на земле́; **work the ~** обраба́тывать (*impf.*) зе́млю; **good farming ~** плодоро́дная по́чва; **a house with some ~** дом с земе́льным уча́стком; **~ hunger** земе́льный го́лод; **~ tax** поземе́льный нало́г; **~ tenure** землевладе́ние. **3.** (*country*) земля́, страна́; (*state*) госуда́рство; **~ of dreams** страна́ грёз; **~ of promise, promised ~** земля́ обетова́нная; **native ~** ро́дина, отчи́зна; край родно́й; оте́чество; **in a foreign ~** за грани́цей; **in the ~ of the living** в живы́х; **no man's ~** ничья́ земля́; (*mil.*) ниче́йная полоса́. **4.** (*property*) земля́, име́ние; **he owns ~** он владе́ет землёй; **his ~s extend for several miles** его́ владе́ния простира́ются на не́сколько миль.

v.t. **1.** (*bring to shore*): **~ a vessel** прив|оди́ть, -ести́ су́дно к бе́регу; **~ cargo** выгружа́ть, вы́грузить груз; **~ passengers** выса́живать, вы́садить пассажи́ров. **2.**: **~ an aircraft** сажа́ть, посади́ть (*or* приземл|я́ть, -и́ть) самолёт. **3.**: **~ a fish** выта́скивать, вы́тащить ры́бу на бе́рег; **a ~ed fish** по́йманная ры́ба. **4.** (*win*) выи́грывать, вы́играть; (*secure*): **he ~ed himself a good job** он пристро́ился на хоро́шую рабо́ту. **5.** (*get, involve*): **that will ~ you in gaol** э́то доведёт вас до тюрьмы́; **he ~ed himself in trouble** он навлёк на себя́ беду́; **he ~ed himself with a lot of work** он загрузи́л себя́ рабо́той. **6.** (*deal*): **I ~ed him one on the nose** я зае́хал ему́ по́ носу (*coll.*).

v.i. **1.** (*of ship*) прист|ава́ть, -а́ть к бе́регу; прича́ли|вать, -ть; (*of passengers*) выса́живаться, вы́садиться; сходи́ть, сойти́ (на бе́рег). **2.** (*of aircraft*) приземл|я́ться, -и́ться; де́лать, с- поса́дку; (*on water*) приводн|я́ться, -и́ться; (*space-craft on moon*) прилун|я́ться, -и́ться; (*on Mars*) примарси́ться (*pf.*). **3.** (*of athlete, after jump*) приземл|я́ться, -и́ться. **4.** (*fall, lit. or fig.*): **she ~ed in trouble** она́ попа́ла в беду́; **we ~ed in a bog** мы угоди́ли в боло́то; **the ball ~ed on his head** мяч попа́л ему́ в го́лову. **5.**: **~ up** (*coll., arrive*) приб|ыва́ть, -ы́ть; **I ~ed up in the wrong street** я очути́лся не на той у́лице.

cpds. **~-agent** *n.* (*steward*) управля́ющий име́нием; (*dealer in property*) аге́нт по прода́же земе́льных уча́стков; **~fall** *n.*: **make a ~fall** под|ходи́ть, -ойти́ к бе́регу; **~-girl** *n.* рабо́тница на фе́рме; **~holder** *n.* землевладе́лец; **~lady** *n.* хозя́йка; **~line** *n.* назе́мная ли́ния свя́зи; **~-locked** *adj.* окружённый су́шей, закры́тый; без вы́хода к мо́рю; **~lord** *n.* хозя́ин; (*owner of ~*) землевладе́лец; (*of building*) до́мовладе́лец; **~lubber** *n.* сухопу́тная кры́са; **~mark** *n.* (*boundary marker*) межево́й столб; (*prominent feature*) заме́тный предме́т на ме́стности; (*from air*) назе́мный опознава́тельный знак; (*from sea*) берегово́й знак; (*mil.*) (назе́мный) ориенти́р; (*turning-point in history etc.*) ве́ха; **~-mine** *n.* фуга́с; **~owner** *n.* землевладе́лец; **~rail** *n.* коросте́ль (*m.*), дерга́ч; **~slide** *n.* (*of hill etc.*) обва́л; (*subsidence*) о́ползень (*m.*); (*pol.*): **they won by a ~slide** они́ одержа́ли реши́тельную побе́ду; **~slip** *n.* обва́л, о́ползень (*m.*); **~sman** *n.* неморя́к; **~-surveying** *n.* (геодези́ческая) съёмка, межева́ние; **~-surveyor** *n.* землеме́р; **~-tax** *n.* земе́льный нало́г.

landau ['lændɔ:] *n.* ландо́ (*indecl.*).

landed ['lændɪd] *adj.* **1.** (*possessing land*) землевладе́льческий; **~ gentry** поме́щики (*m. pl.*). **2.** (*consisting of land*): **~ property** земе́льные владе́ния.

lander ['lændə(r)] *n.* (*aeron.*) спуска́емый аппара́т.

landing ['lændɪŋ] *n.* **1.** (*bringing or coming to earth*) поса́дка, приземле́ние; **~ approach** захо́д на поса́дку; **forced ~** вы́нужденная поса́дка. **2.** (*on water*) приводне́ние; (*on the moon*) прилуне́ние. **3.** (*putting ashore; depositing by air*) вы́садка; (*of goods*) вы́грузка. **4.** (*mil.*) деса́нт, вы́садка деса́нта; **opposed ~** вы́садка (деса́нта) с бо́ем (*or* при сопротивле́нии проти́вника). **5.** (*on stairs*) (ле́стничная) площа́дка.

cpds. **~-craft** *n.* деса́нтное су́дно; деса́нтный (броне)ка́тер; **~-deck** *n.* поса́дочная па́луба; **~-field** *n.* лётное по́ле; **~-gear** *n.* шасси́ (*nt. indecl.*); **~-ground** *n.* взлётно-поса́дочная площа́дка; **~-net** *n.* подсачо́к, сачо́к; **~-party** *n.* деса́нтная гру́ппа, деса́нт; **~-stage** *n.* дебаркаде́р, при́стань; **~-strip** *n.* поса́дочная полоса́.

landscape [ˌlændskeɪp, 'læns-] *n.* (*picture*) пейза́ж; (*scenery*) ландша́фт, вид ме́стности.

cpds. **~-gardening** *n.* садо́во-па́рковая архитекту́ра; **~-painter** *n.* пейзажи́ст; **~-painting** *n.* (*picture*) пейза́ж; (*art*) иску́сство пейза́жа.

landscapist ['lændˌskeɪpɪst, 'lænˌs-] *n.* пейзажи́ст.

landward ['lændwəd] *n.*: **to ~** к бе́регу.

adj.: **on the ~ side** со стороны́ су́ши.

adv. (*also* **~s**) к бе́регу.

lane [leɪn] *n.* **1.** (*narrow street*) переу́лок, у́зкая у́лочка; (*country road*) доро́жка, тропи́нка. **2.** (*between rows of* *people*) прохо́д; **form a ~** вы́строиться (*pf.*). **3.** (*of traffic*) ряд; **get into ~** вста|ва́ть, -ть в ряд; **four-~ highway** автостра́да с четырьмя́ ряда́ми движе́ния. **4.** (*air route*) тра́сса. **5.** (*for shipping*) морско́й путь; (*through ice*) разво́дье. **6.** (*on race-track*, *swimming-pool*) доро́жка; **wrong ~** чужа́я доро́жка.

language [ˈlæŋgwɪdʒ] *n.* язы́к; (*esp. spoken*) речь; **~ and literature** (*as subj. of study*) филоло́гия; **in a foreign ~** на иностра́нном языке́; **they don't speak the same ~** (*fig.*) они́ говоря́т на ра́зных языка́х; **a degree in ~s** дипло́м об оконча́нии филологи́ческого факульте́та; (*words*, *expressions*): **he has a great command of ~** он прекра́сно владе́ет языко́м; **bad ~** сквернесло́вие; **strong ~** си́льные выраже́ния; **science of ~** языкове́дение, языкозна́ние; **native ~** родно́й язы́к; **spoken ~** разгово́рный язы́к; **business ~** делова́я речь; **~ student** (*at university*) фило́лог; **~ laboratory** лингафо́нный кабине́т.

languid [ˈlæŋgwɪd] *adj.* то́мный, вя́лый.

languidness [ˈlæŋgwɪdnɪs] *n.* то́мность, вя́лость.

languish [ˈlæŋgwɪʃ] *v.i.* томи́ться (*impf.*); изныва́ть (*impf.*); **a ~ing look** то́мный взгляд.

languor [ˈlæŋgə(r)] *n.* то́мность, вя́лость; (*pleasant*) исто́ма.

languorous [ˈlæŋgərəs] *adj.* то́мный; по́лный исто́мы.

lank [læŋk] *adj.* **1.** (*tall and lean*) поджа́рый, худоща́вый. **2.**: **~ hair** гла́дкие/прямы́е во́лосы.

lanky [ˈlæŋkɪ] *adj.* долговя́зый; **~ person** верзи́ла (*c.g.*) (*coll.*).

lanolin [ˈlænəlɪn] *n.* ланоли́н.

lantern [ˈlænt(ə)n] *n.* **1.** фона́рь (*m.*); **magic ~** волше́бный фона́рь. **2.** (*of lighthouse*) светова́я ка́мера.

cpds. **~-jawed** *adj.* с впа́лыми щека́ми; **~-lecture** *n.* ле́кция с пока́зом диапозити́вов; **~-slide** *n.* диапозити́в.

lanthanum [ˈlænθənəm] *n.* ланта́н.

lanyard [ˈlænjəd, -jɑːd] *n.* (*cord*) реме́нь (*m.*); (*for securing sail*) та́лреп; (*mil.*) вытяжно́й шнур.

Laos [laʊz, laʊs] *n.* Лао́с.

Laotian [ˈlaʊʃɪən, lɑːˈəʊʃɪən] *n.* (*pers.*) лао́с|ец (*fem.* -ка); лаотя́н|ин (*fem.* -ка); (*language*) лао́сский язы́к.

adj. лао́сский.

lap[1] [læp] *n.* **1.**: **the boy sat on his mother's ~** ма́льчик сиде́л у ма́тери на коле́нях; **the cat climbed on to my ~** ко́шка забрала́сь ко мне на коле́ни; (*fig.*): **in the ~ of the gods** в руце́ бо́жьей; **he lives in the ~ of luxury** ≃ он живёт как у Христа́ за па́зухой. **2.** (*of garment*) пола́, фа́лда, подо́л.

cpds. **~-dog** *n.* боло́нка; **~top** *adj.*: **~top computer** наколе́нный компью́тер.

lap[2] [læp] *n.* **1.** (*coil or turn e.g. of rope*) вито́к, оборо́т; (*of rolled cloth*) руло́н. **2.** (*circuit of race-track*) круг; **he won by 3 ~s** он победи́л, обойдя́ проти́вника на 3 кру́га; **I'm on the last ~** (*fig.*, *have almost finished*) я закругля́юсь; я почти́ ко́нчил.

v.t. **1.** (*wrap*): **~ cloth round sth.** обёр|тывать, -ну́ть что-н. мате́рией; **~ sth. in cloth** зав|ора́чивать, -ерну́ть что-н. в мате́рию; (*fig.*, *surround*, *enfold*) окруж|а́ть, -и́ть. **2.** (*sport*: *be a ~ ahead of*) об|ходи́ть, -ойти́ (*or* об|гоня́ть, -огна́ть) (*кого*) на круг.

lap[3] [læp] *n.* (*sound of waves*) плеск.

v.t. **1.** (*drink with tongue*) лака́ть, вы́-; **the cat ~ped up the milk** ко́шка вы́лакала молоко́. **2.** (*fig.*, *accept eagerly*) жа́дно глота́ть (*impf.*); **he ~ped up their compliments** он жа́дно лови́л их комплиме́нты.

v.i. (*of waves*) плеска́ться (*impf.*); **waves ~ on the beach** во́лны пле́щутся о бе́рег.

lapel [ləˈpel] *n.* ла́цкан, отворо́т.

lapidary [ˈlæpɪdərɪ] *n.* (*gem cutter*) грани́льщик; (*polisher*) шлифова́льщик; (*engraver*) гравёр.

adj. **1.** (*pert. to stone-cutting*) грани́льный; **a ~ inscription** вы́гравированная на ка́мне на́дпись. **2.** (*fig.*) лапида́рный.

lapis lazuli [ˌlæpɪs ˈlæzjuːlɪ, -ˌlaɪ] *n.* лазури́т, ля́пис-лазу́рь.

Lapland [ˈlæplænd] *n.* Лапла́ндия.

Laplander [ˈlæpˌlændə(r)] *n.* лапла́нд|ец (*fem.* -ка).

Lapp [læp] *n.* **1.** (*pers.*) саа́м (*fem.* -ка); лопа́р|ь (*fem.* -ка). **2.** (*also* **~ish:** *language*) саа́мский/лопа́рский язы́к; язы́к саа́ми.

adj. **1.** (*also* **~ish**) лопа́рский, саа́мский. **2.** (*of Lapland*) лапла́ндский.

lapse [læps] *n.* **1.** (*slight mistake*, *slip*) упуще́ние, опло́шность; (*of memory*) прова́л па́мяти; (*of the pen*) опи́ска; (*of the tongue*) обмо́лвка, огово́рка. **2.** (*moral deviation*) просту́пок; (*decline*) паде́ние. **3.** (*leg.*, *ending of right etc.*) прекраще́ние; недействи́тельность. **4.** (*passage of time*) тече́ние; **after the ~ of a month** по истече́нии ме́сяца; (*interval*) промежу́ток.

v.i. **1.** (*decline morally*; *slip back*) пасть (*pf.*); **they ~d into heresy** они́ впа́ли в е́ресь; **he ~d into his old ways** он приня́лся за ста́рое; **~ into idleness** облени́ться (*pf.*); **~ into silence** зам|олка́ть, -о́лкнуть; **a ~d Catholic** бы́вший като́лик. **2.** (*leg.*, *become void*) теря́ть, по- си́лу; (*revert*): **the property ~d to the Crown** име́ние отошло́ к казне́. **3.** (*of time*) про|ходи́ть, -йти́; минова́ть (*impf.*, *pf.*).

lapsus linguae [ˌlæpsəs ˈlɪŋgwaɪ] *n.* обмо́лвка, огово́рка.

lapwing [ˈlæpwɪŋ] *n.* чи́бис, пи́галица.

larboard [ˈlɑːbəd] *n.* ле́вый борт.

larcenous [ˈlɑːsənəs] *adj.*: **with ~ intent** с наме́рением соверши́ть кра́жу.

larceny [ˈlɑːsənɪ] *n.* кра́жа; **grand/petty ~** кру́пная/ме́лкая кра́жа.

larch [lɑːtʃ] *n.* (*tree*) ли́ственница; **(~wood)** древеси́на ли́ственницы.

lard [lɑːd] *n.* лярд, топлёное свино́е са́ло.

v.t. (*cul.*) шпигова́ть, на-; (*fig.*) усна|ща́ть, -сти́ть.

larder [ˈlɑːdə(r)] *n.* кладова́я, кладо́вка.

lares and penates [ˈlɑːriːz] *n.* ла́ры и пена́ты (*pl.*); родны́е пена́ты.

large [lɑːdʒ] *n.*: **at ~** (*free*) на во́ле, на свобо́де; **set at ~** освобо|жда́ть, -ди́ть; (*in general*) целико́м; во всём объёме; в свое́й ма́ссе; **the public at ~** широ́кая пу́блика; **people at ~ were dissatisfied** наро́д в основно́м был недово́лен; (*at length*) простра́нно; (*without particularization*): **he casts imputations at ~** он разбра́сывает обвине́ния напра́во и нале́во; (*coll.*) он обвиня́ет всех чо́хом; **ambassador at ~** (*US*) посо́л по осо́бым поруче́ниям.

adj. большо́й, кру́пный; **a man of ~ sympathies** челове́к большо́го се́рдца; **on a ~ scale** в большо́м/кру́пном масшта́бе; **a criminal on a ~ scale** престу́пник кру́пного кали́бра; **~ handwriting** кру́пный по́черк; **in ~ type** кру́пным шри́фтом; **a ~ landowner** кру́пный землевладе́лец; **a ~ population** многочи́сленное/большо́е населе́ние; (*spacious*) просто́рный; (*considerable*) значи́тельный (*copious*) оби́льный; (*extensive*) широ́кий; (*fat*) по́лный; **as ~ as life** (*fig.*) во всей красе́; **here he is, as ~ as life** он тут как тут; **he turned up as ~ as life** он яви́лся со́бственной персо́ной; **~r than life** бо́лее, чем в натура́льную величину́; (*fig.*) преувели́ченный.

adv.: **by and ~** вообще́ говоря́.

cpds. **~-bore** *adj.* крупнокали́берный; **~-handed** *adj.* (*generous*) ще́дрый; **~-hearted** *adj.* великоду́шный; **~-minded** *adj.* широ́ких взгля́дов; **~-scale** *adj.* крупномасшта́бный; **a ~-scale map** крупномасшта́бная ка́рта.

largely [ˈlɑːdʒlɪ] *adv.* (*to a great extent*) по бо́льшей ча́сти; в значи́тельной сте́пени; (*generously*) ще́дро.

largess(e) [lɑːˈʒes] *n.* щедро́ты (*f. pl.*).

largish [ˈlɑːdʒɪʃ] *adj.* дово́льно большо́й; великова́тый.

largo [ˈlɑːgəʊ] *n.*, *adj.* & *adv.* ла́рго (*indecl.*).

lariat [ˈlærɪət] *n.* арка́н.

lark[1] [lɑːk] *n.* (*bird*) жа́воронок; **rise with the ~** вста|ва́ть, -ть с петуха́ми.

cpd. **~spur** *n.* жи́вокость, шпо́рник.

lark[2] [lɑːk] *n.* (*coll.*), (*prank*) прока́за; (*amusement*) заба́ва; **for a ~** шу́тки ра́ди; **what a ~!** вот потёха!

v.i.: **~ about** резви́ться (*impf.*).

larrikin [ˈlærɪkɪn] *n.* хулига́н.

larrup [ˈlærəp] *v.t.* (*coll.*) поро́ть, вы́-; да|ва́ть, -ть (*кому*) трёпку/по́рку.

larva [ˈlɑːvə] *n.* личи́нка.

laryngeal [lə'rɪndʒɪəl] *adj.* горта́нный.
laryngitis [,lærɪn'dʒaɪtɪs] *n.* ларинги́т.
laryngoscope [lə'rɪŋgə,skəʊp] *n.* ларингоско́п.
larynx ['lærɪŋks] *n.* горта́нь.
Lascar ['læskə(r)] *n.* матро́с-инди́ец.
lascivious [lə'sɪvɪəs] *adj.* похотли́вый.
lasciviousness [lə'sɪvɪəsnɪs] *n.* по́хоть, похотли́вость.
laser ['leɪzə(r)] *n.* ла́зер; (*attr.*) ла́зерный; **~ printer** (*comput.*) ла́зерный при́нтер.
lash[1] [læʃ] *n.* (**eye ~**) ресни́ца.
lash[2] [læʃ] *n.* **1.** (*thong*) реме́нь (*m.*); **he got the ~** он был нака́зан плетью. **2.** (*stroke*) уда́р (плетью); **he got fifty ~es** он получи́л пятьдеся́т уда́ров плетью; (*fig.*): **the ~ of criticism** бич кри́тики; **he felt the ~ of her tongue** он по себе́ знал, како́й у неё о́стрый язы́к.
v.t. **1.** (*with whip; also of wind, rain*) хлест|а́ть, -ну́ть; (*fig.*): **~ o.s. into a fury** разъяр|я́ться, -и́ться; (*with satire, criticism, abuse*) бичева́ть (*impf.*). **2.** (*wave about*): **the dog ~ed its tail** соба́ка би́ла хвосто́м. **3.** (*fasten with rope etc.*) свя́з|ывать, -а́ть; привя́з|ывать, -а́ть.
v.i.: **the rain ~ed against the window** ве́тер хлеста́л в окно́; **he ~ed into his opponent** он набро́сился на своего́ проти́вника.
with advs.: **~ down** *v.t.* привя́з|ывать, -а́ть (*что к чему*); (*naut.*) найто́вить, об-; **~ out** *v.i.* (*with fists*) наки́|дываться, -нуться (*на кого*); (*kick*) ляг|а́ть, -ну́ть; (*verbally*) разра|жа́ться, -зи́ться бра́нью; (*coll., spend lavishly*) сори́ть (*impf.*) деньга́ми; **~ together** *v.i.* свя́з|ывать, -а́ть.
cpd. **~-up** *n.* (*makeshift*) времянка.
lashing ['læʃɪŋ] *n.* (*whipping*) по́рка; (*pl., coll., plenty*): **~s of cream** ма́сса сли́вок.
lass [læs], **-ie** ['læsɪ] *nn.* (*child*) де́вочка; (*young woman*) де́вушка.
lassitude ['læsɪ,tju:d] *n.* уста́лость, утомле́ние, вя́лость.
lasso [læ'su:, 'læsəʊ] *n.* арка́н, лассо́ (*indecl.*).
v.t. арка́нить, за-.
last[1] [lɑ:st] *n.* (*shoemaker's*) коло́дка; **stick to your ~!** (*fig.*) занима́йся свои́м де́лом!; ≃ всяк сверчо́к знай свой шесто́к.
last[2] [lɑ:st] *n.* (*final or most recent pers. or thg.*): **he was the ~ of his line** он был после́дним в роду́; **he was the ~ to go** он ушёл после́дним; **our house is the ~ in the road** наш дом после́дний/кра́йний на у́лице; **the ~ of the wine** оста́тки (*m. pl.*) вина́; **the ~ shall be first** ≃ мно́гие после́дние бу́дут пе́рвыми; **on the ~ of the month** в после́дний день ме́сяца; **breathe one's ~** испусти́ть (*pf.*) после́дний вздох; **look one's ~ at, on** смотре́ть, по- в после́дний раз на+*a.*; **we have seen the ~ of him** мы его́ бо́льше не уви́дим; **he remained impenitent to the ~** он не раска́ялся до са́мого конца́; **at ~** наконе́ц; (*as excl.*) наконе́ц-то!; **at long ~** в конце́ концо́в, наконе́ц.
adj. **1.** (*latest; final; ~ of series*) после́дний; **in the ~ 7 years** в после́дние 7 лет; **at the very ~ moment** в са́мый после́дний моме́нт; **her hat is the ~ word** её шля́па — после́дний крик мо́ды; **the L~ Day, Judgement** Стра́шный суд; Су́дный день; светопреставле́ние; **~ rites, sacrament** причаще́ние пе́ред сме́ртью; **this chair is on its ~ legs** э́тот стул е́ле ды́шит; **~ name** фами́лия; **~ but not least of his talents** после́дний по счёту, но не по ва́жности из его́ тала́нтов; **~ but one** предпосле́дний; **~ but two** тре́тий от конца́; **the ~ thing I heard was that he was getting married** после́днее, что я о нём слы́шал, э́то то, что он собира́ется жени́ться; **~ thing at night** по́здно ве́чером; пре́жде, чем лечь спать; пе́ред сном. **2.** (*preceding, of time*) про́шлый; **in the ~ century/year/month** в про́шлом столе́тии/году́/ме́сяце; **~ week** на про́шлой неде́ле; **~ night we got home late** вчера́ ве́чером мы по́здно верну́лись; **~ night I slept badly** про́шлой но́чью я пло́хо спал; **the week before ~** позапро́шлая неде́ля; **the night before ~** позавчера́ ве́чером. **3.** (*utmost*): **a matter of the ~ importance** де́ло чрезвыча́йной ва́жности. **4.** (*least likely or suitable*): **he is the ~ person I expected to see** вот кого́ ме́ньше всего́ я ожида́л уви́деть; **she is the ~ person to help** от неё ме́ньше всего́ мо́жно ожида́ть по́мощи; **that's the ~ thing I would have expected** э́того я ника́к не ожида́л.
adv. **1.** (*in order*) по́сле всех; **he finished ~** он ко́нчил после́дним. **2.** (*for the ~ time*) в после́дний раз; **when I ~ saw him** когда́ я в после́дний раз ви́дел его́. **3.** (*~ly, in the ~ place*) на после́днем ме́сте; **~ but not least I wish you success** и, наконе́ц, — но отню́дь не в после́днюю о́чередь, — я жела́ю вам успе́ха.
v.i. **1.** (*go on, continue*) дли́ться, про-; прод|олжа́ться, -о́лжиться; **winter ~s six months** зима́ дли́тся шесть ме́сяцев; **will the performance ~ much longer?** до́лго ли ещё продли́тся спекта́кль?; **the rain won't ~ long** дождь ско́ро пройдёт; **if the good weather ~s** е́сли уде́ржится (*or* бу́дет стоя́ть) хоро́шая пого́да. **2.** (*hold out*) выде́рживать, вы́держать; **as long as my health ~s (out)** пока́ у меня́ хва́тит здоро́вья; (*be preserved, survive*) сохран|я́ться, -и́ться; **the tradition has ~ed until today** э́та тради́ция сохрани́лась до настоя́щего вре́мени. **3.** (*of clothes*): **this suit has ~ed well** э́тому костю́му сно́су нет. **4.** (*of the dying*): **he won't ~ long** он до́лго не протя́нет (*coll.*). **5.** (*be sufficient for*) хват|а́ть, -и́ть на+*a.*; **£30 ~s me a week** 30 фу́нтов мне хвата́ет на неде́лю; **the bread won't ~ us today** хле́ба нам на сего́дня не хва́тит.
cpds. **~-ditch** *adj.*: **a ~-ditch stand** упо́рная оборо́на; **~-minute** *adj.* (сде́ланный) в после́днюю мину́ту; **~-named** *adj.* после́дний (из упомя́нутых).
lasting ['lɑ:stɪŋ] *adj.* (*durable, enduring*) про́чный, продолжи́тельный; **~ peace** про́чный мир; **a ~ monument** ве́чный па́мятник; (*persistent, permanent*) постоя́нный; **~ regrets** постоя́нное чу́вство сожале́ния; **leave a ~ impression** произв|оди́ть, -ести́ неизглади́мое впечатле́ние.
lastly ['lɑ:stlɪ] *adv.* в заключе́ние; наконе́ц.
latch [lætʃ] *n.* (*bar*) щеко́лда; (*lock*) защёлка; **on the ~** на щеко́лде/защёлке.
v.t. (*put on ~*) закр|ыва́ть, -ы́ть на щеко́лду.
v.i.: **~ on to** смекну́ть (*pf.*) (*coll.*).
cpd. **~-key** *n.* ключ (от америка́нского замка́); соба́чка; **~-key child** безнадзо́рный ребёнок.
late [leɪt] *adj.* **1.** (*far on in time*) по́здний; **it is ~** по́здно; **it's getting ~** де́ло идёт к но́чи; **in the ~ evening** по́здним ве́чером; **in ~ summer** к концу́ ле́та; **in ~ May** к концу́ ма́я; в после́дних чи́слах ма́я; **the ~ 19th century** коне́ц 19 ве́ка; **~ edition** вече́рний вы́пуск; **keep ~ hours** по́здно ложи́ться (*impf.*) спать; **it is ~ in the day for that** для э́того позднова́то; **~r events** после́дующие собы́тия; **at, by 2 o'clock at the ~st** са́мое по́зднее в 2 часа́. **2.** (*behind time*): **be ~ for the train** оп|а́здывать, -озда́ть на по́езд (**for the theatre** в теа́тр; **for dinner** к у́жину); **he was an hour ~** он опозда́л на ча́с; **the train is running an hour ~** по́езд идёт с опозда́нием в (оди́н) час; по́езд опа́здывает на час; **I was ~ in replying** я опозда́л отве́тить (*or* с отве́том); **plums are ~ this year** сли́вы в э́том году́ поспе́ли по́здно; **~ developer** ≃ заме́дленного разви́тия; **~ riser** лю́бящий подо́льше поспа́ть; **he is a ~ riser** он по́здно встаёт. **3.** (*recent*) неда́вний; после́дний; **in ~ years** за после́дние го́ды; **the ~ war** после́дняя/про́шлая война́; **his ~st book** его́ после́дняя кни́га; **~st news** после́дние изве́стия. **4.** (*former*) пре́жний; (*immediately preceding*) бы́вший; **the ~ government** пре́жнее прави́тельство. **5.** (*deceased*) поко́йный, (ны́не) почи́вший. **6.** (*belated*) запозда́лый; **a few ~ swallows** не́сколько запозда́лых ла́сточек.
adv. по́здно; **better ~ than never** лу́чше по́здно, чем никогда́; **sooner or ~r** ра́но и́ли по́здно; **stay up ~** по́здно ложи́ться (*impf.*); **~ in life** в пожило́м во́зрасте; на ста́рости лет; **a year ~r** спустя́ год; **see you ~r!** уви́димся!; пока́!; **~ into the night** до по́здней но́чи; **of ~** (в/за) после́днее вре́мя.
cpd. **~-night** *adj.* ночно́й (*сеанс и т.п.*).
latecomer ['leɪt,kʌmə(r)] *n.* опозда́вший.
lately ['leɪtlɪ] *adv.* неда́вно; **have you seen him ~?** ви́дели ли вы его́ в после́днее вре́мя?; **I've been working hard ~** после́днее вре́мя я мно́го рабо́тал.

latency ['leɪt(ə)nsɪ] *n.* скры́тое состоя́ние; (*tech.*) лате́нтность.

lateness ['leɪtnɪs] *n.*: **the ~ of the train** опозда́ние по́езда; **despite the ~ of the hour** несмотря́ на по́здний час.

latent ['leɪt(ə)nt] *adj.* скры́тый, лате́нтный; (*chem.*) свя́занный.

lateral ['lætər(ə)l] *adj.* боково́й, горизонта́льный; ~ **section** попере́чный разре́з; ~ **strut** горизонта́льная связь; ~ **road** (*mil.*) рока́дная доро́га.

latest ['leɪtɪst] *adj.* после́дний; са́мый но́вый; **the ~ thing** после́днее сло́во, но́вость, нови́нка; *see also* **late**

latex ['leɪteks] *n.* мле́чный сок, ла́текс.

lath [lɑːθ] *n.* ре́йка, пла́нка; ~ **and plaster** дра́нка и штукату́рка; (*on roof*) обрешётка; ~ **fence** штаке́тник; **as thin as a ~** худо́й как ще́пка.

lathe [leɪð] *n.* тока́рный стано́к.

lather ['lɑːðə(r), 'læðə(r)] *n.* (мы́льная) пе́на; (*on horse*) мы́ло, пе́на; **in a ~** в мы́ле; (*fig., agitated*) в запа́рке.

v.t. мы́лить (*impf.*); намы́ли|вать, -ть; (*coll., thrash*) взду́ть (*pf.*); да|ва́ть, -ть трёпку +*d.*

v.i. (*of soap*) мы́литься; (*of a horse*) покр|ыва́ться, -ы́ться мы́лом.

lathering ['lɑːðərɪŋ, 'læðərɪŋ] *n.* (*coll.*) трёпка, взбу́чка.

lathery ['lɑːðərɪ, 'læðərɪ] *adj.* (*covered with lather*) намы́ленный; (*lathering easily*) мы́лкий; (*of a horse*) взмы́ленный.

Latin ['lætɪn] *n.* **1.** (*language*) латы́нь; лати́нский язы́к; **dog ~** ку́хонная латы́нь; **low ~** вульга́рная латы́нь. **2.** (*inhabitant of Latium*) латиня́нин. **3.** (*Frenchman, Italian etc.*) челове́к рома́нского происхожде́ния.

adj. лати́нский; ~ **America** Лати́нская Аме́рика; ~ **languages/nations** рома́нские языки́/наро́ды; ~ **scholar** латини́ст.

cpd. **~-American** *adj.* латиноамерика́нский.

Latinism ['lætɪ,nɪz(ə)m] *n.* латини́зм.

Latinist ['lætɪnɪst] *n.* латини́ст.

Latinity [læ'tɪnɪtɪ] *n.* (*quality of Latin*) лати́нский стиль.

latish ['leɪtɪʃ] *adj.* позднова́тый.

latitude ['lætɪ,tjuːd] *n.* **1.** (*distance from equator; pl., regions*) широта́; ~ **25° N** 25° се́верной широты́; **high/low ~s** высо́кие/тропи́ческие широ́ты. **2.** (*freedom of action*) свобо́да (де́йствий); (*liberality*) широта́ (взгля́дов); терпи́мость. **3.** (*breadth, extent*) обши́рность.

latitudinal [,lætɪ'tjuːdɪn(ə)l] *adj.* широ́тный.

latitudinarian [lætɪ,tjuːdɪ'neərɪən] *adj.* веротерпи́мый.

latrine [lə'triːn] *n.* убо́рная, отхо́жее ме́сто; (*on ship*) гальюн.

latter ['lætə(r)] *pron. & adj.* после́дний, второ́й; **in the ~ half of June** во второ́й полови́не ию́ня; **the former ... the ~** пе́рвый... второ́й/после́дний; **the ~** то, после́дний.

cpd. **~-day** *adj.* совреме́нный, нове́йший; **L~-day Saints** мормо́ны (*m. pl.*).

latterly ['lætəlɪ] *adv.* (*of late*) (в/за) после́днее вре́мя; (*towards the end*) к концу́, под коне́ц.

lattice ['lætɪs] *n.* решётка; (*attr.; also* **~d**) решётчатый.

Latvia ['lætvɪə] *n.* Ла́твия.

Latvian ['lætvɪən] *n.* (*pers.*) латви́|ец (*fem.* -йка); латы́ш (*fem.* -ка); (*language*) латы́шский язы́к.

adj. латви́йский, латы́шский.

laud [lɔːd] *n.* хвала́; (*pl., eccl.*) хвали́тны (*f. pl.*).

v t. восхвал|я́ть, -и́ть; сла́вить (*impf.*).

laudability [,lɔːdə'bɪlɪtɪ] *n.* похва́льность.

laudable ['lɔːdəb(ə)l] *adj.* похва́льный.

laudanum ['lɔːdnəm, 'lɒd-] *n.* насто́йка о́пия.

laudatory ['lɔːdətərɪ] *adj.* хвале́бный.

laugh [lɑːf] *n.* смех; (*loud ~*) хо́хот; **it was a ~** сме́ху-то бы́ло; **we had a good ~ over it** мы от души́ посмея́лись над э́тим; **he had the last ~** в конце́ концо́в посмея́лся он; **have the ~ on s.o.** ост|авля́ть, -а́вить кого́-н. в дурака́х; **the ~ was on him** он оста́лся в дурака́х; **I could not raise a ~** меня́ э́то ничу́ть не рассмеши́ло; **he joined in the ~** он присоедини́лся к о́бщему сме́ху; **he gave a loud ~** он гро́мко рассмея́лся.

v.t. ~ **to scorn** высме́ивать, вы́смеять; **I ~ed him out of his fears** ~ я рассе́ял сме́хом его́ опасе́ния; **he was ~ed out of court** он был осмея́н; **he was ~ing his head off** он хохота́л как безу́мный.

v.i. смея́ться (*impf.*); хохот|а́ть, -ну́ть; (*begin ~ing*) засмея́ться (*pf.*); **burst out ~ing** рассмея́ться (*pf.*); расхохота́ться (*pf.*); разрази́ться (*pf.*) сме́хом; **I almost burst out ~ing** я чуть бы́ло не пры́снул; **he who ~s last, ~s longest** хорошо́ смеётся тот, кто смеётся после́дним; **he ~s at my jokes** он смеётся, когда́ я шучу́; **who/what are you ~ing at?** над чем/кем вы смеётесь?; **it's nothing to ~ at** ничего́ смешно́го; **I should ~ if he came in** ну и смея́лся бы я, е́сли бы он вошёл; **he ~ed in my face** он рассмея́лся мне в лицо́; **he ~ed fit to burst** (*coll.*) он чуть не ло́пнул со́ смеху; **I ~ed till I cried** я смея́лся до слёз; **he was ~ing up his sleeve** он смея́лся в кула́к (*or* исподтишка́); **he'll soon be ~ing on the other side of his face** ему́ ско́ро бу́дет не до сме́ху; **make s.o. ~** смеши́ть, рас- кого́-н.; **don't make me ~!** (*iron.*) не смеши́те (меня́); **it's enough to make a cat ~** э́то ку́рам на́ смех; **I couldn't help ~ing** я не мог удержа́ться от сме́ха; **I couldn't stop ~ing** я смея́лся так, что не мог останови́ться.

with advs.: ~ **away** *v.t.* прог|оня́ть, -на́ть (*or* рассе́|ивать, -ять) сме́хом; ~ **off** *v.t.*: ~ **it off** отшу́|чиваться, -ти́ться; ~ **sth. off** отде́л|ываться, -аться от чего́-н. шу́ткой; св|оди́ть, -ести́ что-н. на шу́тку.

laughable ['lɑːfəb(ə)l] *adj.* смешно́й, смехотво́рный.

laughing ['lɑːfɪŋ] *n.* смех; **I was in no mood for ~** мне бы́ло не до сме́ху; **I couldn't speak for ~** от сме́ха я не мог произнести́ ни сло́ва; **it is no ~ matter** э́то не шу́точное де́ло; **he burst out ~** он рассмея́лся/расхохота́лся.

cpds. **~-gas** *n.* веселя́щий газ; **~-stock** *n.* посме́шище; **make a ~-stock of s.o.** выставля́ть, вы́ставить кого́-н. на посме́шище.

laughter ['lɑːftə(r)] *n.* смех; (*loud*) хо́хот; **he broke into peals of ~** он разрази́лся раска́тистым сме́хом; **die of, with ~** ум|ира́ть, -ере́ть со́ смеху; смея́ться (*impf.*) до упа́ду; **roar with ~** хохота́ть (*impf.*) во всё го́рло; **rock (or be convulsed) with ~** пока́т|ываться, -и́ться со́ смеху; **split one's sides with ~** над|рыва́ть, -орва́ть живо́тики со́ смеху (*coll.*).

launch[1] [lɔːntʃ] *n.* (*motor-boat*) ка́тер; (*warship's longboat*) ланч.

launch[2] [lɔːntʃ] *n.* (*of ship*) спуск (на́ воду); (*of rocket or spacecraft*) за́пуск; (*of torpedo*) вы́пуск.

v.t. (*set afloat*): ~ **a ship** спус|ка́ть, -ти́ть кора́бль на́ воду; (*send into air*): ~ **a rocket** запус|ка́ть, -ти́ть раке́ту; (*aircraft from flight deck*) катапульти́ровать (*impf., pf.*); (*hurl, discharge*): ~ **a spear** мет|а́ть, -ну́ть (*or* бр|оса́ть, -о́сить) копьё; ~ **a torpedo** выпуска́ть, вы́пустить торпе́ду; (*initiate*): ~ **an attack** нач|ина́ть, -а́ть ата́ку; ~ **a campaign** нач|ина́ть, -а́ть (*or* откр|ыва́ть, -ы́ть) кампа́нию; ~ **an enterprise** пус|ка́ть, -ти́ть предприя́тие.

v.i. пус|ка́ться, -ти́ться; **he ~ed into an argument** он пусти́лся в спор; **we are ~ing (out) on, into a new enterprise** мы начина́ем но́вое де́ло; **I decided to ~ out on a new car** я реши́л разори́ться на но́вый автомоби́ль (*coll.*).

cpds. **~(ing)-pad** *n.* ста́ртовая площа́дка; **~ing-range** *n.* раке́тный полиго́н; **~(ing)-site** *n.* ста́ртовая пози́ция; **~(ing)-tower** *n.* пускова́я вы́шка; **~-vehicle** *n.* раке́та-носи́тель (*m.*).

launder ['lɔːndə(r)] *v.t. & i.* стира́ть(ся), вы́-; **this cloth ~s well** э́та мате́рия хорошо́ стира́ется.

laund(e)rette [lɔːn'dret] *n.* пра́чечная самообслу́живания.

laundress ['lɔːndrɪs] *n.* пра́чка.

laundry ['lɔːndrɪ] *n.* **1.** (*establishment*) пра́чечная; **send to the ~** отд|ава́ть, -а́ть в сти́рку (*or* в пра́чечную); **my shirt came back torn from the ~** в пра́чечной мне порва́ли руба́шку. **2.** (*clothes*) бельё (для сти́рки *or* из сти́рки).

cpd. **~man** *n.* рабо́чий в пра́чечной.

laureate ['lɒrɪət, 'lɔː-] *n.*: **Poet L~** поэ́т-лауреа́т.

laurel ['lɒr(ə)l] *n.* лавр; (*attr.*) лавро́вый; (*fig., pl.*): **reap, win ~s** пожина́ть (*impf.*) ла́вры; **rest on one's ~s** поч|ива́ть, -и́ть на ла́врах; **look to one's ~s** защи|ща́ть, -ти́ть своё пе́рвенство.

laurelled ['lɒr(ə)ld] *adj.* уве́нчанный ла́врами (*or* лавро́вым венко́м).

lava ['lɑ:və] *n.* ла́ва; ~ **bed** пласт ла́вы; ~ **flow** пото́к ла́вы.

lavatory ['lævətərɪ] *n.* (*WC*) убо́рная, туале́т; (*washroom*) умыва́льная (ко́мната); ~ **paper** туале́тная бума́га.

lave [leɪv] *v.t.* (*liter.*) омыва́ть (*impf.*).

lavender ['lævɪndə(r)] *n.* лава́нда; ~ **water** лава́ндовая вода́; **a ~ gown** пла́тье бле́дно-лило́вого цве́та.

lavish ['lævɪʃ] *adj.* **1.** (*generous*) ще́дрый; (*prodigal*) расточи́тельный; **he is ~ in his praise** он щедр на похвалы́; **a ~ reception** бога́тый приём. **2.** (*abundant*) оби́льный.

v.t.: ~ **money on sth.** расточа́ть (*impf.*) де́ньги на что-н.; ~ **praise on s.o.** расточа́ть (*impf.*) похвалы́ кому́-н.; ~ **care on s.o.** окружа́ть (*impf.*) кого́-н. чрезме́рными забо́тами.

lavishness ['lævɪʃnɪs] *n.* ще́дрость; расточи́тельность.

law [lɔ:] *n.* **1.** (*rule or body of rules for society*) зако́н; **the ~ of the land** зако́н страны́; **the bill became ~** законопрое́кт был при́нят; **above the ~** вы́ше зако́на; **by ~** по зако́ну; **within the ~** в ра́мках (*or* без наруше́ния) зако́на; **break, violate the ~** нар|уша́ть, -у́шить зако́н; **keep, observe the ~** соблюда́ть (*impf.*) зако́н; **pass a ~** прин|има́ть, -я́ть зако́н; **his word is ~** его́ сло́во — зако́н; **he is a ~ unto himself** он живёт по со́бственным зако́нам; **necessity knows no ~** нужда́ не зна́ет зако́на; **natural ~** зако́н приро́ды; **the ~ of supply and demand** зако́н спро́са и предложе́ния; **the ~s of the game** пра́вила (*nt. pl.*) игры́. **2.** (*as subject of study, profession, system*) пра́во, юсти́ция; **civil ~** гражда́нское пра́во; **in international ~** по междунаро́дному пра́ву; **declare martial ~** объяв|ля́ть, -и́ть вое́нное положе́ние; ~ **and order** правопоря́док; зако́нность и поря́док; **rule of ~** правопоря́док; ~ **school** юриди́ческая шко́ла; **read, study ~** изуч|а́ть, -и́ть пра́во; **go in for the ~** учи́ться, вы́- на юри́ста; **follow, practise ~** быть юри́стом; **doctor of ~s** до́ктор юриди́ческих нау́к; **court of ~** суд; **L~ Courts** (*building*) Дом правосу́дия. **3.** (*process of ~; ~suit*) суде́бный проце́сс; **go to ~** возбу|жда́ть, -ди́ть суде́бное де́ло; **have the ~ on s.o.** пода́ть (*pf.*) на кого́-н. в суд; **take the ~ into one's own hands** поступ|а́ть, -и́ть самочи́нно. **4.** (*phys. etc.*): ~ **of gravity** зако́н тяготе́ния; ~ **of probability** тео́рия вероя́тностей.

cpds. **~-abiding** *adj.* законопослу́шный; **~-breaker** *n.* правонаруши́тель (*m.*); **~-court** *n.* суд; **~-enforcement** *n.* (*attr.*): **~-enforcement agencies** правоохрани́тельные о́рганы; **~-giver, ~-maker** *nn.* законода́тель (*m.*); **~man** *n.* (*US*) полице́йский, шери́ф; **~suit** *n.* суде́бный проце́сс; **bring a ~suit against s.o.** возбу|жда́ть, -ди́ть (суде́бное) де́ло про́тив кого́-н.

lawful ['lɔ:fʊl] *adj.* зако́нный; **his ~ wedded wife** его́ зако́нная жена́; (*rightful*) правоме́рный.

lawfulness ['lɔ:fʊlnɪs] *n.* зако́нность, закономе́рность.

lawks [lɔ:ks] *int.* (*coll.*) Бо́же мой!; Го́споди!

lawless ['lɔ:lɪs] *adj.* (*of country etc.*) ди́кий, анархи́чный; (*of pers.*) непоко́рный, мяте́жный.

lawlessness ['lɔ:lɪsnɪs] *n.* беззако́нность, беззако́ние; непоко́рность, мяте́жность.

lawn[1] [lɔ:n] *n.* (*area of grass*) газо́н; ~ **tennis** те́ннис.

cpds. **~-mower** *n.* газо́нокоси́лка; **~-sprinkler** *n.* устро́йство для поли́вки газо́нов.

lawn[2] [lɔ:n] *n.* (*linen*) бати́ст.

lawyer ['lɔɪə(r), 'lɔ:jə(r)] *n.* юри́ст; (*advocate, barrister*) адвока́т; (*legal adviser or expert*) законове́д, юриско́нсульт.

lax [læks] *adj.* (*negligent, inattentive*) небре́жный; (*not strict*) нестро́гий; ~ **discipline** сла́бая дисципли́на; ~ **morals** распу́щенные нра́вы.

laxative ['læksətɪv] *n.* слаби́тельное (сре́дство).

adj. слаби́тельный.

lax|ity ['læksɪtɪ], **-ness** ['læksnɪs] *nn.* небре́жность; (*of morals*) распу́щенность; (*of expression*) нето́чность.

lay[1] [leɪ] *n.* (*liter.*) пе́сня, балла́да.

lay[2] [leɪ] *n.* **1.: she's an easy ~** она́ сла́ба на передо́к (*sl.*). **2.** *see also* **lie**[2] *n.*

v.t. **1.** (*put down, deposit*) класть, положи́ть; **he laid his hand on my shoulder** он положи́л ру́ку мне на плечо́; ~ **a child to sleep** укла́дывать, уложи́ть ребёнка (спать); ~ **to rest** (*bury*) хорони́ть, по-; ~ **an egg** нести́, с- яйцо́; (*set in position*): ~ **bricks** класть (*impf.*) кирпичи́; ~ **a foundation** (*lit., fig.*) за|кла́дывать, -ложи́ть фунда́мент; ~ **a carpet** стлать, по- ковёр; ~ **cable/pipes** про|кла́дывать, -ложи́ть ка́бель/тру́бы; ~ **rails** укла́дывать, уложи́ть ре́льсы; ~ **an ambush** устр|а́ивать, -о́ить заса́ду; ~ **a trap** ста́вить, по- лову́шку. **2.** (*fig., place*): ~ **a bet** держа́ть (*impf.*) пари́; ~ **£10 on a horse** ста́вить, по- 10 фу́нтов на ло́шадь; **I'll ~** (*coll.*) пари́ держу́; бьюсь об закла́д; ~ **evidence before s.o.** предъяв|ля́ть, -и́ть кому́-н. доказа́тельства; ~ **the facts before s.o.** дов|оди́ть, -ести́ фа́кты до све́дения кого́-н.; ~ **a charge** предъяв|ля́ть, -и́ть обвине́ние (*кому в чём*); ~ **sth. to s.o.'s charge** вмен|я́ть, -и́ть что-н. в вину́ кому́-н.; ~ **s.o. under an obligation** связа́ть (*pf.*) кого́-н. благода́рностью; **the scene is laid in London** де́йствие происхо́дит в Ло́ндоне. **3.** (*prepare*): ~ **a fire** пригото́вить (*pf.*) всё, что́бы развести́ ого́нь; ~ **the table for dinner** накр|ыва́ть, -ы́ть стол к обе́ду; ~ **plans** сост|авля́ть, -а́вить пла́ны. **4.** (*cause to subside*): ~ **the corn** прим|ина́ть, -я́ть пшени́цу; ~ **the dust** приб|ива́ть, -и́ть пыль; ~ **a ghost** изг|оня́ть, -на́ть ду́ха. **5.** (*cover*) укла́дывать, уложи́ть; покр|ыва́ть, -ы́ть; **a floor laid with linoleum** пол, покры́тый лино́леумом. **6.** (*cause to be*): ~ **bare** (*lit.*) обнаж|а́ть, -и́ть; (*fig., reveal*) раскр|ыва́ть, -ы́ть; ~ **low** (*knock over*) вали́ть, с-; (*overthrow*) низл|ага́ть, -ожи́ть; **he was laid low with a fever** он слёг с лихора́дкой; ~ **o.s. open to attack** подст|авля́ть, -а́вить себя́ под уда́р; ~ **o.s. open to suspicion** навл|ека́ть, -е́чь на себя́ подозре́ние; ~ **waste** опустош|а́ть, -и́ть. **7.:** ~ **by the heels** излови́ть (*pf.*). **8.** (*sl., copulate with*) тра́х|ать, -нуть.

v.i. **1.** (*sc. eggs*) нести́сь (*impf.*). **2.** (*sc. the table*): **she laid for six** она́ накры́ла на шестеры́х. **3.** (*strike*): ~ **about s.o.** колоти́ть, по- кого́-н.; ~ **about one** раздава́ть (*impf.*) уда́ры напра́во и нале́во; ~ **into s.o.** нап|ада́ть, -а́сть на кого́-н.

with advs.: ~ **aside** (*also* ~ **by**) *v.t.* (*lit.*) от|кла́дывать, -ложи́ть; **he laid aside his work** он отложи́л рабо́ту; (*relinquish, abandon*) ост|авля́ть, -а́вить; **you must ~ aside your prejudices** на́до оста́вить/(от)бро́сить предрассу́дки; (*save*) от|кла́дывать, -ложи́ть; ~ **back** *v.t.*: **the dog laid back its ears** соба́ка прижа́ла у́ши; ~ **by** *v.t.* = ~ **aside;** ~ **down** *v.t.* (*on ground, bed etc.*) укла́дывать, уложи́ть; ~ **down one's arms** (*surrender*) скла́дывать, сложи́ть ору́жие; ~ **down a field to grass** пус|ка́ть, -ти́ть по́ле под траву́; (*formulate, prescribe*): ~ **down conditions/rules** устан|а́вливать, -ови́ть (*or* формули́ровать, с-; вырaба́тывать, вы́работать) усло́вия/пра́вила; **he laid it down as a condition that ...** он поста́вил усло́вием, что́бы...; **this is laid down in the regulations** э́то предпи́сано пра́вилами; **he is fond of ~ing down the law** он лю́бит диктова́ть/распоряжа́ться; (*sacrifice*): ~ **down one's life for one's friends** же́ртвовать, по- жи́знью (*or* класть, положи́ть жизнь) за друзе́й; (*begin to build*): ~ **down a ship** за|кла́дывать, -ложи́ть кора́бль; ~ **in** *v.t.* (*stock up with*) загот|а́вливать, (*or* -овля́ть), -о́вить; запас|а́ть, -ти́; запас|а́ться, -ти́сь +*i.*; ~ **off** *v.t.* (*suspend from work*) ув|ольня́ть, -о́лить (со слу́жбы); отстран|я́ть, -и́ть (от рабо́ты); (*coll., desist from*) перест|ава́ть, -а́ть; *v.i.*: ~ **off!** (*coll.*) бро́сь(те)!; отста́нь(те)!; ~ **on** *v.t.* (*provide supply of*) пров|оди́ть, -ести́; **is water laid on here?** здесь есть водопрово́д?; (*coll.*): **he promised to ~ on some drinks** он обеща́л поста́вить вы́пивку; (*arrange*) устр|а́ивать, -о́ить; **it's all laid on** всё устро́ено; (*fig.*): ~ **it on thick** (*coll., of exaggerated praise*) гру́бо льсти́ть (*impf.*); ~ **out** *v.t.* (*arrange for display etc.*) выставля́ть, вы́ставить; ~ **out clothes** выкла́дывать, вы́ложить оде́жду; (*design*) плани́ровать, рас-; (*garden etc.*) разб|ива́ть, -и́ть; (*for burial*): ~ **out a corpse** уб|ира́ть, -ра́ть поко́йника; (*spend*) тра́тить, ис-; (*knock down*) сби|ва́ть, -ть (с ног); ~ **o.s. out to please s.o.** из ко́жи вон лезть (*impf.*), что́бы угоди́ть кому́-н.; ~ **to** *v.i.* (*of ship*) ложи́ться, лечь в дрейф (*or* на курс); ~ **up** *v.t.* (*save, store*) копи́ть, на-; запас|а́ть, -ти́; **you are ~ing up**

trouble for yourself вы лишь навлечёте неприя́тности себе́ на́ голову; (*make inactive*): **my car was laid up all winter** всю зи́му моя́ маши́на простоя́ла; **he was laid up with a broken leg** он был прико́ван к посте́ли из-за сло́манной ноги́.

cpds. **~about** *n.* (*coll.*) бродя́га (*c.g.*), тунея́дец; безде́льник; **~-by** *n.* придоро́жная площа́дка для стоя́нки автомоби́лей; стоя́нка (на обо́чине); **~-off** *n.* (*of workers*) сокраще́ние ка́дров; **~out** *n.* (*arrangement*) расположе́ние; (*of town etc.*) планиро́вка; (*of garden etc.*) разби́вка; (*plan*) чертёж, план.

lay[3] [leɪ] *adj.* **1.** (*opp. clerical*) мирско́й; ~ **brother** беле́ц. **2.** (*opp. professional*): ~ **opinion** мне́ние неспециали́стов.

cpd. **~man** *n.* миря́нин; профа́н; непрофессиона́л, неспециали́ст; **~woman** *n.* мироя́нка, непрофессиона́лка.

layer[1] [ˈleɪə(r)] *n.* (*thickness, stratum*) слой, пласт, насло́ение; (*of ice on road*) ледяна́я ко́рка; (*inserted* ~) прокла́дка; ~ **cake** слоёный пиро́г.

v.t. (*lay or cut in* ~*s*) пластова́ть (*impf.*); насл|а́ивать, -ои́ть.

layer[2] [ˈleɪə(r)] *n.* (*laying hen*) несу́шка; **these hens are good ~s** э́ти ку́ры хорошо́ несу́тся.

layette [leɪˈet] *n.* прида́ное новорождённого.

lay-figure [leɪ] *n.* манеке́н.

laying [leɪɪŋ] *n.* (*of eggs*) кла́дка; (*of cable*) прокла́дка; (*of bricks*) укла́дка; (*of carpet*) расстила́ние; (*of turf*) дерно́вка; (*of rails, pipes*) укла́дка.

cpd. **~-on** *n.*: **~-on of hands** рукоположе́ние.

lazaret(to) [ˌlæzəˈret(əʊ)] *n.* (*leper hospital*) лепрозо́рий; (*quarantine station*) каранти́нное помеще́ние.

Lazarus [ˈlæzərəs] *n.* (*bibl.*) Ла́зарь (*m.*).

laze [leɪz] *v.t. & i.*: ~ **about** слоня́ться (*impf.*) без де́ла; ~ **away the time** безде́льничать (*impf.*).

laziness [ˈleɪzɪnɪs] *n.* лень, ле́ность.

lazy [ˈleɪzɪ] *adj.* лени́вый; **become** ~ разле́н|иваться, -и́ться; **be** ~ лени́ться (*impf.*); **I was too ~ to write to him** я лени́лся (*or* мне бы́ло лень) ему́ писа́ть.

cpds. **~bones** *n.* лентя́й (*fem.* -ка), ло́дырь (*m.*); (*coll.*) лежебо́ка (*c.g.*); **~-tongs** *n.* пантогра́фный захва́т.

lb. [paʊnd(z)] *n.* (*abbr. of* **libra**) фунт.

LCD (*abbr. of* **liquid-crystal display**) ЖКИ, (жидкокристалли́ческий индика́тор).

L/Cpl. [lɑːns ˈkɔːpər(ə)l] *n.* (*abbr. of* **Lance-Corporal**) мла́дший капра́л.

LEA (*abbr. of* **local education authority**) ме́стные о́рганы образова́ния.

lea [liː] *n.* луг.

leach [liːtʃ] *v.t.* выщела́чивать, вы́щелочить.

lead[1] [led] *n.* **1.** (*metal*) свине́ц; (*attr.*) свинцо́вый; ~ **foil** свинцо́вая фольга́; **red** ~ свинцо́вый су́рик; **white** ~ свинцо́вые бели́ла; ~ **poisoning** отравле́ние свинцо́м. **2.** (*black* ~) графи́т; ~ **pencil** (графи́товый) каранда́ш; **the ~ keeps breaking** гри́фель постоя́нно лома́ется. **3.** (*on fishing line*) грузи́ло; (*as ammunition*) дробь; (*bullets*) пу́ли (*f. pl.*). **4.** (*naut., for sounding*) лот; **cast, heave the** ~ бр|оса́ть, -о́сить лот; **swing the** ~ отлы́нивать (*impf.*) от рабо́ты (*coll.*). **5.** (~ **seal**) свинцо́вая пло́мба. **6.** (*typ.*) шпон. **7.** (*pl., on roof or window*) свинцо́вые листы́ (*m. pl.*) для покры́тия кры́ши.

v.t. (*cover with* ~) освинц|о́вывать, -ева́ть.

cpds. **~-free** *adj.* неэтили́рованный; **~sman** *n.* лотово́й; **~works** *n.* свинцопла́вильный заво́д.

lead[2] [liːd] *n.* **1.** (*direction, guidance; initiative*) руково́дство; инициати́ва; **give a ~ to s.o.** под|ава́ть, -а́ть приме́р кому́-н.; **take the** ~ брать, взять на (себя́) руково́дство/инициати́ву; **follow s.o.'s** ~ (*lit., fig.*) сле́довать, по- за кем-н. **2.** (*first place*): **be in the** ~ стоя́ть (*impf.*) во главе́; (*sport*) быть впереди́; вести́ (*det.*); (*fig.*) стоя́ть (*impf.*) во главе́, пе́рвенствовать (*impf.*); **take the** ~ (*sport*) выходи́ть, вы́йти вперёд; **he had a ~ of 10 metres** он опереди́л други́х на 10 ме́тров. **3.** (*clue*): **give s.o. a ~ on sth.** наво|ди́ть, -дести́ кого́-н. на след чего́-н.; **the police are looking for a** ~ поли́ция пыта́ется напа́сть на след. **4.** (*cord, strap*) поводо́к, при́вязь; **'dogs must be kept on a ~'** (*notice*) «соба́к держа́ть на поводке́». **5.** (*elec.*) про́вод (*pl.* -а́). **6.** (*theatr.*) гла́вная роль; актёр, игра́ющий гла́вную роль. **7.** (*cards*) ход; **your ~!** ваш ход!

v.t. **1.** (*conduct*) води́ть (*indet.*), вести́, по- (*det.*), ~ **by the hand** вести́ за́ руку; ~ **a horse by the bridle** вести́ ло́шадь под уздцы́; ~ **s.o. by the nose** вести́ кого́-н. на поводу́; ~ **astray** сбива́ть (*impf.*) с пути́ и́стинного; ~ **captive** взять (*pf.*) в плен; ~ **to the altar** (*of bridegroom*) повести́ (*pf.*) к алтарю́; жени́ться (*impf., pf.*) на+*p.*; **he led his troops into battle** он повёл солда́т в бой; ~ **the way** идти́ (*det.*) во главе́; **he was led off the premises** его́ вы́вели из помеще́ния. **2.** (*fig., bring, incline, induce*): **what led you to this idea?** что навело́ вас на э́ту мысль?; ~ **s.o. to believe** созда́ть (*pf.*) впечатле́ние у кого́-н., что…; **he led us to expect much** он пробуди́л у нас больши́е наде́жды. **3.** (*cause to go, e.g. water*) пров|оди́ть, -ести́. **4.** (*be in charge of*): ~ **an expedition/orchestra** руководи́ть (*impf.*) экспеди́цией/орке́стром; (*direct*) управля́ть (*impf.*) +*i.*; (*command*) кома́ндовать (*impf.*) +*i.*; (*act as chief or head of*) возгл|авля́ть, -а́вить; (*be in the forefront of*): **the choir ~s the procession** хор идёт во главе́ проце́ссии; ~ **the fashion** быть законода́телем мод; **Britain led the world in trade** Великобрита́ния была́ веду́щей торго́вой держа́вой ми́ра. **5.** (*pass, spend*): ~ **an idle life** вести́ (*det.*) пра́здную жизнь; ~ **a wretched existence** влачи́ть (*impf.*) жа́лкое существова́ние. **6.** (*cause to spend or undertake*): ~ **s.o. a dog's life** отравля́ть (*impf.*) жизнь кому́-н.; ~ **s.o. a dance** заст|авля́ть, -а́вить кого́-н. попляса́ть/пому́читься; мане́жить, по- кого́-н. **7.** (*cards*): ~ **trumps** ходи́ть, пойти́ с ко́зыря.

v.i. **1.** (*of a road etc.*) вести́ (*det.*): **all roads ~ to Rome** все доро́ги веду́т в Рим; (*fig.*) вести́; прив|оди́ть, -ести́; **this method will ~ to difficulties** э́тот ме́тод вы́зовет сло́жности. **2.** (*be first or ahead*) быть впереди́; вести́ (*det.*); лиди́ровать (*impf.*); **our team is ~ing by 5 points** на́ша кома́нда впереди́ на пять очко́в. **3.** (*cards*) ходи́ть, пойти́. **4.** (*journalism*): **the Times led with an article on the strike** «Таймс» посвяти́ла свою́ передову́ю статью́ забасто́вке.

with advs.: ~ **away** *v.t.* отв|оди́ть, -ести́; ув|оди́ть, -ести́; ~ **in** *v.t.* вв|оди́ть, -ести́; ~ **off** *v.t.* (*take away*) ув|оди́ть, -ести́; (*start*): **they led off the dance** они́ откры́ли та́нец; *v.i.*: **he led off with an apology** он на́чал с извине́ния; ~ **on** *v.t.* (*lit.*): **he led his troops on to victory** он вёл свои́ войска́ к побе́де; (*encourage*) поощр|я́ть, -и́ть; (*deceive*) обма́н|ывать, -у́ть; (*flirt with*): **she is ~ing him on** она́ его́ завлека́ет; *v.i.*: ~ **on!** вперёд!; ~ **up** *v.i.*: ~ **up to** (*lit.*) подв|оди́ть, -ести́ к+*d.*; (*precede, form preparation for*) подгот|овля́ть, -о́вить; **the events that led up to the war** собы́тия, приве́дшие к войне́; (*direct conversation towards*) нав|оди́ть, -ести́ разгово́р на+*a.*; **what are you ~ing up to?** куда́ вы кло́ните?

cpd. **~-in** *n.* (*introduction*) введе́ние, ввод; (*elec.*) ввод.

leaden [ˈled(ə)n] *adj.* (*lit., fig.*) свинцо́вый.

leader [ˈliːdə(r)] *n.* **1.** (*pol.*) руководи́тель (*m.*), ли́дер; (*rhet.*) вождь (*m.*). **2.** (*of group*) вожа́к; (*of gang*) глава́рь (*m.*). **3.** (*mil.*) команди́р. **4.** (*of orchestra*) пе́рвая скри́пка; (*US, conductor*) дирижёр. **5.** (*front horse in team*) пере́дняя ло́шадь. **6.** (*leading article*) передова́я (статья́), передови́ца.

leadership [ˈliːdərˌʃɪp] *n.* (*role of leader; group of leaders*) руково́дство; (*pre-eminence*) пе́рвенство; (*qualities of a leader*) ли́дерство, инициати́вность.

leading [ˈliːdɪŋ] *adj.* (*foremost*) веду́щий; (*outstanding*) выдаю́щийся; ~ **aircraftman** рядово́й авиа́ции пе́рвого кла́сса; ~ **article** передова́я (статья́), передови́ца; ~ **case** (руководя́щий) суде́бный прецеде́нт; ~ **lady** исполни́тельница гла́вной ро́ли; ~ **light** (*of art, science etc.*) свети́ло, корифе́й; (*of society*) знамени́тость, свети́ло; ~ **question** наводя́щий вопро́с; ~ **seaman** ста́рший матро́с; ~ **topic** злободне́вная те́ма.

cpds. **~-rein** *n.* по́вод; **~-strings** *n. pl.*: **in ~-strings** (*fig.*) на поводу́.

leaf [liːf] *n.* **1.** (*of tree or plant*) лист (*pl.* -ья); **in** ~ покры́тый листво́й; **come into** ~ распус|ка́ться, -ти́ться;

tobacco ~ листово́й таба́к. **2.** (*of book*) лист (*pl.* -ы́); (*fig.*): **take a ~ out of s.o.'s book** брать, взять приме́р с кого́-н.; **turn over a new ~** откр|ыва́ть, -ы́ть но́вую страни́цу; нач|ина́ть, -а́ть но́вую жизнь, испра́виться (*pl.*). **3.** (*of metal etc.*) лист (*pl.* -ы́); **gold ~** листово́е зо́лото; **~ spring** листова́я рессо́ра. **4.** (*of table etc.*) откидна́я доска́; (*inserted section*) вставна́я доска́. **5.** (*of shutter*) ство́рка.

v.t.: **~ over, through** перели́ст|ывать, -а́ть.

v.i. (*come into* ~) распус|ка́ться, -ти́ться.

cpds. **~-green** *adj.* цве́та зелёной листвы́; **~-mould** *n.* ли́ственный перегно́й.

leafage ['li:fɪdʒ] *n.* листва́.

leafless ['li:flɪs] *adj.* безли́стный.

leaflet ['li:flɪt] *n.* **1.** (*bot.*) листо́к. **2.** (*printed*) брошю́рка; (*fold-out*) букле́т; (*pol.*) листо́вка.

leafy ['li:fɪ] *adj.* густоли́ственный.

league[1] [li:g] *n.* (*measure*) лье (*indecl.*).

league[2] [li:g] *n.* (*alliance*) ли́га; **L~ of Nations** Ли́га на́ций; **in ~ with** в сою́зе с+*i.*; (*pej.*) в сго́воре с+*i.*; **be not in the same ~ as s.o.** быть не того́ кла́сса; **football ~** футбо́льная ли́га.

v.i.: **~ together** образо́в|ывать, -а́ть сою́з; (*pej.*) сгов|а́риваться, -ори́ться.

leak [li:k] *n.* (*hole*) течь; **spring a ~** да|ва́ть, -ть течь; **stop a ~** остан|а́вливать, -ови́ть течь; (*escape of fluid*) уте́чка; (*fig.*, *of information*) уте́чка/проса́чивание информа́ции.

v.t. (*fig.*) выдава́ть, вы́дать.

v.i. (*lit.*) течь (*impf.*); протека́ть (*impf.*); прос|а́чиваться, -очи́ться; (*fig.*): **the affair ~ed out** де́ло вы́плыло нару́жу; **take a ~** (*coll.*, *urinate*) отл|ива́ть, -и́ть.

cpd. **~-proof** *adj.* непроница́емый, гермети́ческий.

leakage ['li:kɪdʒ] *n.* (*lit.*, *fig.*) уте́чка.

leaky ['li:kɪ] *adj.* дыря́вый, име́ющий течь; **a ~ pipe** протека́ющая труба́; **these barrels are ~** э́ти бо́чки теку́т; (*coll.*, *indiscreet*) болтли́вый.

lean[1] [li:n] *n.* (*of meat*) по́стная часть.

adj. **1.** (*thin*) то́щий; (*fig.*): **~ years** ску́дные го́ды; **a ~ harvest** ску́дный/плохо́й урожа́й. **2.** (*of meat*) нежи́рный, по́стный.

lean[2] [li:n] *n.* (*inclination*) укло́н, накло́н.

v.t. прислон|я́ть, -и́ть (*что к чему*); оп|ира́ть, -ере́ть (*что обо что*): **~ the ladder against the wall!** прислони́те ле́стницу к стене́!; **he was ~ing his arm on the table** он опира́лся руко́й о стол.

v.i. **1.** (*incline from vertical*) наклон|я́ться, -и́ться; **the tower ~s slightly** ба́шня слегка́ наклони́лась; **the trees are ~ing in the wind** дере́вья кло́нятся от ве́тра; **the L~ing Tower of Pisa** Па́дающая ба́шня в Пи́зе; **sit ~ing backward/forward** сиде́ть (*impf.*), пода́вшись наза́д/вперёд; **he ~s over backwards to help** (*fig.*) он из ко́жи вон ле́зет, что́бы помо́чь; **~ out of the window** высо́вываться, вы́сунуться из окна́; **he ~ed over to her** он наклони́лся к ней; **he was ~ing over my shoulder** он загля́дывал мне че́рез плечо́; **he ~t towards clemency** он был скло́нен к милосе́рдию; **I ~ towards the same opinion** я скло́нен ду́мать то же са́мое. **2.** (*support o.s.*) прислон|я́ться, -и́ться; оп|ира́ться, -ере́ться; **he was ~ing against a tree** он стоя́л, прислони́вшись к де́реву; **he walked ~ing on a stick** он шёл, опира́ясь на трость; **she was ~ing on the table with her elbows** она́ сиде́ла, облокоти́вшись о/на стол; **she was ~ing on his arm** она́ опира́лась на его́ ру́ку; (*fig.*): **he ~s** (*depends*) **on his wife for support** он опира́ется на подде́ржку жены́; **I had to ~** (*coll.*, *put pressure*) **on him to get results** мне пришло́сь нажа́ть на него́, что́бы доби́ться результа́тов.

cpd. **~-to** *n.* односка́тная пристро́йка.

leaning ['li:nɪŋ] *n.* (*inclination*) скло́нность; (*tendency*) пристра́стие.

leanness ['li:nnɪs] *n.* худоба́, истоще́ние.

leap [li:p] *n.* прыжо́к, скачо́к; **take a ~** пры́гнуть (*pf.*); **his heart gave a ~** се́рдце у него́ дро́гнуло/ёкнуло; (*fig.*): **a ~ in the dark** прыжо́к в неизве́стность; **by ~s and bounds** стреми́тельно.

v.t. (~ *over*) переск|а́кивать, -очи́ть (*or* перепры́г|ивать, -нуть) че́рез+*a.*

v.i. пры́г|ать, -нуть; **my heart ~t for joy** у меня́ се́рдце подскочи́ло от ра́дости; **~ to one's feet** вск|а́кивать, -очи́ть; **he ~t** (*fig.*) **at my offer** он так и ухвати́лся за моё предложе́ние.

cpds. **~-frog** *n.* чехарда́; *v.t.* перепры́г|ивать, -нуть че́рез+*a.*; **~-year** *n.* високо́сный год.

learn [lɜ:n] *v.t.* **1.** (*get knowledge of*) учи́ться, на- +*d. or inf.*; изуч|а́ть, -и́ть; (*study*) занима́ться +*i.*; **he ~ed (how) to ride** он научи́лся е́здить верхо́м; (~ *a trade*) обуч|а́ться, -и́ться +*d. or inf.*; **he is ~ing to be an interpreter** он у́чится на перево́дчика; (~ *off or by heart*) учи́ть, вы́-; вы́учиться (*pf.*) +*d.*; **he ~t French** он вы́учился францу́зскому языку́; **where did you ~ Russian?** где вы изуча́ли ру́сский язы́к?; **she is ~ing her part** она́ у́чит/разу́чивает свою́ роль; **he ~t the prayer by heart** он вы́учил моли́тву наизу́сть/назубо́к; **he ~t his lesson** (*fig.*) он получи́л хоро́ший уро́к. **2.** (*be informed*) узн|ава́ть, -а́ть; **I have yet to ~ where we are going** я ещё не зна́ю, куда́ мы пойдём. **3.** (*vulg.*, *teach*) учи́ть, про-; **that'll ~ you** э́то вам бу́дет нау́кой; **I'll ~ him** я покажу́ ему́!; я проучу́ его́.

v.i.: **he ~s slowly** нау́ки ему́ даю́тся тру́дно; он у́чится с трудо́м; **you can ~ from his mistakes** учи́тесь на его́ оши́бках; **I was sorry to ~ of your illness** я с сожале́нием узна́л о ва́шей боле́зни.

learned ['lɜ:nɪd] *adj.* учёный; **my ~ friend** (*Counsel*) мой учёный колле́га; **a ~ society** нау́чное о́бщество.

learner ['lɜ:nə(r)] *n.* начина́ющий; **he is a good ~** он хорошо́ у́чится; (*~-driver*) начина́ющий води́тель (не име́ющий води́тельских прав); шофёр-учени́|к (*fem.* -ца).

learning ['lɜ:nɪŋ] *n.* (*process*) уче́ние; изуче́ние; **~ did not come easily to him** уче́ние ему́ дава́лось нелегко́; (*possession of knowledge*) учёность, эруди́ция; (*body of knowledge*) нау́ка; **seat of ~** оча́г просвеще́ния; **the New L~** (*Renaissance*) Возрожде́ние.

lease [li:s] *n.* аре́нда; **long ~** долгосро́чная аре́нда; **the ~ is running out** срок аре́нды истека́ет; **we took the house on a 20-year ~** мы взя́ли дом в аре́нду на 20 лет; (*fig.*): **the doctors gave him a new ~ of life** врачи́ ему́ продли́ли жизнь; **he took on a new ~ of life** он сло́вно за́ново роди́лся; **the drama has taken on a new ~ of life** иску́сство дра́мы возроди́лось.

v.t. (*of lessee*) арендова́ть (*impf.*, *pf.*); брать, взять в аре́нду/наём; (*of lessor*) сд|ава́ть, -ать в аре́нду.

cpds. **~hold** *n.* аре́нда; владе́ние на права́х аре́нды; **~hold property** арендо́ванная со́бственность; **~holder** *n.* аренда́тор; **~-lend** *n.* ленд-ли́з.

leash [li:ʃ] *n.* при́вязь, поводо́к; (*for hounds*) смычо́к; **let off the ~** (*lit.*) спус|ка́ть, -ти́ть с поводка́; (*fig.*) развяза́ть (*pf.*) ру́ки +*d.*; **hold in ~** (*lit.*, *fig.*) держа́ть (*impf.*) на (коро́тком) поводке́; **strain at the ~** (*fig.*) рва́ться (*impf.*) в бой.

v.t. брать, взять на поводо́к.

least [li:st] *n.*: **~ said, soonest mended** чем ме́ньше ска́зано, тем ле́гче испра́вить де́ло; **to say the ~** мя́гко говоря́; **the ~ he could do is to pay for the damage** он мог бы по кра́йней ме́ре возмести́ть уще́рб; **at ~** по кра́йней ме́ре; са́мое ме́ньшее; не ме́ньше +*g.*; **at the very ~** по ме́ньшей ме́ре; **give me ten at the (very) ~** да́йте мне ми́нимум де́сять; **at ~ once a year** не ре́же, чем раз в год; **he is at ~ as tall as you** он ва́шего ро́ста, а мо́жет быть и вы́ше; **you should at ~ have warned me** вы бы хоть предупреди́ли меня́; **you can at ~ try** попы́тка не пы́тка; **not in the ~** ни в мале́йшей сте́пени, ничу́ть, нисколько; **not in the ~ interested** совсе́м не заинтересо́ван (*pred.*).

adj. (*smallest*) наиме́ньший; минима́льный; **~ common multiple** о́бщее наиме́ньшее кра́тное; **that's the ~ of my worries** э́то меня́ ме́ньше всего́ волну́ет; (*slightest*) мале́йший; **he hasn't the ~ idea about it** он об э́том не име́ет ни мале́йшего поня́тия.

adv. ме́ньше всего́; **I like this the ~ of all his plays** э́та его́ пье́са мне нра́вится ме́ньше всех други́х; **it is the ~ successful of his books** э́то наиме́нее уда́чная из его́ книг; **no-one can complain, you ~ of all** никто́ не мо́жет жа́ловаться, а вы и пода́вно; **with the ~ possible trouble** с наиме́ньшими хло́потами; с наиме́ньшей затра́той сил; **not ~** не в после́днюю о́чередь.

least|ways ['li:stweɪz], **-wise** ['li:stwaɪz] *adv.* (*dial.*) по кра́йней ме́ре.

leather ['leðə(r)] *n.* **1.** ко́жа; **patent ~** лакиро́ванная ко́жа; **imitation ~** кожими́т; **as tough as ~** жёсткий как подо́шва. **2.** (*wash-~*) за́мша; бархо́тка. **3.** (*~ thong*) реме́нь (*m.*).

adj. **1.** (*made of ~*) ко́жаный; **~ jacket** ко́жаная ку́ртка; ко́жанка. **2.** (*pert. to ~*) коже́венный; **~ goods** коже́венный това́р.

v.t. (*thrash*) лупи́ть, от- (*coll.*); поро́ть, вы́-.

cpd. **~-neck** *n.* (*US sl., marine*) солда́т морско́й пехо́ты.

leatherette [,leðə'ret] *n.* кожими́т.

leathering ['leðərɪŋ] *n.* (*thrashing*) трёпка, по́рка (*coll.*).

leathery ['leðərɪ] *adj.* (*tough*) жёсткий; **~ skin** загрубе́вшая ко́жа.

leave [li:v] *n.* **1.** (*permission*) позволе́ние, разреше́ние; **who gave you ~ to go?** кто дал вам разреше́ние уйти́?; **I take ~ to remark** я позво́лю себе́ заме́тить; **by your ~** с ва́шего разреше́ния; **without (so much as) a 'by your ~'** без спро́са/спро́су. **2.** (*~ of absence*) о́тпуск; **he is on ~** он в отпуску́; **when are you going on ~?** когда́ вы ухо́дите в о́тпуск?; **I've come back from ~** я верну́лся из о́тпуска; **he took French ~** он ушёл не прости́вшись (*or* по-англи́йски); **sick ~** о́тпуск по боле́зни; **compassionate ~** (*mil.*) увольне́ние по семе́йным обстоя́тельствам; **~ pass** увольни́тельная запи́ска; отпускно́е свиде́тельство. **3.** (*farewell*): **take (one's) ~ (of s.o.)** про|ща́ться, -сти́ться (с кем-н.); **take ~ of one's senses** с ума́ сойти́ (*pf.*); (*coll.*) рехну́ться (*pf.*).

v.t. **1.** (*allow or cause to remain*) ост|авля́ть, -а́вить; **the wound left a scar** от ра́ны оста́лся шрам; **his words left a deep impression** его́ слова́ произвели́ большо́е впечатле́ние; **I was left with the feeling that ...** у меня́ оста́лось чу́вство, что...; **let us ~ it at that** пусть так; **you can take it or ~ it!** ва́ша во́ля!; **has anyone left a message?** никто́ ничего́ не передава́л?; **he left a wife and three children** по́сле его́ сме́рти жена́ оста́лась одна́ с тремя́ детьми́; **two from five ~s three** пять ми́нус два равня́ется трём; (*with indication of state or circumstances*): **~ me alone!** оста́вьте меня́ (в поко́е)!; **~ my books alone!** не тро́гайте мои́ кни́ги; **~ well alone!** от добра́ добра́ не и́щут; лу́чшее — враг хоро́шего; **it ~s me cold** (*fig.*) э́то меня́ не тро́гает; **I left him in no doubt as to my intention** я ему́ я́сно объясни́л своё наме́рение; **they left him in the lurch** они́ бро́сили его́ в беде́; **it ~s much to be desired** э́то оставля́ет жела́ть мно́го лу́чшего; **~ the door open!** оста́вьте дверь откры́той!; не закрыва́йте дверь!; **he ~s himself open to attack** он ста́вит себя́ под уда́р; **some things are better left unsaid** о не́которых веща́х лу́чше не говори́ть; **she was left a widow** она́ оста́лась вдово́й; **the illness left him weak** по́сле боле́зни у него́ появи́лась сла́бость; (*past p., remaining*): **I have no money left** у меня́ не оста́лось де́нег; **how much milk is there left?** ско́лько оста́лось молока́? **2.** (*~ behind by accident*) заб|ыва́ть, -ы́ть; **I left my umbrella at home** я забы́л зо́нтик до́ма. **3.** (*bequeath*) завеща́ть (*impf., pf.*); ост|авля́ть, -а́вить в насле́дство; **she was left a large inheritance by her uncle** дя́дя оста́вил ей большо́е насле́дство. **4.** (*abandon*) бр|оса́ть, -о́сить; пок|ида́ть, -и́нуть; **he left his wife for another woman** он бро́сил свою́ жену́ ра́ди друго́й же́нщины. **5.** (*relinquish*): **~ hold, go of** выпуска́ть, вы́пустить из рук. **6.** (*commit, entrust*) предост|авля́ть, -а́вить; **I ~ the decision to you** предоставля́ю реше́ние вам; **it was left to him to decide** реша́ть до́лжен был он; **~ it to him** пусть он э́то сде́лает; **~ it to me** я э́тим займу́сь; **he ~s nothing to chance** он чрезвыча́йно осторо́жен; **he was left to himself** он был предоста́влен самому́ себе́. **7.** (*go away from*) выходи́ть, вы́йти из+*g.*; (*by vehicle*) выезжа́ть, вы́ехать из+*g.*; (*by air*) вылета́ть, вы́лететь из+*g.*; (*for vv. used when subj. is a mode of transport, see v.i.*); **I ~ the house at eight** я выхожу́ из дому в во́семь часо́в; **~ the room!** вы́йдите из ко́мнаты; **has your cold left you yet?** у вас прошла́ просту́да?; **the train was an hour late leaving Oxford** по́езд о́тбыл из О́ксфорда с часовы́м опозда́нием; **I left him in good health** когда́ я его́ поки́нул, он был соверше́нно здоро́в; **you ~ the church on your left** це́рковь оста́нется у вас сле́ва; (*come off*): **the train left the rails** по́езд сошёл с ре́льсов; (*rise from*): **~ the table** вст|ава́ть, -ать из-за стола́; (*~ for good, quit*) бр|оса́ть, -о́сить; пок|ида́ть, -и́нуть; **he left his job** он бро́сил свою́ рабо́ту; **our typist left us** на́ша машини́стка уво́лилась; **he left the Communist party** он вы́шел из коммунисти́ческой па́ртии; **has he left the country for good?** он навсегда́ поки́нул страну́?; **he left home at 16** в 16 лет он ушёл и́з дому; **he ~s school this year** он конча́ет шко́лу в э́том году́.

v.i. **1.** (*of pers. on foot*) уходи́ть, уйти́; (*by transport*) уезжа́ть, уе́хать; (*by air*) улет|а́ть, -е́ть; **when do you ~ for the South?** когда́ вы уезжа́ете на юг?; (*~ for good*): **she left** (*her job*) **without giving notice** она́ ушла́ с рабо́ты, не уве́домив нача́льства. **2.** (*of train*) от|ходи́ть, -ойти́; (*of boat*) от|ходи́ть, -ойти́; отпл|ыва́ть, -ы́ть; (*of aircraft*) вылета́ть, вы́лететь.

with advs.: **~ about, ~ around** *v.t.*: **don't ~ your money around** не оставля́йте де́ньги, где попа́ло; **~ aside** *v.t.* ост|авля́ть, -а́вить в стороне́; **leaving expense aside, it's not a practical idea** э́то бесполе́зная зате́я, уж не говоря́ о расхо́дах; **~ behind** *v.t.* ост|авля́ть, -а́вить по́сле себя́; (*forget to take*): **he left his hat behind** он забы́л свою́ шля́пу; (*abandon*): **he was left behind on the island** его́ поки́нули на о́строве; (*bequeath*): **he left behind a tidy sum** он оста́вил изря́дную су́мму; (*outstrip*): **we left him far behind** мы его́ оста́вили далеко́ позади́; **~ down** *v.t.*: **~ the blinds down!** не поднима́йте што́ры!; **~ in** *v.t.*: **we ~ the fire in overnight** у нас ками́н гори́т всю ночь; **he left in all the quotations** он сохрани́л все цита́ты; **~ off** *v.t.* (*not put on*): **I posted the letter but left off the stamp** я отосла́л письмо́, но не прикле́ил ма́рки; (*not wear*): **I ~ off my waistcoat in hot weather** в жару́ я не ношу́ жиле́та; (*stop*) перест|ава́ть, -а́ть +*inf*; конча́ть, ко́нчить +*a.*; **~ off smoking** бр|оса́ть, -о́сить кури́ть; *v.i.* (*halt*) останавливаться, -ови́ться; **where did we ~ off?** на чём мы останови́лись?; **~ on** *v.t.*: **I left the light on** я оста́вил свет включённым; **I left my jacket on** я не снял пиджака́; **~ out** *v.t.*; **she left the washing out in the rain** она́ оста́вила бельё под дождём; (*omit*) пропус|ка́ть, -ти́ть; **~ me out of this!** не втя́гивайте меня́ в э́то!; **I felt left out** я почу́вствовал себя́ ли́шним; **~ over** *v.t.* (*defer*) от|кла́дывать, -ложи́ть; (*pass., remain*): ост|ава́ться, -а́ться; **a lot was left over after dinner** по́сле обе́да оста́лось ещё мно́го еды́.

cpd. **~-taking** *n.* проща́ние, расстава́ние.

leaved [li:vd] *adj.*: **thickly ~** с густо́й листво́й, густоли́ственный.

leaven ['lev(ə)n] *n.* (*lit., fig.*) заква́ска; **of the same ~** (*fig.*) из одного́ те́ста.

v.t. (*lit.*) заква́|шивать, -сить; (*fig.*): **he ~ed his speech with a few jokes** он оживи́л свою́ речь двумя́-тремя́ анекдо́тами.

leavening ['levənɪŋ] *n.* заква́ска.

leavings ['li:vɪŋz] *n.* оста́тки (*m. pl.*); (*of food*) объе́дки (*m. pl.*); (*of drink*) опи́в|ки (*pl., g.* -ок).

Lebanese [,lebə'ni:z] *n.* лива́н|ец (*fem.* -ка).

adj. лива́нский.

Lebanon ['lebə,nən] *n.*: **(the) ~** Лива́н.

lecher ['letʃə(r)] *n.* развра́тник, распу́тник.

lecherous ['letʃərəs] *adj.* развра́тный, распу́тный.

lecherousness ['letʃərəsnɪs] *n.* развра́тность, распу́тство.

lechery ['letʃərɪ] *n.* развра́т.

lectern ['lektɜ:n, -t(ə)n] *n.* анало́й; (*in lecture-room*) пюпи́тр.

lector ['lektɔ:(r)] *n.* доце́нт, преподава́тель (*m.*).

lecture ['lektʃə(r)] *n.* **1.** (*dissertation*) ле́кция; **attend a ~** слу́шать, про- ле́кцию; **give a ~** чита́ть, про- (*or* проче́сть) ле́кцию. **2.** (*reproof*) нота́ция; **give, read s.o. a ~** чита́ть, про- нота́цию кому́-н.

v.t. чита́ть, про- ле́кцию/нота́цию +*d.*

v.i.: **he ~s in Russian** он чита́ет ле́кции по ру́сскому языку́; **he ~s in Roman law** он препода́ёт ри́мское пра́во.

cpd. **~-room** *n.* аудито́рия.

lecturer ['lektʃərə(r)] *n.* (*speaker*) докла́дчик; (*professional* ~) ле́ктор; (*univ.*) препода́ватель (*m.*).

lectureship ['lektʃəʃɪp] *n.* ле́кторство; (*senior* ~) доценту́ра.

LED (*abbr. of* ***light-emitting diode***) СИД, (свето-излуча́ющий дио́д).

ledge [ledʒ] *n.* (*shelf*) пла́нка, по́лочка; (*projection*) вы́ступ; (*edge*) край; (*under water*) шельф, бар.

ledger ['ledʒə(r)] *n.* (*book*) гроссбу́х; (гла́вная) учётная кни́га; **~ shelf** по́лка для счетово́дных книг.

lee [li:] *n.* (*shelter*): **under the ~ of** под защи́той +*g.*; (**~** *side*) подве́тренная сторона́; **~ shore** подве́тренный бе́рег.

cpd. **~way** *n.* дрейф; **make up ~way** (*lit.*) компенси́ровать (*impf.*, *pf.*) снос ве́тром; (*fig.*) навёрст|ывать, -а́ть упу́щенное; **he has much ~way to make up** ему́ предстои́т мно́гое наверста́ть.

leech[1] [li:tʃ] *n.* (*arch.*, *physician*) ле́карь (*m.*).

leech[2] [li:tʃ] *n.* (*worm*) пия́вка; **prescribe ~es** назн|ача́ть, -а́чить пия́вки; **stick like a ~** присоса́ться (*impf.*) как пия́вка.

leek [li:k] *n.* лук-поре́й.

leer [lɪə(r)] *n.* ухмы́лка.

v.i. ухмыл|я́ться, -ну́ться; **~ at** хи́тро/зло́бно смотре́ть, по- на+*a.*, кри́во улыб|а́ться, -ну́ться +*d.*

leery ['lɪərɪ] *adj.* (*sl.*) хи́трый; (*wary*) недове́рчивый.

lees [li:z] *n.* (*lit.*, *fig.*) подо́нки (*m. pl.*); **drain to the ~** (*lit.*) вы́пить (*pf.*) до дна; (*fig.*) испи́ть (*pf.*) ча́шу (*чего*).

leeward ['li:wəd, *naut.* 'lu:əd] *n.* подве́тренная сторона́; **to ~ (of)** на подве́тренной стороне́ (от+*g.*).

adj. подве́тренный; **L~ Islands** Подве́тренные острова́.

adv. под ве́тром.

left [left] *n.* **1.** (*side, direction*): **from the ~** сле́ва; **from ~ to right** сле́ва напра́во; **on the ~ of the street** по ле́вой стороне́ у́лицы; **on, to my ~** (*location or motion*) нале́во от меня́; **on, from my ~** сле́ва от меня́; **he turned to the ~** он поверну́л нале́во. **2.** (**~**-*handed blow*) уда́р ле́вой (руко́й). **3.** (*mil.*: **~** *flank*) ле́вый фланг. **4.** (*pol.*): **the L~** ле́вые (*pl.*) (па́ртии).

adj. ле́вый; **~ hook** ле́вый хук; **~ turn** ле́вый поворо́т; **~ wing** (*pol.*) ле́вое крыло́.

adv. нале́во; **turn ~** св|ора́чивать, -ерну́ть нале́во; **~ turn!** (*mil.*) нале́во!

cpds. **~-hand** *adj.* ле́вый; **~-hand service** (*tennis*) пода́ча ле́вой руко́й; **car with ~-hand drive** маши́на с левосторо́нним управле́нием (*or* с рулём сле́ва); **~-hand screw** винт с ле́вым хо́дом; **~-handed** *adj.* де́лающий всё ле́вой руко́й; **~-handed person** левша́ (*c.g.*); **~-handed blow** уда́р ле́вой руко́й; **~-handed compliment** сомни́тельный комплиме́нт; **~-wing** *adj.* ле́вый, с ле́выми тенде́нциями; **~-winger** *n.* представи́тель (*m.*) ле́вого крыла́ (па́ртии), ле́вый.

leftism ['leftɪz(ə)m] *n.* левизна́, ле́вые взгля́ды (*m. pl.*).

leftist ['leftɪst] *n.* лева́|к (*fem.* -чка).

adj. ле́вый.

leftovers ['left,əʊvəz] *n. pl.* оста́тк|и (*pl. g.* -ов); (*food*) объе́дк|и (*pl. g.* -ов).

leftwards ['leftwədz] *adv.* нале́во, вле́во.

lefty ['leftɪ] *n.* (*coll.*) (*left-handed pers.*) левша́ (*c.g.*); (*pol.*) лева́|к (*fem.* -чка).

leg [leg] *n.* **1.** нога́; (*dim.*) но́жка; (*of bird*) ла́па, ла́пка; **she is all ~s** она́ дли́нная и нескла́дная; **with one's ~s in the air** вверх нога́ми; **he is on his ~s again** (*after illness*) он встал на́ ноги; **I've been on my ~s all day** я был на нога́х це́лый день; **he is on his last ~s** (*dying*) он ды́шит на ла́дан; **the car is on its last ~s** маши́на вот-во́т развали́тся; **I could hardly drag one ~ after another** я едва́ волочи́л но́ги; **get on one's hind ~s** (*of dog etc.*) вста|ва́ть, -ть на за́дние ла́пы; **give s.o. a ~ up** (*lit.*) помо́чь (*pf.*) кому́-н. взобра́ться; (*fig.*, *assist*) ока́з|ывать, -а́ть по́мощь кому́-н.; **pull s.o.'s ~** разы́гр|ывать, -а́ть кого́-н.; подшу́|чивать, -ти́ть над кем-н.; **run s.o. off his ~s** заг|оня́ть, -на́ть кого́-н.; **be run off one's ~s** сб|ива́ться, -и́ться с ног; **shake a ~** (*coll.*, *dance*) танцева́ть (*impf.*); (*coll.*, *get going*) дви́гаться (*impf.*); шевели́ть (*impf.*) нога́ми; **show a ~!** (*coll.*) подъём!; **he hasn't a ~ to stand on** ему́ нет оправда́ния; его́ до́воды не выде́рживают (ни мале́йшей) кри́тики; **stretch one's ~s** размя́ть (*pf.*) но́ги; **take to one's ~s** унести́ (*pf.*) но́ги; бро́ситься (*pf.*) в бе́гство; **walk s.o. off his ~s** заму́чить (*pf.*) кого́-н. ходьбо́й. **2.** (*meat*): **~ of mutton** бара́нья нога́; **~ of pork** о́корок. **3.** (*of furniture etc.*) но́жка. **4.** (*of garment*): **trouser ~** штани́на; (*of sock or stocking*) па́голенок. **5.** (*stage of journey etc.*) эта́п.

v.t.: **~ it** (*coll.*) идти́ (*det.*) пешко́м; **we ~ged it for 20 miles** мы отмаха́ли 20 миль пешко́м.

cpds. **~-pull** *n.* (*coll.*) мистифика́ция, ро́зыгрыш; **~-room** *n.* ме́сто для ног; **~-show** *n.* (*coll.*) фриво́льный эстра́дный та́нец, «пара́д но́жек».

legacy ['legəsɪ] *n.* насле́дство, насле́дие.

legal ['li:g(ə)l] *adj.* **1.** (*pert. to or based on law*) юриди́ческий, правово́й; **~ department** юриди́ческий отде́л; **~ aid bureau** юриди́ческая консульта́ция; **~ obligation** правово́е обяза́тельство; **~ fiction** юриди́ческая фи́кция; **~ practitioner** адвока́т; **~ adviser** юриско́нсульт; **the ~ profession** профе́ссия юри́ста; (*lawyers*) юри́сты, адвока́ты (*both m. pl.*); **take ~ advice** консульти́роваться, про- с юри́стом. **2.** (*permitted or ordained by law*) зако́нный, лега́льный; **~ tender** зако́нное платёжное сре́дство; **~ offence** правонаруше́ние; **within one's ~ rights** в зако́нном пра́ве. **3.** (*involving court proceedings*) суде́бный; **~ action** суде́бный иск; суде́бное де́ло; **take ~ action against** возбу|жда́ть, -ди́ть де́ло про́тив+*g.*; под|ава́ть, -а́ть в суд на+*a.*; **~ costs** суде́бные изде́ржки.

legalism ['li:gə,lɪz(ə)m] *n.* буквое́дство, бюрократи́зм.

legalist ['li:gə,lɪst] *n.* зако́нник.

legalistic [,li:gə'lɪstɪk] *adj.* бюрократи́ческий.

legality [lɪ'gælɪtɪ, li:'g-] *n.* зако́нность, лега́льность.

legalization ['li:gə,laɪ'zeɪʃ(ə)n] *n.* узаконе́ние, легализа́ция; оформле́ние.

legalize ['li:gə,laɪz] *v.t.* узако́ни|вать, -ть; легализи́ровать (*impf.*, *pf.*); оф|ормля́ть, -о́рмить.

legate[1] [lɪ'geɪt] *n.* лега́т.

legate[2] [lɪ'geɪt] *v.t.* завеща́ть (*impf.*, *pf.*)

legatee [,legə'ti:] *n.* насле́дни|к (*fem.* -ца), легата́рий.

legation [lɪ'geɪʃ(ə)n] *n.* представи́тельство, ми́ссия.

legato [lɪ'gɑ:təʊ] *n.* & *adv.* лега́то (*indecl.*).

legend ['ledʒ(ə)nd] *n.* **1.** леге́нда; **famous in ~** воспе́тый в леге́ндах. **2.** (*inscription, explanatory matter*) на́дпись, леге́нда.

legendary ['ledʒəndərɪ] *adj.* легенда́рный.

legerdemain [,ledʒədə'meɪn] *n.* (*sleight of hand*) ло́вкость рук; (*trickery*) надува́тельство; (*trick*) уло́вка.

leger line ['ledʒə(r)] *n.* (*mus.*) доба́вочная лине́йка.

leggings ['legɪŋz] *n.* (*cloth*) гама́ши (*f. pl.*); (*leather*) кра́ги (*f. pl.*)

leggy ['legɪ] *adj.* длинноно́гий.

leghorn ['leghɔ:n, lɪ'gɔ:n] *n.* (*fowl*) леггорн.

legibility [,ledʒɪ'bɪlɪtɪ] *n.* разбо́рчивость, чёткость, удобочита́емость.

legible ['ledʒɪb(ə)l] *adj.* разбо́рчивый, чёткий, удобочита́емый.

legion ['li:dʒ(ə)n] *n.* **1.** (*body of soldiers*) легио́н; **Foreign L~** иностра́нный легио́н; **L~ of Honour** о́рден Почётного легио́на. **2.** (*multitude*) легио́н, тьма; **their name is ~** и́мя им легио́н.

legion|ary ['li:dʒənərɪ], **-naire** [,li:dʒə'neə(r)] *nn.* легионе́р.

legislate ['ledʒɪs,leɪt] *v.i.* изд|ава́ть, -а́ть зако́ны.

legislation [,ledʒɪs'leɪʃ(ə)n] *n.* законода́тельство.

legislative ['ledʒɪslətɪv] *adj.* законода́тельный.

legislator ['ledʒɪs,leɪtə(r)] *n.* законода́тель (*m.*).

legislature ['ledʒɪs,leɪtʃə(r), -lətʃə(r)] *n.* (*authority*) законода́тельная власть; (*assembly*) законода́тельный о́рган; (*institutions*) законода́тельные учрежде́ния.

legitimacy [lɪ'dʒɪtɪməsɪ] *n.* зако́нность.

legitimate[1] [lɪ'dʒɪtɪmət] *adj.* **1.** (*lawful*) зако́нный; **~ sovereign** зако́нный мона́рх; (*proper*): **~ drama** драмати́ческий теа́тр; дра́ма; (*justifiable*): **~ demands**

справедли́вые тре́бования; (*reasonable*, *admissible*) обосно́ванный, допусти́мый. **2.** (*by birth*) законнорождённый.

legitimate[2] [lɪ'dʒɪtɪ,meɪt] *v.t.*, **legitimation** [lɪ,dʒɪtɪ'meɪʃ(ə)n] *n.* = **legitimiz|e, -ation**

legitimist [lɪ'dʒɪtɪmɪst] *n.* легитими́ст.

legitim|ization [lɪ,dʒɪtɪmaɪ'zeɪʃ(ə)n], **-ation** [lɪ,dʒɪtɪ'meɪʃ(ə)n] *nn.* узаконе́ние, легитима́ция.

legitim|ize [lɪ'dʒɪtɪ,maɪz], **-ate** [lɪ'dʒɪtɪ,meɪt] *vv.t.* **1.** узако́ни|вать, -ть. **2.** (*adopt*, *of pers.*) усынов|ля́ть, -и́ть (*внебрачного ребёнка*).

legless ['leglɪs] *adj.* безно́гий.

legume ['legju:m] *n.* (*pod*) стручо́к; (*pl.*, *crops*) бобо́вые (*pl.*).

leguminous [lɪ'gju:mɪnəs] *adj.* бобо́вый, стручко́вый.

Le Havre [lə'hɑ:vrə] *n.* Гавр.

Leipzig ['laɪpsɪg] *n.* Ле́йпциг.

leisure ['leʒə(r)] *n.* свобо́дное вре́мя; досу́г; **at ~** на досу́ге; **at one's ~** (*in free time*) в свобо́дное вре́мя; (*unhurriedly*) не спеша́; **I have ~ for reading** у меня́ есть вре́мя для чте́ния; **~ clothes** дома́шняя оде́жда; **in one's ~ hours** в свобо́дное вре́мя; **~ time** досу́жее вре́мя.

leisured ['leʒəd] *adj.* досу́жий, пра́здный; **the ~ classes** нетрудовы́е кла́ссы.

leisureliness ['leʒəlɪnɪs] *n.* неторопли́вость.

leisurely ['leʒəlɪ] *adj.* неспе́шный, неторопли́вый; **at a ~ pace** споко́йным ша́гом.

adv. не спеша́, ме́дленно.

leitmoti|f, -v ['laɪtməʊ,ti:f] *n.* лейтмоти́в.

lemming ['lemɪŋ] *n.* ле́мминг.

lemon ['lemən] *n.* **1.** (*fruit*, *tree*) лимо́н; (*attr.*) лимо́нный; **~ drop** лимо́нный ледене́ц; **~ squash** лимо́нный сок с со́довой водо́й; **~ squeezer** соковыжима́лка для лимо́на. **2.** (*colour*) лимо́нный цвет. **3.: the answer's a ~** (*coll.*) так не пойдёт!

lemonade [,lemə'neɪd] *n.* лимона́д.

lemon sole ['lemən] *n.* морско́й язы́к.

lemur ['li:mə(r)] *n.* лему́р.

lend [lend] *v.t.* **1.** да|ва́ть, -ть взаймы́; од|а́лживать (*or* -олжа́ть), -олжи́ть; ссу|жа́ть, -ди́ть (*кого чем or что кому*); **~ me £5** одолжи́те мне (*or* да́йте мне взаймы́) пять фу́нтов; **~ me the book for a while** да́йте мне кни́гу на вре́мя; **he lent me the book to read** он дал мне почита́ть э́ту кни́гу. **2.** (*impart*) прид|ава́ть, -а́ть; **their costumes lent a note of gaiety to the scene** их костю́мы придава́ли карти́не жизнера́достный тон. **3.** (*proffer*): **~ an ear to** выслу́шивать, вы́слушать; **~ a hand** (*help*) ока́з|ывать, -а́ть по́мощь (*кому*); (*cooperate*) ока́з|ывать, -а́ть соде́йствие (*кому*); (*help out in difficulty*) выруча́ть, вы́ручить. **4.: ~ o.s. to** (*agree to*) позво́лить (*pf.*) себе́ согласи́ться на+*a.*; (*accommodate o.s. to*) подд|ава́ться, -а́ться на+*a.*; **the novel ~s itself to filming** рома́н подхо́дит для экраниза́ции; (*connive at*) потака́ть (*impf.*) +*d.*; (*indulge in*) пред|ава́ться, -а́ться+*d.*; (*allow of*) допус|ка́ть, -ти́ть; **the affair ~s itself to many interpretations** де́ло мо́жно толкова́ть по-ра́зному; (*be serviceable for*) годи́ться (*impf.*) на+*a.* (*or* для+*g.*).

with advs.: **~ out** *v.t.* (*of library etc.*) выдава́ть, вы́дать на́ дом.

cpd. **~-lease** *n.* ленд-ли́з.

lender ['lendə(r)] *n.* заимода́вец, кредито́р.

lending ['lendɪŋ] *n.* ссу́да; (*of money*) да́ча взаймы́; **he does not approve of ~** он не одобря́ет долго́в; **~ library** библиоте́ка (с вы́дачей книг на́ дом); отде́л абонеме́нта, абонеме́нт.

length [leŋθ, leŋkθ] *n.* **1.** (*dimension*, *measurement*) длина́; **2 metres in ~** 2 ме́тра длино́й; **this material is sold by ~** э́та мате́рия продаётся на ме́тры/я́рды; **he lay at full ~** он лежа́л вы́тянувшись во всю длину́; **he travelled the ~ and breadth of Europe** он изъе́здил Евро́пу вдоль и поперёк. **2.** (*racing etc.*): **the horse won by a ~** ло́шадь опереди́ла други́х на ко́рпус; **they lost (the boat-race) by half a ~** (в состяза́ниях по гре́бле) они́ отста́ли на полко́рпуса. **3.** (*of time*) продолжи́тельность, дли́тельность, срок; **the ~ of the visit was excessive** визи́т затяну́лся; **the chief fault of this film is its ~** гла́вный недоста́ток э́того фи́льма — его́ растя́нутость; **he objected to the ~ of the play** он счита́л, что пье́са сли́шком дли́нная; **seniority by ~ of service** старшинство́ по вы́слуге лет; **I shall be away for a certain ~ of time** меня́ не бу́дет не́которое вре́мя; **~ of the course** (*of study*) срок обуче́ния; **at ~** (*finally*) наконе́ц; (*in detail*) во всех подро́бностях; **he explained at some ~** он объясни́л дово́льно простра́нно; (*for a long time*) до́лго; **he spoke at great ~** он говори́л о́чень до́лго. **4.** (*distance*, *extent*) расстоя́ние; **keep s.o. at arm's ~** (*fig.*) держа́ть (*impf.*) кого́-н. на почти́тельном расстоя́нии; **the ships passed at a cable's ~ apart** суда́ прошли́ друг от дру́га на расстоя́нии ка́бельтова. **5.** (*extent*, *degree*): **go to any ~(s)** идти́ (*det.*) на всё; ни пе́ред чем не остана́вливаться (*impf.*); **he went to great ~s not to offend them** он сде́лал всё возмо́жное, что́бы их не оби́деть; **she went to all ~s to get her own way** она́ из ко́жи ле́зла, что́бы доби́ться своего́; **I will not go the ~ of denying it** я не ста́ну отрица́ть э́того. **6.** (*of vowel or syllable*) долгота́. **7.** (*piece of material*) кусо́к; отре́з.

lengthen ['leŋθ(ə)n, 'leŋkθ(ə)n] *v.t. & i.* удлин|я́ть(ся), -и́ть(ся); **the author ~ed (out) his article** а́втор растяну́л статью́.

lengthening ['leŋθənɪŋ, 'leŋkθənɪŋ] *n.* удлине́ние.

lengthiness ['leŋθɪnɪs, 'leŋkθɪnɪs] *n.* растя́нутость; длинно́ты (*f. pl.*).

length|ways ['leŋθweɪz, 'leŋkθ-], **-wise** ['leŋθwaɪz, 'leŋkθ-] *adv.* (*along its length*): **fold the blanket ~** сложи́те одея́ло вдоль; (*in length*): **this piece measures not quite 3 feet ~** в длину́ в э́том куске́ без ма́лого три фу́та.

lengthy ['leŋθɪ, 'leŋkθɪ] *adj.* дли́нный, затя́нутый; (*in time*) дли́тельный; (*of speech etc.*) растя́нутый, простра́нный.

leniency ['li:nɪənsɪ] *n.* снисхожде́ние; мя́гкость.

lenient ['li:nɪənt] *adj.* (*of pers.*) снисходи́тельный; (*of punishment etc.*) мя́гкий.

Leningrad ['lenɪn,græd] *n.* Ленингра́д; (*attr.*) ленингра́дский.

Leningrader ['lenɪn,grædə(r)] *n.* ленингра́д|ец (*fem.* -ка).

Leninism ['lenɪ,nɪz(ə)m] *n.* ленини́зм.

Leninist ['lenɪ,nɪst] *n.* ле́нинец.

adj. ле́нинский.

lenitive ['lenɪtɪv] *adj.* успока́ивающий.

lenity ['lenɪtɪ] *n.* милосе́рдие.

lens [lenz] *n.* (*anat.*, *opt.*) ли́нза; (*anat.*) хруста́лик гла́за; (*phot.*) объекти́в.

Lent [lent] *n.* вели́кий пост, **~ term** весе́нний триме́стр.

Lenten ['lent(ə)n] *adj.* (*of Lent*) великопо́стный; (*fasting*): **~ fare** по́стный стол.

lentil ['lentɪl] *n.* чечеви́ца; **~ soup** чечеви́чная похлёбка.

lento ['lentəʊ] *adv.* ле́нто (*indecl.*).

Leo ['li:əʊ] *n.* (*astr.*, *hist.*) Лев.

leonine ['li:ə,naɪn] *adj.* льви́ный.

leopard ['lepəd] *n.* леопа́рд; **snow, mountain ~** сне́жный леопа́рд/барс, и́рбис; **the ~ cannot change his spots** ≃ мо́жет ли барс перемени́ть пя́тна свои́?; мо́жет ли челове́к измени́ть свою́ приро́ду?

leopardess ['lepədɪs] *n.* са́мка леопа́рда.

leotard ['li:ə,tɑ:d] *n.* трико́ (*indecl.*), леота́рд

leper ['lepə(r)] *n.* прокажённый.

lepidoptera [,lepɪ'dɒptərə] *n. pl.* чешуекры́лые (*pl.*).

lepidopterous [,lepɪ'dɒptərəs] *adj.* чешуекры́лый.

leprechaun ['leprə,kɔ:n] *n.* гном.

leprosarium [,leprə'seərɪəm] *n.* лепрозо́рий.

leprosy ['leprəsɪ] *n.* прока́за.

leprous ['leprəs] *adj.* (*infected by leprosy*) прокажённый.

lesbian ['lezbɪən] *n.* (*homosexual*) лесбия́нка.

adj. (*geog.*) **L~** лесбо́сский; (*pert. to lesbianism*) лесби́йский.

lesbianism ['lezbɪən,ɪz(ə)m] *n.* лесби́йская любо́вь.

lèse majesté [li:z 'mædʒɪstɪ] *n.* оскорбле́ние мона́рха.

lesion ['li:ʒ(ə)n] *n.* поврежде́ние, пораже́ние.

less [les] *n.* ме́ньшее коли́чество; **you should eat ~** вам сле́дует ме́ньше есть; **I cannot accept ~ than £50** ме́ньше, чем на 50 фу́нтов я не соглашу́сь; **no ~ than £500** не ме́нее пятисо́т фу́нтов; **no more and no ~ than ...** не бо́лее и не ме́нее, как...; **all the ~ because ...** ещё ме́ньше из-за того́, что...; **it is nothing ~ than disgraceful** э́то позо́р и бо́льше ничего́; **he knew it would mean nothing ~ than the sack** он знал, что за э́то ему́ не минова́ть увольне́ния; **in ~ than no time** в одно́ мгнове́ние; **in ~ than an hour** ме́ньше чем за час; **you will see ~ of me in future** впосле́дствии вы не бу́дете ви́деть меня́ так ча́сто; **(I want) ~ of your cheek!** не хами́те!; **the ~ said, the better** чем ме́ньше слов, тем лу́чше; **I don't think any the ~ of him for that** э́то не умаля́ет моего́ мне́ния о нём; **he was a father to them, no ~** он был для них как родно́й оте́ц.

adj. **1.** (*smaller*) ме́ньший; **of ~ importance** ме́ньшей ва́жности; **of ~ magnitude** ме́ньшего разме́ра; **in a ~(er) degree** в ме́ньшей сте́пени; **grow ~** ум|еньша́ться, -е́ньшиться. **2.** (*not so much*) ме́ньше; **there will be ~ danger if we go together** е́сли мы пойдём вме́сте, э́то не бу́дет так опа́сно; **eat ~ meat!** е́шьте ме́ньше мя́са!; **~ noise!** поти́ше! **3.** (*of lower rank*): **no ~ a person than ...** никто́ ино́й, как...

adv. ме́ньше, ме́нее; не так, не сто́лько; **he is ~ intelligent than his sister** он не так умён, как его́ сестра́; **the ~ you think about it the better** чем ме́ньше об э́том ду́мать, тем лу́чше; **~ and ~** всё ме́ньше и ме́ньше; **none the ~** тем не ме́нее; **I do not say he is negligent, still (*or* much) ~ dishonest** я не хочу́ сказа́ть, что он небре́жен, и уж тем бо́лее не обвиня́ю его́ в нече́стности.

prep. ми́нус; **I paid him his wages, ~ what he owed me** я вы́дал ему́ зарпла́ту, вы́чтя из неё су́мму, кото́рую он мне задолжа́л.

lessee [le'siː] *n.* (*of house etc.*) съёмщик; (*of land*) аренда́тор, нанима́тель (*m.*).

lessen ['les(ə)n] *v.t.* & *i.* ум|еньша́ть(ся), -е́ньшить(ся).

lessening ['lesənɪŋ] *n.* уменьше́ние.

lesser ['lesə(r)] *adj.* ме́ньший; (*of plants, animals*) ма́лый; **the ~ brethren** ме́ньшая бра́тия; **the ~ evil** ме́ньшее из двух зол, наиме́ньшее зло; (*trifling*): **the ~ troubles of everyday life** ме́лкие хло́поты повседне́вной жи́зни.

lesson ['les(ə)n] *n.* **1.** уро́к, заня́тие; **English ~s** уро́ки англи́йского языка́; **give ~s in physics** да|ва́ть, -ть уро́ки фи́зики; **~s begin on 1 September** заня́тия начина́ются пе́рвого сентября́; **take ~s** брать (*impf.*) уро́ки; **teach s.o. a ~** (*rebuke, punish*) дать (*pf.*) уро́к кому́-н.; проучи́ть (*pf.*) кого́-н.; **let that be a ~ to you!** да бу́дет э́то вам нау́кой! **2.** (*eccl.*) чте́ние.

lessor [le'sɔː(r)] *n.* арендода́тель (*m.*), сдаю́щий в аре́нду (*or* внаём).

lest [lest] *conj.* что́бы не; **I fear ~ he should see her** я бою́сь, как бы он её не уви́дел.

let[1] [let] *n.* **1.: without ~ or hindrance** беспрепя́тственно. **2.** (*tennis*): **~ ball!** се́тка!

let[2] [let] *n.* (*of property*) аре́нда; **take a house on a long ~** снять (*pf.*) дом на дли́тельный срок.

v.t. (*also* **~ out**) сда|ва́ть, -ть в наём; **the flat is already ~** кварти́ра уже́ сдана́; **'house to ~ furnished'** (*notice*) «сдаётся дом с ме́белью».

v.i.: **this house would ~ easily** э́тот дом сни́мут бы́стро.

let[3] [let] *v.t.* **1.** (*allow*) позв|оля́ть, -о́лить +*d.*; разреш|а́ть, -и́ть +*d.*; **~ me help you** позво́льте вам помо́чь; **why not ~ him try?** да́йте ему́ возмо́жность попро́бовать; **he won't ~ me work** он не даёт мне рабо́тать; **~ s.o. be** ост|авля́ть, -а́вить кого́-н. в поко́е; **~ sth. be** не тро́|гать, -нуть чего́-н.; **~ drop, fall** роня́ть, урони́ть; **~ fly at** (*go for*) **s.o.** напус|ка́ться, -ти́ться на кого́-н.; **~ fly at** (*shoot at*) **sth.** стреля́ть (*impf.*) во что-н.; **~ go** (*relax grip on*) выпуска́ть, вы́пустить из рук; отпус|ка́ть, -ти́ть; **~ go (of) my hand** отпусти́те мою́ ру́ку; **~ o.s. go** увл|ека́ться, -е́чься; (*set free*) выпуска́ть, вы́пустить; **~ things go** вести́ (*det.*) дела́ спустя́ рукава́; (*sell*): **he ~ the chair go for a song** он про́дал стул по дешёвке; (*ignore*): **this was untrue but I ~ it go, pass** э́то бы́ло непра́вдой, но я не стал возража́ть; **~ one's hair grow** отпус|ка́ть, -ти́ть во́лосы; **we ~ the storm pass and then went out** мы пережда́ли грозу́, пото́м вы́шли; **~ slide** пусти́ть (*pf.*) на самотёк (*see also* **~ go**); **~ slip** (*chance etc.*) упус|ка́ть, -ти́ть. **2.** (*cause to*): **~ s.o. have it** (*coll., punish*) суро́во наказа́ть (*pf.*) кого́-н.; **~ s.o. know** да|ва́ть, -ть кому́-н. знать; **I ~ him see he was in the wrong** я дал ему́ поня́ть, что он непра́в; **~ it not be said that we were afraid** да не обвиня́т нас в тру́сости. **3.** (*in imper. or hortatory sense*): **~ me see** (*reflect*) погоди́те; да́йте поду́мать; **~ him do it** пусть он э́то сде́лает; **just ~ him try it!** пусть то́лько попро́бует!; **~ X equal the height of the building** пусть высота́ зда́ния равня́ется X; **~ us drink** вы́пьем(те); дава́й(те) вы́пьем/пить; **~ us pray** помо́лимся; **~ us not be greedy** не бу́дем жа́дничать; **~ them come in** пусть войду́т; **~ there be light** да бу́дет свет. **4.** (**~** *come or go*): **he ~ me into the room** он впусти́л меня́ в ко́мнату; **shall I ~ you into a secret?** хоти́те я раскро́ю вам та́йну?; **he was ~ out of prison** его́ вы́пустили из тюрьмы́. **5.: ~ blood** пус|ка́ть, -ти́ть кровь (*кому*).

with advs.: **~ alone** *v.t.* ост|авля́ть, -а́вить (*кого*) в поко́е; не тро́|гать, -нуть (*чего*); **~ him alone to finish it** не меша́йте ему́ зако́нчить э́то; **~ alone** (*not to mention*) не то́лько что, не говоря́ уже́ о+*p.*; **they haven't got a radio, ~ alone television** у них и ра́дио нет, не то, что телеви́зора; **he can't even walk, ~ alone run** он и ходи́ть-то не мо́жет, а бе́гать и пода́вно; **~ well alone** не вме́шиваться без нужды́; ≃ от добра́ добра́ не и́щут; **~ down** *v.t.* (*lower*) опус|ка́ть, -ти́ть; **~ one's hair down** (*lit.*) распус|ка́ть, -ти́ть во́лосы; (*fig.*) разоткрове́нничаться (*pf.*); **~ s.o. down gently** (*fig.*) щади́ть, по- чьё-н. самолю́бие; (*disappoint*) разочаро́в|ывать, -а́ть; **I feel ~ down** я разочаро́ван; (*fail to support*) подв|оди́ть, -ести́ (*coll.*); **I was badly ~ down** меня́ здо́рово подвели́; **he ~ the side down** (*coll.*) он подвёл свои́х; (*deflate*): **~ down tyres** спус|ка́ть, -ти́ть ши́ны; (*lengthen*): **~ down a dress** выпуска́ть, вы́пустить пла́тье; **~ in** *v.t.* (*admit*) впус|ка́ть, -ти́ть; **the window doesn't ~ in much light** че́рез э́то окно́ проника́ет ма́ло све́та; **my shoes ~ in water** мои́ ту́фли протека́ют; **he ~ himself in** он сам откры́л дверь и вошёл; **he ~ me in for endless trouble** он впу́тал меня́ в бесконе́чные неприя́тности; **what have I ~ myself in for?** во что я ввяза́лся?; **we ~ him in on the secret** мы посвяти́ли его́ в та́йну; (*insert*) вст|авля́ть, -а́вить; (*into garment*) вши|ва́ть, -ть; (*engage*): **~ the clutch in** включ|а́ть, -и́ть сцепле́ние; **~ off** *v.t.* (*discharge*) разря|жа́ть, -ди́ть; **~ off fireworks** запуска́ть (*impf.*) фейерве́рк; (*emit*): **~ off steam** (*lit., fig.*) выпуска́ть, вы́пустить пары́; **~ off a smell** испуска́ть (*impf.*) за́пах; (*allow to dismount*): **~ me off at the next stop** ссади́те меня́ на сле́дующей остано́вке; (*acquit; not punish*) не нака́зывать (*impf.*); поми́ловать (*pf.*); **he was ~ off lightly** он легко́ отде́лался; (*excuse*) про|ща́ть, -сти́ть +*d.*, **they ~ him off his debt** ему́ прости́ли долг; (*liberate*) освобо|жда́ть, -ди́ть; **he ~ them off work for the day** он их освободи́л от рабо́ты на день; *v.i.* (*fire*) вы́стрелить (*pf.*); **~ on** *v.t.* & *i.* (*coll., divulge*) прогов|а́риваться, -ори́ться; **don't ~ on about it** ни сло́ва об э́том!; (*pretend*) прики́|дываться, -нуться; **~ out** *v.t.* выпуска́ть, вы́пустить; **~ the air out of a tyre** вы́пустить (*pf.*) во́здух из ши́ны; спусти́ть (*pf.*) ши́ну; **~ the water out of the bath** вы́пустить/спусти́ть (*both pf.*) во́ду из ва́нны; **~ out a scream** завизжа́ть (*pf.*); взви́згнуть (*pf.*); **~ out a secret** прогов|а́риваться, -ори́ться; проболта́ться (*pf.*); **he ~ out the whole story** он вы́болтал всю исто́рию; **she ~ out the sleeves** она́ вы́пустила рукава́; **~ the fire out** да|ва́ть, -ть поту́хнуть огню́; **~ past** *v.t.* да|ва́ть, -ть пройти́; **~ through** *v.t.* пропус|ка́ть, -ти́ть; **~ up** *v.i.* (*weaken, diminish*) ослаб|ева́ть, -е́ть; (*stop for a while*) приостан|а́вливаться, -ови́ться; (*relax, take a rest*) перед|ыха́ть, -охну́ть; **he never ~s up in his work** он рабо́тает без переды́шки (*or* не поклада́я рук).

cpds. **~-down** *n.* (*disappointment, anticlimax*) разочарова́ние; **~-off** *n.*: **that was a ~-off!** пронесло́!; **~-out** *n.* возмо́жность отступле́ния; **a ~-out clause** усло́вие об освобожде́нии от отве́тственности; **~-up** *n.* (*respite*) переды́шка; остано́вка, прекраще́ние; (*relaxation*) ослабле́ние.

lethal ['liːθ(ə)l] *adj.* (*fatal*) смерте́льный; **a ~ dose**

смерте́льная до́за; (*designed to kill*) смертоно́сный; ~ **gas** смертоно́сный газ; ~ **chamber** ка́мера для усыпле́ния живо́тных.

lethargic [lɪ'θɑ:dʒɪk] *adj.* вя́лый; (*med.*) летарги́ческий.

lethargy ['leθədʒɪ] *n.* вя́лость; летерги́я.

Lethe ['li:θi:] *n.* (*myth.*) Ле́та.

Lett [let] *n.* латы́ш (*fem.* -ка).

letter ['letə(r)] *n.* **1.** (*of alphabet*) бу́ква; **capital** ~ прописна́я бу́ква; **the word is written with a capital** ~ э́то сло́во пи́шется с прописно́й бу́квы; **small** ~ строчна́я бу́ква; **it was written in small ~s** э́то бы́ло напи́сано строчны́ми бу́квами; (*fig., precise detail*): **to the** ~ буква́льно; **the** ~ **of the law** бу́ква зако́на; **he follows the law to the** ~ он соблюда́ет зако́н до после́дней запято́й; **in** ~ **and in spirit** по фо́рме и по существу́. **2.** (*typ.*) ли́тера. **3.** (*written communication*) письмо́; (*official*) паке́т; **registered** ~ заказно́е письмо́; ~ **of credit** аккредити́в; ~ **of introduction** рекоменда́тельное письмо́; ~ **of advice** (*comm.*) уведомле́ние; **~s of credence** вери́тельные гра́моты (*f. pl.*); **~s patent** жа́лованная гра́мота, пате́нт; ~ **of recall** отзывны́е гра́моты. **4.** (*pl., literature*) литерату́ра; **man of ~s** литера́тор; **the profession of ~s** литера́торство, заня́тие литерату́рой.

v.t. **1.** (*impress title on*) отти́с|кивать, -нуть загла́вие на+*a.*; **the title was ~ed in gold** загла́вие бы́ло вы́теснено золоты́ми бу́квами. **2.** (*classify by means of ~s*) пом|еча́ть, -е́тить бу́квами.

cpds. **~-balance** *n.* почто́вые вес|ы́ (*pl., g.* -о́в); **~-bomb** *n.* письмо́, начинённое взрывча́ткой; бо́мба в конве́рте; **~-box** *n.* почто́вый я́щик; **~-card** *n.* письмо́-секре́тка; **~-head(ing)** *n.* (*heading*) ша́пка на фи́рменном бла́нке; (*paper*) фи́рменный бланк; **~press** *n.* (*text, captions*) печа́тный текст; (*printing from raised type*) высо́кая печа́ть; **~-writer** *n.* (*pers.*) тот, кто ведёт перепи́ску; (*manual*) письмо́вник.

lettered ['letəd] *adj.* (*well-read*) начи́танный.

lettering ['letərɪŋ] *n.* (*inscription*) на́дпись; (*impressing of title*) тисне́ние (бу́квами); (*script*) шрифт.

Lettish ['letɪʃ] *n.* латы́шский язы́к.

adj. латы́шский.

lettuce ['letɪs] *n.* (*plant, dish*) сала́т; (*plant*) лату́к; **cabbage** ~ коча́нный сала́т.

leucocyte ['lu:kə,saɪt] *n.* лейкоци́т.

leucorrhoea [,lu:kə'ri:ə] *n.* бе́л|и (*pl., g.* -ей).

leuk(a)emia [lu:'ki:mɪə] *n.* белокро́вие, лейкеми́я.

Levant[1] [lɪ'vænt] *n.*: **the** ~ Лева́нт, Бли́жний Восто́к.

levant[2] [lɪ'vænt] *v.i.* смы́ться (*pf.*) (*coll.*).

Levantine [lɪ'væntaɪn, 'levən-] *n.* леванти́н|ец (*fem.* -ка); жи́тель (*fem.* -ница) Лева́нта.

adj. леванти́йский.

levee[1] ['levɪ, lɪ'vi:] *n.* (*reception*) (у́тренний) приём при дворе́ с прису́тствием одни́х мужчи́н.

levee[2] ['levɪ, lɪ'vi:] *n.* (*US, embankment*) на́бережная.

level ['lev(ə)l] *n.* **1.** (*instrument*) ватерпа́с; у́ровень (*m.*); **spirit** ~ спиртово́й у́ровень. **2.** (*horizontal plane or line*) у́ровень; **on a** ~ **with** на одно́м у́ровне с+*i.*; **out of** ~ не по отве́су; **water finds its own** ~ вода́ в сообща́ющихся сосу́дах стои́т на одно́м у́ровне; **at eye** ~ на у́ровне глаза́; (*fig., coll.*): **on the** ~! че́стно!; **is he on the** ~? мо́жно ли ему́ ве́рить? **3.** (*social etc., standing*): **he found his own** ~ он нашёл подходя́щее для себя́ ме́сто/о́бщество; **students at an advanced** ~ бо́лее продви́нутые студе́нты; **a higher** ~ **of civilization** бо́лее высо́кий у́ровень цивилиза́ции; **subsistence** ~ прожи́точный ми́нимум; **talks at Cabinet** ~ перегово́ры на у́ровне прави́тельства. **4.** (*geog., plain*) равни́на.

adj. (*even*) ро́вный; (*flat*) пло́ский; (*horizontal*) горизонта́льный; ~ **crossing** (железнодоро́жный) перее́зд; **the room was** ~ **with the street** ко́мната была́ на одно́м у́ровне с у́лицей; **the water was** ~ **with the banks** вода́ была́ вро́вень с берега́ми; **draw** ~ **with** наг|оня́ть, -на́ть; **have, keep a** ~ **head** сохраня́ть (*impf.*) споко́йствие; **do one's** ~ **best** че́стно стара́ться (*impf.*).

v.t. **1.** (*make* ~) ур|а́внивать, -овня́ть; вы́ра́внивать, вы́ровнять. **2.** (*raze to ground*) ср|а́внивать, -овня́ть с землёй; **the bump on the runway must be ~led** на́до вы́ровнять буго́р на взлётной площа́дке. **3.** (*geol.*) нивели́ровать (*impf., pl.*). **4.** (*direct, aim*) нав|оди́ть, -ести́; наце́ли|вать, -ть; **they ~led their guns at the enemy positions** они́ наце́лили ору́дия на пози́ции неприя́теля; **she ~led a gun at his head** она́ прице́лилась ему́ в го́лову; (*fig.*) напр|авля́ть, -а́вить (*что против кого*).

with advs.: ~ **down** *v.t.* выра́внивать, вы́ровнять; (*fig.*) нивели́ровать (*impf., pf.*); ~ **off,** ~ **out** *vv.t.* (*smooth out*) сгла́|живать, -дить; (*make* ~, *even, identical*) ур|а́внивать, -овня́ть; *v.i.* (*of aircraft*) выра́вниваться, вы́ровняться; ~ **up** *v.t.* ур|а́внивать, -овня́ть.

cpd. **~-headed** *adj.* тре́звый, рассуди́тельный.

leveller ['levələ(r)] *n.* побо́рник ра́венства; (*hist.*) ле́веллер.

lever ['li:və(r)] *n.* (*lit., fig.*) рыча́г; (*long pole*) ва́га; ~ **watch** а́нкерные часы́.

v.t.: ~ **sth. out** высвобожда́ть, вы́свободить что-н. рычаго́м; ~ **sth. up** подн|има́ть, -я́ть что-н. рычаго́м; **he ~ed the stone into position** он установи́л ка́мень с по́мощью рычага́.

leverage ['li:vərɪdʒ] *n.* (*action*) де́йствие/уси́лие рычага́; ~ **system** рыча́жная переда́ча; **use** ~ **on s.o.** (*fig.*) повлия́ть (*pf.*) на кого́-н.

leveret ['levərɪt] *n.* зайчо́нок.

leviathan [lɪ'vaɪəθ(ə)n] *n.* (*bibl., fig.*) левиафа́н.

levitate ['levɪ,teɪt] *v.t. & i.* подн|има́ть(ся), -я́ть(ся) в во́здух.

levitation [,levɪ'teɪʃ(ə)n] *n.* левита́ция.

Levite ['li:vaɪt] *n.* леви́т.

Leviticus [lɪ'vɪtɪkəs] *n.* Леви́т.

levity ['levɪtɪ] *n.* легкомы́слие.

levy ['levɪ] *n.* **1.** (*collection of taxes etc.*) сбор; (*imposition*) обложе́ние; (*raising*) взима́ние; **capital** ~ нало́г на капита́л. **2.** (*of recruits*) набо́р; **mass** ~ наро́дное ополче́ние; (*body of recruits*) новобра́нцы (*m. pl.*).

v.t. **1.** (*raise*) взима́ть (*impf.*) (*что с кого*). **2.** (*recruit*) наб|ира́ть, -ра́ть. **3.**: ~ **blackmail on s.o.** вымога́ть (*impf.*) де́ньги у кого́-н. путём шантажа́.

lewd [lju:d] *adj.* (*of pers.*) развра́тный; (*of thg.*) са́льный.

lewdness ['lju:dnɪs] *n.* развра́тность; са́льность.

lewisite ['lu:ɪ,saɪt] *n.* люизи́т.

lexical ['leksɪk(ə)l] *adj.* лекси́ческий.

lexicographer [,leksɪ'kɒgrəfə(r)] *n.* лексико́граф.

lexicographical [,leksɪkə'græfɪk(ə)l] *adj.* лексикографи́ческий.

lexicography [,leksɪ'kɒgrəfɪ] *n.* лексикогра́фия.

lexicon ['leksɪkən] *n.* (*dictionary*) слова́рь, лексико́н; (*vocabulary of writer etc.*) ле́ксика.

lexis ['leksɪs] *n.* ле́ксика, слова́рь.

ley [leɪ] *n.* пар, парово́е по́ле; ~ **farming** травопо́льная систе́ма.

Leyden jar ['laɪd(ə)n] *n.* ле́йденская ба́нка.

Lhasa ['lɑ:sə] *n.* Лха́са.

liabilit|y [,laɪə'bɪlɪtɪ] *n.* **1.** (*responsibility*) отве́тственность; **limited ~y company** компа́ния с ограни́ченной отве́тственностью; **admit ~y for sth.** призн|ава́ть, -а́ть себя́ отве́тственным за что-н. **2.** (*obligation*) обяза́тельство; **meet one's ~ies** выполня́ть, вы́полнить обяза́тельства; (*pl., debts*) долги́ (*m. pl.*). **3.** (*burden, handicap*): **he's nothing but a ~y** он про́сто обу́за; **this is a terrible ~y** э́то нам стра́шно меша́ет; **I shall only be a ~y** я бу́ду то́лько поме́хой.

liable ['laɪəb(ə)l] *adj.* **1.** (*answerable*) отве́тственный (за+*a.*). **2.** (*subject*): **he is** ~ **to a heavy fine** его́ мо́гут подве́ргнуть большо́му штра́фу; **she is** ~ **to epileptic fits** она́ подве́ржена эпилепти́ческим припа́дкам; **the words are** ~ **to misconstruction** ничего́ не сто́ит неве́рно истолкова́ть э́ти слова́. **3.** (*apt, likely*): **difficulties are** ~ **to arise** мо́гут возни́кнуть тру́дности; **she is** ~ **to forget it** она́ скло́нна забыва́ть об э́том.

liaise [lɪ'eɪz] *v.i.* (*coll.*) устана́вливать/подде́рживать (*impf.*) связь (с+*i.*).

liaison [lɪ'eɪzɒn] *n.* **1.** (*mil. etc.*) связь; ~ **officer** офице́р свя́зи. **2.** (*love affair*) (любо́вная) связь. **3.** (*phon.*) свя́зывание коне́чного согла́сного с нача́льным гла́сным после́дующего сло́ва.

liana [lɪ'ɑ:nə] *n.* лиа́на.

liar [ˈlaɪə(r)] *n.* лгун (*fem.* -ья); врун (*fem.* -ья).
Lias [ˈlaɪəs] *n.* (*geol.*) лейáс.
liassic [laɪˈæsɪk] *adj.* (*geol.*) лейáсский.
Lib [lɪb] *n.* (*coll.*): **Women's ~** феминистское движéние (*за уравнение женщин в правах с мужчинами*).
libation [laɪˈbeɪʃ(ə)n, lɪ-] *n.* (*drink-offering*) возлия́ние.
libel [ˈlaɪb(ə)l] *n.* клеветá; **~ action** дéло по обвинéнию в клеветé; **publish a ~ against s.o.** печáтать, на- клеветни́ческие заявлéния о ком-н.; **law of ~** закóн о диффамáции.
v.t. клеветáть, о- (*кого*), на- (*на кого*).
libeller [ˈlaɪbələ(r)] *n.* клеветни́|к (*fem.* -ца); пасквиля́нт.
libellous [ˈlaɪbələs] *adj.* клеветни́ческий; (*of books etc.*) пáсквильный.
liberal [ˈlɪbər(ə)l] *n.* либерáл.
adj. **1.** (*generous, open-handed*) щéдрый; (*abundant*) оби́льный. **2.** (*open or broadminded*): **a man of ~ views** человéк ширóких взгля́дов; (*progressive*) передовóй; (*non-specialist*): **a ~ education** гуманитáрное образовáние; **the ~ arts** гуманитáрные наýки. **3.** (*pol.*) либерáльный; **the L~s** либерáльная пáртия.
liberalism [ˈlɪbərəˌlɪz(ə)m] *n.* либерали́зм.
liberality [ˌlɪbəˈrælɪtɪ] *n.* щéдрость; широтá взгля́дов.
liberalization [ˌlɪbərəlaɪˈzeɪʃ(ə)n] *n.* демократизáция, либерализáция.
liberalize [ˈlɪbərəˌlaɪz] *v.t.*: **~ trade** облегч|áть, -и́ть услóвия торгóвли; (*ideas, regime*) либерализи́ровать (*impf., pf.*).
liberate [ˈlɪbəˌreɪt] *v.t.* **1.** освобо|ждáть, -ди́ть; **a mind ~d from prejudice** ум, освобождённый от предрассýдков. **2.** (*chem.*) выделя́ть, вы́делить.
liberation [ˌlɪbəˈreɪʃ(ə)n] *n.* освобождéние; (*chem.*) выделéние.
liberator [ˈlɪbəˌreɪtə(r)] *n.* освободи́тель (*fem.* -ница).
Liberia [laɪˈbɪərɪə] *n.* Либéрия.
Liberian [laɪˈbɪərɪən] *n.* либери́|ец (*fem.* -йка).
adj. либери́йский.
libertarian [ˌlɪbəˈteərɪən] *n.* (*advocate of freedom*) борéц за демократи́ческие свобóды.
libertine [ˈlɪbəˌtiːn, -tɪn, -ˌtaɪn] *n.* (*licentious pers.*) распýтник.
adj. распýщенный.
libertinism [ˈlɪbətiːnˌɪz(ə)m, -tɪnˌɪz(ə)m, -taɪnˌɪz(ə)m] *n.* распýщенность.
libert|y [ˈlɪbətɪ] *n.* **1.** (*freedom*) свобóда; **~y of the subject** свобóда пóдданного; **~y of action** свобóда дéйствий; **~y boat** шлю́пка с увольня́емыми на бéрег; **~y man** матрóс, увольня́емый на бéрег; **at ~y** находя́щийся на свобóде; **you are at ~y to go** вы вольны́ уйти́; **set at ~y** выпускáть, вы́пустить на вóлю/свобóду; **regain one's ~y** (*escape*) вернýть (*pf.*) себé свобóду; (*be released*) быть вы́пущенным на свобóду. **2.** (*licence*) вóльность; **take ~ies** позв|оля́ть, -óлить себé вóльности; **the author takes ~ies with facts** áвтор сли́шком вóльно обращáется с фáктами; **take the ~y** осмéли|ваться, -ться *+inf.*; позв|оля́ть, -óлить себé *+inf.*; **may I take the ~y of asking your name?** позвóльте спроси́ть, как вас зовýт? **3.** (*pl., privileges; rights*) вóльности (*f. pl.*); привилéгии (*f. pl.*).
libidinous [lɪˈbɪdɪnəs] *adj.* похотли́вый.
libido [lɪˈbiːdəʊ, lɪˈbaɪdəʊ] *n.* либи́до (*indecl.*).
Libra [ˈliːbrə, ˈlɪb-, ˈlaɪb-] *n.* (*astron.*) Вес|ы́ (*pl., g.* -óв).
librarian [laɪˈbreərɪən] *n.* библиотéкарь (*m.*).
librarianship [laɪˈbreərɪənʃɪp] *n.* (*post*) дóлжность библиотéкаря; (*technique*) библиотéчное дéло, библиотековéдение.
library [ˈlaɪbrərɪ] *n.* библиотéка; (*reading-room*) читáльный зал; **reference ~** спрáвочная библиотéка; (*attr.*) библиотéчный; **~ ticket** читáтельский билéт.
librettist [lɪˈbretɪst] *n.* либретти́ст.
libretto [lɪˈbretəʊ] *n.* либрéтто (*indecl.*).
Libya [ˈlɪbɪə, ˈlɪbjə] *n.* Ли́вия.
Libyan [ˈlɪbɪən, ˈlɪbjən] *n.* ливи́|ец (*fem.* -йка).
adj. ливи́йский.
licence [ˈlaɪs(ə)ns] (*US also* **license**) *n.* **1.** (*permission*) разрешéние; (*for trade*) лицéнзия; **grant s.o. a ~** выдавáть, вы́дать лицéнзию комý-н. **2.** (*permit, certificate*) свидéтельство; **driving ~** води́тельские правá. **3.** (*freedom*): **poetic ~** поэти́ческая вóльность. **4.** (*licentiousness*) распýщенность.
cpds. **~-holder** *n.* = **licensee; ~-plate** *n.* (*US*) номернóй знак.
license [ˈlaɪs(ə)ns] (*US also* **licence**) *v.t.* **1.** (*permit, authorize*) разреш|áть, -и́ть (*что*); да|вáть, -ть разрешéние на (*что*); **the police would not ~ his gun** поли́ция отказáла емý в разрешéнии на огнестрéльное орýжие. **2.** (*grant permit, permission to*) разреш|áть, -и́ть *+d.*; **a shop ~d to sell tobacco** лáвка, обладáющая лицéнзией на продáжу табáчных издéлий; **~d premises** (*inn*) заведéние, в котóром разрешáется продáжа спиртны́х напи́тков.
licensee [ˌlaɪsənˈsiː] (*also* **license-holder**) *n.* обладáтель (*fem.* -ница) разрешéния/лицéнзии; (*of public house*) хозя́|ин (*fem.* -йка) бáра.
licensing [ˈlaɪsənsɪŋ] *n.* лицензи́рование; **~ hours** часы́ продáжи спиртны́х напи́тков; **~ system** лицензиóнная систéма.
licentiate [laɪˈsenʃɪət, -ʃət] *n.* лиценциáт; обладáтель (*fem.* -ница) диплóма.
licentious [laɪˈsenʃəs] *adj.* распýщенный.
licentiousness [laɪˈsenʃəsnɪs] *n.* распýщенность.
lichee, lychee [ˈlaɪtʃɪ, ˈlɪ-] *n.* личжи́ (*indecl.*), китáйский крыжóвник (*collect.*).
lichen [ˈlaɪkən, ˈlɪtʃ(ə)n] *n.* лишáйник.
lich-gate [ˈlɪtʃgeɪt] = **lych-gate**
licit [ˈlɪsɪt] *adj.* закóнный.
lick [lɪk] *n.* **1.: he gave the stamp a ~** он лизнýл мáрку; **he gave his face a ~ and a promise** (*coll.*) он нáспех ополоснýл лицó. **2.** (*sl., speed*): **he went at a fair ~** он мчáлся очертя́ гóлову.
v.t. **1.** лиз|áть, -нýть; (**~** *all over*) обли́з|ывать, -áть; **~ one's lips/**(*coll.*) **chops** обли́з|ывать, -áть гýбы; обли́з|ываться, -áться; (*fig.*): **~ s.o.'s boots** лизáть (*impf.*) сапоги́ комý-н.; **~ one's wounds** зали́з|ывать, -áть рáны; **~ sth. into shape** прид|авáть, -áть вид чемý-н.; **~ s.o. into shape** обтёс|ывать, -áть когó-н. **2.** (*coll., thrash*) зад|авáть, -áть взбýчку *+d.* **3.** (*coll., defeat*) поб|ивáть, -и́ть.
v.t.: **~ off, ~ up** сли́з|ывать, -áть (*or* -нýть).
cpd. **~spittle** *n.* подхали́м.
lickerish [ˈlɪkərɪʃ] *adj.*: (*greedy*) жáдный; (*lustful*) похотли́вый.
licking [ˈlɪkɪŋ] *n.* (*coll.*): **he took a ~** (*thrashing*) емý достáлась взбýчка; (*was defeated*) он был разби́т в пух и прах.
licorice [ˈlɪkərɪs, -rɪʃ] = **liquorice**
lid [lɪd] *n.* **1.** кры́шка; (*fig.*): **take the ~ off** (*disclose*) вы́тащить (*pf.*) на свет бóжий; **that puts the ~ on it** (*sl.*) э́то конéц! **2.** (*sl., hat*) покры́шка.
lido [ˈliːdəʊ, ˈlaɪ-] *n.* (общéственный) пляж.
lie[1] [laɪ] *n.* (*falsehood*) ложь; **white ~** ложь во спасéние; **tell a ~** лгать, со-; **give the ~ to s.o.** обвин|я́ть, -и́ть когó-н. во лжи; **give the ~ to sth.** опров|ергáть, -éргнуть что-н.
v.t.: **he ~d his way out** он вы́путался с пóмощью лжи.
v.i. лгать, со-; врать, со-/на-; **he ~d to me** он мне солгáл; **~ in one's teeth, throat** нáгло/бессты́дно лгать, со-; **the camera cannot ~** фотогрáфия не (со)врёт.
cpd. **~-detector** *n.* детéктор лжи, полигрáф.
lie[2] [laɪ] *n.* (*also* **lay**): **the ~ of the land** харáктер мéстности; обстанóвка.
v.i. **1.** (*repose*) лежáть, по-; **she lay on the grass all morning** онá всё ýтро пролежáла на травé; **here ~s ...** здесь покóится прах *+g.*; (*remain*): **~ in ambush** находи́ться (*impf.*) в засáде; **~ in wait for s.o.** выжидáть (*impf.*) когó-н. в засáде; **~ low** притаи́ться (*pf.*), затаи́ться (*pf.*); **~ idle** (*of machinery etc.*) прост|áивать, -оя́ть. **2.** (*be; be situated*) находи́ться (*impf.*); быть располóженным; **~ at anchor** стоя́ть (*impf.*) на я́коре; **near us lay a cruiser** недалекó от нас стоя́л крéйсер; **London ~s on the Thames** Лóндон стои́т на Тéмзе; **the town lay in ruins** гóрод лежáл в руи́нах; **the crime lay heavy on his conscience** э́то преступлéние тяжёлым кáмнем лежáло на егó сóвести; **see how the land ~s**

(*fig.*) выявля́ть, вы́явить обстано́вку; узн|ава́ть, -а́ть, как обстои́т де́ло; **the coast ~s open to attack** бе́рег не защищён от нападе́ния. **3.** (*fig.*, *reside*, *rest*): **the choice ~s with you** вы́бор зави́сит от вас; вам выбира́ть; **do you know what ~s behind it all?** вы зна́ете, что за э́тим кро́ется?; **do your interests ~ in that direction?** у вас есть интере́с к тако́го ро́да дела́м?; э́та о́бласть вас интересу́ет?; **she knows where her interests ~** она́ зна́ет свою́ вы́году; **the blame ~s at his door** вина́ на нём; **it ~s with you** от вас зави́сит; **as far as in me ~s** наско́лько э́то от меня́ зави́сит; **I will do all that ~s in my power** сде́лаю всё, что в мои́х си́лах. **4.** (**~ down**) ложи́ться, лечь; приле́чь (*pf.*); **he went and lay on the bed** он лёг на крова́ть; **~ with s.o.** (*carnally*) спать/жить (*impf.*) с кем-н.

with advs.: **~ about, ~ around** валя́ться (*impf.*); быть разбро́санным; (*idle*) болта́ться (*impf.*); **~ ahead** предстоя́ть (*impf.*); **~ back** (*in chair etc.*) отки́|дываться, -нуться; (*take things easy*) сиде́ть (*impf.*) сложа́ ру́ки; **~ down** ложи́ться, лечь; **I shall ~ down for an hour** я приля́гу на час/часо́к; **take an insult lying down** безро́потно прин|има́ть, -я́ть оскорбле́ние; **~ down on the job** (*fig.*, *slack*) лени́ться (*impf.*); (*sl.*) сачкова́ть (*impf.*); **~ in** остава́ться (*impf.*) в посте́ли; не встава́ть (*impf.*); **~ to** (*naut.*) лежа́ть (*impf.*) в дре́йфе; **~ up** (*stay in bed*) остава́ться (*impf.*) в посте́ли; не встава́ть (*impf.*) с посте́ли; (*go into hiding*) скр|ыва́ться, -ы́ться; (*naut.*) находи́ться (*impf.*) в до́ке.

lief [li:f] *adv.* (*arch.*) охо́тно.

liege [li:dʒ] *n.* ле́нник.

adj. ле́нный; **~ lord** сеньо́р.

cpd. **~man** *n.* васса́л.

lien ['li:ən] *n.* пра́во удержа́ния.

lieu [lju:] *n.*: **in ~ of** вме́сто+*g.*

lieutenancy [lef'tenənsɪ] *n.* зва́ние лейтена́нта.

lieutenant [lef'tenənt] *n.* **1.** (*mil.*) лейтена́нт; **first, second ~**: *corresponding to these two Br. Army ranks are the three Russ. Army ranks of* ста́рший лейтена́нт, лейтена́нт *and* мла́дший лейтена́нт. **2.** (*civilian*) замести́тель (*m.*).

cpds. **~-colonel** *n.* подполко́вник; **~-commander** *n.* (*nav.*) капита́н-лейтена́нт; **~-general** *n.* генера́л-лейтена́нт.

life [laɪf] *n.* **1.** (*being alive*) жизнь, (*coll.*) житьё; **a matter of ~ and death** вопро́с жи́зни и сме́рти; **he has the power of ~ and death over his subjects** в его́ рука́х жизнь и смерть его́ по́дданных; **bring back to ~** (*from the dead*) воскре|ша́ть, -си́ть; возвра|ща́ть, -ти́ть к жи́зни; **escape with one's ~** вы́жить (*pf.*), уцеле́ть (*pf.*); **give (or lay down) one's ~ for s.o.** отда́ть/положи́ть (*both pf.*) жизнь за кого́-н.; **lose one's ~** ги́бнуть, по-; **many lives were lost** мно́гие поги́бли; мно́го наро́ду поги́бло; **great loss of ~** мно́го челове́ческих жертв; **run for one's ~ (or for dear ~)** бежа́ть (*det.*) сломя́ го́лову; **save one's ~** спас|а́ться, -ти́сь от сме́рти; **save s.o.'s ~** спасти́ (*pf.*) кого́-н. от сме́рти; спасти́ жизнь кому́-н.; **take ~** убива́ть (*impf.*); **take one's (own) ~** конча́ть, (по)ко́нчить с собо́й; **take one's ~ in one's hands** рискова́ть (*impf.*) жи́знью; **take s.o.'s ~** лиши́ть (*pf.*) кого́-н. жи́зни; **upon my ~!** че́стное сло́во!; ей-Бо́гу!; **not on your ~!** ни за что!; **I couldn't for the ~ of me ...** хоть убе́й, я не мог (бы)...; **insure one's ~** страхова́ть, за- свою́ жизнь; **~ insurance** страхова́ние жи́зни; (*existence*): **this (earthly) ~** земно́е бытие́; **the next ~, ~ beyond the grave** загро́бная/потусторо́нняя жизнь; **~ eternal, everlasting** ве́чная жизнь; **do you believe in a future ~?** вы ве́рите в загро́бную жизнь?; **that's ~!** такова́ жизнь!; **what a ~!** (*pej.*) ра́зве э́то жизнь?; **make ~ easy for s.o.** облегча́ть (*impf.*) кому́-н. жизнь; **with all the pleasure in ~** с превели́ким удово́льствием; (*way or style of ~*) быт; житьё-бытьё; **family ~** дома́шний быт; **country, village ~** дереве́нская жизнь; **he leads a gay ~** он ве́село живёт; **a dog's ~** соба́чья жизнь; **high ~** све́тская жизнь; **low ~** жизнь низо́в; **the simple ~** просто́й/непритяза́тельный о́браз жи́зни; **this is the ~!** вот э́то жизнь!; не жизнь, а ма́сленица; **anything for a quiet ~!** ли́шь бы поко́й!; чем бы дитя́ ни те́шилось, лишь бы не пла́кало; (*department of ~*): **in private/public ~** в ча́стной/обще́ственной жи́зни; **sex ~** полова́я жизнь; **see ~** повида́ть (*pf.*) свет. **2.** (*period, span of ~*): **at my time of ~** в моём во́зрасте; **get the fright of one's ~** перепуга́ться (*pf.*) на́смерть; **have the time of one's ~** прекра́сно проводи́ть (*impf.*) вре́мя; быть счастли́вым как никогда́; наслажда́ться (*impf.*) жи́знью; **he has had a good/quiet ~** он про́жил хоро́шую/споко́йную жизнь; **average expectation of ~** сре́дняя продолжи́тельность жи́зни; **he got ~; he is in for ~** (*coll.*) он получи́л пожи́зненное заключе́ние; **~ annuity** пожи́зненная ре́нта; **~ interest** пра́во на пожи́зненное владе́ние (*чем*); **~ peerage** ли́чное/пожи́зненное пэ́рство; **~ sentence** пригово́р к пожи́зненному заключе́нию; **it was his ~ work** э́то бы́ло трудо́м (всей) его́ жи́зни; (*of inanimate things, durability*) долгове́чность; срок слу́жбы; **these machines have an average ~ of 10 years** сре́дний срок слу́жбы э́тих маши́н 10 лет; **~ of a tyre** пробе́г ши́ны. **3.** (*animation*) жи́вость, оживле́ние; **put some ~ into it!** живе́е!; пошеве́ливайтесь!; **the ~ and soul of the party** душа́ о́бщества; **there's ~ in the old dog yet** есть ещё по́рох в пороховни́цах; **the child is full of ~** ребёнок о́чень живо́й; **there's no ~ in her playing** её игра́ безжи́зненна; **bring (back) to ~** (*after fainting etc.*) прив|оди́ть, -ести́ в чу́вства; (*fig.*) вдохну́ть (*pf.*) жизнь в+*a.*; воскре|ша́ть, -си́ть; **come to ~** (*recover senses*) очну́ться (*pf.*); **the play came to ~ in the third act** к тре́тьему де́йствию пье́са оживи́лась. **4.** (*living things*) жизнь; **is there ~ on Mars?** есть ли жизнь на Ма́рсе?; **animal ~** живо́тный мир; **marine ~** морска́я фа́уна; **still ~** натюрмо́рт; **draw from ~** рисова́ть, на- с нату́ры; **~ model** нату́рщи|к (*fem.* -ца); моде́ль. **5.** (*actuality*): **true to ~** реалисти́чный; **as large as ~** в натура́льную величину́; как живо́й; со́бственной персо́ной; **larger than ~** преувели́ченный; **that's him to the ~!** э́то вы́литый он! **6.** (*chance of living*): **he has nine lives** он живу́чий. **7.** (*biography*) жизнь, биогра́фия; **lives of the saints ~** жития́ святы́х; **the ~ history of a plant** жи́зненный цикл расте́ния; **he told me his ~ story** он пове́дал мне исто́рию свое́й жи́зни; он рассказа́л мне всю свою́ жизнь.

cpds. **~-and-death** *adj.* жи́зненно ва́жный, реша́ющий; **a ~-and-death struggle** борьба́ не на жизнь, а на́ смерть; **~belt** *n.* спаса́тельный круг; **~-blood** *n.* кровь; (*fig.*) жи́зненная си́ла; **~boat** *n.* спаса́тельная ло́дка; **~buoy** *n.* спаса́тельный круг; **~-cycle** *n.* жи́зненный цикл; цикл разви́тия; **~-force** *n.* жи́зненная си́ла; **~-giving** *adj.* живи́тельный; **~-guard, ~-saver** *nn.* спаса́тель (*fem.* -ница) (на пля́же); **~jacket** *n.* спаса́тельная ку́ртка; **~like** *adj.* реалисти́чный; **~-line** *n.* (*naut.*) спаса́тельный коне́ц; (*diver's*) сигна́льный коне́ц; (*palmistry*) ли́ния жи́зни; **~long** *adj.* пожи́зненный; **they were ~long friends** они́ бы́ли друзья́ми всю жизнь; **~-preserver** *n.* (*weapon*) дуби́нка, запо́лненная свинцо́м; **~-saver** *n.* = **~-guard**; (*fig.*) спасе́ние; **~-saving** *n.* спасе́ние; *adj.* спаса́тельный; **~-size(d)** *adj.* в натура́льную величину́; **~-span** *n.* продолжи́тельность/протяже́ние жи́зни; **~-style** *n.* о́браз жи́зни; **~-support** *adj.*: **~-support system** систе́ма жизнеобеспе́чения; **~time** *n.* жизнь; **in s.o.'s ~time** при жи́зни кого́-н.; **the chance of a ~ time** ре́дкий/исключи́тельный слу́чай; **it's a ~time since I saw her** я её не ви́дел це́лую ве́чность.

lifeless ['laɪflɪs] *adj.* (*dead*) мёртвый; (*inanimate*) неживо́й; (*inert, without animation*) безжи́зненный.

lifelessness ['laɪflɪsnɪs] *n.* безжи́зненность.

lifer ['laɪfə(r)] *n.* (*coll.*) (*pers.*) заключённый пожи́зненно; приговорённый к пожи́зненной ка́торге; (*sentence*) пожи́зненное заключе́ние.

lift [lɪft] *n.* **1.** (*act of raising*) подъём; (*extent of rise*) высота́ подъёма; (*aeron., upward pressure*) подъёмная си́ла. **2.** (*transport by air*) возду́шные перево́зки (*f. pl.*). **3.** (*transport of passenger in car etc.*): **give s.o. a ~** подв|ози́ть, -езти́ кого́-н.; (*coll.*) подки́|дывать, -нуть кого́-н.; **he thumbed a ~ to London** он дое́хал на попу́тных маши́нах до Ло́ндона; он дое́хал до Ло́ндона автосто́пом. **4.** (*fig., of spirits*): **the news gave her a ~** от э́той но́вости она́ воспря́ла ду́хом. **5.** (*apparatus*) лифт; (*tech.*) подъёмник; ~ **attendant** лифтёр (*fem.* -ша); ~ **cage** клéтка подъёмника; **take the** ~ подн|има́ться, -я́ться ли́фтом (*or* на ли́фте).

v.t. **1.** (*raise*) подн|има́ть, -я́ть; **he barely ~ed his eyes to her** он едва́ взгляну́л на неё; **she had her face ~ed** ей сде́лали пласти́ческую опера́цию (*or* подтя́жку) лица́; **he did not ~ a finger** (*fig.*) он и па́льцем не пошевельну́л; ~ **one's hand** (*to deal blow*) зама́х|иваться, -ну́ться; ~ **one's hands** (*in prayer*) возд|ева́ть, -е́ть ру́ки; **I would not ~ a hand against him** у меня́ на него́ не подняла́сь бы рука́. **2.** (*dig up*): ~ **potatoes** выка́пывать, вы́копать карто́фель. **3.** (*transport by air*): **the troops were ~ed to Africa** войска́ бы́ли доста́влены в А́фрику по во́здуху. **4.** (*steal*) сперéть (*pf.*) (*coll.*); (*of a plagiarist*) спи́с|ывать, -а́ть, красть, у-; плагии́ровать (*impf.*). **5.** (*remove*): ~ **a ban** сн|има́ть, -ять запре́т.

v.i. (*rise*) подн|има́ться, -я́ться; (*disperse*) рассе́|иваться, -яться; (*cease*) прекра|ща́ться, -ти́ться.

with advs.: ~ **down** *v.t.* снять (*pf.*) и поста́вить (*pf.*) на́ пол (*or* на зе́млю); ~ **off** *v.t.* сн|има́ть, -ять; *v.i.* (*of rocket*) от|рыва́ться, -орва́ться от земли́; ~ **out** *v.t.* вынима́ть, вы́нуть; ~ **up** *v.t.* подн|има́ть, -я́ть; ~ **up one's voice** (*sing*) запе́ть (*pf.*); (*speak*) заговори́ть (*pf.*); (*cry out*) подня́ть (*pf.*) крик; закрича́ть (*pf.*); ~ **up your hearts!** горе́ сердца́!

cpds. **~boy, ~man** *nn.* лифтёр; **~-off** *n.* отры́в от земли́; (*of rocket*) моме́нт схо́да.

ligament ['lɪgəmənt] *n.* свя́зка.

ligature ['lɪgətʃə(r)] *n.* (*med., typ.*) лигату́ра; (*mus.*) ли́га.

light[1] [laɪt] *n.* **1.** свет; **in the** ~ на свету́; **in the ~ of day** при дневно́м све́те; **in artificial** ~ при иску́сственном освеще́нии; **at first** ~ на рассве́те; **this room has a north** ~ в э́той ко́мнате о́кна выхо́дят на се́вер; **stand against the** ~ стоя́ть (*impf.*) про́тив све́та; **get in s.o.'s** ~ заслон|я́ть, -и́ть свет кому́-н.; (*attr.*) светово́й; (*fig.*): **see the ~ (of day)** (*be born*) уви́деть (*pf.*) свет; (*be made public*) быть обнаро́дованным, уви́деть (*pf.*) свет; **see the** ~ (*realize truth*) прозр|ева́ть, -е́ть; **in the ~ of experience** исходя́ из о́пыта; **by the ~ of nature** свои́м умо́м; **bring to** ~ выводи́ть, вы́вести на чи́стую во́ду; раскр|ыва́ть, -ы́ть; **come to** ~ обнару́жи|ваться, -ться; выплыва́ть, вы́плыть; **shed, throw ~ on sth.** прол|ива́ть, -и́ть свет на что-н.; **hide one's ~ under a bushel** зарыва́ть (*impf.*) свой тала́нт в зе́млю; (*brightness*): **northern ~s** се́верное сия́ние; **there was a ~ in his eyes** у него́ блесте́ли глаза́; (*in a picture*): **effects of ~ and shade** эффе́кты све́та и те́ни; светоте́нь; (*lighting*) освеще́ние; **electric** ~ электри́ческое освеще́ние; **in a bad** ~ при плохо́м освеще́нии; (*fig.*): **this book shows him in a bad** ~ э́та кни́га пока́зывает его́ в невы́годном све́те; **there was a ~ in the window** в окне́ был свет; окно́ свети́лось; **put on the** ~ заж|ига́ть, -е́чь свет; (*point of* ~): **the ~s of the town** огни́ го́рода. **2.** (*lamp*) ла́мпа; ~ **bulb** ла́мпочка; **'L~s out!'** «погаси́ть ого́нь/свет!»; (*of car*) фа́ра; **we saw the ~s of a car** мы уви́дели свет автомоби́льных фар; **dip the ~s** переключ|а́ть, -и́ть на бли́жний свет; **navigation ~s** (*of ship*) сигна́льно-отличи́тельные огни́; (*of aircraft*) аэронавигацио́нные огни́; **traffic ~s** светофо́р; **go against the ~s** е́хать (*impf.*) (*or* про|езжа́ть, -е́хать) на кра́сный свет; **give s.o. the green** ~ (*fig.*) да|ва́ть, -ть зелёную у́лицу кому́-н.; **see the red** ~ (*fig.*) зам|еча́ть, -е́тить опа́сность; (*fig.*): **a leading** ~ (*in society*) свети́ло, знамени́тость. **3.** (*flame*) ого́нь (*m.*); **strike a** ~ (*with match*) заж|ига́ть, -е́чь спи́чку; **have you a ~?** нет ли у вас огонька́?; **give me a** ~ да́йте прикури́ть. **4.** (*fig., natural ability*): **according to one's ~s** по ме́ре свои́х спосо́бностей. **5.** (*archit.*) окно́; просве́т.

adj. **1.** (*opp. dark*) све́тлый; **get** ~ рассве|та́ть, -сти́; **we must leave while it's still** ~ нам на́до уйти́ за́светло. **2.** (*in colour*) све́тлый; све́тлого цве́та; **a ~ green** светло-зелёный цвет.

v.t. (*also* ~ **up**) **1.** (*kindle*) заж|ига́ть, -е́чь; ~ **a fire** разв|оди́ть, -ести́ ого́нь; ~ **(up) a cigarette** заку́р|ивать, -и́ть папиро́су. **2.** (*illuminate*) осве|ща́ть, -ти́ть; **the house is lit by electricity** в до́ме электри́ческое освеще́ние; **the town is lit up for the carnival** по слу́чаю карнава́ла в го́роде иллюмина́ция; ~ **the way for s.o.** свети́ть, по- кому́-н.; (*fig.*): **a smile lit up his face** улы́бка озари́ла его́ лицо́; **he was lit up** (*drunk*) он был под му́хой/гра́дусом.

v.i.: ~ **up** (*switch on ~s*) включ|а́ть, -и́ть свет; **~ing-up time** вре́мя для включе́ния фар; (*of the face*) свети́ться, за-; ожив|ля́ться, -и́ться; (*start smoking*) заку́р|ивать, -и́ть.

cpds. **~-emitting** *adj.*: **~-emitting diode** светоизлуча́ющий дио́д, светодио́д; **~house** *n.* мая́к; **~house keeper** смотри́тель (*m.*) маяка́; **~-meter** *n.* экспоно́метр; **~ship** *n.* плаву́чий мая́к; **~-year** *n.* светово́й год.

light[2] [laɪt] *adj.* (*opp. heavy*) лёгкий; ~ **artillery** лёгкая артилле́рия; **a ~ blow** лёгкий уда́р; **our casualties were light** на́ши поте́ри бы́ли незначи́тельны; ~ **coin** неполнове́сная моне́та; ~ **comedy** лёгкая коме́дия; **a ~ crop** ску́дный урожа́й; **a ~ diet** облегчённая дие́та; ~ **of foot** прово́рный; **he needs a ~ hand** с ним ну́жно обраща́ться мя́гко; **with a ~ heart** с лёгким се́рдцем; ~ **industry** лёгкая промы́шленность; **a ~ meal** непло́тная еда́; **we had a ~ meal** мы перекуси́ли; ~ **music** лёгкая му́зыка; ~ **rain** небольшо́й/ме́лкий дождь; ~ **reading** лёгкое чте́ние; **a ~ sentence** мя́гкий пригово́р; **the ship returned** ~ кора́бль верну́лся без гру́за; **a ~ sleep** лёгкий/чу́ткий/неглубо́кий сон; **I am a ~ sleeper** я чу́тко сплю; ~ **soil** ры́хлая по́чва; **traffic is ~ today** сего́дня неинтенси́вное движе́ние; **the bridge is suitable for ~ traffic only** мост годи́тся то́лько для легковы́х маши́н; **in ~ type** све́тлым шри́фтом; **give s.o. ~ weight** обве́|шивать, -сить кого́-н.; **a ~ woman** же́нщина лёгкого поведе́ния; **he made ~ work of it** он легко́ спра́вился с э́тим де́лом; **he made ~ of the difficulties** он преуменьша́л тру́дности; **I was £1** ~ я недосчита́лся одного́ фу́нта.

adv.: **travel** ~ путеше́ствовать (*impf.*) налегке́.

cpds. **~-armed** *adj.* (*with ~ weapons*) легковооружённый; **~-fingered** *adj.* нечи́стый на́ руку; **~-footed** *adj.* прово́рный, легконо́гий; **~-headed** *adj.*: **she felt ~-headed** у неё закружи́лась голова́; **~-hearted** *adj.* (*carefree*) беспе́чный; (*gay*) весёлый; (*thoughtless*) легкомы́сленный; (*of action*) необду́манный; (*joking*) игри́вый, шутли́вый; **~-heartedness** *n.* беспе́чность; **~-weight** *n.* легкове́с; боре́ц/боксёр лёгкого ве́са; (*fig.*) несерьёзный челове́к; *adj.* легкове́сный.

light[3] [laɪt] *v.i.*: ~ **on** (*encounter*) набрести́ (*pf.*) на+*a.*; **his eyes ~ed on her face** его́ взгляд упа́л на её лицо́.

lighten[1] ['laɪt(ə)n] *v.t.* (*make less heavy or easier*) облегч|а́ть, -и́ть; **they ~ed the ship of ballast** они́ сбро́сили балла́ст с корабля́; **it ~ed our task** э́то облегчи́ло на́шу зада́чу; (*mitigate*): **a sentence** смягч|а́ть, -и́ть пригово́р.

v.i.: **his heart ~ed** у него́ ста́ло ле́гче на душе́.

lighten[2] ['laɪt(ə)n] *v.t.* (*illuminate, make brighter*) осве|ща́ть, -ти́ть; просвет|ля́ть, -и́ть.

v.i. **1.** (*grow brighter*) светле́ть, про-; проясн|я́ться, -и́ться. **2.** (*of lightning*) сверк|а́ть, -ну́ть; **it is ~ing** сверка́ет мо́лния.

lighter[1] ['laɪtə(r)] *n.* (*for cigarettes etc.*) зажига́лка; (*for fires etc.*) запа́л.

lighter[2] ['laɪtə(r)] *n.* (*boat*) ли́хтер.

cpd. **~man** *n.* матро́с на ли́хтере.

lighting ['laɪtɪŋ] *n.* освеще́ние.

lightish ['laɪtɪʃ] *adj.* (*of colour*) светлова́тый.

lightly ['laɪtlɪ] *adv.* легко́; **tread** ~ легко́/осторо́жно ступа́ть (*impf.*); **he touched ~ on the past** он слегка́ косну́лся про́шлого; **he jumped ~ to the ground** он ло́вко спры́гнул на зе́млю; **it's not a thing to enter upon** ~ за таки́е дела́ не сле́дует бра́ться необду́манно; **he takes everything** ~ он ничего́ не принима́ет всерьёз; **you have got off** ~ вы легко́ отде́лались; **the accused got off** ~ обвиня́емый отде́лался лёгким наказа́нием.

lightness ['laɪtnɪs] *n.* (*of weight*) лёгкость; (*nimbleness*) ло́вкость; (*mildness*) мя́гкость; (*of colour*) све́тлость, светлота́.

lightning ['laɪtnɪŋ] *n.* мо́лния; **forked** ~ зигзагообра́зная мо́лния; **sheet, summer** ~ зарни́ца; **swift as** ~

молниено́сный; **he was struck by ~** в него́ уда́рила мо́лния.

adj.: **with ~ speed** молниено́сно; **a ~ attack** молниено́сная ата́ка.

cpds. **~-conductor, ~-rod** *nn.* громоотво́д.

lights [laɪts] *n.* (*animal's lungs*) лёгкие (*nt. pl.*).

lightsome [ˈlaɪtsəm] *adj.* (*graceful*) лёгкий, грацио́зный; (*merry*) беспе́чный, весёлый; (*nimble*) подви́жный.

ligneous [ˈlɪgnɪəs] *adj.* древе́сный, деревя́нистый.

lignite [ˈlɪgnaɪt] *n.* лигни́т.

lignum vitae [ˌlɪgnəm ˈvaɪtɪ, ˈviːtaɪ] *n.* гвая́ковое де́рево.

likable [ˈlaɪkəb(ə)l] = **lik(e)able**

like[1] [laɪk] *n.* (*sth. equal or similar*) подо́бное; **did you ever hear the ~ (of it)?** слы́шали ли вы что́-нибудь подо́бное?; как вам э́то нра́вится?; **music, dancing and the ~** му́зыка, та́нцы и тому́ подо́бное; (*pers.*) подо́бный; **we shall not look upon his ~ again** тако́го (челове́ка) мы никогда́ бо́льше не встре́тим; **the ~s of me, us** наш брат; **the ~s of you** ваш брат.

adj. подо́бный, похо́жий; **in ~ manner** подо́бным о́бразом; **we have ~ tastes** у нас схо́дные вку́сы; **as ~ as two peas** похо́жи как две ка́пли воды́; **~ father, ~ son** я́блоко от я́блони недалеко́ па́дает; (*equal*) ра́вный; **~ signs** (*math.*) одина́ковые зна́ки; **~ poles repel each other** одноимённые по́люсы отта́лкиваются. *See also prep. uses.*

adv. **1.** (*probably*): **~ enough, very ~** весьма́ возмо́жно; **(as) ~ as not** верне́е всего́. **2.** (*coll., as it were*) вро́де, похо́же.

prep. **1.** (*similar to, characteristic of*) похо́жий на+*a.*; **she is ~ her mother** она́ похо́жа на мать; **that's just ~ him!** э́то похо́же на него́!; узна́ю его́!; **what's she ~?** что она́ за челове́к?; кака́я она́?; что она́ собо́й представля́ет?; **I don't care for films ~ that** я не люблю́ подо́бных фи́льмов; **a house ~ yours** дом вро́де ва́шего; **don't be ~ that!** (*coll., behave unhelpfully*) бро́сьте!; **there's nothing ~ walking to keep you fit** для здоро́вья нет ничего́ поле́знее, чем ходьба́; ходи́ть пешко́м — лу́чший спо́соб сохрани́ть здоро́вье; **his second book is nothing ~ as good as the first** его́ втора́я кни́га значи́тельно ху́же пе́рвой; **that is nothing ~ enough** э́того не мо́жет хвати́ть; **£500 would be more ~ it** скоре́е фу́нтов 500; **they sold something ~ 1,000 copies** они́ про́дали (что́-то) о́коло 1000 экземпля́ров; **that's something ~ comfort!** вот э́то комфо́рт так комфо́рт!; **look ~** *see* **look** *v.i.* **3.; it smells ~ something burning** па́хнет горе́лым; **it sounds ~ thunder** как бу́дто греми́т гром; **the crowd buzzed ~ a swarm of bees** толпа́ гуде́ла, то́чно рой шмеле́й; **it sounds ~ a good idea** э́то, пожа́луй, хоро́шая иде́я; **he drinks ~ a fish** он пьёт как бо́чка; **don't talk ~ that!** не на́до так говори́ть; **a person ~ that** тако́й челове́к; **he was working ~ anything** он труди́лся изо всех сил; **it's ~ nothing on earth** э́то ни на что не похо́же. **2.** (*inclined towards*): **do you feel ~ going for a walk?** вам (не) хо́чется пройти́сь?; **I don't feel ~ it** мне (что́-то) не хо́чется; **I felt ~ crying** мне хоте́лось пла́кать; я чуть не запла́кал; **I feel ~ an ice-cream** я бы не прочь съесть моро́женое; **I feel ~ nothing on earth** (*dreadful*) я себя́ отврати́тельно чу́вствую.

conj. (*coll.*): **he talks ~ I do** он говори́т так же, как я.

cpd. **~-minded** *adj.* приде́рживающийся тех же взгля́дов; **~-minded person** единомы́шленник.

like[2] [laɪk] *n.*: **~s and dislikes** симпа́тии и антипа́тии (*both f. pl.*); **she has her ~s and dislikes** у неё о́чень определённый вкус.

v.t. (*take pleasure in*) люби́ть (*impf.*), цени́ть (*impf.*); **he ~s living in Paris** ему́ нра́вится жить в Пари́же; **she ~d dancing** она́ люби́ла танцева́ть; **I ~ him** он мне нра́вится; **his parents ~ me** я пришёлся его́ роди́телям по душе́; **I ~ oysters but they don't ~ me** я люблю́ у́стрицы, но пло́хо их переношу́; **we ~d the play** пье́са нам понра́вилась; **how do you ~ that?** как вам э́то нра́вится?; **I ~ that!** (*iron.*) ничего́ себе́!; ну и ну!; **I ~ his impudence** вот э́то наха́льство!; **what don't you ~ about it?** что вас в э́том не устра́ивает?; **I don't ~** (*am reluctant*) **to disturb you** прости́те, что беспоко́ю вас; **(you can) ~ it or lump it!** (*coll.*) нра́вится — не нра́вится, а ничего́ не поде́лаешь; **whether you ~ it or not** во́лей-нево́лей; **would you ~ a drink?** хоти́те вы́пить (чего́-нибудь)?; **if you ~** е́сли хоти́те; **I should ~ to meet him** мне хоте́лось бы познако́миться с ним; **he would ~ to come** он хоте́л бы прийти́; **I would have ~d to** (*or* **would like to have) come** я жале́ю, что не мог прийти́; **I'd ~ to see you do it!** посмотре́л бы я, как э́то у вас получи́лось бы; **I ~ this picture better than that** мне э́та карти́на нра́вится бо́льше, чем та; **I wouldn't ~ there to be any misunderstanding** я хоте́л бы, что́бы меня́ по́няли пра́вильно; **I ~ to think he values my advice** мне хоте́лось бы ду́мать (*or* я наде́юсь), что он це́нит мой сове́т; **I ~ people to tell the truth** (я) люблю́, когда́ (лю́ди) говоря́т пра́вду; **I ~ to be sure** я предпочита́ю знать наверняка́; **how do you ~ your tea?** вы пьёте чай с са́харом/молоко́м (*и т.п.*)?; **as you ~** как уго́дно; **come whenever you ~** приходи́те в любо́е вре́мя; **he was outspoken if you ~, but not rude** он был, е́сли хоти́те, открове́нен, но ника́к не груб; **that was a performance if you ~!** (*a fine one*) вот э́то спекта́кль, э́то я понима́ю!

lik(e)able [ˈlaɪkəb(ə)l] *adj.* симпати́чный.

likelihood [ˈlaɪklɪˌhʊd] *n.* вероя́тность; **in all ~** по всей вероя́тности; **there is little ~ of his coming** ма́ло вероя́тно, что он прие́дет.

likely [ˈlaɪklɪ] *adj.* **1.** (*probable*) вероя́тный; (*plausible*) правдоподо́бный; **a ~ story!** (*iron.*) так я и пове́рил! **2.** (*suitable*) подходя́щий; (*promising*) многообеща́ющий. **3.** (*to be expected*): **he is ~ to come** он вероя́тно придёт; **that is never ~ to happen** э́то вряд ли когда́-нибудь случи́тся.

adv. вероя́тно; **most, very ~** наве́рно; скоре́е всего́; **not ~!** (на)вря́д ли!; как бы не так!; **as ~ as not** вполне́ вероя́тно/возмо́жно; не исключено́.

liken [ˈlaɪkən] *v.t.* упод|обля́ть, -о́бить (*кого/что кому/ чему*); сра́вн|ивать, -и́ть (*кого, что с чем*).

likeness [ˈlaɪknɪs] *n.* **1.** (*resemblance*) схо́дство, подо́бие; **a family ~** фами́льное схо́дство; **in his own image and ~** по своему́ о́бразу и подо́бию. **2.** (*guise*) обли́чие; **in the ~ of** в ви́де +*g.*; под личи́ной +*g.* **3.** (*representation, portrait*) изображе́ние, портре́т.

likewise [ˈlaɪkwaɪz] *adv.* подо́бно.

conj. таки́м же о́бразом.

liking [ˈlaɪkɪŋ] *n.* симпа́тия (*к кому*); расположе́ние (*к чему*); **he has a ~ for quotations** он лю́бит цита́ты; **I took a ~ to him** я почу́вствовал к нему́ симпа́тию; **she has no ~ for this work** э́та рабо́та ей не по душе́; **is the meat done to your ~?** э́то мя́со пригото́влено как вы лю́бите?

lilac [ˈlaɪlək] *n.* сире́нь.

adj. (*pert. to ~*; *~-coloured*) сире́невый.

lilliputian [ˌlɪlɪˈpjuːʃ(ə)n] *adj.* лилипу́тский, миниатю́рный, кро́шечный.

lilt [lɪlt] *n.* (*tune*) напе́в; (*rhythm*) ритм.

v.i.: **a ~ing melody** мелоди́чный напе́в.

lily [ˈlɪlɪ] *n.* ли́лия; **~ of the valley** ла́ндыш.

cpds. **~-livered** *adj.* трусли́вый; **~-pond** *n.* пруд с ли́лиями; **~-white** *adj.* лиле́йный.

limb [lɪm] *n.* **1.** (*of body*; *also fig.*). член; коне́чность; **escape with life and ~** вы́йти (*pf.*) це́лым и невреди́мым; **tear s.o. ~ from ~** раз|рыва́ть, -орва́ть кого́-н. на ча́сти. **2.** (*branch of tree*) сук, ветвь; **out on a ~** (*fig.*) в невы́годном/ опа́сном положе́нии.

limber[1] [ˈlɪmbə(r)] *n.* (*mil.*) передо́к.

limber[2] [ˈlɪmbə(r)] *adj.* (*flexible, pliable*) ги́бкий, пода́тливый; (*nimble*) прово́рный.

v.i.: **~ up** разм|ина́ться, -я́ться.

limbless [ˈlɪmlɪs] *adj.* (*armless*) безру́кий; (*legless*) безно́гий.

limbo [ˈlɪmbəʊ] *n.* **1.** (*relig.*) лимб; преддве́рие а́да. **2.** (*fig.*): **our plans are in ~** неизве́стно, что из на́ших пла́нов полу́чится.

lime[1] [laɪm] *n.* (*fruit*) лайм; **~ juice** сок ла́йма.

lime[2] [laɪm] *n.* (*tree*) ли́па; (*attr.*) ли́повый.

lime[3] [laɪm] *n.* **1.** (*calcium oxide*) и́звесть; **slaked/quick ~** гашёная/негашёная и́звесть; **~ water** известко́вая вода́. **2.** (*bird-~*) пти́чий клей.

v.t. **1.** (*soil*) известкова́ть (*impf.*, *pf.*); уд|обря́ть, -обрить и́звестью. **2.** (*twig*) нама́з|ывать, -ать (пти́чьим) кле́ем; (*bird*) лови́ть, пойма́ть на клей.

cpds. **~-kiln** *n.* печь для обжи́га и́звести; **~light** *n.* (*lit.*) свет ра́мпы; (*fig.*): **be in the ~light** быть знамени́тостью; быть в це́нтре внима́ния; быть на виду́; **come into the ~light** ста|нови́ться, -ть знамени́тостью; **~-pit** *n.* зо́льник; **~stone** *n.* известня́к; (*attr.*) известняко́вый.

limey [ˈlaɪmɪ] *n.* (*US sl.*) англича́нин.

limit [ˈlɪmɪt] *n.* **1.** (*terminal point*) преде́л; (*comm.*) лими́т; **the ~s of endurance** преде́лы выно́сливости; **he exceeded the speed ~** он превы́сил устано́вленную ско́рость; **set, fix a ~ to sth.** устан|а́вливать, -ови́ть преде́л чему́-н.; **lower/upper ~** ми́нимум/ма́ксимум; **that's the ~!** э́то перехо́дит все грани́цы; **he is the (very) ~!** он невозмо́жен!; **without ~** без конца́; (*endlessly*) бесконе́чно; **there is a ~ to what I can stand** моему́ терпе́нию есть преде́л; **his greed knows no ~s** его́ жа́дность не зна́ет преде́лов; **I am willing to help you, within ~s** я гото́в помо́чь вам в преде́лах возмо́жного (*or* в изве́стных преде́лах). **2.** (*border*, *boundary*) грани́ца; **he has gone beyond the ~s of decency** он перешёл грани́цы прили́чия; **city ~s** городска́я черта́; **'off ~s to military personnel'** (*US*) «вход военнослу́жащим запрещён». **3.** (*time ~*) (преде́льный) срок; **next week is our extreme ~** сле́дующая неде́ля для нас кра́йний срок; **age ~** преде́льный во́зраст.

v.t. ограни́чи|вать, -ть (*кого/что чем*); **I shall ~ myself to a single chapter** я ограни́чусь одно́й главо́й; **~ed monarchy** ограни́ченная мона́рхия; **~ed edition** изда́ние, вы́пущенное ограни́ченным тиражо́м; **~ed liability company** компа́ния с ограни́ченной отве́тственностью.

limitation [ˌlɪmɪˈteɪʃ(ə)n] *n.* **1.** (*limiting*, *being limited*) ограниче́ние; (*condition*) огово́рка; (*drawback*) недоста́ток; **he has his ~s** он не лишён недоста́тков. **2.** (*leg.*) да́вность; **statute of ~s** зако́н об и́сковой да́вности.

limitless [ˈlɪmɪtlɪs] *adj.* безграни́чный, беспреде́льный; (*of time*) бесконе́чный.

limn [lɪm] *v.t.* (*arch.*, *liter.*) (живо)писа́ть (*impf.*, *pf.*); изобра|жа́ть, -зи́ть.

limousine [ˈlɪmʊˌziːn, ˌlɪmʊˈziːn, ˈlɪməˌziːn] *n.* лимузи́н.

limp[1] [lɪmp] *n.* хромота́; **he has (*or* walks with) a ~** он хрома́ет/прихра́мывает.

v.i. хрома́ть (*impf.*); **he was ~ing along the street** он ковыля́л по у́лице; (*fig.*): **the plane ~ed back to base** самолёт с трудо́м добра́лся до ба́зы.

limp[2] [lɪmp] *adj.* **1.** (*flexible*) мя́гкий; **a book in ~ covers** кни́га в мя́гком переплёте. **2.** (*without energy*; *flabby*) вя́лый; **I feel ~** я совсе́м без сил; **go ~** обм|яка́ть, -я́кнуть.

limpet [ˈlɪmpɪt] *n.* блю́дечко (*моллюск*); **stick like a ~** приста́ть (*pf.*) как ба́нный лист; **~ mine** магни́тная ми́на.

limpid [ˈlɪmpɪd] *adj.* прозра́чный.

limpidity [ˌlɪmˈpɪdɪtɪ] *n.* прозра́чность.

limy [ˈlaɪmɪ] *adj.* (*sticky*) кле́йкий, вя́зкий; (*of soil*) известко́вый.

linage [ˈlaɪnɪdʒ] *n.* (*number of lines*) коли́чество строк; (*payment*) постро́чная опла́та.

linchpin, lynchpin [ˈlɪntʃpɪn] *n.* чека́; (*fig.*, *of pers. or thg.*) тот/то, на ком/чём всё де́ржится; незамени́мый челове́к; опо́ра.

linctus [ˈlɪŋktəs] *n.* миксту́ра.

linden [ˈlɪnd(ə)n] *n.* ли́па.

line[1] [laɪn] *n.* **1.** (*cord*) верёвка; **hang washing on the ~** разве́сить (*pf.*) бельё на верёвке; (*fishing-~*) ле́ска; **fish with rod and ~** уди́ть (*impf.*) ры́бу; (*plumb-~*) отве́с; (*naut.*, *for sounding*) лот, ло́тлинь (*m.*). **2.** (*wire*, *cable for communication*) ли́ния (свя́зи); ка́бель (*m.*); про́вод; **direct ~** пряма́я ли́ния; **party ~** паралле́льные телефо́ны; **hot ~** (*coll.*) прямо́й про́вод; **the ~ is bad** пло́хо слы́шно; **the ~ is engaged** (*US*, *busy*) ли́ния занята́; **he is on the ~** он говори́т по телефо́ну; он у телефо́на; **give me a ~ to the Ministry** соедини́те меня́ с министе́рством; **an outside ~, please** да́йте го́род, пожа́луйста; **hold the ~!** подожди́те у телефо́на!; не ве́шайте тру́бку!; **lay ~s** про|кла́дывать, -ложи́ть ка́бель. **3.** (*rail.*) ли́ния; **~s of communication** (*mil.*) коммуника́ции (*f. pl.*); **up (down) ~** железнодоро́жная ли́ния, веду́щая в столи́цу (из столи́цы); **main ~** гла́вный путь, магистра́ль; **branch ~** (железнодоро́жная) ве́тка; **he has reached the end of the ~** (*fig.*) он дошёл до ру́чки/то́чки/преде́ла; (*track*) полотно́; ре́льсы (*m. pl.*); (ре́льсовый) путь; **I crossed the ~ by the bridge** я перешёл ли́нию по мосту́. **4.** (*transport system*) ли́ния; **air ~s** возду́шные ли́нии. **5.** (*long narrow mark*) ли́ния, черта́; (*geom.*, geog. *etc.*): **~s of force** силовы́е ли́нии; **date ~** ли́ния су́точного вре́мени; **cross the L~** перес|ека́ть, -е́чь эква́тор; (*imagined straight ~*): **~ of fire** направле́ние стрельбы́; **hang a picture on the ~** ве́шать, пове́сить карти́ну на у́ровне глаз. **6.** (*on face etc.*) скла́дка, морщи́ны; (*on palm*): **~ of fate** ли́ния судьбы́. **7.** (*drawn*, *painted etc.*) штрих; **~ drawing** штрихово́й/каранда́шный рису́нок; **~ engraving** штрихова́я гравю́ра; **purity of ~** чистота́ ли́ний; **in broad ~s** в о́бщих черта́х; **drawn in bold ~s** нарисо́ванный сме́лыми штриха́ми; (*pl.*, *contour*, *outline*, *shape*) ко́нтур, очерта́ние; **~s of a ship** обво́ды (*m. pl.*) корабля́. **8.** (*boundary*, *limit*) грани́ца, преде́л, черта́; **dividing ~** раздели́тельная черта́; (*fig.*): **draw a ~ between** различ|а́ть, -и́ть; **draw the ~** пров|оди́ть, -ести́ грани́цу; **one must draw the ~ somewhere** всему́ есть преде́л; **I draw the ~ at that** на э́то я уж не согла́сен; (*sport*): **the ball went over the ~** мяч перешёл черту́; **at the starting ~** на ста́рте; **toe the ~** (*fig.*) беспрекосло́вно слу́шаться/подчиня́ться (*impf.*); ходи́ть (*indet.*) по ни́точке. **9.** (*row*) ряд, ли́ния; **stand in ~** стоя́ть (*impf.*) в ряд; (*US*, *queue*) стоя́ть (*impf.*) в о́череди; (в)стать (*pf.*) в о́чередь; **in ~ with** в одну́ ли́нию (*or* в ряд) с+*i.*; (*fig.*) в согла́сии/соотве́тствии с+*i.*; **bring into ~** (*fig.*) привле́чь (*pf.*) (*кого*) на свою́ сто́рону; согласо́в|ывать, -а́ть (*что*); **come, fall into ~** согла|ша́ться, -си́ться; (*fig.*) согласова́ться (*impf.*, *pf.*); **be out of ~** (*fig.*) не соотве́тствовать (*impf.*) но́рме; (*mil.*): **in ~** в развёрнутом строю́; **~ of march** похо́дный поря́док; **draw up in ~** стро́ить, по- в ряд; (*nav.*, *aeron.*): **~ abreast** строй фро́нта; **~ ahead** строй в ли́нию, строй кильва́тера. **10.** (*mil.*, *entrenched position*): **front ~** ли́ния фро́нта; **in the front ~** на передово́й; **~s of defence** оборони́тельный рубе́ж; **behind the enemy~s** за расположе́нием (*or* в (бли́жнем) тылу́) проти́вника; **go up the ~** отпр|авля́ться, -а́виться на фронт; **he was beaten all along the ~** (*fig.*) он потерпе́л пораже́ние на всех фронта́х. **11.** (*mil.*, *nav.*: *main*, *not auxiliary*, *formation*): **~ regiment** лине́йный полк; **ship of the ~** лине́йный кора́бль (*abbr.* линко́р). **12.** (*of print or writing*) строка́; **on ~ 10** на строке́ деся́той; **begin a new ~!** начни́те с но́вой строки́!; **read between the ~s** (*fig.*) чита́ть (*impf.*) ме́жду строк; **marriage ~s** свиде́тельство о бра́ке; **send** (*coll. drop*) **s.o. a ~ (or a few ~s)** черкну́ть (*pf.*) кому́-н. не́сколько слов; (*pl.*, *verse*) стихи́ (*m. pl.*); (*pl.*, *actor's part*) роль. **13.** (*lineage*) ли́ния; **in direct ~ of descent** по прямо́й (нисходя́щей) ли́нии; **the last of a long ~ of kings** после́дний в стари́нном короле́вском роду́; **in the male ~** по мужско́й ли́нии. **14.** (*course*, *direction*, *track*) направле́ние, ли́ния; **~ of action** ли́ния поведе́ния/де́йствия; **general ~s of policy** о́бщие направле́ния поли́тики; **take a firm, hard, strong ~** зан|има́ть, -я́ть твёрдую пози́цию; де́йствовать (*impf.*) энерги́чно; стро́го об|ходи́ться, -ойти́сь (*с кем*); **take the ~ of least resistance** пойти́ (*pf.*) по ли́нии наиме́ньшего сопротивле́ния; **follow the party ~** приде́рживаться (*impf.*) парти́йной ли́нии; **take a different ~** зан|има́ть, -я́ть ину́ю пози́цию; **get a ~ on sth.** навести́ (*pf.*) спра́вки о чём-нибудь; **on similar ~s** аналоги́чным о́бразом; на тех же основа́ниях; **you and I are thinking along the same ~s** мы с ва́ми ду́маем в одно́м направле́нии; **on different ~s** по-друго́му; (*principle*): **the business is run on co-operative ~s** предприя́тие де́йствует на кооперати́вных нача́лах. **15.** (*province*, *sphere of activity*): **cards are not in my ~** ка́рточная игра́ — не по мое́й ча́сти; **in the ~ of duty** при исполне́нии служе́бных обя́занностей; **his ~ of business** род его́ заня́тий; **I have friends in the banking**

~ у меня́ есть друзья́ в фина́нсовом ми́ре; **what's your ~?** чем вы занима́етесь?; кака́я у вас профе́ссия? **16.** (*class of goods*) сорт, род, моде́ль (това́ра); **they are bringing in a new ~ in bicycles** они́ вво́дят/внедря́ют но́вую моде́ль велосипе́да; **consumer ~s** потреби́тельские това́ры (*m. pl.*). **17.** (*pl., coll., fortune*): **it was hard ~s on him** (ужа́сно) не повезло́ ему́; **hard ~s!** бедня́га! (*c.g.*).

v.t. **1.** (*mark with ~s*) линова́ть, раз-; **~d paper** лино́ванная бума́га; **his face was deeply ~d** его́ лицо́ бы́ло изборождено́ морщи́нами. **2.** (*form a ~ along*) стоя́ть (*impf.*) (*or* быть расста́вленными) вдоль+*g.*; **police ~d the street** полице́йские стоя́ли по обе́им сторона́м у́лицы; **the road was ~d with trees** доро́га была́ обса́жена дере́вьями.

with adv.: **~ up** *v.t.* (*align*) выстра́ивать, вы́строить в ряд/ли́нию; **they were ~d up against a wall** их вы́строили вдоль стены́; (*coll., arrange*): **I have something ~d up for you** я для вас ко́е-что устро́ил; (*coll., collect*): **he ~d up a lot of votes** он собра́л мно́го голосо́в; *v.i.* выстра́иваться, вы́строиться в ряд/ли́нию; (*queue up*) ста|нови́ться, -ть в о́чередь; (*fig., align o.s.*) присоедин|я́ться, -и́ться (*к кому*).

cpds. **~man** *n.* (*teleg.*) лине́йный надсмо́трщик; **~sman** *n.* (*rail.*) путево́й обхо́дчик; (*sport*) боково́й судья́; **~-up** *n.* (*arrangement, grouping*) расположе́ние, строй; расстано́вка.

line[2] [laɪn] *v.t.* **1.** (*put lining into*) ста́вить, по- на подкла́дку; подб|ива́ть, -и́ть; **~ a coat with silk** поста́вить (*pf.*) пальто́ на шёлковую подкла́дку; подб|ива́ть, -и́ть пальто́ шёлком; **her coat is ~d with silk** у неё пальто́ на шёлковой подкла́дке. **2.** (*fig.*) заст|авля́ть, -а́вить; **the wall was ~d with books** стена́ была́ заста́влена кни́гами; (*fig., fill*): **~ one's pockets** наб|ива́ть, -и́ть себе́ карма́ны; **~ one's stomach** подкреп|ля́ться, -и́ться. **3.** (*tech., of walls etc.*) облиц|о́вывать, -ева́ть.

lineage [ˈlɪnɪɪdʒ] *n.* (*ancestry*) происхожде́ние; (*genealogy*) родосло́вная.

lineal [ˈlɪnɪəl] *adj.* происходя́щий по прямо́й ли́нии (*от кого*).

lineament [ˈlɪnɪəmənt] *n.* черта́; (*pl.*) очерта́ния (*nt. pl.*), ко́нтуры (*m. pl.*).

linear [ˈlɪnɪə(r)] *adj.* лине́йный.

linen [ˈlɪnɪn] *n.* **1.** (*material: smooth*) полотно́; (*coarse*) холст. **2.** (*~ articles*) бельё; (*clothing*) (носи́льное) бельё; (*bed-~*) посте́льное бельё; **table ~** столо́вое бельё; **wash one's dirty ~ in public** (*fig.*) выноси́ть (*impf.*) сор из избы́.

adj. **1.** (*pert. to flax*) льняно́й; **~ industry** льняна́я промы́шленность; **~ cloth** льняно́е полотно́. **2.** (*made of ~*) полотня́ный.

cpds. **~-draper** *n.* торго́вец льняны́ми тка́нями; **~-room** *n.* бельева́я (ко́мната).

liner [ˈlaɪnə(r)] *n.* (*ship*) ла́йнер; **air ~** возду́шный ла́йнер.

ling[1] [lɪŋ] *n.* (*heather*) ве́реск.

ling[2] [lɪŋ] *n.* (*fish*) морска́я щу́ка; морско́й нали́м.

linger [ˈlɪŋgə(r)] *v.i.* (*take one's time*) ме́длить (*impf.*); ме́шкать (*impf.*); **without ~ing a minute** не ме́для ни мину́ты; **she ~ed over her dressing** она́ до́лго одева́лась; **a ~ing death** ме́дленная смерть; (*stay on*) заде́рж|иваться, -а́ться; **~ing disease** затяжна́я боле́знь; **I have ~ing doubts** мои́ сомне́ния не рассе́ялись; **the guests ~ed over their coffee** го́сти засиде́лись за ко́фе; (*dwell at length*): **the speaker ~ed on, over his favourite subject** ора́тор задержа́лся на своём люби́мом предме́те; **she gave him a ~ing glance** она́ посмотре́ла на него́ до́лгим взгля́дом; (*of time: drag*) затя́гиваться (*impf.*); (*continue to live*): **the old man ~ed for another week** стари́к протяну́л ещё одну́ неде́лю.

with advs.: **~ about, ~ around** *v.i.* болта́ться (*impf.*); **~ on** *v.i.* (*of doubt etc.: remain*) ост|ава́ться, -а́ться; (*of customs; be preserved*) сохраня́ться (*impf.*); (*of invalid*) влачи́ть (*impf.*) существова́ние; **~ out** *v.t.*: **~ out one's days** влачи́ть (*impf.*) дни свои́.

lingerie [ˈlæʒərɪ] *n.* да́мское бельё.

lingo [ˈlɪŋgəʊ] *n.* (*pej.*) (иностра́нный) язы́к; (*jargon*) жарго́н.

lingua franca [ˌlɪŋgwə ˈfræŋkə] *n.* сме́шанный язы́к.

lingual [ˈlɪŋgw(ə)l] *adj.* язы́чный.

linguist [ˈlɪŋgwɪst] *n.* (*speaker of foreign languages*): **he is a good ~** ему́ легко́ даю́тся языки́; он о́чень спосо́бен к языка́м; (*philologist*) лингви́ст, языкове́д.

linguistic [lɪŋˈgwɪstɪk] *adj.* лингвисти́ческий, языкове́дческий; **~ problems** пробле́мы языка́.

linguistics [lɪŋˈgwɪstɪks] *n.* лингви́стика, языкозна́ние, языкове́дение.

liniment [ˈlɪnɪmənt] *n.* мазь.

lining [ˈlaɪnɪŋ] *n.* (*of garment*) подкла́дка; (*of walls etc.*) облицо́вка; (*of stomach*) сте́нки (*f. pl.*); **brake ~** тормозна́я прокла́дка; **every cloud has a silver ~** нет ху́да без добра́.

link [lɪŋk] *n.* **1.** (*of chain; also fig.*) звено́; **missing ~** недостаю́щее звено́. **2.** (*cuff-~*) за́понка. **3.** (*connection*) связь.

v.t. (*unite*) соедин|я́ть, -и́ть; (*join*) свя́з|ывать, -а́ть; (*tech., couple*) сцеп|ля́ть, -и́ть; **these notions are not ~ed (to each other)** э́ти поня́тия не свя́заны ме́жду собо́й; **~ arms with s.o.** идти́ (*det.*) по́д руку с кем-н.; **~ one's arm through another's** взять кого́-н. по́д руку.

v.i.: **~ on to sth.** прим|ыка́ть, -кну́ть к чему́-н.; **~ with** (*fit in with*) **sth.** вяза́ться (*impf.*) с чем-н.

with advs.: **~ together** *v.t.* свя́з|ывать, -а́ть; **~ up** *v.t. & i.* соедин|я́ться, -и́ться.

cpds. **~-man** *n.* (*on TV*) веду́щий програ́мму; **~-up** *n.* связь, соедине́ние.

linkage [ˈlɪŋkɪdʒ] *n.* (*chem.*) связь; (*pol.*) **a ~ policy** поли́тика «увя́зок».

links [lɪŋks] *n.* (*golf-~*) по́ле для игры́ в гольф.

linnet [ˈlɪnɪt] *n.* коноплё́нка.

lino [ˈlaɪnəʊ] = **linoleum**

linocut [ˈlaɪnəʊˌkʌt] *n.* гравю́ра на лино́леуме, линогравю́ра.

linoleum [lɪˈnəʊlɪəm] *n.* лино́леум.

linotype [ˈlaɪnəʊˌtaɪp] *n.* линоти́п.

linseed [ˈlɪnsiːd] *n.* льняно́е се́мя; **~ cake** льняны́е жмыхи́ (*m. pl.*); **~ oil** льняно́е ма́сло.

lint [lɪnt] *n.* **1.** (*med.*) ко́рпия; (*gauze*) ма́рля. **2.** (*fluff*) пух.

lintel [ˈlɪnt(ə)l] *n.* при́толока.

lion [ˈlaɪən] *n.* лев; **~'s share** (*fig.*) льви́ная до́ля; **put one's head in the ~'s mouth** (*fig.*) рискова́ть (*impf.*) голово́й; (*fig., celebrity*) све́тский лев, знамени́тость.

cpds. **~-cub** *n.* львёнок; **~-hearted** *adj.* неустраши́мый; **~-hunter** *n.* охо́тник на львов; (*fig.*) челове́к, гоня́ющийся за знамени́тостями.

lioness [ˈlaɪənɪs] *n.* льви́ца.

lionize [ˈlaɪəˌnaɪz] *v.t.*: **~ s.o.** носи́ться (*impf.*) с ке́м-нибудь, как со знамени́тостью.

lip [lɪp] *n.* **1.** губа́ (*dim.* гу́бка); **lower/upper ~** ни́жняя/ве́рхняя губа́; **bite one's ~** (*in vexation*) куса́ть (*impf.*) гу́бы; (*in thought*) заку́с|ывать, -и́ть губу́; **curl one's ~** (*in scorn*) презри́тельно криви́ть, с- гу́бы; **not a word escaped, passed his ~s** он не пророни́л ни сло́ва; **hang on s.o.'s ~s** впи́тывать (*impf.*) ка́ждое сло́во кого́-н.; слу́шать кого́-н. с восто́ргом; смотре́ть кому́-н. в рот; **keep a stiff upper ~** сохран|я́ть, -и́ть самооблада́ние; **lick one's ~s** обли́з|ываться, -ну́ться; **smack one's ~s** чмо́к|ать, -нуть; **I heard it from his own ~s** я слы́шал э́то от него́ самого́; **the news is on everyone's ~s** но́вость у всех на уста́х. **2.** (*edge of cup, wound etc.*) край; (*of ladle*) но́сик. **3.** (*coll., impudence*) де́рзость; **none of your ~!** не дерзи́!; **I won't take any ~ from him!** я ему́ покажу́ дерзи́ть!; пусть он не про́бует мне дерзи́ть.

cpds. **~-read** *v.t. & i.* чита́ть (*impf.*) с губ; **~-reading** *n.* чте́ние с губ; **~-salve** *n.* мазь для смягче́ния губ; **~-service** *n.* неискренние призна́ния/завере́ния; **pay ~-service to sth.** призн|ава́ть, -а́ть что-н. то́лько на слова́х; **~stick** *n.* (*substance*) губна́я пома́да; (*applicator*) па́лочка губно́й пома́ды.

lipped [lɪpd] *adj.* (*of vessel*) с но́сиком; (*of edge*) загну́тый.

comb. form: **thick-~** толстогу́бый.

liquefaction [ˌlɪkwɪˈfækʃ(ə)n] *n.* расплавле́ние; сжиже́ние.

liquefy [ˈlɪkwɪˌfaɪ] *v.t. & i.* (*of metals etc.*) распл|авля́ть(ся),

-а́вить(ся); (*of gas*) сжи́|ма́ть(ся), -ди́ть(ся).

liqueur [lɪ'kjʊə(r)] *n.* ликёр.

cpd. **~-glass** *n.* ликёрная рю́м(оч)ка.

liquid ['lɪkwɪd] *n.* **1.** (*substance*) жи́дкость; **~ measure** ме́ра жи́дкости. **2.** (*phon.*) пла́вный.

adj. **1.** (*in ~ form*) жи́дкий; **~ oxygen** жи́дкий кислоро́д; **~ food** жи́дкая пи́ща. **2.** (*translucent*): **~ eyes** я́сные глаза́; **a ~ sky** прозра́чное не́бо. **3.** (*of sounds*) певу́чий, мелоди́чный, пла́вный. **4.**: **~ assets** ликви́дные акти́вы.

cpd. **~-crystal** *adj.*: **~-crystal display** жидкокристалли́ческий индика́тор.

liquidate ['lɪkwɪ,deɪt] *v.t.* (*all senses*) ликвиди́ровать (*impf., pf.*).

liquidation [,lɪkwɪ'deɪʃ(ə)n] *n.* ликвида́ция; **go into ~** ликвиди́роваться (*impf., pf.*); **~ of debts** погаше́ние долго́в.

liquidator ['lɪkwɪ,deɪtə(r)] *n.* ликвида́тор.

liquidity [lɪ'kwɪdɪtɪ] *n.* жи́дкое состоя́ние; (*fin.*) ликви́дность.

liquidize ['lɪkwɪ,daɪz] *v.t.* (*cul.*) разжи|жа́ть, -ди́ть.

liquidizer ['lɪkwɪ,daɪzə(r)] *n.* (*cul.*) разжижи́тель (*m.*).

liquor ['lɪkə(r)] *n.* **1.** (*alcoholic drink*) (спиртно́й) напи́ток; **in** (*or* **the worse for**) под му́хой; **~ store** ви́нный магази́н. **2.** (*liquid*) жи́дкость.

liqu|orice, lic- ['lɪkərɪs, -rɪʃ] *n.* (*plant*) соло́дка, лакри́чник; (*substance*) лакри́ца.

lira ['lɪərə] *n.* ли́ра.

Lisbon ['lɪzbən] *n.* Лиссабо́н.

lisle [laɪl] *n.* (**~ thread**) фильдеко́с; **~ stockings** фильдеко́совые чулки́.

lisp [lɪsp] *n.* шепеля́вость; **he has** (*or* **speaks with**) **a ~** он шепеля́вит; (*of leaves etc.*) шо́рох.

v.i. шепеля́вить (*impf.*); сюсю́кать (*impf.*).

lissom(e) ['lɪsəm] *adj.* ги́бкий.

list[1] [lɪst] *n.* **1.** (*roll, inventory, enumeration*) спи́сок, пе́речень (*m.*); **black ~** чёрный спи́сок; **casualty ~** спи́сок поте́рь; **on the active ~** на действи́тельной слу́жбе; **enter sth. on a ~** вн|оси́ть, -ести́ что-н. в спи́сок; **make a ~** сост|авля́ть, -а́вить спи́сок; **~ price** цена́ по прейскура́нту. **2.** (*pl., tilting-yard*) аре́на (турни́ра); (*fig.*): **enter the ~s against s.o.** вступ|а́ть, -и́ть в бой с кем-н.

v.t. (*make a ~ of*) сост|авля́ть, -а́вить спи́сок +*g.*; (*enter on a ~*) вн|оси́ть, -ести́ в спи́сок; (*enumerate*) переч|исля́ть, -и́слить; **~ed building** зда́ние, находя́щееся под охра́ной госуда́рства.

list[2] [lɪst] *n.* (*leaning*) крен; накло́н; **have a ~** крени́ться (*impf.*).

v.i. (*of ship*) накреня́ться (*impf.*); крени́ться, на-.

listen ['lɪs(ə)n] *v.i.* слу́шать, по-; **~ to** слу́шать, по- +*a.*; **do you ~ (in) to the radio?** слу́шаете ли вы ра́дио?; (*pay attention; heed to*) прислу́ш|иваться, -аться к+*d.*; **don't ~ to him!** не обраща́йте на него́ внима́ния!; **I was ~ing for the bell** я (напряжённо) ждал звонка́; (*hear out*) выслу́шивать, вы́слушать; **~ to me and then decide** вы́слушайте меня́, а пото́м реша́йте!; (*for a certain time*) прослу́ш|ивать, -ать; **he ~s to the radio all evening** он це́лый ве́чер слу́шает ра́дио; **the doctor ~ed to his heart** врач прослу́шал его́ се́рдце; (*overhear, eavesdrop on*) подслу́ш|ивать, -ать; **he ~ed in on their conversation** он подслу́шал их разгово́р; **~ing-post** пост подслу́шивания.

listener ['lɪsənə(r)] *n.* слу́шатель (*m.*); **he is a good ~** он уме́ет слу́шать; (*to radio*) радиослу́шатель (*m.*).

listing ['lɪstɪŋ] *n.* спи́сок; составле́ние спи́ска.

listless ['lɪstlɪs] *adj.* апати́чный, вя́лый.

listlessness ['lɪstlɪsnɪs] *n.* апа́тия, вя́лость.

litany ['lɪtənɪ] *n.* екте́нья.

liter ['li:tə(r)] = **litre**

literacy ['lɪtərəsɪ] *n.* гра́мотность.

literal ['lɪtər(ə)l] *adj.* **1.** (*of, or expr. in, letters*) бу́квенный; **~ error** опеча́тка, бу́квенная оши́бка. **2.** (*following the text exactly; taking words in primary sense*) буква́льный; **he has a ~ mind** у него́ педанти́чный/прозаи́ческий ум.

literalness ['lɪtərəlnɪs] *n.* буква́льность.

literary ['lɪtərərɪ] *adj.* **1.** (*pert. to literature, books, writing*) литерату́рный; (*of ~ studies*) литературове́дческий; **~ history** исто́рия литерату́ры; **a ~ man** литера́тор; **~ property** литерату́рная со́бственность. **2.** (*of style or vocabulary*) кни́жный.

literate ['lɪtərət] *adj.* гра́мотный.

literati [,lɪtə'rɑ:ti:] *n.* литера́торы (*m. pl.*)

literature ['lɪtərətʃə(r), 'lɪtrə-] *n.* литерату́ра; **student of ~** литературове́д; **study of ~** литературове́дение; (*printed matter*) литерату́ра; кни́ги, брошю́ры и т.п.

lithe [laɪð] *adj.* ги́бкий.

litheness ['laɪðnɪs] *n.* ги́бкость.

lithium ['lɪθɪəm] *n.* ли́тий.

lithograph ['lɪθə,grɑ:f, 'laɪθə-] *n.* литогра́фия; **~ print** литогра́фский о́ттиск.

v.t. литографи́ровать (*impf., pf.*).

lithographer [lɪ'θɒgrəfə(r)] *n.* лито́граф.

lithographic [,lɪθə'græfɪk] *adj.* литогра́фский.

lithography [lɪ'θɒgrəfɪ] *n.* литогра́фия.

Lithuania [,lɪθju:'eɪnɪə, ,lɪθu:-] *n.* Литва́.

Lithuanian [,lɪθju:'eɪnɪən, ,lɪθu:-] *n.* (*pers.*) лито́в|ец (*fem.* -ка); (*language*) лито́вский язы́к.

adj. лито́вский.

litigant ['lɪtɪgənt] *n.* тя́жущаяся сторона́.

litigate ['lɪtɪ,geɪt] *v.i.* суди́ться (*impf.*)

litigation [,lɪtɪ'geɪʃ(ə)n] *n.* тя́жба; суде́бный проце́сс.

litigious [lɪ'tɪdʒəs] *adj.* **1.** (*fond of going to law*) сутя́жнический; **a ~ person** сутя́га (*c.g.*); сутя́жни|к (*fem.* -ца). **2.** (*pert. to litigation*): **~ procedure** процеду́ра суде́бного разбира́тельства.

litmus ['lɪtməs] *n.* ла́кмус; **~ paper** ла́кмусовая бума́га.

litotes [laɪ'təʊti:z] *n.* лито́та.

litre ['li:tə(r)] (*US* **liter**) *n.* литр.

litter ['lɪtə(r)] *n.* **1.** (*refuse*) сор, отбро́с|ы (*pl., g.* -ов). **2.** (*straw etc. for animals*) подсти́лка. **3.** (*newly-born animals*) помёт. **4.** (*hist., means of transport*) паланки́н; (*stretcher*) носи́л|ки (*pl., g.* -ок).

v.t. **1.** (*make untidy*) сори́ть, на-; **he ~ed the room with paper** он разброса́л бума́гу по всей ко́мнате; **the table is ~ed with books** стол зава́лен кни́гами. **2.** (*provide with straw for bedding*): **~ a horse** де́лать, с- подсти́лку для ло́шади.

v.i. (*give birth: of dogs*) щени́ться, о-; (*of pigs*) пороси́ться, о-.

cpds. **~-basket** *n.* му́сорная корзи́на; **~-bin** *n.* му́сорный я́щик.

littérateur [,lɪtərɑ:'tɜ:(r)] *n.* литера́тор.

little ['lɪt(ə)l] *n.* (*not much*) ма́ло, немно́го, немно́жко +*g.*; **there was ~ left** оста́лось ма́ло/немно́го; **it had ~ to do with me** э́то де́ло меня́ ма́ло каса́лось; **our plans came to ~** из на́ших пла́нов ма́ло что получи́лось; **he makes ~ of physical pain** он не бои́тся физи́ческой бо́ли; **he thinks ~ of me** он обо мне ни́зкого/невысо́кого мне́ния; **it takes ~ to make him angry** его́ нетру́дно рассерди́ть; **I see ~ of him now** я тепе́рь ре́дко ви́жу его́; **in ~** в миниатю́ре; **~ or nothing** почти́ ничего́; ма́ло что; **he has done ~ or nothing for us** он нам почти́ ниче́м не помо́г; (*small amount*): **I did what ~ I could** я сде́лал то немно́гое, что мог; **the ~ of his work that remains** то немно́гое, что сохрани́лось из его́ трудо́в; **I'd like a ~ of that salad** я бы хоте́л немно́го/чу́точку э́того сала́та; **he knows a ~ Japanese** он немно́го зна́ет япо́нский; **he knows a ~ of everything** он зна́ет обо всём понемно́гу; **he has done not a ~ to harm us** он нам нема́ло/поря́дком навреди́л; (*short time or distance*): **after a ~ he returned** вско́ре он верну́лся; **won't you stay (for) a ~?** побу́дьте/посиди́те ещё немно́го!; **~ by ~** ма́ло-пома́лу; постепе́нно.

adj. **1.** (*small*) ма́ленький, небольшо́й; **~ finger** мизи́нец; **~ toe** мизи́нец ноги́; **L~ Bear** (*astron.*) Ма́лая Медве́дица; (*expr. by dim., e.g.*); **~ house** до́мик; **~ man** челове́чек. **2.** (*young*): **~ boy** (ма́ленький) ма́льчик; **~ girl** (ма́ленькая) де́вочка; **my ~ brother** мой брати́шка; **~ ones** (*children*) де́т|и (*pl., g.* -е́й); малыши́ (*m. pl.*); де́тки (*f. pl.*); (*animals*) детёныши (*m. pl.*). **3.** (*trivial, unpretentious*) ме́лкий; незначи́тельный; **the ~ things of life** жите́йские ме́лочи (*f. pl.*). **4.** (*not tall or long*) невысо́кий; недли́нный; **he was a ~ man** он был челове́к небольшо́го ро́ста; **I went a ~ way with him** я с ним прошёл не́сколько шаго́в; **wait here for a ~ while** подожди́те здесь немно́жко. **5.** (*small, of quantity*) ма́ло, немно́го, немно́жко +*g.*; **there is ~ butter left** ма́сла оста́лось ма́ло; **he knows ~ Japanese** он пло́хо зна́ет япо́нский; **have a ~ something to eat!** перекуси́те чу́точку!; ску́шайте что́-нибудь!; **it gives me no ~ pleasure** э́то доста́вит мне и́стинное удово́льствие. **6.** (*in var. emotive senses*): **that poor ~ girl!** бедня́жка!; **he's quite the ~ gentleman** э́тот ма́льчик — настоя́щий джентльме́н; **so that's your ~ game!** так вы вон что заду́мали!; **I know your ~ ways** я зна́ю ва́ши шту́чки; зна́ем мы вас!; **I left the ~ woman** (*coll.*) **at home** жена́/ стару́шка оста́лась до́ма; **you ~ liar!** ах ты, лгуни́шка! (*c.g.*).

adv. **1.** (*not much*) ма́ло; **I see him very ~** я ма́ло/ ре́дко с ним ви́жусь; **~ more** ненамно́го/немно́гим бо́льше; **it is ~ more than speculation** э́то но́сит предположи́тельный хара́ктер; **he is ~ better than a thief** он про́сто-на́просто вор; **~ short of madness** су́щее безу́мие; (*not at all*): **~ did he know I was following him** он и не подозрева́л, что я иду́ за ним; **we ~ thought he would go to those lengths** мы ника́к не ожида́ли, что он дойдёт до тако́й кра́йности. **2.** (**a ~**: *slightly, somewhat*) немно́го, немно́жко; **this hat is a ~ too big for me** э́та шля́па мне немно́го велика́; **I was a ~ afraid you would not come** я немно́го боя́лся, что вы не придёте; **he was not a ~ annoyed** он был не на шу́тку раздражён; **I am a ~ happier now** я тепе́рь не́сколько успоко́ился; **she is a ~ over 40** ей немно́гим бо́льше сорока́.

littoral [ˈlɪtər(ə)l] *n.* побере́жье.

adj. прибре́жный.

liturgical [lɪˈtɜːdʒɪk(ə)l] *adj.* литурги́ческий.

liturgy [ˈlɪtədʒɪ] *n.* (*eccl.*) литурги́я.

livable [ˈlɪvəb(ə)l] = **liv(e)able**

live[1] [laɪv] *adj.* **1.** (*living*) живо́й; **~ bait** живе́ц; (*pert. to living pers. or thg.*): **~ birth** рожде́ние живо́го ребёнка; **number of ~ births** число́ живорождённых дете́й; **~ weight** живо́й вес; (*fig.*): **a ~ issue** актуа́льный вопро́с. **2.** (*burning*): **~ coals** горя́щие у́гли. **3.** (*not spent or exploded*): **a ~ match** неиспо́льзованная спи́чка; **~ ammunition** боевы́е патро́ны; **~ rail** токопроводя́щий рельс; **a ~ wire** (*lit.*) про́вод под то́ком/напряже́нием; (*fig.*) челове́к с изю́минкой, «жи́вчик». **4.** (*not recorded*): **~ broadcast** пряма́я переда́ча; (*away from studio*) внестуди́йная переда́ча; **the game was broadcast ~** матч трансли́ровался непосре́дственно со стадио́на.

cpd. **~stock** *n.* дома́шний скот.

live[2] [lɪv] *v.t.* (*spend, experience*) пров|оди́ть, -ести́; прож|ива́ть, -и́ть; **he ~d his whole life there** он там про́жил всю жизнь; **he is living a double life** он ведёт двойну́ю жизнь; **he ~s life to the full** он живёт по́лной жи́знью; **life is not worth living** жить не сто́ит; **~ a lie** жить (*impf.*) по лжи.

v.i. **1.** (*be alive*) жить (*impf.*); (*of habitat*) води́ться, обита́ть (*both impf.*). **2.** (*subsist*): **they ~ on vegetables** они́ пита́ются овоща́ми; **you can't ~ on air** на пи́ще свято́го Анто́ния до́лго не проживёшь; **they ~ off the land** они́ живу́т на подно́жном корму́; **they ~ from hand to mouth** они́ перебива́ются с хле́ба на во́ду; они́ е́ле сво́дят концы́ с конца́ми. **3.** (*depend for one's living*) жить (*impf.*); **he ~s on his wife** он живёт на иждиве́нии жены́; **he ~s on his earnings** он живёт на свои́ за́работки; **they ~ quietly, within their income** они́ живу́т скро́мно, по сре́дствам; **he ~s on, off his friends** он живёт за счёт друзе́й; **he ~s on his reputation** он живёт ста́рым капита́лом; **he ~s by, on his wits** он живёт на сомни́тельные дохо́ды. **4.** (*conduct o.s.*) жить (*impf.*); **he ~s up to his principles/reputation** он стро́го приде́рживается свои́х при́нципов; он не роня́ет свое́й репута́ции; **he ~d up to my expectations** он не обману́л мои́х ожида́ний; **he ~s to himself** он живёт за́мкнуто; **he ~d and died a bachelor** он жил и у́мер холостяко́м; (*arrange one's diet, habits etc.*): **he ~s well** он живёт хорошо́ (*or* на широ́кую но́гу); **two can ~ as cheaply as one** вдвоём жить не доро́же, чем одному́; **~ like a lord** (*or* **a fighting cock**) ката́ться (*impf.*) как сыр в ма́сле. **5.** (*enjoy life*): **now at last I'm really living** вот э́то я называ́ю жи́знью!; **if you've never been to Paris, you haven't ~d** кто в Пари́же не быва́л, тот жи́зни не вида́л. **6.** (*continue alive*): **the doctors think he won't ~** врачи́ ду́мают, что он не вы́живет; **he ~d to a great** (*or* **ripe old**) **age** он дожи́л до глубо́кой ста́рости; **they ~d happily ever after** они́ ста́ли жить-пожива́ть да добра́ нажива́ть; **he ~d to regret it** впосле́дствии он об э́том жале́л; **he did not ~ to finish the work** он у́мер, не заверши́в рабо́ту; **he will ~ to see his grandchildren married** он успе́ет вну́ков жени́ть; **long ~ the Queen!** да здра́вствует короле́ва!; **she has ~d through a great deal** она́ мно́го пережила́; **you, we ~ and learn** век живи́ — век учи́сь; **~ and let ~** сам живи́ и други́м не меша́й; **I have nothing to ~ for** мне не́зачем жить; **he ~s for his work** он живёт свое́й рабо́той; для него́ рабо́та — всё; (*fig., survive*): **his fame will ~ for ever** сла́ва его́ не умрёт. **7.** (*reside*) жить, прожива́ть (*both impf.*); обита́ть (*impf.*); **where do you ~?** где вы живёте; **I ~ at No. 17** я живу́ в до́ме но́мер 17; **the house has a ~d-in appearance** у до́ма обжито́й вид; **he is living with his secretary** он живёт/сожи́тельствует с секрета́ршей; **they are living apart** (*of married couple*) они́ живу́т врозь; они́ разъе́хались; **~ with** (*fig. tolerate*) мири́ться, при- с+*i.*

with advs.: **~ down** *v.t.* загла́|живать, -дить; **he will never ~ down the scandal** ему́ никогда́ не уда́стся загла́дить сканда́л; ему́ никогда́ не забу́дут его́ сканда́льного поведе́ния; **~ in** *v.i.*: **the servants all ~ in/out** вся прислу́га — живу́щая/приходя́щая; **~ on** *v.i.*: **his memory ~s on** па́мять о нём жива́; **~ out** *v.t.* (*survive*): **she will not ~ out the night** она́ не протя́нет до утра́; *v.i.*: **most officers ~ out** бо́льшая часть офице́ров не живёт в каза́рмах; *see also* **~ in**; **~ together** *v.i.*: **are they married or only living together?** они́ жена́ты и́ли так живу́т (*or* сожи́тельствуют)?; **France and Germany have learnt to ~ together** Фра́нция и Герма́ния научи́лись жить в ми́ре; **~ up** *v.t.*: **~ it up** (*coll.*) жить (*impf.*) широко́.

cpd. **~long** *adj.* це́лый; **the ~long day** день-деньско́й.

liv(e)able [ˈlɪvəb(ə)l] *adj.* **1.** (*of house etc.*) го́дный для жилья́. **2.** (*of life*) сно́сный. **3.**: **~-with** (*of pers.*) тако́й, с кото́рым мо́жно ужи́ться.

livelihood [ˈlaɪvlɪˌhʊd] *n.* сре́дства (*nt. pl.*) к существова́нию; **earn, gain one's ~** зараба́тывать (*impf.*) на жизнь; добыва́ть (*impf.*) сре́дства к существова́нию.

liveliness [ˈlaɪvlɪnɪs] *n.* жи́вость, оживлённость.

lively [ˈlaɪvlɪ] *adj.* **1.** (*lit., fig.*) живо́й; **take a ~ interest in sth.** проявля́ть (*impf.*) живо́й интере́с к чему́-н.; (*animated*) оживлённый; **trade was ~** торго́вля шла бо́йко; (*energetic*) живо́й, де́ятельный; (*bright*): **~ colours** я́ркие кра́ски; (*brisk*): **we walked at a ~ pace** мы шли бы́стрым ша́гом; **look ~!** быстре́е!; жи́во!; повора́чивайся! **2.** (*exciting, dangerous*): **make things ~ for s.o.** зада́ть (*pf.*) жа́ру кому́-н.; насоли́ть (*pf.*) кому́-н.

liven [ˈlaɪv(ə)n] *v.t.* & *i.* (*also* **~ up**) ожив|ля́ть(ся), -и́ть(ся).

liver[1] [ˈlɪvə(r)] *n.* (*anat.*) пе́чень; **~ complaint** боле́знь пе́чени; (*food*) печёнка; **~ sausage** ли́верная колбаса́.

cpd. **~-fluke** *n.* печёночная двуу́стка.

liver[2] [ˈlɪvə(r)] *n.*: **loose ~** распу́тник; **fast ~** прожига́тель (*m.*) жи́зни.

liveried [ˈlɪvərɪd] *adj.* ливре́йный.

liver|ish [ˈlɪvərɪʃ], **-y** [ˈlɪvərɪ] *adjs.*: **he is feeling ~y** у него́ поша́ливает пе́чень; (*fig., peevish*) жёлчный.

livery[1] [ˈlɪvərɪ] *n.* (*of servants*) ливре́я; (*of a guild etc.*) фо́рма; (*for horses*) прoко́рм; **~ stable** пла́тная коню́шня.

livery[2] [ˈlɪvərɪ] = **liverish**

livid [ˈlɪvɪd] *adj.* (*of colour*) серова́то-си́ний; ме́ртвенно-бле́дный; (*coll., of temper*): **be ~** черне́ть, по-; **I was ~** я был взбешён.

living [ˈlɪvɪŋ] *n.* **1.** (*process, manner of ~*): **~ conditions** усло́вия жи́зни; **a ~ wage** прожи́точный ми́нимум; **the art of ~** уме́ние жить; **loose ~** распу́тство; **cost of ~** сто́имость жи́зни; **standard of ~** жи́зненный у́ровень. **2.** (*livelihood*) сре́дства (*nt. pl.*) к жи́зни; **earn one's ~** зараб|а́тывать, -о́тать себе́ на жизнь; **he makes his ~ by teaching** он зараба́тывает преподава́нием; **the world owes us a ~** о́бщество обя́зано содержа́ть нас. **3.** (*fare*): **good,**

high ~ богáтый стол; **plain ~** простóй стол. **4.** (*eccl.*) бенефúций.

adj. **1.** (*alive*) живóй; **a ~ language** живóй язы́к; **a ~ death** жáлкое существовáние; **within ~ memory** на пáмяти живýщих; **not a ~ soul** (*as obj.*) ни (однóй) живóй души́; **no man ~ could do better** никтó на свéте не мог бы сдéлать лýчше; (*as n.*) **the ~** живы́е (*pl.*); **he is in the land of the ~** он ещё жив; он ещё не поки́нул э́тот свет. **2.** (*true to life*): **he is the ~ image of his father** он вы́литый отéц. **3.** (*contemporary*): **he is the greatest of ~ writers** он крупнéйший из совремéнных писáтелей.

cpds. **~-room** *n.* гости́ная; **~-space** *n.* жи́зненное прострáнство.

Livy ['lɪvɪ] *n.* Ли́вий.

lizard ['lɪzəd] *n.* я́щерица.

Ljubljana [luːˈbljɑːnə] *n.* Любля́на.

llama ['lɑːmə] *n.* лáма.

Lloyd's [lɔɪdz] *n.*: **~ Register** реги́стр Ллóйда.

lo [ləʊ] *int.* (*arch.*): **~ and behold** и вдруг, о чýдо.

loach [ləʊtʃ] *n.* голéц.

load [ləʊd] *n.* **1.** (*what is carried; burden*) нóша; груз, нагрýзка; тя́жесть; **each one carried his own ~** кáждый нёс свою́ поклáжу; (*fig.*) брéмя; **a ~ of worries** брéмя забóт; **that was a ~ off my mind** у меня́ как горá с плеч; **you have taken a ~ off my mind** от вáших слов мне стáло лéгче. **2.** (*amount carried by vehicle etc.*) груз; **a ~ of bricks** груз кирпичéй; (*fig., coll.*): **it's a ~ of rubbish** э́то сплошнáя чепухá. **3.** (*phys., elec.*) нагрýзка; **test under ~** испы́т|ывать, -áть под нагрýзкой. **4.** (*pl., coll., large amount*) ýйма, мáсса.

v.t. **1.** (*cargo etc.*) грузи́ть, по-; **the goods were ~ed on to the ship** товáры погрузи́ли на корáбль. **2.** (*ship, vehicle etc.*) грузи́ть, на-; нагру|жáть, -зи́ть (*что чем*). **3.** (*fig., with cares etc.*) обремен|я́ть, -и́ть (*кого чем*); **don't ~ yourself with extra work** не взвáливайте на себя́ ли́шнюю рабóту. **4.** (*with gifts, praises etc.*) ос|ыпáть, -ы́пать (*кого чем*). **5.** (*firearm, camera etc.*) заря|жáть, -ди́ть; **he ~ed the camera with film** он заряди́л аппарáт (плёнкой). **6.** (*weight with lead*) нал|ивáть, -и́ть свинцóм; **~ed dice** нáлитые свинцóм кóсти; **the dice were ~ed against him** (*fig.*) все шáнсы бы́ли прóтив негó; егó поражéние бы́ло предрешенó; (*fig.*): **a ~ed question** провокациóнный вопрóс. **7.** (*fill to capacity*): **the bus was ~ed with people** автóбус был перепóлнен. **8.** (*sl.*): **he's ~ed** (*rich*) у негó дéнег кýры не клюю́т; (*drunk*) он нагрузи́лся; (*drugged*) он под кáйфом.

v.i. грузи́ться, на-.

with advs.: **~ down** *v.t.* обремен|я́ть, -и́ть; **~ up** *v.t.* нагру|жáть, -зи́ть; *v.i.* грузи́ться, на-.

cpds. **~-bearing** *adj.*: **~-bearing capacity** грузоподъёмность; **~-carrier** *n.* грузовáя маши́на, грузови́к; **~-displacement, ~-draught** *nn.* водоизмещéние при пóлном грýзе; **~-line** *n.* грузовáя ватерли́ния; **~star, ~stone** *see* **lode-**

loader ['ləʊdə(r)] *n.* (*pers.*) грýзчик.

loading ['ləʊdɪŋ] *n.* **1.** (*of cargo*) погрýзка. **2.** (*of ship, vehicle etc.*) нагрýзка; **~ berth** погрýзочный причáл; **~ hatch** грузовóй люк. **3.** (*of gun, camera etc.*) заря́дка. **4.** (*elec.*) нагрýзка.

loaf[1] [ləʊf] *n.* **1.** (*of bread*) бухáнка; **cottage ~** каравáй; **small ~** бýлка; **half a ~ is better than no bread** ≃ на безры́бье и рак ры́ба; (*~shaped food*): **meat ~** мяснóй рулéт; **sugar ~** сáхарная головá. **2.** (*sl., head*) башкá; **use one's ~** шевели́ть (*impf.*) мозгáми.

loaf[2] [ləʊf] *v.i.* (*coll.; also* **~ about**) лóдырничать, гоня́ть лóдыря (*both impf.*); шатáться (*impf.*) без дéла.

loafer ['ləʊfə(r)] *n.* лóдырь (*m.*); прáздношатáющийся.

loam [ləʊm] *n.* сугли́нок.

loamy ['ləʊmɪ] *adj.* сугли́нистый.

loan [ləʊn] *n.* **1.** (*sum lent*) заём, ссýда; **government ~s** госудáрственные зáймы (*m. pl.*); **he asked for a ~ of £10** он попроси́л 10 фýнтов взаймы́. **2.** (*lending or being lent*): **take on ~; have the ~ of** (*of money*) брать, взять взаймы́; (*of objects*) брать, взять на врéмя (*or* во врéменное пóльзование); **may I have the ~ of this book?** могý ли я взять на врéмя э́ту кни́гу?; **this exhibit is on ~ from the museum** э́тот экспонáт врéменно взят из музéя; **the picture is out on ~** э́та карти́на переданá в други́е рýки.

v.t. одолж|áть, -и́ть; да|вáть, -ть взаймы́.

cpds. **~-collection** *n.* вы́ставка экспонáтов из чáстных коллéкций; **~-translation** *n.* кáлька; **~-word** *n.* заи́мствованное слóво.

lo(a)th [ləʊθ] *pred. adj.*: **he was ~ to do anything** он ничегó не хотéл дéлать; **nothing ~, he went** он отпрáвился с удовóльствием.

loathe [ləʊð] *v.t.* (*detest*) ненави́деть (*impf.*); (*feel disgust for*) чýвствовать/испы́тывать (*impf.*) отвращéние к+*d.*; (*be unable to bear*) быть не в состоя́нии терпéть; **I ~ asking him about it** мне ужáсно неприя́тно егó спрáшивать об э́том.

loathing ['ləʊðɪŋ] *n.* отвращéние; **feel ~ for** испы́тывать (*impf.*) отвращéние к+*d.*

loathsome ['ləʊðsəm] *adj.* отврати́тельный, омерзи́тельный.

lob [lɒb] *n.* (*high-pitched ball*) свечá.

v.t.: **~ a ball** под|авáть, -áть свечý.

lobby ['lɒbɪ] *n.* вестибю́ль (*m.*); (*theatr.*) фойé (*indecl.*); (*in Parliament*) кулуáр|ы (*pl., g.* -ов).

v.t. агити́ровать, (*impf.*) (в кулуáрах).

lobbying ['lɒbɪɪŋ] *n.* агитáция (в кулуáрах).

lobbyist ['lɒbɪɪst] *n.* лобби́ст.

lobe [ləʊb] *n.* (*of liver, brain etc.*) дóля; (*of ear*) мóчка.

lobelia [ləˈbiːlɪə] *n.* лобéлия.

lobotomy [ləˈbɒtəmɪ] *n.* лоботоми́я.

lobster ['lɒbstə(r)] *n.* омáр; **red as a ~** крáсный как рак.

cpd. **~-pot** *n.* вéрша для омáров.

local ['ləʊk(ə)l] *n.* (*inhabitant*) мéстный жи́тель; (*paper*) мéстная газéта; (*train*) мéстный пóезд; (*public house*) мéстный паб, мéстная пивня́.

adj. мéстный; здéшний; (*of that place*) (*coll.*) тáмошний; **~ anaesthetic** мéстный наркóз; **~ authority** мéстные влáсти; **~ colour** мéстный колори́т; **~ government** мéстное самоуправлéние; **~ pain** локализóванная боль; **~ population** коренно́е населéние; **~ showers** ≃ местáми дожди́; **2 o'clock ~ time** два часá по мéстному врéмени; **he is a ~ man** он из здéшних мест; он здéшний.

locale [ləʊˈkɑːl] *n.* мéсто (дéйствия); мéстность.

localism ['ləʊkəˌlɪz(ə)m] *n.* (*local custom or idiom*) мéстный обы́чай; мéстное/областнóе выражéние.

locality [ləʊˈkælɪtɪ] *n.* мéстность; (*neighbourhood*): **there is no cinema in the ~** нигдé побли́зости нет кинó; (*faculty of recognizing places*): **she has a good sense/**(*coll.*) **bump of ~** онá хорошó ориенти́руется (на мéстности).

localization [ˌləʊkəlaɪˈzeɪʃ(ə)n] *n.* локализáция.

localize ['ləʊkəˌlaɪz] *v.t.* локализовáть (*impf., pf.*).

locally ['ləʊkəlɪ] *adv.*: **he is well-known ~** он извéстен в э́тих края́х; **he works ~** он рабóтает побли́зости.

locate [ləʊˈkeɪt] *v.t.* **1.** (*establish in a place*) помe|щáть, -сти́ть; (*designate place of*) назн|ачáть, -áчить мéсто (*чему or для чего*); **be ~d** (*situated*) находи́ться (*impf.*). **2.** (*determine position of*) определ|я́ть, -и́ть мéсто/местоположéние *+g.*; **has the fault been ~d?** нашли́ поврежде́ние?; определи́ли ли мéсто повреждéния?; (*discover*) обнарýжи|вать, -ть; **he ~d the source of the Nile** он нашёл истóки Ни́ла.

location [ləʊˈkeɪʃ(ə)n] *n.* **1.** (*determining of place*) определéние (мéста). **2.** (*position, situation*) местонахождéние, местоположéние. **3.**: **on ~** (*cin.*) на натýре.

locative ['lɒkətɪv] *n. & adj.* (*gram.*) мéстный (падéж).

loch [lɒk, lɒx] *n.* óзеро (*в Шотландии*); **L~ Ness** óзеро Лох-Нéсс.

lock[1] [lɒk] *n.* (*of hair*) лóкон, прядь.

lock[2] [lɒk] *n.* **1.** (*on door or firearm*) замóк; **under ~ and key** под замкóм; **~, stock and barrel** целикóм и пóлностью; (*on door or gate*) запóр; (*on mechanism*) стóпор. **2.** (*of vehicle's wheels*) ýгол поворóта; **full ~** до упóра; **other ~** поворóт в другýю стóрону. **3.** (*wrestling hold*) захвáт. **4.** (*on canal*) шлюз.

v.t. **1.** (*secure; restrict movement of*) зап|ирáть, -ерéть (на замóк); **is the door ~ed?** дверь запертá?; **she ~ed him into the bedroom** онá заперлá егó в спáльне; **I was**

~ed out дверь была́ заперта́, и я не мог войти́. **2.** (*cause to stop moving or revolving*) тормози́ть, за-; **he ~ed the steering** он за́пер руль. **3.** (*engage, interlace*) спле|та́ть, -сти́; **his fingers were ~ed together** он сцепи́л ру́ки; **they were ~ed in an embrace** они́ сжима́ли друг дру́га в объя́тиях.

v.i. **1.: does this chest ~?** э́тот сунду́к запира́ется?; в сундуке́ есть замо́к? **2.** (*become rigid or immovable*) застр|ева́ть, -я́ть. **3.** (*interlace*) перепле|та́ться, -сти́сь; сцеп|ля́ться, -и́ться; **the parts ~ into each other** дета́ли взаи́мно блоки́руются.

with advs.: **~ away** *v.t.* спря́тать (*pf.*) под замо́к; **~ in** *v.t.* зап|ира́ть, -ере́ть (*кого*) в ко́мнате/до́ме *и т.п.*; **he ~ed himself in** он за́перся́ на ключ; **~ out** *v.t.* зап|ира́ть, -ере́ть дверь и не впуска́ть; **the workers were ~ed out** рабо́чих подве́ргли лока́уту; **~ up** *v.t.* зап|ира́ть, -ере́ть на замо́к; (*imprison*) сажа́ть, посади́ть; **he ought to be ~ed up** его́ сле́дует помести́ть в сумасше́дший дом; **his capital is ~ed up in land** весь его́ капита́л в земе́льных владе́ниях; *v.i.*: **when do you ~ up for the night?** в кото́ром часу́ вы ве́чером закрыва́етесь?

cpds. **~-gate** *n.* шлю́зные воро́та; **~jaw** *n.* тризм че́люсти; **~-keeper** *n.* смотри́тель (*m.*) шлю́за; **~out** *n.* лока́ут; **~smith** *n.* сле́сарь (*m.*); **~smith's trade** слеса́рное де́ло; **~-up** *n.*ареста́нтская ка́мера; (*shed*) сара́й.

locker ['lɒkə(r)] *n.* (*cupboard*) шка́фчик; (*naut.*) рунду́к.

cpd. **~-room** *n.* раздева́лка.

locket ['lɒkɪt] *n.* медальо́н.

loco[1] ['ləʊkəʊ] (*coll.*) = **locomotive**

loco[2] ['ləʊkəʊ] *adj.* (*insane*) чо́кнутый (*sl.*).

locomotion [ˌləʊkə'məʊʃ(ə)n] *n.* передвиже́ние.

locomotive [ˌləʊkə'məʊtɪv] *n.* локомоти́в; (*steam*) парово́з; (*electric*) электрово́з; (*diesel*) ди́зель (*m.*), теплово́з; **~ shed** депо́ (*indecl.*).

adj. дви́жущий, двига́тельный; **~ engine** = *n.*

locum (tenens) [ˌləʊkəm 'tiːnenz, 'tenenz] *n.* (*doctor or clergyman*) вре́менный замести́тель (*m.*).

locus ['ləʊkəs, 'lɒkəs] *n.* (*math.*) траекто́рия; **~ of points** геометри́ческое ме́сто то́чек.

locus classicus [ˌləʊkəs 'klæsɪkəs, ˌlɒkəs] *n.* класси́ческая цита́та, наибо́лее подходя́щая в да́нном слу́чае.

locust ['ləʊkəst] *n.* **1.** (*insect*) саранча́ (*also collect.*); **~s and wild honey** (*bibl.*) акри́д|ы (*pl., g.* —) и ди́кий мёд. **2.** (*carob tree*) рожко́вое де́рево. **3.** (*false acacia*) лжеака́ция.

locution [lək'juːʃ(ə)n] *n.* оборо́т (ре́чи), идио́ма.

lode [ləʊd] *n.* ру́дная жи́ла.

cpds. **~star** *n.* (*fig.*) путево́дная звезда́; **~stone** (*also* **loadstone**) *n.* магни́тный железня́к; (*fig.*) магни́т.

lodge [lɒdʒ] *n.* **1.** (*cottage e.g. at entrance to park*) дом приврáтника. **2.** (*porter's apartment*) сторо́жка. **3.** (*hunting* ~) охо́тничий до́мик. **4.** (*freemason's* ~) масо́нская ло́жа. **5.** (*trade union branch*) ме́стная профсою́зная организа́ция. **6.** (*beaver's etc. lair*) нора́.

v.t. **1.** (*accommodate*) да|ва́ть, -ть помеще́ние +*d.*; поме|ща́ть, -сти́ть; **this building can ~ 50** в э́том зда́нии мо́гут размести́ться 50 жильцо́в. **2.** (*deposit*) сда|ва́ть, -ть на хране́ние. **3.** (*fig., enter*): **~ a complaint/appeal** обра|ща́ться, -ти́ться с жа́лобой/апелля́цией; **~ a claim** предъяв|ля́ть, -и́ть прете́нзию; **~ an objection** заяв|ля́ть, -и́ть проте́ст.

v.i. **1.** (*reside*) жить (*impf.*); прожива́ть (*impf.*); **he ~s with us** он наш жиле́ц. **2.** (*become embedded, stuck*) застр|ева́ть, -я́ть; **a bone ~d in his throat** кость застря́ла у него́ в го́рле.

lodgement ['lɒdʒm(ə)nt] *n.* **1.** (*mil.*): **make a ~** захва́т|ывать, -и́ть пози́цию; закреп|ля́ться, -и́ться. **2.** (*deposit; depositing of funds*) депози́т; депони́рование.

lodger ['lɒdʒə(r)] *n.* жил|е́ц (*fem.* -и́ца); (*occupant of flat*) квартира́нт (*fem.* -ка).

lodging ['lɒdʒɪŋ] *n.* (*dwelling-place*) кварти́ра; (*rented accommodation*) наёмная кварти́ра; (*pl.*) меблиро́ванные ко́мнаты (*f. pl.*); **he lives in ~s** он живёт в номера́х; он снима́ет ко́мнату.

loess ['ləʊɪs, lɜːs] *n.* лёсс.

loft [lɒft] *n.* (*room in roof*) черда́к; (*hay-~*) сенова́л; (*pigeon-~*) голубя́тня; (*organ-~*) хо́р|ы (*pl., g.* -ов).

v.t.: **~ a ball** пос|ыла́ть, -ла́ть мяч высоко́/вверх.

loftiness ['lɒftɪnɪs] *n.* (больша́я) высота́; возвы́шенность; (*fig., haughtiness*) высокоме́рие, надме́нность.

lofty ['lɒftɪ] *adj.* (*high*) высо́кий; (*exalted*) возвы́шенный; (*haughty*) высокоме́рный, надме́нный.

log[1] [lɒg] *n.* **1.** (*of wood*) бревно́, чурба́н; (*for fire*) поле́но; **he slept like a ~** он спал как уби́тый; **~ cabin** (бреве́нчатая) хи́жина.

cpds. **~jam** *n.* зато́р; (*fig.*) засто́й, тупи́к; **~-rolling** *n.* перека́тка брёвен; (*fig.*) поли́тика «ты мне — я тебе́».

log[2] [lɒg] *n.* **1.** (*naut., trailed float*) лаг. **2.** (*~-book*) ва́хтенный журна́л; (*of aircraft*) бортово́й журна́л; формуля́р; (*of lorry or car*) формуля́р.

v.t. (*record*) занос|и́ть, -ести́ в ва́хтенный журна́л; регистри́ровать (*impf., pf.*); (*attain*) разв|ива́ть, -и́ть (*скорость по лагу*).

cpds. **~-book** *n.* = *n.* **2.; ~-line** *n.* лагли́нь (*m.*).

log[3] [lɒg] = **logarithm**

loganberry ['ləʊgənbərɪ] *n.* лога́нова я́года (*гибрид малины с ежевикой*).

logarithm ['lɒgəˌrɪð(ə)m] *n.* логари́фм.

logarithmic [ˌlɒgə'rɪðmɪk] *adj.* логарифми́ческий.

loggerhead ['lɒgəˌhed] *n.*: **they are at ~s** они́ в ссо́ре (*or* не в лада́х) друг с дру́гом.

loggia ['ləʊdʒə, 'lɒ-] *n.* ло́джия.

logging ['lɒgɪŋ] *n.* (*cutting into logs*) лесозагото́вка.

logic ['lɒdʒɪk] *n.* ло́гика.

cpd. **~-chopping** *n.* софи́стика.

logical ['lɒdʒɪk(ə)l] *adj.* логи́ческий; (*consistent*) логи́чный, после́довательный.

logician [lə'dʒɪʃ(ə)n] *n.* ло́гик.

logistics [lə'dʒɪstɪks] *n.* (*mil.*) материа́льно-техни́ческое обеспе́чение.

logo ['ləʊgəʊ, 'lɒgəʊ] *n.* эмбле́ма.

loin [lɔɪn] *n.* **1.** (*pl.*) поясни́ца; **gird up one's ~s** препоя́сать (*pf.*) свои́ чре́сла (*bibl.*). **2.** (*joint of meat*) филе́ (*indecl.*).

cpd. **~-cloth** *n.* набе́дренная повя́зка.

Loire [lwɑːr] *n.* Луа́ра.

loiter ['lɔɪtə(r)] *v.i.* (*dawdle*) ме́шкать (*impf.*); заме́шкаться (*pf.*); (*hang about*) шата́ться, окола́чиваться, слоня́ться (*all impf.*) (без де́ла).

loiterer ['lɔɪtərə(r)] *n.* праздношата́ющийся.

loll [lɒl] *v.i.* **1.** (*sit or stand in lazy attitude*) сиде́ть/стоя́ть (*impf.*) развaля́сь. **2.** (*of tongue etc.: hang loose*) выва́ливаться (*impf.*).

lollipop ['lɒlɪˌpɒp] *n.* леден́ец на па́лочке.

lollop ['lɒləp] *v.i.*: **~ along** идти́ (*det.*) вразва́лку.

lolly ['lɒlɪ] *n.* **1.** (*coll.*) = **lollipop. 2.** (*sl., money*) гро́ш|и (*pl., g.* -е́й).

Lombard ['lɒmbɑːd] *n.* (*native of Lombardy*) ломба́рдец; жи́тель (*fem.* -ница) Ломба́рдии; (*hist.*) лангоба́рд.

adj. ломба́рдский; (*hist.*) лангоба́рдский.

Lombardy ['lɒmbədɪ] *n.* Ломба́рдия; **~ poplar** то́поль пирамида́льный *or* италья́нский.

London ['lʌnd(ə)n] *n.* Ло́ндон; **Greater ~** Большо́й Ло́ндон; (*attr.*) ло́ндонский.

Londoner ['lʌndənə(r)] *n.* ло́ндон|ец (*fem.* -ка).

lone [ləʊn] *adj.* одино́кий, уединённый; **~ wolf** (*lit., fig.*) бирю́к; **play a ~ hand** де́йствовать (*impf.*) в одино́чку.

loneliness ['ləʊnlɪnɪs] *n.* одино́чество.

lonely ['ləʊnlɪ] *adj.* **1.** (*solitary, alone*) одино́кий; **feel ~** испы́тывать (*impf.*) одино́чество; чу́вствовать (*impf.*) себя́ одино́ким; **lead a ~ existence** вести́ (*det.*) одино́кий о́браз жи́зни; жить (*impf.*) уединённо/за́мкнуто. **2.** (*isolated*) уединённый.

loner ['ləʊnə(r)] *n.* (*coll.*) бирю́к, одино́чка (*c.g.*).

lonesome ['ləʊnsəm] *adj.* одино́кий; **on one's ~** (*coll.*) оди́н-одинёшенек; **feel ~** тоскова́ть (*impf.*); томи́ться (*impf.*) одино́чеством.

long[1] [lɒŋ] *n.* **1.** (*a ~ time*): **I shan't be away for ~** я уезжа́ю ненадо́лго; я ско́ро верну́сь; **it won't take ~** э́то не займёт мно́го вре́мени; **will you take ~ over it?** вы ско́ро ко́нчите?; **he did not take ~ to answer** он не заме́длил отве́тить; **it is ~ since he was here** он давно́ здесь не́ был; **at the ~est** са́мое бо́льшее. **2.: the ~ and the short of it is that ...** сло́вом, де́ло в том, что… **3.** (~ *syllable*) до́лгий слог.

adj. **1.** (*of space, measurement*) дли́нный; **the table is 2 metres ~** э́тот стол длино́й в 2 ме́тра (*or* име́ет 2 ме́тра длины́); **how ~ is this river?** какова́ длина́ э́той реки́?; **~ form** (*of Russian adj.*) по́лная фо́рма; **~ jump** прыжо́к в длину́; **~ measure** ме́ра длины́; **a ~ mile** до́брая ми́ля; **in the ~ run** в коне́чном ито́ге/счёте; с тече́нием вре́мени; **~ in the tooth** (*fig.*) не пе́рвой мо́лодости; **~ trousers** брю́к|и (*pl., g.* —); **on the ~ wave** на дли́нной волне́. **2.** (*of distance*) да́льний; **a ~ journey** да́льний/до́лгий путь; **a ~ way off** далеко́; **from a ~ way off** издалека́. **3.** (*of time*) до́лгий; **a ~ life** до́лгая жизнь; **a ~ memory** хоро́шая па́мять; **my holiday is 2 weeks ~** мой о́тпуск дли́тся две неде́ли; я име́ю две неде́ли о́тпуска (*or* двухнеде́льный о́тпуск); **~ service** дли́тельная/до́лгая слу́жба; **a quarrel of ~ standing** да́вняя/многоле́тняя ссо́ра; **for a ~ time** до́лго, давно́; надо́лго; **a ~ time ago** мно́го вре́мени тому́ наза́д; давны́м-давно́; **a ~ time before the war** задо́лго до войны́; **it will be a ~ time before we meet again** мы встре́тимся сно́ва ещё не ско́ро; **I had not seen him for many a ~ day** я его́ це́лую ве́чность не ви́дел. **4.** (*prolonged*) дли́тельный; **a ~ illness** затяжна́я боле́знь.

adv. **1.** (*a ~ time*): **I shan't be ~** я ско́ро верну́сь; я не задержу́сь; **he is not ~ for this world** он не жиле́ц на э́том све́те; **she is ~ since dead** она́ давно́ умерла́; **it was ~ past midnight** бы́ло далеко́ за́ полночь; **~ after** (*prep.*) до́лгое вре́мя по́сле+*g.*; **~ before** (*prep.*) задо́лго до+*g.*; **~ after(wards)** до́лгое вре́мя спустя́; гора́здо по́зже/поздне́е; **~ before** (*adv.*) давно́, гора́здо ра́ньше; **these events are ~ past** всё э́то случи́лось давно́; **~ ago** (давны́м-)давно́; **before ~** вско́ре, ско́ро. **2.** (*for a ~ time*): **I have ~ thought so** я давно́ так ду́маю; **how ~ have you been here?** вы здесь давно́?; вы давно́ (сюда́) пришли́/прие́хали?; **~ live the Queen!** да здра́вствует короле́ва! **3.** (*throughout*): **all day ~** це́лый день; день-деньско́й; **all night ~** всю ночь напролёт. **4.: as ~ as I live** пока́ я жив; **stay as ~ as you like** остава́йтесь, ско́лько хоти́те; **as ~ as you don't mind** е́сли вам всё равно́; е́сли вы не возража́ете. **5.: so ~!** пока́! (*coll.*). **6.: no ~er** бо́льше не; **I can't wait much ~er** мно́го до́льше ждать я не могу́.

cpds. **~-awaited** *adj.* долгожда́нный; **~boat** *n.* барка́с; **~bow** *n.* большо́й лук; **~-delayed** *adj.* запозда́лый; **~-distance** *adj.*: **~-distance call** междугоро́дный/междунаро́дный вы́зов; **~-distance train** по́езд да́льнего сле́дования; **~-distance runner** ста́йер, бегу́н на дли́нные диста́нции; **~-drawn-out** *adj.* (*of conversation*) затяну́вшийся; (*of story*) растя́нутый; (*of illness*) затяжно́й; **~-haired** *adj.* длинноволо́сый; **~hand** *n.* обы́чное письмо́ (от руки́); **~-headed** *adj.* (*fig.*) проница́тельный; **~-legged** *adj.* длинноно́гий; **~-lived** *adj.* долгове́чный; **~-lost** *adj.* давно́ поте́рянный/утра́ченный; **~-playing** *adj.* долгоигра́ющий; **~-range** *adj.* (*of gun*) дальнобо́йный; (*of aircraft*) да́льнего де́йствия; (*of forecast, policy etc.*) долгосро́чный; **~shoreman** *n.* порто́вый гру́зчик; **~-sighted** *adj.* дальнозо́ркий; (*fig.*) дальнови́дный; **~-standing** *adj.* стари́нный, долголе́тний; **a ~-standing promise** да́внее обеща́ние; **~-suffering** *n.* долготерпе́ние; *adj.* многострада́льный, долготерпели́вый; **~-term** *adj.* долгосро́чный; (*of plans etc.*) перспекти́вный; **~-wave** *adj.* длинново́лновый; **~-winded** *adj.* (*prolix*) многоречи́вый, многосло́вный.

long² [lɒŋ] *v.i.*: **~ for sth.** жа́ждать (*impf.*) чего́-н.; **we are ~ing for your return** мы ждём не дождёмся ва́шего возвраще́ния; **I ~ed for a drink** я ужа́сно хоте́л пить; я томи́лся жа́ждой; **~ for s.o.** тоскова́ть (*impf.*) по кому́-н.; скуча́ть (*impf.*) по кому́-н.; **~ to do sth.** мечта́ть (*impf.*) что-то де́лать; **he ~ed to get away from town** ему́ не терпе́лось уе́хать из го́рода.

longevity [lɒn'dʒevɪtɪ] *n.* (*of pers.*) долголе́тие; (*of thg.*) долгове́чность.

longing ['lɒŋɪŋ] *n.* жела́ние, жа́жда (*чего*); тоска́ (*по чему*).

adj. тоску́ющий; **he looked at the books with ~ eyes** он смотре́л на кни́ги с вожделе́нием.

longish ['lɒŋɪʃ] *adj.* (*of size*) длиннова́тый; (*of duration*) долгова́тый.

longitude ['lɒŋgɪˌtju:d, 'lɒndʒ-] *n.* долгота́; **at 20° ~ West** на двадца́том гра́дусе за́падной долготы́.

longitudinal [ˌlɒŋgɪ'tju:dɪn(ə)l, ˌlɒndʒ-] *adj.* (*of longitude*) долго́тный; (*lengthwise*) продо́льный.

longw|ays ['lɒŋweɪz], **-ise** ['lɒŋwaɪz] *adv.* в длину́.

loo [lu:] *n.* (*lavatory*) сорти́р (*coll.*); **I need (to use) the ~** мне на́до ко́е-куда́ сбе́гать.

loofah ['lu:fə] *n.* люфа́, лю́ффа.

look [lʊk] *n.* **1.** (*glance*) взгляд; **he gave me a ~** он бро́сил взгляд (*or* взгляну́л) на меня́; **there were angry ~s from the crowd** толпа́ гляде́ла с негодова́нием; **give s.o. a black ~** зло́бно посмотре́ть/взгляну́ть (*pf.*) на кого́-н.; **may I have, take a ~ at your paper?** позво́льте просмотре́ть ва́шу газе́ту. **2.: have, take a ~ at** (*examine*) осм|а́тривать, -отре́ть; рассм|а́тривать, -отре́ть; **the doctor had a good ~ at his throat** до́ктор внима́тельно посмотре́л его́ го́рло; (*fig.*): **we must take a long ~ at these terms** мы должны́ разобра́ться в поста́вленных усло́виях тща́тельно (*or* как сле́дует). **3.: have a ~ for** (*search for*) иска́ть, по-. **4.** (*expression*) выраже́ние; **there was a ~ of horror on his face** его́ лицо́ выража́ло у́жас; **a ~ of pleasure came over her features** выраже́ние удово́льствия разлило́сь по её лицу́. **5.** (*appearance*) вид; **he had an odd ~ about him** у него́ был стра́нный вид; **this house has a homely ~** у э́того до́ма ую́тный вид; **I don't like the ~ of things** пло́хо де́ло!; **he has given the shop a new ~** он совсе́м преобрази́л магази́н; **this is the new ~ in evening wear** вот но́вый силуэ́т вече́рних туале́тов; (*pl., personal appearance*) нару́жность, вне́шность; **~s don't count** по вне́шности не су́дят; не в красоте́ де́ло; **she has good ~s** она́ хороша́ собо́й; **lose one's (good) ~s** дурне́ть, по-.

v.t. **1.** (*inspect, scrutinize*): **~ s.o. in the face, eye** смотре́ть, по- в глаза́ кому́-н.; **don't ~ a gift horse in the mouth** дарёному коню́ зу́бы не смо́трят; **~ s.o. up and down** сме́рить (*pf.*) кого́-н. глаза́ми/взгля́дом. **2.** (*express with eyes*): **she ~ed her thanks** она́ взгля́дом вы́разила благода́рность; **she ~ed daggers at him** она́ зло́бно (*or* со зло́стью) посмотре́ла на него́. **3.** (*have the appearance of*; *see also v.i.* **3.**) вы́глядеть (*impf.*) +*i.*: **he ~s an old man** он вы́глядит старико́м; **he made me ~ a fool** он поста́вил меня́ в дура́цкое положе́ние; **he ~s his age** ему́ вполне́ дашь его́ го́ды; **she is thirty, but she does not ~ it** ей три́дцать, но ей сто́лько не дашь; **he is not ~ing himself** на нём лица́ нет; **you are ~ing yourself again** тепе́рь вы сно́ва ста́ли похо́жи на себя́; **she ~s her best in blue** ей си́нее бо́льше всего́ к лицу́; **I ~ my best after breakfast** я лу́чше всего́ вы́гляжу по́сле за́втрака. **4.** (*with ind. questions*: *observe*) смотре́ть, по-; **~ who's here!** кого́ я ви́жу!; **now ~ what you've done!** смотри́те, что вы наде́лали!; **~ where you're going!** смотри́те, куда́ идёте!

v.i. **1.** (*use one's eyes*; *pay attention*) смотре́ть, по-; **he ~ed out of the window to see if she was coming** он посмотре́л в окно́, не идёт ли она́; **~ over there!** посмотри́те/взгляни́те туда́!; **~ before you leap** ≃ семь раз приме́рь, оди́н отре́жь; не зна́я бро́ду, не су́йся в во́ду; **~ here!** послу́шайте; **~ alive, sharp!** живе́й!; потора́пливайтесь!; смотри́ в о́ба!; не зева́йте!; (*fig., consider*) вду́маться (*impf.*); **when one ~s more closely** при ближа́йшем рассмотре́нии; (*search*) иска́ть, по-. **2.** (*face*) выходи́ть (*impf.*); **the windows ~ on to the garden (street)** о́кна выхо́дят в сад (на у́лицу). **3.** (*appear*; *see also v.i.* **3.**) вы́глядеть (*impf.*) +*i.*; **she is ~ing well** она́ хорошо́ вы́глядит; **everybody ~ed tired** у всех был уста́лый вид; **that ~s tasty** у э́того блю́да аппети́тный вид; **that hat ~s well on you** вам идёт (*or* к лицу́) э́та шля́па; **you would ~ well if he were to refuse** (*iron.*) хорошо́ же вы бу́дете вы́глядеть, е́сли он отка́жется; хоте́л бы я на вас посмотре́ть, е́сли он отка́жется; **it would not ~ well to refuse** отказа́ться бы́ло бы неудо́бно/нело́вко; **he made me ~ small** он меня́ уни́зил; **things ~ black** пло́хо де́ло; **the situation ~s promising** ситуа́ция как бу́дто благоприя́тная/обнадёживающая; **that ~s suspicious** э́то подозри́тельно; **it ~s as if …** ка́жется (, что)…; похо́же на то, что…; **~ like** (*resemble*) вы́глядеть (*impf.*) +*i.*; походи́ть (*impf.*) на+*a.*; **the old man ~s like a tramp** у старика́ вид бродя́ги; **he ~s like his father** он похо́ж на отца́; **she ~s like nothing on earth** она́ Бог зна́ет на что похо́жа; (*give expectation of*): **it ~s like rain** собира́ется (*or* похо́же, что бу́дет) дождь; де́ло (идёт) к дождю́; **it ~s like a fine day** день обеща́ет быть хоро́шим; **it ~s like war** па́хнет войно́й; **'Shall we be late?' — 'It ~s like it'** «Мы опа́здываем?» — «Похо́же (, что так)» (*or* «Весьма́ вероя́тно»); **he ~s like winning** он, ка́жется, вы́йдет победи́телем; похо́же, что он вы́играет.

with preps.: **~ about one** огля́д|ываться, -е́ться; **he ~ed about the room** он обвёл глаза́ми ко́мнату; **~ after** (*follow with eye*) следи́ть (*impf.*) глаза́ми за+*i.*; (*care for*) смотре́ть (*impf.*) за+*i.*; присма́тривать (*impf.*) за+*i.*; уха́живать (*impf.*) за+*i.*; **she has four children to ~ after** на её попече́нии че́тверо дете́й; **he needs ~ing after** он нужда́ется в ухо́де; **he seems well ~ed after** у него́ ухо́женный вид; **he had to ~ after himself** ему́ приходи́лось всё де́лать самому́; **I can ~ after myself** я не нужда́юсь в посторо́нней по́мощи; **~ after yourself!** (*in leave-taking*) береги́те себя́!; (*keep safe*) храни́ть (*impf.*); **I gave my valuables to the bank to ~ after** я сдал свои́ це́нности в банк на хране́ние; (*be responsible for*) вести́ (*det.*); занима́ться (*impf.*) +*i.*; **a lawyer is ~ing after my affairs** мои́ми дела́ми ве́дает юри́ст; **don't worry, I'll ~ after the bill** не беспоко́йтесь, я займу́сь счётом; **~ at** (*direct gaze on*) смотре́ть, по- на+*a.*; **he was ~ing at a book** он смотре́л на кни́гу; **just ~ at the time!** поду́майте, как по́здно!; **it's not worth ~ing at** здесь (и) смотре́ть не́ на что; **he's not much to ~ at** вне́шность у него́ не сли́шком внуши́тельная; вне́шне он ничего́ осо́бенного собо́й не представля́ет; **to ~ at him, you would think …** су́дя по его́ ви́ду, мо́жно поду́мать, что…; **he won't even ~ at milk** он и смотре́ть не хо́чет на молоко́; (*inspect, examine*) смотре́ть, по- на+*a.*; осм|а́тривать, -отре́ть; **the doctor ~ed at the patient** врач осмотре́л больно́го; **I must get my car ~ed at** на́до, что́бы посмотре́ли/прове́рили мою́ маши́ну; **the customs men ~ed at our luggage** тамо́женники осмотре́ли наш бага́ж; (*fig., consider*) вду́маться (*impf.*) в+*a.*; обра|ща́ть, -ти́ть внима́ние на+*a.*, **we must ~ at the matter carefully** на́до как сле́дует поду́мать об э́том де́ле (*or* разобра́ться в э́том вопро́се); **I ~ed down the street** я оки́нул взгля́дом у́лицу; **he ~ed down the page** он пробежа́л страни́цу глаза́ми; **~ for** (*seek*) иска́ть, по-; **he is ~ing for his wife** он и́щет свою́ жену́; **he is ~ing for a wife** он и́щет себе́ жену́; **he is ~ing for a job** он и́щет ме́ста; **he is ~ing for trouble** он рвётся в бой; он ле́зет на рожо́н; (*hope for, expect*) наде́яться (*impf.*) на+*a.*; ожида́ть (*impf.*) +*g.*; **I ~ed for better things from him** я ожида́л от него́ лу́чшего; **we obtained the ~ed-for result** мы доби́лись жела́емого результа́та; **~ in the mirror** смотре́ться, по- в зе́ркало; **~ into** (*lit.*) смотре́ть, по- в+*a.*; (*investigate, examine*) иссле́довать (*impf.*); рассм|а́тривать, -отре́ть; **it is something that needs ~ing at** с э́тим на́до разобра́ться; **I shall ~ into the matter** я займу́сь э́тим вопро́сом; **~ on** (*regard*) счита́ть (*impf.*); **I ~ on him as my son** я счита́ю его́ свои́м сы́ном; он мне всё равно́ что сын; **he ~ed on the remark as an insult** он восприня́л замеча́ние как оскорбле́ние; **he ~s on me with contempt** он меня́ презира́ет; **~ on the bright side** смотре́ть (*impf.*) оптимисти́чески; **~ on to** (*face*) *see* *v.i.* **2.**; **he ~ed out of the window** он посмотре́л в окно́; **he ~ed over the wall** он посмотре́л че́рез стену́; **~ over one's shoulder** огля́|дываться, -ну́ться; **~ over s.o.'s shoulder** смотре́ть, по- кому́-н. че́рез плечо́; **the teacher was ~ing over our homework** учи́тель просма́тривал на́шу дома́шнюю рабо́ту; **he left us to ~ over the house** он оста́вил нас одни́х осма́тривать дом; **~ round** (*inspect*) осм|а́тривать, -отре́ть; **he ~ed through the window** он посмотре́л в окно́; **he ~ed right through** (*ignored*) **me** он смотре́л ми́мо меня́; **they ~ed through** (*examined*) **our papers** они́ просмотре́ли на́ши бума́ги; **he quickly ~ed through the newspaper** он бы́стро пробежа́л глаза́ми газе́ту; **~ to** (*turn to*) обра|ща́ться, -ти́ться к+*d.*; **we ~ed to him for help** мы рассчи́тывали на его́ по́мощь; (*heed*): **~ to one's laurels** стреми́ться (*impf.*) сохрани́ть своё пе́рвенство; **he should ~ to his manners** ему́ сле́дует обрати́ть внима́ние на свои́ мане́ры; **~ upon** *see* **~ at, on**

with advs.: **~ about, ~ around** *v.i.* осм|а́триваться, -отре́ться; иска́ть (*impf.*) (*что*) повсю́ду; **~ ahead** *v.i.* (*lit., fig.*) смотре́ть (*impf.*) вперёд; **~ around** *see* **~ about, ~ round; ~ aside** *v.i.* смотре́ть (*impf.*) в сто́рону; **~ away** *v.i.* отв|ора́чиваться, -ерну́ться; **~ back** *v.i.* (*lit., fig.*) огл|я́дываться, -яну́ться; **once started, there was no ~ing back** раз уж мы на́чали, отступа́ть бы́ло по́здно; **I will ~ back in an hour's time** я ещё раз загляну́ че́рез час; **~ back on** вспомина́ть (*impf.*); припомина́ть (*impf.*); **~ behind** *v.i.* смотре́ть, по- наза́д; **~ down** *v.i.* (*lower one's gaze*) опус|ка́ть, -ти́ть глаза́; **~ down on** смотре́ть (*impf.*) свысока́ на+*a.*; презира́ть (*impf.*); **~ forward** смотре́ть (*impf.*) вперёд; **~ forward to** предвкуша́ть (*impf.*); ждать (*impf.*) +*g.* с нетерпе́нием; **I ~ forward to meeting you** жду с нетерпе́нием, когда́ уви́жусь с ва́ми; **I am so ~ing forward to it** я так жду э́того; **I ~ forward to his arrival** я не дожду́сь его́ прие́зда; **~ in** *v.i.*: **~ in** (*call*) **on s.o.** загля́|дывать, -ну́ть (*or* забе|га́ть, -жа́ть) к кому́-н.; **~ on** *v.i.* наблюда́ть, смотре́ть (*both impf.*); **~ out** *v.t.* (*select*): **I must ~ out some old dresses** мне на́до отобра́ть каки́е-то ста́рые пла́тья; **he ~ed out some examples** он подыска́л не́сколько приме́ров; *v.i.* (*from a window*) смотре́ть, по- в окно́; (*be careful*) быть настороже́; **~ out!** осторо́жно!; **if you don't ~ out you'll lose your ticket** смотри́те, как бы не потеря́ть биле́т!; (*keep one's eyes open*): **she stood at the door ~ing out for the postman** она́ стоя́ла в дверя́х, высма́тривая почтальо́на; **we are ~ing out for a house** мы присма́триваем дом; **~ over** *v.t.* (*scrutinize*) просм|а́тривать, -отре́ть; **~ round, ~ around** *v.i.* (*turn one's head*) огля́|дываться, -ну́ться; озира́ться (*impf.*); (*make an inspection*) осм|а́триваться, -отре́ться; **~ round for** (*seek*) поды́скивать (*impf.*); **~ up** *v.t.* (*visit*) наве|ща́ть, -сти́ть; (**~** *for, seek information on*) оты́ск|ивать, -а́ть; и|ска́ть, разы-; **~ up trains** посмотре́ть (*pf.*) расписа́ние; *v.i.* (*raise one's eyes*) подн|има́ть, -я́ть глаза́ (**at s.o.:** на кого́-н.); (*improve*) ул|учша́ться, -у́чшиться; **things are ~ing up** дела́ иду́т на попра́вку; **~ up to** (*respect*) уважа́ть (*impf.*); **he is ~ed up to by everybody** он по́льзуется всео́бщим уваже́нием; все его́ уважа́ют.

cpds. **~-alike** *n.* двойни́к; **a Prince Charles ~-alike** вы́литый принц Чарлз; **~-in** *n.*: **I didn't get a ~-in** меня́ не подпусти́ли к пирогу́; **~-out** *n.* (*watchman*) наблюда́тель (*m.*); (*post*) наблюда́тельный пункт; (*watch*): **be on the ~-out** быть начеку́ (*or* настороже́ *or* на стра́же); **be on the ~-out for** (*e.g. a house*) присма́тривать (*impf.*) себе́; **be on the ~-out for the enemy** подстерега́ть (*impf.*) неприя́теля; (*prospect*): **it's a poor ~-out for us** у нас перспекти́ва нева́жная; (*concern*): **that's his ~-out** э́то его́ де́ло/забо́та; **~-see** *n.* (*coll.*) бе́глый просмо́тр, бы́стрый взгляд.

looker-on [ˈlʊkə(r)] *n.* зри́тель (*m.*), наблюда́тель (*m.*).

looking-glass [ˈlʊkɪŋˌglɑːs] *n.* зе́ркало; **Alice through the L~** «Али́са в зазерка́лье».

loom[1] [luːm] *n.* тка́цкий стано́к.

loom[2] [luːm] *v.i.* **1.** (*appear indistinctly*; *also* **~ up**) нея́сно вырисо́вываться (*impf.*); мая́чить (*impf.*); **a black shape ~ed in the distance** что-то черне́ло вдали́. **2.** (*impend*) нав|иса́ть, -и́снуть; **~ large** (*threateningly*) прин|има́ть, -я́ть угрожа́ющие разме́ры; (*prominently*): **the risk ~ed large in his mind** мысль об опа́сности его́ пресле́довала неотсту́пно.

loon [luːn] *n.* (*bird*) гага́ра.

loon(y) [ˈluːnɪ] *n.* & *adj.* рехну́вшийся; чо́кнутый (*coll.*).

cpd. **~-bin** *n.* (*sl.*) психбольни́ца

loop [luːp] *n.* **1.** петля́. **2.** (*rail.*; *also* **~-line**) ве́тка. **3.** (*aeron.*) мёртвая петля́. **4.** (*contraceptive*) пружи́нка, петля́.

v.t. **1.** (*form into* ~) де́лать, с- пе́тлю из+*g.* **2.** (*fasten with* ~) закреп|ля́ть, -и́ть петлёй. **3.** ~ **the** ~ (*aeron.*) де́лать, с- мёртвую пе́тлю.

loophole ['lu:phəʊl] *n.* (*in wall*) бойни́ца; (*fig.*) лазе́йка.

loopy ['lu:pɪ] *adj.* рехну́вшийся (*coll.*).

loose [lu:s] *n.*: **on the** ~ в загу́ле; на свобо́де; на во́ле.

adj. **1.** (*free, unconfined, unrestrained*) свобо́дный; **break** ~ вы́рваться (*pf.*) на свобо́ду; (*of a dog*) сорва́ться с цепи́; **let** ~ (*e.g. a dog*) спус|ка́ть, -ти́ть с цепи́; (*e.g. lion, maniac*) выпуска́ть, вы́пустить; ~ **box** денни́к. **2.** (*not fastened or held together*): ~ **papers** отде́льные листы́; ~ **cover** (*on armchair etc.*) чехо́л; **he carries his change** ~ **in his pocket** ме́лочь у него́ пря́мо в карма́не (без кошелька́); **she wears her hair** ~ она́ хо́дит с распу́щенными волоса́ми; (*not packed*) без упако́вки; (*of dry goods*) развесно́й. **3.** (*not secure or firm*): **a** ~ **end** (*of rope*) свобо́дный коне́ц; **at a** ~ **end** (*fig.*) без де́ла; **he was at a** ~ **end** он не знал за что приня́ться; **I have a** ~ **tooth** у меня́ зуб шата́ется; **his tooth came** ~ у него́ зуб расшата́лся; **the nut is** ~ га́йка разболта́лась; **the button is** ~ пу́говица болта́ется; **the screw came, worked** ~ винт развинти́лся; **he has a screw** ~ (*sl.*) у него́ ви́нтика не хвата́ет; **the string is** ~ верёвка сла́бо завя́зана; **the string came** ~ верёвка развяза́лась; **hang** ~ болта́ться (*impf.*). **4.** (*slack*) сла́бо натя́нутый; **with a** ~ **rein** с отпу́щенными вожжа́ми; **ride s.o. with a** ~ **rein** (*fig.*) обраща́ться (*impf.*) с кем-н. снисходи́тельно; дава́ть (*impf.*) кому́-н. во́лю; распуска́ть (*impf.*) кого́-н.; ~ **bowels** поно́с; **are your bowels** ~? у вас расстро́йство (желу́дка)?; **he has a** ~ **tongue** он сли́шком болтли́в; ~ **clothes** широ́кая/просто́рная оде́жда; **a** ~ **collar** свобо́дный во́рот; (*not close-knit*): **a** ~ **build, frame** нескла́дная фигу́ра. **5.** (*not compact or dense*): ~ **soil** ры́хлая по́чва; ~ **weave** ре́дкая ткань; ~ **order** (*mil.*) расчленённый строй. **6.** (*imprecise*): **a** ~ **statement** неопределённое/расплы́вчатое заявле́ние; **a** ~ **translation** приблизи́тельный/во́льный перево́д; **a** ~ **style** небре́жный стиль; ~ **thinking** нечёткость мы́сли. **7.** (*morally lax*) распу́щенный; ~ **living** распу́тство; распу́тный о́браз жи́зни; **a** ~ **woman** распу́тная же́нщина.

v.t. (*release*) освобо|жда́ть, -ди́ть; высвобожда́ть, вы́свободить; отпус|ка́ть, -ти́ть; (*undo*) развя́з|ывать, -а́ть; (*relax*) распус|ка́ть, -ти́ть.

cpds. ~**fitting** *adj.* широ́кий, просто́рный; ~**-leaf** *adj.* со вкладны́ми листка́ми; ~**-leaf binder** скоросшива́тель (*m.*); ~**-limbed** *adj.* ги́бкий; ~**-tongued** *adj.* болтли́вый.

loosen ['lu:s(ə)n] *v.t.* (*tongue*) развя́з|ывать, -а́ть; (*screw*) отви́н|чивать, -ти́ть; (*by shaking or pulling*) расша́т|ывать, -а́ть; (*soil*) разрыхл|я́ть, -и́ть; (*tie, rope, belt etc.*) осл|абля́ть, -а́бить; **the wine** ~**ed his tongue** вино́ развяза́ло ему́ язы́к; ~ **a tooth** расшата́ть (*pf.*) зуб; ~ **one's grip** осла́бить (*pf.*) хва́тку; ~ **discipline** осла́бить дисципли́ну; ~ **one's hold on sth.** выпуска́ть, вы́пустить что-н. из рук; (*bowels*) просл|абля́ть, -а́бить.

looseness ['lu:snɪs] *n.* (*slackness*) сла́бость; (*of morals*) распу́щенность; (*of bowels*) поно́с.

loosestrife ['lu:sstraɪf] *n.* верба́йник.

loot [lu:t] *n.* добы́ча, награ́бленное добро́.

v.t. гра́бить, раз-.

v.i. ун|оси́ть, -ести́ добы́чу.

looter ['lu:tə(r)] *n.* мародёр, граби́тель (*m.*).

looting ['lu:tɪŋ] *n.* мародёрство, грабёж.

lop [lɒp] *v.t.* (*also* ~ **off**) руби́ть (*impf*); отруб|а́ть, -и́ть.

lope [ləʊp] *v.i.* бежа́ть (*det.*) вприпры́жку.

lop-eared ['lɒp,ɪəd] *adj.* вислоу́хий.

lop-sided [lɒp'saɪdɪd] *adj.* кривобо́кий; (*fig.*) неравноме́рный, односторо́нний; **your tie has got** ~ у вас га́лстук на́бок съе́хал.

loquacious [lɒ'kweɪʃəs] *adj.* словоохо́тливый, болтли́вый.

loquaci|ousness [lɒ'kweɪʃəsnɪs], **-ty** [lɒ'kwæsɪtɪ] *n.* словоохо́тливость, болтли́вость.

lord [lɔ:d] *n.* **1.** (*ruler; also fig.*) власти́тель (*m.*), властели́н; ~**s of creation** (*mankind*) род челове́ческий; (*joc., men*) си́льный пол; (*king*) госуда́рь (*m.*); (*feudal* ~) сеньо́р; ~ **of the manor** владе́лец поме́стья; (*magnate*) магна́т; ~ **and master** (*joc., husband*) супру́г и повели́тель (*m.*); (*senior or superior*) хозя́ин; **live like a** ~ жить (*impf.*) припева́ючи; **drunk as a** ~ пьян в сте́льку/как сапо́жник. **2.** (*nobleman*) лорд; **House of L~s** пала́та ло́рдов; ~**s temporal and spiritual** «све́тские» и «духо́вные» ло́рды; **My** ~! мило́рд! **3.** (*God*) Госпо́дь; **Our L~** (*Christ*) Госпо́дь; **L~ have mercy!** Го́споди, поми́луй!; **(the) L~ only knows** Бог (его́) зна́ет; **in the year of our L~ ...** в ...ом году́ от рождества́ Христо́ва; **L~'s day** воскре́сный день; **L~'s Prayer** моли́тва госпо́дня, О́тче наш; **L~'s Supper** Евхари́стия.

v.t.: ~ **it over s.o.** кома́ндовать (*impf.*) кем-н.; помыка́ть (*impf.*) кем-н.

lordly ['lɔ:dlɪ] *adj.* (*magnificent*) пы́шный; (*haughty*) надме́нный.

lordship ['lɔ:dʃɪp] *n.* **1.** (*rule, authority*) власть, владе́ние. **2.: Your L~** ва́ша све́тлость/ми́лость.

lore [lɔ:(r)] *n.* (специа́льные) зна́ния (*nt. pl.*); **bird** ~ зна́ния о пти́цах; (*traditions*) преда́ния (*nt. pl.*).

lorgnette [lɔ:'njet] *n.* лорне́т.

Lorraine [lɒ'reɪn] *n.* Лотари́нгия.

lorry ['lɒrɪ] *n.* грузови́к.

Los Angeles [lɒs 'ændʒɪ,li:z] *n.* Лос-А́нджелес.

los|e [lu:z] *v.t.* **1.** теря́ть, по-; утра́|чивать, -тить; лиш|а́ться, -и́ться +*g.*; **give sth. up for** ~**t** счита́ть (*impf.*) что-н. (безвозвра́тно) пропа́вшим; **the goods were** ~**t in transit** това́ры пропа́ли в пути́; **I** ~**t count of his mistakes** я потеря́л счёт его́ оши́бкам; **I am beginning to** ~**e faith in him** ~ я начина́ю теря́ть ве́ру в него́; **he** ~**t his head** (*fig.*) он потеря́л го́лову; **Charles I** ~**t his head** Карл I был обезгла́влен; ~**e heart** па́|дать, -сть ду́хом; **the plane was** ~**ing height** самолёт теря́л высоту́; **he** ~**t a leg** он потеря́л но́гу, он лиши́лся ноги́; ~**e patience** выходи́ть, вы́йти из терпе́ния; ~**e one's place** (*job*) быть уво́ленным; (*in queue*) теря́ть, по- о́чередь; (*while reading*) сби́ться (*pf.*), потеря́ть (*pf.*) ме́сто; ~**e one's reason** лиш|а́ться, -и́ться рассу́дка; сходи́ть, сойти́ с ума́; ~**e** (*forfeit*) **one's rights** утра́|чивать, -тить свои́ права́; ~**e sight of** (*lit.*) упус|ка́ть, -ти́ть и́з виду; (*fig.*) не уч|и́тывать, -е́сть; заб|ыва́ть, -ы́ть; ~**e one's sight** осле́пнуть (*pf.*); потеря́ть (*pf.*) зре́ние; ~**e one's temper** рассерди́ться (*pf.*); **have you** ~**t your tongue?** вы что — язы́к проглоти́ли?; **I** ~**t touch with him** я потеря́л связь с ним; **we** ~**t track of the time** мы утра́тили вся́кое представле́ние о вре́мени; **he** ~**t the use of his legs** у него́ отняли́сь но́ги; **he** ~**t his voice** он потеря́л/сорва́л го́лос; ~**e one's way** заблуди́ться (*pf.*); **I am trying to** ~**e weight** я стара́юсь похуде́ть; **a** ~**t art** утра́ченное иску́сство; **a** ~**t soul** (*fig.*) пропа́щий челове́к; **I am** ~**t without her** без неё я как без рук; **he was** ~**t to all sense of shame** он утра́тил вся́кий стыд. **2.** (~**e** *by death*): ~**e an old friend** лиши́ться (*pf.*) ста́рого дру́га; **he** ~**t his wife** у него́ умерла́ жена́; **he** ~**t his son in the war** у него́ на войне́ поги́б сын; **she** ~**t the baby** (*by miscarriage*) у неё был вы́кидыш; **the enemy** ~**t 1,000 men** неприя́тель потеря́л ты́сячу челове́к; **be** ~**t** (*perish, die*) ги́бнуть (*impf.*); пог|иба́ть, -и́бнуть; **the ship was** ~**t with all hands** су́дно со всем экипа́жем поги́бло. **3.: be, get** ~**t** (~*e one's way*) заблуди́ться (*pf.*); **get** ~**t!** исче́зни!, кати́сь! (*coll.*); (*fig.*): ~**t in thought** заду́мавшись; ~**e o.s. in sth.** погру|жа́ться, -зи́ться во что́-н. **4.** (*cease to see, understand etc.*): **I've** ~**t you; you've** ~**t me** (*coll., I can't follow you*) я потеря́л нить (ва́шей мы́сли); **be** ~**t** (*disappear*) исч|еза́ть, -е́знуть; проп|ада́ть, -а́сть; **the train was** ~**t to sight** по́езд скры́лся (и́з виду); **the church was** ~**t in the fog** це́рковь скры́лась в тума́не; **what he said was** ~**t in the noise** его́ слова́ потону́ли в шу́ме. **5.** (*fail to use; waste*): ~**e an opportunity** упус|ка́ть, -ти́ть возмо́жность; **he** ~**t no opportunity** он по́льзовался вся́кой возмо́жностью; ~**e time** теря́ть, по- вре́мя; **he** ~**t no time in getting away** он тут же убежа́л, не теря́я вре́мени; **there is not a moment to be** ~**t** нельзя́ теря́ть ни мину́ты (вре́мени); вре́мя не те́рпит; **make up for** ~**t time** наве́рст|ывать, -а́ть упу́щенное вре́мя; **the joke was** ~**t on him** шу́тка не дошла́ до него́. **6.** (*in contest, sport,* *gambling*) проигр|ывать, -áть; **he ~t the argument** егó побили в спóре; **the motion was ~t** предложéние не прошлó; **they ~t the match** они проигрáли; **I ~t my bet** я проигрáл пари. **7.** (*of a clock*) отст|авáть, -áть на+*a.*; **my watch ~es 5 minutes a day** мои часы отстают на 5 минут в день.

v.i. **1.** проигр|ывать, -áть; терять, по-; **fight a ~ing battle** вести (*det.*) безнадёжную борьбу; **they ~t by 3 points** они недобрали трёх очкóв; **he ~t on the deal** в этой сдéлке он остáлся в прóигрыше; **~e out** (*coll.*) потерпéть (*pf.*) неудáчу. **2.** (*of a clock*): **my watch is ~ing** мои часы отстают.

loser ['lu:zə(r)] *n.* (*at a game*) проигрáвший; (*pers. who habitually fails*) неудáчник; **he is a good (bad) ~** он (не) умéет достóйно проигрывать; **come off (*or* be) a ~** остáться (*pf.*) в прóигрыше.

losings ['lu:zɪŋz] *n.* прóигрыш.

loss [lɒs] *n.* **1.** потéря; **~ of sight** потéря зрéния; **~ of heat** теплопотéря; **~ of life** потéри убитыми; человéческие жéртвы (*f. pl.*); **suffer heavy ~es** понести (*pf.*) большие потéри. **2.** (*detriment*) утрáта; **his death was a great ~** егó смерть былá большóй утрáтой; **his resignation is no great ~** егó отстáвка — небольшáя потéря; **it's your ~, not mine** это вáша бедá, не моя. **3.** (*monetary*) убыток; **cover a ~** покр|ывáть, -ыть убыток; **incur ~es** терпéть, по- убытки; **meet a ~** нести (*det.*) убыток; **sell at a ~** прод|авáть, -áть с убытком (*or* в убыток); **dead ~** чистый убыток; (*coll.*, *useless pers. etc.*) пустóе мéсто; **gambling ~es** прóигрыши (*m. pl.*) (в кáртах, на бегáх *и т.п.*). **4.** (*destruction*, *wreck*) гибель. **5.: I am at a ~ to answer** я затрудняюсь ответить; **he was at a ~ what to say** он не нашёлся, что сказáть; **in my presence he was always at a ~** при мне он всегдá терялся.

lot [lɒt] *n.* **1.: decide by ~** реш|áть, -ить жеребьёвкой; **cast ~s** бр|осáть, -óсить жрéбий; **draw ~s** тянуть (*impf.*) жрéбий; (*fig.*, *destiny*) судьбá, учáсть, дóля; **cast in one's ~ with s.o.** связ|ывать, -áть свою судьбу с кем-н.; **it fell to his ~ to go** емý выпал жрéбий (*or* пришлóсь) идти. **2.** (*plot of land*) учáсток; **parking ~** (*US*) стоянка для машин/автомобилей. **3.** (*coll.*, *of persons*) нарóд; **our/your ~** наш/ваш брат; **these children are an extremely dirty ~** эти дéти грязны до невозмóжности. **4.** (*in auction*) пáртия; (*coll.*): **he is a bad ~** он плохóй человéк. **5.: the ~** (*coll.*, *everything*) всё; **that's the ~!** вот и всё! **6. (a ~, ~s:** *a large number*, *amount*) мнóго; мáло ли что; **a ~ of people** мнóго нарóду; мнóгие; мáло ли кто (*+sg. vb.*); **what a ~ of people there were!** скóлько было нарóду!; **I have seen a ~ in my time** на своём векý я мнóгое повидáл; **I don't see a ~ of him nowadays** мы с ним мáло/рéдко видимся ныне; **he has ~s of friends** у негó мнóго друзéй; **~s of times** мáло ли когдá; **there were ~s of apples left** остáлась уйма яблок; **he plays a ~ of football** он мнóго игрáет в футбóл.

adv. **(a ~) 1.** (*often*) чáсто; **we went to the theatre a ~** мы чáсто ходили в теáтр. **2.** (*with comps.: much*) горáздо, сильно; **a ~ worse** горáздо хýже; **a ~ better** кудá лýчше; **the patient became a ~ worse** больнóму стáло намнóго хýже.

loth [ləʊθ] = **lo(a)th**

Lothario [lə'θɑ:rɪəʊ, -'θeərɪəʊ] *n.* (*fig.*) волокита (*m.*), повéса (*m.*), донжуáн.

lotion ['ləʊʃ(ə)n] *n.* примóчка; (*cosmetic*) лосьóн.

lottery ['lɒtərɪ] *n.* лотерéя; **~ ticket** лотерéйный билéт.

lotto ['lɒtəʊ] *n.* лотó (*indecl.*).

lotus ['ləʊtəs] *n.* (*bot.*, *myth.*) лóтос.

cpd. **~-eater** *n.* сибарит.

loud [laʊd] *adj.* грóмкий; (*sonorous*) звучный; (*noisy*) шýмный; (*fig.*): **~ colours** кричáщие/крикливые крáски/цветá.

adv. грóмко; **we laughed ~ and long** мы дóлго и грóмко смеялись; **out ~** вслух.

cpds. **~-hailer** *n.* рýпор; **~-mouthed** *adj.* крикливый; **~speaker** *n.* громкоговоритель (*m.*), динáмик.

loudness ['laʊdnɪs] *n.* грóмкость; звóнкость; (*of colour*) крикливость.

lough [lɒk, lɒx] *n.* óзеро (в Ирлáндии).

Louis ['lu:ɪ] *n.* (*hist.*) Людóвик; **Louis Philippe** Луи Филипп.

lounge [laʊndʒ] *n.* (*in hotel*) фойé (*indecl.*); (*at airport*) зал ожидáния.

v.i. (*sit in relaxed position*) сидéть (*impf.*) развалясь (*or* вразвáлку); (*sit or stand, leaning against sth.*) сидéть/стоять (*impf.*) прислонясь (*к чему*); **~ about** (*idly*) бездéльничать (*impf.*); слоняться (*impf.*); **~ lizard** (*sl.*) свéтский бездéльник; **~ suit** костюм, пиджáчная пáра.

lounger ['laʊndʒə(r)] *n.* шезлóнг.

lour ['laʊə(r)], **lower** ['ləʊə(r)] *v.i.* (*lit.*, *fig.*) насýп|ливаться, -иться; **he ~ed at me** он смотрéл на меня насýпившись; **a ~ing sky** мрáчное нéбо; **a ~ing expression** угрюмое выражéние.

louse [laʊs] *n.* вошь; (*sl.*, *of pers.*) гнида.

v.t. **~ up** (*sl.*) испóртить, испогáнить (*both pf.*).

lousiness ['laʊzɪnɪs] *n.* вшивость; (*fig.*) гнýсность.

lousy ['laʊzɪ] *adj.* **1.** (*infested with lice*) вшивый. **2.** (*sl.*, *disgusting*, *rotten*) паршивый, отвратительный; **he played a ~ trick on me** он мне сдéлал гáдость; он мне подложил свинью; **I feel ~ today** я сегóдня чýвствую себя отвратительно. **3.** (*sl.*): **be ~ with** кишéть (*impf.*) +*i.*; **he is ~ with money** он не знáет, кудá девáть дéньги; у негó дéнег кýры не клюют.

lout [laʊt] *n.* хам.

loutish ['laʊtɪʃ] *adj.* хáмский; неотёсанный.

loutishness ['laʊtɪʃnɪs] *n.* хáмство; неотёсанность.

louv|er, -re ['lu:və(r)] *n.* (*slatted opening*; *also* **~-boards**) жалюзи (*nt. pl. indecl.*); (*skylight*) слуховóе окнó.

lovable ['lʌvəb(ə)l] *adj.* милый, приятный, обаятельный.

lovage ['lʌvɪdʒ] *n.* бороздоплóдник.

love [lʌv] *n.* **1.** любóвь; **mother(ly) ~** материнская любóвь; **he has a ~ of adventure** он большóй любитель приключéний; **feel ~ for, towards s.o.** испытывать (*impf.*) любóвь к комý-н.; **show ~ to s.o.** проявл|ять, -ить любóвь к комý-н.; **for ~ of** из любви к+*d.*; рáди+*g.*; **for the ~ of God** рáди Бóга; **labour of ~** бескорыстный труд; любимое дéло; **he sent you his ~** он просил передáть вам сердéчный привéт; **there is no ~ lost between them** они друг дрýга недолюбливают; **not for ~ or money** ни за что на свéте; **they were playing for ~** они игрáли не на дéньги; **they married for ~** они женились по любви; **be in ~ (with s.o.)** быть влюблённым в когó-н.; **fall in ~ with s.o.** влюб|ляться, -иться в когó-н.; **fall out of love with s.o.** разлюбить (*pf.*) когó-н.; **make ~ to** (*court*) ухáживать (*impf.*) за+*i.*; **make ~** (*have sexual intercourse*) быть близкими; **his ~ was not returned** он любил без взаимности; **unrequited ~** неразделённая любóвь; любóвь без взаимности; **~ affair** ромáн; (*pej.*) любóвная связь; **~ story** ромáн про любóвь; (*in address*): **(my) ~!** (мой) милый!; (моя) милая!; рáдость моя! **2.** (*delightful pers.*, *esp. child*) прéлесть; (*sweetheart*, *mistress*) любимая, милая, возлюбленная; **he has had many ~s** он любил мнóго раз; **an old ~ of mine** моя стáрая (дáвняя) пáссия. **3.** (*zero score*) ноль (*m.*); **~ all** счёт ноль-ноль; **~ game** «сухáя».

v.t. любить (*impf.*); **I ~ the way he smiles** мне ужáсно нрáвится, как он улыбáется; я люблю егó улыбку; **I ~ my work** я люблю мою рабóту; **I ~ walking in the rain** я обожáю гулять под дождём; **he ~s finding fault** он вéчно придирáется; **I'd ~ to go to Italy** мне óчень хотéлось бы съéздить в Итáлию; **I'd ~ you to come** я был бы счáстлив, éсли бы вы пришли; **'Will you come?' — 'Yes. I'd ~ to'** «Вы придёте?» — «Да, с удовóльствием/рáдостью».

cpds. **~-bird** *n.* неразлýчник; (*pl.*, *fig.*) влюблённые; **~-child** *n.* дитя (*nt.*) любви; **~-feast** *n.* вéчеря брáтства; **~-hate** *adj.*: **they have a ~-hate relationship** у них любóвь-нéнависть; **~-in-a-mist** *n.* чернýшка; **~-in-idleness** *n.* анютины глáзки (*m. pl.*); **~-letter** *n.* любóвная записка; **~-lies-bleeding** *n.* щирица; **~-lorn** *adj.* безнадёжно влюблённый; **~-making** *n.* (*intimacy*) физическая близость; **~-match** *n.* брак по любви; **~-nest** *n.* гнёздышко; **~-philtre, ~-potion** *nn.* любóвный напиток; приворóтное зéлье; **~-seat** *n.* крéсло-диван на двоих;

~sick *adj.* снедáемый любóвью; **~-song** *n.* любóвная пéсня; **~-token** *n.* залóг любвѝ.

loveless ['lʌvlɪs] *adj.* нелюбящий, без любвѝ; **a ~ marriage** брак не по любвѝ.

loveliness ['lʌvlɪnɪs] *n.* (*beauty*) красотá; (*attractiveness*) очаровáние.

lovely ['lʌvlɪ] *adj.* (*beautiful*) красѝвый, прекрáсный; (*charming, attractive*) прелéстный, миловѝдный; **we had a ~ time** мы прекрáсно провелѝ врéмя; **~!** (*excellent!*) замечáтельно!; отлѝчно!

lover ['lʌvə(r)] *n.* любóвни|к (*fem.* -ца); (*pl.*) влюблённые; **they became ~s** (*had intercourse*) онѝ сошлѝсь/сблѝзились; **a ~s' quarrel** ≃ мѝлые бранятся, тóлько тéшатся. **2.** (*devotee*) любѝтель (*m.*); поклóнник; охóтник (*до чего*); привéрженец; сторóнник; **~ of good food** гурмáн; **animal ~** любѝтель (*m.*) живóтных.

lovey ['lʌvɪ] *n.* (*coll.*) мѝлый, голýбчик.

loving ['lʌvɪŋ] *n.*: **the child needs a lot of ~** ребёнок нуждáется в любвѝ и лáске.

adj. любящий; **from your ~ father** от любящего тебя отцá; (*tender*) нéжный.

cpds. **~-cup** *n.* кругóвая чáша; **~-kindness** *n.* нéжная забóтливость; милосéрдие.

low[1] [ləʊ] *n.* **1.** (*meteor.*) циклóн. **2.** (*~ point or level*): **the pound fell to an all-time ~** фунт достѝг небывáло нѝзкого ýровня.

adj. **1.** нѝзкий, невысóкий; **the chair is too ~** стул слѝшком нѝзкий/нѝзок; **of ~ stature** невысóкого рóста; **the switch was very ~ down** выключáтель был располóжен óчень нѝзко; **~ dress** (*with ~ neck*) плáтье с нѝзким/глубóким вырезом (*or* с большѝм декольтé); **~ gear** пéрвая скóрость; **the sun was ~ in the sky** сóлнце стоялó нѝзко (над горизóнтом); **~ pressure/voltage** нѝзкое давлéние/напряжéние; **~ blood pressure** понѝженное кровянóе давлéние; **~ tide, water** мáлая водá, отлѝв; **at ~ tide, water** во врéмя отлѝва; **~ visibility** понѝженная/плохáя/слáбая вѝдимость; (*geog.*, *~-lying*) нѝзкий, нѝзменный; **Low Countries** Нидерлáнды, Бéльгия и Люксембýрг; (*of pitch of sound*) нѝзкий; **in a ~ key** (*fig.*) приглушённо, сдéржанно, без шýма; (*of volume of sound*) негрóмкий, тѝхий; **he spoke in a ~ voice** он говорѝл, понѝзив гóлос (*or* тѝхим гóлосом); **keep a ~ profile** вестѝ себя сдéржанно; **I have a ~ opinion of him** я невысóкого/невáжного мнéния о нём; **~ birth** нѝзкое происхождéние. **2.** (*vulgar, common*): **~ life** жизнь низóв; **~ Latin** вульгáрная латынь; **~ language** нѝзменный/вульгáрный язык; **a ~ style** вульгáрный стиль; **~ comedy** нѝзкая комéдия; фарс. **3.** (*base*) нѝзкий, пóдлый; **a ~ trick** пóдлая улóвка; **a ~ scoundrel** отпéтый негодяй; **~ cunning** нѝзкое ковáрство; пóдлые улóвки (*f. pl.*). **4.** (*nearly empty; scanty*): **the river is ~** рекá мелкá/обмелéла; **a ~ attendance** мáлая/плохáя посещáемость; **we are getting ~ on sugar** у нас остаётся маловáто сáхару. **5.** (*poor, depressed*): **be in ~ health** прихвáрывать (*impf.*); **in ~ spirits** в подáвленном настроéнии; **I was feeling ~** я чýвствовал себя невáжно.

adv. нѝзко; **bow ~** отвéсить (*pf.*) нѝзкий поклóн; нѝзко клáняться, поклонѝться; **bring ~** (*fig.*) пов|ергáть, -éргнуть; **lay ~** (*fig.*) низв|ергáть, -éргнуть; **lie ~** (*fig.*) затá|иваться, -ѝться; **stocks are running ~** запáсы кончáются; **sink ~** опус|кáться, -тѝться; **sink ~ in the water** глубокó погру|жáться, -зѝться в вóду; **he sank ~ in my esteem** он нѝзко пал в моѝх глазáх; **I didn't think he would stoop so ~** я не ожидáл, что он падёт так нѝзко.

cpds. **~-alcohol** *adj.* слабоалкогóльный; **~-born** *adj.* нѝзкого происхождéния; **~-bred** *adj.* невоспѝтанный; **~brow** *n.* человéк, обладáющий нерáзвитым вкýсом; *adj.* нерáзвитый, обывáтельский; **~brow tastes** мещáнские вкýсы; **~-calorie** *adj.* малокалорѝйный; **~-down** *n.* (*information*) подноготная (*coll.*); *adj.* пóдлый, сквéрный; **~-fat** *adj.* маложѝрный; **~-frequency** *adj.* низкочастóтный; **~-grade** *adj.* низкосóртный; (*of ore*) бéдный; **~-key** *adj.* (*fig.*) сдéржанный; **~land** *n.* (*usu. pl.*) нѝзменность, низѝна; *adj.* низѝнный; **~-lying** *adj.* нѝзменный; **~-lying areas** нѝзменности (*f. pl.*); **~-necked** *adj.* с нѝзким вырезом; **~-paid** *adj.* малооплáчиваемый; **~-pitched** *adj.* (*of sound*) нѝзкий; нѝзкого тóна; (*of roof*) полóгий; **~-powered** *adj.* маломóщный; **~-profile** *adj.* сдéржанный; тѝхий; **~-spirited** *adj.* унылый, подáвленный; **~-water** *adj.*: **~-water mark** отмéтка ýровня нѝзкой воды; (*fig.*) (нѝзший) предéл.

low[2] [ləʊ] *v.i.* (*of cattle*) мычáть, за-.

lower[1] ['ləʊə(r)] *adj.* нѝжний; **~ case** (*typ.*) стрóчные бýквы (*f. pl.*); **the L~ Chamber, House** нѝжняя палáта; палáта óбщин; **~ deck** нѝжняя пáлуба; **on a ~ floor** (этажóм) нѝже; **the ~ orders** нѝзшие сослóвия; **~ reaches** (*of a river*) низóвь|е, -я; **the ~ regions** (*hell*) преиспóдняя; **~ school** млáдшие клáссы; пéрвая ступéнь.

v.t. **1.** (*e.g. boat, flag*) спус|кáть, -тѝть; (*eyes*) опус|кáть, -тѝть; пот|уплять, -ýпить; (*price*) сн|ижáть, -ѝзить; (*voice*) пон|ижáть, -ѝзить; **a ~ing illness** изнурѝтельная болéзнь. **2.** (*decrease*) ум|еньшáть, -éньшить. **3.** (*debase*) ун|ижáть, -ѝзить.

cpd. **~-class** *adj.* принадлежáщий к нѝзшему сослóвию.

lower[2] ['laʊə(r)] = **lour**

lowermost ['ləʊəməʊst] *adj.* нижáйший; (сáмый) нѝжний.

lowlander ['ləʊləndə(r)] *n.* жѝтель (шотлáндских) низѝн.

lowliness ['ləʊlɪnɪs] *n.* скрóмность, непритязáтельность.

lowly ['ləʊlɪ] *adj.* (*humble*) скрóмный; (*primitive*) нѝзший.

loyal ['lɔɪəl] *adj.* (*faithful*) вéрный; **he is ~ to his comrades** он вéрен товáрищам: (*devoted*) прéданный; **a ~ wife** прéданная женá; **~ supporters of the local team** постоянные болéльщики мéстной комáнды; (*pol., supporting established authority*) верноподданный, благонадёжный.

loyalist ['lɔɪəlɪst] *n.* лоялѝст.

loyalty ['lɔɪəltɪ] *n.* вéрность, прéданность, лояльность; **political ~** политѝческая благонадёжность.

lozenge ['lɒzɪndʒ] *n.* (*shape*) ромб; (*pastille*) таблéтка, лепёшка, пастѝлка.

cpd. **~-shaped** *adj.* ромбовѝдный.

LP (*abbr. of* ***long-playing record***) долгоигрáющая пластѝнка.

LSD *abbr. of* **1.** ***pounds, shillings and pence*** дéн|ьги (*pl., g.* -ег). **2.** (*pharm.*) ***lysergic acid diethylamide*** ЛСД, (диэтиламѝд лизергѝновой кислоты).

Lt [lef'tenənt] *n.* (*abbr. of* **Lieutenant**) л-т, (лейтенáнт).

Ltd. ['lɪmɪtɪd] *adj.* (*comm., abbr. of* ***limited liability company***) с огранѝченной ответственностью.

lubber ['lʌbə(r)] *n.* (*clumsy fellow*) ýвалень (*m.*) (*coll.*); (*seaman*) неóпытный моряк.

lubricant ['lu:brɪkənt] *n.* смáзка, мазь.

lubricat|e ['lu:brɪˌkeɪt] *v.t.* смáз|ывать, -ать; **~ing oil** смáзочное мáсло.

lubrication [ˌlu:brɪ'keɪʃ(ə)n] *n.* смáзывание.

lubricator ['lu:brɪˌkeɪtə(r)] *n.* (*pers.*) смáзчик; (*oil*) смáзка; (*machine component*) лубрикáтор.

lubricious [lu:'brɪʃəs] *adj.* (*lewd*) похотлѝвый.

lubricity [lu:'brɪsɪtɪ] *n.* похотлѝвость.

lucent ['lu:s(ə)nt] *adj.* (*shining*) блестящий; (*transparent*) прозрáчный.

lucerne [lu:'sɜ:n] *n.* люцéрна.

lucid ['lu:sɪd] *adj.* ясный; **he has a ~ mind** у негó ясная головá; **a ~ interval** свéтлый промежýток; прóблеск сознáния.

lucidity [ˌlu:'sɪdɪtɪ] *n.* ясность.

Lucifer ['lu:sɪfə(r)] *n.* (*Satan*) Люцифéр; (*star*) ýтренняя звездá.

luck [lʌk] *n.*: **good/bad ~** счáстье/несчáстье; везéние/невезéние; удáча/неудáча; **good ~!; the best of ~!** желáю счáстья/удáчи/успéха!; **... and good ~ to him** …дай емý Бог; **bad, hard ~!** не повезлó!; **what rotten ~!** какóе невезéние!; **worse ~!** к несчáстью/сожалéнию; увы!; тем хýже (для негó *и т.п.*); **no such ~!** увы, нет; **as ~ would have it** по/к счáстью; (*unfortunately*) по/к несчáстью; как назлó; (*in neutral sense*) получѝлось так, что…; **it was just a matter of ~** это был вопрóс везéния; **just my ~!** такóе уж у меня везéние!; **I had the (good) ~ to be selected** мне посчастлѝвилось попáсть в числó избранных; **he had the bad ~ to break his leg** как на грех, он сломал себе ногу; **we're in ~ ('s way)** нам везёт; **we're out of ~** (нам) не везёт; **he's down on his ~** ему не везёт; **it was a great piece of ~** это была большая/редкая удача; **I did it by sheer ~** мне просто повезло; **a run of (bad) ~** полоса (не)везения; **his ~ is in** ему везёт; **he has the devil's own ~** ему чертовски везёт; **try one's ~** пытать, по- счастья; **push one's ~** искушать (*impf.*) судьбу; **you never know your ~** как знать, вдруг да и посчастливится; **he wears a mascot for ~** он носит талисман на счастье.

luckily ['lʌkɪlɪ] *adv.* к/по счастью; удачно; по счастливому случаю.

luckless ['lʌklɪs] *adj.* (*of pers., unfortunate*) несчастливый, незадачливый; (*unsuccessful*) неудачливый; (*of things or actions*) несчастный, неудачный, злополучный.

lucky ['lʌkɪ] *adj.* **1.** (*of pers.*) счастливый, удачливый; (*of things, actions, events*) удачный; **a ~ person** счастливец, удачник; **~ dog, beggar** счастливчик; **he's ~ in everything** ему во всём везёт; **he's ~ in business** он удачлив в делах; **~ for you he's not here** ваше счастье, что его здесь нет; **you're ~ to be alive** скажи спасибо, что остался в живых; **a ~ shot** удачный выстрел; (*fig., guess*) счастливая догадка; ≃ попал в точку. **2.** (*bringing luck*): **a ~ charm** счастливый талисман.

lucrative ['lu:krətɪv] *adj.* (*profitable*) прибыльный; (*remunerative*) доходный.

lucre ['lu:kə(r)] *n.* прибыль, нажива; **filthy ~** презренный металл.

Lucretius [lu:'kri:ʃɪəs] *n.* Лукреций.

lucubration [ˌlu:kjʊ'breɪʃ(ə)n] *n.* занятия (*nt. pl.*) по ночам; (*product*) плоды (*m. pl.*) ночных раздумий.

Lucullan [lu:'kʌlən, lʊ-] *adj.*: **~ feast** Лукуллов пир.

ludicrous ['lu:dɪkrəs] *adj.* (*absurd*) нелепый; (*laughable*) смехотворный, смешной.

luff [lʌf] *v.t.* прив|одить, -ести к ветру.

v.i. идти (*det.*) в бейдевинд.

Luftwaffe ['lʊftˌvæfə] *n.* люфтваффе (*indecl.*); военно-воздушные силы гитлеровской Германии.

lug[1] [lʌg] *n.* (*projection*) ушко; (*sl., ear*) ухо.

lug[2] [lʌg] *v.t.* (*coll.*) волочить (*impf.*); тащить (*impf.*).

luge [lu:ʒ] *n.* тобогган.

luggage ['lʌgɪdʒ] *n.* багаж; **piece of ~** вещь, место; **left ~ office** камера хранения.

cpds. **~-carrier** *n.* (*e.g. on bicycle*) багажник; **~-label** *n.* багажный ярлык; **~-rack** *n.* (*in train*) сетка/полка для багажа; **~-trolley** *n.* багажная тележка; **~-van** *n.* багажный вагон.

lugger ['lʌgə(r)] *n.* люгер.

lugubrious [lu:'gu:brɪəs, lʊ-] *adj.* (*mournful*) скорбный; (*dismal*) мрачный.

lugubriousness [lu:'gu:brɪəsnɪs, lʊ-] *n.* мрачность.

lugworm ['lʌgwɜ:m] *n.* пескожил.

Luke [lu:k] *n.* (*bibl.*) Лука (*m.*).

lukewarm [lu:k'wɔ:m, 'lu:k-] *adj.* тепловатый, чуть тёплый; комнатной температуры; (*fig., indifferent*) прохладный.

lull [lʌl] *n.* (*in storm, fighting etc.*) затишье; (*in conversation*) пауза, перерыв.

v.t. (*~ to sleep*) убаюк|ивать, -ать; (*allay*) усып|лять, -ить; рассе|ивать, -ять.

lullaby ['lʌləˌbaɪ] *n.* колыбельная (песня).

lumbago [lʌm'beɪgəʊ] *n.* люмбаго (*indecl.*); прострел.

lumbar ['lʌmbə(r)] *adj.* поясничный.

lumber[1] ['lʌmbə(r)] *n.* (*disused furniture etc.*) рухлядь, хлам; (*US, timber*) пиломатериалы (*m. pl.*).

v.t. (*fill, obstruct, make untidy with ~*) завал|ивать, -ить (*что чем*); (*encumber*) обременять (*impf.*); **I'm ~ed with my mother-in-law** тёща у меня на шее.

v.i. (*work on tree-felling etc.*) рубить/валить (*impf.*) деревья; распиливать/заготавливать (*impf.*) лес.

cpds. **~jack, ~man** *nn.* лесоруб; **~-jacket** *n.* (короткая) рабочая куртка; **~-mill** *n.* лесопильный завод; **~-room** *n.* чулан; **~-yard** *n.* склад пиломатериалов.

lumber[2] ['lʌmbə(r)] *v.i.* (*also* **~ along**) двигаться (*impf.*) тяжело; переваливаться (*impf.*).

lumbering[1] ['lʌmbərɪŋ] *n.* лесозаготовка.

lumbering[2] ['lʌmbərɪŋ] *adj.* (*of pers.*) двигающийся тяжело/неуклюже; (*of cart etc.*) громыхающий.

luminary ['lu:mɪnərɪ] *n.* (*lit., fig.*) светило.

luminescence [ˌlu:mɪ'nes(ə)ns] *n.* свечение, люминисценция.

luminescent [ˌlu:mɪ'nes(ə)nt, ˌlju:-] *adj.* светящийся, люминисцентный.

luminosity [ˌlu:mɪ'nɒsɪtɪ, ˌlju:-] *n.* освещённость, яркость.

luminous ['lu:mɪnəs, 'lju:-] *adj.* светящийся; (*bright*) светлый, яркий.

lumme ['lʌmɪ] *int.* (*coll.*) Боже мой!

lump [lʌmp] *n.* **1.** (*of earth, dough etc.*) ком; **~ of clay** ком глины; (*large piece*) (крупный) кусок; **~ of sugar** кусок сахара; **~ sugar** пилёный/кусковой сахар; **~ of ice/snow** глыба льда/снега; **~ of wood** чурбан; **~ in the throat** комок в горле. **2.** (*swelling*) шишка, опухоль. **3.** (*pers.*) дубина (*c.g.*). **4.:** **~ sum** паушальная сумма; единовременная плата; **they get paid a ~ sum** им платят аккордно.

v.t. **1.** **~ together** (*collect into heap*) валить (*impf.*), свал|ивать, -ить в кучу; (*treat alike; place in single category*) ставить (*impf.*) на одну доску; **the passengers were ~ed in with the crew** пассажиров поместили вместе с экипажем. **2.:** **~ it** (*coll., put up with it*) примириться (*pf.*) (*с чем*); **you must ~ it** нравится — не нравится, а придётся проглотить.

cpd. **~-fish** *n.* морской воробей.

lumping ['lʌmpɪŋ] *adj.* (*clumsy*) неуклюжий; (*dull-witted*) тупоумный.

lumpish ['lʌmpɪʃ] *adj.* неуклюжий; тупой, глупый.

lumpy ['lʌmpɪ] *adj.* комковатый.

lunacy ['lu:nəsɪ] *n.* (*insanity*) безумие, сумасшествие; (*leg.*) невменяемость; (*folly*) безумие.

lunar ['lu:nə(r), 'lju:-] *adj.* лунный; **~ rover** луноход.

cpd. **~scape** *n.* лунный ландшафт.

lunatic ['lu:nətɪk] *n.* сумасшедший; душевнобольной.

adj. (*mad*) сумасшедший; **~ asylum** сумасшедший дом; психиатрическая больница; (*foolish, senseless*) безумный; (*eccentric*) чудаческий; **~ fringe** кучка фанатиков; экстремисты (*m. pl.*).

lunation [lu:'neɪʃ(ə)n, lju:-] *n.* лунный месяц.

lunch [lʌntʃ] *n.* (*midday meal*) обед; (второй) завтрак, ленч.

v.t. уго|щать, -стить обедом/завтраком.

v.i. обедать, по-; завтракать, по-.

cpds. **~-break, ~-hour, ~-time** *nn.* обеденный перерыв; **~-party** *n.* званый обед/завтрак.

luncheon ['lʌntʃ(ə)n] *n.* обед.

cpds. **~-meat** *n.* мясной рулет; **~-voucher** *n.* талон на обед.

lung [lʌŋ] *n.* лёгкое; **he has a good pair of ~s** у него зычный голос; **~ cancer** рак лёгк|ого, -их.

cpds. **~-fish** *n.* двоякодышащая рыба; **~-power** *n.* сила голоса.

lunge [lʌndʒ, lju:-] *n.* (*forward movement*) бросок; (*in fencing*) выпад.

v.i. **~ (out) at** (*fencing, boxing etc.*) сделать (*pf.*) выпад на+*a.*

lunik ['lu:nɪk] *n.* лунник.

lupin ['lu:pɪn] *n.* люпин.

lupine ['lu:paɪn] *adj.* волчий.

lupus ['lu:pəs] *n.* волчанка; туберкулёз кожи.

lurch[1] [lɜ:tʃ] *n.*: **leave s.o. in the ~** пок|идать, -инуть кого-н. в беде; подв|одить, -ести кого-н.

lurch[2] [lɜ:tʃ] *n.*: (*stagger*) **the ship gave a ~** корабль дал крен (*or* накренился).

v.i. шататься (*impf.*); пошат|ываться, -нуться; **the drunken man ~ed across the street** пьяный, пошатываясь, перешёл улицу.

lure [ljʊə(r), lʊə(r)] *n.* (*falconry*) приманка; (*bait for fish*) приманка, наживка; (*decoy used in hunting*) вабик; (*fig., enticement*) соблазн; **the ~ of foreign travel** заманчивость заграничных путешествий.

v.t. (*fish*) приман|ивать, -ить; (*persons*) заман|ивать, -ить; завле|кать, -ечь; **a rival firm ~d him away**

конкури́рующая фи́рма переман́ила его́ (к себе́); **I was ~d (on) by the promise of a reward** меня́ соблазни́ла перспекти́ва награ́ды; **they were ~d on to destruction** их замани́ли на (по)ги́бель.
lurid [ˈljʊərɪd, ˈlʊə-] *adj.* (*wan*) (мёртвенно-)бле́дный; ту́склый; (*stormy*) грозово́й; (*gaudy*) крича́щий, аляпова́тый; (*sinister*) зловéщий; (*sensational*): **a ~ novel** бульва́рный рома́н; **~ details** жу́ткие подро́бности.
lurk [lɜːk] *v.i.* прита́|иваться, -и́ться; **~ about** ждать (*impf.*) притаи́вшись; **I have a ~ing sympathy for him** он вызыва́ет у меня́ нево́льное сочу́вствие.
luscious [ˈlʌʃəs] *adj.* (*succulent*) со́чный; (*ripe, also fig.*) наливно́й; (*over-sweet, cloying*) при́торный.
lusciousness [ˈlʌʃəsnɪs] *n.* со́чность, при́торность.
lush[1] [lʌʃ] *n.* (*US, drunkard*) пьянчу́жка (*c.g.*), алка́ш (*sl.*).
lush[2] [lʌʃ] *adj.* пы́шный, роско́шный.
lust [lʌst] *n.* **1.** (*sexual passion*) по́хоть, вожделе́ние; **~s of the flesh** пло́тские позы́вы. **2.** (*craving*): **~ for power** жа́жда вла́сти.
v.i.: **~ for, after s.o.** испы́т|ывать, -а́ть вожделе́ние к кому́-н.; жела́ть (*impf.*) кого́-н.
lustful [ˈlʌstfʊl] *adj.* похотли́вый.
lustfulness [ˈlʌstfʊlnɪs] *n.* похотли́вость.
lustiness [ˈlʌstɪnɪs] *n.* (*health*) здоро́вье; (*vigour*) бо́дрость.
lustre [ˈlʌstə(r)] *n.* (*chandelier*) лю́стра; (*material*) блестя́щая полушерстяна́я мате́рия; (*glaze*) глазу́рь; (*gloss, brilliance*) блеск, гля́нец; (*bright light*) сия́ние; (*splendour, glory*) сла́ва; **add ~ to sth.** прид|ава́ть, -а́ть блеск чему́-н.
lustreless [ˈlʌstərlɪs] *adj.* ту́склый.
lustrous [ˈlʌstrəs] *adj.* (*brilliant*) блестя́щий; (*glossy*) глянцеви́тый.
lusty [ˈlʌstɪ] *adj.* (*healthy*) здоро́вый; (*robust*) здорове́нный; (*vigorous*) бо́дрый.
lutenist [ˈluːtənɪst, ˈljuː-] *n.* игра́ющий на лю́тне.
lute [luːt, ljuːt] *n.* (*mus.*) лю́тня.
Lutheran [ˈluːθərən, ˈljuː-] *n.* лютера́н|ин (*fem.* -ка).
adj. лютера́нский.
Lutheranism [ˈluːθərənˌɪz(ə)m, ˈljuː-] *n.* лютера́нство.
lux [lʌks] *n.* (*phys.*) люкс.
Luxemburg [ˈlʌksəmˌbɜːg] *n.* Лю́ксембу́рг.
adj. люксембу́ргский.
Luxemburger [ˈlʌksəmˌbɜːgə(r)] *n.* люксембу́ржец; жи́тель (*fem.* -ница) Люксембу́рга.
luxuriance [lʌgˈzjʊərɪəns, lʌkˈsj-, lʌgˈʒʊə-] *n.* изоби́лие; бога́тство; пы́шность.
luxuriant [lʌgˈzjʊərɪənt, lʌkˈsj-, lʌgˈʒʊə-] *adj.* (*profuse*) оби́льный; (*of imagination etc.*) бога́тый; (*splendid*) пы́шный; (*of growth*) бу́йный.
luxuriate [lʌgˈzjʊərɪˌeɪt, lʌkˈsj-, lʌgˈʒʊə-] *v.i.* **1.** (*of plants*) бу́йно расти́ (*impf.*). **2.** (*enjoy o.s.*): **~ in sth.** наслажда́ться (*impf.*) чем-н.
luxurious [lʌgˈzjʊərɪəs, lʌkˈsj-, lʌgˈʒʊə-] *adj.* (*sumptuous*) роско́шный; (*splendid*) пы́шный; (*self-indulgent*) расточи́тельный; **live ~ly** роско́шествовать (*impf.*).
luxury [ˈlʌkʃərɪ] *n.* **1.** (*luxuriousness*) ро́скошь; **live in the lap of ~** жить (*impf.*) в ро́скоши; (*pleasure*) удово́льствие. **2.** (*object of ~*) предме́т ро́скоши; **wine is my only ~** еди́нственная ро́скошь, кото́рую я себе́ позволя́ю — э́то вино́; **~ goods** предме́ты ро́скоши; **~ apartment** роско́шная кварти́ра; но́мер-люкс.
LV [ˈlʌntʃ(ə)n ˈvaʊtʃə(r)] *n.* (*abbr. of* **luncheon voucher**) тало́н на обе́д.
lycanthropy [laɪˈkænθrəpɪ] *n.* ликантро́пия.
lycée [ˈliːseɪ] *n.* лице́й.
Lyceum [laɪˈsiːəm] (*hist.*) *n.* лице́й.
lychee [ˈlaɪtʃɪ, ˈlɪ-] = **lichee**
lych-(*also* **lich-**)**gate** [ˈlɪtʃgeɪt] поко́йницкая.
lye [laɪ] *n.* щёлок.
lying[1] [ˈlaɪɪŋ] *n.* (*telling lies*) ложь, враньё.
adj. ло́жный, лжи́вый.
lying[2] [ˈlaɪɪŋ] *n.*: **~ in state** до́ступ к те́лу имени́того поко́йника.
cpd. **~-in** *n.* ро́д|ы (*pl., g.* -ов); послеродово́й пери́од; **~-in hospital** роди́льный дом.
lymph [lɪmf] *n.* (*physiol.*) ли́мфа.
lymphatic [lɪmˈfætɪk] *adj.* лимфати́ческий; (*fig., of pers.*) вя́лый.
lynch [lɪntʃ] *n.*: **~ law** суд/зако́н Ли́нча; самосу́д.
v.t. линчева́ть (*impf., pf.*).
lynchpin [ˈlɪntʃpɪn] = **linchpin**
lynx [lɪŋks] *n.* рысь.
cpd. **~-eyed** *adj.* с о́стрым зре́нием.
Lyra [ˈlaɪərə] *n.* (*astron.*) Ли́ра.
lyre [ˈlaɪə(r)] *n.* ли́ра.
cpd. **~-bird** *n.* пти́ца-ли́ра, лирохво́ст.
lyric [ˈlɪrɪk] *n.* **1.** (*~ poem*) лири́ческое стихотворе́ние; (*pl.*) лири́ческие стихи́ (*m. pl.*); (*~ poetry*) ли́рика. **2.** (*theatr., words of song*) слова́ (*nt. pl.*)/текст пе́сни.
adj. лири́ческий; **~ writer** ли́рик; поэ́т-пе́сенник.
lyrical [ˈlɪrɪk(ə)l] *adj.* лири́ческий; **he waxed ~ about, over ...** он расчу́вствовался, говоря́ о...; **he was ~ in his praise of the play** он с воодушевле́нием расхва́ливал пье́су.
lyricism [ˈlɪrɪˌsɪz(ə)m] *n.* лири́зм.
lyrist [ˈlaɪərɪst] *n.* (*player on lyre*) игра́ющий на ли́ре; (*poet*) лири́ческий поэ́т.
lysol [ˈlaɪsɒl] *n.* лизо́л.

M

m. [ˈmiːtə(r)(z)] *n.* (*abbr. of* **metre(s)**) м, (метр).
MA[1] (*abbr. of* ***Master of Arts***) маги́стр гуманита́рных нау́к.
ma[2] [mɑː] *n.* (*coll.*) ма́ма.
ma'am [mæm, mɑːm, məm] *n.* суда́рыня.
mac [mæk] (*coll.*) = **mac(k)intosh**
macabre [məˈkɑːbr] *adj.* мра́чный, жу́ткий.
macadam [məˈkædəm] *n.* макада́м, щебёночное покры́тие.
macadamia (nut) [ˌmækəˈdeɪmɪə] *n.* кинда́ль (*m.*).
macadamize [məˈkædəmaɪz] *v.t.*: **~d road** доро́га с щебёночным покры́тием.
macaroni [ˌmækəˈrəʊnɪ] *n.* макаро́н|ы (*pl., g.* —).
macaroon [ˌmækəˈruːn] *n.* минда́льное пече́нье.
macaw [məˈkɔː] *n.* а́ра (*m. indecl.*).
Macbeth [məkˈbeθ, mæk-] *n.* Макбе́т.
mace[1] [meɪs] *n.* (*club; staff of office*) булава́; жезл.
cpd. **~-bearer** *n.* булавоно́сец, жезлоно́сец.
mace[2] [meɪs] *n.* (*spice*) муска́т.
macedoine [ˈmæsɪˌdwɑːn] *n.* (*cul.*) маседуа́н; (*fig.*) винегре́т.
Macedon [ˈmæsɪˌdɒn], **-ia** [ˌmæsəˈdəʊnɪə] *nn.* Македо́ния.
Macedonian [ˌmæsəˈdəʊnɪən] *n.* македо́н|ец (*fem.* -ка).
adj. македо́нский.
macerate [ˈmæsəˌreɪt] *v.t.* выма́чивать, вы́мочить; мацери́ровать (*impf., pf.*).
maceration [ˌmæsəˈreɪʃ(ə)n] *n.* выма́чивание, мацера́ция.
Mach (number) [mɑːk, mæk] *n.* число́ М(а́ха).
machete [məˈtʃetɪ, məˈʃetɪ] *n.* мачéте (*indecl.*).
Machiavellian [ˌmækɪəˈvelɪən] *adj.* макиаве́ллевский.
machicolation [məˌtʃɪkəˈleɪʃ(ə)n] *n.* навесна́я бойни́ца.
machination [ˌmækɪˈneɪʃ(ə)n, ˌmæʃ-] *n.* (*usu. pl.*) махина́ции; ко́зни (*f. pl.*); интри́га.
machine [məˈʃiːn] *n.* **1.** (*mechanical device, apparatus*) маши́на, механи́зм; **the ~ age** век маши́н/те́хники; **~ translation** маши́нный перево́д; **~ shop** механи́ческий цех; (*~-tool*) стано́к; **grinding ~** шлифова́льный стано́к. **2.** (*means of transport*) маши́на; (*car*) автомоби́ль (*m.*), маши́на; (*bicycle*) велосипе́д; (*motor-cycle*) мотоци́кл; (*aircraft*) самолёт. **3.** (*controlling organization*) аппара́т; **party ~** парти́йный аппара́т.
v.t. (*on lathe etc.*) обраб|а́тывать, -о́тать (на станке́ *or*

механи́ческим спо́собом); (*on sewing-*~) шить, с- на маши́не.

cpds. **~-gun** *n.* пулемёт; **~-gun fire** пулемётный ого́нь; *v.t.* (*fire at*) обстре́л|ивать, -я́ть; (*shoot down*) расстре́л|ивать, -я́ть; **~-gunner** *n.* пулемётчик; **~-made** *adj.*: **~-made goods** това́р фабри́чного произво́дства; **~-minder** *n.* рабо́чий у станка́; **~-operator** *n.* (*agr.*) механиза́тор; **~-readable** *adj.* (*comput.*) машиночита́емый.

machinery [mə'ʃi:nərɪ] *n.* (*collect., machines*) маши́ны (*f. pl.*), те́хника; (*mechanism*) механи́зм; (*fig.*): **the ~ of government** прави́тельственная структу́ра.

machinist [mə'ʃi:nɪst] *n.* машини́ст; (*sewing-machine operator*) шве́йник, (*fem.*) швея́.

mack [mæk] (*coll.*) = **mac(k)intosh**

mackerel ['mækr(ə)l] *n.* макре́ль, ску́мбрия; **~ sky** не́бо в бара́шках.

mac(k)intosh ['mækɪn,tɒʃ] *n.* непромока́емый плащ, дождеви́к, макинто́ш.

macramé [mə'krɑ:mɪ] *n.* макраме́ (*indecl.*).

macrocephalic [,mækrəʊsɪ'fælɪk] *adj.* большеголо́вый, макроцефа́льный.

macrocosm ['mækrəʊ,kɒz(ə)m] *n.* макроко́см.

macron ['mækrɒn] *n.* знак долготы́.

mad [mæd] *adj.* **1.** (*insane*) сумасше́дший; **he is as ~ as a hatter** он соверше́нно сумасше́дший; **go ~** сходи́ть, сойти́ с ума́; **drive s.o. ~** св|оди́ть, -ести́ кого́-н. с ума́; **this is bureaucracy gone ~** э́то бюрокра́тия, доведённая до безу́мия. **2.** (*of animals*) бе́шеный. **3.** (*wildly foolish*) шально́й; **a ~ escapade** безрассу́дная вы́ходка; **that was a ~ thing to do** поступи́ть так бы́ло про́сто безу́мием; **~ly in love** безу́мно влюблённый; **~ly expensive** безу́мно дорого́й. **4.** (*coll., angry, annoyed*) серди́тый; **~ with anger** вне себя́ от гне́ва; **be, get ~** вы́йти (*pf.*) из себя́; **I was ~ at missing the train** я был вне себя́ из-за того́, что опозда́л на по́езд; **be, get ~ with s.o.** серди́ться, рас- на кого́-н.; **she was ~ with me for breaking the vase** она́ разозли́лась на меня́ за то, что я разби́л ва́зу. **5.: ~ about** (*infatuated with, enthusiastic for*) в восто́рге (*or* без па́мяти) от+*g.*; **she was ~ about him** она́ была́ от него́ без ума́; **the boy is ~ about ice-cream** ма́льчик обожа́ет моро́женое; **his wife was ~ about cats** его́ жена́ была́ поме́шана на ко́шках. **6.: like ~** безу́держно; **I rushed like ~** я помча́лся как угоре́лый; **he is working like ~** он рабо́тает как одержи́мый; **they were shouting like ~** они́ крича́ли благи́м ма́том; **he drove like ~** он е́хал с бе́шеной ско́ростью.

cpds. **~cap** *n.* сорвиголова́ (*c.g.*); *adj.* сумасбро́дный, неи́стовый; **~house** *n.* сумасше́дший дом; **~man** *n.* сумасше́дший; **~woman** *n.* сумасше́дшая.

Madagascar [,mædə'gæskə(r)] *n.* Мадагаска́р.

madam ['mædəm] *n.* (*form of address*) мада́м, суда́рыня; (*coll., brothel-keeper*) мада́м.

madden ['mæd(ə)n] *v.t.* (*persons*) раздраж|а́ть, -и́ть; (*animals*) беси́ть, вз-.

maddening ['mædənɪŋ] *adj.* несно́сный.

madder ['mædə(r)] *n.* (*plant*) маре́на; (*dye*) маре́новый краси́тель, крапп.

Madeira [mə'dɪərə] *n.* Маде́йра; (*wine*) маде́ра.

mademoiselle [,mædəmwə'zel] *n.* мадемуазе́ль; (*governess*) гуверна́нтка-францу́женка.

made-to-measure ['meɪdtə'meʒə(r)] *adj.* сде́ланный (как) на зака́з.

madness ['mædnɪs] *n.* (*insanity*) сумасше́ствие; (*of animals*) бе́шенство; (*folly*) безу́мие.

madonna [mə'dɒnə] *n.* мадо́нна; **~ lily** бе́лая ли́лия.

Madrid [mə'drɪd] *n.* Мадри́д; (*attr.*) мадри́дский.

madrigal ['mædrɪg(ə)l] *n.* мадрига́л.

maelstrom ['meɪlstrəm] *n.* водоворо́т; (*fig.*) вихрь (*m.*).

maenad ['mi:næd] *n.* мена́да.

maestro ['maɪstrəʊ] *n.* маэ́стро (*m. indecl.*).

maffick ['mæfɪk] *v.i.* бу́рно ра́доваться (*impf.*).

Mafia ['mæfɪə, 'mɑ:-] *n.* ма́фия; (*fig.*) кли́ка.

magazine[1] [,mægə'zi:n] *n.* **1.** (*mil. store*) вое́нный склад; (*for arms and ammunition*) склад боеприпа́сов; (*on ship*) порохово́й по́греб; по́греб боеприпа́сов. **2.** (*cartridge chamber*) магази́нная коро́бка; (*attr.*) магази́нный.

magazine[2] [,mægə'zi:n] *n.* (*periodical*) журна́л; (*attr.*) журна́льный.

magenta [mə'dʒentə] *n.* фукси́н.

adj. красновა́то-лило́вого цве́та.

maggot ['mægət] *n.* (*grub*) личи́нка; (*whim, fancy*) причу́да, блажь.

maggoty ['mægətɪ] *adj.* черви́вый.

Magi ['meɪdʒaɪ] *n.*: **the ~** волхвы́ (*m. pl.*); **Adoration of the ~** поклоне́ние волхво́в.

magic ['mædʒɪk] *n.* (*lit., fig.*) ма́гия, волшебство́; **as if by ~** как по волшебству́.

adj. волше́бный, маги́ческий; **~ lantern** волше́бный фона́рь; **~ wand** волше́бная па́лочка.

magical ['mædʒɪk(ə)l] *adj.* феери́ческий, волше́бный.

magician [mə'dʒɪʃ(ə)n] *n.* (*sorcerer*) волше́бник; (*conjurer*) фо́кусник.

magisterial [,mædʒɪ'stɪərɪəl] *adj.* (*of a magistrate*) суде́йский; (*authoritative*) авторите́тный.

magistracy ['mædʒɪstrəsɪ], **magistrature** ['mædʒɪstrə,tjʊə(r)] *nn.* суде́йство; магистрату́ра.

magistrate ['mædʒɪstrət] *n.* судья́ (*m.*) (ни́зшей инста́нции).

Magna C(h)arta [,mægnə 'kɑ:tə] *n.* Вели́кая ха́ртия во́льностей.

magnanimity [,mægnə'nɪmɪtɪ] *n.* великоду́шие.

magnanimous [mæg'nænɪməs] *adj.* великоду́шный.

magnate ['mægneɪt, -nɪt] *n.* магна́т.

magnesia [mæg'ni:ʒə, -ʃə, -zjə] *n.* магне́зия, о́кись ма́гния; **milk of ~** молочко́ магне́зии.

magnesium [mæg'ni:zɪəm] *n.* ма́гний; **~ flare** вспы́шка ма́гния.

magnet ['mægnɪt] *n.* (*lit., fig.*) магни́т.

magnetic [mæg'netɪk] *adj.* магни́тный; **~ tape** магнитоле́нта; (*fig.*): **~ personality** притяга́тельная/магнети́ческая ли́чность.

magnetism ['mægnɪ,tɪz(ə)m] *n.* магнети́зм; (*magnetic properties*) магни́тные сво́йства; (*fig.*) притяга́тельность.

magnetization [,mægnɪtaɪ'zeɪʃ(ə)n] *n.* (*process*) намагни́чивание; (*state*) намагни́ченность.

magnetize ['mægnɪ,taɪz] *v.t.* намагни́|чивать, -тить; (*fig.*) гипнотизи́ровать, за-.

magneto [mæg'ni:təʊ] *n.* магне́то (*indecl.*).

Magnificat [mæg'nɪfɪ,kæt] *n.* Велича́ние (Богоро́дицы).

magnification [,mægnɪfɪ'keɪʃ(ə)n] *n.* увеличе́ние; **a microscope of 50 ~s** микроско́п с пятидесятикра́тным увеличе́нием; (*of a radio signal*) усиле́ние; (*exaggeration*) преувеличе́ние.

magnificence [mæg'nɪfɪs(ə)ns] *n.* великоле́пие.

magnificent [mæg'nɪfɪs(ə)nt] *adj.* великоле́пный.

magnifico [mæg'nɪfɪ,kəʊ] *n.* вельмо́жа (*m.*).

magnify ['mægnɪ,faɪ] *v.t.* (*cause to appear larger*) увели́чи|вать, -ть; **~ing-glass** увеличи́тельное стекло́, лу́па; (*exaggerate*) преувели́чи|вать, -ть; **~ an incident** разд|ува́ть, -у́ть инциде́нт; (*extol*) превозн|оси́ть, -ести́.

magniloquence [mæg'nɪləkwəns] *n.* высокопа́рность, напы́щенность.

magniloquent [mæg'nɪləkwənt] *n.* высокопа́рный, напы́щенный.

magnitude ['mægnɪ,tju:d] *n.* (*size*) величина́; **a star of the first ~** звезда́ пе́рвой величины́; (*importance*) ва́жность; **a matter of the first ~** де́ло первостепе́нной ва́жности.

magnolia [mæg'nəʊlɪə] *n.* магно́лия.

magnum ['mægnəm] *n.* ви́нная буты́ль, вмеща́ющая две ква́рты.

magpie ['mægpaɪ] *n.* соро́ка; (*fig., collector, hoarder*) барахо́льщик.

Magyar ['mægjɑ:(r)] *n.* **1.** (*pers.*) мадья́р (*fem.* -ка); венг|р (*fem.* -е́рка). **2.** (*language*) венге́рский язы́к. **3.** (**~ blouse**) венге́рка.

adj. мадья́рский, венге́рский.

Maharaja(h) [,mɑ:hə'rɑ:dʒə] *n.* махара́джа (*m.*).

Maharani [,mɑ:hə'rɑ:nɪ] *n.* магара́ни (*f. indecl.*).

Mahdi ['mɑ:dɪ] *n.* Махди́ (*m. indecl.*).

mah-jong [mɑ:'dʒɒŋ] *n.* маджо́нг.

mahogany [mə'hɒgənɪ] *n.* (*wood, tree*) кра́сное де́рево; (*colour*) цвет кра́сного де́рева.

Mahomet [mə'hɒmɪt], **-an** [mə'hɒmɪtən] = **Mohammed, -an**

mahout [mə'haʊt] *n.* погóнщик слонóв.

maid [meɪd] *n.* **1.** (*girl, unmarried woman*) дéва, девúца; **old ~** стáрая дéва; **~ of honour** фрéйлина. **2.** (*domestic servant*) прислýга, домрабóтница; (*in hotel*) гóрничная; **~ of all work** прислýга за всё.

cpd. **~servant** *n.* прислýга, служáнка.

maiden ['meɪd(ə)n] *n.* дéва.

adj. **1.** (*of a girl*) дéвúчий; **~ name** дéвичья фамúлия. **2.** (*unmarried*): **~ aunt** незамýжняя тётка. **3.** (*first*): **~ speech** пéрвая речь (новоúзбранного члéна парлáмента); **~ voyage** пéрвый рейс.

cpds. **~hair (fern)** *n.* адиáнтум; **~head** *n.* дéвственность; **~like, ~ly** *adjs.* дéвúчий.

mail[1] [meɪl] *n.* **1.** (*postal system*) пóчта; **by ordinary ~** обы́чной пóчтой; **~ order** почтóвый закáз/перевóд. **2.** (*~-train*) почтóвый пóезд. **3.** (*letters*) пóчта, пúсьма (*nt. pl.*); **has the ~ come?** пóчта былá?; **I had a lot of ~ today** я получúл сегóдня мнóго писéм.

v.t. отпр|авля́ть, -áвить (по пóчте); **where can I ~ this letter?** где тут почтóвый я́щик?; **the firm has me on its ~ing-list** я состою́ в спúске подпúсчиков фúрмы.

cpds. **~bag** *n.* мешóк для почтóвой корреспондéнции; **~-boat** *n.* почтóвый парохóд; **~box** *n.* (*US*) почтóвый я́щик; **~-coach** *n.* почтóвая карéта; **~-order** *adj.* торгýющий по почтóвым закáзам; **~-order firm** торгóво-посы́лочная фúрма; **~-van** *n.* (*road*) почтóвый вагóн; автомобúль, собирáющий и развозя́щий пóчту; (*rail*) почтóвый вагóн.

mail[2] [meɪl] *n.* (*coat of ~*) кольчýга.

mailed [meɪld] *adj.*: **~ fist** (*fig.*) бронúрованный кулáк, воéнная мощь.

maim [meɪm] *v.t.* калéчить, ис-; **he was ~ed for life** он остáлся калéкой на всю жизнь.

main [meɪn] *n.* **1.: in the ~** в основнóм. **2.: with might and ~** изо всех сил. **3.** (*arch., sea*) (откры́тое) мóре. **4.** (*sg. and pl., principal supply line*) магистрáль; (*sewerage*) канализáция; **our house is not on the mains** к нáшему дóму не подведенá канализáция; (*water*) водопровóд; водопровóдная магистрáль; **turn the water off at the ~(s)!** перекрóйте водопровóд; (*gas*) газопровóд; (*electricity*) кáбель (*m.*); **~s supply** электроснабжéние; **the ~s voltage is 250** напряжéние электросéти 250 вольт; **~s radio set** радиоприёмник, рабóтающий от сéти.

adj. **1.** (*principal*) глáвный, основнóй; **~ course** (*of meal*) жаркóе; **~ line** (*rail*) железнодорóжная магистрáль; **the ~ point** основнóй/глáвный пункт, суть; **~ road** магистрáль, глáвная дорóга; **~ street** глáвная ýлица. **2.** (*fully exerted*): **by ~ force** насúльно.

cpds. **~brace** *n.* грóта-брас; **splice the ~brace** (*coll., serve rum ration*) вы́дать (*pf.*) дополнúтельную пóрцию рóма; (*take a drink*) напúться (*pf.*); **~-deck** *n.* глáвная пáлуба; **~land** *n.* (*continent*) матерúк; (*opp. island*): **they live on the ~land** онú живýт на большóй землé; **~mast** *n.* грот-мáчта; **~sail** *n.* грот; **~spring** *n.* (*of watch*) ходовáя пружúна; (*fig.*) глáвная двúжущая сúла; **~stay** *n.* (*naut.*) грóта-штаг; (*fig.*) опóра; **~stream** *n.* (*fig.*) госпóдствующая тендéнция.

mainframe ['meɪnfreɪm] *adj.*: **~ computer** большáя ЭВМ.

mainly ['meɪnlɪ] *adv.* глáвным óбразом.

maintain [meɪn'teɪn] *v.t.* **1.** (*keep up*) поддéрживать (*impf.*); (*preserve*) сохран|я́ть, -úть; (*continue*) продолжáть (*impf.*); **the pilot ~ed a constant speed** пилóт поддéрживал постоя́нную скóрость; **if prices are ~ed** éсли цéны удéржатся на прéжнем ýровне; **law and order must be ~ed** законопоря́док дóлжен соблюдáться; **~ a custom** блюстú (*impf.*) обы́чай; **he ~ed his ground** он стоя́л на своём; **he ~ed silence** он хранúл молчáние. **2.** (*support*) содержáть (*impf.*); **he has a wife and child to ~** емý прихóдится содержáть женý и ребёнка. **3.** (*keep in repair*): **he ~s his car himself** он ремонтúрует свою́ машúну сам. **4.** (*defend*) отст|áивать, -оя́ть; **he ~ed his rights** он отстáивал своú правá. **5.** (*assert as true*) утверждáть (*impf.*); **he ~ed his innocence** он настáивал на своéй невинóвности.

maintenance ['meɪntənəns] *n.* **1.** (*maintaining*) поддержáние; сохранéние; **price ~** поддержáние цен. **2.** (*payment in support of dependants*) содержáние. **3.** (*care or repair of machinery etc.*) технúческое обслýживание; **~ crew** ремóнтная бригáда/комáнда; **~ manual** руковóдство по ухóду и обслýживанию.

maison(n)ette [ˌmeɪzə'net] *n.* (*small house*) кóттедж; (*apartment*) двухэтáжная квартúра.

maître d'hôtel [ˌmetrə dəʊ'tel, ˌmeɪt-] *n.* метрдотéль (*m.*).

maize [meɪz] *n.* кукурýза, маúс.

Maj. ['meɪdʒə(r)] *n.* (*abbr. of* **Major(-)**) м, (майóр).

majestic [mə'dʒestɪk] *adj.* величéственный.

majesty ['mædʒɪstɪ] *n.* (*stateliness*) величéственность; (*title*): **His/Her M~** егó/её велúчество.

majolica [mə'jɒlɪkə, mə'dʒɒl-] *n.* майóлика.

major ['meɪdʒə(r)] *n.* (*rank*) майóр; (*mus.*: **~ key**) мажóр.

adj. **1.** (*greater*) бóльший; **the ~ part** бóльшая часть; (*principal, more important*) глáвный; **~ road** глáвная дорóга; **the ~ part in a play** глáвная роль в пьéсе; **~ premise** большáя посы́лка. **2.** (*significant*) крýпный; **a ~ success** крýпный успéх; **~ advances in science** крýпные/значúтельные успéхи в наýке; **a ~ operation** крýпная оперáция; **a ~ war** большáя войнá. **3.** (*elder*): **Smith M~** Смит стáрший. **4.** (*mus.*) мажóрный; **~ key** мажóрная тонáльность; **~ third** большáя тéрция.

v.i.: **he ~ed in science** (*US*) он специализúровался в фúзике.

cpds. **~-domo** *n.* мажордóм; **~-general** *n.* генерáл-майóр.

Majorca [mə'jɔːkə, -'dʒɔː-] *n.* Мальóрка, Майóрка.

majority [mə'dʒɒrɪtɪ] *n.* **1.** (*greater part or number*) бóльшая часть; большинствó; (*in elections etc.*): **absolute ~** абсолю́тное большинствó; **they gained a ~ of 30** онú получúли на 30 голосóв бóльше; **the government has a ~ of 60** у правúтельства — большинствó в 60 голосóв бóльше, чем у оппозúции; **he won by a large ~** он победúл значúтельным большинствóм (голосóв); **~ verdict** приговóр, за котóрый проголосовáло бóльше половúны прися́жных заседáтелей. **2.** (*full age*) совершеннолéтие; **when will he attain his ~?** когдá он достúгнет совершеннолéтия?

make [meɪk] *n.* (*product of particular firm or pers.*): **a good ~ of car** автомобúль хорóшей мáрки; **is this jam your own ~?** э́то варéнье вáшего сóбственного изготовлéния?

v.t. **1.** (*fashion, create, construct*) дéлать, с-; (*build*) стрóить, по-; **what is this made of?** из чегó э́то сдéлано?; **I'm not made of stone** я не кáменный; **you must think I'm made of money** вы, навéрно, дýмаете, что я дéнежный мешóк; **this chair is made to last** э́тот стул сдéлан прóчно/добрóтно; **they were made for each other** онú бы́ли сóзданы друг для дрýга. **2.** (*sew together*) шить, с-; **a suit made to order** костю́м, сшúтый на закáз. **3.** (*utter*) произн|осúть, -естú; **he made a speech** он произнёс речь; он вы́ступил с рéчью; **she made a remark** онá сдéлала замечáние; **don't ~ a noise** не шумúте; соблюдáйте тишинý; **he made a choking sound** он издáл звук, слóвно поперхнýлся. **4.** (*compile, compose*) сост|авля́ть, -áвить; **~ a list!** состáвьте спúсок!; **have you made your will?** вы состáвили завещáние? **5.** (*bodily movements, etc.: execute*) дéлать, с-; *see also under n. obj.* **6.** (*manufacture, produce*) изгот|овля́ть, -óвить; произв|одúть, -естú; **the factory ~s shoes** завóд изготовля́ет óбувь; **paper is made here** здесь произвóдится бумáга; **he made a good impression** он произвёл хорóшее впечатлéние; **he made a sketch** он сдéлал рисýнок/наброóсок; **~ a film** сн|имáть, -ять фильм. **7.** (*prepare*) готóвить, при-; варúть, с-; **she made breakfast** онá приготóвила зáвтрак; **is the coffee made?** кóфе готóв?; **~ a fire** разв|одúть, -естú огóнь; **~ a bed** (*prepare it for sleeping*) стлать, по- (*or* стелúть, по-) постéль; (*tidy it after use*) уб|ирáть, -рáть постéль. **8.** (*establish, create*): **~ a rule** устан|áвливать, -овúть прáвило; **he ~s a rule of going to bed early** он взял (себé) за прáвило ложúться рáно. **9.** (*equal, result in*) равня́ться (*impf.*) +*d.*; **four plus two ~s six** четы́ре плюс два равня́ется шестú; **this ~s**

the third time you've been late вы уже́ тре́тий раз опа́здываете; **it ~s no difference** всё равно́; **this book ~s pleasant reading** э́ту кни́гу чита́ешь с удово́льствием; (*constitute*) **he ~s a good chairman** он хоро́ший председа́тель; **it ~s (good) sense** э́то разу́мно; (*become, turn out to be*): **she will ~ a good pianist** из неё вы́йдет хоро́шая пиани́стка. **10.** (*construe, understand*) пон|има́ть, -я́ть; **can you ~ anything of it?** вы что́-нибудь тут понима́ете?; **what do you ~ of this sentence?** как вы понима́ете э́то предложе́ние?; (*estimate, consider to be*): **what do you ~ the time?** кото́рый час на ва́ших часа́х?; **what do you ~ that bird to be?** что э́то, по-ва́шему, за пти́ца? **11.: ~ much of: he has not made much of his opportunities** он ма́ло испо́льзовал свои́ возмо́жности; **the author ~s much of his childhood** а́втор придаёт большо́е значе́ние своему́ де́тству; **~ little of** не придава́ть (*impf.*) большо́го значе́ния +*d.*; (*minimize*) преум|еньша́ть, -е́ньшить; **~ the best of** испо́льзовать наилу́чшим о́бразом; **~ the best of a bad job** де́лать, с- хоро́шую ми́ну при плохо́й игре́; **~ the most of** испо́льзовать (*impf., pf.*) максима́льно; **you only have a week, so ~ the most of it** у вас всего́ неде́ля, так что проведи́те её с максима́льной по́льзой. **12.** (*reach*) дост|ига́ть, -и́чь +*g.*; **we made the bridge by dusk** мы добра́лись до моста́, когда́ ста́ло смерка́ться; **we just made the train** мы е́ле поспе́ли на по́езд; **he made it** (*succeeded*) **after three years** он дости́г успе́ха че́рез три го́да; (*gain*) получ|а́ть, -и́ть; **he made a clear profit** он получи́л чи́стую при́быль; (*earn*) зараб|а́тывать, -о́тать; **he ~s a good living** он хорошо́ зараба́тывает; (*ensure*) обеспе́чи|вать, -ть; **this success made his career** э́тот успе́х обеспе́чил ему́ карье́ру; **he's got it made (for him)** (*coll.*) ему́ обеспе́чен успе́х. **13.** (*cause to be*) де́лать, с- +*a. and i.*; **the rain ~s the road slippery** от дождя́ доро́га де́лается ско́льзкой; **she made his life miserable** она́ отрави́ла ему́ жизнь; **she made herself a martyr** она́ преврати́ла себя́ в му́ченицу; **~ s.o. angry** серди́ть, рас- кого́-н.; (*appoint, elect*): **I made him my helper** я сде́лал его́ свои́м помо́щником; **they made him a general** его́ произвели́ в генера́лы; **they made him chairman** его́ вы́брали председа́телем; (*represent as*): **Shakespeare ~s Richard a weak character** Шекспи́р изобража́ет Ри́чарда безво́льным челове́ком. **14.** (*compel, cause to*) заст|авля́ть, -а́вить; побу|жда́ть, -ди́ть; **he made them suffer for it** за э́то он им отплати́л; **he was made to kneel** его́ заста́вили стать на коле́ни; **I'll ~ you pay for this!** вы у меня́ за э́то запла́тите!; **don't ~ me laugh!** не смеши́те меня́!; **the book made me laugh, but it made her cry** меня́ кни́га рассмеши́ла, а её расстро́гала до слёз; **it ~s you think** э́то заставля́ет заду́маться; **look what you made me do!** ≃ всё из-за вас!; смотри́, до чего́ ты меня́ довёл!; **she made believe she was crying** она́ сде́лала вид, бу́дто пла́чет; **he ~s Richard die in 1026** по нему́ выхо́дит, что Ри́чард у́мер в 1026 году́; **~ sth. do, ~ do with sth.** об|ходи́ться, -ойти́сь с чем-н.; **we must ~ do on our pension** мы должны́ обойти́сь одно́й пе́нсией; **can you ~ do without coal for another week?** мо́жете ли вы обойти́сь ещё одну́ неде́лю без угля́?

v.i. **1.** (*with certain preps.: move, proceed*): **~ after** пус|ка́ться, -ти́ться в пого́ню (*or* вслед) за+*i.*; **~ at** (*attack*) напусти́ться (*pf.*) на+*a.*; **~ for** (*head towards*) напр|авля́ться, -а́виться на+*a. or* к+*d.*; (*depart for*) отпр|авля́ться, -а́виться в/на+*a.*; (*assail*) кида́ться, ки́нуться на+*a.*; (*try to get*): **he made for her purse** он попыта́лся стащи́ть у неё кошелёк; (*conduce to*) спосо́бствовать (*impf.*) +*d.*; **~ with** (*US coll., hurry up, get on*): **~ with the drinks!** неси́те скоре́е напи́тки! **2.** (*act, behave*): **he made as if to go** он сде́лал вид, что хо́чет уйти́; **may I ~ so bold as to come in?** позво́льте мне взять на себя́ сме́лость войти́. **3.** (**~** *a profit*): **did you ~ on the deal?** ну как, кре́пко нагре́ли ру́ки на э́той сде́лке? (*coll.*).

with advs.: **~ away** *v.i.* = **~ off; ~ away with** (*get rid of*) изб|авля́ться, -а́виться от+*g.*; (*kill*) прик|а́нчивать, -о́нчить; **~ away with o.s.** (*or* **one's life**) поко́нчить (*pf.*) с собо́й; **~ off** *v.i.* (*hurry away*) сбе|га́ть, -жа́ть; **he made off with all speed** он пусти́лся бежа́ть со всех ног; (*escape, abscond*) скр|ыва́ться, -ы́ться; **the thieves made off with the jewellery** во́ры скры́лись, захвати́в с собо́й драгоце́нности; **~ out** *v.t.* (*write out*): **~ out a bill/cheque** выпи́сывать, вы́писать счёт/чек; **~ out a report** сост|авля́ть, -а́вить отчёт; (*assert, maintain*) утвержда́ть (*impf.*); **they ~ out he was drunk** они́ утвержда́ют, что он был пьян; **you ~ me out to be a liar** по-ва́шему выхо́дит, что я лгу; (*conclude*): **how do you ~ that out?** как э́то у вас получа́ется?; (*argue*): **he made out a good case for it** он привёл ве́ские до́воды в по́льзу э́того; (*understand*) раз|бира́ться, -обра́ться в+*p.*; **I can't ~ him out** я не могу́ его́ поня́ть; **we can't ~ out what he wants** мы ника́к не поймём, чего́ он хо́чет; (*discern, distinguish*) различ|а́ть, -и́ть; *v.i.* (*coll., get on*): **how did he ~ out?** как он спра́вился (с э́той зада́чей)?; **~ over** *v.t.* (*refashion*) переде́л|ывать, -ать; (*transfer*) перев|оди́ть, -ести́; **he made the money over to me** он перевёл де́ньги на моё и́мя; **~ up** *v.t.* (*increase*): **they made up the wall to its former height** они́ достро́или сте́ну до пре́жней высоты́; **he made up the mixture to the right consistency** он развёл смесь до ну́жной консисте́нции; (*complete*): **~ up the complement** сост|авля́ть, -а́вить кома́нду, гру́ппу *и т.п.*; **will you ~ up a four at bridge?** не соста́вите ли вы нам па́ртию в бридж?; (*pay; pay the residue of*) допла́|чивать, -ти́ть; **I shall ~ up the difference out of my own pocket** я доплачу́ ра́зницу из своего́ карма́на; (*repay*) возме|ща́ть, -сти́ть; **we must ~ it up to him somehow** мы должны́ ка́к-то возмести́ть ему́ э́то; (*recover*) навёрст|ывать, -а́ть; (*fig.*): **he quickly made up leeway in his studies** он бы́стро ликвиди́ровал отстава́ние в свои́х заня́тиях; **he made up his losses in a single night** он возмести́л свои́ убы́тки за одну́ ночь; (*prepare,* **~** *ready*) гото́вить, при-/из-; **ask the chemist to ~ up this prescription** попроси́те фармаце́вта пригото́вить лека́рство по э́тому реце́пту; **~ up a bed** заст|ила́ть, -ла́ть (*or* -ели́ть) посте́ль; **~ up a road** асфальти́ровать (*impf., pf.*) доро́гу; **we ~ up the fire before going to bed** пе́ред сном мы разжига́ем ками́н; (*typ.: set up*) наб|ира́ть, -ра́ть; (*sew together*) шить, с-; (*pack up, tie together*): **the parcel was neatly made up** посы́лка была́ аккура́тно упако́вана; (*fig.*): **~ up one's mind** реш|а́ть, -и́ть; **my mind is made up** я при́нял реше́ние; **~ up your mind!** реша́йтесь на что́-нибудь!; (*form, compose; compile*) сост|авля́ть, -а́вить; **what are the qualities which ~ up his character?** каки́е ка́чества определя́ют его́ хара́ктер?; **life is made up of disappointments** жизнь полна́ разочаро́ваний; (*concoct, invent*) выду́мывать; сочин|я́ть, -и́ть; **the whole story was made up** вся э́та исто́рия была́ вы́думана; **he ~s it up as he goes along** он сочиня́ет на ходу́; (*assemble*) соб|ира́ть, -ра́ть; (*settle*) ула́|живать, -дить; **~ (it) up** (*be reconciled*) мири́ться, по-; **let's ~ it up and be friends** дава́йте помири́мся; (*for a stage performance*) гримирова́ть, за-; **he was made up to look the part** его́ загримирова́ли как тре́бовалось для ро́ли; (*with cosmetics*) кра́сить, по-; ма́заться, на-; **she was heavily made up** она́ была́ си́льно накра́шена; *v.i.* (*be reconciled*) мири́ться, по-; (*for the stage*) гримирова́ться, за-; (*use cosmetics*) кра́ситься, на-; **~ up for** (*compensate for*) возме|ща́ть, -сти́ть; **this will ~ up for everything** э́тим всё бу́дет компенси́ровано; **he was lazy at school but he has made up for it since** в шко́ле он лени́лся, но пото́м наверста́л всё (с лихво́й); **~ up to** (*curry favour with*) подли́з|ываться, -а́ться к+*d.*

cpds. **~-believe** *n.*: **he lives in a world of ~-believe** он живёт в ми́ре грёз; **it's all ~-believe** э́то — сплошна́я фанта́зия; **~shift** *n.* вре́менное приспособле́ние/сре́дство; (*attr.*): **a ~shift shelter** на́скоро сколо́ченное укры́тие; время́нка; **a ~shift dinner** на́скоро пригото́вленный обе́д; **~-up** *n.* (*composition*): **there is some cowardice in his ~-up** он не́сколько трусова́т; (*theatr., etc.*) грим; **~-up room** *n.* гримёрная; **put on ~-up** гримирова́ться, за-; (*cosmetics*) космети́ческие това́ры (*m. pl.*); **she wears, uses a lot of ~-up** она́ си́льно кра́сится; **~weight** *n.* дове́сок; противове́с.

maker ['meɪkə(r)] *n.* (*manufacturer*) производи́тель (*m.*), изготови́тель (*m.*); (*relig.*, *creator*): **the M~ of the universe** творе́ц вселе́нной; **he went to meet his M~** он преста́вился.

making ['meɪkɪŋ] *n.* **1.** (*that which makes s.o. successful etc.*; *decisive influence*): **this incident was the ~ of him** благодаря́ э́тому собы́тию, он вы́шел в лю́ди. **2.** (*pl.*, *profits*) за́работок. **3.** (*pl.*, *potential qualities*): **he has all the ~s of a general** у него́ есть все зада́тки, что́бы стать генера́лом. **4.** (*construction*) стро́йка, построе́ние; (*creation*) созда́ние; **the difficulties were not of my ~** э́ти тру́дности возни́кли не из-за меня́; (*compilation*) составле́ние; (*manufacture, production*) изготовле́ние, произво́дство; (*preparation*) приготовле́ние.

malachite ['mælə,kaɪt] *n.* малахи́т; (*attr.*) малахи́товый.

maladjusted [,mælə'dʒʌstɪd] *adj.* (*fig.*, *of pers.*) пло́хо приспосо́бленный; **~ children** трудновоспиту́емые де́ти.

maladjustment [,mælə'dʒʌstmənt] *n.* плоха́я приспособля́емость.

maladministration [,mæləd,mɪnɪ'streɪʃ(ə)n] *n.* плохо́е управле́ние.

maladroit [,mælə'drɔɪt, 'mæl-] *adj.* (*clumsy*) нело́вкий; (*tactless*) беста́ктный.

maladroitness [,mælə'drɔɪtnɪs] *n.* нело́вкость; беста́ктность.

malady ['mælədɪ] *n.* (*lit.*, *fig.*) неду́г, боле́знь.

Malaga ['mæləgə] *n.* (*town*) Мала́га; (*wine*) мала́га.

Malagasy [,mælə'gæsɪ] *n.* (*pers.*) малагаси́|ец (*fem.* -йка); (*language*) малагаси́йский язы́к.

adj. малагаси́йский; **the ~ Republic** Малагаси́йская респу́блика.

malaise [mə'leɪz] *n.* (*bodily discomfort*) недомога́ние; (*disquiet*) беспоко́йство.

malapropism ['mæləprɒ,pɪz(ə)m] *n.* непра́вильное употребле́ние слов.

malapropos [,mælæprə'pəʊ] *adv.* некста́ти, невпопа́д.

malaria [mə'leərɪə] *n.* маляри́я.

malarial [mə'leərɪəl] *adj.* маляри́йный.

malarkey [mə'lɑːkɪ] *n.*: **none of your ~!** конча́йте трепа́ться! (*sl.*).

Malawi [mə'lɑːwɪ] *n.* Мала́ви (*nt. indecl.*).

Malaya [mə'leɪə] *n.* Мала́йя.

Malay(an) [mə'leɪ(ən)] *n.* (*pers.*) мала́|ец (*fem.* -йка); (*language*) мала́йский язы́к.

adj. мала́йский.

Malaysia [mə'leɪzɪə, -ʒə] *n.* Мала́йзия.

malcontent ['mælkən,tent] *n.* & *adj.* недово́льный.

male [meɪl] *n.* (*pers.*) мужчи́на (*m.*); (*animal etc.*) саме́ц.

adj. мужско́й; **~ animal** саме́ц; **~ heir** насле́дник; **~ model** манеке́нщик; **~ nurse** санита́р; **~(-voice) choir** мужско́й хор; (*tech.*): **~ screw** винт, болт, шуру́п.

malediction [,mælɪ'dɪkʃ(ə)n] *n.* прокля́тие.

malefactor ['mælɪ,fæktə(r)] *n.* злоде́й.

maleficent [mə'lefɪs(ə)nt] *adj.* (*hurtful*) па́губный; (*criminal*) престу́пный.

malevolence [mə'levələns] *n.* недоброжела́тельность, злора́дство.

malevolent [mə'levələnt] *adj.* недоброжела́тельный, злора́дный.

malfeasance [mæl'fiːz(ə)ns] *n.* должностно́е преступле́ние.

malformation [,mælfɔː'meɪʃ(ə)n] *n.* непра́вильное образова́ние; уро́дство.

malformed [mæl'fɔːmd] *adj.* непра́вильно/пло́хо сформиро́ванный; уро́дливый.

malfunction [mæl'fʌŋkʃ(ə)n] *n.* неиспра́вная рабо́та, отка́з.

v.i. неиспра́вно де́йствовать (*impf.*).

Mali ['mɑːlɪ] *n.* Мали́ (*nt. indecl.*).

Malian ['mɑːlɪən] *n.* мали́|ец (*fem.* -йка).

adj. мали́йский.

malice ['mælɪs] *n.* **1.** (*ill-will*) зло́ба; **bear ~ to(wards), against s.o.** таи́ть, за- зло́бу на кого́-н. (*or* про́тив кого́-н.); **I bear you no ~** я не пита́ю к вам зло́бы. **2.** (*leg.*, *wrongful intent*): **with ~ aforethought** злоумы́шленно.

malicious [mə'lɪʃəs] *adj.* (*of pers.*) злой; (*of thought, act etc.*) зло́бный; **~ tongues** злы́е языки́; **~ intent** престу́пное наме́рение.

malign [mə'laɪn] *adj.* па́губный.

v.t. (*slander*) клевета́ть, на- на+*a.*; оклевета́ть (*pf.*); (*defame*) поро́чить, о-; черни́ть, о-; **much-~ed** оклевета́нный.

malignancy [mə'lɪgnənsɪ] *n.* зло́бность; (*med.*) злока́чественность.

malignant [mə'lɪgnənt] *adj.* злой, зло́бный; (*med.*) злока́чественный.

malignity [mə'lɪgnɪtɪ] *n.* зло́бность.

malinger [mə'lɪŋgə(r)] *v.i.* симули́ровать (*impf.*, *pf.*) боле́знь.

malingerer [mə'lɪŋgərə(r)] *n.* симуля́нт (*fem.* -ка).

mall [mæl, mɔːl] *n.* алле́я; (*shopping precinct*) торго́вый центр.

mallard ['mælɑːd] *n.* кря́ква.

malleability [,mælɪə'bɪlɪtɪ] *n.* ко́вкость; (*fig.*) пода́тливость.

malleable ['mælɪəb(ə)l] *adj.* (*of metal etc.*) ко́вкий; (*of pers.*) пода́тливый.

mallet ['mælɪt] *n.* деревя́нный молото́к; колоту́шка.

mallow ['mæləʊ] *n.* ма́льва, просвирня́к.

malmsey ['mɑːmzɪ] *n.* мальва́зия.

malnutrition [,mælnjuː'trɪʃ(ə)n] *n.* недоеда́ние; непра́вильное пита́ние.

malodorous [mæl'əʊdərəs] *adj.* злово́нный.

malpractice [mæl'præktɪs] *n.* (*wrongdoing*) противозако́нное де́йствие; (*leg.*, *of physician*) престу́пная небре́жность (врача́); (*leg.*, *abuse of trust*) злоупотребле́ние дове́рием.

malt [mɔːlt, mɒlt] *n.* со́лод; **~ liquor** солодовый напи́ток.

v.t. (*make into ~*) солоди́ть, на-.

cpd. **~house** *n.* солодо́вня.

Malta ['mɔːltə, 'mɒltə] *n.* Ма́льта.

Maltese [mɔːl'tiːz, mɒl-] *n.* (*pers.*) мальти́|ец (*fem.* -йка); (*language*) мальти́йский язы́к.

adj. мальти́йский.

Malthusian [mæl'θjuːzɪən] *n.* мальтузиа́нец.

adj. мальтузиа́нский.

maltreat [mæl'triːt] *v.t.* ду́рно обраща́ться (*impf.*) с+*i.*; **he was jailed for ~ing his children** он был заключён в тюрьму́ за дурно́е обраще́ние с детьми́; **~ books** по́ртить (*impf.*) кни́ги.

maltreatment [mæl'triːtmənt] *n.* дурно́е обраще́ние (*с кем*).

malversation [,mælvə'seɪʃ(ə)n] *n.* злоупотребле́ние по слу́жбе.

mama ['mæmə, mə'mɑː], **mamma** ['mæmə], **mammy** ['mæmɪ] *n.* ма́ма, ма́мочка; **~'s boy** ма́менькин сыно́к.

mamba ['mæmbə] *n.* ма́мба.

mamma ['mæmə] = **mama**

mammal ['mæm(ə)l] *n.* млекопита́ющее (живо́тное).

mammalian [,mæ'meɪlɪən] *adj.* относя́щийся к млекопита́ющим.

mammary ['mæmərɪ] *adj.*: **~ gland** моло́чная железа́.

Mammon ['mæmən] *n.* (*also* **m~**, *fig.*) мам(м)о́на, бога́тство.

mammoth ['mæməθ] *n.* ма́монт.

adj. (*huge*) гига́нтский, грома́дный.

mammy ['mæmɪ] = **mama**

Man[1] [mæn] *n.*: **the Isle of ~** о́стров (*abbr.* о́-в) Мэн.

man[2] [mæn] *n.* **1.** (*person, human being*) челове́к (*pl.* лю́ди); **what can a ~ do?** что (тут) поде́лаешь?; **as one ~** все как оди́н; **to a ~** все до одного́; **any ~ = anybody; no ~ = nobody; ~ about town** све́тский челове́к; **~ in the street** сре́дний челове́к; **a ~ in a thousand** ре́дкостный челове́к; **~ of action** челове́к де́йствия/де́ла; **~ of character** челове́к с хара́ктером; **~ of God** (*saint*) свято́й уго́дник; (*priest*) свяще́нник; **~ of honour** челове́к че́сти; че́стный челове́к; **~ of ideas** изобрета́тельный челове́к; **~ of letters** литера́тор; **~ of mark** выдаю́щийся челове́к; **~ of means** состоя́тельный челове́к; **~ of the moment** челове́к, по́сланный само́й судьбо́й; **~ of peace** миролюби́вый челове́к; **~ of principle** принципиа́льный челове́к; **~ of property** состоя́тельный челове́к; **~ of sense** разу́мный челове́к; **~ of taste** челове́к со вку́сом; **~ of his word** челове́к сло́ва; **~ of few words** немногосло́вный челове́к; **~ of the world** быва́лый челове́к; **he is an Oxford ~** он выпускни́к О́ксфорда; **the inner ~** душа́; вну́треннее «я»; (*joc.*) желу́док; **I feel a**

new ~ я чу́вствую себя́ обновлённым; **he is his own** ~ он сам себе́ хозя́ин; **he's just the** ~ **for the job** он со́здан для э́того; **I'm your** ~ я и́менно тот, кто вам ну́жен; я с ва́ми. **2.** (*mankind*) челове́к, челове́чество; **the rights of** ~ права́ челове́ка; (*typifying an era*): **Renaissance** ~ челове́к эпо́хи Возрожде́ния; **Neanderthal** ~ неандерта́лец. **3.** (*adult male*) мужчи́на (*m.*); **they talked** ~ **to** ~ они́ говори́ли как мужчи́на с мужчи́ной; **I have known him** ~ **and boy** я его́ зна́ю с де́тства; **old** ~ стари́к; **young** ~ молодо́й челове́к; **come to** ~**'s estate** дост|ига́ть, -и́чь совершенноле́тия; (*implying virility or fortitude*): **it will make a** ~ **of him** э́то сде́лает из него́ настоя́щего мужчи́ну; **he bore the pain like a** ~ он терпе́л боль как настоя́щий мужчи́на; **be a** ~**!** бу́дьте мужчи́ной! **4.** (*in address*): **speak up,** ~**!** говори́те же!; **tell me, my (good)** ~ **...** скажи́те мне, дружо́к...; **old** ~ старина́ (*m.*). **5.** (*husband*) муж; **they lived as** ~ **and wife** они́ жи́ли как муж и жена́; **my old** ~**'s a dustman** мой стари́к рабо́тает му́сорщиком. **6.: best** ~ (*at wedding*) ша́фер. **7.** (*servant, esp. valet*) слуга́ (*m.*). **8.** (*pl., soldiers*) солда́ты; (*sailors*) матро́сы; (*employees*) рабо́чие. **9.** (*piece in chess*) фигу́ра; (*in draughts*) ша́шка; (*in other games*) фи́шка.

v.t. **1.** (*mil., equip*) укомплекто́в|ывать, -а́ть ли́чным соста́вом. **2.** (*occupy*) зан|има́ть, -я́ть; ~ **the guns** обслу́живать (*impf.*) ору́дия; **a** ~**ned spacecraft** пилоти́руемый косми́ческий кора́бль.

cpds. ~**-at-arms** *n.* (*arch.*) во́ин, солда́т; ~**-eater** *n.* людое́д; ~**-eating tiger** тигр-людое́д; ~**handle** *v.t.* (*move by manual effort*) та|ска́ть (*indet.*), -щи́ть (*det.*) (вручну́ю); (*treat roughly*) изб|ива́ть, -и́ть; ~**-hater** *n.* мизантро́п, человеконенави́стник; ~**hole** *n.* (*inspection well*) смотрово́й коло́дец; (*naut.*) люк; ~**-hour** *n.* челове́ко-час; ~**-hunt** *n.* ро́зыск, полице́йская обла́ва; ~**kind** *n.* челове́чество; ~**-made** *adj.* иску́сственный; (*text.*) синтети́ческий; ~**-of-war,** ~**-o'-war** *nn.* вое́нный кора́бль; ~**power** *n.* рабо́чая си́ла; ~**servant** *n.* слуга́; ~**-size(d)** *adj.* для взро́слого челове́ка; ~**slaughter** *n.* непредумы́шленное уби́йство; уби́йство по неосторо́жности; ~**-trap** *n.* западня́.

manacle ['mænək(ə)l] *n.* нару́чник; (*pl., fetters, lit., fig.*) око́в|ы (*pl., g.* —).

v.t. над|ева́ть, -е́ть нару́чники *+d.*

manag|e ['mænɪdʒ] *v.t.* **1.** (*control, conduct*) управля́ть, руководи́ть, заве́довать (*all impf. +i.*); **they** ~**ed the business between them** они́ вдвоём управля́ли предприя́тием; **the estate was** ~**ed by his brother** име́нием управля́л его́ брат; ~**e a household** вести́ (*det.*) (дома́шнее) хозя́йство; ~**ing director** дире́ктор-распоряди́тель (*m.*). **2.** (*handle*) владе́ть (*impf.*) *+i.*; **she can** ~**e a bicycle** она́ уме́ет е́здить на велосипе́де; **can you** ~**e the car by yourself?** вы мо́жете са́ми спра́виться с маши́ной?; **I can't** ~**e it** э́то мне не по си́лам. **3.** (*be* ~*er of*): **he has** ~**ed the team for 10 years** он руководи́л кома́ндой в тече́ние десяти́ лет; **the singer was looking for someone to** ~**e him** певе́ц подыскивал себе́ импреса́рио; **who** ~**es this department?** кто заве́дует э́тим отде́лом? **4.** (*cope with*) спр|авля́ться, -а́виться с*+i.*; **I can't** ~**e this work** я не спра́влюсь с э́той рабо́той; э́та рабо́та мне не по плечу́; **can't you** ~**e another sandwich?** неуже́ли вы не оси́лите ещё оди́н бутербро́д? **5.** (*contrive*) суме́ть (*pf.*); умудр|я́ться, -и́ться; ухитр|я́ться, -и́ться; **he** ~**ed to answer** он суме́л отве́тить; **I** ~**ed to convince him** мне удало́сь убеди́ть его́; **he** ~**ed to break his neck** он умудри́лся слома́ть себе́ ше́ю; **can you** ~ **dinner?** вы смо́жете пообе́дать с на́ми?

v.i. (*cope*) спр|авля́ться, -а́виться; **you will never** ~**e on your pension** вы ни за что не проживёте на свою́ пе́нсию; (*get by, make do*) об|ходи́ться, -ойти́сь; **we must** ~**e without bread today** сего́дня нам придётся обойти́сь без хле́ба.

manageable ['mænɪdʒəb(ə)l] *adj.* (*of task etc.*) выполни́мый; **of** ~ **dimensions** удо́бных разме́ров; (*of pers.*) сгово́рчивый; **he is** ~ с ним мо́жно договори́ться.

management ['mænɪdʒmənt] *n.* **1.** (*control, controlling*) управле́ние (*чем*), руково́дство, организа́ция; **estate** ~ управле́ние име́нием; **it was all due to bad** ~ всё де́ло бы́ло в плохо́м управле́нии. **2.** (*handling pers. or thg.*) обраще́ние; уме́ние владе́ть *+i.*; **staff** ~ обраще́ние с ли́чным соста́вом. **3.** (*governing body*) правле́ние; (*managerial staff*) администра́ция; (*senior staff*) дире́кция.

manager ['mænɪdʒə(r)] *n.* **1.** (*controller of business etc.*) заве́дующий (*чем*); нача́льник, дире́ктор, ме́неджер; (*sport*) ста́рший тре́нер; ме́неджер; **sales** ~ заве́дующий отде́лом сбы́та. **2.** (*pers. with administrative skill*) администра́тор; **she is no** ~ (*of housewife*) она́ плоха́я хозя́йка.

manageress [,mænɪdʒə'res] *n.* заве́дующая; **canteen** ~ заве́дующая столо́вой.

managerial [,mænɪ'dʒɪərɪəl] *adj.* администрати́вный; управле́нческий.

manatee [,mænə'ti:] *n.* ламанти́н.

Manchu [mæn'tʃu:] *n.* маньчжу́р (*fem.* -ка).

Manchuria [mæn'tʃʊərɪə] *n.* Маньчжу́рия.

mandarin[1] ['mændərɪn] *n.* **1.** (*official*) мандари́н; (*bureaucrat*) чино́вник; (*pedant*) бо́нза (*m.*). **2.** (*language*) мандари́нское наре́чие кита́йского языка́.

mandarin[2] ['mændərɪn] *n.* (*orange*) мандари́н.

mandate ['mændeɪt] *n.* (*authority*) полномо́чие; (*to govern territory*) манда́т; (*given by voters*) нака́з; (*leg.*) прика́з суда́.

v.t.: ~**d territory** подманда́тная террито́рия.

mandatory ['mændətərɪ] *adj.* (*compulsory*) обяза́тельный; (*hist., pert. to mandates*) манда́тный; ~ **state** госуда́рство-мандата́рий.

mandible ['mændɪb(ə)l] *n.* (*of mammals*) ни́жняя че́люсть; (*of birds*) створка клю́ва; (*of insects*) жва́ло.

mandolin(e) [,mændə'lɪn] *n.* мандоли́на.

mandrake ['mændreɪk] *n.* мандраго́ра.

mandrill ['mændrɪl] *n.* мандри́л.

mane [meɪn] *n.* гри́ва.

manège [mæ'neɪʒ] *n.* мане́ж.

maneuver [mə'nu:və(r)], **-ability** [mə,nu:vrə'bɪlɪtɪ], **-able** [mə'nu:vrəb(ə)l] = **manoeuvre** *etc.*

manful ['mænfʊl] *adj.* му́жественный.

manganese ['mæŋgə,ni:z] *n.* ма́рганец.

adj. ма́рганцевый.

mange [meɪndʒ] *n.* парша́.

mangel(-wurzel) ['mæŋg(ə)l], **mangold** ['mæŋg(ə)ld] *n.* кормова́я свёкла.

manger ['meɪndʒə(r)] *n.* я́сл|и (*pl., g.* -е́й); **dog in the** ~ соба́ка на се́не.

mangle[1] ['mæŋg(ə)l] *n.* (отжи́мный) като́к.

v.t. отж|има́ть, -а́ть.

mangle[2] ['mæŋg(ə)l] *v.t.* (*mutilate*) уро́довать, из-; (*cut to pieces*) кромса́ть, ис-; (*fig.*) иска|жа́ть, -зи́ть.

mango ['mæŋgəʊ] *n.* ма́нго (*indecl.*).

mangosteen ['mæŋgə,sti:n] *n.* мангуста́н.

mangrove ['mæŋgrəʊv] *n.* древоко́рень (*m.*).

mangy ['meɪndʒɪ] *adj.* парши́вый.

manhood ['mænhʊd] *n.* **1.** (*state of being a man; adult status*) возмужа́лость; взро́слость, совершенноле́тие. **2.** (*manly qualities*) му́жественность. **3.** (*the male population*) мужско́е населе́ние.

mania ['meɪnɪə] *n.* ма́ния; (*lit., fig.*) **a** ~ **for work** ма́ния к рабо́те.

maniac ['meɪnɪ,æk] *n.* манья́к; (*fig.*): **football** ~ зая́длый футболи́ст; **speed** ~ люби́тель (*m.*) ско́рости.

adj. (*also* ~**al, manic**) маниака́льный.

manic-depressive ['mænɪk] *adj.* страда́ющий маниака́льно-депресси́вным психо́зом.

manicur|e ['mænɪ,kjʊə(r)] *n.* маникю́р; (*attr.*) маникю́рный.

v.t. де́лать, с- маникю́р *+d.*; **she was** ~**ing her nails** она́ де́лала себе́ маникю́р.

manicurist ['mænɪ,kjʊərɪst] *n.* (*fem.*) маникю́рша.

manifest ['mænɪ,fest] *n.* (*cargo-list*) деклара́ция, манифе́ст.

adj. я́вный, очеви́дный; **he was** ~**ly disturbed** он был я́вно взволно́ван.

v.t. (*show clearly*) я́сно пока́з|ывать, -а́ть; (*exhibit*) прояв|ля́ть, -и́ть; **he** ~**ed a desire to leave** он прояви́л жела́ние уйти́; (*prove*) дока́з|ывать, -а́ть.

manifestation [ˌmænɪfeˈsteɪʃ(ə)n] *n.* проявлéние; (*public demonstration*) манифестáция.
manifesto [ˌmænɪˈfestəʊ] *n.* манифéст.
manifold [ˈmænɪˌfəʊld] *adj.* (*numerous*) многочи́сленный; (*various*) разнообрáзный.
manikin [ˈmænɪkɪn] *n.* (*undersized man*) человéчек; (*dwarf*) кáрлик; (*artist's dummy*) манекéн.
Manila [məˈnɪlə] *n.* Мани́ла.
adj. мани́льский; ~ **paper** мани́льская бумáга.
manioc [ˈmænɪˌɒk] *n.* маниóка.
manipulate [məˈnɪpjʊˌleɪt] *v.t.* (*lit., fig.; also pej.*) манипули́ровать (*impf.*) +*i.*; **he ~d the arguments in his own favour** он умéло орýдовал дóводами в свою пóльзу.
manipulation [məˌnɪpjʊˈleɪʃ(ə)n] *n.* манипуля́ция; ~ **of the stock market** игрá на би́рже.
manipulator [məˈnɪpjʊˌleɪtə(r)] *n.* манипуля́тор.
manlike [ˈmænlaɪk] *adj.* мужскóй; (*of a woman*) мужеподóбная; (*of animal*) похóжий на человéка.
manliness [ˈmænlɪnɪs] *n.* мýжественность.
manly [ˈmænlɪ] *adj.* (*of pers.*) мужскóй; (*bold, resolute*) мýжественный; (*of qualities etc.*) подобáющий мужчи́не.
manna [ˈmænə] *n.* мáнна; **like ~ from heaven** мáнна небéсная.
mannequin [ˈmænɪkɪn] *n.* (*pers.*) манекéнщица; (*dummy*) манекéн.
manner [ˈmænə(r)] *n.* **1.** (*way, fashion, mode*) óбраз; **in, after this ~** таки́м óбразом; **in a ~ of speaking** в нéкотором смы́сле; **he holds his fork in an awkward ~** он неуклю́же дéржит ви́лку; ~ **of proceeding** при́нятый поря́док (*чего*); **adverb of ~** нарéчие óбраза дéйствия; **he made his first speech as to the ~ born** он произнёс свою пéрвую речь, как прирождённый орáтор. **2.** (*pl., ways of life; customs*) обы́чаи (*m. pl.*); нрáвы (*m. pl.*); **comedy of ~s** комéдия нрáвов. **3.** (*personal bearing, style of behaviour*) манéра; **he has a strange ~ of speaking** у негó стрáнная манéра говори́ть; **he has an awkward ~** он дéржится нелóвко; (*style in literature or art*): **after the ~ of Dickens** в сти́ле Ди́ккенса. **4.** (*pl., behaviour*) манéры (*f. pl.*); **good, bad ~s** хорóшие/плохи́е манéры; **it is bad ~s to yawn** зевáть неприли́чно; **the children have good table ~s** дéти умéют себя́ вести́ за столóм; (*polite behaviour*): **have you no ~s?** где вáши манéры?; **have you forgotten your ~s?** вы забы́ли, как нáдо себя́ вести́? **5.** (*kind*): **what ~ of man is he?** что он за человéк?; **all ~ of things** вся́кого рóда вéщи; **by no ~ of means** никóим óбразом.
mannered [ˈmænəd] *adj.* (*showing mannerism*) манéрный.
mannerism [ˈmænəˌrɪz(ə)m] *n.* манéра, манéрность; (*style of art*) маньери́зм.
mannerist [ˈmænəˌrɪst] *n.* (*art*) маньери́ст.
mannerly [ˈmænəlɪ] *adj.* вéжливый.
mannish [ˈmænɪʃ] *adj.* (*of a woman*) похóжая на мужчи́ну; мужеподóбная.
manœuvrability [məˌnuːvrəˈbɪlɪtɪ] (*US* **maneuverability**) *n.* манёвренность.
manœuvrable [məˈnuːvrəb(ə)l] (*US* **maneuverable**) *adj.* манёвренный.
manœuvre [məˈnuːvə(r)] (*US* **maneuver**) *n.* **1.** (*mil.*) манёвр; **on ~s** на манёврах; **the Army is holding ~s** сухопýтные войскá провóдят манёвры. **2.** (*adroit management*) манёвр, махинáция; **the conditions leave us no room for ~** обстанóвка таковá, что маневри́ровать невозмóжно; (*intrigue*) интри́га.
v.t. маневри́ровать (*impf.*) +*i.*; **I ~d him to his chair** мне удалóсь подвести́ егó к стýлу; **he ~d his queen out of a difficult position** он вы́вел ферзя́ из трýдного положéния.
v.i. (*lit., fig.*) маневри́ровать (*impf.*).
manometer [məˈnɒmɪtə(r)] *n.* манóметр.
manor [ˈmænə(r)] *n.* (*estate*) помéстье; **lord of the ~** помéщик; (~-*house*) усáдьба, помéщичий дом.
manorial [məˈnɔːrɪəl] *adj.* манориáльный.
manqué [ˈmɒŋkeɪ] *adj.*: **a poet ~** неудáвшийся поэ́т.
mansard [ˈmænsɑːd] *n.* (~ *roof*) мансáрдная кры́ша; (*garret*) мансáрда.
manse [mæns] *n.* дом пáстора (*в Шотландии*).
mansion [ˈmænʃ(ə)n] *n.* особня́к; **country ~** зáгородный дом; (*pl., house of flats*) многокварти́рный дом.
mantel(piece) [ˈmænt(ə)lˌpiːs] *n.*ками́нная пóлка.
mantilla [mænˈtɪlə] *n.* манти́лья.
mantis [ˈmæntɪs] *n.* **(praying ~)** богомóл.
mantissa [mænˈtɪsə] *n.* манти́сса
mantle [ˈmænt(ə)l] *n.* **1.** (*cloak*) мáнтия; (*fig.*): **he assumed the prophet's ~** он взял на себя́ роль прорóка; **the ~ of the late Prime Minister has fallen on him** он продолжáтель дéла покóйного премьéр-мини́стра. **2.** (*fig., covering*) покрóв. **3.** (*for gas-jet*) кали́льная сéтка.
v.t. & i. (*liter.*): **the fields were ~d with snow** поля́ бы́ли покры́ты снéгом; **an ivy-~d wall** стенá уви́тая плющóм; **her cheeks ~d with blushes** онá зардéлась.
manual [ˈmænjʊəl] *n.* **1.** (*handbook*) руковóдство; (*textbook*) учéбник; (*aid*) посóбие. **2.** (*keyboard*) клавиатýра оргáна.
adj. (*operated by hand*) ручнóй; **~ly** ручны́м спóсобом; (*performed by hand*): ~ **labour** физи́ческий труд.
manufactur|e [ˌmænjʊˈfæktʃə(r)] *n.* изготовлéние; (*on large scale*) произвóдство; **goods of foreign ~e** издéлия инострáнного произвóдства.
v.t. **1.** (*produce*) изгот|овля́ть, -óвить; **~ed goods** промтовáры (*m. pl.*); **~ing industry** обрабáтывающая промы́шленность; **~ing town** промы́шленный гóрод. **2.** (*make up, invent*) фабриковáть, с-.
manumission [ˌmænjʊˈmɪʃ(ə)n] *n.* освобождéние от рáбства.
manumit [ˌmænjʊˈmɪt] *v.t.* отпус|кáть, -ти́ть на вóлю.
manure [məˈnjʊə(r)] *n.* навóз.
v.t. унавó|живать, -зить.
manuscript [ˈmænjʊskrɪpt] *n.* рýкопись; **the book is still in ~** кни́га ещё в рýкописи; (*attr.*) рукопи́сный.
Manx [mæŋks] *n.* (*language*) мэ́нский язы́к; **the ~** (*people*) жи́тели (*m. pl.*) óстрова Мэн.
adj. мэ́нский; ~ **cat** (кóшка-)манкс, бесхвóстая кóшка.
cpds. **~man, ~woman** *nn.* жи́тель(ница) (*or* урожéн|ец, -ка) óстрова Мэн.
many [ˈmenɪ] *adj.* мнóгие; **a good, great ~** большóе коли́чество +*g.*; ~ **people** мнóго людéй; мнóгие (лю́ди); ~ **years passed** прошлó мнóго лет; ~ **a one** мнóгие; ~ **a time, ~ times** мнóго раз; **~'s the time** óчень чáсто, частéнько; **half as ~** вдвóе мéньше; **twice as ~** вдвóе бóльше; **I haven't seen him for ~ a day** я егó давнó не ви́дел; **as, so ~ (as)** стóлько(, скóлько); **not as ~ as** не так мнóго, как; **there were as ~ as forty people there** там бы́ло цéлых сóрок человéк; **not ~** немнóго, не так уж мнóго; **is it right that the ~ should starve?** рáзве справедли́во, чтóбы мáссы голодáли?; ~ **more** горáздо бóльше +*g.*; **one too ~** (*not wanted; in the way*) трéтий ли́шний; **I was one too ~ for him** (*coll.*) я егó перехитри́л; **he's had one too ~** (*coll.*) он вы́пил ли́шнего.
cpds. мнóго...; **~-coloured** *adj.* пёстрый, многоцвéтный; **~-sided** *adj.* (*lit., fig.*) многосторóнний.
Maoism [ˈmaʊɪz(ə)m] *n.* маои́зм.
Maoist [ˈmaʊɪst] *adj.* маои́стский.
Maori [ˈmaʊrɪ] *n.* (*pers.*) мáори (*c.g., indecl.*); (*language*) маори́йский язы́к.
adj. маори́йский.
map [mæp] *n.* кáрта; (*e.g. of rail system*) схéма; **town ~** план гóрода; **this town is right off the ~** э́то совсéм захолýстный городóк; **they wiped the village off the ~** они́ стёрли дерéвню с лицá земли́; **this scandal put the village on the ~** селó получи́ло извéстность из-за э́того скандáла.
v.t.: (*make ~ of*): **this district was first ~ped a hundred years ago** кáрта э́того райóна былá впервы́е состáвлена сто лет назáд; **he ~ped out his route before leaving** он состáвил маршрýт пéред отъéздом; (*fig.*): **he ~ped out his plans** он прики́нул, что емý нýжно дéлать; **~ping pen** рейсфéдер.
cpds. **~-maker** *n.* картóграф; **~-reader** *n.*: **he is an excellent ~-reader** он прекрáсно читáет кáрту; **~-reading** *n.* чтéние карт.
maple [ˈmeɪp(ə)l] *n.* клён; ~ **sugar/syrup** кленóвый сáхар/сирóп.

cpds. **~-leaf** *n.* кленóвый лист; **~-wood** *n.* клён; (*attr.*) кленóвый.
maquette [mə'ket] *n.* макéт.
Maquis [mæ'ki:] *n.* макú (*m. indecl.*).
mar [mɑ:(r)] *v.t.* пóртить, ис-.
marabou ['mærə,bu:] *n.* марабý (*m. indecl.*).
maraschino [,mærə'ski:nəʊ] *n.* мараскúн.
marathon ['mærəθ(ə)n] *n.* (**~ race**) марафóнский бег; **~ runner** марафóнец; (*attr.*): **a ~ effort** гигáнтское усúлие.
maraud [mə'rɔ:d] *v.i.* мародёрствовать (*impf.*, *pf.*).
marauder [mə'rɔ:də(r)] *n.* мародёр.
marble ['mɑ:b(ə)l] *n.* **1.** (*substance*) мрáмор; (*pl.*, *collection of statuary*) коллéкция скульптýр из мрáмора. **2.** (*in child's game*) стеклянный шáрик; **play ~s** игрáть (*impf.*) в шáрики.
adj. (*lit.*, *fig.*) мрáморный.
v.t. раскрá|шивать, -сить под мрáмор; **~d paper** мрáморная бумáга.
cpd. **~-topped** *adj.* с мрáморным вéрхом.
March[1] [mɑ:tʃ] *n.* март; (*attr.*) мáртовский.
march[2] [mɑ:tʃ] *n.* (*hist.*, *frontier area*) погранúчная полосá.
march[3] [mɑ:tʃ] *n.* (*mil.*) марш; **on the ~** в похóде; **~ past** торжéственный марш; **forced ~** форсúрованный марш; **quick/slow ~** бы́стрый/мéдленный марш; (*mus.*): **dead ~** похорóнный марш; **in ~ time** в тéмпе мáрша; (*pol.*) похóд, демонстрáция; **peace ~** похóд за мир; (*fig.*, *distance*): **it was a long day's ~** был длúнный перехóд; **steal a ~ on one** опере|жáть, -дúть; (*fig.*, *progress*): **~ of events** ход собы́тий; **the ~ of time** пóступь врéмени.
v.t. **1.** (*cause to ~*) водúть (*indet.*), вестú, по- стрóем; **he ~ed them up to the top of the hill** он повёл их стрóем на вершúну холмá. **2.** (*cover by ~ing*) про|ходúть, -йтú.
v.i. **1.** (*mil.*) маршировáть (*impf.*, *pf.*); **German troops ~ed into Austria** немéцкие войскá вступúли в Áвстрию; **we watched them ~ past** мы смотрéли, как они прошлú стрóем; **quick ~!** шáгом марш! **2.** (*walk determinedly*): **he ~ed into the room** он смéло вошёл в кóмнату; **with these words he ~ed out** с э́тими словáми он демонстратúвно вы́шел.
with advs.: **~ along** *v.i.*: **they were ~ing along singing** онú маршировáли с пéснями; **~ back** *v.t.*: **I caught him running off and ~ed him back** я поймáл егó, когдá он убегáл, и препроводúл обрáтно; *v.i.*: **they ~ed back to barracks** онú стрóем вернýлись в казáрмы; **~ by** *v.i.* прошагáть (*pf.*) мúмо; **~ in** *v.t.*: **he was ~ed in to see the Head** егó ввелú в кабинéт начáльника; *v.i.*: **when the soldiers ~ed in** когдá солдáты вступúли (в гóрод *и т.п.*); **~ off** *v.t.*: **he was ~ed off to prison** егó препроводúли в тюрьмý; *v.i.*: **she ~ed off in disgust** ей стáло протúвно и онá вы́шла; **~ out** *v.t.*: выводúть, вы́вести *v.i.*: **the workers ~ed out on strike** рабóчие вы́шли на забастóвку; **~ up** *v.i.*: **they ~ed up to the wall** онú прошагáли к стенé; **he ~ed up and hit her** он решúтельно подошёл к ней и удáрил её.
marcher ['mɑ:tʃə(r)] *n.* демонстрáнт (*fem.* -ка).
marching ['mɑ:tʃɪŋ] *n.* похóдное движéние; **~ drill** строевáя подготóвка; **in ~ order** в похóдном порядке; **~ orders** (*mil.*) прикáз о выступлéнии; (*fig.*): **get one's ~ orders** получ|áть, -úть расчёт; **they gave him his ~ orders** онú увóлили егó; **~ song** похóдная пéсня.
marchioness [,mɑ:ʃə'nes, 'mɑ:-] *n.* маркúза.
Mardi Gras [,mɑ:dɪ 'grɑ:] *n.* мáсленица.
mare [meə(r)] *n.* кобы́ла; **~'s nest** (*fig.*) миф, иллю́зия.
margarine [,mɑ:dʒə'ri:n, ,mɑ:gə-, 'mɑ:-] *n.* маргарúн.
marge[1] [mɑ:dʒ] *n.* (*poet.*, *margin*) каймá.
marge[2] [mɑ:dʒ] (*coll.*) = **margarine**
margin ['mɑ:dʒɪn] *n.* **1.** (*edge*, *border*) край; (*of page*) пóле (*usu. pl.*); **in the ~** на полях; **~ release** (*on typewriter*) табулятор полéй. **2.** (*extra amount*) запáс; коэффициéнт; **safety ~** запáс прóчности; **he won by a narrow ~** он победúл с небольшúм преимýществом; **~ of error** допустúмая погрéшность; **they allowed a ~ for mistakes** онú сдéлали дóпуск на ошúбки; **he was allowed a certain ~** емý остáвили кóе-какýю свобóду дéйствий; **profit ~** прúбыль, размéр прúбыли.
marginal ['mɑ:dʒɪn(ə)l] *adj.* **1.** (*written in margin*) (напúсанный) на полях; **~ notes** замéтки (*f. pl.*) (на полях). **2.** (*pert. to an edge or limit*) краевóй; предéльный; **~ utility** предéльная полéзность; **~ land** малоплодорóдная земля; **~ question** второстепéнный вопрóс. **3.** (*minimal*; *barely adequate or perceptible*) минимáльный.
marginalia [,mɑ:dʒɪ'neɪlɪə] *n.* замéтки (*f. pl.*) на полях.
margrave ['mɑ:greɪv] *n.* маркгрáф.
marguerite [,mɑ:gə'ri:t] *n.* нивяник, маргарúтка.
marigold ['mærɪ,gəʊld] *n.* ноготкú (*m. pl.*).
mari|juana, -huana [,mærɪ'hwɑ:nə] *n.* марихуáна.
marina [mə'ri:nə] *n.* марúна (*пристань для яхт*).
marinade [,mærɪ'neɪd, 'mæ-] *n.* маринáд.
v.t. (*also* **marinate**) мариновáть, за-.
marine [mə'ri:n] *n.* **1.** (*fleet*): **mercantile, merchant ~** торгóвый флот. **2.** (*naval infantryman*) солдáт морскóй пехóты; **the M~s** морскáя пехóта; **tell that to the (Horse) M~s!** расскажúте э́то своéй бáбушке! (*coll.*).
adj. морскóй; **~ engineer** судовóй механик; **~ insurance** морскóе страховáние; **~ painting** морскóй пейзáж; **~ stores** судовы́е припáсы.
mariner ['mærɪnə(r)] *n.* мореплáватель (*m.*); **master ~** капитáн, шкúпер; **~'s compass** морскóй кóмпас.
marionette [,mærɪə'net] *n.* марионéтка.
marital ['mærɪt(ə)l] *adj.* (*of marriage*): **~ union** брáчный сою́з; (*of husband or wife*): **~ rights** супрýжеские правá.
maritime ['mærɪ,taɪm] *adj.* (*of the sea*): **~ law** морскóе прáво; **~ powers** морскúе держáвы; (*situated by the sea*): **the M~ Province** (*of the former USSR*) Примóрский край.
marjoram ['mɑ:dʒərəm] *n.* душúца.
mark[1] [mɑ:k] *n.* **1.** (*surface imperfection*; *stain*, *spot etc.*) пятнó; **the horse has a white ~ on its nose** у лóшади на носý бéлое пятнó; (*scratch*) царáпина; (*cut*) порéз; (*scar*) рубéц, шрам; **there were ~s of smallpox on his face** егó лицó бы́ло изры́то óспой. **2.** (*trace*) след; **tyre ~s** следы́ шин; **you have left dirty ~s on the floor** вы наследúли на полý. **3.** (*sign*, *symbol*) знак; **punctuation ~s** знáки препинáния; **question ~** вопросúтельный знак; **as a ~ of goodwill** в знак расположéния; (*indication*, *feature*, *symptom*) прúзнак; **politeness is the ~ of a gentleman** вéжливость — отличúтельная чертá джентльмéна. **4.** (*for purpose of distinction or identification*) мéтка, (*notch*) зарýбка; **~s made on trees** мéтки, сдéланные на дерéвьях; (*fig.*): **make one's ~** выдвигáться, вы́двинуться; **a man of ~** выдаю́щийся человéк; (*as signature*): **he could not write his name but made his ~** он вмéсто пóдписи постáвил крест; (*on an industrial product*) фабрúчная мáрка; (*fig.*, *stamp*): **it bears the ~ of hurried work** вúдно, что э́то дéлалось в спéшке. **5.** (*reference point*) мéтка; **the ~s show the depth of water in feet** отмéтки покáзывают глубинý воды́ в фýтах; (*fig.*, *standard*): **his work was not up to the ~** егó рабóта былá не на высотé; **I'm not quite up to the ~ today** я сегóдня не совсéм в фóрме; **come up to the ~** оправд|ывать, -áть ожидáния; **keep s.o. up to the ~** добивáться (*impf.*) от когó-н. хорóших показáтелей; **overstep the ~** (*fig.*) выходúть, вы́йти за грани́цы дозвóленного. **6.** (*starting-line*) старт; **get off the ~** стартовáть (*impf.*, *pf.*); **quick/slow off the ~** (*fig.*) лёгкий/тяжёлый на подъём; **on your ~s; get set; go!** на старт; внимáние; марш! **7.** (*assessment of performance*) отмéтка; **he always gets good ~s** он всегдá получáет хорóшие отмéтки; **she got top ~s in the exam** онá сдалá (экзáмен) на «отлúчно»; (*unit of assessment*) балл; **they gave him 7 ~s out of 10** он набрáл 7 бáллов из 10; (*fig.*): **I give him full ~s for trying** я высокó ценю́ егó старáтельность; **this is a black ~ against him** э́то емý зачтётся. **8.** (*target*) цель; **hit the ~** (*lit.*, *fig.*) поп|адáть, -áсть в цель; **miss (or fall wide of) the ~** промáх|иваться, -нýться; **his criticism was beside the ~** егó крúтика былá не по существý; **overshoot the ~** (*lit.*) стрелять, вы́стрелить с перелётом; (*fig.*) за|ходúть, -йтú слúшком далекó (*coll.*); пересолúть (*pf.*); **you're way off the ~** вы попáли пáльцем в нéбо (*coll.*).
v.t. **1.** (*stain*, *scar*, *scratch etc.*): **a tablecloth ~ed with coffee stains** скáтерть, забры́зганная кóфе; **the table was**

badly ~ed стол был си́льно запа́чкан; **his face was ~ed with spots** его́ лицо́ бы́ло покры́то прыща́ми; **features ~ed by grief** черты́ лица́, отме́ченные го́рем; (*of animal's coloration etc.*): **the bird was ~ed with white on the throat** у пти́цы была́ бе́лая отме́тина на ше́е. **2.** (*for recognition purposes*) ме́тить, по-; **~ed cards** краплёные ка́рты; **~ing-ink** маркиро́вочные черни́ла; (*with price*): **all the goods are ~ed** на всех това́рах проста́влена цена́. **3.** (*distinguish*): **his reign was ~ed by great victories** его́ ца́рствование бы́ло ознамено́вано вели́кими побе́дами; **this novel ~s him as a great author** э́тот рома́н ста́вит его́ в ряд вели́ких писа́телей; **he called for champagne to ~ the occasion** он заказа́л шампа́нское, что́бы отме́тить (э́то) собы́тие. **4.** (*indicate*) отм|еча́ть, -е́тить; **is our village ~ed on this map?** на́ша дере́вня нанесена́ на э́ту ка́рту?; **the prices are clearly ~ed** це́ны чётко проста́влены; **to ~ his displeasure he remained silent** он храни́л молча́ние в знак недово́льства. **5.** (*record*) запи́с|ывать, -а́ть; (*observe and remember*): **a ~ed man** челове́к, взя́тый на заме́тку; (*promising*) многообеща́ющий челове́к; (*football etc.*: *follow closely*) закр|ыва́ть, -ы́ть; (*notice*; *pay heed to*) зам|еча́ть, -е́тить; **~ you, I don't agree with all he says** заме́тьте, я согла́сен не со всем, что он говори́т; **~ my words!** помяни́те моё сло́во! **6.** (*assign ~s to*; *assess*): **~ an exercise** пров|еря́ть, -е́рить упражне́ние; **the judges ~ed his performance very high** су́дьи высоко́ оцени́ли его́ выступле́ние. **7.: ~ time** (*mil.*) обознача́ть (*impf.*) шаг на ме́сте; **~ time!** на ме́сте ша́гом — марш!; (*fig.*) топта́ться (*impf.*) на ме́сте; тяну́ть (*impf.*) вре́мя.

with advs.: **~ down** *v.t.* (*select*): **they had ~ed him down as their victim** они́ занесли́ его́ в свой чёрный спи́сок; (*reduce price of*): **all the goods were ~ed down for the sale** для распрода́жи це́ны на все това́ры бы́ли сни́жены; (*give low ~ to*): **he was ~ed down for bad spelling** ему́ сни́зили оце́нку за орфографи́ческие оши́бки; **~ in** *v.t.*: **he ~ed in his route on the map** он разме́тил свой маршру́т на ка́рте; **~ off** *v.t.* отм|еча́ть, -е́тить; **an area was ~ed off for the guests** часть мест *и m.n.* была́ отведена́ для госте́й; **~ out** *v.t.*: **a tennis court had been ~ed out** те́ннисный корт был расче́рчен/разме́чен; (*plan*): **their course was ~ed out several weeks in advance** их маршру́т был разрабо́тан не́сколькими неде́лями ра́нее; (*preselect*, *destine*): **he was ~ed out for promotion** его́ реши́ли повы́сить в до́лжности; **cattle ~ed out for slaughter** скот, ото́бранный на убо́й; **~ up** *v.t.* (*raise*; *raise price of*): **prices were ~ed up every month** це́ны повыша́ли ка́ждый ме́сяц; **goods were ~ed up after the budget** це́ны бы́ли повы́шены по́сле объявле́ния фина́нсовой сме́ты; (*record*): **who will ~ up the score?** кто бу́дет запи́сывать счёт?; (*raise ~s of*) зав|ыша́ть, -ы́сить оце́нку +*d*.

cpd. **~-up** *n.* наце́нка.

mark² [mɑ:k] *n.* (*currency*) ма́рка.

marked [mɑ:kt] *adj.* (*distinct*, *noticeable*) заме́тный; **they were ~ly different** они́ суще́ственно отлича́лись друг от дру́га.

marker ['mɑ:kə(r)] *n.* (*recorder of score*) маркёр; (*indicator*) индика́тор; (*flag*) сигна́льный флажо́к; (*beacon*) ма́ркерный (ра́дио)мая́к; (*buoy*) буёк; (*bookmark*) закла́дка; (*tool*) отме́тчик; (*pen*) флома́стер.

market ['mɑ:kɪt] *n.* **1.** (*gathering*; *event*; *place of business*) ры́нок, база́р; **he sends his pigs to ~** он продаёт свои́х свине́й на база́ре; (*attr.*) ры́ночный, база́рный; **~ hall** ры́ночный павильо́н/зал; (*fig.*, *area of sale*): **world ~** мирово́й ры́нок; **the Common M~** О́бщий ры́нок. **2.** (*trade*) торго́вля; **the ~ in wool** торго́вля ше́рстью; (*opportunity for sale*) сбыт; **there is no ~ for these goods** на э́ти това́ры нет спро́са; **they will find a ready ~** они́ легко́ найду́т сбыт. **3.** (*rates of purchase and sale*; *share prices*) це́ны (*f. pl.*); **the ~ is falling** це́ны па́дают; **the coffee ~ is steady** цена́ на ко́фе стаби́льна (*or* де́ржится твёрдо); **play the ~** спекули́ровать (*impf.*) на би́рже; **~ research** изуче́ние конъюнкту́ры/возмо́жностей ры́нка; **~ value** ры́ночная сто́имость. **4.: in the ~ for** (*ready to buy*) обду́мывающий поку́пку (*чего*). **5. on the ~** (*available for purchase*): **he put his house on the ~** он вы́ставил свой дом на прода́жу; **his estate will soon come on to the ~** его́ име́ние ско́ро посту́пит в прода́жу.

v.t. (*sell in ~*) продава́ть (*impf.*); (*put up for sale*) пус|ка́ть, -ти́ть в прода́жу.

cpds. **~-day** *n.* база́рный день; **~-garden** *n.* огоро́д (для выра́щивания овоще́й на прода́жу); **~-gardener** *n.* владе́лец огоро́да; **~-gardening** *n.* това́рное овощево́дство; **~-place** *n.* база́рная пло́щадь; **~ town** *n.* го́род, в кото́ром есть ры́нок.

marketable ['mɑ:kɪtəb(ə)l] *adj.* (*produced for sale*) това́рный; (*selling quickly*) хо́дкий.

marketing ['mɑ:kɪtɪŋ] *n.* (*trade*) торго́вля; (*sale*) сбыт.

marking ['mɑ:kɪŋ] *n.* **1.** (*coloration of animals etc.*) окра́ска. **2.** (*for identification*): **aircraft ~s** опознава́тельные зна́ки (*m. pl.*) самолёта. **3.** (*assessment*) оце́нка.

marksman ['mɑ:ksmən] *n.* стрело́к; **a good ~** ме́ткий стрело́к; (*sniper*) сна́йпер.

marksmanship ['mɑ:ksmən,ʃɪp] *n.* ме́ткая стрельба́; стрелко́вое мастерство́.

marl [mɑ:l] *n.* ме́ргель (*m.*).

marline ['mɑ:lɪn] *n.* марли́нь (*m.*).

cpd. **~-spike** *n.* сва́йка.

marmalade ['mɑ:mə,leɪd] *n.*: **orange ~** апельси́новое/апельси́нное варе́нье.

Marmara ['mɑ:mərə] *n.*: **Sea of ~** Мра́морное мо́ре.

marmoreal [mɑ:'mɔ:rɪəl] *adj.* (*fig.*) мра́морный.

marmoset ['mɑ:mə,zet] *n.* марты́шка.

marmot ['mɑ:mət] *n.* суро́к.

maroon¹ [mə'ru:n] *n.* & *adj.* (*colour*) тёмно-бордо́вый цвет.

maroon² [mə'ru:n] *n.* (*signal*) сигна́льная раке́та.

maroon³ [mə'ru:n] *v.t.* выса́живать, вы́садить на необита́емый о́стров *и m.n.*; (*fig.*, *pass.*) застр|ева́ть, -я́ть; **we were ~ed in Paris** мы застря́ли в Пари́же; **we were ~ed by the tide** мы бы́ли отре́заны прили́вом.

marque [mɑ:k] *n.*: **letters of ~** (*hist.*) ка́перское свиде́тельство.

marquee [mɑ:'ki:] *n.* (больша́я) пала́тка.

marquetry ['mɑ:kɪtrɪ] *n.* маркетри́ (*nt. indecl.*), инкруста́ция по де́реву.

marqu|is ['mɑ:kwɪs], **-ess** ['mɑ:kwɪs] *n.* марки́з.

marquise [mɑ:'ki:z] *n.* марки́за.

marriage ['mærɪdʒ] *n.* **1.** (*ceremony*) сва́дьба; бракосочета́ние. **2.** (*contraction of ~ by man*) жени́тьба; **his ~ to Liza** его́ жени́тьба на Ли́зе; **he made her an offer of ~** он сде́лал ей предложе́ние; **he took her in ~** он взял её в жёны; (*by woman*) вы́ход за́муж; **he gave his daughter in ~** он вы́дал дочь за́муж. **3.** (*married state*) брак, супру́жество; (*of woman*, *also*) заму́жество; **~s are made in heaven** бра́ки заключа́ются на небеса́х; **~ of convenience** брак по расчёту; **they were joined in ~** они́ сочета́лись бра́ком; **their ~ broke up** их брак распа́лся; **relative by ~** сво́йственни|к (*fem.* -ца); ро́дственни|к (*fem.* -ца) по му́жу/жене́. **4.** (*attr.*) бра́чный; **~ bureau** бракопосре́днические аге́нтство; **~ certificate** свиде́тельство о бра́ке; **~ guidance** консульта́ция для вступа́ющих в брак (и состоя́щих в бра́ке; **~ licence** разреше́ние на брак; **~ market** я́рмарка неве́ст; **~ portion** прида́ное; **~ settlement** бра́чный догово́р. **5.** (*fig.*, *union*) сочета́ние.

cpds. **~-bed** *n.* бра́чное/супру́жеское ло́же; **~-broker** *n.* сват; (*fem.*) сва́ха; **~-lines** *n. pl.* свиде́тельство о бра́ке.

marriageable ['mærɪdʒəb(ə)l] *adj.*: **of ~ age** бра́чного во́зраста; **a ~ girl** де́вушка на вы́данье (*coll.*); неве́ста.

married ['mærɪd] *adj.* **1.** (*of man*) жена́тый; (*of woman*) заму́жняя, (*pred.*) за́мужем (за+*i.*); **they are ~** (*to each other*) они́ жена́ты. **2.** (*pert. to marriage*) супру́жеский; **a ~ couple** супру́жеская па́ра; **~ life** супру́жеская жизнь, супру́жество; (*n. pl.*) **young ~s** молодожёны.

marrow ['mærəʊ] *n.* **1.** (*anat.*) (ко́стный) мозг; **I was chilled to the ~** я продро́г до мо́зга косте́й. **2. (vegetable ~)** кабачо́к.

cpds. **~-bone** *n.* мозгова́я кость; **~fat** *n.* мозгово́й горо́х.

marr|y ['mærɪ] *v.t.* **1.** (*of man*) жени́ться (*impf., pf.*) на+*p.*; **he would like to ~ money** он хоте́л бы жени́ться на бога́той (*or* на деньга́х). **2.** (*of woman*) выходи́ть, вы́йти за́муж за+*a.* **3.** (*of parent; give daughter in marriage*) выдава́ть, вы́дать за́муж (*за кого*); (*give son in marriage*) жени́ть (*на ком*). **4.** сочета́ть бра́ком; (*of priest*) венча́ть, об-. **5.** (*fig., join*) сочета́ть (*impf., pf.*) (*devote*): **he was ~ied to his work** он был поглощён свое́й рабо́той.

v.i. (*of man*) жени́ться (*impf., pf.*); (*of woman*) выходи́ть, вы́йти за́муж; (*of couple*) пожени́ться (*pf.*); вступ|а́ть, -и́ть в брак; (*relig.*) венча́ться, об-.

Mars [mɑ:z] *n.* (*myth., astron.*) Марс.

Marsala [mɑ:'sɑ:lə] *n.* марсала́.

Marseillaise [ˌmɑ:seɪ'jeɪz, ˌmɑ:sə'leɪz] *n.* Марселье́за.

Marseilles [mɑ:'seɪ] *n.* Марсе́ль (*m.*).

marsh [mɑ:ʃ] *n.* боло́то; (~*y ground*) боло́тистая ме́стность; (*attr.*) боло́тный; **~ gas** боло́тный газ.

cpds. **~land** *n.* боло́тистая ме́стность; топь; **~mallow** *n.* (*plant*) лека́рственный алте́й; (*confection*) пастила́; **~-marigold** *n.* боло́тная калу́жница.

marshal ['mɑ:ʃ(ə)l] *n.* **1.** (*mil.*) ма́ршал; **air ~** ма́ршал авиа́ции. **2.** (*organizer of ceremonies*) оберцеремонийме́йстер.

v.t. **1.** (*draw up in order*): **~ troops** выстра́ивать, вы́строить войска́; (*fig.*): **~ one's forces** соб|ира́ть, -ра́ть си́лы; **~ facts, arguments** прив|оди́ть, -ести́ фа́кты/до́воды в систе́му. **2.** (*direct*): **~ a crowd** напр|авля́ть, -а́вить толпу́; (*fig.*): **~ public opinion** напр|авля́ть, -а́вить обще́ственное мне́ние; **they were ~led into the dining-room** они́ бы́ли торже́ственно введены́ в столо́вую. **3.** (*rail.*) сортирова́ть (*impf.*); **~ling-yard** сортиро́вочная (ста́нция).

marshy ['mɑ:ʃɪ] *adj.* боло́тистый, то́пкий.

marsupial [mɑ:'su:pɪəl] *n.* су́мчатое живо́тное.

adj. су́мчатый.

mart [mɑ:t] *n.* (*market-place*) ры́нок; (*centre of trade*) торго́вый центр; (*auction-room*) аукцио́нный зал.

marten ['mɑ:tɪn] *n.* куни́ца.

martial ['mɑ:ʃ(ə)l] *adj.* (*military*) вое́нный; **~ arts** спорти́вная борьба́; **~ law** вое́нное положе́ние; (*militant*): **~ spirit** боево́й дух.

Martian ['mɑ:ʃ(ə)n] *n.* марсиа́н|ин (*fem.* -ка).

martin ['mɑ:tɪn] *n.*: **house-~** городска́я ла́сточка; **sand-~** берегова́я ла́сточка.

martinet [ˌmɑ:tɪ'net] *n.* приди́рчивый нача́льник; сторо́нник стро́гой дисципли́ны.

martingale ['mɑ:tɪŋˌgeɪl] *n.* мартинга́л.

martlet ['mɑ:tlɪt] *n.* стриж (чёрный).

martyr ['mɑ:tə(r)] *n.* му́чени|к (*fem.* -ца); (*fig., sufferer*) страда́л|ец (*fem.* -ица); **be a ~ to, for a cause** страда́ть, по- за де́ло; **he is a ~ to gout** он изму́чен пада́грой; **she makes a ~ of herself** она́ стро́ит из себя́ му́ченицу; **he made a ~ of his wife** он заму́чил свою́ жену́.

v.t. му́чить, за-; (*fig.*): **he ~ed himself for the party** он принёс себя́ в же́ртву па́ртии; **she had a ~ed air** у неё был му́ченический вид.

martyrdom ['mɑ:tədəm] *n.* му́ченичество; (*ordeal*) муче́ние; **suffer ~** (*lit., fig.*) быть му́чеником.

martyrology [ˌmɑ:tə'rɒlədʒɪ] *n.* мартиро́лог.

marvel ['mɑ:v(ə)l] *n.* чу́до; **he's a ~** он чуде́сный челове́к; **she is a ~ of patience** она́ само́ терпе́ние; **it's a ~ that he escaped** э́то су́щее чу́до, что ему́ удало́сь спасти́сь; **the medicine worked ~s** лека́рство сотвори́ло чудеса́.

v.t. & i. (*wonder*) диви́ться (*impf.*) +*d.*; удив|ля́ться, -и́ться +*d.* **he ~led that ...** он порази́лся тому́, что...; **I ~ how it was done** я не могу́ себе́ предста́вить, как э́того дости́гли; **~ at** (*be surprised at*) изум|ля́ться, -и́ться +*d.*; (*admire*) восхи|ща́ться, -ти́ться +*i.*

marvellous ['mɑ:vələs] *adj.* (*astonishing*) изуми́тельный; (*splendid*) чуде́сный.

Marxian ['mɑ:ksɪən] *adj.* маркси́стский.

Marxism ['mɑ:ksɪz(ə)m] *n.* маркси́зм.

Marxist ['mɑ:ksɪst] *n.* маркси́ст (*fem.* -ка).

adj. маркси́стский.

Mary ['meərɪ] *n.*: **the Virgin M~** Де́ва Мари́я.

marzipan ['mɑ:zɪˌpæn, -'pæn] *n.* марципа́н.

mascara [mæ'skɑ:rə] *n.* тушь для ресни́ц; **put on ~** подв|оди́ть, -ести́ глаза́/бро́ви.

mascot ['mæskɒt] *n.* талисма́н.

masculine ['mæskjʊlɪn, 'mɑ:s-] *n.* **(~ gender)** мужско́й род; **(~ noun)** существи́тельное мужско́го ро́да.

adj. мужско́й; (*manly*) му́жественный; (*of a woman*) мужеподо́бная; (*pros.*): **~ rhyme** мужска́я ри́фма.

masculinity [ˌmæskjʊ'lɪnɪtɪ] *n.* му́жественность.

maser ['meɪzə(r)] *n.* ма́зер.

mash [mæʃ] *n.* (*for brewing*) су́сло; (*animal fodder*) ме́сиво, болту́шка из отрубе́й; (*potato etc.*) пюре́ (*indecl.*).

v.t. (*brewing*): **~ malt** зава́р|ивать, -и́ть со́лод; (*cul.*): **~ turnips** де́лать, с- пюре́ из ре́пы; **~ed potatoes** карто́фельное пюре́.

mask [mɑ:sk] *n.* ма́ска; **under the ~ of friendship** под личи́ной дру́жбы; **he threw off the ~** (*fig.*) он сбро́сил ма́ску/личи́ну.

v.t. над|ева́ть, -е́ть ма́ску на+*a.*; **~ed men** лю́ди в ма́сках; **~ed ball** маскара́д; (*fig.*) **she ~ed her feelings** она́ скрыва́ла свои́ чу́вства; (*mil.*) маскирова́ть, за-; (*cover*) закр|ыва́ть, -ы́ть.

masochism ['mæsəˌkɪz(ə)m] *n.* мазохи́зм.

masochist ['mæsə'kɪst] *n.* мазохи́ст.

masochistic [ˌmæsə'kɪstɪk] *adj.* мазохи́стский.

mason ['meɪs(ə)n] *n.* (*builder*) ка́менщик; (*stone-dresser*) каменотёс; **(M~, Free~)** масо́н.

Masonic [mə'sɒnɪk] *adj.* масо́нский; **~ lodge** масо́нская ло́жа.

masonry ['meɪsənrɪ] *n.* (*stonework*) ка́менная кла́дка; **(M~, Free~)** масо́нство.

masque [mɑ:sk] *n.* ма́ска.

masquerad|e [ˌmɑ:skə'reɪd, ˌmæs-] *n.* (*lit., fig.*) маскара́д.

v.i.: **he ~ed as a general** он выдава́л себя́ за генера́ла; **he is ~ing under an assumed name** он скрыва́ется под вы́мышленной фами́лией.

mass[1] [mæs] *n.* (*relig.*) ме́сса, литурги́я; (*in Orthodox church*) обе́дня; **high ~** торже́ственная ме́сса; **low ~** ме́сса без пе́ния; **~es were said for his soul** за упоко́й его́ души́ служи́ли обе́дни.

mass[2] [mæs] *n.* **1.** (*phys. etc.*) ма́сса; **in the ~** в ма́ссе, в це́лом; **his body is a ~ of bruises** он весь в синяка́х; **his story was a ~ of lies** его́ расска́з был сплошно́й ло́жью; **a ~ of earth/rock** гру́да земли́/камне́й. **2.** (*large number*) мно́жество; **~es of people** ма́сса наро́ду; **the ~es** (наро́дные/широ́кие) ма́ссы; (*pl., coll., a large amount*): **there's ~es of food** полно́ еды́. **3.** (*greater part*) бо́льшая часть. **4.** (*attr.*) ма́ссовый; **~ destruction** ма́ссовое уничтоже́ние; **~ education** всео́бщее обуче́ние/образова́ние; **the ~ media** сре́дства ма́ссовой информа́ции; **~ meeting** ма́ссовый ми́тинг; **~ number** ма́ссовое число́; **~ observation** опро́с обще́ственного мне́ния; **~ production** ма́ссовое произво́дство.

v.t. соб|ира́ть, -ра́ть; **~ troops** масси́ровать (*impf., pf.*) войска́; **~ed bands** объединённые (вое́нные) орке́стры; **the flowers were ~ed for effect** для созда́ния эффе́кта цветы́ бы́ли со́браны вме́сте.

v.i. соб|ира́ться, -ра́ться; **the clouds are ~ing** собира́ются облака́.

cpd. **~-produce** *v.t.*: **these toys are ~-produced** э́ти игру́шки ма́ссового/сери́йного произво́дства.

massacre ['mæsəkə(r)] *n.* бо́йня; **M~ of the Innocents** Избие́ние младе́нцев.

v.t. переб|ива́ть, -и́ть; (*fig., in sport*) разгроми́ть (*pf.*).

massage ['mæsɑ:ʒ, -sɑ:dʒ] *n.* масса́ж.

v.t. масси́ровать (*impf., pf.*).

masseur [mæ'sɜ:(r)] *n.* массажи́ст.

masseuse [mæ'sɜ:z] *n.* массажи́стка.

massif ['mæsi:f, mæ'si:f] *n.* (го́рный) масси́в.

massive ['mæsɪv] *adj.* масси́вный; (*very considerable, substantial*): **he received ~ support** он получи́л огро́мную подде́ржку.

massy ['mæsɪ] *adj.* масси́вный, соли́дный.

mast[1] [mɑ:st] *n.* (*ship's ~, flagpole, radio ~*) ма́чта; **sail before the ~** служи́ть (*impf.*) просты́м матро́сом.

cpd. **~head** *n.* топ ма́чты; (*of newspaper*) заголо́вок газе́ты.

mast[2] [mɑːst] *n.* (*bot.*) плодоко́рм.
mastectomy [mæs'tektəmɪ] *n.* мастэктоми́я.
master ['mɑːstə(r)] *n.* **1.** (*one in control, boss*) хозя́ин; (*owner*) владе́лец; ~ **of the house** хозя́ин до́ма; **is the ~ in?** до́ма хозя́ин?; **be one's own ~** быть самому́ по себе́; ни от кого́ не зави́сеть; **he is ~ in his own house** он хозя́ин в со́бственном до́ме; **I will show you who's ~** посмо́трим, кто здесь гла́вный; **be ~ of o.s.** владе́ть (*impf.*) собо́й; ~ **of ceremonies** церемонийме́йстер; ~ **of the situation** хозя́ин положе́ния; **like ~, like man** ≃ како́в поп, тако́в прихо́д; (*of a ship*) капита́н; ~ **mariner** капита́н, шки́пер. **2.** (*teacher*) учи́тель (*m.*); **maths ~** учи́тель матема́тики; (*in university*); **M~ of Arts** маги́стр гуманита́рных нау́к; **M~ of a college** глава́ (*m.*) колле́джа. **3.** (*skilled craftsman, expert*) ма́стер; ~ **builder** строи́тель-подря́дчик; **he was a ~ of satire** он был ма́стером сати́ры; **old ~s** (*artists*) ста́рые мастера́; (*paintings*) карти́ны ста́рых мастеро́в; **grand ~** (*chess*) гроссме́йстер; **he made himself ~ of the language** он овладе́л языко́м. **4.** (*original*) по́длинник, моде́ль, оригина́л. **5.** (*pref. to boy's name*) ма́стер, господи́н. **6.** (*attr.*): ~ **bedroom** гла́вная спа́льня; ~ **plan** генера́льный план; ~ **race** ра́са госпо́д; ~ **switch** гла́вный выключа́тель; ~ **touch** рука́ ма́стера.

v.t. **1.** (*gain control of; deal with*) спр|авля́ться, -а́виться с+*i.*; **the problem was easily ~ed** с пробле́мой легко́ удало́сь спра́виться; **can you ~ that horse?** смо́жете вы совлада́ть с э́той ло́шадью? **2.** (*acquire knowledge of, skill in*) овлад|ева́ть, -е́ть +*i.*; **it is a language which can be ~ed in 6 months** э́тим языко́м мо́жно овладе́ть за шесть ме́сяцев. **3.** (*overcome*) овлад|ева́ть, -е́ть +*i.*; ~ **one's feelings** владе́ть, о- свои́ми чу́вствами.

cpds. **~-at-arms** *n.* гла́вный старшина́ корабе́льной поли́ции; **~-hand** *n.* ма́стер, специали́ст; **~-key** *n.* отмы́чка; **~-mind** *n.* (*genius*) ге́ний; (*leader*) руководи́тель (*m.*); *v.t.*: **he ~-minded the plan** он разрабо́тал весь план; **~piece** *n.* шеде́вр; **~-stroke** *n.* гениа́льный ход.
masterful ['mɑːstə,fʊl] *adj.* (*imperious*) вла́стный; (*skilful*) мастерско́й.
masterfulness ['mɑːstə,fʊlnɪs] *n.* вла́стность, деспоти́чность; уве́ренность; мастерство́.
masterly ['mɑːstəlɪ] *adj.* мастерско́й; **in (a) ~ fashion** мастерски́.
mastership ['mɑːstəʃɪp] *n.* (*dominion, control*) главе́нство; (*office of master*) до́лжность дире́ктора *и т.п.*
mastery ['mɑːstərɪ] *n.* **1.** (*authority*) власть; (*supremacy*) госпо́дство; ~ **of the seas** госпо́дство на мо́ре; **gain the ~ of** доб|ива́ться, -и́ться госпо́дства над+*i.* **2.** (*skill*) мастерство́. **3.** (*knowledge*) владе́ние; ~ **of a subject** основа́тельное зна́ние предме́та.
mastic ['mæstɪk] *n.* (*resin*) масти́ка; (*tree*) масти́ковое де́рево.
masticate ['mæstɪ,keɪt] *v.t.* & *i.* жева́ть, раз-.
mastication [,mæstɪ'keɪʃ(ə)n] *n.* жева́ние.
mastiff ['mæstɪf, 'mɑːs-] *n.* масти́фф.
mastitis [mæ'staɪtɪs] *n.* масти́т.
mastodon ['mæstə,dɒn] *n.* мастодо́нт.
mastoid ['mæstɔɪd] *n.* (*growth*) сосцеви́дный отро́сток; (*coll., mastoiditis*) мастоиди́т.
masturbate ['mæstə,beɪt] *v.i.* онани́ровать (*impf.*), мастурби́ровать (*impf.*).
masturbation [,mæstə'beɪʃ(ə)n] *n.* онани́зм, мастурба́ция.
mat[1] [mæt] *n.* **1.** (*floor covering*) ко́врик; (**door-~**) рого́жка, полови́к; **wipe your feet on the ~** вы́трите но́ги о полови́к; **the boss had him on the ~** (*fig., coll.*) хозя́ин дал ему́ нагоня́й. **2.** (*placed under an object to protect surface*) подста́вка.
mat[2] [mæt] *n.* (*tangled mass of hair etc.*) колту́н, клубо́к.

v.t.: **his hair was ~ted with blood** его́ во́лосы сли́плись от кро́ви.
mat[3] [mæt] *adj.* = **mat(t)**
matador ['mætə,dɔː(r)] *n.* матадо́р.
match[1] [mætʃ] *n.* (*for producing flame*) спи́чка; **box of ~es** коро́бка спи́чек; **put a ~ to** заж|ига́ть, -е́чь; подж|ига́ть, -е́чь; **strike a ~** заж|ига́ть, -е́чь спи́чку; чи́ркнуть (*pf.*) спи́чкой; **safety ~es** безопа́сные/обыкнове́нные спи́чки; (*mil., fuse*) запа́льный фити́ль.

cpds. **~board** *n.* шпунтова́я доска́; **~box** *n.* спи́чечная коро́бка; **~lock** *n.* фити́льный замо́к; **~lock gun** фити́льное ружьё; **~stick** *n.*: **he's as thin as a ~stick** он худо́й как ще́пка; **he drew ~stick figures** он рисова́л па́лочных челове́чков; **~wood** *n.* (*splinters*) спи́чечная соло́мка; **make ~wood of** разб|ива́ть, -и́ть вдре́безги; **the ship was smashed to ~wood** кора́бль разби́лся вдре́безги.
match[2] [mætʃ] *n.* **1.** (*equal in strength or ability*) па́ра, ро́вня; под стать +*d.*; **he's no ~ for her** он ей не па́ра; куда́ ему́ с ней равня́ться; **he found, met his ~** он нашёл/встре́тил досто́йного проти́вника; ≃ нашла́ коса́ на ка́мень; **he was more than a ~ for me** он был сильне́е меня́. **2.** (*thg. resembling or suiting another*): **these curtains are a good ~ for the carpet** э́ти занаве́ски подхо́дят к ковру́; **a perfect ~ of colours** прекра́сное сочета́ние цвето́в; **I can't find a ~ for this glove** я не могу́ подобра́ть па́ру к э́той перча́тке; (*of man and woman*): **they are, make a good ~** они́ хоро́шая па́ра. **3.** (*matrimonial alliance*) па́ртия; **she wants to make a good ~ for her daughter** она́ и́щет хоро́шей па́ртии свое́й до́чери; **they decided to make a ~ of it** они́ реши́ли пожени́ться; (*pers. eligible for marriage*): **he would be an excellent ~** он соста́вит отли́чную па́ртию. **4.** (*contest; game*) соревнова́ние, состяза́ние; матч, игра́; **wrestling ~** состяза́ние по борьбе́; **football ~** футбо́льный матч; **doubles ~** па́рная игра́; **the ~ was drawn** игра́ ко́нчилась вничью́; **we lost all our away ~es** мы проигра́ли все и́гры/ма́тчи на чужо́м по́ле.

v.t. **1.** (*equal*) сравня́ться (*impf.*) с+*i.* **2.** (*pit, oppose*) противопост|авля́ть, -а́вить (*кого/что кому/чему*); **no-one was willing to ~ themselves against him** никто́ не хоте́л с ним свя́зываться; **the contestants were well ~ed** уча́стники состяза́ния бы́ли уда́чно подо́браны. **3.** (*suit; correspond to*) под|ходи́ть, -ойти́ к+*d.*; гармони́ровать с+*i.*; **her hat doesn't ~ her dress** у неё шля́па не подхо́дит к пла́тью; **a hat trimmed with velvet to ~** шля́па, отде́ланная ба́рхатом подходя́щего цве́та; **she bought 6 chairs and 6 cushions to ~** она́ купи́ла 6 сту́льев и к ним 6 поду́шек соотве́тствующего цве́та; (*find a ~ for*): **can you ~ this button?** мо́жете ли вы подобра́ть таку́ю же пу́говицу?; **we try to ~ the jobs with the applicants** мы стара́емся подобра́ть подходя́щую рабо́ту для кандида́тов; **they are a well-~ed couple** они́ хоро́шая/подходя́щая па́ра.

v.i. (*correspond: be identical*): **the handbag and gloves don't ~** су́мочка и перча́тки не гармони́руют друг с дру́гом.

cpd. **~-maker** *n.* сват; (*fem.*) сва́ха; (*fig.*) сво́дня (*c.g.*).
matchless ['mætʃlɪs] *adj.* несравне́нный.
mate[1] [meɪt] *n.* **1.** (*companion; coll.) form of address*) брат, друг, ко́реш; (*fellow-worker*) напа́рник; (*schoolfellow*) соучени́к. **2.** (*one of a pair of animals or birds*) саме́ц; (*fem.*) са́мка; (*marriage partner*) супру́г (*fem.* -а). **3.** (*assistant*) помо́щник; **surgeon's ~** ассисте́нт хиру́рга. **4.** (*ship's ~*) помо́щник капита́на; **second ~** второ́й помо́щник.

v.t. & *i.* спа́ри|вать(ся), -ть(ся).
mate[2] [meɪt] *n.* (*chess*) мат; **fool's ~** мат со второ́го хо́да; **~!** шах и мат!

v.t. де́лать, с- мат +*d.*
matelot ['mætləʊ] *n.* (*coll.*) моря́к.
material [mə'tɪərɪəl] *n.* **1.** (*substance*) материа́л; **raw ~(s)** сырьё; (*fig., of pers.*): **he is good officer ~** из него́ вы́йдет хоро́ший офице́р; (*subject matter*): **there is good ~ there for a novel** там есть хоро́ший материа́л для рома́на. **2.** (*fabric, stuff*) мате́рия; **dress ~** платяна́я ткань; **made of waterproof ~** сде́ланный из непромока́емого материа́ла. **3.** (*pl.*): **writing ~s** пи́сьменные принадле́жности.

adj. **1.** (*pert. to matter or material; physical; bodily*) материа́льный; ~ **needs** физи́ческие потре́бности; **the ~ world** материа́льный мир; ~ **nouns** существи́тельные, обознача́ющие вещество́; ~ **pleasures** земны́е ра́дости.

2. (*important, essential*) существе́нный; **a ~ witness** ва́жный свиде́тель; **~ evidence** веще́ственные доказа́тельства; **the position has not changed ~ly** положе́ние по существу́ не измени́лось.

materialism [mə'tɪərɪə,lɪz(ə)m] *n.* (*pej.*) вещи́зм; (*philos.*) материали́зм.

materialist [mə'tɪərɪə,lɪst] *n.* материали́ст.

materialistic [mə,tɪərɪə'lɪstɪk] *adj.* материалисти́ческий.

materialization [mə,tɪərɪəlaɪ'zeɪʃ(ə)n] *n.* (*taking bodily form*) материализа́ция; (*fulfilment*) осуществле́ние; материализа́ция.

materialize [mə'tɪərɪə,laɪz] *v.t.* материализова́ть (*impf., pf.*).

v.i. материализова́ться; (*come to pass, be fulfilled*) осуществ|ля́ться, -и́ться.

matériel [mə,tɪərɪ'el] *n.* (*mil.*) материа́льная часть, те́хника.

maternal [mə'tɜ:n(ə)l] *adj.* (*motherly*) матери́нский; (*on mother's side*): **~ uncle** дя́дя с матери́нской стороны́ (*or* по ма́тери).

maternity [mə'tɜ:nɪtɪ] *n.* матери́нство; (*attr.*): **~ benefit** посо́бие роже́нице; **~ dress** пла́тье для бере́менных; **~ home, hospital** роди́льный дом; **~ nurse** акуше́рка; **the doctor is out on a ~ case** врача́ вы́звали приня́ть ро́ды.

mat(e)y ['meɪtɪ] *adj.* общи́тельный, компане́йский.

math [mæθ] *n.* (*US coll., abbr.*) = **mathematics**

mathematical [,mæθɪ'mætɪk(ə)l] *adj.* математи́ческий.

mathematician [,mæθɪmə'tɪʃ(ə)n] *n.* матема́тик.

mathematics [,mæθɪ'mætɪks] *n.* матема́тика.

maths [mæθs] *n.* (*coll., abbr.*) = **mathematics**

matinée ['mætɪ,neɪ] *n.* дневно́е представле́ние; у́тренник; **~ idol** актёр, по́льзующийся популя́рностью у завя́длых театра́лок.

matins ['mætɪnz] *n.* (за)у́треня.

matriarchy ['meɪtrɪ,ɑ:kɪ] *n.* матриарха́т.

matricide ['meɪtrɪ,saɪd] *n.* (*crime*) матереуби́йство; (*criminal*) матереуби́йство (*c.g.*).

matriculate [mə'trɪkjʊ,leɪt] *v.i.* быть при́нятым в вы́сшее уче́бное заведе́ние.

matriculation [mə,trɪkjʊ'leɪʃ(ə)n] *n.* зачисле́ние в вы́сшее уче́бное заведе́ние.

matrilineal [,mætrɪ'lɪnɪəl] *adj.* по матери́нской ли́нии.

matrimonial [,mætrɪ'məʊnɪəl] *adj.* супру́жеский; бра́чный.

matrimony ['mætrɪmənɪ] *n.* брак; **the bonds of ~** бра́чные у́з|ы (*pl., g.* —).

matrix ['meɪtrɪks] *n.* (*anat., womb*) ма́тка; (*typ. etc., mould*) ма́трица.

matron ['meɪtrən] *n.* **1.** (*elderly married woman*) матро́на. **2.** (*in hospital*) ста́ршая сестра́; сестра́-хозя́йка. **3.** (*in school*) эконо́мка.

matronly ['meɪtrənlɪ] *adj.* подоба́ющий почте́нной же́нщине.

mat(t) [mæt] *adj.* ма́товый; **~ paint** ма́товая кра́ска.

matter ['mætə(r)] *n.* **1.** (*phys., phil*) мате́рия; (*substance*) вещество́. **2.** (*physiol.*): **grey ~** се́рое вещество́; (*pus*) гной. **3.** (*content, opp. form or style*) содержа́ние. **4.** (*material for reading*) материа́лы (*m. pl.*); **printed ~** печа́тный материа́л; (*as category for postal purposes*) ≃ бандеро́ль. **5.** (*material for discussion*) те́ма, предме́т; **the article provided ~ for debate** статья́ дала́ пи́щу для диску́ссии; (*question; issue*) вопро́с; де́ло; **that's quite another ~** э́то совсе́м друго́е де́ло; **a ~ of common knowledge** общеизве́стный факт; **it is a ~ of course** само́ собо́й разуме́ется; **as a ~ of fact** (*to tell the truth*) по пра́вде сказа́ть; (*in reality*) на са́мом де́ле; (*incidentally*) со́бственно (говоря́); **a ~ of some (*or* of slight) importance** ва́жный/второстепе́нный вопро́с; **it is a ~ for the police** э́то де́ло поли́ции; **a hanging ~** уголо́вное преступле́ние; **it's no laughing ~** э́то де́ло не шу́точное; **a ~ of life and death** вопро́с жи́зни и сме́рти; **there's a little ~ of payment** остаётся пустяко́вый вопро́с — вопро́с о платежа́х; **it's a ~ of money** всё де́ло в деньга́х; **that's a ~ of opinion** э́то вопро́с мне́ния; на э́то ка́ждый смо́трит по-сво́ему; э́то как для кого́; **a ~ of principle** де́ло при́нципа; принципиа́льный вопро́с; **a ~ of taste** де́ло вку́са; **it's only a ~ of time before he gives in** ра́но и́ли по́здно он сда́стся; **a ~ of urgency** сро́чное де́ло; (*pl., affairs*) дела́; **money ~s** де́нежные дела́; **as ~s stand** при тепе́решнем положе́нии дел; **to make ~s worse** в доверше́ние ко всем бе́дам. **6.: the ~** (*wrong, amiss*): **what's the ~?** в чём де́ло?; **is (there) anything the ~?** что́-нибудь не ла́дно?; **what's the ~ with him?** что с ним?; **there's nothing the ~ (with me)** (у меня́) всё в поря́дке. **7.** (*importance*): **(it's) no ~** э́то нева́жно; **no ~ what I do, the result will be the same** что бы я ни сде́лал, результа́т бу́дет тот же; **he could not do it, no ~ how he tried** как он ни стара́лся, он не мог э́того сде́лать. **8.: a ~ of** (*about*): **that was a ~ of 40 years ago** э́то дела́ сорокале́тней да́вности; **a ~ of £5** о́коло пяти́ фу́нтов; (*a few*): **he was back again in a ~ of hours** он верну́лся че́рез не́сколько часо́в. **9.: for that ~; for the ~ of that** е́сли уж на то пошло́. **10.: in the ~ of** в отноше́нии +*g.*; относи́тельно+*g.*; что каса́ется +*g.*

v.i. име́ть (*impf.*) значе́ние; **it doesn't ~ to me** э́то не име́ет для меня́ значе́ния; **does it ~ if I come late?** ничего́, е́сли я опозда́ю? **it doesn't ~ much if you come late** ничего́ стра́шного, е́сли вы опозда́ете; **what does it ~ what I say?** ра́зве мои́ слова́ име́ют хоть како́е-то значе́ние?; **what can it possibly ~ to him?** тако́е значе́ние, в конце́ концо́в, э́то име́ет для него́?

cpds. **~-of-course** *adj.* само́ собо́й разуме́ющийся; **~-of-fact** *adj.* приземлённый, лишённый фанта́зии; сухо́й, делово́й, практи́чный.

Matthew ['mæθju:] *n.* (*bibl.*) Матфе́й.

matting ['mætɪŋ] *n.* рого́жка, цино́вка.

mattins ['mætɪnz] = **matins**

mattock ['mætək] *n.* моты́га.

mattress ['mætrɪs] *n.* матра́ц; **air ~** надувно́й матра́ц.

maturation [,mætjʊ'reɪʃ(ə)n] *n.* созрева́ние.

mature [mə'tjʊə(r)] *adj.* **1.** (*of fruit etc., ripe*) спе́лый; (*lit., fig., ripe, developed*) зре́лый; **on ~ consideration** по зре́лом размышле́нии; **a person of ~ years** челове́к зре́лых лет. **2.** (*ready, prepared*) гото́вый. **3.** (*comm., ready for payment*) подлежа́щий опла́те; (*of debt*) подлежа́щий погаше́нию.

v.t. (*crops, wine etc.*) выде́рживать, вы́держать; (*fig.*): **the years have ~d his character** с года́ми его́ хара́ктер установи́лся.

v.i. **1.** (*lit., fig., ripen, develop*) созр|ева́ть, -е́ть; **the grapes ~d in the sun** виногра́д созре́л на со́лнце; **children ~ earlier nowadays** в на́ши дни де́ти развива́ются быстре́е; **his plans have not yet ~d** его́ пла́ны ещё не созре́ли/офо́рмились. **2.** (*become due for payment*): **the policy ~s next year** в бу́дущем году́ наступа́ет срок вы́платы по страхово́му по́лису.

maturity [mə,tjʊər'ɪtɪ] *n.* зре́лость; **reach ~** дост|ига́ть, -и́чь зре́лости; **bring to ~** заверши́ть (*pf.*).

matutinal [,mætju:'taɪn(ə)l, mə'tju:tɪn(ə)l] *adj.* у́тренний.

matzo ['mɑ:tsəʊ] *n.* маца́.

maudlin ['mɔ:dlɪn] *adj.* слюня́во сентимента́льный; плакси́вый во хмелю́.

maul [mɔ:l] *v.t.* **1.** (*of pers.*) изб|ива́ть, -и́ть; **stop ~ing me about!** переста́ньте меня́ терза́ть!; (*of animal*) терза́ть, рас-; **he was ~ed to death by a tiger** его́ растерза́л тигр. **2.** (*fig., by criticism*) громи́ть, раз-; **his last book got a ~ing from the critics** кри́тики разгроми́ли его́ после́днюю кни́гу в пух и прах.

maulstick ['mɔ:lstɪk] *n.* муштабель (*m.*).

maunder ['mɔ:ndə(r)] *v.i.* (*talk idly*) говори́ть (*impf.*) бессвя́зно.

Maundy Thursday ['mɔ:ndɪ] *n.* Страстно́й/Вели́кий Четве́рг.

Mauritania [,mɒrɪ'teɪnɪə] *n.* Маврита́ния.

Mauritanian [,mɒrɪ'teɪnɪən] *n.* маврита́н|ец (*fem.* -ка).

adj. маврита́нский.

Mauritius [mə'rɪʃəs] *n.* Маври́кий.

mausoleum [,mɔ:sə'li:əm] *n.* мавзоле́й.

mauve [məʊv] *n., adj.* розова́то-лило́вый (цвет).

maverick ['mævərɪk] *n.* (*calf*) неклеймёный телёнок; (*fig., dissenter; outsider*) диссиде́нт; изго́й; (*attr.*) неприка́янный.

maw [mɔ:] *n.* утро́ба; (*fig.*) пасть.

mawkish ['mɔ:kɪʃ] *adj.* при́торный.

mawkishness ['mɔ:kɪʃnɪs] *n.* при́торность.
maxilla [mæk'sɪlə] *n.* ве́рхняя че́люсть.
maxillary [mæk'sɪlərɪ] *adj.* верхнечелюстно́й.
maxim ['mæksɪm] *n.* (*aphorism*) афори́зм; (*principle*) при́нцип.
maximize ['mæksɪ,maɪz] *v.t.* максима́льно увели́чи|вать, -ть.
maximum ['mæksɪməm] *n.* ма́ксимум.
adj. максима́льный.
May[1] [meɪ] *n.* **1.** (*month*) май; ~ **Day** Пе́рвое мая; пра́здник Пе́рвого ма́я; ~ **Day parade** первома́йский пара́д. **2.** (*attr.*) ма́йский. **3.** **(m~)** (*hawthorn*) боя́рышник.
cpds. **~-beetle, ~-bug** *nn.* ма́йский жук; **~day** *n.* (*distress signal*) сигна́л бе́дствия; **~fly** *n.* подёнка; **~pole** *n.* ма́йское де́рево.
may[2] [meɪ] *v. aux.* **1.** (*expr. possibility*) мо́жет быть; пожа́луй; **it ~ be true** возмо́жно, э́то пра́вда; **it ~ not be true** возмо́жно, э́то не так; **he ~, might lose his way** он мо́жет заблуди́ться; **he might have lost his way without my help** без моє́й по́мощи он мог бы заблуди́ться; **I was afraid he might have lost his way** я боя́лся, как бы он не заблуди́лся; **you might kill s.o.** вы ещё убьёте кого́-н.; **you ~ well be right** вполне́ возмо́жно, вы и пра́вы; **we ~, might as well stay** почему́ бы нам не оста́ться; **and who ~, might you be?** а кто вы тако́й?; **that's as ~ be** э́то ещё вопро́с; **be that as it ~** как бы то ни́ было. **2.** (*expr. permission*): **~ I come and see you?** мо́жно мне (*or* могу́ я) к вам зайти́?; **you ~ go if you wish** е́сли хоти́те, мо́жете идти́; **you ~ not smoke** нельзя́ кури́ть; **where have you been, ~ I ask?** могу́ я узна́ть, где вы пропада́ли?; **you ~ well** (*with good reason*) **say so** ва́ша пра́вда. **3.** (*expr. suggestion*): **you might call at the butcher's** вы бы зашли́ к мяснику́. **4.** (*expr. reproach*): **you might offer to help!** вы могли́ бы предложи́ть свою́ по́мощь!; **you might have asked my permission** мо́жно бы́ло бы спроси́ть моего́ согла́сия. **5.** (*in subord. clauses, expr. purpose, fear, wish, hope*): **I wrote (so) that you might know** я вам написа́л, что́бы вы зна́ли; **I fear he ~ be dead** я бою́сь, что он у́мер; **I hope he ~ come** наде́юсь, он придёт; **I hoped he might come** я наде́ялся, что он придёт. **6.** (*in main clause, expr. wish or hope*): **~ you live long!** жела́ю вам до́лгой жи́зни!; **~ you live to repent it!** наде́юсь, вы об э́том ещё пожале́ете!; **~ the best man win!** да победи́т сильне́йший!; **~ it please your Majesty** да бу́дет уго́дно ва́шему вели́честву. **7.** (*be able*): **try as I ~, I shall never learn to speak Russian well** как бы я ни стара́лся, я никогда́ не научу́сь хорошо́ говори́ть по-ру́сски.
cpds. **~be** *adv.* мо́жет быть; **might-have-been** *n.* (*pers.*) неуда́чник; (*lost opportunity*) упу́щенная возмо́жность; «е́сли бы да кабы́».
Maya ['mɑ:jə] *n.* (*race*) ма́йя; (*member of race*) ма́йя (*c.g.*); (*language*) язы́к ма́йя.
mayhem ['meɪhem] *n.* нанесённые уве́чья; (*fig.*) разгро́м, погро́м; **commit, cause, create ~** нан|оси́ть, -ести́ уве́чье (*кому*).
mayonnaise [,meɪə'neɪz] *n.* майоне́з.
mayor [meə(r)] *n.* городско́й голова́; мэр.
mayoralty ['meərəltɪ] *n.* (*office*) до́лжность мэ́ра; (*period*): **during his ~** в бы́тность его́ мэ́ром.
mayoress ['meərɪs] *n.* (*mayor's wife*) жена́ мэ́ра; (*female mayor*) же́нщина-мэр.
maze [meɪz] *n.* лабири́нт; (*fig.*) пу́таница.
mazurka [mə'zɜ:kə] *n.* мазу́рка.
Mb ['megə,baɪt(z)] *n.* (*comput., abbr. of* **megabyte(s)**) мегаба́йт.
MBE (*abbr. of* ***Member of the Order of the British Empire***) кавале́р о́рдена Брита́нской импе́рии 5-й сте́пени.
MC (*abbr. of* ***Master of Ceremonies***) конферансье́.
MD *abbr. of* **1.** ***Doctor of Medicine*** до́ктор медици́ны. **2.** ***Managing Director*** дире́ктор-распоряди́тель.
mead[1] [mi:d] *n.* (*drink*) мёд.
mead[2] [mi:d] (*arch.*) = **meadow**
meadow ['medəʊ] *n.* луг.
cpds. **~-grass** *n.* мя́тлик лугово́й; **~-lark** *n.* жа́воронок лугово́й; **~-saffron** *n.* безвреме́нник осе́нний, зимо́вник; **~-sweet** *n.* та́волга; лаба́зник.
meagre ['mi:gə(r)] *adj.* **1.** (*of pers., thin*) худо́й, то́щий. **2.** (*poor, scanty*) ску́дный; **a ~ style** сухо́й стиль; **~ fare** по́стная еда́.
meal[1] [mi:l] *n.* (*ground grain*) мука́ (гру́бого помо́ла).
meal[2] [mi:l] *n.* еда́, тра́пеза; **don't talk during ~s** не разгова́ривайте во вре́мя еды́; **have a good ~** пло́тно пое́сть (*pf.*); **have a light ~** заку́с|ывать, -и́ть; **it's a long time since I had a square ~** я давно́ не ел сы́тно; **don't make a ~ of it** (*coll., fig.*) не раздува́йте из э́того це́лую исто́рию; **we have 3 ~s a day** мы еди́м три ра́за в день; **we have our ~s in the canteen** мы пита́емся в столо́вой; **let's have a ~ out this evening** дава́йте сего́дня поу́жинаем в рестора́не; **shall we ask them round for a ~?** не пригласи́ть ли их отобе́дать/оту́жинать с на́ми?; **evening ~** у́жин; **midday ~** обе́д.
cpds. **~-ticket** *n.* тало́н на обе́д; **~time** *n.*: **at ~-times** за едо́й.
mealie ['mi:lɪ] *n.* поча́ток кукуру́зы; (*pl.*) кукуру́за.
mealy ['mi:lɪ] *adj.* **1.** (*consisting of meal*) мучни́стый; (*resembling meal, floury*): **~ potatoes** рассы́пчатый карто́фель. **2.** (*fig., of complexion*) боле́зненно-бле́дный, мучни́стый.
cpd. **~-mouthed** *adj.* чрезме́рно делика́тный.
mean[1] [mi:n] *n.* (*intermediate or average point, condition etc.*) середи́на; **a happy (*or* the golden) ~** золота́я середи́на; (*math.*) сре́дняя величина́; (*pl., method, resources*) *see* **means**
adj. сре́дний; (*math.*): **~ line** биссектри́са; **Greenwich ~ time** сре́днее вре́мя по Гри́нвичу.
cpds. **~time** *n.*: **in the ~time** ме́жду тем; **~while** *adv.* ме́жду тем, тем вре́менем.
mean[2] [mi:n] *adj.* **1.** (*lowly*) ни́зкий; **of ~ parentage** ни́зкого происхожде́ния. **2.** (*inferior*): **it is clear to the ~est intelligence** э́то да́же дураку́/глупцу́ я́сно; **he is a man of no ~ abilities** он челове́к незауря́дных спосо́бностей. **3.** (*shabby, squalid*): **~ streets** убо́гие у́лицы (*f. pl.*). **4.** (*niggardly*) скупо́й. **5.** (*ignoble; discreditable*) ни́зкий, по́длый, нече́стный. **6.** (*ill-natured, spiteful*) зло́бный; **don't be ~ to him** не обижа́йте его́.
mean[3] [mi:n] *v.t.* **1.** (*intend*) име́ть (*impf.*) в виду́; намерева́ться (*impf.*); **I ~ to solve this problem** я наме́рен реши́ть э́тот вопро́с; **he ~s business** он берётся за де́ло всерьёз; **he ~s mischief** у него́ дурны́е наме́рения; **he ~s well by you** он жела́ет вам добра́; **I ~t no harm** я не жела́л зла; **I ~ you to (*or* that you should) go away** я хочу́, что́бы вы ушли́; **I ~t it as a joke** я хоте́л пошути́ть; **I ~t to leave yesterday, but couldn't** я собира́лся вчера́ уе́хать, но не смог; **I didn't ~ to hurt you** я не хоте́л вас оби́деть; **I didn't ~ you to read it** я не хоте́л, что́бы вы э́то чита́ли. **2.** (*design, destine*) предназн|ача́ть, -а́чить; **I ~ this house for my son** я предназнача́ю э́тот дом для сы́на; **his parents ~t him to be a doctor** роди́тели про́чили его́ в доктора́; **they were ~t for each other** они́ бы́ли со́зданы друг для дру́га; **this letter is ~t for you** э́то письмо́ предназнача́ется вам. **3.** (*of pers., intend to convey*) хоте́ть (*impf.*) сказа́ть; **what do you ~?** что вы э́тим хоти́те сказа́ть; **he ~s what he says** он говори́т то, что ду́мает; он слов на ве́тер не броса́ет; **what do you ~, 'finished'?** как так, зако́нчил?; **do you ~ Charles I or Charles II?** вы говори́те о Ка́рле I и́ли о Ка́рле II?; **what do you ~ by it?** (*how dare you?*) как вы сме́ете? **4.** (*of words etc., signify*) зна́чить (*impf.*), означа́ть (*impf.*); **this sentence ~s nothing to me** э́то предложе́ние ничего́ мне не говори́т; **what is ~t by this word?** как на́до понима́ть э́то сло́во?; **modern music ~s nothing to me** совреме́нная му́зыка мне соверше́нно непоня́тна; **this ~s we can't go** зна́чит, мы не смо́жем пойти́; **her promises don't ~ a thing** её обеща́ния ничего́ не сто́ят; **does my friendship ~ nothing to you?** неуже́ли моя́ дру́жба ничего́ для вас не зна́чит; (*entail, involve*): **organizing a fête ~s a lot of hard work** подгото́вка к пра́зднику тре́бует мно́го уси́лий; (*portend*): **this ~s war** э́то приведёт к войне́; зна́чит, бу́дет война́.
meander [mɪ'ændə(r)] *v.i.* (*of streams, roads etc.*) извива́ться

(*impf.*), ви́ться (*impf.*); **a ~ing river** изви́листая река́; (*of pers., wander along*) броди́ть (*impf.*); (*in speech etc.*) сбива́ться (*impf.*) с мы́слей (в ре́чи *и т.п.*); растека́ться (*impf.*) мы́слью по дре́ву.

meaning ['mi:nɪŋ] *n.* значе́ние; **what is the ~ of this word?** что э́то сло́во означа́ет; **this word can have two ~s** у э́того сло́ва есть два значе́ния; **get the ~ of** пон|има́ть, -я́ть смысл *+g.*; **what is the ~ of this?** (*querying another's action*) что э́то зна́чит?; **he looked at me with ~** он посмотре́л на меня́ многозначи́тельно.

adj. многозначи́тельный.

meaningful ['mi:nɪŋfʊl] *adj.* (*full of meaning*) многозначи́тельный; (*making sense*) содержа́тельный, толко́вый.

meaningless ['mi:nɪŋlɪs] *adj.* бессмы́сленный.

meanness ['mi:nnɪs] *n.* по́длость, ни́зость; ску́пость.

means [mi:nz] *n.* **1.** (*instrument, method*) спо́соб; **a ~ to an end** сре́дство для достиже́ния це́ли; **we shall find ways and ~ of persuading him** мы найдём спо́соб убеди́ть его́; **by fair ~ or foul** все́ми пра́вдами и непра́вдами; **by ~ of** посре́дством*+g.*; с по́мощью *+g.*; **by all (manner of) ~** все́ми сре́дствами; **by all ~** (*US, without fail*) непреме́нно; (*expr. permission*) коне́чно; пожа́луйста; **by all ~ ask him, but he won't come** пригласи́те-то вы его́ пригласи́те, но он всё равно́ не придёт; **by no ~** нико́им о́бразом; **he is by no ~ to be admitted** его́ ни в ко́ем слу́чае нельзя́ пуска́ть сюда́; **it was by no ~ easy** э́то бы́ло отню́дь не легко́. **2.** (*facilities*): **~ of communication** (*transport*) сре́дства сообще́ния; (*telecommunication*) сре́дства свя́зи. **3.** (*resources*) сре́дства; **~ of existence** сре́дства к существова́нию; **a man of ~** челове́к со сре́дствами; **he has private ~** у него́ есть со́бственные сре́дства; **~ test** прове́рка нужда́емости; **live beyond one's ~** жить (*impf.*) не по сре́дствам.

measles ['mi:z(ə)lz] *n.* корь; **German ~** красну́ха; **a child with ~** ребёнок, больно́й ко́рью.

measly ['mi:zlɪ] *adj.* (*coll., miserably small*) жа́лкий.

measurable ['meʒərəb(ə)l] *adj.* измери́мый; **in the ~ future** в обозри́мом бу́дущем; **within ~ limits** в изве́стных преде́лах.

measure ['meʒə(r)] *n.* **1.** (*calculated quantity, size etc.; system of ~ment*) ме́ра; **dry ~** ме́ра сыпу́чих тел; **linear ~** лине́йная ме́ра; **liquid ~** ме́ра жи́дкостей; **clothes made to ~** оде́жда, сши́тая на зака́з; **short ~** (*of weight*) недове́с; (*of length etc.*) недоме́р; **full ~** по́лная ме́ра; (*fig.*): **he repaid my kindness in full ~** он отплати́л мне за мою́ доброту́ сполна́; **it took him less than a day to get the ~ of his new assistant** не прошло́ и дня, как он раскуси́л своего́ но́вого помо́щника. **2.** (*degree, extent*) сте́пень; **his reply showed the ~ of his intelligence** по его́ отве́ту мо́жно бы́ло суди́ть о сте́пени его́ ума́; **his efforts were in large ~ wasted** его́ уси́лия во мно́гом пропа́ли да́ром; **in some ~** до не́которой сте́пени; (*prescribed limit, extent*) преде́л; **she was irritated beyond ~** она́ пришла́ в невероя́тное раздраже́ние; **set ~s to** ограни́чи|вать, -ть. **3.** (*measuring device*): **metre ~** метр; **litre ~** литро́вый ме́рный сосу́д. **4.** (*proceeding, step*) ме́ра, мероприя́тие; **take ~s against** прин|има́ть, -я́ть ме́ры про́тив*+g.*; **adopt severe ~s** примен|я́ть, -и́ть стро́гие ме́ры. **5.** (*law*) зако́н; **pass a ~** приня́ть (*pf.*) зако́н. **6.** (*verse rhythm*) разме́р; (*mus.*) такт; **tread a ~** (*arch.*) танцева́ть (*impf.*). **7.** (*mineral stratum*): **coal ~s** каменноу́гольные пласты́ (*m. pl.*).

v.t. **1.** (*find size etc. of*) ме́рить, с-; изм|еря́ть, -е́рить; **the cloth is ~d in metres** мате́рию измеря́ют в ме́трах; **a ~d mile** ме́рная ми́ля; **he was ~d for a suit** с него́ сня́ли ме́рку для костю́ма; (*fig.*): **I ~d him up and down** я сме́рил его́ взгля́дом; **he offered to ~ his strength against mine** он предложи́л поме́риться со мно́й си́лами; **he fell and ~d his length on the ground** он упа́л и растяну́лся во всю длину́. **2.** (*amount to when ~d*): **the room ~s 12 ft. across** ко́мната шириной в двена́дцать фу́тов.

with advs.: **~ off, ~ out** *vv.t.* отм|еря́ть, -е́рить; **he ~d out a litre of milk** он отме́рил литр молока́; **the football pitch had been ~d out** футбо́льное по́ле бы́ло уже́ разме́чено; **~ up** *v.i.*: **the team has not ~d up to our expectations** кома́нда не оправда́ла на́ших ожида́ний.

measured ['meʒəd] *adj.* **1.** (*rhythmical*) разме́ренный; **~ tread** ме́рная по́ступь. **2.** (*of speech, moderate*) уме́ренный; (*carefully considered*) обду́манный, осторо́жный.

measureless ['meʒələs] *adj.* безме́рный, безграни́чный, неизмери́мый.

measurement ['meʒəmənt] *n.* (*measuring*) измере́ние; (*dimension*) разме́р; **take s.o.'s ~s** снять (*pf.*) ме́рку с кого́-н.; **waist ~** объём та́лии.

meat [mi:t] *n.* мя́со; **one man's ~ is another man's poison** что поле́зно одному́, то друго́му вре́дно; ≃ что ру́сскому здо́рово, то не́мцу смерть; **argument is ~ and drink to him** его́ хле́бом не корми́, дай поспо́рить; **strong ~** (*fig.*) ≃ оре́шек не по зуба́м; **a speech full of ~** содержа́тельная речь.

cpds. **~-axe** *n.* сека́ч; **~-ball** *n.* фрикаде́лька; **~-eating** *adj.* плотоя́дный; **~-pie** *n.* пиро́г с мя́сом; **~-safe** *n.* холоди́льник для хране́ния мя́са.

meaty ['mi:tɪ] *adj.* мяси́стый; (*fig., pithy*) содержа́тельный.

Mecca ['mekə] *n.* (*lit., fig.*) Ме́кка.

mechanic [mɪ'kænɪk] *n.* меха́ник.

mechanical [mɪ'kænɪk(ə)l] *adj.* **1.** (*pert. to machines*) механи́ческий; **~ engineering** машинострое́ние; **a ~ failure** механи́ческое поврежде́ние; **~ly operated** с механи́ческим управле́нием. **2.** (*of pers. or movements: automatic*) машина́льный.

mechanics [mɪ'kænɪks] *n.* (*lit., fig.*) меха́ника.

mechanism ['mekə,nɪz(ə)m] *n.* механи́зм.

mechanistic [,mekə'nɪstɪk] *adj.* (*phil.*) механисти́ческий.

mechanization [,mekənaɪ'zeɪʃ(ə)n] *n.* механиза́ция.

mechanize ['mekə,naɪz] *v.t. & i.* механизи́ровать(ся) (*impf., pf.*).

Med [med] *n.* (*coll., abbr.*): **the ~** Средизе́мное мо́ре.

medal ['med(ə)l] *n.* меда́ль; **the reverse of the ~** (*fig.*) обра́тная сторона́ меда́ли; (*mil. award*) о́рден (*pl.* -а́).

medallion [mɪ'dæljən] *n.* медальо́н.

medallist ['medəlɪst] *n.* (*recipient*) медали́ст (*fem.* -ка); призёр; (*engraver*) медалье́р.

meddle ['med(ə)l] *v.i.*: **~ in** (*interfere in*) вме́ш|иваться, -а́ться в*+a.*; **~ with** (*touch, tamper with*) тро́|гать, -нуть.

meddlesome ['medəlsəm] *adj.* назо́йливый; **he is a ~ person** он всё вре́мя вме́шивается не в свои́ дела́.

Mede [mi:d] *n.*: **laws of the ~s and Persians** (*fig.*) незы́блемые зако́ны.

media ['mi:dɪə] *see* **medium** *n.* **6.**

mediaeval [,medɪ'i:v(ə)l] = **medi(a)eval**

medial ['mi:dɪəl] *adj.* **1.** (*situated in middle*) среди́нный; **~ consonant** согла́сный в середи́не сло́ва. **2.** (*of average size*) сре́дний.

median ['mi:dɪən] *n.* (*math., stat.*) медиа́на; (*anat.*: **~ artery**) среди́нная арте́рия.

adj. среди́нный.

mediate[1] ['mi:dɪət] *adj.* опосре́дствованный.

mediate[2] ['mi:dɪ,eɪt] *v.t.*: **the settlement was ~d by Britain** соглаше́ние бы́ло дости́гнуто при посре́дничестве Великобрита́нии.

v.i. выступа́ть, вы́ступить посре́дником; посре́дничать (*impf.*).

mediation [,mi:dɪ'eɪʃ(ə)n] *n.* посре́дничество.

mediator ['mi:dɪ,eɪtə(r)] *n.* посре́дник.

mediatory ['mi:dɪətərɪ] *adj.* посре́днический.

medic ['medɪk] *n.* (*coll.*) (студе́нт-)ме́дик.

medical ['medɪk(ə)l] *n.* (*coll.*, **~** *examination*): **have a ~** про|ходи́ть, -йти́ медици́нский осмо́тр (*abbr.* медосмо́тр).

adj. медици́нский; враче́бный; (*opp. surgical*) терапевти́ческий; **~ certificate** спра́вка от врача́; **~ history** исто́рия боле́зни; **~ man, practitioner** врач, терапе́вт; **~ officer** офице́р медици́нской слу́жбы; **~ orderly** санита́р; **~ service** медици́нское обслу́живание; **~ unit** санита́рная часть; санча́сть.

medicament [mɪ'dɪkəmənt, 'medɪkəmənt] *n.* лека́рство, медикаме́нт.

medicate ['medɪ,keɪt] *v.t.* (*treat medically*) лечи́ть (*impf.*); (*impregnate*) нас|ыща́ть, -ы́тить лека́рством.

medication [ˌmedɪ'keɪʃ(ə)n] *n.* лечéние.

medicinal [mɪ'dɪsɪn(ə)l] *adj.* (*of medicine*) лекáрственный; (*curative*) целéбный.

medicine ['medsɪn, -dɪsɪn] *n.* **1.** (*science, practice*) медицúна; **practise ~** практиковáть/рабóтать (*impf.*) врачóм. **2.** (*opp. surgery*) терапúя. **3.** (*substance*) лекáрство, срéдство; медикамéнт, микстýра; **he is taking ~ for a cough** он принимáет лекáрство от кáшля; **he took his ~** (*fig., punishment*) **like a man** он проглотúл э́ту пилю́лю как настоя́щий мужчúна; **I gave him a taste of his own ~** (*fig.*) я емý отплатúл той же монéтой.

cpds. **~-ball** *n.* медицинбóл; **~-chest** *n.* аптéчка; **~-glass** *n.* мензýрка; **~-man** *n.* знáхарь (*m.*).

medico ['medɪˌkəʊ] *n.* (*coll.*) мéдик.

medieval [ˌmedɪ'iːv(ə)l] *adj.* средневекóвый.

medievalist [ˌmedɪ'iːv(ə)lɪst] *n.* медиевúст.

mediocre [ˌmiːdɪ'əʊkə(r)] *adj.* посрéдственный.

mediocrity [ˌmiːdɪ'ɒkrɪtɪ] *n.* (*quality; pers.*) посрéдственность.

meditate ['medɪˌteɪt] *v.t.* замышля́ть (*impf.*).

v.i. размышля́ть (*impf.*) (**on:** о+*p.*).

meditation [ˌmedɪ'teɪʃ(ə)n] *n.* размышлéние; **lost in ~** погружённый в размышлéния.

meditative ['medɪtətɪv] *adj.* (*of pers.*) задýмчивый; (*of mind etc.*) созерцáтельный.

Mediterranean [ˌmedɪtə'reɪnɪən] *n.* (**~ Sea**) Средизéмное мóре.

adj. средиземномóрский.

medium ['miːdɪəm] *n.* **1.** (*middle quality*) середúна; **he strikes a happy ~** он придéрживается золотóй середúны. **2.** (*phys., intervening substance*) средá. **3.** (*means, agency*) срéдство; **through the ~ of** посрéдством+*g.* **4.** (*solvent*) растворúтель (*m.*). **5.** (*spiritualist*) мéдиум. **6.** (*means or channel of expression*) срéдство; **the media** (*sc. of communication*) срéдства мáссовой информáции; **one sculptor chooses stone as his ~, another metal** однú скýльпторы предпочитáют рабóтать с кáмнем, другúе — с метáллом.

adj. (*intermediate*) промежýточный; (*average*) срéдний; **a man of ~ height** человéк срéднего рóста.

cpds. **~-sized** *adj.* срéднего размéра; **~-wave** *adj.* средневóлновый.

medlar ['medlə(r)] *n.* мушмулá.

medley ['medlɪ] *n.* смесь; (*mus.*) попуррú (*nt. indecl.*).

medusa [mɪ'djuːsə] *n.* (*zool.*) медýза; **M~** (*myth.*) Медýза.

meed [miːd] *n.* (*liter.*) вознаграждéние.

meek [miːk] *adj.* крóткий.

meekness ['miːknɪs] *n.* крóтость.

meerschaum ['mɪəʃəm] *n.* (*clay*) морскáя пéнка; (*pipe*) пéнковая трýбка.

meet[1] [miːt] *n.* (*of sportsmen, etc.*) сбор.

v.t. **1.** (*encounter*) встр|ечáть, -éтить; **fancy ~ing you!** ну и встрéча!; **well met!** добрó пожáловать!; **~ s.o. halfway** (*fig.*) идтú, пойтú навстрéчу комý-н.; (*greet*): **she met her guests at the door** онá встрéтила гостéй в дверя́х; **a bus ~s all trains** к прихóду кáждого пóезда подаю́т автóбус; **they were met by a hail of bullets** онú бы́ли встрéчены шквáльным огнём; (*make acquaintance of*) знакóмиться, по- с+*i.*; **I met your sister in Moscow** я познакóмился с вáшей сестрóй в Москвé; **(I want you to) ~ my fiancée** я хочý познакóмить вас с моéй невéстой. **2.** (*reach point of contact with*): **where the river ~s the sea** там, где рекá впадáет в мóре; при впадéнии рекú в мóре; **our street ~s the main road by the church** нáша ýлица выхóдит на глáвную дорóгу у цéркви; **there is more in this than ~s the eye** здесь дéло не так прóсто. **3.** (*face*): **they advanced to ~ the enemy** онú продвúнулись навстрéчу протúвнику; **I am ready to ~ your challenge** я готóв приня́ть ваш вы́зов. **4.** (*experience, suffer*): **~ one's death** погúбнуть (*pf.*); **he met misfortune with a smile** он мýжественно переносúл невзгóды. **5.** (*satisfy, answer, fulfil*): **I cannot ~ your wishes** я не могý вы́полнить (*pf.*) вáши трéбования; **the request was met by a sharp refusal** прóсьба натолкнýлась на рéзкий откáз; **I'm afraid your offer does not ~ the case** я бою́сь, вáше предложéние не отвечáет трéбованиям; **how can I ~ my commitments?** как мне вы́полнить свои обя́занности?; **he met all their objections** он учёл все их возражéния. **6.** (*pay, settle*): **~ a bill** уплá|чивать, -тúть по счёту; **this will barely ~ my expenses** э́то с трудóм покрóет мои расхóды.

v.i. **1.** (*of pers., come together*) встр|ечáться, -éтиться; **we seldom ~** мы рéдко встречáемся; **haven't we met before?** мы с вáми не знакóмы?; **I hope to ~ you again soon** я надéюсь скóро с вáми встрéтиться; **till we ~ again** до слéдующей встрéчи; **our eyes met** нáши глазá встрéтились; (*become acquainted*) знакóмиться, по-; **we met at a dance** мы познакóмились на тáнцах. **2.** (*assemble*) соб|ирáться, -рáться; **the council met to discuss the situation** совéт собрáлся, чтóбы обсудúть положéние. **3.** (*of things, qualities etc.: come into contact, unite*) сходúться (*impf.*); **this belt won't ~ round his waist** э́тот пóяс на нём не схóдится; **there are traffic lights where the roads ~** на перекрёстке — светофóр; **the rivers Oka and Volga ~ at Nizhniy Novgorod** Нúжний Нóвгород — мéсто слия́ния рек Окú и Вóлги; **all these qualities met in him** он обладáл всéми э́тими кáчествами; **make (both) ends ~** (*fig.*) св|одúть, -естú концы́ с концáми. **4. ~ with: ~ with difficulties** испы́т|ывать, -áть затруднéния; **I met with much opposition** я натолкнýлся на сúльное сопротивлéние; **~ with approval/refusal** встрéтить (*pf.*) одобрéние/откáз; **he met with an accident** с ним произошёл несчáстный слýчай; (*find by chance*) нат|ыкáться, -кнýться на+*a.*

with advs.: **~ together** *v.i.* соб|ирáться, -рáться; **~ up** *v.i.* (*coll.*): **we met up (or I met up with him) in London** мы встрéтились в Лóндоне.

meet[2] [miːt] *adj.* (*arch., right, proper*) подобáющий; **it is ~ for him** емý подобáет.

meeting ['miːtɪŋ] *n.* **1.** (*encounter*) встрéча; **our ~ was purely accidental** мы встрéтились совершéнно случáйно; (*by arrangement*) свидáние. **2.** (*gathering*) собрáние; **address a ~** выступáть, вы́ступить на собрáнии; (*political ~*) мúтинг; (*session*) заседáние. **3.** (*of waters*) слия́ние. **4.** (*sports ~*) (спортúвное) состязáние; (*race-~*) скáчки (*f. pl.*).

cpds. **~-house** *n.* молúтвенный дом; **~-place** *n.* мéсто встрéчи.

megabyte ['megəˌbaɪt] *n.* (*comput.*) мегабáйт.

megacycle ['megəˌsaɪk(ə)l] *n.* мегагéрц.

megadeath ['megəˌdeθ] *n.* одúн миллиóн убúтых.

megalith ['megəlɪθ] *n.* мегалúт.

megalithic [ˌmegə'lɪθɪk] *n.* мегалитúческий.

megalomania [ˌmegələ'meɪnɪə] *n.* мегаломáния, мáния велúчия.

megalomaniac [ˌmegələ'meɪnɪˌæk] *n.* страдáющий мáнией велúчия.

megalopolis [ˌmegə'lɒpəlɪs] *n.* мегалóполис.

megaphone ['megəˌfəʊn] *n.* мегафóн.

megaton ['megəˌtʌn] *n.* мегатóн.

megawatt ['megəˌwɒt] *n.* мегавáтт.

megohm ['megəʊm] *n.* мегóм.

megrim ['megrɪm] *n.* (*migraine*) мигрéнь; (*pl., low spirits*) уны́ние.

meiosis [maɪ'əʊsɪs] *n.* мейóзис.

melancholia [ˌmelən'kəʊlɪə] *n.* меланхóлия.

melancholy ['melənkəlɪ] *n.* уны́ние.

adj. (*of pers.*) уны́лый; (*of things: saddening*) грýстный, печáльный.

Melanesia [ˌmelə'niːzɪə, -ʃə] *n.* Меланéзия.

Melanesian [ˌmelə'niːzɪən, -ʃ(ə)n] *n.* меланезú|ец (*fem.*, -йка).

adj. меланезúйский.

mélange [meɪ'lɑ̃ʒ] *n.* смесь.

mêlée ['meleɪ] *n.* свáлка.

mellifluous [mɪ'lɪflʊəs] *adj.* медоточúвый.

mellow ['meləʊ] *adj.* **1.** (*of fruit*) спéлый; (*of wine*) вы́держанный. **2.** (*of voice, sound, colour, light*) сóчный. **3.** (*of character: softened*) подобрéвший, смягчúвшийся; (*genial*) добродýшный. **4.** (*coll., tipsy*) подвы́пивший.

v.t.: **fruit ~ed by the sun** плод, созрéвший на сóлнце; **age has ~ed him** гóды смягчúли егó харáктер.

v.i. (*of fruit*) созр|евáть, -éть; посп|евáть, -éть; (*of wine*) станови́ться (*impf.*) вы́держанным; (*of voice*) станови́ться (*impf.*) сочне́е; (*of pers.*) смягч|а́ться, -и́ться; добре́ть, по-.

mellowness ['meləʊnɪs] *n.* спе́лость; вы́держанность; со́чность.

melodic [mɪ'lɒdɪk] *adj.* мелоди́чный.

melodious [mɪ'ləʊdɪəs] *adj.* мелоди́чный; ~ **voice** певу́чий го́лос.

melodiousness [mɪ'ləʊdɪəsnɪs] *n.* мелоди́чность, певу́честь.

melodrama ['meləˌdrɑːmə] *n.* (*lit., fig.*) мелодра́ма.

melodramatic [ˌmelədrə'mætɪk] *adj.* мелодрамати́ческий.

melody ['melədɪ] *n.* (*tune*) мело́дия; (*tunefulness*) мелоди́чность.

melon ['melən] *n.* ды́ня; **(water-~)** арбу́з; **(water-)~ plantation** бахча́.

Melpomene [mel'pɒmɪnɪ] *n.* Мельпоме́на.

melt [melt] *v.t.* **1.** (*reduce to liquid: of ice, snow, butter, wax*) раст|а́пливать, -опи́ть; (*of metal*) пла́вить, рас-. **2.** (*dissolve*) раствор|я́ть, -и́ть. **3.** (*fig., soften*) размягч|а́ть, -и́ть.

v.i. **1.** (*become liquid: of ice, snow, butter, wax*) та́ять, рас-; (*of metal*) пла́виться, рас-. **2.** (*dissolve*) расвор|я́ться, -и́ться. **3.** (*fig., soften*) смягч|а́ться, -и́ться; та́ять, от-; **her heart ~ed at the sight** её се́рдце смягчи́лось при ви́де э́того. **4.** (*change slowly; merge*): **one colour ~ed into another** оди́н цвет переходи́л в друго́й. **5.** (*coll., suffer from heat*): **I'm ~ing!** я весь распла́вился (от жары́).

with advs.: ~ **away** *v.i.* (*lit., fig., disappear*) та́ять, рас-; (*fig., disperse*) рассе́|иваться, -яться; ~ **down** *v.t.* распл|авля́ть, -а́вить.

melting [meltɪŋ] *n.* плавле́ние.

adj. (*fig., of looks*) то́мный.

cpds. **~-point** *n.* температу́ра плавле́ния; **~-pot** *n.* ти́гель (*m.*); (*fig.*): **throw into the ~-pot** подв|ерга́ть, -е́ргнуть коренно́му измене́нию.

member ['membə(r)] *n.* член, уча́стни|к (*fem.* -ца) (о́бщества *и т.п.*); **~s only** вход то́лько для чле́нов; **full ~** полнопра́вный член.

membership ['membəʃɪp] *n.* (*being a member*) чле́нство; (*collect., members*) чле́ны (*m. pl.*); (*number of members*) число́ чле́нов; (*composition*) соста́в; **admission to ~** приня́тие (*в клуб и т.п.*); **~ card** чле́нский биле́т.

membrane ['membreɪn] *n.* перепо́нка, мембра́на.

memento [mɪ'mentəʊ] *n.* сувени́р; **as a ~** на па́мять.

memo ['meməʊ] = **memorandum**

memoir ['memwɑː(r)] *n.* (*brief biography*) (биографи́ческая) заме́тка; (*pl., autobiography*) воспомина́ния (*nt. pl.*), мемуа́р|ы (*pl., g.* -ов); **author of ~s** мемуари́ст.

memorable ['memərəb(ə)l] *adj.* достопа́мятный.

memorandum [ˌmemə'rændəm] *n.* (*written reminder*) запи́ска; (*record of events, facts, transactions etc.*) докладна́я запи́ска; (*dipl.*) мемора́ндум; **memo(randum) book, pad** записна́я кни́жка; блокно́т.

memorial [mɪ'mɔːrɪəl] *n.* (*commemorative object, custom etc.*) па́мятник; (*pl., chronicles*) хро́ника, ле́топись.

adj.: ~ **plaque** мемориа́льная доска́; ~ **service** помина́льная слу́жба.

memorialize [mɪ'mɔːrɪəˌlaɪz] *v.t.* (*commemorate*) увекове́чи|вать, -ть.

memorize ['meməˌraɪz] *v.t.* (*commit to memory*) зап|омина́ть, -о́мнить; (*learn by heart*) зау́ч|ивать, -и́ть (наизу́сть).

memory ['memərɪ] *n.* **1.** (*faculty; its use*) па́мять; **I have a bad ~ for faces** у меня́ плоха́я па́мять на ли́ца; **a ~ like a sieve** дыря́вая па́мять; **search, rack one's ~** ры́ться, по- в па́мяти; **play by, from ~** игра́ть (*impf.*) на па́мять; **lose one's ~** лиш|а́ться, -и́ться па́мяти; **loss of ~** поте́ря па́мяти; **it escapes my ~** я не по́мню э́того; **may I refresh, jog your ~?** позво́льте вам напо́мнить; **in ~ of** в па́мять *+g.*; **sacred to the ~ of ...** свяще́нной па́мяти *+g.*; **... of blessed ~** блаже́нной па́мяти; **within living ~** на па́мяти живу́щих. **2.** (*recollection*) воспомина́ние; **relive old memories** за́ново пережи́ть (*pf.*) про́шлое; **I have a clear ~ of what happened** я я́сно по́мню, что случи́лось. **3.** (*comput.*): ~ **bank, store** маши́нная па́мять; запомина́ющее устро́йство.

menace ['menɪs] *n.* (*threat*) угро́за; (*obnoxious pers.*) (*coll.*) зану́да (*c.g.*).

v.t. угрожа́ть (*impf.*) *+d.*

ménage [meɪ'nɑːʒ] *n.* хозя́йство; **~ à trois** брак втроём.

menagerie [mɪ'nædʒərɪ] *n.* (*lit., fig.*) звери́нец.

mend [mend] *n.* **1.** (*patch*) запла́та; (*darn*) што́пка. **2. be on the ~** идти́ (*det.*) на попра́вку.

v.t. **1.** (*repair; make sound again*) чини́ть, по-; заш|ива́ть, -и́ть; **~ socks** што́пать, за- носки́; **my socks need ~ing** мои́ носки нужда́ются в почи́нке; **the road was ~ed only last week** доро́гу почини́ли то́лько на про́шлой неде́ле. **2.** (*improve, reform*) испр|авля́ть, -а́вить; **that won't ~ matters** э́тим де́лу не помо́жешь; **~ one's ways** испр|авля́ться, -а́виться; **it is never too late to ~** испра́виться никогда́ не по́здно; **~ one's pace** наб|ира́ть, -ра́ть ско́рость.

v.i. (*regain health*) выздора́вливать, вы́здороветь; **his leg is ~ing nicely** его́ нога́ зажива́ет хорошо́.

mendacious [men'deɪʃəs] *adj.* лжи́вый.

mendacity [men'dæsɪtɪ] *n.* лжи́вость.

Mendelian [ˌmen'diːlɪən] *adj.* ме́нделевский.

mendic|ancy ['mendɪkənsɪ], **-ity** [men'dɪsɪtɪ] *nn.* ни́щенство, попроша́йничество.

mendicant ['mendɪkənt] *n. & adj.* ни́щий.

mending ['mendɪŋ] *n.* (*of clothes*) почи́нка, што́пка; **invisible ~** худо́жественная што́пка.

menfolk ['menfəʊk] *n.* мужчи́ны (*m. pl.*).

menhir ['menhɪə(r)] *n.* менги́р, ка́менный столб.

menial ['miːnɪəl] *n.* лаке́й.

adj. лаке́йский; **~ work** чёрная рабо́та.

meningitis [ˌmenɪn'dʒaɪtɪs] *n.* менинги́т.

meniscus [mɪ'nɪskəs] *n.* мени́ск.

menopause ['menəˌpɔːz] *n.* климактери́ческий пери́од, кли́макс.

menses ['mensiːz] *n.* менструа́ции (*f. pl.*).

Menshevik ['menʃəvɪk] *n.* меньшеви́к; (*attr.*) меньшеви́стский.

menstrual ['menstrʊəl] *adj.* менструа́льный.

menstruate ['menstrʊˌeɪt] *v.i.* менструи́ровать (*impf.*).

menstruation [ˌmenstrʊ'eɪʃ(ə)n] *n.* менструа́ция.

mensurable ['mensjʊrəb(ə)l] *adj.* измери́мый.

mensuration [ˌmensjʊə'reɪʃ(ə)n] *n.* измере́ние.

menswear ['menzweə(r)] *n.* мужска́я оде́жда.

mental ['ment(ə)l] *adj.* **1.** (*of the mind*) у́мственный; **~ powers** у́мственные спосо́бности; **he has a ~ age of 7** у него́ у́ровень семиле́тнего ребёнка; **~ deficiency** слабоу́мие; **~ly defective, deficient** у́мственно отста́лый. **2.** (*pert. to ~ illness*) психи́ческий; **~ disease** психи́ческая боле́знь; **~ home, hospital** психиатри́ческая больни́ца; **~ patient** душевнобольно́й. **3.** (*carried out in the mind*) мы́сленный; **~ reservation** мы́сленная огово́рка; **he made a ~ note of the number** он отме́тил но́мер в уме́; **~ arithmetic** у́стный счёт.

mentality [men'tælɪtɪ] *n.* (*capacity*) у́мственные спосо́бности (*f. pl.*); (*level*) у́мственное разви́тие; (*attitude*) пси́хика.

menthol ['menθɒl] *n.* ментол, мя́та.

mentholated ['menθəˌleɪtɪd] *adj.* менто́ловый.

mention ['menʃ(ə)n] *n.* упомина́ние; ссы́лка; **there was a ~ of him in the paper** в газе́те упомина́лось его́ и́мя; **receive a ~** (*be referred to*) быть упомя́нутым; **honourable ~** похва́льный о́тзыв; **he made no ~ whatever of your illness** он ни сло́вом не обмо́лвился о ва́шей боле́зни.

v.t. упом|ина́ть, -яну́ть (*кого/что or о ком/чём*); ссыла́ться, сосла́ться на*+a.*; **I shall ~ it to him** я скажу́ ему́ об э́том; **~ s.o.'s name** наз|ыва́ть, -ва́ть чьё-н. и́мя; **forgive me for ~ing it, but ...** прости́те, что я говорю́ об э́том, но...; **he was ~ed in dispatches** его́ и́мя упомина́лось в спи́ске отличи́вшихся; **don't ~ it!** не́ за что!; ничего́; не сто́ит!; **not to ~** (*or* **without ~ing**) не говоря́ уж о*+p.*; не то́лько что; **yes, now you ~ it** ах да, вы мне напо́мнили.

mentor ['mentɔː(r)] *n.* наста́вник, ме́нтор.

menu ['menjuː] *n.* меню́ (*nt. indecl.*).

MEP (*abbr. of* ***Member of the European Parliament***) депута́т европарла́мента.

Mephistopheles [ˌmefɪ'stɒfɪˌli:z] *n.* Мефисто́фель (*m.*).

mephitic [mɪ'fɪtɪk] *adj.* ядови́тый, вре́дный.

mercantile ['mɜ:kənˌtaɪl] *adj.* торго́вый; **~ marine** торго́вый флот.

mercenary ['mɜ:sɪnərɪ] *n.* наёмник.

adj. (*hired*) наёмный; (*motivated by money*) коры́стный.

merchandise ['mɜ:tʃənˌdaɪz] *n.* това́ры (*m. pl.*).

merchant ['mɜ:tʃ(ə)nt] *n.* **1.** (*trader*) купе́ц; (*attr.*) купе́ческий; **the ~ class** купе́чество; (*with qualifying word*: *dealer*, *tradesman*) торго́вец; **wine ~** торго́вец ви́нами; (*attr.*) торго́вый; **~ ship** торго́вое су́дно; **~ fleet, marine, navy, service** торго́вый флот; **~ bank** комме́рческий банк. **2.** (*coll.*, *in cpds.*: *addict*): **speed-~** лиха́ч.

cpd. **~man** *n.* торго́вое су́дно.

merciful ['mɜ:sɪˌfʊl] *adj.* милосе́рдный, сострада́тельный; **Lord, be ~ to us** Го́споди, сми́луйся над на́ми; **his death was a ~ release** смерть была́ для него́ бла́гом; **~ Heavens!** Бо́же ми́лостивый!; **we were ~ly spared the details** к сча́стью, нас не посвяти́ли во все подро́бности.

mercifulness ['mɜ:sɪfʊlnɪs] *n.* милосе́рдие.

merciless ['mɜ:sɪlɪs] *adj.* беспоща́дный, безжа́лостный.

mercilessness ['mɜ:sɪlɪsnɪs] *n.* беспоща́дность, безжа́лостность.

mercurial [mɜ:'kjʊərɪəl] *adj.* **1.** (*of mercury*) рту́тный; **~ poisoning** отравле́ние рту́тью. **2.** (*of pers.*, *lively*) живо́й; (*volatile*) непостоя́нный, изме́нчивый.

mercuric [mɜ:'kjʊərɪk] *adj.*: **~ chloride** суле́ма; **~ oxide** о́кись рту́ти.

Mercury[1] ['mɜ:kjʊrɪ] *n.* (*myth.*, *astron.*) Мерку́рий.

mercury[2] ['mɜ:kjʊrɪ] *n.* (*metal*) ртуть; **~ column** (*of barometer*) рту́тный столб.

merc|y ['mɜ:sɪ] *n.* **1.** (*compassion*, *forbearance*, *clemency*) милосе́рдие; поща́да; **beg for ~y** проси́ть (*impf.*) поща́ды; **show ~y to** (*or* **have ~y on**) щади́ть, по-; **they were given no ~y** им не́ было поща́ды; **throw o.s. on s.o.'s ~y** сда́ться (*pf.*) на ми́лость кого́-н.; **a verdict of guilty with a recommendation to ~y** верди́кт о вино́вности с рекоменда́цией поми́лования; **act of ~y** акт милосе́рдия; **~y killing** эйтана́зия, умерщвле́ние неизлечи́мых больны́х; **God's ~y** ми́лость Бо́жья; **Lord, have ~y upon us!** Го́споди, поми́луй! **2.** (*power*): **at the ~y of** во вла́сти +*g.*; **they left him to the ~y of fate** они́ оста́вили его́ на произво́л судьбы́; **he was left to X's tender ~ies** его́ оста́вили на ми́лость X'а. **3.** (*blessing*): **it's a ~y he wasn't drowned** сча́стье, что он не утону́л; **one must be thankful for small ~ies** на́до ра́доваться и ма́лому.

mere[1] [mɪə(r)] *n.* (*lake*) о́зеро.

mere[2] [mɪə(r)] *adj.* **1.** (*simple*; *pure*) просто́й; чи́стый; (*absolute*) су́щий; (*no more than*, *nothing but*) не бо́лее чем; всего́ лишь; то́лько; **~ coincidence** просто́е совпаде́ние; **by the ~st chance** по чи́стой случа́йности; **he is the ~st nobody** он су́щее ничто́жество; **it's a ~ trifle** э́то су́щая ме́лочь; **a ~ thousand roubles** кака́я-нибу́дь ты́сяча/тысчёнка рубле́й; **he is a ~ child** он всего́ лишь ребёнок; **they received a ~ pittance** они́ получа́ли су́щие гроши́. **2.** (*single*; *...alone*) оди́н (то́лько); **~ words are not enough** слова́ми де́лу не помо́жешь; **at the ~ thought** при одно́й мы́сли; **the ~ sight of him disgusts me** оди́н его́ вид вызыва́ет у меня́ отвраще́ние.

merely ['mɪəlɪ] *adv.* (*simply*) про́сто; (*only*) то́лько.

meretricious [ˌmerɪ'trɪʃəs] *adj.* мишу́рный.

merganser [mɜ:'gænsə(r)] *n.* крoха́ль (*m.*).

merge [mɜ:dʒ] *v.t.* & *i.* сл|ива́ть(ся), -и́ть(ся); **twilight ~d into darkness** су́мерки смени́лись темното́й.

merger ['mɜ:dʒə(r)] *n.* слия́ние; (*comm.*) объедине́ние.

meridian [mə'rɪdɪən] *n.* (*geog.*) меридиа́н; (*astr. and fig.*) зени́т.

adj. (*of noon*) полу́денный; (*fig.*, *culminating*) кульминацио́нный.

meridional [mə'rɪdɪən(ə)l] *adj.* (*of a meridian*) меридиона́льный; (*of the south*, *esp. of Europe*) ю́жный.

meringue [mə'ræŋ] *n.* мере́нга.

merino [mə'ri:nəʊ] *n.* (*sheep*) мерино́с; (*wool*) мерино́совая шерсть.

merit ['merɪt] *n.* (*deserving quality*, *worth*) досто́инство; **a man of ~** челове́к с несомне́нными досто́инствами; **the suggestion has ~; there is some ~ in the suggestion** в э́том предложе́нии есть свои́ плю́сы; **make a ~ of sth.** ста́вить (*impf.*) что-н. себе́ в заслу́гу; (*action etc. deserving recognition*) заслу́га; **he was rewarded according to his ~s** он был вознаграждён по заслу́гам; (*pl.*, *rights and wrongs*): **one must decide each question on its ~s** на́до реша́ть ка́ждый вопро́с по существу́.

v.t. заслу́ж|ивать, -и́ть.

meritocracy [ˌmerɪ'tɒkrəsɪ] *n.* о́бщество, управля́емое людьми́ с наибо́льшими спосо́бностями.

meritorious [ˌmerɪ'tɔ:rɪəs] *adj.* похва́льный.

merlin ['mɜ:lɪn] *n.* де́рбник, кре́чет.

mermaid ['mɜ:meɪd] *n.* руса́лка.

merman ['mɜ:mæn] *n.* водяно́й трито́н.

merriment ['merɪmənt] *n.* весе́лье.

merry ['merɪ] *adj.* **1.** (*happy*, *full of gaiety*) весёлый; **make ~** (*have fun*) весели́ться, по-; **M~ Christmas!** с Рождество́м (Христо́вым)!

cpds. **~-go-round** *n.* карусе́ль; **~-making** *n.* весе́лье, потёха; **~thought** *n.* ви́лочка.

mesa ['meɪsə] *n.* столо́вая гора́.

mésalliance [meɪ'zælɪˌɑ̃s] *n.* нера́вный брак, мезалья́нс.

mescalin(e) ['meskəˌli:n] *n.* мескали́н.

Mesdames [meɪ'dɑ:m, -'dæm] *n.* (*pl.*) госпожи́ (*f. pl.*).

mesh [meʃ] *n.* **1.** (*space in net etc.*) яче́йка; **~ bag** аво́ська. **2.** (*pl.*, *network*) сеть; (*fig.*, *snares*) се́ти (*f. pl.*). **3.**: **in ~** (*mech.*) сце́пленный.

v.t. (*catch in net*) пойма́ть (*pf.*) в се́ти.

v.i. (*interlock*) зацеп|ля́ться, -и́ться; (*fig.*, *harmonize*, *of people*) найти́ (*pf.*) о́бщий язы́к.

mesmeric [mez'merɪk] *adj.* гипноти́ческий.

mesmerism ['mezməˌrɪz(ə)m] *n.* гипноти́зм.

mesmerist ['mezmərɪst] *n.* гипнотизёр.

mesmerize ['mezməˌraɪz] *v.t.* (*lit.*, *fig.*) гипнотизи́ровать, за-.

mesolithic [ˌmezəʊ'lɪθɪk] *adj.* мезолити́ческий; **~ age** сре́дний ка́менный век.

meson ['mezɒn, 'mi:zɒn] *n.* мезо́н.

Mesozoic [ˌmesəʊ'zəʊɪk] *adj.* мезозо́йский.

mess[1] [mes] *n.* **1.** (*disorder*) беспоря́док; **the room was in a complete ~** ко́мната была́ в соверше́нном беспоря́дке; **make a ~ of** (*spoil*; *bungle*) прова́л|ивать, -и́ть; **he made a ~ of his life** он загуби́л свою́ жизнь. **2.** (*dirt*) грязь; **your shirt is in a ~** у вас руба́шка запа́чкалась; **make a ~ of** (*soil*) па́чкать, за-. **3.** (*confusion*) пу́таница. **4.** (*trouble*) неприя́тность, беда́, го́ре; **get o.s. into a ~** вли́пнуть (*pf.*) (*coll.*).

v.t. (*make dirty*, *esp. with excrement*): **Johnny's ~ed his pants** Джо́нни замара́л штани́шки.

v.i.: **~ with** (*interfere with*) вме́шиваться (*impf.*) в+*a.*

with advs.: **~ about** *v.t.* (*inconvenience*) причиня́ть (*impf.*) неудо́бство +*d.*; *v.i.* (*work half-heartedly or without plan*) ковыря́ться (*impf.*); (*potter*, *idle about*) канители́ться (*impf.*); **~ about with** (*fiddle with*) вози́ться (*impf.*) с+*i.*; **don't ~ about with matches** не игра́йте со спи́чками; **~ up** *v.t.* (*make dirty*) па́чкать, пере-; (*bungle*) прова́л|ивать, -и́ть; (*put into confusion*) перепу́т|ывать, -ать.

mess[2] [mes] *n.* **1.** (*eating-place*) столо́вая; **officers' ~** офице́рский клуб; (*on ship*) каю́т-компа́ния. **2.**: **~ of pottage** (*bibl.*) чечеви́чная похлёбка.

v.i. есть (*impf.*).

cpds. **~-jacket** *n.* обе́денный ки́тель; **~-kit** *n.* столо́вый набо́р; **~mate** *n.* това́рищ по каю́т-компа́нии; **~-tin** *n.* котело́к.

message ['mesɪdʒ] *n.* **1.** (*formal*) сообще́ние; (*informal*) запи́ска, за́пись; **I received a ~ by telephone** мне переда́ли по телефо́ну; **can I take a ~ for him?** что ему́ переда́ть?; **have you got the ~?** (*understood*) до вас дошло́?; поня́тно?; усекли́? **2.** (*writer's theme*) иде́йное содержа́ние; (*prophet's teaching*) уче́ние.

messenger ['mesɪndʒə(r)] *n.* курье́р, связно́й, посы́льный; (*postal ~*) посы́льный, разно́счик.

cpd. **~-boy** *n.* ма́льчик на посы́лках.

Messiah [mɪˈsaɪə] *n.* Месси́я (*m.*).
Messianic [ˌmesɪˈænɪk] *adj.* мессиа́нский.
Messrs [ˈmesəz] *n. pl.* (*abbr. of* **Messieurs**) господ|а́ (*pl. g.* —).
messy [ˈmesɪ] *adj.* (*untidy*) неу́бранный; (*dirty*) гря́зный; (*slovenly*) неря́шливый.
metabolic [ˌmetəˈbɒlɪk] *adj.*: ~ **disease** наруше́ние обме́на веще́ств.
metabolism [mɪˈtæbəˌlɪz(ə)m] *n.* обме́н веще́ств.
metacarpal [ˌmetəˈkɑːpəl] *n.* (*also* ~ **bone**) пя́стная кость.
adj. пя́стный.
metacarpus [ˌmetəˈkɑːpəs] *n.* пясть.
metal [ˈmet(ə)l] *n.* **1.** мета́лл; **ferrous/non-ferrous** ~**s** чёрные/цветны́е мета́ллы. **2.** (**road-**~) щебе́нь (*m.*). **3.** (*pl., rails*) ре́льсы (*m. pl.*); **the train jumped the** ~**s** по́езд сошёл с ре́льсов.
adj. металли́ческий.
v.t.: ~**led road** шоссе́ (*indecl.*).
cpds. ~**-detector** *n.* металлоиска́тель (*m.*); ~**work** *n.* металлообрабо́тка; ~**worker** *n.* металли́ст, сле́сарь (*m.*).
metallic [mɪˈtælɪk] *adj.* металли́ческий.
metalliferous [ˌmetəˈlɪfərəs] *adj.* рудоно́сный.
metallize [ˈmetəˌlaɪz] *v.t.* металлизи́ровать (*impf., pf.*).
metallography [ˌmetəˈlɒgrəfɪ] *n.* металлогра́фия.
metallurgic(al) [ˌmetəˈlɜːdʒɪk(ə)l] *adj.* металлурги́ческий.
metallurgist [meˈtælədʒɪst] *n.* металлу́рг.
metallurgy [mɪˈtælədʒɪ, ˈmetəˌlɜːdʒɪ] *n.* металлу́ргия.
metamorphose [ˌmetəˈmɔːfəʊz] *v.t.* превра|ща́ть, -ти́ть.
metamorphosis [ˌmetəˈmɔːfəsɪs, ˌmetəmɔːˈfəʊsɪs] *n.* метаморфо́за.
metaphor [ˈmetəˌfɔː(r)] *n.* мета́фора; **mixed** ~ сме́шанная мета́фора.
metaphorical [ˌmetəˈfɒrɪk(ə)l] *adj.* метафори́ческий; ~**ly speaking** о́бразно говоря́.
metaphysical [ˌmetəˈfɪzɪk(ə)l] *adj.* метафизи́ческий; ~ **poet** поэ́т метафизи́ческой шко́лы.
metaphysics [ˌmetəˈfɪzɪks] *n.* метафи́зика.
metatarsal [ˌmetəˈtɑːsəl] *n.* (~ **bone**) плюснева́я кость.
adj. плюснево́й.
metatarsus [ˌmetəˈtɑːsəs] *n.* плюсна́.
metathesis [mɪˈtæθɪsɪs] *n.* (*gram., phon.*) перестано́вка букв/зву́ков; метате́за.
mete (out) [miːt] *v.t.* назн|ача́ть, -а́чить; определ|я́ть, -и́ть; выделя́ть, вы́делить.
metempsychosis [ˌmetempsaɪˈkəʊsɪs] *n.* метмпсихо́з, перемеще́ние душ.
meteor [ˈmiːtɪə(r)] *n.* метео́р; ~ **shower** пото́к метео́ров.
meteoric [ˌmiːtɪˈɒrɪk] *adj.* **1.** (*of meteors*) метеори́ческий; (*fig.*): **a** ~ **career** метеори́ческая карье́ра. **2.** (*of the atmosphere*) метеорологи́ческий.
meteorite [ˈmiːtɪəˌraɪt] *n.* метеори́т.
meteorograph [ˈmiːtɪərəˌgrɑːf] *n.* метеоро́граф.
meteoroid [ˈmiːtɪəˌrɔɪd] *n.* метеоро́ид.
meteorological [ˌmiːtɪərəˈlɒdʒɪk(ə)l] *adj.* метеорологи́ческий; ~ **centre, office** слу́жба пого́ды.
meteorologist [ˌmiːtɪəˈrɒlədʒɪst] *n.* метеоро́лог.
meteorology [ˌmiːtɪəˈrɒlədʒɪ] *n.* метеороло́гия.
meter[1] [ˈmiːtə(r)] *n.* (*apparatus*) счётчик; **gas** ~ га́зовый счётчик; **a man came to read the** ~ слу́жащий пришёл снять показа́ния счётчика.
v.t. изм|еря́ть, -е́рить; зам|еря́ть, -е́рить.
meter[2] [ˈmiːtə(r)] = **metre**
methane [ˈmeθeɪn, ˈmiːθeɪn] *n.* мета́н.
method [ˈmeθəd] *n.* (*mode, way*) ме́тод, спо́соб; (*system*) систе́ма, мето́дика; **work without** ~ рабо́тать (*impf.*) без вся́кой систе́мы; **there's** ~ **in his madness** в его́ безу́мии есть систе́ма.
methodical [mɪˈθɒdɪk(ə)l] *adj.* (*systematic*) системати́ческий; (*of regular habits*) методи́чный.
Methodism [ˈmeθəˌdɪz(ə)m] *n.* методи́зм.
Methodist [ˈmeθədɪst] *n.* методи́ст; (*attr.*) методи́стский.
methodological [ˌmeθədəˈlɒdʒɪk(ə)l] *adj.* методологи́ческий.
meths [meθs] (*coll.*) = **methylated spirit**
Methuselah [mɪˈθjuːzələ] *n.* Мафусаи́л.
methyl [ˈmeθɪl, ˈmiːθaɪl] *n.* мети́л; (*attr.*): ~ **alcohol** мети́ловый спирт.
methylated [ˈmeθɪˌleɪtɪd] *adj.*: ~ **spirit** денатура́т.
meticulous [məˈtɪkjʊləs] *adj.* (*punctilious*) тща́тельный, педанти́чный; (*over-scrupulous*) щепети́льный.
meticulousness [məˈtɪkjʊləsnɪs] *n.* тща́тельность, педанти́чность; щепети́льность.
métier [ˈmetjeɪ] *n.* (*profession*) профе́ссия; (*trade*) ремесло́.
metonymy [mɪˈtɒnɪmɪ] *n.* метони́мия.
met|re [ˈmiːtə(r)] (*US* **-er**) *n.* (*unit of length*) метр; (*verse rhythm*) разме́р.
metric [ˈmetrɪk] *adj.* метри́ческий.
metrical [ˈmetrɪk(ə)l] *adj.* (*of, or composed in, metre*) метри́ческий; (*pert. to measurement*) измери́тельный.
metrication [ˌmetrɪˈkeɪʃ(ə)n] *n.* введе́ние метри́ческой систе́мы.
metrics [ˈmetrɪks] *n.* ме́трика.
Metro [ˈmetrəʊ] *n.* метро́ (*indecl.*).
metronome [ˈmetrəˌnəʊm] *n.* метроно́м.
metropolis [mɪˈtrɒpəlɪs] *n.* (*city*) столи́ца; (*country*) метропо́лия.
metropolitan [ˌmetrəˈpɒlɪt(ə)n] *n.* (*eccl.*) митрополи́т.
adj. (*of capital*) столи́чный; (*of country*) относя́щийся к метропо́лии; (*of see*) митрополи́чий.
mettle [ˈmet(ə)l] *n.* (*strength of character*) хара́ктер; **show one's** ~ прояви́ть (*pf.*) свой хара́ктер; (*spirit, combativeness*) боево́е настрое́ние; **her taunts put him on his** ~ её насме́шки пробуди́ли в нём рве́ние.
mettlesome [ˈmetəlsəm] *adj.* (*of pers.*) рья́ный; (*of horse*) рети́вый.
mew[1] [mjuː] *n.* (*of cat*) мяу́канье.
v.i. мяу́к|ать, -нуть.
mew[2] [mjuː] *n.* (*gull*) ча́йка.
mewl [mjuːl] *v.i.* попи́скивать (*impf.*).
mews [mjuːz] *n.* коню́шни (*f. pl.*) (переде́ланные в жило́е помеще́ние).
Mexican [ˈmeksɪkən] *n.* мексика́н|ец (*fem.* -ка).
adj. мексика́нский.
Mexico [ˈmeksɪˌkəʊ] *n.* Ме́ксика; ~ **City** Ме́хико (*m. indecl.*).
mezzanine [ˈmetsəˌniːn, ˈmez-] *n.* антресо́ль, полуэта́ж.
mezzo [ˈmetsəʊ] *adv.* по́лу-; ~ **forte** дово́льно гро́мко.
cpd. ~**-soprano** *n.* ме́ццо-сопра́но (*indecl.*).
mezzotint [ˈmetsəʊtɪnt] *n.* ме́ццо-ти́нто (*nt. & f. indecl.*).
mg. [ˈmɪlɪˌgræm(z)] *n.* (*abbr. of* **milligram(me)(s)**) мг, (миллигра́м).
Mgr. [mɒnˈsiːnjɜː(r)] *n.* (*abbr. of* **Monsignor**) монсеньёр.
MIA (*abbr. of* ***missing in action***) пропа́вший без ве́сти.
M.I.5 (*abbr. of* ***Military Intelligence Section 5***) эм ай 5.
M.I.6 (*abbr. of* ***Military Intelligence Section 6***) эм ай 6.
miaou, miaow [mɪˈaʊ] n. мяу́канье; (*onomat.*) мя́у!
v.i. мяу́кать (*impf.*).
miasma [mɪˈæzmə, maɪ-] *n.* миа́зм|ы (*pl., g.* —).
mica [ˈmaɪkə] *n.* слюда́; (*attr.*) слюдяно́й.
Michael [ˈmaɪk(ə)l] *n.* Михаи́л.
Michaelmas [ˈmɪkəlməs] *n.* Миха́йлов день; ~ **term** (*acad.*) осе́нний тримéстр.
Michelangelo [ˌmaɪk(ə)lˈændʒɪˌləʊ] *n.* Микела́нджело (*m. indecl.*).
mickey [ˈmɪkɪ] *n.* (*sl.*): **take the** ~ **out of s.o.** издева́ться (*impf.*) над кем-н.
Mickey Finn [ˌmɪkɪ ˈfɪn] *n.* (*drink*) ёрш (*sl.*).
Mickey Mouse [ˌmɪkɪ ˈmaʊs] *adj.* (*pej.*) ребя́ческий.
microbe [ˈmaɪkrəʊb] *n.* микро́б.
microbiological [ˌmaɪkrəʊbaɪəˈlɒdʒɪk(ə)l] *adj.* микробиологи́ческий.
microbiologist [ˌmaɪkrəʊbaɪˈɒlədʒɪst] *n.* микробио́лог.
microbiology [ˌmaɪkrəʊbaɪˈɒlədʒɪ] *n.* микробиоло́гия.
microcircuit [ˈmaɪkrəʊˌsɜːkɪt] *n.* микросхе́ма.
microcomputer [ˈmaɪkrəʊkəmˈpjuːtə(r)] *n.* микрокомпью́тер.
microcosm [ˈmaɪkrəˌkɒz(ə)m] *n.* микроко́см.
microdot [ˈmaɪkrəʊˌdɒt] *n.* микрофотосни́мок.
microcomponent [ˌmaɪkrəʊkəmˈpəʊnənt] *n.* микроэлеме́нт.
micro-electronics [ˌmaɪkrəʊɪlekˈtrɒnɪks] *n.* микроэлектро́ника.
microelement [ˌmaɪkrəʊˈelɪmənt] *n.* микроэлеме́нт.
microfiche [ˈmaɪkrəʊˌfiːʃ] *n.* микрофи́ша.
microfilm [ˈmaɪkrəʊfɪlm] *n.* микрофи́льм.

v.t. микрофильми́ровать (*impf.*); де́лать, с- микрофи́льм +*g.*
micrometer [maɪ'krɒmɪtə(r)] *n.* микро́метр.
micron ['maɪkrɒn] *n.* микро́н.
microphone ['maɪkrəˌfəʊn] *n.* микрофо́н.
microscope ['maɪkrəˌskəʊp] *n.* микроско́п.
microscopic [ˌmaɪkrə'skɒpɪk] *adj.* микроскопи́ческий.
microwave ['maɪkrəʊˌweɪv] *n.* микроволна́; (*attr.*) микрово́лновый; ~ **oven** СВЧ-печь, сверхвысокочасто́тная печь.
mid [mɪd] *adj. & pref.*: **in ~ air** (высоко́) в во́здухе; **in ~ career** в разга́р карье́ры; **in ~ Channel** посреди́ Ла-Ма́нша; **in ~ course** посреди́не пути́; **from ~ June to ~ July** с середи́ны ию́ня до середи́ны ию́ля; **she interrupted him in ~ sentence** она́ прервала́ его́ на полусло́ве.
cpds. **~day** *n.* по́лдень (*m.*); *adj.*: **the ~day sun** полу́денное со́лнце; **~land** *adj.* располо́женный внутри́ страны́; **the M~lands** центра́льные гра́фства А́нглии; **~most** *adj.* середи́нный; **~night** *n.* по́лночь; **as black as ~night** чёрный как ночь; **during the ~night hours** в полно́чь; **he was burning the ~night oil** он рабо́тал по ноча́м; он полуно́чничал; **~night sun** полу́но́чное со́лнце; **~summer** *n.* середи́на ле́та; **at ~summer** среди́ ле́та; *adj.* **M~summer Day** Ива́нов день; **M~summer Night's Dream** (*play title*) «Сон в ле́тнюю ночь»; **~summer madness** чи́стое сумасше́ствие/безу́мие; **~way** *adv.* на полпути́; **the M~(dle)-west** *n.* Сре́дний За́пад США; **~winter** *n.* середи́на зимы́.
midden ['mɪd(ə)n] *n.* наво́зная ку́ча.
middle ['mɪd(ə)l] *n.* **1.** середи́на; **in the ~ of** среди́+*g.*; **there is a pain in the ~ of my back** у меня́ боль в поясни́це; **in the ~ of nowhere** Бог зна́ет где; (*of time*): **in the ~ of the night** посреди́ но́чи; **I was in the ~ of getting ready** в тот моме́нт я как раз собира́лся. **2.** (*waist*) та́лия; **he caught her round the ~** он о́бнял/схвати́л её за та́лию. **3.** (*gram.*) сре́дний зало́г.
adj. сре́дний; **in ~ age** в сре́днем во́зрасте; **the M~ Ages** сре́дние века́; **the ~ classes** сре́дние слои́ о́бщества; буржуази́я; **upper/lower ~ class** кру́пная/ме́лкая буржуази́я; **he followed a ~ course** он держа́лся уме́ренного ку́рса; он вы́брал сре́дний путь; **~ distance** сре́дний план; **M~ America** Сре́дняя Аме́рика; **M~ American** сре́дний америка́нец; **M~ East** Бли́жний Восто́к; **M~ English** среднеангли́йский язы́к; **~ finger** сре́дний па́лец; **in ~ life** в середи́не жи́зни; **his ~ name is George** его́ второ́е и́мя — Гео́ргий; **politics is his ~ name** (*coll.*) поли́тика для него́ — всё; **~ school** сре́дняя шко́ла; **~ term** (*logic*) сре́дняя посы́лка; **~ watch** ночна́я ва́хта; **M~ West** = **Mid-west.**
cpds. **~-aged** *adj.* сре́дних лет; немолодо́й; **~-class** *adj.* буржуа́зный; **~man** *n.* посре́дник; **~-of-the-road** *adj.* уме́ренных (полити́ческих) взгля́дов; **~weight** *n. & adj.* (боксёр) сре́днего ве́са.
middling ['mɪdlɪŋ] *adj.* сре́дний, второсо́ртный; **fair to ~** так себе́.
adv. сно́сно, сре́дне; ничего́, так себе́.
middy ['mɪdɪ] (*coll.*) = **midshipman**
midge [mɪdʒ] *n.* кома́р, мо́шка; (*pl., collect.*) мошкара́.
midget ['mɪdʒɪt] *n.* ка́рлик; (*attr.*) ка́рликовый; **~ submarine** сверхма́лая подво́дная ло́дка.
midi ['mɪdɪ] *n.* ми́ди (*юбка и т.д.*).
midpoint ['mɪdˌpɔɪnt] *n.* сре́дняя то́чка.
midriff ['mɪdrɪf] *n.* диафра́гма; ве́рхняя часть живота́.
midshipman ['mɪdʃɪpmən] *n.* ми́чман, гардемари́н.
midst [mɪdst] *n.* середи́на; **in the ~ of** среди́, в разга́р +*g.*, ме́жду+*i.*; **a stranger in our ~** чужо́й среди́ нас.
midwife ['mɪdwaɪf] *n.* акуше́рка; повива́льная ба́бка.
midwifery ['mɪdˌwɪfərɪ] *n.* акуше́рство.
mien [mi:n] *n.* (*liter.*) вид, нару́жность.
miff [mɪf] *v.t.* (*coll.*): **he was ~ed by my remark** моё замеча́ние его́ оби́дело/заде́ло.
might[1] [maɪt] *n.* **1.** (*power to enforce will*) мощь; **~ is right** кто силён, тот и прав. **2.** (*strength*) си́ла; **with (all his) ~ and main** изо всей мо́чи.
might[2] [maɪt] *v. aux. see* **may**
mightiness ['maɪtɪnɪs] *n.* (*power*) мо́щность; (*size*) вели́чие.
mighty ['maɪtɪ] *adj.* **1.** (*powerful*) мо́щный; (*great*) вели́кий; **high and ~** (*pompous, arrogant*) зано́счивый. **2.** (*massive*) грома́дный.
adv. (*US coll.*) о́чень.
mignonette [ˌmɪnjə'net] *n.* резеда́.
migraine ['mi:greɪn, 'maɪ-] *n.* мигре́нь.
migrant ['maɪgrənt] *n.* переселе́нец; (*bird*) перелётная пти́ца.
adj. кочу́ющий; перелётный.
migrate [maɪ'greɪt] *v.i.* пересел|я́ться, -и́ться; мигри́ровать (*impf.*); (*of birds*) соверш|а́ть, -и́ть перелёт.
migration [maɪ'greɪʃ(ə)n] *n.* мигра́ция; перелёт.
migratory [maɪ'greɪtərɪ] *adj.* перелётный.
mike [maɪk] (*coll.*) = **microphone**
milage ['maɪlɪdʒ] = **mil(e)age**
milch [mɪltʃ] *adj.*: **~ cow** до́йная коро́ва.
mild [maɪld] *adj.* мя́гкий; (*of pers.*) кро́ткий, ти́хий; **a ~ reproof** мя́гкий упрёк; **to put it ~ly** мя́гко говоря́; **a ~ day** тёплый день; **a ~ cheese** нео́стрый/мя́гкий сыр; **~ steel** мя́гкая сталь; **~ tobacco** сла́бый таба́к.
mildew ['mɪldju:] *n.* ми́лдью (*nt. indecl.*), ложномучни́стая роса́.
mildness ['maɪldnɪs] *n.* мя́гкость; (*of food etc.*) пре́сность.
mile [maɪl] *n.* ми́ля; **for ~s around** на мно́го миль вокру́г; **30 ~s an hour** 30 миль в час; **he ran the ~ in 4 minutes** он пробежа́л ми́лю за 4 мину́ты; (*fig.*): **I am feeling ~s better** мне намно́го лу́чше; **I was ~s away** я замеча́лся; **it sticks out a ~** э́то броса́ется в глаза́; э́то ви́дно за версту́.
cpd. **~stone** *n.* ка́мень с указа́нием расстоя́ния; (*fig.*) ве́ха.
mil(e)age ['maɪlɪdʒ] *n.* **1.** (*distance in miles*) расстоя́ние в ми́лях; (*of car*) пробе́г автомоби́ля в ми́лях; **~ indicator** счётчик про́йденного пути́. **2.** (*travel expenses*) проездны́е (*pl.*). **3.** (*coll., benefit*) по́льза, вы́года.
miler ['maɪlə(r)] *n.* (*athlete*) бегу́н на диста́нцию в одну́ ми́лю.
milieu [mɪ'ljɜ:, 'mi:ljɜ:] *n.* окруже́ние, среда́.
militancy ['mɪlɪt(ə)nsɪ] *n.* вои́нственность.
militant ['mɪlɪt(ə)nt] *n.* бое́ц, боре́ц; воя́ка (*m.*); активи́ст (*fem.* -ка).
adj. вои́нствующий; **the Church ~** вои́нствующая це́рковь; **~ students** вои́нственно настро́енные студе́нты.
militarism ['mɪlɪtəˌrɪz(ə)m] *n.* милитари́зм.
militarist ['mɪlɪtərɪst] *n.* милитари́ст.
militarize ['mɪlɪtəˌraɪz] *v.t.* милитаризи́ровать (*impf., pf.*), военизи́ровать (*impf., pf.*).
military ['mɪlɪtərɪ] *n.*: **the ~** военнослу́жащие (*m. pl.*), войска́ (*nt. pl.*).
adj. вое́нный; **of ~ age** призывно́го во́зраста; **~ band** вое́нный орке́стр; **~ engineering** вое́нно-инжене́рное де́ло; **a ~ man** военнослу́жащий, вое́нный; **~ service** вое́нная слу́жба; (*as liability*) во́инская пови́нность; **~ training** вое́нная подгото́вка.
militate ['mɪlɪˌteɪt] *v.i.*: **~ against** препя́тствовать (*impf.*) +*d.*; говори́ть (*impf.*) про́тив+*g.*; **his age ~s against him** ему́ меша́ет во́зраст.
militia [mɪ'lɪʃə] *n.* мили́ция.
cpd. **~man** *n.* милиционе́р.
milk [mɪlk] *n.* молоко́; **the ~ of human kindness** сострада́ние; **it's no good crying over spilt ~** слеза́ми го́рю не помо́жешь; (*attr.*) моло́чный; **~ pudding** моло́чный пу́динг; **~ tooth** моло́чный зуб.
v.t. дои́ть, по-; (*fig.*): **they ~ed him of all his cash** они́ вы́жали из него́ все де́ньги.
v.i.: **the cows are ~ing well** коро́вы хорошо́ до́ятся.
cpds. **~-and-water** *adj.* (*fig.*) безли́кий, бесцве́тный, безво́льный, бесхара́ктерный; **~-bar** *n.* кафе́-моло́чная; **~-churn** *n.* маслобо́йка; **~-float** *n.* теле́жка для разво́зки молока́; **~maid** *n.* доя́рка; **~man** *n.* продаве́ц молока́, моло́чник; **~-powder** *n.* порошко́вое молоко́; **~-shake** *n.* моло́чный кокте́йль; **~sop** *n.* тря́пка; мя́мля (*c.g.*); **~-white** *adj.* моло́чно-бе́лый.
milky ['mɪlkɪ] *adj.* моло́чный; **the M~ Way** Мле́чный путь.
mill [mɪl] *n.* (*for grinding corn*) ме́льница; **they put him through the ~** (*fig.*) они́ подве́ргли его́ тяжёлым

испытáниям; (*factory*) фáбрика.

v.t. **1.** (*grind*) молóть, пере-. **2.** (*cut with ~ing-machine*) фрезеровáть (*impf.*); **a coin with a ~ed edge** монéта с насéчкой по краю.

v.i. (*coll.*): **a crowd was ~ing around the entrance** лю́ди толпи́лись у вхóда.

cpds. **~-hand** *n.* фабри́чный/заводскóй рабóчий; **~-pond** *n.* мéльничный пруд; **the sea is like a ~-pond** мóре совершéнно спокóйно; **~-race** *n.* (*trough*) мéльничный лотóк; **~stone** *n.* жёрнов; (*fig.*) кáмень (*m.*) на шéе; **~-wheel** *n.* мéльничное колесó.

millenary [mɪ'lenərɪ] *n.* тысячелéтие.

adj. тысячелéтний.

millennial [mɪ'lenɪəl] *adj.* тысячелéтний.

millennium [mɪ'lenɪəm] *n.* тысячелéтие; (*fig.*) золотóй век.

millepede ['mɪlɪ,pi:d] = **millipede**

miller ['mɪlə(r)] *n.* мéльник.

millet ['mɪlɪt] *n.* прóсо.

milliard ['mɪljəd, -jɑ:d] *n.* миллиáрд.

millibar ['mɪlɪ,bɑ:(r)] *n.* миллибáр.

milligram(me) ['mɪlɪ,græm] *n.* миллигрáм.

millilitre ['mɪlɪ,li:tə(r)] *n.* миллили́тр.

millimetre ['mɪlɪ,mi:tə(r)] *n.* миллимéтр.

milliner ['mɪlɪnə(r)] *n.* (*fem.*) моди́стка.

millinery ['mɪlɪnərɪ] *n.* (*trade*) произвóдство/продáжа дáмских шляп; (*stock-in-trade*) дáмские шля́пки (*f. pl.*).

million ['mɪljən] *n.* & *adj.* миллиóн (+*g.*); **he made a cool ~** он сколоти́л (*coll.*) миллиóнчик; **thanks a ~** (*coll.*) огрóмное спаси́бо; **an inheritance of a ~** миллиóнное наслéдство.

millionaire [,mɪljə'neə(r)] *n.* миллионéр.

millionairess [,mɪljə'neərɪs] *n.* миллионéрша.

millionth ['mɪljənθ] *n.* миллиóнная часть.

adj. миллиóнный.

mill|ipede, -epede ['mɪlɪ,pi:d] *n.* многонóжка.

milometer [maɪ'lɒmɪtə(r)] *n.* счётчик прóйденных миль.

milt [mɪlt] *n.* семенники́ (*m. pl.*).

mime [maɪm] *n.* (*drama; performer*) мим; (*dumb-show*) пантоми́ма.

v.t. (*act by miming*) изобра|жáть, -зи́ть мими́чески; (*mimic*) подражáть (*impf.*) +*d.*; передрáзн|ивать, -и́ть; имити́ровать (*impf.*).

mimeograph ['mɪmɪə,grɑ:f] *n.* мимеóграф.

v.t. печáтать на мимеóграфе.

mimesis [mɪ'mi:sɪs, maɪ-] *n.* мимети́зм, мимикри́я.

mimetic [mɪ'metɪk] *adj.* (*imitative*) подражáтельный; (*biol.*) обладáющий мимикрíей.

mimic ['mɪmɪk] *n.* имитáтор; мими́ческий актёр, мими́ст (*fem.* -ка); **he is a good ~** он обладáет дáром подражáния.

adj. подражáтельный.

v.t. **1.** (*ridicule by imitation*) передрáзн|ивать, -и́ть; пароди́ровать (*impf.*). **2.** (*zool.*) принимáть (*impf.*) защи́тную окрáску +*g.*

mimicry ['mɪmɪkrɪ] *n.* (*imitation*) имити́рование; подражáние (+*d.*); (*zool.*) мимикри́я.

mimosa [mɪ'məʊzə] *n.* мимóза.

min. ['mɪnɪt(z)] *n.* (*abbr. of* **minute(s)**) мин., (мину́та).

minaret [,mɪnə'ret] *n.* минарéт.

minatory ['mɪnətərɪ] *adj.* угрожáющий.

mince [mɪns] *n.* (*chopped meat*) фарш.

v.t. (*chop small*) руби́ть (*impf.*); пропус|кáть, -ти́ть чéрез мясору́бку; **~d beef** фарш из говя́дины; **mincing-machine** мясору́бка; (*fig.*): **he does not ~ matters** он говори́т без обиняков.

v.i. (*behave affectedly*) жемáниться (*impf.*); (*of walk*) семени́ть (*impf.*); **he ~d up to me** он подошёл ко мне семеня́щей похóдкой.

cpds. **~meat** *n.* слáдкая начи́нка для пирожкóв; **they made ~meat of our team** (*fig.*) они́ разгроми́ли нáшу комáнду в пух и прах; **~-pie** *n.* ≃ слáдкий пирожóк.

mincer ['mɪnsə(r)] *n.* мясору́бка.

mind [maɪnd] *n.* **1.** (*intellect*) ум, рáзум; **he has a very good ~** он óчень спосóбный; **you must be out of your ~** вы с умá сошли́; **a triumph of ~ over matter** торжествó ду́ха над матéрией; **his ~ has gone; he has lost his ~** он не в своём умé; **great ~s** вели́кие умы́; **he is one of the best ~s of our time** он оди́н из величáйших/лу́чших умóв нáшего врéмени. **2.** (*remembrance*): **bear in ~** зап|оминáть, -óмнить; **bring to ~** нап|оминáть, -óмнить о+*p.*; **I called his words to ~** я вспóмнил егó словá; **it puts me in ~ of something** э́то мне чтó-то напоминáет; **the tune went clean out of my ~** я нáчисто забы́л э́ту melóдию; **out of sight, out of ~** с глаз долóй — из сéрдца вон; **time out of ~** испокóн векóв. **3.** (*opinion*) мнéние; **he spoke his ~ on the subject** он откровéнно вы́сказался на э́ту тéму; **I gave him a piece of my ~** я емý вы́ложил всё, что ду́мал; **we are of one** (*or* **of the same**) **~** мы одинáкового мнéния; **is he still of the same ~?** он всё ещё тогó же мнéния?; **he doesn't know his own ~** он сам не знáет, чегó он хóчет; **try to keep an open ~!** попытáйтесь сохрани́ть объекти́вный подхóд. **4.** (*intention*) намéрение; **I have a good** (*or* **half a**) **~ not to go** я склóнен не пойти́; **he changed his ~** он передýмал; **I have made up my ~ to stay** я реши́л остáться; **my ~ is made up** я твёрдо реши́л; **I was in two ~s whether to accept the invitation** я колебáлся, приня́ть мне приглашéние или нет. **5.** (*direction of thought or desire*): **she set her ~ on a holiday abroad** ей óчень хотéлось провести́ кани́кулы заграни́цей. **6.** (*thought*) мы́сли (*f. pl.*); **my ~ was on other things** я ду́мал о другóм; **I had something on my ~** меня́ чтó-то тревóжило; **I set his ~ at rest** я егó успокóил; **it took her ~ off her troubles** э́то отвлеклó её от её забóт/невзгóд; **I cannot read his ~** я не могу́ разгадáть егó мы́сли; **I can see him in my ~'s eye** он стои́т у меня́ пéред глазáми. **7.** (*way of thinking*) настроéние; **in his present frame, state of ~** в егó ны́нешнем состоя́нии; **to my ~** на мой взгляд; мне кáжется (*or* я считáю), что. **8.** (*attention*): **he turned his ~ to his work** он сосредотóчился на своéй рабóте; **if you give, set your ~ to your work** éсли вы настрóитесь на рабóту; **keep your ~ on what you are doing** не отвлекáйтесь; **absence of ~** рассéянность; **he showed great presence of ~** он проявля́л огрóмное прису́тствие ду́ха.

v.t. **1.** (*take care, charge of*) присм|áтривать, -отрéть за+*i.*; **~ your own business!** не вмéшивайтесь не в своё дéло! **2.** (*worry about*) забóтиться (*impf.*) о+*p.*; беспокóиться о+*p.*; **never ~ the expense** не ду́майте о расхóдах; **~ your head!** осторóжнее, не ушиби́те гóлову. **3.** (*object to*) возра|жáть, -зи́ть на+*a.*; имéть (*impf.*) что-н. прóтив+*g.*; **I don't ~ the cold** я не бою́сь хóлода; **would you ~ opening the door?** открóйте, пожáлуйста, дверь; **I wouldn't ~ going for a walk** я не прочь прогуля́ться; **I don't ~ going alone** мне всё равнó, я могу́ пойти́ оди́н. **4.** (*heed, note*) прислу́ш|иваться, -аться к+*d.*; слу́шаться (*impf.*) +*g.*; **if I had ~ed his advice** éсли бы я прислу́шался к егó совéту; **~ you lock the door!** не забу́дьте заперéть/закры́ть дверь!

v.i. **1.** (*worry*) беспокóиться (*impf.*); тревóжиться (*impf.*); **we're rather late, but never ~** мы немнóго опáздываем, ну, ничегó!; **but I do ~!** но мне не всё равнó!; **'Where have you been?' — 'Never you ~!'** «Где вы бы́ли? — «Не вáше дéло!». **2.** (*object*) возра|жáть, -зи́ть; **do you ~ if I smoke?** вы не прóтив, éсли я закурю́?; **if you don't ~** с вáшего разрешéния; éсли вас не затрудни́т; **do you ~, you're treading on my foot!** прости́те, вы наступи́ли мне нá ногу. **3.** (*bear sth. in ~*) не заб|ывáть, -ы́ть; **~ you, I don't altogether approve** замéтьте, что я э́то не совсéм одобря́ю; **not a word, ~!** смотри́те, никомý ни словá!

cpds. **~-bending** *adj.* умопомрачи́тельный (*coll.*); **~-reader** *n.* отгáдчик мы́слей; яснови́дящий; **~-reading** *n.* чтéние/угáдывание мы́слей, яснови́дение.

minded ['maɪndɪd] *adj.* **1.** (*disposed*): **I am ~ to go and see him** мне хóчется егó повидáть. **2.** (*as suff. expr. interest*) склóнный к+*d.*; проявля́ющий интерéс к+*d.*; **mathematically-~** с математи́ческими наклóнностями.

mindful ['maɪndfʊl] *adj.* забóтливый; **we must be ~ of the children** мы должны́ ду́мать о дéтях; **I was ~ of his advice**

я по́мнил его́ сове́т; **he was ~ of his duty** он сознава́л свой долг.

mindfulness ['maɪndfʊlnɪs] *n.* забо́тливость.

mindless ['maɪndlɪs] *adj.* **1.** (*without care*) беззабо́тный; **~ of danger** не сознава́я опа́сности. **2.** (*not requiring intelligence*): **~ drudgery** механи́ческий труд. **3.** (*without intelligence*) глу́пый; **~ youths** безмо́зглые юнцы́.

mindlessness ['maɪndlɪsnɪs] *n.* (*unconcern*) беззабо́тность; легкомы́слие; (*stupidity*) глу́пость, безмо́зглость.

mine[1] [maɪn] *n.* **1.** (*excavation*) ша́хта; рудни́к; копь; **(gold-~)** (золото́й) при́иск; **the men went down the ~** рабо́чие спусти́лись в ша́хту; (*fig.*) сокро́вищница; кла́дезь (*m.*); **he is a ~ of information** он неиссяка́емый исто́чник информа́ции. **2.** (*explosive device*) ми́на.

v.t. **1.** (*excavate*); **~ coal/ore** добыва́ть (*impf.*) у́голь/руду́; **coal is ~d** у́голь добыва́ют из под земли́. **2.** (*mil.*) мини́ровать, за-; под|рыва́ть, -орва́ть; **they ~d the approaches to the harbour** они́ замини́ровали подхо́ды к га́вани; **the vessel was ~d** су́дно подорва́ли.

v.i. разраб|а́тывать, -о́тать рудни́к; **they were mining for gold** они́ добыва́ли зо́лото; **the mining industry** го́рная промы́шленность; **a mining town** шахтёрский го́род/посёлок; **mining engineer** го́рный инжене́р.

cpds. **~-detector** *n.* миноиска́тель (*m.*); **~field** *n.* ми́нное по́ле; **~layer** *n.* ми́нный загради́тель; **~laying** *n.* мини́рование; **~sweeper** *n.* ми́нный тра́льщик.

mine[2] [maɪn] *pron.*: **that book is ~** э́то моя́ кни́га; **a friend of ~** (оди́н) мой друг/знако́мый.

adj. (*arch.*): **~ host** мой гостеприи́мный хозя́ин.

miner ['maɪnə(r)] *n.* (*coal-~*) шахтёр; (*gold-~*) золотоиска́тель (*m.*).

mineral ['mɪnər(ə)l] *n.* минера́л, руда́.

adj. минера́льный; **~ oil** нефть; **~ water** минера́льная вода́.

mineralogist [,mɪnə'rælədʒɪst] *n.* минерало́г.

mineralogy [,mɪnə'rælədʒɪ] *n.* минерало́гия.

minestrone [,mɪnɪ'strəʊnɪ] *n.* италья́нский овощно́й суп.

mingle ['mɪŋg(ə)l] *v.t.* сме́ш|ивать, -а́ть.

v.i. сме́шиваться (*impf.*); **~ with** (*frequent*) обща́ться (*impf.*) с+*i.*; враща́ться (*impf.*) среди́+*g.*

mingy ['mɪndʒɪ] *adj.* (*coll.*) скупо́й, прижи́мистый.

mini ['mɪnɪ] *n.* (*garment*) ми́ни (*юбка и т.д.*); (*car*) малолитра́жный автомоби́ль.

miniature ['mɪnɪtʃə(r)] *n.* (*portrait; branch of painting*) миниатю́ра; (*small-scale model*) маке́т; (*fig.*): **she is her mother in ~** она́ вы́литая мать, то́лько в миниатю́ре.

adj. миниатю́рный; **~ camera** малоформа́тный фотоаппара́т.

miniaturist ['mɪnɪtʃərɪst] *n.* миниатюри́ст.

minibus ['mɪnɪ,bʌs] *n.* микроавто́бус.

minicab ['mɪnɪ,kæb] *n.* микротакси́ (*nt. indecl.*).

minim ['mɪnɪm] *n.* (*mus.*) полови́нная но́та

minimal ['mɪnɪm(ə)l] *adj.* (*least possible*) минима́льный; (*minute*) о́чень ма́ленький, наиме́ньший.

minimize ['mɪnɪ,maɪz] *v.t.* (*reduce to minimum*) дов|оди́ть, -ести́ до ми́нимума; (*make light of*) преум|еньша́ть, -е́ньшить.

minimum ['mɪnɪməm] *n.* ми́нимум; (*attr.*) минима́льный; **~ wage** минима́льная за́работная пла́та.

mining ['maɪnɪŋ] *n.* го́рное де́ло, го́рная промы́шленность; *see also* **mine** *v.t.*

minion ['mɪnjən] *n.* (*favourite*) фавори́т, люби́мец; (*servant*) приспе́шник.

miniskirt ['mɪnɪ,skɜːt] *n.* мини-ю́бка.

minister ['mɪnɪstə(r)] *n.* **1.** (*head of government dept.*) мини́стр; **Prime M~** премье́р-мини́стр. **2.** (*in dipl. service*) посла́нник. **3.** (*clergyman*) свяще́нник, па́стор.

v.i.: **~ to** служи́ть (*impf.*) +*d.*; прислу́живать (*impf.*) +*d.*; **he ~ed to her wants** он ей прислу́живал; **a ~ing angel** а́нгел-храни́тель (*m.*).

ministerial [,mɪnɪ'stɪərɪəl] *adj.* министе́рский.

ministration [,mɪnɪ'streɪʃ(ə)n] *n.* (*pl., services*) по́мощь; обслу́живание; (*of a priest*) отправле́ние свяще́нником свои́х обя́занностей.

ministry ['mɪnɪstrɪ] *n.* **1.** (*department of state*) министе́рство. **2.** (*government*) кабине́т мини́стров. **3.** (*relig.*): **he entered the ~** он при́нял духо́вный сан.

mink [mɪŋk] *n.* но́рка; (*attr.*) но́рковый; **~ coat** но́рковое пальто́/манто́.

minnow ['mɪnəʊ] *n.* песка́рь (*m.*).

Minoan [mɪ'nəʊən] *adj.* мино́йский.

minor ['maɪnə(r)] *n.* (*pers. under age*) несовершенноле́тний.

adj. **1.** (*of lesser importance*) второстепе́нный; малозначи́тельный, ме́лкий, небольшо́й; **~ repairs** ме́лкий ремо́нт; **~ suit** (*cards*) мла́дшая масть; **~ term** (*log.*) ма́лая посы́лка. **2.** (*younger*) ме́ньший, мла́дший; **Smith M~** Смит мла́дший. **3.** (*mus.*) мино́рный, ма́лый.

minority [maɪ'nɒrɪtɪ] *n.* **1.** (*being under age*) несовершенноле́тие. **2.** (*smaller number of votes etc.*) меньшинство́, ме́ньшая часть; **you are in the ~** вы в меньшинстве́; **they lost by a ~ of one** они́ получи́ли на оди́н го́лос ме́ньше (и проигра́ли); (*attr.*): **~ report** заявле́ние меньшинства́; **~ group** меньшинство́. **3.** (**~** *nationality*) национа́льное меньшинство́, нацменьшинство́.

Minotaur ['maɪnə,tɔː(r)] *n.* Минота́вр.

minster ['mɪnstə(r)] *n.* кафедра́льный собо́р.

minstrel ['mɪnstr(ə)l] *n.* **1.** (*medieval singer or poet*) менестре́ль (*m.*). **2.** (*esp. pl., public entertainer*) исполни́тели (*m. pl.*) негритя́нских мело́дий и пе́сен (загримиро́ванные не́грами).

minstrelsy ['mɪnstr(ə)lsɪ] *n.* иску́сство менестре́лей.

mint[1] [mɪnt] *n.* (*bot.*) мя́та; **~ sauce** со́ус из мя́ты.

mint[2] [mɪnt] *n.* (*fin.*) моне́тный двор; **he made a ~ of money** он сколоти́л (*coll.*) состоя́ние; (*attr., lit., fig.*) но́венький, но́вый; **a book in ~ condition** новёхонькая кни́га.

v.t. чека́нить (*impf.*); (*fig., invent*) выду́мывать, вы́думать; **a newly-~ed phrase** све́жий оборо́т.

minuet [,mɪnjʊ'et] *n.* менуэ́т.

minus ['maɪnəs] *n.* ми́нус; **two ~es make a plus** (*in multiplication*) ми́нус на ми́нус даёт плюс.

adj. отрица́тельный; **~ sign** (знак) ми́нус; **~ quantity** отрица́тельная величина́.

prep. ми́нус; без+*g.*; **~ 1** ми́нус едини́ца; **he came back ~ an arm** он верну́лся без руки́.

minuscule ['mɪnə,skjuːl] *n.* (*letter*) мину́скул; (*script*) ру́копись, напи́санная мину́скулами.

adj. минуска́льный; о́чень ма́ленький.

minute[1] ['mɪnɪt] *n.* **1.** (*fraction of hour or degree*) мину́та; **he left it to the last ~** он э́то оста́вил до после́дней мину́ты; **the train left several ~s ago** по́езд отошёл не́сколько мину́т наза́д. **2.** (*moment*) мгнове́ние, моме́нт, миг; **I'll come in a ~** я сейча́с/ми́гом приду́; **come here this ~!** сейча́с же иди́ сюда́!; **just a ~** одну́ мину́тку!; **I won't be a ~** я на мину́тку; сейча́с верну́сь!; **I'll tell him the ~ he arrives** как то́лько он придёт, я ему́ скажу́; **he came in and the next ~ he was gone** он пришёл и че́рез секу́нду его́ не́ было; **they left at 2 o'clock to the ~** они́ ушли́ в 2 часа́ ро́вно; **he is always up to the ~ with his news** он всегда́ в ку́рсе после́дних новосте́й. **3.** (*usu. pl., record*) протоко́л; **the ~s of the last meeting** протоко́л после́днего совеща́ния; (*memorandum*) (делова́я) запи́ска.

v.t. вести́ протоко́л +*g.*; запи́с|ывать, -а́ть.

cpds. **~-book** *n.* кни́га протоко́лов; **~-gun** *n.* сигна́льная пу́шка; **~-hand** *n.* мину́тная стре́лка; **~man** *n.* (*US hist.*) солда́т наро́дной мили́ции.

minute[2] [maɪ'njuːt] *adj.* (*tiny*) ме́лкий, кро́хотный; (*detailed*) подро́бный, дета́льный.

minuteness [maɪ'njuːtnɪs] *n.* подро́бность.

minutiae [maɪ'njuːʃɪ,iː, mɪ-] *n.* ме́лочи (*f. pl.*); дета́ли (*f. pl.*).

minx [mɪŋks] *n.* озорни́ца; (*coquette*) коке́тка.

Miocene ['mɪə,siːn] *n.* миоце́н.

adj. миоце́новый.

miracle ['mɪrək(ə)l] *n.* чу́до; **~ play** мира́кль (*m.*); **he escaped by a ~** он чу́дом уцеле́л; **a ~ of ingenuity** чу́до изобрета́тельности.

miraculous [mɪ'rækjʊləs] *adj.* (*supernatural*) сверхъесте́ственный; (*surprising*) чуде́сный; (*miracle-working*) чудотво́рный.

mirage ['mɪrɑːʒ] *n.* (*lit., fig.*) мира́ж.

mire ['maɪə(r)] *n.* трясина; боло́то; **his name was dragged through the ~** его́ смеша́ли с гря́зью.

mirror ['mɪrə(r)] *n.* зе́ркало; ~ **image** (*lit., fig.*) (зерка́льное) отображе́ние; (*fig.*) отображе́ние, изображе́ние.
v.t. отра|жа́ть, -зи́ть; (*fig.*) отобра|жа́ть, -зи́ть; изобра|жа́ть, -зи́ть.
mirth [mɜ:θ] *n.* (*gladness*) весе́лье, ра́дость; (*laughter*) смех.
mirthful ['mɜ:θfʊl] *adj.* весёлый, ра́достный.
mirthless ['mɜ:θlɪs] *adj.* безра́достный.
miry ['maɪərɪ] *adj.* боло́тистый; гря́зный.
misadventure [ˌmɪsəd'ventʃə(r)] *n.* несча́стье, несча́стный слу́чай; **death by** ~ смерть от несча́стного слу́чая.
misalliance [ˌmɪsə'laɪəns] *n.* мезалья́нс.
misandrist [mɪ'zændrɪst] *n.* мужененави́стница.
misanthrope ['mɪzənˌθrəʊp, 'mɪs-] *n.* мизантро́п.
misanthropic [ˌmɪzən'θrɒpɪk, 'mɪs-] *adj.* мизантропи́ческий, человеконенави́стнический.
misanthropy [mɪ'zænθrəpɪ] *n.* мизантро́пия.
misapplication [mɪsˌæplɪ'keɪʃ(ə)n] *n.* непра́вильное испо́льзование (*+g.*); злоупотребле́ние (*+i.*).
misapply [ˌmɪsə'plaɪ] *v.t.* непра́вильно испо́льзовать (*impf., pf.*); злоупотреб|ля́ть, -и́ть *+i.*
misapprehend [ˌmɪsæprɪ'hend] *v.t.* пон|има́ть, -я́ть превра́тно.
misapprehension [ˌmɪsæprɪ'henʃ(ə)n] *n.* превра́тное понима́ние; недоразуме́ние; **I was under a** ~ я заблужда́лся.
misappropriate [ˌmɪsə'prəʊprɪˌeɪt] *v.t.* (незако́нно) присв|а́ивать, -о́ить; соверш|а́ть, -и́ть растра́ту *+g.*
misappropriation [ˌmɪsəˌprəʊprɪ'eɪʃ(ə)n] *n.* незако́нное присвое́ние; растра́та.
misbegotten [ˌmɪsbɪ'gɒt(ə)n] *adj.* (*fig.*) презре́нный, позо́рный.
misbehave [ˌmɪsbɪ'heɪv] *v.i.* ду́рно себя́ вести́ (*det.*).
misbehaviour [ˌmɪsbɪ'heɪvɪə(r)] *n.* дурно́е поведе́ние.
miscalculate [ˌmɪs'kælkjʊˌleɪt] *v.t.* пло́хо рассчи́т|ывать, -а́ть.
v.i. просчи́т|ываться, -а́ться.
miscalculation [ˌmɪskælkjʊ'leɪʃ(ə)n] *n.* просчёт.
miscall [mɪs'kɔ:l] *v.t.* (*call by wrong name*) неве́рно наз|ыва́ть, -ва́ть.
miscarriage ['mɪsˌkærɪdʒ, mɪs'kærɪdʒ] *n.* **1.** (*biol.*) вы́кидыш; **she had a** ~ у неё произошёл вы́кидыш. **2.** (*going astray*) оши́бка; ~ **of goods** недоста́вка това́ров по а́дресу; ~ **of justice** суде́бная оши́бка.
miscarr|y [mɪs'kærɪ] *v.i.* **1.** (*of a woman*) име́ть (*impf.*) вы́кидыш. **2.** (*fail*) терпе́ть (*impf.*) неуда́чу; **his plans ~ied** его́ пла́ны провали́лись. **3.** (*fail to arrive*) не доходи́ть (*impf.*) по а́дресу; **my letters ~ied** мои́ пи́сьма не дошли́ (*or* затеря́лись).
miscast [mɪs'kɑ:st] *v.t.* да|ва́ть, -ть неподходя́щую роль *+d.*; **he was** ~ **as Falstaff** ему́ не сле́довало поруча́ть роль Фальста́фа; **the play was** ~ ро́ли в пье́се бы́ли распределены́ неуда́чно.
miscegenation [ˌmɪsɪdʒɪ'neɪʃ(ə)n] *n.* смеше́ние рас.
miscellanea [ˌmɪsə'leɪnɪə] *n. pl.* литерату́рная смесь; ра́зное.
miscellaneous [ˌmɪsə'leɪnɪəs] *adj.* сме́шанный; разнообра́зный, разношёрстный.
miscellany [mɪ'selənɪ] *n.* смесь, вся́кая вся́чина; **literary** ~ литерату́рный альмана́х/сбо́рник.
mischance [mɪs'tʃɑ:ns] *n.* неуда́ча; невезе́ние; **by** ~ к несча́стью.
mischief ['mɪstʃɪf] *n.* **1.** (*harm, damage*) вред; **put that knife away, or you'll do someone a** ~ убери́те нож, а то кого́-нибудь пора́ните. **2.** (*discord, ill-feeling*) раздо́р; **he is out to make** ~ **between us** он хо́чет нас поссо́рить. **3.** (*naughtiness*) озорство́; прока́зы (*f. pl.*); **he is always getting into** ~ он всегда́ прока́зничает/шали́т; **can't you keep him out of** ~**?** неуже́ли вы не мо́жете удержа́ть его́ от прока́з? **4.** (*mockery*) **his eyes were full of** ~ его́ глаза́ бы́ли полны́ лука́вства. **5.** (*coll., mischievous child*) озорни́к; прока́зник.
cpds. **~-maker** *n.* интрига́н, смутья́н; **~-making** *n.* интри́ги (*f. pl.*), интрига́нство.
mischievous ['mɪstʃɪvəs] *adj.* (*harmful*) вре́дный; (*spiteful, malicious*) злой, зло́бный; (*given to pranks*) озорно́й, шаловли́вый.
misconceive [ˌmɪskən'si:v] *v.t.* непра́вильно пон|има́ть, -я́ть.
misconception [ˌmɪskən'sepʃ(ə)n] *n.* непра́вильное представле́ние/понима́ние.
misconduct[1] [mɪs'kɒndʌkt] *n.* **1.** (*mismanagement*) плохо́е веде́ние (дел). **2.** (*improper conduct*) дурно́е поведе́ние; **professional** ~ наруше́ние профессиона́льной э́тики; должностно́е преступле́ние. **3.** (*adultery*) супру́жеская неве́рность.
misconduct[2] [ˌmɪskən'dʌkt] *v.t.* (*mismanage*) пло́хо вести́ (*det.*) (дела́); ~ **o.s.** ду́рно себя́ вести́ (*det.*).
misconstruction [ˌmɪskən'strʌkʃ(ə)n] *n.* непра́вильное/неве́рное толкова́ние; **his words were open to** ~ его́ слова́ могли́ быть истолко́ваны неве́рно/непра́вильно/превра́тно.
misconstrue [ˌmɪskən'stru:] *v.t.* непра́вильно истолко́в|ывать, -а́ть.
miscount [mɪs'kaʊnt] *n.* непра́вильный подсчёт.
v.t. & i. ошиб|а́ться, -и́ться в подсчёте; обсчи́т|ываться, -а́ться.
miscreant ['mɪskrɪənt] *n.* (*arch., scoundrel*) подле́ц, негодя́й.
miscue [mɪs'kju:] *n.* непра́вильный/плохо́й уда́р (*в бильярде*).
misdate [mɪs'deɪt] *v.t.* непра́вильно дати́ровать (*impf., pf.*)
misdeal [mɪs'di:l] *n.* непра́вильная сда́ча.
v.i. ошиб|а́ться, -и́ться при сда́че карт.
misdeed [mɪs'di:d] *n.* преступле́ние.
misdemeanour [ˌmɪsdɪ'mi:nə(r)] *n.* просту́пок.
misdirect [ˌmɪsdaɪ'rekt, -dɪ'rekt] *v.t.* неве́рно напр|авля́ть, -а́вить; **the letter was ~ed** письмо́ бы́ло непра́вильно адресо́вано; **his efforts were ~ed** его́ уси́лия бы́ли напра́влены по ло́жному пути́; **the jury was ~ed** прися́жным да́ли непра́вильное напу́тствие.
misdirection [ˌmɪsdaɪ'rekʃ(ə)n, -dɪ'rekʃ(ə)n] *n.* непра́вильное указа́ние направле́ния/пути́.
misdoubt [mɪs'daʊt] *v.t.* (*arch.*) **1.** (*have doubts of*): **I** ~ **his loyalty** я сомнева́юсь в его́ ве́рности. **2.** (*suspect*): **I** ~ **that he will betray us** я подозрева́ю, что он нас преда́ст.
mise-en-scène [ˌmi:z ɑ̃ 'sen] *n.* мизансце́на; (*fig., setting, environment*) окружа́ющая обстано́вка.
miser ['maɪzə(r)] *n.* скря́га (*c.g.*), скупе́ц.
miserable ['mɪzərəb(ə)l] *adj.* **1.** (*wretched; unhappy*) жа́лкий, несча́стный. **2.** (*causing wretchedness*) плохо́й, скве́рный; **what** ~ **weather!** кака́я скве́рная пого́да!; **a** ~ **hovel** жа́лкая лачу́га/хиба́рка. **3.** (*mean; contemptible*) **a** ~ **sum (of money)** ничто́жная/ми́зерная су́мма.
miserere [ˌmɪzə'reərɪ, -'rɪərɪ] *n.* (*prayer*) мизере́ре (*indecl.*); «поми́луй мя, Бо́же».
miserliness ['maɪzəlɪnɪs] *n.* ску́пость, ска́редность.
miserly ['maɪzəlɪ] *adj.* скупо́й, ска́редный.
misery ['mɪzərɪ] *n.* **1.** (*suffering; wretchedness*) страда́ние; муче́ние; **he put the dog out of its** ~ он положи́л коне́ц страда́ниям соба́ки; **I was suffering** ~ **from toothache** я не знал, куда́ де́ться от зубно́й бо́ли. **2.** (*extreme poverty*) нищета́, бе́дность. **3.** (*coll., pers. who complains*) зану́да (*c.g.*), ны́тик.
misfire [mɪs'faɪə(r)] *n.* осе́чка.
v.i. да|ва́ть, -ть осе́чку; (*tech., of ignition*) выпада́ть, вы́пасть; **the gun ~d** ружьё да́ло осе́чку; (*fig.*) не состоя́ться (*impf.*); **his plans ~d** его́ план сорва́лся.
misfit ['mɪsfɪt] *n.* (*of clothes*) пло́хо сидя́щее/сши́тое пла́тье; (*pers.*) неприспосо́бленный челове́к; (*failure*) неуда́чник.
misfortune [mɪs'fɔ:tʃu:n, -tju:n] *n.* (*bad luck*) беда́, несча́стье; **I had the** ~ **to lose my purse** я име́л несча́стье потеря́ть кошелёк; **companions in** ~ друзья́ по несча́стью; (*stroke of bad luck*) несча́стье, неуда́ча; **~s never come singly** пришла́ беда́, отворя́й ворота́.
misgive [mɪs'gɪv] *v.t.*: **my mind ~s me** у меня́ дурно́е предчу́вствие.
misgiving [mɪs'gɪvɪŋ] *n.* опасе́ние; дурно́е предчу́вствие.
misgovern [mɪs'gʌv(ə)n] *v.t.* пло́хо управля́ть (*impf.*) *+i.*; пло́хо руководи́ть (*impf.*) *+i.*
misgovernment [mɪs'gʌvənmənt] *n.* плохо́е управле́ние/руково́дство (*чем*).
misguided [mɪs'gaɪdɪd] *adj.*: **I was** ~ **enough to trust him** я име́л неосторо́жность ему́ дове́рить; ~ **enthusiasm**

энтузиа́зм, досто́йный лу́чшего примене́ния.

mishandle [mɪsˈhænd(ə)l] *v.t.* (*ill-treat*) пло́хо/ду́рно обраща́ться (*impf.*) с+*i.*; (*manage inefficiently*) пло́хо вести́ (*det.*) (де́ло).

mishap [ˈmɪshæp] *n.* неуда́ча; неприя́тное происше́ствие.

mishear [mɪsˈhɪə(r)] *v.t.* нето́чно расслы́шать (*pf.*).

mishit [ˈmɪshɪt] *n.* про́мах.

mishmash [ˈmɪʃmæʃ] *n.* (*coll.*) пу́таница, мешани́на.

misinform [ˌmɪsɪnˈfɔːm] *v.t.* непра́вильно информи́ровать (*impf., pf.*).

misinformation [ˌmɪsɪnfəˈmeɪʃ(ə)n] *n.* неве́рная информа́ция.

misinterpret [ˌmɪsɪnˈtɜːprɪt] *v.t.* непра́вильно пон|има́ть, -я́ть; непра́вильно истолко́в|ывать, -а́ть.

misinterpretation [ˌmɪsɪnˌtɜːprɪˈteɪʃ(ə)n] *n.* непра́вильное понима́ние/толкова́ние.

misjudge [mɪsˈdʒʌdʒ] *v.t.* неве́рно оце́н|ивать, -и́ть; **he ~d the distance and fell** он не рассчита́л расстоя́ние и упа́л; **he has been ~d** о нём соста́вили непра́вильное мне́ние; его́ недооцени́ли.

misjudg(e)ment [mɪsˈdʒʌdʒmənt] *n.* непра́вильное мне́ние/сужде́ние.

mislay [mɪsˈleɪ] *v.t.* (*lose*) затеря́ть (*pf.*); (*put in wrong place*) положи́ть (*pf.*) не на ме́сто.

mislead [mɪsˈliːd] *v.t.* (*lit., lead astray*) вести́ (*det.*) по непра́вильному пути́; (*fig., cause to do wrong*) сби|ва́ть, -ть с пути́; (*fig., give wrong impression to*) вв|оди́ть, -ести́ в заблужде́ние; **a ~ing statement** заявле́ние, вводя́щее в заблужде́ние.

mismanage [mɪsˈmænɪdʒ] *v.t.* пло́хо управля́ть (*impf.*) +*i.*; пло́хо руководи́ть (*impf.*) +*i.*

mismanagement [mɪsˈmænɪdʒmənt] *n.* плохо́е управле́ние/руково́дство; (*inefficiency*) нераспоряди́тельность.

misname [mɪsˈneɪm] *v.t.* неве́рно именова́ть (*impf.*).

misnomer [mɪsˈnəʊmə(r)] *n.* непра́вильное назва́ние/и́мя.

misogynist [mɪˈsɒdʒɪnɪst] *n.* женоненави́стник.

misogyny [mɪˈsɒdʒɪnɪ] *n.* женоненави́стничество.

misplace [mɪsˈpleɪs] *v.t.* положи́ть (*pf.*) не на ме́сто.

misplaced [mɪsˈpleɪsd] *adj.* (*out of place*) неуме́стный; (*unfounded*) безоснова́тельный.

misprint [ˈmɪsprɪnt] *n.* опеча́тка.

mispronounce [ˌmɪsprəˈnaʊns] *v.t.* непра́вильно произн|оси́ть, -ести́.

mispronunciation [ˌmɪsprəˌnʌnsɪˈeɪʃ(ə)n] *n.* непра́вильное произноше́ние.

misquotation [mɪsˌkwəʊˈteɪʃ(ə)n] *n.* нето́чная цита́та; искаже́ние цита́ты.

misquote [mɪsˈkwəʊt] *v.t.* нето́чно цити́ровать, про-; **I have been ~d** мои́ слова́ искази́ли.

misread [mɪsˈriːd] *v.t.* (*read incorrectly*) чита́ть, про- непра́вильно; (*misinterpret*) непра́вильно истолко́в|ывать, -а́ть.

misremember [ˌmɪsrɪˈmembə(r)] *v.t. & i.* пло́хо/нето́чно по́мнить (*impf.*).

misrepresent [ˌmɪsreprɪˈzent] *v.t.* иска|жа́ть, -зи́ть; **he ~ed the facts** он искази́л фа́кты; **I was ~ed** меня́ предста́вили в ло́жном све́те.

misrepresentation [ˌmɪsreprɪzenˈteɪʃ(ə)n] *n.* искаже́ние (фа́ктов).

misrule [mɪsˈruːl] *n.* (*bad government*) плохо́е правле́ние; (*lawlessness*) беспоря́док, ана́рхия.

miss[1] [mɪs] *n.* (*failure to hit etc.*) про́мах; **a ~ is as good as a mile** «чуть-чу́ть» не счита́ется; **near ~** (*lit.*) попада́ние/разры́в вблизи́ це́ли; (*fig.*) бли́зкая дога́дка *и т.п.*; **I gave the meeting a ~** я не пошёл на собра́ние.

v.t. **1.** (*fail to hit or catch*): **he ~ed the ball** он пропусти́л мяч; **he ~ed the target** он не попа́л в цель; **the bullet ~ed him by inches** пу́ля чуть-чу́ть его́ не заде́ла; **he ~ed the bus** (*lit.*) он опозда́л на авто́бус; (*fig.*) он упусти́л слу́чай. **2.** (*fig., fail to grasp*) не пон|има́ть, -я́ть; не улови́ть (*pf.*); **you have ~ed the point** вы не по́няли су́ти. **3.** (*fail to secure*): **he ~ed his footing and fell** он оступи́лся и упа́л. **4.** (*fail to hear or see*) не услы́шать (*pf.*); пропус|ка́ть, -ти́ть; **I ~ed your last remark** я прослу́шал ва́ше после́днее замеча́ние; **you must not ~ this film** не пропусти́те э́тот фильм; **you haven't ~ed much** вы немно́го потеря́ли; **it's the corner house; you can't ~ it** э́то углово́й дом — вы его́ не мо́жете не заме́тить. **5.** (*fail to meet*): **you've just ~ed him!** вы с ним чуть-чу́ть размину́лись! **6.** (*escape by chance*) избе|га́ть, -жа́ть; **we just ~ed having an accident** мы чуть не попа́ли в катастро́фу; ещё немно́го и мы попа́ли бы в катастро́фу. **7.** (*discover or regret absence of*): **when did you ~ your purse?** когда́ вы обнару́жили, что у вас нет кошелька́?; **she ~es her husband** она́ скуча́ет по му́жу; **we ~ed you** нам вас недостава́ло; **he won't be ~ed** его́ отсу́тствия не заме́тят; (*sc. lamented*) никто́ не пожале́ет, что его́ нет; **I ~ his talks** я скуча́ю по его́ ле́кциям; **he wouldn't ~ a hundred pounds** что ему́ сто фу́нтов!

v.i. **1.** (*fail to hit target*) прома́х|иваться, -ну́ться; не поп|ада́ть, -а́сть в цель; **he shot at me but ~ed** он вы́стрелил в меня́, но промахну́лся. **2.** (*of an engine*): **it is ~ing on one cylinder** оди́н цили́ндр барахли́т.

with adv.: **~ out** *v.t.* упус|ка́ть, -ти́ть; пропус|ка́ть, -ти́ть; **you have ~ed out the most important thing** вы пропусти́ли/упусти́ли са́мое ва́жное; **I shall ~ out the first course** я не бу́ду есть пе́рвое; *v.i.* (*coll.*): **he ~ed out on all the fun** он пропусти́л са́мое весёлое; **I felt I was ~ing out** я чу́вствовал, что мно́гое упуска́ю.

miss[2] [mɪs] *n.* (*young girl; also voc.*) де́вушка; (**M~**: *as title, abbr. of* **mistress**) мисс.

missal [ˈmɪs(ə)l] *n.* служе́бник, моли́твенник.

missel-thrush [ˈmɪs(ə)l] *n.* дрозд-деря́ба.

misshapen [mɪsˈʃeɪpən] *adj.* уро́дливый, деформи́рованный.

missile [ˈmɪsaɪl] *n.* **1.** (*object thrown*) мета́тельный предме́т. **2.** (*weapon thrown or fired*) снаря́д. **3.** (*rocket weapon*) раке́та; **guided ~** управля́емая раке́та; **ballistic ~** баллисти́ческая раке́та; **~ site** ста́ртовая пози́ция; ста́ртовый ко́мплекс.

missing [ˈmɪsɪŋ] *adj.* недостаю́щий; потеря́вшийся; **there is a page ~** не хвата́ет страни́цы; **he was ~ing for a whole day** он где́-то пропада́л це́лый день; **he went ~** он пропа́л (бе́з вести); **the dead and ~** уби́тые и пропа́вшие бе́з вести; **the ~ link** недостаю́щее звено́.

quasi-prep. (*coll., short of*): **I am ~ two shirt buttons** у меня́ на руба́шке оторва́лись две пу́говицы.

mission [ˈmɪʃ(ə)n] *n.* **1.** (*errand*) поруче́ние; командиро́вка. **2.** (*vocation*) ми́ссия, призва́ние; **his ~ in life** цель его́ жи́зни. **3.** (*mil., sortie or task*) зада́ние. **4.** (*dipl.*) ми́ссия, (*to UN*) делега́ция. **5.** (*relig.*) ми́ссия; миссионе́рская де́ятельность.

missionary [ˈmɪʃənərɪ] *n.* миссионе́р (*fem.* -ка).

adj. миссионе́рский.

missis [ˈmɪsɪz] *n.* (*coll.*) жена́; хозя́йка.

missive [ˈmɪsɪv] *n.* посла́ние.

misspell [mɪsˈspel] *v.t. & i.* непра́вильно написа́ть (*pf.*); сде́лать (*pf.*) орфографи́ческую оши́бку.

misspelling [mɪsˈspelɪŋ] *n.* непра́вильное написа́ние.

misspen|d [mɪsˈspend] *v.t.* (*of funds*) тра́тить, рас-; **a ~t youth** (напра́сно) растра́ченная мо́лодость.

misstate [mɪsˈsteɪt] *v.t.* де́лать, с- ло́жное заявле́ние о+*p.*; предст|авля́ть, -а́вить в ло́жном све́те.

misstatement [mɪsˈsteɪtmənt] *n.* ло́жное заявле́ние.

missus [ˈmɪsəz] = **missis**

missy [ˈmɪsɪ] *n.* (*coll.*) ба́рышня, де́вушка.

mist [mɪst] *n.* (*lit., fig.*) тума́н, ды́мка, мгла.

v.t. & i. затума́ни|вать(ся), -ть(ся); **my glasses have ~ed over** у меня́ запоте́ли очки́.

mistakable [mɪˈsteɪkəb(ə)l] *adj.*: **he is easily ~ for his brother** его́ легко́ приня́ть за бра́та.

mistak|e [mɪˈsteɪk] *n.* оши́бка; заблужде́ние; **by ~e** по оши́бке; **make no ~e (about it)** бу́дьте уве́рены; **he's a villain and no ~e** он моше́нник, в э́том не мо́жет быть сомне́ния.

v.t. (*misunderstand*) ошиб|а́ться, -и́ться в+*p.*; **there is no ~ing his meaning** смысл его́ слов преде́льно я́сен; (*misrecognize*): **he mistook me for my brother** он при́нял меня́ за моего́ бра́та.

mistaken [mɪˈsteɪkən] *adj.* **1.** (*in error*): **if I am not ~** е́сли я не ошиба́юсь. **2.** (*ill-judged; erroneous*) неосмотри́тельный;

ошибочный, неправильный; **a ~ kindness** неуместная любезность.
mister ['mɪstə(r)] *n.* (*coll., as voc.*) мистер, сэр; гражданин.
mistime [mɪs'taɪm] *v.t.* (*action*) сделать (*pf.*) не вовремя; **he ~d his blow** он плохо/не рассчитал удар; (*speech*) сказать (*pf.*) не вовремя; **a ~d remark** неуместное замечание.
mistiness ['mɪstɪnɪs] *n.* туманность.
mistletoe ['mɪs(ə)l,təʊ] *n.* омела белая.
mistral ['mɪstrɑːl, mɪ'strɑːl] *n.* мистраль (*m.*).
mistranslate [,mɪstrænz'leɪt, ,mɪstrɑː-, -s'leɪt] *v.t.* неправильно перев|одить, -ести.
mistranslation [,mɪstrænz'leɪzeɪʃ(ə)n, ,mɪstrɑː-, -s'leɪzeɪʃ(ə)n] *n.* неправильный перевод.
mistress ['mɪstrɪs] *n.* **1.** (*of household etc.*) хозяйка; (*of college*) глава; **~ of the situation** хозяйка положения; **a ~ of needlework** мастерица вышивать; **Britain was ~ of the seas** Британия была владычицей морей. **2.** (*schoolteacher*) учительница. **3.** (*lover*) любовница.
mistrial [mɪs'traɪəl] *n.* неправильное судебное разбирательство.
mistrust [mɪs'trʌst] *n.* недоверие.
v.t. не доверять (*impf.*) +*d.*
mistrustful [mɪs'trʌstfʊl] *adj.* недоверчивый.
misty ['mɪstɪ] *adj.* туманный; (*fig.*) смутный; расплывчатый.
misunder|stand [,mɪsʌndə'stænd] *v.t.* неправильно пон|имать, -ять; **she felt ~stood** она чувствовала, что её не понимают.
misunderstanding [,mɪsʌndə'stændɪŋ] *n.* недоразумение.
misuse[1] [mɪs'juːs] *n.* неправильное употребление; злоупотребление (*чем*); дурное обращение (*с чем*).
misuse[2] [mɪs'juːz] *v.t.* (*use improperly*) неправильно употреб|лять, -ить; (*treat badly*) дурно обращаться (*impf.*) с+*i.*
mite[1] [maɪt] *n.* (*small coin*) полушка; грош; (*fig., small contribution*) лепта; (*bit*) чуточка, капелька; **he was not a ~ ashamed** ему не было ни капельки стыдно; (*small child*) малютка (*c.g.*), крошка.
mite[2] [maɪt] *n.* (*insect*) клещ.
Mithraism ['mɪθreɪ,ɪz(ə)m] *n.* митраизм.
Mithras ['mɪθræs] *n.* Митра (*m.*).
mitigat|e ['mɪtɪ,geɪt] *v.t.* смягч|ать, -ить; облегч|ать, -ить; **~ing circumstances** смягчающие обстоятельства.
mitigation [,mɪtɪ'geɪʃ(ə)n] *n.* смягчение, ослабление; **a plea in ~** ходатайство о смягчении приговора.
mitre[1] ['maɪtə(r)] *n.* (*headgear*) митра.
mitre[2] ['maɪtə(r)] *n.* (*joint*) соединение в ус.
v.t. соедин|ять, -ить в ус.
mitt [mɪt] *n.* (*mitten*) митенка; (*sl., hand*) рука; (*pl. sl., boxing gloves*) боксёрские перчатки (*f. pl.*).
mitten ['mɪt(ə)n] *n.* рукавица, варежка.
mix [mɪks] *n.* смесь; состав; **cake ~** порошок для кекса *и т.п.*
v.t. **1.** (*mingle*) смеш|ивать, -ать; (*combine*) сочетать (*impf.*); **you can't ~ oil and water** масло с водой не смешивается; **I like to ~ business with pleasure** я люблю сочетать приятное с полезным. **2.** (*prepare by ~ing*) смеш|ивать, -ать; переме́ш|ивать, -ать; **~ me a cocktail** приготовьте мне коктейль.
v.i. (*mingle*) смешиваться (*impf.*); (*combine*) сочетаться (*impf.*); **wine and beer don't ~** после вина нельзя пить пиво; (*of persons*) общаться (*impf., pf.*); **she won't ~ with her neighbours** она не хочет общаться с соседями.
with advs.: **~ in** *v.t.* заме́|шивать, -сить; **beat the eggs and ~ in the flour** взбейте яйца и смешайте с мукой; **~ up** *v.t.* (**~** *thoroughly*) (хорошо) переме́|шивать, -сить; (*confuse*) перепут|ывать, -ать; **I ~ed him up with his father** я перепутал его с отцом; **I ~ed up the dates** я перепутал числа; **a ~ed-up child** (*coll.*) трудный ребёнок; (*involve*) впут|ывать, -ать; **I don't want to become ~ed up in the affair** я не хочу ввязываться в это дело.
cpd. **~-up** *n.* недоразумение.
mixed [mɪkst] *adj.* смешанный, перемешанный; **(place for) ~ bathing** общий пляж; **a ~ bunch** (*of flowers*) смешанный букет; (*of people*) разношёрстная компания; **~ doubles** смешанная парная игра; **~ farming** смешанное хозяйство; **I have ~ feelings about it** у меня на этот счёт разноречивые чувства; **~ grill** ассорти (*nt. indecl.*) из жареного мяса; **~ marriage** смешанный брак; **~ metaphor** смешанная метафора; **~ school** школа совместного обучения.
mixer ['mɪksə(r)] *n.* **1.** (*machine*) мешалка, миксер. **2.** (*sociable pers.*): **he is a good ~** он общительный человек. **3.** (*cin. etc.*) микшер; тонмейстер.
mixture ['mɪkstʃə(r)] *n.* (*mixing*) смешивание; (*sth. mixed*) смесь; **cough ~** микстура от кашля; **the ~ as before** (*fig.*) по старым рецептам.
miz(z)en ['mɪz(ə)n] *n.* **(~-sail)** бизань.
cpd. **~-mast** *n.* бизань-мачта.
mizzle ['mɪz(ə)l] *v.i.* (*drizzle*) моросить (*impf.*).
ml. *n. abbr. of* **1. millilitre(s)** ['mɪlɪ,liːtə(r)(z)] мл, миллилитр. **2. mile(s)** [maɪl(z)] миля.
MLR (*abbr. of* ***minimum lending rate***) минимальный ссудный процент.
mm. ['mɪlɪ,miːtə(r)(z)] *n.* (*abbr. of* **millimetre(s)**) мм, (миллиметр).
mnemonic [nɪ'mɒnɪk] *n.* (*aid to memory*) мнемоническая память.
adj. мнемонический.
mo [məʊ] (*coll.*) = **moment**
moan [məʊn] *n.* стон; (*coll., complaint*) стон, нытьё.
v.t. & i. стонать (*impf.*); (*coll., complain*) ныть (*impf.*); (*fig.*) выть (*impf.*); завывать (*impf.*); **the ~ing of the wind** завывание ветра.
moaner ['məʊnə(r)] *n.* нытик (*coll.*).
moat [məʊt] *n.* ров с водой.
v.t.: **a ~ed castle** замок, обнесённый рвом.
mob [mɒb] *n.* **1.** (*rabble, crowd*) толпа. **2.: the ~** (*common people*) толпа; чернь; **~ rule** самосуд; суд Линча.
v.t. нап|адать, -асть на+*a.*; **the singer was ~bed by his fans** певца осаждали поклонники.
mobile ['məʊbaɪl] *n.* подвесная конструкция, «мобайл».
adj. **1.** (*easily moved*) передвижной, переносный; **~ troops** подвижные войска; **~ canteen** автолавка. **2.** (*lively, agile*) подвижный; **~ features** живое лицо.
mobility [mə'bɪlɪtɪ] *n.* подвижность, мобильность.
mobilization [,məʊbɪlaɪ'zeɪʃ(ə)n] *n.* мобилизация.
mobilize ['məʊbɪ,laɪz] *v.t.* мобилизовать (*impf., pf.*); **he ~d all his resources to help us** он мобилизовал все свои ресурсы, чтобы нам помочь.
v.i. мобилизоваться (*impf., pf.*).
mobster ['mɒbstə(r)] *n.* бандит.
moccasin ['mɒkəsɪn] *n.* мокасин.
mocha ['mɒkə] *n.* кофе (*m.*) мокко (*indecl.*).
mock [mɒk] *n.* насмешка, посмешище; **this makes a ~ of all my work** это сводит всю мою работу на нет.
adj. поддельный, фальшивый; **~ battle** учебный бой; **~ examination** предэкзаменационная проверка.
v.t. **1.** (*ridicule*) насмехаться (*impf.*) над+*i.*; издеваться (*impf.*) над+*i.*; высмеивать, высмеять; **they ~ed the teacher** они издевались над учителем. **2.** (*mimic*) передразни|вать, -ть; **~ing-bird** пересмешник. **3.** (*defy*): **the iron bars ~ed his efforts to escape** железная решётка лишала его надежды на побег.
v.i.: **~ at** = **~** *v.t.* **1.**
cpds. **~-heroic;** *adj.* ироикомический; **~-modesty** *n.* ложная скромность; **~-turtle soup** *n.* суп из телячьей головы; **~up** *n.* макет.
mocker ['mɒkə(r)] *n.* насмешни|к (*fem.* -ца).
mockery ['mɒkərɪ] *n.* (*ridicule*) издевательство, осмеяние; **he was held up to ~** над ним издевались; (*parody*) пародия; **the trial was a ~ of justice** суд был пародией на правосудие.
MOD (*abbr. of* ***Ministry of Defence***) Министерство обороны.
mod [mɒd] *n.* (*sl.*) стиляга (*c.g.*), модник.
modal ['məʊd(ə)l] *adj.* (*logic, gram.*) модальный; (*mus.*) ладовый.
modality [mə'dælɪtɪ] *n.* (*in pl.:*) методы (*m. pl.*), приёмы (*m. pl.*), методика.

mode [məʊd] *n.* **1.** (*manner*) ме́тод, спо́соб; ~ **of operation** спо́соб рабо́ты; ~ **of life** о́браз жи́зни. **2.** (*fashion*) мо́да; обы́чай. **3.** (*mus.*) лад; тона́льность.

model ['mɒd(ə)l] *n.* **1.** (*representation*) моде́ль, маке́т, схе́ма; **working** ~ де́йствующая моде́ль; ~ **aircraft** моде́ль самолёта. **2.** (*pattern*) образе́ц, станда́рт; **he made each box on the** ~ **of the first** он сде́лал все коро́бки по образцу́ пе́рвой; **he is a** ~ **of gallantry** он образе́ц гала́нтности; **a** ~ **husband** идеа́льный муж. **3.** (*pers. posing for artist*) нату́рщи|к (*fem.* -ца); **life** ~ жива́я моде́ль. **4.** (*woman displaying clothes etc.*) манеке́нщица; **male** ~ манеке́нщик. **5.** (*dress*) моде́ль. **6.** (*design*) моде́ль, тип; **sports** ~ (*car*) спорти́вный автомоби́ль.

v.t. де́лать, с- моде́ль +*g.*; **he** ~**led her face in wax** он вы́лепил из во́ска её лицо́; **she** ~**led the dress** (*wore it as a* ~) она́ демонстри́ровала пла́тье; **clay** ~**ling** ле́пка из гли́ны; (*fig.*): **delicately** ~**led features** то́нкие черты́ лица́; **he** ~**s himself upon his father** он подража́ет отцу́; он сле́дует приме́ру своего́ отца́; **she** ~**s for a living** она́ рабо́тает манеке́нщицей.

modeller ['mɒdlə(r)] *n.* ле́пщик, моде́льщик.

modem ['məʊdem] *n.* мо́дем.

moderate[1] ['mɒdərət] *n.* уме́ренный челове́к; челове́к, приде́рживающийся уме́ренных взгля́дов.

adj. уме́ренный; сре́дний; ~ **appetite** уме́ренный аппети́т; ~ **drinker** челове́к, пью́щий уме́ренно; ~**ly well dressed** дово́льно хорошо́ оде́тый.

moderat|e[2] ['mɒdə,reɪt] *v.t.* ум|еря́ть, -е́рить; смягч|а́ть, -и́ть; **he** ~**ed his demands** он уме́рил свои́ тре́бования; ~**e your language** выбира́йте выраже́ния.

v.i. **1.** (*become less violent*) смягч|а́ться, -и́ться; **the wind is** ~**ing** ве́тер стиха́ет. **2.** (*preside*) председа́тельствовать (*impf.*).

moderation [,mɒdə'reɪʃ(ə)n] *n.* (*moderating*) сде́рживание; регули́рование; (*moderateness*) уме́ренность, сде́ржанность; **in** ~ уме́ренно.

moderator ['mɒdə,reɪtə(r)] *n.* (*mediator*) арби́тр, посре́дник; (*chairman*) председа́тель (*m.*).

modern ['mɒd(ə)n] *adj.* совреме́нный; ~ **languages** но́вые языки́; ~ **history** но́вая исто́рия.

modernism ['mɒdə,nɪz(ə)m] *n.* модерни́зм.

modernist ['mɒdə,nɪst] *n.* модерни́ст.

modernistic [,mɒdə'nɪstɪk] *adj.* модерни́стский.

modernity [mɒ'dɜ:nɪtɪ] *n.* совреме́нность.

modernization [,mɒdənaɪ'zeɪʃ(ə)n] *n.* модерниза́ция.

modernize ['mɒdə,naɪz] *v.t.* модернизи́ровать (*impf.*, *pf.*).

modest ['mɒdɪst] *adj.* **1.** (*decorous*) благопристо́йный. **2.** (*unassuming, indifferent*) скро́мный, засте́нчивый. **3.** (*not excessive*) скро́мный, уме́ренный.

modesty ['mɒdɪstɪ] *n.* **1.** благопристо́йность. **2.** скро́мность, засте́нчивость; **in all** ~ со всей скро́мностью. **3.** сде́ржанность, уме́ренность.

modicum ['mɒdɪkəm] *n.* о́чень ма́лое коли́чество.

modification [,mɒdɪfɪ'keɪʃ(ə)n] *n.* модифика́ция; видоизмене́ние.

modif|y ['mɒdɪ,faɪ] *v.t.* **1.** (*make changes in*) модифици́ровать (*impf.*); видоизмен|я́ть, -и́ть. **2.** (*make less severe, violent etc.*) смягч|а́ть, -и́ть; ум|еря́ть, -е́рить. **3.** (*gram.*) определ|я́ть, -и́ть; **the adverb** ~**ies the verb** наре́чие определя́ет глаго́л; **a** ~**ied vowel** изменя́емый гла́сный.

modish ['məʊdɪʃ] *adj.* мо́дный.

modiste [mɒ'di:st] *n.* (*dressmaker*) моди́стка; (*milliner*) шля́пница.

modulate ['mɒdjʊ,leɪt] *v.t.* (*vary pitch of; also radio*) модули́ровать (*impf.*).

modulation [,mɒdjʊ'leɪʃ(ə)n] *n.* модуля́ция.

modular ['mɒdjʊlə(r)] *adj.* бло́чный.

module ['mɒdju:l] *n.* (*independent unit*) блок, се́кция; (*spacecraft*) мо́дульный отсе́к; **command** ~ кома́ндный отсе́к; **lunar** ~ лу́нная ка́псула.

modus operandi [,məʊdəs ,ɒpə'rændɪ] *n.* спо́соб де́йствия.

modus vivendi [,məʊdəs vɪ'vendɪ] *n.* мо́дус виве́нди (*indecl.*).

moggy ['mɒgɪ] *n.* (*sl., cat*) ки́с(к)а.

mogul ['məʊg(ə)l] *n.*: **the Great, Grand M**~ (*hist.*) Вели́кий Мого́л; (*fig., tycoon*) магна́т.

mohair ['məʊheə(r)] *n.* мохе́р; (*attr.*) мохе́ровый.

Mohammed, Muhammad [mə'hæməd], **Mahomet** [mə'hɒmɪt] *n.* Муха́ммед, Магоме́т.

Mohammedan, Muhammadan [mə'hæməd(ə)n], **Mahometan** [mə'hɒmɪt(ə)n] *n.* магомета́н|ин (*fem.* -ка).

adj. магомета́нский.

Mohammedanism [mə'hæmədən,ɪz(ə)m] *n.* магомета́нство.

moiety ['mɔɪətɪ] *n.* (*arch.*) полови́на; (*portion*) часть, до́ля.

moire [mwɑ:(r)] *n.* муа́р.

moiré ['mwɑ:reɪ] *adj.* муа́ровый.

moist [mɔɪst] *adj.* вла́жный, сыро́й.

moisten ['mɔɪs(ə)n] *v.t.* увлажн|я́ть, -и́ть; см|а́чивать, -очи́ть; **she** ~**ed the cloth** она́ смочи́ла тря́пку; **he** ~**ed his lips** он облизну́л гу́бы.

moisture ['mɔɪstʃə(r)] *n.* вла́жность, влага.

moisturize ['mɔɪstʃə,raɪz] *v.t.* увлажн|я́ть, -и́ть.

moisturizer ['mɔɪstʃə,raɪzə(r)] *n.* увлажня́ющий крем.

moke [məʊk] *n.* (*sl.*) осёл, иша́к.

molar ['məʊlə(r)] *n.* моля́р, коренно́й зуб.

adj. коренно́й.

molasses [mə'læsɪz] *n.* мела́сса, чёрная па́тока.

mold [məʊld], **-er** ['məʊldə(r)], **-ing** ['məʊldɪŋ], **-y** ['məʊldɪ] = **mould** *etc.*

Moldavia [mɒl'deɪvɪə] *n.* Молда́вия.

Moldavian [mɒl'deɪvɪən] *n.* молдава́н|ин (*fem.* -ка); *adj.* молда́вский.

mole[1] [məʊl] *n.* (*blemish*) ро́динка, борода́вка.

mole[2] [məʊl] *n.* (*zool.*) крот; (*secret agent*) «крот».

cpds. ~**-hill** *n.* крото́вина; ~**skin** *n.* кро́товый мех; *adj.* кро́товый.

mole[3] [məʊl] *n.* (*breakwater*) мол, да́мба.

molecular [mə'lekjʊlə(r)] *adj.* молекуля́рный.

molecule ['mɒlɪ,kju:l] *n.* моле́кула.

molest [mə'lest] *v.t.* прист|ава́ть, -а́ть к+*d.*; зад|ира́ть, -ра́ть.

molestation [,mɒle'steɪʃ(ə)n, ,məʊl-] *n.* пристава́ние.

moll [mɒl] *n.* (*gangster's mistress*) шалашо́вка, мару́ха (*sl.*).

mollify ['mɒlɪ,faɪ] *v.t.* смягч|а́ть, -и́ть; успок|а́ивать, -о́ить.

mollusc ['mɒləsk] *n.* моллю́ск.

mollycoddle ['mɒlɪ,kɒd(ə)l] *n.* не́женка; «ма́менькин сыно́к».

v.t. не́жить (*impf.*); балова́ть, из-.

Moloch ['məʊlɒk] *n.* (*myth.*) Мо́лох.

Molotov cocktail ['mɒlə'tɒf] *n.* буты́лка с зажига́тельной сме́сью.

molt [məʊlt] = **moult**

molten ['məʊlt(ə)n] *adj.* распла́вленный, ли́тый; ~ **metal** распла́вленный мета́лл.

molto ['mɒltəʊ] *adv.* (*mus.*) о́чень.

Moluccas [məʊ'lʌkəz, mə-] *n.* Молу́ккские острова́ (*m. pl.*).

molybdenum [mə'lɪbdɪnəm] *n.* молибде́н.

moment ['məʊmənt] *n.* **1.** (*instant; short period of time*) моме́нт, миг; **this** ~ **(at once)** сию́ мину́ту; **at the right** ~ в подходя́щий моме́нт; **at the last** ~ в после́днюю мину́ту; **he will be here (at) any** ~ **now** он здесь бу́дет с мину́ты на мину́ту; **half, just a** ~**!** оди́н моме́нт; мину́точку!; **it was all done in a** ~ всё бы́ло сде́лано в миг; **he was ready to go at a** ~**'s notice** он был гото́в идти́ по пе́рвому зо́ву; **I am busy at the** ~ я сейча́с за́нят; **at this** ~ в да́нную мину́ту; **only a** ~ **ago** мину́ту наза́д; **at odd** ~**s** ме́жду де́лом; **I would not agree to that for a** ~ я ни за что́ не соглашу́сь с э́тим; я ника́к не могу́ с э́тим согласи́ться; **the** ~ (*as soon as*) **I saw him** как то́лько я его́ уви́дел. **2.** (*mech.*) моме́нт. **3.** (*arch., importance*) ва́жность, значе́ние; **affairs of (great)** ~ ва́жные дела́; дела́ первостепе́нной ва́жности; **it is of no** ~ э́то нева́жно.

momentary ['məʊməntərɪ, -trɪ] *adj.* (*lasting a moment*) момента́льный.

momentous [mə'mentəs] *adj.* ва́жный, знамена́тельный.

momentum [mə'mentəm] *n.* (*phys.*) ине́рция; (*fig., impetus*) дви́жущая си́ла; и́мпульс; **the conspiracy gathered** ~ за́говор разроста́лся.

Monaco ['mɒnə,kəʊ, mə'nɑ:kəʊ] *n.* Мона́ко (*indecl.*).

monad ['mɒnæd, 'məʊ-] *n.* (*phil.*) мона́да.

monarch ['mɒnək] *n.* мона́рх.

monarchic(al) [mə'nɑːkɪk(ə)l] *adj.* монархи́ческий.

monarchism ['mɒnə,kɪz(ə)m] *n.* монархи́зм.

monarchist ['mɒnəkɪst] *n.* монархи́ст.
adj. монархи́стский.

monarchy ['mɒnəkɪ] *n.* мона́рхия.

monastery ['mɒnəstərɪ, -strɪ] *n.* монасты́рь (*m.*).

monastic [mə'næstɪk] *adj.* (*of monasteries*) монасты́рский; ~ **order** мона́шеский о́рден; ~ **life** мона́шеская жизнь.

monasticism [mə'næstɪ,sɪz(ə)m] *n.* мона́шество.

Monday ['mʌndeɪ, -dɪ] *n.* понеде́льник.

Monegasque [,mɒnə'gæsk] *n.* жи́тель (*fem.* -ница) Мона́ко.
adj. мона́кский.

monetarism ['mʌnɪtə,rɪz(ə)m] *n.* монетари́зм.

monetarist ['mʌnɪtə,rɪst] *n.* монетари́ст.
adj. монетари́стский.

monetary ['mʌnɪtərɪ] *adj.* де́нежный; моне́тный; ~ **unit** де́нежная едини́ца; ~ **reform** де́нежная рефо́рма; ~ **fund** валю́тный фонд.

money ['mʌnɪ] *n.* де́н|ьги (*pl. g.* -ег); **ready** ~ нали́чные (*pl.*); **he's after your** ~ он охо́тится за ва́шими деньга́ми; **for** ~ для/ра́ди/из-за де́нег; **they play** (*cards*) **for** ~ они́ игра́ют на де́ньги; **for my** ~ (*fig.*) на мой взгляд; **I got my** ~**'s worth** я получи́л сполна́ за свои́ де́ньги; **he lost** ~ **on the deal** он потеря́л де́ньги на сде́лке; **make** ~ (*become rich*) разбогате́ть (*pf.*); **do you think I'm made of** ~**?** вы ду́маете, у меня́ де́нег полно́?; **he put his** ~ **into the business** он вложи́л свой капита́л в де́ло; **I put my** ~ **on the favourite** я поста́вил на фавори́та; **throw good** ~ **after bad** упо́рствовать (*impf.*) в безнадёжном де́ле; ~ **for jam (*or* for old rope)** (*coll.*) де́ньги, полу́ченные ни за что́; **there's** ~ **in it for you** вы́годное для вас де́ло; **marry (into)** ~ жени́ться (*impf., pf.*) на бога́той/деньга́х; ~ **talks** с деньга́ми всего́ мо́жно доби́ться.
cpds. ~**-box** *n.* копи́лка; ~**-changer** *n.* меня́ла (*m.*); ~**-grubber** *n.* стяжа́тель (*m.*); ~**-grubbing** *adj.* стяжа́тельский; ~**lender** *n.* ростовщи́к; ~**-market** *n.* де́нежный/валю́тный ры́нок; ~**-order** *n.* почто́вый перево́д; ~**-spinner** *n.* (*coll.*) де́нежное де́ло.

moneyed ['mʌnɪd] *adj.*: **a** ~ **man** де́нежный челове́к.

moneyless ['mʌnɪlɪs] *adj.* безде́нежный.

Mongol ['mɒŋg(ə)l] *n.* (*racial type*) монго́л (*fem.* -ка); (**m**~: *sufferer from* ~*ism*) монголо́ид.
adj. (*racial*) монго́льский; (*path.*) монголо́идный.

Mongolia [mɒŋ'gəʊlɪə] *n.* Монго́лия.

Mongolian [mɒŋ'gəʊlɪən] *n.* (*pers.*) монго́л (*fem.* -ка); (*language*) монго́льский язы́к.
adj. монго́льский.

mongolism ['mɒŋgə,lɪz(ə)m] *n.* монголи́зм.

mongoose ['mɒŋguːs] *n.* мангу́ста.

mongrel ['mʌŋgr(ə)l, 'mɒŋ-] *n.* дворня́жка, по́месь, ублю́док; (*fig.*) мети́с (*fem.* -ка).
adj. нечистокро́вный, беспоро́дный.

monitor ['mɒnɪt(ə)r] *n.* **1.** (*in school*) ста́роста (*c.g.*). **2.** (*of broadcasts*) слуха́ч, радиоперехва́тчик; сотру́дник слу́жбы радиопрослу́шивания. **3.** (*detector apparatus*) устано́вка для радиоперехва́та. **4.** (*TV*) видеоконтро́льное устро́йство.
v.t. проверя́ть, контроли́ровать, изуча́ть (*all impf.*); ~ **a treaty** наблюда́ть (*impf.*) за исполне́нием догово́ра.

monitoring ['mɒnɪt(ə),rɪŋ] *n.* монито́ринг, слеже́ние; **environmental** ~ монито́ринг за окружа́ющей средо́й.

monk [mʌŋk] *n.* мона́х.

monkey ['mʌŋkɪ] *n.* обезья́на; ~ **business, tricks** ша́лости (*f. pl.*), проде́лки (*f. pl.*); **he made a** ~ **out of me** (*fig.*) он вы́ставил меня́ на посме́шище; **get one's** ~ **up** (*sl.*) рассерди́ться (*pf.*); **you young** ~**!** ах ты, прока́зник/озорни́к!
v.i. дура́читься (*impf.*); забавля́ться (*impf.*); **stop** ~**ing about with the radio!** переста́ньте копа́ться в приёмнике!
cpds. ~**-jacket** *n.* матро́сская ку́ртка; ~**-nut** *n.* ара́хис; ~**-puzzle** *n.* араука́рия; ~**-wrench** *n.* разводно́й га́ечный ключ.

monochrome ['mɒnə,krəʊm] *n.* однокра́сочное изображе́ние.
adj. монохро́мный.

monocle ['mɒnək(ə)l] *n.* моно́кль (*m.*).

monogamous [mə'nɒgəməs] *adj.* монога́мный, единобра́чный.

monogamy [mə'nɒgəmɪ] *n.* монога́мия, единобра́чие.

monogram ['mɒnə,græm] *n.* моногра́мма.

monograph ['mɒnə,grɑːf] *n.* моногра́фия.

monohull ['mɒnəʊ,hʌl] *n.* однoко́рпусное су́дно.

monolith ['mɒnəlɪθ] *n.* моноли́т.

monolithic [,mɒnə'lɪθɪk] *adj.* (*lit., fig.*) моноли́тный.

monologue ['mɒnə,lɒg] *n.* моноло́г.

monomania [,mɒnə'meɪnɪə] *n.* монома́ния.

monomaniac [,mɒnə'meɪnɪæk] *n.* монома́н.

monophonic [,mɒnə'fɒnɪk] *adj.* монофони́ческий.

monoplane ['mɒnə,pleɪn] *n.* монопла́н.

monopolist [mə'nɒpəlɪst] *n.* монополи́ст.

monopolistic [mə,nɒpə'lɪstɪk] *adj.* монополисти́ческий.

monopolize [mə'nɒpə,laɪz] *v.t.* монополизи́ровать (*impf., pf.*); **he** ~**s the conversation** он не даёт никому́ вста́вить сло́ва.

monopoly [mə'nɒpəlɪ] *n.* монопо́лия.

monorail ['mɒnəʊ,reɪl] *n.* моноре́льс; одноре́льсовая подвесна́я желе́зная доро́га.

monosyllabic [,mɒnəsɪ'læbɪk] *adj.* односло́жный.

monosyllable ['mɒnə,sɪləb(ə)l] *n.* односло́жное сло́во.

monotheism ['mɒnə,θiːɪz(ə)m] *n.* монотеи́зм, единобо́жие.

monotheist ['mɒnəʊ,θiːɪst] *n.* монотеи́ст.

monotheistic [,mɒnəʊθiː'ɪstɪk] *adj.* монотеисти́ческий.

monotone ['mɒnə,təʊn] *n.*: **in a** ~ без вся́кого выраже́ния, моното́нно.

monotonous [mə'nɒtənəs] *adj.* моното́нный.

monotony [mə'nɒtənɪ] *n.* моното́нность, однообра́зие.

monotype ['mɒnə,taɪp] *n.* моноти́п.

monoxide [mə'nɒksaɪd] *n.* одноо́кись; **carbon** ~ о́кись углеро́да.

monsignor(e) [mɒn'siːnjə(r), -'njɔː(r)] *n.* монсеньёр.

monsoon [mɒn'suːn] *n.* (*wind*) муссо́н; (*season*) сезо́н дожде́й.

monster ['mɒnstə(r)] *n.* (*misshapen creature*) уро́д; (*imaginary animal*) чудо́вище; (*pers. of exceptional cruelty etc.*) чудо́вище, и́зверг; (*sth. abnormally large*) грома́дина; (*attr.*) чудо́вищный.

monstrosity [mɒn'strɒsɪtɪ] *n.* (*quality*) уро́дство, чудо́вищность; (*object*) чудо́вище.

monstrous ['mɒnstrəs] *adj.* (*monster-like*) ужа́сный, безобра́зный; (*huge*) грома́дный, исполи́нский; (*outrageous*) чудо́вищный, ужа́сный.

montage [mɒn'tɑːʒ] *n.* (*cinema*) монта́ж; (*composite picture*) фотомонта́ж.

Mont Blanc [mɔ̃ 'blɑ̃] *n.* Монбла́н.

Monte Carlo [,mɒntɪ 'kɑːləʊ] *n.* Мо́нте-Ка́рло (*m. indecl.*).

Montenegrin [,mɒntɪ'niːgrɪn] *n.* черногоре́|ец (*fem.* -ка).
adj. черного́рский.

Montenegro [mɒntɪ'niːgrəʊ] *n.* Черного́рия.

month [mʌnθ] *n.* ме́сяц; **he will never do it in a** ~ **of Sundays** он никогда́ э́того не сде́лает; **the last six** ~**s** после́дние полго́да; **friendship** ~ ме́сячник дру́жбы.

monthly ['mʌnθlɪ] *n.* (*periodical*) ежеме́сячник; (*pl., coll., woman's period*) ме́сячные (*pl.*).
adj. ме́сячный; ~ **ticket** ме́сячный (проездно́й) биле́т.
adv. ежеме́сячно.

Montreal [,mɒntrɪ'ɔːl] *n.* Монреа́ль (*m.*).

monument ['mɒnjʊmənt] *n.* па́мятник; **a** ~ **to Pushkin** па́мятник Пу́шкину; **ancient** ~ дре́вний па́мятник; (*fig. model, example*) образе́ц, приме́р.

monumental [,mɒnjʊ'ment(ə)l] *adj.* увекове́чивающий, монумента́льный; ~ **mason** ма́стер, де́лающий надгро́бные пли́ты; (*fig.*) колосса́льный; **a** ~ **achievement** колосса́льное достиже́ние; **he showed** ~ **ignorance** он прояви́л порази́тельное неве́жество.

moo [muː] *n.* мыча́ние.
v.i. мыча́ть, про-.
cpd. ~**-cow** *n.* (*coll.*) коро́вка.

mooch [muːtʃ] *v.i.* (*coll.*) слоня́ться (*impf.*) (без де́ла).

mood[1] [muːd] *n.* (*state of mind*) настрое́ние; **I am not in the** ~ **for conversation** я не располо́жен к разгово́ру; **he works as the** ~ **takes him** он рабо́тает по настрое́нию;

she is in one of her ~s она́ опя́ть не в ду́хе; **a man of ~s** челове́к настрое́ния.

mood² [mu:d] *n.* (*gram.*) наклоне́ние.

moodiness ['mu:dɪnɪs] *n.* угрю́мость, мра́чность; капри́зность.

moody ['mu:dɪ] *adj.* (*gloomy*) угрю́мый; (*subject to changes of mood*) капри́зный; переме́нчивого настрое́ния.

moon¹ [mu:n] *n.* луна́; (*astron.*) Луна́; (*esp. poet.*) ме́сяц; **is there a ~ tonight?** ночь сего́дня лу́нная?; **new ~** молодо́й ме́сяц, новолу́ние; **the ~ was at the full** бы́ло полнолу́ние; **she is crying for the ~** (*fig.*) ей то́лько пти́чьего молока́ не хвата́ет; (*satellite*) спу́тник; **the ~s of Jupiter** спу́тники Юпи́тера; (*month*): **many ~s ago** давны́м-давно́; **once in a blue ~** раз в год по обеща́нию.

cpds. **~beam** *n.* луч луны́; **~-faced** *adj.* круглоли́цый; **~fall, ~-landing** *nn.* прилуне́ние; **~light** *n.* лу́нный свет; **by ~light** при луне́; **a ~light walk** прогу́лка при луне́; **do a ~light flit** (*sl.*) та́йно съе́хать с кварти́ры (*чтобы не платить за неё*); **~lighter** *n.* (*coll., one who does a second job in evening*) халту́рщик; прираба́тывающий побо́чно/нале́во; **~lighting** *n.* (*coll.*) халту́ра; побо́чный при́работок; **~lit** *adj.* за́литый лу́нным све́том; **~scape** *n.* лу́нный ландша́фт; **~shine** *n.* (*lit.*) лу́нный свет; (*visionary talk etc.*) фанта́зия; бред; (*US, smuggled spirits*) контраба́ндный спирт; **~-shot** *n.* за́пуск на Луну́; **~stone** *n.* лу́нный ка́мень; **~-struck** *adj.* поме́шанный.

moon² [mu:n] *v.t.* & *i.*: **he ~ed away a whole week** он потра́тил впусту́ю це́лую неде́лю; **stop ~ing around the house!** переста́ньте слоня́ться/броди́ть/болта́ться по до́му!

moonless ['mu:nlɪs] *adj.* безлу́нный.

moony ['mu:nɪ] *adj.* (*listless*) вя́лый; (*dreamy*) мечта́тельный.

moor¹ [mʊə(r), mɔ:(r)] *n.* ме́стность, поро́сшая ве́реском.

cpds. **~cock** *n.* саме́ц шотла́ндской куропа́тки; **~fowl** *n.* шотла́ндская куропа́тка; **~hen** *n.* са́мка шотла́ндской куропа́тки; **~land** *n.* ве́ресковая пу́стошь.

Moor² [mʊə(r), mɔ:(r)] *n.* мавр; (*fem.*) маврита́нка.

moor³ [mʊə(r), mɔ:(r)] *v.t.* ста́вить, по- на прича́л; швартова́ть, при-; **the boat was ~ed to a stake** ло́дка была́ зача́лена за ко́лышек.

v.i.: **they ~ed in the harbour** они́ пришвартова́лись в га́вани.

mooring|s ['mʊərɪŋz, 'mɔ:rɪŋz] *n.* (*gear*) мёртвые якоря́; (*place*) ме́сто стоя́нки; прича́л.

cpds. **~-mast** *n.* (*for airship*) прича́льная ма́чта; **~-rope** *n.* шварто́в.

Moorish ['mʊərɪʃ, 'mɔ:rɪʃ] *adj.* маврита́нский; ма́врский.

moose [mu:s] *n.* америка́нский лось.

moot [mu:t] *adj.*: **a ~ point** спо́рный пункт.

v.t.: **the question was ~ed** вопро́с поста́вили на обсужде́ние.

mop¹ [mɒp] *n.* шва́бра; **~ of hair** копна́ воло́с.

v.t. прот|ира́ть, -ере́ть; вытира́ть, вы́тереть; **she ~ped the floor** она́ протёрла пол; **he ~ped his brow** он вы́тер лоб.

with adv.: **~ up** *v.t.* & *i.* (*fig.*): **the profits were quickly ~ped up** вся при́быль бы́стро испари́лась; **~ping-up operations** (*mil.*) прочёсывание райо́на; очи́стка захва́ченной террито́рии от проти́вника.

mop² [mɒp] *v.i.*: **~ and mow** грима́сничать (*impf.*).

mope [məʊp] *v.i.* хандри́ть (*impf.*); ку́кситься (*impf.*).

moped ['məʊped] *n.* мопе́д.

moppet ['mɒpɪt] *n.* малю́тка (*c.g.*).

moquette [mɒ'ket] *n.* ковёр «моке́т»; плюш «моке́т».

moraine [mə'reɪn] *n.* море́на.

moral ['mɒr(ə)l] *n.* **1.** мора́ль; **the ~ of this story is ...** мора́ль сей ба́сни такова́...; **the book points a ~** в кни́ге содержи́тся нравоуче́ние. **2.** (*pl.*) нра́в|ы (*pl., g.* -ов); **loose ~s** свобо́дные нра́вы, распу́щенность; **a man without ~s** безнра́вственный челове́к.

adj. **1.** (*ethical*) мора́льный; нра́вственный; **~ sense** уме́ние отлича́ть добро́ от зла; **~ standards** мора́льные крите́рии/усто́и; **~ philosophy** э́тика. **2.** (*virtuous*) нра́вственный; **he leads a ~ life** он ведёт добродéтельную жизнь. **3.** (*capable of ~ action*): **man is a ~ agent** челове́к — носи́тель эти́ческого нача́ла. **4.** (*conducive to ~ behaviour*) нравоучи́тельный; **a ~ tale** нравоучи́тельный расска́з. **5.** (*non-physical*) мора́льный, духо́вный; **he won a ~ victory** он одержа́л мора́льную побе́ду; **I gave him ~ support** я оказа́л ему́ мора́льную подде́ржку; **he had the ~ courage to refuse** у него́ хвати́ло си́лы ду́ха отказа́ть. **6.** (*virtual*): **it is a ~ certainty that he will win** почти́ наверняка́ он победи́т.

morale [mə'rɑ:l] *n.* мора́льное состоя́ние.

moralist ['mɒrəlɪst] *n.* (*teacher of morality*) моралист.

morality [mə'rælɪtɪ] *n.* **1.** (*moral conduct*) мора́ль. **2.** (*system of morals*) нра́вственность, э́тика. **3.** (**~ play**) моралите́ (*indecl.*).

moralize ['mɒrə,laɪz] *v.i.* морализи́ровать (*impf.*).

morass [mə'ræs] *n.* боло́то; тряси́на.

moratorium [,mɒrə'tɔ:rɪəm] *n.* морато́рий; **impose a ~** объяв|ля́ть, -и́ть морато́рий.

morbid ['mɔ:bɪd] *adj.* **1.** (*pert. to disease*): **~ anatomy** патологи́ческая анато́мия; **~ growth** (злока́чественное) новообразова́ние. **2.** (*unwholesome*) боле́зненный, нездоро́вый.

morbid|ity [mɔ:'bɪdɪtɪ], **-ness** ['mɔ:bɪdnɪs] *n.* боле́зненность.

mordant ['mɔ:d(ə)nt] *adj.* ко́лкий; язви́тельный.

more [mɔ:(r)] *n.* & *adj.* (*greater amount or number*) бо́льше, бо́лее; **a little ~** побо́льше; **he received ~ than I did** он получи́л бо́льше меня́; **~ than enough** предоста́точно; **he got no ~ than his due** он получи́л сто́лько, ско́лько ему́ поло́жено; **you thanked her, which is ~ than I did** вы поблагодари́ли её, чего́ я не сде́лал; (*additional amount or number*) ещё; бо́льше; **~ tea** ещё ча́ю; **I hope to see ~ of you** я наде́юсь ви́деться с ва́ми поча́ще; **and what is ~** а кро́ме того́; и бо́льше того́; **have you any ~ matches?** у вас ещё оста́лись спи́чки?; **there is no ~ soup** бо́льше нет су́па; **twice ~** ещё два ра́за.

adv. бо́льше, бо́лее; (*rather*) скоре́е; **~ or less** бо́лее и́ли ме́нее; **I like beef ~ than mutton** я предпочита́ю говя́дину бара́нине; **he is no ~ a professor than I am** он тако́й же профе́ссор как я; **~ ridiculous** бо́лее смехотво́рный; **she is ~ beautiful than her sister** она́ краси́вее свое́й сестры́; **~ and ~** всё бо́лее и бо́лее; **I became ~ and ~ tired** я всё бо́льше устава́л; **the ~ the better** чем бо́льше, тем лу́чше; **~ than once** не раз; **once ~** сно́ва, опя́ть, ещё раз; **I saw him no ~** я его́ бо́льше не ви́дел; **he is no ~** его́ уже́ нет с на́ми (*or* нет в живы́х); его́ не ста́ло; **'I can't understand this' — 'No ~ can I'** «Я э́того не понима́ю» — «Я то́же»; **all the ~ because ...** тем бо́лее, что...

morel [mə'rel] *n.* (*mushroom*) сморчо́к.

morello [mə'reləʊ] *n.* ви́шня море́ль.

moreover [mɔ:'rəʊvə(r)] *adv.* кро́ме того́; сверх того́.

mores ['mɔ:reɪz, -ri:z] *n.* нра́вы (*m. pl.*).

morganatic [,mɔ:gə'nætɪk] *adj.* морганати́ческий.

morgue [mɔ:g] *n.* морг, мертве́цкая.

moribund ['mɒrɪ,bʌnd] *adj.* умира́ющий, отмира́ющий.

Mormon ['mɔ:mən] *n.* мормо́н (*fem.* -ка).

Mormonism ['mɔ:mən,ɪz(ə)m] *n.* мормони́зм.

morn [mɔ:n] *n.* (*poet.*) у́тро; денни́ца.

morning ['mɔ:nɪŋ] *n.* **1.** у́тро; **in the ~** у́тром; **it began to rain in the ~** дождь пошёл с утра́; **on Monday ~** в понеде́льник у́тром; **next ~** на (сле́дующее) у́тро; **three o'clock in the ~** три часа́ но́чи/пополу́ночи; **this ~** сего́дня у́тром; **from ~ till night** с утра́ до ве́чера; **one ~** в одно́ у́тро; одна́жды у́тром; **when he awoke it was ~** когда́ он просну́лся, света́ло; **good ~!** до́брое у́тро!; с до́брым у́тром!; **~ after** (*coll.*) похме́лье. **2.** (*attr.*) у́тренний; **~ coat** визи́тка; **~ glory** вьюно́к пурпу́рный; **~ sickness** тошнота́ и рво́та бере́менных по утра́м; **~ star** у́тренняя звезда́, Вене́ра.

Moroccan [mə'rɒkən] *n.* марокка́н|ец (*fem.* -ка).

adj. марокка́нский.

Morocco [mə'rɒkəʊ] *n.* Маро́кко (*indecl.*); (**m~**: *leather*) сафья́н, (*attr.*) сафья́новый.

moron ['mɔ:rɒn] *n.* слабоу́мный.

moronic [mə'rɒnɪk] *adj.* слабоу́мный, идио́тский.

morose [mə'rəʊs] *adj.* (*gloomy*) мра́чный; (*unsociable*) необщи́тельный.

moroseness [mə'rəʊsnɪs] *n.* мра́чность; необщи́тельность.

morpheme ['mɔːfiːm] *n.* морфе́ма.

Morpheus ['mɔːfɪəs] *n.*: **in the arms of ~** в объя́тиях Морфе́я.

morph|ia ['mɔːfɪə], **-ine** ['mɔːfiːn] *n.* мо́рфий.

morphological [ˌmɔːfə'lɒdʒɪk(ə)l] *adj.* морфологи́ческий.

morphology [mɔː'fɒlədʒɪ] *n.* морфоло́гия.

morris dance ['mɒrɪs] *n.* мо́ррис (*народный английский танец*).

morrow ['mɒrəʊ] *n.* (*liter.*): **on the ~** на сле́дующий день.

morse [mɔːs] *n.* (**~ code**) а́збука Мо́рзе; **~ key** ключ Мо́рзе.

morsel ['mɔːs(ə)l] *n.* кусо́чек, ка́пелька.

mortal ['mɔːt(ə)l] *n.* сме́ртный.

adj. **1.** (*subject to death*) сме́ртный; **in this ~ life** в э́той преходя́щей жи́зни. **2.** (*leading to death*) смерте́льный, смертоно́сный; **a ~ accident** катастро́фа со смерте́льным исхо́дом; **a ~ wound** смерте́льная ра́на; **~ combat** сме́ртный бой; **they were ~ enemies** они́ бы́ли смерте́льные враги́; **~ sin** сме́ртный грех. **3.** (*extreme*) смерте́льный, ужа́сный; **~ fear** смерте́льный страх; **he was in a ~ hurry** он был в стра́шной спе́шке.

mortality [mɔː'tælɪtɪ] *n.* (*being mortal*; *number or rate of deaths*) сме́ртность; **the ~ rate was high** проце́нт сме́ртности был высо́кий.

mortar[1] ['mɔːtə(r)] *n.* (*building material*) известко́вый раство́р.

v.t. скреп|ля́ть, -и́ть известко́вым раство́ром.

cpd. **~-board** *n.* (*used in building*) со́кол; (*cap*) академи́ческая ша́почка.

mortar[2] ['mɔːtə(r)] *n.* (*bowl*) сту́п(к)а.

mortar[3] ['mɔːtə(r)] *n.* (*mil.*) миномёт.

v.t. обстре́л|ивать, -я́ть миномётным огнём.

cpd. **~-fire** *n.* миномётный ого́нь.

mortgage ['mɔːgɪdʒ] *n.* закла́д; ипоте́ка; (*deed*) закладна́я; **pay off the ~** вы́купить (*pf.*) зало́женный дом; **raise a ~** получ|а́ть, -и́ть заём под закладну́ю.

v.t. за|кла́дывать, -ложи́ть; **the house was ~d for £10,000** дом был зало́жен за 10 000 фу́нтов сте́рлингов.

mortgagee [ˌmɔːgɪ'dʒiː] *n.* залогодержа́тель (*m.*).

mortgag|er ['mɔːgɪdʒə(r)], **-or** [ˌmɔːgɪ'dʒɔː(r)] *n.* должни́к по закладно́й.

mortice ['mɔːtɪs] = **mortise**

mortician [mɔː'tɪʃ(ə)n] *n.* (*US*) похоро́нных дел ма́стер.

mortification [ˌmɔːtɪfɪ'keɪʃ(ə)n] *n.* **1.** (*hurt*, *humiliation*, *grief*) оби́да, униже́ние, оскорбле́ние; (*bitterness*) го́речь. **2.** (*subduing*) подавле́ние, укроще́ние; **~ of the flesh** умерщвле́ние пло́ти. **3.** (*med.*) омертве́ние, некро́з.

mortify ['mɔːtɪˌfaɪ] *v.t.* **1.** (*cause shame or humiliation to*) об|ижа́ть, -и́деть; ун|ижа́ть, -и́зить. **2.** (*cause grief to*) оскорб|ля́ть, -и́ть; **a ~ing defeat** унизи́тельное пораже́ние. **3.** (*embitter*) нап|олня́ть, -о́лнить го́речью. **4.** (*subdue*) под|авля́ть, -ави́ть; укро|ща́ть, -ти́ть; умерщв|ля́ть, -и́ть; **he learnt to ~ the flesh** он научи́лся подавля́ть стра́сти.

v.i. гангренизи́роваться (*impf.*, *pf.*); мертве́ть, о-.

mort|ise, -ice ['mɔːtɪs] *n.* гнездо́; **~ lock** врезно́й замо́к.

v.t. запус|ка́ть, -ти́ть в паз.

mortuary ['mɔːtjʊərɪ] *n.* морг, поко́йницкая.

adj. похоро́нный, погреба́льный.

Mosaic[1] [məʊ'zeɪɪk] *adj.* Моисе́ев; **the ~ law** Моисе́евы зако́ны.

mosaic[2] [məʊ'zeɪɪk] *n.* моза́ика.

adj. мозаи́чный.

Moscow ['mɒskəʊ] *n.* Москва́; (*attr.*) моско́вский; **in the ~ area** под Москво́й.

Moselle [məʊ'zel] *n.* Мо́зель (*m.*); (*wine*) мозельве́йн.

Moses ['məʊzɪz] *n.* Моисе́й.

Moslem ['mɒzləm] = **Muslim**

mosque [mɒsk] *n.* мече́ть.

mosquito [mɒs'kiːtəʊ] *n.* кома́р.

cpd. **~-net** *n.* противомоски́тная се́тка; накома́рник.

moss [mɒs] *n.* (*plant*) мох; (*peat-bog*) торфяно́е боло́то.

cpds. **~-green** *adj.* тёмно-зелёный; **~-grown** *adj.* поро́сший мхом; **~-rose** *n.* му́скусная ро́за.

mossy ['mɒsɪ] *adj.* мши́стый.

most [məʊst] *n.* (*greatest part*) бо́льшая часть; **I was in bed ~ of the time** бо́льшую часть вре́мени я провёл в посте́ли; (*greatest amount*) наибо́льшее коли́чество; **who scored the ~?** кто получи́л наибо́льшее коли́чество очко́в?; **at (the) ~** са́мое бо́льшее; ма́ксимум; максима́льно; не бо́льше (*+g.*, *or* чем...); **£5 at the ~** ма́ксимум 5 фу́нтов; **that is the ~ I can do** э́то ма́ксимум того́, что я могу́ сде́лать; **you must make the ~ of your chances** вам ну́жно наилу́чшим о́бразом испо́льзовать свои́ возмо́жности.

adj.: **the play was boring for the ~ part** в основно́м пье́са была́ ску́чная; **~ people** большинство́ люде́й; **~ of us** большинство́ из нас; **who has the ~ money?** у кого́ бо́льше всех де́нег?

adv. **1.** (*expr. comparison*): **what I ~ desire** чего́ я бо́льше всего́ хочу́; **the ~ beautiful** са́мый краси́вый; **~ accurately** са́мым то́чным о́бразом. **2.** (*very*) о́чень, весьма́, в вы́сшей сте́пени.

mostly ['məʊstlɪ] *adv.* гла́вным о́бразом; **the weather was ~ dull** в основно́м пого́да стоя́ла па́смурная; **his diet was ~ fruit and vegetables** он обы́чно пита́лся фру́ктами и овоща́ми.

MOT (*abbr. of* ***Ministry of Transport***) Министе́рство тра́нспорта; **~ (test)** ≃ листо́к техосмо́тра.

mote [məʊt] *n.* (*speck*) пыли́нка; **he sees the ~ in his brother's eye** (*fig.*) он ви́дит сучо́к в гла́зе бра́та своего́; он ви́дит лишь чужи́е недоста́тки.

motel [məʊ'tel] *n.* автопансиона́т, моте́ль (*m.*).

motet [məʊ'tet] *n.* моте́т.

moth [mɒθ] *n.* мотылёк, ночна́я ба́бочка; **(clothes) ~** (платяна́я) моль.

cpds. **~ball** *n.* нафтали́новый ша́рик; **in ~balls** (*fig.*) на хране́нии; *v.t.* (*fig.*): **the ship was ~balled** кора́бль поста́вили на консерва́цию; **~-eaten** *adj.* (*lit.*) изъе́денный мо́лью; (*fig.*) устаре́вший; обветша́лый; **~-proof** *adj.* молесто́йкий; *v.t.* обраб|а́тывать, -о́тать молесто́йкими вещества́ми.

mother ['mʌðə(r)] *n.* **1.** мать; (*dim.*) ма́ма, ма́тушка; **she was like a ~ to him** она́ была́ ему́ как родна́я мать; **every ~'s son (of them)** все до одного́; **unmarried ~** мать-одино́чка; (*fig. origin*) исто́чник, нача́ло; **necessity is the ~ of invention** (*prov.*) голь на вы́думки хитра́. **2.** (*attr.*) матери́нский; **~ country** ро́дина; **M~ Earth** земля́-корми́лица; мать сыра́ земля́; **~ ship** плаву́чая ба́за; **~ tongue** родно́й язы́к; **~ wit** здра́вый смысл. **3.** (*head of religious community*): **M~ Superior** мать-игу́менья.

v.t. относи́ться (*impf.*) по-матери́нски к+*d.*; уха́живать (*за кем*) как за ребёнком; вск|а́рмливать, -орми́ть; **she ~ed a family of ten** она́ вы́растила десятеры́х дете́й; **a child needs ~ing** ребёнку нужна́ матери́нская забо́та; **M~ing Sunday** матери́нское воскресе́нье.

cpds. **~craft** *n.* уме́ние воспи́тывать дете́й; **~-in-law** *n.* (*wife's mother*) тёща; (*husband's mother*) свекро́вь; **~land** *n.* ро́дина, отчи́зна, оте́чество; **~-of-pearl** *n.* перламу́тр; *adj.* перламу́тровый; **~'s help** *n.* ня́ня.

motherhood ['mʌðəhʊd] *n.* матери́нство.

motherless ['mʌðəlɪs] *adj.* лишённый ма́тери.

motherliness ['mʌðəlɪnɪs] *n.* матери́нская не́жность/забо́тливость.

motherly ['mʌðəlɪ] *adj.* не́жный, забо́тливый.

motif [məʊ'tiːf] *n.* (*in music*, *literature*) лейтмоти́в; гла́вная мысль; (*in painting*) моти́в; (*ornament on dress*) вы́шитое украше́ние.

motion ['məʊʃ(ə)n] *n.* **1.** (*movement*), движе́ние; **perpetual ~** ве́чное движе́ние; **the car was in ~** маши́на дви́галась; **he put the machine in ~** он привёл маши́ну в де́йствие; **he set the plan in ~** он приступи́л к осуществле́нию пла́на; **~ picture** кинофи́льм; (*fig.*) **he went through the ~s of asking my permission** он попроси́л моего́ разреше́ния лишь для профо́рмы. **2.** (*gesture*) телодвиже́ние; жест; **I made a ~ to him to stop** я показа́л ему́ же́стом, что́бы он останови́лся. **3.** (*proposal*) предложе́ние; **the ~ was carried** предложе́ние бы́ло при́нято; **we put the ~ to the vote** мы поста́вили предложе́ние на голосова́ние. **4.** (*evacuation of bowels*) стул, испражне́ние. **5.** (*mechanism of clock etc.*) ход.

v.t. & i.: **he ~ed to them to leave** он показа́л же́стом, что́бы они́ ушли́; **he ~ed to the auctioneer** он дал знак аукциони́сту; **he ~ed the girls to come nearer** он помани́л де́вушек к себе́.

motionless [ˈməʊʃənlɪs] *adj.* неподви́жный.

motivate [ˈməʊtɪˌveɪt] *v.t.* **1.** (*induce*) побу|жда́ть, -ди́ть; толк|а́ть, -ну́ть; **he is highly ~d** у него́ есть мо́щный сти́мул; **he is insufficiently ~d** ему́ не хвата́ет сти́мула. **2.** (*give reasons for*) обосно́в|ывать, -а́ть; мотиви́ровать (*impf., pf.*).

motivation [ˌməʊtɪˈveɪʃ(ə)n] *n.* побужде́ние, сти́мул; (*interest*) заинтересо́ванность; (*giving reasons*) обоснова́ние, мотиви́ровка.

motive [ˈməʊtɪv] *n.* (*inducement, cause*) по́вод, моти́в, побужде́ние; (*motif*) моти́в.

adj. дви́жущий; **~ power/force** дви́жущая си́ла.

motley [ˈmɒtlɪ] *adj.* (*multi-coloured*) разноцве́тный, пёстрый; (*varied*): **a ~ crowd** разноше́рстная/пёстрая толпа́.

moto-cross [ˈməʊtəʊˌkrɒs] *n.* мотокро́сс; **~ racer** мотокроссме́н.

motor [ˈməʊtə(r)] *n.* **1.** (*engine*) дви́гатель (*m.*), мото́р; **electric ~** электродви́гатель (*m.*); **~ oil** авто́л; **~ vehicle** автомоби́ль (*m.*). **2.** **(~-car)** (легково́й) автомоби́ль (*m.*); **~ show** автосало́н; **the ~ trade** торго́вля автомоби́лями. **3.** (*anat.*): **~ nerve** дви́гательный нерв.

v.i. **they ~ed down to the country** они́ пое́хали на автомоби́ле за́ город.

cpds. **~-bicycle, ~-bike** (*coll.*) *nn.* мотоци́кл; **~-boat** *n.* мото́рная ло́дка; **~-car** *n.* автомоби́ль (*m.*); **~-coach** *n.* экскурсио́нный/междугоро́дный авто́бус; **~-cycle** *n.* мотоци́кл; **~-cycle racing** мотого́нки (*f. pl.*); **~-cyclist** *n.* мотоцикли́ст; **~man** *n.* води́тель (*m.*); (*of train*) машини́ст; **~-racing** *n.* автомоби́льные го́нки (*abbr.* автого́нки) (*f. pl.*); **~scooter** *n.* моторо́ллер; **~-ship** *n.* теплохо́д; **~way** *n.* автостра́да, автомагистра́ль.

motorcade [ˈməʊtəˌkeɪd] *n.* (*US*) автоколо́нна; корте́ж автомоби́лей.

motorist [ˈməʊtərɪst] *n.* автомобили́ст (*fem.* -ка).

motorize [ˈməʊtəˌraɪz] *v.t.* моторизова́ть (*impf., pf.*).

mottled [ˈmɒt(ə)ld] *adj.* пятни́стый, кра́пчатый.

motto [ˈmɒtəʊ] *n.* **1.** (*inscription*) эпи́граф; (*her.*) на́дпись на гербе́. **2.** (*maxim*) деви́з; ло́зунг.

moue [muː] *n.* грима́са.

moujik, muzhik [ˈmuːʒɪk] *n.* мужи́к.

mould[1] [məʊld] (*US* **mold**) *n.* (*hollow form for casting etc.*) лите́йная фо́рма; (*for making jellies etc.*) фо́рмочка, фо́рма; (*fig.*): **they are not cast in the same ~** они́ лю́ди ра́зные.

v.t. отлива́ть (*impf.*); формова́ть (*impf.*): **she ~ed the dough into loaves** она́ формова́ла буха́нки из те́ста; **the head was ~ed in clay** голова́ была́ вы́леплена в гли́не; (*fig.*) формирова́ть (*impf.*); **his character was ~ed by experience** его́ хара́ктер сформирова́лся под влия́нием жи́зненного о́пыта.

mould[2] [məʊld] (*US* **mold**) *n.* (*fungus*) пле́сень.

mould[3] [məʊld] (*US* **mold**) *n.* (*loose earth*) взрыхлённая земля́.

moulder[1] [ˈməʊldə(r)] (*US* **molder**) *n.* формо́вщик, лите́йщик.

moulder[2] [ˈməʊldə(r)] (*US* **molder**) *v.i.* расс|ыпа́ться, -ы́паться; разр|уша́ться, -у́шиться; **~ing ruins** ве́тхие разва́лины.

moulding [ˈməʊldɪŋ] (*US* **molding**) *n.* **1.** (*shaping*) формо́вка; отли́вка. **2.** (*archit.*) лепно́е украше́ние.

mouldy [ˈməʊldɪ] (*US* **moldy**) *adj.* (*affected by mould*) запле́сневелый; (*stale*) чёрствый; (*coll., inferior*) скве́рный, парши́вый; (*coll., unwell*) нездоро́вый.

moult [məʊlt] (*US* **molt**) *n.* ли́нька.

v.i. линя́ть (*impf.*); меня́ть (*impf.*) опере́ние.

mound [maʊnd] *n.* (*for burial or fortification*) на́сыпь; курга́н.

mount [maʊnt] *n.* **1.** (*mountain; hill*) возвы́шенность; **M~ Everest** гора́ Эвере́ст. **2.** (*horse*) (верхова́я) ло́шадь. **3.** (*of a picture*) паспарту́ (*nt. indecl.*). **4.** (*glass slide for specimens*) предме́тное стекло́. **5.** (*of a jewel*) опра́ва.

v.t. **1.** (*ascend, get on to*) вз|бира́ться, -обра́ться на+*a.*; подн|има́ться, -я́ться на+*a.*; **he ~ed the hill** он подня́лся на холм; **he ~ed his horse** он сел на ло́шадь; **he ~ed the throne** он взошёл на престо́л; **the stallion ~ the mare** жеребе́ц покры́л кобы́лу. **2.** (*provide with horse*): **we can ~ you** мы мо́жем снабди́ть вас верхово́й ло́шадью; **~ed police** ко́нная поли́ция. **3.** (*put, fix on a ~*) вст|авля́ть, -а́вить в опра́ву; опр|авля́ть, -а́вить; **do you want your photographs ~ed?** вы хоти́те накле́ить фотогра́фии на паспарту́?; **the guns were ~ed** ору́дия бы́ли устано́влены на лафе́ты. **4.** (*set up*): **they ~ed guard over the jewels** они́ охраня́ли драгоце́нности; **the enemy ~ed an offensive** враг предпри́нял наступле́ние. **5.** (*present on stage or for display*) ста́вить, по-; **the play was lavishly ~ed** спекта́кль был пы́шно офо́рмлен.

v.i. **1.** (*increase*) расти́ (*impf.*); (*also* **~ up**) нак|а́пливаться, -опи́ться. **2.**: **the blood ~ed to her cheeks** кровь бро́силась ей в лицо́; **he ~ed and rode off** он вскочи́л в седло́ и ускака́л.

mountain [ˈmaʊntɪn] *n.* **1.** гора́; **he is making a ~ out of a molehill** он де́лает из му́хи слона́. **2.** (*attr.*) го́рный; **~ chain, range** го́рная цепь; **~ sickness** го́рная боле́знь; **~ ash** ряби́на (ликёрная); **~ lion** пу́ма, кугуа́р. **3.** (*fig.*) ма́сса, ку́ча; **a ~ of debts** ма́сса долго́в; **a butter ~** (*glut*) избы́ток ма́сла.

mountaineer [ˌmaʊntɪˈnɪə(r)] *n.* альпини́ст.

mountaineering [ˌmaʊntɪˈnɪərɪŋ] *n.* альпини́зм.

mountainous [ˈmaʊntɪnəs] *adj.* гори́стый; (*huge*) грома́дный.

mountebank [ˈmaʊntɪˌbæŋk] *n.* (ле́карь-)шарлата́н; скоморо́х, фигля́р.

mourn [mɔːn] *v.t.* опла́кивать (*impf.*); **he ~ed the loss of his wife** он скорбе́л по по́воду сме́рти свое́й жены́.

v.i. скорбе́ть (*impf.*); печа́литься (*impf.*); **she ~ed for her child** она́ опла́кивала смерть своего́ ребёнка.

mourner [ˈmɔːnə(r)] *n.* прису́тствующий на похорона́х; (*hired*) пла́кальщи|к (*fem.* -ца).

mournful [ˈmɔːnfʊl] *adj.* ско́рбный, тра́урный.

mourning [ˈmɔːnɪŋ] *n.* **1.** (*grief; respect for the dead*) скорбь; тра́ур; **day of ~** тра́урный день. **2.** (*black clothes*) тра́ур; **she was in deep ~** она́ была́ в глубо́ком тра́уре; **the court went into ~** двор облачи́лся в тра́ур.

cpd. **~-band** *n.* тра́урная повя́зка.

mouse [maʊs] *n.* мышь; (*fig.*) мы́шка, мышо́нок.

v.i. (*of cat*) лови́ть (*impf.*) мыше́й.

cpds. **~-coloured** *adj.* мыши́ного цве́та; **~-trap** *n.* мышело́вка.

mouser [ˈmaʊsə(r)] *n.* мышело́в.

mousse [muːs] *n.* мусс.

moustache [məˈstɑːʃ] (*US* **mustache**) *n.* ус|ы́ (*pl.*, g. -о́в).

mousy [ˈmaʊsɪ] *adj.* **1.** (*timid*) ро́бкий, ти́хий. **2.** (*colour*) мыши́ный.

mouth[1] [maʊθ] *n.* рот; (*dim., e.g. baby's*) ро́тик; **I shouldn't have opened my ~** мне не сле́довало говори́ть; **I have only to open my ~ and he gets annoyed** сто́ит мне то́лько откры́ть рот, как он начина́ет зли́ться; **keep your ~ shut!** молчи́!; пома́лкивай!; **her ~ turned down** она́ ску́ксилась; **he was down in the ~** он ходи́л, как в во́ду опу́щенный; **the word passed from ~ to ~** но́вость передава́лась из уст в уста́; **by word of ~** у́стно; **they live from hand to ~** они́ е́ле сво́дят концы́ с конца́ми; **don't put words into my ~** не припи́сывайте мне того́, что я не говори́л; **you have taken the words out of my ~** вы предвосхи́тили мои́ слова́; я и́менно э́то хоте́л сказа́ть; **you will be laughing on the wrong side of your ~** вы ещё напла́четесь; вам бу́дет не до сме́ха; **the food made his ~ water** при ви́де еды́ у него́ потекли́ слю́нки; (*fig.*): **~ of a bottle** го́рлышко; **~ of a cave** вход в пеще́ру; **~ of a river** у́стье реки́; **~ of a sack** горлови́на мешка́.

cpds. **~-organ** *n.* губна́я гармо́ника; **~piece** *n.* (*of instrument, pipe etc.*) мундшту́к; (*fig., spokesman*) ру́пор; глаша́тай; **~-wash** *n.* полоска́ние для рта; зубно́й эликси́р; **~-watering** *adj.* вку́сный, аппети́тный.

mouth[2] [maʊð] *v.t.*: **the actor ~ed his words** актёр напы́щенно деклами́ровал; **he ~ed the words 'Go away'** «Уйди́те», сказа́л он одни́ми губа́ми.

v.i. беззву́чно шевели́ть (*impf.*) губа́ми; грима́сничать (*impf.*).

mouthful ['maʊθfʊl] *n.* кусо́к, глото́к; (*fig., long word*) тру́дно произноси́мое сло́во; **you spoke a ~!** (*coll.*) ≃ золоты́е слова́!

movable ['mu:vəb(ə)l] *adj.* (*portable*) подвижно́й, портати́вный; (*varying in date*): **~ feast** переходя́щий.

movables ['mu:vəb(ə)lz] *n.* (*furniture etc.*) дви́жимое иму́щество.

move [mu:v] *n.* **1.** (*in games*) ход; **it's your ~** ваш ход!; (*fig.*) посту́пок; ход, шаг. **2.** (*initiation of action or motion*) движе́ние; **it's time we made a ~** нам пора́ дви́гаться; **they made a ~ to go** они́ ста́ли собира́ться уходи́ть; они́ напра́вились к вы́ходу; **get a ~ on!** дви́гайтесь!, поторáпливайтесь!, пошеве́ливайтесь!; **the enemy is on the ~** враг на ма́рше. **3.** (*change of residence*) перее́зд; **when does your ~ take place?** когда́ вы переезжа́ете?

v.t. **1.** (*change position of; put in motion*) дви́гать (*impf.*); передв|ига́ть, -и́нуть; **he ~d his chair nearer the fire** он пододви́нул стул к ками́ну; **~ your books out of the way!** убери́те свои́ кни́ги!; **do you mind moving your car?** бу́дьте любе́зны, переста́вьте свою́ маши́ну; **he couldn't ~ his queen** (*at chess*) он не мог продви́нуть ферзя́; **he never ~d a muscle** он не шевельну́л ни одни́м му́скулом; (*fig.*) он и бро́вью не повёл; **I ~d heaven and earth to get him the job** я сде́лал всё возмо́жное, что́бы устро́ить его́ на э́ту рабо́ту. **2.** (*affect, provoke*) тро́гать (*impf.*); волнова́ть (*impf.*); **the play ~d me deeply** пье́са меня́ глубоко́ взволнова́ла; **the sight ~d him to tears** зре́лище тро́нуло его́ до слёз; **a moving experience** волну́ющее пережива́ние; **he is easily ~d to anger** его́ легко́ рассерди́ть. **3.** (*prompt, induce*) побу|жда́ть, -ди́ть; заст|авля́ть, -а́вить; **I was ~d to intervene** я не мог не вмеша́ться; **he works when the spirit ~s him** он рабо́тает, когда́ у него́ есть настрое́ние. **4.** (*propose*) вн|оси́ть, -ести́ предложе́ние; **I ~ that the meeting be adjourned** я предлага́ю отложи́ть заседа́ние. **5.** (*loosen*): **the laxative ~d his bowels** слаби́тельное поде́йствовало.

v.i. **1.** (*change position; be in motion*) дви́гаться (*impf.*); шевел|и́ться, -ьну́ться; **the lever won't ~** рыча́г не сдвига́ется; **don't ~!** не дви́гайтесь!; **a moving staircase** эскала́тор; **moving pictures** кинокарти́на; **we were certainly moving** (*going fast*) мы бы́стро мча́лись/дви́гались. **2.** (*in games*) ходи́ть (*impf.*); **whose turn is it to ~?** чей ход? **3.** (*change one's residence*) пере|езжа́ть, -е́хать; **moving-day** день перее́зда; **moving-van** фурго́н для перево́зки ме́бели. **4.** (*make progress*) развива́ться (*impf.*); **things began to ~ fast** собы́тия на́чали бы́стро развива́ться; **work ~s slowly** рабо́та идёт ме́дленно; **one must ~ with the times** на́до шага́ть в но́гу со вре́менем. **5.** (*stir*) шевели́ться (*impf.*); **nobody ~d to help him** никто́ не пошевели́лся, что́бы ему́ помо́чь. **6.** (*go about*) враща́ться (*impf.*); **he ~s in exalted circles** он враща́ется в вы́сших сфе́рах. **7.** (*leg., make application*) хода́тайствовать (*impf.*); **I ~ for a new trial** я хода́тайствую о пересмо́тре де́ла.

with advs.: **~ about, ~ around** *v.t.* перест|авля́ть, -а́вить; **they ~d the furniture about** они́ переста́вили ме́бель; **he was ~d about a lot** его́ ча́сто переводи́ли с одно́й до́лжности на другу́ю; *v.i.* пере|езжа́ть, -е́хать; разъезжа́ть (*impf.*); **he ~s about a lot** он мно́го разъезжа́ет; **~ along** *v.i.*: **~ along there, please!** проходи́те, пожа́луйста!; **~ around** *v.t.* = **~ about, ~ round; ~ aside** *v.t. & i.* отодв|ига́ть(ся), -и́нуть(ся); **~ away** *v.t. & i.* удал|я́ть(ся), -и́ть(ся); **~ your hand away!** убери́те ру́ку!; **they ~d away from here** они́ перее́хали отсю́да; **~ back** *v.t.*: **he ~d the books back** (*away from him*) он отодви́нул кни́ги; (*to where they had been*) он поста́вил кни́ги наза́д (на по́лку); *v.i.*: **he ~d** (*stepped*) **back** он отошёл; **they ~d back** (*to where they had lived*) они́ верну́лись (на ста́рую кварти́ру *и т.п.*); **~ forward** *v.t. & i.* дви́|гать(ся), -нуть(ся) вперёд; **~ in** *v.t.*: **troops were ~d in** бы́ли введены́ войска́; *v.i.* (*take up abode*): **they ~d in next door** они́ посели́лись в сосе́днем до́ме; **~ off** *v.i.*: **the train was moving off** по́езд на́чал отходи́ть (*or* тро́нулся); **~ on** *v.t.* продв|ига́ть, -и́нуть; **he ~d the hands** (*of the clock*) **on** он переста́вил стре́лки вперёд; **the police ~d the crowd on** поли́ция заста́вила толпу́ отойти́; *v.i.* продв|ига́ться, -и́нуться; идти́ (*det.*) да́льше; **she stopped and then ~d on** она́ останови́лась, а пото́м опя́ть продолжа́ла путь; **he ~d on to a better job** он перешёл на бо́лее подходя́щую рабо́ту; **~ out** *v.t.*: **the squatters were ~d out** скво́ттеров вы́селили; *v.i.*: **we have to ~ out tomorrow** мы должны́ съе́хать за́втра; **~ over** *v.t.* отодв|ига́ть, -и́нуть; *v.i.* (*e.g. in bed*) передв|ига́ться, -и́нуться; **~ round** *v.t.*: **she ~d the furniture round** она́ переста́вила ме́бель; *v.i.*: **the sails of the windmill ~d round** кры́лья ме́льницы враща́лись; **~ together** *v.t.* сдв|ига́ть, -и́нуть; *v.i.* сходи́ться, сойти́сь; съ|езжа́ться, -е́хаться; **~ up** *v.t.*: **~ up a chair!** пододви́ньте стул!; **he was ~d up into the next class** его́ перевели́ в сле́дующий класс; **they ~d up the reserves** они́ подтяну́ли резе́рвы; *v.i.*: **~ up and let me sit down!** подви́ньтесь и да́йте мне сесть; **prices ~d up** це́ны подняли́сь; **they ~d up in the world** они́ вы́шли в лю́ди.

movement ['mu:vmənt] *n.* **1.** (*state of moving, motion*) движе́ние, перемеще́ние; **his hands were in constant ~** ру́ки у него́ находи́лись в беспреста́нном движе́нии; **what are your ~s today?** како́е у вас сего́дня расписа́ние? **2.** (*of the body or part of it*) жест, телодвиже́ние; **he made a ~ to go** он собра́лся уходи́ть; **with a ~ of his head** движе́нием головы́. **3.** (*mil. evolution*) передвиже́ние. **4.** (*from one place to another*) переселе́ние; **~ of populations** переселе́ние наро́дов. **5.** (*organized activity*): **peace ~** движе́ние за мир. **6.** (*of the bowels*) стул, рабо́та кише́чника. **7.** (*action of novel etc.*) разви́тие де́йствия, сюже́т. **8.** (*mus., rhythm*) темп; **this piece has a lively ~** э́та му́зыка напи́сана в живо́м те́мпе. **9.** (*mus., section of composition*) часть; **slow ~** ме́дленная часть. **10.** (*moving parts*) ход; механи́зм; **a clock's ~** ход часо́в. **11.** (*group united by common purpose*) движе́ние; **the labour ~** рабо́чее движе́ние. **12.** (*comm., fin.: animation*) оживле́ние; **~ of prices** измене́ние в це́нах.

mover ['mu:və(r)] *n.* **1.** (*initiator of idea etc.*) инициа́тор. **2.** (*of proposal*) а́втор предложе́ния. **3. prime ~** первы́чный дви́гатель. **4.** (*US, towing vehicle*) (автомоби́ль-)тяга́ч.

movie ['mu:vɪ] *n.* (*coll.*) фильм, кинокарти́на; **~ mogul** киноделе́ц; **he's gone to the ~s** он пошёл в кино́.

cpds. **~-goer** *n.* люби́тель (*fem.* -ница) кино́; **~-maker** *n.* режиссёр.

moving ['mu:vɪŋ] *adj.* волну́ющий, тро́гательный.

mow[1] [məʊ] *v.t. & i.* коси́ть, с-; **they were ~ing the hay** они́ коси́ли се́но; **he ~ed the lawn** он подстри́г траву́.

with adv.: **~ down** (*fig.*) ск|а́шивать, -оси́ть; **they were ~n down by a burst of machine-gun fire** их скоси́ла пулемётная о́чередь.

mow[2] [məʊ] *v.i. see* **mop**[2]

Mozambican [ˌməʊzæm'bi:kən] *n.* жи́тель (*fem.* -ница) Мозамби́ка.

adj. мозамби́кский.

Mozambique [ˌməʊzæm'bi:k] *n.* Мозамби́к.

MP (*abbr. of* ***Member of Parliament***) член парла́мента.

mpg (*abbr. of* ***miles per gallon***) ми́ли на галло́н бензи́на.

mph (*abbr. of* ***miles per hour***) (*столько-то*) миль в час.

Mr ['mɪstə(r)] *n.* (*abbr. of* **mister**) (*pl.* **Messrs.**) г-н, (господ|и́н, *pl.* -а́); ми́стер; **she is waiting for M~ Right** она́ ждёт своего́ су́женого.

Mrs ['mɪsɪz] *n.* (*abbr. of* **mistress**) (*pl. as sg.*) г-жа, (госпожа́).

MS *abbr. of* **1. manuscript** ['mænjʊskrɪpt] ру́копись. **2.** ***multiple sclerosis*** рассе́янный *or* мно́жественный склеро́з.

Ms [mɪz, məz] *n.* (*pl. as sg.*) миз, г-жа, (госпожа́).

M.Sc. (*abbr. of* ***Master of Science***) маги́стр (есте́ственных нау́к.

Mt. [maʊnt] *n.* (*abbr. of* **Mount**) г, (гора́).

much [mʌtʃ] *n.* & *adj.* мно́гое; мно́го +*g.*; ~ **of what you say is true** мно́гое из того́, что вы говори́те, справедли́во; **I have ~ to tell you** мне есть, что вам рассказа́ть; **I will say this ~** сто́лько (и не бо́льше) я гото́в сказа́ть; **his work is not up to ~** в его́ рабо́те нет ничего́ осо́бенного; **too ~** сли́шком (мно́го); мно́го; **it was too ~ for me** э́то бы́ло для меня́ (уж) сли́шком; **he thinks too ~ of himself** он сли́шком высо́кого мне́ния о себе́; **don't make too ~ of the incident** не придава́йте э́той исто́рии сли́шком большо́го значе́ния; **I couldn't make ~ of the lecture** ле́кция была́ мне не о́чень поня́тна; **I don't see ~ of him** я его́ ре́дко ви́жу; **he doesn't read ~** он ма́ло чита́ет; **he is not ~ of an actor** он актёр о́чень нева́жный; **she is not ~ to look at** она́ далеко́ не краса́вица; **I don't think ~ of this cheese** мне не о́чень нра́вится э́тот сыр; **we are not devoting ~ attention** мы не уделя́ем большо́го внима́ния; мы уделя́ем ма́ло внима́ния; **how ~** ско́лько +*g.*; **very ~** о́чень (мно́го); о́чень си́льно; **as ~ again** ещё сто́лько же; **I thought as ~** я так и ду́мал; **I will do as ~ for you** я вам отплачу́ тем же; **I didn't get as ~ as he** я получи́л ме́ньше его́; **as ~ as to say** как бы говоря́; **it is as ~ my idea as yours** э́то сто́лько же моя́ иде́я, ско́лько ва́ша; **it was as ~ as I could do to stop laughing** я с трудо́м уде́рживался от сме́ха; **so ~** сто́лько +g.; **without so ~ as a 'by your leave'** не сказа́в да́же «с ва́шего позволе́ния»; **a bit ~** (*coll.*) немно́жко-мно́жко.

adv. **1.** (*by far*) гора́здо; ~ **better** гора́здо лу́чше; ~ **the best** гора́здо лу́чше други́х/остальны́х. **2.** (*greatly*) о́чень; нема́ло; **I am ~ obliged to you** премно́го вам обя́зан; **I was ~ amused** мне бы́ло о́чень заба́вно; **it doesn't ~ matter** э́то не име́ет большо́го значе́ния; **it does not differ ~** э́то немно́гим отлича́ется; **so ~ the better** тем лу́чше; **he was not ~ the worse** он не о́чень пострада́л; **I couldn't see him, ~ less speak to him** я не смог его́ уви́деть, не то, что поговори́ть с ним; **how ~ do you love me?** как си́льно ты меня́ лю́бишь?; ~ **to my surprise** к моему́ вели́кому удивле́нию; ~ **as I should like to go** как бы я ни хоте́л пойти́; **not ~!** (*coll.*, *very ~*) о́чень да́же!; а вы как ду́маете?; а как же! **3.** (*about*) приме́рно, почти́; **his condition is ~ the same** его́ состоя́ние приме́рно тако́е же; **they are ~ of a size** они́ почти́ одного́ разме́ра; ~ **of a ~ness** (*coll.*) приме́рно одного́ ка́чества; почти́ одина́ково.

mucilage ['mju:sɪlɪdʒ] *n.* (*US*) клей.

muck [mʌk] (*coll.*) *n.* **1.** (*manure*) наво́з. **2.** (*dirt*) грязь; (*fig.*, *anything disgusting*) дрянь. **3.** (*mess*): **he tried to finish the job and made a ~ of it** он попыта́лся зако́нчить рабо́ту и то́лько загуби́л её.

v.t. (*manure*) унаво́|живать, -зить; (*make dirty*) па́чкать, ис-.

with advs.: ~ **about** *v.t.* (*inconvenience*) причин|я́ть, -и́ть неудо́бство +*d.*; *v.i.*: **he was ~ing about with the radio** он вози́лся с ра́дио; ~ **in** *v.i.*: **if we all ~ in we shall soon get it done** е́сли мы вме́сте за э́то возьмёмся, мы э́то бы́стро сде́лаем; ~ **out** *v.t.*: **he ~ed out the stables** он почи́стил коню́шни; ~ **up** *v.t.* (*make dirty*) загрязн|я́ть, -и́ть; па́чкать, ис-; (*spoil, bungle*) испо́ртить (*pf.*); напорта́чить (*pf.*); **I ~ed up my exam** я завали́л экза́мен.

cpds. **~-cart** *n.* теле́га для перево́зки наво́за; **~-heap** *n.* наво́зная ку́ча; **~-raker** *n.* (*fig.*) выгреба́тель (*m.*) му́сора; **~-raking** *n.* копа́ние в грязи́; **~-sweat** *n.*: **he is in a ~-sweat** он весь в поту́; **~-up** *n.* пу́таница.

mucker ['mʌkə(r)] *n.* (*sl.*) ко́реш, корешо́к.

mucky ['mʌkɪ] *adj.* (*coll.*) гря́зный; пога́ный.

mucous ['mju:kəs] *adj.* сли́зистый; ~ **membrane** сли́зистая оболо́чка.

mucus ['mju:kəs] *n.* слизь.

mud [mʌd] *n.* грязь; сля́коть; **(here's) ~ in your eye!** (*sl.*) бу́дем здоро́вы!; **I am used to having ~ thrown at me** (*fig.*) я привы́к к тому́, что меня́ полива́ют; **his name was ~** (*fig.*) он был опозо́рен; (*attr.*): ~ **flat** вя́зкое дно, обнажа́ющееся при отли́ве; ~ **hut** земля́нка; ~ **pie** кули́чик.

cpds. **~-bath** *n.* грязева́я ва́нна; **~guard** *n.* крыло́; **~-pack** *n.* космети́ческая ма́ска; **~-slinging** *n.* (*fig.*) клевета́.

muddle ['mʌd(ə)l] *n.* **1.** (*mess*; *disorder*) беспоря́док; неразбери́ха; **you have made a ~ of it** вы всё перепу́тали; **things have got into a ~** всё перепу́талось/смеша́лось; **he left everything in a dreadful ~** он оста́вил по́сле себя́ ужа́сный беспоря́док. **2.** (*confusion of mind*) пу́таница; **I was in a ~ over the dates** я запу́тался в да́тах.

v.t. **1.** (*bring into disorder*) перепу́т|ывать, -ать; вн|оси́ть, -ести́ беспоря́док в+*a.*; **you have ~d (up) my papers** вы смеша́ли мои́ бума́ги. **2.** (*confuse*) пу́тать, на-; сби|ва́ть, -ть с то́лку; **don't ~ me (up)** не сбива́йте меня́ с то́лку; **his brain was ~d with drink** по́сле вы́пивки он пло́хо соobpaжа́л.

v.i. ~ **along,** ~ **through** вози́ться (*impf.*); копа́ться (*impf.*); **they ~ed along** они́ де́йствовали наобу́м; **we shall ~ through somehow** мы ко́е-как спра́вимся.

cpds. **~-headed** *adj.* бестолко́вый; **~-headedness** *n.* бестолко́вость.

muddy ['mʌdɪ] *adj.* **1.** (*covered or soiled with mud*) гря́зный, запа́чканный; **a ~ road** гря́зная доро́га; ~ **boots** забры́зганные гря́зью боти́нки. **2.** (*of colours*) нечи́стый, гря́зный. **3.** (*of liquids*) му́тный; **a ~ stream** му́тный руче́й; ~ **coffee** му́тный ко́фе. **4.** (*of complexion*) земли́стый. **5.** (*of ideas etc.*) пу́таный, тума́нный.

v.t. обры́зг|ивать, -ать (*or* забры́зг|ивать, -ать) гря́зью.

muezzin [mu:'ezɪn] *n.* муэдзи́н.

muff[1] [mʌf] *n.* (*for hands*; *also tech.*) му́фта.

muff[2] [mʌf] *v.t.* (*coll.*) ма́зать, про-; пропус|ка́ть, -ти́ть; **he ~ed the catch** он пропусти́л мяч; (*spoil*) по́ртить, ис-; **the actor ~ed his lines** актёр перепу́тал ре́плики.

muffin ['mʌfɪn] *n.* ≃ горя́чая бу́лочка.

muffle ['mʌf(ə)l] *v.t.* **1.** (*wrap up*) ку́тать, за-; **he was ~d up in an overcoat** он заку́тался в пальто́; **~d oars** обмо́танные вёсла. **2.** (*of sound*) глуши́ть, за-; **a ~d peal of bells** приглушённый звон колоколо́в; **~ed voices** приглушённые голоса́.

muffler ['mʌflə(r)] *n.* (*scarf*) кашне́ (*indecl.*), шарф; (*silencer*) глуши́тель (*m.*).

mufti[1] ['mʌftɪ] *n.* (*in Islam*) му́фтий.

mufti[2] ['mʌftɪ] *n.* (*civilian clothes*) шта́тское пла́тье; **in ~** в шта́тском.

mug[1] [mʌg] *n.* (*vessel*) кру́жка; (*sl.*, *face*) мо́рда.

mug[2] [mʌg] *n.* (*simpleton*) балбе́с; **it's a ~'s game** э́то для дурако́в; безнадёжное де́ло.

mug[3] [mʌg] *v.t.*: ~ **up** (*sl.*, *study hard*) зубри́ть, вы-.

mug[4] [mʌg] *v.t.* (*sl.*, *attack*) напада́ть, -а́сть на+*a.*; (*rob*) гра́бить, о-; **~ging** у́личный грабёж, ограбле́ние прохо́жего.

mugger ['mʌgə(r)] *n.* у́личный граби́тель.

muggins ['mʌgɪnz] *n.* (*sl.*, *fool, dupe*) простофи́ля (*c.g.*).

muggy ['mʌgɪ] *adj.* (*damp and warm*) сыро́й и тёплый; (*close*) уду́шливый.

mugwump ['mʌgwʌmp] *n.* (*US sl.*) (*fence-sitter*) неусто́йчивый член организа́ции; (*boss*) ши́шка (*c.g.*).

Muhammad [mə'hæməd], **-an** [mə'hæməd(ə)n] *n.* = **Mohammed, -an**

mulatto [mju:'lætəʊ] *n.* мула́т (*fem.* -ка).

adj. бро́нзовый, сму́глый.

mulberry ['mʌlbərɪ] *n.* (*tree*) ту́товое де́рево, шелкови́ца; (*fruit*) ту́товая я́года; (*attr.*, *colour*) багро́вый.

mulch [mʌltʃ, mʌlʃ] *n.* му́льча.

v.t. мульчи́ровать (*impf.*, *pf.*).

mulct [mʌlkt] *v.t.* (*fine*) штрафова́ть, о-; (*swindle*): **he was ~ed of £5** у него́ вы́манили 5 фу́нтов; его́ нагре́ли (*coll.*) на 5 фу́нтов.

mule[1] [mju:l] *n.* **1.** (*animal*) мул; (*fig.*, *of pers.*) упря́мый осёл. **2.** (*spinning-machine*) мюль-маши́на.

cpd. **~-driver** *n.* пого́нщик му́лов.

mule[2] [mju:l] *n.* (*slipper*) шлёпанец.

muleteer [,mju:lɪ'tɪə(r)] *n.* пого́нщик му́лов.

mulish ['mju:lɪʃ] *adj.* упря́мый.

mull[1] [mʌl] *v.t.* ~ **wine** вари́ть, с- глинтве́йн.

mull[2] [mʌl] *v.t.*: ~ **over** (*ponder*) размышля́ть (*impf.*)

над+*i.*; обду́м|ывать, -ать; (*discuss*) обсу|жда́ть, -ди́ть.

mullah ['mʌlə] *n.* мулла́ (*m.*).

mullet ['mʌlɪt] *n.* кефа́ль.

mulligatawny [ˌmʌlɪgə'tɔ:nɪ] *n.* о́стрый инди́йский суп.

mullion ['mʌljən] *n.* сре́дник; **~ed window** сво́дчатое окно́.

multi- ['mʌltɪ] *comb. form* много…, мульти…

multicoloured ['mʌltɪˌkʌləd] *adj.* многоцве́тный, кра́сочный.

multifaceted [ˌmʌltɪ'fæsɪtɪd] *adj.* многогра́нный.

multifarious [ˌmʌltɪ'feərɪəs] *adj.* разнообра́зный.

multiform ['mʌltɪˌfɔ:m] *adj.* многообра́зный.

multilateral [ˌmʌltɪ'lætər(ə)l] *adj.* многосторо́нний.

multilingual [ˌmʌltɪ'lɪŋgw(ə)l] *adj.* многоязы́чный, разноязы́чный.

multimillionaire [ˌmʌltɪˌmɪljə'neə(r)] *n.* мультимиллионе́р.

multinational [ˌmʌltɪ'næʃən(ə)l] *n.* **(~ company)** междунаро́дная/транснациона́льная корпора́ция.

adj. многонациона́льный; **~ peace-keeping force** многонациона́льные си́лы по поддержа́нию ми́ра.

multipartite [ˌmʌltɪ'pɑ:taɪt] *adj.* многосторо́нний.

multiple ['mʌltɪp(ə)l] *n.* кра́тное число́; **lowest common ~** о́бщее наиме́ньшее кра́тное.

adj. составно́й; многочи́сленный; **~ injuries** многочи́сленные ране́ния; **~ sclerosis** рассе́янный *or* мно́жественный склеро́з; **~ store** фи́рменный магази́н; **~ warhead** многозаря́дная боеголо́вка.

multiplex ['mʌltɪˌpleks] *adj.* составно́й, сло́жный.

multiplication [ˌmʌltɪplɪ'keɪʃ(ə)n] *n.* умноже́ние; **~ table** табли́ца умноже́ния.

multiplicity [ˌmʌltɪ'plɪsɪtɪ] *n.* многочи́сленность, разнообра́зие.

multiplier ['mʌltɪˌplaɪə(r)] *n.* мно́житель (*m.*), коэффицие́нт.

multipl|y ['mʌltɪˌplaɪ] *v.t.* **1.** (*math.*) умн|ожа́ть, -о́жить; **seven ~ied by two** два́жды семь; **66 ~ied by 36** 66 помно́женное на 36. **2.** (*increase*) увели́чи|вать, -ть; мно́жить, по-/у-; **one can ~y instances** мо́жно привести́ мно́жество приме́ров.

v.i. размн|ожа́ться, -о́житься; **rabbits ~ rapidly** кро́лики бы́стро размножа́ются; **increase and ~!** плоди́тесь и размножа́йтесь.

multi-purpose [ˌmʌltɪ'pɜ:pəs] *adj.* многоцелево́й.

multiracial [ˌmʌltɪ'reɪʃ(ə)l] *adj.* многонациона́льный, многора́совый.

multi-storey [ˌmʌltɪ'stɔ:rɪ] *adj.* многоэта́жный.

multitasking [ˌmʌltɪ'tɑ:skɪŋ] *n.* (*comput.*) многозада́чный режи́м (рабо́ты).

multitude ['mʌltɪˌtju:d] *n.* (*great number*) мно́жество, ма́сса; **the ~** (*mass of people*) толпа́; чернь, ма́сса.

multitudinous [ˌmʌltɪ'tju:dɪnəs] *adj.* многочи́сленный, многообра́зный.

multivitamins [ˌmʌltɪ'vɪtəmɪnz] *n. pl.* поливитами́н|ы (*pl.*, *g.* -ов).

mum[1] [mʌm] *n.* (*coll.*, *mother*) маму́ля, ма́ма.

mum[2] [mʌm] *adj.* (*coll.*, *quiet*): **I kept ~ about it** я об э́том пома́лкивал; **~'s the word** молчо́к!; ни сло́ва!

mumble ['mʌmb(ə)l] *n.* бормота́ние.

v.t. & i. (*mutter*) бормота́ть, про-; (*chew with gums*) ша́мкать, про-.

mumbo-jumbo [ˌmʌmbəʊ'dʒʌmbəʊ] *n.* (*idol*) и́дол, фети́ш; (*gibberish*) тараба́рщина.

mummer ['mʌmə(r)] *n.* ря́женый; (*pej.*, *actor*) фигля́р.

mummery ['mʌmərɪ] *n.* (*dumb-show*) пантоми́ма; (*pej.*, *ceremonial*) неле́пый ритуа́л; маскара́д.

mummify ['mʌmɪˌfaɪ] *v.t.* мумифици́ровать (*impf.*, *pf.*).

mummy[1] ['mʌmɪ] *n.* (*embalmed corpse*) му́мия.

mummy[2] ['mʌmɪ] *n.* (*coll.*, *mother*) ма́ма, ма́мочка; **~'s boy, darling** ма́менькин сынок.

mumps [mʌmps] *n.* сви́нка.

munch [mʌntʃ] *v.t. & i.* жева́ть, про-; ча́вкать (*impf.*).

mundane [mʌn'deɪn] *adj.* земно́й, мирско́й, све́тский.

Munich ['mju:nɪk] *n.* Мю́нхен.

municipal [mju:'nɪsɪp(ə)l] *adj.* муниципа́льный, городско́й.

municipality [mju:ˌnɪsɪ'pælɪtɪ] *n.* муниципалите́т.

munificence [mju:'nɪfɪs(ə)ns] *n.* ще́дрость.

munificent [mju:'nɪfɪs(ə)nt] *adj.* ще́дрый.

muniment ['mju:nɪmənt] *n.* гра́мота; докуме́нт.

munition [mju:'nɪʃ(ə)n] *v.t.* обеспе́чи|вать, -ть снаряже́нием.

munitions [mju:'nɪʃ(ə)ns] *n.* снаряже́ние, вооруже́ние; (*attr.*) **~ factory** вое́нный заво́д.

mural ['mjʊər(ə)l] *n.* фре́ска; стенна́я ро́спись.

adj. стенно́й.

murder ['mɜ:də(r)] *n.* уби́йство; **he was accused of ~** его́ обвини́ли в уби́йстве; **a ~ has been committed** совершено́ уби́йство; **~ weapon** ору́дие уби́йства; **~ will out** (*fig.*) ≃ ши́ла в мешке́ не утаи́шь; **he cried blue ~** (*coll.*) он (за)крича́л/вопи́л карау́л (*or* благи́м ма́том); (*fig.*): **the traffic was (sheer) ~** (*coll.*) движе́ние бы́ло стра́шное/смертоуби́йственное.

v.t. уб|ива́ть, -и́ть; **a man was ~ed** уби́ли челове́ка; челове́к уби́т; (*fig.*, *of a bad performance*) по́ртить (*impf.*); губи́ть (*impf.*); **she ~ed the sonata** она́ загуби́ла сона́ту; **he ~s the language** он кове́ркает язы́к.

v.i.: **he ~ed for gain** он соверши́л преднаме́ренное уби́йство с це́лью нажи́вы.

murderer ['mɜ:dərə(r)] *n.* уби́йца (*c.g.*).

murderess ['mɜ:dərɪs] *n.* (же́нщина-)уби́йца.

murderous ['mɜ:dərəs] *adj.* смертоно́сный, уби́йственный; **a ~ glance** уби́йственный взгляд; **the exams are ~** экза́мены уби́йственно трудны́.

murk [mɜ:k] *n.* мрак, темнота́.

murkiness ['mɜ:kɪnɪs] *n.* мра́чность.

murky ['mɜ:kɪ] *adj.* мра́чный, тёмный; **his ~ past** его́ тёмное про́шлое.

murmur ['mɜ:mə(r)] *n.* **1.** (*low sound*) бормота́ние, шёпот; **his voice sank to a ~** он заговори́л шёпотом; его́ го́лос пони́зился до шёпота; **a ~ of conversation** ти́хая бесе́да; **the ~ of bees** жужжа́ние пчёл; **the ~ of the waves** ро́пот волн; **a heart ~** (*med.*) шумы́ (*m. pl.*) в се́рдце. **2.** (*fig.*, *complaint*) ро́пот, ворча́ние; **~s of discontent** выраже́ние (*nt. pl.*) недово́льства; **he paid up without a ~** он заплати́л без зву́ка.

v.t. & i. говори́ть (*impf.*) ти́хо; бормота́ть, про-; шепта́ть, про-; **he ~ed a prayer** он прошепта́л моли́тву; (*complain*) ропта́ть (*impf.*); ворча́ть (*impf.*); **the people ~ed at, against the new laws** наро́д ропта́л по по́воду но́вых зако́нов.

murrain ['mʌrɪn] *n.* я́щур.

Muscat ['mʌskət] *n.* Маска́т; **~ and Oman** Ома́н и Маска́т; **m~ grape** муска́тный виногра́д.

muscatel [ˌmʌskə'tel] *n.* (*wine*) муска́т.

muscle ['mʌs(ə)l] *n.* мы́шца, му́скул; **he didn't move a ~** (*remained motionless*) он не (по)шевельну́лся; он и у́хом не повёл.

v.i. (*coll.*): **he ~d in on the conversation** он ввяза́лся в разгово́р.

cpd. **~man** *n.* сила́ч, геркуле́с; (*bouncer*) вышиба́ла (*m.*).

Muscovite ['mʌskəˌvaɪt] *n.* (*native of old Russia*) москвитя́н|ин (*fem.* -ка); (*native of Moscow*) москви́ч (*fem.* -ка).

adj. моско́вский.

Muscovy ['mʌskəvɪ] *n.* Моско́вия; **Grand Duchy of ~** Вели́кое кня́жество Моско́вское.

muscular ['mʌskjʊlə(r)] *adj.* (*pert. to muscle*) мы́шечный; (*with strong muscles*; *robust*) му́скули́стый; си́льный.

muse[1] [mju:z] *n.* (*myth.*) му́за.

muse[2] [mju:z] *v.i.* размышля́ть (*impf.*); заду́мываться (*impf.*).

museum [mju:'zɪəm] *n.* музе́й; **~ piece** (*lit.*, *fig.*) музе́йный экспона́т; музе́йная ре́дкость.

mush [mʌʃ] *n.* (*pulpy mass*) ка́ша, ка́шица; (*US*, *boiled meal*) ка́ша; (*coll.*, *sentimental writing or music*) сентимента́льщина.

mushroom ['mʌʃrʊm, -ru:m] *n.* гриб; **~ cloud** грибови́дное о́блако; **~ growth** (*fig.*) бы́стрый рост.

v.i. (*pick ~s*) собира́ть (*impf.*) грибы́; (*fig.*, *grow rapidly*) бы́стро распространя́ться (*impf.*); расти́ (*impf.*) как грибы́ под дождём.

mushy ['mʌʃɪ] *adj.* мя́гкий; (*fig.*) слаща́вый.

music ['mju:zɪk] *n.* **1.** му́зыка; **take up ~** заня́ться (*pf.*) му́зыкой; **the lines were put, set to ~ by Brahms** Брамс положи́л стихи́ на му́зыку; **it was ~ to his ears** э́то ласка́ло его́ слух; **you will have to face the ~** (*criticism, outcry*) вам придётся за э́то распла́чиваться. **2.** (*attr.*) **~ centre** музыка́льный комба́йн; **~ lesson** уро́к му́зыки; **~ master, teacher** учи́тель (*m.*) му́зыки. **3.** (*sheet ~, ~al score*) но́ты (*f. pl.*).

cpds. **~-hall** *n.* (*place, entertainment*) мю́зик-хо́лл; **~-hall artist** эстра́дный арти́ст (*fem.* -ка); **~-paper** *n.* но́тная бума́га; **~-room** *n.* музыка́льная ко́мната; **~-stand** *n.* пюпи́тр.

musical ['mju:zɪk(ə)l] *n.* (**~** *comedy*) музыка́льная коме́дия; музыка́льное ревю́ (*indecl.*), опере́тта.

adj. (*pert. to, fond of music*) музыка́льный; **~ box** музыка́льная шкату́лка; **~ chairs** «сту́лья с му́зыкой» (*игра*); **~ glasses** стекля́нная гармо́ника; **a ~ voice** мелоди́чный го́лос; **~ talent** музыка́льность.

musician [mju:'zɪʃ(ə)n] *n.* (*performer*) музыка́нт; (*composer*) компози́тор.

musicianship [mju:'zɪʃənʃɪp] *n.* музыка́льность.

musicologist [,mju:zɪ'kɒlədʒɪst] *n.* музыкове́д.

musicology [,mju:zɪ'kɒlədʒɪ] *n.* музыкове́дение.

musk [mʌsk] *n.* му́скус.

cpds. **~-deer** *n.* му́скусный оле́нь; **~-melon** *n.* ды́ня му́скусная; **~-ox** *n.* му́скусный бык, овцебы́к; **~-rat** *n.* онда́тра, вы́хухоль (*m.*), му́скусная кры́са; **~-rose** *n.* му́скусная ро́за.

musket ['mʌskɪt] *n.* мушке́т.

musketeer [,mʌskɪ'tɪə(r)] *n.* мушкетёр.

musketry ['mʌskɪtrɪ] *n.* (*small arms firing*) стрельба́ из винто́вки.

musky ['mʌskɪ] *adj.* му́скусный, па́хнущий му́скусом.

Muslim ['mʊzlɪm, 'mʌ-], **Moslem** ['mɒzləm], **Mussulman** ['mʌsəlmən] *n.* мусульма́н|ин (*fem.* -ка).

adj. мусульма́нский.

muslin ['mʌzlɪn] *n.* мусли́н, кисея́.

adj. мусли́новый, кисе́йный.

musquash ['mʌskwɒʃ] *n.* (*fur*) мех онда́тры.

muss [mʌs] *v.t.* (*coll.*): **~ up** (*e.g. hair*) взъеро́шить (*pf.*); растрепа́ть (*pf.*).

mussel ['mʌs(ə)l] *n.* двуство́рчатая ра́кушка; ми́дия.

Mussulman ['mʌsəlmən] = **Muslim**

must[1] [mʌst] *n.* (*unfermented grape juice*) муст, виногра́дное су́сло.

must[2] [mʌst] *n.* (*mould*) пле́сень.

must[3] [mʌst] *n.* (*coll., necessary item*): **the Tower of London is a ~ for visitors** тури́сты должны́ непреме́нно посмотре́ть Ло́ндонский Та́уэр.

v. aux. **1.** (*expr. necessity*): **one ~ eat to live** что́бы жить, ну́жно есть; **~ you go so soon?** неуже́ли вам на́до уже́ уходи́ть?; **if you ~, you ~** в конце́ концо́в, ну́жно зна́чит ну́жно; **~ you behave like that?** неуже́ли вы ина́че не мо́жете?; (*expr. obligation*): **you ~ do as you're told** ну́жно слу́шаться; **we ~ not be late** нам нельзя́ опа́здывать; **you ~ not forget to write** непреме́нно напиши́те; **I ~ ask you to leave** я вы́нужден попроси́ть вас уйти́; **I ~ admit** я до́лжен призна́ть; **we ~ see what can be done** сле́дует поду́мать, что здесь мо́жно сде́лать (*or* как помо́чь де́лу). **2.** (*with neg., expr. prohibition*): **cars ~ not be parked here** стоя́нка маши́н запрещена́. **3.** (*expr. certainty or strong probability*): **you ~ be tired** вы, наве́рно, уста́ли; **this ~ be the bus coming now** э́то вероя́тно/наве́рно (*or* должно́ быть), авто́бус; **you ~ have known that** не мо́жет быть, что́бы вы э́того не зна́ли. **4.** (*iron.*): **just as I was leaving, he ~ come and talk to me** то́лько я собра́лся уйти́, он как на беду́ яви́лся и затея́л разгово́р.

mustache [mə'stɑ:ʃ] = **moustache**

mustang ['mʌstæŋ] *n.* муста́нг.

mustard ['mʌstəd] *n.* (*plant; relish*) горчи́ца; **keen as ~** по́лный энтузиа́зма; **~ gas** горчи́чный газ, ипри́т.

cpds. **~-plaster** *n.* горчи́чник; **~-pot** *n.* горчи́чница.

muster ['mʌstə(r)] *n.* **1.** (*mil., assembly*) сбор, смотр. **2.** (*numbers attending a function*) о́бщее число́; **there was a good ~** яви́лось мно́го наро́ду. **3.** (*inspection; roll-call*) пове́рка; перекли́чка; **will his work pass ~?** (*fig.*) его́ рабо́та годи́тся? **4.** (*~-book, ~-roll*) спи́сок ли́чного соста́ва.

v.t. (*summon together*) соз|ыва́ть, -ва́ть; соб|ира́ть, -ра́ть; (*fig.*) **he ~ed up all his courage** он собра́лся с ду́хом.

v.i. (*assemble*) соб|ира́ться, -ра́ться.

mustiness ['mʌstɪnɪs] *n.* за́тхлость; ко́сность, отста́лость.

musty ['mʌstɪ] *adj.* (*mouldy, stale*) запле́сневелый; (*smelling of mould or age*) прокисший, за́тхлый; (*fig., ancient; out-of-date*) ко́сный, отста́лый, устаре́лый.

mutability [,mju:tə'bɪlɪtɪ] *n.* изме́нчивость.

mutable ['mju:təb(ə)l] *adj.* изме́нчивый.

mutant ['mju:t(ə)nt] *adj.* мута́нтный.

mutate [mju:'teɪt] *v.i.* (*biol.*) видоизменя́ться (*impf.*).

mutation [mju:'teɪʃ(ə)n] *n.* измене́ние; (*biol.*) мута́ция.

mutatis mutandis [mu:,tɑ:tɪs mu:'tændɪs, mju:-, -i:s] *adv.* внося́ необходи́мые измене́ния.

mute[1] [mju:t] *n.* **1.** (*dumb pers.*) немо́й. **2.** (*non-speaking actor*) стати́ст. **3.** (*mus.*) сурди́н(к)а.

adj. **1.** (*silent*) безмо́лвный; **he made a ~ appeal** он бро́сил моля́щий взгля́д. **2.** (*dumb*) немо́й. **3.** (*phon., silent*) немо́й, непроизноси́мый (*plosive*) глухо́й.

v.t. приглуш|а́ть, -и́ть; **they played with ~d strings** они́ игра́ли под сурди́нку.

mute[2] [mju:t] *v.i.* (*of birds*) мара́ться (*impf.*).

mutilate ['mju:tɪ,leɪt] *v.t.* уве́чить, из-; кале́чить, ис-; (*fig.*) иска|жа́ть, -зи́ть; **the book was ~d in the film version** в фи́льме содержа́ние кни́ги бы́ло искажено́.

mutilation [,mju:tɪ'leɪʃ(ə)n] *n.* уве́чье; (*fig.*) искаже́ние.

mutineer [,mju:tɪ'nɪə(r)] *n.* мяте́жник.

mutinous ['mju:tɪnəs] *adj.* мяте́жный.

mutiny ['mju:tɪnɪ] *n.* мяте́ж.

v.i. бунтова́ть, взбунтова́ться; под|ыма́ть, -ня́ть мяте́ж.

mutt [mʌt] *n.* (*sl.*) (*stupid pers.*) остоло́п, о́лух; (*dog*) пёс.

mutter ['mʌtə(r)] *n.* бормота́ние; **he spoke in a ~** он бормота́л; **the ~ of thunder** глухи́е раска́ты (*m. pl.*) гро́ма.

v.t. & i. бормота́ть (*impf.*); говори́ть (*impf.*) невня́тно; **he ~ed an apology** он пробормота́л извине́ние; **~ings of discontent** глухо́й ро́пот недово́льства.

mutton ['mʌt(ə)n] *n.* бара́нина; **as dead as ~** мёртвый; **~ dressed as lamb** (*fig.*) молодя́щаяся стару́шка; **return to ones ~s** верну́ться (*pf.*) к те́ме разгово́ра (*or* свои́м бара́нам); **~ chop** бара́нья отбивна́я.

cpd. **~-head** *n.* (*coll.*) бара́н.

mutual ['mju:tʃʊəl, -tjʊəl] *adj.* взаи́мный; **~ admiration society** о́бщество взаи́много восхище́ния/восхвале́ния; **our ~ friend** наш о́бщий друг; **~ insurance company** компа́ния взаи́много страхова́ния.

muzhik ['mu:ʒɪk] = **moujik**

muzzle ['mʌz(ə)l] *n.* **1.** (*animal's*) мо́рда, ры́ло. **2.** (*guard for this*) намо́рдник. **3.** (*of firearm*) ду́ло; **~ velocity** нача́льная ско́рость.

v.t. над|ева́ть, -е́ть намо́рдник на+*a.*; (*fig.*) заст|авля́ть, -а́вить молча́ть; зат|ыка́ть, -кну́ть; **he tried to ~ the press** он пыта́лся заста́вить печа́ть молча́ть.

cpd. **~-loading** *adj.* заряжа́ющийся с ду́ла.

muzzy ['mʌzɪ] *adj.* (*coll.*) нея́сный; тума́нный; (*drunk*) опьяне́вший.

MW ['megə,wɒt(z)] *n.* (*abbr. of* **megawatt(s)**) МВт, (мегава́тт).

my [maɪ] *poss. adj.* мой; (*belonging to speaker*) свой; **I lost ~ pen** я потеря́л свою́ ру́чку; **for ~ part** что каса́ется меня́; **~ own child** мой (со́бственный) ребёнок; **I was all on ~ own** я был оди́н-одинёшенек/одинёхонек (*or* соверше́нно оди́н); **I did it all on ~ own** я сде́лал э́то самостоя́тельно (*or* без посторо́нней по́мощи); (*with words of address*): **~ dear** дорого́й; **~ dear fellow** дорого́й мой; **~ good man/woman** мой друг; (*in exclamations*): **~ goodness!; oh, ~!** Бо́же мой!; **~, ~!** ну и ну́! поду́мать то́лько!

Myanmar [,mi:æn'mɑ:(r)] *n.* Мья́нма.

Mycenae [maɪ'si:ni:] *n.* Мике́н|ы (*pl., g.* —).

Mycenean [,maɪsɪ'ni:ən] *adj.* мике́нский.

mycology [maɪ'kɒlədʒɪ] *n.* миколо́гия.

myna(h) ['maɪnə] *n.* ма́йна.

myopia [maɪ'əʊpɪə] *n.* миопи́я, близору́кость.

myopic [maɪ'ɒpɪk] *adj.* миопи́ческий, близору́кий.

myosotis [,maɪə'səʊtɪs] *n.* незабу́дка.

myriad [ˈmɪrɪəd] *n.* мириа́д|ы (*pl.*, *g.* —); несчётное число́.
adj. несчётный.
myrmidon [ˈmɜːmɪd(ə)n] *n.* (*fig.*) прислу́жник; **~s of the law** блюсти́тели (*m. pl.*) зако́на/поря́дка.
myrrh [mɜː(r)] *n.* (*resin*) ми́рра.
myrtle [ˈmɜːt(ə)l] *n.* мирт.
myself [maɪˈself] *pron.* **1.** (*refl.*) себя́; **I said to ~** я себе́ сказа́л; **I felt pleased with ~** я был дово́лен собо́й. **2.** (*emph.*) сам; **I ~ did it** э́то я сде́лал; **I did it ~** я сам э́то сде́лал; **I did it by ~** (*without help*) я э́то сде́лал сам; **I am not ~ today** я сего́дня немно́го не в фо́рме. **3.** (*after preps.*): **for ~, I prefer tea** что каса́ется меня́, я предпочита́ю чай; **dancing takes me out of ~** та́нцы развлека́ют меня́. **4.** (*representing* I *or* me): **my wife and ~ were there** мы с жено́й бы́ли там.
mysterious [mɪˈstɪərɪəs] *adj.* таи́нственный, зага́дочный.
mystery [ˈmɪstərɪ] *n.* **1.** (*secret*, *secrecy*; *obscurity*) та́йна, секре́т, зага́дка; **the murder remained a ~** э́то уби́йство оста́лось зага́дкой/та́йной; **their origins are wrapped in ~** их происхожде́ние покры́то мра́ком неизве́стности; **don't make a ~ of it** не де́лайте из э́того та́йну. **2.** (*relig.*) та́инство, та́йные обря́ды (*m. pl.*); **~ play** мисте́рия. **3.** (*novel etc.*) детекти́в.
mystic [ˈmɪstɪk] *n.* ми́стик.
adj. (*also* **~al**) мисти́ческий.
mysticism [ˈmɪstɪˌsɪz(ə)m] *n.* мистици́зм, ми́стика.
mystification [ˌmɪstɪfɪˈkeɪʃ(ə)n] *n.* мистифика́ция.
mystify [ˈmɪstɪˌfaɪ] *v.t.* мистифици́ровать (*impf.*, *pf.*); озада́чи|вать, -ть.
mystique [mɪˈstiːk] *n.* таи́нственность, зага́дочность; мисти́ческая/таи́нственная си́ла.
myth [mɪθ] *n.* (*lit.*, *fig.*) миф.
mythic(al) [ˈmɪθɪk(ə)l] *adj.* мифи́ческий.
mythological [ˌmɪθəˈlɒdʒɪk(ə)l] *adj.* мифологи́ческий.
mythologist [mɪˈθɒlədʒɪst] *n.* мифо́лог.
mythology [mɪˈθɒlədʒɪ] *n.* мифоло́гия.
myxomatosis [ˌmɪksəməˈtəʊsɪs] *n.* миксомато́з.

N

nab [næb] *v.t.* (*arrest*) накр|ыва́ть, -ы́ть (*coll.*); (*catch in wrong-doing*) заст|ига́ть, -и́гнуть.
nabob [ˈneɪbɒb] *n.* (*hist.*) набо́б.
nacelle [nəˈsel] *n.* (*aero-engine casing*) кожу́х; (*airship car*) гондо́ла.
nacre [ˈneɪkə(r)] *n.* (*mother-of-pearl*) перламу́тр; (*shellfish*) жемчу́жница.
nacr(e)ous [ˈneɪkrɪəs] *adj.* перламу́тровый.
nadir [ˈneɪdɪə(r), ˈnæd-] *n.* (*astron.*) нади́р; (*fig.*) ни́зшая то́чка; **he was at the ~ of his hopes** он потеря́л вся́кую наде́жду.
nag[1] [næg] *n.* лоша́дка; (*pej.*) кля́ча.
nag[2] [næg] *v.t.* пили́ть (*impf.*); **she ~ged him into going to the theatre** она́ пили́ла его́, пока́ он не согласи́лся пойти́ с ней в теа́тр.
v.i. брюзжа́ть (*impf.*); **~ at s.o.** пили́ть (*impf.*) кого́-н.
nagger [ˈnægə(r)] *n.* брюзга́ (*c.g.*).
nagging [ˈnægɪŋ] *n.* брюзжа́ние; постоя́нные приди́рки (*f. pl.*); (*coll.*) пилёж.
adj. приди́рчивый; (*quarrelsome*) сварли́вый; **a ~ pain** но́ющая боль.
naiad [ˈnaɪæd] *n.* ная́да.
nail [neɪl] *n.* **1.** (*on finger or toe*) но́готь (*m.*); (*dim.*) ногото́к; **bite one's ~s with impatience** куса́ть (*impf.*) но́гти от нетерпе́ния; **you should get your ~s cut** вам сле́дует постри́чь но́гти. **2.** (*metal spike*) гвоздь (*m.*); **he's as hard as ~s** э́то желе́зный челове́к; (*physically*) у него́ желе́зное здоро́вье; (*morally*) у него́ жёсткий хара́ктер; **you've hit the ~ on the head** вы попа́ли в то́чку; **he pays on the ~** он распла́чивается неме́дленно; **a ~ in s.o.'s coffin** (*fig.*) гвоздь (*m.*) в чей-н. гроб.
v.t. **1.** пригво|жда́ть, -зди́ть; приб|ива́ть, -и́ть (*что к чему*); **he ~ed the picture (on) to the wall** он приби́л карти́ну к стене́; **I am ~ing the lid down** я прибива́ю кры́шку; я забива́ю я́щик; **he ~ed the ends together** он сбил края́ (*чего*); **the windows were ~ed up** о́кна бы́ли заколо́чены; (*fig.*): **he stood ~ed to the ground** он стоя́л как вко́панный; его́ сло́вно к земле́ пригвозди́ли; **he ~ed his colours to the mast** он стоя́л на́смерть; он упо́рствовал до конца́. **2.** (*fig.*, *fix*, *arrest*): **his words ~ed my attention** его́ слова́ прикова́ли к себе́ моё внима́ние; (*catch*, *get hold of*): **he ~ed me as I was leaving** он перехвати́л меня́ на вы́ходе; (*pin down*): **he tried to evade the issue but I ~ed him down** он пыта́лся уйти́ от пробле́мы, но я его́ прижа́л к сте́нке; (*confute*): **that lie must be ~ed** э́ту ложь на́до разоблачи́ть.
cpds. **~-brush** *n.* щёт(оч)ка для ногте́й; **~-file** *n.* пи́лка (для ногте́й); **~-head** *n.* шля́пка (гвоздя́); **~-parings** *n. pl.* сре́занные но́гти (*m. pl.*); **~-scissors** *n. pl.* но́жниц|ы (*pl.*, *g.* —) для ногте́й; **~-varnish** *n.* лак для ногте́й.
naive [nɑːˈiːv, naɪˈiːv] *adj.* наи́вный, простоду́шный; простова́тый; (*of art*) примити́вный.
naïveté [nɑːˈiːvteɪ], **naivety** [nɑːˈiːvtɪ, naɪ-] *nn.* наи́вность, простоду́шие, простова́тость.
naked [ˈneɪkɪd] *adj.* го́лый; **strip ~** разд|ева́ть(ся), -е́ть(ся) (догола́); **with ~ swords** с ша́шками наголо́; **~ wire** го́лый про́вод; **~ flame, light** откры́тый ого́нь; (*of natural objects*: *bare*) го́лый; (*defenceless*) безору́жный; (*plain*, *undisguised*, *unadorned*) просто́й, неприкра́шенный; **the ~ truth** го́лая и́стина; **with the ~ eye** невооружённым гла́зом.
nakedness [ˈneɪkɪdnɪs] *n.* нагота́, обнажённость; (*fig.*): **the ~ of his arguments** голосло́вность его́ аргумента́ции.
namby-pamby [ˌnæmbɪˈpæmbɪ] *adj.* мягкоте́лый; слаща́вый, сентимента́льный.
name [neɪm] *n.* **1.** (*esp.* **fore~**) и́мя (*nt.*); (*surname*) фами́лия; (*of pet*) кли́чка; **what is his ~?** как его́ зову́т/фами́лия?; **a man by, of the ~ of ...** челове́к по и́мени/фами́лии...; **your ~ was given me by Ivanov** Ивано́в дал мне ва́шу фами́лию; **a certain doctor, Crippen by ~** не́кий до́ктор по и́мени Кри́ппен; **they are known to me by ~** мне изве́стны их имена́; я зна́ю их понаслы́шке; **he goes by various ~s** он изве́стен под ра́зными фами́лиями; **he knows all the staff by ~** он зна́ет и́мя ка́ждого сотру́дника; **he goes by, under the ~ of Smith** он изве́стен под и́менем Смит; **in heaven's ~** ра́ди Бо́га; **in the ~** (*on behalf*) of от и́мени +*g.*; **in the ~ of common sense** во и́мя здра́вого смы́сла; **in the ~ of the law** и́менем зако́на; **he kept the money in his own ~** он держа́л де́ньги на своё и́мя; **he published the book in his own ~** он изда́л кни́гу под свои́м и́менем (*or* под свое́й фами́лией); **she was his wife in ~ only** она́ была́ его́ жено́й лишь номина́льно; она́ то́лько чи́слилась его́ жено́й; **he lent his ~ to their petition** он поддержа́л пети́цию свои́м авторите́том; **I put my ~ down for a flat** я записа́лся в о́чередь на кварти́ру; **he has a house to his ~** у него́ со́бственный дом; **she hasn't a penny to her ~** у неё за душо́й ни гроша́; **he has £500 to his ~** он мо́жет похва́статься пятьюста́ми фу́нтами; **take s.o.'s ~ in vain** всу́е пом|ина́ть, -яну́ть чьё-н. и́мя; **you may use my ~** мо́жете сосла́ться на меня́. **2.** (*of a thg.*) назва́ние; **what is the ~ of your school?** как называ́ется ва́ша шко́ла?; **this street has changed its ~** э́ту у́лицу переименова́ли. **3.** (*family*): **he upheld the honour of his ~** он поддержа́л честь (своего́) ро́да (*or* свое́й семьи́); **he was the last of his ~** он был после́дний в роду́. **4.** (*personage*): **the great ~s of history** вели́кие истори́ческие ли́чности (*f. pl.*)/де́ятели (*m. pl.*). **5.** (*reputation*) и́мя, репута́ция; **he made a ~ for himself** он со́здал/соста́вил/сде́лал себе́ и́мя; **he**

has a bad ~ у него́ дурна́я сла́ва; **this firm has a** ~ **for honesty** э́та фи́рма изве́стна свое́й че́стностью. **6.: call s.o.** ~**s** руга́ть (*impf.*) кого́-н.

v.t. **1.** (*give* ~ *to*) наз|ыва́ть, -ва́ть; да|ва́ть, -ть и́мя +*d.*; **they haven't yet** ~**d the baby** они́ ещё не да́ли ребёнку и́мя; **he was** ~**d Andrew after his grandfather** его́ назва́ли Андре́ем по де́ду (*or* в честь де́да); **the street is** ~**d after Napoleon** у́лица но́сит и́мя Наполео́на; **the Moscow underground railway was** ~**d after Lenin** моско́вскому метро́ бы́ло присво́ено и́мя Ле́нина; **Cape Kennedy was** ~**d in honour of the President** назва́ние «Мыс Ке́ннеди» бы́ло дано́ в честь президе́нта. **2.** (*recite*): **the pupil** ~**d the chief cities of Europe** учени́к перечи́слил/назва́л гла́вные города́ Евро́пы; (*state, mention*) наз|ыва́ть, -ва́ть; ~ **your price!** назна́чьте це́ну!; **you** ~ **it, we've got it** (*coll.*) чего́ то́лько у нас нет!; (*identify*): **how many stars can you** ~ (*sc. identify*)? ско́лько звёзд вы мо́жете определи́ть?; (*appoint*): **he asked her to** ~ **the day** он проси́л её назна́чить день (сва́дьбы); (*nominate*): **he was** ~**d for the professorship** его́ кандидату́ра была́ вы́двинута на до́лжность профе́ссора; он был назна́чен профе́ссором; (*as an example*) прив|оди́ть, -ести́ (что) в ка́честве приме́ра.

cpds. ~**-day** *n.* имени́н|ы (*pl.*, *g.* —); ~**-dropping** *n.* (*coll.*) ≃ хвастовство́ свои́ми знако́мствами/свя́зями; ~**-part** *n.* загла́вная роль; ~**-plate** *n.* доще́чка/табли́чка с и́менем; ~**sake** *n.* (*with same first* ~) тёзка (*c.g.*); (*with same surname, but unrelated*) однофами́л|ец (*fem.* ица); ~**-tape** *n.* тесьма́ с фами́лией (*для метки белья и т.п.*).

nameless ['neɪmlɪs] *adj.* (*without a name*) безымя́нный; (*unnamed, unmentioned*) нена́званный, неупомя́нутый; **someone who shall be** ~ не́кто, кого́ мы не ста́нем называ́ть по и́мени; (*unmentionable, unspeakable*): ~ **horror** невырази́мый у́жас.

namely ['neɪmlɪ] *adv.* и́менно; то есть.

Namibia [nə'mɪbɪə] *n.* Нами́бия.

Namibian [nə'mɪbɪən] *adj.* намиби́йский.

nancy(-boy) ['nænsɪ] *n.* «девчо́нка», пе́дик (*sl.*).

nankeen [næŋ'ki:n, næn-] *n.* на́нка, кита́йка.

nanny ['nænɪ] *n.* (*nurse*) ня́ня, ня́нька; (*as addressed by child*) ня́нечка.

cpd. ~**-goat** *n.* коза́.

nap[1] [næp] *n.* (*short sleep*) коро́ткий сон; **have, take a** ~ вздремну́ть (*pf.*); **catch s.o.** ~**ping** заста́ть/засти́гнуть (*pf.*) кого́-н. врасплóх.

nap[2] [næp] *n.* (*surface of cloth*) ворс, начёс; (*downy surface*) пушо́к.

v.t. начёс|ывать, -а́ть.

nap[3] [næp] *n.* (*game*) наполео́н; **go** ~ поста́вить (*pf.*) всё на ка́рту.

napalm ['neɪpɑ:m] *n.* напа́лм; (*attr.*) напа́лмовый.

nape [neɪp] *n.* загри́вок.

napery ['neɪpərɪ] *n.* столо́вое бельё.

naphtha ['næfθə] *n.* лигрои́н.

naphthal|ene, -ine ['næfθə,li:n] *n.* нафтали́н.

Napierian [neɪ'pɪərɪən] *adj.* не́перов.

napkin ['næpkɪn] *n.* (**table-**~) салфе́тка.

cpd. ~**-ring** *n.* кольцо́ для салфе́тки.

Naples ['neɪp(ə)lz] *n.* Неа́поль (*m.*).

Napoleon [nə'pəʊlɪən] *n.* Наполео́н; (*coin*) наполеондо́р.

Napoleonic [nə,pəʊlɪ'ɒnɪk] *adj.* наполео́новский; ~ **code** ко́декс Наполео́на.

nappy ['næpɪ] *n.* (*coll.*) пелёнка.

narcissism ['nɑ:sɪ,sɪz(ə)m, nɑ:'sɪs-] *n.* нарцисси́зм, самолюбова́ние, самовлюблённость.

narcissistic [,nɑ:sɪ'sɪstɪk] *adj.* самовлюблённый; любу́ющийся собо́й.

narcissus [nɑ:'sɪsəs] *n.* нарци́сс.

narcosis [nɑ:'kəʊsɪs] *n.* нарко́з.

narcotic [nɑ:'kɒtɪk] *n.* (*drug*) нарко́тик; (*addict*) нарко́ма́н.

adj. наркоти́ческий.

nark[1] [nɑ:k] *n.* (*police decoy or spy; informer*) лега́вый (*coll.*); стука́ч (*coll.*).

nark[2] [nɑ:k] *v.t.* (*sl.*) злить, разо-; ~ **it!** брось!

narrate [nə'reɪt] *v.t.* расска́з|ывать, -а́ть; повествова́ть (*impf.*).

narration [nə'reɪʃ(ə)n] *n.* (*action, story*) расска́з, повествова́ние; (*story*) по́весть.

narrative ['nærətɪv] *n.* (*story*) расска́з, по́весть; (*exposition of facts or circumstances, e.g. in court*) изложе́ние фа́ктов/обстоя́тельств де́ла.

adj. повествова́тельный.

narrator [nə'reɪtə(r)] *n.* расска́зч|ик (*fem.* -ица); (*of folk tales*) сказа́тель (*fem.* -ница).

narrow ['nærəʊ] *n.* (*usu. pl., strait*) у́зкий проли́в.

adj. (*lit., fig.*) **1.** у́зкий; **within** ~ **limits** в у́зких преде́лах/ ра́мках; **a** ~ **circle of acquaintances** те́сный круг знако́мых; ~ **circumstances** стеснённые обстоя́тельства; **a** ~ **mind** ограни́ченный ум; **take a** ~ **view of sth.** у́зко под|ходи́ть, -ойти́ к чему́-н. **2.** (*with little margin*): **a** ~ **majority** незначи́тельное большинство́; **a** ~ **victory** побе́да с небольши́м преиму́ществом; **he had a** ~ **escape from death** он чу́дом избежа́л сме́рти; **he** ~**ly escaped drowning** он чуть не утону́л; **I had a** ~ **squeak** (*coll.*) я дёшево отде́лался. **3.** (*close; precise*): **he was** ~**ly watched** за ним при́стально наблюда́ли.

v.t. сужа́ть, су́|живать, -зить; ~ **one's eyes, gaze** сощу́ри|ваться, -ться; (*limit*) ограни́чи|вать, -ть; **the choice was** ~**ed down to two candidates** вы́бор свёлся к двум кандидату́рам; **this** ~**s the field** (*of search*) э́то сужа́ет круг по́исков.

v.i. (*of river etc.*) су́|живаться, -зиться; **his eyes** ~**ed** он прищу́рился; он сощу́рил глаза́.

cpds. ~**-gauge** *adj.* узкоколе́йный; ~**-minded** *adj.* у́зкий; с предрассу́дками; ~**-mindedness** *n.* у́зость взгля́дов.

narrowness ['nærəʊnɪs] *n.* у́зость, теснота́.

narthex ['nɑ:θeks] *n.* на́ртекс, притво́р.

narwhal ['nɑ:w(ə)l] *n.* нарва́л.

NASA ['næsə] *n.* (*abbr. of* ***National Aeronautics and Space Administration***) НАСА, (Национа́льное управле́ние по аэрона́втике и иссле́дованию косми́ческого простра́нства).

nasal ['neɪz(ə)l] *n.* (*phon.*) носово́й (звук).

adj. **1.** (*of, for the nose*) носово́й; ~ **catarrh** на́сморк; (*of the voice*) гнуса́вый; **speak in a** ~ **voice** говори́ть (*impf.*) в нос; гнуса́вить (*impf.*). **2.** (*phon.*) носово́й.

nasality [,neɪ'zælɪtɪ] *n.* носово́й хара́ктер (зву́ка).

nasalization [,neɪzəlaɪ'zeɪʃ(ə)n] *n.* назализа́ция.

nasalize ['neɪzəlaɪz] *v.t.* произн|оси́ть, -ести́ в нос; **this sound has become** ~**d** э́тот звук преврати́лся в носово́й.

nascent ['næs(ə)nt, 'neɪs-] *adj.* (на)рожда́ющийся.

nastiness ['nɑ:stɪnɪs] *n.* гну́сность, проти́вность.

nasturtium [nə'stɜ:ʃəm] *n.* насту́рция.

nasty ['nɑ:stɪ] *adj.* **1.** (*offensive, e.g. smell or taste*) неприя́тный, проти́вный; **the medicine tastes** ~ у э́того лека́рства неприя́тный/проти́вный вкус; (*repellent, sickening*) отврати́тельный. **2.** (*morally offensive*) ме́рзкий, га́дкий; **a** ~ **piece of work!** (*said of pers.*) ну и мерза́вец!; ну и мерза́вка!; **he has a** ~ **mind** у него́ гря́зное воображе́ние. **3.** (*unkind, spiteful, unpleasant*) злой; **a** ~ **remark** зло́е замеча́ние; **a** ~ **temper** тяжёлый хара́ктер; **he played a** ~ **trick on me** он сыгра́л со мной злу́ю шу́тку; **turn** ~ обозли́ться (*pf.*); (*of the elements*): ~ **weather** скве́рная пого́да; **a** ~ **wind** пронзи́тельный ве́тер; **there's a** ~ **storm brewing** надвига́ется си́льный што́рм. **4.** (*threatening*) опа́сный; **there was a** ~ **look in his eye** его́ вид не предвеща́л ничего́ до́брого. **5.** (*troublesome*): **a** ~ **bout of bronchitis** тяжёлый при́ступ бронхи́та; **he had a** ~ **fall** он неуда́чно упа́л (и расши́бся). **6.** (*difficult*): **that's a** ~ **rock to climb** на э́ту скалу́ нелегко́ взобра́ться; **it's a** ~ **situation to be in** очути́ться в тако́м положе́нии неприя́тно; **that's a** ~ **one!** (*question*) тру́дный вопро́с!; спроси́те поле́гче!; (*insult*) э́то уж чересчу́р!

natal ['neɪt(ə)l] *adj.*: ~ **day** день рожде́ния.

natality [nə'tælɪtɪ] *n.* рожда́емость.

nation ['neɪʃ(ə)n] *n.* на́ция; (*people*) наро́д; (*state*) госуда́рство; (*country*) страна́.

cpd. ~**-wide** *adj.*: **a** ~**-wide search** ро́зыск/по́иски по всей стране́; (*in former USSR*) всесою́зный ро́зыск; ~**-wide poll** всенаро́дный опро́с.

national ['næʃən(ə)l] *n.* (*citizen*) гражд|ани́н (*fem.* -а́нка); (*subject*) по́дданн|ый (*fem.* -ая).

adj. (*of the state*) госуда́рственный; (*of the country or population as a whole*) наро́дный, всенаро́дный; (*central*; *opp. provincial*) центра́льный; (*pert. to a particular nation or ethnic group*) национа́льный; ~ **anthem** госуда́рственный гимн; ~ **debt** госуда́рственный долг; ~ **economy** наро́дное хозя́йство; ~ **elections** всео́бщие вы́боры; ~ **emergency** чрезвыча́йное положе́ние в стране́; ~ **feeling** национали́зм, патриоти́зм; ~ **flag** госуда́рственный флаг; ~ **genius, spirit** дух наро́да; ~ **government** центра́льное прави́тельство; **a** ~ (*all-party*) **government** коалицио́нное прави́тельство; ~ **holiday/income/language** госуда́рственный пра́здник/дохо́д/язы́к; ~ **newspapers** центра́льные газе́ты; ~ **park** запове́дник, национа́льный парк; ~ **service** во́инская пови́нность; ~ **theatre** госуда́рственный теа́тр; ~**ly known** изве́стный всей стране́; **the possibility of solving the problem** ~**ly** возмо́жность разреше́ния вопро́са в общегосуда́рственном масшта́бе.

nationalism ['næʃənə,lɪz(ə)m] *n.* национали́зм.

nationalist ['næʃənə,lɪst] *n.* национали́ст (*fem.* -ка).

adj. (*also* **-ic**) националисти́ческий.

nationality [,næʃə'nælɪtɪ] *n.* (*membership of a nation, country*) по́дданство; гражда́нство; **(of) what** ~ **are you?** како́го вы по́дданства?; како́е у вас по́дданство?; (*ethnic group, e.g. within former USSR*) национа́льность.

nationalization [,næʃənəlaɪ'zeɪʃ(ə)n] *n.* национализа́ция.

nationalize ['næʃənə,laɪz] *v.t.* национализи́ровать (*impf.*, *pf.*); **steel was** ~**d** сталелите́йная промы́шленность была́ национализи́рована.

native ['neɪtɪv] *n.* **1.** (*indigenous inhabitant*) тузе́м|ец (*fem.* -ка); коренно́й жи́тель (*fem.* коренна́я жи́тельница). **2.: a** ~ **of** (*born in*) уроже́н|ец (*fem.* -ка) +*g.*; (*living in*) жи́тель (*fem.* -ница) +*g.*; (*local inhabitant*) жи́тель (*fem.* -ница). **3.** (*of animal*): **the kangaroo is a** ~ **of Australia** кенгуру́ во́дится в Австра́лии; (*of plant*): **the eucalyptus is a** ~ **of Australia** ро́дина эвкали́пта — Австра́лия.

adj. **1.** (*innate*) врождённый, приро́дный. **2.** (*of one's birth*) родно́й; ~ **language** родно́й язы́к; ~ **land** ро́дина, оте́чество; **he returned to his** ~ **haunts** он возврати́лся в родны́е края́ (*or* в родну́ю сто́рону). **3.** (*indigenous, esp. of non-European countries*) тузе́мный; ~ **customs** (тузе́мные/ме́стные) обы́чаи (*m. pl.*); ~ **population** тузе́мное/коренно́е/ме́стное населе́ние; **go** ~ «отузе́миться» (*pf.*) (*coll.*); ~ **plants** ме́стные расте́ния. **4.** (*natural, in natural state*) есте́ственный; (*of minerals*): ~ **gold** саморо́дное зо́лото.

nativity [nə'tɪvɪtɪ] *n.* (*birth of Christ*; *picture of this*) Рождество́ Христо́во; (*of Virgin etc.*) рожде́ние.

NATO ['neɪtəʊ] *n.* (*abbr. of* ***North Atlantic Treaty Organization***) НАТО, (Организа́ция Се́вероатланти́ческого догово́ра); ~ **member** на́товец.

adj. на́товский.

natter ['nætə(r)] (*coll.*) *n.*: **I came in for a** ~ я зашёл поболта́ть.

v.i. болта́ть (*impf.*).

natterjack ['nætə,dʒæk] *n.* (~ **toad**) камышо́вая жа́ба.

natt|y ['nætɪ] *adj.* (*coll.*, *spruce*, *trim*) элега́нтный; **he is** ~**ily dressed** он оде́т с иго́лочки; он элега́нтен, как роя́ль.

natural ['nætʃər(ə)l] *n.* **1.** (*mus. sign*) бека́р. **2.** (*mental defective*) идио́т, слабоу́мный. **3.: he's a** ~ **for the part** он рождён/со́здан для э́той ро́ли.

adj. **1.** (*found in, established by, conforming or pertaining to nature*) есте́ственный, приро́дный; стихи́йный; ~ **death** есте́ственная смерть; **she died a** ~ **death** она́ умерла́ свое́й сме́ртью; ~ **forces** си́лы приро́ды; ~ **gas** приро́дный газ; ~ **history** естествозна́ние; ~ **law** есте́ственное пра́во; ~ **life** земно́е существова́ние; **for the rest of one's** ~ **life** до конца́ жи́зни; ~ **phenomena** явле́ния приро́ды; ~ **resources** приро́дные бога́тства; ~ **sciences** есте́ственные нау́ки; ~ **selection** есте́ственный отбо́р; **in its** ~ **state** (*of land, animals etc.*) в есте́ственном/первобы́тном/приро́дном состоя́нии. **2.** (*normal, ordinary, not surprising*) есте́ственный, норма́льный; **he spoke in his** ~ **voice** он говори́л свои́м обы́чным го́лосом; **his presence seems quite** ~ его́ прису́тствие ка́жется вполне́ есте́ственным; **it is** ~ **for parents to love their children** для роди́телей есте́ственно люби́ть дете́й. **3.** (*unforced, spontaneous*) непринуждённый; (*simple, unaffected*) просто́й; простоду́шный; (*not artificial*) живо́й; (*genuine*) по́длинный. **4.** (*innate*) врождённый, приро́дный; ~ **gifts** приро́дные дарова́ния. **5.** (*destined by nature*): **he is a** ~ **linguist** он прирождённый лингви́ст. **6.** (*illegitimate*) незаконнорождённый. **7.** (*mus.*): **B** ~ си-бека́р.

cpd. ~**-born** *adj.*: **a** ~**-born Englishman** англича́нин по рожде́нию.

naturalism ['nætʃərə,lɪz(ə)m] *n.* натурали́зм.

naturalist ['nætʃərəlɪst] *n.* **1.** (*student of animals etc.*) естествоиспыта́тель (*m.*). **2.** (*in art*) натурали́ст.

naturalistic [,nætʃərə'lɪstɪk] *adj.* натуралисти́ческий.

naturalization [,nætʃərəlaɪ'zeɪʃ(ə)n] *n.* натурализа́ция; акклиматиза́ция.

naturalize ['nætʃərə,laɪz] *v.t.* (*admit to citizenship*) натурализова́ть (*impf.*, *pf.*); (*of animals, plants*: *introduce to another country*) акклиматизи́ровать (*impf.*, *pf.*).

naturally ['nætʃərəlɪ] *adv.* **1.** (*not surprisingly*) есте́ственно; (*of course*) коне́чно. **2.** (*spontaneously, without affectation*) есте́ственно. **3.** (*by nature*) от рожде́ния; по приро́де (свое́й); (*as by instinct*): **he took** ~ **to swimming** пла́вание дало́сь ему́ легко́; он как бу́дто всю жизнь пла́вал; **oratory comes** ~ **to him** он прирождённый ора́тор.

naturalness ['nætʃərəlnɪs] *n.* **1.** (*absence of affectation*) непринуждённость; **behave with** ~ держа́ться (*impf.*) есте́ственно. **2.** (*lifelike quality*): **the portrait lacks** ~ портре́т вы́глядит безжи́зненным.

nature ['neɪtʃə(r)] *n.* **1.** (*force, natural phenomena*) приро́да; **N**~**'s laws** зако́ны приро́ды; **in the course of** ~ есте́ственным хо́дом/путём; **against (*or* contrary to)** ~ противоесте́ственный; ~ **cure** лече́ние путём стимули́рования есте́ственных проце́ссов; ~ **reserve** запове́дник; ~ **study** природове́дение, естествозна́ние; ~ **worship** поклоне́ние приро́де; **paint from** ~ писа́ть (*impf.*) с нату́ры; **one of N**~**'s gentlemen** джентельме́н по приро́де (свое́й); **in a state of** ~ (*e.g. primitive man*) в первобы́тном состоя́нии; (*naked*) в чём мать родила́. **2.** (*of humans or animals*: *character, temperament*) хара́ктер, нату́ра; **a generous** ~ ще́дрый хара́ктер; **he did it out of good** ~ он сде́лал э́то по доброте́ душе́вной; **she was cautious by** ~ она́ была́ от приро́ды осторо́жна; **human** ~ челове́ческая приро́да; **second** ~ втора́я нату́ра; **it was his** ~ **to be proud** он был го́рдым по нату́ре. **3.** (*of things*: *essential quality*) хара́ктер; **the** ~ **of the evidence** хара́ктер доказа́тельств; **by, in the (very)** ~ **of things** по приро́де веще́й; **the** ~ **of gases** сво́йства (*nt. pl.*) га́зов; (*sort, kind*) род; **things of this** ~ тако́го ро́да ве́щи; **our talk was of a confidential** ~ на́ша бесе́да носи́ла конфиденциа́льный хара́ктер; **something in the** ~ **of a disappointment** не́что вро́де разочарова́ния. **4.: relieve** ~ отпр|авля́ть, -а́вить есте́ственные на́добности.

naturism ['neɪtʃə,rɪz(ə)m] *n.* (*nudism*) нуди́зм.

naturist ['neɪtʃərɪst] *n.* (*nudist*) нуди́ст.

naturopath [,neɪtʃərə'pæθ] *n.* натуропа́т.

naturopathy [,neɪtʃə'rɒpəθɪ] *n.* натуропа́тия.

naught [nɔːt] *n.* (*arch. exc. in phrr.*): **bring to** ~ св|оди́ть, -ести́ на нет; **come to** ~ св|оди́ться, -ести́сь к нулю́; ни к чему́ не прив|оди́ть, -ести́; (*peter out*) сходи́ть, сойти́ на нет; **set at** ~ ни во что не ста́вить (*impf.*); *see also* **nought**

naughtiness ['nɔːtɪnɪs] *n.* озорство́.

naughty ['nɔːtɪ] *adj.* **1.** (*e.g. child's behaviour*) озорно́й, капри́зный; **be** ~ озорнича́ть (*impf.*); капри́зничать (*impf.*); **you were** ~ **today** ты сего́дня пло́хо себя́ вёл; **that is** ~ **of you** (*to adult*) э́то нехорошо́ с ва́шей стороны́; **don't be** ~**!** не шали́! **2.** (*risqué*) риско́ванный.

nausea ['nɔːzɪə, -sɪə] *n.* (*physical*) тошнота́; **I was overcome by** ~ меня́ затошни́ло/стошни́ло; (*mental disgust*) отвраще́ние.

nauseat|e ['nɔːzɪˌeɪt, -sɪˌeɪt] *v.t.* **1.** (*physically*) вызыва́ть, вы́звать тошноту́ у+*g.*; **~ing** тошнотво́рный; **I find rich food ~ing** меня́ тошни́т от жи́рной пи́щи. **2.** (*fig.*, *disgust*) вызыва́ть, вы́звать отвраще́ние у+*g.*; прети́ть (*impf.*) +*d.*; **I am ~ed by hypocrisy** мне проти́вно лицеме́рие; **~ing** отврати́тельный.

nauseous ['nɔːzɪəs, -sɪəs] *adj.* тошнотво́рный; (*fig.*) отврати́тельный.

nautical ['nɔːtɪk(ə)l] *adj.* морско́й; **~ mile** морска́я ми́ля.

nautilus ['nɔːtɪləs] *n.* науту́лус, кора́блик.

naval ['neɪv(ə)l] *adj.* **1.** морско́й; (*of the navy*) вое́нно-морско́й; (*of a fleet*) фло́тский; **~ barracks** морска́я каза́рма; **~ base** вое́нно-морска́я ба́за; **~ life** фло́тская жизнь; **~ officer** морско́й офице́р; **~ stores** шки́перское иму́щество. **2.** (*pert. to ships*) корабе́льный, судово́й; **~ architect** инжене́р-судострои́тель (*m.*); **~ yard** вое́нная верфь; судострои́тельный заво́д.

nave[1] [neɪv] *n.* (*of church*) кора́бль (*m.*), неф.

nave[2] [neɪv] *n.* (*of wheel*) ступи́ца.

navel ['neɪv(ə)l] *n.* (*lit.*) пуп, пупо́к; (*fig.*) пуп; **~ orange** апельси́н с ру́бчиком, на́вель (*m.*).

cpds. **~-cord, ~-string** *nn.* пупо́чный кана́тик, пупови́на.

navigability [ˌnævɪgə'bɪlɪtɪ] *n.* судохо́дность.

navigable ['nævɪgəb(ə)l] *adj.* (*of waters*) судохо́дный; (*of vessels*) морехо́дный.

navigate ['nævɪˌgeɪt] *v.t.* **1.** (*of pers.*): **~ a ship/aircraft** управля́ть (*impf.*) кораблём/самолётом; вести́ (*det.*) кора́бль/самолёт; **~ a river/sea** пл|а́вать, -ыть по реке́/мо́рю; (*fig.*): **he ~d the bill through Parliament** он провёл законопрое́кт в парла́менте; **he ~d the difficulties with skill** он уме́ло обходи́л тру́дности. **2.** (*of vessel*): **the yacht easily ~d the locks** я́хта легко́ прошла́ шлю́зы.

v.i. (*in ship*) пла́вать (*indet.*), плыть (*det.*); (*in aircraft*) лета́ть (*indet.*), лете́ть (*det.*); **navigating officer** шту́рман.

navigation [ˌnævɪ'geɪʃ(ə)n] *n.* **1.** (*process*) управле́ние (кораблём, самолётом *и т.п.*). **2.** (*skill*) навига́ция; **~ lights** навигацио́нные огни́. **3.** (*passage of ships*) судохо́дство; **inland ~** речно́е судохо́дство; (*period of possible ~*) навига́ция.

navigator ['nævɪˌgeɪtə(r)] *n.* (*naut.*, *aeron.*) шту́рман, навига́тор; (*hist.*, *explorer*) морепла́ватель (*m.*).

navvy ['nævɪ] *n.* землеко́п; чернорабо́чий.

navy ['neɪvɪ] *n.* **1.** (*naval forces*) вое́нно-морски́е си́лы (*f. pl.*); (*ships of war*) вое́нно-морско́й флот; **merchant ~** торго́вый флот; **~ yard** вое́нная верфь. **2.** (*department of naval affairs*) морско́е ве́домство. **3.** (**~ blue**) тёмно-си́ний цвет

cpd. **~-blue** *adj.* тёмно-си́ний.

nay [neɪ] *n.* (*liter.*): **no-one dared to say him ~** никто́ не смел отказа́ть/возража́ть ему́.

adv. (*arch.*) нет; **he asked, ~ begged us to stay** он проси́л, верне́е, умоля́л нас оста́ться.

Nazareth ['næzərəθ] *n.* Назаре́т; **Jesus of ~** Иису́с из Назаре́та; Иису́с Назаря́нин/Назоре́й.

Nazi ['nɑːtsɪ, 'nɑːzɪ] *n.* наци́ст (*fem.* -ка), ги́тлеровец.

adj. наци́стский, ги́тлеровский.

Nazism ['nɑːtsɪz(ə)m] *n.* наци́зм.

NB (*abbr. of* **nota bene**) нотабе́не.

NCO *n.* = **non-commissioned officer**

Neanderthal [nɪ'ændəˌtɑːl] *n.* (**~ man**) неандерта́лец; неандерта́льский челове́к.

neap [niːp] *n.* (**~ tide**) квадрату́рный прили́в.

Neapolitan [nɪə'pɒlɪt(ə)n] *n.* неаполита́н|ец (*fem.* -ка).

adj. неаполита́нский.

near [nɪə(r)] *adj.* **1.** (*close at hand, in space or time*) бли́зкий; **how ~ is the sea?** (как) бли́зко/далеко́ отсю́да мо́ре?; **the station is quite ~ (to) our house** ста́нция совсе́м бли́зко от на́шего до́ма; **which is the ~est way to the stadium?** как бли́же всего пройти́ к стадио́ну?; **in the ~ future** в ближа́йшем бу́дущем; **spring is ~** бли́зится весна́; **I spoke to the man ~est me** я заговори́л со свои́м ближа́йшим сосе́дом; **the N~ East** Бли́жний Восто́к; **~ sight** близору́кость; (*fig.*): **your guess is ~ the truth** ва́ша дога́дка близка́ к и́стине (*or* недалека́ от и́стины); вы почти́ угада́ли. **2.** (*closely connected*) бли́зкий; **a ~ relative** бли́зкий ро́дственник; **his ~est and dearest** его́ бли́зкие (*pl.*). **3. the ~ side** (*of road or vehicle in Britain*) ле́вая сторона́. **4.** (*narrowly achieved*): **he had a ~ escape** он едва́ избежа́л (*чего*); **a ~ miss** непрямо́е попада́ние; **we won, but it was a ~ thing** мы победи́ли, но с трудо́м. **5.** (*coll.*, *niggardly*) прижи́мистый.

adv. **1.** (*of place or time*) бли́зко; **he was standing ~ at hand (*or* ~ by)** он стоя́л бли́зко/ря́дом; **they looked far and ~** они́ иска́ли повсю́ду; **people came from far and ~** лю́ди прибыва́ли отовсю́ду (*or* со всех концо́в страны́/земли́); **the procession drew ~** проце́ссия приближа́лась; **Christmas is drawing ~** бли́зится Рождество́; **it is ~ (up)on midnight** почти́ по́лночь; **come a little ~er** подойди́те побли́же. **2.** (*fig.*): **I came ~ to believing him** я чуть бы́ло ему́ не пове́рил; **as ~ as I can guess** наско́лько я могу́ суди́ть; **this is as ~ bribery as makes no matter** э́то со́бственно равноси́льно взя́точничеству; **the bus was nowhere ~ full** авто́бус был далеко́ не по́лон; **she is nowhere ~ as old as her husband** она́ далеко́ не так стара́ как муж; она́ гора́здо моло́же му́жа.

v.t. прибл|ижа́ться, -и́зиться к+*d.*; **he is ~ing his end** ему́ ско́ро придёт коне́ц; он при́ смерти.

prep. у, о́коло, близ, бли́зко от (*all* +*g.*); **she sat ~ the door** она́ сиде́ла у/во́зле две́ри; **there are woods ~ the town** о́коло го́рода есть лес; **he lives ~ us** он живёт бли́зко от нас; **~ here** недалеко́ отсю́да; **is there a hotel ~ here?** есть здесь побли́зости гости́ница; **come ~er the fire!** (по)дви́гайтесь к ками́ну; **I'm getting ~ the end of the book** я зака́нчиваю кни́гу; **it must be ~ dinner-time** ско́ро должно́ быть обе́д; **his hopes are ~ fulfilment** ещё немно́го, и наде́жды его́ сбу́дутся; **no-one can come ~ him for skill** никто́ не мо́жет сравни́ться с ним в мастерстве́; **we are no ~er a solution** мы ничу́ть не бли́же к реше́нию.

cpds. **~by** *adj.* располо́женный побли́зости; близлежа́щий, сосе́дний; **~-side** *adj.* (*in Britain*) ле́вый; **~-sighted** *adj.* близору́кий.

nearly ['nɪəlɪ] *adv.* **1.** (*almost*) почти́; **we are ~ there** мы почти́ прие́хали/пришли́; **I was ~ run over** меня́ чуть не задави́ли; **he ~ fell** он чуть бы́ло не упа́л; **there is not ~ enough to eat** еды́ далеко́ не доста́точно. **2.** (*closely, intimately*) бли́зко; **~ related** в бли́зком родстве́.

nearness ['nɪənɪs] *n.* бли́зость.

neat [niːt] *adj.* **1.** (*of appearance*: *tidy*) опря́тный, аккура́тный; (*elegant*) изя́щный; (*well-proportioned*) хорошо́ сложённый; **a ~ figure** изя́щная фигу́рка. **2.** (*clear, precise, e.g. of handwriting, style*) чёткий; (*of wit*: *pointed, well-turned*) ме́ткий; отто́ченный; **a ~ retort** остроу́мная ре́плика. **3.** (*of liquor etc.*, *undiluted*) неразба́вленный; **drink one's whisky ~** пить (*impf.*) чи́стое ви́ски. **4.** (*skilful*) иску́сный, ло́вкий; **he made a ~ job of it** он э́то здо́рово сде́лал.

neatness ['niːtnɪs] *n.* опря́тность; изя́щность, изя́щество; ме́ткость; ло́вкость.

Nebuchadnezzar [ˌnebjuːkəd'nezə(r)] *n.* Навуходоно́сор.

nebula ['nebjʊlə] *n.* (*astron.*) тума́нность; (*med.*) помутне́ние рогово́й оболо́чки; бельмо́.

adj. небуля́рный.

nebular ['nebjʊlə(r)] *adj.* небуля́рный.

nebulosity [ˌnebjʊ'lɒsɪtɪ] *n.* (*cloudiness*) о́блачность; (*fig.*, *vagueness*) тума́нность.

nebulous ['nebjʊləs] *adj.* (*cloudy*) о́блачный; (*fig.*) тума́нный, нея́сный, сму́тный.

necessarily ['nesəsərɪlɪ, -'serɪlɪ] *adv.* обяза́тельно; **it is not ~ true** э́то не обяза́тельно так.

necessar|y ['nesəsərɪ] *n.*: **the ~ies of existence** предме́ты пе́рвой необходи́мости; **I did the ~y** я сде́лал (всё), что ну́жно; (*money*): **I had to find the ~y** мне пришло́сь раскоше́литься (*coll.*).

adj. (*inevitable, inescapable*) неизбе́жный; **a ~y evil** неизбе́жное зло; (*indispensable*) необходи́мый; **food is ~y to life** пи́ща необходи́ма для жи́зни; (*compulsory, obligatory*) необходи́мый, обяза́тельный; **it is ~y to eat in order to live** что́бы жить, необходи́мо пита́ться; **it is**

not ~y to dress for dinner мо́жно не одева́ться к обе́ду; переодева́ться к обе́ду необяза́тельно.

necessitate [nɪ'sesɪˌteɪt] *v.t.* вынужда́ть, вы́нудить; **his illness ~d his retirement** из-за боле́зни он был вы́нужден пода́ть в отста́вку; **the weather ~s a change of plan** из-за пого́ды прихо́дится меня́ть пла́ны; **your proposal ~s borrowing money** е́сли приня́ть ва́ше предложе́ние, придётся занима́ть де́ньги.

necessitous [nɪ'sesɪtəs] *adj.* нужда́ющийся, бе́дный.

necessity [nɪ'sesɪtɪ] *n.* **1.** (*inevitability*) неизбе́жность; **logical ~** логи́чески неизбе́жный вы́вод; **the doctrine of ~** детермени́зм. **2.** (*compulsion, need*) нужда́, необходи́мость; **physical ~** физи́ческая необходи́мость; **of ~** по необходи́мости; **~ knows no law** нужда́ кре́пче зако́на; **in case of ~** в слу́чае необходи́мости; **~ is the mother of invention** голь на вы́думки хитра́. **3.** (*necessary thg.*): **the telephone is a ~** телефо́н не ро́скошь, а предме́т пе́рвой необходи́мости.

neck [nek] *n.* **1.** ше́я; (*dim.*) ше́йка; **I have a stiff ~** мне проду́ло ше́ю; **break s.o.'s ~** свёр|тывать, -ну́ть (*or* слома́ть (*pf.*)) ше́ю кому́-н.; **he got it in the ~** ему́ влете́ло/попа́ло (*coll.*); он получи́л нагоня́й; ему́ да́ли по ше́е; **he's a pain in the ~** он ужа́сная зану́да (*coll.*); **risk one's ~** риск|ова́ть, -ну́ть голово́й; **save one's ~** спасти́ (*pf.*) свою́ го́лову/шку́ру; **stick one's ~ out** (*coll.*) напр|а́шиваться, -оси́ться на неприя́тности; лезть, по- в пе́тлю; ста́вить, по- себя́ под уда́р; **he was up to his ~ in water** он стоя́л по ше́ю в воде́; **he is up to his ~ in debt** он в долгу́ как в шелку́; **he is up to his ~ in work** у него́ рабо́ты по го́рло; **the horse won by a ~** ло́шадь опереди́ла други́х на го́лову; **wring s.o.'s ~** свёр|тывать, -ну́ть ше́ю кому́-н.; **I'll wring his ~** (*fig.*) я ему́ го́лову/ше́ю сверну́; **he was thrown out ~ and crop** его́ вы́толкали в ше́ю; **~ and ~** ноздря́ в ноздрю́; голова́ в го́лову; **~ or nothing** пан и́ли пропа́л. **2.** (*geog., promontory*) мыс; (*isthmus*) перешеек. **3.** (*of var. objects*): **~ of a bottle** го́рлышко буты́лки; **~ of a violin** гриф скри́пки; **~ of a shirt** во́рот руба́шки; **grab s.o. by the ~** хвата́ть, схвати́ть кого́-н. за ши́ворот. **4.** (*sl., impudence*) наха́льство.

v.i. не́жничать (*impf.*); обжима́ться (*impf.*) (*sl.*).

cpds. **~cloth** *n.* га́лстук; ше́йный плато́к; **~lace** *n.* ожере́лье; **~line** *n.* вы́рез (пла́тья); **low ~line** декольте́ (*indecl.*); **~tie** *n.* га́лстук; **~wear** *n.* га́лстуки, воротнички́ (*m. pl.*) *и т.п.*

necking ['nekɪŋ] *n.* не́жничанье, обжима́ние (*coll.*).

necklet ['neklɪt] *n.* коро́ткое ожере́лье; горже́тка.

necrology [ne'krɒlədʒɪ] *n.* (*obituary notice*) некроло́г; (*death-roll*) спи́сок уме́рших.

necromancer ['nekrəʊˌmænsə(r)] *n.* некрома́нт; колду́н.

necromancy ['nekrəʊˌmænsɪ] *n.* некрома́нтия; колдовство́; чёрная ма́гия.

necromantic [ˌnekrəʊ'mæntɪk] *adj.* колдовско́й.

necrophilia [ˌnekrə'fɪlɪə] *n.* некрофи́лия.

necropolis [ne'krɒpəlɪs] *n.* некро́поль (*m.*).

necrosis [ne'krəʊsɪs] *n.* омертве́ние, некро́з.

nectar ['nektə(r)] *n.* (*myth., bot.*) некта́р.

nectarine ['nektərɪn, -ˌri:n] *n.* гла́дкий пе́рсик, нектари́н.

née [neɪ] *adj.* урождённая.

need [ni:d] *n.* (*want, requirement*) нужда́; **be, stand in ~ of** нужда́ться (*impf.*) в+*p.*; **the house is in ~ of repair** дом нужда́ется в ремо́нте; **I have ~ of a rest** мне ну́жен о́тдых; **she feels a ~ for** (*or* **the ~ of**) **company** у неё есть потре́бность в о́бществе; ей не хвата́ет о́бщества; **my ~s are few** у меня́ потре́бности скро́мные; **enough to satisfy one's ~s** доста́точно, что́бы удовлетвори́ть потре́бности; (*emergency*) нужда́; **in one's** (*hour of*) **~** в нужде́; **a friend in ~ is a friend indeed** друзья́ познаю́тся в беде́; (*necessity*) необходи́мость; **if ~ be** в слу́чае необходи́мости; **is there any ~ to hurry?** ра́зве ну́жно торопи́ться?; **there's no ~ to get upset** не́зачем расстра́иваться; **there is no ~ for him to read the whole book** ему́ необяза́тельно прочита́ть всю кни́гу.

v.t. **1.** (*want, require*) нужда́ться (*impf.*) в+*p.*; **the grass ~s cutting** газо́н сле́дует подстри́чь; **the tap ~s a new washer** ну́жно смени́ть прокла́дку в кра́не; **he ~s a haircut** ему́ пора́ (под)стри́чься; **we shall ~ every penny** нам потре́буется/пона́добится ка́ждая копе́йка; **what he ~s is a good hiding** его́ сле́дует хороше́нько вы́пороть; **it only ~s one volunteer and everyone would go** доста́точно вы́зваться одному́, и (за ним) пойду́т все. **2.** (*with inf., be obliged, under necessity*): **~ I come today?** мне ну́жно приходи́ть сего́дня?; **you ~n't do it all tomorrow** вам не обяза́тельно ко́нчить всю рабо́ту за́втра; **one ~s to be on one's guard with him** с ним сле́дует/ну́жно держа́ть у́хо востро́; **it ~s to be done** э́то ну́жно сде́лать; э́то должно́ быть сде́лано; **don't be away longer than you ~** не заде́рживайтесь там до́льше, чем ну́жно/необходи́мо; **~ she have come at all?** на́до ли бы́ло ей приходи́ть вообще́?; **you ~ not have bothered** напра́сно вы беспоко́ились; **I ~ not** (*have no reason to*) мне не́зачем; **he ~ not come** он мо́жет не (*or* он не до́лжен *or* ему́ не на́до) приходи́ть.

v.i. (*be in want*) нужда́ться (*impf.*).

needful ['ni:dfʊl] *n.*: **the ~** (*coll.*) де́н|ьги (*pl., g.* -ег).

adj. необходи́мый.

needle ['ni:d(ə)l] *n.* **1.** (*for sewing etc.*) игла́, иго́лка; **thread a ~** вд|ева́ть, -еть ни́тку в иго́лку; **eye of a ~** (иго́льное) ушко́; **as sharp as a ~** (*fig.*) у́мный, как чёрт; черто́вски проница́тельный; **look for a ~ in a haystack** иска́ть (*impf.*) иго́лку в сто́ге се́на; **gramophone ~** патефо́нная игла́; (*for knitting*) спи́ца; (*instrument pointer*) стре́лка. **2.** (*leaf of conifer*): **pine/fir ~** сосно́вая/ело́вая игла́; (*pl.*) хво́я (*collect.*). **3.** (*obelisk*) обели́ск. **4.** (*coll., irritation*): **get the ~** не́рвничать (*impf.*).

v.t. (*irritate, tease*) подд|ева́ть, -е́ть.

cpds. **~-case** *n.* иго́льник; **~craft** *n.* рукоде́лие; **~woman** *n.* швея́; (*non-professional*) рукоде́льница; **~work** *n.* рукоде́лие, шитьё, вышива́ние.

needless ['ni:dlɪs] *adj.* (*unnecessary*) нену́жный; (*superfluous*) ли́шний; (*inappropriate, uncalled for*) неуме́стный; **~ to say** (само́ собо́й) разуме́ется; **~ to say, we shall return the book** мы, разуме́ется, вернём кни́гу.

needlessness ['ni:dlɪsnɪs] *n.* нену́жность, неуме́стность.

needs [ni:dz] *adv.* (*liter.*): **I ~ must go** я до́лжен идти́; (*iron.*): **he must ~ go just when I want him** ему́, ви́дите ли, на́до уходи́ть и́менно тогда́, когда́ он мне ну́жен; **~ must when the devil drives** про́тив рожна́ не попрёшь; нужда́ кре́пче зако́на.

needy ['ni:dɪ] *adj.* нужда́ющийся; **they are in ~ circumstances** они́ нужда́ются; (*as n.*): **the poor and ~** беднота́.

ne'er [neə(r)] *adv.* (*arch.*) никогда́; **he had ~ a friend in the world** на всём бе́лом све́те не́ было ни одно́й родно́й души́.

cpd. **~-do-well** *n.* безде́льник, него́дник.

nefarious [nɪ'feərɪəs] *adj.* злоде́йский, бесче́стный.

negate [nɪ'geɪt] *v.t.* (*deny*) отрица́ть (*impf.*); отрица́ть существова́ние +*g.*; (*nullify*) св|оди́ть, -ести́ на нет; (*be opposite of; contradict*) опроверга́ть (*impf.*).

negation [nɪ'geɪʃ(ə)n] *n.* (*denial*) отрица́ние; (*nullification*) опроверже́ние; (*contradiction*): **this is a ~ of common sense** э́то противоре́чит здра́вому смы́слу.

negative ['negətɪv] *n.* **1.** (*statement, reply, word*) отрица́ние; **he answered in the ~** он дал отрица́тельный отве́т; **two ~s make an affirmative** отрица́ние отрица́ния равноси́льно утвержде́нию; ми́нус на ми́нус даёт плюс; **a sentence in the ~** отрица́тельное предложе́ние. **2.** (*elec.*) отрица́тельный по́люс. **3.** (*phot.*) негати́в.

adj. **1.** отрица́тельный; **take a ~ attitude** отрица́тельно/негати́вно отн|оси́ться, -ести́сь к (*чему*); **~ sign** (*math.*) знак ми́нус; **~ voice** (*vote*) го́лос про́тив. **2.** (*phot.*) негати́вный.

v.t. (*reject, veto*) отв|ерга́ть, -е́ргнуть; нал|ага́ть, -ожи́ть ве́то/запре́т на+*a.*; (*disprove*) опров|ерга́ть, -е́ргнуть; (*contradict*) противоре́чить (*impf.*) +*d.*

negativism ['negətɪˌvɪz(ə)m] *n.* негативи́зм.

neglect [nɪ'glekt] *n.* **1.** (*failure to attend to*) пренебреже́ние +*i.*; **~ of one's duties** пренебреже́ние свои́ми обя́занностями, хала́тность; ~ **of one's appearance** пренебреже́ние свое́й вне́шностью. **2.** (*lack of care*) запу́щенность; **the wound festered through** ~ ра́на загнои́лась оттого́, что была́ запу́щена; ~ **of one's children** отсу́тствие забо́ты о со́бственных де́тях; **she scolded him for his** ~ **of her** она́ его́ руга́ла за невнима́тельность. **3.** (*failure to notice*; *disregard*) невнима́ние. **4.** (*uncared-for state*) запу́щенность, забро́шенность; **the house was in a state of** ~ дом был запу́щен/забро́шен.

v.t. **1.** (*leave undone*, *let slip*) запус|ка́ть, -ти́ть; забр|а́сывать, -о́сить; **he ~ed his studies** он запусти́л заня́тия; **you ~ed your duty** вы не вы́полнили свой долг; **I shall ~ no opportunity of seeing him** я повида́ю его́ (*or* встре́чусь с ним) при пе́рвой же возмо́жности. **2.** (*leave uncared for*): **he ~s his family** он не забо́тится о семье́; **~ed children** безнадзо́рные/забро́шенные де́ти; **a ~ed garden** запу́щенный/забро́шенный сад; **you have been ~ing me all these months** все э́ти ме́сяцы вы не обраща́ли на меня́ никако́го внима́ния; (*of books*, *writers etc.*): **he is a ~ed composer** он (несправедли́во) забы́тый компози́тор. **3.** (*with inf.*, *fail*, *forget*) заб|ыва́ть, -ы́ть; **he ~ed to wind up the clock** он забы́л завести́ часы́.

neglectful [nɪ'glektfʊl] *adj.* (*careless*, *inattentive*) небре́жный, невнима́тельный; (*remiss*) неради́вый, беспе́чный; **he is ~ of his interests** он не забо́тится о со́бственных интере́сах.

negligée ['neglɪˌʒeɪ] *n.* неглиже́ (*indecl.*); пеньюа́р.

negligence ['neglɪdʒ(ə)ns] *n.* небре́жность, хала́тность; **criminal** ~ престу́пная небре́жность; невнима́тельность; неря́шливость.

negligent ['neglɪdʒ(ə)nt] *adj.* (*careless*) небре́жный; **he is ~ of his duties** он отно́сится небре́жно/хала́тно к свои́м обя́занностям; (*inattentive*) невнима́тельный; (*slovenly*) неря́шливый; **he is ~ in dress/appearance** он одева́ется неря́шливо; у него́ соверше́нно опусти́вшийся вид.

negligible ['neglɪdʒɪb(ə)l] *adj.* незначи́тельный.

negotiable [nɪ'gəʊʃəb(ə)l] *adj.* **1.** ~ **conditions, terms** усло́вия, кото́рые мо́гут служи́ть предме́том перегово́ров. **2.** (*of securities*, *cheques etc.*) подлежа́щий переусту́пке; с пра́вом переда́чи; ~ **securities** оборо́тные це́нные бума́ги. **3.** (*navigable*) проходи́мый; (*of roads*) прое́зжий.

negotiate [nɪ'gəʊʃɪˌeɪt] *v.t.* **1.** (*arrange*) догов|а́риваться, -ори́ться о+*p.*; (*conduct negotiations over*) вести́ (*impf.*) перегово́ры о+*p.*; (*conclude agreement on*) прийти́ (*pf.*) к соглаше́нию о+*p.* **2.** (*convert into cash*): ~ **a cheque** получ|а́ть, -и́ть де́ньги по че́ку; разменя́ть (*pf.*) чек; вы́платить (*pf.*) по че́ку. **3.** (*get over or through*) проб|ира́ться, -ра́ться че́рез+*a.*; ~ **a corner** брать, взять поворо́т; (*fig.*, *surmount*): ~ **an obstacle/difficulty** преодо́л|ева́ть, -е́ть препя́тствие/тру́дность.

v.i. догов|а́риваться, -ори́ться.

negotiation [nɪˌgəʊʃɪ'eɪʃ(ə)n, nɪˌgəʊsɪ'eɪʃ(ə)n] *n.* **1.:** ~ **of terms** обсужде́ние усло́вий; **conduct ~s** вести́ перегово́ры. **2.** ~ **of a bill** переусту́пка/переда́ча ве́кселя. **3.** (*fig.*): ~ **of difficulties** преодоле́ние тру́дностей.

negotiator [nɪ'gəʊʃɪˌeɪtə(r)] *n.* уча́стник перегово́ров; (*representative*) представи́тель (*m.*).

Negress ['ni:grɪs] *n.* негритя́нка.

negritude ['ni:grɪˌtju:d] *n.* принадле́жность к чёрной ра́се.

Negro ['ni:grəʊ] *n.* негр.

adj. негритя́нский.

Negroid ['ni:grɔɪd] *adj.* негро́идный.

Negus[1] ['ni:gəs] *n.* не́гус.

negus[2] ['ni:gəs] *n.* (*drink*) не́гус.

neigh [neɪ] *n.* ржа́ние.

v.i. ржа́ть, за-.

neighbour ['neɪbə(r)] *n.* (*lit.*, *and of countries*, *guests at dinner etc.*) сосе́д (*fem.* -ка); **my next-door** ~ мой ближа́йший сосе́д (по у́лице); **this house and its ~s** э́тот и сосе́дние с ним дома́; **love of one's** ~ любо́вь к бли́жнему; **love thy ~!** возлюби́ бли́жнего своего́!

v.i.: ~ **on** прилега́ть (*impf.*) к+*d.*; сосе́дствовать (*impf.*) +*i.*; **~ing countries** сосе́дние стра́ны; пограни́чные госуда́рства.

neighbourhood ['neɪbəˌhʊd] *n.* **1.** (*locality*) ме́стность, окре́стность; **our ~ is a healthy one** мы живём в здоро́вой ме́стности; (*district*) райо́н; (*vicinity*) сосе́дство; **in the ~ of the park** о́коло (*or* недалеко́ от) па́рка; **in the ~ of 20 tons** приблизи́тельно/приме́рно два́дцать тонн. **2.** (*neighbours*; *community*) сосе́ди (*m. pl.*); окружа́ющие (*pl.*); **he was the laughing-stock of the** ~ он был посме́шищем всей окру́ги.

neighbourliness ['neɪbəlɪnɪs] *n.* добрососе́дское отноше́ние.

neighbourly ['neɪbəlɪ] *adj.* добрососе́дский; **in a ~ fashion** по-сосе́дски; **that's not a ~ thing to do** э́то не по-сосе́дски.

neither ['naɪðə(r), 'ni:ð-] *pron. & adj.* ни тот ни друго́й; ~ **of them knows** ни оди́н (*or* никто́) из них не зна́ет; они́ о́ба не зна́ют; ~ **of them likes it** э́то не нра́вится ни тому́, ни друго́му; **he took ~ side in the argument** в спо́ре он не присоедини́лся ни к той ни к друго́й стороне́ (*or* ни к одно́й из сторо́н).

adv. **1.:** ~ **...** ни... ни; ~ **one thing nor the other** ни ры́ба, ни мя́со; **one must ~ smoke nor spit here** здесь нельзя́ ни кури́ть, ни плева́ть; **he ~ knows nor cares** он не зна́ет и не хо́чет знать; **it's of no interest to you, nor to me** ~ (*sl.*) э́то никому́ не интере́сно — ни вам, ни мне; **that's ~ here nor there** э́то тут ни при чём; ~ **he nor I went** ни он ни я не пошли́. **2.** (*after neg. clause*): **if you don't go, ~ shall I** е́сли вы не пойдёте, то и я не пойду́; **he didn't go and ~ did I** он не пошёл, я то́же.

nelson ['nels(ə)n] *n.* (*wrestling-hold*) не́льсон.

nem. con. [nem 'kɒn] *adv.* (*abbr. of* ***nemine contradicente***) без возраже́ний.

Nemesis ['nemɪsɪs] *n.* (*retribution*) возме́здие, ка́ра.

neoclassical [ˌni:əʊ'klæsɪk(ə)l] *adj.* неоклассѝческий.

neocolonial [ˌni:əʊkə'ləʊnɪəl] *adj.* неоколониали́стский.

neocolonialism [ˌni:əʊkə'ləʊnɪəˌlɪz(ə)m] *n.* неоколониали́зм.

neo-Fascist [ˌni:əʊ'fæʃɪst] *n.* неофаши́ст.

adj. неофаши́стский.

neolithic [ˌni:ə'lɪθɪk] *n.* (*the ~ age*) неоли́т.

adj. неолити́ческий.

neologism [ni:'ɒlədʒˌɪz(ə)m] *n.* неологи́зм.

neon ['ni:ɒn] *n.* нео́н.

adj. нео́новый; ~ **sign** нео́новая рекла́ма.

neonate ['ni:əˌneɪt] *n.* новорождённый.

neophyte ['ni:əˌfaɪt] *n.* неофи́т.

neo-Platonism [ˌni:əʊ'pleɪtəˌnɪz(ə)m] *n.* неоплатони́зм.

neo-Platonist [ˌni:əʊ'pleɪtəˌnɪst] *n.* неоплато́ник.

Neozoic [ˌni:əʊ'zəʊɪk] *adj.* кайнозо́йский.

Nepal [nɪ'pɔ:l] *n.* Непа́л.

Nepal|ese [ˌnepə'li:z], **-i** [nɪ'pɔ:lɪ] *n.* непа́лец; (*fem.*) жи́тельница Непа́ла.

adj. непа́льский.

nephew ['nevju:, 'nef-] *n.* племя́нник.

nephrite ['nefraɪt] *n.* нефри́т.

nephritic [nɪ'frɪtɪk] *adj.* по́чечный.

nephritis [nɪ'fraɪtɪs] *n.* нефри́т.

ne plus ultra [ˌneɪ plʊs 'ʊltrɑ:] *n.* верх (*чего*).

nepotism ['nepəˌtɪz(ə)m] *n.* непоти́зм, кумовство́.

Neptune ['neptju:n] *n.* (*myth.*, *astron.*) Непту́н.

nerd [nɜ:d] *n.* зану́да.

nereid ['nɪərɪɪd] *n.* (*myth.*, *zool.*) нере́йда.

Nero ['nɪərəʊ] *n.* Неро́н.

nerve [nɜ:v] *n.* **1.** нерв; ~ **gas** отравля́ющее вещество́ (*abbr.* ОВ) не́рвно-паралити́ческого де́йствия; ~ **specialist** врач по не́рвным боле́зням, невропато́лог; (*pl.*): **he has ~s of steel** у него́ желе́зные не́рвы; **he doesn't know what ~s are** он не зна́ет, что тако́е не́рвы; **my ~s are bad** у меня́ не́рвы никуда́ не годя́тся; **he's just a bundle of ~s** он про́сто комо́к не́рвов; **he suffers from ~s** у него́ не́рвы не в поря́дке; **he gets on my ~s** он де́йствует мне на не́рвы. **2.** (*courage*, *assurance*) сме́лость; **lose one's** ~ оробе́ть (*pf.*); (*coll.*, *impudence*): **have the ~ to ...** име́ть на́глость +*inf.*; **he's got a** ~ ну и нагле́ц!; **he had the ~ to ask me ...** у него́ хвати́ло ду́ху спроси́ть меня́... **3.** (*sinew*) жи́ла; **strain every ~ to ...** напр|яга́ть, -я́чь все си́лы, что́бы... **4.** (*bot.*) жи́лка.

v.t. (*impart vigour/courage to*) прид|ава́ть, -а́ть си́лы/хра́брости +*d.*; **he ~d himself to make a speech** он собрáлся с дýхом и произнёс речь.

cpds. **~-cell** *n.* нéрвная клéтка; **~-centre** *n.* нéрвный центр; **~-racking** *adj.* дéйствующий на нéрвы; изм́атывающий.

nerveless ['nɜːvlɪs] *adj.* (*inert*) инéртный; (*limp, flabby*) вя́лый; (*powerless*) бесси́льный; (*without feeling*) бесчýвственный; **his arm fell ~ to his side** егó рукá бесси́льно опусти́лась; **he writes in a ~ style** он пи́шет вя́ло/скýчно/безжи́зненно.

nervous ['nɜːvəs] *adj.* **1.** (*pert. to nerves*) нéрвный; **~ system** нéрвная систéма; **~ strain** нéрвное напряжéние; **he had a ~ breakdown** у негó бы́ло нéрвное расстрóйство. **2.** (*highly strung*) нéрвный. **3.** (*agitated*) взволнóванный; **he was ~ before making his speech** он волновáлся/нéрвничал пéред выступлéнием. **4.** (*apprehensive*) нéрвный; **I am ~ of asking him** я не решáюсь спроси́ть егó.

nervousness ['nɜːvəsnɪs] *n.* нéрвность, нервóзность.

nervy ['nɜːvɪ] *adj.* нéрвный, нервóзный; **feel ~** нéрвничать (*impf.*).

nest [nest] *n.* гнездó, (*dim.*) гнёздышко; (*fig.*) **feather one's ~** ≃ наби́ть (*pf.*) себé кармáн; наж|ивáться, -и́ться; нагрéть (*pf.*) рýки; **he feathered his ~ by selling arms** он нажи́лся на торгóвле орýжием; **foul one's own ~** пáкостить (*impf.*) в сóбственном дóме; **~ of tables** комплéкт стóликов, вставля́ющихся оди́н в другóй; **~ of vipers** змеи́ное гнездó.

v.i. **1.** (*of birds*) гнезди́ться (*impf.*). **2.** (*hunt for birds' ~s*) охóтиться (*impf.*) за гнёздами.

cpd. **~-egg** *n.* (*lit.*) подкладнóе яйцó; (*fig., savings*) сбережéния (*nt. pl.*).

nestle ['nes(ə)l] *v.t. & i.*: **~ (one's head/face) against s.o./sth.** приж|имáться, -áться (головóй/лицóм) к комý/чемý-н.; **~ down** устрóиться (*pf.*) поудóбнее; **~ down in bed** свёр|тываться, -нýться калáчиком в постéли; **~ up to s.o.** ласкáться, при- к комý-н.; льнýть, при- к комý-н.

nestling ['neslɪŋ, 'nest-] *n.* птенéц, птéнчик.

net[1] [net] *n.* **1.** (*fruit-~, mosquito-~ etc.*) сéтка; (*snare for birds, fishing-~ and fig.*) сеть, сéти (*f. pl.*); (*hair-~, tennis, cricket-~ etc.*) сéтка; (*butterfly-~*) сачóк. **2.** (*fabric*) тюль (*m.*); **~ curtains** тю́левые занавéски. **3.** (*network, of communications etc.*) сеть.

v.t. **1.** (*fish, birds etc.*) лови́ть, поймáть в сеть/сéти. **2.** (*fruit etc.*) накр|ывáть, -ы́ть сéткой; **3. he ~ted the ball** он заки́нул мяч в сéтку; (*at football*) он заби́л гол.

cpds. **~ball** *n.* баскетбóл; **~work** *n.* сеть.

net[2], **nett** [net] *adj.* чи́стый; **~ income** чи́стый дохóд; **~ weight** чи́стый вес; вес нéтто.

v.t. (*obtain as profit*) срывáть, сорвáть; **he ~ted a handsome profit** он сорвáл соли́дный куш.

nether ['neðə(r)] *adj.* ни́жний; **~ garments** (*joc.*) штан|ы́ (*pl., g.* -óв); **~ regions, world** преиспóдняя.

cpd. **~most** *adj.* сáмый ни́жний.

Netherlander ['neðələndə(r)] *n.* голлáнд|ец (*fem.* -ка).

Netherlandish ['neðələndɪʃ] *adj.* нидерлáндский.

Netherlands ['neðələndz] *n.* Нидерлáнды (*pl., g.* -ов).

nett [net] = **net**[2]

netting ['netɪŋ] *n.* сéтка.

nettle ['net(ə)l] *n.* крапи́ва.

v.t. (*fig.*) зад|евáть, -éть; раздраж|áть, -и́ть.

cpd. **~-rash** *n.* крапи́вница.

neural ['njʊər(ə)l] *adj.* нéрвный.

neuralgia [njʊə'rældʒə] *n.* невралги́я.

neuralgic [njʊə'rældʒɪk] *adj.* невралги́ческий.

neurasthenia [,njʊərəs'θiːnɪə] *n.* неврастени́я.

neurasthenic [,njʊərəs'θenɪk] *adj.* неврастени́ческий, неврастени́чный.

neuritis [njʊə'raɪtɪs] *n.* неври́т.

neurologist [njʊə'rɒlədʒɪst] *n.* неврóлог.

neurology [njʊə'rɒlədʒɪ] *n.* неврологи́я.

neuron ['njʊərɒn] *n.* нейрóн.

neuropath ['njʊərəʊ,pæθ] *n.* невропáт.

neuropathic [,njʊərəʊ'pæθɪk] *adj.* невропатологи́ческий.

neuropathologist [,njʊərəʊpə'θɒlədʒɪst] *n.* невропатóлог.

neuropathology [,njʊərəʊpə'θɒlədʒɪ] *n.* невропатолóгия.

neurosis [njʊə'rəʊsɪs] *n.* неврóз.

neurotic [njʊə'rɒtɪk] *n.* неврастéник.

adj. неврастени́ческий, неврастени́чный.

neuter ['njuːtə(r)] *n.* (*gram., gender*) срéдний род; (*word*) слóво срéднего рóда.

adj. (*gram.*) срéдний; срéднего рóда; (*zool.*) кастри́рованный; (*bot.*) беспóлый.

v.t. кастри́ровать (*impf., pf.*).

neutral ['njuːtr(ə)l] *n.* (*of gears*) холостóй ход; **in ~** в срéднем положéнии.

adj. **1.** (*of state or pers.*) нейтрáльный; **be ~** зан|имáть, -я́ть нейтрáльную пози́цию. **2.** (*of colour etc., indeterminate*) неопределённый, нейтрáльный. **3.** (*chem.*) срéдний. **4.** (*elec.*) нулевóй, нейтрáльный. **5.** (*of gears*) холостóй.

neutralism ['njuːtrə,lɪz(ə)m] *n.* нейтрали́зм.

neutrality [njuː'trælɪtɪ] *n.* нейтралитéт.

neutralization [,njuːtrəlaɪ'zeɪʃ(ə)n] *n.* нейтрализáция.

neutralize ['njuːtrə,laɪz] *v.t.* нейтрализовáть (*impf., pf.*); (*paralyse*) парализовáть (*impf., pf.*).

neutron ['njuːtrɒn] *n.* нейтрóн.

Neva ['niːvə] *n.* Невá.

never ['nevə(r)] *adv.* **1.** никогдá (… не); (*not once*) ни рáзу (… не); **it is ~ too late to mend** испрáвиться никогдá не пóздно; **~ a dull moment!** не соскýчишься!; **you ~ know** как знать?; **~ before** никогдá рáньше; **I have ~ before (or in my life) seen such tomatoes** в жи́зни не ви́дел/ви́дывал таки́х помидóров; **I believed him once, but ~ again** однáжды я емý повéрил, но бóльше никогдá не повéрю; (*emphatic for not*) так и не; **that will ~ do** э́то никудá не годи́тся; **he ~ even tried** он дáже не попрóбовал; **he spoke ~ a word** он не пророни́л ни слóва; **I ~ slept a wink** я глаз не сомкнýл; (*expr. incredulity*) **~!** не мóжет быть!; (*with imper.*): **~ fear!** не бóйтесь!; не беспокóйтесь!; **~ say die!** не отчáивайтесь!; **~ mind** (*don't trouble yourself*) не беспокóйтесь!; (*in answer to apology*) ничегó! **2.** (*expr. surprise*): **surely you ~ told him!** неужéли вы емý сказáли?; **well, I ~ (did)!** не мóжет быть!

cpds. **~-ceasing** *adj.* беспрестáнный, непреры́вный; **~-dying** *adj.* бессмéртный; **~-ending** *adj.* бесконéчный; **it's a ~-ending job** э́той рабóте концá нет; **~-fading** *adj.* (*fig.*) неувядáемый; **~-failing** *adj.* надёжный; **~more** *adv.* никогдá бóльше/впредь; **~-~** *n.*: **~-~ land** (*sc. of plenty*) скáзочная странá изоби́лия; **he bought his car on the ~-~** (*coll.*) он купи́л маши́ну в рассрóчку; **~theless** *adv.* однáко; *conj.* тем не мéнее; **~-to-be-forgotten** *adj.* незабвéнный.

new [njuː] *adj.* **1.** нóвый; **the N~ World** Нóвый Свет; **the N~ Testament** Нóвый завéт; **N~ Year** Нóвый год; *see also* **Year**; **as good as ~** совсéм как нóвый; **what's ~?** что нóвого?; **he became a ~ man** он стал други́м человéком. **2.** (*modern, advanced*) новомóдный; **the ~ diplomacy** совремéнная диплимáтия; **the ~ mathematics** нóвый мéтод преподавáния матемáтики; **the ~est fashions** новéйшие/послéдние мóды. **3.** (*fresh*) молодóй; **~ potatoes** молодóй картóфель; **~ moon** молодóй мéсяц, новолýние; **~ wine** молодóе винó. **4.** (*unaccustomed*): **I am ~ to this work** я в э́том дéле новичóк; (*unfamiliar*) **this work is ~ to me** э́та рабóта для меня́ непривы́чна.

cpds. **~-born** *adj.* новорождённый; **~comer** *n.* новичóк; **he's a ~comer to the village** он посели́лся в э́той дерéвне недáвно; **~-fangled, ~-fashioned** *adjs.* новомóдный; **~-found** *adj.*: **a ~-found interest** нóвое увлечéние (+*i.*); **N~foundland** *n.* Ньюфáундлéнд; (*dog*) ньюфáундленд, водолáз; **~-laid** *adj.* свéжий; **~-mown** *adj.* свежескóшенный; **~-year** *adj.* новогóдний.

newel ['njuːəl] *n.* колóнна винтовóй лéстницы; баля́сина.

New Guinea [njuː 'gɪnɪ] *n.* Нóвая Гвинéя.

newly ['njuːlɪ] *adv.* **1.** (*recently*) недáвно; **~ arrived** недáвно прибы́вший. **2.** (*anew*) вновь; **a ~ painted gate** свежеокрáшенная кали́тка. **3.** (*in a new way*) зáново; по-инóму; по-нóвому.

cpds. **~-built** *adj.* недáвно вы́строенный; **~-wed** *n.*: **the ~-weds** молодожён|ы (*pl., g.* -ов); *adj.* новобрáчный.

newness ['nju:nɪs] *n.* новизна́.

news [nju:z] *n.* **1.** но́вости (*f. pl.*); (*piece of* ~) но́вость; **have you heard the ~?** вы слы́шали но́вость?; **is there any (*or* what's the) ~?** что но́вого?; **what ~ of him?** что слы́шно о нём?; **that's good ~!** рад слы́шать!; вот здо́рово!; сла́ва Бо́гу!; **I had bad ~ from home** я получи́л неуте́шительные ве́сти и́з дому; **he brought bad ~** он принёс дурну́ю весть; **that's no ~ to me!** я э́то и ра́ньше знал; **no ~ is good ~** отсу́тствие весте́й — хоро́шая весть; **we had ~ from him** мы получи́ли от него́ ве́сточку; **have you had ~ of the results?** вам уже́ изве́стны результа́ты? **2.** (*in press or radio*) после́дние изве́стия; **he is in the ~** про него́ пи́шут в газе́тах; **~ agency** аге́нтство печа́ти; **~ bulletin** информацио́нный бюллете́нь; **~ cinema, theatre** кинотеа́тр; «Но́вости дня»; **~ conference** пресс-конфере́нция; **~ flash** э́кстренное сообще́ние.

cpds. **~agent, ~-dealer, ~-vendor** *nn.* продав|е́ц (*fem.* -щи́ца) газе́т; (газе́тный) киоскёр (*fem.* -ша); **~boy** *n.* газе́тчик; **~cast** *n.* после́дние изве́стия (по ра́дио/телеви́дению); **~caster** *n.* ди́ктор; радиокомментáтор; **~-dealer** *n.* = **~agent; ~-girl** *n.* газе́тчица; **~-letter** *n.* информацио́нный бюллете́нь; **~monger** *n.* сплетни|к (*fem.* -ца); **~paper** *n.* газе́та; (*attr.*) газе́тный; **~print** *n.* газе́тная бума́га; **~-reader** *n.* ди́ктор (после́дних изве́стий); **~reel** *n.* кинохро́ника; **~room** *n.* отде́л новосте́й; **~sheet** *n.* информацио́нный листо́к; **~-stand** *n.* газе́тный кио́ск; **~-vendor** *n.* = **~agent; ~worthy** *adj.* интере́сный; представля́ющий интере́с для печа́ти.

newsy ['nju:zɪ] *adj.* (*coll.*) по́лный новосте́й.

newt [nju:t] *n.* трито́н.

Newton ['nju:t(ə)n] *n.* Нью́то́н.

Newtonian [nju:'təʊnɪən] *adj.* нью́то́нов.

New York [nju:' jɔ:k] *n.* Нью-Йо́рк; (*attr.*) нью-йо́ркский.

New Yorker [nju: 'jɔ:kə(r)] *n.* жи́тель (*fem.* -ница) Нью-Йо́рка; уроже́н|ец (*fem.* -ка) Нью-Йо́рка.

New Zealand [nju: 'zi:lənd] *n.* Но́вая Зела́ндия; (*attr.*) новозела́ндский.

next [nekst] *n.* (*in order*): **the week after ~** че́рез неде́лю; **~, please!** сле́дующий!; **~ of kin** ближа́йший ро́дственник; (*letter*): **I will tell you in my ~** сообщу́ в сле́дующем письме́; (*issue*): **to be continued in our ~** продолже́ние в сле́дующем но́мере.

adj. **1.** (*of place*: *nearest*) ближа́йший; (*adjacent*) сосе́дний, сме́жный; **in the ~ house** в сосе́днем до́ме; **the house ~ to ours** дом ря́дом с на́шим; **he lives ~ door** он живёт ря́дом; **he lives ~ door but one to us** он живёт че́рез дом от нас; **~ door to blasphemy** на гра́ни богоху́льства; **the chair was ~ to the fire** стул стоя́л у ками́на. **2. ~ to** (*fig.*, *almost*) почти́; **it was ~ to impossible** бы́ло почти́ невозмо́жно; **I got it for ~ to nothing** я купи́л э́то за бесце́нок. **3.** (*in a series*) очередно́й; (*future*) бу́дущий, сле́дующий; (*past or future*) сле́дующий; **~ day** на друго́й/сле́дующий день; **~ Friday** в (сле́дующую) пя́тницу; **~ October** в октябре́ э́того/бу́дущего го́да; **the ~ day but one was a holiday** э́то бы́ло за́ два дня до пра́здника; **~ week** на бу́дущей/той неде́ле; **~ year** в бу́дущем году́; **the Sunday ~ before Easter** после́днее воскресе́нье пе́ред Па́схой; **~ time we'll go to London** в сле́дующий раз мы пое́дем в Ло́ндон; **better luck ~ time!** мо́жет, в сле́дующий раз бо́льше повезёт!; **the shoes ~ to these in size** ту́фли на оди́н разме́р бо́льше/ме́ньше э́тих; **he is ~ in line** он пе́рвый на о́череди; он сле́дующий; **the ~ thing I knew, I was lying on the floor** в ту же мину́ту я оказа́лся лежа́щим на полу́; **the ~ world** друго́й/потусторо́нний мир.

adv.: **he stood ~ to the fire** он стоя́л во́зле ками́на; **he placed his chair ~ to hers** он поста́вил свой стул ря́дом с её (сту́лом); **what ~?** ещё что!; э́того ещё не хвата́ло!; **what will he do ~?** а тепе́рь что он наду́мает?; **G comes ~ to, ~ after F** «G» сле́дует за «F»; **when I ~ saw him** когда́ я его́ уви́дел в сле́дующий раз; **~ we come to the library** зате́м мы подхо́дим к библиоте́ке.

prep. ря́дом с+*i.*; **he never wears wool ~ (to) his skin** он никогда́ не надева́ет шерсть/шерстяно́е на го́лое те́ло.

cpd. **~-door** *adj.* сосе́дний; **~-door neighbour** ближа́йший сосе́д.

nexus ['neksəs] *n.* связь.

NHS (*abbr. of* ***National Health Service***) Национа́льная слу́жба здравоохране́ния.

Niagara [naɪ'ægərə] *n.*: **~ Falls** Ниага́рский водопа́д.

nib [nɪb] *n.* перо́.

nibble ['nɪb(ə)l] *n.*: **have, take a ~ at sth.** надку́с|ывать, -и́ть что-н.

v.t. поку́сывать (*impf.*); (*at bait*) дёрг|ать, -нуть; (*at grass*) щипа́ть (*impf.*); пощи́пывать (*impf.*); (*of fish*) кл|ева́ть, -ю́нуть.

v.i.: **~ at sth.** грызть (*impf.*) что-н.; (*fig.*): **he ~ed at the offer** он поду́мывал приня́ть э́то предложе́ние.

Nicaragua [,nɪkə'rægjʊə] *n.* Никара́гуа (*indecl.*).

Nicaraguan [,nɪkə'rægjʊən] *n.* никарагуа́н|ец (*fem.* -ка).

adj. никарагуа́нский.

Nice[1] [ni:s] *n.* Ни́цца.

nice[2] [naɪs] *adj.* **1.** (*agreeable*) прия́тный, ми́лый; (*good*) хоро́ший; (*of pers.*) ми́лый, симпати́чный, любе́зный; **they have a ~ (*comfortable*) home** у них ую́тный дом; **that's very ~ of you** э́то о́чень ми́ло с ва́шей стороны́; **this soup tastes ~** э́то вку́сный суп; **the country is looking ~** за́ городом тепе́рь краси́во; **the house was ~ and big** дом был просто́рный; **get the room ~ and tidy!** хороше́нько убери́те ко́мнату!; **the soup was ~ and hot** суп был по-настоя́щему горя́чий; **the children were ~ and clean** де́ти бы́ли чи́стенькие/ухо́женные; (*iron.*): **a ~ state of affairs!** хоро́шенькое де́ло! **2.** (*fastidious, scrupulous*) разбо́рчивый; (*discriminating*): **it calls for ~ judgement** здесь тре́буется всё стара́тельно/хороше́нько взве́сить; (*subtle*) то́нкий; **a ~ shade of meaning** то́нкий смыслово́й отте́нок (*or* отте́нок значе́ния); **~ distinctions** то́нкие разли́чия.

cpd. **~-looking** *adj.* краси́вый, симпати́чный.

nicely ['naɪslɪ] *adv.* (*well, satisfactorily*) хорошо́; **he is getting along ~** у него́ дела́ иду́т хорошо́; (*of progress*) он де́лает успе́хи; (*of invalid*) он поправля́ется; (*agreeably*) прия́тно; (*kindly*) ми́ло; **that will suit me ~** э́то мне вполне́ подойдёт; (*aptly*): **~ put** ме́тко ска́зано.

niceness ['naɪsnɪs] *n.* (*amiability*) любе́зность; (*exactitude*) то́чность.

nicety ['naɪsɪtɪ] *n.* **1.** (*exactness*) то́чность; (*accuracy*) аккура́тность; **to a ~** то́чно. **2.** (*subtle quality*) то́нкость; **a point of great ~** о́чень то́нкий вопро́с. **3.** (*pl.*, *minute distinctions, details*) ме́лкие подро́бности (*f. pl.*).

niche [nɪtʃ, ni:ʃ] *n.* ни́ша; (*fig.*): **he found his ~ in life** он нашёл своё ме́сто (*or* себе́ месте́чко) в жи́зни.

Nicholas ['nɪkələs] *n.* Никола́й.

nick[1] [nɪk] *n.* **1.** (*notch*) зару́бка. **2.** (*prison*) кутýзка (*sl.*). **3.**: **in the ~ of time** в (са́мый) после́дний моме́нт; как раз во́время.

v.t. **1.** (*cut notch in*) де́лать, с- зару́бку на+*p.*; **he ~ed his chin shaving** он поре́зал себе́ подборо́док во вре́мя бритья́. **2.** (*sl., arrest*) задержа́ть, арестова́ть, схвати́ть (*all pf.*). **3.** (*steal*) сти́брить (*pf.*) (*sl.*).

Nick[2] [nɪk] *n.*: **Old ~** чёрт, сатана́ (*m.*).

nickel ['nɪk(ə)l] *n.* (*metal*) ни́кель (*m.*); (*US coin*) пятице́нтовик.

adj. ни́келевый.

v.t. никелирова́ть (*impf., pf.*).

cpds. **~-plated** *adj.* никелиро́ванный; **~-plating** *n.* никелиро́вка.

nick-nack ['nɪknæk] = **knick-knack**

nickname ['nɪkneɪm] *n.* про́звище, кли́чка.

v.t. проз|ыва́ть, -ва́ть +*a.* & *i.*; **he was ~d Shorty** его́ прозва́ли Коро́ты́шкой.

nicotine ['nɪkə,ti:n] *n.* никоти́н; **~ poisoning** отравле́ние никоти́ном.

cpd. **~-stained** *adj.* жёлтый от табака́.

niece [ni:s] *n.* племя́нница.

niello [nɪ'eləʊ] *n.* чернь (*на мета́лле*).

Niemen ['njemen] *n.* Не́ман.

Nietzschean ['ni:tʃɪən] *adj.* ницшеа́нский.

nifty ['nɪftɪ] *adj.* (*sl.*) (*adept*) ло́вкий; (*stylish*) сти́льный.
Niger ['naɪdʒə(r)] *n.* Ни́гер.
Nigeria [naɪ'dʒɪərɪə] *n.* Ниге́рия.
Nigerian [naɪ'dʒɪərɪən] *n.* нигери́|ец (*fem.* -йка).
adj. нигери́йский.
niggard ['nɪgəd] *n.* скря́га (*c.g.*).
niggardliness ['nɪgədlɪnɪs] *n.* ску́пость.
niggardly ['nɪgədlɪ] *adj.* скупо́й.
nigger ['nɪgə(r)] *n.* (*pej.*) чернома́зый (*coll.*); **he's the ~ in the woodpile** в нём вся загво́здка; **he works like a ~** он рабо́тает как вол.
cpd. **~-brown** *adj.* тёмно-кори́чневый.
niggle ['nɪg(ə)l] *v.t.* (*irritate*) задева́ть (*impf.*); поддева́ть (*impf.*).
v.i. (*fuss over detail*) мелочи́ться (*impf.*); (*make trivial complaints*) придира́ться (*impf.*) (к пустяка́м).
niggling ['nɪglɪŋ] *adj.* (*requiring attention to detail*) кропотли́вый; (*petty*) ме́лочный; **~ criticism** ме́лочная кри́тика, приди́рки (*f. pl.*).
nigh [naɪ] (*arch.*) = **near**
night [naɪt] *n.* **1.** ночь; (*waking hours of darkness*) ве́чер; **dark, black as ~** чёрный как смоль; **all ~ (long)** всю ночь (напролёт); **last ~** вчера́ ве́чером; **tomorrow ~** за́втра ве́чером; **at, by ~** но́чью; **at ~s** по ноча́м; **at dead of ~** в глуху́ю ночь; **~ and day** днём и но́чью; **we reached home before ~** мы пришли́ домо́й за́светло; **on Saturday ~** в суббо́ту ве́чером; **on the ~ of the 12th/13th** в ночь с двена́дцатого на трина́дцатое; **good ~!**; (*coll.*) **~-~!** споко́йной но́чи!; **have a good/bad ~ (~'s sleep)** хорошо́/пло́хо спать (*impf.*); **it's my ~ off** э́то мой свобо́дный ве́чер; **stay the ~** ночева́ть, пере-; **turn ~ into day** превра|ща́ть, -ти́ть ночь в день; **the Arabian N~s** (*title*) «Ты́сяча и одна́ ночь»; **work ~s** рабо́тать (*impf.*) по ноча́м; **a ~'s lodging** ночле́г. **2.** (*attr.*) ночно́й; **~ fighter** (*aircraft*) ночно́й истреби́тель; **~ life** ночна́я жизнь (го́рода); **~ nurse** ночна́я сиде́лка; **~ shift** ночна́я сме́на; **in the ~ watches** в бессо́нные но́чи.
cpds. **~-bell** *n.* ночно́й звоно́к; **~-bird** *n.* (*lit.*) ночна́я пти́ца; (*fig.*) полуно́чник, сова́; **~-blindness** *n.* кури́ная слепота́; **~cap** *n.* (*clothing*) ночно́й колпа́к; (*beverage*) стака́н (*чего*) на́ ночь; **~-club** *n.* ночно́й клуб, кафешанта́н; **~-dress** *n.* ночна́я соро́чка/руба́шка; **~fall** *n.* су́мер|ки (*pl.*, *g.* -ек); **by ~fall** к ве́черу; **~-gown** *n.* ночна́я руба́шка; **~jar** *n.* козодо́й; **~-light** *n.* ночни́к; **~-line** *n.* (*fishing*) у́дочка с прима́нкой, поста́вленная на́ ночь; **~-long** *adj.* продолжа́ющийся всю ночь; **~mare** *n.* кошма́р; (*fig.*) у́жас; **have a ~mare** ви́деть (*impf.*) кошма́рный сон; **he had ~mares all through the night** всю ночь ему́ сни́лись кошма́ры; **~marish** *adj.* кошма́рный; **~-owl** *n.* (*fig.*) = **~-bird; ~-porter** *n.* ночно́й швейца́р/портье́ (*m. indecl.*); **~-school** *n.* вече́рняя шко́ла; **~shade** *n.* паслён; **deadly ~shade** со́нная о́дурь; **~-shirt** *n.* ночна́я руба́шка; **~-soil** *n.* нечисто́ты (*f. pl.*); **~-time** *n.* ночно́е вре́мя; **in the ~-time** но́чью; **~-watchman** *n.* ночно́й сто́рож; **~-work** *n.* ночна́я рабо́та.
night|ie, -y ['naɪtɪ] *n.* ночна́я соро́чка.
nightingale ['naɪtɪŋ,geɪl] *n.* солове́й.
nightly ['naɪtlɪ] *adj.* (*happening at night*) ночно́й; (*happening every night*) ежено́щный; **~ performances** ежедне́вные вече́рние представле́ния.
adv. ежено́щно; ка́ждую ночь.
nighty ['naɪtɪ] **1.** = **nightie. 2.: ~-night!** ба́иньки-бай! (*coll.*).
nihilism ['naɪɪ,lɪz(ə)m, 'naɪhɪ,lɪz(ə)m] *n.* нигили́зм.
nihilist ['naɪɪlɪst, 'naɪhɪlɪst] *n.* нигили́ст (*fem.* -ка).
nihilistic [,naɪɪ'lɪstɪk, ,naɪhɪ'lɪstɪk] *adj.* нигилисти́ческий.
nil [nɪl] *n.* нуль (*m.*); **his influence is ~** его́ влия́ние равно́ нулю́.
Nile [naɪl] *n.* Нил; **Blue ~** Голубо́й Нил.
Nilotic [naɪ'lɒtɪk] *adj.* (*geog.*) ни́льский; (*anthrop.*) нилоти́ческий; **~ languages** нило́тские языки́.
nimble ['nɪmb(ə)l] *adj.* (*agile*) прово́рный; (*lively*) живо́й; шу́стрый; (*swift*) бы́стрый; (*dextrous*) ло́вкий; **he is ~ on his feet** он о́чень прово́рен; (*mentally quick, sharp*) бо́йкий, нахо́дчивый; **a ~ wit** бо́йкий ум.
cpds. **~-footed** *adj.* быстроно́гий; **~-witted** *adj.* нахо́дчивый, остроу́мный; **he is ~-witted** он за сло́вом в карма́н не поле́зет.
nimbus ['nɪmbəs] *n.* (*halo*) нимб; (*aureole*) орео́л; (*meteor.*) дождево́е о́блако.
nincompoop ['nɪŋkəm,pu:p] *n.* дура́к, болва́н.
nine [naɪn] *n.* (число́/но́мер) де́вять; (**~ *people***) де́вятеро, де́вять челове́к; **~ each** по девяти́; **in ~s, ~ at a time** по девяти́, девя́тками; (*figure; thg. numbered 9; group of* **~**) девя́тка; (*with var. nn. expr. or understood: cf. examples under* **five**); **dressed (up) to the ~s** разоде́тый в пух и прах.
adj. де́вять +*g. pl.*; **~ twos are eighteen** де́вять на два — восемна́дцать; **a ~ days' wonder** скоропреходя́щая сенса́ция; **~ times out of ten** в девяти́ слу́чаях из десяти́; в грома́дном большинстве́ слу́чаев.
cpds. **~fold** *adj.* девятикра́тный; *adv.* вде́вятеро, в де́вять раз, в девятикра́тном разме́ре; **~pins** *n.* ке́гл|и (*pl.*, *g.* -ей).
nineteen [naɪn'ti:n] *n.* девятна́дцать; **in the 1920s** в двадца́тые го́ды 20-го ве́ка; **talk ~ to the dozen** тарато́рить (*impf.*); треща́ть (*impf.*) без у́молку.
adj. девятна́дцатый.
nineteenth [naɪn'ti:nθ] *n.* (*date*) девятна́дцатое число́; (*fraction*) одна́ девятна́дцатая, девятна́дцатая часть.
adj. девятна́дцатый.
ninetieth ['naɪntɪɪθ] *n.* одна́ девяно́стая; девяно́стая часть.
adj. девяно́стый.
ninet|y ['naɪntɪ] *n.* девяно́сто; **he is in his ~ies** ему́ за девяно́сто; **in the ~ies** (*decade*) в девяно́стых года́х; (*temperature*) за девяно́сто гра́дусов (по Фаренге́йту).
adj. девяно́сто +*g. pl.*; **~y-nine times out of a hundred** в девяно́ста девяти́ слу́чаях из ста.
Nineveh ['nɪnɪvə] *n.* Нине́вия.
ninny ['nɪnɪ] *n.* дурачо́к.
ninth [naɪnθ] *n.* (*date*) девя́тое число́; (*fraction*) одна́ девя́тая; девя́тая часть; (*mus. interval*) но́на.
adj. девя́тый.
nip [nɪp] *n.* **1.** (*pinch*) щипо́к; **he gave her a playful ~ on the cheek** он игри́во ущипну́л её за́ щёку. **2.** (*small bite*) уку́с; **the puppy gave his finger a ~** щено́к кусану́л его́ за па́лец. **3.** (*of frost*): **there's a ~ in the air today** сего́дня (моро́з) пощи́пывает. **4.** (*of liquor etc.*) рю́мочка, глото́к, ка́пелька.
v.t. **1.** (*pinch*) щип|а́ть, -ну́ть; **his fingers were ~ped in the door** ему́ прищеми́ло па́льцы две́рью. **2.** (*bite*) покуса́ть, укуси́ть, кусану́ть (*all pf.*). **3.** (*of frost etc.*) щип|а́ть, -ну́ть; **the blossom was ~ped by the frost** за́морозки поби́ли ра́нний цвет; **~ sth. in the bud** (*fig.*) задуши́ть/подави́ть (*pf.*) что-н. в заро́дыше. **4. ~ off** отку́с|ывать, -и́ть.
v.i. **1.** (*pinch*) щипа́ться (*impf.*); **a crab can ~ quite severely** краб о́чень бо́льно щи́плется. **2.** (*strike cold*) щипа́ть (*impf.*); **the frost ~s hard today** моро́з сего́дня здо́рово щи́плет; **a ~ping wind** секу́щий ве́тер. **3.** (*usu. with advs., move smartly*): **I must ~ along to the shop** мне ну́жно сбе́гать в магази́н; **he ~ped in just ahead of me** он заскочи́л как раз пе́редо мной; **he ~ped off home** он удра́л домо́й; **I'll (just) ~ on ahead** я побегу́ вперёд; **he ~ped out to have a smoke** он вы́скочил покури́ть.
nipper ['nɪpə(r)] *n.* (*claw*) клешня́; (*pl., pincers*) клещ|и́ (*pl.*, *g.* -е́й); (*sl., child*) малы́ш, кро́шка.
nipple ['nɪp(ə)l] *n.* (*of breast*) сосо́к; (*of feeding-bottle*) со́ска; (*tech.*) ни́ппель (*m.*).
nippy ['nɪpɪ] *adj.* **1.** (*nimble*) прово́рный; **look ~!** пошеве́ливайтесь! **2.** (*chilly*): **a ~ wind** ре́зкий ве́тер; **the weather is ~** моро́зит.
nirvana [nɜ:'vɑ:nə, nɪə-] *n.* нирва́на.
nisi ['naɪsaɪ] *conj.*: **decree ~** усло́вный разво́д.
nit [nɪt] *n.* гни́да; (*sl., fool*) дурачо́к.
cpds. **~-pick** *v.i.* (*sl.*) придира́ться (*impf.*) к мелоча́м; **~-picking** *n.* (*sl.*) приди́рки (*f. pl.*), блохоиска́тельство; *adj.* приди́рчивый.
nitrate ['naɪtreɪt] *n.* соль/эфи́р азо́тной кислоты́; нитра́т; **copper ~** азотноки́слая медь.
nitre ['naɪtə(r)] *n.* сели́тра.

nitric ['naɪtrɪk] *adj.* азо́тный; ~ **acid** азо́тная кислота́; ~ **oxide** о́кись азо́та.

nitrogen ['naɪtrədʒ(ə)n] *n.* азо́т.
adj. азо́тный.

nitrogenous [,naɪ'trɒdʒɪnəs] *adj.* азо́тный.

nitroglycerine [,naɪtrəʊ'glɪsərɪn] *n.* нитроглицери́н.

nitrous ['naɪtrəs] *adj.* азо́тистый; ~ **acid** азо́тистая кислота́; ~ **oxide** за́кись азо́та; ~ **gases** нитро́зные га́зы.

nitty-gritty [,nɪtɪ'grɪtɪ] *n.* (*sl.*) суть де́ла; конкре́тные дета́ли (*f. pl.*); «вся ку́хня»; **the** ~ **of politics** полити́ческая ку́хня.

nitwit ['nɪtwɪt] *n.* о́лух (*coll.*).

nix [nɪks] *n.* (*sl.*, *nothing*) ничего́; ни черта́.

no [nəʊ] *n.* (*refusal*) отка́з; (*vote against*) го́лос про́тив; **the** ~**es have it** большинство́ (голосо́в) про́тив.
adj. **1.** (*not any*) никако́й; **there's** ~ **food in the house** в до́ме нет еды́; ~ **two people are alike** нет двух люде́й, схо́дных во всём; нет двух одина́ковых люде́й; все лю́ди ра́зные; **it's** ~ **use complaining** нет (никако́го) смы́сла жа́ловаться; жа́лобы де́лу не помо́гут; ~ **doubt** несомне́нно; ~ **end of sth.** о́чень мно́го чего́-н.; **in** ~ **way** ничу́ть; нисколько; **it's** ~ **go** не вы́йдет/пойдёт (*coll.*); ~ **way** (*coll.*, *certainly not*) нико́им о́бразом; ~ **words can describe ...** слова́ бесси́льны описа́ть...; ≃ ни сло́вом сказа́ть, ни перо́м описа́ть; **under** ~ **pretext** ни под каки́м ви́дом; **there is** ~ **question of that** об э́том не мо́жет быть и ре́чи; **there's** ~ **saying what may happen** мо́жет случи́ться что уго́дно; мо́жно ждать чего́ уго́дно; **they are in** ~ **way alike** они́ ни в чём не похо́жи; ~ **man**, ~ **one** никто́; **I spoke to** ~ **one** я ни с кем не говори́л; ~ **one was there** там никого́ не́ было; ~ **one man can do this** в одино́чку э́то никому́ не под си́лу; *see also* **nobody. 2.** (*not a*; *quite other than*) не; **he's** ~ **fool** он (во́все) не дура́к; он совсе́м не глуп; **he's** ~ **friend of mine** мне он не друг; он мне отню́дь не друг; **it's** ~ **distance at all** э́то совсе́м недалеко́; э́то в двух шага́х; туда́ руко́й пода́ть; **in** ~ **time** в два счёта; **I have** ~ **great regard for him** осо́бого уваже́ния он у меня́ не вызыва́ет. **3.** (*expr. refusal or prohibition*): ~ **children!** то́лько без дете́й!; ~ **surrender!** не сдава́ться!; ~ **smoking** кури́ть воспреща́ется; ~ **talking!** никаки́х разгово́ров!; ~ **entry** вход воспрещён; нет вхо́да.
adv. **1.** (*with comps.*, *not at all*, *in no way*) не; ~ **better than before** ничу́ть не лу́чше, чем ра́ньше; **he is** ~ **better than an animal** он настоя́щее живо́тное; **he is** ~ **less than a scoundrel** он про́сто-на́просто подле́ц; **he gave him** ~ **less than 10,000** он дал ему́ це́лых де́сять ты́сяч; **we met the president**, ~ **less** мы да́же ви́дели само́го президе́нта; **he** ~ **longer lives there** он бо́льше там не живёт; **I have** ~ **more to say** мне бо́льше не́чего сказа́ть; мне не́чего приба́вить; **there is** ~ **more bread** хле́ба бо́льше нет; **he is** ~ **more a professor than I am** он тако́й же профе́ссор, как я; ~ **sooner said than done!** ска́зано — сде́лано!; ~ **sooner had he said it than ...** не успе́л он сказа́ть, как... **2. whether or** ~ так и́ли ина́че; в любо́м слу́чае; **whether he comes or** ~ придёт он и́ли нет.
particle **1.** (*in replies*) нет; **he can never say** ~ **to an invitation** он никогда́ не отка́жется от приглаше́ния; **he will not take** ~ **for an answer** он не при́мет отка́за; он не отсту́пится, пока́ не полу́чит согла́сия; (*after negative statement or question*, *sometimes*) да; **"You don't like him, do you?" — "No, I don't"** «Вам ведь он не нра́вится?» — «Да, не нра́вится»; **"He's not a nice man" — "No, he isn't"** «Он челове́к нева́жный» — «Да, нева́жный». **2.** (*interpolated for emphasis*): **one man cannot lift it**, ~, **nor half a dozen** одному́ э́того не подня́ть, да что одному́ — и шестеры́м не спра́виться. **3.** (*expr. incredulity*) ~! не мо́жет быть!
cpds. ~**-go** *adj.*: **a** ~**-go area** запре́тная о́бласть; ~**-good** *adj.* никчёмный; ~**-man's-land** *n.* ничья́/ниче́йная земля́; нейтра́льная зо́на; ~**-one** *pron.*: *see* **no** *adj.* **1., nobody;** ~**-show** *n.* (*pers.*) неяви́вшийся пассажи́р.

No. ['nʌmbə(r)] *n.* (*abbr. of* **number**) №.

Noah ['nəʊə, nɔː] *n.* Ной; ~**'s ark** Но́ев ковче́г.

nob [nɒb] *n.* (*sl.*, *bigwig*) (больша́я) ши́шка.

nobble ['nɒb(ə)l] *v.t.* (*sl.*) **1.** (*horse*) по́ртить, ис-. **2.** (*bribe*) подкуп|а́ть, -и́ть.

Nobel prize ['nəʊbel, -'bel] *n.* Но́белевская пре́мия.

nobility [nəʊ'bɪlɪtɪ] *n.* (*quality*) благоро́дство; (*titled class*) дворя́нство.

noble ['nəʊb(ə)l] *n.* двор|яни́н (*fem.* -я́нка).
adj. **1.** (*of character or conduct*) благоро́дный; (*expr. high ideals*, *sentiments*): **a** ~ **poem** стихотворе́ние, прони́кнутое высо́кими чу́вствами. **2.** (*belonging to the nobility*) дворя́нский; **of** ~ **birth** дворя́нского происхожде́ния. **3.** (*imposing*, *impressive*) внуши́тельный; (*majestic*) велича́вый, вели́чественный; (*excellent*) превосхо́дный, прекра́сный. **4.** ~ **metal** благоро́дный мета́лл.
cpds. ~**man** *n.* дворяни́н; ~**-minded** *adj.* великоду́шный, благоро́дный; ~**-mindedness** *n.* (душе́вное) благоро́дство; ~**woman** *n.* дворя́нка.

noblesse [nəʊ'bles] *n.*: ~ ***oblige*** положе́ние обя́зывает.

nobody ['nəʊbədɪ] *n.* ничто́жный челове́к, ничто́жество.
pron. (*also* **no(-)one**) никто́ (... не); ~ **knows** никто́ не зна́ет; **there was** ~ **present** никого́ не́ было; **it's** ~**'s business but his own** э́то его́ (со́бственное) де́ло; *see also* **no** *adj.* **1.**

nocturnal [nɒk'tɜːn(ə)l] *adj.* ночно́й.

nocturne ['nɒktɜːn] *n.* ноктю́рн.

nod [nɒd] *n.* киво́к; **give a** ~ **of the head to s.o.** кив|а́ть, -ну́ть голово́й кому́-н.; **he was given the job on the** ~ он получи́л рабо́ту с ходу́; **to pass a motion on the** ~ приня́ть (*pf.*) предложе́ние без голосова́ния; **the land of** ~ (*joc.*) со́нное ца́рство; **on the** ~ (*coll.*, *on credit*) в креди́т.
v.t.: ~ **one's head** кив|а́ть, -ну́ть голово́й; ~ **assent** кивну́ть (*pf.*) в знак согла́сия.
v.i. **1.** кив|а́ть, -ну́ть; **he** ~**ded to me in the street** он кивну́л мне на у́лице; **a** ~**ding acquaintance** ша́почное знако́мство. **2.** (*become drowsy*) клева́ть (*impf.*) но́сом (*coll.*); **he** ~**ded off during the lecture** он задрема́л на ле́кции; **even Homer** ~**s** ≃ и на стару́ху быва́ет проруха.

noddle ['nɒd(ə)l] *n.* (*sl.*, *head*) башка́.

node [nəʊd] *n.* (*bot.*, *phys.*) у́зел; (*astron.*, *math.*) то́чка пересече́ния.

nodule ['nɒdjuːl] *n.* (*bot.*) узело́к; (*med.*) узело́к, узелко́вое утолще́ние.

noggin ['nɒgɪn] *n.* кру́жечка.

nohow ['nəʊhaʊ] *adv.* (*coll.*) ника́к; нико́им о́бразом.

noise [nɔɪz] *n.* **1.** (*din*) шум; **make a** ~ шуме́ть, за-; **don't make so much** ~! не шуми́те!; переста́ньте шуме́ть! **2.** (*sound*) звук; **can you hear a funny** ~? вы слы́шите э́тот стра́нный звук?; **he made sympathetic** ~**s** (*coll.*) он сочу́вственно подда́кивал. **3.: a big** ~ (*coll.*) ши́шка. **4.** (*radio*) поме́хи (*f. pl.*).
v.t.: ~ **abroad** распростран|я́ть, -и́ть.

noiseless ['nɔɪzlɪs] *adj.* бесшу́мный.

noisette [nwɑː'zet] *n.* (*cul.*) ≃ те́фтел|и (*pl.*, *g.* -ей).

noisiness ['nɔɪzɪnɪs] *n.* шумли́вость, гро́мкость.

noisome ['nɔɪsəm] *adj.* (*harmful*) вре́дный; (*fetid*) злово́нный, воню́чий; (*offensive*) омерзи́тельный, ме́рзкий, отврати́тельный.

noisy ['nɔɪzɪ] *adj.* (*of thg.*) шу́мный; **a** ~ **party** шу́мная вечери́нка; **your engine sounds** ~ мото́р у вас что́-то шуми́т; (*of pers.*) шумли́вый; **don't be so** ~! что вы так расшуме́лись?; ~ **laughter** гро́мкий смех.

nomad ['nəʊmæd] *n.* коче́вник; (*attr.*) кочево́й.

nomadic [nəʊ'mædɪk] *adj.* кочево́й; **lead a** ~ **life** кочева́ть (*impf.*); вести́ (*impf.*) кочево́й о́браз жи́зни.

nom de guerre [,nɒm də 'geə(r)], ***nom de plume*** [,nɒm də 'pluːm] *nn.* псевдони́м.

nomenclature [nəʊ'menklətʃə(r), 'nəʊmən,kleɪtʃə(r)] *n.* номенклату́ра.

nominal ['nɒmɪn(ə)l] *adj.* **1.** (*pert. to nn. or names*) имено́й; ~ **roll** именно́й спи́сок. **2.** (*existing in name only*) номина́льный.

nominalism ['nɒmɪnə,lɪz(ə)m] *n.* номинали́зм.

nominalist ['nɒmɪnəlɪst] *n.* номинали́ст.

nominate ['nɒmɪ,neɪt] *v.t.* (*appoint*, *e.g. date*, *place*, *pers.*) назн|ача́ть, -а́чить; (*propose*, *e.g. candidate*) выставля́ть,

вы́ставить кандидату́ру +*g*.
nomination [ˌnɒmɪˈneɪʃ(ə)n] *n.* назначе́ние; выставле́ние кандидату́ры; **how many ~s are there for chairman?** ско́лько вы́ставлено кандида́тов на пост председа́теля?
nominative [ˈnɒmɪnətɪv] *n.* **(~ case)** имени́тельный паде́ж.
adj. имени́тельный.
nominee [ˌnɒmɪˈniː] *n.* кандида́т.
non- [nɒn] *pref.* не…
non-addictive [ˌnɒnəˈdɪktɪv] *adj.* не вызыва́ющий привыка́ния.
nonage [ˈnəʊnɪdʒ, ˈnɒn-] *n.* несовершенноле́тие; (*immaturity*) незре́лость.
nonagenarian [ˌnəʊnədʒɪˈneərɪən, ˌnɒn-] *n.* девяностоле́тний стари́к.
non-aggression [ˌnɒnəˈgreʃ(ə)n] *n.*: **~ pact** догово́р о ненападе́нии.
non-alcoholic [ˌnɒnælkəˈhɒlɪk] *adj.* безалкого́льный.
non-aligned [ˌnɒnəˈlaɪnd] *adj.* (*pol.*) неприсоедини́вшийся (к бло́кам).
non-alignment [ˌnɒnəˈlaɪnmənt] *n.* поли́тика неприсоедине́ния.
non-appearance [ˌnɒnəˈpɪərəns] *n.* (*leg.*) нея́вка в суд.
non-attendance [ˌnɒnəˈtend(ə)ns] *n.* непосеще́ние, нея́вка.
non-believer [ˌnɒnbɪˈliːvə(r)] *n.* неве́рующий.
non-belligerency [ˌnɒnbəˈlɪdʒərənsɪ] *n.* неуча́стие в войне́.
non-belligerent [ˌnɒnbəˈlɪdʒərənt] *n.* & *adj.* не уча́ствующий в войне́; нево́юющий.
nonbiodegradable [ˌnɒnbaɪəʊdɪˈgreɪdəb(ə)l] *adj.* не разлага́емый микроорганизмами.
nonce [nɒns] *n.*: **for the ~** для да́нного слу́чая; на э́то вре́мя; поку́да.
cpd. **~-word** *n.* (*ling.*) окказиона́льное сло́во.
nonchalance [ˈnɒnʃələns] *n.* беззабо́тность; безразли́чие.
nonchalant [ˈnɒnʃələnt] *adj.* (*carefree*) беспе́чный, беззабо́тный; **a ~ manner** развя́зная мане́ра; (*indifferent*) безразли́чный.
non-combatant [nɒnˈkɒmbət(ə)nt] *n.* (*non-fighting soldier*) нестроево́й солда́т; (*pl. civilians*) гражда́нское населе́ние.
adj. небоево́й; (*of units*) нестроево́й.
non-commissioned [ˌnɒnkəˈmɪʃ(ə)nd] *adj.*: **~ officer** сержа́нт; военнослу́жащий сержа́нтского соста́ва.
non-committal [ˌnɒnkəˈmɪt(ə)l] *adj.* (*evasive*) укло́нчивый.
non-compliance [ˌnɒnkəmˈplaɪəns] *n.*: **~ with regulations** несоблюде́ние пра́вил.
non compos mentis [ˌnɒn kɒmpɒs ˈmentɪs] *adj.* невменя́емый.
non-conducting [ˌnɒnkənˈdʌktɪŋ)] *adj.* непроводя́щий.
non-conductor [ˌnɒnkənˈdʌktə(r)] *n.* непроводни́к.
nonconformist [ˌnɒnkənˈfɔːmɪst] *n.* своеобы́чный челове́к; (*pol.*) диссиде́нт, инакомы́слящий; (*relig.*) секта́нт, раско́льник.
adj. своеобы́чный; диссиде́нтский; секта́нтский.
nonconformity [ˌnɒnkənˈfɔːmɪtɪ] *n.* несоблюде́ние (пра́вил), неподчине́ние; (*relig.*) секта́нтство, раско́л.
non-contributary [ˌnɒnkənˈtrɪbjʊtərɪ] *adj.* не тре́бующий взно́сов.
non-cooperation [ˌnɒnkəʊˌɒpəˈreɪʃ(ə)n] *n.* нежела́ние совме́стно рабо́тать; отка́з от сотру́дничества.
non-dairy [ˌnɒnˈdeərɪ] *adj.* безмоло́чный.
non-delivery [ˌnɒndɪˈlɪvərɪ] *n.* (*of mail*) недоста́вка; (*of goods*) неприбы́тие (това́ра).
nondescript [ˈnɒndɪskrɪpt] *adj.* невзра́чный; неопределённого ви́да; се́рый; безли́чный.
none [nʌn] *pron.* (*pers.*) никто́; **~ of us is perfect** никто́ из на́с не явля́ется соверше́нством; ≃ все мы гре́шные; **I saw ~ of the people I wanted to** я не ви́дел никого́ из тех, кого́ хоте́л повида́ть; **it was ~ other than Smith himself** э́то был никто́ ино́й, как Смит; **~ of the people died** ни оди́н челове́к не у́мер; **~ but fools believe it** э́тому ве́рят одни́ дураки́; **he is ~ of your canting hypocrites** он не принадлежи́т к ханжа́м и лицеме́рам; (*thg.*) ничто́; **there is ~ of it left** из э́того ничего́ не оста́лось; **~ of this is mine** из э́того мне ничего́ не принадлежи́т; всё э́то не моё; **~ of the books is red** среди́ э́тих книг — кра́сной ни одно́й; **~ of the houses collapsed** ни оди́н дом не ру́хнул; **~ of the exhibition is worth seeing** на вы́ставке нет ничего́ сто́ящего; **it's better than ~ at all** э́то лу́чше, чем ничего́; **he will accept ~ but the best** он не принима́ет ничего́ второсо́ртного; он на второ́й сорт не согла́сен; **his understanding is ~ of the clearest** у него́ не са́мая я́сная голова́; **he would have ~ of it** он и слу́шать не хоте́л; **~ of that!** э́то не пойдёт!; дово́льно!; **~ of your impudence!** без де́рзостей, пожа́луйста!; **it's ~ of your business** э́то не ва́ше де́ло; **you have money and I have ~** у вас есть де́ньги, а у меня́ нет.
adv.: **I feel ~ the better for seeing the doctor** врач мне ниче́м не помо́г; **he is ~ the worse for his accident** он вполне́ опра́вился по́сле несча́стного слу́чая; **the pay is ~ too high** пла́та отню́дь не высо́кая; **~ the less** тем не ме́нее.
non-effective [ˌnɒnɪˈfektɪv] *adj.* недействи́тельный; (*mil.*) вы́шедший из стро́я по боле́зни (*or* вследствие ране́ния); него́дный к вое́нной слу́жбе.
nonentity [nɒˈnentɪtɪ] *n.* (*pers.*) ничто́жество.
non-essential [ˌnɒnɪˈsenʃ(ə)l] *n.* несуще́ственная вещь.
adj. несуще́ственный.
non-Euclidean [ˌnɒnjuːˈklɪdɪən] *adj.* неэвкли́дов.
non-European [nɒnˌjʊərəˈpɪən] *n.* неевропе́|ец (*fem.* -йка).
adj. неевропе́йский.
non-event [ˌnɒnɪˈvent] *n.* собы́тие сомни́тельной ва́жности.
non-existence [ˌnɒnɪgˈzɪst(ə)ns] *n.* небытие́.
non-existent [ˌnɒnɪgˈzɪst(ə)nt] *adj.* несуществу́ющий.
non-ferrous [nɒnˈferəs] *adj.*: **~ metals** цветны́е мета́ллы.
non-fiction [nɒnˈfɪkʃ(ə)n] *adj.* документа́льный.
non-figurative [nɒnˈfɪgərətɪv, -jʊr] *adj.* **1.** (*literal*) буква́льный, не перено́сный. **2.:** **~ art** абстра́ктное/беспредме́тное иску́сство.
non-flammable [nɒnˈflæməb(ə)l] *adj.* невоспламеня́ющийся.
non-fulfilment [ˌnɒnfʊlˈfɪlmənt] *n.* невыполне́ние.
non-interference [ˌnɒnɪntəˈfɪərəns] *n.* невмеша́тельство.
non-intervention [ˌnɒnɪntəˈvenʃ(ə)n] *n.* невмеша́тельство.
non-iron [nɒnˈaɪən] *adj.* (*of clothes*) немну́щийся.
non-member [nɒnˈmembə(r)] *n.* нечле́н.
non-metal [nɒnˈmet(ə)l] *n.* немета́лл, металло́ид.
non-metallic [ˌnɒnmɪˈtælɪk] *adj.* неметалли́ческий.
non-moral [nɒnˈmɒr(ə)l] *adj.* не относя́щийся к э́тике; амора́льный.
non-negotiable [ˌnɒnnɪˈgəʊʃəb(ə)l] *adj.* (*comm.*) непередава́емый, необраща́ющийся; (*not for discussion*) не подлежа́щий осужде́нию.
non-nuclear [nɒnˈnjuːklɪə(r)] *adj.* нея́дерный; (*pol.*) не применя́ющий я́дерное ору́жие; не располага́ющий я́дерным ору́жием; (*of zone, area*) безъя́дерный; (*of weapons*) обы́чный, нея́дерный.
non-observance [ˌnɒnəbˈzɜːv(ə)ns] *n.* несоблюде́ние, невыполне́ние, наруше́ние.
no-nonsense [ˌnəʊˈnɒns(ə)ns] *adj.* серьёзный, делово́й; стро́гий.
nonpareil [ˈnɒnpər(ə)l, ˌnɒnpəˈreɪl] *n.* (*perfect specimen*) верх соверше́нства; идеа́л; (*typ.*) нонпаре́ль.
non-party [nɒnˈpɑːtɪ] *adj.* беспарти́йный.
non-payment [nɒnˈpeɪmənt] *n.* неупла́та, неплатёж.
nonplus [nɒnˈplʌs] *v.t.* прив|оди́ть, -ести́ в замеша́тельство; сму|ща́ть, -ти́ть.
non-political [ˌnɒnpəˈlɪtɪk(ə)l] *adj.* неполити́ческий.
non-polluting [ˌnɒnpəˈluːtɪŋ] *adj.* не загрязня́ющий окружа́ющую среду́.
non-productive [ˌnɒnprəˈdʌktɪv] *adj.* непроизводи́тельный.
non-profit(-making) [nɒnˈprɒfɪtˌmeɪkɪŋ] *adj.* некомме́рческий; на обще́ственных нача́лах.
non-proliferation [ˌnɒnprəˌlɪfəˈreɪʃ(ə)n] *n.* нераспростране́ние (я́дерного ору́жия).
non-recognition [ˌnɒnrekəgˈnɪʃ(ə)n] *n.* непризна́ние.
non-renewable [ˌnɒnrɪˈnjuːəb(ə)l] *adj.* невозобновля́емый.
non-residence [nɒnˈrezɪd(ə)ns] *n.* непрожива́ние (где-н.).
non-resident [nɒnˈrezɪd(ə)nt] *n.* & *adj.* непрожива́ющий (где-н.); прие́зжий.
non-resistance [ˌnɒnrɪˈzɪst(ə)ns] *n.* непротивле́ние (*кому/чему*).

non-resistant [ˌnɒnrɪ'zɪst(ə)nt] *adj.* не ока́зывающий сопротивле́ния; неусто́йчивый.
non-rigid [nɒn'rɪdʒɪd] *adj.* нежёсткой констру́кции.
non-sectarian [ˌnɒnsek'teərɪən] *adj.* включа́ющий все рели́гии.
nonsense ['nɒns(ə)ns] *n.* (*sth. without meaning*) бессмы́слица; **the sentence seems sheer ~ to me** предложе́ние ка́жется мне соверше́нно бессмы́сленным; (*rubbish*) ерунда́, чепуха́, вздор; **talk ~** говори́ть (*impf.*) ерунду́; нагороди́ть (*pf.*) вздор; нести́ (*impf.*) чушь/дичь. **2.** (*foolish conduct*) глу́пость; **let's have no more ~!** хва́тит валя́ть дурака́!; **what ~ is this?** э́то что за глу́пости!; **~ verse(s)** стишки́ (*m. pl.*) -неле́пицы/-бессмы́слицы (*f pl.*).
nonsensical [nɒn'sensɪk(ə)l] *adj.* бессссмы́сленный, неле́пый, глу́пый.
non sequitur [nɒn 'sekwɪtə(r)] *n.* нелоги́чное заключе́ние.
non-skid [nɒn'skɪd] *adj.* небуксу́ющий.
non-slip [nɒn'slɪp] *adj.* нескóльзкий.
non-smoker [nɒn'sməʊkə(r)] *n.* (*pers.*) некуря́щий; (*compartment*) *see* **non-smóking**
non-smoking [nɒn'sməʊkɪŋ] *adj.*: **~ compartment** купе́ (*indecl.*) для некуря́щих.
non-starter [nɒn'stɑːtə(r)] *n.* (*coll.*) мёртвый но́мер.
non-stick [nɒn'stɪk] *adj.*: **a ~ saucepan** неподгора́ющая кастрю́ля.
non-stop [nɒn'stɒp] *adj.* **1.** (*of train or coach*) безостано́вочный; (*of aircraft or flight*) беспоса́дочный. **2.** (*continuous*) непреры́вный.
adv. **1.** безостано́вочно; беспоса́дочно; без остано́вок. **2.: he talks ~** он говори́т без у́молку.
nonsuit [nɒn'sjuːt, -'suːt] *v.t.*: **~ a plaintiff** прекра|ща́ть, -ти́ть произво́дство гражда́нского де́ла; закры́ть (*pf.*) де́ло.
non-swimmer [nɒn'swɪmə(r)] *n.* не уме́ющий пла́вать.
non-transferable [ˌnɒntræns'fɜːrəb(ə)l] *adj.* не подлежа́щий переда́че (друго́му).
non-U [nɒn'juː] *adj.* ≃ некульту́рный.
non-union [nɒn'juːnɪən] *adj.*: **he employs ~ labour** он принима́ет на рабо́ту нечле́нов профсою́за.
non-violence [nɒn'vaɪələns] *n.* отка́з от примене́ния наси́льственных ме́тодов.
non-violent [nɒn'vaɪələnt] *adj.* ненаси́льственный.
non-white [nɒn'waɪt] *n.* & *adj.* (*of race*) цветно́й.
noodle ['nuːd(ə)l] *n.* (*simpleton*) балда́ (*c.g.*), ду́рень (*m.*).
noodles ['nuːd(ə)lz] *n. pl.* (*cul.*) лапша́.
nook [nʊk] *n.* уголо́к; **I searched every ~ and cranny** я обша́рил ка́ждый уголо́к; (*retreat*) укро́мный уголо́к.
noon [nuːn] *n.* (*also* **~day, ~tide**) по́лдень (*m.*); **at ~** в по́лдень; **12 ~** двена́дцать часо́в дня; (*attr.*) полу́денный, полдне́вный.
noose [nuːs] *n.* (*loop*) петля́; (*lasso*) арка́н; **put one's neck in the ~** (*fig.*) лезть (*impf.*) в пе́тлю.
nor [nɔː(r), nə(r)] *conj.*: **they had neither arms ~ provisions** у них не́ было ни ору́жия, ни провиа́нта; **he can't do it, ~ can I** он не мо́жет э́то сде́лать, да и я то́же; **you are not well, ~ am I** вам нездоро́вится, и мне то́же; **I said I had not seen him, ~ had I** я сказа́л, что не ви́дел его́, и э́то пра́вда; **he had neither the means ~, apparently, the inclination** у него́ не́ было средств — да, похо́же, и жела́ния; **~ will I deny that ...** не ста́ну та́кже отрица́ть, что...; **~ is this all** и э́то ещё не всё.
Nordic ['nɔːdɪk] *adj.* норди́ческий, скандина́вский.
norm [nɔːm] *n.* но́рма, пра́вило.
normal ['nɔːm(ə)l] *adj.* (*regular, standard*) норма́льный; **it is ~ weather for the time of year** э́то обы́ная/норма́льная пого́да для э́того вре́мени го́да; (*usual*) обы́чный; **it's quite ~ for him to arrive late** опа́здывать вполне́ в его́ обы́чае; **I ~ly use the bus** обы́чно я е́ду авто́бусом; (*sane, well-balanced*) норма́льный.
normal|cy ['nɔːməlsɪ], **-ity** [nɔː'mælɪtɪ] *nn.* норма́льность; обы́чное состоя́ние.
normalization [ˌnɔːməlaɪ'zeɪʃ(ə)n] *n.* нормализа́ция.
normalize ['nɔːməˌlaɪz] *v.t.* нормализова́ть (*impf., pf.*).
v.i. нормализова́ться (*impf., pf.*).
Norman ['nɔːmən] *n.* норма́нд|ец (*fem.* -ка).
adj. норма́ндский; **the ~ Conquest** Норма́ндское Завоева́ние А́нглии; **~ French** норма́ндский диале́кт францу́зского языка́; **~ architecture** рома́нский стиль в архитекту́ре.
Normandy ['nɔːməndɪ] *n.* Норма́ндия.
normative ['nɔːmətɪv] *adj.* нормати́вный.
Norse [nɔːs] *n.*: **Old ~** древнескандина́вский язы́к.
adj. норма́ннский.
cpd. **~man** *n.* норма́нн; (*Russ. hist.*) варя́г.
north [nɔːθ] *n.* се́вер; (*naut.*) норд; **the far ~** кра́йний се́вер; **the ~ of England** се́верная часть А́нглии; **the ~ of Europe** се́верные стра́ны (*f. pl.*) Евро́пы; **in the ~** на се́вере; **from the ~** с се́вера; **to the ~** на се́вер; **to the ~ of** к се́веру от+*g.*; се́driнее +*g.*; **magnetic ~** се́верный магни́тный по́люс; **~ by east/west** норд-тень-ост/вест.
adj. се́верный; **N~ America** Се́верная Аме́рика; **N~ American** урожéн|ец (*fem.* -ка) Се́верной Аме́рики; североамерика́нский; **the ~ country** се́верная А́нглия; **N~ Island** о́стров Се́верный; **N~ Pole** Се́верный по́люс; **N~ Sea** Се́верное мо́ре; **N~ star** Поля́рная звезда́.
adv.: **we went ~** мы пое́хали на се́вер; **a line drawn ~ and south** ли́ния, проведённая с се́вера на юг; **~ of a line from A to B** к се́веру от ли́нии, веду́щей от А к Б, (*or* иду́щей от А к Б).
cpds. **~bound** *adj.* иду́щий/дви́жущийся на се́вер; **~countryman** *n.* уроже́нец се́верной А́нглии; **~-east** *n.* се́веро-восто́к; (*naut.*) норд-о́ст; *adj.* (*also* **~-easterly, ~-eastern**) се́веро-восто́чный; **~-east wind** (*also* **~-easter** *n.*) норд-о́ст; *adv.* (*also* **~-easterly, ~-eastward**) к се́веро-восто́ку; на се́веро-восто́к; **~-west** *n.* се́веро-за́пад; (*naut.*) норд-ве́ст; *adj.* (*also* **~-westerly, ~-western**) се́веро-за́падный; **~-west wind** (*also* **~-wester(ly)** *nn.*) норд-ве́ст; *adv.* (*also* **~-westerly, ~-westward**) к се́веро-за́паду; на се́веро-за́пад.
northerly ['nɔːðəlɪ] *n.* (*wind*) се́верный ве́тер.
adj. се́верный.
adv.: **the wind blows ~** ве́тер ду́ет с се́вера; **proceed ~** дви́гаться (*impf.*) к се́веру.
northern ['nɔːð(ə)n] *adj.* се́верный; **~ lights** се́верное сия́ние.
northerner ['nɔːðənə(r)] *n.* северя́н|ин (*fem.* -ка).
northernmost ['nɔːðənˌməʊst] *adj.* са́мый се́верный.
northward ['nɔːθwəd] *n.*: **to ~** к се́веру.
adj. се́верный.
adv. на се́вер.
Norway ['nɔːweɪ] *n.* Норве́гия.
Norwegian [nɔː'wiːdʒ(ə)n] *n.* (*pers.*) норве́ж|ец (*fem.* -ка); (*language*) норве́жский язы́к.
adj. норве́жский.
nose [nəʊz] *n.* **1.** нос; (*dim.*) но́сик; **my ~ is bleeding** у меня́ идёт кровь но́сом; **his ~ is running** у него́ на́сморк/со́пли; **I have a stuffy ~** у меня́ заложи́ло нос; **with one's ~ in the air** (*fig.*) задра́в нос; **as plain as the ~ on your face** я́сно как два́жды два — четы́ре (*or* как на ладо́ни); **bite, snap s.o.'s ~ off** (*fig.*) огрыз|а́ться, -ну́ться на кого́-н.; **blow one's ~** сморка́ться, вы-; **bury one's ~ in a book** уткну́ться (*pf.*) но́сом в кни́гу; **cut off one's ~ to spite one's face** с доса́ды сде́лать (*pf.*) ху́же себе́; **follow one's ~** (*go straight ahead*) идти́ (*det.*) пря́мо (вперёд); (*be guided by instinct*) руково́дствоваться (*impf.*) интуи́цией/чутьём; **hold one's ~** заж|има́ть, -а́ть нос; **keep one's ~ clean** (*coll., avoid trouble*) держа́ться (*impf.*) пода́льше (*от чего*); не высо́вываться (*impf.*); **keep your ~ out of my business!** не су́йте нос не в своё де́ло!; **keep one's ~ to the grindstone** не отрыва́ться (*impf.*) от де́ла; рабо́тать (*impf.*) не поклада́я рук; не дава́ть себе́ переды́шки; **keep s.o.'s ~ to the grindstone** не дава́ть (*impf.*) кому́-н. ни о́тдыху ни сро́ку; **lead s.o. by the ~** вести́ (*det.*) кого́-н. на поводу́; **look down one's ~ at s.o.** смотре́ть, по- свысока́ на кого́-н.; **make a long ~ at s.o.** пока́з|ывать, -а́ть нос кому́-н.; **pay through the ~** плати́ть, за- втридорога; **poke, push, thrust one's ~ into sth.** сова́ть, су́нуть нос во что-н.; **punch s.o. on the ~** да|ва́ть, -ть кому́-н. по́ носу; **put s.o.'s ~ out of joint** ≃ утере́ть (*pf.*) нос кому́-н.; **rub s.o.'s ~ in sth.** ты́кать,

ткнуть кого́-н. но́сом во что-н.; **he can see no further than his ~** он да́льше своего́ но́са не ви́дит; **talk through one's ~** говори́ть (*impf.*) в нос; **turn up one's ~ at sth.** вороти́ть (*impf.*) нос от чего́-н.; **under one's ~** под са́мым но́сом; **he stole the purse from under my ~** он укра́л кошелёк из-под моего́ но́са. **2.** (*sense of smell*; *also fig.*, *flair*) чутьё; **my dog has a good ~** у мое́й соба́ки хоро́шее чутьё; **he has a ~ for gossip** у него́ како́й-то (*or* пря́мо-таки) нюх на спле́тни. **3.** (*of car*, *aircraft etc.*) нос; **they were driving ~ to tail** они́ е́хали вплотну́ю друг за дру́гом; маши́ны шли пло́тной верени́цей. **4.** (*nozzle*) сопло́.

v.t. **1.** (*of animals*, *smell*) чу́ять (*impf.*). **2.** (*nuzzle*) ты́каться, ткну́ться но́сом в+*a*. **3.** **~ one's way** проб|ира́ться, -ра́ться; **the ship ~d her way through the channel** кора́бль осторо́жно пробира́лся по фарва́теру. **4.** **~ into** (*pry*, *meddle*) сова́ться (*or* сова́ть нос) (*impf.*) в+*a*.

with advs.: **~ about** *v.i.* (*sniff*, *smell*) ню́хать (*impf.*); **the dog ~d about the room** соба́ка обню́хивала ко́мнату; **~ out** *v.t.* (*of animals*) учу́ять (*impf.*); оты́ск|ивать, -а́ть чутьём; (*fig.*) разню́х|ивать, -ать; **he will ~ out scandal anywhere** сканда́л он как ню́хом чу́ет.

cpds. **~-bag** *n.* то́рба; **~-bleed** *n.*: **he has frequent ~-bleeds** у него́ ча́сто идёт но́сом кровь; **~-cone** *n.* (*of rocket etc.*) носово́й ко́нус; **~-dive** *n.* пики́рование, пике́ (*indecl.*); **prices took a ~-dive** це́ны ре́зко упа́ли; *v.i.* пики́ровать (*impf.*, *pf.*); **~gay** *n.* (*arch.*) буке́т цвето́в; **~-ring** *n.* (*for bull*) ноздрево́е кольцо́.

noseless [ˈnəʊzlɪs] *adj.* безно́сый.

nosey [ˈnəʊzɪ] = **nosy**

nosh [nɒʃ] *n.* шамо́вка, жратва́ (*sl.*).

nostalgia [nɒˈstældʒɪə, -dʒə] *n.* (*homesickness*) тоска́ по ро́дине; ностальги́я; (*for old times*) тоска́ по про́шлому.

nostalgic [nɒˈstældʒɪk] *adj.* (*pers.*) тоску́ющий; (*thg.*) ностальги́ческий, вызыва́ющий воспомина́ния.

nostril [ˈnɒstrɪl] *n.* ноздря́.

no-strings [nəʊˈstrɪŋz] *adj.* (*coll.*): **~ agreement** безогово́рочный.

nostrum [ˈnɒstrəm] *n.* (*lit.*, *fig.*) панаце́я.

nos|y,-ey [ˈnəʊzɪ] *adj.* (*coll.*) любопы́тный.

not [nɒt] *adv.* **1.** не; **it is my book, ~ yours** э́то моя́ кни́га, а не ва́ша; **~ till after dinner** то́лько по́сле обе́да; **she is ~ here** её здесь нет; **'Are you going to tell him?' — 'N~ I!'** «Вы ему́ ска́жете?» — «То́лько не я!»; **he won't pay you, ~ he!** он ника́к вам не запла́тит, э́то уж пове́рьте!; **I won't go there, ~ I!** я́-то уж не пойду́ туда́. **2.** (*elliptical phrr.*): **guilty or ~, he is my son** вино́вен — невино́вен, а всё равно́ он мой сын; **if it's fine, we'll go, but if ~ we'll stay here** е́сли бу́дет хоро́шая пого́да, мы пое́дем, а нет — (так) оста́немся здесь; **we must hurry, if ~ we may be late** на́до потора́пливаться, а (не) то опозда́ем; **whether or ~** так и́ли ина́че; **I hope ~** наде́юсь, что нет; **'are you afraid?' — 'I should say ~!'** «Вы бои́тесь?» — «Да ничу́ть!». **3.** (**~** *even*): **~ one of them moved** ни оди́н из них не подви́нулся; **there's ~ a drop left** не оста́лось ни еди́ной ка́пли; **~ a day passed without ...** и дня не проходи́ло без (того́, что́бы)...; **'Have you heard any news?' — 'N~ a thing'** «Вы слы́шали каки́е-нибу́дь но́вости?» — «Никаки́х». **4.** (*litotes*): **~ a few** мно́гие, дово́льно мно́го; **~ infrequently** дово́льно ча́сто; **~ unconnected with ...** име́ющий не́которую связь с+*i.*; **'Was he annoyed?' — 'N~ half!'** «Он рассерди́лся?» — «Ещё как!». **5.** (**~** *at all*): **'Do you mind if I smoke?' — 'N~ at all!'** «Вы не возража́ете, е́сли я закурю́?» — «Ниско́лько/ничу́ть»; **'Many thanks!' — 'N~ at all!'** «Большо́е спаси́бо!» — «Не сто́ит! (*or* Пожа́луйста!)»; **it's ~ at all clear** совсе́м/во́все не я́сно. **6.** (*introducing concession*): **it's ~ that I don't want to, I can't** не то что я не хочу́, не могу́; **(it is) ~ that I fear him, but ...** я не то что́бы его́ боя́лся, но...; **I can't do it, ~ but what a younger man might** (ли́чно) я на э́то не спосо́бен, но э́то не зна́чит, что кто́-нибудь помоло́же не мо́жет. **7.** (*var. phrr.*): **~ for the world** ни за что на све́те; **~ on your life** ни в ко́ем слу́чае; и не ду́майте; как (бы) не так; **~ really!** да нет!; не мо́жет быть!; **~ in the least** ничу́ть; ниско́лько; **he's ~ much of an actor** он нева́жный (*or* так себе́) актёр.

notability [ˌnəʊtəˈbɪlɪtɪ] *n.* знамени́тость.

notable [ˈnəʊtəb(ə)l] *n.* знамени́тость.

adj. (*perceptible*) заме́тный; (*worthy of note*, *remarkable*) замеча́тельный; (*eminent*, *outstanding*) ви́дный, выдаю́щийся; (*well-known*) изве́стный; (*celebrated*) знамени́тый; (*noteworthy*) достопримеча́тельный; (*famed*, *renowned*) сла́вящийся, изве́стный (*чем*); **a city ~ for its buildings** го́род, сла́вящийся свое́й архитекту́рой.

notably [ˈnəʊtəblɪ] *adv.* осо́бенно; в осо́бенности; (*perceptibly*) заме́тно.

notary [ˈnəʊtərɪ] *n.* нота́риус.

notation [nəʊˈteɪʃ(ə)n] *n.* нота́ция; **musical ~** но́тное письмо́; **phonetic ~** фонети́ческая транскри́пция.

notch [nɒtʃ] *n.* зару́бка.

v.t. **1.** (*mark with ~*) де́лать, с- зару́бку на+*p*. **2.**: **~ up a point** (*in game*) выи́грывать, вы́играть очко́.

note [nəʊt] *n.* **1.** (*mus.*, *as written*, *sounded or sung*) но́та; (*key of instrument*) кла́виша; **eighth/quarter ~** (*US*) восьма́я/четвёртая но́та; **strike the ~s** брать, взять но́ты; ударя́ть (*impf.*) по кла́вишам; (*fig.*): **he sounded a ~ of warning** он вы́разил опасе́ние; **there was a ~ of irony in his voice** в его́ го́лосе слы́шалась иро́ния; **the ~ of pessimism in his writings** пессимисти́ческая но́тка в его́ сочине́ниях; **strike the right ~** попа́сть (*pf.*) в тон; **strike a false ~** не попа́сть в тон; взять (*pf.*) неве́рный тон; (*characteristic*) черта́; **frankness is the chief ~ in his character** открове́нность — гла́вная черта́ его́ хара́ктера. **2.** (*distinction*): **a family of ~** изве́стная семья́; **a man of ~** ва́жное лицо́. **3.** (*attention*, *notice*) внима́ние; **take ~ of** (*observe*) прин|има́ть, -я́ть во внима́ние; (*heed*) прин|има́ть, -я́ть к све́дению; **worthy of ~** заслу́живающий внима́ния. **4.** (*written record*) за́пись; **make a ~ of sth.** запи́с|ывать, -а́ть что-н.; **he made, took ~s of the lecture** он законспекти́ровал ле́кцию; **he made a ~ in his diary** он сде́лал за́пись в дневнике́; **he spoke from ~s** он говори́л по конспе́кту; **compare ~s** (*fig.*) обме́н|иваться, -я́ться впечатле́ниями. **5.** (*annotation*) примеча́ние; (*in paper*, *book etc.*) заме́тка. **6.** (*communication*) запи́ска; **he left a ~ for you** он оста́вил вам запи́ску; **diplomatic ~** дипломати́ческая но́та; **promissory ~** долгова́я распи́ска. **7.** (*currency*) банкно́т; ба́нковый биле́т.

v.t. **1.** (*observe*, *notice*) зам|еча́ть, -е́тить; (*heed*) обра|ща́ть, -ти́ть внима́ние на+*a*. **2.** **~ down** (*in writing*) запи́с|ывать, -а́ть.

cpds. **~book** *n.* (*pad*) блокно́т, (*exercise-book*) тетра́дь; **~book computer** *n.* компью́тер-блокно́т; **~case** *n.* бума́жник; **~paper** *n.* пи́счая бума́га; **~worthy** *adj.* досто́йный внима́ния; (*of thg.*) достопримеча́тельный.

noted [ˈnəʊtɪd] *adj.* изве́стный, знамени́тый; **~ for his courage** изве́стный свои́м му́жеством.

nothing [ˈnʌθɪŋ] *n.* (*trifle*) ме́лочь, пустя́к; **a mere ~** су́щий пустя́к; **sweet ~s** ми́лый вздор; (*nonentity*) ничто́жество; (*zero*) нуль (*m.*).

pron. ничто́, ничего́; **~ came of it** из э́того ничего́ не вы́шло; **~ I did was right** что бы я ни де́лал, всё (бы́ло) не так; **~ whatever** ро́вно ничего́; **~ worries him** ничто́ не забо́тит его́; **Much Ado about N~** Мно́го шу́ма из ничего́; **he's a politician and ~ more** он поли́тик и ничего́ бо́лее; **~ but peace can save mankind** то́лько мир мо́жет спасти́ челове́чество; **I heard ~ but reproaches** я слы́шал одни́ упрёки; **he is ~ but a liar** он про́сто-на́просто лгун; **it's ~ but robbery** э́то су́щий грабёж; **in ~ but a shirt** в одно́й руба́шке; **he is ~ if not conscientious** чего́-чего́, а добросо́вестности у него́ хвата́ет; **she is ~ to me** она́ мне безразли́чна; **he is ~ without his money** без де́нег он был бы ниче́м; **it's ~ to what I felt** э́то ничто́ по сравне́нию с тем, что мне пришло́сь пережи́ть; **it's ~ to him to work all night** ему́ ничего́ не сто́ит порабо́тать всю ночь; **it's ~ to him what I say** мои́ слова́ для него́ — ничто́; он не обраща́ет ни мале́йшего внима́ния на мои́ слова́; **there's ~ to do (or be done)** не́чего де́лать; **there's**

~ to be ashamed of в э́том ничего́ нет посты́дного; **there's ~ worse than getting wet through** нет ничего́ ху́же, чем промо́кнуть насквозь; **~ doing!** не вы́йдет!; (э́тот) но́мер не пройдёт!; **there was ~ for it but to tell the truth** пришло́сь сказа́ть пра́вду; **there's ~** (*no difficulty*) **to it** э́то пустяки́; **there's ~** (*no truth*) **in it** э́то (сплошна́я) вы́думка; **there's ~** (*no advantage*) **in it for me** мне э́то ничего́ не да́ст; **there's ~ like a hot bath** нет ничего́ лу́чше горя́чей ва́нны; **~ much** ма́ло; **what's wrong? ~ much!** в чём де́ло? Да ни в чём!; что случи́лось? Ничего́ осо́бенного!; **there's ~ wrong with that** ничего́ в э́том плохо́го нет; **bring to ~** св|оди́ть, -ести́ на нет; **our efforts came to ~** из на́ших уси́лий ничего́ не вы́шло; **that music does ~ for me** э́та му́зыка меня́ не тро́гает; **he did ~ to help** он ниче́м не помо́г; **you knew, and did ~ about it** вы зна́ли и ничего́ не сде́лали; **he did ~ but look at her** он то́лько и де́лал, что смотре́л на неё; **you do ~ but complain** вы то́лько и зна́ете, что жа́ловаться; **I feel like ~ (on earth)** я чу́вствую себя́ (пре)отврати́тельно; **I have ~ to do** мне не́чего де́лать; **it has ~ to do with me** э́то меня́ не каса́ется; я здесь ни при чём; э́то от меня́ не зави́сит; **they had ~ to eat** у них не́ было никако́й еды́; **I have ~ against him** я ничего́ про́тив него́ не име́ю; **I have ~ but praise for him** я не могу́ им нахвали́ться; **he has ~ in him** он соверше́нная пусты́шка; **I had ~ to do with him** я с ним ника́к не́ был свя́зан (*or* не име́л никаки́х дел); **he had ~ on** (*was naked*) он был нагишо́м (*or* соверше́нно го́лый); **Miss England has ~ on** (*coll., is inferior to*) **her** Мисс А́нглия ей в подмётки не годи́тся; **the police have ~ on me** (*to my discredit*) у поли́ции ко мне не мо́жет быть никаки́х прете́нзий; **our investigations led to ~** на́ши иссле́дования ни к чему́ не привели́; **I like ~ better than ...** я бо́льше всего́ люблю́...; **he looks like ~ on earth** он вы́глядит соверше́нным пу́галом; **I could make ~ of his statement** я ничего́ не по́нял в его́ заявле́нии; **he made ~ of his illness** он не придава́л значе́ния свое́й боле́зни; **she made ~ of the job** (*was ineffective*) она́ не спра́вилась с де́лом; **~ of the kind** ничего́ подо́бного; **mathematics mean ~ to me** я ничего́ не понима́ю в матема́тике; **does it mean ~ to you that I am unhappy?** а то, что я несча́стен — для вас ничто́?; **to say ~ of the expense** не говоря́ о расхо́дах; **he started from ~** он на́чал с нуля́; **he will stop at ~** он ни пе́ред чем не остано́вится; **he thinks ~ of walking 20 miles** он споко́йно мо́жет пройти́ два́дцать миль пешко́м; **when it first happened I thought ~ of it** когда́ э́то случи́лось в пе́рвый раз, я ниско́лько не́ был взволно́ван; **think ~ of it!** (*replying to thanks etc.*) э́то пустяки́!; ничего́!; **for ~** (*without cause*) ни за́ что, ни про́ что; (*to no purpose*) зря, напра́сно, да́ром; (*free of charge*) (за)да́ром, беспла́тно; **he was not his father's son for ~** неда́ром он был сы́ном своего́ отца́; **thank you for ~!** благодари́м поко́рно!; **she wants for ~** она́ ни в чём не нужда́ется.

adv.: **she is ~ like her sister** она́ совсе́м не похо́жа на сестру́; **this exam is ~ like as hard as the last** э́тот экза́мен гора́здо/куда́ ле́гче предыду́щего; **it is ~ short of scandalous** э́то настоя́щее/су́щее/про́сто безобра́зие.

nothingness [ˈnʌθɪŋnɪs] *n.* (*non-existence*) небытие́; (*insignificance*) ничто́жество.

notice [ˈnəʊtɪs] *n.* **1.** (*intimation*) предупрежде́ние; **give ~ of sth. to s.o.** предупре|жда́ть, -ди́ть кого́-н. о чём-н.; **have ~ of sth.** быть предупреждённым о чём-н.; **~ is hereby given** настоя́щим сообща́ется. **2.** (*time-limit*): **he gave me a week's ~** (*of dismissal*) он предупреди́л меня́ об увольне́нии за неде́лю; **I have to give my employer a month's ~** (*of resignation*) я до́лжен предупреди́ть хозя́ина за ме́сяц (об ухо́де с рабо́ты); **the employees were all given ~** всем слу́жащим объяви́ли об увольне́нии; **the landlord gave the tenant ~ to quit** домовладе́лец предупреди́л съёмщика о расторже́нии контра́кта; **he gave me due/ample ~** он предупреди́л меня́ своевре́менно/заблаговре́менно; **at short ~** в после́днюю мину́ту; в сро́чном поря́дке; не предупреди́в заблаговре́менно; **at a moment's ~** то́тчас, незамедли́тельно; **till further ~** впредь до дальне́йшего/осо́бого уведомле́ния/распоряже́ния; **deposit at short ~** краткосро́чный вклад. **3.** (*written or printed announcement*) объявле́ние, извеще́ние; **obituary ~** (*reporting death*) объявле́ние о сме́рти; (*biographical*) некроло́г; **~s are posted up on the board** объявле́ния вы́вешены на доске́. **4.** (*attention*) внима́ние; **it has come to my ~ that ...** мне ста́ло изве́стно, что...; до меня́ дошли́ све́дения о том, что...; **may I bring to your ~ the fact that ...?** позво́льте обрати́ть ва́ше внима́ние на тот факт, что...; **he took no ~ of me** он не обраща́л на меня́ внима́ния; **he sat up and took ~** он навостри́л у́ши; **take ~ that this is my lowest price** предупрежда́ю, что э́то моя́ кра́йняя цена́; **he considers the matter beneath his ~** он счита́ет э́то де́ло недосто́йным его́ внима́ния. **5.** (*critique*) реце́нзия, о́тзыв; **the play got good ~s** газе́ты да́ли положи́тельные о́тзывы о пье́се.

v.t. **1.** (*observe*) зам|еча́ть, -е́тить; **he didn't even ~ me** он меня́ да́же не заме́тил; **I couldn't help but ~ what she was wearing** я нево́льно обрати́л внима́ние на её наря́д; **I ~d fear in his voice** я почу́вствовал страх в его́ го́лосе; **he ~s things** он наблюда́тельный челове́к; он всё замеча́ет. **2.** (*write account or critique of*) писа́ть, на- отчёт о+*p.*; рецензи́ровать, про-.

cpd. **~-board** *n.* доска́ объявле́ний.

noticeable [ˈnəʊtɪsəb(ə)l] *adj.* заме́тный.

notifiable [ˈnəʊtɪˌfaɪəb(ə)l] *adj.* (*of disease etc.*) подлежа́щий регистра́ции.

notification [ˌnəʊtɪfɪˈkeɪʃ(ə)n] *n.* (*announcement*) объявле́ние, извеще́ние, предупрежде́ние; (*official registration*) регистра́ция.

notif|y [ˈnəʊtɪˌfaɪ] *v.t.* **1.** (*give notice of, announce*) объяв|ля́ть, -и́ть о+*p.*; **he ~ied the loss of his wallet to the police** он заяви́л в поли́цию о пропа́же бума́жника; (*register*) регистри́ровать (*impf., pf.*); **all births must be ~ied** все рожде́ния подлежа́т регистра́ции. **2.** (*inform*) изве|ща́ть, -сти́ть; сообщ|а́ть, -и́ть +*d.*; **I was ~ied of your arrival** меня́ извести́ли о ва́шем (предстоя́щем) прие́зде; **he ~ied me of his address** он сообщи́л мне свой а́дрес.

notion [ˈnəʊʃ(ə)n] *n.* **1.** (*idea, conception*) поня́тие, представле́ние; (*opinion*) мне́ние, взгляд; **I haven't the slightest ~** не име́ю ни мале́йшего поня́тия; **I had no ~ of leaving my country** я и в мы́слях не держа́л покида́ть ро́дину; **the ~ of my resigning is absurd** предположе́ние, что я пойду́ в отста́вку, абсу́рдно; **he got the ~ of selling the house** ему́ пришло́/взбрело́ в го́лову прода́ть дом; **his head is full of stupid ~s** голова́ его́ наби́та дура́цкими иде́ями; **such is the common ~** таково́ общепри́нятое мне́ние. **2.** (*pl., US, small wares*) галантере́я.

notional [ˈnəʊʃən(ə)l] *adj.* (*ostensible, imaginary*) вообража́емый, мни́мый.

notoriety [ˌnəʊtəˈraɪətɪ] *n.* дурна́я сла́ва; **his arrest won him a brief ~** его́ аре́ст со́здал/принёс ему́ на вре́мя печа́льную изве́стность.

notorious [nəʊˈtɔːrɪəs] *adj.* (*well-known*) (обще)изве́стный; **a ~ criminal** изве́стный престу́пник; (*pej.*) пресловýтый; печа́льно изве́стный.

notwithstanding [ˌnɒtwɪθˈstændɪŋ, -wɪðˈstændɪŋ] *adv.* всё-таки.

prep. несмотря́ на+*a.*

conj.: **~ that ...** несмотря́ на то, что...

nougat [ˈnuːgɑː] *n.* нуга́.

nought [nɔːt] *n.* **1.** (*nothing*) = **naught. 2.** (*zero*) нуль (*m.*); **6 from 6 leaves ~** шесть ми́нус шесть равня́ется нулю́. **3.** (*figure 0*) ноль (*m.*); **add a ~** приба́вить (*pf.*) ноль; **~ point one (0.1)** ноль це́лых и одна́ деся́тая.

noun [naʊn] *n.* (и́мя) существи́тельное; **~ declension** склоне́ние существи́тельных.

nourish [ˈnʌrɪʃ] *v.t.* (*lit., fig.*) пита́ть (*impf.*); **~ing food** пита́тельная еда́; **he was ~ed on radical ideas** радика́льные иде́и ему́ привива́ли с де́тства.

nourishment [ˈnʌrɪʃmənt] *n.* пита́ние; **he is able to take ~ again** он сно́ва мо́жет принима́ть пи́щу.

nous [naʊs] *n.* (*common sense*) здра́вый смысл; (*coll.*) смётка.

nouveau riche [ˌnuːvəʊ ˈriːʃ] *n.* нувори́ш.

nova ['nəʊvə] *n.* но́вая звезда́.
Nova Scotia ['nəʊvə 'skəʊʃə] *n.* Но́вая Шотла́ндия.
novel ['nɒv(ə)l] *n.* рома́н.
adj. (*new*) но́вый; (*unusual*) необы́чный.
novelette [ˌnɒvə'let] *n.* (*pej.*) дешёвый рома́н.
novelist ['nɒvəlɪst] *n.* писа́тель (*fem.* -ница); романи́ст (*fem.* -ка).
novella [nə'velə] *n.* по́весть, нове́лла.
novelt|y ['nɒvəltɪ] *n.* (*newness*) новизна́; (*new thg.*) нови́нка; но́вшество; **it was a ~y for him to travel by plane** бы́ло ему́ в нови́нку путеше́стовать самолётом; **the shops were full of Christmas ~ies** магази́ны ломи́лись от но́вых рожде́ственских това́ров.
November [nə'vembə(r)] *n.* ноя́брь (*m.*); (*attr.*) ноя́брьский; **on ~ the fifth** пя́того ноября́.
novice ['nɒvɪs] *n.* **1.** (*relig.*) по́слушни|к (*fem.* -ца). **2.** (*beginner*) нович́ок.
novi|ciate, -tiate [nə'vɪʃɪət] *n.* по́слушничество; (*fig., probation*) иску́с, испыта́ние.
now [naʊ] *adv.* **1.** (*at the present time*) тепе́рь, сейча́с, ны́н(ч)е; в настоя́щее вре́мя; (*opp. previously*): **I'm married ~** я уже́ жена́т; **(it's) ~ or never** тепе́рь и́ли никогда́; **~ and again** вре́мя от вре́мени; **(every) ~ and then** поро́й; **~ he's cheerful, ~ he's sad** он то ве́сел, то гру́стен; **~ he says one thing, ~ another** он говори́т то одно́, то друго́е; (*with preps.*): **before ~** (*hitherto*) до сих пор; (*in the past*) в про́шлом; **by ~** к э́тому вре́мени; **he should be here by ~** он до́лжен бы уже́ быть здесь; **from ~ on** впредь; отны́не; **till (***or* **up to) ~** до сих пор. **2.** (*this time*): **~ you've broken it!** ну, вот вы и слома́ли его́/её!; **~ you're talking!** (*coll.*) э́то друго́е де́ло. **3.** (*at once; at this moment*) сейча́с; **I must go ~** мне пора́ (уходи́ть); **he was here just ~** он то́лько что был здесь; **only ~** то́лько тепе́рь. **4.** (*in historic narrative*) тепе́рь; тогда́; в тот моме́нт; в то вре́мя; (*by then*) к тому́ вре́мени; (*next*) по́сле э́того. **5.** (*introducing new factor or aspect; summing up*) а; так вот; и вот; **~ it turned out that** и вот оказа́лось, что; **~ Barabbas was a robber** э́тот Вара́вва был разбо́йник; **~ there lived a blacksmith in the village** так вот, а в селе́ жил кузне́ц. **6.** (*emphatic*) ну, так, ита́к; **~ you just listen to me** нет, вы послу́шайте, что я вам скажу́; **~ don't get upset** вы то́лько не расстра́ивайтесь; **~ what do you mean by that?** что вы, со́бственно, хоти́те э́тим сказа́ть?; **~ what's the matter with you?** что э́то с ва́ми?; **~ then** ну́-ка; ну-ну́; послу́шайте!; **~ why didn't I think of that?** как же я об э́том не поду́мал?
conj. (*also* **~ that)** по́сле того́, как; **~ you mention it, I do remember** тепе́рь, когда́ вы упомяну́ли об э́том, я вспомина́ю; **~ that I know you better ...** тепе́рь, узна́в вас коро́че...; **~ (that) he has come** раз/поско́льку он пришёл.
nowadays ['naʊəˌdeɪz] *adv.* ны́нче; в на́ше вре́мя; в на́ши дни; в ны́нешние времена́.
nowhere ['nəʊweə(r)] *adv.* нигде́; (*motion*) никуда́; **the horse came in ~** ло́шадь безнадёжно отста́ла; **the house was ~ near the park** дом стоя́л о́чень далеко́ от па́рка; **he was ~ near 60** ему́ ещё бы́ло далеко́ до шести́десяти (лет); **£5 is ~ near enough** пяти́ фу́нтов далеко́ не доста́точно; **this conversation is getting us ~** э́тот разгово́р нас ни к чему́ не приведёт; **a bottle of vodka appeared from ~** отку́да ни возьми́сь, возни́кла буты́лка во́дки; **there's ~ to sit** не́где сесть; **he has ~ to go** ему́ не́куда идти́; **in the middle of ~** у чёрта на кули́чках.
nowise ['nəʊwaɪz] *adv.* (*arch.*) нико́им о́бразом.
nowt [naʊt] *n.* (*dial.*) ничего́.
noxious ['nɒkʃəs] *adj.* (*harmful*) вре́дный, па́губный; (*poisonous*) ядови́тый.
noxiousness ['nɒkʃəsnɪs] *n.* вре́дность.
nozzle ['nɒz(ə)l] *n.* со́пло; **jet ~** форсу́нка; **fire ~** брандспо́йт.
NSPCC (*abbr. of* ***National Society for the Prevention of Cruelty to Children***) Национа́льное о́бщество защи́ты дете́й от жесто́кого обраще́ния.
nth [enθ] *adj.* э́нный; **to the ~ degree** (*fig.*) в вы́сшей сте́пени.
nuance ['nju:ɑ̃s] *n.* отте́нок, нюа́нс.
nub [nʌb] *n.* (*fig., point, gist*) суть.
nubile ['nju:baɪl] *adj.* дости́гшая бра́ного во́зраста.
nuclear ['nju:klɪə(r)] *adj.* **1.** (*phys.*) я́дерный; **~ bomb** термоя́дерная бо́мба; **~ energy** я́дерная эне́ргия; **~ fallout** радиоакти́вные оса́дки (*m. pl.*); **~ fission** я́дерное деле́ние; **~ physics** я́дерная фи́зика; **~ reactor** а́томный реа́ктор; **~ test** испыта́ние термоя́дерного ору́жия; **~ ship** а́томное су́дно; **~ warfare** я́дерная война́; **~ weapons** я́дерное ору́жие. **2.: ~ family** ма́лая/нуклеа́рная семья́.
nucleonic [ˌnju:klɪ'ɒnɪk] *adj.* неукло́нный; **~ warfare** я́дерно-электро́нная война́.
nucleonics [ˌnju:klɪ'ɒnɪks] *n.* нуклео́ника.
nucleus ['nju:klɪəs] *n.* (*phys., fig.*) ядро́; (*biol.*) заро́дыш.
nude [nju:d] *n.* **1.** (*art*) обнажённая (фигу́ра). **2.: in the ~** нагишо́м.
adj. го́лый, обнажённый, наго́й.
nudge [nʌdʒ] *n.* толчо́к ло́ктем; **give s.o. a ~** (*lit., fig.*) подт|а́лкивать, -олкну́ть кого́-н.
v.t. подт|а́лкивать, -олкну́ть.
nudism ['nju:dɪz(ə)m] *n.* нуди́зм.
nudist ['nju:dɪst] *n.* нуди́ст.
nudity ['nju:dɪtɪ] *n.* нагота́.
nugatory ['nju:gətərɪ] *adj.* пусто́й, пустя́чный; (*inoperative*) недействи́тельный.
nugget ['nʌgɪt] *n.* саморо́док.
nuisance ['nju:s(ə)ns] *n.* (*annoyance*) доса́да; (*unpleasantness*) неприя́тность; (*inconvenience*) неудо́бство; **what a ~!** кака́я доса́да!; **that boy is a perfect ~** э́тот мальчи́шка — су́щее наказа́ние; **go away, you are a ~!** уходи́, ты мне меша́ешь!; **commit no ~** (*do not urinate*) безобра́зничать запреща́ется!; **be a ~ to s.o.** (*of pers.*) доса|жда́ть, -ди́ть кому́-н.; (*of thg.*) раздража́ть (*impf.*) кого́-н.; **make a ~ of o.s. to s.o.** надо|еда́ть, -е́сть кому́-н.; **he makes a ~ of himself** он тако́й надое́дливый; с ним возни́ не оберёшься.
null [nʌl] *adj.* **1.** (*invalid*) недействи́тельный; **become ~ and void** утра́|чивать, -тить (зако́нную) си́лу. **2.** (*insignificant, without character*) ничто́жный.
nullification [ˌnʌlɪfɪ'keɪʃ(ə)n] *n.* аннули́рование.
nullify ['nʌlɪˌfaɪ] *v.t.* (*annul*) аннули́ровать (*impf., pf.*); (*bring to nothing*) св|оди́ть, -ести́ к нулю́.
nullity ['nʌlɪtɪ] *n.* **1.** (*invalidity*) недействи́тельность; **~ decree** суде́бное реше́ние о призна́нии бра́ка недействи́тельным. **2.** (*insignificant pers.*) ничто́жество, пусто́е ме́сто.
numb [nʌm] *adj.* **1.** (*of body*) онеме́лый, онеме́вший; (*of extremities*: **~** *with cold*) окочене́лый; **go ~** онеме́ть (*pf.*). **2.** (*of mind, senses*) оцепене́вший; **go ~** оцепене́ть (*pf.*).
v.t.: **my hand was ~ed with cold** моя́ рука́ окочене́ла от хо́лода; **my senses were ~ed with terror** я оцепене́л от у́жаса.
number ['nʌmbə(r)] *n.* **1.** (*numeral*) число́, ци́фра; **odd and even ~s** чётные и нечётные чи́сла; **in round ~s** в кру́глых ци́фрах; кру́глым число́м; приме́рно; **by ~s** (*mil., in drill movements*) по подразделе́ниям. **2.** (*quantity, amount, total*) число́, коли́чество; **the average ~ in a class is 30** сре́дняя чи́сленность кла́сса — 30 челове́к/ ученико́в; **the lift will only hold a certain ~** лифт поднима́ет лишь определённое число́/коли́чество пассажи́ров; **we were 20 in ~** нас бы́ло два́дцать (челове́к); **we must keep the ~s down** на́до бы́ло ограни́чить число́ (*кого, чего*); **there were a large ~ of people there** там бы́ло мно́го наро́ду; **a ~ of professors attended the lecture** не́сколько профессоро́в слу́шали ле́кцию; **a ~ of people thought otherwise** не́которые/ мно́гие ду́мали ина́че; **a small ~ of children** небольша́я гру́ппа дете́й; **they won by force of ~s** они́ победи́ли благодаря́ чи́сленному превосхо́дству; (*company*): **among our ~ there were several students** среди́ нас бы́ло не́сколько уча́щихся; **he was (one) of our ~ at first** внача́ле он был одни́м из на́ших; **times without ~** несчётное число́ раз. **3.** (*identifying*) но́мер; **he was ~ 3 on the list** он шёл тре́тьим но́мером в спи́ске; **look after**

~ **one** (*fig.*) забо́титься (*impf.*) о со́бственной персо́не; **public enemy ~ one** враг но́мер оди́н; **he lives at ~ 5** он живёт в до́ме но́мер 5; **the gentleman in (room) ~ 204** господи́н из но́мера 204; **telephone ~** но́мер телефо́на; **what is your ~?** како́й у вас но́мер?; **you have the wrong ~** вы не туда́ звони́те/попа́ли; **a car's (registration) ~** но́мер автомоби́ля; **catalogue ~** шифр по катало́гу; **he's got your ~** (*fig., has sized you up*) он вас раскуси́л; **he drew a ~ in a raffle** он вы́тащил биле́т в лотере́е; **when your ~ comes up** (*fig.*) когда́ придёт ваш черёд (*or* ва́ша о́чередь); **his ~ is up** (*coll.*) его́ пе́сенка спе́та; (*coll., pers.*): **he's a curious ~** он любопы́тный тип; (*issue of magazine*): **the current ~** после́дний/очередно́й но́мер; **back ~** ста́рый но́мер; (*fig.*): **he's a back ~** он отста́л от жи́зни; **this model is a back ~** э́та моде́ль устаре́ла; **in penny ~s** (*fig., piecemeal*) в/че́рез час по ча́йной ло́жке; (*song or item in stage performance*) но́мер; (*coll., garment*): **she wore a fetching little ~** на ней бы́ло преми́ленькое пла́тьице. **4.** (*bibl.*): **the Book of N~s** Кни́га Чи́сел. **5.** (*gram.*) число́.

v.t. **1.** (*count*) переч|исля́ть, -и́слить; **his days are ~ed** его́ дни сочтены́. **2.** (*give ~ to*) нумерова́ть, за-/пере-; **all the seats are ~ed** все места́ нумеро́ваны; **he ~ed the men off** он сде́лал перекли́чку по номера́м. **3.** (*amount to*) насчи́тываться (*impf.*); **they ~ed sixty all told** их в о́бщей сло́жности насчи́тывалось шестьдеся́т (челове́к); **the town ~s about 50,000 inhabitants** го́род насчи́тывает о́коло пятидесяти ты́сяч жи́телей. **4.** (*include*) вклю-ч|а́ть, -и́ть; **I ~ him among my friends** я счита́ю его́ свои́м дру́гом.

v.i. (*mil., also* **~ off**) рассчи́т|ываться, -а́ться (по поря́дку номеро́в); **'by twos, ~!'** «на пе́рвый-второ́й, рассчита́йся!»

cpd. **~-plate** *n.* номерно́й знак.

numberless [ˈnʌmbəlɪs] *adj.* бесчи́сленный.

numbness [ˈnʌmnɪs] *n.* оцепене́ние.

numbskull [ˈnʌmskʌl] = **numskull**

numeracy [ˈnjuːmərəsɪ] *n.* элемента́рное зна́ние арифме́тики.

numeral [ˈnjuːmər(ə)l] *n.* **1.** ци́фра; **Arabic/Roman ~s** ара́бские/ри́мские ци́фры. **2.** (*gram.*) (и́мя) числи́тельное.

adj. цифрово́й.

numerate [ˈnjuːmərət] *adj.* облада́ющий элемента́рным зна́нием арифме́тики.

numeration [ˌnjuːməˈreɪʃ(ə)n] *n.* нумера́ция.

numerator [ˈnjuːməˌreɪtə(r)] *n.* числи́тель (*m.*).

numerical [njuːˈmerɪk(ə)l] *adj.* чи́сленный, числово́й; **~ superiority** чи́сленное превосхо́дство; **~ly superior** превосходя́щий чи́сленностью; **~ value** числово́е значе́ние.

numerous [ˈnjuːmərəs] *adj.* многочи́сленный; **a ~ company** больша́я компа́ния; **my relatives are not ~** у меня́ не так уж мно́го ро́дственников.

numinous [ˈnjuːmɪnəs] *adj.* мисти́ческий, таи́нственный.

numismatics [ˌnjuːmɪzˈmætɪks] *n.* нумизма́тика.

numismatist [ˌnjuːˈmɪzmətɪst] *n.* нумизма́т.

numskull, numbskull [ˈnʌmskʌl] *n.* тупи́ца (*c.g.*), о́лух.

nun [nʌn] *n.* мона́хиня, мона́шенка.

nuncio [ˈnʌnʃɪəʊ, -sɪəʊ] *n.* па́пский ну́нций.

nunnery [ˈnʌnərɪ] *n.* (же́нский) монасты́рь.

nuptial [ˈnʌpʃ(ə)l] *adj.* сва́дебный.

nuptials [ˈnʌpʃəlz] *n. pl.* сва́дьба.

Nuremberg [ˈnjʊərəmˌbɜːg] *n.* Ню́рнберг.

nurse [nɜːs] *n.* **1.** (*~maid*) ня́ня, ня́нька. **2.** (*wet-~*) корми́лица. **3.** (*of the sick*) ня́нечка, санита́рка, сиде́лка; (*senior ~*) медсестра́; **male ~** санита́р, (*coll.*) медбра́т. **4. put a child out to ~ with s.o.** отд|ава́ть, -а́ть ребёнка кому́-н. на воспита́ние. **5.** (*fig.*): **~ of liberty** колыбе́ль свобо́ды.

v.t. **1.** (*suckle*) корми́ть (*impf.*) (гру́дью); **nursing mother** кормя́щая мать. **2.** (*take charge of; attend to*) уха́живать (*impf.*) за+*i.* **3.** (*hold in one's arms*) держа́ть (*impf.*) на рука́х. **4.** (*fig.*): **~ hopes** леле́ять (*impf.*) наде́жду; **~ a grudge, grievance against s.o.** таи́ть (*impf.*) оби́ду про́тив кого́-н.; **~ one's resources** эконо́мить (*impf.*) сре́дства; **~** (*sit over*) **the fire** сиде́ть (*impf.*) у са́мого ками́на; **~ a young plant** выра́щивать, вы́растить расте́ние; **~ a cold** (сиде́ть (*impf.*) до́ма и) лечи́ться (*impf.*) от на́сморка; **~ one's constituency** обха́живать (*impf.*) избира́телей.

v.i. (*US, feed at the breast*) соса́ть (*impf.*) грудь.

nurs(e)ling [ˈnɜːslɪŋ] *n.* пито́мец.

nursery [ˈnɜːsərɪ] *n.* **1.** (*room*) де́тская. **2.** (*institution etc. for care of young*): **day ~** (дневны́е) я́сл|и (*pl., g.* -ей). **3.:** **~ school** де́тский сад, детса́д; **~ rhyme** де́тские стишки́ (*m. pl.*); де́тская пе́сенка; **~ slopes** (*skiing*) поло́гие спу́ски (*m. pl.*), спу́ски для начина́ющих лы́жников. **3.** (*hort.*) расса́дник, пито́мник.

cpd. **~man** *n.* (*proprietor*) владе́лец пито́мника; (*employee*) рабо́тник пито́мника.

nursing [ˈnɜːsɪŋ] *n.* (*career*) профе́ссия сре́днего медици́нского персона́ла; **take up ~** сде́латься (*pf.*) медици́нской сестро́й; учи́ться (*impf.*) на медсестру́; **~ sister** медсестра́; **~ home** (ча́стная) лече́бница, (ча́стный) санато́рий.

nursling [ˈnɜːslɪŋ] = **nurs(e)ling**

nurture [ˈnɜːtʃə(r)] *n.* (*nourishment*) пита́ние; (*training*) воспита́ние; (*care*) ухо́д.

v.t. (*nourish*) пита́ть (*impf.*); (*rear*) воспи́т|ывать, -а́ть.

nut [nʌt] *n.* **1.** оре́х; **crack ~s** раск|а́лывать, -оло́ть (*or* щёлкать, *impf.*) оре́хи; **a hard ~ to crack** (*fig.*) кре́пкий оре́шек; **he can't sing for ~s** (*coll.*) он соверше́нно не уме́ет петь; по ча́сти пе́ния он пас; **~s (to you)!** (*sl.*) к чёрту!; ещё чего́ захоте́л!; как не так! **2.** (*sl., head*) башка́; **he is off his ~** он спя́тил; **do one's ~** беси́ться, вз-. **3.** (*pl., coll., crazy*): **he is ~s** у него́ не все до́ма; **he is ~s on her** он на ней поме́шан; **he is ~s about motorcycles** он поме́шан на мотоци́клах. **4.** (*for securing bolt*) га́йка; **~s and bolts** (*fig., practical details*) конкре́тные дета́ли.

v.i.: **go ~ting** собира́ть (*impf.*) оре́хи.

cpds. **~-brown** *adj.* кашта́новый; **~-case** *n.* (*sl.*) псих; **the N~cracker** *n.* (*ballet title*) Щелку́нчик; **~crackers** *n. pl.* щипц|ы́ (*pl., g.* -о́в) для оре́хов; **~hatch** *n.* по́ползень (*m.*); **~-house** *n.* психу́шка, дурдо́м (*sl.*); **~shell** *n.* оре́ховая скорлупа́; **in a ~shell** (*fig.*) кра́тко; в двух слова́х; **he put the problem in a ~shell** он кра́тко и чётко сформули́ровал пробле́му; **~-tree** *n.* оре́х(овое де́рево); (*hazel tree*) оре́шник.

nutmeg [ˈnʌtmeg] *n.* муска́тный оре́х.

nutria [ˈnjuːtrɪə] *n.* ну́трия.

nutrient [ˈnjuːtrɪənt] *n.* пита́тельное вещество́.

nutriment [ˈnjuːtrɪmənt] *n.* пи́ща.

nutrition [njuːˈtrɪʃ(ə)n] *n.* пита́ние; (*food*) пи́ща.

nutritional [njuːˈtrɪʃən(ə)l] *adj.* пита́тельный; дие́тный.

nutritionist [njuːˈtrɪʃənɪst] *n.* дието́лог; диетвра́ч; диетсестра́.

nutritious [njuːˈtrɪʃəs] *adj.* пита́тельный.

nutritive [ˈnjuːtrɪtɪv] *adj.* пита́тельный.

nutter [ˈnʌtə(r)] *n.* (*coll.*) сумасше́дший.

nutty [ˈnʌtɪ] *adj.* **1.** (*of taste*) с при́вкусом оре́ха. **2.** (*crazy*) чо́кнутый (*coll.*).

nuzzle [ˈnʌz(ə)l] *v.t. & i.*: **~ (against, into) s.o./sth.** ты́каться, (у)ткну́ться но́сом в кого́-н./что-н.

NY [nju ˈjɔːk] *n.* (*abbr. of* **New York**) Нью-Йо́рк.

nyctalopia [ˌnɪktəˈləʊpɪə] *n.* кури́ная слепота́.

nylon [ˈnaɪlɒn] *n.* нейло́н; (*pl.,* **~** *stockings*) нейло́новые чулки́ (*m. pl.*).

nymph [nɪmf] *n.* **1.** (*myth.*) ни́мфа; **water ~** ная́да; (*Russ.*) руса́лка; **sea ~** нере́йда; **wood ~** дриа́да. **2.** (*zool.*) ни́мфа.

nymphet [ˈnɪmfet, -ˈfet] *n.* нимфе́тка.

nymphomania [ˌnɪmfəˈmeɪnɪə] *n.* нимфома́ния.

nymphomaniac [ˌnɪmfəˈmeɪnɪæk] *n.* нимфома́нка.

nystagmus [nɪˈstægməs] *n.* ниста́гм.

NZ [nju ˈziːlənd] *n.* (*abbr. of* **New Zealand**) Но́вая Зела́ндия; (*attr.*) новозела́ндский.

O

O [əʊ] *n.* (*nought*) нуль (*m.*).
int. o!; ~ **God!** Бо́же!; *see also* **Oh**

oaf [əʊf] *n.* (*awkward lout*) неуклю́жий челове́к; у́валень (*m.*); (*stupid pers.*) ду́рень (*m.*).

oafish ['əʊfɪʃ] *adj.* неуклю́жий; придуркова́тый.

oak [əʊk] *n.* (*tree*; *wood*) дуб; (*attr.*) дубо́вый.
cpds. **~-apple, gall** *nn.* черни́льный оре́шек; **~-wood** *n.* (*copse*) дубо́вая ро́ща, дубня́к, дубра́ва; (*timber*) дуб.

oaken ['əʊkən] *adj.* дубо́вый.

oakum ['əʊkəm] *n.* па́кля.

OAP (*abbr. of* **old-age pensioner**) пенсионе́р (*fem.* -ка) (по ста́рости).

oar [ɔ:(r)] *n.* **1.** весло́; **he pulls a good** ~ он хорошо́ гребёт; **strain at the ~s** налега́ть (*impf.*) на вёсла; **rest on one's ~s** (*lit.*) суши́ть (*impf.*) вёсла; (*fig.*) почи|ва́ть, -и́ть на ла́врах; **put, shove, stick one's ~ into sth** вме́шиваться (*impf.*) в чужи́е дела́; **chained to the** ~ (*fig.*) прико́ванный к тяжёлой рабо́те. **2.** (*rower*) гребе́ц; **he is a good** ~ он хоро́ший гребе́ц; он хорошо́ гребёт.
cpds. **~lock** *n.* уклю́чина; **~sman** *n.* гребе́ц; **~smanship** *n.* иску́сство гребли́; **~swoman** *n.* (же́нщина-)гребе́ц.

oared [ɔ:rd] *adj.* & *comb. form* (-)весе́льный.

oasis [əʊ'eɪsɪs] *n.* оа́зис.

oast [əʊst] *n.* печь для су́шки хме́ля.
cpd. **~house** *n.* суши́лка для хме́ля.

oat [əʊt] *n.* (*in pl.*) овёс; **feel one's ~s** (*coll.*) быть оживлённым; чу́вствовать (*impf.*) свою́ си́лу; **he is off his ~s** (*coll.*) он потеря́л аппети́т; **wild ~s** овсю́г; **sow one's wild ~s** (*fig.*) прож|ига́ть, -е́чь мо́лодость; **he has sown his wild ~s** он уже́ перебеси́лся/остепени́лся.
adj. овся́ный.
cpds. **~-cake** *n.* овся́ная лепёшка; **~meal** *n.* толокно́; овся́ная мука́.

oath [əʊθ] *n.* **1.** прися́га; **on, under** ~ под прися́гой; **~ of allegiance** прися́га на ве́рность; **take, swear an** ~ да|ва́ть, -ть кля́тву; прися|га́ть, -ну́ть; **put s.o. on, under ~; administer an ~ to s.o.** прив|оди́ть, -ести́ кого́-н. к прися́ге. **2.** (*profanity*) прокля́тие, руга́тельство.

OAU (*abbr. of* **Organization of African Unity**) ОАЕ, (Организа́ция африка́нского еди́нства).

Obadiah [,əʊbə'daɪə] *n.* (*bibl.*) А́вдий.

obbligato [,ɒblɪ'gɑ:təʊ] *n.* & *adj.* облига́то (*indecl.*).

obduracy ['ɒbdjʊrəsɪ] *n.* упря́мство; ожесточе́ние.

obdurate ['ɒbdjʊrət] *adj.* (*stubborn*) упря́мый; (*hard-headed*) ожесточённый, чёрствый; (*impertinent*, *unregenerate*) нераска́янный; закорене́лый.

OBE (*abbr. of* **Officer of the Order of the British Empire**) кавале́р о́рдена Брита́нской импе́рии 4-й сте́пени.

obedience [əʊ'bi:dɪəns] *n.* послуша́ние, поко́рность; **~ to rules** повинове́ние пра́вилам; **~ to one's parents** послуша́ние роди́телям; **in ~ to the law** согла́сно зако́ну; в соотве́тствии с зако́ном; **take a vow of ~** да|ва́ть, -ть обе́т послуша́ния; **passive ~** по́лное послуша́ние; повинове́ние.

obedient [əʊ'bi:dɪənt] *adj.* послу́шный, поко́рный; **~ to his wishes** повину́ясь его́ жела́ниям; **your ~ servant** (*arch.*) ваш поко́рный слуга́.

obeisance [əʊ'beɪs(ə)ns] *n.* (*bow*) покло́н; (*curtsey*)ревера́нс; (*fig.*, *homage*) почте́ние, уваже́ние; **do, pay ~ to** выража́ть, вы́разить почте́ние +*d.*

obelisk ['ɒbəlɪsk] *n.* обели́ск.

obelus ['ɒbələs] *n.* кре́стик, обели́ск.

obese [əʊ'bi:s] *adj.* ту́чный, по́лный.

obesity [əʊ'bi:sɪtɪ] *n.* ту́чность, полнота́; (*med.*) ожире́ние.

obey [əʊ'beɪ] *v.t.* (*comply with*): **~ the laws** подчин|я́ться, -и́ться зако́нам; (*be obedient to*): **~ one's parents** слу́шаться, по- роди́телей; (*execute*): **~ an order** выполня́ть, вы́полнить кома́нду/прика́з/приказа́ние; (*act in response to*): **~ an impulse** подда|ва́ться, -а́ться поры́ву.
v.i. повинова́ться (*impf.*, *pf.*).

obfuscate ['ɒbfʌ,skeɪt] *v.t.* (*darken*, *obscure*) затемн|я́ть, -и́ть; (*confuse*) сму|ща́ть, -ти́ть; **~ s.o.'s mind** тума́нить, за- чей-н. рассу́док.

obfuscation [,ɒbfʌs'keɪʃ(ə)n] *n.* затемне́ние, помутне́ние.

obituary [ə'bɪtjʊərɪ] *n.* некроло́г.
adj.: некрологи́ческий.

object[1] ['ɒbdʒɪkt] *n.* **1.** (*material thg.*) предме́т, вещь; **~ lesson** (*lit.*) нагля́дный уро́к; (*fig.*): **he is an ~ lesson in courtesy** он образе́ц ве́жливости; (*coll.*, *spectacle*): **what an ~ you look in that hat!** ну и ви́д(ик) у тебя́ в э́той шля́пе! **2.** (*focus of feeling*, *effort etc.*) предме́т, объе́кт; **an ~ of curiosity** предме́т любопы́тства; **a suitable ~ for study** объе́кт, подходя́щий для изуче́ния. **3.** (*purpose*, *aim*) цель; **what was your ~ in writing?** с како́й це́лью вы писа́ли?; чего́ вы хоте́ли доби́ться ва́шим писа́нием?; **I had no particular ~ in view** я никако́й определённой це́ли не пресле́довал; **I visited him with the ~ of settling my debts** я пошёл к нему́ для того́, что́бы расплати́ться с долга́ми; **his one ~ in life** цель всей его́ жи́зни. **4.** (*consideration*): **money/time is no ~** де́ньги/вре́мя не в счёт. **5.** (*philos.*) объе́кт. **6.** (*gram.*) дополне́ние; **a transitive verb takes a direct ~** перехо́дный глаго́л тре́бует прямо́го дополне́ния.
cpd. **~-finder** *n.* видоиска́тель (*m.*).

object[2] [əb'dʒekt] *v.t.* & *i.* возра|жа́ть, -зи́ть; протестова́ть (*impf.*); выдвига́ть, вы́двинуть возраже́ния (про́тив+*g.*); **I ~ to being treated like this** я не жела́ю, что́бы со мной так обраща́лись; **do you ~ to my smoking?** вас не беспоко́ит, что я курю́?; **I'll open a window if you don't ~** с ва́шего разреше́ния я откро́ю окно́.

objectify [ɒb'dʒektɪ,faɪ] *v.t.* де́лать, с- веще́ственным/предме́тным.

objection [əb'dʒekʃ(ə)n] *n.* возраже́ние, проте́ст; **raise (an) ~ to, against sth.** возра|жа́ть, -зи́ть про́тив чего́-н.; **are there any ~s?** есть возраже́ния?; **~ overruled/sustained** возраже́ние отклоня́ется/принима́ется; **I have no ~ to your going abroad** я не возража́ю (*or* я ничего́ не име́ю) про́тив ва́шей пое́здки за грани́цу.

objectionable [əb'dʒekʃənəb(ə)l] *adj.* (*open to objection*) вызыва́ющий возраже́ние; (*undesirable*; *unpleasant*) нежела́тельный; неприя́тный.

objective [əb'dʒektɪv] *n.* **1.** (*aim*) цель. **2.** (*mil.*) объе́кт, цель. **3.** (*gram.*) объе́ктный паде́ж. **4.** (*lens*) объекти́в.
adj. (*var. senses*) объекти́вный; (*mil.*): **~ point** то́чка встре́чи.

objectivism [əb'dʒektɪ,vɪz(ə)m] *n.* объективи́зм.

objectivity [,ɒbdʒek'tɪvɪtɪ] *n.* объекти́вность.

objector [əb'dʒektə(r)] *n.* возража́ющий; **conscientious ~** челове́к, отка́зывающийся от вое́нной слу́жбы по принципиа́льным соображе́ниям.

objet d'art [,ɒbʒeɪ 'dɑ:] *n.* предме́т иску́сства.

objurgation [,ɒbdʒə'geɪʃ(ə)n] *n.* упрёк, вы́говор.

oblation [əʊ'bleɪʃ(ə)n] *n.* же́ртва; поже́ртвование.

obligate ['ɒblɪ,geɪt] *v.t.* обя́з|ывать, -а́ть.

obligation [,ɒblɪ'geɪʃ(ə)n] *n.* (*promise*, *engagement*) обяза́тельство; (*duty*, *responsibility*) обя́занность; **be under an ~ to s.o.** быть обя́занным кому́-н.; быть в долгу́ пе́ред кем-н.; **fulfil, repay an ~** выполня́ть, вы́полнить обяза́тельство; уплати́ть (*pf.*) долг; отблагодари́ть (*pf.*); **meet one's ~s** покр|ыва́ть, -ы́ть свои́ обяза́тельства; **you are under no ~ to reply** вы не обя́заны отвеча́ть.

obligatory [ə'blɪgətərɪ] *adj.* обяза́тельный.

oblige [ə'blaɪdʒ] *v.t.* **1.** (*bind by promise etc.*; *require*) обя́з|ывать, -а́ть; свя́з|ывать, -а́ть (*кого*) обяза́тельством. **2.** (*compel*) вынужда́ть, вы́нудить; **we are ~d to remind**

you мы вы́нуждены напо́мнить вам; **I am ~d to say** я до́лжен (вам) сказа́ть; **if you do not leave I shall be ~d to call the police** е́сли вы не поки́нете помеще́ние, мне придётся вы́звать поли́цию. **3.** (*do favour to*) обя́з|ывать, -а́ть; **I would be ~d if you would close the door** сде́лайте одолже́ние, закро́йте, пожа́луйста, дверь; **I am much ~d to you** я вам о́чень обя́зан/благода́рен; **can you ~ me with a pen?** не мо́жете ли вы одолжи́ть мне ру́чку?

v.i.: **he ~d with a song** он любе́зно спел пе́сню.

obliging [ə'blaɪdʒɪŋ] *adj.* услу́жливый, любе́зный.

oblique [ə'bli:k] *adj.* **1.** (*slanting*) косо́й; **~ surface** накло́нная пло́скость. **2.** (*gram. and fig.*) ко́свенный. **3.** (*devious*) око́льный; (*sly*) лука́вый, кова́рный.

obliquity [ə'blɪkwɪtɪ] *n.* (*deviousness*) лука́вство, кова́рство.

obliterate [ə'blɪtəˌreɪt] *v.t.* (*lit.*, *fig.*, *erase*, *wipe out*) вычёркивать, вы́черкнуть; ст|ира́ть, -ере́ть; (*destroy*) изгла́|живать, -дить; уничт|ожа́ть, -о́жить.

obliteration [əˌblɪtə'reɪʃ(ə)n] *n.* стира́ние; вычёркивание; уничтоже́ние, изгла́живание.

oblivion [ə'blɪvɪən] *n.* забве́ние; **fall, sink into ~** быть забы́тым (*or* пре́данным забве́нию).

oblivious [ə'blɪvɪəs] *adj.* (*forgetful*) забы́вчивый; **he was ~ of the time** он (соверше́нно) забы́л о вре́мени; **he was ~ to her objections** он был глух к её возраже́ниям.

obliviousness [ə'blɪvɪəsnɪs] *n.* забы́вчивость.

oblong ['ɒblɒŋ] *n.* (*shape*) продолгова́тая фигу́ра; (*object*) продолгова́тый предме́т.

adj. продолгова́тый.

obloquy ['ɒbləkwɪ] *n.* (*defamation*) клевета́; (*reproach*) поноше́ние; **heap ~ on s.o.** (*or* **s.o. with ~**) подв|ерга́ть, -е́ргнуть кого́-н. поноше́ниям.

obnoxious [əb'nɒkʃəs] *adj.* (*offensive*) проти́вный; (*intolerable*) несно́сный.

obnoxiousness [əb'nɒkʃəsnɪs] *n.* проти́вность; несно́сность.

oboe ['əʊbəʊ] *n.* гобо́й.

oboist ['əʊbəʊɪst] *n.* гобоист (*fem.* -ка).

obscene [əb'si:n] *adj.* непристо́йный, неприли́чный.

obscenit|y [əb'senɪtɪ] *n.* непристо́йность; **he was shouting ~ies** он гро́мко выкри́кивал нецензу́рные слова́.

obscurantism [ˌɒbskjʊə'ræntɪz(ə)m] *n.* мракобе́сие, обскуранти́зм.

obscurantist [ˌɒbskjʊə'ræntɪst] *n.* мракобе́с, обскура́нт.

adj. обскуранти́стский.

obscuration [əbˌskjʊə'reɪʃ(ə)n] *n.* помраче́ние; (*astron.*) затме́ние.

obscure [əb'skjʊə(r)] *adj.* **1.** (*not easily understood or clearly expressed*) невразуми́тельный, непоня́тный; нея́сный; невня́тный; **his motives were ~** моти́вы его́ бы́ли нея́сны. **2.** (*remote*; *hidden*) уединённый; скры́тый; **an ~ village** глуха́я дереву́шка; (*inconspicuous*; *little-known*) незаме́тный; малоизве́стный; безве́стный; **an ~ poet** малоизве́стный поэ́т; **a man of ~ origins** челове́к скро́много происхожде́ния. **3.** (*dark*, *sombre*, *dim*, *dull*) тёмный, мра́чный, сму́тный, ту́склый.

v.t. (*darken*; *also fig.*, *make less noticeable or clear*) затемн|я́ть, -и́ть; (*dim the glory of*; *eclipse*) затм|ева́ть, -и́ть; (*conceal from sight*) заслон|я́ть, -и́ть; загор|а́живать, -оди́ть.

obscurity [əb'skjʊərɪtɪ] *n.* (*darkness*, *gloom*) тьма, мрак; (*vagueness*, *lack of clarity*) нея́сность; (*unintelligibility*) непоня́тность; (*being unknown or unheard of*) неизве́стность, безве́стность.

obsequies ['ɒbsɪkwɪz] *n. pl.* погребе́ние, по́хор|оны (*pl.*, *g.* -о́н).

obsequious [əb'si:kwɪəs] *adj.* подобостра́стный, раболе́пный.

obsequiousness [əb'si:kwɪəsnɪs] *n.* подобостра́стие, раболе́пие, подхали́мство.

observable [əb'zɜ:vəb(ə)l] *adj.* заме́тный, различи́мый.

observance [əb'zɜ:v(ə)ns] *n.* **1.** (*of rule*, *law*, *custom etc.*) соблюде́ние. **2.** (*rite*, *ceremony*) обря́д, пра́зднование; (*ritual*) ритуа́л.

observant [əb'zɜ:v(ə)nt] *adj.* **1.** (*attentive*) наблюда́тельный; внима́тельный. **2.**: **~ of the rules** приде́рживающийся пра́вил.

observation [ˌɒbzə'veɪʃ(ə)n] *n.* **1.** (*observing*, *surveillance*) наблюде́ние; **keep s.o. under ~** держа́ть (*impf.*) кого́-н. под наблюде́нием; **come under ~** поп|ада́ть, -а́сть под наблюде́ние; **take ~s of sth.** наблюда́ть (*impf.*) (*or* де́лать (*impf.*) наблюде́ния) над че́м-н.; **he was sent to hospital for ~** его́ положи́ли в больни́цу на обсле́дование; **~ post** наблюда́тельный пункт; **~ car** ваго́н (для тури́стов) с повы́шенной обзо́рностью. **2.** (*quality of being observant*) наблюда́тельность. **3.** (*remark*) замеча́ние, выска́зывание.

observatory [əb'zɜ:vətərɪ] *n.* обсервато́рия.

observe [əb'zɜ:v] *v.t.* **1.** (*notice*) зам|еча́ть, -е́тить; (*see*) ви́деть, у-. **2.** (*watch*) наблюда́ть (*impf.*) за+*i.*; следи́ть (*impf.*) за+*i.*; (*examine*, *study*) изуч|а́ть, -и́ть. **3.** (*keep*, *adhere to*) соблю|да́ть, -сти́; **~ silence** храни́ть (*impf.*) молча́ние. **4.** (*remark*, *comment*) зам|еча́ть, -е́тить. **5.** (*commemorate*) отм|еча́ть, -е́тить. **6.** (*celebrate*) пра́здновать, от-.

observer [əb'zɜ:və(r)] *n.* **1.** (*spectator*, *watcher*) наблюда́тель (*m.*). **2.**: **he is an ~ of old customs** он соблюда́ет ста́рые обы́чаи; он приде́рживается ста́рых обы́чаев.

obsess [əb'ses] *v.t.* завлад|ева́ть, -е́ть (*or* овлад|ева́ть, -е́ть) (чьим-н.) умо́м; (*haunt*) му́чить (*impf.*); **he was ~ed by the thought of failure** он был одержи́м мы́слью о неуда́че; **he is ~ed by money** он поме́шан на деньга́х; **he is ~ed by class prejudice** он весь во вла́сти кла́ссовых предрассу́дков.

obsession [əb'seʃ(ə)n] *n.* (*being obsessed*) одержи́мость; (*fixed idea*) навя́зчивая иде́я; **dieting became an ~ with him** он был одержи́м/поглощён мы́слью о дие́те.

obsess|ive [əb'sesɪv], **-ional** [əb'seʃənəl] *adjs.* навя́зчивый, всепоглоща́ющий.

obsidian [əb'sɪdɪən] *n.* обсидиа́н.

obsolescence [ˌɒbsə'les(ə)ns] *n.* устарева́ние; **planned, built-in ~** запланиро́ванный мора́льный изно́с, запланиро́ванная устаре́лость.

obsolescent [ˌɒbsə'les(ə)nt] *adj.* устарева́ющий; выходя́щий из употребле́ния.

obsolete ['ɒbsəˌli:t] *adj.* устаре́лый; вы́шедший из употребле́ния; **become ~** выходи́ть, вы́йти из употребле́ния; отж|ива́ть, -и́ть; отм|ира́ть, -ере́ть.

obstacle ['ɒbstək(ə)l] *n.* (*physical obstruction*) препя́тствие; **~ race** бег/ска́чки с препя́тствиями; **clear an ~** взять (*pf.*) препя́тствие; (*hindrance*) препя́тствие, поме́ха; **put, throw ~s in s.o.'s way** чини́ть (*impf.*) препя́тствия кому́-н.; **~s to world peace** препя́тствия/поме́хи на пути́ к всеобщему ми́ру.

obstetric(al) [əb'stetrɪk(əl)] *adj.* акуше́рский, родовспомога́тельный.

obstetrician [ˌɒbstə'trɪʃ(ə)n] *n.* акуше́р (*fem.* -ка).

obstetrics [əb'stetrɪks] *n.* акуше́рство.

obstinacy ['ɒbstɪnəsɪ] *n.* упря́мство; насто́йчивость.

obstinate ['ɒbstɪnət] *adj.* (*stubborn*) упря́мый; (*persistent*) насто́йчивый; (*of disease*) упо́рный, трудноизлечи́мый.

obstreperous [əb'strepərəs] *adj.* (*unruly*) бу́йный; (*noisy*) шу́мный.

obstreperousness [əb'strepərəsnɪs] *n.* бу́йность, шумли́вость.

obstruct [əb'strʌkt] *v.t.* меша́ть (*impf.*) +*d.*, препя́тствовать (*impf.*) +*d.*; **~ the road** загра|жда́ть, -ди́ть доро́гу; **~ s.o.'s movement** препя́тствовать, вос- кому́-н.; **~ progress** затрудн|я́ть, -и́ть прогре́сс; **~ the view** заслон|я́ть, -и́ть вид; **~ the light** загор|а́живать, -оди́ть свет.

obstruction [əb'strʌkʃ(ə)n] *n.* загражде́ние, поме́ха; (*hindrance*) препя́тствие; (*difficulty*) затрудне́ние; (*parl.*) обстру́кция.

obstructive [əb'strʌktɪv] *adj.* препя́тствующий; загора́живающий; обструкцио́нный.

obstructiveness [əb'strʌktɪvnɪs] *n.* обструкцио́нность.

obtain [əb'teɪn] *v.t.* **1.** (*receive*) получ|а́ть, -и́ть; **he ~ed a prize** он получи́л приз; **have you ~ed permission?** вы получи́ли разреше́ние. **2.** (*procure*) доб|ыва́ть, -ы́ть; **he ~ed the services of a secretary** он получи́л возмо́жность по́льзоваться услу́гами секретаря́; (*acquire*) приобре|та́ть, -сти́; **this book was ~ed for me by the library** библиоте́ка вы́писала э́ту кни́гу для меня́. **3.** (*attain*) дост|игáть, -и́гнуть +*g.*; **they ~ed good results** они́ дости́гли/доби́лись хоро́ших результа́тов.

v.i. (*be current, prevalent*) примен|я́ться, -и́ться; **these views no longer ~** э́ти взгля́ды уже́ устаре́ли.

obtainable [əb'teɪnəb(ə)l] *adj.* достижи́мый, досту́пный; **is this model still ~?** э́ту моде́ль мо́жно ещё получи́ть?

obtrude [əb'tru:d] *v.t.* навя́з|ывать, -а́ть; **~ o.s. on s.o.** навя́з|ываться, -а́ться кому́-н.

v.i. навя́з|ываться, -а́ться.

obtrusion [əb'tru:ʒ(ə)n] *n.* навя́зывание.

obtrusive [əb'tru:sɪv] *adj.* (*importunate*) навя́зчивый, назо́йливый; (*conspicuous*) броса́ющийся в глаза́.

obtrusiveness [əb'tru:sɪvnɪs] *n.* навя́зчивость, назо́йливость; (*prominence*) заме́тность.

obtuse [əb'tju:s] *adj.* (*lit., fig.*) тупо́й.

obtuseness [əb'tju:snɪs] *n.* ту́пость.

obverse ['ɒbvɜ:s] *n.* (*of a coin etc.*) лицева́я сторона́.

obviate ['ɒbvɪ,eɪt] *v.t.* (*evade, circumvent*) избе|га́ть, -жа́ть +*g.*; (*get rid of*) изб|авля́ться, -а́виться от+*g.*; (*remove*) устран|я́ть, -и́ть.

obvious ['ɒbvɪəs] *adj.* очеви́дный, я́сный; **for an ~ reason** по вполне́ поня́тной причи́не; **an ~ remark** трюи́зм.

obviousness ['ɒbvɪəsnɪs] *n.* очеви́дность, я́сность.

ocarina [,ɒkə'ri:nə] *n.* окари́на.

occasion [ə'keɪʒ(ə)n] *n.* **1.** слу́чай; **on many ~s** во мно́гих слу́чаях; ча́сто; **I was there on one ~** я там был одна́жды; **on ~** (*when the ~ arises*) при слу́чае; (*now and then*) вре́мя от вре́мени, иногда́; **on the ~ of his marriage** по слу́чаю его́ бра́ка; **today is a special ~** сего́дня осо́бый день; **he was dressed for the ~** он был соотве́тственно оде́т; **profit by the ~** воспо́льзоваться (*pf.*) слу́чаем; **choose one's ~** вы́брать (*pf.*) подходя́щий моме́нт; **rise to the ~** оказа́ться (*pf.*) на высоте́ положе́ния. **2.** (*reason, ground*) причи́на, основа́ние; **give ~ to** служи́ть поводом/основа́нием для+*g.*; **I had no ~ to meet him** у меня́ не́ было по́вода встреча́ться с ним; **there is no ~ for laughter** здесь смея́ться не́чему; (*immediate cause*): **the ~ of the strike was one man's dismissal** по́водом к забасто́вке послужи́ло увольне́ние одного́ рабо́чего.

v.t. (*cause*) причин|я́ть, -и́ть; вызыва́ть, вы́звать; **his behaviour ~ed his parents much anxiety** его́ поведе́ние доставля́ло роди́телям мно́го волне́ний; (*be reason for*) служи́ть (*impf.*) по́водом к+*d.*

occasional [ə'keɪʒən(ə)l] *adj.* случа́йный; (*infrequent*) ре́дкий; **~ table** сто́лик.

occasionally [ə'keɪʒən(ə)lɪ] *adv.* (*at times*) поро́й, иногда́, и́зредка; вре́мя от вре́мени; случа́йно.

Occident ['ɒksɪd(ə)nt] *n.* за́пад.

occidental [,ɒksɪ'dent(ə)l] *adj.* за́падный.

occipital [ɒk'sɪpɪt(ə)l] *adj.* заты́лочный.

occiput ['ɒksɪ,pʌt] *n.* заты́лок.

occlude [ə'klu:d] *v.t.* прегра|жда́ть, -ди́ть; закр|ыва́ть, -ы́ть; заку́пори|ва́ть, -ть.

occlusion [ə'klu:ʒ(ə)n] *n.* прегражде́ние, загражде́ние, закры́тие, заку́порка; (*dental*) прику́с (зубо́в).

occult[1] [ɒ'kʌlt, 'ɒkʌlt] *n.*: **the ~** окку́льтные нау́ки (*f. pl.*).

adj. (*secret*) та́йный, сокрове́нный; (*magical*) маги́ческий.

occult[2] [ɒ'kʌlt] *v.t.* (*astron.*) заслон|я́ть, -и́ть; затемн|я́ть, -и́ть.

occultation [,ɒkʌl'teɪʃ(ə)n] *n.* (*astron.*) покры́тие.

occultism [ɒ'kʌl,tɪz(ə)m] *n.* оккульти́зм.

occupancy ['ɒkjʊpənsɪ] *n.* заня́тие; (*taking, holding possession*) завладе́ние; (*holding on lease*) аре́нда, владе́ние.

occupant ['ɒkjʊpənt] *n.* **1.** (*inhabitant*) жи́тель (*fem.* -ница). **2.** (*tenant, lessee*) жиле́ц, аренда́тор, нанима́тель (*m.*), квартиросъёмщик, квартиронанима́тель (*m.*). **3.** (*one who has taken possession, conqueror*) оккупа́нт; захва́тчик. **4.: the ~s of the car** все, кто находи́лись в маши́не; е́хавшие в маши́не.

occupation [,ɒkjʊ'peɪʃ(ə)n] *n.* **1.** (*taking possession*) завладе́ние; **the house is ready for immediate ~** дом гото́в для неме́дленного вселе́ния; (*forcible ~ of building etc.*) захва́т. **2.** (*mil.*) оккупа́ция; **army of ~** оккупацио́нная а́рмия. **3.** (*holding, inhabiting as owner or tenant*) прожива́ние (в до́ме *и т.п.*); (*temporary use*) вре́менное по́льзование (*чем*); (*period of tenure*) пери́од прожива́ния. **4.** (*way of spending time*) заня́тие, время(пре)провожде́ние. **5.** (*employment*) заня́тие; род заня́тий; профе́ссия; **what is his ~?** чем он занима́ется?; кто он по профе́ссии?

occupational [,ɒkjʊ'peɪʃən(ə)l] *adj.* профессиона́льный; **~ disease** профессиона́льное заболева́ние; **~ hazard** риск, свя́занный с хара́ктером рабо́ты; профессиона́льный риск; **~ therapy** трудотерапи́я.

occupier ['ɒkjʊ,paɪə(r)] *n.* (*temporary occupant; dweller*) вре́менный владе́лец; жиле́ц; (*lessee*) аренда́тор, наё́мщик.

occup|y ['ɒkjʊ,paɪ] *v.t.* **1.** (*take over or move into property, house, country etc.; take possession of*) завладе́ть (*pl.*) +*i.*; **the building was ~ied by squatters** зда́ние бы́ло за́нято самово́льно въе́хавшими жильца́ми. **2.** (*be in possession of; hold*) занима́ть (*impf.*); (*mil.*) оккупи́ровать (*impf., pf.*); **all the rooms are ~ied** все ко́мнаты за́няты; **he ~ied the position of treasurer** он занима́л до́лжность казначе́я. **3.** (*take up*): **the bed ~ies most of the room** крова́ть занима́ет бо́льшую часть ко́мнаты; **the whole day was ~ied in shopping** весь день ушёл на хожде́ние по магази́нам; **the work ~ies my whole attention** рабо́та целико́м поглоща́ет меня́. **4.** (*employ*): **he ~ies his time with crossword puzzles** он заполня́ет всё своё вре́мя реше́нием кроссво́рдов; **my day is fully ~ied** мой день по́лностью за́нят; я за́нят весь день; **~y o.s. with sth.** занима́ться (*impf.*) чем-н.

occur [ə'kɜ:(r)] *v.i.* **1.** (*be met, found*) встр|еча́ться, -е́титься. **2.** (*take place*) случа́ться, -и́ться; прои|сходи́ть, -зойти́; **~ again** (*impf.*) повторя́ться (*impf.*). **3.** (*of thought, ideas*) при|ходи́ть, -йти́ на ум; **it ~red to me that ...** мне пришло́ в го́лову, что...

occurrence [ə'kʌrəns] *n.* (*incident, event*) происше́ствие, слу́чай; (*phenomenon*) явле́ние; **an everyday ~** обы́чное явле́ние; (*incidence*): **of frequent ~** ча́сто встреча́ющийся, распространённый.

ocean ['əʊʃ(ə)n] *n.* **1.** океа́н; (*attr.*) океа́нский; **~s and seas** (*collect.*) мирово́й океа́н. **2.** (*coll., pl., vast amount*): **~s of food** ма́сса еды́; **~s of tears** мо́ре слёз.

cpd. **~-going** *adj.* океа́нский.

Oceania [,əʊsɪ'ɑ:nɪə] *n.* Океа́ния.

oceanic [,əʊʃɪ'ænɪk, ,əʊsɪ-] *adj.* океа́нский.

oceanographer [,əʊʃənɒ'grəfə(r)] *n.* океано́граф.

oceanographic [,əʊʃənə'græfɪk] *adj.* океанографи́ческий.

oceanography [,əʊʃə'nɒgrəfɪ] *n.* океаногра́фия.

ocelot ['ɒsɪ,lɒt] *n.* оцело́т.

ochre ['əʊkə(r)] *n.* о́хра.

ochr(e)ous ['əʊkrɪəs] *adj.* охря́ный.

o'clock [ə'klɒk] *adv.*: **two ~** два часа́; **like one ~** (*vigorously, promptly*) в два счёта; как штык (*coll.*).

OCR (*comput.*) (*abbr. of* **optical character recognition**) опти́ческое распознава́ние.

octagon ['ɒktəgən] *n.* восьмиуго́льник.

octagonal [,ɒk'tægən(ə)l] *adj.* восьмиуго́льный.

octahedral [,ɒktə'hi:drəl] *adj.* восьмигра́нный.

octahedron [,ɒktə'hi:drəl, -'hedrəl] *n.* восьмигра́нник, окта́эдр.

octane ['ɒkteɪn] *n.* окта́н; **high-~** *adj.* высокоокта́новый.

octave ['ɒktɪv] *n.* (*mus.*) окта́ва; (*pros.*) окта́ва, восьмисти́шие.

octavo [ɒk'teɪvəʊ, ɒk'tɑ:vəʊ] *n.* форма́т в восьму́ю до́лю листа́.

adj.: **an ~ volume** то́мик ин-окта́во (*or* в одну́ восьму́ю листа́).

octet [ɒk'tet] *n.* окте́т.

October [ɒk'təʊbə(r)] *n.* октя́брь (*m.*); (*attr.*) октя́брьский; **the ~ Revolution** Октя́брьская револю́ция.

octogenarian [,ɒktəʊdʒɪ'neərɪən] *n.* восьмидесятиле́тний стари́к; (*fem.*) восьмидесятиле́тняя стару́ха.

adj. восьмидесятиле́тний.

octopus ['ɒktəpəs] *n.* осьмино́г, спрут.

octosyllabic [,ɒktəʊsɪ'læbɪk] *adj.* восьмисло́жный.

octosyllabics [ˌɒktəʊsɪˈlæbɪks] *n.* восьмисло́жные стихи́ (*m. pl.*).
octroi [ˈɒktrwɑː] *n.* (*duty*) вну́тренняя по́шлина; (*place of levy*) городска́я тамо́жня.
ocular [ˈɒkjʊlə(r)] *adj.* глазно́й; ~ **proof** нагля́дное доказа́тельство.
oculist [ˈɒkjʊlɪst] *n.* окули́ст.
odalisque [ˈəʊdəlɪsk] *n.* одали́ска.
odd [ɒd] *adj.* **1.** (*not even*) нечётный; ~ **numbers** нечётные чи́сла; **houses with ~ numbers** дома́ с нечётными номера́ми. **2.** (*not matching*) непа́рный; **I was wearing ~ socks** я был в ра́зных носка́х. **3.** (*not in a set*) разро́зненный. **4.** (*with some remainder or excess*) с ли́шним; **40 ~** со́рок с ли́шним (*or* с чем-то *or* (*coll.*) с га́ком); **£12 ~** двена́дцать с ли́шним фу́нтов; ~ **change** сда́ча; (*small coins*) ме́лочь. **5.** (*spare, extra*) доба́вочный; ~ **player** запасно́й игро́к; ~ **man out** (*pers. or thg. outside group*) исключе́ние; не принадлежа́щий к да́нному ря́ду. **6.** (*occasional, casual*) случа́йный; ~ **jobs** случа́йная рабо́та; **at ~ times** (*now and then*) поро́й; **he made the ~ mistake** (*coll.*) ему́ случа́лось ошиба́ться; **we picked up an ~ bargain or two** нам удало́сь сде́лать не́сколько уда́чных поку́пок; (*unoccupied*): **in an ~ moment** ме́жду де́лом. **7.** (*strange, queer, unusual*) стра́нный, необы́чный, эксцентри́чный, чудно́й; **his behaviour was very ~** он о́чень стра́нно себя́ вёл.
cpds. **~ball** *n.* (*sl.*) чуда́к, оригина́л; **~job** *n.* (*attr.*): **~-job man** разнорабо́чий; **~-looking** *adj.* стра́нного ви́да; чудно́й.
oddish [ˈɒdɪʃ] *adj.* стра́нный, чудакова́тый.
oddity [ˈɒdɪtɪ] *n.* (*quality*) стра́нность, чудакова́тость; (*pers.*) чуда́|к (*fem.* -чка); (*thg. or event*) причу́дливая вещь; стра́нное/необы́чное явле́ние.
oddly [ˈɒdlɪ] *adv.*: ~ **enough** как (э́то) ни стра́нно; предста́вьте себе́.
oddment [ˈɒdmənt] *n.* (*left-over piece*) оста́ток, обре́зок; (*misc. article*) шту́ка.
oddness [ˈɒdnɪs] *n.* стра́нность.
odds [ɒdz] *n. pl.* **1.** (*difference*) ра́зница; **it makes no ~** нева́жно, всё равно́; **what's the ~?** кака́я ра́зница? **2.** (*balance of advantage*): **the ~ are in our favour** переве́с на на́шей стороне́; **the ~ were against his winning** ша́нсы (*m. pl.*) на вы́игрыш бы́ли про́тив него́; **he won against heavy ~** он вы́играл про́тив значи́тельного превосхо́дства сил; **by long ~** намно́го, значи́тельно, реши́тельно. **3.** (*chances, likelihood*): **the ~ are that he will do so** вероя́тнее всего́, что он и́менно так посту́пит. **4.** (*equalizing allowance*): **give s.o. ~** да|ва́ть, -ть кому́-н. преиму́щество. **5.** (*betting*): **lay, give ~ of 10 to 1** ста́вить (*impf.*) де́сять про́тив одного́; **long ~** нера́вные ша́нсы (*m. pl.*); **short ~** почти́ ра́вные ша́нсы; **it is ~ on that he will win** его́ ша́нсы на вы́игрыш вы́ше, чем у проти́вника; **over the ~** (*fig., excessive*) чересчу́р. **6.** (*variance*): **be at ~ with s.o.** не ла́дить (*impf.*) с кем-н. **7.:** ~ **and ends** (*leftovers*) оста́тки (*m. pl.*); обры́вки (*m. pl.*); (*sundries*) вся́кая вся́чина; (*of material*) обре́зки (*m. pl.*).
ode [əʊd] *n.* о́да.
odious [ˈəʊdɪəs] *adj.* (*hateful*) ненави́стный; (*foul, vile*) гну́сный; (*repulsive*) отврати́тельный, проти́вный.
odiousness [ˈəʊdɪəsnɪs] *n.* гну́сность, отврати́тельность.
odium [ˈəʊdɪəm] *n.* (*hatred*) не́нависть; (*disgust*) отвраще́ние; (*reprobation*) осужде́ние, позо́р; **incur, bear ~** навл|ека́ть, -е́чь на себя́ не́нависть/отвраще́ние; **the affair brought ~ upon his family** де́ло навлекло́ позо́р на его́ семью́.
odometer [əʊˈdɒmɪtə(r)] *n.* одо́метр.
odor|iferous [ˌəʊdəˈrɪfərəs], **-ous** [ˈəʊdərəs] *adjs.* благоуха́ющий, благово́нный.
odour [ˈəʊdə(r)] *n.* (*smell*) за́пах; (*aroma*) арома́т; (*fig., savour, trace*) при́вкус; (*fig., repute, reputation*): **be in good/bad ~ with s.o.** быть в ми́лости/неми́лости у кого́-н.; ~ **of sanctity** (*fig.*) орео́л свя́тости.
odourless [ˈəʊdəlɪs] *adj.* без за́паха.
Odysseus [əˈdiːsɪəs] *n.* Одиссе́й.
Odyssey [ˈɒdɪsɪ] *n.* Одиссе́я; (*fig.*) одиссе́я, приключе́ния (*nt. pl.*).
OED (*abbr. of* ***Oxford English Dictionary***) Большо́й о́ксфордский слова́рь (англи́йского языка́).
oedema [ɪˈdiːmə] *n.* отёк.
Oedipus [ˈiːdɪpəs] *n.* Эди́п; ~ **complex** эди́пов ко́мплекс.
o'er [ˈəʊə(r)] = **over**
oersted [ˈɜːsted] *n.* э́рстед.
oesophagus [iːˈsɒfəgəs] *n.* пищево́д.
oestrogen [ˈiːstrədʒ(ə)n] *n.* эстроге́н.
oestr|us [ˈiːstrəs], **-um** [ˈiːstrəm] *nn.* те́чка.
oeuvre [ˈɜːvr] *n.* труды́ (*m. pl.*); произведе́ния (*nt. pl.*).
of [ɒv, əv] *prep., expr. by g. and/or var. preps.*: **1.** (*origin*): **he is ~ noble descent** он благоро́дного происхожде́ния; **he comes ~ a good family** он происхо́дит из хоро́шей семьи́; **there was one child ~ that marriage** от э́того бра́ка роди́лся оди́н ребёнок; **Lawrence ~ Arabia** Ло́уренс Арави́йский; **that's what comes ~ being careless** вот к чему приво́дит неосторо́жность/небре́жность; **what will become ~ us?** что с на́ми бу́дет? **2.** (*cause*): **he died ~ fright** он у́мер от испу́га (*or* со стра́ху); **he did it ~ necessity** он сде́лал э́то по необходи́мости; ~ **one's own accord** доброво́льно; по со́бственному жела́нию; **it happened ~ itself** э́то произошло́ само́ по себе́. **3.** (*authorship*): **the works ~ Shakespeare** произведе́ния Шекспи́ра. **4.** (*material*): **what is it made ~?** из чего́ э́то сде́лано?; **a house ~ cards** ка́рточный до́мик. **5.** (*composition*): **a bunch ~ keys** свя́зка ключе́й; **a family ~ 8** семья́ из восьми́ челове́к (*or* в во́семь челове́к); **a work ~ 250 pages** рабо́та в 250 страни́ц; **a loan ~ £20** заём в 20 фу́нтов; **an error ~ 10 roubles** оши́бка в/на де́сять рубле́й. **6.** (*contents*): **a bottle ~ milk** (*full*) буты́лка молока́; (*with some milk in it*) буты́лка с молоко́м. **7.** (*qualities, characteristics*): **a man ~ strong character** челове́к си́льного хара́ктера (*or* с си́льным хара́ктером); **a man ~ ability** спосо́бный челове́к. **8.** (*description*): **a case ~ smallpox** слу́чай (чёрной) о́спы; **an accusation ~ theft** обвине́ние в кра́же; **a vow ~ friendship** кля́тва в дру́жбе; **an act ~ violence** акт наси́лия; **the King ~ Denmark** да́тский коро́ль; **a man ~ 80** челове́к восьми́десяти лет; восьмидесятиле́тний стари́к. **9.** (*identity, definition*): **the name ~ George** и́мя Гео́ргий; **the city ~ Rome** (го́род) Рим; **the Port ~ London** Ло́ндонский порт; **that fool ~ a driver** э́тот глу́пый води́тель; **a letter ~ introduction** рекоменда́тельное письмо́; **a letter ~ complaint** письмо́ с жа́лобой; **your letter ~ the 14th** ва́ше письмо́ от 14-го (числа́); **the affair ~ the missing papers** де́ло о пропа́вших докуме́нтах. **10.** (*objective*): **a lover ~ music** люби́тель (*m.*) му́зыки; **love ~ study** любо́вь к заня́тиям; **the use ~ a car** по́льзование маши́ной; **a view ~ the river** вид на́ реку; **a copy ~ the letter** ко́пия (с) письма́. **11.** (*subjective*): **the love ~ a mother** любо́вь ма́тери; матери́нская любо́вь. **12.** (*possession, belonging*): **the property ~ the state** госуда́рственная со́бственность; **a thing ~ the past** де́ло про́шлого. **13.** (*partitive*): **some ~ us** не́которые/ко́е-то из нас; **5 ~ us** пя́теро из нас; **a quarter ~ an hour** че́тверть ча́са; **that he ~ all men should do it!** ме́ньше всего́ мо́жно бы́ло э́того ожида́ть от него́!; **most ~ all** осо́бенно; бо́льше всего́/всех; ~ **all the cheek!** ну и на́глость!; **here ~ all places you expect punctuality** где-где́, а здесь, каза́лось бы, мо́жно бы́ло рассчи́тывать на то́чность; **a friend ~ ours** оди́н из на́ших знако́мых; **a great friend ~ ours** большо́й наш друг; **this wine is none ~ the best** э́то вино́ не из лу́чших; **he is ~ the same opinion** он того́ же мне́ния. **14.** (*concerning*): **we talked ~ politics** мы говори́ли о поли́тике; **that is true ~ every case** э́то приложи́мо ко всем слу́чаям; **what ~ it?** что из того́?; ну и что? **15.** (*during*): ~ **an evening** ве́чером; по вечера́м; ~ **late years** в после́дние го́ды. **16.** (*separation, distance, direction*): **within 10 miles ~ London** в десяти́ ми́лях от Ло́ндона; **north ~** к се́веру от+*g.*; се́вернее +*g.* **17.** (*on the part* ~): **it was good ~ you** бы́ло о́чень ми́ло с ва́шей стороны́. **18.** (*intensive*): **the Holy ~ Holies** свята́я святы́х. **19.** (*when dependent on preceding v. or adj., see under this word*).

off [ɒf] *n.* (*start of race*): **they were waiting for the ~** они́ жда́ли сигна́ла к ста́рту.

adj. **1.** (*nearer to centre of road*): **on the ~ side** (*in Britain*) на пра́вой стороне́ доро́ги. **2.** (*improbable*): **I went on the ~ chance of finding him in** я пошёл туда́ на аво́сь — вдруг заста́ну (его́). **3.** (*spare*): **during an ~ moment** ме́жду де́лом. **4.** (*substandard*): **it was one of my ~ days** в тот день я был не в са́мой лу́чшей фо́рме. **5.** (*inactive*): **the ~ season** мёртвый сезо́н. **6.: ~ licence** пате́нт на прода́жу спиртны́х напи́тков на вы́нос.

adv. (*for phrasal vv. with* **off** *see relevant v. entries*) **1.** (*away*): **two miles ~** в двух ми́лях отту́да/отсю́да; **the elections are still two years ~** до вы́боров ещё два го́да; **~ with you!** марш отсю́да!; пойди́те прочь!; **he's ~ to France tomorrow** он за́втра уезжа́ет во Фра́нцию; **it's time I was ~; I must be ~** мне пора́ (уходи́ть); **~ we go!** пошли́!; **they're ~!** (*racing*) старту́ют!; **~ with his head!** го́лову с плеч! **2.** (*removed*): **hats ~!** (*fig.*) ша́пки доло́й; **he is going to have his beard ~** он собира́ется сбрить бо́роду. **3.** (*disconnected*; *not available*): **the light is ~** свет отключён; **the electricity was ~** электри́чество бы́ло отключено́; **are the brakes ~?** вы отпусти́ли тормоза́?; **the ice-cream is ~** моро́женое ко́нчилось; **the ~ position** (*of switch etc.*) положе́ние выключе́ния; «отключено́». **4.** (*ended*, *cancelled*): **their engagement is ~** их помо́лвка расто́ргнута; **the match is ~** матч отменён. **5.** (*not working*): **day ~** выходно́й (день); **today is my day ~** я (*or* у меня́) сего́дня выходно́й; **night ~** свобо́дный ве́чер; **he was ~ sick** он не́ был на рабо́те по боле́зни; **he was always taking time ~** он постоя́нно брал отгу́лы; **I'm ~ now till Monday** меня́ не бу́дет до понеде́льника. **6.** (*of food*: *not fresh*; *tainted*): **the fish is ~** ры́ба испо́ртилась (*or* с душко́м (*coll.*)). **7.** (*theatr.*): **noises ~** шум за сце́ной. **8.** (*coll.*, *ill-behaved*): **I thought it a bit ~ when he left me to pay the bill** по-мо́ему, бы́ло не о́чень краси́во с его́ стороны́ оста́вить меня́ распла́чиваться. **9.** (*supplied*): **they are quite well ~** они́ вполне́ обеспе́чены; **how are you ~ for money?** как у вас с деньга́ми? **10.: ~ and on** (*intermittently*) с переры́вами; вре́мя от вре́мени; от слу́чая к слу́чаю; от ра́за к ра́зу.

prep. (*from*; *away from*; *up or down from*): **the car went ~ the road** маши́на съе́хала с доро́ги; **~ the beaten track** по непрото́ренной доро́ге; **just ~ the High Street** неподалёку от гла́вной у́лицы; **~ balance** несбаланси́рованный; неусто́йчивый; **~ centre** смещённый от це́нтра; асимметри́чный; **~ work** не на рабо́те; **~ colour** (*out of sorts*) нездоро́вый; не в фо́рме; (*risqué*) риско́ванный; **he fell ~ the ladder** он упа́л с ле́стницы; **he took 50p ~ the price** он сни́зил це́ну на пятьдеся́т пенсов; он сба́вил с цены́ пятьдеся́т пе́нсов; **I picked it up ~ the floor** я по́днял э́то с по́лу; **they were eating ~ the same plate** они́ е́ли из одно́й таре́лки; **I won £5 ~ him** (*coll.*) я вы́играл у него́ пять фу́нтов; **the ship lay ~ the coast** су́дно стоя́ло неподалёку от бе́рега; **I broke the spout ~ the teapot** я отби́л но́сик у ча́йника; **he has been walking me ~ my feet** мы с ним сто́лько ходи́ли пешко́м, что я валю́сь с ног; **I was run ~ my feet** я сби́лся с ног; **~ form** не в фо́рме; **he was ~ his game** он был не в лу́чшей фо́рме; **he must be ~ his head** он, должно́ быть, спя́тил; **he got ~ the point** он сби́лся с те́мы; (*disinclined for*): **he is ~ his food** он потеря́л аппети́т; **I'm ~ smoking** мне надое́ло кури́ть; (*have given it up*) я бро́сил кури́ть.

offal ['ɒf(ə)l] *n.* **1.** (*of meat*) потроха́ (*m. pl.*); (*entrails*) требуха́. **2.** (*refuse*, *garbage*) отбро́сы (*m. pl.*). **3.** (*of grain*) о́труб|и (*pl.*, *g.* -ей).

off-beat ['ɒfbi:t] *n.* (*mus.*) неуда́рная но́та.

adj. (*fig.*) необы́чный; нешабло́нный, оригина́льный, эксцентри́чный.

off-centre [ɒf'sentə(r)] *adj.* смещённый от це́нтра.

off-colour [ɒf'kʌlə(r)] *adj.* (*risqué*) риско́ванный.

offence [ə'fens] (*US* **offense**) *n.* **1.** (*wrong-doing*) просту́пок; (*crime*) преступле́ние; **an ~ against the law** наруше́ние зако́на; **commit an ~** соверш|а́ть, -и́ть правонаруше́ние. **2.** (*affront*; *wounded feeling*; *annoyance*) оби́да; **cause, give ~ to** оскорб|ля́ть, -и́ть; **take ~ at** об|ижа́ться, -и́деться на+*a.*; **quick to take ~** оби́дчивый; **no ~ (meant)!** не в оби́ду бу́дет ска́зано! **3.** (*attack*) нападе́ние.

offend [ə'fend] *v.t.* **1.** (*give offence to*; *wound*) об|ижа́ть, -и́деть; **I hope you won't be ~ed** наде́юсь, вы не оби́дитесь; **are you ~ed with me?** вы на меня́ (не) оби́делись? **2.** (*outrage*) оскорб|ля́ть, -и́ть; **it ~s my sense of decency** э́то оскорбля́ет моё чу́вство прили́чия.

v.i. греши́ть (*impf.*); **his statement ~s against the truth** его́ заявле́ние греши́т про́тив и́стины; **~ against the law** нар|уша́ть, -у́шить зако́н; **he deleted the ~ing words** он вы́черкнул слова́, вы́звавшие возраже́ния.

offender [ə'fendə(r)] *n.* (*against law*) правонаруши́тель (*m.*); престу́пник; **first ~** соверши́вший преступле́ние впервы́е.

offense [ə'fens] = **offence**

offensive [ə'fensɪv] *n.* нападе́ние; (*mil.*) наступле́ние; **take** (*or* **go over to**) **the ~** пере|ходи́ть, -йти́ в наступле́ние; (*fig.*) зан|има́ть, -я́ть наступа́тельную пози́цию.

adj. **1.** (*causing offence*) оскорби́тельный; (*of pers.*) проти́вный. **2.** (*repulsive*) отврати́тельный. **3.** (*aggressive*) агресси́вный. **4.** (*mil.*) наступа́тельный; **~ weapon** наступа́тельное ору́жие.

offer ['ɒfə(r)] *n.* **1.** предложе́ние; **make an ~** де́лать, с- предложе́ние; **decline an ~** отклон|я́ть, -и́ть предложе́ние; **submit an ~** предст|авля́ть, -а́вить предложе́ние. **2.: on ~** в прода́же.

v.t. предл|ага́ть, -ожи́ть; **~ one's hand** (*lit.*) протя́|гивать, -ну́ть ру́ку; (*in marriage*) де́лать, с- предложе́ние; предл|ага́ть, -ожи́ть ру́ку; **he ~ed me a drink** он предложи́л мне вы́пить; **I was ~ed a lift** меня́ предложи́ли подвезти́; **the job ~s good prospects** э́то перспекти́вная рабо́та; **they are ~ing a reward** объя́влено вознагражде́ние; **may I ~ my congratulations?** позво́льте вас поздра́вить?; **~ sth. for sale** выставля́ть, вы́ставить что-н. на прода́жу; **~ an opinion** выража́ть, вы́разить (*or* выска́зывать, вы́сказать) своё мне́ние; **~ an apology** прин|оси́ть, -ести́ извине́ния; **~ one's services** предложи́ть (*pf.*) свои́ услу́ги; **he did not ~ to help** он не предложи́л помо́чь; **~ resistance** ока́з|ывать, -а́ть сопротивле́ние; **~ (up) a sacrifice** прин|оси́ть, -ести́ (*что*) в же́ртву; **~ prayers** возн|оси́ть, -ести́ моли́твы.

v.i.: **as opportunity ~s** как предста́вится (удо́бный) слу́чай; при (удо́бном) слу́чае.

offering ['ɒfərɪŋ] *n.* **1.** предложе́ние. **2.** (*of a sacrifice*) жертвоприноше́ние; (*thg. or creature offered*) подноше́ние, же́ртва. **3.** (*contribution*) поже́ртвование.

offertory ['ɒfətərɪ, -trɪ] *n.* (*collection*) церко́вные поже́ртвования (*nt. pl.*).

off-hand [ɒf'hænd, 'ɒfhænd] *adj.* (*also* **off-handed**) развя́зный, бесцеремо́нный.

adv. сра́зу, без подгото́вки.

office ['ɒfɪs] *n.* **1.** (*position of responsibility*; *service*) до́лжность, слу́жба; **honorary ~** почётная слу́жба; **the party in ~** па́ртия, находя́щаяся у вла́сти; **he held ~ for 10 years** он занима́л пост де́сять лет; **take** (*or* **enter upon**) **~** вступ|а́ть, -и́ть в до́лжность; **run for ~** (*US*) выставля́ть, вы́ставить свою́ кандидату́ру; **leave, resign one's ~** уйти́ (*pf.*) с до́лжности; **term of ~** срок полномо́чий. **2.** (*duty*) обя́занность, фу́нкция; **it is my ~ to check the accounts** в мои́ обя́занности вхо́дит проверя́ть счета́. **3.** (*premises*) конто́ра, канцеля́рия; (*private ~*, *also doctor's or dentist's*) кабине́т; **~ block** администрати́вное зда́ние; **~ equipment** оргте́хника; **~ hours** часы́ рабо́ты; рабо́чее/служе́бное вре́мя; **I must be at the ~** мне на́до быть на слу́жбе. **4.** (*department*, *agency*) бюро́ (*indecl.*); отде́л, департа́мент; управле́ние, ве́домство; **Home/Foreign O~** Министе́рство вну́тренних/иностра́нных дел; **Record O~** Госуда́рственный архи́в; **International Labour O~** Междунаро́дное бюро́ труда́; **~ expenses** расхо́ды на канцеля́рские принадле́жности; **booking ~** биле́тная ка́сса; **editorial ~** реда́кция; **publishing ~** изда́тельство; **enquiry ~** спра́вочное бюро́; **lost property ~** бюро́/стол нахо́док; **recruiting ~** призывно́й пункт; **branch ~** филиа́л, отделе́ние. **5.** (*usu.*

pl., *service*, *assistance*) услу́га; **through his good ~s** благодаря́ его́ посре́дничеству. **6.** (*rite*) обря́д; **the last ~s** погреба́льный обря́д; **O~ for the Dead** заупоко́йная слу́жба, панихи́да. **7.** (*pl.*, *subsidiary rooms*): **the house has 5 main rooms and the usual ~s** в до́ме 5 основны́х ко́мнат и разли́чные слу́жбы.

cpds. **~-boy** *n.* рассы́льный; посы́льный; **~-work** *n.* канцеля́рская рабо́та; **~-worker** *n.* (контo̓рский) слу́жащий; канцеля́рский рабо́тник.

officer ['ɒfɪsə(r)] *n.* **1.** (*in armed forces*) офице́р; (*pl.*, *collect.*) офице́рский соста́в; **commanding ~** команди́р; **~s' mess** офице́рская столо́вая; **~ of the day** дежу́рный офице́р; **first ~** (*naval*) пе́рвый помо́щник капита́на. **2.** (*official*) должностно́е лицо́, чино́вник; **the highest ~s of state** вы́сшие сано́вники госуда́рства; **medical ~ of health** санита́рный инспе́ктор; **consular ~** ко́нсульский рабо́тник; **customs ~** тамо́женный чино́вник; **scientific research ~** нау́чный сотру́дник; **~s of a club** руково́дство (*or* чле́ны правле́ния) клу́ба.

v.t. комплектова́ть (*or* укомплекто́вывать), у- офице́рским соста́вом.

official [ə'fɪʃ(ə)l] *n.* должностно́е лицо́, чино́вник, слу́жащий; **government ~s** прави́тельственные чино́вники; госуда́рственные слу́жащие.

adj. (*relating to an office*) служе́бный, должностно́й; **~ duties** служе́бные обя́занности; **~ position** служе́бное положе́ние; (*formal*): **an ~ style** форма́льный стиль; (*authoritative*) официа́льный; **~ language** официа́льная терминоло́гия; (*of a country*) госуда́рственный язы́к; **~ly I am not here** официа́льно меня́ здесь нет.

officialdom [ə'fɪʃəldəm] *n.* чино́вничество, бюрократи́ческий аппара́т.

officialese [əfɪʃə'li:z] *n.* казённый язы́к; бюрократи́ческий жарго́н.

officiate [ə'fɪʃɪ,eɪt] *v.i.*: **~ for s.o.** исполня́ть (*impf.*) обя́занности кого́-н.; **~ at a wedding** соверша́ть (*impf.*) обря́д бракосочета́ния; **~ as host** быть за хозя́ина; **~ as chairman** председа́тельствовать (*impf.*).

officious [ə'fɪʃəs] *adj.* (*over-zealous*) чрезме́рно (*or* не в ме́ру) усе́рдный/услу́жливый; (*interfering*) навя́зчивый, назо́йливый.

officiousness [ə'fɪʃəsnɪs] *n.* навя́зывание свои́х услу́г; чрезме́рное рве́ние; «администрати́вный восто́рг».

offing ['ɒfɪŋ] *n.* (*naut.*) откры́тое мо́ре; **in the ~** (*naut.*) в виду́ бе́рега; (*fig.*) в перспекти́ве.

off-key [ɒf'ki:] *adj.* (*lit.*, *fig.*) фальши́вый.

off-line [ɒf'laɪn] *adj.* (*comput.*) автоно́мный.

off-load ['ɒfləʊd, ɒf'ləʊd] *v.t.* разгру|жа́ть, -зи́ть.

off-peak ['ɒfpi:k] *adj.* непи́ковый; **~ hours** часы́ зати́шья.

offprint ['ɒfprɪnt] *n.* о́ттиск.

off-putting ['ɒfpʊtɪŋ] *adj.* (*coll.*) отта́лкивающий.

off-season ['ɒfsi:z(ə)n] *n.* межсезо́нье.

adj. несезо́нный.

offset ['ɒfset] *n.* (*compensation*) возмеще́ние; (*typ.*) офсе́т.

v.i. (*compensate for*) возме|ща́ть, -сти́ть; (*neutralize*) противостоя́ть (*impf.*) +*d.*; (*typ.*) печа́тать, на- офсе́тным спо́собом.

offshoot ['ɒfʃu:t] *n.* побе́г; (*fig.*) о́трасль; бокова́я ветвь.

offshore ['ɒfʃɔ:(r)] *adj.* (*close to shore*) прибре́жный; (*abroad*) загрaни́чный; **~ wind** берегово́й ве́тер; **~ fishery** морско́й рыболо́вный про́мысел.

off-side [ɒf'saɪd] *n.* (*football*) положе́ние вне игры́; офса́йд.

offspring ['ɒfsprɪŋ] *n.* пото́мок, о́тпрыск; (*pl.*) пото́мство; (*fig.*) плод.

off-stage [ɒf'steɪdʒ] *adj.*: **~ whisper** шёпот за кули́сами.

off-the-cuff [,ɒfðə'kʌf] *adj.* импровизи́рованный.

off-the-peg [,ɒfðə'peg] *adj.* гото́вый (*об одежде*).

off-the-record [,ɒfðə'rekɔ:d] *adj.* неофициа́льный.

off-the-shelf [,ɒfðə'ʃelf] *adj.* станда́ртный, типово́й.

off-white ['ɒfwaɪt] *adj.* серова́то-бе́лый.

often ['ɒf(ə)n, 'ɒft(ə)n] *adv.* ча́сто; **every so ~** вре́мя от вре́мени; **as ~ as not** нере́дко; **more ~ than not** бо́льшей ча́стью, в большинстве́ слу́чаев; **not ~** не ча́сто, ре́дко, ма́ло когда́.

ogee ['əʊdʒi:, -'dʒi:] *n.* си́нус; гусёк; S-обра́зная крива́я.

ogival [əʊ'dʒaɪv(ə)l] *adj.* оживáльный, стре́льчатый.

ogive ['əʊdʒaɪv, -'dʒaɪv] *n.* стре́лка сво́да; стре́льчатый свод.

ogle ['əʊg(ə)l] *v.t.* не́жно погля́д|ывать, -е́ть на+*a.*; стро́ить (*impf.*) гла́зки +*d.*

ogre ['əʊgə(r)] *n.* велика́н-людое́д.

ogress ['əʊgrɪs] *n.* велика́нша-людое́дка.

oh [əʊ] *int.* о!, ах!; (*expr. surprise*, *fright*, *pain*) ой!; **~ yes, ~ really?** (нет,) пра́вда; неуже́ли?; да?; **~ for a drink!** ах, как хо́чется пить!

ohm [əʊm] *n.* ом.

ohmmeter ['əʊm,mi:tə(r)] *n.* омме́тр.

oho [əʊ'həʊ] *int.* ого́.

oil [ɔɪl] *n.* **1.** ма́сло; **mineral/vegetable ~** минера́льное/расти́тельное ма́сло; **fixed/volatile ~s** жи́рные/эфи́рные масла́; **cod-liver ~** ры́бий жир; **engine ~** маши́нное ма́сло; **fuel ~** мазу́т; **burn the midnight ~** рабо́тать (*impf.*) по ноча́м; **pour ~ on the flames** подл|ива́ть, -и́ть ма́сла в ого́нь; **pour ~ on troubled waters** успок|а́ивать, -о́ить волне́ния/стра́сти; умиротворя́ть (*impf.*). **2.** (*petroleum*) нефть; **strike ~** обнару́жить/найти́ (*pf.*) месторожде́ние не́фти; (*fig.*, *attain success*) напа́сть (*pf.*) на жи́лу; неожи́данно разбогате́ть (*pf.*). **3.** (*painting*) ма́сляная кра́ска; **paint in ~s** писа́ть (*impf.*) ма́слом.

v.t. (*lubricate*) сма́з|ывать, -ать; **~ the wheels** (*fig.*) ула́дить де́ло; (*bribe*) да|ва́ть, -ть взя́тку; «подма́зать» (*pf.*); (*treat with ~*) пропи́т|ывать, -а́ть ма́слом; **~ed silk** прорези́ненный шёлк; **well ~ed** (*drunk*) нагрузи́вшись (*coll.*), навеселе́.

cpds. **~-bearing** *adj.* нефтено́сный; **~-cake** *n.* жмых; **~-can** *n.* маслёнка; **~cloth** *n.* клеёнка; (*linoleum*) лино́леум; **~-colour** *n.* ма́сляная кра́ска; **~field** *n.* месторожде́ние не́фти; **~-fired** *adj.*: **~-fired central heating** нефтяно́е центра́льное отопле́ние; **~-heater** *n.* парафи́новая пе́чка; **~-lamp** *n.* кероси́новая ла́мпа; **~man** *n.* нефтепромы́шленник; **~-paint** *n.* ма́сляная кра́ска; **~-painting** *n.* (*activity*) жи́вопись; (*object*) ма́сло, холст, карти́на; **she's no ~-painting** она́ далеко́ не краса́вица; **~-paper** *n.* вощáнка; **~-press** *n.* маслобо́йный пресс; **~-resistant** *adj.* маслоупо́рный; **~-rig** *n.* нефтяна́я вы́шка; **~skin** *n.* (*material*) клеёнка; (*garment*) непромока́емый костю́м; **~-slick** *n.* плёнка не́фти (*or* нефтяно́е пятно́) на воде́; **~stone** *n.* точи́льный ка́мень; **~-tank** *n.* нефтяна́я цисте́рна; **~-tanker** *n.* (*ship*) та́нкер; (*vehicle*) нефтево́з; **~-well** *n.* нефтяна́я сква́жина.

oiliness ['ɔɪlɪnɪs] *n.* масляни́стость, вя́зкость; (*fig.*) еле́йность.

oily ['ɔɪlɪ] *adj.* **1.** ма́сляный, вя́зкий; **~ cheese** масляни́стый сыр. **2.** (*fig.*, *fawning*, *unctuous*) еле́йный.

ointment ['ɔɪntmənt] *n.* мазь.

OK, okay [əʊ'keɪ] (*coll.*) *n.* одобре́ние, разреше́ние, «добро́».

adj.: **it's ~** ничего́; годи́тся; **it's ~ by me** я согла́сен; **it looks ~ to me** по-мо́ему, ничего́; **an ~ expression** прие́млемое выраже́ние.

adv.: **the meeting went off ~** собра́ние прошло́ благополу́чно.

v.t.: **he ~ed the proposal** он одо́брил э́то предложе́ние.

int. ла́дно!; хорошо́!; идёт!; слу́шаюсь.

okapi [əʊ'kɑ:pɪ] *n.* ока́пи (*m. indecl.*).

okay [əʊ'keɪ] = **OK**

okra ['əʊkrə, 'ɒkrə] *n.* о́кра.

old [əʊld] *n.* **1.: the ~** (*people*) стари́ки́ (*m. pl.*); **young and ~** (*everyone*) стар и млад. **2.: of ~** в пре́жнее вре́мя; в пре́жние времена́; **from of ~** и́сстари; **in days of ~** в старину́; **men of ~** лю́ди, жи́вшие в старину́.

adj. **1.** ста́рый, стари́нный; **~ age** ста́рость; **~ age pension** пе́нсия по ста́рости; **~ man** (*also coll.*, *husband or father*) стари́к; **~ woman** (*also coll.*, *wife*) стару́ха; **~ lady** ста́рая да́ма, стару́ха; **~ folk** старики́; **~ folk's home** дом для престаре́лых; **~ maid** ста́рая де́ва; **on the ~ side** в лета́х/года́х; **grow ~** ста́риться, со-. **2.** (*characteristic of old people*) ста́рческий; **he has an ~ face** у него́ старообра́зное лицо́; **an ~ head on young shoulders** му́дрый не по лета́м. **3.** (*expr. age in years etc.*): **how ~ is** he? сколько ему́ лет?; **he is ~ enough to know better** в его во́зрасте пора́ бы понима́ть, что к чему́; **he is ~ enough to be her father** он ей в отцы́ годи́тся; **my son is 4 years ~** моему́ сы́ну четы́ре го́да; **he could read at 4 years ~** в четы́ре го́да он уже́ чита́л; **a four-year-~** (*child*) четырёхле́тний ребёнок; (*horse*) четырёхле́тка; **this newspaper is two weeks ~** э́та газе́та двухнеде́льной да́вности. **4.** (*practised, experienced*) о́пытный; (*inveterate*) закорене́лый; **he is an ~ hand at such things** он в таки́х дела́х ма́стер (*or* соба́ку съел); **he is ~ in crime** он закорене́лый престу́пник. **5.** (*coll., expr. familiarity*): **~ man, chap, fellow** старина́ (*m.*), стари́к; **~ boy, thing** дружо́к, дружи́ще (*m.*); **the ~ man** (*employer*) стари́к, хозя́ин, шеф, «сам»; **we had a good, fine, high ~ time** мы хорошо́/здо́рово провели́ вре́мя. **6.** (*coll., whatever*): **any ~ time** когда́ уго́дно; **he dresses any ~ how** он одева́ется, как попа́ло (*or* Бог/чёрт зна́ет как). **7.** (*dating from the past; ancient; longstanding*) стари́нный, давни́шний; **an ~ family** стари́нный род; **one of the ~ school** челове́к ста́рого зака́ла; **that story is as ~ as the hills** э́тот расска́з стар как мир; **they are ~ friends** они́ стари́нные/да́вние друзья́; **the ~ guard** ста́рая гва́рдия; **the O~ World** Ста́рый Свет; **the O~ Testament** Ве́тхий заве́т; **he was paying off ~ scores** он своди́л ста́рые счёты. **8.** (*former*) бы́вший, пре́жний; **an ~ boy** (*of school*) бы́вший учени́к; выпускни́к; **~-boy network** круг бы́вших однока́шников; **the good ~ days** до́брое ста́рое вре́мя; **the ~ country** ро́дина (отцо́в); **O~ English/German** (*language*) древнеангли́йский/древненеме́цкий (язы́к); **O~ French** старофранцу́зский; **~ ways** стари́нные обы́чаи; **~ master** (*artist*) живопи́сец эпо́хи до XVIII (восемна́дцатого) ве́ка; (*painting*) произведе́ние иску́сства эпо́хи до XVIII ве́ка; **see the ~ year out** встр|еча́ть, -е́тить Но́вый год. **9.** (*worn, shabby*) поно́шенный, потрёпанный; **I was wearing my ~est clothes** я был в са́мом поно́шенном из мои́х костю́мов.

cpds. **~-clothes-man** *n.* старьёвщик; **~-established** *adj.* да́вний, давни́шний, стари́нный; **~-fashioned** *adj.* старомо́дный; (*obsolete*) устаре́лый; **~-maidish** *adj.* староде́вичий, чо́порный; **he is rather ~-maidish** в нём есть что́-то от ста́рой де́вы; **~-time** *adj.* стари́нный; **~-timer** *n.* старожи́л; **~-womanish** *adj.* стару́шечий; **~-world** *adj.* (*ancient*) стари́нный; (*belonging to former days*) старосве́тский.

olden ['əʊld(ə)n] *adj.* (*arch.*) ста́рый, бы́лой; **in ~ days, times** в бы́лые времена́.

olde-worlde ['əʊldɪ] *adj.* (*coll.*) стилизо́ванный под старину́.

oldish ['əʊldɪʃ] *adj.* старова́тый.

oleaginous [ˌəʊlɪ'ædʒɪnəs] *adj.* (*oily*) масляни́стый; (*yielding oil*) ма́сличный.

oleander [ˌəʊlɪ'ændə(r)] *n.* олеа́ндр.

oleograph ['əʊlɪəˌgrɑːf] *n.* олеогра́фия.

oleomargarine [ˌəʊlɪəʊˌmɑːdʒə'riːn, -'mɑːdʒərɪn, -ˌmɑːgə'riːn] *n.* олеомаргари́н.

O level ['əʊ lev(ə)l] *n.* (*Br.*) экза́мен (по програ́мме сре́дней шко́лы) на обы́чном у́ровне.

olfactory [ɒl'fæktərɪ] *adj.* обоня́тельный; **~ organ** о́рган обоня́ния.

oligarch ['ɒlɪˌgɑːk] *n.* олига́рх.

oligarchic(al) [ˌɒlɪ'gɑːkɪk((ə)l)] *adj.* олигархи́ческий.

oligarchy ['ɒlɪˌgɑːkɪ] *n.* олига́рхия.

olive ['ɒlɪv] *n.* **1.** (*tree*) масли́на; оли́вковое де́рево; **Mount of O~s** гора́ Елео́нская; (*fruit*) масли́на, оли́вка. **2.** (*colour*) оли́вковый цвет.

adj. оли́вковый; **hold out an ~ branch** (*fig.*) стара́ться, по- ула́дить де́ло ми́ром; **~ oil** оли́вковое ма́сло.

Olympiad [ə'lɪmpɪˌæd] *n.* олимпиа́да.

Olympian [ə'lɪmpɪən] *n.* (*godlike pers.; participant in Olympic games*) олимпи́ец.

adj. олимпи́йский.

Olympic [ə'lɪmpɪk] *adj.* олимпи́йский; **~ games, ~s** Олимпи́йские и́гры.

Olympus [ə'lɪmpəs] *n.* Оли́мп.

Oman [əʊ'mɑːn] *n.* Ома́н; **Trucial ~** (*hist.*) Ома́н Догово́рный.

ombudsman ['ɒmbʊdzmən] *n.* о́мбудсман (*чиновник, рассматривающий претензии граждан к правительственным служащим*).

omega ['əʊmɪgə] *n.* оме́га.

omelet(te) ['ɒmlɪt] *n.* омле́т; **you can't make an ~ without breaking eggs** ≃ лес ру́бят — ще́пки летя́т.

omen ['əʊmən, -men] *n.* предзнаменова́ние; (*sign*) знак.

v.t. предвеща́ть (*impf.*).

ominous ['ɒmɪnəs] *adj.* злове́щий.

omission [ə'mɪʃ(ə)n] *n.* **1.** про́пуск. **2.** упуще́ние.

omit [ə'mɪt] *v.t.* **1.** (*leave out*) пропус|ка́ть, -ти́ть. **2.** (*neglect*) упус|ка́ть, -ти́ть; **I ~ted to lock the door** я забы́л запере́ть дверь.

omnibus ['ɒmnɪbəs] *n.* **1.** автобус. **2.** (**~** *volume*) одното́мник. **3.** (*attr.*): **~ resolution** резолю́ция по ря́ду вопро́сов; **~ bill** законопрое́кт по ра́зным статья́м.

omnipotence [ɒm'nɪpət(ə)ns] *n.* всемогу́щество.

omnipotent [ɒm'nɪpət(ə)nt] *adj.* всемогу́щий.

omnipresence [ˌɒmnɪ'prez(ə)ns] *n.* вездесу́щность.

omnipresent [ˌɒmnɪ'prez(ə)nt] *adj.* вездесу́щий.

omniscience [ɒm'nɪsɪəns, -ʃɪəns] *n.* всеве́дение.

omniscient [ɒm'nɪsɪənt, -ʃɪənt] *adj.* всеве́дущий.

omnivorous [ɒm'nɪvərəs] *adj.* (*lit., fig.*) всея́дный.

on [ɒn] *adv.* (*for phrasal vv. with* **on**, *see relevant v. entries*). **1.** (*expr. continuation*): **straight ~** пря́мо; **and so ~** и так да́лее; **from now ~** (начина́я) с э́того дня; **read ~!** продолжа́йте чита́ть!; чита́йте да́льше!; **he looked at me and then walked ~** он взгляну́л на меня́ и пошёл да́льше (*or* продолжа́л свой путь); **we walked ~ and ~** мы всё шли и шли; **he went ~ (and ~) about his dog** он без конца́ говори́л о свое́й соба́ке; **what is he ~ about?** (*coll.*) о чём э́то он?; **he was ~ at me to lend him my bicycle** он (всё) пристава́л ко мне, что́бы я одолжи́л ему́ мой велосипе́д; (*expr. extension*): **further ~** да́льше; **later ~** по́зже; **a garage has been built ~ (to the house)** (к до́му) пристро́или гара́ж. **2.** (*placed, fixed, spread etc.* **~** *sth.*): **the kettle is ~** ча́йник стои́т/поста́влен; **the light-switch is ~** свет включён; **he had his glasses ~** он был в очка́х; он наде́л очки́; на нём бы́ли очки́; **your badge is ~ upside-down** у вас (*or* вы нацепи́ли) значо́к вверх нога́ми. **3.** (*arranged, available*): **what's ~ this week?** (*at theatre*) что идёт/даю́т на э́той неде́ле?; **what's ~ tonight?** (*TV*) кака́я сего́дня програ́мма?; что сего́дня пока́зывают?; **he is ~** (*performing*) **tonight** он выступа́ет сего́дня (ве́чером); **have you anything ~ next week?** у вас что́-нибудь наме́чено на бу́дущей неде́ле?; вы бу́дете за́няты на сле́дующей неде́ле?; **is the match still ~?** матч не отмени́ли/отменён?; **breakfast is ~ from 8 to 10** за́втрак подаю́т с восьми́ до десяти́ часо́в. **4.** (*turned, switched* **~**): **the radio was ~ full blast** ра́дио бы́ло включено́ на всю мощь; **the tap was left ~** кран был не вы́ключен; забы́ли вы́ключить кран; **leave the light ~!** не гаси́те свет!; **is the brake ~?** то́рмоз включён? **5.** (**~** *stage*): **you're ~ next!** сле́дующий вы́ход — ваш! **6.** (*expr. contact*): **I've been ~ to him this morning** (*by telephone*) я говори́л с ним (по телефо́ну) сего́дня у́тром; **he's ~ to a good thing** (*coll.*) ему́ повезло́; **he was ~ to it in a flash** (*coll.*) он сра́зу схвати́л (*or* вник в) суть (де́ла); **the police are ~ to him** (*coll.*) поли́ция его́ раскуси́ла. **7.: you're ~!** (*coll., I accept your offer, bet etc.*) идёт!; **it's not ~** (*coll., feasible*) не вы́йдет/пройдёт.

prep. (*for some senses see also* **upon**) **1.** (*expr. position*): **~ the table** на столе́; **Rostov-~-Don** Росто́в-на-Дону́; (*supported by*): **stand ~ one leg** стоя́ть (*impf.*) на одно́й ноге́; **he walks ~ crutches** он хо́дит на костыля́х; **the look ~ his face** выраже́ние его́ лица́; (*as means of transport*): **ride ~ a donkey** е́хать (*det.*) верхо́м на осле́; **~ horseback** верхо́м; **~ foot** пешко́м; **I came ~ the bus** я прие́хал авто́бусом; (**~** *one's pers.*): **I have no money ~ me** у меня́ нет при себе́ де́нег; **a gun was found ~ him** у него́ нашли́ ору́жие; (*over the surface of; along*): **the fly was crawling ~ the ceiling** му́ха по́лзала по потолку́; **the boat floated ~ the current** ло́дка плыла́ по тече́нию; (*expr. relative position, with* **left, right, side, hand** *etc.*): **~ all sides** со всех сторо́н; повсю́ду; **~ my left** сле́ва от меня́; **~ my**

part с моéй стороны́; ~ **the one hand ...** ~ **the other (hand)** с однóй стороны́... с другóй (стороны́); ~ **either side of the street** по óбе стóроны ýлицы; **he walked** ~ **the other side of the street** он шёл по противополóжной сторонé ýлицы; **uncle** ~ **the father's side** дя́дя со стороны́ отцá. **2.** (*expr. final position of movement or action*): **she threw her gloves** ~**(to) the floor** онá брóсила перчáтки нá пол; **he sat down** ~ **the sofa** он сел на дивáн; **they went** ~ **deck** они́ вы́шли на пáлубу; **the windows open** ~ **(to) the garden** óкна выхóдят в сад. **3.** (*expr. point of contact*): **he hit me** ~ **the head** он удáрил меня́ по головé; **I hit my head** ~ **a stone** я удáрился головóй о кáмень; **I cut my finger** ~ **the glass** я порéзал себé пáлец о стеклó; **he kissed her** ~ **the lips** он поцеловáл её в гýбы; **he knocked** ~ **the door** он постучáл в дверь; **I cut my finger** ~ **a knife** я порéзал себé пáлец ножóм; **she dried her hands** ~ **a towel** онá вы́терла рýки полотéнцем; **her dress caught** ~ **a nail** онá зацепи́лась плáтьем за гвоздь. **4.** (*of musical instrument*): **he played a tune** ~ **the fiddle** он сыгрáл мелóдию на скри́пке. **5.** (*of a medium of communication*): ~ **the radio/telephone/television** по рáдио/телефóну/телеви́зору. **6.** (*expr. membership*): **she is** ~ **the committee** онá член комитéта; **we have no one over 40** ~ **our staff** у нас в штáте нет никогó стáрше сорокá лет. **7.** (*expr. time*): ~ **that same day** в тот же день; ~ **Tuesday** во втóрник; ~ **time** вóвремя; своеврéменно; тóчно по расписáнию; ~ **the instant** тóтчас; ~ **the next day** на слéдующий день; ~ **this occasion** на э́тот раз; ~ **the 8th of May** восьмóго мáя; ~ **the morning of the 8th of May** ýтром восьмóго мáя; ~ **a winter morning** зи́мним ýтром; ~ **Tuesdays** по втóрникам; ~ **our holidays we work on a farm** во врéмя óтпуска мы рабóтаем на фéрме; ~ **the occasion of his death** по слýчаю егó смéрти. **8.** (*at the time of*; *immediately after*): ~ **his arrival** по егó приéзде; ~ **my return** когдá я вернýлся/вернýсь; **cash** ~ **delivery** оплáта по достáвке; ~ **seeing him she ran off** уви́дев егó, онá убежáла; ~ **this I spoke** тогдá я вы́сказался; ~ **his father's death** по смéрти отцá; (*during*): ~ **my way home** по дорóге домóй; ~ **his rounds** во врéмя (егó) обхóда; ~ **examination** при осмóтре. **9.** (*concerning*): **an article** ~ **Pushkin** статья́ о Пýшкине; **decisions** ~ **reparations** решéния по репарáциям; **a poem** ~ **X's death** стихотворéние на смерть X'а; ~ **that subject** на э́ту тéму, по э́той тéме, над э́той тéмой, по э́тому пóводу. **10.** (*on the strength, basis of*): **he was acquitted** ~ **my evidence** он был оправдáн на оснóве мои́х показáний; ~ **easy terms** на льгóтных услóвиях; **workers** ~ **part time** рабóчие, зáнятые непóлный рабóчий день; ~ **half-pay** с сохранéнием полови́ны оклáда. **11.** (*expr. direction of effort*): **work** ~ **a book** рабóта над кни́гой; **work** ~ **building a house** рабóта поострóйке дóма; **I spent two hours** ~ **that job** я потрáтил на э́ту рабóту два часá; **he spent £500** ~ **his daughter's wedding** он потрáтил пятьсóт фýнтов на свáдьбу дóчери. **12.** (*at the expense of*): **drinks are** ~ **me** я угощáю; **the joke was** ~ **me** шýтка обернýлась прóтив меня́; **he lives** ~ **his friends** он живёт за счёт друзéй. **13.** (*by means of*): **he lives** ~ **slender means** он живёт на скýдные срéдства; **he lives** ~ **fish** он питáется ры́бой; **the machine runs** ~ **oil** маши́на рабóтает на мáсле. **14.** (*imposed* ~): **a tax** ~ **tobacco** пóшлина на табáчные издéлия.

onanism [ˈəʊnəˌnɪz(ə)m] *n.* онани́зм.

on-board [ˈɒnbɔːd] *adj.* бортовóй.

once [wʌns] *adv.* **1.** (оди́н) раз; **he read the letter only** ~ он прочитáл письмó тóлько оди́н раз; ~ **is enough** одногó рáза (вполнé) достáточно; ~ **bitten twice shy** ≃ обжёгшись на молокé, бýдешь дуть и нá воду; пýганая ворóна кустá бои́тся; ~ **six is six** оди́ножды шесть — шесть; **it happened only that** ~ э́то случи́лось в тот еди́нственный раз; **more than** ~ не раз; ~ **a day** (оди́н) раз в день; ~ **every 6 weeks** кáждые шесть недéль; **just (for) this** ~ на э́тот раз, в ви́де исключéния; тóлько в э́тот оди́н-еди́нственный раз; хотя́ бы на э́тот раз; **for** ~ на сей раз; в ви́де исключéния; ~ **again, more** ещё раз; ~ **and again; (every)** ~ **in a while** (*occasionally*) и́зредка; врéмя от врéмени; **for** ~ **in a way, while** на э́тот раз; ~ **(and) for all** (*finally*) раз (и) навсегдá; ~ **or twice** нéсколько раз; **not** ~ ни рáзу, никогдá. **2.** (*whenever, as soon as*): ~ **he understands this** как тóлько он поймёт э́то; ~ **you hesitate you are lost** стóит заколебáться и ты пропáл. **3.** (*at one time, formerly*) нéкогда; однó врéмя; однáжды; когдá-то; как-то; ~ **upon a time there was** (давны́м-давнó) жил-был; (*on one occasion in the past*) однáжды. **4.:** **at** ~ (*immediately*) сейчáс же; срáзу же; тóтчас; немéдленно; (*simultaneously*) в то же врéмя; **don't all talk at** ~! не говори́те все срáзу/вмéсте!; **all at** ~ (*suddenly*) внезáпно/вдруг.

conj. see adv. **2.**

cpds. ~**-famous** *adj.* нéкогда прослáвленный; ~**-over** *n.* (*coll.*): **give s.o./sth. the** ~**-over** бéгло осм|áтривать, -отрéть когó/что-н.

oncology [ɒŋˈkɒlədʒɪ] *n.* онколóгия.

oncoming [ˈɒnˌkʌmɪŋ] *adj.* приближáющийся, наступáющий.

on-duty [ˈɒndjuːtɪ] *adj.* дежýрный.

one [wʌn] *n.* **1.** (*number*) оди́н; (*in counting*): ~, **2, 3** раз/оди́н, два, три; (*figure 1*) едини́ца; числó оди́н; **minus** ~ ми́нус едини́ца; **a row of** ~**s** ряд едини́ц; **they came in, by** ~**s and twos** они́ входи́ли по одинóчке и пó двое; **5** ~**s are 5** пя́тью оди́н — пять; ~ **or two** (*several*) нéсколько; (*a few*) немнóго; ~ **in 10** оди́н из десяти́; на дéсять человéк (тóлько) оди́н; **he scored** ~ **out of 10** он получи́л однó очкó из десяти́ (возмóжных); **ten to** ~ **he will forget** стáвлю дéсять прóтив одногó — он забýдет; **he's** ~ **in a thousand** таки́х, как он — оди́н на ты́сячу; **last but** ~ предпослéдний; ~ **and a half** полторá +*g*.; **go** ~ **better than s.o.** превзойти́ (*pf.*) когó-н.; **he was** ~ **too many for me** он был сильнéе меня́; я с ним не мог спрáвиться; **you're** ~ **up on me** (у вас) очкó в вáшу пóльзу; вы меня́ опереди́ли. **2.** (*in a series*): **Part O**~ часть пéрвая, I часть (*read as* пéрвая часть); **Volume O**~ том пéрвый, I том (*read as* пéрвый том); **Act I** дéйствие пéрвое; **room** ~ кóмната (нóмер) оди́н; пéрвая кóмната; пéрвый нóмер; **a no. 1** (*bus*) пéрвый нóмер; **he looks after number** ~ (*i.e. himself*) он забóтится (лишь) о самóм себé. **3.** (*hour*) час; **I'll see you at** ~ я вас уви́жу в час; **it was past** ~ шёл вторóй час; **quarter/half past** ~ чéтверть/полови́на вторóго; **at a quarter to** ~ (в) без чéтверти час; ~ **o'clock** (*a.m.*) час нóчи; (*p.m.*) час дня. **4.** (*age*): **he's only** ~ емý всегó/тóлько гóд(ик). **5.** (*expr. unity or identity*): **he is a scholar and a musician all in** ~ он и учёный и музыкáнт; **we are at** ~ **in thinking ...** мы соглáсны в том, что...; **it's all** ~ **to me** мне безразли́чно (*or* всё равнó). **6.** (*being, person, creature*): **the Evil O**~ чёрт, дья́вол, нечи́стый; **little** ~**s** дéти; **our loved** ~**s** нáши бли́зкие; **the bird feeds its young** ~**s** пти́ца кóрмит свои́х птенцóв; **he fought like** ~ **possessed** он борóлся, как одержи́мый; **he is not** ~ **to refuse** он не такóв, чтóбы отказáться; **what a** ~ **you are for making excuses!** вы мáстер находи́ть предлóги; **he is** ~ **who never complains** он не из тех, кто жáлуется; **believe** ~ **who has tried it** повéрьте óпытному человéку; ~ **who speaks German** человéк, котóрый (*or* тот, кто) говори́т по-немéцки. **7.** (*member of a group*) оди́н; ~ **of my friends** оди́н из мои́х друзéй; **he was** ~ **of the first to arrive** он пришёл одни́м из пéрвых; **many a** ~ мнóгие; ~ **of the women** ктó-то из жéнщин; **the** ~ **with the beard** тот(, котóрый) с бородóй; **which** ~ **of you did it?** кто из вас э́то сдéлал?; ~ **and all** все как оди́н; **I for** ~ **don't believe him** что касáется меня́, то я не вéрю емý; ~ **of these days** кáк-нибудь на днях; **he is not** ~ **of our customers** э́то не наш клиéнт; он не из нáших клиéнтов; он не принадлежи́т к нáшим клиéнтам; **not** ~ **of them** ни оди́н из них; никтó из них; ~ **another** друг дрýга; ~ **after the other;** ~ **by** ~ оди́н за други́м; **(the)** ~ **... the other ...** оди́н/тот... другóй...; ~ **each** по одномý; ~ **at a time** по одномý/одинóчке; по óчереди; не все рáзом; ~ **of a kind** (*unique specimen*) ýникум; (*unique*) уникáльный. **8.** (*referring to category specified or understood*): **Do you play the piano? There's** ~ **in the study** Игрáете ли вы на роя́ле? В кабинéте есть роя́ль; **which book do you want, the red or the green** ~**?** какýю кни́гу вы хоти́те, крáсную и́ли зелёную?; **'Take my pen!' — 'Thanks, I have ~'** «Возьми́те мою́ ру́чку!» — «Спаси́бо, у меня́ есть»; **other people have a mother, but I haven't ~** у други́х мать есть, а у меня́ нет; **this pencil is better than that ~** э́тот каранда́ш лу́чше того́; **this book is more interesting than the ~ I read yesterday** э́та кни́га интере́снее чем та, кото́рую я чита́л вчера́; **I gave him ~** (*blow*) **on the chin** я дал ему́ по че́люсти (*or* в зу́бы); **that's ~ in the eye for you/him** (*fig.*) получи́л!; **we had ~** (*drink*) **for the road** мы вы́пили на доро́жку; **let's have a quick ~!** пропу́стим по одно́й! (*coll.*); **he had ~ too many** он вы́пил ли́шнего.

pron.: **~ never knows** никогда́ не зна́ешь; кто его́ зна́ет?; **~ doesn't say that in Russian** по-ру́сски так не говоря́т; **~ can say anything nowadays** в на́ше вре́мя мо́жно всё говори́ть; **how can ~ do it?** как э́то сде́лать?; **cut off ~'s nose** навреди́ть (*pf.*) самому́ себе́; **~ gets used to anything** челове́к ко всему́ привыка́ет; **~'s own** свой (со́бственный).

adj. **1.** оди́н; (*sometimes untranslated, e.g.*) **price ~ rouble** цена́ рубль; (*with pluralia tantum*) одни́; **~ watch** одни́ часы́; **~ hundred and ~** сто оди́н; **not ~ man in a hundred will understand you** на со́тню ни одного́ (челове́ка) не сы́щется, кто бы вас по́нял; **I have ~ or two things to do** у меня́ есть ко́е-каки́е дела́. **2.** (*only*) еди́нственный; **the ~ way to do it** еди́нственный спо́соб э́то сде́лать; **the ~ thing I detest is ...** бо́льше всего́ я ненави́жу...; (*single*): **no ~ man can lift it** одному́ э́то ника́к не подня́ть; **with ~ accord** единоду́шно; **they spoke with ~ voice** они́ говори́ли в оди́н го́лос; **~ and undivided** еди́ный и недели́мый; (*united*): **be made ~** (*in marriage*) пожени́ться (*pf.*), сочета́ться (*impf., pf.*) бра́ком. **3.** (*the same*) тот же са́мый; **all in ~ direction** всё в том же (са́мом) направле́нии; **at ~ and the same time** в одно́ и то же вре́мя. **4.** (*particular but unspecified*): **at ~ time** когда́-то; одно́ вре́мя; не́когда; **~ evening** ка́к-то/одна́жды ве́чером; **~ day** (*in past*) одна́жды; (*in future*) когда́-нибудь; **~ fine day** в оди́н прекра́сный день. **5.** (*a certain*) не́кий; **we bought the house from ~ Jones** мы купи́ли дом у не́коего Джо́нса. **6.** (*opp. other*): **I'll go ~ way and you go the other** я пойду́ в одну́ сто́рону, а вы — в другу́ю; я пойду́ одно́й доро́гой, а вы — друго́й; **neither ~ thing nor the other** ни то́ ни сё; **(just) ~ thing after another** не одно́, так друго́е; **for ~ thing, I'm not ready** во-пе́рвых, я не гото́в.

cpds. **~-act** *adj.* одноа́ктный; **~-armed** *adj.* однору́кий; **~-armed bandit** (*sl.*) иго́рный автома́т; **~-eyed** *adj.* одногла́зый; **~-horse** *adj.*: **~-horse town** захолу́стный городи́шко; **~-legged** *adj.* одноно́гий; **~-man** *adj.* (*seating ~ man*) одноме́стный; **~-man exhibition, show** персона́льная вы́ставка; **~-man business** единоли́чное предприя́тие; **~-night** *adj.*: **~-night stand** (*theatr.*) еди́нственное представле́ние; **~-off, ~-shot** *adjs.* (*coll.*) уника́льный, еди́нственный; в одно́м экземпля́ре; ра́зовый, однора́зовый; единовре́менный; **~-piece** *adj.* це́льный, состоя́щий из одного́ куска́; **~-sided** *adj.* (*asymmetrical*) ассиметри́чный; (*prejudiced*) однобо́кий, односторо́нний, пристра́стный; **~-time** *adj.* бы́вший; было́й; *see also* **~-off**; **~-to-one** *adj.* с отноше́нием одного́ к одному́; **~-track** *adj.* (*rail*) одноколе́йный; (*fig.*): **~-track mind** у́зкий кругозо́р; **~-upmanship** *n.* уме́ние взять верх над проти́вником; **~-way** *adj.*: **~-way traffic** односторо́ннее движе́ние; **~-way street** у́лица с односторо́нним движе́нием; **~-way ticket** биле́т в одну́ сто́рону (*or* в одно́м направле́нии).

oneiromancy [əˈnaɪrəˌmænsɪ] *n.* толкова́ние снов.

oneness [ˈwʌnnɪs] *n.* еди́нство.

onerous [ˈɒnərəs, ˈəʊn-] *adj.* обремени́тельный, тя́гостный, хлопотный.

onerousness [ˈɒnərəsnɪs, ˈəʊn-] *n.* обремени́тельность, тя́гостность.

oneself [wʌnˈself] *pron.* (*refl.*) себя́, ...ся; **talk to ~** говори́ть (*impf.*) с сами́м собо́й; **sit by ~** сиде́ть (*impf.*) в стороне́/одино́честве; **for ~** самостоя́тельно; **cooking for ~ is a bore** ску́чно гото́вить для одного́/самого́ себя́ (*or* для себя́ одного́); **see for ~** убеди́ться самому́ ли́чно.

ongoing [ˈɒnˌgəʊɪŋ] *adj.* теку́щий; проходя́щий сейча́с; для́щийся.

onion [ˈʌnjən] *n.* лу́ковица; (*pl., collect.*) лук (ре́пчатый); **spring ~s** зелёный лук; (*attr.*) лу́ковый; **~ dome** ку́пол-лу́ковка; **he knows his ~s** (*sl.*) он в своём де́ле соба́ку съел.

cpd. **~-skin** *n.* лу́ковичная шелуха́.

on-line [ɒnˈlaɪn] *adj.* (*comput.*) неавтоно́мный.

onlooker [ˈɒnˌlʊkə(r)] *n.* зри́тель (*m.*); наблюда́тель (*m.*); (*witness*) свиде́тель (*m.*); **~s see most of the game** со стороны́ видне́е.

only [ˈəʊnlɪ] *adj.* еди́нственный; **one and ~** оди́н еди́нственный; **she was an ~ child** она́ была́ еди́нственным ребёнком; **~ children are usually self-centred** еди́нственные де́ти (у роди́телей) обы́чно эгоцентри́чны; **this ring is the ~ one of its kind** э́то кольцо́ — еди́нственное в своём ро́де; **she is not the ~ one** она́ не исключе́ние; **I was the ~ one there** кро́ме меня́ там никого́ не́ было; **he was the ~ one to object** он оди́н возража́л; **~ women attended the meeting** на заседа́нии бы́ли одни́ же́нщины; **~ a month ago** не да́лее как ме́сяц тому́ наза́д; **the ~ thing is, I can't afford it** но то́лько я не могу́ себе́ э́то позво́лить; де́ло лишь в том, что мне э́то не по сре́дствам; **the ~ thing for 'flu is to go to bed** про́тив гри́ппа есть лишь одно́ сре́дство — отлежа́ться (в посте́ли).

adv. то́лько; всего́; **I have ~ just arrived** я то́лько что при́был; **he was ~ just in time** он чуть (бы́ло) не опозда́л; он едва́ успе́л; **if ~ you knew** е́сли бы вы то́лько зна́ли; **I am ~ too pleased** я о́чень рад; **it is ~ too true** увы́, э́то пра́вда/так; **the engine started, ~ to stop again** мото́р завёлся, но тут же загло́х; **not ~ that!** ма́ло того́!; **the soup was ~ warm** суп был то́лько что тёплый.

conj. но; **I would go myself, ~ I'm tired** я пошёл бы сам, но я уста́л; **he's a good speaker, ~ he shouts a lot** он хоро́ший ора́тор, то́лько вот сли́шком кричи́т.

cpd. **~-begotten** *adj.* единоро́дный.

on-off [ˈɒnˈɒf] *adj.*: **~-off switch** выключа́тель (*m.*); руби́льник.

onomastic [ˌɒnəˈmæstɪk] *adj.* ономасти́ческий.

onomatopoeia [ˌɒnəˌmætəˈpiːə] *n.* звукоподража́ние.

onomatopoeic [ˌɒnəˌmætəˈpiːɪk] *adj.* звукоподража́тельный.

onrush [ˈɒnrʌʃ] *n.* на́тиск; (*attack*) ата́ка.

on-screen [ɒnˈskriːn] *adj.* (*comput.*) экра́нный; **~ graphics** экра́нная гра́фика.

onset [ˈɒnset] *n.* на́тиск, ата́ка, поры́в; (*beginning*) нача́ло, наступле́ние.

onshore [ˈɒnʃɔː(r)] *adj.*: **~ wind** морско́й ве́тер, ве́тер с мо́ря.

on-site [ˈɒnsaɪt] *adj.* на места́х/ме́сте.

onslaught [ˈɒnslɔːt] *n.* стреми́тельная/я́ростная ата́ка; реши́тельная борьба́.

onto [ˈɒntuː] = **on** *prep.* **2.**

ontological [ˌɒntəˈlɒdʒɪk(ə)l] *adj.* онтологи́ческий.

ontology [ɒnˈtɒlədʒɪ] *n.* онтоло́гия.

onus [ˈəʊnəs] *n.* бре́мя, отве́тственность; **~ of proof** бре́мя дока́зывания.

onward [ˈɒnwəd] *adj.* продвига́ющийся; **~ movement** движе́ние вперёд.

adv. (*also* **~s**) вперёд; **from now ~** впредь, отны́не; **from then ~** с тех пор; с той поры́; (*in future*) с того́ вре́мени.

onyx [ˈɒnɪks] *n.* о́никс.

oodles [ˈuːd(ə)lz] *n.* (*coll.*) ма́сса, у́йма; **~ of money** ку́ча де́нег.

oolite [ˈəʊəˌlaɪt] *n.* ооли́т.

oolitic [ˌəʊəˈlɪtɪk] *adj.* ооли́товый.

oomph [ʊmf] *n.* пика́нтность, шик.

oops! [uːps, ʊps] *int.* (*coll.*) ой!

ooze [uːz] *n.* (*slime*) ил, ти́на; (*wet mud*) ли́пкая грязь; (*exudation*) просა́чивание.

v.t. (*emit*): **the wound ~d blood** из ра́ны сочи́лась кровь; (*fig.*): **he ~d self-confidence** от него́ так и несло́ самоуве́ренностью.

v.i. (*flow slowly*) ме́дленно течь (*impf.*); (*in drops*) сочи́ться (*impf.*); (*fig.*): ~ **away** уб|ыва́ть, -ы́ть; **his strength ~d away** си́лы покида́ли его́; **the secret ~d out** та́йна постепе́нно просочи́лась.

opacity [əˈpæsɪtɪ] *n.* **1.** непрозра́чность; (*obscurity*) затенённость. **2.** (*obscurity of meaning*) нея́сность; (*of thought*) сму́тность. **3.** (*dullness of mind*) ту́пость.

opal [ˈəʊp(ə)l] *n.* опа́л.

adj. опа́ловый; ~ **glass** моло́чное/ма́товое стекло́.

opal|escent [ˌəʊpəˈles(ə)nt], **-ine** [ˈəʊpəˌlaɪn] *adjs.* опа́ловый.

opaque [əʊˈpeɪk] *adj.* непрозра́чный; (*dark, obscure*) тёмный; (*obtuse, dull-witted*) тупо́й, глу́пый.

opaqueness [əʊˈpeɪknɪs] *n.* непрозра́чность; темнота́; ту́пость, глу́пость.

op-art [ɒpˈɑːt] *n.* оп-иску́сство.

op. cit. [ɒp ˈsɪt] (*abbr. of* ***opere citato***) в цити́рованном труде́.

OPEC [ˈəʊpek] *n.* (*abbr. of* ***Organization of Petroleum-Exporting Countries***) ОПЕК, (Организа́ция стран-экспортёров не́фти).

open [ˈəʊpən] *n.* **1.** (~ *space*; ~ *air*) откры́тое простра́нство; **in the** ~ под откры́тым не́бом; на откры́том во́здухе. **2.** (*fig.*): **bring sth. into the** ~ выводи́ть, вы́вести что-н. на чи́стую во́ду; **come into the** ~ выявля́ться, вы́явиться; (*be frank*) быть открове́нным.

adj. **1.** откры́тый; **in the** ~ **air** на откры́том во́здухе; **receive, welcome with** ~ **arms** (*fig.*) встр|еча́ть, -е́тить тепло́/раду́шно (*or* с распростёртыми объя́тиями); ~ **boat** беспа́лубное су́дно; **you can read him like an** ~ **book** его́ нетру́дно/легко́ раскуси́ть; **keep one's bowels** ~ следи́ть (*impf.*) за (своевре́менным) де́йствием кише́чника; ~ **car/carriage** откры́тая маши́на/каре́та; ~ **city** откры́тый го́род; ~ **competition** откры́тое состяза́ние; откры́тый чемпиона́т; ~ **contempt** я́вное презре́ние; **in** ~ **country** в непересечённой ме́стности; среди́ поле́й и луго́в; **in** ~ **court** в откры́том суде́бном заседа́нии; ~ **day** (*at school*) день откры́тых двере́й; ~ **drain** откры́тая (водо)сто́чная труба́; **keep one's ears** ~ прислу́шиваться (*impf.*); навостри́ть (*pf.*) у́ши; **with** ~ **eyes** (*or* **one's eyes** ~) с откры́тыми глаза́ми; (*fig.*) созна́тельно; ~ **flower** распусти́вшийся цвето́к; ~ **ground** незащищённый грунт; **with an** ~ **hand** ще́дрой руко́й; ~ **hostility** откры́тая/неприкры́тая вражда́; **they keep** ~ **house** у них откры́тый/гостеприи́мный дом; ~ **letter** откры́тое письмо́; ~ **market** во́льный ры́нок; **have an** ~ **mind on sth.** не име́ть предвзя́того мне́ния по да́нному вопро́су; **with** ~ **mouth** с откры́тым ртом; ~ **prison** тюрьма́ откры́того ти́па; **an** ~ **question** откры́тый/нерешённый вопро́с; **on the** ~ **road** на большо́й доро́ге; **an** ~ **scandal** публи́чный сканда́л; **on the** ~ **sea** в откры́том мо́ре; ~ **season** охо́тничий сезо́н; ~ **secret** секре́т полишине́ля; ~ **space** незагоро́женное ме́сто; ~ **ticket** биле́т без ограниче́ния сро́ка по́льзования; ~ **warfare** откры́тая война́; ~ **winter** мя́гкая зима́; ~ **wound** откры́тая/незажи́вшая ра́на; **break** ~ (*v.t.*) вскры|ва́ть, -ть; распеча́т|ывать, -ать; взл|а́мывать, -ома́ть; **the door flew** ~ дверь распахну́лась; **he threw the window** ~ он распахну́л окно́; **we left the matter** ~ мы оста́вили вопро́с откры́тым. **2.** (*accessible, available*) досту́пный; **the road is** ~ **to traffic** доро́га откры́та для движе́ния; **the chairman threw the debate** ~ председа́тель объяви́л пре́ния откры́тыми; **the post is still** ~ ме́сто ещё не за́нято; ~ **to attack** уязви́мый; ~ **to question** спо́рный; ~ **to misinterpretation** спосо́бный вы́звать непра́вильное толкова́ние; ~ **to offer** гото́вый рассмотре́ть предложе́ние; ~ **to argument** гото́вый вы́слушать до́воды. **3.** (*generous*) ще́дрый; (*hospitable*) гостеприи́мный. **4.** (*frank*) открове́нный; **he is as** ~ **as the day** э́то откры́тая душа́. **5.** (*phon.*) откры́тый.

v.t. **1.** откр|ыва́ть, -ы́ть; (*unseal*) распеча́т|ывать, -ать; (*unwrap*) разв|ора́чивать, -ерну́ть; (*book, newspaper*) раскр|ыва́ть, -ы́ть; ра|скла́дывать, -зложи́ть; (*vein; parcel at customs etc.*) вскр|ыва́ть, -ы́ть; (*bottle*) откупо́ри|вать, -ть; ~ **the bowels** оч|ища́ть, -и́стить кише́чник; ~ **wide** (*e.g. door*) распа́х|ивать, -ну́ть; **he ~ed his mouth wide** он широко́ откры́л рот; **don't** ~ **your umbrella indoors** не раскрыва́йте зо́нтик в ко́мнате. **2.** (*fig.*): **she ~ed her heart to me** она́ откры́ла мне ду́шу; **I ~ed his eyes to the situation** я откры́л ему́ глаза́ на положе́ние дел; **he ~ed an account** он откры́л счёт; **the secretary ~ed the debate** секрета́рь откры́л пре́ния; **the enemy ~ed fire** неприя́тель откры́л ого́нь; **we ~ed negotiations** мы приступи́ли к перегово́рам; **a new business has been ~ed** осно́вано но́вое предприя́тие. **3.: a road was ~ed through the forest** че́рез лес проложи́ли доро́гу; **they are planning to** ~ **a mine** они́ собира́ются заложи́ть ша́хту; **many acres were ~ed to cultivation** (бы́ло) распа́хано мно́жествоземе́ль.

v.i. **1.** откр|ыва́ться, -ы́ться; (*unfold*, ~ *wide*) раскр|ыва́ться, -ы́ться; **the heavens ~ed** (*fig.*) дождь поли́л, как из ведра́. **2.** (*fig., begin*) нач|ина́ться, -а́ться; **the play ~s with a long speech** пье́са начина́ется дли́нным моноло́гом; **the new play ~s on Saturday** но́вая пье́са идёт с суббо́ты; в суббо́ту — премье́ра но́вой пье́сы; **when does the school** ~ **again?** когда́ возобновля́ются заня́тия в шко́ле?; **I shall** ~ **by reading the minutes** я начну́ с чте́ния протоко́ла. **3.** (*of door, room etc.*): **the study ~s into the drawing-room** кабине́т сообща́ется с гости́ной; **the windows** ~ **on to a courtyard** о́кна выхо́дят во двор.

with advs.: ~ **out** *v.i.*: **the river ~s out** река́ расширя́ется; **the roses ~ed out** ро́зы распусти́лись; (*become communicative*) раскр|ыва́ться, -ы́ться; ~ **up** *v.t.*: ~ **up!** (*command to open*) откро́йте дверь!; **he ~ed up the boot (of the car)** он откры́л/раскры́л бага́жник; (*territory*) осв|а́ивать, -о́ить; **his stories** ~ **up a new world** его́ расска́зы раскрыва́ют но́вый мир; *v.i.*: **he ~ed up about his visit** он открове́нно рассказа́л о свое́й пое́здке; **a machine-gun ~ed up** на́чал стреля́ть пулемёт.

cpds. **~-air** *adj.*: **~-air life** жизнь на откры́том во́здухе; **~-armed** *adj.* с распростёртыми объя́тиями; **an ~-armed welcome** раду́шный приём; **~cast** *adj.*: **~cast mining** откры́тая разрабо́тка; откры́тые го́рные рабо́ты; **~ended** *adj.* (*fig.*) не име́ющий зара́нее предусмо́тренных ограниче́ний; бессро́чный; **~-eyed** *adj.* с широко́ раскры́тыми глаза́ми; (*watchful*) бди́тельный; с откры́тыми глаза́ми; *adv.* созна́тельно; **~-handed** *adj.* ще́дрый; **~-heart** *adj.*: **~-heart operation** опера́ция, проводи́мая на отключённом се́рдце; **~-hearted** *adj.* с откры́той душо́й; (*sincere*) чистосерде́чный; (*generous*) великоду́шный; **~-hearth** *adj.*: **~-hearth furnace** марте́новская печь; **~-minded** *adj.* непредубеждённый; **~-mouthed** *adj.* рази́нувший рот от удивле́ния; **~-work** *n.* ажу́рная рабо́та/стро́чка; мере́жка; *adj.* ажу́рный.

opener [ˈəʊpənə(r), ˈəʊpnə(r)] *n.* (*for cans etc.*) консе́рвный нож; (*coll.*) открыва́лка (*also for bottles*).

opening [ˈəʊpənɪŋ, ˈəʊpnɪŋ] *n.* **1.** (*vbl. senses*) откры́тие, раскры́тие, вскры́тие. **2.** (*aperture*) отве́рстие; щель; прохо́д. **3.** (*football: gap in defence*) окно́. **4.** (*beginning*) нача́ло, вступле́ние; (*initial part*) вступи́тельная часть. **5.** (*job*) ме́сто, вака́нсия. **6.** (*favourable opportunity*) удо́бный слу́чай; благоприя́тная возмо́жность. **7.** (*chess*) дебю́т.

adj. (*initial*) нача́льный, пе́рвый; (*introductory*) вступи́тельный; ~ **remarks** вступи́тельные замеча́ния; ~ **night** премье́ра; (*working*): ~ **hours** рабо́чие часы́; часы́ рабо́ты.

openly [ˈəʊpənlɪ] *adv.* откры́то; (*frankly*) открове́нно; (*publicly*) публи́чно, откры́то.

openness [ˈəʊpənnɪs] *n.* (*frankness*) открове́нность; (*liberality of mind*) широта́ (кругозо́ра); непредубеждённость; восприи́мчивость.

opera [ˈɒpərə] *n.* о́пера; **at/to the** ~ в о́пере/о́перу; (*branch of art*) о́перное иску́сство.

cpds. **~-glass(es)** *n.* (театра́льный) бино́кль; **~-hat** *n.* шапокля́к, складно́й цили́ндр; **~-house** *n.* о́перный теа́тр; **~-singer** *n.* о́перный певе́ц, о́перная певи́ца.

operable [ˈɒpərəb(ə)l] *adj.* **1.** (*med.*) опера́бельный. **2.** (*workable*) де́йствующий, функциони́рующий.

operate ['ɒpəˌreɪt] *v.t.* **1.** (*control work of*) управля́ть (*impf.*) +*i.*; эксплуати́ровать (*impf.*); **he ~s a lathe** он рабо́тает на тока́рном станке́; **the company ~s three factories** э́та компа́ния управля́ет тремя́ фа́бриками; **the machine is ~d by electricity** э́та маши́на рабо́тает на электри́честве. **2.** (*bring into motion*) прив|оди́ть, -ести́ в движе́ние. **3.** (*put into effect*): **we ~ a simple system** мы применя́ем просту́ю систе́му.

v.i. **1.** (*work, act*) рабо́тать (*impf.*); де́йствовать (*impf.*); **the brakes failed to ~** тормоза́ отказа́ли. **2.** (*produce effect or influence*) ока́з|ывать, -а́ть влия́ние (на+*a.*); де́йствовать, по-. **3.: ~ on** (*surg.*) опери́ровать (*impf.*, *pf.*) (**for:** по по́воду +*g.*). **4.** (*mil.*) де́йствовать (*impf.*); опери́ровать (*impf.*, *pf.*).

operatic [ˌɒpə'rætɪk] *adj.* о́перный.

operating ['ɒpəˌreɪtɪŋ] *adj.* **1.** (*surg.*): **~ room, theatre** операцио́нная; **~ surgeon** опери́рующий хиру́рг; **~ table** операцио́нный стол. **2.: ~ costs** эксплуатацио́нные расхо́ды.

operation [ˌɒpə'reɪʃ(ə)n] *n.* **1.** (*action, effect*) де́йствие; рабо́та; функциони́рование; **bring into ~** прив|оди́ть, -ести́ в де́йствие; **come into ~** нач|ина́ть, -а́ть де́йствовать; **go out of ~** выходи́ть, вы́йти из стро́я. **2.** (*force, validity*) си́ла. **3.** (*process*) проце́сс, опера́ция. **4.** (*control, making work*) управле́ние, эксплуата́ция. **5.** (*business transaction*) опера́ция; (*speculation*) спекуля́ция. **6.** (*mil.*) опера́ция, де́йствие; **combined ~s** совме́стные де́йствия; **~s room** кома́ндный пункт. **7.** (*med.*) опера́ция; хирурги́ческое вмеша́тельство; **an ~ for appendicitis** опера́ция аппендици́та; **an ~ for cancer** опера́ция (по по́воду) ра́ка; **perform an ~** де́лать, с- (*or* произв|оди́ть, -ести́) опера́цию. **8.** (*math.*) де́йствие.

operational [ˌɒpə'reɪʃən(ə)l] *adj.* **1.** (*mil.*) операти́вный; **~ message** боево́е донесе́ние/сообще́ние; **~ unit** боево́е подразделе́ние. **2. the fleet is ~** флот в состоя́нии боево́й гото́вности; **the factory is fully ~** заво́д по́лностью гото́в к эксплуата́ции. **3.** (*needed for operating*): **~ data** рабо́чие да́нные.

operative ['ɒpərətɪv] *n.* (*machine operator*) квалифици́рованный рабо́чий, стано́чник, меха́ник; (*artisan*) реме́сленник.

adj. **1.** (*working, operating*) де́йствующий; (*having force*) действи́тельный; (*effective*) де́йственный; **become ~** (*of law etc.*) входи́ть, войти́ в си́лу; **~ part of a resolution** резолюти́вная часть реше́ния. **2.** (*practical*) операти́вный; (*of surgical operations*) операцио́нный, операти́вный.

operator ['ɒpəˌreɪtə(r)] *n.* **1.** (*one who works a machine*) управля́ющий (маши́ной); опера́тор. **2.** (*telephonist*) телефони́ст (*fem.* -ка); (*W/T* ~) телеграфи́ст (*fem.* -ка); (*radio* ~) ради́ст (*fem.* -ка), связи́ст (*fem.* -ка). **3.** (*comm.*) деле́ц; (*pej.*) спекуля́нт.

operetta [ˌɒpə'retə] *n.* опере́тта.

ophidian [əʊ'fɪdɪən] *n.* змея́.

ophthalmia [ɒf'θælmɪə] *n.* офтальми́я.

ophthalmic [ɒf'θælmɪk] *adj.* глазно́й.

ophthalmologist [ˌɒfθæl'mɒlədʒɪst] *n.* офтальмо́лог.

ophthalmology [ˌɒfθæl'mɒlədʒɪ] *n.* офтальмоло́гия.

ophthalmoscope [ɒf'θælməˌskəʊp] *n.* офтальмоско́п.

opiate ['əʊpɪət] *n.* опиа́т; (*fig.*) о́пиум.

opine [əʊ'paɪn] *v.t.* (*express opinion*) выска́зывать, вы́сказать мне́ние, что...; (*hold opinion*) приде́рживаться (*impf.*) того́ мне́ния, что...

opinion [ə'pɪnjən] *n.* (*judgement, belief*) мне́ние; (*view*) взгляд; **public ~** обще́ственное мне́ние; **in the ~ of** по мне́нию +*g.*; **in my ~** по моему́ мне́нию, по-мо́ему, на мой взгляд; **be of the ~ that ...** держа́ться (*impf.*) того́ мне́ния, что...; полага́ть (*impf.*) (*or* счита́ть (*impf.*)), что...; **change one's ~** меня́ть (*impf.*), перемени́ть (*pf.*) мне́ние; **form an ~** сост|авля́ть, -а́вить себе́ мне́ние; **that is a matter of ~** э́то зави́сит от то́чки зре́ния; на э́то существу́ют разли́чные мне́ния; **~ poll** опро́с обще́ственного мне́ния; (*estimate*): **have a high/low ~ of** быть высо́кого/невысо́кого мне́ния о+*p.*; (*conviction*) убежде́ние; **act up to one's ~s** поступ|а́ть, -и́ть в соотве́тствии со свои́ми убежде́ниями (*or* согла́сно свои́м убежде́ниям); (*expert judgment*) заключе́ние; **I wish to get another ~** я хоте́л бы пригласи́ть (ещё одного́) специали́ста.

opinionated [ə'pɪnjəˌneɪtɪd] *adj.* догмати́чный; упо́рствующий в свои́х взгля́дах.

opisometer [ˌɒpɪ'sɒmɪtə(r)] *n.* курвиме́тр.

opium ['əʊpɪəm] *n.* о́пиум; **~ den** прито́н кури́льщиков о́пиума.

opossum [ə'pɒsəm] *n.* опо́ссум.

opponent [ə'pəʊnənt] *n.* оппоне́нт, проти́вник.

adj. противополо́жный; (*antagonistic*) вражде́бный.

opportune ['ɒpəˌtju:n] *adj.* (*timely*) своевре́менный, уме́стный; (*suitable*) подходя́щий; благоприя́тный.

opportunism [ˌɒpə'tju:nɪz(ə)m, 'ɒpə-] *n.* оппортуни́зм.

opportunist [ˌɒpə'tju:nɪst] *n.* оппортуни́ст.

adj. оппортунисти́ческий.

opportunit|y [ˌɒpə'tju:nɪtɪ] *n.* (*favourable circumstance*) удо́бный слу́чай; (*good chance*) благоприя́тная возмо́жность; **as ~y offers** при слу́чае; **there were few ~ies of, for hearing music** почти́ не́ было возмо́жности слу́шать му́зыку; **I had no ~y to thank him** у меня́ не́ было возмо́жности поблагодари́ть его́; **the legacy afforded/gave him an ~y to travel** насле́дство предоста́вило/дало́ ему́ возмо́жность путеше́ствовать; **ring me up if you get the ~y!** позвони́те, е́сли бу́дет возмо́жность (*or* предста́вится слу́чай); **I made an ~y to meet him** я нашёл предло́г встре́титься с ним; **he seized, took the ~y to ...** он воспо́льзовался слу́чаем, что́бы...; **he let slip a golden ~y** он упусти́л блестя́щую возмо́жность.

oppos|e [ə'pəʊz] *v.t.* **1.** (*set against or in contrast to*) противопост|авля́ть, -а́вить (*что чему*); **two ~ed ideas** две противополо́жные иде́и; **as ~ed to** в отли́чие от+*g.*; **I am firmly ~ed to the idea** я реши́тельно про́тив э́той иде́и. **2.** (*set o.s. against*) восст|ава́ть, -а́ть (*or* возра|жа́ть, -зи́ть *or* выступа́ть, вы́ступить) про́тив+*g.*; проти́виться, вос- +*d.*; **the ~ing side** проти́вная сторона́; (*sport*) кома́нда проти́вника; **they were ~ed by enemy forces** им противостоя́ли си́лы проти́вника; (*show opposition to*) ока́з|ывать, -а́ть сопротивле́ние +*d.*; сопротивля́ться (*impf.*) +*d.*; (*reject; propose rejection of*) отклон|я́ть, -и́ть; **he ~ed my request** он отклони́л мою́ про́сьбу; **the motion was ~ed by a majority** предложе́ние бы́ло отклонено́ большинство́м (голосо́в).

opposite ['ɒpəzɪt] *n.* противополо́жность; **he was quite the ~ of what I expected** он оказа́лся по́лной противополо́жностью того́, что я ожида́л; **just the ~** пряма́я/по́лная противополо́жность; как раз наоборо́т.

adj. противополо́жный; **the ~ sex** противополо́жный пол; **his house is ~ ours** его́ дом (стои́т) напро́тив на́шего; **in the ~ direction** в обра́тном направле́нии; **~ poles** (*elec.*) разноимённые по́люсы; **~ number** лицо́, занима́ющее таку́ю же до́лжность в друго́м ве́домстве *и т.п.*

adv. напро́тив.

prep. (на)про́тив+*g.*; **put a tick ~ your name** поста́вьте га́лочку про́тив ва́шей фами́лии.

opposition [ˌɒpə'zɪʃ(ə)n] *n.* **1.** (*placing or being placed opposite*) противопоставле́ние; **they found themselves in ~ (to each other)** они́ оказа́лись в противополо́жных лагеря́х. **2.** (*contrast*) противополо́жность. **3.** (*resistance, contrary action*) сопротивле́ние, противоде́йствие, оппози́ция; **the infantry encountered heavy ~** пехо́та встре́тила си́льное сопротивле́ние; **he offered no ~** он не оказа́л никако́го сопротивле́ния; **he acted in ~ to my wishes** он поступи́л вопреки́ мои́м жела́ниям. **4.** (*pol.*) оппози́ция; **the Leader of the O~** ли́дер оппози́ции; **the party was in ~** па́ртия находи́лась в оппози́ции. **5.** (*astron.*) противостоя́ние.

oppositionist [ˌɒpə'zɪʃənɪst] *n.* оппозиционе́р.

oppress [ə'pres] *v.t.* **1.** (*of a ruler or government*) угнета́ть (*impf.*); притесн|я́ть, -и́ть; подав|ля́ть, -и́ть. **2.** (*weigh down; weary*) удруч|а́ть, -и́ть; томи́ть (*impf.*); **feel ~ed with the heat** томи́ться (*impf.*) от жары́; **be ~ed with grief** быть удручённым го́рем.

oppression [ə'preʃ(ə)n] *n.* **1.** (*oppressing*) угнете́ние, гнёт, притесне́ние, тира́ния; (*being oppressed*) угнетённость. **2.** (*heaviness, languor*) пода́вленность.

oppressive [ə'presɪv] *adj.* угнета́ющий, давя́щий; (*tyrannical*) деспоти́ческий; (*burdensome*) тя́гостный; (*wearisome*) утоми́тельный; ~ **weather** угнета́ющая/ду́шная пого́да.

oppressor [ə'presə(r)] *n.* угнета́тель (*m.*).

opprobrious [ə'prəʊbrɪəs] *adj.* (*injurious*) оскорби́тельный; (*shameful*) позо́рный.

opprobrium [ə'prəʊbrɪəm] *n.* (*reproach*) напа́дки (*m. pl.*); негодова́ние, возмуще́ние; (*shame, disgrace*) позо́р.

opt [ɒpt] *v.i.*: ~ **for** выбира́ть, вы́брать; ~ **out of** уклон|я́ться, -и́ться от+*g.*; (доброво́льно) выбыва́ть, вы́быть из+*g.*; устран|я́ться, -и́ться от+*g.*

optative [ɒp'teɪtɪv, 'ɒptətɪv] *n.* (~ **mood**) оптати́в; жела́тельное наклоне́ние.
adj. оптати́вный.

optic ['ɒptɪk] *n.* **1.** (*lens*) ли́нза. **2.** (*joc., eye*) глаз.
adj. зри́тельный, опти́ческий, глазно́й; ~ **angle** у́гол зре́ния; ~ **nerve** зри́тельный нерв.

optical ['ɒptɪk(ə)l] *adj.* опти́ческий, зри́тельный; ~ **illusion** опти́ческий обма́н; обма́н зре́ния.

optician [ɒp'tɪʃ(ə)n] *n.* о́птик.

optics ['ɒptɪks] *n.* о́птика.

optimism ['ɒptɪ,mɪz(ə)m] *n.* оптими́зм.

optimist ['ɒptɪmɪst] *n.* оптими́ст (*fem.* -ка).

optimistic [,ɒptɪ'mɪstɪk] *adj.* оптимисти́ческий, оптимисти́чный.

optimum ['ɒptɪməm] *adj.* оптима́льный.

option ['ɒpʃ(ə)n] *n.* **1.** (*choice*) вы́бор; **soft** ~ лёгкий вы́бор; ли́ния наиме́ньшего сопротивле́ния; **I have no ~ but to ...** у меня́ нет друго́го вы́бора, как...; **keep, leave one's ~s open** ост|авля́ть, -а́вить вы́бор за собо́й; не свя́з|ывать, -а́ть себя́ (оконча́тельно). **2.** (*right of choice*) пра́во вы́бора; **I have an ~ on the house** я облада́ю преиму́щественным пра́вом на поку́пку э́того до́ма; **at buyer's** ~ по усмотре́нию покупа́теля. **3.** (*stock exchange etc.*) опцио́н; ~ **price** курс пре́мий.

optional ['ɒpʃən(ə)l] *adj.* необяза́тельный, факультати́вный; ~ **(bus) stop** остано́вка по тре́бованию.

optometrist [ɒp'tɒmɪtrɪst] *n.* о́птик.

opulence ['ɒpjʊləns] *n.* бога́тство, оби́лие, изоби́лие.

opulent ['ɒpjʊlənt] *adj.* (*wealthy*) бога́тый; (*abundant*) оби́льный.

opus ['əʊpəs, 'ɒp-] *n.* **1.** (*mus.*) о́пус. **2.: magnum** ~ са́мое кру́пное (*or* гла́вное) произведе́ние (а́втора *и т.п.*).

or[1] [ɔ:(r)] *n.* (*her.*) золото́й цвет.

or[2] [ɔ:(r), ə(r)] *conj.* **1.** и́ли; **will you be here ~ not?** вы здесь бу́дете и́ли нет?; **he came for a day ~ two** он прие́хал на день-друго́й; **two ~ three** два-три. **2.** (~ *else*) и́ли, ина́че; и́ли же; а (не) то; **take the book now, ~ I'll give it to s.o. else** возьми́те кни́гу сейча́с, а не то я её отда́м кому́-нибудь друго́му; **wear your coat ~ you'll catch cold** наде́ньте пальто́, ина́че (*or* а то) просту́дитесь; **we must hurry ~ we'll be late** ну́жно потора́пливаться, а то опозда́ем; **do as I say ~ else!** де́лай что ска́зано и́ли пеня́й на себя́! **3.: there were 20 ~ so people present** там бы́ло челове́к 20 (*or* о́коло двадцати́ челове́к). **4.: storm ~ no storm, I shall go** гроза́ не гроза́, пойду́.

oracle ['ɒrək(ə)l] *n.* (*hist., fig.*) ора́кул; **work the ~** (*fig.*) нажа́ть (*pf.*) на та́йные пружи́ны; (*oracular statement*) прорица́ние, предсказа́ние.

oracular [ə'rækjʊlə(r)] *adj.* (*prophetic*) проро́ческий; (*ambiguous*) двусмы́сленный; (*obscure*) зага́дочный.

oral ['ɔ:r(ə)l] *n.* у́стный экза́мен.
adj. (*by word of mouth*) у́стный; (*pert. to mouth*) стоматологи́ческий; ~ **cavity** ротова́я по́лость; ~ **history** изу́стная исто́рия; ~ **sex** ора́льный секс.

orange ['ɒrɪndʒ] *n.* **1.** (*fruit*) апельси́н; **blood ~** (апельси́н-)королёк; (*attr.*) апельси́новый (*see also cpds.*); **Seville ~** помера́нец. **2.** (*tree*) апельси́новое де́рево; ~ **marmalade** апельси́новое варе́нье. **3.** (*colour*) ора́нжевый цвет. **4.: William of O~** Вильге́льм Ора́нский; **O~ Free State** (*hist.*) Ора́нжевая Респу́блика.
adj. (*colour*) ора́нжевый.
cpds. **~-blossom** *n.* флёрдора́нж; помера́нцевые цветы́ (*m. pl.*); **~-juice** *n.* апельси́новый сок; **O~man** *n.* оранжи́ст; **~-peel** *n.* апельси́нная ко́рка; (*dried*) апельси́нная це́дра; (*candied*) апельси́нный цука́т; **~-pip** *n.* зёрнышко апельси́на; **O~woman** *n.* оранжи́стка.

orangeade [,ɒrɪndʒ'eɪd] *n.* оранжа́д.

orangery ['ɒrɪndʒərɪ] *n.* оранжере́я (для выра́щивания апельси́новых дере́вьев).

orang-utan [ɔ:,ræŋu:'tæn] *n.* орангута́нг.

orate [ɔ:'reɪt] *v.i.* ора́торствовать (*impf.*).

oration [ɔ:'reɪʃ(ə)n, ə-] *n.* речь.

orator ['ɒrətə(r)] *n.* ора́тор.

oratorical [,ɒrə'tɒrɪk(ə)l] *adj.* ора́торский; (*rhetorical*) ритори́ческий.

oratorio [,ɒrə'tɔ:rɪəʊ] *n.* орато́рия.

oratory ['ɒrətərɪ] *n.* (*rhetoric*) красноре́чие, рито́рика; (*chapel*) моле́льня.

orb [ɔ:b] *n.* (*globe, sphere*) шар, сфе́ра; (*heavenly body*) небе́сное свети́ло; (*part of regalia*) держа́ва; (*poet., eye*) о́ко.

orbit ['ɔ:bɪt] *n.* **1.** (*of planet etc.*) орби́та; (*circuit completed by space vehicle*) вито́к. **2.** (*eye-socket*) глазна́я впа́дина; орби́та, глазни́ца. **3.** (*fig., sphere of action*) сфе́ра де́ятельности, орби́та.
v.t. (*put into* ~) выводи́ть, вы́вести на орби́ту.
v.i. (*move in* ~) враща́ться (*impf.*) по орби́те.

orbital ['ɔ:bɪt(ə)l] *adj.* (*astron.*) орбита́льный; (*of road*) окружно́й; (*of eye*) глазно́й.

Orcadian [ɔ:'keɪdɪən] *n.* жи́тель (*fem.* -ница) Оркне́йских острово́в; оркне́|ец (*fem.* -йка).
adj. оркне́йский.

orchard ['ɔ:tʃəd] *n.* (фрукто́вый) сад; **cherry ~** вишнёвый сад.

orchestra ['ɔ:kɪstrə] *n.* **1.** орке́стр; **full ~** симфони́ческий орке́стр; **string ~** стру́нный орке́стр; ~ **pit** оркестро́вая я́ма; ~ **stalls** парте́р. **2.** (*Gk. theatre*) орхе́стра.

orchestral [,ɔ:'kestr(ə)l] *adj.* оркестро́вый.

orchestrate ['ɔ:kɪ,streɪt] *v.t.* оркестрова́ть (*impf., pf.*); (*fig.*) организова́ть, с-; компонова́ть, с-.

orchestration [,ɔ:kɪ'streɪʃ(ə)n] *n.* оркестро́вка.

orchid ['ɔ:kɪd] *n.* орхиде́я.

orchidaceous [,ɔ:kɪ'deɪʃəs] *adj.* орхиде́йный.

ordain [ɔ:'deɪn] *v.t.* **1.** (*eccl.*) посвя|ща́ть, -ти́ть в духо́вный сан; **he was ~ed priest** он был посвящён в свяще́нники. **2.** (*destine, decree*) предпи́с|ывать, -а́ть.

ordeal [ɔ:'di:l] *n.* **1.** (*hist.*) «суд бо́жий». **2.** (*trying experience*) мыта́рство, му́ка; тяжёлое испыта́ние.

order ['ɔ:də(r)] *n.* **1.** (*arrangement*) поря́док; (*sequence, succession*) после́довательность; ~ **of the day** (*agenda*) пове́стка дня; **in alphabetical ~** в алфави́тном поря́дке; **in ~ of size** по разме́ру; **in ~ of importance** по сте́пени ва́жности; **out of ~, not in the right ~** не по поря́дку; не в поря́дке; не на (том) ме́сте; **put sth. in ~** прив|оди́ть, -ести́ что-н. в поря́док. **2.** (*mil. formation*) строй; **battle ~** боево́й поря́док; **in close/open/extended ~** в со́мкнутом/разо́мкнутом/расчленённом строю́. **3.** (*result of arrangement or control*): **everything is in ~** всё в поря́дке; **he keeps his books in (good) ~** он соде́ржит свои́ кни́ги в поря́дке; (*settled state*): **keep ~** подде́рживать (*impf.*) (*or* соблю|да́ть, -сти́) поря́док; **restore ~** восстан|а́вливать, -ови́ть поря́док; **law and ~** правопоря́док, зако́нность; (*efficient state*) поря́док, испра́вность; **out of ~** неиспра́вный, в плохо́м состоя́нии; **the bell is out of ~** звоно́к не рабо́тает (*or* в неиспра́вности); **he got the typewriter into working ~** он почини́л (*or* привёл в поря́док) маши́нку; (*healthy state*) поря́док; хоро́шее состоя́ние; **his liver is out of ~** у него́ с пе́ченью не в поря́дке. **4.** (*procedure*) поря́док; (*procedural rules*) регла́мент; **call s.o. to ~** приз|ыва́ть, -ва́ть кого́-н. к поря́дку; **call a meeting to ~** откры́ть (*pf.*) заседа́ние; **maintain, keep ~ (in the hall)** обеспе́чи|вать, -ть соблюде́ние поря́дка (в за́ле); следи́ть (*impf.*) за поря́дком; **O~!** к поря́дку!; регла́мент!; **he raised a point of ~** он проси́л сло́во (*or* вы́ступил) по поря́дку веде́ния заседа́ния; **the motion is in** ~ предложе́ние прие́млемо; **is it in** ~ **to ask questions?** подаётся ли задава́ть вопро́сы?; **am I in** ~? в поря́дке ли моё заявле́ние?; **out of** ~ в наруше́ние процеду́ры. **5.** (*command, instruction*) прика́з, распоряже́ние, поруче́ние; **by** ~ **of the president** по поруче́нию/прика́зу президе́нту; **give an, the** ~ отд|ава́ть, -а́ть прика́з; **I won't take** ~**s from you** вы мной не распоряжа́йтесь/кома́ндуйте; **obey** ~**s** подчин|я́ться, -и́ться прика́зу; **till further** ~**s** до дальне́йшего распоряже́ния; **under s.o.'s** ~**s** под кома́ндой кого́-н.; **get one's marching** ~**s** (*dismissal*) (*fig.*) получи́ть (*pf.*) отста́вку; (*warrant*) о́рдер (*pl.* -а́); ~ **to view (a house)** смотрово́й о́рдер. **6.** (*direction to supply*) зака́з (на+*a.*); **on** ~ по зака́зу; **is on** ~ зака́зан; **put in an** ~ **for** зака́з|ывать, -а́ть; **fill, fulfil an** ~ выполня́ть, вы́полнить зака́з; **I am having a suit made to** ~ я шью себе́ костю́м на зака́з; **that's a tall** ~ (*fig.*) э́то нелёгкая/тру́дная зада́ча; мно́гого захоте́л! **7.** (*direction to bank*): **standing** ~ прика́з о регуля́рных платежа́х; (*pl., parl.*) пра́вила (*nt. pl.*) процеду́ры. **8.** (*direction to Post Office*): **money/postal** ~ де́нежный/почто́вый перево́д. **9.** (*social group, stratum*) социа́льная гру́ппа; слой; **lower** ~**s** просто́й наро́д. **10.** (*pl., eccl.*): **holy** ~**s** духо́вный сан; **confer** ~**s on** рукопол|ага́ть, -ожи́ть; **take** ~**s** ста|нови́ться, -ть духо́вным лицо́м. **11.** (*distinction; insignia*) о́рден (*pl.* -а́); **O**~ **of Lenin** о́рден Ле́нина; **he was awarded the O**~ **of the Garter** его́ награди́ли о́рденом Подвя́зки. **12.** (*kind, sort, category*) сорт, род; **talent of another** ~ тала́нт ино́го поря́дка; (*math.*) поря́док; **a sum of the** ~ **of £10** су́мма поря́дка десяти́ фу́нтов; (*biol.*) отря́д; (*archit.*) о́рдер (*pl.* -ы), о́рден (*pl.* -ы). **13.** (*of chivalry or relig.*) о́рден (*pl.* -ы). **14.: in** ~ **to** (для того́,) что́бы +*inf.*; **in** ~ **that** (для того́,) что́бы +*past tense.*

v.t. **1.** (*arrange, regulate*) прив|оди́ть, -ести́ в поря́док; **he** ~**s his affairs well** у него́ дела́ в безукори́зненном поря́дке; (*mil.*): ~ **arms!** к ноге́! **2.** (*command*) прика́з|ывать, -а́ть; распоряж|а́ться, -ди́ться; **he** ~**ed an enquiry** он приказа́л (*or* дал распоряже́ние) провести́ рассле́дование; **he** ~**ed the soldiers to leave** он приказа́л солда́там разойти́сь; **he** ~**ed the gates to be closed** он приказа́л закры́ть воро́та; **he was** ~**ed home** ему́ приказа́ли верну́ться (*or* его́ отосла́ли) домо́й. **3.** (*prescribe*) пропи́с|ывать, -а́ть. **4.** (*reserve; request; arrange for supply of*) зака́з|ывать, -а́ть. **5.:** ~ **s.o. about** кома́ндовать (*impf.*) +*i.*; **I don't like being** ~**ed about** я не люблю́, когда́ мно́ю кома́ндуют/распоряжа́ются.

cpds. ~**-book** *n.* кни́га зака́зов; ~**-form** *n.* бланк зака́за.

orderliness [ˈɔːdəlɪnɪs] *n.* (*order*) поря́док; (*methodical nature*) аккура́тность; (*good behaviour*) хоро́шее поведе́ние.

orderly [ˈɔːdəlɪ] *n.* (*mil., runner*) ордина́рец, связно́й; (*mil., attendant in barracks*) дневальный; (*in hospital*) санита́р.

adj. **1.** (*methodical, neat, tidy*) аккура́тный, опря́тный. **2.** (*quiet; well-behaved*) ти́хий, послу́шный. **3.** (*organized*) организо́ванный. **4.** (*mil.*): ~ **officer** дежу́рный офице́р; ~ **room** помеще́ние для су́точного наря́да.

ordinal [ˈɔːdɪn(ə)l] *n.* (~ *number*) поря́дковое числи́тельное.

ordinance [ˈɔːdɪnəns] *n.* ука́з; (*decree*) декре́т.

ordinand [ˈɔːdɪnənd] *n.* ожида́ющий рукоположе́ния.

ordinariness [ˈɔːdɪnərɪnɪs] *n.* обы́чность, зауря́дность.

ordinary [ˈɔːdɪnərɪ] *n.* **1.: out of the** ~ необы́чный, незауря́дный. **2.: in** ~ постоя́нный; **Surgeon-in-**~ **to the King/Queen** лейб-ме́дик; **professor-in-**~ ордина́рный профе́ссор.

adj. (*usual*) обы́чный; (*average, common*) обыкнове́нный; (*simple*) просто́й; (*normal*) норма́льный; (*commonplace*) зауря́дный; ~ **seaman** мла́дший матро́с.

ordination [ˌɔːdɪˈneɪʃ(ə)n] *n.* (*eccl.*) рукоположе́ние (в духо́вный сан).

ordnance [ˈɔːdnəns] *n.* (*artillery*) артилле́рия; (*military stores and material*) артиллери́йско-техни́ческое и вещево́е снабже́ние; ~ **survey** (*mapping*) вое́нно-топографи́ческая съёмка; (*department*) госуда́рственное картографи́ческое управле́ние.

ordure [ˈɔːdjʊə(r)] *n.* (*dung*) наво́з; (*filth*) грязь.

ore [ɔː(r)] *n.* руда́.

cpds. ~**-bearing** *adj.* рудоно́сный; ~**-field** *n.* ру́дный бассе́йн.

oread [ˈɔːrɪˌæd] *n.* ореа́да; го́рная ни́мфа.

organ [ˈɔːgən] *n.* **1.** (*mus.*) орга́н, (*attr.*) орга́нный; **American** ~ фисгармо́ния; **mouth** ~ губна́я гармо́ника, (*coll.*) гармо́шка; **street** ~ шарма́нка. **2.** (*biol., pol. etc.*) о́рган.

cpds. ~**-blower** *n.* (*pers.*) раздува́льщик мехо́в (у орга́на); ~**-grinder** *n.* шарма́нщик; ~**-loft** *n.* хо́р|ы (*pl., g.* -ов); галере́я; ~**-pipe** *n.* орга́нная труба́; ~**-stop** *n.* реги́стр орга́на.

organd|ie, -y [ˈɔːgəndɪ, -ˈgændɪ] *n.* органди́ (*f. indecl.*); (гру́бая) кисея́.

organic [ɔːˈgænɪk] *adj.* **1.** органи́ческий; ~ **whole** еди́ное це́лое. **2.** (*organized*) организо́ванный.

organism [ˈɔːgəˌnɪz(ə)m] *n.* органи́зм.

organist [ˈɔːgənɪst] *n.* органи́ст.

organization [ˌɔːgənaɪˈzeɪʃ(ə)n] *n.* организа́ция.

organize [ˈɔːgəˌnaɪz] *v.t.* организо́в|ывать, -а́ть; устр|а́ивать, -о́ить; ста́вить по-; **it took him a long time to get** ~**d** он до́лгое вре́мя не мог собра́ться; **she is an** ~**d person** она́ челове́к организо́ванный.

organizer [ˈɔːgəˌnaɪzə(r)] *n.* организа́тор.

orgasm [ˈɔːgæz(ə)m] *n.* орга́зм.

orgiastic [ˌɔːdʒɪˈæstɪk] *adj.* (*fig.*) разну́зданный.

orgy [ˈɔːdʒɪ] *n.* о́ргия; (*fig.*) разгу́л; **an** ~ **of concerts** бесконе́чная цепь конце́ртов.

oriel [ˈɔːrɪəl] *n.* э́ркер; ~ **window** э́ркерное окно́.

orient [ˈɔːrɪənt] *n.* восто́к.

adj. (*poet.*) восто́чный.

v.t. = **orient(ate)**

oriental [ˌɔːrɪˈent(ə)l, ˌɒr-] *adj.* восто́чный; ~ **studies** востокове́дение, ориентали́стика.

orientalism [ˌɔːrɪˈentəlɪz(ə)m, ˌɒr-] *n.* ориентали́зм.

orientalist [ˌɔːrɪˈentəlɪst, ˌɒr-] *n.* востокове́д, ориентали́ст.

orient(ate) [ˈɒrɪenˌteɪt, ˈɔːr-] *v.t.* (*determine position of*) определ|я́ть, -и́ть местонахожде́ние +*g.*; ~ **o.s.** ориенти́роваться (*impf., pf.*).

orientation [ˌɒrɪenˈteɪʃ(ə)n, ˌɔːr-] *n.* (*lit., fig.*) ориентиро́вка, ориента́ция.

orienteering [ˌɔːrɪenˈtɪərɪŋ, ˌɒr-] *n.* ориенти́рование на ме́стности.

orifice [ˈɒrɪfɪs] *n.* (*aperture*) отве́рстие; (*mouth*) у́стье.

oriflamme [ˈɒrɪˌflæm] *n.* орифла́мма.

origin [ˈɒrɪdʒɪn] *n.* (*beginning, source*) нача́ло, исто́чник; (*derivation, extraction*) происхожде́ние; **he is of peasant** ~ он вы́ходец из крестья́н.

original [əˈrɪdʒɪn(ə)l] *n.* **1.** по́длинник; **a copy of the** ~ ко́пия с по́длинника/оригина́ла; **I am reading Tolstoy in the** ~ я чита́ю Толсто́го в по́длиннике; **X was the** ~ **of Ivanov** (*in the novel*) X явля́ется прототи́пом Ивано́ва. **2.** (*eccentric*) оригина́л, чуда́к.

adj. **1.** (*first, earliest*) первонача́льный; ~ **sin** первоpо́дный грех; **the** ~ **inhabitants** иско́нные жи́тели. **2.** (*archetypal; genuine*) по́длинный; ~ **manuscript** по́длинная ру́копись. **3.** (*constructive, inventive*) оригина́льный; **an** ~ **mind** изобрета́тельный/самобы́тный ум. **4.** (*novel, fresh*) но́вый, све́жий; своеобра́зный.

originality [əˌrɪdʒɪˈnælɪtɪ] *n.* по́длинность; оригина́льность, своеобра́зие, изобрета́тельность, самобы́тность.

originally [əˈrɪdʒɪnəlɪ] *adv.* (*in the first place*) первонача́льно, исхо́дно; (*in origin*) по происхожде́нию.

originate [əˈrɪdʒɪˌneɪt] *v.t.* **1.** (*cause to begin, initiate*) причин|я́ть, -и́ть; зав|оди́ть, -ести́; вв|оди́ть, -ести́; дав|а́ть, -ть нача́ло +*d.* **2.** (*create*) созд|ава́ть, -а́ть; поро|жда́ть, -ди́ть.

v.i. брать, взять нача́ло; (*arise*) возн|ика́ть, -и́кнуть; зав|оди́ться, -ести́сь; **the quarrel** ~**d in a remark of mine** ссо́ра возни́кла из-за моего́ замеча́ния.

origination [əˌrɪdʒɪˈneɪʃ(ə)n] *n.* (*source, origin*) нача́ло, происхожде́ние; (*creation*) исто́к, исто́чник, созда́ние.

originator [əˈrɪdʒɪˌneɪtə(r)] *n.* (*initiator*) инициа́тор; (*author*) а́втор; (*creator*) созда́тель (*m.*); (*inventor*) изобрета́тель (*m.*); (*sender of message*) отправи́тель (*m.*).

oriole ['ɔːrɪəʊl] *n.* иволга.
Orion [ə'raɪən] *n.* (*astron.*) Орио́н.
orison ['ɒrɪz(ə)n] *n.* (*arch.*) моле́ние.
Orkney ['ɔːknɪ] *n.*: **the ~s** (*also* **the ~ Islands**) Оркне́йские острова́ (*m. pl.*); (*attr.*) оркне́йский.
ormolu ['ɔːmə,luː] *n.* золочёная бро́нза; ме́бель с украше́ниями из золочёной бро́нзы.
ornament[1] ['ɔːnəmənt] *n.* **1.** (*adornment, embellishment*) украше́ние. **2.** (*decorative article or feature*) орна́мент; (*fig.*): **he is an ~ to the school** го́рдость шко́лы. **3.** (*pl., eccl.*) церко́вная у́тварь. **4.** (*mus.*) орname̕нтика.
ornament[2] ['ɔːnə,ment] *v.t.* укр|аша́ть, -а́сить.
ornamental [,ɔːnə'ment(ə)l] *adj.* орнамента́льный; (*decorative*) декорати́вный.
ornamentation [,ɔːnəmen'teɪʃ(ə)n] *n.* украше́ние.
ornate [ɔː'neɪt] *adj.* бога́то укра́шенный; (*of style*) витиева́тый, цвети́стый.
ornithological [,ɔːnɪθə'lɒdʒɪk(ə)l] *adj.* орнитологи́ческий.
ornithologist [,ɔːnɪ'θɒlədʒɪst] *n.* орнито́лог.
ornithology [,ɔːnɪ'θɒlədʒɪ] *n.* орнитоло́гия.
orotund ['ɒrə,tʌnd, 'ɔːr-] *adj.* (*of voice*) зву́чный, полнозву́чный; (*of style*) высокопа́рный; (*pretentious*) напы́щенный.
orphan ['ɔːf(ə)n] *n.* сирота́ (*c.g.*).
adj. сиро́тский.
v.t. лиш|а́ть, -и́ть (*кого*) роди́телей; де́лать, с- сирото́й; **an ~ed child** осироте́вший ребёнок.
orphanage ['ɔːfənɪdʒ] *n.* прию́т для сиро́т.
orphanhood ['ɔːfənhʊd] *n.* сиро́тство.
Orpheus ['ɔːfɪəs] *n.* Орфе́й.
orris ['ɒrɪs] *n.* (*bot.*) каса́тик флоренти́йский.
cpd. **~-root** *n.* фиа́лковый ко́рень; порошо́к из фиа́лкового ко́рня.
orthodox ['ɔːθə,dɒks] *adj.* ортодокса́льный, правове́рный; (*relig.*): **the O~ Church** правосла́вная це́рковь.
orthodoxy ['ɔːθə,dɒksɪ] *n.* ортодокса́льность, правове́рность; (*relig.*) правосла́вие.
orthographic(al) [,ɔːθə'græfɪk((ə)l)] *adj.* орфографи́ческий.
orthography [ɔː'θɒgrəfɪ] *n.* правописа́ние, орфогра́фия.
orthopaedic [,ɔːθə'piːdɪk] *adj.* ортопеди́ческий.
orthopaedics [,ɔːθə'piːdɪks] *n.* ортопе́дия.
orthopaedist [,ɔːθə'piːdɪst] *n.* ортопе́д.
orthotics [ɔː'θɒtɪks] *n.* биопротези́рование.
ortolan ['ɔːtələn] *n.* садо́вая овся́нка.
oryx ['ɒrɪks] *n.* сернобы́к.
Oscar ['ɒskə(r)] *n.* (*cin.*) пре́мия О́скара.
cpds. **~-winner** *n.* лауреа́т пре́мии О́скара; **~-winning** *adj.*: **~-winning picture** фильм, получи́вший О́скара.
oscillate ['ɒsɪ,leɪt] *v.t.* кача́ть (*impf.*).
v.i. (*swing*) кача́ться (*impf.*); (*fluctuate*) колеба́ться (*impf.*); (*elec., radio; also fig.*) колеба́ться (*impf.*).
oscillation [,ɒsɪ'leɪʃ(ə)n] *n.* колеба́ние; (*elec.*) осцилля́ция.
oscillator ['ɒsɪ,leɪtə(r)] *n.* осцилля́тор; (*radio*) генера́тор.
oscillatory [ɒ'sɪlətərɪ, 'ɒsɪ,leɪtərɪ] *adj.* колеба́тельный.
oscillograph [ə'sɪlə,grɑːf] *n.* осцилло́граф.
oscilloscope [ə'sɪlə,skəʊp] *n.* осциллоско́п.
osier ['əʊzɪə(r)] *n.* (*plant*) и́ва; (*shoot*) лоза́.
adj. и́вовый.
cpd. **~-bed** *n.* ивня́к.
Oslo ['ɒzləʊ] *n.* О́сло (*m. indecl.*).
osmium ['ɒzmɪəm] *n.* о́смий.
osmosis [ɒz'məʊsɪs] *n.* о́смос.
osmotic [ɒz'mɒtɪk] *adj.* осмоти́ческий.
osprey ['ɒspreɪ, -prɪ] *n.* (*zool.*) скопа́.
osseous ['ɒsɪəs] *adj.* (*of bone*) костяно́й; (*bony*) кости́стый.
ossification [,ɒsɪfɪ'keɪʃ(ə)n] *n.* окостене́ние; (*fig.*) очерствле́ние, окостене́ние.
ossif|y ['ɒsɪ,faɪ] *v.t. & i.* превра|ща́ть(ся), -ти́ть(ся) в кость; (*fig.*) заст|ыва́ть, -ы́ть; очерстве́ть, окосне́ть, окостене́ть (*all pf.*); **his opinions ~ied with age** с во́зрастом он закосне́л в свои́х убежде́ниях.
ossuary ['ɒsjʊərɪ] *n.* склеп; (*cave*) пеще́ра с костя́ми; (*urn*) кремацио́нная у́рна.
Ostend [ɒs'tend] *n.* Осте́нде (*m. indecl.*).
ostensibl|e [ɒ'stensɪb(ə)l] *adj.* (*for show*) показно́й; (*professed*) мни́мый; **he called ~y to thank me** он пришёл я́кобы для того́, что́бы поблагодари́ть меня́.
ostentation [,ɒsten'teɪʃ(ə)n] *n.* (*display*) выставле́ние напока́з; (*boasting*) хвастовство́, бахва́льство.
ostentatious [,ɒsten'teɪʃəs] *adj.* показно́й, хвастли́вый.
osteoarthritis [,ɒstɪəʊɑː'θraɪtɪs] *n.* остеоартри́т.
osteopath ['ɒstɪə,pæθ] *n.* остеопа́т.
osteopathic [,ɒstɪə'pæθɪk] *adj.* остеопати́ческий.
osteopathy [,ɒstɪ'ɒpəθɪ] *n.* остеопа́тия.
ostler ['ɒslə(r)] (*US* **hostler**) *n.* ко́нюх.
ostracism ['ɒstrə,sɪz(ə)m] *n.* (*hist., fig.*) острaки́зм; (*fig.*) изгна́ние (из о́бщества).
ostracize ['ɒstrə,saɪz] *v.t.* подв|ерга́ть, -е́ргнуть острaки́зму; изг|оня́ть, -на́ть.
ostrich ['ɒstrɪtʃ] *n.* (*also fig.*) стра́ус; (*attr.*) стра́усовый; **a digestion like an ~** лужёный желу́док.
other ['ʌðə(r)] *pron.* друго́й, ино́й; **the ~** (*liter., pers. referred to*) тот; **one (thing) or the ~** одно́ из двух; **~s may disagree with you** ины́е мо́гут с ва́ми не согласи́ться; **as an example to ~s** в приме́р други́м/про́чим; **'~s'** (*in classification*) про́чие; **one after the ~** оди́н за други́м; **we talked of this, that and the ~** мы говори́ли о том, о сём; **the money belongs to one or ~ of them** де́ньги принадлежа́т кому́-то из них; **someone or ~ has left the gate open** кто́-то оста́вил кали́тку откры́той; **some day or ~** когда́-нибудь, ка́к-нибудь; **I will get there somehow or ~** я уж ка́к-нибудь туда́ доберу́сь; **I want this book and no ~** я хочу́ и́менно э́ту кни́гу; **it was none ~ than Mr. Brown** э́то был не кто ино́й, как сам г-н Бра́ун; **no one ~ than he** никто́ кро́ме него́; **I could do no ~ than agree** мне не остава́лось ничего́ друго́го, как согласи́ться; (*expr. reciprocity*): **they were in love with each ~** они́ бы́ли влюблены́ друг в дру́га; **they got in each ~'s way** они́ друг дру́гу меша́ли; (*pl., additional ones; more*) ещё *+g.*; **let me see some ~s** покажи́те ещё каки́е-нибудь!; **there are no ~s** други́х нет; (*remaining ones*): **the ~s had already gone** остальны́е уже́ ушли́; **why this day of all ~s?** почему́ и́менно сего́дня?
adj. **1.** друго́й; **on the ~ hand** с друго́й стороны́; **open your ~ eye** откро́йте второ́й глаз; **on the ~ side of the road** на той стороне́ доро́ги; **the ~ world** тот свет; **the ~ side of the moon** обра́тная сторона́ луны́; **we must find some ~ way** мы должны́ изыска́ть друго́й спо́соб; **there was no ~ place to go** бо́льше идти́ бы́ло не́куда; **some ~ time** в друго́й раз. **2.** (*additional*) ещё *+g.*; **how many ~ children have you?** ско́лько у вас ещё дете́й? **3.** (*remaining*) остально́й; **we shall visit the ~ museums tomorrow** мы посети́м остальны́е музе́и за́втра; **~ things being equal** при про́чих ра́вных усло́виях. **4.: the ~ day** на днях; **every ~** ка́ждый второ́й; **every ~ day** че́рез день. **5.: ~ ranks** (*mil.*) серж́антско-рядово́й соста́в.
adv.: see **otherwise** *adv.* **1.**
cpd. **~-worldly** *adj.* не от ми́ра сего́; потусторо́нний.
otherness ['ʌðənɪs] *n.* непохо́жесть, отли́чие.
otherwise ['ʌðə,waɪz] *adj.*: **the matter is quite ~** де́ло обстои́т совсе́м не так.
adv. **1.** (*in a different way*) по-друго́му, други́м спо́собом, ина́че; **I was ~ engaged** я был за́нят други́м (де́лом); **~ known as ...** та́кже имену́емый *+i.*; он же; **I could do no ~ (*or* other)** я не мог поступи́ть ина́че; **they do not influence him ~ (*or* other) than by example** они́ де́йствуют на него́ то́лько приме́ром. **2.** (*in other respects or circumstances*): в други́х отноше́ниях; **the house is cold but ~ comfortable** дом холо́дный, но в остально́м удо́бный; **I will go if you do, but not ~** я пойду́ то́лько, е́сли вы то́же пойдёте. **3.** (*if not, or else*): **I went, ~ I would have missed them** я пошёл, ина́че я бы их не заста́л; **shut the windows, ~ the rain will come in** закро́йте о́кна, а то дождём намо́чит. **4.: the merits or ~ of the plan** досто́инства и́ли недоста́тки э́того пла́на.
cpd. **~-minded** *adj.* инакомы́слящий.
otiose ['əʊʃɪəʊs, 'əʊt-, -əʊz] *adj.* нену́жный, ли́шний.
otitis [ə'taɪtɪs] *n.* оти́т.
Ottawa ['ɒtəwə] *n.* Отта́ва.

otter ['ɒtə(r)] *n.* вы́дра; **sea ~** морско́й бобр.
cpd. **~-hound** *n.* вы́дровая соба́ка.

Otto ['ɒtəʊ] *n.* (*hist.*) Отто́н.

Ottoman ['ɒtəmən] *n.* **1.** (*hist.*) оттома́н. **2.** (*sofa*) оттома́нка, тахта́.
adj. оттома́нский.

oubliette [ˌu:blɪ'et] *n.* потайна́я, подзе́мная темни́ца.

ouch [aʊtʃ] *int.* ой!, ай!

ought [ɔ:t] *v. aux.* **1.** (*expr. duty*): **you ~ to go there** вы должны́ (*or* вам сле́дует) туда́ пойти́; **you ~ to have gone yesterday** вам сле́довало пойти́ туда́ вчера́; **he ~ never to have done it** он ни в ко́ем слу́чае не до́лжен был так поступа́ть. **2.** (*expr. desirability*): **you ~ to see that film** вы (непреме́нно) должны́ посмотре́ть э́тот фильм; **you ~ to have seen his face** на́до бы́ло ви́деть его́ лицо́; **I told him the house ~ to be painted** я сказа́л ему́, что сле́дует покра́сить дом. **3.** (*expr. probability*) вероя́тно; **if he started early he ~ to be there by now** е́сли он отпра́вился ра́но, то он, вероя́тно (*or* должно́ быть), сейча́с уже́ там; **it ~ not to take you long** э́то не должно́ заня́ть у вас мно́го вре́мени.

ouija-board ['wi:dʒə] *n.* планше́тка для спирити́ческих сеа́нсов.

ounce[1] [aʊns] *n.* (*weight*) у́нция; (*fig.*): **he hasn't an ~ of sense** у него́ нет ни ка́пли здра́вого смы́сла; **an ~ of practice is worth a pound of theory** день пра́ктики сто́ит го́да тео́рии.

ounce[2] [aʊns] *n.* (*zool.*) и́рбис.

our ['aʊə(r)] *poss. adj.* наш; **O~ Father** О́тче наш; **O~ Lady** Бо́жья ма́терь, Пресвята́я де́ва; **in ~ midst** среди́ нас, в на́шей среде́; **in ~ opinion** (*i.e. of the writer, editor*) по на́шему мне́нию.

ours ['aʊəz] *pron. & pred. adj.* наш; **~ is a blue car** на́ша маши́на си́няя; **this tree is ~** э́то де́рево на́ше (*or* принадлежи́т нам); **this government of ~** э́то на́ше прави́тельство; **if you are short of chairs, borrow one of ~** е́сли у вас не хвата́ет сту́льев, возьми́те у нас; **the money is not ~ to give away** мы не име́ем пра́ва распоряжа́ться э́тими деньга́ми.

ourselves [aʊə'selvz] *pron.* **1.** (*refl.*) себя́; **we washed ~** мы умы́лись; (*after preps.*): **we can only depend on ~** мы мо́жем полага́ться то́лько на себя́ (сами́х); **we were not satisfied with ~** мы бы́ли недово́льны собо́й. **2.** (*emph.*) са́ми; **we ~ were not present** са́ми мы не прису́тствовали. **3.: by ~** (*alone*) са́ми по себе́; **we can't do it by ~** (*without aid*) мы не мо́жем сде́лать э́то са́ми/одни́.

oust [aʊst] *v.t.* вытесня́ть, вы́теснить; (*expel*) выгоня́ть, вы́гнать; (*eject*) выселя́ть, вы́селить.

out [aʊt] *pred. adj. & adv.* (*for phrasal vv. see relevant v. entries*) **1.** (*away from home, office, room, usual place etc.*): **he is ~** его́ нет до́ма; **he is, was ~ for lunch** он ушёл обе́дать; **let's have dinner ~!** пойдёмте обе́дать в рестора́н!; **it was the maid's night ~** у прислу́ги был свобо́дный ве́чер; **the jury was ~ for 2 hours** прися́жные совеща́лись два часа́; **the book was ~** (*of the library*) кни́га была́ вы́дана (*or* на рука́х); **the children are ~** (*of school*) **early today** сего́дня дете́й ра́но отпусти́ли; (*of expulsion*): **the crowd were shouting 'Stevens ~!'** толпа́ крича́ла: «доло́й Сти́венса!» (*or* «Сти́венса вон!»); **the workers are ~** (*on strike*) рабо́чие басту́ют; **~!** (*at tennis*) нет! **2.** (**~** *of doors*) на дворе́; на у́лице; **it is quite warm ~ today** сего́дня на дворе́ тепло́; **we sleep ~ on fine nights** в пого́жие но́чи мы спим на во́здухе; **he was ~ and about all day** он был на нога́х весь день; **we were ~ in the garden** мы бы́ли в саду́; **the police are ~ looking for him** поли́ция разы́скивает его́ (повсю́ду); (*fig., intent*): **they are ~ to get him** они́ (во что бы то ни ста́ло) наме́рены его́ пойма́ть; **he is ~ for my blood** он жа́ждет мое́й кро́ви; **he is ~ for what he can get** он блюдёт свои́ интере́сы. **3.** (*extracted*): **you will feel better when the tooth is ~** вы себя́ почу́вствуете лу́чше, когда́ вам удаля́т зуб. **4.** (*open*): **the blossom is ~** цветы́ распусти́лись; (*visible*): **the moon came ~** луна́ показа́лась; вы́плыла луна́; **the stars are ~** звёзды вы́сыпали; **the sun will be ~ this afternoon** по́сле полу́дня пока́жется/поя́вится со́лнце; (*revealed*): **the secret is, was ~** секре́т раскры́лся (*or* стал всем изве́стен); **murder will ~** ≃ ши́ла в мешке́ не утаи́шь; **~ with it!** отвеча́йте!; говори́те же, что́ у вас на душе́!; (*published, issued*): **my book is ~ at last** моя́ кни́га вы́шла, наконе́ц, из печа́ти; **when will the results be ~?** когда́ объя́вят результа́ты?; **there is a warrant ~ for his arrest** име́ется о́рдер на его́ аре́ст. **5.** (*with superl.*): **whisky is the best thing ~ for a cold** ви́ски — лу́чшее сре́дство от просту́ды. **6.** (*at departure*): **will you see me ~?** вы меня́ прово́дите (до двере́й)?; **on the voyage ~** на пути́ туда́; **he stumbled on the way ~** выходя́, он споткну́лся; (*at a distance*): **he is ~ in the Far East** он на Да́льнем Восто́ке; **~ at sea** в откры́том мо́ре; **when they were four days ~** на четвёртый день пла́вания; **the tide is ~** сейча́с отли́в. **7.** (*coll.*, **~** *of favour, fashion*): **short hair is ~** коро́ткая стри́жка не в мо́де; (*inadmissible*): **that idea is ~ for a start** э́та иде́я исключа́ется с са́мого нача́ла; (*astray, wrong*): **be ~ in one's calculations** ошиб|а́ться, -и́ться в расчётах; **I wasn't far ~** я не на мно́го оши́бся; **my watch is 10 minutes ~** мои́ часы́ отстаю́т/спеша́т/(*coll.*) врут на де́сять мину́т. **8.** (*ended, over*): **before the week is ~** до оконча́ния неде́ли; (*to the end*): **I let him have his sleep ~** я дал ему́ вы́спаться; (*extinguished*): **the fire is ~** ого́нь поту́х; (*conflagration*) пожа́р ко́нчился; **lights ~!** гаси́те свет!; **sound 'lights ~'** сыгра́ть (*pf.*) зо́рю; (*unconscious*) без созна́ния; **he was ~ (for the count)** он был в нока́уте; **she was ~ for about five minutes** она́ лежа́ла без чувств о́коло пяти́ мину́т; **two drinks and he is ~** ему́ доста́точно двух рю́мок, что́бы впасть в бесчу́вствие. **9.: ~ and ~** соверше́нно, по́лностью; **~ and away** безусло́вно, несравне́нно. **10.: ~ of** (*movement*): **he fell ~ of the window** он вы́пал из окна́; **as they came ~ of the theatre** когда́ они́ вы́шли из теа́тра; **he leapt ~ of bed** он вскочи́л с посте́ли; **the soldiers came ~ of the firing-line** солда́ты вы́шли из-под огня́; (*material*): **made ~ of silk** (сши́тый) из шёлка, шёлковый; (*horse-breeding*): **~ of Lady Grey** сын (кобы́лы) Ле́ди Грей; (*from among*): **2 students ~ of 40** два студе́нта из сорока́; **one week ~ of ten** одна́ неде́ля из десяти́; (*motive*): **~ of pity/love/respect** из жа́лости/ любви́/уваже́ния (*к кому/чему*); **~ of grief/joy** с го́ря/ ра́дости; **~ of boredom** от/со ску́ки; (*outside*): **~ of danger** вне опа́сности; **~ of doors** на у́лице, на дворе́, на во́здухе; **~ of hours** вне рабо́чего вре́мени; не в приёмные часы́; **~ of (its) place** не на ме́сте; **it's ~ of the question** об э́том не мо́жет быть и ре́чи; **~ of town** за́ городом; **he is ~ of town** его́ нет в го́роде; он уе́хал; **~ of this world** (*coll.*) умопомрачи́тельный, неслы́ханный; восхити́тельный; **he was never ~ of England** он никогда́ не выезжа́л из А́нглии; **feel ~ of it** чу́вствовать (*impf.*) себя́ чужи́м (*or* ни при чём); (*not conforming or amenable to*): **~ of condition** не в фо́рме; **~ of control** вне контро́ля; **~ of fashion** не в мо́де; **get ~ of hand** вы́йти (*pf.*) из-под контро́ля; отби́ться (*pf.*) от рук; **~ of sorts** не в свое́й таре́лке; не в ду́хе/настрое́нии; **~ of step** не в но́гу; **~ of tune** расстро́енный; не в тон; (*without*): **~ of breath** запыха́вшийся; **~ of patience** вы́веденный из терпе́ния; **~ of work** безрабо́тный; **we are ~ of sugar** у нас ко́нчился са́хар; (*origin*): **a scene ~ of a play** сце́на из пье́сы; **he paid for it ~ of his salary** он заплати́л за э́то из свое́й зарпла́ты; (*so as to give up or lose*): **he was talked ~ of the idea** его́ отговори́ли от э́той зате́и; **I have been cheated ~ of £50** меня́ наду́ли на 50 фу́нтов.

outage ['aʊtɪdʒ] *n.* переры́в, безде́йствие.

out-and-out [ˌaʊtənd'aʊt] *adj.* соверше́нный, по́лный, отъя́вленный.

outback ['aʊtbæk] *n.* глушь.

outbalance [aʊt'bæləns] *v.t.* переве́|шивать, -сить.

outbid [aʊt'bɪd] *v.t.* **1.** (*at auction*): **~ s.o.** предл|ага́ть, -ожи́ть бо́лее высо́кую це́ну, чем кто-н. **2.** (*surpass*) прев|осходи́ть, -зойти́.

outboard ['aʊtbɔ:d] *adj.* забо́ртный; **~ motor** подвесно́й мото́р.
adv.: за бо́ртом.

outbound ['aʊtbaʊnd] *adj.* выходя́щий/уходя́щий в рейс.

outbreak ['aʊtbreɪk] *n.* (*of disease, anger etc.*) вспы́шка; ~ **of hostilities** нача́ло вое́нных де́йствий.

outbuilding ['aʊt,bɪldɪŋ] *n.* надво́рное строе́ние, надво́рная постро́йка.

outburst ['aʊtbɜːst] *n.* (*of rage etc.*) вспы́шка, взры́в, поры́в; (*of applause or laughter*) взрыв.

outcast ['aʊtkɑːst] *n.* (*exile*) изгна́нник, отве́рженный, отщепе́нец; (*homeless pers.*) (бездо́мный) бродя́га (*m.*).

adj. и́згнанный, отве́рженный; бездо́мный, бесприю́тный.

outclass [aʊt'klɑːs] *v.t.* прев|осходи́ть, -зойти́.

outcome ['aʊtkʌm] *n.* (*result*) результа́т; (*issue*) исхо́д; (*consequence*) (по)сле́дствие.

outcrop ['aʊtkrɒp] *n.* (*geol.*) обнаже́ние поро́д; (*fig.*) выявле́ние.

v.i. обнажи́ться (*impf.*) (*or* выходи́ть (*impf.*)) на пове́рхность.

outcry ['aʊtkraɪ] *n.* (*noise*) крик, вы́крик; (*protest*) проте́ст; (обще́ственное) негодова́ние.

outdated [aʊt'deɪtɪd] *adj.* устаре́лый, устаре́вший.

outdistance [aʊt'dɪst(ə)ns] *v.t.* перег|оня́ть, -на́ть.

outdo [aʊt'duː] *v.t.* прев|осходи́ть, -зойти́.

outdoor ['aʊtdɔː(r)] *adj.*: ~ **games** и́гры на откры́том во́здухе; подвижны́е и́гры; ~ **clothes** ве́рхнее пла́тье; **an ~ type** люби́тель (*m.*) приро́ды (*or* спорти́вных игр); ~ **aerial** вне́шняя/нару́жная анте́нна.

outdoors [aʊt'dɔːz] *n.*: **the great ~** ма́тушка приро́да.

adv. на откры́том во́здухе, на дворе́; (*expr. motion*) на во́здух.

outer ['aʊtə(r)] *n.* (*on target*) (попада́ние в) «молоко́»; **he scored an ~** он попа́л в молоко́; он промахну́лся.

adj. (*external*) вне́шний; **the ~ world** вне́шний мир; (*turned to the outside*) нару́жный; (*further away*): ~ **space** ко́смос; **the ~ suburbs** да́льние предме́стья.

outermost ['aʊtə,məʊst] *adj.* са́мый да́льний от це́нтра.

outface [aʊt'feɪs] *v.t.* (*defy*) смути́ть (*pf.*); сконфу́зить (*pf.*).

outfall ['aʊtfɔːl] *n.* (*of river*) у́стье.

outfield ['aʊtfiːld] *n.* (*outlying land*) отдалённое по́ле.

outfit ['aʊtfɪt] *n.* **1.** (*set of equipment*) снаряже́ние, компле́кт; (*of tools etc.*) инструме́нт, набо́р, прибо́р; (*of clothes*) костю́м. **2.** (*organized group*) ба́нда (*coll.*); (*mil. unit*) (воен)ча́сть; во́инская/войскова́я часть.

outfitter ['aʊt,fɪtə(r)] *n.*: **gentlemen's ~** владе́лец магази́на мужско́й оде́жды.

outflank [aʊt'flæŋk] *v.t.* об|ходи́ть, -ойти́ (*or* охва́т|ывать, -и́ть) фланг +*g.*; (*fig., outwit*) перехитри́ть (*pf.*).

outflow ['aʊtfləʊ] *n.* истече́ние; (*e.g. of gold*) уте́чка.

outfox [aʊt'fɒks] *v.t.* (*coll.*) перехитри́ть (*pf.*).

out-general [aʊt'dʒenər(ə)l] *v.t.* превзойти́ (*pf.*) в вое́нном иску́сстве.

outgoing ['aʊt,gəʊɪŋ] *adj.* **1.** (*departing*): ~ **ship** уходя́щее су́дно; ~ **mail** исходя́щая по́чта; **the ~ president** прези-де́нт, чей срок на посту́ истека́ет. **2.** (*sociable*): **an ~ personality** общи́тельный/лёгкий хара́ктер; ужи́вчивый челове́к.

outgoings ['aʊt,gəʊɪŋz] *n.* расхо́ды (*m. pl.*), изде́ржки (*f. pl.*).

outgrow [aʊt'grəʊ] *v.t.* **1.** (*grow taller than*) перераст|а́ть, -и́; (*grow too large for*) выраста́ть, вы́расти из+*g.*; **my family has ~n our house** наш дом стал те́сен для мое́й семьи́. **2.** (*discard with time*) отде́л|ываться, -аться от (*чего*) с во́зрастом; выраста́ть, вы́расти из+*g.*

outgrowth ['aʊtgrəʊθ] *n.* **1.** (*of plants etc.*) наро́ст. **2.** (*result, development*) проду́кт, результа́т. **3.** (*off-shoot*) о́тпрыск.

outgun [aʊt'gʌn] *v.t.* дост|ига́ть, -и́чь огнево́го превосхо́дства над+*i.*; ~ **the enemy** подав|ля́ть, -и́ть артилле́рию проти́вника.

outhouse ['aʊthaʊs] *n.* надво́рное строе́ние; (*US*) убо́рная во дворе́.

outing ['aʊtɪŋ] *n.* прогу́лка, экску́рсия; (*on foot*) похо́д; (*picnic*) пикни́к.

outlandish [aʊt'lændɪʃ] *adj.* дико́винный, чудно́й.

outlast [aʊt'lɑːst] *v.t.* (*outlive*) переж|ива́ть, -и́ть.

outlaw ['aʊtlɔː] *n.* лицо́, объя́вленное вне зако́на.

v.t. объяв|ля́ть, -и́ть вне зако́на.

outlawry ['aʊtlɔːrɪ] *n.* объявле́ние/положе́ние вне зако́на.

outlay ['aʊtleɪ] *n.* (*expenses*) изде́ржки (*f. pl.*), затра́ты (*f. pl.*); ~ **on clothes** расхо́ды (*m. pl.*) на оде́жду.

outlet ['aʊtlet, -lɪt] *n.* **1.** (*lit.*) выходно́е/выпускно́е отве́рстие. **2.** (*fig., comm.*) сбыт. **3.** (*for energies etc.*) отду́шина, вы́ход. **4.** (*elec.*) ште́псельная розе́тка.

outline ['aʊtlaɪn] *n.* **1.** (*contour*) очерта́ние, ко́нтур, а́брис; (*attr.*) ко́нтурный; **in ~** в о́бщих черта́х. **2.** (*draft, sketch, summary*) набро́сок, эски́з; о́черк. **3.** (*scheme; schedule*) план, схе́ма, конспе́кт.

v.t. **1.** (*drawing*) нарисова́ть (*pf.*) ко́нтур (*чего*). **2.** (*give an ~ of*) нам|еча́ть, -е́тить в о́бщих черта́х; набр|а́сывать, -оса́ть.

outlive [aʊt'lɪv] *v.t.* переж|ива́ть, -и́ть.

outlook ['aʊtlʊk] *n.* **1.** (*prospect, lit., fig.*) вид, перспекти́ва; **the ~ for trade is good** перспекти́вы для торго́вли хоро́шие; (*weather etc.*) прогно́з. **2.** (*point of view*) то́чка зре́ния; (*mental horizon*) кругозо́р.

outlying ['aʊt,laɪɪŋ] *adj.* отдалённый, удалённый.

outmanoeuvre [,aʊtmə'nuːvə(r)] (*US* **outmaneuver**) *v.t.* (*fig.*) перехитри́ть (*pf.*).

outmatch [aʊt'mætʃ] *v.t.* прев|осходи́ть, -зойти́.

outmoded [aʊt'məʊdɪd] *adj.* старомо́дный, немо́дный.

outnumber [aʊt'nʌmbə(r)] *v.t.* прев|осходи́ть, -зойти́ (*кого, что*) чи́сленно.

out-of-date [,aʊtəv'deɪt] *adj.* устаре́лый; старомо́дный.

out-of-fashion [,aʊtəv'fæʃən] *adj.* старомо́дный, немо́дный.

out-of-print [,aʊtəv'prɪnt] *adj.* распро́данный, разоше́дшийся; ~ **books** букинисти́ческие кни́ги.

out-of-the-way [,aʊtəv,ðə'weɪ] *adj.* **1.** (*remote*) отдалённый, удалённый. **2.** (*obscure*) малоизве́стный, малоупотреби́-тельный; экзоти́ческий, эксцентри́чный. **3.** (*out of place*) неуме́стный.

out-of-work [,aʊtəv'wɜːk] *adj.* безрабо́тный.

outpace [aʊt'peɪs] *v.t.* об|гоня́ть, -огна́ть.

out-patient ['aʊt,peɪʃ(ə)nt] *n.* амбулато́рный больно́й; ~ **department** амбулато́рия, поликли́ника; ~ **treatment** амбулато́рное лече́ние.

outplay [aʊt'pleɪ] *v.t.* обы́гр|ывать, -а́ть.

outpost ['aʊtpəʊst] *n.* (*mil.*) аванпо́ст; (*settlement*) отдалённое поселе́ние.

outpouring ['aʊt,pɔːrɪŋ] *n.* излия́ние.

output ['aʊtpʊt] *n.* **1.** (*production*) вы́пуск, проду́кция, произво́дство; **literary ~** литерату́рная проду́кция; (*of mine*) добы́ча; (*of power station*) мо́щность; (*of computer*) выходя́щая информа́ция. **2.** (*productivity*) производи́тельность.

outrage ['aʊtreɪdʒ] *n.* безобра́зие, оскорбле́ние; наруше́ние прили́чий.

v.t. (*offend, insult*) оскорб|ля́ть, -и́ть; (*rape*) изнаси́ловать (*pf.*).

outrageous [aʊt'reɪdʒəs] *adj.* безобра́зный, возмути́тельный, вопию́щий, сканда́льный; ~ **prices** возмути́тельные це́ны; **an ~ remark** возмути́тельное замеча́ние.

outré ['uːtreɪ] *adj.* экстрава́гантный.

outreach [aʊt'riːtʃ] *v.t.* (*surpass*) прев|осходи́ть, -зойти́.

outrider ['aʊt,raɪdə(r)] *n.* (*usu. pl.*) полице́йский эско́рт.

outrigger ['aʊt,rɪgə(r)] *n.* (*rowlock*) выносна́я уклю́чина; (*boat*) аутри́гер.

outright ['aʊtraɪt] *adj.* (*open, direct*) прямо́й, откры́тый; (*positive*) соверше́нный; **an ~ scoundrel** отъя́вленный моше́нник; **he gave an ~ denial** он категори́чески отрица́л (свою́ вину́ *и т.п.*).

adv. (*openly, right out*) пря́мо, откры́то; (*at once*) сра́зу; (*once and for all*) раз (и) навсегда́; **own sth. ~** владе́ть (*impf.*) чем-н. по́лностью.

outrival [aʊt'raɪv(ə)l] *v.t.* прев|осходи́ть, -зойти́.

outrun [aʊt'rʌn] *v.t.* (*outstrip*) опере|жа́ть, -ди́ть; (*run farther than*) перег|оня́ть, -на́ть.

outsell [aʊt'sel] *v.t.*: ~ **s.o.** прод|ава́ть, -а́ть бо́льше, чем кто-н.

outset ['aʊtset] *n.* нача́ло; **at the ~** внача́ле; **from the ~** с са́мого нача́ла.

outshine [aʊt'ʃaɪn] *v.t.* (*lit., fig.*) затм|ева́ть, -и́ть.

outside [aʊt'saɪd, 'aʊtsaɪd] *n.* нару́жная сторона́; (*outer surface*) вне́шняя пове́рхность; **from ~** извне́; **from, on**

the ~ снару́жи; **the door opens from the ~** дверь открыва́ется снару́жи; **they covered the ~ of the door** они́ оби́ли дверь снару́жи; **the ~ of the house needs painting** нару́жные сте́ны до́ма нужда́ются в покра́ске; **at the (very) ~** са́мое бо́льшее.

adj. **1.** (*external, exterior*) нару́жный, вне́шний; **~ repairs** нару́жный ремо́нт; **~ broadcast** внестуди́йная переда́ча; **~ measurements** габари́тные разме́ры. **2.** (*extreme*) кра́йний; **he has an ~ chance of winning** есть совсе́м небольша́я вероя́тность, что он вы́играет; у него́ есть небольшо́й/ничто́жный шанс на вы́игрыш; **~ left/right** (*sport*) ле́вый/пра́вый кра́йний. **3.** (*not belonging*) посторо́нний, вне́шний; **~ help** по́мощь извне́; посторо́нняя по́мощь; **the ~ world** вне́шний мир.

adv. снару́жи; извне́; (*to the ~*) нару́жу; (*out of doors*) на у́лице; на дворе́; (*in the open air*) на откры́том во́здухе.

prep. **1.** вне+*g.*; (*beyond bounds of*) за преде́лами +*g.*; **~ the door/window** за две́рью/окно́м; **he went ~ the house** он вы́шел и́з дому во двор; **it is ~ my field** э́то не вхо́дит в мою́ компете́нцию; э́то вне мое́й юрисди́кции. **2.** (*apart from*) за исключе́нием +*g.*; **he has no interests ~ his work** вне/кро́ме рабо́ты его ничего́/ничто́ не интересу́ет.

outsider [aʊt'saɪdə(r)] *n.* посторо́нний; (*non-specialist*) дилета́нт, неспециали́ст, профа́н; (*in contest, lit., fig.*) тёмная лоша́дка, аутса́йдер; (*cad*) невоспи́танный челове́к, хам.

outsize ['aʊtsaɪz] *n.* разме́р бо́льше станда́ртного.

adj. нестанда́ртный; больши́х разме́ров.

outskirts ['aʊtskɜ:ts] *n.* (*of town*) окра́ина, предме́стье.

outsmart [aʊt'smɑ:t] *v.t.* (*coll.*) перехитри́ть (*pf.*).

outspoken [aʊt'spəʊkən] *adj.* прямо́й, открове́нный.

outspread [aʊt'spred, 'aʊtspred] *adj.* распростёртый.

outstanding [aʊt'stændɪŋ] *adj.* (*prominent, eminent*) выдаю́щийся; (*still to be done*) невы́полненный; (*unpaid*): **~ accounts** невы́плаченные счета́.

outstare [aʊt'steə(r)] *v.t.* сму|ща́ть, -ти́ть при́стальным взгля́дом.

outstay [aʊt'steɪ] *v.t.* (*other guests*) переси́|живать, -де́ть; **~ one's welcome** загости́ться (*pf.*); заси́|живаться, -де́ться; злоупотреб|ля́ть, -и́ть гостеприи́мством.

outstretched ['aʊtstretʃd, aʊt'stretʃd] *adj.* протя́нутый, растяну́вшийся.

outstrip [aʊt'strɪp] *v.t.* (*lit., fig.*) опере|жа́ть, -ди́ть; об|гоня́ть, -огна́ть; перег|оня́ть, -на́ть.

outtalk [aʊt'tɔ:k] *v.t.* говори́ть (*impf.*) до́льше, чем (*кто*); заговори́ть (*pf.*).

out-tray ['aʊttreɪ] *n.* корзи́нка/я́щик для исходя́щих бума́г.

outvie [aʊt'vaɪ] *v.t.* прев|осходи́ть, -зойти́.

outvote [aʊt'vəʊt] *v.t.*: **~ s.o.** наб|ира́ть, -ра́ть бо́льше голосо́в, чем кто-н.; **the proposal was ~d** предложе́ние провали́ли при голосова́нии.

outward ['aʊtwəd] *adj.* (*external*) нару́жный, вне́шний; **~ calm** вне́шнее споко́йствие; **~ form** вне́шность; (*visible*) ви́димый; **to all ~ appearances** су́дя (*or* наско́лько мо́жно суди́ть) по вне́шности; по всем при́знакам; (*superficial*) пове́рхностный.

adv.: **~ bound** выходя́щий/уходя́щий в пла́вание/рейс.

outwardly ['aʊtwədlɪ] *adv.* вне́шне, снару́жи; (*at sight*) на вид.

outwards ['aʊtwədz] *adv.* нару́жу.

outwear [aʊt'weə(r)] *v.t.* (*wear out*) изн|а́шивать, -оси́ть.

outweigh [aʊt'weɪ] *v.t.* переве́|шивать, -сить.

outwit [aʊt'wɪt] *v.t.* перехитри́ть (*pf.*).

outwork ['aʊtwɜ:k] *n.* (*mil.*) вне́шнее/передово́е укрепле́ние.

outworn [aʊt'wɔ:n] *adj.* (*lit.*) изно́шенный; (*of ideas etc.*) устаре́лый, изби́тый.

ouzel ['u:z(ə)l] *n.* чёрный дрозд.

oval ['əʊv(ə)l] *n.* ова́л.

adj. ова́льный.

ovarian [ə'veərɪən] *adj.* яи́чниковый.

ovary ['əʊvərɪ] *n.* яи́чник.

ovation [əʊ'veɪʃ(ə)n] *n.* ова́ция.

oven ['ʌv(ə)n] *n.* духово́й шкаф, духо́вка; (*baker's, industrial*) печь.

cpd. **~ware** *n.* огнеупо́рная посу́да.

over[1] ['əʊvə(r)] *n.* (*cricket*) се́рия бросќов.

over[2] ['əʊvə(r)] *adv.* (*for phrasal vv. with* **over** *see relevant v.*) **1.** (*across; to, on the other side*): **~ there** (вон) там; **~ against** (*opposite*) про́тив/напро́тив+*g.*; (*compared to*) по сравне́нию с+*i.*; **I asked him ~** я пригласи́л его́ (к себе́); **he's ~!** (*has jumped clear*) он перепры́гнул!; он взял высоту́!; **~ (to you)!** (*said by radio operator*) перехожу́ на приём!; **see ~** (*instruction to reader*) см. на оборо́те!; (*to the ground*): **one push and ~ I went!** толчо́к — и я растяну́лся на земле́! **2.** (*covering surface*): **all ~** (*everywhere*) повсю́ду; **hills covered ~ with trees** холмы́, сплошь покры́тые дере́вьями; **your shoes are all ~ mud** ва́ши ту́фли все в грязи́; **the whole world ~** по всему́ ми́ру; во всём ми́ре; **I felt hot and cold all ~** меня́ (всего́) броса́ло в жар и хо́лод; **that's John all ~** э́то типи́чный Джон; **John is his father all ~** Джон — вы́литый оте́ц. **3.** (*at an end*): **the meeting is ~** собра́ние ко́нчилось; **the holidays are half ~** уже́ прошла́/минова́ла полови́на кани́кул; **I shall be glad to get it ~ (with)** сла́ва Бо́гу, де́ло идёт к концу́; **it's all ~ with their marriage** с их супру́жеской жи́знью поко́нчено; **the doctor could see it was all ~ with him** врачу́ бы́ло я́сно, что он безнадёжен. **4.** (*also* **~ again:** *for a second time; once more*) опя́ть, сно́ва, ещё раз; **~ and ~ again** ты́сячу раз; **he read it three times ~** он три́жды э́то перечита́л; **if I had my life ~ again** е́сли б мне довело́сь прожи́ть жизнь за́ново. **5.** (*in excess*): **sums of £5 and ~** су́ммы в 5 фу́нтов и вы́ше; **the parcel weighs 2 pounds or ~** посы́лка ве́сит два фу́нта, е́сли не бо́льше (*or* а то и бо́льше); **I had £3 (left) ~** у меня́ ещё остава́лось три фу́нта.

prep. **1.** (*above*): **a roof ~ one's head** кры́ша над голово́й; **the threat hanging ~ them** нави́сшая над ни́ми угро́за; **a seagull flew ~ us** над на́ми пролете́ла ча́йка; (*expr. division*): **five ~ two** (*math.*) пять дробь два; **1 ~ 2** одна́ втора́я; (*fig.*): **the lecture was ~ their heads** ле́кция была́ вы́ше их понима́ния; **his voice was heard ~ the crowd** его́ го́лос раздава́лся над толпо́й. **2.** (*to the far side of*): **a bridge ~ the river** мост че́рез ре́ку; **he climbed ~ the fence** он переле́з че́рез забо́р; **~ the sea** за́ море; **~ the hills** за го́ры; **I threw the ball ~ the wall** я переки́нул мяч че́рез сте́ну; **he jumped ~ the puddles** он перепры́гнул (че́рез) лу́жи; **he swam ~ the river** он переплы́л ре́ку; **he looked ~ his shoulder** он огляну́лся; **he read the letter ~ my shoulder** он чита́л письмо́, загля́дывая че́рез моё плечо́; **he looked at her ~ his spectacles** он смотре́л на неё пове́рх очко́в; (*down from*): **he fell ~ the cliff** он упа́л со скалы́; (*against*): **he tripped ~ a stone** он споткну́лся о ка́мень. **3.** (*on the far side of*): **he lives ~ the ocean** он живёт по ту сто́рону океа́на (*or* за океа́ном); **he lives ~ the way** он живёт че́рез у́лицу; **she is ~ the operation** опера́ция у неё прошла́ благополу́чно. **4.** (*resting on; covering*): **he carried a raincoat ~ his arm** он шёл, переки́нув плащ че́рез ру́ку; **he pulled his cap ~ his eyes** он надви́нул ша́пку на глаза́; **crossing one leg ~ the other** переки́нув но́гу за́ ногу; **a change came ~ him** с ним произошла́ переме́на; **what has come ~ you?** что с ва́ми случи́лось?; (*across, ~ the surface of*): **~ the whole country** по всей стране́; **a flush spread ~ her face** кра́ска залила́ её лицо́ (*or* разлила́сь по её лицу́); **all ~ the world** во всём ми́ре; по всему́ све́ту; **the news was all ~ town** но́вость разошла́сь по го́роду; **he was all ~ me** (*coll., of flattery, attention*) он засы́пал меня́ комплиме́нтами. **5.** (*more than*): **~ a year ago** бо́льше/свы́ше го́да тому́ наза́д; **he can't be ~ 60** ему́ (ника́к) не бо́льше шести́десяти (лет); **~ and above his wages** в добавле́ние к его́ зарпла́те; **~ and above that** (*moreover*) к тому́ же; **children ~ 5** де́ти ста́рше пяти́ лет; **~ 600** шестьсо́т с ли́шним; **~ age** превыша́ющий возрастно́й преде́л; (*superior to in rank*): **a general is ~ a colonel** генера́л вы́ше полко́вника. **6.** (*in command, charge, control of*): **he was ruler ~ several tribes** он был вождём не́скольких племён; **I have two people ~ me** на́до мной ещё два нача́льника; **have you no control ~ your dog?** вы что, не мо́жете спра́виться со своей собакой?; **he has an advantage ~ me** у него передо мной преимущество; **a victory ~ the forces of reaction** победа над силами реакции. **7.** (*as long as*): **can you stay ~ the whole week?** можете ли вы остаться на всю/целую неделю?; **I can only stay ~ Saturday night** я могу остаться только до утра воскресенья; (*during*): **much has happened ~ the past two years** за последние два года много чего произошло. **8.** (*near; leaning, bending ~*): **they were sitting ~ the fire** они сидели у камина; **I stood ~ him while he finished it** я не отходил от него, пока он не кончил. **9.** (*while engaged in*): **he takes too long ~ his work** он слишком долго возится со своей работой; **he fell asleep ~ the job** он заснул за работой; (*while consuming*): **we chatted ~ a bottle of wine** мы болтали за бутылкой вина. **10.** (*on the subject of; because of*): **he laughed ~ our misfortune** он смеялся над нашей бедой; **it's no good crying ~ spilt milk** теперь уж поздно слёзы лить; слезами горю не поможешь; **he gets angry ~ nothing** он злится из-за пустяков; **a quarrel ~ money** ссора из-за денег. **11.** (*through the medium of*): **I heard it ~ the radio** я слышал это по радио.

over-abundance [ˌəʊvərəˈbʌnd(ə)ns] *n.* избыток, излишество.

over-abundant [ˌəʊvərəˈbʌnd(ə)nt] *adj.* избыточный, излишний.

overact [ˌəʊvərˈækt] *v.t. & i.* переигр|ывать, -ать.

over-active [ˌəʊvərˈæktɪv] *adj.* сверхактивный.

over-activity [ˌəʊvərækˈtɪvɪtɪ] *n.* повышенная активность.

overall [ˈəʊvərˌɔːl] *n.* рабочий халат; (*pl.*) комбинезон.
adj. (*total*) полный; (*general*) (все)общий; **~ dimensions** габаритные/предельные размеры.
adv. (*taken as a whole*) в целом.

over-ambitious [ˌəʊvəræmˈbɪʃəs] *adj.* чересчур честолюбивый.

over-anxiety [ˌəʊvəræŋˈzaɪɪtɪ] *n.* чрезмерное волнение.

over-anxious [ˌəʊvərˈæŋkʃəs] *adj.* слишком обеспокоенный; **~ mother** излишне заботливая мать.

overarching [ˌəʊvərˈɑːtʃɪŋ] *adj.* (*all-embracing*) всеобъемлющий, всеохватывающий.

overarm [ˈəʊvərˌɑːm] *adj. & adv.*: **~ stroke** оверарм.

overawe [ˌəʊvərˈɔː] *v.t.* внуш|ать, -ить благоговейный страх +*d.*

overbalance [ˌəʊvəˈbæləns] *v.t.* (*knock over*) опроки|дывать, -нуть; (*capsize*) перев|орачивать, -ернуть; (*outweigh*) переве|шивать, -сить.
v.i. терять, по- равновесие.

overbear [ˌəʊvəˈbeə(r)] *v.t.* одол|евать, -еть; подав|лять, -ить; **an ~ing manner** властная манера.

overblown [ˌəʊvəˈbləʊn] *adj.* (*of flower etc.*) осыпающийся; **an ~ beauty** перезрелая красавица.

overboard [ˈəʊvəˌbɔːd] *adv.*: **man ~!** человек за бортом!; **throw ~** (*lit.*) выкидывать, выкинуть за борт; (*fig.*) бр|осать, -осить.

over-bold [ˌəʊvəˈbəʊld] *adj.* слишком смелый; (*rash*) опрометчивый.

overbook [ˌəʊvəˈbʊk] *v.t.*: **the trip** (*etc.*) **was ~ed** билетов было продано больше, чем мест.

overbuild [ˌəʊvəˈbɪld] *v.t. & i.* (чрезмерно) застр|аивать, -оить.

overburden [ˌəʊvəˈbɜːd(ə)n] *v.t.* перегру|жать, -зить.

over-busy [ˌəʊvəˈbɪzɪ] *adj.* (*overworked*) перегруженный.

over-careful [ˌəʊvəˈkeəfʊl] *adj.* чрезмерно осторожный.

overcast [ˈəʊvəˌkɑːst] *adj.* (*of sky*) покрытый облаками; (*of weather*) хмурый.

over-cautious [ˌəʊvəˈkɔːʃəs] *adj.* чрезмерно осторожный/робкий; излишне предусмотрительный.

overcharge [ˌəʊvəˈtʃɑːdʒ] *n.* (*of money*) завышенная цена; (*elec.*) перезаряд.
v.t. & i. запр|ашивать, -осить чрезмерную цену у (*кого*); (*elec.*) перезаря|жать, -дить; (*fig.*) перегру|жать, -зить.

overcloud [ˌəʊvəˈklaʊd] *v.t.* заст|илать, -лать облаками/тучами; (*fig.*) омрач|ать, -ить.

overcoat [ˈəʊvəˌkəʊt] *n.* пальто (*indecl.*); (*mil.*) шинель.

overcome [ˌəʊvəˈkʌm] *v.t. & i.* (*prevail over, get the better of*) преодол|евать, -еть; (*be victorious over*) побе|ждать, -дить; (*of emotion*) охват|ывать, -ить; **he was ~ by rage** он был охвачен яростью; **~ by the sight** растроганный зрелищем; (*of heat*) изнур|ять, -ить; (*of hunger*) истощ|ать, -ить.

over-confidence [ˌəʊvəˈkɒnfɪd(ə)ns] *n.* самонадеянность, самоуверенность.

over-confident [ˌəʊvəˈkɒnfɪd(ə)nt] *adj.* самонадеянный, самоуверенный; **he was ~ of success** он был слишком уверен в успехе.

overcook [ˌəʊvəˈkʊk] *v.t.* пережар|ивать, -ить; перевар|ивать, -ить.

over-critical [ˌəʊvəˈkrɪtɪk(ə)l] *adj.* чрезмерно суровый.

overcrop [ˌəʊvəˈkrɒp] *v.t.* истощ|ать, -ить.

overcrowd [ˌəʊvəˈkraʊd] *v.t.* переп|олнять, -олнить.

over-curious [ˌəʊvəˈkjʊərɪəs] *adj.* чрезмерно любопытный.

overdevelop [ˌəʊvədɪˈveləp] *v.t.* (*phot.*) передерж|ивать, -ать (при проявлении); **~ed** чрезмерно развитый; преувеличенный.

overdo [ˌəʊvəˈduː] *v.t.* (*overcook*) пережари|вать, -ть; **the comic scenes were ~ne** они переборщили в комических сценах; **~ it** переб|арщивать, -орщить; перес|аливать, -олить; переусердствовать (*pf.*) (*в чём*); **don't ~ it** (*work too hard*) не перенапрягайтесь/переутомляйтесь.

overdose [ˈəʊvəˌdəʊs] *n.* передозировка; **she died of an ~** она умерла от чрезмерной дозы (*наркотика и т.п.*).

overdraft [ˈəʊvəˌdrɑːft] *n.* овердрафт, перерасход; превышение кредита.

overdraw [ˌəʊvəˈdrɔː] *v.t.* **1.: ~ one's account** прев|ышать, -ысить кредит; **I am £100 ~n** я превысил кредит в банке на 100 фунтов; у меня на счету 100 фунтов дефицита. **2.** (*exaggerate*): **his characters are ~n** его персонажи карикатурны.

overdress [ˌəʊvəˈdres] *v.t. & i.*: **she ~es (*or* is ~ed)** она одевается/одета слишком нарядно.

overdrive [ˈəʊvəˌdraɪv] *n.* (*of vehicle*) ускоряющая передача.
v.t. (*pers.*) переутом|лять, -ить; (*horse*) заг|онять, -нать.

overdue [ˌəʊvəˈdjuː] *adj.* запоздалый; **the train is ~** поезд запаздывает; **recognition of his services is long ~** давно пора признать его заслуги; **the baby is 2 weeks ~** ребёнок должен был родиться две недели тому назад; (*of payment*) просроченный.

over-eager [ˌəʊvərˈiːgə(r)] *adj.* слишком усердный/ревностный/нетерпеливый.

over-eagerness [ˌəʊvərˈiːgənɪs] *n.* излишнее усердие; излишняя поспешность/горячность.

overeat [ˌəʊvərˈiːt] *v.i.* пере|едать, -есть; объ|едаться, -есться.

over-emotional [ˌəʊvəɪˈməʊʃən(ə)l] *adj.* слишком эмоциональный.

over-emphasize [əʊvərˈemfəˌsaɪz] *v.t.* излишне подчёрк|ивать, -нуть.

over-emphatic [ˌəʊvəremˈfætɪk] *adj.* с излишним нажимом.

over-enthusiasm [ˌəʊvərɪnˈθjuːzɪˌæz(ə)m, -ˈθuːzɪˌæz(ə)m] *n.* чрезмерный энтузиазм.

over-enthusiastic [ˌəʊvərɪnˌθjuːzɪˈæstɪk, -θuːzɪˈæstɪk] *adj.* с излишним энтузиазмом; **he was not ~** он не был в восторге.

overestimate[1] [ˌəʊvərˈestɪˌmeɪt] *n.* слишком высокая оценка.

overestimate[2] [ˌəʊvərˈestɪˌmeɪt] *v.t.* переоцен|ивать, -ить.

over-excite [ˌəʊvərɪkˈsaɪt] *v.t.* крайне возбу|ждать, -дить.

over-excitement [ˌəʊvərɪkˈsaɪtmənt] *n.* перевозбуждение.

over-exert [ˌəʊvərɪgˈzɜːt] *v.t.* перенапр|ягать, -ячь.

over-exertion [ˌəʊvərɪgˈzɜːʃ(ə)n] *n.* пернапряжение.

over-expose [ˌəʊvərɪkˈspəʊz] *v.t.* (*phot.*) передерж|ивать, -ать.

over-exposure [ˌəʊvərɪkˈspəʊzjə(r)] *n.* передержка; (*fig.*) чрезмерная реклама.

over-familiar [ˌəʊvəfəˈmɪlɪə(r)] *adj.* слишком фамильярный.

over-familiarity [ˌəʊvəfəˌmɪlɪˈærɪtɪ] *n.* чрезмерная фамильярность.

overfeed [ˌəʊvəˈfiːd] *v.t.* перек|армливать, -ормить.

overfeeding [ˌəʊvəˈfiːdɪŋ] *n.* перекармливание.

overfish [ˌəʊvəˈfɪʃ] *v.i.* истощ|ать, -ить запасы рыбы.

overflight [ˈəʊvəˌflaɪt] *n.* перелёт.

overflow [ˈəʊvəˌfləʊ] *n.* (*flowing ~*) разлив; (*superfluity*) избыток; (*outlet*) сливное отверстие.
v.t. & i. перел|иваться, -иться (*через что*); **the river ~s**

its banks река́ разлива́ется (*or* выхо́дит из берего́в); **~ing with** перепо́лненный +*i.*; (*fig.*) преиспо́лненный +*g./i.*

overfly [ˌəʊvəˈflaɪ] *v.t.* перелет|а́ть, -е́ть че́рез+*a.*

overfond [ˌəʊvəˈfɒnd] *adj.*: **I am not ~ of skating** я не сли́шком-то люблю́ ката́ться на конька́х.

overfondness [ˌəʊvəˈfɒndnɪs] *n.* чрезме́рное увлече́ние.

overfulfil [ˌəʊvəfʊlˈfɪl] (*US* **-l**) *v.t.* перев|ыполня́ть, -ы́полнить.

overfulfilment [ˌəʊvəfʊlˈfɪlmənt] (*US* **-ll-**) *n.* перевыполне́ние.

overfull [ˌəʊvəˈfʊl] *adj.* перепо́лненный (+*i.*).

over-generous [ˌəʊvəˈdʒenərəs] *adj.* сли́шком ще́дрый.

overglaze [ˈəʊvəˌgleɪz] *n.* ве́рхний слой глазу́ри.

overground [ˈəʊvəˌgraʊnd] *adj.* надзе́мный.

overgrow [ˌəʊvəˈgrəʊ] *v.t.* зараст|а́ть, -и́; **the garden was ~n with nettles** сад заро́с крапи́вой.

overgrowth [ˌəʊvəˈgrəʊθ] *n.* (*excessive growth*) чрезме́рный рост (*of weeds etc.*) за́росль.

overhand [ˈəʊvəˌhænd] *adj.* & *adv.* (*delivery of ball*) производи́мый све́рху вниз.

overhang [ˈəʊvəˌhæŋ] *n.* вы́ступ.

v.t. & *i.* выступа́ть, выдава́ться (*both impf.*) над+*i.*; (*fig.*) нав|иса́ть, -и́снуть над+*i.*

over-hasty [ˌəʊvəˈheɪstɪ] *adj.* опроме́тчивый; сли́шком поспе́шный.

overhaul [ˈəʊvəˌhɔːl] *n.* (техни́ческий/медици́нский) осмо́тр; (*reconditioning*) восстановле́ние; (*thorough repair*) капита́льный ремо́нт.

v.t. **1.** осм|а́тривать, -отре́ть; восстан|а́вливать, -ови́ть; ремонти́ровать, от-. **2.** (*overtake*) дог|оня́ть, -на́ть.

overhead [ˈəʊvəˌhed] *n.* (*usu. pl.*) накладны́е расхо́ды (*m. pl.*).

adj. **1.** (*above ground level*): **~ projector** графопрое́ктор; **~ railway** надзе́мная желе́зная доро́га; **~ wires, lines** возду́шные провода́; **~ crane** мостово́й кран. **2.** (*comm.*): **~ charges, costs** накладны́е расхо́ды.

adv. наверху́; (*above one's head*) над голово́й; (*in the sky*) на не́бе.

overhear [ˌəʊvəˈhɪə(r)] *v.t.* (*intentionally*) подслу́ш|ивать, -ать; (*accidentally*) нечая́нно услы́шать (*pf.*).

overheat [ˌəʊvəˈhiːt] *v.t.* & *i.* перегр|ева́ть(ся), -е́ть(ся).

over-indulge [ˌəʊvərɪnˈdʌldʒ] *v.t.* (*spoil*) сли́шком балова́ть, из-.

v.i.: **~ in sth.** злоупотребля́ть (*impf.*) чем-н.

over-indulgence [ˌəʊvərɪnˈdʌldʒəns] *n.* чрезме́рное баловство́; злоупотребле́ние (+*i*).

over-indulgent [ˌəʊvərɪnˈdʌldʒənt] *adj.* потака́ющий; сли́шком снисходи́тельный.

overjoyed [ˌəʊvəˈdʒɔɪd] *adj.* вне себя́ от ра́дости; о́чень счастли́вый.

overkill [ˈəʊvəkɪl] *n.* многокра́тное уничтоже́ние; (*fig.*) ≃ пу́шками по воробья́м.

over-kind [ˌəʊvəˈkaɪnd] *adj.* сли́шком до́брый.

overladen [ˌəʊvəˈleɪd(ə)n] *adj.* перегру́женный.

overland [ˈəʊvəˌlænd] *adj.* сухопу́тный.

adv. по су́ше.

overlap [ˈəʊvəˌlæp] *n.* (*tech.*) перекры́тие; (*fig.*) части́чное совпаде́ние.

v.t. покр|ыва́ть, -ы́ть части́чно.

v.i. заходи́ть (*impf.*) (оди́н на друго́й); (*coincide*) (части́чно) совпада́ть (*impf.*); **my holidays ~ with yours** мой о́тпуск части́чно совпада́ет с ва́шим.

overlapping [ˌəʊvəˈlæpɪŋ] *n.* параллели́зм, дубли́рование, повторе́ние.

adj. паралле́льный, части́чно дубли́рующий.

overlay [ˈəʊvəˌleɪ] *n.* покры́тие.

v.i. покр|ыва́ть, -ы́ть.

overleaf [ˌəʊvəˈliːf] *adv.* на оборо́те страни́цы.

overleap [ˌəʊvəˈliːp] *v.t.* перепры́г|ивать, -нуть (че́рез) +*a.*

overl|ie [ˌəʊvəˈlaɪ] *v.t.* лежа́ть (*impf.*) над+*i.*; **~ying** ве́рхние сло́и; **she ~ay the baby** она́ заспала́ ребёнка.

overload [ˈəʊvəˌləʊd] *n.* перегру́зка.

v.t. перегру|жа́ть, -зи́ть.

over-long [ˌəʊvəˈlɒŋ] *adj.* сли́шком дли́нный/до́лгий.

adv. сли́шком до́лго.

overlook [ˌəʊvəˈlʊk] *v.t.* **1.** (*look down on*) смотре́ть, посве́рху на+a.; (*tower above*): **the mountains ~ the sea** го́ры возвыша́ются над мо́рем. **2.** (*open on to*) выходи́ть (*impf.*) на+*a.*; **our house is not ~ed** наш дом защищён от посторо́нних взгля́дов; **a view ~ing the lake** вид на о́зеро. **3.** (*superintend*) смотре́ть (*impf.*) за+*i.* **4.** (*fail to notice*) просмотре́ть (*pl.*); прогляде́ть (*pf.*); пропус|ка́ть, -ти́ть; **the mistake was completely ~ed** никто́ не заме́тил оши́бки; **you've ~ed one important thing** вы упусти́ли и́з виду одно́ ва́жное обстоя́тельство; **he was ~ed** (*not promoted*) его́ обошли́. **5.** (*excuse*) про|ща́ть, -сти́ть; **I will ~ his mistakes** я не бу́ду заде́рживаться на его́ оши́бках.

overlord [ˈəʊvəˌlɔːd] *n.* (*suzerain*) сюзере́н; (*master*) повели́тель (*m.*).

overly [ˈəʊvəlɪ] *adv.* сли́шком, чересчу́р.

overman [ˌəʊvəˈmæn] *v.t.*: **the department is ~ned** в отде́ле разду́ты шта́ты; отде́л перегру́жен людьми́.

overmanning [ˌəʊvəˈmænɪŋ] *n.* раздува́ние шта́тов.

overmantel [ˈəʊvəˌmænt(ə)l] *n.* резно́е украше́ние над ками́ном.

overmaster [ˌəʊvəˈmɑːstə(r)] *v.t.* покор|я́ть, -и́ть; подчин|я́ть, -и́ть.

overmastering [ˌəʊvəˈmɑːstərɪŋ] *adj.* непреодоли́мый.

over-modest [ˌəʊvəˈmɒdɪst] *adj.* чересчу́р скро́мный.

over-much [ˌəʊvəˈmʌtʃ] *adv.* сли́шком мно́го; чрезме́рно.

overnight [ˌəʊvəˈnaɪt] *adj.*: **~ preparations** подгото́вка накану́не; **an ~ stay** ночёвка, ночле́г; **~ bag** доро́жная су́мка, саквоя́ж.

adv. (*on the previous evening*) накану́не ве́чером; (*through the night*) всю ночь; (*during the night*) за́ ночь; **stay ~** ночева́ть, за-; (*fig.*) **he rose to fame ~** сла́ва пришла́ к нему́ внеза́пно.

overpass [ˈəʊvəˌpɑːs] *n.* путепрово́д, эстака́да, виаду́к.

overpay [ˌəʊvəˈpeɪ] *v.t.* перепла́|чивать, -ти́ть.

overpayment [ˌəʊvəˈpeɪmənt] *n.* перепла́та.

over-peopled [ˌəʊvəˈpiːp(ə)ld] *adj.* перенаселённый.

overpersuade [ˌəʊvəpəˈsweɪd] *v.t.* переубе|жда́ть, -ди́ть.

overplay [ˌəʊvəˈpleɪ] *v.t.* (*overact*) перeигр|ывать, -а́ть; (*overemphasize*) прид|ава́ть, -а́ть чрезме́рное значе́ние +*d.*; **~ one's hand** (*fig.*) переоце́н|ивать, -и́ть свои́ возмо́жности.

overplus [ˈəʊvəˌplʌs] *n.* избы́ток, изли́шек.

overpopulated [ˌəʊvəˈpɒpjʊˌleɪtɪd] *adj.* перенаселённый.

overpopulation [ˌəʊvəpɒpjʊˈleɪʃ(ə)n] *n* перенаселе́ние.

overpower [ˌəʊvəˈpaʊə(r)] *v.t.* одол|ева́ть, -е́ть; **~ing grief** сокруша́ющее го́ре; **I found the heat ~ing** я изнемога́л от жары́; мне бы́ло нестерпи́мо жа́рко.

overpraise [ˌəʊvəˈpreɪz] *v.t.* перехва́л|ивать, -и́ть.

over-produce [ˌəʊvəprəˈdjuːs] *v.t.* перепроизв|оди́ть, -ести́.

over-production [ˌəʊvəprəˈdʌkʃ(ə)n] *n.* перепроизво́дство.

overrate [ˌəʊvəˈreɪt] *v.t.* переоце́н|ивать, -и́ть.

overreach [ˌəʊvəˈriːtʃ] *v.t.* (*outwit*) перехитри́ть (*pf.*); **~ o.s.** (*defeat one's object*) зарва́ться (*pf.*); заходи́ть, зайти́ сли́шком далеко́.

over-react [ˌəʊvərɪˈækt] *v.i.* реаги́ровать (*impf.*) чрезме́рно ре́зко.

over-refined [ˌəʊvərɪˈfaɪnd] *adj.* чрезме́рно утончённый/рафини́рованный.

over|ride [ˌəʊvəˈraɪd] *v.t.* (*e.g. enemy country*) вт|орга́ться, -о́ргнуться в+*a.*; **he ~rode my objections** он отве́рг/отмёл мои́ возраже́ния; он не посчита́лся с мои́ми возраже́ниями; **~riding** основно́й, первостепе́нный; гла́вный, реша́ющий; **an ~riding objection** неопровержи́мое возраже́ние.

overrider [ˈəʊvəˌraɪdə(r)] *n.* клык ба́мпера.

over-ripe [ˌəʊvəˈraɪp] *adj.* перезре́лый.

overrule [ˌəʊvəˈruːl] *v.t.* (*annul*) аннули́ровать (*impf.*, *pf.*); отмен|я́ть, -и́ть; **~ a claim/objection** отв|erга́ть, -е́ргнуть (*or* отклон|я́ть, -и́ть) прете́нзию/возраже́ние; **I was ~d** моё возраже́ние отве́ргли.

overrun [ˌəʊvəˈrʌn] *v.t.* **1.** (*of river*) зал|ива́ть, -и́ть. **2.** (*of enemy*) соверш|а́ть, -и́ть набе́г на+*a.* **3.** (*of vermin, weeds etc.*: *infest*): **the garden is ~ with weeds** сад заро́с сорняка́ми; **the house is ~ with rats** дом киши́т кры́сами. **4.** (*go beyond*): **the speaker overran his time** выступа́ющий превы́сил регла́мент. **5.** (*typ.*) перебр|а́сывать, -о́сить.

v.i.: **the bath is ~ning** ва́нна перелива́ется/переполня́ется (че́рез край); **the broadcast is ~ning by 20 minutes** переда́ча идёт на 20 мину́т до́льше поло́женного вре́мени.

overseas [ˈəʊvəˌsiːz] *adj.* замо́рский; (*foreign*) заграни́чный; **~ trade** вне́шняя торго́вля; **~ shipment** отпра́вка за грани́цу.

adv. за́ мо́рем; **go ~** е́хать (*det.*), по- за́ мо́ре.

oversee [ˌəʊvəˈsiː] *v.t.* надзира́ть (*impf.*) за+*i.*

overseer [ˈəʊvəˌsiːə(r)] *n.* надсмо́трщик, надзира́тель (*m.*).

oversell [ˌəʊvəˈsel] *v.t.* прод|ава́ть, -а́ть сверх свои́х запа́сов; (*fig.*) преувели́чи|вать, -ть досто́инства +*g.*; перехва́л|ивать, -и́ть.

over-sensitive [ˌəʊvəˈsensɪtɪv] *adj.* чересчу́р чувстви́тельный.

over-sensitiveness [ˌəʊvəˈsensɪtɪvnɪs] *n.* чрезме́рная чувстви́тельность.

over-serious [ˌəʊvəˈsɪərɪəs] *adj.* чересчу́р серьёзный.

over-sexed [ˌəʊvəˈsekst] *adj.* сладостра́стный; чрезме́рно чу́вственный; эроти́чный; легковозбуди́мый.

overshadow [ˌəʊvəˈʃædəʊ] *v.t.* (*lit., fig.*) заслон|я́ть, -и́ть; затм|ева́ть, -и́ть.

overshoe [ˈəʊvəˌʃuː] *n.* гало́ша.

overshoot [ˈəʊvəˌʃuːt] *n.* (*aeron.*) перелёт при поса́дке.

v.t.: **~ the mark** (*lit.*) взять (*pf.*) вы́ше це́ли; (*fig.*) преувели́чи|вать, -ть; перес|а́ливать, -оли́ть; зайти́ (*pf.*) сли́шком далеко́.

v.i.: **the plane overshot on landing** самолёт перелете́л при поса́дке.

oversight [ˈəʊvəˌsaɪt] *n.* (*failure to notice*) недосмо́тр, упуще́ние; (*supervision*) надзо́р.

over-simplification [ˌəʊvəsɪmplɪfɪˈkeɪʃ(ə)n] *n.* сли́шком большо́е упроще́ние; вульгариза́ция.

over-simplify [ˌəʊvəˈsɪmplɪˌfaɪ] *v.t.* сли́шком упро|ща́ть, -сти́ть.

oversize(d) [ˈəʊvəˌsaɪzd] *adj.* о́чень/сли́шком большо́го разме́ра.

oversleep [ˌəʊvəˈsliːp] *v.i.* заспа́ться, проспа́ть (*both pf.*).

oversleeve [ˈəʊvəˌsliːv] *n.* нарука́вник.

overspend [ˌəʊvəˈspend] *v.i.* тра́тить (*impf.*) сли́шком мно́го.

overspill [ˈəʊvəspɪl] *n.* (*of population*) избы́ток населе́ния; **~ town** го́род-спу́тник.

overstate [ˌəʊvəˈsteɪt] *v.t.* преувели́ч|ивать, -ить; разд|ува́ть, -у́ть.

overstatement [ˈəʊvəˌsteɪtmənt] *n.* преувеличе́ние.

overstay [ˌəʊvəˈsteɪ] *v.t.*: **~ one's welcome** загости́ться (*pf.*); злоупотреб|ля́ть, -и́ть гостеприи́мством.

oversteer [ˈəʊvəˌstɪə(r)] *n.* изли́шнее/чрезме́рное повора́чивание (*автомобиля*).

overstep [ˌəʊvəˈstep] *v.t.* переступ|а́ть, -и́ть (*что or границы чего*).

overstock [ˌəʊvəˈstɒk] *v.t.* (*with goods*) переп|олня́ть, -о́лнить това́ром; **the market is ~ed** ры́нок зава́лен/заби́т това́ром.

over-strain [ˌəʊvəˈstreɪn] *n.* перенапряже́ние.

v.t. перенапр|яга́ть, -я́чь; (*over-exert*) переутом|ля́ть, -и́ть.

over-stress [ˌəʊvəˈstres] *v.t.* изли́шне подчёрк|ивать, -ну́ть.

overstrung [ˌəʊvəˈstrʌŋ] *adj.* (*of pers., nerves etc.*) перенапряжённый; **he is ~** он нахо́дится в не́рвном напряже́нии; у него́ натя́нуты не́рвы.

oversubscribe [ˌəʊvəsəbˈskraɪb] *v.t.*: **the loan has been ~d** подпи́ска на заём превы́сила устано́вленную су́мму.

overt [əʊˈvɜːt, ˈəʊvɜːt] *adj.* (*open*) откры́тый; (*obvious, evident*) я́вный, очеви́дный.

overtak|e [ˌəʊvəˈteɪk] *v.t.* (*catch up with*) дог|оня́ть, -на́ть; (*outstrip*) об|гоня́ть, -огна́ть; перег|оня́ть, -на́ть; **no ~ing!** обго́н запрещён!; **misfortune overtook him** его́ пости́гло несча́стье; **we were ~en by a shower** ли́вень засти́г нас врасплох.

overtax [ˌəʊvəˈtæks] *v.t.* (*lit.*) обремен|я́ть, -и́ть чрезме́рными нало́гами; (*strength, patience etc.*) истощ|а́ть, -и́ть.

overthrow[1] [ˈəʊvəˌθrəʊ] *n.* (*ruin, destruction*) ниспроверже́ние; (*defeat*) пораже́ние.

overthrow[2] [ˌəʊvəˈθrəʊ] *v.t.* (*lit., fig.*) ниспров|ерга́ть, -е́ргнуть; пора|жа́ть, -зи́ть; (*subvert*) св|ерга́ть, -е́ргнуть; побе|жда́ть, -ди́ть.

overtime [ˈəʊvəˌtaɪm] *n.* сверхуро́чное вре́мя; (*work*) сверхуро́чная рабо́та, перерабо́тка.

adv. сверхуро́чно.

overtired [ˌəʊvəˈtaɪəd] *adj.* переутомлённый.

overtone [ˈəʊvəˌtəʊn] *n.* оберто́н; (*fig., also*) отте́нок.

overtop [ˌəʊvəˈtɒp] *v.t.* возв|ыша́ться, -ы́ситься над+*i.*

overtrump [ˌəʊvəˈtrʌmp] *v.t.* перекр|ыва́ть, -ы́ть ста́ршим ко́зырем.

overture [ˈəʊvəˌtjʊə(r)] *n.* **1.** (*mus.*) увертю́ра. **2.** (*pl.*): **peace ~s** ми́рные предложе́ния, ми́рная инициати́ва.

overturn [ˌəʊvəˈtɜːn] *v.t. & i.* опроки́|дывать(ся), -нуть(ся).

overvalue [ˌəʊvəˈvæljuː] *v.t.* ста́вить, по- завы́шенную це́ну на+*a.*

overview [ˈəʊvəˌvjuː] *n.* обзо́р.

overweening [ˌəʊvəˈwiːnɪŋ] *adj.* (*arrogant*) высокоме́рный; **~ ambition/pride** чрезме́рное тщесла́вие/высокоме́рие.

overweight [ˈəʊvəˌweɪt] *n.* изли́шек ве́са.

adj. ве́сящий бо́льше но́рмы; **he is several pounds ~** у него́ не́сколько фу́нтов ли́шнего ве́са; он ве́сит на не́сколько фу́нтов бо́льше но́рмы; **~ luggage** (опла́чиваемый) изли́шек багажа́.

overwhelm [ˌəʊvəˈwelm] *v.t.* (*weigh down*) подав|ля́ть, -и́ть; (*submerge*) погру|жа́ть, -зи́ть; (*in battle*) сокруш|а́ть, -и́ть; (*fig.*): **his kindness ~ed me** я был ошеломлён/пода́влен его́ доброто́й; **I was ~ed with joy** моё се́рдце перепо́лнилось ра́достью; **~ing majority** подавля́ющее большинство́.

overwind [ˌəʊvəˈwaɪnd] *v.t.*: **~ a watch** перекрути́ть (*pf.*) пружи́ну у часо́в.

overwork [ˌəʊvəˈwɜːk] *n.* (*overstrain*) перенапряже́ние, переутомле́ние.

v.t. & i. переутом|ля́ть(ся), -и́ть(ся); (*fig.*): **that phrase has been ~ed** э́то выраже́ние зата́скано.

overwrite [ˌəʊvəˈraɪt] *v.i.* (*write too elaborately*) писа́ть (*impf.*) вы́чурно.

overwrought [ˌəʊvəˈrɔːt] *adj.* сли́шком возбуждённый, не́рвничающий; **she is ~** у неё не́рвное истоще́ние.

Ovid [ˈɒvɪd] *n.* Ови́дий.

oviduct [ˈəʊvɪˌdʌkt] *n.* яйцево́д.

oviform [ˈəʊvɪˌfɔːm] *adj.* яйцеви́дный.

ovine [ˈəʊvaɪn] *adj.* ове́чий.

oviparous [əʊˈvɪpərəs] *adj.* яйцено́сный.

ovipositor [ˌəʊvɪˈpɒzɪtə(r)] *n.* яйцекла́д.

ovoid [ˈəʊvɔɪd] *adj.* яйцеви́дный.

ovulate [ˈɒvjʊˌleɪt] *v.i.* овули́ровать (*impf., pf.*).

ovulation [ˌɒvjʊˈleɪʃ(ə)n] *n.* овуля́ция.

ovum [ˈəʊvəm] *n.* яйцо́.

owe [əʊ] *v.t. & i.* **1.** (*be under obligation to pay*) быть до́лжным +*d.*; **you ~ us £50** вы должны́ нам 50 фу́нтов; **I ~d him a large sum** я был до́лжен ему́ большу́ю су́мму; **I ~ you for the ticket** я вам до́лжен за биле́т; **he ~s 4 roubles** за ним оста́лось четы́ре рубля́; **he still ~s for last year** у него́ ещё задо́лженность за про́шлый год; **you ~ it to yourself to take a holiday** вам необходи́мо взять о́тпуск. **2.** (*be indebted for*) быть обя́занным (*кому чем*); **I ~ it to you that I am still alive** я обя́зан вам жи́знью; **he ~s his success to hard work** свои́м успе́хом он обя́зан неуста́нной рабо́те.

owing [ˈəʊɪŋ] *adj.* **1.** (*yet to be paid*) причита́ющийся; **there is 2 roubles ~ to you from me** вам причита́ется два рубля́ с меня́. **2.**: **~ to** (*attributable to; caused by*) по причи́не +*g.*; всле́дствие+*g.*; (*thanks to*) благодаря́+*d.*; (*on account of, because of*) из-за+*g.*; **~ to fog we were late** из-за тума́на мы опозда́ли.

owl [aʊl] *n.* сова́; **barn ~** сипу́ха; **little ~** домо́вый сыч; **tawny ~** нея́сыть.

owlet [ˈaʊlɪt] *n.* совёнок.

owlish [ˈaʊlɪʃ] *adj.* глупова́тый.

own [əʊn] *pron.*: **come into one's ~** доби́ться (*pf.*) призна́ния; **get one's ~ back on s.o.** поквита́ться (*pf.*) с кем-н.; **hold one's ~** стоя́ть (*impf.*) на своём; **on one's ~** (*alone*) в одино́честве; (*unaided, independently*) самостоя́тельно, незави́симо, сам (по себе́).

adj. со́бственный, свой; **my ~ house** мой со́бственный дом; **this house is not my ~** э́тот дом мне не принадлежи́т;

I want a dog of, for my very ~ я хочу́ соба́ку, кото́рая бы принадлежа́ла мне одному́; **my time is my ~** я хозя́ин своего́ вре́мени; **may I have it for my ~?** мо́жно мне взять э́то насовсе́м?; **can I have a room of my ~?** мо́жно получи́ть отде́льную ко́мнату?; **a flavour all its ~** осо́бенный арома́т; **with one's ~ hand** собственнору́чно; **he died by his ~ hand** он поко́нчил с собо́й; он поко́нчил самоуби́йством; **he had reasons of his ~** у него́ бы́ли (на то) свои́ причи́ны; **he has nothing of his ~** он ничего́ не име́ет; **I love truth for its ~ sake** я люблю́ пра́вду ра́ди пра́вды; **name your ~ price!** назови́те свою́ це́ну!; **of one's ~ accord** по со́бственному побужде́нию; доброво́льно; **he is his ~ master** он сам себе́ хозя́ин; **she makes all her ~ clothes** она́ сама́ себя́ обшива́ет; **my ~ father** мой родно́й оте́ц; **he was ~ brother to the Prime Minister** он приходи́лся родны́м бра́том премье́р-мини́стру.

v.t. **1.** (*have as property*) владе́ть +*i.*; **who ~s this bag?** чья э́то су́мка; **the land was ~ed by my father** (э́та) земля́ принадлежа́ла моему́ отцу́. **2.** (*acknowledge, admit*) призн|ава́ть, -а́ть; **he would not ~ his faults** он не признава́л за собо́й недоста́тков; **he refused to ~ the child** он отка́зывался призна́ть отцо́вство.

v.i.: **~ to sth.; ~ up** призн|ава́ться, -а́ться в чём-н.; **I ~ to having told a lie** я признаю́сь, что солга́л.

owner ['əunə(r)] *n.* владе́лец; хозя́|ин (*fem.* -йка); **at ~'s risk** на отве́тственность владе́льца; **joint ~** совладе́лец.

cpd. **~-occupier** *n.* домо... *or* квартировладе́лец.

ownerless ['əunəlɪs] *adj.* бесхо́зный, без хозя́ина.

ownership ['əunəʃɪp] *n.* со́бственность, пра́во со́бственности; владе́ние; **joint ~** о́бщая со́бственность, сосо́бственность.

ox [ɒks] *n.* бык; (*castrated*) вол.

cpds. **~-bow** *n.* (*geog.*) слепо́й рука́в реки́; **~hide** *n.* воло́вья шку́ра; **~tail** *n.* воло́вий/бы́чий хвост; **~-tongue** *n.* воло́вий/бы́чий язы́к.

oxalic [ɒk'sælɪk] *adj.* щаве́левый.

Oxbridge ['ɒksbrɪdʒ] *n.* (*coll.*) О́ксфорд и Ке́мбридж (университе́ты).

Oxford ['ɒksfəd] *n.* О́ксфорд; (*attr.*) оксфо́рдский; **~ man** оксфо́рдец; **~ University** Оксфо́рдский университе́т.

oxidation [,ɒksɪ'deɪʃ(ə)n] = **oxidization**

oxide ['ɒksaɪd] *n.* о́кись.

oxidization [,ɒksɪ,daɪ'zeɪʃ(ə)n] *n.* окисле́ние.

oxidize ['ɒksɪ,daɪz] *v.t.* окисл|я́ть, -и́ть.

Oxonian [ɒk'səunɪən] *n.* **1.** студе́нт (*fem.* -ка) Оксфо́рдского университе́та; око́нчивш|ий (*fem.* -ая) Оксфо́рдский университе́т; преподава́тель (*fem.* -ница) Оксфо́рдского университе́та. **2.** оксфо́рдец (*fem.* жи́тельница О́ксфорда).

adj. оксфо́рдский.

oxyacetylene [,ɒksɪə'setɪ,li:n] *adj.* кислоро́дно-ацетиле́новый.

oxygen ['ɒksɪdʒ(ə)n] *n.* кислоро́д; **~ mask** кислоро́дная ма́ска; **~ tent** кислоро́дная пала́тка.

oxygenate ['ɒksɪdʒə,neɪt, ɒk'sɪ-] *v.t.* нас|ыща́ть, -ы́тить кислоро́дом.

oxygenation [,ɒksɪdʒə'neɪʃ(ə)n] *n.* насыще́ние кислоро́дом.

oxygenous [ɒk'sɪdʒɪnəs] *adj.* кислоро́дный.

oxymoron [,ɒksɪ'mɔ:rɒn] *n.* оксю́морон.

oyez [əu'jes, -'jez] *int.* (*arch.*) слу́шайте!

oyster ['ɔɪstə(r)] *n.* у́стрица; **the world is his ~** весь мир к его́ услу́гам.

cpds. **~-bed** *n.* у́стричный садо́к; **~-catcher** *n.* (*zool.*) кули́к-соро́ка.

Oz [ɒz] *n.* (*coll.*) Австра́лия.

oz. [auns(ɪz)] *n.* (*abbr. of* **ounce(s)**) у́нция.

ozone ['əuzəun] *n.* озо́н; **~ layer** озо́нный слой.

cpd. **~-friendly** *adj.* не разруша́ющий слой озо́на.

P

P [pi:] *n.*: **we must mind our ~'s and Q's** на́до быть осторо́жным; на́до соблюда́ть прили́чия.

p. *n. abbr. of* **1. penny** ['penɪ] (*pl.* ***pence***) пе́нни (*nt. indecl.*), пенс. **2. page** [peɪdʒ] стр, (страни́ца).

PA (*abbr. of* ***personal assistant***) ли́чный секрета́рь.

pa [pɑ:] *n.* (*coll.*) па́па (*m.*).

p.a. [pər 'ænəm] *adv.* (*abbr. of* ***per annum***) в год.

pabulum ['pæbjʊləm] *n.*: **mental ~** пи́ща для ума́.

pace[1] [peɪs] *n.* **1.** (*step*) шаг. **2.** (*speed of progression*): **mend, quicken one's ~** уск|оря́ть, -о́рить шаг; **keep ~ with** посп|ева́ть, -е́ть за+*i.*; **the train moved at a snail's ~** по́езд дви́гался с черепа́шьей ско́ростью; (*fig.*): **the slowest pupil sets the ~ for the whole class** са́мый отста́лый учени́к задаёт темп всему́ кла́ссу; **London tempted him to go the ~** в Ло́ндоне он вёл бу́рный о́браз жи́зни. **3.** (*gait, esp. of horse*) аллю́р, по́ступь; **he put the horse through its ~s** он пуска́л ло́шадь ра́зными аллю́рами.

v.t. **1.** (*measure out, traverse in ~s*) шага́ть (*impf.*); **he ~d the floor** он расха́живал по ко́мнате; **I ~d out the distance ~** я изме́рил расстоя́ние шага́ми. **2.** (*set the ~ for*) за|дава́ть, -а́ть темп +*d.*; лиди́ровать (*бегуна*).

v.i. ходи́ть (*indet.*); расха́живать (*impf.*); **he ~d up and down** он ходи́л взад и вперёд.

cpd. **~-maker** *n.* ли́дер, задаю́щий темп; (*cardiac aid*) ритмиза́тор се́рдца.

pace[2] ['pɑ:tʃeɪ, 'peɪsɪ] *prep.*: **~ the critics** с позволе́ния кри́тиков.

pachyderm ['pækɪ,dɜ:m] *n.* толстоко́жее (живо́тное).

pacific [pə'sɪfɪk] *n.*: **the P~ (Ocean)** Ти́хий океа́н; (*attr.*) тихоокеа́нский; **the P~ Islands** Океа́ния.

adj. (*peaceful, calm*) споко́йный; (*promoting peace*) миролюби́вый.

pacification [,pæsɪfɪ'keɪʃ(ə)n] *n.* успокое́ние; умиротворе́ние.

pacificatory [pə'sɪfɪkətərɪ] *adj.* успокои́тельный; умиротворя́ющий.

pacifier ['pæsɪ,faɪə(r)] *n.* (*one who soothes*) успокои́тель (*m.*); (*bringer of peace*) миротво́рец; (*US, child's dummy*) со́ска, пусты́шка.

pacifism ['pæsɪ,fɪz(ə)m] *n.* пацифи́зм.

pacifist ['pæsɪfɪst] *n.* пацифи́ст; (*attr.*) пацифи́стский.

pacify ['pæsɪ,faɪ] *v.t.* (*soothe; appease*) успок|а́ивать, -о́ить; умиротвор|я́ть, -и́ть; (*rebels etc.*) усмир|я́ть, -и́ть.

pack [pæk] *n.* **1.** (*bundle*) тюк; (*carried on back*) вьюк, у́зел. **2.** (*packet; packaged quantity of goods*) па́чка, паке́т. **3.** (*collection*) набо́р; **it's all a ~ of lies** э́то сплошна́я ложь; **a ~ of thieves** ша́йка воро́в. **4.** (*animals*): **~ of hounds** сво́ра го́нчих; **~ of wolves** ста́я волко́в. **5.** (*Rugby forwards*) нападе́ние. **6.** (*cards*) коло́да. **7.** (**~-ice**) пак.

v.t. **1.** (*put into container*) упако́в|ывать, -а́ть; запако́в|ывать, -а́ть; укла́дывать, уложи́ть; **~ed lunch** за́втрак в паке́те, кото́рый беру́т с собо́й; (*for preservation*) консерви́ровать, за-. **2.** (*put into small space*) наб|ива́ть, -и́ть; **they were ~ed like sardines** они́ наби́лись как се́льди в бо́чке. **3.** (*cover for protection in transit etc.*) уплотн|я́ть, -и́ть; **the glass is ~ed in cotton wool** стекло́ упако́вано в ва́ту. **4.** (*fill*) зап|олня́ть, -о́лнить; **he ~ed his bags and left** он упакова́л ве́щи и уе́хал; **the hall was ~ed** зал был наби́т. **5.: ~ a jury/committee** под|бира́ть, -обра́ть соста́в жюри́/комите́та. **6.: he ~s a punch** (*coll.*) у него́ си́льный уда́р.

v.i. **1.** (**~ one's clothes**) упако́в|ываться, -а́ться. **2.**

(*crowd together*): **they ~ed into the car** они́ вти́снулись в автомоби́ль. **3.: send s.o. ~ing** прогна́ть (*pf.*) кого́-н.

with advs.: ~ **away** *v.t.* от|кла́дывать, -ложи́ть; **I ~ed my overcoat away for the summer** я убра́л своё пальто́ на ле́то; ~ **down** *v.t.* уплотн|я́ть, -и́ть; **the soil should be ~ed down firmly** грунт сле́дует хороше́нько утрамбова́ть; ~ **in** *v.t.*: **she took her bag and ~ed everything in** она́ взяла́ су́мку и всё в неё упакова́ла; (*fig., accomplish in given time*): **I'm only going for a week, so I have a lot to ~ in** я е́ду то́лько на неде́лю, и потому́ моё вре́мя бу́дет о́чень уплотнено́; (*coll., stop, give up*) прекра|ща́ть, -ти́ть; **he's ~ing in his job** он броса́ет рабо́ту; ~ **it in, will you!** бро́сьте, пожа́луйста; *v.i.*: **it was a small car but they all ~ed in somehow** автомоби́ль был ма́ленький, но все ко́е-как в него́ вти́снулись; ~ **off** *v.t.* (*dispatch*) отгру|жа́ть, -зи́ть; отпр|авля́ть, -а́вить; **the goods were ~ed off yesterday** това́р был отгружён/отпра́влен вчера́; **she ~ed the children off to school** она́ отпра́вила дете́й в шко́лу; *v.i.* (*depart*): **he ~ed off to London** он махну́л (*coll.*) в Ло́ндон; ~ **on** *v.t.*: ~ **on sail** подня́ть (*pf.*) все паруса́; ~ **out** *v.t.*: **the hall was ~ed out** зал был запо́лнен до отка́за; ~ **up** *v.t.*: **have the presents been ~ed up yet?** пода́рки уже́ упако́ваны?; (*coll., stop*): **I ~ed up smoking last year** я бро́сил кури́ть в про́шлом году́; *v.i.*: **we spent the day ~ing up** мы це́лый день скла́дывались; (*coll., stop working*): **the workmen ~ed up at 5** рабо́чие смота́лись в 5 часо́в; **the engine ~ed up** мото́р отказа́л.

cpds. **~-drill** *n.* наказа́ние марширо́вкой с по́лной вы́кладкой; **~-horse** *n.* вью́чная ло́шадь; **~-ice** *n.* пак; па́ковый лёд; **~-saddle** *n.* вью́чное седло́; **~-thread** *n.* бечёвка, шпага́т.

package ['pækɪdʒ] *n.* посы́лка, паке́т; (*fig.*): ~ **deal** ко́мплексная сде́лка.

v.t. упак|о́вывать, -ова́ть; (*fig.*): **a ~ tour** организо́ванная тури́стская пое́здка; ко́мплексное турне́ (*indecl.*).

packer ['pækə(r)] *n.* (*pers.; firm*) упако́вщик.

packet ['pækɪt] *n.* **1.** (*small parcel; carton*) па́чка; паке́т. **2.** (*coll., large sum of money*): **that must have cost him a ~** э́то, наве́рное, ему́ сто́ило у́йму де́нег; **it cost me a ~** э́то мне влете́ло/ста́ло в копе́ечку.

packing ['pækɪŋ] *n.* **1.** (*action, process*) упако́вка; **I have all my ~ to do to-night** я до́лжен упакова́ть все ве́щи сего́дня ве́чером. **2.** (*material*) упако́вочный материа́л; (*seal for pipes etc.*) уплотни́тельный материа́л.

cpds. **~-case** *n.* я́щик для упако́вки; **~-needle** *n.* упако́вочная игла́; **~-thread** *n.* бечёвка.

pact [pækt] *n.* пакт.

pad [pæd] *n.* **1.** (*small cushion*) поду́шечка; (*for protection*) прокла́дка; **he played with ~s on his shins** он игра́л в щитка́х; (*to give shape*) подкладны́е пле́чики (*m. pl.*). **2.** (*block of paper*) блокно́т. **3.** (*of animal's foot*) ла́па. **4.** (*launching platform*) пусково́й/ста́ртовый стол; пусква́я площа́дка. **5.** (*sl., bed, sleeping quarters*) ко́мната, убе́жище, приста́нище, свой у́гол.

v.t. **1.** (*provide with padding*): **~ded cell** пала́та, оби́тая во́йлоком; ~ **shoulders** подкладны́е пле́чики (*nt. pl.*). **2.** (*fig., also ~ out*) перегру|жа́ть, -зи́ть; разб|авля́ть, -а́вить; **his essays are ~ded out with quotations** его́ о́черки перегру́жены цита́тами.

v.i. (*coll., move softly*) дви́гаться (*impf.*) бесшу́мно.

padding ['pædɪŋ] *n.* (*lit.*) наби́вка, подби́вка; (*fig.*) многосло́вие; длинно́ты (*f. pl.*); «вода́».

paddle[1] ['pæd(ə)l] *n.* (*oar*) гребо́к; байда́рочное весло́; (*~-shaped implement*) скребо́к; (*blade of ~-wheel*) пли́ца.

v.t. & i. грести́ (*impf.*); **I learned to ~ my own canoe** (*fig.*) я научи́лся де́йствовать самостоя́тельно.

cpds. **~-steamer** *n.* колёсный парохо́д; **~-wheel** *n.* гребно́е колесо́.

paddl|e[2] ['pæd(ə)l] *n.*: **the children have gone for a ~e** де́ти пошли́ поплеска́ться в воде́.

v.i. (*walk in shallow water*) шлёпать (*impf.*) по воде́; **~ing-pool** де́тский бассе́йн-лягуша́тник.

paddock ['pædək] *n.* (*small field, esp. for horses*) вы́гул, па́стбище; (*at racecourse*) па́ддок.

Paddy[1] ['pædɪ] *n.* (*coll., Irishman*) Пэ́дди (*m. indecl.*), ирла́ндец.

paddy[2] ['pædɪ] *n.* (*growing rice*) рис-сыре́ц.

cpd. **~-field** *n.* (заливно́е) ри́совое по́ле.

paddy[3]**(whack)** ['pædɪ] *n.* (*coll., fit of temper*) я́рость.

padlock ['pædlɒk] *n.* вися́чий замо́к.

v.t. ве́шать, пове́сить замо́к на+*a.*

padre ['pɑːdrɪ, -dreɪ] *n.* (*coll.*) па́дре (*m. indecl.*).

paean ['piːən] *n.* пеа́н.

p(a)ederast ['pedə,ræst], **-y** ['pedə,ræstɪ] = **pederast, -y**

paediatric [,piːdɪ'ætrɪk] *adj.* педиатри́ческий.

paediatrician [,piːdɪə'trɪʃ(ə)n] *n.* педиа́тр.

paediatrics [,piːdɪ'ætrɪks] *n.* педиатри́я.

paedophile ['piːdə,faɪl] *n.* педофи́л.

paedophilia [,piːdə'fɪlɪə] *n.* педофили́я.

paella [paɪ'elə] *n.* (*cul.*) паэ́лья.

pagan ['peɪgən] *n.* язы́чник.

adj. язы́ческий.

paganism ['peɪgən,ɪz(ə)m] *n.* язы́чество.

page[1] [peɪdʒ] *n.* (*of a book etc.; also fig.*) страни́ца; (*typ.*) полоса́; ~ **proof** корректу́ра в листа́х; вёрстка (*collect.*).

v.t. нумерова́ть, про- страни́цы (*книги и т.п.*).

page[2] [peɪdʒ] *n.* (*boy servant, attendant*) паж.

v.t.: **please have Mr. Smith ~d** пожа́луйста, вы́зовите господи́на Сми́та.

pageant ['pædʒ(ə)nt] *n.* (*sumptuous spectacle*) церемо́ния, проце́ссия; (*open-air enactment of historical events*) представле́ние, де́йство.

pageantry ['pædʒəntrɪ] *n.* пы́шность, пара́дность.

paginate ['pædʒɪ,neɪt] *v.t.* нумерова́ть, пере- страни́цы +*g.*

pagination [,pædʒɪ'neɪʃ(ə)n] *n.* пагина́ция.

pagoda [pə'gəʊdə] *n.* па́года.

pah [pɑː] *int.* фу!, тьфу!

pail [peɪl] *n.* бадья́, ведро́.

pailful ['peɪlfʊl] *n.*: ~ **of water** ведро́ воды́.

paill(i)asse ['pælɪ,æs] = **palliasse**

pain [peɪn] *n.* **1.** (*suffering*) боль; **he is in great ~** у него си́льная боль; **he cried out in ~** он вскри́кнул от бо́ли; **her words caused me ~** её слова́ причини́ли мне боль; (*particular or localized*): **where do you feel the ~?** где вы чу́вствуете боль?; **he had severe stomach ~s** у него́ бы́ли о́стрые бо́ли в желу́дке; **she felt her (labour) ~s coming on** она́ чу́вствовала приближе́ние схва́ток; **he is a ~ in the neck** (*coll.*) он де́йствует на не́рвы. **2.** (*pl., trouble, effort*) стара́ния (*nt. pl.*), хло́п|оты (*pl., g.* -о́т); **she spared no ~s to make us comfortable** она́ не жале́ла уси́лий, что́бы нам бы́ло удо́бно; **he takes great ~s over every picture** он му́чится над ка́ждой карти́ной; **he was at ~s to show us everything** он позабо́тился о том, что́бы показа́ть нам всё; **you will get nothing for your ~s** вы ничего́ не полу́чите за свои́ труды́. **3.** (*penalty*): **he goes there on ~ of his life (*or* on ~ of death)** он идёт туда́ под стра́хом сме́рти.

v.t. причин|я́ть, -и́ть боль +*d.*; **does your tooth ~ you?** у вас боли́т зуб?; **it ~s me to have to say this** мне бо́льно э́то говори́ть; **a ~ed expression** оби́женное выраже́ние лица́; **a ~ed silence** тя́гостное молча́ние.

cpd. **~-killer** *n.* болеутоля́ющее (сре́дство).

painful ['peɪnfʊl] *adj.* (*to body or mind*) боле́зненный, мучи́тельный, причиня́ющий боль; **it is my ~ duty to tell you ...** мой тя́гостный долг сообщи́ть вам, что ...

painfulness ['peɪnfʊlnɪs] *n.* боле́зненность, мучи́тельность.

painless ['peɪnlɪs] *adj.* безболе́зненный.

painlessness ['peɪnlɪsnɪs] *n.* безболе́зненность.

painstaking ['peɪnz,teɪkɪŋ] *adj.* стара́тельный, усе́рдный; кропотли́вый.

paint [peɪnt] *n.* кра́ска; **wet ~!** осторо́жно, окра́шено!; **that door could do with a touch of ~** э́ту дверь хорошо́ бы подкра́сить; **a stone hit the car and took the ~ off** в маши́ну попа́л ка́мень и поцара́пал кра́ску; (*cosmetic*) румя́н|а (*pl., g.* —), косме́тика; (*theatr.*) грим.

v.t. & i. **1.** (*portray in colours*) рисова́ть (*impf.*); писа́ть, на- кра́сками; **he ~s** он худо́жник; он занима́ется жи́вописью; (*fig., in words*) распи́с|ывать, -а́ть; **he's not as black as he is ~ed** не так уж он плох, как его́ изобража́ют. **2.** (*cover or adorn with* ~) кра́сить, по-; **the house is ~ed white** дом вы́крашен в бе́лый цвет; **she never ~s her face** она́ никогда́ не кра́сится; ~ **the lily** (*fig.*) ≃ переборщи́ть (*pf.*); переусе́рдствовать (*pf.*); **they ~ed the town red** (*fig.*) они загуля́ли (*or* устро́или кутёж); **~ed lady** (*butterfly*) репе́йница.

with advs.: ~ **in** *v.t.* впи́с|ывать, -а́ть; ~ **out** *v.t.* закра́|шивать, -сить.

cpds. **~-box** *n.* набо́р кра́сок; **~-brush** *n.* кисть; **~-remover** *n.* раствори́тель (*m.*), смы́вка; **~-roller** *n.* краси́льный ва́лик; **~work** *n.* кра́ска.

painter[1] [ˈpeɪntə(r)] *n.* (*artist*) худо́жник; (*decorator*) маля́р.

painter[2] [ˈpeɪntə(r)] *n.* (*rope*) фа́линь (*m.*); **cut the** ~ (*fig.*) отдел|я́ться, -и́ться (*от чего*).

painterly [ˈpeɪntəlɪ] *adj.* худо́жественный, живопи́сный.

painting [ˈpeɪntɪŋ] *n.* **1.** (*profession*) жи́вопись; **he took up** ~ он заня́лся́ жи́вописью. **2.** (*work of art*) карти́на. **3.** (*cosmetics*) косме́тика; (*theatr.*) грим.

pair [peə(r)] *n.* па́ра; **I have only one ~ of hands** у меня́ всего́ две ру́ки (*or* па́ра рук); **I have found one boot, but its ~ is missing** я нашёл оди́н боти́нок, а па́рного нет; **the happy** ~ счастли́вая па́ра; **they walked along in ~s** они́ шли па́рами; **a carriage and** ~ каре́та, запряжённая па́рой (ло́шадей); ~ **of scissors** но́жниц|ы (*pl., g.* —); **one ~ of scissors** одни́ но́жницы; ~ **of spectacles** очк|и́ (*pl., g.* -о́в); **two ~s of trousers** дво́е (*or* две па́ры) брюк.

v.t. (*unite*) спа́ри|вать, -ть; (*mate*) случ|а́ть, -и́ть.

with adv.: ~ **off** *v.t. & i.* разб|ива́ть(ся), -и́ть(ся) на па́ры; (*coll., marry*) жени́ться (*impf., pf.*), пожени́ться (*pf.*).

pajamas [pɪˈdʒɑːməz, pə-] = **pyjamas**

Paki [ˈpækɪ] *n.* (*coll., pej.*) пакиста́н|ец (*fem.* -ка).

adj. пакиста́нский.

Pakistan [ˌpɑːkɪˈstɑːn, ˌpækɪ-] *n.* Пакиста́н.

Pakistani [ˌpɑːkɪˈstɑːnɪ, ˌpækɪ-] *n.* пакиста́н|ец (*fem.* -ка).

adj. пакиста́нский.

pal [pæl] (*coll.*) *n.* ко́реш, кореšо́к; **he was a real ~ to me** он был мне настоя́щим дру́гом; **be a ~ and lend me a cigarette** будь дру́гом, дай мне сигаре́ту.

v.i.: ~ **up** подружи́ться (*pf.*).

palace [ˈpælɪs] *n.* (*residence; splendid building*) дворе́ц; (*hall of entertainment*) зал.

paladin [ˈpælədɪn] *n.* (*hist.*) палади́н; (*fig., champion*) ры́царь (*m.*).

palaeographer [ˌpælɪˈɒgrəfə(r)] *n.* палео́граф.

palaeographic [ˌpælɪəˈgræfɪk] *adj.* палеографи́ческий.

palaeography [ˌpælɪˈɒgrəfɪ] *n.* палеогра́фия.

palaeolithic [ˌpælɪəʊˈlɪθɪk] *adj.* палеолити́ческий.

palaeontologist [ˌpælɪɒnˈtɒlədʒɪst, ˌpeɪlɪ-] *n.* палеонто́лог.

paleontology [ˌpælɪɒnˈtɒlədʒɪ, ˌpeɪlɪ-] *n.* палеонтоло́гия.

Palaeozoic [ˌpælɪəʊˈzəʊɪk] *n.* палеозо́й.

adj. палеозо́йский.

palan|quin, -keen [ˌpælənˈkiːn] *n.* паланки́н.

palatable [ˈpælətəb(ə)l] *adj.* вку́сный; (*fig.*) прие́млемый.

palatal [ˈpælət(ə)l] *n.* (*phon.*) палата́льный звук.

adj. палата́льный.

palatalization [ˌpælətəlaɪˈzeɪʃ(ə)n] *n.* палатализа́ция, смягче́ние.

palatalize [ˈpælətəˌlaɪz] *v.t.* палатализи́ровать (*impf.*); смягч|а́ть, -и́ть.

palate [ˈpælət] *n.* (*roof of mouth*) нёбо; (*lit., fig. taste*) вкус.

palatial [pəˈleɪʃ(ə)l] *adj.* роско́шный, великоле́пный.

palatinate [pəˈlætɪˌneɪt] *n.* палатина́т; **the P~** (*in Germany*) Пфальц.

Palatine [ˈpæləˌtaɪn] *adj.* гра́фский; **count** ~ пфальцгра́ф; **county** ~ пфальцгра́фство.

palaver [pəˈlɑːvə(r)] *n.* (*coll.*) перегово́ры (*pl., g.* -ов).

v.i. трепа́ться (*impf.*) (*coll.*).

pale[1] [peɪl] *n.* (*stake*) кол; (*boundary*) черта́; **his conduct puts him beyond the** ~ (*fig.*) его́ поведе́ние перехо́дит все грани́цы; ~ **of settlement** (*hist.*) черта́ осе́длости.

pale[2] [peɪl] *adj.* **1.** (*of complexion*) бле́дный; **she turned** ~ она́ побледне́ла; (*of colours*) све́тлый; ~ **ale** све́тлое пи́во; ~ **blue** све́тло-голубо́й. **2.** (*dim*) бле́дный, ту́склый; **a ~ reflection of its former glory** бле́дная тень бы́лой сла́вы.

v.i. бледне́ть, по-; (*fig.*) тускне́ть, по-; **the event ~d into insignificance** э́то собы́тие отошло́ на за́дний план.

cpds. **~face** *n.* (*white man*) челове́к бе́лой ра́сы; **~faced** *adj.* бледноли́цый.

paleness [ˈpeɪlnɪs] *n.* бле́дность.

Palestine [ˈpælɪˌstaɪn] *n.* Палести́на.

Palestinian [ˌpælɪˈstɪnɪən] *n.* палести́н|ец (*fem.* -ка).

adj. палести́нский.

palette [ˈpælɪt] *n.* (*lit., fig.*) пали́тра.

cpd. **~-knife** *n.* мастихи́н.

palfrey [ˈpɔːlfrɪ] *n.* (да́мская) верхова́я ло́шадь.

palimpsest [ˈpælɪmpˌsest] *n.* палимпсе́ст.

palindrome [ˈpælɪnˌdrəʊm] *n.* палиндро́м.

palindromic [ˌpælɪnˈdrɒmɪk] *adj.* палиндроми́ческий.

paling [ˈpeɪlɪŋ] *n.* палиса́д, частоко́л.

palinode [ˈpælɪˌnəʊd] *n.* палино́дия.

palisade [ˌpælɪˈseɪd] *n.* частоко́л.

palish [ˈpeɪlɪʃ] *adj.* бледнова́тый.

pall[1] [pɔːl] *n.* покро́в; (*fig.*) покро́в, пелена́; **a ~ of smoke hung over the city** о́блако ды́ма висе́ло над го́родом.

cpd. **~-bearer** *n.* несу́щий гроб.

pall[2] [pɔːl] *v.i.* при|еда́ться, -е́сться (*+d.*); ~ **on** наску́чи|вать, -ть *+d.*

Pallas [ˈpæləs] *n.* Палла́да.

pallet [ˈpælɪt] *n.* (*straw bed*) соло́менный тюфя́к.

palliasse, paill(i)asse [ˈpælɪˌæs] *n.* тюфя́к.

palliate [ˈpælɪˌeɪt] *v.t.* (*alleviate*) облегч|а́ть, -и́ть; (*extenuate*) смягч|а́ть, -и́ть.

palliation [ˌpælɪˈeɪʃ(ə)n] *n.* облегче́ние; смягче́ние; **I say this, not in ~ of my action** я говорю́ э́то не для того́, что́бы оправда́ть своё поведе́ние.

palliative [ˈpælɪətɪv] *n.* паллиати́в.

adj. паллиати́вный; смягча́ющий.

pallid [ˈpælɪd] *adj.* бле́дный.

pallor [ˈpælə(r)] *n.* бле́дность.

pally [ˈpælɪ] *adj.* (*coll.*) сво́йский, обходи́тельный.

palm[1] [pɑːm] *n.* (*tree*) па́льма; (*branch, symbol of victory*) па́льмовая ветвь; **P~ Sunday** ве́рбное воскресе́нье; **he carried, bore off the** ~ ему́ доста́лась па́льма пе́рвенства.

cpd. **~-oil** *n.* па́льмовое ма́сло; (*fig., bribe-money*) взя́тка.

palm[2] [pɑːm] *n.* (*of hand*) ладо́нь; **if you cross the Gypsy's ~ with silver she will read your hand** позолоти́те цыга́нке ру́чку, она́ вам погада́ет; **he greased the doorman's** ~ (*bribed him*) он подма́зал портье́; **he has an itching** ~ (*fig.*) у него́ ру́ки загребу́щие.

v.t.: ~ **sth. off on s.o.** (*or* **s.o. off with sth.**) подс|о́вывать, -у́нуть что-н. кому́-н.; **the baker tried to ~ off a stale loaf on me** бу́лочник хоте́л мне сбыть чёрствый хлеб.

palmary [ˈpɑːmərɪ] *adj.* превосхо́дный.

palmist [ˈpɑːmɪst] *n.* хирома́нт (*fem.* -ка).

palmistry [ˈpɑːmɪstrɪ] *n.* хирома́нтия.

palmy [ˈpɑːmɪ] *adj.* (*fig.*) счастли́вый; **in my ~ days** в мои́ счастли́вые/золоты́е дни.

palpable [ˈpælpəb(ə)l] *adj.* осяза́емый; ощути́мый; **a ~ swelling** прощу́пываемая о́пухоль; **a ~ error** я́вная оши́бка.

palpate [pælˈpeɪt] *v.t.* ощу́пывать (*impf.*); пальпи́ровать (*impf.*).

palpitate [ˈpælpɪˌteɪt] *v.i.* (*pulsate*) пульси́ровать (*impf.*); (*tremble*) трепета́ть (*impf.*).

palpitation [ˌpælpɪˈteɪʃ(ə)n] *n.* сердцебие́ние; **just to watch him gave me ~s** оди́н его́ вид приводи́л меня́ в тре́пет.

pals|y [ˈpɔːlzɪ, ˈpɒl-] *n.* парали́ч.

v.t. (*fig.*) парализова́ть (*impf.*); **he was ~ied with fear** его́ парализова́л страх.

palter [ˈpɔːltə(r), ˈpɒl-] *v.i.* (*equivocate*) хитри́ть, с-.

paltriness [ˈpɔːltrɪnɪs, ˈpɒl-] *n.* ме́лочность, ничто́жность.

paltry [ˈpɔːltrɪ, ˈpɒl-] *adj.* (*worthless*) ничто́жный; (*petty, mean*) ме́лкий; (*contemptible*) презре́нный.

pampas [ˈpæmpəs] *n.* пампа́с|ы (*pl., g.* -ов).

cpd. **~-grass** *n.* трава́ пампа́сная.

pamper [ˈpæmpə(r)] *v.t.* балова́ть, из-; **she ~ed herself and stayed in bed all morning** она́ не́жилась в посте́ли всё у́тро.

pamphlet [ˈpæmflɪt] *n.* (*treatise*) памфле́т; (*printed leaflet*) брошю́ра.

pamphleteer [ˌpæmflɪ'tɪə(r)] *n.* памфлети́ст.

pan[1] [pæn] *n.* **1.** (*kitchen utensil; sauce*~) кастрю́ля; (**frying-**~) сковорода́. **2.** (*of scales*) ча́шка. **3.** (*of water-closet*) унита́з. **4.** (*ore-washing screen*) лото́к, поддо́н.

v.t. **1.** (*coll., criticize severely*) разн|оси́ть, -ести́. **2.** (*also* ~ **out:** *wash gravel etc.*) пром|ыва́ть, -ы́ть.

v.i. (*fig.*): **everything** ~**ned out well** де́ло вы́шло как нельзя́ лу́чше.

cpds. ~**cake** *n.* блин; ола́дья; **the ground was as flat as a** ~**cake** земля́ была́ соверше́нно пло́ская; ~**handle** *n.* (*US*) у́зкий вы́ступ земли́; *v.t.* & *i.* (*US*) попроша́йничать (*impf.*); ~**-lid** *n.* кры́шка (кастрю́ли); ~**tile** *n.* жело́бчатая черепи́ца.

pan[2] [pæn] *n.* (*camera movement*) панорами́рование.

v.t. панорами́ровать (*impf.*).

v.i. (*of camera*) повора́чиваться (*impf.*).

Pan[3] [pæn] *n.* (*myth.*) Пан.

cpd. **p**~**-pipes** *n. pl.* фле́йта Па́на.

pan-[4] [pæn] *comb. form* пан...

panacea [ˌpænə'si:ə] *n.* панаце́я.

panache [pə'næʃ] *n.* (*fig.*) рисо́вка.

Panama ['pænəˌmɑ:] *n.* Пана́ма; ~ **hat** пана́ма.

Panamanian [ˌpænə'meɪnɪən] *n.* жи́тель (*fem.* -ница) Пана́мы.

adj. пана́мский.

Pan-American [ˌpænə'merɪkən] *adj.* панамерика́нский.

panchromatic [ˌpænkrəʊ'mætɪk] *adj.* панхромати́ческий.

pancreas ['pæŋkrɪəs] *n.* поджелу́дочная железа́.

pancreatic ['pæŋkrɪ'ætɪk] *adj.* панкреати́ческий.

panda ['pændə] *n.* па́нда; ~ **car** ≃ канаре́йка.

pandemic [pæn'demɪk] *n.* пандеми́я.

adj. всео́бщий.

pandemonium [ˌpændɪ'məʊnɪəm] *n.* (*uproar, confusion*) смяте́ние, шум, столпотворе́ние.

pander ['pændə(r)] *n.* (*procurer*) сво́дник; (*accomplice*) посо́бник.

v.i. (*procure*) сво́дничать (*impf.*); (*minister*) потво́рствовать (*impf.*); потака́ть (*impf.*); **this newspaper** ~**s to the lowest tastes** э́та газе́та угожда́ет са́мым ни́зменным вку́сам.

Pandora's box [pæn'dɔ:rəz] *n.* я́щик Пандо́ры.

pane [peɪn] *n.* око́нное стекло́.

panegyric [ˌpænɪ'dʒɪrɪk] *n.* панеги́рик.

adj. панегири́ческий.

panel ['pæn(ə)l] *n.* **1.** (*of door etc.*) пане́ль. **2.** (*of cloth*) вста́вка. **3.** (*register*) спи́сок; ~ **doctor** врач страхка́ссы; **I am on Dr Jones's** ~ я в спи́ске до́ктора Джо́нса. **4.** (*group of speakers*) коми́ссия, жюри́ (*nt. indecl.*); ~ **game** виктори́на. **5.** (*for instruments*) пульт; **control** ~ пульт управле́ния.

panelling ['pænəlɪŋ] *n.* пане́льная обши́вка; филёнка.

panellist ['pænəlɪst] *n.* уча́стник диску́ссии; член жюри́.

Pan-European [ˌpænjʊrə'pɪən] *adj.* панъевропе́йский.

pang [pæŋ] *n.* **1.** (*physical*) боль; ~**s of hunger** му́ки го́лода; **birth** ~**s** родовы́е схва́тки (*f. pl.*). **2.** (*mental*) му́ки (*f. pl.*); **a** ~ **of conscience** угрызе́ние со́вести.

pangolin [pæŋ'gəʊlɪn] *n.* я́щер.

panic ['pænɪk] *n.* па́ника; ~ **measures** отча́янные ме́ры.

v.t. (*coll.*): **they were** ~**ked into surrender** они́ впа́ли в па́нику и сдали́сь.

v.i. впа|да́ть, -сть в па́нику; паникова́ть (*impf.*).

cpds. ~**-monger** *n.* паникёр; ~**-stricken** *adj.* охва́ченный па́никой.

panicky ['pænɪkɪ] *adj.* (*coll.*) пани́ческий.

panjandrum [pæn'dʒændrəm] *n.* «ши́шка» (*coll.*).

pannier ['pænɪə(r)] *n.* (*basket*) корзи́на; (*part of skirt*) кринoли́н.

pannikin ['pænɪkɪn] *n.* кру́жка, ми́сочка.

panoplied ['pænəplɪd] *adj.* во всеору́жии.

panoply ['pænəplɪ] *n.* доспе́х|и (*pl., g.* -ов).

panorama [ˌpænə'rɑ:mə] *n.* (*lit., fig.*) панора́ма.

panoramic [ˌpænə'ræmɪk] *adj.* панора́мный.

pansy ['pænzɪ] *n.* (*flower*) аню́тины гла́з|ки (*pl., g.* -ок); (*coll., homosexual*) «пе́дик».

adj. (*coll., effeminate*) женоподо́бный.

pant [pænt] *v.i.* тяжело́ дыша́ть (*impf.*); пыхте́ть (*impf.*); зад|ыха́ться, -охну́ться; ~ **for** (*fig.*) вздыха́ть (*impf.*) о+*p.*

pantaloon [ˌpæntə'lu:n] *n.* **1.** (*clown*) Пантало́не (*m. indecl.*), кло́ун. **2.** (*pl., hist.*) пантало́н|ы (*pl., g.* —); (*coll., trousers*) штан|ы́ (*pl., g.* -о́в).

pantechnicon [pæn'teknɪkən] *n.* (*warehouse*) склад; (*van*) фурго́н.

pantheism ['pænθɪˌɪz(ə)m] *n.* пантеи́зм.

pantheist ['pænθɪˌɪst] *n.* пантеи́ст.

pantheistic [ˌpænθɪ'ɪstɪk] *adj.* пантеисти́ческий.

pantheon ['pænθɪən] *n.* (*lit., fig.*) пантео́н.

panther ['pænθə(r)] *n.* панте́ра; (*US*) пу́ма.

panties ['pæntɪz] *n.* (*children's*) штани́ш|ки (*pl., g.* -ек); (*women's*) тру́сик|и (*pl., g.* -ов).

panto ['pæntəʊ] (*coll.*) = **pantomine**

pantograph ['pæntəˌgrɑ:f] *n.* пантóграф.

pantomime ['pæntəˌmaɪm] *n.* (*entertainment*) пантоми́ма; фее́рия; (*dumb show*) пантоми́ма.

pantry ['pæntrɪ] *n.* кладова́я.

pants [pænts] *n.* (*underwear*) трус|ы́ (*pl., g.* -о́в); (*long*) кальсо́н|ы (*pl., g.* —); (*coll. or US, trousers*) брю́к|и (*pl., g.* —); штан|ы́ (*pl., g.* -о́в); ~ (*or* **pant**) **suit** (же́нский) брю́чный костю́м.

pantyhose ['pæntɪˌhəʊz] *n.* колго́т|ки (*pl., g.* -ок).

panzer ['pæntsə(r), 'pænz-] *adj.* бронета́нковый.

pap [pæp] *n.* (*soft food*) каши́ца.

papa [pə'pɑ:] *n.* па́па (*m.*).

papacy ['peɪpəsɪ] *n.* па́пство.

papal ['peɪp(ə)l] *adj.* па́пский; **P**~ **States** (*hist.*) па́пская о́бласть.

papaw, pawpaw [pə'pɔ:] *n.* **1.** (*Carica papaya*) папа́йя. **2.** (*Asimina*) азими́на.

paper ['peɪpə(r)] *n.* **1.** бума́га; **it seemed a good scheme on** ~ на бума́ге план вы́глядел хорошо́; **you must get that idea down on** ~ (*or* **commit ... to** ~) вы должны́ э́ту мысль записа́ть; **I had hardly put pen to** ~ я то́лько бы́ло приня́лся писа́ть; (*attr.*): ~ **bag** бума́жный мешо́к; ~ **napkin** бума́жная салфе́тка; **a** ~ **tiger** «бума́жный тигр»; **a** ~ **vote was taken** проведено́ пи́сьменное голосова́ние. **2.** (**news**~) газе́та; **what do the** ~**s say?** что пи́шут газе́ты?; **he wants to get his name in the** ~**s** он хо́чет попа́сть в газе́ту; (*attr.*): ~ **round** доста́вка газе́т на́ дом; ~ **shop** газе́тный кио́ск. **3.** (*currency*) банкно́ты (*f. pl.*), бума́жные де́н|ьги (*pl., g.* -ег). **4.** (*pl., documents*) докуме́нты (*m. pl.*), бума́ги (*f. pl.*); **ship's** ~**s** судовы́е докуме́нты; **he sent in his** ~**s** он по́дал в отста́вку. **5.** (**examination** ~) экзаменацио́нная рабо́та; сочине́ние. **6.** (*essay, lecture*) докла́д. **7.** (**wall**~) обо́|и (*pl., g.* -ев).

v.t. (*put wall*~ *on*) окле́и|вать, -ть обо́ями.

with adv.: ~ **over** *v.t.* заклéи|вать, -ть бума́гой; (*fig.*): **his speech merely** ~**ed over the cracks in the party** его́ речь была́ лишь попы́тка затушева́ть раско́л в па́ртии.

cpds. ~**back** *n.* кни́га в бума́жном/мя́гком переплёте; ~**-boy** *n.* разно́счик газе́т; ~**-chase** *n.* игра́ «за́яц и соба́ки»; ~**-clip** *n.* канцеля́рская скре́пка; ~**-hanger** *n.* обо́йщик; ~**-knife** *n.* листоре́з; ~**-mill** *n.* бума́жная фа́брика; ~**-weight** *n.* пресс-папье́ (*indecl.*); ~**-work** *n.* канцеля́рская рабо́та.

papier mâché [ˌpæpjeɪ 'mæʃeɪ] *n.* папье́-маше́ (*indecl.*).

papist ['peɪpɪst] *n.* (*pej.*) папи́ст; като́лик.

papistry ['peɪpɪstrɪ] *n.* (*pej.*) папи́зм; католици́зм.

papoose [pə'pu:s] *n.* инде́йский ребёнок.

paprika ['pæprɪkə, pə'pri:kə] *n.* кра́сный/стручко́вый пе́рец, па́прика.

Papua ['pæpjʊə] *n.* Па́пуа (*indecl.*).

Papuan ['pæpjʊən] *n.* папуа́с (*fem.* -ка).

adj. папуа́сский.

papyrus [pə'paɪərəs] *n.* папи́рус.

par [pɑ:(r)] *n.* **1.** (*equality*) ра́венство; **this is on a** ~ **with his other work** э́то на у́ровне други́х его́ рабо́т. **2.** (*recognized or face value*) цена́; **above** ~ вы́ше номина́льной цены́; **at** ~ по номина́льной цене́; **below** ~ ни́же номина́льной цены́. **3.** (*standard, normal condition*) норма́льное состоя́ние; **I feel below** ~ **today** я себя́ сего́дня нева́жно чу́вствую; ~ **for the course** (*fig., coll.*) сре́дняя но́рма.

para [ˈpærə] (*coll.*) *abbr. of* **1. paratrooper** парашюти́ст-деса́нтник, авиадеса́нтник. **2. paragraph** абза́ц.

parable [ˈpærəb(ə)l] *n.* при́тча.

parabola [pəˈræbələ] *n.* пара́бола.

parabolic [ˌpærəˈbɒlɪk] *adj.* (*math.*) параболи́ческий.

parachute [ˈpærəˌʃu:t] *n.* парашю́т; (*attr.*): ~ **flare** освети́тельная раке́та; ~ **jump/landing** прыжо́к/приземле́ние с парашю́том; ~ **mine** парашю́тная ми́на; ~ **troops** возду́шно-деса́нтные войска́.

v.t.: **the stores were ~d to the ground** припа́сы бы́ли сбро́шены с парашю́том.

v.i.: **the pilot ~d out of the aircraft** пило́т вы́бросился из самолёта с парашю́том.

cpds. **~-jumper** *n.* парашюти́ст; **~-jumping** *n.* прыжки́ (*m. pl.*) с парашю́том.

parachutist [ˈpærəˌʃu:tɪst] *n.* парашюти́ст.

parade [pəˈreɪd] *n.* **1.** (*display*) пока́з; **fashion** ~ пока́з мод; **he makes a ~ of his virtues** он щеголя́ет свои́ми доброде́телями. **2.** (*muster of troops*) пара́д; **they were on ~ all morning** у них всё у́тро была́ строева́я подгото́вка. **3.** (*~-ground*) плац. **4.** (*public promenade*) промена́д.

v.t. (*display*) выставля́ть, вы́ставить напока́з; (*muster*) стро́ить, вы́-/по-.

v.i. (*muster*) стро́иться, вы́-/по-; (*march in procession*) ше́ствовать (*impf.*); маршироaccess (*impf.*).

cpds. **~-dress** *n.* пара́дное пла́тье; **~-ground** *n.* плац.

paradigm [ˈpærəˌdaɪm] *n.* паради́гма.

paradise [ˈpærəˌdaɪs] *n.* рай; **bird of ~** ра́йская пти́ца; **a ~ on earth** рай земно́й; **he is living in a fool's ~** он живёт в ми́ре иллю́зий.

paradis(i)al [ˈpærəˌdaɪs(ə)l] *adj.* ра́йский.

paradox [ˈpærəˌdɒks] *n.* парадо́кс.

paradoxical [ˌpærəˈdɒksɪk(ə)l] *adj.* парадокса́льный.

paraffin [ˈpærəfɪn] *n.* **1.** (~ *oil*) кероси́н; ~ **lamp** кероси́новая ла́мпа. **2.** (~ *wax*) парафи́н; **liquid** ~ парафи́новое ма́сло.

paragon [ˈpærəgən] *n.* образе́ц.

paragraph [ˈpærəˌgrɑ:f] *n.* абза́ц; (*newspaper item*) заме́тка.

v.t. раздел|я́ть, -и́ть на абза́цы.

Paraguay [ˈpærəˌgwaɪ] *n.* Парагва́й.

Paraguayan [ˌpærəˈgwaɪən] *n.* парагва́|ец (*fem.* -йка).

adj. парагва́йский.

parakeet [ˈpærəˌki:t] *n.* длиннохво́стый попуга́й.

parallax [ˈpærəˌlæks] *n.* паралла́кс.

parallel [ˈpærəˌlel] *n.* **1.** (*line or direction*) паралле́льная ли́ния; **in ~** паралле́льно; (*of latitude*) паралле́ль. **2.** (*fig., similar thg.; comparison*) паралле́ль; **one cannot draw a ~ between the two wars** невозмо́жно провести́ паралле́ль ме́жду э́тими двумя́ во́йнами.

adj. паралле́льный; ~ **bars** (паралле́льные) бру́сь|я (*pl., g.* -ев); (*analogous, similar*) аналоги́чный.

v.t. (*produce a ~ to*) подыска́ть (*pf.*) паралле́ль +*d.*; (*compare*) сра́вн|ивать, -и́ть; пров|оди́ть, -ести́ паралле́ль ме́жду +*i.*; (*correspond to*) соотве́тствовать (*impf.*) +*d.*

parallelepiped [ˌpærəlelˈepɪˌped, -ləˈpaɪpɪd] *n.* параллелепи́пед.

parallelism [ˈpærəlelˌɪz(ə)m] *n.* (*lit., fig.*) параллели́зм.

parallelogram [ˌpærəˈleləˌgræm] *n.* параллелогра́мм.

paralyse [ˈpærəˌlaɪz] *v.t.* (*lit., fig.*) парализова́ть (*impf., pf.*).

paralysis [pəˈrælɪsɪs] *n.* (*lit., fig.*) парали́ч.

paralytic [ˌpærəˈlɪtɪk] *n.* парали́тик.

adj. (*lit.*) паралити́ческий, парализо́ванный; (*incapably drunk*) парализо́ванный; (*feeble, inept*) не́мощный, хи́лый.

paramedic [ˌpærəˈmedɪk] *n.* медрабо́тник без вы́сшего образова́ния.

parameter [pəˈræmɪtə(r)] *n.* (*math.; also fig., aspect, factor*) пара́метр.

paramilitary [ˌpærəˈmɪlɪtərɪ] *adj.* полувое́нный; военизи́рованный.

paramount [ˈpærəˌmaʊnt] *adj.* первостепе́нный; **his influence was ~** он име́л огро́мное/всеси́льное влия́ние.

paramour [ˈpærəˌmʊə(r)] *n.* любо́вни|к (*fem.* -ца).

paranoia [ˌpærəˈnɔɪə] *n.* парано́йя.

paranoi|d [ˈpærəˌnɔɪd], **-ac** [ˌpærəˈnəʊɪk, -ˈnɔɪɪk] *nn.* парано́ик.

adjs. парано́идный, параноите́ческий.

paranormal [ˌpærəˈnɔ:m(ə)l] *adj.* паранорма́льный.

parapet [ˈpærəpɪt] *n.* (*low wall*) парапе́т; (*trench defence*) бру́ствер.

paraphernalia [ˌpærəfəˈneɪlɪə] *n.* (*belongings*) ли́чные ве́щи (*f. pl.*), принадле́жности (*f. pl.*); (*trappings*) атрибу́ты (*m. pl.*), причинда́л|ы (*pl., g.* -ов).

paraphrase [ˈpærəˌfreɪz] *n.* переска́з.

v.t. переска́з|ывать, -а́ть.

paraplegia [ˌpærəˈpli:dʒə] *n.* параплеги́я.

paraplegic [ˌpærəˈpli:dʒɪk] *adj.* парализо́ванный.

paraquat [ˈpærəkwɒt] *n.* параква́т.

parasite [ˈpærəˌsaɪt] *n.* парази́т; (*fig.*) парази́т; туне́ядец.

parasitic [ˌpærəˈsɪtɪk] *adj.* (*lit., fig.*) паразити́ческий.

parasol [ˈpærəˌsɒl] *n.* зо́нтик (от со́лнца).

paratrooper [ˈpærəˌtru:pə(r)] *n.* парашюти́ст-деса́нтник, авиадеса́нтник.

paratroops [ˈpærəˌtru:ps] *n.* парашю́тно-деса́нтные войска́ (*nt. pl.*).

paratyphoid [ˌpærəˈtaɪfɔɪd] *n.* парати́ф.

parboil [ˈpɑ:bɔɪl] *v.t.* обва́р|ивать, -и́ть кипятко́м.

parcel [ˈpɑ:s(ə)l] *n.* **1.** (*package*) паке́т, посы́лка; ~ **post** почто́во-посы́лочная слу́жба. **2.** (*arch., portion*) часть; **a ~ of land** уча́сток земли́; **part and ~** составна́я/неотъе́млемая часть (*чего*).

v.t. (*pack up; also ~* **up**) пакова́ть, у-; (*divide; also ~* **out**) дроби́ть, раз-.

parch [pɑ:tʃ] *v.t.* иссуш|а́ть, -и́ть; перес|ыха́ть, -о́хнуть; **the ground was ~ed** земля́ вы́сохла; **his throat was ~ed with thirst** у него́ от жа́жды пересо́хло в го́рле; **my lips are ~ed** у меня́ запекли́сь гу́бы.

parchment [ˈpɑ:tʃmənt] *n.* (*skin, manuscript, type of paper*) перга́мент.

pardon [ˈpɑ:d(ə)n] *n.* **1.** извине́ние, проще́ние; **I beg your ~** (*apology*) прошу́ проще́ния; (*request for repetition*) повтори́те, пожа́луйста!; прости́те, не расслы́шал. **2.** (*leg.*) поми́лование; **they were granted a free ~** их поми́ловали.

v.t. (*forgive*) про|ща́ть, -сти́ть; (*excuse*) извин|я́ть, -и́ть; **if you'll ~ the expression** извини́те за выраже́ние; (*leg.*) поми́ловать (*pf.*).

pardonabl|e [ˈpɑ:dənəb(ə)l] *adj.* прости́тельный; **she was ~y proud of her son** она́, вполне́ заслу́женно, горди́лась свои́м сы́ном.

pare [peə(r)] *v.t.* (*trim*) стричь, обо-; (*peel*) чи́стить, по-; (*reduce; also ~* **away, ~ down**) ур|е́зывать, -е́за́ть, (*pf.*) -е́зать.

paregoric [ˌpærɪˈgɒrɪk] *n.* болеутоля́ющее/успока́ивающее сре́дство.

adj. болеутоля́ющий.

parent [ˈpeərənt] *n.* (*father or mother*) роди́тель (*fem.* -ница); **our first ~s** (*Adam and Eve*) на́ши прароди́тели; (*fig., origin*) исто́чник; (*attr., original*) первонача́льный; **~ firm** компа́ния-учреди́тель; **~ stock** (*bot.*) корнева́я по́росль.

parentage [ˈpeərəntɪdʒ] *n.* происхожде́ние; отцо́вство, матери́нство; **he is of mixed ~** он происхо́дит от сме́шанного бра́ка.

parental [pəˈrent(ə)l] *adj.* роди́тельский.

parenthes|is [pəˈrenθəsɪs] *n.* вво́дное сло́во/предложе́ние; (*pl.*) кру́глые ско́бки (*f. pl.*); **in ~es** в ско́бках.

parenthetic(al) [ˌpærənˈθetɪkəl] *adj.* вво́дный.

parenthetically [ˌpærənˈθetɪkəlɪ] *adv.* ме́жду де́лом/про́чим, в ви́де отступле́ния.

parenthood [ˈpeərənthʊd] *n.*: **planned ~** (иску́сственное) ограниче́ние соста́ва семьи́.

par excellence [ˌpɑ:r eksəˈlɑ̃s] *adv.*: **this is the fashionable quarter ~** э́то са́мый что ни на есть мо́дный райо́н.

pariah [pəˈraɪə, ˈpærɪə] *n.* (*lit. fig.*) па́рия (*c.g.*).

cpd. **~-dog** *n.* дворня́жка.

paring [ˈpeərɪŋ] *n.* (*peeling*) очище́ние; (*trimming: of nails etc.*) стри́жка; (*slicing: of cheese etc.*) нареза́ние; **nail ~s** обре́зки (*m. pl.*) ногте́й.

pari passu [ˌpɑ:rɪ ˈpæsu:, ˌpærɪ] *adv.* наравне́, паралле́льно.

Paris [ˈpærɪs] *n.* (*geog.*) Пари́ж; (*myth.*) Пари́с.

parish [ˈpærɪʃ] *n.* (*eccles.*) прихо́д; (*civil*) о́круг; ~ **clerk** псало́мщик; ~ **council** прихо́дский сове́т; ~ **register** прихо́дская метри́ческая кни́га.

parishioner [pəˈrɪʃənə(r)] *n.* прихожа́н|ин (*fem.* -ка).

Parisian [pəˈrɪzɪən] *n.* парижа́н|ин (*fem.* -ка).
adj. пари́жский.

Parisienne [ˌpærɪzjˈen] *n.* парижа́нка.

parity [ˈpærɪtɪ] *n.* (*equality*) ра́венство; (*analogy*) анало́гия; **by ~ of reasoning** по анало́гии.

park [pɑːk] *n.* **1.** (*public garden*) парк. **2.** (*protected area of countryside*) запове́дник; национа́льный парк. **3.** (*grounds of country mansion*) уго́д|ья (*pl.*, *g.* -ий). **4.** (*for vehicles etc.*) стоя́нка, парк.
v.t. паркова́ть, за-; ост|авля́ть, -а́вить; (*coll.*, *stow*, *dispose*) скла́дывать, сложи́ть; **you can ~ your things in my room** вы мо́жете бро́сить свои́ ве́щи в мое́й ко́мнате; **he ~ed himself in the best chair** он усе́лся в лу́чшее кре́сло.
v.i. паркова́ться, за-; ста́вить, по- маши́ну (на стоя́нку); (*coll.*) устро́иться (*pf.*); расположи́ться (*pf.*).
cpd. **~-keeper** *n.* сто́рож (при па́рке).

parka [ˈpɑːkə] *n.* па́рка.

parking [ˈpɑːkɪŋ] *n.* (авто)стоя́нка; **'no ~!'** «стоя́нка запрещена́!»
cpds. **~-light** *n.* подфа́рник; **~-lot** *n.* стоя́нка; ме́сто стоя́нки; **~-meter** *n.* стоя́ночный счётчик; счётчик на стоя́нке.

Parkinson's disease [ˈpɑːkɪns(ə)nz] *n.* боле́знь Паркинсо́на.

Parkinson's law [ˈpɑːkɪns(ə)nz] *n.* зако́н Паркинсо́на.

parky [ˈpɑːkɪ] *adj.* (*coll.*) холоднова́тый.

parlance [ˈpɑːləns] *n.* язы́к; мане́ра выраже́ния; **in common ~** в просторе́чии.

parley [ˈpɑːlɪ] *n.* перегово́р|ы (*pl.*, *g.* -ов).
v.i. догова́риваться (*impf.*).

parliament [ˈpɑːləmənt] *n.* парла́мент; **P~ met** парла́мент собра́лся; **P~ is sitting** парла́мент заседа́ет; **P~ rose** парла́мент око́нчил заседа́ние; **the Queen opened P~** короле́ва откры́ла се́ссию парла́мента.

parliamentarian [ˌpɑːləmenˈteərɪən] *n.* (*member of parliament*) парламента́рий.

parliamentary [ˌpɑːləˈmentərɪ] *adj.* парла́ментский, парламента́рный.

parlour [ˈpɑːlə(r)] *n.* (*in house*) гости́ная; **~ tricks** све́тские тала́нты; (*in inn*) зал; (*for official reception*) приёмная; (*US*, *for clients*) ателье́ (*indecl.*), кабине́т, сало́н; **beauty ~** косметй́ческий кабине́т/сало́н; **funeral ~** похоро́нное бюро́ (*indecl.*); **ice-cream ~** кафе́-моро́женое.
cpds. **~-game** *n.* фа́нт|ы (*pl.*, *g.* -ов); **~-maid** *n.* го́рничная.

parlous [ˈpɑːləs] *adj.* (*arch.*, *joc.*) стра́шный.

Parmesan [ˌpɑːmɪˈzæn, ˈpɑː-] *n.* **(~ cheese)** сыр пармеза́н.

Parnassian [pɑːˈnæsɪən] *adj.* парна́сский.

parochial [pəˈrəʊkɪəl] *adj.* прихо́дский; (*fig.*) ограни́ченный, у́зкий.

parochialism [pəˈrəʊkɪəˌlɪz(ə)m] *n.* ограни́ченность, у́зкость.

parodist [ˈpærədɪst] *n.* пароди́ст.

parody [ˈpærədɪ] *n.* паро́дия.
v.t. пароди́ровать (*impf.*, *pf.*).

parole [pəˈrəʊl] *n.* че́стное сло́во; **he was released on ~** его́ освободи́ли под че́стное сло́во.
v.t. освобо|жда́ть, -ди́ть под че́стное сло́во (*or* на пору́ки).

paroxysm [ˈpærəkˌsɪz(ə)m] *n.* пароксй́зм; (*of anger*, *laughter*) при́ступ.

parquet [ˈpɑːkɪ, -keɪ] *n.* парке́т.

parricidal [ˌpærɪˈsaɪdəl] *adj.* отцеуби́йственный.

par|ricide [ˈpærɪˌsaɪd], **pat-** [ˈpætrɪˌsaɪd] *nn.* (*pers.*) отцеуби́йца (*c.g.*); (*crime*) отцеуби́йство.

parrot [ˈpærət] *n.* (*lit.*, *fig.*) попуга́й.
v.t. повтор|я́ть, -и́ть как попуга́й.
cpd. **~-fashion** *adv.* как попуга́й.

parry [ˈpærɪ] *v.t.* отра|жа́ть, -зи́ть (уда́р).

parse [pɑːz] *v.t.* & *i.* де́лать, с- граммати́ческий разбо́р (*чего*).

parsec [ˈpɑːsek] *n.* парсе́к.

Parsee [pɑːˈsiː] *n.* парс.

parsimonious [ˌpɑːsɪˈməʊnɪəs] *adj.* скупо́й, прижи́мистый.

parsimony [ˈpɑːsɪmənɪ] *n.* ску́пость.

parsley [ˈpɑːslɪ] *n.* петру́шка.

parsnip [ˈpɑːsnɪp] *n.* пастерна́к.

parson [ˈpɑːs(ə)n] *n.* па́стор; **~'s nose** (*of fowl*) «архиере́йский нос», кури́ная гу́зка.

parsonage [ˈpɑːsənɪdʒ] *n.* пастора́т.

part [pɑːt] *n.* **1.** часть; (*portion*) до́ля; **the greater ~** (*majority*) бо́льшая часть; **for the most ~** бо́льшей ча́стью; по бо́льшей ча́сти; **in ~** части́чно, отча́сти; **this book is good in ~s** э́та кни́га хороша́ места́ми; **inquisitiveness is ~ of being young** мо́лодости сво́йственно любозна́тельность; **~ and parcel** *see* **parcel** *n.* **2.**; (*equal division*): **he received a fifth ~ of the estate** он получи́л пя́тую до́лю состоя́ния; **the glass was three ~s full** стака́н был нали́т на три че́тверти; (*instalment*): **the journal comes out in weekly ~s** журна́л выхо́дит еженеде́льными вы́пусками; (*component*): **spare ~s** запасны́е ча́сти; (*gram.*): **~s of speech** ча́сти ре́чи; **principal ~s of a verb** основны́е фо́рмы (*f. pl.*) глаго́ла. **2.** (*share*, *contribution*) уча́стие; **take ~ in** прин|има́ть, -я́ть уча́стие в+*p.*; **I'll have no ~ in it** я не бу́ду принима́ть в э́том уча́стия; **I have done my ~** я сде́лал своё де́ло (*or* свою́ часть рабо́ты). **3.** (*actor's role or lines*) роль; **he is only playing a ~** он про́сто игра́ет; **luck played a large ~ in his success** уда́ча сыгра́ла большу́ю роль в его́ успе́хе. **4.** (*side in dispute etc.*) сторона́; **take s.o.'s ~** вст|ава́ть, -ать на чью-н. сто́рону; **there will be no objection on his ~** с его́ стороны́ возраже́ний не бу́дет; **for my ~** с мое́й стороны́, что каса́ется меня́; **he took my criticism in good ~** он не оби́делся на мою́ кри́тику. **5.** (*region*) места́ (*nt. pl.*), край; **in our ~ of the world** в на́ших края́х; **I'm a stranger in these ~s** я в э́тих места́х чужо́й; **do you know these ~s?** зна́ете вы э́ти края́? **6.** (*mus.*) па́ртия; **it is a difficult ~ to sing** э́ту па́ртию тру́дно спеть; **a song for four ~s** пе́сня на четы́ре го́лоса. **7.** (*pl.*, *abilities*) спосо́бности (*f. pl.*); **a man of ~s** спосо́бный челове́к. **8.** (*pl.*, *genitals*): **private ~s** половы́е о́рганы (*m. pl.*).
adv. части́чно, ча́стью, отча́сти; **the wall is ~ brick and ~ stone** стена́ сло́жена части́чно из кирпича́, части́чно из ка́мня.
v.t. раздел|я́ть, -и́ть; **he ~ed the fighters** он разня́л деру́щихся/драчуно́в; **the policeman ~ed the crowd** толпа́ расступи́лась пе́ред полице́йским; **his hair was ~ed in the middle** его́ во́лосы бы́ли расчёсаны на прямо́й пробо́р; **he ~s it at the side** он но́сит пробо́р сбо́ку; **we ~ed company** (*went different ways*) мы разошли́сь/разъе́хались; (*ended our relationship*) мы расста́лись; (*differed*) мы разошли́сь во мне́ниях.
v.i. расст|ава́ться, -а́ться; **they ~ed friends** они́ расста́лись друзья́ми; **she has ~ed from her husband** она́ разошла́сь с му́жем; **he hates to ~ with his money** он страх как не лю́бит расстава́ться с деньга́ми.
cpds. **~-owner** *n.* совладе́лец; **~-song** *n.* хорова́я пе́сня; **~-time** *adj.*, *adv.* на непо́лной ста́вке; с непо́лной нагру́зкой; **~-work** *n.* кни́га, выходя́щая отде́льными вы́пусками; **~-worn** *adj.* слегка́ поно́шенный.

partake [pɑːˈteɪk] *v.i.* **1.** (*take a share*) прин|има́ть, -я́ть уча́стие; **they partook of our meal** они́ пое́ли с на́ми. **2.** (*fig.*, *savour*): **his manner ~s of insolence** его́ поведе́ние грани́чит с на́глостью.

parterre [pɑːˈteə(r)] *n.* (*in garden*) цветни́к; (*theatr.*) парте́р.

parthenogenesis [ˌpɑːθɪnəʊˈdʒenɪsɪs] *n.* партеногене́з

Parthenon [ˈpɑːθəˌnɒn, -nən] *n.* Парфено́н.

Parthian [ˈpɑːθɪən] *adj.*: **a ~ shot, shaft** парфя́нская стрела́.

partial [ˈpɑːʃ(ə)l] *adj.* **1.** (*opp. total*) части́чный; **~ eclipse** непо́лное затме́ние. **2.** (*biased*) пристра́стный. **3.: ~ to** (*fond of*) неравноду́шный к+*d.*

partiality [ˌpɑːʃɪˈælɪtɪ] *n.* (*bias*) пристра́стность; (*fondness*) скло́нность (*к кому/чему*).

participant [pɑːˈtɪsɪpənt] *n.* уча́стник.

participate [pɑːˈtɪsɪˌpeɪt] *v.i.* (*take part*) уча́ствовать (*impf.*).

participation [pɑːˌtɪsɪˈpeɪʃ(ə)n] *n.* уча́стие.

participle [ˈpɑːtɪˌsɪp(ə)l] *n.* прича́стие; **present and past ~s** прича́стия настоя́щего и проше́дшего вре́мени.

particle [ˈpɑːtɪk(ə)l] *n.* **1.** части́ца, крупи́ца; **a ~ of dust** пыли́нка; **she hasn't a ~ of sense** у неё нет ни ка́пли здра́вого смы́сла. **2.** (*gram.*) неизменя́емая части́ца.

particoloured [ˈpɑːtɪˌkʌləd] *adj.* разноцве́тный.

particular [pəˈtɪkjʊlə(r)] *n.* ча́стность; **in ~** в ча́стности; **they agreed down to the smallest ~** они́ соглаша́лись во всём до мельча́йших подро́бностей; (*pl.*) да́нные (*pl.*); **let me take down your ~s** разреши́те мне записа́ть ва́ши да́нные; **they sent me ~s of the house** они́ присла́ли мне (подро́бное) описа́ние до́ма.

adj. **1.** (*specific, special*) осо́бенный, осо́бый; **for no ~ reason** без осо́бой причи́ны. **2.** (*detailed*) обстоя́тельный; **a ~ account** обстоя́тельный/дета́льный отчёт. **3.** (*fastidious*) привере́дливый; **I am not ~ what I eat** я неразбо́рчив в еде́; **she is not ~ about her dress** ей всё равно́, что наде́ть.

particularism [pəˈtɪkjʊləˌrɪz(ə)m] *n.* приве́рженность; (*pol.*) партикуляри́зм.

particularity [pəˌtɪkjʊˈlærɪtɪ] *n.* специ́фика.

particularize [pəˈtɪkjʊləˌraɪz] *v.t.* переч|исля́ть, -и́слить.

v.i. вда|ва́ться, -ться в подро́бности.

particularly [pəˈtɪkjʊlәlɪ] *adv.* осо́бенно.

parting [ˈpɑːtɪŋ] *n.* **1.** (*leave-taking*) проща́ние; **a kiss at ~** поцелу́й на проща́ние; **a ~ gift** проща́льный пода́рок. **2.** (*separation*) расстава́ние; проща́ние; **at the ~ of the ways** (*lit., fig.*) на распу́тье. **3.** (*of the hair*) пробо́р.

parti pris [ˌpɑːtɪ ˈpriː] *n.* предвзя́тое мне́ние.

parti|san, -zan [ˈpɑːtɪˌzæn] *n.* **1.** (*zealous supporter*) приве́рженец; **you say that in a ~ spirit** вы говори́те пристра́стно. **2.** (*resistance fighter*) партиза́н (*fem.* -ка).

partisanship [ˈpɑːtɪˌzænʃɪp] *n.* приве́рженность.

partition [pɑːˈtɪʃ(ə)n] *n.* (*division*) разде́л; **the ~ of Poland** разде́л По́льши; (*dividing structure*) перегоро́дка; (*compartment*) отделе́ние, се́кция.

v.t. дели́ть, раз-/по-; **~ off** отгор|а́живать, -оди́ть.

partitive [ˈpɑːtɪtɪv] *adj.* (*gram.*) раздели́тельный.

partly [ˈpɑːtlɪ] *adv.* части́чно, отча́сти.

partner [ˈpɑːtnə(r)] *n.* (*cards, dancing etc.*) партнёр (*fem.* -ша); (*comm.*): **senior ~ in the firm** гла́вный компаньо́н фи́рмы; **~s in crime** соуча́стники (*m. pl.*) преступле́ния; (*in marriage*) супру́г (*fem.* -а).

v.t. (*be ~ to*) быть партнёром +*g*.

partnership [ˈpɑːtnəʃɪp] *n.* това́рищество; компа́ния; партнёрство; **to go into ~ (with)** войти́ (*pf.*) в партнёрство (с+*i.*); **marriage is a ~ for life** брак — сою́з на всю жизнь.

partridge [ˈpɑːtrɪdʒ] *n.* куропа́тка.

parturition [ˌpɑːtjʊˈrɪʃ(ə)n] *n.* ро́д|ы (*pl., g.* -ов).

party [ˈpɑːtɪ] *n.* **1.** (*political group*) па́ртия; **he puts ~ before country** он ста́вит интере́сы па́ртии вы́ше интере́сов ро́дины; **~ politics** парти́йная поли́тика; **the ~ system** парти́йная систе́ма. **2.** (*group with common interests or pursuits*) компа́ния, гру́ппа; **we travelled abroad in a ~** мы пое́хали за грани́цу гру́ппой; **we need one more to make up the ~** нам ну́жен ещё оди́н челове́к, что́бы соста́вить компа́нию. **3.** (*social gathering*) вечери́нка, приём; **~ dress** вече́рнее пла́тье; **he lacks the ~ spirit** он не компане́йский челове́к. **4.** (*outing*) экску́рсия. **5.** (*participant in contract etc.*) сторона́; **the wife was the injured ~** жена́ была́ пострада́вшей стороно́й; **I won't be ~ to such a scheme** я не приму́ уча́стия в э́той зате́е. **6.** (*joc., pers.*) осо́ба. **7.** (*attr., shared*): **~ line** (*telephone*) о́бщий телефо́нный про́вод; **~ wall** брандма́уер.

cpd. **~-coloured** *adj.* = **particoloured**

parvenu [ˈpɑːvəˌnuː] *n.* парвеню́ (*m. indecl.*).

paschal [ˈpæsk(ə)l] *adj.* пасха́льный.

Pas de Calais [pɑː də kæˈleɪ] *n.* Па-де-Кале́ (*indecl.*).

pas de deux [pɑː də ˈdɜː] *n.* па-де-де́ (*m., nt. indecl.*).

pasha [ˈpɑːʃə] *n.* паша́ (*m.*).

pass [pɑːs] *n.* **1.** (*qualifying standard in exam*) сда́ча экза́мена; **he got a ~ in French** он сдал францу́зский; он прошёл по-францу́зскому; **a bare ~** сда́ча экза́мена без отли́чия. **2.** (*situation*) положе́ние; **things reached a pretty ~** дела́ при́няли скве́рный оборо́т. **3.** (*arch.*): **it came to ~** так случи́лось/произошло́. **4.** (*permit, document*) про́пуск (*pl.* -а́); **free ~** свобо́дный вход; контрама́рка. **5.** (*transfer of ball in game*) пас, переда́ча. **6.** (*movement of hand*) пасс. **7.** (*lunge, thrust*) вы́пад; (*coll., amorous approach*): **he made a ~ at her** он к ней пристава́л. **8.** (*mountain defile*) уще́лье, перева́л; **he sold the ~** (*fig.*) он соверши́л преда́тельство. **9.** (*at cards*) пас.

v.t. **1.** (*go by*) про|ходи́ть, -йти́ ми́мо +*g.*; **he ~es the shop on his way to work** он прохо́дит ми́мо магази́на по доро́ге на рабо́ту; **I ~ed him in the street** я прошёл ми́мо него́ на у́лице. **2.** (*overtake*) об|гоня́ть, -огна́ть. **3.** (*go, get through*) про|ходи́ть, -йти́; **not a word ~ed his lips** он не произнёс ни сло́ва; **will your car ~ the test** пройдёт ли ва́ша маши́на испыта́ние?; **~ an exam** сдать/вы́держать (*pf.*) экза́мен. **4.** (*spend*) пров|оди́ть, -ести́; **he ~ed a pleasant evening there** он провёл там прия́тный ве́чер. **5.** (*surpass, exceed*) прев|ыша́ть, -ы́сить; **it ~es all reason** э́то выхо́дит за преде́лы разу́много. **6.** (*examine and accept*) пропус|ка́ть, -ти́ть; **only one candidate was ~ed by the board** коми́ссия утверди́ла то́лько одного́ кандида́та; (*approve, sanction*) од|обря́ть, -о́брить. **7.** (*hand over*) перед|ава́ть, -а́ть; **~ (me) the salt, please!** переда́йте мне соль, пожа́луйста! **8.** (*utter*) произн|оси́ть, -ести́; **he refrained from ~ing judgement** он воздержа́лся выноси́ть сужение; **the judge ~ed sentence** судья́ вы́нес пригово́р; **we met and ~ed the time of day** мы встре́тились и поздоро́вались. **9.** (*cause to circulate*) пус|ка́ть, -ти́ть в обраще́ние; **he was accused of ~ing forged notes** его́ обвини́ли в распростране́нии фальши́вых де́нег. **10.** (*cause to go, move*): **he ~ed his eye over the goods** он просмотре́л това́ры; **he ~ed a rope round her waist** он обвяза́л её та́лию верёвкой; **~ a ball** перед|ава́ть, -а́ть (*or* бр|оса́ть, -о́сить) мяч. **11.** (*excrete*) испус|ка́ть, -ти́ть; **he could not ~ water** он не мог мочи́ться.

v.i. **1.** (*proceed, move*) про|ходи́ть, -йти́; перепр|авля́ться, -а́виться; **he ~ed by the window** он прошёл ми́мо окна́; **he ~ed through the door** он прошёл в/че́рез дверь; **~ along (down) the car!** проходи́те да́льше; **she ~ed out of sight** она́ исче́зла и́з виду; **his name will ~ into oblivion** его́ и́мя забу́дется (*or* ка́нет в Ле́ту); (*get through*): **let me ~!** да́йте мне пройти́; (*circulate*) перед|ава́ться, -а́ться; **the magazine ~ed from hand to hand** журна́л передава́лся из рук в ру́ки; (*in opposite directions*) минова́ть (*impf., pf.*); **they ~ed without speaking** они́ мо́лча прошли́ ми́мо друг дру́га; (*fig., live*): **he has ~ed through many misfortunes** он пе́режил мно́го несча́стий. **2.** (*overtake*) об|гоня́ть, -огна́ть; **~ing prohibited for 2 miles** обго́н запрещён на две ми́ли. **3.** (*go by, elapse*) про|ходи́ть, -йти́; **the procession ~ed** проце́ссия прошла́ ми́мо; **time ~es slowly** вре́мя прохо́дит ме́дленно; **six years have ~ed since then** с тех пор прошло́ шесть лет. **4.** (*change*) превра|ща́ться, -ти́ться; **day ~es into night** день перехо́дит в ночь; **his mood ~ed from fear to anger** в нём страх смени́лся я́ростью. **5.** (*be said or done*) прои|сходи́ть, -зойти́; **did you hear what ~ed between them?** вы зна́ете, что произошло́ ме́жду ни́ми? **6.** (*go without comment*): **his words ~ed unnoticed** его́ слова́ прошли́ незаме́ченными; на его́ слова́ никто́ не обрати́л внима́ния; **let it ~!** не на́до об э́том говори́ть! **7.** (*come to an end*) про|ходи́ть, -йти́; прекра|ща́ться, -ти́ться; **the pain will ~** боль пройдёт. **8.** (*qualify in exam etc.; be valid, accepted, recognized*) про|ходи́ть, -йти́; **he ~es for an expert** он счита́ется специали́стом; **he ~ed under a false name** он жил под чужо́й фами́лией. **9.** (*at cards*) пасова́ть, с-.

with advs.: **~ along** *v.i.* про|ходи́ть, -йти́; **~ away** *v.i.* (*vanish*) прекра|ща́ться, -ти́ться; исч|еза́ть, -е́знуть; (*die*) сконча́ться (*pf.*); **~ by** *v.t. & i.* про|ходи́ть, -йти́ ми́мо; **~ down** *v.t.* перед|ава́ть, -а́ть; **the custom was ~ed down from father to son** обы́чай передава́лся от отца́ к сы́ну; *v.i.* пере|ходи́ть, -йти́; **~ off** *v.t.* (*dismiss*): **he ~ed off the whole affair as a joke** он обрати́л всё де́ло в шу́тку; (*palm off, get rid of*) подс|о́вывать, -у́нуть; сбы|ва́ть, -ть; (*falsely represent*): **he ~es himself off as a foreigner** он выдаёт себя́ за иностра́нца; **he tried to ~ off the picture as genuine** он выдава́л карти́ну за по́длинник; *v.i.* (*go away*) прекра|ща́ться, -ти́ться; **the pain was slow to ~ off** боль проходи́ла ме́дленно; (*be carried through*) про|ходи́ть, -йти́; **the wedding ~ed off without a hitch** сва́дьба прошла́ без сучка́ без задо́ринки; **~ on** *v.t.* перед|ава́ть, -а́ть; (*charge, tax etc.*) пере|кла́дывать, -ложи́ть (*на кого*); *v.i.* про|ходи́ть, -йти́; **let us ~ on to other topics** дава́йте перейдём/переключи́мся на други́е те́мы; (*euph., die*) сконча́ться (*pf.*); **~ out** *v.i.* (*qualify, graduate*) про|ходи́ть, -йти́; **~ing-out parade** пара́д выпускнико́в; (*coll., lose consciousness*) теря́ть, по- созна́ние; **~ over** *v.t.* (*hand over*) перед|ава́ть, -а́ть; (*omit; overlook, ignore*) пропус|ка́ть, -ти́ть; **we shall ~ over your previous offences** мы не бу́дем инкримини́ровать вам предыду́щие наруше́ния; **he was ~ed over for a younger man** они́ ему́ предпочли́ бо́лее молодо́го челове́ка; *v.i.* про|ходи́ть, -йти́; **the storm ~ed over** буря́ пронесла́сь (и ушла́); (*euph., die*) сконча́ться (*pf.*); **~ round** *v.t.* перед|ава́ть, -а́ть; **~ the hat round** пусти́ть (*pf.*) ша́пку по кру́гу; **~ through** *v.t.* прод|ева́ть, -е́ть; **~ up** *v.t.* (*hand up*) под|ава́ть, -а́ть; (*coll., refuse*) отка́з|ываться, -а́ться от +*g.*

cpds. **~-book** *n.* ба́нковская кни́жка; **~-key** *n.* отмы́чка; **P~over** *n.* евре́йская Па́сха; **~word** *n.* паро́ль (*m.*).

passable ['pɑːsəb(ə)l] *adj.* (*affording passage*) проходи́мый, прое́зжий; (*tolerable*) сно́сный.

passage ['pæsɪdʒ] *n.* **1.** (*going by*) прохо́д; **the ~ of time** тече́ние вре́мени; (*going across, over*) перее́зд; перелёт; **a bird of ~** перелётная пти́ца; (*transition, change*) перехо́д; (*going through, way through*) прохо́д; **the police forced a ~ through the crowd** поли́ция проложи́ла себе́ путь че́рез толпу́; (*right to go through*) пра́во прохо́да. **2.** (*crossing by ship etc.*) рейс; **have you booked your ~?** вы заказа́ли биле́т на парохо́д?; **we had a rough ~** на́ше пла́вание бы́ло бу́рным; (*fig.*): **the bill had a rough ~** законопрое́кт был при́нят по́сле бу́рного обсужде́ния; **work one's ~** отраб|а́тывать, -о́тать свой прое́зд. **3.** (*passing of law etc.*) проведе́ние. **4.** (*corridor*) коридо́р. **5.** (*alley*) прохо́д. **6.** (*coll., duct in body*) прохо́д, прото́к; **back ~** (*rectum*) за́дний прохо́д; (*pl., breathing tubes*) дыха́тельные пут|и́ (*pl., g.* -е́й). **7.** (*literary excerpt*) ме́сто, отры́вок, текст; (*mus.*) пасса́ж. **8.** (*pl., interchange*) сты́чка. **9.: ~ of arms** (*lit.*) схва́тка, бой; (*fig.*) сты́чка.

cpd. **~-way** *n.* коридо́р; прохо́д.

passé ['pæseɪ] *adj.* (*past one's prime*) увя́дший.

passenger ['pæsɪndʒə(r)] *n.* **1.** пассажи́р; седо́к; **~ train** пассажи́рский по́езд; **~ seat** ме́сто ря́дом с води́телем. **2.** (*coll. one not pulling his weight*) балла́ст, «слаба́к».

passe-partout [ˌpæspɑːˈtuː, ˌpɑːs-] *n.* (*key*) отмы́чка; (*picture-framing method*) паспарту́ (*nt. indecl.*).

passer-by [ˌpɑːsəˈbaɪ] *n.* прохо́жий.

passim ['pæsɪm] *adv.* везде́, повсю́ду.

passing ['pɑːsɪŋ] *n.* **1.** (*going by*) прохожде́ние; **I just called in ~** я зашёл мимохо́дом; **I will mention in ~** я заме́чу попу́тно (*or* ме́жду про́чим). **2.** (*death*) смерть, кончи́на.

adj. (*transient*): **a ~ fancy** мимолётное увлече́ние; **the ~ fashion** преходя́щая мо́да.

adv. (*arch. exceedingly*) чрезвыча́йно.

cpds. **~-bell** *n.* похоро́нный звон; **~-note** *n.* (*mus.*) перехо́дная но́та.

passion ['pæʃ(ə)n] *n.* **1.** (*strong emotion; sexual feeling*) страсть; **his ~s were quickly aroused** его́ бы́ло нетру́дно разъяри́ть; (*burst of anger*) взрыв; **fly into a ~** при|ходи́ть, -йти́ в я́рость; **he was in a towering ~** он ужа́сно серди́лся; (*enthusiasm*) пыл; **she has a ~ for Bach** она́ стра́стно увлечена́ му́зыкой Ба́ха. **2.** (*relig.*): **the P~** стра́сти Госпо́дни (*f. pl.*); кре́стные му́ки (*f. pl.*); **P~ play** библе́йская мисте́рия; **the St. Matthew P~** Стра́сти по Матве́ю.

passionate ['pæʃənət] *adj.* (*having strong emotions*) стра́стный, пы́лкий; (*sexually ardent*) стра́стный; (*impassioned of language etc.*) пы́лкий, горя́чий, стра́шный.

passionately ['pæʃənətlɪ] *adv.* стра́стно, пы́лко; **he is ~ fond of golf** он энтузиа́ст го́льфа.

passionless ['pæʃənlɪs] *adj.* бесстра́стный.

passive ['pæsɪv] *n.* (*gram.*) пасси́вная фо́рма, страда́тельный зало́г.

adj. пасси́вный; (*gram.*) пасси́вный, страда́тельный.

passiv|eness ['pæsɪvnɪs], **-ity** [pæ'sɪvɪtɪ] *nn.* пасси́вность.

passport ['pɑːspɔːt] *n.* (*lit.*) па́спорт; (*fig.*) ключ, путёвка; **hard work is the ~ to success** усе́рдие — зало́г успе́ха.

past [pɑːst] *n.* **1.** про́шлое; **courtesy is a thing of the ~** ве́жливость вы́шла из мо́ды; **you are living in the ~** вы живёте в про́шлом; **one cannot undo the ~** нельзя́ зачеркну́ть про́шлое; (**~ *life, career***): **a woman with a ~** же́нщина с про́шлым; **he tried to live down his ~** он стара́лся перечеркну́ть своё про́шлое. **2.** (*gram.*) проше́дшее вре́мя.

adj. **1.** (*bygone*) мину́вший, про́шлый; **that is all ~ history** всё э́то уже́ исто́рия; (*pred., gone by*) ми́мо; **the time for that is ~** вре́мя для э́того давно́ минова́ло; **that is all ~ and done with** с э́тим поко́нчено; **what's ~ is ~** де́ло про́шлое. **2.** (*preceding*) про́шлый; **for the ~ few days** за после́дние не́сколько дней; **during the ~ week** за э́ту неде́лю; **for some time ~** за после́днее вре́мя. **3.** (*gram.*) проше́дший; **~ participle** прича́стие проше́дшего вре́мени; **~ tense** проше́дшее вре́мя. **4.: a ~ master** непревзойдённый ма́стер.

adv. ми́мо; **the soldiers marched ~** солда́ты прошли́ ми́мо; **he pushed ~** он протолка́лся/проби́лся.

prep. **1.** (*after*) по́сле +*g.*; **it is ~ eight o'clock** тепе́рь девя́тый час; **ten ~ one** де́сять мину́т второ́го; **he lived to be ~ eighty** ему́ бы́ло за во́семьдесят, когда́ он у́мер. **2.** (*by*) ми́мо+*g.*; **he drove ~ the house** он прое́хал ми́мо до́ма; **he hurried ~ me** он пробежа́л ми́мо меня́. **3.** (*to or on the far side of*) за+*a./i.*; **you've gone ~ the turning** вы прое́хали поворо́т; **his house is ~ the church** его́ дом за це́рковью. **4.** (*beyond, exceeding*) свы́ше+*g.*, сверх+*g.*; **I am ~ caring** тепе́рь мне уже́ всё равно́; **the pain was ~ endurance** боль была́ нестерпи́ма; **he was a fine actor, but he's ~ it now** (*coll.*) когда́-то он был хоро́шим актёром, но э́то в про́шлом; **this is ~ a joke** э́то перехо́дит грани́цы шу́ток; **he is ~ praying for** он безнадёжен; **I wouldn't put it ~ him to steal the money** я ду́маю, что он спосо́бен укра́сть де́ньги.

pasta ['pæstə] *n.* макаро́н|ы (*pl., g.* —).

paste [peɪst] *n.* (*soft dough*) те́сто; (*malleable mixture; savoury preparation*) па́ста; (*adhesive*) клей; (*gem substitute*) страз.

v.t. **1.** (*stick*) накле́|ивать, -ить; **the notice was ~ed up on the wall** объявле́ние бы́ло прикле́ено к стене́; **she ~d the pictures into her album** она́ вкле́ила карти́нки в альбо́м; **his name had been ~d over** его́ и́мя закле́или. **2.** (*sl., beat*) устр|а́ивать, -о́ить взбу́чку +*d.*; **their team got a good pasting** их кома́нда получи́ла хоро́шую взбу́чку.

cpd. **~board** *n.* карто́н.

pastel ['pæst(ə)l] *n.* (*crayon*) пасте́ль; **~ shades** пасте́льные кра́ски; (*drawing in ~*) рису́нок пасте́лью.

pastern ['pæst(ə)n] *n.* путова́я кость.

pasteurization [ˌpɑːstjəraɪˈzeɪʃ(ə)n, -tʃəraɪˈzeɪʃ(ə)n, ˌpæst-] *n.* пастериза́ция.

pasteurize ['pɑːstjəˌraɪz, -tʃəˌraɪz, 'pæst-] *v.t.* пастеризова́ть (*impf., pf.*).

pastiche [pæ'stiːʃ] *n.* (*literary imitation*) стилиза́ция (под+*a.*); подде́лка.

pastille ['pæstɪl] *n.* пасти́лка.

pastime ['pɑːstaɪm] *n.* (прия́тное) время(пре)провожде́ние.

pastor ['pɑːstə(r)] *n.* па́стор.

pastoral ['pɑːstər(ə)l] *n.* (*literary or artistic work*) пастора́ль; (*bishop's letter*) посла́ние.

adj. (*pert. to shepherds or country life*) пастора́льный; (*pert. to clergy*) па́сторский.

pastor|ate ['pɑːstərət], **-ship** ['pɑːstəʃɪp] *nn.* пастора́т.

pastry ['peɪstrɪ] *n.* (*baked dough*) конди́терские изде́лия; (*tart, cake*) пиро́жное.

cpd. **~-cook** *n.* конди́тер.

pasturage ['pɑːstʃərɪdʒ] *n.* (*grazing*) па́стбище; (*herbage for cattle etc.*) подно́жный корм; (*grazing land*) вы́пас.

pasture ['pɑ:stjə(r)] *n.* = **pasturage; the sheep were put out to** ~ овéц вы́гнали на пáстбище.
v.t. (*put to graze*) пасти́ (*impf.*).
pasty[1] ['pæstɪ] *n.* пирожóк, расстегáй.
pasty[2] ['peɪstɪ] *adj.* (*like paste*) тестообрáзный; (*palefaced*) блéдный.
pat[1] [pæt] *n.* **1.** (*light touch or sound*) хлопóк; шлепóк; **he deserves a** ~ **on the back** (*fig.*) он заслу́живает одобрéния/похвалы́. **2.** (*small mass*): **the butter was served in** ~**s** мáсло пóдали крóхотными кусóчками.
v.t. подхлóп|ывать, -ать; (*a dog*) глáдить, по-; **he** ~**ted my shoulder** он похлóпал меня́ по плечу́; **I can't help** ~**ting myself on the back** я не могу́ не похвали́ть себя́.
pat[2] [pæt] *adv.* (*appositely*) кстáти; **his answer came** ~ он отвéтил без колебáния; **he had his lesson off** ~ он знал урóк назубóк; **stand** ~ (*stick to one's decision or bet*) стоя́ть (*impf.*) на своём; (*at cards etc.*) оставáться (*impf.*) при свои́х; не брать (*impf.*) при́купа.
cpds. ~**-a-cake** *n.* (*child's game*) лáдуш|ки, (*pl., g.* -ек); ~**-ball** *n.* вя́лый тéннис.
Patagonia [,pætə'gəʊnɪə] *n.* Патагóния.
patch [pætʃ] *n.* **1.** (*covering over hole*) заплáта; **he wore** ~**es on his elbows** на локтя́х у негó бы́ли заплáты; (*over wound*) плáстырь (*m.*); (*over eye*) повя́зка; (*fig., coll.*): **the film is not a** ~ **on the book** фильм — ничтó по сравнéнию с кни́гой. **2.** (*decorative facial spot*) му́шка. **3.** (*superficial mark or stain*) пятнó; (*distinctive area*) клочóк; ~**es of blue sky** клочки́ голубóго нéба; **we ran into a fog** ~ мы попáли в тумáн; **there were** ~**es of ice on the road** на дорóге местáми былá гололéдица; (*fig.*): **he has struck a bad** ~ ему́ не везёт; **the play was amusing in** ~**es** местáми пьéса былá забáвной. **4.** (*piece of ground*) учáсток. **5.** (*scrap, remnant*) отрéзок.
v.t. (*mend*) латáть, за-.
with advs.: ~ **over** *v.t.* латáть, за-; ~ **up** *v.t.* (*lit.*) чини́ть, по-; задéл|ывать, -ать; (*fig.*) мири́ть, по-; **the quarrel was soon** ~**ed up** ссóра былá вскóре улáжена.
cpds. ~**-pocket** *n.* накладнóй кармáн; ~**work** *n.* лоску́тное шитьё; ~**work quilt** лоску́тное одея́ло; (*lit.*) латáние; (*fig.*) мешани́на.
patchouli [pə'tʃu:lɪ, 'pætʃʊlɪ] *n.* пачу́л|и (*pl., g.* -ей).
patchy ['pætʃɪ] *adj.* (*marked with patches*) пятни́стый; (*fig., of uneven quality*) неоднорóдный, разнорóдный, нерóвный.
pate[1] [peɪt] *n.* (*arch.*) башкá.
pâté[2] ['pæteɪ] *n.* паштéт; ~ ***de foie gras*** гуси́ный паштéт.
patella [pə'telə] *n.* патéлла.
patent ['peɪt(ə)nt, 'pæt-] *n.* патéнт; **P**~ **Office** патéнтное бюрó.
adj. **1.** (*giving entitlement*): **letters** ~ жáлованная грáмота; привилéгия. **2.** (*protected by* ~) патентóванный; ~ **leather** лакирóванная кóжа, лак; ~**-leather shoes** лакирóванные ту́фли. **3.** (*coll., well-contrived, ingenious*) изобретáтельный. **4.** (*obvious*) очеви́дный.
v.t. патентовáть, за-.
patentee [,peɪtən'ti:] *n.* патентообладáтель (*m.*).
pater ['peɪtə(r)] *n.* (*coll.*) отéц, папáша (*m.*).
paterfamilias [,peɪtəfə'mɪlɪ,æs] *n.* главá (*m.*) семьи́.
paternal [pə'tɜ:n(ə)l] *adj.* **1.** (*fatherly*) отцóвский, отéческий; ~ **instinct** отцóвский инсти́нкт; **he is very** ~ **towards her** по отношéнию к ней он дéржится весьмá покрови́тельственно; (*fig.*): ~ **government** прави́тельство, отéчески относя́щееся к нарóду. **2.** (*related through father*) рóдственный по отцу́; ~ **grandmother** бáбушка со стороны́ отцá.
paternalism [pə'tɜ:nə,lɪz(ə)m] *n.* покрови́тельственное попечéние.
paternity [pə'tɜ:nɪtɪ] *n.* отцóвство; (*fig., source, authorship*) áвторство.
paternoster [,pætə'nɒstə(r)] *n.* (*Lord's prayer*) «Óтче наш».
path [pɑ:θ] *n.* (*track for walking*) тропá, тропи́нка; дорóжка; ~ **through the woods** леснáя тропá/тропи́нка; **garden** ~ садóвая дорóжка; (*fig.*) путь (*m.*); **the police made a** ~ **for him through the crowd** поли́ция проложи́ла ему́ прохóд в толпé; **if ever he crosses my** ~ éсли он когдá-нибудь встрéтится мне на пути́; **he swept aside all who stood in his** ~ он сметáл всех, кто стоя́л на егó пути́; **on our** ~ **through life** на нáшем жи́зненном пути́; **he followed the** ~ **of duty** он вéрно слéдовал дóлгу; **our** ~**s diverged** нáши дорóги разошли́сь; (*course, trajectory*) траектóрия; **the** ~ **of a bullet** траектóрия полёта пу́ли.
cpds. ~**finder** *n.* (*explorer*) исслéдователь (*m.*); (*aircraft*) самолёт наведéния; ~**way** *n.* тропá, путь (*m.*).
pathetic [pə'θetɪk] *adj.* (*arousing pity*) печáльный, жáлкий, трóгательный; (*coll., wretchedly inadequate*) жáлкий.
pathless ['pɑ:θlɪs] *adj.* бездорóжный.
pathological [,pæθə'lɒdʒɪk(ə)l] *adj.* патологи́ческий.
pathologist [pə'θɒlədʒɪst] *n.* патóлог.
pathology [pə'θɒlədʒɪ] *n.* паталóгия.
pathos ['peɪθɒs] *n.* пáфос.
patience ['peɪʃ(ə)ns] *n.* **1.** терпéние; **he would try the** ~ **of Job** он вы́вел бы из терпéния дáже áнгела; **I have no** ~ **with him** он меня́ вывóдит из терпéния; **I am out of** (*or* **have lost**) ~ **with him** я потеря́л с ним вся́кое терпéние; **my** ~ **is exhausted** моё терпéние кóнчилось. **2.** (*card game*) пасья́нс.
patient ['peɪʃ(ə)nt] *n.* пациéнт, больнóй.
adj. терпели́вый.
patina ['pætɪnə] *n.* пати́на.
patio ['pætɪəʊ] *n.* пáтио (*indecl.*), дво́рик.
patois ['pætwɑ:] *n.* мéстный гóвор.
patriarch ['peɪtrɪ,ɑ:k] *n.* (*male head of tribe*) старéйшина (*m.*); (*venerable old man*) патриáрх; (*eccl.*) патриáрх.
patriarchal [,peɪtrɪ'ɑ:k(ə)l] *adj.* патриархáльный.
patriarchate ['peɪtrɪ,ɑ:kət] *n.* (*eccl.*) патриáршество.
patriarchy ['peɪtrɪ,ɑ:kɪ] *n.* патриáрхия, патриархáт.
patrician [pə'trɪʃ(ə)n] *n.* (*Roman noble*) патри́ций; (*aristocrat*) аристокрáт.
adj. патрициáнский; аристократи́ческий.
patricide ['pætrɪ,saɪd] = **parricide**
patrimonial [,pætrɪ'məʊnɪəl] *adj.* наслéдственный.
patrimony ['pætrɪmənɪ] *n.* (*inheritance from father*) отцóвское наслéдие; (*fig.*) наслéдие.
patriot ['peɪtrɪət, 'pæt-] *n.* патриóт.
patriotic [,peɪtrɪ'ɒtɪk, ,pæt-] *adj.* патриоти́ческий.
patriotism ['peɪtrɪət,ɪz(ə)m, 'pæt-] *n.* патриоти́зм.
patrol [pə'trəʊl] *n.* **1.** (*action*) патрули́рование; **on** ~ в дозóре; ~ **car** (полицéйская) патру́льная маши́на; ~ **vessel** сторожевóе су́дно. **2.** (*of aircraft*) барражи́рование. **3.** (~*ling body*) патру́ль (*m.*); (~*ling official*) патру́льный.
v.t. & i. патрули́ровать (*impf.*).
cpd. ~**man** *n.* (*road scout*) патру́льный; (*US, policeman*) полицéйский.
patron ['peɪtrən] *n.* **1.** (*supporter, protector*) покрови́тель (*m.*); **a** ~ **of the arts** покрови́тель искýсств, меценáт; ~ **saint** святóй засту́пник, святáя засту́пница. **2.** (*customer*) (постоя́нный) клиéнт, покупáтель (*m.*).
patronage ['pætrənɪdʒ] *n.* (*support, sponsorship*) покрови́тельство, шéфство; (*right of appointment*) прáво назначéния на дóлжность; ('*protection*', *influence*) покрови́тельство; (*coll.*) блат; (*customer's support*) постоя́нная клиенту́ра; (*patronizing manner*) покрови́тельственные манéры (*f. pl.*).
patroness ['peɪtrənɪs] *n.* покрови́тельница, патронéсса.
patroniz|e ['pætrə,naɪz] *v.t.* (*support, encourage*) покрови́тельствовать (*impf.*) +*d.*; (*visit as customer*) постоя́нно посещáть (*impf.*); (*treat condescendingly*) отн|оси́ться, -ести́сь свысокá к+*d.*; ~**ing airs** покрови́тельственные манéры (*f. pl.*).
patronymic [,pætrə'nɪmɪk] *n.* (*Russ.*) óтчество.
patter[1] ['pætə(r)] *n.* (*of salesman, conjurer etc.*) скороговóрка.
v.i. (*talk glibly*) тараторить (*impf.*).
patter[2] ['pætə(r)] *n.* (*tapping sound*) посту́кивание; тóпот, стук.
v.i. барабáнить (*impf.*); топотáть (*impf.*); **the rain** ~**ed on the windows** дождь барабáнил в óкна; **her footsteps** ~**ed down the hall** её шаги́ простучáли по зáлу.
pattern ['pæt(ə)n] *n.* **1.** (*laudable example*) образéц; **a** ~ **of virtue** образéц добродéтели; (*attr.*) образцóвый. **2.** (*model for production*) вы́кройка; **dress** ~ вы́кройка (плáтья).

3. (*sample of cloth etc.*) обра́зчик. **4.** (*design*) моде́ль. **5.** (*arrangement, system*) о́браз, мане́ра; **new ~s of behaviour** но́вые но́рмы (*f. pl.*) поведе́ния; **events are following the usual ~** собы́тия сле́дуют обы́чным путём.

v.t. **1.** (*model*) копи́ровать, с-; **~ a dress on a Paris model** скопи́ровать пла́тье с пари́жской моде́ли; **he ~ed himself on his father** он брал приме́р со своего́ отца́. **2.** (*decorate with design*) укр|аша́ть, -а́сить; **a ~ed dress** пла́тье в узо́рах (*or* с узо́рами).

patty ['pætı] *n.* пирожо́к; котле́та.

cpd. **~-pan** *n.* про́тивень (*m.*).

paucity ['pɔːsıtı] *n.* нехва́тка, недоста́точность, ску́дость.

Paul ['pɔːl] *n.* Па́вел; **~ Pry** чрезме́рно любопы́тный челове́к.

paunch [pɔːntʃ] *n.* брюшко́, пу́зо.

paunchy ['pɔːntʃı] *adj.* пуза́тый.

pauper ['pɔːpə(r)] *n.* бедня́к.

pauperism ['pɔːpə,rız(ə)m] *n.* нищета́.

pauperization [,pɔːpəraı'zeıʃ(ə)n] *n.* пауперииза́ция.

pauperize ['pɔːpəraız] *v.t.* дов|оди́ть, -ести́ до нищеты́.

pause [pɔːz] *n.* (*intermission, temporary halt*) переры́в; переды́шка; **my remarks gave him ~** мои́ замеча́ния смути́ли его́; (*in speaking, reading, mus.*) па́уза.

v.i. остан|а́вливаться, -ови́ться; **she scarcely ~d for breath** она́ не переводи́ла дыха́ния; **if you ~ to think** е́сли заду́маться.

pavan(e) [pə'vɑːn] *n.* (*mus.*) пава́на.

pave [peıv] *v.t.* мости́ть, вы́-; **~d road** мощёная доро́га; **the road to hell is ~d with good intentions** благи́ми наме́рениями вы́мощена доро́га в ад; (*fig.*): **his proposal ~d the way for an understanding** его́ предложе́ние откры́ло путь к взаимопонима́нию.

pavement ['peıvmənt] *n.* **1.** (*footway*) тротуа́р; **~ artist** худо́жник, рису́ющий на тротуа́ре. **2.** (*paved floor*) пол, вы́ложенный моза́йкой.

pavilion [pə'vıljən] *n.* (*building for sport or tournament*) павилио́н; (*large tent*) шатёр.

paving ['peıvıŋ] *n.* (*paved way*) мостова́я; (*act of ~*) моще́ние у́лиц.

cpd. **~-stone** *n.* брусча́тка, булы́жник.

paw [pɔː] *n.* ла́па; (*coll.*): **take your ~s off me!** ру́ки прочь!

v.t. (*touch with ~*) тро́гать, по- ла́пой; **the horse ~ed the ground** конь бил копы́тами; (*handle, fondle clumsily*) ла́пать (*impf., pf.*).

pawky ['pɔːkı] *adj.* лука́вый; ирони́ческий.

pawl [pɔːl] *n.* (*lever*) защёлка.

pawn[1] [pɔːn] *n.* (*chessman, also fig.*) пе́шка.

pawn[2] [pɔːn] *n.* (*pledge*) зало́г, закла́д; **in ~** зало́женный; **he took his watch out of ~** он вы́купил часы́ из ломба́рда.

v.t. за|кла́дывать, -ложи́ть.

cpds. **~broker** *n.* ростовщи́к; **~shop** *n.* ломба́рд.

pawpaw ['pɔːpɔː] = **papaw**

pax [pæks] *n.* **1.** (*peace*) мир; ***P~ Romana*** мир, навя́занный ри́мской импе́рией. **2.** (*schoolboy's truce-word*) чур меня́!; хва́тит!

pay [peı] *n.* пла́та, (*coll.*) зарпла́та; жа́лование; **~ clerk** бухга́лтер-расчётчик; **a ~ cut** сниже́ние зарпла́ты; **a ~ increase** повыше́ние зарпла́ты; **on half ~** на полови́нной ста́вке; **he is in the ~ of the enemy** он на слу́жбе у врага́.

v.t. **1.** (*give in return for sth.*) плати́ть, за-, у-; **she always ~s cash** она́ всегда́ пла́тит нали́чными; **he has paid the penalty for his greed** он поплати́лся за свою́ жа́дность; (*contribute*): **everyone must ~ his share** ка́ждый до́лжен внести́ свою́ до́лю; **I'll ~ the difference** я доплачу́; **~ one's fare** плати́ть, за- за прое́зд; опла́|чивать, -ти́ть прое́зд. **2.** (*remunerate, recompense*) опла́|чивать, -ти́ть +*d.*; **they are paid by the hour** они́ получа́ют почасову́ю опла́ту; **we are paid on Fridays** мы получа́ем зарпла́ту по пя́тницам; **he who ~s the piper calls the tune** кто пла́тит музыка́нту, тот и зака́зывает му́зыку; **he was paid in his own coin** ему́ отплати́ли той же моне́той; **there will be the devil to ~** пото́м хлопо́т не оберёшься; бу́дет грандио́зный сканда́л. **3.** (*settle, ~ for*) упла́|чивать, -ти́ть; **the defendant must ~ costs** обвиня́емый до́лжен уплати́ть суде́бные изде́ржки; **he paid his way through college** он сам зараба́тывал себе́ на вы́сшее обуче́ние. **4.** (*bestow, render*): **~ attention to me!** послу́шайте меня́!; **~ s.o. a compliment** де́лать, с- кому́-н. комплиме́нт; **~ heed to** обра|ща́ть, -ти́ть внима́ние на+*a.*; **~ one's respects to** свиде́тельствовать, за- своё почте́ние +*d.*; **~ s.o. a visit** наве|ща́ть, -сти́ть кого́-н. **5.** (*benefit, profit*): **it will ~ you to wait** вам сто́ит подожда́ть.

v.i. **1.** (*give money*) распла́|чиваться, -ти́ться; **he ~s on the nail** он пла́тит неме́дленно; **I paid through the nose for it** я заплати́л за э́то бе́шеные де́ньги. **2.** (*suffer*) поплати́ться (*pf.*); **you'll ~ dearly for this** вы за э́то до́рого запла́тите; **he paid for his carelessness** он пострада́л из-за своего́ легкомы́слия. **3.** (*yield a return*) окуп|а́ться, -и́ться; дава́ть (*impf.*) при́быль; (*fig.*) име́ть смысл; опра́вд|ывать, -а́ть себя́; **the business is ~ing handsomely** де́ло прино́сит прекра́сный дохо́д; де́ло прекра́сно окупа́ется; **it ~s to advertise** рекла́ма окупа́ется.

with advs.: **~ back** *v.t.* (*return*) возвра|ща́ть, -ти́ть (*also* верну́ть); **he paid back every penny** он верну́л всё до после́дней копе́йки; (*reimburse*): **he paid me back in person** он самоли́чно верну́л мне де́ньги; (*have revenge on*): **I'll ~ you back for this** я вам за э́то отплачу́; **~ in** *v.t.* вн|оси́ть, -ести́; **~ off** *v.t.* рассчи́т|ываться, -а́ться с+*i.*; **the workers were paid off** с рабо́чими рассчита́лись; **I have paid off my debts** я расплати́лся со свои́ми долга́ми; **he is ~ing off old scores** он сво́дит ста́рые счёты; (**~** *wages and discharge*) рассчи́т|ывать, -а́ть; (*bribe*) подкупа́ть (*pf.*); *v.i.* (*bring profit*) окуп|а́ться, -и́ться; **~ out** *v.t.* (*expend, make payment of*) выпла́чивать, вы́платить; (*rope etc.*) отпус|ка́ть, -ти́ть; трави́ть (*impf.*); **~ over** *v.t.* перепла́|чивать, -ти́ть; **~ up** *v.t.* (*settle*) выпла́чивать, вы́платить; **a paid-up account** закры́тый счёт; *v.i.* (**~** *amount due*) рассчи́т|ываться, -а́ться сполна́; **~ up and look pleasant!** выкла́дывай де́нежки и улыба́йся!

cpds. **~-day** *n.* платёжный день; (*coll.*) день зарпла́ты, получ́ка; **~-desk** *n.* ка́сса; **~load** *n.* (*of vehicle*) поле́зный груз; (*of missile*) поле́зная нагру́зка; **~master** *n.* касси́р; **P~master-General** гла́вный казначе́й; **~-off** *n.* (*settlement*) вы́плата; (*profit, reward*) награ́да; (*bribe*) взя́тка, бакши́ш; (*coll., climax, e.g. of a joke*) развя́зка; **~-packet** *n.* за́работок, (*coll.*) полу́чка; **~roll, ~-sheet** *nn.* платёжная ве́домость; **there are 500 men on the ~roll** в платёжной ве́домости (*or* в шта́те) чи́слится 500 челове́к.

payable ['peıəb(ə)l] *adj.* опла́чиваемый; подлежа́щий упла́те.

payee [peı'iː] *n.* получа́тель (*fem.* -ница) (де́нег).

payer ['peıə(r)] *n.* плате́льщи|к (*fem.* -ца).

payment ['peımənt] *n.* (*paying, sum paid*) опла́та; платёж; (*of debt etc.*) упла́та; **prompt ~ is requested** про́сят неме́дленно уплати́ть; **he made a cash ~ of £50** он заплати́л 50 фу́нтов нали́чными; (*requital*): **this is in ~ of your services** э́то вознагражде́ние за ва́ши услу́ги.

PC *abbr. of* **1.** ***Police Constable*** полице́йский, конста́бль. **2.** ***personal computer*** ПК, (персона́льный компью́тер).

p.d.q. (*sl.*) (*abbr. of* **pretty damn quick**) поживе́е, «как из пу́шки».

PE (*abbr. of* **physical education**) физкульту́ра; **~ class** уро́к физкульту́ры.

pea [piː] *n.* горо́шина; (*pl., collect.*) горо́х; **they are as like as two ~s** они́ похо́жи как две ка́пли воды́; **~ soup** горохово́й суп; **split ~s** лущёный горо́х.

cpds. **~-green** *adj.* я́рко-зелёный; **~nut** *n.* земляно́й оре́х, ара́хис; **~nut butter** па́ста из тёртого ара́хиса; оре́ховая па́ста; **~nuts** *n. pl.* (*US sl., trifling amount*) гроши́ (*m. pl.*); **~-shooter** *n.* тру́бка для стрельбы́ горо́хом; **~-souper** *n.* (*coll., fog*) густо́й тума́н.

peace [piːs] *n.* **1.** (*freedom from war*) мир; **~ with honour** почётный мир; **our countries are at ~ again** ме́жду на́шими стра́нами сно́ва устано́влен мир; (*treaty*): **the ~ of Paris** пари́жский мир; **~ talks** ми́рные перегово́ры; (*fig.*): **make one's ~ with s.o.** помири́ться (*pf.*) с кем-н. **2.** (*freedom from civil disorder*) споко́йствие; поря́док; **they were bound over to keep the ~** им предписа́ли соблюда́ть поря́док; **breach of the ~** наруше́ние обще́ственного поря́дка; **Justice of the P~** мирово́й судья́. **3.** (*rest, quiet*) споко́йствие, поко́й; **~ be with you!** мир вам!; **may he rest in ~** мир пра́ху его́; **she found ~** (*died*) **at last** она́, наконе́ц, отпра́вилась на поко́й; **can we have some ~ and quiet?** нельзя́ ли поти́ше?; **~ of mind** споко́йствие ду́ха; **he never gives me a moment's ~** он мне не даёт ни мину́ты поко́я; **he held his ~** (*arch.*) он пребыва́л в молча́нии.

cpds. **~-keeping** *adj.*: **~-keeping force** войска́ (*nt. pl.*) по поддержа́нию ми́ра; **~-loving** *adj.* миролюби́вый; **~maker** *n.* миротво́рец; **~-offering** *n.* искупи́тельная же́ртва; (*fig.*) зада́бривание; **~-pipe** *n.* тру́бка ми́ра; **~time** *n.* ми́рное вре́мя.

peaceable ['pi:səb(ə)l] *adj.* миролюби́вый, ми́рный.

peaceful ['pi:sfʊl] *adj.* ми́рный; **~ coexistence** ми́рное сосуществова́ние; **a ~ end** (*death*) ми́рная кончи́на.

peach[1] [pi:tʃ] *n.* **1.** (*fruit*) пе́рсик; **~ blossom** пе́рсиковый цвет. **2.** (*tree*) пе́рсиковое де́рево. **3.** (*coll., superb specimen*) «пе́рвый сорт». **4.** (*coll., attractive girl*) красо́тка.

peach[2] [pi:tʃ] *v.i.* стуча́ть, на- (*на кого*) (*sl.*).

peacock ['pi:kɒk] *n.* павли́н; **~ blue** перели́вчатый си́ний цвет.

peahen ['pi:hen] *n.* са́мка павли́на, па́ва.

peajacket ['pi:ˌdʒækɪt] *n.* бушла́т, тужу́рка.

peak[1] [pi:k] *n.* **1.** (*mountain top*) пик, верши́на. **2.** (*point of beard*) кли́нышек. **3.** (*of cap*) козырёк. **4.** (*of ship*) концево́й отсе́к. **5.** (*fig., highest point, maximum*) пик; **~ load** (*elec.*) максима́льная нагру́зка; **his excitement reached its ~** его́ возбужде́ние дости́гло преде́ла; **~ hours** часы́ пик; **~ viewing hours** наибо́лее популя́рные часы́ для пока́за телепереда́ч.

v.i.: **demand ~ed** спрос дости́г вы́сшей то́чки.

peak[2] [pi:k] *v.i.* (*waste away*) ча́хнуть, за-.

peaked [pi:kd] *adj.* **1.** остроконе́чный; **~ cap** (фо́рменная) фура́жка. **2.** (*haggard; also* **peaky**) осу́нувшийся; изможднённый.

peaky ['pi:kɪ] *adj.* = **peaked 2.**

peal [pi:l] *n.* (*of bells*) звон, трезво́н; (*of thunder*) гро́хот, раска́т; (*of laughter*) взрыв.

v.t.: **~ bells** трезво́нить (*impf.*).

v.i. (*of bells*) трезво́нить (*impf.*); (*of thunder*) греме́ть, про-; (*of laughter*) разд|ава́ться, -а́ться.

pear [peə(r)] *n.* **1.** (*fruit*) гру́ша. **2.** (*tree*) гру́шевое де́рево, гру́ша. **3.**: **prickly ~** опу́нция.

pearl [pɜ:l] *n.* жемчу́жина; (*pl., collect.*) же́мчуг; **cast ~s before swine** мета́ть (*impf.*) би́сер пе́ред сви́ньями; **(mother-of-)~ buttons** перламу́тровые пу́говицы.

cpds. **~-barley** *n.* перло́вая крупа́; **~-diver, ~-fisher** *nn.* лове́ц/иска́тель (*m.*) же́мчуга.

pearly ['pɜ:lɪ] *adj.* похо́жий на же́мчуг; жемчу́жного цве́та, жемчу́жный.

peasant ['pez(ə)nt] *n.* крестья́н|ин (*fem.* -ка).

peasantry ['pezəntrɪ] *n.* крестья́нство.

pease pudding [pi:z] *n.* горо́ховый пу́динг, горо́ховая запека́нка.

peat [pi:t] *n.* торф.

cpd. **~-bog** *n.* торфяно́е боло́то.

pebble ['peb(ə)l] *n.* голы́ш; га́лька; булы́жник; **~ lens** ли́нза из го́рного хрусталя́; **she's not the only ~ on the beach** таки́х как она́ пруд пруди́.

cpd. **~-dash** *n.* грави́йная набро́ска; *adj.* грави́йный.

pebbly ['peblɪ] *adj.* покры́тый га́лькой.

pecan ['pi:kən] *n.* оре́х-пека́н.

peccadillo [ˌpekə'dɪləʊ] *n.* грешо́к.

peck[1] [pek] *n.* (*fig., large amount*) ма́сса, ку́ча.

peck[2] [pek] *n.* (*made by beak*) клево́к; (*fig., hasty kiss*): **he gave her a ~ on the cheek** он чмо́кнул её в щёку.

v.t. клева́ть, клю́нуть; поклева́ть (*pf.*).

v.i. (*fig.*): **she ~ed at her food** она́ едва́ дотро́нулась до еды́; **~ing order** ≃ неофициа́льная иера́рхия.

pecker ['pekə(r)] *n.* (*sl.*): **keep your ~ up!** не ве́шай но́са!

peckish ['pekɪʃ] *adj.* (*coll.*) голо́дный.

pectoral ['pektər(ə)l] *adj.* грудно́й.

peculiar [pɪ'kju:lɪə(r)] *adj.* **1.** (*exclusive, distinctive*) осо́бенный, своеобра́зный; **this custom is ~ to the English** э́то чи́сто англи́йский обы́чай. **2.** (*particular*) осо́бенный; **a building of ~ interest** зда́ние, представля́ющее осо́бый интере́с. **3.** (*strange*) стра́нный; **his behaviour was rather ~** он вёл себя́ дово́льно стра́нно.

peculiarity [pɪˌkju:lɪ'ærɪtɪ] *n.* (*characteristic*) сво́йство; осо́бенность; (*oddity*) стра́нность.

pecuniary [pɪ'kju:nɪərɪ] *adj.* де́нежный.

pedagogic(al) [ˌpedə'gɒgɪk((ə)l), -'gɒdʒɪk((ə)l)] *adj.* педагоги́ческий.

pedagogue ['pedəˌgɒg] *n.* педаго́г.

pedagogy ['pedəˌgɒdʒɪ, -ˌgɒgɪ] *n.* педаго́гика.

pedal ['ped(ə)l] *n.* педа́ль.

v.t. & i. (*of cyclist*) е́хать (*det.*) (на велосипе́де); (*of organist*) наж|има́ть, -а́ть (на) педа́ль.

cpd. **~-cycle** *n.* велосипе́д.

pedalo ['pedəˌləʊ] *n.* морско́й/во́дный велосипе́д.

pedant ['ped(ə)nt] *n.* педа́нт.

pedantic [pɪ'dæntɪk] *adj.* педанти́чный.

pedantry ['ped(ə)ntrɪ] *n.* педанти́чность.

peddle ['ped(ə)l] *v.t.* торгова́ть (*impf.*) вразно́с; **he ~s his wares in every town** он разво́зит свои́ това́ры по всем города́м; (*fig.*): **she likes to ~ gossip** она́ лю́бит разноси́ть спле́тни.

peddler ['pedlə(r)] = **pedlar**

pe|derast, pae- ['pedəˌræst] *n.* педера́ст.

pe|derasty, pae- ['pedəˌræstɪ] *n.* педера́стия.

pedestal ['pedɪst(ə)l] *n.* (*of column or statue*) пьедеста́л; **he set her on a ~** (*fig.*) он вознёс её на пьедеста́л; (*of desk etc.*) основа́ние.

pedestrian [pɪ'destrɪən] *n.* пешехо́д.

adj. **1.** (*of or for walking*) пешехо́дный; **~ crossing** перехо́д; **~ footpath** пешехо́дная доро́жка. **2.** (*fig., prosaic*) прозаи́ческий, прозаи́чный, ску́чный.

pedestrianization [pɪˌdestrɪəˌnaɪ'zeɪʃ(ə)n] *n.* созда́ние пешехо́дных зон.

pedestrianize [pɪ'destrɪəˌnaɪz] *v.t.* запре|ща́ть, -ти́ть автомоби́льное движе́ние.

pediatric [ˌpi:dɪ'ætrɪk], **-ian** [ˌpi:dɪə'trɪʃ(ə)n], **-s** [ˌpi:dɪ'ætrɪks] = **paediatric** *etc.*

pedicab ['pedɪˌkæb] *n.* велосипе́д-такси́.

pedicure ['pedɪˌkjʊə(r)] *n.* (*chiropody*) педикю́р; (*chiropodist*) ма́стер по педикю́ру; педикю́рша.

pedigree ['pedɪˌgri:] *n.* (*genealogical table*) родосло́вная; (*line of descent*) происхожде́ние; (*ancient descent*): **a man of ~** челове́к с хоро́шей родосло́вной; (*fig., of word etc.*) этимоло́гия; (*attr.*): **~ cattle** племенно́й скот.

pediment ['pedɪmənt] *n.* фронто́н.

pedlar ['pedlə(r)] (*US* **peddler**) *n.* разно́счик, коробе́йник.

pedometer [pɪ'dɒmɪtə(r)] *n.* шагоме́р.

pee [pi:] (*coll.*) *n.* (*urination*) пи-пи́ (*nt. indecl.*); (*urine*) моча́.

v.i. мочи́ться, по-.

peek [pi:k] (*coll.*) *n.* взгляд укра́дкой.

v.i. взгля́|дывать, -ну́ть; **~ in** загля́|дывать, -ну́ть; **~ out** выгля́дывать, вы́глянуть.

peel [pi:l] *n.* (*thin skin e.g. of apple or potato*) кожура́, шелуха́; (*rind of orange etc.*) ко́рка.

v.t. **1.** (*remove skin from*) оч|ища́ть, -и́стить; (*fig.*): **he kept his eyes ~ed** (*coll.*) он смотре́л в о́ба. **2.** (*remove from surface*) сн|има́ть, -ять; **he ~ed the stamp off the envelope** он откле́ил ма́рку от конве́рта.

v.i. **1.** (*lose skin, bark etc.*) шелуши́ться (*impf.*); **the sun makes my arms ~** у меня́ шелуша́тся пле́чи от со́лнца; **the walls were ~ing with the damp** сте́ны облезли от сы́рости. **2.** (*come away from surface; also* **~ away, ~ off**) слез|а́ть, -ть; обл|еза́ть, -е́зть; **the paint has begun to ~ (off)** кра́ска начала́ сходи́ть.

with advs.: **~ away** *v.t.* сн|има́ть, -ять; *v.i.* = **peel** *v.i.* **2.**; **~ off** *v.t.*: **he ~ed off his clothes and dived in** он сбро́сил с себя́ оде́жду и нырну́л; *v.i.* (*lit.*) = **peel** *v.i.* **2.**; (*fig., detach o.s. from group*) выходи́ть, вы́йти из стро́я; **the aircraft ~ed off to attack** самолёт вы́рвался из стро́я для ата́ки.

peeler ['pi:lə(r)] *n.* (*device for peeling*) шелуши́тель (*m.*).

peeling ['pi:lɪŋ] *n.* кожура́, шелуха́; **potato ~s** карто́фельные очи́стки (*f. pl.*).

peep[1] [pi:p] *n.* **1.** (*furtive or hasty look*) взгляд укра́дкой; **~ing Tom** ≃ любопы́тная Варва́ра; **take, have a ~ at** взгляну́ть (*pf.*) на+*a.* **2.** (*first appearance*) про́блеск; **at ~ of day, dawn** на рассве́те.

v.i. погля́д|ывать, -е́ть; **he ~ed in at the window** он загляну́л в окно́; **during the morning the sun ~ed out** у́тром вы́глянуло со́лнце.

cpds. **~-hole** *n.* глазо́к; **~-show** *n.* кинетоско́п.

peep[2] [pi:p] *n.* (*chirp*) писк, чири́канье; (*fig.*): **I couldn't get a ~ out of him** я не мог из него́ ни сло́ва вы́жать.

v.i. пища́ть, пи́скнуть; чири́к|ать, -нуть.

peer[1] [pɪə(r)] *n.* **1.** (*equal*) ро́вня́; **you will not find his ~** вы не найдёте ему́ ра́вного; **this wine is without ~** э́то вино́ несравне́нно; **~ group** гру́ппа све́рстников; **~ group pressure** группово́й нажи́м. **2.** (*noble*) лорд, пэр; **he was made a ~** его́ возвели́ в ло́рды; ему́ пожа́ловано зва́ние ло́рда.

peer[2] [pɪə(r)] *v.i.* (*look closely*) всм|а́триваться, -отре́ться (в+*a.*).

peerage ['pɪərɪdʒ] *n.* (*body of peers*) сосло́вие пэ́ров; (*rank*) пэ́рство, ти́тул пэ́ра.

peeress ['pɪərɪs] *n.* супру́га пэ́ра; же́нщина, име́ющая ти́тул пэ́ра.

peerless ['pɪəlɪs] *adj.* несравне́нный.

peeve [pi:v] (*coll.*) *n.* (*grievance*) прете́нзия.

v.t.: **he looks ~d** у него́ недово́льный вид.

peevish ['pi:vɪʃ] *adj.* брюзгли́вый; каприз́ный.

peewit, pewit ['pi:wɪt] *n.* чи́бис.

peg [peg] *n.* ко́лышек; **(clothes-~)** крючо́к; **(hat-, coat-~)** ве́шалка; **he buys his clothes off the ~** он покупа́ет гото́вую оде́жду; **(tent-~)** ко́лышек для натя́гивания пала́тки; (*fig.*): **he is a square ~ in a round hole** он не на своём ме́сте; **it provided a ~ to hang a discourse on** э́то послужи́ло по́водом для выступле́ния; **he should be taken down a ~** его́ ну́жно осади́ть; с него́ на́до сбить спесь.

v.t. (*fasten*) прикреп|ля́ть, -и́ть; (*comm., fix level of*): **~ prices** замор|а́живать, -о́зить це́ны.

with advs.: **~ away** *v.i.* вка́лывать (*impf.*); корпе́ть (*impf.*) (*coll.*); **~ down** *v.t.* (*lit.*) укреп|ля́ть, -и́ть; (*fig., restrict*) свя́з|ывать, -а́ть; **~ out** *v.t.* (*mark with ~s*): **he ~ged out his claim** (*lit.*) он отме́тил грани́цы своего́ уча́стка; (*fig.*) он закрепи́л своё пра́во; (*hang out with ~s*): **~ out the clothes** разве́|шивать, -сить оде́жду; *v.i.* (*sl., expire*) выдыха́ться, вы́дохнуться; умере́ть (*pf.*).

cpds. **~-board** *n.* стенд; **~-leg** *n.* (*leg*) деревя́нная нога́; (*pers.*) челове́к с деревя́нной ного́й; **~-top** *n.* куба́рь (*m.*), волчо́к; **~-top trousers** брю́ки, широ́кие в бёдрах и у́зкие внизу́.

peignoir ['peɪnwɑ:(r)] *n.* пеньюа́р.

pejorative [pɪ'dʒɒrətɪv, 'pi:dʒə-] *adj.* уничижи́тельный, пренебрежи́тельный.

peke [pi:k] (*coll.*) = **pekin(g)ese 2.**

Pekin(g) ['pi:kɪn, 'pi:kɪŋ] *n.* Пеки́н.

Pekin(g)ese [,pi:kɪ'ni:z] *n.* **1.** (*pers.*) жи́тель (*fem.* -ница) Пеки́на. **2.** (*dog*) кита́йский мопс, пекине́с.

pelagic [pɪ'lædʒɪk] *adj.* пелаги́ческий; **~ whaling** морско́й лов кито́в.

pelargonium [,pelə'gəʊnɪəm] *n.* пеларго́ния.

pelican ['pelɪkən] *n.* пелика́н; **~ crossing** перехо́д с автомати́ческим светофо́ром.

pelisse [pɪ'li:s] *n.* (*officer's*) гуса́рский ме́нтик.

pellet ['pelɪt] *n.* ша́рик; (*pill*) пилю́ля; (*small shot*) пу́лька.

pell-mell [pel'mel] *adv.* впереме́шку; беспоря́дочно; **his words came out ~** он говори́л сби́вчиво.

pellucid [pɪ'lu:sɪd, -'lju:sɪd] *adj.* прозра́чный.

pelmet ['pelmɪt] *n.* ламбреке́н.

pelt[1] [pelt] *n.* (*skin*) ко́жа, шку́ра.

pelt[2] [pelt] *n.*: **at full ~** по́лным хо́дом.

v.t. (*assail*) швыр|я́ть, -ну́ть; забр|а́сывать, -о́сить; **they ~ed him with stones/insults** они́ заброса́ли его́ камня́ми/оскорбле́ниями.

v.i. стуча́ть, по-; бараба́нить (*impf.*); **the rain was ~ing down** дождь бараба́нил вовсю́.

pelvic ['pelvɪk] *adj.* та́зовый; **~ girdle** та́зовый по́яс.

pelvis ['pelvɪs] *n.* таз.

pemmican ['pemɪkən] *n.* пеммика́н.

pen[1] [pen] *n.* (*writing instrument*) перо́ (*strictly* 'nib, quill'), ру́чка (*strictly* '**~-holder**'); **he never puts ~ to paper** он никогда́ не берётся за перо́; (*fig.*): **he makes his living by his ~** он живёт литерату́рным трудо́м; **he has a witty ~** он пи́шет остроу́мно.

v.t. писа́ть, на-; сочин|я́ть, -и́ть.

cpds. **~-and-ink** *adj.* нарисо́ванный перо́м; **a ~-and-ink drawing** рису́нок перо́м/ту́шью; **~-friend** *n.* корреспонде́нт (*fem.* -ка); **~holder** *n.* ру́чка; **~knife** *n.* перочи́нный но́ж(ик); **~manship** *n.* каллигра́фия; **~-name** *n.* (литерату́рный) псевдони́м; **~-nib** *n.* перо́ (пи́счее); **~-portrait** *n.* литерату́рный портре́т; **~-pusher** *n.* (*coll.*) писа́ка (*c.g.*).

pen[2] [pen] *n.* (*enclosure*) заго́н; **submarine ~** укры́тие для подво́дных ло́док.

v.t. (*also* **~ in, ~ up**) зап|ира́ть, -ере́ть.

penal ['pi:n(ə)l] *adj.*: **~ code** уголо́вный ко́декс; **~ colony** штрафна́я коло́ния; **~ laws** уголо́вное пра́во; **~ offence** уголо́вное преступле́ние; **~ servitude** ка́торжные/исправи́тельно-трудовы́е рабо́ты.

penalize ['pi:nə,laɪz] *v.t.* (*make punishable*) нака́з|ывать, -а́ть; (*subject to penalty*) штрафова́ть, о-; нака́з|ывать, -а́ть; **he was ~d for a foul** он был нака́зан за гру́бую игру́.

penalty ['penəltɪ] *n.* (*lit., fig.*) наказа́ние; **on, under ~ of death** под стра́хом сме́ртной ка́зни; **he paid the ~ of his folly** он поплати́лся за со́бственное безрассу́дство; (*sport*) штрафно́е очко́; **~ area** штрафна́я площа́дка; **~ kick** пена́льти (*m.*); одиннадцатиметро́вый уда́р.

penance ['penəns] *n.* епитимья́; покая́ние; **he must do ~ for his sins** он до́лжен замоли́ть/искупи́ть свои́ грехи́.

pence [pens] *n. see* **penny**

penchant ['pɑ̃ʃɑ̃] *n.* скло́нность (*к чему*); симпа́тия (*к кому*).

pencil ['pensɪl] *n.* каранда́ш; **coloured ~** цветно́й каранда́ш; **eyebrow ~** каранда́ш для брове́й; **a ~ drawing** рису́нок карандашо́м.

v.t. рисова́ть, на-; **~led eyebrows** подрисо́ванные бро́ви; **he ~led** (*reserved provisionally*) **a cabin** он сде́лал предвари́тельный зака́з на каю́ту; **the corrections were ~led in** попра́вки бы́ли внесены́ карандашо́м.

pendant ['pend(ə)nt] *n.* **1.** (*hanging ornament*) подве́ска; брело́к; **~s on a chandelier** подве́ски на лю́стре. **2.** (*complement, counterpart*) дополне́ние, па́ра.

pendent ['pend(ə)nt] *adj.* (*lit., hanging*) свиса́ющий, вися́чий; (*fig., incomplete, in suspense*) нерешённый.

pendentive [pen'dentɪv] *n.* па́рус сво́да/ку́пола.

pending ['pendɪŋ] *adj.* рассма́триваемый; нерешённый; **~ tray, file** я́щик для бума́г, отло́женных для рассмотре́ния; па́пка «К рассмотре́нию».

prep. **1.** (*during*) во вре́мя+*g.*; в тече́ние+*g.* **2.** (*until*) до+*g.*; в ожида́нии+*g.*

pendulous ['pendjʊləs] *adj.* подвесно́й.

pendulum ['pendjʊləm] *n.* ма́ятник; **swing of the ~** (*fig.*) кача́ние ма́ятника.

penetrability [,penɪtrə'bɪlɪtɪ] *n.* проница́емость.

penetrable ['penɪtrəb(ə)l] *adj.* проница́емый.

penetrate ['penɪ,treɪt] *v.t.* **1.** (*pierce, find access to*) прон|ика́ть, -и́кнуть в+*a.*; **the bullet ~d his brain** пу́ля прони́кла ему́ в мозг; **they ~d the enemy's defences** они́ прорвали́сь че́рез оборо́ну проти́вника; (*see through*): **our eyes could not ~ the darkness** мы не могли́ ничего́ разгляде́ть в темноте́; (*fig.*) разга́д|ывать, -а́ть; **I soon ~d his designs** я вско́ре раскуси́л его́ наме́рения. **2.** (*pervade*) прон|ика́ть, -и́кнуть; прони́з|ывать, -а́ть; **the smell ~d the whole house** за́пах распространи́лся по всему́ до́му.

v.i. **1.** (*make one's way*) вт|орга́ться, -о́ргнуться; **Livingstone ~d into the interior of Africa** Ливингсто́н прони́к вглубь А́фрики. **2.** (*be heard clearly*): **his voice ~d into the next room** его́ го́лос доноси́лся в сосе́днюю ко́мнату.

penetrating ['penɪ,treɪtɪŋ] *adj.* си́льный; о́стрый; **a ~ mind** проница́тельный/о́стрый ум; **a ~ voice** пронзи́тельный го́лос.

penetration [ˌpenɪˈtreɪʃ(ə)n] *n.* (*penetrating*) проника́ние; **peaceful ~** (*of a country*) ми́рное проникнове́ние; (*mil.*, *breach of defences*) проры́в; (*mental acumen*) проница́тельность; (*sexual*) соити́е.

penguin [ˈpeŋgwɪn] *n.* пингви́н.

penicillin [ˌpenɪˈsɪlɪn] *n.* пеницилли́н.

peninsula [pɪˈnɪnsjʊlə] *n.* полуо́стров.

peninsular [pɪˈnɪnsjʊlə(r)] *adj.* полуостровно́й; **the P~ War** война́ на Пирене́йском полуо́строве.

penis [ˈpiːnɪs] *n.* пе́нис, (мужско́й) член.

penitence [ˈpenɪt(ə)ns] *n.* раска́яние.

penitent [ˈpenɪt(ə)nt] *n.* ка́ющийся гре́шник.
adj. раска́ивающийся.

penitential [ˌpenɪˈtenʃ(ə)l] *adj.* покая́нный.

penitentiary [ˌpenɪˈtenʃərɪ] *n.* (*house of correction*) исправи́тельный дом; (*prison*) тюрьма́.
adj. исправи́тельный.

pennant [ˈpenənt] *n.* флажо́к, вы́мпел.

penniless [ˈpenɪlɪs] *adj.* без гроша́.

pennon [ˈpenən] *n.* флажо́к, вы́мпел.

penny [ˈpenɪ] *n.* пе́нни (*nt. indecl.*), пенс; (*US coin*) цент; **a ~ for your thoughts** о чём вы заду́мались?; **in for a ~, in for a pound** ≃ взя́вшись за гуж, не говори́, что не дюж; **he turned up like a bad ~** ≃ то́лько его́ не хвата́ло; **he found a way of turning an honest ~** он нашёл че́стный за́работок; **that cost a pretty ~** э́то влете́ло в копе́ечку; **at last the ~ has dropped!** (*coll.*) наконе́ц-то дошло́; **I must (go and) spend a ~** (*coll.*) мне ну́жно кой-куда́; **in ~ numbers** (*fig.*, *small quantities*) в ма́леньком коли́честве; **~ wise and pound foolish** крохобо́р в мелоча́х и расточи́телен в кру́пном.
cpds. **~-a-liner** *n.* писа́ка (*c.g.*); **~-farthing** *n.* (*bicycle*) велосипе́д-пау́к; **~-in-the-slot machine** *n.* автома́т.

penologist [piːˈnɒlədʒɪst] *n.* пено́лог; тюрьмове́д.

penology [piːˈnɒlədʒɪ] *n.* пеноло́гия; тюрьмове́дение.

pension [ˈpenʃ(ə)n] *n.* пе́нсия; **old-age, retirement ~** пе́нсия по ста́рости; **war ~** вое́нная пе́нсия; **widow's ~** вдо́вья пе́нсия.
v.t. назн|ача́ть, -а́чить пе́нсию *+d.*
with adv.: **~ off** *v.t.* ув|ольня́ть, -о́лить на пе́нсию.

pension [pɑ̃sjɔ̃] *n.* (*boarding-house*) пансио́н; ***en ~* rates** по́лный пансио́н.

pensionable [ˈpenʃənəb(ə)l] *adj.*: **he is a ~ employee** он име́ет пра́во на пе́нсию; **his job is ~** э́то рабо́та даёт ему́ пра́во на пе́нсию.

pensionary [ˈpenʃənərɪ] *n.* пенсионе́р.
adj. пенсио́нный.

pensioner [ˈpenʃənə(r)] *n.* пенсионе́р.

pensive [ˈpensɪv] *adj.* заду́мчивый.

pensiveness [ˈpensɪvnɪs] *n.* заду́мчивость.

pent [pent] *adj.* за́пертый; **~-up feelings** пода́вленные чу́вства.

pentacle [ˈpentək(ə)l] *n.* пентагра́мма, маги́ческий пятиуго́льник.

pentagon [ˈpentəgən] *n.* пятиуго́льник; **the P~** (*U.S. War Dept.*) Пентаго́н.

pentagram [ˈpentəˌgræm] *n.* пентагра́мма, маги́ческий пятиуго́льник.

pentameter [penˈtæmɪtə(r)] *n.* пента́метр.

Pentateuch [ˈpentəˌtjuːk] *n.* пятикни́жие.

pentathlete [penˈtæθliːt] *n.* пятибо́рец.

pentathlon [penˈtæθlən] *n.* пятибо́рье.

Pentecost [ˈpentɪˌkɒst] *n.* пятидеся́тница.

Pentecostal [ˌpentɪˈkɒst(ə)l] *adj.* пятидеся́тнический.

Pentecostalist [ˌpentɪˈkɒstəlɪst] *n.* пятидеся́тни|к (*fem.* -ца).

penthouse [ˈpenthaʊs] *n.* (*sloping roof*) наве́с; (*US*, *apartment on roof*) мезони́н; особня́к, выстроенный на кры́ше небоскрёба.

pentode [ˈpentəʊd] *n.* пенто́д.

penultimate [pɪˈnʌltɪmət] *adj.* предпосле́дный.

penumbra [pɪˈnʌmbrə] *n.* полуте́нь.

penurious [pɪˈnjʊərɪəs] *adj.* бе́дный; ску́дный.

penury [ˈpenjʊrɪ] *n.* нужда́; ску́дность.

peon [ˈpiːən] *n.* (*labourer*) пео́н, подёнщик.

peonage [ˈpiːənɪdʒ] *n.* батра́чество.

peony [ˈpiːənɪ] *n.* пио́н.

people [ˈpiːp(ə)l] *n.* **1.** (*race, nation*) наро́д; **the ~s of the former Soviet Union** наро́ды бы́вшего Сове́тского Сою́за; **government of the ~, by the ~, for the ~** власть наро́да, для наро́да, осуществля́емая наро́дом; **~'s republic** наро́дная респу́блика. **2.** (*proletariat*) наро́д; **the common ~** просто́й наро́д; **a man of the ~** челове́к из наро́да; **he rose from the ~** он вы́шел из наро́да. **3.** (*inhabitants*) жи́тели (*m. pl.*); (*workers*) слу́жащие (*pl.*); (*citizens*) гра́ждане (*m. pl.*). **4.** (*persons grouped by class, place etc.*): **poor ~** бедняки́ (*m. pl.*); **country ~** се́льские жи́тели; **young ~** молодёжь; **old ~** старики́ (*m. pl.*); **our ~** на́ши. **5.** (*relatives, parents*) родны́е (*pl.*). **6.** (*persons in general*) лю́ди (*pl.*, *g.* -е́й); **few ~** ма́ло люде́й; **four ~** четы́ре челове́ка; че́тверо; **there were 20 ~ present** прису́тствовало 20 челове́к; **many, most ~ will object** большинство́ бу́дет про́тив; **~ say he's mad** говоря́т, что он сумасше́дший; **he doesn't care what ~ say** ему́ всё равно́, что о нём говоря́т.
v.t. засел|я́ть, -и́ть; **a thickly-~d district** густонаселённый райо́н; (*fig.*): **the town is ~d with memories** го́род по́лон воспомина́ний.

pep [pep] (*coll.*) *n.* бо́дрость ду́ха; **put some ~ into it!** веселе́е!; живе́е!; **~ pill** стимуля́тор, стимули́рующая пилю́ля (*наркотик*); **~ talk** «нака́чка».
v.t. (*usu.* **~ up**) подбодр|я́ть, -и́ть; стимули́ровать (*impf.*, *pf.*).

pepper [ˈpepə(r)] *n.* (*condiment*) пе́рец; (*capsicum plant or pod*) стручко́вый пе́рец.
v.t. **1.** (*sprinkle or season with ~*) пе́рчить, на-/по-. **2.** (*fig.*, *sprinkle*) усе́|ивать, -ять. **3.** (*fig.*, *pelt*) забр|а́сывать, -о́сить; **he was ~ed with questions** его́ заброса́ли вопро́сами.
cpds. **~-and-salt** *n.* (*cloth*) тка́цкий рису́нок «пе́рец и соль»; *adj.* (*colour*) кра́пчатый; **~-box, ~-castor,** *nn.* пе́речница; **~corn** *n.* пе́речное зерно́, перчи́нка; (*fig.*, *rent*) номина́льная аре́ндная пла́та; **~-mill** *n.* ме́льница (для пе́рца); **~mint** *n.* (*plant*; *its essence*) мя́та пе́речная; (*flavoured sweet*) мя́тный ледене́ц; **~-pot** *n.* = **~-box**

peppery [ˈpepərɪ] *adj.* (*of food*) напе́рченный; (*fig.*, *irascible*) вспы́льчивый.

pepsin [ˈpepsɪn] *n.* пепси́н.

peptic [ˈpeptɪk] *adj.* пепти́ческий, пищевари́тельный; **~ ulcer** я́зва желу́дка.

per [pɜː(r)] *prep.* **1.** (*for each*) в+*a.*; на+*a.*; с+*g.*; **60 miles ~ hour** 60 миль в час; **grams ~ square centimetre** гра́ммы на оди́н квадра́тный сантиме́тр; **they collected 20 pence ~ man** они́ собра́ли по 20 пе́нсов с челове́ка. **2.** (*by means of*) по+*d.*; че́рез+*a.* **3.: as ~ usual** (*coll.*) по обыкнове́нию.

peradventure [pərədˈventʃə(r), ˌpɜr-] *n.*: **beyond a ~** без сомне́ния.

perambulate [pəˈræmbjʊˌleɪt] *v.t.* расха́живать (*impf.*) по+*d.*

perambulation [pəˌræmbjʊˈleɪʃ(ə)n] *n.* прогу́лка; обхо́д.

perambulator [pəˈræmbjʊˌleɪtə(r)] *n.* де́тская коля́ска.

per annum [pər ˈænəm] *adv.* в год.

percale [pəˈkeɪl] *n.* перка́ль (*f. or m.*).

per capita [pə ˈkæpɪtə] *adv.* на ду́шу.

perceivable [pəˈsiːvəb(ə)l] *adj.* ощути́мый.

perceive [pəˈsiːv] *v.t.* (*with mind*) пон|има́ть, -я́ть; пост|ига́ть, -и́гнуть, -и́чь; (*through senses*) чу́вствовать, по-; ощу|ща́ть, -ти́ть.

per cent, percent [pə ˈsent] *n.* проце́нт; **three ~** три проце́нта.
adv. проце́нт, на со́тню.

percentage [pəˈsentɪdʒ] *n.* (*rate per cent*) проце́нтное содержа́ние; (*proportion*) проце́нтное отноше́ние, проце́нт; (*share in profits*) до́ля, часть; (*US coll.*, *profit*) вы́года.

perceptibility [pəˌseptɪˈbɪlɪtɪ] *n.* ощути́мость.

perceptibl|e [pəˈseptɪb(ə)l] *adj.* ощути́мый; **he was ~y moved** он был заме́тно растро́ган.

perception [pəˈsepʃ(ə)n] *n.* (*process or faculty of perceiving*) восприя́тие, ощуще́ние; (*quality of discernment*) осозна́ние; понима́ние; (*phil.*) перце́пция.

perceptive [pə'septɪv] *adj.* восприи́мчивый; проница́тельный.
perceptiveness [pə'septɪvnɪs] *n.* восприи́мчивость, проница́тельность.
perch[1] [pɜːtʃ] *n.* (*zool.*) о́кунь (*m.*).
perch[2] [pɜːtʃ] *n.* (*of bird*) насе́ст, жё́рдочка; (*fig.*): **he was knocked off his ~** ему́ сби́ли го́нор (*coll.*).
v.t. & i. сади́ться (*impf.*) на насе́ст; устр|а́иваться, -о́иться; **birds ~ on the boughs** пти́цы садя́тся на ве́тви; **he ~ed (himself) on a stool** он присе́л на табуре́т; **a town ~ed on a hill** го́род, прилепи́вшийся на верши́не холма́.
perchance [pə'tʃɑːns] *adv.* (*arch. or joc.*) быть мо́жет, случа́йно.
percipience [pə'sɪpɪəns] *n.* спосо́бность восприя́тия.
percipient [pə'sɪpɪənt] *adj.* воспринима́ющий.
percolate ['pɜːkə,leɪt] *v.t.* про|ходи́ть, -йти́ че́рез+*a.*; **the water ~s every crevice** вода́ проника́ет че́рез ка́ждую щель.
v.i. прос|а́чиваться, -очи́ться; **water ~s through sand** вода́ прохо́дит сквозь песо́к; **I'm waiting for the coffee to ~** я жду, пока́ ко́фе профильтру́ется; (*fig.*): **the news ~d at last** но́вости наконе́ц просочи́лись.
percolator ['pɜːkə,leɪtə(r)] *n.* (*cul.*) кофе́йник, перколя́тор, кофева́рка.
per contra [pɜː 'kɒntrə] *adv.* с друго́й стороны́; наоборо́т.
percussion [pə'kʌʃ(ə)n] *n.* **1.** (*striking*) уда́р; **~ cap** уда́рный писто́н; **~ fuse** взрыва́тель (*m.*) уда́рного де́йствия. **2.** (**~ instruments**) уда́рные инструме́нты (*m. pl.*).
percussionist [pə'kʌʃ(ə)nɪst] *n.* уда́рник.
per diem [pə 'diːem, 'daɪem] *adv.* в день.
perdition [pə'dɪʃ(ə)n] *n.* ги́бель.
peregrination [,perɪgrɪ'neɪʃ(ə)n] *n.* стра́нствование.
peregrine ['perɪgrɪn] *n.* (**~ falcon**) со́кол; сапса́н.
peremptory [pə'remptərɪ, 'perɪm-] *adj.* (*imperious*) повели́тельный; непререка́емый; (*leg.*) императи́вный; **~ challenge** (*leg.*) отво́д (прися́жного) без указа́ния причи́ны.
perennial [pə'renɪəl] *n.* (*plant*) многоле́тнее расте́ние; **hardy ~** (*lit.*) выно́сливый многоле́тник; (*fig.*) навя́зший в зуба́х вопро́с.
adj. (*lasting throughout year*) длящийся кру́глый год; (*enduring*) (веко)ве́чный; (*regularly repeated*) регуля́рно повторя́ющийся.
perestroika [,pere'strɔːkə] *n.* перестро́йка.
perfect[1] ['pɜːfɪkt] *n.* (*gram.*) перфе́кт; **the future ~** бу́дущее совершё́нное вре́мя.
adj. **1.** (*entire, complete; absolute*) соверше́нный, по́лный; **I felt a ~ fool** я почу́вствовал себя́ по́лным/фо́рменным дурако́м; **the child was a ~ nuisance** ребё́нок всем до сме́рти надое́л; **that is ~ nonsense** э́то по́лный абсу́рд; э́то абсолю́тная чепуха́; **you have a ~ right to your opinion** вы име́ете по́лное пра́во приде́рживаться своего́ мне́ния; **a ~ stranger** совсе́м чужо́й (челове́к); **I am ~ly sure of it** я соверше́нно уве́рен в э́том. **2.** (*faultless*) соверше́нный; безупре́чный; **a ~ diamond** безупре́чный алма́з; **he speaks ~ English** он в соверше́нстве говори́т по-англи́йски; (*thoroughly accomplished*) соверше́нный; **the actors were word-~** актё́ры зна́ли роль назубо́к; (*corresponding to an ideal*) соверше́нный, идеа́льный; (*corresponding to definition; archetypal*): **a ~ circle** то́чный круг; **he committed the ~ murder** он соверши́л класси́ческое уби́йство. **3.** (*exact, precise*) абсолю́тный; **~ pitch** (*mus.*) абсолю́тный слух; (*corresponding to requirements*) безупре́чный; **the dress is a ~ fit** пла́тье прекра́сно сиди́т; **that is a ~ instance of what I mean** э́то как нельзя́ лу́чше подтвержда́ет то, что я име́ю в виду́. **4.** (*gram.*) перфе́ктный, соверше́нный; **~ tense** перфе́кт; **~ participle** прича́стие проше́дшего вре́мени. **5.** (*mus.*): **~ fifth** чи́стая кви́нта.
perfect[2] [pə'fekt] *v.t.* (*complete; accomplish, achieve*) заверш|а́ть, -и́ть; выполня́ть, вы́полнить; (*bring to highest standard*) соверше́нствовать, у-.
perfection [pə'fekʃ(ə)n] *n.* **1.** (*perfecting*) заверше́ние, соверше́нствование. **2.** (*faultlessness, excellence*) соверше́нство; **she dances to ~** она́ безупре́чно танцу́ет. **3.** (*ideal or its embodiment*) зако́нченность; **the ~ of beauty** верх красоты́; (*highest pitch*) вы́сшая сте́пень (*чего*).
perfectionism [pə'fekʃə,nɪz(ə)m] *n.* стремле́ние к соверше́нству.
perfectionist [pə'fekʃənɪst] *n.* взыска́тельный челове́к; добива́ющийся соверше́нства; (*towards o.s.*) взыска́тельный к себе́ челове́к.
perfective [pə'fektɪv] *n.* (*gram.*) соверше́нный вид.
adj. соверше́нный; в соверше́нном ви́де.
perfervid [pə'fɜːvɪd] *adj.* пы́лкий.
perfidious [,pɜː'fɪdɪəs] *adj.* вероло́мный, кова́рный.
perfid|iousness [,pɜː'fɪdɪəsnɪs], **-y** ['pɜːfɪdɪ] *nn.* вероло́мство, кова́рность.
perforate ['pɜːfə,reɪt] *v.t.* перфори́ровать (*impf.*); **a ~d appendix** прободно́й аппе́ндикс.
v.i.: **the appendix ~d** произошло́ прободе́ние аппе́ндикса.
perforation [,pɜːfə'reɪʃ(ə)n] *n.* (*piercing*) перфора́ция, просве́рливание; (*row of pierced holes*) перфори́рованный ряд.
perforce [pə'fɔːs] *adv.* во́лей-нево́лей.
perform [pə'fɔːm] *v.t.* **1.** (*carry out*) выполня́ть, вы́полнить; исп|олня́ть, -о́лнить. **2.** (*enact*) исп|олня́ть, -о́лнить; **Hamlet will be ~ed next week** «Га́млета» даю́т на сле́дующей неде́ле; **~ing rights** права́ на постано́вку/исполне́ние; **he ~ed conjuring tricks** он показа́л фо́кусы.
v.i. **1.** (*act, play instrument etc.*) игра́ть, сыгра́ть; (*execute tricks*): **~ing seal** дрессиро́ванный тюле́нь. **2.** (*function*): **my car ~s well on hills** моя́ маши́на хорошо́ идё́т в го́ру.
performance [pə'fɔːməns] *n.* **1.** (*execution*) исполне́ние, выполне́ние, проведе́ние; **in the ~ of his duty** при исполне́нии до́лга. **2.** (*achievement, feat*) де́йствие; **that was a fine ~ of his!** (*iron.*) хорошо́ же он себя́ прояви́л! **3.** (*of a machine, vehicle etc.*) ход, характери́стика. **4.** (*public appearance*) выступле́ние. **5.** (*of play etc.*) представле́ние; постано́вка; спекта́кль (*m.*); (*of music*) исполне́ние. **6.** (*coll., tedious process, fuss*): **he made a ~ of it** он из э́того устро́ил це́лую исто́рию.
performer [pə'fɔːmə(r)] *n.* исполни́тель (*m.*); **he is a fine ~ on the flute** он прекра́сно игра́ет на фле́йте.
perfume ['pɜːfjuːm] *n.* (*odour*) благоуха́ние; (*fluid*) дух|и́ (*pl., g.* -о́в).
v.t. (*impart odour to*) де́лать, с- благоуха́нным; (*apply scent to*) души́ть, на-.
perfumer [pə'fjuːmə(r)] *n.* парфюме́р.
perfumery [pə'fjuːmərɪ] *n.* (*business*) парфюме́рная промы́шленность; (*shop*) парфюме́рия; (*wares*) парфюме́рные това́ры (*m. pl.*).
perfunctoriness [pə'fʌŋktərɪnɪs] *n.* пове́рхностность; небре́жность.
perfunctory [pə'fʌŋktərɪ] *adj.* пове́рхностный; небре́жный.
pergola ['pɜːgələ] *n.* пе́ргола.
perhaps [pə'hæps] *adv.* мо́жет быть; возмо́жно; пожа́луй; **~ not** мо́жет быть и нет; **there is no ~ about it** э́то несомне́нно.
pericardium [,perɪ'kɑːdɪəm] *n.* перика́рд.
peridot ['perɪ,dɒt] *n.* перидо́т.
perigee ['perɪ,dʒiː] *n.* периге́й.
perihelion [,perɪ'hiːlɪən] *n.* периге́лий.
peril ['perɪl] *n.* опа́сность; риск; **he goes in ~ of his life** его́ жизнь в постоя́нной опа́сности; **you come inside at your ~** вход (сюда́) риско́ван.
perilous ['perɪləs] *adj.* опа́сный; риско́ванный.
perimeter [pə'rɪmɪtə(r)] *n.* (*of a geom. figure*) пери́метр; (*of an airfield etc.*) вне́шняя грани́ца; (*of a defensive position*) вне́шний обво́д (*or* пере́дний край) кругово́й оборо́ны; **~ defence** кругова́я оборо́на.
period ['pɪərɪəd] *n.* **1.** пери́од; **the ~ of the sun's revolution** пери́од обраще́ния со́лнца; **she has ~s of depression** у неё́ быва́ют пери́оды депре́ссии; **at no ~ in his life was he ever happy** он никогда́ в жи́зни не́ был сча́стлив; **he will be away for a long ~** его́ не бу́дет до́лгое вре́мя. **2.** (*previous age*) эпо́ха; **she wore the dress of the ~** она́ была́ оде́та в сти́ле эпо́хи; **~ furniture** сти́льная/стари́нная ме́бель; **a ~ play** пье́са, рису́ющая нра́вы

определённой эпо́хи. **3.** (*session of instruction*) уро́к. **4.** (*course of disease*) ста́дия. **5.** (*menses*) ме́сячные (*pl.*). **6.** (*sentence*) фра́за; (*pl., rhetorical language*) рито́рика. **7.** (*full stop*) то́чка; коне́ц; **the war put a ~ to his studies** война́ положи́ла коне́ц его́ заня́тиям.
periodic [ˌpɪərɪˈɒdɪk] *adj.* периоди́ческий, очередно́й; **~ table** (*chem.*) периоди́ческая табли́ца.
periodical [ˌpɪərɪˈɒdɪk(ə)l] *n.* периоди́ческое изда́ние; (*pl.*) перио́дика.
adj. = **periodic**
periodicity [ˌpɪərɪəˈdɪsɪtɪ] *n.* периоди́чность.
peripatetic [ˌperɪpəˈtetɪk] *adj.* (*itinerant*) бродя́чий.
peripheral [pəˈrɪfər(ə)l] *n.* (*comput.*) перифери́йное устро́йство.
adj. (*lit.*) перифери́йный; (*fig., not central to a subject*) несуще́ственный; побо́чный.
periphery [pəˈrɪfərɪ] *n.* окру́жность; (*lit., fig.*) перифери́я.
periphrasis [pəˈrɪfrəsɪs] *n.* перифра́з.
periphrastic [ˌperɪˈfræstɪk] *adj.* перифрасти́ческий.
periscope [ˈperɪˌskəʊp] *n.* периско́п.
periscopic [ˌperɪˈskɒpɪk] *adj.* перископи́ческий; **~ sight** периско́пный прице́л.
perish [ˈperɪʃ] *v.t.*: **we were ~ed with cold** мы про́сто погиба́ли от хо́лода; **strong sun will ~ rubber** си́льные со́лнечные лучи́ разруша́ют рези́ну.
v.i. **1.** пог|иба́ть, -и́бнуть; **they shall ~ by the sword** они́ поги́бнут от меча́; **... or ~ in the attempt** ≃ пан и́ли пропа́л; **~ the thought!** Бо́же упаси́! **2.: the rubber has ~ed** рези́на пришла́ в него́дность.
perishable [ˈperɪʃəb(ə)l] *adj.* тле́нный, непро́чный, скоропо́ртящийся; (*pl., as n.*) скоропо́ртящийся това́р.
perisher [ˈperɪʃə(r)] *n.* (*sl.*) ничто́жество; (*child*) прока́зник.
perishing [ˈperɪʃɪŋ] *adj.* (*coll.*) (*cold*): **it's ~ here** здесь а́дский хо́лод; (*wretched*) ужа́сный, стра́шный.
peristyle [ˈperɪˌstaɪl] *n.* перисти́ль (*m.*).
peritoneum [ˌperɪtəˈniːəm] *n.* брюши́на.
peritonitis [ˌperɪtəˈnaɪtɪs] *n.* перитони́т.
periwig [ˈperɪwɪg] *n.* (пу́дреный) пари́к.
periwinkle [ˈperɪˌwɪŋk(ə)l] *n.* (*mollusc*) литори́на; (*plant*) барви́нок.
perjure [ˈpɜːdʒə(r)] *v.t.*: **~ o.s.** да|ва́ть, -ть ло́жное показа́ние под прися́гой; **a ~d witness** лжесвиде́тель (*fem.* -ница).
perjurer [ˈpɜːdʒərə(r)] *n.* лжесвиде́тель (*fem.* -ница).
perjury [ˈpɜːdʒərɪ] *n.* лжесвиде́тельство; **commit ~ = perjure o.s.**
perk[1] [pɜːk] *n.* (*coll.*) = **perquisite**
perk[2] [pɜːk] *v.t.* **1.** (*move smartly*): **the dog ~ed up its tail** соба́ка задрала́ хвост; **he ~ed his head over the fence** он вы́сунул го́лову че́рез забо́р. **2.: ~ up** (*smarten*) приукра́|шивать, -сить; ожив|ля́ть, -и́ть; (*of taste*) припр|авля́ть, -а́вить.
v.i.: **I hope the weather ~s up** (*coll.*) наде́юсь, что пого́да пола́дится.
perkiness [ˈpɜːkɪnɪs] *n.* бо́йкость, весёлость.
perky [ˈpɜːkɪ] *adj.* (*of dog etc.*) живо́й, бо́йкий; (*cheerful*) весёлый.
perm [pɜːm] *n.* (*coll., permanent wave*) перманéнт.
v.t.: **she had her hair ~ed** она́ сде́лала себе́ перманéнтную зави́вку.
permafrost [ˈpɜːməˌfrɒst] *n.* ве́чная мерзлота́.
permalloy [ˈpɜːməˌlɔɪ] *n.* пермалло́й.
permanence [ˈpɜːmənəns] *n.* неизме́нность.
permanency [ˈpɜːmənənsɪ] *n.* **1.** = **permanence. 2.** (*sth. permanent*) обы́денное явле́ние; (*job*) постоя́нное заня́тие.
permanent [ˈpɜːmənənt] *adj.* постоя́нный; **~ wave** зави́вка «перманéнт»; **~ way** ве́рхнее строе́ние пути́.
permanganate [pɜːˈmæŋgəˌneɪt, -nət] *n.* пермангана́т; **~ of potash** марганцовоки́слый ка́лий.
permeability [ˌpɜːmɪəˈbɪlɪtɪ] *n.* проница́емость.
permeable [ˈpɜːmɪəb(ə)l] *adj.* проница́емый.
permeate [ˈpɜːmɪˌeɪt] *v.t. & i.* пропи́т|ывать, -а́ть; прон|ика́ть, -и́кнуть в+*a.*; прос|а́чиваться, -очи́ться в+*a.*
permeation [ˌpɜːmɪˈeɪʃ(ə)n] *n.* (*lit., fig.*) проникнове́ние, проса́чивание.
Permian [ˈpɜːmɪən] *adj.* пе́рмский.
per mille [pɜː ˈmɪlɪ] *adv.* на ты́сячу.
permissibility [pəˌmɪsɪˈbɪlɪtɪ] *n.* допусти́мость.
permissible [pəˈmɪsɪb(ə)l] *adj.* допусти́мый, позволи́тельный.
permission [pəˈmɪʃ(ə)n] *n.* позволе́ние, разреше́ние; **you must get ~ to go there** что́бы пойти́ туда́, необходи́мо разреше́ние; **she has my ~ to stay** я разреша́ю ей оста́ться; **with your ~ I'll leave** с ва́шего позволе́ния я ухожу́.
permissive [pəˈmɪsɪv] *adj.*: **~ society** о́бщество вседозво́ленности.
permissiveness [pəˈmɪsɪvnɪs] *n.* вседозво́ленность.
permit[1] [ˈpɜːmɪt] *n.* разреше́ние, про́пуск (*pl.* -а́); **work ~** разреше́ние на рабо́ту; **residence ~** вид на жи́тельство.
permit[2] [pəˈmɪt] *v.t.* разреш|а́ть, -и́ть; **smoking ~ted** кури́ть разреша́ется; **if I may be ~ted to speak** е́сли мне бу́дет позво́лено вы́сказаться.
v.i.: **if circumstances ~** е́сли обстоя́тельства позво́лят; **weather ~ting** е́сли пого́да позво́лит; **the situation ~s of no delay** ситуа́ция не те́рпит отлага́тельства.
permutation [ˌpɜːmjʊˈteɪʃ(ə)n] *n.* пермута́ция.
pernicious [pəˈnɪʃəs] *adj.* па́губный, вре́дный; **~ anaemia** злока́чественное малокро́вие.
perniciousness [pəˈnɪʃəsnɪs] *n.* па́губность.
pernickety [pəˈnɪkɪtɪ] *adj.* (*coll.*) приверéдливый.
perorate [ˈperəˌreɪt] *v.i.* (*declaim*) разглаго́льствовать (*impf.*).
peroration [ˌperəˈreɪʃ(ə)n] *n.* (*conclusion*) заключе́ние ре́чи.
peroxide [pəˈrɒksaɪd] *n.* пе́рекись; **hydrogen ~** пе́рекись водоро́да; **a ~ blonde** кра́шеная блонди́нка.
v.t. обесцве́|чивать, -тить.
perpend [pəˈpend] *v.t.* взве́шивать, обду́мывать (*both impf.*).
perpendicular [ˌpɜːpənˈdɪkjʊlə(r)] *n.* перпендикуля́р; **out of the ~** невертика́льный; (*plumb-line*) отве́сная ли́ния.
adj. (*at right angles*) перпендикуля́рный; (*vertical*) вертика́льный.
perpetrate [ˈpɜːpɪˌtreɪt] *v.t.* соверш|а́ть, -и́ть; учин|я́ть, -и́ть; **he ~d a frightful pun** он остря́пал/вы́дал потряса́ющий каламбу́р.
perpetration [ˌpɜːpɪˈtreɪʃ(ə)n] *n.* соверше́ние.
perpetrator [ˈpɜːpɪˌtreɪtə(r)] *n.* вино́вный; престу́пник.
perpetual [pəˈpetjʊəl] *adj.* ве́чный; **~ motion** ве́чное движе́ние; (*for life*) бессро́чный, пожи́зненный.
perpetuate [pəˈpetjʊˌeɪt] *v.t.* увекове́чи|вать, -ть.
perpetuation [pəˌpetjʊˈeɪʃ(ə)n] *n.* увекове́чение.
perpetuity [ˌpɜːpɪˈtjuːɪtɪ] *n.* ве́чность; **in ~** навсегда́, (на)ве́чно.
perplex [pəˈpleks] *v.t.* (*puzzle*) озада́чи|вать, -ть; (*complicate*) усложн|я́ть, -и́ть; запу́т|ывать, -ать.
perplexity [pəˈpleksɪtɪ] *n.* (*bewilderment*) озада́ченность, недоуме́ние; (*cause of bewilderment*) запу́танность.
perquisite [ˈpɜːkwɪzɪt] *n.* льго́та; (*pl.*) побо́чные преиму́щества.
perry [ˈperɪ] *n.* гру́шевый сидр.
per se [pɜː ˈseɪ] *adv.* само́ по себе́.
persecute [ˈpɜːsɪˌkjuːt] *v.t.* пресле́довать (*impf.*).
persecution [ˌpɜːsɪˈkjuːʃ(ə)n] *n.* пресле́дование; **~ mania** ма́ния пресле́дования.
persecutor [ˈpɜːsɪˌkjuːtə(r)] *n.* пресле́дователь (*m.*).
perseverance [ˌpɜːsɪˈvɪərəns] *n.* упо́рство; насто́йчивость.
persever|e [ˌpɜːsɪˈvɪə(r)] *v.i.*: **you must ~e in (at, with) your work** вы должны́ упо́рно продолжа́ть свою́ рабо́ту; **he is very ~ing** он о́чень стара́телен.
Persia [ˈpɜːʃə] *n.* Пе́рсия.
Persian [ˈpɜːʃ(ə)n] *n.* (*pers.*) перс (*fem.* -ия́нка); (*language*) перси́дский язы́к.
adj. перси́дский; **~ Gulf** Перси́дский зали́в.
persiflage [ˈpɜːsɪˌflɑːʒ] *n.* подшу́чивание.
persimmon [pɜːˈsɪmən] *n.* хурма́.
persist [pəˈsɪst] *v.i.* **1.** (*resist dissuasion*) упо́рствовать (*impf.*); **he ~ed in his opinion** он упо́рствовал в своём мне́нии; он упо́рно отста́ивал своё мне́ние; **he ~ed in coming with me** он настоя́л на том, что́бы пойти́ со мно́й. **2.** (*continue to exist, remain*) сохран|я́ться, -и́ться; **the custom ~s to this day** э́тот обы́чай сохрани́лся по сей

день; **fog will ~ all day** тума́н подéржится весь день.

persistence [pə'sɪst(ə)ns] *n.* (*obstinacy*) упо́рство; (*continuation*) продолже́ние; живу́честь.

persistent [pə'sɪst(ə)nt] *adj.* **1.** (*obstinate*) упо́рный. **2.** (*slow to go or change*) усто́йчивый, постоя́нный.

person ['pɜːs(ə)n] *n.* **1.** (*individual*) челове́к; осо́ба; **a young ~** молода́я осо́ба; **out of bounds to all ~s whatsoever** вход воспрещён абсолю́тно всем; **not a single ~ was injured** ра́неных нé было совсе́м; (*of particular category*) лицо́; **a very important ~** о́чень ва́жное/значи́тельное лицо́; **displaced ~s** перемещённые ли́ца; (*relig.*) лицо́, ипоста́сь; **the three ~s of the Trinity** три ипоста́си Тро́ицы. **2.** (*body*) лицо́; **an offence against the ~** преступле́ние про́тив ли́чности; **freedom of the ~** свобо́да ли́чности; **the great man appeared in ~** вели́кий челове́к яви́лся со́бственной персо́ной; **the Church was there in the ~ of Father X** це́рковь была́ предста́влена отцо́м X. **3.** (*gram.*) лицо́; **first ~ singular** пе́рвое лицо́ еди́нственного числа́.

persona [pɜː'səʊnə] *n.* вне́шняя сторона́ ли́чности; **~ (non) grata** персо́на (нон) гра́та (*indecl.*).

personable ['pɜːsənəb(ə)l] *adj.* привлека́тельный.

personage ['pɜːsənɪdʒ] *n.* (*important pers.*) ли́чность, персо́на; (*in a play*) персона́ж.

personal ['pɜːsən(ə)l] *adj.* ли́чный; **this letter is ~ to me** э́то ли́чное письмо́ мне; **she is a ~ acquaintance of mine** я её ли́чно зна́ю; **she has great ~ charm** у неё большо́е ли́чное обая́ние; **~ column** (*of newspaper*) ли́чная коло́нка; **~ estate** (*leg.*) дви́жимое иму́щество; **they were selected by ~ interview** их отобра́ли путём индивидуа́льного собесе́дования; **~ pronoun** ли́чное местоиме́ние; **~ stereo** во́кмен, пле́ер; **don't make ~ remarks!** не переходи́те на ли́чности!

personality [ˌpɜːsə'nælɪtɪ] *n.* **1.** (*individual existence or identity*) индивидуа́льность. **2.** (*distinctive ~, character*) ли́чность; **a strong ~** си́льная ли́чность; **dual ~** раздвое́ние ли́чности; **~ cult** культ ли́чности. **3.** (*public figure*) де́ятель (*m.*), изве́стная ли́чность. **4.** (*pl.*, *offensive remarks*) вы́пады (*m. pl.*).

personalize ['pɜːsənəˌlaɪz] *v.t.* прин|има́ть, -я́ть на свой счёт; вноси́ть, -ести́ ли́чный элеме́нт в+*a.*; **~d stationery** (*marked with initials etc.*) имённая пи́счая бума́га.

personally ['pɜːsənəlɪ] *adv.* ли́чно; **he was ~ involved** он был ли́чно заме́шан; **don't take it ~!** не принима́йте э́то на свой счёт!; **~ I prefer this** ли́чно я предпочита́ю э́то.

personalty ['pɜːsənəltɪ] *n.* (*leg.*) дви́жимость.

personate ['pɜːsəˌneɪt] *v.t.* (*act the part of*) игра́ть, сыгра́ть роль +*g.*; (*pretend to be*) выдава́ть (*impf.*) себя́ за+*a.*

personation [ˌpɜːsə'neɪʃ(ə)n] *n.* воплоще́ние; (*leg.*) персона́ция.

personification [pəˌsɒnɪfɪ'keɪʃ(ə)n] *n.* олицетворе́ние; **he is the ~ of selfishness** он воплощённый эгои́зм.

personif|y [pə'sɒnɪˌfaɪ] *v.t.* (*give personal attributes to*) олицетвор|я́ть, -и́ть; (*exemplify*) вопло|ща́ть, -ти́ть; **she was kindness ~ied** она́ была́ воплоще́нием доброты́.

personnel [ˌpɜːsə'nel] *n.* персона́л; штат; ка́дры (*m. pl.*); **~ officer** рабо́тник отде́ла ка́дров; **~ department** отде́л ка́дров.

perspective [pə'spektɪv] *n.* **1.** (*system of representation*) перспекти́ва; **the roof is out of ~** (*in a drawing*) кры́ша изображена́ вне перспекти́вы; (*fig.*): **you must see, get things in (their right) ~** на́до ви́деть ве́щи в их и́стинном све́те. **2.** (*vista*) вид; (*fig.*) перспекти́вы (*f.pl.*).

adj. перспекти́вный; **~ drawing** чертёж в перспекти́ве.

perspex ['pɜːspeks] *n.* плексигла́с.

perspicacious [ˌpɜːspɪ'keɪʃəs] *adj.* проница́тельный.

perspicacity [ˌpɜːspɪ'kæsɪtɪ] *n.* проница́тельность.

perspicuous [pə'spɪkjʊəs] *adj.* я́сный, поня́тный.

perspicu|ousness [pə'spɪkjʊəsnɪs], **-ity** [ˌpəspɪ'kjuːɪtɪ] *nn.* я́сность, поня́тность.

perspiration [ˌpɜːspɪ'reɪʃ(ə)n] *n.* (*sweating*) поте́ние; (*sweat*) пот.

perspire [pə'spaɪə(r)] *v.i.* поте́ть, вс-.

persuadable [pə'sweɪdəb(ə)l] *adj.* внуша́емый; поддаю́щийся убежде́нию.

persuade [pə'sweɪd] *v.t.* **1.** (*convince*) убе|жда́ть, -ди́ть; **I ~d him of my innocence** я убеди́л его́ в мое́й невино́вности. **2.** (*induce*) угов|а́ривать, -ори́ть; **he was ~d to sing** его́ уговори́ли спеть.

persuader [pə'sweɪdə(r)] *n.* увещева́тель (*m.*).

persuasion [pə'sweɪʒ(ə)n] *n.* (*persuading*) убежде́ние; (*persuasiveness*) убеди́тельность; (*conviction*) убежде́ние; (*denomination*) вероисповеда́ние.

persuasive [pə'sweɪsɪv] *adj.* убеди́тельный; (*of pers.*) облада́ющий да́ром убежде́ния.

persuasiveness [pə'sweɪsɪvnɪs] *n.* убеди́тельность.

pert [pɜːt] *adj.* де́рзкий, наха́льный.

pertain [pə'teɪn] *v.i.* (*belong*) принадлежа́ть (*impf.*); (*be appropriate*) под|ходи́ть, -ойти́; подоба́ть (*impf.*); (*relate*) относи́ться (*impf.*) (*к кому/чему*).

pertinacious [ˌpɜːtɪ'neɪʃəs] *adj.* упря́мый, неусту́пчивый.

pertinac|iousness [ˌpɜːtɪ'neɪʃəsnɪs], **-ity** [ˌpɜːtɪ'næsɪtɪ] *nn.* упря́мство, неусту́пчивость.

pertinence ['pɜːtɪnəns] *n.* уме́стность.

pertinent ['pɜːtɪnənt] *adj.* уме́стный; подходя́щий.

pertness ['pɜːtnɪs] *n.* де́рзость, наха́льство.

perturb [pə'tɜːb] *v.t.* трево́жить, вс-; волнова́ть, вз-.

perturbation [ˌpɜːtə'beɪʃ(ə)n] *n.* встрево́женность; волне́ние.

Peru [pə'ruː] *n.* Перу́ (*f. indecl.*).

peruke [pə'ruːk] *n.* (пу́дреный) пари́к.

perusal [pə'ruːzəl] *n.* (внима́тельное) чте́ние.

peruse [pə'ruːz] *v.t.* внима́тельно чита́ть, про-; (*examine*) рассм|а́тривать, -отре́ть.

Peruvian [pə'ruːvɪən] *n.* перуа́н|ец, (*fem.* -ка).

adj. перуа́нский.

pervade [pə'veɪd] *v.t.* наполня́ть (*impf.*); пропи́тывать (*impf.*).

pervasion [pə'veɪʒ(ə)n] *n.* распростране́ние; наполне́ние.

pervasive [pə'veɪsɪv] *adj.* прони́зывающий, распространённый.

pervasiveness [pə'veɪsɪvnɪs] *n.* распростране́ние.

perverse [pə'vɜːs] *adj.* (*unreasonable*) превра́тный; (*persistent in wrongdoing*) поро́чный, извращённый.

pervers|eness [pə'vɜːsnɪs], **-ity** [pə'vɜːsɪtɪ] *nn.* превра́тность; извращённость.

perversion [pə'vɜːʃ(ə)n] *n.* (*distortion, misrepresentation*) искаже́ние; (*corruption, leading astray*) извраще́ние; (*sexual deviation*) извраще́ние, перве́рсия.

pervert[1] ['pɜːvɜːt] *n.* (*sexual deviant*) извраще́нец; (*renegade*) отсту́пник.

pervert[2] [pə'vɜːt] *v.t.* (*misapply*) извра|ща́ть, -ти́ть; (*corrupt*) развра|ща́ть, -ти́ть.

pervious ['pɜːvɪəs] *adj.* (*allowing passage; permeable*) проходи́мый; досту́пный; (*receptive*) восприи́мчивый.

peseta [pə'seɪtə] *n.* песе́та.

pesky ['peskɪ] *adj.* (*US coll.*) доку́чливый, зану́дливый.

peso ['peɪsəʊ] *n.* пе́со (*indecl.*).

pessary ['pesərɪ] *n.* песса́рий.

pessimism ['pesɪˌmɪz(ə)m] *n.* пессими́зм.

pessimist ['pesɪmɪst] *n.* пессими́ст.

pessimistic [ˌpesɪ'mɪstɪk] *adj.* пессимисти́ческий, пессимисти́чный.

pest [pest] *n.* (*harmful creature*) вреди́тель (*m.*); **insect ~s** вре́дные насеко́мые; (*of pers.*) зану́да (*c.g.*).

pester ['pestə(r)] *v.t.* докуча́ть (*impf.*); **he keeps ~ing me for money** он всё пристаёт ко мне насчёт де́нег; **she ~ed her father to take her with him** она́ пристава́ла к отцу́, что́бы он взял её с собо́й.

pesticide ['pestɪˌsaɪd] *n.* пестици́д.

pestiferous [pe'stɪfərəs] *adj.* тлетво́рный, па́губный; (*of pers.*) доку́чливый.

pestilence ['pestɪləns] *n.* чума́.

pestilent ['pestɪlənt] *adj.* смертоно́сный; (*fig.*) губи́тельный.

pestilential [ˌpestɪ'lenʃ(ə)l] *adj.* чумно́й; па́губный.

pestle ['pes(ə)l] *n.* пе́стик.

pet[1] [pet] *n.* **1.** (*animal, bird etc.*) дома́шнее/ко́мнатное/люби́мое живо́тное; **~ food** корм для дома́шних живо́тных; **~ shop** зоомагази́н. **2.** (*favourite*) люби́м|ец (*fem.* -ица), ба́ловень (*m.*); **teacher's ~** люби́мчик учи́теля; **his ~ subject** его́ излю́бленная те́ма; **onions**

are my ~ aversion я бо́льше всего́ не люблю́ лук; **~ name** ласка́тельное/уменьши́тельное и́мя.

v.t. (*treat with affection*) балова́ть, из-; (*fondle*) ласка́ть, при-.

v.i. (*coll.*, *fondle each other*) обжима́ться (*impf.*).

pet[2] [pet] *n.* (*ill-humour, sulk*) дурно́е настрое́ние.

petal ['pet(ə)l] *n.* лепесто́к.

petard [pɪ'tɑ:d] *n.* пета́рда; **he was hoist with his own ~** он попа́л в со́бственную лову́шку; он сде́лал э́то на свою́ же го́лову.

Peter[1] ['pi:tə] *n.* Пётр; **he is robbing ~ to pay Paul** у одного́ берёт, а другому́ даёт; со Спа́са дерёт, да на Нико́лу кладёт.

peter[2] ['pi:tə(r)] *v.i.*: **~ out** (*run dry, low*) исс|яка́ть, -я́кнуть; **the track ~ed out** след постепе́нно заглóх.

petit bourgeois [ˌpə'tɪ 'bʊəʒwɑ:] *adj.* мелкобуржуа́зный.

petite [pə'ti:t] *adj.* ма́ленькая (*f.*), миниатю́рная (*f.*).

petite bourgeoisie [pə'ti:t ˌbʊəʒwɑ:'zi:] *n.* ме́лкая буржуази́я.

petit four [ˌpetɪ 'fɔ:(r)] *n.* петифу́р.

petition [pɪ'tɪʃ(ə)n] *n.* проше́ние; (*formal request*) пети́ция; (*application to court*) хода́тайство.

v.t. & i. под|ава́ть, -а́ть проше́ние +*d.*; хода́тайствовать, по-.

petitioner [pɪ'tɪʃənə(r)] *n.* проси́тель (*m.*); (*in a divorce suit*) исте́ц.

petits pois [ˌpetɪ 'pwɑ:] *n.* ме́лкий горо́шек.

petrel ['petr(ə)l] *n.* буреве́стник; **stormy ~** (*lit.*) качу́рка ма́лая; (*fig.*) буреве́стник.

petrification [ˌpetrɪfɪ'keɪʃ(ə)n] *n.* (*lit.*) петрифика́ция, окамене́ние; (*fig.*) оцепене́ние.

petrif|y ['petrɪˌfaɪ] *v.t.* (*lit.*) превра|ща́ть, -ти́ть в ка́мень; (*fig.*) прив|оди́ть, -ести́ в оцепене́ние; **I was ~ied** я остолбене́л/оцепене́л.

petrochemicals [ˌpetrəʊ'kemɪk(ə)ls] *n. pl.* хими́ческие проду́кты (*m. pl.*) из нефтяно́го сырья́.

petrodollar ['petrəʊˌdɒlə(r)] *n.* нефтедо́ллар.

petrol ['petr(ə)l] *n.* бензи́н; **fill up with ~** запр|авля́ться, -а́виться бензи́ном; **~ bomb** буты́лка с зажига́тельной сме́сью; **~ can** кани́стра для бензи́на; **~ engine** бензи́новый дви́гатель; **~ pump** бензонасо́с; **~ pump attendant** слу́жащий бензоколо́нки; **~ station** бензоколо́нка; **~ tank** бензоба́к; **~ tanker** бензово́з.

petroleum [pɪ'trəʊlɪəm] *n.* нефть; **the ~ industry** нефтяна́я промы́шленность; **~ jelly** вазели́н.

petrologist [pɪ'trɒlədʒɪst] *n.* петро́граф.

petrology [pɪ'trɒlədʒɪ] *n.* петроло́гия, петрогра́фия.

petticoat ['petɪˌkəʊt] *n.* ни́жняя ю́бка; **~ government** ба́бье ца́рство.

pettifogger ['petɪˌfɒgə(r)] *n.* сутя́га, крючкотво́р.

pettifogging ['petɪˌfɒgɪŋ] *n.* сутя́жничество, крючкотво́рчество.

adj. сутя́жнический.

pettiness ['petɪnɪs] *n.* ме́лочность.

pettish ['petɪʃ] *adj.* оби́дчивый, раздражи́тельный.

petty ['petɪ] *adj.* **1.** (*trivial*) ме́лкий, малова́жный. **2.** (*small-minded*) ме́лочный. **3.** (*of small amounts*): **~ cash** де́ньги на ме́лкие расхо́ды; **~ theft** ме́лкая кра́жа. **4.**: **~ officer** (*nav.*) старшина́ (*m.*).

petulance ['petjʊləns] *n.* раздражи́тельность, нетерпели́вость.

petulant ['petjʊlənt] *adj.* раздражи́тельный, нетерпели́вый.

petunia [pɪ'tju:nɪə] *n.* пету́ния.

pew [pju:] *n.* отгоро́женное ме́сто в це́ркви; **take a ~!** (*coll.*) приса́живайтесь!

pewit ['pi:wɪt] = **peewit**

pewter ['pju:tə(r)] *n.* (*alloy*) сплав о́лова с други́м мета́ллом; (*vessels made of ~*) оловя́нная посу́да.

adj. оловя́нный.

pfennig ['pfenɪg, 'fenɪg] *n.* пфе́нниг.

phaeton ['feɪt(ə)n] *n.* фаэто́н.

phalanx ['fælæŋks] *n.* (*hist.*) фала́нга; (*anat.*) фала́нга па́льца.

phalarope ['fæləˌrəʊp] *n.* плаву́нчик.

phallic ['fælɪk] *adj.* фалли́ческий; **~ symbol** изображе́ние/си́мвол фа́ллоса.

phallus ['fæləs] *n.* фа́ллос.

phantasm ['fænˌtæz(ə)m] *n.* (*ghost*) фанто́м, при́зрак.

phantasmagoria [ˌfæntæzmə'gɔ:rɪə] *n.* фантасмаго́рия.

phantasmal [ˌfæn'tæzm(ə)l] *adj.* при́зрачный.

phantasy ['fæntəsɪ, -zɪ] = **fantasy**

phantom ['fæntəm] *n.* **1.** (*ghost*) при́зрак, фанто́м; (*attr.*) при́зрачный. **2.** (*illusion*): **a ~ of the imagination** плод фанта́зии.

Pharaoh ['feərəʊ] *n.* фарао́н.

Pharaonic [ˌfeəreɪ'ɒnɪk] *adj.* фарао́новский.

Pharisaical [ˌfærɪ'seɪɪk(ə)l] *adj.* (*fig.*) фарисе́йский; (*fig.*) ха́нжеский.

Pharisaism ['færɪseɪˌɪz(ə)m] *n.* фарисе́йство; (*fig.*) ханжество́.

Pharisee ['færɪˌsi:] *n.* фарисе́й; (*fig.*) ханжа́ (*c.g.*).

pharmaceutical [ˌfɑ:mə'sju:tɪk(ə)l] *adj.* фармацевти́ческий; **~ chemist** фармаце́вт, апте́карь (*m.*).

pharmaceutics [ˌfɑ:mə'sju:tɪks] *n.* фармаци́я, апте́чное де́ло.

pharmacist ['fɑ:məsɪst] *n.* фармаце́вт.

pharmacologist [ˌfɑ:mə'kɒlədʒɪst] *n.* фармако́лог.

pharmacology [ˌfɑ:mə'kɒlədʒɪ] *n.* фармаколо́гия.

pharmacopoeia [ˌfɑ:məkə'pi:ə] *n.* фармакопе́я.

pharmacy ['fɑ:məsɪ] *n.* (*dispensing*) апте́чное де́ло; (*dispensary*) апте́ка.

pharyng(e)al [ˌfærɪŋ'dʒi:əl] *adj.* гло́точный.

pharyngitis [ˌfærɪŋ'dʒaɪtɪs] *n.* фаринги́т.

pharynx ['færɪŋks] *n.* зев; гло́тка.

phase [feɪz] *n.* фа́за; (*stage*) ста́дия; (*aspect*) аспе́кт; **be in (out of) ~ with** (не) совпада́ть с+*i.*

v.t.: **a ~d withdrawal** поэта́пный вы́вод; **~ out** (*e.g. weapons, bases*) сн|има́ть, -я́ть с вооруже́ния (по эта́пам); св|ёртывать, -ерну́ть; ликвиди́ровать (*impf., pf.*).

Ph.D. (*abbr. of* ***Doctor of Philosophy***) сте́пень кандида́та нау́к.

pheasant ['fez(ə)nt] *n.* фаза́н.

phenomenal [fɪ'nɒmɪn(ə)l] *adj.* (*perceptible*) ощуща́емый; (*extraordinary, prodigious*) феномена́льный.

phenomenon [fɪ'nɒmɪnən] *n.* (*object of perception*) фено́мен, явле́ние; (*remarkable pers. or thg.*) фено́мен, чу́до; **infant ~** чу́до-ребёнок, вундерки́нд.

phew [fju:] *int.* (*expr. astonishment*) ну и ну!; **~, what a crowd!** ну и толпа́!; (*discomfort*): **~, isn't it hot!** уф, ну и жара́!; (*weariness*): **~, what a day it's been!** уф, ну и денёк вы́дался; (*disgust*): **~, that meat's bad!** фу, э́то мя́со испо́рчен!; (*relief*): **~, that was a near one!** ф-фу/уф, пронесло́! (*coll.*).

phial ['faɪəl] *n.* пузырёк.

philander [fɪ'lændə(r)] *v.i.* флиртова́ть (*impf.*).

philanderer [fɪ'lændərə(r)] *n.* волоки́та (*c.g.*), ловела́с.

philanthropic [ˌfɪlən'θrɒpɪk] *adj.* филантропи́ческий.

philanthropist [fɪ'lænθrəpɪst] *n.* филантро́п.

philanthropy [fɪ'lænθrəpɪ] *n.* филантро́пия.

philatelic [ˌfɪlə'telɪk] *adj.* филателисти́ческий.

philatelist [ˌfɪ'lætəlɪst] *n.* филатели́ст.

philately [fɪ'lætəlɪ] *n.* филатели́я.

philharmonic [ˌfɪlhɑ:'mɒnɪk] *n.* (**~** *society*) филармо́ния.

adj. филармони́ческий.

philippic [fɪ'lɪpɪk] *n.* (*fig.*) обличи́тельная речь, фили́ппика.

Philippine ['fɪlɪˌpi:n] *adj.* филиппи́нский; **the ~s** (*islands*) Филиппи́н|ы (*pl., g.* —).

Philistine ['fɪlɪˌstaɪn] *n.* (*bibl.*) филисти́млянин; (*fig.*) фили́стер, обыва́тель (*m.*).

adj. обыва́тельский.

Philistinism ['fɪlɪstɪˌnɪz(ə)m] *n.* фили́стерство.

Phillips ['fɪlɪps] *n.* (*propr.*): **~ screwdriver** крестова́я отвёртка.

philological [ˌfɪlə'lɒdʒɪk(ə)l] *adj.* языкове́дческий, филологи́ческий.

philologist [fɪ'lɒlədʒɪst] *n.* языкове́д; фило́лог.

philology [fɪ'lɒlədʒɪ] *n.* языкове́дение; филоло́гия.

philosopher [fɪ'lɒsəfə(r)] *n.* фило́соф; (*pers. of equable temperament*) фило́соф, невозмути́мый челове́к.

philosophic(al) [ˌfɪlə'sɒfɪk(ə)l] *adj.* (*both senses*) филосо́фский.

philosophize [fɪ'lɒsəˌfaɪz] *v.i.* филосо́фствовать (*impf.*).

philosophy [fɪ'lɒsəfɪ] *n.* филосо́фия; (*equability*) филосо́фская невозмути́мость.
philtre ['fɪltə(r)] *n.* любо́вный напи́ток.
phlebitis [flɪ'baɪtɪs] *n.* флеби́т.
phlebotomy [flɪ'bɒtəmɪ] *n.* вскры́тие ве́ны.
phlegm [flem] *n.* (*secretion*) мокро́та; (*fig.*) флегмати́чность.
phlegmatic [fleg'mætɪk] *adj.* флегмати́чный.
phobia ['fəʊbɪə] *n.* фо́бия, страх.
Phoenicia [fə'nɪʃɪə, fə'ni:-] *n.* Финики́я.
Phoenician [fə'nɪʃ(ə)n, fə'ni:-] *n.* финики́ян|ин (*fem.* -ка).
adj. финики́йский.
phoenix ['fi:nɪks] *n.* (*bird*) фе́никс; (*fig., paragon*) образе́ц соверше́нства.
phone [fəʊn] (*see also* **telephone**) *n.* телефо́н; (*attr.*) телефо́нный; ~ **card** ка́рточка для телефо́нного автома́та.
v.t. & i. звони́ть, по- (*кому*).
with advs.: ~ **back** *v.t. & i.* сде́лать (*pf.*) отве́тный телефо́нный звоно́к; перезвони́ть (*pf.*); ~ **up** *v.t. & i.* позвони́ть (*pf.*) (*кому*).
cpd. ~**-in** *n.* програ́мма «звони́те — отвеча́ем».
phoneme ['fəʊni:m] *n.* фоне́ма.
phonetic [fə'netɪk] *adj.* фонети́ческий.
phonetician [,fəʊnɪ'tɪʃ(ə)n], **phoneticist** [fə'netɪsɪst] *n.* фонети́ст.
phonetics [fə'netɪks] *n.* фоне́тика.
phon(e)y ['fəʊnɪ] (*sl.*) *n.* (*pers.*) шарлата́н, обма́нщик; (*thg.*) подде́лка, фальши́вка, ли́па.
adj. подде́льный, фальши́вый, ли́повый; **'the ~ war'** (*hist.*) «стра́нная война́».
phonograph ['fəʊnə,grɑ:f] *n.* (*US, gramophone*) граммофо́н, патефо́н.
phonological [,fəʊnə'lɒdʒɪk(ə)l, ,fɒn-] *adj.* фонологи́ческий.
phonologist [fə'nɒlədʒɪst] *n.* фоно́лог.
phonology [fə'nɒlədʒɪ] *n.* фоноло́гия.
phony ['fəʊnɪ] = **phon(e)y**
phooey ['fu:ɪ] *int.* (*sl.*) фу!
phosgene ['fɒzdʒi:n] *n.* фосге́н.
phosphate ['fɒsfeɪt] *n.* фосфа́т.
phosphorescence [,fɒsfə'res(ə)ns] *n.* фосфоресце́нция.
phosphorescent [,fɒsfə'res(ə)nt] *adj.* фосфоресци́рующий.
phosphoric [,fɒs'fɒrɪk] *adj.* фосфори́ческий.
phosphorous ['fɒsfərəs] *adj.* фо́сфористый.
phosphorus ['fɒsfərəs] *n.* фо́сфор.
photo ['fəʊtəʊ] *n.* (*coll.*) фо́то (*indecl.*), сни́мок; ~ **call,** ~ **opportunity** сеа́нс фотосъёмки.
cpds. ~**copier** *n.* фотокопирова́лный аппара́т; ~**-copy** *n.* фотоко́пия, светоко́пия; *v.t.* сн|има́ть, -ять фотоко́пию +*g*; ~**-finish** *n.* фотофи́ниш; ~**fit** *n.* фотокомпози-цио́нный портре́т.
photoelectric [,fəʊtəʊɪ'lektrɪk] *adj.* фотоэлектри́ческий.
photogenic [,fəʊtəʊ'dʒenɪk, -'dʒi:nɪk] *adj.* (*photographing well*) фотогени́чный.
photograph ['fəʊtə,grɑ:f] *n.* фотогра́фия.
v.t. фотографи́ровать, с-.
v.i.: **she ~s well** она́ хорошо́ выхо́дит на фотогра́фиях.
photographer [fə'tɒgrəfə(r)] *n.* фото́граф.
photographic [,fəʊtə'græfɪk] *adj.* фотографи́ческий.
photography [fə'tɒgrəfɪ] *n.* фотогра́фия, фотосъёмка.
photogravure [,fəʊtəʊgrə'vjʊə(r)] *n.* фотогравю́ра.
photostat ['fəʊtəʊ,stæt] *n.* фотоко́пия.
v.t. сн|има́ть, -ять фотоко́пию +*g*.
phototypesetter [,fəʊtəʊ'taɪp,setə(r)] *n.* (*phototypesetting machine*) фотонабо́рный аппара́т.
phrase [freɪz] *n.* (*group of words or mus. notes*) фра́за; (*expression*) оборо́т, словосочета́ние; **empty ~s** пусты́е слова́.
v.t. **1.** (*express in words*) формули́ровать, с-. **2.** (*mus.*) фрази́ровать (*impf.*).
cpd. ~**-book** *n.* разгово́рник.
phraseological [,freɪzɪə'lɒdʒɪk(ə)l] *adj.* фразеологи́ческий.
phraseology [,freɪzɪ'ɒlədʒɪ] *n.* фразеоло́гия.
phrenetic [frɪ'netɪk] *adj.* исступлённый.
phrenologist [frɪ'nɒlədʒɪst] *n.* френо́лог.
phrenology [frɪ'nɒlədʒɪ] *n.* френоло́гия.

phut [fʌt] *adv.* (*coll.*): **the balloon went ~** ша́рик ло́пнул.
phylloxera [,fɪlɒk'sɪərə, fɪ'lɒksərə] *n.* филлоксе́ра.
phylum ['faɪləm] *n.* (*biol.*) фи́люм.
physic ['fɪzɪk] *n.* (*medical practice*): **a doctor of ~** до́ктор медици́ны; (*medicine*) лека́рство.
physical ['fɪzɪk(ə)l] *adj.* физи́ческий; **~ properties** физи́ческие сво́йства; **the ~ universe** материа́льный мир; **it is a ~ impossibility** э́то физи́чески невозмо́жно; (*relating to the body*): **~ beauty** физи́ческая красота́; **~ education/training** физи́ческое воспита́ние/трениро́вка; физкульту́ра; **~ exercises** гимнасти́ческие упражне́ния; заря́дка; **~ly handicapped** физи́чески неполноце́нный; **have you had your ~ (examination)?** вы бы́ли на медици́нском осмо́тре?
physician [fɪ'zɪʃ(ə)n] *n.* врач.
physicist ['fɪzɪsɪst] *n.* фи́зик.
physics ['fɪzɪks] *n.* фи́зика.
physiognomist [,fɪzɪ'ɒnəmɪst] *n.* (*judge of character from face*) физиономи́ст.
physiognomy [,fɪzɪ'ɒnəmɪ] *n.* физионо́мия; (*of country etc.*) о́блик.
physiographic(al) [,fɪzɪə'græfɪk((ə)l)] *adj.* физиографи́ческий.
physiography [,fɪzɪ'ɒgrəfɪ] *n.* физиогра́фия.
physiological [,fɪzɪə'lɒdʒɪk(ə)l] *adj.* физиологи́ческий.
physiologist [,fɪzɪ'ɒlədʒɪst] *n.* физио́лог.
physiology [,fɪzɪ'ɒlədʒɪ] *n.* физиоло́гия.
physiotherapist [,fɪzɪəʊ'θerəpɪst] *n.* физиотерапе́вт.
physiotherapy [,fɪzɪəʊ'θerəpɪ] *n.* физиотерапи́я.
physique [fɪ'zi:k] *n.* телосложе́ние.
pi[1] [paɪ] *n.* (*geom.*) число́ «пи».
pi[2] [paɪ] *adj.* (*sl., pious*) на́божный.
pianissimo [,pɪə'nɪsɪ,məʊ] *n., adj. & adv.* пиани́ссимо (*indecl.*).
pianist ['pɪənɪst] *n.* пиани́ст (*fem.* -ка).
piano[1] [pɪ'ænəʊ] *n.* фортепья́но (*indecl.*), роя́ль (*m.*); (*upright*) пиани́но (*indecl.*); **~ accordion** аккордео́н; **~ lessons** уро́ки игры́ на фортепья́но.
cpds. ~**forte** *n.* фортепья́но (*indecl.*); ~**-player** *n.* пиани́ст; (*instrument*) пиано́ла; ~**-stool** *n.* табуре́т для пиани́ста; ~**-tuner** *n.* настро́йщик.
piano[2] [pɪ'ænəʊ] *adj. & adv.* (*mus.*) пиа́но; **a ~ passage** пасса́ж «пиа́но»; (*fig.*): **he seemed ~ today** он что́-то сего́дня прити́х.
pianola [pɪə'nəʊlə] *n.* пиано́ла.
piastre [pɪ'æstə(r)] *n.* пиа́стр.
piazza [pɪ'ætsə] *n.* (*square*) пло́щадь, ры́нок; (*US, verandah*) вера́нда.
pibroch ['pi:brɒx, -brɒk] *n.* вариа́ции (*f. pl.*) для волы́нки.
pica ['paɪkə] *n.* (*typ.*) ци́церо (*m. indecl.*).
picador ['pɪkə,dɔ:(r)] *n.* пикадо́р.
picaresque [,pɪkə'resk] *adj.* авантю́рно-плутовско́й.
picayune [,pɪkə'ju:n] *adj.* (*US coll.*) ничто́жный.
piccalilli [,pɪkə'lɪlɪ] *n.* марино́ванные о́вощ|и (*pl., g.* -е́й).
piccaninny, pickaninny [,pɪkə'nɪnɪ] *n.* негритёнок.
piccolo ['pɪkə,ləʊ] *n.* пи́кколо (*indecl.*).
pick [pɪk] *n.* **1.** (*~axe*) кирка́, кайло́. **2.** (*probing instrument, e.g. dentist's*) про́бник. **3.** (*selection*) отбо́р, вы́бор; **take your ~!** выбира́йте!; **I had first ~** мне пе́рвому доста́лось; **the ~ of the bunch** са́мое лу́чшее/отбо́рное.
v.t. **1.** (*pluck, gather*) соб|ира́ть, -ра́ть; **they were ~ing apples** они́ собира́ли я́блоки; **don't ~ the flowers!** не рви́те цветы́!; **she ~ed the thread from her dress** она́ сняла́ ни́тку с пла́тья. **2.** (*extract contents of*): **he is ~ing your brains** он испо́льзует ва́ши иде́и/позна́ния; **his pocket was ~ed in the crowd** в толпе́ ему́ зале́зли в карма́н. **3.** (*remove flesh from*) обгл|а́дывать, -ода́ть; **the birds ~ed the bones clean** пти́цы склева́ли всё мя́со с косте́й; **I have a bone to ~ with you** (*fig.*) у меня́ к вам кру́пный разгово́р. **4.** (*probe*) ковыря́ть (*impf.*); **it's not nice to ~ one's teeth** ковыря́ть в зуба́х некраси́во; **stop ~ing your nose!** не ковыря́й в носу́!; (*probe to open*) откр|ыва́ть, -ы́ть отмы́чкой; **the lock has been ~ed** замо́к взло́ман. **5.** (*pull apart*) щипа́ть, о(б)-; **criminals were made to ~ oakum** заключённых поста́вили щипа́ть па́клю; (*fig.*): **he ~ed my argument to pieces** он разнёс

мою аргумента́цию в пух и прах. **6.** (*make by* ~*ing*): **he ~ed a hole in the cloth** он продыря́вил мате́рию; **he ~s holes in everything I say** он придира́ется ко вся́кому моему́ сло́ву. **7.** (*select*) выбира́ть, вы́брать; **he ~ed his words carefully** он тща́тельно подбира́л слова́; **she ~ed her way through the mud** она́ осторо́жно ступа́ла по гря́зи; **the captains ~ed sides** капита́ны подобра́ли соста́в кома́нд; **can you ~ the winner?** мо́жете ли вы зара́нее угада́ть победи́теля?; **he's trying to ~ a quarrel** он и́щет по́вода для ссо́ры.

v.i. (*select*) выбира́ть, вы́брать; **you mustn't ~ and choose** вы сли́шком уж разбо́рчивы.

with preps.: **the invalid ~ed at** (*trifled with*) **his food** инвали́д поковыря́л еду́ ви́лкой; **she's always ~ing at** (*nagging*) **me** она́ ве́чно ко мне придира́ется; **why do you always ~ on** (*single out*) **the same boy?** почему́ вы всегда́ выбира́ете одного́ и того́ же ма́льчика?

with advs.: **~ off** *v.t.* (*pluck*) срыва́ть, сорва́ть; (*shoot by deliberate aim*) подстрели́ть (*pf.*); **~ out** *v.t.* (*select*): **he ~ed out the best for himself** са́мое лу́чшее он вы́брал для себя́; (*distinguish*): **I ~ed him out in the crowd** я узна́л его́ в толпе́; **the pattern was ~ed out in red** кра́сный узо́р выделя́лся (на фо́не); (*play note by note*): **she can ~ out tunes by ear** она́ подбира́ет мело́дии по слу́ху; **~ over** *v.t.* (*examine*) переб|ира́ть, -ра́ть; **~ up** *v.t.* (*lift*) подн|има́ть, -я́ть; **he ~ed himself up off the ground** он подня́лся с земли́; **he ~ed up his bag** он взял свою́ су́мку; (*acquire*, *gain*) приобре|та́ть, -сти́; **he has ~ed up an American accent** он приобрёл америка́нский акце́нт; **he could barely ~ up a livelihood** он с трудо́м зараба́тывал себе́ на жизнь; **he went there to ~ up information** он пошёл туда́ раздобы́ть све́дения; **I ~ed up a bargain at the sale** я сде́лал вы́годную поку́пку на распрода́же; **he ~ed her up on the street corner** он подцепи́л (*coll.*) её на перекрёстке; **where can I have ~ed up this germ?** где я мог подцепи́ть э́ту инфе́кцию?; **the car began to ~ up speed** маши́на начала́ набира́ть ско́рость; **can you ~ up Moscow on your radio?** вы мо́жете пойма́ть Москву́ на своём приёмнике?; (*provide transport for*) брать (*impf.*), под|бира́ть, -обра́ть; **the train stops to ~ up passengers** по́езд остана́вливается, что́бы забра́ть пассажи́ров; **I never ~ up hitch-hikers** я никогда́ не беру́ «голосу́ющих» на доро́гах; (*collect*): **I ~ her up from school on my way home from work** я забира́ю её из шко́лы, возвраща́ясь домо́й по́сле рабо́ты; (*apprehend*) задерж|ивать, -а́ть; **the culprit was ~ed up by the police** престу́пник был задёржан поли́цией; (*regain*) приобре|та́ть, -сти́; **he soon ~ed up spirits** он вско́ре повеселе́л; (*resume*) возобнов|ля́ть, -и́ть; **he ~ed up the thread where he had left off** он возобнови́л бесе́ду с того́ ме́ста, где останови́лся; *v.i.* (*recover health*) попр|авля́ться, -а́виться; **he soon ~ed up after his illness** он бы́стро опра́вился по́сле боле́зни; (*improve*) ул|учша́ться, -у́чшиться; **trade is ~ing up** торго́вля оживля́ется; (*gain speed*): **after a slow start the engine ~ed up** по́сле ме́дленного ста́рта мото́р зарабо́тал как сле́дует; (*become acquainted*) знако́миться, по-; **who has he ~ed up with now?** с кем он тепе́рь завёл знако́мство?

cpds. **~axe** *n.* киркомоты́га; **~lock** *n.* (*instrument*) отмы́чка; **~-me-up** *n.* тонизи́рующее сре́дство; **~pocket** *n.* вор-карма́нник; **~-up** *n.* (*microphone*) да́тчик; (*of record-player*) ада́птер; (*van*) пика́п; (*casual acquaintance*) случа́йное знако́мство, (*sl.*) «кадр»; (*acceleration*) ускоре́ние.

pick-a-back ['pɪkəˌbæk], **piggy-back** ['pɪgɪˌbæk] *advs.* на спине́; на зако́рках.

pickaninny [ˌpɪkə'nɪnɪ] = **piccaninny**

picker ['pɪkə(r)] *n.* (*of fruit etc.*) сбо́рщи|к (*fem.* -ца).

picket ['pɪkɪt] *n.* **1.** (*pointed stake*) кол; **~ fence** частоко́л. **2.** (*also* **picquet:** *small body of troops*) заста́ва, карау́л. **3.** (*of strikers*) пике́т; (*individual*) пике́тчик.

v.t. **1.** (*secure with stakes*) обн|оси́ть, -ести́ частоко́лом; **the horse was ~ed nearby** ло́шадь была́ привя́зана неподалёку. **2.** (*guard*): **the camp was securely ~ed** ла́герь надёжно охраня́лся. **3.** (*deploy as guards*): **he ~ed his men round the house** он вы́ставил свои́х люде́й охраня́ть дом. **4.** (*mount guards on*): **the enemy has ~ed the bridge** враг вы́ставил карау́л у мо́ста́. **5.** (*deny entry to*) пикети́ровать (*impf.*); **the workers are ~ing the factory** рабо́чие пикети́руют фа́брику.

picking ['pɪkɪŋ] *n.* **1.** (*gathering*) собира́ние, сбор. **2.: ~ and stealing** воровство́. **3.** (*pl.*, *remains*) оста́тки (*m. pl.*); объе́дки (*m. pl.*). **4.** (*pl.*, *profits*) пожи́ва.

pickle ['pɪk(ə)l] *n.* **1.** (*preservative*) марина́д; рассо́л; **I have a rod in ~ for him** (*fig.*) я держу́ для него́ ро́згу нагото́ве. **2.** (*usu. pl.*, *preserved vegetables*) соле́нья (*pl.*); **mustard ~(s)** пи́кул|и (*pl.*, *g.* -ей) в горчи́чном со́усе. **3.** (*coll.*, *predicament*, *mess*) беда́; **he came home in a sorry ~** он пришёл домо́й в плаче́вном состоя́нии. **4.** (*coll.*, *mischievous child*) озорни́к, шалу́н.

v.t. **1.** маринова́ть, за-; **~d herrings** марино́ванная селёдка. **2.: he came home ~d** он пришёл домо́й под гра́дусом/га́зом (*sl.*).

picky ['pɪkɪ] *adj.* (*US coll.*) разбо́рчивый, приди́рчивый.

picnic ['pɪknɪk] *n.* пикни́к; (*fig.*, *coll.*, *sth. easily done*) удово́льствие; **it was no ~** э́то бы́ло нелёгкое де́ло.

v.i. за́втракать, по- на траве́.

cpds. **~-basket** *n.* корзи́нка для пикника́; **~-flask** *n.* фля́жка для пикника́.

picnicker ['pɪknɪkə(r)] *n.* уча́стник пикника́.

picquet ['pɪkɪt] = **picket** *n.* **2.**

Pict [pɪkt] *n.* пикт.

pictograph ['pɪktəˌgrɑːf] *n.* пиктогра́мма.

pictorial [pɪk'tɔːrɪəl] *n.* иллюстри́рованное изда́ние.

adj. изобрази́тельный; (*illustrated*) иллюстри́рованный.

picture ['pɪktʃə(r)] *n.* **1.** (*depiction*; *pictorial composition*) карти́на; **~s** (*in general*) жи́вопись; **~ hat** ≃ наря́дная шля́пка; **~ postcard** худо́жественная откры́тка; откры́тка с ви́дом; (*illustration*) изображе́ние; (*portrait*) портре́т, ко́пия; (*fig.*): **she is the very ~ of her mother** она́ вы́литая мать; (*drawing*) рису́нок; (*image on TV screen*) карти́н(к)а. **2.** (*beautiful object*) карти́нка. **3.** (*embodiment*) олицетворе́ние; **he looks the ~ of health** он олицетворе́ние здоро́вья. **4.** (*coll.*, *of information*): **he will soon put you in the ~** он вско́ре объясни́т вам, что к чему́; **don't fail to keep me in the ~** не забу́дьте держа́ть меня́ в ку́рсе де́ла. **5.** (*film*) (кино)фи́льм, карти́на; (*pl.*, *cinema show*, *cinema*) кино́ (*indecl.*); **what's on at the ~s?** что идёт в кино́?

v.t. (*depict*) опи́с|ывать, -а́ть; изобра|жа́ть, -зи́ть; **~ to yourself** вообрази́те/предста́вьте себе́.

cpds. **~-book** *n.* кни́жка с карти́нками; **~-card** *n.* (*court card*) фигу́рная ка́рта; **~-gallery** *n.* карти́нная галлере́я; **~-house, ~-palace, ~-theatre** *nn.* кинотеа́тр; **~-writing** *n.* пиктографи́ческое письмо́.

picturesque [ˌpɪktʃə'resk] *adj.* (*of scenery*, *buildings etc.*) живопи́сный; (*of language*) о́бразный; (*of pers.*) колори́тный.

piddle ['pɪd(ə)l] *v.i.* (*coll.*) мочи́ться, по-.

piddling ['pɪdlɪŋ] *adj.* (*coll.*, *trifling*) пустя́чный.

pidgin ['pɪdʒɪn], **pigeon** ['pɪdʒɪn, -dʒ(ə)n] *n.*: **that's not my ~** э́то не моя́ забо́та; **~ English** упрощённый гибри́дный вариа́нт англи́йского языка́.

pie[1] [paɪ] *n.* (*pastry with filling*) пиро́г, пирожо́к; (*fig.*): **~ in the sky** пиро́г на том све́те; **it's as easy as ~** э́то плёвое де́ло (*coll.*); **he has a finger in the ~** он заме́шен в э́том де́ле.

cpds. **~-crust** *n.* ко́рочка (пирога́); **~-eyed** *adj.* (*sl.*) пья́ный.

pie[2] [paɪ] *n.* (*typ.*) сыпь.

piebald ['paɪbɔːld] *n.* пе́гая ло́шадь.

adj. пе́гий.

piece [piːs] *n.* **1.** (*portion*, *fragment*, *bit*) кусо́к; **a ~ of bread** кусо́к хле́ба; **a ~ of cake** (*lit.*) кусо́к то́рта; (*coll.*, *sth. easily accomplished*) ле́гче лёгкого; **a ~ of coal** кусо́к у́гля; (*small*) уголёк; **a ~ of paper** листо́к бума́ги; **(all) of a ~ with** в соотве́тствии с+*i.*; **all in one ~** неразо́бранный; (*fig.*, *unharmed*) це́лый и невреди́мый; **the dish lay in ~s** блю́до разби́лось на куски́; **the record was smashed to ~s** пласти́нка разби́лась вдре́безги; **he took the watch to**

~s он разобра́л часы́; **he was left to pick up the ~s** (*fig.*) его́ оста́вили расхлёбывать ка́шу; **he went to ~s under interrogation** он раскололся на допро́се; **he went to ~s after his wife's death** он совсе́м рассы́пался по́сле сме́рти жены́. **2.** (*small area*) уча́сток; **a ~** (*plot*) **of land** уча́сток земли́; **a ~** (*sheet*) **of water** водоём, пруд. **3.** (*example, instance*) образе́ц; **a ~ of news** но́вость; **here's a ~ of luck!** вот э́то уда́ча!; **may I give you a ~ of advice?** мо́жно дать вам сове́т?; **I gave him a ~ of my mind** я его́ отчита́л. **4.** (*unit of material*) шту́ка, кусо́к; **this cloth is sold by the ~** э́тот материа́л продаётся отре́зами. **5.** (*single composition*) произведе́ние; **a ~ of music** пье́са; **a ~ of verse** стихотворе́ние; **the child said its ~** ребёнок повтори́л, что вы́учил наизу́сть. **6.** (*object of art or craft*) произведе́ние иску́сства; вещь, вещи́ца; **there were some nice ~s at the sale** на распрода́же бы́ло не́сколько хоро́ших веще́й; **~ of furniture** ме́бель; **three-~ suite** дива́н с двумя́ кре́слами; **museum ~** (*lit.*) музе́йная вещь; (*fig.*) музе́йная ре́дкость; **a beautiful ~ of work** великоле́пная рабо́та; **nasty ~ of work** (*coll.*) проти́вный тип. **7.** (*one of a set*): **he set out the ~s on the chessboard** он расста́вил фигу́ры на ша́хматной доске́; **a 52-~ dinner service** обе́денный серви́з из пяти́десяти двух предме́тов. **8.** (*coin*) моне́та; **a ten-cent ~** моне́та в де́сять це́нтов; **~ of eight** пе́со (*indecl.*). **9.** (*instrument*) инструме́нт; **a six-~band** сексте́т. **10.** (*sl., woman, girl*) де́вушка, «бабёнка».

v.t. (*make up from ~s*) соб|ира́ть, -ра́ть из кусо́чков; (*join*) соедин|я́ть, -и́ть.

with advs.: **~ out** *v.t.* восп|олня́ть, -о́лнить; **~ together** *v.t.* соедин|я́ть, -и́ть; (*fig.*) свя́з|ывать, -а́ть; **~ up** *v.t.* чини́ть, по-.

cpds. **~-goods** *n. pl.* шту́чный това́р; **~meal** *adj.* части́чный; *adv.* по частя́м; уры́вками; **~-rates** *n. pl.* сде́льная опла́та; **~-work** *n.* сде́льщина; **~-worker** *n.* сде́льщик.

pièce de résistance [ˌpjes də reɪˈziːstɑ̃s] *n.* (*cul.*) гла́вное блю́до; (*fig.*) достопримеча́тельность.

pied [paɪd] *adj.* пёстрый; **P~ Piper** ду́дочник в пёстром костю́ме.

pied à terre [ˌpjeɪdɑːˈteə(r)] *n.* приста́нище.

pier [pɪə(r)] *n.* **1.** (*structure projecting into sea*) пирс; (*breakwater*) волноло́м; (*landing stage*) мол. **2.** (*bridge support*) бык. **3.** (*masonry between windows*) просте́нок.

cpd. **~-glass** *n.* трюмо́ (*indecl.*).

pierc|e [pɪəs] *v.t.* прок|а́лывать, -оло́ть; **she had her ears ~ed** ей прокколо́ли у́ши; **~ing cold** прони́зывающий хо́лод; **a ~ing cry** пронзи́тельный крик; **a ~ing gaze** проница́тельный взгляд.

v.i. прон|ика́ть, -и́кнуть; проб|ива́ться, -и́ться; **they ~ed through the enemy lines** они́ прорвали́сь сквозь ли́нии укрепле́ний врага́.

pierrot [ˈpɪərəʊ, ˈpjerəʊ] *n.* (*minstrel*) пьеро́ (*m. indecl.*).

pietà [ˌpɪeˈtɑː] *n.* пиета́, плач Богома́тери.

pietism [ˈpaɪəˌtɪz(ə)m] *n.* (*exaggerated piety*) чрезме́рное благоче́стие.

piety [ˈpaɪɪtɪ] *n.* на́божность.

piffle [ˈpɪf(ə)l] *n.* (*coll.*) вздо́р, чепуха́.

piffling [ˈpɪflɪŋ] *adj.* (*coll., trifling*) ничто́жный, пустя́чный.

pig [pɪg] *n.* **1.** (*animal*) свинья́; **~s might fly** быва́ет, что сви́ньи лета́ют; **he bought a ~ in a poke** он купи́л кота́ в мешке́; (*greedy or disagreeable pers.*): **he made a ~ of himself** он нажра́лся, как свинья́. **2.** (*mass of iron*) брусо́к.

v.t. & i. **1.** (*farrow*) порос|и́ться, о-. **2.** жить (*impf.*) по-сви́нски; **they had to ~ (it) together in a small room** им пришло́сь тесни́ться в кро́шечной ко́мнате.

cpds. **~-headed** *adj.* тупо́й; **~-iron** *n.* чугу́н в чу́шках; **~skin** *n.* свина́я ко́жа; **~-sticker** *n.* (*hunter*) охо́тник на кабано́в; (*knife*) большо́й нож; **~-sticking** *n.* охо́та на кабано́в; **~sty** *n.* (*lit., fig.*) свина́рник; **~tail** *n.* коси́чка; **~wash** *n.* помо́|и (*pl., g.* -ев).

pigeon[1] [ˈpɪdʒɪn, -dʒ(ə)n] *n.* го́лубь (*m.*); **carrier, homing ~** почто́вый го́лубь; **clay ~** гли́няная лета́ющая мише́нь.

cpds. **~-breasted, ~-chested** *adjs.* с цыпля́чьей гру́дью; **~hole** *n.* (*compartment*) отделе́ние для бума́г; *v.t.* (*fig.*) от|кла́дывать, -ложи́ть в до́лгий я́щик; **~-toed** *adj.* косола́пый.

pigeon[2] [ˈpɪdʒɪn, -dʒ(ə)n] = **pidgin**

piggery [ˈpɪgərɪ] *n.* **1.** (*sty*) свина́рник, хлев; (*farm*) свинофе́рма. **2.** (*piggishness*) сви́нство.

piggy [ˈpɪgɪ] *n.* (*piglet; greedy child*) поросёнок.

adj. свино́й, порося́чий.

cpds. **~-back** *adv.* = **pick-a-back; ~-bank** *n.* копи́лка.

pig|let [ˈpɪglɪt], **-ling** [ˈpɪglɪŋ] *nn.* поросёнок.

pigment [ˈpɪgmənt] *n.* пигме́нт.

pigmentation [ˌpɪgmənˈteɪʃ(ə)n] *n.* пигмента́ция.

pigmented [ˈpɪgməntɪd] *adj.* пигменти́рованный.

pigmy [ˈpɪgmɪ] = **pygmy**

pike [paɪk] *n.* (*weapon*) копьё; (*fish*) щу́ка.

cpd. **~staff** *n.*: **plain as a ~staff** я́сный как день.

pila|ff [pɪˈlæf], **-u** [pɪˈlaʊ] *n.* пила́в, плов.

pilaster [pɪˈlæstə(r)] *n.* пиля́стр(а).

pilau [pɪˈlaʊ] = **pilaff**

pilchard [ˈpɪltʃəd] *n.* сарди́н(к)а.

pile[1] [paɪl] *n.* (*stake, post*) сва́я.

cpd. **~-driver** *n.* копёр.

pile[2] [paɪl] *n.* **1.** (*heap*) ку́ча, гру́да; **funeral ~** погреба́льный костёр; (*coll., of money*): **he made his ~** он на́жил состоя́ние; (*coll., any large quantity*) ку́ча, ма́сса. **2.** (*massive building*) зда́ние. **3.** (*elec.*) батаре́я. **4.: atomic ~** а́томный реа́ктор.

v.t. **1.** (*heap up*) свал|ивать, -и́ть в ку́чу; **the soldiers ~d arms** солда́ты соста́вили винто́вки в ко́злы; **he ~d coal on to the fire** он подбро́сил у́гля в ками́н. **2.** (*load*) нагру|жа́ть, -зи́ть; **the table was ~d high with dishes** стол ломи́лся от я́ств.

with advs.: **~ in** *v.i.* (*coll., crowd into a vehicle etc.*) заб|ира́ться, -ра́ться; наб|ива́ться, -и́ться; **~ on** *v.t.* нава́л|ивать, -и́ть; (*fig.*) преувели́чи|вать, -ть; **don't ~ it on!** бро́сьте залива́ть! (*coll.*); **~ up** *v.t.* накоп|ля́ть, -и́ть; *v.i.* (*accumulate*) нагромо|жда́ться, -зди́ться; **work keeps piling up** рабо́та всё вре́мя прибавля́ется; (*crash*) разб|ива́ться, -и́ться.

cpd. **~-up** *n.* (*crash*) столкнове́ние не́скольких маши́н.

pile[3] [paɪl] *n.* (*down, soft hair*) шерсть, во́лос; (*nap on cloth, carpet etc.*) ворс.

pile[4] [paɪl] *n.* (*usu. pl., haemorrhoid*) геморро́й.

pilfer [ˈpɪlfə(r)] *v.t. & i.* ворова́ть (*impf.*), таска́ть (*impf.*).

pilfer|age [ˈpɪlfərɪdʒ], **-ing** [ˈpɪlfərɪŋ] *nn.* ме́лкая кра́жа.

pilferer [ˈpɪlfərə(r)] *n.* ме́лкий жу́лик, вори́шка (*c.g.*).

pilgrim [ˈpɪlgrɪm] *n.* пилигри́м, palо́мник; **P~ Fathers** «отцы́-пилигри́мы»; англи́йские колони́сты, посели́вшиеся в Аме́рике в 1620 году́.

pilgrimage [ˈpɪlgrɪmɪdʒ] *n.* пало́мничество; **they went on a ~ to Lourdes** они́ отпра́вились на пало́мничество в Лурд.

pill [pɪl] *n.* **1.** пилю́ля, табле́тка; **take ~s** прин|има́ть, -я́ть пилю́ли; (*fig.*): **a bitter ~** го́рькая пилю́ля; **contraceptive ~** противозача́точная пилю́ля; **she is on the ~** она́ принима́ет (противозача́точные) табле́тки. **2.** (*sl., ball*) мяч.

cpd. **~box** *n.* (*receptacle*) коро́бочка для табле́ток; (*mil., emplacement*) долговре́менное огнево́е сооруже́ние (*abbr.* ДОС); (*hat*) шля́пка без поле́й.

pillage [ˈpɪlɪdʒ] *n.* мародёрство, грабёж.

v.t. & i. мародёрствовать (*impf.*); гра́бить.

pillager [ˈpɪlɪdʒə(r)] *n.* мародёр.

pillar [ˈpɪlə(r)] *n.* (*column*) столб; (*support*) опо́ра; **he was driven from ~ to post** он мета́лся с ме́ста на ме́сто; (*fig.*) столп; **P~s of Hercules** Геркуле́совы столпы́; **~s of society** столпы́ о́бщества.

cpd. **~-box** *n.* (стоя́чий) почто́вый я́щик.

pillion [ˈpɪljən] *n.* (*on motor-cycle*) за́днее сиде́нье; **she rode ~** она́ е́хала на за́днем сиде́нье мотоци́кла.

pillory [ˈpɪlərɪ] *n.* позо́рный столб.

v.t. (*fig.*) пригво|жда́ть, -зди́ть к позо́рному столбу́.

pillow [ˈpɪləʊ] *n.* поду́шка.

v.t.: **~ one's head** класть, положи́ть го́лову (на+*a.*); **he ~ed his head in his hands** он подпёр го́лову руко́й.

cpds. **~-case, ~-slip** *nn.* на́волочка; **~-fight** *n.* дра́ка поду́шками.

pilot ['paɪlət] *n.* **1.** (*of vessel*) ло́цман; **drop the ~** (*fig.*) отка́з|ываться, -а́ться от ве́рного сове́тчика; (*of aircraft*) лётчик, пило́т; **~ officer** лейтена́нт авиа́ции. **2.** (*attr.*, *fig.*) про́бный, о́пытный; **~ scheme** экспериме́нт.
v.t. (*lit.*, *fig.*) пилоти́ровать (*impf.*); напр|авля́ть, -а́вить.
cpds. **~-balloon** *n.* шар-пило́т; **~-boat** *n.* ло́цманское су́дно, ло́цманский бот; **~-fish** *n.* ры́ба-ло́цман; **~-light** *n.* (*for gas indicator*) га́зовая горе́лка; контро́льная/сигна́льная ла́мпа.

pilotage ['paɪlətɪdʒ] *n.* пилота́ж.

pilotless ['paɪlətlɪs] *adj.* беспило́тный.

pim(i)ento [ˌpɪmɪ'entəʊ, pɪm'jentəʊ] *n.* (*sweet pepper*) пиме́нт, пе́рец души́стый.

pimp [pɪmp] *n.* (*pander*) сво́дник; (*ponce*) сутенёр.
v.i. сво́дничать (*impf.*).

pimpernel ['pɪmpəˌnel] *n.* о́чный цвет.

pimple ['pɪmp(ə)l] *n.* прыщ, пры́щик.

pimply ['pɪmplɪ] *adj.* прыща́вый.

PIN [pɪn] *n.* (*abbr. of* ***personal identification number***) персона́льный код.

pin [pɪn] *n.* **1.** була́вка; шпи́лька; **for two ~s I'd knock you down** ещё немно́го, и я вас сту́кну; **I don't care a ~ for your advice** мне наплева́ть на ваш сове́т; **she was as neat as a new ~** она́ была́ оде́та с иго́лочки; **you could have heard a ~ drop** мо́жно бы́ло услы́шать, как му́ха пролети́т; **~s and needles** (*tingling sensation*) колотьё по́сле до́лгого сиде́нья; **I've got ~s and needles in my leg** у меня́ нога́ затекла́. **2.** (*securing peg*) прище́пка. **3.** (*pl.*, *coll.*, *legs*) но́ги (*f. pl.*); **he's shaky on his ~s** он пло́хо де́ржится на нога́х.
v.t. **1.** (*fasten*) прик|а́лывать, -оло́ть; **she ~ned a rose to her dress** она́ приколо́ла ро́зу к пла́тью; (*fig.*): **~ accusation, blame on s.o.** сва́л|ивать, -и́ть вину́ на кого́-н.; **I ~ my faith on the captain** я возлага́ю все наде́жды на капита́на. **2.** (*immobilize*) приж|има́ть, -а́ть; **the bandits ~ned him against the wall** банди́ты прижа́ли его́ к стене́; **he was ~ned beneath the vehicle** его́ придави́ло маши́ной; **his arms were ~ned behind him** ему́ связа́ли ру́ки за спино́й.
with advs.: **~ down** *v.t.* (*lit.*) прик|а́лывать, -оло́ть; (*fig.*, *commit to an action or opinion*) прип|ира́ть, -ере́ть к сте́нке; **~ on** *v.t.* прик|а́лывать, -оло́ть; **~ together** *v.t.* ск|а́лывать, -оло́ть; скреп|ля́ть, -и́ть; **~ up** *v.t.* прик|а́лывать, -оло́ть; пове́сить (*pf.*); **she ~ned up her hair** она́ заколо́ла во́лосы.
cpds. **~ball, ~-table** *nn.* (*game*, *machine*) пинбо́л, кита́йский билья́рд; **~ball machine** билья́рд-автома́т; **~cushion** *n.* поду́шечка для иго́лок и була́вок; **~head** *n.* (*sl.*, *stupid pers.*) болва́н, тупи́ца (*c.g.*); **~-money** *n.* де́ньги на ме́лкие расхо́ды; **~point** *n.* (*lit.*) остриё була́вки; *v.t.* (*fig.*) то́чно определ|я́ть, -и́ть; ука́з|ывать, -а́ть па́льцем; **~-prick** *n.* (*lit.*) була́вочный уко́л; (*fig.*) «шпи́лька», ме́лкий уко́л; **~-stripe** (*suit*) *n.* костю́м в то́нкую све́тлую поло́ску; **~-table** *n.* = **~ball**; **~-up** *n.* фотогра́фия красо́тки в журна́ле; **~-up girl** красо́тка.

pinafore ['pɪnəˌfɔː(r)] *n.* фа́ртук, пере́дник; **~ dress** пла́тье-сарафа́н.

pince-nez ['pænsneɪ, pæs'neɪ] *n.* пенсне́ (*indecl.*).

pincer ['pɪnsə(r)] *n.* **1.** (*of crustacean*) клешня́. **2.** (*pl.*) щипц|ы́ (*pl.*, *g.* -о́в); клещ|и́ (*pl.*, *g.* -е́й); **~ movement** (*mil.*) захва́т в клещи́.

pinch [pɪntʃ] *n.* **1.** (*nip*) щипо́к; **he gave her a ~ on the cheek** он ущипну́л её за щёку; (*fig.*, *constraint*) сжа́тие; **he felt the ~ of poverty** он оказа́лся в тиска́х нужды́; **at a ~; if it comes to the ~** в кра́йнем слу́чае; е́сли придётся ту́го. **2.** (*small amount*) щепо́тка; **a ~ of snuff** поню́шка табаку́; **you must take that with a ~ of salt** (*fig.*) вы не должны́ э́тому ве́рить.
v.t. **1.** (*nip*, *squeeze*) прищем|ля́ть, -и́ть; ущипну́ть (*pf.*); **his fingers were ~ed in the door** он прищеми́л па́льцы две́рью; **that's where the shoe ~es** (*fig.*) вот в чём загво́здка; (*fig.*): **his face was ~ed with cold** моро́з щипа́л ему́ лицо́; **I have often been ~ed for money** я ча́сто страда́л от недоста́тка де́нег. **2.** (*steal*) стяну́ть (*pf.*), стащи́ть (*pf.*) (*coll.*). **3.** (*arrest*, *charge*) «заца́пать» (*pf.*) (*sl.*).
v.i. (*be niggardly*) скупи́ться, по-; отка́зывать (*impf.*) себе́ (*в чём*); **she had to ~ and scrape to make ends meet** ей приходи́лось эконо́мить на всём для того́, что́бы своди́ть концы́ с конца́ми.

pinchbeck ['pɪntʃbek] *n.* томпа́к.
adj. томпа́ковый; (*fig.*) подде́льный.

pine[1] [paɪn] *n.* **1.** (*conifer*) сосна́. **2.** (*~apple*) анана́с.
cpds. **~apple** *n.* анана́с; **~-cone** *n.* сосно́вая ши́шка; **~-marten** *n.* америка́нская куни́ца; **~-needle** *n.* хво́я; **~wood** *n.* сосно́вая древеси́на.

pin|e[2] [paɪn] *v.i.* **1.** (*languish*, *waste*) ча́хнуть, за-; томи́ться (*impf.*); **she is ~ing away** она́ ча́хнет. **2.** (*long*): **~e for** жа́ждать +*g*; **I ~e for sea air** так хо́чется подыша́ть морски́м во́здухом.

pineal ['pɪnɪəl, 'paɪ-] *adj.* шишкови́дный.

ping [pɪŋ] *n.* свист, писк.
v.i. св|исте́ть, -и́стнуть; пи́скнуть (*pf.*).

ping-pong ['pɪŋpɒŋ] *n.* пинг-по́нг.

pinion[1] ['pɪnjən] *n.* (*end of wing*) оконе́чность пти́чьего крыла́; (*poet.*, *wing*) крыло́.
v.t. (*immobilize by cutting wing*) подр|еза́ть, -е́зать кры́лья +*g.*; (*bind arms of*) свя́з|ывать, -а́ть ру́ки +*g.*

pinion[2] ['pɪnjən] *n.* (*cog-wheel*) шестерня́.

pink[1] [pɪŋk] *n.* (*flower*) гвозди́ка; (*colour*) ро́зовый цвет; (*perfection*): **he is in the ~ (of health)** он пы́шет здоро́вьем; (*foxhunter's coat*) кра́сный камзо́л.
adj. (*of colour*) ро́зовый; (*of pol. shade of opinion*) «ро́зовый», ле́вый.

pink[2] [pɪŋk] *v.t.* (*prick with sword*) прок|а́лывать, -оло́ть; (*decorate by perforation*) укр|аша́ть, -а́сить ды́рочками; **~ing shears** фесто́нные но́жницы.

pink[3] [pɪŋk] *v.i.* (*of engine*) стуча́ть (*impf.*).

pinnace ['pɪnɪs] *n.* команди́рский ка́тер.

pinnacle ['pɪnək(ə)l] *n.* (*of building*) шпиц; (*fig.*) верши́на.

pinny ['pɪnɪ] *n.* (*coll.*) пере́дничек.

pint [paɪnt] *n.* пи́нта; **~ jug** кувши́н ёмкостью в пи́нту.
cpd. **~-sized** *adj.* (*fig.*) ма́ленький, кро́хотный.

pioneer [ˌpaɪə'nɪə(r)] *n.* (*one who is first in the field*) пионе́р, нова́тор, первооткрыва́тель (*m.*); (*mil.*) сапёр; **P~ Corps** сапёрно-строи́тельные ча́сти.
v.t. & i. быть пионе́ром (*в чём*); про|кла́дывать, -ложи́ть путь; **~ing** *adj.* нова́торский; первопрохо́дческий.

pious ['paɪəs] *adj.* на́божный.

pip [pɪp] *n.* **1.** (*fruit seed*) се́мечко; зёрнышко. **2.** (*fowl disease*) типу́н; **this weather gives me the ~** (*sl.*) пого́да нагоня́ет на меня́ тоску́. **3.** (*high-pitched sound*) писк; (*teleph.*) гудо́к, сигна́л. **4.** (*spot on playing-card etc.*) очко́. **5.** (*coll.*, *star on officer's uniform*) звёздочка.
v.t. (*sl.*, *defeat*) прова́л|ивать, -и́ть; **he was ~ped at the post** его́ обогна́ли в после́днюю мину́ту; (*hit with shot*) подстре́л|ивать, -и́ть.
cpd. **~-squeak** *n.* (*coll.*) ничто́жество.

pipe [paɪp] *n.* **1.** (*conduit*) труба́. **2.** (*mus. instrument*) свире́ль; ду́дка; (*bosun's whistle*) бо́цманская ду́дка; (*bagpipe*) волы́нка. **3.** (*shrill voice or sound*) вопль (*m.*); писк; (*note of bird*) свист; пе́ние. **4.** (*for smoking*) тру́бка; **he lit a ~ and smoked it** он закури́л тру́бку; **your ~ has gone out** ва́ша тру́бка поту́хла; **~ of peace** тру́бка ми́ра; **put that in your ~ and smoke it!** (*coll.*) намота́йте э́то себе́ на ус! **5.** (*cask of wine*) бо́чка (вмести́мостью в 105 галло́нов).
v.t. **1.** (*also v.i.*) (*play on ~*) игра́ть, сыгра́ть на свире́ли/ду́дке/волы́нке. **2.** (*lead*, *summon by piping*) свиста́ть (*impf.*); **he ~d all hands on deck** он свиста́л всех наве́рх. **3.** (*utter in shrill voice*) пища́ть, пи́скнуть. **4.** (*decorate cake*) покр|ыва́ть, -ы́ть кре́мом; (*ornament dress*) отде́л|ывать, -ать ка́нтом. **5.** (*convey by ~s*) пус|ка́ть, -ти́ть по тру́бам; **a ~d water supply** водопрово́д.
with advs.: **~ down** *v.i.* (*restrain o.s.*) сба́вить (*pf.*) тон (*coll.*); **~ up** (*coll.*, *start to sing*, *play*, *speak*) запе́ть (*pf.*); пода́ть (*pf.*) го́лос.
cpds. **~-clay** *n.* бе́лая гли́на; тру́бочная гли́на; *v.t.* бели́ть, по- тру́бочной гли́ной; **~-dream** *n.* пуста́я/несбы́точная мечта́; **~line** *n.* трубопрово́д, нефтепрово́д; (*fig.*) коммуникацио́нная ли́ния; **in the ~line** (*fig.*) на

подхóде; **~-rack** *n.* подстáвка для трýбок; **~-tobacco** *n.* трýбочный табáк.

piper ['paɪpə(r)] *n.* дýдочник; (*bag* ~) волы́нщик; **he who pays the ~ calls the tune** кто плáтит, тот и распоряжáется.

pipette [pɪ'pet] *n.* пипéтка.

piping ['paɪpɪŋ] *n.* (*system of pipes*) трубопровóд; (*ornamental cord*) кант; (*cake decoration*) глазýрь, крем; (*playing of pipes*) игрá свирéли *и т.п.*

adj. (*of voice etc.*) пронзи́тельный.

adv.: ~ **hot** с пы́лу, с жáру.

pipistrel(le) [,pɪpɪ'strel] *n.* летýчая мышь.

pipkin ['pɪpkɪn] *n.* гли́няный горшóчек.

pippin ['pɪpɪn] *n.* пепи́н(ка).

piquancy ['pi:kənsɪ, -kɑ:nsɪ] *n.* (*lit.*, *fig.*) пикáнтность.

piquant ['pi:kənt, -kɑ:nt] *adj.* (*lit.*, *fig.*) пикáнтный.

pique [pi:k] *n.* досáда; **in a fit of ~** в поры́ве раздражéния.

v.t. (*hurt the pride of*) уязв|ля́ть, -и́ть; (*stimulate*) возбу|ждáть, -ди́ть; ~ **o.s. on** горди́ться (*impf.*) +*i.*

piqué ['pi:keɪ] *n.* пикé (*indecl.*).

piquet [pɪ'ket] *n.* пикéт.

piracy ['paɪrəsɪ] *n.* пирáтство; (*infringement of copyright*) нарушéние áвторского прáва.

piragua [pɪ'rægwə] *n.* пирóга.

pirate ['paɪərət] *n.* (*sea-robber*) пирáт; (*ship*) пирáтский корáбль; (*infringer of copyright*) наруши́тель (*m.*) áвторского прáва; (*unauthorized broadcaster*) радиопирáт.

v.t. (*literary etc. work*) публиковáть, о- в нарушéние áвторских прав.

piratical [,paɪə'rætɪk(ə)l] *adj.* пирáтский.

pirouette [,pɪrʊ'et] *n.* пируэ́т.

v.i. дéлать (*impf.*) пируэ́ты; сдéлать (*pf.*) пируэ́т.

pis aller [,pi:z æ'leɪ] *n.* послéднее срéдство; **as a ~** на худóй конéц; в крáйнем слýчае.

piscatorial [,pɪskə'tɔ:rɪəl] *adj.* рыболóвный.

Pisces ['paɪsi:z, 'pɪski:z] *n.* Ры́бы (*f. pl.*).

piscicultural [,pɪsɪ'kʌltʃər(ə)l] *adj.* рыбовóдный.

pisciculture ['pɪsɪ,kʌltʃə(r)] *n.* рыбовóдство.

pisé ['pi:zeɪ] *n.* гли́на с грáвием.

pish [pɪʃ] *int.* фи!, фу!

piss [pɪs] *n.* (*vulg.*) мочá; ~ **artist** забулды́га *c.g.*; **take the ~ (out of)** насмехáться (над+*i.*) (*impf.*).

v.t.: ~ **the bed** мочи́ться, по- в кровáть; ~ **blood** мочи́ться, по- крóвью.

v.i. мочи́ться (*impf.*); ~ **off!** отцепи́сь!; провáливай!

cpds. **~-taker** *n.* насмéшник; **~-taking** *n.* насмехáтельство; **~-up** *n.* выпивóн.

pissed [pɪsd] *adj.* (*vulg.*, *drunk*) пья́ный в стéльку.

pistachio [pɪ'stɑ:ʃɪəʊ] *n.* фистáшка.

pistil ['pɪstɪl] *n.* пéстик.

pistol ['pɪst(ə)l] *n.* пистолéт; **he was held up at ~ point** егó задержáли, угрожáя пистолéтом.

cpd. **~-shot** *n.* пистолéтный вы́стрел.

piston ['pɪst(ə)n] *n.* пóршень (*m.*); (*mus.*) пистóн.

cpds. **~-engine** *n.* поршневóй двигáтель; **~-ring** *n.* поршневóе кольцó; **~-rod** *n.* поршневóй шток.

pit[1] [pɪt] *n.* **1.** (*excavation*) я́ма; **gravel from the ~** грáвий из карьéра. **2.** (*coal-mine*) шáхта; **he works down the ~** он на подзéмных рабóтах в шáхте; ~ **pony** шáхтная лóшадь. **3.** (*covered hole, trap*) западня́, ловýшка; **the ~** (*hell*) преиспóдняя; ад. **4.** (*depression*) углублéние, я́мка; ~ **of the stomach** подлóжечная я́мка. **5.** (*scar*) óспина, ряби́на. **6.** (*theatr.*) оркестрóвая я́ма; ~ **stalls** партéр. **7.** (*on motor-racing circuit*) ремóнтная я́ма, смотровáя канáва.

v.t. **1.** (*oppose*): **he ~ted his wits against the law** он пытáлся обойти́ закóн. **2.** (*scar*): **his face was ~ted by smallpox** егó лицó бы́ло изры́то óспой.

cpds. **~fall** *n.* (*lit.*, *fig.*) западня́, капкáн; **~head** *n.* надшáхтное здáние; **~man** *n.* (*miner*) шахтёр; **~-prop** *n.* рудни́чная стóйка.

pit[2] [pɪt] (*US*) *n.* (*fruit-stone*) кóсточка.

v.t. (*remove stones from*) вынимáть, вы́нуть кóсточки из+*g.*

pit-a-pat ['pɪtə,pæt] *n.* биéние, трéпет.

adv. с биéнием/трéпетом; **her heart went ~** её сéрдце затрепетáло; **she ran ~ down the stairs** онá бы́стро — топ-топ-топ — сбежáла вниз по лéстнице.

pitch[1] [pɪtʃ] *n.* **1.** (*plunging motion of ship*) (килевáя) кáчка; (*lurch forward*) бросóк. **2.** (*throw*) бросóк; (*delivery of ball*) подáча. **3.** (*area for games*) пóле, площáдка. **4.** (*spot where trader or entertainer operates*) (постоя́нное/обы́чное) мéсто. **5.** (*of voice or instrument*) высотá. **6.** (*height, intensity, degree*) ýровень (*m.*), стéпень; **excitement reached fever ~** всех тряслó от возбуждéния; **things came to such a ~ that ...** дéло дошлó до тогó, что... **7.** (*slope of roof*) уклóн, скат.

v.t. **1.** (*set up, erect*): **they ~ed camp for the night** они́ разби́ли лáгерь нá ночь; **a ~ed battle** генерáльное сражéние. **2.** (*throw*) бр|осáть, -óсить; **he was ~ed on to his head** он удáрился головóй о зéмлю; (*fig.*): **he was ~ed into the centre of events** он очути́лся в сáмом цéнтре собы́тий. **3.** (*mus.*): **the song is ~ed too high for me** пéсня сли́шком высокá для моегó гóлоса. **4.** (*coll.*, *tell*) расскáз|ывать, -áть; **he ~ed a plausible yarn** он вы́дал правдоподóбную истóрию.

v.i. (*of ship*): **the ship was ~ing** корáбль качáло; (*of pers.*, *fall or lurch forwards*) пáдать, упáсть; (*fig.*) набр|áсываться, -óситься; **he ~ed into the work** он окунýлся в рабóту; **he ~ed into me** он брóсился на меня́; **he ~ed on the easiest solution** он ухвати́лся за сáмое лёгкое решéние.

with advs.: ~ **in** *v.i.* (*join in with vigour*) горячó/энерги́чно взя́ться (*pf.*) (*за что*); ~ **out** *v.t.* выбрáсывать, вы́бросить; выки́дывать, вы́кинуть; **the car overturned and the occupants were ~ed out** автомоби́ль переверну́лся, и пассажи́ров вы́швырнуло из негó.

cpd. **~fork** *n.* (сенны́е) ви́л|ы (*pl.*, *g.* —).

pitch[2] [pɪtʃ] *n.* (*bituminous substance*) смолá; ~ **darkness** тьма кромéшная.

cpds. **~-black** *adj.* чёрный как смоль; **~blende** *n.* уранини́т; **~-dark** *adj.*: **it is ~-dark here** здесь темны́м-темнó; **~-pine** *n.* соснá жёсткая.

pitcher ['pɪtʃə(r)] *n.* (*jug*) кувши́н; (*at baseball*) подающий.

pitchy ['pɪtʃɪ] *adj.* смоли́стый.

piteous ['pɪtɪəs] *adj.* жáлкий; жáлобный.

pith [pɪθ] *n.* (*plant tissue*) паренхи́ма; сердцеви́на; (*spinal cord*) спиннóй мозг; (*essential part*) суть; (*vigour, force*) энéргия, си́ла.

pithy ['pɪθɪ] *adj.* (*fig.*) сжáтый; содержáтельный.

pitiable ['pɪtɪəb(ə)l] *adj.* несчáстный; (*contemptible*) жáлкий.

pitiful ['pɪtɪ,fʊl] *adj.* (*compassionate*) жáлостливый; (*arousing pity*) жáлостный; (*contemptible*) жáлкий.

pitiless ['pɪtɪlɪs] *adj.* безжáлостный.

pitilessness ['pɪtɪlɪsnɪs] *n.* безжáлостность.

pittance ['pɪt(ə)ns] *n.* «жáлкие гроши́» (*m. pl.*).

pitter-patter ['pɪtə,pætə(r)] *n.* & *adv.* топ-тóп, тук-тýк.

v.i. постýкивать (*impf.*).

pituitary [pɪ'tju:ɪtərɪ] *n.* (**~ gland**) мозговóй придáток; гипофи́з.

pit|y ['pɪtɪ] *n.* **1.** (*compassion*) жáлость; **have, take ~y on** сжáлиться (*pf.*) над+*i.*; **I feel ~y for him** мне егó óчень жáлко; **he married her out of ~y** он жени́лся на ней из жáлости; **for ~y's sake!** (*expr. impatience*) Гóсподи Бóже мой! **2.** (*cause for regret*) жаль; **what a ~y!** как жáлко!; **more's the ~y** тем хýже; **it's a great ~y** (*or* **a thousand ~ies**) óчень, óчень жаль; **the ~y of it is that ...** сáмое грýстное в э́том то, что...

v.t. жалéть, по-; **she is much to be ~ied** её óчень жаль.

Pius ['paɪəs] *n.* Пий.

pivot ['pɪvət] *n.* тóчка вращéния; (*fig.*) тóчка опóры.

v.i. вращáться (*impf.*); вертéться (*impf.*); **everything ~s on his decision** всё упирáется в егó решéние.

pivotal ['pɪvətəl] *adj.* осевóй; центрáльный; (*fig.*) основнóй.

pixel ['pɪks(ə)l] *n.* (*comput.*) элемéнт изображéния.

pixilated ['pɪksɪ,leɪtɪd] *adj.* (*sl.*) чóкнутый.

pix|y, -ie ['pɪksɪ] *n.* эльф.

pizazz [ˌpɪ'zæz] *n.* огонёк, аза́рт.
pizza ['piːtsə] *n.* пи́цца; ~ **parlour** пиццери́я.
pizzeria [ˌpiːtsə'riːə] *n.* пиццери́я.
pizzicato [ˌpɪtsɪ'kɑːtəʊ] *n. adj. & adv.* пиццика́то (*indecl.*).
pl. ['plʊər(ə)l] *n.* (*abbr. of* **plural**) мн. ч., (мно́жественное число́).
placard ['plækɑːd] *n.* плака́т; (*advertising performance*) афи́ша.
v.t. (*display* ~*s on*) разве́|шивать, -сить плака́ты на+*p.*; (*advertise with* ~*s*) реклами́ровать (*impf.*, *pf.*).
placate [plə'keɪt, 'plæ-, 'pleɪ-] *v.t.* умиротвор|я́ть, -и́ть; успок|а́ивать, -о́ить.
placatory [plə'keɪtərɪ] *adj.* задабривающий; умиротворя́ющий.
place [pleɪs] *n.* **1.** ме́сто; **I have put my money in a safe** ~ я положи́л де́ньги в надёжное ме́сто; **all over the** ~ (*everywhere*) повсю́ду; (*in confusion*) повсю́ду, в беспоря́дке; (*correct, appropriate* ~): **everything is in** ~ всё на ме́сте; **there's a time and a** ~ **for everything** всему́ своё вре́мя и ме́сто; **her hair was out of** ~ её причёска растрепа́лась; **your laughter is out of** ~ ваш смех неуме́стен; **that put him in his** ~ э́то поста́вило его́ на ме́сто; (*reserved, occupied* ~): **he took his** ~ **in the queue** он за́нял ме́сто в о́череди; (*seat*): **he gave up his** ~ **to a lady** он уступи́л своё ме́сто да́ме; **take your** ~**s!** займи́те свои́ места́!; (*fig., position*): **put yourself in my** ~ поста́вьте себя́ на моё ме́сто; **in your** ~ **I would go** на ва́шем ме́сте я бы пошёл; (*at table*): **six** ~**s were laid** стол был накры́т на шесть персо́н; на столе́ бы́ло шесть прибо́ров; (*fig.*): **take** ~ (*occur*) име́ть (*impf.*) ме́сто; **when will the race take** ~? когда́ состоя́тся го́нки?; **take the** ~ **of** (*replace*) замен|я́ть, -и́ть; **give** ~ **to** смен|я́ться, -и́ться +*i.*; **her tears gave** ~ **to smiles** её слёзы смени́лись улы́бкой; **in** ~ **of** вме́сто+*g.* **2.** (*locality; specific area or point*) ме́сто; **in** ~**s** (*here and there*) места́ми; **we visited all the** ~**s of interest** мы осмотре́ли все интере́сные места́; **small** ~**s are not marked on the map** ме́лкие пу́нкты не обозна́чены на ка́рте; **there's no** ~ **like home** в гостя́х хорошо́, а до́ма лу́чше; **I have a sore** ~ **on my lip** у меня́ боля́чка на губе́. **3.** (*building; domicile*) дом; жили́ще; ~ **of worship** моли́твенный дом; **his** ~ **of work** ме́сто его́ рабо́ты; ~**s of entertainment** места́ развлече́ний; **he has a little** ~ **in the country** у него́ небольшо́й за́городный до́мик; **come round to my** ~! заходи́те ко мне! **4.** (*employment*) ме́сто, слу́жба; **he will have to seek another** ~ ему́ придётся иска́ть друго́е ме́сто. **5.** (*point or passage in book etc.*) ме́сто, страни́ца; **I put in a pencil to mark my** ~ я заложи́л страни́цу карандашо́м; **he closed the book and lost his** ~ он закры́л кни́гу и забы́л, где останови́лся. **6.** (*position in race or contest*): **our team took first** ~ на́ша кома́нда заняла́ пе́рвое ме́сто; **he backed the horse for a** ~ он поста́вил на ло́шадь в расчёте, что она́ займёт одно́ из пе́рвых мест; (*stage, position in series*): **in the first** ~ во-пе́рвых. **7.** (*math.*): **correct to three** ~**s of decimals** с то́чностью до тре́тьего десяти́чного зна́ка.
v.t. **1.** (*stand*) ста́вить, по-; (*lay*) класть, положи́ть; (*set*) сажа́ть, посади́ть; (*dispose*) разме|ща́ть, -сти́ть; расс|тавля́ть, -а́вить. **2.** (*appoint*) поме|ща́ть, -сти́ть. **3.** (*comm.*) поме|ща́ть, -сти́ть (*деньги и т.п.*); **I** ~**d an order with them** я помести́л у них зака́з; **£500 was** ~**d to his credit** на его́ счёт бы́ло поло́жено 500 фу́нтов; **how can we** ~ (*find a buyer for*) **this stock?** как бы сбыть э́тот това́р? **4.** (*repose*) возл|ага́ть, -ожи́ть (*надежды и т.п.*); **no-one** ~**s any confidence in his reports** его́ сообще́ния не вызыва́ют не у кого́ дове́рия. **5.** (*identify*) определ|я́ть, -и́ть; **I know those lines, but I cannot** ~ **them** мне знако́мы э́ти стро́чки, но я не могу́ вспо́мнить, отку́да они́.
cpds. ~**-kick** *n.* уда́р по неподви́жному мячу́; ~**-mat** *n.* ≃ салфе́тка под столо́вый прибо́р; ~**-name** *n.* географи́ческое назва́ние; ~**s** (*collect.*) топони́мика.
placebo [plə'siːbəʊ] *n.* (*med.*) безвре́дное (не ока́зывающее де́йствия) лека́рство.
placement ['pleɪsmənt] *n.* размеще́ние; (*seating order*) расса́дка.
placenta [plə'sentə] *n.* плаце́нта.
placet ['pleɪset] *n.* го́лос «за».
placid ['plæsɪd] *adj.* споко́йный, безмяте́жный.
placidity [plə'sɪdɪtɪ] *n.* споко́йствие, безмяте́жность.
plagiarism ['pleɪdʒəˌrɪz(ə)m] *n.* плагиа́т.
plagiarist ['pleɪdʒərɪst] *n.* плагиа́тор.
plagiarize ['pleɪdʒəˌraɪz] *v.t. & i.* занима́ться (*impf.*) плагиа́том; **he** ~**d my book** его́ рабо́та целико́м спи́сана с моей кни́ги.
plague [pleɪg] *n.* **1.** (*pestilence*) чума́. **2.** (*infestation*) бе́дствие; **a** ~ **of rats** наше́ствие крыс. **3.** (*annoyance*) напа́сть, чума́, «зара́за».
v.t. (*afflict*) нас|ыла́ть, -ла́ть чуму́/бе́дствие на+*a.*; (*pester*) докуча́ть (*impf.*) +*d.*
cpd. ~**-spot** *n.* (*on skin*) чумно́е пятно́; (*district*) зачумлённая ме́стность; (*fig.*) расса́дник зара́зы.
plaice [pleɪs] *n.* ка́мбала.
plaid [plæd] *n.* (*garment*) плед.
plain [pleɪn] *n.* равни́на.
adj. **1.** (*clear, evident*) я́сный, я́вный; **it is as** ~ **as the nose on one's face** э́то я́сно как день; **her distress was** ~ **to see** она́ я́вно страда́ла; **it was** ~ **sailing from then on** с тех пор всё пошло́ как по ма́слу. **2.** (*easy to understand*) я́сный, поня́тный; **the telegram was sent in** ~ **language** телегра́мму да́ли откры́тым те́кстом; **why can't you speak** ~ **English?** почему́ вы не говори́те просты́м языко́м? **3.** (*straightforward, candid*) прямо́й; **I am a** ~ **man** я челове́к просто́й; **I will be** ~ **with you** я бу́ду с ва́ми открове́нен; ~ **speaking hurts nobody** никогда́ не меша́ет говори́ть без обиняко́в; ~ **dealing** че́стность, прямота́. **4.** (*simple, ordinary, unembellished, not coloured*) просто́й, скро́мный, неприхотли́вый, безыску́сный; ~ **clothes** (*opp. to uniform*) шта́тское (пла́тье); ~ **food** проста́я пи́ща; ~ **living** скро́мная жизнь; ~ **words** просты́е слова́. **5.** (*unattractive*) некраси́вый; **a** ~ **Jane** некраси́вая де́вушка, дурну́шка.
adv. я́сно, про́сто.
cpds. ~**-chant,** ~**-song** *nn.* одното́нный напе́в; ~**-clothes** *adj.* оде́тый в шта́тское; ~**-clothes man** сы́щик, переоде́тый полице́йский, шпик; ~**-spoken** *adj.* открове́нный.
plainness ['pleɪnnɪs] *n.* (*candour*) прямота́, открове́нность; (*simplicity*) простота́, скро́мность, неприхотли́вость, безыску́сность; (*unattractiveness*) непривлека́тельность.
plaint [pleɪnt] *n.* (*leg., accusation*) жа́лоба; (*poet., lamentation*) се́тование, стена́ние.
plaintiff ['pleɪntɪf] *n.* исте́ц.
plaintive ['pleɪntɪv] *adj.* печа́льный, гру́стный.
plait [plæt] *n.* коса́; **she wears her hair in a** ~ она́ но́сит ко́су.
v.t. запле|та́ть, -сти́.
plan [plæn] *n.* план; (*drawing, diagram*) чертёж; ~**s were drawn up** бы́ли соста́влены пла́ны; (*map*) ка́рта; **a** ~ **of the city** план го́рода; (*schedule*): **all went according to** ~ всё прошло́ по пла́ну (*or* как бы́ло наме́чено); (*project*) прое́кт; **five-year** ~ пятиле́тний план; **master** ~ генера́льный план; **they made** ~**s for the future** они́ стро́или пла́ны на бу́дущее; (*system*) за́мысел; **on the instalment** ~ в рассро́чку; **an open-**~ **house** дом откры́той планиро́вки.
v.t. **1.** (*make a* ~ *of*) плани́ровать, за-. **2.** (*arrange, design*) проекти́ровать (*impf.*); ~**ned economy** пла́новая эконо́мика.
v.i. намерева́ться (*impf.*); **where are you** ~**ning to go this year?** куда́ вы собира́етесь е́хать в э́том году́?; **we must** ~ **ahead** на́до ду́мать о бу́дущем.
planchette [plɑːn'ʃet] *n.* планше́тка (для спирити́ческих сеа́нсов).
plane¹ [pleɪn] *n.* (*tree*) плата́н.
plane² [pleɪn] *n.* (*tool*) руба́нок, струг, калёвка.
v.t. & i. строга́ть, вы́-.
with advs.: ~ **away,** ~ **down** *v.t.* состру́г|ивать, -а́ть.
plane³ [pleɪn] *n.* **1.** (*flat surface*) пло́скость. **2.** (*aeroplane*) самолёт. **3.** (*fig., level*) у́ровень (*m.*); **her thoughts are on a higher** ~ у неё бо́лее высо́кий строй мы́слей. **4.:** ~ **sailing** (*naut.*) пла́вание по локсодро́мии; (*fig.*) несло́жное де́ло.
adj. пло́ский, плоскостно́й.

planet ['plænɪt] *n.* плане́та.

planetarium [ˌplænɪ'teərɪəm] *n.* планета́рий.

planetary ['plænɪtərɪ] *adj.* плане́тарный, плане́тный.

plangent ['plændʒ(ə)nt] *adj.* (*plaintive*) зауны́вный.

plank [plæŋk] *n.* доска́; **the pirates made him walk the ~** пира́ты сбро́сили его́ в мо́ре; (*fig., item in election programme*) пункт предвы́борной платфо́рмы.
v.t. (*coll., also* **plunk**): **he ~ed down his money on the table** он вы́ложил де́ньги на стол.
cpd. **~-bed** *n.* на́р|ы (*pl., g.* —).

planking ['plæŋkɪŋ] *n.* обши́вка доска́ми; насти́л; (*planks*) до́ски (*f. pl.*).

plankton ['plæŋkt(ə)n] *n.* планкто́н.

planner ['plænə(r)] *n.* планови́к, организа́тор; проектиро́вщик.

planning ['plænɪŋ] *n.* плани́рование; **long-term ~** перспекти́вное плани́рование; **family ~** (иску́сственное) ограниче́ние соста́ва семьи́.

plant [plɑ:nt] *n.* **1.** (*vegetable organism*) расте́ние; **~ diseases** боле́зни расте́ний; **house ~** ко́мнатное расте́ние; **~ life** жизнь расте́ний. **2.** (*industrial fixtures or machinery*) обору́дование. **3.** (*factory*) заво́д. **4.** (*swindle, hoax*) надува́тельство, подво́х. **5.** (*coll., article placed to incriminate; incrimination*) сфабрико́ванная ули́ка.
v.t. **1.** (*put in ground or water to grow*) сажа́ть, посади́ть; се́ять; **I have ~ed out the cabbages** я вы́садил капу́сту в грунт. **2.** (*furnish with ~s*) заса́|живать, -ди́ть; **the beds were ~ed with roses** гря́дки бы́ли заса́жены ро́зами. **3.** (*fig., establish, settle*): **the colony was ~ed 300 years ago** э́та коло́ния была́ осно́вана 300 лет наза́д; **he ~ed a doubt in my mind** он посе́ял во мне сомне́ние; **he ~ed himself in front of the fire** он стал пе́ред са́мим ками́ном; **~ a blow** нанести́ (*pf.*) то́чный уда́р; **~ evidence** подстр|а́ивать, -о́ить ули́ки; **the enemy ~ed a spy in our midst** враг засла́л шпио́на в на́ши ряды́.

plantain ['plæntɪn] *n.* (*herb*) подоро́жник; (*tropical tree*) ди́кий бана́н.

plantation [plæn'teɪʃ(ə)n, plɑ:n-] *n.* (*area of planted trees*) насажде́ния (*pl.*); (*estate*) планта́ция.

planter ['plɑ:ntə(r)] *n.* (*plantation owner*) планта́тор; (*agric. machine*) се́ялка; (*container for plants*) я́щик для расса́ды.

plantigrade ['plæntɪˌgreɪd] *adj.* стопоходя́щий.

plaque [plæk, plɑ:k] *n.* (*tablet*) табли́чка, доще́чка; (*badge*) значо́к, бля́ха.

plash [plæʃ] *n.* (*splashing sound*) плеск, вплеск.
v.i. плес|ка́ть, -ну́ть; плеска́ться (*impf.*).

plasm(a) ['plæzmə] *n.* (*fluid*) пла́зма; **blood ~** кровяна́я пла́зма.

plaster ['plɑ:stə(r)] *n.* **1.** (*for coating walls etc.*) штукату́рка; **~ cast** ги́псовый сле́пок; **~ of Paris** гипс; **~ saint** (*fig.*) свято́й, безгре́шный. **2.** (*med.*) пла́стырь (*m.*).
v.t. **1.** (*coat with ~*) штукату́рить, о(т)-; (*fig.*) па́чкать, за-; **his boots were ~ed with mud** его боти́нки бы́ли обле́плены гря́зью. **2.** (*cover with sticking-~*) на|кла́дывать, -ложи́ть пла́стырь на+*a.*; (*fig.*): **the trunk was ~ed with labels** сунду́к был весь обле́плен накле́йками. **3.: get ~ed** (*sl., drunk*) нализа́ться (*pf.*); упи́ться (*pf.*).

plasterer ['plɑ:stərə(r)] *n.* штукату́р.

plastic ['plæstɪk] *n.* пла́стик, пластма́сса; (*pl.*) пла́стика (*sg.*).
adj. **1.** (*made of ~*) пластма́ссовый; **~ bomb** пла́стиковая бо́мба. **2.** (*pert. to moulding; sculptural*) лепно́й; скульпту́рный; **the ~ arts** пласти́ческие иску́сства; **~ surgery** пласти́ческая хирурги́я. **3.** (*malleable*) пласти́чный; (*fig., susceptible to influence*) пода́тливый.

plasticine ['plæstɪˌsi:n] *n.* пластили́н.

plasticity [ˌplæs'tɪsɪtɪ] *n.* пласти́чность.

plate [pleɪt] *n.* **1.** (*shallow dish*) таре́лка; **side ~** таре́лка для хле́ба; **a ~ of cold meat** блю́до с холо́дным мя́сом; (*fig.*): **he has a lot on his ~** у него́ дел по го́рло (*coll.*); **the game was handed to him on a ~** ему́ преподнесли́ побе́ду на блю́дечке; **collection ~** блю́до для поже́ртвований. **2.** (*collect., metal tableware*) посу́да; **silver ~** сере́бряная посу́да. **3.** (*sheet of metal, glass etc.*) лист, полоса́; **a ~ on the door gave the doctor's name** на две́ри была́ табли́чка с фами́лией до́ктора; **the battery has zinc ~s** батаре́я име́ет ци́нковые пласти́ны; (*metal in this form*) броня́; **armour ~** броневы́е пли́ты (*f. pl.*). **4.** (*phot.*) фотопласти́нка; **half ~** полуто́новое клише́ (*indecl.*). **5.** (*lithographic*) гальваноклише́ (*indecl.*); (*illustration*) вкладна́я иллюстра́ция. **6.** (*typ.*) стереоти́п. **7.** (**dental ~**) вставна́я че́люсть, (зубно́й) проте́з. **8.** (*cup as racing prize*) ку́бок. **9.** (*rail.*) ре́льсовая накла́дка.
v.t. **1.** (*cover with metal ~s*) плакирова́ть (*impf.*). **2.** (*coat with layer of metal*) покр|ыва́ть, -ы́ть мета́ллом; **silver-~d spoons** посеребрённые ло́жки.
cpds. **~-glass** *adj.* из зерка́льного стекла́; **~layer** *n.* путево́й рабо́чий; **~-rack** *n.* суши́лка для посу́ды.

plateau ['plætəʊ] *n.* плато́ (*indecl.*).

plateful ['pleɪtfʊl] *n.* (по́лная) таре́лка (*чего*).

platen ['plæt(ə)n] *n.* (*of typewriter*) ва́лик.

platform ['plætfɔ:m] *n.* **1.** (*at station*) платфо́рма, перро́н; **at ~ No. 3** на платфо́рме № 3; **~ ticket** перро́нный биле́т. **2.** (*for speakers*) трибу́на; (*fig., pol.*) (полити́ческая) платфо́рма.

plating ['pleɪtɪŋ] *n.* покры́тие, обши́вка.

platinum ['plætɪnəm] *n.* пла́тина; **~ blonde** «пла́тиновая» (о́чень све́тлая) блонди́нка.

platitude ['plætɪˌtju:d] *n.* пло́скость, бана́льность.

platitudinous [ˌplætɪ'tju:dɪnəs] *adj.* пло́ский, бана́льный.

Plato ['pleɪtəʊ] *n.* Плато́н.

Platonic [plə'tɒnɪk] *adj.* платони́ческий.

platoon [plə'tu:n] *n.* взвод.

platter ['plætə(r)] *n.* блю́до; **cold ~** холо́дное ассорти́ (*indecl.*).

platypus ['plætɪpəs] *n.* утконо́с.

plaudit ['plɔ:dɪt] *n.* (*usu. pl.*) аплодисме́нт|ы (*pl., g.* -ов); похвала́ (*sg.*).

plausibility [ˌplɔ:zɪ'bɪlɪtɪ] *n.* вероя́тность, правдоподо́бие.

plausible ['plɔ:zɪb(ə)l] *adj.* правдоподо́бный.

play [pleɪ] *n.* **1.** (*recreation, amusement*) игра́; **all work and no ~ makes Jack a dull boy** Джек в дру́жбе с де́лом, в ссо́ре с безде́льем — бедня́га Джек не знако́м с весе́льем; **the children were at ~** де́ти игра́ли; **mathematics is child's ~ to him** матема́тика для него́ — де́тские игру́шки; **it was said in ~** э́то бы́ло ска́зано ра́ди заба́вы; **~ on words** игра́ слов. **2.** (*gambling*) аза́ртная игра́. **3.** (*conduct of game etc.*) игра́; мане́ра игры́; **there was a lot of rough ~** бы́ло мно́го гру́бой игры́; **I am here to see fair ~** я слежу́ за тем, что́бы игра́ вела́сь по пра́вилам; **the police suspect foul ~** поли́ция подозрева́ет, что де́ло нечи́сто. **4.** (*state of being played with*): **the ball was out of ~** мяч был вне игры́. **5.** (*turn or move in game*) ход; **it's your ~** ваш ход. **6.** (*fig., action*) де́йствие, де́ятельность; **all his strength was brought into ~** он моболизова́л все свои́ си́лы; **the ~ of market forces** возде́йствие фа́кторов ры́нка. **7.** (*dramatic work*) пье́са, спекта́кль (*m.*); **their quarrel was as good as a ~** их ссо́ра была́ заба́вным зре́лищем. **8.** (*visual effect*) игра́; перели́вы (*m. pl.*); **the ~ of light on the water** игра́ све́та на воде́. **9.** (*free movement*) люфт, свобо́дный ход; **there is too much ~ in the brake pedal** тормо́зная педа́ль име́ет сли́шком большо́й свобо́дный ход. **10.** (*fig., scope*) во́ля; просто́р; **she allowed her curiosity free ~** она́ дала́ во́лю своему́ любопы́тству; **he made much ~ with the fact that I was unmarried** он осо́бенно упира́л на то, что я не жена́т.
v.t. **1.** (*perform, take part in*) игра́ть, сыгра́ть в+*a.*; **~ football** игра́ть (*impf.*) в футбо́л; **~ the game!** (*fig., abide by the rules*) игра́йте по пра́вилам!; **he wouldn't ~ ball** (*coll., cooperate*) он не хоте́л сотру́дничать; **~ it cool** (*coll.*) сохраня́ть (*impf.*) хладнокро́вие; **~ it long** (*coll.*) тяну́ть (*impf.*) вре́мя. **2.** (*perform on*) игра́ть, сыгра́ть на+*p.*; **can you ~ the piano?** вы игра́ете на роя́ле?; **he ~s second fiddle** (*fig.*) он игра́ет втору́ю скри́пку. **3.** (*cause to be heard*) исп|олня́ть, -о́лнить; **they ~ed their favourite records** они́ поста́вили/проигра́ли свои́ люби́мые пласти́нки; **he ~ed it by ear** (*fig., of extempore action*) он де́йствовал по интуи́ции. **4.** (*perpetrate*): **he is always ~ing tricks on me** он всегда́ надо мно́й подшу́чивает; **my memory ~s tricks** па́мять меня́ подво́дит; **you will ~ that joke once too often** вы когда́-нибудь доигра́етесь. **5.**

(*enact role of*) игра́ть, сыгра́ть; **I ~ed Horatio** я игра́л Гора́цио; **she loves to ~ the great lady** она́ лю́бит изобража́ть из себя́ гранд-да́му; **~ the man!** бу́дьте мужчи́ной!; **stop ~ing the fool!** переста́ньте валя́ть дурака́; **this will ~ havoc with our plans** э́то расстро́ит на́ши пла́ны; **~ truant** прогу́л|ивать, -я́ть заня́тия/уро́ки. **6.** (*enact drama of*) дава́ть (*impf.*); дава́ть представле́ние +*g.*; **they are ~ing Othello** (в теа́тре) даю́т/идёт «Оте́лло». **7.** (*contend against*): **will you ~ me at chess?** вы сыгра́ете со мной в ша́хматы? **8.** (*angling*: *keep on end of line*) выва́живать (*impf.*). **9.** (*cards*): **he ~ed the ace** он пошёл с туза́; **he ~ed his trump card** (*fig.*) он пусти́л в ход ко́зырь; **he ~ed his cards well** (*fig.*) он де́йствовал уме́ло. **10.** (*use as ~er*): **they ~ed Jones at full back** Джо́нса поста́вили игра́ть защи́тником. **11.** (*strike, propel*) уд|аря́ть, -а́рить; (*fig.*): **he ~ed it off the cuff** он импровизи́ровал на ходу́; **he ~ed the affair skilfully** он иску́сно провёл де́ло. **12.** (*direct*) напр|авля́ть, -а́вить; **the firemen ~ed their hoses on to the blaze** пожа́рники напра́вили брандспо́йты на пла́мя.

v.i. **1.** игра́ть, сыгра́ть; (*amuse o.s., have fun*) забавля́ться (*impf.*); резви́ться (*impf.*); **they were ~ing at soldiers** они́ игра́ли в войну́; **you're not trying, you're just ~ing at it!** вы не рабо́таете, а в бирю́льки игра́ете!; **what are you ~ing at?** что за игру́ вы ведёте?; **she ~ed on his vanity** она́ сыгра́ла на его́ тщесла́вие; **he is fond of ~ing on words** он лю́бит каламбу́ры; **she is ~ing with his affections** она́ игра́ет его́ чу́вствами; **I am ~ing with the idea of resigning** я поду́мываю об отста́вке; **he ~ed with his glasses while he was talking** разгова́ривая, он верте́л в рука́х очки́; **don't ~ with fire!** (*fig.*) не игра́йте с огнём!; **run away and ~!** пойди́ поигра́й!; (*take part in game or sport*): **they ~ed to win** они́ игра́ли с аза́ртом; **two can ~ at that game!** (*fig.*) посмо́трим ещё, чья возьмёт!; **I have always ~ed fair with you** я всегда́ поступа́л с ва́ми че́стно; (*gamble*) **what shall we ~ for?** по ско́льку бу́дем игра́ть/ста́вить?; **he is ~ing for high stakes** (*fig.*) он игра́ет по-кру́пному; (*perform music*): **it's an old instrument but it ~s well** э́то ста́рый инструме́нт, но у него́ хоро́ший звук; (*on stage etc.*): **they ~ed to full houses** они́ игра́ли при по́лном за́ле; **~ to the gallery** (*fig.*) иска́ть (*impf.*) дешёвой популя́рности; игра́ть (*impf.*) на пу́блику; (*move, be active*): **a smile ~ed on her lips** улы́бка игра́ла на её губа́х; **a breeze ~ed in the trees** ветеро́к шелесте́л в дере́вьях; **the light ~ed on the water** на воде́ игра́ли светов́ые бли́ки; **the fountains were ~ing** би́ли фонта́ны. **2.** (*be directed*): **searchlights ~ed on the aircraft** проже́кторы бы́ли напра́влены на самолёт; **the guns ~ed on the enemy's lines** пу́шки обстре́ливали пози́ции врага́. **3.** (*of ground or pitch*): **the pitch ~ed well until the rain came** по́ле бы́ло в хоро́шем состоя́нии, пока не начался́ дождь. **4.** (*strike ball*) де́лать, с- бросо́к; (*fig.*): **he ~ed into my hands** он сыгра́л мне на́ руку.

with advs.: **~ about, ~ around** *v.i.* игра́ть (*impf.*); резви́ться (*impf.*); **the children were ~ing about in the garden** де́ти резви́лись в саду́; **~ back** *v.t.* воспроизв|оди́ть, -ести́; прослу́ш|ивать, -ать; **the tape was ~ed back** плёнку проигра́ли; **~ down** *v.t.* (*fig., minimize*) преум|еньша́ть, -е́ньшить; **I ~ed down his faults in my report** в своём отчёте я части́чно обошёл его́ недоста́тки; **~ o.s. in** *v.i.* разы́гр|иваться, -а́ться; входи́ть, войти́ в игру́/рабо́ту; **~ off** *v.t.* (*replay*): **the drawn game must be ~ed off next week** ничья́ должна́ быть переи́грана на сле́дующей неде́ле; (*set in opposition*) натра́в|ливать, -и́ть (*кого на кого*); **he ~ed his rivals off against one another** он стра́вливал свои́х сопе́рников ме́жду собо́й; **~ out** *v.t.* (*~ to the end, to a result*) доигр|ывать, -а́ть; (*pass., be exhausted*) выдыха́ться, вы́дохнуться; **~ over** *v.t.* переигр|ивать, -а́ть; **may I ~ over my new composition?** мо́жно вам проигра́ть моё но́вое произведе́ние?; **~ through** *v.t.* сыгра́ть (*pf.*) (целико́м); **the conductor made them ~ the movement through again** дирижёр заста́вил их сыгра́ть/проигра́ть э́ту часть за́ново; **~ up** *v.t.* (*give emphasis, importance to*) обы́гр|ивать, -а́ть; **he ~ed up the advantages of the scheme** он обыгра́л преиму́щества пла́на; (*coll., give trouble to*) му́чить, за-; **Tommy has been ~ing me up all morning** То́мми досажда́л мне всё у́тро; **my car is ~ing me up again** моя́ маши́на опя́ть барахли́т; *v.i.* (*exert o.s. in game*) стара́ться, по-; **~ up, boys!** нажми́, ребя́та!; (*misbehave*) распус|ка́ться, -ти́ться; **the boys ~ up when their father is away** ма́льчики распуска́ются, когда́ отца́ нет до́ма; **~ up to** (*support*) подде́рж|ивать, -а́ть; (*on stage*) поды́гр|ивать, -а́ть +*d.*; **the cast ~ed up to the leading lady** тру́ппа поды́грывала веду́щей актри́се; (*humour*) подда́кивать (*impf.*); **she ~s up to her husband** она́ подда́кивает своему́ му́жу; (*give flattering attention to*) льсти́ть (*impf.*) +*d.*; подли́зываться (*impf.*) к+*d.*

cpds. **~-acting** *n.* (*fig.*) притво́рство, на́игрыш; **~back** *n.* воспроизведе́ние; **~bill** *n.* (*poster*) театра́льная афи́ша; **~-box** *n.* я́щик для игру́шек; **~boy** *n.* пове́са (*m.*), донжуа́н; **~fellow, ~mate** *nn.*: **the child needs a ~fellow** ребёнку на́до с ке́м-то игра́ть; **~goer** *n.* театра́л; **~-going** *n.* посеще́ние теа́тра; **~ground** *n.* (*at school*) площа́дка для игр; шко́льный двор; (*fig.*) излю́бленное ме́сто развлече́ния; **~group** *n.* дошко́льная гру́ппа (малыше́й); **~house** *n.* теа́тр; **~mate** *n.* = **~fellow**; **~-off** *n.* реша́ющая встре́ча; повто́рная встре́ча после ничье́й; **~-pen** *n.* де́тский мане́ж; **~school** *n.* де́тский сад; **~-suit** *n.* спорти́вный костю́м; **~thing** *n.* (*lit., fig.*) игру́шка; **~time** *n.* вре́мя о́тдыха; шко́льная переме́на; **~wright** *n.* драмату́рг.

player [ˈpleɪə(r)] *n.* **1.** (*of game*) игро́к; спортсме́н; (*cricket*) профессиона́льный игро́к; **~s and gentlemen** профессиона́лы и люби́тели. **2.** (*actor*) актёр. **3.** (*musician*): **a ~ on the clarinet** кларнети́ст. **4.** (*record-~*) прои́грыватель (*m.*).

cpd. **~-piano** *n.* пиано́ла.

playful [ˈpleɪfʊl] *adj.* игри́вый, шаловли́вый.

playfulness [ˈpleɪfʊlnɪs] *n.* игри́вость.

playing [ˈpleɪɪŋ] *n.* игра́.

cpds. **~-card** *n.* игра́льная ка́рта; **~-field** *n.* спорти́вное по́ле.

playlet [ˈpleɪlɪt] *n.* пье́ска.

plaza [ˈplɑːzə] *n.* пло́щадь.

PLC, plc (*abbr. of* ***public limited company***) обще́ственная компа́ния с ограни́ченной отве́тственностью.

plea [pliː] *n.* **1.** (*leg.*) заявле́ние в суде́; аргуме́нт, возраже́ние; **he entered a ~ of guilty** он призна́л себя́ вино́вным. **2.** (*excuse*) предло́г; **on the ~ of ill-health** под предло́гом боле́зни. **3.** (*request, appeal*) про́сьба.

plead [pliːd] *v.t.* **1.** (*argue for*) защи|ща́ть, -ти́ть; **he had a lawyer to ~ his case** его́ де́ло вёл адвока́т; **he ~ed the cause of the pensioners** он защища́л интере́сы пенсионе́ров. **2.** (*offer as excuse*) ссыла́ться, сосла́ться на+*a.*; **the defendant ~ed insanity** подсуди́мый сосла́лся на невменя́емость; **I must ~ ignorance of the facts** к сожале́нию, я не в ку́рсе де́ла. **3.** (*declare o.s.*): **my client ~s (not) guilty** мой клие́нт (не) признаёт себя́ вино́вным.

v.i. **1.** (*address court as advocate*) выступа́ть, вы́ступить в суде́. **2.** (*appeal, entreat*) приз|ыва́ть, -ва́ть; умоля́ть (*impf.*); **the prisoners ~ed for mercy** заключённые проси́ли о поми́ловании; **he ~ed with me to stay** он умоля́л меня́ не уходи́ть.

pleading [ˈpliːdɪŋ] *n.* выступле́ние защи́ты; хода́тайство; **special ~** тенденцио́зный подбо́р фа́ктов/аргуме́нтов.

pleasance [ˈplez(ə)ns] *n.* (*arch.*) сад, парк.

pleasant [ˈplez(ə)nt] *adj.* прия́тный; **I made myself ~ to them** я с ни́ми держа́лся как мо́жно любе́знее.

pleasantness [ˈplezəntnɪs] *n.* любе́зность.

pleasantry [ˈplezəntrɪ] *n.* (*joke*) шу́тка; (*amiable interchange*) любе́зность.

please [pliːz] *v.t.* нра́виться, по- +*d.*; дост|авля́ть, -а́вить удово́льствие +*d.*; **it ~s the eye** э́то ра́дует глаз; **his attitude ~s me** меня́ ра́дует его́ пози́ция; **I was not very ~d at, by, with the results** я был не о́чень дово́лен результа́тами; **I feel better, I'm ~d to say** рад сообщи́ть, что я чу́вствую себя́ лу́чше; **as ~d as Punch** (*coll.*) рад-радёшенек; **I was ~d to note** мне бы́ло прия́тно отме́тить; **I shall be ~d to attend** я бу́ду рад приня́ть уча́стие; **he was ~d to criticize me** (*iron.*) он почёл за бла́го сде́лать мне замеча́ния; **~ God we shall arrive in time!** дай Бог, что́бы мы прие́хали во́-время!; **~ yourself** как вам бу́дет уго́дно; **he ~s himself what he does** он поступа́ет, как ему́ заблагорассу́дится.

v.i. **1.** (*give pleasure*) уго|жда́ть, -ди́ть; **she is very anxious to ~** она́ о́чень стара́ется угоди́ть. **2.** (*think fit*) изво́лить (*impf.*); **do as you ~** де́лайте, как хоти́те; **he comes just when he ~s** он прихо́дит, когда́ ему́ взду́мается/заблагорассу́дится. **3.** (*polite request*): **~ shut the door** пожа́луйста, закро́йте дверь; **won't you ~ sit down?** пожа́луйста, сади́тесь; **~ do try the jam** прошу́ вас, попро́буйте варе́нья; **~ forgive our long silence** о́чень про́сим извини́ть нас за до́лгое молча́ние; **if you ~** е́сли вам уго́дно; о́чень вас прошу́; пожа́луйста, бу́дьте так добры́; (*iron.*): **he's taken a day's leave, if you ~** предста́вьте себе́ (*or* поду́майте то́лько), он взял выходно́й.

pleasing [ˈpli:zɪŋ] *adj.* прия́тный.

pleasurable [ˈpleʒərəb(ə)l] *adj.* доставля́ющий удово́льствие.

pleasure [ˈpleʒə(r)] *n.* **1.** (*enjoyment*) удово́льствие; **lead a life of ~** жить (*impf.*) в своё удово́льствие; **he is travelling for ~** он путеше́ствует для своего́ со́бственного удово́льствия; **it's a ~!** (*sc. to oblige*) рад служи́ть!; **it gives me great ~ to see you** мне о́чень прия́тно вас ви́деть; **may I have the ~ (of a dance)?** разреши́те пригласи́ть вас (на та́нец)?; **he takes ~ in teasing her** ему́ доставля́ет удово́льствие подтру́нивать над ней; **they take their ~s sadly** им и ра́дость не в ра́дость. **2.** (*will, desire*) жела́ние; **at your ~** по ва́шему жела́нию; **we await your ~** к ва́шим услу́гам; **he was detained during her Majesty's ~** он был заде́ржан до осо́бого распоряже́ния коро́ны.

cpds. **~-boat** *n.* прогу́лочный ка́тер; **~-ground** *n.* сад, парк; **~-lover** *n.* охо́тник до удово́льствий; **~-seeking** *adj.* и́щущий удово́льствий.

pleat [pli:t] *n.* скла́дка.

v.t. плиссирова́ть (*impf.*); **~ed skirt** плиссиро́ванная ю́бка; ю́бка в скла́дку.

plebeian [plɪˈbi:ən] *n.* плебе́й.

adj. плебе́йский.

plebiscite [ˈplebɪsɪt, -saɪt] *n.* плебисци́т.

plebs [plebz] *n.* плебс.

plectrum [ˈplektrəm] *n.* плектр.

pledge [pledʒ] *n.* **1.** (*thg. left as earnest of intent; token*) зало́г. **2.** (*promise*) обе́т, обеща́ние; **he has signed the (*temperance*) ~** он дал заро́к не пить. **3.: goods in ~** това́ры в зало́ге; **take out of ~** выкупа́ть, вы́купить (из закла́да).

v.t. **1.** (*give as security*) отд|ава́ть, -а́ть в зало́г; (*pawn*) за|кла́дывать, -ложи́ть; **~ o.s.** обя́з|ываться, -а́ться; руча́ться, поручи́ться; **I ~ my word** даю́ сло́во; руча́юсь. **2.** (*enjoin*): **I ~d him to secrecy** я взял с него́ сло́во не говори́ть (об э́том).

Pleiades [ˈplaɪə,di:z] *n.* Плея́д|ы (*pl., g.* —).

Pleistocene [ˈpleɪstə,si:n] *n.* плейстоце́н.

plenary [ˈpli:nərɪ] *adj.*: **~ powers** неограни́ченные полномо́чия; **~ session** плена́рное заседа́ние, пле́нум.

plenipotentiary [,plenɪpəˈtenʃərɪ] *n.* полномо́чный представи́тель.

adj. полномо́чный, неограни́ченный.

plenitude [ˈplenɪ,tju:d] *n.* (*fullness*) полнота́; (*abundance*) изоби́лие.

plenteous [ˈplentɪəs] *adj.* (*abundant*) оби́льный; (*productive*) урожа́йный.

plentiful [ˈplentɪ,fʊl] *adj.* изоби́льный, оби́льный.

plenty [ˈplentɪ] *n.* **1.** (*abundance*) изоби́лие; **there was food in ~** еда́ была́ в изоби́лии. **2.** (*large quantity or number*) мно́жество; **he has ~ of money** у него́ по́лно де́нег; **we have ~ of time to spare** у нас мно́го вре́мени в запа́се. **3.** (*sufficient*) доста́ток; **that will be ~** э́того бу́дет предоста́точно.

adv. (*coll., amply*) вполне́.

plenum [ˈpli:nəm] *n.* пле́нум.

pleonasm [ˈpli:ə,næz(ə)m] *n.* плеона́зм.

pleonastic [,pli:əˈnæstɪk] *adj.* плеонасти́ческий.

plesiosaurus [,pli:sɪəˈsɔ:rəs] *n.* плезиоза́вр.

plethora [ˈpleθərə] *n.* (*med.*) полнокро́вие; (*fig., over-abundance*) избы́ток.

pleurisy [ˈplʊərɪsɪ] *n.* плеври́т.

plexus [ˈpleksəs] *n.* сплете́ние; **solar ~** со́лнечное сплете́ние.

pliability [,plaɪəˈbɪlɪtɪ] *n.* ги́бкость; (*fig.*) ги́бкость, усту́пчивость.

pliable [ˈplaɪəb(ə)l] *adj.* ги́бкий; (*fig.*) ги́бкий, усту́пчивый.

pliant [ˈplaɪənt] *adj.* ги́бкий; (*fig.*) ги́бкий, пода́тливый.

pliers [ˈplaɪəz] *n.* щипц|ы́ (*pl., g.* -о́в); кле́щ|и́ (*pl., g.* -е́й).

plight[1] [plaɪt] *n.* незави́дное положе́ние.

plight[2] [plaɪt] *v.t.* (*arch.*): **they ~ed their troth** они́ покляли́сь в ве́рности; **~ed lovers** помо́лвленные (*pl.*), обручённые (*pl.*).

plimsoll [ˈplɪms(ə)l] *n.* **1.** (*light shoe*): **~s** паруси́новые ту́фли (*f. pl.*); кроссо́в|ки (*pl., g.* -ок); та́почки (*f. pl.*). **2.: P~ line** грузова́я ма́рка.

plinth [plɪnθ] *n.* пли́нтус.

Pliocene [ˈplaɪə,si:n] *n.* плиоце́н.

PLO (*abbr. of* ***Palestine Liberation Organization***) ООП, (Организа́ция освобожде́ния Палести́ны).

plod [plɒd] *n.* (*walk*) тяжёлая по́ступь; (*work*) тяжёлая рабо́та.

v.t. & i. тащи́ться (*impf.*); **the labourer ~ded his way home** рабо́чий уста́ло тащи́лся домо́й; (*fig.*): **~ away at sth.** корпе́ть (*impf.*) над чем-н.

plodder [ˈplɒdə(r)] *n.* (*fig.*) труд́яга (*c.g.*); работя́га (*c.g.*).

plonk [plɒŋk] *n.* (*sl., cheap wine*) дешёвое вино́, бормоту́ха.

v.t. (*coll., put down heavily*) гро́х|ать, -нуть; ба́х|ать, -нуть; **he ~ed himself in an armchair** он плю́хнулся в кре́сло.

plop [plɒp] *n.* бульк.

adv.: **fall ~** булты́хну́ться (*pf.*).

v.t. & i. шлёпнуть(ся) (*pf.*).

int. бух!

plosive [ˈpləʊsɪv] *n.* взрывно́й звук.

adj. взрывно́й.

plot [plɒt] *n.* **1.** (*piece of ground*) уча́сток (земли́). **2.** (*outline of play etc.*) фа́була, сюже́т. **3.** (*conspiracy*) за́говор.

v.t. **1.** (*make plan of*) плани́ровать, за-. **2.** (*record*) нан|оси́ть, -ести́. **3.** (*measure out: also* **~ out**) разб|ива́ть, -и́ть. **4.** (*conspire to achieve*): **they ~ted his ruin** они́ гото́вили ему́ ги́бель.

v.i. (*conspire*) вына́шивать (*impf.*) за́говор.

plough [plaʊ] (*US* **plow**) *n.* **1.** плуг; **we have 100 acres under ~** у нас 100 а́кров па́шни (*or* па́хотной земли́); **he put his hand to the ~** (*fig.*) он взя́лся/приня́лся за де́ло; **(snow-~)** снегоочисти́тель (*m.*). **2.: the P~** (*astron.*) Больша́я Медве́дица.

v.t. **1.** паха́ть, вс-; **he is ~ing the sand** (*fig.*) он тра́тит си́лы впусту́ю; **he ~s a lonely furrow** (*fig.*) он де́йствует в одино́чку; (*fig.*): **he ~ed his way through the mud** он шлёпал по грязи́. **2.** (*coll., fail*) прова́л|ивать, -и́ть.

v.i. **1.** (*fig.*) продв|ига́ться, -и́нуться; **the ship ~ed through the waves** кора́бль рассека́л во́лны; **I ~ed through the book** я с трудо́м оси́лил кни́гу. **2.** (*coll., fail in exam*) прова́л|иваться, -и́ться.

with advs.: **~ back** *v.t.*: **profits are ~ed back** при́быль вкла́дывается в де́ло; **~ in** *v.t.* запа́х|ивать, -а́ть.

cpds. **~boy** *n.* па́рень (*m.*) «от сохи́»; **~land** *n.* па́хотная земля́; **~man** *n.* па́харь (*m.*); **~share** *n.* плу́жный ле́мех.

plover [ˈplʌvə(r)] *n.* ржа́нка.

plow [plaʊ] = **plough**

ploy [plɔɪ] *n.* (*manoeuvre*) уло́вка.

pluck [plʌk] *n.* **1.** (*pull, twitch*) дёрганье. **2.** (*of an animal*) ли́вер. **3.** (*coll., courage*) сме́лость, отва́га.

v.t. **1.** (*pull off, pick*) срыва́ть, сорва́ть; соб|ира́ть, -ра́ть. **2.** (*strip of feathers*) ощи́п|ывать, -а́ть. **3.** (*cause to vibrate by twitching*) щипа́ть (*pf.*); **~ed instrument** щипко́вый инструме́нт. **4.** (*twitch, pull at; also v.i.*) дёр|гать, -нуть.

with advs.: ~ **off** *v.t.* выдёргивать, вы́дернуть; ~ **out** *v.t.* выщи́пывать, вы́щипать; ~ **up** *v.t.*: ~ **up courage** собра́ться (*pf.*) с ду́хом.

plucky ['plʌkɪ] *adj.* (*coll.*) сме́лый, отва́жный, реши́тельный.

plug [plʌg] *n.* **1.** (*stopper, e.g. of bath*) про́бка, заты́чка, сто́пор; **(wax) ear-~** заты́чка для уше́й. **2.** (*elec. connector*) ви́лка; (*socket*) розе́тка. **3.** (*spark-~*) запа́льная свеча́. **4.** (*of WC*): **he pulled the ~** он спусти́л во́ду. **5.** (*of tobacco*) жева́тельный таба́к. **6.** (*coll., advertisement*) рекла́ма.

v.t. (*stop up*) заку́пори|вать, -ть; (*connect with elec. ~*) включ|а́ть, -и́ть; (*coll., boost*) реклами́ровать (*impf., pf.*); (*US sl., shoot*) застрели́ть (*pf.*).

with advs.: ~ **away** *v.i.* (*coll., persevere*) корпе́ть (*impf.*); ~ **in** *v.t.* включ|а́ть, -и́ть; ~ **up** *v.t.* заку́пори|вать, -ть.

cpds. **~-in** *adj.* вставно́й; **~-ugly** *n.* (*US sl.*) держимо́рда (*m.*), хулига́н.

plum [plʌm] *n.* **1.** (*fruit, tree*) сли́ва. **2.** (*raisin*) изю́м; кори́нка; ~ **cake** кекс с кори́нкой; ~ **duff** варёный пу́динг с кори́нкой; ~ **pudding** плам-пу́динг. **3.** (*fig., prized object or possession*) «жи́рный кусо́к», «сли́в|ки» (*pl., g.* -ок); ла́комый кусо́чек; **a ~ job** тёплое месте́чко.

plumage ['plu:mɪdʒ] *n.* опере́ние.

plumb [plʌm] *n.* отве́с, грузи́ло; **out of ~** накло́нный, отве́сный.

adj. (*vertical*) вертика́льный.

adv. (*exactly*) то́чно; (*US sl., utterly*) соверше́нно, совсе́м.

v.t. (*sound*) изм|еря́ть, -е́рить ло́том; (*fig.*) прон|ика́ть, -и́кнуть в+*a.*; **he ~ed the depths of absurdity** он дошёл до по́лного абсу́рда.

cpds. **~-line** *n.* отве́с, отве́сная ли́ния; **~-rule** *n.* лине́йка с отве́сом.

plumbago [plʌm'beɪgəʊ] *n.* (*graphite*) графи́т.

plumber ['plʌmə(r)] *n.* водопрово́дчик.

plumbing ['plʌmɪŋ] *n.* (*occupation*) слеса́рно-водопрово́дное де́ло; (*installation*) водопрово́д, санте́хника.

plume [plu:m] *n.* **1.** (*feather*) перо́; **in borrowed ~s** ≃ воро́на в павли́ньих пе́рьях; **a ~ of smoke** стру́йка ды́ма; дымо́к. **2.** (*in headdress*) султа́н, плюма́ж.

v.t.: **the bird ~s its feathers** пти́ца охора́шивается (*or* чи́стит пёрышки); (*fig.*): **he ~s himself on his skill** он кичи́тся свои́м мастерство́м.

plummet ['plʌmɪt] *n.* свинцо́вый груз; грузи́ло, тя́жесть.

v.i. об|рыва́ться, -орва́ться; (*fig.*): **shares ~ed** а́кции ре́зко упа́ли.

plummy ['plʌmɪ] *adj.* (*coll., of voice*) со́чный.

plump[1] [plʌmp] *adj.* (*rounded, chubby*) пу́хлый, окру́глый; (*fattish*) по́лный.

v.t.: ~ **up 1.** (*fatten*) вск|а́рмливать, -орми́ть; де́лать, с- пу́хлым. **2.**: **she ~ed up the cushions** она́ взби́ла поду́шки.

v.i.: ~ **out** разд|ава́ться, -а́ться; толсте́ть, рас-; **her cheeks have ~ed out** у неё округли́лись щёки.

plump[2] [plʌmp] *adj.* (*blunt*) прямо́й.

v.t. (*drop; usu.* ~ **down**) бу́х|ать, -нуть; швыр|я́ть, -ну́ть.

v.i. (*fall heavily; usu.* ~ **down**) шлёп|аться, -нуться; (*make one's choice*) реш|а́ть, -и́ть; **I ~ for the roast beef** я — за ро́стбиф.

plunder ['plʌndə(r)] *n.* (*looting*) грабёж; (*loot*) добы́ча.

v.t. & i. гра́бить, о-; расх|ища́ть, -и́тить.

plunge [plʌndʒ] *n.* **1.** (*dive*) ныря́ние; (*fig.*): **he took the ~** он реши́л: была́ не была́. **2.** (*violent movement*) бросо́к.

v.t. погру|жа́ть, -зи́ть; **the room was ~d into darkness** ко́мната погрузи́лась во мрак; **he ~d his hands into water** он опусти́л ру́ки в во́ду; **they were ~d into despair** они́ бы́ли пове́ргнуты в отча́яние.

v.i. **1.** (*dive*) окун|а́ться, -у́ться; (*fig.*): **a plunging neckline** глубо́кий вы́рез на пла́тье. **2.** (*lunge forward*) бр|оса́ться, -о́ситься (вперёд); **the horse ~d forward** ло́шадь рвану́лась вперёд; **the ship ~d through the waves** кора́бль шёл, рассека́я во́лны; (*fig.*) погру|жа́ться, -зи́ться; **he ~d into the work** он погрузи́лся в рабо́ту. **3.** (*sl., gamble heavily*) аза́ртно игра́ть (*impf.*).

plunger ['plʌndʒə(r)] *n.* плу́нжер.

plunk [plʌŋk] = **plank** *v.t.*

pluperfect [plu:'pɜ:fɪkt] *n.* давнопроше́дшее вре́мя.

adj. давнопроше́дший.

plural ['plʊər(ə)l] *n.* мно́жественное число́.

adj. **1.** (*gram.*) мно́жественный. **2.** (*multiple*) многочи́сленный; неодноро́дный; **a ~ society** плюралисти́ческое о́бщество.

pluralism ['plʊərəˌlɪz(ə)m] *n.* плюрали́зм.

plurality [plʊə'rælɪtɪ] *n.* (*plural state*) мно́жественность; (*large number*) мно́жество; (*pluralism*) совмести́тельство; (*relative majority*) относи́тельное большинство́.

plus [plʌs] *n.* **1.** (*symbol*) знак плюс. **2.** (*additional or positive quantity*) доба́вочное коли́чество.

adj. (*additional, extra*) доба́вочный; (*math., elec.*) положи́тельный.

prep. плюс; ~ **or minus** плюс-ми́нус.

cpd. **~-fours** *n. pl.* брю́к|и (*pl., g.* —) гольф.

plush [plʌʃ] *n.* плюш.

adj. (*made of ~*) плю́шевый; (*sl., sumptuous; also* **plushy**) шика́рный.

Pluto ['plu:təʊ] *n.* (*myth., astron.*) Плуто́н.

plutocracy [plu:'tɒkrəsɪ] *n.* плутокра́тия.

plutocrat ['plu:təˌkræt] *n.* плутокра́т.

plutocratic [ˌplu:tə'krætɪk] *adj.* плутократи́ческий.

plutonium [plu:'təʊnɪəm] *n.* плуто́ний.

ply[1] [plaɪ] *n.* (*layer*) слой, пласт; (*strand*) слой; **three-~ cable** трёхсло́йный/трёхжи́льный ка́бель.

cpd. **~wood** *n.* фане́ра; *adj.* фане́рный.

ply[2] [plaɪ] *v.t.* **1.** (*manipulate*): **she plied her needle** она́ занима́лась шитьём; **they plied the oars** они́ налега́ли на вёсла. **2.** (*work at*): **he plies an honest trade** он зараба́тывает на хлеб че́стным трудо́м. **3.** (*keep supplied*) по́тчевать (*impf.*); **I was plied with food** меня́ усе́рдно корми́ли; **they plied him with questions** они́ засы́пали его́ вопро́сами.

v.i. курси́ровать (*impf.*).

PM (*abbr. of* **Prime Minister**) премье́р-мини́стр.

p.m. (*abbr. of* **post meridiem**) попо́лудни; **at 5 p.m.** в 5 ч. дня.

PMT (*abbr. of* **premenstrual tension**) предменструа́льный невро́з.

pneumatic [nju:'mætɪk] *adj.* пневмати́ческий; возду́шный.

pneumonia [nju:'məʊnɪə] *n.* воспале́ние лёгких, пневмони́я.

PO *abbr. of* **1. Post Office** по́чта. **2. postal order** почто́вый перево́д. **3. Petty Officer** старшина́ (во фло́те).

po [pəʊ] (*coll.*) *n.* ночно́й горшо́к.

cpd. **~-faced** *adj.* надме́нный, презри́тельный, чва́нный.

poach[1] [pəʊtʃ] *v.t.* (*cul.*): ~ **eggs** вари́ть, с- (яйцо́-)пашо́т.

poach[2] [pəʊtʃ] *v.t. & i.*: ~ **game** браконье́рствовать (*impf.*); охо́титься (*or* уди́ть ры́бу) (*both impf.*) в чужи́х владе́ниях; **you are ~ing on my preserves** (*lit., fig.*) вы вме́шиваетесь в мои́ дела́; вы вторга́етесь в мои́ владе́ния; (*fig.*): ~ **(a ball)** (*e.g. at tennis*) перехва́т|ывать, -и́ть мяч.

poacher ['pəʊtʃə(r)] *n.* браконье́р.

pocket ['pɒkɪt] *n.* **1.** (*in clothing*) карма́н; **put your pride in your ~** спря́чьте го́рдость в карма́н; **I am always dipping into my ~ for him** мне прихо́дится всегда́ дава́ть ему́ де́ньги; **they live in each other's ~s** они́ неразлу́чны; **he has the chairman in his ~** председа́тель у него́ в рука́х. **2.** (*money resources*): **your ~ will suffer** пострада́ет ваш карма́н; э́то уда́рит по ва́шему карма́ну; **he was in ~ at the end of the day** под коне́ц дня он был в вы́игрыше; **I shall be out of ~** я бу́ду в про́игрыше; у меня́ бу́дет убы́ток; **out-of-~ expenses** расхо́ды, опла́чиваемые нали́чными. **3.** (*at billiards*) лу́за. **4.** (*small area*): ~ **of resistance** оча́г сопротивле́ния; **~s of unemployment** райо́ны безрабо́тицы. **5.**: **air ~** возду́шная я́ма; возду́шный мешо́к. **6.** (*geol.*) карма́н, гнездо́. **7.** (*attr., miniature*) карма́нный; ~ **edition** карма́нное изда́ние; ~ **battleship** «карма́нный» линко́р.

v.t. **1.** класть, положи́ть в карма́н; (*fig., appropriate*) прикарма́ни|вать, -ть. **2.: he ~ed the ball** (*billiards*) он загна́л шар в лу́зу. **3.: he had to ~ the insult** ему́ пришло́сь проглоти́ть оби́ду.

cpds. **~-book** *n.* (*notebook*) записна́я кни́жка; (*wallet*) бума́жник; **~-handkerchief** *n.* носово́й плато́к; **~-knife** *n.* карма́нный но́ж(ик); **~-money** *n.* карма́нные де́н|ьги (*pl.*, *g.* -ег); **~-size(d)** *adj.* карма́нного форма́та; миниатю́рный.

pocketful [ˈpɒkɪtˌfʊl] *n.* по́лный карма́н (*чего*).

pock-marked [ˈpɒkmɑːkt] *adj.* рябо́й.

pod [pɒd] *n.* (*seed vessel*) стручо́к.

v.t. (*shell*) лущи́ть (*impf.*).

podgy [ˈpɒdʒɪ] *adj.* то́лстенький, призе́мистый; (*of face*) пу́хлый, толстощёкий.

podium [ˈpəʊdɪəm] *n.* (*archit.*) по́диум, по́дий; (*rostrum*) трибу́на; возвыше́ние.

poem [ˈpəʊɪm] *n.* стихотворе́ние; (*long narrative*) поэ́ма.

poet [ˈpəʊɪt] *n.* поэ́т.

poetaster [ˌpəʊɪˈtæstə(r)] *n.* рифмоплёт.

poetess [ˈpəʊɪtɪs] *n.* поэте́сса.

poetic [pəʊˈetɪk] *adj.* поэти́ческий; **~ licence** поэти́ческая во́льность; **~ justice** справедли́вое возме́здие.

poetical [pəʊˈetɪk(ə)l] *adj.* поэти́ческий, поэти́чный; **~ works** поэти́ческие произведе́ния.

poetry [ˈpəʊɪtrɪ] *n.* (*also fig.*) поэ́зия; (*poetical work*) стих|и́ (*pl.*, *g.* -о́в); (*poetical quality*) поэти́чность.

pogrom [ˈpɒgrəm, -rɒm] *n.* погро́м.

poignancy [ˈpɔɪnjənsɪ] *n.* острота́, ре́зкость.

poignant [ˈpɔɪnjənt] *adj.* (*of taste etc.*) о́стрый, те́рпкий; (*painfully moving*) о́стрый, ре́зкий, го́рький.

point [pɔɪnt] *n.* **1.** (*sharp end*) остриё; **not to put too fine a ~ on it** (*fig.*) без обиняко́в; не делика́тничая; говоря́ напрями́к. **2.** (*tip*) ко́нчик. **3.** (*promontory*) мыс. **4.** (*dot*) то́чка; **full ~** то́чка; **decimal ~** (*in Russian usage*) запята́я (*отделяющая десятичную дробь от целого числа*); **two ~ five (2.5)** две це́лых и пять деся́тых; **forty-five ~ nought (45.0)** со́рок пять и ноль деся́тых; **36.6** (*human temperature Centigrade*) три́дцать шесть и шесть. **5.** (*mark*, *position*) ме́сто, пункт; **~ of contact** (*lit.*, *fig.*) то́чка соприкоснове́ния; **~ of departure** отправна́я/исхо́дная то́чка; **~ of intersection** то́чка пересече́ния; **~ of view** то́чка зре́ния; **they have reached the ~ of no return** возвра́та наза́д для них уже́ нет. **6.** (*moment*) моме́нт; **at this ~ he turned round** тут он поверну́лся; **I was on the ~ of leaving** я уже́ собра́лся уходи́ть; **at the ~ of death** при́ сме́рти; **when it came to the ~, he refused** в реша́ющий моме́нт он отказа́лся. **7.** (*mark on scale*) отме́тка, деле́ние; (*unit*) едини́ца; **boiling-~** то́чка кипе́ния; **up to a ~** до изве́стной сте́пени. **8.** (*of the compass*) страна́ све́та. **9.** (*unit of evaluation*, *score*) пункт, очко́; **they won on ~s** они́ вы́играли по очка́м; **he can give me ~s in boxing** он даст мне мно́го очко́в вперёд в бо́ксе; **he tried to score a ~ off me** (*lit.*) он попыта́лся меня́ обста́вить. **10.** (*chief idea*, *meaning*, *purpose*) суть, де́ло, вопро́с, смысл; **that is beside the ~** не в э́том суть/де́ло; **he carried his ~** он отстоя́л свою́ то́чку зре́ния; он провёл свою́ иде́ю; **come to the ~** дойти́ (*pf.*) до гла́вного/су́ти де́ла; **that's just the ~** вот и́менно; в то́м-то и де́ло; **I don't see the ~ of the joke** я не по́нял, в чём соль э́того анекдо́та; э́та шу́тка мне непоня́тна; **you have a ~ there** тут вы пра́вы; то́же ве́рно; **a case in ~** нагля́дный приме́р; **in ~ of fact** в действи́тельности; факти́чески; **his remarks lack ~** его́ замеча́ния недоста́точно конкре́тны; **I made a ~ of seeing him** я счёл необходи́мым повида́ться с ним; **you missed the ~** вы не по́няли су́ти де́ла; **there was no ~ in staying** не име́ло смы́сла остава́ться; **that's not the ~** не в э́том суть; **off the ~** некста́ти; **he is off the ~** он говори́т не по существу́; **I see your ~** я вас понима́ю; **what's the ~ of it?** како́й в э́том смысл? **11.** (*item*) пункт; **we agree on certain ~s** по не́которым пу́нктам мы схо́димся; **I explained the theory ~ by ~** я разъясни́л тео́рию по пу́нктам; **I suppose we can stretch a ~** я полага́ю, мы мо́жем сде́лать ски́дку; **it is a ~ of honour with him** для него́ э́то вопро́с че́сти; **~ of order** вопро́с к поря́дку веде́ния; **that is a ~ in his favour** э́то говори́т в его́ по́льзу. **12.** (*quality*, *trait*) черта́; **the plan has its good ~s** э́тот план не лишён досто́инств; **the weak ~ of the argument** сла́бое ме́сто в аргумента́ции; **singing is not my strong ~** я не силён в пе́нии. **13.** (*pl.*, *rail.*) стре́лочный перево́д; стре́лки (*f. pl.*). **14.** (*typ.*) то́чка, пункт. **15.** (*action of dog*) сто́йка.

v.t. **1.** (*aim*) ука́з|ывать, -а́ть; пока́з|ывать, -а́ть; **he ~ed a gun at her** он навёл на неё пистоле́т; **he ~ed a finger at her** он указа́л па́льцем на неё. **2.** (*sharpen*) точи́ть, за-. **3.** (*give force to*) заостр|я́ть, -и́ть. **4.** (*fill with mortar*): **~ brickwork** расш|ива́ть, -и́ть швы кла́дки.

v.i. ука́з|ывать, -а́ть; **the sign ~ed to the station** доро́жный знак ука́зывал направле́ние к ста́нции; **everything ~s to his guilt** всё ука́зывает на его́ вину́; (*of a dog*) де́лать, с- сто́йку.

with adv.: **~ out** *v.t.* ука́з|ывать, -а́ть на+*a.*; подч|ёркивать, -еркну́ть; **he ~ed out my mistakes** он указа́л мне на мои́ оши́бки.

cpds. **~-blank** *adj.* (*lit.*) прямо́й; (*fig.*) категори́ческий; *adv.* пря́мо, в упо́р; **~-duty** *n.* обя́занности (*f. pl.*) полице́йского-регулиро́вщика; **~sman** *n.* стре́лочник; **~-to-~** *n.* (*race*) кросс по пересечённой ме́стности.

pointed [ˈpɔɪntɪd] *adj.* **1.** (*e.g. a stick*) остроконе́чный. **2.** (*significant*, *directed against s.o.*) о́стрый, ко́лкий; подчёркнутый; **she gave me a ~ look** она́ на меня́ многозначи́тельно посмотре́ла.

pointer [ˈpɔɪntə(r)] *n.* **1.** (*rod*) ука́зка. **2.** (*of balance etc.*) стре́лка, указа́тель (*m.*). **3.** (*indication*, *hint*) намёк. **4.** (*dog*) по́йнтер.

pointillism [ˈpwæntɪˌlɪz(ə)m] *n.* пуантили́зм.

pointing [ˈpɔɪntɪŋ] *n.* (*of wall etc.*) расши́вка швов.

pointless [ˈpɔɪntlɪs] *adj.* (*purposeless*, *useless*) бессмы́сленный; **a ~ joke** пло́ская шу́тка; **it is ~ to argue with him** спо́рить с ним бессмы́сленно.

poise [pɔɪz] *n.* (*equilibrium*) равнове́сие; (*carriage*) оса́нка; (*self-possession*) уравнове́шенность, самооблада́ние.

v.t. уде́рж|ивать, -а́ть в равнове́сии; **he is ~d to attack** он гото́в к нападе́нию.

poison [ˈpɔɪz(ə)n] *n.* яд, отра́ва; **he hates me like ~** он меня́ смерте́льно ненави́дит.

v.t. (*lit.*, *fig.*) отрав|ля́ть, -и́ть; **he has food ~ing** он отрави́лся.

cpds. **~-gas** *n.* ядови́тый газ; **~-ivy** *n.* сума́х ядоно́сный/укореня́ющийся; **~-pen** *adj.*: **~-pen letter** анони́мка.

poisoner [ˈpɔɪzənə(r)] *n.* отрави́тель (*fem.* -ница).

poisonous [ˈpɔɪzənəs] *adj.* ядови́тый; (*fig.*) вре́дный; (*vicious*) злой, ядови́тый; (*coll.*, *repulsive*) проти́вный.

poke [pəʊk] *n.* (*prod*) толчо́к; **give the fire a ~!** повороши́те/пошуру́йте у́гли/дрова́; **he gave me a ~ in the ribs** он толкну́л меня́ в бок.

v.t. **1.** (*prod*) ты́кать, ткнуть. **2.** (*thrust*) пиха́ть (*impf.*); сова́ть (*impf.*); **he ~d his stick through the fence** он просу́нул па́лку че́рез забо́р; **he ~d his tongue out** он вы́сунул язы́к; **he ~s his nose into other people's business** он суёт нос не в своё де́ло; **he ~d fun at me** он насмеха́лся надо мно́й. **3.** (*cause by prodding*): **the boy ~d a hole in his drum** ма́льчик продыря́вил бараба́н.

v.i.: **he ~d about among the rubbish** он ры́лся в му́соре.

poke-bonnet [ˈpəʊkˌbɒnɪt] *n.* да́мская шля́пка с козырько́м.

poker [ˈpəʊkə(r)] *n.* **1.** (*for a fire*) кочерга́; **gas ~** га́зовая зажига́лка. **2.** (*game*) по́кер.

cpds. **~-face** *n.* бесстра́стное/ка́менное лицо́; **~-faced** *adj.* с ка́менным выраже́нием лица́; **~-work** *n.* выжига́ние по де́реву.

poky [ˈpəʊkɪ] *adj.* (*coll.*) те́сный, убо́гий.

Poland [ˈpəʊlənd] *n.* По́льша.

polar [ˈpəʊlə(r)] *adj.* **1.** (*of or near either Pole*) поля́рный; **~ bear** бе́лый медве́дь; **~ exploration** иссле́дование поля́рных райо́нов. **2.** (*elec.*) поля́рный, по́люсный. **3.** (*geom.*) поля́рный.

polarity [pəˈlærɪtɪ] *n.* (*lit.*, *fig.*) поля́рность.

polarization [ˌpəʊləraɪˈzeɪʃ(ə)n] *n.* (*lit.*, *fig.*) поляриза́ция.

polarize [ˈpəʊləˌraɪz] *v.t.* & *i.* (*lit.*, *fig.*) поляризова́ть(ся) (*impf.*).

pole[1] [pəʊl] *n.* (*of the earth; also elec. and fig.*) по́люс; **an expedition to the P~** экспеди́ция к по́люсу; **he and his sister are ~s apart** они́ с сестро́й — две противополо́жности.
cpd. **~-star** *n.* Поля́рная звезда́.
pole[2] [pəʊl] *n.* (*post, rod etc.*) столб, шест; **up the ~** (*sl.*) (*crazy*) не в своём уме́; (*in difficulties*) в тяжёлом положе́нии.
cpds. **~-jumping, ~-vault** *nn.* прыжки́ (*m. pl.*) с шесто́м; **~-vaulter** *n.* шестови́к.
Pole[3] [pəʊl] *n.* (*pers.*) поля́к (*fem.* по́лька).
pole-axe ['pəʊlæks] *n.* (*old weapon*) секи́ра; (*butcher's implement*) топо́р.
v.t. заб|ива́ть, -и́ть (*скот*).
polecat ['pəʊlkæt] *n.* лесно́й хорёк.
polemic [pə'lemɪk] *n.* поле́мика; спор.
adj. (*also* **~al**) полеми́ческий, спо́рный.
polemicist [pə'lemɪsɪst] *n.* полеми́ст; спо́рщик.
police [pə'li:s] *n.* поли́ция, (*in former USSR*) мили́ция; **~ constable** полице́йский, (*in Britain*) консте́бль (*m.*); **~ force** поли́ция; **a ~ state** полице́йское госуда́рство.
v.t. соблюда́ть (*impf.*) поря́док и дисципли́ну в+*p.*; (*of pers.*) держа́ть (*impf.*) в струне́.
cpds. **~-court** *n.* полице́йский суд; **~-magistrate** *n.* судья́, председа́тельствующий в полице́йском суде́; **~man** *n.* полисме́н, полице́йский; (*in former USSR*) милиционе́р; **~-officer** *n.* полице́йский; **~-station** *n.* (полице́йский) уча́сток; мили́ция, отделе́ние мили́ции; **~woman** *n.* же́нщина-полице́йский/милиционе́р.
policlinic [,pɒlɪ'klɪnɪk] *n.* поликли́ника.
policy ['pɒlɪsɪ] *n.* (*planned course of action*) поли́тика, курс; (*statecraft*) поли́тика; (*insurance*) страхово́й по́лис.
cpd. **~-holder** *n.* держа́тель (*m.*) страхово́го по́лиса.
polio(myelitis) [,pəʊlɪəʊ,maɪə'laɪtɪs] *n.* полиомиели́т.
polish[1] ['pɒlɪʃ] *n.* **1.** (*smoothness, brightness*) полиро́вка. **2.** (*substance used for ~ing*) политу́ра. **3.** (*act of ~ing*) полиро́вка; **I must give my shoes a ~** я до́лжен почи́стить ту́фли. **4.** (*fig., refinement*) то́нкость; лоск.
v.t. полирова́ть, от-; (*fig.*) шлифова́ть, от-; **~ed** (*behaviour etc.*) све́тский, ве́жливый.
with advs.: **~ off** *v.t.* (*coll., finish*) разде́латься (*pf.*) с+*i.*; **I must ~ off this letter** я до́лжен поко́нчить с э́тим письмо́м; **he ~ed off the cake** он бы́стро распра́вился с пирого́м; **~ up** *v.t.* (*lit., give gloss to*) прид|ава́ть, -а́ть лоск +*d.*; **she ~ed up the silver** она́ почи́стила серебро́; (*fig., improve*) соверше́нствовать, у-; **I must ~ up my French** мне ну́жно освежи́ть (в па́мяти) францу́зский язы́к.
Polish[2] ['pəʊlɪʃ] *n.* (*language*) по́льский язы́к.
adj. по́льский.
polisher ['pɒlɪʃə(r)] *n.* (*workman*) поли́ровщик; (*machine*) полирова́льная маши́на.
Politburo ['pɒlɪt,bjʊərəʊ] *n.* политбюро́ (*indecl.*).
polite [pə'laɪt] *adj.* ве́жливый, учти́вый, воспи́танный; **~ society** хоро́шее/культу́рное о́бщество.
politeness [pə'laɪtnɪs] *n.* ве́жливость, учти́вость, воспи́танность.
politic ['pɒlɪtɪk] *adj.* **1.** (*prudent*) благоразу́мный. **2.: the body ~** госуда́рство, полити́ческая систе́ма.
political [pə'lɪtɪk(ə)l] *adj.* полити́ческий; (*pert. to internal politics*) внутриполити́ческий; **~ science** политоло́гия.
politician [,pɒlɪ'tɪʃ(ə)n] *n.* поли́тик; (*pej.*) поли́тик, политика́н.
politics ['pɒlɪtɪks] *n.* поли́тика; **party ~** парти́йная поли́тика; **he went into ~ as a young man** он вступи́л на полити́ческое по́прище в мо́лодости; (*political views*) полити́ческие взгля́ды (*m. pl.*); **what are his ~?** каковы́ его́ полити́ческие убежде́ния?
polity ['pɒlɪtɪ] *n.* (*form of government*) госуда́рственное устро́йство; (*organized society, state*) госуда́рство.
polka ['pɒlkə, 'pəʊlkə] *n.* по́лька.
cpd. **~-dot** *n.* (*pattern*) узо́р в горо́шек; (*attr.*): **~-dot dress** пла́тье в горо́шек.
poll[1] [pəʊl] *n.* (*voting process*) голосова́ние; **the country will go to the ~s in May** страна́ бу́дет голосова́ть (*or* в стране́ бу́дут вы́боры) в ма́е; (*list of voters/candidates*) спи́сок избира́телей/кандида́тов; **he came head of the ~** он получи́л наибо́льшее коли́чество/число́ голосо́в; (*counting of votes*) подсчёт голосо́в; (*number of votes*) коли́чество по́данных голосо́в; **there was a light/heavy ~** акти́вность избира́телей была́ ни́зкой/высо́кой; (*opinion canvass*) опро́с.
v.t. **1.** (*receive*): **he ~ed 60,000 votes** он получи́л 60 000 голосо́в. **2.** (*take votes of*): **they ~ed the meeting** они́ поста́вили вопро́с на голосова́ние.
cpd. **~-tax** *n.* поду́шный нало́г.
poll[2] [pɒl] *n.* (*coll., parrot*) «по́пка» (*m.*).
pollard ['pɒləd] *n.* подстри́женное де́рево; (*attr.*) подстри́женный.
v.t. подстр|ига́ть, -и́чь (*дерево*).
pollen ['pɒlən] *n.* цвето́чная пыльца́.
pollinate ['pɒlɪ,neɪt] *v.t.* опыл|я́ть, -и́ть.
pollination [,pɒlɪ'neɪʃ(ə)n] *n.* опыле́ние.
polling ['pəʊlɪŋ] *n.* голосова́ние.
cpds. **~-booth** *n.* каби́на для голосова́ния; **~-day** *n.* день вы́боров; **~-station** *n.* избира́тельный уча́сток.
pollster ['pəʊlstə(r)] *n.* лицо́, производя́щее опро́с обще́ственного мне́ния.
pollutant [pə'lu:tənt] *n.* загрязни́тель (*m.*); поллюта́нт.
pollute [pə'lu:t] *v.t.* загрязн|я́ть, -и́ть; (*fig.*) оскверн|я́ть, -и́ть.
pollution [pə'lu:ʃ(ə)n] *n.* загрязне́ние; **environmental ~** загрязне́ние окружа́ющей среды́; (*fig.*) оскверне́ние.
polo ['pəʊləʊ] *n.* по́ло (*indecl.*).
cpd. **~-neck** (*sweater*) *n.* сви́тер с закры́тым высо́ким воротнико́м; «водола́зка».
polonaise [,pɒlə'neɪz] *n.* полоне́з.
polonium [pə'ləʊnɪəm] *n.* поло́ний.
poltergeist ['pɒltə,gaɪst] *n.* полтерге́йст.
poltroon [pɒl'tru:n] *n.* (*arch.*) трус.
polyandry ['pɒlɪ,ændrɪ] *n.* полиа́ндрия, многому́жие.
polyanthus [,pɒlɪ'ænθəs] *n.* при́мула высо́кая.
polyclinic ['pɒlɪ,klɪnɪk] *n.* поликли́ника.
polygamist [pə'lɪgəmɪst] *n.* полигами́ст.
polygamous [pə'lɪgəməs] *adj.* полига́мный.
polygamy [pə'lɪgəmɪ] *n.* полига́мия, многобра́чие.
polyglot ['pɒlɪ,glɒt] *n.* полигло́т.
adj. многоязы́чный.
polygon ['pɒlɪgən, -,gɒn] *n.* многоуго́льник.
polygonal [pə'lɪgən(ə)l] *adj.* многоуго́льный.
polygraph ['pɒlɪ,grɑ:f] *n.* полигра́ф.
polymath ['pɒlɪ,mæθ] *n.* эруди́т; всесторо́нне осведомлённый челове́к.
polymer ['pɒlɪmə(r)] *n.* полиме́р.
Polynesia [,pɒlɪ'ni:ʒə] *n.* Полине́зия.
Polynesian [,pɒlɪ'ni:ʒ(ə)n] *n.* полинези́|ец; (*fem.* -йка).
adj. полинези́йский.
polyp ['pɒlɪp] *n.* (*zool., med.*) поли́п.
polyphonic [,pɒlɪ'fɒnɪk] *adj.* полифони́ческий.
polyphony [pə'lɪfənɪ] *n.* полифони́я.
polypus ['pɒlɪpəs] *n.* поли́п.
polystyrene [,pɒlɪ'staɪə,ri:n] *n.* полистиро́л.
polysyllabic [,pɒlɪsɪ'læbɪk] *adj.* многосло́жный.
polysyllable ['pɒlɪ,sɪləb(ə)l] *n.* многосло́жное сло́во.
polytechnic [,pɒlɪ'teknɪk] *n.* полите́хникум.
adj. политехни́ческий.
polytheism ['pɒlɪθi:,ɪz(ə)m] *n.* полите́изм.
polytheist ['pɒlɪ,θi:ɪst] *n.* полите́ист.
polytheistic [,pɒlɪθi:'ɪstɪk] *adj.* политеисти́ческий.
polythene ['pɒlɪ,θi:n] *n.* полиэтиле́н; (*attr.*) полиэтиле́новый.
polyunsaturated [,pɒlɪʌn'sætʃə,reɪtɪd] *adj.*: **~ fats** полинасы́щенные жиры́.
pom [pɒm] (*coll.*) = **pomeranian**
pomade [pə'mɑ:d] *n.* пома́да.
v.t. пома́дить, на-.
pomander [pə'mændə(r)] *n.* ша́рик с аромати́ческими тра́вами.
pomegranate ['pɒmɪ,grænɪt, 'pɒm,grænɪt] *n.* грана́т.
Pomeranian [,pɒmə'reɪnɪən] *n.* (*dog*) шпиц.
pommel ['pʌm(ə)l] *n.* (*of saddle*) лука́; (*of sword*) голо́вка.
v.t. = **pummel**

pomp [pɒmp] *n.* пы́шность, по́мпа.
pompano [pɒm'pɑːnəʊ] *n.* трохино́тус.
Pompey ['pɒmpɪ] *n.* Помпе́й.
pom-pom ['pɒmpɒm] *n.* (*mil.*) малокали́берная зени́тная устано́вка.
pompon ['pɒmpɒn] *n.* (*tuft*) помпо́н.
pomposity [pɒm'pɒsɪtɪ] *n.* помпё́зность; (*of pers.*) напы́щенность.
pompous ['pɒmpəs] *adj.* помпё́зный; (*of pers.*) напы́щенный.
ponce [pɒns] *n.* (*coll.*) сутенё́р.
v.i.: ~ **about/around** шикова́ть (*impf.*), выпе́ндриваться (*impf.*).
poncho ['pɒntʃəʊ] *n.* наки́дка «по́нчо», (*indecl.*).
pond [pɒnd] *n.* пруд.
cpds. **~-life** *n.* прудова́я фа́уна; **~weed** *n.* рдест.
ponder ['pɒndə(r)] *v.t.* обду́м|ывать, -ать; взве́|шивать, -сить.
v.i. размышля́ть (*impf.*).
ponderable ['pɒndərəb(ə)l] *adj.* (*fig.*) весо́мый, значи́тельный.
ponderous ['pɒndərəs] *adj.* (*heavy*) тяжё́лый; (*bulky*) масси́вный; (*of style etc.*) тяжё́лове́сный.
pong [pɒŋ] *n.* (*coll.*) вонь, злово́ние.
poniard ['pɒnjəd] *n.* коро́ткий кинжа́л.
v.t. зак|а́лывать, -оло́ть кинжа́лом.
pontiff ['pɒntɪf] *n.* (*high priest*) первосвяще́нник; (*bishop*) епи́скоп; **supreme ~** (*the Pope*) па́па ри́мский.
pontifical [pɒn'tɪfɪk(ə)l] *adj.* епи́скопский, епископа́льный; (*fig.*) догмати́ческий.
pontificals [pɒn'tɪfɪkəls] *n.* (*vestments*) архиере́йское облаче́ние.
pontificate [pɒn'tɪfɪkət] *n.* (*office*) понтифика́т.
v.i. (*fig.*, *lay down the law*) веща́ть (*impf.*).
pontoon [pɒn'tuːn] *n.* **1.** (*boat*) понто́н; **~ bridge** понто́нный мост. **2.** (*card game*) два́дцать одно́.
pony ['pəʊnɪ] *n.* (*horse*) по́ни (*m. indecl.*); (*sl.*, *£25*) два́дцать пять фу́нтов сте́рлингов.
cpd. **~-tail** *n.* «ко́нский хвост».
poodle ['puːd(ə)l] *n.* пу́дель (*m.*).
poof (ter) [pʊf, 'pʊftə(r)] *n.* (*sl.*) го́мик.
poofy ['pʊfɪ] *adj.* (*sl.*) женоподо́бный.
pooh [puː] *int.* фу!; уф!
pooh-pooh [puː'puː] *v.t.* фы́ркать (*impf.*) на+*a.*; относи́ться (*impf.*) пренебрежи́тельно к+*d.*
pool[1] [puːl] *n.* (*small body of water*) пруд; (*puddle*) лу́жа; **(swimming-~)** бассе́йн; (*still place in river*) за́водь.
pool[2] [puːl] *n.* **1.** (*total of staked money*) пу́лька; совоку́пность ста́вок; **football ~s** футбо́льный тотализа́тор. **2.** (*business arrangement*) пул. **3.** (*common reserve*) о́бщий фонд. **4.** (*billiards game*) пул. **5.: typing ~** машинопи́сное бюро́ (*indecl.*).
v.t. объедин|я́ть, -и́ть в о́бщий фонд; **we ~ed our resources** мы объедени́ли на́ши ресу́рсы.
cpd. **~-room** *n.* билья́рдная.
poop [puːp] *n.* (*of ship*) корма́.
pooped [puːpt] *adj.* изнурё́нный, вы́дохшийся.
poor [pʊə(r)] *n.* (*collect.*: **the ~**) бедняки́ (*m. pl.*), бе́дные (*pl.*); **the ~ ye have always with you** (*bibl.*) ни́щих всегда́ име́ете с собо́й.
adj. **1.** (*indigent*) бе́дный. **2.** (*unfortunate*, *deserving of sympathy*) бе́дный, несча́стный; **the ~ fellow has nowhere to sleep** бедня́ге не́где переночева́ть; **~ little chap!** бедня́жка! **3.** (*small*, *scanty*) ску́дный; плохо́й; **a ~ supply** плохо́е снабже́ние; **a ~ harvest** ни́зкий урожа́й; **a ~ response** сла́бый о́тклик. **4.** (*of low quality*) плохо́й; **~ soil** бе́дная, неплодоро́дная по́чва; **~ health** сла́бое здоро́вье. **5.** (*miserable*, *spiritless*) несча́стный, жа́лкий.
cpds. **~-box** *n.* кру́жка для сбо́ра в по́льзу бе́дных; **~-house** *n.* богаде́льня; **~-spirited** *adj.* ро́бкий, малоду́шный.
poorly ['pʊəlɪ] *adj.* нездоро́вый; **are you feeling ~?** вам нездоро́вится?
adv. бе́дно; пло́хо; **his parents are ~ off** его́ роди́тели живу́т бе́дно; **this book is ~ written** э́та кни́га пло́хо напи́сана.
poorness ['pʊənɪs] *n.* (*poor quality*) бе́дность; недоста́точность; **the ~ of the soil** ску́дость/неплодоро́дность по́чвы.
pop[1] [pɒp] *n.* (*explosive sound*) щё́лк, треск; (*coll.*, *gaseous drink*) шипу́чий напи́ток; (*sl.*, *pawn*): **in ~** в закла́де.
adv.: **the balloon went ~** ша́рик ло́пнул; **the cork went ~** про́бка ло́пнула.
v.t. **1.** (*cause to explode*): **~ a balloon** проколо́ть (*pf.*) ша́рик. **2.** (*put suddenly*) сова́ть, су́нуть; **he ~ped his head through the window** он вы́сунул го́лову из окна́; **~ the question** (*coll.*) сде́лать (*pf.*) предложе́ние. **3.** (*sl.*, *pawn*) за|кла́дывать, -ложи́ть.
v.i. (*make explosive sound*) тре́скаться (*impf.*); **the sound of a cork ~ping** звук вы́стрелившей про́бки; (*shoot*) стрельну́ть (*pf.*), (*coll.*) пульну́ть (*pf.*); **they were ~ping away at the target** они́ пали́ли по мише́ни.
with advs. (*coll.*): **they ~ped in for a drink** они́ заскочи́ли/забежа́ли вы́пить; **I am ~ping off home now** ну, я побежа́л домо́й; **he ~ped off** (*died*) **last week** на про́шлой неде́ле он отда́л концы́ (*sl.*); **his eyes ~ped out** он вы́лупил глаза́; **I'll ~ over to the shop** я сбе́гаю в магази́н.
cpds. **~corn** *n.* по́пкорн; возду́шная кукуру́за; **~-eyed** *adj.* пучегла́зый; **~-gun** *n.* пуга́ч.
pop[2] [pɒp] *n.* (*coll.*, *abbr. of* **popular 2.**) (*music*) поп-му́зыка.
adj.: **~ art** поп-иску́сство; **~ artist** поп-худо́жник; **~ concert** поп-конце́рт; **~ singer** поп-пев|е́ц (*fem.* -и́ца); исполни́тель (*fem.* -ница) поп-му́зыки.
pop[3] [pɒp] *n.* (*US coll.*, *father*) па́пка, ба́тька (*both m.*).
pope [pəʊp] *n.* (*bishop of Rome*) па́па (*m.*); (*Orthodox priest*) поп.
popery ['pəʊpərɪ] *n.* (*pej.*) папи́зм.
popinjay ['pɒpɪn,dʒeɪ] *n.* (*conceited pers.*) вообража́ла (*c.g.*); (*fop*) фат, хлыщ.
popish ['pəʊpɪʃ] *adj.* (*pej.*) католи́ческий.
poplar ['pɒplə(r)] *n.* то́поль (*m.*).
poplin ['pɒplɪn] *n.* popли́н.
poppa ['pɒpə] *n.* (*US coll.*) па́пка, па́па, ба́тя, папа́ня (*all m.*).
poppet ['pɒpɪt] *n.* (*as term of endearment*) кро́шка, малы́шка; **she is a ~** она́ пре́лесть.
poppy ['pɒpɪ] *n.* мак; (*attr.*) ма́ковый.
cpds. **~-head** *n.* коро́бочка/голо́вка ма́ка; **~-seed** *n.* мак.
poppycock ['pɒpɪ,kɒk] *n.* чепуха́ (*coll.*).
popsy ['pɒpsɪ] *n.* кро́шка, ку́колка (*coll.*).
populace ['pɒpjʊləs] *n.* (*the masses*) ма́ссы (*f. pl.*); (*mob*) чернь.
popular ['pɒpjʊlə(r)] *adj.* **1.** (*of the people*) наро́дный; **~ front** наро́дный фронт. **2.** (*suited to the needs*, *tastes etc. of the people*): **the ~ press** ма́ссовая пре́сса/печа́ть; **~ prices** общедосту́пные це́ны; **~ science** нау́чно-популя́рная литерату́ра; **~ song** популя́рная пе́сня. **3.** (*generally liked*) по́льзу́ющийся о́бщей симпа́тией; **she is ~ at school** её́ лю́бят в шко́ле; **he is ~ with the ladies** он име́ет успе́х у же́нщин; **he is not ~ with his colleagues** колле́ги его́ недолю́бливают.
popularity [,pɒpjʊ'lærɪtɪ] *n.* популя́рность; успе́х.
popularization [,pɒpjʊləraɪ'zeɪʃ(ə)n] *n.* популяриза́ция.
popularize ['pɒpjʊlə,raɪz] *v.t.* популяризи́ровать (*impf.*).
popularly ['pɒpjʊləlɪ] *adv.*: **he was ~ supposed to be a magician** в наро́де его́ счита́ли волше́бником.
populate ['pɒpjʊ,leɪt] *v.t.* насел|я́ть, -и́ть; засел|я́ть, -и́ть.
population [,pɒpjʊ'leɪʃ(ə)n] *n.* населе́ние; жи́тели (*m. pl.*).
populism ['pɒpjʊlɪz(ə)m] *n.* (*Russ. hist.*) наро́дничество.
populist ['pɒpjʊlɪst] *n.* (*Russ. hist.*) наро́дник.
adj. попули́стский, наро́днический.
populous ['pɒpjʊləs] *adj.* многолю́дный, густонаселё́нный.
porcelain ['pɔːsəlɪn] *n.* фарфо́р; (*attr.*) фарфо́ровый.
porch [pɔːtʃ] *n.* (*covered entrance*) подъе́зд, по́ртик; (*US*, *verandah*) вера́нда, балко́н.
porcine ['pɔːsaɪn] *adj.* свино́й.
porcupine ['pɔːkjʊ,paɪn] *n.* дикобра́з.
pore[1] [pɔː(r)] *n.* по́ра.
pore[2] [pɔː(r)] *v.i.*: **he likes to ~ over old books** он лю́бит сиде́ть над ста́рыми кни́гами.

pork [pɔ:k] *n.* свини́на; ~ **chop** свина́я отбивна́я котле́та; ~ **pie** пиро́г со свини́ной.

cpd. ~-**butcher** *n.* свинобо́ец.

porker ['pɔ:kə(r)] *n.* отко́рмленный на убо́й поросёнок.

pork|y ['pɔ:kɪ] *n.* (*sl.*): **tell ~ies** лить/отлива́ть (*impf.*) пу́ли.

porn(o) ['pɔ:nəʊ] *n.* (*coll.*) порногра́фия.

pornographer [pɔ:'nɒgrəfə(r)] *n.* челове́к, распространя́ющий порногра́фию.

pornographic [ˌpɔ:nə'græfɪk] *adj.* порнографи́ческий.

pornography [pɔ:'nɒgrəfɪ] *n.* порногра́фия.

porosity [pɔ:'rɒsɪtɪ] *n.* по́ристость.

porous ['pɔ:rəs] *adj.* по́ристый.

porphyry ['pɔ:fɪrɪ] *n.* порфи́р.

porpoise ['pɔ:pəs] *n.* морска́я свинья́.

porridge ['pɒrɪdʒ] *n.* овся́ная ка́ша; **save your breath to cool your** ~ ≃ сиди́ и пома́лкивай; держи́ язы́к за зуба́ми.

porringer ['pɒrɪndʒə(r)] *n.* ми́сочка.

port[1] [pɔ:t] *n.* (*harbour*) порт, га́вань; **P~ of London** Ло́ндонский порт; ~ **of call** порт захо́да; (*fig.*) приста́нище; **free** ~ во́льная га́вань; **any ~ in a storm** (*fig.*) в бу́рю люба́я га́вань хороша́.

port[2] [pɔ:t] *n.* (*left side*) ле́вый борт; **hard to ~!** ле́во руля́!; **on the ~ bow** сле́ва по́ носу.

port[3] [pɔ:t] *n.* (*wine*) портве́йн.

port[4] [pɔ:t] *n.* (*mil.*) строева́я сто́йка с ору́жием; ~ **arms!** на грудь!

portability [ˌpɔ:tə'bɪlɪtɪ] *n.* портати́вность.

portable ['pɔ:təb(ə)l] *adj.* портати́вный.

portage ['pɔ:tɪdʒ] *n.* перено́ска, перево́з; перепра́ва во́локом.

v.t. перепр|авля́ть, -а́вить во́локом.

portal ['pɔ:t(ə)l] *n.* порта́л.

portcullis [pɔ:t'kʌlɪs] *n.* опускна́я решётка.

portend [pɔ:'tend] *v.t.* предвеща́ть (*impf.*).

portent ['pɔ:tent, -t(ə)nt] *n.* (*omen*) предзнаменова́ние; (*marvel*) чу́до.

portentous [pɔ:'tentəs] *adj.* (*prophetic*) ве́щий; (*significant*) многозначи́тельный; (*pompous*) напы́щенный.

porter ['pɔ:tə(r)] *n.* **1.** (*carrier of luggage etc.*) носи́льщик. **2.** (*US, sleeping car attendant*) проводни́к. **3.** (*door-keeper*) швейца́р; **~'s lodge** до́мик привра́тника; дво́рницкая. **4.** (*type of beer*) по́ртер.

porterage ['pɔ:tərɪdʒ] *n.* перено́ска, доста́вка.

portfolio [pɔ:t'fəʊlɪəʊ] *n.* **1.** (*case*) портфе́ль (*m.*), па́пка. **2.** (*of investments*) пе́речень (*m.*) це́нных бума́г. **3.** (*ministerial office*) портфе́ль (*m.*); **minister without ~** мини́стр без портфе́ля.

porthole ['pɔ:thəʊl] *n.* иллюмина́тор.

portico ['pɔ:tɪˌkəʊ] *n.* по́ртик.

portière [ˌpɔ:tɪ'eə(r)] *n.* портье́ра.

portion ['pɔ:ʃ(ə)n] *n.* (*part, share*) часть; до́ля; (*of food*) по́рция; (*dowry*) прида́ное; (*lot*) до́ля.

v.t. (*divide*) дели́ть, раз-; ~ **out** (*distribute*) произв|оди́ть, -ести́ разде́л +*g*.

portionless ['pɔ:ʃənlɪs] *adj.*: **a ~ girl** бесприда́нница.

portliness ['pɔ:tlɪnɪs] *n.* доро́дство, полнота́, ту́чность.

portly ['pɔ:tlɪ] *adj.* доро́дный, по́лный, ту́чный.

portmanteau [pɔ:t'mæntəʊ] *n.* складно́й саквоя́ж.

portrait ['pɔ:trɪt] *n.* портре́т.

portraitist ['pɔ:trɪtɪst] *n.* портрети́ст.

portraiture ['pɔ:trɪtʃə(r)] *n.* портре́тная жи́вопись; описа́ние, характери́стика.

portray [pɔ:'treɪ] *v.t.* (*depict, describe*) рисова́ть, на- портре́т +*g.*; (*act part of*) игра́ть, сыгра́ть; созда́ть (*pf.*) о́браз +*g.*

portrayal [pɔ:'treɪəl] *n.* изображе́ние, о́браз.

Portugal ['pɔ:tjʊg(ə)l] *n.* Португа́лия.

Portuguese [ˌpɔ:tjʊ'gi:z, ˌpɔ:tʃ-] *n.* **1.** (*pers.*) португа́л|ец (*fem.* -ка); **the P~** (*pl.*) португа́льцы (*m. pl.*). **2.** (*language*) португа́льский язы́к.

adj. португа́льский.

pose [pəʊz] *n.* (*of body or mind*) по́за.

v.t. (*put in desired position*) ста́вить, по- в по́зу; (*put forward, propound*) предл|ага́ть, -ожи́ть; изл|ага́ть, -ожи́ть; **this ~s an awkward problem** э́то создаёт серьёзную пробле́му.

v.i. **1.** (*take up a position or attitude*) пози́ровать (*impf.*); **they ~d for the photograph** они́ пози́ровали для фотогра́фии; **he ~s as an expert** он выдаёт себя́ за знатока́/специали́ста. **2.** (*behave in an affected way*) рисова́ться (*impf.*).

poser ['pəʊzə(r)] *n.* (*problem*) загво́здка, закавы́ка.

poseur [pəʊ'zɜ:(r)] *n.* позёр.

posh [pɒʃ] *adj.* (*coll.*) шика́рный, фешене́бельный.

posit ['pɒzɪt] *v.t.* (*postulate*) постули́ровать (*impf.*).

position [pə'zɪʃ(ə)n] *n.* **1.** (*place occupied by s.o. or sth.*) ме́сто; **he took up his ~ by the door** он за́нял своё ме́сто у две́ри; (*mil.*) пози́ция; **the enemy's ~s were stormed** пози́ции врага́ бы́ли взя́ты шту́рмом. **2.** (*situation, circumstances*) положе́ние; **the ~ is desperate** положе́ние отча́янное; **that puts me in an awkward ~** э́то ста́вит меня́ в неудо́бное положе́ние; **I am not in a ~ to say** я не в состоя́нии сказа́ть. **3.** (*posture*) по́за; **he assumed a sitting ~** он при́нял сидя́чую по́зу. **4.** (*mental attitude, line of argument*) пози́ция; **allow me to state my ~** разреши́те мне вы́сказать свою́ то́чку зре́ния. **5.** (*place in society, status*) положе́ние; **he is a man of wealth and ~** у него́ есть и де́ньги и положе́ние. **6.** (*post, employment*) до́лжность, ме́сто; **I am looking for a ~ as tutor** я ищу́ ме́сто репети́тора.

v.t. (*place in ~*) ста́вить, по-; поме|ща́ть, -сти́ть; (*determine ~ of*) разме|ща́ть, -сти́ть.

positive ['pɒzɪtɪv] *n.* (*gram.*) положи́тельная сте́пень; (*math.*) положи́тельная величина́; (*phot.*) позити́в.

adj. **1.** (*definite, explicit*) несомне́нный, определённый; **to my ~ knowledge he has not seen her** я то́чно зна́ю, что он её не ви́дел; **proof ~** несомне́нное доказа́тельство. **2.** (*convinced, certain*) уве́ренный, убеждённый; **are you ~ you saw him?** вы уве́рены, что ви́дели его́?; **I am quite ~ on that point** я в э́том абсолю́тно убеждён. **3.** (*assertive*) самоуве́ренный. **4.** (*practical, helpful*) положи́тельный; **a ~ suggestion** де́льное предложе́ние. **5.** (*downright*) абсолю́тный, зако́нченный; **he is a ~ fool** он зако́нченный дура́к. **6.** (*gram., math., elec.*) положи́тельный; **a ~ charge** положи́тельный заря́д; **the ~ sign** знак плюс. **7.** (*phot.*) позити́вный.

positively ['pɒzɪtɪvlɪ] *adv.* несомне́нно, я́сно, абсолю́тно; **his opinions were ~ expressed** его́ сужде́ния бы́ли вы́ражены я́сно/категори́чески; **'Are you warm enough?' — 'Positively!'** «Вам тепло́?» — «О, да!»; **she was ~ rude to me** она́ была́ со мной про́сто груба́.

positivism ['pɒzɪtɪˌvɪz(ə)m] *n.* позитиви́зм.

positivist ['pɒzɪtˌvɪst] *n.* позитиви́ст.

positron ['pɒzɪˌtrɒn] *n.* позитро́н.

posse ['pɒsɪ] *n.* отря́д полице́йских.

possess [pə'zes] *v.t.* **1.** (*own, have*) владе́ть (*impf.*) +*i.*; облада́ть (*impf.*) +*i.*; **all I ~ is yours** всё, что я име́ю, — ва́ше. **2.** (*keep control of, maintain*): ~ **o.s. in patience** сохраня́ть (*impf.*) споко́йствие. **3.**: ~ **o.s. of** (*acquire*) приобре|та́ть, -сти́; **the thief ~ed himself of my purse** вор присво́ил себе́ мой кошелёк. **4.**: **be ~ed of** (*endowed with*) быть наделённым +*i*. **5.** (*dominate, influence*) овлад|ева́ть, -е́ть; захва́т|ывать, -и́ть; **witches were thought to be ~ed by the devil** счита́лось, что ве́дьмы одержи́мы дья́волом; **he is ~ed by one idea** он одержи́м одно́й иде́ей; **whatever ~ed him to do that?** что его́ заста́вило/дёрнуло поступи́ть таки́м о́бразом? **6.** (*sexually*) овладе́ть (*pf.*) +*i*.

possession [pə'zeʃ(ə)n] *n.* **1.** (*ownership, occupation*) владе́ние; **she came into ~ of a fortune** она́ получи́ла состоя́ние в насле́дство; **they took ~ of the house** они́ ста́ли владе́льцами до́ма; **the documents are in my ~** докуме́нты в мои́х рука́х; **he is in full ~ of his senses** он в здра́вом уме́; **~ is nine points of the law** владе́ние иму́ществом почти́ равно́ пра́ву на него́. **2.** (*property*) иму́щество, со́бственность. **3.** (*territory*) владе́ния (*nt. pl.*); **Britain's overseas ~s** замо́рские/заокеа́нские владе́ния Великобрита́нии. **4.** (*diabolic etc.*) одержи́мость. **5.** (*sexual*) облада́ние.

possessive [pə'zesɪv] *n.* (*gram.*) притяжа́тельный паде́ж.

adj. **1.** (*gram.*) притяжа́тельный. **2.** (*of pers.*) со́бственнический, хва́ткий; (*jealous*) ревни́вый; **she is a ~ mother** она́ вла́стная мать.

possessiveness [pə'zesıvnıs] *n.* ревни́вость.

possessor [pə'zesə(r)] *n.* (*owner*) владе́лец, облада́тель (*m.*); (*holder*) факти́ческий владе́лец.

possibilit|y [ˌpɒsı'bılıtı] *n.* возмо́жность; (*likelihood*) вероя́тность, вероя́тие; **there is no ~y of his coming** возмо́жность его́ прихо́да исключена́; **it is within the bounds of ~y** э́то в преде́лах возмо́жности; (*pl.*, *potentiality*) возмо́жности (*f. pl.*); перспекти́вы (*f. pl.*); **the idea has great ~ies** э́та иде́я открыва́ет больши́е возмо́жности.

possible ['pɒsıb(ə)l] *n.* (~ *choice*) возмо́жное.

adj. **1.** возмо́жный; (*achievable*) осуществи́мый; **as soon as ~** как мо́жно скоре́е; **I have done everything ~ to help** я сде́лал всё возмо́жное, что́бы помо́чь. **2.** (*tolerable*, *reasonable*) терпи́мый, сно́сный; **he is the only ~ man for the job** он еди́нственный челове́к, кото́рый подхо́дит для э́той рабо́ты.

possibly ['pɒsıblı] *adv.* **1.** (*in accordance with what is possible*) возмо́жно; вероя́тно; **how can I ~ do that?** как же я могу́ э́то сде́лать? **2.** (*perhaps*) возмо́жно; мо́жет быть.

possum ['pɒsəm] *n.* (*coll.*) опо́ссум; **play ~** (*fig.*) прики́дываться (*impf.*) бесчу́вственным.

post[1] [pəʊst] *n.* (*of wood, metal etc.*) столб; **starting ~** ста́ртовый столб; **winning ~** столб у фи́ниша; **whipping ~** позо́рный столб.

v.t. (*display publicly*) выве́шивать, вы́весить; объяв|ля́ть, -и́ть; **'~ no bills'** «выве́шивать объявле́ния воспреща́ется»; **the results will be ~ed (up) on the board** результа́ты бу́дут вы́вешены на доске́; **the ship was ~ed as missing** су́дно бы́ло объя́влено пропа́вшим бе́з вести.

post[2] [pəʊst] *n.* (*mail*) по́чта; **by ~** по́чтой; по по́чте; **by return of ~** с обра́тной по́чтой; **parcel ~** почто́во-посы́лочная слу́жба; **I must take these letters to the ~** я до́лжен отнести́ э́ти пи́сьма на по́чту; **if you hurry you will catch the ~** е́сли вы поспеши́те, то успе́ете до отпра́вки по́чты; **has the ~ come yet?** по́чта уже́ была́?; **the letter came by the first ~** письмо́ пришло́ с у́тренней по́чтой.

v.t. **1.** (*dispatch by mail*) отпр|авля́ть, -а́вить по по́чте. **2.** (*book-keeping*) перен|оси́ть, -ести́ в гроссбу́х; зан|оси́ть, -ести́ в бухга́лтерские кни́ги; (*fig.*) изве|ща́ть, -сти́ть; **keep me ~ed (of events)** держи́те меня́ в ку́рсе (дел)!

cpds. **~-bag** *n.* су́мка почтальо́на; **~-box** *n.* почто́вый я́щик; **~card** *n.* откры́тка; **picture ~card** худо́жественная откры́тка; **~code** *n.* почто́вый и́ндекс; **~-free** *adj.* опла́ченный отправи́телем; *adv.* опла́чено; **~-haste** *adv.* о́чень бы́стро; **~man** *n.* почтальо́н; **~mark** *n.* почто́вый ште́мпель; *v.t.* ста́вить, по- почто́вый ште́мпель на+*a./p.*; **~master** *n.* почтме́йстер; нача́льник почто́вого отделе́ния; **~mistress** *n.* нача́льница почто́вого отделе́ния; **~-office** *n.* по́чта; (*branch office*) отделе́ние свя́зи; (*main office*) почта́мт; **~-paid** *adj.* с опла́ченными почто́выми расхо́дами; *adv.* опла́чено.

post[3] [pəʊst] *n.* **1.** (*place of duty*) пост; **at one's ~** на посту́. **2.** (*fort*) форт. **3.** (*trading station*) торго́вый пост; факто́рия. **4.** (*appointment*, *job*) до́лжность. **5.** (*bugle-call*): **last ~** пове́стка пе́ред вече́рней заре́й.

v.t. **1.** (*assign to place of duty*) назн|ача́ть, -а́чить на до́лжность. **2.** (*mil.*) прикомандиро́в|ывать, -а́ть.

post- [pəʊst] *pref.* по…, после…, пост…

postage ['pəʊstıdʒ] *n.* почто́вый сбор; почто́вые расхо́ды (*m. pl.*).

cpd. **~-stamp** *n.* почто́вая ма́рка.

postal ['pəʊst(ə)l] *adj.* почто́вый; **~ order** де́нежный почто́вый перево́д; **~ tuition** зао́чное обуче́ние; **Universal P~ Union** Междунаро́дный почто́вый сою́з.

post-date [pəʊst'deıt] *v.t.* дати́ровать (*impf.*) пере́дним (*or* бо́лее по́здним) число́м.

poster ['pəʊstə(r)] *n.* (*placard*) афи́ша, плака́т; **(bill-~)** раскле́йщик афи́ш.

cpd. **~-paint** *n.* плака́тная кра́ска.

poste restante [ˌpəʊst re'stɑ̃t] *n.* до востре́бования.

posterior [pɒ'stıərıə(r)] *n.* зад.

adj. (*subsequent*) после́дующий; (*behind*) за́дний.

posterity [pɒ'sterıtı] *n.* (*descendants*) пото́мство; (*future generations*) после́дующие поколе́ния (*nt. pl.*); **go down to ~** войти́ (*pf.*) в века́.

postern ['pɒst(ə)n, 'pəʊ-] *n.* за́дняя дверь; бокову́й вход.

post-graduate [pəʊst'grædjʊət] *n.*: **~ student** аспира́нт (*fem.* -ка); **~ studies** аспиранту́ра.

posthumous ['pɒstjʊməs] *adj.* посме́ртный; **~ child** ребёнок, рождённый по́сле сме́рти отца́.

postil(l)ion [pɒ'stıljən] *n.* форе́йтор.

Post-Impressionist [ˌpəʊstım'preʃənıst] *n.* постимпрессиони́ст.

post-mortem [pəʊst'mɔːtəm] *n.* (*on dead body*) вскры́тие тру́па, аутопси́я; (*coll.*, *on game etc.*) разбо́р (*игры/матча и т.п.*).

post-natal [pəʊst'neıt(ə)l] *adj.* послеродово́й.

postpone [pəʊst'pəʊn, pə'spəʊn] *v.t.* отсро́чи|вать, -ть; от|кла́дывать, -ложи́ть.

postponement [pəʊst'pəʊnmənt, pə'spəʊnmənt] *n.* отсро́чка, откла́дывание.

post-prandial [pəʊst'prændıəl] *adj.* послеобе́денный.

postscript ['pəʊstskrıpt, 'pəʊskrıpt] *n.* постскри́птум.

postulate[1] ['pɒstjʊlət] *n.* постула́т.

postulate[2] ['pɒstjʊˌleıt] *v.t.* постули́ровать (*impf.*).

posture ['pɒstʃə(r)] *n.* (*physical attitude*) по́за; (*carriage of body*) оса́нка; (*situation*, *condition*) положе́ние.

v.i.: **she ~d in front of the glass** она́ пози́ровала пе́ред зе́ркалом.

posturer ['pɒstʃərə(r)] *n.* позёр.

post-war [pəʊst'wɔː(r), 'pəʊst-] *adj.* послевое́нный.

posy ['pəʊzı] *n.* буке́т цвето́в.

pot[1] [pɒt] *n.* **1.** (*vessel*) горшо́к; **a ~ of jam** ба́нка варе́нья; **~s and pans** ку́хонная посу́да/у́тварь; **a ~ of tea** ча́йник с зава́ренным ча́ем; **~ plant** горшо́чное расте́ние; **~ roast** тушёное мя́со; (*fig.*): **he wrote to keep the ~ boiling** он писа́л ра́ди за́работка; **it's the ~ calling the kettle black** ≃ са́м-то ты хоро́ш!; чья бы коро́ва мыча́ла…; **his work is going to ~** (*coll.*) его́ рабо́та идёт насма́рку; **come and take ~ luck with us!** ≃ чем бога́ты, тем и ра́ды!; **a watched ~ never boils** кто над ча́йником стои́т, у того́ он не кипи́т. **2.** (*coll.*, *usu. pl.*, *large sum*): **~s of money** ку́ча де́нег. **3.** (*coll.*, *pers. of importance*): **big ~** «ши́шка». **4.** (*coll.*, *prize cup*) ку́бок. **5.** (*coll.*, *paunch*) пу́зо.

v.t. **1.** (*e.g. preserves*) консерви́ровать, за-; **~ted meat** консерви́рованное мя́со. **2.** (*e.g. plants*) сажа́ть, посади́ть в горшо́к; **~ting shed** помеще́ние для переса́дки расте́ний. **3.** (*fig.*, *abridge*) сокра|ща́ть, -ти́ть; уре́з|ывать, -ать; **~ted history** кра́ткая исто́рия. **4.** (*billiards*) заг|оня́ть, -на́ть в лу́зу. **5.: ~ a baby** (*coll.*) сажа́ть, посади́ть ребёнка на горшо́к. **6.** (*kill with a ~-shot*) подстре́л|ивать, -и́ть.

v.i.: **he was ~ting away at the ducks** он стреля́л по у́ткам науга́д (*or* не це́лясь).

cpds. **~-bellied** *adj.* пуза́тый; **~-belly** *n.* брю́хо, пу́зо; **~-boiler** *n.* (*book etc.*) халту́ра; **~-boy** *n.* слуга́ (*m.*) в тракти́ре; **~-herb** *n.* (съедо́бная) зе́лень; **~hole** *n.* (*in road surface*) вы́боина, ры́твина; (*in rocks*) котлови́на, му́льда; **~-holer** *n.* (спортсме́н-)спелео́лог; **~-holing** *n.* спелеоло́гия; **~-hook** *n.* (*for hanging pots*) крюк; (*fig.*, *curved stroke*) закорю́(ч)ка; **~-house** *n.* каба́к; пивна́я; **~-hunter** *n.* «охо́тник за приза́ми»; **~-roast** *v.t.* туши́ть, с-; **~-shot** *n.* неприце́льный вы́стрел.

pot[2] [pɒt] *n.* (*coll.*, *marijuana*) дурь, тра́вка, анаша́; **~ smoker** анаши́ст.

potash ['pɒtæʃ] *n.* пота́ш.

potassium [pə'tæsıəm] *n.* ка́лий; (*attr.*) ка́лиевый.

potation [pə'teıʃ(ə)n] *n.* питьё.

potato [pə'teıtəʊ] *n.* (*collect.*, *and pl.*) карто́фель (*m.*), (*coll.*) карто́шка; (*single ~*) карто́фелина; **mashed ~es** карто́фельное пюре́ (*indecl.*); **~ crop** урожа́й карто́феля; **~ crisps** хрустя́щий карто́фель.

poteen [pɒ'tiːn] *n.* ирла́ндский самого́н.

potency ['pəʊt(ə)nsı] *n.* си́ла; власть; эффекти́вность; (*sexual*) поте́нция.

potent ['pəʊt(ə)nt] *adj.* (*powerful*) си́льный, могу́щественный; (*efficacious*) эффекти́вный.

potentate ['pəʊtən,teɪt] *n.* повели́тель (*m.*), властели́н.

potential [pə'tenʃ(ə)l] *n.* потенциа́л.

adj. потенциа́льный.

potentialit|y [pə,tenʃɪ'ælɪtɪ] *n.* потенциа́льность; **he has great ~ies** у него́ больши́е зада́т|ки (*pl.*, *g.* -ов)/возмо́жности.

pother ['pɒðə(r)] *n.* шум, сумато́ха.

potion ['pəʊʃ(ə)n] *n.* насто́йка, сна́добье; **love ~** приворо́тное зе́лье; любо́вный напи́ток.

potpourri [pəʊ'pʊərɪ, -'riː] *n.* (*lit.*, *fig.*) попурри́ (*nt. indecl.*).

potsherd ['pɒtʃɜːd] *n.* черепо́к.

pottage ['pɒtɪdʒ] *n.* (*arch.*) похлёбка; **mess of ~** (*Bibl.*) чечеви́чная похлёбка.

potter[1] ['pɒtə(r)] *n.* гонча́р; **~'s wheel** гонча́рный круг.

potter[2] ['pɒtə(r)] *v.i.* (*e.g. in garden*) копа́ться (*impf.*), ковыря́ться (*impf.*); **he ~ed along the road** он плёлся по доро́ге.

pottery ['pɒtərɪ] *n.* (*ware*) кера́мика; (*craft*) гонча́рное де́ло; (*workshop*) гонча́рня.

potty[1] ['pɒtɪ] *n.* (*coll.*, *chamber-pot*) горшо́чек.

potty[2] ['pɒtɪ] *adj.* (*trifling*) ме́лкий, пустяко́вый; (*crazy*) чо́кнутый (*coll.*).

pouch [paʊtʃ] *n.* су́мка, мешо́чек; **ammunition ~** патро́нная су́мка; **tobacco ~** кисе́т; (*container for documents etc.*) па́пка; **diplomatic ~** (*US*) дипломати́ческая по́чта; (*kangaroo's*) су́мка; (*fig.*, *loose skin*) мешо́к.

v.t. (*put into ~*) класть, положи́ть в су́мку.

pouf(fe) [puːf] *n.* (*seat*) пуф.

poulterer ['pəʊltərə(r)] *n.* торго́вец пти́цей и ди́чью.

poultice ['pəʊltɪs] *n.* припа́рка.

v.t. ста́вить, по- припа́рки на+*a.*

poultry ['pəʊltrɪ] *n.* дома́шняя пти́ца (*collect.*).

cpds. **~-farm** *n.* птицефе́рма; **~-farmer** *n.* птицево́д; **~farming** *n.* птицево́дство; **~-house** *n.* пти́чник; **~man** *n.* птицево́д; торго́вец дома́шней пти́цей; **~-run** *n.* пти́чий волье́р; **~-yard** *n.* пти́чий двор.

pounce [paʊns] *n.* (*swoop*) налёт, прыжо́к.

v.i. набр|а́сываться, -оси́ться; **the cat ~d on the mouse** ко́шка бро́силась на мы́шь; (*fig.*) кида́ться, наки́нуться (*на кого/что*); (*find fault*) прид|ира́ться, -ра́ться; **he ~d on every mistake** он цепля́лся за мале́йшую оши́бку.

pound[1] [paʊnd] *n.* **1.** (*weight*) фунт; **butter is 60p a ~** ма́сло сто́ит 60 пе́нсов за фунт; **he insisted on his ~ of flesh** он безжа́лостно потре́бовал выполне́ния сде́лки. **2.** (*money*) фунт (сте́рлингов); **a five-~ note** банкно́та в 5 фу́нтов сте́рлингов; **20p in the ~** два́дцать проце́нтов.

pound[2] [paʊnd] *n.* (*enclosure*) заго́н.

pound[3] [paʊnd] *v.t.* **1.** (*crush*) бить, раз-; **the ship was ~ed on the rocks** кора́бль уда́рило о ска́лы. **2.** (*thump*) колоти́ть (*impf.*); **she ~ed him with her fists** она́ колоти́ла его́ кулака́ми; **the pianist was ~ing out a tune** пиани́ст бараба́нил по кла́вишам.

v.i. **1.** (*thump*): **the guns were ~ing away** ору́дия пали́ли вовсю́; **he ~ed at the door** он колоти́л в дверь; **his feet ~ed on the stairs** он то́пал по ле́стнице; **her heart was ~ing with excitement** её се́рдце колоти́лось от волне́ния. **2.** (*run heavily*) мча́ться/нести́сь (*both impf.*) с гро́хотом.

poundage ['paʊndɪdʒ] *n.* (*payment per lb.*) по́шлина с ве́са; (*postal charge*) пла́та за де́нежный перево́д.

-pounder ['paʊndə(r)] *comb. form*: **he caught a three~** (*fish*) он пойма́л ры́бу ве́сом в три фу́нта; (*gun firing shot of — pounds*) **100~** ≃ 152-мм пу́шка.

pour [pɔː(r)] *v.t.* лить (*impf.*); нал|ива́ть, -и́ть; **will you ~ me (out) a cup of tea?** нале́йте мне, пожа́луйста, ча́шку ча́я; **who will ~** (*the tea*)? кто бу́дет разлива́ть чай?; (*fig.*): **he ~ed scorn on the idea** он вы́смеял э́ту иде́ю; **he tried to ~ oil on troubled waters** он пыта́лся остуди́ть стра́сти; **he ~ed cold water on my suggestion** он раскритикова́л моё предложе́ние.

v.i. ли́ться (*impf.*); **water ~ed from the roof** вода́ струи́лась с кры́ши; **sweat ~ed off his brow** с него́ кати́лся пот; (*fig.*): **the crowd ~ed out of the theatre** толпа́ повали́ла из теа́тра; (*of rain*) лить (*impf.*) как из ведра́; **it's going to ~** бу́дет ли́вень; **it was ~ing with rain** шёл проливно́й дождь; **it was a ~ing wet day** весь день ли́ло как из ведра́; **it never rains but it ~s** (*fig.*) беда́ не прихо́дит одна́; пришла́ беда́ — открыва́й воро́та.

with advs. (*fig.*): **letters ~ed in** пи́сьма так и посы́пались; **she ~ed out a tale of woe** она́ излила́ своё го́ре; **his words ~ed out in a flood** слова́ лили́сь из него́ пото́ком.

pourer ['pɔːrə(r)] *n.*: **who's going to be ~?** кто бу́дет разлива́ть?; **this jug is a good ~** из э́того кувши́на удо́бно разлива́ть/налива́ть.

pout [paʊt] *n.* наду́тые гу́бы (*f. pl.*).

v.i. над|ува́ть, -у́ть гу́бы; ду́ться, на-.

pouter ['paʊtə(r)] *n.* (*pigeon*) зоба́стый го́лубь.

poverty ['pɒvətɪ] *n.* бе́дность, нищета́; **on the ~ line** на гра́ни нищеты́; (*fig.*) нехва́тка; отсу́тствие; **~ of ideas** ску́дость мы́слей.

cpd. **~-stricken** *adj.* (*lit.*) ни́щий; (*fig.*) захуда́лый, убо́гий.

POW (*abbr. of **prisoner of war***) военнопле́нный.

powder ['paʊdə(r)] *n.* (*chem.*, *med. etc.*) порошо́к; (*cosmetic*) пу́дра; (*explosive*) по́рох; **keep your ~ dry** (*fig.*) держи́те по́рох сухи́м; **it's not worth ~ and shot** (*fig.*) ≃ овчи́нка вы́делки не сто́ит.

v.t. **1.** (*reduce to ~*) превра|ща́ть, -ти́ть в порошо́к; **~ed milk** порошко́вое/сухо́е молоко́. **2.** (*apply ~ to*) пу́дрить, на-.

cpds. **~-blue** *adj.* зеленова́то-голубо́й; **~-flask**, **~-horn** *nn.* порохо́вница; **~-magazine** *n.* порохово́й по́греб; **~-puff** *n.* пухо́вка; **~-room** *n.* да́мская (туале́тная) ко́мната.

powdery ['paʊdərɪ] *adj.* порошкообра́зный; рассы́пчатый.

power ['paʊə(r)] *n.* **1.** (*ability*, *capacity*) си́ла, мощь; **I will do all in my ~** я сде́лаю всё, что в мои́х си́лах; **it is not within my ~** э́то не в мое́й вла́сти; **purchasing ~** покупа́тельная спосо́бность; **his voice has great carrying ~** у него́ о́чень зво́нкий го́лос; **his ~s of resistance are low** у него́ сла́бая сопротивля́емость; **this ring has the ~ to make you invisible** э́то кольцо́ облада́ет сво́йством де́лать челове́ка неви́димым; **the ~ to express one's thoughts** спосо́бность выража́ть свои́ мы́сли. **2.** (*pl.*, *faculties*): **he is a man of considerable ~s** он наделён больши́ми спосо́бностями; **he was at the height of his ~s** он был в расцве́те сил; **his ~s are failing** его́ си́лы угаса́ют; **the task is beyond his ~s** зада́ча ему́ не по си́лам. **3.** (*vigour*, *strength*) эне́ргия; **more ~ to your elbow!** (*coll.*) жела́ю уда́чи! **4.** (*energy*, *force*) эне́ргия; **electric ~** электроэне́ргия; **there was a ~ cut** электроэне́ргию вре́менно отключи́ли; **the machine is on full ~** маши́на рабо́тает на по́лную мо́щность. **5.** (*authority*, *control*) власть; **I have him in my ~** он в мое́й вла́сти; **he has no ~ over me** у него́ нет на́до мной вла́сти; **France was at the height of her ~** Фра́нция находи́лось в расцве́те своего́ могу́щества; **in ~** у вла́сти; **out of ~** не у вла́сти; **the party in ~** пра́вящая па́ртия; **balance of ~** равнове́сие сил; **~ politics** поли́тика с пози́ции си́лы. **6.** (*right*, *authorization*) пра́во; **the judge exceeded his ~s** судья́ превы́сил свои́ полномо́чия; **the committee has ~ to co-opt members** комите́т име́ет пра́во коопти́ровать чле́нов. **7.** (*influential pers. or organization*) си́ла; **he is a great ~ for good** его́ влия́ние весьма́ благотво́рно; **the ~s that be** си́льные (*pl.*) ми́ра сего́. **8.** (*state*) держа́ва; **the Great P~s** вели́кие держа́вы. **9.** (*supernatural force*) си́ла; **the ~s of darkness** си́лы тьмы; **merciful ~s!** си́лы небе́сные! **10.** (*coll.*, *large number or amount*) мно́жество; **this medicine has done me a ~ of good** э́то лека́рство принесло́ мне огро́мную по́льзу. **11.** (*math.*) сте́пень; **two to the ~ of ten** два в деся́той сте́пени; **the fourth ~ of ten** четвёртая сте́пень деся́тки. **12.** (*magnifying capacity*) си́ла увеличе́ния.

v.t. (*supply with energy*) снаб|жа́ть, -ди́ть силовы́м дви́гателем; **an aircraft ~ed by four jets** самолёт с четырьмя́ реакти́вными дви́гателями.

cpds. **~-boat** *n.* мото́рный ка́тер; **~-dive** *n.* пики́рование с рабо́тающим мото́ром; **~-driven** *adj.* с механи́ческим приво́дом; **~-house** *n.* силова́я ста́нция; **~-lathe** *n.* механи́ческий тока́рный стано́к; **~-plant**, **~-station** *nn.* электроста́нция; **~-point** *n.* электроввод, штéпсельная розéтка.

powerful ['paʊəˌfʊl] *adj.* сúльный, мóщный; **a ~ voice** сúльный гóлос; **a ~ argument** мóщный/убедúтельный дóвод; **a ~ nation** могýщественный нарóд; **a ~ speech** яркая/впечатлúющая речь.

powerless ['paʊəlɪs] *adj.* бессúльный; **I was ~ to move** я был не в состоя́нии двúнуться; **he is ~ in the matter** он бессúлен чтó-либо сдéлать.

powwow ['paʊwaʊ] (*coll.*) *n.* собрáние, говорúльня.

v.i. совещáться (*impf.*).

pox [pɒks] *n.* (*coll.*) сúфилис.

pp. ['peɪdʒɪz] *n.* (*abbr. of* **pages**) стр, (стрáницы).

PR *abbr. of* **1.** ***public relations*** *see* **public** *adj.* **1.**. **2.** ***proportional representation*** пропорционáльное представúтельство.

practicability [ˌpræktɪkə'bɪlɪtɪ] *n.* целесообрáзность.

practicable ['præktɪkəb(ə)l] *adj.* (*feasible*) осуществúмый, реáльный.

practical ['præktɪk(ə)l] *adj.* **1.** (*concerned with practice*) практúческий; **a ~ joke** рóзыгрыш, шýтка; **play a ~ joke on** разы́гр|ывать, -áть; **he is a ~ man** он практúческий человéк; **you must be ~ about it** вы должны́ смотрéть на э́то с практúческой тóчки зрéния. **2.** (*useful in practice, workable, feasible*) осуществúмый; **this is not a ~ suggestion** э́то предложéние нереáльно. **3.** (*virtual*) фактúческий, настоя́щий; **it is a ~ impossibility** э́то практúчески невозмóжно.

practicality [ˌpræktɪ'kælɪtɪ] *n.* практúчность.

practically ['præktɪkəlɪ] *adv.* **1.** (*in a practical manner*) практúчески; **look at a question ~** смотрéть на вопрóс с практúческой тóчки зрéния. **2.** (*almost*) практúчески, фактúчески; в сýщности, почтú.

practice ['præktɪs] *n.* **1.** (*performance*) прáктика; **the idea will not work in ~** э́та идéя на прáктике неосуществúма; **he put his plan into ~** он осуществúл свой план. **2.** (*regular or habitual performance*) обы́чай, обыкновéние; **he makes a ~ of early rising** он взял себé за прáвило рáно вставáть; **my usual ~ is to tip** я имéю обыкновéние давáть чаевы́е; **borrowing money is a bad ~** брать дéньги в долг — сквéрная привы́чка; **this ~ must stop** э́ту прáктику нáдо прекратúть; **sharp ~** мошéнничество, махинáции (*f. pl.*); **put into ~** осуществ|ля́ть, -úть. **3.** (*repeated exercise*) упражнéние, тренирóвка; **~ makes perfect** нáвык мáстера стáвит; **your game needs more ~** вам нáдо бóльше тренúроваться; **I am badly out of ~** я давнó не упражня́лся/практиковáлся. **4.** (*work of doctor, lawyer etc.*) прáктика; **the ~ of medicine** медицúнская прáктика; **he is in ~ in York** он имéет прáктику в Йóрке.

v.t. & *i.*: = **practise**

practician [præk'tɪʃ(ə)n] *n.* прáктик.

practis|e ['præktɪs] (*US* **practice**) *v.t.* **1.** (*perform habitually*) дéлать, с- по привы́чке; **you should ~e what you preach** вáши словá не должны́ расходúться с дéлом; (*for exercise*): **you should ~e this stroke** вам нýжно отрабóтать э́тот удáр; (*sport game etc.*) упражня́ться (*impf.*) в+*p.*; (*instrument*): **she was ~ing the piano** онá упражня́лась на роя́ле. **2.** (*a profession etc.*) практиковáть (*impf.*); **a ~ing physician** практикýющий врач.

v.i. **1.** упражня́ться (*impf.*); тренировáться (*impf.*). **2.** **~e on** (*exploit*) испóльзовать (*pf.*); злоупотреб|ля́ть, -úть; **he ~ed upon my good nature** он воспóльзовался моéй добротóй.

practitioner [præk'tɪʃənə(r)] *n.* (*med.*) практикýющий врач; **general ~** участкóвый врач.

praetorian [priː'tɔːrɪən] *adj.* преториáнский; **~ guard** преториáнцы (*m. pl.*).

pragmatic(al) [præg'mætɪk(əl)] *adj.* прагматúческий.

pragmatism ['prægməˌtɪz(ə)m] *n.* прагматúзм.

pragmatist ['prægmətɪst] *n.* прагмáтик.

Prague [prɑːg] *n.* Прáга; (*attr.*) прáжский.

prairie ['preərɪ] *n.* прéрия.

cpds. **~-chicken** *n.* луговóй тéтерев; **~-dog** *n.* луговáя собáчка.

praise [preɪz] *n.* похвалá; **his work is beyond ~** егó рабóта вы́ше вся́кой похвалы́; **he spoke in ~ of sport** он говорúл о пóльзе спóрта; **he sang his master's ~s** он пел дифирáмбы своемý хозя́ину; **he was loud in her ~s** он осыпáл её похвалáми; **~ be (to God)!** слáва Бóгу!

v.t. (*voice approval, admiration of*) хвалúть, по-; (*give glory to*) восхвал|я́ть, -úть.

cpd. **~worthy** *adj.* достóйный похвалы́; похвáльный.

pram [prɑːm] *n.* (*coll.*) = **perambulator**

prance [prɑːns] *n.* (*leap*) скачóк.

v.i. (*of horse*) гарцевáть (*impf.*); (*of pers.*) (*coll.*) форсúть (*impf.*).

prang [præŋ] *n.* авáрия, столкновéние.

prank [præŋk] *n.* вы́ходка, продéлка; **he is up to his ~s again** он опя́ть за свой прокáзы; **play ~s on** разы́грывать (*impf.*); **play a ~ on** разыгрáть (*pf.*).

prankster ['præŋkstə(r)] *n.* шутнúк, прокáзник.

prat [præt] *n.* дуралéй.

prate [preɪt] *v.i.* трепáться (*impf.*).

pratique [præ'tiːk] *n.* свидéтельство о сня́тии карантúна.

prattle ['præt(ə)l] *n.* болтовня́; лéпет.

v.i. болтáть (*impf.*); лепетáть, про-.

prattler ['prætlə(r)] *n.* болтýн.

prawn [prɔːn] *n.* кревéтка.

pray [preɪ] *v.t.* **1.** (*supplicate*) молúть (*impf.*); умол|я́ть, -úть; **~ God he comes in time** дай Бог, чтóбы он пришёл вóвремя. **2.** (*arch., ellipt.*) пожáлуйста; **what, ~, is the meaning of that?** какóй в э́том смысл, скажúте на мúлость?

v.i. молúться, по-; **the farmers ~ed for rain** фéрмеры молúли о дождé; **we will ~ for the Queen** мы бýдем молúться за королéву; **he is past ~ing for** он пропáщий человéк; егó пéсенка спéта.

prayer ['preə(r)] *n.* **1.** (*act of praying*) молéние. **2.** (*formula, petition*) молúтва; **the Lord's P~** Óтче наш, молúтва госпóдня; **say one's ~s** молúться, по-. **3.** (*entreaty*) прóсьба, мольбá. **4.** (*also pl., form of worship*) богослужéние.

cpds. **~-book** *n.* молúтвенник; **~mat, ~-rug** *nn.* молúтвенный кóврик; **~-meeting** *n.* молúтвенное собрáние; **~-wheel** *n.* молúтвенное колесó.

prayerful ['preəˌfʊl] *adj.* (*pers.*) богомóльный, нáбожный.

pre- [priː] *pref.* (*beforehand, in advance*) до..., пред...; зарáнее; (*dating from before*) до...

preach [priːtʃ] *v.t.* проповéдовать (*impf.*); **go out and ~ the gospel!** идúте и несúте лю́дям Евáнгелие!; **he ~ed the virtue of thrift** он проповéдовал бережлúвость.

v.i. (*deliver sermon*) читáть прóповедь; (*give moral advice*) поучáть (*impf.*); **~ to the converted** ≃ ломúться (*m. pf.*) в открытую дверь.

preacher ['priːtʃə(r)] *n.* проповéдник.

preachify ['priːtʃɪˌfaɪ] *v.i.* (*coll.*) проповéдовать (*impf.*); читáть (*impf.*) нотáции.

preamble [priː'æmb(ə)l, 'priː-] *n.* преáмбула.

pre-arrange [ˌpriːə'reɪndʒ] *v.t.* организóв|ывать, -áть зарáнее; **at a ~d signal** по услóвленному знáку/сигнáлу.

pre-arrangement [ˌpriːə'reɪndʒmənt] *n.* предварúтельная подготóвка/договорённость.

prebend ['prebənd] *n.* пребéнда.

prebendary ['prebəndərɪ] *n.* пребендáрий.

precarious [prɪ'keərɪəs] *adj.* **1.** (*uncertain*) ненадёжный; **a ~ foothold** ненадёжная опóра; **~ health** слáбое здорóвье; **he makes a ~ living** он едвá зарабáтывает на жизнь. **2.** (*dangerous, risky*) опáсный, рискóванный.

precaution [prɪ'kɔːʃ(ə)n] *n.* предосторóжность, предусмотрúтельность; **it is wise to take ~s against fire** разýмно приня́ть мéры предосторóжности прóтив (*or* на слýчай) пожáра.

precautionary [prɪ'kɔːʃənərɪ] *adj.* предупредúтельный; **~ measures** мéры предосторóжности.

preced|e [prɪ'siːd] *v.t.* (*take ~ence of, come before*) предшéствовать (*impf.*) +*d.*; (*walk ahead of*): **he was ~ed by his wife** женá шла впередú егó.

v.i.: **in the ~ing sentence** в предыдýщем предложéнии.

precedence ['presɪd(ə)ns] *n.* **1.** (*priority, superiority*) первоочерёдность, приоритéт; **this question takes ~** э́тот вопрóс дóлжен рассмáтриваться в пéрвую óчередь. **2.** (*right of preceding others*) старшинствó.

precedent ['presɪd(ə)nt] *n.* прецеде́нт; **there is no ~ for this** э́то не име́ет прецеде́нта; **create, set a ~** созд|ава́ть, -а́ть (*or* устан|а́вливать, -ови́ть) прецеде́нт.
precentor [prɪ'sentə(r)] *n.* ре́гент хо́ра.
precept ['pri:sept] *n.* наставле́ние; предписа́ние.
preceptor [prɪ'septə(r)] *n.* наста́вник.
precession [prɪ'seʃ(ə)n] *n.*: **~ of the equinoxes** предваре́ние равноде́нствий.
pre-Christian [pri:'krɪstɪən] *adj.* дохристиа́нский.
precinct ['pri:sɪŋkt] *n.* **1.** (*enclosed space*) двор. **2.** (*pl., environs*) окре́стности (*f. pl.*). **3.** (*area of restricted access*): **pedestrian ~** уча́сток у́лицы то́лько для пешехо́дов; **shopping ~** торго́вый пасса́ж. **4.** (*US, police or electoral district*) уча́сток.
preciosity [,preʃɪ'ɒsɪtɪ] *n.* изы́сканность, изощрённость.
precious ['preʃəs] *adj.* **1.** (*of great value*) драгоце́нный; **~ stones/metals** драгоце́нные ка́мни (*m. pl.*)/мета́ллы (*m. pl.*); (*as endearment*) люби́мый; **my ~** мой ненагля́дный. **2.** (*affected, over-refined*) мане́рно-изы́сканный. **3.** (*coll., very great*) огро́мный; **it cost a ~ sight more** э́то сто́ило намно́го доро́же; **he is a ~ rascal** он настоя́щий моше́нник; (*iron.*) драгоце́нный; **a ~ friend!** хоро́ш друг!
adv. (*coll.*) о́чень, здо́рово; **I got ~ little for the ring** я получи́л за кольцо́ о́чень ма́ло; **there is ~ little hope** наде́жды почти́ нет.
preciousness ['preʃəsnɪs] *n.* (*value*) драгоце́нность; (*affectation*) мане́рность.
precipice ['presɪpɪs] *n.* про́пасть, обры́в; **fall over a ~** сорва́ться (*pf.*) с обры́ва.
precipitate[1] [prɪ'sɪpɪtət] *n.* оса́док.
adj. (*headlong*) стреми́тельный; (*rash*) опроме́тчивый, скоропали́тельный.
precipitate[2] [prɪ'sɪpɪ,teɪt] *v.t.* **1.** (*throw down*) низв|ерга́ть, -е́ргнуть; (*fig.*) вв|ерга́ть, -е́ргнуть; **the country was ~d into war** страну́ вве́ргнули в войну́. **2.** (*bring on rapidly*) уск|оря́ть, -о́рить. **3.** (*chem.*) оса|жда́ть, -ди́ть.
precipitation [prɪ,sɪpɪ'teɪʃ(ə)n] *n.* (*rain etc.*) оса́д|ки (*pl., g.* -ов); (*rashness, haste*) стреми́тельность, поспе́шность.
precipitous [prɪ'sɪpɪtəs] *adj.* (*steep*) обры́вистый, круто́й; (*hasty*) поспе́шный.
precipitousness [prɪ'sɪpɪtəsnɪs] *n.* (*steepness*) обры́вистость, крутизна́; (*haste*) скоропали́тельность, поспе́шность.
précis ['preɪsi:] *n.* кра́ткое изложе́ние, конспе́кт.
precise [prɪ'saɪs] *adj.* (*exact*) то́чный, аккура́тный, пунктуа́льный; (*punctilious*) тща́тельный.
precisely [prɪ'saɪslɪ] *adv.* то́чно; (*with numbers or quantities*) ро́вно; **at ~ two o'clock** ро́вно в два часа́; **~ nothing** ро́вно ничего́; (*as reply: 'quite so'*) соверше́нно ве́рно; вот и́менно.
preciseness [prɪ'saɪsnɪs] *n.* то́чность; чёткость.
precision [prɪ'sɪʒ(ə)n] *n.* то́чность; аккура́тность, пунктуа́льность; **~ bombing** прице́льное бомбомета́ние; **~ instrument** то́чный прибо́р.
preclude [prɪ'klu:d] *v.t.* предотвра|ща́ть, -ти́ть; исключ|а́ть, -и́ть.
precocious [prɪ'kəʊʃəs] *adj.* (*of fruit*) скороспе́лый; (*of pers.*) ра́но разви́вшийся; (*coll.*) из молоды́х да ра́ний.
precoci|ousness [prɪ'kəʊʃəsnɪs], **-ty** [prɪ'kɒsɪtɪ] *nn.* скороспе́лость; ра́ннее разви́тие.
precognition [,pri:kɒg'nɪʃ(ə)n] *n.* предви́дение.
preconceived [,pri:kən'si:vd] *adj.* предвзя́тый.
preconception [,pri:kən'sepʃ(ə)n] *n.* предвзя́тое мне́ние.
pre-condition [,pri:kən'dɪʃ(ə)n] *n.* предвари́тельное усло́вие.
precursor [pri:'kɜ:sə(r)] *n.* предше́ственник, предве́стник, предте́ча (*c.g.*).
pre-date [pri:'deɪt] *v.t.* (*antedate*) дати́ровать за́дним (*or* бо́лее ра́нним) число́м; (*precede*) предше́ствовать +*d.*
predator ['predətə(r)] *n.* хи́щник.
predatory ['predətərɪ] *adj.* хи́щный, хи́щнический, граби́тельский.
predecease [,pri:dɪ'si:s] *v.t.*: **he ~d her** он у́мер ра́ньше её.
predecessor ['pri:dɪ,sesə(r)] *n.* предше́ственник; **this car is bigger than its ~** э́то маши́на бо́льше ста́рой/пре́жней.
predestination [pri:,destɪ'neɪʃ(ə)n] *n.* предопределе́ние.
predestine [pri:'destɪn] *v.t.* предопредел|я́ть, -и́ть.
predeterminate [,pri:dɪ'tɜ:mɪnət] *adj.* предопределённый, предрешённый.
predetermination [,pri:dɪtɜ:mɪ'neɪʃ(ə)n] *n.* предопределе́ние.
predetermine [,pri:dɪ'tɜ:mɪn] *v.t.* предреш|а́ть, -и́ть.
predicament [prɪ'dɪkəmənt] *n.* тру́дная ситуа́ция, (*coll.*) переплёт; **that puts me in a ~** э́то ста́вит меня́ в тру́дное положе́ние.
predicate[1] ['predɪkət] *n.* (*gram.*) сказу́емое; (*log.*) предика́т.
predicate[2] ['predɪ,keɪt] *v.t.* утвер|жда́ть, -ди́ть.
predication [,predɪ'keɪʃ(ə)n] *n.* предика́ция, утвержде́ние.
predicative [prɪ'dɪkətɪv] *adj.* предикати́вный.
predict [prɪ'dɪkt] *v.t.* предска́з|ывать, -а́ть.
predictable [prɪ'dɪktəb(ə)l] *adj.* предсказу́емый.
prediction [prɪ'dɪkʃ(ə)n] *n.* предсказа́ние.
predictor [prɪ'dɪktə(r)] *n.* (*mil.*) прибо́р управле́ния артиллери́йским зени́тным огнём.
predigest [,pri:daɪ'dʒest] *v.t.* (*fig.*) адапти́ровать (*impf.*); разжёвывать (*impf.*).
predilection [,pri:dɪ'lekʃ(ə)n] *n.* пристра́стие, скло́нность (**for:** к+*d.*).
predispose [,pri:dɪ'spəʊz] *v.t.* предраспол|ага́ть, -ожи́ть; **I am ~d in his favour** я предрасполо́жен к нему́; **my mother is ~d to rheumatism** моя́ мать предрасполо́жена к ревмати́зму.
predisposition [,pri:dɪspə'zɪʃ(ə)n] *n.* предрасположе́ние, скло́нность (*к чему*).
predominance [prɪ'dɒmɪnəns] *n.* (*control; superiority*) превосхо́дство; госпо́дство; (*preponderance*) преоблада́ние.
predominant [prɪ'dɒmɪnənt] *adj.* (*without rival*) преоблада́ющий, превосходя́щий; (*preponderant, conspicuous*) домини́рующий.
predominate [prɪ'dɒmɪ,neɪt] *v.i.* преоблада́ть (*impf.*); домини́ровать (*impf.*).
pre-eminence [pri:'emɪnəns] *n.* преиму́щество, превосхо́дство.
pre-eminent [pri:'emɪnənt] *adj.* превосходя́щий, выдаю́щийся.
pre-empt [pri:'empt] *v.t.* (*buy up*) скуп|а́ть, -и́ть; (*appropriate*) присв|а́ивать, -о́ить; завлад|ева́ть, -е́ть +*i.*; (*forestall*) предупре|жда́ть, -ди́ть.
pre-emption [pri:'empʃ(ə)n] *n.* ску́пка; присвое́ние; завладе́ние (*чем*).
pre-emptive [pri:'emptɪv] *adj.* опережа́ющий; **~ strike** упрежда́ющий уда́р.
preen [pri:n] *v.t.* (*of bird*): **~ one's feathers** чи́стить (*impf.*) пе́рья/пёрышки; (*of pers.*) прихор|а́шиваться, -о́шиться; (*fig.*): **he ~s himself on his good looks** он горди́тся свое́й вне́шностью.
pre-existence [,pri:ɪg'zɪstəns] *n.* предсуществова́ние.
pre-existent [,pri:ɪg'zɪstənt] *adj.* предсуществу́ющий.
prefabricate [pri:'fæbrɪ,keɪt] *v.t.*; **~d house** (*coll.*, **prefab**) сбо́рный дом.
prefabrication [pri:,fæbrɪ'keɪʃ(ə)n] *n.* изготовле́ние дета́лей для сбо́рки.
preface ['prefəs] *n.* (*written*) предисло́вие; (*spoken*) вво́дное сло́во; (*fig.*) вступле́ние, проло́г.
v.t. де́лать, с- вступле́ние к+*d.*; предпос|ыла́ть, -ла́ть; **he ~d his remarks with a quotation** он на́чал свои́ замеча́ния с цита́ты.
prefatory ['prefətərɪ] *adj.* вступи́тельный, вво́дный.
prefect ['pri:fekt] *n.* **1.** (*official*) префе́кт. **2.** (*at school*) ста́рший учени́к, ста́роста (*c.g.*), префе́кт.
prefecture ['pri:fektjʊə(r)] *n.* префекту́ра.
prefer [prɪ'fɜ:(r)] *v.t.* **1.** (*like better*) предпоч|ита́ть, -е́сть; **I ~ fish to meat** я предпочита́ю ры́бу мя́су. **2.** (*promote*) продв|ига́ть, -и́нуть. **3.** (*submit*): **~ charges** выдвига́ть, вы́двинуть обвине́ния.
preferable ['prefərəb(ə)l] *adj.* предпочти́тельный; **it's not a comfortable bed, but it's ~ to sleeping on the floor** э́та крова́ть не о́чень удо́бна, но на ней всё же лу́чше спать, чем на полу́.
preference ['prefərəns] *n.* **1.** (*greater liking*) предпочте́ние; **he has a ~ for silk ties** он пита́ет сла́бость к шёлковым га́лстукам; **have you any ~?** что вы предпочита́ете?; **I chose this in ~ to the other** я предпочёл э́то тому́; **we**

cannot give you ~ over everyone else мы не мо́жем дать вам предпочте́ние пе́ред все́ми други́ми; (*preferred thg.*) вы́бор. **2.** (*econ.*) льго́тная тамо́женная по́шлина.

preferential [ˌprefəˈrenʃ(ə)l] *adj.* предпочти́тельный; льго́тный.

preferment [prɪˈfɜːmənt] *n.* продвиже́ние по слу́жбе.

prefigure [priːˈfɪgə(r)] *v.t.* служи́ть (*impf.*) прототи́пом +*g.*

prefix [ˈpriːfɪks] *n.* (*at beginning of word*) приста́вка, пре́фикс; (*title such as* 'Mr') обраще́ние, ти́тул.

v.t. присоедин|я́ть, -и́ть (*приставку к слову*).

pregnancy [ˈpregnənsɪ] *n.* бере́менность.

pregnant [ˈpregnənt] *adj.* бере́менная; **become ~** забере́менеть (*pf.*); (*fig.*) чрева́тый; **words ~ with meaning** слова́, испо́лненные смы́сла; **a ~ silence** многозначи́тельное молча́ние.

pre-heat [priːˈhiːt] *v.t.* предвари́тельно подогр|ева́ть, -е́ть.

prehensile [priːˈhensaɪl] *adj.* хвата́тельный.

prehistoric [ˌpriːhɪˈstɒrɪk] *adj.* доистори́ческий.

prehistory [ˌpriːˈhɪstərɪ] *n.* предысто́рия.

pre-human [priːˈhjuːmən] *adj.* существова́вший до появле́ния челове́ка.

prejudge [priːˈdʒʌdʒ] *v.i.* предреш|а́ть, -и́ть.

prejudgement [priːˈdʒʌdʒmənt] *n.* предреше́ние.

prejudice [ˈpredʒʊdɪs] *n.* **1.** (*preconceived opinion*) предубежде́ние, предрассу́док. **2.** (*detriment*) уще́рб, вред. **3.** (*prejudgement*): **without ~** без уще́рба (для+*g.*); (*leg.*) не отка́зываясь от свои́х прав.

v.t. **1.** (*cause to have a ~*) предубе|жда́ть, -ди́ть; **you are ~d against him** вы предубежде́ны про́тив него́. **2.** (*impair validity of*) нан|оси́ть, -ести́ уще́рб +*d.*; **he ~d his reputation** он подпо́ртил себе́ репута́цию.

prejudicial [ˌpredʒʊˈdɪʃ(ə)l] *adj.* (*detrimental*) вре́дный; ущемля́ющий; нанося́щий уще́рб +*d.*

prelacy [ˈpreləsɪ] *n.* прела́тство.

prelate [ˈprelət] *n.* прела́т.

prelim [ˈpriːlɪm, prɪˈlɪm] *n.* (*coll.*) вступи́тельный экза́мен; (*pl.*, *typ.*) сбо́рный лист.

preliminary [prɪˈlɪmɪnərɪ] *n.* предготови́тельное мероприя́тие.

adj. предвари́тельный.

prelude [ˈpreljuːd] *n.* (*mus.*) прелю́дия; (*fig.*): **this was the ~ to the storm** э́то был пе́рвый гром пе́ред бу́рей.

v.t. (*serve as ~ to*) служи́ть (*impf.*) вступле́нием к+*d.*

premarital [priːˈmærɪt(ə)l] *adj.* добра́чный.

premature [ˈpreməˌtjʊə(r), -ˈtjʊə(r)] *adj.* преждевре́менный; **~ birth** преждевре́менные ро́д|ы (*pl.*, *g.* -ов); **~ baby** недоно́шеный младе́нец; **~ decision** необду́манное/поспе́шное реше́ние.

premeditate [priːˈmedɪˌteɪt] *v.t.*: **~d murder** преднаме́ренное уби́йство.

premeditation [priːˌmedɪˈteɪʃ(ə)n] *n.* преднаме́ренность.

premenstrual [priːˈmenstrʊəl] *adj.* предменструа́льный.

premier [ˈpremɪə(r)] *n.* премье́р-мини́стр.

adj. пе́рвый; гла́вный.

première [ˈpremɪˌeə(r)] *n.* премье́ра; **the film had its ~ last night** э́тот фильм был впервы́е пока́зан вчера́.

premiership [ˈpremɪəʃɪp] *n.* премье́рство.

premise[1] [ˈpremɪs] *n.* **1.** (*log.*, *also* **premiss**) посы́лка. **2.** (*pl.*, *house and land*) помеще́ние; **drinks are to be consumed on the ~s** напи́тки продаю́тся распи́вочно; **licensed ~s** помеще́ние, в кото́ром разрешена́ прода́жа спиртны́х напи́тков.

premise[2] [prɪˈmaɪz] *v.t.* предпос|ыла́ть, -ла́ть.

premiss [ˈpremɪs] = **premise**[1]

premium [ˈpriːmɪəm] *n.* **1.** (*reward*) награ́да; **this will put a ~ on dishonesty** э́то бу́дет поощря́ть нече́стных люде́й. **2.** (*amount paid for insurance*) (страхова́я) пре́мия. **3.** (*additional charge or payment*) припла́та. **4.: at a ~** вы́ше номина́ла; с при́былью; (*in demand*) по́льзующийся спро́сом.

premonition [ˌpreməˈnɪʃ(ə)n, ˌpriː-] *n.* предчу́вствие.

premonitory [prɪˈmɒnɪtərɪ] *adj.* предупрежда́ющий, предостерега́ющий.

pre-natal [priːˈneɪt(ə)l] *adj.* предродово́й.

preoccupation [priːˌɒkjʊˈpeɪʃ(ə)n] *n.* (*mental absorption*) озабо́ченность, поглощённость; (*absorbing subject*) забо́та; **his one ~ is making money** его́ еди́нственная забо́та — де́лать де́ньги.

preoccup|y [priːˈɒkjʊˌpaɪ] *v.t.* забо́тить, о-; **the match ~ied his thoughts** матч занима́л все его́ мы́сли; **he was too ~ied to pay attention** он не обрати́л внима́ния, так как был сли́шком поглощён свои́ми мы́слями.

pre-ordain [ˌpriːɔːˈdeɪn] *v.t.* предназн|ача́ть, -а́чить.

prep [prep] *n.* (*coll.*, *school work*) приготовле́ние уро́ков; (*work set*) ≃ уро́к(и) на́ дом.

adj. (*coll.*): **~ school** (ча́стная) приготови́тельная шко́ла.

pre-packed [priːˈpækd] *adj.* расфасо́ванный.

preparation [ˌprepəˈreɪʃ(ə)n] *n.* **1.** (*process of preparing or being prepared*) приготовле́ние; **she was packing in ~ for the journey** она́ укла́дывала ве́щи, гото́вясь к пое́здке; **a second edition is in ~** гото́вится второ́е изда́ние; (*pl.*, *preparatory measures*): **~s are well under way** подгото́вка идёт вовсю́; **he made ~s to leave** он стал гото́виться к отъе́зду. **2. (medicine)** лека́рство.

preparatory [prɪˈpærətərɪ] *adj.* подготови́тельный.

adv.: **~ to** пре́жде чем (+*inf.*); до того́, как (+*finite v.*).

prepare [prɪˈpeə(r)] *v.t.* гото́вить (*impf.*); пригот|а́вливать, -о́вить; подгот|а́вливать, -о́вить; **she ~d a meal** она́ пригото́вила еду́; **I was ~d for the worst** я был гото́в к са́мому ху́дшему; **the tutor ~d him for his exams** учи́тель гото́вил его́ к экза́менам; **he ~d his speech in advance** он подгото́вил свою́ речь зара́нее; **they ~d** (*fitted out*) **an expedition** они оснасти́ли экспеди́цию.

v.i. подгот|а́вливаться, -о́виться; пригот|а́вливаться, -о́виться; **they ~d for an attack** они́ подгото́вились к ата́ке (неприя́теля).

preparedness [prɪˈpeərɪdnɪs] *n.* гото́вность.

prepa|y [priːˈpeɪ] *v.t.* опла́|чивать, -ти́ть зара́нее; **~id telegram** телегра́мма с опла́ченным отве́том.

preponderance [prɪˈpɒndərəns] *n.* переве́с, преиму́щество.

preponderant [prɪˈpɒndərənt] *adj.* име́ющий переве́с; преоблада́ющий.

preponderate [prɪˈpɒndəˌreɪt] *v.i.* переве́|шивать, -сить; преоблада́ть (*impf.*).

preposition [ˌprepəˈzɪʃ(ə)n] *n.* предло́г.

prepositional [ˌprepəˈzɪʃənəl] *adj.* предло́жный.

prepossess [ˌpriːpəˈzes] *v.t.* предраспол|ага́ть, -ожи́ть; **his appearance is not ~ing** у него́ нераспологáющая вне́шность; **the jury were ~ed in his favour** прися́жные бы́ли предрасполо́жены к нему́.

prepossession [ˌpriːpəˈzeʃ(ə)n] *n.* предрасположе́ние.

preposterous [prɪˈpɒstərəs] *adj.* неле́пый.

Pre-Raphaelite [priːˈræfəˌlaɪt] *n.* прерафаэли́т.

prerequisite [priːˈrekwɪzɪt] *n.* предпосы́лка.

pre-revolutionary [ˌpriːˌrevəˈluːʃənərɪ] *adj.* дореволюцио́нный.

prerogative [prɪˈrɒgətɪv] *n.* (*of ruler, etc.*) прерогати́ва; (*privilege*) привиле́гия.

Pres. [ˈprezɪd(ə)nt] *n.* (*abbr. of* **President**) президе́нт.

presage [ˈpresɪdʒ] *n.* (*portent*) предзнаменова́ние, при́знак; (*presentiment*) предчу́вствие.

v.t. (*portend*) предвеща́ть (*impf.*); (*forebode*) предчу́вствовать (*impf.*).

presbyter [ˈprezbɪtə(r)] *n.* пресви́тер; (*in early Church*) старе́йшина (*m.*).

Presbyterian [ˌprezbɪˈtɪərɪən] *n.* пресвитериа́н|ин (*fem.* -ка).

adj. пресвитериа́нский.

presbytery [ˈprezbɪtərɪ] *n.* (*body of presbyters*) пресвите́рия; (*priest's house*) дом свяще́нника при це́ркви.

prescience [ˈpresɪəns] *n.* предви́дение.

prescient [ˈpresɪənt] *adj.* предви́дящий.

prescind [prɪˈsɪnd] *v.i.*: **~ from** выпуска́ть, вы́пустить и́з виду; абстраги́роваться (*impf.*, *pf.*) +*g.*

prescribe [prɪˈskraɪb] *v.t.* **1.** (*lay down, impose*) предпи́с|ывать, -а́ть; **penalties ~d by the law** ме́ры наказа́ния, предусмо́тренные зако́ном. **2.** (*med.*) пропи́с|ывать, -а́ть.

prescription [prɪˈskrɪpʃ(ə)n] *n.* **1.** (*prescribing*) предпи́сывание; распоряже́ние. **2.** (*doctor's direction*) реце́пт. **3.** (*leg.*) пра́во да́вности; **positive ~** приобрете́ние пра́ва по да́вности; **negative ~** утéря пра́ва по сро́ку да́вности.

prescriptive [prɪ'skrɪptɪv] *adj.* **1.** (*giving directions*) предпи́сывающий. **2.** (*leg.*): ~ **right** пра́во, осно́ванное на да́вности.

preselect [ˌpri:sɪ'lekt] *v.t.*: ~ **a gear** (*on car*) изб|ира́ть, -ра́ть переда́чу (в автомоби́ле) для после́дующего её включе́ния.

preselective [ˌpri:sɪ'lektɪv] *adj.*: ~ **gearbox** преселекти́вная коро́бка переда́ч.

presence ['prez(ə)ns] *n.* **1.** (*being present*) прису́тствие; ~ **of mind** прису́тствие ду́ха; **I was summoned to his** ~ я был вы́зван к нему́; **he was calm in the** ~ **of danger** он остава́лся споко́йным пе́ред лицо́м опа́сности; **a military** ~ вое́нное прису́тствие; континге́нт войск; **saving your** ~ при всём к вам уваже́нии. **2.** (*carriage, bearing*) оса́нка.

cpd. ~**-chamber** *n.* приёмный зал.

present[1] ['prez(ə)nt] *n.* **1.** (*time now at hand*) настоя́щее (вре́мя); **there's no time like the** ~ ≃ лови́ моме́нт; **at** ~ сейча́с; **for the** ~ пока́; **he lives in the** ~ он живёт сего́дняшним днём. **2.** (*gram.*, ~ **tense**) настоя́щее вре́мя.

adj. **1.** (*at hand*) прису́тствующий; ~ **company excepted** о прису́тствующих не говоря́т; **no one else was** ~ никого́ бо́льше не́ было; **all** ~ **and correct** все налицо́; всё в поря́дке; ~ **to the senses** осознава́емый, ощути́мый. **2.** (*in question, under consideration*) да́нный, настоя́щий; **in the** ~ **case** в да́нном слу́чае; **the** ~ **writer** пи́шущий э́ти стро́ки. **3.** (*existent, prevalent*) настоя́щий, тепе́решний; (*available, to hand*) име́ющийся; **at the** ~ **time** в настоя́щее вре́мя; сейча́с; **the** ~ **fashion** совреме́нная мо́да; **the** ~ **holder of the title** ны́нешний облада́тель ти́тула; **under** ~ **circumstances** в ны́нешних усло́виях; в да́нных (*or* при сложи́вшихся) обстоя́тельствах; ~ **value** (*of an object*) тепе́решняя цена́. **4.** (*gram.*) настоя́щий; ~ **participle** прича́стие настоя́щего вре́мени.

cpd. ~**-day** *adj.* совреме́нный, ны́нешний.

present[2] ['prez(ə)nt] *n.* (*gift*) пода́рок, дар; **I will make you a** ~ **of this shawl** я вам подарю́ э́ту шаль.

present[3] [prɪ'zent] *n.* (*mil.*) взя́тие на карау́л.

v.t. **1.** (*tender, offer, put forward*) дари́ть, по-; вруч|а́ть, -и́ть; **he** ~**ed his compliments** он засвиде́тельствовал своё уваже́ние/почте́ние; **the little girl** ~**ed a bouquet** де́вочка преподнесла́ буке́т цвето́в; **the waiter** ~**ed the bill** официа́нт предста́вил счёт; **he** ~**ed his case well** он хорошо́ изложи́л свои́ до́воды; **he** ~**ed himself for duty** он яви́лся на слу́жбу; **as soon as an opportunity** ~**s itself** как то́лько предста́вится слу́чай; (*give, furnish*): **she** ~**ed her husband with a son** она́ подари́ла му́жу сы́на; **I was** ~**ed with a choice** мне предоста́вили вы́бор. **2.** (*introduce*) предст|авля́ть, -а́вить; **may I** ~ **my wife?** разреши́те предста́вить мою́ жену́; **she was** ~**ed at court** она́ была́ предста́влена ко двору́. **3.** (*put on stage*) пока́з|ывать, -а́ть; **this play was first** ~**ed in New York** э́ту пье́су пе́рвый раз показа́ли/поста́вили в Нью-Йо́рке; **'International Films** ~ **...'** фильм... произво́дства компа́нии «Интерне́шнл фильмс». **4.** (*exhibit*): **his face** ~**ed a strange appearance** его́ лицо́ вы́глядело стра́нно; **the situation** ~**s a threat** положе́ние чрева́то опа́сностью; **he** ~**ed a bold front** он напусти́л на себя́ хра́брый вид. **5.** (*mil.*): ~ **arms** брать, взять на карау́л; (*as command*) на карау́л!

presentable [prɪ'zentəb(ə)l] *adj.* прили́чный, респекта́бельный.

presentation [ˌprezən'teɪʃ(ə)n] *n.* **1.** (*making a present*) подноше́ние, вруче́ние; ~ **copy** (*of a book*) да́рственный экземпля́р. **2.** (*introduction, esp. at court*) представле́ние; **sales** ~ презента́ция това́ра. **3.** (*theatr.*) пока́з, постано́вка. **4.** (*production, submission*) предъявле́ние; **the cheque is payable on** ~ чек бу́дет опла́чен по предъявле́нии. **5.** (*exposition*) пода́ча.

presentiment [prɪ'zentɪmənt, -'sentɪmənt] *n.* предчу́вствие; **he had a** ~ **of danger** он предчу́вствовал опа́сность.

presently ['prezəntlɪ] *adv.* (*soon*) вско́ре; (*US, at present*) сейча́с, в настоя́щее вре́мя, в да́нный моме́нт.

preservation [ˌprezə'veɪʃ(ə)n] *n.* **1.** (*act of preserving*) сохране́ние, консерви́рование; ~ **of life** сохране́ние жи́зни; ~ **of food** консерви́рование проду́ктов; (*of monuments, etc.*) охра́на. **2.** (*state of being preserved*) сохра́нность; **the building is in a fine state of** ~ э́то зда́ние прекра́сно сохрани́лось.

preservative [prɪ'zɜ:vətɪv] *n.* (*in food*) консерва́нт.

preserve [prɪ'zɜ:v] **1.** (*jam*) варе́нье. **2.** (*area for protection of game, etc.*) запове́дник; (*fig.*): **this subject is his private** ~ э́то его́ о́бласть.

v.t. **1.** (*save; protect from harm*) сохран|я́ть, -и́ть; **his presence of mind** ~**d him from a worse fate** прису́тствие ду́ха уберегло́ его́ от ху́дшей у́части; **God** ~ **us!** упаси́ нас Бог/Госпо́дь! **2.** (*keep from decomposition, etc.*) консерви́ровать, за-. **3.** (*of game, etc.*) охраня́ть (*impf.*) от браконье́рства; **fishing is** ~**d in this river** лови́ть ры́бу в э́той реке́ запреща́ется. **4.** (*keep alive, youthful etc.*) сохран|я́ть, -и́ть; **his name will be** ~**d for ever** его́ и́мя оста́нется в века́х; **she is well** ~**d** она́ хорошо́ сохрани́лась; **he is a well-**~**d eighty** он хорошо́ сохрани́лся для его́ восьми́десяти лет. **5.** (*maintain*) подде́рж|ивать, -а́ть; храни́ть, со-; **he** ~**d his dignity** он сохрани́л своё досто́инство; **she** ~**d a discreet silence** она́ благоразу́мно храни́ла молча́ние.

preside [prɪ'zaɪd] *v.i.* председа́тельствовать (*impf.*); **the mayor** ~**d over the council** мэр председа́тельствовал на заседа́нии сове́та; **Father** ~**d at table** оте́ц сиде́л во главе́ стола́.

presidency ['prezɪdənsɪ] *n.* президе́нтство.

president ['prezɪd(ə)nt] *n.* (*of State etc.*) президе́нт; (*of college*) ре́ктор, дире́ктор; (*US, of company, bank etc.*) дире́ктор, глава́ (*c.g.*).

presidential [ˌprezɪ'denʃ(ə)l] *adj.* президе́нтский; дире́кторский.

presidium [prɪ'sɪdɪəm, -'zɪdɪəm] *n.* прези́диум.

press [pres] *n.* **1.** (*act of* ~*ing*): **he gave her hand a** ~ он пожа́л ей ру́ку; **she gave his trousers a** ~ она́ погла́дила ему́ брю́ки. **2.** (*machine for* ~*ing*) пресс. **3.** (*printing-machine*) пресс; печа́тный стано́к; **his new book is in the** ~ его́ но́вая кни́га нахо́дится в печа́ти; **we go to** ~ **tomorrow** за́втра но́мер идёт в набо́р/печа́ть; **newspaper hot from the** ~ све́жий но́мер газе́ты; **stop** ~ **(news)** э́кстренное сообще́ние; **'stop** ~**'** (*heading*) «в после́днюю мину́ту». **4.** (*printing or publishing house*) изда́тельство. **5.** (*newspaper world*) печа́ть, пре́сса; ~ **agency** аге́нство печа́ти; газе́тная аге́нство; ~ **agent** аге́нт по дела́м печа́ти; ~ **campaign** кампа́ния в печа́ти; ~ **conference** пресс-конфере́нция; ~ **release** сообще́ние для печа́ти; (*newspaper reaction*) о́тклик, реце́нзия; **a good** ~ **helps to sell a book** хоро́шие о́тклики в печа́ти спосо́бствуют сбы́ту кни́ги; **the bill had a bad** ~ пре́сса недоброжела́тельно встре́тила э́тот законопрое́кт. **6.** (*crowd*) толчея́, толпа́. **7.** (*pressure*) спе́шка; ~ **of business** неотло́жные дела́. **8.** (*cupboard*) шкаф.

v.t. **1.** (*exert physical pressure on*) наж|има́ть, -а́ть; нада́в|ливать, -и́ть; ~ **the trigger/button** нажа́ть (*pf.*) куро́к/кно́пку; **he** ~**ed the button** (*initiated action*) он дал де́лу ход. **2.** (*push*) приж|има́ть, -а́ть; **he** ~**ed his nose against the window** он прижа́л нос к окну́. **3.** (*compress, etc.*) гла́дить, по-; утю́жить, от-; **my suit needs** ~**ing** мой костю́м нужда́ется в утю́жке; **the villagers are** ~**ing the grapes** жи́тели дере́вни да́вят виногра́д; **the juice** ~**ed from a lemon** сок из вы́жатого лимо́на; ~**ed beef** мясны́е консе́рв|ы (*pl., g.* -ов). **4.** (*clasp, embrace*) приж|има́ть, -а́ть; **she** ~**ed the child to her bosom** она́ прижа́ла ребёнка к груди́; **he** ~**ed her hand** он пожа́л ей ру́ку. **5.** (*fig., sustain vigorously*): **our team** ~**ed home its attack** на́ша кома́нда наседа́ла; **he** ~**ed his claim** он наста́ивал на своём тре́бовании. **6.** (*fig., harry, exert pressure on*) тесни́ть (*impf.*); **our forces were hard** ~**ed** враг си́льно тесни́л на́ши войска́; **he was hard** ~**ed for an answer** он не нашёл, что отве́тить; **I was** ~**ed for time** у меня́ бы́ло вре́мени в обре́з. **7.** (*urge, importune*): **they** ~**ed me to stay** они́ угова́ривали меня́ оста́ться; **he** ~**ed me for a decision** он торопи́л меня́ с реше́нием. **8.** (*urge acceptance of*) навя́зывать (*impf.*); **he** ~**ed money on me** он уси́ленно предлага́л мне де́ньги. **9.** (*recruit forcibly*) наси́льно вербова́ть, за-; **every available chair was** ~**ed into service** все име́ющиеся в распоряже́нии сту́лья пошли́ в ход.

v.i.: **if you ~ too hard, the pencil will break** е́сли сли́шком нажима́ть, каранда́ш слома́ется; (*fig.*): **his responsibilities ~ed heavily upon him** он был пода́влен свои́ми обя́занностями; **time ~es** вре́мя не те́рпит.

with advs.: **~ back** *v.t.* отбр|а́сывать, -о́сить; оттесн|я́ть, -и́ть; **~ down** *v.t.* приж|има́ть, -а́ть; прида́в|ливать, -и́ть; **~ forward** *v.i.* прот|а́лкиваться, -олкну́ться (вперёд); **~ on** *v.i.* потора́пливаться (*impf.*); **~ on regardless!** продолжа́йте в том же ду́хе несмотря́ ни на что!; **~ out** *v.t.* выжима́ть, вы́жать; **~ up** *v.t.* тесни́ть (*impf.*).

cpds. **~-button** *n.* нажи́мная кно́пка; **~-button warfare** «кно́почная война́»; **~-clipping, ~-cutting** *nn.* газе́тная вы́резка; **~-gallery** *n.* места́ для представи́телей пре́ссы/печа́ти; **~-gang** *n.* (*hist.*) отря́д вербо́вщиков во флот; *v.t.* наси́льно вербова́ть во флот; (*fig.*) ока́з|ывать, -а́ть давле́ние на+*a.*; **~man** *n.* журнали́ст, газе́тчик, репортёр; **~-mark** *n.* шифр; **~-stud** *n.* кно́пка (*одёжная*); **~-up** *n.* отжи́м; **do ~-ups** отжима́ться (*impf.*) (на полу́).

presser ['presə(r)] *n.* глади́льщик.

pressing[1] ['presɪŋ] *n.* (*of clothing*) гла́жка, утю́жка.

pressing[2] ['presɪŋ] *adj.* (*urgent*) спе́шный, неотло́жный; (*insistent*) настоя́тельный, насто́йчивый.

pressure ['preʃə(r)] *n.* **1.** давле́ние; **the tyre ~s are low** давле́ние в ши́нах ни́зкое; **~ cabin** гермети́ческая каби́на; **~ suit** пневмокостю́м; (*fig.*) напряже́ние; **they are working at high ~** они́ рабо́тают о́чень напряжённо. **2.** (*compulsive influence*) давле́ние, возде́йствие; **bring ~ to bear on** прин|ужда́ть, -у́дить; **they brought ~ to bear on him to sign** они прину́дили его́ подписа́ться; **put ~ on** наж|има́ть, -а́ть на+*a.*; **the police put ~ on him** поли́ция оказа́ла нажи́м/давле́ние на него́; **~ group** ≃ инициати́вная гру́ппа; **under ~ of poverty** под гнётом нищеты́.

cpds. **~-cooker** *n.* скорова́рка; **~-gauge** *n.* мано́метр.

pressurize ['preʃə,raɪz] *v.t.* **1.** герметизи́ровать (*impf.*); **~d cabin** гермети́ческая каби́на. **2.** (*fig.*) ока́з|ывать, -а́ть давле́ние на+*a.*; **he was ~d into writing a confession** его́ заста́вили написа́ть призна́ние.

prestidigitation [,prestɪ,dɪdʒɪ'teɪʃ(ə)n] *n.* пока́зывание фо́кусов.

prestidigitator [,prestɪ'dɪdʒɪ,teɪtə(r)] *n.* фо́кусник.

prestige [pre'stiːʒ] *n.* прести́ж.

prestigious [pre'stɪdʒəs] *adj.* (*having prestige*) влия́тельный, авторите́тный, уважа́емый.

prestissimo [pre'stɪsɪ,məʊ] *n.*, *adj.* & *adv.* прести́ссимо (*indecl.*).

presto[1] ['prestəʊ] *n.*, *adj.* & *adv.* (*mus.*) пре́сто (*indecl.*).

presto[2] ['prestəʊ] *int.*: **(hey) ~!** гопля́!

pre-stressed [priː'strest] *adj.* предвари́тельно напряжённый.

presumable [prɪ'zjuːməb(ə)l] *adj.* предпологáемый, вероя́тный.

presumably [prɪ'zjuːməblɪ] *adv.* вероя́тно; на́до полага́ть, что...

presume [prɪ'zjuːm] *v.t.* **1.** (*assume, take for granted*) полага́ть (*impf.*); **you are married, I ~?** я полага́ю, что вы жена́ты? **2.** (*with inf.*: *venture*) позв|оля́ть, -о́лить себе́; осме́ли|ваться, -ться; **I would not ~ to argue with you** я не возьму́ на себя́ сме́лость с ва́ми спо́рить.

v.i.: **~ on** (*take liberties with*): **he ~d on my good nature** он злоупотреби́л мое́й доброто́й.

presumption [prɪ'zʌmpʃ(ə)n] *n.* **1.** (*assumption*) предположе́ние, (*leg.*) презу́мпция; **~ of innocence** презу́мпция невино́вности; **I left on the ~ he would follow** я ушёл, предполага́я, что он после́дует за мной; **the ~ is that he is lying** на́до исходи́ть из того́, что он врёт; **there is a strong ~ against it** есть серьёзные основа́ния про́тив. **2.** (*arrogance, boldness*) самонаде́янность.

presumptive [prɪ'zʌmptɪv] *adj.* предположи́тельный, предполага́емый; **~ father** предполага́емый оте́ц; **~ evidence** показа́ния, осно́ванные на дога́дках.

presumptuous [prɪ'zʌmptjʊəs] *adj.* самонаде́янный, самоуве́ренный.

presumptuousness [prɪ'zʌmptjʊəsnɪs] *n.* самонаде́янность, самоуве́ренность.

presuppose [,priːsə'pəʊz] *v.t.* (зара́нее) предпол|ага́ть, -ожи́ть; допус|ка́ть, -ти́ть.

presupposition [priː,sʌpə'zɪʃ(ə)n] *n.* предположе́ние, допуще́ние; исхо́дная предпосы́лка.

pre-tax [priː'tæks] *adj.* начи́сленный до вы́чета нало́гов; **~ profits** при́быль до нало́га.

pretence [prɪ'tens] (*US* **pretense**) *n.* **1.** (*pretending, make-believe*) притво́рство; **he made a ~ of reading the newspaper** он притвори́лся, что чита́ет газе́ту; **he obtained money by false ~s** он раздобы́л де́ньги обма́нным путём. **2.** (*pretext, excuse*) предло́г, отгово́рка; **he called under the ~ of asking advice** он зашёл под предло́гом спроси́ть сове́та. **3.** (*claim*) прете́нзия; **I make no ~ to scholarship** я не претенду́ю на учёность. **4.** (*ostentation*) претенцио́зность; **a man without ~** челове́к без прете́нзий.

pretend [prɪ'tend] *v.t.* & *i.* **1.** (*make believe*) притворя́ться (*impf.*); де́лать вид; **she is ~ing to be asleep** она́ притворя́ется, что спит; **let's ~ to be pirates!** дава́йте игра́ть в пира́тов! **2.** (*claim*) претендова́ть (*impf.*); **I don't ~ to understand Einstein** я не претенду́ю на то, что понима́ю Эйнште́йна; **they both ~ed to the throne** они́ о́ба претендова́ли на престо́л.

pretender [prɪ'tendə(r)] *n.* претенде́нт, самозва́нец.

pretense [prɪ'tens] = **pretence**

pretension [prɪ'tenʃ(ə)n] *n.* **1.** (*claim*) притяза́ние, прете́нзия; **I make no ~ to literary style** я во́все не претенду́ю на литерату́рный стиль. **2.** (*pretentiousness*) претенцио́зность.

pretentious [prɪ'tenʃəs] *adj.* претенцио́зный; показно́й.

pretentiousness [prɪ'tenʃəsnɪs] *n.* претенцио́зность.

preterite ['pretərɪt] *n.* прете́рит.

adj. прете́ритный.

pretermission [,priːtə'mɪʃ(ə)n] *n.* (*omission, neglect*) упуще́ние; небре́жность; (*breaking off*) вре́менное прекраще́ние.

pretermit [,priːtə'mɪt] *v.t.* (*omit to mention*) пропус|ка́ть, -ти́ть; (*omit to do*) пренебр|ега́ть, -е́чь +*i.*; (*discontinue*) прер|ывать, ва́ть.

preternatural [,priːtə'nætʃər(ə)l] *adj.* сверхъесте́ственный.

pretext ['priːtekst] *n.* предло́г, отгово́рка; **on, under the ~ of** под предло́гом +*g.*

prettify ['prɪtɪ,faɪ] *v.t.* укр|аша́ть, -а́сить.

prettiness ['prɪtɪnɪs] *n.* милови́дность; пре́лесть, привлека́тельность.

pretty ['prɪtɪ] *n.*: **my ~!** моя́ пре́лесть!

adj. **1.** (*attractive*) краси́вый, хоро́шенький. **2.** (*pleasant*) прия́тный, хоро́ший; **he has a ~ wit** он о́чень остроу́мен. **3.** (*iron.*) хоро́шенький, весёленький; **a ~ mess you have made of it!** ну и ка́шу вы завари́ли! **4.** (*considerable*) значи́тельный; изря́дный; **this will cost you a ~ penny** э́то вам обойдётся в копе́ечку.

adv. **1.** (*fairly*) доста́точно, дово́льно; **I have ~ well finished my work** я почти́ что зако́нчил свою́ рабо́ту; **~ much** о́чень, в значи́тельной сте́пени; почти́. **2.: he is sitting ~** он непло́хо устро́ился.

cpd. **~-~** *adj.* (*of pers.*) смазли́вый, ку́кольный; (*of thg.*) как карти́нка; как конфе́тка.

pretzel ['prets(ə)l] *n.* кренделёк.

prevail [prɪ'veɪl] *v.i.* **1.** (*win*) торжествова́ть (*impf.*); **truth will ~** пра́вда восторжеству́ет; **~ over** одол|ева́ть, -е́ть. **2.** (*be widespread*) преоблада́ть (*impf.*), госпо́дствовать (*impf.*): **~ing winds** преоблада́ющие ве́тры; **the fashion still ~s** э́та мо́да ещё госпо́дствует; **calm ~s** цари́т споко́йствие. **3.: ~ on** (*persuade*) убе|жда́ть, -ди́ть; **I ~ed on him to stop smoking** я уговори́л его́ бро́сить кури́ть.

prevalence ['prevələns] *n.* распростране́ние.

prevalent ['prevələnt] *adj.* распространённый.

prevaricate [prɪ'værɪ,keɪt] *v.i.* уклоня́ться (*impf.*) от отве́та; увил|ивать, -ьну́ть.

prevarication [prɪ,værɪ'keɪʃ(ə)n] *n.* уклоне́ние от отве́та; увилива́ние.

prevent [prɪ'vent] *v.t.* предотвра|ща́ть, -ти́ть; предохран|я́ть, -и́ть; меша́ть, по- +*d.*; препя́тствовать, вос- +*d.*; не дать (*pf.*) +*d.*; **illness ~ed him from coming** боле́знь помеша́ла емý прийтú.

preventable [prɪ'ventəb(ə)l] *adj.* не неизбéжный.

preventative [prɪ'ventətɪv] = **preventive**

prevention [prɪ'venʃ(ə)n] *n.* предотвращéние, предохранéние; ~ **is better than cure** предупреждéние — лýчше лечéния.

prevent|ive [prɪ'ventɪv], **-ative** [prɪ'ventətɪv] *n.* предупредúтельная мéра.

adj. предупредúтельный; ~ **detention** превентúвное заключéние; ~ **medicine** профилактúческая медицúна, профилáктика.

preview ['pri:vju:] *n.* (предварúтельный) просмóтр, премьéра, вернисáж.

v.t. предварúтельно просм|áтривать, -отрéть.

previous ['pri:vɪəs] *adj.* **1.** (*earlier*, *former*) предыдýщий; **on a ~ occasion** в предыдýщем слýчае; **on the ~ day** зá день до э́того. **2.** (*coll.*, *premature*, *hasty*) преждеврéменный; **you are a little ~** вы немнóго поспешúли.

adv.: ~ **to** прéжде+*g.*, до+*g.*; ~ **to that he was in the army** до э́того он был в áрмии.

previously ['pri:vɪəslɪ] *adv.* **1.** (*earlier*) зарáнее, рáньше; **I arrived two days ~** я приéхал нá два днá рáньше. **2.** (*formerly*): ~ **he had lived with his brother** до э́того он жил со своúм брáтом.

prevision [prɪ'vɪʒ(ə)n] *n.* предвúдение.

pre-war [pri:'wɔ:(r), 'pri:wɔ:(r)] *adj.* предвоéнный, довоéнный.

prey [preɪ] *n.* добы́ча; **bird of ~** хúщная птúца; (*fig.*) жéртва; **he fell an easy ~ to their cunning** он оказáлся лёгкой жéртвой их ковáрства; **she was a ~ to anxiety** её одолевáло/мучúло беспокóйство.

v.i. охóтиться (*impf.*); **owls ~ on mice** сóвы охóтятся на мышéй; (*fig.*): **he ~ed upon credulous women** он обмáнывал довéрчивых жéнщин; **the crime ~ed upon his mind** (совершённое) преступлéние не давáло емý покóя.

price [praɪs] *n.* **1.** ценá; **asking ~** запрáшиваемая ценá; **he bought it at cost ~** он купúл э́то по себестóимости; **what is the ~ of eggs?** скóлько стóят я́йца?; **there is a ~ on his head** объ́явлена наградá за егó гóлову; **every man has his ~** все лю́ди продáжны; **they wanted peace at any ~** им нýжен бы́л мир любóй ценóй; **I wouldn't have your job at any ~** я бы не согласúлся на вáшу рабóту ни за какúе дéньги; **he got the job, but at a ~** он получúл рабóту, но дорогóй ценóй. **2.** (*value*) цéнность; **a pearl of great ~** жемчýжина большóй цéнности; **good health is beyond ~** хорóшее здорóвье — бесцéнный дар. **3.** (*betting odds*) шáнсы (*m. pl.*); **what ~ the favourite?** каковá вы́плата за фаворúта?; **what ~ honour?** чегó тепéрь стóит честь?

v.t. **1.** (*fix ~ of*) назн|ачáть, -áчить ценý на+*a.*; **he will ~ himself out of the market** он завышáет цéну и теря́ет покупáтелей. **2.** (*enquire ~ of*) прицéн|иваться, -úться к+*d.*

cpds. **~-control** *n.* контрóль (*m.*) над ценáми; **~-list** *n.* прейскурáнт; **~-tag** *n.* ярлы́к (с указáнием ценьı́).

priceless ['praɪslɪs] *adj.* (*invaluable*) бесцéнный; (*coll.*, *most amusing*) бесподóбный.

pricey ['praɪsɪ] *adj.* (*coll.*) дорогóй.

prick [prɪk] *n.* **1.** шип; колю́чка; (*puncture*) прокóл; (*fig.*): **the ~s of conscience** угрызéния (*nt. pl.*) сóвести. **2.** (*mark made by ~ing*) укóл. **3.** (*arch.*, *goad*): **it is no use kicking against the ~s** зачéм лезть на рожóн? **4.** (*penis*) хуй (*vulg.*).

v.t. колóть, у-; **her laughter ~ed the bubble of his self-esteem** её смех уязвúл егó самолю́бие; (*fig.*) терзáть (*impf.*); **my conscience has been ~ing me** меня́ мýчила сóвесть.

v.i. колóться, у-.

with advs.: ~ **off**, ~ **out** *v.t.* пикировáть (*impf.*); перес|áживать, -адúть; ~ **up** *v.t.*: ~ **up one's ears** (*of animal or pers.*) навострúть (*pf.*) ýши.

prickle ['prɪk(ə)l] *n.* (*thorn*) колю́чка, шип; (*of hedgehog etc.*) иглá.

v.t. & i. колóть(ся), у-.

prickly ['prɪklɪ] *adj.* (*having spines or thorns*) колю́чий; (*causing a prickling sensation*) кóлкий; (*fig.*, *easily offended*) обúдчивый.

pride [praɪd] *n.* **1.** (*self-esteem*, *conceit*) гóрдость; (*pej.*) спесь; (*amour-propre*) амбúция; ~ **goes before a fall** горды́ня до добрá не доведёт; **pocket, swallow one's ~** поступúться (*pf.*) своúм самолю́бием. **2.** (*consciousness of worth*; *dignity*) чýвство сóбственного достóинства; **proper ~** самоуважéние; **I have too much ~ to accept charity** гóрдость не позволя́ет мне прúнять мúлостыню; **false ~** лóжная гóрдость, тщеслáвие; **he takes ~ in his work** он гордúтся своéй рабóтой. **3.** (*object of satisfaction*): **the yacht was his ~ and joy** э́та я́хта былá егó гóрдостью и рáдостью. **4.** (*prime*) расцвéт; **in the ~ of his youth** в расцвéте мóлодости. **5.** (*primacy*): **his book takes ~ of place** егó кнúге принадлежúт почётное мéсто. **6.**: **a ~ of lions** стáя львов.

v.t.: ~ **o.s. on** гордúться (*impf.*) +*i.*; **she ~s herself on her cooking** онá гордúтся своúм кулинáрным искýсством.

prie-dieu [pri:'djɜ:] *n.* скамéечка для молúтвы.

priest [pri:st] *n.* (*of Christian church*) свящéнник, священнослужúтель (*m.*); (*of non-Christian religion*) жрец; **high ~** верхóвный жрец.

cpds. **~craft** *n.* вмешáтельство духовéнства в мирскýю жизнь; **~-ridden** *adj.* (находя́щийся) в подчинéнии у духовéнства.

priestess ['pri:stɪs] *n.* жрúца.

priesthood ['pri:sthʊd] *n.* (*office*) свящéнство; (*clergy*) духовéнство; (*non-Christian*) жрéчество.

priestly ['pri:stlɪ] *adj.* свящéннический; жрéческий.

prig [prɪg] *n.* педáнт; (*hypocrite*) ханжá (*c.g.*).

priggish ['prɪgɪʃ] *adj.* педантúчный; хáнжеский.

priggishness ['prɪgɪʃnɪs] *n.* педантúчность; хáнжествó.

prim [prɪm] *adj.* (*also ~ and proper*) чóпорный.

prima [ˌpri:mə] *adj.*: **~ ballerina** прúма-балерúна; **~ donna** (*lit.*) примадóнна, дúва; (*fig.*) примадóнна.

primacy ['praɪməsɪ] *n.* (*pre-eminence*) главéнство; (*office of primate*) сан архиепúскопа.

primaeval [praɪ'mi:v(ə)l] = **primeval**

prima facie [ˌpraɪmə 'feɪʃi:] *adj.*: **~ evidence** доказáтельство, достáточное при отсýтствии опровержéния.

adv. на пéрвый взгляд.

primal ['praɪm(ə)l] *adj.* (*original*) первоначáльный; (*chief*) глáвный.

primarily ['praɪmərɪlɪ, -'meərɪlɪ] *adv.* (*originally*) первоначáльно; (*principally*, *essentially*) в основнóм; глáвным óбразом; в пéрвую óчередь.

primary ['praɪmərɪ] *n.* (*US*) предварúтельное предвы́борное собрáние; предварúтельные вы́бор|ы (*pl.*, *g.* -ов).

adj. **1.** (*original*) первоначáльный; **~ school** начáльная шкóла. **2.** (*fundamental*, *basic*, *principal*) основнóй; **~ colours** основны́е цветá; **of ~ importance** первостепéнной вáжности; **~ meaning** основнóе/первúчное значéние.

primate ['praɪmeɪt] *n.* (*archbishop*) примáс; (*mammal*) примáт.

prime [praɪm] *n.* **1.** (*perfection*, *best part*) расцвéт; **in the ~ of life** в расцвéте сил; **he is past his ~** егó лýчшие дни остáлись позадú. **2.** (*first or earliest part*) начáло. **3.** (~ *number*) простóе числó.

adj. **1.** (*principal*) глáвный; **~ minister** премьéр-минúстр. **2.** (*excellent*) первоклáссный; **~ beef** первосóртная говя́дина. **3.** (*fundamental*) основнóй; **~ cost** себестóимость; **~ mover** (*source of motive power*) первúчный двúгатель; (*fig.*) зачúнщик; **~ number** простóе числó.

v.t. **1.** (*firearm*) заря|жáть, -дúть; (*engine*, *pump*) запр|авля́ть, -áвить. **2.** (*supply with facts etc.*) инструктúровать (*impf.*, *pf.*); натáск|ивать, -áть. **3.** (*fill with food or drink*) накормúть (*pf.*); напоúть (*pf.*). **4.** (*cover with first coat of paint etc.*) грунтовáть (*impf.*).

primer[1] ['praɪmə(r)] *n.* **1.** (*school-book*) буквáрь (*m.*). **2.** (*for igniting*) запáл, кáпсюль (*m.*). **3.** (*paint*) грунтóвка.

primer[2] ['praɪmə(r)] *n.* (*size of type*) шрифт в 18 пýнктов.

prim|eval, -aeval [praɪ'mi:v(ə)l] *adj.* первобы́тный, первоздáнный.

priming ['praɪmɪŋ] *n.* (*firing charge*) заправка, залúвка;

(*paint*) грунт, грунто́вка.

primitive ['prɪmɪtɪv] *n.* (*painter*) примитиви́ст; (*painting*) примити́в.

adj. (*earliest*) первобы́тный; ~ **man** первобы́тный челове́к; (*unsophisticated, simple*) примити́вный, несло́жный.

primness ['prɪmnɪs] *n.* чо́порность.

primogenitor [,praɪməʊ'dʒenɪtə(r)] *n.* прароди́тель (*m.*), пра́щур.

primogeniture [,praɪməʊ'dʒenɪtʃə(r)] *n.* первоpо́дство.

primordial [praɪ'mɔ:dɪəl] *adj.* первичный, иско́нный, первобы́тный; (*fundamental*) основно́й.

primrose ['prɪmrəʊz] *n.* **1.** (*flower*) при́мула; **the ~ path** ≃ путь наслажде́ний. **2.** (*colour*) бле́дно-жёлтый цвет.

Primus ['praɪməs] *n.* (*propr.*) **(~ stove)** при́мус.

prince [prɪns] *n.* **1.** князь (*m.*); (*son of royalty*) принц, (*arch.*) короле́вич; **P~ of Wales/Denmark** принц Уэ́льский/Да́тский; **~ consort** принц-супру́г; **~ of the Church** кардина́л, князь це́ркви. **2.** (*fig.*): **the P~ of Peace** Христо́с; **the ~ of darkness** сатана́ (*m.*); **~ of poets** царь (*m.*) поэ́тов; **merchant ~** кру́пный коммерса́нт; **~ of rogues** коро́ль жу́ликов.

princedom ['prɪnsdəm] *n.* сан при́нца; кня́жество.

princeling ['prɪnslɪŋ] *n.* (*pej.*) князёк.

princely ['prɪnslɪ] *adj.* (*pert. to a prince*) кня́жеский, короле́вский; (*generous*) благоро́дный; (*splendid*) кня́жеский, ца́рственный.

princess [prɪn'ses] *n.* (*wife of non-royal prince*) княги́ня; (*their daughter*) княжна́; (*daughter or daughter-in-law of sovereign*) принце́сса, (*arch.*) короле́вна; **~ royal** ста́ршая дочь короля́/короле́вы.

principal ['prɪnsɪp(ə)l] *n.* **1.** (*head of college etc.*) дире́ктор, ре́ктор. **2.** (*pers. for whom another acts*) довери́тель (*m.*). **3.** (*chief participant in crime*) гла́вный престу́пник. **4.** (*in duel*) дуэли́ст. **5.** (*pl., chief actors*) веду́щие исполни́тели (*m. pl.*). **6.** (*sum of money*) капита́л.

adj. гла́вный, основно́й.

principality [,prɪnsɪ'pælɪtɪ] *n.* кня́жество.

principally ['prɪnsɪpəlɪ] *adv.* гла́вным о́бразом; преиму́щественно.

principle ['prɪnsɪp(ə)l] *n.* при́нцип, нача́ло; **the ~ of the wheel** при́нцип колеса́; **Archimedes' ~** зако́н Архиме́да; **the first ~s of geometry** осно́вы (*f. pl.*) геоме́трии; **I agree in ~** в при́нципе я согла́сен; **I object to it on ~** я возража́ю про́тив э́того из при́нципа; **a man of ~** принципиа́льный челове́к.

prink [prɪŋk] *v.t.* наря|жа́ть, -ди́ть; **she ~ed herself up at the mirror** она́ наряжа́лась/прихора́шивалась пе́ред зе́ркалом.

v.i. наря|жа́ться, -ди́ться.

print [prɪnt] *n.* **1.** (*mark made on surface by pressure*) след; отпеча́ток; **the police took his ~s** поли́ция сня́ли у него́ отпеча́тки па́льцев. **2.** (*letters, etc.*) шрифт; печа́ть; **~ run** тира́ж; **he looked forward to seeing his name in ~** он предвкуша́л моме́нт появле́ния своего́ и́мени в печа́ти; **the book is in ~** кни́га ещё в прода́же; **the book is out of ~** кни́га распро́дана. **3.** (*picture*) гравю́ра, эста́мп, репроду́кция. **4.** (*phot.*) отпеча́ток. **5.** (*cotton fabric*) си́тец; **a ~ dress** си́тцевое пла́тье.

v.t. **1.** (*impress*) печа́тать, на-/от-; (*fig.*) запечатл|ева́ть, -е́ть; **her face was ~ed on his memory** её лицо́ запечатле́лось у него́ в па́мяти. **2.** (*produce by ~ing process; copy photographically*) печа́тать, на-/от-; **this undertaking is not worth the paper it is ~ed on** э́то обяза́тельство не сто́ит бума́ги, на кото́рой оно́ напи́сано; **where did you get it ~ed?** где вам э́то напеча́тали? **3.** (*write in imitation of ~*) писа́ть, на- печа́тными бу́квами. **4.** (*mark with coloured design*) наб|ива́ть, -и́ть.

with advs.: **~ off, ~ out** *v.t.* (*phot.*) де́лать, с- фотоотпеча́тки +*g*.

cpds. **~-out** *n.* (*by computer*) распеча́тка (с) ЭВМ; **~-seller** *n.* продаве́ц гравю́р и эста́мпов.

printable ['prɪntəb(ə)l] *adj.* (*fit to print*) досто́йный напеча́тания.

printer ['prɪntə(r)] *n.* (*operator of press*) печа́тник, типо́граф; (*type-setter*) набо́рщик; **~'s copy** оригина́л для набо́ра; **~'s devil** учени́к (ма́льчик) на побегу́шках в типогра́фии; (*owner of printing business*) типо́граф; (*comput.*) при́нтер; (*teleprinter*) телепри́нтер.

printing ['prɪntɪŋ] *n.* (*act or process*) печа́тание; (*trade*) печа́тное де́ло; (*material printed in one operation*) печа́тное изда́ние.

cpds. **~-ink** *n.* печа́тная кра́ска; **~-machine** *n.* печа́тная маши́на; **~-office** *n.* типогра́фия; **~-press** *n.* печа́тный стано́к.

prior[1] ['praɪə(r)] *n.* (*eccl.*) прио́р, настоя́тель (*m.*).

prior[2] ['praɪə(r)] *adj.* (*earlier*) пре́жний; (*more important*) первоочередно́й; **he has a ~ claim to your attention** он мо́жет претендова́ть на ва́ше внима́ние в пе́рвую о́чередь.

adv.: **~ to** до+*g*.

prioress ['praɪərɪs] *n.* настоя́тельница.

prioritize [praɪ'ɒrɪtaɪz] *v.t.* устан|а́вливать, -ови́ть очерёдность; распредел|я́ть, -и́ть приорите́ты.

priorit|y [praɪ'ɒrɪtɪ] *n.* приорите́т; поря́док очерёдности; **safety is our first, highest, top ~y** безопа́сность — на́ша са́мая неотло́жная забо́та; **have you got your ~ies right?** пра́вильно ли вы оцени́ли, что бо́лее и что ме́нее ва́жно?

priory ['praɪərɪ] *n.* монасты́рь (*m.*).

pri|se, -ze [praɪz] *v.t.* взл|а́мывать, -oма́ть; **the box was ~d open** я́щик взлома́ли; **he ~d up the paving-stone** он по́днял булы́жник с по́мощью рычага́; (*fig.*) разн|има́ть, -я́ть; **they ~d the combatants apart** они́ разня́ли деру́щихся.

prism ['prɪz(ə)m] *n.* при́зма.

prismatic [prɪz'mætɪk] *adj.* призмати́ческий.

prison ['prɪz(ə)n] *n.* **1.** тюрьма́; **he is in ~ for murder** он в тюрьме́ за уби́йство; **he was sent to ~ for a year** его́ посади́ли в тюрьму́ на́ год. **2.** (*attr.*) тюре́мный; **~ camp** исправи́тельно-трудово́й ла́герь; **~ clothes** аре́стантская оде́жда; **~ sentence** тюре́мный срок.

cpd. **~-breaking** *n.* побе́г из тюрьмы́.

prisoner ['prɪznə(r)] *n.* **1.** (*detained by civil authorities*) заключённый; **~ at the bar** подсуди́мый; (*fig.*) пле́нник; **he was a ~ to his habits** он был пле́нником свои́х привы́чек. **2.** (*~ of war*) военнопле́нный; **they were all taken ~** их всех взя́ли в плен.

prissy ['prɪsɪ] *adj.* чо́порный, жема́нный, вы́чурный.

pristine ['prɪsti:n, 'prɪstaɪn] *adj.* (*former*) пре́жний, было́й; (*fresh, pure*) чи́стый, нетро́нутый.

prithee ['prɪði:] *int.* (*arch.*) молю́/прошу́ вас.

privacy ['prɪvəsɪ, 'praɪ-] *n.* (*seclusion*) уедине́ние, уединённость; **this is an invasion of my ~** э́то — вмеша́тельство в мою́ ли́чную/ча́стную жизнь; (*avoidance of publicity*) секре́тность; **he told me in the strictest ~ that ...** он мне сказа́л стро́го по секре́ту, что...

private ['praɪvət, -vɪt] *n.* **1.** (*soldier*) рядово́й. **2.**: **in ~** в у́зком кругу́; в ча́стной жи́зни; **he drinks a great deal in ~** он мно́го пьёт в одино́чку; **can we discuss this in ~?** мо́жно нам поговори́ть об э́том с глазу на глаз?

adj. **1.** (*personal*) ча́стный, ли́чный; **my ~ affairs** мои́ ли́чные дела́; **~ enterprise** ча́стное предпринима́тельство, (*a particular concern*) ча́стное предприя́тие; **in ~ life** в ли́чной жи́зни; **~ means** ли́чное состоя́ние; **~ property** ча́стная со́бственность; **for ~ reasons** по ли́чным причи́нам; **~ secretary** ли́чный секрета́рь. **2.** (*not open to the general public*) закры́тый; **~ view** закры́тый просмо́тр, вернисаж. **3.** (*secret*) та́йный, секре́тный; **for your ~ ear** стро́го ме́жду на́ми; **~ parts** половы́е о́рганы. **4.** (*without official status*) ча́стный; неофициа́льный; прива́тный; **in one's ~ capacity** как ча́стное лицо́; **~ eye** (*coll.*) ча́стный сы́щик, детекти́в; **~ member** (*of Parliament*) депута́т парла́мента, не входя́щий в прави́тельство; **a doctor in ~ practice** ча́стный врач.

privateer [,praɪvə'tɪə(r)] *n.* (*vessel, captain*) ка́пер.

privateering [,praɪvə'tɪərɪŋ] *n.* ка́перство.

privation [praɪ'veɪʃ(ə)n] *n.* (*loss*) утра́та; лише́ние; (*hardship*) лише́ние; нужда́.

privatization [ˌpraɪvəˌtaɪ'zeɪʃ(ə)n] *n.* приватиза́ция.

privatize ['praɪvəˌtaɪz] *v.t.* приватизи́ровать.

privet ['prɪvɪt] *n.* бирючи́на.

privilege ['prɪvɪlɪdʒ] *n.* привиле́гия; **the ~ of birth** привиле́гия по рожде́нию; (*in Parliament*) депута́тская неприкоснове́нность; **breach of ~** наруше́ние прав парла́мента; (*fig.*): **it was a ~ to listen to him** слу́шать его́ бы́ло исключи́тельным удово́льствием.
v.t. да|ва́ть, -ть привиле́гию +*d.*; **I was ~d to be there** я име́л сча́стье/честь там быть.

privileged ['prɪvɪlɪdʒd] *adj.* привилегиро́ванный.

privy ['prɪvɪ] *n.* (*latrine*) убо́рная.
adj. **1.** (*secret*) ча́стный, прива́тный, скры́тый; **~ parts** (*arch.*) полов́ые о́рганы. **2.** (*pert. to the sovereign*): **P~ Council** та́йный сове́т; **the ~ purse** су́ммы, ассигно́ванные на ли́чные расхо́ды мона́рха. **3.**: **~ to** прича́стный к+*d.*; посвящённый в+*a.*; **he was ~ to her intentions** он был посвящён в её пла́ны.

prize[1] [praɪz] *n.* **1.** (*reward for merit etc.*) приз; (*esp. monetary*) пре́мия; награ́да. **2.** (*fig., goal*) предме́т жела́ний; **the ~s of life** жи́зненные бла́га. **3.** (*attr., awarded as prize*) призово́й; (*~-winning*) премиро́ванный; **~ poem** поэ́ма, удосто́енная пре́мии; (*coll., egregious*) отъя́вленный; **he is a ~ idiot** он патенто́ванный дура́к.
v.t. высоко́ цени́ть (*impf.*); **he ~s his honour above everything** он це́нит свою́ честь бо́льше всего́ остально́го.
cpds. **~-fight** *n.* матч боксёров-профессиона́лов; **~fighter** *n.* боксёр-профессиона́л; **~-ring** *n.* ринг; **~-winner** *n.* призёр (*fem. coll.* -ша).

prize[2] [praɪz] *n.* (*taken at sea*) приз, трофе́й; (*fig., windfall*) нахо́дка, добы́ча.
cpd. **~-money** *n.* призовы́е де́н|ьги (*pl., g.* -ег).

prize[3] [praɪz] = **prise**

pro[1] [prəʊ] *n.* (*point in favour*): **~s and cons** до́воды «за» и «про́тив».
prep. (*coll., in favour of*) за+*a.*; **are you ~ the bill?** вы за э́тот законопрое́кт?

pro[2] [prəʊ] *n.* (*coll., professional actor, sportsman etc.*) профессиона́л (*fem.* -ка).

PRO[3] (*abbr. of* **public relations officer**) *see* **public** *adj.* **1.**

probability [ˌprɒbə'bɪlɪtɪ] *n.* вероя́тность; **in all ~** по всей вероя́тности; **there is a strong ~ that ...** весьма́ вероя́тно, что...

probable ['prɒbəb(ə)l] *n.* (*candidate*) си́льный кандида́т.
adj. вероя́тный.

probate ['prəʊbeɪt, -bət] *n.* (*proving of will*) утвержде́ние завеща́ния; **~ has been granted** завеща́ние бы́ло утверждено́; (*copy of will*) заве́ренная ко́пия завеща́ния.

probation [prə'beɪʃ(ə)n] *n.* **1.** (*testing of candidate etc.*) испыта́ние; (*period of test*) стажиро́вка; испыта́тельный срок; **he was on ~ for two years** он прошёл двухле́тний испыта́тельный срок. **2.** (*leg.*) испыта́тельный срок, усло́вное освобожде́ние; **he was put on ~** он получи́л усло́вный пригово́р; **~ officer** должностно́е лицо́, осуществля́ющее надзо́р за усло́вно осуждённым.

probationary [prə'beɪʃənərɪ] *adj.* испыта́тельный; **~ sentence** усло́вный пригово́р.

probationer [prə'beɪʃənə(r)] *n.* (*trainee*) стажёр; практика́нт; (*offender on probation*) усло́вно осуждённый.

probative ['prəʊbətɪv] *adj.* доказа́тельный; слу́жащий доказа́тельством.

probe [prəʊb] *n.* (*instrument*) зонд; (*fig., investigation*) рассле́дование; (*space exploration*): **moon ~** испыта́тельный полёт на Луну́; (*spacecraft*) иссле́довательская/зонди́рующая ракe ́та.
v.t. & i. зонди́ровать (*impf.*); (*fig., also*) иссле́довать (*impf., pf.*); **it would be unwise to ~ too deeply into the matter** неблагоразу́мно пыта́ться вни́кнуть сли́шком глубоко́ в э́то де́ло.

probity ['prəʊbɪtɪ, 'prɒ-] *n.* че́стность; **a man of ~** челове́к безукори́зненной че́стности.

problem ['prɒbləm] *n.* пробле́ма, вопро́с; **he was faced with the ~ of moving house** пе́ред ним вста́ла пробле́ма перее́зда; **~ child** тру́дный ребёнок; **~ play** пробле́мная пье́са; (*math. etc.*) зада́ча; **chess ~** ша́хматная зада́ча.

problematic(al) [ˌprɒblə'mætɪk(əl)] *adj.* проблемати́чный.

proboscis [prəʊ'bɒsɪs] *n.* (*of elephant etc.*) хо́бот; (*of insect*) хобото́к; (*joc., nose*) дли́нный нос.

pro-British [ˌprəʊ'brɪtɪʃ] *adj.* пробрита́нский.

procedural [prə'siːdjərəl, -dʒərəl] *adj.* процеду́рный.

procedure [prə'siːdjə(r), -dʒə(r)] *n.* процеду́ра; **rules of ~** пра́вила процеду́ры, регла́мент; пра́вила вну́треннего распоря́дка; свод процессуа́льных норм.

proceed [prə'siːd, prəʊ-] *v.i.* **1.** (*go on*) прод|олжа́ть, -о́лжить. **2.** (*start*): **she ~ed to lay the table** она́ приняла́сь накрыва́ть на стол; **shall we ~ to business?** перейдём к де́лу? **3.** (*make one's way*) отпр|авля́ться, -а́виться. **4.** (*originate*) исходи́ть (*impf.*); **the evils that ~ from war** несча́стья, вызыва́емые войно́й; **the noise appeared to ~ from the next room** каза́лось, что шум исхо́дит из сосе́дней ко́мнаты. **5.** (*take legal action*): **will you ~ against him?** вы собира́етесь возбуди́ть де́ло про́тив него́?

proceeding [prə'siːdɪŋ] *n.* **1.** (*piece of conduct*) посту́пок; (*pl., conduct*) поведе́ние; (*pl., activity*) де́ятельность. **2.** (*pl., records of society etc.*) труды́ (*m. pl.*), запи́ски (*f. pl.*). **3.** (*pl., legal action*) суде́бное де́ло; судопроизво́дство; разбира́тельство; **he took ~s against his employer** он возбуди́л (суде́бное) де́ло про́тив своего́ работода́теля.

proceeds ['prəʊsiːdz] *n.* вы́ручка, дохо́д; **the ~ will go to charity** вы́рученная су́мма пойдёт на благотвори́тельные це́ли.

process[1] ['prəʊses] *n.* **1.** проце́сс. **2.** (*course*) тече́ние, ход; **in ~ of time** с тече́нием вре́мени; **the house is in ~ of construction** дом стро́ится. **3.** (*method of manufacture etc.*) проце́сс; спо́соб. **4.** (*leg., summons*) вы́зов в суд; **a ~ will be served on him** его́ вы́зовут в суд.
v.t. **1.** (*treat in special way*) обраб|а́тывать, -о́тать; **~ed cheese** пла́вленый сыр. **2.** (*subject to routine handling*) оф|ормля́ть, -о́рмить; **it will take a week to ~ your request** потре́буется неде́ля, что́бы рассмотре́ть ва́шу про́сьбу.

process[2] ['prəʊses] *v.i.* (*coll., walk in procession*) уча́ствовать (*impf.*) в проце́ссии.

procession [prə'seʃ(ə)n] *n.* проце́ссия, ше́ствие; **walk in ~** дефили́ровать (*impf.*); идти́ (*det.*) ма́ршем.

processor ['prəʊsesə(r)] *n.* (*comput.*) проце́ссор.

proclaim [prə'kleɪm] *v.t.* (*announce*) провозгла|ша́ть, -си́ть; (*reveal*): **his accent ~ed him (to be) a foreigner** его́ акце́нт выдава́л в нём иностра́нца.

proclamation [ˌprɒklə'meɪʃ(ə)n] *n.* провозглаше́ние; обнаро́дование.

proclivity [prə'klɪvɪtɪ] *n.* скло́нность, накло́нность.

proconsul [prəʊ'kɒns(ə)l] *n.* замести́тель (*m.*) ко́нсула; (*Rom. hist.*) проко́нсул; (*governor*) губерна́тор.

procrastinate [prəʊ'kræstɪˌneɪt] *v.i.* ме́длить (*impf.*); тяну́ть (*impf.*) вре́мя/кани́тель.

procrastination [prəʊˌkræstɪ'neɪʃ(ə)n] *n.* промедле́ние, кани́тель.

procreate ['prəʊkrɪˌeɪt] *v.t. & i.* произв|оди́ть, -ести́ (пото́мство).

procreation [ˌprəʊkrɪ'eɪʃ(ə)n] *n.* воспроизведе́ние; (*of people*) деторожде́ние; (*of animals*) размноже́ние.

Procrustean [prəʊ'krʌstɪən] *adj.*: **~ bed** прокру́стово ло́же.

proctor ['prɒktə(r)] *n.* **1.** (*university official*) про́ктор, надзира́тель (*m.*). **2.** (*leg.*) адвока́т; **Queen's/King's P~** чино́вник Высо́кого суда́, ве́дающий дела́ми о разво́дах.

procurable [prə'kjʊərəb(ə)l] *adj.* досту́пный.

procurator ['prɒkjʊˌreɪtə(r)] *n.* **1.** (*magistrate*) пове́ренный; **public ~** прокуро́р; **~ fiscal** прокуро́р (*в Шотландии*). **2.** (*proxy*) дове́ренное лицо́.

procure [prə'kjʊə(r)] *v.t.* **1.** (*obtain*) дост|ава́ть, -а́ть. **2.** (*bring about*): **he ~d his wife's death** он подстро́ил смерть жены́; **he ~d her dismissal** он доби́лся того́, что её уво́лили.
v.i. (*act as procurer*) сво́дничать (*impf.*).

procurement [prə'kjʊəmənt] *n.* приобрете́ние, получе́ние; (*of equipment etc.*) поста́вка.

procurer [prəˈkjʊərə(r)] *n.* поставщи́к; (*pimp*) сво́дник.
procuress [prəˈkjʊərɪs] *n.* сво́дница, сво́дня.
prod [prɒd] *n.* тычо́к.
v.t. ты́кать (*impf.*); (*fig.*) подстрека́ть (*impf.*); **he has to be ~ded into action** его́ прихо́дится подта́лкивать; **I ~ded his memory** я заста́вил его́ напря́чь па́мять.
prodigal [ˈprɒdɪg(ə)l] *n.* мот, транжи́ра (*c.g.*).
adj. (*wasteful*) расточи́тельный; **the P~ Son** блу́дный сын; (*lavish*) ще́дрый; **he is ~ of advice** он ще́дро раздаёт сове́ты.
prodigality [ˌprɒdɪˈgælɪtɪ] *n.* расточи́тельность, мотовство́; ще́дрость.
prodigious [prəˈdɪdʒəs] *adj.* (*amazing*) потряса́ющий; (*enormous*) огро́мный.
prodigy [ˈprɒdɪdʒɪ] *n.* чу́до; **infant ~** вундерки́нд; **a ~ of learning** (*pers.*) кла́дезь (*m.*) прему́дрости.
produce[1] [ˈprɒdju:s] *n.* проду́кты (*m. pl.*).
produce[2] [prəˈdju:s] *v.t.* **1.** (*make, manufacture*) выраба́тывать, вы́работать; произв|оди́ть, -ести́; выпуска́ть, вы́пустить. **2.** (*bring about*) вызыва́ть, вы́звать; прин|оси́ть, -ести́; **this method ~s good results** э́тот ме́тод даёт хоро́шие результа́ты. **3.** (*bring forward*) предст|авля́ть, -а́вить; **can you ~ proof of your words?** мо́жете ли вы предста́вить что́-либо в доказа́тельство правоты́ ва́ших слов? **4.** (*bring out, into view*) предъяв|ля́ть, -и́ть; дост|ава́ть, -а́ть; **you must ~ a ticket** вы должны́ предъяви́ть биле́т. **5.** (*also v.i., yield, bear*) прин|оси́ть, -ести́; произв|оди́ть, -ести́; **France ~s the best wine** Фра́нция произво́дит лу́чшее вино́; **this soil ~s good crops** э́то по́чва даёт хоро́ший урожа́й; **his wife ~d an heir** его́ жена́ родила́ насле́дника; **our hens ~ well** ку́ры у нас хорошо́ несу́тся; **our country has ~d many great men** на́ша страна́ дала́ ми́ру мно́го вели́ких люде́й. **6.** (*compose, write*) созд|ава́ть, -а́ть. **7.** (*bring before public*) ста́вить, по-; **the opera was first ~d in Vienna** э́ту о́перу впервы́е поста́вили в Ве́не; (*cin.*) выпуска́ть, вы́пустить. **8.** (*geom.*): **~ a line** прод|олжа́ть, -о́лжить ли́нию.
producer [prəˈdju:sə(r)] *n.* **1.** (*of goods*) производи́тель (*m.*). **2.** (*stage, TV*) режиссёр, постано́вщик. **3.** (*film*) продю́сер. **4.**: **~ gas** генера́торный газ.
product [ˈprɒdʌkt] *n.* (*article produced*) проду́кт; (*result*) результа́т, плод; (*math.*) произведе́ние.
production [prəˈdʌkʃ(ə)n] *n.* **1.** (*manufacture*) проду́кция; **mass ~** ма́ссовая проду́кция; **~ line** пото́чная ли́ния. **2.** (*yield*) производи́тельность. **3.** (*composing; composition*) произведе́ние. **4.** (*stage, film*) постано́вка.
productive [prəˈdʌktɪv] *adj.* (*tending to produce*) производи́тельный; **money is not always ~ of happiness** де́ньги не всегда́ прино́сят сча́стье; (*producing commodities of value*): **~ labour** производи́тельный труд; (*yielding well, fertile*) плодоро́дный; **a ~ author** плодови́тый а́втор; (*efficient*) продукти́вный.
productivity [ˌprɒdʌkˈtɪvɪtɪ] *n.* (*rate of production*) производи́тельность; (*productiveness, efficiency*) продукти́вность.
prof [prɒf] (*coll.*) = **professor 2.**
profanation [ˌprɒfəˈneɪʃ(ə)n] *n.* профана́ция, оскверне́ние.
profane [prəˈfeɪn] *adj.* (*secular*) мирско́й; (*uninitiated*) непосвящённый; (*heathen*) язы́ческий; (*irreverent*) богоху́льный.
v.t. профани́ровать (*impf., pf.*); оскверн|я́ть, -и́ть.
profanity [prəˈfænɪtɪ] *n.* (*irreverence*) богоху́льство; (*swearing*) скверносло́вие.
profess [prəˈfes] *v.t.* **1.** (*claim to have or feel*) откры́то заяв|ля́ть, -и́ть; **he ~es an interest in architecture** он заявля́ет, что интересу́ется архитекту́рой. **2.** (*claim, admit, pretend*) претендова́ть (*impf.*); **I don't ~ to know much about music** я не претенду́ю на больши́е позна́ния в му́зыке; **he ~es to be an expert at chess** он выдаёт себя́ за первокла́ссного шахмати́ста. **3.** (*affirm belief in*) испове́довать (*impf.*). **4.** (*practice*): **he ~es medicine** он занима́ется медици́ной. **5.** (*teach as professor*) преподава́ть (*impf.*).
professed [prəˈfest] *adj.* **1.** (*self-declared*) откры́тый, я́вный. **2.** (*alleged, ostensible*) мни́мый. **3.** (*monk*) при́нявший по́стриг; **a ~ nun** мона́хиня, да́вшая обе́т.
professedly [prəˈfesɪdlɪ] *adv.* (*ostensibly*) притво́рно, я́кобы.
profession [prəˈfeʃ(ə)n] *n.* **1.** (*occupation*) профе́ссия; **he is a teacher by ~** он по профе́ссии учи́тель; **the ~** (*i.e. actors*) актёры (*m. pl.*); **the oldest ~** древне́йшая профе́ссия. **2.** (*declaration; admission*) заявле́ние; завере́ние; **~s of love** завере́ния любви́.
professional [prəˈfeʃən(ə)l] *n.* (*expert practitioner*) профессиона́л; (*sportsman*) спортсме́н-профессиона́л.
adj. профессиона́льный; **~ people** ли́ца свобо́дных профе́ссий.
professionalism [prəˈfeʃənəˌlɪz(ə)m] *n.* профессионали́зм.
professor [prəˈfesə(r)] *n.* **1.** (*one who professes*): **a ~ of Christianity** испове́дующий христиа́нство. **2.** (*teacher*) профе́ссор.
professorial [ˌprɒfɪˈsɔ:rɪəl] *adj.* профе́ссорский.
professorship [prəˈfesəʃɪp] *n.* профе́ссорство.
proffer [ˈprɒfə(r)] *n.* предложе́ние.
v.t. предл|ага́ть, -ожи́ть; **he ~ed his hand** он протяну́л ру́ку.
proficiency [prəˈfɪʃ(ə)nsɪ] *n.* мастерство́, уме́ние.
proficient [prəˈfɪʃ(ə)nt] *adj.* уме́лый; **she is ~ at typing** она́ хорошо́ печа́тает; **he is ~ in the art of flattery** он иску́сный льстец.
profile [ˈprəʊfaɪl] *n.* (*side view, esp. of face*) про́филь (*m.*); **seen in ~** в про́филь; (*fig.*) пози́ция; **to adopt a low/high ~** де́йствовать сде́ржанно/акти́вно; **he kept a low ~** он стара́лся не выделя́ться; (*biographical sketch*) биографи́ческий о́черк.
profit [ˈprɒfɪt] *n.* **1.** (*advantage*) по́льза, вы́года; **he discovered to his ~ that ...** он узна́л к со́бственной вы́годе, что...; **you will gain no ~ from resistance** вы ничего́ не добьётесь сопротивле́нием; **he studied to little ~** уче́ние не принесло́ ему́ почти́ никако́й по́льзы; **there is no ~ in further discussion** продолжа́ть диску́ссию бесполе́зно; **with ~** вы́годно. **2.** (*pecuniary gain*) при́быль; **he made a ~ out of the deal** он получи́л при́быль на э́той сде́лке; **he sold the land at a ~** он про́дал зе́млю с вы́годой; **they keep hens for ~** они́ разво́дят кур ра́ди де́нег; **the ~ motive** пого́ня за при́былью; **~ and loss account** счёт при́былей и убы́тков.
v.t. прин|оси́ть, -ести́ по́льзу +*d.*; **what will it ~ him?** что э́то ему́ даст?
v.i. по́льзоваться, вос- (+*i.*); извле|ка́ть, -е́чь по́льзу (из+*g.*); **he has not ~ed from his experience** он не воспо́льзовался свои́м о́пытом; **I ~ed by your advice** ваш сове́т пошёл мне на по́льзу; **he ~ed by his wife's death** смерть жены́ была́ ему́ вы́годна.
cpd. **~-sharing** *n.* уча́стие в при́были.
profitability [ˌprɒfɪtəˈbɪlɪtɪ] *n.* поле́зность, дохо́дность, при́быльность, рента́бельность.
profitable [ˈprɒfɪtəb(ə)l] *adj.* (*advantageous*) поле́зный, вы́годный; (*lucrative*) дохо́дный, при́быльный, рента́бельный.
profiteer [ˌprɒfɪˈtɪə(r)] *n.* спекуля́нт.
v.i. спекули́ровать (*impf.*).
profiteering [ˌprɒfɪˈtɪərɪŋ] *n.* спекуля́ция.
adj. спекуля́нтский.
profiterole [prəˈfɪtəˌrəʊl] *n.* (*cul.*) профитро́ль *m.*
profitless [ˈprɒfɪtlɪs] *adj.* бесполе́зный; беспло́дный.
profligacy [ˈprɒflɪgəsɪ] *n.* распу́тство; расточи́тельность.
profligate [ˈprɒflɪgət] *n.* развра́тник; расточи́тель (*m.*).
adj. (*dissolute*) распу́тный; (*extravagant*) расточи́тельный.
pro forma [prəʊ ˈfɔ:mə] *adj.*: **~ invoice** приме́рная/ориентиро́вочная/предвари́тельная факту́ра.
adv. phr. для профо́рмы.
profound [prəˈfaʊnd] *adj.* глубо́кий; **~ ignorance** по́лное неве́жество; **he took a ~ interest in it** он проявля́л огро́мный интере́с к э́тому; **a ~ subject** сло́жный предме́т; **a ~ writer** серьёзный писа́тель.
profundity [prəˈfʌndɪtɪ] *n.* глубина́; (*fig.*) серьёзность.
profuse [prəˈfju:s] *adj.* (*plentiful*) оби́льный; (*lavish*) ще́дрый, расточи́тельный; **he apologized ~ly** он рассы́пался в извине́ниях.

profuseness [prəˈfjuːsnɪs] *n.* оби́лие.
profusion [prəˈfjuːʒ(ə)n] *n.* изоби́лие.
progenitor [prəʊˈdʒenɪtə(r)] *n.* пpapoди́тель (*m.*), пре́док; (*predecessor*) предше́ственник.
progeny [ˈprɒdʒɪnɪ] *n.* пото́мство.
pro-German [ˌprəʊˈdʒɜːmən] *n.* германофи́л (*fem.* -ка).
adj. германофи́льский, пронеме́цкий.
progesterone [prəʊˈdʒestəˌrəʊn] *n.* прогестеро́н.
prognathous [prɒgˈneɪθəs, ˈprɒgnəθəs] *adj.* прогнати́ческий.
prognosis [prɒgˈnəʊsɪs] *n.* прогно́з.
prognostic [prɒgˈnɒstɪk] *n.* предзнаменова́ние.
adj. предвеща́ющий.
prognosticate [prɒgˈnɒstɪˌkeɪt] *v.t.* предска́з|ывать, -а́ть; предвеща́ть (*impf.*).
prognostication [prɒgˌnɒstɪˈkeɪʃ(ə)n] *n.* предсказа́ние; (*omen*) предзнаменова́ние.
program(me) [ˈprəʊgræm] *n.* **1.** програ́мма; (*radio, TV*) переда́ча; (*plan*) план; **what's (on) the ~ for tonight?** каки́е у нас пла́ны на ве́чер?; **he has a full ~ tomorrow** за́втра он по́лностью за́нят. **2.** (*computer instructions*) программи́рование.
v.t. (*make plan of*) сост|авля́ть, -а́вить програ́мму +*g.*; (*supply data to*) программи́ровать, за-.
progress[1] [ˈprəʊgres] *n.* **1.** (*forward movement*) движе́ние вперёд; **the horses made slow ~** ло́шади дви́гались ме́дленно. **2.** (*advance, development*) прогре́сс; **~ report** докла́д о хо́де рабо́ты; **the invalid is making good ~** больно́й поправля́ется; **a meeting is in ~** идёт заседа́ние; **preparations are in ~** веду́тся приготовле́ния.
progress[2] [prəˈgres] *v.i.* прогресси́ровать (*impf.*); ул|учша́ться, -у́чшиться; **how are things ~ing?** как иду́т дела́?; **he has hardly ~ed at all with his studies** он не сде́лал почти́ никаки́х успе́хов в учёбе.
progression [prəˈgreʃ(ə)n] *n.* (*progress*) продвиже́ние; (*math.*) прогре́ссия; (*mus.*) прогре́ссия, секве́нция.
progressive [prəˈgresɪv] *n.* прогресси́вный челове́к.
adj. **1.** (*favouring progress*) прогресси́вный, передово́й. **2.** (*gradual*) поступа́тельный, постепе́нный. **3.** (*of disease etc.*) прогресси́рующий. **4.:** **~ tense** (*gram.*) продо́лженное вре́мя, континуати́в.
prohibit [prəˈhɪbɪt] *v.t.* запре|ща́ть, -ти́ть; **smoking ~ed** кури́ть воспреща́ется.
prohibition [ˌprəʊhɪˈbɪʃ(ə)n, ˌprəʊɪˈb-] *n.* запреще́ние; (*of sale of intoxicants*) запреще́ние прода́жи спиртны́х напи́тков, сухо́й зако́н.
prohibitionism [ˌprəʊhɪˈbɪʃənˈɪz(ə)m, ˌprəʊɪˈb-] *n.* прогибициони́зм.
prohibitionist [ˌprəʊhɪˈbɪʃənɪst, ˌprəʊɪˈb-] *n.* прогибициони́ст.
prohibitive [prəʊˈhɪbɪtɪv] *adj.* запрети́тельный, запреща́ющий; **~ prices** недосту́пные це́ны.
prohibitory [prəˈhɪbɪtərɪ] *adj.* запреща́ющий.
project[1] [ˈprɒdʒekt] *n.* прое́кт, план; (*industrial etc. plant*) новостро́йка.
project[2] [prəˈdʒekt] *v.t.* **1.** (*devise*) проекти́ровать, за-. **2.** (*throw, impel*) выбра́сывать, вы́бросить. **3.** (*of light*) испус|ка́ть, -ти́ть; (*of shadow*) отбр|а́сывать, -о́сить. **4.** (*with projector; also math.*) проекти́ровать, с-; проеци́ровать (*impf., pf.*). **5.** (*fig.*): **he ~ed himself into the future** он мы́сленно перенёсся в бу́дущее; **a good actor can ~ himself into a role** хоро́ший актёр мо́жет по́лностью войти́ в (свою́) роль.
v.i. (*protrude*) выдава́ться (*impf.*); выступа́ть (*impf.*); **~ing teeth** торча́щие зу́бы; **a ~ing balcony** нависа́ющий балко́н.
projectile [prəˈdʒektaɪl] *n.* снаря́д.
adj. мета́тельный; **~ force** дви́жущая си́ла.
projection [prəˈdʒekʃ(ə)n] *n.* **1.** (*planning*) проекти́рование. **2.** (*throwing, propulsion*) отбра́сывание. **3.** (*cin.*) прое́кция (изображе́ния); **~ room** (кино)проекцио́нная каби́на. **4.** (*psych., geom.*) прое́кция; **Mercator's ~** мерка́торская прое́кция. **5.** (*protrusion*) вы́ступ; (*protruding part*) выдаю́щаяся часть.
projectionist [prəˈdʒekʃənɪst] *n.* (*of film etc.*) киномеха́ник.
projector [prəˈdʒektə(r)] *n.* (*planner*) проектиро́вщик; планови́к; (*apparatus*) прое́ктор.
prolapse [ˈprəʊlæps] *n.* прола́пс, выпаде́ние.
v.i. выпада́ть, вы́пасть.
prole [prəʊl] *n.* (*coll.*) пролета́рий; «трудя́га» (*c.g.*).
prolegomena [ˌprəʊlɪˈgɒmɪnə] *n.* пролегоме́н|ы (*pl., g.* -ов).
proletarian [ˌprəʊlɪˈteərɪən] *n.* пролета́рий.
adj. пролета́рский.
proletariat [ˌprəʊlɪˈteərɪət] *n.* пролетариа́т.
pro-life [prəʊˈlaɪf] *adj.* защища́ющий «пра́во на жизнь».
pro-lifer [prəʊˈlaɪfə(r)] *n.* защи́тни|к (*fem.*-ца) «пра́ва на жизнь».
proliferate [prəˈlɪfəˌreɪt] *v.i.* пролифери́ровать (*impf., pf.*); размн|ожа́ться, -о́житься; (*fig.*) распростран|я́ться, -и́ться.
proliferation [prəˌlɪfəˈreɪʃ(ə)n] *n.* пролифера́ция; (*fig.*) распростране́ние.
prolific [prəˈlɪfɪk] *adj.* (*lit.*) плодоро́дный; оби́льный; (*fig.*) плодови́тый; **~ of ideas** порожда́ющий иде́ю за иде́ей.
prolix [ˈprəʊlɪks, prəˈlɪks] *adj.* многосло́вный, ну́дный.
prolixity [ˌprəʊˈlɪksɪtɪ, prəˈlɪksɪtɪ] *n.* многосло́вие, ну́дность.
prologue [ˈprəʊlɒg] *n.* проло́г.
prolong [prəˈlɒŋ] *v.t.* продл|ева́ть, -и́ть; **he ~ed his leave by a day** он продли́л свой о́тпуск на оди́н день; **a ~ed argument** затяну́вшийся спор.
prolongation [ˌprəʊlɒŋˈgeɪʃ(ə)n] *n.* продле́ние; пролонга́ция; (*lengthening*) продолже́ние; удлине́ние.
prom [prɒm] (*coll.*) = **promenade** *n.* **2.**
promenade [ˌprɒməˈnɑːd] *n.* **1.** (*walk for pleasure etc.*) прогу́лка; **~ concert** промена́дный конце́рт. **2.** (*place of pedestrian resort*) ме́сто для гуля́ния. **3.** (*US, students' ball*) бал (*в колледже*).
v.i. гуля́ть, по-; прогу́л|иваться, -я́ться.
Promethean [prəˈmiːθɪən] *adj.* промете́ев.
Prometheus [prəˈmiːθɪəs] *n.* Промете́й.
prominence [ˈprɒmɪnəns] *n.* (*importance*) ви́дное положе́ние.
prominent [ˈprɒmɪnənt] *adj.* **1.** (*projecting*) выступа́ющий. **2.** (*conspicuous*) заме́тный; **a ~ feature in the landscape** характе́рная черта́ пейза́жа. **3.** (*important, distinguished*) выдаю́щийся.
promiscuity [ˌprɒmɪˈskjuːɪtɪ] *n.* неразбо́рчивость; распу́щенность.
promiscuous [prəˈmɪskjʊəs] *adj.* неразбо́рчивый, огу́льный; (*sexually*) распу́щенный.
promise [ˈprɒmɪs] *n.* **1.** (*assurance*) обеща́ние; **he gave his solemn ~ never to steal again** он твёрдо/торже́ственно обеща́л (*or* дал сло́во) бо́льше не ворова́ть; **he kept his ~** он сдержа́л своё обеща́ние; **~s are made to be broken** на то и обеща́ния, что́бы их наруша́ть; **breach of ~** наруше́ние обеща́ния. **2.** (*ground for expectation*) наде́жда; **he shows ~** он подаёт наде́жды; **a writer of ~** многообеща́ющий писа́тель.
v.t. & i. **1.** (*undertake, assure*) обеща́ть, по-; **he ~d to be here by 7** он обеща́л быть здесь в 7 часо́в; **I ~d myself a quiet evening ~** я реши́л споко́йно провести́ ве́чер; **it will not be easy, I ~ you** уверя́ю вас, что э́то бу́дет нелегко́; **the P~d Land** (*bibl.*) земля́ обетова́нная. **2.** (*give grounds for expecting*): **the clouds ~ rain** ту́чи предвеща́ют дождь; **it ~s to be a warm day** день обеща́ет быть тёплым; **the scheme ~s well** э́тот план вы́глядит многообеща́ющим; **the boy ~s well** ма́льчик подаёт больши́е наде́жды.
promising [ˈprɒmɪsɪŋ] *adj.* перспекти́вный; многообеща́ющий, подаю́щий наде́жды.
promissory [ˈprɒmɪsərɪ] *adj.*: **~ note** долгово́е обяза́тельство.
promontory [ˈprɒməntərɪ] *n.* мыс.
promote [prəˈməʊt] *v.t.* **1.** (*raise to higher rank*) продв|ига́ть, -и́нуть; пов|ыша́ть, -ы́сить в чи́не; **he was ~d (to the rank of) sergeant** ему́ присво́или зва́ние сержа́нта. **2.** (*establish*) учре|жда́ть, -ди́ть; осно́в|ывать, -а́ть. **3.** (*encourage, support*) поощр|я́ть, -и́ть; подде́рж|ивать, -а́ть; соде́йствовать, по- +*d.* **4.** (*publicize to boost sales*) реклами́ровать (*impf.*); соде́йствовать прода́же +*g.*
promoter [prəˈməʊtə(r)] *n.* (*patron*) покрови́тель (*m.*); **company ~** учреди́тель/основа́тель (*m.*) компа́нии.
promotion [prəˈməʊʃ(ə)n] *n.* (*in rank*) продвиже́ние, повыше́ние; (*encouragement, support*) поощре́ние, подде́ржка, соде́йствие; (*publicizing*) рекла́ма.

prompt[1] [prɒmpt] *n.* (*theatr.*) подска́зка.

v.t. & i. **1.** (*assist memory of*) подска́з|ывать, -а́ть +*d.*; (*theatr.*) суфли́ровать +*d.* **2.** (*impel, induce*) побу|жда́ть, -ди́ть; **he was ~ed by mercy** он де́йствовал из жа́лости.

cpd. **~-book** *n.* суфлёрский экземпля́р пье́сы.

prompt[2] [prɒmpt] *adj.* бы́стрый; **he was ~ in coming forward** он сра́зу же (*or* тут же) откли́кнулся; **he arrived ~ly at 9** он прие́хал то́чно в де́вять; **a ~ answer** неме́дленный отве́т; **~ payment** своевре́менная упла́та; неме́дленный платёж.

prompter ['prɒmptə(r)] *n.* суфлёр.

prompt|itude ['prɒmp,tıtju:d], **-ness** ['prɒmptnıs] *nn.* быстрота́, гото́вность.

promulgate ['prɒməl,geıt] *v.t.* обнаро́довать (*impf.*); провозгла|ша́ть, -си́ть.

promulgation [,prɒməl'geıʃ(ə)n] *n.* обнаро́дование, провозглаше́ние.

prone [prəʊn] *adj.* **1.** (*face downwards*) лежа́щий ничко́м. **2.:** **~ to** (*disposed, liable to*) скло́нный к+*d.*; **he is ~ to make mistakes** ему́ сво́йственно ошиба́ться; **I am ~ to accidents** со мной ве́чно что́-то случа́ется.

proneness ['prəʊnnıs] *n.* скло́нность.

prong [prɒŋ] *n.* зубе́ц.

pronominal [prəʊ'nɒmın(ə)l] *adj.* местоиме́нный.

pronoun ['prəʊnaʊn] *n.* местоиме́ние.

pronounc|e [prə'naʊns] *v.t.* **1.** (*declare*) объяв|ля́ть, -и́ть; **~e judgement** (*leg.*) выноси́ть, вы́нести суде́бное реше́ние; **~e a curse on** прокл|ина́ть, -я́сть; **the doctor ~ed him out of danger** до́ктор объяви́л, что он вне опа́сности; **he ~ed himself in favour of the bill** он вы́сказался в по́льзу законопрое́кта. **2.** (*utter*) произн|оси́ть, -ести́; выгова́ривать (*impf.*); **how is this word ~ed?** как произно́сится э́то сло́во?

v.i. **1.** (*give one's opinion*) выска́зываться, вы́сказаться; **the jury ~ed for the defendant** прися́жные оправда́ли подсуди́мого. **2.:** **a ~ing dictionary** слова́рь произноше́ния, орфоэпи́ческий слова́рь.

pronounceable [prə'naʊnsəb(ə)l] *adj.* удобопроизноси́мый.

pronounced [prə'naʊnst] *adj.* (*decided*) я́вный; ре́зко вы́раженный; **the play was a ~ success** пье́са я́вно име́ла успе́х; **he walks with a ~ limp** он си́льно/заме́тно хрома́ет.

pronouncement [prə'naʊnsmənt] *n.* заявле́ние; выска́зывание.

pronto ['prɒntəʊ] *adv.* (*sl.*) жи́во, бы́стро.

pronunciamento [prə,nʌnsıə'mentəʊ] *n.* пронунсиаме́нто (*indecl.*).

pronunciation [prə,nʌnsı'eıʃ(ə)n] *n.* произноше́ние, вы́говор.

proof [pru:f] *n.* **1.** доказа́тельство; **this is ~ positive of his guilt** э́то несомне́нно дока́зывает его́ вину́; **as, in ~ of his good intentions** в доказа́тельство его́ до́брых наме́рений. **2.** (*demonstration*): **is it capable of ~?** э́то доказу́емо? **3.** (*test, trial*) испыта́ние; прове́рка; **his courage was put to the ~** его́ сме́лость подве́рглась испыта́нию; **the ~ of the pudding is in the eating** ≃ обо всём су́дят по результа́там; не попро́буешь, не узна́ешь. **4.** (*of alcoholic liquor*) кре́пость. **5.** (*typ.*) корректу́ра; (*from engraving*) про́бный о́ттиск с гравю́ры.

adj. **1.** (*of tried or prescribed strength*) устано́вленной кре́пости; **~ spirit** раство́р спи́рта определённой кре́пости. **2.** (*impenetrable, resistant*): **~ against bullets** пуленепроница́емый; **~ against weather** непромока́емый, погодоусто́йчивый; (*fig.*): **~ against temptation** не поддаю́щийся искуше́нию.

v.t. (*waterproof*) де́лать, с- непроница́емым.

cpds. **~-read** *v.t. & i.* чита́ть, про- (*or* держа́ть) корректу́ру; **~-reader** *n.* корре́ктор; **~-reading** *n.* счи́тка; чте́ние корректу́ры; **~-sheet** *n.* корректу́ра.

prop[1] [prɒp] *n.* (*support*) сто́йка; подпо́рка; (*fig.*) опо́ра; подде́ржка.

v.t. **1.** подп|ира́ть, -ере́ть; **~ open a door** подп|ира́ть, -ере́ть дверь, что́бы она́ не захло́пнулась; **he sat ~ped up in bed** он сиде́л в крова́ти, опира́ясь на поду́шки; **~ the ladder against the wall!** приста́вьте ле́стницу к стене́! **2.** (*fig.*) подде́рж|ивать, -а́ть.

prop[2] [prɒp] *n.* (*coll., theatr.*) бутафо́рия, реквизи́т.

prop[3] [prɒp] (*coll.*) = **propeller**

propaganda [,prɒpə'gændə] *n.* пропага́нда; (*attr.*) пропага́ндный, пропаганди́ческий.

propagandist [,prɒpə'gændıst] *n.* пропаганди́ст.

propagandize [,prɒpə'gændaız] *v.t.* пропаганди́ровать (*impf.*).

propagate ['prɒpə,geıt] *v.t.* (*multiply by reproduction*) размн|ожа́ть, -о́жить; разв|оди́ть, -ести́; (*disseminate*) распростран|я́ть, -и́ть; (*transmit; extend operation of*) перед|ава́ть, -а́ть.

v.i. размн|ожа́ться, -о́житься.

propagation [,prɒpə'geıʃ(ə)n] *n.* размноже́ние; (*fig.*) распростране́ние.

propagator ['prɒpə,geıtə(r)] *n.* распространи́тель (*fem.* -ница).

propane ['prəʊpeın] *n.* пропа́н.

propel [prə'pel] *v.t.* прив|оди́ть, -ести́ в движе́ние; **~ling pencil** выдвижно́й каранда́ш; автомати́ческий каранда́ш, автокаранда́ш.

propell|ant, -ent [prə'pelənt] *nn.* дви́жущая си́ла; (*fuel*) раке́тное то́пливо.

propeller [prə'pelə(r)] *n.* дви́житель (*m.*); (*of ship*) винт (корабля́); (*of aircraft*) пропе́ллер, (возду́шный) винт.

propensity [prə'pensıtı] *n.* предрасполо́женность, скло́нность.

proper ['prɒpə(r)] *adj.* **1.** (*belonging especially*) сво́йственный; прису́щий. **2.** (*suitable, appropriate*) подходя́щий, ну́жный; **at the ~ time** в своё вре́мя; **they did the ~ thing by him** с ним обошли́сь по справедли́вости. **3.** (*decent, respectable*) (благо)присто́йный, прили́чный. **4.** (*correct, accurate*) пра́вильный; **in the ~ sense of the word** в настоя́щем/прямо́м смы́сле сло́ва. **5.** (*gram.*): **~ noun** и́мя со́бственное. **6.** (*strictly so called*): **within the sphere of architecture ~** в о́бласти со́бственно архитекту́ры. **7.** (*coll. thorough*) соверше́нный, по́лный; **his room was in a ~ mess** в его́ ко́мнате цари́л по́лный беспоря́док.

properly ['prɒpəlı] *adv.* (*correctly*) подоба́юще; как сле́дует; до́лжным о́бразом; **~ speaking** со́бственно говоря́; **you must be ~ dressed** вы должны́ оде́ться подоба́ющим о́бразом.

propertied ['prɒpətıd] *adj.* име́ющий со́бственность; иму́щий; **the ~ classes** иму́щие кла́ссы; землевладе́льцы.

propert|y ['prɒpətı] *n.* **1.** (*possession(s)*) со́бственность; иму́щество; **a man of ~y** со́бственник; **the news is common ~y** но́вость изве́стно всем; **real ~y** недви́жимая со́бственность; **~y qualification** иму́щественный ценз. **2.** (*house; estate*) дом; име́ние. **3.** (*ownership*) пра́во со́бственности. **4.** (*attribute, quality*) сво́йство; **this plant has healing ~ies** э́то расте́ние облада́ет целе́бными сво́йствами. **5.** (*theatr.*) бутафо́рия, реквизи́т.

cpds. **~man, ~-master** *nn.* реквизи́тор.

prophecy ['prɒfısı] *n.* предсказа́ние, проро́чество.

prophesy ['prɒfı,saı] *v.t. & i.* предска́з|ывать, -а́ть; проро́чить, на-.

prophet ['prɒfıt] *n.* проро́к, предсказа́тель (*m.*).

prophetess ['prɒfıtıs] *n.* проро́чица; предсказа́тельница.

prophetic [prə'fetık] *adj.* проро́ческий.

prophylactic [,prɒfı'læktık] *n.* профилакти́ческое сре́дство.

adj. профилакти́ческий.

prophylaxis [,prɒfı'læksıs] *n.* профила́ктика.

propinquity [prə'pıŋkwıtı] *n.* (*closeness*) бли́зость, сосе́дство; (*kinship*) родство́.

propitiate [prə'pıʃı,eıt] *v.t.* (*appease*) умиротвор|я́ть, -и́ть; ут|еша́ть, -е́шить; (*win favour of*) сниска́ть (*pf.*) благоскло́нность +*g.*

propitiation [prə,pıʃı'eıʃ(ə)n] *n.* умиротворе́ние; утеше́ние.

propitiatory [prə'pıʃıətərı] *adj.* утеша́ющий; примири́тельный.

propitious [prə'pıʃəs] *adj.* (*benevolent*) благожела́тельный; (*favourable*) благоприя́тный.

proponent [prə'pəʊnənt] *n.* пропаганди́ст, побо́рник (*чего*).

proportion [prə'pɔ:ʃ(ə)n] *n.* **1.** (*comparative part*) пропо́рция, часть. **2.** (*ratio*) пропо́рция, соотноше́ние; **the ~ of blacks to whites is high** пропорциона́льно чёрных гора́здо бо́льше, чем бе́лых; **in ~** пропорциона́льно, соразме́рно. **3.** (*math., equality of ratios*) пропо́рция. **4.** (*due relation*) соразме́рность; **keep a sense of ~** сохрани́ть (*impf.*) чу́вство ме́ры; **his ambitions are out of all ~** его́ честолю́бие выхо́дит за вся́кие ра́мки. **5.** (*pl., dimensions*) разме́р, разме́ры (*m. pl.*); **a house of stately ~s** дом внуши́тельных разме́ров.

v.t. соразм|еря́ть, -е́рить; дози́ровать (*impf.*).

proportional [prəˈpɔːʃən(ə)l] *adj.* пропорциона́льный.

proportionate [prəˈpɔːʃənət] *adj.* соразме́рный; **payment will be ~ to effort** опла́та бу́дет соотве́тствовать затра́ченным уси́лиям.

proposal [prəˈpəuz(ə)l] *n.* предложе́ние.

propose [prəˈpəuz] *v.t.* **1.** (*offer suggestion or plan of*) предл|ага́ть, -ожи́ть; вн|оси́ть, -ести́ предложе́ние; **he ~d (marriage) to her** он сде́лал ей предложе́ние. **2.** (*nominate, put forward*) выдвига́ть, вы́двинуть; **his name was ~d for secretary** его́ выдвига́ли на пост секретаря́. **3.** (*offer as toast*): **his health was ~d** провозгласи́ли тост за его́ здоро́вье. **4.** (*intend*) предпол|ага́ть, -ожи́ть; **I ~ to leave tomorrow** я собира́юсь/наме́рен е́хать за́втра.

v.i. (*make plans*) намерева́ться (*impf.*); **man ~s, God disposes** челове́к предполага́ет, а Бог располага́ет.

proposition [ˌprɒpəˈzɪʃ(ə)n] *n.* **1.** (*statement*) заявле́ние. **2.** (*proposed scheme*) предложе́ние. **3.** (*coll., undertaking, problem etc.*) де́ло; **he is a tough ~** с ним тру́дно име́ть де́ло. **4.** (*coll., immoral proposal*) гну́сное предложе́ние.

propound [prəˈpaund] *v.t.* предл|ага́ть, -ожи́ть на обсужде́ние; изл|ага́ть, -ожи́ть.

proprietary [prəˈpraɪətərɪ] *adj.* со́бственнический; (*pert. to a firm*) фи́рменный; **~ medicines** патенто́ванные лека́рства; **~ rights** пра́во со́бственности; **he adopted a ~ attitude towards her** он относи́лся к ней, как к свое́й со́бственности.

proprietor [prəˈpraɪətə(r)] *n.* владе́лец, хозя́ин.

proprietress [prəˈpraɪətrɪs] *n.* владе́лица, хозя́йка.

propriet|y [prəˈpraɪɪtɪ] *n.* (*fitness*) уме́стность; (*correctness of behaviour or morals*) пра́вильность; (благо)присто́йность; (*pl., rules of behaviour*) **the ~ies must be observed** на́до соблюда́ть пра́вила прили́чия.

propulsion [prəˈpʌlʃ(ə)n] *n.* движе́ние вперёд; **jet ~** реакти́вное движе́ние.

propulsive [prəˈpʌlsɪv] *adj.* дви́жущий вперёд; **~ force** дви́жущая си́ла.

pro rata [prəu ˈrɑːtə, ˈreɪtə] *adv.* пропорциона́льно; в соотве́тствии (*с чем*).

pro-rector [ˌprəuˈrektə] *n.* проре́ктор.

prorogation [ˌprərəuˈgeɪʃ(ə)n] *n.* пророга́ция (парла́мента).

prorogue [prəˈrəug] *v.t.* назн|ача́ть, -а́чить переры́в в рабо́те (*парламента и т.п.*).

prosaic [prəˈzeɪɪk, prəu-] *adj.* прозаи́ческий.

proscenium [prəˈsiːnɪəm, prəu-] *n.* просце́ниум.

proscribe [prəˈskraɪb] *v.t.* (*deprive of legal protection*) объяв|ля́ть, -и́ть вне зако́на; (*denounce, condemn*) осу|жда́ть, -ди́ть.

proscription [prəˈskrɪpʃ(ə)n] *n.* изгна́ние; опа́ла.

prose [prəuz] *n.* **1.** про́за; (*attr.*) прозаи́ческий; **~ writers** (писа́тели-)проза́ики; **~ poem** стихотворе́ние в про́зе; (*fig.*) про́за, прозаи́чность. **2.** (*piece set for translation*) отры́вок для перево́да.

v.i. (*talk tediously*) распространя́ться (*impf.*) (*о чём*).

prosecute [ˈprɒsɪˌkjuːt] *v.t.* **1.** (*continue*) прод|олжа́ть, -о́лжить. **2.** (*carry on*) занима́ться (*impf.*) +*i.*; **he ~d the inquiry with vigour** он энерги́чно повёл рассле́дование. **3.** (*leg.*) возбу|жда́ть, -ди́ть де́ло про́тив+*g.*; **trespassers will be ~d** нару́шители бу́дут пресле́доваться по зако́ну.

prosecution [ˌprɒsɪˈkjuːʃ(ə)n] *n.* **1.** (*pursuit*) веде́ние; **in the ~ of his duty** при исполне́нии свои́х обя́занностей. **2.** (*carrying on legal proceedings*) обвине́ние; предъявле́ние и́ска. **3.** (*prosecuting party*) обвине́ние; **counsel for the ~** обвини́тель (*m.*) (в уголо́вном проце́ссе).

prosecutor [ˈprɒsɪˌkjuːtə(r)] *n.* обвини́тель (*m.*); **Public P~** госуда́рственый обвини́тель, прокуро́р.

proselyte [ˈprɒsɪˌlaɪt] *n.* прозели́т (*fem.* -ка).

proselytize [ˈprɒsɪlɪˌtaɪz] *v.t.* (*convert*) обра|ща́ть, -ти́ть в другу́ю ве́ру.

prosiness [ˈprəuzɪnɪs] *n.* ну́дность.

prosodic [prəˈsɒdɪk] *adj.* просоди́ческий.

prosody [ˈprɒsədɪ] *n.* просо́дия.

prospect[1] [ˈprɒspekt] *n.* **1.** (*extensive view*) вид, панора́ма; (*fig., mental scene*) перспекти́ва. **2.** (*expectation, hope*) перспекти́ва; **there is no ~ of success** нет наде́жды на успе́х; **a job without ~s** рабо́та без перспекти́в; **I have nothing in ~ at present** в настоя́щее вре́мя у меня́ нет ничего́ в перспекти́ве. **3.** (*coll., possible customer*) потенциа́льный покупа́тель/зака́зчик.

prospect[2] [prəˈspekt] *v.t.* иссле́довать (*impf.*); разве́д|ывать, -ать.

v.i.: **they were ~ing for gold** они́ иска́ли зо́лото.

prospective [prəˈspektɪv] *adj.* **1.** (*applicable to future*) бу́дущий; предпологáемый; **the law is ~** зако́н не име́ет обра́тной си́лы. **2.** (*expected*) ожида́емый. **3.** (*future*) бу́дущий.

prospector [prəˈspektə(r)] *n.* разве́дчик, стара́тель (*m.*).

prospectus [prəˈspektəs] *n.* проспе́кт.

prosper [ˈprɒspə(r)] *v.t.* благоприя́тствовать +*d.*; **may Heaven ~ you!** да помо́жет вам Бог!

v.i. преусп|ева́ть, -е́ть; процвета́ть (*impf.*); **cheats never ~** обма́н до добра́ не доведёт.

prosperity [prɒˈsperɪtɪ] *n.* процвета́ние.

prosperous [ˈprɒspərəs] *adj.* процвета́ющий, зажи́точный.

prostaglandin [ˌprɒstəˈglændɪn] *n.* простагланди́н.

prostate [ˈprɒsteɪt] *n.* проста́та; **~ disease** боле́знь предста́тельной железы́.

prosthesis [ˈprɒsθɪsɪs, -ˈθiːsɪs] *n.* проте́з.

prosthetic [prɒsˈθetɪk] *adj.* проте́зный.

prostitute [ˈprɒstɪˌtjuːt] *n.* проститу́тка.

v.t.: **~ o.s.** зан|има́ться, -я́ться проститу́цией; (*fig.*) торгова́ть (*impf.*) собо́й; **he ~d his talents** он прода́л/загуби́л свой тала́нт.

prostitution [ˌprɒstɪˈtjuːʃ(ə)n] *n.* (*lit., fig.*) проститу́ция.

prostrate[1] [ˈprɒstreɪt] *adj.* **1.** (*lying face down*) распростёртый; лежа́щий ничко́м. **2.** (*overcome, overthrown*) пове́рженный; **she was ~ with grief** она́ была́ сло́млена го́рем. **3.** (*exhausted*) измождённый.

prostrate[2] [prɒˈstreɪt, prə-] *v.t.* **1.** (*lay flat on ground*) опроки́|дывать, -нуть; **trees were ~d by the gale** бу́ря повали́ла дере́вья; **he ~d himself before the altar** он пал ниц пе́ред алтарём. **2.** (*overcome*) изнур|я́ть, -и́ть; **they were ~d by the heat** жара́ их изнури́ла.

prostration [prɒˈstreɪʃ(ə)n, prə-] *n.* (*lying flat*) распростёртое положе́ние; (*exhaustion*) изнеможе́ние; прострáция.

prosy [ˈprəuzɪ] *adj.* ну́дный.

protagonist [prəuˈtægənɪst] *n.* (*chief actor*) гла́вный геро́й; (*in contest etc.*) протагони́ст; (*advocate*) побо́рник.

protean [ˈprəutɪən, -ˈtiːən] *adj.* многообра́зный, изме́нчивый.

protect [prəˈtekt] *v.t.* **1.** (*keep safe, guard*) охран|я́ть, -и́ть; предохран|я́ть, -и́ть; **the house is well ~ed against fire** дом хорошо́ защищён от огня́. **2.** (*fit with safety device*) обезопа́сить (*pf.*). **3.** (*shelter*) защи|ща́ть, -ти́ть; огра|жда́ть, -ди́ть; **it is government policy to ~ the farmer** поли́тика прави́тельства — защища́ть (интере́сы) фе́рмера.

protection [prəˈtekʃ(ə)n] *n.* **1.** (*defence*) защи́та; **his clothing afforded him no ~ from the cold** оде́жда была́ ему́ плохо́й защи́той от хо́лода; **~ money** о́ткуп от вымога́телей. **2.** (*shelter*) огражде́ние. **3.** (*care*) попече́ние; **under my ~** на моём попече́нии. **4.** (*patronage*) покрови́тельство. **5.** (*assurance, security*) обеспе́чение. **6.** (*protective pers. or thg.*) защи́тник. **7.** (*econ.*) протекциони́зм.

protectionism [prəˈtekʃ(ə)ˌnɪz(ə)m] *n.* протекциони́зм.

protectionist [prəˈtekʃ(ə)nɪst] *n.* сторо́нник протекциони́зма.

protective [prəˈtektɪv] *adj.* защи́тный; **~ colouring** защи́тная окра́ска; **~ custody** содержа́ние под стра́жей; **~ tariff** протекцио́ный тари́ф.

protector [prəˈtektə(r)] *n.* (*pers.*) защи́тник; (*hist., regent*) ре́гент, проте́ктор; (*protective device*) защи́тное приспособле́ние.

protectorate [prəˈtektərət] *n.* (*protected territory*) протектора́т; (*regency*) ре́гентство.

protectress [prəˈtektrɪs] *n.* защи́тница.

protégé [ˈprɒtɪˌʒeɪ, -teˌʒeɪ, ˈprəu-] *n.* протеже́ (*c.g., indecl.*).

protein [ˈprəutiːn] *n.* протеи́н; бело́к.

pro tempore [prəu ˈtempərɪ], **pro tem** [prəu ˈtem] (*coll.*) *adv.* вре́менно, пока́.

protest[1] ['prəʊtest] *n.* протéст; возражéние; **enter, lodge a ~** заяви́ть (*pf.*) протéст; **he made no ~** он не протестовáл; **without ~** не протестýя; **~ march** марш протéста; **~ vote** гóлос, пóданный в знак протéста.

protest[2] [prə'test] *v.t.* **1.** (*affirm*) утверждáть (*impf.*); **he continued to ~ his innocence** он продолжáл отстáивать свою́ невинóвность. **2.** (*US, object to*) возражáть/протестовáть (*impf.*) прóтив+*g*. **3.** (*comm.*) опротест|óвывать, -овáть.

v.i.: **I ~ against being called a liar** я протестýю прóтив тогó, чтóбы меня́ называ́ли лжецóм; **the prisoners ~ed about their food** заключённые бы́ли недовóльны тюрéмной пи́щей и устрóили протéст; **they ~ed against the decision** они́ опротестовáли решéние.

Protestant ['prɒtɪst(ə)nt] *n.* протестáнт.

adj. протестáнтский.

Protestantism ['prɒtɪstənt,ɪz(ə)m] *n.* протестáнтство.

protestation [,prɒtɪ'steɪʃ(ə)n] *n.* (*affirmation*) (торжéственное) заявлéние; (*protest*) протéст.

protest|er, -or [prəʊ'testə(r)] *nn.* протестýющий.

protestingly [prəʊ'testɪŋlɪ] *adv.* протестýющим тóном.

protocol [,prəʊtə'kɒl] *n.* (*agreement*; *etiquette*) протокóл.

proton ['prəʊtɒn] *n.* протóн.

protoplasm ['prəʊtə,plæz(ə)m] *n.* протоплáзма.

prototype ['prəʊtə,taɪp] *n.* прототи́п; óпытный образéц.

protozoa [,prəʊtə'zəʊə] *n.* протозóа (*pl. indecl.*), простéйшие (*nt. pl.*).

protract [prə'trækt] *v.t.* затя́|гивать, -нýть; **a ~ed visit** затянýвшийся визи́т; **a ~ed war** затяжнáя войнá.

protractor [prə'træktə(r)] *n.* транспорти́р, угломéр.

protrud|e [prə'tru:d] *v.t.* высóвывать, вы́сунуть.

v.i. выдавáться (*impf.*); **~ing teeth** торчáщие зýбы.

protrusion [prə'tru:ʒ(ə)n] *n.* высóвывание; вы́ступ.

protuberance [prə'tju:bərəns] *n.* вы́пусклость, óпухоль, ши́шка.

protuberant [prə'tju:bərənt] *adj.* вы́пуклый, выдаю́щийся.

proud [praʊd] *adj.* гóрдый; **he is a ~ man** он гордéц; **he was too ~ to complain** он был сли́шком горд, чтóбы жáловаться; **he was ~ of his garden** он горди́лся своúм сáдом; **he was the ~ father of twins** он был счастли́вым отцóм двойни́; **this is a ~ day for the school** э́то торжéственный/рáдостный день для шкóлы; (*arrogant*) надмéнный; (*splendid*) величáвый, гордели́вый; **the fleet was a ~ sight** флот вы́глядел велúчественно великолéпно.

adv.: **it was a sumptuous meal: they did us ~** они́ нас угости́ли на слáву.

provable ['pru:vəb(ə)l] *adj.* доказýемый.

prove [pru:v] *v.t.* **1.** (*demonstrate*) докáз|ывать, -áть; обоснóв|ывать, -áть; **he ~d his worth many times over** он показáл себя́ в вы́сшей стéпени достóйным человéком; **he cannot be ~d guilty** нельзя́ доказáть, что он винóвен; **he needs to ~ himself to others** емý надо утверди́ть себя́ в глазáх други́х. **2.** (*put to the test*) испы́т|ывать, -áть; **the exception ~s the rule** исключéние подтверждáет прáвило; **proving-ground** (*mil.*) испытáтельный полигóн. **3.** (*leg.*): **~ a will** утверди́ть (*pf.*) завещáние.

v.i. (*turn out*) окáз|ываться, -áться; **the alarm ~d (to be) a hoax** тревóга оказáлась лóжной; **the play ~d a success** пьéса имéла успéх; **the report ~d true** сообщéние подтверди́лось; **he ~d to have been right** получи́лось, что он был прав.

proven ['pru:v(ə)n, 'prəʊ-] *adj.* докáзанный; **not ~** (*Sc.*) «винá не докáзана».

provenance ['prɒvɪnəns] *n.* происхождéние.

Provençal [,prɒvɒn'sɑ:l, ,prɒvɑ̃'sæl] *n.* (*pers.*) провансáл|ец (*fem.* -ка); (*language*) провансáльский язы́к.

adj. провансáльский, провáнский.

Provence [prɒ'vɑ̃s] *n.* Прованс.

provender ['prɒvɪndə(r)] *n.* (*fodder*) фурáж; (*joc., food*) пи́ща.

proverb ['prɒvɜ:b] *n.* послóвица; **(the Book of) P~s** Кни́га при́тчей Соломóновых.

proverbial [prə'vɜ:bɪəl] *adj.* **1.** (*pert. to provs.*) провербиáльный; **~ wisdom** нарóдная мýдрость; **he spends money like the ~ fool** он трáтит дéньги, как послéдний дурáк. **2.** (*notorious*) общеизвéстный; **he is ~ly unpunctual** егó непунктуáльность вошлá в поговóрку.

provide [prə'vaɪd] *v.t.* **1. ~ s.o. with sth.** обеспéчи|вать, -ть когó-н. чем-н.; снаб|жáть, -ди́ть когó-н. чем-н.; **who will ~ the food?** кто позабóтится о пи́ще?; **they are well ~d with money** у них достáточно дéнег; **students must ~ their own textbooks** студéнты обя́заны приобретáть учéбники сáми; **the tale ~d much amusement** расскáз всех óчень развесели́л; **the Lord will ~** Бог подáст. **2.** (*prescribe*) предусм|áтривать, -отрéть.

v.i. (*prepare o.s.*) пригот|áвливаться, -óвиться; **~ against one's old age** обеспéчить (*pf.*) себя́ к стáрости; **she had three children to ~ for** на её содержáнии бы́ло трóе детéй.

provid|ed [prə'vaɪdɪd], **-ing** [prə'vaɪdɪŋ] *conjs.* при услóвии, что; éсли.

providence ['prɒvɪd(ə)ns] *n.* **1.** (*foresight, thrift*) предусмотри́тельность. **2.** (*divine care*): **he escaped by a special ~** егó спаслó (тóлько) провидéние; (**P~:** *God*) провидéние, прóмысл бóжий.

provident ['prɒvɪd(ə)nt] *adj.* предусмотри́тельный; расчётливый.

providential [,prɒvɪ'denʃ(ə)l] *adj.* (*lucky*) счастли́вый; **it was ~ that you came** вас сам Бог послáл.

provider [prə'vaɪdə(r)] *n.* снабжéнец; поставщи́к; **her husband is a good ~** её муж хорошó обеспéчивает семью́.

providing [prə'vaɪdɪŋ] = **provided**

province ['prɒvɪns] *n.* **1.** (*division of country*) óбласть, прови́нция. **2.: the ~s** прови́нция; перифери́я; **in the ~s** на местáх/перифери́и. **3.** (*sphere, department*) компетéнция; óбласть; **that is outside my ~** э́то вне моéй компетéнции. **4.** (*eccl.*) епáрхия.

provincial [prə'vɪnʃ(ə)l] *n.* (*pers. from provinces*) провинциáл (*fem.* -ка).

adj. (*lit., fig.*) провинциáльный; **~ governor** губернáтор прови́нции.

provincialism [prə'vɪnʃə,lɪz(ə)m] *n.* провинциáльность; (*in language etc.*) диалекти́зм.

provision [prə'vɪʒ(ə)n] *n.* **1.** (*supplying*) снабжéние. **2.** (*pl., supplies, esp. food*) прови́зия; съестны́е припáсы (*m. pl.*); **~s merchant** оптóвый торгóвец продовóльствием. **3.** (*preparation*) обеспéчение; **their father had made ~ for them** отéц обеспéчил их на бýдущее. **4.** (*item of agreement, law etc.*) услóвие; положéние.

v.t. снаб|жáть, -ди́ть продовóльствием.

provisional [prə'vɪʒən(ə)l] *n.*: **the P~s** Врéменное крылó ИРА.

adj. врéменный; (*approximate*) ориентирóвочный; **he gave ~ consent** он дал предвари́тельное соглáсие; **~ government** врéменное прави́тельство; **P~ IRA** Врéменное крылó ИРА.

proviso [prə'vaɪzəʊ] *n.* услóвие, оговóрка; **with the ~ that ...** с услóвием (*or* с оговóркой), что; **subject to this ~** при э́том услóвии.

provocation [,prɒvə'keɪʃ(ə)n] *n.* **1.** (*challenge, incitement*) вы́зов; **he swears on the slightest ~** он ругáется по малéйшему пóводу; **I did it under ~** меня́ спровоци́ровали на э́то. **2.** (*ruse*) провокáция.

provocative [prə'vɒkətɪv] *adj.* вызывáющий; провокациóнный; **his remarks were ~ of laughter** егó замечáния вы́звали смех; **she gave him a ~ smile** онá улыбнýлась на негó зазывáюще; **race is a ~ subject** рáсовая тéма всегдá вызывáет полéмику.

provoke [prə'vəʊk] *v.t.* (*cause, arouse*; *challenge*) вызывáть, вы́звать; провоци́ровать, с-. **2.** (*impel*) побу|ждáть, -ди́ть. **3.** (*anger*) серди́ть, рас-; раздраж|áть, -и́ть; **he is easily ~d** егó легкó вы́вести из себя́.

provoking [prə'vəʊkɪŋ] *adj.* раздражáющий, досáдный.

provost ['prɒvəst] *n.* (*head of college*) рéктор; (*Sc. dignitary*) мэр; **~-marshal** начáльник воéнной поли́ции.

prow [praʊ] *n.* нос (*сýдна, самолёта*).

prowess ['praʊɪs] *n.* дóблесть, отвáга; (*skill*) мастерствó, умéние.

prowl [praʊl] *n.*: **cats on the ~ after mice** ко́шки, высма́тривающие мыше́й.
v.t.: **thieves ~ the streets** во́ры шныря́ют по у́лицам.
v.i. кра́сться (*impf.*); **wolves were ~ing outside the tent** во́лки ры́скали вокру́г пала́тки.
prox. [prɒks] *adj.* (*abbr. of* ***proximo***) сле́дующего ме́сяца.
proximate ['prɒksɪmət] *adj.* ближа́йший, непосре́дственный.
proximity [prɒk'sɪmɪtɪ] *n.* бли́зость; сосе́дство; **in (close) ~ to** вблизи́/поблизо́сти от+*g.*, ря́дом с+*i.*; **~ fuse** радиовзрыва́тель (*m.*).
proxy ['prɒksɪ] *n.* **1.** (*authorization*) полномо́чие, дове́ренность; **they voted (married) by ~** они́ голосова́ли (заключи́ли брак) по дове́ренности. **2.** (*substitute*) замести́тель (*m.*); **he stood ~ for his brother** он представля́л своего́ бра́та; (*attr.*): **~ vote** голосова́ние по дове́ренности.
prude [pru:d] *n.* ханжа́ (*c.g.*).
prudence ['pru:d(ə)ns] *n.* благоразу́мие; предусмотри́тельность.
prudent ['pru:d(ə)nt] *adj.* благоразу́мный; предусмотри́тельный.
prudential [pru:'denʃ(ə)l] *adj.* расчётливый.
prudery ['pru:dərɪ] *n.* (притво́рная) стыдли́вость.
prudish ['pru:dɪʃ] *adj.* стыдли́вый; ха́нжеский.
prudishness ['pru:dɪʃnɪs] *n.* (напускна́я) стыдли́вость; ха́нжество́.
prune[1] [pru:n] *n.* чернosли́в.
prun|e[2] [pru:n] *v.t.* **1.** (*trim*) обр|еза́ть, -е́зать; подр|еза́ть, -е́зать; **~ing-hook** прививо́чный нож; **~ing-shears** сека́тор; садо́вые но́жницы; (*fig.*) сокра|ща́ть, -ти́ть; **the department was ~ed of superfluous staff** весь изли́шний штат в отде́ле сократи́ли. **2.** (*simplify*) упро|ща́ть, -сти́ть.
prurienc|e ['prʊərɪəns], **-y** ['prʊərɪənsɪ] *nn.* похотли́вость; зуд.
prurient ['prʊərɪənt] *adj.* похотли́вый.
pruritus [prʊə'raɪtəs] *n.* зуд.
Prussia ['prʌʃə] *n.* Пру́ссия.
Prussian ['prʌʃ(ə)n] *n.* прусса́|к (*fem.* -чка).
adj. пру́сский; **~ blue** берли́нская лазу́рь.
prussic ['prʌsɪk] *adj.* циа́нистый; **~ acid** сини́льная кислота́.
pry [praɪ] *v.i.* (*peer*) погля́д|ывать, -е́ть; подсм|а́тривать, -отре́ть; (*interfere*) вме́шиваться (*impf.*).
PS (*abbr. of* **postscript**) постскри́птум, припи́ска.
psalm [sɑ:m] *n.* псало́м.
psalmist ['sɑ:mɪst] *n.* псалми́ст.
psalmody ['sɑ:mədɪ, 'sæl-] *n.* псалмо́дия.
psalter ['sɔ:ltə(r), 'sɒl-] *n.* псалты́рь (*f. or m.*).
psaltery ['sɔ:ltərɪ, 'sɒl-] *n.* псалтерио́н.
PSBR (*abbr. of* ***Public Sector Borrowing Requirement***) потре́бность госуда́рственного се́ктора в сре́дствах для покры́тия дефици́та.
psephologist [se'fɒlədʒɪst, pse-] *n.* псефо́лог.
psephology [se'fɒlədʒɪ, pse-] *n.* псефоло́гия.
pseud [sju:d] *n.* позёр.
pseudo ['sju:dəʊ] *adj.* фальши́вый.
pseudo- ['sju:dəʊ] *comb. form* псе́вдо…, лже…
pseudonym ['sju:dənɪm] *n.* псевдони́м.
pseudonymous [sju:'dɒnɪməs] *adj.* пи́шущий/напи́санный под псевдони́мом.
pshaw [pʃɔ:, ʃɔ:] *int.* фи!, фу!, тьфу!
psittacosis [ˌsɪtə'kəʊsɪs] *n.* пситтако́з.
psoriasis [sə'raɪəsɪs] *n.* псориа́з.
psst [pst] *int.* хм-хм (*чтобы привлечь внимание*).
psych [saɪk] *v.t.*: **~ o.s. up** настр|а́ивать, -о́ить себя́.
Psyche[1] ['saɪkɪ] *n.* (*myth.*) Психе́я.
psyche[2] ['saɪkɪ] *n.* душа́; дух.
psychedelic [ˌsaɪkɪ'delɪk] *adj.* психедели́ческий; зау́мный.
psychiatric [ˌsaɪkɪ'ætrɪk] *adj.* психиатри́ческий.
psychiatrist [saɪ'kaɪətrɪst] *n.* психиа́тр.
psychiatry [saɪ'kaɪətrɪ] *n.* психиатри́я.
psychic ['saɪkɪk] *n.* экстрасе́нс.
adj. **1.** = **psychical. 2.** (*susceptible to occult influence*) ≃ ясновидящий.
psychical ['saɪkɪk(ə)l] *adj.* (*of the soul or mind*) душе́вный; (*of non-physical phenomena*) психи́ческий.
psychoanalyse [ˌsaɪkəʊ'ænəˌlaɪz] *v.t.* психоанализи́ровать (*impf., pf.*).
psychoanalysis [ˌsaɪkəʊə'nælɪsɪs] *n.* психоана́лиз.
psychoanalyst [ˌsaɪkəʊ'ænəlɪst] *n.* психоанали́тик.
psychoanalytic [ˌsaɪkəʊˌænə'lɪtɪk] *adj.* психоаналити́ческий.
psycholinguistics [ˌsaɪkəʊlɪŋ'gwɪstɪks] *n.* психолингви́стика.
psychological [ˌsaɪkə'lɒdʒɪk(ə)l] *adj.* психологи́ческий; **he arrived at the ~ moment** он появи́лся в са́мое подходя́щее вре́мя; **~ warfare** психологи́ческая война́.
psychologist [saɪ'kɒlədʒɪst] *n.* психо́лог.
psychology [saɪ'kɒlədʒɪ] *n.* психоло́гия; (*coll., mental processes*) пси́хика.
psychopath ['saɪkəˌpæθ] *n.* психопа́т (*fem.* -ка).
psychopathic [ˌsaɪkə'pæθɪk] *adj.* психопати́ческий; **he is ~** он психопа́т.
psychopathology [ˌsaɪkəʊpə'θɒlədʒɪ] *n.* психопатоло́гия.
psychopathy [saɪ'kɒpəθɪ] *n.* психопа́тия.
psychosis [saɪ'kəʊsɪs] *n.* психо́з.
psychosomatic [ˌsaɪkəʊsə'mætɪk] *adj.* психозомати́ческий.
psychotherapeutic [ˌsaɪkəʊθerə'pju:tɪk] *adj.* психотерапевти́ческий.
psychotherapist [ˌsaɪkəʊ'θerəpɪst] *n.* психотерапе́вт.
psychotherapy [ˌsaɪkəʊ'θerəpɪ] *n.* психотерапи́я.
psychotic [saɪ'kɒtɪk] *adj.* психо́зный, психоти́ческий, душевнобольно́й.
PT (*abbr. of* ***physical training***) физи́ческая подгото́вка.
pt. [paɪnt(z)] *n.* (*abbr. of* **pint(s)**) пи́нта.
PTA (*abbr. of* ***parent-teacher association***) Ассоциа́ция учи́телей и роди́телей.
ptarmigan ['tɑ:mɪgən] *n.* шотла́ндский те́терев.
Pte ['praɪvət] *n.* (*abbr. of* **Private**) рядово́й.
pterodactyl [ˌterə'dæktɪl] *n.* птерода́ктиль (*m.*).
PTO (*abbr. of* ***please turn over***) см. на об., (смотри́ на оборо́те).
Ptolemaic [ˌtɒlɪ'meɪɪk] *adj.*: **~ system** Птолеме́ева систе́ма ми́ра.
Ptolemy ['tɒlɪmɪ] *n.* Птолеме́й.
ptomaine ['təʊmeɪn] *n.* птомаи́н; **~ poisoning** отравле́ние тру́пным я́дом.
pub [pʌb] *n.* (*coll.*) пивна́я; бар; каба́к.
cpd. **~-crawl** *n.* (*coll.*) шата́ние по пивны́м/ба́рам.
puberty ['pju:bətɪ] *n.* полова́я зре́лость.
pubes ['pju:bi:z] *n.* лобко́вая о́бласть.
pubescence [pju:'bes(ə)ns] *n.* полово́е созрева́ние.
pubescent [pju:'bes(ə)nt] *adj.* дости́гший полово́й зре́лости.
pubic ['pju:bɪk] *adj.* лобко́вый, ло́нный; **~ hair** во́лосы на лобке́.
pubis ['pju:bɪs] *n.* лобко́вая/ло́нная кость.
public ['pʌblɪk] *n.* **1.** (*community*) обще́ственность; наро́д; **the British ~** англи́йский наро́д; **the library is open to the ~** вход в библиоте́ку свобо́дный; **members of the (general) ~** представи́тели обще́ственности (*or* широ́кой пу́блики). **2.** (*section of community*) пу́блика; **the theatre-going ~** театра́льная пу́блика. **3.** (*audience*) пу́блика; **he refuses to appear before the ~** он отка́зывается публи́чно выступа́ть; **I have never spoken in ~** я никогда́ не выступа́л публи́чно; **my ~** (*of an actor*) моя́ аудито́рия; мои́ зри́тели (*m. pl.*). **4.** (*coll.*, **~ house**) пивна́я; бар.
adj. **1.** (*pert. to people in general*) обще́ственный; **~ opinion** обще́ственное мне́ние; **a matter of ~ concern** де́ло, представля́ющее обще́ственный интере́с; **he is in the ~ eye** он нахо́дится в по́ле зре́ния обще́ственности; **~ health** здравоохране́ние; **it is ~ knowledge** э́то общеизве́стно; **~ relations** взаимоотноше́ние (организа́ции) с клиенту́рой (и о́бществом в це́лом); рекла́ма; **~ relations officer** нача́льник/сотру́дник отде́ла информа́ции (и рекла́мы); **in the ~ interest** в интере́сах о́бщества/госуда́рства; **~ enemy** враг наро́да. **2.** (*pert. to politics or the state*) обще́ственный, госуда́рственный; **a ~ man, figure** обще́ственный де́ятель; **he entered ~ life** он заня́лся обще́ственной де́ятельностью; **he held ~ office** он занима́л (вы́борную) госуда́рственную до́лжность; **~ record office** госуда́рственный архи́в; **in**

the ~ service на госуда́рственной слу́жбе; **~ prosecutor** обще́ственный прокуро́р; **~ spirit** обще́ственное созна́ние. **3.** (*accessible to all*; *shared by the community*) публи́чный, общедосту́пный, общенаро́дный; **~ convenience** обще́ственная убо́рная; **~ holiday** устано́вленный зако́ном пра́здник; **~ library** публи́чная библиоте́ка; **~ utilities** коммуна́льные услу́ги; **~ works** обще́ственные рабо́ты; предприя́тия обще́ственного по́льзования. **4.** (*done openly*, *in view of others*) публи́чный, гла́сный; откры́тый; **~ inquiry** публи́чное рассле́дование; **he made it ~** он пре́дал э́то гла́сности; **~ speaking** ора́торское иску́сство; **he does a lot of ~ speaking** он ча́сто выступа́ет публи́чно; **~ address system** громкоговори́тели (*m. pl.*); систе́ма трансляцио́нного радиовеща́ния; **~ protest** откры́тый проте́ст.

cpds. **~-house** *n.* пивна́я, бар; **~-spirited** *adj.* патриоти́чески настро́енный; дви́жимый интере́сами обще́ственности.

publican ['pʌblɪkən] *n.* (*keeper of public-house*) содержа́тель (*m.*) ба́ра; (*hist.*, *tax-gatherer*) сбо́рщик нало́гов, (*bibl.*) мы́тарь (*m.*).

publication [ˌpʌblɪ'keɪʃ(ə)n] *n.* (*of news etc.*) публика́ция, опубликова́ние; (*issuing of written work*, *photograph etc.*) изда́ние, вы́ход, вы́пуск; (*published work*) изда́ние; произведе́ние.

publicist ['pʌblɪsɪst] *n.* (*writer on current topics*) публици́ст.

publicity [pʌb'lɪsɪtɪ] *n.* **1.** (*public notice*, *dissemination*) гла́сность; **an actress seeking ~** актри́са, добыва́ющаяся рекла́мы; **the report was given full ~** сообще́ние получи́ло широ́кую огла́ску. **2.** (*advertisement*) реклами́рование; **~ agent** аге́нт по рекла́ме; **~ campaign** рекла́мная кампа́ния.

publicize ['pʌblɪˌsaɪz] *v.t.* реклами́ровать (*impf.*); огла|ша́ть, -си́ть.

publish ['pʌblɪʃ] *v.t.* **1.** (*make generally known*) публикова́ть, о-; огла|ша́ть, -си́ть. **2.** (*announce formally*) официа́льно объяв|ля́ть, -и́ть. **3.** (*issue copies of*) печа́тать, на-; изд|ава́ть, -а́ть, выпуска́ть, вы́пустить; **be ~ed** выходи́ть, вы́йти (из печа́ти).

publishable ['pʌblɪʃəb(ə)l] *adj.* могу́щий быть напеча́танным/и́зданным; приго́дный для печа́ти.

publisher ['pʌblɪʃə(r)] *n.* изда́тель (*m.*).

publishing ['pʌblɪʃɪŋ] *n.* изда́тельское де́ло; **~ house** изда́тельство.

puce [pju:s] *adj.* краснова́то-кори́чневый.

puck [pʌk] *n.* (*in ice-hockey*) ша́йба.

pucker ['pʌkə(r)] *n.* (*fold*, *crease*) скла́дка; (*wrinkle*) морщи́на.

v.t. & *i.* мо́рщить(ся), на-; **his brow was ~ed** он насу́пился; **this coat ~s up at the shoulders** э́то пальто́ морщи́т в плеча́х.

puckish ['pʌkɪʃ] *adj.* прока́зливый.

pud [pʊd] (*coll.*) = **pudding**

pudding ['pʊdɪŋ] *n.* пу́динг, запека́нка; (*sweet course*) сла́дкое; **black ~** кровяна́я колбаса́; **~ face** (*coll.*) то́лстая, невырази́тельная физионо́мия.

puddle ['pʌd(ə)l] *n.* (*pool*) лу́жа.

v.t. (*metall.*) пудлингова́ть (*impf.*).

pudenda [pju:'dendə] *n.* (же́нские) нару́жные половы́е о́рганы (*m. pl.*).

pudgy ['pʌdʒɪ] *adj.* пу́хлый; ни́зенький и то́лстый.

puerile ['pjʊəraɪl] *adj.* де́тский, инфанти́льный.

puerility [pjʊə'rɪlɪtɪ] *n.* инфанти́льность.

puerperal [pju:'ɜ:pər(ə)l] *adj.* роди́льный; **~ fever** роди́льная горя́чка.

Puerto Rican [ˌpwɜ:təʊ 'ri:kən] *n.* пуэртори́кан|ец (*fem.* -ка).

adj. пуэрто-рика́нский.

Puerto Rico [ˌpwɜ:təʊ 'ri:kəʊ] *n.* Пуэ́рто-Ри́ко (*indecl.*).

puff [pʌf] *n.* **1.** (*of breath*) вы́дох. **2.** (*of smoke*, *steam etc.*) дымо́к, клуб; **he took a ~ at his cigar** он затяну́лся сига́рой. **3.** (*sound*) пыхте́ние. **4.** (*of air or wind*) струя́ во́здуха. **5.** (*coll.*, *publicity*) ду́тая рекла́ма, похвала́. **6.** (*cake*) сло́йка; слоёный пирожо́к.

v.t. **1.** (*breathe out*) выдыха́ть, вы́дохнуть; **he ~ed smoke in my face** он пусти́л дым мне в лицо́. **2.** (*make out of breath*): **I was ~ed after the climb** у меня́ сде́лалась оды́шка по́сле подъёма. **3.**: **~ out, up** над|ува́ть, -у́ть; расп|уха́ть, -у́хнуть; **his hand was ~ed up** его́ рука́ распу́хла; **he ~ed out his chest with pride** он го́рдо вы́пятил грудь. **4.** (*praise extravagantly*) чрезме́рно расхва́л|ивать, -и́ть.

v.i. **1.** (*come out in ~s*) клуби́ться (*impf.*). **2.** (*breathe quickly*): **he was ~ing and panting** он не мог отдыша́ться; он пыхте́л. **3.** (*emit smoke*) дыми́ться (*impf.*); **he ~ed away at his pipe** он попы́хивал тру́бкой.

cpd. **~-ball** *n.* дождеви́к.

puffer(-train) ['pʌfə(r)] *n.* (*coll.*) ту-ту́ (*nt. indecl.*).

puffin ['pʌfɪn] *n.* ту́пик, топо́рик.

puffy ['pʌfɪ] *adj.* (*swollen*) одутлова́тый.

pug [pʌg] *n.* мопс.

cpd. **~-nosed** *adj.* курно́сый.

pugilism ['pju:dʒɪˌlɪz(ə)m] *n.* кула́чный бой.

pugilist ['pju:dʒɪlɪst] *n.* боксёр.

pugilistic [ˌpju:dʒɪ'lɪstɪk] *adj.* кула́чный.

pugnacious [pʌg'neɪʃəs] *adj.* драчли́вый, вои́нственный.

pugnacity [pʌg'næsɪtɪ] *n.* драчли́вость, вои́нственность.

puissance ['pju:ɪs(ə)ns, 'pwɪs-] *n.* (*arch.*) могу́щество, мощь.

puissant ['pju:ɪs(ə)nt, 'pwi:s-, 'pwɪs-] *adj.* (*arch.*) могу́щественный, мо́щный.

puke [pju:k] *v.i.* блева́ть (*impf.*); **he ~d** его́ вы́рвало; (*vulg.*) он сблевну́л.

pukka ['pʌkə] *adj.* (*coll.*) настоя́щий.

pulchritude ['pʌlkrɪˌtju:d] *n.* красота́.

pule [pju:l] *v.i.* пища́ть (*impf.*); скули́ть (*impf.*).

pull [pʊl] *n.* **1.** (*tug*) тя́га; дёрганье; **he gave a ~ on the rope** он дёрнул (за) верёвку. **2.** (*swig*) глото́к; **he took a ~ at the bottle** он сде́лал глото́к из буты́лки. **3.** (*inhalation of smoke*) затя́жка; **he took a ~ at his pipe** он затяну́лся тру́бкой. **4.** (*coll.*, *row*) гре́бля; **let's go for a ~ on the lake!** дава́йте поката́емся по о́зеру! **5.** (*handle*) ру́чка; шнуро́к. **6.** (*force*, *effort*) напряже́ние; **the tide exerts a strong ~** прили́в облада́ет большо́й си́лой; **it was a long hard ~ up the hill** взобра́ться на́ гору сто́ило больши́х уси́лий. **7.** (*coll.*, *advantage*) преиму́щество; **you have the ~ over me** у вас пе́редо мной преиму́щество. **8.** (*coll.*, *influence*) блат; **he has a lot of ~** у него́ больши́е свя́зи. **9.** (*print*, *rough proof*) про́бный о́ттиск. **10.** (*at cricket or golf*) уда́р с ле́вым укло́ном.

v.t. **1.** (*draw towards one*, *tug*, *jerk*) тяну́ть, по-; тащи́ть, под-; **the boy ~ed his sister's hair** ма́льчик дёрнул сестру́ за́ волосы; **he ~ed me by the sleeve** он потяну́л меня́ за рука́в. **2.** (*obtain by ~ing*): **the barman ~ed a glass of beer** барме́н нацеди́л стака́н пи́ва. **3.** (*fig.*): **he is good at ~ing strings** он ма́стер нажима́ть на кно́пки; **~ s.o.'s leg** разы́гр|ивать, -а́ть кого́-н.; **she ~ed a face at him** она́ ско́рчила ему́ грима́су; **he ~ed a long face** у него́ вы́тянулась физионо́мия; **he is trying to ~ a fast one** он стара́ется нас объего́рить (*coll.*). **4.** (*extract*, *pluck*) выта́скивать, вы́тащить; выдёргивать, вы́дернуть; **~ a tooth** вырыва́ть, вы́рвать зуб; **she ~ed all the flowers** она́ сорвала́ все цветы́; **he ~ed a gun on me** он вы́хватил пистоле́т и навёл его́ на меня́. **5.** (*propel by ~ing*) тяну́ть, по-; **the carriage was ~ed by horses** каре́та была́ запряжена́ лошадьми́; **he is not ~ing his weight** (*lit.*, *in rowing*) он не налега́ет на вёсла; (*fig.*) он рабо́тает вполси́лы. **6.** (*rowing*): **he ~s a good oar** он хорошо́ гребёт. **7.** (*restrain*) сде́рж|ивать, -а́ть; **the jockey ~ed his horse** жоке́й придержа́л своего́ коня́; **he ~ed his punches** (*lit.*, *fig.*) он уда́рил вполси́лы. **8.** (*strain*, *e.g. muscle*) растя́|гивать, -ну́ть.

v.i. **1.** (*exert drawing force*) тяну́ть, по-; **they ~ed on the rope** они́ потяну́ли за верёвку; **he ~ed at the bell** он дёрнул звоно́к; **the boatman ~ed hard at, on the oars** ло́дочник усе́рдно налега́л на вёсла; **the horse ~ed against the bit** ло́шадь натяну́ла удила́; **the engine is ~ing well** мото́р хорошо́ тя́нет. **2.** (*suck*) тяну́ть, по-; **he ~ed on his pipe** он потя́гивал тру́бку. **3.** (*propel boat*, *car etc.*) е́хать, про-; **he had to ~ across the road** ему́ на́до бы́ло перее́хать на другу́ю сто́рону; **~ for the shore!** греби́те к бéрегу! **4.** (*move under propulsion*) двúгаться (*impf.*); **the car is ~ing to the left** машúну занóсит влéво; **the train ~ed out of the station** пóезд отошёл от стáнции.

with advs.: ~ **about** *v.t.* таскáть (*impf.*) тудá и сюдá; **the dog ~ed the cushion about** собáка теребúла подýшку; ~ **apart** *v.t.* (*also* ~ **to pieces**) раз|рывáть, -орвáть на кускú; (*fig., criticize severely*) разн|осúть, -естú в пух и прах; ~ **aside** *v.t.* оття́|гивать, -нýть; ~ **away** *v.t.*: **he ~ed his hand away** он убрáл рýку; *v.i.* (*move off*) от|рывáться, -орвáться; **the boat ~ed away from the quay** лóдка отплылá от прúстани; (*gain ground*) **the favourite quickly ~ed away** фаворúт бы́стро оторвáлся от остальны́х; ~ **back** *v.t.* оттá|скивать, -щúть; оття́|гивать, -нýть; **he ~ed her back from the window** он оттащúл её от окнá; ~ **back the curtains!** отдёрните/открóйте занавéски!; *v.i.*: **when she saw his gun she ~ed back** увúдев егó пистолéт, онá отпря́нула; ~ **down** *v.t.* (*lower by ~ing*) спус|кáть, -тúть; ~ **down the blinds!** опустúте штóры!; **he ~ed the branch down** он нагнýл вéтку; **he was attacked and ~ed down** на негó напáли и повалúли егó на зéмлю; (*demolish*) сн|осúть, -естú; (*debilitate*) осл|абля́ть, -áбить; ~ **in** *v.t.* (*retract*) втя́|гивать, -нýть; (*curtail*) сокра|щáть, -тúть; (*haul on, draw towards one*) тащúть, вы́-; тянýть, по-; **the rope was ~ed in** верёвку натянýли; **he ~ed in his horse** он осадúл лóшадь; (*coll., arrest*) арестóв|ывать, -áть; **he ~s in £50 a week** он получáет 50 фýнтов в недéлю; **I was ~ed in to help in the search** меня́ застáвили при́нять учáстие в рóзыске; *v.i.* (*drive or move to a standstill*) остан|áвливаться, -овúться; **the train ~ed in** пóезд подошёл к перрóну; **he ~ed in to the kerb** он подъéхал к тротуáру; (*drive or move towards near side of road*): **he ~ed in to avoid a collision** он прижáлся к обóчине, чтóбы избежáть столкновéния; ~ **off** *v.t.* (*remove, detach*) стя́|гивать, -нýть; сн|имáть, -ять; **he ~ed the buttons off** он сорвáл/оторвáл пýговицы; **he ~ed his shoes off** он стащúл тýфли; (*coll., achieve*) успéшно заверш|áть, -úть; **he ~ed off the three first prizes** он сорвáл три пéрвых прúза; **if he ~s it off** éсли у негó вы́йдет/вы́горит; *v.i.* трóгаться (*impf.*); **the car ~ed off in a hurry** машúна бы́стро отъéхала; ~ **on** *v.t.* натя́|гивать, -нýть; **he ~ed his socks on** он натянýлноскú; ~ **out** *v.t.* (*extract*) вытáскивать, вы́тащить; **he ~ed out his watch** он вы́тащил часы́; **he ~ed out the drawer** он вы́двинул я́щик; **the weeds should be ~ed out** сорнякú нáдо вы́дернуть/вы́полоть; (*withdraw*) выводúть, вы́вести; **the troops should be ~ed out** войскá слéдует вы́вести; *v.i.* (*drive or move away*) от|ходúть, -ойтú; **he caught the train as it was ~ing out** он вскочúл в пóезд на ходý; (*of driving manœuvres*) отъ|езжáть, -éхать; **he ~ed out to overtake** он вы́шел на обгóн; (*withdraw*): **the troops had to ~ out** войскáм пришлóсь вы́йти из бóя; **the drawer won't ~ out** я́щик не выдвигáется; **he ~ed out** (*of the business*) он отказáлся от учáстия в э́том дéле; ~ **round** *v.t.* вылéчивать, вы́лечить; **the brandy will soon ~ you round** конья́к скóро приведёт вас в чýвство; *v.i.* (*recover*) попр|авля́ться, -áвиться; **he will ~ round in a day or so** он придёт в себя́ (*or* поправится) чéрез день-другóй; (*reverse direction*) разв|орáчиваться, -ернýться; ~ **through** *v.t.* (*lit.*) протá|скивать, -щúть; (*fig.*) спас|áть, -тú; **the doctor ~ed him through** дóктор егó спас; **he dreaded the exam but his determination ~ed him through** он ужáсно боя́лся экзáмена, но решúлся сдать и сдал; *v.i.* (*recover from illness*) попр|авля́ться, -áвиться; **he was gravely ill, but ~ed through somehow** он был тяжелó бóлен, но кóе-как сумéл поправиться; (*surmount difficulties, survive*): **we shall ~ through in the end** в концé концóв мы вы́крутимся; ~ **together** *v.t.*: ~ **yourself together!** возьмúте себя́ в рýки!; держúте себя́ в рукáх!; *v.i.* (*fig.*) сраб|áтываться, -óтаться; сходúться, сойтúсь; **if we all ~ together, we shall win** объединúвшись, мы победúм; **the oarsmen ~ed together as one man** гребцы́ налеглú на вёсла как одúн человéк; ~ **up** *v.t.* (*uproot*) вырывáть, вы́рвать; **the plant had been ~ed up by the roots** растéние вы́рвали с кóрнем; (*raise*) вытя́гивать, вы́тянуть; **he ~ed himself up to his full height** он вы́прямился во весь рост; **you must ~ your socks up** (*fig., coll.*) вам нáдо засучúть рукавá; (*draw nearer*) придв|игáть, -úнуть; ~ **up a chair!** придвúньте стул!; (*bring to a halt*) остан|áвливать, -овúть; (*reprimand*) отчúт|ывать, -áть; *v.i.* (*come to a halt*) остан|áвливаться, -овúться; **don't get off the bus until it ~s up** не выходúте из автóбуса до пóлной остановки; (*improve one's position*) подтя́|гиваться, -нýться; **he ~ed up to second place** он вы́шел на вторóе мéсто.

cpds. **~-in** *n.* (*driver's cafe*) закýсочная, забегáловка; **~-out** *n.* (*folded illustration*) вклéйка большóго формáта; (*detachable section*) вклáдка; **~-out** *n.* вы́вод, отвóд; ~ **of troops** вы́вод войск; **~over** *n.* пулóвер; **~-through** *n.* протúрка (*орудия*); **~-up** *n.* = **~-in**; (*gymnastic exercise*) подтя́гивание.

pullet ['pʊlɪt] *n.* молóдка, молодáя кýрочка.

pulley ['pʊlɪ] *n.* шкив; блок.

cpd. **~-block** *n.* полиспáст.

pullulate ['pʌljʊ,leɪt] *v.i.* (*multiply*) расплодúться (*pf.*); (*teem*) изобúловать (*impf.*).

pulmonary ['pʌlmənərɪ] *adj.* лёгочный.

pulp [pʌlp] *n.* **1.** (*of fruit*) мя́коть. **2.** (*of animal tissue*) пýльпа. **3.** (*of wood, rags etc. for making paper*) древéсная мáсса, пýльпа. **4.** (*fig.*) кащúца; бесфóрменная мáсса; **his arm was crushed to a ~** емý раздробúло рýку; ~ **literature** макулатýра.

v.t. (*make into ~*) превра|щáть, -тúть в пýльпу; (*remove ~ from*) оч|ищáть, -úстить от мя́коти.

pulpit ['pʊlpɪt] *n.* амвóн, кáфедра; (*fig.*) трибýна.

pulpy ['pʌlpɪ] *adj.* мясúстый; сóчный.

pulsar ['pʌlsɑː(r)] *n.* пульсáр.

pulsate [pʌl'seɪt, 'pʌl-] *v.i.* пульсúровать (*impf.*).

pulsation [pʌl'seɪʃ(ə)n] *n.* пульсáция.

puls|e[1] [pʌls] *n.* пульс; **the doctor took his ~e** врач пощýпал емý пульс; **what is your ~e rate?** какóй у вас пульс?; (*fig.*) пульсáция, биéние; **he has his finger on the nation's ~e** он знáет, чем ды́шит странá; **the music stirred his ~e** мýзыка егó взволновáла; (*of music*) ритм.

v.i. пульсúровать (*impf.*); биться (*impf.*); **it sent the blood ~ing through his veins** э́то зажглó егó/емý кровь.

pulse[2] [pʌls] *n.* (*collect., legumes*) бобóвые (растéния).

pulverize ['pʌlvə,raɪz] *v.t.* **1.** (*reduce to powder*) размельч|áть, -úть; (*fig., smash, demolish*) сокруш|áть, -úть. **2.** (*divide into spray*) распыл|я́ть, -úть.

v.i. распыля́ться (*impf.*).

pulverizer ['pʌlvə,raɪzə(r)] *n.* (*crusher*) дробúлка; (*spray*) пульверизáтор.

puma ['pjuːmə] *n.* пýма, кугуáр.

pumice ['pʌmɪs] *n.* (**~-stone**) пéмза.

v.t. шлифовáть (*impf.*) (пéмзой).

pummel, pommel ['pʌm(ə)l] *v.t.* колотúть, по-; тузúть, от-.

pump[1] [pʌmp] *n.* насóс, пóмпа; ~ **attendant** (*at filling station*) слýжащий бензоколóнки.

v.t. **1.** (*transfer by ~ing*) качáть, на-; **they ~ed water out of the hold** онú вы́качали вóду из трю́ма; **we have a ~ed water supply** водá подаётся к нам насóсами; **the tyre needs more air ~ing into it** шúну нáдо подкачáть; (*fig.*): **I had maths ~ed into me at school** в меня́ вдáлбливали матемáтику в шкóле. **2.** (*affect or empty by ~ing*) выкáчивать, вы́качать; **the well had been ~ed dry** кóлодец пóлностью осушúли; (*fig.*): **I ~ed him for information** я егó выспрáшивал; я вывéдывал у негó свéдения. **3.** (*agitate as in ~ing*): **he ~ed my arm up and down** он дóлго тряс мне рýку. **4.** (*also ~ up: inflate*) накáч|ивать, -áть; **bicycle tyres should be ~ed hard** велосипéдные шúны должны́ быть тýго накáчаны.

cpd. **~-room** *n.* бювéт; зал для питья́ минерáльной воды́.

pump[2] [pʌmp] *n.* (*shoe*) тýфля-лóдочка.

pumpernickel ['pʌmpə,nɪk(ə)l, 'pʊ-] *n.* немéцкий ржанóй хлеб.

pumpkin ['pʌmpkɪn] *n.* ты́ква.

pun [pʌn] *n.* игрá слов, каламбýр.

v.i. игрáть словáми, каламбýрить (*impf.*).

punch[1] [pʌntʃ] *n.* **1.** (*blow with fist*) удáр кулакóм; **I gave him a ~ on the nose** я дал емý пó носу. **2.** (*fig., energy*) энéргия; **his performance lacked ~** он игрáл вя́ло (*or* без изю́минки); егó игрé недоставáло огня́. **3.** (*tool for perforating e.g. paper*) перфорáтор, компóстер; (*for stamping designs*) пуансóн.

v.t. **1.** (*hit with fist*) уд|аря́ть, -áрить кулакóм; **I'd like to ~ your face** я бы охóтно дал вам по физиономи́и; **he was ~ed on the chin** он получи́л кулакóм в чéлюсть. **2.** (*perforate*) компости́ровать (*impf.*); **the conductor ~ed our tickets** кондýктор прокомпости́ровал/проби́л нáши билéты; **~ holes** проб|ивáть, -и́ть отвéрстия; **the bolts must be ~ed out** болты́ нýжно вы́бить; **~ed card** перфокáрта.

cpds. **~-ball, ~ing-ball** *nn.* пенчингбóл; подвеснáя грýша; **~-drunk** *adj.* ошарáшенный, обалдéлый; **~-line** *n.* кульминациóнный пункт; **~-up** *n.* дрáка, потасóвка.

punch[2] [pʌntʃ] *n.* (*beverage*) пунш.

cpd. **~-bowl** *n.* чáша для пýнша.

Punch[3] [pʌntʃ] *n.* (*puppet character*) Панч, Петрýшка (*m.*); **~ and Judy show** кýкольное (я́рмарочное) представлéние; **he was as pleased as ~** он расплывáлся от удовóльствия.

punctilio [pʌŋk'tɪlɪəʊ] *n.* формáльность; педанти́зм.

punctilious [pʌŋk'tɪlɪəs] *adj.* педанти́чный; скрупулёзный.

punctiliousness [pʌŋk'tɪlɪəsnɪs] *n.* педанти́чность; скрупулёзность.

punctual ['pʌŋktjʊəl] *adj.* пунктуáльный, тóчный; **let us try to be ~ for meals** давáйте не опáздывать к столý.

punctuality [,pʌŋktjʊ'ælɪtɪ] *n.* пунктуáльность, тóчность.

punctuate ['pʌŋktjʊ,eɪt] *v.t.* (*insert punctuation marks in*) стáвить, по- знáки препинáния в+*a.*; (*fig.*, *interrupt*, *intersperse*) прер|ывáть, -вáть; **his speech was ~d with cheers** егó речь прерывáлась вóзгласами одобрéния.

punctuation [,pʌŋktjʊ'eɪʃ(ə)n] *n.* пунктуáция; **~ mark** знак препинáния.

puncture ['pʌŋktʃə(r)] *n.* прокóл; **his bicycle had a ~** он проткнýл ши́ну своегó велосипéда.

v.t. прок|áлывать, -олóть; (*fig.*): **his pride was ~d** егó гóрдость былá уязвленá.

v.i.: **these tyres ~ easily** э́ти ши́ны легкó прокáлываются.

pundit ['pʌndɪt] *n.* учёный индýс; (*authority*, *expert*) знатóк, специали́ст; дóка (*coll.*, *m.*).

pungency ['pʌndʒ(ə)nsɪ] *n.* остротá; éдкость.

pungent ['pʌndʒ(ə)nt] *adj.* (*of smell or taste*) óстрый; (*of speech*, *humour etc.*) óстрый, éдкий.

Punic ['pju:nɪk] *adj.* пуни́ческий.

punish ['pʌnɪʃ] *v.t.* **1.** (*inflict penalty on*) накáз|ывать, -áть; **the thief was ~ed by a fine** на вóра наложи́ли штраф. **2.** (*inflict penalty for*): **theft was severely ~ed** за крáжу сурóво карáли. **3.** (*tax strength of*) изнур|я́ть, -и́ть; изм|áтывать, -отáть; **he set a ~ing pace** он зáдал уби́йственный темп. **4.** (*treat roughly*): **England were ~ed in the second half** англичáнам всы́пали во вторóм тáйме. **5.** (*coll.*, *make inroads on*): **he ~ed the meat pie** он набрóсился на мяснóй пирóг.

punishable ['pʌnɪʃəb(ə)l] *adj.*: **treason is ~ by death** измéна карáется смéртной кáзнью.

punishment ['pʌnɪʃmənt] *n.* (*penalty*) взыскáние; наказáние; (*rough treatment*) сурóвое обращéние; **his opponent came in for severe ~** егó проти́внику здóрово досталóсь.

punitive ['pju:nɪtɪv] *adj.* карáтельный; **~ taxation** сурóвое налогообложéние.

Punjab [pʊn'dʒɑ:b, 'pʊnjɑ:b] *n.* Пенджáб.

Punjabi [pʊn'dʒɑ:bɪ] *n.* (*pers.*) пенджáб|ец (*fem.* -ка); (*language*) язы́к пенджáби.

adj. пенджáбский.

punk [pʌŋk] *n.* **1.** (*admirer of ~ rock*) панк. **2.** (*rotten wood*) гни́лое дéрево; (*as tinder*) трут.

adj. **1.** пáнковый. **2.** (*sl.*, *inferior*) никуды́шный, дряннóй.

punkah ['pʌŋkə] *n.* подвéшенное опахáло; электровентиля́тор под потолкóм.

punnet ['pʌnɪt] *n.* корзи́н(оч)ка.

punster ['pʌnstə(r)] *n.* каламбури́ст.

punt[1] [pʌnt] *n.* (*boat*) плоскодóнный я́лик.

v.i. плыть (*impf.*), оттáлкиваясь шестóм.

punt[2] [pʌnt] *n.* (*kick*) удáр ногóй.

v.t. & *i.* уд|аря́ть, -áрить ногóй.

punt[3] [pʌnt] *v.i.* (*at cards*) понти́ровать (*impf.*); (*at races*) стáвить, по- на лóшадь.

punter ['pʌntə(r)] *n.* (*at cards*) понтёр; (*at races*) игрóк.

puny ['pju:nɪ] *adj.* (*undersized*, *feeble*) тщеду́шный; хи́лый.

pup [pʌp] *n.* **1.** (*young dog*) щенóк; **the bitch is in ~** сýка ожидáет щеня́т; **you've been sold a ~** (*fig.*, *coll.*) вас провели́. **2.** (*conceited youth*) щенóк; молокосóс.

pupa ['pju:pə] *n.* кýколка.

pupate [pju:'peɪt] *v.i.* окýкли|ваться, -ться.

pupil ['pju:pɪl, -p(ə)l] *n.* **1.** (*one being taught*) учени́к. **2.** (*ward under age*) подопéчный. **3.** (*of eye*) зрачóк.

cpd. **~-teacher** *n.* студéнт-практикáнт.

pupil(l)age ['pju:pɪlɪdʒ] *n.* (*state of being a ward*) малолéтство; (*being under instruction*) учени́чество.

pupillary ['pju:pɪlərɪ] *adj.* (*anat.*) зрачкóвый.

puppet ['pʌpɪt] *n.*: **glove ~** кýкла; **string ~** марионéтка; (*fig.*) марионéтка; **~ state** марионéточное госудáрство.

cpd. **~-play, ~-show** *nn.* кýкольное представлéние, кýкольный спектáкль.

puppy ['pʌpɪ] *n.* **1.** (*young dog*) щенóк; **~ fat** дéтская пýхлость; **~ love** дéтская любóвь. **2.** (*conceited youth*) щенóк; молокосóс.

purblind ['pɜ:blaɪnd] *adj.* подслеповáтый; (*fig.*) недальнови́дный.

purchasable ['pɜ:tʃɪsəb(ə)l, -tʃəsəb(ə)l] *adj.* имéющийся в продáже.

purchase ['pɜ:tʃɪs, -tʃəs] *n.* **1.** (*buying*) кýпля; **~ price** покупнáя ценá. **2.** (*thing bought*) покýпка; **she came home laden with ~s** онá вернýлась домóй, нагрýженная покýпками. **3.** (*value*; *return from land*) стóимость; дохóд с земли́; **sold at 20 years' ~** прóдано за стóимость, рáвную двадцатикрáтному годовóму дохóду; **his life is not worth a day's ~** он и дня не проживёт. **4.** (*lever*, *leverage*) рычáг; зажи́м, захвáт.

v.t. (*buy*) покупáть, купи́ть; приобре|тáть, -сти́; **his life was dearly ~d** он дóрого заплати́л за свою́ жизнь; **the purchasing power of the pound** покупáтельная спосóбность фýнта (стéрлингов).

cpds. **~-money** *n.* покупны́е дéн|ьги (*pl.*, *g.* -ег); **~-tax** *n.* налóг на покýпку.

purchaser ['pɜ:tʃɪsə(r), -tʃəsə(r)] *n.* покупáтель (*fem.* -ница).

purdah ['pɜ:də] *n.* **1.** (*curtain*) зáнавес, отделя́ющий жéнскую полови́ну; (*covering body*) чадрá. **2.** (*segregation of women*) затвóрничество жéнщин; (*fig.*) затвóрничество; **he went into ~ for several days** он уедини́лся на нéсколько дней.

pure [pjʊə(r)] *adj.* (*in var. senses*) чи́стый; (*unmixed*) беспри́месный; (*of unmixed race or descent*) чистокрóвный; **~ mathematics** теорети́ческая/чи́стая матемáтика; **~ in heart** чистосердéчный; **~ taste** безупрéчный вкус; **it was a ~ accident** э́то былá чи́стая случáйность; **that is laziness ~ and simple** э́то прóсто-нáпросто лень.

cpd. **~-bred** *adj.* чистокрóвный.

purée ['pjʊəreɪ] *n.* пюрé (*indecl.*).

purely ['pjʊəlɪ] *adv.* (*blamelessly*) чи́сто; (*entirely*) чи́сто, совершéнно, вполнé.

pureness ['pjʊənɪs] = **purity**

purgation [pɜ:'geɪʃ(ə)n] *n.* очищéние; (*of bowels*) очищéние кишéчника.

purgative ['pɜ:gətɪv] *n.* слаби́тельное срéдство.

adj. (*aperient*) слаби́тельный, очисти́тельный; (*purificatory*) очищáющий.

purgatorial [,pɜ:gə'tɔ:rɪəl] *adj.* очисти́тельный.

purgatory ['pɜ:gətərɪ] *n.* чисти́лище; (*fig.*) ад.

purge [pɜ:dʒ] *n.* **1.** (*clearance*; *cleansing*) очищéние; очи́стка; (*pol.*) чи́стка; репрéссии (*f. pl.*). **2.** (*medicine*) слаби́тельное.

v.t. **1.** (*lit.*, *fig.*, *cleanse*) оч|ищáть, -и́стить; **he was ~d of his sins** емý отпусти́ли грехи́; **a medicine to ~ the bowels** слаби́тельное для очищéния кишéчника; **he ~d himself of all suspicion** он очи́стил себя́ от всех подозрéний; **the party was ~d of its rebels** пáртию очистили от бунтовщиков. **2.** (*lit., fig., remove by cleansing; also* ~ **away, off, out**): **the stains were ~d out** пятна отчистили/вывели; **he ~d his contempt (of court)** он поплатился за неуважение к суду.

purification [ˌpjʊərɪfɪˈkeɪʃ(ə)n] *n.* очистка, очищение; **the P~ (of the Virgin Mary)** Сретение господне.

purificatory [ˈpjʊrɪfɪˌkeɪtərɪ] *adj.* очистительный, очищающий.

purify [ˈpjʊərɪˌfaɪ] *v.t.* оч|ищать, -истить; (*relig.*) соверш|ать, -шить обряд очищения.

purism [ˈpjʊərɪz(ə)m] *n.* пуризм.

purist [ˈpjʊərɪst] *n.* пурист.

puritan [ˈpjʊərɪt(ə)n] *n.* (*lit., fig.*) пуритан|ин (*fem.* -ка).
adj. пуританский.

puritanical [ˌpjʊərɪˈtænɪk(ə)l] *adj.* пуританский.

puritanism [ˈpjʊərɪtənˌɪz(ə)m] *n.* пуританизм.

purity [ˈpjʊərɪtɪ] *n.* (*var. senses*) чистота; (*absence of adulteration*) беспримесность; (*of race or descent*) чистокровность.

purl[1] [pɜːl] *n.* (*knitting*) оборотное двухлицевое вязание.
v.i. вязать (*impf.*) петлей наизнанку.

purl[2] [pɜːl] *n.* (*sound of brook*) журчание.
v.i. журчать (*impf.*).

purler [ˈpɜːlə(r)] *n.* (*coll.*) падение; **he tripped and came a ~** он споткнулся и полетел головой вниз.

purlieus [ˈpɜːljuːz] *n. pl.* (*limits*) границы (*f. pl.*); пределы (*m. pl.*); (*outskirts*) окрестности (*f. pl.*), окраина.

purloin [pəˈlɔɪn] *v.t.* присв|аивать, -оить; пох|ищать, -итить.

purple [ˈpɜːp(ə)l] *n.* **1.** (*colour*) пурпур; фиолетовый цвет. **2.** (**the ~**: *robes of emperor etc.*) порфира; **born in the ~** (*fig.*) знатного рода; **he was raised to the ~** он стал кардиналом.
adj. пурпурный; лиловый; фиолетовый; багровый; **P~ Heart** (*drug*) «красное сердечко»; (*US mil. decoration*) алое сердце; **~ patch, passage** цветистый/пышний пассаж; **he turned ~ with rage** он побагровел от ярости.
v.t. & i. обагр|ять(ся), -ить(ся).

purplish [ˈpɜːplɪʃ] *adj.* багрянистый.

purport[1] [ˈpɜːpɔːt] *n.* смысл; суть.

purport[2] [pəˈpɔːt] *v.t.* подразумевать (*impf.*); **this book is not all it ~s to be** эта книга не совсем такая, какой она претендует быть.

purpose [ˈpɜːpəs] *n.* **1.** (*design, aim, intention*) цель, намерение; **what was your ~ in coming?** с какой целью вы пришли?; **this tool will serve my ~** этот инструмент мне подойдёт; **a novel with a ~** нравоучительный/тенденциозный роман; **for what ~ are they meeting?** какова цель их встречи?; **for practical ~s the war is over** война практически окончена; **the box had been used for various ~s** ящик использовали для различных целей; **he went there of set ~** он пошёл туда преднамеренно (*or* с определённой целью); **on ~** нарочно, специально; **I left the gate open on ~** я специально оставил ворота открытыми; **so far he has said nothing to the ~** пока он ничего не сказал путного (*or* по существу); **I went there to no ~** я напрасно туда ходил; **she went out with the ~ of buying clothes** она вышла с намерением купить одежду. **2.** (*determination, resolve*) целеустремлённость.
v.t. (*liter.*) иметь целью; замышлять (*impf.*); **what do you ~ to achieve?** какие цели вы себе ставите?; чего вы добиваетесь?

purposeful [ˈpɜːpəsˌfʊl] *adj.* целеустремлённый, целенаправленный.

purposeless [ˈpɜːpəslɪs] *adj.* бесцельный; бессмысленный.

purposely [ˈpɜːpəslɪ] *adv.* нарочно, (пред)намеренно, специально.

purposive [ˈpɜːpəsɪv] *adj.* целевой; (*determined*) решительный.

purr [pɜː(r)] *n.* (*of cat*) мурлыканье; (*of engine etc.*) урчание.
v.i. (*of cat; also fig.*) мурлыкать (*impf.*); (*of engine etc.*) урчать (*impf.*).

purse [pɜːs] *n.* **1.** (*bag for money*) кошелёк; **his ~ was a good deal lighter by the end of the evening** к концу вечера его кошелёк изрядно опустел; (*US, handbag*) сум(оч)ка. **2.** (*fig., monetary resources*) ден|ьги (*pl., g.* -ег); **the public ~** казна; **the privy ~** суммы (*f. pl.*), ассигнованные на личные расходы монарха. **3.** (*sum collected or offered as prize or gift*) денежный приз.
v.t. морщить, с-; **he ~d (up) his lips** он поджал губы.
cpds. **~-proud** *adj.* гордящийся своим богатством; **~-strings** *n. pl.*: **her husband holds the ~-strings** (*fig.*) её муж распоряжается деньгами (*or* контролирует расходы).

purser [ˈpɜːsə(r)] *n.* судовой казначей.

pursuance [pəˈsjuːəns] *n.* выполнение; **in ~ of one's duties** по долгу службы.

pursuant [pəˈsjuːənt] *adj.*: **~ to** в соответствии с+*i.*; **~ to your instructions** согласно вашим указаниям.

pursue [pəˈsjuː] *v.t.* (*hunt, chase, beset*) преследовать (*impf.*). **2.** (*strive after, aim at*) добиваться (*impf.*) +*g.* **3.** (*carry out, engage in*) следовать (*impf.*) +*d.*; **the policy ~d by the government** политика, проводимая правительством. **4.** (*continue*) прод|олжать, -олжить.

pursuer [pəˈsjuːə(r)] *n.* преследователь (*m.*).

pursuit [pəˈsjuːt] *n.* **1.** (*chase*) преследование; погоня; **he escaped, with the police in hot ~** он бежал, преследуемый полицией по пятам; **~ aircraft** самолёт-истребитель. **2.** (*following, seeking*) поиск|и (*pl., g.* -ов); **he will stop at nothing in ~ of his ends** он не остановится ни перед чем для достижения своих целей. **3.** (*profession or recreation*) занятие.

pursy [ˈpɜːsɪ] *adj.* (*short-winded*) страдающий одышкой; (*corpulent*) тучный.

purulence [ˈpjuːrʊləns] *n.* нагноение.

purulent [ˈpjuːrʊlənt] *adj.* гнойный.

purvey [pəˈveɪ] *v.t.* (*supply*) снаб|жать, -дить (*кого чем*).
v.i. (*supply provisions*) пост|авлять, -авить продовольствие.

purveyance [pəˈveɪəns] *n.* поставка.

purveyor [pəˈveɪə(r)] *n.* поставщи|к (*fem.* -ца).

purview [ˈpɜːvjuː] *n.* (*range, scope*) сфера; область действия; **these matters fall within my ~** эти дела входят в мою компетенцию.

pus [pʌs] *n.* гной.

push [pʊʃ] *n.* **1.** (*act of propulsion*) толчок; **he closed the door with a ~** он захлопнул дверь; **my car won't start; can you give me a ~?** моя машина не заводится, вы можете её подтолкнуть? **2.** (*coll., dismissal*) увольнение; **they have given me the ~** меня выгнали. **3.** (*self-assertion*) напористость; **in this job you need plenty of ~** в этой работе надо быть очень предприимчивым. **4.** (*vigorous effort*) нажим; **we must make a ~ to be there by 8** мы должны поднажать, чтобы поспеть туда к восьми (часам); **the enemy's ~ was successful** натиск врага был успешным. **5.: at a ~; if it comes to the ~** (*coll.*) на худой конец; в крайнем случае.
v.t. **1.** (*propel; exert pressure to move*) толк|ать, -нуть; пих|ать, -нуть; **stop ~ing me!** перестаньте меня толкать!; **he ~es all the dirty jobs on to me** он всю грязную работу спихивает/сваливает на меня. **2.** (*fig., urge, impel*) подт|алкивать, -олкнуть; **he had to ~ himself to finish the job** ему пришлось приналечь, чтобы закончить работу; **I didn't want to go, I was ~ed into it** я не хотел идти, меня на это ввязали. **3.** (*force*) прот|алкивать, -олкнуть; **he ~ed his fist through the window** он просунул кулак в окно; **I ~ed my way through the crowd** я протиснулся сквозь толпу. **4.** (*press*) наж|имать, -ать; **~ the button and the bell will ring** нажмите кнопку, и звонок зазвонит. **5.** (*put under pressure*) оказ|ывать, -ать давление на+*a.*; **I am ~ed for time** у меня времени в обрез. **6.** (*exploit*): **the enemy ~ed their advantage to the utmost** неприятель использовал своё преимущество до конца; **don't ~ your luck!** (*coll.*) не испытываете судьбу! **7.** (*promote, advertise*) рекламировать (*impf.*); проталкивать (*impf.*).
v.i. **1.** (*exert force*) толкаться (*impf.*); **it's like ~ing against a brick wall** это всё равно, что биться лбом о стену; **~ hard at the door!** толкните дверь посильнее!; **don't ~!** не толкайтесь!; не напирайте! **2.** (*force one's way*) прот|алкиваться, -олкнуться; **he ~ed between us** он протиснулся между нами; **they all ~ed into the room** они все ввалились в комнату; **I had to ~ through the crowd** мне пришлось протискиваться сквозь толпу; **he ~ed past me** он пролез вперёд, оттолкнув меня.

with advs.: ~ **about** *v.t.* (*coll.*) потрепа́ть (*pf.*); помя́ть (*pf.*); **he was seized by the gang and ~ed about** хулига́ны пойма́ли его́ и поколоти́ли; ~ **along** *v.t.* (*lit.*): **the boy was ~ing his barrow along** ма́льчик кати́л та́чку; (*fig.*) спеши́ть, по-; пот|ара́пливать, -оропи́ть; **the work is going slowly; see if you can ~ it along** рабо́та идёт ме́дленно; мо́жет, вы суме́ете её ускорить; *v.i.* (*coll.*) убира́ться (*impf.*); **it's getting late, I must ~ along** стано́вится по́здно, мне пора́ в путь; ~ **around** *v.t.* переставля́ть (*impf.*); передвига́ть (*impf.*); (*fig.*) кома́ндовать (*impf.*) (*кем*); **I won't be ~ed around** я не позво́лю кома́ндовать над собо́й; ~ **aside** *v.t.* отт|а́лкивать, -олкну́ть; ~ **away** *v.t.* = ~ **aside;** *v.i.*: **they ~ed away from the shore** они́ отплы́ли от бе́рега; ~ **back** *v.t.* (*repulse*) отбр|а́сывать, -о́сить; (*move away*) отодв|ига́ть, -и́нуть; **she ~ed back the bedclothes** она́ отки́нула одея́ло; **he ~ed back his glasses** он сдви́нул очки́ на лоб; (*coll., swallow*) прогл|а́тывать, -оти́ть; **he ~ed back two whiskies** он опроки́нул два стака́нчика ви́ски; ~ **down** *v.t.* вали́ть, по-; **every time he tried to stand up he was ~ed down** при ка́ждой попы́тке встать его́ вали́ли с ног; ~ **forward** *v.t.* толк|а́ть, -ну́ть вперёд; *v.i.* (*make progress*) продв|ига́ться, -и́нуться (вперёд); **tomorrow we can ~ forward again with our work** за́втра мы опя́ть нава́лимся на рабо́ту; ~ **in** *v.t.* вт|а́лкивать, -олкну́ть; **have you ~ed the plug fully in?** вы по́лностью воткну́ли ви́лку?; *v.i.* втира́ться, втере́ться; **don't ~ in!** (*intrude*) не ле́зьте; ~ **off** *v.t.* отт|а́лкивать, -олкну́ть; **in the struggle his hat was ~ed off** в потасо́вке ему́ сби́ли шля́пу; **they ~ed the boat off from shore** они́ оттолкну́ли ло́дку от бе́рега; *v.i.* (*in a boat*) отт|а́лкиваться, -олкну́ться от бе́рега; (*coll., leave*) см|ыва́ться, -ы́ться; ~ **on** *v.i.* продв|ига́ться, -и́нуться вперёд; **next day they ~ed on again** на сле́дующий день они́ продолжа́ли путь; ~ **out** *v.t.*: **plants are ~ing out new leaves** у расте́ний распуска́ются но́вые ли́стья; **he opened the door and ~ed me out** он откры́л дверь и вы́толкнул меня́; *v.i.* выдава́ться (*impf.*) вперёд; **they ~ed out to sea** они́ вы́шли в мо́ре; ~ **over** *v.t.* опроки́|дывать, -нуть; **I was nearly ~ed over in the rush** в толкотне́ меня́ чуть не сби́ли с ног; ~ **past** *v.i.* прот|а́лкиваться, -олкну́ться; ~ **through** *v.t.* (*lit., fig.*) прот|а́лкивать, -олкну́ть; **the bill was ~ed through against opposition** законопрое́кт протолкну́ли, несмотря́ на оппози́цию; *v.i.* проти́|скиваться, -снуться; **he saw a gap in the crowd and ~ed through** он уви́дел разры́в в толпе́ и вти́снулся в него́; ~ **to** *v.t.* (*close*) закр|ыва́ть, -ы́ть; ~ **together** *v.t.* (*e.g. books on a shelf*) сдв|ига́ть, -и́нуть; ~ **up** *v.t.* сдв|ига́ть, -и́нуть; подн|има́ть, -я́ть кве́рху; (*increase*) увели́чи|вать, -ть; *v.i.*: **he ~ed up against me** он прижа́лся ко мне.

cpds. **~-bike** *n.* (*coll.*) велосипе́д; **~-button** *n.* нажи́мная кно́пка; **~-button warfare** «кно́почная» война́; **~-cart** *n.* ручна́я теле́жка; **~-chair** *n.* прогу́лочная коля́ска; **~over** *n.* (*sl., someone easily overcome*) пода́тливый челове́к; (*coll.*) слаба́к; (*sl., something easily accomplished*) па́ра пустяко́в; **~-up** *n.* (*exercise*) выжима́ние в упо́ре; **do ~-ups** отжима́ться (*impf.*) на рука́х.

pusher [ˈpʊʃə(r)] *n.* **1.** (*aircraft*) самолёт с толка́ющим винто́м. **2.** (*forceful pers.*) пробивно́й ма́лый; напо́ристый челове́к. **3.** (*sl., drug ~*) наркоделе́ц; зверёк.

pushful [ˈpʊʃfʊl] *adj.* предприи́мчивый, пробивно́й; *see also* **pushing**

pushfulness [ˈpʊʃfʊlnɪs] *n.* предприи́мчивость; (*self assertion*) насты́рность.

push|ing [ˈpʊʃɪŋ], **-y** [ˈpʊʃɪ] *adjs.* насты́рный, назо́йливый.

pusillanimity [ˌpjuːsɪləˈnɪmɪtɪ] *n.* малоду́шие.

pusillanimous [ˌpjuːsɪˈlænɪməs] *adj.* малоду́шный.

puss [pʊs] *n.* (*cat*) ко́шечка, ки́ска; **~, ~!** кис-ки́с!; (*coll., girl*) ко́шечка.

cpd. **~-moth** *n.* ночна́я ба́бочка; ночно́й мотылёк.

pussy [ˈpʊsɪ] *n.* ки́са, ки́ска, ко́тик, ко́ш(еч)ка.

cpds. **~-cat** *n.* ко́шечка; **~foot** *v.i.* (*move stealthily*) кра́сться (*impf.*) по-коша́чьи; (*coll., behave cautiously*) виля́ть (*impf.*); темни́ть (*impf.*); **~-willow** *n.* и́ва-шелю́га кра́сная, ве́рба.

pustule [ˈpʌstjuːl] *n.* пу́стула; прыщ.

put [pʊt] *v.t.* **1.** (*move into a certain position*) класть, положи́ть; (*stand*) ста́вить, по-; (*set*) сажа́ть, посади́ть; **~ the glasses on the tray!** поста́вьте стака́ны на подно́с; **he is trying to ~ it across you** (*coll.*) он пыта́ется вас провести́; **the boy ~ the cat down the well** ма́льчик бро́сил кота́ в коло́дец; **~ the money in your pocket!** положи́те де́ньги в карма́н; **he ~ his hands in his pockets** он засу́нул ру́ки в карма́ны; **~ a nail in the wall** вбить (*pf.*) гвоздь в сте́ну; **I'll ~ you in the best bedroom** я вас помещу́ в са́мой лу́чшей ко́мнате; **~ some milk in my tea!** нале́йте мне молока́ в чай!; **don't ~ sugar in my tea!** не клади́те са́хару в чай; **he was ~ in prison** его́ посади́ли в тюрьму́; **I ~ myself in your hands** я отдаю́ себя́ в ва́ши ру́ки; **~ yourself in my place!** поста́вьте себя́ на моё ме́сто; **I ~ him in his place** (*fig.*) я поста́вил его́ на ме́сто; **he ~ the papers into the drawer** он убра́л/положи́л бума́ги в я́щик стола́; **they ~ a satellite into orbit** они́ вы́вели спу́тник на орби́ту; **I ~ the matter into the hands of my lawyer** я поручи́л э́то де́ло своему́ адвока́ту; **the thief ~ his hand inside my pocket** вор засу́нул ру́ку мне в карма́н; **they are sure to ~ him inside** (*i.e. prison*) его́ наверняка́ поса́дят; **don't ~ your daughter on the stage** не пуска́йте дочь на сце́ну; **I asked her to ~ a patch on my trousers** я попроси́л её залата́ть мои́ брю́ки; **he ~ me on my way** он показа́л мне доро́гу; **she ~ the clothes on the line** она́ разве́сила бельё; **she ~ a cloth on the table** она́ накры́ла стол ска́тертью; **she ~ her daughter on to the swing** она́ посади́ла дочь на каче́ли; **I'll ~ you on to a good thing** (*coll.*) я дам вам хоро́ший сове́т; **a cloche was ~ over the plants** расте́ния бы́ли накры́ты стекля́нным колпако́м; **he ~ a shawl round her shoulder** он накры́л её пле́чи ша́лью; **~ it there!** (*shake hands*) дай пять (*coll.*); **the postman ~ a letter through the box** почтальо́н опусти́л письмо́ в я́щик; **they ~ the horse to the cart** ло́шадь запрягли́ в теле́гу; **she ~ the children to bed** она́ уложи́ла дете́й; **he was ~ to a good school** его́ определи́ли в хоро́шую шко́лу; **he ~ the glass to his lips** он поднёс стака́н к губа́м; **~ a napkin under the plate!** подложи́те салфе́тку под таре́лку!; **the sweep ~ his brush up the chimney** трубочи́ст засу́нул щётку в дымохо́д; **where did I ~ that book** куда́ я дел ту кни́гу? **2.** (*move with force; thrust*) вонз|а́ть, -и́ть; **she ~ a knife between his ribs** она́ вонзи́ла ему́ нож ме́жду рёбер; **he ~ a bullet through his head** он пусти́л себе́ пу́лю в лоб; **he ~ his fist through the window** он проби́л окно́ кулако́м. **3.** (*bring into a certain state or relationship*): **his alibi ~s him above suspicion** благодаря́ а́либи он стои́т вне подозре́ния; **that ~s me at a disadvantage** э́то ста́вит меня́ в невы́годное положе́ние; **he ~ me at my ease** с ним я почу́вствовал себя́ свобо́дно; **that will ~ the whole project at risk** э́то поста́вит весь план под угро́зу; **he ~ his past behind him** он порва́л со свои́м про́шлым; **they ~ him in a terrible fright** его́ запуга́ли до сме́рти; **the dinner ~ him in a good mood** обе́д привёл его́ в хоро́шее расположе́ние ду́ха; **you ~ me in mind of your mother** вы напомина́ете мне ва́шу мать; **the least thing ~s him in a rage** любо́й пустя́к приво́дит его́ в я́рость; **he likes to ~ people in the wrong** он лю́бит ука́зывать други́м на оши́бки; **that ~s us level** (*at game etc.*) тепе́рь мы квиты́; **his cold ~ him off his food** из-за просту́ды ему́ не хоте́лось есть; **his antics ~ me off my game** его́ проде́лки меша́ли мне игра́ть; **he was ~ on oath** его́ привели́ к прися́ге; **the bark of the dog ~ him on his guard** лай соба́ки предостерёг его́; **the workers were ~ on short time** рабо́чих перевели́ на сокращённую неде́лю; **he was ~ out of countenance** он смути́лся; **he ~ the poor creature out of its misery** он изба́вил бедня́гу от страда́ний; **he ~ me right on this point** в э́том он меня́ попра́вил; **the boiler needs to be ~ right** на́до почини́ть коло́нку; **the examiner ~ him through it** (*tested severely*) экзамена́тор его́ как сле́дует погоня́л (*coll.*); **he ~ my suggestion to the test** он подве́рг моё предложе́ние испыта́нию; **he was ~ to death** его казни́ли; **let's ~ it to the vote** поста́вим вопро́с на голосова́ние; **I was ~ to great expense** меня́ ввели́ в огро́мный расхо́д; **I am sorry to ~ you to inconvenience** прости́те, что я причиня́ю вам неудо́бства; **I was hard ~ to it not to laugh** я с трудо́м уде́рживался от сме́ха; **your generosity ~s me to shame** ва́ша ще́дрость заставля́ет меня́ красне́ть; **the villagers were ~ to the sword** жи́телей дере́вни пре́дали мечу́; (*impose, bring in*): **the tax ~s a heavy burden on the rich** нало́г ложи́тся тяжёлым бре́менем на бога́тых; **~ an end to** прекра|ща́ть, -ти́ть; положи́ть (*pf.*) коне́ц *+d.*; **he ~ an end to his life** он поко́нчил с собо́й; **he ~ the blame on me** он свали́л вину́ на меня́; **the government ~ a tax on wealth** прави́тельство ввело́ нало́г на состоя́ние; (*set, arrange*): **~ in order** прив|оди́ть, -ести́ в поря́док; **the party should ~ its house in order** па́ртии сле́дует навести́ поря́док в свои́х ряда́х; **he tried to ~ matters right** он стара́лся попра́вить дела́; (*appoint, set*) назн|ача́ть, -а́чить; **~ s.o. in charge of** ста́вить, по- кого́-н. во главе́ *+g.*; (*apply*): **if you ~ your mind to it** е́сли вы займётесь э́тим всерьёз; **he ~s his knowledge to good use** он испо́льзует свои́ зна́ния с то́лком; (*offer, present*): **they ~ their house on the market** они́ объяви́ли о прода́же до́ма; **the play has never been ~ on (the stage) before** э́ту пье́су никогда́ ра́ньше не ста́вили; (*instil, inspire*) всел|я́ть, -и́ть; вдохну́ть (*pf.*); **a glass of brandy will ~ new life into you** рю́мка коньяку́ прида́ст вам но́вую си́лу; (*stake*) ста́вить, по-; (*invest*) вкла́дывать, вложи́ть; поме|ща́ть, -сти́ть; **I should ~ the money into property** я бы помести́л де́ньги в недви́жимость; (*make s.o. succumb or resort to*): **he ~ his opponent to flight** он обрати́л своего́ проти́вника в бе́гство; **take a tablet to ~ you to sleep** прими́те табле́тку, что́бы усну́ть; **the dog had to be ~ to sleep** соба́ку пришло́сь усыпи́ть. **4.** (*write; mark*) писа́ть, на-; ста́вить, по- (*знак и т.п.*); **I cannot ~ my name to that document** я не могу́ подписа́ть тако́й докуме́нт; **this ~ paid to his ambitions** э́то положи́ло коне́ц его́ наде́ждам. **5.** (*of price etc.*): **he ~s a high value on courtesy** он высоко́ це́нит ве́жливость; **I wouldn't care to ~ a price on it** я бы предпочёл не называ́ть то́чную це́ну; **a price was ~ on his head** за его́ го́лову был объя́влен вы́куп; **I would ~ her (age) at about 65** я бы дал ей лет 65; **I wouldn't ~ it past him to be lying** с него́ ста́нется и совра́ть. **6.** (*submit, propound*) выдвига́ть, вы́двинуть; зад|ава́ть, -а́ть; **may I ~ a suggestion?** мо́жно мне внести́ предложе́ние?; **I ~ it to you that ...** ра́зве вы мо́жете отрица́ть, что..? **7.** (*express; present*) изл|ага́ть, -ожи́ть; **how can I ~ it?** как бы э́то сказа́ть?; **the case can be ~ in a few words** де́ло мо́жно изложи́ть в не́скольких слова́х; **will you ~ that in writing?** вы мо́жете изложи́ть/подтверди́ть э́то на бума́ге?; **I can't ~ it into words** я не могу́ вы́разить э́то слова́ми; **how would you ~ that in English?** как вы э́то ска́жете (*or* как э́то бу́дет) по-англи́йски?; **that's ~ting it mildly!** мя́гко говоря́! **8.** (*translate*) перев|оди́ть, -ести́; **it was difficult to ~ his speech into French** бы́ло тру́дно перевести́ его́ речь на францу́зский. **9.** (*mus., set*): **his poems have been ~ to music many times** его́ стихи́ бы́ли мно́го раз поло́жены на му́зыку. **10.** (*hurl*): **~ting the shot** толка́ние ядра́.

v.i. **1.** (*impose*): **don't let him ~ upon you** смотри́те, что́бы он вам на ше́ю не сел. **2. ~ to sea** (*of vessel or crew*) уходи́ть, уйти́ в мо́ре.

with advs.: **~ about** *v.t.* (*spread*) распростран|я́ть, -и́ть; **the news was ~ about that he was missing** разнёсся/распространи́лся слух, что он пропа́л; (*turn round*): **he ~ the boat about** он разверну́л ло́дку; (*inconvenience*) причин|я́ть, -и́ть неудо́бство/хло́поты *+d.*; *v.i.* пов|ора́чиваться, -ерну́ться; **~ across** *v.t.* (*convey over river, road etc.*) перепр|авля́ть, -а́вить; **the ferry will ~ you across to the other bank** паро́м перевезёт вас на друго́й бе́рег; (*make clear, communicate*) объясн|я́ть, -и́ть; **he failed to ~ his idea across** ему́ не удало́сь поясни́ть свою́ мысль/иде́ю; **~ aside** *v.t.* (*lay to one side; save*) от|кла́дывать, -ложи́ть; (*ignore*): **these objections cannot be ~ aside** мы обя́заны приня́ть во внима́ние э́ти возраже́ния; **~ away** *v.t.* (*tidy*) уб|ира́ть, -ра́ть; (*save*) от|кла́дывать, -ложи́ть; (*renounce*) отка́з|ываться, -а́ться от*+g.*; изб|авля́ться, -а́виться от*+g.*; **I ~ away childish things** я поко́нчил с де́тством; (*coll., eat*): **it's amazing how much that boy can ~ away** про́сто удиви́тельно, ско́лько э́тот ма́льчик мо́жет съесть/(*coll.*)сло́пать; (*coll., ~ into confinement*) упря́тать (*pf.*) (за решётку; в сумасше́дший дом); (*kill*): **our dog had to be ~ away** нам пришло́сь усыпи́ть соба́ку; **~ back** *v.t.* (*replace, restore*) класть, положи́ть на ме́сто; **they ~ the deposed king back on the throne** они́ сно́ва возвели́ све́ргнутого короля́ на престо́л; (*move backwards*) передв|ига́ть, -и́нуть (*or* перест|авля́ть, -а́вить) наза́д; (*of clock*) перев|оди́ть, -ести́ наза́д; (*retard, delay*) заде́рж|ивать, -а́ть; **heavy rains ~ back the harvest** си́льные дожди́ задержа́ли созрева́ние (*or* убо́рку) урожа́я; (*postpone*) от|кла́дывать, -ложи́ть; *v.i.* возвра|ща́ться, -ти́ться; **the ship was forced to ~ back to port** кораблю́ пришло́сь верну́ться/возврати́ться в порт; **~ by** *v.t.* (*save*) от|кла́дывать, -ложи́ть; **~ down** *v.t.* (*place on ground etc.*) класть, положи́ть на зе́млю; **~ your gun down!** бро́сьте ору́жие!; опусти́те ружьё!; **he ~ his head down and was soon asleep** он положи́л го́лову на поду́шку и вско́ре засну́л; **~ one's foot down** (*be firm*) стоя́ть (*impf.*) на своём; (*accelerate*) нажа́ть (*pf.*) на газ; (*allow to alight*): **the bus stopped to ~ down passengers** авто́бус останови́лся, что́бы вы́садить пассажи́ров; (*place in storage*): **I ~ down a supply of port** я сде́лал запа́с портве́йна; (*make deposit of*) вн|оси́ть, -ести́ (*задаток*); (*lower, reduce*) сн|ижа́ть, -и́зить; (*bring in to land*): **the pilot ~ his machine down safely** пило́т благополу́чно посади́л маши́ну; (*coll., swallow*): **he can ~ down 6 pints in a row** он мо́жет опроки́нуть шесть кру́жек (пи́ва) зара́з; (*repress*) подав|ля́ть, -и́ть; **the rebellion was quickly ~ down** восста́ние бы́ло бы́стро пода́влено; **his aim is to ~ down crime** его́ цель — искорени́ть престу́пность; **his cheerfulness will not be ~ down** его́ жизнера́достность неиссяка́ема; **I ~ him down** (*coll.*) я осади́л его́; (*write down*) запи́с|ывать, -а́ть; **let me ~ your name down before I forget** дава́йте я запишу́ ва́шу фами́лию, пока́ не забы́л; **you may ~ me down for £5** я даю́ 5 фу́нтов; **~ these groceries down to my account** запиши́те э́ти проду́кты на мой счёт; (*consider*) счита́ть (*impf.*); **I would ~ her down as about 25** я дал бы ей лет 25; **I ~ him down as a braggart** я при́нял его́ за хвастуна́; (*attribute*) припи́с|ывать, -а́ть; (*kill, of animals*) усып|ля́ть, -и́ть; умерщв|ля́ть, -и́ть; **~ forth** *v.t.* (*exert*) напр|яга́ть, -я́чь; (*produce*): **the trees are ~ting forth new leaves** на дере́вьях распуска́ются но́вые ли́стья; **~ forward** *v.t.* (*advance*): **the clocks are ~ forward in spring** весно́й часы́ перево́дят вперёд; **we must ~ our best foot forward** мы должны́ поднажа́ть (*coll.*); (*propose*) выдвига́ть, вы́двинуть; **he ~ forward a theory** он вы́двинул тео́рию; **his name was ~ forward** была́ вы́двинута его́ кандидату́ра; (*bring nearer*) передв|ига́ть, -и́нуть вперёд; **the meeting has been ~ forward to Tuesday** собра́ние перенесли́ на вто́рник; **~ in** *v.t.* (*cause to enter; insert*) вст|авля́ть, -а́вить; **he ~ his head in at the window** он всу́нул го́лову в окно́; **have you ~ the joint in yet?** вы уже́ поста́вили мя́со в духо́вку?; **to make a call you must ~ in a coin** что́бы позвони́ть по телефо́ну, на́до опусти́ть моне́ту; (*instal*) вст|авля́ть, -а́вить; **I had to have a new engine ~ in** мне пришло́сь поста́вить но́вый мото́р; **they are ~ting in the telephone** они́ ста́вят себе́ телефо́н; им/нам (*и т.п.*) ста́вят телефо́н; (*elect to office*) изб|ира́ть, -ра́ть; **we helped to ~ the Conservatives in** мы помогли́ консерва́торам прийти́ к вла́сти; (*contribute*): **I ~ in a word for him** я вста́вил за него́ слове́чко; (*submit, present*) под|ава́ть, -а́ть; **he is ~ting in a claim for damages** он предъявля́ет иск об убы́тках; **I ~ in an application** я пода́л заявле́ние; **~ in an appearance** появ|ля́ться, -и́ться; (*work*): **I ~ in 6 hours today** я сего́дня отрабо́тал 6 часо́в; *v.i.* (*of boat or crew*) за|ходи́ть, -йти́ в порт; **the ship ~ in at Gibraltar** кора́бль зашёл в Гибралта́р; (*apply*): **she ~ in for a job as secretary** она́ подала́ заявле́ние на до́лжность секретаря́ (*or* ме́сто секрета́рши); **~ off** *v.t.* (*postpone*) от|кла́дывать, -ложи́ть; отсро́чи|вать, -ть; **never ~ off**

till tomorrow what you can do today никогда́ не откла́дывай на за́втра то, что мо́жешь сде́лать сего́дня; **that is simply ~ting off the evil day** э́то зна́чит то́лько оття́гивать час распла́ты; (*cancel engagement with*) отмен|я́ть, -и́ть встре́чу с+*i.*; (*postpone*): **I shall have to ~ you off till next week** мне придётся перенести́ встре́чу с ва́ми на сле́дующую неде́лю; (*fob off*): **he ~ me off with promises** он отде́лался от меня́ обеща́ниями; (*deter*) отпу́г|ивать, -ну́ть; **we were ~ off by the weather** мы переду́мали из-за пого́ды; (*repel*) отт|а́лкивать, -олкну́ть; **I was ~ off by his tactlessness** меня́ оттолкну́ла/покоро́била его́ беста́ктность; (*distract*): **I can't recite if you keep ~ting me off** я не могу́ деклами́ровать, когда́ вы меня́ отвлека́ете; (*allow to alight*): **will you ~ me off at the next stop?** вы мо́жете вы́садить меня́ на сле́дующей остано́вке?; *v.i.* (*leave shore*) отча́ли|вать, -ть; **~ on** *v.t.* (*clothes etc.*) над|ева́ть, -е́ть; **you should ~ more clothes on** вы должны́ потепле́е оде́ться; (*place in position*): **when the pot is full, ~ the lid on** когда́ кастрю́ля напо́лнится, накро́йте её кры́шкой; **~ the potatoes on (to boil)!** поста́вьте (вари́ть) карто́шку!; (*add*) приб|авля́ть, -а́вить; **he ~ more coal on** он подбро́сил у́гля; **he ~ on a spurt** он рвану́лся (вперёд); (*assume*): **he ~ on an air of innocence** он напусти́л на себя́ неви́нный вид; **her modesty is all ~ on** её скро́мность наи́гранна; **she is fond of ~ting on airs** она́ лю́бит ва́жничать; (*increase*) увели́чи|вать, -ть; **the ship ~ on steam** кора́бль увели́чил ско́рость; **you're ~ting on weight** вы полне́ете; (*light, radio etc.*) включ|а́ть, -и́ть; (*make available*) примен|я́ть, -и́ть; **they are ~ting on extra trains** они пуска́ют дополни́тельные поезда́; (*present*) ста́вить, по-; **the children are ~ting on a play** де́ти ста́вят пье́су; **she ~ on a first-class meal** она́ пригото́вила отли́чный обе́д/у́жин; **~ on an act; ~ it on** (*coll.*) лома́ть (*impf.*) коме́дию; (*advance*) передв|ига́ть, -и́нуть вперёд; **watches should be ~ on an hour** часы́ на́до перевести́ на час вперёд; (*stake*) ста́вить, по-; (*coll., overcharge*): **some hotels ~ it on during the season** не́которые гости́ницы деру́т высо́кую це́ну во вре́мя ле́тнего сезо́на; (*tease, 'kid'*): **he's ~ting you on** он вас разы́грывает; **~ out** *v.t.*: (*thrust out, eject*): **he ~ out his own eyes** он вы́колол себе́ глаза́; **his family was ~ out into the street** его́ семью́ вы́бросили на у́лицу; (*place outside door*) выставля́ть, вы́ставить за дверь; **~ the cat out** вы́пустите ко́шку!; (*extend, protrude*): **~ your tongue out!** покажи́те язы́к!; **he ~ out his hand in welcome** он протяну́л ру́ку для приве́тствия; **she opened the window and ~ her head out** она́ откры́ла окно́ и вы́сунула го́лову; **the snail ~ out its horns** ули́тка вы́пустила ро́жки; (*arrange so as to be seen*) выкла́дывать, вы́ложить; **the shopkeeper ~ out his best wares** ла́вочник вы́ложил/вы́ставил свой лу́чший това́р; **the valet ~ out my clothes** камерди́нер вы́ложил мою́ оде́жду; (*hang up outside*) выве́шивать, вы́весить; **~ out the flags!** вы́весите фла́ги!; **she ~ the washing out to dry** она́ разве́сила бельё суши́ться; (*produce*) выпуска́ть, вы́пустить; **this firm ~s out shoddy goods** э́та фи́рма выпуска́ет дрянно́й това́р; **the tree ~s out blossom** де́рево цветёт; (*issue*) выпуска́ть, вы́пустить; **they ~ out invitations** они́ разосла́ли приглаше́ния; (*send away for a purpose*) отпр|авля́ть, -а́вить; от|сыла́ть, -осла́ть; **repairs are done here, not ~ out** ремо́нт веду́т на ме́сте — никуда́ не отсыла́ют; **the horse was ~ out to stud** жеребца́/кобы́лу пусти́ли на пле́мя; (*extinguish*) туши́ть, по-; гаси́ть, по-; **~ the lights out!** потуши́те свет!; **~ your cigarette out!** погаси́те сигаре́ту!; **~ out the fire before going to bed!** потуши́те ого́нь (в ками́не) пе́ред тем, как идти́ спать; **the firemen ~ out the blaze** пожа́рные потуши́ли пла́мя; (*dislocate*) вы́вихнуть (*pf.*); (*disconcert*) нерви́ровать (*impf.*); (*inconvenience*) наруш|а́ть, -и́ть пла́ны +*g.*; **would it ~ you out to come at 3?** вас не затрудни́т прийти́ в 3 часа́?; (*vex*) раздраж|а́ть, -и́ть; (*lend out at interest*) да|ва́ть, -ть под проце́нты; **he has £1,000 ~ out at 5%** он дал ты́сячу фу́нтов под 5 проце́нтов; (*allow to alight*) опус|ка́ть, -ти́ть; **I asked the driver to ~ me out at the station** я попроси́л шофёра вы́садить меня́ у ста́нции; *v.i.*: **the lifeboat ~ out to sea** спаса́тельная шлю́пка вы́шла в мо́ре; **~ over** *v.t.* (*convey*) перед|ава́ть, -а́ть; **he ~ over his meaning effectively** он хорошо́ изложи́л свою́ мысль; **he is trying to ~ one over on you** (*coll.*) он пыта́ется вас одура́чить; **~ through** *v.t.* (*transact*) осуществ|ля́ть, -и́ть; выполня́ть, вы́полнить; **he ~ through a successful deal** он проверну́л вы́годную сде́лку; (*connect by telephone*) соедин|я́ть, -и́ть; **~ together** *v.t.* (*bring close or into contact*) соедин|я́ть, -и́ть; скреп|ля́ть, -и́ть; (*assemble*) сост|авля́ть, -а́вить; (*construct from components*) соб|ира́ть, -ра́ть; **he ~ the clock together again** он собра́л часы́; (*collect*) соб|ира́ть, -ра́ть; **~ your things together ready for the journey!** соберите ве́щи в доро́гу!; **better than all the rest ~ together** лу́чше всех остальны́х вме́сте взя́тых; **~ up** *v.t.* (*raise, hold up*) подн|има́ть, -я́ть; **~ up your hand if you know the answer!** кто зна́ет отве́т, подними́те ру́ку!; **~ your hands up!; ~ them up!** (*coll.*) ру́ки вверх!; **~ one's feet up** полёживать (*impf.*); **he ~s my back up** (*coll.*) он меня́ раздража́ет/бе́сит; (*display*) выставля́ть, вы́ставить; **a warning was ~ up where the cliff had fallen** у ме́ста обва́ла скалы́ бы́ло вы́ставлено предупрежде́ние; (*erect*) воздв|ига́ть, -и́гнуть; стро́ить, по-; **this house was ~ up in six weeks** э́тот дом постро́или за шесть неде́ль; **shall we ~ the curtains up?** бу́дем ве́шать занаве́ски?; (*increase*) пов|ыша́ть, -е́сить; **~ up prices** подн|има́ть, -я́ть це́ны; (*offer*) выдвига́ть, вы́двинуть; **she ~ up a prayer for his safety** она́ моли́лась, что́бы с ним ничего́ не случи́лось; **he ~ up no resistance** он не оказа́л сопротивле́ния; **I ~ up a suggestion** я внёс предложе́ние; **our men ~ up a good show** на́ши лю́ди хорошо́ себя́ показа́ли/прояви́ли; **the house was ~ up for sale** объяви́ли о прода́же до́ма; (*pack*) пакова́ть, у-/за-; **the tomatoes are ~ up in boxes** помидо́ры уло́жены в я́щики; **will you ~ up some sandwiches for us?** вы мо́жете дать нам с собо́й бутербро́ды?; (*propose*) выдвига́ть, вы́двинуть (в кандида́ты); **they ~ up three candidates** они́ вы́двинули трёх кандида́тов; (*supply*) вн|оси́ть, -ести́; **I will ~ up £1,000 to support him** я внесу́ ты́сячу фу́нтов в его́ по́льзу; (*stow away; sheathe*) уб|ира́ть, -ра́ть; пря́тать, с-; **~ up your sword!** вложи́те меч в но́жны!; (*cause to fly up*): **~ up game** подн|има́ть, -я́ть дичь; **the beaters ~ up some partridges** заго́нщики по́дняли куропа́ток; (*accommodate*): **he ~ me up for the night** я переночева́л у него́; (*coll., introduce*): **I ~ him up to that trick** я его́ научи́л э́тому приёму/трю́ку; (*coll., prompt*): **who ~ him up to it, I wonder?** интере́сно, кто его́ надоу́мил?; *v.i.* (*stand for election*) баллоти́роваться (*impf.*); выдвига́ть, вы́двинуть свою́ кандидату́ру; (*stay*) остан|а́вливаться, -ови́ться; ночева́ть, пере-; (*tolerate*) мири́ться, при- (*с кем/чем*); **I won't ~ up with any nonsense** я не потерплю́ никаки́х глу́постей.

cpds. **~-down** *n.* (*snub*) ре́зкость; **~-off** *n.* (*evasion*) уло́вка; отгово́рка; **~-on** *n.* (*teasing remark*) насме́шка, ро́зыгрыш; **~-up** *adj.*: **a ~-up job** подстро́енное де́ло; **~-upon** *adj.* оби́женный, трети́руемый.

putative ['pju:tətɪv] *adj.* мни́мый, предполага́емый.

putrefaction [,pju:trɪ'fækʃ(ə)n] *n.* гние́ние; разложе́ние.

putrefy ['pju:trɪ,faɪ] *v.i.* гнить, с-; разл|ага́ться, -ожи́ться.

putrescence [pju:'tres(ə)ns] *n.* гние́ние.

putrescent [pju:'tres(ə)nt] *adj.* гнию́щий; разлага́ющийся.

putrid ['pju:trɪd] *adj.* (*decomposed*) гнило́й; (*coll., unpleasant*) отврати́тельный.

putsch [potʃ] *n.* путч.

putt [pʌt] *n.* уда́р, загоня́ющий мяч в лу́нку (*гольф*).

v.i. гнать (*det.*) мяч в лу́нку; **~ing-green** лужа́йка вокру́г лу́нки (*гольф*).

puttee ['pʌtɪ] *n.* обмо́тка; (*US, legging*) кра́га.

putty ['pʌtɪ] *n.* зама́зка; шпаклёвка.

v.t. шпаклева́ть (*impf.*).

puzzle ['pʌz(ə)l] *n.* зага́дка; (*for entertainment*) головоло́мка.

v.t. озада́чи|вать, -ть; прив|оди́ть, -ести́ в недоуме́ние; **don't ~ your brains over it** не лома́йте себе́ го́лову над э́тим.

v.i.: **he ~d over the problem all night** он всю ночь би́лся над э́той зада́чей.

with adv.: ~ **out** *v.t.* разгада́ть (*pf.*); найти́ (*pf.*) реше́ние +*g.*

puzzlement [ˈpʌzəlmənt] *n.* замеша́тельство.

PVC (*abbr. of* ***polyvinyl chloride***) ПХВ, (полихлорвини́л).

pye-dog [ˈpaɪdɒg] *n.* бродя́чая соба́ка, дворня́жка (в Индии).

pygmy, pigmy [ˈpɪgmɪ] *n.* пигме́й.

pyjamas [pɪˈdʒɑːməz, pə-] (*US* **pajamas**) *n.* пижа́ма; ~ **trousers** пижа́мные штаны́.

pylon [ˈpaɪlən, -lɒn] *n.* столб, пило́н.

pylorus [paɪˈlɔːrəs] *n.* привра́тник желу́дка, пило́рус.

Pyongyang [ˈpjɒŋˈjæŋ] *n.* Пхенья́н.

pyorrh(o)ea [ˌpaɪəˈriːə] *n.* пиоре́я.

pyramid [ˈpɪrəmɪd] *n.* (*lit., fig.*) пирами́да.

pyramidal [pɪˈræmɪd(ə)l] *adj.* пирамида́льный, пирами́дный.

pyre [ˈpaɪə(r)] *n.* погреба́льный костёр.

Pyrenean [ˌpɪrəˈniːən] *adj.* пирене́йский.

Pyrenees [ˌpɪrəˈniːz] *n.* Пирене́|и (*pl., g.* -ев).

pyrites [paɪˈraɪtiːz] *n.* серни́стые мета́ллы (*m. pl.*).

pyromania [ˌpaɪərəʊˈmeɪnɪə] *n.* пирома́ния.

pyromaniac [ˌpaɪərəʊˈmeɪnɪˌæk] *n.* пирома́н.

pyrotechnic [ˌpaɪərəʊˈteknɪk] *adj.* пиротехни́ческий.

pyrotechnics [ˌpaɪərəʊˈteknɪks] *n.* (*art of making fireworks*) пироте́хника; (*firework display; also fig.*) фейерве́рк.

Pyrrhic [ˈpɪrɪk] *adj.*: **a ~ victory** пи́ррова побе́да.

Pythagoras [paɪˈθægərəs] *n.* Пифаго́р; **~' theorem** теоре́ма Пифаго́ра.

python [ˈpaɪθ(ə)n] *n.* пито́н.

pythoness [ˈpaɪθənɪs] *n.* пи́фия; веще́нья.

pyx [pɪks] *n.* (*eccl.*) дарохрани́тельница; (*at Royal Mint*) я́щик для про́бной моне́ты.

Q

Qatar [kæˈtɑː] *n.* Ка́тар.

QC (*abbr. of* ***Queen's Counsel***) адвока́т вы́сшего ра́нга.

QED (*abbr. of* ***quod erat demonstrandum***) что и тре́бовалось доказа́ть.

q.t. (*abbr. of* **quiet**) **to do sth. on the ~** сде́лать по-ти́хому.

qua [kwɑː] *prep.* как, в ка́честве +*g.*

quack[1] [kwæk] *n.* (*sound*) кря́канье.

v.i. кря́кать (*impf.*).

cpd. **~-~** *n.* (*coll., duck*) кря-кря́ (*indecl.*).

quack[2] [kwæk] *n.* (*bogus doctor etc.*) шарлата́н; **~ medicine** шарлата́нское сна́добье/сре́дство.

quackery [ˈkwækərɪ] *n.* шарлата́нство.

quad [kwɒd] (*coll.*) **1.** = **quadrangle. 2.** = **quadruplet**

quadrangle [ˈkwɒdˌræŋg(ə)l] *n.* (*courtyard*) четырёхуго́льный двор.

quadrangular [ˌkwɒdˈræŋgjʊlə(r)] *adj.* четырёхуго́льный.

quadrant [ˈkwɒdrənt] *n.* (*of circle*) квадра́нт; (*instrument*) се́кторный ру́мпель.

quadraphonic [ˌkwɒdrəˈfɒnɪk] *adj.* квадрофони́ческий.

quadratic [kwɒˈdrætɪk] *adj.* квадра́тный.

quadrilateral [ˌkwɒdrɪˈlætər(ə)l] *n.* четырёхуго́льник.

adj. четырёхсторо́нный.

quadrille [kwɒˈdrɪl] *n.* (*dance*) кадри́ль.

quadroon [kwɒˈdruːn] *n.* квартеро́н.

quadruped [ˈkwɒdrʊˌped] *n.* четвероно́гое (живо́тное).

quadruple [ˈkwɒdrʊp(ə)l] *n.* учетверённое коли́чество.

adj. **1.** (*fourfold*) учетверённый; **his income is ~ mine** его́ дохо́д бо́льше моего́ в четы́ре ра́за. **2.** (*quadripartite*) четырёхсторо́нний. **3.** (*mus.*): **~ time** четырёхча́стный такт.

v.t. учетвер|я́ть, -и́ть.

v.i. увели́|чиваться, -ться в четы́ре ра́за.

quadruplets [ˈkwɒdrʊplɪts, ˈkwɒˈdruːplɪts] *n.* четверня́; **she gave birth to ~** она́ родила́ четверню́ (*or* четверы́х близнецо́в).

quadruplicate[1] [kwɒˈdruːplɪkət] *n.*: **copy this in ~** напеча́тайте э́то в четырёх экземпля́рах.

adj. четырёхкра́тный.

quadruplicate[2] [kwɒˈdruːplɪˌkeɪt] *v.t.* учетвер|я́ть, -и́ть.

quaff [kwɒf, kwɑːf] *v.t. & i.* пить, вы- за́лпом.

quagmire [ˈkwɒgˌmaɪə(r), ˈkwæg-] *n.* боло́то.

quail[1] [kweɪl] *n.* пе́репел.

quail[2] [kweɪl] *v.i.* тру́сить, с-; па́дать (*impf.*) ду́хом.

quaint [kweɪnt] *adj.* причу́дливый, чудно́й, курьёзный; **he has some ~ notions** он челове́к со стра́нными поня́тиями.

quaintness [ˈkweɪntnɪs] *n.* причу́дливость, курьёзность.

quak|e [kweɪk] *n.* (*coll., earth~*) землетрясе́ние.

v.i. дрожа́ть (*impf.*); содрог|а́ться, -ну́ться; **I woke up ~ing with fright** я просну́лся, дрожа́ от стра́ха; **~ing-grass** трясу́нка.

Quaker [ˈkweɪkə(r)] *n.* ква́кер (*fem.* -ша); (*attr.*) ква́керский.

qualification [ˌkwɒlɪfɪˈkeɪʃ(ə)n] *n.* **1.** (*modification, limiting factor*) ограниче́ние, огово́рка; **without ~** безогово́рочно. **2.** (*required quality*) квалифика́ция. **3.** (*description*) оце́нка, характери́стика.

qualifier [ˈkwɒlɪˌfaɪə(r)] *n.* (*gram.*) определи́тель (*m.*).

qualif|y [ˈkwɒlɪˌfaɪ] *v.t.* **1.** (*render fit*) де́лать, с- приго́дным; **I am not ~ied to advise you ~** я недоста́точно компете́нтен, что́бы дава́ть вам сове́ты; **his age ~ies him for the vote** по во́зрасту он име́ет пра́во го́лоса; **~ying examination** отбо́рочный экза́мен; **he is a ~ied doctor** он дипломи́рованный врач. **2.** (*limit, modify*) ум|еньша́ть, -е́ньшить; ум|еря́ть, -е́рить; **I must ~y my statement** я до́лжен сде́лать огово́рку; **I gave the idea my ~ied approval** я одо́брил э́ту иде́ю с не́которыми огово́рками. **3.** (*describe*) оце́н|ивать, -и́ть; определ|я́ть, -и́ть; **adjectives ~y nouns** прилага́тельные определя́ют существи́тельные.

v.i.: **he will ~y after three years** че́рез три го́да он полу́чит дипло́м; **will you ~y for a pension?** бу́дет ли вам причита́ться пе́нсия?

qualitative [ˈkwɒlɪtətɪv, -ˌteɪtɪv] *adj.* ка́чественный.

quality [ˈkwɒlɪtɪ] *n.* **1.** (*degree of merit*) ка́чество; **of poor ~** ни́зкого ка́чества; **a high-~ fabric** высокока́чественная ткань; **we consider ~ before quantity** мы ста́вим ка́чество вы́ше коли́чества; (*excellence*) доброка́чественность; **~ goods** высокока́чественные това́ры. **2.** (*faculty, characteristic, attribute*) ка́чество, сво́йство; **he has the ~ of inspiring confidence** он облада́ет сво́йством внуша́ть дове́рие; **he gave us a taste of his ~** он показа́л, на что он спосо́бен; **he has many good qualities** у него́ мно́го це́нных ка́честв; **her voice has a shrill ~** у неё визгли́вый го́лос. **3.** (*high rank*): **people of ~**; **the ~** вы́сшее о́бщество; знать.

adj. (высоко)ка́чественный; **~ newspapers** «соли́дные» газе́ты.

qualm [kwɑːm, kwɔːm] *n.* **1.** (*queasy feeling*) тошнота́. **2.** (*misgiving*) сомне́ние, колеба́ние; **~s of conscience** угрызе́ния (*nt. pl.*) со́вести.

quandary [ˈkwɒndərɪ] *n.* затрудни́тельное положе́ние; **I was in a ~ which way to go** я был в затрудне́нии (*or* не знал), како́й вы́брать путь.

quango [ˈkwæŋgəʊ] *n.* (*coll.*) полуавтоно́мная организа́ция.

quantify [ˈkwɒntɪˌfaɪ] *v.t.* (*determine quantity of*) определ|я́ть, -и́ть коли́чество +*g.*; (*express as quantity*) выража́ть, вы́разить коли́чественно.

quantitative [ˈkwɒntɪtətɪv, -ˌteɪtɪv] *adj.* коли́чественный.

quantit|y [ˈkwɒntɪtɪ] *n.* **1.** (*measurable property*) коли́чество. **2.** (*thg. having ~y*) величина́; число́; **unknown ~y** (*math.*) неизве́стное; (*pers.*) челове́к-зага́дка. **3.** (*sum or amount*) до́ля; часть; **she buys in small ~ies** она́ покупа́ет понемно́гу; (*considerable sum or amount*) большо́е коли́чество; **there is a ~y of work left undone** оста́лось мно́го недоде́ланной рабо́ты. **4.** (*of vowel*) долгота́.

quantum [ˈkwɒntəm] *n.* (*amount*) коли́чество, су́мма;

(*phys.*) квант; ~ **leap** ква́нтовый скачо́к; ~ **theory** ква́нтовая тео́рия.

quarantine [ˈkwɒrən,tiːn] *n.* каранти́н; **dogs are kept in ~ for 6 months** соба́к де́ржат 6 ме́сяцев в каранти́не.
v.t. содержа́ть (*impf.*) в каранти́не.

quark [kwɑːk] *n.* кварк.

quarrel [ˈkwɒr(ə)l] *n.* **1.** (*altercation, contention*) ссо́ра; **he loves to pick a ~** он лю́бит ссо́риться; **they made up their ~** они́ помири́лись. **2.** (*cause for complaint*) по́вод для ссо́ры; **I have no ~ with him on that score** у меня́ нет к нему́ прете́нзии по э́тому по́воду.
v.t. (*contend, dispute*) ссо́риться, по-; (*take issue*) спо́рить, по-; **I cannot ~ with his logic** я не могу́ не согласи́ться с его́ ло́гикой.

quarrelsome [ˈkwɒrəlsəm] *adj.* сварли́вый.

quarry[1] [ˈkwɒrɪ] *n.* (*object of pursuit; prey*) добы́ча; пресле́дуемый зверь.

quarr|y[2] [ˈkwɒrɪ] *n.* (*for stone etc.*) каменоло́мня.
v.t. (*extract*) доб|ыва́ть, -ы́ть.
v.i. (*fig.*) ры́ться (*impf.*); **he has ~ied in the library for his evidence** он переры́л библиоте́ку в по́исках доказа́тельств.
with advs.: **the hillside has been almost ~ied away** почти́ весь склон холма́ разрабо́тан; **this marble was ~ied out by hand** э́тот мра́мор добы́ли вручну́ю.
cpd. **~yman** *n.* каменобо́ец, каменотёс.

quart [kwɔːt] *n.* ква́рта.

quarter [ˈkwɔːtə(r)] *n.* **1.** (*fourth part*) че́тверть; (*of hour*): **a ~ to six** без че́тверти шесть; **a ~ past six** че́тверть седьмо́го; **an hour and a ~** час с че́твертью; **a ~ of an hour later** на пятна́дцать мину́т по́зже; **the clock strikes the ~s** часы́ бьют ка́ждые пятна́дцать мину́т; (*lunar period*): **the first ~ of the moon** пе́рвая че́тверть Луны́; (*of year*) кварта́л; **(court of) ~ sessions** суд кварта́льных се́ссий; **we pay a ~'s rent in advance** мы пла́тим квартпла́ту за (оди́н) кварта́л вперёд. **2.** (*of carcase*) четверти́на (ту́ши); **fore/hind ~s** пере́дняя/за́дняя часть; **the dog got up on its hind ~s** соба́ка вста́ла на за́дние ла́пы. **3.** (*US coin*) два́дцать пять це́нтов. **4.** (*her.*) че́тверть (геральди́ческого щита́). **5.** (*measure of grain etc.*) ква́ртер, че́тверть. **6.** (*point of compass*) страна́ све́та; (*fig., direction, place*) ме́сто; **the boys came running from every ~** ма́льчики бежа́ли со всех сторо́н; **you will get no sympathy from that ~** вы не должны́ ожида́ть сочу́вствия с его́/её стороны́; **there is a belief in certain ~s that ...** в не́которых круга́х счита́ется, что... **7.** (*district of town*) кварта́л; **residential ~** жило́й кварта́л; **the Latin Q~** Лати́нский кварта́л. **8.** (*pl., lodgings*) каза́рмы (*f. pl.*); кварти́ры (*f. pl.*); **the army went into winter ~s** а́рмия перешла́ на зи́мние кварти́ры; **he took up his ~s with a local family** он посели́лся у кого́-то из ме́стных жи́телей. **9.: at close ~s** в те́сном сосе́дстве, вблизи́; **they were fighting at close ~s** они́ вели́ бли́жный бой; **when I saw him at close ~s I was appalled** я ужасну́лся, когда́ уви́дел его́ вблизи́. **10.** (*mercy*) поща́да; **the enemy was forced to cry ~** врагу́ пришло́сь проси́ть поща́ды; **no ~ was asked and none was given** никто́ поща́ды не проси́л, никто́ поща́ды не дава́л.
v.t. **1.** (*divide into four*) дели́ть, раз- на четы́ре ча́сти; **traitors were hanged, drawn and ~ed** преда́телей веша́ли и четвертова́ли; (*her.*) дели́ть (*impf.*) (*щит*) на че́тверти; поме|ща́ть, -сти́ть (*новый герб*) в одно́й из четверте́й щита́. **2.** (*put into lodgings*) расквартиро́в|ывать, -а́ть; **where are you ~ed?** где вы останови́лись/посели́лись?
cpds. **~-back** *n.* защи́тник; **~-day** *n.* день, начина́ющий кварта́л; **~-deck** *n.* квартерде́к; (*fig., officers*) офице́рский соста́в; **~-final** *n.* четвертьфина́л; **~-hour** *n.* че́тверть ча́са; **~-hourly** *adv.* ка́ждый че́тверть ча́са; **~-light** *n.* ма́лое боково́е окно́; **~master** *n.* квартирме́йстер; **Q~master General** ≃ генера́льный квартирме́йстер, нача́льник квартирме́йстерской слу́жбы; **~master sergeant** сержа́нт-квартирме́йстер; **~-mile** *n.* че́тверть ми́ли; **~-miler** *n.* бегу́н на че́тверть ми́ли; **~-tone** *n.* (*mus.*) интерва́л в че́тверть то́на.

quartering [ˈkwɔːtərɪŋ] *n.* (*dividing into four*) деле́ние на четы́ре; (*lodging*) расквартирова́ние; (*her.*) разделе́ние герба́/щита́.

quarterly [ˈkwɔːtəlɪ] *n.* (*periodical*) ежекварта́льное изда́ние.
adj. кварта́льный; **~ payment** покварта́льная вы́плата; вы́плата раз в три ме́сяца.
adv. ежекварта́льно; раз в три ме́сяца; по четвертя́м (го́да).

quartet(te) [kwɔːˈtet] *n.* кварте́т.

quarto [ˈkwɔːtəʊ] *n.* (*size of paper*) (ин-)ква́рто (*indecl.*); (*book of ~ sheets*) кни́га форма́та ин-ква́рто.

quartz [kwɔːts] *n.* кварц; (*attr.*) ква́рцевый.

quasar [ˈkweɪzɑː(r), -sɑː(r)] *n.* квза́р.

quash [kwɒʃ] *v.t.* (*cancel*) отмен|я́ть, -и́ть; аннули́ровать (*impf., pf.*); (*crush*) подав|ля́ть, -и́ть.

quasi- [ˈkweɪzaɪ, ˈkwɑːzɪ] *comb. form* квази...; полу...

quassia [ˈkwɒʃə] *n.* (*tree*) ка́ссия; (*drug*) отва́р из ка́ссии.

quatercentenary [,kwætəsenˈtiːnərɪ] *n.* четырёхсотле́тие.
adj. четырёхсотле́тний.

quaternary [kwəˈtɜːnərɪ] *n.* (*geol.*: **~ system**) четверти́чный пери́од.
adj. **1.** (*of four parts*) состоя́щий из четырёх часте́й. **2.** (*geol.*) четверти́чный.

quatrain [ˈkwɒtreɪn] *n.* четверости́шие.

quatrefoil [ˈkætrə,fɔɪl] *n.* четырёхли́стник.

quattrocento [,kwætrəʊˈtʃentəʊ] *n.* кватроче́нто (*indecl.*); XV (пятна́дцатый) век.

quaver [ˈkweɪvə(r)] *n.* **1.** (*trembling tone*) дрожа́ние; **there was a ~ in his voice** его́ го́лос дрожа́л. **2.** (*mus.*) восьма́я но́та.
v.i. дрожа́ть (*impf.*); вибри́ровать (*impf.*).

quay [kiː] *n.* прича́л; на́бережная.
cpd. **~side** *n.* при́стань.

queasiness [ˈkwiːzɪnɪs] *n.* тошнота́; (*fig.*) щепети́льность, со́вестливость.

queasy [ˈkwiːzɪ] *adj.* **1.** (*inclined to sickness*) подве́рженный тошноте́; **my stomach feels a little ~** меня́ немно́го тошни́т; **he turned ~ at the sight of food** ему́ сде́лалось пло́хо при ви́де еды́. **2.** (*fig., fastidious, over-scrupulous*) щепети́льный, со́вестливый.

Quebec [kwɪˈbek] *n.* Квебе́к; (*attr.*) квебе́кский.

queen [kwiːn] *n.* **1.** короле́ва; **~ consort** супру́га пра́вящего короля́; **~ dowager** вдо́вствующая короле́ва; **~ mother** короле́ва-мать; **Q~ Anne is dead** (*prov.*) ≃ откры́л Аме́рику! **2.** (*fig.*) боги́ня, короле́ва, цари́ца; **Q~ of the May** короле́ва ма́я; **beauty ~** короле́ва красоты́; **~ of cities** коро́ль городо́в; царь-го́род; **Britain was ~ of the seas** А́нглия была́ влады́чицей море́й. **3.** (**~** *bee*, **~** *wasp*, **~** *ant*) ма́тка. **4.** (*at chess*) ферзь (*m.*), короле́ва; **~'s pawn** фе́рзевая пе́шка. **5.** (*at cards*) да́ма; **~ of hearts** черво́нная да́ма; да́ма черве́й. **6.: Q~'s Bench** (*hist.*) Суд короле́вской скамьи́; **Q~'s Counsel** адвока́т вы́сшего ра́нга; **he can't speak the Q~'s English** он не уме́ет пра́вильно говори́ть по-англи́йски; **Q~'s evidence** обвиня́емый, облича́ющий свои́х соо́бщников; *see also* **king. 7.** (*sl., homosexual*) гомосексуали́ст.
v.t. **1.: she ~ed it over the other girls** она́ разы́грывала принце́ссу пе́ред подру́гами. **2.** (*chess*): **~ a pawn** пров|оди́ть, -ести́ пе́шку в ферзи́.

queenly [ˈkwiːnlɪ] *adj.* ца́рственный, короле́вский.

queer [kwɪə(r)] *n.* (*sl., homosexual*) педера́ст, (*coll.*) пе́дик.
adj. (*strange, odd*) стра́нный; чудакова́тый; **he's a ~ customer** он стра́нный тип; **he is ~ in the head** у него́ не все до́ма; (*causing suspicion*) подозри́тельный, сомни́тельный; **he is up to something ~** он замышля́ет что́-то подозри́тельное; **he found himself in Q~ Street** он попа́л в беду́; (*unwell*) недомога́ющий; **the heat is making me feel ~** мне нехорошо́ от жары́; (*homosexual*) гомосексуа́льный.
v.t. по́ртить, ис-.

queerness [ˈkwɪənɪs] *n.* стра́нность; чудакова́тость.

quell [kwel] *v.t.* подав|ля́ть, -и́ть.

quench [kwentʃ] *v.t.* (*extinguish*) гаси́ть, по-; туши́ть, по-; (*slake*): **~ one's thirst** утол|я́ть, -и́ть жа́жду; (*fig., suppress*) подав|ля́ть, -и́ть; (*tech., cool in water*) зака́л|ивать, -и́ть.

quenchless ['kwentʃlɪs] *adj.* неугаси́мый; неутоли́мый.
quern [kwɜːn] *n.* ручна́я ме́льница.
querulous ['kwerʊləs] *adj.* ворчли́вый.
querulousness ['kwerʊləsnɪs] *n.* ворчли́вость.
quer|y ['kwɪərɪ] *n.* (*question*) вопро́с; **~y, where did he go?** спра́шивается, куда́ он пошёл?; (*question mark*) вопроси́тельный знак.

v.t. **1.** (*ask, inquire*) осв|едомля́ться, -е́домиться; допы́тыватся (*impf.*). **2.** (*call in question*) выража́ть, вы́разить сомне́ние в+*p.*; **he ~ied my reasons for coming** он усомни́лся в причи́нах моего́ прихо́да.

quest [kwest] *n.* по́иски (*m. pl.*); **the ~ for happiness** пого́ня за сча́стьем; **he went in ~ of food** он отпра́вился на по́иски еды́.

v.i. иска́ть (*impf.*); разы́скивать (*impf.*).

question ['kwestʃ(ə)n] *n.* **1.** (*interrogation; problem*) вопро́с; **stop asking ~s!** переста́ньте задава́ть вопро́сы!; **I put the ~ to him** я за́дал ему́ вопро́с; **he popped the ~** (*coll.*) **over dinner** он сде́лал ей предложе́ние за у́жином; **a leading ~** наводя́щий вопро́с; **a good ~!** зако́нный/толко́вый вопро́с!; **beg the ~** исходи́ть (*impf.*) из того́, что ещё не дока́зано; приводи́ть (*impf.*) в ка́честве аргуме́нта спо́рное предложе́ние; обходи́ть (*impf.*) принципиа́льный вопро́с; **it is only a ~ of finding the money** де́ло то́лько за тем, что́бы раздобы́ть де́ньги; **the ~ of the hour** злободне́вный вопро́с; **the ~ is, can we afford it?** вопро́с в том, мо́жем ли мы э́то себе́ позво́лить?; **a holiday is out of the ~** об о́тпуске не мо́жет быть и ре́чи; **that's not the ~** не в э́том де́ло; **the man in ~** челове́к, о кото́ром идёт речь; **his wishes do not come into ~** его́ жела́ния тут ни при чём; **the ~ does not arise** тако́го вопро́са не возника́ет. **2.** (*doubt, objection*) сомне́ние; **his statements were called in ~** его́ заявле́ния бы́ли поста́влены под сомне́ние; **his veracity is open to ~** его́ правди́вость ещё под вопро́сом; **I make no ~ that you are telling the truth** я не сомнева́юсь в том, что вы говори́те пра́вду; **without, beyond ~** бесспо́рно; **he allowed my claims without ~** он удовлетвори́л мои́ тре́бования без еди́ного вопро́са; **there is no ~ but that he will succeed** (*or* **of his not succeeding**) его́ успе́х не подлежи́т сомне́нию. **3.** (*arch., torture*): **the prisoners were put to the ~** заключённых подве́ргли пы́тке.

v.t. **1.** (*interrogate*) допр|а́шивать, -оси́ть; **I ~ed him closely on his theory** я подро́бно расспра́шивал его́ о его́ тео́рии; **he is wanted for ~ing by the police** поли́ция разы́скивает его́ для допро́са. **2.** (*cast doubt on*) сомнева́ться (*impf.*) в+*p.*; осп|а́ривать, -о́рить.

cpds. **~-mark** вопроси́тельный знак; **~-master** *n.* веду́щий виктори́ну (*or* в виктори́не).

questionable ['kwestʃənəb(ə)l] *adj.* (*doubtful*) сомни́тельный; ненадёжный; (*disreputable*) сомни́тельный, подозри́тельный.
questioner ['kwestʃənə(r)] *n.* интервьюе́р.
questionnaire [ˌkwestʃə'neə(r), ˌkestjə-] *n.* анке́та, вопро́сник.
queue [kjuː] *n.* о́чередь; **he was trying to jump the ~** он пыта́лся влезть без о́череди; **get to the back of the ~!** ста́ньте в о́чередь!

v.i. (*also* **~ up**) станови́ться (*impf.*) в о́чередь.

quibbl|e ['kwɪb(ə)l] *n.* софи́зм, увёртка.

v.i. уви́л|ивать, -ьну́ть; **a ~ing argument** уклóнчивый до́вод; **I won't ~e over 20p** я не бу́ду пререка́ться из-за двадцати́ пе́нсов.

quibbler ['kwɪblə(r)] *n.* казуи́ст, крючкотво́р.
quick [kwɪk] *n.* **1.: the ~** (*arch., live persons*) живы́е (*pl.*). **2.: he bit his nails to the ~** он искуса́л но́гти до кро́ви; **his words cut me to the ~** его́ слова́ заде́ли меня́ за живо́е.

adj. **1.** (*rapid*) бы́стрый, ско́рый; **he set off at a ~ pace** он пошёл бы́стрым ша́гом; **this is the ~est way home** э́то са́мая коро́ткая доро́га домо́й; **be ~ about it!** потороп́итесь!, живе́й!; **he is a ~ worker** он бы́стро рабо́тает; **there were three shots in ~ succession** три вы́стрела раздали́сь оди́н за други́м; **~ march!** ша́гом — марш!; **the soldiers were marching in ~ time** солда́ты шли бы́стрым ша́гом; **we got there in double ~ time** мы добрали́сь туда́ в два счёта; **there's just time for a ~ one** (*drink*) мы как раз успе́ем пропусти́ть по ма́ленькой. **2.** (*lively, prompt*) бы́стрый; живо́й; (*of mind*) сообрази́тельный, шу́стрый; **a ~ child** живо́й/сообрази́тельный ребёнок; **you need a ~ eye at tennis** в те́ннисе ну́жен бы́стрый глаз; **he is ~ at figures** он бы́стро счита́ет; **~ of foot** подви́жный; **he has a ~ temper** он вспы́льчив; **she is ~ to take offence** она́ о́чень оби́дчива.

adv. бы́стро; **~, get a doctor!** скоре́е позови́те врача́!; **I'll come as ~ as I can** я приду́, как то́лько смогу́; **she replied, as ~ as lightning** она́ отве́тила мгнове́нно.

cpds. **~-change** *adj.*: **~-change artist** актёр-трансформа́тор; **~-eared** *adj.* облада́ющий о́стрым слу́хом; **~-firing** *adj.* скорostре́льный; **~-freeze** *v.t.* бы́стро замор|а́живать, -о́зить; **~-frozen** *adj.* быстрозаморо́женный; **~lime** *n.* нега́шеная и́звесть; **~sand(s)** *n.* зыбу́чий песо́к; **~set** *adj.*: **a ~set hedge** жива́я и́згородь; **~silver** *n.* ртуть; (*fig., attr.*) живо́й, подви́жный; **~step** *n.* (*dance*) куик-сте́п; **~-tempered** *adj.* вспы́льчивый; **~-witted** *adj.* смышлёный, нахо́дчивый.

quicken ['kwɪkən] *v.t.* (*make quicker*) уск|оря́ть, -о́рить; **he ~ed his pace** он приба́вил ша́гу; (*stimulate*) возбу|жда́ть, -ди́ть.

v.i. **1.** (*become quicker*) уск|оря́ться, -о́риться; **her pulse ~ed** её пульс уско́рился/участи́лся. **2.: the child ~ed in her womb** ребёнок шевельну́лся у неё под се́рдцем.

quickie ['kwɪkɪ] *n.* (*coll.*) что́-то сде́ланное на ско́рую ру́ку; (*in quiz*) кра́ткий вопро́с.
quickness ['kwɪknɪs] *n.* быстрота́; (*of eye, ear etc.*) острота́; (*of hand*) прово́рство; (*of mind*) сообрази́тельность; (*of temper*) вспы́льчивость.
quid[1] [kwɪd] *n.* (*coll., £1*) фунт (сте́рлингов).
quid[2] [kwɪd] *n.* (*of tobacco*) кусо́к прессо́ванного табака́.
quid pro quo [ˌkwɪd prəʊ 'kwəʊ] *n.* услу́га за услу́гу.
quiescence [kwɪ'es(ə)ns] *n.* неподви́жность; безде́йствие.
quiescent [kwɪ'es(ə)nt] *adj.* неподви́жный; безде́йствующий; дре́млющий.
quiet ['kwaɪət] *n.* (*stillness, silence*) тишина́; **absolute ~ reigned** цари́ло по́лное споко́йствие; (*repose*) поко́й, споко́йствие, мир; **I was glad to have an hour's ~** я был рад ча́су поко́я; **there is peace and ~ in the countryside** в дере́вне тишина́ и поко́й.

adj. **1.** (*making little or no sound*) ти́хий; бесшу́мный; **~ footsteps** неслы́шные/бесшу́мные шаги́; **a ~ car** бесшу́мная маши́на; **a ~ room** ти́хий но́мер; **be ~!** помолчи́те!; **can't you keep ~?** не мо́жете ли вы помолча́ть?; **this will keep him ~ for a bit** э́то его́ на вре́мя утихоми́рит; **the baby was ~ at last** наконе́ц младе́нец утих. **2.** (*making little motion*) ти́хий; неподви́жный; **a ~ sea** споко́йное мо́ре. **3.** (*undisturbed*) споко́йный; ми́рный; **we had a ~ night** ночь прошла́ споко́йно; **now I can go to bed with a ~ mind** тепе́рь я могу́ спать споко́йно. **4.** (*of gentle or inactive disposition*) споко́йный; ти́хий. **5.** (*unobtrusive*) нея́ркий; **~ colours** приглушённые/споко́йные цвета́; **a ~ dress** скро́мное/нея́ркое пла́тье. **6.** (*private; concealed*) та́йный; скры́тый; **keep it ~!** об э́том молчо́к!; **on the ~** (*secretly*) тайко́м; втихомо́лку; (*in confidence*) под секре́том. **7.** (*informal, unostentatious*) скро́мный.

v.t. успок|а́ивать, -о́ить.

int. ти́ше!

quieten ['kwaɪət(ə)n] *v.t.* & *i.* (*also* **~ down**) успок|а́ивать(ся), -о́ить(ся).
quietism ['kwaɪəˌtɪz(ə)m] *n.* квиети́зм.
quietist ['kwaɪətɪst] *n.* квиети́ст; (*attr., also* **~ic**) квиети́ческий.
quietness ['kwaɪətnɪs] *n.* (*stillness*) тишина́; (*repose*) поко́й; (*of manner, character*) невозмути́мость, споко́йствие.
quietude ['kwaɪɪˌtjuːd] *n.* (*liter.*) поко́й, споко́йствие.
quietus [kwaɪ'iːtəs] *n.* (*arch., death*) конч́ина; **he received his ~** ему́ пришёл коне́ц; **give the ~ to** положи́ть (*pf.*) коне́ц +*d*.
quiff [kwɪf] *n.* чёлка; (*tuft*) зачёс.
quill [kwɪl] *n.* (*feather*) пти́чье перо́; (**~ pen**) гуси́ное перо́; (*of porcupine*) игла́ (дикобра́за).

quilt [kwɪlt] *n.* стёганое одея́ло.
v.t. стега́ть, вы-/про-; **a ~ed dressing-gown** стёганый хала́т.
quin [kwɪn] (*coll.*) = **quintuplet**
quince [kwɪns] *n.* (*fruit, tree*) айва́; (*attr.*) айво́вый.
quincentenary [ˌkwɪnsenˈtiːnərɪ] *n.* пятисотле́тие.
quinine [ˈkwɪniːn, -ˈniːn] *n.* хини́н.
quinquagenarian [ˌkwɪŋkwədʒɪˈneərɪən] *n.* челове́к пяти́-десяти лет.
adj. пятидесятиле́тний.
quinquennial [kwɪnˈkwenɪəl] *adj.* пятиле́тний.
quinquennium [kwɪnˈkwenɪəm] *n.* пятиле́тие.
quinsy [ˈkwɪnzɪ] *n.* флегмоно́зная анги́на.
quintal [ˈkwɪnt(ə)l] *n.* це́нтнер, квинта́л.
quintessence [kwɪnˈtes(ə)ns] *n.* квинтэссе́нция.
quintessential [ˌkwɪntɪˈsenʃ(ə)l] *adj.* наибо́лее суще́ственный; коренно́й.
quintet(te) [kwɪnˈtet] *n.* квинте́т.
quintuple [ˈkwɪntjʊp(ə)l] *n.* пятикра́тное коли́чество.
adj. пятикра́тный.
v.t. увели́чи|вать(ся), -ть(ся) в пять раз.
quintuplet [ˈkwɪntjʊplɪt, -ˈtjuːplɪt] *n.* оди́н из пяти́ близнецо́в.
quip [kwɪp] *n.* острота́, кра́сное словцо́.
v.i. остри́ть, с-.
quire [ˈkwaɪə(r)] *n.* (*of paper*) десть.
quirk [kwɜːk] *n.* (*oddity*) причу́да; **through some ~ of fate** по капри́зу судьбы́; (*flourish*) завито́к, вы́верт.
quirky [ˈkwɜːkɪ] *adj.* с причу́дами.
quisling [ˈkwɪzlɪŋ] *n.* кви́слинг, преда́тель (*m.*).
quit [kwɪt] *adj.*: **we are ~ of the obligation** мы свобо́дны от обяза́тельства; **we are well ~ of him** к сча́стью, мы от него́ изба́вились.
v.t. **1.** (*leave*) ост|авля́ть, -а́вить. **2.** (*coll., stop*) прекра|ща́ть, -ти́ть; бр|оса́ть, -о́сить; **the men ~ work** рабо́чие прекрати́ли рабо́ту; (*US*): **~ grumbling!** бро́сьте ворча́ть! **3.:** **~** (*acquit*) **o.s.** вести́ (*impf.*) себя́.
v.i. **1.** (*leave premises, job etc.*): **the tenant was asked to ~** жильца́ попроси́ли съе́хать с кварти́ры; **the maid was given notice to ~** го́рничную предупреди́ли об увольне́нии. **2.** (*leave off*) перест|ава́ть, -а́ть.
quite [kwaɪt] *adv.* **1.** (*entirely*) совсе́м, соверше́нно, вполне́; **I ~ agree** я вполне́ согла́сен; **~ right!** соверше́нно ве́рно!; **~ so!**; **~!** безусло́вно!, несомне́нно!, ве́рно!, (вот) и́менно!; **have you ~ finished?** ну, вы ко́нчили?; **this is ~ the best book** э́то безусло́вно са́мая хоро́шая кни́га; **that is ~ another matter** э́то совсе́м друго́е де́ло; **pink is ~ the thing this year** ро́зовый цвет мо́ден в э́том году́; **it's not ~ the thing (to do)** э́то не совсе́м при́нято; **I am not ~ myself today** я немно́го не в себе́ сего́дня. **2.** (*to a certain extent*) дово́льно, вполне́; **it is ~ cold here** зде́сь дово́льно хо́лодно; **I ~ like cycling** я не прочь поката́ться на велосипе́де; **it took me ~ a long time** э́то о́тняло у меня́ дово́льно мно́го вре́мени; **~ a few** дово́льно мно́го; нема́ло.
quits [kwɪts] *pred. adj.*: **I will be ~ with you yet** я ещё с ва́ми расквита́юсь; **now we are ~** тепе́рь мы квиты́; **he decided to cry ~** он реши́л пойти́ на мирову́ю.
quittance [ˈkwɪt(ə)ns] *n.* освобожде́ние.
quitter [ˈkwɪtə(r)] *n.* (*coll.*) (*coward*) трус; (*shirker*) прогу́льщик.
quiver[1] [ˈkwɪvə(r)] *n.* (*for arrows*) колча́н.
quiver[2] [ˈkwɪvə(r)] *n.* (*vibration*) дрожь.
v.i. дрожа́ть, за-; трясти́сь, за-.
qui vive [kiː ˈviːv] *n.*: **on the ~** наготове, начеку́, настороже́.
Quixote [ˈkwɪksət] *n.*: **Don ~** Дон-Кихо́т; (*as generic*) донкихо́т.
quixotic [kwɪkˈsɒtɪk] *adj.* донкихо́тский.
quiz [kwɪz] *n.* (*interrogation*) опро́с; (*test of knowledge*) се́рия вопро́сов; (*entertainment*) виктори́на.
v.t. (*interrogate*) выспра́шивать, выспросить; (*make fun of*) подшу́|чивать, -ти́ть над+*i.*; (*regard with curiosity*) разгля́д|ывать, -е́ть.
cpd. **~-master** *n.* веду́щий виктори́ну (*or* в виктори́не).
quizzical [ˈkwɪzɪk(ə)l] *adj.* насме́шливый, ирони́ческий.
quod [kwɒd] *n.* (*prison*) тюря́га (*sl.*).
quoin [kɔɪn] *n.* углово́й ка́мень кла́дки.
quoit [kɔɪt] *n.* мета́тельное кольцо́; **~s** (*game*) мета́ние коле́ц в цель.
quondam [ˈkwɒndæm] *adj.* (*liter.*) бы́вший, пре́жний.
quorum [ˈkwɔːrəm] *n.* кво́рум.
quota [ˈkwəʊtə] *n.* кво́та, но́рма.
quotable [ˈkwəʊtəb(ə)l] *adj.* досто́йный повторе́ния.
quotation [kwəʊˈteɪʃ(ə)n] *n.* **1.** (*quoting*) цити́рование; **~ marks** кавы́ч|ки (*pl., g.* -ек); **double ~ marks** кавы́чки в два штриха́; (*passage quoted*) цита́та. **2.** (*estimate of cost*) цена́, расце́нка.
quot|e [kwəʊt] *n.* **1.** (*coll., quotation*) цита́та. **2.** (*pl., coll., quotation marks*) кавы́ч|ки (*pl., g.* -ек).
v.t. **1.** (*repeat words of*) цити́ровать, про-; **he is always ~ing Shakespeare** он всегда́ цити́рует Шекспи́ра; **can I ~e you on that?** могу́ ли я сосла́ться на ва́ши слова́?; '**~ … unquote**' «откры́ть кавы́чки… закры́ть кавы́чки». **2.** (*adduce*) ссыла́ться, сосла́ться на+*a.*; **can you ~ an instance?** мо́жете ли вы́ привести́ приме́р? **3.:** **~ a price** назн|ача́ть, -а́чить це́ну; **this is the best price I can ~ you** э́то са́мая лу́чшая цена́, каку́ю я могу́ вам предложи́ть.
quoth [kwəʊθ] *v.t.* (*arch., pret.*) промо́лвил.
quotidian [kwɒˈtɪdɪən] *n.* (**~ fever**) маляри́я с ежедне́вными при́ступами.
adj. ежедне́вный.
quotient [ˈkwəʊʃ(ə)nt] *n.* ча́стное; **intelligence ~** коэффицие́нт врождённых у́мственных спосо́бностей.
q.v. (*abbr. of* ***quod vide***) см., (смотри́) (*там-то*).

R

R [ɑː(r)] *n.*: **the three ~s** ≃ азы́ (*m. pl.*) нау́ки.
rabbi [ˈræbaɪ] *n.* равви́н.
rabbinical [rəˈbɪnɪk(ə)l] *adj.* равви́нский.
rabbit [ˈræbɪt] *n.* **1.** (*rodent*) кро́лик; **~ punch** подзаты́льник. **2.** (*poor performer at game*) мази́ла (*c.g.*), слаба́к (*coll.*). **3.:** **Welsh ~** (*also* **rarebit**) грено́к с сы́ром; **breed like ~s** размножа́ться (*impf.*) как кро́лики.
v.i. **1.** (*hunt ~s*) охо́титься (*impf.*) на за́йцев. **2.** (*babble*) трепа́ться (*impf.*) (*coll.*).
cpds. **~-hole** *n.* кро́личья нора́; **~-hutch** *n.* кро́личья кле́тка; **~-warren** *n.* крольча́тник; (*fig.*) лабири́нт.
rabble [ˈræb(ə)l] *n.* сброд, чернь.
cpds. **~-rouser** *n.* демаго́г; **~-rousing** *n.* демаго́гия.
Rabelaisian [ˌræbəˈleɪzɪən] *adj.* раблезиа́нский.
rabid [ˈræbɪd, ˈreɪ-] *adj.* **1.** (*affected with rabies*) бе́шеный, больно́й водобоя́знью. **2.** (*furious, violent*) бе́шеный, я́ростный. **3.** (*extremist*): **a ~ socialist** оголте́лый социали́ст.
rabies [ˈreɪbiːz] *n.* бе́шенство, водобоя́знь.
RAC (*abbr. of* ***Royal Automobile Club***) Короле́вский автомоби́льный клуб.
raccoon [rəˈkuːn] = **racoon**
race[1] [reɪs] *n.* **1.** (*contest*) бег на ско́рость, го́нка; забе́г; **(horse-)~s** ска́чки (*f. pl.*); **~ walker** скорохо́д; **how many horses are in the first ~?** ско́лько лошаде́й уча́ствуют в пе́рвом забе́ге?; **a racing man** завсегда́тай тотализа́тора; **let's have a ~** дава́йте побежи́м наперего́нки; **it was a ~ against time** вре́мени бы́ло в обре́з; (*fig.*): **his ~ is almost run** его́ жизнь бли́зится к зака́ту. **2.** (*swift current*) бы́стрый пото́к.
v.t. **1.** (*compete in speed with*): **I'll ~ you to the corner** посмо́трим, кто быстре́е добежи́т до угла́. **2.** (*cause to

compete in ~): **how often do you ~ your horses?** как ча́сто ва́ши ло́шади уча́ствуют в ска́чках? **3.** (*cause to move fast*): **they ~d the bill through** они́ в спе́шном поря́дке протащи́ли билль че́рез парла́мент; **~ an engine** форси́ровать (*impf.*, *pf.*) дви́гатель; перегру|жа́ть, -зи́ть мото́р.

v.i. **1.** (*compete in speed*) состяза́ться (*impf.*) в ско́рости. **2.** (*participate in horse-racing*) уча́ствовать (*impf.*) в ска́чках. **3.** (*move at speed*) нести́сь (*impf.*); мча́ться, по-; **the propeller was racing** пропе́ллер сли́шком раскрути́лся.

cpds. **~-card** *n.* програ́мма ска́чек; **~course** *n.* ипподро́м; **~horse** *n.* скакова́я ло́шадь; **~-meeting** *n.* день (*m.*) ска́чек; **~-track** *n.* тре́к; автомотодро́м.

race[2] [reɪs] *n.* пле́мя (*nt.*), род; **the human ~** род людско́й; **a ~ apart** осо́бая ра́са; (*breed*) род, поро́да; (*descent*) происхожде́ние; (*ethnic*) ра́са; (*attr.*) ра́совый.

raceme [rəˈsiːm] *n.* гроздь (*m.*), кисть.

racer [ˈreɪsə(r)] *n.* (*pers.*) го́нщик, (*rider*) нае́здник; (*horse*) скакова́я ло́шадь; (*car, yacht etc.*) го́ночная маши́на/я́хта *и т.п.*

rachitic [rəˈkɪtɪk] *adj.* рахити́чный.

racial [ˈreɪʃ(ə)l] *adj.* ра́совый.

raci|alism [ˈreɪʃəˌlɪz(ə)m], **-sm** [ˈreɪsɪz(ə)m] *nn.* раси́зм.

raci|alist [ˈreɪʃəˌlɪst], **-st** [ˈreɪsɪst] *nn.* раси́ст.

raciness [ˈreɪsɪnɪs] *n.* острота́, пря́ность, те́рпкость.

racis|m [ˈreɪsɪz(ə)m], **-t** [ˈreɪsɪst] = **racialis|m, -t**

rack[1] [ræk] *n.* **1.** (*frame*) сто́йка с по́лками; стелла́ж; (*for fodder*) я́сл|и (*pl., g.* -ей); (*plate-~*) подста́вка для посу́ды; (*hat-~*) ве́шалка; (*luggage-~ for travellers*) се́тка. **2.** (*toothed bar*) зубча́тая ре́йка; **~(-and-pinion) railway** зубча́тая желе́зная доро́га.

rack[2] [ræk] *n.* (*instrument of torture*) ды́ба; **he was put on the ~** (*lit.*) его́ вздёрнули на ды́бу; **I was on the ~** (*fig.*) **all the time he was away** всё вре́мя, что его́ не́ было, я был как на иго́лках.

v.t. **1.** (*torture*) му́чить, и́з-; терза́ть, ис-; **he was ~ed with pain** он ко́рчился от бо́ли; (*fig.*): **I ~ed my brains for an answer** я лома́л го́лову над отве́том. **2.** (*shake violently*): **the cough ~ed his whole body** всё его́ те́ло сотряса́лось от ка́шля. **3.** (*exact excessive rent from*) драть (*impf.*); об|дира́ть, -одра́ть.

cpd. **~-rent** *n.* граби́тельская аре́ндная/кварти́рная пла́та.

rack[3] [ræk] (*also* **wrack**) *n.* (*drifting clouds*) несу́щиеся облака́.

rack[4] [ræk] (*also* **wrack**) *n.* (*destruction*): **everything went to ~ and ruin** всё пошло́ пра́хом.

rac|ket[1], **-quet** [ˈrækɪt] *n.* **1.** (*for tennis etc.*) раке́тка. **2.: squash ~s** сквош.

cpd. **~-press** *n.* зажи́м для раке́тки.

racket[2] [ˈrækɪt] *n.* **1.** (*din, uproar*) шум, гам, гро́хот. **2.** (*hectic activity*) го́нка, горя́чка, сумато́ха; (*social*) вихрь (*m.*) удово́льствий; разгу́л, прожига́ние жи́зни. **3.: I could never stand the ~** (*pace*) я бы не вы́держал тако́го те́мпа жи́зни; **I refused to stand the ~** (*take the blame*) я отказа́лся отвеча́ть за э́то. **4.** (*coll., dishonest scheme or system*) жу́льническое предприя́тие, надува́тельство, афе́ра; (*extortion*) вымога́тельство.

v.i. (*usu.* **~ about**) (*lead gay life*) весели́ться (*impf.*); пуска́ться (*impf.*) в разгу́л; (*move noisily*) шуме́ть (*impf.*).

racketeer [ˌrækɪˈtɪə(r)] *n.* афери́ст, рэкети́р.

raconteur [ˌrækɒnˈtɜː(r)] *n.* хоро́ший расска́зчик; анекдо́тчик.

rac|oon, -coon [rəˈkuːn] *n.* ено́т.

racquet [ˈrækɪt] = **racket**[1]

racy [ˈreɪsɪ] *adj.* (*piquant, lively*) о́стрый, пря́ный; **a ~ style** бо́йкий/я́ркий стиль; **a ~ flavour** те́рпкий при́вкус; **~ of the soil** самобы́тный, кондо́вый.

RADA [ˈrɑːdə] *n.* (*abbr. of* ***Royal Academy of Dramatic Art***) Короле́вская акаде́мия театра́льного иску́сства.

radar [ˈreɪdɑː(r)] *n.* (*system*) радиолока́ция; (*apparatus*) радиолока́тор, рада́р; (*attr.*) рада́рный, радиолокацио́нный.

raddle [ˈræd(ə)l] *n.* кра́сная о́хра.

v.t.: **~d cheeks** нарумя́ненные щёки.

radial [ˈreɪdɪəl] *adj.* радиа́льный; (*anat.*) лучево́й.

radiance [ˈreɪdɪəns] *n.* сия́ние, блеск; **the sun's ~** со́лнечное сия́ние.

radiant [ˈreɪdɪənt] *adj.* **1.** (*lit., fig.*) сия́ющий; **she was ~ with youth** она́ блиста́ла мо́лодостью; **she was ~ with happiness** она́ сия́ла от сча́стья; **he is in ~ health** он пы́шет здоро́вьем. **2.** (*transmitted by radiation*) лучи́стый; **~ heat** теплово́е излуче́ние.

radiate [ˈreɪdɪˌeɪt] *v.t. & i.* излуч|а́ть(ся), -и́ть(ся); (*fig.*): **his face ~d happiness** его́ лицо́ свети́лось ра́достью.

radiation [ˌreɪdɪˈeɪʃ(ə)n] *n.* радиа́ция, излуче́ние; **~ treatment** радиотерапи́я; **~ sickness** лучева́я боле́знь; (*fig.*) сия́ние.

radiator [ˈreɪdɪˌeɪtə(r)] *n.* (*heating device*) батаре́я, радиа́тор; (*portable*) электронагрева́тель (*m.*), рефле́ктор; (*of car*) радиа́тор.

radical [ˈrædɪk(ə)l] *n.* (*math., philol.*) ко́рень (*m.*); (*pol.*) радика́л.

adj. (*fundamental*) коренно́й; (*pol.*) радика́льный; (*math.*) относя́щийся к ко́рню; (*philol., bot.*) корнево́й.

radicalism [ˈrædɪkəˌlɪz(ə)m] *n.* радикали́зм.

radio [ˈreɪdɪəʊ] *n.* (*means of communication*) ра́дио (*indecl.*); (*broadcasting system*) радиовеща́ние; (*receiving/transmitting apparatus*) радиоприёмник/радиопереда́тчик; (*message sent by ~*) радиогра́мма; **~ beacon** радиомая́к; **~ car** радиофици́рованный автомоби́ль; **~ cassette (recorder)** магнито́ла; **~ compass** радиоко́мпас; **~ direction finding** радиопеленга́ция; **~ ham** радиолюби́тель (*m.*); **~ programme** радиопереда́ча; **~ silence** радиомолча́ние.

v.t. **1.** (*send by ~*) перед|ава́ть, -а́ть (по ра́дио). **2.** (*contact by ~*) ради́ровать (*pf.*) +*d.*

radioactive [ˌreɪdɪəʊˈæktɪv] *adj.* радиоакти́вный.

radioactivity [ˌreɪdɪəʊækˈtɪvɪtɪ] *n.* радиоакти́вность.

radiocarbon [ˌreɪdɪəʊˈkɑːbən] *n.* радиоакти́вный углеро́д; **~ dating** датиро́вка радиоуглеро́дным ме́тодом.

radiogram [ˈreɪdɪəʊˌgræm] *n.* (*picture*) рентгеногра́мма; (*telegram*) радиогра́мма; (*gramophone with radio*) радио́ла.

radiograph [ˈreɪdɪəʊˌgrɑːf] *n.* (*instrument*) актино́метр.

radiographic [ˌreɪdɪəˈgræfɪk] *adj.* радиографи́ческий.

radiography [ˌreɪdɪˈɒgrəfɪ] *n.* радиогра́фия.

radiolocation [ˌreɪdɪəʊləˈkeɪʃ(ə)n] *n.* радиолока́ция.

radiologist [ˌreɪdɪˈɒlədʒɪst] *n.* радио́лог, рентгено́лог.

radiotherapy [ˌreɪdɪəʊˈθerəpɪ] *n.* лучева́я терапи́я.

radish [ˈrædɪʃ] *n.* реди́ска.

radium [ˈreɪdɪəm] *n.* ра́дий.

radius [ˈreɪdɪəs] *n.* ра́диус; (*anat.*) лучева́я кость; **within a ~ of** в ра́диусе +*g.*

radix [ˈreɪdɪks] *n.* основа́ние систе́мы счисле́ния.

radome [ˈreɪdəʊm] *n.* (*aeron.*) ко́жух/обтека́тель (*m.*) анте́нны.

RAF (*abbr. of* ***Royal Air Force***) ВВС (*f. pl.*) (вое́нно-возду́шные си́лы) Великобрита́нии.

raffia [ˈræfɪə] *n.* ра́ффия.

raffish [ˈræfɪʃ] *adj.* (*dissipated*) беспу́тный; (*in appearance*) потрёпанный.

raffle [ˈræf(ə)l] *n.* лотере́я.

v.t. (*also* **~ off**) разы́гр|ывать, -а́ть в лотере́е.

raft [rɑːft] *n.* (спла́вной) плот.

rafter [ˈrɑːftə(r)] *n.* стропи́ло.

raftsman [ˈrɑːftsmən] *n.* спла́вщик ле́са; (*ferryman*) паро́мщик.

rag[1] [ræg] *n.* **1.** (*small, esp. torn, piece of cloth*) тря́пка, лоску́т; **they tore his shirt to ~s** они́ разорва́ли его́ руба́шку в кло́чья; (*pl., torn or tattered clothing*) лохмо́ть|я (*pl., g.* -ев); отре́пья (*nt. pl.*); **he went about in ~s** он ходи́л, как оборва́нец; **his coat is in ~s** его́ пальто́ изно́шено до дыр. **2.** (*pej. or joc., garment*) тря́пки (*f. pl.*); **I haven't a ~ to wear** мне соверше́нно не́чего наде́ть; **the ~ trade** (*coll.*) шве́йная промы́шленность; **glad ~s** (*coll.*) пара́дное облаче́ние. **3.** (*pej., newspaper*) газетёнка. **4.** (*fig., shred, scrap*) обры́вки, оста́тки (*both m. pl.*); **he couldn't provide a ~ of evidence** он не мог привести́ ни мале́йшего доказа́тельства; **the meat was cooked to ~s** мя́со соверше́нно вы́варилось.

cpds. **~-(and-bone-)man** *n.* старьёвщик; **~bag** *n.* (*lit.*) мешо́к для лоскуто́в; (*fig.*) вся́кая вся́чина; **~-doll** *n.*

тряпи́чная ку́кла; **~-paper** *n.* тряпи́чная бума́га; **~-picker** *n.* старьёвщик; **~tag (and bobtail)** *n.* подо́нки (*m. pl.*), сброд; **~time** *n.* ре́гтайм.

rag[2] [ræg] *n.* (*students' prank*) подтру́нивание, проказы (*f. pl.*).

v.t. (*play prank on; tease*) разыгр|ывать, -а́ть; изводи́ть (*impf.*); **he took a lot of ~ging at school** в шко́ле его́ здо́рово изводи́ли.

ragamuffin [ˈrægə,mʌfɪn] *n.* оборва́нец.

rag|e [reɪdʒ] *n.* **1.** (*violent anger*) я́рость, гнев; **he flew into a ~e** он пришёл в я́рость; (*fig.*): **the ship was exposed to the full ~e of the storm** кора́бль испыта́л всю я́рость бу́ри. **2.** (*dominant fashion*): **short skirts were all the ~e** коро́ткие ю́бки бы́ли тогда́ после́дним кри́ком мо́ды.

v.i.: **he ~ed at his wife** он наки́нулся на свою́ жену́; **the wind ~ed all day** ве́тер бушева́л весь день; **a ~ing torrent** бушу́ющий пото́к; **a ~ing thirst** мучи́тельная жа́жда.

ragged [ˈrægɪd] *adj.* **1.** (*torn, frayed*) рва́ный, потрёпанный; (*wearing torn clothes*) обо́рванный. **2.** (*rough or uneven in outline*): **a ~ beard** косма́тая борода́; **~ clouds** рва́ные облака́. **3.** (*wanting polish or uniformity*): **their singing is ~** они́ пою́т нестро́йно.

raggle-taggle [ˈrægəl,tæg(ə)l] *adj.* разношёрстный, беспоря́дочный.

raglan [ˈræglən] *n.* пальто́ (*indecl.*) регла́н.

ragout [ræˈguː] *n.* рагу́ (*nt. indecl.*).

raid [reɪd] *n.* налёт, набе́г, рейд; **he was killed during a ~ on London** он был уби́т во вре́мя налёта на Ло́ндон; **the police made a ~ on the club** поли́ция нагря́нула в клуб; **there was a ~ on the bank** произошло́ ограбле́ние ба́нка; **there was a ~ on sterling** была́ сде́лана попы́тка подорва́ть курс фу́нта; **the boys made a ~ on the pantry** мальчи́шки зале́зли в чула́н с проду́ктами.

v.t.: **our bombers ~ed Hamburg** на́ши бомбардиро́вщики соверши́ли налёт на Га́мбург; **the flat was ~ed in his absence** в его́ отсу́тствие кварти́ру огра́били; **he had to ~ his savings** ему́ пришло́сь воспо́льзоваться ча́стью свои́х сбереже́ний.

raider [ˈreɪdə(r)] *n.* (*aeron.*) уча́стник налёта; (*criminal*) налётчик, граби́тель (*m.*).

rail[1] [reɪl] *n.* **1.** (*bar for protection, support etc.*) перекла́дина, ре́йка; (*of staircase*) пери́л|а (*pl., g.* —); **~ fence** огра́да; **the horse was forced to the ~s** ло́шадь оказа́лась прижа́той к огра́де (ипподро́ма); **they were leaning over the ship's ~** они́ стоя́ли, облокоти́вшись о борт па́лубы. **2.** (*of railway or tram track*) рельс; **live ~** конта́ктный рельс; **the train ran off the ~s** по́езд сошёл с ре́льсов; (*fig.*): **after his wife's death he went off the ~s** он был соверше́нно вы́бит из коле́и сме́ртью жены́; (*railway transport*): **by ~** по́ездом; **~ fares are going up** сто́имость прое́зда по желе́зной доро́ге повыша́ется.

v.t.: **~ in** огор|а́живать, -оди́ть; **~ off** отгор|а́живать, -оди́ть.

cpds. **~car** *n.* дрези́на; **~head** *n.* коне́чная/вы́грузочная ста́нция; **~road** *n.* (*US*) желе́зная доро́га; *v.t.* (*coll.*): **they were ~roaded into agreement** их с хо́ду втяну́ли в соглаше́ние; **the bill was ~roaded through the House** билль протащи́ли че́рез парла́мент; **~way** *n.* (*track, system, company*) желе́зная доро́га; **model ~way** игру́шечная желе́зная доро́га; (*attr.*) железнодоро́жный; **~wayman** *n.* железнодоро́жник.

rail[2] [reɪl] *v.i.* (*liter.*) руга́ться (*impf.*); **he ~ed at me** он стал на меня́ ора́ть; **it's no use ~ing against the system** како́й смы́сл поноси́ть систе́му?

railing(s) [ˈreɪlɪŋs] *n.* и́згородь, огра́да.

raillery [ˈreɪlərɪ] *n.* (добродушное) подтру́нивание/подшу́чивание.

raiment [ˈreɪmənt] *n.* (*liter.*) одея́ние.

rain [reɪn] *n.* дождь (*m.*); **I was caught in the ~** я попа́л под дождь; **don't go out in the ~** не выходи́те под дождь; **I think I felt a drop of ~** вро́де начина́ет накра́пывать; **a shower of ~** ли́вень (*m.*); **a light ~ was falling** мороси́л до́ждик; **let's have a drink to keep the ~ out** что́-то ста́ло холода́ть, не пора́ ли нам поддА́ть?; **~ or shine** в любу́ю пого́ду; **as right as ~** в по́лном поря́дке; **the ~s start in July** дожди́ начина́ются в ию́ле; **a ~ of bullets** град пуль; **a ~ of congratulations** пото́к поздравле́ний.

v.t.: **it is ~ing cats and dogs** льёт как из ведра́; (*fig.*): **she ~ed blows on his head** она́ колоти́ла его́ по голове́.

v.i.: **it is ~ing** дождь идёт; **it was ~ing hard** шёл си́льный/проливно́й дождь; **it never ~s but it pours** пришла́ беда́ — отворя́й ворота́; (*fig.*): **tears ~ed down her cheeks** слёзы гра́дом кати́лись по её щека́м.

with advs.: **~ in** *v.i.*: **it is ~ing in under the door** дождь подтека́ет под дверь; **~ off** *v.t.*: **the match was ~ed off** матч был со́рван из-за́ дождя́; **~ out** *v.t.*: **the storm ~ed itself out** гроза́ отбушева́ла и улегла́сь.

cpds. **~bow** *n.* ра́дуга; **her dress was all the colours of the ~bow** её пла́тье отлива́ло все́ми цвета́ми ра́дуги; **~-cloud** *n.* ту́ча; **~coat** *n.* плащ; **~drop** *n.* ка́пля дождя́; **~fall** *n.* оса́дк|и (*pl., g.* -ов); **~-gauge** *n.* дождоме́р; **~-maker** *n.* ≃ шама́н/колду́н, наклика́ющий дождь; **~proof** *adj.* непромока́емый; **~storm** *n.* гроза́; **~-water** *n.* дождева́я вода́; **~wear** *n.* непромока́емая оде́жда и о́бувь.

rainforest [ˈreɪn,fɒrɪst] *n.* тропи́ческий лес.

rainy [ˈreɪnɪ] *adj.* дождли́вый; **you should save for a ~ day** вы должны́ откла́дывать на чёрный день.

raise [reɪz] *n.* (*US, rise in salary*) приба́вка; (*increase in stake or bid*) повыше́ние.

v.t. **1.** (*lift; cause to rise*) подн|има́ть, -я́ть; **the anchor was ~d** я́корь был по́днят; **he barely ~d his eyes** он почти́ не поднима́л глаз; **will all in favour ~ their hand** все, кто «за», подними́те ру́ки; **he ~d his hat** он приподнял шля́пу; **the ship was ~d from the sea-bed** кора́бль был по́днят со дна; **a little yeast will ~ the dough** что́бы те́сто подняло́сь, ну́жно немно́го дрожже́й; (*make higher*) пов|ыша́ть, -ы́сить; **I ~d the temperature to 80°** я повы́сил температу́ру до 80°; **the government ~d the duty on tobacco** прави́тельство повы́сило по́шлину на таба́к; **the news ~d my hopes** изве́стие укрепи́ло мои́ наде́жды; **the stakes were ~d** ста́вки бы́ли повы́шены; **I'll ~ you** я повыша́ю ста́вку; (*make louder, more vehement*): **don't ~ your voice** не повыша́йте го́лоса; **voices were ~d in anger** раздали́сь гне́вные голоса́; (*cause to stand*): **I ~d him from his knees** я помо́г ему́ подня́ться с коле́н; (*arouse*): **the heat ~d blisters on his skin** от жары́ он весь покры́лся волдыря́ми; **the carriage ~d a cloud of dust** каре́та подняла́ о́блако пы́ли; **Lazarus was ~d from the dead** Ла́зарь был воскрешён из мёртвых; (*fig.*): **he ~d Cain, hell** он устро́ил стра́шный сканда́л; (*elevate*): **he was ~d to the peerage** его́ произвели́ в пэ́ры; (*erect*): **they ~d the standard of revolt** они́ по́дняли флаг восста́ния; **a monument was ~d to his memory** ему́ был воздви́гнут па́мятник. **2.** (*bring up*): **may I ~ one question?** мо́жно мне зада́ть вопро́с?; **the issue will never be ~d** э́тот вопро́с никогда́ не бу́дет по́днят; **several objections were ~d** бы́ло сде́лано не́сколько возраже́ний; (*evoke*): **his words hardly ~d a laugh** почти́ никто́ не засмея́лся в отве́т; **this ~d a blush on her cheek** э́то заста́вило её покрасне́ть; **you ~d a doubt in my mind** вы зарони́ли мне в ду́шу сомне́ние; (*summon up*): **I couldn't ~ a smile** я не мог себя́ заста́вить улыбну́ться; **he could hardly ~ the energy to get up** он е́ле собра́лся с си́лами, что́бы встать. **3.** (*give voice to*): **she ~d the alarm** она́ подняла́ трево́гу; **they ~d a hue and cry** они́ ста́ли зва́ть на по́мощь. **4.** (*collect, procure*): **she ~d money for charity** она́ собрала́ де́ньги на благотвори́тельные це́ли; **I tried to ~ a loan** я попыта́лся взять де́ньги в долг; **he couldn't ~ enough money for a meal** он не смог раздобы́ть доста́точно де́нег, что́бы пое́сть; (*levy*): **the king ~d an army** коро́ль собра́л а́рмию. **5.** (*rear*): **they ~d a family** они́ вы́растили дете́й; **sheep are ~d on the downs** ове́ц разво́дят в холми́стых райо́нах; (*grow, cultivate*): **he ~d a fine crop of turnips** он вы́растил хоро́ший урожа́й ре́пы. **6.** (*siege etc.*) сн|има́ть, -ять.

raisin [ˈreɪz(ə)n] *n.* изю́минка; (*pl., collect.*) изю́м.

raison d'être [,reɪzɔ̃ ˈdetr] *n.* смысл, разу́мное основа́ние.

raj [rɑːdʒ] *n.* (*hist.*) брита́нское правле́ние в И́ндии.

rajah [ˈrɑːdʒə] *n.* ра́джа (*m.*).

rake[1] [reɪk] *n.* (*implement*) гра́бл|и (*pl.*, *g.* -ей); **croupier's** ~ лопа́точка крупье́; **as thin as a** ~ худо́й как ще́пка.

v.t.: **he** ~**d the soil level** он разрыхли́л грунт; **the paths were** ~**d clean** доро́жки бы́ли расчи́щены; (*fig.*): **the guns** ~**d the ship** су́дно бы́ло обстре́ляно продо́льным огнём.

v.i. (*fig.*): **he** ~**d among his papers** он переворошил свои́ бума́ги.

with advs.: ~ **in** *v.t.*: **he** ~**d in the money** (*fig.*) он загреба́л де́ньги лопа́той; ~ **out** *v.t.* выгреба́ть, вы́грести; **she** ~**d out the ashes** она́ вы́гребла пе́пел; ~ **together** *v.t.* сгре|ба́ть, -сти́ в ку́чу; ~ **up** *v.t.* сгре|ба́ть, -сти́; (*fig.*): **why** ~ **up an old quarrel?** заче́м вороши́ть ста́рую ссо́ру?

cpd. ~**-off** *n.* (*coll.*) магары́ч; комиссио́нные (*pl.*).

rake[2] [reɪk] *n.* (*arch.*, *dissolute pers.*) пове́са (*m.*), распу́тни|к (*fem.* -ца).

rake[3] [reɪk] *n.* (*slope*) у́гол накло́на.

v.t.: **the ship's funnels are** ~**d** тру́бы корабля́ устано́влены накло́нно.

rakish [ˈreɪkɪʃ] *adj.* (*jaunty*) щеголова́тый; у́харский; **his hat was set at a** ~ **angle** он носи́л ша́пку (ли́хо) набекре́нь.

rallentando [ˌrælənˈtændəʊ] *n.*, *adj.* & *adv.* раллента́ндо.

rall|y [ˈrælɪ] *n.* **1.** (*assembly*) сбор, слёт, ми́тинг. **2.** (*recovery*, *revival*) восстановле́ние сил; попра́вка. **3.** (*at tennis etc.*) переки́дка. **4.** (*motor race*) автора́лли; ~**y driver** авторалли́ст.

v.t. **1.** (*reassemble*) соб|ира́ть, -ра́ть (в строй); спл|а́чивать, -оти́ть. **2.** (*revive*): **his words** ~**ied their spirits** его́ слова́ воодушеви́ли их. **3.** (*chaff*) поддра́зн|ивать, -и́ть.

v.i. **1.** (*reassemble*) соб|ира́ться, -ра́ться; спл|а́чиваться, -оти́ться; **they** ~**ied round the leader** они́ сплоти́лись вокру́г вождя́; **they** ~**ied to the cause** де́ло сплоти́ло их. **2.** (*revive*): **he** ~**ied from his illness** он опра́вился от боле́зни; **the market** ~**ied** ры́нок воспря́нул.

RAM [ræm] *n.* (*comput.*) (*abbr. of* **random-access memory**) ЗУПВ, (запомина́ющее устро́йство с произво́льной вы́боркой).

ram [ræm] *n.* **1.** (*male sheep*) бара́н. **2.** (*astron.*: **the R**~) Ове́н. **3.** (*battering-*~) тара́н.

v.t. **1.** (*drive or compress by force*): **stakes were** ~**med into the ground** ко́лья бы́ли вби́ты в зе́млю; **the soil was** ~**med down** грунт был утрамбо́ван; **he** ~**med his clothes into a drawer** он запихну́л свою́ оде́жду в я́щик (комо́да); (*fig.*): **he** ~**med the point home** он вдолби́л им свою́ мысль; **why do you** ~ **my faults down my throat?** заче́м вы мне ты́чете мои́ми недоста́тками? **2.** (*strike with force*): **the ship** ~**med the bridge** (*by accident*) кора́бль наскочи́л на мост; **he** ~**med the enemy flagship** он протара́нил фла́гман проти́вника.

cpds. ~**-jet** *n.* самолёт с прямото́чным возду́шно-реакти́вным дви́гателем; ~**rod** *n.* шо́мпол.

Ramadan [ˈræməˌdæn] *n.* (*relig.*) рамаза́н.

rambl|e [ˈræmb(ə)l] *n.* прогу́лка.

v.i. **1.** (*walk for pleasure*) прогу́л|иваться, -я́ться. **2.** (*of plants*) ползти́, ви́ться (*both impf.*). **3.** (*fig.*, *of speech or writing*) болта́ть (*impf.*) языко́м; бубни́ть (*impf.*); **a** ~**ing speaker** раски́дчивый ора́тор; (*of sick pers.*) загова́риваться (*impf.*). **4.**: **a** ~**ing house** разбро́санный дом.

rambler [ˈræmblə(r)] *n.* (*hiker*) люби́тель пешехо́дного тури́зма; (*discursive speaker*) пустоме́ля (*c.g.*); (*kind of rose*) выо́щаяся ро́за.

rambling [ˈræmblɪŋ] *n.* пешехо́дный тури́зм.

ramification [ˌræmɪfɪˈkeɪʃ(ə)n] *n.* разветвле́ние; (*offshoot*) ответвле́ние.

ramif|y [ˈræmɪˌfaɪ] *v.t.* & *i.* развев|ля́ть(ся), -и́ть(ся); **a** ~**ied system of railways** разветвлённая систе́ма желе́зных доро́г.

ramp[1] [ræmp] *n.* (*slope*) скат, укло́н.

ramp[2] [ræmp] *n.* (*coll.*, *swindle etc.*) обдира́ловка, вымога́тельство.

rampage [ˈræmpeɪdʒ] *n.* бу́йство, разгу́л.

v.i. бу́йствовать, буя́нить (*both impf.*).

rampageous [ræmˈpeɪdʒəs] *adj.* бу́йный, нейстовый.

rampant [ˈræmpənt] *adj.* **1.** (*her.*): **lion** ~ взды́бленный лев. **2.** (*violent*, *rabid*) я́рый, огoлте́лый. **3.** (*unchecked*, *widespread*) свире́пствующий, безу́держный; **disease was** ~ боле́знь свире́пствовала. **4.** (*rank*, *luxuriant*) бу́йный, пы́шный.

rampart [ˈræmpɑːt] *n.* крепостно́й вал; парапе́т; (*fig.*) опло́т.

ramshackle [ˈræmˌʃæk(ə)l] *adj.* (*e.g. house*) обветша́лый; (*e.g. car*) разби́тый.

ranch [rɑːntʃ] *n.* ра́нчо (*indecl.*), фе́рма.

v.t. разв|оди́ть, -ести́.

rancher [ˈrɑːntʃə(r)] *n.* владе́лец ра́нчо; скотово́д.

rancid [ˈrænsɪd] *adj.* прого́рклый, ту́хлый.

rancorous [ˈræŋkərəs] *adj.* озло́бленный, злопа́мятный.

rancour [ˈræŋkə(r)] *n.* зло́ба, озло́бленность; злопа́мятство.

rand [rænd] *n.* (*currency*) ранд.

random [ˈrændəm] *n.*: **at** ~ наобу́м, науга́д, науда́чу; **shoot at** ~ стреля́ть (*impf.*) не це́лясь; **he hit out at** ~ он бил, куда́ придётся.

adj. случа́йный; сде́ланный на аво́сь; ~ **bullet** шальна́я пу́ля; ~ **choice** случа́йный вы́бор; ~ **paving** моще́ние без подбо́ра камне́й; ~ **remark** случа́йное замеча́ние.

randy [ˈrændɪ] *adj.* распу́тный, похотли́вый.

ranee [ˈrɑːnɪ] = **rani**

range [reɪndʒ] *n.* **1.** (*row*, *line*, *series*) цепь, ряд; **a** ~ **of mountains** го́рная цепь; **a** ~ **of buildings** ряд зда́ний. **2.** (*grazing area*) неугоро́женое па́стбище; (*hunting ground*) охо́тничье уго́дье. **3.** (*area for firing*, *bombing etc.*) полиго́н; **rifle** ~ стре́льбище; тир; ~ **practice** уче́бная стрельба́. **4.** (*area of distribution of species*) ареа́л, зо́на обита́ния. **5.** (*operating distance*) да́льность, ра́диус; **the missile has a** ~ **of 1,000 miles** ра́диус де́йствия раке́ты — 1000 миль; ~ **of a transmitter** да́льность де́йствия переда́тчика; ~ **of an aircraft** да́льность полёта самолёта; **the enemy was out of** ~ **of our guns** враг был вне досяга́емости на́ших ору́дий; **wait till he is within** ~ подпусти́те его́ на расстоя́ние вы́стрела. **6.** (*distance to target*) расстоя́ние, да́льность; **they fired at close** ~ они́ стреля́ли с бли́зкого расстоя́ния; **find the** ~ определ|я́ть, -и́ть расстоя́ние. **7.** (*limit of audibility or visibility*) преде́л, -ы; **beyond the** ~ **of vision** вне преде́лов ви́димости. **8.** (*extent*; *distance between limits*) диапазо́н; **her voice has a remarkable** ~ у неё замеча́тельный диапазо́н; **a wide** ~ **of temperature** широ́кий диапазо́н температу́р. **9.** (*selection*) набо́р; (*assortment*) ассортиме́нт; **this fabric comes in a wide** ~ **of colours** э́та ткань выпуска́ется са́мых разли́чных цвето́в. **10.** (*scope*): **the subject is outside my** ~ э́тот вопро́с — не по мое́й ча́сти. **11.** (*cooking-stove*) ку́хонная плита́.

v.t. **1.** (*place in row*) распол|ага́ть -ожи́ть (*or* выстра́ивать, вы́строить) в ряд; **they** ~**d themselves against the wall** они́ вы́строились вдоль стены́; **the troops were** ~**d along the river-bank** войска́ бы́ли размещены́ вдоль бе́рега реки́. **2.** (*traverse*): **wolves** ~**d the prairie** во́лки ры́скали по сте́пи; **police** ~**d the woods** (*in their search*) поли́ция прочёсывала лес; **ships** ~**d the seas** корабли́ борозди́ли моря́.

v.i. **1.** (*wander*, *roam*): **tigers** ~**d through the jungle** ти́гры броди́ли по джу́нглям. **2.** (*extend*) простира́ться (*impf.*); **my research** ~**s over a wide field** мои́ иссле́дования охва́тывают широ́кую о́бласть. **3.** (*vary between limits*) колеба́ться (*impf.*); **prices** ~ **from £10 to £50** це́ны коле́блются от десяти́ до пяти́десяти фу́нтов. **4.** (*of guns etc.*, *carry*): **the gun** ~**s over 5 miles** дальнобо́йность пу́шки — 5 миль.

cpd. ~**-finder** *n.* дальноме́р.

ranger [ˈreɪndʒə(r)] *n.* (*guard of forest or parkland*) лесни́чий, лесни́к, объе́здчик; (*pl.*, *mounted troops*) ко́нная охра́на.

rangy [ˈreɪndʒɪ] *adj.* (*of pers.*) длинноно́гий, поджа́рый.

ran|i, -ee [ˈrɑːnɪ] *n.* ра́ни (*f. indecl.*).

rank[1] [ræŋk] *n.* **1.** (*row*) ряд; (*taxi-*~) стоя́нка такси́. **2.** (*line of soldiers*) шере́нга; **in the front** ~ (*lit.*) в пе́рвой шере́нге; (*fig.*, *pre-eminent*) в пе́рвых ряда́х; **the men broke** ~**(s)** солда́ты нару́шили строй; **an artist of the first** ~ первокла́ссный худо́жник; **among the** ~**s of the unemployed** в ряда́х безрабо́тных. **3.** (*usu. pl.*, *common* *soldiers*): ~ **and file** (*mil. etc.*) рядовы́е; **he rose from the ~s** он вы́служился из рядовы́х; **he was reduced to the ~s** его́ разжа́ловали в рядовы́е. **4.** (*in armed forces*) зва́ние, чин; **he has the ~ of captain** он име́ет чин капита́на; **other ~s** сержа́нтско-рядово́й соста́в. **5.** (*official position*) служе́бное положе́ние; (*social position*): **he attained high ~** он дости́г высо́кого положе́ния; **persons of ~** высокопоста́вленные лю́ди; **~ and fashion** вы́сшее о́бщество; **people of all ~s of society** представи́тели всех слоёв о́бщества.

v.t. (*class, assess*) классифици́ровать (*impf., pf.*); **he was ~ed among the great poets** его́ причисля́ли к вели́ким поэ́там.

v.i. (*have a place*): **a major ~s above a captain** майо́р — вы́ше капита́на по чи́ну; **a high-~ing officer** ста́рший офице́р; **France ~s among the great powers** Фра́нция вхо́дит в число́ вели́ких держа́в.

rank[2] [ræŋk] *adj.* **1.** (*too luxuriant, coarse*) бу́йный, пы́шный; **~ vegetation** бу́йная расти́тельность; **the roses are growing ~** ро́зы сли́шком бу́йно разросли́сь; **a garden ~ with weeds** сад, заро́сший сорняка́ми. **2.** (*foul to smell or taste; offensive*): **the skunk gives off a ~ odour** от ску́нса исхо́дит злово́ние. **3.** (*loathsome, corrupt*) гну́сный. **4.** (*gross*) чрезме́рный; **~ indecency** ди́кая непристо́йность; **~ injustice** вопию́щая несправедли́вость; **~ nonsense** су́щая чепуха́; **~ poison** настоя́щая отра́ва, чи́стый яд; **~ treason** на́глая изме́на.

rank-and-file ['ræŋkənd,faɪl] *adj.* рядово́й.

ranker ['ræŋkə(r)] *n.* (*private soldier*) рядово́й.

rankle ['ræŋk(ə)l] *v.i.* (*fester*) гнои́ться (*impf.*); (*give pain*) боле́ть (*impf.*); **the insult ~d in his memory** его́ жгло воспомина́ние об оби́де.

rankness ['ræŋknɪs] *n.* (*excess*) изоби́лие, чрезме́рность; (*offensiveness*) гну́сность.

ransack ['rænsæk] *v.t.* **1.** (*search*) обша́ри|вать, -ть; переры́ть (*pf.*); **I ~ed my memory** я перевороши́л свою́ па́мять. **2.** (*plunder*) гра́бить, раз-.

ransom ['rænsəm] *n.* вы́куп; **he was held to ~** (*lit.*) за него́ тре́бовали вы́куп; (*fig.*) его́ шантажи́ровали; **it is worth a king's ~** (*fig.*) э́то не име́ет цены́.

v.t. (*pay ~ for*) плати́ть, за- вы́куп за+*a.*

rant [rænt] *n.* тира́да; разглаго́льствование.

v.i. вити́йствовать; разглаго́льствовать (*both impf.*).

ranter ['ræntə(r)] *n.* фразёр, краснобай.

rap [ræp] *n.* **1.** (*light blow*) лёгкий уда́р, стук; **I heard a ~ at the window** я услы́шал стук в окно́; **he received a ~ on the knuckles** (*fig., reproof*) ему́ да́ли по рука́м; **I don't care a ~** мне наплева́ть. **2.** (*blame*): **who will take the ~ for this?** кто бу́дет за э́то отдува́ться? (*coll.*).

v.t. слегка́ уд|аря́ть, -а́рить по+*d.*

v.i. ст|уча́ть, -у́кнуть; посту́|кивать, -ча́ть; **he ~ped on the door** он постуча́л в дверь.

with adv.: **~ out** *v.t.* (*utter brusquely*) говори́ть (*impf.*) отры́висто; **he ~ped out his orders** он выкри́кивал свой приказа́ния.

rapacious [rə'peɪʃəs] *adj.* жа́дный, а́лчный, ненасы́тный.

rapacity [rə'pæsɪtɪ] *n.* жа́дность, а́лчность, ненасы́тность.

rape[1] [reɪp] *n.* изнаси́лование; (*fig.*): **the ~ of Czechoslovakia** наси́льственный захва́т Чехослова́кии.

v.t. наси́ловать, из-; (*fig.*) надруга́ться (*pf.*) над+*i.*

rape[2] [reɪp] *n.* (*bot.*) рапс.

Raphael ['ræfeɪəl] *n.* (*bibl.*) Рафаи́л; (*painter*) Рафаэ́ль (*m.*).

rapid ['ræpɪd] *n.* (*pl.*) речно́й поро́г; **shoot ~s** преодол|ева́ть, -е́ть поро́ги.

adj. (*swift*) бы́стрый, ско́рый; (*steep*) круто́й.

rapidity [rə'pɪdɪtɪ] *n.* быстрота́, ско́рость.

rapier ['reɪpɪə(r)] *n.* рапи́ра.

cpd. **~-thrust** (*lit.*) уко́л рапи́рой; (*fig., of repartee*) остроу́мный вы́пад; уда́р в то́чку.

rapine ['ræpaɪn, -pɪn] *n.* (*liter.*) грабёж.

rapist ['reɪpɪst] *n.* наси́льник.

rapport [ræ'pɔː(r)] *n.* взаимопонима́ние, конта́кт; **he and I are in ~** мы с ним отли́чно ла́дим.

rapporteur [,ræpɔː'tɜː(r)] *n.* докла́дчик.

rapprochement [ræ'prɒʃmɑ̃] *n.* сближе́ние.

rapscallion [ræp'skæljən] *n.* прощелы́га (*c.g.*), моше́нник.

rapt [ræpt] *adj.* (*enraptured*) восхищённый; (*absorbed*) поглощённый; **he was ~ in contemplation** он был погружён в разду́мье; **she listened with ~ attention** она́ слу́шала, затаи́в дыха́ние.

rapture ['ræptʃə(r)] *n.* восто́рг; **she went into ~s over the play** она́ была́ в (ди́ком) восто́рге от пье́сы.

rapturous ['ræptʃərəs] *adj.* восто́рженный.

rare[1] [reə(r)] *adj.* **1.** (*not dense*): **a ~ atmosphere** разрежённая атмосфе́ра. **2.** (*uncommon*) ре́дкий; **it is ~ for him to smile** он ре́дко улыба́ется; **this flower is ~ in Britain** э́тот цвето́к ре́дко встреча́ется в Великобрита́нии. **3.** (*remarkably good*): ре́дкостный; **we had a ~ old time** (*coll.*) мы на ре́дкость хорошо́ провели́ вре́мя; **he has a ~ wit** он на ре́дкость остроу́мен.

rare[2] [reə(r)] *adj.* (*undercooked*) недожа́ренный; **a ~ steak** бифште́кс с кро́вью.

rarebit ['reəbɪt] = **rabbit** *n.* **3.**

raref|action [,reərɪ'fækʃ(ə)n], **-ication** [,reərɪfɪ'keɪʃ(ə)n] *nn.* разреже́ние, разрежённость.

rarefy ['reərɪ,faɪ] *v.t.* разре|жа́ть, -ди́ть; разжижа́ть (*impf.*); (*fig.*) утонч|а́ть, -и́ть; рафини́ровать (*impf., pf.*).

v.i. разре|жа́ться, -ди́ться; разжижа́ться (*impf.*).

rarely ['reəlɪ] *adv.* ре́дко, неча́сто, и́зредка.

raring ['reərɪŋ] *adj.* (*coll.*): **he was ~ to go** ему́ не терпе́лось приступи́ть к де́лу.

rarity ['reərɪtɪ] *n.* (*uncommonness, infrequency*) ре́дкость; (*thg. valued for this*) (больша́я) ре́дкость.

rascal ['rɑːsk(ə)l] *n.* (*rogue*) моше́нник, плут; (*mischievous child*) шалу́н.

rascally ['rɑːskəlɪ] *adj.* моше́ннический, нече́стный.

rase [reɪz] = **raze**

rash[1] [ræʃ] *n.* сыпь; **he broke out in a ~** у него́ вы́ступила сыпь; (*fig.*): **there was a ~ of new building** но́вые зда́ния вы́росли как грибы́ (по́сле дождя́).

rash[2] [ræʃ] *adj.* поспе́шный, опроме́тчивый, необду́манный.

rasher ['ræʃə(r)] *n.* ло́мтик (беко́на, ветчины́).

rashness ['ræʃnɪs] *n.* поспе́шность, опроме́тчивость, необду́манность.

rasp [rɑːsp] *n.* (*file*) тёрка, ра́шпиль (*m.*); (*grating sound*) скре́жет.

v.t. (*scrape*) скрести́, скобли́ть, тере́ть (*all impf.*).

v.i. скрежета́ть (*impf.*); **a ~ing voice** скрипу́чий го́лос.

with advs.: **~ away, ~ off** *v.t.* соска́бл|ивать, -и́ть; ст|а́чивать, -очи́ть; **~ out** *v.t.* (*e.g. an order*) га́ркнуть, прохрипе́ть (*both pf.*).

raspberry ['rɑːzbərɪ] *n.* **1.** (*fruit*) мали́на (*collect.*); **a ~** я́года мали́ны; **~ cane** куст мали́ны; **~ jam** мали́новое варе́нье. **2.** (*sl, sound or gesture of derision*): **he blew me a ~** он показа́л мне нос.

Rasta ['ræstə] *n.* & *adj.* = **Rastafarian**

Rastafarian [,ræstə'feərɪən] *n.* растафа́ри (*c.g. indecl.*).

adj. растафа́ри.

raster ['ræstə(r)] *n.* растр.

rat [ræt] *n.* **1.** (*rodent*) кры́са; **he looked like a drowned ~** он походи́л на мо́крую ку́рицу; **I smell a ~** я чу́ю подво́х; здесь что́-то нечи́сто; **~s!** (*coll., nonsense*) чушь! **2.** (*traitor to cause*) изме́нник, ренега́т.

v.i. **1.** (*hunt ~s*) лови́ть (*impf.*) крыс. **2.**: **~ on** (*break faith with, desert*) **s.o.** измен|я́ть, -и́ть кому́-н.

cpds. **~-catcher** *n.* крысоло́в; **~-race** *n.*: **we are all in the ~-race** мы все бо́ремся за ме́сто под со́лнцем; **~-trap** *n.* крысоло́вка.

ratable ['reɪtəb(ə)l] = **rat(e)able**

rat-a-tat [,rætə'tæt] = **rat-tat**

ratchet ['rætʃɪt] *n.* (*toothed mechanism*) храпово́й механи́зм, храпови́к; **(~-wheel)** храпово́е колесо́.

rate[1] [reɪt] *n.* **1.** (*numerical proportion*) но́рма, разме́р; ста́вка; **~ of exchange** курс обме́на; **~ of interest** проце́нтная ста́вка; **bank ~** учётная ста́вка ба́нка; **birth ~** рожда́емость; **death ~** сме́ртность. **2.** (*speed*) ско́рость; **at a steady ~** с постоя́нной ско́ростью; **we shall never get there at this ~** при таки́х те́мпах мы туда́ никогда́ не доберёмся; **~ of climb** скороподъёмность. **3.** (*price*) расце́нка, тари́ф; **his ~s are high** он до́рого берёт; **the letter ~ goes up every year** тариф на пи́сьма повыша́ется ежего́дно. **4.** (*tax on property etc.*) ме́стный/коммуна́льный нало́г; **water ~** пла́та за водоснабже́ние. **5.: at any ~** (*in any case*) во вся́ком слу́чае; **at that ~** (*on that basis, if that is so*) **you will never succeed** в тако́м слу́чае вы никогда́ не добьётесь успе́ха.

v.t. **1.** (*estimate, consider*) оце́н|ивать, -и́ть; **how do you ~ my chances?** как вы оце́ниваете мои́ ша́нсы?; **do you ~ him among your friends?** счита́ете ли вы его́ свои́м дру́гом? **2.** (*assess for purposes of levy*) оце́н|ивать, -и́ть (*or* классифици́ровать (*impf., pf.*)) в це́лях налогообложе́ния. **3.** (*deserve*): **he ~s a prize** он заслу́живает награ́ды.

v.i. коти́роваться (*impf.*); **~ as** (*be considered*) счита́ться (*impf.*) +*i.*; **he ~s high in my esteem** я его́ о́чень ценю́/уважа́ю.

cpds. **~-collector** *n.* сбо́рщик ме́стных нало́гов; **~payer** *n.* плате́льщик ме́стных/коммуна́льных нало́гов.

rate[2] [reɪt] *v.t.* (*liter., scold*) отчи́т|ывать, -а́ть; брани́ть (*impf.*).

rat(e)able ['reɪtəb(ə)l] *adj.* подлежа́щий обложе́нию нало́гом/нало́гами.

rather ['rɑːðə(r)] *adv.* **1.** (*by preference or choice*): **I would ~ die than consent** я скоре́е умру́, чем соглашу́сь; **I'd ~ have coffee** я предпочёл бы ко́фе; **I'd ~ not say** я лу́чше промолчу́; **~ than annoy him, she agreed** она́ согласи́лась, что́бы не серди́ть его́. **2.** (*more truly or precisely*) скоре́е, верне́е; **last night, or ~ this morning** вчера́ ве́чером, и́ли, верне́е/точне́е (сказа́ть), сего́дня у́тром; **she is shy ~ than unsociable** она́ скоре́е засте́нчива, чем необщи́тельна; **a year ~ than a term** год, а не семе́стр. **3.** (*somewhat*) дово́льно, не́сколько; **the result was ~ surprising** результа́т был дово́льно неожи́данным; **he is ~ stupid** он како́й-то глу́пый; **he is ~ taller than his brother** он немно́го вы́ше своего́ бра́та; **his style is ~ heavy** у него́ тяжелова́тый стиль; **it is ~ a pity** а жаль всё же; **I ~ think you are mistaken** а мне сдаётся, что вы ошиба́етесь; **the effect was ~ spoiled** эффе́кт был не́сколько подпо́рчен. **4.** (*coll., assuredly*) ещё бы!

ratification [,rætɪfɪ'keɪʃ(ə)n] *n.* ратифика́ция.

ratify ['rætɪ,faɪ] *v.t.* ратифици́ровать (*impf., pf.*).

rating[1] ['reɪtɪŋ] *n.* **1.** (*of property etc.*) оце́нка; (*assessment of worth*) определе́ние сто́имости; (*of vehicles etc.*) классифика́ция. **2.** (*sailor*) матро́с, специали́ст рядово́го и́ли старши́нского соста́ва.

rating[2] ['reɪtɪŋ] *n.* (*scolding*) нагоня́й.

ratio ['reɪʃɪəʊ] *n.* отноше́ние, соотноше́ние; коэффицие́нт; **in inverse ~ to** обра́тно пропорциона́льный +*d.*

ratiocinate [,rætɪ'ɒsɪ,neɪt, ,ræʃɪ-] *v.i.* рассужда́ть (*impf.*) логи́чески.

ratiocination [,rætɪ,ɒsɪ'neɪʃ(ə)n, ,ræʃɪ-] *n.* логи́ческие рассужде́ния.

ration ['ræʃ(ə)n] *n.* рацио́н, паёк; **~ book** продово́льственная/промтова́рная кни́жка; **~ card** продово́льственная ка́рточка; **iron ~s** неприкоснове́нный запа́с; **they were on short ~s** они́ бы́ли на ску́дном пайке́; (*pl., food*) продово́льствие, дово́льствие.

v.t.: **they were ~ed to one loaf a week** их паёк своди́лся к одно́й буха́нке в неде́лю; **meat was severely ~ed** мя́со бы́ло стро́го нормиро́вано.

rational ['ræʃən(ə)l] *adj.* (*based on reason*) разу́мный; (*endowed with reason*) разу́мный, мы́слящий; (*math.*) рациона́льный.

rationale [,ræʃə'nɑːl] *n.* основна́я причи́на; логи́ческое обоснова́ние.

rationalism ['ræʃənə,lɪz(ə)m] *n.* рационали́зм.

rationalist ['ræʃənəlɪst] *n.* рационали́ст.

rationalistic [,ræʃənə'lɪstɪk] *adj.* рационалисти́ческий.

rationality [,ræʃə'nælɪtɪ] *n.* разу́мность, рациона́льность.

rationalization [,ræʃənəlaɪ'zeɪʃ(ə)n] *n.* (*explanation*) обоснова́ние, разу́мное объясне́ние; (*justification*) оправда́ние; (*improvement*) рационализа́ция.

rationalize ['ræʃənə,laɪz] *v.t.* (*give or find reasons for*) обосно́в|ывать, -а́ть; разу́мно объясн|я́ть, -и́ть; опра́вд|ывать, -а́ть; (*make more efficient*) рационализи́ровать (*impf., pf.*).

rattan [rə'tæn] *n.* (*palm*) па́льма рота́нговая; (*material*) рота́нг; (*cane*) трость.

rat-tat(-tat) [,rættæt'tæt] (*also* **rat-a-tat**) *n.* тук-ту́к.

ratter ['rætə(r)] *n.* (*rat-catcher*) крысоло́в; (*traitor, deserter*) ренега́т, перебе́жчик.

rattle ['ræt(ə)l] *n.* **1.** (*sound*) треск, гро́хот; **the ~ of machine-guns** пулемётная дробь; (*of hail*) стук; (*of crockery*) гро́хот. **2.** (*child's toy*) погрему́шка. **3.** (*for sports fans etc.*) трещо́тка. **4.** (*of conversation*) болтовня́.

v.t. **1.** (*cause to ~*): **he ~d the money-box** он встряхну́л копи́лку; **the wind ~d the windows** о́кна дребезжа́ли от ве́тра. **2.** (*coll., agitate*): **he is not easily ~d** его́ нелегко́ вы́вести из равнове́сия.

v.i.: **the hail ~d on the roof** град бараба́нил по кры́ше; **the car ~d over the stones** маши́на громыха́ла по камня́м.

with advs.: **he ~d off a list of names** он вы́палил це́лый спи́сок фами́лий; **he ~d on about his family** он продолжа́л тарато́рить о свое́й семье́.

cpds. **~-brain, ~-pate** *nn.* пустоголо́вый челове́к; трепло́ (*c.g.*); **~-brained, ~-pated** *adjs.* пустоголо́вый; **~snake** *n.* грему́чая змея́; **~trap** *n.* драндуле́т, колыма́га.

rattling ['rætlɪŋ] *adj. & adv.* (*coll.*): **he set off at a ~ pace** он бо́дро зашага́л; **we had a ~ (good) time** мы шика́рно провели́ вре́мя.

ratty ['rætɪ] *adj.* (*coll.*) злой, раздражи́тельный; **don't get ~ with me!** не огрыза́йся!

raucous ['rɔːkəs] *adj.* ре́зкий, хри́плый, ре́жущий у́хо.

raunchy ['rɔːntʃɪ] *adj.* (*US coll.*) распу́тный, похотли́вый.

ravage ['rævɪdʒ] *n.* (*usu. pl.*) разруше́ние, опустоше́ние; (*fig.*): **the ~s of time** следы́ (*m. pl.*) вре́мени.

v.t. & i. **1.** (*plunder*) гра́бить, раз-; опустош|а́ть, -и́ть; **the troops ~d the countryside** войска́ разгра́били весь райо́н. **2.** (*devastate, damage*): **the fire ~d through the town** ого́нь бушева́л по всему́ го́роду; (*fig.*): **her face was ~d by suffering** на её лице́ была́ печа́ть страда́ния.

rave [reɪv] *n.* (*coll., enthusiastic review*) восто́рженный о́тзыв.

v.t.: **he ~d himself hoarse** он докрича́лся до хрипоты́.

v.i. (*in delirium*) бре́дить (*impf.*); (*fig., in anger*) неи́стовствовать (*impf.*); (*in delight*): **they ~d about the play** они́ бы́ли в восто́рге от пье́сы (*see also* **raving**).

ravel ['ræv(ə)l] *v.t. & i.* запу́т|ывать(ся), -ать(ся); спу́т|ывать(ся), -ать(ся); **the wool became ~led (up)** ни́тки спу́тались.

with advs.: **~ out** *v.t.* распу́т|ывать, -ать; **~ up** *v.t.* пу́тать (*or* запу́тывать), за-.

raven[1] ['reɪv(ə)n] *n.* во́рон.

cpd. **~-haired** *adj.* с волоса́ми цве́та во́ронова крыла́.

raven[2] ['reɪv(ə)n] *v.t.* (*liter.*) пож|ира́ть, -ра́ть.

v.i. (*prowl*) ры́скать (*impf.*) в по́исках добы́чи.

ravenous ['rævənəs] *adj.* прожо́рливый, хи́щный; **a ~ beast** хи́щник; **a ~ appetite** во́лчий аппети́т; **I am ~** я го́лоден как волк.

raver ['reɪvə(r)] *n.* (*pleasure-seeker*) гуля́ка (*c.g.*), кути́ла (*c.g.*).

ravine [rə'viːn] *n.* овра́г, лощи́на.

raving ['reɪvɪŋ] *n.* бред; **the ~s of an idiot** бред сумасше́дшего.

adj. & adv. **1.** (*insane*): **a ~ lunatic** бу́йно поме́шанный; **you must be ~ mad** ты совсе́м спя́тил. **2.: a ~ beauty** сногсшиба́тельная краса́вица; **a ~ success** оглуши́тельный успе́х.

ravioli [,rævɪ'əʊlɪ] *n.* равио́ли (*nt. and pl. indecl.*).

ravish ['rævɪʃ] *v.t.* (*enchant*) обольщ|а́ть, -сти́ть; восхи|ща́ть, -ти́ть; **a ~ing view** восхити́тельный вид.

raw [rɔː] *n.*: **my remarks touched him on the ~** мои́ слова́ заде́ли его́ за живо́е.

adj. **1.** (*uncooked*) сыро́й, све́жий; **I prefer my fruit ~** я предпочита́ю све́жие фру́кты. **2.** (*in natural state, unprocessed*) необрабо́танный; **~ data** необрабо́танные да́нные; **~ materials** сырьё; **~ spirit** чи́стый спирт; **~ sugar** нерафини́рованный са́хар. **3.** (*callow, inexperienced*) зелёный, нео́пытный; ~ **recruits** необстре́лянные солда́ты. **4.** (*unprotected by skin, sensitive*): **a ~ wound** свéжая/незажи́вшая ра́на; **the wind has made my face ~** у меня́ обве́трилось лицо́. **5.** (*artistically crude*) гру́бый, топо́рный. **6.** (*of weather*) промо́зглый, сыро́й; холо́дный и вла́жный. **7.** (*harsh*) суро́вый; **he got a ~ deal** (*coll.*) с ним суро́во обошли́сь.

cpds. **~-boned** *adj.* костля́вый; **~hide** *n.* сде́ланный из недублёной ко́жи.

rawness [ˈrɔːnɪs] *n.* **1.** (*lack of experience*) нео́пытность. **2.** (*sensitivity of skin*) чувстви́тельность ко́жи (*при раздражении, ссадине и т.п.*). **3.** (*crudity*) гру́бость, топо́рность. **4.** (*of weather*) промо́зглость, сы́рость, вла́жность.

ray[1] [reɪ] *n.* (*lit., fig.*) луч; **the sun's ~s** со́лнечные лучи́; **a ~ of hope** луч/про́блеск наде́жды.

ray[2] [reɪ] *n.* (*fish*) скат.

rayon [ˈreɪɒn] *n.* иску́сственный шёлк, виско́за.

raze, rase [reɪz] *v.t.* **1.** (*demolish*) разр|уша́ть, -у́шить до основа́ния; **the city was ~d to the ground** го́род сравня́ли с землёй. **2.** (*efface*) ст|ира́ть, -ере́ть; вычёркивать, вы́черкнуть; **his name was ~d from her memory** его́ и́мя стёрлось у неё в па́мяти.

razor [ˈreɪzə(r)] *n.* бри́тва; **electric ~** электробри́тва; **open, cut-throat ~** опа́сная бри́тва; **safety ~** безопа́сная бри́тва.

cpds. **~-bill** *n.* гага́рка; **~-blade** *n.* ле́звие; **~-edge** *n.* (*fig.*) остриё ножа́; **on a ~-edge** на краю́ про́пасти.

razzia [ˈræzɪə] *n.* набе́г, налёт.

razzle(-dazzle) [ˈræzəl,dæz(ə)l] *n.* (*sl.*) кутёж, гуля́нка; **they have gone on the ~** они́ загуля́ли.

RC (*abbr. of* ***Roman Catholic***) като́лик.

Rd. [rəʊd] *n.* (*abbr. of* **road**) ул., (у́лица).

RE (*abbr. of* ***Religious Education***) религио́зное обуче́ние.

re[1] [reɪ, riː] *n.* (*mus.*) ре (*indecl.*).

re[2] [riː, rɪ, re] *prep.* по де́лу +*g.*; каса́тельно+*g.*

reach [riːtʃ] *n.* **1.** (*stretching movement*): **he made a ~ for the railing** он протяну́л ру́ку к пери́лам; (*extent of this*) разма́х/длина́ руки́; **tennis requires a good ~** для те́нниса ну́жен большо́й разма́х руки́; **the apples were beyond their ~** они́ не могли́ дотяну́ться до я́блок; (*fig.*): **we are within easy ~ of London** от нас легко́ добра́ться до Ло́ндона; **the subject is above my ~** э́то вы́ше моего́ понима́ния. **2.** (*stretch of river etc.*): **the upper ~es of the Thames** верхо́вья (*nt. pl.*) Те́мзы.

v.t. **1.** (*attain, fetch with outstretched hand*) дотя́|гиваться, -ну́ться до+*g.*; **I can just ~ the shelf** я е́ле-е́ле могу́ дотяну́ться до по́лки; **please ~ me that book** доста́ньте мне, пожа́луйста, э́ту кни́гу. **2.** (*arrive at*) дост|ига́ть, -и́гнуть +*g.*; **we shall ~ town in 5 minutes** мы бу́дем в го́роде че́рез 5 мину́т; **the ladder will not ~ the window** ле́стница не доста́нет до окна́; **your letter ~ed me only yesterday** ва́ше письмо́ дошло́ до меня́ то́лько вчера́; **a rumour ~ed my ears** до меня́ дошёл слух; **~ agreement** прийти́ (*pf.*) к соглаше́нию; **~ a conclusion** прийти́ (*pf.*) к заключе́нию. **3.** (*make contact with*): **can I ~ you by telephone?** с ва́ми мо́жно связа́ться по телефо́ну? **4.** (*rise or sink to*): **his genius ~ed new heights** его́ ге́ний дости́г небыва́лых высо́т; **the pound ~ed a new low** курс фу́нта (сте́рлингов) упа́л ещё ни́же, чем когда́-нибудь пре́жде.

v.i. **1.** (*stretch out hand*) тяну́ться, по- руко́й; **he ~ed for his rifle** он потяну́лся к винто́вке. **2.** (*extend*) простира́ться, тяну́ться (*both impf.*); **his voice ~ed to the back of the hall** его́ го́лос был слы́шен в конце́ за́ла; **the park ~es from here to the river** парк тя́нется отсю́да до реки́; (*fig.*): **his income will not ~ to it** его́ дохо́дов до э́того не хва́тит.

with advs.: **~ down** *v.t.* (*fetch down*) дост|ава́ть, -а́ть; сн|има́ть, -ять; брать, взять; *v.i.*: **he ~ed down and picked up the coin** он нагну́лся и по́днял моне́ту; **the well ~es down for over 100 feet** коло́дец ухо́дит вглубь бо́лее чем на 100 фу́тов; **~ forward** *v.i.*: **he ~ed forward to save her** он протяну́л ру́ку, что́бы удержа́ть её; **~ out** *v.i.*: **he ~ed out to catch the ball** он протяну́л ру́ки, что́бы пойма́ть мяч; **~ up** *v.i.* (*stretch hand up*) протяну́ть (*pf.*) ру́ку вверх; (*rise*) **the tree ~es up to the sky** де́рево тя́нется к не́бу.

cpd. **~-me-downs** *n. pl.* (*coll.*) гото́вая оде́жда.

reachable [ˈriːtʃəb(ə)l] *adj.* достижи́мый.

react [rɪˈækt] *v.i.* реаги́ровать (*impf., pf.*); (*have an effect*) вызыва́ть, вы́звать реа́кцию; влия́ть (*impf.*); **applause ~s upon a speaker** аплодисме́нты воодушевля́ют ора́тора; **these two influences ~ on each other** э́ти два влия́ния взаимоде́йствуют; (*chem.*): **acids ~ together** кисло́ты вступа́ют в реа́кцию; (*respond*) реаги́ровать (*impf.*); отв|еча́ть, -е́тить (на+*a.*); **animals ~ to kindness** живо́тные реаги́руют на ла́ску; **she ~ed by bursting into tears** в отве́т она́ распла́калась; **the enemy ~ed with a bombardment** враг отве́тил на э́то бомбардиро́вкой; (*act in opposition*) проти́виться, вос-; сопротивля́ться (*impf.*).

reaction [rɪˈækʃ(ə)n] *n.* (*var. senses*) реа́кция; **my first ~ was one of disbelief** снача́ла э́то вы́звало у меня́ недове́рие; **chain ~** цепна́я реа́кция.

reactionary [rɪˈækʃənərɪ] *n.* реакционе́р.

adj. реакцио́нный.

reactivate [rɪˈæktɪ,veɪt] *v.t.* реактиви́ровать (*impf., pf.*); вдохну́ть (*pf.*) но́вую жизнь в+*a.*

reactivation [rɪ,æktɪˈveɪʃ(ə)n] *n.* реактива́ция; возобновле́ние де́ятельности.

reactive [rɪˈæktɪv] *adj.* реакти́вный.

reactivity [,rɪækˈtɪvɪtɪ] *n.* реакти́вность.

reactor [rɪˈæktə(r)] *n.* (*tech.*) реа́ктор.

read [riːd] *n.* чте́ние; **a good ~** (*book*) интере́сная/захва́тывающая кни́га; **I shall have a ~ and then go to bed** я немно́го почита́ю и ля́гу спать.

v.t. **1.** (*peruse*) чита́ть, про- *or* проче́сть; **have you ~ this book?** вы чита́ли э́ту кни́гу?; **he can ~ several languages** он уме́ет чита́ть на не́скольких языка́х; **he ~ the letter to himself** он прочёл письмо́ про себя́; **this author is widely ~** э́того а́втора мно́го чита́ют; **can you ~ music?** вы уме́ете игра́ть по но́там?; вы разбира́ете но́ты?; **he was ~ing his head off** он зачи́тывался; **Johnny learnt to ~ the time** Джо́нни научи́лся понима́ть вре́мя по часа́м; **~ the letter to me!** прочита́йте мне письмо́!; **he likes being ~ to** он лю́бит, когда́ ему́ чита́ют; **the bill was ~** (*parl.*) ≃ билль был обсуждён; **she ~ herself to sleep** она́ чита́ла, пока́ не усну́ла; **he ~ himself hoarse** он охри́п от чте́ния; **he ~ himself into the subject** он вчита́лся в э́тот предме́т. **2.** (*discern, make out*): **he ~ my thoughts** он чита́л мои́ мы́сли; **he can ~ shorthand** он уме́ет расшифро́вывать стеногра́ммы; **she had her hand ~** ей погада́ли по руке́; **you ~ too much into my words** вы вкла́дываете в мои́ слова́ то, чего́ в них нет; **you (have) ~ too much into the text** вы вы́читали из те́кста то, чего́ в нём нет. **3.** (*interpret*): **do not ~ my silence as consent** не прими́те моё молча́ние за согла́сие; **I ~ his letter as a refusal** я расце́ниваю/истолко́вываю его́ письмо́ как отка́з. **4.** (*take as correct*): **for X ~ Y** вме́сто X (*or* напеча́тано X) сле́дует чита́ть У; **this editor ~s X for Y** э́тот реда́ктор замени́л У на X; **for Copperfield ~ Dickens** напи́сано Ко́пперфильд, а подразумева́ется Ди́ккенс. **5.** (*study*) изуча́ть (*impf.*); **he is ~ing law** он у́чится на юриди́ческом факульте́те. **6.** (*examine*): **~ a meter** сн|има́ть, -ять показа́ния счётчика; **~ proofs** держа́ть (*impf.*) корректу́ру; пра́вить, вы- вёрстку. **7.** (*indicate, register*) *see v.i.* **2.**

v.i. **1.**: **he can neither ~ nor write** он не уме́ет ни чита́ть, ни писа́ть; **I ~ about it in the papers** я прочёл об э́том в газе́тах; **have you ~ of him before?** вы чита́ли о нём ра́ньше?; **you must ~ between the lines** (*fig.*) сле́дует чита́ть ме́жду срок; **he ~ down the advertisement columns** он прочита́л разде́л объявле́ний; **she ~s to the children at bedtime** она́ чита́ет де́тям пе́ред сном. **2.** (*consist of specified words etc.*): **the text ~s '500'** в те́ксте напи́сано «500»; **the document ~s as follows** докуме́нт гласи́т сле́дующее; **the letter ~s ...** в письме́ говори́тся/ска́зано...; **how does the sentence ~ now?** как тепе́рь звучи́т/сформули́ровано э́то предложе́ние?; **the passage ~s thus** э́то ме́сто чита́ется так; **the thermometer ~s 20° below** термо́метр пока́зывает ми́нус 20°. **3.** (*produce* *effect when read*): **this ~s like a threat** э́то звучи́т как угро́за; **the play ~s well** пье́са хорошо́ чита́ется. **4.** (*study*): **he is ~ing for the exam** он гото́вится к экза́мену.

with advs.: **~ back** *v.t.* повтор|я́ть, -и́ть; **the operator ~ the telegram back** телефони́ст(ка) повтори́л(а) телегра́мму; **~ in** *v.t.*: **~ o.s. in** вчи́тываться (*impf.*); **~ off** *v.t.* (*e.g. list*) прочи́т|ывать, -а́ть; (*from dial etc.*) сн|има́ть, -ять (*показания*); счи́т|ывать, -а́ть; **~ out** *v.t.* прочи́т|ывать, -а́ть; огла|ша́ть, -си́ть; **the results were ~ out** бы́ли оглашены́ результа́ты; **~ over** *v.t.* перечи́т|ывать, -а́ть; прочи́т|ывать, -а́ть; **I finished my essay and ~ it over** я зако́нчил своё сочине́ние и перечита́л его́; **I ~ the letter over to him** я прочёл ему́ письмо́; **~ through** *v.t.* прочи́т|ывать, -а́ть; **have you ~ his letter through?** вы прочита́ли его́ письмо́ до конца́?; **~ up** *v.t.* подчита́ть (*pf.*); чита́ть (*impf.*) для подгото́вки; **he ~ up the subject** он подчита́л ко́е-что по э́тому предме́ту.

cpd. **~-out** *n.* вы́вод/вы́дача да́нных.

readability [ˌri:də'bɪlɪtɪ] *n.* (*legibility*) разбо́рчивость, удобочита́емость; (*interest*) чита́бельность.

readable ['ri:dəb(ə)l] *adj.* **1.** (*legible*) разбо́рчивый, удобочита́емый. **2.** (*teleg.*): **are my signals ~?** мои́ сигна́лы расшифро́ваны/при́няты? **3.** (*enjoyable*) (*coll.*) интере́сный, чита́бельный; **this is a ~ novel** э́тот рома́н хорошо́ чита́ется.

readdress [ˌri:ə'dres] *v.t.* переадресо́в|ывать, -а́ть.

reader ['ri:də(r)] *n.* **1.** (*of books etc.*) чита́тель (*fem.* -ница); **he is a fast ~** он бы́стро чита́ет; **~'s slip** (*in library*) чита́тельское тре́бование; **publisher's ~** рецензе́нт (изда́тельства). **2.** (*university teacher*) ≃ ста́рший преподава́тель; доце́нт. **3.** (*textbook*) хрестома́тия; кни́га для чте́ния; **child's ~** буква́рь (*m.*); **a Russian ~** хрестома́тия по ру́сскому языку́.

readership ['ri:dəʃɪp] *n.* (*readers*) круг чита́телей; (*university post*) до́лжность ста́ршего преподава́теля; доценту́ра.

readily ['redɪlɪ] *adv.* (*willingly*) охо́тно; (*without difficulty*) легко́, без труда́.

readiness ['redɪnɪs] *n.* (*prompt compliance*) гото́вность, охо́та; (*facility, resourcefulness*) нахо́дчивость; (*prepared state*) гото́вность; **reinforcements were held in ~** подкрепле́ния бы́ли приведены́ в состоя́ние гото́вности.

reading ['ri:dɪŋ] *n.* **1.** (*act or pursuit*) чте́ние; **his exploits make interesting ~** его́ похожде́ния чита́ются с интере́сом; **a man of wide ~** начи́танный челове́к. **2.** (*version*) вариа́нт, формулиро́вка; **there is a variant ~** есть друго́й вариа́нт те́кста. **3.** (*interpretation*) толкова́ние; **what is your ~ of events?** как вы оце́ниваете собы́тия? **4.** (*of instrument*) показа́ние; **the gauge showed a high ~** показа́ния индика́тора бы́ли высо́кими. **5.** (*of proofs, or part in play*) счи́тка; (*recital*) публи́чное чте́ние, деклама́ция; **a ~ from the New Testament** чте́ние из Но́вого заве́та. **6.** (*stage in passage of bill*) чте́ние; **the motion was rejected on the second ~** предложе́ние бы́ло отве́ргнуто при второ́м чте́нии.

cpds. **~-desk** *n.* пюпи́тр; **~-lamp** *n.* насто́льная ла́мпа; **~-room** *n.* чита́льный зал, чита́льная.

readjust [ˌri:ə'dʒʌst] *v.t.* попр|авля́ть, -а́вить; испр|авля́ть, -а́вить; приспос|а́бливать, -о́бить; **he ~ed his tie** он попра́вил га́лстук; **they had to ~ their attitude** им пришло́сь пересмотре́ть свои́ пози́ции.

v.i.: **after the war he found it hard to ~** по́сле войны́ ему́ тру́дно бы́ло приспосо́биться.

readjustment [ˌri:ə'dʒʌstmənt] *n.* приспособле́ние, регулиро́вка, перестро́йка; **the speedometer needs ~** спидо́метр на́до отрегули́ровать; **the war brought about a complete ~** война́ вы́звала по́лную перестро́йку жи́зни.

ready ['redɪ] *n.*: **he held his rifle at the ~** он держа́л винто́вку в положе́нии для стрельбы́.

adj. (*prepared; in a fit state*) гото́вый (*к чему*); пригото́вленный, подгото́вленный; **I'm just getting ~** я почти́ гото́в; **she got the children ~ for school** она́ собрала́ дете́й в шко́лу; **~! go!** внима́ние — марш!; **she was ~ to drop with fatigue** она́ па́дала с ног от уста́лости; (*willing*) гото́вый, проявля́ющий гото́вность; **I am ~ to admit I was wrong** гото́в призна́ть, что я был непра́в; **he is ~ for anything** он гото́в ко всему́ (*or* на всё); (*quick, facile*) скло́нный; **you are very ~ to find fault** вы ве́чно придира́етесь; **he is always ~ with an excuse** у него́ всегда́ найдётся отгово́рка; **a ~ wit** нахо́дчивость; (*available*) (име́ющийся) нагото́ве; **~ money** нали́чные де́ньги.

adv.: **they sell meat ~ cooked** там продаётся мясна́я кулина́рия.

cpds. **~-made** *adj.* гото́вый; (*fig.*) изби́тый, шабло́нный; **~-to-wear** *adj.* гото́вый; **~-witted** *adj.* нахо́дчивый, сообрази́тельный.

reaffirm [ˌri:ə'fɜ:m] *v.t.* (вновь) подтвер|жда́ть, -ди́ть.

reaffirmation [ri:æfə'meɪʃ(ə)n] *n.* (повто́рное) подтвержде́ние.

reafforestation [ˌri:əfɒrɪ'steɪʃ(ə)n] = **reforestation**

reagent [ri:'eɪdʒ(ə)nt] *n.* (*chem.*) реакти́в.

real[1] [ri:l] *n.* (*hist., coin*) реа́л.

real[2] [ri:l] *n.*: **for ~** (*coll.*) по-настоя́щему; всерьёз.

adj. (*actual*) реа́льный; реа́льно существу́ющий; настоя́щий; (*genuine*) по́длинный; (*sincere*) и́скренний, неподде́льный; (*substantial, fundamental*) реа́льный, суще́ственный; **was it ~ or a dream?** э́то бы́ло во сне и́ли наяву́?; **in ~ life** в жи́зни; **~ silver** настоя́щее/чи́стое серебро́; **the ~ McCoy** (*coll.*) са́мый настоя́щий; ≃ не придерёшься; **that is not the ~ reason** настоя́щая причи́на не в том; **a ~ gentleman** настоя́щий джентльме́н; **that's what I call a ~ car!** вот э́то маши́на — ничего́ не ска́жешь!; **I have a ~ admiration for him** я им и́скренне восхища́юсь; **he has a ~ grievance** его́ прете́нзии обосно́ваны; **the ~ point is ...** суть вопро́са в том, что...; (*leg.*): **~ estate** недви́жимость.

adv. (*US coll.*): **we had a ~ nice time** мы здо́рово провели́ вре́мя.

realign [ˌri:ə'laɪn] *v.t.* перестр|а́ивать, -о́ить.

realignment [ˌri:ə'laɪnmənt] *n.* перестро́йка.

realism ['ri:əˌlɪz(ə)m] *n.* (*var. senses*) реали́зм.

realist ['rɪəlɪst] *n.* реали́ст (*fem.* -ка)

realistic [rɪə'lɪstɪk] *adj.* (*practical*) реалисти́чный, практи́чный; (*in art etc.*) реалисти́ческий.

reality [rɪ'ælɪtɪ] *n.* реа́льность, существова́ние, действи́тельность; **in ~** в/на са́мом де́ле; в действи́тельности; **it is time he was brought back to ~** ему́ на́до откры́ть глаза́ на фа́кты (*or* спусти́ться на зе́млю); (*sincerity*) и́скренность; (*verisimilitude*) реалисти́чность; по́длинность, достове́рность.

realization [ˌrɪəlaɪ'zeɪʃ(ə)n] *n.* (*recognition*) осозна́ние; (*achievement*) осуществле́ние; (*conversion into money*) реализа́ция, прода́жа.

realize ['rɪəlaɪz] *v.t.* **1.** (*be aware of*) осозн|ава́ть, -а́ть; (*grasp mentally*) сообра|жа́ть, -зи́ть; **he ~d his mistake at once** он сра́зу же осозна́л свою́ оши́бку; **I ~ what you must think of me** представля́ю, что вы обо мне ду́маете; **do you ~ what you have done?** вы понима́ете, что вы сде́лали?; **I didn't ~ you wanted it** до меня́ не дошло́ (*or* мне бы́ло невдомёк), что э́то вам ну́жно. **2.** (*convert into fact*) осуществ|ля́ть, -и́ть; **I will help you to ~ your ambition** я помогу́ вам осуществи́ть ва́ши стремле́ния; **her worst fears were ~d** оправда́лись её са́мые ху́дшие опасе́ния. **3.** (*convert into money*) реализо́в|ывать, -а́ть; превра|ща́ть, -ти́ть в де́ньги. **4.** (*fetch*) выруча́ть, вы́ручить; **the sale ~d over £5,000** при прода́же бы́ло вы́ручено бо́лее пяти́ ты́сяч фу́нтов. **5.** (*amass, gain*) получ|а́ть, -и́ть; **they ~d an enormous profit** они́ получи́ли огро́мную при́быль.

really ['rɪəlɪ] *adv.* действи́тельно; в/на са́мом де́ле; по-настоя́щему; то́чно; **do you ~ mean it?** вы серьёзно?; **he is ~ not such a bad fellow** на са́мом де́ле он не тако́й уж плохо́й челове́к; **did that ~ happen last year?** ра́зве э́то случи́лось в про́шлом году́?; **I am ~ sorry for you** мне вас и́скренне жаль; **I ~ think you should stay** по-мо́ему, вам непреме́нно ну́жно оста́ться; **~, you should be more careful** пра́во же, вам сле́дует быть осторо́жнее; **~?** (*expr. surprise*) серьёзно?, неуже́ли?; (*acknowledging information*) да?, пра́вда?; **~!** (*expr. indignation*) ну, зна́ете!

realm [relm] *n.* королéвство; (*fig.*) сфéра; **peer of the ~** пэр (Великобритáнии); **coin of the ~** ходя́чая монéта; **out of the ~** (*leg.*) за предéлами страны́; (*fig.*): **you are entering the ~s of fancy** вы переносúтесь/вступáете в цáрство фантáзии.

realtor ['ri:əltə(r)] *n.* (*US*) агéнт по продáже недвúжимости.

realty ['ri:əltɪ] *n.* (*leg.*) недвúжимость.

ream [ri:m] *n.* (*quantity of paper*) стопá (= *480 листам*); (*fig.*): **he wrote ~s of nonsense** он написáл бéздну вся́кой чепухú.

reanimate [ri:'ænɪ,meɪt] *v.t.* ож|ивля́ть, -úть; воскре|шáть, -сúть.

reanimation [ri:,ænɪ'meɪʃ(ə)n] *n.* оживлéние, воскрешéние.

reap [ri:p] *v.t. & i.* жать, с-; пож|инáть, -áть; **~ing-hook** серп; **~ing-machine** жáтка; (*fig.*): **he is ~ing where he has not sown** он пожинáет плоды́ чужóго трудá; **he is ~ing the fruits of his folly** он пожинáет плоды́ своéй глýпости.

reaper ['ri:pə(r)] *n.* **1.** (*labourer*) жн|ец (*fem.* -úца); **Death the R~** стáрая с косóй. **2.** (*machine*) жáтка.

reappear [,ri:ə'pɪə(r)] *v.i.* снóва появ|ля́ться, -úться.

reappearance [,ri:ə'pɪərəns] *n.* нóвое появлéние; возрождéние.

reappoint [,ri:ə'pɔɪnt] *v.t.* повтóрно назн|ачáть, -áчить.

reappointment [,ri:ə'pɔɪntmənt] *n.* повтóрное назначéние.

reappraisal [,ri:ə'preɪzəl] *n.* переоцéнка.

reappraise [,ri:ə'preɪz] *v.t.* пересм|áтривать, -отрéть; зáново оцéн|ивать, -úть; переоцéн|ивать, -úть.

rear[1] [rɪə(r)] *n.* **1.** зáдняя чáсть, сторонá; **the kitchen is at the ~ of the house** кýхня — в зáдней чáсти дóма. **2.** (*of army etc.*) тыл; хвост колóнны; **they were attacked in the ~** их атаковáли с ты́ла; **~ services** слýжба ты́ла; **he was a slow runner and always brought up the ~** он плóхо бежáл и всегдá окáзывался в хвостé. **3.** (*coll., buttocks*) зад, зáдница.

adj.: **~ entrance** чёрный ход; **~ wheel** зáднее колесó.

cpds. **~-admiral** *n.* контр-адмирáл; **~guard** *n.* арьергáрд; **~guard action** арьергáрдный бой; **~most** *adj.* сáмый зáдний; послéдний.

rear[2] [rɪə(r)] *v.t.* **1.** (*raise, erect*) воздв|игáть, -úгнуть; **a monument was ~ed on the spot** на э́том мéсте был воздвúгнут пáмятник; **jealousy ~ed its head** (в нём *и т.п.*) зашевелúлась рéвность. **2.** (*bring up*) растúть (*or* вырáщивать), вы́-; воспúт|ывать, -áть; **the children were ~ed by foster-parents** детéй воспитáли/вы́растили приёмные родúтели; (*breed*) разв|одúть, -естú; **cattle are ~ed on the plains** скот развóдят на равнúнах.

v.i. (*also* **~ up**) ста|новúться, -ть на дыбы́; **the horse ~ed in terror** лóшадь (в)сталá на дыбы́ от испýга.

re-arise [,ri:ə'raɪz] *v.i.* снóва возн|икáть, -úкнуть; возро|ждáться, -дúться.

rearm [ri:'ɑ:m] *v.t. & i.* перевоорýж|áть(ся), -úть(ся).

rearmament [ri:'ɑ:məmənt] *n.* перевооружéние.

rearrange [,ri:ə'reɪndʒ] *v.t.* перестр|áивать -óить; перест|авля́ть, -áвить; передв|игáть, -úнуть.

rearrangement [,ri:ə'reɪndʒmənt] *n.* перестанóвка, перестрóйка, перегруппирóвка.

rearward ['rɪəwəd] *n.* тыл; **in the ~** в тылý; **to the ~ of** позадú+*g.*

adj. тыловóй, зáдний.

rearwards ['rɪəwədz] *adv.* назáд; в тыл; на попя́тную.

reascend [,ri:ə'send] *v.t. & i.* снóва подн|имáться, -я́ться; снóва восходúть, взойтú (на+*a.*).

reascent [,ri:ə'sent] *n.* повтóрный подъём; нóвое восхождéние.

reason ['ri:z(ə)n] *n.* **1.** (*cause, ground*) причúна; **he refused to give his ~s** он отказáлся объяснúть; **there is ~ to believe that ...** есть основáния полагáть, что...; **that is no ~ for thinking ...** э́то не даёт основáния дýмать, что...; **with ~** обоснóванно; **for no good ~** без уважúтельной причúны; **he resigned for ~s of health** он увóлился по состоя́нию здорóвья; **for the simple ~ that ...** по той простóй причúне, что...; **give back the money, or I'll know the ~ why** отдáй дéньги, а то пожалéешь; **he was excused by ~ of his age** егó освободúли, приня́в во внимáние вóзраст. **2.** (*intellectual faculty*) рáзум, рассýдок; **he lost his ~** он лишúлся рассýдка. **3.** (*good sense, moderation*) благоразýмие; **he will not listen to ~** он не прислýшивается к гóлосу рáзума; **he was brought to ~** егó удалóсь образýмить; **his actions are without rhyme or ~** в егó постýпках нет никакóго смы́сла; **it stands to ~** разумéется; **I will do anything in ~** я сдéлаю всё в предéлах разýмного; **there is ~ in what you say** то, что вы говорúте, разýмно/резóнно.

v.t. **1.** (*argue, contend*) докáзывать (*impf.*). **2.** (*express logically*): **a ~ed argument** обоснóванный дóвод. **3.** (*persuade by argument*) убе|ждáть, -дúть; **he ~ed her out of her fears** он убедúл её, что её стрáхи необоснóваны. **4.: ~ out** (*solve by ~ing*) разгáд|ывать, -áть.

v.i.: **it is useless to ~ with him** егó бесполéзно убеждáть; лóгика на негó не дéйствует.

reasonable ['ri:zənəb(ə)l] *adj.* **1.** (*sensible, amenable to reason*) (благо)разýмный. **2.** (*moderate*) умéренный, приéмлемый; **he has a ~ chance of success** у негó неплохúе шáнсы на успéх. **3.** (*of price*) недорогóй; **the charges are ~** (онú) берýт недóрого; **the shoes are quite ~** тýфли стóят недóрого.

reasonableness ['ri:zənəb(ə)lnɪs] *n.* благоразýмие, рассудúтельность; (*of prices*) умéренность.

reasoning ['ri:zənɪŋ] *n.* рассуждéние, аргументáция; **the ~ faculty, powers of ~** спосóбность рассуждáть.

reassemble [,ri:ə'semb(ə)l] *v.t.* снóва соб|ирáть, -рáть; (*tech.*) переб|ирáть, -рáть.

v.i. снóва соб|ирáться, -рáться; снóва встр|ечáться, -éтиться.

reassembly [,ri:ə'semb(ə)lɪ] *n.* (*of committee etc.*) возобновлённое заседáние (пóсле переры́ва); (*tech.*) перебóрка.

reassert [,ri:ə'sɜ:t] *v.t.* снóва подтвер|ждáть, -дúть; снóва выдвигáть, вы́двинуть; **~ o.s.** самоутверждáться (*impf.*).

reassertion [,ri:ə'sɜ:ʃ(ə)n] *n.* повтóрное заверéние, подтверждéние.

reassess [,ri:ə'ses] *v.t.* переоцéн|ивать, -úть.

reassessment [,ri:ə'sesmənt] *n.* переоцéнка.

reassign [,ri:ə'saɪn] *v.t.* назн|ачáть, -áчить на другóе мéсто; перев|одúть, -естú; перераспредел|я́ть, -úть.

reassignment [,ri:ə'saɪnmənt] *n.* перевóд, перераспределéние.

reassume [,ri:ə'sju:m] *v.t.* снóва брать, взять (*or* прин|имáть, -я́ть) на себя́.

reassumption [,ri:ə'sʌmpʃ(ə)n] *n.* повтóрное принятие (на себя́).

reassurance [,ri:ə'ʃʊərəns] *n.* (повтóрное) заверéние, подтверждéние.

reassur|e [,ri:ə'ʃʊə(r)] *v.t.* успок|áивать, -óить; подбодр|я́ть, -úть; зав|еря́ть, -éрить; **I can ~e you on that point** я могý успокóить вас на э́тот счёт; **his words were most ~ing** егó словá звучáли сáмым ободря́ющим óбразом.

reattach [,ri:ə'tætʃ] *v.t.* снóва прикреп|ля́ть, -úть; (*mil.*) переподчин|я́ть, -úть.

reattachment [,ri:ə'tætʃmənt] *n.* повтóрное прикреплéние; (*mil.*) переподчинéние.

Réaumur ['reɪəʊ,mjʊə(r)] *n.* Реомю́р.

reawaken [,ri:ə'weɪkən] *v.t.* снóва пробу|ждáть, -дúть; возро|ждáть, -дúть.

reawakening [,ri:ə'weɪkənɪŋ] *n.* нóвое пробуждéние; возрождéние.

rebarbative [rɪ'bɑ:bətɪv] *adj.* оттáлкивающий, непривлекáтельный.

rebate ['ri:beɪt] *n.* (*discount*) скúдка; вы́чет.

rebel[1] ['reb(ə)l] *n.* (*against government*) повстáнец, мятéжник; бунтовщú|к (*fem.* -ца), бунтáрь (*m.*); (*attr.*) повстáнческий; бунтáрский.

rebel[2] [rɪ'bel] *v.i.* восст|авáть, -áть; бунтовáть, взбунтовáться; **the tribes ~led against the government** племенá восстáли прóтив правúтельства; **such treatment would make anyone ~** прóтив такóго обращéния кто угóдно взбунтýется.

rebellion [rɪ'beljən] *n.* восстáние, мятéж, бунт.

rebellious [rɪ'beljəs] *adj.* (*in revolt*) восстáвший, мятéжный, повстáнческий; (*disobedient*) строптúвый, непокóрный.

rebelliousness [rɪ'beljəsnɪs] *n.* бунтáрство, непослушáние, непокóрность.

rebind [riːˈbaɪnd] *v.t.* зáново перепле|тáть, -стú.
rebirth [riːˈbɜːθ, ˈriː-] *n.* вторóе рождéние, возрождéние, воскресéние.
rebore [riːˈbɔː(r)] *v.t.* раст|áчивать, -очúть.
reborn [riːˈbɔːn] *adj.* возрождённый, возродúвшийся, перерождúвшийся.
rebound[1] [rɪˈbaʊnd] *n.* отскóк, рикошéт; **on the ~** рикошéтом; (*fig.*): **he married her on the ~** он женúлся на ней с досáды.
rebound[2] [rɪˈbaʊnd] *v.i.* отск|áкивать, -очúть; **the ball ~ed against the wall** мяч отскочúл от стены́; (*fig.*): **your action may ~ on yourself** э́то мóжет обернýться прóтив вас самúх.
rebuff [rɪˈbʌf] *n.* отпóр, рéзкий откáз, попрáние.
v.t.: **she ~ed his advances** онá пресеклá егó заúгрывания; **the enemy's attack was ~ed** атáка неприя́теля былá отбúта/отраженá.
rebuild [riːˈbɪld] *v.t.* снóва стрóить, по-; перестр|áивать, -óить; застр|áивать, -óить; реконструúровать (*impf., pf.*).
rebuke [rɪˈbjuːk] *n.* упрёк, укóр; вы́говор, замечáние.
v.t. упрек|áть, -нýть; укоря́ть (*impf.*); дéлать, с- замечáние/вы́говор +*d*.
rebus [ˈriːbəs] *n.* рéбус.
rebut [rɪˈbʌt] *v.t.* опров|ергáть, -éргнуть; отв|ергáть, -éргнуть.
rebuttal [rɪˈbʌtəl] *n.* опровержéние.
recalcitrance [rɪˈkælsɪtrəns] *n.* непокóрность, непослушáние.
recalcitrant [rɪˈkælsɪtrənt] *adj.* непокóрный, непослýшный; с нóровом.
recalculate [riːˈkælkjʊˌleɪt] *v.t.* пересчúт|ывать, -áть.
recalculation [riːˌkælkjʊˈleɪʃ(ə)n] *n.* пересчёт.
recall [ˈriːkɔl] *n.* **1.** (*summons to return*) óтзыв; (*signal to return*) сигнáл к возвращéнию; (*bringing back*): **the letters are lost beyond ~** э́ти пúсьма бесслéдно исчéзли. **2.** (*recollection*) воспоминáние; пáмять; **total ~** пóлное восстановлéние в пáмяти.
v.t. **1.** (*summon back*) от|зывáть, -озвáть; **the ambassador was ~ed** послá отозвáли; **he was ~ed from furlough** егó вы́звали из óтпуска. **2.** (*bring back to mind*) нап|оминáть, -óмнить; **this ~s my childhood to me** э́то напоминáет мне дéтство; **I ~ed his words** я вспóмнил егó словá; **can you ~ where you lost the bag?** вы мóжете припóмнить, где вы остáвили сýмку? **3.** (*revoke*) отмен|я́ть, -úть; брать, взять обрáтно; **the order was ~ed** прикáз отменúли.
recant [rɪˈkænt] *v.t. & i.* публúчно кáяться, рас- (*в чём*); отр|екáться, -éчься (*от чего*).
recantation [ˌriːkænˈteɪʃ(ə)n] *n.* отречéние; публúчное покая́ние.
recap [ˈriːkæp] (*coll.*) *n.* повторéние.
v.t. & i. = **recapitulate**
recapitulate [ˌriːkəˈpɪtjʊˌleɪt] *v.t.* повтор|я́ть, -úть; резюмúровать (*impf., pf.*).
recapitulation [ˌriːkəˌpɪtjʊˈleɪʃ(ə)n] *n.* повторéние; резюмé (*indecl.*); суммúрование.
recapture [riːˈkæptʃə(r)] *n.* повтóрный захвáт; взя́тие обрáтно.
v.t. взять (*pf.*) обрáтно; поймáть (*pf.*); **the prisoner was ~d** заключённого поймáли; (*fig.*) восстан|áвливать, -овúть в пáмяти; **I tried to ~ my first impressions** я пытáлся восстановúть свои́ пéрвые впечатлéния.
recast [riːˈkɑːst] *v.t.* **1.** (*cast again, e.g. a gun*) отл|ивáть, -úть зáново. **2.** (*rewrite, rephrase*) перерабá|тывать, -óтать; испр|авля́ть, -áвить. **3.** (*remodel, refashion*) передéл|ывать, -ать; перестр|áивать, -óить. **4.** (*change cast*) перераспредел|я́ть, -úть рóли в (*пьесе*).
recce [ˈrekɪ] (*coll.*) = **reconnaissance**
reced|e [rɪˈsiːd] *v.i.* **1.** (*move back*) отступ|áть, -úть; от|ходúть, -ойтú; **the tide was ~ing** водá спадáла; начался́ отлúв; **~ing hair** редéющие вóлосы. **2.** (*slope back*) отклоня́ться (*impf.*) назáд; **a ~ing chin** срéзанный подборóдок; **a ~ing cliff** навúсшая скалá. **3.** (*fig., withdraw*) от|ходúть, -ойтú. **4.** (*decline*) пон|ижáться, -úзиться; **~ing prices** снижáющиеся цéны.
receipt [rɪˈsiːt] *n.* **1.** (*receiving*) получéние; **on ~ of the news** по получéнии извéстия; **I am in ~ of your letter** Вáше письмó мнóю полýчено. **2.** (*pl., money received*) дéнежные поступлéния. **3.** (*written acknowledgement*) распúска, квитáнция.
v.t.: **~ a bill** распúс|ываться, -áться на счёте.
receive [rɪˈsiːv] *v.t.* **1.** (*get, be given*) получ|áть, -úть; **your letter will ~ attention** вáше письмó бýдет рассмóтрено; **he ~d a warm welcome** емý оказáли тёплый приём; **he ~d injuries** он получúл ранéния; **he ~d severe punishment** он подвéргся сурóвому наказáнию; **information has not yet been ~d** свéдения ещё не поступúли; **that is not the impression I ~d** у меня́ создалóсь инóе впечатлéние; **they ~d the sacrament** онú причастúлись; **he ~s stolen goods** он укрывáет крáденое. **2.** (*admit*) прин|имáть, -я́ть; допус|кáть, -тúть; **I am not receiving guests** я не принимáю гостéй; **he was ~d into the Church** егó прúняли в лóно цéркви; (*give reception to, greet*) прин|имáть, -я́ть; **he was ~d with open arms** егó встрéтили с распростёртыми объя́тиями; **how was your speech ~d?** как бы́ло встрéчено вáше выступлéние?; **how did he ~ the news?** как он восприня́л э́ту нóвость? **3.** (*hold, contain*) вме|щáть, -стúть. **4.** (*accept as true, accurate etc.*) призн|авáть, -áть прáвильным; **~d religion** госпóдствующая релúгия; **~d pronunciation** норматúвное произношéние. **5.** (*bear weight or impact of*): **he ~d the bullet in his shoulder** пýля попáла емý в плечó. **6.** (*obtain signals from*): **are you receiving me?** вы меня́ слы́шите?; **can you ~ the third programme?** ваш приёмник берёт трéтью прогрáмму?; **broadcast receiving licence** лицéнзия на пóльзование радиоприёмником.
receiver [rɪˈsiːvə(r)] *n.* **1.** получáтель (*m.*); (*of stolen goods*) укрывáтель (*m.*) крáденого. **2.** (**official ~**) ликвидáтор, управля́ющий кóнкурсной мáссой. **3.** (**telephone ~**) (телефóнная) трýбка; **lift the ~** подн|имáть, -я́ть трýбку; **replace the ~** класть, положúть трýбку. **4.** (**radio ~**) (радио)приёмник.
recension [rɪˈsenʃ(ə)n] *n.* пересмóтренное издáние; испрáвленный вариáнт; редáкция.
recent [ˈriːs(ə)nt] *adj.* **1.** (*occurring lately*) недáвний; **within ~ memory** за послéднее врéмя. **2.** (*modern*) совремéнный.
recently [ˈriːsəntlɪ] *adv.* недáвно, на днях, за послéднее врéмя; **until quite ~** ещё совсéм недáвно.
receptacle [rɪˈseptək(ə)l] *n.* вместúлище, приёмник.
reception [rɪˈsepʃ(ə)n] *n.* **1.** (*of guests etc.*) приём; **they are having a ~** онú даю́т приём; **~ area** (*of camp etc.*) лáгерь приёма пополнéния; **~ centre** приёмник; **~ clerk** (*in hotel, hospital*) (*also* **~ist**) регистрáтор, дежýрный; (*in a business firm*) секретáр|ь (*fem.* -ша) по приёму посетúтелей; **~ desk** (*in hotel*) регистрáция, контóрка портьé; (*in hospital*) регистратýра; **~ room** приёмная. **2.** (*greeting, display of feeling*) встрéча, приём; **he was given a great ~** емý устрóили великолéпный приём; **his book had a lukewarm ~** егó кнúга былá встрéчена хóлодно. **3.** (*of ideas etc.*) восприя́тие. **4.** (*of radio signals*) приём; **~ is good in this area** в э́том райóне хорóший приём.
receptionist [rɪˈsepʃənɪst] *see* **reception 1.**
receptive [rɪˈseptɪv] *adj.* восприúмчивый.
receptivity [ˌriːsepˈtɪvɪtɪ] *n.* восприúмчивость.
recess [rɪˈses, ˈriːses] *n.* **1.** (*vacation*) переры́в; **Parliament has gone into ~** парлáмент распýщен на канúкулы. **2.** (*alcove, niche*) нúша, алькóв. **3.** (*secret place*) тайнúк; укрóмный уголóк; **in the ~es of the heart** в глубинé душú.
v.t. (*set back*) отодв|игáть, -úнуть назáд.
v.i. (*adjourn*): **the court ~ed** был объя́влен переры́в в заседáнии судá.
recession [rɪˈseʃ(ə)n] *n.* (*withdrawal*) ухóд, отступлéние; (*slump*) спад.
recessional [rɪˈseʃən(ə)l] *n.* послéднее песнопéние (*перед концом службы*).
recessive [rɪˈsesɪv] *adj.*: **~ characteristic** (*biol.*) рецессúвный прúзнак.
recharge [riːˈtʃɑːdʒ] *v.t.* перезаря|жáть, -дúть; **he ate to ~ his energies** он ел, чтóбы восстановúть свои́ сúлы.
recherché [rəˈʃeəʃeɪ] *adj.* (*choice*) изы́сканный, тóнкий; (*far-fetched*) вы́чурный.

rechristen [riːˈkrɪs(ə)n] *v.t.* (*fig.*) переименóв|ывать, -áть.

recidivism [rɪˈsɪdɪvˌɪz(ə)m] *n.* рецидúв.

recidivist [rɪˈsɪdɪvɪst] *n.* рецидивúст.

recipe [ˈresɪpɪ] *n.* (*lit.*, *fig.*) рецéпт; **a ~ for happiness** секрéт счáстья.

recipient [rɪˈsɪpɪənt] *n.* получáтель (*fem.* -ница); (*med.*, *also*) реципиéнт.

reciprocal [rɪˈsɪprək(ə)l] *n.* (*math.*) обрáтная величинá.

adj. (*mutual*) взаúмный (*also gram.*), обоюдный; (*inversely corresponding*) обрáтный.

reciprocate [rɪˈsɪprəˌkeɪt] *v.t.* отв|ечáть, -éтить взаúмностью; **she ~ed his feelings** онá отвечáла емý взаúмностью; **they ~ed presents** онú обменя́лись подáрками.

v.i. **1.** (*move back and forth*) двúгаться (*impf.*) взад и вперёд; **~ing engine** поршневóй двúгатель. **2.** (*make a return*) отплá|чивать, -тúть; отвечáть (*impf.*) тем же; **I bought him a drink and he ~ed** я угостúл егó винóм, а он — меня́.

reciprocation [rɪˌsɪprəˈkeɪʃ(ə)n] *n.* отвéтное дéйствие; обмéн.

reciprocity [ˌresɪˈprɒsɪtɪ] *n.* взаúмность; взаимодéйствие; обмéн.

recital [rɪˈsaɪt(ə)l] *n.* (*narration*) изложéние; повествовáние; (*entertainment*) сóльный концéрт; **song ~** сóльный вокáльный концéрт.

recitation [ˌresɪˈteɪʃ(ə)n] *n.* декламáция; **there is to be a ~ from Shakespeare** бýдут читáть отры́вки из Шекспúра; **we heard a ~ of her troubles** мы услы́шали подрóбный расскáз о её несчáстьях.

recitative [ˌresɪtəˈtiːv] *n.* речитатúв.

recite [rɪˈsaɪt] *v.t.* (*declaim from memory*) декламúровать, про-; (*enumerate*) переч|исля́ть, -úслить.

reck [rek] *v.t.* (*arch.*) забóтиться (*impf.*); **he ~ed nothing of danger** он не счита́лся с опáсностью.

reckless [ˈreklɪs] *adj.* безрассýдный, опромéтчивый; отчáянный; **a ~ disregard of consequences** бездýмное пренебрежéние послéдствиями; **he drove ~ly** он неосторóжно вёл машúну; **a ~ spender** мот.

recklessness [ˈreklɪsnɪs] *n.* безрассýдность, опромéтчивость, отчáянность.

reckon [ˈrekən] *v.t.* **1.** (*calculate*) считáть, вы́-; **he never ~s the cost** он никогдá не учúтывает расхóдов; **charges are ~ed from the first of the month** плáта исчисля́ется с пéрвого числá кáждого мéсяца. **2.** (*consider*, *rate*) считáть (*impf.*); **do you ~ him to be a great writer?** вы считáете егó велúким писáтелем? **3.** (*coll.*, *opine*) полагáть (*impf.*); **I ~ he will win** я дýмаю, что он победúт.

v.i. **1.** (*count*) считáть (*impf.*); **he is a man to be ~ed with** с такúм человéком, как он, нýжно считáться; **he ~ed without the English climate** он не взял в расчёт англúйский клúмат. **2.** (*rely*, *depend*) рассчúтывать (*impf.*) (*на кого/что*); **he ~ed on making a clear profit** он рассчúтывал на чúстую прúбыль. **3.** (*settle account*) (*lit.*, *fig.*) рассчúт|ываться, -áться; (*fig.*) расквитáться (*pf.*).

reckoner [ˈrekənə(r)] *n.*: **ready ~** сбóрник вычислúтельных таблúц.

reckoning [ˈrekənɪŋ] *n.* **1.** (*calculation*) счёт, вычислéние; **dead ~** (*nav.*, *aeron.*) навигациóнное счислéние; **he is out in his ~** он ошúбся в расчётах. **2.** (*account*) расплáта; **day of ~** (*fig.*) час расплáты; **there will be a heavy ~ to pay** расплáта предстоúт тя́жкая.

reclaim [rɪˈkleɪm] *n.* = **reclamation; beyond ~** неисправúмый.

v.t. **1.** (*reform*) испр|авля́ть, -áвить. **2.** (*civilize*) перевоспúт|ывать, -áть. **3.** (*bring under cultivation*) осв|áивать, -óить. **4.** (*demand return of*) трéбовать, по- обрáтно.

reclamation [ˌrekləˈmeɪʃ(ə)n] *n.* **1.** исправлéние, улучшéние. **2.** перевоспитáние. **3.** освоéние.

réclame [ˈreɪklɑːm] *n.* реклáма, рекламúрование.

reclassification [riːˌklæsɪfɪˈkeɪʃ(ə)n] *n.* перевóд в другýю категóрию; реклассификáция, пересортирóвка.

reclassify [riːˈklæsɪˌfaɪ] *v.t.* перев|одúть, -естú в другýю категóрию; пересортирóв|ывать, -áть; переклассифицúровать (*impf.*, *pf.*).

recline [rɪˈklaɪn] *v.t.* откú|дывать, -úнуть ; **she ~d her head on his shoulder** онá склонúла гóлову емý на плечó; **he ~d his head against the back of the chair** он сидéл, откúнув гóлову на спúнку крéсла.

v.i. (полу)лежáть (*impf.*); возлежáть (*impf.*); **they ~d on the ground** онú разлеглúсь на землé; **he ~d against the mantelpiece** он стоя́л, прислонúвшись к камúну; **reclining nude** лежáщая обнажённая.

reclothe [riːˈkləʊð] *v.t.* снóва од|евáть, -éть; од|евáть, -éть в нóвое.

recluse [rɪˈkluːs] *n.* затвóрник, отшéльник.

recognition [ˌrekəgˈnɪʃ(ə)n] *n.* **1.** (*knowing again*) опознавáние; **he changed beyond ~** он изменúлся до неузнавáемости. **2.** (*acknowledgement*) признáние; **the ~ of Communist China** признáние коммунистúческого Китáя; **he received a cheque in ~ of his services** он получúл чек в знак признáния егó услýг.

recognizable [ˈrekəgˌnaɪzəb(ə)l] *adj.* опознавáемый.

recognizance [rɪˈkɒgnɪz(ə)ns] *n.* (*bond*) ≃ обязáтельство, дáнное в судé; (*sum pledged*) залóг.

recognize [ˈrekəgˌnaɪz] *v.t.* **1.** (*know again*) узн|авáть, -áть; **I could barely ~ him** я егó éле узнáл. **2.** (*acknowledge*) призн|авáть, -áть; **he was ~d as the lawful heir** он был прúзнан закóнным наслéдником.

recoil [ˈriːkɔɪl] *n.* отскóк; отдáча.

v.i. **1.** (*shrink back*) отпря́нуть (*pf.*); отпры́г|ивать, -нуть; отшáт|ываться, -нýться; **the sight made him ~ with horror** зрéлище застáвило егó отпря́нуть в ýжасе. **2.** (*of gun*) откáт|ываться, -úться; (*of rifle*) отд|авáть, -áть. **3.** (*rebound*) удáрить (*pf.*) рикошéтом; (*fig.*) отра|жáться, -зúться (*на ком*); **his scheme ~ed on his own head** он попáл в сéти, котóрые сам расстáвил.

recollect [ˌrekəˈlekt] *v.t.* всп|оминáть, -óмнить; прип|оминáть, -óмнить.

recollection [ˌrekəˈlekʃ(ə)n] *n.* пáмять; воспоминáние; **to the best of my ~** наскóлько я пóмню; **the music brought back ~s of the past** мýзыка оживúла в пáмяти прóшлое.

recommence [ˌriːkəˈmens] *v.t.* возобнов|ля́ть, -úть; нач|инáть, -áть снóва.

v.i. возобнов|ля́ться, -úться.

recommend [ˌrekəˈmend] *v.t.* **1.** (*speak well of*; *suggest as suitable*) рекомендовáть (*impf.*, *pf.*), от-/по- (*pf.*); совéтовать, по-; **he was ~ed for promotion** егó вы́двинули на повышéние. **2.** (*make acceptable*): **his appearance did not ~ him** егó нарýжность не располагáла (к немý). **3.** (*advise*) рекомендовáть, по- *+d.*; совéтовать, по- *+d.* **4.** (*commend*) вв|еря́ть, -éрить; поруч|áть, -úть; **the child was ~ed to their care** ребёнка отдáли на их попечéние.

recommendation [ˌrekəˌmenˈdeɪʃ(ə)n] *n.* рекомендáция; **I bought the shares on your ~** я купúл áкции по вáшей рекомендáции; **my ~ would be to sell them** я бы посовéтовал продáть их; **that is no ~ of him** э́то не говорúт в егó пóльзу.

recompense [ˈrekəmˌpens] *n.* компенсáция; **in ~ for your help** в вознаграждéние за вáшу пóмощь.

v.t. компенсúровать (*impf.*, *pf.*); **he was amply ~d for his trouble** егó щéдро вознаградúли за егó усúлия; **his losses were barely ~d** емý едвá возместúли убы́тки.

reconcilable [ˈrekənˌsaɪləb(ə)l] *adj.* (*compatible*) совместúмый (*с чем*).

reconcile [ˈrekənˌsaɪl] *v.t.* **1.** (*make friendly*) мирúть, по-; **they finally became ~d** онú, наконéц, помирúлись. **2.** (*settle*, *compose*) улá|живать, -дить; **their differences were ~d** онú улáдили своú разноглáсия. **3.** (*cause to agree*, *make compatible*) совме|щáть, -стúть; согласóв|ывать, -áть; **how can you ~ this with your principles?** как же э́то сочетáется с вáшими прúнципами? **4.** (*resign*): **~ o.s.** смир|я́ться, -úться (*с чем*); примир|я́ться, -úться (*с чем*); **you must ~ yourself to a life of poverty** вы должны́ примирúться с пожúзненной бéдностью.

reconcil|ement [ˈrekənˌsaɪlmənt], **-iation** [ˌrekənˌsɪlɪˈeɪʃ(ə)n] *nn.* примирéние; улáживание.

recondite [ˈrekənˌdaɪt, rɪˈkɒn-] *adj.* (*obscure*) заýмный, малоизвéстный; (*of subject*, *specialized*) извéстный ýзкому крýгу.

recondition [ˌriːkənˈdɪʃ(ə)n] *v.t.* ремонти́ровать, от-.

reconnaissance [rɪˈkɒnɪs(ə)ns] *n.* разве́дка; ~ **party** разве́дывательная гру́ппа; разве́дывательный отря́д.

reconnoitre [ˌrekəˈnɔɪtə(r)] *v.t. & i.* разве́дывать (*impf.*); производи́ть (*impf.*) разве́дку.

reconquer [riːˈkɒŋkə(r)] *v.t.* отвоёв|ывать, -а́ть.

reconquest [riːˈkɒŋkwest] *n.* возвраще́ние, возвра́т (поте́рянной террито́рии *и т.п.*).

reconsider [ˌriːkənˈsɪdə(r)] *v.t.* пересм|а́тривать, -отре́ть.
v.i. переду́мать (*pf.*).

reconsideration [ˌriːkənˌsɪdəˈreɪʃ(ə)n] *n.* пересмо́тр; измене́ние реше́ния; **on ~ he decided to stay** поду́мав, он реши́л оста́ться.

reconstitute [riːˈkɒnstɪˌtjuːt] *v.t.* воспроизв|оди́ть, -ести́.

reconstitution [ˌriːkɒnstɪˈtjuːʃ(ə)n] *n.* воспроизведе́ние, воссозда́ние.

reconstruct [ˌriːkənˈstrʌkt] *v.t.* перестр|а́ивать, -о́ить; реконструи́ровать (*impf., pf.*); (*fig.*) воспроизв|оди́ть, -ести́; **the police ~ed the crime** поли́ция воспроизвела́ карти́ну преступле́ния.

reconstruction [ˌriːkənˈstrʌkʃ(ə)n] *n.* перестро́йка, реконстру́кция; (*of acts etc.*) воспроизведе́ние, воссозда́ние.

reconvene [ˌriːkənˈviːn] *v.t.* соз|ыва́ть, -ва́ть вновь.
v.i. соб|ира́ться, -ра́ться вновь.

reconversion [ˌriːkənˈvɜːʃ(ə)n] *n.* (*e.g. of currency*) реконве́рсия; (*of industry*) перево́д на ми́рные ре́льсы.

reconvert [ˌriːkənˈvɜːt] *v.t.* пров|оди́ть, -ести́ реконве́рсию +*g.*; (*industry*) перев|оди́ть, -ести́ на ми́рные ре́льсы.

record[1] [ˈrekɔːd] *n.* **1.** (*written note, document*) за́пись, учёт; **the teacher keeps a ~ of attendance** учи́тель ведёт учёт посеща́емости; **weather ~s** регистра́ция метеорологи́ческих да́нных; **~s department** отде́л учёта; **R~ Office** госуда́рственный архи́в. **2.** (*state of being recorded, esp. as evidence*) за́пись; **it is a matter of ~** э́то зафикси́ровано/зарегистри́ровано; **it is on ~ that you lost every game** изве́стно, что вы проигра́ли все ма́тчи; **it was the hottest day on ~** э́то был са́мый жа́ркий день из ра́нее зафикси́рованных; **I went on ~ as opposing the plan** в протоко́ле бы́ло отме́чено, что я про́тив э́того пла́на; **this is off the ~** э́то не должно́ быть пре́дано огла́ске. **3.** (*relic of past*) па́мятник; **~s of past civilizations** па́мятники про́шлых цивилиза́ций. **4.** (*chronicle*) ле́топись; **the film provides an interesting ~ of the war** э́тот фильм интере́сен как ле́топись войны́. **5.** (*past achievement*) про́шлое; **attendance ~** посеща́емость; **he has an honourable ~ of service** у него́ безупре́чный послужно́й спи́сок; **this firm has a bad ~ for strikes** э́та фи́рма изве́стна многочи́сленными забасто́вками; **his ~ is against him** его́ про́шлое говори́т про́тив него́; **the defendant had a (criminal) ~** у обвиня́емого ра́нее име́лись суди́мости. **6.** (*sound recording*) (грам)пласти́нка; **long-playing ~** долгоигра́ющая пласти́нка; **is that symphony on ~?** запи́сана ли э́та симфо́ния на пласти́нку?; **they made a new ~ of the song** вы́пустили ещё одну́ за́пись э́той пе́сни. **7.** (*best performance*) реко́рд; **world ~** реко́рд ми́ра; **she set up a new ~ for the mile** она́ установи́ла но́вый реко́рд в бе́ге на одну́ ми́лю; **England held the ~ for some years** э́тот реко́рд принадлежа́л А́нглии не́сколько лет; **he will easily beat the ~** он легко́ побьёт реко́рд; **equal a ~** повтор|я́ть, -и́ть реко́рд; (*attr.*) реко́рдный, небыва́лый; **we shall have a ~ apple crop** у нас бу́дет реко́рдный урожа́й я́блок; **he set off at a ~ pace** он с ме́ста разви́л реко́рдную ско́рость; **cars have had ~ sales** про́дано реко́рдное коли́чество маши́н.
cpds. **~-breaking** *adj.* реко́рдный; **~-holder** *n.* рекордсме́н (*fem.* -ка); **~-player** *n.* прои́грыватель (*m.*).

record[2] [rɪˈkɔːd] *v.t.* **1.** (*set down in writing, or fig.*) запи́с|ывать, -а́ть; протоколи́ровать, за-; **the book ~s his early years** в кни́ге отражены́ его́ молоды́е го́ды; **the ~ing angel** а́нгел, отмеча́ющий до́брые дела́ и грехи́. **2.** (*on tape, film etc.*) запи́с|ывать, -а́ть (на плёнку); **the camera ~ed his features** фотоаппара́т запечатле́л его́ черты́. **3.** (*of instrument: register*) регистри́ровать, за-; **the thermometer ~ed zero** термо́метр пока́зывал ноль.

recorder [rɪˈkɔːdə(r)] *n.* (*magistrate*) реко́рдер; (*apparatus*) магнитофо́н; (*mus.*) (англи́йская) фле́йта.

recording [rɪˈkɔːdɪŋ] *n.* (*putting on record*) за́пись, регистра́ция; (*registering of sound or TV*) звукоза́пись; видеоза́пись; (*recorded performance etc.*) за́пись.

recount[1] [riːˈkaʊnt] *n.* (*second count*) пересчёт.
v.t. пересчи́т|ывать, -а́ть.

recount[2] [rɪˈkaʊnt] *v.t.* (*narrate*) расска́з|ывать, -а́ть.

recoup [rɪˈkuːp] *v.t.* **1.** (*leg., deduct*) уде́рж|ивать, -а́ть. **2.** (*recover*): **~ one's losses** возвраща́ть, верну́ть поте́рянное. **3.** (*compensate*) возме|ща́ть, -сти́ть (*что кому*); компенси́ровать (*impf., pf.*) (*кого за что*).

recourse [rɪˈkɔːs] *n.* прибе́жище; вы́ход; **your only ~ is legal action** вам ничего́ не остаётся де́лать, как обрати́ться в суд; **have ~ to** приб|ега́ть, -е́гнуть к+*d.*

recover[1] [rɪˈkʌvə(r)] *v.t.* **1.** (*regain, retrieve*) получ|а́ть, -и́ть обра́тно; доста́ть (*pf.*), верну́ть (*pf.*); **he tried to ~ his losses** он пыта́лся верну́ть поте́рянное; **you will never ~ lost time** вы никогда́ не наверста́ете упу́щенного вре́мени; **he quickly ~ed his health** он бы́стро вы́здоровел; **will he ~ the use of his legs?** смо́жет ли он когда́-нибудь сно́ва ходи́ть?; **she never ~ed consciousness** она́ так и не пришла́ в созна́ние; **he ~ed his appetite** к нему́ возврати́лся аппети́т; **she was badly shocked, but ~ed herself** она́ была́ си́льно потрясена́, но пото́м пришла́ в себя́; **he staggered, but ~ed himself** он оступи́лся, но сохрани́л равнове́сие; (*win back*) отвоёв|ывать, -а́ть; **much land has been ~ed from the sea** мно́го су́ши отвоёвано у мо́ря. **2.** (*secure by legal process*) взы́ск|ивать, -а́ть в суде́бном поря́дке; **an action to ~ damages** иск о возмеще́нии уще́рба.
v.i. **1.** (*revive*) попр|авля́ться, -а́виться; опр|авля́ться, -а́виться; **has he quite ~ed (from his illness)?** оконча́тельно ли он опра́вился от боле́зни?; **I have quite ~ed** я по́лностью вы́здоровел; **it took me some time to ~ from my astonishment** я до́лго не мог прийти́ в себя́ от удивле́ния; **we must help the country to ~** мы должны́ помо́чь стране́ сно́ва встать на́ ноги. **2.** (*leg.*) возме|ща́ть, -сти́ть по суду́; **plaintiff shall ~** (*sc. damages*) надлежи́т возмести́ть убы́тки, понесённые истцо́м.

recover[2] [riːˈkʌvə(r)] *v.t.* сно́ва покр|ыва́ть, -ы́ть; перекр|ыва́ть, -ы́ть; **the chair needs ~ing** стул на́до оби́ть на́ново.

recovery [rɪˈkʌvərɪ] *n.* **1.** (*regaining possession; reclamation*) возвра́т; возмеще́ние; **the ~ of your money will take time** пройдёт вре́мя, пре́жде чем вы полу́чите свои́ де́ньги обра́тно; **the ~ of marshland** осуше́ние боло́т. **2.** (*revival; restoration to health*) выздоровле́ние; оздоровле́ние; **he made a rapid ~** он бы́стро попра́вился; **his business made a ~** его́ дела́ пошли́ на попра́вку. **3.** (*rehabilitation; restoration to use*) восстановле́ние; ремо́нт; **~ vehicle** авари́йный автомоби́ль.

recreant [ˈrekrɪənt] *n.* (*liter.*) (*apostate*) отсту́пник; (*coward*) трус.
adj. отсту́пнический; трусли́вый, малоду́шный.

recreate [ˈrekrɪˌeɪt] *v.t.* (*refresh*) восстан|а́вливать, -ови́ть си́лы +*g.*; обнов|ля́ть, -и́ть.

re-create [ˌriːkrɪˈeɪt] *v.t.* вновь созд|ава́ть, -а́ть; воссозд|ава́ть, -а́ть.

recreation [ˌrekrɪˈeɪʃ(ə)n] *n.* о́тдых; развлече́ние; **I need ~** мне на́до отдохну́ть/отвле́чься; **he plays chess for ~** он отдыха́ет, игра́я в ша́хматы; ша́хматы для него́ о́тдых; **~ ground** спортплоща́дка; площа́дка для игр.

recriminate [rɪˈkrɪmɪˌneɪt] *v.t.* отв|еча́ть, -е́тить обвине́нием на обвине́ние.

recrimination [rɪˌkrɪmɪˈneɪʃ(ə)n] *n.* встре́чное обвине́ние; **they indulged in mutual ~s** они́ броса́ли друг дру́гу обвине́ния.

recriminatory [rɪˈkrɪmɪnətərɪ] *adj.*: **he made a ~ speech** он вы́ступил с контробвине́ниями.

recrudesce [ˌriːkruːˈdes, ˌrek-] *v.i.* возобнов|ля́ться, -и́ться; ожив|ля́ться, -и́ться.

recrudescence [ˌriːkruːˈdesəns, ˌrek-] *n.* (*of illness*) втори́чное заболева́ние; (*fig.*) рециди́в; но́вая вспы́шка.

recrudescent [ˌriːkruːˈdesənt, ˌrek-] *adj.* возобнови́вшийся; повто́рный.

recruit [rɪ'kru:t] *n.* (*mil.*) новобра́нец; **raw ~** (*fig.*) новичо́к; (*new member*) но́вый член/уча́стник; **our task is to win ~s for the cause** на́ша зада́ча — привле́чь как мо́жно бо́льше люде́й к о́бщему де́лу.

v.t. **1.** (*enlist*) вербова́ть, за-; наб|ира́ть, -ра́ть; приз|ыва́ть, -ва́ть; **~ing sergeant** сержа́нт по вербо́вке на вое́нную слу́жбу. **2.** (*build up*): **he is ~ing his strength** он понемно́гу восстана́вливает свои́ си́лы.

recruitment [rɪ'kru:tmənt] *n.* вербо́вка; комплектова́ние ли́чным соста́вом.

rectangle ['rek,tæŋg(ə)l] *n.* прямоуго́льник.

rectangular [rek'tæŋgʊlə(r)] *adj.* прямоуго́льный.

rectification [,rektɪfɪ'keɪʃ(ə)n] *n.* (*correction*) исправле́ние, попра́вка; (*chem.*) ректифика́ция; (*elec.*) выпрямле́ние.

rectifier ['rektɪ,faɪə(r)] *n.* (*elec.*) выпрями́тель (*m.*), дете́ктор.

rectif|y ['rektɪ,faɪ] *v.t.* **1.** (*correct*) испр|авля́ть, -а́вить; **I am trying to ~y the situation** я пыта́юсь испра́вить положе́ние; **he ~ied his statement** он уточни́л своё заявле́ние; **many abuses were ~ied** мно́го несправедли́востей бы́ло устранено́. **2.** (*chem.*) ректифици́ровать (*impf., pf.*). **3.** (*elec.*) выпрямля́ть, вы́прямить.

rectilinear [,rektɪ'lɪnɪə(r)] *adj.* прямолине́йный.

rectitude ['rektɪ,tju:d] *n.* че́стность, прямота́.

recto ['rektəʊ] *n.* лицева́я сторона́.

rector ['rektə(r)] *n.* (*clergyman*) ≃ прихо́дский свяще́нник; (*of university*) ре́ктор.

rectory ['rektərɪ] *n.* дом прихо́дского свяще́нника.

rectum ['rektəm] *n.* пряма́я кишка́.

recumbent [rɪ'kʌmbənt] *adj.* лежа́чий, лежа́щий; **in a ~ posture** в лежа́чем положе́нии.

recuperate [rɪ'ku:pə,reɪt] *v.i.* попр|авля́ться, -а́виться.

recuperation [rɪ,ku:pə'reɪʃ(ə)n] *n.* восстановле́ние сил; выздоровле́ние.

recur [rɪ'kɜ:(r)] *v.i.* **1.** (*occur repeatedly*) повтор|я́ться, -и́ться; **a ~ring headache** хрони́ческие головны́е бо́ли (*f. pl.*); **it is a ~ring problem** э́то постоя́нно возника́ющая пробле́ма; **~ring decimal** периоди́ческая десяти́чная дробь. **2.** (*return*) возвра|ща́ться, -ти́ться; **the thought often ~s to me** э́та мысль ча́сто меня́ посеща́ет.

recurrence [rɪ'kʌrəns] *n.* повторе́ние; возвра́т.

recurrent [rɪ'kʌrənt] *adj.* повторя́ющийся.

recusancy ['rekjʊz(ə)nsɪ] *n.* неподчине́ние вла́сти; неповинове́ние.

recusant ['rekjʊz(ə)nt] *n.* нонконформи́ст; бунта́рь (*m.*).

adj. нонконформи́стский; бунта́рский.

recycle [ri:'saɪk(ə)l] *v.t.* рециркули́ровать (*impf., pf.*); **~d paper** бума́га из ути́ля.

recycling [ri:'saɪklɪŋ] *n.* повто́рное испо́льзование, перерабо́тка.

red [red] *n.* **1.** кра́сный цвет; **his ~s are too bright** у него́ сли́шком я́ркие отте́нки кра́сного; **the article made me see ~** (*fig.*) статья́ привела́ меня́ в бе́шенство; (*of clothes*): **~ doesn't suit her** кра́сное ей не идёт; **she was dressed in ~** она́ была́ оде́та в кра́сное; (*billiards*): **he went in off the ~** он сыгра́л своего́ от кра́сного шара́. **2.** (*debit side of account*) долг, задо́лженность; **my account is in the ~** у меня́ задо́лженность в ба́нке; **how can I get out of the ~?** как мне вы́йти из долго́в? **3.** (*coll., Communist*) «кра́сный».

adj. **1.** кра́сный; а́лый; **her eyes were ~ with weeping** её глаза́ покрасне́ли от слёз; **she went ~ in the face** она́ покрасне́ла; **he was ~ with anger** он покрасне́л от гне́ва; **was my face ~!** (*coll.*) ну, и оскanда́лился же я!; **his hands were ~ with the blood of his victims** его́ ру́ки бы́ли обагрены́ кро́вью жертв; **let's go out and paint the town ~!** (*coll.*) (дава́й) пойдём поку́тим!; **R~ Admiral** (*butterfly*) ба́бочка-адмира́л; **R~ Cross** Кра́сный Крест; **~ deer** благоро́дный оле́нь; **R~ Ensign** флаг торго́вого фло́та Великобрита́нии; **~ flag** (*danger signal*) кра́сный флажо́к; (*pol.*) кра́сный флаг, кра́сное зна́мя; **~ hat** (*of cardinal*) кра́сная ша́пка; **~ heat** кра́сное кале́ние; **R~ Indian** краснoко́жий, инде́ец; (*adj.*) краснoко́жий; **~ lead** (*min.*) свинцо́вый су́рик; **~ light** (*warning signal*) сигна́л опа́сности; (*fig.*) **he has seen the ~ light at last** он наконе́ц почу́ял опа́сность; (*sign of brothel*) кра́сный фона́рь; **~ light district** кварта́л публи́чных домо́в; **~ meat** чёрное мя́со; **it was like a ~ rag to a bull** э́то поде́йствовало, как кра́сная тря́пка на быка́; **the R~ Sea** Кра́сное мо́ре; **~ tape** (*fig.*) канцеля́рская волоки́та. **2.** (*coll., Soviet*): **the R~ Air Force** сове́тские вое́нно-возду́шные си́лы.

cpds. **~-blooded** *adj.* (*fig.*) энерги́чный; му́жественный; **~breast** *n.* мали́новка; **R~ brick** *n.* ≃ провинциа́льный университе́т; **~cap** *n.* (*mil. policeman*) вое́нный полице́йский; (*US, porter*) носи́льщик; **~-cheeked** *adj.* краснощёкий; **~coat** *n.* (*hist.*) «кра́сный мунди́р», брита́нский солда́т; **~currant** *n.* кра́сная сморо́дина; **~-eyed** *adj.* (*from weeping*) с глаза́ми, кра́сными от слёз; **~-haired** *adj.* рыжеволо́сый; **~-handed** *adj.*: **he was caught ~-handed** его́ пойма́ли на ме́сте преступле́ния (*or* с поли́чным); **~head** *n.* ры́жий челове́к; **~-headed** *adj.* ры́жий; **~-hot** *adj.* раскалённый докрасна́; (*fig.*) (*fervent*) горя́чий, пы́лкий; **a ~-hot socialist** пла́менный социали́ст; (*exciting*): **~-hot news** сенсацио́нное сообще́ние; **~-letter** *adj.* пра́здничный; **it was a ~-letter day for me** э́то бы́ло для меня́ пра́здником; **~skin** *n.* (*coll.*) краснoко́жий; **~wood** *n.* (*bot.*) кра́сное де́рево.

redden ['red(ə)n] *v.t.* окра́|шивать, -сить в кра́сный цвет; багряни́ть (*impf.*).

v.i. красне́ть, по-; покр|ыва́ться, -ы́ться багря́нцем.

reddish ['redɪʃ] *adj.* краснова́тый.

redecorate [ri:'dekə,reɪt] *v.t.* отде́л|ывать, -ать; ремонти́ровать, от-.

redecoration [ri:,dekə'reɪʃ(ə)n] *n.* отде́лка; ремо́нт.

redeem [rɪ'di:m] *v.t.* **1.** (*get back, recover*) выкупа́ть, вы́купить; восстан|а́вливать, -ови́ть; **the mortgage was ~ed** зало́г был вы́плачен; **he was able to ~ his honour** он смог восстанови́ть свою́ честь. **2.** (*fulfil*) выполня́ть, вы́полнить; **he ~ed his promise** он вы́полнил обеща́ние. **3.** (*purchase freedom of*) выкупа́ть, вы́купить; **the slaves were ~ed** рабо́в вы́купили; **Christ came to ~ sinners** Христо́с пришёл искупи́ть грехи́ люде́й. **4.** (*compensate*) искуп|а́ть, -и́ть; компенси́ровать (*impf., pf.*); **he has one ~ing feature** у него́ есть одно́ положи́тельное ка́чество.

redeemable [rɪ'di:məb(ə)l] *adj.* (*subject to purchase*) подлежа́щий вы́купу/погаше́нию.

redeemer [rɪ'di:mə(r)] *n.* спаси́тель, избави́тель, искупи́тель (*all m.*).

redefine [,ri:dɪ'faɪn] *v.t.* определ|я́ть, -и́ть за́ново.

redefinition [,ri:defɪ'nɪʃ(ə)n] *n.* но́вое определе́ние; но́вая формулиро́вка.

redemption [rɪ'dempʃ(ə)n] *n.* **1.** (*repurchase*) вы́куп. **2.** (*fulfilment*): **~ of a promise** выполне́ние обеща́ния. **3.** (*deliverance, salvation*) искупле́ние; **past ~** без наде́жды на спасе́ние. **4.** (*reform*) исправле́ние.

redemptive [rɪ'demptɪv] *adj.* искупи́тельный, искупа́ющий.

redeploy [,ri:dɪ'plɔɪ] *v.t. & i.* передислоци́ровать(ся) (*impf., pf.*); перегруппиро́в|ывать(ся), -а́ть(ся); (*of resources*) перераспредел|я́ть, -и́ть.

redeployment [,ri:dɪ'plɔɪmənt] *n.* передислока́ция; перегруппиро́вка; перераспределе́ние.

re-design [,ri:dɪ'zaɪn] *v.t.* перепланиро́вать (*pf.*), за́ново (с)конструи́ровать (*pf.*).

redevelop [,ri:dɪ'veləp] *v.t.* (*e.g. an area*) перестр|а́ивать, -о́ить; застр|а́ивать, -о́ить.

redevelopment [,ri:dɪ'veləpmənt] *n.* перестро́йка; застро́йка; **~ area** райо́н застро́йки.

rediffuse [,ri:dɪ'fju:z] *v.t.* (ре)трансли́ровать (*impf., pf.*).

rediffusion [,ri:dɪ'fju:ʒ(ə)n] *n.* (*broadcasting system*) (ре)трансля́ция.

redintegrate [rɪ'dɪntɪ,greɪt] *v.t.* восстан|а́вливать, -ови́ть; воссоедин|я́ть, -и́ть.

redintegration [rɪ,dɪntɪ'greɪʃ(ə)n] *n.* восстановле́ние, воссоедине́ние.

redirect [,ri:daɪ'rekt, -dɪ'rekt] *v.t.* (*e.g. letters*) переадресо́в|ывать, -а́ть; (*re-route*): **the traffic was ~ed** тра́нспорт был напра́влен по друго́му маршру́ту; **he ~ed me to the station** он напра́вил меня́ обра́тно на ста́нцию; (*fig.*): **his efforts were ~ed to a new goal** его́ уси́лия бы́ли обращены́ на другу́ю цель.

redirection [ˌri:daɪˈrekʃ(ə)n, -dɪˈrekʃ(ə)n] *n.* переадресова́ние; перебро́ска.

rediscover [ˌri:dɪˈskʌvə(r)] *v.t.* откр|ыва́ть, -ы́ть за́ново.

rediscovery [ˌri:dɪˈskʌvərɪ] *n.* за́ново сде́ланное откры́тие.

redistribute [ˌri:dɪˈstrɪˌbju:t, *disp.* ri:ˈdɪs-] *v.t.* перераспредел|я́ть, -и́ть.

redistribution [ˌri:dɪˌstrɪˈbju:ʃ(ə)n] *n.* перераспределе́ние.

redo [ri:ˈdu:] *v.t.* переде́л|ывать, -а́ть; (*redecorate*) ремонти́ровать, от-.

redolent [ˈredələnt] *adj.*: ~ (*fig.*, *suggestive*) **of** отдаю́щий (*чем*), напомина́ющий (*что*).

redouble [ri:ˈdʌb(ə)l] *v.t. & i.* **1.** (*increase*) удв|а́ивать(ся), -о́ить(ся); уси́ли|вать(ся), -ть(ся); увели́чи|вать(ся), -ть(ся); **he ~d his efforts** он удво́ил свои́ уси́лия; **the cheers ~d** ова́ция оси́лилась. **2.** (*at bridge*) втори́чно удв|а́ивать, -о́ить (ста́вку).

redoubt [rɪˈdaʊt] *n.* реду́т.

redoubtable [rɪˈdaʊtəb(ə)l] *adj.* гро́зный; устраша́ющий.

redound [rɪˈdaʊnd] *v.i.*: ~ **to** спосо́бствовать (*impf.*) +*d.*; соде́йствовать (*impf.*) +*d.*; **this will ~ to your credit** э́то укрепи́т ва́шу репута́цию.

redraft [ri:ˈdrɑ:ft] *n.* но́вый прое́кт; но́вая формулиро́вка.

v.t. перепи́с|ывать, -а́ть.

redress [rɪˈdres] *n.* возмеще́ние; **I shall seek ~** я бу́ду добива́ться компенса́ции.

v.t. испр|авля́ть, -а́вить; возме|ща́ть, -сти́ть; **their victory ~ed the balance of forces** их побе́да восстанови́ла равнове́сие сил; **her grievances were ~ed** её жа́лобы бы́ли удовлетворены́.

reduce [rɪˈdju:s] *v.t.* **1.** (*make less or smaller*) ум|еньша́ть, -е́ньшить; сокра|ща́ть, -ти́ть; **we must ~ our expenditure** мы должны́ сократи́ть расхо́ды; **in ~d circumstances** в стеснённых обстоя́тельствах; **their numbers were ~d to five** их число́ уме́ньшилось до пяти́; **exercise will ~ your weight** заря́дка помо́жет вам сба́вить вес; (*lower*) сн|ижа́ть, -и́зить; сб|авля́ть, -а́вить; **'~ speed now'** «води́тель, притормози́!»; **all prices are ~d** все це́ны сни́жены; **his temperature is much ~d** у него́ температу́ра значи́тельно пони́зилась; (*shorten*) сокра|ща́ть, -ти́ть; укор|а́чивать, -оти́ть; **his sentence was ~d to 6 months** ему́ сократи́ли при́говор до шести́ ме́сяцев; (*make narrower*) сужа́ть, су́зить; (*weaken*) осл|абля́ть, -а́бить; (*demote*) пон|ижа́ть, -и́зить в до́лжности; **he was ~d to the ranks** его́ разжа́ловали в рядовы́е. **2.** (*bring*, *compel*) дов|оди́ть, -ести́ (*до чего*); вынужда́ть, вы́нудить; **the film ~d her to tears** фильм расстро́гал её до слёз; **I was ~d to silence** мне пришло́сь промолча́ть; **the teacher ~d the class to order** учи́тель навёл поря́док в кла́ссе; **the rebels were ~d to submission** мяте́жников заста́вили прекрати́ть сопротивле́ние; **the family was ~d to begging** семья́ была́ обречена́ на нищету́; **this ~s your argument to absurdity** э́то лиша́ет ваш до́вод вся́кого смы́сла. **3.** (*convert*) превра|ща́ть, -ти́ть; **the proposition, ~d to its simplest terms** предложе́ние в преде́льно упрощённом ви́де; **all fractions can be ~d to decimals** все дро́би мо́жно перевести́ в десяти́чные; **the logs were ~d to ashes** поле́нья сгоре́ли дотла́; **he was ~d to a skeleton** он преврати́лся в скеле́т. **4.** (*force to surrender*) подчин|я́ть, -и́ть; покор|я́ть, -и́ть.

v.i. **1.** (*become less*) сн|ижа́ться, -и́зиться; ум|еньша́ться, -е́ньшиться; **interest is paid at a reduced rate** проце́нт выпла́чивается по пони́женной ста́вке. **2.** (*lose weight*) худе́ть (*impf.*); соблюда́ть (*impf.*) дие́ту для похуде́ния; **a reducing diet** дие́та для поте́ри ве́са; **I'm trying to ~** я стара́юсь похуде́ть. **3.** (*be equivalent*) равня́ться (*impf.*); **31/2 yards ~s to 126 inches** три с полови́ной я́рда — э́то 126 дю́ймов.

reducible [rɪˈdju:sɪb(ə)l] *adj.*: **these facts are ~ to natural causes** э́ти фа́кты мо́гут быть объяснены́ есте́ственными причи́нами; **the prices are ~** (*can be lowered*) це́ны мо́жно пони́зить. **2.** (*math.*) своди́мый.

reductio ad absurdum [rɪˌdʌktɪəʊ æd æbˈzɜ:dəm] *n.* доведе́ние до абсу́рда.

reduction [rɪˈdʌkʃ(ə)n] *n.* **1.** (*decrease*) сокраще́ние; сниже́ние; **a ~ in numbers** коли́чественное сокраще́ние; **price ~s** сниже́ние цен; **is there a ~ for children?** есть ли ски́дка для дете́й?; **~ in rank** пониже́ние в зва́нии; **~ of armaments** сокраще́ние вооруже́ний; **~ of temperature** сниже́ние температу́ры; (*shortening*) сокраще́ние; (*narrowing*) суже́ние; (*demotion*) пониже́ние; **~ to the ranks** разжа́лование (в солда́ты). **2.** (*conversion*) перево́д; превраще́ние. **3.** (*reduced copy of picture etc.*) уме́ньшенная ко́пия.

redundanc|e [rɪˈdʌnd(ə)ns], **-y** [rɪˈdʌnd(ə)nsɪ] *nn.* (*superfluity*) изли́шек, избы́точность; (*in work-force*) безрабо́тица; **there will be ~ies in the building industry** в строи́тельной промы́шленности ожида́ется большо́е сокраще́ние.

redundant [rɪˈdʌnd(ə)nt] *adj.* изли́шний, избы́точный; **the last sentence is ~** после́днее предложе́ние изли́шне; **many workers were made ~** мно́гих рабо́чих уво́лили.

reduplicate [rɪˈdju:plɪˌkeɪt] *v.t.* удв|а́ивать, -о́ить (*also gram.*); удв|а́ивать, -о́ить.

reduplication [rɪˌdju:plɪˈkeɪʃ(ə)n] *n.* удвое́ние.

re-echo [ri:ˈekəʊ] *v.t.* отра|жа́ть, -зи́ть (*or* повтор|я́ться, -и́ться) э́хом; откл|ика́ться, -и́кнуться.

reed [ri:d] *n.* **1.** (*bot.*) тростни́к, камы́ш; **~ thatch** соло́менная кры́ша; **he proved a broken ~** (*fig.*) оказа́лось, что на него́ нельзя́ опере́ться. **2.** (*mus.*) свире́ль; **~ stop** (*of organ*) орга́нный реги́стр с язычко́выми тру́бками; **the ~s** (*of an orchestra*) деревя́нные трубковы́е инструме́нты (*m. pl.*).

re-edit [ri:ˈedɪt] *v.t.* за́ново отредакти́ровать (*pf.*).

re-educate [ri:ˈedjʊˌkeɪt] *v.t.* перевоспи́т|ывать, -а́ть.

re-education [ri:ˌedjʊˈkeɪʃ(ə)n] *n.* перевоспита́ние.

reedy [ˈri:dɪ] *adj.* **1.** (*full of reeds*) тростнико́вый; заро́сший тростнико́м. **2.** (*of sounds*) пронзи́тельный.

reef[1] [ri:f] *n.* (*geog.*) риф; подво́дная скала́.

reef[2] [ri:f] *n.* (*naut.*) риф.

v.t.: **~ a sail** брать, взять ри́фы.

cpd. **~-knot** *n.* ри́фовый/прямо́й у́зел.

reefer[1] [ˈri:fə(r)] *n.* (*jacket*) бушла́т.

reefer[2] [ˈri:fə(r)] *n.* (*sl.*, *marijuana cigarette*) сигаре́та с марихуа́ной.

reek [ri:k] *n.* (*foul smell*) вонь; (*smoke*, *vapour*) пары́ (*m. pl.*).

v.i. воня́ть, про-; **his clothes ~ed of tobacco** от его́ оде́жды несло́ табако́м; (*fig.*) попа́хивать, па́хнуть (*both impf.*); **the affair ~s of corruption** де́ло па́хнет корру́пцией.

reel[1] [ri:l] *n.* (*winding device*) кату́шка; руло́н; **a ~ of thread, cotton** кату́шка ни́ток; **a ~ of film for a camera** кату́шка плёнки для фотоаппара́та; (*fig.*): **he sang three songs off the ~** он еди́ным ду́хом пропе́л три пе́сни.

v.t. нам|а́тывать, -ота́ть.

with advs.: **the fisherman ~ed in the line** рыба́к смота́л у́дочку; **the guide ~ed off a lot of dates** гид вы́палил це́лый ряд истори́ческих дат.

reel[2] [ri:l] *n.* (*stagger*) шата́ние, колеба́ние.

v.i. кружи́ться (*impf.*); верте́ться (*impf.*); **he ~ed under the blow** он зашата́лся от уда́ра; **it makes the mind ~** от э́того голова́ кру́гом идёт; **the drunkard went ~ing home** шата́ясь, пья́ница поплёлся домо́й.

reel[3] [ri:l] *n.* (*dance*) рил; хорово́д.

re-elect [ˌri:ɪˈlekt] *v.t.* переизб|ира́ть, -ра́ть.

re-election [ˌri:ɪˈlekʃ(ə)n] *n.* переизбра́ние.

re-eligible [ˌri:ˈelɪdʒɪb(ə)l] *adj.* переизбира́емый.

re-embark [ˌri:ɪmˈbɑ:k] *v.t.* (*pers.*) вновь сажа́ть, посади́ть; (*cargo*) вновь грузи́ть, по- (на кора́бль *и т.п.*).

v.i. возвра|ща́ться, -ти́ться на́ борт.

re-embarkation [ˌri:ɪmˌbɑ:ˈkeɪʃ(ə)n] *n.* возвраще́ние на́ борт; поса́дка (по́сле стоя́нки).

re-emerge [ˌri:ɪˈmɜ:dʒ] *v.i.* вновь появ|ля́ться, -и́ться.

re-emergence [ˌri:ɪˈmɜ:dʒəns] *n.* появле́ние вновь.

re-emphasis [ri:ˈemfəsɪs] *n.* повто́рное подчёркивание.

re-emphasize [ri:ˈemfəˌsaɪz] *v.t.* подчёрк|ивать, -ну́ть сно́ва (*or* ещё раз).

re-enact [ˌri:ɪˈnækt] *v.t.* вновь вв|оди́ть, -ести́ в де́йствие.

re-enactment [ˌri:ɪˈnæktmənt] *n.* повто́рный ввод в де́йствие.

re-engage [ˌri:ɪnˈgeɪdʒ] *v.t.*: **he ~d the clutch** он вновь включи́л сцепле́ние; **the workers were laid off and then**

~d рабо́чих уво́лили, а пото́м вновь при́няли на рабо́ту; **they are ~d** (*to be married*) они́ обручи́лись сно́ва.
re-engagement [ˌriːɪnˈgeɪdʒmənt] *n.* **1.** (*of clutch, gearing etc.*) повто́рное включе́ние. **2.** (*of soldiers*) оставле́ние на сверхсро́чной слу́жбе. **3.** (*of workers*) восстановле́ние на рабо́те. **4.** (*of couple*) возобновле́ние помо́лвки.
re-enlist [ˌriːɪnˈlɪst] *v.i.* поступ|а́ть, -и́ть на сверхсро́чную слу́жбу.
re-enlistment [ˌriːɪnˈlɪstmənt] *n.* поступле́ние на сверхсро́чную слу́жбу.
re-enter [riːˈentə(r)] *v.i.* сно́ва входи́ть, войти́ в+*a.*; возвраща́ться, верну́ться в+*a.*
re-entrant [riːˈentrənt] *adj.* (*geom.*) входя́щий.
re-entry [riːˈentrɪ] *n.* вхожде́ние/вступле́ние за́ново; **~ module** возвраща́емый отсе́к; **~ into the atmosphere** возвра́т в атмосфе́ру.
re-equip [ˌriːɪˈkwɪp] *v.t.* переосна|ща́ть, -сти́ть.
re-equipment [ˌriːɪˈkwɪpmənt] *n.* переоснаще́ние.
re-establish [ˌriːɪˈstæblɪʃ] *v.t.* восстан|а́вливать, -ови́ть.
re-establishment [ˌriːɪˈstæblɪʃmənt] *n.* восстановле́ние.
re-examination [ˌriːɪgˌzæmɪˈneɪʃ(ə)n] *n.* повто́рное рассмотре́ние; переэкзамено́вка.
re-examine [ˌriːɪgˈzæmɪn] *v.t.* вновь рассм|а́тривать, -отре́ть; пересм|а́тривать, -отре́ть; (*acad.*) втори́чно экзаменова́ть, про-.
re-export [riːˈekspɔːt] *n.* реэ́кспорт.
v.t. реэкспорти́ровать (*impf., pf.*).
ref [ref] (*coll.*) = **referee 2.**
reface [riːˈfeɪs] *v.t.* за́ново отде́л|ывать, -ать.
refashion [riːˈfæʃ(ə)n] *v.t.* перемодели́ровать (*impf., pf.*); переина́чи|вать, -ть.
refectory [rɪˈfektərɪ, ˈrefɪktərɪ] *n.* тра́пезная; столо́вая.
refer [rɪˈfɜː(r)] *v.t.* **1.** (*pass on, direct*) от|сыла́ть, -осла́ть; напр|авля́ть, -а́вить; **the clerk ~red me to the manager** слу́жащий отосла́л меня́ к нача́льнику; **the dispute was ~red to the UN** спор был пе́редан на рассмотре́ние ООН; **the note ~s the reader to the appendix** примеча́ние отсыла́ет чита́теля к приложе́нию; **the motion was ~red back** предложе́ние бы́ло возвращено́ для но́вого рассмотре́ния. **2.** (*ascribe, assign*) припи́с|ывать, -а́ть; **he ~red his success to his wife's support** он припи́сывал свой успе́х подде́ржке жены́.
v.i. **1.** (*have recourse*) спр|авля́ться, -а́виться; **he ~red to the dictionary** он спра́вился со словарём; **the speaker ~red to his notes** ора́тор загляну́л в конспе́кт. **2.** (*allude*): **~ to** упом|ина́ть, -яну́ть; подразумева́ть (*impf.*); **all his writings ~ to the war** все его́ произведе́ния посвящены́ войне́; **are you ~ring to me?** вы име́ете в виду́ меня́?
referee [ˌrefəˈriː] *n.* **1.** (*arbitrator*) арби́тр. **2.** (*at games*) судья́ (*m.*); рефери́ (*m. indecl.*). **3.** (*pers. supplying testimonial*) поручи́тель (*m.*).
v.t. & i.: **he agreed to ~ the match** он согласи́лся суди́ть матч; **~ing** суде́йство.
reference [ˈrefərəns] *n.* **1.** (*referring for decision, consideration etc.*) отсы́лка; **he acted without ~ to his superiors** он де́йствовал без консульта́ции с нача́льством; **terms of ~** компете́нция, круг полномо́чий, веде́ние. **2.** (*relation*) отноше́ние; **success has little ~ to merit** заслу́ги далеко́ не всегда́ определя́ют успе́х; **with ~ to your letter** в связи́ с ва́шим письмо́м. **3.** (*allusion*) упомина́ние, ссы́лка; **he made frequent ~ to our agreement** он ча́сто ссыла́лся на на́ше соглаше́ние; **the book contains many ~s to the Queen** в кни́ге ча́сто упомина́ется короле́ва. **4.** (*in text*) ссы́лка, сно́ска; **~ mark** (*asterisk etc.*) знак сно́ски. **5.** (*referring for information*) спра́вка; **you should make ~ to a dictionary** вам сле́дует обрати́ться к словарю́; **work of ~, ~ book** спра́вочник; насто́льная кни́га; **~ library** спра́вочная библиоте́ка. **6.** (*testimonial*) о́тзыв, рекоменда́ция; (*pers. supplying ~*) поручи́тель (*m.*); **he gave his professor as a ~** он назва́л профе́ссора в ка́честве своего́ поручи́теля.
v.t. (*provide book etc. with ~s*) снаб|жа́ть, -ди́ть примеча́ниями.
referendum [ˌrefəˈrendəm] *n.* рефере́ндум.
referral [rɪˈfɜːr(ə)l] *n.* направле́ние.
refill[1] [ˈriːfɪl] *n.* (*of fuel*) (до)запра́вка; (*of drink*) доли́тая рю́мка; (*for pen etc.*) запасно́й сте́ржень.
refill[2] [riːˈfɪl] *v.t.* нап|олня́ть, -о́лнить вновь; **may I ~ your glass?** позво́льте подли́ть?
v.i. запр|авля́ться, -а́виться.
refine [rɪˈfaɪn] *v.t.* **1.** (*purify*) оч|ища́ть, -и́стить; **~d sugar** са́хар-рафина́д. **2.** (*make more elegant or cultured*) соверше́нствовать, у-; **~d manners** утончённые/изы́сканные мане́ры.
refinement [rɪˈfaɪnmənt] *n.* **1.** (*purification*) очище́ние, очи́стка. **2.** (*of feeling, taste etc.*) утончённость, то́нкость; (*of breeding or manners*) благовоспи́танность; **lack of ~** неотёсанность. **3.** (*subtle or ingenious manifestation*) утончённость; **a ~ of torture** изощрённость пы́тки.
refinery [rɪˈfaɪnərɪ] *n.* (*oil*) нефтеочисти́тельный заво́д.
refit[1] [ˈriːfɪt] *n.* ремо́нт, переоборудование.
refit[2] [riːˈfɪt] *v.t.* чини́ть, по-; переобору́довать (*impf., pf.*); ремонти́ровать, от-.
reflate [riːˈfleɪt] *v.i.* (*econ.*) пров|оди́ть, -ести́ рефля́цию.
reflation [riːˈfleɪʃ(ə)n] *n.* рефля́ция.
reflect [rɪˈflekt] *v.t.* **1.** (*light, heat etc.*) отра|жа́ть, -зи́ть; **light is ~ed from a white surface** свет отража́ется от бе́лой пове́рхности; (*fig., express, reveal*): **her thoughts were ~ed in her face** все её мы́сли отража́лись на её лице́; (*fig., bring, result in*): **this behaviour ~s credit on his parents** тако́е поведе́ние де́лает честь его́ роди́телям. **2.** (*consider*) размышля́ть (*impf.*); разду́мывать (*impf.*); **I ~ed how fortunate I had been** я поду́мал о том, как мне повезло́.
v.i. **1.** (*produce a reflection*) отра|жа́ться, -зи́ться; **is the light ~ing in your eyes?** вам свет не бьёт в глаза́?; (*fig., bring discredit*): **your behaviour ~s on us all** ва́ше поведе́ние кладёт пятно́ на нас всех; **I do not wish to ~ on your honesty** я не хочу́ броса́ть тень на ва́шу честь. **2.** (*ponder*) заду́маться (*pf.*) (над+*i.*).
refle|ction, -xion [rɪˈflekʃ(ə)n] *n.* **1.** (*of light, heat etc.*) отраже́ние; **she saw his ~ in the mirror** она́ уви́дела его́ отраже́ние в зе́ркале. **2.** (*consideration*) размышле́ние; рефле́ксия; **he acts without ~** он де́йствует неосмотри́тельно; **she was lost in ~** она́ была́ погружена́ в свои́ мы́сли; **on ~, I may have been wrong** по размышле́нии я реши́л, что, возмо́жно, я был непра́в. **3.** (*expression of idea*) соображе́ние; замеча́ние. **4.** (*expression of blame*) порица́ние; **I intended no ~ on you** я не собира́лся вас порица́ть. **5.** (*cause of credit or discredit*): **it is a ~ on my honour** э́то задева́ет мою́ честь.
reflective [rɪˈflektɪv] *adj.* (*of a surface*) отража́ющий; (*thoughtful*) мы́слящий; заду́мчивый.
reflector [rɪˈflektə(r)] *n.* рефле́ктор.
reflex [ˈriːfleks] *n.* (**~ action**) рефле́кс.
adj. отражённый; рефлекто́рный; **~ camera** зерка́льный фотоаппара́т.
reflexion [rɪˈflekʃ(ə)n] = **reflection**
reflexive [rɪˈfleksɪv] *adj.* возвра́тный.
reflexologist [ˌriːflekˈsɒlədʒɪst] *n.* рефлексотерапе́вт.
refloat [riːˈfləʊt] *v.t.* подн|има́ть, -я́ть (*затонувшее судно*); сн|има́ть, -ять с ме́ли.
reflorescence [ˌriːflɔːˈresəns] *n.* повто́рное цвете́ние.
reflux [ˈriːflʌks] *n.* отли́в, отто́к.
reforestation [riːˌfɒrɪˈsteɪʃ(ə)n] *n.* восстановле́ние лесны́х масси́вов.
reform [rɪˈfɔːm] *n.* (*improvement, correction*) рефо́рма; **~ school** исправи́тельная шко́ла.
v.t. **1.** (*change for the better*) реформи́ровать (*impf., pf.*); **he is a ~ed character** он соверше́нно испра́вился. **2.** (*correct*) испр|авля́ть, -а́вить; **~ abuses** устран|я́ть, -и́ть злоупотребле́ния.
re-form [riːˈfɔːm] *v.t.* (*reshape, form again*) пере-формиро́в|ывать, -а́ть.
v.i. перестр|а́иваться, -о́иться; **the soldiers ~ed into two ranks** солда́ты перестро́ились в две шере́нги.
reformation [ˌrefəˈmeɪʃ(ə)n] *n.* (*change, improvement*) преобразова́ние; **the R~** Реформа́ция.
re-formation [ˌriːfɔːˈmeɪʃ(ə)n] *n.* (*forming again*) пере-формирова́ние.

reformative [rɪ'fɔ:mətɪv] *adj.* исправи́тельный.

reformatory [rɪ'fɔ:mətərɪ] *n.* исправи́тельное заведе́ние.
adj. исправи́тельный.

reformer [rɪ'fɔ:mə(r)] *n.* реформа́тор; преобразова́тель (*m.*); **the R~s** (*hist.*) реформа́торы це́ркви.

refract [rɪ'frækt] *v.t.* прелом|ля́ть, -и́ть.

refraction [rɪ'frækʃ(ə)n] *n.* преломле́ние; рефра́кция.

refractor [rɪ'fræktə(r)] *n.* рефра́ктор.

refractory [rɪ'fræktərɪ] *n.* огнеупо́рный материа́л.
adj. **1.** (*of pers.*) упря́мый, непослу́шный, неуправля́емый. **2.** (*of illness*) упо́рный; не поддаю́щийся лече́нию. **3.** (*fire-resisting*) огнеупо́рный.

refrain[1] [rɪ'freɪn] *n.* рефре́н, припе́в; **they joined in the ~** они́ подхвати́ли припе́в.

refrain[2] [rɪ'freɪn] *v.i.* сдéрж|иваться, -а́ться; возде́рж|иваться, -а́ться; **I could hardly ~ from laughing** я е́ле сде́рживался от сме́ха; **I ~ed from comment** я воздержа́лся от замеча́ний/коммента́риев.

refresh [rɪ'freʃ] *v.t.* освеж|а́ть, -и́ть; **I woke ~ed** сон освежи́л меня́; **~ o.s.** (*with food and drink*) подкреп|ля́ться, -и́ться; **let me ~ your memory** позво́льте напо́мнить вам; **the batteries need ~ing** батаре́и ну́жно подзаряди́ть.

refresher [rɪ'freʃə(r)] *n.* **1.** (**~ course**) курс переподгото́вки (*or* повыше́ния квалифика́ции). **2.** (*fee*) дополни́тельный гонора́р. **3.** (*coll.*, *drink*) вы́пивка.

refreshing [rɪ'freʃɪŋ] *adj.* освежа́ющий; **~ innocence** подкупа́ющая наи́вность; **he was ~ly frank** его́ и́скренность была́ умили́тельна.

refreshment [rɪ'freʃmənt] *n.* **1.** (*reinvigoration*) восстановле́ние сил. **2.** (*food or drink*) еда́; питьё; **won't you take some ~?** не хоти́те ли подкрепи́ться/закуси́ть?; **~s are served on the train** в по́езде мо́жно перекуси́ть; **~ room** буфе́т.

refrigerate [rɪ'frɪdʒə,reɪt] *v.t.* замор|а́живать, -о́зить.

refrigeration [rɪ,frɪdʒə'reɪʃ(ə)n] *n.* замора́живание.

refrigerator [rɪ'frɪdʒə,reɪtə(r)] *n.* холоди́льник.

refuel [ri:'fju:əl] *v.i.* поп|олня́ть, -о́лнить запа́сы то́плива; дозапра́виться (*pf.*).

refuge ['refju:dʒ] *n.* **1.** (*shelter*) убе́жище; приста́нище; **the cat took ~ beneath the table** кот спря́тался под столо́м; **he sought ~ from his pursuers** он иска́л убе́жище, что́бы укры́ться от пресле́дователей; (*fig.*) утеше́ние; спасе́ние; **take ~ in lies** приб|ега́ть, -е́гнуть ко лжи; **she took ~ in silence** она́ отма́лчивалась. **2.** (*traffic island*) острово́к безопа́сности.

refugee [,refjʊ'dʒi:] *n.* бе́жен|ец (*fem.* -ка); **political ~** политэмигра́нт.

refulgence [rɪ'fʌldʒ(ə)ns] *n.* сия́ние, сверка́ние.

refulgent [rɪ'fʌldʒ(ə)nt] *adj.* сия́ющий, сверка́ющий.

refund[1] ['ri:fʌnd] *n.* возмеще́ние убы́тков; **they gave me a ~** мне верну́ли де́ньги.

refund[2] [rɪ'fʌnd] *v.t.* (*pay back*) возвраща́ть, верну́ть (*деньги*); (*reimburse*) возме|ща́ть, -сти́ть.

refurbish [ri:'fɜ:bɪʃ] *v.t.* поднов|ля́ть, -и́ть; отде́л|ывать, -ать.

refurnish [ri:'fɜ:nɪʃ] *v.t.* за́ново меблирова́ть (*impf.*, *pf.*).

refusal [rɪ'fju:z(ə)l] *n.* отка́з; **he would take no ~** он не при́нял отка́за; **when I sell the house I will give you first ~** когда́ я бу́ду продава́ть дом, я предложу́ его́ вам в пе́рвую о́чередь.

refuse[1] ['refju:s] *n.* му́сор; **~ collection** убо́рка му́сора; **~ dump** сва́лка.

refuse[2] [rɪ'fju:z] *v.t.* & *i.* (*decline to give or grant*) отка́з|ывать, -а́ть (*кому в чём*); (*reject*) отв|ерга́ть, -е́ргнуть; (*decline sth. offered*) отка́з|ываться, -а́ться от+*g.*; **the request was ~d** в про́сьбе бы́ло отка́зано; **the invitation was ~d** приглаше́ние не бы́ло при́нято; **they ~d me permission** мне не́ дали разреше́ния; **children were ~d admittance** дете́й не впусти́ли; **it is an offer not to be ~d** тако́е предложе́ние не сле́дует отклоня́ть; **he proposed to her and was ~d** он сде́лал ей предложе́ние и получи́л отка́з; **the horse ~d (the fence)** пе́ред барье́ром ло́шадь заарта́чилась.

refusenik [rɪ'fju:znɪk] *n.* отка́зни|к (*fem.* -ца).

refutable [rɪ'fju:təb(ə)l] *adj.* опровержи́мый.

refutation [,refjʊ'teɪʃ(ə)n] *n.* опроверже́ние.

refute [rɪ'fju:t] *v.t.* опров|ерга́ть, -е́ргнуть.

regain [rɪ'geɪn] *v.t.* **1.** (*recover*) получ|а́ть, -и́ть обра́тно; **the prisoners ~ed their freedom** у́зники вновь обрели́ свобо́ду; **he never ~ed consciousness** он так и не пришёл в созна́ние; **he ~ed his footing** он сно́ва нащу́пал опо́ру ного́й; (*mil.*, *recapture*) отвоёв|ывать, -а́ть. **2.** (*reach again*) сно́ва дост|ига́ть, -и́гнуть; **they ~ed the shore** они́ вновь дости́гли бе́рега.

regal ['ri:g(ə)l] *adj.* короле́вский.

regale [rɪ'geɪl] *v.t.* уго|ща́ть, -сти́ть; по́тчевать (*impf.*).

regalia [rɪ'geɪlɪə] *n.* рега́ли|и (*pl.*, *g.* -й).

regard [rɪ'gɑ:d] *n.* **1.** (*gaze*) взгляд. **2.** (*point of attention, respect*) отноше́ние; **in this ~** в э́том отноше́нии; **in, with ~ to your request** что каса́ется ва́шей про́сьбы. **3.** (*heed*) внима́ние; **he pays no ~ to my warnings** он не прислу́шивается к мои́м предупрежде́ниям; **he acted without ~ for decency** поступа́я таки́м о́бразом, он забы́л о поря́дочности. **4.** (*consideration*) внима́ние, забо́та; **he paid no ~ to her feelings** он не счита́лся с её чу́вствами. **5.** (*esteem*) уваже́ние (к+*g.*); **he holds your opinion in high ~** он о́чень высоко́ це́нит ва́ше мне́ние. **6.** (*pl.*, *greetings*) приве́т, покло́н; (*formula at end of letter*) с приве́том; **my mother sends you her ~s** моя́ мать шлёт вам приве́т; **give him my warmest ~s** переда́йте ему́ от меня́ серде́чный приве́т.
v.t. **1.** (*look at*) разгля́д|ывать, -е́ть; **he ~ed me with hostility** он разгля́дывал меня́ с неприя́знью. **2.** (*view mentally, consider*) расце́н|ивать, -и́ть; сч|ита́ть, -есть; **I ~ his behaviour with suspicion** я отношу́сь к его́ посту́пкам с подозре́нием; **he was ~ed as a hero** его́ счита́ли геро́ем. **3.** (*give heed to*) счита́ться (*impf.*) с+*i.*; **he seldom ~s my advice** он ре́дко принима́ет мои́ сове́ты. **4.** (*respect, esteem*) уважа́ть (*impf.*); **we all ~ him highly** мы все его́ о́чень уважа́ем. **5.** (*concern*): **this does not ~ me** э́то меня́ не каса́ется; **as ~s, ~ing** относи́тельно/каса́тельно+*g.*; что каса́ется +*g.*; насчёт+*g.*; **he is careless as ~s money** он легкомы́слен в де́нежных дела́х.

regardful [rɪ'gɑ:dfʊl] *adj.*: **he was ~ of my advice** он внял моему́ сове́ту.

regardless [rɪ'gɑ:dlɪs] *adj.* невнима́тельный (к+*d.*); **~ of expense** не счита́ясь с расхо́дами; **he pressed on ~** (*coll.*) он рва́лся вперёд, невзира́я ни на что.

regatta [rɪ'gætə] *n.* рега́та.

regency ['ri:dʒənsɪ] *n.* ре́гентство; **R~ architecture** архитекту́ра эпо́хи ре́гентства.

regenerate[1] [rɪ'dʒenərət] *adj.* возрождённый.

regenerate[2] [rɪ'dʒenə,reɪt] *v.t.* & *i.* возро|жда́ть(ся), -ди́ть(ся).

regeneration [rɪ,dʒenə'reɪʃ(ə)n] *n.* перерожде́ние, возрожде́ние.

regent ['ri:dʒ(ə)nt] *n.* ре́гент; **Prince R~** принц-ре́гент.

reggae ['regeɪ] *n.* ре́гги (*m. indecl.*).

regicide ['redʒɪ,saɪd] *n.* (*crime*) цареуби́йство; (*criminal*) цареуби́йца (*c.g.*).

regime, régime [reɪ'ʒi:m] *n.* режи́м, строй; **under the old ~** при ста́ром режи́ме.

regimen ['redʒɪ,men] *n.* (*set of rules*) режи́м; поря́док; (*med.*, *esp. diet*) режи́м, дие́та.

regiment[1] ['redʒɪmənt] *n.* полк; (*fig.*, *large number*) мно́жество, (це́лый) легио́н.

regiment[2] ['redʒɪ,ment] *v.t.* муштрова́ть (*impf.*); помыка́ть (*impf.*) +*i.*

regimental [,redʒɪ'ment(ə)l] *adj.* полково́й.

regimentals [,redʒɪ'ment(ə)ls] *n.* обмундирова́ние; **they paraded in full ~s** они́ маршировáли в по́лной фо́рме.

regimentation [,redʒɪmən'teɪʃ(ə)n] *n.* регимента́ция, стро́гая регламента́ция; муштра́.

Regina [rɪ'dʒaɪnə] *n.* (*leg.*): **~ v. Brown** де́ло по обвине́нию Бра́уна.

region ['ri:dʒ(ə)n] *n.* райо́н, о́бласть; регио́н; **the Arctic ~s** А́рктика (*sg.*); **the nether, lower ~s** ад, преиспо́дняя; (*of body*) по́лость; **the abdominal ~** брюшна́я по́лость; **in the ~ of the heart** в о́бласти се́рдца; (*fig.*) о́бласть, сфе́ра; **his income is in the ~ of £5,000** он получа́ет приблизи́тельно 5000 фу́нтов.

regional [ˈriːdʒənəl] *adj.* райо́нный, областно́й; региона́льный; **a ~ accent** ме́стный акце́нт/вы́говор.

register [ˈredʒɪstə(r)] *n.* **1.** (*record, list*) рее́стр; за́пись; (*in school*) журна́л; **hotel ~** регистрацио́нная кни́га; **~ of voters** спи́сок избира́телей; **parish ~** прихо́дская кни́га; **~ office** = **registry 2.. 2.** (*compass of voice or instrument*) реги́стр. **3.** (*linguistic level*) стилисти́ческий у́ровень. **4.** (*mechanical recording device*) счётчик; **cash ~** ка́ссовый аппара́т, ка́сса. **5.** (*draught regulator*) задви́жка.

v.t. **1.** (*enter on official record*) регистри́ровать, за-; оф|ормля́ть, -о́рмить; **all cars must be ~ed** все маши́ны должны́ быть зарегистри́рованы; **~ed letter** заказно́е письмо́. **2.** (*make mental note of*) отм|еча́ть, -е́тить; зап|омина́ть, -о́мнить; **his mind did not ~ the fact** э́тот факт не запечатле́лся у него́ в уме́. **3.** (*of an instrument: record*) пока́з|ывать, -а́ть; отм|еча́ть, -е́тить; **the thermometer ~ed 20°C** термо́метр пока́зывал 20 гра́дусов по Це́льсию. **4.** (*express*) выража́ть, вы́разить; **the audience ~ed their disapproval** пу́блика вы́разила своё недово́льство; **her face ~ed surprise** на её лице́ отрази́лось удивле́ние.

v.i. **1.** (*record one's name*) регистри́роваться, за-. **2.** (*coll., correspond to sth. known*): **your name doesn't ~ with him** ва́ше и́мя ничего́ ему́ не говори́т. **3.** (*be impressed on memory*): **his words ~ed with me** его́ слова́ запа́ли мне в па́мять.

registrar [ˌredʒɪsˈtrɑː(r), ˈredʒ-] *n.* (*keeper of records*) рабо́тник регистрату́ры; (*head of register office*) заве́дующий (райо́нного) отделе́ния за́гса; (*of university etc.*) регистра́тор, секрета́рь (*m.*).

registration [ˌredʒɪˈstreɪʃ(ə)n] *n.* регистра́ция; **~ of letters** отпра́вка пи́сем заказно́й по́чтой; **~ number of a car** (регистрацио́нный) но́мер маши́ны.

registry [ˈredʒɪstrɪ] *n.* **1.** (*registration*) регистра́ция. **2.** (*office for keeping records*) регистрату́ра; **they were married at a ~** они расписа́лись в за́гсе; они́ зарегистри́ровались; **servant's ~** бюро́ по приписа́нию ме́ста для прислу́ги.

regress [rɪˈgres] *v.i.* дви́гаться (*impf.*) в обра́тном направле́нии.

regression [rɪˈgreʃ(ə)n] *n.* возвраще́ние (к+*d.*); (*decline*) упа́док.

regressive [rɪˈgresɪv] *adj.* регресси́вный.

regret [rɪˈgret] *n.* сожале́ние; **I found to my ~ that I was late** я обнаружи́л, к своему́ сожале́нию, что опозда́л; **I have no ~s** я ни о чём не жале́ю; **he could not attend, and sent his ~s** он переда́л, что не мо́жет прийти́ и про́сит его́ извини́ть.

v.t. **1.** (*feel sorrow for*) сожале́ть (*impf.*); **I ~ losing my temper** я сожале́ю, что вы́шел из себя́; **I ~ to say ...** к сожале́нию, я до́лжен сказа́ть...; **it is to be ~ted that ...** к сожале́нию...; мо́жно то́лько пожале́ть, что...; **you will live to ~ this** вы ещё пожале́ете об э́том. **2.** (*feel loss of*): **he died ~ted by all** он у́мер, все́ми опла́канный; **he ~s his lost opportunities** он (со)жале́ет об утра́ченных возмо́жностях.

regretful [rɪˈgretfʊl] *adj.* опеча́ленный; по́лный сожале́ния.

regrettable [rɪˈgretəb(ə)l] *adj.* приско́рбный; досто́йный сожале́ния.

regroup [riːˈgruːp] *v.t. & i.* перегруппиро́в|ывать(ся), -а́ть(ся).

regular [ˈregjʊlə(r)] *n.* **1.** (**~ soldier**) солда́т регуля́рной а́рмии. **2.** (*coll.*, **~ customer**) завсегда́тай; постоя́нный посети́тель.

adj. **1.** (*orderly in appearance, symmetrical*) пра́вильный, регуля́рный; **~ features** пра́вильные черты́; **a ~ hexagon** пра́вильный шестиуго́льник. **2.** (*steady, unvarying, systematic*) регуля́рный, норма́льный; **~ breathing** споко́йное дыха́ние; **a ~ pulse** ритми́чный пульс; **he approached with ~ steps** он подошёл разме́ренным ша́гом; **are your bowels ~?** у вас регуля́рный стул?; **I have no ~ work** у меня́ нет постоя́нной рабо́ты; **he keeps ~ hours** у него́ чёткий/стро́гий режи́м; (*in order*) очередно́й. **3.** (*conventional, proper*) при́нятый, устано́вленный; **this is the ~ procedure** такова́ при́нятая/обы́чная процеду́ра; тако́в поря́док. **4.** (*gram.*) пра́вильный. **5.** (*properly appointed*) регуля́рный; ка́дровый; **~ army** регуля́рная/постоя́нная а́рмия. **6.** (*coll., thorough, real*) су́щий, настоя́щий; **she is a ~ nuisance** она́ ужа́сная зану́да. **7.** (*US, ordinary, standard*) регуля́рный, обы́чный. **8.** (*US, likeable*): **a ~ guy** (*coll.*) сла́вный ма́лый.

regularity [ˌregjʊˈlærɪtɪ] *n.* (*symmetry*) пра́вильность; (*systematic occurrence*) регуля́рность.

regularize [ˈregjʊləˌraɪz] *v.t.* упоря́дочи|вать, -ть.

regulate [ˈregjʊˌleɪt] *v.t.* **1.** (*control*) регули́ровать (*impf.*); **the police ~d the traffic** поли́ция регули́ровала движе́ние. **2.** (*adapt to requirements*) контроли́ровать, про-; регули́ровать (*impf.*). **3.** (*adjust*) регули́ровать, от-; (*clock*) выверя́ть, вы́верить.

regulation [ˌregjʊˈleɪʃ(ə)n] *n.* **1.** (*control*) регули́рование; упорядоче́ние. **2.** (*adjustment*) вы́верка, регулиро́вка. **3.** (*rule*) пра́вило; **the ~s say we must wear black** согла́сно/по пра́вилам/уста́ву мы должны́ ходи́ть в чёрном. **4.** (*attr., standard*) устано́вленный; **uniform of the ~ colour** фо́рма устано́вленного цве́та; **a ~ haircut** стри́жка в соотве́тствии с уста́вом.

regulator [ˈregjʊˌleɪtə(r)] *n.* регуля́тор, стабилиза́тор.

regurgitate [rɪˈgɜːdʒɪˌteɪt] *v.t.* отры́г|ивать, -ну́ть.

regurgitation [rɪˌgɜːdʒɪˈteɪʃ(ə)n] *n.* отры́гивание.

rehabilitate [ˌriːhəˈbɪlɪˌteɪt] *v.t.* (*restore to efficiency*) восстан|а́вливать, -ови́ть работоспосо́бность +*g.*; (*re-educate*) перевоспи́т|ывать, -а́ть; (*exculpate*) реабилити́ровать (*impf., pf.*).

rehabilitation [ˌriːhəˌbɪlɪˈteɪʃ(ə)n] *n.* трудоустро́йство; перевоспита́ние; реабилита́ция.

rehash [ˈriːhæʃ] *n.* перекро́йка; перетасо́вка.

v.t. перекр|а́ивать, -о́ить; перетасова́ть (*pf.*).

rehear [riːˈhɪə(r)] *v.t.*: **the case will be ~d** де́ло бу́дет слу́шаться повто́рно.

rehearsal [rɪˈhɜːs(ə)l] *n.* **1.** (*practice*) репети́ция; **dress ~** генера́льная репети́ция. **2.** (*recitation, list*) перечисле́ние.

rehearse [rɪˈhɜːs] *v.t.* (*practise*) репети́ровать, от-; (*recite, recount*) переч|исля́ть, -и́слить.

rehouse [riːˈhaʊz] *v.t.* пересел|я́ть, -и́ть.

Reich [raɪx] *n.* рейх.

reign [reɪn] *n.* ца́рствование, власть; **in the ~ of Peter the Great** в ца́рствование Петра́ Вели́кого; (*fig.*) власть, госпо́дство; **~ of terror** (*hist.*) (якоби́нский) терро́р.

v.i. ца́рствовать (*impf.*); (*fig.*) цари́ть (*impf.*); **silence ~ed** цари́ла тишина́; **~ing beauty** пе́рвая краса́вица.

re-ignite [ˌriːɪgˈnaɪt] *v.t.* вновь разж|ига́ть, -е́чь.

reimburse [ˌriːɪmˈbɜːs] *v.t.* возме|ща́ть, -сти́ть (*что кому*); опла́|чивать, -ти́ть (*что кому*).

reimbursement [ˌriːɪmˈbɜːsmənt] *n.* возмеще́ние, возвраще́ние.

reimpose [ˌriːɪmˈpəʊz] *v.t.* восстан|а́вливать, -ови́ть; сно́ва вв|оди́ть, -ести́.

reimposition [ˌriːɪmpəˈzɪʃ(ə)n] *n.* восстановле́ние.

Reims [riːmz] *n.* Реймс.

rein [reɪn] *n.* по́вод (*pl.* -á *or* пово́дья), вожжа́; **he gave his horse the ~(s)** он отпусти́л пово́дья; **he drew ~ outside the door** он останови́л ло́шадь у вхо́да; (*fig.*): **his wife holds the ~s** его́ жена́ верхово́дит в до́ме; **you are giving ~ to your imagination** у вас разыгра́лось воображе́ние; **we must keep a tight ~ on our spending** мы должны́ стро́го контроли́ровать на́ши расхо́ды.

v.t. (*fig.*) держа́ть (*impf.*) в узде́; **~ in a horse** приде́рж|ивать, -а́ть ло́шадь.

reincarnate [ˌriːɪnˈkɑːneɪt] *v.t.* перевопло|ща́ть, -ти́ть.

reincarnation [ˌriːɪnkɑːˈneɪʃ(ə)n] *n.* перевоплоще́ние.

reindeer [ˈreɪndɪə(r)] *n.* се́верный оле́нь.

reinfect [ˌriːɪnˈfekt] *v.t.* вновь зара|жа́ть, -зи́ть.

reinfection [ˌriːɪnˈfekʃ(ə)n] *n.* повто́рное зараже́ние.

reinforce [ˌriːɪnˈfɔːs] *v.t.* усили|вать, -ть; **the army was ~d** а́рмия получи́ла подкрепле́ние; **this ~s my argument** э́то подкрепля́ет мои́ до́воды; **~d concrete** железобето́н.

reinforcement [ˌriːɪnˈfɔːsmənt] *n.* усиле́ние; (*of concrete*) арми́рование; (*pl., troops*) подкрепле́ние.

reinsert [ˌriːɪnˈsɜːt] *v.t.* вв|оди́ть, -ести́ вновь.

reinsertion [ˌriːɪnˈsɜːʃ(ə)n] *n.* втори́чный ввод.

reinstate [ˌriːɪnˈsteɪt] *v.t.* восстан|а́вливать, -ови́ть в права́х/до́лжности.

reinstatement [ˌriːɪnˈsteɪtmənt] *n.* восстановле́ние в права́х/до́лжности.

reinsurance [ˌriːɪnˈʃʊərəns] *n.* (*lit.*, *fig.*) перестрахо́вка.

reinsure [ˌriːɪnˈʃʊə(r)] *v.t.* (*lit.*, *fig.*) перестрахо́в|ывать, -а́ть.

reinter [ˌriːɪnˈtɜː(r)] *v.t.* перезахорони́ть (*pf.*).

reinterment [ˌriːɪnˈtɜːrmənt] *n.* перезахороне́ние.

reinterpret [ˌriːɪnˈtɜːprɪt] *v.t.* интерпрети́ровать (*pf.*) по-но́вому.

reinterpretation [ˌriːɪnˌtɜːprɪˈteɪʃ(ə)n] *n.* но́вая интерпрета́ция.

reintroduce [ˌriːɪntrəˈdjuːs] *v.t.* вновь вв|оди́ть, -ести́.

reintroduction [ˌriːɪntrəˈdʌkʃ(ə)n] *n.* повто́рное введе́ние.

reinvest [ˌriːɪnˈvest] *v.t.* & *i.* сно́ва поме|ща́ть, -сти́ть (капита́л).

reinvestment [ˌriːɪnˈvestmənt] *n.* повто́рное инвести́рование.

reinvigorate [ˌriːɪnˈvɪgəˌreɪt] *v.t.* вдохну́ть (*pf.*) но́вые си́лы в+*a*.

reissue [riːˈɪʃuː, -sjuː] *n.* переизда́ние; повто́рный вы́пуск.

v.t. переизд|ава́ть, -а́ть; сно́ва выпуска́ть, вы́пустить.

reiterate [riːˈɪtəˌreɪt] *v.t.* повтор|я́ть, -и́ть; тверди́ть (*impf.*).

reiteration [riːˌɪtəˈreɪʃ(ə)n] *n.* повторе́ние.

reject[1] [ˈriːdʒekt] *n.* (*discarded article*) брак; (*man unfit for mil. service*) при́знанный него́дным к вое́нной слу́жбе.

reject[2] [rɪˈdʒekt] *v.t.* **1.** (*throw away*) отбр|а́сывать, -о́сить. **2.** (*refuse to accept*) отв|ерга́ть, -е́ргнуть; отклон|я́ть, -и́ть; (*candidate*) забаллоти́ровать (*pf.*); **my offer was ~ed out of hand** моё предложе́ние сра́зу же отклони́ли; **I ~ your accusation** я не принима́ю ва́ше обвине́ние; **a ~ed suitor** отве́ргнутый покло́нник; **he was ~ed by the board** он не прошёл коми́ссию; **his stomach ~s food** его́ желу́док не принима́ет пи́щу.

rejection [rɪˈdʒekʃ(ə)n] *n.* (*casting out*) брако́вка; (*refusal to accept*) отка́з, отклоне́ние; **~ slip** уведомле́ние реда́кции об отка́зе напеча́тать произведе́ние.

rejoice [rɪˈdʒɔɪs] *v.t.* ра́довать, об-.

v.i. ра́доваться, об- (*чему*); **he ~s in the name of Eustace** его́ награди́ли и́менем Евста́хий.

rejoicing [rɪˈdʒɔɪsɪŋ] *n.* весе́лье, ра́дость.

rejoin[1] [riːˈdʒɔɪn] *v.t.* **1.** (*join together again*) вновь присоедин|я́ть, -и́ть. **2.** (*return to*) присоедин|я́ться, -и́ться вновь +*d.*; прим|ыка́ть, -кну́ть вновь к+*d.*; **he ~ed his regiment** он верну́лся в свой полк; **he ~ed his companions** он присоедини́лся к друзья́м.

rejoin[2] [rɪˈdʒɔɪn] *v.t.* & *i.* (*answer*) отв|еча́ть, -е́тить; возра|жа́ть, -зи́ть.

rejoinder [rɪˈdʒɔɪndə(r)] *n.* отве́т; возраже́ние.

rejuvenate [rɪˈdʒuːvɪˌneɪt] *v.t.* омол|а́живать, -оди́ть.

rejuvenation [rɪˌdʒuːvɪˈneɪʃ(ə)n] *n.* омоложе́ние.

rekindle [riːˈkɪnd(ə)l] *v.t.* разж|ига́ть, -е́чь вновь.

v.i. вновь разгор|а́ться, -е́ться.

relapse [rɪˈlæps] *n.* повторе́ние; рециди́в; **she suffered a ~** она́ сно́ва заболе́ла; **~ from virtue** отхо́д от пути́ и́стинного.

v.i. сно́ва преда́ться (*pf.*) (*чему*); сно́ва впасть (*pf.*) (*в какое-н. состояние*); **he ~d into bad ways** он сно́ва сби́лся с пути́; он (сно́ва) взя́лся за ста́рое; **she ~d into silence** она́ (сно́ва) замолча́ла.

relate [rɪˈleɪt] *v.t.* **1.** (*narrate*) расска́з|ывать, -а́ть о+*p.*; **strange to ~** как э́то ни стра́нно. **2.** (*establish relation between*) свя́з|ывать, -а́ть (*что с чем*); сопост|авля́ть, -а́вить (*что с чем*); устан|а́вливать, -ови́ть связь/отноше́ние (ме́жду+*i.*); *see also* **related**

v.i. **1.** (*be relevant*) относи́ться (*impf.*) (к+*d.*); име́ть (*impf.*) отноше́ние (к+*d.*). **2.** (*establish contact*): **he does not ~ well to people** он пло́хо схо́дится с людьми́.

related [rɪˈleɪtɪd] *adj.* **1.** (*logically connected*) (взаи́мно) свя́занный (с+*i.*). **2.** (*by blood or marriage*): **he is ~ to the royal family** он в родстве́ с короле́вской семьёй; **he and I are ~** мы с ним ро́дственники; **we are distantly ~** мы в да́льнем родстве́.

relatedness [rɪˈleɪtɪdnɪs] *n.* отноше́ние.

relation [rɪˈleɪʃ(ə)n] *n.* **1.** (*narration*) изложе́ние, расска́з. **2.** (*connection*, *correspondence*) отноше́ние, зави́симость; **in, with ~ to** что каса́ется +*g.*; относи́тельно+*g.*; **the cost bears no ~ to the results** расхо́ды несоизмери́мы с результа́тами. **3.** (*pl.*, *dealings*) отноше́ния (*nt. pl.*); **international ~s** междунаро́дные отноше́ния; **they broke off diplomatic ~s** они́ порва́ли дипломати́ческие отноше́ния; **public ~s officer** нача́льник/сотру́дник отде́ла информа́ции и рекла́мы; **sexual ~s** половы́е сноше́ния; **~s are strained between them** у них натя́нутые отноше́ния. **4.** (*kinsman*, *kinswoman*) ро́дственни|к (*fem.* -ца); (*pl.*) родня́ (*sg.*); **a near, close ~** бли́зкий ро́дственник; **~s by marriage** ро́дственники по му́жу/жене́; сво́йственники.

relationship [rɪˈleɪʃənʃɪp] *n.* (*relevance*) связь, отноше́ние; (*association*, *liaison*) взаимоотноше́ния (*nt. pl.*), связь; (*kinship*) родство́.

relative [ˈrelətɪv] *n.* (*kinsman*, *kinswoman*) ро́дственни|к (*fem.* -ца).

adj. **1.** (*comparative*) относи́тельный, сравни́тельный; **he is a ~ newcomer** он здесь относи́тельно неда́вно; (*not absolute*) относи́тельный, усло́вный; **beauty is a ~ term** красота́ — поня́тие относи́тельное; **~ly speaking** вообще́ говоря́. **2.**: **~ to** (*having reference to*) каса́ющийся +*g.*; относя́щийся к+*d.*; **the facts ~ to the situation** обстоя́тельства, относя́щиеся к де́лу. **3.** (*gram.*): **~ pronoun** относи́тельное местоиме́ние.

relativism [ˈrelətɪˌvɪz(ə)m] *n.* релятиви́зм.

relativity [ˌreləˈtɪvɪtɪ] *n.* относи́тельность; **theory of ~** тео́рия относи́тельности.

relax [rɪˈlæks] *v.t.* рассл|абля́ть, -а́бить; **he ~ed his grip** он разжа́л ру́ку; **we must not ~ our efforts** мы не должны́ ослабля́ть уси́лий; **the rules may be ~ed** распоря́док мо́жет быть ме́нее жёстким; **do not ~ your attention** не ослабля́йте внима́ние; **a ~ing climate** кли́мат, де́йствующий расслабля́юще.

v.i. (*weaken*) осл|абева́ть, -а́бнуть; (*rest*) рассл|абля́ться, -а́биться; отдыха́ть (*impf.*); **I like to ~ in the sun** я люблю́ посиде́ть/поваля́ться на со́лнце; **the atmosphere ~ed** атмосфе́ра разряди́лась.

relaxation [riːlækˈseɪʃ(ə)n] *n.* **1.** (*slackening*) спад; уменьше́ние; смягче́ние; **~ of discipline** ослабле́ние дисципли́ны. **2.** (*recreation*) о́тдых, развлече́ние; **take one's ~** отдыха́ть (*impf.*). **3.** (*relief of tension*) разря́дка.

relay [ˈriːleɪ] *n.* **1.** (*fresh team*) сме́на; (*pl.*): **they worked in ~s** они́ рабо́тали посме́нно. **2.** (**~ race**) эстафе́тный бег. **3.** (*elec.*) реле́ (*indecl.*). **4.** (*retransmitting device*) ретрансля́ция; **~ station** ретрансляцио́нная ста́нция.

v.t. (*retransmit*) ретрансли́ровать (*impf.*, *pf.*).

re-lay [riːˈleɪ] *v.t.* пере|кла́дывать, -ложи́ть.

relearn [riːˈlɜːn] *v.t.* вы́учить (*pf.*) за́ново.

release [rɪˈliːs] *n.* **1.** (*liberation*, *deliverance*) освобожде́ние; **~ from prison** освобожде́ние из тюрьмы́; **death was a happy ~ for him** смерть изба́вила его́ от тя́жких страда́ний. **2.** (*document authorizing ~*) свиде́тельство/докуме́нт об освобожде́нии. **3.** (*letting go*, *unfastening*) освобожде́ние; **~ of bombs** сбра́сывание бомб. **4.** (*device for doing this*) спуск; **carriage ~** (*of typewriter*) освобожде́ние каре́тки; **~ button** спускова́я кно́пка. **5.** (*publication*, *issue*) вы́пуск; **press ~** сообще́ние для печа́ти; **the latest ~s** (*films*) нови́нки (*f. pl.*) экра́на; **this film is on general ~** э́тот фильм в широ́ком прока́те.

v.t. **1.** (*liberate*) освобо|жда́ть, -ди́ть; изб|авля́ть, -а́вить. **2.** (*unfasten*, *let go*) отпус|ка́ть, -ти́ть; выпуска́ть, вы́пустить; **do not ~ the brake** не отпуска́йте то́рмоз; **he ~d her hand** он отпусти́л её ру́ку. **3.** (*make over*, *surrender*) отд|ава́ть, -а́ть; **he ~d his right to the property** он отказа́лся от прав на иму́щество. **4.** (*issue for circulation*) выпуска́ть, вы́пустить; **the news was ~d** сообще́ние бы́ло пре́дано огла́ске; **the film was ~d** фильм был вы́пущен (на экра́ны).

relegate [ˈrelɪˌgeɪt] *v.t.* от|сыла́ть, -осла́ть; низв|оди́ть, -ести́; **the team was ~d to the second division** кома́нду перевели́ во второ́й разря́д; **his works have been ~d to oblivion** его́ произведе́ния бы́ли пре́даны забве́нию.

relegation [ˌrelɪˈgeɪʃ(ə)n] *n.* пониже́ние, перево́д (в бо́лее ни́зкий класс *и т.п.*).

relent [rɪˈlent] *v.i.* смягч|а́ться, -и́ться; подобре́ть (*pf.*); **the storm ~ed** бу́ря ути́хла; **his sufferings made her ~** его́ страда́ния разжа́лобили её.

relentless [rɪ'lentlɪs] *adj.* (*merciless*) безжáлостный; (*implacable*) неумоли́мый; ~ **persecution** жестóкие гонéния; (*persistent*) упóрный, неуклóнный; ~ **efforts** неослáбные уси́лия.

relentlessness [rɪ'lentlɪsnɪs] *n.* безжáлостность; неумоли́мость.

relet [ri:'let] *v.t.* сда|вáть, -ть снóва.

relevance ['relɪv(ə)ns] *n.* отношéние к дéлу; умéстность, релевáнтность.

relevant ['relɪv(ə)nt] *adj.* относя́щийся к дéлу; умéстный, релевáнтный; ~ **to** относя́щийся к+*d*.

reliability [rɪ,laɪə'bɪlɪtɪ] *n.* надёжность; достовéрность.

reliable [rɪ'laɪəb(ə)l] *adj.* надёжный; (*of a source*, *statement etc.*) достовéрный.

reliance [rɪ'laɪəns] *n.* (*trust*) довéрие; **I place great ~ upon him** я емý óчень доверя́ю; я óчень на негó надéюсь/полагáюсь.

reliant [rɪ'laɪənt] *adj.* (*dependent*) зави́симый, зави́сящий; **they are completely ~ on their pension** они́ пóлностью зави́сят от своéй пéнсии.

relic ['relɪk] *n.* **1.** (*of saint etc.*) рели́квия; (*pl.*) мóщ|и (*pl.*, *g.* -éй). **2.** (*survival from past*) рели́квия; (*custom etc.*) пережи́ток. **3.** (*pl.*, *residue*) остáток.

relict ['relɪkt] *n.* (*leg.*, *widow*) вдовá.

relief [rɪ'li:f] *n.* **1.** (*alleviation*, *deliverance*) облегчéние; **the medicine brought some ~** лекáрство принеслó нéкоторое облегчéние; **she heaved a sigh of ~** онá издалá вздох облегчéния; **it was a great ~ to me** у меня́ отлеглó от сéрдца. **2.** (*abatement*) снижéние, смягчéние; ~ **of urban traffic congestion** разгрýзка городскóго трáнспорта; ~ **road** вспомогáтельная дорóга. **3.** (*assistance to poor*, *distressed etc.*) посóбие; ~ **agency** организáция по оказáнию пóмощи; **famine ~** пóмощь голодáющим; **eligible for public ~** имéющий прáво на госудáрственное посóбие; **he had to go on ~** емý пришлóсь перейти́ на посóбие; **a ~ fund for flood victims** фонд пóмощи жéртвам наводнéния. **4.** (*liberation*) освобождéние; (*raising of siege*) сня́тие осáды. **5.** (*replacement*) смéна (дежýрных); (*pers.*) смéна; дежýрный, заступáющий на пост. **6.** (*contrast*) перемéна, контрáст; **a blank wall without ~** глухáя рóвная стенá; **Shakespeare introduces comic ~** Шекспи́р прибегáет к коми́ческой разря́дке. **7.** (*sculpture etc.*) рельéф; **high/low ~** горельéф/барельéф; **in high ~** óчень вы́пукло; ~ **design** рельéфный узóр; ~ **map** рельéфная кáрта; (*fig.*) чёткость, рельéфность; **the facts stand out in full ~** фáкты представля́ются самоочеви́дными.

relieve [rɪ'li:v] *v.t.* **1.** (*alleviate*) облегч|áть, -и́ть; **I was ~d to get your letter** я был рад получи́ть вáше письмó; **it ~s the monotony** э́то внóсит разнообрáзие. **2.** (*bring assistance to*) при|ходи́ть, -йти́ на пóмощь +*d*.; выручáть, вы́ручить. **3.** (*unburden*) освобо|ждáть, -ди́ть (*когó от чегó*); **this ~s me of the necessity to speak** э́то освобождáет меня́ от необходи́мости говори́ть; **swearing ~s one's feelings** когдá вы́ругаешься, станóвится лéгче; **he ~d himself** (*urinated*) **against the wall** он помочи́лся у стéнки; **may I ~ you of your bags?** позвóльте мне взять вáши чемодáны; **the thief ~d him of his watch** вор стащи́л у негó часы́. **4.** (*replace on duty*) смен|я́ть, -и́ть; **you will be ~d at 10 o'clock** вас смéнят в 10 часóв.

religion [rɪ'lɪdʒ(ə)n] *n.* рели́гия, вéра; вероисповéдание; **she makes a ~ of housework** онá дéлает культ из домáшнего хозя́йства.

religious [rɪ'lɪdʒəs] *n.* ≃ монáх; (*pl.*) чёрное духовéнство.

adj. **1.** (*of religion*) религиóзный; (*devout*; *practising religion*) религиóзный, нáбожный; (*of a monastic order*) монáшеский. **2.** (*fig.*, *scrupulous*): **he attended every meeting ~ly** он добросóвестно/неукосни́тельно/свя́то посещáл все собрáния.

reline [ri:'laɪn] *v.t.* меня́ть, смени́ть подклáдку у+*g*. (*or* на+*p*.).

relinquish [rɪ'lɪŋkwɪʃ] *v.t.* (*give up*, *abandon*) ост|авля́ть, -áвить; **she ~ed all hope** онá остáвила вся́кую надéжду; **I ~ed the habit** я брóсил э́ту привы́чку; (*surrender*) сд|авáть, áть; остав|ля́ть, -áвить; **he ~ed his claims** он отказáлся от свои́х трéбований; (*let go*) разж|имáть, -áть; осл|абля́ть, -áбить; **the dog ~ed its hold** собáка разжáла зýбы.

relinquishment [rɪ'lɪŋkwɪʃmənt] *n.* оставлéние, сдáча, откáз (*от чегó*).

reliquary ['relɪkwərɪ] *n.* рáка, ковчéг.

relish ['relɪʃ] *n.* **1.** (*appetizing flavour*) вкус, при́вкус. **2.** (*fig.*, *attractive quality*) прéлесть, привлекáтельность; **sport lost its ~ for me** спорт потеря́л для меня́ свою́ прéлесть; **he enjoys the ~ of danger** егó влечёт опáсность; (*zest*, *liking*) смак, пристрáстие; **he ate with ~** он ел с аппети́том; **I have no ~ for travel** у меня́ нет тя́ги к путешéствиям. **3.** (*sauce*, *garnish*) припрáва; маринáд.

v.t. получ|áть, -и́ть удовóльствие от+*g*.; **I could ~ a steak** я бы с удовóльствием съел бифштéкс; **you will not ~ what I have to say** то, что я скажý, не придётся вам по вкýсу.

relive [ri:'lɪv] *v.t.* переж|ивáть, -и́ть вновь.

reload [ri:'ləʊd] *v.t.* (*a vehicle etc.*) нагру|жáть, -зи́ть зáново; (*a weapon*) перезаря|жáть, -ди́ть.

relocate [,ri:ləʊ'keɪt] *v.t.* & *i.* переме|щáть(ся), -сти́ть(ся); перебази́ровать(ся) (*pf.*).

relocation [,ri:ləʊ'keɪʃən] *n.* перемещéние.

reluctance [rɪ'lʌkt(ə)ns] *n.* нежелáние; неохóта; нерасположéние.

reluctant [rɪ'lʌkt(ə)nt] *adj.* неохóтный; **she was ~ to leave home** ей не хотéлось покидáть дом; **he followed with ~ steps** он неохóтно тащи́лся слéдом.

rely [rɪ'laɪ] *v.i.* полагáться (*impf.*); надéяться (*impf.*) (*both* на+*a*.); **you can ~ on me** вы мóжете на меня́ положи́ться; **~ upon it, he will come** он придёт, бýдьте увéрены.

remain [rɪ'meɪn] *v.i.* ост|авáться, -áться; **little ~ed of the original building** от первоначáльного здáния почти́ ничегó не остáлось; **it only ~s for me to thank you** мне тóлько остаётся вас поблагодари́ть; **that ~s to be seen** поживём — уви́дим; ну, мы э́то ещё посмóтрим; (*stay*) пребывáть (*impf.*); **he ~ed a week in Paris** он прóбыл недéлю в Пари́же; **her face will ~ in my memory** её лицó остáнется в моéй пáмяти; **he ~ed silent** он храни́л молчáние; **his servants ~ed faithful to him** слýги остáлись вéрны емý; **these things ~ the same** э́ти вéщи не меня́ются; **please ~ seated!** пожáлуйста, не вставáйте!; **one thing ~s certain** однó безуслóвно я́сно; **I ~ yours truly** остаю́сь прéданный Вам.

remainder [rɪ'meɪndə(r)] *n.* **1.** (*residue*, *rest*) остáт|ок, -ки; **he is selling the ~ of his estate** он продаёт остáвшуюся часть своегó помéстья; (*of people*) остальны́е (*pl.*). **2.** (*arith.*) остáток. **3.** (*of book left unsold*) нераспрóданный тирáж. **4.** (*leg.*) послéдующее иму́щественное прáво.

v.t. уцен|я́ть, -и́ть нераспрóданный тирáж; **the book was ~ed** кни́га былá уцененá.

remains [rɪ'meɪnz] *n.* остáтки (*m. pl.*), остáнк|и (*pl.*, *g.* -ов); **the ~ of daylight** остáтки дневнóго свéта; **the ~ of a meal** остáтки еды́; (*ruins*) развáлин|ы (*pl.*, *g.* —); (*corpse*): **the ~s were cremated** остáнки бы́ли сожжены́.

remake ['ri:meɪk] *n.* (*e.g. of a film*) пересня́тый фильм; передéлка.

v.t. передéл|ывать, -ать.

remand [rɪ'mɑ:nd] *n.* возвращéние (арестóванного) под стрáжу; ~ **home** исправи́тельный дом для несовершеннолéтних.

v.t.: **he was ~ed in custody** егó отослáли обрáтно под стрáжу.

remark [rɪ'mɑ:k] *n.* **1.** (*notice*) наблюдéние; **it is worthy of ~** э́то достóйно внимáния; **it passed without ~** э́то прошлó незамéченным. **2.** (*spoken observation*) замечáние; **he made rude ~s about my clothes** он отпускáл невéжливые замечáния по пóводу моéй одéжды.

v.t. **1.** (*observe*) отм|ечáть, -éтить. **2.** (*comment*) зам|ечáть, -éтить; **'you are late,' he ~ed** «Вы опоздáли» — замéтил он.

v.i. выскáзываться, вы́сказаться; **he ~ed upon your absence** он отмéтил вáше отсýтствие.

remarkable [rɪ'mɑ:kəb(ə)l] *adj.* (*extraordinary*) удиви́тельный;

замеча́тельный; (*notable*): **this year has been ~ for its lack of rain** э́то был на ре́дкость сухо́й год.

remarriage [ri:ˈmærɪdʒ] *n.* (вступле́ние в) но́вый брак.

remarry [ri:ˈmærɪ] *v.t.* (*of man*) вновь жени́ться (*pf.*) на+*p.*; (*of woman*) вновь вы́йти (*pf.*) (за́муж) за+*a.*

v.i. вступ|а́ть, -и́ть в но́вый брак.

remediable [rɪˈmi:dɪəb(ə)l] *adj.* поправи́мый, излечи́мый.

remedial [rɪˈmi:dɪəl] *adj.* исправля́ющий, лече́бный; (*educ.*) корректи́вный; **~ work** рабо́та с отстаю́щими.

remed|y [ˈremɪdɪ] *n.* **1.** (*cure*) сре́дство, лека́рство; **a ~y for warts** сре́дство про́тив борода́вок; **the ~y for superstition is knowledge** лу́чшее лекарство от суеве́рия — зна́ние. **2.** (*redress*) возмеще́ние; (*legal recourse*) сре́дство суде́бной защи́ты.

v.t. выле́чивать, вы́лечить; испр|авля́ть, -а́вить; **this cannot ~y the situation** э́то не попра́вит положе́ния; **these ills must be ~ied** э́ти недоста́тки должны́ быть испра́влены.

remember [rɪˈmembə(r)] *v.t.* **1.** (*keep in the memory*) по́мнить (*impf.*); уде́рживать/храни́ть (*impf.*) в па́мяти; **I ~ her as a girl** я по́мню её де́вочкой; **don't ~ it against me** не зли́тесь на меня́ за э́то. **2.** (*recall*) вспо|мина́ть, -о́мнить; прип|омина́ть, -о́мнить; **I can't ~ his name** я не могу́ вспо́мнить его́ и́мя; **I ~ you saying it** я по́мню, что вы э́то сказа́ли; **not that I can ~** наско́лько я по́мню, нет; **he ~ed himself in time** он во́время опо́мнился. **3.** (*not forget; be mindful of*) не забыва́ть/забы́ть, име́ть (*impf.*) в виду́; **~ to turn out the light** не забу́дьте погаси́ть свет; **~ me in your prayers** помяни́те меня́ в свои́х моли́твах; **you should ~ your place** вы должны́ по́мнить своё ме́сто; **~ you are still a young man** не забыва́йте, что вы ещё мо́лоды. **4.** (*implying gift or gratuity*): **~ the waiter!** не забу́дьте дать официа́нту на чай!; **he ~ed her in his will** он упомяну́л её в своём завеща́нии. **5.** (*convey greetings*): **~ me to your mother** кла́няйтесь ва́шей ма́тушке; переда́йте приве́т ва́шей ма́тери.

remembrance [rɪˈmembrəns] *n.* **1.** (*memory; recollection*) па́мять; воспомина́ние; **in ~ of** в па́мять о+*p.*; **it put me in ~ of my youth** э́то напо́мнило мне мо́лодость; **to the best of my ~** наско́лько я по́мню; **a service in ~ of the dead** помина́льная слу́жба; **R~ Day** день па́мяти поги́бших (в пе́рвую и втору́ю мировы́е во́йны). **2.** (*memento*) сувени́р. **3.** (*pl., greetings*) приве́т; **give my kind ~s to your wife** переда́йте серде́чный приве́т ва́шей жене́.

remilitarization [ri:ˌmɪlɪtəˌraɪˈzeɪʃ(ə)n] *n.* ремилитариза́ция.

remilitarize [ri:ˈmɪlɪtəˌraɪz] *v.t.* ремилитаризи́ровать (*impf., pf.*).

remind [rɪˈmaɪnd] *v.t.* нап|омина́ть, -о́мнить (*кому что or о чём or inf.*); **he ~s me of my father** он напомина́ет мне отца́; **I was ~ed of the last time we met** э́то напо́мнило мне о на́шей после́дней встре́че; **he ~ed me to buy bread** он напо́мнил мне купи́ть хле́ба; **that ~s me!** кста́ти!; **don't let me have to ~ you again** не заставля́йте меня́ напомина́ть вам ещё раз; **visitors are ~ed that there is no admission after 6** посети́телей про́сят име́ть в виду́, что впуск прекраща́ется в 6 часо́в.

reminder [rɪˈmaɪndə(r)] *n.* напомина́ние; **I sent him a ~** я посла́л ему́ пи́сьменное напомина́ние; **he needs a gentle ~** ему́ на́до осторо́жно напо́мнить.

reminisce [ˌremɪˈnɪs] *v.i.* пред|ава́ться, -а́ться воспомина́ниям.

reminiscence [ˌremɪˈnɪs(ə)ns] *n.* **1.** (*memory*) воспомина́ние; **he wrote ~s of the war** он написа́л вое́нные мемуа́ры. **2.** (*similarity*) схо́дство; черта́, напомина́ющая (*кого/что*).

reminiscent [ˌremɪˈnɪs(ə)nt] *adj.* **1.** (*recalling the past*) вспомина́ющий, напомина́ющий; **I found him in ~ mood** я заста́л его́ погружённым в воспомина́ния; **she had a ~ look** у неё был заду́мчивый вид. **2.:** **~** (*suggestive*) **of** напомина́ющий; **his music is ~ of Brahms** его́ му́зыка напомина́ет Бра́мса.

remiss [rɪˈmɪs] *adj.* хала́тный; неради́вый.

remission [rɪˈmɪʃ(ə)n] *n.* **1.** (*forgiveness*) проще́ние; **~ of sins** отпуще́ние грехо́в. **2.** (*discharge*): **~ of a debt** освобожде́ние от до́лга. **3.** (*abatement, decrease*) уменьше́ние; **~ of effort** ослабле́ние уси́лий; **the noise went on without ~** шум не умолка́л.

remissness [rɪˈmɪsnɪs] *n.* хала́тность; неради́вость.

remit[1] [ˈri:mɪt, rɪˈmɪt] *n.* (*terms of reference*) зада́чи (*f. pl.*), компете́нция.

remit[2] [rɪˈmɪt] *v.t.* **1.** (*forgive*) про|ща́ть, -сти́ть; отпус|ка́ть, -ти́ть (*грехи*). **2.** (*excuse payment of*) освобо|жда́ть, -ди́ть (*кого*) от+*g.*; **~ a tax** сн|има́ть, -ять нало́г. **3.** (*slacken, mitigate*) ум|еньша́ть, -е́ньшить; осл|абля́ть, -а́бить. **4.** (*send, transfer*) перес|ыла́ть, -ла́ть; перев|оди́ть, -ести́ (*деньги*). **5.** (*refer for decision*) от|сыла́ть, -осла́ть.

v.i. (*abate*) осл|абля́ться, -а́биться; прекра|ща́ться, -ти́ться.

remittance [rɪˈmɪt(ə)ns] *n.* (*sending of money*) перево́д де́нег; (*money sent*) де́нежный перево́д; переводи́мые де́н|ьги (*pl., g.* -ег).

remitter [rɪˈmɪtə(r)] *n.* (*sender of money*) отправи́тель (*m.*) де́нежного перево́да.

remnant [ˈremnənt] *n.* (*remains*) оста́ток; (*trace*) след; (*of cloth*) оста́ток; (*survival*) пережи́ток.

remodel [ri:ˈmɒd(ə)l] *v.t.* переде́л|ывать, -ать.

remonstrance [rɪˈmɒnstrəns] *n.* проте́ст; ремонстра́ция.

remonstrate [ˈremənˌstreɪt] *v.i.* протестова́ть (*impf.*); возра|жа́ть, -зи́ть; (*urge*): **he ~d with me** он увещева́л меня́.

remorse [rɪˈmɔ:s] *n.* **1.** (*repentance; regret*) угрызе́ния (*nt. pl.*) со́вести; **do you feel no ~ for what you did?** вас не му́чит со́весть, что вы так поступи́ли? **2.** (*compunction*) жа́лость; **without ~** безжа́лостно.

remorseful [rɪˈmɔ:sfʊl] *adj.* по́лный раска́яния.

remorseless [rɪˈmɔ:slɪs] *adj.* безжа́лостный.

remote [rɪˈməʊt] *adj.* отдалённый, да́льный, глухо́й; **a ~ village** глухо́е село́; **a ~ ancestor** далёкий пре́док; **~ control** дистанцио́нное управле́ние; **there is a ~ possibility of its happening** не совсе́м исключено́, что э́то случи́тся; **I haven't the ~st idea** не име́ю ни мале́йшего поня́тия; **he was not even ~ly interested** он не прояви́л ни мале́йшего интере́са (к+*d.*).

cpd. **~-controlled** *adj.* радиоуправля́емый.

remould[1] [ˈri:məʊld] *n.* (*tyre*) ши́на с восстано́вленным проте́ктором.

remould[2] [ri:ˈməʊld] *v.t.* лепи́ть, вы- за́ново; (*fig.*) преобра|жа́ть, -зи́ть.

remount[1] [ˈri:maʊnt] *n.* (*horse*) запасна́я/ремо́нтная ло́шадь; (*horses*) ремо́нтные ло́шади, ко́нский ремо́нт.

remount[2] [ri:ˈmaʊnt] *v.t.* **1.** (*climb again*): **he ~ed the ladder** он сно́ва подня́лся на ле́стницу; **he ~ed his horse** он сно́ва сел на ло́шадь; **we ~ed the hill** мы сно́ва подняли́сь на холм. **2.** (*provide fresh horses for*) меня́ть, по- лошаде́й +*d.* **3.** (*a photograph etc.*) перекле́ить (*pf.*) на друго́е паспарту́.

v.i. сно́ва сади́ться/сесть на ло́шадь.

removable [rɪˈmu:vəb(ə)l] *adj.* (*detachable*) съёмный; (*from office*) устрани́мый, сменя́емый.

removal [rɪˈmu:v(ə)l] *n.* (*taking away*) удале́ние; (*from office etc.*) смеще́ние, отстране́ние; (*of obstacles etc.*) устране́ние; (*of furniture*) перево́зка; **~ firm** трансаге́нтство; **~ men** перево́зчики ме́бели.

remove [rɪˈmu:v] *n.* **1.** (*degree of distance*) удале́ние; **this is only one ~ from treason** от э́того то́лько оди́н шаг до изме́ны. **2.** (*move to higher class*) перехо́д/перево́д в сле́дующий класс.

v.t. **1.** (*take away, off*) уб|ира́ть, -ра́ть; ун|оси́ть, -ести́; **the maid ~d the tea-things** го́рничная убрала́ ча́йную посу́ду; **how can I ~ these stains?** как мо́жно вы́вести э́ти пя́тна?; **the boy was ~d from school** ма́льчика забра́ли из шко́лы; **he ~d his hat** он снял шля́пу; **this will ~ all your doubts** э́то рассе́ет все ва́ши сомне́ния. **2.** (*dismiss*) сме|ща́ть, -сти́ть; **he was ~d from office** его́ сня́ли с рабо́ты. **3.** (*eliminate*) устран|я́ть, -и́ть. **4.** (*separate*): *see* **removed**

v.i. (*move house*) пере|езжа́ть, -е́хать.

removed [rɪˈmu:vd] *p.p.* **1.** (*distant*) далёкий, отдалённый; **what you have heard is not far ~ from the truth** то, что вы слы́шали, не так далеко́ от и́стины. **2.** (*of relationships*) да́льний; **first cousin once ~** (*cousin's child*) ребёнок двою́родного бра́та (*or* двою́родной сестры́); (*parents cousin*) двою́родный дя́дя, двою́родная тётя.

remover [rɪ'mu:və(r)] *n.* **(furniture-~)** перево́зчик ме́бели.

remunerate [rɪ'mju:nə,reɪt] *v.t.* (*pers.*) вознагра|жда́ть, -ди́ть; (*work*) опла́|чивать, -ти́ть.

remuneration [rɪ,mju:nə'reɪʃ(ə)n] *n.* вознагражде́ние; опла́та.

remunerative [rɪ'mju:nərətɪv] *adj.* (*well-rewarded*) вы́годный, хорошо́ опла́чиваемый.

rena|issance [rɪ'neɪs(ə)ns, rə'n-, -sɑ̃s], **-scence** [rɪ'næs(ə)ns] *n.* (*hist.*) Ренесса́нс, Возрожде́ние; **R~ art** иску́сство эпо́хи Возрожде́ния; (*revival*) возрожде́ние.

renal ['ri:n(ə)l] *adj.* по́чечный.

rename [ri:'neɪm] *v.t.* переимено́в|ывать, -а́ть.

renascence [rɪ'næs(ə)ns] = **renaissance**

renascent [rɪ'næs(ə)nt] *adj.* возрожда́ющийся.

rend [rend] *v.t.* **1.** (*tear apart*) раз|рыва́ть, -орва́ть; раз|дира́ть, -одра́ть; **the country was rent by civil war** страну́ раздира́ла гражда́нская война́; **an explosion rent the air** взрыв сотря́с во́здух. **2.** (*tear away*) от|рыва́ть, -орва́ть; от|дира́ть, -одра́ть.

render ['rendə(r)] *v.t.* **1.** (*give when required or due*) возд|ава́ть, -а́ть; отд|ава́ть, -а́ть; **let us ~ thanks to God** возблагодари́м же Бо́га; **we are told to ~ good for evil** нас у́чат плати́ть добро́м за зло; **~ unto Caesar (the things that are Caesar's)** ке́сарево ке́сарю; **doctors ~ valuable service** врачи́ де́лают поле́зное де́ло; **I was called on to ~ assistance** меня́ попроси́ли оказа́ть по́мощь. **2.** (*present, submit*) предст|авля́ть, -а́вить; **the tradesman ~ed his account** торго́вец предъяви́л свой счёт; **you must ~ an account of your expenditure** вы должны́ отчита́ться в свои́х расхо́дах. **3.** (*perform, portray*) исп|олня́ть, -о́лнить; **the sonata was beautifully ~ed** сона́та была́ прекра́сно испо́лнена; **the artist ~ed his expression faithfully** худо́жник ве́рно улови́л выраже́ние его́ лица́. **4.** (*translate*) перев|оди́ть, -ести́. **5.** (*cause to be*): **he was ~ed speechless** он онеме́л; **the car accident ~ed him helpless** в результа́те автомоби́льной катастро́фы он оста́лся инвали́дом. **6.** (*melt and clarify*) топи́ть, пере-. **7.** (*cover with plaster*) штукату́рить, от-.

rend|ering ['rendərɪŋ], **-ition** [ren'dɪʃ(ə)n] *nn.* (*performance*) исполне́ние, тракто́вка; (*translation*) перево́д.

rendezvous ['rɒndɪ,vu:, -deɪ,vu:] *n.* (*meeting*) рандеву́ (*nt. indecl.*), свида́ние; (*place*) ме́сто свида́ния; (*mil.*) сбор.

v.i. встр|еча́ться, -е́титься.

rendition [ren'dɪʃ(ə)n] = **rendering**

renegade ['renɪ,geɪd] *n.* ренега́т, отсту́пник.

adj. ренега́тский, отсту́пнический.

reneg(u)e [rɪ'ni:g, -'neg, -'neɪg] *v.i.*: **he ~d on his promise** он нару́шил своё обеща́ние; (*US, at cards*) = **revoke** *v.i.*

renew [rɪ'nju:] *v.t.* **1.** (*replace*) обн|овля́ть, -о́вить; замен|я́ть, -и́ть; **she ~ed the water in his glass** она́ поменя́ла ему́ во́ду в стака́не; **the trees ~ed their leaves** дере́вья покры́лись но́вой листво́й. **2.** (*restore, mend*) восстан|а́вливать, -ови́ть; **with ~ed vigour** с удво́енной эне́ргией; с но́выми си́лами. **3.** (*repeat, continue*) возобнов|ля́ть, -и́ть; **the game was ~ed** игра́ возобнови́лась; **your subscription needs ~ing** вам ну́жно возобнови́ть/продли́ть перепи́ску.

renewable [rɪ'nju:əb(ə)l] *adj.* могу́щий быть обновлённым/продлённым; **~ resources** возобновля́емые ресу́рсы; **the lease is ~ next year** срок аре́нды сле́дует продли́ть в сле́дующем году́; (*replaceable*) замени́мый; **a pencil with ~ leads** каранда́ш с запасны́ми гри́фелями.

renewal [rɪ'nju:əl] *n.* (*replacement*) обновле́ние; заме́на; (*restoration*) восстановле́ние; (*resumption*) возобновле́ние, продле́ние.

rennet ['renɪt] *n.* (*curdled milk*) сычу́жина.

renounc|e [rɪ'naʊns] *v.t.* **1.** (*surrender*) отка́з|ываться, -а́ться от+*g.*; отр|ека́ться, -е́чься от+*g.*; **he ~ed the world** он отрёкся от ми́ра. **2.** (*repudiate*) отв|ерга́ть, -е́ргнуть. **3.** (*abandon, discontinue*) отка́з|ываться, -а́ться от+*g.*; **they ~ed their attempt to reach the summit** они́ отказа́лись от попы́тки взобра́ться на верши́ну; **~ing all thought of gain** соверше́нно не ду́мая о вы́годе.

renouncement [rɪ'naʊnsmənt] *n.* (*surrender*) отрече́ние, отка́з; (*repudiation*) отрица́ние.

renovate ['renə,veɪt] *v.t.* (*renew*) обнов|ля́ть, -ови́ть; восстан|а́вливать, -ови́ть; (*repair*) поднов|ля́ть, -и́ть; ремонти́ровать, от-.

renovation [,renə'veɪʃ(ə)n] *n.* обновле́ние; восстановле́ние; (*repair*) реконстру́кция; ремо́нт; **the builders carried out ~s** строи́тели произвели́ ремо́нт.

renovator ['renə,veɪtə(r)] *n.* реставра́тор.

renown [rɪ'naʊn] *n.* сла́ва; изве́стность; **a preacher of ~** пропове́дник, по́льзующийся большо́й изве́стностью; **he won ~ on the battlefield** он завоева́л сла́ву на по́ле бо́я.

renowned [rɪ'naʊnd] *adj.* просла́вленный, изве́стный; **he is ~ for his eloquence** он сла́вится свои́м красноре́чием.

rent[1] [rent] *n.* (*tear, split*) дыра́; проре́ха; **a ~ in the clouds** просве́т в ту́чах.

rent[2] [rent] *n.* (*for premises*) наёмная/аре́ндная пла́та; (*of land*) аре́ндная пла́та; (*of a flat*) квартпла́та; (*of telephone*) пла́та за телефо́н; **she pays a high, heavy ~ for her flat** она́ о́чень мно́го пла́тит за кварти́ру; **I pay £50 a week in ~** я плачу́ 50 фу́нтов в неде́лю за кварти́ру; **the ~ is fixed at £50** аре́ндная пла́та устано́влена в разме́ре пятидесяти фу́нтов; **I shall charge you ~ for the use of my car** я бу́ду брать с вас пла́ту за по́льзование мои́м автомоби́лем.

v.t. **1.** (*occupy or use for ~*) арендова́ть (*impf.*); сн|има́ть, -ять в наём. **2.** (*let out for ~*) сд|ава́ть, -ать в наём; **~ed accommodation** сня́тое жильё. **3.** (*be let*): **these old houses ~ cheap** э́ти ста́рые дома́ сдаю́тся дёшево.

cpds. **~-book** *n.* кни́га учёта аре́ндной пла́ты; **~-collector** *n.* сбо́рщик кварти́рной пла́ты; **~-free** *adj.* & *adv.* освобождённый (*or* с освобожде́нием) от кварти́рной пла́ты; **~-roll** *n.* (*register*) спи́сок владе́ний и дохо́дов от сда́чи в аре́нду.

rentable ['rentəb(ə)l] *adj.* приго́дный к сда́че внаём; могу́щий быть сда́нным в аре́нду.

rental ['rent(ə)l] *n.* (*income from rents*) ре́нтный дохо́д; (*rate of rent*) разме́р аре́ндной пла́ты.

renter ['rentə(r)] *n.* (*payer*) нанима́тель (*m.*), аренда́тор; (*payee*) наймода́тель (*m.*), арендода́тель (*m.*).

rentier ['rɑ̃tɪ,eɪ] *n.* рантье́ (*m. indecl.*).

renumber [ri:'nʌmbə(r)] *v.t.* перенумеро́в|ывать, -а́ть.

renunciation [rɪ,nʌnsɪ'eɪʃ(ə)n] *n.* (*surrender*) отка́з, отрече́ние; (*repudiation*) отрица́ние; (*self-denial*) самоотрече́ние.

reoccupation [ri:,ɒkjʊ'peɪʃ(ə)n] *n.* (*of territory*) повто́рный захва́т; (*of a building etc.*) повто́рное заселе́ние.

reoccupy [ri:'ɒkjʊ,paɪ] *v.t.* вновь зан|има́ть, -я́ть; вновь оккупи́ровать (*impf., pf.*).

reopen [ri:'əʊpən] *v.t.* вновь/сно́ва откр|ыва́ть, -ы́ть; возобнов|ля́ть, -и́ть; **she ~ed the window** она́ сно́ва откры́ла окно́; **the discussion was ~ed** диску́ссия возобнови́лось; **I intend to ~ my bank account** я собира́юсь вновь откры́ть ба́нковский счёт.

v.i.: **the shops will ~ after the holidays** по́сле пра́здников магази́ны откро́ются сно́ва.

reorder [ri:'ɔ:də(r)] *n.* повто́рный/возобновлённый зака́з.

v.t. (*rearrange*) перестр|а́ивать, -о́ить; (*renew order for*) повтор|я́ть, -и́ть (*or* возобнов|ля́ть, -и́ть) зака́з на+*a.*

reorganization [ri:,ɔ:gə,naɪ'zeɪʃ(ə)n] *n.* реорганиза́ция.

reorganize [ri:'ɔ:gə,naɪz] *v.t.* реорганизо́в|ывать, -а́ть.

rep[1], **-p, -s** [rep] *n.* (*text.*) репс.

rep[2] [rep] (*coll.*) = **representative** *n.*

rep[3] [rep] (*coll.*) = **repertory 2.**

repaint [ri:'peɪnt] *v.t.* перекра́|шивать, -сить.

repair[1] [rɪ'peə(r)] *n.* **1.** (*restoring to sound condition*) ремо́нт; **minor/running ~s** ме́лкий/теку́щий ремо́нт; **'~s while you wait'** «ремо́нт в прису́тствии зака́зчика»; **the shop is closed for ~s** магази́н на ремо́нте (*or* закры́т на ремо́нт); **the road is under ~** доро́гу ремонти́руют; **my shoes need ~** мне ну́жно почини́ть ту́фли; **~ shop** ремо́нтная мастерска́я. **2.** (*good condition*) го́дность, испра́вность; **the house is in good ~** дом в хоро́шем состоя́нии; **the car is out of ~** маши́на неиспра́вна.

v.t. **1.** (*mend, renovate*) ремонти́ровать, от-; (*restore*) восстан|а́вливать, -ови́ть. **2.** (*make amends for*): **I should like to ~ my omission** я бы хоте́л испра́вить упуще́ние.

repair[2] [rɪˈpeə(r)] *v.i.* (*betake o.s.*) отпр|авля́ться, -а́виться; напр|авля́ться, -а́виться.

repairable [rɪˈpeərəb(ə)l] *adj.* поддаю́щийся ремо́нту/исправле́нию.

repairer [rɪˈpeərə(r)] *n.* ма́стер, ремо́нтник.

reparable [ˈrepərəb(ə)l] *adj.* поправи́мый, исправи́мый; восполни́мый.

reparation [ˌrepəˈreɪʃ(ə)n] *n.* компенса́ция; возмеще́ние уще́рба; **he made ~ for his fault** он загла́дил свою́ вину́; (*pl.*, *compensation for war damage*) (вое́нные) репара́ции (*f. pl.*).

repartee [ˌrepɑːˈtiː] *n.* остроу́мный отве́т; **gift of ~** нахо́дчивость, остроу́мие.

repast [rɪˈpɑːst] *n.* (*liter.*) тра́пе́за; (*banquet*) пи́ршество.

repatriate[1] [riːˈpætrɪˌeɪt] *n.* репатриа́нт (*fem.* -ка).

repatriate[2] [riːˈpætrɪˌeɪt] *v.t.* репатрии́ровать (*impf.*, *pf.*).

repatriation [riːˌpætrɪˈeɪʃ(ə)n] *n.* репатриа́ция.

repay [riːˈpeɪ] *v.t.* выпла́чивать, вы́платить; отпла́|чивать, -ти́ть; (*recompense*) возме|ща́ть, -сти́ть; **how can I ~ you?** как я могу́ вас отблагодари́ть?; **I shall ~ him in kind** я отплачу́ ему́ тем же (*or* той же моне́той); **I repaid his visit** я нанёс ему́ отве́тный визи́т; **I repaid his blows with interest** я как сле́дует дал ему́ сда́чи.

v.i.: **God will ~** Бог возда́ст.

repayable [riːˈpeɪəb(ə)l] *adj.* подлежа́щий упла́те/погаше́нию.

repayment [riːˈpeɪmənt] *n.* вы́плата, возмеще́ние.

repeal [rɪˈpiːl] *n.* отме́на, аннули́рование.

v.t. аннули́ровать (*impf.*, *pf.*).

repeat [rɪˈpiːt] *n.* повторе́ние; **~ order** повто́рный зака́з.

v.t. **1.** (*say or do again*) повтор|я́ть, -и́ть; **he is always ~ing himself** он постоя́нно повторя́ется; **the language he used will not bear ~ing** он употреби́л слова́, кото́рые и повтори́ть неприли́чно; **after ~ed attempts** по́сле неоднокра́тных попы́ток; **don't ~ what I have told you** не говори́те никому́ того́, что я вам сказа́л. **2.** (*recite*) говори́ть (*impf.*) наизу́сть; деклами́ровать (*impf.*); **~ one's lesson** отв|еча́ть, -е́тить уро́к.

v.i. **1.** (*recur*) повтор|я́ться, -и́ться; встреча́ться (*impf.*); **0.3 ~ing** (*math.*) 0 це́лых и 3 в перио́де. **2.** (*of food*): **onions ~ on me** (*coll.*) у меня́ отры́жка от лу́ка. **3.**: **~ing rifle** магази́нная винто́вка.

repeatable [rɪˈpiːtəb(ə)l] *adj.* (*of goods etc.*) обы́чный, станда́ртный, ма́ссового произво́дства.

repeatedly [rɪˈpiːtɪdlɪ] *adv.* неоднокра́тно, многокра́тно, то и де́ло.

repeater [rɪˈpiːtə(r)] *n.* (*watch*) час|ы́ (*pl.*, *g.* -о́в) с репети́ром; (*firearm*) магази́нное ору́жие.

repêchage [ˌrepɪˈʃɑːʒ] *n.* (*sport*) дополни́тельные соревнова́ния для включе́ния в фина́л.

repel [rɪˈpel] *v.t.* **1.** (*phys.*) отт|а́лкивать, -олкну́ть. **2.** (*repulse*) от|гоня́ть, -огна́ть; отб|ива́ть, -и́ть; **the attack was ~led** ата́ка была́ отби́та; **measures to ~ the enemy** ме́ры для оказа́ния отпо́ра врагу́; **she ~led his advances** она́ отве́ргла его́ уха́живания. **3.** (*be repulsive to*) отта́лкивать (*impf.*); вызыва́ть, вы́звать отвраще́ние у+*g.*

repellent [rɪˈpelənt] *n.*: **insect ~** сре́дство от насеко́мых.

adj. (*repulsive*) отта́лкивающий; вызыва́ющий отвраще́ние.

repent [rɪˈpent] *v.t. & i.* ка́яться (*impf.*); раска́|иваться, -яться (*в чём*); сокруша́ться (*impf.*) (*о чём*); **he will live to ~ (of) his folly** он когда́-нибу́дь пожале́ет о своём безрассу́дстве.

repentance [riːˈpəntəns] *n.* раска́яние.

repentant [riːˈpəntənt] *adj.* ка́ющийся, раска́ивающийся; **he is not in the least ~** он ниско́лько не раска́ивается.

repeople [riːˈpiːp(ə)l] *v.t.* вновь засел|я́ть, -и́ть.

repercussion [ˌriːpəˈkʌʃ(ə)n] *n.* (*recoil*) отда́ча; (*of sound*) о́тзвук; (*fig.*) резона́нс; после́дствия (*nt. pl.*); **this event will have wide ~s** э́то собы́тие бу́дет име́ть далеко́ иду́щие после́дствия.

repertoire [ˈrepəˌtwɑː(r)] *n.* репертуа́р.

repertory [ˈrepətərɪ] *n.* **1.** (*repertoire*) репертуа́р. **2.** (*also* **rep**, *coll.*): **~ company** постоя́нная гру́ппа с определённым репертуа́ром; **~ theatre** репертуа́рный теа́тр. **3.** (*fig.*, *store*) запа́с.

repetition [ˌrepɪˈtɪʃ(ə)n] *n.* **1.** (*repeating*, *recurrence*) повторе́ние; **let there be no ~ of this** что́бы э́того бо́льше не́ было. **2.** (*saying by heart*) повторе́ние наизу́сть. **3.** (*replica*) ко́пия.

repetiti|ous [ˌrepɪˈtɪʃəs], **-ve** [rɪˈpetɪtɪv] *adjs.* повторя́ющийся; изоби́лующий повторе́ниями.

rephrase [riːˈfreɪz] *v.t.* перефрази́ровать (*impf.*, *pf.*).

repine [rɪˈpaɪn] *v.i.* томи́ться (*impf.*); изныва́ть (*impf.*).

replace [rɪˈpleɪs] *v.t.* **1.** (*put back*, *return*) класть, положи́ть (*or* ста́вить, по-) на ме́сто; возвра|ща́ть, -ти́ть; **~ the receiver** положи́ть телефо́нную тру́бку; **he ~d the money he had stolen** он верну́л укра́денные де́ньги. **2.** (*provide substitute for*) замен|я́ть, -и́ть; **the vase cannot be ~d** э́то уника́льная ва́за. **3.** (*take the place of*; *succeed*) заме|ща́ть, -сти́ть; **he ~d me as secretary** он замеща́л/смени́л меня́ в до́лжности секретаря́.

replaceable [rɪˈpleɪsəb(ə)l] *adj.* заменя́емый, замени́мый.

replacement [rɪˈpleɪsmənt] *n.* (*restitution*) возмеще́ние; (*provision of substitute or successor*) замеще́ние, заме́на; (*substitute*, *successor*) заме́на; прее́мни|к (*fem.* -ца).

replant [riːˈplɑːnt] *v.t.* сно́ва заса́|живать, -ди́ть; переса́|живать, -ди́ть; **the shrubs were ~ed wider apart** кусты́ бы́ли переса́жены с бо́льшими интерва́лами.

replay[1] [ˈriːpleɪ] *n.* (*of a game*) переигро́вка; (*of a record etc.*) (повто́рное) прои́грывание, повто́р.

replay[2] [riːˈpleɪ] *v.t.* переигр|ывать, -а́ть; (повто́рно) прои́гр|ывать, -а́ть.

replenish [rɪˈplenɪʃ] *v.t.* поп|олня́ть, -о́лнить; дозапр|авля́ть, -а́вить.

replenishment [rɪˈplenɪʃmənt] *n.* пополне́ние; дозапра́вка.

replete [rɪˈpliːt] *adj.* напо́лненный, перепо́лненный; сы́тый, насы́щенный, бога́тый (*чем*); **~ with food** нае́вшийся вдо́воль.

repletion [rɪˈpliːʃ(ə)n] *n.* (*satiety*) сы́тость, насыще́ние; **full to ~** по́лный до отка́за.

replica [ˈreplɪkə] *n.* то́чная ко́пия, дублика́т.

reply [rɪˈplaɪ] *n.* отве́т; **in** (*or* **by way of**) **~** в отве́т (на+*a.*); **I rang but there was no ~** я звони́л, но никто́ не отве́тил; **~ paid** с опла́ченным отве́том.

v.i. отв|еча́ть, -е́тить; **the enemy replied with a burst of gunfire** проти́вник отве́тил оруди́йным огнём.

repoint [riːˈpɔɪnt] *v.t.* за́ново расш|ива́ть, -и́ть швы кирпи́чной кла́дки.

repolish [riːˈpɒlɪʃ] *v.t.* за́ново полирова́ть, от-.

repopulate [riːˈpɒpjʊˌleɪt] *v.t.* за́ново засел|я́ть, -и́ть.

repopulation [riːˌpɒpjʊˈleɪʃ(ə)n] *n.* втори́чное заселе́ние.

report [rɪˈpɔːt] *n.* **1.** (*account*, *statement*) докла́д, отчёт; **newspaper ~** сообще́ние, изве́стие, репорта́ж; **school ~** отчёт об успева́емости; **progress ~** отчёт о хо́де выполне́ния; **the policeman made a full ~** полице́йский соста́вил подро́бный протоко́л. **2.** (*common talk*, *rumour*) молва́, слух; **we have only ~s to go on** наш еди́нственный исто́чник — слу́хи; **by all ~s, he is doing well** по всем све́дениям он процвета́ет. **3.** (*sound of explosion or shot*) звук взры́ва/вы́стрела.

v.t. **1.** (*give news or account of*) сообщ|а́ть, -и́ть; сост|авля́ть, -а́вить отчёт о+*p.*; перед|ава́ть, -а́ть; де́лать, с- репорта́ж о+*p.*; **it has been ~ed that ...** сообща́лось, что...; **he was ~ed missing** он счита́лся пропа́вшим бе́з вести; **he ~ed having lost the money** он заяви́л о поте́ре де́нег; **the trial was ~ed in the press** проце́сс освеща́лся в печа́ти; (*gram.*): **~ed** (*indirect*) **speech** ко́свенная речь. **2.** (*inform against*, *make known*) жа́ловаться, по- на+*a.*; **I shall ~ you for insolence** я пожа́луюсь на вас за ва́шу де́рзость.

v.i. **1.** (*give information*) до|кла́дывать, -ложи́ть; де́лать, с- докла́д; предст|авля́ть, -а́вить отчёт; да|ва́ть, -ть репорта́ж; **they ~ well of the prospects** они́ даю́т благоприя́тный о́тзыв о перспекти́вах. **2.** (*present o.s.*) яв|ля́ться, -и́ться (*куда-н.*); приб|ыва́ть, -ы́ть (*куда-н.*); **he was told to ~ to headquarters** ему́ бы́ло ве́лено яви́ться в штаб; **~ing time** (*at airport*) вре́мя я́вки пассажи́ров.

reportage [ˌrepɔːˈtɑːʒ] *n.* репорта́ж.

reportedly [rɪˈpɔːtɪdlɪ] *adv.* по сообще́ниям; (*allegedly*) я́кобы.

reporter [rɪˈpɔ:tə(r)] *n.* репортёр.

repose [rɪˈpəʊz] *n.* (*rest, sleep*) о́тдых, переды́шка; **her face is beautiful in ~** её лицо́ прекра́сно, когда́ споко́йно; (*restfulness, tranquillity*) поко́й, безмяте́жность, гармо́ния.

v.t. (*lay down*) класть, положи́ть; (*fig., place*): **he ~s confidence in her** он ей целико́м доверя́ет.

v.i. **1.** (*take one's rest*) отд|ыха́ть, -охну́ть; лечь (*pf.*) отдохну́ть. **2.** (*lie*) лежа́ть (*impf.*); поко́иться (*impf.*); **his remains ~ in the churchyard** его́ прах поко́ится на кла́дбище. **3.** (*be based*) осно́вываться (*impf.*); **his argument ~s on a falsehood** его́ до́воды осно́ваны на ло́жной предпосы́лке.

repository [rɪˈpɒzɪtərɪ] *n.* (*receptacle*) храни́лище, вмести́лище; (*store*) склад; (*fig.*): **he is a ~ of information** он неиссяка́емый исто́чник информа́ции; **she is the ~ of all my secrets** я поверя́ю ей все свои́ та́йны.

repossess [ˌri:pəˈzes] *v.t.* из|ыма́ть, -ъя́ть за неплатёж.

repossession [ˌri:pəˈzeʃ(ə)n] *n.* (*in hire-purchase*) изъя́тие иму́щества, взя́того в рассро́чку.

repp [rep] = **rep**[1]

reprehend [ˌreprɪˈhend] *v.t.* де́лать, с- вы́говор +*d.*; осу|жда́ть, -ди́ть.

reprehensible [ˌreprɪˈhensɪb(ə)l] *adj.* досто́йный осужде́ния; предосуди́тельный.

represent [ˌreprɪˈzent] *v.t.* **1.** (*portray*) изобра|жа́ть, -зи́ть; **what does this picture ~?** что изображено́ на э́той карти́не? **2.** (*symbolize, correspond to*) символизи́ровать (*impf., pf.*), изобража́ть (*impf.*), обознача́ть (*impf.*); **one inch on the map ~s a mile** оди́н дюйм на ка́рте равня́ется одно́й ми́ле. **3.** (*make clear, point out*): **they ~ed their case** они́ изложи́ли свои́ до́воды. **4.** (*make out*): **he ~ed himself as an expert** он выдава́л себя́ за знатока́. **5.** (*play the part of*): **she ~ed Cleopatra** она́ игра́ла Клеопа́тру. **6.** (*speak or act for*) представля́ть (*impf.*); **he ~s Britain at the UN** он представля́ет Великобрита́нию в ООН; **who ~s the defendant?** кто явля́ется защи́тником обвиня́емого?

representation [ˌreprɪzenˈteɪʃ(ə)n] *n.* **1.** (*portrayal*) изображе́ние. **2.** (*statement of one's case*): **diplomatic ~s** дипломати́ческие представле́ния. **3.** (*performance*) представле́ние. **4.** (*delegation, deputizing*) представи́тельство; **proportional ~** пропорциона́льное представи́тельство.

representational [ˌreprɪzenˈteɪʃən(ə)l] *adj.*: **~ art** репрезентати́вное (*or* предме́тно-изобрази́тельное) иску́сство.

representative [ˌreprɪˈzentətɪv] *n.* представи́тель (*m.*), **House of R~s** пала́та представи́телей.

adj. показа́тельный, типи́чный; **a ~ collection** представи́тельная колле́кция; **~ government** представи́тельное прави́тельство; **he is ~ of his age** он типи́чный представи́тель свое́й эпо́хи.

repress [rɪˈpres] *v.t.* **1.** (*put down, curb*) подав|ля́ть, -и́ть; угнета́ть (*impf.*); **the revolt was ~ed** восста́ние бы́ло пода́влено. **2.** (*restrain*) сде́рж|ивать, -а́ть; **I could not ~ my laughter** я не мог удержа́ться от сме́ха; **a ~ed personality** пода́вленная ли́чность.

repression [rɪˈpreʃ(ə)n] *n.* (*suppression*) подавле́ние; репре́ссия; (*repressed impulse etc.*): **he is full of ~s** он ужа́сно закомплексо́ван.

repressive [rɪˈpresɪv] *adj.* репресси́вный.

reprieve [rɪˈpri:v] *n.* (*leg.*): отсро́чка приведе́ния в исполне́ние (сме́ртного) пригово́ра; (*fig.*) переды́шка, вре́менное облегче́ние.

v.t.: **the murderer was ~ed** казнь уби́йцы отсро́чили.

reprimand [ˈreprɪˌmɑ:nd] *n.* вы́говор, замеча́ние.

v.t. де́лать, с- вы́говор/замеча́ние +*d.*

reprint[1] [ˈri:prɪnt] *n.* но́вое изда́ние; перепеча́тка; репри́нт, репри́нтное изда́ние.

reprint[2] [ri:ˈprɪnt] *v.t.* переизд|ава́ть, -а́ть; перепеча́т|ывать, -ать.

v.i.: **the book is ~ing** кни́га переиздаётся.

reprisal [rɪˈpraɪz(ə)l] *n.* отве́тный уда́р; отве́тное де́йствие, отме́стка; **by way of ~** в отме́стку.

reproach [rɪˈprəʊtʃ] *n.* **1.** (*rebuke*) упрёк, уко́р; **his honesty is above ~** он безупре́чно че́стен; **he gave me a look of ~** он посмотре́л на меня́ с укори́зной; **~es were heaped upon him** его́ засы́пали упрёками. **2.** (*disgrace*) позо́р; **he brought ~ on himself** он себя́ опозо́рил; **these slums are a ~ to the council** э́ти трущо́бы слу́жат уко́ром для ме́стных власте́й.

v.t. упрек|а́ть, -ну́ть; укоря́ть (*impf.*); **he ~ed his wife with extravagance** он упрекну́л жену́ в расточи́тельстве; **I have nothing to ~ myself for** мне не́ в чем себя́ упрекну́ть; (*fig.*): **his eyes ~ed me** я прочита́л упрёк в его́ глаза́х.

reproachful [rɪˈprəʊtʃfʊl] *adj.* укори́зненный.

reprobate [ˈreprəˌbeɪt] *n.* негодя́й, нечести́вец.

adj. нечести́вый; безнра́вственный.

v.t. порица́ть (*impf.*).

reprobation [ˌreprəˈbeɪʃ(ə)n] *n.* порица́ние.

reproduce [ˌri:prəˈdju:s] *v.t.* **1.** (*copy, imitate*) воспроизв|оди́ть, -ести́; **the artist has ~d your features well** худо́жник хорошо́ воспроизвёл ва́ши черты́; (*of pictures*) репродуци́ровать (*impf., pf.*). **2.** (*beget*): **living things ~ their kind** живы́е существа́ размножа́ются. **3.** (*renew, grow again*) восстан|а́вливать, -ови́ть.

v.i. **1.** (*recreate sounds*): **this record-player ~s well** у э́того прои́грывателя хоро́шее ка́чество звуча́ния. **2.** (*of animals*) размн|ожа́ться, -о́житься.

reproducible [ˌri:prəˈdju:sɪb(ə)l] *adj.* воспроизводи́мый.

reproduction [ˌri:prəˈdʌkʃ(ə)n] *n.* воспроизведе́ние; (*of picture*) репроду́кция; (*begetting of offspring*) размноже́ние.

reproductive [ˌri:prəˈdʌktɪv] *adj.* воспроизводи́тельный; (*biol.*) полово́й; **~ organs** о́рганы размноже́ния.

reprography [rɪˈprɒgrəfɪ] *n.* репрогра́фия.

reproof [rɪˈpru:f] *n.* порица́ние; вы́говор; **he spoke in ~ of our motives** он осуди́л на́ши побужде́ния; **the teacher administered a sharp ~** учи́тель сде́лал ре́зкое замеча́ние.

re-proof [ri:ˈpru:f] *v.t.* (*e.g. a coat*) вновь пропи́т|ывать, -а́ть водоотта́лкивающим соста́вом.

reproval [rɪˈpru:vəl] *n.* вы́говор, порица́ние.

reprove [rɪˈpru:v] *v.t.* отчи́т|ывать, -а́ть; де́лать, с- вы́говор +*d.*

reps [reps] = **rep**[1]

reptile [ˈreptaɪl] *n.* пресмыка́ющееся; (*fig., of pers.*) пресмыка́ющийся, подхали́м.

reptilian [repˈtɪlɪən] *adj.* (*fig.*) пресмыка́ющийся, по́длый.

republic [rɪˈpʌblɪk] *n.* респу́блика; **People's R~** наро́дная респу́блика; **R~ of South Africa** Ю́жно-Африка́нская Респу́блика; (*fig.*) мир, ца́рство; **the ~ of letters** литерату́рный мир.

republican [rɪˈpʌblɪkən] *n.* республика́нец; **R~** (*US*) член Республика́нской па́ртии.

adj. республика́нский.

republicanism [rɪˈpʌblɪkənɪz(ə)m] *n.* республикани́зм.

republication [ˌrɪpʌblɪˈkeɪʃ(ə)n] *n.* переизда́ние.

republish [ri:ˈpʌblɪʃ] *v.t.* переизд|ава́ть, -а́ть.

repudiate [rɪˈpju:dɪˌeɪt] *v.t.* отв|ерга́ть, -е́ргнуть; отр|ека́ться, -е́чься от+*g.*; **I ~ your accusation** я отверга́ю ва́ше обвине́ние; **he ~s the authority of the law** он не признаёт вла́сти зако́на; **he ~d his responsibility** он отказа́лся от отве́тственности.

repudiation [rɪˌpju:dɪˈeɪʃ(ə)n] *n.* отрече́ние; отрица́ние; отка́з.

repugnance [rɪˈpʌgnəns] *n.* (*antipathy*) отвраще́ние; (*contradiction*) противоре́чие.

repugnant [rɪˈpʌgnənt] *adj.* (*distasteful*) отврати́тельный; (*incompatible*) противореча́щий.

repulse [rɪˈpʌls] *n.* отпо́р, отраже́ние; **the enemy suffered a ~** враг был отбро́шен наза́д.

v.t. (*drive back*) отб|ива́ть, -и́ть; (*rebuff, refuse*) отт|а́лкивать, -олкну́ть; отв|ерга́ть, -е́ргнуть.

repulsion [rɪˈpʌlʃ(ə)n] *n.* **1.** (*aversion*) отвраще́ние, омерзе́ние. **2.** (*phys.*) отта́лкивание.

repulsive [rɪˈpʌlsɪv] *adj.* **1.** (*disgusting*) отврати́тельный, омерзи́тельный. **2.** (*phys.*) отта́лкивающий.

repurchase [ri:ˈpɜ:tʃɪs] *n.* поку́пка ра́нее про́данного това́ра.

v.t. вновь покупа́ть, купи́ть (ра́нее про́данный това́р).

reputable [ˈrepjʊtəb(ə)l] *adj.* почте́нный, уважа́емый.

reputation [ˌrepjʊˈteɪʃ(ə)n] *n.* **1.** (*name*) репута́ция; **he has a ~ for courage** он сла́вится хра́бростью; **he lived up to his ~** он показа́л, что сла́ва о нём была́ справедли́вой. **2.** (*respectability*) до́брое и́мя; **persons of ~** почте́нные лю́ди; **a tarnished ~** запя́тнанная репута́ция.

repute [rɪˈpjuːt] *n.* (*reputation*) репута́ция; **I know him by ~** я зна́ю о нём понаслы́шке; (*good reputation, renown*) до́брое и́мя; **an artist of ~** худо́жник с и́менем.

v.t.: **he is ~d to be rich** он счита́ется бога́тым; говоря́т, что он бога́т; **the ~d father** предполага́емый оте́ц.

reputedly [rɪˈpjuːtɪdlɪ] *adv.* по о́бщему мне́нию.

request [rɪˈkwest] *n.* про́сьба; **at my ~** по мое́й про́сьбе; **~ stop** остано́вка по тре́бованию; **details sent on ~** подро́бная информа́ция высыла́ется по тре́бованию; **I have a ~ to make of you** у меня́ к вам про́сьба; **you shall have your ~** ва́ша про́сьба бу́дет удовлетворена́; **put in a ~ for** пода́ть (*pf.*) заявле́ние/зая́вку на+*a.*; **a programme of ~s** конце́рт по зая́вкам; **this book is in great ~** на э́ту кни́гу большо́й спрос.

v.t. проси́ть, по-; **he ~ed to be allowed to remain** он попроси́л разреше́ния оста́ться; **that is all I ~ of you** э́то всё, чего́ я от вас прошу́; **passengers are ~ed not to smoke** пассажи́ров про́сят не кури́ть; **may I ~ you to leave?** бу́дьте любе́зны удали́ться; **may I ~ the pleasure of a dance?** разреши́те пригласи́ть вас на та́нец.

requiem [ˈrekwɪˌem] *n.* ре́квием, панихи́да.

require [rɪˈkwaɪə(r)] *v.t.* **1.** (*need*) нужда́ться (*impf.*) в+*p.*; тре́бовать (*impf.*) +*g.*; **your car ~s repair** ва́ша маши́на нужда́ется в ремо́нте; **when do you ~ the job to he done?** к како́му сро́ку должна́ быть завершена́ рабо́та?; **it ~d all his skill to ...** ему́ пона́добилось примени́ть всё своё уме́ние, что́бы...; **all that is ~d is a little patience** всё, что тре́буется, э́то немно́го терпе́ния; **the matter ~s some thought** над э́тим на́до поду́мать. **2.** (*demand, order*) тре́бовать, по- +*g.*; прика́з|ывать, -а́ть; **my attendance is ~d by law** по зако́ну я обя́зан прису́тствовать; **what do you ~ of me?** что вы от меня́ хоти́те?; **I have done all that is ~d** я сде́лал всё, что тре́буется; **the situation ~s me to be present** ситуа́ция тре́бует моего́ прису́тствия.

requirement [rɪˈkwaɪəmənt] *n.* **1.** (*need*) нужда́; потре́бность; **I have few ~s** мои́ потре́бности невелики́. **2.** (*demand*) тре́бование; усло́вие.

requisite [ˈrekwɪzɪt] *n.* необходи́мая вещь.

adj. необходи́мый.

requisition [ˌrekwɪˈzɪʃ(ə)n] *n.* **1.** (*official demand*) тре́бование; (*mil.*) реквизи́ция. **2.** (*service, use*) испо́льзование; **every car was brought into ~** все маши́ны бы́ли реквизи́рованы; **the dictionary was in constant ~** словарём постоя́нно по́льзовались.

v.t. реквизи́ровать (*impf., pf.*); **houses were ~ed for billets** дома́ бы́ли реквизи́рованы для размеще́ния солда́т.

requital [rɪˈkwaɪtəl] *n.* воздая́ние, вознагражде́ние; возме́здие; **in ~ of his services** в вознагражде́ние за его́ услу́ги; **he made full ~** он по́лностью рассчита́лся.

requite [rɪˈkwaɪt] *v.t.* вознагра|жда́ть, -ди́ть; отпла́|чивать, -ти́ть; **his kindness was ~d with ingratitude** за доброту́ ему́ отплати́ли неблагода́рностью; **he was ~d for his services** он был вознаграждён за свои́ услу́ги.

re-read [riːˈriːd] *v.t.* перечи́т|ывать, -а́ть.

reredos [ˈrɪədɒs] *n.* запресто́льный экра́н (в це́ркви).

re-route [riːˈruːt] *v.t.* измен|я́ть, -и́ть маршру́т/тра́ссу +*g.*

re-run [ˈriːrʌn] *n.* (*of film etc.*) повто́рный пока́з фи́льма.

v.t.: **the race was ~** состоя́лся повто́рный забе́г; **he reran the tape** он ещё раз проигра́л плёнку.

resaddle [riːˈsæd(ə)l] *v.t.* перес|ёдлывать, -едла́ть.

resale [riːˈseɪl] *n.* перепрода́жа.

rescind [rɪˈsɪnd] *v.t.* аннули́ровать (*impf., pf.*); отмен|я́ть, -и́ть.

rescission [rɪˈsɪʒ(ə)n] *n.* аннули́рование, отме́на.

rescript [riːˈskrɪpt] *n.* рескри́пт.

rescue [ˈreskjuː] *n.* спасе́ние, вы́ручка; **he came to my ~** он пришёл мне на по́мощь/вы́ручку; **I had forgotten our guest's name, but she came to my ~** я забы́л и́мя на́шего го́стя, но она́ мне подсказа́ла; **a ~ attempt** попы́тка спасти́ (*кого/что*); **~ vessel** спаса́тельная ло́дка.

v.t. спас|а́ть, -ти́; **all the crew were ~d** всю кома́нду спасли́; **I ~ d the letter from the dustbin** я вы́удил э́то письмо́ из му́сорного я́щика.

rescuer [ˈreskjuːə(r)] *n.* спаси́тель (*fem.* -ница); избави́тель (*fem.* -ница).

reseal [riːˈsiːl] *v.t.* вновь запеча́т|ывать, -ать.

research [rɪˈsɜːtʃ, *disp.* ˈriːsɜːtʃ] *n.* изуче́ние, иссле́дование, изыска́ние; по́иски (*m. pl.*); **~ and development** нау́чно-иссле́довательская рабо́та; **~ library** нау́чно-техни́ческая библиоте́ка; **~ assistant, worker** нау́чный сотру́дник/рабо́тник; **~ satellite** иссле́довательский спу́тник.

v.t. & i. иссле́довать (*impf., pf.*); **he is ~ing the subject** он изуча́ет/разраба́тывает э́ту те́му; **the book is well ~ed** за э́той кни́гой чу́вствуется больша́я рабо́та.

researcher [rɪˈsɜːtʃə(r)] *n.* иссле́дователь (*fem.* -ница), учёный.

reseat [riːˈsiːt] *v.t.* **1.**: **the chair has been ~ed** у сту́ла замени́ли сиде́нье. **2.** (*seat again*) переса́|живать, -ди́ть; **she ~ed herself more comfortably** она́ усе́лась поудо́бнее.

resell [riːˈsel] *v.t.* перепрод|ава́ть, -а́ть.

resemblance [rɪˈzembləns] *n.* схо́дство; **he bears a strong ~ to his father** он о́чень похо́ж на своего́ отца́.

resemble [rɪˈzemb(ə)l] *v.t.* походи́ть (*impf.*) на+*a.*; име́ть (*impf.*) схо́дство с+*i.*

resent [rɪˈzent] *v.t.* возму|ща́ться, -ти́ться +*i.*; негодова́ть (*impf.*) на+*a.*; **I ~ your interfering in my affairs** мне о́чень не нра́вится, что вы вме́шиваетесь в мои́ дела́.

resentful [rɪˈzentfʊl] *adj.* возмущённый, негоду́ющий.

resentment [rɪˈzentmənt] *n.* возмуще́ние; негодова́ние; **I bear no ~ against him** я на него́ не в оби́де.

reservation [ˌrezəˈveɪʃ(ə)n] *n.* **1.** (*limitation, exception*) огово́рка; **mental ~** мы́сленная огово́рка. **2.** (*booking*) (предвари́тельный) зака́з; зака́занное/заброни́рованное ме́сто. **3.** (*for tribes etc.*) резерва́ция; (*for game*) запове́дник.

reserve [rɪˈzɜːv] *n.* **1.** (*store*) запа́с, резе́рв; **a ~ of food** запа́с еды́/продово́льствия; **gold ~s** золоты́е запа́сы; **he has great ~s of energy** у него́ большо́й запа́с эне́ргии; **he has a little money in ~** у него́ припасено́/отло́жено немно́го де́нег; **~ bank** резе́рвный банк. **2.** (*mil.*) резе́рв; **the R~** резе́рвные ча́сти (*f. pl.*). **3.** (*~ player*) запасно́й (игро́к). **4.** (*area*): **game ~** охо́тничий запове́дник. **5.** (*limitation, restriction*) огово́рка; **I accept your statement without ~** я принима́ю ва́ше заявле́ние без огово́рок; **he fixed a ~ price on his house** он установи́л отправну́ю це́ну на свой дом. **6.** (*reticence*) сде́ржанность; **I managed to break through his ~** мне удало́сь преодоле́ть его́ за́мкнутость.

v.t. **1.** (*hold back, save*) бере́чь, с-; прибер|ега́ть, -е́чь; **~ your strength for tomorrow** береги́те си́лы на за́втрашний день. **2.**: **~ judgement** (*leg.*) от|кла́дывать, -ложи́ть реше́ние; **I prefer to ~ judgement** я предпочита́ю пока́ не выска́зываться; **~ a right** сохран|я́ть, -и́ть (*or* резерви́ровать (*impf., pf.*)) пра́во. **3.** (*set aside*) резерви́ровать, за-; (*book*) зака́з|ывать, -а́ть; брони́ровать, за-. **4.** (*destine*) предназн|ача́ть, -а́чить; **a great future is ~d for him** ему́ угото́вано большо́е бу́дущее.

reserved [rɪˈzɜːvd] *adj.* **1.** (*booked, set aside*) зака́занный (зара́нее); **~ seats** (*in train*) плацка́ртные места́. **2.** (*reticent, uncommunicative*) сде́ржанный, за́мкнутый.

reservist [rɪˈzɜːvɪst] *n.* резерви́ст.

reservoir [ˈrezəˌvwɑː(r)] *n.* (*for water*) водохрани́лище, водоём; (*for other fluids*) резервуа́р, бачо́к; (*of a fountain pen*) резервуа́р; (*fig., store*) сокро́вищница, исто́чник.

reset [riːˈset] *v.t.* **1.** (*sharpen again*) подрегули́ровать (*pf.*). **2.** (*e.g. a watch*) перест|авля́ть, -а́вить; (*trap etc.*) сно́ва ста́вить, по-. **3.** (*place in position again*) впр|авля́ть, -а́вить; вновь вст|авля́ть, -а́вить; **the doctor ~ his arm** врач впра́вил ему́ ру́ку; **the diamond was ~** брilliáнт вста́вили в но́вую опра́ву.

resettle [riːˈset(ə)l] *v.t.* (*land*) сно́ва засел|я́ть, -и́ть; (*people*) пересел|я́ть, -и́ть.

v.i. пересел|я́ться, -и́ться.

resettlement [riːˈsetəlmənt] *n.* (*of territory*) повтóрное заселéние; (*of refugees etc.*) переселéние; (*reemployment*) трудоустрóйство (*демобилизованных и т.п.*).

reshape [riːˈʃeɪp] *v.t.* прид|авáть, -áть нóвую фóрму +*d.*; (*fig.*) видоизмен|ять, -ить; перекр|áивать, -оúть.

reship [riːˈʃɪp] *v.t.* (*reload*) перегру|жáть, -зúть.

reshipment [riːˈʃɪpmənt] *n.* перегрýзка.

reshuffle [riːˈʃʌf(ə)l] *n.* (*cards*) перетасóвка; (*fig.*) перестанóвка, перетря́ска.

v.t. перетасóв|ывать, -áть; (*fig.*) произвестú (*pf.*) перестанóвку/перетря́ску в+*p.*

reside [rɪˈzaɪd] *v.i.* **1.** (*live*) проживáть (*impf.*); пребывáть (*impf.*). **2.:** ~ (*inhere, be vested*) **in** принадлежáть (*impf.*) +*d.*; быть присýщим +*d.*; **supreme authority ~s in the President** президéнт облечён вы́сшей влáстью.

residence [ˈrezɪd(ə)ns] *n.* **1.** (*residing*) проживáние, пребывáние; **take up ~** въ|езжáть, -éхать (в официáльную резидéнцию); **the students are in ~ again** студéнты вернýлись в общежúтие. **2.** (*home, mansion*) дом, резидéнция.

residency [ˈrezɪdənsɪ] *n.* резидéнция (*посла и т.п.*).

resident [ˈrezɪd(ə)nt] *n.* **1.** (*permanent inhabitant*) (постоя́нный) жúтель; (*in hotel*) постоя́лец. **2.** (*government agent*) резидéнт.

adj. **1.** (*residing*) постоя́нно проживáющий; **the ~ population** постоя́нное населéние. **2.** (*inherent*) присýщий, свóйственный.

residential [ˌrezɪˈdenʃ(ə)l] *adj.*: ~ **qualifications for voting** избирáтельный ценз осéдлости; **a ~ area** жилóй райóн.

residual [rɪˈzɪdjʊəl] *adj.* остáточный, остáвшийся.

residuary [rɪˈzɪdjʊərɪ] *adj.* (*leg.*): ~ **legatee** наслéдник имýщества, очúщенного от долгóв и завещáтельных откáзов.

residue [ˈrezɪˌdjuː] *n.* **1.** (*remainder*) остáток. **2.** (*leg.*) наслéдство, очúщенное от долгóв и завещáтельных откáзов.

residuum [rɪˈzɪdjʊəm] *n.* (*chem.*) остáток, осáдок.

resign [rɪˈzaɪn] *v.t.* **1.** (*give up*) откáз|ываться, -áться от+*g.*; **I have ~ed all claim to the money** я отказáлся от вся́ких притязáний на э́ти дéньги; **he ~ed his post as Chancellor** он пóдал в отстáвку с постá кáнцлера; **they ~ed all hope** онú остáвили вся́кую надéжду. **2.** (*hand over*): **he ~ed the children to her care** он остáвил детéй на её попечéние. **3.** (*reconcile*): **he ~ed himself to defeat** он смирúлся с поражéнием; **he was ~ed to being alone** он примирúлся с одинóчеством.

v.i. под|авáть, -áть (*or* уходúть, уйтú) в отстáвку; уходúть, уйтú с рабóты; **he ~ed from the government** он вы́шел из правúтельства.

resignation [ˌrezɪgˈneɪʃ(ə)n] *n.* **1.** (*surrender*) сдáча. **2.** (*resigning of office*) отстáвка; **he handed in his ~** он пóдал заявлéние об отстáвке/ухóде; **his ~ was accepted** егó отстáвка былá принятá. **3.** (*acceptance of fate*) покóрность, смирéние.

resigned [rɪˈzaɪnd] *adj.* покóрный, безрóпотный, смирúвшийся (с+*i.*).

resilience [rɪˈzɪlɪəns] *n.* эластúчность, упрýгость; (*fig.*) вынóсливость, живýчесть, жизнеспосóбность.

resilient [rɪˈzɪlɪənt] *adj.* эластúчный, упрýгий; (*fig.*) неунывáющий; вынóсливый, живýчий.

resin [ˈrezɪn] *n.* смолá; канифóль.

resinous [ˈrezɪnəs] *adj.* смолúстый.

resist [rɪˈzɪst] *v.t.* **1.** (*oppose*) сопротивля́ться (*impf.*) +*d.*; противúться (*impf.*) +*d.*; **he ~ed arrest** он сопротивля́лся арéсту; **all their attacks were ~ed** все их атáки бы́ли отбúты; **it will do you no good to ~ authority** сопротивлéние влáстям не принесёт вам пóльзы. **2.** (*be proof against*) не поддавáться (*impf.*) +*d.*; противостоя́ть (*impf.*) +*d.*; **this metal ~s acid** э́тот метáлл не окисля́ется. **3.** (*refrain from*) воздéрж|иваться, -áться от+*g.*; **I could not ~ the temptation to smile** я не мог удержáться от улы́бки; **she cannot ~ chocolates** онá не мóжет устоя́ть пéред шоколáдом; **he can never ~ a joke** он не мóжет не пошутúть.

resistance [rɪˈzɪst(ə)ns] *n.* **1.** (*opposition*) сопротивлéние; **they offered stout ~** онú оказáли упóрное сопротивлéние; **he took the line of least ~** он пошёл по лúнии наимéньшего сопротивлéния; **I broke down his ~** я сломúл егó сопротивлéние; **(~ movement)** движéние сопротивлéния. **2.** (*power to withstand*) сопротивля́емость; **she has no ~ against cold** у неё нет никакóй сопротивля́емости к хóлоду. **3.** (*elec.*) сопротивлéние.

resistant [rɪˈzɪst(ə)nt] *adj.* сопротивля́ющийся; стóйкий; **~ to all entreaty** глухóй ко всем мольбáм; **~ to heat** жаростóйкий.

resister [rɪˈzɪstə(r)] *n.* сопротивля́ющийся, учáстни|к (*fem.* -ца) движéния сопротивлéния.

resistor [rɪˈzɪstə(r)] *n.* резúстор; катýшка сопротивлéния.

re-sit [riːˈsɪt] *v.t.*: ~ **an examination** пересдавáть (*impf.*) экзáмен; **permission to ~ physics** разрешéние на пересдáчу фúзики.

re-sole [riːˈsəʊl] *v.t.* стáвить, по- нóвые подмётки на+*a.*

resolute [ˈrezəˌluːt, -ˌljuːt] *adj.* решúтельный; пóлный решúмости.

resolution [ˌrezəˈluːʃ(ə)n, -ˈljuːʃ(ə)n] *n.* **1.** (*firmness of purpose*) решúтельность, решúмость. **2.** (*vow*): **New Year ~** новогóдний зарóк; новогóднее обещáние самомý себé. **3.** (*expression of opinion or intent*) резолю́ция; **they passed a ~ to go on strike** онú прúняли решéние начáть забастóвку. **4.** (*of doubt, discord etc.*) (раз)решéние. **5.** (*separation into components; analysis*) разложéние, расщеплéние. **6.** (*mus.*) разрешéние.

resolve [rɪˈzɒlv] *n.* (*determination*) решúтельность, решúмость; (*vow, intention*) решéние; намéрение.

v.t. & i. **1.** (*decide, determine*) реш|áть, -úть; прин|имáть, -я́ть решéние; **I have ~d to spend less** я решúл трáтить мéньше дéнег; **it was ~d** бы́ло решенó; **they ~d to elect a new president** онú постановúли избрáть нóвого президéнта. **2.** (*settle*) (раз)решáть, -úть; **all doubts were ~d** все сомнéния бы́ли разрешены́/рассéяны; **their quarrel was ~d** их спор разрешúлся. **3.** (*break up, re-form*) разл|агáть, -ожúть; превра|щáть, -тúть; **the distant shape ~d itself into a tower** нея́сный силуэ́т вдалú оказáлся бáшней.

resonance [ˈrezənəns] *n.* резонáнс, гул.

resonant [ˈrezənənt] *adj.* звучáщий, звóнкий.

resort [rɪˈzɔːt] *n.* **1.** (*recourse*): **without ~ to force** не прибегáя к насúлию; **in the last ~** в крáйнем слýчае. **2.** (*expedient*) надéжда; спасúтельное срéдство; **an operation was the only ~** оперáция былá едúнственной надéждой. **3.** (*frequented place*): **a ~ of businessmen** излю́бленное мéсто бизнесмéнов; **holiday ~** курóрт; **seaside ~** морскóй курóрт.

v.i. **1.** (*have recourse*) приб|егáть, -éгнуть (к+*d.*). **2.** (*go in numbers or frequently*) бывáть (*impf.*) (*где*); **~ to** посе|щáть, -тúть; **townsfolk ~ to the country every Sunday** кáждое воскресéнье горожáне устремля́ются зá город.

re-sort [riːˈsɔːt] *v.t.* пересортирóв|ывать, -áть.

resound [rɪˈzaʊnd] *v.i.* звучáть (*impf.*); **the hall ~ed with voices** в зáле раздавáлись голосá; (*fig.*) гремéть, про-; **their fame ~ed throughout Europe** их слáва гремéла по всей Еврóпе; **a ~ing success** шýмный успéх.

resource [rɪˈsɔːs, -ˈzɔːs] *n.* **1.** (*available supply; stock*) запáсы (*m. pl.*); ресýрсы (*m. pl.*); **the country's natural ~s** естéственные ресýрсы страны́; **we must make the most of our ~s** мы должны́ наилýчшим óбразом испóльзовать нáши ресýрсы; **I came to the end of my ~s** я исчéрпал все свои запáсы/возмóжности; **he was left to his own ~s** он мог положúться тóлько на самогó себя́. **2.** (*leisure occupation*) óтдых, развлечéние. **3.** (*ingenuity*) нахóдчивость; **a man of ~** нахóдчивый человéк.

resourceful [rɪˈsɔːsfʊl, -ˈzɔːsfʊl] *adj.* изобретáтельный, нахóдчивый.

resourcefulness [rɪˈsɔːsfʊlnɪs, -ˈzɔːsfʊlnɪs] *n.* изобретáтельность, нахóдчивость.

respect [rɪˈspekt] *n.* **1.** (*esteem, deference*) уважéние; **he won their ~** он завоевáл их уважéние; **he is held in great ~** егó óчень уважáют; **I have the greatest ~ for his opinion** я óчень считáюсь с егó мнéнием; **with ~, I cannot agree** при всём уважéнием к вам, я не могý согласúться. **2.**

(*consideration, attention*): **we must have, pay ~ to public opinion** нам на́до счита́ться с обще́ственным мне́нием; **without ~ of persons** невзира́я на ли́ца. **3.** (*reference, relation*) отноше́ние, каса́тельство; **in ~ of, with ~ to** что каса́ется +*g.*; **his writing is admirable in ~ of style** что каса́ется сти́ля, он пи́шет превосхо́дно. **4.** (*pl., polite greetings*) приве́т; **give my ~s to her** переда́йте ей от меня́ приве́т; **he came to pay his ~s** он пришёл засвиде́тельствовать своё почте́ние.

v.t. **1.** (*treat with consideration or esteem; defer to*) уважа́ть (*impf.*); почита́ть (*impf.*); **my wishes were ~ed** мои́ пожела́ния бы́ли учтены́. **2.** (*relate to*): **the law ~ing young persons** зако́н, каса́ющийся молодёжи.

respectability [rɪˌspektəˈbɪlɪtɪ] *n.* респекта́бельность.

respectable [rɪˈspektəb(ə)l] *adj.* **1.** (*estimable*) досто́йный уваже́ния; **he acted from ~ motives** он де́йствовал из благоро́дных побужде́ний. **2.** (*qualifying for social approval*) респекта́бельный; **your clothes are not quite ~** вы не о́чень прили́чно оде́ты; **he comes of a ~ family** он из хоро́шей/прили́чной семьи́. **3.** (*of some merit, size or importance*) прили́чный; **he earns a ~ salary** он зараба́тывает прили́чные де́ньги; **he is quite a ~ painter** он вполне́ прили́чный худо́жник.

respecter [rɪˈspektə(r)] *n.*: **God is no ~ of persons** Бог не лицеприя́тен; **X is no ~ of persons** X де́йствует, невзира́я на ли́ца.

respectful [rɪˈspektfʊl] *adj.* почти́тельный; **they kept (at) a ~ distance** они́ держа́лись на почти́тельном расстоя́нии; **yours ~ly** с уваже́нием.

respective [rɪˈspektɪv] *adj.* соотве́тственный; **we went off to our ~ rooms** мы разошли́сь по свои́м ко́мнатам; **the boys and girls were taught woodwork and sewing ~ly** ма́льчиков и де́вочек учи́ли соотве́тственно столя́рному де́лу и шитью́.

respiration [ˌrespɪˈreɪʃ(ə)n] *n.* дыха́ние; **he was given artificial ~** ему́ сде́лали иску́сственное дыха́ние.

respirator [ˈrespɪˌreɪtə(r)] *n.* (*gas-mask*) противога́з, респира́тор; (*med.*) прибо́р для дли́тельного иску́сственного дыха́ния.

respiratory [rɪˈspɪrətərɪ, ˈrespəˌreɪtərɪ] *adj.* респира́торный, дыха́тельный.

respite [ˈrespaɪt, -pɪt] *n.* **1.** (*relief, rest*) переды́шка; **I worked without ~** я рабо́тал без переды́шки; **they gave us no ~** они́ не дава́ли нам передохну́ть. **2.** (*temporary reprieve*) отсро́чка.

resplendent [rɪˈsplend(ə)nt] *adj.* блиста́тельный, ослепи́тельный.

respond [rɪˈspɒnd] *v.i.* **1.** (*reply*) отв|еча́ть, -е́тить (на+*a.*); **he ~ed with a blow** он отве́тил уда́ром. **2.** (*react*) реаги́ровать, от- (на+*a.*); от|зыва́ться, -озва́ться (на+*a.*); **his illness is ~ing to treatment** его́ боле́знь поддаётся лече́нию.

respondent [rɪˈspɒnd(ə)nt] *n.* (*leg.*) отве́тчи|к (*fem.* -ца).

response [rɪˈspɒns] *n.* **1.** (*reply*) отве́т; **he made no ~** он ничего́ не отве́тил; **in ~ to your enquiry** в отве́т на ваш запро́с. **2.** (*reaction*) реа́кция, о́тклик; **my appeal met with no ~** моё обраще́ние не вы́звало никако́го о́тклика; **there was little ~ from the audience** аудито́рия реаги́ровала сла́бо. **3.** (*eccl.*): **sung ~s** отве́тствие хо́ра.

responsibilit|y [rɪˌspɒnsɪˈbɪlɪtɪ] *n.* **1.** (*being responsible*) отве́тственность; **I take full ~y for my actions** я беру́ на себя́ по́лную отве́тственность за свои́ де́йствия; **he acted on his own ~y** он де́йствовал на свой страх и риск; **I decline all ~y** я отка́зываюсь от вся́кой отве́тственности; **he has a position of great ~y** он занима́ет о́чень отве́тственную до́лжность. **2.** (*charge, duty*) обя́занность, отве́тственность; **a family is a great ~y** семья́ накла́дывает большу́ю отве́тственность; **he was relieved of his ~ies** он был освобождён от исполне́ния обя́занностей.

responsible [rɪˈspɒnsɪb(ə)l] *adj.* **1.** (*liable, accountable*) отве́тственный; **~ government** отве́тственное прави́тельство; **he is ~ to me for keeping the accounts** в вопро́сах бухгалте́рии он подчиня́ется мне; **she is ~ for cleaning my room** убо́рка моей ко́мнаты вхо́дит в её обя́занности; (*to blame*): **he was held ~ for the loss** его́ обвини́ли в э́той пропа́же; **who was ~ for breaking the window?** кто разби́л окно́?; (*to be thanked*): **Churchill was ~ for our victory** на́ша побе́да — заслу́га Че́рчилля. **2.** (*trustworthy*) надёжный. **3.** (*involving responsibility*) ва́жный; **a ~ post** отве́тственный пост.

responsive [rɪˈspɒnsɪv] *adj.* отзы́вчивый, восприи́мчивый; чу́ткий.

rest[1] [rest] *n.* **1.** (*sleep; relaxation in bed*) сон; о́тдых; **you need a good night's ~** вам на́до как сле́дует вы́спаться; **I'm going (up) to have a ~** я пойду́ приля́гу; я приля́гу отдохну́ть. **2.** (*inactive, immobile or undisturbed state*) поко́й; **day of ~** де́нь о́тдыха; **I set his mind at ~** я его́ успоко́ил; **the ball came to ~** мяч останови́лся; **he brought the van to ~** он останови́л автофурго́н; **he was laid to ~** (*buried*) его́ похорони́ли. **3.** (*intermission of work, activity etc.*) переды́шка; **they took a short ~** они́ сде́лали небольшу́ю переды́шку; **he gave his horse a ~** он дал коню́ отдохну́ть; **why don't you give drinking a ~?** (*coll.*) отдохну́л бы ты мале́нько от питья́. **4.** (*lodging house, shelter*) ме́сто о́тдыха, клуб; **seamen's ~** морско́й клуб. **5.** (*prop, support*) опо́ра; (*for telephone*) рыча́г; (*for billiard cue*) сто́йка. **6.** (*mus.*) па́уза.

v.t. **1.** (*give ~ to*) да|ва́ть, -ть о́тдых +*d.*; **he ~ed his horse** он дал коню́ отдохну́ть; **God ~ his soul!** ца́рствие ему́ небе́сное!; **the land was ~ed for a year** земля́ год лежа́ла под па́ром; **are you quite ~ed?** вы хорошо́ отдохну́ли?; **a soft light ~s the eyes** при мя́гком освеще́нии глаза́ отдыха́ют. **2.** (*place for support*) класть, положи́ть (на+*a.*); прислон|я́ть, -и́ть (*что к чему*); **she ~ed her elbows on the table** она́ положи́ла ло́кти на стол; **he ~ed his chin on his hand** он подпира́л подборо́док руко́й; **he ~ed his gaze on the horizon** он не отрыва́ясь смотре́л на горизо́нт; **~ the ladder against the wall!** прислони́те ле́стницу к сте́нке; (*fig., base*) обосно́в|ывать, -а́ть; **he ~s his case on the right of ownership** он стро́ит свои́ доказа́тельства на пра́ве со́бственности; **he is ~ing his hopes on fine weather** он наде́ется на хоро́шую пого́ду.

v.i. **1.** (*relax; take repose*) лежа́ть (*impf.*); отд|ыха́ть, -охну́ть; **may he ~ in peace!** мир пра́ху его́!; **(last) ~ing-place** моги́ла; **I could not ~ until I'd told you the news** я не мог успоко́иться, пока́ не подели́лся с ва́ми но́востью. **2.** (*fig., remain*) ост|ава́ться, -а́ться; **the matter cannot ~ there** э́то де́ло нельзя́ так оста́вить; **the decision ~s with you** реше́ние зави́сит от вас; **~ assured I will do all I can** я сде́лаю всё возмо́жное, мо́жете не сомнева́ться. **3.** (*be supported*) опира́ться (*impf.*) (*на что*); поко́иться (*impf.*) (*на чём*); **the bridge ~s on 4 piers** мост поко́ится на четырёх опо́рах; **there was a bicycle ~ing against the wall** у стены́ стоя́л велосипе́д; (*fig.*) осно́вываться (*impf.*); **your argument ~s on a fallacy** ваш до́вод исхо́дит из оши́бочного утвержде́ния. **4.** (*linger; alight*) поко́иться (*impf.*); ост|ава́ться, -а́ться; **the light ~ed on her face** её лицо́ бы́ло освещено́. **5.** (*lie fallow*) остава́ться (*impf.*) под па́ром. **6.** (*US leg.*): **the defence ~s** защи́те не́чего доба́вить.

cpds. **~-cure** *n.* лече́ние поко́ем; (*fig.*) рабо́та — не бей лежа́чего; **~-day** *n.* выходно́й/нерабо́чий день; **~-home** *n.* санато́рий, дом о́тдыха; **~-house** *n.* гости́ница; **~-room** *n.* (*US, lavatory*) туале́т, убо́рная.

rest[2] [rest] *n.* (*remainder*) оста́ток; (*remaining things, people*) остальны́е (*pl.*); **and all the ~ of it** и всё про́чее; **for the ~** в остально́м.

restart [riːˈstɑːt] *v.t.* вновь нач|ина́ть, -а́ть; сно́ва зав|оди́ть, -ести́ (*машину*).

restate [riːˈsteɪt] *v.t.* (*repeat*) вновь заяв|ля́ть, -и́ть; утвержда́ть (*impf.*); (*reformulate*) за́ново формули́ровать, с-.

restatement [riːˈsteɪtmənt] *n.* повто́рное заявле́ние; но́вая формулиро́вка.

restaurant [ˈrestəˌrɒnt, -ˌrɔ̃] *n.* рестора́н.

restaurateur [ˌrestərəˈtɜː(r)] *n.* владе́лец рестора́на.

restful [ˈrestfʊl] *adj.* успоко́ительный, успока́ивающий; **a ~ light** мя́гкий свет; **he has a ~ manner** с ним (о́чень) споко́йно.

restitution [ˌrestɪ'tju:ʃ(ə)n] *n.* возвраще́ние, возмеще́ние; **~ of conjugal rights** восстановле́ние супру́жеских прав; **he was forced to make ~** его́ заста́вили возмести́ть убы́тки.

restive ['restɪv] *adj.* (*of horse*) норови́стый; (*of pers.*) стропти́вый; (*restless*) беспоко́йный.

restless ['restlɪs] *adj.* беспоко́йный, непосе́дливый, неугомо́нный; **I feel ~** мне что-то не сиди́тся; **she spent a ~ night** она́ провела́ беспоко́йную/бессо́нную ночь.

restlessness ['restlɪsnɪs] *n.* беспоко́йство, непосе́дливость, неугомо́нность.

restock [ri:'stɒk] *v.i.* поп|олня́ть, -о́лнить запа́сы.

restoration [ˌrestə'reɪʃ(ə)n] *n.* **1.** (*return*) восстановле́ние; **~ of property** возвраще́ние иму́щества; **~ to health** восстановле́ние здоро́вья. **2.** (*refurbishment; renewal*) реставра́ция; **church ~** реставра́ция це́ркви; **~ of a text** восстановле́ние те́кста. **3.** (*model or drawing of lost object etc.*) реконстру́кция. **4.** (*hist.*) реставра́ция; **R~ drama** дра́ма эпо́хи Ка́рла II.

restorative [rɪ'stɒrətɪv] *n.* тонизи́рующее/укрепля́ющее сре́дство.

restore [rɪ'stɔ:(r)] *v.t.* **1.** (*give, bring or put back*) возвра|ща́ть, -ти́ть (*or* верну́ть); восстан|а́вливать, -ови́ть; **the book was ~d to the library** кни́гу верну́ли в библиоте́ку; **he was ~d to his former post** его́ восстанови́ли на пре́жней рабо́те; **he wants to ~ the old custom** он хо́чет возроди́ть ста́рый обы́чай; **it ~s my confidence** э́то вселя́ет в меня́ но́вую уве́ренность; **he was soon ~d to health** его́ здоро́вье вско́ре восстанови́лось; **his spirits were ~d by the sight** э́то зре́лище верну́ло ему́ хоро́шее настрое́ние; **order was ~d** поря́док был восстано́влен. **2.** (*reconvert to original state*) реставри́ровать (*impf., pf.*); восстан|а́вливать, -ови́ть; **these pictures have been ~d** э́ти карти́ны реставри́рованы; **the text has been ~d** текст восстано́влен.

restorer [rɪ'stɔ:rə(r)] *n.* реставра́тор; восстанови́тель (*m.*).

restrain [rɪ'streɪn] *v.t.* сде́рж|ивать, -а́ть; обу́зд|ывать, -а́ть; **it needed four men to ~ him** пона́добилось четы́ре челове́ка, что́бы удержа́ть его́; **I could not ~ my laughter** я не мог удержа́ться от сме́ха; **his manner was ~ed** он был сде́ржан.

restraint [rɪ'streɪnt] *n.* **1.** (*self-control*) сде́ржанность, самооблада́ние; невозмути́мость. **2.** (*physical*) ограниче́ние свобо́ды движе́ния. **3.** (*constraint*) ограниче́ние; **the ~s of poverty** тиск|и́ (*pl., g.* -о́в) бе́дности/нужды́; **without ~** без ограниче́ний; свобо́дно.

restrict [rɪ'strɪkt] *v.t.* ограни́чи|вать, -ть; **free travel is ~ed to pensioners** беспла́тный прое́зд распространя́ется то́лько на пенсионе́ров; **speed is ~ed to 30 mph** ско́рость ограни́чена до тридцати́ миль в час; **his vision was ~ed by trees** ему́ бы́ло пло́хо ви́дно из-за дере́вьев; **~ed area** райо́н ограни́ченной ско́рости движе́ния; (*US mil.*) райо́н, закры́тый для военнослу́жащих.

restriction [rɪ'strɪkʃ(ə)n] *n.* ограниче́ние; **a speed ~ was first imposed and then lifted** снача́ла ввели́ ограниче́ние ско́рости, пото́м сня́ли; **you can drink without ~** мо́жно пить ско́лько уго́дно.

restrictive [rɪ'strɪktɪv] *adj.* ограничи́тельный; **~ practices in industry** ме́ры по ограниче́нию конкуре́нции и́ли произво́дства.

restyle [ri:'staɪl] *v.t.* переде́л|ывать, -ать; измен|я́ть, -и́ть стиль *+g.*

result [rɪ'zʌlt] *n.* результа́т, сле́дствие; **he died as a ~ of his injuries** он у́мер от ран; **his efforts were without ~** его́ уси́лия бы́ли безрезульта́тны/беспло́дны ; (*of a sum or problem*) результа́т, отве́т.

v.i. **1.** (*arise, come about*) сле́довать (*impf.*) (*из чего*); **this ~s from negligence** э́то сле́дствие небре́жности. **2.** (*issue, end*) конча́ться, ко́нчиться (*+i.*); **the quarrel ~ed in bloodshed** ссо́ра ко́нчилась кровопроли́тием.

resultant [rɪ'zʌlt(ə)nt] *n.* (*phys.*, **~ force**) равноде́йствующая си́ла.

adj. равноде́йствующий; (*consequent*) вытека́ющий (*из чего*).

resume [rɪ'zju:m] *v.t.* (*renew*) возобнов|ля́ть, -и́ть; (*continue*) прод|олжа́ть, -о́лжить; **to ~ my story** я продо́лжу свой расска́з; (*take again*) вновь обре|та́ть, -сти́; **he ~d his seat** он верну́лся на своё ме́сто; **they ~d control** они́ восстанови́ли контро́ль; **he ~d command** он сно́ва при́нял кома́ндование (*чем*).

v.i.: **let us ~ after lunch** продо́лжим по́сле обе́да.

résumé ['rezjʊˌmeɪ] *n.* резюме́ (*indecl.*).

resumption [rɪ'zʌmpʃ(ə)n] *n.* (*renewal*) возобновле́ние; (*continuation*) продолже́ние; (*reacquisition*) возвраще́ние; получе́ние обра́тно.

resurface [ri:'sɜ:fɪs] *v.t.* меня́ть, смени́ть покры́тие *+g.*

v.i. (*of a submarine*) всплы|ва́ть, -ть.

resurgence [rɪ'sɜ:dʒ(ə)ns] *n.* возрожде́ние, воскреше́ние.

resurgent [rɪ'sɜ:dʒ(ə)nt] *adj.* возрожда́ющийся.

resurrect [ˌrezə'rekt] *v.t.* **1.** (*raise from the dead*) воскр|еса́ть, -е́снуть. **2.** (*exhume*) выка́пывать, вы́копать (*труп*). **3.** (*fig., rediscover, revive*) возро|жда́ть, -ди́ть; воскре|ша́ть, -си́ть.

resurrection [ˌrezə'rekʃ(ə)n] *n.* воскресе́ние; выка́пывание (*трупа*); (*fig.*) возрожде́ние, воскреше́ние.

resuscitate [rɪ'sʌsɪˌteɪt] *v.t.* прив|оди́ть, -ести́ в созна́ние; (*fig.*) возвра|ща́ть, -ти́ть к жи́зни; воскре|ша́ть, -си́ть.

resuscitation [rɪˌsʌsɪ'teɪʃ(ə)n] *n.* приведе́ние в созна́ние; (*fig.*) возвраще́ние к жи́зни; воскреше́ние.

retail ['ri:teɪl] *n.* ро́зничная прода́жа; **goods sold (by) ~ are dearer** това́ры, продаю́щиеся в ро́зницу, сто́ят доро́же; **~ prices** ро́зничные це́ны.

v.t. (*sell by ~*) прод|ава́ть, -а́ть в ро́зницу; (*recount details of*) переска́з|ывать, -а́ть.

v.i. продава́ться (*impf.*) в ро́зницу.

retailer ['ri:teɪlə(r)] *n.* ро́зничный торго́вец.

retain [rɪ'teɪn] *v.t.* **1.** (*keep, continue to have*) уде́рживать (*impf.*); сохран|я́ть, -и́ть. **2.** (*keep in place*) подде́рж|ивать, -а́ть; **~ing wall** подпо́рная стена́. **3.** (*secure services of*) нан|има́ть, -я́ть; **~ing fee** предвари́тельный гонора́р адвока́ту.

retainer [rɪ'teɪnə(r)] *n.* **1.** (*hist.*) васса́л; (*servant*) слуга́ (*m.*). **2.** (*fee*) предвари́тельный гонора́р.

retake[1] ['ri:teɪk] *n.* (*cin.*) дубль (*m.*), повто́рная съёмка.

retake[2] [ri:'teɪk] *v.t.* **1.** (*recapture*) сно́ва брать, взять; **the city was ~n** го́род был сно́ва захва́чен. **2.** (*take back*) от|бира́ть, -обра́ть. **3.** (*film etc.*) пересн|има́ть, -я́ть.

retaliate [rɪ'tælɪˌeɪt] *v.i.* отпла́|чивать, -ти́ть той же моне́той; мстить, ото- (*кому за что*).

retaliation [rɪˌtælɪ'eɪʃ(ə)n] *n.* отпла́та, возме́здие.

retaliatory [rɪ'tæljətərɪ] *adj.* отве́тный, кара́тельный.

retard [rɪ'tɑ:d] *v.t.* зам|едля́ть, -е́длить; **the ignition needs to be ~ed** ну́жно переста́вить на бо́лее по́зднее зажига́ние; **a ~ed child** у́мственно отста́лый ребёнок.

retardation [ˌri:tɑ:'deɪʃ(ə)n] *n.* замедле́ние, запа́здывание.

retch [retʃ, ri:tʃ] *v.i.* ту́житься (*impf.*) при рво́те; рыга́ть (*impf.*).

retell [ri:'tel] *v.t.* переска́з|ывать, -а́ть.

retention [rɪ'tenʃ(ə)n] *n.* уде́рживание, сохране́ние; **~ of urine** заде́ржка мочи́.

retentive [rɪ'tentɪv] *adj.*: **a ~ memory** це́пкая па́мять; **a soil ~ of moisture** по́чва, сохраня́ющая вла́гу.

retentiveness [rɪ'tentɪvnɪs] *n.* (*of memory*) це́пкость.

rethink [ri:'θɪŋk] *v.t.* пересм|а́тривать, -отре́ть.

reticence ['retɪs(ə)ns] *n.* молчали́вость; скры́тность.

reticent ['retɪs(ə)nt] *adj.* молчали́вый; скры́тный.

reticulated [rɪ'tɪkjʊleɪtɪd] *adj.* се́тчатый.

reticulation [rɪˌtɪkjʊ'leɪʃ(ə)n] *n.* се́тчатый узо́р.

retina ['retɪnə] *n.* сетча́тка.

retinue ['retɪˌnju:] *n.* сви́та; эско́рт.

retir|e [rɪ'taɪə(r)] *v.t.* ув|ольня́ть, -о́лить; **he was ~ed on a pension** его́ отпра́вили на пе́нсию.

v.i. **1.** (*withdraw*) удал|я́ться, -и́ться; **she wishes to ~e from the world** она́ хо́чет уйти́ из ми́ра; **in company he ~es into himself** когда́ круго́м лю́ди, он ухо́дит в себя́; **she ~ed (to bed) early** она́ ра́но легла́ (спать); **he has a ~ing disposition** он засте́нчивый челове́к; (*mil.*) отступ|а́ть, -и́ть. **2.** (*from employment*) уходи́ть, уйти́ в отста́вку; **when will you reach ~ing age?** когда́ вы дости́гнете пенсио́нного во́зраста?

retired [rɪ'taɪəd] *adj.* **1.** (*in retirement*) (находя́щийся) на пе́нсии; в отста́вке; **a ~ officer** отставно́й офице́р; **the ~ list** спи́сок офице́ров, находя́щихся в отста́вке. **2.** (*secluded*) уединённый.

retirement [rɪ'taɪəmənt] *n.* (*withdrawal*) отхо́д; (*seclusion*) уедине́ние; (*end of employment*) отста́вка, вы́ход на пе́нсию (*or* в отста́вку); **in ~** в отста́вке; **~ age** пенсио́нный во́зраст.

retool [ri:'tu:l] *v.t.* переобору́довать (*impf., pf.*).

retort[1] [rɪ'tɔ:t] *n.* (*vessel*) рето́рта.

retort[2] [rɪ'tɔ:t] *n.* (*reply*) возраже́ние; ре́зкий отве́т; отве́тный вы́пад.

v.t. & i. отв|еча́ть, -е́тить ре́зко (тем же); пари́ровать (*impf., pf.*).

retouch [ri:'tʌtʃ] *n.* ре́тушь.

v.t. ретуши́ровать, от-/под-.

retoucher [ri:'tʌtʃə(r)] *n.* ретушёр.

retrace [rɪ'treɪs] *v.t.* просле́|живать, -ди́ть; (*in memory*) восстан|а́вливать, -ови́ть в па́мяти; **~ one's steps** возвраща́ться, верну́ться тем же путём; (*reconstruct, rehearse*) переч|исля́ть, -и́слить.

retract [rɪ'trækt] *v.t.* **1.** (*draw in*) втя́|гивать, -ну́ть. **2.** (*withdraw*) отр|eка́ться, -е́чься от+*g.*; отка́з|ываться, -а́ться от+*g.*; **I ~ my statement** я беру́ наза́д своё заявле́ние.

v.i. втя́|гиваться, -ну́ться.

retractable [rɪ'træktəb(ə)l] *adj.*: **~ undercarriage** убира́ющееся шасси́.

retractation [rɪ,træk'teɪʃ(ə)n] = **retraction**

retraction [rɪ'trækʃ(ə)n] *n.* (*drawing in*) втя́гивание; (*withdrawal; also* **retractation**) отрече́ние, отка́з (от+*g.*).

retrain [ri:'treɪn] *v.t.* переподгот|а́вливать, -о́вить.

retranslate [,ri:trænz'leɪt, -s'leɪt, ,ri:trɑ:n-] *v.t.* (*back-translate*) де́лать, с- обра́тный перево́д +*g.*

retranslation [,ri:trænz'leɪʃ(ə)n, -s'leɪʃ(ə)n, ,ri:trɑ:n-] *n.* (*back-translation*) обра́тный перево́д; (*into third language*) перево́д не с оригина́ла.

retransmission [,ri:trænz'mɪʃ(ə)n, -s'mɪʃ(ə)n, ,ri:trɑ:n-] *n.* ретрансми́ссия, ретрансля́ция.

retransmit [,ri:trænz'mɪt, -s'mɪt, ,ri:trɑ:n-] *v.t.* ретрансли́ровать (*impf., pf.*).

retread [ri:'tred] *v.t.*: **~ a tyre** восстан|а́вливать, -ови́ть проте́ктор (ши́ны).

retreat [rɪ'tri:t] *n.* **1.** (*withdrawal*) отступле́ние, отхо́д; **the army was in full ~** а́рмия отступа́ла по всему́ фро́нту; **he beat a hasty ~** он бы́стро пошёл на попя́тную; **they sounded the ~** они́ да́ли сигна́л к отхо́ду. **2.** (*secluded place*) убе́жище.

v.i. (*withdraw*) удал|я́ться, -и́ться; (*recede*): **a ~ing chin** сре́занный подборо́док.

retrench [rɪ'trentʃ] *v.t.* сокра|ща́ть, -ти́ть; уре́з|ывать, -ать.

v.i. (*economize*) эконо́мить, с-.

retrenchment [rɪ'trentʃmənt] *n.* сокраще́ние расхо́дов.

retrial [ri:'traɪəl] *n.* повто́рное слу́шание де́ла.

retribution [,retrɪ'bju:ʃ(ə)n] *n.* возме́здие, ка́ра.

retributive [rɪ'trɪbjʊtɪv] *adj.* кара́ющий, кара́тельный.

retrievable [rɪ'tri:vəb(ə)l] *adj.* восстанови́мый; (*reparable*) поправи́мый.

retrieval [rɪ'tri:vəl] *n.* **1.** (*recovery, getting back*) возвраще́ние; **the money is lost beyond ~** де́ньги потеря́ны безвозвра́тно; (*of birds etc. by dogs*) поно́ска; (*tech., of information*) по́иск. **2.** (*recollection, restoration, revival*) восстановле́ние. **3.** (*making good, repair*) исправле́ние.

retrieve [rɪ'tri:v] *v.t.* **1.** (*get back, recover*) брать, взять обра́тно; доста́ть (*pf.*), верну́ть (*pf.*); (*of dogs; also v.i.*) приноси́ть (*impf.*) (*дичь*). **2.** (*restore*) восстан|а́вливать, -ови́ть. **3.** (*put right, make amends for*) испр|авля́ть, -а́вить.

retriever [rɪ'tri:və(r)] *n.* охо́тничья по́иско́вая соба́ка.

retroactive [,retrəʊ'æktɪv] *adj.* име́ющий обра́тное де́йствие (*or* обра́тную си́лу).

retrocede [,retrəʊ'si:d] *v.t.* сно́ва уступ|а́ть, -и́ть.

retrocession [,retrə'seʃ(ə)n] *n.* обра́тная усту́пка.

retrograde ['retrə,greɪd] *adj.* дви́жущийся в обра́тном направле́нии; **~ motion** обра́тное движе́ние; (*fig.*) реакцио́нный.

retrogress [,retrə'gres] *v.i.* (*go back*) дви́гаться (*impf.*) наза́д; (*decline*) ух|удша́ться, -у́дшиться; регресси́ровать (*impf.*).

retrogression [,retrə'greʃ(ə)n] *n.* (*backward movement*) обра́тное движе́ние; (*decline*) регре́сс.

retrogressive [,retrə'gresɪv] *adj.* обра́тный; регресси́рующий.

retro-rocket ['retrəʊ,rɒkɪt] *n.* тормозна́я ракéта, ракéта с обра́тной тя́гой.

retrospect ['retrə,spekt] *n.* взгляд в про́шлое; **in ~** ретроспекти́вно; **the journey was pleasant in ~** пото́м об э́том путеше́ствии бы́ло прия́тно вспомина́ть.

retrospection [,retrə'spekʃ(ə)n] *n.* размышле́ния (*nt. pl.*) о про́шлом; ретроспе́кция.

retrospective [,retrə'spektɪv] *adj.* (*regarding the past*) ретроспекти́вный; обращённый в про́шлое; (*applying to the past*) относя́щийся к про́шлому; **a ~ law** зако́н, име́ющий обра́тную си́лу.

retroussé [rə'tru:seɪ] *adj.* вздёрнутый, курно́сый.

re-try [ri:'traɪ] *v.t.* (*leg., case*) слу́шать (*impf.*) за́ново; (*pers.*) суди́ть (*impf.*) сно́ва.

returf [ri:'tɜ:f] *v.t.* за́ново покр|ыва́ть, -ы́ть дёрном.

return [rɪ'tɜ:n] *n.* **1.** (*coming or going back*) возвраще́ние; **point of no ~** (*aeron.*) крити́ческая то́чка; (*fig.*) черта́, за кото́рой (уже́) нет возвра́та (наза́д); **there was no ~ of the symptoms** симпто́мы не повтори́лись; **by ~ (of post)** обра́тной по́чтой; **many happy ~s (of the day)!** с днём рожде́ния!; **~ fare** сто́имость обра́тного прое́зда. **2.** (**~ ticket**) обра́тный биле́т. **3.** (*turnover*) оборо́т; (*profit*) при́быль; **he got a good ~ on his investment** он получи́л хоро́ший дохо́д от вло́женных де́нег. **4.** (*giving, sending, putting, paying back*) отда́ча, возвра́т, опла́та; **the ~ of a ball** возвра́т мяча́; **~ match** отве́тный матч; **the ~ of a candidate** избра́ние кандида́та в парла́мент. **5.** (*reciprocation*): **in ~ (for)** взаме́н (+*g.*); (*in response to*) в отве́т (на+*a.*). **6.** (*report*) отчёт, ра́порт; **income tax ~** нало́говая деклара́ция/ве́домость; **election ~s** результа́т вы́боров.

v.t. **1.** (*give, send, put, pay back*) возвра|ща́ть, -ти́ть (*or* верну́ть); **I ~ed the book to the shelf** я поста́вил кни́гу обра́тно на по́лку; **he ~ed the ball accurately** он хорошо́ отби́л мяч; **she ~ed my compliment** она́ сде́лала мне отве́тный комплиме́нт; **he ~ed the blow with interest** его́ отве́тный уда́р был ещё сильне́е; **his affection was not ~ed** он не по́льзовался взаи́мностью; **he ~ed good for evil** он отплати́л добро́м за зло; **he was ~ed by a narrow majority** он прошёл (в парла́мент) с незначи́тельным большинство́м; **~ing officer** (*pol.*) уполномо́ченный по вы́борам. **2.** (*say in reply*) отв|еча́ть, -е́тить; возра|жа́ть, -зи́ть. **3.** (*declare*) до|кла́дывать, -ложи́ть; заяв|ля́ть, -и́ть; **the jury ~ed a verdict of guilty** прися́жные призна́ли обвиня́емого вино́вным.

v.i. возвра|ща́ться, -ти́ться (*or* верну́ться); **he left, never to ~** он ушёл/уе́хал навсегда́.

returnable [rɪ'tɜ:nəb(ə)l] *adj.* подлежа́щий возвра́ту/обме́ну.

reunion [ri:'ju:njən, -nɪən] *n.* (*reuniting*) воссоедине́ние, объедине́ние; (*meeting of old friends etc.*) встре́ча; **family ~** сбор всей семьи́.

reunite [,ri:ju:'naɪt] *v.t. & i.* воссоедин|я́ть(ся), -и́ть(ся).

reusable [ri:'ju:zəb(ə)l] *adj.* многокра́тного по́льзования.

re-use[1] [ri:'ju:s] *n.* повто́рное/но́вое испо́льзование.

re-use[2] [ri:'ju:z] *v.t.* сно́ва испо́льзовать (*impf., pf.*).

Rev.[1] ['revərənd] *n.* = **Reverend**

rev[2] [,revə'lu:ʃ(ə)n] *n.* (*coll.*) = **revolution 2.**

v.t. & i. (*also* **~ up**) увели́чи|вать, -ть оборо́ты (мото́ра).

revaluation [ri:,vælju:'eɪʃ(ə)n] *n.* (*of currency*) ревальва́ция.

revalue [ri:'vælju:] *v.t.* ревальви́ровать (*impf., pf.*).

revamp [ri:'væmp] *v.t.* (*fig.*) поднов|ля́ть, -и́ть; приукра́|шивать, -сить.

revanchist [rɪ'væntʃɪst] *n.* реванши́ст.

adj. реванши́стский.

reveal [rɪ'vi:l] *v.t.* обнару́жи|вать, -ть; пока́з|ывать, -а́ть; **he would not ~ his name** он не хоте́л назва́ть своё и́мя; **he ~ed himself to be the father** он объяви́л себя́ отцо́м; **this account is very ~ing** э́тот отчёт о́чень показа́телен;

~ed religion богооткрове́нная рели́гия; **it was evening before the sun ~ed itself** со́лнце показа́лось то́лько к ве́черу; **she wore a ~ing dress** она́ была́ в откры́том пла́тье.

reveille [rɪˈvælɪ, rɪˈvelɪ] *n.* у́тренняя заря́; побу́дка.

revel [ˈrev(ə)l] *n.* гуля́нка, кутёж; **the ~s went on all night** гуля́нка шла всю ночь.

v.i. **1.** (*make merry*) пирова́ть (*impf.*); кути́ть (*impf.*). **2.** (*take delight*) наслажда́ться (*impf.*) (+*i.*); упива́ться (*impf.*) (+*i.*); **she ~s in gossip** она́ обожа́ет спле́тни.

revelation [ˌrevəˈleɪʃ(ə)n] *n.* откры́тие, открове́ние (*also fig., surprise*); (*bibl.*, **R~(s)**) открове́ние Иоа́нна Богосло́ва; апока́липсис.

reveller [ˈrevələ(r)] *n.* кути́ла (*m.*), гуля́ка (*m.*).

revelry [ˈrevəlrɪ] *n.* попо́йка, разгу́л, гульба́.

revenge [rɪˈvendʒ] *n.* **1.** (*retaliatory action*) месть; **he took his ~ on me** он мне отомсти́л. **2.** (*vindictive feeling*) мсти́тельность; **I acted out of ~** я э́то сде́лал из ме́сти. **3.** (*in games*) рева́нш; **they gave their opponents their ~** они́ да́ли свои́м проти́вникам возмо́жность отыгра́ться.

v.t. мстить, ото- (*кому за кого/что*); **he ~d the wrong done him** он отомсти́л за нанесённую ему́ оби́ду; **he ~d himself on his enemies** он отомсти́л свои́м врага́м.

revengeful [rɪˈvendʒfʊl] *adj.* мсти́тельный; жа́ждущий ме́сти.

revenue [ˈrevəˌnjuː] *n.* дохо́д; (*of state*) госуда́рственные дохо́ды; **Inland R~** фина́нсовое/нало́говое управле́ние.

reverberate [rɪˈvɜːbəˌreɪt] *v.t.* отра|жа́ть, -зи́ть.

v.i. (*of sound etc.*) отра|жа́ться, -зи́ться; (*fig.*): **the news ~d** э́та но́вость произвела́ фуро́р.

reverberation [rɪˌvɜːbəˈreɪʃ(ə)n] *n.* отраже́ние, реверберáция; (*fig.*) о́тклик, о́тзвук.

revere [rɪˈvɪə(r)] *v.t.* почита́ть (*impf.*); чтить (*impf.*); глубоко́ уважа́ть (*impf.*).

reverence [ˈrevərəns] *n.* **1.** (*awe, respect*) почита́ние, почте́ние; **they have no ~ for tradition** у них нет никако́го уваже́ния к тради́циям. **2.** (*bow; curtsy*) покло́н; рева́нс. **3.: your R~** ва́ше преподо́бие.

v.t. почита́ть (*impf.*); чтить (*impf.*).

reverend [ˈrevərənd] *adj.*: **the R~ John Smith** его́ преподо́бие Джон Смит; **the ~ gentleman is mistaken** его́ преподо́бие заблужда́ется.

reverent(ial) [ˌrevəˈrenʃ(ə)l] *adj.* почти́тельный, благогове́йный.

reverie [ˈrevərɪ] *n.* мечта́ние, мечта́, грёза; **she was lost in ~** она́ погрузи́лась в мечта́ния.

reversal [rɪˈvɜːsəl] *n.* (*annulment*) отме́на; (*conversion into opposite*) по́лная переме́на, поворо́т на 180° (сто во́семьдесят гра́дусов); переворо́т; **a ~ of fortune** превра́тность судьбы́; (*phot.*) обраще́ние.

reverse [rɪˈvɜːs] *n.* **1.** (*opposite*) противополо́жность; **the ~ is true** де́ло обстои́т как раз наоборо́т; **he was the ~ of happy** он был отню́дь не рад; **I am not ill, quite the ~** я не бо́лен — совсе́м наоборо́т. **2.** (**~ gear**): **he put the car into ~** он включи́л за́дний ход; (*fig.*): **he was forced to put his plans into ~** ему́ пришло́сь пойти́ на попя́тную. **3.** (*of coin*) обра́тная сторона́; ре́шка. **4.** (*misfortune; defeat*) неуда́ча; пораже́ние; прова́л.

adj. обра́тный, противополо́жный; **in ~ order** в обра́тном поря́дке; **stamps have gum on the ~ side** с обра́тной стороны́ ма́рки покры́ты клеем; **in ~ gear** за́дним хо́дом; **~ image** обра́тное/перевёрнутое изображе́ние.

v.t. **1.** (*turn round, invert*) пов|ора́чивать, -ерну́ть обра́тно; **the situation was ~d** ситуа́ция кру́то измени́лась; **he ~d himself** (*his statement, attitude etc.*) он кру́то измени́л свою́ пози́цию. **2.** (*annul*) отмен|я́ть, -и́ть; **he ~d his decision** он пересмотре́л своё реше́ние. **3.** (*drive backwards*): **he ~d (the car) into a wall** он дал за́дний ход и вре́зался в сте́ну.

v.i. **1.** (*of driver*) да|ва́ть, -ть за́дний ход. **2.** (*of vehicle*): **the car ~s well** маши́на хорошо́ идёт за́дним хо́дом; **reversing light** фона́рь (*m.*) за́днего хо́да. **3.** (*in waltzing*) вальси́ровать/кружи́ться (*impf.*) в обра́тную сто́рону.

reversible [rɪˈvɜːsɪb(ə)l] *adj.* (*of process etc.*) обрати́мый; (*that can be turned inside out*) двусторо́нний.

reversion [rɪˈvɜːʃ(ə)n] *n.* **1.** (*return*) возвраще́ние (к пре́жнему состоя́нию); **~ to type** атави́зм. **2.** (*of property or rights*) обра́тный перехо́д (иму́щества) к первонача́льному владе́льцу. **3.** (*sum payable on death*) страхо́вка, выпла́чиваемая по́сле сме́рти.

revert [rɪˈvɜːt] *v.i.* возвра|ща́ться, -ти́ться; **the fields have ~ed to scrub** поля́ вновь поросли́ куста́рником; **he ~ed to his old ways** он взя́лся за ста́рое; **~ing to your original question** возвраща́ясь к ва́шему первонача́льному вопро́су; (*of property, rights etc.*) пере|ходи́ть, -йти́ (*к прежнему владельцу*); **his land ~ed to the state** его́ земля́ перешла́ к госуда́рству.

revet [rɪˈvet] *v.t.* облиц|о́вывать, -ева́ть.

revetment [rɪˈvetmənt] *n.* облицо́вка, обши́вка.

revictual [riːˈvɪt(ə)l] *v.i.* попо́лнить (*pf.*) запа́сы продово́льствия.

review [rɪˈvjuː] *n.* **1.** (*re-examination, survey, revision*) пересмо́тр, просмо́тр; **the decision is subject to ~** реше́ние подлежи́т пересмо́тру; **the matter is under constant ~** к э́тому вопро́су постоя́нно возвраща́ются. **2.** (*retrospect*) пересмо́тр; воспомина́ние; **a ~ of the year's events** обзо́р собы́тий го́да. **3.** (*of mil. forces etc.*) пара́д. **4.** (*of book etc.*) реце́нзия, о́тзыв. **5.** (*periodical*) периоди́ческое изда́ние, обозре́ние.

v.t. **1.** (*reconsider, re-examine*) пересм|а́тривать, -отре́ть. **2.** (*survey mentally*) мы́сленно обозр|ева́ть, -е́ть; **he ~ed his chances of success** он проанализи́ровал/взве́сил свои́ ша́нсы на успе́х. **3.** (*inspect*) просм|а́тривать, -отре́ть. **4.** (*write critical account of*) рецензи́ровать, от-/про-; **the film was well ~ed** фильм получи́л хоро́шие реце́нзии.

v.i.: **he ~s for the Times** он реце́нзент газе́ты «Таймс».

reviewer [rɪˈvjuːə(r)] *n.* реценз́ент, кри́тик.

revile [rɪˈvaɪl] *v.t.* оскорб|ля́ть, -и́ть; поноси́ть (*impf.*); брани́ть (*impf.*).

revise [rɪˈvaɪz] *n.* испра́вленный текст.

v.t. пересм|а́тривать, -отре́ть; испр|авля́ть, -а́вить; перераб|а́тывать, -о́тать; **~d and enlarged edition** испра́вленное и допо́лненное изда́ние; **I ~d my opinion of him** я измени́л своё мне́ние о нём.

v.i.: **I must ~ for the exams** я до́лжен повтори́ть материа́л (*or* гото́виться) к экза́менам.

reviser [rɪˈvaɪzə(r)] *n.* реда́ктор.

revision [rɪˈvɪʒ(ə)n] *n.* пересмо́тр, реви́зия; (*checking*) прове́рка, перерабо́тка, редакту́ра; (*for exams*) повторе́ние.

revisionism [rɪˈvɪʒəˌnɪz(ə)m] *n.* ревизиони́зм.

revisionist [rɪˈvɪʒənɪst] *n.* ревизиони́ст.

revisit [riːˈvɪzɪt] *v.t.* посе|ща́ть, -ти́ть сно́ва.

revitalization [riːˌvaɪtəlaɪˈzeɪʃ(ə)n] *n.* оживле́ние.

revitalize [riːˈvaɪtəˌlaɪz] *v.t.* вновь ожив|ля́ть, -и́ть.

revival [rɪˈvaɪv(ə)l] *n.* (*return to consciousness, health etc.*) возвраще́ние созна́ния; восстановле́ние здоро́вья; **a sudden ~ in spirits** внеза́пный подъём ду́ха; **a ~ of interest** оживле́ние интере́са; (*return to use, knowledge, popularity*) возрожде́ние; **the ~ of old customs** возрожде́ние ста́рых обы́чаев; **the ~ of learning** Возрожде́ние, Ренесса́нс; **(religious ~)** возрожде́ние ве́ры; (*of play*) возобновле́ние.

revivalism [rɪˈvaɪvəˌlɪz(ə)m] *n.* евангели́зм; уче́ние возрожде́нцев.

revivalist [rɪˈvaɪvəlɪst] *n.* евангели́ст (*fem.* -ка); возрожде́нец.

revive [rɪˈvaɪv] *v.t.* возро|жда́ть, -ди́ть; ожив|ля́ть, -и́ть; **a glass of brandy ~d her** рю́мка коньяку́ привела́ её в чу́вство; **their hopes were ~d** они́ вновь обрели́ наде́жду; **can you ~ the fire?** вы мо́жете сно́ва разже́чь ого́нь?; **the opera was recently ~d** э́ту о́перу неда́вно поста́вили сно́ва.

v.i. возро|жда́ться, -ди́ться; (*regain vigour*) ожив|а́ть, -и́ть; **his spirits ~d** он приободри́лся; (*regain consciousness*) при|ходи́ть, -йти́ в себя́/чу́вство.

revocable [ˈrevəkəb(ə)l] *adj.* могу́щий быть отменённым.

revocation [ˌrevəˈkeɪʃ(ə)n] *n.* отме́на, аннули́рование.

revoke [rɪˈvəʊk] *n.* отме́на; рено́нс (*при наличии требуемой масти*).

v.t. отмен|я́ть, -и́ть; аннули́ровать (*impf., pf.*).
v.i. (*at cards*; *US also* **reneg(u)e**) пойти́ (*pf.*) с друго́й ма́сти при нали́чии тре́буемой.

revolt [rɪˈvəʊlt] *n.* восста́ние; бунт; **the peasants were in ~** крестья́не восста́ли.
v.t. вызыва́ть, вы́звать отвраще́ние у+*g.*; **a ~ing sight** отврати́тельное зре́лище.
v.i. восст|ава́ть, -а́ть; бунтова́ть(ся), взбунтова́ться; **common sense ~s at it** здра́вый смысл восстаёт про́тив э́того.

revolution [ˌrevəˈluːʃ(ə)n] *n.* **1.** (*revolving*) враще́ние; **the ~ of the earth** враще́ние земли́. **2.** (*one complete rotation*; *coll.* **rev**) оборо́т; **at 60 ~s per minute** при шести́десяти оборо́тах в мину́ту. **3.** (*pol., fig.*) револю́ция.

revolutionary [ˌrevəˈluːʃənərɪ] *n.* революционе́р.
adj. революцио́нный.

revolutionize [ˌrevəˈluːʃəˌnaɪz] *v.t.* (*stir up to revolution*, *transform*) революционизи́ровать (*impf., pf.*).

revolv|e [rɪˈvɒlv] *v.t.* (*fig.*): **he ~ed the problem in his mind** он всесторо́нне обду́мал пробле́му.
v.i. враща́ться (*impf.*); **~ing doors** враща́ющиеся две́ри; (*fig.*): **he thinks everything ~es around him** он мнит себя́ це́нтром вселе́нной.

revolver [rɪˈvɒlvə(r)] *n.* револьве́р.

revue [rɪˈvjuː] *n.* обозре́ние, ревю́ (*nt. indecl.*).

revulsion [rɪˈvʌlʃ(ə)n] *n.* **1.** (*sudden change*) внеза́пное измене́ние; **a ~ in popular feeling** перело́м в обще́ственном мне́нии. **2.** (*disgust*) отвраще́ние.

reward [rɪˈwɔːd] *n.* **1.** (*recompense*) награ́да (за+*a.*); **without thought of ~** не ду́мая о вознагражде́нии. **2.** (*sum offered*) пре́мия; де́нежное вознагражде́ние; **there was a ~ (out) for his capture** была́ объя́влена награ́да за его́ пои́мку.
v.t. (воз)награ|жда́ть, -ди́ть; **it was a ~ing task** де́ло сто́ило того́; **our patience was ~ed** на́ше терпе́ние бы́ло вознаграждено́.

rewind [riːˈwaɪnd] *v.t.* перем|а́тывать, -ота́ть; (*a watch*) (сно́ва) зав|оди́ть, -ести́.

re-wire [riːˈwaɪə(r)] *v.t.*: **~ a house** обнов|ля́ть, -и́ть прово́дку в до́ме.

reword [riːˈwɜːd] *v.t.* выража́ть, вы́разить другими слова́ми; переформули́ровать (*impf., pf.*).

rewrite[1] [ˈriːraɪt] *n.* перерабо́танный текст.

rewrite[2] [riːˈraɪt] *v.t.* перепи́с|ывать, -а́ть.

Rex [reks] *n.* (*leg.*): **~ v. Brown** де́ло по обвине́нию Бра́уна.

Reykjavik [ˈreikjəˌviːk] *n.* Ре́йкьявик.

rhapsodize [ˈræpsəˌdaɪz] *v.i.* (*fig.*) восторга́ться (*impf.*); говори́ть (*impf.*) с упое́нием.

rhapsod|y [ˈræpsədɪ] *n.* (*mus.*) рапсо́дия; (*fig.*): **he went into ~ies over her dress** он пел дифира́мбы её туале́ту.

rheostat [ˈriːəˌstæt] *n.* реоста́т.

rhesus [ˈriːsəs] *n.* **(~ monkey)** ре́зус; **R~ factor** ре́зус-фа́ктор; **R~-negative** ре́зус-отрица́тельный.

rhetoric [ˈretərɪk] *n.* (*art of speech*) рито́рика; ора́торское иску́сство; (*pej.*) краснобა́йство, фразёрство.

rhetorical [rɪˈtɒrɪk(ə)l] *adj.* ритори́ческий; **~ question** ритори́ческий вопро́с.

rhetorician [ˌretəˈrɪʃ(ə)n] *n.* ри́тор; ора́тор.

rheumatic [ruːˈmætɪk] *n.* (*sufferer from rheumatism*) ревма́тик; (*pl., coll., rheumatism*) ревмати́зм.
adj. ревмати́ческий; **~ fever** ревмати́зм.

rheumaticky [ruːˈmætɪkɪ] *adj.* (*coll.*) страда́ющий ревмати́змом.

rheumatism [ˈruːməˌtɪz(ə)m] *n.* ревмати́зм.

rheumatoid [ˈruːməˌtɔɪd] *adj.* ревмато́идный, ревмати́ческий; **~ arthritis** ревмати́ческий полиартри́т, суставно́й ревмати́зм.

Rhine [raɪn] *n.* Рейн; **~ wine** ре́йнское вино́.
cpds. **~land** *n.* Ре́йнская о́бласть; **r~stone** *n.* го́рный хруста́ль.

rhino [ˈraɪnəʊ] *n.* **1.** = **rhinoceros. 2.** (*money*) ба́шл|и (*pl., g.* -ей) (*sl.*).

rhinoceros [raɪˈnɒsərəs] *n.* носоро́г.

rhizome [ˈraɪzəʊm] *n.* ризо́ма.

Rhodes [rəʊdz] *n.* Ро́дос.

Rhodesia [rəʊˈdiːʃə] *n.* Роде́зия.

Rhodesian [rəʊˈdiːʃən] *n.* родези́|ец (*fem.* -йка).
adj. родези́йский.

rhododendron [ˌrəʊdəˈdendrən] *n.* рододе́ндрон.

rhomboid [ˈrɒmbɔɪd] *n.* (*geom.*) ромбо́ид.
adj. (*also* **-al**) ромбови́дный.

rhombus [ˈrɒmbəs] *n.* (*geom.*) ромб.

Rhone [rəʊn] *n.* Ро́на.

rhubarb [ˈruːbɑːb] *n.* **1.** реве́нь (*m.*). **2.** (*sl., confused shouting*) гвалт; «гур-гу́р», «ва́ра, ва́ра»; (*US sl., dispute*) перебра́нка.

rhumb-line [rʌm] *n.* локсодро́мия.

rhyme [raɪm] *n.* ри́фма; **think of a ~ for 'love'** приду́майте ри́фму к сло́ву «любо́вь»; **he wrote the greeting in ~** он написа́л приве́тствие в стиха́х; **there is no ~ or reason in it** в э́том нет никако́го смы́сла; (*poem*) стих; **nursery ~** де́тский стишо́к; (*pl., verse*) стихи́ (*m. pl.*), поэ́зия.
v.t. & i. рифмова́ть(ся) (*impf.*); **you can't ~ those two words** э́ти два сло́ва не рифму́ются; **~ed verses** рифмо́ванный стих; **rhyming dictionary** слова́рь рифм; (*compose verse*) сочиня́ть (*impf.*) стихи́.

rhymester [ˈraɪmstə(r)] *n.* рифмоплёт, стихоплёт.

rhythm [ˈrɪð(ə)m] *n.* ритм; **~ section** (*of a band*) уда́рные инструме́нты.

rhythmic(al) [ˈrɪðmɪk(əl)] *adj.* ритми́чный, ритми́ческий; **rhythmic gymnastics** худо́жественная гимна́стика.

RI (*abbr. of* ***religious instruction***) религио́зное обуче́ние.

rial [ˈriːɑːl] *n.* (*unit of currency*) риа́л.

rib [rɪb] *n.* **1.** (*anat.*) ребро́; **he dug me in the ~s** он толкну́л меня́ в бок; **spare ~s** (*of meat*) рёбрышки (*nt. pl.*); (*of leaf*) жи́лка. **2.** (*ship's timber*) шпанго́ут, ребро́.
v.t. (*sl., tease*) разы́гр|ывать, -а́ть.

ribald [ˈrɪb(ə)ld] *adj.* непристо́йный, скабрёзный; бессты́дный.

ribaldry [ˈrɪbəldrɪ] *n.* непристо́йность, скабрёзность; скверносло́вие.

riband [ˈrɪbənd] = **ribbon**

ribbed [rɪbd] *adj.*: **~ cloth** ру́бчатая ткань.

ribbon [ˈrɪbən] (*also* **riband**) *n.* ле́нта, тесьма́; **hair ~** ле́нта; **campaign ~** ле́нта уча́стника кампа́нии; (*fig.*): **~ development** ле́нточная застро́йка; **his clothes were torn to ~s** его́ оде́жда была́ разо́рвана в кло́чья.

riboflavin [ˌraɪbəʊˈfleɪvɪn] *n.* рибофлави́н.

rice [raɪs] *n.* рис; **boiled ~** ри́совая ка́ша.
cpds. **~field** *n.* ри́совое по́ле; **~-paper** *n.* ри́совая бума́га.

rich [rɪtʃ] *n.* (*collect.*, **the ~**) бога́тые (*pl.*).
adj. **1.** (*wealthy*) бога́тый. **2.** (*fertile, abundant*) плодоро́дный; **a ~ soil** плодоро́дная/ту́чная по́чва; **a land ~ in minerals** земля́, бога́тая ископа́емыми; **he struck it ~** (*coll.*) он напа́л на жи́лу. **3.** (*valuable, plentiful*) оби́льный; **a ~ harvest** бога́тый урожа́й. **4.** (*costly, splendid*) це́нный, бога́тый, роско́шный. **5.** (*of food*) сдо́бный, жи́рный. **6.** (*of colours*) густо́й. **7.** (*of sounds or voices*) густо́й, со́чный. **8.** (*coll., amusing*) потёшный, умори́тельный. **9.** (*of fuel*): **a ~ mixture** бога́тая смесь.

riches [ˈrɪtʃɪz] *n.* бога́тство, оби́лие; (*fig.*): **the ~ of the soil** сокро́вища (*nt. pl.*) земли́/не́др.

richly [ˈrɪtʃlɪ] *adv.*: **she was ~ dressed** она́ была́ бога́то оде́та; **his punishment was ~ deserved** он вполне́ заслужи́л тако́е наказа́ние.

richness [ˈrɪtʃnɪs] *n.* бога́тство, оби́лие; (*of food*) сдо́бность, жи́рность.

Richter scale [ˈrɪktə] *n.* шкала́ Ри́хтера.

rick[1] [rɪk] *n.* (*stack*) стог.

rick[2] [rɪk] (*also* **wrick**) *v.t.* растя́|гивать, -ну́ть; вы́вихнуть (*pf.*); **I ~ed my neck** я нело́вко поверну́л ше́ю.

rickets [ˈrɪkɪts] *n.* рахи́т.

rickety [ˈrɪkɪtɪ] *adj.* (*suffering from rickets*) рахити́чный; (*fragile, unsteady*) ша́ткий, неусто́йчивый.

rickshaw [ˈrɪkʃɔː] *n.* ри́кша.

ricochet [ˈrɪkəˌʃeɪ, -ˌʃet] *n.* рикоше́т; **~ fire** стрельба́ на рикоше́тах.
v.i. рикошети́ровать (*impf.*); бить (*impf.*) рикоше́том.

rid [rɪd] *v.t.* освобо|жда́ть, -ди́ть; изб|авля́ть, -а́вить; **he ~ the country of beggars** он изба́вил страну́ от ни́щих; **get ~ of** изб|авля́ться, -а́виться от+*g.*; (*coll.*) спла́вить (*pf.*);

we were glad to be, get ~ of him мы бы́ли ра́ды от него́ изба́виться; **you are well ~ of that car** сла́ва Бо́гу, что вы изба́вились от э́той маши́ны.

riddance [ˈrɪd(ə)ns] *n.* избавле́ние; устране́ние; **good ~ to him!** ≃ ска́тертью доро́га!

riddle[1] [ˈrɪd(ə)l] *n.* зага́дка; (*mystery*) та́йна; **he set me a ~ to solve** он за́дал мне зага́дку; **he talks in ~s** он говори́т зага́дками; **the ~ of the universe** та́йна вселе́нной.

riddle[2] [ˈrɪd(ə)l] *n.* (*sieve*) решето́.

v.t. (*pierce all over*) решети́ть, из-; **he was ~d with bullets** пу́ли изрешети́ли его́ те́ло; (*fig.*): **~d with disease** насквозь больно́й; **they ~d his arguments** они́ разби́ли его́ до́воды в пух и прах; **the manuscript is ~d with errors** ру́копись пестри́т оши́бками.

ride [raɪd] *n.* **1.** (*journey on horseback*) прогу́лка верхо́м; (*by vehicle*) пое́здка, езда́; **it is only a 5-minute ~ to the station** до ста́нции всего́ 5 мину́т езды́. **2.** (*excursion*) прогу́лка; **let's go for a ~ into the country** дава́йте съе́здим за́ город ра́ди прогу́лки; **he took me for a ~** (*lit.*) он прокати́л меня́; (*coll.*, *cheated*) он меня́ разыгра́л.

v.t. & *i.* **1.** (*on horseback*) е́здить (*indet.*), е́хать, по- (верхо́м) (на+*p.*); ката́ться (*impf.*) (верхо́м) (на+*p.*); (*gallop*) скака́ть (*impf.*); **she ~s a horse well** она́ хорошо́ е́здит верхо́м (*or* на ло́шади); **he rode his horse at the fence** он напра́вил ло́шадь к барье́ру; **he rode his horse over the fence** он перемахну́л на ло́шади че́рез забо́р; **the jockey rode a good race** жоке́й хорошо́ скака́л; **do you ~?** вы е́здите верхо́м?; **he ~s to hounds** он охо́тится верхо́м с соба́ками; **he is riding for a fall** он допрыга́ется; **he rode roughshod over her feelings** он соверше́нно не счита́лся с её чу́вствами. **2.** (*on a vehicle*) е́здить (*indet.*), е́хать, по- (на+*p.*); **I ~ a bicycle to work** я е́зжу на рабо́ту на велосипе́де. **3.** (*of ships etc.*) плыть (*impf.*) (по+*d.*); **the ship rode the waves** кора́бль рассека́л во́лны; **the ship was riding at anchor** кора́бль стоя́л на я́коре; **the moon is riding high** луна́ плывёт высоко́; **let it ~** (*fig.*) ну и пусть! **4.** (*of a horse or vehicle*) кати́ться (*impf.*); идти́ (*det.*); **this car ~s comfortably** в э́той маши́не удо́бно е́здить.

with advs.: **~ away** *v.i.* отъ|езжа́ть, -е́хать; уезжа́ть, уе́хать; **~ down** *v.t.* (*pursue and catch up with*) дог|оня́ть, -на́ть; наст|ига́ть, -и́чь верхо́м; (*knock down by riding at s.o.*) дави́ть (*impf.*); топта́ть (*impf.*); **~ out** *v.t.*: **the ship rode out the storm** кора́бль вы́держал на́тиск бу́ри; **we shall ~ out our present troubles** мы переживём ны́нешние тру́дности; *v.i.* соверш|а́ть, -и́ть прогу́лку; **~ up** *v.i.* (*approach on horseback*) подъ|езжа́ть, -е́хать верхо́м; (*of clothing*) лезть (*impf.*) вверх.

rider [ˈraɪdə(r)] *n.* **1.** (*horseman*) вса́дни|к (*fem.* -ца), нае́здни|к (*fem.* -ца); (*cyclist*) велосипеди́ст (*fem.* -ка). **2.** (*clause*) дополне́ние; добавле́ние; попра́вка.

riderless [ˈraɪdəlɪs] *adj.* без вса́дника.

ridge [rɪdʒ] *n.* **1.** край; спи́нка; **the ~ of a roof** конёк кры́ши. **2.** (*of soil*) гре́бень (*m.*); **~ cultivation** гребнево́й посе́в. **3.** (*of high land*) го́рный хребе́т/кряж.

cpd. **~-pole** *n.* распо́рка, растя́жка; конько́вый брус.

ridicule [ˈrɪdɪˌkju:l] *n.* осмея́ние, насме́шка; **he was an object of ~** он был предме́том насме́шек; **I don't like being held up to ~** не люблю́, когда́ из меня́ де́лают посме́шище; **you will lay yourself open to ~** вы вы́ставите себя́ на посме́шище.

v.t. осме́ивать (*impf.*); подн|има́ть, -я́ть на́ смех.

ridiculous [rɪˈdɪkjʊləs] *adj.* смехотво́рный; неле́пый; **don't be ~!** не говори́те глу́постей!

ridiculousness [rɪˈdɪkjʊləsnɪs] *n.* смехотво́рность; неле́пость.

riding [ˈraɪdɪŋ] *n.* верхова́я езда́.

cpds. **~-breeches** *n. pl.* бри́дж|и (*pl.*, *g.* -ей) для верхово́й езды́; **~-habit** *n.* амазо́нка; **~-master** *n.* бере́йтор; инстру́ктор по верхово́й езде́; **~-school** *n.* шко́ла верхово́й езды́.

rife [raɪf] *adj.* распространённый; **superstition was ~** суеве́рия бы́ли широко́ распространены́; **the country was ~ with rumours** в стране́ ходи́ло мно́жество слу́хов.

riffle [ˈrɪf(ə)l] *v.t.* & *i.*: **he ~d (through) the pages** он бы́стро перелиста́л страни́цы.

riffraff [ˈrɪfræf] *n.* подо́нки (*m. pl.*) о́бщества; сброд, шпана́.

rifle [ˈraɪf(ə)l] *n.* винто́вка; **~ regiment** пехо́тный/стрелко́вый полк; (*pl.*, **~** *troops*) стрелко́вая часть; стрелки́ (*m. pl.*).

v.t. **1.** (*cut grooves in*) нареза́ть (*impf.*) кана́л (*ствола*). **2.** (*plunder*) гра́бить, о-; очи́стить (*pf.*).

cpds. **~man** *n.* стрело́к; **~-range** *n.* (*for shooting practice*) тир, стре́льбище; (*distance*) да́льность руже́йного вы́стрела; **~-shot** *n.* вы́стрел из винто́вки.

rift [rɪft] *n.* **1.** тре́щина, щель; **a ~ in the clouds** просве́т в ту́чах. **2.** (*fig.*; *also* **~ in the lute**) разла́д.

cpd. **~-valley** *n.* ри́фтовая доли́на; доли́на прова́ла.

rig [rɪg] *n.* **1.** (*naut.*) приспособле́ние, осна́стка; па́русное вооруже́ние. **2.** (*dress*) оде́жда; **in full ~** при по́лном пара́де. **3.** (*for drilling*) бурова́я вы́шка.

v.t. **1.** (*fit out*) осна|ща́ть, -сти́ть; снаря|жа́ть, -ди́ть. **2.** (*manipulate*, *conduct fraudulently*): **the elections were ~ged** результа́ты вы́боров бы́ли подтасо́ваны; **a ~ged match** догово́рный матч.

with advs.: **~ out** *v.t.* снаря|жа́ть, -ди́ть; наря|жа́ть, -ди́ть; **she ~ged the boys out with new clothes** она́ вы́рядила ма́льчиков в но́вую оде́жду; **~ up** (на́скоро) *v.t.* соору|жа́ть, -ди́ть.

cpd. **~-out** *n.* наря́д.

Riga [ˈri:gə] *n.* Ри́га; (*attr.*) ри́жский.

rigging [ˈrɪgɪŋ] *n.* такела́ж, осна́стка.

right [raɪt] *n.* **1.** (*what is just, fair*) правота́; справедли́вость; **~, not might, must triumph** должна́ восторже́ствовать справедли́вость; **the child must learn the difference between ~ and wrong** ребёнка сле́дует научи́ть отлича́ть добро́ от зла́; **I know I am in the ~** я зна́ю, что я прав. **2.** (*entitlement*) пра́во; **as of ~** как полага́ющийся по пра́ву; **in his, her own ~** сам, в своём пра́ве, по себе́; **stand on one's ~s** наст|а́ивать, -оя́ть на свои́х права́х; **stand up for one's ~s** отст|а́ивать, -оя́ть свои́ права́; **by ~ of conquest** по пра́ву завоева́теля; **the house is hers by ~** дом принадлежи́т ей по зако́ну; **she accepts everything as hers by ~** она́ всё принима́ет так, бу́дто ей э́то поло́жено по пра́ву; **by ~s** по справедли́вости; че́стно говоря́; **by ~s he should be at work** вообще́-то ему́ поло́жено быть на рабо́те; **~ of way** пра́во прохо́да/прое́зда; **the divine ~ of kings** пра́во пома́занника бо́жьего; **bill of ~s** билль (*m.*) о права́х. **3.** (*pl.*, *correct state*): **I have yet to find out the ~s and wrongs of the case** мне ещё предстои́т разобра́ться, кто тут прав и кто винова́т; **he put the engine to ~s** он привёл мото́р в поря́док; **he tried to set the world to ~s** он пыта́лся переде́лать мир. **4.** (*~-hand side etc.*) пра́вая сторона́; **on, to the ~** напра́во; **on, from the ~** спра́ва; **most countries drive on the ~** в большинстве́ стран правосторо́ннее движе́ние; **my father is on the ~ of the photograph** мой оте́ц нахо́дится на фотогра́фии спра́ва; **the enemy's ~** пра́вый фланг проти́вника. **5.** (*pol.*): **the R~** пра́вые (*pl.*); **politicians of the R~** полити́ческие де́ятели пра́вого крыла́. **6.** (*boxing*) уда́р пра́вой.

adj. **1.** (*just, morally good*) пра́вый, справедли́вый; **I try to do what is ~** я стара́юсь поступа́ть че́стно; **he did the ~ thing by her** он с ней че́стно поступи́л; **you were ~ to refuse** вы сде́лали пра́вильно, что отказа́лись; **it is only ~ to tell you ...** я счита́ю свои́м до́лгом сказа́ть вам, что…; **that is only ~ and proper** так тому́ и сле́дует быть; **it is not ~ that he should be accused** его́ обвиня́ют несправедли́во. **2.** (*correct, true, required*) пра́вильный, ве́рный, ну́жный; **the ~ use of words** пра́вильное употребле́ние слов; **the ~ man in the ~ place** челове́к на своём ме́сте; **she is waiting for Mr R~** она́ всё ещё ждёт при́нца; **the ~ road** пра́вильный путь; **that's not the ~ way to do it** э́то де́лается не так; **what is the ~ time?** вы мо́жете сказа́ть то́чное вре́мя?; **he tried to keep on the ~ side of the teacher** он стара́лся не по́ртить отноше́ния с учи́телем; **~ side up** в пра́вильном положе́нии; **he is on the ~ side of forty** ему́ ещё нет сорока́; **that's ~!** пра́вильно!; ве́рно!; справедли́во ска́зано!; (*iron.*) пра́вильно!; ну и удружи́л!; **let's get it ~, are you on my side or not?** дава́йте разберёмся, на моéй вы сторонé или́ нет?; **I tried to put him ~** я пытáлся вы́вести егó из заблуждéния; **I set him ~ on a few points** я емý кóе-что разъясни́л; **he's a Frenchman, ~ enough** да, он францýз — уж э́то тóчно. **3.** (*in order, good health*) испрáвный; здорóвый; **can you put my watch ~?** вы мóжете почини́ть мои́ часы́?; **these matters must be put ~** э́ти делá нýжно улáдить; **this medicine will soon put you ~** от э́того лекáрства вы скóро попрáвитесь; **I feel as ~ as rain** я себя́ прекрáсно чýвствую; **he's not quite ~ in the head** у негó не все дóма; **he was not in his ~ mind** он был не в своём умé; **everything will turn out ~ in the end** всё в концé концóв улáдится; **are you all ~?** всё в порядке?; (*expr. doubt*) вам нехорошó?; вам плóхо?; **all ~, I'll come with you!** лáдно, я пойдý с вáми!; **all ~, I admit it!** лáдно уж, признаю́сь; **it's all ~ with me** я не возражáю; **~!** (*expr. agreement or consent*) вéрно!; хорошó!; **~ you are** хорошó!; (*coll.*) идёт!; есть такóе дéло; **4.** (*opp. left*) прáвый; **on my ~ hand** напрáво от меня́; **he is my ~ arm** (*fig.*) он моя́ прáвая рукá; **he made a ~ turn** он повернýл напрáво. **5.: ~ angle** прямóй ýгол; **at ~ angles to** под прямы́м ýглом к+*d*. **6.** (*thorough*): **you've made a ~ mess of it** ну, надéлали вы тут делóв (*coll.*).

adv. **1.** (*straight*) прямо; **carry ~ on!** всё врéмя пря́мо!; **he went ~ to the point** он срáзу перешёл к дéлу; **the wind is ~ behind us** вéтер дýет нам пря́мо в спи́ну; **the plane flew ~ overhead** самолёт пролетéл пря́мо над головóй. **2.** (*exactly*) тóчно; **the shot was ~ on target** удáр попáл пря́мо в цель; **I was there ~ on the stroke of one** я пришёл рóвно в час, минýта в минýту; **~ here/there** (*US*) пря́мо здесь/там; **~ now** (*US*) сейчáс; в дáнный момéнт. **3.** (*immediately*) срáзу (же); **~ away** срáзу (же), немéдленно, сию́ минýту. **4.** (*all the way, completely*) пóлностью; **he turned ~ round** он повернýлся кругóм; **the ship was ~ off course** корáбль совершéнно сбился с кýрса; **they climbed ~ to the top** они́ взобрали́сь на сáмую верши́ну; **the apples were rotten ~ through** я́блоки совсéм сгни́ли; **he drank it ~ up** он вы́пил всё (зáлпом); **I went ~ back to the beginning** я вернýлся к сáмому начáлу; **he came ~ up to me** он подошёл ко мне вплотнýю. **5.** (*justly; correctly, properly*) справедли́во; прáвильно; **he can do nothing ~** у негó ничегó не лáдится; **have I guessed ~?** я угадáл?; **nothing goes ~ for him** у негó всё идёт не так; **if I remember ~** éсли мне не изменя́ет пáмять; **it serves you ~** поделóм вам; так вам и нáдо. **6.** (*arch., very*) óчень; **you know ~ well ...** вы отли́чно знáете… **7.** (*in titles*): **R~ Honourable** достопочтéнный. **8.** (*of direction*) напрáво; **eyes ~!** равнéние напрáво!; **he owes money ~ and left** он кругóм в долгáх; **~, left and centre** кругóм, всю́ду.

v.t. **1.** (*restore to correct position*) вырáвнивать, вы́ровнять; **the boat ~ed itself** лóдка вы́ровнялась; (*fig., correct*) испр|авля́ть, -áвить; **the fault will ~ itself** э́то испрáвится самó собóй. **2.** (*make reparation for*) возме|щáть, -сти́ть; **this wrong must be ~ed** э́ту несправедли́вость нýжно устрани́ть.

cpds. **~about** *n.*: **they sent him to the ~about** (*fig.*) они́ егó вы́проводили; *adj. & adv.*: **~about turn** поворóт кругóм (*or* на 180°); **~-angled** *adj.* прямоугóльный; **~-hand** *adj.* прáвый; **~-hand drive** правосторóннее управлéние; **~-hand man** правофлангóвый; (*fig.*) вéрный помóщник; **~-hand screw** винт с прáвой нарéзкой; **~-hand turn** прáвый поворóт; **~-handed** *adj.* дéлающий всё прáвой рукóй; **~-hander** *n.* (*blow*) удáр прáвой рукóй; (*pers.*) правшá (*coll., c.g.*); **~-minded** *adj.* благонамéренный; разýмный; **~-mindedness** *n.* благонамéренность; разýмность; **~-wing** *adj.* прáвых взгля́дов; **~-winger** *n.* (*pol.*) прáвый; человéк прáвых взгля́дов.

righteous ['raɪtʃəs] *adj.* прáведный; **~ indignation** справедли́вое негодовáние.

righteousness ['raɪtʃəsnɪs] *n.* прáведность.

rightful ['raɪtfʊl] *adj.* закóнный, правомéрный.

rightist ['raɪtɪst] *n. & adj.* прáвый; (человéк) прáвых взгля́дов.

rightly ['raɪtlɪ] *adv.* **1.** (*correctly, properly*) прáвильно; **~ or wrongly, I believe he is lying** прав я и́ли неправ, но я дýмаю, он врёт. **2.** (*justly*) справедли́во; **he was punished, and ~ so** он был накáзан, и поделóм.

rightness ['raɪtnɪs] *n.* справедли́вость.

righto ['raɪtəʊ, raɪ'təʊ] (*int.*) хорошó!; лáдно!

rigid ['rɪdʒɪd] *adj.* жёсткий, негнýщийся; (*fig.*) кóсный, неги́бкий; **~ discipline/economy** стрóгая дисципли́на/ экономия.

rigidity [ˌrɪ'dʒɪdɪtɪ] *n.* жёсткость; (*fig.*) кóсность, неги́бкость.

rigmarole ['rɪgməˌrəʊl] *n.* пустáя болтовня́, пустозвóнство.

rigor ['rɪgə(r), 'raɪgɔː(r)] *n.* ознóб; оцепенéние; **~ mortis** трýпное окоченéние; (*US*) = **rigour**

rigorous ['rɪgərəs] *adj.* (*strict*) стрóгий; (*severe, harsh*) сурóвый, безжáлостный.

rigour ['rɪgə(r)] *n.* стрóгость; сурóвость, безжáлостность; **with all the ~ of the law** по всей стрóгости закóна; **the ~s of winter** сурóвость зимы́.

rile [raɪl] *v.t.* (*coll.*) серди́ть, рас-; раздраж|áть, -и́ть; **it ~d him to lose the game** егó зли́ло, что он проигрáл.

rill [rɪl] *n.* ручеёк.

rim [rɪm] *n.* обод; край; **~ of a wheel** óбод колесá; **~ of a cup** край чáшки; **spectacles with steel ~s** очки́ в стальнóй опрáве.

v.t. обр|амля́ть, -áмить; **her eyes were red-~med** у неё бы́ли воспалены́ глазá/вéки.

rime [raɪm] *n.* (*frost*) и́ней, и́зморозь.

rimless ['rɪmlɪs] *adj.* не имéющий óбода; без опрáвы; **~ spectacles** пенснé (*indecl.*).

rind [raɪnd] *n.* (*bark*) корá; (*of melon, cheese*) кóрка; (*of bacon*) кожурá, шкýрка.

rinderpest ['rɪndəˌpest] *n.* чумá рогáтого скотá.

ring[1] [rɪŋ] *n.* **1.** (*ornament, implement*) кольцó; (*with stone; signet-~*) пéрстень (*m.*); **engagement ~** кольцó, подáренное при помóлвке; **wedding ~** обручáльное кольцó. **2.** (*circle*) кольцó, круг; **~s of a tree** годовы́е кóльца дéрева; **he was blowing smoke ~s** он пускáл кóльца ды́ма; **they stood in a ~** они́ стáли в круг; **he had ~s under his eyes** у негó бы́ли тёмные круги́ под глазáми; **he made ~s round me** (*fig.*) он заткнýл меня́ зá пояс. **3.** (*conspiracy*) шáйка, бáнда, кли́ка; **spy ~** шпиóнская организáция. **4.** (*of circus, boxing etc.*) арéна, ринг; **he retired from the ~** (*from a boxing career*) он брóсил бокс. **5.** (*of cooker*) конфóрка.

v.t. **1.** (*encompass*) окруж|áть, -и́ть; **the singer was ~ed (round) by admirers** певи́цу окружи́ли поклóнники. **2.** (*put ~ on*): **the birds have been ~ed** птиц окóльцевали. **3.** (*put ~ around*): **his name was ~ed in pencil** егó и́мя бы́ло обведенó карандашóм. **4.** (*cut into ~s, e.g. fruit*) рéзать, на- кружкáми.

cpds. **~-bark** *v.t.* окольц|óвывать, -евáть (*дерево*); **~-dove** *n.* вити́тень (*m.*); **~-fence** *n.* огрáда; **~-finger** *n.* безымя́нный пáлец; **~leader** *n.* главáрь (*m.*), заши́нщик; **~-master** *n.* инспéктор манéжа; **~-road** *n.* кольцевáя дорóга; **~side** *n.* пéрвые ряды́ (*m. pl.*) (вокрýг арéны); **he had a ~side seat** (*lit.*) он сидéл в пéрвых рядáх; (*fig.*) он находи́лся в гýще собы́тий; **~worm** *n.* стригýщий лишáй.

ring[2] [rɪŋ] *n.* **1.** звон; звук; **the ~ of a coin** звон монéты; **the ~ of his voice** звук егó гóлоса; (*fig.*): **it has the ~ of truth** э́то звучи́т правдоподóбно. **2.** (*sound of bell*) звонóк; **there was a ~ at the door** в дверь позвони́ли. **3.** (*telephone call*) звонóк; **give me a ~ tomorrow** позвони́те мне зáвтра.

v.t. **1.** звони́ть, по- в+*a.*; **the postman rang the bell** почтальóн позвони́л в дверь; **they rang a peal** они́ звони́ли в колоколá; (*fig.*): **he rang the bell with his last book** (*coll.*) послéдняя кни́га принеслá емý успéх; **that ~s a bell** да, да, припоминáю; **he rang the changes on his theme** он тверди́л однó и то же на рáзные лады́. **2.** (*telephone, also ~ up*) звони́ть, по- +*d.*; **will you ~ me when you get home?** вы мне позвони́те, когдá прибýдете домóй? **3.** (*mark by ~ing*): **the bell ~s the half-hours** кóлокол звони́т кáждые полчасá.

v.i. **1.** звони́ть, по-; **the bells are ~ing** звоня́т колоколá;

the bell rang for dinner позвони́ли к обе́ду; **the telephone rang** зазвони́л телефо́н; **my ears are ~ing** у меня́ звени́т в уша́х; **his voice was still ~ing in my ears** его́ го́лос всё ещё звуча́л у меня́ в уша́х; (*fig.*): **his words ~ true** его́ слова́ звуча́т правдоподо́бно; **did you ~, Madam?** вы меня́ вызыва́ли, суда́рыня? **2.** (*telephone*) звони́ть, по-; **we must ~ for the doctor** мы должны́ вы́звать врача́ (по телефо́ну). **3.** (*resound*) огла|ша́ться, -си́ться; разноси́ться (*impf.*); **the house rang with the sound of children's voices** де́тские голоса́ разноси́лись по всему́ до́му; **the town rang with his praises** его́ сла́вил весь го́род.

with advs.: **they rang down/up the curtain** за́навес опусти́ли/по́дняли; **~ off** пове́сить (*pf.*) тру́бку; **the bells rang out the old year and rang in the new** колоко́льным зво́ном проводи́ли ста́рый год и встре́тили но́вый; **a shot rang out** разда́лся вы́стрел; **someone rang (up) for you this morning** вам кто-то звони́л у́тром.

ringlet [ˈrɪŋlɪt] *n.* (*curl*) ло́кон, завито́к.

rink [rɪŋk] *n.* като́к.

rinse [rɪns] *n.* (*action of rinsing*) полоска́ние; (*hair-dye*) сре́дство для подкра́шивания воло́с.

v.t. полоска́ть, вы́-; спол|а́скивать, -осну́ть; **~ out your mouth!** прополощи́те рот!; **she ~d out the cup** она́ сполосну́ла ча́шку.

Rio (de Janeiro) [ˈriːəʊ (də dʒəˈnɪərəʊ)] *n.* Ри́о-де-Жане́йро (*m. indecl.*).

Rio Grande [ˈriːəʊ ˈgrænd, ˈgrændɪ] *n.* Ри́о-Гра́нде (*f. indecl.*).

riot [ˈraɪət] *n.* **1.** (*brawl*) беспоря́дки (*m. pl.*); **there was a ~ in the theatre** в теа́тре разрази́лся сканда́л. **2.** (*revolt*) мяте́ж, бунт; **the R~ Act** зако́н об охра́не обще́ственного поря́дка; (*fig.*): **the teacher read the ~ act to his class** учи́тель сде́лал вы́говор всему́ кла́ссу. **3.** (*fig.*): **the students ran ~ with delight** студе́нты беси́лись от ра́дости; **his latest play was a ~** его́ после́дняя пье́са име́ла потряса́ющий успе́х; **he was a prey to a ~ of emotions** он не мог совлада́ть с нахлы́нувшими на него́ чу́вствами; **she allowed her fancy to run ~** она́ дала́ по́лную во́лю воображе́нию; **the plague ran ~** чума́ свире́пствовала; **the weeds are running ~** сорняки́ бу́йно разраста́ются; **the garden was a ~ of colour** сад пестре́л все́ми кра́сками.

v.i. **1.** (*brawl, rebel*) бесчи́нствовать (*impf.*); бу́йствовать (*impf.*); **the crowd ~ed in the streets** толпа́ бесчи́нствовала на у́лицах. **2.** (*fig.*) прожига́ть (*impf.*) жизнь.

rioter [ˈraɪətə(r)] *n.* бунта́рь (*m.*), мяте́жник.

riotous [ˈraɪətəs] *adj.* (*rebellious*) мяте́жный; (*wildly enthusiastic*) безу́держный, шу́мный; **~ laughter** безу́держный смех; **~ living** разгу́льная жизнь.

riotousness [ˈraɪətəsnɪs] *n.* неи́стовство, безу́держность.

RIP (*abbr. of* **rest in peace**) мир пра́ху (*кого*).

rip[1] [rɪp] *n.* (*tear*) разре́з, проре́ха.

v.t. рвать, разо-; расп|а́ривать, -оро́ть; **he ~ped his trousers on a nail** он разорва́л брю́ки о гвоздь; **he ~ped open the envelope** он разорва́л конве́рт; **he ~ped off the lid** он сорва́л кры́шку; **they ~ped out his appendix** ему́ удали́ли аппе́ндикс; **~ off** (*coll., steal*) об|дира́ть, -одра́ть.

v.i. **1.** (*tear*) рва́ться, разо-; **the cloth ~ped right across** мате́рия разорва́лась попола́м. **2.** (*rush along*) мча́ться, про-; **let her ~!** жми на всю кату́шку! (*coll.*); **he lost his temper and let ~ at me** он вы́шел из себя́ и крыл меня́ после́дними слова́ми; **I just let things ~** я реши́л: будь что бу́дет!

cpds. **~-cord** *n.* вытяжно́й трос; **~-off** *n.* (*sl.*) воровство́, моше́нничество; **it's a ~-off** э́то обдира́ловка; *adj.* граби́тельский; **~-roaring, ~-snorting** *adjs.* (*coll.*) бу́йный, шумли́вый; **~-saw** *n.* продо́льная пила́.

rip[2] [rɪp] *n.* (*coll., rake*) распу́тник, пове́са (*m.*).

riparian [raɪˈpeərɪən] *adj.* прибре́жный.

ripe [raɪp] *adj.* **1.** (*ready for gathering, eating or use*) спе́лый, зре́лый; **the corn is ~** зерно́ созре́ло; **~ cheese** вы́держанный сыр; **~ lips** а́лые/по́лные гу́бы; (*fig.*): **~ judgement** му́дрость, зре́лые сужде́ния; **he lived to a ~ old age** он до́жил до глубо́кой ста́рости. **2.** (*ready, suitable*) гото́вый, созре́вший; **land ~ for development** земля́, ожида́ющая застро́йки; **the time is ~ for action** пришло́ вре́мя де́йствовать.

ripen [ˈraɪpən] *v.t.* зреть (*or* созрева́ть), со-.

v.i. де́латься, с- зре́лым; **their friendship ~ed into love** их дру́жба переросла́ в любо́вь.

ripeness [ˈraɪpnɪs] *n.* спе́лость, зре́лость.

riposte [rɪˈpɒst] *n.* (*fencing*) отве́тный уда́р; (*verbal*) нахо́дчивый отве́т.

v.i. пари́ровать, от- уда́р; нахо́дчиво отв|еча́ть, -е́тить.

ripping [ˈrɪpɪŋ] *adj.* (*coll.*) великоле́пный, потряса́ющий; **we had a ~ (good) time** мы здо́рово повесели́лись.

ripple [ˈrɪp(ə)l] *n.* рябь, зыбь, круг; (*fig.*): **his words caused a ~ of laughter** его́ слова́ вы́звали лёгкий смешо́к; **he showed not a ~ of emotion** он не вы́казал никаки́х чувств.

v.t. & i. покр|ыва́ть(ся), -ы́ть(ся) ря́бью; (*fig.*): **her hair ~d over her shoulders** во́лосы струи́лись по её плеча́м; **her voice ~d** её го́лос журча́л.

rise [raɪz] *n.* **1.** (*upward slope*) подъём; **we came to a ~ in the road** мы подошли́ к подъёму доро́ги. **2.** (*area of higher ground*) холм, возвы́шенность. **3.** (*fig., ascent*) подъём; восхожде́ние; **the ~ and decline of capitalism** подъём и упа́док капитали́зма. **4.** (*increase*) повыше́ние, увеличе́ние; **a ~ in temperature** повыше́ние температу́ры; **they asked for a ~** они попроси́ли об увеличе́нии зарпла́ты; **a ~ in the cost of living** удорожа́ние жи́зни; **unemployment is on the ~** безрабо́тица растёт. **5.** (*in angling*): **he waited all day for a ~** он весь день ждал клёва; (*fig.*): **he is taking a ~ out of you** он вас провоци́рует/дра́знит. **6.** (*vertical height of step*) высота́ (ступе́ньки). **7.** (*origin*): **give ~ to** вызыва́ть, вы́звать.

v.i. **1.** (*get up from bed*) вста|ва́ть, -ть (на́ ноги); **I rose at 6** я встал в 6; (*from seated or kneeling position*) вста|ва́ть, -ть; подн|има́ться, -я́ться; **they rose from the table** они́ подняли́сь из-за стола́; **the House rose at 10** пала́та зако́нчила рабо́ту в 10; **he rose to his full height** он встал во весь рост; **the horse rose (up) on its hind legs** ло́шадь вста́ла на дыбы́; (*into the air*) подн|има́ться, -я́ться; (*fig.*): **you should ~ above petty jealousy** вы должны́ быть вы́ше ме́лкой за́висти; (*from the dead*) воскр|еса́ть, -е́снуть; **Christ is ~n** Христо́с воскре́с; (*above the horizon*) восходи́ть, взойти́; **when the sun ~s** когда́ восхо́дит со́лнце; (*fig., appear*) возн|ика́ть, -и́кнуть; **a picture rose in my mind** в моём воображе́нии возни́к о́браз; **the rising generation** подраста́ющее поколе́ние; (*to the surface*) выходи́ть, вы́йти на пове́рхность; **the fish won't ~** ры́ба не клюёт; (*fig.*): **he rose to my bait** он попа́лся на мою́ у́дочку; **he will always ~ to the occasion** он не растеря́ется в любо́й ситуа́ции; **his gorge rose at the sight** при ви́де э́того он почу́вствовал отвраще́ние. **2.** (*slope upwards*) подн|има́ться, -я́ться; **on rising ground** на скло́не/возвыше́нии; (*tower*): **the cliffs rose sheer above them** над ни́ми кру́то возвыша́лись ска́лы; **wooded mountains rose before us** перед на́ми вста́ли леси́стые го́ры; **a range of hills rose on our left** сле́ва от нас тяну́лась гряда́ холмо́в. **3.** (*increase in amount*) возраста́ть (*impf.*); увели́чи|ваться, -ться; **rising costs** увели́чивающие расхо́ды; (*in level*): **the waters are rising** вода́ поднима́ется/прибыва́ет; **rising tide** нараста́ющий прили́в; **the bread has ~n** хлеб подня́лся; **the temperature is rising** температу́ра повыша́ется; (*in price*) пов|ыша́ться, -ы́ситься в цене́; дорожа́ть, по-/вз-; (*in pitch*) уси́ли|вать, -ть; **his voice rose in anger** в гне́ве он повы́сил го́лос; **his voice rose to a shriek** го́лос его́ сорва́лся на крик; (*in intensity or animation*) увели́чи|ваться, -ться; **the wind is rising** ве́тер поднима́ется/уси́ливается/крепча́ет; **her colour rose** она́ покрасне́ла; **his spirits rose** его́ настрое́ние улу́чшилось; (*in importance or rank*) продв|ига́ться, -и́нуться; **he hopes to ~ in the world** он наде́ется сде́лать карье́ру; **a rising lawyer** подаю́щий наде́жды адвока́т; **he rose from the ranks** (*mil.*) он вы́служился из рядовы́х; он вы́двинулся в офице́ры; **he rose to international fame** он приобрёл мирову́ю изве́стность; (*in age*): **he is rising 40** ему́ под со́рок. **4.** (*spring, originate*) брать, взять нача́ло;

возн|ика́ть, -и́кнуть; **the Severn ~s in Wales** Се́верн берёт своё нача́ло в Уэ́льсе. **5.** (*rebel*) восст|ава́ть, -а́ть; **the people rose (up) in arms** наро́д восста́л с ору́жием в рука́х.

riser [ˈraɪzə(r)] *n.* **1.: he is an early ~** он встаёт с петуха́ми. **2.** (*of staircase*) по́дступень.

risible [ˈrɪzɪb(ə)l] *adj.* (*pert. to laughing*) смешли́вый; (*laughable*) смешно́й, смехотво́рный.

rising [ˈraɪzɪŋ] *n.* **1.** (*getting up*) подъём; **I believe in early ~** я счита́ю, что встава́ть на́до ра́но. **2.** (*of the sun, moon etc.*) восхо́д. **3.** (*rebellion*) восста́ние.

risk [rɪsk] *n.* риск; **he takes many ~s** он лю́бит рискова́ть; **he ran the ~ of defeat** он рискова́л потерпе́ть пораже́ние; **at the ~ of one's life** риску́я жи́знью; **at owner's ~** на риск владе́льца; **you go at your own ~** вы идёте туда́ на свой страх и риск; **I spoke at the ~ of offending him** несмотря́ на то, что он мо́жет оби́деться, я реши́л вы́сказаться; **he is a security ~** он неблагонадёжен.

v.t. **1.** (*expose to ~*) рискова́ть (*impf.*); **he ~ed his life to save her** он спас её, риску́я жи́знью. **2.** (*take the chance of*) риск|ова́ть, -ну́ть (*чем*); **shall we ~ it?** ну что, рискнём?; **we must ~ getting caught** мы риску́ем попа́сться, но вы́хода нет.

risky [ˈrɪskɪ] *adj.* риско́ванный, опа́сный.

risotto [rɪˈzɒtəʊ] *n.* ризо́тто (*m. indecl.*).

risqué [ˈrɪskeɪ, -ˈkeɪ] *adj.* риско́ванный, сомни́тельный.

rissole [ˈrɪsəʊl] *n.* ру́бленая котле́та.

rite [raɪt] *n.* обря́д, ритуа́л, церемо́ния; **the ~s of hospitality** обы́чаи гостеприи́мства; **last ~s** (*extreme unction*) собо́рование; (*funeral*) похоро́нный обря́д; прово́д|ы (*pl., g.* -ов) в после́дний путь.

ritual [ˈrɪtjʊəl] *n.* ритуа́л, обря́дность; (*book*) служе́бник, тре́бник; **he makes a ~ of eating** он де́лает из еды́ культ.

adj. ритуа́льный; (*fig., invariable*) обяза́тельный, неизме́нный.

ritualism [ˈrɪtjʊəˌlɪz(ə)m] *n.* приве́рженность к ритуа́лам/обря́дности.

ritualist [ˈrɪtjʊəlɪst] *n.* ритуали́ст.

ritualistic [ˌrɪtjʊəˈlɪstɪk] *adj.* ритуалисти́ческий.

ritzy [ˈrɪtzɪ] *adj.* (*coll.*) (*US*) шика́рный.

rival [ˈraɪv(ə)l] *n.* сопе́рник; **~s in love (or for power)** сопе́рники в любви́ (*or* в борьбе́ за власть); **he has many business ~s** у него́ мно́го конкуре́нтов; **he was without a ~ as chef** он был непревзойдённым по́варом.

adj. сопе́рничающий; **television is a ~ attraction to reading** телеви́зор — (мо́щный) конкуре́нт чте́ния; **the ~ team** кома́нда проти́вника.

v.t. сопе́рничать (*impf.*) c+*i.*; **I cannot hope to ~ your skill** я не беру́сь сопе́рничать с ва́ми в уме́нии.

rivalry [ˈraɪvəlrɪ] *n.* сопе́рничество, конкуре́нция; **the teams were in friendly ~** ме́жду кома́ндами существова́ло дру́жеское сопе́рничество; **let us not enter into ~** заче́м нам сопе́рничать?

rive [raɪv] *v.t.* (*liter.*) раз|рыва́ть, -орва́ть; срыва́ть, сорва́ть; сдира́ть (*impf.*); (*split*): **trees ~n by lightning** дере́вья, расколо́тые мо́лнией.

river [ˈrɪvə(r)] *n.* река́; (*attr.*) речно́й; **up/down ~** вверх/вниз по реке́; (*fig.*): **the streets were ~s of blood** у́лицы преврати́лись в пото́ки кро́ви.

cpds. **~-basin** *n.* бассе́йн реки́; **~-bed** *n.* ру́сло реки́; **~side** *n.* прибре́жная полоса́; *adj.* прибре́жный, стоя́щий на берегу́ реки́.

riverain [ˈrɪvəˌren] *adj.* речно́й, прибре́жный.

rivet [ˈrɪvɪt] *n.* заклёпка.

v.t. клепа́ть (*impf.*); склёп|ывать, -а́ть; (*fig.*) устрем|ля́ть, -и́ть (*взгляд/внимание*); **his eyes were ~ed on her** его́ взгляд был прико́ван к ней.

riveting [ˈrɪvɪtɪŋ] *adj.* (*coll.*) захва́тывающий, прико́вывающий внима́ние.

Riviera [ˌrɪvɪˈeərə] *n.* Ривье́ра.

rivière [riːvˈjeə(r), ˈrɪvɪˌeə(r)] *n.* ожере́лье из не́скольких ни́тей.

rivulet [ˈrɪvjʊlɪt] *n.* речу́шка, руче́й.

Riyadh [rɪˈjɑːd] *n.* Эр-Рия́д.

riyal [ˈriːɑːl] *n.* (*unit of currency*) риа́л.

RN (*abbr. of* ***Royal Navy***) англи́йский ВМФ, (вое́нно-морско́й флот).

roach [rəʊtʃ] *n.* (*fish*) плотва́; **(cock~)**育 тарака́н.

road [rəʊd] *n.* **1.** (*thoroughfare*) доро́га; (*attr.*) доро́жный (*see also cpds.*); **main ~** гла́вная доро́га; **~ accident** автомоби́льная/доро́жная катастро́фа; **~ junction** пересече́ние доро́г, перекрёсток; **~ sense** «чу́вство доро́ги»; **~ works** доро́жные-ремо́нтные рабо́ты; **my car is parked off the ~** я поста́вил маши́ну на обо́чине; **the car has been off the ~ for a month** маши́на проста́ивает це́лый ме́сяц; **we have been on the ~ for hours** мы е́дем уже́ мно́го часо́в; **he is on the ~** (*of a salesman*) он в отъе́зде; (*of an actor*) он на гастро́лях; (*of a tramp*) он скита́ется по доро́гам; **they live just up the ~ from us** они́ живу́т в двух шага́х от нас на той же у́лице; **the ~ has been up since Sunday** доро́гу ремонти́руют с воскресе́нья; **one for the ~** проща́льная рю́мка, посошо́к на доро́гу. **2.** (*fig.*) путь (*m.*), доро́га; **he is on the ~ to recovery** он на пути́ к выздоровле́нию; **there is no royal ~ to learning** путь к зна́ниям нелёгок. **3.** (*coll., way*): **get out of my ~!** прочь с доро́ги!; **you are getting in my ~** вы мне меша́ете; **I want to get these jobs out of the ~** я хочу́ разде́латься с э́тими дела́ми. **4. (~stead)** рейд.

cpds. **~-bed** *n.* полотно́ доро́ги; **~-block** *n.* загражде́ние на доро́ге; **~-book** *n.* доро́жный спра́вочник; **~-hog** *n.* плохо́й води́тель, лиха́ч; **~house** *n.* придоро́жный рестора́н; **~man** *n.* доро́жный рабо́чий; **~-map** *n.* доро́жная ка́рта; **~-metal** *n.* щебёнка; **~side** *n.* обо́чина доро́ги; **~stead** *n.* рейд; **~-test** (*of a car*) *n.* доро́жное испыта́ние; *v.t.* испы́т|ывать, -а́ть (*машину*) в пробе́ге; **~way** *n.* доро́га, прое́зжая часть; **~worthiness** *n.* приго́дность для езды́ по доро́гам; **~worthy** *adj.* приго́дный для езды́ по доро́гам (*or* к эксплуата́ции).

roam [rəʊm] *v.t. & i.* броди́ть, стра́нствовать, скита́ться (*all impf.*); **he ~ed the streets** он броди́л по у́лицам.

roan[1] [rəʊn] *n.* (*leather*) замени́тель сафья́на для переплётов.

roan[2] [rəʊn] *adj.* ча́лый.

roar [rɔː(r)] *n.* (*of animal*) рёв, рык; (*loud human cry*) крик; вопль (*m.*); **he gave a ~ of anger** он изда́л я́ростный вопль; **there were ~s of laughter** разда́ли́сь взры́вы хо́хота; **he set the table in a ~** он заста́вил весь стол покати́ться со сме́ха; (*of wind or sea*) рёв; (*of engine*) гро́хот, гул.

v.t. & i. реве́ть (*impf.*); рыча́ть (*impf.*); **the audience ~ed approval** пу́блика реве́ла от восто́рга (*or* шу́мно выража́ла одобре́ние); **they ~ed themselves hoarse** они́ охри́пли от кри́ка; **he ~ed his head off** он ора́л изо всей мо́чи; **the lion ~ed** лев зарыча́л; **he ~ed with laughter** он надрыва́лся от сме́ха; он хохота́л во всё го́рло; **shops are doing a ~ing trade** в магази́нах това́ры иду́т нарасхва́т.

roast [rəʊst] *n.* жарко́е; кусо́к мя́са для жа́рки; **cold ~** холо́дное жа́реное мя́со.

v.t. жа́рить, под-; печь, ис-; **~ beef** жа́реная говя́дина; **~ed coffee beans** поджа́ренные кофе́йные зёрна; **he ~ed himself in front of the fire** он гре́лся у ками́на.

v.i. гре́ться (*impf.*); **switch off the fire, I'm ~ing** вы́ключите пе́чку, я весь изжа́рился.

roaster [ˈrəʊstə(r)] *n.* (*oven*) жаро́вня; (*chicken*) цыплёнок для жаре́нья.

rob [rɒb] *v.t.* красть, обо-; гра́бить, о-; **I have been ~bed** меня́ обокра́ли/огра́били; **the bank was ~bed** банк огра́били; **they ~bed him of his watch** они́ укра́ли у него́ часы́; (*fig., deprive*) лиш|а́ть, -и́ть.

robber [ˈrɒbə(r)] *n.* граби́тель (*m.*), вор.

robbery [ˈrɒbərɪ] *n.* грабёж; **~ with violence** грабёж с наси́лием; **there has been a ~** произошло́ ограбле́ние; **to charge such a price is daylight ~** запроси́ть таку́ю це́ну — грабёж средь бе́ла дня.

robe [rəʊb] *n.* ма́нтия; (*US, dressing-gown; also* **bath-~**) (купа́льный) хала́т.

v.t.: **~d in black** облачённый в чёрное.

v.i. облач|а́ться, -и́ться.

robin (redbreast) ['rɒbɪn] *n.* мали́новка.

robot ['rəʊbɒt] *n.* (*lit.*, *fig.*) ро́бот; (*attr.*) автомати́ческий.

robotics [rəʊ'bɒtɪks] *n.* робо(то)те́хника.

robust [rəʊ'bʌst] *adj.* (*of pers.*, *physique*) кре́пкий, си́льный; (*of health*) хоро́ший, кре́пкий; (*of appetite*) здоро́вый; (*of an object*, *mechanism etc.*) про́чный.

robustness [rəʊ'bʌstnɪs] *n.* здоро́вье; си́ла; кре́пость, про́чность.

roc [rɒk] *n.* пти́ца Рух.

rock[1] [rɒk] *n.* (*solid part of earth's crust*) го́рная поро́да; **they dug down a foot and struck ~** они́ вы́копали я́му в фут глубины́ и наткну́лись на ска́льную поро́ду; **a house built on ~** дом, постро́енный на скале́ (*or* ска́льном гру́нте); (*large stone*) скала́, утёс; (*boulder*) валу́н; **the ship ran upon the ~s** кора́бль наскочи́л на ска́лы; **the firm is on the ~s** (*coll.*) фи́рма прогоре́ла; (*US*, *stone*, *pebble*) ка́мень (*m.*), булы́жник; **whisky on the ~s** (*coll.*) ви́ски со льдом.

cpds. **~-bed** *n.* пласт ка́менной поро́ды; **~-bottom** *n.* (*lit.*) коренна́я подстила́ющая поро́да; (*fig.*): **at ~-bottom prices** по са́мым ни́зким це́нам; **~-cake** *n.* бу́лочка/пече́нье из круто́го те́ста; **~-climber** *n.* скалола́з; **~-climbing** *n.* скалола́зание; **~-crystal** *n.* го́рный хруста́ль; **~-drill** *n.* перфора́тор; **~-garden** *n.* (*also* **~ery**) альпина́рий; **~-plant** *n.* альпи́йское расте́ние; **~-ribbed** *adj.* (*fig.*) твёрдый, непоколеби́мый; **~-salmon** *n.* нали́м; **~-salt** *n.* ка́менная соль.

rock[2] [rɒk] *n.* (*music*) рок.

v.t. (*sway gently*) кач|а́ть, -ну́ть; ука́ч|ивать, -а́ть; **the nurse ~ed the baby to sleep** ня́ня укача́ла/убаю́кала ребёнка; **the boat was ~ed by the waves** ло́дка покача́лась на во́лна́х; **don't ~ the boat!** (*coll.*) ле́гче на поворо́тах!; (*shake*) трясти́, по-; **the earthquake ~ed the house** дом шата́лся от землетрясе́ния; **the news ~ed the city** но́вость потрясла́ го́род.

v.i. (*sway gently*) кача́ться (*impf.*); **the trees ~ed in the wind** дере́вья раска́чивались на ветру́; **~ing-chair** кача́лка; **~ing-horse** конь (*m.*)-кача́лка; **he ~ed with laughter** он тря́сся от сме́ха.

cpd. **~-'n'-roll** *n.* рок-н-ро́лл.

rocker ['rɒkə(r)] *n.* **1.** (*of cradle etc.*; *chair*) кача́лка. **2.** (*biker*) ро́кер. **3.: go off one's ~** рехну́ться (*pf.*) (*coll.*).

rockery ['rɒkərɪ] = **rock-garden**

rocket ['rɒkɪt] *n.* **1.** (*projectile*) раке́та; **~ range** раке́тный полиго́н; **~ site** ста́ртовая площа́дка, полиго́н. **2.** (*reprimand*): **he got a ~ from the boss** он получи́л взбу́чку (*coll.*) от нача́льника.

v.i. (*fig.*): **prices ~ed (up)** це́ны ре́зко подскочи́ли.

cpd. **~-propelled** *adj.* раке́тный.

rocketry ['rɒkɪtrɪ] *n.* раке́тная те́хника.

rocky ['rɒkɪ] *adj.* **1.** (*of or like rock*; *full of rocks*) скали́стый, камени́стый; **the R~ Mountains, the Rockies** (*coll.*) Скали́стые го́ры (*f. pl.*); **a ~ road** (*fig.*) терни́стый путь. **2.** (*shaky*, *unsteady*) неусто́йчивый, ша́ткий.

rococo [rə'kəʊkəʊ] *n.* рококо́ (*indecl.*).

adj. в сти́ле рококо́; (*fig.*) вы́чурный.

rod [rɒd] *n.* **1.** (*slender stick*) прут; (*fishing-~*) у́дочка; **he fished with ~ and line** он лови́л ры́бу у́дочкой; (*instrument of chastisement*) ро́зга, хлыст; **spare the ~ and spoil the child** пожале́ешь ро́згу — испо́ртишь ребёнка; **he is making a ~ for his own back** он сам себе́ ро́ет я́му; **I have a ~ in pickle for him** я держу́ для него́ ро́згу нагото́ве; **he ruled the people with a ~ of iron** он пра́вил желе́зной руко́й. **2.** (*metal bar*) сте́ржень (*m.*); **curtain ~** металли́ческий карни́з.

rodent ['rəʊd(ə)nt] *n.* грызу́н.

rodeo ['rəʊdɪəʊ, rə'deɪəʊ] *n.* роде́о (*indecl.*).

rodomontade [ˌrɒdəmɒn'teɪd] *n.* бахва́льство.

roe[1] [rəʊ] *n.* (*hard ~*) икра́; (*soft ~*) моло́к|и (*pl.*, *g.* —).

roe[2] [rəʊ] *n.* (*deer*) косу́ля.

cpd. **~buck** *n.* косу́ля-саме́ц.

roentgen ['rʌntjən] *n.* рентге́н.

roger ['rɒdʒə(r)] *int.* (*sl.*) вас по́нял!; ла́дно!; бу́дет сде́лано!; поря́док!

rogue [rəʊg] *n.* **1.** (*dishonest pers.*) жу́лик, моше́нник; **~s' gallery** архи́в фотосни́мков престу́пников. **2.** (*mischievous or waggish pers.*) шалу́н, прока́зник, озорни́к. **3.** (*animal*): **~ elephant** слон-отше́льник.

rogu|ery ['rəʊgərɪ], **-ishness** ['rəʊgɪʃnɪs] *nn.* (*villainy*) жу́льничество, моше́нничество; (*mischief*) ша́лость, прока́зы (*f. pl.*), озорство́.

roguish ['rəʊgɪʃ] *adj.* (*villainous*) жулнова́тый; (*playful*) шаловли́вый, прока́зливый, озорно́й.

roguishness ['rəʊgɪʃnɪs] = **roguery**

roister ['rɔɪstə(r)] *v.i.* бесчи́нствовать (*impf.*); беснова́ться.

roisterer ['rɔɪstərə(r)] *n.* кути́ла (*m.*).

role [rəʊl] *n.* (*lit.*, *fig.*) роль, амплуа́ (*nt. indecl.*); **he played (in) the ~ of Hamlet** он исполня́л роль Га́млета; **title ~** загла́вная роль; **he assumed the ~ of leader** он взял на себя́ роль ли́дера.

roll [rəʊl] *n.* **1.** (*of cloth*, *paper*, *film etc.*) руло́н. **2.** (*register*, *list*) рее́стр, спи́сок; **~ of honour** спи́сок уби́тых на войне́; **the lawyer was struck off the ~s** адвока́та лиши́ли пра́ва пра́ктики; **the sergeant called the ~** сержа́нт сде́лал перекли́чку. **3.** (*other material in cylindrical form*) ка́тышек, ва́лик. **4.** (*of bread*) бу́лочка. **5.** (*oscillating or revolving motion*) враще́ние; колыха́ние; пока́чивание; **the ~ of the ship** пока́чивание корабля́; **he walked with a slight ~** он ходи́л слегка́ вразва́лку; **the pilot executed a ~** (*aeron.*) пило́т вы́полнил двойно́й переворо́т; **the dog had a ~ on the grass** соба́ка повaля́лась на траве́. **6.** (*rumbling sound*) раска́т; бой бараба́на; **a ~ of thunder** раска́т гро́ма; **a ~ of drums** бараба́нная дробь.

v.t. **1.** (*move by revolving*) ката́ть (*indet.*), кати́ть (*det.*), по-; **the logs were ~ed down the hill** брёвна скати́ли с холма́; (*wind*) завёр|тывать, -ну́ть; **he had a scarf ~ed round his neck** он обмота́л ше́ю ша́рфом; (*rotate*) враща́ть (*impf.*); **~ one's eyes** враща́ть (*impf.*) глаза́ми. **2.** (*flatten by use of cylinder*) ката́ть, рас-; раска́тывать (*impf.*); **she was ~ing pastry** она́ раска́тывала те́сто; **the lawn needs ~ing** траву́ на́доуката́ть; **~ing-mill** прока́тный стан; **~ing-pin** ска́лка; **~ed gold** накладно́е зо́лото. **3.** (*shape into cylinder or sphere*) свёр|тывать, -ну́ть; свора́чивать (*impf.*); (*e.g. cigarette*) скру́|чивать, -ти́ть; **I ~ my own (cigarettes)** я де́лаю самокру́тки; **he carried a ~ed newspaper** он шёл со свёрнутой газе́той; **the hedgehog ~ed itself (up) into a ball** ёж сверну́лся в клубо́к; **help me ~ this ball of wool** помоги́те мне смота́ть э́тот клубо́к ше́рсти; **she was nurse and housemaid ~ed into one** она́ была́ одновре́менно и за ня́ньку и за прислу́гу. **4.: he cannot ~ his r's** он карта́вит; **he ~s his r's** он раска́тисто произно́сит звук «р»; он произно́сит «р» с вибра́цией.

v.i. **1.** (*move by revolving*; *revolve*) кати́ться (*impf.*); ска́тываться (*impf.*); **the coin ~ed under the table** моне́та закати́лась под стол; **the car began to ~ downhill** маши́на начала́ кати́ться вниз; **tears ~ed down her cheeks** слёзы кати́лись по её щека́м; **the carriage ~ed along the drive** экипа́ж кати́лся по алле́е; **we must keep the wheels of industry ~ing** мы должны́ соде́йствовать рабо́те промы́шленности; **set, start the ball ~ing** (*fig.*) откры́ть (*pf.*) диску́ссию; **~ing stock** подвижно́й соста́в. **2.** (*tumble about*, *wallow*) валя́ться (*impf.*); **porpoises were ~ing in the waves** дельфи́ны кувы́ркались в во́лна́х; **he is ~ing in money** он купа́ется в деньга́х. **3.** (*sway*, *rock*) кача́ться (*impf.*); колыха́ться (*impf.*); **the ship began to ~** парохо́д на́чало кача́ть; **~ing gait** похо́дка вразва́лку. **4.** (*undulate*): **waves were ~ing on to the shore** во́лны нака́тывались на бе́рег; **~ing sea** волну́ющееся мо́ре; **~ing countryside** холми́стая ме́стность. **5.** (*be flattened*): **the dough ~s well** те́сто легко́ раска́тывается. **6.** (*make deep vibrating sound*) греме́ть (*impf.*); грохота́ть (*impf.*); **thunder ~ed in the hills** по холма́м прокати́лся гром.

with advs.: **~ about** *v.i.* валя́ться; **~ along** *v.i.*: **we were ~ing along at 30 m.p.h.** маши́на кати́лась со ско́ростью 30 миль в час; **~ away** *v.i.*: **the mists ~ed away** тума́н рассе́ялся; **~ back** *v.t.* отка́т|ывать, -и́ть наза́д; **let's ~ back the carpet and dance!** дава́йте свернём/скатáем ковёр и потанцу́ем!; *v.i.*: **the cart ~ed back** теле́жка откати́лась наза́д; **~ by** *v.i.*: **the bus ~ed by** авто́бус проéхал мúмо; **how the years ~ by!** как бы́стро кáтятся гóды!; **~ down** *v.t.* скáт|ывать, -úть вниз; **~ down the blinds!** опустúте жалюзú!; **stones ~ed down by the river** кáмни, перекáтываемые рекóй; **~ in** *v.i.*: **contributions began to ~ in** нáчали поступáть взнóсы; **he ~ed in half-an-hour late** он подкатúл/подрулúл (*coll.*) с опоздáнием на полчасá; **~ off** *v.t.*: **please ~ off a dozen copies** бýдьте добры́, отпечáтайте 12 экземпля́ров (*or* сдéлайте 12 óттисков); *v.i.* скáт|ываться, -úться; **he ~ed off the bed** он скатúлся с кровáти; **~ on** *v.t.*: **she ~ed on her stockings** онá натянýла чулкú; *v.i.*: **the years are ~ing on** гóды идýт; **~ on summer!** (*coll.*) скорéй бы наступúло лéто!; **~ out** *v.t.* (*e.g. carpet, pastry*) раскáт|ывать, -áть; **they ~ed out the chorus** припéв дрýжно подхватúли; *v.i.*: **the organ notes ~ed out** лилúсь звýки оргáна; **she dropped her basket and everything ~ed out** онá уронúла корзúнку, и всё из неё вы́катилось; **~ over** *v.t.* перев|орáчивать, -ернýть; опрокú|дывать, -нуть; **I ~ed the stone over** я переврнýл кáмень; *v.i.* ворóчаться (*impf.*); **he ~ed over and went to sleep again** он перевернýлся на другóй бок и снóва заснýл; **~ up** *v.t.* свёр|тывать, -нýть; **~ up the curtain** подня́ть (*pf.*) зáнавес; **he ~ed himself up in a blanket** он завернýлся в одея́ло; **they ~ed up the enemy's flank** онú оттеснúли неприя́теля с флáнга; *v.i.*: **he ~ed up to me** (*fig.*) он подкатúл ко мне; **~ up! ~ up!** налетáй; не проходúте мúмо!

cpds. **~-call** *n.* переклúчка; **~-collar** *n.* отложнóй воротнúк; **~-collar jersey** фуфáйка с высóким гóрлом; **~-film** *n.* рóликовая фотоплёнка; **~-neck (pullover)** *n.* водолáзка; **~-on** *n.* (*woman's garment*) эластúчный пóяс; **~-top (desk)** *n.* бюрó с деревя́нной штóрой.

roller [ˈrəʊlə(r)] *n.* **1.** рóлик; катóк; **garden ~** садóвый катóк. **2.** (*wave*) волнá, вал.

cpds. **~-bearing** *n.* рóликовый подшúпник; **~-coaster** *n.* америкáнские гóры (*f. pl.*); **~-skate** *n.* (*pl.*) рóлики (*m. pl.*); *v.i.* катáться (*indet.*) на рóликах; **~-towel** *n.* полотéнце на рóлике.

rollick [ˈrɒlɪk] *v.i.* резвúться (*impf.*); веселúться (*impf.*); **we had a ~ing time** мы здóрово повеселúлись.

roly-poly [ˌrəʊlɪˈpəʊlɪ] *n.* пýдинг с варéнием; (*fig., plump child*) «пóнчик»; пýхлый ребёнок.

ROM [rɒm] *n. comput.* (*abbr. of* ***read only memory***) ПЗУ, (постоя́нное запоминáющее устрóйство).

Roman [ˈrəʊmən] *n.* **1.** (*citizen of anc. Rome*) рúмлян|ин (*fem.* -ка). **2.** (**~ Catholic**) катóлик. **3.** (**r~: type**) *see adj.*

adj. **1.** (*of Rome*) рúмский; **the ~ alphabet** латúнский алфавúт; **~ candle** рúмская свечá; **the ~ Empire** Рúмская импéрия; **r~ script, type** латúнский шрифт; латúнская грáфика; (*opp. italics*) прямóй шрифт; (*opp. bold*) свéтлый шрифт. **2.** (*relig.*) католúческий; **~ Catholicism** католúчество.

romance [rəʊˈmæns, *also disp.* ˈrəʊ-] *n.* **1.: R~ languages** ромáнские языкú; **R~ philologist** романúст. **2.** (*medieval tale*) ры́царский ромáн. **3.** (*tale, episode, love affair*) ромáн. **4.** (*romantic atmosphere, glamour*) ромáнтика. **5.** (*mus.*) ромáнс.

v.i. приукрá|шивать, -сить прáвду; фантазúровать (*impf.*).

romancer [rəʊˈmænsə(r)] *n.* фантазёр, вы́думщик.

Romanesque [ˌrəʊməˈnesk] *n. & adj.* ромáнский (стиль).

Romania, R(o)umania [rəʊˈmeɪnɪə] *n.* Румы́ния.

Romanian, R(o)umanian [rəʊˈmeɪnɪən] *n.* (*pers.*) румы́н (*fem.* -ка); (*language*) румы́нский язы́к.

adj. румы́нский.

Romanic [rəʊˈmænɪk] *adj.* (*neo-Latin*) ромáнский.

Romanism [ˈrəʊməˌnɪz(ə)m] *n.* (*pej., Catholicism*) католицúзм.

Romanist [ˈrəʊmənɪst] *n.* (*pej.*) кат|óлик (*fem.* -олúчка).

Romanize [ˈrəʊmənaɪz] *v.t.* романизúровать (*impf., pf.*).

Romansh [rəʊˈmænʃ, -ˈmɑːnʃ] *n. & adj.* ретороманский (язы́к).

romantic [rəʊˈmæntɪk] *n.* ромáнтик.

adj. романтúческий, романтúчный; **the R~ movement** романтúзм.

romanticism [rəʊˈmæntɪˌsɪz(ə)m] *n.* романтúзм.

romanticist [rəʊˈmæntɪsɪst] *n.* ромáнтик.

romanticize [rəʊˈmæntɪˌsaɪz] *v.i.* романтизúровать (*impf., pf.*).

Romany [ˈrɒmənɪ, ˈrəʊ-] *n.* (*Gypsy*) цыгáн (*fem.* -ка); (*language*) цыгáнский язы́к.

adj. цыгáнский.

Rome [rəʊm] *n.* **1.** (*city or state*) Рим; **~ was not built in a day** не срáзу Москвá стрóилась; Рим не срáзу стрóился; **when in ~, do as ~ does** ≃ в чужóй монасты́рь, со своúм устáвом не хóдят; с вóлками жить — по-вóлчьи выть. **2.** (*Church of ~*) рúмско-католúческая цéрковь.

Romish [ˈrəʊmɪʃ] *adj.* (*pej.*) рúмско-католúческий.

romp [rɒmp] *n.* (*boisterous play*) возня́; (*lively child*) сорванéц.

v.i. резвúться (*impf.*); **the horse ~ed home** лóшадь с лёгкостью вы́играла скáчки; **he ~ed through his exams** он шутя́ сдал экзáмены.

rompers [ˈrɒmpəz] *n.* (*also* **romper suit**) ползунк|ú (*pl., g.* -óв); дéтский комбинезóн.

rondo [ˈrɒndəʊ] *n.* рóндо (*indecl.*).

roneo [ˈrəʊnɪəʊ] *n.* ронеóграф, множúтельный аппарáт.

v.t. печáтать, на- на ронеóграфе; размн|ожáть, -óжить.

rood [ruːd] *n.* (*arch., cross*) крест, распя́тие.

cpd. **~-screen** *n.* крéстная перегорóдка, отделя́ющая клúрос от нéфа.

roof [ruːf] *n.* кры́ша, крóвля; **the water-tank is in the ~** бак для воды́ стоúт под кры́шей; **you have a ~ over your head** у вас есть кры́ша над головóй; **I will not have him under my ~** я не хочý находúться с ним под однóй кры́шей; **the audience raised the ~** стéны сотрясáлись от аплодисмéнтов; **~ of the mouth** нёбо.

v.t. кры́ть, по-; наст|илáть, -лáть кры́шу на+*p.*; **~ed with slates** кры́тый шúфером; **~ing-felt** крóвельный картóн; толь (*m.*).

cpds. **~-garden** *n.* сад на кры́ше; **~-rack** *n.* багáжник (на кры́ше автомобúля); **~-tree** *n.* стропúльная ногá.

rook [rʊk] *n.* (*bird*) грач; (*chess piece*) турá, ладья́.

v.t. (*swindle*) обмáн|ывать, -ýть; (*overcharge*) обсчúт|ывать, -áть.

rookery [ˈrʊkərɪ] *n.* грачóвник; (*of seals etc.*) лéжбище.

rookie [ˈrʊkɪ] *n.* (*sl.*) новобрáнец, новичóк.

room [ruːm, rʊm] *n.* **1.** кóмната; **a four-~(ed) flat** четырёхкóмнатная квартúра; **~ service** обслýживание в нóмере; **~ and board** пóлный пансиóн; (*pl., apartments*) квартúра, кóмнаты (*f. pl.*); **private ~** (*in restaurant*) отдéльный кабинéт; **language ~** (*in school*) кабинéт инострáнных языкóв; **~ clerk** (*US*) дежýрный (в гостúнице). **2.** (*space*) мéсто, прострáнство; **the small table will take up no ~** мáленький стóлик займёт немнóго мéста; **there's plenty of ~** полнó мéста; **standing ~ only** тóлько стоя́чие местá; **there was no ~ to turn round in** нéгде бы́ло повернýться; **is there ~ for one more?** ещё одúн человéк уся́дется?; (*fig.*): **he was promoted to make ~ for his juniors** егó повы́сили, чтóбы продвúнуть молоды́х. **3.** (*scope, opportunity*) возмóжность; **it leaves no ~ for doubt** э́то не оставля́ет никакúх сомнéний; **there is ~ for improvement in your work** вáша рабóта моглá бы быть и лýчше.

v.i.: **we ~ed together in Paris** в Парúже мы жúли в однóй квартúре; **~ing-house** меблирóванные кóмнаты (*f. pl.*).

cpd. **~-mate** *n.* товáрищ по кóмнате.

roomer [ˈruːmə(r), ˈrʊmə(r)] *n.* (*US, lodger*) квартирáнт, жилéц.

roomful [ˈruːmfʊl, ˈrʊmfʊl] *n.* пóлная кóмната.

roomy [ˈruːmɪ] *adj.* простóрный, вместúтельный.

roost [ruːst] *n.* куря́тник, насéст; **go to ~** садúться, сесть на насéст; (*fig.*): **he rules the ~ here** он тут верховóдит/ распоряжáется.

v.i. (*of birds*) ус|áживаться, -éсться на насéст; **his curses came home to ~** егó прокля́тия пáли на егó же гóлову.

rooster [ˈruːstə(r)] *n.* петýх.

root [ruːt] *n.* **1.** (*of plant*) кóрень (*m.*); **the tree was torn up by the ~s** дéрево вы́рвали с кóрнем; **take, strike ~** пус|кáть, -тúть кóрни; **the idea took ~ in his mind** э́та мысль засéла емý в гóлову; **poverty must be removed ~**

and branch нищету́ ну́жно искорени́ть. **2.** (*cul.*, *med.*): **~s** коре́нь|я (*pl.*, *g.* -ев); **~ plant** корнепло́д; **~ crop** корнепло́дная культу́ра. **3.** (*of tooth*, *tongue*, *hair etc.*) ко́рень (*m.*). **4.** (*fig.*, *source*, *basis*) причи́на; **~ cause** основна́я причи́на; **money is the ~ of all evil** де́ньги — ко́рень зла; **he got to the ~ of the problem** он добра́лся до су́ти де́ла; **envy lies at the ~ of all his actions** за́висть лежи́т в осно́ве всех его́ де́йствий; **the quarrel had its ~s deep in the past** конфли́кт уходи́л корня́ми в далёкое про́шлое; **this strikes at the very ~ of democracy** э́то подрыва́ет са́мую осно́ву демокра́тии. **5.** (*math.*, *philol.*) ко́рень (*m.*); **square ~** квадра́тный ко́рень (из+*g.*).

v.t. **1.: the seedling ~ed itself** са́женец приви́лся (*or* пусти́л ко́рни). **2.** (*fig.*): **I have a ~ed objection to being disturbed** я о́чень не люблю́, когда́ мне меша́ют; **he is a man of deeply ~ed prejudices** он челове́к с укорени́вшимися предрассу́дками. **3.** (*transfix*): **he stood ~ed to the ground** он стоя́л как вко́панный.

v.i. **1.** (*take ~*) укорен|я́ться, -и́ться. **2.** (*of pigs etc.*, *also* **rootle**) ры́ться (*impf.*); рыть (*impf.*) зе́млю; **the dog was ~ing for an old bone** соба́ка отка́пывала ста́рую кость. **3.: ~ for** (*US*, *support*) боле́ть (*impf.*) за+*a.* (*coll.*).

with advs.: **~ about** *v.i.* (*lit.*, *fig.*) ры́ться (*impf.*); **~ out** *v.t.* (*lit.*, *fig.*, *extirpate*) вырыва́ть, вы́рвать с ко́рнем; (*fig.*, *also*) уничт|ожа́ть, -о́жить; (*lit.*, *fig.*, *dig out*) откопа́ть (*pf.*); **~ up** *v.t.* вырыва́ть, вы́рвать с ко́рнем.

rootle [ˈruːt(ə)l] = **root** *v.i.* **2.**

rootless [ruːtlɪs] *adj.* **1.** (*unfounded*) беспо́чвенный, необосно́ванный. **2.** (*of pers.*) безро́дный, без ро́ду, без корне́й, без пле́мени.

rope [rəʊp] *n.* (*cord*, *cable*) верёвка, кана́т; (*fig.*): **money for old ~** лёгкая нажи́ва; **give him enough ~ and he'll hang himself** да́йте ему́ во́лю и он сам себя́ загу́бит; **he knows the ~s** он в ку́рсе де́ла; он зна́ет все ходы́ и вы́ходы; он зна́ет, что к чему́; (*string*, *skein*) ни́тка, вя́зка; **a ~ of onions** вя́зка лу́ка; **a ~ of pearls** ни́тка же́мчуга; **a ~ of hair** жгут воло́с.

v.t. привя́з|ывать, -а́ть (*что к чему*).

with advs.: **~ in** *v.t.* (*coll.*, *enlist*) втя́|гивать, -ну́ть; **I was ~d in to help** меня́ запрягли́ в э́то де́ло; **~ off** *v.t.* отгор|а́живать, -оди́ть верёвкой/кана́том; **~ together** *v.t.*: **the climbers were ~d together** альпини́сты бы́ли свя́заны верёвкой; **~ up** *v.t.* перевя́з|ывать, -а́ть.

cpds. **~-dancer** *n.* кана́тный плясу́н; **~-end** *n.* коне́ц тро́са; **~-ladder** *n.* верёвочная ле́стница.

ropy [ˈrəʊpɪ] *adj.* (*stringy*) вя́зкий, тягу́чий; (*sl.*, *of poor quality*) никуды́шный.

ro-ro [ˈrəʊrəʊ] *adj.*: **~ ship** су́дно «ро-ро́», ро́лкер.

rorqual [ˈrɔːkw(ə)l] *n.* кит полоса́тик, ро́рквал.

rosary [ˈrəʊzərɪ] *n.* чёт|ки (*pl.*, *g.* -ок).

rose [rəʊz] *n.* **1.** ро́за; **Wars of the R~s** война́ А́лой и Бе́лой ро́зы; **there is no ~ without a thorn** нет ро́зы без шипо́в; (*fig.*): **her path was strewn with ~s** её путь был усы́пан ро́зами; **life was no bed of** (*or* **not all**) **~s for him** у него́ была́ отню́дь не сла́дкая жизнь; **this will put the ~s back into your cheeks** э́то вернёт вам здоро́вье и све́жесть; **under the ~** (*fig.*) по секре́ту, втихомо́лку. **2.** (*colour*) ро́зовый цвет. **3.** (*sprinkler*) спри́нклерная розе́тка.

cpds. **~-bed** *n.* клу́мба с ро́зами; **~bud** *n.* буто́н ро́зы; **a ~bud mouth** гу́бы, как лепестки́ ро́зы; **~-bush** *n.* ро́зовый куст; **~-coloured** *adj.* ро́зовый; **he sees the world through ~-coloured spectacles** он смо́трит на мир че́рез ро́зовые очки́; **~-garden** *n.* роза́рий; **~-pink** *n.* розова́тый отте́нок; *adj.* розова́тый; **~-red** *n.* цвет кра́сной ро́зы; *adj.* кра́сный как ро́за; **~-tree** *n.* шта́мбовая ро́за; **~-water** *n.* ро́зовая вода́; **~-window** *n.* окно́-розе́тка; **~wood** *n.* палиса́ндровое/ро́зовое де́рево.

rosé [ˈrəʊzeɪ] *n.* (*wine*) ро́зовое вино́.

roseate [ˈrəʊzɪət] *adj.* ро́зовый; све́тлый.

rosemary [ˈrəʊzmərɪ] *n.* розмари́н.

rosette [rəʊˈzet] *n.* розе́тка.

Rosicrucian [ˌrəʊzɪˈkruːʃ(ə)n] *n.* розенкре́йцер.

rosin [ˈrɒzɪn] *n.* канифо́ль.

v.t. нат|ира́ть, -ере́ть канифо́лью.

roster [ˈrɒstə(r), ˈrəʊstə(r)] *n.* гра́фик; рее́стр; расписа́ние.

rostrum [ˈrɒstrəm] *n.* трибу́на; ка́федра.

rosy [ˈrəʊzɪ] *adj.* ро́зовый; **~ cheeks** румя́ные щёки; (*fig.*) ра́достный, ра́дужный.

rot [rɒt] *n.* **1.** (*decay*) гние́ние; гниль; (*fig.*, *deterioration*): **the ~ set in** начала́сь полоса́ неуда́ч; начался́ разла́д; **stop the ~** пресе́чь (*pf.*) зло в ко́рне. **2.** (*disease of sheep*) копы́тная гниль. **3.** (*coll.*, *nonsense*) вздор, чушь; **don't talk ~!** бро́сьте чепуху́ моло́ть!

v.t. по́ртить, ис-.

v.i. **1.** (*decay*) гнить, с-; по́ртиться, ис-; (*fig.*) разл|ага́ться, -ожи́ться; **the tree was ~ting away** де́рево гни́ло. **2.** (*coll.*) нести́ (*det.*) вздор.

int. **~!** чушь!; бред!

cpd. **~-gut** *n.* (*liquor*) не вино́, а отра́ва; «сучо́к».

rota [ˈrəʊtə] *n.* гра́фик; рее́стр; (шта́тное) расписа́ние.

rotary [ˈrəʊtərɪ] *adj.* враща́ющийся; **~ motion** враща́тельное движе́ние; **~ press** ротацио́нная печа́тная маши́на; **~ pump** ротацио́нный насо́с.

rotate [rəʊˈteɪt] *v.t.* & *i.* **1.** (*revolve*) враща́ть(ся) (*impf.*). **2.** (*arrange or recur in rotation*) чередова́ть(ся) (*impf.*); **the duties (were) ~d every six weeks** дежу́рства чередова́лись ка́ждые шесть неде́ль; **the chairmanship ~s** председа́тели поочерёдно выполня́ют свои́ фу́нкции.

rotation [rəʊˈteɪʃ(ə)n] *n.* **1.** (*revolving*) враще́ние; оборо́т. **2.** (*regular succession*) чередова́ние; **~ of crops** севооборо́т; **they did guard duty in ~** они́ поочерёдно несли́ карау́льную слу́жбу.

rotatory [ˈrəʊtətərɪ, -ˈteɪtərə] *adj.* враща́тельный; враща́ющийся.

rote [rəʊt] *n.*: **he learnt the poem by ~** он вы́учил/вы́зубрил стихотворе́ние наизу́сть; **perform duties by ~** механи́чески выполня́ть обя́занности.

rotor [ˈrəʊtə(r)] *n.* (*of electric motor*) ро́тор; (*of helicopter*) несу́щий винт.

rotten [ˈrɒt(ə)n] *adj.* (*decayed*, *putrid*) гнило́й, прогни́вший; **~ eggs** ту́хлые я́йца; (*morally corrupt*) разложи́вшийся; испо́рченный; (*worthless*) никуды́шный; **a ~ idea** дура́цкая иде́я; (*very disagreeable*, *unfortunate*) отврати́тельный; **what a ~ shame!** э́то про́сто безобра́зие!; оби́дно до слёз!; **I'm feeling ~** я себя́ пога́но чу́вствую.

rottenness [ˈrɒtənnɪs] *n.* испо́рченность, разложе́ние.

rotter [ˈrɒtə(r)] *n.* (*sl.*) подле́ц, подо́нок.

rotund [rəʊˈtʌnd] *adj.* (*spherical*) округлённый; (*corpulent*, *plump*) по́лный; (*sonorous*, *grandiloquent*) зву́чный, высокопа́рный.

rotunda [rəʊˈtʌndə] *n.* рото́нда.

rotundity [rəʊˈtʌndɪtɪ] *n.* округлённость; полнота́; зву́чность, высокопа́рность.

r(o)uble [ˈruːb(ə)l] *n.* рубль (*m.*); (*note*) рублёвка, рублёвая бума́жка.

roué [ˈruːeɪ] *n.* пове́са (*m.*).

rouge [ruːʒ] *n.* (*cosmetic*) румя́н|а (*pl.*, *g.* —); губна́я пома́да.

v.t. & *i.* румя́нить(ся), на-.

rough [rʌf] *n.* **1.** (*~ things or circumstances*) тру́дности (*f. pl.*); **you must take the ~ with the smooth** на́до сто́йко переноси́ть превра́тности судьбы́. **2.** (*~ ground*, *esp. on golfcourse*) неро́вная пове́рхность; **he played the ball on to the ~** он посла́л мяч на неро́вный уча́сток по́ля. **3.** (*unfinished state*): **I saw the poem in the ~** я ви́дел поэ́му в черновике́. **4.** (*ruffian*, *rowdy*) грубия́н, хулига́н.

adj. **1.** (*opp. smooth*, *even*, *level*) шерохова́тый, неро́вный; **his skin was ~ to the touch** у него́ была́ горша́вая на о́щупь ко́жа; **the next few miles were ~ going** зате́м на протяже́нии не́скольких миль доро́га была́ уха́бистой/труднопроходи́мой. **2.** (*opp. calm*, *gentle*, *orderly*) бу́рный; **~ water** бу́рные во́ды; **the wind is getting ~** ве́тер крепча́ет; **their team played a ~ game** их кома́нда игра́ла гру́бо; **a ~ crowd** хамова́тая пу́блика; **the students were ~ly handled by the police** поли́ция гру́бо обраща́лась со студе́нтами; **the bill had a ~ passage** законопрое́кт прошёл с трудо́м (*or* со скри́пом, *coll.*). **3.** (*uncomfortable*, *arduous*) тру́дный; **he had a ~ time** ему́ пришло́сь ту́го; **they gave him a ~ ride** (*fig.*) они́ ему́ показа́ли, почём фунт ли́ха; **he is not capable of ~ work** тяжёлая рабо́та не для него́; **~ luck!** вот невезе́ние! **4.** (*of sounds*: *harsh*) ре́зкий. **5.** (*crude*) гру́бый; **they meted out ~ justice** наказа́ние вы́несли суро́вое; **a ~ and ready meal** еда́, пригото́вленная на ско́рую ру́ку. **6.** (*unfinished, rudimentary*) чернової́; **a ~ sketch** черново́й набро́сок; **a ~ diamond** (*lit.*) неогранённый алма́з; (*fig.*) неотшлифо́ванный алма́з. **7.** (*inexact, approximate*) приблизи́тельный; **at a ~ guess** по приблизи́тельной оце́нке; **this will give you a ~ idea** э́то даст вам о́бщее представле́ние; **~ly speaking** гру́бо говоря́.

adv.: **they treated him ~** (*coll.*) с ним гру́бо обраща́лись; **he is inclined to play ~** он допуска́ет гру́бую игру́.

v.t.: **~ it** (*coll.*) жить (*impf.*) без удо́бств.

with advs.: **~ out** *v.t.* (*e.g. a plan*) набр|а́сывать, -оса́ть; **~ up** *v.t.*: **don't ~ up my hair!** не еро́шьте мне во́лосы!

cpds. **~-and-tumble** *n.* дра́ка; сумато́ха; заварýха; *adj.* беспоря́дочный; **~cast** *n.* га́лечная штукату́рка; *adj.* (*lit.*) гру́бо оштукату́ренный; (*fig.*) грубова́тый, неотёсанный; **~-hew** *v.t.* гру́бо обтёс|ывать, -а́ть; **~-hewn** *adj.* (*fig.*) неотёсанный, некульту́рный; **~house** *n.* (*coll.*) шум; сканда́л, база́р; **~-neck** *n.* (*coll.*) хулига́н; **~-rider** *n.* (*horse-breaker*) бере́йтор; **~shod** *adj.* подко́ванный на шипы́; *adv.* (*fig.*): **he rode ~shod over their feelings** он гру́бо попира́л их чу́вства; **~-spoken** *adj.* гру́бый; гру́бо выража́ющийся.

roughage [ˈrʌfɪdʒ] *n.* гру́бая пи́ща; гру́бые корма́.

roughen [ˈrʌf(ə)n] *v.t.* & *i.* де́лать(ся), с- гру́бым/шерохова́тым.

roughness [ˈrʌfnɪs] *n.* **1.** (*to touch*) шерохова́тость. **2.** (*unevenness*) неро́вность. **3.** (*of water etc.*) волне́ние. **4.** (*crudity, coarseness*) гру́бость. **5.** (*harshness of sound*) ре́зкость.

roulette [ruːˈlet] *n.* руле́тка; **~ wheel** колесо́ руле́тки.

Roumania [ruːˈmeɪnɪə], **-n** [ruːˈmeɪnɪən] = **Romania, -n**

round [raʊnd] *n.* **1.** (*circular or ~ed object*) круг, окру́жность; (*slice*) ло́мтик. **2.** (*3-dimensional form*): **a statue in the ~** кру́глая ста́туя; **theatre in the ~** кру́глая сце́на в це́нтре за́ла. **3.** (*regular circuit or cycle*) цикл; обхо́д; круговоро́т; **the daily ~** повседне́вные дела́; **milk ~** ежедне́вная доста́вка молока́; **the doctor is on his ~s** до́ктор нахо́дится на обхо́де; **he made, went the ~ of the sentries** он соверши́л обхо́д часовы́х; **a ~ of pleasures** вихрь (*m.*) наслажде́ний; **the news went the ~ of the village** но́вость обошла́ всю дере́вню; **a ~ of golf** па́ртия го́льфа. **4.** (*stage in contest*) тур, эта́п, ра́унд; **he was knocked out in the third ~** он получи́л нока́ут в тре́тьем ра́унде; **the team got through to the final ~** кома́нда вы́шла в фина́л. **5.** (*set, series, burst*): **he bought a ~ of drinks** он поста́вил по стака́нчику всем прису́тствующим; **a ~ of applause** взрыв аплодисме́нтов; **a ~ of wage claims** очередно́е тре́бование повыше́ния зарпла́ты. **6.** (*of ammunition*) патро́н; компле́кт вы́стрела; **dummy ~** учёбный/холосто́й патро́н. **7.** (*song*) ро́ндо (*indecl.*). **8.** (*dance*) хорово́д; кругово́й та́нец.

adj. **1.** (*circular, spherical, convex*) кру́глый; **~ shoulders** суту́лые пле́чи, суту́лость. **2.** (*involving circular motion*) кругово́й; **~ game** игра́ с неограни́ченным коли́чеством уча́стников; **~ dance** хорово́д; **~ robin** проше́ние с по́дписями, располо́женными в кружо́к; **~ trip** пое́здка в о́ба конца́. **3.** (*of numbers*) кру́глый; **a ~ dozen** це́лая дю́жина; **in ~ numbers** в кру́глых ци́фрах. **4.** (*considerable*) кру́пный, значи́тельный; **a good ~ sum** поря́дочная/кру́гленькая су́мма; **at a ~ pace** кру́пным аллю́ром. **5.** (*outspoken*) прямо́й; **a ~ oath** кре́пкое руга́тельство.

adv. (*for phrasal vv. with* **round** *see relevant v. entries*): **all the year ~** кру́глый год; **he slept the clock ~** он проспа́л весь день; **the tree is six feet ~** э́то де́рево шесть фу́тов в окру́жности; **better all ~** лу́чше во всех отноше́ниях; **taking it all ~** принима́я во внима́ние всё; **he went a long way ~** он сде́лал изря́дный крюк; **he was ~ at our house** он зашёл к нам; **she ordered the car ~** она́ веле́ла пода́ть маши́ну (к подъе́зду).

v.t. **1.** (*make ~*) округл|я́ть, -и́ть; **a well-~ed phrase** гла́дкая фра́за. **2.** (*go ~*) огиба́ть, обогну́ть; об|ходи́ть, -ойти́ круго́м; **we ~ed the corner** мы заверну́ли/сверну́ли за́ угол; **the patient ~ed the corner** больно́й пошёл на попра́вку; **the ship ~ed the Cape** кора́бль обогну́л мыс До́брой Наде́жды.

v.i. **1.** (*become ~ or plump*) округл|я́ться, -и́ться. **2.** (*turn aggressively*): **he ~ed on me with abuse** он обру́шился на меня́ с бра́нью; **he ~ed on his pursuers** он набро́сился на свои́х пресле́дователей.

with advs.: **~ off** *v.t.* (*smooth*) выра́внивать, вы́ровнять; (*bring to a conclusion*) заверш|а́ть, -и́ть; **~ out** *v.t.* закругл|я́ть, -и́ть; заверш|а́ть, -и́ть; *v.i.*: **her figure was beginning to ~ out** её фигу́ра начала́ округля́ться; **~ up** *v.t.* сгоня́ть, согна́ть; **the cattle were ~ed up** скот согна́ли; **the courier ~ed up the party** гид собра́л свою́ гру́ппу; (*arrest*) арест|о́вывать, -ова́ть.

prep. **1.** (*encircling*) вокру́г, круго́м, о́коло (*all +g.*); **~ the world** вокру́г све́та; **they sat ~ the table** они́ сиде́ли вокру́г стола́; **the earth revolves ~ the sun** земля́ враща́ется вокру́г со́лнца; **he worked ~ the clock** он рабо́тал круглосу́точно (*or* кру́глые су́тки). **2.** (*to or at all points of*): **he looked ~ the room** он осмотре́л (всю) ко́мнату; **we walked ~ the garden** мы гуля́ли по са́ду; **they went ~ the galleries** они обошли карти́нные галере́и. **3. ~ the corner** за угло́м, (*of motion*) за́ угол. **4.** (*about, based on*): **he wrote a book ~ his experience** он описа́л свой о́пыт в кни́ге. **5.** (*approximately*) о́коло+*g.*; **he got there ~ (about) midday** он добра́лся туда́ о́коло полу́дня.

cpds. **~about** *n.* (*merry-go-round*) карусе́ль; (*traffic island*) кольцева́я тра́нспортная развя́зка; (*on road sign*) кругово́е движе́ние; *adj.* око́льный, кру́жный, кружно́й; (*fig.*) ко́свенный, обхо́дный; **R~head** *n.* круглоголо́вый, пурита́нин; **~house** *n.* (*of ship*) кормова́я ру́бка; **~-shouldered** *adj.* суту́лый; **~sman** *n.* доста́вщик; (*US*) полице́йский инспе́ктор; **~-table** *n.* (*attr.*): **~-table conference** конфере́нция кру́глого стола́; **~-the-clock** *adj.* круглосу́точный; **~-up** *n.* (*of news*) сво́дка новосте́й; (*of cattle*) заго́н скота́; (*raid*) обла́ва.

roundel [ˈraʊnd(ə)l] *n.* (*circular panel or window*) кру́глое окно́; (*medallion*) медальо́н.

roundelay [ˈraʊndɪˌleɪ] *n.* коро́тенькая пе́сенка.

rounders [ˈraʊndəs] *n.* англи́йская лапта́.

roundness [ˈraʊndnɪs] *n.* окру́глость.

rouse [raʊz] *v.t.* **1.** (*wake*) буди́ть, раз-. **2.** (*stimulate to action, interest etc.*) подстрека́ть (*impf.*); побу|жда́ть, -ди́ть; **he ~d himself and went to work** он взял себя́ в ру́ки и пошёл на рабо́ту; **I could ~ no spark of sympathy** я не мог вы́звать (в себе́) ни ка́пли сочу́вствия; **a rousing chorus** волну́ющий припе́в. **3.** (*provoke to anger*) возбу|жда́ть, -ди́ть; выводи́ть, вы́вести из себя́; **he is terrible when ~d** в гне́ве он ужа́сен.

v.i. пробу|жда́ться, -ди́ться.

rout[1] [raʊt] *n.* (*defeat*) разгро́м; (*disorderly retreat*) бе́гство; **the enemy were put to ~** враг был разгро́млен.

v.t. разб|ива́ть, -и́ть на́голову; разгроми́ть (*pf.*); обра|ща́ть, -ти́ть в бе́гство.

rout[2] [raʊt] *v.t.*: **~ out** (*drag out*) выта́скивать, вы́тащить; (*disclose*) обнару́жи|вать, -ть.

route [ruːt, *mil. also* raʊt] *n.* маршру́т; тра́сса; **in column of ~** (*mil.*) в похо́дной коло́нне.

v.t. отпр|авля́ть, -а́вить по маршру́ту; разраб|а́тывать, -о́тать маршру́т +*g.*

cpd. **~-march** *n.* похо́дный марш.

routine [ruːˈtiːn] *n.* **1.** (*regular course of action*) заведённый поря́док; режи́м; пра́ктика; форма́льность; (*attr.*) регуля́рный; очередно́й; теку́щий; повседне́вный. **2.** (*artiste's act*) но́мер, выступле́ние; **a dance ~** танцева́льный но́мер.

rov|e [rəʊv] *v.i.* скита́ться (*impf.*); **he has a ~ing disposition** он лю́бит стра́нствовать; **she has a ~ing eye** она́ так и стреля́ет глаза́ми; **a ~ing correspondent** разъездно́й корреспонде́нт; **~ing thoughts** блужда́ющие мы́сли.

rover [ˈrəʊvə(r)] *n.* (*wanderer*) бродя́га (*m.*); скита́лец.

row[1] [rəʊ] *n.* (*line*) ряд; **they stood in a ~** они стоя́ли в ряд; **the houses were built in ~s** дома́ бы́ли постро́ены ряда́ми; **seats in the front ~** места́ в пе́рвом ряду́; **a hard ~ to hoe** (*fig.*) тру́дная зада́ча.

row[2] [rəʊ] *n.* (*by boat*) прогу́лка на ло́дке; **we went (out) for a ~** мы пошли́ поката́ться на ло́дке.

v.t.: **he ~ed the boat in to shore** он привёл ло́дку к бе́регу; **we were ~ed across the river** нас перепра́вили/перевезли́ че́рез ре́ку на ло́дке; **Oxford were ~ing 40 (strokes) to the minute** кома́нда О́ксфорда де́лала со́рок гребко́в в мину́ту.

v.i. грести́ (*impf.*); **~ out** грести́ (*impf.*) от бе́рега; **the boat ~s well** ло́дка хорошо́ идёт; **~(ing)-boat** гребна́я шлю́пка.

row[3] [raʊ] *n.* **1.** (*noise, commotion*) шум; **I can't work with this ~ going on** я не могу́ рабо́тать в тако́м шу́ме; **don't make (such) a ~!** не шуми́те!; **the tenants kicked up a ~** (*made a noise; protested*) жильцы́ по́дняли шум. **2.** (*argument, quarrel*) ссо́ра; спор; **I had a ~ with the neighbours** я поруга́лся с сосе́дями. **3.** (*disgrace*): **I shall get into a ~ if I'm late** мне здо́рово доста́нется, е́сли я опозда́ю.

v.i. (*quarrel*) ссо́риться, по-; руга́ться (*impf.*).

rowan ['rəʊən, 'raʊ-] *n.* ряби́на.

rowdiness ['raʊdɪnɪs] *n.* бесчи́нство; хулига́нство.

rowdy ['raʊdɪ] *n.* буя́н, скандали́ст; хулига́н.

adj. гру́бый, шу́мный.

rowdyism ['raʊdɪ,ɪz(ə)m] *n.* гру́бость, хулига́нство.

rowel ['raʊəl] *n.* колёсико (шпо́ры).

rowlock ['rɒlək, 'rʌlək] *n.* уклю́чина.

royal ['rɔɪəl] *n.* (*coll., member of a ~ family*) член короле́вской семьи́.

adj. **1.** (*of the reigning family; kingly*) короле́вский, ца́рский; **of the blood ~** короле́вской кро́ви; **the R~ Family** короле́вская семья́; **His R~ Highness** его́ короле́вское высо́чество; **the R~ Navy** англи́йский вое́нно-морско́й флот; **~ blue** я́рко-си́ний цвет. **2.** (*magnificent*) великоле́пный; **we were ~ly entertained** нас принима́ли по-ца́рски.

royalism ['rɔɪəlɪz(ə)m] *n.* рояли́зм.

royalist ['rɔɪəlɪst] *n.* рояли́ст (*fem.* -ка).

adj. рояли́стский.

royalty ['rɔɪəltɪ] *n.* **1.** (*royal pers. or persons*) чле́н(ы) короле́вской семьи́. **2.** (*mineral rights; payment for these*) (пла́та за) пра́во разрабо́тки недр. **3.** (*payment to owner of patent or copyright*) а́вторский гонора́р; отчисле́ния (*pl.*) а́втору пье́сы *и т.п.*

RP (*abbr. of* **received pronunciation**) нормати́вное произноше́ние.

rpm (*abbr. of* **revolutions per minute**) оборо́ты (*m. pl.*) в мину́ту.

RSC (*abbr. of* ***Royal Shakespeare Company***) Короле́вская шекспи́ровская тру́ппа.

RSPB (*abbr. of* ***Royal Society for the Protection of Birds***) Короле́вское о́бщество защи́ты птиц.

RSPCA (*abbr. of* ***Royal Society for the Prevention of Cruelty to Animals***) Короле́вское о́бщество защи́ты живо́тных от жесто́кого обраще́ния.

RSVP (*abbr. of* ***répondez, s'il vous plaît***) бу́дьте любе́зны отве́тить.

Rt. Hon. [raɪt 'ɒnərəb(ə)l] *n.* (*abbr. of* ***Right Honourable***) высокочти́мый.

rub [rʌb] *n.* **1.** (*act of ~bing*) натира́ние; стира́ние; **she gave the mirror a ~ with a cloth** она́ протёрла зе́ркало тря́пкой. **2.** (*snag*): **there's the ~!** в то́м-то и загво́здка!

v.t. тере́ть (*impf.*); пот|ира́ть, -ере́ть; нат|ира́ть, -ере́ть; **the dog ~bed its head against my legs** соба́ка тёрлась голово́й о мои́ но́ги; **Johnny ~bed his knee on the wall** Джо́нни ободра́л коле́но о сте́нку; **he ~bed the skin off his knees** он стёр ко́жу на коле́нях; **he ~bed himself (dry) with a towel** он до́суха вы́терся полоте́нцем; **he ~bed his hands with soap** он намы́лил ру́ки; **he ~bed his hands with satisfaction** он потира́л ру́ки от удово́льствия; **the Maoris ~ noses in greeting** ма́ори тру́тся носа́ми в знак приве́тствия; **there is no need to ~ my nose in it** (*fig.*) не́зачем ты́кать меня́ но́сом; **he ~s shoulders with the great** он обща́ется с больши́ми людьми́; **~ the oil well into your skin** на́до хороше́нько втере́ть ма́сло в ко́жу; **the elbows of his coat were ~bed** рукава́ его́ пальто́ пообтёрлись на локтя́х.

v.i. тере́ться (*impf.*); **mind you don't ~ against the wet paint** бу́дьте осторо́жны и не запа́чкайтесь кра́ской.

with advs.: **~ along** *v.i.* ла́дить (*impf.*); уж|ива́ться, -и́ться; выпу́тываться, вы́путаться; **~ down** *v.t.* обт|ира́ть, -ере́ть; **he ~bed his horse down** он основа́тельно почи́стил ло́шадь; **~ in** *v.t.* вт|ира́ть, -ере́ть; вд|а́лбливать, -олби́ть; **the liniment should be ~bed in** мазь сле́дует втира́ть; **it was my fault; don't ~ it in!** моя́ вина́! но ско́лько мо́жно упрека́ть?; **~ off** *v.t.* ст|ира́ть, -ере́ть; **all the shine was ~bed off** весь блеск сошёл/стёрся; *v.i.*: **her happiness ~bed off on those around her** её сча́стье передава́лось тем, кто её окружа́л; **~ on** *v.t.* (*e.g. ointment*) на|кла́дывать, -ложи́ть; **~ out** *v.t.* отт|ира́ть, -ере́ть; ст|ира́ть, -ере́ть; (*murder*) приши́ть (*pf.*) (*sl.*); *v.i.*: **this ink will not ~ out** э́ти черни́ла не стира́ются; **~ over** *v.t.* прот|ира́ть, -ере́ть; **if the glass mists up, ~ it over** е́сли стекло́ запоте́ет, протри́те его́; **~ through** *v.i.* **his trousers had ~bed through at the knees** его́ брю́ки протёрлись на коле́нях; **~ together** *v.t.*: **he lit the fire by ~bing two sticks together** он развёл костёр, добы́в ого́нь тре́нием; **~ up** *v.t.* нач|ища́ть, -и́стить; полирова́ть, от-; **she ~bed up the silver** она́ начи́стила/почи́стила серебро́; **you ~bed him up the wrong way** вы к нему́ не так подошли́; **I must ~ up my French** мне ну́жно освежи́ть францу́зский.

rub-a-dub ['rʌbə,dʌb] *n.* бараба́нный бой; трам-там-та́м.

rubato [ru:'bɑ:təʊ] *n., adj. & adv.* руба́то (*indecl.*).

rubber[1] ['rʌbə(r)] *n.* **1.** (*substance*) рези́на; **~ band** рези́нка; **~ goods** (*contraceptives*) противозача́точные сре́дства; **~ plant** каучуконо́с; фи́кус каучуконо́сный. **2.** (*eraser*) ла́стик, рези́нка. **3.** (*US sl., condom*) презервати́в. **4.** (*pl., galoshes*) кало́ши (*f. pl.*).

cpds. **~neck** (*sl.*) *n.* зева́ка (*c.g.*); *v.i.* глазе́ть (*impf.*); **~-stamp** *v.t.* (*coll.*) подпи́с|ывать, -а́ть не гля́дя.

rubber[2] ['rʌbə(r)] *n.* (*cards*) ро́ббер.

rubberized ['rʌbə,raɪzd] *adj.* прорези́ненный, обло́женный рези́ной, гуммиро́ванный.

rubbing ['rʌbɪŋ] *n.* (*tracing*) копиро́вка притира́нием.

rubbish ['rʌbɪʃ] *n.* (*refuse, trash*) му́сор; хлам; (*nonsense*) чепуха́, вздор.

cpds. **~-bin** *n.* му́сорное ведро́; **~-cart** *n.* мусорово́з; **~-dump, ~-tip** *nn.* му́сорная я́ма.

rubbishy ['rʌbɪʃɪ] *adj.* никуда́ не го́дный; дрянно́й.

rubble ['rʌb(ə)l] *n.* булы́жник, щёбень (*m.*).

rubella [ru:'belə] *n.* красну́ха.

Rubicon ['ru:bɪ,kɒn] *n.*: **he crossed the ~** он перешёл Рубико́н.

rubicund ['ru:bɪ,kʌnd] *adj.* румя́ный.

ruble ['ru:b(ə)l] = **r(o)uble**

rubric ['ru:brɪk] *n.* заголо́вок; ру́брика.

ruby ['ru:bɪ] *n.* руби́н; (*attr.*) руби́новый.

ruck[1] [rʌk] *n.* (*crowd*) чернь; се́рая ма́сса.

ruck[2] [rʌk] *n.* (*wrinkle*) морщи́на.

v.t. & i.: **~ up** соб|ира́ть(ся), -ра́ть(ся) скла́дками; мо́рщить(ся), с-.

rucksack ['rʌksæk, 'rʊk-] *n.* рюкза́к.

ructions ['rʌkʃ(ə)ns] *n.* (*sl.*) завару́ха, сканда́л.

rudder ['rʌdə(r)] *n.* (*of vessel*) руль (*m.*), штурва́л; (*of aircraft*) руль направле́ния.

rudderless ['rʌdəlɪs] *adj.* без руля́; (*fig.*) без руля́ и без ветри́л.

ruddy ['rʌdɪ] *adj.* **1.** (*glowing, reddish*) румя́ный; **a ~ face** румя́ное лицо́; **~ health** цвету́щее здоро́вье; **a ~ glow** я́рко-кра́сный цвет. **2.** (*as expletive*) прокля́тый, чо́ртов.

rude [ru:d] *adj.* **1.** (*impolite, offensive*) гру́бый; невоспи́танный; **don't make ~ remarks!** не груби́те!; **he was ~ to the teacher** он нагруби́л учи́теля. **2.** (*indecent*) гру́бый, непристо́йный. **3.** (*startling, violent*) ре́зкий; **a ~ shock** внеза́пный уда́р; **I had a ~ awakening** (*fig.*) меня́ пости́гло го́рькое разочарова́ние. **4.** (*primitive, roughly made*) топо́рный; гру́бо сде́ланный. **5.** (*in natural state*) необрабо́танный; ~ **ore** необогащённая/рядова́я руда́. **6.** (*vigorous*) кре́пкий, си́льный; **in ~ health** кре́пкого здоро́вья.

rudeness [ˈru:dnɪs] *n.* (*impoliteness*) гру́бость, невоспи́танность.

rudiment [ˈru:dɪmənt] *n.* **1.** (*in pl., elements, first principles*) элемента́рные зна́ния; (*beginnings, first trace*) зача́тки (*m. pl.*); **he has not even the ~s of common sense** у него́ нет ни ка́пли здра́вого смы́сла. **2.** (*imperfectly developed organ*) рудимента́рный о́рган.

rudimentary [ˌru:dɪˈmentərɪ] *adj.* (*elementary*) элемента́рный; (*undeveloped*) рудимента́рный, зача́точный.

rue[1] [ru:] *n.* (*bot.*) ру́та.

rue[2] [ru:] *v.t.* (*liter.*) сожале́ть (*impf.*); **you will ~ it** вы об э́том пожале́ете; **he lived to ~ the day** пришло́ вре́мя, когда́ он про́клял тот день.

rueful [ˈru:fʊl] *adj.* печа́льный, удручённый.

ruff[1] [rʌf] *n.* (*frill*) жабо́ (*indecl.*); (*on bird's neck*) кольцо́ пе́рьев вокру́г ше́и пти́цы.

ruff[2] [rʌf] *n.* (*bird*) турухта́н.

ruffian [ˈrʌfɪən] *n.* головоре́з, банди́т.

ruffianly [ˈrʌfɪənlɪ] *adj.* банди́тский.

ruffle [ˈrʌf(ə)l] *n.* (*ornamental frill*) обо́рка.

v.t.: **a breeze ~d the surface of the lake** от ве́тра о́зеро покры́лось ря́бью; **she ~d his hair** она́ взъеро́шила ему́ во́лосы; **the bird ~d up its feathers** пти́ца взъеро́шила пе́рья; **he never gets ~d** он всегда́ невозмути́м; его́ невозмо́жно вы́вести из себя́.

rug [rʌg] *n.* **1.** (*mat*) ковёр; **sweep sth. under the ~** (*fig.*) стыдли́во ута́ивать (*impf.*) что-н.; зама́зать/скрыть/замаскирова́ть (*pf.*) что-н. неприя́тное. **2.** (*wrap*) плед.

Rugby (football) [ˈrʌgbɪ] *n.* ре́гби (*nt. indecl.*).

rugged [ˈrʌgɪd] *adj.* **1.** (*rough, uneven*) неро́вный; **a ~ coast** скали́стый бе́рег. **2.** (*irregular, strongly-marked*) гру́бый; **~ features** ре́зкие черты́. **3.** (*unrefined*) неотшлифо́ванный, гру́бый. **4.** (*austere, harsh*) тяжёлый, тру́дный. **5.** (*sturdy*) кре́пкий, твёрдый.

ruggedness [ˈrʌgɪdnɪs] *n.* неро́вность; гру́бость; твёрдость.

rugger [ˈrʌgə(r)] (*coll.*) = **Rugby (football)**

Ruhr [rʊə(r)] *n.* (*river*) Рур; (*region*) Ру́рская о́бласть.

ruin [ˈru:ɪn] *n.* **1.** (*downfall*) ги́бель, круше́ние; **the ~ of his hopes** круше́ние его́ наде́жд; **ambition led to his** (*or* **brought him to**) **~** честолю́бие погуби́ло его́; **~ stared him in the face** ему́ грози́ло разоре́ние. **2.** (*collapsed or destroyed state; building in this state*) разва́лины, руи́ны (*both f. pl.*); **the house fell into ~** дом соверше́нно развали́лся (*or* преврати́лся в гру́ду разва́лин); **ancient ~s** дре́вние руи́ны (*f. pl.*); **his life lay in ~s** его́ жизнь была́ загу́блена. **3.** (*destroying agency*) поги́бель; **he will be the ~ of us** он нас погу́бит.

v.t. разр|уша́ть, -у́шить; уничт|ожа́ть, -о́жить; губи́ть, по-; **he was ~ed** (*in business*) он разори́лся; **this will ~ my chances** э́то подорвёт мои́ ша́нсы; **the effect was ~ed** никако́го эффе́кта не получи́лось; **the rain ~ed my suit** дождь испо́ртил мой костю́м; **a ~ed building** разру́шеное зда́ние.

ruination [ˌru:ɪˈneɪʃ(ə)n] *n.* ги́бель; разоре́ние.

ruinous [ˈru:ɪnəs] *adj.* (*disastrous*) губи́тельный; (*in ruins*) разру́шенный; (*expensive*) разори́тельный.

rule [ru:l] *n.* **1.** (*regulation; recognized principle*) пра́вило; **keep, stick to the ~s of the game** соблюда́ть (*impf.*) пра́вила игры́; **~ of the road** пра́вила (*pl.*) у́личного движе́ния; **he does everything by ~** он де́лает всё по пра́вилам; **smoking is against the ~s** кури́ть не разреша́ется; **work** (*n.*) **to ~** замедле́ние те́мпа рабо́ты (*род итальянской забастовки*); **by ~ of thumb** куста́рным спо́собом; на глазо́к. **2.** (*normal practice; custom*) привы́чка, обы́чай; **my ~ is never to start an argument** мой при́нцип — никогда́ не затева́ть спор; **as a ~** как пра́вило; **he makes it a ~ to rise early** он взял за пра́вило встава́ть ра́но. **3.** (*government, sway*) правле́ние, госпо́дство; **~ of law** власть зако́на; **under foreign ~** под иностра́нным влады́чеством. **4.** (*measuring-stick*) лине́йка.

v.t. **1.** (*govern*) управля́ть (*impf.*) +*i.*; руководи́ть (*impf.*) +*i.*; **she ~s her husband** она́ кома́ндует му́жем; **don't be ~d by prejudice** не поддава́йтесь предрассу́дкам. **2.** (*decree, decide*) постан|овля́ть, -ови́ть; **the chairman ~d the motion out of order** председа́тель отклони́л предложе́ние, как наруша́ющее регла́мент; **the umpire ~d that the ball was not out** судья́ объяви́л, что мяч не́ был в а́уте. **3.**: **a ~d exercise book** тетра́дь в лине́йку; **~d paper** лино́ванная бума́га.

v.i. (*hold sway*) пра́вить (*impf.*); управля́ть (*impf.*); **ruling classes** пра́вящие кла́ссы; **ruling passion** всепоглоща́ющая страсть.

with advs.: **~ off** *v.t.* отдел|я́ть, -и́ть черто́й; **~ out** *v.t.* (*exclude*) исключ|а́ть, -и́ть; **I would not ~ out the possibility** я не исключа́ю тако́й возмо́жности.

ruler [ˈru:lə(r)] *n.* (*reigning pers.*) прави́тель (*m.*); (*measuring-stick*) лине́йка.

ruling [ˈru:lɪŋ] *n.* (*decree; decision*) постановле́ние; реше́ние.

rum[1] [rʌm] *n.* ром.

cpd. **~runner** *n.* контрабанди́ст спиртны́х напи́тков.

rum[2] [rʌm] *adj.* (*coll.*) чудно́й; **he is a ~ customer** он стра́нный тип; **a ~ go!** стра́нные дели́шки!

Rumania [ru:ˈmeɪnɪə], **-n** [ru:ˈmeɪnɪən] = **Romania, -n**

rumba [ˈrʌmbə] *n.* ру́мба.

v.i. танцева́ть, про- ру́мбу.

rumbl|e [ˈrʌmb(ə)l] *n.* громыха́ние, гул.

v.t. (*coll., unmask, discover*) ви́деть (*impf.*) (*кого/что*) насквозь.

v.i. громыха́ть (*impf.*); греме́ть, за-/про-; **thunder was ~ing in the distance** вдалеке́ греме́л гром; **a tractor ~ed along** громыха́я, прошёл тра́ктор.

rumbustious [rʌmˈbʌstʃəs] *adj.* (*coll.*) шумли́вый, шу́мный.

ruminant [ˈru:mɪnənt] *n.* жва́чное живо́тное.

adj. жва́чный.

ruminate [ˈru:mɪˌneɪt] *v.i.* (*chew the cud*) жева́ть (*impf.*) жва́чку; (*ponder*) разду́мывать (*impf.*).

rumination [ˌru:mɪˈneɪʃ(ə)n] *n.* жева́ние жва́чки; (*fig.*) размышле́ние.

rummage [ˈrʌmɪdʒ] *n.* (*search*) о́быск; (*old articles*) старьё; **~ sale** барахо́лка; распрода́жа поде́ржанных веще́й.

v.t. обы́ск|ивать, -а́ть; **the ship was ~d by Customs** тамо́женники произвели́ досмо́тр корабля́.

v.i. ры́ться (*impf.*); **he ~d (about) for his matches** он всю́ду ры́лся в по́исках спи́чек.

rummy [ˈrʌmɪ] *n.* (*card game*) ре́ми-бридж.

rumour [ˈru:mə(r)] *n.* слух; то́лк|и (*pl., g.* -ов); **~ has it that ...** хо́дят слу́хи, что...; **there were ~s of war** ходи́ли слу́хи, что бу́дет война́.

v.t.: **it was ~ed that ...** ходи́ли слу́хи, что...; **the ~ed visit** визи́т, о кото́ром прошёл слух.

rump [rʌmp] *n.* кресте́ц; (*fig., remnant*) оста́тки (*m. pl.*).

cpd. **~-steak** *n.* ромште́кс; вы́резка.

rumple [ˈrʌmp(ə)l] *v.t.* мять, по-; трепа́ть, по-; еро́шить, взъ-; **her dress was ~d** её пла́тье помя́лось; **don't ~ my hair!** не трепи́те мне во́лосы!

rumpus [ˈrʌmpəs] *n.* шум, гам; сканда́л; **~ room** ко́мната для игр и развлече́ний.

run [rʌn] *n.* **1.** (*action of ~ning*) бег, пробе́г; **he went for a ~ before breakfast** он сде́лал пробе́жку пе́ред за́втраком; **he took a ~ and jumped across the brook** он разбежа́лся и перепры́гнул че́рез руче́й; **he started off at a ~** он побежа́л (с ме́ста); **the prisoner made a ~ for it** заключённый бежа́л/удра́л; **the general had the enemy on the ~** генера́л обрати́л проти́вника в бе́гство; **the prisoner is on the ~** заключённый нахо́дится в бега́х; **she has been on the ~ all morning** она́ была́ в бега́х всё у́тро; **he had a good ~ for his money** (*fig.*) он не зря стара́лся; его́ уси́лия окупи́лись. **2.** (*trip, journey, route*) пое́здка, рейс, маршру́т; **we went for a ~ in the country** мы съе́здили за́ город; **it is a fast ~ from here to London** отсю́да мо́жно бы́стро добра́ться до Ло́ндона; **the driver was not on his usual ~** води́тель рабо́тал не на своём обы́чном маршру́те; **the train did the ~ in 3 hours** по́езд дошёл за три часа́; **the ship was on a trial ~** кора́бль находи́лся в испыта́тельном ре́йсе. **3.** (*continuous stretch*) пери́од; отре́зок вре́мени; **the government had a long ~ in office** прави́тельство до́лго остава́лось у вла́сти; **he**

had a ~ of good luck у него́ была́ полоса́ везе́ния; **the play had a long ~** пье́са шла до́лго; **in the long ~** в коне́чном счёте. **4.** (*score at cricket etc.*) очко́. **5.** (*tendency, sequence*) направле́ние; **the ~ of the hills is from east to west** гряда́ холмо́в тя́нется с восто́ка на за́пад. **6.** (*demand*) спрос; **there is a ~ on this book** э́та кни́га по́льзуется больши́м спро́сом. **7.** (*ordinary kind*): **his talents are out of the common ~** он незауря́дно тала́нтлив; **~ of the mill** обы́чный/сре́дний сорт. **8.** (*for fowls etc.*) заго́н. **9.** (*use, access*): **he gave me the ~ of his library** он предоста́вил мне всю свою́ библиоте́ку. **10.** (*mus., rapid scale passage*) рула́да, пасса́ж. **11.** (*cards in numerical sequence*) ка́рты (*f. pl.*), иду́щие подря́д по досто́инству. **12.** (*ladder in stocking etc.*) спусти́вшаяся пе́тля.

v.t. **1.** (*cause to ~*): **he ran a horse in the Derby** он вы́ставил свою́ ло́шадь на Де́рби; **you will ~ yourself short of breath** вы задохнётесь от бе́га; **he nearly ran me off my legs** он меня́ так загна́л, что я на нога́х не стоя́л. **2.** (*execute, perform*): **he ran a good race** он хорошо́ пробежа́л (диста́нцию); **the heats were ~ yesterday** забе́ги состоя́лись вчера́; **he likes ~ning errands** ему́ нра́вится быть на побегу́шках. **3.** (*cover, traverse*) бежа́ть (*det.*), про-; **he can ~ the mile in under a minute** он мо́жет пробежа́ть ми́лю ме́ньше, чем за мину́ту; **I'd ~ a mile to avoid him** я бы от него́ за версту́ убежа́л; **the illness has to ~ its course** боле́знь должна́ пройти́ все эта́пы; **her children are ~ning the streets** её де́ти бе́гают по у́лицам (как беспризо́рные); **the canoe ran the rapids** каноэ́ прошло́ че́рез поро́ги. **4.** (*expose o.s. to*) подв|ерга́ться, -е́ргнуться +*d.*; **he ~s the risk of being caught** он риску́ет быть по́йманным; **he ran it too fine** он оста́вил (*времени/денег*) в обре́з. **5.** (*hunt, pursue*) пресле́довать (*impf.*); трави́ть (*impf.*); **the hounds ran the fox to earth** соба́ки загна́ли лису́ в но́ру; **I ran him to earth in his study** наконе́ц я насти́г его́ в кабине́те; **I won, but he ran me very close** я вы́играл у него́, но с больши́м трудо́м. **6.** (*convey in car*) подв|ози́ть, -езти́ (*or* подбр|а́сывать, -о́сить) (на маши́не); **shall I ~ you home?** хоти́те, я подвезу́ вас домо́й?; **I'll ~ you to the station** я подброшу́ вас к ста́нции. **7.** (*smuggle*) пров|ози́ть, -езти́ контраба́ндой. **8.** (*cause to go*): **they ran the ship aground** они́ посади́ли кора́бль на мель; **he ran the car into the garage** он загна́л маши́ну в гара́ж; **he ran the car into a tree** он вре́зался в де́рево; **he ran his fingers over the keys** он пробежа́л (*or* бы́стро провёл) па́льцами по кла́вишам; **he ran his eye over the page** он пробежа́л глаза́ми страни́цу; **I shall ~ (water into) the bath** я напущу́ воды́ в ва́нну; я пригото́влю ва́нну; **he ran a sword through his enemy's body** он пронзи́л врага́ мечо́м. **9.** (*operate*) управля́ть (*impf.*) +*i.*; эксплуати́ровать (*impf.*); **who is ~ning the shop?** кто ве́дает ла́вкой?; **he ~s a small business** у него́ своё небольшо́е де́ло; **she ~s the house single-handed** она́ сама́ ведёт хозя́йство; **he ran the engine for a few minutes** он завёл мото́р на не́сколько мину́т; **they ran extra trains** они́ пусти́ли дополни́тельные поезда́; **can you afford to ~ a car?** вы в состоя́нии держа́ть маши́ну?; **he thinks he ~s the show** (*fig.*) он ду́мает, что он здесь гла́вный. **10.:** **he is ~ning a temperature** у него́ температу́ра.

v.i. **1.** (*move quickly, hurry*) бе́гать (*indet.*); бежа́ть (*det.*), по-; **I ran after him** я побежа́л за ним; **I had to ~ for the train** мне пришло́сь бежа́ть, что́бы поспе́ть на по́езд; **he ran for his life** он удира́л изо всех сил (*or* во весь дух); **~ for it!** беги́!; (*coll.*) дуй!; **he came ~ning to my aid** он бро́сился ко мне на по́мощь; **~ and see who's at the door!** сбе́гай посмотри́, кто пришёл!; **she ~s after every man she meets** она́ гоня́ется за всеми мужчи́нами. **2.** (*compete*) соревнова́ться (*impf.*); **he is ~ning in the 100 metres** он бежи́т стометро́вку; (*fig.*): **he ran for president** он баллоти́ровался в президе́нты. **3.** (*come by chance*) столкну́ться (*pf.*) (с+*i.*); натолкну́ться (*pf.*) (на+*a.*); **I ran into, across an old friend** я случа́йно встре́тил ста́рого това́рища. **4.** (*of ship etc.*): **the vessel ran ashore** су́дно вы́бросило на бе́рег (*or* приткну́лось к бе́регу); **they were ~ning before the wind** они́ плы́ли с попу́тным ве́тром; **they had to ~ into port** им пришло́сь зайти́ в порт. **5.** (*of public transport*) ходи́ть (*indet.*); **there are no trains ~ning** поезда́ не хо́дят. **6.** (*of machines etc.: function*) де́йствовать (*impf.*); **most cars ~ on petrol** большинство́ маши́н рабо́тает/хо́дит на бензи́не; **leave the engine ~ning!** не выключа́йте мото́р! **7.** (*of objects in motion*): **it ~s on wheels** э́то дви́гается на колёсах; (*fig.*): **life ~s smoothly for him** его́ жизнь течёт гла́дко. **8.** (*of liquid, sand etc.: flow*) течь, протека́ть, струи́ться (*all impf.*); **the water is ~ning** кран откры́т; **the floor was ~ning with water** пол был зали́т водо́й; **wine ran like water** вино́ лило́сь реко́й; **tears/sweat ran down his face** слёзы кати́лись (*or* пот струи́лся) по его́ щека́м; **the tide ~s strong** си́льный прили́в; **the river is ~ning high** вода́ в реке́ подняла́сь; **I hit him till the blood ran** я бил его́, пока́ не показа́лась кровь; **my eyes are ~ning** у меня́ слезя́тся глаза́; **his nose was ~ning** у него́ текло́ из носу; (*fig.*): **feelings ran high** стра́сти разгоре́лись; **prices are ~ning high** це́ны поднима́ются. **9.** (*become, grow*) станови́ться (*impf.*); **the well ran dry** коло́дец вы́сох; **supplies were ~ning low** запа́сы бы́ли на исхо́де; **he ran short of money** у него́ не остава́лось де́нег; **his blood ran cold** у него́ кровь засты́ла в жи́лах. **10.** (*develop unchecked*): **the garden is ~ning wild** сад бу́рно разраста́ется; **she lets her children ~ wild** её де́ти расту́т без присмо́тра; **the lettuces ran to seed** сала́т пошёл в семена́; **he is ~ning to fat** у него́ появля́ется жиро́к; **don't let good food ~ to waste** не переводи́те зря хоро́шую пи́щу. **11.** (*of colour, ink etc.: spread*) линя́ть, по-; **if you wash this dress the dye will ~** е́сли вы постира́ете э́то пла́тье, оно́ полиня́ет. **12.** (*of emotions, thought etc.: travel*): **the news ran like wildfire** но́вость распространи́лась с молниено́сной быстрото́й; **a tremor ran through the crowd** толпа́ затрепета́ла; **a pain ran up his arm** у него́ стрельну́ло в руке́; **the thought ran through his head** у него́ промелькну́ла мысль; **his thoughts were ~ning on a certain woman** его́ мы́сли возвраща́лись к одно́й же́нщине; **my eyes ran over the page** я пробежа́л глаза́ми страни́цу; **the tune kept ~ning through my head** э́та мело́дия всё вре́мя звуча́ла у меня́ в уша́х. **13.** (*extend, stretch*) тяну́ться (*impf.*); простира́ться (*impf.*); **the gardens ~ down to the river** сады́ тя́нутся до реки́; **a road ~ning along the river** доро́га, иду́щая вдоль реки́; **a fence ~s round the field** по́ле огоро́жено забо́ром; **the first volume ~s to 500 pages** в пе́рвом то́ме 500 страни́ц; **his biography ran into six editions** его́ биогра́фия вы́держала шесть изда́ний; **his income ~s into five figures** он получа́ет бо́льше десяти́ ты́сяч; **it will ~ to a lot of money** э́то бу́дет сто́ить больши́х де́нег; **our funds will not ~ to it** на́ших де́нег на э́то не хва́тит. **14.** (*continue; remain in operation*) быть действи́тельным; **the lease has seven years to ~** догово́р о на́йме действи́телен ещё семь лет; **the play has been ~ning for five years** пье́са идёт пять лет; **it ~s in their family** э́то у них насле́дственное. **15.** (*become unwoven*) спуска́ться (*impf.*); **these stockings will not ~** на э́тих чулка́х пе́тли не спуска́ются. **16.** (*of narrative or verse*) гласи́ть (*impf.*); **I forget how the line (of poetry) ~s** я забы́л, как звучи́т э́та строка́; **so the story ~s** так говоря́т; **her reply ran true to form** отве́т был типи́чным для неё.

further phrr. with preps.: **~ into** (*collide with*) налете́ть (*impf.*) на+*a.*; столкну́ться (*pf.*) с+*i.*; **he ran into a lamp-post** он налете́л на фона́рный столб; (*encounter, incur*): **he ran into debt** он зале́з/влез в долги́; **if you ~ into danger** е́сли вам бу́дет угрожа́ть опа́сность; **the plan ran into difficulties** план натолкну́лся на тру́дности; **~ over, through** (*review; rehearse*) повтор|я́ть, -и́ть; **I will ~ over the main points** я повторю́ (*or* ещё раз перечи́слю) гла́вные пу́нкты; **shall I ~ over the part with you?** дава́йте пройдём ва́шу роль вме́сте; **he ran through his mail** он просмотре́л по́чту; **~ through** (*spend*) тра́тить, по-; **he ran through a small fortune** он истра́тил це́лое состоя́ние.

with advs.: **~ about** *v.i.* бе́гать (*indet.*); **let the children ~ about** пусть де́ти побе́гают; **~ along** *v.i.*: **I must ~ along** мне на́до бежа́ть; **~ along and play!** иди́ поигра́й!;

~ around *v.i.*: **she is ~ning around with a married man** она́ кру́тит с жена́тым (челове́ком); **he had me ~ning around in circles** он меня́ соверше́нно сбил с то́лку; **~ away, ~ off** *v.i.* убе|га́ть, -жа́ть; уд|ира́ть, -ра́ть; **he ran away with his employer's daughter** он сбежа́л с хозя́йской до́чкой; **he ran away with the game** он шутя́ вы́играл па́ртию; **entertaining ~s away with a lot of money** принима́ть госте́й сто́ит де́нег; **don't ~ away with the idea that I am against you** не внуша́йте себе́, что я име́ю что-ли́бо про́тив вас; **the horse ran away with him** ло́шадь его́ понесла́; **he lets his tongue ~ away with him** он сли́шком распуска́ет язы́к; **~ back** *v.t.*: **he ran the tape back** он перемота́л плёнку наза́д; *v.i.*: **he ran back to apologize** он прибежа́л наза́д, что́бы извини́ться; **the car ran back down the hill** маши́на откати́лась наза́д по́д гору; **let us ~ back over the argument** дава́йте повтори́м доказа́тельство по пу́нктам; **~ down** *v.t.*: **the ship ran down a rowing-boat in the fog** в тума́не кора́бль наткну́лся на шлю́пку; **the cyclist was ~ down by a lorry** грузови́к сбил велосипеди́ста; **don't ~ your battery down** не тра́тьте батере́ю; **she is always ~ning down her neighbours** она́ ве́чно поно́сит сосе́дей; **you look very ~ down** у вас о́чень утомлённый вид; **the police ran the murderer down in London** поли́ция насти́гла уби́йцу в Ло́ндоне; **it took him all day to ~ the reference down** це́лый день шёл у него́ на наведе́ние спра́вки; **it is their policy to ~ down production** их поли́тика напра́влена к свёртыванию произво́дства; *v.i.* остан|а́вливаться, -ови́ться; **the clock ran down** у часо́в ко́нчился заво́д; **the labour force is ~ning down** рабо́чая си́ла сокраща́ется; **~ in** *v.t.*: **he is ~ning in his car** он обка́тывает свою́ маши́ну; **the police ran him in** его́ заца́пала поли́ция (*coll.*); **~ off** *v.t.*: **I ran off the water from the tank** я вы́пустил во́ду из ба́ка; **he can ~ off an article in half an hour** он мо́жет настрочи́ть статью́ за полчаса́; **can you ~ off 100 more copies?** вы мо́жете сде́лать/отпеча́тать ещё 100 экземпля́ров?; **the heats will be ~ off today** забе́ги состоя́тся сего́дня; *v.i.* убе|га́ть, -жа́ть; уд|ира́ть, -ра́ть; **he ran off with the jewels** он сбежа́л с драгоце́нностями; (*see also* **~ away**); **~ on** *v.t.* (*typ. etc.*) наб|ира́ть, -ра́ть в одну́ строку́ (*or* в подбо́р); *v.i.* прод|олжа́ться, -о́лжиться; **the lecture ran on for two hours** ле́кция продолжа́лась два часа́; **~ out** *v.t.*: **he ran the rope out** он протяну́л верёвку; **he was ~ out of the country** его́ изгна́ли из страны́; *v.i.* (*lit.*) выбега́ть, вы́бежать; (*come to an end*) конча́ться, ко́нчиться; **supplies are ~ning out** запа́сы конча́ются; **he will soon ~ out of money** у него́ ско́ро ко́нчатся де́ньги; **he ran out of ideas** у него́ исся́кли иде́и; **our tea ran out** у нас вы́шел чай; **time is ~ning out** вре́мя истека́ет; **the tide was ~ning out** начался́ отли́в; **the pier ~s out into the sea** мол выдаётся в мо́ре; **~ over** *v.t.* задави́ть (*pf.*); **he was ~ over by a car** его́ задави́ла маши́на; *v.i.*: **the bath ran over** ва́нна перели́лась че́рез край; **the (boiling) milk ran over** молоко́ убежа́ло; **~ through** *v.t.*: **yield, or I will ~ you through!** сдава́йтесь, а то я вас заколю́!; **the teacher ran my mistakes through with his pencil** учи́тель зачеркну́л мои́ оши́бки карандашо́м; **~ together** *v.t.*: **he ~s his words together** он глота́ет слова́; **~ up** *v.t.*: **~ up the flag** подня́ть (*pf.*) флаг; **she ran up a dress** она́ (бы́стро) смастери́ла пла́тье; **he ran up a shed** он сооруди́л сара́й; **he ran up a bill at the tailor's** он задолжа́л портно́му; *v.i.*: **she ran up to tell me the news** она́ прибежа́ла, что́бы сообщи́ть мне но́вость; **he ran up against a snag** он натолкну́лся на препя́тствие.

cpds. **~about** *n.* (*car*) небольшо́й автомоби́ль; малолитра́жка; **~around** *n.* (*coll.*, *excuses*) отгово́рки (*f. pl.*); **~away** *n.* (*fugitive*) бегле́ц; (*attr.*): **a ~away horse** ло́шадь, кото́рая понесла́; **~away inflation** безу́держная инфля́ция; **~-down** *n.* (*reduction*) сокраще́ние; (*summary*) кра́ткое изложе́ние; конспе́кт; **give me a ~-down on events** скажи́те мне кра́тко, что произошло́; **~-off** *n.* (*deciding heat*) дополни́тельная игра́; (*copy from stencil etc.*) ко́пия, отпеча́ток; (*diversion of water*) сток; **~-up** *n.* (*run preparatory to action*) разбе́г; (*fig.*): **the ~-up to the election** предвы́борная пора́/кампа́ния; **~way** *n.* (*aeron.*) взлётно-поса́дочная полоса́ (*abbr.* ВПП).

rune [ruːn] *n.* ру́на.

rung [rʌŋ] *n.* (*of ladder*) ступе́нька; (*fig.*): **he reached the topmost ~ of his profession** он дости́г верши́ны в свое́й профе́ссии; (*of chair*) перекла́дина.

runic [ˈruːnɪk] *adj.* руни́ческий.

runnel [ˈrʌn(ə)l] *n.* (*rivulet*) ручеёк; (*gutter*) кана́ва, сток.

runner [ˈrʌnə(r)] *n.* **1.** (*athlete*) бегу́н; **front ~** ли́дер; **long-distance ~** ста́йер; **marathon ~** марафо́нец. **2.** (*horse in race*) рыса́к, (бегова́я) ло́шадь. **3.** (*messenger*; *scout*) посы́льный курье́р. **4.** (*part which assists sliding motion*): **curtain ~** кольцо́ для занаве́ски; **sledge ~** по́лоз. **5.** (*narrow cloth*; *strip of carpet*) доро́жка. **6.** (*bot.*, *shoot*) побе́г; **~ bean** фасо́ль о́гненная.

cpd. **~-up** *n.* уча́стник/кандида́т, заня́вший второ́е ме́сто.

running [ˈrʌnɪŋ] *n.* **1.** (*sport*, *exercise*) бе́ганье, бег; **I shall take up ~** я займу́сь бе́гом; **~ shoes** беговик|и́ (*pl.*, *g.* -о́в). **2.** (*pace*) ход; **the favourite made all the ~** фавори́т вёл бег; **she made the ~ in the conversation** она́ задава́ла тон в разгово́ре. **3.** (*contest*) состяза́ние; **they are out of the ~ for the Cup** они́ вы́были из соревнова́ний на ку́бок; **he is in the ~ for Prime Minister** он мо́жет стать премье́р-мини́стром. **4.** (*operation*) управле́ние (*чем*), эксплуата́ция.

adj. **1.** (*performed while ~*) бегу́щий; **he took a ~ kick at the ball** он уда́рил мяч с разбе́га; **~ jump** прыжо́к с разбе́га; **~ fight** отхо́д с боя́ми. **2.** (*performed while events proceed*) теку́щий; **~ commentary** репорта́ж (по хо́ду де́йствия). **3.** (*continuous*) непреры́вный; **a ~ fire of questions** непреры́вный пото́к вопро́сов. **4.** (*in succession*) подря́д, кря́ду; **he won three times ~** он вы́играл три ра́за подря́д. **5.** (*flowing*): **~ water** (*in nature*) прото́чная вода́; (*domestic*) водопрово́д; **hot and cold ~ water** горя́чая и холо́дная вода́; (*oozing liquid*) гноя́щийся, слезя́щийся; **a ~ sore** гноя́щаяся боля́чка; **a ~ nose** сопли́вый нос, на́сморк. **6.** (*sliding*) скользя́щий; **a ~ knot** затяжно́й у́зел.

cpd. **~-board** *n.* подно́жка.

runny [ˈrʌnɪ] *adj.* теку́чий, жи́дкий; **a ~ egg** жи́дкое яйцо́; **a ~ nose** мо́крый нос, на́сморк.

runt [rʌnt] *n.* (*undersized animal*) низкоро́слое живо́тное; (*of pers.*, *pej.*) ка́рлик.

rupee [ruːˈpiː] *n.* ру́пия.

rupture [ˈrʌptʃə(r)] *n.* **1.** (*breaking*, *bursting*) проры́в; перело́м. **2.** (*hernia*) гры́жа. **3.** (*breach*, *quarrel*) разры́в, разла́д.

v.t. **1.** (*burst*, *break*) прор|ыва́ть, -ва́ть; **he ~d a blood-vessel** он повреди́л кровено́сный сосу́д. **2. ~ o.s.** над|рыва́ться, -орва́ться. **3.** (*sever*) пор|ыва́ть, -ва́ть; **their relationship was ~d** они́ порва́ли вся́кие отноше́ния.

v.i. раз|рыва́ться, -орва́ться; прекра|ща́ться, -ти́ться.

rural [ˈrʊər(ə)l] *adj.* се́льский; **~ dean** благочи́нный.

ruse [ruːz] *n.* уло́вка, ухищре́ние.

rush[1] [rʌʃ] *n.* (*bot.*) тростни́к.

cpd. **~light** *n.* лучи́на.

rush[2] [rʌʃ] *n.* **1.** (*precipitate movement*) стреми́тельное движе́ние; **the ~ of water** пото́к/напо́р воды́; **a ~ of blood to the head** прили́в кро́ви к голове́; **he made a ~ for the goal** он бро́сился к воро́там; (*bustle*) спе́шка; (*increase in activity*, *buying etc.*): **a ~ of business** оживле́ние в торго́вле; **the Christmas ~** предрожде́ственская суета́/су́толока; **the gold ~** золота́я лихора́дка; **a ~ job** спе́шная рабо́та; **in the ~ hour** в часы́ пик. **2.** (*first print of film*) отсня́тый материа́л, (*in pl.*) «пото́ки» (*m. pl.*).

v.t. **1.** (*speed*, *hurry*) торопи́ть, по-; **troops were ~ed to the front** войска́ бы́ли сро́чно перебро́шены на фронт; **a doctor was ~ed to the scene** на ме́сто происше́ствия сро́чно доста́вили врача́; **the order was ~ed through** зака́з бы́стро проверну́ли; **I refuse to be ~ed into a decision** я отка́зываюсь принима́ть реше́ние в спе́шке; **I was ~ed off my feet** (*exhausted*) я сби́лся с ног; (**~ed into sth.**) мне заморо́чили го́лову; **I must ~ off a letter** я до́лжен бы́стренько настрочи́ть письмо́. **2.** (*charge*) брать, взять шту́рмом; **they ~ed the enemy lines** они́ захвати́ли вра́жеские пози́ции стреми́тельным нати́ском; **the audience ~ed the platform** пу́блика хлы́нула на эстра́ду; **he ~ed the fence** он сли́шком стреми́тельно взял барье́р. **3.** (*charge in money*): **how much did they ~ you for that?** ско́лько с вас содра́ли за э́то? (*coll.*).

v.i. мча́ться, по-; бр|оса́ться, -о́ситься; кида́ться, ки́нуться; **she is always ~ing about** она́ ве́чно но́сится; она́ ве́чно в бега́х; **he ~ed after me** он бро́сился за мной; **the train ~ed by** по́езд промча́лся ми́мо; **he ~ed in and out** он заскочи́л на мину́тку; **he ~ed into print** он поспеши́л напеча́таться; **she ~ed off without saying goodbye** она́ убежа́ла, не попроща́вшись; **they ~ed to congratulate her** они́ бро́сились её поздравля́ть; **the blood ~ed to her face** кровь бро́силась ей в лицо́; **don't ~ to conclusions** не де́лайте поспе́шных вы́водов; **a ~ing wind** поры́вистый ве́тер.

rusk [rʌsk] *n.* суха́рь (*m.*).

russet ['rʌsɪt] *adj.* краснова́то-кори́чневый.

Russia ['rʌʃə] *n.* Росси́я; **Holy ~** Святая Русь.

Russian ['rʌʃ(ə)n] *n.* **1.** (*pers. of Russ. nationality*) ру́сск|ий (*fem.* -ая); (*pers. of Russ. citizenship*) россия́н|ин (*fem.* -ка); **the ~s** ру́сские (*pl.*). **2.** (*language*) ру́сский язы́к; **do you speak ~?** вы говори́те по-ру́сски?

adj. ру́сский; (*pol., hist., also*) росси́йский; **~ studies** руси́стика; **~ salad** винегре́т; сала́т-оливье́ (*indecl.*); **~ wolfhound** ру́сская борза́я.

cpd. **~-speaking** *adj.* русскоязы́чный; зна́ющий/изучи́вший ру́сский язы́к; владе́ющий ру́сским языко́м.

Russianize ['rʌʃənaɪz] *v.t.* русифици́ровать (*impf., pf.*).

Russicism [rʌsɪ'sɪz(ə)m] *n.* руси́зм.

Russification ['rʌsɪfɪ'keɪʃ(ə)n] *n.* русифика́ция.

Russify ['rʌsɪˌfaɪ] *v.t.* русифици́ровать (*impf., pf.*).

Russo-Japanese ['rʌsəʊˌdʒæpə'ni:z] *adj.*: **~ War** ру́сско-япо́нская война́.

Russophile ['rʌsəʊˌfaɪl] *n.* русофи́л (*fem.* -ка).

Russophobia [ˌrʌsəʊ'fəʊbɪə] *n.* русофо́бия.

rust [rʌst] *n.* (*on metal; plant disease*) ржа́вчина.

v.t. покр|ыва́ть, -ы́ть ржа́вчиной.

v.i. ржа́веть, за-; покр|ыва́ться, -ы́ться ржа́вчиной.

cpd. **~-proof** *adj.* нержаве́ющий.

rustic ['rʌstɪk] *n.* деревéнский жи́тель, деревéнщина (*c.g.*).

adj. (*countrified*) деревéнский, сéльский; (*unrefined*) неотёсанный, гру́бый; (*of rough workmanship*) гру́бо срабо́танный; **a ~ bridge** мост из нетёсаного лéса.

rusticate ['rʌstɪˌkeɪt] *v.t.* (*suspend*) врéменно исключа́ть (*impf.*) (*студента из университета*); (*archit.*) рустова́ть (*impf.*).

rustication [ˌrʌstɪ'keɪʃ(ə)n] *n.* (*suspension*) врéменное исключéние (студéнта из университéта); (*archit.*) рустóвка.

rusticity [rʌs'tɪsɪtɪ] *n.* деревéнские обы́чаи (*m. pl.*); простота́; неотёсанность.

rustiness ['rʌstɪnɪs] *n.* ржа́вчина; (*fig.*) отста́лость; (*hoarseness*) хри́плость.

rustle ['rʌs(ə)l] *n.* шéлест, шóрох.

v.t. **1.** (*cause to ~*) шелестéть (*impf.*) +*i.*; шурша́ть (*impf.*) +*i.*; **don't ~ the newspaper** не шелести́те газéтой. **2.** (*US sl., steal*) красть, у-. **3.: ~ up** (*coll.*) разы́ск|ивать, -а́ть; **can you ~ up some food?** вы мóжете раздобы́ть чегó-нибу́дь поéсть?

v.i. шелестéть (*impf.*); шурша́ть (*impf.*).

rustler ['rʌslə(r)] *n.* (*US*) конокра́д; вор, угоня́ющий скот.

rustless ['rʌstlɪs] *adj.* нержавéющий.

rusty ['rʌstɪ] *adj.* ржа́вый, заржа́вленный; (*fig.*): **his dinner-jacket was ~ with age** егó смóкинг порыжéл от ста́рости; (*out of practice*): **my German is ~** я подзабы́л немéцкий; (*hoarse*): **his voice was ~** у негó был скрипу́чий/хри́плый гóлос.

rut[1] [rʌt] *n.* (*wheel-track*) колея́, вы́боина; (*fig.*) рути́на; **it is easy to get into a ~** легкó погря́знуть в рути́не.

v.t.: **a deeply ~ted road** дорóга, изры́тая глубóкими колея́ми.

rut[2] [rʌt] *n.* (*sexual excitement*) гон; **in ~** в охóте.

v.i. быть в охóте; **the ~ting season** врéмя спа́ривания/слу́чки.

Ruth [ru:θ] *n.* (*bibl.*) Руфь.

Ruthenia [ru:'θi:nɪə] *n.* (*hist.*) Малорóссия; **Subcarpathian ~** Подкарпа́тская Русь.

Ruthenian [ru:'θi:nɪən] *n.* руси́н (*fem.* -ка).

adj. руси́нский.

ruthenium [ru:'θi:nɪəm] *n.* рутéний.

ruthless ['ru:θlɪs] *adj.* безжа́лостный, жестóкий.

ruthlessness ['ru:θlɪsnɪs] *n.* безжа́лостность, жестóкость.

Rwanda [rʊ'ændə] *n.* Руа́нда.

rye [raɪ] *n.* рожь; **~ bread** ржанóй хлеб; **(~ whisky)** ржанóе ви́ски (*indecl.*).

S

Saar [sɑ:(r)] *n.* Саа́р; **~land** Саа́рская óбласть.

sabbath ['sæbəθ] *n.* **1.** (*Jewish*) суббóта; (*Christian*) воскресéнье. **2. witches' ~** шаба́ш ведьм.

sabbatical [sə'bætɪk(ə)l] *n.* (**~** *year, term*) *see adj.*

adj. **1.** суббóтний; воскрéсный. **2.: ~ leave** твóрческий/академи́ческий óтпуск.

Sabine ['sæbaɪn] *n.*: **Rape of the ~s** похищéние сабиня́нок.

sable[1] ['seɪb(ə)l] *n.* (*zool.*) сóболь (*m.*); (*fur*) сóболь, собóлий мех.

adj. собóлий, соболи́ный.

sable[2] ['seɪb(ə)l] (*liter.*) *n.* (*colour*) чёрный цвет.

adj. чёрный, воронóй; (*funereal*) мра́чный, тра́урный.

sabot ['sæbəʊt, 'sæbəʊ] *n.* деревя́нный башма́к, сабó (*indecl.*).

sabotage ['sæbəˌtɑ:ʒ] *n.* саботáж, дивéрсия, вреди́тельство; **acts of ~** диверсиóнные а́кты.

v.t. саботи́ровать (*impf., pf.*); (*damage*) повре|жда́ть, -ди́ть; (*fig., disrupt*) срыва́ть, сорва́ть.

saboteur [ˌsæbə'tɜ:(r)] *n.* саботáжник, диверса́нт, вреди́тель (*m.*).

sabre ['seɪbə(r)] *n.* са́бля; (*fencing*) эспадрóн.

v.t. руби́ть (*impf.*) са́блей.

cpds. **~-cut** *n.* (*blow*) са́бельный уда́р; (*wound, scar*) са́бельная ра́на; **~-fencer** *n.* сабли́ст; **~-rattling** *n.* (*fig.*) бряца́ние ору́жием; **~-toothed** *adj.* саблезу́бый.

sabretache ['sæbəˌtæʃ] *n.* та́шка.

sac [sæk] *n.* (*biol.*) мешóчек, су́мка; (*med.*) киста́, мешóчек.

saccharin ['sækərɪn] *n.* сахари́н.

saccharine ['sækəˌri:n] *adj.* са́харный, сахари́стый; (*fig.*) слаща́вый, при́торный.

sacerdotal [ˌsækə'dəʊt(ə)l] *adj.* свящéннический, жрéческий.

sachet ['sæʃeɪ] *n.* сашé (*indecl.*).

sack[1] [sæk] *n.* **1.** (*bag*) мешóк; (**~** *dress*) сак. **2.** (*coll., dismissal*): **get the ~** быть увóленным; получ|а́ть, -и́ть расчёт; **give s.o. the ~** ув|ольня́ть, -óлить когó-н.; рассчи́т|ывать, -а́ть когó-н. **3.** (*US, bed*): **hit the ~** отпр|авля́ться, -а́виться на боковую (*coll.*).

v.t. **1.** (*put into ~s; also* **~ up**) нас|ыпа́ть, -ы́пать в мешки́. **2.** (*coll., dismiss*) рассчи́т|ывать, -а́ть.

cpds. **~cloth** *n.* мешкови́на; (*hair shirt*) власяни́ца; **wear ~cloth and ashes** (*fig.*) посыпа́ть (*impf.*) пéплом главу́; ка́яться (*impf.*); **~-race** *n.* бег в мешка́х.

sack[2] [sæk] *n.* (*plundering*) разграблéние.

v.t. (*also* **put to ~**) гра́бить, раз-; пред|ава́ть, -а́ть разграблéнию; отд|ава́ть, -а́ть на разграблéние.

sack[3] [sæk] *n.* (*hist., wine*) испа́нское бéлое сухóе винó.

sackful ['sækfʊl] *n.* пóлный мешóк (*чего*); **by the ~** (цéлыми) мешка́ми.

sacking ['sækɪŋ] *n.* (*text.*) мешкови́на, дерю́га.

sacral ['seɪkr(ə)l] *adj.* (*anat.*) крестцо́вый; (*relig.*) обря́довый, ритуа́льный.

sacrament ['sækrəmənt] *n.* **1.** (*sacred act or rite*) та́инство. **2.** (*Eucharist*): **the Holy S~** свято́е прича́стие; святы́е дары́ (*m. pl.*); те́ло Госпо́дне; **take, receive the ~** прича|ща́ться, -сти́ться. **3.** (*oath*) кля́тва, обе́т.

sacramental [ˌsækrə'ment(ə)l] *adj.* сакрамента́льный; **~ wine** вино́ для прича́стия.

sacred ['seɪkrɪd] *adj.* свяще́нный, свято́й; **~ books** свяще́нные кни́ги; **~ music** духо́вная му́зыка; **~ duty** свяще́нный долг; **nothing is ~ to him** для него́ нет ничего́ свято́го; **~ cow** (*fig.*) (неприкоснове́нная) святы́ня; **~ to the memory of my wife** незабве́нной па́мяти моей́ супру́ги.

sacredness ['seɪkrɪdnɪs] *n.* свя́тость.

sacrifice ['sækrɪˌfaɪs] *n.* (*lit.*, *fig.*) же́ртва; (*act of relig. ~*) жертвоприноше́ние; **make a ~ of sth.** прин|оси́ть, -ести́ что-н. в же́ртву; же́ртвовать, по- чем-н.; **they made ~s for their children** они́ мно́гим же́ртвовали ра́ди дете́й; **at the ~ of his health** же́ртвуя здоро́вьем, в уще́рб со́бственному здоро́вью; **at the ~ of one's principles** поступи́вшись свои́ми при́нципами; **he sold his house at a ~** он про́дал свой дом с убы́тками.

v.t. (*lit.*, *at altar*) прин|оси́ть, -ести́ (*кого/что*) в же́ртву; (*give up*, *surrender*) же́ртвовать, по- +*i.*; **he ~d truth to his own interests** он принёс и́стину в же́ртву свои́м интере́сам.

sacrificial [ˌsækrɪ'fɪʃ(ə)l] *adj.* же́ртвенный.

sacrilege ['sækrɪlɪdʒ] *n.* святота́тство, кощу́нство.

sacrilegious [ˌsækrɪ'lɪdʒəs] *adj.* святота́тственный, кощу́нственный.

sacristan ['sækrɪst(ə)n] *n.* ри́зничий.

sacristy ['sækrɪstɪ] *n.* ри́зница.

sacrosanct ['sækrəʊˌsæŋkt] *adj.* свяще́нный, неприкоснове́нный.

sacrum ['seɪkrəm] *n.* кресте́ц.

sad [sæd] *adj.* **1.** гру́стный, печа́льный; **I feel ~** мне гру́стно; **with a ~ heart** с тяжёлым се́рдцем; **a ~ event** печа́льное собы́тие; **it is ~ to hear you say that** приско́рбно э́то слы́шать; (*regrettable*, *lamentable*) приско́рбный; **it is ~ that you failed the exams** о́чень жаль, что вы провали́лись на экза́менах; **a ~ mistake** доса́дная оши́бка; **he came to a ~ end** он пло́хо ко́нчил. **2.** (*liter.*): **he is a ~ rascal** он неисправи́мый пове́са; **he writes ~ stuff** он пи́шет ужа́сно пло́хо/скве́рно. **3.** (*fig.*, *of colours*) ту́склый, серова́тый. **4.: you are ~ly mistaken** вы жесто́ко ошиба́етесь; **the garden was ~ly neglected** сад был доне́льзя запу́щен.

sadden ['sæd(ə)n] *v.t.* печа́лить, о-.

saddle ['sæd(ə)l] *n.* **1.** седло́; (*of shaft horse's harness*) седёлка; **be in the ~** (*lit.*) е́хать верхо́м; (*fig.*, *in control*) верхово́дить (*impf.*). **2.** (*of animal's back*) седлови́на, (*as meat*) седло́. **3.** (*in hills*) седлови́на.

v.t. **1.** седла́ть, о-. **2.** (*fig.*, *burden with task*, *guilt etc.*): **~ s.o. with sth.** взва́л|ивать, -и́ть что-н. на кого́-н. (*or* на ше́ю кому́-н.); **he was ~d with his relatives** он был обременён ро́дственниками; у него́ на ше́е сиде́ли ро́дственники.

cpds. **~back** *n.* (*geog.*) седлови́на; **~-bag** *n.* седе́льный вьюк; **~-blanket** *n.* потни́к; **~-bow** *n.* седе́льная лу́ка; **~-cloth** *n.* чепра́к; **~-girth** *n.* подпру́га; **~-horse** *n.* верхова́я ло́шадь; **~-strap** *n.* вью́чный реме́нь.

saddler ['sædlə(r)] *n.* седе́льник, шо́рник.

saddlery ['sædlərɪ] *n.* (*activity*) шо́рное де́ло, шо́рничество; (*workshop*) шо́рная мастерска́я.

Sadducee ['sædjʊˌsiː] *n.* саддуке́й.

sadism ['seɪdɪz(ə)m] *n.* сади́зм.

sadist ['seɪdɪst] *n.* сади́ст (*fem.* -ка).

sadistic [sə'dɪstɪk] *adj.* сади́стский.

sadness ['sædnɪs] *n.* грусть, печа́ль, тоска́; **a look of ~** печа́льный вид.

s.a.e. (*abbr. of* ***stamped addressed envelope***) конве́рт с ма́ркой и обра́тным а́дресом.

safari [sə'fɑːrɪ] *n.* сафа́ри (*nt. indecl.*); охо́тничья экспеди́ция; **on ~** на охо́те; **~ park** «сафа́ри» зоопа́рк.

safe[1] [seɪf] *n.* сейф; несгора́емый шкаф/я́щик; (*meat-~*) холоди́льник.

safe[2] [seɪf] *adj.* **1.** (*affording security*, *not dangerous*) безопа́сный; (*reliable*) надёжный; **put the money in a ~ place!** спря́чьте де́ньги в надёжное ме́сто!; **in ~ custody** под надёжной охра́ной; **in s.o.'s ~ keeping** у кого́-н. на сохране́нии; **is it ~ to leave him (alone)?** не опа́сно/стра́шно его́ оставля́ть одного́?; **to be on the ~ side** на вся́кий слу́чай, для (бо́льшей) ве́рности; **is she ~ on a bicycle?** не стра́шно ей дове́рить велосипе́д?; **is the dog ~ with children?** де́тям не опа́сно игра́ть с э́той соба́кой? **2.** (*free from danger*): **we are ~ from attack** мы мо́жем не опаса́ться нападе́ния; **he is ~ from his enemies** он недосяга́ем для враго́в; **three inoculations will make you ~** три приви́вки — и вы бу́дете в по́лной безопа́сности; **we are ~ as houses here** мы здесь как за ка́менной стено́й; **perfectly ~** в по́лной сохра́нности; (*unhurt*, *undamaged*): **we saw them home ~ and sound** мы доста́вили их домо́й це́лыми и невреди́мыми (*or* в це́лости и сохра́нности). **3.** (*cautious*, *moderate*) осторо́жный; **better ~ than sorry** бережёного (и) Бог бережёт; **I decided to play ~** я реши́л не рискова́ть. **4.** (*certain*): **he is a ~ winner** он наверняка́ вы́играет; у него́ ве́рный вы́игрыш; **it's a ~ bet** мо́жно быть уве́ренным.

cpds. **~-conduct** *n.* (*document*) охра́нная гра́мота; **~-deposit** *n.* храни́лище с се́йфами; **~guard** *n.* охра́на, страхо́вка, гара́нтия (от+*g.*); *v.t.* гаранти́ровать (*impf.*, *pf.*); охран|я́ть, -и́ть.

safely ['seɪflɪ] *adv.* **1.** (*unharmed*) благополу́чно, в сохра́нности; **the parcel arrived ~** посы́лка пришла́ в це́лости и сохра́нности (*or* неповреждённой). **2.** (*for safety*): **I put the bottle ~ away** я убра́л буты́лку от беды́/греха́ пода́льше. **3.** (*by a safe margin*): **they won the match ~** они́ вы́играли матч с лёгкостью. **4.** (*with confidence*): **I can ~ say that ...** я могу́ с уве́ренностью сказа́ть, что...

safeness ['seɪfnɪs] *n.* (*security*): **a feeling of ~** чу́вство безопа́сности; (*of building*, *investment etc.*) надёжность.

safety ['seɪftɪ] *n.* безопа́сность; **endanger s.o.'s ~** грози́ть/угрожа́ть (*both impf.*) чьей-н. безопа́сности; рискова́ть (*impf.*) безопа́сностью кого́-н.; подверга́ть (*impf.*) кого́-н. опа́сности; **our ~ was threatened** на́ша безопа́сность была́ под угро́зой; **they sought ~ in flight** они́ пыта́лись спасти́сь бе́гством; **there is ~ in numbers** ≃ на миру́ и смерть красна́; безопа́снее де́йствовать сообща́; **~ first** осторо́жность пре́жде всего́; **play for ~** избега́ть (*impf.*) ри́ска; **road ~** безопа́сность у́личного движе́ния; безопа́сность движе́ния по доро́гам; **~ curtain** (*theatr.*) противопожа́рный за́навес; **~ factor** коэффицие́нт безопа́сности; **~ film** безопа́сная (невоспламеня́ющаяся) киноплёнка; **~ glass** безоско́лочное стекло́; **~ lamp** (*mining*) ру́дничная ла́мпа; **~ measures, precautions** ме́ры безопа́сности; **~ match** (безопа́сная) спи́чка; **~ net** страхо́вочная се́тка; **~ razor** безопа́сная бри́тва.

cpds. **~-belt** *n.* привязно́й реме́нь; **~-catch** *n.* (*on gun etc.*) предохрани́тель (*m.*); **~-fuse** *n.* (*for explosive*) огнепрово́дный шнур; (*elec.*) (пла́вкий) предохрани́тель (*m.*); **~-pin** *n.* англи́йская була́вка; **~-valve** *n.* предохрани́тельный кла́пан; (*fig.*): **rowing provided a ~-valve for his energies** заня́тия гре́блей дава́ли вы́ход его́ эне́ргии.

saffron ['sæfrən] *n.* (*substance*) шафра́н; (*colour*) шафра́нный/шафра́новый цвет.

adj. шафра́нный, шафра́новый.

sag [sæg] *n.* (*of gate etc.*) оседа́ние, переко́с; (*of ceiling*) проги́б.

v.i. (*of gate etc.*) ос|еда́ть, -е́сть; покоси́ться (*pf.*); (*of rope*, *curtain*) пров|иса́ть, -и́снуть; (*of ladder*, *ceiling*) прог|иба́ться, -ну́ться; **the ceiling ~s in the middle** потоло́к прови́с посереди́не; (*of garment*) отв|иса́ть, -и́снуть; (*of cheeks*, *breasts*) обв|иса́ть, -и́снуть; **a ~ging chin** отви́слый подборо́док; (*fig.*, *of prices*) па́дать, упа́сть.

saga ['sɑːgə] *n.* са́га; (*fig.*): **he told me the ~ of his escape** он пове́дал мне (фантасти́ческую) исто́рию своего́ побе́га.

sagacious [sə'geɪʃ(ə)s] *adj.* **1.** (*of pers.*) му́дрый, здравомы́слящий; (*of animal*) у́мный. **2.** (*perspicacious*) проница́тельный, прозорли́вый; (*of action*: *far-sighted*) дальнови́дный, му́дрый.

sagacity [sə'gæsɪtɪ] *n.* му́дрость, здравомы́слие, ум; проница́тельность, прозорли́вость; дальнови́дность.

sage[1] [seɪdʒ] *n.* **1.** (*bot.*) шалфе́й. **2.** (~ **green**) сeroва́то-зелёный цвет.

sage[2] [seɪdʒ] *n.* (*wise man*) мудре́ц.
adj. му́дрый; (*iron.*) глубокомы́сленный.

Sagittarius [,sædʒɪ'teərɪəs] *n.* Стреле́ц.

sago ['seɪgəʊ] *n.* са́го (*indecl.*); ~ **palm** са́говая па́льма.

Sahara [sə'hɑːrə] *n.* Саха́ра; (*fig.*) пусты́ня.

sahib [sɑːb, 'sɑːhɪb] *n.* (*arch.*) господи́н; джентльме́н.

sail [seɪl] *n.* **1.** па́рус; **hoist** ~ ста́вить, по- (*or* подн|има́ть, -я́ть) паруса́; **lower the** ~**s** спус|ка́ть, -ти́ть паруса́; **under** ~ под паруса́ми; **in full** ~ на всех паруса́х; **get under** (*or* **set**) ~ вы́йти (*pf.*) в пла́вание; **make, set** ~ **for** отпр|авля́ться, -а́виться к+*d.* (*or* в+*a.*); **take in** (*or* **shorten**) ~ (*lit.*) уб|авля́ть, -а́вить паруса́; (*fig.*) ограни́чи|вать, -ть свои́ стремле́ния; **carry** ~ нести́ (*det.*) паруса́; **crowd** ~ форси́ровать (*impf.*, *pf.*) паруса́ми; **strike** ~ убра́ть (*pf.*) паруса́. **2.** (*ship*): **there wasn't a** ~ **in sight** не́ было ви́дно ни одного́ су́дна/корабля́. **3.** (*collect.*): **a fleet of 50** ~ флот из пяти́десяти (па́русных) корабле́й. **4.** (*voyage or excursion on water*) пла́вание; **go for a** ~ отпр|авля́ться, -а́виться в пла́вание; **it is 7 days'** ~ **from here** э́то в семи́ днях пла́вания отсю́да. **5.** (*of windmill*) крыло́. **6.** (*dorsal fin*) спинно́й плавни́к.
v.t. **1.** (*of pers. or ship, travel over*) пла́вать (*indet.*); плыть, про- (*det.*) по+*d.*; **he has** ~**ed the seven seas** он исходи́л все моря́ (и океа́ны); **we** ~**ed 150 miles** мы проплы́ли/прошли́ 150 миль. **2.** (*control navigation of*) управля́ть (*impf.*) +*i.*; ~ **toy boats** пуска́ть (*impf.*) кора́блики.
v.i. **1.** пл|а́вать (*indet.*), -ыть (*det.*), поплы́ть (*pf.*); **the new yacht** ~**s well** у но́вой я́хты хоро́ший ход; ~ **close to the wind** (*lit.*) идти́/плыть (*det.*) кру́то к ве́тру; (*fig.*) вступ|а́ть, -и́ть на опа́сный путь; **the ship** ~**ed into harbour** кора́бль вошёл в га́вань (*or* пришёл в порт); **we** ~**ed out to sea** мы вы́шли в мо́ре; **they** ~**ed up the coast** они́ плы́ли вдоль бе́рега. **2.** (*start a voyage*) отпл|ыва́ть, -ы́ть; (*of freight*): **the goods** ~**ed from London yesterday** това́р был отпра́влен из Ло́ндона вчера́. **3.** (*fig.*, *move gracefully*, *smoothly*) плыть (*impf.*); пла́вно дви́гаться (*impf.*); пропл|ыва́ть, -ы́ть; **he** ~**ed through** (*made light work of*) **the exams** он с лёгкостью (*or* без труда́) вы́держал экза́мены; ~ **into** (*coll.*, *attack*) набр|а́сываться, -о́ситься на+*a.*; обру́ши|ваться, -ться на+*a.* **4.** (*of birds*) пари́ть (*impf.*); (*of clouds*) нести́сь (*det.*); **the clouds** ~**ed by** проноси́лись облака́.
cpds. ~**cloth** *n.* паруси́на; ~**-maker** *n.* па́русный ма́стер; ~**plane** *n.* планёр.

sailboard ['seɪlbɔːd] *n.* виндсёрфер, доска́ под па́русом.

sailboarder ['seɪlbɔːdə(r)] *n.* виндсёрфинги́ст.

sailboarding ['seɪlbɔːdɪŋ] *n.* виндсёрфинг.

sailer ['seɪlə(r)] *n.*: **a fast, good** ~ быстрохо́дное су́дно; хоро́ший ходо́к.

sailing ['seɪlɪŋ] *n.* **1.** (*act of* ~) (море)пла́вание; (*navigation*) морехо́дство, судохо́дство; (*directing a vessel*) кораблевожде́ние; (*as sport*) па́русный спорт. **2.** (*departure*) отхо́д, отплы́тие; (*voyage*) рейс; **list of** ~**s** расписа́ние парохо́дного движе́ния; ~ **orders** прика́з о вы́ходе в мо́ре. **3.** (*fig.*, *progress*): **it was plain** ~ всё шло как по ма́слу.
cpds. ~**-boat** *n.* па́русная ло́дка; ~**-master** *n.* шту́рман; ~**-ship** *n.* па́русное су́дно, па́русник.

sailor ['seɪlə(r)] *n.* **1.** (*seaman*) моря́к, матро́с; морепла́ватель (*m.*), морехо́д; ~**'s cap** (матро́сская) бескозы́рка; ~**s' home** общежи́тие/гости́ница для матро́сов; ~ **jacket** матро́ска. **2.: he is a bad** ~ он пло́хо перено́сит ка́чку (на мо́ре).

sailoring ['seɪlərɪŋ] *n.* морска́я слу́жба.

sailorly ['seɪləlɪ] *adj.* подоба́ющий моряку́.

sainfoin ['seɪnfɔɪn, 'sæn-] *n.* эспарце́т.

saint [seɪnt, sənt] *n.* свято́й, пра́ведник; **my** ~**'s day** мои́ имени́н|ы (*pl.*, *g.* —); **patron** ~ свято́й покрови́тель (*fem.* свята́я покрови́тельница); засту́пни|к (*fem.* -ца); **it's enough to try the patience of a** ~ э́то и а́нгела из терпе́ния вы́ведет; **S**~ **Bernard** (*dog*) сенберна́р; **S**~ **John's wort** зверобо́й; **S**~ **Helena** о́стров свято́й Еле́ны; **S**~ **Kitts** Сент-Кри́стофер; **S**~ **Lawrence river** река́ свято́го Лавре́нтия; **S**~ **Louis** (*city*) Сент-Лу́ис; **S**~ **Lucia** Сент-Люси́я; **S**~ **Petersburg** Санкт-Петербу́рг; **S**~ **Valentine's Day** день свято́го Валенти́на; **S**~ **Vitus's dance** пля́ска свято́го Ви́та; **All S**~**s (Day)** пра́здник всех святы́х.
cpd. ~**like** *adj.* свято́й, а́нгельский.

sainthood ['seɪnthʊd] *n.* свя́тость.

saintliness ['seɪntlɪnɪs] *n.* свя́тость, безгре́шность.

saintly ['seɪntlɪ] *adj.* свято́й; безгре́шный.

St Petersburg [sənt' piːtəz,bɜːg] *n.* Санкт-Петербу́рг; (*attr.*) (санкт-)петербу́ргский.

St Petersburger [sənt' piːtəz,bɜːgə(r)] *n.* (санкт-)петербу́рж|ец (*fem.* -а́нка).

sake[1] [seɪk] *n.*: **for the** ~ **of** ра́ди+*g.*; **for God's, heaven's, goodness** ~ ра́ди Бо́га (*or* всего́ свято́го); **for one's own** ~ для себя́; из-за себя́ самого́; **for all our** ~**s** ра́ди нас всех; **he was persecuted for the** ~ **of his opinions** его́ пресле́довали за убежде́ния; **art for art's** ~ иску́сство для иску́сства; **for old times'** ~ в па́мять про́шлого; **he talks for the** ~ **of talking** он говори́т так про́сто, чтоб поболта́ть.

sake[2] ['sɑːkɪ] *n.* (*Japanese drink*) сакэ́ (*nt. indecl.*).

Sakhalin [,sæxə'liːn] *n.* Сахали́н.

salaam [sə'lɑːm] *n.* селя́м.

salable ['seɪləb(ə)l] = **sal(e)able**

salacious [sə'leɪʃəs] *adj.* (*indecent*) непристо́йный.

salacity [sə'læsɪtɪ] *n.* непристо́йность.

salad ['sæləd] *n.* **1.** сала́т; **fruit** ~ фру́кты в сиро́пе; **Russian** ~ винегре́т; сала́т-оливье́ (*indecl.*). **2.** (*fig.*): **in my** ~ **days** в по́ру мое́й ра́нней ю́ности; когда́ я был зелёным юнцо́м.
cpds. ~**-bowl** *n.* сала́тница; ~**-dressing** *n.* запра́вка (к сала́ту); ~**-oil** *n.* оли́вковое/прова́нское ма́сло.

salamander ['sælə,mændə(r)] *n.* салама́ндра.

salami [sə'lɑːmɪ] *n.* копчёная колбаса́; саля́ми (*f. indecl.*).

sal ammoniac [,sæl ə'məʊnɪ,æk] *n.* нашаты́рь (*m.*).

salaried ['sælərɪd] *adj.* (*pers.*) слу́жащий; (*post*) опла́чиваемый.

salary ['sælərɪ] *n.* окла́д, зарпла́та.

sale [seɪl] *n.* **1.** прода́жа, сбыт; **be on, for** ~ име́ться (*impf.*) в прода́же; **'house for** ~**'** (*as notice*) «продаётся дом»; **he found a quick, ready** ~ **for his work** он нашёл для свои́х изде́лий хоро́ший ры́нок сбы́та; **put up for** ~ выставля́ть, вы́ставить на прода́жу; **the** ~**s were enormous** спрос был колосса́льный; **cash** ~ прода́жа за нали́чный расчёт; **there is no** ~ **for these goods** на э́ти това́ры нет спро́са; ~ (*selling*) **price** прода́жная цена́; ~**s clerk** (*US*, *shop assistant*) продав|е́ц (*fem.* -щи́ца); ~**s department** отде́л сбы́та; ~**s manager** ме́неджер по сбы́ту; ~**s talk** рекла́ма, реклами́рование; ~**s tax** нало́г на про́данный това́р. **2.** (*event*): **auction** ~ прода́жа с аукцио́на; (*clearance* ~) распрода́жа; ~ (*reduced*) **price** сни́женная цена́, цена́ со ски́дкой.
cpds. ~**-room** *n.* аукцио́нный зал; ~**sgirl,** ~**slady** *nn.* = ~**swoman;** ~**sman** *n.* (*in shop*) продаве́ц; (*travelling door-to-door*) коммивояжёр; торго́вый аге́нт; ~**smanship** *n.* уме́ние/иску́сство продава́ть; ~**swoman,** ~**slady,** ~**sgirl** *nn.* (*in shop*) продавщи́ца.

sal(e)able ['seɪləb(ə)l] *adj.* хо́дкий.

Salic ['sælɪk, 'seɪ-] *adj.* сали́ческий; ~ **law** Сали́ческая пра́вда.

salicylic [,sælɪ'sɪlɪk] *adj.* салици́ловый.

salient ['seɪlɪənt] *n.* (*in fortifications*) вы́ступ; (*in line of attack or defence*) вы́ступ, клин.
adj. (*jutting out*) выдаю́щийся, выступа́ющий; (*fig.*) выдаю́щийся, вы́пуклый, я́ркий.

saline ['seɪlaɪn] *n.* (*marsh etc.*) солонча́к; (*solution*) соляно́й раство́р; (*med.*) физиологи́ческий раство́р.
adj. солёный, соляно́й; ~ **spring** солёный исто́чник; ~ **baths** соляны́е ва́нны; ~ **solution** соляно́й раство́р.

salinity [səˈlɪnɪtɪ] *n.* солёность.
saliva [səˈlaɪvə] *n.* слюна́.
salivary [səˈlaɪvərɪ, ˈsælɪvərɪ] *adj.* слю́нный.
salivate [ˈsælɪˌveɪt] *v.i.* выделя́ть, вы́делить слюну́.
salivation [ˌsælɪˈveɪʃ(ə)n] *n.* слюнотече́ние.
sallow[1] [ˈsæləʊ] *n.* (*bot.*) и́ва, раки́та.
sallow[2] [ˈsæləʊ] *adj.* боле́зненно-жёлтый; оли́вковый.
sallowness [ˈsæləʊnɪs] *n.* желтизна́; оли́вковый цвет.
sally [ˈsælɪ] *n.* **1.** (*mil.*) вы́лазка; (*fig., excursion*) прогу́лка, экску́рсия, похо́д. **2.** (*witty remark*) остро́та, остроу́мная вы́ходка, ре́плика.
v.i.: ~ **forth, out** (*mil.*) де́лать, с- вы́лазку; (*fig.*) отпр|авля́ться, -а́виться.
salmon [ˈsæmən] *n.* лосо́сь (*m.*); сёмга; ~ **trout** тайме́нь (*m.*); ку́мжа.
adj. **1.** лососёвый. **2.** (*colour*) ора́нжево-ро́зовый; цве́та сомо́н.
salon [ˈsælɒn, -lɔ̃] *n.* сало́н, ателье́ (*indecl.*).
saloon [səˈluːn] *n.* (*on ship*) сало́н, каю́т-компа́ния; **billiard** ~ билья́рдная; ~ **(bar)** бар; ~ **(car)** седа́н.
salsify [ˈsælsɪfɪ, -ˌfaɪ] *n.* козлоборо́дник.
SALT[1] [sɔːlt, sɒlt] *n.* (*abbr. of* ***Strategic Arms Limitation Talks***) перегово́ры по ОСВ (ограниче́нию стратеги́ческих вооруже́ний); ~ **II** перегово́ры по ОСВ-2.
salt[2] [sɔːlt, sɒlt] *n.* **1.** соль; **bath ~s** аромати́ческие со́ли (*f. pl.*) для ва́нны; **cooking** ~ пова́ренная соль; **rock** ~ ка́менная соль; **sea** ~ морска́я соль; **smelling ~s** ню́хательная соль; **table** ~ столо́вая соль; **in** ~ (*pickled*) солёный; **he is not worth his** ~ он никчёмный челове́к; **take sth. with a grain of** ~ отн|оси́ться, -ести́сь скепти́чески к чему́-н.; **rub** ~ **into s.o.'s wounds** (*fig.*) растрав|ля́ть, -и́ть (*or* сы́пать (*impf.*) соль на) чьи-н. ра́ны; **the** ~ **of the earth** соль земли́. **2.: old** ~ (*sailor*) (ста́рый) морско́й волк.
adj. (*salty, salted*) солёный; (*pert. to production of* ~) соляно́й; ~ **tears** го́рькие слёзы; ~ **water** морска́я вода́; ~ **beef** солони́на.
v.t. **1.** (*cure in brine*) соли́ть, за-; **~ed meat** солони́на. **2.** (*sprinkle with* ~) соли́ть, по-; ~ **the street** пос|ыпа́ть, -ы́пать у́лицу со́лью. **3.** ~ **away, down** (*fig., coll., put in safe keeping*) копи́ть, на-; класть/скла́дывать (*impf.*) в кубы́шку. **4.** (*fig., flavour*): **his conversation was ~ed with humour** разгово́р его́ был сдо́брен изря́дной до́зой ю́мора.
cpds. **~-cellar** *n.* соло́нка; **~-glaze** *n.* соляна́я глазу́рь; **~-lake** *n.* солёное о́зеро; **~-lick** *n.* соляно́й уча́сток/исто́чник; **~-marsh** *n.* солонча́к; **~-mine** *n.* соляна́я ша́хта; **~-pan** *n.* соляно́е о́зеро; (*vessel*) ва́рница; **~-spoon** *n.* ло́жечка для со́ли; **~-water** *adj.*: **~-water fish** морска́я ры́ба; **~-water lake** солёное о́зеро; **~-works** *n.* солева́рня.
saltiness [ˈsɔːltɪnɪs, ˈsɒl-] *n.* солёность.
saltire [ˈsɔːlˌtaɪə(r)] *n.* андре́евский крест.
saltpetre [ˌsɒltˈpiːtə(r), ˌsɔːlt-] *n.* сели́тра.
salty [ˈsɔːltɪ, ˈsɒl-] *adj.* (*lit., fig.*) солёный; **too** ~ пересо́ленный.
salubrious [səˈluːbrɪəs, səˈljuː-] *adj.* (*healthy*) здоро́вый; (*curative*) целе́бный, цели́тельный.
salutary [ˈsæljʊtərɪ] *adj.* (*beneficial*) благотво́рный; **a** ~ **warning** поле́зное предупрежде́ние; (*salubrious*) целе́бный, цели́тельный.
salutation [ˌsæljuːˈteɪʃ(ə)n] *n.* приве́тствие.
salute [səˈluːt, -ˈljuːt] *n.* **1.** (*mil., naut.*) отда́ние че́сти; во́инское приве́тствие; **give, make a** ~ отд|ава́ть, -а́ть честь; **acknowledge, return a** ~ отв|еча́ть, -е́тить на приве́тствие; **take the** ~ прин|има́ть, -я́ть пара́д; (*with guns*) салю́т; **a** ~ **of 6 guns** салю́т из шести́ за́лпов; (*in fencing*) салю́т, приве́тствие. **2.** (*fig.*) приве́тствие, дань (*кому*).
v.t. **1.** отд|ава́ть, -а́ть честь (*кому*); салютова́ть (*impf., pf.*) (*кому/чему*); **they ~d the Queen's birthday with 21 guns** они́ произвели́ салю́т из двадцати́ одного́ ору́дия в честь дня рожде́ния короле́вы. **2.** (*greet*) приве́тствовать (*impf., pf.*); (*meet*) встр|еча́ть, -е́тить.
v.i. отд|ава́ть, -а́ть честь.
Salvadorean [ˌsælvəˈdɔːrɪən] *n.* сальвадо́р|ец (*fem.* -ка).
adj. сальвадо́рский.
salvage [ˈsælvɪdʒ] *n.* **1.** (*saving ship or property*) спасе́ние (иму́щества); (*what is saved*) спасённое иму́щество; спасённый груз *и т.п.*; (~ *money*) вознагражде́ние/награ́да за спасённое иму́щество. **2.** (*saving waste paper, metal etc.*) сбор ути́ля (*or* ути́ль-сырья́).
v.t. (*also* **salve**) спас|а́ть, -ти́; сохран|я́ть, -и́ть.
salvation [sælˈveɪʃ(ə)n] *n.* спасе́ние (души́), избавле́ние; **he must work out his own** ~ пусть выпу́тывается как мо́жет; **S~ Army** А́рмия спасе́ния; (*pers. or thg. that saves*) спаси́тель (*m.*), избави́тель (*m.*); спасе́ние; **you have been the ~ of him** вы его́ спасли́; **work was my** ~ рабо́та была́ мои́м еди́нственным спасе́нием.
salve[1] [sælv, sɑːv] *n.* (*lit.*) целе́бная мазь; (*lit., fig.*) бальза́м.
v.t. (*anoint*) сма́з|ывать, -ать; (*fig., soothe; smooth over*) врачева́ть (*impf.*); успок|а́ивать, -о́ить; сгла́|живать, -дить.
salve[2] [sælv, sɑːv] = **salvage** *v.t.*
salver [ˈsælvə(r)] *n.* (серебряный) подно́с.
salvo [ˈsælvəʊ] *n.* (*of guns*) залп; **fire a** ~ да|ва́ть, -ть залп; (*of bombs*) бо́мбовый уда́р; (*of applause*) взрыв аплодисме́нтов.
sal volatile [ˌsæl vɒˈlætɪlɪ] *n.* ню́хательная соль.
Samaritan [səˈmærɪt(ə)n] *n.* самаритя́н|ин (*fem.* -ка); **good** ~ до́брый самаритя́нин.
adj. самаритя́нский.
samba [ˈsæmbə] *n.* са́мба.
Sam Browne [sæm ˈbraʊn] *n.* офице́рская портупе́я.
same [seɪm] *pron. & adj.* **1.** тот же (са́мый); тако́й же; оди́н (и тот же); (*unvarying*) одина́ковый, неизме́нный, ро́вный; **they are one and the** ~ **person** э́то оди́н и тот же челове́к; **not the** ~ друго́й; **this** ~ э́тот са́мый/же; **is that the** ~ **man we saw yesterday**? э́то тот же челове́к, кото́рого мы ви́дели вчера́?; **I lived in the** ~ **house as he** я жил в одно́м до́ме с ним; **we are the** ~ **age** мы одни́х лет (*or* одного́ во́зраста *or* рове́сники); **he chose the** ~ **career as his father** он вы́брал ту же профе́ссию, что и его́ оте́ц; **the** ~ **weapons as are used today** то же са́мое ору́жие, како́е употребля́ется (и) в на́ши дни; **in the** ~ **way** таки́м/подо́бным же о́бразом; **at the** ~ **time** в то же вре́мя, одновреме́нно, вме́сте; (*however*) ме́жду тем; **at the** ~ **time every evening** ка́ждый ве́чер в оди́н и тот же час; **men and women receive the** ~ **wages** мужчи́ны и же́нщины получа́ют одина́ковую зарпла́ту; **his books seem all the** ~ **to me** все его́ кни́ги ка́жутся мне на одно́ лицо; **it's all the** ~ **to me** мне всё равно́; **the village looks just the** ~ **as ever (it did)** дере́вня вы́глядит тако́й же, как всегда́ (*or* на вид ничу́ть не измени́лась); **I'm not the** ~ **man that I was** я не тако́й, как (*or* каки́м был) пре́жде; **it comes to the** ~ **thing** э́то одно́ и то же; э́то всё равно́/еди́но; (*coll.*) так на так; **I'd do the** ~ **again** я бы то́чно так поступи́л и тепе́рь; ~ **again, please!** то же са́мое, пожа́луйста!; **... and the** ~ **to you!** ... и вам та́кже (*or* того́ же)!
adv.: **I don't feel the** ~ **towards him** я стал к нему́ ина́че относи́ться; я к нему́ охладе́л; **all the** ~ (*nevertheless*) всё-таки; всё равно́; всё же; **just the** ~ (*despite that*) тем не ме́нее; ~ **here!** я то́же!
sameness [ˈseɪmnɪs] *n.* (*identity*) одина́ковость, то́ждество; (*similarity*) схо́дство, подо́бие; (*uniformity*) единообра́зие; (*monotony*) однообра́зие.
samisen [ˈsæmɪsɪn] *n.* сямисэ́н.
Samoa [səˈməʊə] *n.* Само́а (*nt. indecl.*).
Samoan [səˈməʊən] *n.* (*pers.*) самоа́н|ец, (*fem.* -ка); (*language*) самоа́нский язы́к.
adj. самоа́нский.
samovar [ˈsæməˌvɑː(r)] *n.* самова́р.
Samoyed [ˈsæməˌjed] *n.* (*pers.*) не́н|ец (*fem.* -ка); (*language*) не́нецкий язы́к; (*dog*) ла́йка.
sampan [ˈsæmpæn] *n.* сампа́н.
sample [ˈsɑːmp(ə)l] *n.* (*comm., fig.*) образе́ц, обра́зчик, приме́р; (*med.*) про́ба; **take a** ~ **of sth.** *see v.t.*
v.t. брать, взять образе́ц +*g.*; (*wine, food etc.*) про́бовать,

по-; (*try out*) испро́бовать (*pf.*); испы́т|ывать, -а́ть.

sampler[1] ['sɑːmplə(r)] *n.* (*taster*) дегуста́тор.

sampler[2] ['sɑːmplə(r)] *n.* (*embroidery*) ≃ вы́шивка.

sampling ['sɑːmplɪŋ] *n.* (*in statistics*) вы́борка; (*attr.*) вы́борочный.

Samson ['sæms(ə)n] *n.* Самсо́н.

samurai ['sæmʊˌraɪ, -jʊˌraɪ] *n.* самура́й.

sanatorium [ˌsænə'tɔːrɪəm] (*US* **sanitarium**) *n.* санато́рий; **at a ~** в санато́рии.

sanctification [ˌsæŋktɪfɪ'keɪʃ(ə)n] *n.* освяще́ние; оправда́ние.

sanctify ['sæŋktɪˌfaɪ] *v.t.* освя|ща́ть (*or* святи́ть), -ти́ть; (*justify*) опра́вд|ывать, -а́ть.

sanctimonious [ˌsæŋktɪ'məʊnɪəs] *adj.* ха́нжеский; **~ person** ханжа́ (*c.g.*), свято́ша (*c.g.*).

sanctimoniousness [ˌsæŋktɪ'məʊnɪəsnɪs] *n.* ха́нжество.

sanction ['sæŋkʃ(ə)n] *n.* **1.** (*authorization*, *permission*) са́нкция; **official ~ has not been given** официа́льной са́нкции (*or* официа́льного разреше́ния) нет; (*approval*) одобре́ние; **without his ~** без его́ согла́сия. **2.** (*penalty*) ме́ра наказа́ния. **3.** (*moral*, *relig.*, *pol.*) са́нкция.

v.t. (*authorize*) санкциони́ровать (*impf.*, *pf.*); (*ratify*) утвер|жда́ть, -ди́ть; (*approve*) од|обря́ть, -о́брить.

sanctity ['sæŋktɪtɪ] *n.* (*holiness*, *saintliness*) свя́тость; (*inviolability*) неприкоснове́нность.

sanctuary ['sæŋktjʊərɪ] *n.* **1.** (*holy place*) святи́лище. **2.** (*part of church*) алта́рь (*m.*). **3.** (*asylum*, *refuge*) убе́жище; **violate ~** нар|уша́ть, -у́шить пра́во убе́жища. **4.** (*for wild life*) запове́дник; **bird ~** пти́чий запове́дник.

sanctum ['sæŋktəm] *n.* святи́лище; (*fig.*, *'den'*) прибе́жище.

sand [sænd] *n.* **1.** песо́к; **grain of ~** песчи́нка; **a house built on ~** (*fig.*) дом, воздви́гнутый/постро́енный на песке́; **the ~s are running out** дни сочтены́; бли́зится коне́ц. **2.** (*pl.*, *beach*) (песча́ный) пляж; **numberless as the ~s of the sea** бесчи́сленные как песчи́нки на морско́м берегу́.

v.t. (*sprinkle with ~*) пос|ыпа́ть, -ы́пать песко́м; (*polish with ~*) прот|ира́ть, -ере́ть песко́м.

cpds. **~bag** *n.* мешо́к с песко́м, балла́стный мешо́к; *v.t.*: **the entrance was ~bagged** вход был защищён мешка́ми с песко́м; **~bank** *n.* песча́ная о́тмель/ба́нка; **~-bar** *n.* песча́ная о́тмель (в у́стье реки́); **~-bed** *n.* песча́ный пласт; **~-blast** *n.* песча́ная струя́; пескостру́йный аппара́т; *v.t.* обраб|а́тывать, -о́тать из пескоду́вки (*or* песча́ной струёй); **~-box** (*rail.*) *n.* песо́чница; **~boy** *n.*: **happy as a ~boy** беззабо́тный; **~-castle** *n.* за́мок из песка́ (*or* на песке́); **~-dune** *n.* дю́на; **~-eel** *n.* песчи́нка; **~-glass** *n.* песо́чные час|ы́ (*pl.*, *g.* -о́в); **~-hill** *n.* дю́на; **~man** *n.* ≃ дрёма, дремо́та; **~-martin** *n.* берегова́я ла́сточка; **~paper** *n.* шку́рка, нажда́чная бума́га; *v.t.* чи́стить, от- (*or* шлифова́ть, от-) шку́ркой; **~piper** *n.* песо́чник; **~-pit** *n.* (*quarry*) песча́ный карье́р; (*for children*) песо́чница; **~-shoes** *n. pl.* спорти́вные та́почки (*f. pl.*); **~stone** *n.* песча́ник; **~storm** *n.* песча́ная бу́ря, саму́м.

sandal[1] ['sænd(ə)l] *n.* (*footwear*) санда́лия, сандале́та.

sandal[2] ['sænd(ə)l] *n.* (**~ wood**) санда́л.

cpd. **~-tree** *n.* санда́ловое де́рево.

sandalled ['sændəld] *adj.*: **her feet were ~** её но́ги бы́ли обу́ты (*or* она́ была́ обу́та) в санда́лии; она́ была́ в санда́лиях.

sandwich ['sænwɪdʒ, -wɪtʃ] *n.* бутербро́д; **ham ~** бутербро́д с ветчино́й; **open ~** откры́тый бутербро́д (с одни́м куско́м хле́ба); **~ bar** бутербро́дная.

v.t. (*insert*) вти́с|кивать, -нуть; (*squeeze*) сти́с|кивать, -нуть; вти́с|кивать, -нуть; заж|има́ть, -а́ть; **his car was ~ed between two lorries** его́ маши́на была́ зажа́та ме́жду двумя́ грузовика́ми.

cpds. **~-boards** *n. pl.* рекла́мные щиты́ (*m. pl.*); **~ course** *n.* курс обуче́ния, чередую́щий тео́рию с пра́ктикой; **~-man** *n.* челове́к-рекла́ма.

sandy ['sændɪ] *adj.* **1.** (*consisting of sand*) песча́ный; (*containing or resembling sand*) песо́чный. **2.** (*of hair or pers.*) рыжева́тый.

sane [seɪn] *adj.* (*opp. mad*) норма́льный, психи́чески здоро́вый; (*sensible*) здра́вый; здравомы́слящий; разу́мный.

San Francisco [ˌsæn fræn'sɪskəʊ] *n.* Сан-Франци́ско (*m. indecl.*).

sang-froid [sɑ̃'frwɑː] *n.* хладнокро́вие, невозмути́мость.

sangria [sæŋ'griːə] *n.* сангри́я.

sanguinary ['sæŋgwɪnərɪ] *adj.* крова́вый; (*bloodthirsty*) кровожа́дный.

sanguine ['sæŋgwɪn] *adj.* **1.** (*of complexion etc.*) румя́ный. **2.** (*of temperament*) сангвини́ческий; (*optimistic*) оптимисти́ческий; **I am ~ that we shall succeed** я уве́рен в успе́хе; **I am ~ about the plan** я споко́ен за э́тот прое́кт.

Sanhedri|n ['sænɪdrɪn], **-m** ['sænɪdrɪm] *n.* синедрио́н.

sanitarium [ˌsænɪ'teərɪəm] = **sanatorium**

sanitary ['sænɪtərɪ] *adj.* санита́рный, гигиени́ческий, гигиени́чный; **~ arrangements** сану́зел; **~ engineering** санте́хника; **~ inspector** санинспе́ктор; **~ towel** гигиени́ческая (ма́рлевая) поду́шка; **~ ware** унита́зы (*m. pl.*).

sanitation [ˌsænɪ'teɪʃ(ə)n] *n.* (*conditions*) санита́рное состоя́ние; санита́рные усло́вия; (*sewage system*) канализацио́нная систе́ма; **the houses had no indoor ~** в дома́х не́ было канализа́ции.

sanity ['sænɪtɪ] *n.* (*mental health*) психи́ческое здоро́вье; душе́вное равнове́сие; (*reasonableness*) здравомы́слие, благоразу́мие.

sanserif [sæn'serɪf] *n.* гроте́сковый шрифт (без засе́чек).

Sanskrit ['sænskrɪt] *n.* санскри́т; **in ~** на санскри́те.

adj. санскри́тский.

Santa Claus ['sæntə ˌklɔːz] *n.* ≃ Дед Моро́з, рожде́ственский дед.

sap[1] [sæp] *n.* (*of plants*) сок; (*fig.*) жизнь; жи́зненные си́лы (*f. pl.*).

v.t. (*drain of ~*) суши́ть, вы́-; (*fig.*): **~ s.o.'s strength** под|рыва́ть, -орва́ть (*or* истощ|а́ть, -и́ть) чьи-н. си́лы.

cpd. **~wood** *n.* за́болонь.

sap[2] [sæp] *n.* (*mil*, *trench*) са́па; кры́тая транше́я.

v.t. (*mil.*) подк|а́пывать, -опа́ть; под|рыва́ть, -ры́ть; (*of action by water*) подм|ыва́ть, -ы́ть; разм|ыва́ть, -ы́ть; (*fig.*, *undermine*) под|рыва́ть, -орва́ть.

sap[3] [sæp] *n.* (*sl.*, *simpleton*) проста́к.

sapience ['seɪpɪəns] *n.* му́дрость.

sapient ['seɪpɪənt] *adj.* (*wise*) му́дрый.

sapless ['sæplɪs] *adj.* иссо́хший.

sapling ['sæplɪŋ] *n.* (*tree*) молодо́е де́ревце.

sapper ['sæpə(r)] *n.* (*mil.*) сапёр; (*pl.*) инжене́рные войска́.

Sapphic ['sæfɪk] *n.* (*verse*) сафи́ческая строфа́; (*pl.*) сафи́ческие стихи́ (*m. pl.*).

adj. сафи́ческий; (*Lesbian*) лесби́йский, сафи́ческий.

sapphire ['sæfaɪə(r)] *n.* (*stone*) сапфи́р; (*colour*) лазу́рь.

adj. сапфи́рный; лазу́рный, сапфи́ровый.

Sappho ['sæfəʊ] *n.* Сафо́ (*f. indecl.*).

sappy ['sæpɪ] *adj.* со́чный; (*fig.*) по́лный жи́зненных сил; в соку́.

saraband ['særəˌbænd] *n.* сараба́нда.

Saracen ['særəs(ə)n] *n.* сараци́н (*fem.* -ка).

adj. сараци́нский.

Sarah ['seərə] *n.* (*bibl.*) Са́рра.

Sarajevo [ˌsærə'jeɪvəʊ] *n.* Сара́ево.

sarcasm ['sɑːˌkæz(ə)m] *n.* сарка́зм.

sarcastic [sɑː'kæstɪk] *adj.* саркасти́ческий.

sarcoma [sɑː'kəʊmə] *n.* сарко́ма.

sarcophagus [sɑː'kɒfəgəs] *n.* саркофа́г.

sardine [sɑː'diːn] *n.* сарди́н(к)а; **packed like ~s** (наби́ты) как се́льди в бо́чке.

Sardinia [sɑː'dɪnɪə] *n.* Сарди́ния.

Sardinian [sɑː'dɪnɪən] *n.* (*pers.*) сарди́н|ец; (*fem.*) жи́тельница/уроже́нка Сарди́нии.

adj. сарди́нский.

sardonic [sɑː'dɒnɪk] *adj.* сардони́ческий.

sardonyx ['sɑːdənɪks] *n.* сардо́никс.

sari ['sɑriː] *n.* са́ри (*f. indecl.*).

sarong [sə'rɒŋ] *n.* саро́нг.

sarsaparilla [ˌsɑːsəpə'rɪlə] *n.* сарсапари́ль (*m.*).

sartorial [sɑː'tɔːrɪəl] *adj.* (*pert. to tailoring*) портня́жный; **~ elegance** изя́щество в оде́жде; уме́ние одева́ться.

SAS (*abbr. of* ***Special Air Service***) спецслу́жба ВВС.

sash[1] [sæʃ] *n.* (*round waist*) куша́к, по́яс; (*over shoulder*) (о́рденская) ле́нта.

sash[2] [sæʃ] *n.* (*of window*) скользя́щая ра́ма (окна́).
cpd. **~-window** *n.* подъёмное окно́.
Satan ['seɪt(ə)n] *n.* сатана́ (*m.*).
Satanic [sə'tænɪk] *adj.* сатани́нский, а́дский.
Satanism ['seɪtə,nɪz(ə)m] *n.* сатани́зм.
satchel ['sætʃ(ə)l] *n.* су́мка, ра́нец; (шко́льный) портфе́ль.
sate [seɪt] *v.t.* (*liter.*) нас|ыща́ть, -ы́тить; **~d with pleasure** пресы́щенный наслажде́ниями.
sateen [sæ'ti:n] *n.* сати́н.
satellite ['sætə,laɪt] *n.* **1.** (*moon, artefact*) спу́тник, сателли́т; **manned ~** обита́емый спу́тник; спу́тник с экипа́жем на борту́; **~ town** го́род-спу́тник; **~ (radio) link-up** радиомо́ст; **~ (TV) link-up** телемо́ст; **~ television broadcasting** косми́ческое телеви́дение. **2.** (*fig.*) сателли́т, приспе́шник.
adj. вспомога́тельный, подчинённый.
satiate ['seɪʃɪ,eɪt] *v.t.* нас|ыща́ть, -ы́тить.
satiety [sə'taɪɪtɪ] *n.* насыще́ние, сы́тость; (*over abundance*) пресыще́ние; **to ~** до́сыта, вдо́сталь, до отва́ла/отка́за.
satin ['sætɪn] *n.* а́тлас.
adj. атла́сный.
cpds. **~-paper** *n.* сатини́рованная/атла́сная бума́га; **~wood** *n.* атла́сное де́рево.
satinet(te) [,sætɪ'net] *n.* сатине́т.
satiny ['sætɪnɪ] *adj.* атла́сный, шелкови́стый.
satire ['sætaɪə(r)] *n.* сати́ра.
satiric(al) [sə'tɪrɪk(ə)l] *adj.* сатири́ческий.
satirist ['sætərɪst] *n.* сати́рик.
satirize ['sætɪ,raɪz] *v.t.* высме́ивать, вы́смеять.
satisfaction [,sætɪs'fækʃ(ə)n] *n.* **1.** удовлетворе́ние, удовлетворённость; (*pleasure*) удово́льствие; дово́льство; прия́тное созна́ние; **the work was done to my entire ~** я был по́лностью удовлетворён вы́полненной рабо́той; **I wanted to know for my own ~** я про́сто хоте́л удостове́риться; **the results give cause for ~** результа́ты вполне́ удовлетвори́тельны; **you have the ~ of knowing you are right** вы мо́жете утеша́ться созна́нием со́бственной правоты́; **he did not conceal his ~ at the outcome** он не скрыва́л (свое́й) ра́дости по по́воду исхо́да де́ла. **2.** (*in duel*) сатисфа́кция, удовлетворе́ние. **3.** (*payment of debt*) упла́та, погаше́ние; (*fig.*) распла́та; **make ~ for sins** искупи́ть (*pf.*) грехи́. **4.** (*compensation*) компенса́ция.
satisfactory [,sætɪs'fæktərɪ] *adj.* удовлетвори́тельный, хоро́ший, прия́тный; (*successful*) уда́чный; (*convincing*) убеди́тельный.
satisf|y ['sætɪs,faɪ] *v.t.* **1.** удовлетвор|я́ть, -и́ть; **the compromise ~ies everyone** компроми́сс удовлетворя́ет всех; **this solution ~ies all the requirements** э́то реше́ние удовлетворя́ет/отвеча́ет/соотве́тствует всем тре́бованиям; **~y one's hunger** утол|я́ть, -и́ть го́лод; **nothing ~ies him** ниче́м ему́ не угоди́шь; **he ~ied the examiners** он вы́держал экза́мен; **I was more than ~ied with the response** я был бо́лее чем дово́лен о́ткликом; **you must be ~ied with what you have** вам придётся дово́льствоваться тем, что у вас есть; **a ~ied customer** дово́льный клие́нт; **he won't be ~ied until he has had an accident** он то́лько тогда́ успоко́ится, когда́ попадёт в беду́ (*or* сде́лается же́ртвой несча́стного слу́чая). **2.** (*justify*): **the result ~ied our expectations** результа́т оправда́л на́ши ожида́ния. **3.** (*convince*) убе|жда́ть, -ди́ть; **I ~ied him of my innocence** я убеди́л его́ в мое́й невино́вности; **I ~ied myself of his honesty** я убеди́лся в его́ че́стности; **you may be ~ied that it is so** (вы) мо́жете не сомнева́ться, что э́то так. **4.** (*pay*): **~y a debt** пога|ша́ть, -си́ть долг. **5.** (*fulfil*): **~y an obligation** выполня́ть, вы́полнить обяза́тельство. **6.** (*meet*): **~y s.o.'s objections** отв|оди́ть, -ести́ чьи-н. возраже́ния. **7.** (*of food*): **a ~ying lunch** сы́тный обе́д.
satrap ['sætræp] *n.* сатра́п.
satrapy ['sætrəpɪ] *n.* сатра́пия.
saturate ['sætʃə,reɪt, -tjʊ,reɪt] *v.t.* нас|ыща́ть, -ы́тить; **the carpet became ~d with water** ковёр пропита́лся водо́й; **I was ~d** (*wet through*) я весь промо́к; **~d solution** насы́щенный раство́р.
saturation [,sætʃə'reɪʃ(ə)n, -tjʊ'reɪʃ(ə)n] *n.* насыще́ние, насы́щенность; **~ bombing** площадно́е бомбомета́ние со сплошны́м пораже́нием; (*over-abundance*) пресыще́ние.
Saturday ['sætə,deɪ, -dɪ] *n.* суббо́та; (*attr.*) суббо́тний; **on ~ evening** в суббо́ту ве́чером; **Holy ~** Вели́кая суббо́та.
Saturn ['sæt(ə)n] *n.* (*astron., myth.*) Сату́рн; **~'s rings** ко́льца (*nt. pl.*) Сату́рна.
saturnalia [,sætə'neɪlɪə] *n.* сатурна́лии (*f. pl.*).
Saturnian [sə'tɜ:nɪən] *adj.* (*pros.*) сатурни́ческий.
saturnine ['sætə,naɪn] *adj.* мра́чный, угрю́мый.
satyr ['sætə(r)] *n.* сати́р.
sauce [sɔ:s] *n.* (*cul.*) со́ус; (*fig., piquancy*) припра́ва, пика́нтность; (*coll., impertinence*) де́рзость; **none of your ~!** не дерзи́!
cpds. **~-boat** *n.* со́усник; **~pan** *n.* кастрю́ля.
saucer ['sɔ:sə(r)] *n.* блю́дце; **cup and ~** ча́шка с блю́дцем; **flying ~** лета́ющее блю́дце.
cpd. **~-eyed** *adj.* с глаза́ми, как пло́шки.
saucy ['sɔ:sɪ] *adj.* де́рзкий, задо́рный, озорно́й; **a ~ little hat** коке́тливая шля́пка.
Saudi ['saʊdɪ] *n.* сау́дов|ец (*fem.* -ка).
adj. сау́довский; **~ Arabia** Сау́довская Ара́вия.
sauerkraut ['saʊə,kraʊt] *n.* ки́слая/ква́шеная капу́ста.
sauna ['sɔ:nə] *n.* (*also* **~ bath**) са́уна, фи́нская (парна́я) ба́ня.
saunter ['sɔ:ntə(r)] *n.* (*stroll*) прогу́лка; **at a ~** неторопли́во, не спеша́.
v.i. идти́ (*det.*) не торопя́сь; **~ up and down** проха́живаться, прогу́ливаться, флани́ровать (*all impf.*).
saurian ['sɔ:rɪən] *adj.* относя́щийся к я́щерицам/я́щерам.
sausage ['sɒsɪdʒ] *n.* соси́ска; (*large Continental type*) колбаса́.
cpds. **~-meat** *n.* колба́сный фарш; **~-roll** *n.* соси́ска, запечённая в бу́лочке; **~-skin** *n.* колба́сная кожура́/ко́жица.
sauté ['səʊteɪ] *n.* & *adj.* соте́ (*indecl.*).
sauve qui peut [,səʊv ki: 'pɜ:] *n.* беспоря́дочное бе́гство.
savage ['sævɪdʒ] *n.* дика́р|ь (*fem.* -ка); (*fig., brute*) зверь (*m.*), грубия́н.
adj. **1.** (*primitive*) ди́кий, первобы́тный. **2.** (*of animals: fierce*) свире́пый. **3.** (*of attack, blow etc.*) жесто́кий, я́ростный; **his book was ~ly attacked in the press** его́ кни́га подве́рглась свире́пым напа́дкам в пре́ссе.
v.t. (жесто́ко) искуса́ть (*pf.*); (*fig.*) растерза́ть (*pf.*).
savage|ness ['sævɪdʒnɪs], **-ry** ['sævɪdʒrɪ] *nn.* ди́кость; свире́пость; жесто́кость.
savanna(h) [sə'vænə] *n.* сава́нна.
savant ['sæv(ə)nt, sæ'vɑ̃] *n.* (кру́пный) учёный.
sav|e [seɪv] *n.* (*football etc.*): **the goalkeeper made a brilliant ~e** врата́рь блестя́ще отби́л нападе́ние/уда́р.
v.t. **1.** (*rescue, deliver*) спас|а́ть, -ти́; изб|авля́ть, -а́вить; **he ~ed my life** он спас мне жизнь; **she was ~ed from drowning** её во́время вы́тащили из воды́; ей не да́ли утону́ть; **he ~ed the situation** он спас положе́ние; **he thought only of ~ing his own skin** он ду́мал лишь о спасе́нии со́бственной шку́ры; **~e appearances** соблюда́ть (*impf.*) ви́димость/прили́чия; (*protect, preserve*): **God ~e the Queen!** Бо́же, храни́ короле́ву!; **~e face** сохрани́ть/спасти́ (*pf.*) лицо́. **2.** (*put by*) бере́чь, с-; от|кла́дывать, -ложи́ть; копи́ть, на-; **I ~ed (up) £50 towards a holiday** я скопи́л 50 фу́нтов на о́тпуск/кани́кулы; **~e me something to eat!** оста́вьте/приберегите мне что́-нибудь пое́сть!; (*collect*) соб|ира́ть, -ра́ть; (*avoid using or spending*) эконо́мить, с-; **~e expense** избе|га́ть, -жа́ть затра́т; **he took the bus to ~e time** он пое́хал авто́бусом, что́бы сэконо́мить вре́мя; **he is ~ing himself (*or* his strength) for the next race** он бережёт си́лы для сле́дующего соревнова́ния; **we will ~e the cake for tomorrow** прибережём пиро́г на за́втра; (*obviate need for, expense of etc.*): **that will ~e me £100** я сэконо́млю на э́том сто фу́нтов; **it ~ed me a lot of time** э́то мне сберегло́ мно́го вре́мени; **it will ~e you trouble if you come with me** е́сли вы пойдёте со мно́й, э́то изба́вит вас от ли́шних хлопо́т; **I ~ed him the trouble of replying** я изба́вил его́ от необходи́мости отвеча́ть.
v.i. эконо́мить, с-; **he is ~ing up for a bicycle** он

откла́дывает/ко́пит де́ньги (*or* он ко́пит) на велосипе́д.

prep. (*liter.*) кро́ме+*g.*; без+*g.*; **I know nothing of him ~e that he is rich** я ничего́ о нём не зна́ю, кро́ме того́, что он бога́т; **all the men ~e one** все кро́ме одного́ (челове́ка).

saveloy ['sævə,lɔɪ] *n.* сервела́т.

saver ['seɪvə(r)] *n.* **1.** (*investor*) вкла́дчик. **2.: this method is a ~ of time and money** э́тот ме́тод эконо́мит и вре́мя и де́ньги.

saving ['seɪvɪŋ] *n.* **1.** (*salvation, rescue*) спасе́ние; **penicillin led to the ~ of many lives** пеницилли́н мно́гим спас жизнь. **2.** (*economy*) эконо́мия; **a ~ of millions of pounds** эконо́мия в миллио́ны фу́нтов. **3.** (*pl., money laid by*) сбереже́ния (*nt. pl.*); **they live on their ~s** они́ живу́т на свои́ сбереже́ния; **~s bank** сберега́тельная ка́сса; **he had to draw on his ~s** ему́ пришло́сь прибе́гнуть к свои́м сбереже́ниям.

adj. **1.** (*salutary*) спаси́тельный; **~ grace** (*fig.*) положи́тельное/спаси́тельное сво́йство. **2. ~ clause** огово́рка.

prep. (*liter.*) **1.** (*except*) кро́ме+*g.* **2.** (*without offence to*): **~ your presence** при всём уваже́нии к вам; не в оби́ду бу́дет ска́зано.

saviour ['seɪvjə(r)] *n.* спаси́тель (*m.*).

savoir-faire [,sævwɑː 'feə(r)] *n.* сметли́вость.

savoir-vivre [,sævwɑː 'viːvrə] *n.* воспи́танность, такт.

savory ['seɪvərɪ] *n.* садо́вый ча́бер.

savour ['seɪvə(r)] *n.* (*lit., fig.*) при́вкус; **life lost its ~ for me** жизнь потеря́ла для меня́ вся́кую пре́лесть.

v.t. (*sample*) про́бовать, по-; (*enjoy*) смакова́ть (*impf., pf.*).

v.i.: **~ of** отзыва́ть/отдава́ть (*impf.*) +*i.*; **the letter ~s of jealousy** в письме́ сквози́т ре́вность.

savoury ['seɪvərɪ] *adj.* пика́нтный, о́стрый; **~ omelette** омле́т с о́строй припра́вой; (*fig.*): **a not very ~ district** непригля́дный райо́н.

savoy [sə'vɔɪ] *n.*: **~ (cabbage)** саво́йская капу́ста.

savvy ['sævɪ] *n.* смека́лка (*coll.*).

v.i.: **~?** поня́тно?; дошло́?

saw[1] [sɔː] *n.* (*tool*) пила́; **circular ~** кру́глая/циркуля́рная пила́.

v.t. пили́ть (*impf.*); распи́л|ивать, -и́ть.

v.i. пили́ть (*impf.*); **this wood ~s easily** э́то де́рево хорошо́ пи́лится; **he ~ed away on the violin** он пили́л себе́ на скри́пке.

with advs.: **~ down** *v.t.* спи́л|ивать, -и́ть; **~ off** *v.t.* отпи́л|ивать, -и́ть; **he ~ed off the branch he was sitting on** (*fig.*) он подруби́л сук, на кото́ром сиде́л; **~n-off shotgun** обре́з; **~ up** *v.t.* распи́л|ивать, -и́ть.

cpds. **~-blade** *n.* полотно́ пилы́; **~bones** *n.* (*coll.*) хиру́рг, костопра́в; **~dust** *n.* опи́л|ки (*pl., g.* -ок); **~fish** *n.* ры́ба-пила́; **~fly** *n.* пили́льщик; **~-frame** *n.* лесопи́льная ра́ма; **~mill** *n.* лесопи́лка; лесопи́льный заво́д; **~-tooth** *n.* зуб (пилы́); *adj.* зу́бчатый.

saw[2] [sɔː] *n.* (*maxim*) посло́вица, погово́рка.

sawyer ['sɔːjə(r)] *n.* пи́льщик.

sax [sæks] (*coll.*) = **saxophone**

saxifrage ['sæksɪ,freɪdʒ] *n.* камнело́мка.

Saxon ['sæks(ə)n] *n.* (*hist.*) сакс; (*native of Saxony*) саксо́н|ец (*fem.* -ка).

adj. саксо́нский.

Saxony ['sæksənɪ] *n.* Саксо́ния.

saxophone ['sæksə,fəʊn] *n.* саксофо́н.

say [seɪ] *n.* (*expression of opinion*): **let s.o. have his ~** да|ва́ть, -ть кому́-н. вы́сказаться; **I have said my ~** я вы́сказал/сказа́л всё, что име́л/собира́лся сказа́ть; **we had no ~ in the matter** на́шего мне́ния в э́том де́ле не спра́шивали; **he likes to have a ~** он хо́чет, что́бы счита́лись с его́ мне́нием.

v.t. & i. **1.** говори́ть, сказа́ть; **he ~s I am lazy** он говори́т, что я лени́в; **would you ~ I was right?** как по-ва́шему, я прав?; **why can't he ~ what he means?** почему́ он не ска́жет пря́мо, что он име́ет в виду́?; **just ~ the word and I'll go** то́лько скажи́те (сло́во), и я пойду́; **he was asked to ~ something** (*or* **a few words**) его́ попроси́ли сказа́ть не́сколько слов; **~ a good word for** замо́лвить (*pf.*) слове́чко за+*a.*; **as who should ~, as much as to ~** как бы говоря́; **he said as much** он приме́рно так и сказа́л; **how do you ~ this in English?** как э́то сказа́ть по-англи́йски?; **I must ~** призна́ться; не́чего сказа́ть; **I'll have something to ~ to you about this** на э́тот счёт я име́ю вам ко́е-что сказа́ть; **she is said to be rich** говоря́т, она́ бога́та; **the tree is said to be 100 years old** э́то де́рево счита́ется столе́тним; счита́ется/говоря́т, что э́тому де́реву сто лет; **there is much to be said on both sides** здесь мо́жно мно́го сказа́ть и за и про́тив; о́бе стороны́ по-сво́ему пра́вы; **there is much to be said for beginning now** мно́гое говори́т за то, что́бы начина́ть тепе́рь; **there is no more to be said** бо́льше не́чего сказа́ть; **the said Jones** вышеупомя́нутый Джонс; **~ no more!, enough said!** (*coll.*) (всё) поня́тно!; я́сно!; **what have you got to ~ for yourself?** что вы мо́жете сказа́ть в своё оправда́ние?; **he has plenty to ~ for himself** у него́ хорошо́ подве́шен язы́к; **he has little to ~ for himself** (*is taciturn*) он не о́чень(-то) разгово́рчив; из него́ ли́шнего (сло́ва) не вы́тянешь; **there's no ~ing where they might be** кто зна́ет (*or* неизве́стно), где они́ (нахо́дятся); **it's hard to ~ why** тру́дно сказа́ть, почему́; **I couldn't rightly ~** пра́во, не зна́ю; **I dare ~** пожа́луй, наве́рное, вероя́тно; **how can you ~ such a thing?** как вы мо́жете так(о́е) говори́ть?; **I wouldn't (go so far as to) ~ that** э́того я бы не сказа́л; **didn't I ~ so?** а я что сказа́л?; **I'll ~!** (*coll.*) (*yes indeed*) ещё бы!; **you said it!; you can ~ that again!** (*coll.*) золоты́е слова́!; вот и́менно!; то́-то и оно́!; ещё бы!; **you don't ~ (so)!** (*coll.*) неуже́ли?; не мо́жет быть!; **I'm not ~ing** не скажу́; **~ when!** скажи́те, когда́ дово́льно!; **when all is said and done** в конце́ концо́в, в коне́чном счёте; **he spoke for an hour but didn't ~ much** он (про)говори́л би́тый/це́лый час, а ничего́ (почти́) не сказа́л; **I can't ~ much for his English** я невысо́кого мне́ния о его́ зна́нии англи́йского языка́; **it ~s something, much for his honesty** э́то свиде́тельствует о его́ че́стности; **it ~s something for him that he apologized** то, что он извини́лся, говори́т в его́ по́льзу; **~ you are sorry!** проси́ прощéния!; **~ good-morning to s.o.** здоро́ваться, по- с кем-н.; **that is to ~** (*in other words; viz.*) то есть; ина́че говоря́; (*at least*) по кра́йней ме́ре; **so to ~** так сказа́ть; **I ~!** (**US ~!**) (*attracting attention*) послу́шай(те)!; зна́ете что?; (*expr. surprise*) смотри́те!; поду́майте!; вот э́то да!; ух ты!; **so he ~s** е́сли ему́ ве́рить; **~s you!** так я тебе́ и пове́рил! (*coll.*); **it goes without ~ing** (само́ собо́й) разуме́ется; слов нет; **not to say ...** что́бы не сказа́ть...; **to ~ nothing of** (*not to mention*) не говоря́ (уж) о+*p.*; **well said!** хорошо́ ска́зано!; **one would ~ he was asleep** по-ви́димому, он спит; **so ~ all of us** мы все того́ же мне́ния. **2.** (*suppose, assume*): **(let's) ~; shall we ~** ска́жем; допу́стим; (*for instance*) наприме́р; к приме́ру; приме́рно; **I will give you, ~, £100** я вам дам, ска́жем, сто фу́нтов; **~ he were here, what then?** допу́стим, он был бы (*or* ну, а е́сли бы он был) здесь, что тогда́?; **~ it were true** предположи́м, что так. **3.** (*of inanimate objects: state, indicate*): **what does it ~ in the instructions?** как говори́тся в инстру́кции?; **the Bible ~s** в би́блии говори́тся/напи́сано/ска́зано; би́блия у́чит; **what does the Times ~?** что говори́т/пи́шет «Таймс»?; **the signpost ~s London** на указа́теле напи́сано «Ло́ндон»; **the clock ~s 5 o'clock** часы́ пока́зывают пять; **the notice ~s the museum is closed** объявле́ние гласи́т, что музе́й закры́т; **it ~s here he was killed in an accident** здесь говори́тся/напи́сано/утвержда́ется, что/бу́дто он поги́б в катастро́фе; **the law ~s you must pay a fine** по зако́ну вам сле́дует уплати́ть штра́ф. **4.** (*formulate, express*): **~ a prayer** помоли́ться (*pf.*); произнести́ (*pf.*) (*or* чита́ть, про-) моли́тву; **~ mass** служи́ть, от- обе́дню; **he said his lesson to the teacher** он отве́тил уро́к учи́телю. **5.** (*of reactions*): **~ yes** (*agree*) **to sth.** согла|ша́ться, -си́ться на что-н.; **~ yes** (*accept invitation*) приня́ть (*pf.*) приглаше́ние; (*grant request*) дать (*pf.*) согла́сие; согласи́ться (*pf.*); **~ no** (*refuse invitation*) отказа́ться (*pf.*) от приглаше́ния; (*refuse request*) отказа́ть(ся) (*pf.*); **what do you ~ to a glass of beer?** как насчёт кру́жечки пи́ва?; **I could not ~ him nay** я не мог ему́ отказа́ть; **what would you ~ to a game of cards?** а не сыгра́ть ли нам в ка́рты?

with advs.: **~ away!, ~ on!** *vv.i.* дава́й говори́!; говори́, говори́!; **~ out** *v.t.* & *i.* (*express fully, candidly*) вы́сказать(ся) (*pf.*) (открове́нно).

cpd. **~-so** *n.* (*power of decision*) реша́ющий го́лос; (*mere assertion*): **I would not believe it on his ~-so** я бы не стал ве́рить ему́ на́ слово.

saying ['seɪɪŋ] *n.* (*adage*) погово́рка; **as the ~ goes** как говори́тся; **it was a ~ of his that ...** он люби́л говори́ть, что...; (*utterance*): **the ~s of Confucius** выска́зывания (*nt. pl.*) Конфу́ция.

sc. ['saɪlɪ,set, 'ski:lɪ,ket] = **scilicet**

scab [skæb] *n.* боля́чка; (*on putrid wound*) струп; (*mange*) чесо́тка; (*coll., blackleg*) штрейкбре́хер.

v.i. (*also* **~ over**) затя́|гиваться, -ну́ться; покр|ыва́ться, -ы́ться стру́пьями.

scabbard ['skæbəd] *n.* но́ж|ны (*pl., g.* -ен).

scabby ['skæbɪ] *adj.* (*covered with scabs*) покры́тый боля́чками/стру́пьями; (*mangy*) чесо́точный.

scabies ['skeɪbi:z] *n.* чесо́тка.

scabious ['skeɪbɪəs] *n.* скабио́за.

scabrous ['skeɪbrəs] *adj.* (*indecent*) скабрёзный.

scaffold ['skæfəʊld, -f(ə)ld] *n.* **1.** эшафо́т, пла́ха; **die on the ~** пог|иба́ть, -и́бнуть на эшафо́те; **go to (*or* mount) the ~** идти́, пойти́ на эшафо́т/пла́ху; **send to the ~** отпр|авля́ть, -а́вить на эшафо́т. **2.** = **~ing**

v.t. обстр|а́ивать, -о́ить леса́ми.

scaffolding ['skæfəʊldɪŋ, -fəldɪŋ] *n.* лес|а́ (*pl., g.* -о́в).

cpd. **~-pole** *n.* сто́йка (лесо́в).

scald [skɔ:ld, skɒld] *n.* ожо́г.

v.t. **1.** ошпа́ри|вать, -ть; **I ~ed my hand** я ошпа́рил себе́ ру́ку; **the child was ~ed to death** ребёнок у́мер от ожо́гов; **~ing water** круто́й кипято́к; **~ing tears** жгу́чие слёзы; **the tea was ~ing hot** чай был обжига́юще горя́чий. **2. ~ milk** подогр|ева́ть, -е́ть молоко́, не доводя́ до кипе́ния; пастеризова́ть (*impf., pf.*) молоко́.

scale[1] [skeɪl] *n.* **1.** (*of fish, reptile etc.*) чешу́йка; (*pl., collect.*) чешуя́. **2.** (*bot.*) шелуха́. **3.** (*on teeth*) ка́мень (*m.*). **4. the ~s fell from his eyes** (*liter.*) пелена́ спа́ла с его́ глаз.

v.t.: **~ a fish** чи́стить, по- ры́бу; **~ metal** сн|има́ть, -ять ока́лину с мета́лла; **~ a boiler** сн|има́ть, -ять на́кипь с котла́.

v.i. **1.** (*form* ~; *also* **~ over**) образо́в|ывать, -а́ть ока́лину/на́кипь. **2.** (*come off in flakes; also* **~ off**) шелуши́ться (*impf.*); отп|ада́ть, -а́сть.

cpd. **~-armour** *n.* пласти́нчатая броня́.

scale[2] [skeɪl] *n.* **1.** (*of balance*) ча́ш(к)а (весо́в); **turn the ~** (*lit.*); **he turned the ~ at 80 kg** он ве́сил во́семьдесят килогра́ммов; (*fig.*): **this battle turned the ~ in our favour** э́то сраже́ние склони́ло ча́шу весо́в в на́шу сто́рону; **throw sth. into the ~** бр|оса́ть, -о́сить что-н. на ча́шу весо́в. **2.** (*pl., weighing machine*) вес|ы́ (*pl., g.* -о́в); **hold the ~s even** (*fig.*) суди́ть (*impf.*) беспристра́стно.

cpd. **~-beam** *n.* коромы́сло весо́в.

scale[3] [skeɪl] *n.* **1.** (*grading*) шкала́; **~ of charges** шкала́ расцено́к; **centigrade ~** шкала́ Це́льсия; **social ~** обще́ственная ле́стница; (*math.*): **~ of notation** систе́ма обозначе́ния. **2.** (*of map, and fig.*) масшта́б; **draw sth. to ~** черти́ть, на- что-н. в масшта́бе; **~ drawing** масшта́бный чертёж; **on a large/small ~** в большо́м/ма́лом масшта́бе; **we live on a small ~** мы живём скро́мно. **3.** (*size*) разме́р. **4.** (*mus.*) га́мма, звукоря́д; **practise one's ~s** разы́гр|ывать, -а́ть га́ммы.

v.t. **1.** (*climb*): **~ a wall** влез|а́ть, -ть (*or* залез|а́ть, -ть) на сте́ну; **~ a mountain** вз|бира́ться, -обра́ться на́ гору; **~ the heights of wisdom** дост|ига́ть, -и́чь верши́н прему́дрости.

with advs.: **~ down** *v.t.* пон|ижа́ть, -и́зить; сн|ижа́ть, -и́зить; ум|еньша́ть, -е́ньшить; (*fig.*) сокра|ща́ть, -ти́ть; **~ up** *v.t.* пов|ыша́ть, -ы́сить; увели́чи|вать, -ть.

scaleless ['skeɪllɪs] *adj.* бесчешу́йный.

scalene ['skeɪli:n] *adj.* неравносторо́нний.

scallion ['skæljən] *n.* лук-шало́т.

scallop ['skɒləp] *n.* (*mollusc*) гребешо́к; (*ornamental edging*) фесто́н.

v.t. отде́л|ывать, -ать фесто́нами; **~ed handkerchief** носово́й плато́к с фесто́нами.

cpd. **~-shell** *n.* ра́ковина гребешка́.

scallywag ['skælɪ,wæg], **scalawag** ['skælə,wæg] *n.* моше́нник, негодя́й; озорни́к.

scalp [skælp] *n.* ко́жа головы́; (*American Indian trophy*) скальп; **be out for (*or* after) s.o.'s ~** (*fig.*) жа́ждать (*impf.*) чьей-н. кро́ви.

v.t. скальпи́ровать (*impf., pf.*).

scalpel ['skælp(ə)l] *n.* ска́льпель (*m.*).

scalper ['skælpə(r)] *n.* спекуля́нт.

scaly ['skeɪlɪ] *adj.* (*with scales*) чешу́йчатый; (*flaking*) шелуша́щийся.

scam [skæm] *n.* (*sl.*) обма́н.

scamp [skæmp] *n.* шалу́н, пове́са (*m.*).

v.t. де́лать, с- ко́е-как/халту́рно.

scamper ['skæmpə(r)] *n.* (*quick run*) поспе́шное бе́гство; **he ran off at a ~** он побежа́л стремгла́в; (*gallop*) гало́п.

v.i. бе́гать (*indet.*); **the dog ~ed off** соба́ка отскочи́ла; **the class ~ed through Shakespeare** класс гало́пом пробежа́л по Шекспи́ру.

scampi ['skæmpɪ] *n.* креве́тки (*f. pl.*).

scan [skæn] *v.t.* **1.** (*pros.*) сканди́ровать, про-. **2.** (*survey*) обв|оди́ть, -ести́ взгля́дом/глаза́ми; (*stare at*) при́стально смотре́ть (*impf.*) на+*a.*; **he ~ned my face** он испыту́юще взгляну́л мне в лицо́; (*glance through*) пробе|га́ть, -жа́ть (глаза́ми). **3.** (*TV*) разл|ага́ть, -ожи́ть (изображе́ние); скани́ровать (*impf.*).

v.i. (*pros.*) сканди́роваться (*impf.*); **his verses don't ~** его́ стихи́ хрома́ют.

scandal ['skænd(ə)l] *n.* (*disgrace*) сканда́л, позо́р, безобра́зие; (*malicious gossip*) спле́тни (*f. pl.*); **create a ~, give rise to ~** вызыва́ть, вы́звать возмуще́ние; да|ва́ть, -ть по́вод к спле́тням; **it is a ~** э́то безобра́зие/возмути́тельно; **she was the ~ of the neighbourhood** она́ была́ при́тчей во язы́цех; **talk ~** спле́тничать (*impf.*); **School for S~** «Шко́ла злосло́вия».

scandalize ['skændə,laɪz] *v.t.* шоки́ровать (*impf.*).

scandalmonger ['skænd(ə)l,mʌŋgə(r)] *n.* спле́тни|к (*fem.* -ца).

scandalmongering ['skænd(ə)l,mʌŋgərɪŋ] *n.* спле́тни (*f. pl.*).

scandalous ['skændələs] *adj.* (*disgraceful*) позо́рный, безобра́зный, возмути́тельный; (*defamatory*) клеветни́ческий; (*fond of scandal*): **she has a ~ tongue** у неё злой язы́к.

Scandinavia [,skændɪ'neɪvɪə] *n.* Скандина́вия.

Scandinavian [,skændɪ'neɪvɪən] *n.* скандина́в *or* скандина́в|ец (*fem.* -ка).

adj. скандина́вский.

scanner ['skænə(r)] *n.* **1.** (*comput., med.*) ска́нер. **2.** (*TV*) развёртывающее устро́йство.

scansion ['skænʃ(ə)n] *n.* сканди́рование; (*metre*) разме́р.

scant [skænt] *adj.* (*inadequate*) недоста́точный; (*meagre*) ску́дный; **with ~ courtesy** бесцеремо́нно; **with ~ regard for my feelings** не счита́ясь с мои́ми чу́вствами.

scanty ['skæntɪ] *adj.* ску́дный (*see also* **scant**); **~ attire** ску́дная оде́жда; **~ audience** немногочи́сленная аудито́рия; **~ attendance** плоха́я посеща́емость; **~ hair** ре́дкие во́лосы.

scapegoat ['skeɪpgəʊt] *n.* козёл отпуще́ния.

scapegrace ['skeɪpgreɪs] *n.* шалопа́й, пове́са (*m.*).

scapula ['skæpjʊlə] *n.* лопа́тка.

scar[1] [skɑ:(r)] *n.* шрам, рубе́ц; (*fig.*) след.

v.t. (*mark with ~*) ра́нить, из-; **a face ~red with smallpox** ря́бое лицо́; лицо́, изры́тое о́спой; (*scratch*) цара́пать, о-/по-.

v.i. (*form ~; also* **~ over**) зарубц|о́вываться, -ева́ться.

scar[2] [skɑ:(r)], **scaur** [skɔ:(r)] *n.* утёс.

scarab ['skærəb] *n.* скарабе́й.

scarce [skeəs] *adj.* (*insufficient*) недоста́точный; (*scanty*) ску́дный; (*rare*) ре́дкий; **coal is ~ here** у́голь здесь в дефици́те; **butter was ~ during the war** во вре́мя войны́ не хвата́ло ма́сла; **good craftsmen are growing ~** хоро́шие мастера́ встреча́ются всё ре́же; **money is ~ with them** у них с деньга́ми ту́го; **make o.s.** ~ (*coll.*, *make off*) уб|ира́ться, -ра́ться (подобру́-поздоро́ву).

scarcely ['skeəslı] *adv.* **1.** (*barely*) едва́; почти́ не; **she is** ~ **17** ей едва́ испо́лнилось семна́дцать лет; **I** ~ **know him** я его́ почти́ не зна́ю; я едва́ с ним знако́м; (*only just*) то́лько; **I had** ~ **entered the room when the bell rang** то́лько я вошёл в ко́мнату, как зазвони́л телефо́н. **2.** (*surely not*): **you can** ~ **believe her** неуже́ли вы ей ве́рите?; **I** ~ **know what to say** пра́во, я не зна́ю, что сказа́ть; **you will** ~ **maintain that ...** вряд ли вы ста́нете (*or* не ста́нете же вы) утвержда́ть, что…

scarcity ['skeəsıtı] *n.* **1.** (*insufficiency*, *dearth*) недоста́ток, нехва́тка, дефици́т; **it was a time of great** ~ э́то бы́ло вре́мя больши́х лише́ний. **2.** (*rarity*) ре́дкость; ~ **value** сто́имость, определя́емая дефици́том.

scare [skeə(r)] *n.* (*fright*) испу́г; **give s.o. a** ~ пуга́ть, ис- кого́-н.; **you did give me a** ~ как вы меня́ напуга́ли!; (*alarm*, *panic*) па́ника; **the news created a** ~ но́вость вы́звала па́нику; **war** ~ вое́нный психо́з; нави́сшая угро́за войны́; ~ **headlines** сенсацио́нные заголо́вки.

v.t. пуга́ть, ис-; **I felt** ~**d** я боя́лся; **they were** ~ **stiff** они́ до́ смерти перепуга́лись.

v.i.: **he does not** ~ **easily** (*coll.*) он неро́бкого деся́тка.

with advs.: ~ **away,** ~ **off** *vv.t.* отпу́г|ивать, -ну́ть; спугну́ть (*pf.*).

cpds. ~**crow** *n.* пу́гало, (огоро́дное) чу́чело; ~**monger** *n.* паникёр (*fem.* -ша).

scarf [skɑːf] *n.* шарф.

scarify ['skeərıˌfaı] *v.t.* (*surg.*, *agric.*) скарифици́ровать (*impf.*, *pf.*); (*fig.*, *criticize*) жесто́ко раскритикова́ть (*pf.*).

scarlet ['skɑːlıt] *n.* а́лый цвет.

adj. а́лый; **turn** ~ (*blush*) гу́сто покрасне́ть (*pf.*); ~ **fever** скарлати́на; ~ **runner** фасо́ль о́гненная; ~ **woman** блу́дница.

scarp [skɑːp] *n.* (*steep slope*) круто́й отко́с; (*of fortification*) эска́рп.

scarper ['skɑːpə(r)] *v.i.* (*coll.*) = **scram**

scary ['skeərı] *adj.* (*coll.*) (*frightening*) жу́ткий; (*timid*) пугли́вый, ро́бкий.

scathing ['skeıðıŋ] *adj.* ре́зкий, е́дкий, язви́тельный.

scatological [skætə'lɒdʒık(ə)l] *adj.* (*obscene*) сорти́рный.

scatter ['skætə(r)] *v.t.* **1.** (*throw here and there*) разбр|а́сывать, -оса́ть; (*sprinkle*) расс|ыпа́ть, -ы́пать; пос|ыпа́ть, -ы́пать; ~ **seed** разбр|а́сывать, -оса́ть семена́; **toys were** ~**ed all over the room** игру́шки бы́ли разбро́саны по всей ко́мнате; **he** ~**ed his papers over the floor** (*or* ~**ed the floor with his papers**) он разброса́л свои́ бума́ги по всему́ по́лу; **they are** ~**ing gravel on the road** они́ посыпа́ют доро́гу гра́вием. **2.** (*pass.*): **the area is** ~**ed with small hamlets** по э́той ме́стности полно́ ма́леньких дереву́шек; ~**ed villages** раски́данные (там и тут) сёла. **3.** (*lit.*, *fig.*, *drive away*, *disperse*) раз|гоня́ть, -огна́ть; рассе́|ивать, -ять; **a shot** ~**ed the birds** вы́стрел распуга́л птиц; **a wind** ~**ed the clouds** ве́тер рассе́ял облака́; **a rough surface** ~**s the light** шерохова́тая пове́рхность рассе́ивает свет; **a thinly** ~**ed population** ре́дкое населе́ние; **in** ~**ed instances** в отде́льных слу́чаях.

v.i. (*disperse*) расс|ыпа́ться, -ы́паться; рассе́|иваться, -яться; (*move off*) ра|сходи́ться, -зойти́сь; **the crowd** ~**ed** толпа́ разбежа́лась; **the birds** ~**ed** пти́цы разлете́лись.

cpds. ~**-brain** *n.* вертопра́х; ~**-brained** *adj.* ве́треный.

scatty ['skætı] *adj.* (*coll.*) чо́кнутый, тро́нутый.

scaur [skɔː(r)] = **scar**[2]

scavenge ['skævındʒ] *v.i.* ры́ться/копа́ться (*impf.*) в отбро́сах; ходи́ть (*impf.*) по помо́йкам.

scavenger ['skævındʒə(r)] *n.* (*animal*) живо́тное, пита́ющееся па́далью; **the jackal is the** ~ **of the plain** шака́л — му́сорщик степе́й; (*bird*) стервя́тник; (*pers.*) му́сорщик.

scenario [sı'nɑːrıəʊ, -'neərıəʊ] *n.* сцена́рий; (*fig.*) вариа́нт, сцена́рий; **a worst-case** ~ наиху́дший вариа́нт *or* сцена́рий.

scene [siːn] *n.* **1.** (*stage*) сце́на; (*fig.*): **appear on the** ~ появ|ля́ться, -и́ться; **quit the** ~ сойти́ (*pf.*) со сце́ны. **2.** (*place of action*) ме́сто де́йствия; **the** ~ **is laid in London** де́йствие происхо́дит в Ло́ндоне. **3.** (*place*) ме́сто; **the** ~ **of the disaster/crime** ме́сто катастро́фы/преступле́ния; ~ **of operations** (*mil.*) теа́тр вое́нных де́йствий; **change of** ~ переме́на обстано́вки. **4.** (*subdivision of play*) сце́на; **the duel** ~ сце́на дуэ́ли; (*fig.*, *episode*, *incident*): ~**s of country life** сце́ны из се́льской жи́зни; **make a** ~ устр|а́ивать, -о́ить (*or* зака́т|ывать, -и́ть) сце́ну (*кому*). **5.** (*set*, *décor*) декора́ция; (*fig.*): **behind the** ~**s** за кули́сами. **6.** (*view*, *landscape*): **a** ~ **of destruction** карти́на разруше́ния; **a desolate** ~ карти́на запусте́ния. **7.** (*milieu*): **(on) the pop music** ~ в ми́ре поп-му́зыки.

cpds. ~**-painter** *n.* худо́жник-декора́тор; ~**-shifter** *n.* рабо́чий сце́ны.

scenery ['siːnərı] *n.* (*theatr.*) декора́ции (*f. pl.*); (*landscape*) пейза́ж, вид.

scenic ['siːnık] *adj.* сцени́ческий, сцени́чный, театра́льный; карти́нный, живопи́сный; ~ **attraction** привлека́тельное ме́сто; ~ **beauty** живопи́сность (ландша́фта); ~ **railway** америка́нские го́ры (*f. pl.*).

scent [sent] *n.* **1.** (*odour*) за́пах, арома́т, благоуха́ние. **2.** (*perfume*) дух|и́ (*pl.*, *g.* -о́в); **use, apply** ~ души́ться, на-. **3.** (*sense of smell*; *lit.*, *fig.*) чутьё, нюх. **4.** (*trail*) след; **get on** (*or* **pick up**) **the** ~ нап|ада́ть, -а́сть на след; **lose the** ~ теря́ть, по- след; (*fig.*): **he threw the police off the** ~ он сбил поли́цию со сле́да; **be thrown off the** ~ сб|ива́ться, -и́ться со сле́да; **he put them on a false** ~ он напра́вил их по ло́жному пути́.

v.t. **1.** (*discern by smell*; *also fig.*) чу́ять, по-; **he** ~**ed treachery** он почу́ял/заподо́зрил изме́ну. **2.** (*sniff*) ню́хать, по-. **3.** (*impart odour to*): **roses** ~ **the air** ро́зы распространя́ют благоуха́ние; **a** ~**ed rose** благоуха́нная ро́за; ~**ed soap** души́стое мы́ло.

cpds. ~**-bottle** *n.* пузырёк/флако́н (для) духо́в; ~**-spray** *n.* духи́-спре́й (*indecl.*), духи́ в аэрозо́ле.

scentless ['sentlıs] *adj.* без за́паха, лишённый арома́та.

sceptic ['skeptık] (*US* **skeptic**) *n.* ске́птик.

sceptical ['skeptık(ə)l] (*US* **skeptical**) *adj.* скепти́ческий; скепти́чески настро́енный (к+*d.*).

scepticism ['skeptıˌsız(ə)m] (*US* **skepticism**) *n.* скептици́зм.

sceptre ['septə(r)] *n.* ски́петр; **wield the** ~ ца́рствовать (*impf.*); пра́вить (*impf.*).

schadenfreude ['ʃɑːdənˌfrɔıdə] *n.* злора́дство.

schedule ['ʃedjuːl, 'ske-] *n.* **1.** (*list*) спи́сок, пе́речень (*m.*); ~ **of charges** тари́ф ста́вок/расце́нок. **2.** (*plan*, *timetable*) план, расписа́ние; **flight** ~ расписа́ние самолётов; **work** ~ гра́фик рабо́ты; **according to** ~ соотве́тственно пла́ну; **a full** ~ больша́я програ́мма; **be behind** ~ зап|а́здывать, -озда́ть; **be up to** ~ не отст|ава́ть, -а́ть (от гра́фика); **be ahead of** ~ опере|жа́ть, -ди́ть гра́фик; **before** ~ ра́ньше вре́мени; **on** ~ во́время/то́чно.

v.t. **1.** (*tabulate*) сост|авля́ть, -а́вить спи́сок +*g.*; **the house is** ~**d for demolition** дом (пред)назна́чен на снос; ~**d prices** устано́вленные це́ны; **a** ~**d flight** регуля́рный рейс. **2.** (*time*; *plan*) рассчи́т|ывать, -а́ть; нам|еча́ть, -е́тить; **we are** ~**d to finish by May** по пла́ну мы должны́ ко́нчить к ма́ю; **the train is** ~**d to leave at noon** (по расписа́нию) по́езд отхо́дит в по́лдень.

schema ['skiːmə] *n.* схе́ма.

schematic [skı'mætık, skiː-] *adj.* схемати́ческий; (*stereotyped*) схемати́чный.

schematize ['skiːməˌtaız] *v.t.* схематизи́ровать (*impf.*, *pf.*).

schem|e [skiːm] *n.* **1.** (*arrangement*) поря́док; **in the** ~**e of things** в поря́дке веще́й; **colour** ~**e** цветова́я га́мма; сочета́ние кра́сок. **2.** (*plan*) прое́кт, план, програ́мма. **3.** (*plot*) про́иск|и (*pl.*, *g.* -ов), за́мысел.

v.i. интригова́ть (*impf.*); **he was** ~**ing to escape** он замышля́л побе́г; **they were** ~**ing for power** они́ плели́ интри́ги, что́бы пробра́ться к вла́сти.

schemer ['skiːmə(r)] *n.* интрига́н (*fem.* -ка).

scherzo ['skeəˌtsəʊ] *n.* ске́рцо (*indecl.*).

schism ['sız(ə)m, 'skı-] *n.* раско́л; схи́зма.

schismatic [sız'mætık, skız-] *n.* раско́льник.

adj. раско́льнический.

schist [ʃıst] *n.* сла́нец.

schizo ['skɪtsəʊ] *n.* (*coll.*) ши́зик.
schizoid ['skɪtsɔɪd] *n.* шизо́ид.
adj. шизо́идный.
schizophrenia [ˌskɪtsə'friːnɪə] *n.* шизофрени́я.
schizophrenic [ˌskɪtsə'frenɪk, -'friːnɪk] *n.* шизофре́н|ик (*fem.* -и́чка).
adj. шизофрени́ческий.
schmaltz [ʃmɔːlts, ʃmælts] *n.* (*sl.*) сентимента́льщина.
schmaltzy ['smɔːltsɪ, 'smæltsɪ] *adj.* (*sl.*) сентимента́льный, при́торный, слаща́вый; слезли́вый, сопли́вый, «сплошны́е со́пли».
schnapps [ʃnæps] *n.* шнапс.
schnitzel ['ʃnɪtz(ə)l] *n.* шни́цель (*m.*).
schnorkel ['ʃnɔːk(ə)l] = **snorkel**
scholar ['skɒlə(r)] *n.* **1.** (*learned pers.*) учёный-гуманита́р; **Latin** ~ латини́ст; **Greek** ~ знато́к гре́ческого языка́, эллини́ст; **he is no** ~ учёный из него́ нева́жный. **2.** (*learner*) учени́к; **he proved an apt** ~ он оказа́лся спосо́бным ученико́м. **3.** (*holder of ~ship*) стипендиа́т (*fem.* -ка).
scholarly ['skɒləlɪ] *adj.* учёный, эруди́рованный, академи́ческий; **he has a** ~ **mind** у него́ нау́чный склад ума́.
scholarship ['skɒləʃɪp] *n.* (*erudition*) учёность, эруди́ция; (*scholarly method or outlook*) академи́ческий/нау́чный подхо́д; (*grant*) стипе́ндия; **memorial** ~ именна́я стипе́ндия.
scholastic [skə'læstɪk] *adj.* **1.** (*hist.*) схоласти́ческий. **2.** академи́ческий; ~ **institution** уче́бное заведе́ние.
scholasticism [skə'læstɪˌsɪz(ə)m] *n.* схола́стика.
school[1] [skuːl] *n.* **1.** (*place of education*) шко́ла; (*incl. higher education*) уче́бное заведе́ние; **at** ~ в шко́ле; **go to** ~ ходи́ть (*indet.*) в шко́лу; учи́ться (*impf.*) в шко́ле; **go to** ~ **to s.o.** (*fig.*) учи́ться (*impf.*) у кого́-н.; **teach** ~ (*US*) учи́тельствовать (*impf.*); **start** ~ поступ|а́ть, -и́ть (*or* пойти́ (*pf.*)) в шко́лу; **leave** ~ (*complete course*) конча́ть, ко́нчить шко́лу; (*abandon* ~) бр|оса́ть, -о́сить шко́лу; **where were you at** ~? где вы учи́лись?; **we were at** ~ **together** мы вме́сте учи́лись; **of** ~ **age** шко́льного во́зраста; ~ **fees** пла́та за обуче́ние; ~ **report** шко́льный та́бель; **boarding** ~ шко́ла-интерна́т; **boys'/girls'** ~ мужска́я/же́нская шко́ла; **public** ~ (*in UK*) (привилегиро́ванная) ча́стная шко́ла; (*in US*) (беспла́тная) сре́дняя шко́ла; **nursery** ~ де́тский сад; **primary** ~ нача́льная шко́ла; **secondary, high** ~ сре́дняя шко́ла; **junior/senior** ~ шко́ла пе́рвой/второ́й ступе́ни; **evening, night** ~ вече́рняя шко́ла; **military** ~ вое́нное учи́лище; **trade** ~ профессиона́льное учи́лище; **vocational** ~ профессиона́льно-техни́ческое учи́лище; ~ **of art** худо́жественное учи́лище; ~ **of dancing** шко́ла та́нцев; (*research centre*) институ́т; (*department of university, branch of study*): ~ **of law** юриди́ческая ка́федра, юриди́ческий факульте́т; (*pl., examination*) выпускны́е экза́мены (*m. pl.*). **2.** (*lessons*) заня́тия (*nt. pl.*); **there will be no** ~ **today** сего́дня заня́тий/уро́ков не бу́дет; ~ **finishes at 4** заня́тия/уро́ки конча́ются в 4. **3.** (*range of classes*): **the lower/middle/upper** ~ мла́дшие/сре́дние/ста́ршие кла́ссы (*m. pl.*). **4.** (*of art, manners etc.*): **the Impressionist** ~ импрессионисти́ческая шко́ла; **he is one of the old** ~ он челове́к ста́рой шко́лы (*or* ста́рого зака́ла); **there is a** ~ **of thought which says ...** существу́ет тече́ние, согла́сно кото́рому.... **5.** (*attr.*) шко́льный, уче́бный. *See also cpds.*
v.t. обуч|а́ть, -и́ть; ~ **one's temper** обу́здывать (*impf.*) свой хара́ктер; сде́рживать (*impf.*) свой темпера́мент; **~ed by adversity** проше́дший суро́вую шко́лу нужды́/лише́ний; ~ **a horse** объ|езжа́ть, -е́здить ло́шадь.
cpds. **~-bag** *n.* шко́льная су́мка; шко́льный ра́нец/портфе́ль; **~-board** *n.* ≃ райо́нный отде́л наро́дного образова́ния (*abbr.* РОНО); **~-book** *n.* уче́бник; **~boy** *n.* шко́льник; **~boy slang** шко́льный/учени́ческий жарго́н; **~certificate** *n.* аттеста́т зре́лости; **~children** *n.* шко́льники (*m. pl.*); **~-days** *n.*: **I read this author in my ~-days** я э́того а́втора чита́л на шко́льной скамье́ (*or* ещё шко́льником); **my ~-days ended when I was 15** моему́ уче́нию пришёл коне́ц, когда́ мне бы́ло 15 лет; **~fellow, ~mate** *nn.* соучени́|к (*fem.* -ца), шко́льный това́рищ; **~girl** *n.* шко́льница; **~-inspector** *n.* шко́льный инспе́ктор; **~-leaver** *n.* выпускни́|к (*fem.* -ца); **~-leaving** *adj.*: **~-leaving age** во́зраст, до кото́рого обуче́ние обяза́тельно; **~-leaving certificate** аттеста́т зре́лости; **~man** *n.* (*hist.*) схола́ст(ик); **~-marm** *n.* (*coll.*) (се́льская) учи́тельница; **~master** *n.* учи́тель (*m.*); **~mastering** *n.* = **~teaching**; **~mate** *n.* = **~fellow**; **~mistress** *n.* учи́тельница; **~pupil** *n.* учени́|к (*fem.* -ца); шко́льни|к (*fem.* -ца); **~room** *n.* класс; кла́ссная ко́мната; **~teacher** *n.* учи́тель (*fem.* -ница); **~teaching, ~mastering** *nn.* (*as profession*) педаго́гика; **he took up ~teaching** он пошёл в учителя́ (*or* сде́лался педаго́гом/учи́телем); (*activity*) препода́вание; **~-time** *n.* (*lesson-time*) уче́бное вре́мя.
school[2] [skuːl] *n.* (*of fish etc.*) кося́к.
schooling ['skuːlɪŋ] *n.* (*education*) (об)уче́ние; (*training*) подгото́вка; **he had little** ~ ему́ не довело́сь мно́го учи́ться; **who is paying for her** ~? кто опла́чивает (*or* пла́тит за) её обуче́ние?
schooner ['skuːnə(r)] *n.* (*naut.*) шху́на; (*glass*) бока́л, стака́н.
sciatic [saɪ'ætɪk] *adj.* седа́лищный.
sciatica [saɪ'ætɪkə] *n.* и́шиас.
science ['saɪəns] *n.* **1.** (*systematic knowledge*) нау́ка; **pure/applied** ~ чи́стая/прикладна́я нау́ка; **moral** ~ э́тика; **social** ~ обще́ственные нау́ки. **2.** (*natural ~s*) есте́ственные нау́ки; ~ **fiction** нау́чная фанта́стика. **3.** (*skill, e.g. in boxing*) иску́сство.
scientific [ˌsaɪən'tɪfɪk] *adj.* нау́чный; ~ **calculator** компью́тер-калькуля́тор; ~ **knowledge** нау́чное зна́ние; ~ **method** нау́чный ме́тод; **he plays a ~game** он игра́ет по-нау́чному.
scientist ['saɪəntɪst] *n.* учёный(-есте́ственник).
sci-fi ['saɪfaɪ] *n.* (*coll.*) НФ (нау́чная фанта́стика).
adj. нау́чно-фантасти́ческий.
scilicet ['saɪlɪˌset, 'skiːlɪˌket] *adv.* (*abbr. of* **scire licet**) т.е., (то есть).
Scilly ['sɪlɪ] *n.*: **Isles of** ~ острова́ (*m. pl.*) Си́лли (*indecl.*).
scimitar ['sɪmɪtə(r)] *n.* ятага́н.
scintilla [sɪn'tɪlə] *n.* (*fig.*) чу́точка, крупи́ца, ка́пля; **there is not a** ~ **of evidence** нет (реши́тельно) никаки́х доказа́тельств.
scintillat|e ['sɪntɪˌleɪt] *v.i.* (*lit., fig.*) и́скриться (*impf.*); блиста́ть (*impf.*); **a book ~ing with wit** кни́га, и́скрящаяся остроу́мием.
scintillation [ˌsɪntɪ'leɪʃ(ə)n] *n.* сверка́ние, блеск; мерца́ние.
sciolist ['saɪəlɪst] *n.* дилета́нт (*fem.* -ка).
scion ['saɪən] *n.* (*of plant*) побе́г; (*descendant*) о́тпрыск, пото́мок.
Scipio ['skɪpɪˌəʊ, 'sɪpɪ-] *n.* Сципио́н.
scirocco [sɪ'rɒkəʊ] = **sirocco**
scissor|s ['sɪzəz] *n.* (*also in wrestling, gymnastics*) но́жниц|ы (*pl., g.* —); **~s and paste** (*fig.*) компиля́ция, «режь и клей».
cpds. **~-bill** *n.* клёст; **~-case** *n.* футля́р для но́жниц; **~-grinder** *n.* точи́льщик; **~grip, ~-hold** *nn.* но́жницы.
sclerosis [sklɪə'rəʊsɪs] *n.* склеро́з; **multiple** ~ рассе́янный склеро́з.
sclerotic [sklɪə'rɒtɪk] *adj.* склероти́ческий, склероти́чный.
scoff[1] [skɒf] *n.* (*taunt*) насме́шка; (*laughing-stock*) посме́шище.
v.i. смея́ться, (*coll.*) зубоска́лить (*both impf.*); ~ **at** издева́ться/глуми́ться/насмеха́ться (*all impf.*) над+*i.*; **he ~ed at danger** он смея́лся над опа́сностью; **be ~ed at** быть мише́нью насме́шек, подверга́ться (*impf.*) насме́шкам; **he was ~ed at** над ним смея́лись.
scoff[2] [skɒf] *n.* (*food*) жратва́ (*sl.*).
v.t. & i. жрать, со-.
scoffer ['skɒfə(r)] *n.* насме́шник, зубоска́л.
scold [skəʊld] *n.* сварли́вая ба́ба.
v.t. брани́ть, вы-; руга́ть, об-; отчи́т|ывать, -а́ть.
v.i. брани́ться, ворча́ть, брюзжа́ть (*all impf.*).
scolding ['skəʊldɪŋ] *n.* брань; **I gave him a good** ~ я дал ему́ хоро́ший нагоня́й; я его́ как сле́дует отчита́л.

scollop [ˈskɒləp] = **scallop**
sconce [skɒns] *n.* (*candlestick*) подсве́чник; (*on wall bracket*) бра (*nt. indecl.*).
scone [skɒn, skəʊn] *n.* ≃ бу́лочка.
scoop [sku:p] *n.* **1.** (*for grain etc.*) сово́к; (*for liquids*) ковш; (*for food*) ло́жка. **2.:** ~ **neckline** глубо́кое, кру́глое декольте́ (*indecl.*). **3.** (*journ.*) ≃ сенса́ция.
v.t. **1.** (*lift with* ~) че́рп|ать, -ну́ть; заче́рп|ывать, -ну́ть; выче́рпывать, вы́черпать. **2.** (*make by* ~*ing*) выда́лбливать, вы́долбить; **he ~ed out a hole in the sand** он вы́рыл я́му в песке́. **3.** (*make a profit of*) срыва́ть, сорва́ть куш; **he is ~ing in £100 a week** он загреба́ет по сто фу́нтов в неде́лю; ~ **the pool** забра́ть/вы́играть (*pf.*) все взя́тки. **4.** (*journ.*) обст|авля́ть, -а́вить; **they ~ed the other papers on this story** они́ обскака́ли други́е газе́ты с э́той сенса́цией/но́востью.
scoot [sku:t] *v.i.* уд|ира́ть, -ра́ть (*coll.*).
scooter [ˈsku:tə(r)] *n.* (*child's*) самока́т; (*motor* ~) моторо́ллер.
scope [skəʊp] *n.* **1.** (*range, sweep*) разма́х, охва́т; **an undertaking of wide** ~ предприя́тие с широ́ким разма́хом; **this is beyond my** ~ э́то вне мое́й компете́нции; **does the work fall within his** ~**?** э́та рабо́та вхо́дит в сфе́ру его́ де́ятельности?; **this is beyond the** ~ **of our enquiry** э́то выхо́дит за преде́лы/ра́мки на́шего рассле́дования. **2.** (*outlet, vent*): **the game offers** ~ **for the children's imagination** э́та игра́ даёт просто́р де́тскому воображе́нию; **the project provided** ~ **for his abilities** э́тот прое́кт дал ему́ возмо́жность разверну́ть свои́ спосо́бности; **he seeks** ~ **for his energies** он и́щет де́ла, где бы приложи́ть свою́ эне́ргию; **they gave him full** ~ ему́ предоста́вили по́лную свобо́ду де́йствий.
scorbutic [skɔ:ˈbju:tɪk] *adj.* цинго́тный.
scorch [skɔ:tʃ] *v.t.* (*burn, dry up*) жечь, с-; **~ed earth policy** страте́гия вы́жженной земли́; (*clothes etc.*) подпа́л|ивать, -и́ть; **the long summer ~ed the grass** за до́лгое ле́то трава́ вы́горела.
v.i. (*drive or ride at high speed*) жа́рить (*impf.*) (на всю кату́шку) (*coll.*).
cpd. **~-mark** *n.* подпа́лина, ожо́г.
scorcher [ˈskɔ:tʃə(r)] *n.* (*coll., hot day*) зно́йный день.
score [skɔ:(r)] *n.* **1.** (*notch*) зару́бка; (*deep scratch*) глубо́кая цара́пина; (*weal on skin*) рубе́ц. **2.** (*arch., account*) счёт; **pay one's** ~ упла́|чивать, -ти́ть по счёту; распла́|чиваться, -ти́ться; **death pays all ~s** смерть всё примиря́ет; **pay off old ~s** (*fig.*) св|оди́ть, -ести́ ста́рые счёты; расквита́ться (*pf.*). **3.** (*in games*) счёт; **what's the** ~**?** како́й счёт?; **make a good** ~ сыгра́ть (*pf.*) с хоро́шим счётом; **keep the** ~ вести́ (*det.*) счёт; **know the** ~ (*fig., coll.*) быть в ку́рсе; знать (*impf.*), что к чему́. **4.** (*mus.*): **(full)** ~ партиту́ра; **piano/vocal** ~ па́ртия фортепиа́но/го́лоса. **5.** (*twenty*) два́дцать; **a** ~ **of people** челове́к два́дцать; **~s of people** мно́жество наро́ду; **three** ~ **and ten** (*arch.*) се́мьдесят; **~s of times** мно́го раз; ча́сто; **workers are leaving in their ~s** рабо́чие то́лпами оставля́ют рабо́ту. **6.** (*grounds*) причи́на, основа́ние, по́вод; **on the** ~ **of ill health** по причи́не плохо́го здоро́вья; **you need have no fear on that** ~ на э́то счёт вы мо́жете не беспоко́иться. **7.** (*retort*) уда́чная ре́плика. **8.** (*good fortune*) уда́ча.
v.t. **1.** (*notch*) изре́з|ывать, -ать; **a face ~d with wrinkles** лицо́, изборождённое морщи́нами; (*incise*): ~ **a line** провести́ (*pf.*) ли́нию (ножо́м *и т.п.*); (*mark, deface*): **the article was ~d with corrections** статья́ была́ испещрена́ попра́вками; ~ **out, through** вычёркивать, вы́черкнуть; зачёрк|ивать, -ну́ть; (*scratch*) цара́пать, ис-; (*preparatory to cutting*) разм|еча́ть, -е́тить. **2.** (*mark up*) ста́вить, по- в счёт; запи́с|ывать, -а́ть в долг. **3.** (*win*) выи́грывать, вы́играть; ~ **a goal** (*football*) заб|ива́ть, -и́ть гол; ~ **tricks** (*at cards*) брать, взять взя́тки; **he ~d a success with his first book** его́ пе́рвая кни́га принесла́ ему́ успе́х; **a goal ~s six points** за оди́н гол засчи́тывается 6 очко́в. **4.** (*mus., orchestrate*) оркестрова́ть (*impf., pf.*); (*arrange*) аранжи́ровать (*impf., pf.*).
v.i. **1.** (*keep score*) вести́ (*impf.*) счёт; (*win point*) выи́грывать, вы́играть очко́; **they failed to** ~ они́ не вы́играли ни одного́ очка́; **the centre-forward ~d** центр нападе́ния заби́л гол. **2.** (*secure advantage; have good luck*) выи́грывать, вы́играть; **that's where he ~s** вот на чём он вы́играет; вот в чём его́ си́ла/преиму́щество; ~ **off s.o.** вы́смеять/подде́ть (*pf.*) кого́-н.
cpds. **~-keeper** *n.* судья́-секрета́рь (*m.*); **~-sheet** *n.* суде́йский протоко́л.
scorer [ˈskɔ:rə(r)] *n.* **1.** (*keeper of score*) счётчик. **2.: the captain was the** ~ **of that goal** тот гол заби́л капита́н.
scorn [skɔ:n] *n.* презре́ние; **laugh to** ~ высме́ивать, вы́смеять.
v.t. презира́ть (*impf.*); пренебр|ега́ть, -е́чь +*i.*; **he ~ed the danger** он презре́л опа́сность; **he ~ed such methods** он гнуша́лся подо́бными сре́дствами.
scornful [ˈskɔ:nfʊl] *adj.* (*of pers.*) надме́нный; **he was** ~ **of the idea** он отнёсся к э́той иде́е с презре́нием; (*of glance etc.*) презри́тельный.
Scorpio [ˈskɔ:pɪəʊ] *n.* Скорпио́н.
scorpion [ˈskɔ:pɪən] *n.* скорпио́н.
Scot [skɒt] *n.* шотла́нд|ец (*fem.* -ка); (*hist.*) скотт.
Scotch[1] [skɒtʃ] *n.* **1.** (*ling.*) шотла́ндский го́вор. **2.** (*whisky*) шотла́ндское ви́ски (*indecl.*). **3. the** ~ шотла́ндцы (*m. pl.*).
adj. шотла́ндский; ~ (*propr.*) **tape** кле́йкая ле́нта, скотч.
cpds. **~man** *n.* шотла́ндец; **~woman** *n.* шотла́ндка.
scotch[2] [skɒtʃ] *v.t.* **1.** (*arch.*) ра́нить (*impf., pf.*); кале́чить, ис-; обезвр|е́живать, -е́дить. **2.** (*fig.*): **he ~ed the rumour** он опрове́рг слух.
scot-free [ˈskɒtfri:] *adv.*: **go** ~ (*unharmed*) ост|ава́ться, -а́ться невреди́мым; (*unpunished*) ост|ава́ться, -а́ться безнака́занным.
Scotland [ˌskɒtlənd] *n.* Шотла́ндия.
Scots [skɒts] *n.* (*ling.*) шотла́ндский го́вор.
adj. шотла́ндский.
cpds. **~man** *n.* шотла́ндец; **~woman** *n.* шотла́ндка.
Scot(t)icism [ˈskɒtɪˌsɪz(ə)m] *n.* шотланди́зм.
Scottish [ˈskɒtɪʃ] *adj.* шотла́ндский.
scoundrel [ˈskaʊndr(ə)l] *n.* подле́ц, мерза́вец.
scour[1] [ˈskaʊə(r)] *n.* **1.** (*cleansing*) чи́стка; **give sth. a good** ~ вы́чистить (*pf.*) что-н. хороше́нько. **2.** (*action of current*) размы́в.
v.t. **1.** (*cleanse*): ~ **a saucepan** чи́стить, вы́- кастрю́лю; ~ **a dish** нач|ища́ть, -и́стить блю́до. **2.** (*of water*) пром|ыва́ть, -ы́ть. **3.** (*purge*) проч|ища́ть, -и́стить. **4.** (*remove by* ~*ing; also* ~ **away, off**) отт|ира́ть, -ере́ть.
scour[2] [ˈskaʊə(r)] *v.t.* (*range in search or pursuit*) ры́скать, об-; **he ~ed the town for his daughter** он обе́гал весь го́род в по́исках до́чери.
v.i. ры́скать (*impf.*).
scourer [ˈskaʊrə(r)] *n.* (*for saucepans etc.*) металли́ческая мо́чалка; ёж.
scourge [skɜ:dʒ] *n.* (*whip; also fig., pers.*) бич; (*misfortune*) бич, крест, бе́дствие.
v.t. (*flog*) сечь, вы́-; (*chastise*) бичева́ть (*impf.*); кара́ть, по-.
Scouse [skaʊs] *n.* (*coll.*) **1.** ливерпу́льский диале́кт. **2.** ливерпу́л|ец (*fem.* -ка).
adj. ливерпу́льский.
Scouser [ˈskaʊsə(r)] (*coll.*) = **Scouse** *n.* **2.**
scout[1] [skaʊt] *n.* **1.** (*mil.*) разве́дчик (*also ship, aircraft*); ~ **car** разве́дывательный автомоби́ль. **2.** (*Boy S*~) бойска́ут. **3.** (*coll., fellow*): **he's a good** ~ он хоро́ший ма́лый/па́рень.
v.i. (*reconnoitre*) разве́дывать (*impf.*); **he is out ~ing** он в разве́дке; (*coll., search*) разы́скивать (*impf.*); **I have been ~ing about for a present** я обыска́л все магази́ны в по́исках пода́рка; (*belong to S~ movement*): **my son is keen on ~ing** мой сын увлека́ется бойска́утской де́ятельностью.
cpd. **~master** *n.* нача́льник отря́да бойска́утов.
scout[2] [skaʊt] *v.t.* (*reject*) отв|ерга́ть, -е́ргнуть (с презре́нием).
scow [skaʊ] *n.* ба́ржа́, ба́рка.
scowl [skaʊl] *n.* серди́тый/хму́рый взгляд.

v.i. **1.: he ~ed at me** он свирéпо посмотрéл на меня́; **a ~ing face** хму́рое/нахму́ренное лицó. **2.** (*fig., of sky*) хму́риться, на-; (*of cliffs etc.*) нав|исáть, -и́снуть.

Scrabble[1] ['skræb(ə)l] *n.* (*propr.*) скрэбл (≃ Эруди́т).

scrabble[2] ['skræb(ə)l] *v.i.*: **~ about** шáрить (*impf.*); **~ about for sth.** разы́скивать (*impf.*) что-н.

scrag [skræg] *n.*: **~ end of mutton** барáнья шéя.

v.t. (*coll., rough up*) трепáть, по-.

scraggy ['skrægɪ] *adj.* костля́вый, тóщий; чáхлый.

scram [skræm] *v.i.* (*sl.*): **I told him to ~** я велéл емý убирáться; **~!** провáливай!; кати́сь!

scramble ['skræmb(ə)l] *n.* **1.** (*climb with hands and feet*) карáбканье. **2.** (*motor cycle race*) мотокрóсс. **3.** (*struggle to get sth.*) свáлка; (*fig.*) борьбá, схвáтка; **there was a ~ for the ball** произошлá схвáтка/борьбá за мяч; **it was a ~ to get ready in time** мы собрáли́сь с трудóм, чтóбы поспéть вóвремя; **the ~ for office** борьбá за дóлжность/местá.

v.t.: **~ eggs** жáрить, под- яи́чницу-болтýнью.

v.i. **1.** (*clamber*) карáбкаться, вс-; вз|бирáться, -обрáться; **we ~d through the bracken** мы продрáлись чéрез зáросли пáпоротника; **the boys ~d over the wall** мáльчики перелéзли чéрез забóр; **I ~d into my clothes** я поспéшно натянýл (на себя́) одéжду; **he ~d into the car** он влез/залéз в маши́ну. **2.** (*fig.*) борóться (*impf.*); **the passengers ~d for seats** пассажи́ры ри́нулись занимáть местá. **3.** (*sl., of pilots or aircraft: take off*) взлет|áть, -етéть по тревóге.

scrambler ['skræmblə(r)] *n.* (*telephone*) засекрéчиватель (*m.*); автомати́ческое шифровáльное устрóйство.

scrap[1] [skræp] *n.* **1.** (*small piece*) кусóчек; (*of metal*) облóмок; (*of cloth*) обрéзок; лоскýт; (*fragment*) обры́вок; **~s of knowledge/conversation** обры́вки (*m. pl.*) знáний/разговóра; **~s of paper** клочки́ (*m. pl.*) бумáги; **there's not a ~ of evidence** нет никаки́х (*or* каки́х бы то ни́ было) доказáтельств. **2.** (*pl., waste food*) объéдк|и (*pl., g.* -ов); **they found a few ~s of food** они́ нашли́ кóе-каки́е остáтки пи́щи; **we dined off ~s** мы поýжинали тем, что остáлось от вчерáшнего обéда. **3.** (*waste material, refuse*) ути́ль (*m.*); утильсырьё; (**~** *metal*) (металли́ческий) лом, металлолóм.

v.t. **1.** (*make into ~*) обра|щáть, -ти́ть в лом; (*machines etc.*) отд|авáть, -áть (*or* пус|кáть, -ти́ть) на слом. **2.** (*coll., discard*) выбрáсывать, вы́бросить; бракoвáть, за-; сда|вáть, -ть в архи́в.

cpds. **~-book** *n.* альбóм для вырезок; **~-heap** *n.* свáлка; **throw sth. on the ~-heap** (*lit., fig.*) выбрáсывать, вы́бросить что-н. на свáлку; **~-iron** *n.* желéзный лом; **~-merchant** *n.* старьёвщик; торгóвец утилём; **~-value** *n.* стóимость (*чего*) на слом; **~-yard** *n.* склад лóма; пункт приёма металлолóма/ути́ля; склад вторсырья́.

scrap[2] [skræp] *n.* (*coll., fight*) дрáка, сты́чка, потасóвка; **have a ~** дрáться, по-; сцеп|ля́ться, -и́ться; вздóрить, по-; **he is always ready for a ~** он стрáшный забия́ка.

v.i. дрáться (*impf.*).

scrape [skreɪp] *n.* **1.** (*action*) скоблéние, чи́стка; (*of pen*) скрип; (*of foot*) шáрканье; **give a carrot a ~** почи́стить (*pf.*) морко́вь. **2.** (*coll., awkward predicament*) передéлка; **get into a ~** вли́пнуть (*pf.*) (в истóрию) (*coll.*).

v.t. **1.** (*abrade*) скобли́ть, вы́-; (*graze*) ссá|живать, -ди́ть; **I ~d my hand on the wall** я ссади́л/ободрáл себé рýку о стéну. **2.** (*clean*) выскáбливать (*or* скобли́ть), вы́скоблить; **~ one's shoes** соск|áбливать, -обли́ть (*or* сч|ищáть, -и́стить *or* соскре|бáть, -сти́) грязь с подóшв; **he ~d his plate clean** он подчи́стил всю тарéлку (*or* всё с тарéлки). **3.: ~ one's feet** шáркать (*impf.*) ногáми. **4.: ~ a living** кóе-как своди́ть (*impf.*) концы́ с концáми. **5.: ~ acquaintance with s.o.** завя́з|ывать, -зáть знакóмство с кем-н.

v.i. **1.** (*rub*): **my hand ~d against the wall** я ссади́л себé рýку о стéну; **his car ~d against a tree** егó маши́на задéла дéрево; он поцарáпал маши́ну о дéрево. **2.** (*get through*): **he ~d into the university** он с грехóм пополáм прошёл в университéт; **she just ~d into the final** ей едвá удалóсь вы́йти в финáл. **3.: bow and ~** раболéпствовать, подхали́мничать, расшáркиваться (*all impf.*) (*перед кем*). **4.** (*on violin*) пили́кать (*impf.*).

with advs.: **~ along** (*also* **scratch along**), **~ by** *v.i.* (*get by*) проб|ивáться, -и́ться; пробавля́ться (*impf.*); **we can just ~ along** мы кóе-как перебивáемся; **~ down** *v.t.* выскáбливать, вы́скоблить; **~ in** *v.i.*: **the room was full but we just ~d in** кóмната былá биткóм наби́та, но нам кóе-как удалóсь вти́снуться; **~ off** *v.t.* соск|áбливать, -обли́ть; соскре|бáть, -сти́; **~ out** *v.t.* выскребáть, вы́скрести; выгребáть, вы́грести; (*hollow or carve out*) выдáлбливать, вы́долбить; (*bowl etc.*) выскáбливать, вы́скоблить; **~ through** *v.i.* проти́с|киваться, -нуться; **she ~d through (her exam)** онá с трудóм (*or* со скри́пом *or* с грехóм пополáм) вы́держала экзáмен; **~ together** *v.t.* (*money etc.*) наскре|бáть, -сти́; **~ up** *v.t.*: **he ~d up enough money for the concert** он наскрёб дéньги на концéрт.

scraper ['skreɪpə(r)] *n.* (*implement*) скребóк; (*for cleaning shoes*) скобá; (*road-making machine*) скрéпер.

scrappy ['skræpɪ] *adj.* **1.** (*uncoordinated; miscellaneous*) разрóзненный; **a ~ essay** легковéсное сочинéние; **a ~ education** повéрхностное образовáние. **2.** (*fragmentary*) отры́вочный. **3.** (*meagre*) скýдный.

scratch [skrætʃ] *n.* **1.** (*mark*) царáпина. **2.** (*noise*) царáпанье, чи́рканье. **3.** (*wound*) царáпина, ссáдина; **without a ~** (*fig.*) без малéйшей царáпины. **4.** (*act of ~ing*): **give one's head a ~** почесáть (*pf.*) гóлову. **5.** (*starting line*) старт; (*fig.*): **come up to ~** быть на высотé (положéния); дéлать (*impf.*) то, что полóжено; **bring up to ~** дов|оди́ть, -ести́ до трéбуемого состоя́ния; **start from ~** нач|инáть, -áть с начáла/нуля́.

adj. (*haphazard*) случáйный; (*heterogeneous*) разношёрстный; **~ crew** случáйная комáнда; **~ dinner** импровизи́рованный обéд; обéд, приготóвленный на скóрую рýку.

v.t. **1.** царáп|ать, о-; **~ o.s.** поцарáпаться (*pf.*); **he merely ~ed the surface of the problem** он затрóнул/освети́л вопрóс весьмá повéрхностно; **he ~ed letters on the wall** он нацарáпал бýквы на стенé; **the dog ~ed a hole in the lawn** собáка вы́скребла/вы́рыла я́мку в газóне. **2.** (*to relieve itching*) чесáть, по-; **~ one's head** чесáть (*impf.*) гóлову; **he was ~ing his head over the problem** (*fig.*) он ломáл гóлову над э́той задáчей; **you ~ my back and I'll ~ yours** (*fig.*) ты — мне, я — тебé; кукýшка хвáлит петухá за то, что хвáлит он кукýшку; рукá рýку мóет. **3.** (*erase*) вычёркивать, вы́черкнуть; (*withdraw*): **~ a horse** сн|имáть, -ять лóшадь с соревновáния; (*cancel*): **~ an agreement** аннули́ровать (*impf., pf.*) соглашéние.

v.i. **1.** (*of pers., ~ o.s.*) чесáться, по-. **2.** (*of animal*): **does your cat ~?** вáша кóшка царáпается? **3.** (*of pen*) царáпать (*impf.*). **4.** (*coll., withdraw from race*) откáз|ываться, -áться от учáстия в бегáх.

with advs.: **~ about, ~ around** *vv.i.*: **the chickens ~ed around for food** кýры копоши́лись в землé в пóисках пи́щи; **he had to ~ around for evidence** емý с трудóм удалóсь наскрести́ доказáтельства/ули́ки; **~ along** *v.i.* = **scrape along**; **~ out** *v.t.* (*erase*) вычёркивать, вы́черкнуть; зачёрк|ивать, -нýть; (*with knife*) вырезáть, вы́резать; **~ s.o.'s eyes out** вы́царапать (*pf.*) глазá комý-н.; **~ up** *v.t.* (*disinter*): **the dog ~ed up its bone** собáка вы́рыла/вы́копала свою́ кость; (*collect with difficulty*) наскре|бáть, -сти́.

cpd. **~-pad** *n.* блокнóт для замéток.

scratchy ['skrætʃɪ] *adj.* (*of pen: squeaky*) скрипýчий; (*catching in paper*) царáпающий.

scrawl [skrɔːl] *n.* карáкули (*f. pl.*); (*fig.*) небрéжная запи́ска, (*coll.*) писýлька.

v.t. черк|áть, -нýть.

v.i. писáть (*impf.*) карáкулями; **a ~ing hand** неразбóрчивый/размáшистый/небрéжный пóчерк.

scrawny ['skrɔːnɪ] *adj.* костля́вый.

scream [skriːm] *n.* **1.** пронзи́тельный крик; (*shriek*) вопль (*m.*); (*high-pitched ~*) визг; (*of bird*) крик, клёкот, клик; (*of fright, pain*) вопль (*m.*), крик; **~s of laughter** взры́вы (*m. pl.*) хо́хота/сме́ха; **a child's ~** визг ребёнка. **2.** (*coll., funny affair*): **it was a ~!** (э́то была́) умо́ра, да и то́лько!; **he is a perfect ~** он настоя́щий ко́мик.

v.t.: **the sergeant ~ed an order** сержа́нт вы́крикнул кома́нду; **the baby was ~ing its head off** ребёнок надрыва́лся от кри́ка; **she ~ed herself red in the face** она́ побагрове́ла от кри́ка.

v.i. **1.** вопи́ть (*impf.*); **he was ~ing for help** он взыва́л о по́мощи; **you will ~ with laughter** вы живо́тики надорвёте; **he made us ~** он заста́вил нас буква́льно визжа́ть/выть от сме́ха; **the film is ~ingly funny** фильм умори́тельно смешно́й. **2.** (*of bird*) (пронзи́тельно) крича́ть, за-; вскри́к|ивать, -нуть; (*of eagle, hawk etc.*) клекота́ть (*impf.*). **3.** (*of inanimate objects*): **the brakes ~ed as he turned the corner** тормоза́ завизжа́ли на поворо́те.

scree [skri:] *n.* камени́стая о́сыпь.

screech [skri:tʃ] *n.* пронзи́тельный крик, визг; скрип, скре́жет.

v.i. пронзи́тельно крича́ть, за-/про-; (*of gears, tyres etc.*) скрежета́ть (*impf.*); скрипе́ть (*impf.*).

cpd. **~-owl** *n.* сипу́ха.

screechy ['skri:tʃɪ] *adj.* визгли́вый.

screed [skri:d] *n.* (*document*) дли́нное, ску́чное посла́ние; (*harangue*) тира́да.

screen [skri:n] *n.* **1.** (*partition*) перегоро́дка. **2.** (*furniture*) ши́рма. **3.** (*shelter, protection*) прикры́тие, заслóн, заве́са; **behind a ~ of trees** под прикры́тием дере́вьев; (*cover*) покро́в; **under the ~ of night** под покро́вом но́чи; **a ~ of cavalry** кавалери́йский заслóн; **a ~ of indifference** ма́ска равноду́шия. **4.** (*elec.*) изоля́ция. **5.** (*on window*) се́тка. **6.** (*display board*) щит. **7.** (*cin., TV*) экра́н; **~ adaptation** экраниза́ция; **she went for a ~ test** она́ прошла́ про́бную съёмку; **~ size** разме́р экра́на (по диагона́ли).

v.t. **1.** (*shelter*) заслон|я́ть, -и́ть; прикр|ыва́ть, -ы́ть; (*protect*) защи|ща́ть, -ти́ть; огра|жда́ть, -ди́ть; **he is ~ing her** он выгора́живает её. **2.** (*hide*) укр|ыва́ть, -ы́ть; **the house was ~ed from view** дом был укры́т от взо́ров. **3.** (*separate*) отгор|а́живать, -оди́ть; **we ~ed off the kitchen from the dining-room** мы отгороди́ли (ши́рмой) ку́хню от столо́вой. **4.** (*sift; lit., fig.*) просе́|ивать, -ять. **5.** (*fig., investigate*): **they were ~ed before going abroad** пе́ред отъе́здом за грани́цу они́ прошли́ прове́рку (на благонадёжность). **6.** (*show on ~*) пока́з|ывать, -а́ть; (*make film of*) экранизи́ровать (*impf., pf.*). **7.** (*elec.*) экранизи́ровать (*impf., pf.*).

cpds. **~-play** *n.* сцена́рий; **~-writer** *n.* сценари́ст, кинодрамату́рг, теледрамату́рг.

screw [skru:] *n.* **1.** винт, болт, шуру́п; (*female ~*) га́йка; **he has a ~ loose** у него́ ви́нтика не хвата́ет (*coll.*); **put the ~s on** (*fig.*) наж|има́ть, -а́ть на+*a.*; ока́з|ывать, -а́ть давле́ние на+*a.*; зави́н|чивать, -ти́ть га́йки. **2.** (*turn of ~*): **give it another ~** ещё раз(о́к) поверни́те. **3.** (*propeller*) винт. **4. ~ of tobacco** завёртка/закру́тка табаку́. **5.** (*coll., miser*) скря́га (*c.g.*), скупердя́й. **6.** (*wages*): **he gets a good ~** он получа́ет хоро́шие ба́шли за свою́ рабо́ту (*sl.*). **7.** (*prison warder*) вертуха́й (*sl.*).

v.t. **1.** зави́н|чивать, -ти́ть; **the cap is ~ed tight** кры́шка кре́пко зави́нчена; **the cupboard was ~ed to the wall** шкаф был приви́нчен к стене́; **I ~ed the bolt into the post** я ввинти́л болт в столб. **2.** (*fig., turn*): **I had to ~ my neck round to see him** я чуть не вы́вернул ше́ю, что́бы уви́деть его́; **I'll ~ his neck** (*coll.*) я сверну́ ему́ ше́ю. **3.** (*copulate with*) тра́х|ать, -нуть (*sl.*).

v.i.: **the handles ~ into the drawer** ру́чки приви́нчиваются к я́щику; **this piece ~s on to that** э́тот кусо́к приви́нчивается к тому́.

with advs.: **~ down** *v.t. & i.* приви́н|чивать(ся), -ти́ть(ся); **~ off** *v.t. & i.* отви́н|чивать(ся), -ти́ть(ся); **~ on** *v.t. & i.* нави́н|чивать(ся), -ти́ть(ся); **his head is ~ed on the right way** он сообража́ет; у него́ голова́ (хорошо́) ва́рит; у него́ (есть) голова́ на плеча́х; **~ out** *v.t.* (*coll., extort*) выжима́ть, вы́жать; **I managed to ~ the truth out of him** мне удало́сь вы́жать/вы́тянуть из него́ пра́вду; **~ together** *v.t.*: **he ~ed the boards together** он скрепи́л до́ски винта́ми/ви́нтиками; **~ up** *v.t.* зави́н|чивать, -ти́ть; (*crumple*) ко́мкать, с-; **~ up one's eyes** щу́рить, со-/при-глаза́; **a face ~ed up with pain** лицо́, искажённое бо́лью (*or* от бо́ли); **~ o.s. up, ~ up one's courage** собра́ться (*pf.*) с ду́хом; набра́ться (*pf.*) хра́брости; (*sl., spoil*) напорта́чить (*pf.*); зава́л|ивать, -и́ть.

cpds. **~ball** *n.* (*sl.*) чо́кнутый, сумасбро́д; **~-cap, ~-top** *nn.* нави́нчивающаяся кры́шка; **~driver** *n.* отвёртка; **~-propeller** *n.* винт; **~-top** *n.* = **~-cap; ~-valve** *n.* винтово́й кла́пан.

screwy ['skru:ɪ] *adj.* (*sl., crazy*) тро́нутый, чо́кнутый; **a ~ idea** неле́пая/дура́цкая иде́я.

scribbl|e ['skrɪb(ə)l] *n.* кара́кули (*f. pl.*).

v.t. & i. **1.** (*make marks (on)*) черка́ть (*coll.* чёркать), ис-; черти́ть, ис-; **the children ~ed all over the wall** де́ти исчерка́ли/исчерти́ли всю сте́ну. **2.** (*write hastily*) черка́ть, на-; **I ~ed a note to him** я черкну́л ему́ запи́ску; (*write untidily*) каля́кать, на-; (*of amateur writing*) пописывать (*impf.*); **~e verses** кропа́ть (*impf.*) стишки́; **~ing-pad, block** блокно́т для заме́ток.

scribbler ['skrɪblə(r)] *n.* (*fig., poor author*) писа́ка (*c.g.*), бумагомара́тель (*m.*).

scribe [skraɪb] *n.* (*hist.*) писе́ц; (*bibl.*) кни́жник; (*hack*) писа́ка (*c.g.*).

scrimmage ['skrɪmɪdʒ] (*also* **scrum(mage)**) *n.* **1.** (*tussle*) сва́лка. **2.** (*Rugby football*) схва́тка вокру́г мяча́.

v.i. дра́ться (*impf.*); сгру́диться (*coll.*) (*pf.*) вокру́г мяча́.

scrimp [skrɪmp] = **skimp**

scrimshank ['skrɪmʃæŋk] *v.i.* сачкова́ть (*impf.*); отлы́нивать (*impf.*) от обя́занностей (*coll.*).

scrimshanker ['skrɪm,ʃæŋkə(r)] *n.* сачо́к (*coll.*).

scrip [skrɪp] *n.* (*comm.*) вре́менный сертифика́т на владе́ние а́кциями.

script [skrɪpt] *n.* **1.** (*handwriting*) ру́копись; (*writing system*) письмо́, пи́сьменность, гра́фика; **in Cyrillic ~** кири́ллицей. **2.** (*typeface*) шрифт. **3.** (*text*) текст, сцена́рий. **4.** (*leg.*) по́длинник.

v.t.: **~ed discussion** зара́нее подгото́вленная диску́ссия.

cpd. **~-writer** *n.* сценари́ст, кинодрамату́рг, радиодрамату́рг, теледрамату́рг.

scriptorium [,skrɪp'tɔ:rɪəm] *n.* (*hist.*) помеще́ние для перепи́ски ру́кописей.

scriptural ['skrɪptʃər(ə)l, -tʃʊər(ə)l] *adj.* библе́йский; **a ~ quotation** цита́та из би́блии.

scripture ['skrɪptʃə(r)] *n.* писа́ние; **Holy S~** свяще́нное писа́ние; **in the ~s** в би́блии; (*as school subject*) зако́н бо́жий; **~ lesson** уро́к зако́на бо́жьего.

scrivener ['skrɪvənə(r)] *n.* (*hist.*) писе́ц.

scrofula ['skrɒfjʊlə] *n.* золоту́ха.

scrofulous ['skrɒfjʊləs] *adj.* золоту́шный.

scroll [skrəʊl] *n.* (*roll of parchment*) сви́ток; (*archit.*) завито́к, волю́та.

cpd. **~-work** *n.* орна́мент из завитко́в.

Scrooge [skru:dʒ] *n.* скря́га (*c.g.*); **don't be such a ~!** не будь таки́м скря́гой!

scrotum ['skrəʊtəm] *n.* мошо́нка.

scroung|e [skraʊndʒ] *v.t.* (*cadge*) стрел|я́ть, -ьну́ть (*coll.*); (*take illicitly*) стяну́ть; сти́брить; стащи́ть (*all pf., coll.*).

v.i. **1.** (*search about*) ры́скать (*impf.*); **they were ~ing for food** они́ ры́скали в по́исках пи́щи. **2.** (*cadge*) попроша́йничать (*impf.*); кля́нчить (*impf.*). **3.** (*avoid duties*) тунея́дствовать (*impf.*); паразити́ровать (*impf.*).

scrounger ['skraʊndʒə(r)] *n.* попроша́йка (*c.g.*); **social ~** тунея́дец.

scrub[1] [skrʌb] *n.* (*brushwood*) кустáрник; (*area*) за́росли (*f. pl.*).

scrub[2] [skrʌb] *n.*: **give sth. a ~** почи́стить (*pf.*) что-н.

v.t. **1.** (*rub hard*) скрести́ (*impf.*); тере́ть (*impf.*); чи́стить, по-; дра́ить, на-; **~ the floor** мыть, вы- пол; **~ paint off one's hands** сч|ища́ть, -и́стить кра́ску с рук; **~bing brush** жёсткая щётка. **2.** (*sl., cancel*) отмен|я́ть, -и́ть.

with advs.: **~ down** *v.t.*: **he ~bed down the walls** он вы́мыл сте́ны; **~ off** *v.t.* отм|ыва́ть, -ы́ть; **~ out** *v.t.*: **she ~bed out the kitchen** она́ вы́скребла ку́хню до́чиста; **the pans were ~bed out** кастрю́ли бы́ли вы́чищены.

scrubber ['skrʌbə(r)] *n.* (*sl.*) шлю́ха, потаску́ха.

scrubby ['skrʌbɪ] *adj.* (*of land*) поро́сший кустарнико́м; (*of plant etc., stunted*) ча́хлый; (*of chin*) небри́тый.

scruff[1] [skrʌf] *n.*: **take s.o. by the ~ of the neck** хвата́ть, схвати́ть кого́-н. за ши́ворот/загри́вок.

scruff[2] [skrʌf] *n.* неря́ха, растрёпа.

scruffy ['skrʌfɪ] *adj.* (*coll.*) неопря́тный, парши́вый; **a ~ performance** парши́вое исполне́ние.

scrum(mage) ['skrʌmɪdʒ] = **scrimmage**

scrumptious ['skrʌmpʃəs] *adj.* (*coll.*) о́чень вку́сный; **these pears are ~** э́ти гру́ши пря́мо объеде́ние.

scrunch [skrʌntʃ] *v.t.* (*coll.*) = **crunch**

scruple ['skru:p(ə)l] *n.* **1.** (*unit of weight*) скру́пул. **2.** (*of conscience*) сомне́ния (*nt. pl.*) (нра́вственного хара́ктера); **he will tell lies without ~** он врёт без зазре́ния (со́вести); **have ~s about doing sth.** со́веститься, по- сде́лать что-н.; **have no ~s** не стесня́ться (*impf.*) ниче́м; **he had no ~ about telling me everything** он не постесня́лся мне всё рассказа́ть.

v.i. стесня́ться (*impf.*); со́веститься, по-; **I would not ~ to accept the money** я бы с лёгкой со́вестью при́нял де́ньги.

scrupulous ['skru:pjʊləs] *adj.* (*of sensitive conscience*) щепети́льный, добросо́вестный; (*accurate, punctilious*) тща́тельный, скрупулёзный, педанти́чный; **~ care** педанти́чная тща́тельность; **~ cleanliness** абсолю́тная чистота́; **~ honesty** скрупулёзная/безупре́чная че́стность; **he is none too ~** он не отлича́ется щепети́льностью.

scrupulousness ['skru:pjʊləsnɪs] *n.* щепети́льность, добросо́вестность; тща́тельность; скрупулёзность.

scrutineer [,skru:tɪ'nɪə(r)] *n.* член счётной коми́ссии (на вы́борах).

scrutinize ['skru:tɪ,naɪz] *v.t.* (*examine*) рассм|а́тривать, -отре́ть; (*stare at*) при́стально/испыту́юще смотре́ть (*impf.*) на+*a*.

scrutiny ['skru:tɪnɪ] *n.* **1.** (*searching gaze*) внима́тельный/испыту́ющий взгляд. **2.** (*close investigation*) тща́тельное рассле́дование/рассмотре́ние/иссле́дование; **his record does not bear ~** его́ про́шлое/поведе́ние далеко́ не безупре́чно. **3.** (*of votes*) прове́рка пра́вильности подсчёта избира́тельных бюллете́ней.

scuba ['sku:bə, 'skju:-] *n.* ску́ба, аквала́нг; **~ diver** плове́ц/ныря́льщик со ску́бой.

scud [skʌd] *v.i.* нести́сь, про-; пробе|га́ть, -жа́ть; (*naut.*) идти́ (*det.*) под ве́тром.

scuff [skʌf] *v.t.*: ~ (*wear away*) **one's shoes** истрёп|ывать, -а́ть (*or* трепа́ть, об-) о́бувь.

v.i. (*shuffle*) ша́ркать (*impf.*).

scuffle ['skʌf(ə)l] *n.* потасо́вка, схва́тка.

v.i. дра́ться (*impf.*); схва́т|ываться, -и́ться.

scull [skʌl] *n.* (*oar*) па́рное весло́; (*at stern of boat*) кормово́е весло́; (*boat*) = **sculler**

v.t. & i.: **~ a boat** грести́ (*impf.*) па́рными вёслами; (*with stern-oar*) грести́ кормовы́м весло́м, гала́нить (*impf.*).

sculler ['skʌlə(r)] *n.* (*pers.*) гребе́ц; (*boat; also* **scull**) па́рная ло́дка; я́лик.

scullery ['skʌlərɪ] *n.* судомо́йня.

cpd. **~-maid** *n.* судомо́йка.

scullion ['skʌljən] *n.* (*arch.*) ку́хонный мужи́к.

sculpt [skʌlpt] *v.t. & i.* (*coll.*) = **sculpture** *v.t., v.i.*

sculptor ['skʌlptə(r)] *n.* ску́льптор.

sculptress ['skʌlptrɪs] *n.* же́нщина-ску́льптор; **she is a ~** она́ ску́льптор.

sculptural ['skʌlptʃərəl] *adj.* скульпту́рный, пласти́ческий; **~ beauty** пласти́чная/холо́дная красота́.

sculpture ['skʌlptʃə(r)] *n.* (*art, product*) скульпту́ра.

v.t. (*also* **sculpt**) ва́ять, из-; (*model in clay etc.*) лепи́ть, вы́-; (*in stone*) высека́ть, вы́сечь; (*in wood*) ре́зать, вы́-.

v.i. быть/рабо́тать (*impf.*) ску́льптором.

scum [skʌm] *n.* на́кипь, пе́на; (*fig.*) подо́нки (*m. pl.*); **~ of the earth** подо́нки о́бщества.

v.t. (*skim*) сн|има́ть, -ять на́кипь/пе́ну с+*g*.

v.i. (*form ~*) образо́в|ывать, -а́ть на́кипь/пе́ну.

scumbag ['skʌmbæg] *n.* (*sl.*) подо́нок, па́дла.

scumble ['skʌmb(ə)l] *n.* лессиро́вка, то́нкий слой кра́ски.

v.t. лессирова́ть (*impf., pf.*).

scunner ['skʌnə(r)] *n.* (*sl.*): **take a ~ at** почу́вствовать (*pf.*) отвраще́ние (*or* о́струю неприя́знь) к+*d*.

scupper ['skʌpə(r)] *n.* шпига́т.

v.t. (*sink*) потопи́ть (*pf.*); (*fig., coll.*) разби́ть (*pf.*) (в пух и прах); разгроми́ть (*pf.*); **we're ~ed** мы поги́бли.

scurf [skɜ:f] *n.* пе́рхоть.

scurfy ['skɜ:fɪ] *adj.*: **my hair is ~** у меня́ (в волоса́х) пе́рхоть.

scurrility [skʌ'rɪlɪtɪ] *n.* непристо́йность.

scurrilous ['skʌrɪləs] *adj.* (*indecent*) непристо́йный; (*abusive*) оскорби́тельный.

scurry ['skʌrɪ] *n.* суета́, спе́шка; **there was a ~ towards the exit** все бро́сились к вы́ходу; **the ~ of mice under the floor** возня́ мыше́й по́д полом.

v.i. (*also* **~ about**) суетли́во дви́гаться/бе́гать (*both impf.*); снова́ть (*impf.*); **~ through one's work** на́спех проде́лать (*pf.*) рабо́ту.

with advs.: **~ away, ~ off** *vv.i.* убе|га́ть, -жа́ть; (*disperse*) разбе|га́ться, -жа́ться.

scurvied ['skɜ:vɪd] *adj.* цинго́тный.

scurvy ['skɜ:vɪ] *n.* цинга́.

adj. (*arch.*) по́длый; **~ fellow** подле́ц; **~ trick** подво́х; **play a ~ trick on s.o.** подложи́ть (*pf.*) свинью́ кому́-н.

scut [skʌt] *n.* коро́ткий хво́ст(ик).

scutcheon ['skʌtʃ(ə)n] = **escutcheon**

scuttle[1] ['skʌt(ə)l] *n.* (*for coal*) ведёрко/я́щик для у́гля́.

scuttle[2] ['skʌt(ə)l] *n.* (*hurried flight*) стреми́тельное бе́гство; (*fig.*) малоду́шное отступле́ние.

v.i. дви́гаться/бе́гать (*both impf.*); ю́ркнуть (*pf.*); снова́ть (*impf.*).

scuttle[3] ['skʌt(ə)l] *v.t.* (*sink*) топи́ть, по-; затоп|ля́ть, -и́ть.

Scylla [,sɪlə] *n.* Сци́лла; **between ~ and Charybdis** ме́жду Сци́ллой и Хари́бдой.

scythe [saɪð] *n.* коса́.

v.t. коси́ть, с-.

Scythian ['sɪðɪən] *n.* скиф (*fem.* -ка).

adj. ски́фский.

SDI (*abbr. of* ***strategic defense initiative***) СОИ, (стратеги́ческая оборо́нная инициати́ва).

sea [si:] *n.* мо́ре; **at ~** (*lit.*) в мо́ре; **he is at ~** он нахо́дится в пла́вании; **(all) at ~** (*fig.*) озада́чен, растéрян (*pred.*); в недоуме́нии; **he is at ~** он ничего́ не понима́ет/смы́слит, он растéрян; **beyond the ~** за́ морем; **dominions beyond the ~s** замо́рские владе́ния; **by ~** мо́рем; **by the ~** у мо́ря, на мо́ре; **go to ~** (*become a sailor*) идти́ (*det.*), пойти́ (*pf.*) в моряки́; **on the ~** (*in ship*) в мо́ре; **ships sail on the ~** корабли́ пла́вают по́ морю; (*situated on coast*) на мо́ре; **put to ~** (*of ship*) выходи́ть, вы́йти в мо́ре; **the ~ covers three-quarters of the world's surface** моря́ покрыва́ют три че́тверти пове́рхности земно́го ша́ра; **open ~** откры́тое мо́ре; **freedom of the ~s** свобо́да море́й; **on the high ~s** в откры́том мо́ре; **inland ~** закры́тое мо́ре; **sail the seven ~s** пла́вать (*indet.*) по моря́м-океа́нам; объе́здить (*pf.*) весь свет; **a heavy ~** си́льное волне́ние; (*wave*) больша́я волна́; **half ~s over** (*drunk*) вы́пивши, под му́хой (*coll.*); **~s of blood** мо́ре кро́ви; **a ~ of troubles** мо́ре невзго́д/бед; **a ~ of faces** мо́ре лиц; (*attr.*): **~ air** морско́й во́здух; **~ journey, voyage, trip** морско́е путеше́ствие; морска́я прогу́лка, пое́здка по́ морю; **S~ Lord** морско́й лорд (*член главного морского штаба*); **~ mile** морска́я ми́ля; **~ power** морска́я мощь; (*nation*) морска́я держа́ва.

cpds. **~-anchor** *n.* плаву́чий я́корь; **~-anemone** *n.* акти́ния; **~-bathing** *n.* морски́е купа́ния; **~-bed** *n.* морско́е дно; **~-bird** *n.* морска́я пти́ца; **~-biscuit** *n.* суха́рь (*m.*), гале́та; **~board** *n.* примо́рье, (*attr.*) примо́рский; **~-boat** *n.*: **a good ~-boat** су́дно с хоро́шими морехо́дными ка́чествами; **~-born** *adj.* (*of Venus*) пенорождённая; **~-borne** *adj.* (*of trade*) морско́й; (*of goods*) перевози́мый мо́рем; **~-breeze** *n.* ве́тер с мо́ря; **~-calf** *n.* тюле́нь (*m.*); **~-captain** *n.* капита́н да́льнего пла́вания; знамени́тый флотово́дец; **~-change** *n.*

(чуде́сное/радика́льное) преображе́ние; **~-chest** *n.* матро́сский сундучо́к; **~-coast** *n.* морско́й бе́рег; **~-cock** *n.* (*naut.*) кингсто́н, забо́ртный кла́пан; **~-cook** *n.* кок; **son of a ~-cook** ≃ су́кин сын; **~-cow** *n.* морж; **~-cucumber** *n.* морско́й огуре́ц; **~-dog** *n.* (*old sailor*) (ста́рый) морско́й волк; **~-elephant** *n.* морско́й слон; **~farer** *n.* морепла́ватель (*m.*); **~faring** *n.* морепла́вание; *adj.* мореходный; **~faring** (*also* **~going**) **man** моря́к, морепла́ватель (*m.*); **~-fight** *n.* морско́й бой; **~-fish** *n.* морска́я ры́ба; **~-fog** *n.* тума́н, иду́щий с мо́ря; **~food** *n.* проду́кты мо́ря, морски́е проду́кты (*m. pl.*); **~food restaurant** ры́бный рестора́н; **~-fowl** *n.* морска́я пти́ца; **~-front** *n.* примо́рский бульва́р, на́бережная; **~-girt** *adj.* опоя́санный моря́ми; **~-god** *n.* морско́е божество́; **~going** *adj.* (*of ship*) мореходный; (*of pers.*) = **~faring;** **~-green** *adj.* цве́та морско́й волны́; **~gull** *n.* (*also* **~-mew**) ча́йка; **~-horse** *n.* морско́й конёк; **~-kale** *n.* морска́я капу́ста; **~-lane** *n.* морско́й путь; (*pl.*) морски́е коммуника́ции (*f. pl.*); **~-lawyer** *n.* придира (*c.g.*), критика́н; **~-legs** *n. pl.*: **find, get one's ~legs** прив|ыка́ть, -ы́кнуть к ка́чке; **~-level** *n.* у́ровень (*m.*) мо́ря; **~-lion** *n.* морско́й лев; **~man** *n.* моря́к, матро́с; **able ~man** матро́с; **~manship** *n.* иску́сство морепла́вания; **practical ~manship** морска́я пра́ктика; **~-mark** *n.* навигацио́нный знак; ориенти́р на берегу́; **~-mew** *n.* = **~gull;** **~-monster** *n.* морско́е чудо́вище; **~plane** *n.* гидросамолёт; **~port** *n.* морско́й порт; порто́вый го́род; **~quake** *n.* моретрясе́ние; **~-room** *n.* простра́нство для маневри́рования; **~-rover** *n.* пира́т; **~-salt** *n.* морска́я соль; **~scape** *n.* морско́й пейза́ж, мари́на; **~-scout** *n.* морско́й бойска́ут; **~-serpent** *n.* морско́й змей; **~-shell** *n.* морска́я ра́ковина; **~-shore** *n.* морско́й бе́рег, взмо́рье; **~sick** *adj.*: **I was ~sick** меня́ укача́ло; **~sickness** *n.* морска́я боле́знь; **~side** *n.* морско́е побере́жье; **we stayed at the ~side** мы жи́ли/бы́ли на мо́ре/взмо́рье; **he likes the ~side** он лю́бит е́здить на мо́ре; *adj.* примо́рский; **a ~side resort** морско́й куро́рт; **~-to-~** *adj.*: **~-to-~ missile** раке́та кла́сса «кора́бль-кора́бль»; **~trout** *n.* океани́ческая сельдь; **~-urchin** *n.* морско́й ёж; **~-wall** *n.* да́мба; сте́нка на́бережной; **~-water** *n.* морска́я вода́; **~-way** *n.* (*inland waterway*) судохо́дное ру́сло; фарва́тер; вну́тренний во́дный путь; **~weed** *n.* морска́я во́доросль; **~worthiness** *n.* мореходность, го́дность к пла́ванию; **~worthy** *adj.* мореходный, го́дный к пла́ванию.

seal[1] [si:l] *n.* (*zool.*) тюле́нь (*m.*); **(fur-~)** ко́тик.

v.i. охо́титься (*impf.*) на тюле́ней.

cpds. **~-fishery** *n.* тюле́ний/ко́тиковый про́мысел; **~-rookery** *n.* тюле́нье ле́жбище; **~skin** *n.* тюле́нья шку́ра; тюле́ний/ко́тиковый мех.

seal[2] [si:l] *n.* **1.** (*on document etc.*) печа́ть; **wax ~** сургу́чная печа́ть; **leaden ~** пло́мба; **affix, set one's ~ to sth.** ста́вить, по- свою́ печа́ть на что-н.; скреп|ля́ть, -и́ть что-н. печа́тью; **set the ~ on** заверш|а́ть, -и́ть; **he set the ~ of approval on our action** он одо́брил/санкциони́ровал на́ши де́йствия; **under my hand and ~** за мое́й собственноручно́й по́дписью и с приложе́нием печа́ти; **under ~ of secrecy** под секре́том; **~ of confession** та́йна и́споведи; **fix a (leaden) ~ on** пломбирова́ть, за-. **2.** (*gem, stamp etc. for ~ing*) печа́тка.

v.t. **1.** (*affix ~ to*) при|кла́дывать, -ложи́ть печа́ть к+*d.*; **the treaty has been signed and ~ed** догово́р подпи́сан и скреплён печа́тями; **~ed orders** секре́тный прика́з; **~ing-wax** сургу́ч. **2.** (*confirm*): **~ a bargain** закреп|ля́ть, -и́ть сде́лку. **3.** (*close securely; stop up*) запеча́т|ывать, -ать; пло́тно/на́глухо закр|ыва́ть, -ы́ть; **a ~ed envelope** запеча́танный конве́рт; **they ~ed (up) all the windows** они́ зама́зали/заде́лали все о́кна; **the police ~ed off all exits from the square** поли́ция отре́зала/загороди́ла все вы́ходы с пло́щади (*or* оцепи́ла пло́щадь); **my lips are ~ed** у меня́ запеча́таны уста́; **that is a ~ed book to me** э́то для меня́ кни́га за семью́ печа́тями. **4.** (*set mark on; destine*) нал|ага́ть, -ожи́ть печа́ть на+*a.*; **his fate is ~ed** его́ у́часть решена́.

sealer ['si:lə(r)] *n.* (*pers.*) охо́тник на тюле́ней; (*ship*) зверобо́йное су́дно.

sealery ['si:lərɪ] *n.* тюле́нье ле́жбище.

seam [si:m] *n.* шов, рубе́ц; (*of ship*) паз; **burst at the ~s** ло́п|аться, -нуть по шву; **come apart at the ~s** (*lit., fig.*) треща́ть (*impf.*) по швам; (*geol.*) пласт.

v.t.: **a face ~ed with lines** лицо́, изборождённое морщи́нами.

seamless ['si:mlɪs] *adj.* без шва; из одного́ куска́; **~ stockings** чулки́ без шва.

seamstress, sempstress ['semstrɪs] *n.* швея́.

seamy ['si:mɪ] *adj.*: **the ~ side of life** изна́нка жи́зни.

seance ['seɪɑ̃s] *n.* спирити́ческий сеа́нс.

sear [sɪə(r)] *adj.* (*also* **sere**) увя́дший, пожелте́вший, жёлтый, вы́сохший.

v.t. (*scorch*) опал|я́ть, -и́ть; (*cauterize*) приж|ига́ть, -е́чь; (*make callous*) притуп|ля́ть, -и́ть; **his soul was ~ed by injustice** несправедли́вость иссуши́ла ему́ ду́шу.

search [sɜ:tʃ] *n.* **1.** (*quest*) по́иск (*usu. pl.*); **make a ~ for s.o./sth.** иска́ть (*impf.*) кого́-н./что-н.; **a man in ~ of a wife** челове́к, и́щущий себе́ жену́; **he went in ~ of his wife** он пошёл иска́ть жену́ (*or* за жено́й). **2.** (*examination*) о́быск; **the police carried out a ~ of the house** поли́ция произвела́ о́быск в до́ме; **customs ~** тамо́женный досмо́тр; **right of ~** пра́во о́быска (*судов*).

v.t. **1.** (*examine*) обы́ск|ивать, -а́ть; **we were ~ed at the airport** мы прошли́ осмо́тр в аэропорту́; (*rummage through*) обша́ри|вать, -ть; **I ~ed every drawer for my notes** я обша́рил/перерыл все я́щики в по́исках свои́х заме́ток. **2.** (*peer at, scan*) обв|оди́ть, -ести́ взгля́дом; **he ~ed my face** он останови́л на мне испыту́ющий взгляд; он пытли́во (по)смотре́л на меня́. **3.** (*fig., scrutinize*): **~ one's heart** загляну́ть (*pf.*) себе́ в ду́шу; **~ your memory!** напряги́те свою́ па́мять!; **I ~ed my conscience** я спроси́л свою́ со́весть; я допроси́л себя́ с пристра́стием. **4.** (*penetrate*) прон|ика́ть, -и́кнуть; **a ~ing wind** прони́зывающий ве́тер; **~ing questions** подро́бные вопро́сы; **a ~ing enquiry** тща́тельное рассле́дование. **5.**: **~ me!** (*coll.*) я почём зна́ю!; поня́тия не име́ю!

v.i. иска́ть (*impf.*); пров|оди́ть, -ести́ о́быск; **~ after, for** разы́скивать (*impf.*); отыскивать (*impf.*); **~ into the cause of sth.** иссле́довать (*impf.*) причи́ну чего́-н.; **~ out** (*find*) отыска́ть, разыска́ть, обнару́жить (*all pf.*); **~ through** просм|а́тривать, -отре́ть; **I ~ed through my desk for the letter** я перерыл весь пи́сьменный стол в по́исках письма́; **he ~ed through all his papers for the contract** он перебра́л все свои́ бума́ги в по́исках догово́ра.

cpds. **~light** *n.* проже́ктор; **~-party** *n.* по́иско́вая па́ртия/гру́ппа; по́иско́вый отря́д; **~-warrant** *n.* о́рдер на о́быск.

searcher ['sɜ:tʃə(r)] *n.* иска́тель (*fem.* -ница).

season ['si:z(ə)n] *n.* **1.** сезо́н; **the four ~s** четы́ре вре́мени го́да; **in the rainy ~** в сезо́н дожде́й; **compliments of the ~!** с пра́здником!; **strawberries are in ~** сейча́с поспе́ла клубни́ка; **blackberries are out of ~** сейча́с ежеви́ке не сезо́н; **at the height of the ~** в разга́р сезо́на; **holiday ~** сезо́н отпуско́в; **close/open ~** вре́мя, когда́ охо́та запрещена́/разрешена́; **a word in ~** своевре́менное (*or* во́время сказанное) слове́чко; во́время сде́ланный намёк; **in and out of ~** кста́ти и некста́ти; беспреста́нно; не перестава́я; (*period*) пери́од, пора́; **a ~ of inaction** пери́од/пора́ безде́йствия. **2. (~ ticket)** сезо́нный/проездно́й (биле́т); (*for concerts etc.*) абонеме́нт.

v.t. **1.** (*mature: of timber, wine etc.*) выде́рживать, вы́держать. **2.** (*acclimatize, inure*) приуч|а́ть, -и́ть; **he ~ed himself to cold** он приучи́л себя́ к хо́лоду; **a ~ed drinker** ма́стер пить; **~ed troops** о́пытные/испы́танные войска́. **3.** (*spice*) припр|авля́ть, -а́вить; ожив|ля́ть, -и́ть; **a highly ~ed dish** о́строе (*or* о́чень пика́нтное) блю́до.

seasonable ['si:zənəb(ə)l] *adj.* (*suited to the season*) соотве́тствующий сезо́ну; (*opportune*) своевре́менный.

seasonal ['si:zən(ə)l] *adj.* сезо́нный.

seasoning ['si:zənɪŋ] *n.* (*cul.*) припра́ва; (*of timber, wine*) выде́рживание.

seat [si:t] *n.* **1.** сиде́нье; (*chair*) стул; (*bench*) скамья́, скамейка; (*saddle*) седло́; ~ **of judgement** суди́лище. **2.** (*place in vehicle, theatre etc.*) ме́сто; **take one's** ~ зан|има́ть, -я́ть ме́сто; **please take a** ~! сади́тесь, пожа́луйста!; **keep one's** ~ ост|ава́ться, -а́ться на ме́сте; не поднима́ться с ме́ста; **keep my** ~ **for me!** посторожи́те моё ме́сто!; **he booked a** ~ он заказа́л биле́т; **take a back** ~ (*fig.*) от|ходи́ть, -ойти́ на за́дний план; стуш|ёвываться, -ева́ться. **3.** (*of chair*) сиде́нье; **the** ~ **of the chair fell through** у сту́ла провали́лось сиде́нье. **4.** (*backside*) зад, седа́лище; (*of trousers*) зад (у) брюк; **he wore out the** ~ **of his trousers** он просиде́л брю́ки. **5.** (*site, location, headquarters*): ~ **of government** местопребыва́ние прави́тельства; ~ **of an organization** штаб-кварти́ра организа́ции; ~ **of war** теа́тр вое́нных де́йствий; ~ **of the passions** средото́чие страсте́й; **the liver is the** ~ **of the disease** боле́знь локализо́вана/гнезди́тся в пе́чени; ~ **of learning** нау́чный центр. **6.** (*mansion*) уса́дьба, поме́стье. **7.** (*parl.*) ме́сто в парла́менте; **have a** ~ **in parliament** быть чле́ном парла́мента; **lose one's** ~ не быть переи́збранным в парла́мент; **vacate one's** ~ сложи́ть (*pf.*) депута́тские полномо́чия; **he has a** ~ **on the committee** он член комите́та. **8.: he has a good** ~ **on a horse** у него́ хоро́шая поса́дка; он хорошо́ сиди́т на ло́шади.

v.t. **1.** (*make sit*) сажа́ть, посади́ть; ~ **o.s.** сади́ться, сесть; ус|а́живаться, -е́сться; **be** ~**ed!** сади́тесь!; прошу́ сади́ться; **he remained** ~**ed** он продолжа́л сиде́ть; он не подня́лся с ме́ста; **I found them** ~ **ed round the fire** я нашёл их сидя́щими вокру́г ками́на. **2.** (*provide with* ~*s*) вме|ща́ть, -сти́ть; **the hall** ~**s over a thousand** зал вмеща́ет бо́льше ты́сячи челове́к; **this table** ~**s twelve** за э́тот стол мо́жно посади́ть двена́дцать челове́к. **3.** (*mend* ~ *of*) чини́ть, по- сиде́нье +*g.*

cpd. ~**-belt** *n.* (привязно́й) реме́нь.

seating ['si:tɪŋ] *n.* **1.** (*allocation of places*) расса́живание; расса́дка; (*placing at table*) размеще́ние госте́й за столо́м; **the** ~ **arrangements were inadequate** мест не хвата́ло. **2.** (*seats*) (сидя́чие) места́; ~ **capacity** число́ сидя́чих мест; **additional** ~ **for 50 had to be provided** пришло́сь доба́вить 50 сидя́чих мест. **3.** (*material for filling seat*) наби́вка.

SEATO ['si:təʊ] *n.* (*abbr. of* ***South-East Asia Treaty Organization***) СЕАТО, (Организа́ция догово́ра Юго-Восто́чной А́зии).

seaward ['si:wəd] *adj.* (*of breeze etc.*) берегово́й; ~ **tide** отли́в.

adv. (*also* ~**s, to** ~) к мо́рю.

sebaceous [sɪ'beɪʃəs] *adj.* са́льный.

sec. [sɪ'kɒnd(z)] *n.* (*abbr. of* **second(s)**) сек., (секу́нда).

secant ['si:kənt, 'se-] *n.* се́канс.

secateurs [,sekə'tɜ:z] *n. pl.* садо́вые но́жниц|ы (*pl., g.* —); сека́тор.

secede [sɪ'si:d] *v.i.* отл|ага́ться, -ожи́ться; отдел|я́ться, -и́ться; выходи́ть, вы́йти (из+*g.*).

secession [sɪ'seʃ(ə)n] *n.* отложе́ние; отделе́ние (от+*g.*); вы́ход (из+*g.*); **War of S**~ гражда́нская война́ в США.

secessionist [sɪ'seʃənɪst] *n.* сепарати́ст.

seclude [sɪ'klu:d] *v.t.*: ~ **from public gaze** укр|ыва́ть, -ы́ть от взо́ров пу́блики; ~ **o.s. from society** удал|я́ться, -и́ться от о́бщества; **a** ~**d life** уединённая жизнь; **a** ~**d spot** укро́мный уголо́к.

seclusion [sɪ'klu:ʒ(ə)n] *n.* уедине́ние, изоля́ция, уединённость; **to live in** ~ жить (*impf.*) в одино́честве.

second[1] ['sekənd] *n.* **1.** второ́й; **you are the** ~ **to ask me that** вы уже́ второ́й челове́к, кото́рый меня́ об э́том спроси́л/спра́шивает; ~ **in command** замести́тель (*m.*) команди́ра; **on the** ~ **of May** второ́го ма́я; **he came (in) a good** ~ (*in race*) он пришёл к фи́нишу почти́ одновреме́нно с пе́рвым; (*honours degree*) дипло́м второ́й сте́пени. **2.** (*in duel, boxing etc.*) секунда́нт; ~**s out of the ring!** секунда́нты за ринг! **3.** (*pl., imperfect goods*) второсо́ртный това́р; **these plates are** ~**s** э́ти таре́лки брако́ванные/нестанда́ртные. **4.** (*measure of time or angle, also mus.*) секу́нда; **wait a** ~! одну́ секу́нду!; ~**(s) hand** (*of clock*) секу́ндная стре́лка.

adj. второ́й, друго́й; **Charles the S**~ Карл Второ́й; ~ **childhood** ста́рческое слабоу́мие; **he is in his** ~ **childhood** он впал в де́тство; **on the** ~ **(*US* third) floor** на тре́тьем этаже́; **the** ~ **largest city** второ́й по величине́ го́род; ~ **nature** втора́я нату́ра; ~ **person singular** второ́е лицо́ еди́нственного числа́; **he addressed her in the** ~ **person singular** он обраща́лся к ней на ты; **he came in** ~ он за́нял второ́е ме́сто; **in the** ~ **place** во-вторы́х; **for the** ~ **time** втори́чно, второ́й раз; **he did it at the** ~ **time of asking** его́ пришло́сь два́жды проси́ть, пре́жде чем он э́то сде́лал; (*additional*) доба́вочный; ~ **ballot** перебаллотиро́вка; ~ **chamber** ве́рхняя пала́та; ~ **helping** доба́вка; **France was a** ~ **home to him** Фра́нция была́ ему́ (*or* для него́) второ́й ро́диной; ~ **name** фами́лия; **you need a** ~ **pair of boots** вам нужна́ втора́я/запасна́я па́ра боти́нок; **he has** ~ **sight** он яснови́дец; ~ **string** (*fig.*) втора́я скри́пка; ~ **teeth** постоя́нные зу́бы; **have** ~ **thoughts** переду́мать, разду́мать (*pf.*); **I am having** ~ **thoughts** я начина́ю колеба́ться; **on** ~ **thoughts** поразмы́слив; по зре́лом размышле́нии; **do, say sth. a** ~ **time** повтор|я́ть, -и́ть что-н.; **get one's** ~ **wind** обрести́ (*pf.*) второ́е дыха́ние; (*subordinate; comparable*): ~ **to none** непревзойдённый; **he is** ~ **to none** он никому́ не усту́пит; **their taste is** ~ **to none** у них безукори́зненный вкус; ~ **cousin** трою́родный брат (*fem.* трою́родная сестра́); **play** ~ **fiddle** игра́ть (*impf.*) втору́ю скри́пку; **learn sth. at** ~ **hand** узна́ть (*pf.*) что-н. понаслы́шке (*or* из вторы́х рук); ~ **lieutenant** мла́дший лейтена́нт; ~ **officer** помо́щник капита́на; **he thinks he is a** ~ **Tolstoy** он вообража́ет себя́ вторы́м Толсты́м; **the** ~ **violins** вторы́е скри́пки.

v.t. (*support*) подде́рж|ивать, -а́ть; ~ **words with deeds** подкреп|ля́ть, -и́ть слова́ дела́ми.

cpds. ~**-best** *adj.* не са́мый лу́чший; (*inferior*) второразря́дный, второсо́ртный; не лу́чшего ка́чества; *adv.*: **come off** ~**-best** терпе́ть, по- пораже́ние; ~**-class** *n.* (*degree*) дипло́м второ́й сте́пени; (*of travel*) второ́й класс; *adj.* второкла́ссный; ~**-class cabin** каю́та второ́го кла́сса; ~**-class citizens** гра́ждане второ́го со́рта; ~**-class hotel** второразря́дная гости́ница; *adv.*: **we travel** ~**-class** мы е́здим вторы́м кла́ссом; ~**-floor,** ~**-storey** *adjs.* на тре́тьем этаже́; ~**-generation** *adj.* второ́го поколе́ния; ~**-hand** *n. see* **second** *n.* **4.**; *adj.* (*previously used*) поде́ржанный; ~**-hand bookshop** букинисти́ческий магази́н; (*indirect*): ~**-hand information** информа́ция из вторы́х рук; *adv.*: **I bought the car** ~**-hand** я купи́л маши́ну как поде́ржанную; ~**-rate** *adj.* (*of goods*) второсо́ртный; непервокла́ссный; (*mediocre*) посре́дственный; ~**-rater** *n.* посре́дственность; ~**-storey** *n.* = ~**-floor**

second[2] [sɪ'kɒnd] *v.t.* (*mil., admin.*) откомандиро́в|ывать, -а́ть.

secondary ['sekəndərɪ] *adj.* **1.** (*opp. primary*) втори́чный; ~ **school** сре́дняя шко́ла. **2.** (*subordinate*) второстепе́нный.

secondly ['sekəndlɪ] *adv.* во-вторы́х.

secrecy ['si:krɪsɪ] *n.* та́йна; (*of document*) секре́тность; **he promised** ~ он обеща́л храни́ть та́йну; **can we rely on his** ~? мо́жно ли положи́ться на его́ молча́ние/скро́мность?; **he swore me to** ~ он взял с меня́ кля́тву/сло́во молча́ть; он заста́вил меня́ покля́сться не разглаша́ть (та́йну); **the troops were dispatched with absolute** ~ перебро́ска войск осуществля́лась в по́лной та́йне.

secret ['si:krɪt] *n.* та́йна; (*in personal relations*) секре́т; **keep a** ~ храни́ть, со- секре́т; **let s.o. into a** ~ посвя|ща́ть, -ти́ть кого́-н. в та́йну; **he has no** ~**s from me** у меня́ от него́ нет секре́тов; **I make no** ~ **of it** я э́того не скрыва́ю; **state** ~ госуда́рственная та́йна; **open** ~ всем изве́стный секре́т; секре́т полишине́ля; всему́ све́ту по секре́ту; **in** ~ в та́йне, по секре́ту; **the** ~ **of health is temperance** возде́ржанность — зало́г здоро́вья; **the** ~ **of success is to keep on trying** секре́т успе́ха в упо́рстве.

adj. **1.** та́йный; **top** ~ (*as inscription*) соверше́нно секре́тно; **keep sth.** ~ держа́ть (*impf.*) что-н. в та́йне; ~ **agent** разве́дчик, шпио́н; ~ **ballot** та́йное голосова́ние; ~ **police** та́йная поли́ция; ~ **service** секре́тная слу́жба;

развéдка; агентýра; **the court met in ~ session** судéбное заседáние происходи́ло за закры́тыми дверя́ми; **~ sign** услóвный знак; **~ society** тáйное óбщество; (*hidden*) потайнóй, скры́тый; **~ staircase** потайнáя лéстница; (*clandestine*) подпóльный; (*furtive*) скры́тый; (*remote*) укрóмный; **a ~ valley** уединённая доли́на; (*undisclosed*): **my ~ ambition** моя́ сокровéнная мечтá; **I was ~ly glad to see him** в глубинé души́ я был рад егó ви́деть.

secretaire [ˌsekrɪ'teə(r)] *n.* секретéр.

secretarial [ˌsekrɪ'teərɪəl] *adj.* секретáрский.

secretariat [ˌsekrə'teərɪət] *n.* секретариáт.

secretary ['sekrɪtərɪ, 'sekrətrɪ] *n.* секретáр|ь (*fem., coll., typist etc.* -ша); **permanent (under-)~** вы́сший чинóвник министéрства; постоя́нный замести́тель (*m.*) мини́стра; **S~-General** Генерáльный Секретáрь; **S~ of State** (*UK*) мини́стр; (*US*) госудáрственный секретáрь, мини́стр инострáнных дел; **private ~** ли́чный секретáрь.

cpd. **~-bird** *n.* секретáрь (*m.*).

secretaryship ['sekrɪtərɪʃɪp, 'sekrətrɪʃɪp] *n.* дóлжность секретаря́.

secrete [sɪ'kri:t] *v.t.* **1.** (*physiol. etc.*) выделя́ть, вы́делить. **2.** (*conceal*) укр|ывáть, -ы́ть; пря́тать, с-; **~ o.s.** укр|ывáться, -ы́ться; пря́таться, с-.

secretion [sɪ'kri:ʃ(ə)n] *n.* **1.** выделéние, секрéция. **2.** сокры́тие, укрывáние; (*of stolen goods*) укрывáтельство.

secretive ['si:krɪtɪv] *adj.* скры́тный, зáмкнутый; **he was ~ about his job** он ничегó не (*or* мáло) расскáзывал о своéй рабóте.

secretiveness ['si:krɪtɪvnɪs] *n.* скры́тность.

sect [sekt] *n.* сéкта.

sectarian [sek'teərɪən] *n.* сектáнт (*fem.* -ка).

adj. сектáнтский.

section ['sekʃ(ə)n] *n.* **1.** (*separate or distinct part*) сéкция; **built in ~s** сбóрный, разбóрный; (*severed portion*) кусóк; **~ of the day** часть дня; **~ of the population** часть/слой населéния; **residential ~** жилáя часть/сéкция; жилóй учáсток; **~ of a journey** этáп пути́; **~ of a book/speech** раздéл кни́ги/рéчи; (*mil.*) отделéние; (*department*) отдéл, отделéние; (*segment of fruit*) дóлька; (*~-mark, i.e.* §) парáграф. **2.** (*geom. etc.*) разрéз; **~ drawing** чертёж в разрéзе; сечéние. **3.** (*microscopic ~*) срез. **4.** (*surg.*) сечéние, вскры́тие.

sectional ['sekʃən(ə)l] *adj.* **1.** секциóнный. **2.** (*pert. to a section of the community etc.*) группов́ой. **3.** (*made in parts*) сбóрный, разбóрный, составнóй. **4.**: **~ arrangement of material** распределéние материáла по отдéлам. **5.** (*of drawings, plans etc.*) в разрéзе; **~ elevation** разрéз; **~ plan of a building** план здáния в разрéзе.

sectionalism ['sekʃənəˌlɪz(ə)m] *n.* группóвщи́на; сектáнтство, мéстничество.

sector ['sektə(r)] *n.* **1.** (*geom.*) сéктор. **2.** (*mil., rail. etc.*) учáсток. **3.** (*econ.*): **the public/private ~** общéственный/ чáстный сéктор.

secular ['sekjʊlə(r)] *adj.* **1.** (*this-worldly*) мирскóй; **~ affairs** мирски́е делá; (*non-ecclesiastical, lay*) свéтский; **the ~ arm** свéтский суд; **~ education** свéтское образовáние. **2.** (*non-monastic*): **~ clergy** бéлое духовéнство. **3.** (*long-lasting*) (вéко)вéчный.

secularism ['sekjʊləˌrɪz(ə)m] *n.* секуляри́зм.

secularization [ˌsekjʊləraɪ'zeɪʃ(ə)n] *n.* секуляризáция.

secularize ['sekjʊləˌraɪz] *v.t.* секуляризовáть (*impf., pf.*).

secure [sɪ'kjʊə(r)] *adj.* **1.** (*free from care*) спокóйный; **feel ~ about sth.** не беспокóиться (*impf.*) о чём-н.; быть спокóйным за что-н. (*or* относи́тельно чегó-н.); **he left, ~ in the knowledge that I would support him** он ушёл, увéренный (*or* со спокóйной увéренностью) в моéй поддéржке. **2.** (*safe*): **the bridge did not seem ~** мост не казáлся/представля́лся надёжным/прóчным; **the doors are ~** двéри зáперты как слéдует; **the ladder is ~** лéстница стои́т прóчно; **the town was ~ against attack** гóрод был хорошó защищён от нападéния; **~ from interruption** свобóдный от помéх; (*reliable*) надёжный; **make ~** закреп|ля́ть, -и́ть; (*assured*): **a ~ income** обеспéченный/вéрный дохóд; **our victory is ~** побéда за нáми; (*well-founded*): **a ~ assumption** обоснóванное предположéние.

v.t. **1.** (*make safe or fast*) закреп|ля́ть, -и́ть; застрахóв|ывать, -áть; убер|егáть, -éчь; **~ a town against assault** укрепи́ть (*pf.*) оборóну (*or* обеспéчить (*pf.*) безопáсность) гóрода от нападéния; **~ one's valuables** класть, положи́ть свои́ цéнные вéщи в надёжное мéсто; **~ a prisoner** свя́з|ывать, -áть плéнного. **2.** (*guarantee, insure*) страховáть, за-; **he ~d himself against every risk** он застраховáл себя́ от вся́кого ри́ска; **Magna Carta ~d the liberties of Englishmen** Вели́кая хáртия закрепи́ла вóльности англичáн. **3.** (*obtain*) дост|авáть, -áть; заруч|áться, -и́ться +*i.*

security [sɪ'kjʊərɪtɪ] *n.* **1.** (*safety*) безопáсность; **~ against attack** безопáсность от нападéния; **~ device** предохрани́тель (*m.*); **S~ Council** Совéт Безопáсности; **~ guard** охрáнник; **he is a ~ risk** он неблагонадёжен; **I feel a sense of ~ in his presence** егó присýтствие даёт мне чýвство увéренности/защищённости. **2.** (*safeguard, guarantee*) гарáнтия; **~ against thieves** гарáнтия от ворóв. **3.** (*pledge, promise*) залóг, гарáнтия; **~ for a loan** гарáнтия зáйма; заклáд; (*of pers.*) поручи́тель (*m.*). **4.** (*pl., bonds*) цéнные бумáги (*f. pl.*).

sedan [sɪ'dæn] *n.* **(~ chair)** паланки́н; (*US, saloon car*) седáн.

sedate[1] [sɪ'deɪt] *adj.* степéнный, уравновéшенный.

sedate[2] [sɪ'deɪt] *v.t.* да|вáть, -ть успокои́тельное +*d.*

sedateness [sɪ'deɪtnɪs] *n.* степéнность.

sedation [sɪ'deɪʃ(ə)n] *n.* успокоéние; **under ~** под дéйствием успокои́тельных.

sedative ['sedətɪv] *n.* успокои́тельное (срéдство); (*sleeping drug*) снотвóрное (срéдство).

adj. успокáивающий, успокои́тельный; **have a ~ effect** дéйствовать успокáивающе.

sedentary ['sedəntərɪ] *adj.* (*of posture etc.*) сидя́чий; **a ~ way of life** сидя́чий óбраз жи́зни; (*of pers.*) неподви́жный, малоподви́жный.

sedge [sedʒ] *n.* осóка.

cpd. **~-warbler** *n.* камышóвка-барсучóк.

sediment ['sedɪmənt] *n.* осáдок, отстóй.

sedimentary [ˌsedɪ'mentərɪ] *adj.* осáдочный.

sedimentation [ˌsedɪmen'teɪʃ(ə)n] *n.* (*process*) осаждéние; отложéние осáдка; (*sediment*) осáдок.

sedition [sɪ'dɪʃ(ə)n] *n.* (*incitement*) подстрекáтельство к мятежý; подрывнáя дéятельность; (*rebellion*) мятéж.

seditious [sɪ'dɪʃəs] *adj.* мятéжный, подстрекáтельский.

seduce [sɪ'dju:s] *v.t.* **1.** (*lead astray*) соблазн|я́ть, -и́ть; оболь|щáть, -сти́ть; **he was ~d by wealth** он польсти́лся на богáтство. **2.** (*a woman*) совра|щáть, -ти́ть; соблазн|я́ть, -и́ть.

seducer [sɪ'dju:sə(r)] *n.* соблазни́тель (*m.*); обольсти́тель (*m.*), соврати́тель (*m.*).

seduction [sɪ'dʌkʃ(ə)n] *n.* (*act of ~*) обольщéние; (*temptation, enticement*) соблáзн.

seductive [sɪ'dʌktɪv] *adj.* соблазни́тельный; **~ smile** обольсти́тельная улы́бка; (*persuasive*) убеди́тельный.

seductiveness [sɪ'dʌktɪvnɪs] *n.* соблазни́тельность.

seductress [sɪ'dʌktrɪs] *n.* обольсти́тельница.

sedulous ['sedjʊləs] *adj.* (*diligent*) прилéжный; (*assiduous*) усéрдный; (*painstaking*) старáтельный.

sedulousness ['sedjʊləsnɪs] *n.* прилежáние; усéрдие; старáтельность.

see[1] [si:] *n.* (*territory*) епáрхия; (*office*) кáфедра; **the Holy S~** пáпский престóл.

see[2] [si:] *v.t.* **1.** ви́деть; **nothing could be ~n** ничегó нé было ви́дно; **the house cannot be ~n from the road** дом с дорóги не ви́ден/ви́дно; **he is not to be ~n** егó не видáть/ ви́дно; **nothing was ~n of him** о нём нé было ни слýху ни дýху; **I saw her arrive** я ви́дел, как она прибылá; **I saw him approach(ing) the house** я ви́дел, как он подходи́л к дóму; **did you ~ anyone leaving?** вы ви́дели, чтóбы ктó-нибудь выходи́л (*or* когó-нибудь выходя́щим) (оттýда)?; **I saw the boy beaten** я ви́дел, как изби́ли мáльчика; **I have never ~n such a thing** ничегó подóбного я не видáл/ ви́дел; **I never saw such rudeness** я в жи́зни не встречáлся с такóй грýбостью; **most people want to be ~n in the**

best light лю́ди обы́чно хотя́т предста́ть в наилу́чшем све́те; ~ **red** (*coll.*) взбеси́ться (*pf.*); прийти́ (*pf.*) в я́рость/бе́шенство; **I thought I was ~ing things** мне каза́лось, что я бре́жу; **I ~ things differently now** я тепе́рь ина́че смотрю́ на ве́щи; (*in newspaper etc.*): **I ~ our team has won** ока́зывается, на́ша кома́нда победи́ла. **2.** (*look at, watch*) смотре́ть, по- на+*a.*; осм|а́тривать, -отре́ть; ~ **p. 4** см. стр. 4; **let me ~ that** да́йте мне на э́то взгляну́ть; **let me ~ your letter** покажи́те мне ва́ше письмо́; **the film is worth ~ing** э́тот фильм сто́ит посмотре́ть; ~ **what you've done!** смотри́те, что вы наде́лали!; ~ **the sights, town** осм|а́тривать, -отре́ть достопримеча́тельности; **you must ~ Westminster Abbey** вам необходи́мо побыва́ть в Вестми́нстерском абба́тстве (*or* посети́ть Вестми́нстерское абба́тство); **we saw Hamlet yesterday** мы вчера́ бы́ли на «Га́млете». **3.** (*experience*): **he has ~n life** (*or* **the world**) он вида́л/ви́дывал ви́ды; **the house has ~n many changes** дом претерпе́л/повида́л мно́го переме́н; **he has ~n five reigns** он пережи́л пять ца́рствований; **she will never ~ 50 again** ей перевали́ло за пятьдеся́т; **I thought I would never (live to) ~ the day when ...** я не ду́мал, что доживу́ до того́, что́бы... **4.** (*imagine*) предст|авля́ть, -а́вить себе́ (*что*); **can you ~ him apologizing?** мо́жете себе́ предста́вить его́ прося́щим извине́ния? **5.** (*ascertain by looking; find out*) посмотре́ть, узна́ть, вы́яснить (*all pf.*); ~ **for o.s.** убеди́ться (*pf.*) самому́/ли́чно; **(go and) ~ who it is** посмотри́те, кто там; **if you watch me you'll ~ how it's done** смотри́те на меня́ и поймёте, как э́то де́лается; **shall I ~ if I can help them?** мо́жет (быть), им на́до помо́чь?; **I'll ~ if I can get tickets** я постара́юсь/попро́бую доста́ть биле́ты; **that remains to be ~n** э́то ещё неизве́стно. **6.** (*discern, comprehend*) пон|има́ть, -я́ть; **as I ~ it** по-мо́ему; на мой взгляд; **he saw his mistake at once** он сра́зу же по́нял свою́ оши́бку; **I ~ how it is** мне поня́тно, как обстоя́т дела́; **I don't ~ what good that is** я не ви́жу, кака́я от э́того по́льза; **you ~ now why I hesitated** тепе́рь вы понима́ете, отчего́ я колеба́лся; **as far as I can ~** наско́лько я понима́ю; **what does he ~ in her?** что то́лько он в ней ви́дит/нахо́дит?; **(do) you ~?** (вы) понима́ете?; **you ~, I was an only child** ви́дите ли, я был еди́нственным ребёнком; **don't you ~?** неуже́ли вы не понима́ете?; **from this it can be ~n** из э́того сле́дует; **it can be ~n at a glance** э́то я́сно с пе́рвого взгля́да; **so I ~** сам ви́жу; понима́ю; оно́ и ви́дно. **7.** (*consider*) ду́мать, по-; **I'll ~** я поду́маю; посмо́трим; **let me ~!** погоди́те/посто́йте!; **~ing that ...** ввиду́ того́, что...; поско́льку...; так как... **8.** (*come across, meet*) ви́деть, у-; встр|еча́ть, -е́тить; (*coll.*) повстреча́ть (*pf.*); **1920 saw him in Greece** 1920 (ты́сяча девятьсо́т двадца́тый) год заста́л его́ в Гре́ции; (*associate*) ви́деться (*impf.*), встреча́ться (*impf.*) (с кем); **they stopped ~ing each other** они́ разошли́сь (*or* переста́ли встреча́ться); (*visit*) посе|ща́ть, -ти́ть; наве|ща́ть, -сти́ть; **we went to ~ our friends** мы сходи́ли/съе́здили к на́шим друзья́м; мы посети́ли на́ших друзе́й; **come and ~ me, us sometime** заходи́те ка́к-нибудь; **(I'll) be ~ing you!** до ско́рого!; пока́! (*coll.*); ~ **you on Tuesday!** до вто́рника! **9.** (*interview, consult*): **I went to ~ him about a job** я зашёл к нему́ поговори́ть о рабо́те; **can I ~ you for a moment?** мо́жно вас на мину́тку?; **you should ~ a doctor** вам сле́дует обрати́ться/наве́даться к (*or* показа́ться) врачу́; **he went to ~ a lawyer** он пошёл посове́товаться/поговори́ть с адвока́том; **you can't ~ Mr. Smith today** г-н Смит вас сего́дня приня́ть не мо́жет; (*receive; grant interview to*) прин|има́ть, -я́ть; **the doctor will ~ you now** до́ктор при́мет вас сейча́с. **10.** (*escort, conduct*) прово|жа́ть, -ди́ть; **he saw her to the door** он проводи́л её до две́ри; **I saw her across the road** я перевёл её че́рез у́лицу; (*provide for*): **£5 should ~ you to the end of the week** пяти́ фу́нтов должно́ хвати́ть вам до конца́ неде́ли; **she saw him through college** она́ помогла́ ему́ око́нчить университе́т. **11.** (*ensure*) следи́ть, про-; ~ **that it is done** смотри́те, что́бы э́то бы́ло сде́лано/вы́полнено; ~ **(to it) that the door is locked** проследи́те, что́бы за́перли дверь.

v.i. ви́деть, у-; **cats ~ best at night** ко́шки ви́дят лу́чше всего́ в темноте́; **can you ~ from where you are?** вам отту́да ви́дно?; **as far as the eye can ~** наско́лько хвата́ет/ви́дит глаз; **he cannot ~** (*is blind*) он не ви́дит; он слеп; **~ing eye** (*dog*) соба́ка-проводни́к слепо́го, соба́ка-поводы́рь (*m.*); **~ing is believing** пока́ не увижу́, не пове́рю; **he will never be able to ~ again** он (оконча́тельно) осле́п; **I am ~ing double** у меня́ в глаза́х двои́тся; **go and ~ for yourself!** пойди́те и убеди́тесь са́ми!; ~ **if you can ...** попро́буйте...; **she could ~ into the future** она́ уме́ла загля́дывать в бу́дущее; **may I ~ inside?** мо́жно загляну́ть внутрь?; **they asked to ~ over, round the house** они́ проси́ли позво́лить им осмотре́ть дом; **he could not ~ over the hedge** и́згородь заслоня́ла ему́ вид; **we saw through his tricks** мы раскуси́ли его́ шту́чки; ~ **through s.o.** раску́с|ывать, -и́ть кого́-н.; ви́деть (*impf.*) кого́-н. насквозь́; **I couldn't ~ to read** бы́ло сли́шком темно́ (что́бы) чита́ть. **2.** (*imper., look*): ~, **here he comes!** вот и он! **3.** (*make provision; take care; give attention*) забо́титься, по- (*о чём*); (*arrange, organize*) ста́вить, по-; **I shall ~ about the luggage** я позабо́чусь о бага́же (*or* займу́сь багажо́м); **she ~s to the laundry** она́ ве́дает сти́ркой; сти́рка в её ве́дении; **I have to ~ to the children** мне прихо́дится смотре́ть за детьми́; **the garden needs ~ing to** са́дом сле́дует заня́ться; сад запу́щен; **I saw to it that ...** я устро́ил так, что...; **he saw to it that I got the money** он позабо́тился о том, что́бы я получи́л де́ньги.

with advs.: ~ **back** *v.t.*: **as it was late I offered to ~ her back** так как бы́ло по́здно, я предложи́л проводи́ть её (домо́й *и т.п.*); ~ **in** *v.t.*: **they came to ~ the boat in** они́ пришли́ (, что́бы) встре́тить парохо́д; **we saw the New Year in** мы встре́тили Но́вый год; ~ **off** *v.t.*: **we saw them off at the station** мы проводи́ли их на по́езд; ~ **out** *v.t.* пров|оди́ть, -ести́ до вы́хода; **I can ~ myself out** ≃ я сам найду́ доро́гу; **we saw the play out** оста́лись/досиде́ли до конца́ пье́сы; **he saw out** (*survived*) **all his children** он пережи́л всех свои́х дете́й; ~ **through** *v.t.*: **who will ~ the job through?** кто доведёт де́ло до конца́?; **his courage will ~ him through** благодаря́ своему́ му́жеству он вы́держит все испыта́ния.

cpd. **~-through** *adj.* прозра́чный.

seed [si:d] *n.* **1.** (*lit., fig.*) се́мя (*nt.*), зерно́; зёрнышко, се́мечко; (*collect.*) семена́ (*nt. pl.*); **sow ~(s) in the ground** се́ять, по- семена́ в грунт; **go, run to ~** (*lit.*) идти́, пойти́ в семена́; (*fig., of pers.*) захире́ть, опусти́ться, обрю́згнуть (*all pf.*). **2.** (*semen*) се́мя (*nt.*), спе́рма. **3.** (*bibl., offspring, descendants*) пото́мки (*m. pl.*), пото́мство (*nt.*); ~ **of Abraham** се́мя Авраа́мово. **4.** (*sport*: **~ed player**) отбо́рный/просе́янный игро́к; **he is number 3 ~** он просе́ян за № 3.

v.t. **1.** (*remove ~ from*) оч|ища́ть, -и́стить от зёрнышек; **~ed raisins** изю́м без ко́сточек. **2.** (*sow or sprinkle with ~*) се́ять, по-; зас|ева́ть, -е́ять; **a newly ~ed lawn** свежезасе́янный газо́н. **3.** (*sport*) отбира́ть (*impf.*); **~ed player** = **seed** *n.* **4.**

v.i. (*shed ~*) роня́ть (*impf.*) семена́.

cpds. **~-bearing** *adj.* семяно́сный; **~-bed** *n.* гряда́ с расса́дой; (*fig.*) расса́дник, оча́г; **~-box** *n.* я́щик для расса́ды; **~-cake** *n.* пече́нье/кекс с тми́ном; **~-corn** *n.* посевно́е зерно́; **~-pearl** *n.* ме́лкий же́мчуг; **~-potatoes** *n.* семенно́й карто́фель; **~sman** *n.* торго́вец семена́ми; **~-time** *n.* посевно́й сезо́н.

seedless ['si:dlɪs] *adj.* бессемя́нный.

seedling ['si:dlɪŋ] *n.* се́янец; (*pl.*) расса́да (*collect.*).

seedy ['si:dɪ] *adj.* (*shabby*) потрёпанный; **he looks ~** у него́ невзра́чный вид; (*sleazy*) захуда́лый; (*out of sorts*) не в фо́рме; **I feel ~** я себя́ нева́жно/парши́во чу́вствую.

seek [si:k] *v.t.* **1.** (*look for*) иска́ть (*impf.*) +*a./g. of concrete/abstract object*; ~ **a quarrel** иска́ть (*impf.*) (по́вода для) ссо́ры; ~ **one's fortune** пыта́ть (*impf.*) сча́стья; **~ing a better position** в по́исках лу́чшего ме́ста; ~ **out** разыска́ть (*pf.*); отыска́ть (*pf.*); (*enquire into*) иска́ть (*impf.*); **they were ~ing the causes of cancer** они́ иссле́довали (*or* пыта́лись обнару́жить) причи́ны ра́ка;

the reason is not far to ~ за объяснéнием далекó ходи́ть не нáдо; **efficient leaders are far to ~** спосóбных руководи́телей днём с огнём не сы́щешь; (*ask for*): **~ advice** проси́ть (*impf.*) совéта; обра|щáться, -ти́ться за совéтом; совéтоваться, по-; **~ an explanation** трéбовать, по- объяснéния; **~ pardon** добивáться/проси́ть (*impf.*) прощéния. **2.** (*attempt*) старáться, по-; пытáться, по-; **they sought to kill him** они́ хотéли/пытáлись егó уби́ть; они́ покушáлись/посягáли на егó жизнь.

v.i.: **~ after sth.** стреми́ться (*impf.*) к чемý-н.; **a sought-after person** (чрезвычáйно) популя́рная ли́чность; **~ for sth.** искáть (*impf.*) что-н./чегó-н.

seeker ['si:kə(r)] *n.*: **an earnest ~ after truth** рéвностный искáтель и́стины.

seem [si:m] *v.i.* казáться, по-; предст|авля́ться, -áвиться; **it ~s to me** мне кáжется/сдаётся; по-мóему; **I don't ~ to like him** почемý-то он мне (*or* он мне чем-то) не нрáвится; **I ~ to see him still** он так и стои́т у меня́ пéред глазáми; **I ~ed to hear a voice** мне послы́шался чей-то гóлос; **it ~s like yesterday** как бýдто э́то бы́ло вчерá; **he is not what he ~s** он не такóй, как кáжется; **she ~s young** онá вы́глядит мóлодо; **it ~s cold today** сегóдня, кáжется, хóлодно; сегóдня как бýдто хóлодно; **he and I can't ~ to get on together** мы с ним чтó-то никáк не полáдим; **it ~s nobody knew** кáжется, никтó об э́том не знал; **it would ~** по-ви́димому; казáлось бы; **it would ~ that he stole the money** нáдо полагáть, что он укрáл дéньги; **so it ~s** нáдо полагáть; как бýдто так; **so we are to get nothing, it ~s** итáк, выхóдит, мы ничегó не полýчим.

seeming ['si:mɪŋ] *n.*: **to outward ~** внéшне; сýдя по внéшности.

adj. (*apparent*) кáжущийся, внéшний; (*affected*) напускнóй; **a ~ friend** мни́мый друг; **~ly** по-ви́димому; как бýдто.

seemliness ['si:mlɪnɪs] *n.* прили́чие; (благо)пристóйность.

seemly ['si:mlɪ] *adj.* подобáющий, прили́чный, прили́чествующий, пристóйный.

seep [si:p] *v.i.* (*also* **~ out, through**) прос|áчиваться, -очи́ться; (*leak*) прот|екáть, -éчь.

seepage ['si:pɪdʒ] *n.* течь, утéчка, просáчивание.

seer ['si:ə(r), sɪə(r)] *n.* прови́дец, прорóк.

seersucker ['sɪə,sʌkə(r)] *n.* лёгкая крéповая ткань.

seesaw ['si:sɔ:] *n.* (доскá-)качéл|и (*pl.*, *g.* -ей); подкидна́я доскá; **~ contest** состязáние, проходя́щее с перемéнным успéхом; **~ policy** неустóйчивая/непослéдовательная поли́тика.

v.i. (*play on* ~) качáться, по- на доскé/качéлях; (*fig.*, *oscillate*) колебáться (*impf.*).

seeth|e [si:ð] *v.i.* (*of liquids, and fig.*) бурли́ть (*impf.*); **the country is ~ing with discontent** странá бурли́т от недовóльства; **he ~ed with anger** он кипéл негодовáнием; **the streets were ~ing with people** ýлицы кишéли нарóдом.

segment ['segmənt] *n.* сегмéнт, отрéзок; (*of fruit*) дóлька.

v.t. & i. дели́ть(ся), раз- на сегмéнты.

segmentation [,segmən'teɪʃ(ə)n] *n.* сегментáция.

segregate ['segrɪgət] *v.t.* отдел|я́ть, -и́ть; выделя́ть, вы́делить; раздел|я́ть, -и́ть; изоли́ровать (*impf., pf.*).

segregation [,segrɪ'geɪʃ(ə)n] *n.* (*separation*) отделéние, выделéние, изоля́ция; (*racial*) (рáсовая) сегрегáция.

segregationist [,segrɪ'geɪʃ(ə)nɪst] *n.* сторóнник сегрегáции.

seign|eur [seɪ'njɜ:(r)], **-ior** ['seɪnjə(r)] *n.* (*hist.*) сеньóр; **grand ~** вельмóжа (*m.*).

Seine[1] [seɪn] *n.* Сéна.

seine[2] [seɪn] *n.* нéвод; рыболóвная сеть.

v.i. лови́ть (*impf.*) ры́бу нéводом/сетя́ми.

seisin ['si:zɪn] *n.* (*hist.*) владéние недви́жимостью.

seismic ['saɪzmɪk] *adj.* сейсми́ческий.

seismograph ['saɪzmə,grɑ:f] *n.* сейсмóграф.

seismography [saɪz'mɒgrəfɪ] *n.* сейсморгáфия.

seismological [saɪzmə'lɒdʒɪk(ə)l] *adj.* сейсмологи́ческий.

seismometer [saɪz'mɒmɪtə(r)] *n.* сейсмóметр.

seizable ['si:zəb(ə)l] *adj.* (*of goods etc.*) подлежáщий конфискáции.

seize [si:z] *v.t.* **1.** (*grasp; lay hold of*) хватáть, схвати́ть; **he ~d the boy by the arm** он схвати́л мáльчика зá руку; **they ~d the thief** они́ поймáли вóра; **he ~d** (*hold of*) **the rope** он схвати́л (*or* ухвати́лся за) верёвку; **he was ~d by apoplexy** егó хвати́л удáр; (*fig., comprehend*): **he ~d the point at once** он срáзу схвати́л суть дéла; **I can't quite ~ your meaning** я не совсéм понимáю/ухвáтываю/улáвливаю вáшу мысль; (*fig., make use of*): **~ an opportunity** ухвати́ться (*pl.*) за возмóжность; пóльзоваться, вос- слýчаем. **2.** (*take possession of*) захвáт|ывать, -и́ть; **~ a fortress** брать, взять крéпость; **~ power** захвáт|ывать, -и́ть власть; (*fig., strike, affect*) охвáт|ывать, -и́ть; **he was ~d by a feeling of remorse** егó охвати́ло/обуя́ло раскáяние. **3.** (*impound, arrest*) нал|агáть, -ожи́ть арéст на+*a.*; конфисковáть (*impf., pf.*).

v.i. **1. ~ (up)on** ухвати́ться за+*a.*; **they ~d upon the chance** они́ ухвати́лись за предстáвившийся слýчай; **he ~d upon my remark** он прицепи́лся к мои́м словáм. **2.** (*jam; also* **~ up**) за|едáть, -éсть; застр|евáть, -я́ть.

seizure ['si:ʒə(r)] *n.* (*capture*) захвáт; (*confiscation*) конфискáция; (*attack of illness*) припáдок; (*stroke*) удáр; сердéчный при́ступ.

seldom ['seldəm] *adv.* рéдко; **~ if ever** крáйне рéдко; почти́ никогдá; мóжно сказáть, никогдá.

select [sɪ'lekt] *adj.* и́збранный, изы́сканный, элитáрный; **~ circles** и́збранное óбщество; и́збранные круги́; **~ committee** осóбый комитéт; **a ~ club** клуб для и́збранных.

v.t. выбирáть, вы́брать; от|бирáть, -обрáть; под|бирáть, -обрáть; изб|ирáть, -рáть; **~ed works** и́збранные сочинéния; **~ed fruit** отбóрные фрýкты.

selection [sɪ'lekʃ(ə)n] *n.* **1.** (*choice*) вы́бор; **make a ~ of** выбирáть, вы́брать (мéжду+*i.*); **there was a wide, great ~** был большóй вы́бор; (*biol.*): **natural ~** естéственный отбóр. **2.** (*assortment*) подбóр; набóр; **a ~ of summer clothes** ассортимéнт лéтней одéжды; (*number of selected items*) подбóрка; **a ~ from Faust** отры́вки (*m. pl.*) из óперы «Фáуст».

selective [sɪ'lektɪv] *adj.* разбóрчивый; (*radio*) селекти́вный; избирáтельный; **~ service** (*US*) вóинская пови́нность для отдéльных грáждан (по отбóру).

selectivity [,sɪlek'tɪvɪtɪ, ,sel-, ,si:l-] *n.* разбóрчивость; избирáтельность.

selector [sɪ'lektə(r)] *n.* **1.** (*pers.*) отбóрщик. **2.** (*teleph.*) селéктор; **~ gear** избирáтельный аппарáт; (*radio*) рýчка настрóйки; **band ~** переключáтель (*m.*) диапазóнов.

selenite ['selɪ,naɪt] *n.* селени́т.

selenium [sɪ'li:nɪəm] *n.* селéн.

self [self] *n.* **1.** (*individuality, essence*) сýщность; (*personality*) ли́чность; (*ego*) (сóбственное) «я» (*indecl.*); **his own, very ~** он сам; **we get a glimpse of his very ~** мы мóжем заглянýть в сáмую егó сýщность; **I am not my former ~** я ужé не тот, что прéжде; **he refused to listen to his better ~** он оставáлся глух к призы́вам сóвести; **my other ~** моё вторóе «я». **2.** (*one's own interest*): **he has no thought of ~** он не дýмает о себé; **he always puts ~ first** он себя́ не забывáет. **3.** (*comm.: o.s.*): **cheque made out to '~'** чек, вы́писанный на сóбственное и́мя (*or* на себя́); **a ticket for ~ and friend** входнóй билéт на два лицá.

self- [self] *comb. form* само…; себя…; свое…

self-abasement [,selfə'beɪsmənt] *n.* самоунижéние, самоуничижéние.

self-absorbed [,selfəb'zɔ:bd] *adj.* поглощённый собóй.

self-abuse [,selfə'bju:s] *n.* онани́зм.

self-acting [self'æktɪŋ] *adj.* автомати́ческий.

self-addressed [,selfə'drest] *adj.* адресóванный на сóбственное и́мя; **~ envelope** (прилагáемый к письмý) конвéрт с обрáтным áдресом отправи́теля.

self-adhesive [,selfəd'hi:sɪv] *adj.* самозаклéивающийся.

self-adjustment [,selfə'dʒʌstmənt] *n.* автомати́ческая регулирóвка; (*of pers.*) приспособлéние к обстанóвке.

self-admiration [self,ædmə'reɪʃ(ə)n] *n.* самолюбовáние.

self-admiring [self,əd'maɪərɪŋ] *adj.* любýющийся/восхищáющийся собóй.

self-advertisement [,selfəd'vɜ:tɪsmənt] *n.* саморекла́ма.

self-affirmation [self,æfə'meɪʃ(ə)n] *n.* самоутвержде́ние.
self-aggrandizement [,selfə'grændɪzmənt] *n.* самовозвели́чивание.
self-analysis [,selfə'næləsɪs] *n.* самоана́лиз.
self-appointed [,selfə'pɔɪntɪd] *adj.* самозва́нный.
self-approbation [self,æprə'beɪʃ(ə)n], **-approval** [,selfə'pru:v(ə)l] *nn.* самодово́льство.
self-assertion [,selfə'sɜ:ʃ(ə)n] *n.* самоутвержде́ние.
self-assertive [,selfə'sɜ:tɪv] *adj.* самоутвержда́ющийся.
self-assurance [,selfə'ʃʊərəns] *n.* уве́ренность (в себе́); (*pej.*) самоуве́ренность; самонаде́янность.
self-assured [,selfə'ʃʊəd] *adj.* (само)уве́ренный; самонаде́янный.
self-awareness [,selfə'weənɪs] *n.* самосозна́ние.
self-binder [self'baɪndə(r)] *n.* жнея́-сноповяза́лка.
self-centred [self'sentəd] *adj.* эгоцентри́ческий, эгоцентри́чный.
self-coloured [self'kʌləd] *adj.* одноцве́тный; натура́льного цве́та.
self-command [,selfkə'mɑ:nd] *n.* самооблада́ние.
self-condemnation [self,kɒndem'neɪʃ(ə)n] *n.* самоосужде́ние.
self-condemned [,selfkən'demd] *adj.* осуждённый сами́м собо́й; нево́льно вы́давший себя́.
self-confessed [,selfkən'fest] *adj.* открове́нный; признаю́щий себя́ (*виновным*).
self-confidence [self'kɒnfɪd(ə)ns] *n.* уве́ренность (в себе́); (*pej.*) самоуве́ренность; самонаде́янность.
self-confident [self'kɒnfɪd(ə)nt] *adj.* уве́ренный (в себе́); (*pej.*) самоуве́ренный; самонаде́янный.
self-congratulation [,selfkəŋ,grætjʊ'leɪʃ(ə)n] *n.* самодово́льство.
self-conscious [self'kɒnʃəs] *adj.* **1.** (*awkward*) нело́вкий; (*shy*) засте́нчивый; (*embarrassed*) смущённый. **2.** (*phil.*) самосознаю́щий.
self-consciousness [self'kɒnʃəsnɪs] *n.* нело́вкость, засте́нчивость; (*phil.*) самосозна́ние.
self-consistent [,selfkən'sɪst(ə)nt] *adj.* после́довательный.
self-constituted [self'kɒnstɪ,tju:tɪd] *adj.* самозва́нный.
self-contained [,selfkən'teɪnd] *adj.* (*independent, of pers.*) самостоя́тельный, незави́симый; (*of accommodation*) отде́льный, изоли́рованный.
self-contempt [,selfkən'tempt] *n.* презре́ние к самому́ себе́.
self-contradiction [self,kɒntrə'dɪkʃ(ə)n] *n.* вну́треннее противоре́чие.
self-contradictory [self,kɒntrə'dɪktərɪ] *adj.* (вну́тренне) противоречи́вый; противоре́чащий самому́ себе́.
self-control [,selfkən'trəʊl] *n.* самооблада́ние; **he had to exercise** ~ он до́лжен был прояви́ть самооблада́ние; **he regained his** ~ к нему́ верну́лось самооблада́ние.
self-controlled [,selfkən'trəʊld] *adj.* с самооблада́нием.
self-convicted [,selfkən'vɪktɪd] *adj.* скомпромети́ровавшийся.
self-critical [self'krɪtɪk(ə)l] *adj.* самокрити́чный.
self-criticism [self'krɪtɪ,sɪz(ə)m] *n.* самокри́тика.
self-deceit [,selfdɪ'si:t], **-deception** [,selfdɪ'sepʃ(ə)n] *nn.* самообма́н.
self-defeating [,selfdɪ'fi:tɪŋ] *adj.* сам себя́ сводя́щий на нет.
self-defence [,selfdɪ'fens] *n.* самооборо́на, самозащи́та; **in** ~ для самооборо́ны; в поря́дке самозащи́ты.
self-deluded [,selfdɪ'lu:dɪd, -'lju:dɪd] *adj.* сам себя́ вве́дший в заблужде́ние.
self-delusion [,selfdɪ'lu:ʒ(ə)n, -'lju:ʒ(ə)n] *n.* самообма́н, самообольще́ние.
self-denial [,selfdɪ'naɪəl] *n.* самоотрече́ние; **practise** ~ отка́зывать (*impf.*) себе́ во мно́гом; ограни́чивать (*impf.*) себя́.
self-denying [,selfdɪ'naɪɪŋ] *adj.* возде́рж(ан)ный, бескоры́стный, самоотве́рженный.
self-depreciation [,selfdɪ,pri:ʃɪ'eɪʃ(ə)n] *n.* самоуничиже́ние.
self-destruct [,selfdɪ'strʌkt] *v.i.* (*tech.*) самоликвиди́роваться (*impf., pf.*).
self-destruction [,selfdɪ'strʌkʃ(ə)n] *n.* самоуничтоже́ние; (*suicide*) самоуби́йство; (*tech.*) самоликвида́ция.
self-determination [,selfdɪ,tɜ:mɪ'neɪʃ(ə)n] *n.* самоопределе́ние.
self-discipline [self'dɪsɪplɪn] *n.* вну́тренняя дисципли́на.
self-disparagement [,selfdɪ'spærɪdʒmənt] *n.* умале́ние со́бственного досто́инства.
self-disparaging [,selfdɪ'spærɪdʒɪŋ] *adj.* самоуничижи́тельный.
self-distrust [,selfdɪ'strʌst], **-doubt** [self'daʊt] *nn.* неве́рие в себя́.
self-drive [self'draɪv] *n.*: ~ **car hire** прока́т автомаши́н.
self-educated [self'edju:,keɪtɪd] *adj.*: **a** ~ **man, woman** самоу́чка (*c.g.*)
self-education [,self,edju:'keɪʃ(ə)n] *n.* самообразова́ние.
self-effacement [,selfɪ'feɪsmənt] *n.* скро́мность; стремле́ние держа́ться в тени́.
self-effacing [,selfɪ'feɪsɪŋ] *adj.* скро́мный; держа́щийся в тени́.
self-employed [,selfɪm'plɔɪd] *adj.* рабо́тающий не по на́йму; обслу́живающий своё со́бственное предприя́тие; принадлежа́щий к свобо́дной профе́ссии.
self-esteem [,selfɪ'sti:m] *n.* самолю́бие.
self-evident [self'evɪd(ə)nt] *adj.* очеви́дный; само́ собо́й разуме́ющийся.
self-examination [,selfɪg,zæmɪ'neɪʃ(ə)n] *n.* самоана́лиз.
self-existent [,selfɪg'zɪst(ə)nt] *adj.* самостоя́тельный.
self-explanatory [,selfɪk'splænətərɪ] *adj.* не тре́бующий разъясне́ний.
self-expression [,selfɪk'spreʃ(ə)n] *n.* самовыраже́ние.
self-feeding [self'fi:dɪŋ] *adj.* (*of boiler etc.*) с автомати́ческой пода́чей.
self-fertilization [self,fɜ:tɪlaɪ'zeɪʃ(ə)n] *n.* самоопыле́ние; самооплодотворе́ние.
self-fertilizing [self'fɜ:tɪ,laɪzɪŋ] *adj.* самоопыля́ющийся; самооплодотворя́ющийся.
self-forgetful [,selffə'getfʊl] *adj.* бескоры́стный; беззаве́тный.
self-forgetfulness [,selffə'getfʊlnɪs] *n.* бескоры́стие.
self-fulfilment [,selffʊl'fɪlmənt] *n.* реализа́ция свои́х возмо́жностей.
self-glorification [self,glɔ:rɪfɪ'keɪʃ(ə)n] *n.* самовосхвале́ние.
self-governing [self'gʌvənɪŋ] *adj.* самоуправля́ющийся.
self-government [self'gʌvənmənt] *n.* самоуправле́ние.
self-help [self'help] *n.* самопо́мощь.
self-image [self'ɪmɪdʒ] *n.* со́бственное представле́ние о себе́.
self-immolation [,selfɪmə'leɪʃ(ə)n] *n.* самосожже́ние; (*fig.*) самопоже́ртвование.
self-importance [,selfɪm'pɔ:t(ə)ns] *n.* самомне́ние.
self-important [,selfɪm'pɔ:t(ə)nt] *adj.* ва́жный, ва́жничающий.
self-imposed [,selfɪm'pəʊzd] *adj.* доброво́льный; доброво́льно взя́тый на себя́.
self-improvement [,selfɪm'pru:vmənt] *n.* самосоверше́нствование.
self-induction [,selfɪn'dʌkʃ(ə)n] *n.* самоинду́кция.
self-indulgence [,selfɪn'dʌldʒ(ə)ns] *n.* избало́ванность; потака́ние свои́м сла́бостям; потво́рство свои́м жела́ниям.
self-indulgent [,selfɪn'dʌldʒ(ə)nt] *adj.* избало́ванный; потака́ющий свои́м сла́бостям; потво́рствующий свои́м жела́ниям.
self-inflicted [,selfɪn'flɪktɪd] *adj.* (*of penance*) доброво́льный; (*of wound, injury*) нанесённый самому́ себе́.
self-instruction [,selfɪn'strʌkʃ(ə)n] *n.* самообразова́ние.
self-interest [self'ɪntrəst, -trɪst] *n.* со́бственный интере́с; коры́сть; **he acted from** ~ он де́йствовал из коры́стных побужде́ний.
self-interested [self'ɪntrəstɪd, -trɪstɪd] *adj.* коры́стный, корыстолюби́вый.
self-invited [,selfɪn'vaɪtɪd] *adj.* непро́шенный, незва́ный.
selfish ['selfɪʃ] *adj.* эгоисти́ческий, эгоисти́чный, коры́стный; ~ **person** эгои́ст (*fem.* -ка).
selfishness ['selfɪʃnɪs] *n.* эгоисти́чность, эгои́зм.
self-justification [self,dʒʌstɪfɪ'keɪʃ(ə)n] *n.* самоопра́вда́ние.
self-knowledge [self'nɒlɪdʒ] *n.* самопозна́ние.
selfless ['selflɪs] *adj.* самоотве́рженный, беззаве́тный.
selflessness ['selflɪsnɪs] *n.* самоотве́рженность, беззаве́тность.
self-loading [self'ləʊdɪŋ] *adj.* (*of weapon*) самозаря́дный.
self-locking [self'lɒkɪŋ] *adj.* самоблокиру́ющийся.
self-love [self'lʌv] *n.* себялю́бие, эгои́зм.
self-made ['selfmeɪd] *adj.*: **a** ~ **man** челове́к, вы́бившийся из низо́в.

self-mastery [selfˈmɑːstərɪ] *n.* самооблада́ние; владе́ние собо́й.
self-murder [selfˈmɜːdə(r)] *n.* самоуби́йство.
self-neglect [ˌselfnɪˈglekt] *n.* (*slovenliness*) опу́щенность, неопря́тность.
self-perpetuating [ˌselfpəˈpetjuːˌeɪtɪŋ] *adj.* мо́гущий продолжа́ться бесконе́чно; упо́рно держа́щийся за власть.
self-pity [selfˈpɪtɪ] *n.* жа́лость к себе́.
self-pitying [selfˈpɪtɪɪŋ] *adj.* испо́лненный жа́лостью к себе́.
self-portrait [selfˈpɔːtrɪt] *n.* автопортре́т.
self-possessed [ˌselfpəˈzest] *adj.* наделённый самооблада́нием; хладнокро́вный, невозмути́мый; со́бранный.
self-possession [ˌselfpəˈzeʃ(ə)n] *n.* самооблада́ние, хладнокро́вие, невозмути́мость.
self-praise [selfˈpreɪz] *n.* самохва́льство, бахва́льство; ~ **is no recommendation** самоpекла́ма — ещё не рекоменда́ция.
self-preservation [selfˌprezəˈveɪʃ(ə)n] *n.* самосохране́ние.
self-propelled [ˌselfprəˈpeld] *adj.* самохо́дный.
self-realization [selfˌrɪəlaɪˈzeɪʃ(ə)n] *n.* разви́тие свои́х спосо́бностей.
self-recording [ˌselfrɪˈkɔːdɪŋ] *adj.* самопи́шущий, саморегистри́рующий.
self-regard [ˌselfrɪˈgɑːd] *n.* **1.** (*concern for o.s.*) себялю́бие. **2.** = **self-respect**
self-regulating [selfˈregjʊˌleɪtɪŋ] *adj.* саморегули́рующийся.
self-reliance [ˌselfrɪˈlaɪəns] *n.* самостоя́тельность, незави́симость.
self-reliant [ˌselfrɪˈlaɪənt] *adj.* полага́ющийся на себя́.
self-renunciation [ˌselfrɪˌnʌnsɪˈeɪʃ(ə)n] *n.* самоотрече́ние.
self-reproach [ˌselfrɪˈprəʊtʃ] *n.* самоосужде́ние, самобичева́ние.
self-respect [ˌselfrɪˈspekt] *n.* уваже́ние к себе́; самоуваже́ние; чу́вство со́бственного досто́инства.
self-restraint [ˌselfrɪˈstreɪnt] *n.* сде́ржанность.
self-righteous [selfˈraɪtʃəs] *adj.* ха́нжеский, фарисе́йский.
self-righteousness [selfˈraɪtʃəsnɪs] *n.* ха́нжество, фарисе́йство.
self-rule [selfˈruːl] *n.* самоуправле́ние.
self-ruling [selfˈruːlɪŋ] *adj.* самоуправля́ющийся.
self-sacrifice [selfˈsækrɪˌfaɪs] *n.* самопоже́ртвование.
self-sacrificing [selfˈsækrɪˌfaɪsɪŋ] *adj.* самоотве́рженный.
selfsame [ˈselfseɪm] *adj.* тот же са́мый; оди́н и тот же.
self-satisfaction [selfˌsætɪsˈfækʃ(ə)n] *n.* самодово́льство.
self-satisfied [selfˈsætɪsˌfaɪd] *adj.* дово́льный собо́й; самодово́льный.
self-sealing [selfˈsiːlɪŋ] *adj.* самоуплотня́ющийся, самозаклéивающийся.
self-seeking [ˈselfˌsiːkɪŋ] *adj.* своекоры́стный.
self-service [selfˈsɜːvɪs] *n.* самообслу́живание; ~ **store** магази́н самообслу́живания.
self-sown [selfˈsəʊn] *adj.* самосе́вный.
self-starter [selfˈstɑːtə(r)] *n.* автомати́ческий ста́ртер; самопу́ск.
self-styled [ˈselfstaɪld] *adj.* самозва́ный.
self-sufficiency [ˌselfsəˈfɪʃənsɪ] *n.* (*of pers.*) самостоя́тельность, самонаде́янность; (*econ.*) самообеспе́ченнность, автарки́я.
self-sufficient [ˌselfsəˈfɪʃ(ə)nt] *adj.* самостоя́тельный, самонаде́янный; (*econ.*) самообеспе́ченный, автарки́ческий.
self-supporting [ˌselfsəˈpɔːtɪŋ] *adj.* (*of pers.*) самостоя́тельный, незави́симый; (*of business*) самоокупа́ющийся; **the country is ~ in oil** страна́ спосо́бна обеспе́чить себя́ не́фтью.
self-taught [selfˈtɔːt] *adj.*: **a ~ man, woman** самоу́чка (*c.g.*); **English ~** (*as title*) самоучи́тель (*m.*) англи́йского языка́.
self-torture [selfˈtɔːtʃə(r)] *n.* самоистяза́ние.
self-will [selfˈwɪl] *n.* своево́лие.
self-willed [selfˈwɪld] *adj.* своево́льный.
self-winding [selfˈwaɪndɪŋ] *adj.* с автомати́ческим заво́дом.
sell [sel] *n.* **1.** (*manner of ~ing*): **hard ~** навя́зывание това́ра. **2.** (*coll., deception, disappointment*) обма́н; доса́да.
v.t. **1.** прод|ава́ть, -а́ть; торгова́ть (*impf.*) +*i.*; **I'll ~ you this carpet for £20** я вам прода́м/уступлю́ э́тот ковёр за 20 фу́нтов; **I can't remember what I sold it for** я не по́мню, ско́лько я за э́то взял; ~ **short** (*coll., disparage*) умаля́ть (*impf.*) досто́инства +*g.*; **~ing price** прода́жная цена́; **this shop ~s stamps** в э́том магази́не продаю́тся/име́ются почто́вые ма́рки; (*offer dishonourably for gain*): **he sold himself to the highest bidder** он продался тому́, кто бо́льше заплати́л; **traitors who sold their country** преда́тели, прода́вшие ро́дину. **2.** (*coll., put across*): **he was unable to ~ his idea to the management** ему́ не удало́сь убеди́ть правле́ние приня́ть его́ предложе́ние; **~ o.s.** (*present o.s. to advantage*) под|ава́ть, -а́ть себя́; пока́з|ывать, -а́ть това́р лицо́м. **3.: he is sold on the idea** (*coll.*) он твёрдо де́ржится за э́ту иде́ю. **4.** (*coll., cheat, disappoint*): **I've been sold again** меня́ опя́ть наду́ли/обста́вили.
v.i. **1.** (*of pers.*): **you were wise to ~ when you did** вы во́время прода́ли свой това́р. **2.** (*of goods*): **the house sold for £9,000** за дом вы́ручили 9000 фу́нтов; **the record is ~ing like hot cakes** э́ту пласти́нку покупа́ют/беру́т нарасхва́т; **his book ~s well** кни́га хорошо́ идёт; **tennis-balls ~ best in summer** ле́том на те́ннисные мячи́ спрос вы́ше; **wheat is not ~ing** пшени́ца пло́хо продаётся; **these pens ~ at 30p each** э́ти ру́чки сто́ят (*or* продаю́тся за) 30 пе́нсов шту́ка.
with advs.: ~ **back** *v.t.*: **I sold the car back to him for less than I paid for it** я перепро́дал ему́ маши́ну с убы́тком; ~ **off** *v.t.* прод|ава́ть, -а́ть со ски́дкой; **they sold off the goods at a reduced price** они́ распро́дали това́р по сни́женной цене́; ~ **out** *v.t.*: **he sold out his share of the business** он про́дал свою́ до́лю в де́ле; *v.i.* **the book sold out** э́та кни́га разошла́сь; **the shop sold out of cigarettes** они́ про́дали все папиро́сы в магази́не; **they have sold out of tickets** все биле́ты про́даны; **they were accused of ~ing out to the enemy** их обвиня́ли в том, что они́ продали́сь врагу́; ~ **up** *v.t.* (*a debtor*): **he was sold up** его́ иму́щество пошло́ с молотка́ в счёт долго́в; *v.i.* (~ *one's possessions*) распрода́ть (*pf.*) своё иму́щество.
cpd. **~-out** *n.* распрода́жа; **the play was a ~-out** пье́са прошла́ с аншла́гом; (*betrayal*) изме́на, преда́тельство.
seller [ˈselə(r)] *n.* продав|е́ц (*fem.* -щи́ца); торго́в|ец (*fem.* -ка); **~'s market** ры́ночная конъюнкту́ра, вы́годная для продавца́.
Sellotape [ˈseləˌteɪp] *n.* (*propr.*) липу́чка (*coll.*), скотч.
selv|age [ˈselvɪdz], **-edge** [ˈselvedʒ] *n.* кро́мка.
semantic [sɪˈmæntɪk] *adj.* семанти́ческий, смыслово́й.
semantics [sɪˈmæntɪks] *n.* сема́нтика.
semaphore [ˈseməˌfɔː(r)] *n.* семафо́р; ручна́я сигнализа́ция.
v.t. & i. сигнализи́ровать (*impf., pf.*) флажка́ми.
semblance [ˈsembləns] *n.* (*appearance*) вид; нару́жность; ви́димость; **under the ~ of** под ви́дом +*g.*; в о́бразе +*g.*; **he put on a ~ of anger** он притвори́лся рассе́рженным; **the ~ of victory** ви́димость побе́ды; (*likeness*) подо́бие, схо́дство.
semelfactive [ˌseməlˈfæktɪv] *adj.* (*gram.*) однокра́тный.
semen [ˈsiːmən] *n.* се́мя (*nt.*), спе́рма.
semester [sɪˈmestə(r)] *n.* семе́стр.
semi [ˈsemɪ] *n.* (*coll.*) = **~-detached house.**
pref. полу…
cpds. **~-annual** *adj.* полугодово́й; **~-automatic** *adj.* полуавтомати́ческий; **~-barbarous** *adj.* полуди́кий; **~-basement** *n.* полуподва́л; **~breve** *n.* це́лая но́та; **~-circle** *n.* полукру́г; **~-circular** *adj.* полукру́глый; полукру́жный; **~-civilized** *adj.* полуди́кий; **~colon** *n.* то́чка с запято́й; **~-conductor** *n.* полупроводни́к; **~-conscious** *adj.* в полузабытьи́; **~-consciousness** *n.* полузабытьё; **~-darkness** *n.* полутьма́; **~-desert** *n.* полупусты́ня; **~-detached** *n.*: **~-detached house** (*coll., abbr.* **semi**) оди́н из двух особняко́в, име́ющих о́бщую сте́ну; **~-final** *n.* полуфина́л; **~-finalist** *n.* полуфинали́ст (*fem.* -ка); **~-finished** *adj.*: **~finished article** полуфабрика́т; **~-invalid** *adj.* полубольно́й; **~-literate** *adj.* полугра́мотный; **~-monthly** *adj.* двухнеде́льный; **~-nude** *adj.* полуго́лый; **~-official** *adj.* полуофициа́льный; официо́зный; **~-official newspaper**

официо́з; **~-precious** *adj.*: **~-precious stone** самоцве́т; **~quaver** *n.* шестна́дцатая но́та; **~-rigid** *adj.* полужёсткий; **~-skilled** *adj.* полуквалифици́рованный; **~-solid** *adj.* полутвёрдый; **~tone** *n.* полуто́н; **~-trailer** *n.* полуприце́п; **~vowel** *n.* полугла́сный (звук); **~-weekly** *adj.* & *adv.* (*twice a week*) (выходя́щий) два́жды в неде́лю.

seminal ['semɪn(ə)l] *adj.* **1.** семенно́й; **~ fluid** семенна́я жи́дкость. **2.** (*fig.*) плодотво́рный.

seminar ['semɪˌnɑː(r)] *n.* семина́р.

seminarist ['semɪnərɪst] *n.* семинари́ст.

seminary ['semɪnərɪ] *n.* семина́рия.

Semite ['siːmaɪt, 'sem-] *n.* семи́т (*fem.* -ка).

Semitic [sɪ'mɪtɪk] *adj.* семити́ческий.

semolina [ˌsemə'liːnə] *n.* ма́нная крупа́, ма́нка.

sempstress ['semstrɪs] = **seamstress**

Sen. ['senətə(r)] *n.* (*abbr. of* **Senator**) сена́тор.

senate ['senɪt] *n.* сена́т; (*univ.*) сове́т.

senator ['senətə(r)] *n.* сена́тор.

senatorial [ˌsenə'tɔːrɪəl] *adj.* сена́торский.

send [send] *v.t.* **1.** (*dispatch*) пос|ыла́ть, -ла́ть; отпр|авля́ть, -а́вить; **they ~ their goods all over the world** они́ рассыла́ют свои́ това́ры по всему́ све́ту; **he sent me a book** он присла́л мне кни́гу; **I shall ~ you to bed** я отпра́влю тебя́ спать; **the teacher sent him out of the room** учи́тель вы́ставил/вы́гнал его́ из кла́сса; **I will ~ help to them** я им подбро́шу подкрепле́ние; **~ me word of your arrival** извести́те меня́ о ва́шем прибы́тии; **he was sent to a good school** его́ помести́ли/устро́или в хоро́шую шко́лу. **2.** (*cause to move*; *propel*): **~ the ball to s.o.** под|ава́ть, -а́ть мяч кому́-н.; **he sent a stone through the window** он запусти́л ка́мнем в окно́; **~ s.o. packing** (*or* **about his business**) прогна́ть/вы́гнать/вы́проводить/спрова́дить (*all pf.*) кого́-н.; **the blow sent him flying** уда́р сбил его́ с ног; (*fig.*, *drive*): **~ s.o. mad** св|оди́ть, -ести́ кого́-н. с ума́; **his voice sent everyone to sleep** его́ го́лос наводи́л на всех сон; **the garden sent her into raptures** сад привёл её в восто́рг. **3.** (*of divine agent*): **a judgement sent of God** наказа́ние, ниспо́сланное Бо́гом; **God ~s rain** Бог ниспосыла́ет дождь.

v.i.: **I sent for a catalogue** я заказа́л/вы́писал катало́г; **he sent for a doctor** он вы́звал врача́; он посла́л за врачо́м; **I shall wait till I am sent for** я бу́ду ждать, пока́ меня́ не позову́т; **~ to us for details** обраща́йтесь за подро́бностями к нам.

with advs.: **~ across** *v.t.* перепр|авля́ть, -а́вить; **~ along** *v.t.* пос|ыла́ть, -ла́ть; **~ away** *v.t.* от|сыла́ть, -осла́ть; **the manager sent them away contented** они́ ушли́ от дире́ктора дово́льные; *v.i.*: **~ away for sth.** выпи́сывать, вы́писать что-н. (из друго́го ме́ста); **~ back** *v.t.* (*pers.*) пос|ыла́ть, -ла́ть наза́д; (*thg.*) от|сыла́ть, -осла́ть; (*of light etc.*: *reflect*) отра|жа́ть, -зи́ть; **~ down** *v.t.* (*cause to fall*) пон|ижа́ть, -и́зить; (*expel from college*) исключ|а́ть, -и́ть; **a glut sent prices down** затова́ривание привело́ к паде́нию цен; **~ forth** *v.t.* (**~ out**) высыла́ть, вы́слать; (*emit*) испус|ка́ть, -ти́ть; **~ in** *v.t.*: **he sent in his bill** он посла́л счёт; **~ in one's name** (*enrol*) запи́с|ываться, -а́ться; **~ in one's name as a candidate** выставля́ть, вы́ставить свою́ кандидату́ру; **~ in a report** предст|авля́ть, -а́вить отчёт; **~ in paintings for a competition** предст|авля́ть, -а́вить карти́ны на ко́нкурс; **~ off** *v.t.* (*dispatch*) отпр|авля́ть, -а́вить; **he was sent off by the referee** судья́ удали́л его́ с по́ля; **we went to the airport to ~ him off** мы отпра́вились в аэропо́рт проводи́ть его́; **~ on** *v.t.* (*forward*) перес|ыла́ть, -ла́ть; **~ out** *v.t.* высыла́ть, вы́слать; **he was sent out as a missionary** его́ посла́ли миссионе́ром; (*distribute*) ра|ссыла́ть, -зосла́ть; **invitations were sent out** приглаше́ния бы́ли разо́сланы; (*emit*): **~ out rays** испуска́ть (*impf.*) лучи́; **~ out heat** выделя́ть, вы́делить тепло́; **~ out signals** посыла́ть (*impf.*) сигна́лы; *v.i.*: **we sent out for some beer** мы посла́ли за пи́вом; **~ round** *v.t.* **I sent round a note** я посла́л запи́ску; *v.i.*: **he sent round to see how I was** он посла́л ко мне узна́ть, как я чу́вствую себя́; **~ up** *v.t.*: **~ up a rocket** запус|ка́ть, -ти́ть раке́ту; **~ up s.o.'s temperature** подня́ть (*pf.*) у кого́-н. температу́ру; **~ up prices** подн|има́ть, -я́ть це́ны; (*coll.*, *ridicule*) высме́ивать, вы́смеять.

cpds. **~-off** *n.* про́воды (*pl. g.* -ов); **he got a marvellous ~-off from his friends** друзья́ устро́или замеча́тельные про́воды; **~-up** *n.* (*coll.*, *parody*, *satire*) паро́дия, па́сквиль (*m.*), сати́ра.

sender ['sendə(r)] *n.* отправи́тель (*m.*); (*of mail*, *also*) адреса́нт; **return to ~** возврати́ть (*pf.*) отправи́телю.

Seneca ['senɪkə] *n.* Сене́ка (*m.*).

Senegal ['senɪ'gɔːl] *n.* Сенега́л.

Senegalese [ˌsenɪgə'liːz] *n.* сенега́л|ец (*fem.* -ка).

adj. сенега́льский.

senescence [sɪ'nesəns] *n.* старе́ние.

senescent [sɪ'nesənt] *adj.* старе́ющий.

seneschal ['senɪʃ(ə)l] *n.* (*hist.*) сенеша́ль (*m.*).

senile ['siːnaɪl] *adj.* ста́рческий; **~ decay** ста́рческая дря́хлость; (*of pers.*) дря́хлый; **become ~** дряхле́ть, о-; впасть (*pf.*) в ста́рческое слабоу́мие.

senility [sɪ'nɪlɪtɪ] *n.* дря́хлость; ста́рческое слабоу́мие.

senior ['siːnɪə(r)] *n.*: **he is my ~ by 5 years** он на пять лет ста́рше меня́; (*pl.* **~** *pupils*, *students*) старшекла́ссники, старшеку́рсники (*both m. pl.*).

adj. ста́рший (во́зрастом, года́ми, чи́ном); **I am several years ~ to him** я на не́сколько лет ста́рше его́; **~ citizen** челове́к пенсио́нного во́зраста; пожило́й челове́к; **~ common room** профе́ссорская; **~ partner** глава́ фи́рмы, гла́вный компаньо́н; **~ school** (*higher classes*) шко́ла второ́й ступе́ни; **Johnson ~** Джо́нсон-ста́рший; Джо́нсон-оте́ц.

seniority [ˌsiːnɪ'ɒrɪtɪ] *n.* старшинство́.

senna ['senə] *n.* ка́ссия; александри́йский лист.

Señor [sen'jɔː(r)], **-a** [sen'jɔːrə], **-ita** [ˌsenjə'riːtə] *nn.* сеньо́р, -а, -и́та.

sensation [sen'seɪʃ(ə)n] *n.* **1.** (*feeling*) ощуще́ние; **~ of awe** чу́вство благогове́ния; **lose all ~** по́лностью потеря́ть (*pf.*) чувстви́тельность; **he had a ~ of giddiness** он почу́вствовал головокруже́ние. **2.** (*exciting event*; *excitement*) сенса́ция; **the wedding was a great ~** сва́дьба была́ настоя́щей сенса́цией; **this paper deals largely in ~** э́та газе́та преиму́щественно гоня́ется за сенса́циями.

sensational [sen'seɪʃən(ə)l] *adj.* сенсацио́нный.

sensationalism [sen'seɪʃənəˌlɪz(ə)m] *n.* (*pursuit of sensation*) пого́ня за сенса́циями.

sense [sens] *n.* **1.** (*faculty*) чу́вство; **the five ~s** пять чувств; **sixth ~** шесто́е чу́вство; **keen, quick ~s** о́строе чу́вство/чутьё; **a dull ~ of smell** притупле́нное обоня́ние; **a keen ~ of hearing** о́стрый слух; **the pleasures of ~** чу́вственные наслажде́ния. **2.** (*feeling*; *perception*; *appreciation*) чу́вство, ощуще́ние; **he felt a ~ of injury** он испыта́л чу́вство оби́ды; **have you no ~ of shame?** у вас стыда́ нет?; **~ of beauty** эстети́ческое чу́вство; **~ of honour/duty** чу́вство че́сти/до́лга; **~ of proportion** чу́вство ме́ры; **~ of direction** уме́ние ориенти́роваться; **~ of humour** чу́вство ю́мора; **~ of failure** ощуще́ние неуда́чи. **3.** (*pl.*, *sanity*) ум; **take leave of one's ~s** сходи́ть, сойти́ с ума́; **bring s.o. to his ~s** наст|авля́ть, -а́вить кого́-н. на ум; прив|оди́ть, -ести́ кого́-н. в чу́вство; **come to one's ~s** бра́ться, взя́ться за ум. **4.** (*pl.*, *consciousness*): **come to one's ~s** при|ходи́ть, -йти́ в себя́. **5.** (*common ~*) здра́вый смысл; **a man of ~** (благо)разу́мный челове́к; **talk ~** говори́ть (*impf.*) де́ло; **he has more ~ than to ...** он не так глуп (*or* он сли́шком умён), что́бы...; **he had the ~ to call the police** он догада́лся (*or* у него́ хвати́ло ума́) вы́звать поли́цию; **what would be the ~ of going any further?** како́й смысл продолжа́ть?; **there is a lot of ~ in what you say** то, что вы говори́те, вполне́ справедли́во. **6.** (*meaning*) смысл, значе́ние; **in a ~** в изве́стном/не́котором смы́сле; до изве́стной/не́которой сте́пени; **in every ~** во всех отноше́ниях; **in no ~** нико́им о́бразом; ни в како́м отноше́нии; **make ~ of** пон|има́ть, -я́ть; раз|бира́ться, -обра́ться в+*p.*; **it makes ~** э́то разу́мно; **it makes no ~** э́то бессмы́сленно/неле́по; (*cannot be true*) э́то(го) не мо́жет быть. **7.** (*prevailing* *sentiment*): **take the ~ of the meeting** определ|я́ть, -и́ть настрое́ние собра́ния; **the ~ of the meeting was that ...** собра́ние пришло́ к заключе́нию, что... **8.** (*math. etc.*: *direction*) направле́ние.

v.t. чу́вствовать, по-; ощу|ща́ть, -ти́ть.

senseless ['senslıs] *adj.* **1.** (*foolish*) бессмы́сленный, бестолко́вый, дура́цкий. **2.** (*unconscious*) бесчу́вственный; **knock s.o. ~** оглуш|а́ть, -и́ть кого́-н.; **he fell ~ on the floor** он упа́л без чувств (*or* за́мертво) на́ пол.

senselessness ['senslısnıs] *n.* бессмы́сленность; бессозна́тельность.

sensibilit|y [ˌsensı'bılıtı] *n.* чувстви́тельность (*e.g. to kindness* к доброте́); **~y of a writer** то́нкость/чутьё писа́теля; **offend, wound s.o.'s ~ies** ра́нить (*impf.*, *pf.*) чьё-н. самолю́бие; оскорб|ля́ть, -и́ть чью-н. чувстви́тельность.

sensible ['sensıb(ə)l] *adj.* **1.** (*perceptible*) ощути́мый; (*appreciable*) заме́тный. **2.** (*showing good sense*) (благо)разу́мный; **that was ~ of you** вы хорошо́ сде́лали; **~ shoes** практи́чная о́бувь. **3.:** **be ~ of** (*be aware of*, *recognize*, *appreciate*) (о)сознава́ть (*impf.*).

sensibleness ['sensıbəlnıs] *n.* благоразу́мие.

sensitive ['sensıtıv] *adj.* чувстви́тельный, восприи́мчивый, чу́ткий; **eyes ~ to light** глаза́, чувстви́тельные к све́ту; **don't be so ~!** вы сли́шком оби́дчивы!; (*sharp*): **~ ears** о́стрый слух; (*of instruments*): **~ balance** то́чные весы́; (*tender*): **~ skin** не́жная/(легко)раздражи́мая ко́жа; (*painful*): **~ tooth** больно́й зуб; (*potentially embarrassing*): **a ~ topic** щекотли́вая/делика́тная те́ма; (*phot.*): **~ paper** светочувстви́тельная бума́га; (*econ.*): **~ market** неусто́йчивый ры́нок.

sensitivity [ˌsensı'tıvıtı] *n.* чувстви́тельность, восприи́мчивость; чу́ткость, то́чность; светочувстви́тельность; неусто́йчивость.

sensitize ['sensıˌtaız] *v.t.* (*phot.*) де́лать, с- светочувстви́тельным.

sensor ['sensə(r)] *n.* (*tech.*) да́тчик; чувстви́тельный элеме́нт.

sensory ['sensərı] *adj.* сенсо́рный; **~ deprivation** выключе́ние о́рганов чувств; сенсо́рная деприва́ция.

sensual ['sensjʊəl, 'senʃʊəl] *adj.* чу́вственный (*also of mouth etc.*); пло́тский, сладостра́стный.

sensualist ['sensjʊəlıst, 'senʃʊəlıst] *n.* сластолю́бец; эпикуре́ец.

sensuality [ˌsensjʊ'ælıtı, ˌsenʃʊ-] *n.* чу́вственность, сладостра́стие.

sensuous ['sensjʊəs] *adj.* чу́вственный; эстети́ческий.

sensuousness ['sensjʊəsnıs] *n.* чу́вственность.

sentence ['sent(ə)ns] *n.* **1.** (*gram.*) предложе́ние. **2.** (*leg.*) пригово́р; **~ of death** сме́ртный пригово́р; **be under ~ of death** быть приговорённым к сме́рти; **pass ~ on** (*of judge*) выноси́ть, вы́нести пригово́р +*d.*; (*fig.*) осу|жда́ть, -ди́ть.

v.t. пригов|а́ривать, -ори́ть; **he was ~d to penal servitude** его́ приговори́ли к ка́торжным рабо́там.

sententious [sen'tenʃəs] *adj.* дидакти́чный, сентенцио́зный; **my father is very ~** мой оте́ц большо́й охо́тник поуча́ть.

sententiousness [sen'tenʃəsnıs] *n.* дидакти́чность, сентенцио́зность.

sentient ['senʃ(ə)nt] *adj.* наделённый чувстви́тельностью.

sentiment ['sentımənt] *n.* **1.** (*feeling*) чу́вство; **have friendly ~s towards s.o.** пита́ть (*impf.*) дру́жеские чу́вства к кому́-н.; **my ~s towards your brother** мои́ чу́вства (*or* моё отноше́ние) к ва́шему бра́ту; **animated by noble ~s** воодушевлённый благоро́дными чу́вствами; (*tendency to be swayed by feeling*): **appeal to ~** взыва́ть (*impf.*) (*or* апелли́ровать (*impf.*, *pf.*)) к эмо́циям/чу́вствам. **2.** (*opinion*) мне́ние; то́чка зре́ния; **those are my ~s** тако́во моё мне́ние (по э́тому по́воду). **3.** (*sentimentality*) сентимента́льность.

sentimental [ˌsentı'ment(ə)l] *adj.* сентимента́льный; **of ~ value** дорого́й как па́мять.

sentimentalism [ˌsentı'ment(ə)l] *n.* сентиментали́зм.

sentimentalist [ˌsentı'mentəlıst] *n.* сентимента́льный челове́к.

sentimentality [ˌsentımen'tælıtı] *n.* сентимента́льность.

sentimentalize [ˌsentı'mentəlaız] *v.t.* прид|ава́ть, -а́ть (*чему*) сентимента́льную окра́ску.

v.i.: **~ over the past** относи́ться (*impf.*) сентимента́льно к про́шлому; разводи́ть (*impf.*) сентиме́нты относи́тельно про́шлого.

sentinel ['sentın(ə)l] *n.* (*guard*) часово́й; (*outpost*) сторожево́й пост; **stand ~ over sth.** (*fig.*) стоя́ть (*impf.*) на стра́же чего́-н.; охраня́ть (*impf.*) что-н.

sentry ['sentrı] *n.* (*guard*) часово́й; (*post*) карау́льный пост; **stand ~** стоя́ть (*impf.*) на часа́х; **go on ~** заступ|а́ть, -и́ть на дежу́рство; **come off ~** смен|я́ться, -и́ться с дежу́рства; **~ duty** карау́льная слу́жба.

cpds. **~-box** *n.* бу́дка часово́го; **~-go** *n.* карау́льная слу́жба.

Seoul [səʊl] *n.* Сеу́л.

sepal ['sep(ə)l, 'siː-] *n.* чашели́стик.

separable ['sepərəb(ə)l] *adj.* отдели́мый; **~ verb** (*in Ger.*) глаго́л с отделя́емой приста́вкой.

separate[1] ['sepərət] *adj.* отде́льный, осо́бый; **under ~ cover** отде́льно; **he entered my name in a ~ column** он занёс мою́ фами́лию в осо́бую графу́; **a ~ peace** сепара́тный мир; **two ~ questions** два самостоя́тельных/ра́зных вопро́са; **they are living ~ly** они́ живу́т врозь/разде́льно.

separate[2] ['sepəˌreıt] *v.t.* (*set apart*) отдел|я́ть, -и́ть; (*disunite*, *part*) разлуч|а́ть, -и́ть; **he is ~d from his family** он разлучён со свое́й семьёй; (*distinguish*): **~ truth from error** отлича́ть/отделя́ть (*both impf.*) и́стину от заблужде́ния; **~ chaff from grain** оч|ища́ть, -и́стить зерно́ от мяки́ны; **~ milk** сепари́ровать (*impf.*, *pf.*) молоко́.

v.i. **1.** (*become detached*) отдел|я́ться, -и́ться; (*come untied*) развя́з|ываться, -а́ться; (*come unstuck*) откле́и|ваться, -тся. **2.** (*part company*) расст|ава́ться, -а́ться; разлуч|а́ться, -и́ться. **3.** (*of man and wife*) ра|сходи́ться, -зойти́сь; разъ|езжа́ться, -е́хаться.

separation [ˌsepə'reıʃ(ə)n] *n.* отделе́ние, разделе́ние; разлуче́ние; расстава́ние; разлу́ка; **~ of milk** сепари́рование молока́; **~ of cream** сня́тие сли́вок; (*of spouses*) разде́льное жи́тельство супру́гов.

separat(ion)ist ['sepərətıst] *n.* сепарати́ст (*fem.* -ка).

separator ['sepəˌreıtə(r)] *n.* (*machine*) сепара́тор.

sepia ['siːpıə] *n.* (*fluid*; *colour*; **~ drawing**) се́пия.

sepoy ['siːpɔı] *n.* сипа́й.

sepsis ['sepsıs] *n.* се́псис; зараже́ние кро́ви.

September [sep'tembə(r)] *n.* сентя́брь (*m.*).

adj. сентя́брьский.

septennial [sep'tenıəl] *adj.* семиле́тний.

septet(te) [sep'tet] *n.* септе́т.

septic ['septık] *adj.* септи́ческий; **the wound has gone ~** ра́на загнои́лась; **~ sore throat** стрептоко́ковая анги́на; **~ tank** перегнива́тель (*m.*).

septic(a)emia [ˌseptı'siːmıə] *n.* зараже́ние кро́ви.

septuagenarian [ˌseptjʊədʒı'neərıən] *n.* семидесятиле́тний стари́к (*fem.* семидесятиле́тняя стару́ха).

adj. семидесятиле́тний.

Septuagesima [ˌseptjʊə'dʒesımə] *n.* девя́тое воскресе́нье пе́ред Па́схой.

Septuagint ['septjʊəˌdʒınt] *n.* свяще́нное писа́ние в перево́де семи́десяти двух толко́вников.

sepulchral [sı'pʌlkr(ə)l] *adj.* (*of a tomb*): **~ stone** моги́льный ка́мень; (*for burial*): **~ vault** погреба́льный склеп; **~ voice** замоги́льный го́лос.

sepulchre ['sepəlkə(r)] *n.* гробни́ца, моги́ла; **the Holy S~** гроб госпо́день; **whited ~** (*fig.*) лицеме́р; гроб пова́пленный.

sepulture ['sepəltʃə(r)] *n.* погребе́ние.

sequel ['siːkw(ə)l] *n.* **1.** (*result*, *consequence*) (по)сле́дствие; **in the ~** впосле́дствии, в результа́те. **2.** (*of novel etc.*) продолже́ние (+*g.*).

sequence ['siːkwəns] *n.* **1.** (*succession*) после́довательность; ряд; поря́док; **in logical/historical ~** в логи́ческой/истори́ческой (*or* хронологи́ческой) после́довательности; **in rapid ~** оди́н за други́м; **~ of events** ход/после́довательность собы́тий; **~ of the seasons** сме́на времён го́да; (*gram.*): **~ of tenses** после́довательность времён; **a ~ of bad harvests** полоса́ плохи́х урожа́ев; неурожа́йные го́ды, оди́н за други́м. **2.** (*part of film*) эпизо́д. **3.** (*cards*) три и́ли бо́лее ка́рты одно́й ма́сти в непреры́вной после́довательности. **4.** (*mus.*) секве́нция.

sequester [sɪ'kwestə(r)] *v.t.* **1.** (*isolate, detach*) изоли́ровать (*impf., pf.*); **~ o.s. from the world** удал|я́ться, -и́ться от ми́ра; **a ~ed village** уединённая дере́вня; **he leads a ~ed life** он ведёт уединённый о́браз жи́зни. **2.** (*leg. etc.*: *seize, confiscate*; *also* **sequestrate**) секвестрова́ть (*impf., pf.*); конфискова́ть (*impf., pf.*).

sequestrate [sɪ'kwestreɪt, 'si:kwɪ-] = **sequester** *v.t.* **2.**

sequestration [,si:kwɪ'streɪʃ(ə)n] *n.* секвестра́ция; **~ of property** аре́ст иму́щества.

sequin ['si:kwɪn] *n.* (*coin*) цехи́н; (*spangle*) блёстка.

sequoia [sɪ'kwɔɪə] *n.* секво́йя.

seraglio [se'rɑ:lɪəʊ, sɪ-] *n.* сера́ль (*m.*).

seraph ['serəf] *n.* серафи́м.

seraphic [sə'ræfɪk] *adj.* а́нгельский, ангелоподо́бный; (*e.g. smile*) блаже́нный.

Serb [sɜ:b] *n.* серб (*fem.* -ка).

Serbia ['sɜ:bɪə] *n.* Се́рбия.

Serbian ['sɜ:bɪən] *n.* (*native*) серб (*fem.* -ка); (*language*) се́рбский язы́к.
adj. се́рбский.

Serbo-Croat(ian) [,sɜ:bəʊkrəʊ'eɪʃ(ə)n] *n.* серб(ск)охорва́тский язы́к.
adj. серб(ск)охорва́тский.

sere [sɪə(r)] = **sear** *adj.*

serenade [,serə'neɪd] *n.* серена́да.
v.t. & i. петь, с- серена́ду (*кому*); исп|олня́ть, -о́лнить серена́ду (*для кого*).

serendipity [,serən'dɪpɪtɪ] *n.* счастли́вая спосо́бность де́лать неожи́данные откры́тия.

serene [sɪ'ri:n, sə'ri:n] *adj.* **1.** (*of sky*) я́сный; (*of weather*) ти́хий; (*of sea*) безмяте́жный; (*of pers.*: *behaviour, appearance*) (с)поко́йный; **her face wore a ~ look** её лицо́ выража́ло споко́йствие; (*of things*: *trouble-free*): **all ~!** всё в поря́дке! (*coll.*). **2.**: **His S~ Highness** его́ све́тлость.

serenity [sɪ'renɪtɪ, sə'r-] *n.* споко́йствие; тишина́; безмяте́жность.

serf [sɜ:f] *n.* крепостно́й.

serfdom ['sɜ:fdəm] *n.* крепостни́чество; крепостно́е пра́во.

serge [sɜ:dʒ] *n.* са́ржа.

sergeant ['sɑ:dʒ(ə)nt] *n.* сержа́нт.
cpd. **~-major** *n.* старшина́ (*m.*).

serial ['sɪərɪəl] *n.* (*publication*) периоди́ческое изда́ние; (*story etc.*) рома́н, публику́ющийся/выходя́щий отде́льными вы́пусками; (*TV*) многосери́йный телефи́льм; сериа́л.
adj. **1.** (*forming series*) поря́дковый; **~ number** поря́дковый но́мер; **in ~ order** по поря́дку. **2.** (*issued in instalments*): **~ story** по́весть с продолже́ниями; **~ film** фильм в не́скольких се́риях; **~ rights** а́вторское пра́во на сериализа́цию.

serialization [,sɪərɪəlaɪ'zeɪʃ(ə)n] *n.* сериализа́ция.

serialize ['sɪərɪə,laɪz] *v.t.* (*publish, screen etc. in successive parts*) изд|ава́ть, -а́ть вы́пусками/се́риями.

seriatim [,sɪərɪ'eɪtɪm, ,ser-] *adv.* по пу́нктам.

sericulture ['serɪ,kʌltʃ(ə)r] *n.* шелково́дство.

series ['sɪəri:z, -rɪz] *n.* **1.** (*set*; *succession*) се́рия; **a ~ of lectures** цикл ле́кций; **in ~** по поря́дку; (*number*) ряд; **a ~ of questions** ряд вопро́сов; **a ~ of failures** полоса́ неуда́ч. **2.** (*math., chem.*) ряд. **3.** (*geol.*) сви́та. **4.** (*elec.*) после́довательное соедине́ние; **the lamps are connected in ~** ла́мпы соединя́ются после́довательно. **5.** (*TV*) многосери́йная програ́мма.

serif ['serɪf] *n.* засе́чка.

serio-comic [,sɪərɪəʊ'kɒmɪk] *adj.* трагикоми́ческий; полусерьёзный.

serious ['sɪərɪəs] *adj.* **1.** (*thoughtful, earnest*) серьёзный; **a ~ child** заду́мчивый ребёнок; **I am ~ about this** я э́то говорю́ всерьёз; **you can't be ~** вы шу́тите; **give sth. ~ thought** серьёзно обду́м|ывать, -ать что-н.; **take sth. ~ly** прин|има́ть, -я́ть что-н. всерьёз; **to be ~**; **~ly** (*joking apart*) шу́тки в сто́рону. **2.** (*important*; *not slight*) серьёзный, суще́ственный, ва́жный; **a ~ charge** серьёзное/тя́жкое обвине́ние; **a ~ play** пробле́мная пье́са; **he had a ~ accident** с ним случи́лась серьёзная ава́рия; он попа́л в тяжёлую катастро́фу; **he is ~ly ill** он серьёзно/тяжело́/опа́сно бо́лен; **you are making a ~ mistake** вы соверша́ете серьёзную оши́бку.
cpd. **~-minded** *adj.* серьёзный.

seriousness ['sɪərɪəsnɪs] *n.* серьёзность, ва́жность; **in all ~** без шу́ток; со всей серьёзностью.

serjeant-at-arms ['sɑ:dʒ(ə)nt] *n.* парла́ментский при́став.

sermon ['sɜ:mən] *n.* про́поведь; **the S~ on the Mount** Наго́рная про́поведь; **preach a ~** чита́ть, про- про́поведь; **he read me a ~ on laziness** он прочита́л мне нота́цию по по́воду ле́ни.

sermonize ['sɜ:mə,naɪz] *v.t. & i.* чита́ть (*impf.*) про́поведь/мора́ль (*кому*); морализи́ровать (*impf., pf.*).

serpent ['sɜ:pənt] *n.* змея́; (*bibl.*) змий.

serpentine ['sɜ:pən,taɪn] *n.* (*min.*) змееви́к.
adj. (*snake-like*) змееви́дный; (*sinuous*) изви́листый, извива́ющийся; (*subtle, profound*): **~ wisdom** зме́иная му́дрость; (*cunning*) кова́рный.

serrated [se'reɪtɪd] *adj.* зу́бчатый, зазу́бренный; с зу́бчиками.

serried ['serɪd] *adj.*: **in ~ ranks** со́мкнутыми ряда́ми; плечо́м к плечу́.

serum ['sɪərəm] *n.* сы́воротка.

servant ['sɜ:v(ə)nt] *n.* (*male, also fig.*) слуга́ (*m.*); **your humble ~** ваш поко́рный слуга́; **~s' quarters** помеще́ние для прислу́ги; (*maid* **~**) служа́нка, прислу́га, домрабо́тница; **civil ~** госуда́рственный слу́жащий; **public ~s** должностны́е ли́ца.
cpd. **~-girl** *n.* служа́нка.

serve [sɜ:v] *n.* (*at tennis*) пода́ча; **whose ~ is it?** чья пода́ча?
v.t. **1.** (*be servant to*; *give service to*) служи́ть (*impf.*) +*d.*; **he ~d his country well** он ве́рно служи́л ро́дине; **one cannot ~ two masters** нельзя́ служи́ть двум господа́м; **if my memory ~s me (aright)** е́сли па́мять мне не изменя́ет; (*assist in operating*): **~ a gun** обслу́живать (*impf.*) ору́дие; (*fertilize*): **~ a mare** покр|ыва́ть, -ы́ть кобы́лу. **2.** (*meet needs of, satisfy, look after*): **~ a purpose** служи́ть (*impf.*) це́ли; **this box has ~d its purpose** э́та коро́бка сослужи́ла свою́ слу́жбу; **it ~d his interests to keep quiet** ему́ бы́ло вы́годно молча́ть; **these tools will ~ my needs** э́ти инструме́нты вполне́ мне подхо́дят; (*suffice*): **this sum will ~ him for a year** э́тих де́нег ему́ хва́тит на́ год; (*provide service to*) обслу́ж|ивать, -и́ть; **the railway ~s all these villages** желе́зная доро́га обслу́живает все э́ти сёла. **3.** (*supply with food, goods etc.*) под|ава́ть, -а́ть +*d.*; **the waiter ~d us with vegetables** официа́нт по́дал (нам) о́вощи; **persons under 18 cannot be ~d** ли́ца моло́же восемна́дцати лет не обслу́живаются; **the shop-keeper refused to ~ me with butter** ла́вочник отказа́лся отпусти́ть мне ма́сла; **are you being ~d?** вас кто́-нибудь обслу́живает? **4.** (*proffer*) под|ава́ть, -а́ть; **fish is ~d with sauce** ры́ба подаётся с со́усом; **dinner is ~d** обе́д по́дан (*or* на столе́); **~ a ball** под|ава́ть, -а́ть мяч; **~ a summons** вруч|а́ть, -и́ть (*кому*) (суде́бную) пове́стку. **5.** (*fulfil, go through*): **~ one's apprenticeship** про|ходи́ть, -йти́ вы́учку; **~ one's sentence** отб|ыва́ть, -ы́ть срок; **he ~d his time (in army/prison)** он отслужи́л/отбы́л срок. **6.** (*treat*): **he ~d me badly** он ду́рно со мной обошёлся; **it ~s him right** так ему́ и на́до; подело́м (ему́).
v.i. служи́ть (*impf.*); **he ~d in the army** он служи́л в а́рмии; **he ~d in the First World War** он воева́л в пе́рвую мирову́ю войну́; **~ on a jury** быть прися́жным; **she ~s in a shop** она́ рабо́тает в магази́не; **he ~d at table** он прислу́живал за столо́м; **I ~d under him** я служи́л под его́ нача́лом/кома́ндованием; **the plank ~d as a bench** доска́ служи́ла ла́вкой/скамьёй; **the bag isn't very good, but it will ~** мешо́к не осо́бенно хоро́ший, но сойдёт; **a tool which ~s several purposes** инструме́нт, слу́жащий для разли́чных це́лей; **it ~s to show the folly of his claims** э́то пока́зывает всю неле́пость его́ прете́нзий; **it will ~ to remind him of his obligations** э́то послу́жит ему́ напомина́нием о его́ обяза́тельствах; **when occasion ~s** когда́ представля́ется слу́чай; при слу́чае.
with advs.: **~ out** *v.t.* (*distribute*) разд|ава́ть, -а́ть; (*retaliate on*) отпла́|чивать, -ти́ть +*d.*; **~ up** *v.t.* под|ава́ть, -а́ть; (*fig.*): **the papers ~ up the same old news every day**

газе́ты ка́ждый день пи́шут об одно́м и том же.

server ['sɜːvə(r)] *n.* (*at tennis*) подаю́щий.

service[1] ['sɜːvɪs] *n.* **1.** (*employment*) слу́жба; **take s.o. into one's ~** нан|има́ть, -я́ть кого́-н.; **she went into domestic ~** она́ пошла́ в прислу́ги; **my car has seen long ~** моя́ маши́на прослужи́ла мно́го лет; **length of ~** стаж, вы́слуга лет. **2.** (*branch of public work*): **public, civil ~** госуда́рственная слу́жба; **he is in the civil ~** он нахо́дится на госуда́рственной слу́жбе; **he entered the diplomatic ~** он поступи́л на дипломати́ческую слу́жбу; **medical ~** слу́жба здравоохране́ния; (*mil.*) медици́нская слу́жба; **intelligence, secret ~** разве́дка; **military ~** вое́нная слу́жба; **do one's military ~** отб|ыва́ть, -ы́ть во́инскую пови́нность; **which ~ is he in?** в како́м ро́де войск он слу́жит?; **the Senior S~** (брита́нский) военномо́рско́й флот; **on active ~** на действи́тельной слу́жбе; **on detached ~** в командиро́вке; **the (fighting) ~s** вооружённые си́лы (*f. pl.*); **long ~** сверхсро́чная слу́жба; **~ dress** повседне́вное обмундирова́ние; **~ pay** окла́д военнослу́жащего; **~ record** послужно́й спи́сок; **~ rifle** боева́я винто́вка. **3.** (*person's disposal*) услу́га; **at your ~** к ва́шим услу́гам; **on His, Her Majesty's S~** (*on letter*) прави́тельственное (письмо́). **4.** (*work done for s.o. or sth.*): **will you do me a ~?** мо́жно вас попроси́ть об услу́ге; **he has given good ~** он служи́л добросо́вестно; **offer one's ~s** предложи́ть (*pf.*) свои́ услу́ги; **~ of (*or* ~s to) the cause of peace** служе́ние де́лу ми́ра; **I need the ~s of a lawyer** мне нужна́ юриди́ческая по́мощь; (*by hotel staff etc.*): **the ~ is poor in that restaurant** в (э́)том рестора́не обслу́живание никуда́ не годи́тся; **~ charge** пла́та за обслу́живание; **~ flat** кварти́ра с обслу́живанием; **~ hatch** разда́точная; **~ lift** грузово́й лифт. **5.** (*assistance*) по́льза; **can I be of ~ to you?** могу́ я быть вам поле́зен?; **what ~ will that be to you?** кака́я вам от э́того по́льза? **6.** (*system to meet public need*): **postal ~** почто́вая слу́жба; **bus ~** авто́бусное обслу́живание; **municipal ~s** коммуна́льные услу́ги (*f. pl.*); **~ pipe** домово́й ввод; **~ entrance** служе́бный вход; **a frequent train ~ to London** ча́стые поезда́ в Ло́ндон. **7.** (*attention to, maintenance of*) техобслу́живание; **~ station** бензоколо́нка. **8.** (*eccl.*) слу́жба, обря́д; **divine ~** богослуже́ние; **take the/a ~** отпр|авля́ть, -а́вить богослуже́ние; **marriage/burial ~** венча́ние/отпева́ние. **9.** (*set of dishes*) серви́з. **10.** (*in tennis*) пода́ча; **~ court** по́ле пода́чи. **11.** (*leg.*): **~ of a writ** вруче́ние суде́бного предписа́ния.

v.t.: **~ a vehicle** пров|оди́ть, -ести́ осмо́тр и теку́щий ремо́нт маши́ны.

cpd. **~man** *n.* военнослу́жащий.

service[2] ['sɜːvɪs] *n.* (**~ tree**) ряби́на.

serviceability [ˌsɜːvɪsə'bɪlɪtɪ] *n.* го́дность, приго́дность.

serviceable ['sɜːvɪsəb(ə)l] *adj.* (*useful*) поле́зный, го́дный, приго́дный; (*durable*) про́чный.

serviette [ˌsɜːvɪ'et] *n.* салфе́тка.

servile ['sɜːvaɪl] *adj.* (*pert. to slavery; slavish*) ра́бский, ра́бий; **~ imitation** ра́бское подража́ние (+*d.*); (*of pers. or behaviour*) раболе́пный, подобостра́стный.

servility [ˌsɜː'vɪlɪtɪ] *n.* ра́бство; подобостра́стие.

serving ['sɜːvɪŋ] *n.* (*of food*) по́рция.

servitude ['sɜːvɪˌtjuːd] *n.* ра́бство; **penal ~** ка́торжные рабо́ты (*f. pl.*).

servo-mechanism ['sɜːvəʊˌmekəˌnɪsəm] *n.* сервомехани́зм; следя́щая систе́ма.

servo-motor ['sɜːvəʊˌməʊtə(r)] *n.* серводви́гатель (*m.*); сервоприво́д.

sesame ['sesəmɪ] *n.* кунжу́т, сеза́м; **open ~!** сеза́м, откро́йся!

session ['seʃ(ə)n] *n.* **1.** заседа́ние; (*period*) се́ссия; **the House is in ~** пала́та сейча́с заседа́ет; **the committee went into secret ~** дальне́йшее обсужде́ние комите́т провёл при закры́тых дверя́х. **2.** (*University year*) уче́бный год; (*term*) семе́стр.

sessional ['seʃənəl] *adj.* (*univ.*): **~ course of lectures** годи́чный курс ле́кций.

set [set] *n.* **1.** (*collection; outfit*) набо́р; компле́кт; колле́кция; (*number of persons or things*) ряд; се́рия; (*of accessories*) принадле́жности (*f. pl.*); **~ of tools** инструме́нт, набо́р инструме́нтов; **~ of bells** набо́р колоколо́в; **complete ~ of stamps** по́лный компле́кт ма́рок; **~ of golf-clubs** компле́кт клю́шек для го́льфа; **~ of pieces for piano** сбо́рник пьес для фортепья́но; **chess ~** ша́хмат|ы (*pl., g.* —); **~ of drawing instruments (and box)** гото́ва́льня; **~ of furniture** ме́бельный гарниту́р; **toilet ~** туале́тный прибо́р; **dinner ~** столо́вый серви́з; **~ of (natural) teeth** зу́бы (*m. pl.*); (*dentures*) зубно́й проте́з; **~ of rules** свод пра́вил; **~ of circumstances** стече́ние/совоку́пность обстоя́тельств; **~ of questions** се́рия вопро́сов; **~ of lectures** курс/цикл ле́кций; **~ of ideas** систе́ма иде́й; **~ of players** кома́нда игроко́в; **~ of dancers** гру́ппа танцо́ров. **2.** (*receiving apparatus*): **wireless ~** радиоприёмник; **television ~** телеви́зор; **battery ~** батаре́йный радиоприёмник. **3.** (*tennis*) сет, па́ртия; **~ point** сет-бо́л. **4.** (*math.*) мно́жество; **theory of ~s** тео́рия мно́жеств. **5.** (*coterie*) круг, кружо́к; компа́ния; **the racing ~** завсегда́таи (*m. pl.*) бего́в; **the smart ~** фешене́бельное о́бщество; законода́тели (*m. pl.*) мод; **a ~ of thieves** ба́нда/ша́йка воро́в. **6.** (*direction, drift*): **the ~ of the current/wind** направле́ние тече́ния/ве́тра; (*tendency*): **the ~ of public opinion** напра́вленность обще́ственного мне́ния; **mental ~** скла́д ума́. **7.** (*warp, displacement, deflection*) отклоне́ние, накло́н; **the tower has a ~ to the right** ба́шня наклони́лась впра́во. **8.** (*posture, attitude*): **the ~ of his head** поса́дка его́ головы́; **I knew him by the ~ of his hat** я (сра́зу) узна́л его́ по его́ мане́ре носи́ть шля́пу (набекре́нь). **9.** (*pointing stance of dog*) сто́йка; **make a (dead) ~ at** (*attack*) нап|ада́ть, -а́сть на+*a.*; **she made a dead ~ at him** (*made herself attractive*) она́ ста́ла его́ завлека́ть. **10.**: **~ of sun** захо́д со́лнца. **11.** (*seedling; shoot*) са́женец; побе́г. **12.** (*badger's burrow*) нора́. **13.** (*theatr.*) декора́ция. **14.** (*cin.*): **on the ~** на съёмочной площа́дке.

adj. **1.** (*fixed*): **a ~ stare** неподви́жный взгляд; **a ~ smile** засты́вшая улы́бка; **of ~ purpose** умы́шленно; **a man of ~ purpose** целеустремлённый челове́к; **he has ~ opinions** у него́ (раз и навсегда́) установи́вшиеся взгля́ды; **he is ~ in his ways** он закосне́л в свои́х привы́чках; **~ phrase** клише́ (*indecl.*), шабло́нное выраже́ние; **the weather is ~ fair** (хоро́шая) пого́да установи́лась; (*prearranged*): **at the ~ time** в устано́вленное вре́мя; **~ dinner** ко́мплексный обе́д; **~ piece** (*literary etc.*) образцо́вое произведе́ние; (*prescribed*): **~ books** обяза́тельная/рекомендо́ванная литерату́ра; (*prepared*): **a ~ speech** подгото́вленная ре́чь; (*obligatory*): **a ~ subject** обяза́тельный предме́т. **2.** (*coll., ready*): **all ~?** гото́вы?; **we were all ~ to go** мы совсе́м уже собра́лись идти́. **3.** (*resolved*): **he is ~ on going to the cinema** он настро́ился идти́ в кино́; **he was dead ~ against the idea** он на́мертво встал про́тив э́того предложе́ния.

v.t. **1.** (*lay*) класть, положи́ть; (*place*) разме|ща́ть, -сти́ть; распол|ага́ть, -ожи́ть; **he ~ his hand on my shoulder** он положи́л мне ру́ку на плечо́; **she ~ the plates on the table** (*separately*) она́ расста́вила таре́лки на столе́; (*in a pile*) она́ поста́вила (всю) сто́пку таре́лок на стол; **they ~ a tasty meal before us** они́ по́дали нам вку́сное угоще́ние; (*arrange*; **~ out**) расст|авля́ть, -а́вить; **12 chairs were ~ round the table** вокру́г стола́ бы́ло расста́влено двена́дцать сту́льев; (*apply*) при|кла́дывать, -ложи́ть; **he ~ the cup to his lips** он пригу́бил ча́шку; он поднёс ча́шку ко рту; **~ eyes on** посмотре́ть (*pf.*) на+*a.*; взгляну́ть (*pf.*) на+*a.*; **I have never ~ eyes on him since** с тех пор я его́ бо́льше не ви́дел; **~ one's face against** ни за что не соглаша́ться (*impf.*) на+*a.*; **~ fire to** подж|ига́ть, -е́чь; **~ foot on** наступ|а́ть, -и́ть на+*a.*; **he ~ foot on these shores** он при́был в э́ти края́; **he will never ~ foot in my house** я его́ никогда́ на поро́г не пущу́; **where man has never ~ foot** где не ступа́ла нога́ челове́ка; **~ one's hand to** приня́ться (*pf.*) за+*a.*; **~ (a) light to** заж|ига́ть, -е́чь спи́чкой; **~ one's name to a document** расписа́ться (*pf.*) на докуме́нте; **as I was ~ting pen to paper** то́лько я на́чал писа́ть; **~ in the ground** сажа́ть, посади́ть; **a safe was ~ in the wall** в сте́ну был встро́ен сейф. **2.** (*adjust, prepare*) ста́вить, по-; **I always ~ my watch by the station clock** я всегда́ ста́влю часы́ по станцио́нным; **they ~ a trap for him** они́ поста́вили ему́ лову́шку; **~ sail** подн|има́ть, -я́ть па́рус; ста́вить, по- паруса́; (*start a voyage*) отпл|ыва́ть, -ы́ть; пус|ка́ться, -ти́ться в пла́вание; **~ the table** накр|ыва́ть, -ы́ть (на) стол; **~ a saw** разв|оди́ть, -ести́ пилу́; **~ a razor** пра́вить, вы́- бри́тву. **3.** (*make straight or firm*): **~ a bone** впр|авля́ть, -а́вить кость; **~ s.o.'s hair** укла́дывать, уложи́ть кому́-н. во́лосы; **~ting lotion** жи́дкость для укла́дки воло́с; **the wind will ~ the mortar** на ветру́ раство́р затверде́ет/засты́нет. **4.** (*fig., apply*): **~ one's heart on** стра́стно жела́ть (*impf.*) +*g.*; настро́иться (*pf.*) на+*a.*; **~ one's mind on, to sth.** сосредото́читься (*pf.*) на чем-н.; настро́иться (*pf.*) на что-н.; **~ one's hopes on** возл|ага́ть, -ожи́ть наде́жды на+*a.*; **~ a price on** (*assign a price to*) назна́чить (*pf.*) це́ну на+*a.*; **~ a price on s.o.'s head** назн|ача́ть, -а́чить (*or* объяв|ля́ть, -и́ть) це́ну за чью-н. го́лову; оце́н|ивать, -и́ть чью-н. го́лову/жизнь; **~ the seal on** (*fig.*) оконча́тельно реши́ть/утверди́ть (*pf.*); **~ store by** (высоко́) цени́ть (*impf.*); **~ one's teeth** сти́снуть (*pf.*) зу́бы. **5.** (*make or put into specified state*) прив|оди́ть, -ести́; **he will ~ things right** он приведёт всё в поря́док; он всё нала́дит; **he ~ the boat in motion** он привёл ло́дку в движе́ние; **~ sth. afloat** спус|ка́ть, -ти́ть что-н. на́ воду; **~ at liberty** освобо|жда́ть, -ди́ть; **~ s.o. at ease; ~ s.o.'s mind at ease, rest** успок|а́ивать, -о́ить (*or* ут|еша́ть, -е́шить *or* об|одря́ть, -о́дрить) кого́-н.; **~ at naught** ни во что не ста́вить (*impf.*); **~ s.o. on his feet** (*lit., fig.*) поста́вить (*pf.*) кого́-н. на́ ноги; **~ on foot** нача́ть (*pf.*); зате́ять (*pf.*); **~ on fire** подж|ига́ть, -е́чь; (*incite*): **he ~ his dog on me** он натрави́л на меня́ соба́ку; **he ~ the police after (*or* on to) the criminal** он донёс в поли́цию на престу́пника; **she is trying to ~ me against you** она́ стара́ется восстанови́ть/настро́ить меня́ про́тив вас; (*weigh*): **against the cost can be ~ the advantage** при всей дорогови́зне (э́того) сле́дует по́мнить и вы́году. **6.** (*cause; compel*): **I ~ him to sweeping the floor** я веле́л ему́ подмести́ пол; **he ~ them to work at Greek** он усади́л их за гре́ческий язы́к; **I ~ him to copy the picture** я поручи́л ему́ скопи́ровать карти́ну. **7.** (*start*): **the smoke ~ her coughing** от ды́ма она́ зака́шлялась; **his remarks ~ them laughing** его́ замеча́ния рассмеши́ли их; **I ~ him talking about Russia** я навёл его́ на разгово́р о Росси́и; **a programme to ~ you thinking** програ́мма, кото́рая даёт пи́щу для размышле́ния. **8.** (*present, pose*) зад|ава́ть, -а́ть; **his absence ~s us a problem** его́ отсу́тствие ста́вит нас в тру́дное положе́ние; **you have ~ me a difficult task** вы поста́вили передо мной тру́дную зада́чу. **9.** (*establish*): **~ the pace/tone** зад|ава́ть, -а́ть темп/тон; **he is ~ting his children a bad example** он подаёт свои́м де́тям дурно́й приме́р. **10.** (*compile*): **~ an exam paper** сост|авля́ть, -а́вить вопро́сы для пи́сьменного экза́мена. **11.:** **~ sth. to music** класть, положи́ть что-н. на му́зыку; **he ~ new words to an old tune** он написа́л но́вые слова́ на ста́рый моти́в. **12.** (*insert for adornment etc.*) вст|авля́ть, -а́вить (*во что*); **they ~ the top of the wall with broken glass** они́ уты́кали верх стены́ би́тым стекло́м; **a sky ~ with stars** усе́янное звёздами не́бо. **13.** (*situate*): **he ~ the scene in Paris** ме́стом де́йствия он избра́л Пари́ж; **the scene is ~ in London** де́йствие происхо́дит в Ло́ндоне. **14.:** **~ a jewel** опр|авля́ть, -а́вить драгоце́нный ка́мень. **15.** (*typ.*) наб|ира́ть, -ра́ть.

v.i. **1.** (*of sun*) сади́ться, сесть; **we saw the sun ~ting** мы ви́дели зака́т/захо́д со́лнца; (*of stars; also fig.*) за|ходи́ть, -йти́. **2.** (*of fruit, blossom*) завя́з|ываться, -а́ться. **3.** (*become firm or solid*) затверд|ева́ть, -е́ть; тверде́ть (*impf.*); густе́ть, за-; (*of jelly*) заст|ыва́ть, -ы́ть; (*of cement, concrete etc.*) схва́т|ываться, -и́ться. **4.** (*of face or eyes*) заст|ыва́ть, -ы́ть. **5.** (*of current*) определ|я́ться, -и́ться; идти́ (*det.*). **6.** (*of a dog*) де́лать, с- сто́йку.

with preps.: **~ about (doing) sth.** прин|има́ться, -я́ться за что-н.; приступи́ть (*pf.*) к чему́-н.; заня́ться (*pf.*) чем-н.; **~ about** (*beat up*) **s.o.** отде́лать (*pf.*) кого́-н.; **~ after** (*try to overtake*) **s.o.** пус|ка́ться, -ти́ться вдого́нку за кем-н.; **~ (up)on s.o.** нап|ада́ть, -а́сть на кого́-н.; **~ s.o. to work** усади́ть (*pf.*) кого́-н. за рабо́ту; дать (*pf.*) рабо́ту кому́-н.; заста́вить (*pf.*) кого́-н. рабо́тать.

with advs.: **~ apart, ~ aside** *vv.t.* (*allocate*) выделя́ть, вы́делить; (*reserve, save*) от|кла́дывать, -ложи́ть; **a day ~ aside for revision** день, отведённый/вы́деленный для прове́рки; (*disregard*): **I ~ aside personal feelings** я отбро́сил все ли́чные чу́вства; **~ting aside my expenses** не счита́я мои́х расхо́дов; (*quash*) раст|орга́ть, -о́ргнуть; аннули́ровать (*impf., pf.*); отмен|я́ть, -и́ть; **the court's verdict was ~ aside** реше́ние суда́ бы́ло отменено́; **~ a claim aside** отклон|я́ть, -и́ть иск; **~ back** *v.t.* (*lit.*) отодв|ига́ть, -и́нуть; **a house ~ back from the road** дом, стоя́щий в стороне́ от доро́ги; **the horse ~ back its ears** ло́шадь прижа́ла у́ши; **~ one's shoulders back** распр|авля́ть, -а́вить пле́чи; **~ the clock back** перев|оди́ть, -ести́ часы́ наза́д; (*fig.*) поверну́ть (*pf.*) колесо́ исто́рии вспять; (*hinder, delay, damage*) заме́длить (*pf.*); затормози́ть (*pf.*); отбро́сить (*pf.*) наза́д; нанести́ (*pf.*) уро́н +*d.*; **his refusal ~ back our interests** его́ отка́з нанёс уще́рб на́шим интере́сам; (*coll., cost*): **the trip ~ him back a few pounds** пое́здка обошла́сь ему́ в не́сколько фу́нтов; **~ by** *v.t.* (*put by*) от|кла́дывать, -ложи́ть; **~ down** *v.t.* (*put down*) класть, положи́ть; ста́вить, по-; **he ~ down his knapsack on the steps** он (снял и) поста́вил свой рюкза́к на ступе́ньку; (*allow to alight*) выса́живать, вы́садить; **the bus ~ us down at the gate** авто́бус вы́садил нас у воро́т; (*make statement or record*): **he ~ down his complaint in writing** он изложи́л свою́ жа́лобу в пи́сьменном ви́де; **she ~ down her impressions in a diary** она́ заноси́ла/запи́сывала свои́ впечатле́ния в дневни́к; **he ~ himself down as a student** он записа́лся студе́нтом; **they ~ him down as a rogue** они́ записа́ли его́ в негодя́и; **his failure was ~ down to laziness** счита́ли, что он провали́лся (то́лько) из-за свое́й ле́ни; **~ forth** *v.t.* (*propound, declare*) изл|ага́ть, -ожи́ть; формули́ровать, с-; *v.i.* (*leave*) отпр|авля́ться, -а́виться; **~ in** *v.t.* (*insert*) вст|авля́ть, -а́вить; **~ in a sleeve** вш|ива́ть, -и́ть рука́в; (*indent, e.g. a paragraph*) нача́ть (*pf.*) с о́тступа/абза́ца; *v.i.* (*take hold*): **winter is ~ting in** наступа́ет зима́; **the rain ~ in early** до́ждь начался́ ра́но; **the tide is ~ting in** начина́ется прили́в; **a new fashion ~ in** появи́лась но́вая мо́да; **~ off** *v.t.* (*cause to explode*): **they were ~ting off fireworks** они́ пуска́ли фейерве́рк; **~ off a rocket** запус|ка́ть, -ти́ть раке́ту; (*cause, stimulate*): **his arrest ~ off a wave of protest** его́ аре́ст вы́звал волну́ проте́стов; (*enhance*): **the ribbon will ~ off your complexion** ле́нта оттени́т цвет ва́шего лица́; **her dress ~s off her figure** пла́тье подчёркивает её фо́рмы; **the frame ~s off the picture** карти́на в э́той ра́ме выи́грывает (*or* хорошо́ смо́трится); (*compensate*) возме|ща́ть, -сти́ть; компенси́ровать (*impf., pf.*); **~ off gains against losses** баланси́ровать, с- при́были и убы́тки; (*cause to start*): **the story ~ them off laughing** э́тот расска́з заста́вил их расхохота́ться; *v.i.* (*leave*) пойти́, пое́хать (*both pf.*); **we are ~ting off on a journey** мы отправля́емся в путеше́ствие; **the horse ~ off at a gallop** ло́шадь пусти́лась гало́пом; **they ~ off in pursuit** они́ ки́нулись вдого́нку; **he ~ off running** он бро́сился бежа́ть; **~ out** *v.t.* (*arrange, display*) распол|ага́ть, -ожи́ть; выставля́ть, вы́ставить (на обозре́ние); ра|скла́дывать, -зложи́ть; (*plant out*) выса́живать, вы́садить; (*expound*) изл|ага́ть, -ожи́ть; *v.i.* (*leave*) пойти́, пое́хать (*both pf.*); отпр|авля́ться, -а́виться; **they ~ out for Warsaw** они́ отпра́вились/о́тбыли в Варша́ву; (*attempt*): **he ~ out to conquer Europe** он заду́мал/вознаме́рился покори́ть (всю) Евро́пу; **~ to** *v.i.* (*make a start*) прин|има́ться, -я́ться; (*begin to fight or argue*) сцепи́ться (*pf.*); схвати́ться (*pf.*); **~ together** *v.t.* сост|авля́ть, -а́вить (вме́сте); (*compare*) сопост|авля́ть, -а́вить; **~ up** *v.t.* (*erect*) устан|а́вливать, -ови́ть; **a statue was ~ up in his honour** в его́ честь установи́ли ста́тую; (*form*): **~ up a committee** организова́ть (*impf., pf.*) (*or* учре|жда́ть, -ди́ть) комите́т; (*found, establish*): **~ up a school** учре|жда́ть, -ди́ть шко́лу; **he ~ up a new record** он установи́л но́вый реко́рд; **~ up house** зажи́ть (*pf.*) свои́м до́мом; **they ~ up house together** они́ ста́ли жить вме́сте; **~ up shop** откры́ть (*pf.*) ла́вку; основа́ть (*pf.*) де́ло; **he ~ his mistress up in a flat** он обста́вил кварти́ру для свое́й любо́вницы; (*claim, put forward*): **he ~s himself up to be a scholar** он изобража́ет из себя́ учёного; **he was ~ up as a claimant to the throne** его́ про́чили на трон; (*provide*): **I am ~ up with novels for the winter** я обеспе́чен рома́нами на всю зи́му; (*give voice to*): **~ up a cry** подн|има́ть, -я́ть крик; (*cause*): **smoking ~s up an irritation** куре́ние раздража́ет сли́зистую оболо́чку; (*restore to health*): **a holiday will ~ you up** о́тдых вас поста́вит на́ ноги (*or* восстано́вит ва́ши си́лы); **well ~ up** кре́пкого телосложе́ния; (*typ.*) наб|ира́ть, -ра́ть; *v.i.* **he ~ up as a butcher** он откры́л/завёл мясну́ю ла́вку (*or* мясно́й магази́н); **~ up in business** организова́ть (*impf., pf.*) своё де́ло; **~ up as a man of letters** вступи́ть (*pf.*) на литерату́рное по́прище.

cpds. **~back** *n.* (*delay*) заде́ржка; (*reverse*) неуда́ча; (*difficulty*) тру́дность, затрудне́ние; **he met with many ~backs** у него́ бы́ло мно́го неуда́ч; **~-off** *n.* (*compensation*) противове́с; **~-out** *n.* (*beginning*): **at the first ~-out** в са́мом нача́ле; **~-square** *n.* уго́льник; **~-to** *n.* (*fight*) схва́тка; **have a ~-to** схва́т|ываться, -и́ться; сцеп|ля́ться, -и́ться; **~up** *n.* (*coll., arrangement*) поря́дки (*m. pl.*); устро́йство; обстано́вка.

settee [se'ti:] *n.* (небольшо́й) дива́н.

setter ['setə(r)] *n.* (*dog*) се́ттер.

setting ['setɪŋ] *n.* **1.** (*of sun etc.*) захо́д, зака́т. **2.** (*of gems*) опра́ва. **3.** (*background*) фон, обстано́вка, окруже́ние. **4.** (*theatr.*) декора́ции (*f. pl.*) и костю́мы (*m. pl.*); оформле́ние. **5.** (*mus.*) му́зыка на слова́. **6.** (*at table*) прибо́р.

settle[1] ['set(ə)l] *n.* скамья́; скамья́-ларь (*m.*).

settle[2] ['set(ə)l] *v.t.* **1.** (*place securely; put to rest*): **~ o.s. in an armchair** (удо́бно) ус|а́живаться, -е́сться в кре́сло; **~ an invalid among pillows** уса́|живать, -ди́ть больно́го на поду́шках; **~ children for the night** укла́дывать, уложи́ть дете́й на́ ночь. **2.** (*install, establish*) поме|ща́ть, -сти́ть; устр|а́ивать, -о́ить; **he ~d his daughter in a large house** он посели́л дочь в большо́м до́ме. **3.** (*calm*) успок|а́ивать, -о́ить; **he gave me sth. to ~ my stomach** он дал мне желу́дочное лека́рство (*or* сре́дство для пищеваре́ния). **4.** (*reconcile*) ула́|живать, -дить; **their differences were soon ~d** их разногла́сия бы́ли ско́ро ула́жены; **the dispute was ~d out of court** спор был ула́жен полюбо́вно. **5.** (*dispel*): **he ~d their doubts** он разве́ял/рассе́ял их сомне́ния. **6.** (*decide*) реш|а́ть, -и́ть; **that ~s it** э́то реша́ет де́ло; ну, тогда́ не́ о чем спо́рить; **let's ~ the matter** дава́йте ко́нчим с э́тим де́лом; **~ it amongst yourselves!** вы ка́к-нибудь са́ми договори́тесь!; **the terms of the agreement were ~d** бы́ли вы́работаны усло́вия соглаше́ния; **nothing is ~d yet** ещё ничего́ (оконча́тельно) не решено́. **7.** (*put in order*) прив|оди́ть, -ести́ в поря́док; **~ one's estate** де́лать, с- завеща́ние. **8.** (*pay*): **~ a bill** заплати́ть (*pf.*) по счёту; **~ a debt** погаси́ть (*pf.*) долг; **~ old scores** (*fig.*) св|оди́ть, -ести́ ста́рые счёты; расквита́ться (*pf.*). **9.** (*bestow legally*) закреп|ля́ть, -и́ть (*что за кем*); **he ~d an annuity on her** он назна́чил ей ежего́дную ре́нту; (*bequeath*) оста́вить (*pf.*); завеща́ть (*pf.*). **10.** (*colonize*) засел|я́ть, -и́ть; (*transport to new home*) посел|я́ть, -и́ть.

v.i. **1.** (*sink down; come to rest*) ос|еда́ть, -е́сть; **the foundations have ~d** фунда́мент осе́л; **the dust will soon ~** (*fig.*) шуми́ха ско́ро уля́жется; **the excitement ~d** стра́сти ути́хли/улегли́сь; (*of ship*) погру|жа́ться, -зи́ться в во́ду; (*alight*) ус|а́живаться, -е́сться; **a fly ~d on his nose** у него́ на носу́ усе́лась му́ха; **the butterfly ~d on a leaf** ба́бочка се́ла на лист; **dust ~d on everything** повсю́ду осе́ла пыль. **2.** (*become fixed, stable, established*) устан|а́вливаться, -ови́ться; **the weather has ~d at last** наконе́ц-то пого́да установи́лась; **the wind ~d in the east** установи́лся восто́чный ве́тер; **darkness ~d on the land** вся страна́ погрузи́лась во мрак; **the cold ~d on my, his chest** простý́да засе́ла в груди́. **3.** (*become comfortable, accustomed; also* **~ down**): **the dog ~d in its basket** соба́ка улегла́сь в свое́й корзи́нке; **I could not ~ to my work for the noise** я не мог (норма́льно) рабо́тать из-за шу́ма; **he never ~s to anything for long** он ни на чём подо́лгу не мо́жет задержа́ться. **4.** (*make one's home*) посел|я́ться, -и́ться; обосно́в|ываться, -а́ться; ос|еда́ть, -е́сть. **5.** (*pay*) распла́|чиваться, -ти́ться; (*come to terms*) догов|а́риваться, -ори́ться; **I'll ~ for half the profits** (на худо́й коне́ц) я соглашу́сь на полови́ну при́были. **6.** (*decide*) остан|а́вливаться, -ови́ться (*на чём*); **they could not ~ on a name for their son** они́ не могли́ останови́ться ни на одно́м и́мени для сы́на; **have you ~d where to go?** вы реши́ли, куда́ е́хать?

with advs.: **~ back** *v.i.* (*in one's chair*) отки́нуться (*pf.*); **~ down** *v.t.*: **the nurse ~d the patient down for the night** ня́нечка/сестра́ пригото́вила больно́го ко сну; *v.i.* (*in home, job etc.*) обосно́в|ываться, -ова́ться; устр|а́иваться, -о́иться; (*adopt sober ways*) остепен|я́ться, -и́ться; (*at school*) привы́кнуть (*pf.*) к шко́ле; (*become quiet*) успок|а́иваться, -о́иться; **since the strike things have ~d down** по́сле забасто́вки всё пришло́ в но́рму; **we ~d down for the night** мы улегли́сь спать; (*give full attention*): **now we can ~ down to our game** тепе́рь мо́жно заня́ться на́шей игро́й; **I can't ~ down to read with the radio on** я не могу́ (споко́йно) чита́ть, когда́ включено́ ра́дио; **he ~d down to write letters** он приня́лся/усе́лся писа́ть пи́сьма; **~ in** *v.t. & i.* всел|я́ть(ся), -и́ть(ся); водвор|я́ть(ся), -и́ть(ся); **~ up** *v.t.* упла́|чивать, -ти́ть; **he ~d up the account** он оплати́л счёт; **~ up one's affairs** ула́|живать, -дить свои́ дела́; *v.i.* распла́|чиваться, -ти́ться (*с кем*).

settled ['setəld] *adj.* (*fixed, stable*) усто́йчивый; (*permanent*) постоя́нный; **a man of ~ habits** челове́к с укорени́вшимися привы́чками; (*determined*) определённый; **it is my ~ intention to remain** я твёрдо наме́рен оста́ться; (*staid*) степе́нный; (*composed*) споко́йный; уравнове́шенный.

settlement ['setəlmənt] *n.* **1.** (*settling people*) поселе́ние; (*populating country*) заселе́ние. **2.** (*colony*) поселе́ние; **penal ~** ка́торжная/исправи́тельная коло́ния; (*settled place*) посёлок. **3.** (*arranging*) ула́живание. **4.** (*solution*) урегули́рование; реше́ние; (*agreement*) соглаше́ние; **reach a ~** дост|ига́ть, -и́чь соглаше́ния; **arrange a ~ with s.o.** догов|а́риваться, -ори́ться с кем-н. о соглаше́нии; **judicial ~** урегули́рование в суде́бном поря́дке. **5.** (*leg.*): **deed of ~** акт распоряже́ния иму́ществом (в чью-н. по́льзу); **~ of one's estate** (*making will*) составле́ние завеща́ния. **6.** (*payment*) упла́та, расчёт; **~ of an account** упла́та по счёту; **~ day** день платежа́. **7.** (*of building etc.*) оседа́ние; (*of soil*) оса́дка. **8.: Act of S~** (*Eng. hist.*) зако́н о престолонасле́дии.

settler ['setlə(r)] *n.* поселе́нец.

seven ['sev(ə)n] *n.* (число́/но́мер) семь; (**~** *people*) се́меро, семь челове́к; **we ~, the ~ of us** мы се́меро/всемеро́м; **~ each** по семи́; **in ~s, ~ at a time** по семи́, семёрками; (*figure; thg. numbered 7; group of* **~**) семёрка; (*with var. nn. expr. or understood: cf. examples under* **five**).

adj. семь +*g. pl.*; (*for people and pluralia tantum, also*) се́меро +*g. pl.*; **~ twos are fourteen** се́мью (*or* семь на) два — четы́рнадцать; **the S~ Years' War** Семиле́тняя война́; **sail the ~ seas** пла́вать (*indet.*) по всем моря́м и океа́нам.

cpds. **~fold** *adj.* семикра́тный; *adv.* все́меро, в семь раз; **~-league** *adj.*: **~-league boots** семими́льные сапоги́; **~-year** *adj.* семиле́тний.

seventeen [ˌsevən'ti:n] *n. & adj.* семна́дцать +*g. pl.*

seventeenth [ˌsevən'ti:nθ] *n.* (*date*) семна́дцатое (число́); (*fraction*) семна́дцатая часть; одна́ семна́дцатая.

adj. семна́дцатый.

seventh ['sev(ə)nθ] *n.* **1.** (*date*) седьмо́е (число́). **2.** (*fraction*) седьма́я часть; одна́ седьма́я. **3.** (*mus.*) се́птима.

adj. седьмо́й; **in the ~ heaven** на седьмо́м не́бе.

seventieth ['sevəntɪɪθ] *n.* семидеся́тая часть; одна́ семидеся́тая.

adj. семидеся́тый.

sevent|y ['sevəntɪ] *n.* се́мьдесят; **he is in his ~ies** ему́ за се́мьдесят; ему́ восьмо́й деся́ток; **in the ~ies** (*decade*) в семидеся́тых года́х; в семидеся́тые го́ды; (*temperature*) за се́мьдесят гра́дусов.

sever ['sevə(r)] *v.t.* отдел|я́ть, -и́ть; разлуч|а́ть, -и́ть; **~ a**

rope перер|еза́ть, -е́зать верёвку; **he ~ed his opponent's arm** он отруби́л ру́ку проти́внику; **~ one's connection with** пор|ыва́ть, -ва́ть связь с+*i.*; **~ o.s. from the Church** отп|ада́ть, -а́сть от це́ркви; **~ diplomatic relations** раз|рыва́ть, -орва́ть дипломати́ческие отноше́ния.

v.i. раз|рыва́ться, -орва́ться; порва́ться (*pf.*).

several ['sevr(ə)l] *pron.*: **~ of my friends** не́которые/ины́е/ко́е-кто из мои́х друзе́й; **I have four cups but I need ~ more** у меня́ есть четы́ре ча́шки, но мне на́до бы ещё не́сколько (штук).

adj. **1.** (*quite a few*) не́сколько +*g. pl.*; **myself and ~ others** я и ко́е-кто ещё. **2.** (*separate*) отде́льный; **they all go their ~ ways** ка́ждый из них идёт свои́м путём; **~ly** по отде́льности; по одному́; **jointly and ~ly** совме́стно и по́рознь.

severance ['sevərəns] *n.* отделе́ние, разры́в; **~ pay** выходно́е посо́бие; компенса́ция при увольне́нии.

severe [sɪ'vɪə(r)] *adj.* **1.** (*stern, strict, austere*) стро́гий, суро́вый; **he is his own ~st critic** стро́же всех себя́ су́дит он сам; **~ rebuke** стро́гий вы́говор; **~ punishment** суро́вое наказа́ние. **2.** (*violent*) си́льный; **a ~ frost** си́льный/жесто́кий/лю́тый моро́з; **~ pain** си́льная боль; **she had a ~ cold** у неё был си́льный на́сморк; **there was ~ fighting** шли жесто́кие бои́. **3.** (*exacting*): **a ~ test** суро́вая прове́рка; **~ competition** жесто́кая/о́страя конкуре́нция. **4.** (*serious*) тяжёлый; серьёзный; **~ illness** тяжёлая боле́знь; **a ~ shortage of water** о́страя нехва́тка воды́. **5.** (*unadorned*) стро́гий, суро́вый.

severity [sɪ'verɪtɪ] *n.* стро́гость, суро́вость; серьёзность; тя́жесть.

Seville ['sevɪl] *n.*: **~ orange** помера́нец, го́рький апельси́н.

sew [səʊ] *v.t. & i.* шить, с-; **~ a button on to a dress** приш|ива́ть, -и́ть пу́говицу к пла́тью; **~n** (*of a book*) сброшюро́ванный.

with adv.: **~ up** *v.t.* заш|ива́ть, -и́ть; **~ up buttonholes** обмёт|ывать, -а́ть пе́тли; (*coll., finish dealing with*) поко́нчить (*pf.*) с+*i.*

sewage ['su:ɪdʒ, 'sju:-] *n.* сто́чные во́ды (*f. pl.*); нечисто́ты (*f. pl.*); **~ farm** поля́ (*nt. pl.*) ороше́ния.

sewer ['su:ə(r), 'sju:-] *n.* (*conduit*) сто́чная труба́; **main ~** магистра́льная канализацио́нная труба́; **~ rat** кры́са.

sewerage ['su:ərɪdʒ, 'sju:-] *n.* канализа́ция.

sewing ['səʊɪŋ] *n.* (*process, material*) шитьё; (*attr.*) шве́йный; **~ needle** шве́йная игла́; **~ class** уро́к рукоде́лия; кружо́к кро́йки и шитья́.

cpd. **~-machine** *n.* шве́йная маши́на.

sex [seks] *n.* **1.** пол; **the fair, gentle ~** прекра́сный пол; **the weaker ~** сла́бый пол; **the sterner ~** си́льный пол; **without distinction of age or ~** без разли́чия по́ла и во́зраста; (*attr.*) полово́й; **~ antagonism** антагони́зм поло́в; **the ~ act** полово́й акт; **~ appeal** физи́ческая привлека́тельность; **~ change** опера́ция по измене́нию по́ла; **~ kitten** «ко́шечка»; **~ life** полова́я жизнь; **~ maniac** сексуа́льный манья́к, эротома́н (*fem.* -ка). **2.** (*sexual activity*) секс; (*sexual intercourse*) полово́е сноше́ние; **have ~ with s.o.** (*coll.*) име́ть (*impf.*) сноше́ние с кем-н.

v.t. (*determine ~ of*) определ|я́ть, -и́ть пол +*g.*

cpds. **~pot** *n.* (*coll.*) секс-бо́мба; **~-starved** *adj.* испы́тывающий сексуа́льный го́лод.

sexagenarian [ˌseksədʒɪ'neərɪən] *n.* шестидесятиле́тний стари́к (*fem.* шестидесятиле́тняя стару́ха).

adj. шестидесятиле́тний.

Sexagesima [ˌseksə'dʒesɪmə] *n.* восьмо́е воскресе́нье пе́ред Па́схой.

sexagesimal [ˌseksə'dʒesɪm(ə)l] *adj.* шестидесятери́чный.

sexcentenary [ˌseksen'ti:nərɪ] *n.* шестисотле́тие.

sexennial [sek'senɪəl] *adj.* (*lasting 6 years*) шестиле́тний.

sexiness ['seksɪnɪs] *n.* сексуа́льность, чу́вственность.

sexism ['seksɪz(ə)m] *n.* дискримина́ция же́нщин; пренебрежи́тельное отноше́ние к же́нщине.

sexist ['seksɪst] *n.* женофо́б.

adj. женоненави́стнический.

sexless ['sekslɪs] *adj.* беспо́лый; (*lacking sexual appeal or feeling*) асексуа́льный.

sexologist [sek'sɒlədʒɪst] *n.* сексо́лог.

sexology [sek'sɒlədʒɪ] *n.* сексоло́гия.

sextant ['sekst(ə)nt] *n.* секста́нт.

sextet [seks'tet] *n.* сексте́т.

sexton ['sekst(ə)n] *n.* понома́рь (*m.*); церко́вный сто́рож; моги́льщик.

sextuple ['seksˌtju:p(ə)l] *adj.* шестикра́тный.

sexual ['seksjʊəl, -ʃʊəl] *adj.* полово́й.

sexuality [ˌseksjʊ'ælɪtɪ, -ʃʊ'ælɪtɪ] *n.* сексуа́льность.

sexy ['seksɪ] *adj.* (*coll.*) сексуа́льный, чу́вственный, эроти́ческий.

Seychelles [seɪ'ʃel, -'ʃelz] *n.*: **the ~** Сейше́льские острова́ (*m. pl.*).

sh [ʃ] *int.* шш!; тсс!

shabbiness ['ʃæbɪnɪs] *n.* потёртость; изно́шенность; убо́гость, убо́жество; по́длость, ни́зость.

shabby ['ʃæbɪ] *adj.* **1.** (*of clothes*) поно́шенный; потрёпанный; (*of furniture*) вы́тертый; (*of pers. appearance*): **he looks ~** у него́ потёртый/потрёпанный вид; (*of buildings, streets etc.*) убо́гий, захуда́лый. **2.** (*of behaviour*) ни́зкий, по́длый; **a ~ trick** гну́сная шу́тка.

cpd. **~-genteel** *adj.* ≃ стара́ющийся замаскирова́ть свою́ бе́дность.

shack [ʃæk] *n.* лачу́га.

v.i.: **~ up with s.o.** (*sl.*) сожи́тельствовать (*impf.*) с кем-н.

shackle ['ʃæk(ə)l] *n.* (*pl., fetters*) око́в|ы (*pl., g.* —); (*fig.*): **the ~s of convention** ра́мки (*f. pl.*) прили́чий.

v.t. (*lit., fetter*) зако́в|ывать, -а́ть в кандалы́; (*impede*) ско́в|ывать, -а́ть; стесня́ть (*impf.*).

shad [ʃæd] *n.* шэд.

shaddock ['ʃædək] *n.* помпе́льмус, пуме́ло, грейпфру́т.

shade [ʃeɪd] *n.* **1.** (*unilluminated area*) тень; **put in(to) the ~** (*fig.*) затм|ева́ть, -и́ть; **light and ~** (*in picture*) свет и те́ни; (*partial darkness*) полумра́к; **the ~s of night were falling** наступи́ли су́мерки. **2.** (*tint, nuance*) отте́нок; **the same colour in a lighter ~** тот же цвет, (но) светле́е; (*fig.*): **~s of meaning** отте́нки (*m. pl.*) значе́ния; **all ~s of opinion** са́мые ра́зные убежде́ния. **3.** (*slight amount*): **a ~ better** немно́го/ка́пельку (*or* чуть-чу́ть) лу́чше. **4.** (*of lamp*) абажу́р. **5.** (*eye-~*) козырёк. **6.** (*US, blind*) што́ра. **7.** (*pl.*, **the ~s** *i.e. Hades*) ца́рство тене́й.

v.t. **1.** (*screen from light*) затен|я́ть, -и́ть; (*shield from light etc.*) заслон|я́ть, -и́ть; **he ~d his eyes with his hand** он заслони́л глаза́ руко́й (от све́та); **a bench ~d from the wind** скамья́, защищённая от ве́тра. **2.** (*restrict light of*) прикр|ыва́ть, -ы́ть. **3.** (*make gloomy, usu. fig.*) омрач|а́ть, -и́ть. **4.** (*drawing*) тушева́ть, за-.

v.i.: **one colour ~s into another** оди́н цвет (постепе́нно) перехо́дит в друго́й.

shadiness ['ʃeɪdɪnɪs] *n.* тени́стость.

shading ['ʃeɪdɪŋ] *n.* (*in drawing*) тушёвка.

shadow ['ʃædəʊ] *n.* тень; **in the ~ of a tree** в тени́ де́рева; **he has ~s under his eyes** у него́ (чёрные/тёмные) круги́ под глаза́ми; **he was a ~ of his former self; he was worn to a ~** от него́ оста́лась одна́ тень; **cast a ~ on** отбр|а́сывать, -о́сить (*or* бр|оса́ть, -о́сить) тень на+*a.*; (*fig.*) омрач|а́ть, -и́ть; **under the ~ of** (*protection*) под се́нью +*g.*; (*threat*) под угро́зой +*g.*; **he is afraid of his own ~** он бо́ится со́бственной те́ни; **may your ~ never grow less** жела́ю вам здра́вствовать до́лгие го́ды!; **there is not a ~ of doubt** нет ни те́ни/мале́йшего сомне́ния; **catch at ~s** гоня́ться (*impf.*) за при́зраками; **~ cabinet** «тенево́й кабине́т»; **~ factory** предприя́тие, кото́рое легко́ перево́дится с ми́рного произво́дства на вое́нное.

v.t. **1.** (*darken, cast ~ over*) осен|я́ть, -и́ть. **2.** (*foreshadow*) предвеща́ть (*impf.*). **3.** (*watch and follow secretly*) (та́йно) следи́ть/сле́довать (*impf.*) за+*i.*

cpd. **~-boxing** *n.* трениро́вочный бой; (*fig.*) показна́я борьба́; ви́димость борьбы́.

shadowy ['ʃædəʊɪ] *adj.* (*shady*) тени́стый; (*dim*) нея́сный; (*vague*) сму́тный; (*hazy*) тума́нный.

shady ['ʃeɪdɪ] *adj.* **1.** (*affording shade*) тени́стый; (*in shadow*) тенево́й; **~ side** тенева́я сторона́. **2.** (*suspect*) сомни́тельный, тёмный; **~ enterprise** сомни́тельное/тёмное де́ло.

shaft [ʃɑːft] *n.* **1.** (*of lance or spear*) дре́вко. **2.** (*arrow*) стрела́; (*fig.*) вы́пад. **3.** (*of light*) луч; ~ **of lightning** вспы́шка мо́лнии. **4.** (*stem, stalk*) сте́бель (*m.*); (*trunk*) ствол. **5.** (*of column*) сте́ржень (*m.*); (*of chimney*) труба́. **6.** (*of tool*) черено́к, ру́чка, рукоя́тка; (*of axe*) топори́ще. **7.** (*one of a pair on cart etc.*) огло́бля; (*central ~ between horses*) ды́шло. **8.** (*tech., rod*) вал; (*axle*) ось. **9.** (*of mine*) ша́хта; ствол ша́хты; **sink a ~** проходи́ть, -йти́ ша́хту.
cpd. **~-horse** *n.* коренни́к.

shag[1] [ʃæg] *n.* (*tobacco*) махо́рка.

shag[2] [ʃæg] *n.* (*bird*) длиннохво́стый бакла́н.

shagginess [ˈʃægɪnɪs] *n.* косма́тость, лохма́тость, взлохма́ченность.

shaggy [ˈʃægɪ] *adj.* (*of hair*) косма́тый, лохма́тый, взлохма́ченный; (*of pers., hairy*) волоса́тый.

shagreen [ʃæˈgriːn] *n.* шагре́нь, шагре́невая ко́жа.

shah [ʃɑː] *n.* шах.

shake [ʃeɪk] *n.* **1.** встря́ска; **give s.o./sth. a ~** встря́х|ивать, -ну́ть кого́-н./что-н.; **give o.s. a ~** встря́х|иваться, -ну́ться; **give the rug a ~** (*to clean it*) вытря́хивать, вы́тряхнуть ко́врик; **he answered with a ~ of the head** в отве́т он покача́л голово́й. **2.** (*tremble*): **with a ~ in his voice** с дро́жью в го́лосе. **3.** (*mus.*) трель. **4.** (*coll., moment*): **in a brace of ~s** вмиг, в оди́н миг. **5.** (*coll.*): **this book is no great ~s** э́та кни́га — ничего́ осо́бенного; э́та кни́га та́к себе (*or* нева́жная); **he was no great ~s with a pen** он не сли́шком бо́йко владе́л перо́м.
v.t. **1.** тря|сти́, -хну́ть; сотряс|а́ть, -ти́ (*что, чем*); **I shook him by the shoulder** я тряхну́л/потря́с его́ за плечо́; **I shook his hand** (*in greeting*) я пожа́л ему́ ру́ку; **they shook hands** они́ пожа́ли друг дру́гу ру́ки; они́ обменя́лись рукопожа́тием; **I shook the boy** я стал трясти́ мальчи́шку; **he shook the cocktail** он сбил кокте́йль; **he shook his head** он (отрица́тельно) покача́л голово́й; **she shook the duster** она́ вы́тряхнула тря́пку; **~ before using** (*instructions on bottle*) пе́ред употребле́нием взба́лтывать; **the blast shook the windows** от взры́ва задрожа́ли стёкла; **his steps shook the room** от его́ шаго́в трясла́сь вся ко́мната; **~ one's fist at s.o.** грози́ть, по- кому́-н. кулако́м; **~ a leg** (*coll.*) (*dance*) пляса́ть (*impf.*); (*hurry*) потора́пливаться (*impf.*). **2.** (*shock*) потряс|а́ть, -ти́; **she was ~n by the news** э́та но́вость её потрясла́; **it has ~n his health** э́то подорва́ло его́ здоро́вье; **he is much ~n after his illness** боле́знь си́льно его́ подкоси́ла; (*morally*) колеба́ть, по-; **he was ~n out of his complacency** его́ самодово́льства как не быва́ло; **it shook my composure** э́то вы́вело меня́ из споко́йствия; **his faith was ~n** его́ ве́ра была́ поколе́блена; **the prosecutor could not ~ the witness** прокуро́ру не удало́сь сбить свиде́теля; **my confidence in him was ~n** моё дове́рие к нему́ бы́ло подо́рвано.
v.i. **1.** (*vibrate*) трясти́сь (*impf.*); сотряса́ться (*impf.*); **the trees ~ in the wind** дере́вья кача́ются на ветру́; **the room ~s as he walks** ко́мната сотряса́ется от его́ шаго́в. **2.** (*tremble*) дрожа́ть, за-; **he was shaking with cold** он дрожа́л от хо́лода; **he was shaking with fever** его́ трясла́ лихора́дка; **his hands shook** его́ ру́ки дрожа́ли; **~ in one's shoes** трясти́сь/дрожа́ть (*impf.*) от стра́ха; **he shook with laughter** он (за)тря́сся от сме́ха; **her voice shook with emotion** её го́лос (за)дрожа́л/прерыва́лся от волне́ния.
with advs.: **~ back** *v.t.*: **she shook back her hair** она́ отки́нула во́лосы наза́д; **~ down** *v.t.*: **he shook down the apples from the tree** он сбил я́блоки с де́рева; (*cause to settle*) утряс|а́ть, -ти́; **he shook down the grain in the sack** он утря́с зерно́ в мешке́; *v.i.* (*settle, of grain etc.*) утряс|а́ться, -ти́сь; (*coll., of pers.*) распол|ага́ться, -ожи́ться; **we will ~ down on the floor** мы устро́имся/уля́жемся на полу́; (*settle in*) осв|а́иваться, -о́иться; **he will soon ~ down at the new school** он ско́ро осво́ится в но́вой шко́ле; **~ off** *v.t.* (*lit.*) стря́х|ивать, -ну́ть; **she shook off the rain from her hair** она́ стряхну́ла с воло́с ка́пли дождя́; **~ off the dust from one's feet** (*fig.*) отряхну́ть (*pf.*) прах от ног свои́х; (*fig., of pursuers, illness, habit etc.*) отде́л|ываться, -аться от+*g.*; изб|авля́ться, -а́виться от+*g.*; **~ off the yoke** сбро́сить (*pf.*) и́го; **~ out** *v.t.*: **~ out a blanket** вытря́хивать, вы́тряхнуть одея́ло; **~ up** *v.t.* встря́х|ивать, -ну́ть; (*mix by shaking*): **~ up a medicine** взболта́ть (*pf.*) лека́рство; **~ up a cocktail** сбить (*pf.*) кокте́йль; (*restore to shape*): **~ up a pillow** взби|ва́ть, -ть поду́шку; (*coll., rouse*): **he decided to ~ up his staff** он реши́л расшевели́ть свои́х подчинённых.
cpds. **~down** *n.* (*makeshift bed*) импровизи́рованная посте́ль; **~-out, ~-up** *nn.* встря́ска; перемеще́ние должностны́х лиц; коренны́е переме́ны (*f. pl.*).

shaker [ˈʃeɪkə(r)] *n.* (*for cocktails*) ше́йкер; (*relig.*) ше́кер.

Shakespeare [ˈʃeɪkspɪə(r)] *n.* Шекспи́р.

Shakespearian [ʃeɪkˈspɪərɪən] *adj.* шекспи́ровский; **~ scholar** шекспирове́д.

shako [ˈʃeɪkəʊ] *n.* ки́вер.

shaky [ˈʃeɪkɪ] *adj.* ша́ткий, нетвёрдый; **a ~ bridge/table** ша́ткий мост/стол; **his credit was ~** у него́ не́ было твёрдого креди́та; **his position in the party is ~** у него́ в па́ртии ша́ткое/непро́чное положе́ние; **he is on ~ ground** (*fig.*) у него́ под нога́ми зы́бкая по́чва; **~ handwriting** дрожа́щий по́черк; **a ~ gait** нетвёрдая похо́дка; **a ~ voice** дрожа́щий го́лос; **his English is ~** он нетвёрд в англи́йском; **he felt ~ in the saddle** он неуве́ренно чу́вствовал себя́ в седле́; **I feel ~ today** мне сего́дня нездоро́вится; я сего́дня чу́вствую себя́ нева́жно.

shale [ʃeɪl] *n.* сла́нец.

shall [ʃæl, ʃ(ə)l] *v. aux.* (*see also* **should**) **1.** (*in 1st pers.*) *usu. translated by future tense*: **I ~ go** я пойду́. **2.** (*interrog.*): **~ I wait?** мне подожда́ть?; **~ we close the window?** закры́ть окно́?; **~ we have dinner now?** не пообе́дать ли нам сейча́с? **3.** (*in 2nd and 3rd pers., expr. promise*): **you ~ have an apple** полу́чишь (*or* бу́дет тебе́) я́блоко. **4.** (*mandatory*): **I say you ~ go** я прика́зываю вам пойти́; **thou shalt not kill** не убий́; **the committee ~ elect its chairman** председа́тель избира́ется чле́нами комите́та.

shallop [ˈʃæləp] *n.* ладья́; я́лик, шлюп.

shallot [ʃəˈlɒt] *n.* (лук-)шало́т.

shallow [ˈʃæləʊ] *n.* (*~ place*) ме́лкое ме́сто; (*shoal*) мель; **in the ~s** на мели́/о́тмели.
adj. ме́лкий; **~ water** ме́лкая вода́; **~ soil** неглубо́кая по́чва; (*fig.*): **~ mind** пове́рхностный/неглубо́кий ум; **~ talk** пусто́й разгово́р.
cpd. **~-brained, ~-witted** *adjs.* пусто́й, легкомы́сленный.

shallowness [ˈʃæləʊnɪs] *n.* (*of water etc.*) ме́лкость; (*of character*) пове́рхностность; (*of conversation*) пустота́, вздо́рность.

shaly [ˈʃeɪlɪ] *adj.* сланцева́тый.

sham [ʃæm] *n.* **1.** (*pretence*) притво́рство; **his illness is only a ~** он то́лько притворя́ется больны́м; (*hypocrisy*) лицеме́рие; **her life is one long ~** вся её жизнь — сплошно́е лицеме́рие. **2.** (*counterfeit*) подде́лка; **this diamond is a ~** э́тот бриллиа́нт подде́льный; (*deceit*) обма́н. **3.** (*of pers.*) притво́рщик; лицеме́р.
adj. **1.** (*feigned*) притво́рный; **~ illness** мни́мая боле́знь; **~ battle, fight** (*mil.*) уче́бный бой. **2.** (*counterfeit*) подде́льный; бутафо́рский.
v.t. (*feign, simulate*) притвор|я́ться, -и́ться +*i.*; симули́ровать (*impf., pf.*); **~ sleep/stupidity** притвор|я́ться, -и́ться (*or* прики́|дываться, -нуться) спя́щим/простако́м.
v.i.: **he is ~ming** он притворя́ется.

shaman [ˈʃæmən] *n.* шама́н.

shamanism [ˈʃæməˌnɪz(ə)m] *n.* шама́нство.

shamble [ˈʃæmb(ə)l] *n.* неуклю́жая похо́дка
v.i.: **~ along** тащи́ться (*impf.*); ковыля́ть (*impf.*); **~ in** притащи́ться (*pf.*); **he ~d up to us** он приковыля́л к нам.

shambles [ˈʃæmb(ə)lz] *n.* (*slaughter-house*) бо́йня; (*coll., mess*) беспоря́док, каварда́к; **he made a ~ of the job** он завали́л всё де́ло.

shambolic [ʃæmˈbɒlɪk] *adj.* хаоти́ческий, сумбу́рный.

shame [ʃeɪm] *n.* **1.** (*sense of guilt or inferiority; capacity for this*) стыд; **he is quite without ~** у него́ совсе́м нет стыда́; **put to ~** пристыди́ть (*pf.*); **he hung his head for ~** ему́ ста́ло сты́дно, и он опусти́л го́лову; **to my ~ I must confess ...** к своему́ стыду́ до́лжен призна́ться...; **for ~!; ~ on you!** стыди́(те)сь! **2.** (*disgrace*) позо́р, срам; **bring**

~ on опозóрить (*pf.*); навлéчь (*pf.*) позóр на+*a.*; **cry ~ on s.o.** грóмко возмущáться (*impf.*) кем-н.; **it's a ~ to laugh at him** стыдно/нехорошó над ним смеяться. **3.** (*sth. regrettable*) жáлость, досáда; **what a ~!** как жаль!

v.t. **1.** (*cause to feel ashamed*) сму|щáть, -тить; **he ~d me into apologizing** он меня пристыдил/усóвестил, и я извинился. **2.** (*disgrace*) позóрить, о-; посрам|лять, -ить.

cpd. **~faced** *adj.* пристыжённый.

shameful ['ʃeɪmfʊl] *adj.* позóрный, постыдный; **~ act** безобрáзие.

shameless ['ʃeɪmlɪs] *adj.* бесстыдный; **~ person** бесстыдни|к (*fem.* -ца); (*unscrupulous*) бессóвестный; (*indecent*) непристóйный.

shamelessness ['ʃeɪmlɪsnɪs] *n.* бесстыдство.

shammy ['ʃæmɪ] *n.*: **~ leather** зáмша.

shampoo [ʃæm'pu:] *n.* шампýнь (*m.*).

v.t. мыть, вы- (*головy*).

shamrock ['ʃæmrɒk] *n.* бéлый клéвер; кислица; трилистник.

shandy ['ʃændɪ] *n.* смесь пива с лимонáдом; смесь простóго пива с имбирным.

Shanghai [ʃæŋ'haɪ] *n.* Шанхáй.

v.t. (*sl.*): спои́ть (*pf.*) и увезти матрóсом на сýдно.

shank [ʃæŋk] *n.* **1.** (*leg*) ногá; **on S~s's pony, mare** (*coll.*) на свои́х (на) двои́х. **2.** (*shin*) гóлень.

shantung [ʃæn'tʌŋ] *n.* чесучá; (*attr.*) чесучóвый.

shanty[1] ['ʃæntɪ] *n.* (*hut*) хибáрка; **~ town** трущóбный посёлок.

shanty[2] ['ʃæntɪ] *n.* (*song*) ≃ матрóсская пéсня.

shape [ʃeɪp] *n.* **1.** (*configuration, outward form*) фóрма; (*outline*) очертáние; **take ~** (*become clear*) проясн|яться, -иться; обре|тáть, -сти фóрму; выражáться, выразиться; склáдываться, сложиться; **lose one's ~** (*figure*) распл|ывáться, -ыться; полнéть, рас-; толстéть, рас-; **give ~ to** прид|авáть, -áть фóрму +*d.*; (*appearance, guise*) вид, óбраз; **a cloud in the ~ of a bear** óблако в виде медвéдя; **a monster in human ~** чудóвище в человéческом óбразе; **we have a leader in the ~ of Mr. X** мы обрели лидера в лицé г-на X; **I have had no answer in any ~ or form** я не получил решительно никакóго отвéта. **2.** (*vague figure*): **strange ~s appeared in the dark** в темнотé являлись стрáнные óбразы. **3.** (*order*) порядок; **put** (*coll., knock, lick*) **sth. into ~** прив|одить, -ести что-н. в порядок; (*condition*) состояние; **he was in poor ~** он был в плохóм состоянии (*or* плохóй фóрме); **in good ~** в пóлном порядке; в фóрме; **he is exercising to get into ~** он тренирýется, чтóбы обрести спортивную фóрму. **4.** (*mould*) фóрма.

v.t. прид|авáть, -áть фóрму +*d.*; **her face was delicately ~d** у неё были тóнкие черты лицá; **~d like a heart** сердцевидный; **~d like a cone** конусообрáзный; (*from wood*) вырезáть, вырезать; (*from clay*) лепить, вы-/с-; **~ a coat to the figure** шить, с- пальтó по фигýре; (*fig.*): **~ s.o.'s character** формировáть, с- чей-н. харáктер; **the war ~d his destiny** войнá определила егó судьбý; **~ one's life** устр|áивать, -óить свою жизнь; **~ a plan** созд|авáть, -áть план; **~ one's course** устан|áвливать, -овить (*or* брать, взять) курс; (*adapt*) приспос|áбливать, -óбить (*что к чему*).

v.i.: **the boy is shaping well** мáльчик развивáется/формирýется вполнé удовлетворительно; **the affair is shaping well** дéло идёт на лад; **as things are shaping** éсли так пойдёт дáльше.

with adv.: **~ up** *v.i.* (*take ~*) склáдываться, сложиться.

shapeless ['ʃeɪplɪs] *adj.* бесфóрменный.

shapeliness ['ʃeɪplɪnɪs] *n.* красотá, пропорционáльность; (*of pers.*) стрóйность; хорóшее телосложéние.

shapely ['ʃeɪplɪ] *adj.* хорошó сложённый; стрóйный; **a ~ leg** стрóйная нóжка.

shaper ['ʃeɪpə(r)] *n.* **1.** (*machine tool*) поперéчно-строгáльный станóк. **2.: ~ of our destinies** творéц нáших сýдеб; **the ~ of the plan** создáтель (*m.*) плáна.

shard[1] [ʃɑ:d] *n.* (*entom.*) надкрылье.

shard[2] [ʃɑ:d] *n.* (*potsherd*) черепóк.

share[1] [ʃeə(r)] *n.* **1.** (*part*) часть; (*portion, received or held*) дóля; **lion's ~** львиная дóля; **fair ~** причитáющаяся дóля (*кому*); **he has his ~ of conceit** он не лишён самомнéния; **have, take a ~ in sth.** учáствовать (*impf.*) (*or* прин|имáть, -ять учáстие) в чём-н.; **go ~s with s.o.** входить, войти в пай с кем-н.; **going ~s** на паях. **2.** (*contribution*) вклад; **he had a large ~ in bringing this about** егó роль в достижéнии этого былá весьмá сущéственна; **he had no ~ in the plot** он нé был причáстен к зáговору. **3.** (*of capital*) áкция; **ordinary ~s** áкции на предъявителя; **preference ~s** привилегирóванные áкции; **we hold 1,000 ~s in the company** нам принадлежит тысяча áкций этой компáнии; **~ certificate** акционéрное свидéтельство.

v.t. делить, раз- (*что с кем*); **he ~s all his secrets with me** (*or* **I ~ all his secrets**) он дéлиться со мной всéми своими тáйнами; **~ an office with s.o.** рабóтать (*impf.*) с кем-н. в однóй кóмнате; **~ the same book** совмéстно пóльзоваться (*impf.*) однóй книгой; (**~ *in***) раздел|ять, -ить; **he ~s my opinion** он разделяет моё мнéние; **we must all ~ the blame** мы все несём отвéтственность за это.

v.i.: **I ~ in your grief** я разделяю вáше гóре; **~ and ~ alike** всё нáдо делить пóровну.

with adv.: **~ out** *v.t.* (*divide*) делить, раз-; раздел|ять, -ить; (*allocate*) распредел|ять, -ить; разд|авáть, -áть.

cpds. **~-cropper** *n.* издóльщик; **~-cropping** *n.* издóльная систéма; **~holder** *n.* акционéр; **~-list** *n.* курсовóй бюллетéнь; **~-out** *n.* делёж.

share[2] [ʃeə(r)] *n.* (*of plough*) лéмех.

shark [ʃɑ:k] *n.* (*also fig.*) акýла; (*swindler*) мошéнник, шýлер.

cpd. **~skin** *n.* акýлья кóжа; шагрéнь.

sharp [ʃɑ:p] *n.* (*mus.*) диéз.

adj. **1.** (*edged, pointed, clear-cut; also fig., of senses, sensations etc.*) óстрый, остроконéчный, рéзкий; **~ knife** óстрый нож; **~ pencil** óстрый (*or* хорошó оттóченный) карандáш; **~ chin** óстрый подборóдок; **~ features** рéзкие черты лицá; **the roofs stood out ~ly against the sky** крыши чётко вырисóвывались на фóне нéба; (*keen, alert*): **~ eyes** óстрое зрéние; **~ ears** тóнкий слух; **~ wits** óстрый ум; **he is ~** он хитёр; **a ~ child** смышлёный ребёнок; **keep a ~ look-out** смотрéть (*impf.*) в óба; (*of sounds*): **~ voice** рéзкий гóлос; **~ cry** пронзительный крик; (*severe*): **he made a ~ retort** он рéзко возразил; **a ~ remark** кóлкое замечáние; **~ temper** рéзкий харáктер; **~ tongue** злой/óстрый язык; **~ frost** сильный морóз; **~ wind** рéзкий вéтер; **~ attack of fever** сильный/óстрый приступ лихорáдки; **~ pain** óстрая боль; **~ remorse** жестóкое раскáяние; (*to the taste*): **~ dish** óстрое блюдо; **~ wine** тéрпкое винó. **2.** (*abrupt*) крутóй, рéзкий; **~ turn** крутóй поворóт; **a ~ drop in the temperature** рéзкое падéние температýры; **a ~ rise in prices** рéзкий подъём цен. **3.** (*brisk, lively*): **~'s the word!** быстрéнько! пошевéливайся!; **there was a ~ struggle** произошлá энергичная схвáтка. **4.** (*artful*) хитрый; **~ practice** мошéнничество; **he was too ~ for me** он перехитрил меня. **5.** (*mus.*): **F ~** фа (*nt. indecl.*) диéз.

adv. **1.** (*at a ~ angle*): **turn ~ right** крýто повернýть (*pf.*) напрáво. **2.** (*punctually*): **at four o'clock ~** тóчно/рóвно в четыре (часá). **3.** (*coll.*): **look ~!** быстрéе!; **we must look ~** нáдо поторáпливаться/торопиться. **4.** (*mus.*): **he sings ~** он поёт слишком высокó.

cpds. **~-edged** *adj.* óстрый; **~-eyed** *adj.* зóркий; **~-featured** *adj.* с рéзкими чертáми (лицá); **~-set** *adj.* (*hungry*) голóдный; **~shooter** *n.* мéткий стрелóк; снáйпер; **~-sighted** *adj.* зóркий; **~-tempered** *adj.* раздражительный; **~-witted** *adj.* с óстрым умóм.

sharpen ['ʃɑ:pən] *v.t.* **1.** (*knife etc.*) заостр|ять, -ить; точить, от-/на-; (*pencil*) точить, от-; **my razor needs ~ing** моя бритва притупилась. **2.** (*fig.*): **hunger ~ed his wits** гóлод сдéлал егó изворóтливым; **a long walk ~s one's appetite** длительная прогýлка спосóбствует аппетиту. **3.** (*mus.*) пов|ышáть, -ысить на полутóн.

sharpener ['ʃɑ:pənə(r)] *n.* (*whetstone*) точило; (**pencil-~**) точилка.

sharper ['ʃɑ:pə(r)] *n.* шýлер.

sharpish [ˈʃɑːpɪʃ] *adv.* (*coll., quickly*) бы́стренько.

sharpness [ˈʃɑːpnɪs] *n.* острота́; (*of voice etc.*) ре́зкость; (*of outline, photograph etc.*) отчётливость, чёткость; (*astringency*) те́рпкость, е́дкость.

shatter [ˈʃætə(r)] *v.t.* разб|ива́ть, -и́ть (вдре́безги); **the explosion ~ed the house** от взры́ва дом разлете́лся в ще́пки; (*of health or nerves*) расстр|а́ивать, -о́ить; **I was ~ed by the news** (*coll.*) я был потрясён|уби́т э́той но́востью.

shattering [ˈʃætərɪŋ] *adj.* (*coll.*) потряса́ющий.

shave [ʃeɪv] *n.* **1.** бритьё; **give s.o. a ~** бри́ть, по- кого́-н.; **have a ~** побри́ться (*pf.*); **these blades give you a good ~** э́тими ле́звиями хорошо́ бри́ться. **2.** (*coll., escape*): **we had a close, narrow ~** мы бы́ли на волосо́к от ги́бели.

v.t. **1. ~ one's chin/beard** вы́брить (*pf.*) подборо́док; брить (*impf.*) бо́роду; **~ a customer** бри́ть, по- клие́нта; **~ o.s.** бри́ться, по-; **~n** (*of chin*) бри́тый; (*of monk*) постри́женный. **2.** (*pare, of wood etc.*) строга́ть, вы́-. **3.** (*pass close to*) чуть не заде́ть (*pf.*).

v.i.: **he does not ~ every day** он бре́ется не ка́ждый день; **my razor does not ~ properly** моя́ бри́тва пло́хо бре́ет.

with adv.: **~ off** *v.t.* сбри|ва́ть, -ть.

shaver [ˈʃeɪvə(r)] *n.* **1.** (*razor*) бри́тва; **electric ~** электробри́тва. **2.** (*coll.*): **young ~** парнёк.

shaving [ˈʃeɪvɪŋ] *n.* **1.** (*action*) бритьё; **~ is compulsory in the army** в а́рмии полага́ется бри́ться. **2.** (**~s**, *of wood or metal*) стру́жка.

cpds. **~-brush, ~-cream, ~-soap** *nn.* ки́сточка/крем/мы́ло для бритья́.

shawl [ʃɔːl] *n.* шаль; **head ~** головно́й плато́к.

she [ʃiː] *n.* **1.: is the baby a he or a ~?** э́тот младе́нец ма́льчик и́ли де́вочка? **2.** (*female animal*) са́мка; су́ка *и т.п.*

pron. она́; та; **it was ~ who did it** э́то она́ сде́лала; **~ and I** мы с ней.

cpds. **~-ass** *n.* осли́ца; **~-bear** *n.* медве́дица; **~-devil** *n.* ве́дьма; **~-goat** *n.* коза́; **~-wolf** *n.* волчи́ца.

sheaf [ʃiːf] *n.* (*of corn*) сноп; **~ of arrows** пук/пучо́к стрел; **~ of papers** па́чка/свя́зка бума́г.

shear [ʃɪə(r)] *n.* (*pl., pair of ~s*) (садо́вые) но́жниц|ы (*pl., g.* —).

v.t. ре́зать, раз-/от-; (*sheep*) стри́чь, о-; (*fig.*): **shorn of his authority** лишённый вла́сти.

v.i.: **they are ~ing next week** ове́ц бу́дут стричь на той неде́ле.

with adv.: **~ off** *v.t.* отр|еза́ть, -е́зать.

shearer [ˈʃɪərə(r)] *n.* стрига́льщик.

shearing [ˈʃɪərɪŋ] *n.* стри́жка.

sheath [ʃiːθ] *n.* (*of weapon*) но́жны (*pl., g.* но́жен); (*condom*) презервати́в.

cpd. **~-knife** *n.* фи́нка; охо́тничий нож.

sheathe [ʃiːð] *v.t.* **1.: ~ one's sword** вкла́дывать, вложи́ть меч в но́жны. **2.** (*tech., encase*) обш|ива́ть, -и́ть; заключ|а́ть, -и́ть в оболо́чку.

sheathing [ˈʃiːðɪŋ] *n.* обши́вка; (*of cable*) оболо́чка; (*layer of boards*) опа́лубка.

shed[1] [ʃed] *n.* сара́й; **open ~** наве́с; (*railway*) депо́ (*indecl.*); (*for aircraft*) анга́р, э́ллинг.

shed[2] [ʃed] *v.t.* **1.** сбр|а́сывать, -о́сить; **trees ~ their leaves** дере́вья роня́ют ли́стья; **stags ~ their antlers** оле́ни сбра́сывают рога́; (*of animals*) **~ hair, feathers, skin** линя́ть (*impf.*); **~ one's clothes** разд|ева́ться, -е́ться; сн|има́ть, -ять (*or* ски́|дывать, -нуть *or* сбр|а́сывать, -о́сить) оде́жду. **2.** (*cause to flow*) прол|ива́ть, -и́ть; **he ~ his blood for his country** он пролива́л кровь (*or* о́тдал жизнь) за ро́дину; **no tears were ~ at his death** никто́ не жале́л о его́ сме́рти. **3.** (*diffuse*): **~ light on** (*lit., fig.*) бр|оса́ть, -о́сить свет на+*a.*; **this ~s light on his disappearance** э́то пролива́ет/броса́ет свет на его́ исчезнове́ние; **~ warmth around** излуча́ть (*impf.*) тепло́. **4.** (*elec.*): **~ load** сокра|ща́ть, -ти́ть нагру́зку.

shedding [ˈʃedɪŋ] *n.*: **~ of leaves** листопа́д; опада́ние ли́стьев; **~ of skin** ли́нька; **~ of blood** кровопроли́тие, проли́тие кро́ви; **there was much ~ of tears** бы́ло про́лито нема́ло слёз.

sheen [ʃiːn] *n.* (*gloss*) лоск; (*brightness*) блеск, сия́ние.

sheep [ʃiːp] *n.* **1.** овца́; **keep ~** держа́ть (*impf.*) ове́ц; **separate the ~ from the goats** (*fig.*) отдели́ть (*pf.*) ове́ц от ко́злищ; **make ~'s eyes at** броса́ть (*impf.*) не́жные/влюблённые взгля́ды на+*a.*; **they followed him like ~** они́ шли за ним, как ста́до бара́нов; **wolf in ~'s clothing** волк в ове́чьей шку́ре; **the black ~ of the family** вы́родок (в семье́); **I felt like a lost ~** я чу́вствовал себя́ совсе́м поте́рянным; **as well be hanged for a ~ as a lamb** семь бед — оди́н отве́т; **lost ~** заблу́дшая овца́. **2.** (*fig.*) ро́бкий, засте́нчивый челове́к.

cpds. **~-dip** *n.* раство́р для купа́ния ове́ц; **~-dog** *n.* овча́рка; **~-farm** *n.* овцево́дческая фе́рма; **~-farmer** *n.* овцево́д; **~-farming** *n.* овцево́дство; **~-fold** *n.* овча́рня; **~-pen** *n.* заго́н (для ове́ц); **~-run, ~-walk** *nn.* ове́чье па́стбище; **~shank** *n.* (*naut.*) ко́лышка; **~-shearer** *n.* стрига́льщик; **~-shearing** *n.* стри́жка ове́ц; **~skin** *n.* овчи́на; ове́чья шку́ра; бара́нья ко́жа; **~skin coat** дублёнка; *adj.* овчи́нный; **~-walk** *n.* = **~-run**

sheepish [ˈʃiːpɪʃ] *adj.* (*shy*) ро́бкий; (*embarrassed*) сконфу́женный; глупова́тый.

sheer[1] [ʃɪə(r)] *adj.* **1.** (*mere, absolute*) соверше́нный, просто́й, су́щий, я́вный; **~ waste of time** бессмы́сленная/бесполе́зная тра́та вре́мени; **~ nonsense** соверше́нная бессмы́слица; су́щая чепуха́; **~ accident** чи́стая случа́йность; **from ~ habit** про́сто по привы́чке; **it is ~ madness** э́то про́сто сумасше́ствие; **by ~ force of will** исключи́тельно благодаря́ си́ле во́ли. **2.** (*precipitous*) отве́сный; перпендикуля́рный; **a ~ drop** круто́й обры́в. **3.** (*text., diaphanous*) прозра́чный; (*lightweight*) лёгкий.

adv.: **the bird rose ~ into the air** пти́ца взлете́ла пря́мо вверх.

sheer[2] [ʃɪə(r)] *v.i.*: **~ away, off** (*depart*) от|ходи́ть, -ойти́; **he ~ed off the subject** он уклони́лся от э́той те́мы.

sheet[1] [ʃiːt] *n.* **1.** (*bed-linen*) простыня́; **get between the ~s** (*fig.*) заб|ира́ться, -ра́ться в посте́ль; **as white as a ~** бле́дный как полотно́. **2.** (*flat piece*): лист (*pl.* -ы́); **printer's ~** печа́тный лист; **~ of notepaper** листо́к пи́счей бума́ги; **~ of snow** пелена́ сне́га; **~ of water/ice** полоса́ воды́/льда; **the rain came down in ~s** дождь лил как из ведра́; **~ metal** листово́й мета́лл; **~ music** но́ты (*f. pl.*); **~ lightning** зарни́ца; **a clean ~** (*fig.*) не запя́тнанная репута́ция.

sheet[2] [ʃiːt] *n.* (*naut., rope*) шкот; **haul in the ~s** выбира́ть, вы́брать шко́ты; **three ~s in the wind** (*drunk*) вдрызг пья́ный (*coll.*).

cpds. **~-anchor** *n.* (*naut.*) запасно́й я́корь; (*fig.*) я́корь (*m.*) спасе́ния; **~-bend** *n.* шко́товый у́зел.

sheeting [ˈʃiːtɪŋ] *n.* (*text.*) просты́нное полотно́.

sheik(h) [ʃeɪk] *n.* шейх.

sheik(h)dom [ˈʃeɪkdəm] *n.* владе́ния (*nt. pl.*) ше́йха.

shekel [ˈʃek(ə)l] *n.* си́кель (*m.*); сре́бреник; (*pl., joc.*) гроши́ (*m. pl.*).

sheldrake [ˈʃeldreɪk] *n.* пега́нка.

shelf [ʃelf] *n.* **1.** по́лка; **set of shelves** по́лки; **on the ~** (*past working age*) отстранённый от (*or* не у) дел; (*of unmarried woman*): **she is on the ~** она́ ста́рая де́ва. **2.** (*ledge of rock etc.*) вы́ступ, усту́п; (*reef*) риф; (*sandbank*) о́тмель.

cpds. **~-life** *n.* срок хране́ния *or* го́дности; **~-mark** *n.* шифр, по́лочный и́ндекс; **~-room** *n.* (свобо́дное) ме́сто на по́лках.

shell [ʃel] *n.* **1.** (*of mollusc etc.*) ра́ковина, раку́шка; (*of tortoise*) щит, па́нцырь (*m.*); (*of egg, nut*) скорлупа́; **chickens in the ~** невы́лупившиеся цыпля́та; **come out of one's ~** (*fig.*) выходи́ть, вы́йти из свое́й скорлупы́; **retire into one's ~** (*fig.*) зам|ыка́ться, -кну́ться в свое́й скорлупе́; (*pod of pea etc.*) кожура́. **2.** (*outer walls of building, ship*) кожура́. **3.** (*frame of vehicle etc.*) карка́с. **4.** (*light boat*) лёгкая го́ночная ло́дка. **5.** (*fig., outward semblance*) (одна́) ви́димость (*чего*). **6.** (*explosive case, cartridge*) ги́льза; (*of bomb*) оболо́чка; (*missile*) снаря́д.

v.t. **1.: ~ peas** лущи́ть, об- горо́х; **~ eggs** чи́стить, о- я́йца. **2.** (*bombard*) обстре́л|ивать, -я́ть (артиллери́йскими снаря́дами).

with advs.: ~ **off** *v.i.* (*of metal, paint etc.*) шелуши́ться (*impf.*); ~ **out** *v.i.* раскоше́ли|ваться, -ться (*coll.*).

cpds. ~**fire** *n.* артиллери́йский ого́нь; ~**fish** *n.* (*mollusc*) моллю́ск; (*crustacean*) ракообра́зное; ~**-hole** *n.* пробо́ина; ~**proof** *adj.* брониро́ванный; ~**-shock** *n.* контýзия; ~**-shocked** *adj.* контýженный; страда́ющий вое́нным невро́зом; ~**-work** *n.* изде́лие (*or pl.*) из ра́ковин.

shellac [ʃə'læk] *n.* шелла́к.

v.t. покр|ыва́ть, -ы́ть шелла́ком.

shelter ['ʃeltə(r)] *n.* **1.** (*protection*) прикры́тие, укры́тие, защи́та; **under, in the ~ of a tree** под защи́той де́рева; ~ **from the rain** укры́тие от дождя́; **take ~ from** укр|ыва́ться, -ы́ться от+*g.*; **the wall gave us ~ from the wind** стена́ укры́ла/защити́ла нас от ве́тра; **when he was homeless we gave him ~** когда́ емý не́где бы́ло жить, мы да́ли емý приста́нище (*or* приюти́ли его́). **2.** (*building etc. providing ~*) прию́т, приста́нище, убе́жище; (*bomb-~*) (бомбо)убе́жище.

v.t. **1.** (*provide refuge for*) приюти́ть (*pf.*); (*screen from above*) укр|ыва́ть, -ы́ть; (*from side*) прикр|ыва́ть, -ы́ть; **the trees ~ the house from the wind** дере́вья защища́ют/укрыва́ют дом от ве́тра; **a ~ed valley** защищённая от ве́тра доли́на. **2.** (*protect, defend*) обер|ега́ть, -е́чь; **he was ~ed from criticism** его́ защища́ли от кри́тики; **he led a ~ed life** он жил без забо́т и трево́г; **a ~ed industry** покрови́тельствуемая о́трасль промы́шленности.

v.i. укр|ыва́ться, -ы́ться; **we were ~ing from the rain** мы укрыва́лись от дождя́; **he ~s behind his superiors** он пря́чется за́ спину нача́льства.

shelve[1] [ʃelv] *v.t.* **1.** (*put on shelf*) класть, положи́ть (*or*, *standing*: ста́вить, по-) на по́лку; ~ **books** расст|авля́ть, -а́вить кни́ги по по́лкам. **2.** (*fit with ~s*): ~ **a cupboard** вст|авля́ть, -а́вить в шкаф по́лки. **3.** (*fig., put aside*): ~ **a plan** от|кла́дывать, -ложи́ть прое́кт (в до́лгий я́щик); (*retire*) отстран|я́ть, -и́ть (*кого*) от дел; отпр|авля́ть, -а́вить (*кого*) на пе́нсию.

shelve[2] [ʃelv] *v.i.* (*of ground*) отло́го спуска́ться (*impf.*).

shemozzle [ʃɪ'mɒz(ə)l] *n.* (*sl.*) ссо́ра, сканда́л.

sheol ['ʃi:əʊl, -ɒl] *n.* преиспо́дняя.

shepherd ['ʃepəd] *n.* **1.** пасту́х; ~ **boy** подпа́сок, пастушо́к; ~**'s crook** по́сох. **2.** (*eccles.*) па́стырь (*m.*); **the Good S~** до́брый пасты́рь.

v.t. **1.** (*tend*) пасти́ (*impf.*). **2.** (*marshal*): **she~ed the children across the road** она́ перевела́ дете́й че́рез доро́гу; **the tourists were ~ed into the museum** тури́стов повели́ в музе́й.

shepherdess ['ʃepədɪs] *n.* пасту́шка.

sherbet ['ʃɜ:bət] *n.* шербе́т.

sheriff ['ʃerɪf] *n.* шери́ф.

sherry ['ʃerɪ] *n.* хе́рес; ~ **glass** рю́мка для хе́реса.

Shetland ['ʃetlənd] *n.*: **the ~s** (*also* **the ~ Islands**) Шетла́ндские острова́ (*m. pl.*).

shew [ʃəʊ] *see* **show**

shiatsu [ʃɪ'ætsu:] *n.* то́чечный масса́ж.

shibboleth ['ʃɪbə,leθ] *n.* (*bibl.*) шибболе́т; (*fig., pej.*) ло́зунг.

shield [ʃi:ld] *n.* **1.** (*armour; also her., biol.*) щит; (*fig., protector*) защи́та; защи́тник. **2.** (*screen*) экра́н; (*on machine*) предохрани́тельный щит.

v.t. заслон|я́ть, -и́ть; защи|ща́ть, -ти́ть; (*fig.*) огра|жда́ть, -ди́ть; покр|ыва́ть, -ы́ть.

cpd. ~**-bearer** *n.* щитоно́сец.

shift [ʃɪft] *n.* **1.** (*change of position etc.*) сдвиг, измене́ние, перемеще́ние; **there was a ~ in public opinion** в обще́ственном мне́нии произошёл сдвиг; ~ **of the wind** измене́ние ве́тра ~ **of fire** (*mil.*) перено́с огня́; **there has been a ~ of emphasis to ...** акце́нт перенесён на...; **consonant ~** передвиже́ние/перебо́й согла́сных. **2.** (*of workers*) сме́на; **work (in) ~s** рабо́тать (*impf.*) посме́нно; **I have done my ~ for today** сего́дня я отрабо́тал свою́ сме́ну; **he is on the night ~** он (рабо́тает) в ночно́й сме́не. **3.** (*liter., device, scheme*) уло́вка, хи́трость; **as a desperate ~** как кра́йнее сре́дство; **make ~ to** ухитр|я́ться, -и́ться +*inf.*; изловчи́ться (*pf.*); **make ~ without sth.** об|ходи́ться, -ойти́сь, без чего́-н. **4.** (*type of dress*) пла́тье «руба́шка». **5.** (*US, gear-change*) переключе́ние (ско́рости).

v.t. (*move*) дви́|гать, -нуть; **I can't ~ this screw** (*make it turn*) не могу́ поверну́ть/завинти́ть/отвинти́ть э́тот винт; (*transfer*) переме|ща́ть, -сти́ть; ~ **the furniture** перест|авля́ть, -а́вить (*or* передв|ига́ть, -и́нуть) ме́бель; ~ **the scene** (*theatr.*) меня́ть (*impf.*) декора́ции; ~ **key** смени́ть (*pf.*) реги́стр; ~ **responsibility for sth. to s.o. else** пере|кла́дывать, -ложи́ть (*or* сва́л|ивать, -и́ть) отве́тственность за что-н. на кого́-н. друго́го; (*remove*) уб|ира́ть, -ра́ть; **this rubbish has to be ~ed** э́тот му́сор/хлам на́до убра́ть отсю́да; (*change*) меня́ть (*impf.*); **the river ~s its course** река́ меня́ет ру́сло; **he ~ed his weight to the other foot** он перенёс вес на другу́ю но́гу; ~ **one's lodgings** смени́ть (*pf.*) кварти́ру; ~ **one's ground** (*in argument*) (из)меня́ть (*impf.*)/промени́ть (*pf.*) пози́цию; зан|има́ть, -я́ть но́вую пози́цию.

v.i. **1.** переме|ща́ться, -сти́ться; **the scene ~s to Paris** де́йствие перено́сится в Пари́ж; (*change seat*) перес|а́живаться, -е́сть; (*move house*) пере|езжа́ть, -е́хать; ~ **to another bed** переле́чь (*pf.*) на другу́ю крова́ть; ~ **from one foot to another** перемина́ться (*impf.*) с ноги́ на́ ногу; **the wind ~ed** ве́тер перемени́лся; **the wind is ~ing to the south** ве́тер перехо́дит на ю́жный; **the cargo is ~ing in the hold** груз скользи́т по трю́му; ~**ing sands** дви́жущиеся пески́. **2.** (*manage*): **I can ~ for myself** я обойду́сь/спра́влюсь без посторо́нней по́мощи.

cpds. ~**-work** *n.* сме́нная рабо́та; ~**-worker** *n.* рабо́тающий посме́нно.

shiftless ['ʃɪftlɪs] *adj.* беспо́мощный, неуме́лый.

shifty ['ʃɪftɪ] *adj.*: **a ~ fellow** ско́льзкий тип; хи́трый ма́лый; ~ **eyes** бе́гающие гла́зки (*m. pl.*).

Shiite ['ʃi:aɪt] *n.* шии́т; ~ **Muslim** мусульма́нин-шии́т.

adj. шии́тский.

shillela(g)h [ʃɪ'leɪlə, -lɪ] *n.* дуби́нка.

shilling ['ʃɪlɪŋ] *n.* ши́ллинг.

shilly-shally ['ʃɪlɪ,ʃælɪ] *v.i.* колеба́ться (*impf.*).

shimmer ['ʃɪmə(r)] *n.* мерца́ние, сла́бый неро́вный свет.

v.i. мерца́ть (*impf.*); блесте́ть (*impf.*).

shin [ʃɪn] *n.* го́лень; **he barked his ~s** он уда́рился ного́й; ~ **of beef** (*cul.*) говя́жья ру́лька, голя́шка.

v.t. (*coll.*): ~ **up a tree** вскара́бк|иваться, -аться на де́рево; ~ **over a wall** перел|еза́ть, -е́зть че́рез сте́ну; ~ **down a drain-pipe** спус|ка́ться, -ти́ться по водосто́чной трубе́.

cpds. ~**-bone** *n.* большеберцо́вая кость; ~**-guards** *n. pl.* (защи́тные) кра́ги (*f. pl.*); щитки́ (*m. pl.*).

shindy ['ʃɪndɪ] *n.* шум, сканда́л, сумато́ха, сва́лка; (*fuss*) исто́рия; **kick up a ~** подн|има́ть, -я́ть шум; зат|ева́ть, -е́ять (*or* устр|а́ивать, -о́ить) сканда́л.

shin|e [ʃaɪn] *n.* **1.** (*brightness*) блеск; (*gloss, lustre*) гля́нец, лоск; **give the silver a ~e** чи́стить, по- серебро́; **put a ~e on one's shoes** нав|оди́ть, -ести́ гля́нец на ту́фли; **the rain took the ~e out of her hair** по́сле дождя́ её во́лосы потускне́ли. **2.: rain or ~e** в любу́ю пого́ду. **3.** (*US coll.*): **take a ~e to s.o.** увле́чься (*pf.*) кем-н.

v.t. **1.** (*polish*) чи́стить, вы́-; ~**e shoes** чи́стить, по- ту́фли. **2.:** ~**e a light in s.o.'s face** осве|ща́ть, -ти́ть фонарём чьё-н. лицо́; напр|авля́ть, -а́вить фона́рь на чьё-н. лицо́.

v.i. **1.** (*emit, radiate light*) свети́ть(ся) (*impf.*); (*brightly*) сия́ть (*impf.*); **the sun ~es** со́лнце сия́ет; **the moon was ~ing on the lake** луна́ освеща́ла (*or* лу́нный свет озаря́л) о́зеро; **a lamp was ~ing in the window** в окне́ свети́лась/горе́ла ла́мпа; (*fig.*): **his face shone with happiness** его́ лицо́ сия́ло от сча́стья (*or* сча́стьем); ~**ing eyes** сия́ющие глаза́. **2.** (*glitter, glisten*) блиста́ть (*impf.*); блес|те́ть, -ну́ть; **the armour shone in the sun** броня́ блесте́ла на со́лнце. **3.** (*fig., excel*) блиста́ть (*impf.*); блесте́ть (*impf.*); **he does not ~e in conversation** собесе́дник он не блестя́щий; **he is a ~ing example of industry** он явля́ет собо́й замеча́тельный приме́р трудолю́бия.

shiner ['ʃaɪnə(r)] *n.* (*black eye*) фона́рь (*m.*) (*sl.*).

shingle[1] ['ʃɪŋg(ə)l] *n.* (*pebbles*) га́лька.

shingle[2] ['ʃɪŋg(ə)l] *n.* **1.** (*wooden tile*) (кро́вельная) дра́нка (*sg. or collect.*); (*pl.*) гонт (*collect.*). **2.** (*US, sign-board*) вы́веска. **3.** (*hair-style*) коро́ткая (да́мская) стри́жка.

v.t. **1.** (*cover with* ~*s*) крыть, по- гóнтом. **2.** (*hairdressing*) кóротко стричь, по-.

shingles ['ʃɪŋg(ə)lz] *n.* (*med.*) опоя́сывающий лиша́й.

shingly ['ʃɪŋglɪ] *adj.* покры́тый га́лькой.

Shinto(ism) ['ʃɪntəʊ(ɪz(ə)m)] *n.* шинтои́зм.

shiny ['ʃaɪnɪ] *adj.* **1.** (*polished, glistening*) начи́щенный, блестя́щий; **she has** ~ **cheeks** у неё лосня́тся щёки; ~ **boots** начи́щенные до блéска боти́нки. **2.** (*through wear*) лосня́щийся; **his coat was** ~ **with age** его́ пиджа́к лосни́лся от ста́рости.

ship [ʃɪp] *n.* кора́бль (*m.*); су́дно; **on board** ~ на борту́ корабля́; (*motion*) на́ борт; ~**'s articles** догово́р о на́йме на су́дно; ~**'s biscuit** галéта (*m.*); ~**'s captain** капита́н торго́вого су́дна; шки́пер; ~**'s chandler** судово́й поставщи́к; ~**'s company, crew** экипа́ж корабля́; ~**'s papers** судовы́е докумéнты; **when my** ~ **comes in** (*fig.*) когда́ я разбогатéю; **like** ~**s that pass in the night** (разошли́сь) как в мóре корабли́; **take** ~ сади́ться, сесть на кора́бль.

v.t. **1.** (*take on board*) грузи́ть, по-; (*passengers*) произв|оди́ть, -ести́ поса́дку +*g.*; ~ **crew** нан|има́ть, -я́ть кома́нду. **2.** (*dispatch*) отпр|авля́ть, -а́вить. **3.:** ~ **oars** класть, положи́ть вёсла в ло́дку; (*as order*) суши́ вёсла!; ~ **rudder** навé|шивать, -сить руль; ~ **mast** устан|а́вливать, -ови́ть ма́чту; ~ **water** да|ва́ть, -ть течь; ~ **a sea** прин|има́ть, -я́ть во́ду.

v.i.: **he** ~**ped as a steward** он поступи́л на су́дно официа́нтом.

cpds. ~**board** *n.*: **on** ~**board** на борту́; на кораблé; ~**-breaker** *n.* подря́дчик по сло́му ста́рых судо́в; ~**-broker** *n.* судово́й ма́клер; ~**builder** *n.* судострои́тель (*m.*), кораблестрои́тель (*m.*); ~**building** *n.* судостроéние, кораблестроéние; (*attr.*) судострои́тельный; ~**-canal** *n.* кана́л для морски́х судо́в; ~**load** *n.* судово́й груз; грузовмести́мость; ~**mate** *n.* това́рищ (по пла́ванию); ~**-owner** *n.* судовладéлец; ~**shape** *adj.* & *adv.* аккура́тный; в по́лном поря́дке; **get everything** ~**shape** прив|оди́ть, -ести́ всё в по́лный поря́док; ~**way** *n.* ста́пель (*m.*); ~**wreck** *n.* кораблекрушéние; (*fig., ruin*) крах, крушéние; *v.t.*: **be** ~**wrecked** терпéть, по- кораблекрушéние; (*fig.*): **make** ~**wreck of** разру́шить (*pf.*); **their hopes were** ~**wrecked** их надéжды бы́ли разби́ты; ~**wright** *n.* корабéльный пло́тник; ~**yard** *n.* верфь; судострои́тельный заво́д.

shipment ['ʃɪpmənt] *n.* **1.** (*loading*) погру́зка; (*dispatch*) отпра́вка. **2.** (*goods shipped*) па́ртия това́ра.

shipper ['ʃɪpə(r)] *n.* грузоотправи́тель (*m.*).

shipping ['ʃɪpɪŋ] *n.* **1.** = **shipment 1.**. **2.** (*transport*) перево́зка; ~ **charges** пла́та за перево́зку. **3.** (*collect., ships*) тонна́ж; **movement of** ~ движéние судо́в; **unsuitable for** ~ неподходя́щий для судохо́дства.

cpds. ~**-agent** *n.* экспеди́тор; ~**-company** *n.* судохо́дная компа́ния; ~**-office** *n.* тра́нспортная конто́ра.

shire ['ʃaɪə(r)] *n.* гра́фство.

shirk [ʃɜ:k] *v.t.* уклон|я́ться, -и́ться (*or* увил|ивать, -ьну́ть) от+*g.*; **he** ~**s responsibility** он уклоня́ется от отвéтственности; **he has been** ~**ing school** он прогу́ливал шко́лу.

v.i. ло́дырничать (*impf.*); гоня́ть (*impf.*) ло́дыря.

shirker ['ʃɜ:kə(r)] *n.* ло́дырь (*m.*).

shirred [ʃɜ:rd] *adj.* (*US*): ~ **eggs** яйцо́-пашо́т.

shirt [ʃɜ:t] *n.* руба́шка; соро́чка (*also* = **undershirt**); (*woman's, also*) блу́зка; (*fig.*): **he hasn't a** ~ **to his back** он гол как соко́л; **he will have the** ~ **off your back** он вас обдерёт как ли́пку; **keep your** ~ **on!** (*coll.*) споко́йно!; успоко́йтесь!; **put one's** ~ **on** (*fig., stake all on*) ста́вить, по- всё на+*a.*; **stuffed** ~ (*fig., coll.*) напы́щенное ничто́жество.

cpds. ~**-button** *n.* пу́говица от руба́шки; ~**-collar** *n.* воротни́к руба́шки; ~**-front** *n.* мани́шка; ~**-sleeve** *n.*: **in** ~**-sleeves** без пиджака́; ~**-tail** *n.* низ/подо́л руба́шки; ~**-waist** *n.* англи́йская блу́зка; ~**-waist dress** англи́йское пла́тье.

shirting ['ʃɜ:tɪŋ] *n.* руба́шечная ткань.

shirty ['ʃɜ:tɪ] *adj.* (*sl.*) раздражённый; **get** ~ раздраж|а́ться, -и́ться.

shish kebab [ʃɪʃ kɪ'bæb] *n.* шиш-кеба́б.

shit [ʃɪt] *n.* говно́ (*vulg.*).

v.i. срать, по- (*vulg.*).

shiver[1] ['ʃɪvə(r)] *n.* дрожь; **a** ~ **ran up his spine** дрожь пробежа́ла у него́ по спинé; **it sent a** ~ **down my back** у меня́ от э́того мура́шки пробежа́ли по спинé; **it gives me the** ~**s to think of it** от одно́й мы́сли об э́том меня́ броса́ет в дрожь.

v.i. дрожа́ть (*impf.*); **he was** ~**ing with cold** он дрожа́л от хо́лода.

shiver[2] ['ʃɪvə(r)] *n.* (*fragment*) оско́лок; **the glass broke into** ~**s** стекло́ разби́лось вдрéбезги.

v.t. & *i.* разб|ива́ть(ся), -и́ть(ся) вдрéбезги.

shivery ['ʃɪvərɪ] *adj.*: **I feel** ~ меня́ зноби́т/позна́бливает.

shoal[1] [ʃəʊl] *n.* (*shallow*) мелково́дье; (*sandbank*) мель, о́тмель, ба́нка; (*fig.*) скры́тая опа́сность.

v.i. мелéть (*impf.*).

shoal[2] [ʃəʊl] *n.* (*of fish*) ста́я, дося́к (ры́бы); (*great number*) ма́сса, мно́жество; **he gets letters in** ~**s** он получа́ет у́йму пи́сем.

v.i. (*of fish*) собира́ться (*impf.*) в косяки́.

shock[1] [ʃɒk] *n.* **1.** (*violent jar or blow*) толчо́к, уда́р; **the (earthquake)** ~ **was felt throughout the country** (подзéмный) толчо́к ощуща́лся по всей странé; **I got an electric** ~ меня́ уда́рило то́ком; ~ **treatment therapy** шокотерапи́я; ~ **wave** взрывна́я волна́. **2.:** ~ **tactics** (*mil.*) та́ктика сокруши́тельных уда́ров; (*fig.*); внеза́пные/неожи́данные дéйствия ~ **troops** уда́рные войска́. **3.** (*disturbing impression*) потрясéние; **he recovered from the** ~ он отпра́вился от потрясéния; **the news gave him a** ~ но́вость потрясла́ его́; (*distressing surprise*): **his death was a great** ~ **to her** его́ смерть яви́лась для неё больши́м уда́ром. **4.** (*med.*) шок; **treat s.o. for** ~ лечи́ть (*impf.*) кого́-н. от шо́ка; **he is suffering from** ~ он нахо́дится в состоя́нии шо́ка (*or* в шо́ковом состоя́нии).

v.t. **1.** (*by electricity etc.*) уд|аря́ть, -а́рить. **2.** (*distress, outrage*): **I was** ~**ed to hear of the disaster** я был потрясён сообщéнием о катастро́фе; **I was** ~**ed by his ingratitude** я был возмущён его́ неблагода́рностью. **3.** (*offend sense of decency*) шоки́ровать (*impf.*); **a** ~**ed expression** выражéние у́жаса; **he is not easily** ~**ed** его́ ниче́м не удиви́шь.

cpds. ~**-absorber** *n.* амортиза́тор; ~**-brigade** *n.* уда́рная брига́да; ~**proof** *adj.* (*of instrument*) ударосто́йкий, вибросто́йкий; ~**-worker** *n.* уда́рни|к (*fem.* -ца).

shock[2] [ʃɒk] *n.* (*of corn*) копна́; скирд, скирда́; (*of hair*) копна́ воло́с.

v.t. копни́ть (*impf.*); ста́вить (*impf.*) в ко́пны/скирды́; скирдова́ть (*impf.*).

cpd. ~**-headed** *adj.* с копно́й воло́с; косма́тый.

shocker ['ʃɒkə(r)] *n.* (*coll.*): **the picture was a** ~ (*very bad*) карти́на никуда́ (*or* ни к чёрту) не годи́лась; **he likes reading** ~**s** он лю́бит чита́ть бульва́рные рома́ны.

shocking ['ʃɒkɪŋ] *adj.* (*disturbing*) потряса́ющий; (*disgusting*) возмути́тельный; (*improper*) неприли́чный; (*scandalous*) сканда́льный; (*coll., very bad*) ужа́сный; **he carried on something** ~ (*vulg.*) он рвал и мета́л; **he has a** ~ **temper** он ужа́сно вспы́льчивый; **he is** ~**ly late** он ужа́сно запа́здывает.

shoddy ['ʃɒdɪ] *n.* (*text.*) шо́дди (*nt. indecl.*), дешёвка.

adj. дрянно́й, халту́рный, низкопро́бный.

shoe [ʃu:] *n.* **1.** ту́фля; полуботи́нок; (*US*) боти́нок; **put one's** ~**s on**; над|ева́ть, -éть ту́фли; об|ува́ться, -у́ться; **put s.o.'s** ~**s on** об|ува́ть, -у́ть кого́-н.; **take one's** ~**s off** сн|има́ть, -ять ту́фли; **change one's** ~**s** перемени́ть (*pf.*) о́бувь; **she had no** ~**s on** она́ была́ разу́та/босико́м; **she never wore** ~**s** она́ всегда́ ходи́ла босико́м; (*fig.*): **he is ready to step into my** ~**s** он гото́в заня́ть (*or* заступи́ть на) моё мéсто; **I wouldn't be in his** ~**s** я бы не хотéл быть на его́ мéсте (*or* оказа́ться в его́ шку́ре); **he knows where the** ~ **pinches** ≃ он зна́ет, где соба́ка зары́та (*or* в чём беда́); **another pair of** ~**s** друго́й коленко́р; совсéм друго́е дéло. **2.** (**horse**~) подко́ва; **cast, throw a** ~

раско́в|ываться, -а́ться; (*of brake*) коло́дка.

v.t. (*horse*) подко́в|ывать, -а́ть; **shod** (*of pers.*) обу́тый.

cpds. **~black** *n.* чи́стильщик (сапо́г); **~-brush** *n.* сапо́жная щётка; **~-buckle** *n.* пря́жка на ту́флях; **~horn** *n.* рожо́к (для о́буви); **~-lace** *n.* шнуро́к; **~-leather** *n.* сапо́жная ко́жа; **save ~-leather** бере́чь (*impf.*) (*or* не трепа́ть (*impf.*) зря) о́бувь; **~maker** *n.* сапо́жник; **be a ~maker** сапо́жничать (*impf.*); **~making** *n.* сапо́жное ремесло́; **~-shop** *n.* обувно́й магази́н; **~-string** *n.* шнуро́к; **live on a ~-string** ко́е-как перебива́ться (*impf.*); **the business is run on a ~-string** э́то де́ло ведётся с минима́льным капита́лом; **~-tree** *n.* коло́дка.

shoeless [ˈʃuːlɪs] *adj.* разу́тый; босо́й; не име́ющий обуви.

shoo [ʃuː] *v.t.*: **~ away, ~ off** отпу́г|ивать, -ну́ть; от|гоня́ть, -огна́ть.

int. (*to birds*) к(ы)ш!; (*to cats*) брысь!

shoot [ʃuːt] *n.* **1.** (*bot.*) росто́к, побе́г. **2.** (*~ing expedition*) охо́та; (*~ing party*) охо́тники (*m. pl.*); (*land for ~ing*) охо́тничье уго́дье. **3.** (*chute*) жёлоб. **4.: the whole ~** (*coll.*) всё.

v.t. **1.** (*discharge, fire*): **he shot an arrow from his bow** он пусти́л стрелу́ из лу́ка; он вы́стрелил из лу́ка; **he shot a stone from a sling** он метну́л ка́мень из пращи́; **these guns ~ rubber bullets** э́ти ру́жья стреля́ют рези́новыми пу́лями; (*fig.*): **~ a glance at s.o.** ки́нуть/бро́сить (*pf.*) взгляд на кого́-н.; стрельну́ть (*pf.*) глаза́ми в кого́-н.; **~ a line** (*sl.*) врать (*impf.*); трави́ть (*impf.*). **2.** (*kill*) застрели́ть (*pf.*); (*wound*) ра́нить (*impf.*, *pf.*); **he was shot while trying to escape** он был уби́т при попы́тке к бе́гству; **he was shot dead** он был сражён на́смерть (*or* уби́т напова́л); **~ s.o. in the back** вы́стрелить (*pf.*) кому́-н. в спину́; **~ s.o. through the leg** простре́л|ивать, -и́ть кому́-н. но́гу; **he was shot in the head** пу́ля попа́ла ему́ в го́лову; **~ game** стреля́ть (*impf.*) дичь; **we are going duck ~ing tomorrow** мы за́втра отправля́емся стреля́ть (*or* охо́титься на) у́ток; (*execute*) расстре́л|ивать, -я́ть; **he will be shot for treason** он бу́дет расстре́лян (*or* его́ расстреля́ют) за изме́ну. **3.** (*propel*): **~ the ball into the net** пос|ыла́ть, -ла́ть (*or* запус|ка́ть, -ти́ть) мяч в се́тку; **~ dice** броса́ть (*impf.*) ко́сти; игра́ть (*impf.*) в ко́сти; **he was shot over the horse's head** он перелете́л че́рез го́лову ло́шади; **they shot the grain into a lorry** они́ ссы́пали зерно́ в грузови́к; **~ a bolt** (*on door*) задв|ига́ть, -и́нуть засо́в; **he has shot his bolt** (*fig.*) он сде́лал всё, что мог; он вы́дохся. **4.: ~ rapids** нести́сь (*impf.*) по стремни́не; **~** (*be carried rapidly under*) **a bridge** проноси́ться (*impf.*) под мосто́м. **5.** (*cin.*): **~ a film** сн|има́ть, -ять фильм; **~ a scene** засня́ть (*pf.*) эпизо́д. **6.: get shot of sth.** (*coll.*) отде́л|ываться, -аться от чего́-н.

v.i. **1.** (*fire, of pers. or weapon*) стрел|я́ть, -ьну́ть; вы́стрелить (*pf.*); **the archers shot low** лу́чники стреля́ли по́низу; **the police shot to kill** полице́йские стреля́ли, не щадя́ жи́зни; **he was shot at twice** в него́ два́жды стреля́ли/вы́стрелили; **he is out ~ing** он на охо́те; **this rifle ~s well** э́та винто́вка прекра́сно стреля́ет; **a ~ing war** «горя́чая»/настоя́щая война́. **2.** (*dart*) прон|оси́ться, -ести́сь; **a meteor shot across the sky** по не́бу пронёсся метео́р; **the car shot ahead** маши́на рвану́лась вперёд; **he shot out of the doorway** он вы́скочил из подъе́зда; **a pain shot up his arm** он ощути́л стреля́щую боль в руке́; **a ~ing pain** стреля́ющая/дёргающая боль; **a ~ing star** па́дающая звезда́; **the flames shot upward** пла́мя взмы́ло вверх. **3.** (*of plants*) пус|ка́ть, -ти́ть побе́ги. **4.** (*football etc.*): бить (*impf.*) по мячу́; **~!** бей!; (*coll., speak*) валя́й говори́! **5.** (*cin.*): **they were ~ing all morning** они́ всё у́тро снима́ли.

with advs.: **~ away** *v.t.*: **he had a leg shot away** снаря́дом ему́ оторва́ло но́гу; **he shot away all his ammunition** он расстреля́л все свои́ боеприпа́сы; **~ down** *v.t.*: **we shot down five enemy aircraft** мы сби́ли пять самолётов проти́вника; **the prisoners were shot down** пле́нных расстреля́ли; (*coll., demolish in argument*) переспо́рить (*pf.*); **~ off** *v.i.* (*coll., leave hurriedly*) вы́лететь (*pf.*) (пу́лей); **~ out** *v.t.* (*extend*): **he shot out his hand** он стреми́тельно протяну́л ру́ку; (*coll.*): **~ it out** (*fight decisive battle*) дать (*pf.*) реши́тельный бой; *v.i.* вырыва́ться, вы́рваться; **a car shot out of a side-street** из переу́лка вы́летела маши́на; **~ up** *v.t.* (*terrorize by gunfire*) терроризи́ровать (*impf.*, *pf.*) стрельбо́й; *v.i.* (*grow rapidly*) бы́стро расти́, вы-; (*of child*) вытя́гиваться, вы́тянуться; (*of prices etc.*) подск|а́кивать, -очи́ть; взмы|ва́ть, -ть; **twenty hands shot up** взвило́сь два́дцать рук.

shooting [ˈʃuːtɪŋ] *n.* (*marksmanship*) стрельба́; (*sport*) охо́та.

cpds. **~-box** *n.* охо́тничий до́мик; **~-brake** *n.* фурго́нчик; **~-gallery** *n.* тир; **~-jacket** *n.* охо́тничья ку́ртка; **~-match** *n.*: **the whole ~-match** вся ку́ча; всё хозя́йство (*coll.*); **~-party** *n.* гру́ппа охо́тников; (*occasion*) охо́та; **~-range** *n.* тир; (*outdoor*) стре́льбище, полиго́н; **~-stick** *n.* трость-табуре́т.

shop [ʃɒp] *n.* **1.** магази́н; (*small ~*) ла́вка; **keep (a) ~** держа́ть (*impf.*) ла́вку; **set up ~** откр|ыва́ть, -ы́ть ла́вку; **shut up ~** закр|ыва́ть, -ы́ть ла́вку (*fig.*, ла́вочку); **all over the ~** (*everywhere*) повсю́ду; (*in confusion*) в беспоря́дке; **talk ~** разгова́ривать/говори́ть (*impf.*) о (свои́х профессиона́льных) дела́х; вводи́ть (*impf.*) (узко)профессиона́льные те́мы в о́бщий разгово́р; **you've come to the wrong ~** (*fig.*) вы оши́блись а́дресом; не на тако́вского напа́ли. **2.** (*work~*) мастерска́я, цех; **on the ~ floor** в цеха́х; среди́ рядовы́х рабо́чих; **closed ~** предприя́тие, принима́ющее на рабо́ту то́лько чле́нов профсою́за; **~ steward** цехово́й ста́роста.

v.t. (*inform on*) стуча́ть, на- (*sl.*) на+*a.*

v.i. де́лать, с- поку́пки; **we go ~ping in the market** мы хо́дим за поку́пками на ры́нок; **she ~ped around** она́ ходи́ла по магази́нам и прице́нивалась.

cpds. **~-assistant** *n.* продав|е́ц (*fem.* -щи́ца); **~-girl** *n.* продавщи́ца; **~keeper** *n.* ла́вочни|к (*fem.* -ца); **~-lifter** *n.* магази́нный вор; **~-lifting** *n.* воровство́ с прила́вка (*or* в магази́нах); **~-soiled, ~worn** *adjs.* лежа́лый; **~-walker** *n.* дежу́рный администра́тор универма́га; **~-window** *n.* витри́на; **~-window display** вы́ставка това́ров в витри́не; **~worn** *adj.* = **~-soiled**

shopper [ˈʃɒpə(r)] *n.* покупа́тель (*fem.* -ница).

shopping [ˈʃɒpɪŋ] *n.* поку́пки (*f. pl.*); **do one's ~** де́лать, с- поку́пки; **~ centre** торго́вый центр.

cpds. **~-bag, ~-basket** *nn.* су́мка для проду́ктов; хозя́йственная су́мка.

shore¹ [ʃɔː(r)] *n.* бе́рег; **on the ~** на берегу́; **set foot on ~** ступ|а́ть, -и́ть на бе́рег; **in ~** у бе́рега; **distant ~s** да́льние берега́/края́; **he returned to his native ~s** он возврати́лся к родны́м берега́м; **~ leave** о́тпуск/вольне́ние на бе́рег.

cpd. **~-based** *adj.* бази́рующийся на берегу́; **~-based aircraft** самолёт берегово́й авиа́ции.

shore² [ʃɔː(r)] *v.t.*: **~ up** подп|ира́ть, -ере́ть; крепи́ть (*impf.*).

shoreward [ˈʃɔːwəd] *adv.* (*also* **~s**) (по направле́нию) к бе́регу.

short [ʃɔːt] *n.* **1.** (*~ film*) короткометра́жный фильм. **2.** (*~ circuit*) коро́ткое замыка́ние. **3.** (*~ drink*) рю́мочка пе́ред едо́й. **4.** (*pl.*, *~ trousers*) тру́сик|и (*pl.*, *g.* -ов), шо́рт|ы (*pl.*, *g.* -ов).

adj. **1.** коро́ткий; (*of ~ duration*) кра́ткий, краткосро́чный, недо́лгий; (*of stature*) невысо́кого ро́ста; **a ~ way** коро́ткий путь; (*small*) небольшо́й; **a ~ distance away, a ~ way off** недалеко́, неподалёку; **this dress is too ~** э́то пла́тье сли́шком коротко́; **your coat is ~ in the arms** у ва́шего пиджака́ рукава́ коротковаты́; **~ steps** ме́лкие шаги́; **the days are getting ~er** дни стано́вятся коро́че; **the ~est distance** кратча́йшее расстоя́ние; **for a ~ time** на коро́ткое вре́мя; **in a ~ time** вско́ре; **a ~ time ago** неда́вно; **a ~ life** недо́лгая/коро́ткая жизнь; **time is ~** вре́мени ма́ло; вре́мя на исхо́де (*or* не те́рпит); **~ circuit** коро́ткое замыка́ние; **~ cut** (*route*) кратча́йший путь; (*fig.*): **there are no ~ cuts in science** нет лёгких путе́й в нау́ке; **win by a ~ head** опереди́ть (*pf.*) ме́ньше чем на го́лову; **~ list** спи́сок наибо́лее подходя́щих кандида́тов; **a ~ memory** коро́ткая па́мять;

in ~ order (*US, at once*) тóтчас; **at ~ range** с бли́зкого расстоя́ния; **~ story** расска́з; **be on ~ time** рабо́тать (*impf.*) непо́лную неде́лю (*or* на полста́вке); **take the ~ view** быть недальнови́дным; **~ vowel** кра́ткий гла́сный; **make ~ work of sth.** бы́стро распр|авля́ться, -а́виться с чем-н.; **I want my hair cut ~** я хочу́ ко́ротко постри́чься; **have a '~ back and sides'** стри́чься (*impf.*) ко́ротко под бокс. **2.** (*concise, brief*): **in ~** коро́че говоря́; (одни́м) сло́вом; **for ~** сокращённо; для кра́ткости; **they call him Jim for ~** дома́шние/до́ма его́ называ́ют Джи́мом. **3.** (*curt, sharp*) ре́зкий; **he has a ~ temper** он вспы́льчив; **be ~ with s.o.** говори́ть (*impf*). с кем-н. су́хо. **4.** (*insufficient*): **~ delivery** недоста́ча при доста́вке; **in ~ supply** дефици́тный; **give s.o. ~ change** обсчи́т|ывать, -а́ть кого́-н.; **give s.o. ~ weight** обве́|шивать, -сить кого́-н.; **I am 2 roubles ~** у меня́ не хвата́ет двух рубле́й. **5.: be ~ of sth.** (*lacking*) испы́тывать (*impf.*) недоста́ток в чём-н.; не име́ть доста́точно чего́-н.; **be ~ of breath** запыха́ться (*impf.*); **they are ~ of bricks** у них не хвата́ет кирпича́; **it was little ~ of a miracle** э́то бы́ло почти́ чу́до; **he is 3 days ~ of 70** че́рез три дня ему́ бу́дет се́мьдесят. **6.: ~ of** (*except*) кро́ме+*g.*; **all aid ~ of war** вся́ческая по́мощь, кро́ме непосре́дственного уча́стия в вое́нных де́йствиях. **7.** (*of pastry*) рассы́пчатый, песо́чный.

adv. **1.** (*abruptly*): **he stopped ~** он вдруг останови́лся; (*while speaking*) он вдруг замолча́л; **he tried to cut me ~** он стара́лся прерва́ть меня́ на полусло́ве; **the sound of his voice pulled, brought me up ~** звук его́ го́лоса привёл меня́ в чу́вство. **2.** (*not far enough*): **the ball fell ~** мяч не долете́л. **3. ~ of** (*without reaching*): **come, fall ~ of a target** не дост|ига́ть, -и́чь це́ли; **the play fell ~ of my expectations** пье́са не оправда́ла мои́х наде́жд; **their proposals fell ~ of our requirements** их предложе́ния не удовлетворя́ли на́шим тре́бованиям; **go ~ of sth.** ограни́чи|вать, -ть себя́ в чём-н.; **we ran ~ of potatoes** у нас вы́шла (вся) карто́шка; **I was taken ~** у меня́ живо́т схвати́ло (*coll.*). **4.** (*comm.*): **sell ~** (*at a loss*) торгова́ть (*impf.*) в убы́ток; **sell s.o. ~** (*fig., disparage*) отзыва́ться (*impf.*) о ком-н. пренебрежи́тельно.

v.t. (*elec.*): **I ~ed the battery** я замкну́л батаре́ю.

cpds. **~bread, ~cake** *nn.* песо́чное пече́нье; **~-change** *v.t.* (*coll.*) обсчи́т|ывать, -а́ть; недода́ть (*pf.*) сда́чу +*d.*; **~-circuit** *v.t.* зам|ыка́ть, -кну́ть на́коротка; (*fig.*) обойти́ (*pf.*) (кого); **~coming** *n.* недоста́ток; **~-dated** *adj.* (*comm.*) краткосро́чный; **~fall** *n.* недоста́ток, нехва́тка, дефици́т; **~-flowering** *adj.* короткоцветко́вый; **~-haired** *adj.* с коро́ткой стри́жкой; (*of animals*) коротко-ше́рстый; **~hand** *n.* стеногра́фия; **~hand typist** (машини́стка)-стенографи́стка; **take down in ~hand** стеногра-фи́ровать, за-; **~-handed** *adj.*: **we are ~-handed** у нас не хвата́ет люде́й/рабо́тников; **~horn** *n.* шортго́рн; **~-list** *v.t.* зан|оси́ть, -ести́ в спи́сок наибо́лее подходя́щих кандида́тов; **~-lived** *adj.* недолгове́чный, мимолётный; **~-range** *adj.* (*of gun*) с небольшо́й да́льностью стрельбы́; (*of missile*) бли́жнего де́йствия; (*of forecast*) краткосро́чный; **~-sighted** *adj.* (*lit., fig.*) близору́кий; **~-sightedness** *n.* близору́кость; **~-sleeved** *adj.* (*shirt*) с коро́ткими рукава́ми; **~-spoken** *adj.* немногосло́в-ный, неразгово́рчивый; **~-staffed** *adj.* неукомплекто́-ванный шта́тами; страда́ющий недоста́тком рабо́чих рук; **~-tempered** *adj.* вспы́льчивый; **~-term** *adj.* краткосро́чный, кратковре́менный; **~-waisted** *adj.* с высо́кой та́лией; **~-wave** *adj.* коротково́лновый; **~-winded** *adj.*: **be ~-winded** страда́ть (*impf.*) оды́шкой.

shortage ['ʃɔ:tɪdʒ] *n.* недоста́ток, нехва́тка, дефици́т.

shorten ['ʃɔ:t(ə)n] *v.t. & i.* укор|а́чивать(ся), -оти́ть(ся); сокра|ща́ть(ся), -ти́ть(ся) (**by an inch:** на дюйм).

shortening ['ʃɔ:tənɪŋ] *n.* (*cul.*) жир.

shortly ['ʃɔ:tlɪ] *adv.* **1.** (*soon*) ско́ро; **~ before** незадо́лго до+*g.*; **~ after** вско́ре по́сле+*g.* **2.** (*briefly*) кра́тко; **to put it ~** ко́ротко говоря́; вкра́тце. **3.** (*sharply*) ре́зко.

shortness ['ʃɔ:tnɪs] *n.* коро́ткость; (*of vowel*) кра́ткость; **~ of sight** близору́кость; **~ of breath** оды́шка; **~ of temper** вспы́льчивость, раздражи́тельность; **~ of time** нехва́тка вре́мени.

shot [ʃɒt] *n.* **1.** (*missile*): **putting the ~** (*sport*) толка́ние ядра́; (*pellet*) дроби́нка; (*collect.*) дробь. **2.** (*discharge of firearm*) вы́стрел; **fire a ~** де́лать, с- вы́стрел; стрел|я́ть, -ьну́ть; вы́стрелить (*pf.*); **he hit it at the first ~** он попа́л с пе́рвого вы́стрела/ра́за; **take a ~ at** стрельну́ть (*pf.*) по+*d.*; **like a ~** (*rapidly*) в одну́ мину́ту; (*eagerly*) охо́тно; с удово́льствием/ра́достью; (*without hesitation*) не разду́мывая; **he was off like a ~** он вы́бежал стреми́тельно/пу́лей; (*fig.*): **a long ~** натя́жка; слепа́я дога́дка; сме́лое предположе́ние; **have a ~** попыта́ться (*pf.*); **don't make ~s at the question** не отвеча́йте науга́д; **a ~ in the dark** случа́йная дога́дка; **not by a long ~** нико́им о́бразом. **3.** (*stroke, at games etc.*) уда́р; **he made some beautiful ~s** он сде́лал не́сколько превосхо́дных уда́ров; **(good) ~!** молоде́ц! **4.** (*of pers.*) стрело́к; **he's a good ~** он хоро́ший стрело́к; **I'm not much of a ~** стрело́к я не ахти́ како́й; **crack ~** ме́ткий стрело́к; **big ~** туз, (ва́жная) ши́шка (*coll.*). **5.** (*phot.*) сни́мок; (*cin.*) кадр; **long ~** кадр, сня́тый о́бщим пла́ном. **6.** (*small dose*) небольша́я до́за; **~ of liquor** глото́к спиртно́го; (*injection*) уко́л; **~ in the arm** (*fig., stimulus, encouragement*) сти́мул.

cpds. **~-blasting** *n.* дробестру́йная обрабо́тка; **~gun** *n.* дробови́к; **~gun marriage** вы́нужденный брак; ≃ жени́ться (*impf., pf.*) из-под па́лки.

should [ʃʊd, ʃəd] *v. aux.* **1.** (*conditional*): **I ~ say** я бы сказа́л; **I ~ have thought so** каза́лось бы; **~ he die** е́сли он умрёт; **I ~n't think so** не ду́маю; **if I were you I ~n't ...** на ва́шем ме́сте я не стал бы...; **~ he be dismissed** в слу́чае его́ увольне́ния. **2.** (*expr. duty*): **you ~ tell him** вы должны́ ему́ сказа́ть; вам сле́дует ему́ сказа́ть; **why ~ I listen to you?** с како́й ста́ти ста́ну я вас слу́шать?; **there is no reason why you ~ do that** у вас нет никаки́х основа́ний/причи́ны так поступа́ть. **3.** (*expr. probability or expectation*): **we ~ be there by noon** мы должны́ бы поспе́ть туда́ к полу́дню; **they ~ be there by now** они́, ве́рно, уже́ при́были; **how ~ I know?** а я почём зна́ю?; отку́да мне знать? **why ~ you think that?** почему́ вы так ду́маете? **4.** (*expr. future in the past*): **I told him I ~** (*would*) **be going** я ему́ сказа́л, что пойду́. **5.** (*expr. purpose*): **I lent him the book so that he ~ study better** я одолжи́л ему́ э́ту кни́гу, что́бы он полу́чше занима́лся; **I am anxious that it ~ be done at once** мне ва́жно, что́бы э́то бы́ло сде́лано сра́зу; **he suggested that I ~ go** он предложи́л мне уйти́. **6.** (*subjunctive use*): **I am surprised that he ~ be so foolish** не ожида́л я, что он ока́жется столь неразу́мен.

shoulder ['ʃəʊldə(r)] *n.* плечо́; **shrug one's ~s** пож|има́ть, -а́ть плеча́ми; **the coat is narrow across the ~s** пиджа́к у́зок/жмёт в плеча́х; **slung across the ~** перебро́шенный че́рез плечо́; **~ to ~** плечо́м к плечу́; **have round ~s** быть суту́лым; суту́литься (*impf.*); **dislocate one's ~** выви́хивать, вы́вихнуть плечо́; **stand head and ~s above the rest** (*lit., fig.*) быть на́ голову вы́ше остальны́х; **have broad ~s** име́ть (*impf.*) широ́кие пле́чи; (*fig.*) быть двужи́льным/надёжным; быть в состоя́нии вы́нести мно́гое; **I gave it to him straight from the ~** я рубану́л ему́ пря́мо сплеча́; **an old head on young ~s** не по лета́м у́мный; **put, set one's ~ to the wheel** (*fig.*) (при)нале́чь (*pf.*); энерги́чно взя́ться (*pf.*) за де́ло; **give s.o. the cold ~** встр|еча́ть, -е́тить кого́-н. хо́лодно; обре́зать (*pf.*) кого́-н.; **lay the blame on s.o.'s ~s** сва́л|ивать, -и́ть вину́ на кого́-н. **2.** (*of meat*) лопа́тка. **3.** (*of mountain*) усту́п. **4.** (*of road*) обо́чина.

v.t. **1.** (*lit.*): **~ a heavy load** взва́л|ивать, -и́ть на себя́ тяжёлый груз; **~ a rifle** брать, взять винто́вку на плечо́; **~ arms!** на плечо́! к плечу́!; (*fig.*): **~ responsibility** брать, взять на себя́ отве́тственность. **2.** (*push with ~*): **~ s.o. aside (*or* out of the way)** отпи́х|ивать, -ну́ть кого́-н.; **~ (one's way) through a crowd** прот|а́лкиваться, -олкну́ться сквозь толпу́.

cpds. **~-belt** *n.* портупе́я; (*bandolier*) патронта́ш; **~-blade** *n.* лопа́тка; **~-board** *n.* (*mil.*) пого́н; **~-high** *adj.*: **the grass was ~-high** трава́ была́ (*кому*) по плечо́; *adv.*: **carry s.o. ~-high** носи́ть, нести́ кого́-н. на плеча́х; **~-holster** *n.* кобура́ пистоле́та, носи́мая под мы́шкой; **~-knot** *n.*

аксельба́нт; ~**-pad** *n.* пле́чико, подкладно́е плечо́; ~**-strap** *n.* (*mil.*) пого́н; (*of knapsack*) реме́нь (*m.*), ля́мка; (*of undergarment*) брете́лька.

shout [ʃaʊt] *n.* крик.

v.t. выкри́кивать, вы́крикнуть; **he ~ed himself hoarse** он накрича́лся до хрипоты́; он крича́л до хрипоты́; он охри́п от кри́ка.

v.i. кр|ича́ть, за-, -и́кнуть; **he ~ed with laughter** он надрыва́лся от сме́ха; **don't ~ at me** не кричи́те на меня́; **~ for s.o.** кри́кнуть (*pf.*) кого́-н.; гро́мко звать, по- кого́-н.; **~ for help** крича́ть, за- карау́л; звать, по- на по́мощь; **it's all over bar the ~ing** мо́жно праздновáть побе́ду; **the ~ing died down** кри́ки ути́хли.

with advs.: **~ down** *v.t.* перекрича́ть (*pf.*); **he was ~ed down** крича́ли так, что он не смог говори́ть; **~ out** *v.t.*: **he ~ed out our names** он вы́крикнул на́ши фами́лии; *v.i.* закрича́ть (*pf.*).

shove [ʃʌv] *n.* толчо́к; **give s.o. a ~** пихну́ть/толкну́ть (*pf.*) кого́-н.

v.t. толк|а́ть, -ну́ть; **~ sth. into one's pocket** сова́ть/ су́нуть (*or* зас|о́вывать, -у́нуть) что-н. себе́ в карма́н; **he ~d a paper in front of me** он су́нул мне под нос каку́ю-то бума́жку; **he ~d his way forward** он проти́снулся вперёд.

with advs.: **~ aside, ~ away** *vv.t.* отт|а́лкивать, -олкну́ть; отпи́х|ивать, -ну́ть; **~ down** *v.t.* ст|а́лкивать, -олкну́ть; **~ off** *v.i.* (*naut.*) отт|а́лкиваться, -олкну́ться от бе́рега; (*leave*) кати́ться (*impf.*).

shovel [ˈʃʌv(ə)l] *n.* лопа́та, сово́к.

v.t.: **~ coal into a cellar** сбр|а́сывать, -о́сить у́голь в подва́л; **~ earth out of a trench** вынима́ть, вы́нуть зе́млю из кана́вы; **~ snow off a path** сгре|ба́ть, -сти́ снег с доро́жки; **~ potatoes into one's mouth** уплета́ть (*impf.*) карто́шку.

with advs.: **~ out** *v.t.* выгреба́ть, вы́грести; **~ up** *v.t.* сгре|ба́ть, -сти́.

show, (*arch.*) **shew** [ʃəʊ] *n.* **1.** (*manifestation*): **a ~ of hands** голосова́ние подня́тием рук; **make a ~ of force** демонстри́ровать, про- си́лу; **make a ~ of learning** пока́з|ывать, -а́ть свою́ учёность; **make a ~ of generosity** сде́лать (*pf.*) ще́дрый жест; **~ trial** показа́тельный проце́сс; (*semblance*) ви́димость; **there is a ~ of reason in his words** его́ слова́ мо́гут показа́ться разу́мными; **offer a ~ of resistance** ока́з|ывать, -а́ть сопротивле́ния для ви́да. **2.** (*exhibition*) пока́з, вы́ставка; **fashion ~** вы́ставка/пока́з мод; **be on ~** быть вы́ставленным; **dog/ flower ~** вы́ставка соба́к/цвето́в; **do sth. for ~** де́лать, с- что-н. для ви́да/ви́димости (*or* напока́з); (*ostentation*) пы́шность, пара́дность. **3.** (*entertainment*) представле́ние; **~ business** театра́льное де́ло; **let's go to a ~** пойдёмте в теа́тр; (*fig.*): **steal the ~** переключи́ть (*pf.*) всё внима́ние на себя́; **put up a good ~** хорошо́ себя́ прояви́ть (*pf.*); **good ~!** здо́рово!; **bad ~!** не повезло́!; кака́я неуда́ча! **4.** (*concern*) де́ло; **run the ~** вести́ (*det.*) де́ло; хозя́йничать (*impf.*); **give the ~ away** вы́дать (*pf.*) секре́т; проговори́ться (*pf.*).

v.t. **1.** (*disclose, reveal, offer for inspection*) пока́з|ывать, -а́ть; **he ~ed his true colours** он показа́л своё и́стинное лицо́; **this dress will not ~ the dirt** на э́том пла́тье грязь не бу́дет заме́тна; э́то пла́тье нема́ркое; **he has not ~n his face since Friday** он не пока́зывал но́са с пя́тницы; **~ fight** сопротивля́ться (*impf.*); не поддава́ться (*impf.*); рва́ться (*impf.*) в бой; **~ one's hand** (*lit., fig.*) раскр|ыва́ть, -ы́ть ка́рты; **~ a leg** (*sl.*) вст|ава́ть, -ать с посте́ли; **he has nothing to ~ for his efforts** он зря стара́лся; у него́ ничего́ не получи́лось; **have sth. to ~ for one's money** тра́тить, по- де́ньги не впусту́ю; **he ~ ed signs of tiring** он на́чал заме́тно устава́ть; **~ o.s.** (*appear*) появ|ля́ться, -и́ться; пока́з|ываться, -а́ться; **he ~ed himself unfit to govern** он прояви́л свою́ неспосо́бность управля́ть; **his clothes ~ signs of wear** у его́ оде́жды слегка́ поно́шенный вид; **~** (*bare*) **one's teeth** (*of animals*) ска́литься, о-; (*fig.*) пока́з|ывать, -а́ть зу́бы/ко́гти. **2.** (*exhibit publicly*) выставля́ть (*impf.*); (*a film*) демонстри́ровать (*impf., pf.*); **this film has been ~n twice already** э́тот фильм уже́ два́жды шёл/пока́зывали; **what are they ~ing at the theatre?** что идёт в теа́тре? **3.** (*display, manifest*) ока́з|ывать, -а́ть; **he ~ed a preference** он оказа́л предпочте́ние; **he ~ed confidence in her** он оказа́л ей дове́рие; **~ willing** (*coll.*) прояви́ть (*pf.*) гото́вность; **he ~ed bravery** он прояви́л му́жество; **he ~ed no mercy** он был беспоща́ден; **his work ~s originality** его́ рабо́та дово́льно оригина́льна; **it ~s his good taste** э́то свиде́тельствует о его́ хоро́шем вку́се; **~ one's paces** (*fig.*) показа́ть (*pf.*), на что приго́ден/годи́шься. **4.** (*point out*) ука́з|ывать, -а́ть на+*a.*; **he ~ed me where I went wrong** он указа́л мне на оши́бку; (*reach by precept*): **he ~ed me how to play** он показа́л мне, как игра́ть; (*demonstrate, prove*) дока́з|ывать, -а́ть; (*explain, illustrate*) объясн|я́ть, -и́ть. **5.** (*conduct*) прово|жа́ть, -ди́ть; **he ~ed me to the door** он проводи́л меня́ до двере́й; **he ~ed me the door** (*turned me out*) он указа́л мне на дверь; **I ~ed him round the garden** я показа́л ему́ сад; я поводи́л его́ по са́ду.

v.i. **1.** (*be visible*) видне́ться (*impf.*); **the stain will not ~** пятно́ не бу́дет заме́тно; **the buds are just ~ing** по́чки чуть показа́лись; **the clouds ~ed white in the distance** вдали́ беле́ли облака́; **the light ~ed through the curtain** свет просве́чивал сквозь занаве́ску. **2.** (*exhibit pictures etc.*): **he is ~ing in London next spring** сле́дующей весно́й он выставля́ется в Ло́ндоне. **3.** (*be exhibited*): **what films are ~ing?** каки́е иду́т фи́льмы?

with advs.: **~ in** *v.t.* вв|оди́ть, -ести́ в ко́мнату/дом; **~ off** *v.t.* (*display to advantage*): **the frame ~s off the picture** в э́той ра́мке карти́на хорошо́ смо́трится; (*boastfully*) щеголя́ть, по- +*i.*; **he likes to ~ off his wit** он лю́бит блесну́ть остроу́мием; *v.i.*: **the child is ~ing off** ребёнок рису́ется; **~ out** *v.t.* пров|оди́ть, -ести́ к вы́ходу; вы́вести (*pf.*) (*из чего*); **~ through** *v.i.*: **light ~s through** свет проника́ет; **~ up** *v.t.* (*make conspicuous*) сде́лать (*pf.*) заме́тным; подчёрк|ивать, -ну́ть; (*expose*) разоблач|а́ть, -и́ть; изоблич|а́ть, -и́ть; *v.i.* (*coll., appear*) появ|ля́ться, -и́ться; **he will ~ up at six** он поя́вится в шесть; (*be conspicuous*): **the flowers ~ed up against the white background** цветы́ выделя́лись на бе́лом фо́не.

cpds. **~-boat** *n.* плаву́чий теа́тр; **~-business** *n.* театра́льное де́ло, индустри́я развлече́ний; **~-case** *n.* витри́на; **~-down** *n.* про́ба сил; оконча́тельная прове́рка; **~girl** *n.* хори́стка, актри́са на вы́ходах; **~-ground** *n.* ме́сто, вы́деленное для я́рмарок; **~-jumping** *n.* ≃ ко́нные состяза́ния, показа́тельные прыжки́ (*m. pl.*); **~man** *n.* антрепренёр; (*circus manager*) хозя́ин ци́рка; **~manship** *n.* (*fig.*) уме́ние показа́ть това́р лицо́м; **~-off** *n.* хвастуни́шка (*c.g.*) (*coll.*); **~-piece** *n.* образе́ц; **~-place** *n.* достопримеча́тельность; **~-room** *n.* демонстрацио́нный зал; **~-stopper** *n.* (*coll.*) ≃ гвоздь програ́ммы.

shower [ˈʃaʊə(r)] *n.* **1.** (*of rain/snow*) кратковре́менный дождь/снег; **heavy ~** ли́вень (*m.*); проливно́й дождь; **April ~s** апре́льские дожди́ (*m. pl.*). **2.** (*of hail, also fig.*) град; **a ~ of invitations** град приглаше́ний. **3.** (**~-bath**) душ; **take a ~** прин|има́ть, -я́ть душ.

v.t. **1.** (*with water etc.*) залива́ть (*impf.*). **2.** (*with bullets etc.*) ос|ыпа́ть, -ы́пать гра́дом (пуль *и т. п.*); **he ~ed me with questions** он засы́пал/закида́л меня́ вопро́сами; **he ~ed abuse on me** он осы́пал меня́ оскорбле́ниями.

v.i. **1.** (*of rain etc.*) лить(ся) (*impf.*) (ли́внем). **2.** (*fig.*) сы́паться (*impf.*); **arrows ~ed down on them** на них обру́шился град стрел. **3.** (*have a ~-bath*) прин|има́ть, -я́ть душ.

cpds. **~-bath** *n.* душ; **~-cap** *n.* рези́новая ша́почка; **~-curtain** *n.* за́навес для ва́нны; **~-room** *n.* душева́я.

showery [ˈʃaʊərɪ] *adj.* дождли́вый.

showing [ˈʃəʊɪŋ] *n.*: **he made a poor ~** он произвёл нева́жное впечатле́ние; **on present ~** по да́нным, каки́ми мы располага́ем; согла́сно име́ющимся показа́ниям; **on your own ~** по ва́шему со́бственному призна́нию.

showy [ˈʃəʊɪ] *adj.* показно́й; **a ~ hat** бро́ская шля́па.

shrapnel [ˈʃræpn(ə)l] *n.* шрапне́ль.

shred [ʃred] *n.* **1.** (*of cloth*) клочо́к; **tear to ~s** раз|рыва́ть,

-орва́ть в кло́чки/кло́чья; (*fig.*): **they tore his argument to ~s** они́ по́лностью опроки́нули его́ до́воды; **he tore her reputation to ~s** он навсегда́ испо́ртил ей репута́цию; (*small piece*) кусо́к; **cut into ~s** разр|еза́ть, -е́зать на куски́. **2.** (*fig., scrap, bit*): **there is not a ~ of truth in what he says** в том, что он говори́т, (нет) ни крупи́цы/ка́пли пра́вды.

v.t. (*tear*) разр|ыва́ть, -орва́ть; (*cut*) разр|еза́ть, -е́зать; **~ cabbage** шинкова́ть (*impf.*) капу́сту.

shredder [ˈʃredə(r)] *n.* (*for vegetables*) тёрка; (*for documents*) бумагоре́зка; (*tech.*) дезинтегра́тор.

shrew [ʃruː] *n.* (*zool.*) землеро́йка; (*woman*) сварли́вая же́нщина; **Taming of the S~** «Укроще́ние стропти́вой».

shrewd [ʃruːd] *adj.* проница́тельный, ло́вкий, сообрази́тельный; (*astute*) сме́тливый, де́льный, ло́вкий; (*subtle*): **a ~ critic** то́нкий кри́тик; **a ~ frost** жесто́кий/си́льный моро́з; **a ~ blow** жесто́кий уда́р.

shrewdness [ˈʃruːdnɪs] *n.* проница́тельность, ло́вкость, сообрази́тельность, смётка.

shrewish [ˈʃruːɪʃ] *adj.* сварли́вый.

shriek [ʃriːk] *n.* визг; **~s of laughter could be heard** раздава́лись взры́вы сме́ха; **give a ~** взвизгнуть (*pf.*); завизжа́ть (*pf.*).

v.t. визгли́во выкри́кивать, вы́крикнуть.

v.i. визжа́ть, взви́згнуть; пронзи́тельно крича́ть, вскри́кнуть; вопи́ть, за-.

shrift [ʃrɪft] *n.*: **they gave him short ~** они́ с ним бы́стро разде́лались/распра́вились.

shrike [ʃraɪk] *n.* сорокопу́т.

shrill [ʃrɪl] *adj.* пронзи́тельный; (*fig.*) визгли́вый, крикли́вый.

v.i.: **a whistle ~ed** разда́лся пронзи́тельный свист.

shrimp [ʃrɪmp] *n.* креве́тка; (*fig., undersized pers.*) коротышка (*c.g.*).

v.i. лови́ть (*impf.*) креве́ток.

shrine [ʃraɪn] *n.* (*casket with relics*) ра́ка; (*tomb*) гробни́ца; (*chapel*) часо́вня; (*lit., fig., hallowed place*) святы́ня, храм.

shrink [ʃrɪŋk] *v.t.*: **hot water will ~ this fabric** от горя́чей воды́ э́тот материа́л ся́дет; **his face was shrunken with age** его́ лицо́ бы́ло морщи́нистым от ста́рости.

v.i. **1.** (*of clothes*) сади́ться, сесть; **my shirt has shrunk** моя́ руба́шка се́ла; (*of wood*) сс|ыха́ться, -о́хнуться. **2.** (*grow smaller*) сокра|ща́ться, -ти́ться; **~ing resources** сокраща́ющиеся ресу́рсы; **the streams have shrunk from drought** от за́сухи ре́ки обмеле́ли. **3.** (*recoil, retreat*) отпря́нуть (*pf.*); **he shrank (back) from the fire** он отпря́нул от огня́; **he will not ~ from danger** он не отсту́пит пе́ред опа́сностью; **I ~ from meeting him** я бою́сь встреча́ться с ним.

shrinkage [ˈʃrɪŋkɪdʒ] *n.* **1.** (*of clothes, metal*) уса́дка; (*in drying*) усу́шка. **2.** (*of resources*) сокраще́ние.

shrivel [ˈʃrɪv(ə)l] *v.t.* (*dry up*) высу́шивать, вы́сушить; (*wrinkle*) мо́рщить, с-; **the sun ~led the leaves** от со́лнца ли́стья смо́рщились.

v.i. (*dry up*) высыха́ть, вы́сохнуть; исс|ыха́ть, -о́хнуть; (*wrinkle up*) смо́рщи|ваться, -ться; (*wither*) ув|яда́ть, -я́нуть.

shroud [ʃraʊd] *n.* **1.** (*for the dead*) са́ван; (*of Christ*) плащани́ца. **2.** (*naut.*) ва́нта.

v.t. (*obscure, lit. & fig.*) оку́т|ывать, -ать.

Shrovetide [ˈʃrəʊvtaɪd] *n.* ма́сленица.

Shrove Tuesday [ʃrəʊv] *n.* вто́рник на ма́сленой неде́ле.

shrub [ʃrʌb] *n.* (*bot.*) куст.

shrubbery [ˈʃrʌbərɪ] *n.* кустáрник.

shrug [ʃrʌg] *n.* пожима́ние плеча́ми; **with a ~ (of the shoulders)** пожа́в плеча́ми.

v.t. & i.: **~ (one's shoulders)** пож|има́ть, -а́ть плеча́ми; **~ sth. off** отстран|я́ть, -и́ть что-н. от себя́; игнори́ровать (*impf., pf.*) что-н.

shuck [ʃʌk] *n.* (*pod*) стручо́к.

v.t. лущи́ть, об-.

shudder [ˈʃʌdə(r)] *n.* дрожь; **a ~ passed over him; he gave a ~** он вздро́гнул; **it gives me the ~s** от э́того у меня́ мура́шки по спине́ (бе́гают).

v.i. дрожа́ть, за-; содрог|а́ться, -ну́ться; **he was ~ing with cold** он дрожа́л от хо́лода; **I ~ to think of it** содрога́юсь при одно́й мы́сли об э́том.

shuffle [ˈʃʌf(ə)l] *n.* **1.** (*movement*) ша́ркание; **he walks with a ~** он ша́ркает нога́ми; (*dance step*) шафл. **2.** (*of cards*) тасо́вка. **3.** (*equivocation*) виля́ние.

v.t. **1. ~ one's feet** ша́ркать (*impf.*) нога́ми. **2.: ~ cards** тасова́ть, с- ка́рты; **s.o. has ~d my papers (around)** кто́-то ры́лся в мои́х бума́гах.

v.i. **1.: ~ along, about** волочи́ть (*impf.*) но́ги; (*fig.*): **~ through one's work** халту́рить (*pf.*). **2.** (*prevaricate*) увиливать (*impf.*). **3.: ~ out of a difficulty** вы́вернуться (*pf.*).

with advs.: **~ off** *v.t.*: **~ off responsibility** пере|кла́дывать, -ложи́ть отве́тственность на други́х; **~ on** *v.t.*: **~ on one's clothes** наки́нуть (*pf.*) оде́жду.

shun [ʃʌn] *v.t.* избега́ть (*impf.*) +*g.*

shunt [ʃʌnt] *n.* (*elec.*) шунт.

v.t. **1.** (*rail., fig.*) перев|оди́ть, -ести́; **~ line** запа́сный путь. **2.** (*elec.*) шунти́ровать (*impf., pf.*). **3.** (*postpone, shelve*) класть, положи́ть под сукно́.

v.i. маневри́ровать (*impf.*); **~ing-yard** сортиро́вочная ста́нция.

shunter [ˈʃʌntə(r)] *n.* (*rail.*) стре́лочник; (*engine*) маневро́вый электрово́з.

shush [ʃʊʃ, ʃʌʃ] *v.t.* ши́к|ать, -нуть на+*a.*

v.i. (*be silent*) замолча́ть (*pf.*); (*call for silence*) шипе́ть.

int. шш!

shut [ʃʌt] *adj.* (*coll.*): **be, get ~ of** отде́л|ываться, -аться (*or* изб|авля́ться, -а́виться) от+*g.*

v.t. **1.** (*close*) закр|ыва́ть, -ы́ть; затвор|я́ть, -и́ть; **the door was ~ tight** дверь была́ пло́тно закры́та/затворена́; **~ the door on s.o.** (*or* **in s.o.'s face)** захло́пнуть (*pf.*) дверь пе́ред кем-н.; **~ the door on a proposal** отв|ерга́ть, -е́ргнуть предложе́ние; **~ a drawer** задв|ига́ть, -и́нуть я́щик; **he ~ his heart to pity** он гнал от себя́ вся́кую жа́лость; **~ one's mind to** игнори́ровать (*impf.*); отка́зываться (*impf.*) ду́мать о+*p.*; **~ one's mouth** (*stop talking*) замолча́ть (*pf.*); **he learnt to keep his mouth ~** он научи́лся держа́ть язы́к за зуба́ми; (*lock*) зап|ира́ть, -ере́ть; (*keep by force*): **they ~ the dog in the house** они́ за́перли соба́ку в до́ме; **he was ~ out of the room** его́ не пуска́ли в ко́мнату; (*fold up*): **~ a fan** сложи́ть (*pf.*) ве́ер; **~ an umbrella** закры́ть (*pf.*) зо́нтик. **2.** (*trap*): **~ one's finger in a drawer** прищеми́ть (*pf.*) па́лец я́щиком стола́; **my raincoat got ~ in the door** мой плащ прищеми́ло две́рью.

v.i. закр|ыва́ться, -ы́ться.

with advs.: **~ down** *v.t.*: **~ down the lid** захло́пнуть (*pf.*) кры́шку; **they are ~ting the factory down** фа́брику закрыва́ют; *v.i.* закр|ыва́ться, -ы́ться; **~ in** *v.t.* (*surround*) окруж|а́ть, -и́ть; **our house is ~ in by trees** наш дом со всех сторо́н окружён дере́вьями; **I got ~ in** я оказа́лся взаперти́; **~ off** *v.t.* (*stop supply of*) отключ|а́ть, -и́ть; **the gas was ~ off** газ был отключён; (*switch off*) выключа́ть, вы́ключить; (*isolate*) изоли́ровать (*impf., pf.*); **deafness ~s one off** глухота́ на́чисто отреза́ет челове́ка от окружа́ющего ми́ра; **~ out** *v.t.* (*exclude*) исключ|а́ть, -и́ть; (*fence off*) загор|а́живать, -оди́ть; **those trees ~ out the view** э́ти дере́вья заслоня́ют вид; **~ out light/noise** не пропус|ка́ть, -ти́ть све́та/шу́ма; **I closed the curtains to ~ out the light** я задёрнул занаве́ску, что́бы не проника́л свет; **~ to** *v.t. & i.* (пло́тно) закр|ыва́ть(ся), -ы́ть(ся); захло́п|ываться, -нуться; **the door ~ to behind me** дверь за мной захло́пнулась; **~ up** *v.t.* (*close*) зап|ира́ть, -ере́ть; **he ~ up the box** он за́пер шкату́лку; **their house is ~ up for the winter** дом у них заколо́чен на́ зиму; (*confine*): **the boy was ~ up in his room** ма́льчик был за́перт в ко́мнате; **she had to stay ~ up for hours** ей приходи́лось сиде́ть взаперти́ часа́ми; **~ up in prison** сажа́ть, посади́ть в тюрьму́; (*silence*): **they soon ~ him up** они́ ско́ро заста́вили его́ замолча́ть; *v.i.* (*close*): **these flowers ~ up at dusk** э́ти цветы́ закрыва́ются в су́мерки; (*be, become silent*) молча́ть, за-; **~ up!** заткни́сь!; заткни́ гло́тку! (*coll.*).

cpds. **~-down** *n.* закры́тие; **~-eye** *n.*: **time we got some ~-eye** пора́ на бокову́ю (*coll.*).

shutter [ˈʃʌtə(r)] *n.* **1.** (*on window*) ста́вень (*m.*); **put up the ~s** (*fig.*) закр|ыва́ть, -ы́ть ла́вочку. **2.** (*phot.*) затво́р.

v.t. закр|ыва́ть, -ы́ть ста́внями.

shuttle [ˈʃʌt(ə)l] *n.* (*for weaving*) челно́к; (*fig.*) ~ **service** движе́ние (поездо́в, авто́бусов *и т п*) в о́ба конца́; ~ **diplomacy** челно́чная диплома́тия; **space** ~ косми́ческий челно́к/паро́м.

v.i. снова́ть (*impf.*).

cpd. ~**cock** *n.* вола́н.

shy[1] [ʃaɪ] *n.* (*coll.*) (*throw*) бросо́к; **have a ~ at sth.** запус|ка́ть, -ти́ть ка́мнем (*и т п*) во что-н.; (*fig.*, *attempt*) попы́тка; **he had a ~ at the exam** он попыта́л своё сча́стье на экза́мене.

v.t. (*coll.*) бр|оса́ть, -о́сить.

shy[2] [ʃaɪ] *adj.* (*bashful*) засте́нчивый; (*timid*) ро́бкий, пугли́вый; (*reserved*) сде́ржанный; (*inhibited*) стесни́тельный; **be ~ of s.o.** робе́ть (*impf.*) пе́ред кем-н.; **fight ~ of** избега́ть (*impf.*) +*g.*; бе́гать (*impf.*) от+*g.*

v.i. **1.** (*of horse*) отпря́|дывать, -нуть; ~ **at a fence** отка́з|ываться, -а́ться пе́ред препя́тствием. **2.** (*of pers.*): ~ **away from sth.** робе́ть, о- пе́ред чем-н.; отпря́нуть (*pf.*) от чего́-н.

Shylock [ˈʃaɪlɒk] *n.* (*fig.*) бессерде́чный ростовщи́к, кровопи́йца (*c.g.*).

shyness [ˈʃaɪnɪs] *n.* засте́нчивость, ро́бость, сде́ржанность, стесни́тельность.

shyster [ˈʃaɪstə(r)] *n.* крючкотво́р (*coll.*).

Siam [ˈsaɪæm, saɪˈæm] *n.* Сиа́м.

Siamese [ˌsaɪəˈmiːz] *n.* **1.** (*pers.*) сиа́м|ец (*fem.* -ка). **2.** (*language*) сиа́мский язы́к. **3.** (~ **cat**) сиа́мская ко́шка.

adj. сиа́мский; ~ **twins** сиа́мские близнецы́ (*m. pl.*).

Siberia [saɪˈbɪərɪə] *n.* Сиби́рь.

Siberian [saɪˈbɪərɪən] *n.* сибиря́|к (*fem.* -чка).

adj. сиби́рский.

sibilance [ˈsɪbɪləns] *n.* присви́стывание.

sibilant [ˈsɪbɪlənt] *n.* свистя́щий звук.

adj. свистя́щий.

sibling [ˈsɪblɪŋ] *n.* родно́й брат, родна́я сестра́; ~**s** де́ти одни́х роди́телей.

sibyl [ˈsɪbɪl] *n.* (*hist.*) сиви́лла.

sibylline [ˈsɪbɪˌlaɪn] *adj.* зага́дочный; **the S~ books** Сиви́ллины кни́ги (*f. pl.*).

sic [sɪk] *adv.* так!

siccative [ˈsɪkətɪv] *n.* сиккати́в; суши́льное вещество́.

Sicilian [sɪˈsɪljən, -lɪən] *n.* сицили́|ец (*fem.* -йка).

adj. сицили́йский.

Sicily [ˈsɪsɪlɪ] *n.* Сици́лия.

sick [sɪk] *n.* (*collect.*: **the** ~) больны́е (*pl.*).

adj. **1.** (*unwell*) больно́й; **fall ~** забол|ева́ть, -е́ть; **he is a ~ man** он больно́й челове́к; **go, report ~** (*mil.*) до|кла́дывать, -ложи́ть о свое́й боле́зни; **he is off ~** он на бюллете́не; (*fig.*): **he ~ at heart** тоскова́ть (*impf.*). **2.** (*nauseated*): **I feel ~** меня́ тошни́т/мути́т; **I am going to be ~** меня́ сейча́с вы́рвет; **he was ~** его́ вы́рвало; (*fig.*): **it makes me ~ to hear you say that** у́ши вя́нут, когда́ вы говори́те тако́е. **3.:** ~ **of: I am ~ to death of her** она́ мне надое́ла до́ смерти; **we are ~ (and tired) of doing nothing** нам надое́ло безде́льничать; **he was ~ of the sight of food** ему́ сам вид еды́ опроти́вел; он не мог смотре́ть на еду́ без отвраще́ния. **4.:** ~ **at: he was ~ at being beaten** он был удручён свои́м пораже́нием; **I am ~ at the thought of having to leave home** у меня́ се́рдце щеми́т от одно́й мы́сли о расстава́нии с (родны́м) до́мом. **5.:** ~ **for: they were ~ for a sight of home** они́ жа́ждали уви́деть родно́й дом хотя́ бы одни́м глазко́м. **6.:** ~ **joke** мра́чная шу́тка; ~ **humour** чёрный ю́мор.

v.t.: ~ **up** (*coll.*): **he ~ed up the onions** его́ вы́рвало лу́ком.

cpds. ~**-bay** *n.* (корабе́льный) лазаре́т; ~**-bed** *n.* посте́ль больно́го; **he has only just risen from a ~-bed** он то́лько (что) подня́лся (*or* встал на́ ноги) по́сле боле́зни; ~**-benefit** *n.* посо́бие по боле́зни; ~**-leave** *n.* о́тпуск по боле́зни; **he is on ~-leave** он на бюллете́не; ~**-list** *n.* спи́сок больны́х; **he is on the ~-list** он бо́лен/бюллете́нит; ~**-parade** *n.* амбулато́рный/враче́бный приём; ~**-pay** *n.* опла́та по бюллете́ню; ~**-room** *n.* ко́мната больно́го; медици́нский кабине́т, кабине́т врача́.

sicken [ˈsɪkən] *v.t.* (*lit.*): **the sight of blood ~s me** меня́ тошни́т от ви́да кро́ви; (*fig.*, *disgust*, *repel*) вызыва́ть, вы́звать отвраще́ние у (*кого*); ~**ing** отврати́тельный, проти́вный.

v.i. **1.** (*become ill*) забол|ева́ть, -е́ть; **he is ~ing for influenza** он заболева́ет гри́ппом. **2.** (*feel sick*): **I ~ at the sight of meat** меня́ тошни́т/мути́т от ви́да мя́са. **3.** (*grow weary*) прес|ыща́ться, -ы́титься (*чем*); **he ~ed of their quarrels** ему́ надое́ли их ссо́ры.

sickle [ˈsɪk(ə)l] *n.* серп; **a ~ moon** серп луны́, лу́нный серп; молодо́й ме́сяц.

sickly [ˈsɪklɪ] *adj.* (*unhealthy*) боле́зненный; (*puny*) хи́лый; (*unwell*) нездоро́вый; (*inducing nausea*) тошнотво́рный; (*mawkish*) слаща́вый; ~ **smile** крива́я улы́бка.

sickness [ˈsɪknɪs] *n.* (*ill-health*) нездоро́вье; (*disease*) боле́знь; **sleeping ~** со́нная боле́знь; (*vomiting*) рво́та; (*nausea*) тошнота́.

side [saɪd] *n.* **1.** сторона́; **on this ~** на э́той стороне́; по э́ту сто́рону; **on (along) both ~s** по обе́им сторона́м; **on either ~** с обе́их сторо́н; **on all ~s** со всех сторо́н; **from every ~** со всех сторо́н, отовсю́ду; **on the right/left ~** спра́ва/сле́ва; **put on one ~** (*defer*, *shelve*) от|кла́дывать, -ложи́ть; **stand to one ~** посторони́ться, по-; **move to one ~** отодв|ига́ться, -и́нуться; **take s.o. to one ~** отвести́ (*pf.*) кого́-н. в сторо́нку; **on the ~** (*coll.*, *additionally*) по совмести́тельству; (*illicitly*) нале́во; **get, keep on the right ~ of s.o.** распол|ага́ть, -ожи́ть кого́-н. к себе́; быть на хоро́шем счету́ у кого́-н.; **he is on the wrong ~ of 50** ему́ за 50. **2.** (*edge*) край; **on the ~ of the page** на краю́ (*or* на поля́х) страни́цы; **by the ~ of the lake** на берегу́ о́зера; **the ~s of a ditch** сте́нки (*f. pl.*) рва; **on the ~ of the mountain** на скло́не горы́; ~ **of a ship** борт корабля́. **3.** (*of room*, *table*) коне́ц. **4.** (*of the body*) бок; **I have a pain in my ~** у меня́ боли́т бок; **split one's ~s** (*with laughter*) хохота́ть (*impf.*) до упа́ду; живо́тики над|рыва́ть, -орва́ть (от сме́ха); **this dress needs letting out at the ~s** э́то пла́тье на́до вы́пустить в бока́х; **at my ~** ря́дом со мной; **he sat by her ~** он сиде́л во́зле/по́дле неё; **he always had a gun at his ~** он всегда́ име́л при себе́ револьве́р; **they were standing ~ by ~** они́ стоя́ли ря́дом/рядко́м. **5.** (*of meat*) край; **a ~ of beef/pork** полови́на говя́жьей/свино́й ту́ши. **6.** (*of a building*) бокова́я стена́; **he went round the ~ of the house** он обогну́л дом; ~ **entrance** боково́й вход. **7.** (*of cloth*): **right ~** лицева́я сторона́; лицо́; **wrong ~** вверх нога́ми; **wrong ~ out** наизна́нку; (*of packages etc.*): **right ~ up** пра́вильно; **this ~ up** э́той стороно́й вверх; (*as inscription*) верх; **wrong ~ up** вверх нога́ми; (*of paper*) страни́ца; **his essay ran to six ~s** он написа́л сочине́ние на шести́ страни́цах. **8.** (*aspect*): **I can see the funny ~ of the affair** я ви́жу смешну́ю сто́рону де́ла; **try to look on the bright ~!** стара́йтесь быть оптими́стом!; **hear both ~s (of the case)** выслу́шивать, вы́слушать о́бе то́чки зре́ния. **9.: on the long/short ~** длинова́тый/коротковáтый; **the weather is on the cool ~** пого́да дово́льно прохла́дная. **10.** (*party*, *faction*) сторона́; **which ~ are you on?** вы на чьей стороне́?; **win s.o. over to one's ~** привл|ека́ть, -е́чь кого́-н. на свою́ сто́рону; **take ~s with s.o.** прин|има́ть, -я́ть (*or* ста|нови́ться, -ть на) чью-н. сто́рону. **11.** (*team*) кома́нда; **pick ~s** под|бира́ть, -обра́ть кома́нду; **let the ~ down** (*fig.*) подв|оди́ть, -ести́ това́рищей. **12.** (*lineage*): **on the mother's/father's ~** с матери́нской/отцо́вской стороны́; по матери́нской/отцо́вской ли́нии. **13.** (*coll.*, *pretentiousness*) чва́нство, высокоме́рие; **put on ~** ва́жничать (*impf.*). **14.** (*attr.*) боково́й; *see also cpds.*

v.i.: ~ **with s.o.** прин|има́ть, -я́ть чью-н. сто́рону; прим|ыка́ть, -кну́ть к кому́-н.

cpds. ~**-arms** *n.* ли́чное ору́жие; ~**board** *n.* буфе́т, серва́нт; ~**boards,** ~**burns** *nn.* (*coll.*) ба́к|и (*pl.*, *g.* —); ~**-car** *n.* коля́ска; ~**-dish** *n.* гарни́р, сала́т; ~**-drum** *n.* ма́лый бараба́н; ~**-effect** *n.* побо́чное де́йствие; ~**-face** *adv.* (*in profile*) в про́филь; ~**-glance** *n.*: **with a ~-glance at him** и́скоса на него́ взгляну́в; ~**-issue** *n.* побо́чный/второсте́пенный вопро́с; ~**kick** *n.* (*US*, *coll.*) прия́тель (*m.*), ко́реш; ~**light** *n.* (*on car*) боково́й фона́рь; (*on* *ship*) (бортово́й) отличи́тельный ого́нь; (*fig.*): **throw a ~light on a subject** прол|ива́ть, -и́ть дополни́тельный свет на предме́т; **~line** *n.* (*work*) побо́чная рабо́та; (*goods*) неосновно́й това́р; (*football*) боковая ли́ния по́ля; **~long** *adv.* и́скоса; **~-plate** *n.* ма́ленькая таре́лка; **~-road** *n.* просёлочная доро́га; **~-saddle** *n.* да́мское седло́; **~-show** *n.* (*lit., fig.*) интерме́дия; **~-slip** *n.* (*aeron.*) скольже́ние на крыло́; **~-splitting** *adj.* умори́тельный; **~-step** *n.* шаг в сто́рону; *v.t.* (*fig.*) уклон|я́ться, -и́ться от+*g.*; об|ходи́ть, -ойти́; **~-street** *n.* переу́лок; **~-stroke** *n.* пла́вание на боку́; **~-table** *n.* приставно́й стол; стол для заку́сок; **~-track** *n.* запа́сный путь; разъе́зд; *v.t.* (*rail.*) перев|оди́ть, -ести́ на запа́сный путь; (*postpone*) от|кла́дывать, -ложи́ть; (*distract*): **I meant to finish the job, but I was ~-tracked** я собира́лся зако́нчить (э́ту) рабо́ту, да меня́ отвлекли́/сби́ли; **~-view** *n.* вид сбо́ку, про́филь (*m.*); **~walk** *n.* (*US*) тротуа́р; **~wall** *n.* (*of tyre*) бокови́на; **~ways** *adj.* боково́й; **crabs have a ~ways motion** кра́бы дви́жутся бо́ком; *adv.* (*to one ~*) вбок; (*of motion*) бо́ком; **~ways on to sth.** перпендикуля́рно к чему́-н.; **~-whiskers** *n.* бакенба́рд|ы (*pl., g.* —); **~-wind** *n.* боково́й ве́тер; (*fig.*) **by a ~-wind** око́льным путём.

sidereal [saɪ'dɪərɪəl] *adj.* звёздный.

siding ['saɪdɪŋ] *n.* запа́сный путь.

sidle ['saɪd(ə)l] *v.i.*: **~ up to s.o.** под|ходи́ть, -ойти́ к кому́-н. бочко́м; подкра́|дываться, -сться к кому́-н.

siege [si:dʒ] *n.* оса́да, блока́да; **lay ~ to** оса|жда́ть, -ди́ть; **raise a ~** сн|има́ть, -ять оса́ду; **withstand a ~** выде́рживать, вы́держать оса́ду; **~-gun** *n.* оса́дное ору́дие.

sienna [sɪ'enə] *n.* сие́на; **burnt/raw ~** жжёная/натура́льная сие́на.

sierra [sɪ'erə] *n.* го́рная цепь.

siesta [sɪ'estə] *n.* сие́ста.

sieve [sɪv] *n.* си́то; **he has a memory like a ~** у него́ голова́ дыря́вая.

v.t. просе́|ивать, -ять.

sift [sɪft] *v.t.* просе́|ивать, -ять; **~ out sand from gravel** отсе́|ива́ть, -ять песо́к от гра́вия; **~ sugar on to a cake** пос|ыпа́ть, -ы́пать пече́нье са́харом; (*fig.*): **~ the facts** рассм|а́тривать, -отре́ть (*or* тща́тельно анализи́ровать (*pf., impf.*)) фа́кты.

v.i. (*percolate*) прон|ика́ть, -и́кнуть; **the sand ~s into one's shoes** песо́к попада́ет в ту́фли; **the snow was ~ing down** снег сы́пался на зе́млю.

sigh [saɪ] *n.* вздох; **heave a ~ of relief** взд|ыха́ть, -охну́ть с облегче́нием.

v.i. взд|ыха́ть, -охну́ть; **he ~ed for peace and quiet** он вздыха́л по тишине́ и поко́ю; **the wind ~ed in the trees** ве́тер посви́стывал среди́ ветве́й.

sight [saɪt] *n.* **1.** (*faculty*) зре́ние; **long ~** дальнозо́ркость; (*fig.*) дальнови́дность; **short ~** (*lit., fig.*) близору́кость; (*fig.*) недальнови́дность; **second ~** ясновиде́ние; **lose one's ~** теря́ть, по- зре́ние; сле́пнуть, о-; **lose the ~ of one eye** сле́пнуть, о- на оди́н глаз; **I know her by ~** я зна́ю её в лицо́. **2.** (*seeing, being seen*) вид; **I can't bear the ~ of him** я его́ ви́деть не могу́; **I laughed at the ~ of his face** я расхохота́лся, взгляну́в на его́ лицо́; **catch ~ of** заме́тить (*pf.*); **I got a ~ of the procession** мне удало́сь (ме́льком) уви́деть ше́ствие; **I kept him in ~** я не спуска́л с него́ глаз; я не выпуска́л его́ из по́ля зре́ния; **lose ~ of** теря́ть, по- (*or* упус|ка́ть, -ти́ть) и́з виду; **he was lost to ~** он скры́лся и́з виду; **at first ~** с пе́рвого взгля́да; на пе́рвый взгляд; **love at first ~** любо́вь с пе́рвого взгля́да; **at first ~ it looked like suicide** на пе́рвый взгляд э́то каза́лось самоуби́йством; **he can read music at ~** он уме́ет игра́ть с листа́; **they were ordered to shoot at ~** им приказа́ли стреля́ть без предупрежде́ния; (*range of vision*): **come into ~** пока́з|ываться, -а́ться; появ|ля́ться, -и́ться; **in ~** на виду́; **the end is in ~** ви́ден коне́ц; **they were (with)in ~ of land** бе́рег был бли́зок; **put out of ~** пря́тать, с-; уб|ира́ть, -ра́ть; **keep out of ~** не пока́з|ывать(ся), -а́ть(ся) (на глаза́); **he would not let her out of his ~** он её с глаз не спуска́л; **(get) out of my ~!** с глаз мои́х доло́й!; **out of ~, out of mind** с глаз доло́й, из се́рдца вон. **3.** (*view, opinion*) мне́ние; **all are equal in the ~ of God** пе́ред Бо́гом все равны́; **in the ~ of the law** юриди́чески; **guilty in the ~ of the law** вино́вный пе́ред лицо́м зако́на; **find favour in s.o.'s ~** сниска́ть (*pf.*) чьё-н. расположе́ние. **4.** (*spectacle*) вид, зре́лище; **a ~ for sore eyes** прия́тное зре́лище; жела́нный гость; **a ~ for the gods** зре́лище, досто́йное бого́в; **see the ~s** осм|а́тривать, -отре́ть достопримеча́тельности; **what a ~ you are!** ну и вид(ик) у вас!; **he looked a perfect ~** он был похо́ж на пу́гало. **5.** (*coll., great deal*) ма́сса; у́йма; **he looked a ~ better for his holiday** он гора́здо/ значи́тельно/(на)мно́го лу́чше вы́глядел по́сле о́тдыха. **6.** (*aiming device*) приц́ел; (*focusing device*) визи́р; **take a ~ on** прице́ли|ваться, -ться в+*a.*; **get sth. into one's ~s** брать, взять на прице́л что-н.; **he set his ~s on becoming a professor** он ме́тил в профессора́. **7.** (*attr.*): **a ~ draft** ве́ксель (*m.*) на предъяви́теля; **~ unseen** не гля́дя; за глаза́; **~ translation** перево́д с листа́.

v.t. **1.** (*spot after searching*): **they ~ed game** они́ вы́смотрели дичь; **I ~ed her amidst the crowd** я заме́тил её в толпе́; **the sailors ~ed land** матро́сы уви́дели зе́млю. **2.** (*aim*): **~ a gun at a target** нав|оди́ть, -ести́ ору́дие на цель.

cpds. **~-reading** *n.* (*mus.*) игра́ с листа́; **~seeing** *n.* осмо́тр достопримеча́тельностей; **~seer** *n.* тури́ст (*fem.* -ка); экскурса́нт (*fem.* -ка).

sighted ['saɪtɪd] *adj.* (*not blind*) зря́чий.

sightless ['saɪtlɪs] *adj.* слепо́й.

sign [saɪn] *n.* **1.** (*mark; gesture*) знак; **make the ~ of the cross** крести́ться, пере-; **he made a ~ for me to approach** он сде́лал мне знак подойти́; **~s of the zodiac** зна́ки (*m. pl.*) зодиа́ка; **deaf-and-dumb ~s** а́збука глухонемы́х; **~ language** ручна́я/дакти́льная а́збука; (*symbol*) си́мвол; **plus/minus ~** плюс/ми́нус; **equals ~** знак ра́венства. **2.** (*indication*) при́знак; **there is no ~ of progress** нет никаки́х при́знаков прогре́сса; **there's still no ~ of him** его́ всё нет и нет; **the plant showed ~s of growth** расте́ние обнару́жило при́знаки ро́ста; **he showed no ~ of recognizing me** по его́ ви́ду мо́жно бы́ло поду́мать, что он меня́ не узна́л; **~ of the times** зна́мение вре́мени; (*trace*) след; **the house showed ~s of the fire** дом нёс на себе́ следы́ пожа́ра. **3.** (*portent*) приме́та. **4.** (*~-board*) вы́веска; **inn ~** вы́веска тракти́ра; **neon ~** нео́новая рекла́ма.

v.t. & i. **1.** подпи́с|ывать(ся), -а́ть(ся); распи́с|ываться, -а́ться; ста́вить, по- свою́ по́дпись; **I ~ed for the parcel** я расписа́лся в получе́нии паке́та. **2.** (*communicate by ~*) под|ава́ть, -а́ть знак; **she ~ed to the others to leave** она́ подала́ остальны́м знак уйти́.

with advs.: **~ away** *v.t.* отд|ава́ть, -а́ть; **he ~ed away his inheritance** он подписа́л отка́з от насле́дства; **~ off** *v.i.* (*at end of broadcast*) дать (*pf.*) знак оконча́ния переда́чи; **~ on, ~ up** *vv.t. & i.* нан|има́ть(ся), -я́ть(ся); **the sailors ~ed on for a single voyage** матро́сы наняли́сь на одно́ пла́вание; **the club ~ed up a new goalkeeper** клуб на́нял но́вого вратаря́.

cpds. **~board** *n.* вы́веска; **~-painter** *n.* живопи́сец вы́весок; **~post** *n.* указа́тель (*m.*).

signal[1] ['sɪgn(ə)l] *n.* **1.** (*conventional sign, official message*) сигна́л; **distress ~** сигна́л бе́дствия; **he gave the ~ to advance** он дал сигна́л наступа́ть; **the driver gave a hand ~** води́тель (*m.*) дал ручно́й сигна́л; (*rail.*) семафо́р; **the ~s are against us** семафо́р закры́т; (*for road traffic*) светофо́р. **2.** (*indication*): **his rising was a ~ that the meeting was over** он встал, дав э́тим поня́ть, что собра́ние око́нчено; **this was a ~ for the crowd to start shouting** э́то яви́лось для толпы́ сигна́лом, и подня́лся крик. **3.** (*pl., mil.*): **~s troops** войска́ свя́зи.

v.t.: **~ an order** перед|ава́ть, -а́ть прика́з; **the ship ~led its position** су́дно сигнализи́ровало своё местонахожде́ние; **I ~ed** (*motioned to*) **him to come nearer** я по́дал ему́ знак подойти́ побли́же; я помани́л его́ к себе́.

v.i. сигнализи́ровать (*impf., pf.*).

cpds. **~-box** *n.* сигна́льная бу́дка; блокпо́ст; **~man** *n.* (*rail.*) стре́лочник; (*mil.*) связи́ст; (*nav.*) сигна́льщик.

signal[2] [ˈsɪgn(ə)l] *adj.*: ~ **success** блестя́щий успе́х; ~ **failure** полне́йший прова́л.

signalize [ˈsɪgnəˌlaɪz] *v.t.* ознамено́в|ывать, -а́ть; отм|еча́ть, -е́тить.

signaller [ˈsɪgnələ(r)] *n.* сигна́льщик; (*mil.*) связи́ст.

signatory [ˈsɪgnətərɪ] *n.* подписа́вшаяся сторона́; подписа́вшийся.

adj.: ~ **powers** держа́вы, подписа́вшие догово́р.

signature [ˈsɪgnətʃə(r)] *n.* **1.** по́дпись. **2.** (*mus.*): **key** ~ ключ; ~ **tune** музыка́льная ша́пка. **3.** (*typ.*) сигнату́ра.

signet [ˈsɪgnɪt] *n.* печа́тка; ~ **ring** кольцо́ с печа́ткой.

significance [sɪgˈnɪfɪkəns] *n.* (*meaning, import*) значе́ние; (*sense*) смысл; **of no real** ~ без осо́бого значе́ния; **an event of great** ~ собы́тие большо́й ва́жности.

significant [sɪgˈnɪfɪkənt] *adj.* значи́тельный; (*important*) ва́жный; ~ **changes** суще́ственные измене́ния; (*expressive*): **a** ~ **look** многозначи́тельный взгляд.

signification [ˌsɪgnɪfɪˈkeɪʃ(ə)n] *n.* значе́ние; смысл.

signif|y [ˈsɪgnɪˌfaɪ] *v.t.* **1.** (*make known*) выража́ть, вы́разить; **we** ~**ied our approval** мы вы́разили своё одобре́ние. **2.** (*portend*) предвеща́ть (*impf.*); **few people realized what this event** ~**ied** ма́ло кто сознава́л, что предвеща́ло э́то собы́тие. **3.** (*mean*) означа́ть (*impf.*).

v.i. (*be of importance*) зна́чить (*impf.*); **it does not** ~**y** э́то нева́жно.

Signor [ˈsiːnjɔː(r)], **-a** [siːnˈjɔːrə], **-ina** [ˌsiːnjəˈriːnə] *nn.* синьо́р, -а, -и́на.

Sikh [siːk, sɪk] *n.* сикх.

adj. си́кхский.

Sikhism [ˈsiːkɪz(ə)m, ˈsɪk-] *n.* сикхи́зм.

silage [ˈsaɪlɪdʒ] *n.* си́лос.

v.t. силосова́ть, за-.

silence [ˈsaɪləns] *n.* молча́ние; безмо́лвие; тишина́; ~ **is golden** молча́ние — зо́лото; ~ **gives consent** молча́ние — знак согла́сия; **in** ~ мо́лча; ~**!** ти́хо!; молча́ть!; **break** ~ нар|уша́ть, -у́шить молча́ние; **keep** ~ храни́ть (*impf.*) молча́ние; (*coll.*) пома́лкивать (*impf.*); **call for** ~ приз|ыва́ть, -ва́ть к тишине́; **reduce s.o. to** ~ заста́вить (*pf.*) кого́-н. (за)молча́ть.

v.t. (*pers.*) заст|авля́ть, -а́вить замолча́ть; (*thg.*) заглуш|а́ть, -и́ть.

silencer [ˈsaɪlənsə(r)] *n.* глуши́тель (*m.*).

silent [ˈsaɪlənt] *adj.* (*saying nothing*) безмо́лвный; **the** ~ **majority** молчали́вое большинство́; **keep** ~ молча́ть (*impf.*); **keep** ~ **about sth.** ум|а́лчивать, -олча́ть о чём-н.; **history is** ~ **on this matter** исто́рия об э́том ума́лчивает; **fall, become** ~ замолча́ть (*pf.*), умо́лкнуть (*pf.*); (*taciturn*) молчали́вый; (*mute*) немо́й; ~ **film** немо́й фильм; (*not pronounced*) непроизноси́мый; (*noiseless*) бесшу́мный.

silhouette [ˌsɪluːˈet] *n.* силуэ́т; **a portrait in** ~ силуэ́тное изображе́ние, силуэ́т.

v.t.: **the dome was** ~**d against the sky** на не́бе вырисо́вывался силуэ́т ку́пола.

silica [ˈsɪlɪkə] *n.* кремнезём; (*quartz*) кварц.

silicate [ˈsɪlɪˌkeɪt] *n.* силика́т.

silicon [ˈsɪlɪkən] *n.* кре́мний; ~ **chip** кре́мневая микропласти́нка, чип.

silicone [ˈsɪlɪˌkəʊn] *n.* силокса́н.

silicosis [ˌsɪlɪˈkəʊsɪs] *n.* силико́з.

silk [sɪlk] *n.* **1.** шёлк; (*attr.*) шёлковый; ~ **stockings** шёлковые чулки́; ~ **hat** цили́ндр. **2.** (*pl., garments*) шелка́ (*m. pl.*). **3.** (*pl., for embroidery*) шёлк; шёлковые ни́тки (*f. pl.*).

cpds. ~**-breeder** *n.* шелково́д; ~**-growing** *n.* шелково́дство; ~**-screen** *adj.*: ~**-screen printing** шёлкогра́фия; ~**worm** *n.* ту́товый шелкопря́д; шелкови́чный червь.

silken [ˈsɪlkən] *adj.* (*made of silk*) шёлковый; (*resembling* ~) шелкови́стый; (*fig.*) = **silky**

silky [ˈsɪlkɪ] *adj.* шелкови́стый; (*fig., of voice etc.*) медоточи́вый.

sill [sɪl] *n.* (*of window*) подоко́нник; (*of door*) поро́г.

silliness [ˈsɪlɪnɪs] *n.* глу́пость.

silly [ˈsɪlɪ] *n.* глупы́ш (*coll., fem.* -ка, глу́пенькая); дурачо́к (*fem.* ду́рочка).

adj. **1.** (*foolish*) глу́пый; **do/say sth.** ~ сде́лать/сказа́ть/сморо́зить (*pf.*) глу́пость; **how** ~ **of me to forget!** как глу́по бы́ло с моей стороны́ забы́ть! **2.** (*imbecile*) слабоу́мный; **the noise is driving me** ~ э́тот шум меня́ с ума́ сведёт.

silo [ˈsaɪləʊ] *n.* (*tower; pit*) си́лосная ба́шня/я́ма; (*for missile*) ста́ртовая ша́хта.

v.t. силосова́ть, за-.

silt [sɪlt] *n.* ил.

v.t. & i. (*usu.* ~ **up**) зайли|ва́ть(ся), -ть(ся); (*fig.*) накоп|ля́ть(ся), -и́ть(ся).

Silurian [saɪˈljʊərɪən] *adj.* силури́йский.

sil|van, syl- [ˈsɪlv(ə)n] *adj.* лесно́й, леси́стый.

silver [ˈsɪlvə(r)] *n.* **1.** (*metal;* ~**ware;** ~ **coins**) серебро́; **table** ~ столо́вое серебро́; **clean the** ~ чи́стить, по/на- серебро́; **a pocketful of** ~ по́лный карма́н серебра́. **2.** (*colour*) сере́бряный цвет.

adj. (*made of* ~) сере́бряный; (*resembling* ~) серебри́стый; ~ **age** сере́бряный век; ~ **birch** бе́лая берёза; ~ **fir** бе́лая/благоро́дная пи́хта; ~ **fox** черно-бу́рая лиси́ца; ~ **hair** серебри́стые во́лосы; седина́; ~ **jubilee** сере́бряный юбиле́й; двадцатипятиле́тие; ~ **paper** фо́льга; ~ **sand** то́нкий бе́лый песо́к; ~ **spoon** сере́бряная ло́жка; ~ **wedding** сере́бряная сва́дьба.

cpds. ~**-grey** *adj.* серебри́сто-се́рый; ~**-haired** *adj.* седо́й; ~**-plated** *adj.* серебрёный, посеребрённый; гальванизи́рованный серебро́м; ~**point** *n.* (*stylus*) сере́бряный каранда́ш; ~**side** *n.* (*of beef*) ссек; ~**smith** *n.* сере́бряных дел ма́стер; ~**-tongued** *adj.* красноречи́вый; ~**ware** *n.* серебро́; изде́лия (*nt. pl.*) из серебра́.

silvery [ˈsɪlvərɪ] *adj.* серебри́стый.

silviculture [ˈsɪlvɪˌkʌltʃə(r)] *n.* лесово́дство.

simian [ˈsɪmɪən] *adj.* (*of apes*) обезья́ний; (*ape-like*) обезьяноподо́бный.

similar [ˈsɪmɪlə(r)] *adj.* **1.** (*alike*) схо́дный; **the hats are** ~ **in appearance** шля́пы с ви́ду о́чень похо́жи. **2.:** ~ **to** похо́жий на+*a.*; подо́бный +*d.*; **your car is** ~ **to mine** у вас така́я же маши́на, как у меня́; ~ **triangles** подо́бные треуго́льники.

similarity [ˌsɪmɪˈlærɪtɪ] *n.* схо́дство; **points of** ~ черты́ (*f. pl.*) схо́дства; о́бщие черты́; (*geom.*) подо́бие; **his features bear a** ~ **to his father's** он похо́ж на отца́ лицо́м.

similarly [ˈsɪmɪləlɪ] *adv.* так же; таки́м же о́бразом.

simile [ˈsɪmɪlɪ] *n.* сравне́ние.

similitude [sɪˈmɪlɪˌtjuːd] *n.* схо́дство; подо́бие; ви́димость; **in the** ~ **of** наподо́бие +*g.*

simmer [ˈsɪmə(r)] *n.*: **bring to a** ~ дов|оди́ть, -ести́ до лёгкого кипе́ния.

v.t. кипяти́ть (*impf.*) на ме́дленном огне́.

v.i. слегка́ кипе́ть (*impf.*); (*fig.*): ~ **with indignation** кипе́ть (*impf.*) негодова́нием; ~ **down** (*fig.*) от|ходи́ть, -ойти́; успок|а́иваться, -о́иться; ост|ыва́ть, -ы́ть; **he** ~**ed down** он успоко́ился/осты́л; **his rage** ~**ed down** его́ гнев осты́л.

simony [ˈsaɪmənɪ, ˈsɪm-] *n.* симони́я.

simoom [sɪˈmuːm], **simoon** [sɪˈmuːn] *n.* саму́м.

simper [ˈsɪmpə(r)] *n.* жема́нная улы́бка.

v.i. жема́нно улыб|а́ться, -ну́ться.

simple [ˈsɪmp(ə)l] *n.* (*medicinal herb*) лека́рственное расте́ние.

adj. **1.** просто́й; **I am not so** ~ **as to believe that** я не так прост, что́бы пове́рить э́тому; ~ **fracture** просто́й перело́м; **as** ~ **as ABC** про́ще просто́го; **it's as** ~ **as that** то́лько и всего́; вот и всё; и вся недолга́. **2.** (*easy*) лёгкий; **the dress is** ~ **to make** э́то пла́тье легко́ сшить. **3.** (*math.*): ~ **equation** уравне́ние пе́рвой сте́пени.

cpds. ~**-hearted** *adj.* простоду́шный; и́скренний; ~**-minded** *adj.* (*unsophisticated*) бесхи́тростный; (*feeble-minded*) глу́пый, глупова́тый.

simpleton [ˈsɪmp(ə)lt(ə)n] *n.* проста́|к (*fem.* -чка).

simplicity [sɪmˈplɪsɪtɪ] *n.* простота́; (*easiness*) лёгкость; **the game is** ~ **itself** э́та игра́ ле́гче лёгкого.

simplification [ˌsɪmplɪfɪˈkeɪʃ(ə)n] *n.* упроще́ние.

simplify ['sɪmplɪ,faɪ] *v.t.* упро|щáть, -сти́ть; облегч|áть, -и́ть.
simplistic [sɪm'plɪstɪk] *adj.* (чрезмéрно) упрощённый.
simply ['sɪmplɪ] *adv.* прóсто; **the weather was ~ dreadful** погóда былá прямо ужáсная; **I ~ couldn't manage to come** я никáк не мог прийти́; **it's ~ that I don't like him** прóсто-нáпросто мне он не нрáвиться.
simulacrum [,sɪmjʊ'leɪkrəm] *n.* подóбие, ви́димость.
simulate ['sɪmjʊ,leɪt] *v.t.* (*feign*) симули́ровать (*impf., pf.*); изобра|жáть, -зи́ть; (*pretend to be*) притвор|я́ться, -и́ться +*i.*; (*wear guise of, resemble*) упод|обля́ться, -óбиться +*d.*; (*imitate for training purposes*) воспроизв|оди́ть, -ести́; моделíровать (*impf., pf.*); имити́ровать (*impf., pf.*).
simulated ['sɪmjʊ,leɪtɪd] *adj.* поддéльный, искýственный; **~ flight** модели́рованный/услóвный полёт.
simulation [,sɪmjʊ'leɪʃ(ə)n] *n.* симуля́ция; воспроизведéние; модели́рование; имити́рование.
simulator ['sɪmjʊ,leɪtə(r)] *n.* (*pers.*) симуля́нт, притвóрщик; (*device*) модели́рующее/имити́рующее устрóйство.
simultaneity [,sɪməltə'neɪɪtɪ] *n.* одновремéнность, синхрóнность.
simultaneous [,sɪməl'teɪnɪəs] *adj.* одновремéнный, синхрóнный; **~ interpreting** синхрóнный перевóд.
sin [sɪn] *n.* **1.** грех; **original ~** перворóдный грех; **the seven deadly ~s** семь смéртных грехóв; **~s of omission and commission** грехи́ дéянием и недéянием; **forgiveness of ~s** отпущéние грехóв; **live in ~** жить (*impf.*) в незакóнном брáке; **for my ~s** за грехи́ мои́; **like ~** (*coll.*) ужáсно; **as ugly as ~** стрáшен как смéртный грех. **2.** (*offence*): **~ against propriety** нарушéние прили́чий; **it's a ~ to stay indoors** грешнó сидéть дóма.
v.i. греши́ть, со-; **more ~ned against than ~ning** скорéе жéртва, чем винóвный.
Sinai ['saɪnɑɪ] *n.* Сина́й.
since [sɪns] *adv.* **1.** (*from that time*) с тех пор; **he has been here ever ~** с тoй пóры он здесь так и остáлся; **ever before or ~** когдá-либо рáньше и́ли потóм; **he was healthier in the army than ever before or ~** он никогдá нé был так здорóв, как когдá служи́л в áрмии. **2.** (*in the intervening time*): **the theatre has ~ been rebuilt** с тех пор (*or* позднée) теáтр перестрóили; **he was wounded but has ~ recovered** он был рáнен, но успéл прáвиться. **3.** (*liter., ago*) (томý) назáд.
prep. c+*g.*; **nothing has happened ~ Christmas** с Рождествá ничегó не произошлó; **~ my last letter** с тех пор, как я писáл послéдний раз; **~ our talk** после нáшего разговóра; **~ yesterday** со вчерáшнего дня; **~ when have you been fond of music?** с каки́х пор вы стáли люби́ть мýзыку?
conj. **1.** (*from, during the time when*): **how long is it ~ we last met?** скóлько врéмени прошлó с нáшей послéдней встрéчи?; **I have moved house ~ I saw you** я переéхал с тех пор, как мы с вáми ви́делись. **2.** (*seeing that*) так как, поскóльку; **~ you ask, we're going to be married** мы собирáемся жени́ться, éсли хоти́те знать.
sincere [sɪn'sɪə(r)] *adj.* и́скренний; **he was ~ in what he said** он э́то говори́л и́скренне; **a ~ friend** и́стинный друг; **yours ~ly** и́скренне Ваш.
sincerity [sɪn'serɪtɪ] *n.* и́скренность.
sine [saɪn] *n.* си́нус.
sinecure ['saɪnɪ,kjʊə(r), 'sɪn-] *n.* синекýра.
sine die [,saɪnɪ 'daɪɪ, ,sɪneɪ 'di:eɪ] *adv.* на неопределённый срок; без назначéния нóвой дáты.
sine qua non [,sɪneɪ kwɑ: 'nəʊn] *n.* непремéнное/обязáтельное.
sinew ['sɪnju:] *n.* **1.** (*tendon*) сухожи́лие; (*pl., muscles*) жи́лы (*f. pl.*); (*pl., strength*) си́ла; **a man of mighty ~s** двужи́льный человéк. **2.** (*fig., resources*) ресýрсы (*m. pl.*).
sinewy ['sɪnju:ɪ] *adj.* (*muscular*): **~ arms** мýскулистые/жи́листые рýки; (*tough*): **~ meat** жи́листое мя́со.
sinful ['sɪnfʊl] *adj.* грéшный, грехóвный.
sinfulness ['sɪnfʊlnɪs] *n.* грехóвность.
sing [sɪŋ] *v.t.* петь, с-/про-; **~ a baby to sleep** убаю́к|ивать, -ать ребёнка пéнием; (*fig.*): **~ s.o.'s praises** восхваля́ть (*impf.*) когó-н.; петь (*impf.*) хвалý комý-н.
v.i. петь, с-; (*a role, song etc.*) исп|олня́ть, -óлнить; **~ in tune** петь (*impf.*) прáвильно; **~ out of tune** петь (*impf.*) фальши́во; фальши́вить, с-; **she sang to the guitar** онá пéла под гитáру; **~ small** (*coll.*) сбáвить (*pf.*) тон; присмирéть (*pf.*); **Homer sang of the Trojan War** Гомéр воспевáл Троя́нскую войнý; **my ears are ~ing** у меня́ звени́т в ушáх; **a bullet sang over his head** пýля просвистéла над егó головóй.
with advs.: **~ out** *v.i.* (*coll., shout*) кри́кнуть (*pf.*); закричáть (*pf.*); **~ up** *v.i.* петь, за- грóмче.
cpd. **~-song** *n.* **1.** (*impromptu ~ing*) импровизи́рованный (вокáльный) концéрт; **we had a ~-song** мы попéли. **2.** (*rising and falling speech*) певýчая речь; *adj.*: **in a ~-song voice** певýчим гóлосом.
Singapore [,sɪŋə'pɔ:(r), ,sɪŋgə-] *n.* Сингапýр.
Singaporean [,sɪŋə'pɔ:rɪən, ,sɪŋgə-] *n.* сингапýр|ец (*fem.* -ка).
adj. сингапýрский.
singe [sɪndʒ] *n.* ожóг.
v.t. пали́ть (*or* опáливать), о-; **~ one's wings** (*fig.*) опáл|ивать, -и́ть кры́лья; обж|игáться, -éчься; **have one's hair ~d** подпали́ть (*pf.*) вóлосы.
v.i.: **something is ~ing** чтó-то гори́т; пáхнет палёным.
singer ['sɪŋə(r)] *n.* пев|éц (*fem.* -и́ца).
cpd. **~-songwriter** *n.* шансонье́ (*m. indecl.*).
Singhalese [,sɪŋghə'li:z, ,sɪŋgə'li:z] = **Sinhalese**
singing ['sɪŋɪŋ] *n.* пéние; **she has a good ~ voice** у неё хорóший гóлос.
single ['sɪŋg(ə)l] *n.* (*ticket*) билéт в оди́н конéц; (*pl., of tennis etc.*) одинóчная игрá.
adj. **1.** (*one*) оди́н; (*only one*) еди́нственный, еди́ный; **not a ~ man moved** ни оди́н человéк не дви́нулся; **a ~ idea occupied his mind** однá еди́нственная мысль занимáла егó ум; **I haven't met a ~ soul** я ни еди́ной дýши не встрéтил; **he didn't say a ~ word** он не произнёс ни (одногó) слóва; **in ~ file** гуськóм; **~ line** (*rail.*) одноколéйная дорóга; **~ quotes** кавы́чки в оди́н штрих; (*for or involving one pers.*): **~ bed** односпáльная кровáть; **~ room** одинóчный нóмер; **~ combat** единобóрство; (*taken individually*): **every ~ one of his pupils passed** все егó учени́ки до еди́ного прошли́. **2.** (*unmarried*) холостóй; незáмужняя; **lead a ~ life** вести́ (*det.*) холостýю жизнь; **~ father** отéц-одинóчка; **~ mother** мать-одинóчка; **she stayed ~ all her life** онá до концá своéй жи́зни так и не вы́шла зáмуж. **3.** (*consistent*): **with a ~ mind** послéдовательно; целеустремлённо.
v.t.: **~ out**: **he was ~d out** егó вы́делили; **he ~d out the largest plums** он отобрáл сáмые крýпные сли́вы.
cpds. **~-barrelled** *adj.* одноствóльный; **~-breasted** *adj.* однобóртный; **~-decker** *n.* (*bus*) одноэтáжный автóбус; **~-entry** *adj.* (*comm.*): **~-entry bookkeeping** простáя бухгалтéрия; **~-handed** *adj.* & *adv.* (*unaided*) без посторóнней пóмощи; **~-hearted** *adj.* (*sincere*) прямодýшный; **~-line** *adj.*: **~-line traffic** движéние в оди́н ряд; **~-minded** *adj.* прéданный одномý дéлу; целеустремлённый; **~-seater** *n.* (*plane*) одномéстный самолёт; **~-sex** *adj.*: **~-sex school** шкóла раздéльного обучéния; **~-track** *adj.* (*rail.*) одноколéйный.
singleness ['sɪŋgəlnɪs] *n.*: **~ of purpose** целеустремлённость.
singlet ['sɪŋglɪt] *n.* мáйка.
singleton ['sɪŋg(ə)lt(ə)n] *n.* (*cards*) еди́нственная кáрта дáнной мáсти.
singly ['sɪŋglɪ] *adv.* (*separately*) врозь; в отдéльности; **these articles are sold ~** э́ти вéщи продаю́тся поштýчно.
singular ['sɪŋgjʊlə(r)] *n.* (*gram.*) еди́нственное числó.
adj. **1.** (*gram.*) еди́нственный. **2.** (*rare, unusual*) необычáйный; (*odd*) стрáнный. **3.** (*outstanding*) чрезвычáйный; **she was ~ly beautiful** онá былá необычáйно/исключи́тельно хорошá.
singularity [,sɪŋgjʊ'lærɪtɪ] *n.* (*peculiarity*) осóбенность; (*uncommonness; oddness*) необы́чность; стрáнность.
singularize ['sɪŋgjʊlə,raɪz] *v.t.* (*distinguish*) выделя́ть, вы́делить.
Sin|halese [,sɪnhə'li:z, ,sɪnə'li:z], **Sing-** [,sɪŋghə'li:z, ,sɪŋgə'li:z] *n.* (*pers.*) сингáлец, сингáл (*fem.* -ка); (*language*) сингáльский язы́к.
adj. сингáльский.
sinister ['sɪnɪstə(r)] *adj.* **1.** зловéщий; **a ~ plot** ковáрный

зáговор; **a ~ character** тёмная ли́чность. **2.: bar ~** (*fig.*) незаконнорождённость.

sink [sɪŋk] *n.* **1.** (*in kitchen etc.*) ра́ковина. **2.** (*cesspool*) клоа́ка; (*fig.*): **~ of iniquity** верте́п.

v.t. **1.: ~ a ship** топи́ть, по- су́дно; (*coll., fig.*): **~ a plan** провали́ть (*pf.*) план; **we're sunk** (*coll.*) мы поги́бли!; (*immerse*): **sunk in thought** погружённый в размышле́ния. **2.** (*lower*) опус|ка́ть, -ти́ть; **she sank her head on to the pillow** она́ опусти́ла го́лову на поду́шку; **he sank his voice to a whisper** он пони́зил го́лос до шёпота; (*drink down*): **he can ~ a pint in ten seconds** он спосо́бен вы́хлестнуть (*coll.*) пи́нту (пи́ва) за де́сять секу́нд. **3.** (*set aside, forget, ignore*): **let us ~ our differences** забу́дем на́ши разногла́сия!; **he sank his own interests in the common good** он поступи́лся со́бственными интере́сами ра́ди о́бщих. **4.** (*drive, plunge*): **~ a post six feet into the earth** вк|а́пывать, -опа́ть столб в зе́млю на шесть фу́тов; **~ a pile** погру|жа́ть, -зи́ть сва́ю; (*fig.*): **the dog sank its teeth into his leg** соба́ка вонзи́ла зу́бы в его́ но́гу. **5.** (*invest*) вкла́дывать, вложи́ть; **he sank all his capital in property** он вложи́л весь капита́л в недви́жимость. **6.** (*excavate*): **~ a well** рыть, вы- (*or* углуб|ля́ть, -и́ть) коло́дец; **~ a shaft** про|ходи́ть, -йти́ ша́хтный ствол. **7.** (*engrave*): **~ a die** выреза́ть, вы́-штамп.

v.i. **1.** (*in water etc.*) тону́ть, за-; погру|жа́ться, -зи́ться; идти́ (*det*), пойти́ ко дну; **the ship sank with all hands** су́дно затону́ло вме́сте со всем экипа́жем; **he sank to his knees in mud** он по коле́но провали́лся в грязь; **the bather sank like a stone** купа́льщик ка́мнем пошёл ко дну; **~ or swim** ли́бо пан, ли́бо пропа́л; **he was left to ~ or swim** его́ бро́сили на произво́л судьбы́. **2.** (*disappear*) исч|еза́ть, -е́знуть; скр|ыва́ться, -ы́ться; (*below the horizon*) па́дать, упа́сть; за|ходи́ть, -йти́; **the sun ~s in the west** со́лнце захо́дит на за́паде. **3.** (*subside, of water*) спа|да́ть, -сть; (*of building or soil*) ос|еда́ть, -е́сть. **4.** (*abate*) ослаб|ева́ть, -е́ть. **5.** (*get lower*) па́дать, упа́сть; **his voice sank** его́ го́лос упа́л; **prices were ~ing** це́ны (ре́зко) па́дали/снижа́лись. **6.** (*fall*): **his head sank back on the pillow** его́ голова́ отки́нулась на поду́шку; **she sank into a coma** она́ впа́ла в комато́зное состоя́ние; **I sank into a deep sleep** я погрузи́лся в глубо́кий сон; (*fig.*): **he has sunk in my estimation** он упа́л в мои́х глаза́х; **my heart sank** у меня́ упа́ло се́рдце; **his spirits sank** он пал ду́хом; **they sank into poverty** они́ впа́ли в нищету́. **7.** (*become hollow*) впа|да́ть, -сть; **his cheeks have sunk** его́ щёки впа́ли. **8.** (*percolate, penetrate*) впи́т|ываться, -а́ться; вп|ива́ться, -и́ться; **the dye ~s into the fabric** кра́ска впи́тывается в ткань; **the rain sank into the dry ground** дождь пропита́л суху́ю зе́млю; (*fig.*): **~ into the ground** провали́ться (*pf.*) сквозь зе́млю; **the lesson sank into his mind** уро́к ему́ хорошо́ запо́мнился; **his words sank in** его́ слова́ не прошли́ да́ром. **9.** (*approach death*): **he is ~ing** он угаса́ет.

sinker ['sɪŋkə(r)] *n.* (*lead weight*) грузи́ло.

sinking ['sɪŋkɪŋ] *n.* (*of ship*) потопле́ние; (*of one's strength*) поте́ря сил; ослабе́ние; (*of voice*) пониже́ние (го́лоса); (*of a well etc.*) выка́пывание; (*of debt*) погаше́ние; **~ fund** фонд погаше́ния.

sinless ['sɪnlɪs] *adj.* безгре́шный.

sinner ['sɪnə(r)] *n.* гре́шни|к (*fem.* -ца).

Sino- ['saɪnəʊ] *comb. form* кита́йско-...

sinologist [saɪ'nɒlədʒɪst, sɪ-] *n.* китаи́ст, сино́лог.

sinology [saɪ'nɒlədʒɪ, sɪ-] *n.* китаеве́дение.

sinuosity [,sɪnjʊ'ɒsɪtɪ] *n.* изви́лина, изви́листость.

sinuous ['sɪnjʊəs] *adj.* (*serpentine*) изви́листый; (*undulating*) волни́стый.

sinus ['saɪnəs] *n.* (*anat.*) па́зуха; **frontal ~es** ло́бные па́зухи.

sinusitis [,saɪnə'saɪtɪs] *n.* синуси́т.

Sioux [su:] *n.* си́у (*m. indecl.*).

sip [sɪp] *n.* глото́к; **have, take a ~ of** глотну́ть (*pf.*); вы́пить (*pf.*) глото́к +*g.*

v.t. потя́гивать (*impf.*).

si|phon, sy- ['saɪf(ə)n] *n.* сифо́н.

v.t. **~ off, out** выка́чивать, вы́качать сифо́ном; (*fig.*) перек|а́чивать, -ача́ть.

v.i. ст|ека́ть, -ечь.

sir [sɜ:(r)] *n.* (*form of address; title*) сэр, су́дарь (*m.*), господи́н; **Dear S~** (*in letters*) Многоуважа́емый господи́н.

v.t. велича́ть (*impf.*) сэ́ром.

sire ['saɪə(r)] *n.* **1.** (*father*) оте́ц; (*ancestor*) пре́док. **2.** (*stallion etc.*) производи́тель (*m.*). **3.** (*Your Majesty*) ва́ше вели́чество.

v.t. произвести́ (*pf.*) на свет; **the stallion ~d twenty foals** от э́того жеребца́ родило́сь 20 жереба́т; **~d by** рождённый от+*g.*

siren ['saɪərən] *n.* (*myth., fig.*) сире́на; (*hooter*) сире́на, гудо́к; **~ suit** комбинезо́н (из тёмной тка́ни).

Sirius ['sɪrɪəs] *n.* Си́риус.

sirloin ['sɜ:lɔɪn] *n.* филе́ (*indecl.*); филе́йная часть (ту́ши).

sirocco, scirocco [sɪ'rɒkəʊ] *n.* сиро́кко (*m. indecl.*).

sisal ['saɪs(ə)l] *n.* сиза́ль (*m.*).

siskin ['sɪskɪn] *n.* чиж, чи́жик.

sissy ['sɪsɪ] *n.* (*coll.*) «девчо́нка», не́женка (*c.g.*); ма́менькин сыно́к; (*coll.*) слаба́к.

adj. изне́женный, женоподо́бный.

sister ['sɪstə(r)] *n.* сестра́; **full ~** родна́я сестра́; (*nun*): **S~ of Mercy** сестра́ милосе́рдия; (*nursing ~*) (ста́ршая) медици́нская сестра́; (*attr.*): **~ nations** бра́тские стра́ны; **~ ship** однoти́пное су́дно.

cpd. **~-in-law** *n.* (*brother's wife*) неве́стка; (*husband's sister*) золо́вка; (*wife's sister*) своя́ченица.

sisterhood ['sɪstə,hʊd] *n.* (*relig.*) се́стринская общи́на.

sisterly ['sɪstəlɪ] *adj.* се́стринский.

Sistine Chapel ['sɪsti:n, 'sɪstaɪn] *n.* Сиксти́нская капе́лла.

Sisyphean [,sɪzɪ'fi:ən] *adj.*: **a ~ task** сизи́фов труд.

sit [sɪt] *v.t.* **1.** (*seat*) сажа́ть, посади́ть; уса́|живать, -ди́ть; **they sat the old lady by the fire** стару́шку посади́ли у огня́; (*of several persons*) расса́|живать, -ди́ть; **I don't know if I can ~ you all round the table** бою́сь, что вы все не поме́ститесь за э́тим сто́лом; **~ you/yourself down!** (*coll.*) сади́тесь! **2.: he ~s his horse well** он хорошо́ де́ржится в седле́. **3.** (*undergo*): **~ an examination** держа́ть/сдава́ть (*impf.*) экза́мен.

v.i. **1.** (*take a seat*) сади́ться, сесть. **2.** (*be seated*) сиде́ть (*impf.*); **he can't ~ still** ему́ не сиди́тся (на ме́сте); **~** (*stay*) **at home** сиде́ть (*impf.*) до́ма; **~ tight** (*stick to one's position*) не сдава́ться (*impf.*); не уступа́ть (*impf.*); держа́ться (*impf.*) (своего́); **~ on** (*coll., snub*) **s.o.** осади́ть (*pf.*) кого́-н.; **~ on a committee** быть чле́ном комите́та; **~ on sth.** (*shelve it*) класть (*impf.*) что-н. под сукно́; (*of hens*: **~** *on eggs*) выси́живать (*impf.*) цыпля́т; (*of birds: perch*) сиде́ть (*impf.*); **~ting duck, target** (*fig.*) лёгкая мише́нь; гото́вая же́ртва. **3.** (*pose*): **~ to an artist** пози́ровать (*impf.*) худо́жнику; **~ for one's photograph** фотографи́роваться (*impf*). **4.** (*hold meeting; be in session*) заседа́ть (*impf.*); **the committee ~s at 10** заседа́ние комите́та начина́ется в 10 часо́в; **he sat on the committee** он был чле́ном комите́та; **~ on a case** разбира́ть (*impf.*) де́ло. **5.** (*be candidate*): **~ for an exam** держа́ть (*impf.*) экза́мен; **~ for a constituency** представля́ть (*impf.*) о́круг в парла́менте. **6.** (*of clothes: fit, hang*): **his coat does not ~ properly on his shoulders** его́ пиджа́к пло́хо сиди́т в плеча́х. **7.** (*weigh*): **the large dinner sat heavily on my stomach** от оби́льного у́жина я испы́тывал тя́жесть в желу́дке; **his principles ~ lightly on him; he ~s loosely to his principles** он не сли́шком(-то) стеснён свои́ми при́нципами. **8.: the wind ~s in the east** ве́тер ду́ет с восто́ка.

with advs.: **~ back** *v.i.* (*lit.*) отки́|дываться, -нуться; (*fig., relax effort*) безде́йствовать (*impf.*); **~ down** *v.t.* сажа́ть, посади́ть; уса́|живать, -ди́ть; *v.i.* сади́ться, сесть; (*for a moment*) прис|а́живаться, -е́сть; **~ down under an insult** (безро́потно) сн|оси́ть, -ести́ оскорбле́ние; **~ in** *v.i.* (*occupy premises in protest*) зан|има́ть, -я́ть помеще́ние в знак проте́ста; **~ in** (*deputize*) **for s.o.** замеща́ть (*impf.*) кого́-н.; (*act as baby-sitter*) сиде́ть (*impf.*) с (чужи́м) ребёнком; **~ in on a meeting** прису́тствовать (*impf.*) на собра́нии; **~ out** *v.t.* (*take no* *part in*): **I have decided to ~ this one** (*dance*) **out** я реши́л пропусти́ть э́тот та́нец; (*stay to end of*) выси́живать, вы́сидеть; (*outstay*) переси|живать, -де́ть; *v.i.* (~ *outdoors*) сиде́ть (*impf.*) на во́здухе; ~ **through** *v.t.*: **we sat through the concert** мы вы́сидели весь конце́рт; ~ **up** *v.i.* (*from lying position*): **he sat up in bed** он приподня́лся (и сел) в посте́ли; (*straighten one's back*) сиде́ть (*impf.*) пря́мо; вы́прямиться (*pf.*); (*not go to bed*) заси́|живаться, -де́ться; **we sat up all night with the invalid** мы просиде́ли всю ночь с больны́м; **don't ~ up for me** не жди́те меня́, ложи́тесь спать; (*coll., be startled*): **the news made him ~ up** э́та но́вость его́ огоро́шила.

cpds. **~-down** *adj.*: **a ~-down strike** сидя́чая забасто́вка; **~-in** *n.* демонстрати́вное заня́тие помеще́ния; **~-upon** *n.* (*coll.*) за́дница.

sitcom ['sɪtkɒm] *n.* (*coll.*) коме́дия положе́ний.

site [saɪt] *n.* (*place*) ме́сто; (*position*) положе́ние; (*location*) местоположе́ние, местонахожде́ние; **building ~** строи́тельный уча́сток.

v.t. **1.** (*arrange, dispose*) распол|ага́ть, -ожи́ть. **2.** (*choose ~ of*) выбира́ть, вы́брать ме́сто для+*g.* **3.** (*locate*): **the house is ~d on a slope** дом располо́жен на скло́не горы́/холма́.

sitter ['sɪtə(r)] *n.* **1.** (*pers. sitting for portrait*) моде́ль; тот/та, кто пози́рует худо́жнику (*и т.п.*) для портре́та. **2.** (*hen*) насе́дка. **3.** (*baby-~*) ≃ приходя́щая ня́ня. **4.** (*sth. easily done*) па́ра пустяко́в (*coll.*).

sitting ['sɪtɪŋ] *n.* **1.** сиде́ние. **2.** (*session*) заседа́ние; **the first ~ for lunch is at 12 o'clock** за́втрак для пе́рвой о́череди подаётся в 12 часо́в; **at one ~** в оди́н присе́ст. **3.** (*posing*) пози́рование; **two ~s** два сеа́нса.

cpd. **~-room** *n.* гости́ная.

situate ['sɪtjʊˌeɪt] *v.t.* поме|ща́ть, -сти́ть; распол|ага́ть, -ожи́ть.

situated ['sɪtjʊˌeɪtɪd] *adj.* **1.** (*of buildings etc.*) располо́женный; **a pleasantly ~ house** дом, располо́женный в краси́вой ме́стности. **2.** (*of pers.*): **I am awkwardly ~** я нахожу́сь в затрудни́тельном положе́нии; **this is how I am ~** таковы́ мои обстоя́тельства; **how are you ~ for money?** как у вас (обстои́т) с деньга́ми?

situation [ˌsɪtjʊ'eɪʃ(ə)n] *n.* **1.** (*place*) ме́сто; (*position*) местоположе́ние. **2.** (*circumstances*) обстано́вка, положе́ние, ситуа́ция; **what is the ~?** каково́ положе́ние дел?; какова́ обстано́вка? **3.** (*job*) пост, ме́сто; **~s vacant** (*as column heading*) вака́нтные до́лжности; тре́буется рабо́чая си́ла.

six [sɪks] *n.* (число́/но́мер) шесть; (~ *people*) ше́стеро, шесть челове́к; **we ~, the ~ of us** мы ше́стеро/вшестеро́м; **~ each** по шести́; **in ~es, ~ at a time** по шести́, шестёрками; (*figure; thg. numbered 6; group of ~*) шестёрка; (*with var. nn. expr. or understood: cf. also examples under* **five**): **it is ~ of one and half a dozen of the other** э́то одно́ и то же; что в лоб, что по́ лбу; оди́н друго́го сто́ит; **everything is at ~es and sevens** всё вверх дном; **the news knocked me for ~** э́та но́вость меня́ огоро́шила (*coll.*); **he threw a ~** (*dice*) у него́ вы́пала шестёрка; **double ~** (*domino*) ду́пель (*m.*) шесть.

adj. шесть +*g. pl.*; **~ feet high** шесть фу́тов высото́й; (*for people and pluralia tantum also*) ше́стеро +*g. pl.*; **~ fives are thirty** ше́стью (*or* шесть на) пять — три́дцать; **~ times as good** вше́стеро (*or* в шесть раз) лу́чше.

cpds. **~fold** *adj.* шестикра́тный; *adv.* вше́стеро; в шесть раз; **~-foot** *adj.* шестифу́товый; **~-shooter** *n.* шестизаря́дный револьве́р; **~-sided** *adj.* шестисторо́нний, шестигра́нный.

sixteen [ˌsɪks'ti:n, 'sɪks-] *n. & adj.* шестна́дцать (+*g. pl.*).

sixteenth [ˌsɪks'ti:nθ, 'sɪks-] *n.* **1.** (*date*) шестна́дцатое (число́). **2.** (*fraction*) шестна́дцатая часть; одна́ шестна́дцатая.

adj. шестна́дцатый.

sixth [sɪksθ] *n.* **1.** (*date*) шесто́е (число́). **2.** (*fraction*) шеста́я часть; одна́ шеста́я; **five ~s** пять шесты́х. **3.** (*mus.*) се́кста.

adj. шесто́й; **in the ~ form** в ста́ршем кла́ссе; **~ sense** шесто́е чу́вство.

sixthly ['sɪksθlɪ] *adv.* в-шесты́х.

sixtieth ['sɪkstɪɪθ] *n.* шестидеся́тая часть; одна́ шестидеся́тая.

adj. шестидеся́тый.

sixt|y ['sɪkstɪ] *n.* шестьдеся́т; **he is in his ~ies** ему́ за шестьдеся́т (лет); он на седьмо́м деся́тке; **in the ~ies** (*decade*) в шестидеся́тых года́х; в шестидеся́тые го́ды; (*temperature*) за шестьдеся́т гра́дусов (по Фаренге́йту).

adj. шестьдеся́т +*g. pl.*

sizable ['saɪzəb(ə)l] = **siz(e)able**

size[1] [saɪz] *n.* **1.** (*dimension, magnitude*) разме́р; величина́; **what is the ~ of the house?** какова́ пло́щадь э́того до́ма?; **what ~ will the army be?** какова́ бу́дет чи́сленность а́рмии?; **a dog of enormous ~** огро́мная соба́ка; **these books are all the same ~** э́ти кни́ги все одного́ форма́та; **a wave the ~ of a house** волна́, величино́й/высото́й с дом; **that's about the ~ of it** (*coll.*) та́к-то обстои́т де́ло; **cut s.o. down to ~** (*coll.*) ста́вить, по- кого́-н. на ме́сто. **2.** (*of clothes etc.*): **~ 4** четвёртый разме́р/но́мер; **what is your ~?; what ~ do you take?** како́й у вас но́мер?; **the dress is just her ~** э́то пла́тье как раз её разме́ра; **I take ~ 10 in shoes** я ношу́ (*or* у меня́) со́рок второ́й но́мер о́буви; **these are three ~s too big** э́ти на три но́мера велики́; **they are made in several ~s** они́ быва́ют разли́чных разме́ров.

v.t. **1.** сорти́ровать, рас- по разме́ру. **2.**: **~ s.o. up** оце́н|ивать, -и́ть кого́-н.; сост|авля́ть, -а́вить о ком-н. мне́ние; **~ up the situation** определи́ть/взве́сить (*pf.*) обстано́вку.

size[2] [saɪz] *n.* (*for glazing paper, walls etc.*) клей, грунт; (*for textile*) шлихта.

v.t.: **~ a wall** окле́и|вать, -ть сте́ну; **~ paper** прокле́и|вать, -ть бума́гу; **~ cloth** шлихтова́ть (*impf.*) сукно́; **~ canvas** грунтова́ть, за- холст.

siz(e)able ['saɪzəb(ə)l] *adj.* значи́тельного разме́ра; поря́дочный, изря́дный.

sizzl|e ['sɪz(ə)l] *n.* шипе́ние.

v.i. шипе́ть (*impf.*); **a ~ing hot day** зно́йный (*or* о́чень жа́ркий) день.

skate[1] [skeɪt] *n.* (*ice-~*) конёк; **get one's ~s on** (*lit.*) над|ева́ть, -е́ть коньки́; (*fig., hurry*) потора́пливаться (*impf.*); (**roller-~**) ро́лик; ро́ликовый конёк.

v.i. **1.** (*on ice*) ката́ться/бе́гать (*both indet.*) на конька́х; (*on roller-~s*) ката́ться (*indet.*) на ро́ликах; **~ on thin ice** (*fig.*) прик|аса́ться, -осну́ться к щекотли́вой те́ме; игра́ть (*impf.*) с огнём; **~ over, round sth.** (*fig.*) каса́ться, косну́ться чего́-н. вскользь; об|ходи́ть, -ойти́ что-н. **2.** (*slide, skid*) скользи́ть (*impf.*) (по пове́рхности).

cpds. **~board** *n.* ро́ликовая *or* ро́ллинговая доска́; **~boarder** *n.* скейтборди́ст (*fem.* -ка); **~boarding** *n.* скейтбординг.

skate[2] [skeɪt] *n.* (*fish*) скат.

skater ['skeɪtə(r)] *n.* конькобе́ж|ец (*fem. also* -ка).

skating ['skeɪtɪŋ] *n.* бег/ката́ние на конька́х; конькобе́жный спорт; **free(-style) ~** произво́льное ката́ние; **pair ~** па́рное ката́ние.

cpd. **~-rink** *n.* като́к.

skedaddle [skɪ'dæd(ə)l] (*coll.*) *n.*: **there was a general ~** все бро́сились врассыпну́ю.

v.i. улепёт|ывать, -ну́ть (*coll.*); **~!** кати́сь! (*coll.*)

skein [skeɪn] *n.* (*of wool etc.*) мото́к пря́жи.

skeletal ['skelɪtəl] *adj.* скеле́тный, скелетообра́зный, скелетоподо́бный.

skeleton ['skelɪt(ə)n] *n.* **1.** скеле́т, костя́к; **~ in the cupboard** (*fig.*) семе́йная та́йна; **~ at the feast** (*fig.*) «мертве́ц». **2.** (*fig., outline*) костя́к, схе́ма. **3.** (*framework*) скеле́т, о́стов, карка́с, костя́к. **4.** (*emaciated pers.*) ко́жа да ко́сти. **5.** (*attr.*): **~ crew/staff** минима́льный экипа́ж/штат; **~ key** отмы́чка.

skep [skep], **skip** [skɪp] *n.* (*basket*) плетёнка; (*beehive*) (соло́менный) у́лей; (*tub*) бадья́.

skeptic ['skeptɪk], **-al** ['skeptɪk(ə)l] = **sceptic, -al**

sketch [sketʃ] *n.* **1.** (*artistic*) эски́з, набро́сок, зарисо́вка. **2.** (*verbal account*) (бе́глый) о́черк. **3.** (*play*) скетч.

v.t. (*draw, lit., fig.*) набр|а́сывать, -оса́ть; **he ~ed in the details** он наброса́л дета́ли; **he ~ed out his plans** он обрисова́л свои́ пла́ны в о́бщих черта́х.

v.i. рисова́ть (*impf.*); де́лать (*impf.*) набро́ски.

cpds. **~-block, ~-book** *nn.* альбо́м; блокно́т; **~-map** *n.* схемати́ческая ка́рта.

sketching ['sketʃɪŋ] *n.* рисова́ниеески́зов; рабо́та над набро́сками.

sketchy ['sketʃɪ] *adj.* (*in outline*) схемати́ческий, схемати́чный; (*superficial*) пове́рхностный; (*fragmentary*) отры́вочный, эски́зный, небре́жный.

skew [skju:] *n.*: **on the ~** кри́во, ко́со, на́искось, наискосо́к.
adj. (*coll.* **~-whiff**) косо́й; (*math.*) асимметри́чный.
cpd. **~bald** *adj.* пе́гий.

skewer ['skju:ə(r)] *n.* ве́ртел.
v.t. наса́|живать, -ди́ть на ве́ртел; (*fig.*) пронз|а́ть, -и́ть.

ski [ski:] *n.* лы́жа.
v.i. ходи́ть (*indet.*) на лы́жах.
cpds. **~-boots** *n. pl.* лы́жные боти́нки (*m. pl.*); **~-joring** *n.* лы́жная буксиро́вка за ло́шадью; **~-jump** *n.* лы́жный трампли́н; **~-jumping** *n.* прыжки́ (*m. pl.*) на лы́жах с трампли́на; **~-lift** *n.* подъёмник; **~-pants** *n. pl.* лы́жные брю́к|и (*pl., g.* —); **~-run, ~-track** *nn.* лыжня́.

skid [skɪd] *n.* **1.** (*slipping, e.g. of engine-wheel*) буксова́ние; **go into a ~** забуксова́ть (*pf.*); (*of car*) зано́с; юз; **the car went into a ~** маши́ну занесло́. **2.** (*braking device*) тормозна́я коло́дка. **3.** (*supporting piece of timber etc.*): **put the ~s under** (*fig.*) уск|оря́ть, -о́рить коне́ц/паде́ние (кого).
v.i. (*of wheels*) буксова́ть, за-; (*of car*) пойти́ (*pf.*) ю́зом; *see also n.* **1.**
cpds. **~-chain** *n.* цепь противоскольже́ния; **~-lid** *n.* (*sl.*) шлем мотоцикли́ста; **~-proof** *adj.* неподдающийся зано́су; нескользя́щий; **~-row** *n.* (*US*) райо́н алкаше́й (*coll.*) и бродя́г.

skier ['ski:ə(r)] *n.* лы́жник.

skiff [skɪf] *n.* я́лик, скиф-одино́чка.

skiing ['ski:ɪŋ] *n.* лы́жный спорт.

skilful ['skɪlfʊl] (*US* **skillful**) *adj.* иску́сный, уме́лый, ло́вкий, о́пытный; (*in sport*) техни́чный.

skill [skɪl] *n.* иску́сство; (*competence*) уме́ние; (*dexterity*) ло́вкость; (*technique*) мастерство́, снаро́вка.

skilled [skɪld] *adj.* иску́сный; (*highly-trained*) квалифици́рованный, о́пытный; **~ labour** квалифици́рованная рабо́та.

skillet ['skɪlɪt] *n.* кастрю́лька на но́жках с дли́нной ру́чкой; (*US*) сковорода́.

skillful ['skɪlfʊl] = **skilful**

skim [skɪm] *adj.*: **~ milk** снято́е молоко́.
v.t. **1.**: **~ a liquid** сн|има́ть, -ять на́кипь с жи́дкости; **~ milk** сн|има́ть, -ять сли́вки (с молока́). **2.** (*remove*): **~ the grease from, off the soup** сн|има́ть, -ять жир с су́па; **~ the cream off sth.** (*fig.*) сн|има́ть, -ять сли́вки/пе́нки с чего́-н. **3.** (*move lightly over*): **~ the ground** лете́ть (*det.*) над са́мой землёй. **4.** (*scan through*) пробе|га́ть, -жа́ть; (*book etc.*) чита́ть (*impf.*) «по диагона́ли»; (*touch on*) бе́гло каса́ться, косну́ться вопро́са.

skimmer ['skɪmə(r)] *n.* **1.** (*ladle*) шумо́вка. **2.** (*for milk*) сепара́тор.

skimp [skɪmp] *v.t.* скупи́ться (*impf.*) на+*a.*; **~ one's work** халту́рить, с-; манки́ровать (*impf., pf.*) рабо́той.
v.i. эконо́мничать (*impf.*).

skimpy ['skɪmpɪ] *adj.* (*meagre*) ску́дный; (*of clothes: short or tight*) те́сный, у́зкий.

skin [skɪn] *n.* **1.** ко́жа; **clear ~** чи́стая ко́жа; **dark ~** сму́глая/тёмная ко́жа; **~ disease** ко́жная боле́знь; **take the ~ off one's knees** сдира́ть, содра́ть ко́жу на коле́нях; ссади́ть (*pf.*) (*or* ободра́ть (*pf.*)) коле́ни; **it's no ~ off my nose** (*coll.*) а мне́-то что?; **he has a thick ~** (*fig.*) он толстоко́жий, у него́ то́лстая ко́жа; **strip to the ~** разд|ева́ться, -е́ться донага́; **I got soaked to the ~** я промо́к до (после́дней) ни́тки; **get under s.o.'s ~** (*annoy intensely*) раздража́ть (*impf.*) кого́-н.; де́йствовать кому́-н. на не́рвы; беси́ть (*impf.*) кого́-н.; **I nearly jumped out of my ~** я так и подскочи́л от неожи́данности; **fear for one's ~** дрожа́ть (*impf.*) за свою́ шку́ру; **save one's ~** спас|а́ть, -ти́ свою́ шку́ру; **escape by the ~ of one's teeth** чу́дом спасти́сь (*pf.*); **he was all ~ and bone** от него́ оста́лась одна́ ко́жа да ко́сти. **2.** (*of animal: hide*) шку́ра; **leopard ~** шку́ра леопа́рда; **rabbit ~** кро́личья шку́рка; (*fur*) мех (*pl.* -а́). **3.** (*for wine etc.*) мех (*pl.* -и́). **4.** (*of fruit*) кожура́; (*of grape*) ко́жица; (*of sausage*) кожура́, ко́жица; **orange/lemon ~** апельси́нная/лимо́нная ко́рка. **5.** (*of ship, aeroplane*) обши́вка. **6.** (*on liquid etc.*) пе́нка.
v.t. **1.** (*remove ~ from*) сн|има́ть, -ять шку́ру с+*g.*; свежева́ть, о-; **~ s.o. alive** сдира́ть, содра́ть с кого́-н. ко́жу за́живо. **2.** (*remove peel, rind from*) сн|има́ть, -ять кожуру́ с+*g.*; чи́стить, о-; **keep one's eyes ~ned** (*coll.*) смотре́ть (*impf.*) в о́ба. **3.** (*graze*) об|дира́ть, -одра́ть; **she ~ned her knee** она́ ободра́ла/ссади́ла себе́ коле́но. **4.** (*fleece*) об|ира́ть, -обра́ть; **they ~ned him of every penny** его́ обобра́ли до ни́тки.
v.i. (*also* **~ over**) зарубц|о́вываться, -ева́ться; заж|ива́ть, -и́ть.
cpds. **~-deep** *adj.* пове́рхностный; **~-diver** *n.* аквалангист; лёгкий водола́з; **~-diving** *n.* подво́дное пла́вание (с аквала́нгом); **~-flick** *n.* (фильм-)порну́шка (*coll.*); **~flint** *n.* скря́га (*c.g.*); **~-food** *n.* пита́тельный крем (для ко́жи); **~-graft** *n.* ко́жный транспланта́т; **~-grafting** *n.* переса́дка/транспланта́ция ко́жи; **~head** *n.* (*Br.*) «бритоголо́вый»; **~-tight** *adj.* в обтя́жку.

skinful ['skɪnfʊl] *n.*: **he had a ~** он как сле́дует нагрузи́лся (*coll.*).

skinner ['skɪnə(r)] *n.* (*furrier*) меховщи́к, скорня́к.

skinny ['skɪnɪ] *adj.* то́щий.
cpd. **~-dipping** *n.* (*US*) (*coll.*) купа́ние нагишо́м.

skint [skɪnt] *adj.*: **I'm ~** у меня́ ни копья́/шиша́ (нет) (*sl.*).

skip[1] [skɪp] *n.* скачо́к, прыжо́к.
v.t. (*fig.*) пропус|ка́ть, -ти́ть; **he ~ped the class** он пропусти́л/прогуля́л уро́к; **he ~ped a class** (*went up 2 classes*) он перескочи́л че́рез класс; **~ it!** (*coll.*) хва́тит!; нева́жно!
v.i. **1.** (*use ~ping-rope*) скака́ть (*impf.*) (че́рез верёвочку); **~ping rope** скака́лка; (*jump*): **she ~ped for joy** она́ подпры́гнула от ра́дости; **he ~ped across the brook** он перескочи́л (че́рез) руче́й. **2.** (*coll., go quickly or casually*): **he ~ped off without telling anyone** он ускака́л, никому́ ничего́ не сказа́в; **he ~ped from subject to subject** он переска́кивал с предме́та на предме́т; **I ~ped through the preface** я пробежа́л предисло́вие (глаза́ми); я бы́стро посмотре́л предисло́вие.

skip[2] [skɪp] = **skep**

skipper ['skɪpə(r)] *n.* (*captain*) шки́пер, капита́н.

skirl [skɜ:l] *n.*: **the ~ of pipes** звук волы́нки.

skirmish ['skɜ:mɪʃ] *n.* (*mil., fig.*) сты́чка; (коро́ткая) перестре́лка, схва́тка; **a ~ of wits** борьба́/состяза́ние умо́в.
v.i. (*mil.*) перестре́ливаться (*impf.*); (*fig.*) сцеп|ля́ться, -и́ться.

skirt [skɜ:t] *n.* (*garment; part of dress*) ю́бка; (*woman*) ба́ба (*coll.*); (*edge of forest*) опу́шка.
v.t. (*pass along edge of*): **we ~ed the crowd** мы обошли́ толпу́; **the ship ~ed the coast** су́дно шло вдоль бе́рега; (*form border of*): **the road ~s the forest** доро́га огиба́ет лес; **~ing-board** пли́нтус.
v.i.: **~ round** (*fig., avoid*) об|ходи́ть, -ойти́.

skit [skɪt] *n.* паро́дия, скетч, сати́ра (на+*a.*).

skittish ['skɪtɪʃ] *adj.* (*of horse etc.*) норови́стый; пугли́вый; (*of pers.*) капри́зный, игри́вый, коке́тливый.

skittle ['skɪt(ə)l] *n.* ке́гля; (*pl., game*) ке́гли (*f. pl.*); **it's not all beer and ~s** не всё заба́вы да развлече́ния.
cpd. **~-alley** *n.* кегельба́н.

skive [skaɪv] *v.t.* (*leather*) разр|еза́ть, -е́зать; слои́ть, рас-.
v.i. (*evade duty*) сачкова́ть (*impf.*) (*sl.*).

skiver ['skaɪvə(r)] *n.* сачо́к (*sl.*).

skivvy ['skɪvɪ] *n.* (*coll., pej.*) служа́нка.

skua ['skju:ə] *n.* помо́рник.

skuld|uggery, skulld- [skʌl'dʌgərɪ] надува́тельство, моше́нничество.

skulk [skʌlk] *v.i.* (*hide*) скрыва́ться, (*impf.*); пря́таться (*impf.*); (*lurk*) зата́иваться (*impf.*); (*slink*) кра́сться (*impf.*).

skull [skʌl] *n.* че́реп; **~ and cross bones** че́реп со скре́щенными костя́ми; **he has a thick ~** (*fig.*) он настоя́щий ме́дный лоб; **I tried to get it into his ~** я пыта́лся втемя́шить э́то ему́ (в го́лову).

cpd. ~**-cap** *n.* ермо́лка; (*Central Asian*) тюбете́йка; (*worn by Orthodox priests*) скуфе́йка, скуфья́.

skullduggery [skʌl'dʌgərɪ] *n.* = **skulduggery**

skunk [skʌŋk] *n.* воню́чка, ску́нс; (*fur*) ску́нсовый мех; (*coll., pers.*) подле́ц, подо́нок.

sky [skaɪ] *n.* **1.** не́бо; **there wasn't a cloud in the** ~ на не́бе не́ было ни о́блачка; **sleep under the open** ~ спать (*impf.*) под откры́тым не́бом; **praise s.o. to the skies** превозн|оси́ть, -ести́ кого́-н. до небе́с. **2.** (*climate*) кли́мат; **under warmer skies** в бо́лее тёплых края́х.

v.t.: ~ **a ball** высоко́ запусти́ть (*pf.*) мяч.

cpds. ~**-blue** *adj.* (небе́сно-)голубо́й; лазу́рный; ~**diver** *n.* парашюти́ст(-спортсме́н) (*fem.* -ка(-спортсме́нка)); ~**diving** *n.* парашю́тный спорт, парашюти́зм; затяжны́е прыжки́ с парашю́том; ~**-high** *adv.* высоко́ в во́здух; (*fig.*) до небе́с; до са́мого не́ба; **go** ~**-high** (*explode*) взлете́ть (*pf.*) на во́здух; ~**jack** *n.* уго́н (самолёта); *v.t.* уг|оня́ть, -на́ть; ~**jacker** *n.* уго́нщик (самолёта); ~**lark** *n.* полево́й жа́воронок; *v.i.* (*frolic etc.*) резви́ться (*impf.*); дура́читься (*impf.*); ~**light** *n.* ве́рхний свет; фона́рь (*m.*); ~**line** *n.* горизо́нт; силуэ́т; ~**-pilot** *n.* (*coll.*) свяще́нник, капелла́н; ~**-rocket** *n.* сигна́льная раке́та; *v.i.* (*fig.*) стреми́тельно подня́ться (*pf.*); бы́стро расти́ (*pf.*); ~**scraper** *n.* небоскрёб; ~**-sign** *n.* светова́я рекла́ма; ~**-wave** *n.* волна́, отражённая от ве́рхних слоёв атмосфе́ры; ~**-wave communication** связь на отражённой волне́; ~**way** *n.* возду́шная тра́сса; авиатра́сса; ~**-writing** *n.* прочёрчивание самолётом бу́квенных знако́в; возду́шная рекла́ма.

skywards ['skaɪwədz] *adv.* к не́бу; ввысь; вверх.

slab [slæb] *n.* (*of stone etc.*) плита́; ~ **of concrete** бето́нная плита́; (*of cake etc.*) кусо́к; (*of soap*) бруто́к; кусо́к.

slack[1] [slæk] *n.* **1.** (*loose part of rope, sail*) слабина́; **pull in (*or* take in, up) the** ~ подтя́|гивать, -ну́ть (*or* выбира́ть, вы́брать) слабину́; натя́|гивать, -ну́ть верёвку. **2.** (*pl., trousers*) (широ́кие) брю́к|и (*pl., g.* —). **3.** (~ *period of trade*) зати́шье.

adj. **1.** (*sluggish, slow*): **I feel** ~ **this morning** я сего́дня не в настрое́нии; **trade is** ~ торго́вля идёт вя́ло; в торго́вле засто́й; **demand is** ~ спрос небольшо́й; **at a** ~ **speed** (*of machine*) ти́хим хо́дом; ~ **water** стоя́ние прили́ва/отли́ва. **2.** (*of pers., lax*) расхля́банный; (*negligent*) небре́жный; **be** ~ **in one's work** хала́тно относи́ться (*impf.*) к рабо́те; рабо́тать (*impf.*) спустя́ рукава́; **grow** ~ распус|ка́ться, -ти́ться. **3.** (*loose; not taut*): ~ **rope** прови́сшая верёвка; ~ **muscles** дря́блые мы́шцы, дря́блая мускулату́ра; **ride with a** ~ **rein** е́хать (*det.*), отпусти́в пово́дья. **4.** (*quiet, inactive*): ~ **season, period** мёртвый сезо́н; зати́шье. **5.**: ~ **lime** гашёная и́звесть.

v.t. (*rope, sail, rein*) отпус|ка́ть, -ти́ть; осл|абля́ть, -а́бить.

v.i. **1.** (*also* ~ **off**) = **slacken** *v.i.* **2.** (*be indolent*) ло́дырничать (*impf.*); безде́льничать (*impf.*); гоня́ть (*impf.*) ло́дыря; **we** ~**ed off towards five** к пяти́ часа́м мы сба́вили темп (рабо́ты). **3.** ~ **up** (*reduce speed*) уб|авля́ть, -а́вить ско́рость; зам|едля́ть, -е́длить ход.

slack[2] [slæk] *n.* (*coal*) у́гольная ме́лочь/пыль.

slacken ['slækən] *v.t.* **1.** (*rope, rein*) отпус|ка́ть, -ти́ть; осл|абля́ть, -а́бить; (*sail*) приспус|ка́ть, -ти́ть; (*screw*) осл|абля́ть, -а́бить. **2.** (*diminish*): ~ **one's efforts** осл|абля́ть, -а́бить уси́лия; ~ **speed** уб|авля́ть, -а́вить ско́рость; зам|едля́ть, -е́длить ход.

v.i. **1.** (*also* **slack**) (*of rope*) пров|иса́ть, -и́снуть; (*of sail*) обв|иса́ть, -и́снуть; (*of screw, nut*) ослабе́ть (*pf.*); (*of knot*) развя́з|ываться, -а́ться. **2.** (*die down*): **demand is** ~**ing** спрос уменьша́ется; **the storm is** ~**ing** бу́ря стиха́ет.

slacker ['slækə(r)] *n.* ло́дырь (*m.*); безде́льни|к (*fem.* -ца).

slackness ['slæknɪs] *n.* небре́жность, расхля́банность.

slag [slæg] *n.* шлак.

cpd. ~**-heap** *n.* гру́да шла́ка.

slake [sleɪk] *v.t.* **1.** (*liter.*): ~ **one's thirst** утол|я́ть, -и́ть жа́жду. **2.**: ~ **lime** гаси́ть, по- и́звесть.

slalom ['slɑ:ləm] *n.* сла́лом.

slam [slæm] *n.* **1.**: **I heard the** ~ **of a door** я слы́шал, как хло́пнула дверь. **2.** (*cards*): **grand/little** ~ большо́й/ма́лый шлем.

v.t. **1.** (*shut with a bang*): ~ **a door** хло́пнуть (*pf.*) две́рью; **he** ~**med the door to** он захло́пнул дверь; ~ **the lid of a trunk** захло́п|ывать, -нуть кры́шку сундука́. **2.** (*other violent or sudden action*): **he** ~**med the brakes on** он ре́зко затормози́л; **he** ~**med the box down on the table** он шва́ркнул коро́бку о стол; он швырну́л коро́бку на стол. **3.** (*defeat resoundingly*) разнести́ (*pf.*).

v.i. **1.** (*of door etc.*) захло́п|ываться, -нуться. **2.**: **he** ~**med out of the room** он вы́скочил/вы́летел из ко́мнаты.

slammer ['slæmə(r)] *n.* (*sl.*) тюря́га.

slander ['slɑ:ndə(r)] *n.* клевета́.

v.t. клевета́ть, на- на+*a.*; оклевета́ть (*pf.*); поро́чить, о-; черни́ть, о-.

slanderer ['slɑ:ndərə(r)] *n.* клеветни́|к (*fem.* -ца).

slanderous ['slɑ:ndərəs] *adj.* клеветни́ческий; ~ **person** клеветни́|к (*fem.* -ца).

slang [slæŋ] *n.* жарго́н; сленг; **thieves'** ~ воровско́е арго́ (*indecl.*); ~ **word** жарго́нное сло́во.

v.t. обруга́ть (*pf.*); ~**ing match** перебра́нка.

slangy ['slæŋɪ] *adj.* жарго́нный, вульга́рный; (*of pers.*) употребля́ющий жарго́н.

slant [slɑ:nt] *n.* **1.** (*oblique position*): **he wears his hat on the** ~ он но́сит шля́пу набекре́нь. **2.** (*coll., point of view*) то́чка зре́ния; **my trip gave me a new** ~ **on things** по́сле пое́здки я на всё взгляну́л по-но́вому.

adj. косо́й.

v.t. **1.** (*incline*) наклон|я́ть, -и́ть. **2.** (*fig., distort*) иска|жа́ть, -зи́ть; **a** ~**ed article** тенденцио́зная статья́.

v.i.: **his handwriting** ~**s to the right** он пи́шет с накло́ном впра́во; **the** ~**ing rays of the sun** косы́е лучи́ со́лнца.

cpd. ~**-eyed** *adj.* с раско́сыми глаза́ми.

slantwise ['slɑ:ntwaɪz] *adv.* вкось, ко́со, накло́нно.

slap [slæp] *n.* шлепо́к; **she gave the boy a good** ~ она́ дала́ ма́льчику зво́нкий шлепо́к; ~ **in the face** (*lit., fig.*) пощёчина; ~ **on the back** (*fig.*) поздравле́ние; ~ **and tickle** обжима́ние (*coll.*).

adv.: **the ball hit me** ~ **in the eye** мяч попа́л мне пря́мо в глаз; **he ran** ~ **into a post** он вре́зался в (*or* налете́л на) столб; **he hit the target** ~ **in the middle** он попа́л в са́мое я́блоко мише́ни.

v.t. **1.** (*smack*) шлёпать, от-; ~ **s.o.'s face** дать (*pf.*) кому́-н. пощёчину; ~ **s.o. on the back** хло́п|ать, -нуть кого́-н. по спине́. **2.** (*apply with force or carelessly*): **they** ~**ped a fine on him** ему́ влепи́ли штраф; **the paint was** ~**ped on** кра́ска была́ нало́жена ко́е-как. **3.**: ~ **down** бр|оса́ть, -о́сить; **he** ~**ped down the money on the counter** он бро́сил/шва́ркнул|швырну́л де́ньги на прила́вок; (*rebuke*) оса|жда́ть, -ди́ть.

cpds. ~**-bang** *adv.* со всего́ разма́ха; очертя́ го́лову; ~**dash** *adj.* (*of pers.*) бесшаба́шный; (*of work*) поспе́шный, небре́жный; *adv.* (*hastily*) поспе́шно; (*anyhow*) ко́е-как; (*coll.*) тяп-ля́п, тяп да ляп; ~**-happy** *adj.* обалде́лый; бесшаба́шный; ~**stick** *n.* шутовство́, пая́сничание; ~**stick comedy** (дешёвый) фарс; ~**-up** *adj.* (*coll.*) шика́рный.

slash [slæʃ] *n.* (*slit*) разре́з; (*wound*) ра́на; (*stroke*): **he made a** ~ **with his sword** он взмахну́л са́блей.

v.t. **1.** (*wound with knife etc.*) ра́нить, по-; (*with sword*) руби́ть (*impf.*). **2.** (*cut slits in*) разр|еза́ть, -е́зать; ~**ed sleeves** рукава́ с разре́зом. **3.** (*lash; fig., criticize*) бичева́ть (*impf.*); ~**ing criticism** ре́зкая/разгро́мная/беспоща́дная кри́тика. **4.** (*reduce*): ~ **prices** ре́зко сн|ижа́ть, -и́зить це́ны; ~ **a budget** ре́зко сокра|ща́ть, -ти́ть (*or* уре́з|ывать, -ать) бюдже́т.

slat [slæt] *n.* пла́нка; перекла́дина; (*of blind*) пласти́нка.

slate [sleɪt] *n.* **1.** (*material*) сла́нец; ~ **quarry** сла́нцевый карье́р. **2.** (*piece of* ~ *for roofing*) ши́ферная пли́тка; **a house roofed with** ~**s** дом, кры́тый ши́фером. **3.** (*for schoolwork*) гри́фельная доска́; (*fig.*): **start with a clean** ~ нач|ина́ть, -а́ть с нача́ла (*or* но́вую жизнь); **wipe a debt off the** ~ списа́ть (*pf.*) долг; **wipe the** ~ **clean** поко́нчить (*pf.*) с про́шлым; забы́ть (*pf.*) было́е.

v.t. **1.** (*cover with* ~*s*) крыть, по- ши́фером; **2.** (*US, nominate*) занести́ (*pf.*) в спи́сок кандида́тов; (*arrange*) назн|ача́ть, -а́чить. **3.** (*scold, criticize*) разн|оси́ть, -ести́;

a good slating хоро́шая нахлобу́чка/головомо́йка.
cpds. **~-coloured** *adj.* синева́то-се́рый; **~-pencil** *n.* гри́фель (*m.*).
slater ['sleɪtə(r)] *n.* (*of roofs*) кро́вельщик.
slattern ['slæt(ə)n] *n.* неря́ха, грязну́ля (*both c.g.*).
slatternliness ['slætənlɪnɪs] *n.* неря́шливость.
slatternly ['slætənlɪ] *adj.* неря́шливый.
slaty ['sleɪtɪ] *adj.* (*colour*) синева́то-се́рый.
slaughter ['slɔ:tə(r)] *n.* избие́ние, резня́; ма́ссовое уби́йство; (*of animals*) убо́й.
v.t. **1.** (*pers.*) изб|ива́ть, -и́ть; устр|а́ивать, -о́ить резню́ +*g.*; (*coll.*, *defeat heavily*) разб|ива́ть, -и́ть впух и впрах. **2.** (*animals*) ре́зать, за-.
cpd. **~house** *n.* (ското)бо́йня.
slaughterer ['slɔ:tərə(r)] *n.* мясни́к (на бо́йне); (*fig.*) живодёр, пала́ч.
Slav [slɑ:v] *n.* слав|яни́н (*fem.* -я́нка); **the ~s** славя́не.
adj. славя́нский.
Slavdom ['slɑ:vdəm] *n.* славя́нство; славя́не (*pl.*, *collect.*).
slave [sleɪv] *n.* раб (*fem.* -ы́ня); нево́льни|к (*fem.* -ца); **willing ~** поко́рный/доброво́льный раб; **she makes a ~ of her daughter** она́ помыка́ет до́черью; она́ де́ржит дочь в ра́бском повинове́нии; **he works like a ~** он рабо́тает, как вол; **~ of fashion** раб мо́ды; **~ to duty/passion** же́ртва до́лга/стра́сти; **~ to drink** алкого́лик; **~ labour** ра́бский труд; (*forced labour*) поднево́льный труд.
v.i.: **~ at sth.** корпе́ть (*impf.*) над чем-н.; **~ away** тяну́ть (*impf.*) ля́мку.
cpds. **~-driver** *n.* надсмо́трщик (рабо́в); (*fig.*) безжа́лостный нача́льник, погоня́ла (*c.g.*), эксплуата́тор; **~-ship** *n.* нево́льничий кора́бль; **~-trade** *n.* работорго́вля; **~-trader** *n.* работорго́вец.
slaver[1] ['sleɪvə(r)] *n.* (*pers.*) работорго́вец; (*ship*) нево́льничий кора́бль.
slaver[2] ['slævə(r)] *n.* (*spittle*) слю́ни (*f. pl.*).
v.i. пуска́ть (*impf.*) слю́ни.
slavery ['sleɪvərɪ] *n.* ра́бство.
slavey ['sleɪvɪ] *n.* (*coll.*) ≃ прислу́га (за всё).
Slavic ['slɑ:vɪk] *adj.* славя́нский.
Slavicist ['slɑ:vɪsɪst] = **Slavist**
slavish ['sleɪvɪʃ] *adj.* ра́бский; ра́бий, уго́дливый; **~ imitation** ра́бское подража́ние (+*d.*).
Slavist ['slɑ:vɪst] *n.* слави́ст.
Slavonic [slə'vɒnɪk] *n.* славя́нский язы́к; **Church ~** церковнославя́нский язы́к; **~ studies** слави́стика.
adj. славя́нский.
Slavophil(e) ['slɑ:vəʊfɪl; -,faɪl] *n.* славянофи́л.
adj. славянофи́льский.
slay [sleɪ] *v.t.* (*liter.*) уб|ива́ть, -и́ть; сра|жа́ть, -зи́ть.
slayer ['sleɪə(r)] *n.* уби́йца (*c.g.*).
sleazy ['sli:zɪ] *adj.* (*squalid*) захуда́лый, убо́гий.
sled(ge) [sledʒ] = **sleigh**
sledge-hammer ['sledʒ,hæmə(r)] *n.* кува́лда; кузне́чный мо́лот; **~ blows** (*fig.*) сокруши́тельные уда́ры.
sleek [sli:k] *adj.* (*of animal or its coat, fur*) гла́дкий, лоснящийся; (*of person's hair*) прили́занный.
v.t. (*also* **~ down**) пригла́|живать, -дить; прили́з|ывать, -а́ть.
sleekness ['sli:knɪs] *n.* гла́дкость; прили́занность.
sleep [sli:p] *n.* сон; **light/deep/sound ~** лёгкий/глубо́кий/кре́пкий сон; **have a ~** поспа́ть (*pf.*); сосну́ть (*pf.*); вздремну́ть (*pf.*); **have one's ~ out** высыпа́ться, вы́спаться; **sleep the ~ of the just** спать (*impf.*) сном пра́ведника; **go** (*coll.*, *drop off*) **to ~** зас|ыпа́ть, -ну́ть; **I couldn't get to ~** я не мог усну́ть; мне не спа́ло́сь; **I didn't have a wink of ~ all night** я глаз не сомкну́л всю ночь; **send to ~** усып|ля́ть, -и́ть; **put a child to ~** укла́дывать, уложи́ть ребёнка (спать); **we had our dog put to ~** нам пришло́сь соба́ку усыпи́ть; **I need 8 hours' ~ a night** мне тре́буется/ну́жно 8 часо́в, что́бы вы́спаться; **he talks/walks in his ~** он говори́т/хо́дит во сне; **I shan't lose any ~ over it** я (по э́тому по́воду) пла́кать не ста́ну; **my foot has gone to ~** я но́гу отсиде́л; у меня́ затекла́ нога́; **winter ~** (*of animal*) зи́мняя спя́чка.
v.t. (*provide* **~ing room for**): **you can ~ ten people here** здесь мо́жно уложи́ть де́сять челове́к; **the hotel ~s 200** гости́ница рассчи́тана на 200 челове́к.
v.i. спать (*impf.*); (*spend the night*) ночева́ть (*impf.*); **~ well!** (жела́ю вам) (с)поко́йной но́чи!; **~ like a top, log** спать (*impf.*) как уби́тый (*or* без за́дних ног *or* мёртвым сном); **I don't ~ well** у меня́ плохо́й сон; **I can't ~** я не могу́ засну́ть; **his bed had not been slept in** его́ посте́ль была́ не смя́та; **~ on a decision** отложи́ть (*pf.*) реше́ние до утра́; **better ~ on it!** у́тро ве́чера мудрене́е (*prov.*); **he slept through the alarm** он проспа́л всю трево́гу; **is he ~ing with her?** он с ней спит/живёт?; **S~ing Beauty** Спя́щая Краса́вица; **~ing partner** пасси́вный партнёр; компаньо́н, акти́вно не уча́ствующий в де́ле; **let ~ing dogs lie** (*prov.*) не буди́ ли́хо, когда́ спит ти́хо.
with advs.: **~ around** *v.i.* (*be promiscuous*) спать (*impf.*) с кем попа́ло; **~ away** *v.t.*: **he slept the time away** он проспа́л всё э́то вре́мя; **~ in** *v.i.* (*intentionally*) поспа́ть (*pf.*) вво́лю; от|сыпа́ться, -оспа́ться; заспа́ться; (*oversleep*) прос|ыпа́ть, -па́ть; заспа́ться (*pf.*); (*at place of work*) ночева́ть (*impf.*) на рабо́те; **~ off** *v.t.*: **~ off a hangover** проспа́ться (*pf.*) (по́сле попо́йки); **~ off a headache** хороше́нько проспа́ться (*pf.*), что́бы прошла́ головна́я боль; **~ on** *v.i.*: **he is tired, let him ~ on** он уста́л, не буди́те его́ (*or* пусть спит); **~ out** *v.i.* (*out of doors*) спать (*impf.*) под откры́тым не́бом; (*away from home*) ночева́ть (*impf.*) не до́ма (*or* в гостя́х); **~** (*sc. live*) **together** *v.i.* жить (*impf.*).
cpds. **~-walker** *n.* луна́тик; **~-walking** *n.* лунати́зм.
sleeper ['sli:pə(r)] *n.* (*pers.*): **he is a light/heavy ~** он чу́тко/кре́пко спит; (*rail support*) шпа́ла; (*sleeping-car*) спа́льный ваго́н.
sleepiness ['sli:pɪnɪs] *n.* сонли́вость.
sleeping ['sli:pɪŋ] *n.*: **~ accommodation** ночле́г; ме́сто для ночёвки.
cpds. **~-bag** *n.* спа́льный мешо́к; **~-car** *n.* спа́льный ваго́н; **~-draught** *n.* снотво́рное; **~-pill** *n.* снотво́рная табле́тка; **~-quarters** *n.* спа́льное помеще́ние; **~-sickness** *n.* со́нная боле́знь; **~-suit** *n.* де́тский спа́льный комбинезо́н.
sleepless ['sli:plɪs] *adj.* бессо́нный; бо́дрствующий; **~ vigilance** неусы́пная бди́тельность.
sleeplessness ['sli:plɪsnɪs] *n.* бессо́нница.
sleepy ['sli:pɪ] *adj.* (*lit.*, *fig.*) со́нный; сонли́вый, вя́лый; **I feel ~** мне хо́чется (*or* я хочу́) спать; у меня́ слипа́ются глаза́; **I grew ~** меня́ разбира́л сон; меня́ клони́ло ко сну; **make s.o. ~** наг|оня́ть, -на́ть сон на кого́-н.; (*fig.*): **this is a ~ place** здесь со́нное ца́рство.
cpd. **~head** *n.* со́ня (*c.g.*).
sleet [sli:t] *n.* дождь (*m.*) со сне́гом; крупа́.
v.i.: **it is ~ing** сы́плет крупа́.
sleeve [sli:v] *n.* **1.** рука́в; **pluck s.o.'s ~** дёр|гать, -нуть кого́-н. за рука́в; **roll up one's ~s** (*lit.*, *fig.*) засу́ч|ивать, -и́ть рукава́; **have, keep sth. up one's ~** (*fig.*) име́ть (*impf.*) что-н. про запа́с (*or* нагото́ве); **laugh up one's ~** посме́иваться (*impf.*) в кула́к. **2.** (*aeron.*, **wind-~**) ветроуказа́тель (*m.*); ветряно́й ко́нус. **3.** (*record cover*) конве́рт.
sleeveless ['sli:vlɪs] *adj.* безрука́вный; **~ vest** безрука́вка.
sleigh [sleɪ], **sled(ge)** [sledʒ] *nn.* (*children's*) са́н|ки (*pl.*, *g.* -ок); сала́з|ки (*pl.*, *g.* -ок); (*for transport*) са́н|и (*pl.*, *g.* -е́й).
v.i. ката́ться (*indet.*) в/на саня́х (*or* на са́нках/сала́зках).
cpds. **~-bell** *n.* бубе́нчик, колоко́льчик (на саня́х); **~-dog** *n.* ездова́я/упряжна́я соба́ка.
sleight-of-hand [slaɪt] *n.* ло́вкость рук.
slender ['slendə(r)] *adj.* **1.** (*thin*; *narrow*) то́нкий; (*of pers.*, *slim*) стро́йный. **2.** (*scanty*) ску́дный; **~ means** ску́дные сре́дства; **~ hope** сла́бая наде́жда; **he has a ~ acquaintance with the law** у него́ (весьма́) пове́рхностное знако́мство с зако́ном.
slenderness ['slendənɪs] *n.* то́нкость, стро́йность.
sleuth [slu:θ] *n.* сы́щик.
cpd. **~-hound** *n.* (соба́ка-)ище́йка.
slew [slu:] **(US slue)** *v.t.* & *i.* (*also* **~ round**) кру́то пов|ора́чивать(ся), -ерну́ть(ся).
slice [slaɪs] *n.* **1.** (*of bread*) ломо́ть (*m.*); **cut bread into ~s** нар|еза́ть, -е́зать хлеб ломтя́ми; (*of meat*) ло́мтик; (*of*

fruit) кусо́к, до́ля. **2.** (*portion, share*) часть, до́ля; **the play is a ~ of life** э́та пье́са — сле́пок с жи́зни. **3.** (*for fish etc.*) ры́бный/широ́кий нож; лопа́точка (для то́рта).

v.t. **1.** нар|еза́ть, -е́зать ло́мтиками; **~d bread** (предвари́тельно) наре́занный хлеб. **2.** (*golf*): **~ the ball** ср|еза́ть, -е́зать мяч.

with advs.: **~ off** *v.t.* отр|еза́ть, -е́зать; **~ up** *v.t.* нар|еза́ть, -е́зать.

slick [slɪk] *n.* (*patch of oil etc.*) плёнка.

adj. (*skilful; smart*) ло́вкий, бо́йкий; (*smooth, also fig.*) гла́дкий; (*slippery*) ско́льзкий.

slicker ['slɪkə(r)] *n.* пройдо́ха (*c.g.*); **city ~** городско́й хлыщ (*coll.*).

slid|e [slaɪd] *n.* **1.** (*act of ~ing*) скольже́ние; **have a ~e** поката́ться (*pf.*), прокати́ться (*pf.*) (*по льду, с горки и т.п.*). **2.** (*track on ice*) като́к; (*on snow-covered hill*) ледяна́я го́рка. **3.** (*chute*) спуск, жёлоб. **4.** (*of microscope*) предме́тное стекло́. **5.** (*for projection on screen*) диапозити́в, слайд. **6.** (*hair-~e*) зако́лка.

v.t.: **~e a drawer into place** задв|ига́ть, -и́нуть я́щик; **he ~ the bottle (over) to me** он пододви́нул буты́лку ко мне; **~e sth. into s.o.'s hand** сова́ть, су́нуть что-н. кому́-н. в ру́ку; **he ~ his hand into his pocket** он (незаме́тно) су́нул ру́ку в карма́н.

v.i. **1.** скользи́ть (*impf.*); **~ing door** задвижна́я дверь; **~ing roof** сдвига́ющаяся кры́ша; **~ing seat** скользя́щее сиде́ние; (*down or off*): **the papers ~ off my lap** бума́ги соскользну́ли у меня́ с коле́н; **the book ~ out of my hand** кни́га вы́скользнула из мои́х рук; **his trousers ~ to the ground** у него́ спусти́лись брю́ки; **the dagger ~es into its scabbard** кинжа́л вкла́дывается в но́жны. **2.** (*as pastime*) скользи́ть (*impf.*); ката́ться (*indet.*); **the boy ~ down the banisters** ма́льчик скати́лся по пери́лам. **3.** (*fig.*): **he ~ into the room** он проскользну́л в ко́мнату; **~e over a delicate subject** об|ходи́ть, -ойти́ щекотли́вую те́му; **the years ~e by** вре́мя лети́т; го́ды прохо́дят; **let sth. ~e** пус|ка́ть, -ти́ть что-н. на самотёк; **~ing scale** скользя́щая шкала́.

cpds. **~e-controls** *n. pl.* движко́вые регуля́торы; **~e-rule** *n.* логарифми́ческая лине́йка; **~e-valve** *n.* золотни́к.

slight[1] [slaɪt] *n.* (*disrespect*) неуваже́ние, пренебреже́ние; (*offence, injury*) оби́да; **put a ~ on s.o.** нанести́ (*pf.*) оби́ду кому́-н.; вы́казать (*pf.*) неуваже́ние к кому́-н.

v.t. об|ижа́ть, -и́деть; нан|оси́ть, -ести́ оби́ду +*d.*; выка́зывать, вы́казать неуваже́ние +*d.*; трети́ровать (*impf.*).

slight[2] [slaɪt] *adj.* **1.** (*frail*) хру́пкий; (*slender*) то́нкий. **2.** (*light; not serious*) лёгкий; **she has a ~ cold** у неё небольшо́й на́сморк; **~ concussion** лёгкая конту́зия. **3.** (*inconsiderable*) незначи́тельный; (*small*): **there is a ~ risk of infection** есть не́которая опа́сность зарази́ться; **the risk is ~** опа́сность невелика́; **he paid me ~ attention** он не обраща́л на меня́ почти́ никако́го внима́ния. **4.**: **~est** мале́йший; **this is not the ~est use** от э́того ро́вно никако́й по́льзы; **'Do you mind fresh air?' — 'Not in the ~est'** «Вы не возража́ете, что откры́то окно?» — «Ничу́ть!»; **he is not to blame in the ~est** он ни в мале́йшей сте́пени не винова́т.

slightly ['slaɪtlɪ] *adv.* слегка́; **I know them ~** я с ни́ми немно́го знако́м; **I know them only ~** я их почти́ не зна́ю; **he was ~ injured** он слегка́ пострада́л; он получи́л лёгкое ране́ние (*or* лёгкий уши́б); **~ younger** немно́го/чуть моло́же.

slim [slɪm] *adj.* (*slender*) то́нкий; (*small*): **on the ~mest of evidence** на основа́нии сомни́тельных да́нных; **a ~ chance of success** сла́бая наде́жда на успе́х.

v.i. худе́ть, по-; сбра́сывать (*impf.*) (ли́шний) вес; **~ming exercises** гимна́стика, спосо́бствующая похуде́нию (*or* поте́ре ве́са).

slime [slaɪm] *n.* (*mud*) ил; (*viscous substance*) слизь.

slimy ['slaɪmɪ] *adj.* **1.** сли́зистый; (*sticky*) вя́зкий; (*slippery*) ско́льзкий. **2.** (*fig., of pers.*) гну́сный, ско́льзкий.

sling [slɪŋ] *n.* **1.** (*for missile*) праща́. **2.** (*bandage*) пе́ревязь, косы́нка; **his arm was in a ~** у него́ рука́ была́ на пе́ревязи. **3.** (*of rifle*) руже́йный реме́нь.

v.t. **1.** (*throw*) швыр|я́ть, -ну́ть; **~ s.o. out of the room** вы́швырнуть (*pf.*) кого́-н. из ко́мнаты. **2.** (*cast by means of ~*) мет|а́ть, -ну́ть. **3.** (*suspend*) подве́|шивать, -сить; **he slung the rifle over his shoulder** он переки́нул винто́вку че́рез плечо́; (*hoist with ~*): **the crates were slung on board** я́щики по́дняли на́ борт; **~ one's hook** мота́ть (*impf.*); см|а́тываться, -ота́ться (*sl.*).

cpd. **~-shot** *n.* (*US*) рога́тка.

slink [slɪŋk] *v.i.*: **~ off, away** потихо́ньку от|ходи́ть, -ойти́; уйти́ (*pf.*), поджа́вши хвост.

slinky ['slɪŋkɪ] *adj.*: **a ~ dress** пла́тье в обтя́жку; **a ~ walk** кра́дущаяся похо́дка.

slip [slɪp] *n.* **1.** (*landslip*) обва́л. **2.** (*mishap, error*) оши́бка (по небре́жности); **there's many a ~ ('twixt cup and lip)** ≃ не скажи́ «гоп», пока́ не перескочи́шь/перепры́гнешь; **I made a ~** я оши́бся; я дал про́мах/ма́ху; **~ of the tongue/pen** огово́рка/опи́ска. **3.**: **he gave his pursuers the ~** он ускользну́л/улизну́л от пресле́дователей. **4.** (*loose cover*) чехо́л; **pillow ~** на́волочка (для поду́шки). **5.** (*petticoat*) комбина́ция; (ни́жняя) соро́чка. **6.** (*of paper*) ка́рточка; поло́ска бума́ги; **printer's ~s** (*galleys*) гра́нки (*f. pl.*), о́ттиски (*m. pl.*). **7.** (*plant cutting*) побе́г, черено́к, отро́сток; **a ~ of a girl** девчу́шка. **8.** (**~way**) ста́пель (*m.*), слип, э́ллинг; **the ship is still on the ~s** кора́бль ещё не сошёл со стапеле́й. **9.** (*pl., theatr.*) кули́сы (*f. pl.*).

v.t. **1.** (*slide; pass covertly*): **she ~ped her little hand into mine** она́ вложи́ла свою́ ру́чку в мою́; **he ~ped the ring on to her finger** он наде́л ей на па́лец кольцо́; **I ~ped the waiter a coin** я су́нул официа́нту моне́тку. **2.** (*slide out of; escape from*): **the dog ~ped its collar** соба́ка вы́тащила го́лову из оше́йника; **it ~ped my memory/mind** э́то у меня́ вы́скочило из па́мяти/головы́. **3.** (*release; drop*): **they ~ped the anchor** они́ сня́ли́сь с я́коря; **the cow ~ped its calf** коро́ва ски́нула телёнка; **I ~ped the dog from its leash ~** я спусти́л соба́ку с поводка́.

v.i. **1.** (*fall; slide*): **she ~ped on the ice** она́ поскользну́лась на льду; **the blanket ~ped off the bed** одея́ло соскользну́ло с посте́ли; **~ped disc** смещённый межпозвонко́вый диск; **she let the plate ~** она́ урони́ла таре́лку (на́ пол); (*fig.*): **I let him ~ through my fingers** я дал ему́ ускользну́ть от меня́; я упусти́л его́; **he let the opportunity ~** он упусти́л возмо́жность; **the remark ~ped out** э́то замеча́ние случа́йно сорва́ло́сь у него́ (*и т.п.*) с языка́; **he is ~ping** (*losing his grip*) у него́ слабе́ет хва́тка. **2.** (*move quickly and/or unnoticed*): **he ~ped away** он незаме́тно ушёл; **she ~ped out of the room** она́ вы́скользнула из ко́мнаты; **I'll ~ across to the pub** я сбе́гаю в пивну́ю; **the years are ~ping by** го́ды ухо́дят; **an error ~ped in** вкра́лась оши́бка; **he ~ped into the room** он незаме́тно вошёл/прони́к в ко́мнату; **he unconsciously ~ped into French** он машина́льно (*or*, сам не замеча́я,) перешёл на францу́зский; **I'll ~ into another dress** я (бы́стренько) переоде́нусь; **~ through** проскользну́ть (*pf.*) (че́рез+*a.*).

with adv.: **~ up** *v.i.*: **he ~ped up and hurt his back** он поскользну́лся и повреди́л себе́ спи́ну; **I ~ped up in my calculations** я оши́бся в подсчётах; (*fig.*) я просчита́лся; **I ~ped up there** я дал ма́ху.

cpds. **~-carriage, ~-coach** *nn.* ваго́н, отцепля́емый на ста́нции без остано́вки по́езда; **~-knot** *n.* скользя́щий затяжно́й у́зел; **~shod** *adj.* (*fig.*) небре́жный, неря́шливый, халту́рный; **~-slop** *n.* (*sentimentality*) сентимента́льный вздор; (*weak drink*) бурда́; **~-stream** *n.* (*aeron.*) спу́тная струя́ за винто́м; **~-up** *n.* оши́бка, про́мах, недосмо́тр; **~way** *n.* ста́пель (*m.*), слип, э́ллинг.

slipper ['slɪpə(r)] *n.* (дома́шняя) ту́фля; та́почка; (*step-in*) шлёпанец.

v.t. отшлёпать (*pf.*) ту́флей.

slipperiness ['slɪpərɪnɪs] *n.* ско́льзкость.

slippery ['slɪpərɪ] *adj.* **1.** ско́льзкий; **he is on a ~ slope** (*fig.*) он ка́тится по накло́нной пло́скости. **2.** (*fig., evasive, shifty*) увёртливый, ско́льзкий; (*unreliable*) ненадёжный.

slippy ['slɪpɪ] *adj.*: **look ~!** пошеве́ливайся! (*coll.*).

slit [slɪt] *n.* (*cut*) проре́з; (*slot*) щель, щёлка; **~ trench** щель; **a ~ skirt** ю́бка с разре́зом.

v.t.: ~ **open an envelope** вскрыть/разорвáть (*both pf.*) конвéрт; ~ **s.o.'s throat** перерéзать (*pf.*) комý-н. глóтку.
cpd. **~-eyed** *adj.* узкоглáзый.

slither ['slɪðə(r)] *v.i.*: ~ **about in the mud** скользи́ть (*impf.*) по гря́зи; **they ~ed down the hill** они́ скати́лись с холмá; **he ~ed down the pole** он соскользну́л (вниз) по шестý.

sliver ['slɪvə(r), 'slaɪvə(r)] *n.* (*of wood*) щéпка, лучи́на.
v.t. & i. расщеп|ля́ть(ся), -и́ть(ся).

slivovitz ['slɪvəvɪts] *n.* сливя́нка.

slob [slɒb] *n.* (*sl.*) недотёпа (*c.g.*).

slobber ['slɒbə(r)] *v.i.* (*lit., fig.*) распускáть (*impf.*) слю́ни.

sloe [sləʊ] *n.* тёрн.
cpds. **~-eyed** *adj.* ≃ с глазáми как ви́шни; **~-gin** *n.* сливя́нка; сли́вовая настóйка.

slog [slɒg] *n.* (*hit*) си́льный удáр; (*arduous work*) тяжёлая/утоми́тельная рабóта.
v.t.: ~ **s.o. in the jaw** дать (*pf.*) комý-н. в зýбы; ~ **a ball** (си́льно/крéпко) удáрить (*pf.*) по мячý.
v.i.: ~ **at the ball** бить (*impf.*) по мячý; **he was ~ging along the road** он упóрно шагáл по дорóге; **he is ~ging away at Latin** он корпи́т над латы́нью (*coll.*).

slogan ['sləʊgən] *n.* (*motto, watchword*) лóзунг, деви́з; (*in advertising*) реклáмная фóрмула.

sloop [slu:p] *n.* шлюп.

slop [slɒp] *n.* **1.** (*liquid food*) жи́дкая пи́ща; (*thin gruel*) размазня́; (*poor soup etc.*) бурдá; жи́дкая похлёбка. **2.** (*pl., waste liquid*) помó|и (*pl., g.* -ев). **3.** (*fig., sentimental utterance*) слезли́вые излия́ния, сантимéнт|ы (*pl., g.* -ов).
v.t. **1.** (*spill, splash*): ~ **beer over the table** расплёск|ивать, -áть пи́во по столý; ~ **tea into the saucer** вы́плеснуть (*pf.*) чай на блю́дце; ~ **paint on the wall** заля́п|ывать, -ать стéну крáской. **2.**: ~ **out a prison cell** выноси́ть, вы́нести парáшу; ~ **down the decks** драи́ть, на- пáлубу.
v.i.: ~ **about** плескáться (*impf.*).
cpds. **~-basin** *n.* полоскáтельница; **~-pail** *n.* (помóйное) ведрó.

slope [sləʊp] *n.* **1.** наклóн, склон, уклóн, покáтость; (*upward*) подъём; (*downward*) спуск, скат; **mountain ~s** гóрные склóны; **the house was on the ~ of the hill** дом стоя́л на склóне горы́; **the table is on a ~** стол стои́т наклóнно. **2.** (*mil.*): **the ~** положéние с винтóвкой на плечó.
v.t.: ~ **a roof** стáвить, по- кры́шу с уклóном; ~ **arms!** на плечó!
v.i. **1.**: ~ **back(wards)/forwards** покоси́ться (*pf.*) назáд/вперёд; **her handwriting ~s backwards** у неё пóчерк с наклóном влéво; ~ **down** спускáться (*impf.*); ~ **up(wards)** поднимáться (*impf.*); **a sloping roof** покáтая кры́ша. **2.**: ~ **off** см|áтываться, -отáться; уд|ирáть, -рáть (*coll.*).

sloppiness ['slɒpɪnɪs] *n.* (*untidiness*) неря́шливость; (*sentimentality*) сентиментáльность.

sloppy ['slɒpɪ] *adj.* **1.** (*of food*) жи́дкий. **2.** (*of road: muddy, slushy*) гря́зный, сля́котный. **3.** (*of floor, table*) забры́зганный, замы́зганный, зáлитый (чем-н.). **4.** (*careless; slovenly*) неря́шливый. **5.** (*sentimental*) сентиментáльный; ~ **sentiment** лóжная чувстви́тельность.

slosh [slɒʃ] *v.t.* (*pour clumsily*) плеснýть (*pf.*); (*hit*) отдубáсить (*pf.*) (*coll.*).
v.i. ~ (*splash*) **about** плескáться (*impf.*).

sloshed [slɒʃt] *adj.* (*drunk*) в дыми́ну пья́ный (*sl.*).

slot [slɒt] *n.* **1.** паз, отвéрстие; **put a coin in the ~** опус|кáть, -ти́ть монéту в автомáт. **2.** (*coll., suitable place or job*): **we found a ~ for him as junior editor** мы подыскáли емý мéсто млáдшего редáктора. **3.** (*in timetable*) клéтка.
v.t. **1.**: ~ **together** спл|áчивать, -оти́ть в паз. **2.**: ~ **one part into another** вдв|игáть, -и́нуть однý часть в другýю; **we ~ted a song recital into the programme** мы вставили в прогрáмму исполнéние пéсен; **the graduates were ~ted into jobs** выпускникóв устрóили на рабóту.
v.i. ~ **in** вст|авля́ться, -áвиться.
cpds. **~-machine** *n.* (торгóвый/игóрный) автомáт; **~-meter** *n.* (*e.g. for gas*) счётчик(-автомáт).

sloth [sləʊθ] *n.* **1.** (*zool.*) лени́вец. **2.** (*idleness*) лень, лéность.

slothful ['sləʊθfʊl] *adj.* лени́вый.

slothfulness ['sləʊθfʊlnɪs] *n.* лéность.

slouch [slaʊtʃ] *n.* **1.** (*of walk*) разви́нченная похóдка; (*stoop*) сутýлость. **2.**: **he's no ~ as a comedian** он кóмик хоть кудá! (*coll.*).
v.i. (*stoop*) сутýлиться (*impf.*); ~ **about the house** слоня́ться (*impf.*) по дóму; ~ **along** ходи́ть (*indet.*), идти́ (*det.*) неуклю́же.
cpd. **~-hat** *n.* шля́па с опýщенными поля́ми.

slough[1] [slaʊ] *n.* (*quagmire*) топь, болóто.

slough[2] [slʌf] *n.* (*cast skin*) сбрóшенная кóжа.
v.t. (*of snake etc.*): ~ **its skin** сбр|áсывать, -óсить кóжу; (*fig.*): ~ **(off)** изб|авля́ться, -áвиться от+*g.*

Slovak ['sləʊvæk] *n.* (*pers.*) словá|к (*fem.* -чка); (*language*) словáцкий язы́к.
adj. словáцкий.

Slovakia ['sləʊvækɪə] *n.* Словáкия.

sloven ['slʌv(ə)n] *n.* неря́ха (*c.g.*).

Sloven|e ['sləʊvi:n, slə'vi:n], **-ian** [sləʊ'vi:nɪən, slə'vi:nɪən] *nn.* (*pers.*) словéн|ец (*fem.* -ка); (*language*) словéнский язы́к.
adj. словéнский.

Slovenia [sləʊ'vi:nɪə, slə'vi:nɪə] *n.* Словéния.

slovenliness ['slʌvənlɪnɪs] *n.* неря́шливость.

slovenly ['slʌvənlɪ] *adj.* неря́шливый.

slow [sləʊ] *adj.* **1.** мéдленный; (*dilatory*) медли́тельный; ~ **train** почтóвый пóезд; ~ **march** строевóй марш; **he is a ~ walker** он мéдленно хóдит; ~ **motion** замéдленное движéние; **in ~ motion** замéдленной съёмкой; **in a ~ oven** на мéдленном огнé; **be ~ over sth.** мéдлить (*impf.*) с чем-н.; **~ly but surely** мéдленно, но вéрно; ~ **poison** мéдленно дéйствующий яд; **he was not ~ to defend himself** он не замéдлил вы́ступить в своЮ защи́ту; **he is ~ in the uptake** он тýго соображáет. **2.** (*of clock*): **my watch is 10 minutes ~** мои́ часы́ отстаю́т на дéсять минýт; **you must be ~** вáши часы́, должнó быть, отстаю́т. **3.** (*dull-witted*) тупóй. **4.** (*not lively*): **the film was rather ~** фильм был довóльно скýчным; **business is ~** делá идýт вя́ло. **5.** (*phot., of film*) малочувстви́тельный.
adv. мéдленно; **go ~** (*of workers*) устрáивать (*impf.*) италья́нскую забастóвку; **the doctor told him to go ~** врач велéл емý берéчься.
v.t. (*also* ~ **down**, ~ **up**) зам|едля́ть, -éдлить; **he ~ed (the car) down** он сбáвил скóрость; **his illness ~ed him down** болéзнь застáвила егó сбáвить темп.
v.i. (*also* ~ **down**, ~ **up**) зам|едля́ться, -éдлиться; (*of car or driver*) сб|авля́ть, -áвить скóрость; зам|едля́ть, -éдлить ход.
cpds. **~coach** *n.* копýн, копýша (*c.g.*); **~-down** *n.* замедлéние; **~-match** *n.* огнепровóдный шнур; **~-moving** *adj.* мéдленный; **~-witted** *adj.* тупóй; **~-worm** *n.* веретéница, слепозмéйка.

slowness ['sləʊnɪs] *n.* мéдленность.

sludge [slʌdʒ] *n.* (*mud*) грязь; (*sediment*) осáдок, отстóй; (*sewage*) нечистóт|ы (*pl., g.* —); **(~-ice)** сáло, мéлкий лёд.
cpd. **~-pump** *n.* желóнка, грязевóй насóс.

sludgy ['slʌdʒɪ] *adj.* гря́зный.

slue [slu:] = **slew**

slug [slʌg] *n.* (*zool.*) слизня́к; (*bullet*) пýля; (*typ.*) шпон; (*US sl., short drink*) глотóк, рю́мочка.
v.t. (*US, hit*) = **slog**

slugabed ['slʌgə,bed], **sluggard** ['slʌgəd] *nn.* лентя́й, сóня (*c.g.*), лежебóка (*c.g.*).

sluggish ['slʌgɪʃ] *adj.* **1.** вя́лый; **he has a ~ liver** у негó побáливает пéчень; ~ **market** вя́лый ры́нок; ~ **circulation** вя́лое кровообращéние; (*slow-moving*) мéдленный, медли́тельный; **a ~ stream** мéдленная рéчка. **2.** (*lazy*) лени́вый.

sluggishness ['slʌgɪʃnɪs] *n.* вя́лость, лéность, лень.

sluice [slu:s] *n.* **1.** (*floodgate*) шлюз. **2.** (*for washing ore*) жёлоб.
v.t. (*provide with ~(s)*) шлюзовáть (*impf., pf.*); (*flood with water*) зал|ивáть, -и́ть; (*rinse, wash down*) окáт|ывать, -и́ть (*кого/что чем*); мыть (*or* вытекáть), про-; опол|áскивать, -оснýть.

v.i.: (*of water: pour out*) течь (*or* вытека́ть), вы́-; **rain was sluicing down** шёл проливно́й дождь.

cpds. **~-gate, ~-valve** *nn.* шлюз.

slum [slʌm] *n.* трущо́ба; **~ clearance** расчи́стка трущо́б; снос ве́тхих зда́ний.

v.i. (*visit ~s*) посеща́ть (*impf.*) трущо́бы; обсле́довать (*impf.*, *pf.*) трущо́бы.

cpd. **~-dweller** *n.* трущо́бный жи́тель, обита́тель (*m.*) трущо́бы.

slumber ['slʌmbə(r)] *n.* дремо́та; **disturb s.o.'s ~s** нар|уша́ть, -у́шить чей-н. сон.

v.i. дрема́ть, за-.

slump [slʌmp] *n.* (*fall in prices etc.*) паде́ние; (*trade recession*) засто́й, кри́зис; ре́зкое паде́ние цен.

v.i. **1.** (*of pers., fall, sink*) сва́л|иваться, -и́ться; **he ~ed to the ground** он свали́лся/бу́хнулся на зе́млю. **2.** (*of price, output, trade*) ре́зко па́дать, упа́сть.

slur [slɜː(r)] *n.* **1.** (*mus. sign*) ли́га. **2.** (*stigma*) пятно́; **put, cast a ~ on s.o.** поро́чить, о- кого́-н.; очерн|я́ть, -и́ть кого́-н.; **it is no ~ on his reputation** э́то нико́им о́бразом не броса́ет тень на его́ репута́цию.

v.t. **1.** (*pronounce indistinctly*) говори́ть (*impf.*) невня́тно/нечленоразде́льно; бормота́ть (*impf.*). **2.** (*mus., sing, play legato*) петь/игра́ть (*impf.*) лега́то; (*mark with ~*) свя́з|ывать, -а́ть ли́гой. **3.**: **~ over** сма́з|ывать, -ать; смягч|а́ть, -и́ть.

slurp [slɜːp] (*coll.*) *v.t. & i.* ча́вкать (*impf.*).

slurry ['slʌrɪ] *n.* жи́дкое цеме́нтное те́сто; жи́дкая гли́на; жи́дкий строи́тельный раство́р.

slush [slʌʃ] *n.* **1.** сля́коть. **2.** (*fig., sentiment*) сентимента́льный вздор. **3.** (*US*): **~ fund** фонд для по́дкупа госуда́рственных чино́вников.

slushy ['slʌʃɪ] *adj.* сля́котный, мо́крый; сентимента́льный.

slut [slʌt] *n.* неря́ха; (*trollop*) потаску́ха.

sluttish ['slʌtɪʃ] *adj.* неря́шливый; распу́щенный.

sly [slaɪ] *adj.* (*mischievous*) лука́вый; (*cunning*) хи́трый; **on the ~** укра́дкой; потихо́ньку; **he's a ~ dog** он плут(и́шка) (*m.*); у него́ всё ши́то-кры́то.

cpd. **~boots** *n.* (*coll.*) плут (*fem.* -о́вка).

slyness ['slaɪnɪs] *n.* лука́вость, лука́вство; хи́трость.

smack[1] [smæk] *n.* **1.** (*sound*) хлопо́к; **he brought his hand down with a ~ on the table** он (гро́мко) хло́пнул руко́й по́ столу; **~ of the lips** чмо́канье; **~ of a whip** щёлканье кнута́/хлыста́. **2.** (*blow, slap*) шлепо́к; **~ in the face** пощёчина; **~ in the eye** (*fig.*) (неожи́данный) уда́р; пощёчина. **3.** (*loud kiss*) зво́нкий поцелу́й. **4.**: **have a ~ at** (*attempt*) **sth.** (*coll.*) попро́бовать (*pf.*) что-н.

adv. пря́мо; **he went ~ into the wall** он вре́зался пря́мо в сте́ну.

v.t. **1.** (*slap*) хло́п|ать, -нуть; **~ a naughty child** шлёпать, от- капри́зного ребёнка; **he needs a good ~ing** его́ сле́дует хороше́нько отшлёпать. **2.**: **~ one's lips** чмо́к|ать, -нуть (губа́ми); причмо́к|ивать, -нуть.

smack[2] [smæk] *n.* (*taste, tinge, trace*) при́вкус.

v.i.: **~ of** (*lit., fig.*) отдава́ть (*impf*) +*i.*; **his manner ~s of conceit** его́ мане́ра (держа́ться) не лишена́ самодово́льства.

smack[3] [smæk] *n.* (*naut.*) смак, рыболо́вный шлюп.

smacker ['smækə(r)] *n.* (*sl.*) (*blow*) шлепо́к; (*kiss*) зво́нкий поцелу́й; (*£1*) фунт; (*$1*) до́ллар.

small [smɔːl] *n.* **1.**: **~ of the back** поясни́ца. **2.** (*pl., coll., articles of laundry*) ме́лочь.

adj. **1.** ма́лый, ма́ленький, небольшо́й; (*of eggs, berries, jewels etc.*) ме́лкий; **~ change** ме́лкие де́ньги; **a ~ sum of money** небольша́я су́мма (де́нег); **a ~ family** небольша́я/ма́ленькая семья́; **a ~ number of friends** ку́чка друзе́й; **~ claims court** суд ме́лких тяжб; **~ craft** (*vessels*) ме́лкие суда́/ло́дки; **~ print** ме́лкий шрифт; **~ handwriting** ме́лкий/убо́ристый по́черк; **~ intestine** то́нкая кишка́; (*not big enough*): **this coat is too ~ for** (*or* **is ~ on**) **me** э́то пальто́ мне мало́; (*of stature*) невысо́кий; невысо́кого ро́ста; **he is the ~est** он ни́же всех ро́стом; он са́мый ма́ленький; **make s.o. look ~** (*fig.*) ун|ижа́ть, -и́зить кого́-н.; **I felt very ~** я (по)чу́вствовал себя́ соверше́нно уничто́женным; (*of age*): **~ boy** ма́ленький ма́льчик; **he is too ~ to go to school** он ещё не доро́с до шко́лы; (*of time*): **in the ~ hours** под у́тро. **2.** (*liter., no great*): **he paid ~ attention to me** он ма́ло обраща́л на меня́ внима́ния; **he has ~ cause for satisfaction** у него́ немно́го/ма́ло основа́ний быть дово́льным; **to my no ~ surprise** к моему́ нема́лому удивле́нию; **they lost, and ~ wonder** они́ проигра́ли, и не удиви́тельно! **3.** (*unimportant, of ~ value*) ме́лкий, незначи́тельный; **~ beer** (*fig.*) ме́лочи (*f. pl.*); пустяки́ (*m. pl.*); **~ fry** (*fig.*) ме́лкая со́шка, мелюзга́; **I have no time for such ~ matters** у меня́ нет вре́мени для таки́х пустяко́в; **one must be thankful for ~ mercies** бу́дем благода́рны (и) за ма́лое; **~ talk** све́тский разгово́р. **4.** (*modest, humble*) скро́мный; **he rose from ~ beginnings** он на́чал с ма́лого; **great and ~ alike** вели́кие и ма́лые равно́. **5.** (*petty, mean*) ме́лкий, ме́лочный.

adv.: **chop sth. up ~** ме́лко наруби́ть (*pf.*) что-н.; **sing ~** подж|има́ть, -а́ть хвост; сба́вить (*pf.*) тон.

cpds. **~-arms** *n.* стрелко́вое ору́жие; **~-bore** *adj.* малокали́берный; **~holder** *n.* (*tenant*) ме́лкий арендá́тор; (*owner*) ме́лкий землевладе́лец/со́бственник; **~holding** *n.* уча́сток ме́лкого аренда́тора; небольшо́е земе́льное владе́ние; **~-minded** *adj.* ме́лочный; **~pox** *n.* о́спа; **~-scale** *adj.* ме́лкий; миниатю́рный; в ма́леньком масшта́бе; **~-sword** *n.* рапи́ра, шпа́га; **~-time** *adj.* пустя́чный, пустяко́вый; второсо́ртный, незначи́тельный; **~-town** *adj.* провинциа́льный.

smarm [smɑːm] *v.t.*: **~ down one's hair** (*coll.*) прилиз|ывать, -а́ть во́лосы.

smarmy ['smɑːmɪ] *adj.* (*coll.*) льсти́вый, еле́йный, вкра́дчивый.

smart[1] [smɑːt] *n.* (*liter., pain*) боль; (*of grief*) (серде́чная/душе́вная) боль; го́ре; (*effect of insult*) (о́страя) оби́да.

v.i. **1.** (*of wound or part of body*) жечь (*impf.*); са́днить (*impf.*); **smoke makes the eyes ~** дым ест глаза́; **my eyes are ~ing** у меня́ глаза́ щи́плет. **2.** (*of pers.*): **he ~ed under, from the insult** он испы́тывал о́строе чу́вство оби́ды; **~ for sth.** поплати́ться (*pf.*) за что-н.; **you shall ~ for this** вам за э́то доста́нется/попадёт.

smart[2] [smɑːt] *adj.* **1.** (*sharp, severe*) ре́зкий, суро́вый, о́стрый; **a ~ rebuke** ре́зкая о́тповедь; **a ~ box on the ear** здоро́вая оплеу́ха; **he got a ~ rap on the knuckles** (*lit., fig.*) его́ как сле́дует уда́рили по рука́м (*or* проучи́ли). **2.** (*brisk, prompt*): **he walked off at a ~ pace** он удали́лся бы́стрым ша́гом; **he saluted ~ly** он бра́во отда́л честь. **3.** (*bright, alert*): **a ~ lad** живо́й/шу́стрый ма́лый. **4.** (*clever, ingenious, cunning*) ло́вкий, бо́йкий; **he is ~ at repartee** он за сло́вом в карма́н не поле́зет; **he was too ~ for me** он меня́ перехитри́л; я не мог его́ перехитри́ть. **5.** (*cheeky*): **he answered back ~ly** он де́рзко отве́тил. **6.** (*neat, tidy*) опря́тный. **7.** (*elegant, stylish*): **a ~ hat** элега́нтная шля́пка; **the ~ set** фешене́бельное о́бщество; **you look ~** у вас о́чень изя́щный вид.

cpds. **~-alec(k), ~-alick** (*US* **~y-pants**) *nn.* самоуве́ренный нагле́ц; наха́л (*fem.* -ка).

smarten ['smɑːt(ə)n] *v.t.* (*also* **~ up**): **~ o.s. up** принаря|жа́ться, -ди́ться; прихора́шиваться (*impf.*); (*a room, house, ship etc.*) прив|оди́ть, -ести́ в поря́док; нав|оди́ть, -ести́ блеск в+*p*.

v.i.: **~ up** (*in appearance or dress*): **he has ~ed up** он привёл себя́ в поря́док.

smartness ['smɑːtnɪs] *n.* (*briskness*) бо́йкость; (*elegance*) элега́нтность.

smash [smæʃ] *n.* **1.** (*crash, collision*): **the vase fell with a ~** ва́за с гро́хотом упа́ла; **he gave his head an awful ~ on the pavement** он си́льно уда́рился голово́й о тротуа́р; **there has been a ~ on the motorway** на автостра́де произошло́ столкнове́ние; **many businesses were ruined in the ~** э́то банкро́тство разори́ло/погуби́ло мно́жество предприя́тий. **2.** (*blow with fist*) си́льный уда́р; (*at tennis etc.*) смэш; уда́р по мячу́ све́рху вниз. **3.**: **~ hit** (*coll., play, film etc.*) боеви́к; (*song*) мо́дная пе́сенка; шля́гер.

adv. пря́мо; **he drove ~ through the shop window** он так и вре́зался в витри́ну.

v.t. **1.** (*shatter*) разб|ива́ть, -и́ть; **the bowl was ~ed to bits** ва́за разби́лась вдре́безги (*or* разлете́лась на ме́лкие кусо́чки); **his theory was ~ed** его́ тео́рия была́ разби́та в пух и прах; (*defeat*): **~ an enemy** разгроми́ть (*pf.*) проти́вника; (*ruin financially*) разор|я́ть, -и́ть. **2.** (*drive with force*): **he ~ed his fist into my face** он с си́лой уда́рил меня́ кулако́м по лицу́; **he ~ed the ball over the net** си́льным уда́ром он посла́л мяч че́рез се́тку.

v.i. **1.** (*be broken*) разб|ива́ться, -и́ться. **2.** (*crash, collide*) вр|еза́ться, -е́заться; **the car ~ed into a wall** маши́на вре́залась в сте́ну; **the ship ~ed against the rocks** су́дно наскочи́ло на ска́лы.

with advs.: **~ down** *v.t.* (*e.g. a wall*) сн|оси́ть, -ести́; вали́ть, по-; **~ in** *v.t.* прол|а́мывать, -оми́ть; взл|а́мывать, -ома́ть; **I'll ~ your face in** я тебе́ мо́рду разобью́; **~ up** *v.t.*: **~ up the furniture** разлома́ть (*pf.*) всю ме́бель; **~ up the crockery** переби́ть (*pf.*) всю посу́ду; **~ up one's car** (*in collision*) разби́ть (*pf.*) маши́ну.

cpds. **~-and-grab** *adj.*: **~-and-grab (raid)** (граби́тельский) налёт на витри́ну магази́на; **~-up** *n.* (*collision*) столкнове́ние.

smasher ['smæʃə(r)] *n.* (*coll., s.o. or sth. splendid*) не́что замеча́тельное/снogсшиба́тельное.

smashing ['smæʃɪŋ] *adj.* **1.**: **~ blow** сокруши́тельный уда́р; **~ defeat** (по́лный) разгро́м; тяжёлое пораже́ние. **2.** (*coll.*): **a ~ film** замеча́тельный/потряса́ющий фильм; **we had a ~ time** мы изуми́тельно провели́ вре́мя.

smattering ['smætərɪŋ] *n.*: **he has a ~ of German** он чуть-чуть зна́ет неме́цкий; он зна́ет по-неме́цки два-три сло́ва.

smear [smɪə(r)] *n.* **1.** (*blotch*) пятно́; (*microscope specimen*) мазо́к; **a ~ of dirty fingers on the window** отпеча́ток гря́зных па́льцев на окне́. **2.** (*coll., slander*) клевета́; **~ campaign** клеветни́ческая кампа́ния.

v.t. **1.** (*daub*) ма́зать, на-; разма́з|ывать, -ать; **he ~ed grease paint on his face** (*or* **~ed his face with greasepaint**) он наложи́л грим (себе́) на лицо́ (*or* загримирова́лся); **I ~ed my trousers with paint** я испа́чкал брю́ки кра́ской. **2.** (*blur, e.g. a drawing*) разма́з|ывать, -ать. **3.** (*defame*) черни́ть, о-; поро́чить, о-.

smell [smel] *n.* **1.** (*faculty*) обоня́ние; **a keen sense of ~** то́нкое обоня́ние/чутьё; **I lost my sense of ~** я утра́тил чу́вство обоня́ния; я переста́л распознава́ть за́пахи; (*in animals*) чутьё. **2.** (*odour*) за́пах; **what a** (*sc. bad*) **~!** ну и вонь!; **this flower has no ~** э́тот цвето́к не име́ет за́паха (*or* не па́хнет); **garlic has a pungent ~** у чеснока́ е́дкий за́пах; **there was a ~ of burning** па́хло га́рью/горе́лым. **3.** (*inhalation*): **have, take a ~ of, at** поню́хать (*pf.*).

v.t. **1.** (*perceive ~ of*; *also fig.*) чу́ять (*impf.*); **can you ~ onions?** вы чу́вствуете за́пах лу́ка?; **I can't ~ anything** я не чу́вствую никако́го за́паха; **I ~ something burning** я слы́шу за́пах га́ри; **I ~ a rat** чу́ю недо́брое; **I smelt danger** я почу́вствовал опа́сность. **2.** (*sniff*) ню́хать, по-; **just ~ this rose** то́лько поню́хайте э́ту ро́зу; **~ing salts** ню́хательная соль. **3.**: **~ out** (*lit., fig.*) проню́х|ивать, -ать.

v.i. **1.** (*sniff*): **the dog was ~ing at the lamp-post** соба́ка (об)ню́хала фона́рь. **2.** (*emit ~*) па́хнуть (*impf.*); издава́ть (*impf.*) арома́т; **the soup ~s good** суп хорошо́/вку́сно па́хнет; **the room smelt of polish** в ко́мнате па́хло политу́рой; **his breath ~s** у него́ ду́рно па́хнет изо рта; **the fish began to ~** ры́ба ста́ла пова́нивать/попа́хивать. **3.**: **~ of** (*fig., suggest*) отд|ава́ть, -а́ть *+i.*; **opinions that ~ of heresy** мне́ния, грани́чащие с е́ресью; **his writing ~s of the lamp** у него́ вы́мученный слог; **it ~s of dishonesty** здесь не всё чи́сто.

smelly ['smelɪ] *adj.* попа́хивающий; ду́рно па́хнущий; воню́чий.

smelt[1] [smelt] *n.* (*fish*) ко́рюшка.

smelt[2] [smelt] *v.t.* (*ore*) пла́вить (*impf.*); (*metal*) выплавля́ть, вы́плавить.

smew [smju:] *n.* лу́ток.

smidgen ['smɪdʒ(ə)n] *n.* (*US coll.*) чуто́к.

smile [smaɪl] *n.* улы́бка; **he greeted me with a ~** он встре́тил меня́ улы́бкой; **give s.o. a ~** улыбну́ться (*pf.*) кому́-н.; **he gave a faint ~** он сла́бо улыбну́лся; **force a ~** вы́давить (*pf.*) из себя́ улы́бку; **she was all ~s** у неё был сия́ющий вид; она́ вся сия́ла.

v.t. **1.** (*express by ~*): **he ~d farewell** он улыбну́лся на проща́ние; **she ~d her approval/forgiveness** она́ улыбну́лась в знак одобре́ния/проще́ния. **2.**: **he ~d a frosty smile** он улыбну́лся ледяно́й улы́бкой.

v.i. улыб|а́ться, -ну́ться; усмех|а́ться, -ну́ться; **what are you smiling at?** чему́ вы улыба́етесь?; **they ~d at his claims** его́ прете́нзии каза́лись им смешны́ми; **her ignorance made him ~** её неве́жество вы́звало у него́ улы́бку; **keep smiling!** не унывай́!; **a smiling face** улыба́ющееся лицо́; (*habitual*) улы́бчивое лицо́; **~ on** (*fig.*): **fortune ~ed on him** сча́стье ему́ улыба́лось.

smirch [smɜ:tʃ] *n.* пятно́.

v.t. (*lit., fig.*) пятна́ть, за-; (*fig.*) позо́рить, о-; поро́чить, о-.

smirk [smɜ:k] *n.* жема́нная/самодово́льная улы́бка.

v.i. ухмыля́ться (*impf.*).

smit|e [smaɪt] *v.t.* **1.** (*arch. or joc., strike*) уд|аря́ть, -а́рить. **2.** (*afflict*) пора|жа́ть, -зи́ть; **~ten with the plague** поражённый чумо́й; **his conscience smote him** его́ кольну́ла со́весть; **he was ~ten with remorse** его́ охвати́ло раска́яние; **he was ~ten by her charms** он был покорён её ча́рами.

v.i. (*arch., strike*): **~e (up)on** би́ться (*impf.*) о+*a.*

smith [smɪθ] *n.* **(black~)** кузне́ц.

smithereens [ˌsmɪðə'ri:nz] *n.* (*coll.*): **to ~** вдре́безги.

smithy ['smɪðɪ] *n.* ку́зница.

smock [smɒk] *n.* (*child's*) де́тский хала́тик; (*woman's*) ко́фта; (*peasant's*) (крестья́нская) блу́за.

smocking ['smɒkɪŋ] *n.* фигу́рные бу́ф|ы (*pl., g.* —), ме́лкие сбо́рки (*f. pl.*).

smog [smɒg] *n.* смог.

smoke [sməʊk] *n.* **1.** дым; **clouds of ~** клубы́ (*m. pl.*) ды́ма; **like ~** (*coll., quickly, easily*) в оди́н миг; с лёгкостью; ле́гче лёгкого; **there's no ~ without fire** нет ды́ма без огня́; **emit ~** дыми́ть (*impf.*); **the ~ gets in my eyes** дым разъеда́ет мне глаза́; **~ was pouring out** дым (так и) вали́л; **go up in ~** (*lit.*) сгор|а́ть, -е́ть; (*fig., come to nothing*; *also* **end in ~**) ко́нчиться (*pf.*) ниче́м; **~ abatement** борьба́ с задымлённостью. **2.**: **have a ~** покури́ть (*pf.*); **they broke off for a ~** они́ устро́или переку́р. **3.** (*pl., coll.*) сига́ры и сигаре́ты (*f. pl.*); (*coll.*) ку́рево.

v.t. **1.** (*preserve or darken with ~*) копти́ть, за-; **~d fish** копчёная ры́ба; **~d glass** закопчёное стекло́. **2.** (*fumigate*) оку́р|ивать, -и́ть; **~ out** (*wasps etc.*) выку́ривать, вы́курить; (*fig., unmask*) разоблач|а́ть, -и́ть. **3.** (*tobacco etc.*) кури́ть, вы́-; **~ o.s. sick** накури́ться (*pf.*) до одуре́ния.

v.i. **1.** (*emit ~*; *of chimney, fireplace etc.*) дыми́ть (*impf.*); (*of fire or burning substance*) дыми́ться (*impf.*); кури́ться (*impf.*); **smoking ruins** дымя́щиеся руи́ны. **2.** (*of pers.*: **~ tobacco etc.**) кури́ть (*impf.*); **he ~s like a chimney** он дыми́т без конца́ (*or* как парово́з).

cpds. **~-bomb** *n.* дымова́я бо́мба; **~-dried** *adj.* копчёный; **~-screen** *n.* (*lit., fig.*) дымова́я заве́са; **~-stack** *n.* труба́.

smokeless ['sməʊklɪs] *adj.* безды́мный; **~ zone** безды́мная городска́я зо́на.

smoker ['sməʊkə(r)] *n.* **1.** (*pers.*) куря́щий; кури́льщи|к (*fem.* -ца); **a heavy ~** зая́длый кури́льщик. **2.** (*coll., carriage*) ваго́н для куря́щих.

smoking ['sməʊkɪŋ] *n.* (*of food*) копче́ние; (*of tobacco etc.*) куре́ние; **No S~** кури́ть воспреща́ется; **I gave up ~** я бро́сил кури́ть.

cpds. **~-carriage, ~-compartment** *nn.* ваго́н/купе́ (*indecl.*) для куря́щих; **~-mixture** *n.* (*of pipe tobacco*) тру́бочный таба́к; **~-room** *n.* кури́тельная (ко́мната); **~-room talk** разгово́р «не для дам» (*or* «для куря́щих»).

smoky ['sməʊkɪ] *adj.* ды́мный; дымя́щийся; (*of colour*) ды́мчатый; (*blackened by smoke*) закопте́лый.

smolder ['sməʊldə(r)] = **smo(u)lder**

smooch [smu:tʃ] *v.i.* (*sl.*) обнима́ться, целова́ться (*both impf.*)

smooth [smu:ð] *adj.* **1.** (*even, level*) гла́дкий, ро́вный; **a ~ chin** гла́дкий/бри́тый (*or* гла́дко вы́бритый) подборо́док; **a ~ road** ро́вная доро́га; **the tyre became ~ with wear**

шина сделалась совершенно гладкой от долгой службы; **we must take the rough with the ~ ≃** не всё коту масленица; **a ~ sea** спокойное море; **a ~ paste** тесто без комков; **we had a ~ ride in the train** поезд шёл ровно; **it was a ~ voyage** море было спокойное; **everything went off ~ly** всё прошло без сучка и задоринки. **2.** (*not harsh to ear or taste*): **~ breathing** ровное дыхание; **~ verse** гладкие стихи (*m. pl.*); **~ vodka** мягкая водка; **~ wine** нетерпкое вино. **3.** (*of pers.: equable, unruffled*): **he replied ~ly** он спокойно ответил; **~ manners** мягкие манеры; **he has a ~ tongue** он говорит гладко; он мастер говорить; (*flattering*) льстивый; (*insinuating*) вкрадчивый.

v.t. **1.** (*make level*) выравнивать, выровнять. **2.** (*arrange neatly, flatten*) пригла|живать, -дить; **~ing-iron** утюг. **3.** (*make easy*) смягч|ать, -ить; **he ~ed the way for his successor** он облегчил путь для своего преемника.

with advs.: **~ away** *v.t.*: **he ~ed away our difficulties** он устранил наши затруднения; **~ down** *v.t.*: **~ down one's dress** одёр|гивать, -нуть платье; **he ~ed his hair down** он пригладил волосы; **he was angry but I managed to ~ him down** он был сердит, но мне удалось его успокоить; **~ off** *v.t.*: **~ off sharp edges** обт|ачивать, -очить острые края; **~ out** *v.t.*: **she ~ed out the folds in the tablecloth** она разгладила складки на скатерти; **his face looks ~ed out** (*after sleep etc.*) у него стал более свежий вид; он посвежел; **~ over** *v.t.* смягч|ать, -ить; **~ things over** ула|живать, -дить дело.

cpds. **~-bore** *adj.* гладкоствольный; **~-faced** *adj.* (*beardless*) безбородый; (*shaven*) чисто выбритый; (*ingratiating*; *also* **~-spoken**) вкрадчивый; **~-tongued** *adj.* сладкоречивый, льстивый.

smoothie ['smu:ðɪ] *n.*: **he is a ~** он без мыла куда хочет влезет (*coll.*).

smoothness ['smu:ðnɪs] *n.* гладкость.

smorgasbord ['smɔ:gəs,bɔ:d] *n.* «шведский» стол.

smother ['smʌðə(r)] *n.* (*cloud of dust etc.*) облако пыли *и т. п.*

v.t. **1.** (*suffocate*) душить, за-; **the princes were ~ed in the Tower** принцы были задушены в Тауэре; **he was ~ed by fumes** он задохнулся от испарений; **~** (*extinguish*) **a fire** тушить, по- огонь. **2.** (*cover*): **the furniture was ~ed in dust** мебель была покрыта густым слоем пыли; **she ~ed the child with kisses** она осыпала ребёнка поцелуями; **strawberries ~ed in cream** клубника, залитая сливками. **3.** (*suppress, conceal*) подав|лять, -ить; **~ing a yawn** подавляя/сдерживая зевок; **they ~ed his cries** они заглушили его крики; **~ (up) a crime** зам|инать, -ять преступление.

v.i. зад|ыхаться, -охнуться.

smoulder ['sməʊldə(r)], **(US) smolder** *v.i.* (*lit., fig.*) тлеть (*impf.*); **~ing leaves** тлеющие листья; **~ing hatred** затаённая ненависть.

smudge [smʌdʒ] *n.* пятно; **you have a ~ on your cheek** вы чем-то вымазали/испачкали щёку.

v.t. (*blur*) смаз|ывать, -ать; (*smear*) мазать, вы-.

v.i.: **the drawing ~s easily** рисунок легко смазывается.

smudgy ['smʌdʒɪ] *adj.* запачканный.

smug [smʌg] *adj.* самодовольный.

smuggle ['smʌg(ə)l] *v.t.* пров|озить, -езти контрабандой; (*fig.*) **he was ~d into the house** его тайком провели в дом; **I was able to ~ out a letter** мне удалось тайком переправить письмо.

smuggler ['smʌglə(r)] *n.* контрабандист (*fem.* -ка).

smuggling ['smʌglɪŋ] *n.* контрабанда.

smugness ['smʌgnɪs] *n.* самодовольство.

smut [smʌt] *n.* **1.** (*of soot etc.*) сажа. **2.: talk ~** нести (*det.*) похабщину. **3.** (*fungous disease*) головня.

smutty ['smʌtɪ] *adj.*: **~ face** грязное/запачканное лицо; **~ joke** похабный анекдот.

snack [snæk] *n.* закуска; **have a ~** закус|ывать, -ить.

cpd. **~-bar** *n.* закусочная, буфет.

snaffle ['snæf(ə)l] *n.* уздечка, трензель (*m.*); **ride s.o. on the ~** (*fig.*) деликатно руководить (*impf.*) кем-н.

v.t. (*appropriate, steal*) стянуть, стибрить, урвать (*all pf.*) (*sl.*).

snafu [snæ'fu:] *n.* (*US coll.*) неразбериха, путаница.

snag [snæg] *n.* **1.** (*on tree*) сучок. **2.** (*broken tooth*) сломанный зуб. **3.** (*on river-bed*) коряга. **4.** (*obstacle*) препятствие; (*difficulty*) затруднение; (*hidden*) загвоздка.

v.t. (*catch against*) зацепиться (*pf.*) за+*a.*

snail [sneɪl] *n.* улитка; **go at a ~'s pace** тащиться (*impf.*) как черепаха.

snake [sneɪk] *n.* змея; **grass ~** уж; **~ in the grass** (*fig.*) скрытый враг; змея подколодная.

v.i.: **the road ~s through the mountains** дорога вьётся меж гор.

cpds. **~bite** *n.* укус змеи; змеиный укус; **~-charmer** *n.* заклинатель (*m.*) змей.

snaky ['sneɪkɪ] *adj.* (*perfidious*) коварный; (*venomous*) ядовитый.

snap [snæp] *n.* **1.** (*noise*) щелчок, щёлканье; **the box shut with a ~** коробка (громко *or* с треском) защёлкнулась; (*of sth. breaking*) треск; **there was a ~ and the plank broke** раздался треск и доска сломалась; (*bite*): **the dog made a ~ at him** собака пыталась его укусить. **2.** (*fastener*) кнопка. **3.** (*vigour, zest*) живость, огонь (*m.*), огонёк, изюминка; **put some ~ into it!** живее! **4.** (*coll., photograph*) (любительский) снимок; **take a ~ of** сн|имать, -ять. **5.** (*spell*): **a cold ~** внезапное похолодание.

adj.: **~ decision** скоропалительное решение; **~ answer** ответ с кондачка (*coll.*); **they took a ~ vote** они устроили голосование экспромтом; **~ strike** забастовка, объявленная без предупреждения.

v.t. **1.** (*make ~ping noise with*) щёлк|ать, -нуть +*i.*; **he ~ped his fingers in my face** он щёлкнул пальцами перед моим носом; **~ one's fingers at** (*fig., defy*) плевать (*impf.*) на+*a.* **2.** (*break*) разл|амывать, -омать; **he ~ped the stick in two** он разломал палку надвое. **3.** (*coll., photograph*) сн|имать, -ять.

v.i. **1.** (*make biting motion*): **~ at** отгрыз|аться, -нуться на+*a.*; (*speak sharply*) наброситься (*pf.*) на+*a.*; **don't ~ at me!** не кричите на меня! **2.** (*snatch*): **~ at an opportunity** ухватиться (*pf.*) за возможность. **3.** (*make ~ping sound*) щёлк|ать, -нуть; (*of fastener*) защёлк|иваться, -нуться. **4.** (*break*) треснуть (*pf.*); **the rope ~ped** верёвка оборвалась. **5.** (*move smartly*): **~ to attention** вытянуться (*pf.*) во фронт; **~ out of it!** (*coll.*) брось!; **~ into it!** (*coll.*) давай!

with advs.: **~ down** *v.t.*: **he ~ped the lid down** он защёлкнул/захлопнул крышку; **~ off** *v.t. & i.* (*break off*) отл|амывать(ся), -омать(ся), -омить(ся); **~ s.o.'s head off** (*coll.*) об|рывать, -орвать кого-н.; **~ up** *v.t.* (*snatch*) сцапать (*pf.*); (*buy eagerly*) расхват|ывать, -ать; **the tickets were ~ped up straight away** билеты тут же расхватали.

cpds. **~dragon** *n.* львиный зев; **~-fastener** *n.* кнопка; **~shot** *n.* (любительский) снимок.

snappish ['snæpɪʃ] *adj.* раздражительный; (*of dog*) злой, кусачий.

snappy ['snæpɪ] *adj.* (*brisk*) живой; **make it ~!** (по)живее!; (*coll., neat, elegant*) шикарный.

snare [sneə(r)] *n.* (*noose*) силок; (*trap*) западня, ловушка; **lay, set a ~ for s.o.** ставить, по- ловушку кому-н.; **be caught in a ~** поп|адать, -асть в ловушку; **a ~ and a delusion** сплошной обман.

v.t. ловить, поймать в западню/ловушку.

cpd. **~-drum** *n.* барабан со струнами.

snarl[1] [snɑ:l] *n.* (*growl*) рычание; **he answered with a ~** он зарычал в ответ.

v.t. & i. рычать, за-.

snarl[2] [snɑ:l] *n.* (*tangle*) спутанный клубок.

v.t. запут|ывать, -ать; (*fig.*): **the arrangements were ~ed up** всё было перепутано.

snatch [snætʃ] *n.* **1.** (*act of ~ing*): **make a ~ at sth.** хвататься (*pf.*) за что-н. **2.** (*short spell*): **sleep in ~es** спать (*impf.*) урывками. **3.** (*fragment*) обрывок; **I overheard ~es of their conversation** я подслушал обрывки их разговора. **4.** (*coll., robbery*) налёт.

v.t. **1.** (*seize*) хватать, схватить; **~ sth. from s.o.** урвать (*pf.*) что-н. у кого-н.; **~ sth. out of s.o.'s hands** (*or* **away from s.o.**) выхватывать, выхватить (*or* вырывать, вырвать) что-н. у кого́-н. (из рук); **don't ~!** не хвата́й!; **~ an opportunity** воспо́льзоваться (*pf.*) слу́чаем; **~ a kiss** сорва́ть (*pf.*) поцелу́й; **the wind ~ed off my hat** ве́тер сорва́л с меня́ шля́пу; **she ~ed up her handbag** она́ схвати́ла свою́ су́мочку. **2.** (*obtain with difficulty*) ур|ыва́ть, -ва́ть; **we ~ed a hurried meal** мы на́скоро перекуси́ли; **I managed to ~ a few hours' sleep** мне удало́сь урва́ть не́сколько часо́в сна.

v.i. хвата́ть (*impf.*); **~ at sth.** хвата́ться, схвати́ться за что-н.

snazzy ['snæzɪ] *adj.* (*coll.*) шика́рный, эффе́ктный.

sneak [sni:k] *n.* подле́ц; (*in school*) я́беда (*c.g.*).

v.t. стащи́ть (*pf.*); **~ a look at sth.** взгляну́ть (*pf.*) на что-н. укра́дкой (*or* одни́м глазко́м).

v.i. **1.** (*creep, move silently*) кра́сться (*impf.*); **~ into a room** прокра́|дываться, -сться в ко́мнату; **~ out of a room** выходи́ть, вы́йти укра́дкой (*or* выска́льзывать, вы́скользнуть) из ко́мнаты; **he ~ed off round the corner** он скры́лся за угло́м; (*fig.*): **~ out of responsibility** ускольз|а́ть, -ну́ть от отве́тственности. **2.** (*tell tales*): **~ on s.o.** я́бедничать, на- на кого́-н.

cpd. **~-thief** *n.* ме́лкий вор, вори́шка (*m.*).

sneakers ['sni:kəz] *n.* (*coll.*) полуке́д|ы (*pl.*, *g.* -ов/—).

sneaking ['sni:kɪŋ] *adj.* (*furtive*): **he gave her a ~ glance** он укра́дкой взгляну́л на неё; (*persistent, lingering*): **~ feeling** та́йное подозре́ние; **I have a ~ affection for her** у меня́ к ней сла́бость.

sneer [snɪə(r)] *n.* (*contemptuous smile*) презри́тельная усме́шка; (*taunt*) глумле́ние.

v.i. усмех|а́ться, -ну́ться; **~ at** насмеха́ться (*impf.*) над+*i.*; (*in words*) глуми́ться (*impf.*) над+*i.*; **a ~ing voice** насме́шливый/ехи́дный го́лос.

sneerer ['snɪərə(r)] *n.* насме́шни|к (*fem.* -ца).

sneeze [sni:z] *n.* чиха́нье; (*coll.*) чих; **I felt a ~ coming and couldn't stop it** я чу́вствовал, что сейча́с чихну́, и не мог сдержа́ться.

v.i. чих|а́ть, -ну́ть; **£50 is not to be ~d at** 50 фу́нтов — не шу́тка (*or* на земле́ не валя́ются).

snick [snɪk] *n.* (*notch*) зару́бка; (*cut*) надре́з.

snicker ['snɪkə(r)] *n.* (*whinny*) ржа́ние; (*snigger*) хихи́канье.

v.i. ржать (*impf.*); хихи́к|ать, -нуть.

snide [snaɪd] *adj.* (*coll.*) ехи́дный.

sniff [snɪf] *n.* (*inhalation*) вдох; **one ~ is sufficient to kill** сто́ит э́то вдохну́ть, как сра́зу умрёшь; **take a ~ at, of sth.** поню́хать (*pf.*) что-н.; **get a ~ of fresh air** подыша́ть (*pf.*) све́жим во́здухом; **give a ~** (*of contempt*) фы́рк|ать, -нуть; (*to stop nose running etc.*) шмы́г|ать, -ну́ть (но́сом).

v.t. (*inhale*) вд|ыха́ть, -охну́ть; (*smell at*) ню́хать, по-.

v.i. **1.** (*because of tears, cold etc.*) шмы́г|ать, -ну́ть (но́сом); (*in contempt*) фы́рк|ать, -нуть. **2.:** **~ at** ню́хать, по-; **the dog ~ed at the lamp-post** соба́ка (об)ню́хала фона́рь; **the offer is not to he ~ed at** тако́е предложе́ние не ка́ждый день де́лают.

sniffle ['snɪf(ə)l] *n.* сопе́ние; (*pl.*) на́сморк.

v.i. шмы́г|ать, -ну́ть (но́сом).

sniffy ['snɪfɪ] *adj.* (*coll.*) презри́тельный.

snigger ['snɪgə(r)] *n.* хихи́канье.

v.i. хихи́к|ать, -нуть.

snip [snɪp] *n.* (*act of ~ping*) ре́зание; (*piece cut off*) обре́зок; кусо́к; (*coll., bargain*) (больша́я) уда́ча.

v.t. (*clip, trim*) подр|еза́ть, -е́зать; (*cut*): **~ out a piece of cloth** выре́зывать, вы́резать (*or* кроить, рас-) кусо́к мате́рии; **~ off a bud** ср|еза́ть, -е́зать по́чку.

snipe[1] [snaɪp] *n.* (*bird*) бека́с.

snip|e[2] [snaɪp] *v.i.* (*mil.*) стреля́ть (*impf.*) из укры́тия; (*fig.*): **he is always ~ing at the Church** он ве́чно напада́ет на це́рковь.

sniper ['snaɪpə(r)] *n.* сна́йпер.

snippet ['snɪpɪt] *n.* (*of material*) лоску́т, лоскуто́к; (*pl.*, *of news etc.*) обры́вки (*m. pl.*).

snitch [snɪtʃ] *v.t.* (*coll., filch*) сти́брить, стяну́ть (*both pf.*) (*coll.*).

snivel ['snɪv(ə)l] *v.i.* (*run at the nose*) распус|ка́ть, -ти́ть со́пли; (*whine*) хны́кать (*impf.*); распус|ка́ть, -ти́ть ню́ни.

sniveller ['snɪv(ə)lə(r)] *n.* ны́тик.

snob [snɒb] *n.* сноб.

snobbery ['snɒbərɪ] *n.* сноби́зм.

snobbish ['snɒbɪʃ] *adj.* снобистский.

snood [snu:d] *n.* (*hair-net*) се́тка (для воло́с).

snook [snu:k] *n.*: **cock a ~ at** пока́з|ывать, -а́ть (дли́нный) нос +*d.*

snooker ['snu:kə(r)] *n.* сну́кер.

v.t. (*sl., defeat*) разби́ть (*pf.*), разгроми́ть (*pf.*).

snoop [snu:p] *v.i.* (*coll.*) подгля́дывать/подсма́тривать/ вынюхивать (*impf.*) чужи́е та́йны.

snooper ['snu:pə(r)] *n.* челове́к, сую́щий нос в чужи́е дела́.

snooty ['snu:tɪ] *adj.* (*coll.*) задира́ющий нос, вообража́ющий.

snooze [snu:z] (*coll.*) *n.*: **have, take a ~** вздремну́ть (*pf.*); всхрапну́ть (*pf.*).

v.i. дрема́ть (*impf.*).

snore [snɔ:(r)] *n.* храп.

v.i. храпе́ть, за-; всхрапну́ть (*pf.*).

snorer ['snɔ:rə(r)] *n.* храпу́н (*fem.* -ья).

snorkel ['snɔ:k(ə)l] *n.* шно́ркель (*m.*).

snort [snɔ:t] *n.* (*of contempt*) фы́ркание; (*of horse*) храпе́ние.

v.i. фы́рк|ать, -нуть; кря́к|ать, -нуть (от доса́ды).

snorter ['snɔ:tə(r)] *n.* (*sl.*): **I wrote him a ~** (*rebuke*) я его́ (хороше́нько) отчита́л в письме́.

snot [snɒt] *n.* (*vulg.*) со́пли (*f. pl.*).

snotty ['snɒtɪ] *adj.* (*vulg.*, **~-nosed**) сопли́вый; (*sl., annoyed*) серди́тый; раздражённый.

snout [snaʊt] *n.* **1.** (*of animal*) мо́рда; (*of pig*) ры́ло. **2.** (*nozzle*) сопло́.

snow [snəʊ] *n.* снег; **driven ~** позёмка; **there was a fall of ~** вы́пал снег; **the roads are deep in ~** все доро́ги в сугро́бах; **the ~ is turning to rain** снег перехо́дит в дождь; **S~ Maiden** Снегу́рочка.

v.i.: **it is ~ing** снег идёт.

with advs.: **~ in, ~ up** *vv.t.*: **the road is ~ed up** доро́гу занесло́ сне́гом; **we were ~ed in** наш дом занесло́ сне́гом; **~ under** *v.t.* (*fig.*): **I was ~ed under with letters** я был зава́лен (*or* меня́ засы́пали) пи́сьмами; **we are ~ed under with work** мы зава́лены рабо́той.

cpds. **~ball** *n.* снежо́к; *v.i.* игра́ть (*impf.*) в снежки́; (*fig., increase*) расти́ (*impf.*), как сне́жный ком; **~-blind** *adj.* ослеплённый сверка́ющим сне́гом; **be ~-blind** страда́ть (*impf.*) сне́жной слепото́й; **~-blindness** *n.* сне́жная слепота́; **~-blink** *n.* ледяно́й о́тблеск; **~-boots** *n. pl.* (тёплые) бо́ты (*m. pl.*); **~-bound** *adj.* (*of pers.*) не могу́щий вы́браться (и́з дому) из-за сне́жных зано́сов; (*of place*) занесённый сне́гом; **~-capped, ~-clad, ~-covered** *adjs.* покры́тый сне́гом; **~-drift** *n.* сугро́б; **~drop** *n.* подсне́жник; **~fall** *n.* снегопа́д; **~-fence** *n.* снегозащи́тное загражде́ние; снегово́й щит; **~-field** *n.* сне́жное по́ле; **~flake** *n.* снежи́нка; (*pl.*) (сне́жные) хло́пья; **~gauge** *n.* снегоме́р; **~-goggles** *n. pl.* сне́жные очк|и́ (*pl.*, *g.* -о́в); **~-leopard** *n.* сне́жный барс, и́рбис; **~-line** *n.* снегова́я ли́ния; **~man** *n.* сне́жная ба́ба; **~-mobile** *n.* мотоса́н|и, аэроса́н|и (*pl.*, *g.* -е́й); снегохо́д; **~-plough** *n.* снегоочисти́тель (*m.*); **~-shoes** *n. pl.* снегосту́пы (*m. pl.*); **~-shovel** *n.* лопа́та для сне́га; **~-slip** *n.* лави́на, сне́жный обва́л; **~storm** *n.* мете́ль, вью́га; **~-white** *adj.* белосне́жный; **S~-White** Снегу́рочка.

snowy ['snəʊɪ] *adj.* **1.:** **~ roofs** заснéженные кры́ши; **~ weather** сне́жная пого́да. **2.** (*white*): **~ hair** белосне́жные во́лосы; **~ owl** бе́лая сова́.

snub[1] [snʌb] *n.* (*rebuff, slight*) афро́нт.

v.t. оса́|живать, -ди́ть.

snub[2] [snʌb] *adj.*: **~ nose** вздёрнутый нос.

cpd. **~-nosed** *adj.* курно́сый.

snuff[1] [snʌf] *n.* ню́хательный таба́к; **pinch of ~** поню́шка; **take ~** ню́хать (*impf.*) таба́к; **he is up to ~** (*shrewd*) его́ (на мяки́не) не проведёшь (*coll.*).

cpds. **~-box** *n.* табаке́рка; **~-coloured** *adj.* таба́чный.

snuff[2] [snʌf] *v.t.* **1.** (*also* **~ out**) туши́ть, по-; (*fig.*) гаси́ть, по-; **~ it** (*die*) загну́ться (*pf.*), дать (*pf.*) ду́ба (*sl.*). **2.:** **~ a candle** сн|има́ть, -ять нага́р со свечи́.

snuffle ['snʌf(ə)l] *n.* сопе́ние; **I have the ~s** (*coll.*) у меня́ и́з носу течёт.

v.i. сопе́ть (*impf.*).

snug [snʌg] *adj.* (*cosy*) ую́тный; (*adequate for comfort*): **a ~ income** прили́чный дохо́д; (*close-fitting*): **a ~ jacket** облега́ющая ку́ртка.

snuggery ['snʌgərɪ] *n.* (*coll.*) уголо́к.

snuggle ['snʌg(ə)l] *v.i.*: **~ down in bed** свёр|тываться, -ну́ться (клубко́м/клубо́чком/кала́чиком (*or* в клубо́(че)к)) в посте́ли; **~ up to s.o.** приж|има́ться, -а́ться к кому́-н.

so[1] [səʊ] *n.* (*mus.*) = **so(h)**

so[2] [səʊ] *adv.* **1.** так; **is that ~?** пра́вда?; **~ it is (~ I am etc.)!** действи́тельно!; так оно́ и есть!; (и) в са́мом де́ле; **isn't that ~?** не так ли?; **that being ~** раз так; **I'm ~ glad to see you** я так рад вас ви́деть; **would you be ~ kind as to visit her?** бу́дьте так добры́, навести́те её; **they are ~ bad as to be worthless** они́ насто́лько пло́хи, что про́сто никуда́ не годя́тся; **he is not ~ silly as to ask her** он не насто́лько глуп, что́бы проси́ть её; **he was ~ overworked that ...** он был до тако́й сте́пени перегружён, что...; **not ~ very ...** не так уж...; **ever ~ little** са́мая ма́лость; **if he loves her ever ~ little** е́сли он хоть ско́лько-нибудь её лю́бит; **it is ever ~ easy** э́то про́ще просто́го (*or* о́чень легко́); **every ~ often** вре́мя от вре́мени; **~ be it!** пусть так!; быть по сему́!; **~ far** (*up to now*) пока́, поку́да; до сих пор; **~ far as I know** наско́лько я зна́ю; **~ far ~ good** пока́ всё хорошо́; де́ло подвига́ется непло́хо; **and ~ forth, on** и так да́лее; **just ~** вот и́менно!; ве́рно!; (*in good order*) в ажу́ре; **~ long!** (*au revoir*) пока́! (*coll.*); **~ long as** (*provided that*) е́сли то́лько; **~ many** сто́лько *+g.*; **thank you ~ much!** большо́е спаси́бо!; **(at) ~ much per person** по сто́льку-то с челове́ка; **~ much for his advice** вот и весь его́ сове́т!; **~ much ~ that** насто́лько, что; **~ much the worse/better** тем ху́же/лу́чше; **he is not ~ much discontented as unsatisfied** он скоре́е неудовлетворён, чем недово́лен; **he left without ~ much as a nod** он ушёл, да́же не кивну́в голово́й (на проща́ние); **~ to say, speak** так сказа́ть; **~ what** ну и что (же)? **2.** (*also*) то́же; **(and) ~ do I** и я то́же. **3.** (*consequently, accordingly*) ита́к, поэ́тому; ста́ло быть; зна́чит; **he is ill, (and) ~ he can't come** он нездоро́в, так что не мо́жет прийти́; **~ you did see him after all** ита́к, вы всё-таки его́ ви́дели; **it was late, ~ I went home** бы́ло по́здно, и (поэ́тому) я пошёл домо́й. **4.** (*that the foregoing is true or will happen*): **I suppose/hope ~** я ду́маю/наде́юсь, что да; **do you think ~?** вы так ду́маете?; **'I told you ~!' — '~ you did!'** «я вам говори́л» — «Да, ве́рно». **5.: ~ as to** (*in order to*) (с тем), что́бы *+inf.*; (*in such a way as to*) так, что́бы. **6.** (*thereabouts*): **there were 100 or ~ people there** там бы́ло приме́рно сто челове́к (*or* о́коло ста челове́к).

cpds. **~-and-~** *pron.* (*pers.*) тако́й-то; (*pej.*) тако́й-сяко́й; **he's a mean old ~-and-~** он невероя́тный скря́га; **he told me to do ~-and-~** он сказа́л мне, что́бы я сде́лал то́-то (и то́-то); **~-called** *adj.* так называ́емый; **~-so** *adj. & adv.* ничего́; так себе́.

soak [səʊk] *n.* **1.** (*~ing*): **give the clothes a thorough ~!** пусть бельё подо́льше помо́кнет! **2.** (*sl., hard drinker*) пья́ница (*c.g.*); пьяну́жка (*c.g.*).

v.t. **1.** (*steep*) выма́чивать, вы́мочить; **she ~s the laundry overnight** она́ зама́чивает бельё на́ ночь; **he ~ed his bread in milk** он разма́чивал хлеб в молоке́. **2.** (*wet through*): **the shower ~ed me to the skin** дождь промочи́л меня́ до ни́тки. **3.** (*fig., immerse*): **he ~ed himself in Roman history** он с голово́й ушёл в исто́рию Ри́ма. **4.** (*coll., extort money from*): **~ the rich!** выка́чивайте побо́льше де́нег из бога́тых!

v.i. **1.** (*remain immersed*) мо́кнуть (*impf.*). **2.** (*drain, percolate*) впи́т|ываться, -а́ться; прос|а́чиваться, -очи́тся; **the rain ~ed into the ground** дождь пропита́л по́чву; **the water ~ed through my shoes** вода́ просочи́лась в мои́ ту́фли. **3.** (*coll., drink heavily*) пья́нствовать (*impf.*).

with advs.: **~ off** *v.t.*: **~ off dirt** отм|а́чивать, -очи́ть грязь; **~ up** *v.t.* (*lit., fig.*) впи́т|ывать, -а́ть.

soaker ['səʊkə(r)] *n.* (*heavy rain*) ли́вень (*m.*).

soaking ['səʊkɪŋ] *n.*: **he got a ~** он здо́рово промо́к.

adj. & adv.: **you are ~ (wet)** вы промо́кли насквозь́; **it was a ~ (wet) day** весь день лило́ (как из ведра́).

soap [səʊp] *n.* мы́ло; **cake, tablet of ~** кусо́к мы́ла; **household, washing ~** хозя́йственное мы́ло; **soft ~** (*coll., flattery*) лесть.

v.t. мы́лить, на-; **~ o.s.** намы́ли|ваться, -ться.

cpds. **~-box** *n.* я́щик из-под мы́ла; **~-box orator** у́личный ора́тор; **~-bubble** *n.* мы́льный пузы́рь; **~-dish** *n.* мы́льница; **~-flakes** *n. pl.* мы́льные хло́пь|я (*pl., g.* -ев); **~-opera** *n.* «мы́льная о́пера», телесериа́л; **~-powder** *n.* стира́льный порошо́к; **~stone** *n.* мы́льный ка́мень, стеати́т; **~-suds** *n. pl.* мы́льная пе́на; обмы́лк|и (*pl., g.* -ов); **~-works** *n.* мылова́ренный заво́д.

soapy ['səʊpɪ] *adj.* **1.** (*covered with soap*): **~ face** намы́ленное лицо́. **2.** (*resembling, containing, consisting of soap*) мы́льный; **~ water** мы́льная вода́; **a ~ taste** при́вкус мы́ла; мы́льный при́вкус. **3.** (*unctuous*) еле́йный, вкра́дчивый.

soar [sɔː(r)] *v.i.* **1.** (*of birds*) пари́ть, вос-; высоко́ взлет|а́ть, -е́ть; взмы|ва́ть, -ть. **2.** (*fig., rise, tower*) возн|оси́ться, -ести́сь; **~ing ambition** непоме́рное честолю́бие. **3.** (*of prices*) (ре́зко) пов|ыша́ться, -ы́ситься; возраст|а́ть, -и́. **4.** (*of glider*) плани́ровать, с-.

s.o.b. (*abbr. of* ***son of a bitch***) (*US*) су́кин сын (*coll.*).

sob [sɒb] *n.* всхлип, всхли́пывание.

v.t.: **she ~bed out her grief** облива́ясь слеза́ми, она́ пове́дала своё го́ре; **~ one's heart out** (отча́янно) рыда́ть (*impf.*); го́рько пла́кать (*impf.*); **she ~bed herself to sleep** она́ пла́кала, пока́ не усну́ла; она́ засну́ла в слеза́х.

v.i. всхли́п|ывать, -нуть.

cpds. **~-story** *n.* (*coll.*) жа́лкие слова́; душещипа́тельная исто́рия; **~-stuff** *n.* сентимента́льщина.

sober ['səʊbə(r)] *adj.* **1.** (*not drunk, temperate*) тре́звый. **2.** (*not fanciful*) здра́вый; **a man of ~ judgement** челове́к тре́звого ума́; **no man in his ~ senses would have said that** ни оди́н здравомы́слящий челове́к не сказа́л бы э́того. **3.** (*of colour*) споко́йный; **~ly dressed** нося́щий непро́скую/скро́мную оде́жду.

v.t. (*usu.* **~ down, ~ up**) отрезв|ля́ть, -и́ть; вытрезвля́ть, вы́трезвить; **this had a ~ing effect on them** э́то поде́йствовало на них отрезвля́юще; **~ing-up station** (*in former USSR*) вытрезви́тель (*m.*).

v.i. остепен|я́ться, -и́ться; отрезв|ля́ться, -и́ться; **~ up** протрезви́ться (*pf.*).

cpds. **~-minded** *adj.* рассуди́тельный; (*balanced*) уравнове́шенный; **~sides** *n.* (*sedate pers.*) суха́рь (*m.*), неулы́ба (*c.g.*) (*both coll.*).

sobriety [sə'braɪɪtɪ] *n.* тре́звость.

so|briquet ['səʊbrɪ,keɪ], **sou-** ['suːbrɪ,keɪ] *n.* про́звище, кли́чка.

soccer ['sɒkə(r)] *n.* футбо́л; **~ fan** футбо́льный боле́льщик; **~ match** футбо́льный матч; **~ player** футболи́ст.

sociability [,səʊʃə'bɪlɪtɪ] *n.* общи́тельность.

sociable ['səʊʃəb(ə)l] *adj.* общи́тельный, компане́йский.

social ['səʊʃ(ə)l] *n.* вечери́нка.

adj. **1.** (*pert. to the community*) обще́ственный, социа́льный; **~ contract** обще́ственный догово́р; **S~ Democrat** социа́л-демокра́т; **~ reform** социа́льные рефо́рмы; **~ science** социоло́гия; **~ sciences** обще́ственные нау́ки; **~ security** социа́льное обеспе́чение; **~ services** систе́ма социа́льного обслу́живания; **~ worker** рабо́тни|к (*fem.* -ца) сфе́ры социа́льных пробле́м. **2.** (*pert. to ~ relationships*): **one's ~ equals** себе́ подо́бные (в социа́льной иера́рхии); **~ advancement** продвиже́ние по обще́ственной ле́стнице. **3.** (*convivial*): **~ gathering** дру́жеская встре́ча; **~ evening** вечери́нка; **I have met him ~ly** я встреча́лся с ним в о́бществе; я встреча́л его́ в гостя́х.

cpd. **~-democratic** *adj.* социа́л-демократи́ческий.

socialism ['səʊʃə,lɪz(ə)m] *n.* социали́зм.

socialist ['səʊʃəlɪst] *n.* социали́ст (*fem.* -ка).

adj. социалисти́ческий.

socialite ['səʊʃə,laɪt] *n.* све́тская знамени́тость.

socialization [,səʊʃəlaɪ'zeɪʃ(ə)n] *n.* социализа́ция, национализа́ция, обобществле́ние.

socialize [ˈsəʊʃəˌlaɪz] *v.t.* обобществ|ля́ть, -и́ть; национализи́ровать (*impf., pf.*); **~d medicine** госуда́рственное медици́нское обслу́живание.

v.i. (*coll., go about socially*) вести́ (*impf.*) све́тский о́браз жи́зни; (*maintain social relations*) подде́рживать (*impf.*) све́тское обще́ние (с кем-н.).

society [səˈsaɪətɪ] *n.* о́бщество; (*association*) о́бщество, объедине́ние, организа́ция; (*e.g. students'*) клуб, кружо́к; **high ~** вы́сшее о́бщество; **~ gossip** све́тские спле́тни; све́тская болтовня́; **S~ of Friends** «О́бщество друзе́й», ква́керы (*m. pl.*).

sociological [ˌsəʊsɪəˈlɒdʒɪk(ə)l, ˌsəʊʃɪ-] *adj.* социологи́ческий.

sociologist [ˌsəʊsɪˈɒlədʒɪst, ˌsəʊʃɪ-] *n.* социо́лог.

sociology [ˌsəʊsɪˈɒlədʒɪ, ˌsəʊʃɪ-] *n.* социоло́гия.

sock[1] [sɒk] *n.* **1.** (*short stocking*) носо́к; **pull up one's ~s** (*lit.*) подтя́|гивать, -ну́ть носки́; (*fig.*) подтяну́ться (*pf.*); засучи́ть (*pf.*) рукава́; **put a ~ in it** заткну́ться (*pf.*) (*sl.*); **ankle ~s** коро́ткие носо́чки (*m. pl.*). **2.** (*inner sole*) сте́лька.

sock[2] [sɒk] (*sl.*) *n.* (*blow*) уда́р; **give s.o. a ~ on the nose** да|ва́ть, -ть кому́-н. по́ носу.

v.t.: **I ~ed him in the jaw** я дал ему́ в мо́рду.

socket [ˈsɒkɪt] *n.* **1.** (*anat.*) впа́дина; **eye ~** глазна́я впа́дина, глазни́ца; **wrench s.o.'s arm out of its ~** вы́вернуть (*pf.*) кому́-н. ру́ку. **2.** (*for plug*) розе́тка; (*for bulb*) патро́н.

cpd. **~-joint** *n.* шарни́рное соедине́ние.

socle [ˈsəʊk(ə)l] *n.* цо́коль (*m.*).

Socrates [ˈsɒkrəˌtiːz] *n.* Сокра́т.

Socratic [səˈkrætɪk] *adj.* сокра́товский; **~ method** эвристи́ческий ме́тод.

sod[1] [sɒd] *n.* дёрн; **under the ~** (*in one's grave*) в сыро́й земле́; в моги́ле.

sod[2] [sɒd] *n.* (*sl.*) сво́лочь (*f.*); **silly ~** идио́т; **S~'s Law** зако́н по́длости, зако́н бутербро́да.

v.i. **~ off: I told him to ~ off** я его́ посла́л; **~ off!** иди́ на...!

soda [ˈsəʊdə] *n.* **1.** со́да; углеки́слый на́трий; **baking ~** со́да для пече́ния; **caustic ~** е́дкий натр; **washing ~** стира́льная со́да. **2.** (**~-water**) со́довая/газиро́ванная вода́; газиро́вка.

cpds. **~-bread** *n.* хлеб, вы́печенный на со́де; **~-fountain** *n.* сатура́тор; сто́йка, где продаётся газиро́вка; **~-siphon** *n.* сифо́н для газиро́ванной воды́; **~water** *n.* со́довая/газиро́ванная вода́; газиро́вка.

sodality [səʊˈdælɪtɪ] *n.* бра́тство; о́бщина.

sodden [ˈsɒd(ə)n] *adj.* (*drenched*) промо́кший; (*steeped*) пропи́танный; **he was ~ with drink** он отупе́л от вы́питого; он напи́лся до одуре́ния.

sodium [ˈsəʊdɪəm] *n.* на́трий.

sodomite [ˈsɒdəˌmaɪt] *n.* педера́ст, гомосексуали́ст; скотоло́жец.

sodomy [ˈsɒdəmɪ] *n.* педера́стия, гомосексуали́зм; (*bestiality*) скотоло́жство.

sofa [ˈsəʊfə] *n.* дива́н.

Sofia [ˈsəʊfɪə] *n.* Софи́я.

soft [sɒft] *adj.* **1.** мя́гкий; **~ colour** нея́ркий цвет; **~ cover** (*of book*) мя́гкий переплёт; **~ goods** тексти́льные изде́лия; **~ furnishings** драпиро́вки (*f. pl.*); **a ~ light** мя́гкий свет; **~ palate** мя́гкое нёбо, нёбная занаве́ска; **~ pencil** мя́гкий каранда́ш; **~ rain** лёгкий до́ждик; **~ soil** ры́хлая по́чва; **~ toy** мягконабивна́я игру́шка; **~ water** мя́гкая вода́; **~ drink** безалкого́льный напи́ток; **~ drugs** нарко́тики, не вызыва́ющие привыка́ния; **~ fruit** я́года; **~ pedal** ле́вая педа́ль; **~** (*gentle*) **voice** мя́гкий/не́жный/ла́сковый голос; **~** (*low-pitched*) **voice** ти́хий го́лос; **~ sign** (*gram.*) мя́гкий знак. **2.** (*gentle, compassionate*) мя́гкий, кро́ткий; отзы́вчивый; **have a ~ spot for s.o.** пита́ть (*impf.*) сла́бость к кому́-н.; (*indulgent*) нестро́гий; **she is too ~ with her children** она́ недоста́точно строга́ с детьми́. **3.** (*flabby*) дря́блый, изне́женный. **4.** (*coll., easy*): **he has a ~ job** у него́ лёгкая рабо́та (*or* рабо́та «не бей лежа́чего»). **5.** (*coll., ~ in the head, stupid*) глупова́тый. **6.: ~ currency** необрати́мая валю́та. **7.** (*phot.*) неконтра́стный.

cpds. **~-boiled** *adj.*: **~-boiled egg** яйцо́ всмя́тку; **~-footed** *adj.* мя́гко ступа́ющий; с мя́гкой/ти́хой по́ступью; **~-headed** *adj.* глупова́тый; **~-hearted** *adj.* мягкосерде́чный, отзы́вчивый; **~-pedal** *v.t.* (*fig.*) смягча́ть (*impf.*); сма́зывать (*impf.*); **~-soap** *v.t.* (*coll.*) льстить (*impf.*) +*d.*; **~-spoken** *adj.* с мя́гким го́лосом; медоточи́вый; **~ware** *n.* (*comput.*) програ́ммное обеспе́чение; **~-witted** *adj.* слабоу́мный, придуркова́тый; **~wood** *n.* мя́гкая древеси́на.

soften [ˈsɒf(ə)n] *v.t.* смягч|а́ть, -и́ть; (*of voice*) пон|ижа́ть, -и́зить; (*enfeeble*) изне́жи|вать, -ть.

v.i. смягч|а́ться, -и́ться; **~ing of the brain** размягче́ние мо́зга.

with adv.: **~ up** *v.t.*: **the enemy front was ~ed up by bombardment** ли́ния проти́вника была́ обрабо́тана артогнём; **~ s.o. up** (*fig.*) осл|абля́ть, -а́бить чьё-н. сопротивле́ние.

softener [ˈsɒf(ə)nə(r)] *n.* (*for water etc.*) (с)мягчи́тель (*m.*).

softness [ˈsɒftnɪs] *n.* мя́гкость.

softy [ˈsɒftɪ] *n.* (*coll., weakling*) тря́пка, слаба́к; (*nincompoop*) дурачо́к.

soggy [ˈsɒgɪ] *adj.*: **~ bread** пло́хо пропечённый хлеб; **~ ground** размо́кшая/сыра́я/отсыре́вшая земля́.

so(h) [səʊ] *n.* (*mus.*) соль (*nt. indecl.*).

soi-disant [ˌswɑːdiːˈzɑ̃] *adj.* так называ́емый, мни́мый, самозва́нный.

soigné [ˈswɑːnjeɪ] *adj.* хо́леный; элега́нтный.

soil[1] [sɔɪl] *n.* **1.** (*earth*) по́чва; **~ science** почвове́дение. **2.** (*fig., country*) земля́; **he returned to his native ~** он возврати́лся на родну́ю зе́млю; **on foreign ~** на иностра́нной террито́рии; на чужо́й земле́.

soil[2] [sɔɪl] *v.t.* па́чкать, за-/ис-/вы́-; **~ed linen** гря́зное бельё; **I would not ~ my hands with it** я не хочу́ мара́ть ру́ки э́тим.

v.i.: **this fabric ~s easily** э́то о́чень ма́ркий материа́л.

cpd. **~-pipe** *n.* канализацио́нная труба́.

soirée [ˈswɑːreɪ] *n.* зва́ный ве́чер, суаре́ (*indecl.*).

sojourn [ˈsɒdʒ(ə)n, -dʒɜːn, ˈsʌ-] (*liter.*) *n.* (вре́менное) пребыва́ние.

v.i. пребыва́ть, (вре́менно) жить, прожива́ть, находи́ться (*all impf.*).

solace [ˈsɒləs] *n.* утеше́ние, отра́да; **books were his only ~** кни́ги бы́ли его́ еди́нственной утéхой.

v.t. ут|еша́ть, -е́шить.

solar [ˈsəʊlə(r)] *adj.* со́лнечный; **~ flare** протубера́нец; **~ plexus** со́лнечное сплете́ние; **~ system** со́лнечная систе́ма.

solarium [səˈleərɪəm] *n.* соля́рий.

solder [ˈsəʊldə(r), ˈsɒ-] *n.* припо́й.

v.t. пая́ть (*impf.*); **~ sth. to sth.** припа́|ивать, -я́ть что-н. к чему́-н.; **~ together** спа́|ивать, -я́ть; **~ing-iron** пая́льник.

soldier [ˈsəʊldʒə(r)] *n.* солда́т; (*liter.*) бо́ец, боре́ц; **play at ~s** игра́ть (*impf.*) в солда́тики; **toy ~s** оловя́нные солда́тики; **the Unknown S~** Неизве́стный солда́т; **play, come the old ~** (*fig.*) поуча́ть (*impf.*); кома́ндовать (*impf.*) (на права́х бо́лее о́пытного челове́ка); **~ of fortune** (*mercenary*) наёмник, наёмный солда́т, кондотье́р; **private ~** рядово́й, бо́ец; **a great ~** вели́кий полково́дец; **every inch a ~** и́стинный во́ин (*or* до мо́зга косте́й).

v.i. служи́ть (*impf.*) (в а́рмии); **~ on** (*fig., persevere doggedly*) не сдава́ться (*impf.*).

cpd. **~-like** *see next.*

soldierly [ˈsəʊldʒəlɪ] *adj.* вое́нный; (*in appearance; also* **soldier-like**) с вое́нной вы́правкой; по-солда́тски.

soldiery [ˈsəʊldʒərɪ] *n.* солдатня́.

sole[1] [səʊl] *n.* (*fish*) морско́й язы́к, соль (*f.*).

sole[2] [səʊl] *n.* (*of foot*) ступня́, подо́шва; (*of shoe*) подо́шва, подмётка.

v.t. подш|ива́ть, -и́ть; подб|ива́ть, -и́ть; **~ a shoe** ста́вить, по- подмётку.

sole[3] [səʊl] *adj.* (*only*) еди́нственный; **~ agent** еди́нственный представи́тель; (*exclusive*) исключи́тельный; **he has ~ management of the estate** управле́ние име́нием лежи́т по́лностью на нём.

solecism [ˈsɒlɪˌsɪz(ə)m] *n.* (*of language*) солеци́зм; гру́бая (граммати́ческая) оши́бка; (*of behaviour*) просту́пок про́тив хоро́шего то́на.

solely ['səʊllɪ] *adv.* то́лько, еди́нственно, исключи́тельно; **he is ~ responsible** отве́тственность лежи́т на нём одно́м.

solemn ['sɒləm] *adj.* торже́ственный; (*serious*) серьёзный, ва́жный; **he put on a ~ face** он сде́лал серьёзное лицо́; (*pompous*) напы́щенный; ва́жный.

solemnity [sə'lemnɪtɪ] *n.* торже́ственность; (*gravity*) ва́жность; (*of appearance*) серьёзность; (*ceremony*) торжество́, церемо́ния.

solemnization [sɒləmnaɪ'zeɪʃ(ə)n] *n.* пра́зднование; **~ of marriage** церемо́ния бракосочета́ния; венча́ние.

solemnize ['sɒləm,naɪz] *v.t.* (*perform*) соверш|а́ть, -и́ть; (*celebrate*) пра́здновать, от-; торже́ственно отм|еча́ть, -е́тить; (*make solemn*) прида|ва́ть, -а́ть торже́ственность +*d.*

solenoid ['səʊlə,nɔɪd, 'sɒl-] *n.* солено́ид.

sol-fa ['sɒlfɑ:] *n.* сольфе́джио (*indecl.*).

solicit [sə'lɪsɪt] *v.t.* **1.** (*petition, importune*): **~ s.o.'s help** проси́ть, по- кого́-н. о по́мощи. **2.** (*ask for*): **~ favours of s.o.** выпра́шивать (*impf.*) у кого́-н. ми́лости; **events ~ his attention** собы́тия тре́буют его́ внима́ния. **3.** (*accost*) прист|ава́ть, -а́ть к+*d.*

v.i. (*of prostitute*) пристава́ть (*impf.*) к мужчи́нам.

solicitation [sə,lɪsɪ'teɪʃ(ə)n] *n.* про́сьба, хода́тайство.

solicitor [sə'lɪsɪtə(r)] *n.* адвока́т, юриско́нсульт.

solicitous [sə'lɪsɪtəs] *adj.* забо́тливый, внима́тельный; **she is ~ for, about your safety** она́ забо́тится о ва́шей безопа́сности.

solicitude [sə'lɪsɪ,tju:d] *n.* забо́тливость; (*anxiety*) забо́та, трево́га.

solid ['sɒlɪd] *n.* (*phys.*) твёрдое те́ло; **regular ~** пра́вильное (геометри́ческое) те́ло; (*pl.*, *food*) твёрдая пи́ща.

adj. **1.** (*not liquid or fluid*) твёрдый; **~ food** твёрдая пи́ща; **~ fuel** твёрдое то́пливо; **become ~** тверде́ть, за-. **2.** (*not hollow*) масси́вный; **~ sphere** масси́вный шар; **~ tyre** масси́вная ши́на; **he is ~ from the neck up** у него́ не голова́, а коча́н капу́сты. **3.** (*homogeneous*): **~ silver** чи́стое серебро́. **4.** (*unbroken*): **12 hours' ~ sleep** 12 часо́в непреры́вного сна; **6 hours' ~ work** 6 часо́в безостано́вочной рабо́ты; **a ~ line** сплошна́я черта́; **it rained for 3 ~ days** дождь лил три дня подря́д; **I waited for a ~ hour** я прожда́л це́лый/би́тый час. **5.** (*firmly built, substantial*) про́чный; **a man of ~ build** челове́к кре́пкого/пло́тного телосложе́ния. **6.** (*sound, reliable*) соли́дный; надёжный; **a ~ business** соли́дное де́ло; **~ arguments** основа́тельные до́воды; **he had no ~ ground for his action** у него́ не́ было ве́ских/убеди́тельных основа́ний для тако́го посту́пка; **~ good sense** настоя́щий здра́вый смы́сл. **7.** (*unanimous, united*) единоду́шный; **the meeting was ~(ly) against him** собра́ние единоду́шно вы́ступило про́тив него́; **the party is ~ for peace** па́ртия сплочена́ в стремле́нии к ми́ру. **8.** (*pert. to ~s*): **~ geometry** стереоме́трия; **~(-state) physics** фи́зика твёрдых тел; **~ foot** куби́ческий фут; **~ angle** теле́сный/простра́нственный у́гол.

solidarity [,sɒlɪ'dærɪtɪ] *n.* солида́рность; **~ of purpose/ interests** еди́нство це́лей/интере́сов; **~ of feeling** единоду́шие.

solidification [sə,lɪdɪfɪ'keɪʃ(ə)n] *n.* отвердева́ние.

solidify [sə'lɪdɪ,faɪ] *v.t.* де́лать, с- твёрдым.

v.i. тверде́ть, за-; заст|ыва́ть, -ы́ть.

solidity [sə'lɪdɪtɪ] *n.* твёрдость; (*sturdiness*) про́чность; (*reliability*) надёжность; (*soundness*) основа́тельность; (*unity*) еди́нство.

solidus ['sɒlɪdəs] *n.* (*stroke*) дробь; коса́я/дели́тельная черта́.

soliloquize [sə'lɪlə,kwaɪz] *v.t.* говори́ть/рассужда́ть (*impf.*) с сами́м собо́й; произноси́ть (*impf.*) моноло́г.

soliloquy [sə'lɪləkwɪ] *n.* моноло́г; разгово́р с сами́м собо́й.

solipsism ['sɒlɪp,sɪz(ə)m] *n.* солипси́зм.

solipsist ['sɒlɪpsɪst] *n.* солипси́ст.

solitaire ['sɒlɪ,teə(r)] *n.* (*gem*) солите́р; (*US, card game*) солите́р, пасья́нс.

solitary ['sɒlɪtərɪ] *n.* (*recluse*) отше́льни|к (*fem.* -ца).

adj. (*secluded*) уединённый; (*lonely*) одино́кий; **~ confinement** одино́чное заключе́ние; (*single*) едини́чный, еди́ный; **a ~ instance** едини́чный слу́чай; **he didn't win a ~ prize** он не вы́играл ни одного́ при́за.

solitude ['sɒlɪ,tju:d] *n.* (*being alone; lonely place*) уедине́ние; (*loneliness*) одино́чество.

solo ['səʊləʊ] *n.* **1.** (*mus.*) со́ло (*indecl.*), со́льный но́мер, со́льное выступле́ние; **music for ~ flute** со́льная му́зыка для фле́йты. **2.** (*aeron.*) одино́чный полёт.

adj. со́льный; (*aeron.*) одино́чный.

adv. (*alone*): **fly ~** выполня́ть, вы́полнить одино́чный полёт.

soloist ['səʊləʊɪst] *n.* соли́ст (*fem.* -ка).

Solomon ['sɒləmən] *n.* Соломо́н; (*fig.*) настоя́щий/су́щий Соломо́н, мудре́ц; **judgement of ~** Соломо́ново реше́ние, Соломо́нов суд.

solstice ['sɒlstɪs] *n.* солнцестоя́ние.

solubility [,sɒljʊ'bɪlɪtɪ] *n.* раствори́мость.

soluble ['sɒljʊb(ə)l] *adj.* (*dissolvable*) раствори́мый; (*solvable*) разреши́мый; поддаю́щийся реше́нию.

solution [sə'lu:ʃ(ə)n, -'lju:ʃ(ə)n] *n.* **1.** (*dissolving*) растворе́ние; (*result of this*) раство́р; **strong/weak ~** кре́пкий/сла́бый раство́р; **rubber ~** рези́новый клей. **2.** (*solving; answer*) реше́ние, вы́ход, отве́т; **the only ~ is not to answer** еди́нственно пра́вильное реше́ние — не отвеча́ть.

solve [sɒlv] *v.t.*: **~ an equation/problem** реш|а́ть, -и́ть уравне́ние/зада́чу; **~ a mystery** реш|а́ть, -и́ть зага́дку; распу́т|ывать, -ать (*or* разга́д|ывать, -а́ть) та́йну; **~ a difficulty** на|ходи́ть, -йти́ вы́ход из затрудне́ния.

solvency ['sɒlv(ə)nsɪ] *n.* платежеспосо́бность.

solvent ['sɒlv(ə)nt] *n.* раствори́тель (*m.*); **~ abuse** токсикома́ния; **~ abuser** токсикома́н.

adj. (*chem.*) растворя́ющий; (*fin.*) платежеспосо́бный.

Somali [sə'mɑ:lɪ] *n.* (*pers.*) сомали́|ец (*fem.* -йка); (*language*) язы́к сомали́.

adj. сомали́йский.

Somalia [sə'mɑ:lɪə] *n.* Сомали́ (*nt.*); Сомали́йская Респу́блика.

somatic [sə'mætɪk] *adj.* теле́сный, сомати́ческий.

sombre ['sɒmbə(r)] *adj.* (*gloomy*) угрю́мый; (*dismal*) мра́чный; (*overcast*) па́смурный.

sombreness ['sɒmbənɪs] *n.* угрю́мость; мра́чность; па́смурность.

sombrero [sɒm'breərəʊ] *n.* сомбре́ро (*indecl.*).

some [sʌm] *pron.* **1.** (*of persons*): **~ say yes, ~ say no** кто говори́т да, кто — нет; одни́ говоря́т да, други́е — нет; **~ left and others stayed** одни́ ушли́, други́е оста́лись; **~ (people) were late** ко́е-кто опозда́л; **~ one way, ~ the other** кто куда́; **~ of these girls** ко́е-кто/не́которые из э́тих де́вушек. **2.** (*of thgs., an indefinite quantity or number*): **I have ~ already** у меня́ уже́ есть; **have ~ more!** возьми́те ещё!; **those are nice apples; can I have ~?** каки́е хоро́шие я́блоки — мо́жно (мне) взять па́рочку? **3.** (*a part*) часть; **I have ~ of the documents** часть докуме́нтов у меня́ есть; **~ of the morning** часть утра́; **I agree with ~ of what you said** я согла́сен ко́е с чем из того́, что вы сказа́ли; я части́чно согла́сен с тем, что вы сказа́ли. **4.** (*coll.*): **and then ~!** (*more than that*) ещё как!

adj. **1.** (*definite though unspecified*) како́й-то; **~ fool has locked the door** како́й-то дура́к за́пер дверь; **I read it in ~ book (or other)** я чита́л э́то в како́й-то/одно́й кни́ге; **one must make ~ (sort of) attempt** на́до сде́лать хоть каку́ю-нибудь попы́тку; **first ~ books, then others** снача́ла одни́ кни́ги, пото́м други́е; **~ day, ~ time** когда́-нибудь; **is this ~ kind of joke?** э́то что — своего́ ро́да шу́тка?; **we shall find ~ way round the difficulty** мы найдём како́й-нибудь (*or* тот и́ли ино́й) вы́ход из тру́дного положе́ния. **2.** (*no matter what*) како́й-нибудь, како́й-либо; **he is looking for ~ work** он и́щет (каку́ю-нибудь) рабо́ту; **if I could find at least ~ place to stay the night!** найти́ бы мне хоть како́й-нибудь ночле́г! **3.** (*one or two*) ко́е-каки́е (*pl.*); (*a certain amount or number of: may be untranslated or expr. by g.*): **I bought ~ envelopes** я купи́л конве́ртов; **I gave him ~ advice** я ему́ ко́е-что посове́товал; **~ more** ещё (+*g.*); **~ distance away** на не́котором расстоя́нии; **for ~ time now** с не́которого вре́мени; **~ books** не́сколько книг; **~ (length of) time** дово́льно продолжи́тельное вре́мя; **~ children learn easily** ины́м де́тям уче́ние даётся легко́ (*or* легко́ учи́ться); **it takes ~ courage to ...** тре́буется нема́ло му́жества, что́бы...; **that takes ~ doing** э́то не та́к-то легко́; **~ work is pleasant** быва́ет/встреча́ется/попада́ется прия́тная рабо́та. **4.** (*in ~ sense or degree*; *to a certain extent*): **that is ~ proof** э́то в како́й-то сте́пени мо́жет служи́ть доказа́тельством; **it served as ~ guide to his intentions** э́то в не́которой/изве́стной сте́пени ука́зывало на его́ наме́рения. **5.** (*approximately*) приме́рно, о́коло; **we waited ~ 20 minutes** мы жда́ли мину́т два́дцать (*or* о́коло двадцати́ мину́т). **6.** (*coll.*, *expr. admiration etc.*) вот э́то; вот так; **~ speed!** вот э́то ско́рость!; **~ heat!** ну и жара́, не́чего сказа́ть!; **he's ~ doctor!** э́то настоя́щий врач!; вот э́то врач, э́то я понима́ю!; (*iron.*) вот ещё; вот... то́же; **~ joke, that was!** шу́тка называ́ется!; **~ surprise!** то́же мне сюрпри́з!; **~ painter!** ничего́ себе́ (*or* хоро́ш) худо́жник!

somebody [ˈsʌmbədɪ] *n.*: **a ~** челове́к с положе́нием, ва́жная персо́на, «ши́шка».

pron. (*also* **someone**) (*in particular*) кто́-то; не́кто; **there is ~ in the cellar** в по́гребе кто́-то есть; (*no matter who*) кто́-нибудь, кто́-либо; **I want ~ to help me** я хочу́, что́бы кто́-нибудь мне помо́г; **~ else can do it** кто́-нибудь друго́й мо́жет э́то сде́лать; пусть э́то сде́лает кто́-нибудь друго́й.

somehow [ˈsʌmhaʊ] *adv.* ка́к-нибудь; так и́ли ина́че; тем и́ли ины́м о́бразом; **we shall manage ~** мы ка́к-нибудь спра́вимся; **he found out my name ~** он каки́м-то о́бразом узна́л, как меня́ зову́т; (*for some reason*): **~ I never liked him** он мне почему́-то никогда́ не нра́вился.

someone [ˈsʌmwʌn] = **somebody** *pron.*

someplace [ˈsʌmpleɪs] (*US*) = **somewhere**

somersault [ˈsʌməˌsɒlt] *n.* са́льто (*indecl.*); **turn a double ~** де́лать, с- двойно́е са́льто.

v.i. кувырк|а́ться, -ну́ться.

something [ˈsʌmθɪŋ] *pron.* (*definite*) что́-то, не́что; (*indefinite*) что́-нибудь, что́-либо; **I must get ~ to eat** я до́лжен что́-нибудь перехвати́ть; **he lost ~ or other** он что́-то тако́е потеря́л; **she lectures in ~ or other** она́ чита́ет ле́кции по како́му-то (там) предме́ту; **I have seen ~ of his work** я ви́дел ко́е-каки́е из его́ рабо́т; **he is ~ of a liar** он непро́чь совра́ть; **there is ~ in what you say** в том, что вы говори́те, есть определённый смысл; **there is ~ about him** в нём что́-то тако́е есть; **she speaks with ~ of an accent** она́ говори́т с лёгким акце́нтом; **it is ~ of an improvement** э́то не́который прогре́сс; **won't you take a drop of ~?** нали́ть вам рю́мочку?; **it is ~ to have got so far** сла́ва Бо́гу, хоть сто́лько сде́лали; **you have ~ there** в э́том вы пра́вы; **he thinks he is ~** он высо́кого мне́ния о себе́; **we managed to see ~ of each other** нам удава́лось вре́мя от вре́мени встреча́ться; **I think I'm on to ~** ка́жется, я нащу́пал путь (*or* напа́л на след); **she has a cold or ~** у неё то ли просту́да, то ли ещё что́-то; **he is a surgeon or ~** он хиру́рг и́ли что́-то в э́том ро́де.

adv.: **he left ~ like a million** он оста́вил что́-то поря́дка миллио́на; **his house looks ~ like a prison** его́ дом сма́хивает на тюрьму́; **now that's ~ like a cigar!** вот э́то настоя́щая сига́ра!; **~ awful** (*vulg.*, *frightfully*) ужа́сно.

sometime [ˈsʌmtaɪm] *adj.* (*liter.*) бы́вший.

adv. когда́-то, когда́-нибудь, когда́-либо; **~ soon** ско́ро; **come and see us ~** приходи́те к нам ка́к-нибудь.

sometimes [ˈsʌmtaɪmz] *adv.* иногда́; **~ ... ~ ...** то... то...

somewhat [ˈsʌmwɒt] *pron.*: **he is ~ of a connoisseur** он в не́котором ро́де знато́к.

adv. ка́к-то, не́сколько, дово́льно; **he is ~ off-hand** он де́ржится ка́к-то небре́жно; **he was ~ hard to follow** его́ бы́ло дово́льно тру́дно понима́ть; **the book loses ~ in translation** кни́га не́сколько прои́грывает в перево́де.

somewhere [ˈsʌmweə(r)] *adv.* **1.** (*US also* **someplace**) где́-то, где́-нибудь, где́-либо; **~ else** где́-то в друго́м ме́сте; где́-то ещё; (*motion*) куда́-то; **I am going ~ tomorrow** я за́втра ко́е-куда́ иду́; **the noise came from ~ over there** звук разда́лся где́-то там; **'~'** (*to lavatory*) ко́е-куда́. **2.** (*approximately*) о́коло+*g.*; **it is ~ about 6 o'clock** сейча́с что́-то о́коло шести́.

Somme [sɒm] *n.* Со́мма.

somnambulism [sɒmˈnæmbjʊˌlɪz(ə)m] *n.* лунати́зм, сомнамбули́зм.

somnambulist [sɒmˈnæmbjʊlɪst] *n.* луна́т|ик (*fem.* -и́чка); сомна́мбул (*fem.* -а).

somnolence [ˈsɒmnələns] *n.* сонли́вость.

somnolent [ˈsɒmnələnt] *adj.* (*drowsy*) со́нный, сонли́вый; (*inducing sleep*) снотво́рный.

son [sʌn] *n.* сын (*pl.* -овья́, (*rhet.*) -ы́); **~ and heir** сын и насле́дник; **S~ of Man** Сын челове́ческий; **S~ of God** Сын бо́жий; **~s of the fatherland** сыны́ оте́чества; **~ of the soil** сын земли́; **~ of a bitch** (*sl.*) су́кин сын; (*as form of address*): **(my) ~** сыно́к.

cpd. **~-in-law** *n.* зять (*m.*).

sonant [ˈsəʊnənt] *n.* зво́нкий согла́сный.

sonar [ˈsəʊnə(r)] *n.* гидролока́тор.

sonata [səˈnɑːtə] *n.* сона́та; **~ form** сона́тная фо́рма.

sonatina [ˌsɒnəˈtiːnə] *n.* сонати́на.

sonde [sɒnd] *n.* зонд.

son et lumière [ˌsɒneɪˈluːmjeə(r)] *n.* светозвукоспекта́кль (*m.*).

song [sɒŋ] *n.* **1.** (*singing*) пе́ние; **burst into ~** запе́ть (*pf.*); зали́ться (*pf.*) пе́сней. **2.** (*words set to music*; *also bird's ~*) пе́сня; **S~ of S~s** Песнь пе́сней; **marching ~** похо́дная пе́сня; **drinking ~** засто́льная пе́сня; **give us a ~!** спо́йте нам!; **make a ~ (and dance) about sth.** (*coll.*) подн|има́ть, -я́ть шум из-за чего́-н.; **he bought it for a ~** он э́то купи́л за бесце́нок.

cpds. **~-bird** *n.* пе́вчая пти́ца; **~-book** *n.* пе́сенник; **~writer** *n.* пе́сенник.

songster [ˈsɒŋstə(r)] *n.* (*bird*) пе́вчая пти́ца.

songstress [ˈsɒŋstrɪs] *n.* певи́ца.

sonic [ˈsɒnɪk] *adj.* звуково́й; **~ bang, boom** сверхзвуково́й хлопо́к.

sonnet [ˈsɒnɪt] *n.* соне́т.

sonny [ˈsʌnɪ] *n.* (*coll.*) сыно́к, сыно́чек.

sonority [səˈnɒrɪtɪ] *n.* зву́чность.

sonorous [ˈsɒnərəs, səˈnɔːrəs] *adj.* зву́чный.

soon [suːn] *adv.* **1.** (*in a short while*) ско́ро, вско́ре; **it will ~ be dark** ско́ро стемне́ет; **he ~ recovered** он вско́ре попра́вился; **~ after** че́рез коро́ткое вре́мя; **write ~!** напиши́те поскоре́е!; **as ~ as possible** как мо́жно скоре́е. **2.** (*early*) ра́но; **we arrived too ~** мы при́были сли́шком ра́но; **how ~ can you come?** когда́ вы мо́жете прибы́ть?; **the ~er the better** чем ра́ньше, тем лу́чше; **~er or later** ра́но и́ли по́здно. **3.**: **as ~ as** как то́лько; **as ~ as I saw him, I recognized him** я узна́л его́, как то́лько уви́дел; я его́ сра́зу узна́л; **no ~er had he arrived than he wanted to borrow money** не успе́л он прибы́ть, как стал проси́ть де́нег взаймы́; **no ~er said than done** ска́зано — сде́лано. **4.** (*willingly*): **I would as ~ stay at home** я предпочёл бы оста́ться до́ма; **I would ~er die than permit it** я скоре́е умру́, чем допущу́ э́то; **what would you ~er do, go now or wait?** что вы предпочита́ете — уйти́ и́ли подожда́ть?

soot [sʊt] *n.* са́жа, ко́поть.

sooth [suːθ] *n.* (*arch.*) пра́вда; **~ to say** по пра́вде сказа́ть/говоря́.

cpd. **~sayer** *n.* предсказа́тель (*fem.* -ница).

sooth|e [suːð] *v.t.* (*calm*, *pacify*) успок|а́ивать, -о́ить; **she ~ed the baby to sleep** она́ убаю́кала ребёнка; **in a ~ing tone** успока́ивающе; (*relieve*, *lighten*) облегч|а́ть, -и́ть; **~ing lotion** успока́ивающая примо́чка; (*gratify*, *appease*) те́шить (*impf.*); **my words ~ed his vanity** мои́ слова́ успоко́или его́ самолю́бие.

sooty [ˈsʊtɪ] *adj.* (*blackened with soot*) закопчённый, закопте́лый; покры́тый ко́потью; (*black as soot*) чёрный как са́жа; (*containing*, *consisting of soot*): **~ deposit** слой са́жи; **~ atmosphere** по́лный ко́поти во́здух.

sop [sɒp] *n.* **1.** (*of bread*) кусо́к хле́ба, обмакну́тый во что-н.; (*crouton*) грено́к. **2.** (*fig.*) пода́чка, взя́тка; **as a ~ to his pride** что́бы поте́шить его́ самолю́бие; **throw a ~ to Cerberus** задо́брить (*pf.*) Це́рбера.

v.t. **1.** (*soak*) обма́к|ивать, -ну́ть; мак|а́ть, -ну́ть; мочи́ть, на-. **2.** ~ **up** (*mop up*) подт|ира́ть, -ере́ть. **3.** (*drench*) пром|а́чивать, -очи́ть.

v.i.: **the shirt was ~ping wet** руба́шка промо́кла насквозь́; **we got ~ping wet** мы промо́кли до ни́тки.

Sophia ['səʊfɪə] *n.* (*hist.*) Со́фья.

sophism ['sɒfɪz(ə)m] *n.* софи́зм, софи́стика.

sophist ['sɒfɪst] *n.* софи́ст.

sophistic(al) [sə'fɪstɪk(ə)l] *adj.* софи́стский; скло́нный к софи́стике.

sophisticate[1] [sə'fɪstɪkət] *n.* искушённый челове́к.

sophisticate[2] [sə'fɪstɪˌkeɪt] *v.t.* **1.** (*complicate*) усложн|я́ть, -и́ть; **~d techniques** сло́жная/изощрённая те́хника; **~d weapons** совреме́нные ви́ды ору́жия. **2.** (*mislead*) запу́т|ывать, -ать. **3.** (*refine*) утонч|а́ть, -и́ть; (*make less natural, simple*) лиш|а́ть, -и́ть простоты́/есте́ственности; **~d taste** утончённый/изощрённый вкус; **~d manners** изы́сканные мане́ры. **4.** (*distort*) превра́тно истолко́в|ывать, -а́ть; (*adulterate*) разб|авля́ть, -а́вить.

sophistication [səˌfɪstɪ'keɪʃ(ə)n] *n.* (*refinement*) утончённость, искушённость.

sophistry ['sɒfɪstrɪ] *n.* софи́стика.

Sophocles ['sɒfəˌkliːz] *n.* Софо́кл.

sophomore ['sɒfəˌmɔː(r)] *n.* (*US*) студе́нт-второку́рсник.

soporific [ˌsɒpə'rɪfɪk] *n.* снотво́рное (сре́дство).

adj. снотво́рный, усыпля́ющий.

soppy ['sɒpɪ] *adj.* (*coll.*) (*wet*) промо́кший; (*sentimental*) сентимента́льный, слюня́вый.

soprano [sə'prɑːnəʊ] *n.* (*voice, singer, part*) сопра́но (*f. & nt. indecl.*); (*attr.*) сопра́нный; **boy** ~ ди́скант.

sorbet ['sɔːbeɪ, -bɪt] *n.* шербе́т.

sorcerer ['sɔːsərə(r)] *n.* колду́н, волше́бник; маг.

sorceress ['sɔːsərɪs] *n.* колду́нья, волше́бница; (*witch*) ве́дьма.

sorcery ['sɔːsərɪ] *n.* колдовство́, волшебство́.

sordid ['sɔːdɪd] *adj.* (*squalid, poor*) убо́гий, жа́лкий; (*filthy*) гря́зный; **a ~ affair** гну́сная исто́рия; (*low, base*) по́длый; **~ desires** ни́зменные жела́ния.

sordidness ['sɔːdɪdnɪs] *n.* убо́гость, убо́жество; грязь; по́длость; (*meanness*) ни́зость.

sordine [sɔː'diːn] *n.* сурди́н(к)а.

sore [sɔː(r)] *n.* боля́чка, я́зва; (*wound*) ра́на; (*graze*) сса́дина; (*inflammation*) воспале́ние; (*fig.*): **re-open old ~s** береди́ть, раз- ста́рые ра́ны; **time heals old ~s** вре́мя заживля́ет (ста́рые) ра́ны.

adj. **1.** (*painful*): **a ~ tooth** больно́й зуб; **I have a ~ (*grazed*) knee** я ссади́л себе́ коле́но; **he has a ~ throat** у него́ боли́т го́рло; **my feet are ~ with walking** я мно́го ходи́л и натёр себе́ но́ги; **I woke up with a ~ head** я просну́лся с головно́й бо́лью; **it is a ~ point with him** э́то у него́ больно́е ме́сто; **touch s.o. on a ~ place, spot** (*fig.*) заде́ть (*pf.*) кого́-нибудь за живо́е. **2.** (*grieved, sorrowful*): **a ~ heart** тяжёлое се́рдце. **3.** (*coll., aggrieved*) раздражённый, оби́женный; **he was ~ at not being invited** он был зол (*or* оби́делся), что его́ не позва́ли. **4.** (*acute, extreme*) кра́йний; **he is in ~ need of money** он кра́йне нужда́ется в деньга́х; **I was ~ly tempted** у меня́ бы́ло си́льное искуше́ние.

adv. (*arch.*) кра́йне.

soreness ['sɔːnɪs] *n.* (*painfulness, discomfort*) боль; (*grudge*) оби́да.

sorghum ['sɔːgəm] *n.* со́рго (*indecl.*).

sorority [sə'rɒrɪtɪ] *n.* же́нская организа́ция/общи́на.

sorrel[1] ['sɒr(ə)l] *n.* (*bot.*) щаве́ль (*m.*).

sorrel[2] ['sɒr(ə)l] *n.* (*horse*) гнеда́я ло́шадь.

adj. гнедо́й.

sorrow ['sɒrəʊ] *n.* (*sadness, grief*) печа́ль; (*extreme* ~) скорбь; **more in ~ than in anger** скоре́й с тоско́й, чем с гне́вом; (*regret*) сожале́ние; **express ~ for** выража́ть, вы́разить сожале́ние о+*p.*; **to my ~** к моему́ огорче́нию; (*sad experience*) го́ре; **all these ~s broke his heart** все э́ти го́рести/невзго́ды сломи́ли его́.

v.i. горева́ть (*impf.*); **~ for, over s.o.** опла́кивать (*impf.*) кого́-н.

sorrowful ['sɒrəʊˌfʊl] *adj.* печа́льный, ско́рбный.

sorry ['sɒrɪ] *adj.* **1.** (*regretful*): **be ~ for sth.** сожале́ть (*impf.*) о чём-н.; **I was ~ I had to do it** я (со)жале́л, что пришло́сь так поступи́ть; **I should be ~ for you to think ...** мне не хоте́лось бы, что́бы вы ду́мали...; **aren't you ~ for what you've done?** вы не раска́иваетесь в том, что наде́лали?; **say you're ~!** попроси́ проще́ния!; **you'll be ~ for this one day** когда́-нибудь вы об э́том пожале́ете; **I'm ~ to hear it** приско́рбно слы́шать; **we were ~ to hear of your father's death** с гру́стью узна́ли мы о сме́рти ва́шего отца́; **~!** винова́т!; прости́те!; извини́те!; **I'm ~ I came** и сам не рад, что пришёл; **~, I'm busy** извини́те, но я за́нят; **~, but ...** к сожале́нию...; увы́,... **2.** (*expr. pity, sympathy*): **feel ~ for s.o.** испы́тывать (*impf.*) жа́лость к кому́-н.; жале́ть (*impf.*) кого́-н.; сочу́вствовать (*impf.*) кому́-н.; **it's the children I feel ~ for** кого́ мне жаль — э́то дете́й; **feel ~ for o.s.** быть испо́лненным жа́лости к себе́; испо́лниться (*pf.*) жа́лостью к себе́. **3.** (*wretched, pitiful*) жа́лкий; **in a ~ state** в жа́лком состоя́нии; **a ~ excuse** жа́лкое оправда́ние.

sort [sɔːt] *n.* **1.** (*kind, class, category, species*) род, сорт, разря́д, вид; **we have all ~s of books (*or* books of every ~)** у нас вся́кого ро́да кни́ги; **people of that ~** тако́го ро́да лю́ди; **books of different ~s** кни́ги разли́чного ро́да; **that's the ~ of book I want** и́менно таку́ю кни́гу мне и на́до; **a new ~ of bicycle** но́вый тип велосипе́да; **he is not the ~ (of person) to complain** он не тако́го ро́да челове́к, что́бы жа́ловаться; он не из тех, кто жа́луется; **what ~ of man is he?** что он за челове́к?; **a good ~** хоро́ший челове́к/ма́лый; **what ~ of music do you like?** каку́ю му́зыку вы лю́бите?; **coffee of a ~** так называ́емый ко́фе; **nothing of the ~** ничего́ подо́бного; **a ~ of war** своего́ ро́да (*or* своеобра́зная) война́; **a ~ of novel; a novel of a ~** како́й-то рома́н; не́что вро́де рома́на; **a book of ~s** так себе́ кни́га; **different ~s of goods** това́ры ра́зного ро́да; **people are divided into two ~s** лю́ди де́лятся на два разря́да; **people of all ~s** лю́ди вся́кого разбо́ра; **what ~ of people does he think we are?** за кого́ он нас принима́ет? **2.** (*manner*): **in some ~** (*liter.*) не́которым о́бразом. **3.**: **~ of** (*coll.*) вро́де, как бы; в о́бщем-то; в не́котором ро́де; **he ~ of suggested I took him with me** он как бы дал мне поня́ть, что хо́чет пойти́ со мно́й. **4.**: **out of ~s** не в ду́хе; **I have felt out of ~s all day** я весь день чу́вствую себя́ нева́жно. **5.** (*pl., typ.*) ли́теры (*f. pl.*).

v.t. раз|бира́ть, -обра́ть; **they ~ed themselves into groups of six** они́ разби́лись на гру́ппы по шести́/шесть челове́к; (*grain, coal etc.*) сортирова́ть (*impf., pf.*).

v.i. (*liter., agree*): **his actions ~ed ill with his protestations** его́ посту́пки не вяза́лись с его́ заявле́ниями.

with adv.: **~ out** *v.t.* (*select*) от|бира́ть, -обра́ть; (*separate*) отдел|я́ть, -и́ть; (*arrange, classify*) раз|бира́ть, -обра́ть; (*fig., put in order*): **I have to go home to ~ things out** мне ну́жно пойти́ домо́й и во всём разобра́ться; **everything will ~ itself out** всё нала́дится/образу́ется; **I leave the rest for you to ~ out** в остально́м разберётесь са́ми; **let me ~ myself out** да́йте мне прийти́ в себя́; (*coll., deal with, punish*): **they began to fight but a policeman came along and ~ed them out** они́ зате́яли бы́ло дра́ку, но подошёл полице́йский и навёл поря́док.

sorter ['sɔːtə(r)] *n.* сортиро́вщик.

sortie ['sɔːtɪ] *n.* (*sally*) вы́лазка; (*flight*) вы́лет; **~ into space** вы́ход в ко́смос.

SOS *n.* (ра́дио)сигна́л бе́дствия.

sot [sɒt] *n.* пья́ница (*c.g.*), пьянчу́жка (*c.g.*).

sottish ['sɒtɪʃ] *adj.* тупо́й.

sotto voce [ˌsɒtəʊ 'vəʊtʃɪ] *adv.* вполго́лоса; пони́зив го́лос.

soubrette [suː'bret] *n.* субре́тка.

soubriquet ['suːbrɪˌkeɪ] = **sobriquet**

soufflé ['suːfleɪ] *n.* суфле́ (*indecl.*).

sough [saʊ, sʌf] *v.i.* стона́ть (*impf.*); свисте́ть (*impf.*).

soul [səʊl] *n.* **1.** душа́; **All S ~s' Day** день поминове́ния усо́пших; **commend one's ~ to God** отда́ть (*pf.*) Бо́гу ду́шу; **lost ~** поги́бшая душа́; **I wonder how he keeps body and ~ together** непоня́тно, как он сво́дит концы́ с конца́ми; **throw o.s. body and ~ into sth.** всей душо́й отд|ава́ться, -а́ться (*or* пред|ава́ться, -а́ться) чему́-н.; **his whole ~ revolted against the prospect** подо́бная перспекти́ва возмуща́ла его́ до глубины́ души́; **he cannot call his ~ his own** он не сме́ет пи́кнуть; **he puts his heart and ~ into his work** он всю ду́шу вкла́дывает в свою́ рабо́ту; **upon my ~!** ей-Бо́гу! **2.** (*animating spirit*): **he was the life and ~ of the party** он был душо́й о́бщества; (*inspiration*): **his pictures lack ~** его́ карти́нам недостаёт души́; в его́ карти́нах нет жи́зни. **3.** (*personification*): **he is the ~ of honour** э́то/он воплощённая/сама́ че́стность. **4.** (*personage*): **the greatest ~s of antiquity** велича́йшие лю́ди дре́вности. **5.** (*pers.*): **there wasn't a ~ in sight** не ви́дно бы́ло ни души́; **the ship went down with 200 ~s** су́дно затону́ло с двумяста́ми ду́шами на борту́; **a simple ~** проста́я душа́; **the poor ~ lost her way** бедня́жка заблуди́лась; **don't make a noise, there's a good ~!** не шуми́, будь добр! **6.** (*music*) со́ул.

cpds. **~-destroying** *adj.* иссуша́ющий ду́шу; **~-mate** *n.* задуше́вный друг; задуше́вная подру́га; **~-stirring** *adj.* волну́ющий, захва́тывающий.

soulful ['səʊlfʊl] *adj.* то́мный.

soulless ['səʊllɪs] *adj.* безду́шный.

sound[1] [saʊnd] *n.* **1.** звук; (*of rain, sea, wind etc.*) шум; **not a ~ was heard** не́ было слы́шно ни зву́ка; **catch the ~ of sth.** ул|а́вливать, -ови́ть звук чего́-н.; **I hear the ~ of voices** я слы́шу голоса́ (*or* звук голосо́в); **vowel ~s** гла́сные зву́ки; **~ barrier** звуково́й барье́р; **~ effects** шумовы́е эффе́кты; **~ effects man** шумёр; **~ engineer** звукоопера́тор. **2.** (*hearing range*): **within ~ of** в зо́не слы́шимости *+g.* **3.: I don't like the ~ of it** мне э́то (что́-то) не нра́вится.

v.t. **1.** (*cause to ~*) звони́ть, по- *+a.*; **they ~ed the bell** они́ позвони́ли в ко́локол; **~ a trumpet** труби́ть, по-; **~ the horn** (*of a car*) сигна́лить, про-; да|ва́ть, -ть гудо́к. **2.** (*play on trumpet etc.*): **~ the retreat/reveille** труби́ть, за-/про- отступле́ние/подъём; **~ the alarm** бить, за- трево́гу; **he ~ed her praises** он пел ей хвалу́; он вовсю́ её расхва́ливал. **3.** (*pronounce*) произн|оси́ть, -ести́; **the 'K' is not ~ed** «K» не произно́сится. **4.** (*test*): **the doctor ~ed his chest** до́ктор прослу́шал его́ лёгкие/се́рдце.

v.i. **1.** (*emit sound; convey effect by sound*) звуча́ть, про-; **the trumpets ~ed** раздали́сь зву́ки труб; **this key won't ~** э́та кла́виша не звучи́т. **2.** (*give impression*) каза́ться, по-; **his voice ~s as if he has a cold** по го́лосу ка́жется (*or* мо́жно поду́мать), что он просту́жен; у него́ просту́женный го́лос; **it ~ed as if someone was running** по доноси́вшимся зву́кам каза́лось, что кто́-то бежи́т; **it ~s like thunder** похо́же на гром; **the statement ~s improbable** э́то заявле́ние ка́жется маловероя́тным; **the idea ~ed all right at first** понача́лу э́та мысль показа́лась вполне́ прие́млемой.

with adv.: **~ off** *v.i.* (*coll., of pers.*) шуме́ть (*impf.*); разглаго́льствовать (*impf.*).

cpds. **~-film** *n.* звуково́й фильм; **~-man** *n.* аку́стик; **~-proof** *adj.* звуконепроница́емый; **~-recording** *n.* за́пись зву́ка, звукоза́пись; **~-track** *n.* звуково́е сопровожде́ние; **~-wave** *n.* звукова́я волна́.

sound[2] [saʊnd] *n.* (*strait*) проли́в.

sound[3] [saʊnd] *n.* (*probe*) зонд.

v.t. (*measure*) изм|еря́ть, -е́рить; **they are ~ing the (depth of the) ocean** они́ измеря́ют глубину́ океа́на; (*fig.*): **she ~ed the depths of misery** она́ испи́ла ча́шу до дна. **2.: ~ the atmosphere** зонди́ровать (*impf.*) атмосфе́ру; (*fig.*): **~ (out) s.o. (*or* s.o.'s intentions, opinions)** зонди́ровать, по- кого́-н.

sound[4] [saʊnd] *adj.* **1.** (*healthy*) здоро́вый; **~ in body and mind** здоро́вый те́лом и душо́й (*or* физи́чески и духо́вно); **of ~ mind** в здра́вом уме́ (и твёрдой па́мяти); **~ in wind and limb** в по́лном здра́вии; **his heart is as ~ as a bell** се́рдце у него́ (здоро́вое) как у быка́; (*in good condition*) испра́вный; **~ fruit** неиспо́рченные фру́кты; **~ timber** добро́тный/кре́пкий лесоматериа́л. **2.** (*correct, logical*) здра́вый; **a ~ argument** убеди́тельный до́вод; **his ideas are not very ~** его́ ника́к не назовёшь здравомы́слящим челове́ком. **3.** (*financially stable*) соли́дный; (*solvent*) платёжеспосо́бный. **4.** (*thorough*) хоро́ший; **he needs a ~ slapping** его́ ну́жно хороше́нько отшлёпать; **he slept ~ly** он кре́пко спал; **he was ~ly thrashed** он был здо́рово изби́т; он был изби́т как сле́дует.

sounder ['saʊndə(r)] *n.* (*naut.*) лот.

sounding[1] ['saʊndɪŋ] *n.* (*measurement*) измере́ние глубины́; зонди́рование.

cpds. **~-balloon** *n.* шар-зо́нд; **~-line** *n.* ло́тлинь (*m.*).

sounding[2] ['saʊndɪŋ] *adj.* (*resonant*) зву́чный; (*fig., empty of meaning*): **~ promises** гро́мкие обеща́ния; **~ rhetoric** треску́чие фра́зы.

sounding-board ['saʊndɪŋ,bɔːd] *n.* наве́с ка́федры; де́ка, резона́тор; (*fig.*) ру́пор.

soundless ['saʊndlɪs] *adj.* беззву́чный.

soundness ['saʊndnɪs] *n.* здоро́вье; про́чность; здра́вость; обосно́ванность; разу́мность.

soup[1] [suːp] *n.* суп; **mushroom/vegetable ~** грибно́й/овощно́й суп; **beetroot ~** борщ; **cabbage ~** щи (*pl., g.* щей); **he is in the ~** он влип; он в пи́ковом положе́нии (*coll.*).

cpds. **~-kitchen** *n.* беспла́тная столо́вая для нужда́ющихся; **~-ladle** *n.* поло́вник; **~-plate** *n.* глубо́кая таре́лка; **~-spoon** *n.* столо́вая ло́жка; **~-tureen** *n.* су́пница.

soup[2] [suːp] *v.t.* (*coll.*): **~ed-up** с надду́вом.

soupçon ['suːpsɔ̃] *n.* толи́ка, чу́точка, при́вкус; са́мая ма́лость; намёк (на*+a.*); отте́нок.

sour ['saʊə(r)] *adj.* **1.** (*of fruit etc.*) ки́слый; **~ grapes!** (*fig.*) зе́лен виногра́д! **2.** (*of milk*) прокис́ший, ски́сший; **go, turn ~** ск|иса́ть, -и́снуть; свёр|тываться, -ну́ться; **~ cream** смета́на. **3.** (*of soil*) ки́слый, сыро́й. **4.** (*of pers.*) мра́чный, озло́бленный.

v.t.: **thunder will ~ the milk** в грозу́ молоко́ свёртывается/свора́чивается; **disappointments ~ed his temper** от постоя́нных неуда́ч у него́ испо́ртился хара́ктер.

v.i. ск|иса́ть, -и́снуть; свёр|тываться (*or* свора́чиваться), -ну́ться; (*fig.*) по́ртиться, ис-.

cpd. **~puss** *n.* кисля́й (*coll.*).

source [sɔːs] *n.* **1.** (*of stream etc.*) исто́к; **he traced the river to its ~** он прошёл по реке́ до са́мого верхо́вья. **2.** (*fig.*) исто́чник; **reliable ~s of information** надёжные исто́чники информа́ции; **~ of infection** исто́чник зара́зы.

cpd. **~-book** *n.* сбо́рник докуме́нтов.

sourness ['saʊənɪs] *n.* кислота́; ки́слый вкус.

souse [saʊs] *v.t.* **1.** (*put in pickle*) соли́ть, за-; **~d herrings** солёная/марино́ванная сельдь. **2.** (*plunge or soak in liquid*) мочи́ть, на-/за-; окун|а́ть, -у́ть; обма́к|ивать, -ну́ть. **3.** (*p.p., sl., drunk*) пья́ный в сте́льку.

soutane [suː'tɑːn] *n.* сута́на.

south [saʊθ] *n.* юг; (*naut.*) зюйд; **in the ~** на ю́ге; **to the ~ of** к ю́гу от (*or* ю́жнее) *+g.*; **from the ~** с ю́га.

adj. ю́жный; **on a ~ wall** на ю́жной стене́; на стене́, обращённой к ю́гу; **~ wind** ю́жный ве́тер; ве́тер с ю́га; **S~ Africa** Ю́жная А́фрика; **Republic of S~ Africa** Ю́жно-Африка́нская Респу́блика; **S~ America** Ю́жная Аме́рика; **S~ American** (*n.*) южноамерика́н|ец (*fem.* -ка); (*adj.*) южноамерика́нский; **S~ Island** о́стров Ю́жный; **S~ Pole** Ю́жный по́люс; **the S~ Seas** ю́жная часть Ти́хого океа́на; **S~ Sea Islands** Океа́ния.

adv.: **the ship sailed due ~** су́дно шло пря́мо на юг; **our village is ~ of London** на́ша дере́вня нахо́дится к ю́гу от Ло́ндона.

cpds. **~-east** *n.* ю́го-восто́к; (*naut.*) зюйд-о́ст; *adj.* (*also* **~-easterly, ~-eastern, ~-eastward**) ю́го-восто́чный; *adv.* (*also* **~-easterly, ~-eastwards**) на ю́го-восто́к; **~-easter(ly)** *n.* (*wind*) ю́го-восто́чный ве́тер; зюйд-о́ст; **~-~-east** *n.* (*naut.*) зюйд-зюйд-о́ст; **~-~-west** *n.* (*naut.*) зюйд-зюйд-ве́ст; **~-west** *n.* ю́го-за́пад; (*naut.*) зюйд-ве́ст; *adj.* (*also* **~-westerly, ~-western, ~westward**) ю́го-за́падный; *adv.* (*also* **~-westerly, ~-westwards**) на ю́го-за́пад; **~-wester(ly)** *n.* (*wind*) ю́го-за́падный ве́тер; зюйд-ве́ст.

southerly ['sʌðəlɪ] *n.* (*wind*) ю́жный ве́тер.

adj. ю́жный.

southern ['sʌð(ə)n] *adj.* ю́жный; **~most** са́мый ю́жный.
southerner ['sʌðənə(r)] *n.* южа́н|ин (*fem.* -ка).
southward ['saʊθwəd] *adj.* ю́жный.
adv. (*also* **~s**) на юг; к ю́гу, в ю́жном направле́нии.
souvenir [ˌsuːvə'nɪə(r)] *n.* сувени́р; **as a ~** на па́мять.
sou'wester [saʊ'westə(r)] *n.* (*wind*) ю́жный ве́тер; (*hat*) зюйдве́стка, клеёнчатая ша́пка.
sovereign ['sɒvrɪn] *n.* (*ruler*) госуда́р|ь (*fem.* -ыня); (*coin*) совере́н.
adj. **1.** (*supreme*) верхо́вный. **2.** (*having ~ power; royal*) сувере́нный; **~ rights** сувере́нные права́; **a ~ state** сувере́нное госуда́рство. **3.: a ~ remedy** превосхо́дное сре́дство.
sovereignty ['sɒvrɪntɪ] *n.* суверените́т.
Soviet ['səʊvɪət, 'sɒ-] *n.* сове́т; **the Supreme ~** Верхо́вный Сове́т; **the ~s** (*coll.*) Сове́тское прави́тельство; Сове́тский Сою́з.
adj. сове́тский; **the ~ Union** Сове́тский Сою́з; **Union of ~ Socialist Republics** Сою́з Сове́тских Социалисти́ческих Респу́блик.
Sovietize ['səʊvɪətaɪz, 'sɒ-] *v.t.* советизи́ровать (*impf., pf.*).
sow[1] [saʊ] *n.* (*pig*) свинья́; **breeding ~** свинома́тка.
sow[2] [səʊ] *v.t.* **1.** (*seed*) се́ять, по-; (*fig.*): **he is ~ing (the seeds of) dissension** он се́ет раздо́р (*or* семена́ раздо́ра). **2.** (*ground*): зас|е́ивать (*or* -ева́ть), -е́ять; **a field ~n with maize** по́ле, засе́янное кукуру́зой.
sower ['səʊə(r)] *n.* (*pers.*) се́ятель (*m.*); (*machine*) се́ялка.
sowing ['səʊɪŋ] *n.* посе́в, засе́в.
soya ['sɔɪə] *n.* (*also* (*US*) **soy**) со́я.
adj. со́евый; **~ bean** со́евый боб; **~ milk** со́евое молоко́.
sozzled ['sɒz(ə)ld] *adj.* (*sl.*) пья́ный в сте́льку.
spa [spɑː] *n.* во́ды (*f. pl.*); куро́рт с минера́льными исто́чниками; **~ water** минера́льная вода́.
space [speɪs] *n.* **1.** (*expanse*) простра́нство, просто́р; **he was staring into ~** он уста́вился/смотре́л в одну́ то́чку; **vanish into ~** (*fig.*) испар|я́ться, -и́ться. **2.** (*cosmic, outer ~*) косми́ческое/мирово́е простра́нство; ко́смос; **they were the first to put a man into ~** они́ пе́рвыми запусти́ли челове́ка в ко́смос; (*attr.*) косми́ческий; **~ age** косми́ческий век; **~ shuttle** косми́ческий челно́к/паро́м; косми́ческий лета́тельный аппара́т многокра́тного испо́льзования; **~ travel, flight** косми́ческий полёт; **~ walk** прогу́лка в ко́смосе; *see also cpds.* **3.** (*distance, interval*) расстоя́ние; (*typ.*) интерва́л. **4.** (*of time, distance*): **after a short ~** че́рез не́которое вре́мя; вско́ре; **for the ~ of a mile** на протяже́нии ми́ли; **for a ~ of four weeks** на протяже́нии четырёх неде́ль; **in the ~ of a hour** за час; в тече́ние ча́са. **5.** (*area; room*) ме́сто; **blank ~** пусто́е ме́сто; **in the ~ provided** на ука́занном ме́сте; **for want of ~** из-за недоста́тка ме́ста.
v.t. (*also* **~ out**): **the posts were ~d six feet apart** столбы́ бы́ли располо́жены на расстоя́нии шести́ фу́тов друг от дру́га; **payments can be ~d** вы́плату мо́жно производи́ть в рассро́чку; (*typ.*) наб|ира́ть, -ра́ть в разря́дку.
cpds. **~-bar** *n.* кла́виша для интерва́ла; **~craft** (*also* **~-ship**) *nn.* косми́ческий кора́бль; **~man** *n.* космона́вт; **~-probe** *n.* косми́ческий полёт; **~-ship** *n.* = **~craft; ~-suit** *n.* скафа́ндр (космона́вта); **~-time** *n.* простра́нство-вре́мя; **~woman** *n.* же́нщина-космона́вт, космопла́вательница.
spacial ['speɪʃəl] *adj.* простра́нственный.
spacing ['speɪsɪŋ] *n.* **1.** распределе́ние. **2.** (*typ., between letters*) разря́дка; (*between lines*) межстро́чие, интерва́л; **type in double ~** печа́тать (*impf.*) че́рез два интерва́ла.
spacious ['speɪʃəs] *adj.* **1.** (*roomy*) просто́рный; (*vast, extensive*) общи́рный; (*capacious*) помести́тельный, вмести́тельный. **2.** (*fig.*) раздо́льный.
spaciousness ['speɪʃəsnɪs] *n.* просто́рность, просто́р; общи́рность, вмести́тельность.
spade [speɪd] *n.* **1.** (*tool*) лопа́та; **call a ~ a ~** называ́ть (*impf.*) ве́щи свои́ми имена́ми. **2.** (*cards*) пи́ка; (*pl.*) пи́ки, пи́ковая масть; **queen of ~s** пи́ковая да́ма.
v.t.: **~ up** вы́копать (*pf.*).
cpd. **~-work** *n.* (*fig.*) (кропотли́вая) подготови́тельная рабо́та.
spadeful ['speɪdfʊl] *n.* (це́лая) лопа́та (*чего*).
spaghetti [spə'getɪ] *n.* спаге́тти (*nt. indecl.*).
Spain [speɪn] *n.* Испа́ния.
spam [spæm] *n.* колба́сный фарш.
span [spæn] *n.* **1.** (*distance between supports*): **~ of an arch of a bridge** пролёт а́рки/моста́. **2.** (*of time*) промежу́ток/пери́од вре́мени; **~ of life** продолжи́тельность жи́зни; **attention ~** психологи́ческий объём внима́ния. **3.: wing ~** разма́х кры́льев. **4.** (*distance between thumb and finger*) пядь.
v.t. **1.** (*extend across*) перекр|ыва́ть, -ы́ть; **the bridge ~s the river** мост переки́нут че́рез ре́ку; (*fig.*): **the movement ~s almost two centuries** э́то движе́ние охва́тывает почти́ два столе́тия. **2.** (*measure with fingers*) изм|еря́ть, -е́рить пядя́ми.
cpd. **~-roof** *n.* двуска́тная кры́ша.
spandrel ['spændrɪl] *n.* антрво́льт; па́зуха сво́да.
spangle ['spæŋg(ə)l] *n.* блёстка.
v.t. укр|аша́ть, -а́сить блёстками; **the heavens ~d with stars** не́бо, усы́панное звёздами.
Spaniard ['spænjəd] *n.* испа́н|ец (*fem.* -ка).
spaniel ['spænj(ə)l] *n.* спание́ль (*m.*).
Spanish ['spænɪʃ] *n.* **1.** (*language*) испа́нский (язы́к). **2.: the ~** (*collect.*) испа́нцы (*m. pl.*).
adj. испа́нский; **~ fly** шпа́нская му́шка, шпа́нка.
spank [spæŋk] *n.* шлепо́к; **give a child a ~** шлёпнуть (*pf.*) ребёнка.
v.t. шлёп|ать, -нуть (*or* пошлёпать).
spanking ['spæŋkɪŋ] *n.*: **give a child a ~** нашлёпать/отшлёпать (*pf.*) ребёнка.
adj.: **go at a ~ pace** нести́сь/мча́ться (*impf.*) (во всю).
spanner ['spænə(r)] *n.* (га́ечный) ключ; **throw a ~ into the works** (*fig.*) ≃ вставля́ть (*impf.*) па́лки в колёса.
spar[1] [spɑː(r)] *n.* **1.** (*naut.*) ранго́утное де́рево; (*yard*) реёк. **2.** (*aeron.*) лонжеро́н.
spar[2] [spɑː(r)] *n.* (*min.*) шпат.
spar[3] [spɑː(r)] *n.* (*boxing*) спа́рринг; трениро́вочный/во́льный бой.
v.i. **1.** дра́ться (*impf.*) на кулака́х; бокси́ровать (*impf.*); **~ring-match** трениро́вочный матч; **~ring partner** партнёр для трениро́вки. **2.** (*fig., argue*) спо́рить (*impf.*); препира́ться (*impf.*).
spare [speə(r)] *n.* **1.** (**~ part**) запасна́я часть, запча́сть. **2.** (**~** *wheel*) запасно́е колесо́. **3.** (*of rope*): **take up the ~** натя́|гивать, -ну́ть слабину́.
adj. **1.** (*scanty*) ску́дный; **~ diet** ску́дное пита́ние. **2.** (*lean*) худоща́вый, сухоща́вый. **3.** (*excess, extra*) ли́шний; **~ room** ко́мната для госте́й; **~ time** свобо́дное вре́мя; **~ cash** ли́шние де́ньги; (*additional, reserve*) запасно́й, запа́сный, резе́рвный; **~ parts** запасны́е ча́сти, запча́сти; **~ wheel** запасно́е колесо́; **~ tyre** запасна́я ши́на; (*coll., of fat*) брюшко́.
v.t. **1.** (*withhold use of*) жале́ть, по-; **he ~d no pains/expense to …** он не жале́л уси́лий/расхо́дов, что́бы… **2.** (*dispense with, do without*) об|ходи́ться, -ойти́сь без+*g.*; **we cannot ~ him** мы не мо́жем обойти́сь без него́; мы не мо́жем его́ отпусти́ть. **3.** (*afford*): **can you ~ a cigarette?** нет ли у вас ли́шней сигаре́ты?; **can you ~ me 10 roubles?** мо́жете ли вы дать мне де́сять рубле́й?; **I can ~ you only a few minutes** я могу́ удели́ть вам то́лько не́сколько мину́т. **4. to ~** (*available, left over*): **I have no time to ~** у меня́ нет ли́шнего вре́мени; **we got there with an hour to ~** когда́ мы при́были, у нас оказа́лся це́лый час в запа́се; **three yards to ~** три я́рда ли́шних; **they have enough and to ~** у них бо́лее чем доста́точно; у них ско́лько уго́дно (*чего*). **5.** (*show mercy, leniency to*) щади́ть, по-; **the conquerors ~d no one** победи́тели не (по)щади́ли никого́; **~ s.o.'s life** сохрани́ть (*pf.*) кому́-н. жизнь; **if I am ~d** е́сли бу́ду жив; **I tried to ~ his feelings** я стара́лся щади́ть его́ чу́вства; **~ o.s.** (*reserve strength*) бере́чь (*impf.*) свои́ си́лы; (*take things easily*) щади́ть (*impf.*) себя́. **6.** (*save from*) изб|авля́ть, -а́вить (*кого от чего*); **I want to ~ you any unpleasantness** я хочу́ изба́вить

вас от возмо́жных неприя́тностей; **I will ~ you the trouble of replying** я изба́влю вас от необходи́мости отвеча́ть; **~ us the details** изба́вьте нас от подро́бностей!; пожа́луйста, без подро́бностей!

cpd. **~-ribs** *n. pl.* свины́е рёбрышки (*nt. pl.*).

sparing ['speərɪŋ] *adj.* (*moderate*) уме́ренный; **be ~ with the sugar!** не клади́те сли́шком мно́го са́хару; (*frugal*) скупо́й; **~ of words/praise** скупо́й на слова́/похвалы́; (*scanty, meagre*) ску́дный; (*careful*) бережли́вый; (*economical*) эконо́мный.

spark [spɑːk] *n.* **1.** и́скра; **strike ~s from a flint** высека́ть, вы́сечь и́скры из кремня́; (*fig.*): **if they get together the ~s will fly** е́сли они́ сойду́тся, непреме́нно сце́пятся; **he showed not a ~ of interest** он не прояви́л ни те́ни/мале́йшего интере́са; **he hasn't a ~ of intelligence** у него́ нет ни ка́пли соображе́ния. **2.** (*pl., coll., ship's radio operator*) ради́ст.

v.t. (*also* **~ off:** *cause*) вызыва́ть, вы́звать.

v.i. искри́ть (*impf.*); дать (*pf.*) и́скру.

cpds. **~-arrester** *n.* искрогаси́тель (*m.*); искроулови́тель (*m.*); **~-coil** *n.* индукцио́нная кату́шка; **~-gap** *n.* искрово́й промежу́ток; **~(ing)-plug** *n.* запа́льная свеча́.

sparkle ['spɑːk(ə)l] *n.* сверка́ние, блеск, блиста́ние; блёстка, и́скорка; **a ~ came into his eyes** у него́ глаза́ засверка́ли/заблесте́ли; (*of wine etc.*) шипе́ние, искре́ние; **the wine lost its ~** вино́ утра́тило искри́стость.

v.i. сверка́ть, за-; и́скриться (*impf.*); (*flash*) блесте́ть, за-; **her eyes ~d** у неё глаза́ сверка́ли/блесте́ли; (*of wit*) сверк|а́ть, -ну́ть; (*of wine*) игра́ть (*impf.*); и́скриться (*impf.*); **sparkling wine** шипу́чее/игри́стое вино́.

sparkler ['spɑːklə(r)] *n.* (*coll., diamond*) алма́з.

sparrow ['spærəʊ] *n.* воробе́й.

cpd. **~-hawk** *n.* я́стреб-перепеля́тник; пустельга́ воробьи́ная.

sparse [spɑːs] *adj.* ре́дкий; (*scattered*) разбро́санный; **~ly populated** малонаселённый; **~ vegetation** ску́дная расти́тельность.

spars|eness ['spɑːsnɪs], **-ity** ['spɑːsɪtɪ] *nn.* ску́дость.

Sparta ['spɑːtə] *n.* Спа́рта.

Spartan ['spɑːt(ə)n] *n.* спарта́н|ец (*fem.* -ка).

adj. спарта́нский.

spasm ['spæz(ə)m] *n.* (*of muscles*) спа́зм(а), су́дорога; (*mental or physical reaction*) поры́в, при́ступ, припа́док; **a ~ of coughing** при́ступ ка́шля; **~s of grief** взры́вы отча́яния; **he works in ~s** он рабо́тает наско́ками.

spasmodic [spæz'mɒdɪk] *adj.* **1.** (*med.*) спазмати́ческий; (*convulsive*) су́дорожный. **2.** (*intermittent*) перемежа́ющийся; преры́вистый.

spastic ['spæstɪk] *n.* парали́тик.

adj. спасти́ческий.

spat[1] [spæt] *n.* (*US coll.*) размо́лвка; лёгкая ссо́ра.

v.i. брани́ться, по-.

spat[2] [spæt] *n.* (*pl.*) коро́ткие ге́тры (*f. pl.*).

spate [speɪt] *n.* разли́в; наводне́ние; (*fig.*) пото́к; **the river is in ~** река́ взду́лась.

spatial ['speɪʃ(ə)l] *adj.* простра́нственный.

spatter ['spætə(r)] (*also* **splatter**) *v.t.* бры́згать, за-; **~ed with mud** забры́зганный гря́зью.

spatula ['spætjʊlə] *n.* шпа́тель (*m.*), лопа́точка.

spatulate ['spætjʊlət] *adj.* лопатообра́зный.

spavin ['spævɪn] *n.* ко́стный шпат.

spavined ['spævɪnd] *adj.* страда́ющий (ко́стным) шпа́том.

spawn [spɔːn] *n.* **1.** (*of fish etc.*) икра́; **mushroom ~** грибни́ца. **2.** (*pej., offspring*) отро́дье.

v.t. (*of fish etc.*) мета́ть (*impf.*); (*fig., pej.*) плоди́ть, на-/рас-; поро|жда́ть, -ди́ть.

v.i. (*reproduce*) мета́ть (*impf.*) икру́; (*pej., multiply*) плоди́ться, рас-.

spay [speɪ] *v.t.* удал|я́ть, -и́ть яи́чники у+*g*.

speak [spiːk] *v.t.* **1.** (*say, pronounce, utter*) говори́ть, сказа́ть; произн|оси́ть, -ести́; **he didn't ~ a word** он не произнёс ни сло́ва; **he spoke his lines clearly** он чётко/вня́тно произнёс свой текст; он отчека́нил свою́ роль; **~ words of wisdom** изр|ека́ть, -е́чь му́дрость; (*give utterance to, express*) выска́зывать, вы́сказать; **~ the truth** говори́ть, сказа́ть пра́вду; **~ one's mind** открове́нно выска́зывать, вы́сказать своё мне́ние; *see also* **spoken. 2.** (*converse in*): **he ~s Russian well** он хорошо́/свобо́дно/прекра́сно говори́т по-ру́сски (*or* владе́ет ру́сским языко́м); **they were ~ing French** они́ разгова́ривали/говори́ли по-францу́зски; **he ~s six languages** он владе́ет шестью́ языка́ми; он говори́т на шести́ языка́х.

v.i. говори́ть, по-; (*converse*) разгова́ривать (*impf.*); вести́ (*indet.*) разгово́р; **I was ~ing to him yesterday** я говори́л/разгова́ривал с ним вчера́; **they are not on ~ing terms** они́ в ссо́ре; они́ бо́льше не разгова́ривают; **he is on ~ing terms with her again** он помири́лся с ней; (*make a speech*) произн|оси́ть, -ести́ речь; **I am not used to ~ing in public** я не привы́к публи́чно выступа́ть; **he spoke for the motion** он вы́сказался за предложе́ние; **a ~ing likeness of George** вы́литый Джордж; **~ing clock** говоря́щие часы́; **~ing-trumpet** ру́пор; **~ing-tube** перегово́рная тру́бка; **'Smith ~ing'** (*on telephone*) «(с ва́ми) говори́т Смит»; «Смит у телефо́на»; **'~ing'** (*on telephone*) «э́то я»; «слу́шаю»; **actions ~ louder than words** не по слова́м су́дят, а по дела́м; **she could not ~ for joy** она́ была́ вне себя́ от ра́дости; **this calls for some plain ~ing** сле́дует, ви́дно, объясни́ться начистоту́; **I must ~ to him about his manners** мне на́до бу́дет поговори́ть с ним о его́ мане́рах; **so to ~** так сказа́ть; **roughly, broadly ~ing** в о́бщих/основны́х черта́х; приблизи́тельно, приме́рно; **strictly ~ing** стро́го говоря́; **~ing as a father** как оте́ц; **in a manner of ~ing** е́сли мо́жно так вы́разиться; **the facts ~ for themselves** фа́кты говоря́т (са́ми) за себя́; **~ing for myself** что каса́ется меня́; **~ for yourself!** не говори́те за други́х!; **let him ~ for himself** не подска́зывайте!; пусть сам ска́жет!; **~ well, highly of s.o.** хвали́ть, по- кого́-н.; **he is well spoken of** о нём хорошо́ отзыва́ются/говоря́т; **~ of** (*mention, refer to*) упом|ина́ть, -яну́ть о (*ком/чём*); каса́ться, косну́ться (*чего*); **~ing of money, can you lend me a pound?** кста́ти о деньга́х — не дади́те ли вы мне фунт взаймы́?; **nothing to ~ of** ничего́ осо́бенного; **he has no wealth to ~ of** его́ состоя́ние весьма́ незначи́тельно; **the flat is too small, not to ~ of the noise** э́та кварти́ра сли́шком мала́, и к тому́ же ещё здесь о́чень шу́мно; (*indicate, proclaim*): **everything about her spoke of refined taste** всё в ней ука́зывало на изы́сканный вкус (*or* говори́ло об изы́сканном вку́се); (*announce intention of*): **he ~s of retiring next year** он погова́ривает об ухо́де в отста́вку в бу́дущем году́.

with advs.: **~ out** *v.i.* (*express o.s. plainly*) выска́зываться, вы́сказаться открове́нно; **~ up** *v.i.* (**~** *louder*) говори́ть (*impf.*) погро́мче; (*express support*): **~ up for s.o.** подде́рж|ивать, -а́ть кого́-н.

speaker ['spiːkə(r)] *n.* **1.: the ~ was a man of about 40** говоря́щему бы́ло лет со́рок. **2.: a Russian ~** челове́к, владе́ющий ру́сским языко́м; **he is a native Russian ~** его́ родно́й язы́к — ру́сский. **3.** (*public* ~) ора́тор, докла́дчик, выступа́ющий. **4.** (*parl.*) спи́кер. **5. (loud-~)** громкоговори́тель (*m.*), ру́пор.

spear ['spɪə(r)] *n.* копьё, дро́тик; (*for fish*) гарпу́н, острога́.

v.t. пронз|а́ть, -и́ть копьём; **~ fish** бить (*impf.*) ры́бу острого́й.

cpds. **~head** *n.* (*lit.*) наконе́чник/остриё копья́; (*fig.*) передово́й отря́д; аванга́рд; *v.t.*: **~head a movement** возгл|авля́ть, -а́вить движе́ние; **~man** *n.* копьено́сец, копе́йщик; **~mint** *n.* (*bot.*) мя́та колоси́стая/курча́вая; (*chewing-gum*) мя́тная жва́чка; жева́тельная рези́нка.

spec[1] [spek] *n.* (*coll.*): **it turned out a good ~** э́то оказа́лось вы́годной опера́цией; **he went there on ~** он пошёл туда́ наудачу.

spec[2] [spek] *n.* (*coll., specification*) специфика́ция.

special ['speʃ(ə)l] *n.* (*edition*) э́кстренный вы́пуск; (*train*) по́езд специа́льного назначе́ния; дополни́тельный по́езд.

adj. **1.** осо́бый, осо́бенный, специа́льный, определённый; **~ to** сво́йственный +*d*.; **this book is of ~ interest to me** э́та кни́га представля́ет осо́бый интере́с для меня́; **for a ~ purpose** со специа́льной це́лью; **~ agent** аге́нт по осо́бым поруче́ниям; **a ~ case** осо́бый слу́чай; **my ~ chair** мой люби́мый стул; **~ course/subject** специа́льный курс/предме́т; ~ **correspondent** специа́льный корреспонде́нт; ~ **hospital** специализи́рованная больни́ца; ~ **licence** (*for marriage*) разреше́ние на венча́ние без оглаше́ния. **2.** (*specific, definite*) определённый; **do you want to come at any ~ time?** вы хоти́те зара́нее договори́ться о вре́мени прихо́да? **3.** (*extraordinary*) э́кстренный; ~ **train** по́езд специа́льного назначе́ния; э́кстренный по́езд; ~ **edition** э́кстренный вы́пуск; ~ **delivery** сро́чная доста́вка.

cpd. **~-purpose** *adj.* осо́бого/специа́льного назначе́ния.

specialist ['speʃəlɪst] *n.* специали́ст (*fem.* -ка) (по+*d.*).

speciality [,speʃɪ'ælɪtɪ] (*US* **specialty**) *n.* **1.** (*characteristic*) осо́бенность, специ́фика. **2.** (*pursuit*) о́бласть специализа́ции; **make a ~ of sth.** специализи́роваться (*impf., pf.*) в чём-н.; **what is his ~?** кто он по специа́льности? **3.** (*product, recipe etc.*): ~ **of the house** фи́рменное блю́до.

specialization [,speʃəlaɪ'zeɪʃ(ə)n] *n.* специализа́ция.

specialize ['speʃə,laɪz] *v.t.* **1.** (*make specific, individual*) специализи́ровать (*impf., pf.*); **~d knowledge** специа́льные позна́ния. **2.** (*biol.*): **~d organ** специа́льный/осо́бый о́рган.

v.i. (*be or become specialist*) специализи́роваться (*impf., pf.*) (по+*d.*; в+*p.*).

specially ['speʃəlɪ] *adv.* **1.** (*individually*) осо́бо; **he was ~ mentioned** о нём упомяну́ли осо́бо. **2.** (*for specific purpose*): специа́льно; ~ **selected** специа́льно ото́бранный. **3.** (*exceptionally*): осо́бенно, исключи́тельно; **be ~ careful** быть осо́бенно осторо́жным/внима́тельным.

specialty ['speʃəltɪ] = **speciality**

specie ['spi:ʃi:, -ʃɪ] *n.* металли́ческие де́н|ьги (*pl., g.* -ег); **pay in ~** плати́ть, за- зво́нкой моне́той.

species ['spi:ʃɪz, -ʃi:z, 'spi:s-] *n.* **1.** (*biol.*) (биологи́ческий) вид; **our** (*or* **the (human)**) ~ челове́ческий род; **origin of ~** происхожде́ние ви́дов. **2.** (*kind*) вид, род, разнови́дность.

specific [spɪ'sɪfɪk] *n.* (специфи́ческое) сре́дство/лека́рство.

adj. **1.** (*definite*) определённый, конкре́тный, осо́бенный; **he has no ~ aim** у него́ нет никако́й определённой це́ли; **a ~ statement** конкре́тное утвержде́ние. **2.** (*distinct*) специфи́ческий, осо́бый. **3.** (*biol.*) видово́й. **4.** (*phys.*): ~ **gravity** уде́льный вес. **5.** (*med.*) специфи́ческий. **6.** (*peculiar*) характе́рный; **the style is ~ to that school of painters** э́тот стиль характе́рен для той шко́лы жи́вописи.

specification [,spesɪfɪ'keɪʃ(ə)n] *n.* (*for construction etc.*) специфика́ция, детализа́ция; прое́ктное зада́ние; (*of patent*) специфика́ция; техни́ческие усло́вия (*abbr.* ТУ).

specif|y ['spesɪ,faɪ] *v.t.* **1.** (*name expressly*) определ|я́ть, -и́ть; уточн|я́ть, -и́ть; (*enumerate*) переч|исля́ть, -и́слить; **unless otherwise ~ied** е́сли нет ины́х указа́ний. **2.** (*include in specification*) специфици́ровать (*impf., pf.*); детализи́ровать (*impf., pf.*).

specimen ['spesɪmən] *n.* **1.** (*example; sample*) экземпля́р; образе́ц, обра́зчик; (*individual of species*) о́собь; **zoological ~s** зоологи́ческие о́соби; **a museum ~** музе́йный экспона́т; ~ **page** про́бная страни́ца; ~ **of urine** моча́ для ана́лиза. **2.** (*unusual pers., thg.*) тип, субъе́кт; **a queer ~** чуда́к; стра́нный субъе́кт.

specious ['spi:ʃəs] *adj.* благови́дный; **a ~ argument** вне́шне убеди́тельный до́вод; **a ~ person** лицеме́р (*fem.* -ка).

speciousness ['spi:ʃəsnɪs] *n.* благови́дность.

speck [spek] *n.* (*dot*) кра́пинка; (*of dirt or decay*) пя́тнышко; ~ **of dust** пя́тнышко; **the ship was a ~ on the horizon** кора́бль каза́лся то́чкой на горизо́нте.

speckle ['spek(ə)l] *v.t.* покр|ыва́ть, -ы́ть кра́пинками.

speckled ['spek(ə)ld] *adj.* кра́пчатый; пятни́стый; ~ **hen** пёстрая/ряба́я ку́рица.

specs [speks] *n.* (*coll.*) = **spectacle 2.**

spectacle ['spektək(ə)l] *n.* **1.** (*public show; sight*) зре́лище; **he is a sad ~** он явля́ет собо́й жа́лкое зре́лище; у него́ жа́лкий вид; **he made a ~ of himself** он вы́ставил себя́ на посме́шище. **2.** (*pl., glasses*) очк|и́ (*pl., g.* -о́в); **he sees everything through rose-coloured ~s** он ви́дит всё в ро́зовом све́те; он смо́трит на всё сквозь ро́зовые очки́.

spectacled ['spektək(ə)ld] *adj.* в очка́х, нося́щий очки́; (*of animal*) очко́вый.

spectacular [spek'tækjʊlə(r)] *n.* эффе́ктное зре́лище.

adj. эффе́ктный, импоза́нтный.

spectator [spek'teɪtə(r)] *n.* (*onlooker*) зри́тель (*fem.* -ница); (*observer*) наблюда́тель (*fem.* -ница).

spectral ['spektr(ə)l] *adj.* при́зрачный; (*phys.*) спектра́льный.

spectre ['spektə(r)] *n.* привиде́ние, при́зрак.

spectrograph ['spektrəʊ,grɑ:f] *n.* спектро́граф.

spectrometer [spek'trɒmɪtə(r)] *n.* спектро́метр.

spectroscope ['spektrə,skəʊp] *n.* спектроско́п.

spectroscopic [,spektrə'skɒpɪk] *adj.* спектроскопи́ческий.

spectroscopy [,spek'trɒskəpɪ] *n.* спектроскопи́я.

spectrum ['spektrəm] *n.* **1.** (*phys.*) спектр; ~ **analysis** спектра́льный ана́лиз. **2.** (*fig.*) диапазо́н.

speculate ['spekjʊ,leɪt] *v.i.* **1.** (*meditate*) размышля́ть (*impf.*) (*о чем*); разду́мывать (*impf.*) (*над чем*); (*conjecture*) де́лать (*impf.*) предположе́ния, гада́ть (*impf.*). **2.** (*risk, invest money*) спекули́ровать (*impf.*), игра́ть (*impf.*) на би́рже; **he ~s in oil shares** он спекули́рует нефтяны́ми а́кциями.

speculation [,spekjʊ'leɪʃ(ə)n] *n.* (*meditation*) размышле́ние; (*conjecture*) предположе́ние; дога́дка; (*investment*) спекуля́ция; ~ **on the Exchange** игра́ на би́рже.

speculative ['spekjʊlətɪv] *adj.* (*meditative*) умозри́тельный, теорети́ческий; (*conjectural*) предположи́тельный, гипотети́ческий; (*risky*) риско́ванный; (*comm.*) спекуляти́вный.

speculator ['spekjʊ,leɪtə(r)] *n.* спекуля́нт (*fem.* -ка).

speech [spi:tʃ] *n.* **1.** (*faculty, act of speaking; also gram.*) речь; **lose the power of ~** лиш|а́ться, -и́ться да́ра ре́чи; **a ready flow of ~** пла́вная речь; **freedom of ~** свобо́да сло́ва; **have ~ with** говори́ть, по- с+*i.*; ~ **is silver, silence golden** сло́во — серебро́, молча́ние — зо́лото; **direct/indirect ~** пряма́я/ко́свенная речь; **parts of ~** ча́сти ре́чи; **figure of ~** о́бразное выраже́ние; ритори́ческая фигу́ра. **2.** (*manner of speaking*) речь, го́вор; (*pronunciation*) произноше́ние, вы́говор; **he is slow of ~** у него́ заме́дленная речь; ~ **therapy** логопе́дия. **3.** (*public address*) речь; (ора́торское) выступле́ние; **make a ~** произн|оси́ть, -ести́ речь; выступа́ть, вы́ступить с ре́чью; **set ~** зара́нее соста́вленная речь. **4.** (*language*) речь; язы́к; го́вор.

cpds. **~-day** *n.* акт; а́ктовый день; **~-writer** *n.* «речеви́к».

speechify ['spi:tʃɪ,faɪ] *v.i.* ора́торствовать (*impf.*); разглаго́льствовать (*impf.*) (*coll.*).

speechless ['spi:tʃlɪs] *adj.* (*wordless*) немо́й; (*temporarily unable to speak*) онеме́вший; безмо́лвный; **I was ~ with surprise** я онеме́л (*or* я лиши́лся да́ра ре́чи) от удивле́ния.

speed [spi:d] *n.* **1.** (*rapidity*) быстрота́, ско́рость; (*rate of motion*) ско́рость; **with all possible ~** как мо́жно скоре́е; в срочне́йшем поря́дке; с преде́льной быстрото́й; **at full, top ~** на по́лной ско́рости; по́лным хо́дом; **gain, gather ~** наб|ира́ть, -ра́ть ско́рость; **lose ~** теря́ть, по- ско́рость; **my bicycle has four ~s** мой велосипе́д име́ет четы́ре ско́рости; **he was travelling at ~** он е́хал с большо́й ско́ростью; ~ **limit** дозво́ленная ско́рость; преде́л ско́рости. **2.** (*stimulant*) «спид».

v.t. **1.** (*send off*): ~ **a parting guest** прово|жа́ть, -ди́ть уходя́щего го́стя; ~ **an arrow from the bow** вы́пустить (*pf.*) стрелу́ из лу́ка. **2.** (*also* ~ **up:** *accelerate*) уск|оря́ть, -о́рить; **the train service has been ~ed up** по но́вому расписа́нию поезда́ хо́дят быстре́е; **measures to ~ production** ме́ры по повыше́нию те́мпа произво́дства. **3.** (*increase revolutions of*): ~ **an engine** увели́чи|вать, -ть число́ оборо́тов мото́ра.

v.i. мча́ться, про-; нести́сь, про-; **he was fined for ~ing** его́ оштрафова́ли за превыше́ние ско́рости.

cpds. **~-boat** *n.* быстрохо́дный ка́тер, гли́ссер; **~way** *n.* го́ночный трек; **~way racing** спидве́й, скоростны́е мотого́нки (*f. pl.*); **~way rider** мотого́нщик; **~well** *n.* верони́ка.

speedometer [spi:'dɒmɪtə(r)] *n.* спидо́метр.

speedy ['spi:dɪ] *adj.* (*rapid*) ско́рый, бы́стрый, прово́рный; (*hasty*) поспе́шный; (*prompt, undelayed*) ско́рый, немéдленный; **he wished me a ~ return** он пожелáл мне скóрого возвращéния; **they took ~ action against him** они́ при́няли срóчные мéры прóтив негó.

speleological [ˌspiːlɪəˈlɒdʒɪk(ə)l, ˌspe-] *adj.* спелеологи́ческий.

speleologist [ˌspiːlɪˈɒlədʒɪst, ˌspe-] *n.* спелеóлог; исслéдователь (*m.*) пещéр.

speleology [ˌspiːlɪˈɒlədʒɪ, ˌspe-] *n.* спелеолóгия.

spell[1] [spel] *n.* **1.** (*magical formula; its effect*) заклинáние; чáр|ы (*pl., g.* —); колдовствó; **cast a ~ over** околдóв|ывать, -áть; заколдóв|ывать, -áть; очарóв|ывать, -áть; **break the ~** разр|ушáть, -ýшить чáры. **2.** (*fascination*) обая́ние, очаровáние; **he fell under the ~ of her beauty** он подпáл под обая́ние её красоты́.

cpd. **~-bound** *adj.* очарóванный, зачарóванный; **he held the audience ~-bound** он зачаровáл слýшателей.

spell[2] [spel] *n.* **1.** (*bout, turn*) смéна, períод; **a ~ of work** перúод рабóты; **take a ~** поработать (*pf.*); **shall I take a ~ at the wheel?** смени́ть ли мне вас у руля́? **2.** (*interval*) перúод; промежýток врéмени; **I slept for a ~** я поспáл нéкоторое врéмя; **we had a ~ of good luck** у нас былá полосá везéния; **we're in for a ~ of fine weather** ожидáется полосá хорóшей погóды. **3.** (*period of rest*): **take a ~** отдохнýть (*pf.*).

spell[3] [spel] *v.t.* **1.** (*write or name letters in sequence*) произн|оси́ть, -ести́ (*or* писáть, на-) (*что*) по бýквам; **how do you ~ your name?** как пи́шется вáша фами́лия?; **he cannot ~ his own name** он не мóжет прáвильно писáть свою́ фами́лию; **I wish you would learn to ~** когдá вы наýчитесь писáть без оши́бок? **2.** (*usu.* **~ out:** *decipher slowly*) с трудóм раз|бирáть, -обрáть (по бýквам); (*fig., make explicit*) разжёв|ывать, -áть. **3.** (*of letters: make up*) сост|авля́ть, -áвить (по бýквам); **what do these letters ~?** какóе слóво составля́ют э́ти бýквы? **4.** (*fig., signify*) означáть (*impf.*); **these changes ~ disaster** э́ти перемéны суля́т несчáстье. **5.** (*relieve*) смен|я́ть, -и́ть.

v.i. писáть (*impf.*) прáвильно/грáмотно; **we do not pronounce as we ~** мы произнóсим не так, как пи́шем.

speller [ˈspelə(r)] *n.*: **he is a poor ~** у негó хромáет орфогрáфия; он с орфогрáфией не в ладáх.

spelling [ˈspelɪŋ] *n.* правописáние, орфогрáфия; **I am not certain of the ~ of this word** я не увéрен в правописáнии э́того слóва.

cpd. **~-bee** *n.* состязáние по орфогрáфии.

spen|d [spend] *v.t.* **1.** (*pay out*) трáтить, ис-; расхóдовать, из-; **how much have you ~t?** скóлько вы израсхóдовали?; **she ~ds too much on clothes** онá сли́шком мнóго трáтит на тря́пки/наря́ды; **~d a penny** (*coll., use lavatory*) пойти́ (*pf.*) кóе-кудá. **2.** (*consume, expend, exhaust*) истощ|áть, -и́ть; расхóдовать, из-; **~d o.s.** истощ|áться, -и́ться; вы́мотаться (*pf.*); выдыхáться, вы́дохнуться; **he ~t his strength to no avail** он потрáтил свои́ си́лы безрезультáтно; **the storm ~t itself** бýря улеглáсь/ути́хла; **he is completely ~t** он вы́мотался вконéц; **a ~t bullet** пýля на излёте. **3.** (*pass*) пров|оди́ть, -ести́; **we ~t some hours looking for a hotel** у нас ушлó (*or* мы потрáтили) нéсколько часóв на пóиски гости́ницы; **a well-~t life** с тóлком (*or* не напрáсно) прóжитая жизнь; **she ~t her life in good works** онá всю свою́ жизнь посвяти́ла дóбрым делáм; **how do you ~d your leisure?** как вы провóдите свой досýг?; **the night is far ~t** ночь на исхóде.

v.i. (**~** *money*) трáтиться, по-; **~ding-money** кармáнные дéньги; **they went on a ~ding spree** они́ пошли́ транжи́рить дéньги.

cpd. **~dthrift** *n.* мот (*fem.* -óвка); транжи́р (*fem.* -ка); транжи́ра (*c.g.*); расточи́тель (*fem.* -ница); *adj.* расточи́тельный.

spender [ˈspendə(r)] *n.*: **a lavish ~** щéдрый человéк.

sperm [spɜːm] *n.* спéрма; (**~ whale**) кашалóт.

spermaceti [ˌspɜːməˈsetɪ] *n.* спермацéт.

spermatozoon [ˌspɜːmətəʊˈzəʊɒn] *n.* сперматозóид.

spew [spjuː] *v.t.* выблёвывать, вы́блевать; (*lit., fig.*) изрыг|áть, -нýть; **a machine-gun ~ing out bullets** пулемéт, полива́ющий (неприя́теля) огнём.

v.i. блевáть, сблевнýть.

sphere [sfɪə(r)] *n.* **1.** сфéра; (*globe*) шар, глóбус. **2.** (*fig.*) сфéра, óбласть/пóле (дéятельности); **outside my ~** вне моéй компетéнции; **~ of influence** сфéра влия́ния.

spherical [ˈsferɪk(ə)l] *adj.* сфери́ческий, шарообрáзный.

spheroid [ˈsfɪərɔɪd] *n.* сферóид.

spheroidal [sfɪəˈrɔɪd(ə)l] *adj.* сфероидáльный, шарови́дный.

sphincter [ˈsfɪŋktə(r)] *n.* сфи́нктер.

sphinx [sfɪŋks] *n.* сфинкс.

sphygmomanometer [ˌsfɪgməʊməˈnɒmɪtə(r)] *n.* сфигмóметр.

spice [spaɪs] *n.* **1.** спéция, пря́ность, припрáва. **2.** (*fig., smack, dash*) при́вкус; при́месь; оттéнок; **his story lacked ~** егó расскáзу не хватáло изю́минки.

v.t. припр|авля́ть, -áвить; **highly-~d dishes** óстрые/пря́ные блю́да.

spick [spɪk] *adj.*: **~ and span** (*clean, tidy*) сверкáющий чистотóй; (*smart*) элегáнтный; (*brand-new*) совершéнно нóвый, новёхонький, с иголóчки.

spicy [ˈspaɪsɪ] *adj.* ароматн́ичный, аромáтный, пря́ный; (*fig.*) пикáнтный, солёный.

spider [ˈspaɪdə(r)] *n.* паýк; **~'s web** паути́на.

cpds. **~-crab** *n.* морскóй паýк; **~man** *n.* верхолáз; **~-monkey** *n.* паукообрáзная обезья́на.

spidery [ˈspaɪdərɪ] *adj.*: **~ writing** тóнкий витиевáтый пóчерк; **~ legs** дли́нные, тóнкие нóги, «спи́чки» (*f. pl.*).

spiel [ʃpiːl] (*US sl.*) *n.* заговáривание зубóв.

spiffing [ˈspɪfɪŋ] *adj.* (*coll.*) шикáрный.

spi(f)flicate [ˈspɪflɪˌkeɪt] *v.t.* раздолбáнить (*pf.*) (*coll.*).

spigot [ˈspɪgət] *n.* прóбка, вту́лка.

spike [spaɪk] *n.* **1.** остриё, косты́ль (*m.*); (*on fence*) зубéц; (*for papers etc.*) накóлка; (*on shoe*) шип, гвоздь (*m.*); **~ heels** «гвóздики» (*m. pl.*), «шпи́льки» (*f. pl.*); (*pl., coll.*) (*spiked running shoes*) шипóвки. **2.** (*bot.*) кóлос.

v.t. **1.** (*fasten with ~s*) приб|ивáть, -и́ть гвоздя́ми. **2.** (*furnish with ~s*) снаб|жáть, -ди́ть гвоздя́ми/шипáми; **~d boots** боти́нки (*m. pl.*) на шипáх; **~d helmet** островéрхая кáска. **3.**: **~ s.o.'s guns** (*fig.*) расстр|áивать, -óить чьи-н. зáмыслы.

spikenard [ˈspaɪknɑːd] *n.* нард.

spiky [ˈspaɪkɪ] *adj.* **1.** (*set with spikes*) усáженный остриями. **2.** (*in form of spike*) остроконéчный; заострённый. **3.** (*fig., of pers.*) колю́чий.

spill[1] [spɪl] *n.* (*of wood*) лучи́на; (*of paper*) жгут из бумáги.

spill[2] [spɪl] *n.*: **have a ~** (*fall, e.g. from a horse*) упáсть (*pf.*); свали́ться (*pf.*).

v.t. **1.** (*accidentally*) прол|ивáть, -и́ть; расплёск|ивать, -áть; **I spilt a glass of water on her dress** я проли́л стакáн воды́ на её плáтье; **without ~ing a drop** не расплескáв ни кáпли; **~ salt** расс|ыпáть, -ы́пать (*or* прос|ыпáть, -ы́пать) соль. **2.** (*intentionally*) прол|ивáть, -и́ть; (*fig.*): **~ the beans** (*coll.*) прогов|áриваться, -ори́ться; разб|áлтывать, -олтáть секрéт; **~ s.o.'s blood** прол|ивáть, -и́ть чью-н. кровь; уб|ивáть, -и́ть когó-н.; **much ink has been spilt on this question** на э́тот вопрóс извели́ немáло бумáги. **3.** (*throw out, down*): **they were spilt on to the road** их вы́бросило из экипáжа/маши́ны; **his horse spilt him** лóшадь сбрóсила егó.

v.i. (*of liquids*) разл|ивáться, -и́ться; расплёск|иваться, -áться; (*of salt etc.*) расс|ыпáться, -ы́паться; прос|ыпáться, -ы́паться.

with advs.: **~ out** *v.i.* выливáться, вы́литься; выплёскиваться, вы́плеснуться; **~ over** *v.i.* перел|ивáться, -и́ться (чéрез край).

cpds. **~-over** *n.* (*of population*) избы́точное населéние; **~way** *n.* водосли́в, водосбрóс.

spillage [ˈspɪlɪdʒ] *n.* утéчка, утрýска.

spillikins [ˈspɪlɪkɪnz] *n.* бирю́льки (*f. pl.*).

spin [spɪn] *n.* **1.** (*whirl, twisting motion*) кружéние, верчéние, вращéние; **go into a ~** завертéться (*pf.*); **his head was in a ~** у негó головá шла крýгом. **2.** (*aeron.*) штóпор; **go into a ~** войти́ (*pf.*) в штóпор; **in a flat ~** (*coll.*) в пóлной растéрянности. **3.** (*of ball*) вращéние; **put ~ on a ball** закрý|чивать, -ти́ть мяч. **4.** (*of coin*): **it all turned on the ~ of a coin** всё зави́село от жрéбия. **5.** (*outing*) корóткая прогýлка; **go for a ~ in the car** прокати́ться/покатáться (*both pf.*) на маши́не.

v.t. **1.** (*yarn, wool etc.*) прясть, с-; сучи́ть, с-; **~ning-wheel** (само)пря́лка; **~ning-machine** пряди́льная маши́на; **~ a yarn** (*fig.*) расска́з|ывать, -а́ть исто́рию; трави́ть (*impf.*) (*coll.*); **the spider ~s its web** пау́к плетёт паути́ну; **spun silk** шёлковая пря́жа; *see also* **spun. 2.** (*cause to revolve*) верте́ть, за-; крути́ть, за-; кружи́ть, за-; **~ a coin** подбр|а́сывать, -о́сить моне́тку; **~ a top** пус|ка́ть, -ти́ть волчо́к.

v.i. верте́ться, за-; крути́ться, за-; кружи́ться, за-; (*of compass needle or suspended object*) враща́ться (*impf.*); (*of wheel*) бы́стро враща́ться/крути́ться (*impf.*); (*of pers.*): **the blow sent him ~ning against the wall** уда́р швырну́л его́ (*or* уда́ром его́ отшвырну́ло) к стене́; **my head is ~ning** у меня́ голова́ идёт кру́гом.

with advs.: **~ out** *v.t.*: **~ out a story** растя́|гивать, -ну́ть расска́з; **~ round** *v.t.* & *i.* бы́стро пов|ора́чивать(ся), -ерну́ть(ся) (круго́м).

cpds. **~-drier** *n.* механи́ческая суши́лка, центрифу́га; **~-off** *n.* (*coll.*) побо́чный результа́т; вне́шние эффе́кты (*m. pl.*); дополни́тельный дохо́д.

spina bifida [ˌspaɪnə 'bɪfɪdə] *n.* расщепле́ние ости́стых отро́стков позвоно́чника.

spinach ['spɪnɪdʒ, -ɪtʃ] *n.* шпина́т.

spinal ['spaɪn(ə)l] *adj.* спинно́й; **~ column** позвоно́чный столб, позвоно́чник, спинно́й хребе́т; **~ cord** спинно́й мозг; **~ injury** поврежде́ние позвоно́чника.

spindle ['spɪnd(ə)l] *n.* (*of spinning-wheel*) веретено́; (*of spinning machine*) ось, вал; (*axis, rod*) ось, шпи́ндель (*m.*).

cpds. **~-legged** *adj.* (*of pers.*) длинноно́гий, тонконо́гий (*coll.*); (*of table etc.*) на то́нких но́жках; **~-shanks** *n.* голена́стый (челове́к) (*coll*).

spindly ['spɪndlɪ] *adj.* дли́нный и то́нкий.

spindrift ['spɪndrɪft] *n.* бры́зг|и (*pl., g.* —) морско́й воды́; морска́я пе́на.

spine [spaɪn] *n.* **1.** (*backbone*) позвоно́чный столб, позвоно́чник, спинно́й хребе́т; (*of fish*) хребе́т. **2.** (*of hedgehog etc.*) игла́, колю́чка. **3.** (*of plant*) игла́, колю́чка, шип. **4.** (*of book*) корешо́к.

cpd. **~-chilling** *adj.* жу́ткий; вызыва́ющий у́жас/содрога́ние.

spineless ['spaɪnlɪs] *adj.* (*invertebrate*) беспозвоно́чный; (*fig.*) бесхребе́тный, бесхара́ктерный, мягкоте́лый.

spinet [spɪ'net, 'spɪnɪt] *n.* спине́т.

spinnaker ['spɪnəkə(r)] *n.* спи́накер.

spinner ['spɪnə(r)] *n.* (*pers.*) пряди́льщи|к (*fem.* -ца); пря́ха; (*machine*) пряди́льная маши́на.

spinneret ['spɪnəˌret] *n.* пряди́льный о́рган.

spinney ['spɪnɪ] *n.* за́росль, ро́ща.

spinster ['spɪnstə(r)] *n.* (*old maid*) ста́рая де́ва; (*leg., unmarried woman*) незаму́жняя же́нщина.

spinsterhood ['spɪnstəhʊd] *n.* стародеви́чество.

spiny ['spaɪnɪ] *adj.* (*covered with spines*) покры́тый и́глами/шипа́ми/колю́чками; (*prickly*) колю́чий.

spiral ['spaɪər(ə)l] *n.* спира́ль; **the smoke ascended in a ~** дым поднима́лся ко́льцами; **wage-price ~** спира́ль зарпла́ты и цен.

adj. спира́льный; **~ balance** пружи́нные весы́; **~ staircase** винтова́я ле́стница.

v.i.: **the plane ~led down to earth** самолёт произвёл спира́льный спуск на зе́млю; **the crime rate is ~ling upwards** престу́пность ре́зко возраста́ет.

spirant ['spaɪərənt] *n.* спира́нт.

spire ['spaɪə(r)] *n.* (*of church etc.*) шпиль (*m.*), шпиц.

spirit ['spɪrɪt] *n.* **1.** (*soul, immaterial part of man*) душа́; духо́вное нача́ло; **the ~ is willing but the flesh is weak** дух бодр, плоть же не́мощна; **I shall be with you in ~** душо́й я бу́ду с ва́ми. **2.** (*immoral, incorporeal being*) дух; **the Holy S~** Свято́й Дух; **evil ~** злой дух; **as the ~ moves one** по наи́тию; (*apparition, ghost*) привиде́ние; **raise a ~** вызыва́ть, вы́звать ду́ха; **believe in ~s** ве́рить (*impf.*) в ду́хов/привиде́ния. **3.** (*living being*) ум, ли́чность; **one of the greatest ~s of his time** оди́н из велича́йших умо́в своего́ вре́мени; **leading ~** душа́, руководи́тель (*m.*), вождь (*m.*). **4.** (*mental or moral nature*) хара́ктер; **a man of unbending ~** челове́к непрекло́нного хара́ктера (*or* несгиба́емой во́ли); непрекло́нный челове́к; **the poor in ~** ни́щие ду́хом. **5.** (*courage*) хра́брость; **show some ~** прояв|ля́ть, -и́ть му́жество/хара́ктер; **a man of ~** челове́к с хара́ктером; си́льный ду́хом челове́к; **he infused ~ into his men** он вселя́л му́жество в солда́т; (*vivacity*) жи́вость; **he played the piano with ~** он вдохнове́нно игра́л на роя́ле. **6.** (*mental, moral attitude*) дух, смысл; **take sth. in the wrong ~** не так восприн|има́ть, -я́ть что-н.; **it depends on the ~ in which it is done** всё зави́сит от того́, с каки́м наме́рением э́то сде́лано; **in a ~ of mischief** шу́тки ра́ди; для ро́зыгрыша; **enter into the ~ of Christmas** прон|ика́ться, -и́кнуться ду́хом Рождества́. **7.** (*real meaning, essence*) су́щность, суть; существо́ де́ла; **the ~ of the law** дух зако́на; **I followed the ~ of his instructions** я де́йствовал в ду́хе его́ указа́ний. **8.** (*mental or moral tendency, influence*) дух, тенде́нция; **the ~ of the age** дух вре́мени. **9.** (*pl., humour*) настрое́ние; **he was in high ~s** он был в припо́днятом настрое́нии; **his ~s are low** он в пода́вленном настрое́нии; **keep one's ~s up** мужа́ться (*impf.*); не па́дать (*impf.*) ду́хом; **recover one's ~s** приободр|я́ться, -и́ться; **raise s.o.'s ~s** подбодр|я́ть, -и́ть кого́-н.; ободр|я́ть, -и́ть кого́-н.; подн|има́ть, -я́ть дух у кого́-н. **10.** (*industrial alcohol*) спирт, алкого́ль (*m.*); (*pl., alcoholic drink*) спиртно́й напи́ток; **he never touches ~s** он не пьёт (*or* не берёт в рот) спиртно́го. **11.** (*solution in alcohol*) спиртово́й раство́р; **~s of salt** хлористо-водоро́дная (соляна́я) кислота́.

v.t. **~ away, off** (та́йно) похи́тить, умыкну́ть (*both pf.*).

cpds. **~-gum** *n.* театра́льный клей; гримирова́льный лак; **~-lamp** *n.* спирто́вка; **~-level** *n.* ватерпа́с, спиртово́й у́ровень; **~-rapping** *n.* столоверче́ние, спирити́зм, медиуми́зм; **~-world** *n.* загро́бный мир; ца́рство тене́й.

spirited ['spɪrɪtɪd] *adj.* живо́й, оживлённый, воодушевлённый; энерги́чный, сме́лый, жизнера́достный; **a ~ reply** бо́йкий отве́т; **a ~ horse** горя́чий конь.

spiritless ['spɪrɪtlɪs] *adj.* безжи́зненный, ро́бкий; (*listless*) вя́лый, сла́бый; **a ~ style** бле́дный стиль.

spiritual ['spɪrɪtjʊəl] *n.* (*song*) спи́ричуэл, негритя́нский духо́вный гимн.

adj. **1.** (*incorporeal*) при́зрачный, бестеле́сный. **2.** (*pert. to soul, spirit*) духо́вный; **~ life** духо́вная жизнь; (*fig.*): **Italy is his ~ home** Ита́лия — его́ духо́вная ро́дина. **3.** (*unworldly*) возвы́шенный, одухотворённый; **~ mind** возвы́шенный ум. **4.** (*inspired by Holy Spirit*): **~ gift** боже́ственный дар; **~ songs** духо́вные пе́сни. **5.** (*ecclesiastical*): **~ court** церко́вный суд; **~ father** духо́вный оте́ц; **lords ~** «ло́рды духо́вные», англика́нские епи́скопы-чле́ны пала́ты ло́рдов.

spiritualism ['spɪrɪtjʊəˌlɪz(ə)m] *n.* спирити́зм.

spiritualist ['spɪrɪtjʊəlɪst] *n.* спири́т (*fem.* -ка).

spiritualistic [ˌspɪrɪtjʊə'lɪstɪk] *adj.* (*of communication with spirits*) спирити́ческий.

spirituality [ˌspɪrɪtjʊ'ælɪtɪ] *n.* одухотворённость.

spirituous ['spɪrɪtjʊəs] *adj.* (*of drink*) спиртно́й, алкого́льный.

spirt [spɜːt] = **spurt**[2]

spit[1] [spɪt] *n.* (*for roasting*) ве́ртел; (*of land*) коса́, стре́лка; (*underwater bank*) о́тмель.

v.t. (*put ~ through*) наса́|живать, -ди́ть на ве́ртел; (*pierce*) пронз|а́ть, -и́ть; прот|ыка́ть, -кну́ть.

spit[2] [spɪt] *n.* **1.** (*spittle*) слюна́. **2.: the ~ and** (*or* **~ting**) **image of his father** то́чная ко́пия своего́ отца́; вы́литый оте́ц. **3.: ~ and polish** выли́зывание, надра́ивание.

v.t. (*also* **~ out**) выплёвывать, вы́плюнуть; **~ blood** ха́ркать (*impf.*) кро́вью; (*fig.*): **he spat out threats** он разрази́лся угро́зами.

v.i. **1.** пл|ева́ть, -ю́нуть; (*habitually*) плева́ться (*impf.*); **he spat in my face** он плю́нул мне в лицо́; (*of cat etc.*) фы́рк|ать, -нуть. **2.** (*of pen*) бры́з|гать, -нуть. **3.** (*of fire*) рассыпа́ть (*impf.*) и́скры. **4.** (*coll., rain*) мороси́ть (*impf.*); бры́згать (*impf.*).

cpd. **~fire** *n.* (*pers.*) злю́чка (*c.g.*), «по́рох».

spite [spaɪt] *n.* **1.** (*ill-will*) зло́ба, злость; **out of ~** назло́; по зло́бе; (*grudge*): **have a ~ against s.o.** име́ть (*impf.*)

зуб про́тив/на кого́-н. **2.: in ~ of** несмотря́ на+*a.*; **I smiled in ~ of myself** я нево́льно улыбну́лся.

v.t.: **he does it to ~ me** он де́лает э́то мне назло́ (*or* что́бы досади́ть мне).

spiteful ['spaɪtfʊl] *adj.* зло́бный, недоброжела́тельный, злора́дный; **a ~ remark** зло́бное/язви́тельное/ехи́дное замеча́ние.

spitefulness ['spaɪtfʊlnɪs] *n.* зло́бность, недоброжела́тельность, злора́дство.

Spitsbergen ['spɪts,bɜːgən] *n.* Шпицбе́рген.

spittle ['spɪt(ə)l] *n.* плево́к; слюна́.

spittoon [spɪ'tuːn] *n.* плева́тельница.

spiv [spɪv] *n.* (*sl.*) ме́лкий спекуля́нт; жу́лик, жук.

splash [splæʃ] *n.* **1.** (*action, effect*) плеск, всплеск; бры́зг|и (*pl., g.* —); **he fell into the water with a ~** он с пле́ском бултыхну́лся в во́ду; **the stone made a huge ~** ка́мень упа́л с гро́мким пле́ском; **make a ~** (*fig., attract attention*) наде́лать (*pf.*) шу́му; произв|оди́ть, -ести́ сенса́цию. **2.** (*sound*) плеск, всплеск; **the ~ of waves** плеск волн. **3.** (*liquid*): **I felt a ~ of rain** на меня́ упа́ли ка́пли дождя́; **put a ~ of soda in my whisky** плесни́те мне ка́плю со́довой в ви́ски. **4.** (*of blood, mud etc.*) пятно́; **a ~ of colour** кра́сочное пятно́.

v.t. **1.** бры́зг|ать, -нуть (*чем на что*); забры́зг|ивать, -ать (*что чем*); **he ~ed paint on her dress** он забры́згал её пла́тье кра́ской; **she was ~ing her feet in the water** она́ болта́ла/плеска́лась нога́ми в воде́; **they were ~ing water at one another** они́ бры́згали друг в дру́га водо́й; **~ one's way through mud** шлёпать, про- по гря́зи. **2.** (*coll., fig.*): **the news was ~ed in all the papers** все газе́ты раструби́ли э́ту но́вость; **he likes to ~ his money about** он лю́бит броса́ться/сори́ть деньга́ми.

v.i. **1.** (*of liquid etc.*) разбры́зг|иваться, -аться; плеска́ться (*impf.*); **the mud ~ed up her legs** гря́жью забры́згало ей все но́ги. **2.** (*move or fall with ~*): **he ~ed into the water** он бултыхну́лся/шлёпнулся/плю́хнулся в во́ду; **the ducks ~ed about in the pond** у́тки плеска́лись в пруду́; **the falling tree ~ed into the lake** де́рево с пле́ском упа́ло в о́зеро; **the cows ~ed through the river** коро́вы тяжело́ шли че́рез ре́ку; **the fish ~ed on the end of the line** ры́ба би́лась/трепыха́лась на крючке́; **the capsule ~ed down in the Pacific** ка́псула приводни́лась в Ти́хом океа́не.

int. плюх!

cpds. **~-back** *n.* щито́к; **~-board** *n.* (*over or beside wheel of vehicle*) крыло́; грязево́й щито́к; **~-down** *n.* приводне́ние.

splat [splæt] *n.* наще́льная ре́йка.

splatter ['splætə(r)] *n., v.t. & i.* = **spatter**

splay [spleɪ] *n.* ско́шенный проём окна́ *и т. п.*

v.t. (*spread wide*): **~ one's legs** раски́|дывать, -нуть но́ги.

cpds. **~-foot** *n.* косола́пость; **~-footed** *adj.* косола́пый.

spleen [spliːn] *n.* (*anat.*) селезёнка; (*fig., ill-temper, spite*) раздраже́ние, зло́ба; **vent one's ~ on s.o.** срыва́ть, сорва́ть зло́бу на ком-н.

splendid ['splendɪd] *adj.* (*magnificent*) великоле́пный; (*luxurious*) роско́шный; (*excellent*) прекра́сный, отли́чный; (*impressive, remarkable*) удиви́тельный, замеча́тельный; **~!** замеча́тельно!; **a ~ opportunity for revenge** прекра́сный слу́чай отомсти́ть; **what a ~ idea** замеча́тельная/прекра́сная мысль!

splendiferous [splen'dɪfərəs] *adj.* (*coll.*) прекра́снейший.

splendour ['splendə(r)] *n.* (*brilliance*) блеск; (*grandeur, magnificence*) великоле́пие, пы́шность; (*greatness*) вели́чие, благоро́дство.

splenetic [splɪ'netɪk] *adj.* **1.** (*med.*) селезёночный. **2.** (*of pers.*) раздражи́тельный, брюзгли́вый, сварли́вый, жёлчный.

splice [splaɪs] *v.t.* **1.** (*rope*) ср|а́щивать, -асти́ть; сплe|та́ть, -сти́. **2.** (*wood*) соедин|я́ть, -и́ть внахлёстку/внакро́й. **3.: get ~d** (*sl., marry*) пожени́ться (*pf.*).

splint [splɪnt] *n.* (*for broken bone*) лубо́к, ши́на.

v.t. на|кла́дывать, -ложи́ть ши́ну на+*a.*

splinter ['splɪntə(r)] *n.* **1.** (*of wood*) лучи́на, ще́пка, щепа́, зано́за; (*of stone, metal, glass*) оско́лок; **get a ~ in one's finger** занози́ть (*pf.*) па́лец. **2.** (*fig.*): **~ group** отколо́вшаяся (полити́ческая) группиро́вка/фра́кция.

v.t. & i. расщеп|ля́ть(ся), -и́ть(ся); раск|а́лывать(ся), -оло́ть(ся).

cpd. **~-proof** *adj.*: **~-proof glass** безоско́лочное стекло́.

split [splɪt] *n.* **1.** раска́лывание; (*crack, fissure*) тре́щина, щель, расще́лина. **2.** (*fig., schism, disunion*) раско́л. **3.: do the ~s** де́лать, с- шпага́т.

v.t. **1.** коло́ть, рас-; расщеп|ля́ть, -и́ть; **~ting the atom** расщепле́ние а́тома; (*crack open, rupture*) раск|а́лывать, -оло́ть; **~ s.o.'s skull** проломи́ть (*pf.*) кому́-н. че́реп; **I have a ~ lip** у меня́ губа́ тре́снула; (*fig.*): **~ one's sides** над|рыва́ться, -орва́ться (*or coll.* над|рыва́ть, -орва́ть живо́тики) от сме́ха; **~ hairs** крохобо́рствовать (*impf.*); спо́рить (*impf.*) о пустяка́х/мелоча́х. **2.** (*divide*) раздел|я́ть, -и́ть; (*share*) дели́ть, по-; **they ~ the money into three** (*or* **three ways**) они́ раздели́ли де́ньги на́ три ча́сти; **the job was ~ between us** мы подели́ли рабо́ту ме́жду собо́й; **they ~ the proceeds** они́ подели́ли дохо́ды; **~ a bottle of wine with s.o.** расп|ива́ть, -и́ть буты́лку вина́ с кем-н.; раздави́ть (*pf.*) буты́лочку; **~ the left-wing vote** расколо́ть (*pf.*) голоса́ ле́вых. **3.** (*cause dissension in*) разъедин|я́ть,-и́ть; **the party was ~ by factions** па́ртия расколо́лась на фра́кции; **~ infinitive** расщеплённый инфинити́в; **~ peas** лущёный/ко́лотый горо́х; **~ personality** раздвое́ние ли́чности; **~ ring** разрезно́е кольцо́ (для ключе́й); **~ second** (кака́я-то) до́ля секу́нды; мгнове́ние.

v.i. **1.** (*of hard substance*) раск|а́лываться, -оло́ться; расщеп|ля́ться, -и́ться; тре́снуть (*pf.*); (*divide*) раздел|я́ться, -и́ться; **the wood ~** де́рево тре́снуло; **the ship ~ in two** кора́бль расколо́лся на́двое; **the boat ~ on a reef** ло́дка разби́лась о риф; **~ open** взл|а́мываться, -ома́ться; (*of soft, thin substance*) раз|рыва́ться, -орва́ться; порва́ться (*pf.*); **her dress ~ at the seam** её пла́тье разорва́лось по шву; **my head is ~ting** (*fig.*) у меня́ голова́ трещи́т/раска́лывается (от бо́ли). **2.** (*become disunited*) разъедин|я́ться, -и́ться; раск|а́лываться, -оло́тся. **3.: ~ on s.o.** (*sl.*) вы́дать (*pf.*) кого́-н.

with advs.: **~ off** *v.t. & i.* отк|а́лывать(ся), -оло́ть(ся); **~ off a branch from a tree** отл|а́мывать, -ома́ть/-оми́ть ве́тку от де́рева; **~ up** *v.t. & i.* (*lit.*) раск|а́лывать(ся), -оло́ть(ся); (*separate*) ра|сходи́ться, -зойти́сь; **we ~ up into two groups** мы разби́лись на две гру́ппы; **he and his wife ~ up** они́ с жено́й разошли́сь; **the meeting ~ up at 6** собра́ние ко́нчилось в 6 часо́в.

splitter [splɪtə(r)] *n.* (*pol.*) раско́льник, фракционе́р.

splodge [splɒdʒ] = **splotch**

splosh [splɒʃ] (*coll.*) = **splash** *v.t. & i.*

splotch [splɒtʃ], **splodge** [splɒdʒ] (*coll.*) *n.* (гря́зное) пятно́, мазо́к.

v.t. замы́зг|ивать, -ать.

splurge [splɜːdʒ] *v.i.* (*coll.*) кути́ть (*impf.*); броса́ться (*impf.*) деньга́ми.

splutter ['splʌtə(r)] *n.* (*noise*) треск, треща́ние; (*speech*) бы́страя/сби́вчивая речь; лопота́ние.

v.t. & i. (*also* **sputter**) говори́ть (*impf.*) захлёбываясь (*or* бы́стро и сби́вчиво); бры́згаться (*impf.*) слюно́й при разгово́ре.

spoil [spɔɪl] *n.* **1.** (*booty*) добы́ча; награ́бленное добро́; **~s of war** трофе́и (*m. pl.*); вое́нная добы́ча; **share in the ~s** (*fig.*) получ|а́ть, -и́ть свою́ до́лю добы́чи. **2.** (*profit*) при́быль; (*benefit*) вы́года.

v.t. **1.** (*impair, injure, ruin*) по́ртить, ис-; губи́ть, по-; **the rain ~t our holiday** дождь испо́ртил нам о́тпуск; **eating sweets will ~ your appetite** конфе́ты испо́ртят вам аппети́т; **the crops were ~t by rain** дождь погуби́л урожа́й; **~ s.o.'s pleasure** отрав|ля́ть, -и́ть чью-н. ра́дость; **~ s.o.'s plans** срыва́ть, сорва́ть чьи-н. пла́ны; **he ~t his chances of success** он сам подорва́л свои́ ша́нсы на успе́х. **2.** (*over-indulgence*) балова́ть, из-; **a ~t child** избало́ванный ребёнок. **3.** (*arch., plunder*) гра́бить, о-/раз-; разор|я́ть, -и́ть.

v.i. **1.** (*deteriorate*) ух|удша́ться, -у́дшиться; (*go bad, rotten etc.*) по́ртиться, ис-. **2.** (*be eager*): **he is ~ing for**

a fight он так и ле́зет в дра́ку.

cpd. **~-sport** *n.* тот, кто по́ртит удово́льствие други́м.

spoilage ['spɔɪlɪdʒ] *n.* (*of food*) испо́рченные проду́кты (*m. pl.*); гниль; (*typ.*) брако́ванные о́ттиски (*m. pl.*).

spoiler ['spɔɪlə(r)] *n.* **1.** (*plunderer*) граби́тель (*m.*); мародёр. **2.** (*aeron. etc.*) интерце́птор, прерыва́тель (*m.*) пото́ка, спо́йлер.

spoke [spəʊk] *n.* **1.** (*of wheel*) спи́ца. **2.** (*rung*) перекла́дина, гря́дка (стремя́нки). **3.** (*fig.*): **put a ~ in s.o.'s wheel** вст|авля́ть, -а́вить кому́-н. па́лки в колёса.

cpd. **~shave** *n.* ско́бель (*m.*); криволине́йный струг.

spoken ['spəʊkən] *adj.* у́стный; **the ~ word** у́стная речь; **the ~ language** разгово́рный язы́к; **~ feelings** чу́вства, вы́раженные слова́ми; **these words are to be ~, not sung** э́ти слова́ сле́дует не петь, а про́сто произноси́ть.

spokesman ['spəʊksmən] *n.* представи́тель (*m.*), делега́т; (*public relations officer*) сотру́дник отде́ла информа́ции; **~ for defence** докла́дчик по вопро́сам оборо́ны; **act as ~ for s.o.** выступа́ть, вы́ступить от и́мени кого́-н.

spokesperson ['spəʊks,pɜ:s(ə)n] = **spokesman** *or* **spokeswoman**

spokeswoman ['spəʊks,wʊmən] *n.* представи́тельница, делега́тка, докла́дчица; сотру́дница отде́ла информа́ции.

spoliation [,spəʊlɪ'eɪʃ(ə)n] *n.* грабёж, разграбле́ние.

spondee ['spɒndi:] *n.* сponде́й.

sponge [spʌndʒ] *n.* **1.** (*zool.*; *toilet article*) гу́бка; **throw in, up the ~** (*fig.*) призн|ава́ть, -а́ть себя́ побеждённым; (*sponge-like, absorbent substance*) гу́бчатое/по́ристое вещество́. **2.** (*fig., parasite*) нахле́бник, прижива́льщик, парази́т.

v.t.: **~ a child's face** обт|ира́ть, -ере́ть ребёнку лицо́ гу́бкой; **~ o.s. down** обт|ира́ться, -ере́ться гу́бкой; **~ a car (down)** вытира́ть, вы́тереть маши́ну (гу́бкой); **~ a wound** обм|ыва́ть, -ы́ть ра́ну.

v.i. (*fig.*) жить (*impf.*) на чужо́й счёт; паразити́ровать (*impf.*); **he ~s on his brother** он сиди́т на ше́е у бра́та.

with advs.: **~ off** *v.t.* ст|ира́ть, -ере́ть гу́бкой; **~ up** *v.t.* (*absorb*) вытира́ть, вы́тереть.

cpds. **~-bag** *n.* су́мка для туале́тных принадле́жностей; **~-cake** *n.* бискви́т; **~-cloth** *n.* ткань эпо́нж; хлопчатобума́жная ва́фельная ткань; **~-rubber** *n.* рези́новая гу́бка.

sponger ['spʌndʒə(r)] *n.* парази́т, нахле́бник, прижива́льщик.

spongy ['spʌndʒɪ] *adj.* гу́бчатый; (*porous*) по́ристый, ноздрева́тый; (*e.g. moss, carpet*) мя́гкий; (*of ground*) то́пкий.

sponsor ['spɒnsə(r)] *n.* **1.** (*guarantor*) поручи́тель (*fem.* -ница); (*of new member etc.*) рекоменда́тель (*fem.* -ница). **2.** (*at baptism*) крёстный оте́ц, крёстная мать; **stand ~ to a child** крести́ть (*impf.*, *pf.*) ребёнка. **3.** (*TV etc.*) зака́зчик рекла́мы, рекламода́тель (*m.*).

v.t. руча́ться, поручи́ться за+*a.*; рекомендова́ть (*impf.*, *pf.*); (*e.g. a law or resolution*) вн|оси́ть, -ести́; (*on TV etc.*) субсиди́ровать (*impf.*, *pf.*); финанси́ровать (*impf.*, *pf.*).

sponsorship ['spɒnsəʃɪp] *n.* поручи́тельство, пору́ка, гара́нтия.

spontaneity [,spɒntə'ni:ɪtɪ, -'neɪɪtɪ] *n.* спонта́нность, стихи́йность, непосре́дственность, непринуждённость.

spontaneous [spɒn'teɪnɪəs] *adj.* спонта́нный, доброво́льный, стихи́йный; инстинкти́вный; (*unaffected*) непосре́дственный, непринуждённый; **~ combustion** самовозгора́ние; **~ generation** самозарожде́ние.

spoof [spu:f] (*sl.*) *n.* (*hoax*) ро́зыгрыш, мистифика́ция; (*parody*) паро́дия.

v.t. над|ува́ть, -у́ть; разы́гр|ивать, -а́ть; пароди́ровать, с-.

spook [spu:k] *n.* (*joc.*) привиде́ние, при́зрак, дух.

spooky ['spu:kɪ] *adj.* (*frightening*) жу́ткий; (*sinister*) злове́щий.

spool [spu:l] *n.* шпу́лька, кату́шка.

v.t. нам|а́тывать, -ота́ть на кату́шку.

spoon[1] [spu:n] *n.* ло́жка; **they fed him with a ~** его́ корми́ли с ло́жки; **he was born with a silver ~ in his mouth** он роди́лся в соро́чке.

v.t. (*also* **~ up**) че́рпать, вы́-.

cpds. **~-bait** *n.* блесна́; **~bill** *n.* колпи́ца; **~feed** *v.t.* (*lit.*) корми́ть (*impf.*) с ло́жки; (*fig.*): **~-feed a pupil** ня́нчиться (*impf.*) с ученико́м; всё разжёвывать (*impf.*) ученику́; **~-feed industry** иску́сственно подде́рживать (*impf.*) промы́шленность.

spoon[2] [spu:n] *v.i.* (*sl.*) аму́риться (*impf.*); любе́зничать (*impf.*).

spoonerism ['spu:nə,rɪz(ə)m] *n.* перевёртыш.

spoonful ['spu:nfʊl] *n.* (по́лная) ло́жка (*чего*).

spoor [spʊə(r)] *n.* след.

sporadic [spə'rædɪk] *adj.* споради́ческий.

spore [spɔ:(r)] *n.* спо́ра.

sport [spɔ:t] *n.* **1.** (*outdoor pastime(s)*) спорт; (*pl.*) спорт, ви́ды (*m. pl.*) спо́рта; **indoor ~s** ви́ды спо́рта для закры́тых помеще́ний; **go in for ~** зан|има́ться, -я́ться спо́ртом; **have good ~** (*shooting*) уда́чно поохо́титься (*pf.*); **~s car** спорти́вный автомоби́ль; **~s coat, jacket** спорти́вная ку́ртка; **~s editor** заве́дующий спорти́вным отде́лом газе́ты. **2.** (*pl., athletic events*) спорти́вные и́гры (*f. pl.*); **~s day** день спорти́вных состяза́ний. **3.** (*jest, fun*) шу́тка, заба́ва; (*ridicule*) насме́шка; **say sth. in ~** сказа́ть (*pf.*) что-н. в шу́тку; **make ~ of** смея́ться, над-над+*i.*; подшу́|чивать, -ти́ть над+*i.* **4.** (*plaything, butt*) игру́шка; **he became the ~ of circumstance** он стал игру́шкой обстоя́тельств. **5.** (*coll., good fellow*) молодчи́на (*m.*); **be a ~!** будь челове́ком! **6.** (*biol.*) мута́ция.

v.t.: **~ a rose in one's button-hole** щеголя́ть (*impf.*) ро́зой в петли́це; **everyone ~ed their medals** все нацепи́ли свои́ меда́ли.

v.i. (*frolic*) резви́ться (*impf.*).

cpds. **~sman** *n.* спортсме́н; (*fig.*) че́стный/поря́дочный челове́к; **~smanlike** *adj.* че́стный, поря́дочный, благоро́дный; **~smanship** *n.*: **he showed ~smanship** он прояви́л себя́ настоя́щим спортсме́ном; **~swoman** *n.* спортсме́нка.

sporting ['spɔ:tɪŋ] *adj.* **1.** (*addicted to sport*) спорти́вный; **he was not a ~ man** он не́ был спортсме́ном. **2.** (*sportsmanlike*) че́стный, поря́дочный; (*enterprising*) предприи́мчивый; **that's very ~ of you** э́то с ва́шей стороны́ благоро́дно; **a ~ chance** наде́жда, не́который шанс; **a ~ offer** вы́годное (*or* вполне́ сто́ящее) предложе́ние.

sportive ['spɔ:tɪv] *adj.* шутли́вый, весёлый, игри́вый.

sporty ['spɔ:tɪ] *adj.* (*gay, rakish*) лихо́й, удало́й.

spot [spɒt] *n.* **1.** (*patch, speck*) пятно́, пя́тнышко, кра́пинка; **a white dog with brown ~s** бе́лая соба́ка с кори́чневыми пя́тнами; **come out in ~s** (*rash*) покры́ться (*pf.*) сы́пью; **knock ~s off s.o.** (*coll.*) за́просто одоле́ть (*pf.*) кого́-н. **2.** (*stain*) пятно́; **there were ~s of blood on his shirt** на его́ руба́шке бы́ли пя́тна кро́ви; (*fig.*): **without a ~ on his reputation** с не запя́тнанной репута́цией. **3.** (*pimple*) пры́щ(ик). **4.** (*place*) ме́сто; **the police were on the ~ within minutes** поли́ция прибыла́ на ме́сто (уже́) че́рез не́сколько мину́т; **he was killed on the ~** он был уби́т на ме́сте (*or* сра́зу); **running on the ~** бег на ме́сте; **his question put me on the ~** (*coll.*) его́ вопро́с поста́вил меня́ в затрудни́тельное положе́ние; **we were in a (tight) ~** нам пришло́сь ту́го; **~ check** вы́борочная прове́рка; **sore ~** (*lit., fig.*) больно́е ме́сто; **weak ~** сла́бое ме́сто; **he has a soft ~ for her** он пита́ет к ней сла́бость. **5.** (*coll., small amount*): **I must have a ~ to eat** мне ну́жно перекуси́ть; **I am due for a ~ of leave** мне полага́ется небольшо́й/коро́ткий о́тпуск; **I have a ~ of work to do** мне ну́жно немно́го порабо́тать; **~ of bother** небольша́я неприя́тность; (*drop*): **I felt a few ~s of rain** я почу́вствовал, как на меня́ упа́ло не́сколько ка́пель дождя́. **6.** (*attr., comm.*): **~ cash** нали́чный расчёт; неме́дленная опла́та нали́чными; **~ price** цена́ при усло́вии неме́дленной упла́ты. **7.**: **~ on** (*coll., exactly right*) в са́мую то́чку.

v.t. **1.** (*mark, stain*) запа́чкать (*pf.*); зака́пать (*pf.*); **his books were ~ted with ink** его́ кни́ги бы́ли запа́чканы/забры́зганы черни́лами; (*p.p., covered, decorated with ~s*) пятни́стый, кра́пчатый; **a ~ted tie** га́лстук в кра́пинку. **2.** (*coll., notice*) зам|еча́ть, -е́тить;

(*recognize*) узн|ава́ть, -а́ть; опозн|ава́ть, -а́ть; **I ~ted him as the murderer** я опозна́л в нём уби́йцу; **I ~ted him as an American** я (то́тчас) угада́л в нём америка́нца; (*catch sight of*) уви́деть (*pf.*); **I ~ted my friend in the crowd** я (вдруг) уви́дел в толпе́ своего́ прия́теля; (*detect*) обнару́жи|вать, -ть; (*single out*) определ|я́ть, -и́ть; **he ~ted the winner** он угада́л победи́теля.

v.i. **1.: this silk ~s easily** э́тот шёлк о́чень ма́ркий. **2.: it is ~ting with rain** накра́пывает (дождь).

cpd. **~light** *n.* освети́тельный проже́ктор; (*fig.*): **turn the ~light on sth.** привле́чь (*pf.*) внима́ние к чему́-н.; **be in (*or* hold) the ~light** быть в це́нтре (*or* це́нтром) внима́ния; *v.t.* (*lit., fig.*) осве|ща́ть, -ти́ть; (*fig.*) выделя́ть, вы́делить.

spotless ['spɒtlɪs] *adj.* сверка́ющий чистото́й; без еди́ного пя́тнышка; **the room was ~** ко́мната сверка́ла чистото́й; **a ~ly white shirt** белосне́жная руба́шка; (*fig.*) незапя́тнанный, безупре́чный.

spotty ['spɒtɪ] *adj.* (*of colour*) пятни́стый, пёстрый; (*of uneven quality*) неро́вный; (*pimply*) прыщева́тый.

spouse [spaʊz, spaʊs] *n.* супру́г (*fem.* -а).

spout [spaʊt] *n.* **1.** (*of vessel*) но́сик; (*of pump*) рука́в; (*for rain-water*) водосто́чная труба́; жёлоб. **2.** (*jet of water etc.*) струя́; столб воды́; (*of whale*) ды́хало. **3.** (*sl.*): **up the ~** (*in pawn*) в закла́де/ломба́рде; (*in a mess*) в безнадёжном состоя́нии.

v.t. **1.: a whale ~s water** кит выбра́сывает/испуска́ет струю́ воды́; **a volcano ~ing lava** вулка́н, изверга́ющий ла́ву; **the chimney ~ed smoke** труба́ выбра́сывала клубы́ ды́ма. **2.** (*coll., declaim*) разглаго́льствовать (*impf.*); **~ poetry** деклами́ровать, про- стихи́.

v.i. **1.** струи́ться (*impf.*); бить (*impf.*); ли́ться (*impf.*) пото́ком; (*of whale*) выбра́сывать, вы́бросить струю́ воды́. **2.** (*fig., coll., make speeches*) ора́торствовать (*impf.*).

sprain [spreɪn] *n.* растяже́ние свя́зок/сухожи́лий.

v.t.: **~ one's wrist/ankle** растяну́ть (*pf.*) запя́стье/щи́колотку.

sprat [spræt] *n.* шпро́та, ки́лька; **throw out a ~ to catch a mackerel** ≃ риск|ова́ть, -ну́ть ма́лым ра́ди большо́го.

sprawl [sprɔːl] *n.* небре́жная/неуклю́жая по́за; **urban ~** рост городо́в за счёт се́льской ме́стности.

v.i. **1.** растяну́ться (*pf.*); **send s.o. ~ing** сбить (*pf.*) кого́-н. с ног. **2.** (*straggle*) разва́л|иваться, -и́ться; раскоря́читься (*pf.*); **the words ~ed across the page** слова́ кара́кулями расползли́сь по всей страни́це.

spray[1] [spreɪ] *n.* (*bot.*) ве́тка, побе́г.

spray[2] [spreɪ] *n.* **1.** (*water droplets*) бры́зг|и (*pl., g.* —); **the water turned to ~** вода́ распыли́лась. **2.** (*liquid preparation*) жи́дкость для пульвериза́ции; **chemical ~** ядохимика́т для опры́скивания. **3.** (*device for ~ing; also ~er*) разбры́згиватель (*m.*); распыли́тель (*m.*); пульвериза́тор; **~ can** аэрозо́льный балло́н.

v.t. (*apply ~ to*) опры́ск|ивать, -ать; (*apply in the form of ~*) распыл|я́ть, -и́ть; **he ~ed paint on to the ceiling** он покра́сил потоло́к с по́мощью распыли́теля.

cpd. **~-gun** *n.* распыли́тель (*m.*).

sprayer ['spreɪə(r)] = **spray** *n.* **3.**

spread [spred] *n.* **1.** (*extension*) протяже́ние, протяжённость, простира́ние; (*expansion*) распростране́ние; экспа́нсия; расшире́ние; (*increase*) увеличе́ние; **~ of sail** па́русность, пло́щадь па́русности; **~ of wings** разма́х кры́льев; **~ of an arch** ширина́ а́рки; **have, develop a middle-age ~** полне́ть, по- с во́зрастом; отрасти́ть (*pf.*) брюшко́. **2.** (*dissemination*) распростране́ние. **3.** (*difference between prices etc.*) ра́зница, разры́в. **4.** (*coll., feast*) пир, пи́ршество. **5.** (*cul.*) па́ста. **6.** (*typ.*) разворо́т.

v.t. **1.** (*extend*) распростран|я́ть, -и́ть; (*unfold*) ра|скла́дывать, -зложи́ть; развёр|тывать, -ну́ть; (*cover*) расст|ила́ть, -ели́ть (*or* разостла́ть); **she ~ a cloth on the table** она́ расстели́ла ска́терть на столе́; **~ butter on bread (*or* bread with butter)** нама́з|ывать, -ать ма́сло на хлеб (*or* хлеб ма́слом); **~ a net** раски́|дывать, -нуть сеть; **~ manure over a field** разбр|а́сывать, -оса́ть наво́з по́ полю; **the tree ~ its branches** де́рево раски́нуло свои́ ве́тви; **the bird ~ its wings** пти́ца распростёрла кры́лья; **~ one's wings** (*fig.*) распр|авля́ть, -а́вить кры́лья; **the river ~ its waters over the fields** река́ разлила́сь по луга́м; **the peacock ~ its tail** павли́н распусти́л хвост; **~ (out) a map** ра|скла́дывать, -зложи́ть ка́рту. **2.** (*diffuse*) распростран|я́ть, -и́ть; **he ~ the rumour** он распространи́л слух; **his name ~ fear in our hearts** его́ и́мя вселя́ло в на́ши сердца́ страх. **3.: ~ o.s.** (*lounge*) раски́|дываться, -нуться; (*expatiate*) распростран|я́ться, -и́ться.

v.i. **1.** распростран|я́ться, -и́ться; расстила́ться (*impf.*); **the news soon ~** но́вость/весть бы́стро распространи́лась; **the course ~s over a year** курс рассчи́тан на оди́н год; **the river ~s to a width of a mile** река́ достига́ет ми́ли в ширину́; **a valley ~s out behind the hill** за холмо́м расстила́ется доли́на; **his name ~ throughout the land** его́ сла́ва разошла́сь по всей стране́; его́ и́мя облете́ло всю страну́; **the fire is ~ing** пожа́р разраста́ется; **the fire ~ to the next barn** ого́нь переки́нулся на сосе́дний сара́й; **a flush ~ over her face** кра́ска залила́ её лицо́; **a smile ~ over his face** его́ рот растяну́лся в улы́бке; **~ing trees** раски́дистые дере́вья. **2.** (*disperse*) рассе́|иваться, -яться.

cpds. **~-eagle** *v.t.* распла́ст|ывать, -а́ть; положи́ть (*pf.*) плашмя́; **~sheet** *n.* (*comput.*) крупноформа́тная (электро́нная) табли́ца.

spreading ['spredɪŋ] *adj.* (*branchy*) разве́систый.

spree [spriː] *n.* (*coll.*) весе́лье, кутёж; **have a ~, go on the ~** кути́ть (*impf.*); **we had a rare old ~** мы здо́рово покути́ли; мы покути́ли на сла́ву.

sprig [sprɪg] *n.* (*twig, shoot*) ве́точка, побе́г; (*as ornament*) узо́р в ви́де ве́точки; (*fig., scion*) о́тпрыск.

sprightliness ['spraɪtlɪnɪs] *n.* жи́вость, бо́йкость, ре́звость.

sprightly ['spraɪtlɪ] *adj.* оживлённый, живо́й, бо́йкий, ре́звый.

spring[1] [sprɪŋ] *n.* (*season*) весна́; **in ~** весно́й; (*attr.*) весе́нний; **~ flowers** весе́нние цветы́; **~ onion** зелёный лук; **~ tide** сизиги́йный прили́в.

cpds. **~-clean** *n.* генера́льная (*обычно весенняя*) убо́рка; *v.t. & i.* произв|оди́ть, -ести́ генера́льную убо́рку; **~time** *n.* весна́, весе́нняя пора́.

spring[2] [sprɪŋ] *n.* **1.** (*leap*) прыжо́к, скачо́к; **make, take a ~** пры́гнуть (*pf.*); скакну́ть (*pf.*). **2.** (*elasticity*) упру́гость, эласти́чность; **he has a ~ in his step** у него́ упру́гая похо́дка; (*resilience*) ги́бкость; **his mind lost its ~** его́ ум утра́тил ги́бкость. **3.** (*elastic device*) пружи́на; (*attr.*) пружи́нный; **~ balance** пружи́нные весы́, безме́н; **~ bed** крова́ть на пружи́нах; **~ mattress** пружи́нный матра́ц; (*leaf ~ of vehicle*) рессо́ра. **4.** (*of water*) исто́чник, ключ, родни́к; **hot ~s** горя́чие исто́чники; **~ water** ключева́я/роднико́вая вода́; (*fig.*) исто́чник, моти́в; побуди́тельная причи́на; **~s of action** моти́вы (*m. pl.*) де́йствия.

v.t. **1.** (*cause to act*): **~ a trap** захло́пнуть (*pf.*) лову́шку; **~ a mine** вз|рыва́ть, -орва́ть ми́ну; (*produce suddenly*): **~ a surprise on s.o.** заст|ига́ть, -и́чь кого́-н. врасплох́; **he sprang a proposal on me, us** он вы́ступил с неожи́данным предложе́нием. **2.** (*split*) раск|а́лывать, -оло́ть; **I have sprung my racket** моя́ раке́тка тре́снула. **3.** (*rouse*): **~ game** подн|има́ть, -я́ть дичь. **4.: ~ a leak** да|ва́ть, -ть течь; **the tub sprang a leak** бо́чка протекла́. **5.** (*provide with ~s*) подрессо́ри|вать, -ть; **the carriage is well sprung** у каре́ты хоро́шие рессо́ры. **6.** (*coll., procure escape of*): **he was sprung from prison** ему́ организова́ли побе́г из тюрьмы́.

v.i. **1.** (*leap*) пры́г|ать, -нуть; скак|а́ть, -ну́ть; **~ to one's feet** вск|а́кивать, -очи́ть на́ ноги; **~ over a fence** переск|а́кивать, -очи́ть че́рез забо́р; **~ forward** выска́кивать, вы́скочить вперёд; **~ backward** отпря́нуть (*pf.*); **~ to s.o.'s help** бр|оса́ться, -о́ситься (*or* ри́нуться, *pf.*) кому́-н. на по́мощь; **~ into action** энерги́чно приня́ться (*pf.*) за де́ло; **~ out of bed** вск|а́кивать, -очи́ть с посте́ли; **~ at s.o.** набр|а́сываться, -о́ситься на кого́-н.; **the lid sprang open** кры́шка внеза́пно откры́лась; **where did you ~ from?** (*coll.*) отку́да вы взяли́сь? **2.** (*of liquid*) бить (*impf.*); **water ~s from the earth** из земли́ бьёт ключ; **the blood sprang to her cheeks** кровь бро́силась ей в лицо́. **3.** (*come into being*) появ|ля́ться, -и́ться; возн|ика́ть, -и́кнуть; **he ~s from an old family** он происхо́дит из стари́нного ро́да; **sprung from the people** вы́ходец из наро́да; **a breeze sprang up** подня́лся лёгкий ветеро́к; **weeds ~ up on all sides** сорняки́ прораста́ют повсю́ду; **a belief sprang up that ...** появи́лось мне́ние, что...; **his actions ~ from jealousy** его́ посту́пки вы́званы/продикто́ваны ре́вностью. **4.** (*of timber, warp*) коро́биться, по-.

cpd. **~board** *n.* (*lit., fig.*) трампли́н.

springbok ['sprɪŋbɒk] *n.* газе́ль антидо́рка, прыгу́н.

springiness ['sprɪŋɪnɪs] *n.* упру́гость, эласти́чность, ги́бкость.

springlike ['sprɪŋlaɪk] *adj.* весе́нний.

springy ['sprɪŋɪ] *adj.* упру́гий, эласти́чный, ги́бкий, пружи́нистый.

sprinkle ['sprɪŋk(ə)l] *n.*: **a ~ of rain** до́ждик; небольшо́й дождь; **a ~ of snow** (лёгкий) снежо́к; **with a ~ of salt** слегка́ подсо́ленный.

v.t.: **~ sth. with water, ~ water on sth.** бры́згать, по- что-н. водо́й; **~ sth. with salt/sand, ~ salt/sand on sth.** пос|ыпа́ть, -ы́пать что-н. со́лью/песко́м.

v.i.: **it was sprinkling with rain** накра́пывал дождь.

sprinkler ['sprɪŋklə(r)] *n.* разбры́згиватель (*m.*).

sprinkling ['sprɪŋklɪŋ] *n.* (*fig.*): **there was a ~ of children in the audience** в аудито́рии находи́лось небольшо́е коли́чество дете́й.

sprint [sprɪnt] *n.* спринт.

v.t. & i. спринтова́ть (*impf.*); бежа́ть (*det.*) с максима́льной ско́ростью.

sprinter ['sprɪntə(r)] *n.* спри́нтер.

sprite [spraɪt] *n.* эльф, фе́я.

sprocket ['sprɒkɪt] *n.* (цепна́я) звёздочка.

cpd. **~-wheel** *n.* цепно́е/зубча́тое колесо́.

sprog [sprɒg] *n.* (*sl.*) «щено́к».

sprout [spraʊt] *n.* (*shoot*) росто́к, побе́г, отро́сток; (*pl.*, **Brussels ~s**) брюссе́льская капу́ста.

v.t. (*of animal*): **~ horns** отра́|щивать, -сти́ть рога́; (*of pers.*): **~ a moustache** отпус|ка́ть, -ти́ть (*or* отра́|щивать, -сти́ть) усы́.

v.i. (*of plant*) пус|ка́ть, -ти́ть ростки́; (*of seed*) прораст|а́ть, -и́.

spruce[1] [spru:s] *n.* (*tree*) ель.

spruce[2] [spru:s] *adj.* аккура́тный, опря́тный, наря́дный; **he looked ~** у него́ был щеголева́тый вид.

v.t.: **~ up** нав|оди́ть, -ести́ красоту́/блеск на+*a.*; прив|оди́ть, -ести́ в поря́док; **~ o.s. up** прихора́шиваться (*pf.*); привести́ (*pf.*) себя́ в поря́док.

spry [spraɪ] *adj.* живо́й, подви́жный, проворный.

spud [spʌd] *n.* (*tool*) моты́га; (*sl., potato*) карто́шка, карто́фелина.

v.t. (*usu.* **~ out, up**) моты́жить (*impf.*); оку́чи|вать, -ть.

spume [spju:m] *n.* пе́на, на́кипь.

v.i. пе́ниться (*impf.*).

spun [spʌn] *adj.* пря́деный; **~ yarn** кручёная пря́жа; **~ gold** канители́; **~ glass** стекля́нная нить.

spunk [spʌŋk] *n.* (*coll., mettle*) отва́га, му́жество, темпера́мент.

spunky ['spʌŋkɪ] *adj.* (*coll.*) му́жественный, отва́жный.

spur [spɜ:(r)] *n.* **1.** (*on rider's heel, cock's leg*) шпо́ра; **put, set ~s to a horse** пришпо́рить (*pf.*) ло́шадь/коня́; **win one's ~s** (*fig.*) доби́ться (*pf.*) призна́ния; приобрести́ (*pf.*) и́мя/изве́стность. **2.** (*fig.*) побужде́ние, сти́мул; **competition provided a ~ to his studies** конкуре́нция служи́ла для него́ (дополни́тельным) сти́мулом к прилежа́нию; **on the ~ of the moment** под влия́нием мину́ты; экспро́мтом. **3.** (*of mountain range*) отро́г, усту́п. **4.** (*branch road etc.*) (подъездна́я) ве́тка. **5.** (*bot.*) спорынья́.

v.t. **1.** (*prick with ~s*) пришпо́ри|вать, -ть. **2.** (*fig., stimulate*) побу|жда́ть, -ди́ть; под|гоня́ть, -огна́ть; (*urge*) пон|ужда́ть, -у́дить; **her words ~red him (on) to action** её слова́ побуди́ли/подстрекну́ли его́ к де́йствию; **~red on by ambition** подгоня́емый честолю́бием. **3.** (*furnish with ~s*) снаб|жа́ть, -ди́ть шпо́рами; **booted and ~red** (*fig.*) в по́лной гото́вности.

v.i.: **~ on, forward** спеши́ть (*impf.*); мча́ться (*impf.*).

spurious ['spjʊərɪəs] *adj.* подде́льный, фальши́вый, подло́жный; **~ sentiment** притво́рное чу́вство.

spurn [spɜ:n] *v.t.* (*repel*) отт|а́кливать, -олкну́ть ного́й; (*refuse with disdain*) отв|ерга́ть, -е́ргнуть.

spurt[1] [spɜ:t] *n.* (*sudden effort*) поры́в; (*in race*) рыво́к; **put on a ~** рвану́ться (*pf.*).

v.i. рвану́ться (*pf.*); **~ into the lead** вырыва́ться, вы́рваться вперёд.

spurt[2], **spirt** [spɜ:t] *n.* (*jet*) струя́.

v.t. пус|ка́ть, -ти́ть струёй.

v.i. бить (*impf.*) струёй; хлы́нуть (*pf.*); **the water ~ed into the air** вода́ заби́ла струёй; **blood ~ed from the wound** из ра́ны хлы́нула кровь.

sputnik ['spʊtnɪk, 'spʌt-] *n.* (иску́сственный) спу́тник.

sputter ['spʌtə(r)] *v.t. & i.* **1.** = **splutter. 2.** (*crackle*) треща́ть (*impf.*); (*sizzle, hiss*) шипе́ть (*impf.*); **the candle ~ed out** свеча́ с шипе́нием пога́сла; **the fat was ~ing in the pan** жир на сковоро́дке шипе́л и стреля́л; **my pen keeps ~ing** моя́ ру́чка всё вре́мя де́лает кля́ксы.

sputum ['spju:təm] *n.* слюна́, мокро́та.

spy [spaɪ] *n.* шпио́н; **police ~** шпик.

v.t. (*liter., discern*) разгля́д|ывать, -е́ть; **~ land** уви́деть (*pf.*) зе́млю; **~ out the land** (*fig.*) зонди́ровать (*impf.*) по́чву.

v.i. (*engage in espionage*) шпио́нить (*impf.*); **~ on s.o.** подгля́дывать (*impf.*) за кем-н.

cpds. **~glass** *n.* подзо́рная труба́; **~hole** *n.* глазо́к.

spying ['spaɪɪŋ] *n.* шпиона́ж; подгля́дывание.

Sq. [skweə(r)] *n.* (*abbr. of* **Square**) пл., (пло́щадь).

squabble ['skwɒb(ə)l] *n.* перебра́нка, пререка́ние; ссо́ра из-за пустяко́в.

v.i. пререка́ться (*impf.*) (*с кем*); вздо́рить, по-.

squabbler ['skwɒblə(r)] *n.* люби́тель (*fem.* -ница) повздо́рить.

squad [skwɒd] *n.* **1.** (*mil.*) гру́ппа, кома́нда, отделе́ние; (*gun crew*) оруди́йный расчёт; **punishment ~** штрафна́я кома́нда; **awkward ~** взвод новобра́нцев; новички́ (*m. pl.*); **~ drill** строевы́е заня́тия. **2.** (*gang, group*) отря́д; рабо́чая брига́да; **flying ~** (*of police*) лету́чий отря́д.

squadron ['skwɒdrən] *n.* (*mil.*) эскадро́н; (*nav.*) эска́дра, соедине́ние; (*aeron.*) эскадри́лья; **fighter ~** эскадри́лья истреби́телей.

cpd. **~-leader** *n.* майо́р авиа́ции.

squalid ['skwɒlɪd] *adj.* гря́зный, ни́щенский, убо́гий; (*sordid, base*) ни́зкий, ни́зменный, гну́сный; **a~ quarrel** гну́сные дря́зги.

squalidness ['skwɒlɪdnɪs] = **squalor**

squall [skwɔ:l] *n.* (*gust, storm*) шквал, гроза́; **encounter a ~** поп|ада́ть, -а́сть в бу́рю; **a ~ of rain** ли́вень (*m.*).

v.i. (*cry*) вопи́ть, за-; пронзи́тельно крича́ть, за-; (*sing loudly*) горла́нить (*impf.*).

squally ['skwɔ:lɪ] *adj.* шква́листый; **~ weather** дождли́вая ве́треная пого́да.

squal|or ['skwɒlə(r)], **-idness** ['skwɒlɪdnɪs] *nn.* убо́жество; ни́зость, гну́сность.

squander ['skwɒndə(r)] *v.t.* пром|а́тывать, -ота́ть; растра́|чивать, -тить; транжи́рить, рас-; **he ~ed his fortune** он промота́л своё состоя́ние; **he is ~ing his talents** он растра́чивает свои́ тала́нты.

squanderer ['skwɒndərə(r)] *n.* расточи́тель (*fem.* -ница).

square [skweə(r)] *n.* **1.** квадра́т; **the map was divided into ~s** ка́рта была́ разделена́ на квадра́ты. **2.** (*on chessboard etc.*) кле́тка, по́ле; **we are back to ~ one** (*fig.*) мы верну́лись в исхо́дное положе́ние; начина́й всё снача́ла!; сно́ва — здо́рово! **3.** (*scarf*) ше́йный плато́к. **4.** (*open space in town*) пло́щадь; **Red S~** Кра́сная пло́щадь; (*with central garden*) сквер; (*barrack-~*) уче́бный плац. **5.** (*US, block of buildings*) кварта́л. **6.** (*drawing instrument*) уго́льник, науго́льник; **out of ~** ко́со, нерo̸вно, неперпендикуля́рно; **on the ~** (*fig.*) (*adj.*) поря́дочный, че́стный; (*adv.*) че́стно, без обма́на. **7.** (*math.*) квадра́т; **find the ~ of 72** возвести́ (*pf.*) 72 в квадра́т(ную сте́пень).

8. (*mil. formation*) каре́ (*indecl.*). 9. (*sl.*, *conventional or old-fashioned pers.*) мещани́н, обыва́тель (*m.*), фили́стер; челове́к отста́лых взгля́дов.

adj. 1. (*geom.*, *math.*) квадра́тный; ~ **metre** квадра́тный метр; ~ **number** квадра́т це́лого числа́; ~ **root** квадра́тный ко́рень (из+*g.*); (*right-angled*) прямоуго́льный; **with** ~ **corners** с прямы́ми угла́ми; (*of shape*) квадра́тный, углова́тый; ~ **dance** кадри́ль; ~ **shoulders** прямы́е/широ́кие пле́чи. 2. (*even*, *balanced*) то́чный; в поря́дке; **get one's accounts** ~ прив|оди́ть, -ести́ свои́ счета́ в поря́док; **all** ~ (*in order*) всё в поря́дке; (*even scoring*) с ра́вным счётом; **we are all** ~ мы кви́ты; у нас по́ровну. 3. (*thorough*) по́лный, реши́тельный; **a** ~ **meal** оби́льная еда́. 4. (*fair*, *honest*) че́стный, прямо́й, справедли́вый; ~ **dealing** че́стное веде́ние дел; **he got a** ~ **deal** с ним поступи́ли по справедли́вости. 5. (*sl.*, *conventional*, *old-fashioned*) отста́лый, фили́стерский.

adv. 1. (*at right angles*) перпендикуля́рно. 2. (*straight*) пря́мо; (*firmly in position*): **set sth.** ~ **to the wall** ста́вить, по- что-н. вплотну́ю к стене́; **he sat** ~ **on his chair** он пря́мо сиде́л на своём сту́ле. 3. (*honestly*) че́стно, пря́мо, непосре́дственно. 4.: **ten feet** ~ де́сять фу́тов в ширину́ и де́сять в длину́.

v.t. 1. (*make* ~) прид|ава́ть, -а́ть квадра́тную фо́рму +*d.*; обтёс|ывать, -а́ть по науго́льнику; ~ **the circle** (*fig.*) найти́ (*pf.*) квадрату́ру кру́га. 2. (*divide into* ~*s*) графи́ть, раз- на квадра́ты; ~**d paper** графлёная бума́га; бума́га в кле́тку; миллиметро́вка. 3. (*math.*) возв|оди́ть, -ести́ в квадра́т (*or* во втору́ю сте́пень); **3** ~**d is 9** квадра́т трёх ра́вен (*or* три в квадра́те равно́) девяти́; **A** ~**d** А квадра́т; А в квадра́те; А во второ́й сте́пени. 4. (*straighten*) выпрямля́ть, вы́прямить; ~ **one's shoulders** распр|авля́ть, -а́вить пле́чи; ~ **one's elbows** выставля́ть, вы́ставить ло́кти. 5. (*settle*) ула́|живать, -дить; ~ **accounts** св|оди́ть, -ести́ счёты; (*pay*) опла́|чивать, -ти́ть (*счёт*); (*coll.*, *satisfy*) ублаж|а́ть, -и́ть; удовлетвор|я́ть, -и́ть; (*bribe*) подкуп|а́ть, -и́ть. 6. (*reconcile*) согласо́в|ывать, -а́ть (*что с чем*); приспос|а́бливать, -о́бить (*что к чему*).

v.i. 1. (*agree*) согласо́в|ываться, -а́ться; ~ **with** вяза́ться/сходи́ться (*both impf.*) с+*i.*; **this statement does not** ~ **with the facts** э́то заявле́ние не соотве́тствует фа́ктам. 2.: ~ **up to s.o.** (*with fists*) изгот|а́вливаться, -о́виться к бо́ю. 3.: ~ **up** (*settle accounts*) **with s.o.** поквита́ться (*pf.*) с кем-н.

cpds. ~**-bashing** *n.* (*coll.*) муштра́ на плацу́, шаги́стика; ~**-built** *adj.* корена́стый; ~**-necked** *adj.* (*of dress*) с квадра́тным вы́резом; с вы́резом каре́; ~**-rigged** *adj.* с прямы́м па́русным вооруже́нием; ~**-sail** *n.* прямо́й па́рус; ~**-shouldered** *adj.* широкопле́чий; ~**-toed** *adj.* с тупы́м носко́м; (*fig.*) чо́порный.

squash[1] [skwɒʃ] *n.* (*crush*) да́вка, толчея́; (*crowd*) толпа́; (*crushed mass*) ка́ша, ме́сиво, мезга́; (*drink*) фрукто́вый напи́ток; (~ **rackets**) сквош, ракетбо́л.

v.t. 1. (*crush*) дави́ть, раз-; разда́в|ливать, -и́ть; сплю́щи|вать, -ть; (*compress*) сж|има́ть, -ать; **I** ~**ed the fly against the wall** я раздави́л му́ху на стене́; **the tomatoes were** ~**ed** помидо́ры подави́лись. 2. (*crowd*): **the conductor** ~**ed us into the bus** конду́ктор вти́снул нас в авто́бус; **we were** ~**ed so tightly, we couldn't move** бы́ло так те́сно, что мы шевельну́ться не могли́. 3. (*quash*): **we must** ~ **this rumour** на́до ликвиди́ровать (*impf.*, *pf.*) э́тот слух; **the rebellion was** ~**ed** мяте́ж был пода́влен; (*silence by retort*): **I felt** ~**ed** я чу́вствовал себя́ обескура́женным.

v.i. (*crowd*) потесни́ться (*pf.*); **they** ~**ed up to make room for me** они́ потесни́лись, что́бы дать мне ме́сто; **they** ~**ed through the door** они́ проти́снулись в дверь.

squash[2] [skwɒʃ] *n.* (*bot.*) ты́ква, кабачо́к.

squat [skwɒt] *n.* (*posture*) сиде́нье на ко́рточках; (*coll.*, *unauthorized occupation*) незако́нное вселе́ние.

adj. призе́мистый.

v.i. 1. (*of pers.*) сиде́ть (*impf.*) на ко́рточках; ~ **down** сади́ться (*impf.*) на ко́рточки; присе́сть (*pf.*); (*of animals*) прип|ада́ть, -а́сть к земле́. 2. (*of unauthorized occupation*) сели́ться, по- самово́льно.

squatter ['skwɒtə(r)] *n.* (*illegal occupant*) сква́ттер.

squaw [skwɔ:] *n.* же́нщина, жена́ (*у индейцев*).

squawk [skwɔ:k] *n.* пронзи́тельный крик.

v.i. пронзи́тельно крича́ть, за-.

squeak [skwi:k] *n.* 1. (*of mouse etc.*) писк, взвизг. 2. (*of hinge etc.*) скрип, визг. 3. (*coll.*, *sound*): **I don't want to hear another** ~ **out of you!** и что́бы бо́льше ни сло́ва! 4. (*coll.*, *escape*): **he had a narrow** ~ он был на волоске́ от ги́бели; он чу́дом спа́сся.

v.i. 1. (*of pers. or animal*) пища́ть, за-. 2. (*of object*) скрипе́ть (*impf.*), скри́пнуть (*pf.*). 3. (*turn informer*; *also* **squeal**) стуча́ть, на- (*sl.*).

squeaker ['skwi:kə(r)] *n.* (*device*) пища́лка; (*informer*; *also* **squealer**) стука́ч (*sl.*).

squeaky ['skwi:kɪ] *adj.* пискли́вый, визгли́вый; скрипу́чий.

squeal [skwi:l] *n.* визг.

v.i. визжа́ть, за-; (*coll.*, *protest loudly*) подн|има́ть, -я́ть шум; (*sl.*, *turn informer*) = **squeak** *v.i.* 3.

squealer ['skwi:lə(r)] = **squeaker**

squeamish ['skwi:mɪʃ] *adj.* 1. (*easily nauseated*) подве́рженный тошноте́; **a** ~ **feeling** чу́вство тошноты́; **feel** ~ чу́вствовать, по- тошноту́; **blood makes me feel** ~ меня́ тошни́т от кро́ви. 2. (*sensitive*, *scrupulous*) щепети́льный, разбо́рчивый, брезгли́вый, делика́тный; **one can't afford to be** ~ **in politics** щепети́льность в поли́тике — ро́скошь.

squeamishness ['skwi:mɪʃnɪs] *n.* щепети́льность.

squeegee ['skwi:dʒi:] *n.* рези́новая шва́бра; (*phot.*) рези́новый ва́лик для нака́тывания фотоотпеча́тков.

squeeze [skwi:z] *n.* 1. (*pressure*) сжа́тие, пожа́тие; **he gave the sponge a** ~ он вы́жал гу́бку; **he gave her a** ~ он кре́пко о́бнял её; **he gave my hand a** ~ он пожа́л мне ру́ку. 2. (*sth.* ~*d out*): **a** ~ **of lemon** не́сколько ка́пель лимо́нного со́ка. 3. (*crowding*, *crush*) теснота́, да́вка; **we got in, but it was a tight** ~ нам удало́сь вти́снуться, но бы́ло о́чень те́сно. 4. (*fin.*) нажи́м; ограниче́ние креди́та; **the Government introduced a credit** ~ прави́тельство ввело́ креди́тную рестри́кцию.

v.t. 1. (*compress*) сж|има́ть, -ать; сда́в|ливать, -и́ть; **he** ~**d his fingers in the door** он прищеми́л па́льцы две́рью; ~ **moist clay** мять (*or* размина́ть), раз- сыру́ю гли́ну; (*to extract moisture etc.*) выжима́ть, вы́жать; **he** ~**d the lemon dry** он вы́жал лимо́н; **juice** ~**d out of an orange** сок, вы́жатый из апельси́на; (*fig.*): **a usurer** ~**s his victims** ростовщи́к выжима́ет со́ки из свои́х жертв; (*extort*): ~ **money out of s.o.** вымога́ть (*impf.*) де́ньги у кого́-н.; ~ **a confession from s.o.** вынужда́ть, вы́нудить кого́-н. призна́ться; вырыва́ть, вы́рвать призна́ние у кого́-н. 2. (*force*, *crowd*, *cram*) запи́х|ивать, -а́ть; впи́х|ивать, -нуть; вти́с|кивать, -нуть. 3.: ~ **one's way** = *v.i.*

v.i. проти́с|киваться, -каться (*or* -нуться); прот|а́лкиваться, -олка́ться (*or* -олкну́ться).

cpd. ~**-box** *n.* (*coll.*) гармо́шка, концерти́но.

squeezer ['skwi:zə(r)] *n.* (соко)выжима́лка.

squelch [skweltʃ] *n.* хлю́панье.

v.i. хлю́п|ать, -нуть; **we** ~**ed through the mud** мы хлю́пали по гря́зи.

squib [skwɪb] *n.* 1. (*firework*) пета́рда, шути́ха; **damp** ~ (*fig.*) прова́л. 2. (*lampoon*) памфле́т, па́сквиль (*m.*).

squid [skwɪd] *n.* кальма́р.

squiffy ['skwɪfɪ] *adj.* (*sl.*) подвы́пивший.

squiggle ['skwɪg(ə)l] *n.* загогу́лина; кара́куля.

squiggly ['skwɪglɪ] *adj.* волни́стый, изо́гнутый.

squint [skwɪnt] *n.* 1. косогла́зие; **she has a** ~ **in her right eye** она́ коси́т на пра́вый глаз. 2. (*coll.*, *glance*) взгляд (и́скоса/укра́дкой); **let's have a** ~ **at the paper** дава́йте посмо́трим, что там в газе́те.

adj. косо́й, косогла́зый.

v.i. 1. коси́ть (*impf.*). 2. (*half-shut eyes*) щу́риться (*impf.*); прищу́ри|ваться, -ться. 3.: ~ **at sth.** смотре́ть, по- и́скоса/укра́дкой на что-н.

cpd. ~**-eyed** *adj.* косо́й, косогла́зый; (*fig.*, *malevolent*) зло́бный, недоброжела́тельный.

squire ['skwaɪə(r)] *n.* землевладе́лец, поме́щик, сквайр.

v.t. сопровожда́ть (*impf.*).

squirearchy ['skwaɪə,rɑ:kɪ] *n.* (*class*) землевладе́льцы (*m. pl.*), поме́щики (*m. pl.*).

squirm [skwɜ:m] *n.* извива́ться (*impf.*); ко́рчиться (*impf.*); **he ~ed under her sarcasm** его́ коро́било от её насме́шек; **the child was ~ing on its seat** ребёнок верте́лся/ёрзал на сту́ле; **he made me ~ with embarrassment** он меня́ так смути́л, что я не знал, куда́ де́ться.

squirrel ['skwɪr(ə)l] *n.* бе́лка; (**~ fur**) бе́личий мех; бе́лка.

squirt [skwɜ:t] *n.* **1.** (*jet*) струя́. **2.** (*instrument*) шприц; спринцо́вка. **3.** (*coll.*, *of pers.*) ничто́жество.

v.t. пры́с|кать, -нуть; **~ water in the air** пус|ка́ть, -ти́ть струю́ воды́ в во́здух; **~ scent from atomizer** бры́згать, по- духа́ми из пульвериза́тора.

v.i. бить (*impf.*) струёй; разбры́зг|иваться, -аться.

Sri Lanka [,ʃri: 'læŋkə, ʃrɪ'læŋkə, ,sr-] *n.* Шри Ла́нка́.

Sri Lankan [ʃri: 'læŋkən, ʃrɪ'læŋkən, sr-] *n.* жи́тель (*fem.* -ница) Шри Ла́нки́.

SS *abbr. of* **1. steamship** парохо́д. **2.** (*hist.*) ***Schutz-Staffel***: **~ man** эсэ́совец.

St. *abbr. of* **1. street** ул., (у́лица). **2. Saint** св., (Свят|о́й, -а́я).

stab [stæb] *n.* **1.** уда́р (о́стрым ору́жием); **~ in the back** (*fig.*) нож/уда́р в спи́ну. **2.** (*fig.*, *sharp pain*) внеза́пная о́страя боль; уко́л; **he felt a ~ of conscience** он почу́вствовал уко́л(ы) со́вести. **3.** (*coll.*, *attempt*): **I'll have a ~ at it** попро́бую.

v.t. **1.** (*wound*): **~ s.o. in the chest with a knife** нан|оси́ть, -ести́ кому́-н. уда́р в грудь ножо́м; вса́|живать, -ди́ть (*or* вонз|а́ть, -и́ть) кому́-н. нож в грудь; (*coll.*) пырну́ть (*pf.*) кого́-н. в грудь ножо́м; **the police are investigating a ~bing incident** поли́ция ведёт сле́дствие по по́воду происше́дшей поножо́вщины. **2.** (*plunge*): **he ~bed a knife into the table** он всади́л/вонзи́л нож в стол. **3.** (*fig.*): **her reproaches ~bed him to the heart** её упрёки пронзи́ли его́ в са́мое се́рдце.

v.i. **1.: ~ at s.o.** бро́ситься (*pf.*) на кого́-н. с ножо́м. **2.** (*of pain etc.*) стреля́ть (*impf.*).

stability [stə'bɪlɪtɪ] *n.* стаби́льность, усто́йчивость, про́чность; (*steadfastness*) твёрдость, постоя́нство; (*nav.*, *aeron.*) осто́йчивость.

stabilization [,steɪbɪ,laɪ'zeɪʃ(ə)n] *n.* стабилиза́ция, упро́чение.

stabilize ['steɪbɪ,laɪz] *v.t.* стабилизи́ровать (*impf.*, *pf.*); де́лать, с- усто́йчивым; (*nav.*, *aeron.*) обеспе́чи|вать, -ть осто́йчивость *+g.*

stabilizer ['steɪbɪ,laɪzə(r)] *n.* (*nav.*, *aeron.*) стабилиза́тор; стабилизи́рующее устро́йство.

stable[1] ['steɪb(ə)l] *n.* **1.** коню́шня, хлев. **2.** (*group of horses*) ло́шади (*f. pl.*) одно́й коню́шни; (*racing*) скаковы́е ло́шади одного́ владе́льца; **from the same ~** (*fig.*) из той же плея́ды, из того́ же изда́тельства *и т.п.*

v.t. ста́вить, по- в коню́шню; содержа́ть (*impf.*) в коню́шне.

cpds. **~-boy, ~-lad** *nn.* помо́щник ко́нюха; **~-companion** *n.* ло́шадь той же коню́шни; (*fig.*) однока́шник; **~man** *n.* ко́нюх.

stable[2] ['steɪb(ə)l] *adj.* (*firm*, *strong*, *fixed*) про́чный, кре́пкий; (*of currency*) стаби́льный, усто́йчивый, сто́йкий; **a ~ job** постоя́нная рабо́та.

stabling ['steɪblɪŋ] *n.* коню́шни (*f. pl.*).

staccato [stə'kɑ:təʊ] *n.* & *adv.* стакка́то (*indecl.*).

adj. отры́вистый.

stack [stæk] *n.* **1.** (*of hay etc.*) стог; скирда́; омёт. **2.** (*pile*): **~ of wood** шта́бель (*m.*) дров, поле́нница; **~ of papers** ки́па/сто́пка бума́г; **~ of plates** стопа́ таре́лок; **~ of rifles** винто́вки, соста́вленные в ко́злы. **3.** (*coll.*, *usu. pl.*, *large amount*) ма́сса, ку́ча, гру́да; **he has ~s of money** у него́ ку́ча де́нег; **a ~ of work** ма́сса рабо́ты; **I've a ~ of letters to write** мне на́до написа́ть ку́чу пи́сем; **a ~ of unanswered letters** во́рох неотве́ченных пи́сем; **we have ~s of time** у нас полно́ вре́мени; (*coll.*) вре́мени у нас ваго́н. **4.** (*chimney*) дымова́я труба́; (*group of chimneys*) ряд дымовы́х труб.

v.t. **1.: ~ hay** мете́ть (*impf.*) се́но в стог; скирдова́ть (*impf.*) се́но; **~ books on the floor** ста́вить, по- кни́ги сто́пками на полу́; **~ wood** скла́дывать, сложи́ть дрова́ штабеля́ми; **~ plates** сост|авля́ть, -а́вить таре́лки стопо́й (*or* в сто́пку); **~ arms!** (*mil.*) соста́вь! **2.: ~ the cards** подтасо́в|ывать, -а́ть ка́рты; **the cards were ~ed against him** (*fig.*) всё бы́ло про́тив него́. **3.: ~ aircraft** эшелони́ровать (*impf.*, *pf.*) самолёты пе́ред захо́дом на поса́дку.

stadium ['steɪdɪəm] *n.* стадио́н.

staff [stɑ:f] *n.* **1.** (*for walking etc.*) по́сох, па́лка; (*pole*) столб; (*fig.*): **bread is the ~ of life** хлеб — осно́ва жи́зни; **you are the ~ of his old age** вы его́ опо́ра в ста́рости. **2.** (*emblem of office*) жезл; **pastoral ~** епи́скопский по́сох. **3.** (*shaft*, *handle*) дре́вко. **4.** (*body of assistants*, *employees*) штат; ли́чный соста́в; **~ of a hospital** больни́чный персона́л; **~ of a faculty** сотру́дники (*m. pl.*) ка́федры; **editorial ~** сотру́дники реда́кции; **teaching ~** преподава́тельский соста́в; **~ room** (*at school*) учи́тельская; **~ meeting** педагоги́ческий сове́т; **the department is short of ~** в отде́ле не хвата́ет сотру́дников/рабо́тников. **5.** (*mil.*) штаб; **General S~** генера́льный штаб; **~ college** акаде́мия генера́льного шта́ба; **~ officer** штабно́й офице́р; **~ sergeant** штаб-сержа́нт; **~ work** администрати́вная/штабна́я рабо́та. **6.** (*mus.*) но́тный стан.

v.t. укомплекто́в|ывать, -а́ть (*что or* штат *чего*).

stag [stæg] *n.* (*deer*) оле́нь(*m.*)-саме́ц.

cpds. **~-beetle** *n.* жук-оле́нь (*m.*); **~-party** *n.* (*coll.*) холостя́цкая вечери́нка, мальчи́шник.

stage [steɪdʒ] *n.* **1.** (*platform in theatre*) сце́на, эстра́да, подмо́стк|и (*pl. g.* -ов); **front of the ~** авансце́на; (*landing-~*) схо́дни (*f. pl.*). **2.** (*of microscope*) предме́тный сто́лик. **3.** (*theatr.*) сце́на, подмо́стки; (*as profession*) теа́тр, сце́на; **go on the ~** идти́, пойти́ на сце́ну; **quit the ~** ост|авля́ть, -а́вить (*or* пок|ида́ть, -и́нуть) сце́ну; **put a play on the ~** ста́вить, по- пье́су; **he writes for the ~** он пи́шет для теа́тра; **a ~ Englishman** театра́льный штамп англича́нина. **4.** (*attr.*): **~ direction** рема́рка; **~ door** служе́бный/актёрский вход (в теа́тр); **~ effect** сцени́ческий/театра́льный эффе́кт; **~ fever** страсть к теа́тру/сце́не; **~ fright** страх пе́ред пу́бликой; волне́ние пе́ред выступле́нием; **~ whisper** театра́льный шёпот. **5.** (*fig.*, *scene of action*) аре́на, по́прище, сце́на; **he quitted the ~ of politics** он поки́нул полити́ческую аре́ну; **a larger ~ opened before him** пе́ред ним откры́лось бо́лее широ́кое по́прище. **6.** (*phase*, *point*) пери́од, ста́дия, эта́п, ступе́нь; **the war reached a critical ~** война́ вступи́ла в крити́ческую фа́зу; **at this ~ he was interrupted** на э́том ме́сте его́ переби́ли; **she was in the last ~ of consumption** она́ находи́лась в после́дней ста́дии чахо́тки; **the baby has reached the talking ~** ребёнок на́чал говори́ть (*or* заговори́л); **negotiations reached their final ~** наступи́л заверша́ющий эта́п перегово́ров; **I shall do it in ~s** я сде́лаю э́то постепе́нно. **7.** (*section of route or journey*) перего́н, эта́п; (*stopping place between sections*) остано́вка, ста́нция; **we travelled by easy ~s** мы путеше́ствовали/е́хали не спеша́ (*or* с ча́стными остано́вками). **8.** (*of rocket*) ступе́нь.

v.t.: **~ a play** ста́вить, по- пье́су; (*organize*) устр|а́ивать, -о́ить; организова́ть (*impf.*, *pf.*).

cpds. **~-coach** *n.* почто́вый дилижа́нс; **~craft** *n.* драматурги́ческое мастерство́; мастерство́ режиссёра/актёра; **~-hand** *n.* рабо́чий сце́ны; **~-manage** *v.t.* ста́вить, по- (*спектакль*); режисси́ровать, с-; (закули́сно) руководи́ть *+i.*; **~-manager** *n.* режиссёр, постано́вщик; **~-struck** *adj.*: **she is ~-struck** она́ заболе́ла сце́ной.

stager ['steɪdʒə(r)] *n.*: **old ~** стре́ляный воробе́й.

stagey ['steɪdʒɪ] = **stagy**

stagger ['stægə(r)] *n.* **1.** шата́ние, поша́тывание. **2.** (*pl.*, **the ~s**) (*of horses*) ко́лер; (*of sheep*) вертя́чка.

v.t. **1.** (*cause to ~*): **a ~ing blow** сокруши́тельный уда́р. **2.** (*disconcert*) потряс|а́ть, -ти́; пора|жа́ть, -зи́ть; ошелом|ля́ть, -и́ть; **we were ~ed by the news** мы бы́ли потрясены́/поражены́ э́той но́востью; **~ing success** потряса́ющий успе́х; **~ing misfortune** ужаса́ющее несча́стье. **3.** (*arrange in zigzag order*) распол|ага́ть, -ожи́ть в ша́хматном поря́дке. **4.: ~ working hours, holidays etc.** распределя́ть (*impf.*) часы́ рабо́ты, отпуска́ *и т.п.*; **the work is ~ed in three shifts** рабо́та разби́та на́ три сме́ны.

v.i. шата́ться (*impf.*); поша́тываться (*impf.*); **they ~ed down the street** они́ шли по у́лице поша́тываясь; **a ~ing gait** шата́ющаяся/неве́рная/ковыля́ющая похо́дка.

staging ['steɪdʒɪŋ] *n.* **1.** (*platform*) подмо́стк|и (*pl., g.* -ов), лес|а́ (*pl., g.* -о́в). **2.** (*of play*) постано́вка. **3.: ~ post** (*aeron.*) промежу́точный аэродро́м.

stagnant ['stægnənt] *adj.* **1.** (*of water*) стоя́чий. **2.** (*sluggish*) засто́йный, ине́ртный, вя́лый, ко́сный.

stagnate [stæg'neɪt] *v.i.* **1.** (*of water*) заст|а́иваться, -оя́ться. **2.** (*fig.*) косне́ть, за-; **trade is stagnating** торго́вля в упа́дке.

stagnation [stæg'neɪʃ(ə)n] *n.* (*of water*) засто́й, засто́йность; (*fig.*) засто́й; (*econ.*) стагна́ция.

stagy ['steɪdʒɪ] *adj.* театра́льный; аффекти́рованный.

staid [steɪd] *adj.* степе́нный; положи́тельный.

stain [steɪn] *n.* **1.** пятно́; **remove a ~** выводи́ть, вы́вести пятно́. **2.** (*for colouring wood etc.*) протра́ва, краси́тель (*m.*); **wood ~** протра́ва, мори́лка. **3.** (*fig., moral defect*) пятно́, позо́р; **cast a ~ on** запятна́ть (*pf.*); **without a ~ on his character** с незапя́тнанной репута́цией.

v.t. **1.** (*discolour, soil*) пятна́ть, за-; па́чкать, за-/ис-; **water will not ~ the carpet** вода́ не оставля́ет пя́тен на ковре́. **2.** (*colour with dye etc.*) окра́|шивать, -сить; подцве́|чивать, -ти́ть; протра́в|ливать (*or* протрав|ля́ть), -и́ть; **~ed glass** цветно́е стекло́; **~ed-glass window** витра́ж; **~ wood** мори́ть, за- де́рево. **3.** (*fig.*) пятна́ть, за-.

v.i. (*cause ~s*) оставля́ть (*impf.*) пя́тна; (*be subject to ~ing*) па́чкаться (*impf.*); быть ма́рким.

stainless ['steɪnlɪs] *adj.* **1.** (*unblemished*) чи́стый; (*fig.*) незапя́тнанный, безупре́чный. **2.: ~ steel** нержаве́ющая сталь.

stair [steə(r)] *n.* **1.** (*step*) ступе́нька. **2.** (*pl.,* **~case**) ле́стница; **flight of ~s** ле́стничный марш; **he ran up the ~s** он взбежа́л по ле́стнице; **he ran down the ~s** он сбежа́л с ле́стницы.

cpds. **~-carpet** *n.* доро́жка (для ле́стницы); **~case, ~way** *nn.* ле́стница; ле́стничная кле́тка; **spiral ~case** винтова́я ле́стница; **~head** *n.* ве́рхняя площа́дка ле́стницы; **~-rod** *n.* пру́тик, укрепля́ющий ле́стничный ковёр; **~way** *n.* = **~case; ~-well** *n.* ле́стничная кле́тка; ле́стничный коло́дец.

stake [steɪk] *n.* **1.** (*post*) столб, кол (*pl.* ко́лья); сто́йка, прико́л; **row of ~s** частоко́л; **the plants were tied to ~s** расте́ния бы́ли подвя́заны к ко́лышкам; **he was burnt at the ~** его́ сожгли́ на костре́; **pull up ~s** (*fig.*) сня́ться (*pf.*) с ме́ста. **2.** (*wager; money deposited*) ста́вка, закла́д; (*pl.* **~ race**) ска́чки (*f. pl.*) на приз; **hold the ~s** прин|има́ть, -я́ть закла́д; **play for high ~s** игра́ть (*impf.*) по большо́й; (*fig.*) поста́вить (*pf.*) всё на ка́рту. **3.** (*interest, share*) интере́с, до́ля; **he has a ~ in the country** он кро́вно заинтересо́ван в процвета́нии страны́/кра́я. **4.: his reputation was at ~** его́ репута́ция была́ поста́влена на ка́рту; **his life is at ~** на ка́рту поста́влена его́ жизнь.

v.t. **1.** (*support with ~*) укреп|ля́ть, -и́ть (*or* подп|ира́ть, -ере́ть) коло́м/сто́йкой. **2.** (*wager*) ста́вить, по-; (*risk, gamble*) рискова́ть (*impf.*) +*i.*; **he ~d his fortune on one race** он поста́вил всё своё состоя́ние на оди́н забе́г; **I would ~ my reputation on his honesty** за его́ че́стность я гото́в поручи́ться свое́й че́стью.

with advs.: **~ off** *v.t.* отгор|а́живать, -оди́ть; **~ out** *v.t.*: **~ out a boundary** отм|еча́ть, -е́тить ве́хами грани́цу; **~ (out) one's claim** (*lit.*) застолби́ть (*pf.*) уча́сток; (*fig.*): **he ~d (out) his claim to a seat at the conference** он заяви́л о своём наме́рении уча́ствовать в конфере́нции.

cpds. **~-holder** *n.* посре́дник; **~-net** *n.* зако́л; зако́льный не́вод.

Stakhanovism [stə'kɑːnə,vɪz(ə)m] *n.* стаха́новщина.

Stakhanovite [stə'kɑːnə,vaɪt] *n.* стаха́новец.

adj. стаха́новский.

stalactite ['stælək,taɪt, stə'læk-] *n.* сталакти́т.

stalagmite ['stæləg,maɪt] *n.* сталагми́т.

stale[1] [steɪl] *n.* (*animal's urine*) моча́.

v.i. сочи́ться, по-.

stale[2] [steɪl] *adj.* **1.** (*not fresh*) несве́жий; **~ bread** чёрствый хлеб; **~ egg** лежа́лое яйцо́; (*of air*) спёртый, за́тхлый; **the room smells ~** в ко́мнате за́тхлый во́здух. **2.** (*lacking novelty, tedious*) изби́тый, устаре́вший; **a ~ joke** изби́тая шу́тка; **~ news** устаре́вшая но́вость. **3.** (*out of condition*) вы́дохшийся; **a ~ athlete** перетренирова́вшийся спортсме́н; **go ~** вы́дохнуться (*pf.*); утра́тить (*pf.*) спорти́вную фо́рму; **he got ~ at his work** он заки́с на свое́й рабо́те.

v.i.: **pleasures that never ~** ра́дости, кото́рые никогда́ не приеда́ются.

stalemate ['steɪlmeɪt] *n.* (*chess*) пат; (*fig., impasse*) тупи́к, безвы́ходное положе́ние.

v.t. де́лать, с- пат +*d.*; (*fig.*) загна́ть (*pf.*) в тупи́к, поста́вить (*pf.*) в безвы́ходное положе́ние.

staleness ['steɪlnɪs] *n.* (*of food*) залежа́лость; (*of bread*) чёрствость; (*of air, room etc.*) спёртость, за́тхлость; (*of joke etc.*) изби́тость; (*of news*) устаре́лость.

Stalinism ['stɑːlɪ,nɪz(ə)m] *n.* сталини́зм.

Stalinist ['stɑːlɪnɪst] *n.* сталини́ст (*fem.* -ка).

adj. сталини́стский.

stalk[1] [stɔːk] *n.* (*stem*) сте́бель (*m.*); черешо́к; (*cabbage-~*) кочеры́жка; (*of wine-glass*) но́жка.

stalk[2] [stɔːk] *n.* (*imposing gait*) широ́кая, велича́вая по́ступь; (*hunting*) обла́ва.

v.t. (*game, pers.*) высле́живать, вы́следить; **~ing-horse** (*fig.*) личи́на, предло́г.

v.i. (*stride*) ше́ствовать (*impf.*); го́рдо выступа́ть (*impf.*); **he ~ed up to me** он церемо́нно/торже́ственно подошёл ко мне; (*fig.*): **famine ~ed (through) the land** го́лод ше́ствовал по стране́.

stall[1] [stɔːl] *n.* **1.** (*for animal*) сто́йло. **2.** (*in market etc.*) ларёк, пала́тка; прила́вок; **book ~** кио́ск; (*in street*) (кни́жный) разва́л; **flower ~** цве́точный ларёк; **newspaper ~** газе́тный кио́ск. **3.** (*pl., theatr.*) парте́р, кре́сла (*nt. pl.*). **4.** (*of engine*) заглуха́ние мото́ра; (*of aircraft*) срыв пото́ка.

v.t. **1.** (*place in ~*) ста́вить, по- в сто́йло; (*keep in ~*) содержа́ть (*impf.*) в сто́йле. **2.: ~ an engine** (неча́янно) заглуш|а́ть, -и́ть мото́р.

v.i. **1.** (*get stuck*) застр|ева́ть, -я́ть; ув|яза́ть, -я́знуть. **2.** (*of engine*) гло́хнуть, за-; (*aeron.*) теря́ть, по- ско́рость при сры́ве пото́ка; **~ing speed** ско́рость сры́ва/сва́ливания; крити́ческая ско́рость полёта.

cpds. **~-fed** *adj.* отко́рмленный, упи́танный; **~-holder** *n.* владе́лец ларька́.

stall[2] [stɔːl] *v.t.* (*block, delay*) заде́рж|ивать, -а́ть.

v.i. (*play for time*) тяну́ть, волы́нить, кани́телить (*all impf.*).

stallion ['stæljən] *n.* жеребе́ц.

stalwart ['stɔːlwət] *n.* (*pol.*) активи́ст (*fem.* -ка); **one of the old ~s** настоя́щий ветера́н из ста́рой гва́рдии.

adj. (*robust*) ро́слый, дю́жий; (*staunch*) отва́жный, до́блестный.

stamen ['steɪmən] *n.* тычи́нка.

stamina ['stæmɪnə] *n.* выно́сливость, вы́держка.

stammer ['stæmə(r)] *n.* заика́ние; **person with a ~** заи́ка (*c.g.*); **speak with a ~** заика́ться (*impf.*); говори́ть (*impf.*) с запи́нкой.

v.t. произн|оси́ть, -ести́ (*что*), заика́ясь; бормота́ть, про-.

v.i. заика́ться (*impf.*); запина́ться (*impf.*).

stammerer ['stæmərə(r)] *n.* заи́ка (*c.g.*).

stamp [stæmp] *n.* **1.** (*of foot*) то́пот, то́панье; **with a ~ of the foot** то́пнув ного́й. **2.** (*instrument*) ште́мпель (*m.*), штамп, печа́ть, клеймо́. **3.** (*impress, mark*) печа́ть, клеймо́; о́ттиск, отпеча́ток; (*postage etc.*) ма́рка; **S~ Act** (*hist.*) зако́н о ге́рбовом сбо́ре. **4.** (*characteristic, mark*) печа́ть, отпеча́ток; **his work bears the ~ of genius** его́ рабо́та отме́чена печа́тью ге́ния; **of the same ~** одного́ (*or* того́ же) ти́па; **he is not a man of that ~** он челове́к не тако́го скла́да.

v.t. **1.** (*imprint*) штампова́ть (*impf.*); штемпелева́ть (*impf.*); клейми́ть, за-; отти́с|кивать, -нуть; **a document ~ed with the date** докуме́нт с проштемпелёванной да́той; **a design ~ed in metal** рису́нок, отти́снутый на мета́лле; **the maker's name is ~ed on the goods** на това́ре проста́влено фабри́чное клеймо́; **he ~ed his name on the flyleaf** он поста́вил штамп со свое́й фами́лией на фо́рзаце. **2.** (*affix ~ to*): **~ an envelope** накле́и|вать, -ть ма́рку на конве́рт; **~ a receipt** ста́вить, по- печа́ть на квита́нции. **3.** (*ore etc.*) дроби́ть (*impf.*). **4.** (*imprint on mind*) запечатл|ева́ть, -е́ть; **the scene is ~ed on my memory** э́та сце́на запечатле́лась в мое́й па́мяти. **5.** (*distinguish, characterize*): **his manners ~ him as a boor** его́ мане́ры изоблича́ют в нём невե́жу; **this chapter alone ~s it as a work of genius** уже́ по одно́й э́той главе́ ви́дно, что кни́га напи́сана ге́нием. **6.** (*beat on ground*): **~ one's feet** то́пать (*impf.*) нога́ми; **~ the snow from one's shoes** сби|ва́ть, -ть снег с боти́нок.

v.i. (*feet*) то́п|ать, -нуть.

with adv.: **~ out** *v.t.*: (*lit.*): **~ out a fire** заглуши́ть/затопта́ть (*pf.*) ого́нь; (*exterminate, destroy*) уничт|ожа́ть, -о́жить; истреб|ля́ть, -и́ть; (*suppress*) подав|ля́ть, -и́ть; **the revolt was quickly ~ed out** восста́ние бы́ло ско́ро пода́влено; **~ out an epidemic** потуши́ть/искорени́ть (*pf.*) эпиде́мию.

cpds. **~-album** *n.* альбо́м для ма́рок; **~-collecting** *n.* филатели́я; **~-collector** *n.* филатели́ст (*fem.* -ка); **~-dealer** *n.* торго́вец ма́рками; держа́тель (*m.*) филателисти́ческого магази́на; **~-duty** *n.* ге́рбовый сбор; **~-machine** *n.* автома́т по прода́же почто́вых ма́рок; **~-paper** *n.* ге́рбовая бума́га.

stampede [stæm'pi:d] *n.* (*of cattle*) бе́гство врассыпну́ю; (*of people*) ма́ссовое (пани́ческое) бе́гство.

v.t. обра|ща́ть, -ти́ть в бе́гство.

v.i. (*of cattle*) разбе|га́ться, -жа́ться врассыпну́ю; (*of people*) обра|ща́ться, -ти́ться в (пани́ческое) бе́гство.

stance [stɑ:ns, stæns] *n.* пози́ция; **take up a ~** зан|има́ть, -я́ть пози́цию.

stanch [stɑ:ntʃ, stɔ:ntʃ], **staunch** [stɔ:ntʃ, stɑ:ntʃ] *v.t.*: **~ a wound** остан|а́вливать, -ови́ть кровотече́ние из ра́ны.

stanchion ['stɑ:nʃ(ə)n] *n.* подпо́рка, опо́ра, столб, сто́йка, коло́нна; (*for confining cattle*) стано́к.

stand [stænd] *n.* **1.** (*support, e.g. for teapot*) подста́вка; (*of lamp*) но́жка; (*for radio etc.*) ту́мба; (*for bicycles*) стелла́ж; (*for telescope*) штати́в. **2.** (*stall*) ларёк, сто́йка; (*for display*) стенд, щит. **3.** (*raised structure, e.g. for spectators*) трибу́на. **4.** (*for taxis etc.*) стоя́нка. **5.** (*halt*) остано́вка; **bring, come to a ~** остан|а́вливать(ся), -ови́ть(ся). **6.** (*position*) ме́сто; **take one's ~ on the platform** зан|има́ть, -я́ть ме́сто на сце́не/эстра́де; (*fig.*): **take one's ~ on a principle** ста|нови́ться, -ть на принципиа́льную то́чку зре́ния; **take a firm ~** зан|има́ть, -я́ть твёрдую пози́цию; **make a ~ against s.o.** ока́з|ывать, -а́ть сопротивле́ние кому́-н.; **the retreating enemy made a ~** отступа́ющий непри́ятель дал бой; **make a ~ for** вы́ступить (*pf.*) в защи́ту +*g.* **7.** (*theatr., stop for performance*): **one-night ~** однодне́вные гастро́ли (*f. pl.*). **8.**: **~ of trees** лесонасажде́ние; **~ of wheat** пшени́ца на корню́.

v.t. **1.** (*place, set*) ста́вить, по-; **he stood the ladder against the wall** он прислони́л/приста́вил ле́стницу к стене́; **the teacher stood him in the corner** учи́тель поста́вил его́ в у́гол; **he stood the box on end** он поста́вил я́щик стойма́ (*or* на попа́). **2.** (*bear, tolerate, endure*) терпе́ть, вы́-; выноси́ть, вы́нести; перен|оси́ть, -ести́; **how does he ~ the pain?** как он перено́сит боль?; **she can't ~ him** она́ его́ не выно́сит (*or* терпе́ть не мо́жет); **I can't ~ cold** я не выношу́ хо́лода; **he can't ~ being kept waiting** он терпе́ть не мо́жет, когда́ его́ заставля́ют ждать; (*withstand*) выде́рживать, вы́держать; **your coat won't ~ much rain** ва́ше пальто́ не вы́держит си́льного дождя́; **his plays have stood the test of time** его́ пье́сы вы́держали испыта́ние вре́менем. **3.** (*not yield*): **~ one's ground** не уступ|а́ть, -и́ть. **4.** (*undergo*) подв|ерга́ться +*d.*; **~ one's trial** отв|еча́ть, -е́тить пе́ред судо́м. **5.**: **he doesn't ~ a chance** у него́ нет никако́й наде́жды. **6.** (*provide at one's own expense*) уго|ща́ть, -сти́ть (*кого чем*); поста́вить (*pf.*) (*что кому*); **he stood drinks all round** он угости́л ка́ждого (стака́ном, кру́жкой *и т. п.*); он поста́вил всем по стака́ну *и т. п.*

v.i. **1.** (*be or stay in upright position*) стоя́ть (*impf.*); **she was too weak to ~** она́ не держа́лась на нога́х от сла́бости; **he kept me ~ing** он не предложи́л мне сесть; **when it comes to mathematics he leaves me ~ing** в матема́тике мне за ним не угна́ться; **~ing room only** (*theatr.*) сидя́чих мест нет; **a ~ing ovation** бу́рная ова́ция; **don't ~ in the rain!** не сто́йте под дождём (*or* на дождю́)!; **he left the car ~ing in the rain** он оста́вил маши́ну под дождём; **she let the plant ~ in the sun** она́ вы́ставила цвето́к на со́лнце; **the sight of the corpse made my hair ~ on end** при ви́де тру́па у меня́ во́лосы ста́ли ды́бом; **he is old enough to ~ on his own feet** он доста́точно взро́слый, что́бы быть самостоя́тельным; **he hasn't a leg to ~ on** у него́ нет ни мале́йших (*or* нет никаки́х) доказа́тельств; **I could do that ~ing on my head** я мог бы э́то сде́лать ле́вой ного́й; **I shan't ~ in your way** я вам не ста́ну меша́ть; **~ still!** не дви́гайтесь!; **he can't ~ still for a moment** он ни мину́ты не посиди́т споко́йно; **time seemed to be ~ing still** каза́лось, вре́мя останови́лось. **2.** (*with indication of height*): **he ~s six feet tall** рост у него́ шесть фу́тов. **3.** (*continue, remain*): **our house will ~ for another fifty years** наш дом простои́т ещё пятьдеся́т лет; **~ fast, firm** держа́ться (*impf.*) непоколеби́мо/твёрдо; **we shall ~ or fall together** у нас одна́ судьба́; бу́дем держа́ться вме́сте до конца́; **not a stone was left ~ing** ка́мня на ка́мне не оста́лось; *see also* **standing. 4.** (*hold good*) ост|ава́ться, -а́ться в си́ле. **5.** (*be situated*) стоя́ть (*impf.*); находи́ться; (*impf.*); **a house once stood here** когда́-то здесь стоя́л дом; **tears stood in her eyes** слёзы стоя́ли у неё в глаза́х; **sweat stood on his brow** пот вы́ступил у него́ на лбу. **6.** (*find o.s., be*): **he stood convicted of murder** суд призна́л его́ вино́вным в уби́йстве; **we ~ in need of help** мы нужда́емся в по́мощи; **they ~ under heavy obligations** они́ взя́ли на себя́ серьёзные обяза́тельства; **I will ~ godfather to him** я бу́ду его́ крёстным; **I ~ corrected** я признаю́ свою́ оши́бку; **the price ~s higher than ever** цена́ сейча́с вы́ше, чем когда́-либо; **this is how matters ~** вот как обстои́т де́ло; **as matters ~** при да́нном положе́нии веще́й; в настоя́щих/ны́нешних обстоя́тельствах; **I shall leave the text as it ~s** я не бу́ду пра́вить текст; **how do we ~ for money?** как у нас (обстои́т) с деньга́ми?; **the umbrella stood me in good stead** зо́нтик мне весьма́ пригоди́лся. **7.** (*rise to one's feet*) вста|ва́ть, -ть. **8.** (*come to a halt*) остан|а́вливаться, -ови́ться; **~ still** не дви́гаться (*impf.*); быть неподви́жным; **~ and deliver!** кошелёк и́ли жизнь! **9.** (*assume or move to specified position*): **I'll ~ here** я ста́ну сюда́; **we had to ~ in a queue** нам пришло́сь постоя́ть в о́череди; **he stood on tiptoe** он встал на цы́почки; **he (went and) stood on the tarpaulin** он ступи́л/наступи́л на брезе́нт; **I (went and) stood by the table** я стал у стола́; **~ back!** (пода́йтесь) наза́д!; отойди́те!; **~ clear of the doors!** отойди́те от двере́й!; **the soldiers stood to attention** бойцы́ вста́ли в сто́йку «сми́рно»; **~ at ease!** во́льно! **10.** (*remain motionless*): **the machinery is ~ing idle** станки́ проста́ивают; **let the tea ~!** да́йте ча́ю отстоя́ться!

with preps.: **nothing ~s between him and success** ничто́ не препя́тствует его́ успе́ху; **we will ~ by** (*support*) **you** мы вас подде́ржим; **I ~ by what I said** я не отступа́юсь от свои́х слов; **~ for office** выставля́ть, вы́ставить свою́ кандидату́ру; **~ for Parliament** баллоти́роваться (*impf.*) (*or* выставля́ть (*impf.*) свою́ кандидату́ру) в парла́мент; **we ~ for freedom** мы стои́м за свобо́ду; **'Mg' ~s for magnesium** «Mg» обознача́ет ма́гний; **I will not ~ for such impudence** я не потерплю́ тако́й де́рзости; **the ship stood off the shore** су́дно держа́лось на расстоя́нии от бе́рега; **don't ~ on ceremony** не стесня́йтесь!; пожа́луйста, без церемо́ний!; **his father stood over him till the work was finished** оте́ц стоя́л у него́ над душо́й, пока́ он не зако́нчил рабо́ту; **it ~s to reason** (само́ собо́й) разуме́ется; не подлежи́т сомне́нию; **he ~s to win/lose**

£1,000 его́ ждёт вы́игрыш/про́игрыш в ты́сячу фу́нтов; **this amount ~s to your credit** э́та су́мма нахо́дится на ва́шем счету́; **~ to arms** приня́ть (*pf.*) боеву́ю гото́вность; **~ to one's promise** сдержа́ть (*pf.*) обеща́ние; **how do you ~ with your boss?** как к вам отно́сится ваш нача́льник?; вы на хоро́шем счету́ у нача́льника?

with advs.: **~ about, ~ around** *vv.i.* (*of one pers.*) болта́ться (*impf.*); (*of a group*) стоя́ть (*impf.*) круго́м; **don't ~ about in the corridor!** не торчи́те (*coll.*) в коридо́ре!; **~ aside** *v.i.* (*remain aloof*) стоя́ть (*impf.*) в стороне́; (*move to one side*) посторони́ться (*pf.*); **~ back** *v.i.*: **the house ~s back from the road** дом не стои́т на доро́ге; **he stood back to admire the picture** он отошёл наза́д, что́бы полюбова́ться карти́ной; **he ~s back in favour of others** он уступа́ет ме́сто други́м; **~ by** *v.i.* (*be ready*) быть/стоя́ть (*impf.*) нагото́ве; **the troops were ordered to ~ by** войска́м приказа́ли стоя́ть нагото́ве; **~ by to fire!** пригото́виться к стрельбе́!; (*be spectator*): **I could not ~ by and see her ill-treated** я не мог смотре́ть безуча́стно, как над не́ю издева́ются; **~ down** *v.i.* (*of witness*) ко́нчить (*pf.*) дава́ть показа́ния; (*of candidate*): **he stood down in favour of his brother** он снял свою́ кандидату́ру в по́льзу бра́та; **the guard was stood down** карау́л сня́ли; **~ in** *v.i.* (*substitute*): **~ in for s.o. else** замен|я́ть, -и́ть кого́-н. друго́го; (*naut.*): **the ship was ~ing in to the shore** су́дно подходи́ло к бе́регу; **~ off** *v.t.*: **~ off workers** вре́менно ув|ольня́ть, -о́лить рабо́чих; *v.i.*: **we stood off a mile from the harbour** мы находи́лись в (одно́й) ми́ле от га́вани; **~ out** *v.i.* (*be prominent, conspicuous*) выделя́ться (*impf.*); выдава́ться (*impf.*); **his house ~s out from all the others** его́ дом си́льно отлича́ется от сосе́дних; **his work ~s out from the others'** его́ рабо́та ре́зко выделя́ется среди́ про́чих; **his mistakes ~ out a mile** (*coll.*) его́ оши́бки за версту́ видны́ (*or* броса́ются в глаза́); (*show resistance*): **~ out against tyranny** сопротивля́ться (*impf.*) деспоти́зму; боро́ться (*impf.*) с деспоти́змом; (*hold out*): **~ out for one's claims** наста́ивать (*impf.*) на свои́х тре́бованиях; **~ over** *v.i.* (*be postponed*) быть отло́женным; **~ to** *v.i.* (*mil.*): **~ to!** в ружьё!; **~ up** *v.t.*: **he stood his bicycle up against the wall** он прислони́л свой велосипе́д к стене́; (*coll.*): **his girl-friend stood him up** его́ подру́га не пришла́ на свида́ние; *v.i.*: **he stood up as I entered** он встал, когда́ я вошёл; **he ~s up for his rights** он отста́ивает свои́ права́; **he stood up bravely to his opponent** он му́жественно сопротивля́лся проти́внику; **he ~s up to the pace** он выде́рживает темп; **this steel ~s up to high temperatures** э́та сталь выде́рживает высо́кие температу́ры.

cpds. **~by** *n.* (*state of readiness*) гото́вность; (*dependable thg. or pers.*) надёжная опо́ра; испы́танное сре́дство; **~by generator** запа́сный/резе́рвный генера́тор; **~-down** *n.* (*mil.*) отбо́й; **~-in** *n.* замести́тель (*fem.* -ница); **~-offish** *adj.* (*aloof*) сде́ржанный, за́мкнутый; (*haughty*) надме́нный, высокоме́рный; **~point** *n.* то́чка зре́ния; **~still** *n.* остано́вка, безде́йствие; **come to a ~still** останови́ться (*pf.*); засто́пориться (*pf.*); **at a ~still** на мёртвой то́чке, на то́чке замерза́ния; **bring to a ~still** останови́ть (*pf.*); засто́порить (*pf.*); **trade is at a ~still** торго́вля нахо́дится в засто́е; **many factories are at a ~still** мно́го фа́брик безде́йствует; **the matter is temporarily at a ~still** де́ло пока́ что не дви́жется; **~-to** *n.* (*mil.*) боева́я гото́вность; **~-up** *adj.*: **~-up collar** стоя́чий воротни́к; **~-up supper** у́жин а-ля-фурше́т; **~-up fight** кула́чный бой.

standard [ˈstændəd] *n.* **1.** (*flag*) зна́мя, штанда́рт; **raise the ~ of revolt** подн|има́ть, -я́ть зна́мя восста́ния. **2.** (*norm, model*) станда́рт, но́рма, образе́ц, этало́н; **come up to ~** соотве́тствовать (*impf.*) тре́буемому у́ровню; **set a high/low ~** устан|а́вливать, -ови́ть высо́кие/ни́зкие тре́бования; **~ of education** у́ровень (*m.*) образова́ния; **~ of living** жи́зненный у́ровень; **his work falls short of accepted ~s** его́ рабо́та не соотве́тствует существу́ющим тре́бованиям; **by American ~s** по америка́нским крите́риям; **by any ~** по любы́м но́рмам; **work of a high ~** рабо́та высо́кого ка́чества/у́ровня; **below ~** ни́же но́рмы; **there is no absolute ~ of morality** не существу́ет абсолю́тной но́рмы мора́ли; **gold ~** золото́й станда́рт; **~ of comparison** этало́н, мери́ло. **3.** (*shaft, pole*) коло́нна, сто́йка, подста́вка. **4.** (*in school*) класс в нача́льной шко́ле.

adj. **1.** станда́ртный, норма́льный; **of ~ size** станда́ртного разме́ра. **2.** (*model, basic*) нормати́вный, образцо́вый; (*general*) типово́й; **~ English** литерату́рный/нормати́вный англи́йский язы́к; **~ authors** (писа́тели-)кла́ссики; **a ~ reference work** авторите́тный спра́вочник; **~ gauge** норма́льная ширина́ колеи́. **3.**: **~ lamp** стоя́чая ла́мпа, торше́р.

cpd. **~-bearer** *n.* знамено́сец.

standardization [ˌstændədaɪˈzeɪʃ(ə)n] *n.* стандартиза́ция, нормализа́ция.

standardize [ˈstændəˌdaɪz] *v.t.* стандартизи́ровать (*impf., pf.*); норми́ровать (*impf., pf.*).

standee [stænˈdiː] *n.* стоя́щий пассажи́р; зри́тель (*m.*) на стоя́чих места́х.

standing [ˈstændɪŋ] *n.* **1.** (*rank, reputation*) положе́ние, репута́ция; вес; **a person of high ~** челове́к с положе́нием/и́менем; высокопоста́вленное лицо́. **2.** (*duration*) продолжи́тельность; **a custom of long ~** стари́нный обы́чай. **3.** (*length of service*) стаж.

adj.: **~ army** постоя́нная а́рмия; **~ committee** постоя́нный комите́т; **~ corn** хлеб на корню́; **~ invitation** приглаше́ние приходи́ть в любо́е вре́мя; **~ joke** дежу́рная шу́тка; **~ jump** прыжо́к с ме́ста; **~ order** (*to banker*) прика́з о регуля́рных платежа́х; (*to newsagent etc.*) постоя́нный зака́з; **~ orders** пра́вила процеду́ры; **~ type** нерассы́панный/сохранённый набо́р; **~ water** стоя́чая вода́.

stannic [ˈstænɪk] *adj.*: **~ acid** оловя́нная кислота́.

stanza [ˈstænzə] *n.* строфа́; станс.

staple[1] [ˈsteɪp(ə)l] *n.* (*metal bar or wire*) скоба́, ушко́, пе́тля; (*for papers*) скре́пка; (*on door*) скоба́, пробо́й.

v.t.: **~ papers together** скреп|ля́ть, -и́ть бума́ги скре́пкой.

staple[2] [ˈsteɪp(ə)l] *n.* **1.** (*principal commodity*) основно́й това́р/проду́кт; **the ~s of that country** основна́я проду́кция э́той страны́; **~s of British industry** основны́е ви́ды проду́кции брита́нской промы́шленности. **2.** (*chief material*) осно́ва; **~ of diet** осно́ва пита́ния; **~ of conversation** гла́вная те́ма разгово́ра. **3.** (*raw material*) сырьё. **4.** (*of cotton, wool*) волокно́, шта́пель (*m.*); шта́пельное волокно́.

adj. основно́й, гла́вный.

v.t. (*wool etc.*) сортирова́ть (*impf.*); штапелирова́ть (*impf.*).

stapler [ˈsteɪplə(r)] *n.* (*for paper*) сшива́тель (*m.*), ста́плер.

star [stɑː(r)] *n.* **1.** звезда́; **fixed ~** неподви́жная звезда́; **falling, shooting ~** па́дающая звезда́; **North, Pole S~** Поля́рная звезда́; **S~ of David** звезда́ Дави́да; **we slept under the ~s** мы спа́ли под откры́тым не́бом; **he was born under a lucky ~** он роди́лся под счастли́вой звездо́й; **his ~ was in the ascendant** он преуспева́л; **thank one's lucky ~s** благодари́ть (*impf.*) судьбу́ (*or* свою́ звезду́). **2.** (*famous actor etc.*) звезда́, свети́ло; **film ~** кинозвезда́; **the ~ of the show** звезда́ спекта́кля; **~ turn** гвоздь програ́ммы; **~ pupil** звезда́ кла́сса. **3.** (*~-shaped object, e.g. decoration*) звезда́; (*asterisk*) звёздочка. **4.** (*fig.*): **I saw ~s** у меня́ и́скры из глаз посы́пались. **5.**: **the S~s and Stripes** госуда́рственный флаг США.

v.t. **1.** (*adorn with ~s*) укр|аша́ть, -а́сить звёздами; **~red with jewels** уве́шанный драгоце́нными камня́ми. **2.** (*mark with asterisk*) отм|еча́ть, -е́тить звёздочкой.

v.i.: **~ in a film** игра́ть (*impf.*) гла́вную роль в фи́льме; выступа́ть (*impf.*) в гла́вной ро́ли фи́льма.

cpds. **~fish** *n.* морска́я звезда́; **~light** *n.* свет звёзд; **by ~light** при све́те звёзд; **a ~light night** звёздная ночь; **~lit** *adj.* освещённый све́том звёзд; **~-spangled** *adj.* усе́янный звёздами; **the S~-spangled Banner** Звёздное зна́мя.

starboard [ˈstɑːbəd] *n.* пра́вый борт.

adj. пра́вый; **~ side** пра́вый борт, пра́вая сторона́; **~**

wind ветер с правого борта.

v.t.: ~ **the helm** положить (*pf.*) право руля.

starch [stɑːtʃ] *n.* крахмал; (*fig.*, *stiffness*, *formality*) чопорность, церемонность.

v.t. крахмалить, на-.

starchiness ['stɑːtʃɪnɪs] *n.* мучнистость; (*fig.*) чопорность, церемонность.

starchy ['stɑːtʃɪ] *adj.* (*containing starch*) мучнистый, крахмалистый; (*stiffened*) накрахмаленный; (*fig.*) чопорный, церемонный.

stardom ['stɑːdəm] *n.*: **rise to** ~ сделаться/стать (*pf.*) звездой; занять (*pf.*) ведущее положение.

stare [steə(r)] *n.* пристальный взгляд; **set** ~ застывший взгляд; **vacant** ~ пустой (*or* ничего не выражающий) взгляд; **give s.o. a** ~ уставиться (*pf.*) на кого-н.; **with a** ~ **of amazement** широко открыв глаза от изумления; **a** ~ **of horror** взгляд, полный ужаса.

v.t.: ~ **s.o. in the face** смотреть, по- на кого-н. в упор; ~ **s.o. out of countenance** смутить (*pf.*) кого-н. пристальным взглядом; пристально смотреть/глядеть (*impf.*) на кого-н.; **ruin** ~**s him in the face** он находится на краю гибели; ему грозит неминуемое разорение; **the letter was staring me in the face** письмо лежало у меня под носом; ~ **s.o. up and down** смерить (*pf.*) кого-н. взглядом; ~ **s.o. into silence** одним взглядом заставить (*pf.*) кого-н. замолчать.

v.i. глазеть (*impf.*); широко раскрыть (*pf.*) глаза; таращить, вы- (*or* пялить (*impf.*)) глаза; ~ **at s.o.** пристально смотреть/глядеть (*impf.*) на кого-н.; ~ **into s.o.'s face** уставиться (*or* пялить (*impf.*) глаза) на кого-н.; **he** ~**d rudely at me** он вызывающе/дерзко/нагло уставился на меня; **don't** ~**!** не таращь глаза!; **I** ~**d at him in astonishment** я вытаращил на него глаза от изумления; ~ **into space** устрем|лять, -ить взор в пространство; смотреть (*impf.*) невидящим взглядом.

staring ['steərɪŋ] *adj.* (*of eyes*) пристальный; широко раскрытый; (*of colours*) кричащий, вызывающий.

stark [stɑːk] *adj.* **1.** (*stiff*, *rigid*) застывший, окоченевший. **2.** (*desolate*, *bare*) голый, бесплодный, пустынный; **a** ~ **winter landscape** суровый зимний пейзаж. **3.** (*sharply evident*) явный; **in** ~ **contrast** в вопиющем противоречии. **4.** (*sheer*) полный, абсолютный.

adv. совершенно; ~ **staring mad** абсолютно сумасшедший; ~ **naked** совершенно голый; в чём мать родила.

starless ['stɑːlɪs] *adj.* беззвёздный.

starlet ['stɑːlɪt] *n.* молодая киноактриса.

starling ['stɑːlɪŋ] *n.* скворец.

starry ['stɑːrɪ] *adj.* **1.**: ~ **night** звёздная ночь; ~ **sky** покрытое/усеянное звёздами небо. **2.**: ~ **eyes** лучистые глаза.

cpd. ~**-eyed** *adj.* (*fig.*) романтичный, увлекающийся; видящий всё в розовом свете.

START [stɑːt] *n.* (*abbr. of* ***Strategic Arms Reduction Talks***) переговоры о сокращении стратегических вооружений.

start [stɑːt] *n.* **1.** (*sudden movement*) вздрагивание, содрогание; **give a** ~ **of joy/surprise** вздрогнуть (*pf.*) от радости/удивления; **give s.o. a** ~ испугать (*pf.*) кого-н.; **he woke with a** ~ он вздрогнул и проснулся; **he works by fits and** ~**s** он работает урывками/неравномерно. **2.** (*beginning*) начало; (*of journey*) отправление; (*of engine etc.*) пуск, запуск; (*aeron.*) взлёт; (*of race*) старт; **make a** ~ **on sth.** нач|инать, -ать что-н.; положить (*pf.*) начало чему-н.; **we made an early** ~ мы рано выступили в путь; **make a fresh** ~ нач|инать, -ать сызнова; **he made a fresh** ~ **(in life)** он начал новую жизнь; **at the (very)** ~ в (самом) начале; **for a** ~ для начала; **from** ~ **to finish** с начала до конца; **false** ~ (*sport*) фальстарт; **we made a false** ~ мы ошиблись в самом начале; **get off to a good** ~ удачно начать (*pf.*). **3.** (*advantage in race etc.*): **he was given 10 yards'** ~ ему дали фору в 10 ярдов; **get the** ~ **of s.o.** опере|жать, -дить кого-н.

v.t. **1.** (*begin*) нач|инать, -ать; **he** ~**s work early** он рано начинает работать; **it is** ~**ing to rain** начинается дождь; **when does she** ~ **school?** когда она пойдёт в школу?; **we** ~**ed our journey** мы пустились в путь; **he** ~**ed life as a watchman** он начал свою трудовую жизнь сторожем (*or* со сторожа); **she** ~**ed crying** она расплакалась; *with many vv., the pf. formed with* за- *means 'to start …ing'*. **2.** (*set in motion*): ~ **a clock** зав|одить, -ести часы; ~ **an engine** запус|кать, -тить (*or* зав|одить, -ести) мотор; ~**ing handle** пусковая/заводная рукоятка. **3.** (*in race*): ~ **the runners** да|вать, -ть старт бегунам. **4.** (*assist in* ~*ing*): ~ **s.o. in life** пом|огать, -очь кому-н. встать на ноги. **5.** (*rouse*): ~ **game** подн|имать, -ять дичь; ~ **a hare** (*fig.*) увлечь (*pf.*) разговор в сторону. **6.** (*initiate*): ~ **a business** осно́в|ывать, -ать предприятие; **he** ~**ed business in a small way** он завёл небольшое дело; ~ **a school** откр|ывать, -ыть школу; ~ **a conversation** нач|инать, -ать (*or* зат|евать, -еять) разговор; ~ **a fire** (*arson*) устроить (*pf.*) пожар; (*for warmth etc.*) развести (*pf.*) костёр/огонь; **what** ~**ed the fire?** из-за чего начался пожар?; ~ **a fund** осно́в|ывать, -ать фонд; ~ **a movement** положить (*pf.*) начало (какому-н.) движению; ~ **a rumour** (рас)пус|кать, -тить слух; **now you've** ~**ed something!** ну, вот, ты заварил кашу!; **do you want to** ~ **something?** (*i.e. fight*) ты нарываешься на драку? **7.** (*broach*): ~ **a bottle of wine** поч|инать, -ать бутылку вина; ~ **a subject (of conversation)** завести (*pf.*) разговор о чём-н.; **we** ~**ed French** мы начали заниматься французским. **8.** (*cause to begin*): **the wine** ~**ed him talking** вино развязало ему язык; **my remark** ~**ed him talking about the war** моё замечание заставило его заговориться о войне; **this** ~**ed me thinking** это заставило меня задуматься; **the smoke** ~**ed me coughing** от дыма я закашлялся. **9.** (*warp*) коробить, по-; **the damp** ~**ed the timbers** балки покоробились от сырости.

v.i. **1.** (*make sudden movement*) вздр|агивать, -огнуть; содрог|аться, -нуться; ~ **back** отпрянуть (*pf.*); ~ **from one's sleep** вздрогнуть и проснуться (*pf.*); ~ **from one's chair (***or* **to one's feet)** вскочить (*pf.*) со стула (*or* на ноги); **tears** ~**ed from his eyes** у него слёзы брызнули из глаз; (*of timber*) коробиться, по-; ~ **at the seams** ра|сходиться, -зойтись по швам. **2.** (*begin*) нач|инаться, -аться; (*come into being*, *arise*) появ|ляться, -иться; возн|икать, -икнуть; **it** ~**ed raining** пошёл/начался дождь; **we had to** ~ **again from scratch** пришлось начать всё сначала; **he** ~**ed as a locksmith at £5 a week** он начал свою трудовую деятельность слесарем с жалованием в пять фунтов в неделю; **there were 12 of us to** ~ **with** сначала/сперва нас было 12 человек; **to** ~ **with, you should write to him** прежде всего (*or* во-первых,) вы должны написать ему; **what will you have (***eat***) to** ~ **with?** что вы возьмёте на закуску?; что вы сначала будете есть?; **prices** ~ **at £10** цены от десяти фунтов и выше; ~**ing price** (*at auction*) отправная цена. **3.** (*set out*) отпр|авляться, -авиться; **when do you** ~ **for the office?** во сколько вы уходите на работу?; **he** ~**ed back the next day** на следующий день он пустился в обратный путь; ~**ing point** (*of journey*) отправной пункт; (*of race*) старт; (*fig.*) отправная/исходная точка. **4.** (*in race*) стартовать (*impf.*, *pf.*); ~**ing-gate** барьер на старте; ~**ing-pistol** стартовый пистолет; ~**ing-post** стартовый столб. **5.** (*of engine etc.*): **the car** ~**ed without any trouble** машина завелась без труда; **you should always** ~ **in first gear** стартовать всегда следует на первой скорости.

with advs.: ~ **in** *v.i.*: ~ **in on sth.** (*coll.*) браться, взяться (*or* прин|иматься, -яться) за что-н.; ~ **in on** (*coll.*, *scold*) **s.o.** выбранить (*pf.*) кого-н.; ~ **off** *v.t.*: **he** ~**ed the class off on Virgil** он познакомил учеников с Вергилием; **what** ~**ed him off on that craze?** откуда у него (появилось) это увлечение?; почему он начал этим увлекаться?; **don't** ~ **him off, or he'll never stop** не заводите его, а то он никогда не остановится; *v.i.* (*leave*) пойти, поехать (*both pf.*); **he** ~**ed off with a general introduction** он начал с общего вступления; **she** ~**ed off by apologizing for being late** она начала с извинений за своё опоздание; **he** ~**ed off on the wrong foot** (*coll.*) он неудачно начал; он с самого начала был неправ; **he** ~**ed off in second gear** он стартовал на второй скорости; ~ **out** *v.i.* (*leave*) отпр|авля́ться, -а́виться; пойти́, пое́хать (*both pf.*); (*intend*) соб|ира́ться, -ра́ться; **he ~ed out to reform society** он собира́лся измени́ть о́бщество; **~ up** *v.t.*: **~ up an engine** запус|ка́ть, -ти́ть (*or* зав|оди́ть, -ести́) мото́р; **~ up a conversation** зате́ять/завести́ (*pf.*) разгово́р; **~ up a business** основа́ть/учреди́ть (*pf.*) предприя́тие/де́ло; *v.i.* (*spring to one's feet*) вск|а́кивать, -очи́ть; **he ~ed up at the suggestion** он так и подскочи́л, услы́шав тако́е предложе́ние; (*come into being*) появ|ля́ться, -и́ться; возн|ика́ть, -и́кнуть; **a new firm is ~ing up in the town** в го́роде открыва́ется но́вая фи́рма.

starter ['stɑ:tə(r)] *n.* **1.** (*giving signal for race*) (судья́-)ста́ртер. **2.** (*competitor*) старту́ющий; уча́стник состяза́ния; (*horse*) уча́стник забе́га. **3.** (*device for starting engine etc.*) ста́ртер, пуска́тель (*m.*); пусково́й прибо́р. **4.** (*pl., coll., first course*) заку́ска.

startle ['stɑ:t(ə)l] *v.t.* (*alarm*) трево́жить, вс-; (*scare*) вспу́г|ивать, -ну́ть; (*cause to start*): **~ s.o. out of his sleep** ре́зко разбуди́ть (*pf.*) кого́-н.; **I was ~d when you shouted** я так и вздро́гнул, когда́ вы закрича́ли; **you ~d me** вы меня́ испуга́ли; **the news ~d him out of his apathy** но́вость вы́вела его́ из апа́тии.

startling ['stɑ:tlɪŋ] *adj.* порази́тельный; (*staggering*) потряса́ющий; (*alarming*) пуга́ющий; **nothing ~** ничего́ осо́бенного/выдаю́щегося.

starvation [stɑ:'veɪʃ(ə)n] *n.* го́лод, голода́ние; **death by ~** голо́дная смерть; **die of ~** ум|ира́ть, -ере́ть от го́лода (*or* с го́лоду); **~ diet** голо́дная дие́та; **~ wage** ни́щенский за́работок; ни́щенское жа́лование.

starv|e [stɑ:v] *v.t.* мори́ть, у-/за- (го́лодом); лиш|а́ть, -и́ть пи́щи; **~e s.o. out (*or* into submission)** взять (*pf.*) кого́-н. измо́ром; (*fig.*): **the child was ~ed of affection** ребёнок страда́л от отсу́тствия любви́.

v.i. **1.** (*go hungry*) голода́ть (*impf.*); **a ~ing child** голода́ющий ребёнок; **I'm ~ing** я ужа́сно проголода́лся!; я го́лоден как волк!; **~e to death** ум|ира́ть, -ере́ть с го́лоду. **2.** (*fig.*): **his mind is ~ing for knowledge** его́ ум жа́ждет зна́ний.

stash [stæʃ] *v.t.* (*coll.*): **he has £1,000 ~ed away** у него́ припря́тана ты́сяча фу́нтов.

state[1] [steɪt] *n.* **1.** (*condition*) состоя́ние, положе́ние; **in a poor ~ of health** в плохо́м состоя́нии здоро́вья; **~ of affairs** положе́ние дел; **people of every ~ of life** лю́ди ра́зного зва́ния; **~ of mind** настрое́ние; душе́вное состоя́ние; **in an untidy ~** в беспоря́дке; **what a (dirty) ~ you're in!** на кого́ вы похо́жи!; **he was in quite a ~** он был в ужа́сном возбужде́нии (*excitement*)/волне́нии (*anxiety*); **the country is in a ~ of war** страна́ находи́ться в состоя́нии войны́; **what is the ~ of play?** како́й счёт?; (*fig.*) как обстоя́т дела́? **2.** (*country, community, government*) госуда́рство; **affairs, matters of ~** госуда́рственные дела́; **police ~** полице́йское госуда́рство; **United S~s** Соединённые Шта́ты (Аме́рики) (*abbr.* США); **S~ Department** (*US*) госуда́рственный департа́мент, миинсте́рство иностра́нных дел; **S~s General** Генера́льные шта́ты; **~ control** госуда́рственный контро́ль; **~ trial** суд над госуда́рственным престу́пником. **3.** (*rank, dignity*) положе́ние; (*pomp*) великоле́пие, ро́скошь; **live in ~** жить (*impf.*) в ро́скоши; **lie in ~** быть вы́ставленным для торже́ственного проща́ния; **the Queen drove in ~ through London** короле́ва торже́ственно прое́хала по Ло́ндону; **~ coach** пара́дная каре́та; **~ apartments** пара́дные поко́и (*m. pl.*); **~ visit** госуда́рственный визи́т; **~ ball** торже́ственный бал.

cpds. **~-aided** *adj.* получа́ющий дота́цию/субси́дию/ посо́бие от госуда́рства; **~craft** *n.* = **statesmanship; state-of-the-art** *adj.* совреме́нный, нове́йший; **~room** *n.* (*on ship*) каю́та; **S~side** *adj. & adv.* (*US coll.*) (находя́щийся) в США; **~sman** *and cpds., see separate entries.*

state[2] [steɪt] *v.t.* (*declare; say clearly*) заяв|ля́ть, -и́ть; сказа́ть (*pf.*); утвержда́ть (*impf.*); сообщ|а́ть, -и́ть о+*p.*; **he ~d his intentions** он заяви́л о свои́х наме́рениях; **I have seen it ~d that ...** я чита́л, что/бу́дто...; (*indicate*) ука́з|ывать, -а́ть; наз|ыва́ть, -ва́ть; **as ~d above** как ука́зано вы́ше; (*specify*): **at the ~d time** в озна́ченное вре́мя; **at ~d intervals** че́рез устано́вленные промежу́тки; (*announce*) объяв|ля́ть, -и́ть; (*expound*) изл|ага́ть, -ожи́ть; разъясн|я́ть, -и́ть; **the plaintiff ~d his case** исте́ц изложи́л своё де́ло.

statehood ['steɪthʊd] *n.* ста́тус госуда́рства; госуда́рственность.

stateless ['steɪtlɪs] *adj.* не име́ющий гражда́нства; **~ person** апатри́д (*fem.* -ка).

stateliness ['steɪtlɪnɪs] *n.* вели́чественность, велича́вость.

stately ['steɪtlɪ] *adj.* вели́чественный, велича́вый.

statement ['steɪtmənt] *n.* (*declaration*) заявле́ние; **make, publish a ~** сде́лать/опубликова́ть (*pf.*) заявле́ние; (*exposition*) изложе́ние; (*utterance*) выска́зывание; (*communication*) сообще́ние; (*fin.*) отчёт, бала́нс; **~ of account** вы́писка счёта; **~ of expenses** отчёт о расхо́дах.

statesman ['steɪtsmən] *n.* госуда́рственный де́ятель.

statesmanlike ['steɪtsmənlaɪk] *adj.* досто́йный госуда́рственного де́ятеля.

state|smanship ['steɪtsmənʃɪp], **-craft** ['steɪtkrɑ:ft] *nn.* иску́сство управле́ния госуда́рством; госуда́рственная му́дрость.

static ['stætɪk] *n.* **1.** (*~ electricity*) стати́ческое электри́чество. **2.** (*as radio interference: also* **~s**) (атмосфе́рные) поме́хи (*f. pl.*).

adj. **1.** (*stationary*) неподви́жный, стациона́рный; **~ water tank** стациона́рный во́дный резервуа́р. **2.** (*opp. dynamic*) стати́ческий, стати́чный.

statics ['stætɪks] *n.* **1.** ста́тика. **2.** = **static** *n.* **2.**

station ['steɪʃ(ə)n] *n.* **1.** (*assigned place*) пост, ме́сто, пози́ция; **take up one's ~** зан|има́ть, -я́ть пост/пози́цию. **2.** (*establishment, base, headquarters*) ста́нция; **broadcasting ~** радиоста́нция; **bus ~** авто́бусная ста́нция; **coastguard ~** пост берегово́й оборо́ны; **filling ~** запра́вочный пункт, бензоколо́нка; **fire ~** пожа́рное депо́ (*indecl.*); **lifeboat ~** спаса́тельная ста́нция; **naval ~** вое́нно-морска́я ба́за; **police ~** полице́йский уча́сток; (*in former USSR*) отделе́ние мили́ции; **power ~** электроста́нция. **3.** (*rail.*) ста́нция; (*large, mainline ~*) вокза́л; **goods ~** това́рная ста́нция; (*attr.*) станцио́нный. **4.** (*position in life, rank*) положе́ние; зва́ние; **he married beneath his ~** он соверши́л мезалья́нс; **a man of humble ~** челове́к ни́зкого зва́ния; **the duties of his ~** обя́занности, свя́занные с его́ положе́нием. **5.** (*surv.*) геодези́ческий пункт. **6.** (*eccl.*): **~s of the Cross** остано́вки Христа́ на кре́стном пути́; кальва́рии (*f. pl.*). **7.** (*Austr., sheep-farm*) овцево́дческая фе́рма.

v.t. распол|ага́ть, -ожи́ть; **she ~ed herself at a window** она́ расположи́лась у окна́; **~ a guard at the gate** выставля́ть, вы́ставить карау́л у воро́т; (*mil.*) разме|ща́ть, -сти́ть; дислоци́ровать (*impf., pf.*); **the regiment is ~ed in the south** полк стои́т на ю́ге; **~ing** (*disposition*) **of troops** дислока́ция войск; **~ troops** дислока́ция войск.

cpds. **~-keeping** *n.* (*naut.*) сохране́ние ме́ста в строю́; **~-master** *n.* нача́льник ста́нции; **~-wagon** *n.* автомоби́ль-фурго́н; пика́п.

stationary ['steɪʃənərɪ] *adj.* **1.** (*not moving; at rest*) неподви́жный, стоя́щий неподви́жно. **2.** (*fixed*) закреплённый, стациона́рный; **~ engine** стациона́рный дви́гатель; **~ troops** ме́стные войска́. **3.** (*unchanging, constant*) постоя́нный, неизме́нный; **prices are now ~** це́ны стабилизова́лись; **the population remained ~** чи́сленность населе́ния оста́лась неизме́нной.

stationer ['steɪʃənə(r)] *n.* торго́вец писчебума́жными/ канцеля́рскими принадле́жностями.

stationery ['steɪʃənərɪ] *n.* писчебума́жные/канцеля́рские принадле́жности (*f. pl.*); **S~ Office** прави́тельственное изда́тельство (*в Лондоне*).

statistical [stə'tɪstɪk(ə)l] *adj.* статисти́ческий.

statistician [,stætɪ'stɪʃ(ə)n] *n.* стати́стик.

statistics [stə'tɪstɪks] *n.* статисти́ческие да́нные; (*science*) стати́стика.

statuary ['stætjʊərɪ] *n.* скульпту́ра.

adj. скульпту́рный; ~ **art** вая́ние, скульпту́ра; ~ **marble** мра́мор, приго́дный для скульпту́ры.

statue ['stætju:, 'stætʃu:] *n.* ста́туя, извая́ние; **put up a ~ to s.o.** воздви́гнуть (*pf.*) ста́тую в честь кого́-н.

statuesque [ˌstætjʊ'esk, ˌstætʃʊ'esk] *adj.* велича́вый, вели́чественный.

statuette [ˌstætjʊ'et, ˌstætʃʊ'et] *n.* статуэ́тка.

stature ['stætʃə(r)] *n.* **1.** (*height*) рост; **of low (*or* short of) ~** ни́зкого ро́ста. **2.** (*fig.*) масшта́б, кали́бр; **a man of ~** челове́к кру́пного кали́бра.

status ['steɪtəs] *n.* **1.** (*position, rank*) положе́ние, ста́тус, прести́ж; **official ~** официа́льное положе́ние; **civil ~** гражда́нское состоя́ние; (*professional reputation*) репута́ция; (*superior position*): **the possession of land confers ~** облада́ние земе́льной со́бственностью придаёт челове́ку вес в о́бществе; **~ symbol** показа́тель положе́ния в о́бществе. **2. ~ quo** ста́тус-кво́ (*indecl.*).

statute ['stætju:t] *n.* стату́т; (*law*) зако́н; (*legislative document*) законода́тельный акт; (*regulations, ordinance*) уста́в; **~ (*or* statutory) law** стату́тное пра́во; пи́саный зако́н; **~ of limitations** зако́н о да́вностных сро́ках; **University ~s** уста́в университе́та.

cpd. **~-book** *n.* свод зако́нов.

statutory ['statjʊtərɪ] *adj.* устано́вленный зако́ном; **~ company** компа́ния, учреждённая специа́льным зако́ном; **~ law** *see under* **statute; ~ minimum** определённый зако́ном ми́нимум; **~ offence** дея́ние, кара́емое по зако́ну.

staunch[1] [stɔ:ntʃ, stɑ:ntʃ] *adj.* (*faithful, trusty*) ве́рный; (*loyal*) лоя́льный; (*reliable*) надёжный; (*devoted*): **a ~ socialist** непреклóнный/убеждённый социали́ст.

sta(u)nch[2] [stɔ:ntʃ, stɑ:ntʃ] *v.t.* = **stanch**

staunchness ['stɔ:ntʃnɪs, 'stɑ:ntʃnɪs] *n.* ве́рность, лоя́льность, надёжность, пре́данность.

stave [steɪv] *n.* (*of cask*) клёпка, боча́рная доска́; (*rung of ladder*) перекла́дина; (*stanza*) строфа́; (*mus.*) но́тный стан.

v.t. **1.** (*also* **~ in:** *break in*): **~ in a cask** проб|ива́ть, -и́ть бо́чку; **~ in the side of a boat** прол|а́мывать, -оми́ть борт ло́дки; **~ in a door** проб|ива́ть, -и́ть дыру́ в две́ри. **2.: ~ off** предотвра|ща́ть, -ти́ть.

stay[1] [steɪ] *n.* **1.** (*sojourn*) пребыва́ние; **I am making a short ~ in London** я задержу́сь ненадо́лго в Ло́ндоне; **a ~ of 2 weeks** двухнеде́льное пребыва́ние; **I enjoyed my ~ with you** я прекра́сно провёл вре́мя у вас (*or* у вас погости́л). **2.** (*restraint*): **a ~ upon his activity** вре́менное ограниче́ние его́ де́ятельности. **3.** (*suspension*) отсро́чка; **~ of execution** отсро́чка исполне́ния.

v.t. **1.** (*check*) остан|а́вливать, -ови́ть; препя́тствовать, вос- *+d.*; **~ one's hunger** утоли́ть (*pf.*) го́лод; (*coll.*) замори́ть (*pf.*) червячка́; (*restrain*) сде́рж|ивать, -а́ть; **~ one's hand** возде́рж|иваться, -а́ться от де́йствий; (*delay*) от|кла́дывать, -ложи́ть; отсро́чи|вать, -ть; **~ court proceedings** приостанови́ть (*pf.*) слу́шание де́ла. **2.** (*last out*): **~ the course** выде́рживать, вы́держать до конца́.

v.i. **1.** (*stop, put up*) остан|а́вливаться, -ови́ться; (*as guest*) гости́ть (*impf.*); **which hotel will you ~ at?** в како́й гости́нице вы остано́витесь?; **we are** (*sc. at present*) **~ing with friends** мы останови́лись/гости́м у друзе́й; **we ~ed in Vienna for 3 weeks** мы про́бы́ли в Ве́не три неде́ли. **2.** (*remain*) ост|ава́ться, -а́ться; не уходи́ть (*impf.*); **~ here while I find out** побу́дьте/жди́те здесь, пока́ я разузна́ю; **I ~ed awake all night** я всю ночь не спал; **~ at home** сиде́ть (*impf.*) до́ма; **~ in bed** не встава́ть (*impf.*) (с посте́ли); **~ in the background** держа́ться (*impf.*) в тени́; **they don't like ~ing at home** им не сиди́тся до́ма; **the children ~ed away from school** де́ти прогуля́ли шко́лу; **I ~ed away from work** я не пошёл на рабо́ту; **he made them ~ behind after school** он задержа́л их в шко́ле по́сле уро́ков; **my hair won't ~ down** у меня́ во́лосы ника́к не ложа́тся; **the food would not ~ down** (его́) желу́док не принима́л пи́щи; **can you ~ for, to tea?** вы мо́жете оста́ться к ча́ю?; **he ~ed for the night** он оста́лся ночева́ть; **I am ~ing in today** сего́дня я не выхожу́ (*or* я сижу́ до́ма); **my (hair) set doesn't ~ in for two days** моя́ приче́ска не де́ржится и двух дней; **I hope the rain will ~ off** наде́юсь, что дождь не начнётся; **if you want to lose weight, ~ off starchy foods** е́сли хоти́те похуде́ть, возде́рживайтесь от мучно́го; **he ~ed on at the university** он оста́лся при университе́те; **my hat won't ~ on** у меня́ шля́па не де́ржится (на голове́); **she is allowed to ~ out till midnight** ей разреша́ют возвраща́ться домо́й в 12 часо́в но́чи; **the men are threatening to ~ out** (*on strike*) рабо́чие угрожа́ют продолже́нием забасто́вки; **he ~ed to dinner** он оста́лся обе́дать; **if we ~ together we shan't get lost** е́сли мы бу́дем держа́ться вме́сте, не заблу́димся; **~ up late** не ложи́ться (*impf.*) (спать) допоздна́; **I need a belt to make my trousers ~ up** мне ну́жен по́яс, что́бы не спада́ли брю́ки; **fine weather has come to ~** про́чно установи́лась хоро́шая пого́да; **nothing ~s clean for long** всё в конце́ концо́в па́чкается; **these flowers won't ~ put** э́ти цветы́ (в ва́зе) не стоя́т (*or* па́дают); **~ put!** (*coll.*) ни с ме́ста! **3.** (*endure in race etc.*): **he has no ~ing-power** у него́ нет никако́й выно́сливости.

cpd. **~-at-home** *n.* домосе́д (*fem.* -ка).

stay[2] [steɪ] *n.* **1.** (*naut.*) штаг. **2.** (*prop, support*) опо́ра, сто́йка, подпо́рка, подко́с; (*moral support*) опо́ра, подде́ржка; **the ~ of her old age** её опо́ра в ста́рости. **3.** (*pl., corset*) корсе́т.

v.t. (*prop up*) подп|ира́ть, -ере́ть.

stayer ['steɪə(r)] *n.* выно́сливый челове́к; выно́сливая ло́шадь *и т.п.*

STD (*abbr. of* ***subscriber trunk dialling***) автомати́ческая междугоро́дная телефо́нная связь.

stead [sted] *n.* (*liter.*): **stand s.o. in good ~** сослужи́ть (*pf.*) кому́-н. хоро́шую слу́жбу; **in s.o.'s ~** вме́сто кого́-н.

steadfast ['stedfɑ:st, 'stedfəst] *adj.* (*firm, stable*): **~ in danger** сто́йкий в опа́сности; **~ policy** твёрдая поли́тика; (*faithful*): **~ in love** ве́рный в любви́; (*reliable*) надёжный; (*unwavering*) непоколеби́мый; **~ of purpose** целеустремлённый.

steadfastness ['stedfɑ:stnɪs, 'stedfəstnɪs] *n.* сто́йкость, твёрдость; ве́рность; непоколеби́мость; надёжность; целеустремлённость.

steadiness ['stedɪnɪs] *n.* (*sureness*) уве́ренность; (*resolution*) реши́тельность, непоколеби́мость; (*of gaze*) твёрдость (взгля́да); (*regularity*) равноме́рность; (*stability*) усто́йчивость.

steady ['stedɪ] *adj.* **1.** (*firmly fixed, balanced, supported*) про́чный, усто́йчивый, твёрдый; **he made the table ~** он попра́вил стол, что́бы он не кача́лся; **keep the camera ~!** не дви́гайте аппара́т!; **the ladder must be held ~** на́до кре́пко держа́ть ле́стницу; **he has a ~ hand** у него́ твёрдая рука́; **sailors must be ~ on their legs** матро́сы должны́ твёрдо держа́ться на нога́х; (*unfaltering*): **~ in one's principles** непреклóнный в свои́х при́нципах; **a ~ faith** непоколеби́мая ве́ра; **a ~ gaze** при́стальный взгляд. **2.** (*uniform*) равноме́рный; (*even*) ро́вный; (*constant*) постоя́нный; (*uninterrupted*) непреры́вный; **at a ~ pace** ро́вным ша́гом; **a ~ breeze** усто́йчивый ве́тер; **he works steadily** он упо́рно рабо́тает; **~ demand** постоя́нный спрос; **his health shows a ~ improvement** его́ здоро́вье стано́вится всё лу́чше; **the barometer is ~** баро́метр установи́лся; **a ~ flow of water** непреры́вный пото́к воды́. **3.** (*of pers., staid, sober*) степе́нный, уравнове́шенный. **4.** (*in exhortations*): **~!** осторо́жно!; **~ on!** ле́гче на поворо́тах!; (*naut.*): **~ as she goes!** так держа́ть!

adv.: **go ~ with s.o.** (*coll.*) гуля́ть/дружи́ть (*impf.*) с кем-н.

v.t. **1.** (*strengthen, secure*) укрепл|я́ть, -и́ть; закрепл|я́ть, -и́ть; **the doctor gave him sth. to ~ his nerves** до́ктор дал ему́ лека́рство для успокое́ния не́рвов. **2.: ~ a boat** прив|оди́ть, -ести́ ло́дку в равнове́сие. **3.** (*sober, settle*) остепен|я́ть, -и́ть; **marriage steadied him** жени́тьба остепени́ла его́.

v.i. **1.** (*regain equilibrium*) выра́вниваться, вы́ровняться. **2.** (*become fixed, firm*): **prices are ~ing** це́ны выра́вниваются; **the market is ~ing** це́ны на ры́нке стано́вятся усто́йчивыми. **3.** (*of pers.: settle down*) остепен|я́ться, -и́ться.

steak [steɪk] *n.* (*of beef*) бифштéкс (натурáльный); **fillet ~** вы́резка.

cpd. **~-house** *n.* бифштéксная; ресторáн, специализи́рующийся на бифштéксах.

steal [sti:l] *v.t.* **1.** ворова́ть, с-; красть, у-; **it is wrong to ~** ворова́ть нехорошó; **I had my handbag stolen** у меня́ укрáли сýмку. **2.** (*fig.*): **~ a glance at s.o.** взглянýть (*pf.*) укрáдкой на когó-н.; **~ s.o.'s heart (away)** похи́тить (*pf.*) чьё-н. сéрдце; **~ a march on** предупреди́ть/опереди́ть (*pf.*) (*кого в чём*); **~ the show** затми́ть (*pf.*) всех остальны́х; оказáться (*pf.*) в цéнтре внимáния; ≃ заткнýть (*pf.*) всех зá пояс; **~ s.o.'s thunder** перехвати́ть (*pf.*) чью-н. слáву; **receive stolen goods** скупáть (*impf.*) крáденый товáр.

v.i. **1.** (*thieve*) ворова́ть (*impf.*); **he accused me of ~ing** он обвини́л меня́ в воровствé; **he was caught ~ing** егó поймáли с поли́чным. **2.** (*move secretly or silently*) крáсться (*impf.*); **he stole round to the back door** он прокрáлся к зáдней двéри; **he stole up to her** он подкрáлся к ней; **the sun's rays stole across the lawn** сóлнечные лучи́ скользнýли по лужáйке; **light ~s through the chinks** свет пробивáется сквозь щéли; **a sense of peace stole over him** чýвство покóя овладéло им.

stealth [stelθ] *n.*: **by ~** тайкóм, укрáдкой, втихомóлку.

stealthy ['stelθɪ] *adj.*: **~ glance** взгляд укрáдкой; **~ tread** крáдущаяся похóдка; **~ whisper** приглушённый шёпот.

steam [sti:m] *n.* пар; **full ~ ahead!** пóлный вперёд!; **get up ~** (*lit.*) разв|оди́ть, -ести́ пáры́; (*fig.*) набрáться (*pf.*) сил; **let off ~** (*lit.*) выпускáть, вы́пустить пáры́; (*fig.*) дать (*pf.*) вы́ход чýвствам; **run out of ~** (*fig.*) выдыхáться, вы́дохнуться; **under one's own ~** (*fig.*) сам, свои́ми си́лами, самостоя́тельно; **~ iron** паровóй утю́г; **~ train** пóезд с паровóй тя́гой; **~ turbine** паровáя турби́на (*see also cpds.*).

v.t. **1.** (*cook with ~*) вари́ть, с- на парý; пáрить (*impf.*); **~ed fish** пáреная ры́ба; ры́ба на парý. **2.** (*treat with ~*): **~ a stamp off an envelope** отпáри|вать, -ть мáрку с конвéрта; **the envelope had been ~ed open** ктó-то отклéил конвéрт над пáром. **3.** (*cover with ~*): **the carriage windows were ~ed up** вагóнные óкна запотéли; **get ~ed up** завести́сь (*pf.*) (*coll.*).

v.i. **1.** (*give out ~ or vapour*) выделя́ть (*impf.*) пар/испарéния; пус|кáть, -ти́ть пар; **the kettle is ~ing on the stove** чáйник кипи́т на плитé; **a horse ~s after a hard gallop** пóсле бы́строй езды́ от лóшади вали́т пар; **he wiped his ~ing brow** он вы́тер вспотéвший лоб. **2.** (*move by ~*): **the boat ~ed into the harbour** корáбль вошёл в гáвань; **the train ~ed out** паровóз отошёл от стáнции. **3.: ~ up** запот|евáть, -éть.

cpds. **~-bath** *n.* паровáя бáня; **~boat** *n.* парохóд; **~boiler** *n.* паровóй котёл; **~-coal** *n.* парови́чный ýголь; **~-driven** *adj.* с паровы́м дви́гателем; **~-engine** *n.* паровáя маши́на; (*on road*) локомоби́ль (*m.*); **~-gauge** *n.* манóметр; **~-hammer** *n.* паровóй мóлот; **~-heat** *n.* отдавáемое пáром тепло́; теплотá конденсáции; **~jacket** *n.* паровáя рубáшка; **~-power** *n.* энéргия пáра; **~-roller** *n.* паровóй катóк; *v.t.* (*lit.*) уплотн|я́ть -и́ть; укáт|ывать, -áть; трамбовáть, -у; (*fig.*) сокруш|áть, -и́ть; **~-roller all opposition** подави́ть (*pf.*) вся́ческое сопротивлéние; **~ship** *n.* парохóд; **~-shovel** *n.* паровóй экскавáтор.

steamer ['sti:mə(r)] *n.* (*ship*) парохóд; (*for cooking*) паровáрка.

steamy ['sti:mɪ] *adj.* (*vaporous*) парообрáзный; (*saturated with steam*) насы́щенный парáми; (*of atmosphere*) (*coll.*) пáркий; (*covered with steam*) запотéлый, запотéвший.

stearin ['stɪərɪn] *n.* стеари́н.

steed [sti:d] *n.* (*poet.*) конь (*m.*).

steel [sti:l] *n.* **1.** сталь; (*attr.*) стальнóй; **~ engraving** гравю́ра на стáли; **~ foundry** сталелитéйный завóд/цех; **~ industry** сталелитéйная промы́шленность; **~ wool** ёж(ик); **cold ~** (*weapons*) холóдное орýжие; (*fig.*): **muscles/nerves of ~** стальны́е/желéзные мы́шцы/нéрвы; **a grip of ~** желéзная хвáтка. **2.** (*for sharpening knives*) точи́ло; (*for striking spark*) огни́во.

v.t. (*fig., harden*): **~ o.s.** (*or* **one's heart**) ожесточ|áться, -и́ться; ожесточ|áть, -и́ть сéрдце/дýшу (*против чего*); **his heart was ~ed against pity** егó сéрдцу жáлость былá чуждá.

cpds. **~-blue** *adj.* си́ний со стальны́м отли́вом; **~-clad, ~-plated** *adjs.* брониро́ванный; закóванный/одéтый в броню́; обши́тый стáлью; **~work** *n.* стальны́е издéлия; стальнáя констрýкция; **~-works** *n.* сталелитéйный завóд; **~yard** *n.* безмéн.

steely ['sti:lɪ] *adj.* (*fig., unyielding*) непреклóнный; (*stern*) сурóвый.

steep[1] [sti:p] *n.* (*liter., precipice*) крýча, крутизнá, обры́в.

adj. **1.** крутóй; **the stairs were ~** лéстница былá крутáя; **the ground fell ~ly away** земля́ крýто обрывáлась; (*fig.*): **there has been a ~ decline in trade** в торгóвле произошёл крутóй спад. **2.** (*coll., excessive*) чрезмéрный, непомéрный; **we had to pay a ~ price** нам э́то стáло в копéечку; (*exaggerated*): **his story seems a bit ~** егó расскáз отдаёт фантáстикой; (*unreasonable*): **I thought his conduct a bit ~** егó поведéние показáлось мне довóльно нáглым.

steep[2] [sti:p] *v.t.* **1.** (*soak*) мочи́ть (*impf.*); зам|áчивать, -очи́ть; пропи́т|ывать, -áть; **his hands are ~ed in blood** у негó рýки по лóкоть в крови́. **2.** (*fig., pass. or refl., be immersed*) погру|жáться, -зи́ться (*во что*) **he ~ed himself in the study of the classics** он погрузи́лся в изучéние клáссиков; (*be sunk*) погр|язáть, -я́знуть (*в чем*); **he was ~ed in crime** он погря́з в преступлéниях; **~ed in ignorance** погря́зший в невéжестве.

steeple ['sti:p(ə)l] *n.* колокóльня; шпиц, шпиль (*m.*).

cpds. **~chase** *n.* стипл-чéз; скáчки (*f. pl.*)/бег с препя́тствиями; **~chaser** *n.* (*pers.*) учáстник бéга с препя́тствиями; **~jack** *n.* верхолáз.

steepness ['sti:pnɪs] *n.* крутизнá.

steer[1] [stɪə(r)] *n.* (*animal*) вол, вычóк.

steer[2] [stɪə(r)] *v.t.* **1.** (*ship, vehicle etc.*) прáвить (*impf.*) +*i.*; управля́ть (*impf.*) +*i.* **2.: ~ a course** держáть (*impf.*) курс. **3.** (*pers., activity etc.*) вести́ (*det.*); напр|авля́ть, -áвить; **he ~ed the visitors to their seats** он провёл гостéй на их местá; **he ~ed his country to prosperity** он привёл свою́ странý к процветáнию; **I tried to ~ the conversation away from the subject of death** я пытáлся увести́ разговóр от тéмы смéрти; **~ing committee** прези́диум, руководя́щий комитéт.

v.i. **1.** (*of steersman*) прáвить (*impf.*) рулём; (*of ship, vehicle etc.*): **the car ~s well** э́ту маши́ну легкó вести́; **the ship refused to ~** корáбль не повиновáлся рулю́. **2.** (*of pers.*): **he was ~ing for the hospital** он напрáвился к больни́це; **~ clear of** избегáть (*impf.*) +*g.*; сторони́ться (*impf.*) +*g.*

steerage ['stɪərɪdʒ] *n.* (*steering*) рулевóе управлéние; (*part of ship*) четвёртый класс.

cpd. **~-way** *n.* наимéньшая скóрость хóда, при котóрой сýдно слýшается руля́.

steering ['stɪərɪŋ] *n.* управлéние (*чем*); управля́ющий механи́зм.

cpds. **~-column** *n.* рулевáя колóнна; **~-gear** *n.* (*naut.*) рулевóе устрóйство; (*aeron.*) рулевóй механи́зм; (*of vehicle*) управля́ющий механи́зм; **~-wheel** *n.* (*of car*) руль (*m.*); (*naut.*) штурвáл.

steersman ['stɪəzmən] *n.* рулевóй, штýрман.

stele [sti:l, 'sti:lɪ] *n.* (*archaeol., bot.*) стéла.

stellar ['stelə(r)] *adj.* звёздный.

stellated [ste'leɪtɪd] *adj.* (*bot.*) звёздчатый.

stem[1] [stem] *n.* **1.** (*bot.*) стéбель (*m.*); **fruit-bearing ~** плодонóжка; (*of shrub or tree*) ствол. **2.** (*of wine-glass*) нóжка; (*of mus. note*) пáлочка, шéйка, штиль (*m.*); (*of tobacco-pipe*) черенóк; (*of watch*) вáлик. **3.** (*gram.*) оснóва. **4.** (*branch of family*) ветвь; ли́ния родствá. **5.: from ~ to stern** от нóса до кормы́.

v.i. прои|сходи́ть, -зойти́ (*от/из чего*).

stem[2] [stem] *v.t.* **1.** (*lit., fig., check, stop*) остан|áвливать, -ови́ть; (*dam up*) запрý|живать, -ди́ть; (*fig., arrest, delay*) задéрж|ивать, -áть. **2.** (*make headway against*) идти́ (*det.*)

про́тив+*g.*; сопротивля́ться (*impf.*) +*d.*; **the ship was able to ~ the current** кораблю́ удало́сь преодоле́ть тече́ние; **he succeeded in ~ming the tide of popular indignation** ему́ удало́сь сбить волну́ всео́бщего возмуще́ния.

cpd. **~-turn** *n.* (*ski movement*) поворо́т на лы́жах упо́ром.

Sten [sten] *n.* (**~ gun**) пулемёт Сте́на.

stench [stentʃ] *n.* вонь (*no pl.*), смрад (*no pl.*); злово́ние.

stencil ['stensɪl] *n.* (*~-plate*) трафаре́т, шабло́н; (*pattern*) трафаре́т; узо́р по трафаре́ту; (*waxed sheet*) воско́вка.

v.t. **1.: ~ a pattern** рисова́ть, на- узо́р по трафаре́ту; **~ letters** выводи́ть, вы́вести (*or* нан|оси́ть, -ести́) бу́квы по трафаре́ту. **2.** (*ornament by ~ling*) трафаре́тить (*impf.*).

stenographer [ste'nɒgrəfə(r)] *n.* стено́граф (*fem.* -и́стка).

stenographic [ˌstenə'græfɪk] *adj.* стенографи́ческий.

stenography [ste'nɒgrəfɪ] *n.* стенографи́я.

stentorian [ˌsten'tɔːrɪən] *adj.* громово́й, зы́чный.

step [step] *n.* **1.** (*movement, distance, sound, manner of ~ping*) шаг; **take a ~ forward/back** сде́лать (*pf.*) шаг вперёд/наза́д; **at every ~** на ка́ждом шагу́; **~ by ~** шаг за ша́гом; постепе́нно; **turn one's ~s towards home** напра́вить (*pf.*) стопы́ домо́й; **it is only a short ~ to my house** до моего́ до́ма всего́ два шага́; **within a few ~s of the hotel** в двух шага́х от гости́ницы; **the station is a goodish ~ from here** до ста́нции отсю́да не так уж бли́зко (*or* поря́дочное расстоя́ние); **that is a good ~ towards success** э́то ве́рный шаг к успе́ху; **watch your ~!** (*lit., fig.*) осторо́жно!; **I heard ~s** я слы́шал шаги́; **I recognized your ~** я узна́л звук ва́ших шаго́в. **2.** (*fig., action*) шаг, ме́ра; **make a false ~** де́лать, с- ло́жный/неве́рный шаг; оступ|а́ться, -и́ться; **take ~s towards** предприня́ть (*pf.*) шаги́ к+*d.*; приня́ть (*pf.*) ме́ры к+*d.*; **my first ~ will be to cut prices** я пе́рвым де́лом добью́сь сниже́ния цен; **what's the next ~?** а тепе́рь что сле́дует де́лать? **3.** (*trace of foot*) след; **tread in s.o.'s ~s** сле́довать (*impf.*) по стопа́м кого́-н.; (*fig.*): **I followed in his ~s** я сле́довал по его́ стопа́м; **retrace one's ~s** возвраща́ться, верну́ться по про́йденному пути́. **4.** (*rhythm of ~*): **keep in ~ with** (*lit., fig.*) идти́ (*det.*) в но́гу с+*i.*; **fall into ~ behind s.o.** выра́внивать, вы́ровнять шаг по кому́-н.; **fall into ~** (*fig., conform*) подчин|я́ться, -и́ться; **change ~** смени́ть (*pf.*) но́гу; **fall, get out of ~** сби́ться (*pf.*) с ноги́; **he is out of ~** (*lit., fig.*) он идёт не в но́гу; **bring into ~** выра́внивать, вы́ровнять шаг по кому́-н. **5.** (*raised surface*) ступе́нь, присту́пок; **mind the ~!** осторо́жно — ступе́нька!; (*of staircase etc.*) ступе́нька; (*of ladder*) перекла́дина, ступе́нька; (*of vehicle*) подно́жка; (*in ice*) усту́п; **flight of ~s** ряд ступе́ней; марш (ле́стницы); (*in front of house*) крыльцо́; **fall/run down the ~s** скати́ться/сбежа́ть (*pf.*) по ступе́нькам. **6.** (*pl., ~-ladder; also* **pair of ~s**) стремя́нка; складна́я ле́стница. **7.** (*stage, degree*) ста́дия, ступе́нь, сте́пень; **I cannot follow the ~s of his argument** я не могу́ уследи́ть за хо́дом его́ рассужде́ния; (*advancement*): **when do you get your next ~ up?** когда́ вы полу́чите сле́дующее повыше́ние? **8.** (*dance ~*) па (*nt. indecl.*).

v.t. **1.: ~ a few yards** де́лать, с- не́сколько шаго́в. **2.: ~ a mast** (*naut.*) ста́вить, по- ма́чту (в степс).

v.i. шаг|а́ть, -ну́ть; ступ|а́ть, -и́ть; **~ high** высоко́ подн|има́ть, -я́ть но́ги; **~ this way, please** пройди́те сюда́, пожа́луйста!; **~ping-stone** ка́мень для перехо́да (*через ручей и т. п.*); (*fig.*) трампли́н; **a ~ping-stone to success** ступе́нь к успе́ху; **he ~ped into his car** он сел в маши́ну; **she ~ped into a fortune** на неё свали́лось огро́мное состоя́ние; **~ into the breach** (*fig.*) ри́нуться (*pf.*) на по́мощь; **he ~ped off the train** он сошёл с по́езда; **someone ~ped on my foot** кто́-то наступи́л мне на́ ногу; **~ on s.o.'s toes** (*fig.*) наступи́ть (*pf.*) на чью-н. люби́мую мозо́ль; **~ on it!** (*coll.*) жми!; пошеве́ливайся!; газу́й!; **I ~ped out of his way** я уступи́л ему́ доро́гу; **he ~ped over the threshold** он перешагну́л через поро́г.

with advs.: **~ aside** *v.i.* посторони́ться (*pf.*); (*fig.*) уступи́ть (*pf.*) (доро́гу) друго́му; **~ back** *v.i.* отступ|а́ть, -и́ть; уступ|а́ть, -и́ть; **~ down** *v.t.* (*elec.*) пон|ижа́ть, -и́зить (*напряжение*); *v.i.*: **he ~ped down off the ladder** он спусти́лся/сошёл с ле́стницы; **he ~ped down in favour of a more experienced man** он уступи́л ме́сто бо́лее о́пытному челове́ку; **~ forward** *v.i.*: **the police asked for witnesses to ~ forward** поли́ция проси́ла свиде́телей заяви́ть о себе́; **~ in** *v.i.*: **won't you ~ in for a moment?** мо́жет, зайдёте на мину́тку?; (*intervene*) вмеш|иваться, -а́ться; **~ off** *v.i.* (*start marching*): **~ off with the left foot** сде́лать (*pf.*) шаг с ле́вой ноги́; **he ~ped off on the wrong foot** (*fig.*) он с са́мого нача́ла де́йствовал не так; **~ out** *v.i.* вы́йти (*pf.*) (ненадо́лго); (*walk fast*): **we had to ~ out to get there on time** нам пришло́сь приба́вить ша́гу, что́бы попа́сть туда́ во́время; **~ up** *v.t.* (*increase*) пов|ыша́ть, -ы́сить; уси́ли|вать, -ть; (*electr.*) пов|ыша́ть, -ы́сить (*напряжение*); *v.i.*: **he ~ped up to the platform** он подошёл к трибу́не.

cpds. **~-by-~** *adj.* постепе́нный; (*pol., mil.*) поэта́пный; **~-ins** *n. pl.* шлёпанц|ы (*pl., g.* -ев); **~-ladder** *n.* = **~** *n.* **6.**; **~-rocket** *n.* ступе́нчатая раке́та.

step- [step] *comb. form*: **~brother** *n.* сво́дный брат; **~child** *n.* (*boy*) па́сынок; (*girl*) па́дчерица; **~daughter** *n.* па́дчерица; **~father** *n.* о́тчим; **~mother** *n.* ма́чеха; **~sister** *n.* сво́дная сестра́; **~son** *n.* па́сынок.

Stephen ['stiːv(ə)n] *n.* Степа́н; (*bibl.*) Стефа́н.

steppe [step] *n.* степь; (*attr.*) степно́й; **~ dweller, ~ horse** степня́к.

stereo ['sterɪəʊ, 'stɪə-] *n.* (*~phonic system*) стерео-фони́ческая систе́ма; **personal ~** пле́йер.

stereography [ˌsterɪ'ɒgrəfɪ] *n.* стереогра́фия.

stereophonic [ˌsterɪəʊ'fɒnɪk, ˌstɪə-] *adj.* стереофони́ческий.

stereoscope ['sterɪəˌskəʊp, 'stɪə-] *n.* стереоско́п.

stereoscopic [ˌsterɪə'skɒpɪk, ˌstɪə-] *adj.* стереоскопи́ческий; **~ telescope** стереотруба́.

stereotype ['sterɪəʊˌtaɪp, 'stɪə-] *n.* (*typ.*) стереоти́п; (*fig.*) шабло́н; (*attr.*) стереоти́пный.

v.t. стереотипи́ровать (*impf., pf.*); печа́тать, на- со стереоти́па; (*fig.*) прид|ава́ть, -а́ть шабло́нность +*d.*; **~d phrase** шабло́нная фра́за.

sterile ['steraɪl] *adj.* **1.** (*barren, unproductive, lit., fig.*) неплодоро́дный; беспло́дный; (*fig.*) безрезульта́тный. **2.** (*free from germs*) стери́льный, стерилизо́ванный.

sterility [stə'rɪlɪtɪ] *n.* (*lit., fig., unfruitfulness*) беспло́дность, беспло́дие; (*freedom from germs*) стери́льность.

sterilization [ˌsterɪlaɪ'zeɪʃ(ə)n] *n.* стерилиза́ция.

sterilize ['sterɪˌlaɪz] *v.t.* стерилизова́ть (*impf., pf.*).

sterilizer ['sterɪˌlaɪzə(r)] *n.* стерилиза́тор.

sterlet ['stɜːlɪt] *n.* сте́рлядь.

sterling ['stɜːlɪŋ] *n.* сте́рлинг; фунт сте́рлингов; **~ area** сте́рлинговая зо́на.

adj. **1.** (*of coin, metal etc.*) сте́рлинговый, полноце́нный; **pound ~** фунт сте́рлингов; **~ silver** серебро́ устано́вленной про́бы. **2.** (*fig., of solid worth*): **a ~ person** челове́к по́длинного благоро́дства.

stern[1] [stɜːn] *n.* **1.** (*of ship*) корма́; (*attr.*) кормово́й, за́дний; **~ foremost, on** кормо́й вперёд. **2.** (*rump*) зад; (*coll., of pers.*) за́д(ница).

cpds. **~-post** *n.* ахтерште́вень (*m.*); **~-sheets** *n. pl.* кормово́й решётчатый люк; **~-way** *n.* за́дний ход.

stern[2] [stɜːn] *adj.* (*strict, harsh*) стро́гий; (*severe*) суро́вый; (*inflexible*) непрекло́нный.

sternal ['stɜːn(ə)l] *adj.* груди́нный.

sternness ['stɜːnnɪs] *n.* стро́гость, суро́вость.

sternum ['stɜːnəm] *n.* груди́на.

sternutation [ˌstɜːnjʊ'teɪʃ(ə)n] *n.* чиха́нье.

steroid ['stɪərɔɪd, 'ste-] *n.* стеро́ид.

stertorous ['stɜːtərəs] *adj.* хрипя́щий.

stet [stet] *v.i.* (*as imper.*) оста́вить (как бы́ло)!; не пра́вить!

stethoscope ['steθəˌskəʊp] *n.* стетоско́п.

v.t. выслу́шивать, вы́слушать стетоско́пом.

stevedore ['stiːvəˌdɔː(r)] *n.* до́кер; порто́вый гру́зчик.

stew[1] [stjuː] *n.* **1.** (*cul.*) тушёное мя́со. **2.** (*coll.*): **get into a ~** разволнова́ться (*pf.*); **be in a ~** быть в большо́м волне́нии.

v.t. (*meat, fish, vegetables*) туши́ть, по-; **~ed mutton** тушёная бара́нина; (*fruit*) вари́ть (*impf.*); **~ed fruit** компо́т; **the tea is ~ed** чай перестоя́лся; ≃ чай ве́ником па́хнет.

v.i. **1.** (*of meat, fish, vegetables*) туши́ться (*impf.*); (*of fruit*) вари́ться (*impf.*); **let him ~ in his own juice** пусть ва́рится в со́бственном соку́ (*coll.*). **2.** (*feel oppressed by heat*) изнемога́ть (*impf.*) от жары́.

cpds. **~-pan, ~-pot** *nn.* ме́лкая кастрю́ля; соте́йник.

stew[2] [stju:] *n.* (*fishpond*) ры́бный садо́к.

stew[3] [stju:] *n.* (*arch., pl., brothel*) публи́чный дом.

steward ['stju:əd] *n.* (*of estate, club etc.*) управля́ющий, эконо́м; (*of race-meeting, show etc.*) распоряди́тель (*m.*); (*on ship*) стю́ард, официа́нт, коридо́рный; (*on plane*) стю́ард, бортпроводни́к.

stewardess [ˌstju:ə'des, 'stju:ədɪs] *n.* (*on ship*) стюарде́сса, го́рничная, официа́нтка; (*on plane*) стюарде́сса, бортпроводни́ца.

stewardship ['stju:ədʃɪp] *n.* управле́ние; до́лжность управля́ющего/эконо́ма/распоряди́теля; **give an account of one's ~** отчи́т|ываться, -а́ться в своём управле́нии.

stick[1] [stɪk] *n.* **1.** (*for support, punishment*) па́лка; **(walking-~)** трость, тро́сточка; (*pl., for kindling*) хво́рость; (*for driving cattle*) хворости́нка; **(hockey-~ *etc.*)** клю́шка; (*baton*) (дирижёрская) па́лочка; (*fig.*): **they left us a few ~s of furniture** они́ оста́вили нам ко́е-что из ме́бели; **they live in the ~s** (*sl.*) они́ живу́т в захолу́стье; **he got the ~ for it** за э́то его́ взду́ли; **get hold of the wrong end of the ~** превра́тно поня́ть (*pf.*) что-н.; **he was as cross as two ~s** он был зол как чёрт; **the big ~** (*fig.*) поли́тика большо́й дуби́нки; **~-and-carrot policy** поли́тика кнута́ и пря́ника; **I had him in a cleft ~** я его́ загна́л в тупи́к; **he's a dry old ~** он соверше́нный суха́рь. **2.** (*~shaped object*): **~ of chalk** мело́к; **~ of shaving-soap** мы́льная па́лочка; **~ of sealing-wax** па́лочка сургуча́; **~ of celery/rhubarb** сте́бель (*m.*) сельдере́я/ревеня́; **~ of chocolate** шокола́дный бато́нчик; **~ of dynamite** па́лочка динами́та; **~ of bombs** се́рия бомб; **~ insect** па́лочник.

stick[2] [stɪk] *v.t.* **1.** (*insert point of*) втыка́ть, воткну́ть; **I stuck a pin in the map** я воткну́л була́вку в ка́рту; (*thrust*): **~ one's spurs into a horse's flanks** вонз|а́ть, -и́ть шпо́ры в бока́ ло́шади. **2.** (*pierce*) пронз|а́ть, -и́ть; **~ s.o. with a bayonet** прот|ыка́ть, -кну́ть кого́-н. штыко́м; **~ a pig** зак|а́лывать, -оло́ть свинью́. **3.** (*cause to adhere*) прикле́и|вать, -ть (*что к чему*); накле́и|вать, -ть (*что на что*); **the stamp was stuck on upside down** ма́рка была́ накле́ена вверх нога́ми; (*affix*): **~ a notice on the door** ве́шать, пове́сить объявле́ние на дверь. **4.** (*coll., put*): **~ that book on the shelf** су́ньте э́ту кни́гу на по́лку; **he stuck his head round the door** он просу́нул го́лову в дверь; **with his hands stuck in his pockets** (за)су́нув ру́ки в карма́ны; **~ it on the bill!** припиши́те к счёту! **5.** (*coll., endure*) терпе́ть, вы́-; выноси́ть, вы́нести; **I can't ~ her nagging** я не выношу́ её ворча́ния/пиле́ния; **I couldn't ~ it any longer** я бо́льше не мог терпе́ть; мне ста́ло невтерпёж/невмоготу́. **6.: be stuck, get stuck** *see v.i.* **5.. 7.** (*coll. uses of pass. with preps.*): **be stuck on** (*captivated by*): **he is stuck on her** он к ней присо́х; он в неё втю́рился (*coll.*); **get stuck into** (*make serious start on*) всерьёз за что-н. прин|има́ться, -я́ться; **be stuck with** (*unable to get rid of*) быть не в состоя́нии отде́латься от чего́-н.

v.i. **1.** (*be implanted*): **a dagger ~ing in his back** кинжа́л, торча́щий у него́ в спине́; **there's a nail ~ing into my heel** гвоздь впива́ется мне в пя́тку. **2.** (*remain attached, adhere*) прил|ипа́ть, -и́пнуть (*к чему*); прикле́и|ваться, -ться; **the stamps ~ to my fingers** ма́рки ли́пнут/прилипа́ют к мои́м па́льцам; **this envelope won't ~** э́тот конве́рт не закле́ивается; **these pages have stuck (together)** э́ти страни́цы сли́плись; **~ing-plaster** ли́пкий пла́стырь; **they couldn't make the charge ~** они́ ниче́м не смогли́ подкрепи́ть своего́ обвине́ния; **the nickname stuck** э́то про́звище так и удержа́лось (за ним *и т.п.*). **3.** (*cling, cleave*): **he stuck at it till the job was finished** он упо́рно труди́лся, пока́ не око́нчил рабо́ту; **~ to a task** рабо́тать не покладая́ рук; **~ to one's guns** не сдава́ть (*impf.*) пози́ций; **~ to the point** держа́ться (*impf.*) бли́же к де́лу; **~ to one's principles** ост|ава́ться, -а́ться ве́рным свои́м при́нципам; **~ to one's word** держа́ть, с- сло́во; **I lent him the book and he stuck to it** я одолжи́л ему́ кни́гу, а он её зачита́л; **the accused stuck to his story** обвиня́емый упо́рно стоя́л на своём; **~ by s.o.** подде́рж|ивать, -а́ть кого́-н. **4.** (*coll., stay*): **are you going to ~ at home all day?** вы собира́етесь торча́ть до́ма весь день?; **he ~s in the bedroom all day** он це́лый день не выхо́дит из спа́льни. **5.** (*also* **be stuck, get stuck:** *become embedded, fixed, immobilized*) застр|ева́ть, -я́ть; **~ in the mud** зав|яза́ть, -я́знуть в грязи́; **the needle stuck in the groove** иго́лка застря́ла в боро́здке; **the drawer ~s** я́щик не выдвига́ется; **her zipper stuck** у неё застря́ла (застёжка-)мо́лния; **can you help with this problem? I'm stuck** помоги́те мне, пожа́луйста, с зада́чей — я с ней завя́з (*or* она́ не получа́ется); **when I recited the poem I didn't get stuck at all** я ни ра́зу не запну́лся, когда́ деклами́ровал стихи́; **he got a bone stuck in his throat** у него́ в го́рле застря́ла кость; **one thing ~s in my mind** одно́ у меня́ застря́ло/засе́ло в па́мяти; **he will ~ at nothing to gain his ends** он не остано́вится ни пе́ред чем, что́бы доби́ться своего́.

with advs.: **~ around** *v.i.* (*coll.*) не уходи́ть (*impf.*); **~ down** *v.t.* (*coll., write down*): **~ my name down for a pound** подпиши́те меня́ на оди́н фунт!; (*seal*): **have you stuck the envelope down?** вы закле́или конве́рт?; **~ on** *v.t.* (*affix*) прикле́и|вать, -ть; (*coll., add*): **the shop stuck another 50p on** (*sc. the price*) в магази́не наки́нули ещё 50 пе́нсов; **your article is a bit short, can you ~ on another paragraph?** ва́ша статья́ коротковáта — не мо́жете ли вы приба́вить ещё оди́н абза́ц?; **~ out** *v.t.*: **~ one's tongue out** высо́вывать, вы́сунуть язы́к; **~ one's head out** высо́вываться, вы́сунуться; **~ out one's chest** выпя́чивать, вы́пятить грудь; **~ one's neck out** (*fig.*) выска́кивать (*impf.*); высо́вываться (*impf.*); лезть (*impf.*) на рожо́н; **they stuck out flags from the windows** они́ вы́весили фла́ги из о́кон; (*endure*): **how long can they ~ it out?** как до́лго они́ продержа́тся?; *v.i.* (*project*) торча́ть (*impf.*); **his ears ~ out** у него́ торча́т у́ши; **a nail is ~ing out of the wall** в стене́ гвоздь торчи́т; **his intentions stuck out a mile** (*coll.*) за версту́ бы́ло ви́дно, чего́ он хо́чет; (*hold out*): **~ out for higher wages** наста́ивать (*impf.*) на повыше́нии зарпла́ты; **~ together** *v.t.* (*with glue*) скле́и|вать, -ть; *v.i.*: **good friends ~ together** настоя́щие друзья́ стоя́т друг за дру́га (горо́й); **~ up** (*coll.*) *v.t.* (*place on end*) ста́вить, по- торчко́м (*or* на попа́); **our neighbours stuck up a fence** на́ши сосе́ди вы́строили/поста́вили забо́р; **the traitors' heads were stuck up on poles** го́ловы преда́телей насади́ли на ко́лья; **~ up a notice** ве́шать, пове́сить объявле́ние; (*raise*): **~ 'em up!** (*coll.*) ру́ки вверх!; *v.i.* (*protrude upwards*) торча́ть (*impf.*); стоя́ть (*impf.*) торчко́м; **his hair was ~ing up** у него́ во́лосы торча́ли во все сто́роны; **~ up for** (*coll.*) (*support*) подде́рж|ивать, -а́ть; (*defend*) выступа́ть, вы́ступить в защи́ту +*g.*; заступ|а́ться, -и́ться за (*кого*); **~ up to s.o.** (*coll.*) (*offer resistance*) не сдава́ться (*impf.*) (*or* сопротивля́ться, *impf.*) кому́-н.

cpds. **~-in-the-mud** *n.* рутинёр; ко́сный челове́к; **~-jaw** *n.* (*toffee*) тяну́чка (*coll.*); **~-up** *n.* (*coll.*) налёт, ограбле́ние.

sticker ['stɪkə(r)] *n.* (*label*) накле́йка, этике́тка; (*hard worker*) работя́га (*c.g.*).

stickiness ['stɪkɪnɪs] *n.* ли́пкость, кле́йкость, вя́зкость, тягу́честь.

stickleback ['stɪk(ə)lˌbæk] *n.* ко́люшка.

stickler ['stɪklə(r)] *n.* побо́рник; **he's a ~ for correct grammar** в вопро́сах грамма́тики он педа́нт.

sticky ['stɪkɪ] *adj.* **1.** кле́йкий, ли́пкий; (*viscous*) вя́зкий, тягу́чий; **the path was ~ after the rain** тропи́нка была́ ско́льзкой по́сле дождя́; **the jam made my fingers ~** мои́ па́льцы сде́лались ли́пкими от варе́нья; **come to a ~ end** (*coll.*) пло́хо ко́нчить (*pf.*). **2.** (*of pers., difficult, unamenable*) непокла́дистый; **he was ~ about giving me leave** он ника́к не хоте́л дать мне о́тпуск.

stiff [stɪf] *n.* (*sl.*) (*corpse*) труп; **big ~** (*fool*) болва́н; кру́глый дура́к.

adj. **1.** (*not flexible or soft*) жёсткий, неги́бкий; **~ collar** жёсткий воротничо́к. **2.** (*not working smoothly*) туго́й; **~ hinges** туги́е пе́тли; **this lid is ~ (to unscrew)** кры́шка с трудо́м отви́нчивается. **3.** (*of pers. or parts of body*) онеме́лый, окостене́лый, одеревене́лый; **I have a ~ neck** у меня́ ше́я онеме́ла; мне наду́ло в ше́ю; **he has a ~ leg** у него́ нога́ пло́хо сгиба́ется; **I feel ~** я не могу́ ни согну́ться, ни разогну́ться; **I was ~ with cold** я соверше́нно окочене́л; **keep a ~ upper lip** (*fig.*) быть твёрдым; проявля́ть (*impf.*) вы́держку; не распуска́ть (*impf.*) ню́ни. **4.** (*forceful*) си́льный; **the garrison put up a ~ resistance** гарнизо́н отча́янно сопротивля́лся; **a ~ breeze** кре́пкий ве́тер; **a ~ drink** хоро́ший глото́к спиртно́го. **5.** (*hard to stir or mould*) густо́й; **~ clay** густа́я гли́на; **~ dough** круто́е те́сто. **6.** (*difficult, severe*): **a ~ examination** тру́дный/нелёгкий экза́мен; **a ~ climb** тру́дный/тяжёлый подъём; **a ~ price** непоме́рно высо́кая цена́; **this book is ~ going** э́та кни́га чита́ется с трудо́м; **he got a ~ sentence** ему́ вы́несли суро́вый пригово́р. **7.** (*formal, constrained*) натя́нутый, чо́порный; холо́дный; сухо́й; принуждённый; **he gave a ~ bow** он отве́сил церемо́нный покло́н. **8.** (*pred., coll.*): **he was scared ~** он перепуга́лся на́смерть; **I was bored ~** я чуть не у́мер со ску́ки.

cpd. **~-necked** *adj.* (*stubborn*) упря́мый.

stiffen ['stɪf(ə)n] *v.t.* (*make rigid*) прид|ава́ть, -а́ть жёсткость +*d.*; **collars ~ed with starch** накрахма́ленные воротнички́. **2.** (*make viscous*) сгу|ща́ть, -сти́ть. **3.** (*make resolute*) прид|ава́ть, -а́ть твёрдость +*d.* **4.** (*strengthen*) укреп|ля́ть, -и́ть.

v.i. (*become rigid*) де́латься, с- жёстким; кочене́ть, о-; костене́ть, о-; (*become viscous, thick*) сгу|ща́ться, -сти́ться; густе́ть, за-; (*become stronger*) кре́пнуть (*impf.*); де́латься, с- кре́пче; **the breeze ~ed** ве́тер крепча́л; **opposition is ~ing** сопротивле́ние кре́пнет.

stiffener ['stɪf(ə)nə(r)] *n.* (*for paste, dough*) загусти́тель (*m.*); (*drink*) рю́мочка; глото́к спиртно́го.

stiffness ['stɪfnɪs] *n.* жёсткость; су́хость; одеревене́лость; тру́дность; чо́порность; принуждённость.

stifl|e ['staɪf(ə)l] *v.t.* (*smother, suffocate*) души́ть, за-; **it is ~ing in here** здесь ду́шно; **~ing heat** удуша́ющая жара́. **2.** (*e.g. rebellion, feelings, hopes, sobs*) подав|ля́ть, -и́ть; **~e flames** туши́ть, за- ого́нь; **~e complaints** прес|ека́ть, -е́чь жа́лобы; **~e one's laughter** сде́рж|ивать, -а́ть смех.

v.i. зад|ыха́ться, -охну́ться.

stigma ['stɪgmə] *n.* **1.** (*imputation, stain*) позо́р, пятно́; **he will bear the ~ of the trial all his life** э́тот проце́сс опозо́рит его́ навсегда́ (*or* на всю жизнь); **he bore the ~ of illegitimacy** он нёс на себе́ клеймо́ незаконнорождённости. **2.** (*relig., med.*) сти́гма, стигма́т. **3.** (*bot.*) ры́льце.

stigmatization ['stɪgmətaɪ'zeɪʃ(ə)n] *n.* клейме́ние.

stigmatize ['stɪgməˌtaɪz] *v.t.* клейми́ть, за-; поноси́ть (*impf.*).

stile [staɪl] *n.* (*steps*) переłáз.

stiletto [stɪ'letəʊ] *n.* стиле́т; **~ heels** гво́здики (*m. pl.*); шпи́льки (*f. pl.*).

still[1] [stɪl] *n.* (*for distilling*) перего́нный куб; виноку́ренная устано́вка.

cpd. **~-room** *n.* (*for distilling*) помеще́ние для перего́нки; (*store-room*) кладова́я.

still[2] [stɪl] *n.* **1.** (*liter.*): **in the ~ of night** в ночно́й тиши́. **2.** (*cin.*) (рекла́мный) кадр.

adj. **1.** (*quiet, hushed, calm*) ти́хий, безмо́лвный; **a ~ evening** ти́хий/безве́тренный ве́чер; **become ~** ум|олка́ть, -о́лкнуть; **the ~ small voice of conscience** ти́хий/негро́мкий го́лос со́вести. **2.** (*motionless*) неподви́жный; **sit/stand ~** сиде́ть/стоя́ть (*impf.*) споко́йно; **keep ~!** не шевели́тесь!; споко́йно!; (*US*) (за)молчи́те!; (*to a child*) не верти́сь!; сиди́ ти́хо!; **he is never ~ for a moment** он мину́ты не сиди́т споко́йно; **~ life** (*art*) натюрмо́рт. **3.** (*of wine*) неигри́стый. **4.** (*of water*) гла́дкий, споко́йный; **~ waters run deep** в ти́хом о́муте че́рти во́дятся.

adv. **1.** (*even now, then; as formerly*) (всё) ещё; и сейча́с/тогда́; по-пре́жнему; **he ~ doesn't understand** он до сих пор не понима́ет. **2.** (*nevertheless*) тем не ме́нее, всё-таки, всё равно́. **3.** (*with comp.: even, yet*) ещё.

v.t. (*calm*) успок|а́ивать, -о́ить; утихоми́ри|вать, -ть (*coll.*); **their fears were ~ed** их стра́хи бы́ли развея́ны; (*console*) ут|еша́ть, -е́шить; (*soothe*) утол|я́ть, -и́ть.

cpds. **~-birth** *n.* рожде́ние мёртвого плода́; **~-born** *adj.* мертворождённый.

stillness ['stɪlnɪs] *n.* тишина́.

stilt [stɪlt] *n.* **1.** ходу́ля; **walk on ~s** ходи́ть (*indet.*) на ходу́лях. **2.** (*supporting building*) сва́я.

stilted ['stɪltɪd] *adj.* (*of style etc.*) напы́щенный, высокопа́рный.

stimulant ['stɪmjʊlənt] *n.* побуди́тель (*m.*), сти́мул; (*med.*) стимуля́тор, стимули́рующее сре́дство; (*alcohol*) возбужда́ющий, стимули́рующий.

adj. возбужда́ющий, стимули́рующий.

stimulat|e ['stɪmjʊˌleɪt] *v.t.* **1.** (*rouse, incite*) побу|жда́ть, -ди́ть (*кого + inf. or к чему*); стимули́ровать (*impf., pf.*); **the conversation had a ~ing effect on him** разгово́р приободри́л/подбодри́л его́. **2.** (*excite, arouse*) возбу|жда́ть, -ди́ть; **the story ~ed my curiosity** расска́з возбуди́л моё любопы́тство; **his interest was ~ed** у него́ возни́к интере́с; **light ~es the optic nerve** свет раздража́ет зри́тельный нерв. **3.** (*increase*): **this ~es the action of the heart** э́то уси́ливает серде́чную де́ятельность; **in order to ~e production** в це́лях стимули́рования произво́дства.

stimulation [ˌstɪmjʊ'leɪʃ(ə)n] *n.* (*urging*) побужде́ние; поощре́ние; (*excitement*) возбужде́ние.

stimulus ['stɪmjʊləs] *n.* сти́мул, толчо́к; (*incentive*) побужде́ние; (*motive force*) побуди́тельная/дви́жущая си́ла; раздражи́тель (*m.*).

sting [stɪŋ] *n.* **1.** (*of insect etc.*) жа́ло; **a ~ in the tail** (*fig.*) ≃ скры́тая шпи́лька; **a jest with a ~ in it** язви́тельная шу́тка. **2.** (*of plant*) жгу́чий волосо́к; (*of nettle*) ожо́г. **3.** (*by insect*) уку́с; **I got a ~ on my leg** меня́ что́-то ужа́лило/укуси́ло в но́гу; **his face is covered with ~s** у него́ всё лицо́ иску́сано. **4.** (**~ing pain**) о́страя/жгу́чая боль; (*fig.*): **the ~s of remorse** угрызе́ния (*nt. pl.*) со́вести.

v.t. **1.** (*of insect etc.*) жа́лить, у-; **he was stung by a bee** его́ ужа́лила пчела́; **what stung you?** кто вас ужа́лил?; (*of plant*) обж|ига́ть, -е́чь; жечь (*impf.*); **the nettles stung his feet** крапи́ва жгла ему́ но́ги; **~ing-nettle** (жгу́чая) крапи́ва. **2.** (*of pain, smoke etc.*) обж|ига́ть, -е́чь; **our faces were stung by the hail** град стега́л нам лицо́; **a ~ing slap on the face** жесто́кая пощёчина. **3.** (*pain mentally*) терза́ть (*impf.*); **the reproaches stung him** упрёки уязви́ли его́; **he was stung by remorse** его́ охвати́ло раска́яние; **~ing words** язви́тельные слова́; **her laughter stung him to the quick** её насме́шка заде́ла его́ за живо́е. **4.** (*coll., overcharge, swindle*) облапо́шить/нагре́ть (*both pf., coll.*).

v.i. **1.** (*of insect etc.*) жа́литься (*impf.*); (*of plant*) же́чься (*impf.*). **2.** (*feel pain or irritation*) жечь (*impf.*); **the blow made his hand ~** ему́ жгло ру́ку от уда́ра; **the smoke made my eyes ~** дым ел мне глаза́.

cpd. **~-ray** (*also* **stingaree**) *n.* скат.

stingless [stɪŋlɪs] *adj.* не име́ющий жа́ла; без жа́ла.

stingy ['stɪndʒɪ] *adj.* **1.** (*of pers.*) скупо́й; (*coll.*) ска́редный. **2.** (*meagre*) ску́дный.

stink [stɪŋk] *n.* **1.** вонь, злово́ние. **2.** (*coll.*): **raise (*or* kick up) a ~ about sth.** подня́ть (*pf.*) шум (*or* устро́ить (*pf.*) сканда́л) по како́му-н. по́воду.

v.t.: **~ out** выку́ривать, вы́курить.

v.i. воня́ть (*impf.*); смерде́ть (*impf.*); **the room ~s of onions** в комна́те воня́ет лу́ком; **~ing corpses** злово́нные тру́пы; **a ~ing cellar** воню́чий подва́л; (*fig.*): **he ~s of money (*or* is ~ing rich)** ≃ у него́ де́нег ку́ры не клюю́т; **the suggestion stank in his nostrils** э́то предложе́ние вы́звало у него́ отвраще́ние/омерзе́ние.

stinker ['stɪŋkə(r)] *n.* (*coll.*) **1.** (*pers.*) мерза́вец, га́дина. **2.** (*difficult task*) тру́дная зада́ча. **3.** (*severe letter*) суро́вое письмо́, о́тповедь.

stinkhorn ['stɪŋkhɔːn] *n.* (*bot.*) весёлка.

stint [stɪnt] *n.* **1.** (*liter., restriction*): **without ~** без преде́ла/ограниче́ний; неограни́ченно. **2.** (*fixed amount of work*) уро́к; **do one's daily ~** выполня́ть, вы́полнить дневно́й уро́к.

v.t. ограни́чи|вать, -ть (*кого в чем*); скупи́ться, по- на+*a.*; **he did not ~ his praise** он не скупи́лся на похвалы́; **he ~s himself for his children** он отка́зывает себе́ ра́ди дете́й.

stipend ['staɪpend] *n.* (*of clergyman*) жа́лованье; (*of student*) стипе́ндия.

stipendiary [staɪ'pendjərɪ, stɪ-] *n.* стипендиа́т; (*magistrate*) пла́тный магистра́т (*в отличие от мирового судьи*).

adj. получа́ющий жа́лованье/стипе́ндию.

stipple ['stɪp(ə)l] *n.* (*method of shading*) то́чечный пункти́р; (*engraving/painting*) гравиро́вка/рисова́ние пункти́ром.

v.t. гравирова́ть, на- в пункти́рной мане́ре; изобра|жа́ть, -зи́ть пункти́ром.

stipulate ['stɪpjʊ,leɪt] *v.t.* обусло́в|ливать, -ить; огов|а́ривать, -ори́ть; **it is ~d that the landlord shall be responsible for repairs** оговорено́, что за ремо́нт отвеча́ет владе́лец; **at the ~d time** в обусло́вленное вре́мя.

v.i.: **~ for** выгова́ривать, вы́говорить себе́ (*право на что*).

stipulation [,stɪpjʊ'leɪʃ(ə)n] *n.* (*stipulating*) обусло́вливание; (*condition*) усло́вие.

stir [stɜː(r)] *n.* **1.** (*act of ~ring*) разме́шивание, поме́шивание; **give one's tea a ~** помеша́ть (*pf.*) чай. **2.** (*commotion; movement*) волне́ние, движе́ние; **there was a ~ in the crowd** толпа́ заволнова́лась; **a ~ of warm wind** дунове́ние тёплого ве́тра; **there was not a ~ in the sea** мо́ре бы́ло неподви́жно. **3.** (*sensation*) шум, сенса́ция; **the news caused a ~** э́то изве́стие наде́лало мно́го шу́му.

v.t. **1.** (*cause to move*): **the wind ~s the trees** ве́тер колы́шет дере́вья; **~ the fire** шурова́ть, по- (*or* вороши́ть, по-) у́голь в ками́не; **no one ~red a finger to help me** никто́ па́лец о па́лец не уда́рил (*or* никто́ и па́льцем не шевельну́л), что́бы помо́чь мне; **~ your stumps!** (*coll.*) пошеве́ливайся!; **~ one's tea** разме́ш|ивать, -а́ть чай; **~ the soup** меша́ть, по- суп. **2.** (*arouse, affect, agitate*) возбу|жда́ть, -ди́ть; пробу|жда́ть, -ди́ть; волнова́ть, вз-; **her plea ~red him to pity** её мольба́ пробуди́ла в нём жа́лость; **he made a ~ring speech** он вы́ступил с волну́ющей ре́чью.

v.i.: **something ~red in the undergrowth** что-то (за)шевели́лось в куста́х; **the wind ~red in the trees** ве́тер шелесте́л в дере́вьях; **the cat lay without ~ring** ко́шка лежа́ла, не шелохну́вшись; **he didn't ~ out of his bed** он не вылеза́л из посте́ли; **don't ~ out of the house** не выходи́те и́з дому.

with adv.: **~ up** *v.t.* (*mix*) взб|а́лтывать, -олта́ть; сме́ш|ивать, -а́ть; (*arouse*): **~ up an interest in sth.** пробу|жда́ть, -ди́ть интере́с к чему́-н.; **~ up strife** разд|ува́ть, -у́ть ссо́ру; **~ up rebellion** се́ять (*impf.*) сму́ту; занима́ться (*impf.*) подстрека́тельством.

stirrup ['stɪrəp] *n.* стре́мя (*nt.*).

cpds. **~-cup** *n.* проща́льный ку́бок, «посошо́к»; **~-leather, ~-strap** *nn.* пу́тлище; **~-pump** *n.* ручно́й огнетуши́тель.

stitch [stɪtʃ] *n.* **1.** (*sewing etc.*) стежо́к; (*med.*) шов; **she makes neat ~es** она́ де́лает аккура́тные стежки́; **she learnt a new ~** она́ осво́ила но́вую вя́зку; **put ~es in a wound** на|кла́дывать, -ложи́ть швы на ра́ну; **a ~ in time** своевре́менная ме́ра; **without a ~ (of clothing)** в чём мать родила́; **every ~ on him was soaked** он промо́к/вы́мок до ни́тки. **2.** (*knitting*) петля́; **take up a ~** подн|има́ть, -я́ть пе́тлю; **drop a ~** спус|ка́ть, -ти́ть пе́тлю. **3.** (*pain in side*) ко́лотье в боку́; **he had us in ~es** (*coll.*) он нас чуть не умори́л со́ смеху.

v.t. (*sew together*) сши|ва́ть, -ть; (*esp. med.*) заш|ива́ть, -и́ть; (*bookbinding*) брошюрова́ть, с-.

with advs.: **~ on** *v.t.* приш|ива́ть, -и́ть; **~ up** *v.t.* (*a garment*) сши|ва́ть, -ть; (*a wound*) заш|ива́ть, -и́ть.

stoat [stəʊt] *n.* горноста́й (в ле́тнем меху́).

stock [stɒk] *n.* **1.** (*tree-trunk, stump*) ствол; пень (*m.*). **2.** (*handle, base etc.*): **~ of a rifle** руже́йная ло́жа; **~ of a plough** ру́чка плу́га. **3.** (*lineage*) семья́, род, происхожде́ние; **he comes of good ~** он из хоро́шей семьи́. **4.** (*resources, store, supply*) запа́с, инвента́рь (*m.*); **lay in a ~ of flour** сде́лать (*pf.*) запа́с муки́; запасти́сь (*pf.*) муко́й; **in ~** в ассортиме́нте; **have sth. in ~** име́ть что-н. в нали́чии; **he has a great ~ of information** у него́ огро́мный запа́с све́дений; **the ~ of human knowledge** су́мма челове́ческих зна́ний; **take ~** (*lit.*) инвентаризова́ть (*impf., pf.*); **take ~ of** (*fig., appraise*) крити́чески оце́н|ивать, -и́ть; (*weigh up*) взве́|шивать, -сить; рассм|а́тривать, -отре́ть. **5.** (*of farm*): **(live) ~** скот, поголо́вье скота́. **6.** (*raw material*) сырьё; **paper ~** бума́жное сырьё. **7.** (*cul.*) (кре́пкий) бульо́н. **8.** (*comm.*) а́кции (*f. pl.*); акционе́рный капита́л; фо́нды (*m. pl.*); **hold ~** владе́ть (*impf.*) а́кциями; держа́ть (*impf.*) а́кции; **S~ Exchange** би́ржа; (*fig., reputation*): **his ~ stood high, then fell to nothing** сперва́ его́ а́кции бы́ли о́чень высо́ки, пото́м упа́ли. **9.** (*pl., for confining offenders*) коло́дки (*f. pl.*). **10.** (*pl., for supporting ship*) ста́пель (*m.*); **be on the ~s** стоя́ть (*impf.*) на ста́пел|е/-ях; (*fig.*) быть в рабо́те. **11.** (*neckband*) шарф. **12.** (*bot.*) левко́й.

adj. **1.** (*kept in ~, available*) име́ющийся в нали́чии; **~ sizes in hats** станда́ртные разме́ры шляп. **2.** (*regularly used, hackneyed*) обы́чный, изби́тый, шабло́нный.

v.t. **1.** (*equip, furnish with ~*) снаб|жа́ть, -ди́ть (*что чем*); обору́довать (*impf., pf.*); **the garden was well ~ed with vegetables** в огоро́де бы́ло поса́жено мно́го овоще́й. **2.** (*keep in ~*) держа́ть (*impf.*); име́ть (*impf.*) в нали́чии.

v.i.: **~ up: we ~ed up with fuel for the winter** мы запасли́сь то́пливом на́ зиму.

cpds. **~-account, ~-book** *nn.* счёт капита́ла/това́ра; **~-breeder** *n.* животново́д; **~broker** *n.* (биржево́й) ма́клер; **~broking** *n.* биржевы́е опера́ции (*f. pl.*); **~-farm** *n.* скотово́дческая фе́рма; **~-farmer** *n.* скотово́д; **~-farming** *n.* скотово́дство; **~fish** *n.* вя́леная треска́; **~holder** *n.* акционе́р; **~-in-trade** *n.* запа́с това́ров; това́рная нали́чность; **books are a scholar's ~-in-trade** кни́ги явля́ются ору́диями произво́дства учёного; **promises are the politician's ~-in-trade** обеща́ния — непреме́нный арсена́л политика́на; **~jobber** *n.* биржево́й ма́клер; спекуля́нт; **~jobbery, ~jobbing** *nn.* ажиота́ж; биржевы́е спекуля́ции; **~list** *n.* спи́сок това́ров в ассортиме́нте; **~man** *n.* скотово́д; **~-market** *n.* фо́ндовая би́ржа; **~pile** *n.* материа́льный резе́рв, запа́с; *v.t.* запас|а́ть, -ти́ +*a. or g.*; запас|а́ться, -ти́сь +*i.*; **~pot** *n.* кастрю́лька, в кото́рой ва́рится и храни́тся кре́пкий бульо́н; **~-raising** *n.* животново́дство, скотово́дство; **~-still** *adv.* неподви́жно; **~-taking** *n.* инвентариза́ция; **closed for ~-taking** закры́то на учёт; (*fig.*) обзо́р, оце́нка, крити́ческий ана́лиз; **~yard** *n.* скотоприго́нный двор.

stockade [stɒ'keɪd] *n.* частоко́л.

Stockholm ['stɒkhəʊm] *n.* Стокго́льм.

stockinet(te) [,stɒkɪ'net] *n.* трикота́ж; (*attr.*) трикота́жный.

stocking ['stɒkɪŋ] *n.* чуло́к (*also of horse*); **in one's ~(ed) feet** в одни́х чулка́х/носка́х; без о́буви.

stockist ['stɒkɪst] *n.* ро́зничный продаве́ц (*определённых товаров*).

stocky ['stɒkɪ] *adj.* корена́стый, призе́мистый.

stodge [stɒdʒ] (*coll.*) *n.* (*heavy food*) тяжёлая/сы́тная еда́; (*unimaginative pers.*) бесцве́тный челове́к.

v.t.: **he ~d himself with bread** он наби́л себе́ желу́док хле́бом.

stodginess ['stɒdʒɪnɪs] *n.* (*fig.*) тяжелове́сность, ну́дность.

stodgy ['stɒdʒɪ] *adj.* (*of food*) тяжёлый; (*coll., of pers., style etc.*) тяжелове́сный, ну́дный; гру́зный, неповоро́тливый.

stoic ['stəʊɪk] *n.* (*of either sex*) сто́ик.

adj. сто́йческий.

stoical ['stəʊɪk(ə)l] *adj.* сто́йческий.

stoicism ['stəʊɪ,sɪz(ə)m] *n.* стоици́зм.

stoke [stəʊk] *v.t.* (*also ~ up*) шурова́ть (*impf.*); (*put more fuel on*) загру|жа́ть, -зи́ть (*топку*); забр|а́сывать, -о́сить то́пливо в+*a.*; (*keep going*): **~ the fire** подде́рживать (*impf.*) ого́нь.

v.i. **1.** (*act as ~r*) топи́ть (*impf.*). **2.**: **~ up** подде́рж|ивать, -а́ть ого́нь; шурова́ть (*impf.*); (*coll., eat heavily*) наж|ира́ться, -ра́ться.

cpds. **~hold** *n.* кочега́рка; **~-hole** *n.* отве́рстие то́пки.

stoker ['stəʊkə(r)] *n.* кочега́р, истопни́к.

stole [stəʊl] *n.* (*eccl.*) епитрахи́ль, ора́рь (*m.*); (*woman's*) ≃ паланти́н.

stolid ['stɒlɪd] *adj.* (*impassive*) бесстра́стный; (*dull*) тупо́й; (*phlegmatic*) флегмати́чный; (*sluggish*) вя́лый.

stolidity [stɒ'lɪdɪtɪ] *n.* бесстра́стность, бесстра́стие; ту́пость; флегмати́чность; вя́лость.

stomach ['stʌmək] *n.* **1.** (*internal organ*) желу́док; **a pain in the ~** боль в животе́; **he had a ~ upset** у него́ бы́ло расстро́йство желу́дка; **on a full ~** сра́зу по́сле еды́; на по́лный желу́док; **on an empty ~** натоща́к; на пусто́й желу́док; **a strong ~** хоро́шее пищеваре́ние; **you need a strong ~ to read this report** нужны́ желе́зные не́рвы, что́бы прочита́ть э́тот отчёт; **it turns my ~** меня́ тошни́т от э́того; мне э́то прети́т/проти́вно; **in the pit of the ~** под ло́жечкой. **2.** (*external part of body*; *belly*) живо́т, брю́хо; **someone kicked me in the ~** кто́-то пнул меня́ в живо́т; **he is getting a large ~** у него́ на́чало появля́ться брюшко́; **crawl on one's ~** по́лз|ать, -ти́ на животе́. **3.** (*appetite*): **I have no ~ for rich food** я не люблю́ жи́рного. **4.** (*fig.*, *desire*) жела́ние, охо́та; (*spirit*, *courage*) дух, хра́брость; **he has no ~ for fighting** дра́ться у него́ сме́лости не хвата́ет.

v.t. **1.** (*digest*) перева́р|ивать, -и́ть; (*be able to eat*): **he could ~ nothing but bread and milk** он не́ был в состоя́нии есть ничего́, кро́ме хле́ба с молоко́м. **2.** (*fig.*, *tolerate*): **~ an insult** прогл|а́тывать, -оти́ть оби́ду; **I can't ~ him** я его́ не перева́риваю/переношу́; я его́ выноси́ть/терпе́ть не могу́.

cpds. **~-ache** *n.* ко́лик|и (*pl.*, *g.* —) в животе́; **~-pump, ~-tube** *nn.* желу́дочный зонд.

stomach|al ['stʌməkəl], **-ic** [stə'mækɪk] *adjs.* желу́дочный.

stomp [stɒmp] *v.i.* (*coll.*, *tread heavily*) то́пать, про-.

stone [stəʊn] *n.* **1.** ка́мень (*m.*) (*pl.* ка́мни, каме́нья); **meteoric ~** аэроли́т; **throw ~s** броса́ться (*impf.*) камня́ми; **throw a ~ at s.o.** бр|оса́ть, -о́сить ка́мнем в кого́-н.; **break ~s** бить (*pf.*) ще́бень (*m.*); **I have a ~ in my shoe** у меня́ в боти́нке ка́мешек; **trip over a ~** спот|ыка́ться, -кну́ться о ка́мень; **leave no ~ unturned** (*fig.*) пусти́ть (*pf.*) всё в ход; испо́льзовать (*impf.*, *pf.*) все возмо́жные сре́дства; приложи́ть (*pf.*) все стара́ния; **a rolling ~ gathers no moss** кому́ на ме́сте не сиди́тся, тот добра́ не наживёт; **his house is within a ~'s throw of here** до его́ до́ма отсю́да руко́й пода́ть. **2.** (*gem*): **precious ~** драгоце́нный ка́мень (*pl.* ка́мни). **3.** (*rock*, *material*): **built of local ~** постро́енный из ме́стного ка́мня; **harden into ~** камене́ть, о-; **Portland ~** портла́ндский ка́мень, портла́ндская поро́да; **he has a heart of ~** у него́ не се́рдце, а ка́мень; **S~ Age** ка́менный век; **S~ Age man** челове́к ка́менного ве́ка; **~ circle** кро́млех. **4.** (*of plum etc.*) ко́сточка. **5.** (*med.*) ка́мень (*m.*, *pl.* ка́мни); **he underwent an operation for ~** ему́ сде́лали опера́цию по по́воду камне́й. **6.** (*weight*) сто́ун, стон (*6,35 кг.*).

adj. ка́менный.

v.t. **1.** (*pelt with ~s*) поб|ива́ть, -и́ть камня́ми; **~ the crows!** мать родна́я! (*coll.*). **2.** (*line*, *face with ~*) облиц|о́вывать, -ева́ть ка́мнем; (*pave*) мости́ть, вы́-ка́мнем. **3.** (*remove ~s from*): **~ cherries** оч|ища́ть, -и́стить ви́шни от ко́сточек. **4. ~d** (*drunk*) в сте́лку/вдрызг пья́ный (*coll.*); (*with drugs*) одуре́вший/одурма́ненный нарко́тиком/ами; под ке́йфом (*coll.*).

cpds. **~-blind** *adj.* соверше́нно слепо́й; **~chat** *n.* черного́рлый чека́н; **~-coal** *n.* антраци́т; **~-cold** *adj.* холо́дный как лёд; **~-dead** *adj.* мёртвый; **~-deaf** *adj.* соверше́нно глухо́й; **~-fruit** *n.* костя́нка, ко́сточковый плод; **~-ground** *adj.* размо́лотый жернова́ми; **~mason** *n.* ка́менщик; **~-pit** *n.* каменоло́мня, карье́р; **~-saw** *n.* камнере́зная пила́; **~wall** *v.i.* (*fig.*, *refuse to be drawn*) отма́лчиваться (*impf.*); **~ware** *n.* гонча́рные/керами́ческие изде́лия; **~work** *n.* (*masonry*) ка́менная кла́дка.

stony ['stəʊnɪ] *adj.* камени́стый; (*fig.*, *unfeeling*) ка́менный; из ка́мня.

cpds. **~-broke** *adj.* (*coll.*) вконе́ц разорённый; **~-hearted** *adj.* жестокосе́рдный.

stooge [stu:dʒ] (*sl.*) *n.* (*comedian's foil*) партнёр ко́мика; (*deputy of low standing*) подставно́е лицо́, марионе́тка.

v.i.: **~ around** болта́ться (*impf.*); окола́чиваться (*impf.*) (*coll.*).

stook [stu:k, stʊk] *n.* копна́ (се́на).

stool [stu:l] *n.* **1.** (*seat*) табуре́т(ка); **piano ~** враща́ющийся табуре́т (у роя́ля); **~ of repentance** скамья́ покая́ния; **fall between two ~s** оказа́ться (*pf.*) ме́жду двух сту́льев. **2. (foot~)** скаме́ечка (для ног). **3.** (*lavatory*): **go to ~** испражн|я́ться, -и́ться; (*faeces*) стул.

cpd. **~-pigeon** *n.* (*pers.*) насе́дка, стука́ч (*fem.* -ка) (*coll.*).

stoop [stu:p] *n.* суту́лость; **he walks with a ~** он суту́лится при ходьбе́.

v.t.: **~ one's shoulders** суту́лить (*impf.*) пле́чи.

v.i. **1.** (*of posture*) суту́литься, с-; **walk with a ~ing gait** суту́литься при ходьбе́; (*bend down*) наг| иба́ться, -ну́ться; сгиба́ться, согну́ться. **2.** (*condescend*) сни|сходи́ть, -зойти́; (*lower o.s.*) ун|ижа́ться, -и́зиться; **he never ~ed to lying** он никогда́ не унижа́лся до лжи; **I wouldn't ~ so low** я не паду́ так ни́зко.

stop [stɒp] *n.* **1.** (*halt*, *halting-place*) остано́вка; **come to a ~** останови́ться (*pf.*); **put a ~ to** положи́ть (*pf.*) коне́ц +*d.*; **the traffic was brought to a ~** на у́лице образова́лась про́бка; **the train goes to London without a ~** по́езд идёт до Ло́ндона без остано́вок; **bus ~** авто́бусная остано́вка. **2.** (*stay*) остано́вка, (кра́ткое) пребы́вание; **we made a short ~ in Paris** мы останови́лись ненадо́лго в Пари́же. **3.** (*punctuation mark*) знак препина́ния; **full ~** то́чка; (*in telegram*) то́чка (*abbr.* тчк); (*fig.*): **come to a full ~** прийти́ (*pf.*) к концу́; по́лностью прекрати́ться (*pf.*); **bring to a full ~** по́лностью прекрати́ть (*pf.*). **4.** (*mus.*, *on string*) лад; (*of organ*) реги́стр; **pull out all the ~s** (*fig.*) нажа́ть (*pf.*) на все кно́пки. **5.** (*phot.*) диафра́гма. **6.** (*phon.*) взрывно́й согла́сный (звук).

v.t. **1.** (*also* **~ up:** *close*, *plug*, *seal*) закр|ыва́ть, -ы́ть; зат|ыка́ть, -кну́ть; заде́л|ывать, -ать; **he ~ped his ears when I spoke** он заткну́л у́ши, когда́ я говори́л; **he ~ped his ears to my request** он был глух к мое́й про́сьбе; **I ~ped his mouth with a bribe** я заткну́л ему́ рот взя́ткой; **the dentist ~ped three of my teeth** зубно́й врач запломбирова́л мне три зу́ба; **the drain-pipe is ~ped (up)** дрена́жная труба́ засори́лась; **we can ~ the leak with a rag** мы мо́жем заткну́ть течь тря́пкой; **~ a gap** (*fig.*) зап|олня́ть, -о́лнить пробе́л. **2.** (*arrest motion of*) остан|а́вливать, -ови́ть; **he ~ped the car** он останови́л маши́ну; **he ~ped the engine** (*intentionally*) он вы́ключил/заглуши́л мото́р; (*inadvertently*) у него́ загло́х мото́р; **he was running too fast to ~ himself** он бежа́л так бы́стро, что не мог останови́ться; **I ~ped the first taxi that came along** я взял пе́рвое попа́вшееся такси́; **the thief was ~ped by a policeman** вор был заде́ржан полице́йским; **~ thief!** держи́ во́ра!; **he ~ped the blow with his arm** он отрази́л уда́р руко́й; **~ a bullet** (*coll.*) быть уби́тым/ра́ненным пу́лей. **3.** (*arrest progress of*, *bring to an end*) остан|а́вливать, -ови́ть; заде́рж|ивать, -а́ть; прекра|ща́ть, -ти́ть; **the frost ~ped the growth of the plants** моро́з останови́л рост расте́ний; **the bank ~ped payment** банк прекрати́л платежи́; **rain ~ped play** дождь сорва́л игру́; **it ought to be ~ped** э́тому на́до положи́ть коне́ц; (*suspend*) приостан|а́вливать, -ови́ть; **I ~ped the cheque** я приостанови́л платёж по э́тому че́ку; **production was ~ped for a day** произво́дство бы́ло остано́влено на оди́н день; (*cancel*) отмен|я́ть, -и́ть; **all leave has been ~ped** все отпуска́ отменены́; (*cut off*, *disallow*, *~ provision of*): **they ~ped £20 out of his wages** у него́ удержа́ли 20 фу́нтов из зарпла́ты; **my father ~ped my allowance** оте́ц переста́л выделя́ть мне де́ньги; (*electricity etc.*) выключа́ть, вы́ключить. **4.** (*prevent*, *hinder*): **~ s.o. from** уде́рж|ивать, -а́ть кого́-н. от+*g.*; не дать (*pf.*) (*кому +inf*); **I tried to ~ him (from) telling her** я пыта́лся помеша́ть ему́ сказа́ть ей; **what's ~ ping you?** за чем (же) де́ло ста́ло?; **what is to ~ me going?** что мне помеша́ет пойти́?

5. (*interrupt*) прер|ыва́ть, -ва́ть; **once he gets talking no one can ~ him** когда́ он разговори́тся, его́ невозмо́жно останови́ть (*or* его́ уже́ не остано́вишь). **6.** (*with gerund: discontinue, leave off*) перест|ава́ть, -а́ть +*inf.*; прекра|ща́ть, -ти́ть +*n. obj.*; **~ teasing the cat!** переста́ньте дразни́ть ко́шку!; **~ telling me what to do!** дово́льно/хва́тит учи́ть меня́ жить!; **they ~ped talking when I came in** когда́ я вошёл, они́ умо́лкли. **7.** (*mus.*): **~ a string** заж|има́ть, -а́ть струну́.

v.i. **1.** (*come to a halt*) остан|а́вливаться, -ови́ться; **he ~ped short, dead** он останови́лся как вко́панный; **he did not ~ at murder** он не останови́лся пе́ред уби́йством; **a ~ping train** по́езд, иду́щий с остано́вками; **~!** сто́йте!; **~ a minute!** погоди́те мину́ту!; **the clock has ~ped** часы́ стоя́т/останови́лись. **2.** (*in speaking*) зам|олка́ть, -о́лкнуть; **he ~ped talking** он замолча́л; **he ~ped to light his pipe** он сде́лал па́узу, что́бы раскури́ть тру́бку. **3.** (*cease activity*) перест|ава́ть, -а́ть; конча́ть, ко́нчить; **he ~ped reading** он переста́л/бро́сил чита́ть; **he ~ped smoking** он бро́сил кури́ть; **~ that!** конча́й!; переста́нь!; хва́тит!; дово́льно!; бро́сьте! **4.** (*come to an end*) прекра|ща́ться, -ти́ться; конча́ться, ко́нчиться; перест|ава́ть, -а́ть; **their correspondence ~ped** перепи́ска ме́жду ни́ми оборвала́сь; **the rain ~ped** дождь ко́нчился/переста́л/прошёл; **the road ~ped suddenly** доро́га вдруг ко́нчилась. **5.** (*stay*): **~ at a hotel** остан|а́вливаться, -ови́ться в гости́нице; **~ at home** ост|ава́ться, -а́ться до́ма; **don't ~ out too long** не заде́рживайтесь надо́лго (*or* сли́шком до́лго).

with advs.: **~ by** *v.i.* за|ходи́ть, -йти́; (*in a vehicle*) за|езжа́ть, -е́хать; **~ off, ~ over** *vv.i.* остан|а́вливаться, -ови́ться; **~ up** *v.t.* = **~** *v.t.* **1.**; *v.i.*: **we ~ped up late to welcome him** мы не расходи́лись спать допоздна́, что́бы приве́тствовать его́.

cpds. **~-cock** *n.* запо́рный кран; **~gap** *n.* (*pers.*) вре́менно заменя́ющий; (*thg.*) заты́чка; вре́менная ме́ра; **it will serve as a ~gap** э́то сойдёт на вре́мя; **~-go** *adj.*: **~-go policy** поли́тика «стой-иди́»; **~-lamp, ~-light** *nn.* (*on vehicle*) стоп-сигна́л; **~-light** (*of traffic lights*) кра́сный свет; **~-off, ~-over** *nn.* остано́вка (в пути́); **~-press** *n.* «в после́днюю мину́ту»; э́кстренное сообще́ние (*в газете*); **~valve** *n.* запо́рный ве́нтиль; сто́порный кла́пан; **~-watch** *n.* секундоме́р (с остано́вом).

stoppage [ˈstɒpɪdʒ] *n.* **1.** (*of work etc.*) прекраще́ние, остано́вка, забасто́вка; (*interruption*) перебо́й; **~ of pay** прекраще́ние вы́платы/зарпла́ты **~ of leave** отме́на отпуско́в. **2.** (*obstruction*) засоре́ние, заку́порка; **intestinal ~** засоре́ние желу́дка.

stopper [ˈstɒpə(r)] *n.* (*of bottle etc.*) про́бка; **put a ~ on** (*fig., coll.*) положи́ть (*pf.*) коне́ц +*d.*

v.t. (*also* **~ up:** *cork*) заку́пори|вать, -ть; зат|ыка́ть, -кну́ть.

stopping [ˈstɒpɪŋ] *n.* (*in tooth*) пло́мба.

storage [ˈstɔːrɪdʒ] *n.* (*storing*) хране́ние; (*method*): **in cold ~** в холоди́льнике; **put into cold ~** (*fig.*) отложи́ть (*pf.*) в до́лгий я́щик (*or* под сукно́); (*space*): **put sth. in(to) ~** сда|ва́ть, -ть что-н. на хране́ние; **take sth. out of ~** брать, взять что-н. со скла́да; (*cost, charge*) пла́та за хране́ние; (*of computer*) накопи́тель (*m.*); запомина́ющее устро́йство; па́мять.

cpds. **~-battery** *n.* аккумуля́торная батаре́я; **~-tank** *n.* запасно́й резервуа́р|бак.

store [stɔː(r)] *n.* **1.** (*stock, reserve*) запа́с, резе́рв, припа́с; (*abundance*) изоби́лие; **~ of food** запа́с прови́зии; **a great ~ of information** огро́мный запа́с све́дений; **lay in ~s of butter** де́лать, с- запа́сы ма́сла; **he has a surprise in ~ for you** у него́ для вас припасён сюрпри́з; **the next day had a surprise in ~ for us all** сле́дующий день преподнёс нам всем сюрпри́з. **2.** (*pl., supplies*): **military ~s** вое́нное иму́щество; **naval ~s** корабе́льные припа́с|ы (*pl., g.* -ов); шки́перское иму́щество. **3.** (*warehouse*) склад, пакга́уз, храни́лище; **put furniture in ~** сда|ва́ть, -ть ме́бель на хране́ние. **4.** (*US, shop*) магази́н, ла́вка; **department, multiple ~(s)** универма́г; **general ~(s)** магази́н сме́шанных това́ров. **5.** (*value, significance*) значе́ние; **set ~ by** прид|ава́ть, -а́ть значе́ние +*d.*; **he sets no great ~ by his life** он не сли́шком дорожи́т (свое́й) жи́знью.

adj. (*kept in ~*) запа́сный, запасно́й.

v.t. **1.** (*furnish, stock*) снаб|жа́ть, -ди́ть (*что чем*); нап|олня́ть, -о́лнить (*что чем*); **his mind is ~d with knowledge** он мно́го зна́ет; он зна́ющий челове́к. **2.** (**~ up**, *set aside*) запас|а́ть, -ти́; нак|а́пливать (*or* нак|опля́ть), -опи́ть. **3.** (*deposit in ~*) сда|ва́ть, -ть на хране́ние; **he ~d his car for the winter** он законсерви́ровал маши́ну на́ зиму. **4.** (*hold*) вме|ща́ть, -сти́ть; **the shed will ~ all the coal we need** в сара́й мо́жно засы́пать сто́лько у́гля, ско́лько нам ну́жно.

cpds. **~house** *n.* склад, кладова́я, амба́р; **~keeper** *n.* (*mil., nav.*) кладовщи́к, батале́р; (*shopkeeper*) ла́вочник; **~-room** *n.* кладова́я; **~-ship** *n.* тра́нспорт снабже́ния.

storey [ˈstɔːrɪ] *n.* (*US* **story**) эта́ж; **a house of 5 ~s** пятиэта́жный дом; **add a ~ (to the house)** надстр|а́ивать, -о́ить эта́ж; **top ~** ве́рхний эта́ж; **upper ~** (*joc., brain*) черда́к (*coll.*).

storied [ˈstɔːrɪd] *adj.* (*liter.*) ска́зочный, легенда́рный; ове́янный леге́ндами.

stork [stɔːk] *n.* а́ист.

storm [stɔːm] *n.* **1.** бу́ря, урага́н; (*thunder ~*) гроза́; (*snow ~*) мете́ль, вью́га, бура́н; **cyclonic ~** цикло́н; **magnetic ~** магни́тная бу́ря; **~ in a teacup** (*fig.*) бу́ря в стака́не воды́. **2.** (*naut.*) (жесто́кий) шторм; (*meteor.*) урага́н. **3.** (*upheaval*): **the ~ of revolution** революцио́нный вихрь; **~ and stress** (*hist.*) «бу́ря и на́тиск». **4.** (*fig., hail, shower, volley*) град, ли́вень (*m.*), залп; **a ~ of arrows/bullets** град стрел/пуль; (*of emotion etc.*): **~ of applause** взрыв аплодисме́нтов; **~ of abuse** град оскорбле́ний; **~ of anger/laughter/indignation** взрыв гне́ва/сме́ха/негодова́ния. **5.** (*assault*) штурм; **take a town by ~** брать, взять го́род шту́рмом; **take an audience by ~** покори́ть/захвати́ть (*pf.*) слу́шателей/аудито́рию/пу́блику.

v.t. (*mil.*) штурмова́ть (*impf.*); брать, взять при́ступом.

v.i. (*of wind etc.*) свире́пствовать (*impf.*); бушева́ть (*impf.*); (*fig., rage*) бушева́ть (*impf.*); мета́ть (*impf.*) гро́мы и мо́лнии; **~ at s.o.** крича́ть, на- на кого́-н.; **he ~ed out of the room** он вы́бежал из ко́мнаты в гне́ве.

cpds. **~-beaten, ~-tossed** *adjs.* потрёпанный бу́рей; **~-belt** *n.* по́яс бурь; **~-bound** *adj.* заде́ржанный што́рмом; **~-centre** *n.* центр цикло́на; (*fig., centre, focus of disturbance*) оча́г волне́ний/беспоря́дков; **~-cloud** *n.* грозова́я ту́ча; (*fig.*) ту́чи (*f. pl.*) над голово́й; **~-cone** *n.* штормово́й сигна́льный ко́нус; **~-lantern** *n.* фона́рь (*m.*) «мо́лния»; **~proof** *adj.* буреусто́йчивый; спосо́бный вы́держать шторм/бу́рю; **~-sail** *n.* штормово́й па́рус; **~-tossed** *adj.* = **~-beaten**; **~-trooper** *n.* штурмови́к; **~-troops** *n.* штурмовы́е войска́, штурмовы́е ча́сти (*f. pl.*); **~-window** *n.* зи́мняя ра́ма.

stormy [ˈstɔːmɪ] *adj.* штормово́й; бу́рный (*also fig.*); **~ wind** штормово́й ве́тер; **~ weather** непого́да; **a ~ sky** грозово́е не́бо; **a ~ sunset** предвеща́ющий бу́рю зака́т; **~ petrel** букреве́стник.

story[1] [ˈstɔːrɪ] *n.* **1.** (*tale, account, history*) ска́зка, расска́з, исто́рия; **tell a ~** расска́з|ывать, -а́ть ска́зку; **short ~** расска́з, нове́лла; **long short ~** по́весть; **funny ~** анекдо́т; **a good ~** заба́вная исто́рия; **they all tell the same ~** они́ все говоря́т одно́ и то же; **it's a long ~** э́то до́лгая пе́сня; э́то дли́нная исто́рия; **to cut a long ~ short** коро́че говоря́; одни́м сло́вом; **that's quite another ~** э́то совсе́м друго́е де́ло; **his ~ is an eventful one** его́ жизнь/биогра́фия была́ бога́та собы́тиями; **it's the old, old ~** э́то ве́чная исто́рия; **the ~ goes** говоря́т; преда́ние гласи́т. **2.** (*newspaper report*) отчёт, статья́. **3.** (*plot*) фа́була, сюже́т. **4.** (*coll., untruth*) исто́рия, вы́думка, ложь; **tell a ~** врать, на-; **he tells stories** он враль.

cpds. **~-book** *n.* сбо́рник ска́зок/расска́зов; **the affair had a ~-book ending** у э́той исто́рии коне́ц как в ска́зке; **~-line** *n.* фа́була; **~-teller** *n.* ска́зочни|к (*fem.* -ца), новелли́ст (*fem.* -ка), расска́зчи|к (*fem.* -ца); (*coll., liar*) вы́думщи|к (*fem.* -ца), лгун (*fem.* -ья); враль (*m.*), врун (*fem.* -ья).

story[2] ['stɔːrɪ] *n.* = **storey**

stoup [stuːp] *n.* **1.** (*flagon*) графи́н, буты́ль. **2.** (*eccl.*) ча́ша со свято́й водо́й.

stout [staʊt] *n.* (*beer*) кре́пкий по́ртер.

adj. **1.** (*strong*) кре́пкий, про́чный. **2.** (*resolute*) реши́тельный; (*sturdy*) си́льный; (*staunch*) сто́йкий; **a ~ fellow** бра́вый ма́лый; **a ~ fighter** бое́ц; **a ~ heart** сто́йкость, му́жество; **offer ~ resistance** ока́з|ывать, -а́ть упо́рное сопротивле́ние. **3.** (*corpulent*) по́лный, доро́дный; **get, grow ~** полне́ть, по-/рас-.

cpd. **~-hearted** *adj.* сто́йкий, му́жественный.

stoutness ['staʊtnɪs] *n.* кре́пость, про́чность; реши́тельность, сто́йкость, му́жество; полнота́, ту́чность.

stove [stəʊv] *n.* печь, пе́чка; (*for cooking*) ку́хонная плита́; (*hothouse*) тепли́ца.

cpd. **~-pipe** *n.* дымохо́д; **~-pipe hat** (*US*) цили́ндр.

stow [stəʊ] *v.t.* **1.** (*pack*) укла́дывать, уложи́ть; **I ~ed the trunk (away) in the attic** я убра́л сунду́к на черда́к; (*fill*) загру|жа́ть, -зи́ть (*что чем*); (*naut.*): **~ the anchor** уб|ира́ть, -ра́ть я́корь. **2.** (*sl., stop*): **~ it!** брось!; хва́тит!; **~ that nonsense!** брось/конча́й э́ти глу́пости!

v.i. **~ away** (*on ship*) е́хать (*det.*) за́йцем.

cpd. **~away** *n.* безбиле́тный пассажи́р, «за́яц».

stowage ['stəʊɪdʒ] *n.* (*action*) укла́дка, скла́дывание; (*space*) скла́дочное ме́сто, кладова́я; (*charge*) пла́та за укла́дку.

strabismus [strə'bɪzməs] *n.* страби́зм, косогла́зие.

straddle ['stræd(ə)l] *v.t.* охва́т|ывать, -и́ть; осёдл|ывать, -а́ть; **~ a fence** сиде́ть (*impf.*) верхо́м на забо́ре; (*fig.*): **their shots ~d the target** они́ захвати́ли цель в ви́лку; **my holiday ~s two weeks** мой о́тпуск прихо́дится на коне́ц одно́й неде́ли и нача́ло друго́й.

v.i. (*stand/sit with feet apart*) стоя́ть/сиде́ть (*impf.*), широко́ расста́вив но́ги.

strafe [strɑːf, streɪf] *v.t.* бомбардирова́ть (*impf.*); обстре́л|ивать, -я́ть.

straggl|e ['stræg(ə)l] *v.i.*: **the children ~ed home from school** де́ти бре́ли/тащи́лись из шко́лы домо́й; **a wisp of hair ~ed** небольша́я прядь воло́с вы́билась из приче́ски; **a ~ing line of houses** беспоря́дочный ряд домо́в; **a ~ing line of soldiers** беспоря́дочная цепо́чка солда́т; **a bush with ~ing shoots** куст с торча́щими побе́гами.

straggler ['stræglə(r)] *n.* (*soldier*) отста́вший солда́т; (*ship*) отста́вшее су́дно.

straggly ['stræglɪ] *adj.* беспоря́дочный, растрёпанный.

straight [streɪt] *n.* **1.** (*of racecourse*): **the ~** (после́дняя) пряма́я. **2.**: **out of the ~** косо́й, криво́й. **3.** (*at cards*) ка́рты, подо́бранные подря́д по досто́инству; «поря́док», «стрит».

adj. **1.** прямо́й; (*not bent*) неизо́гнутый; **in a ~ line** пря́мо в ряд; **she had ~ hair** у неё бы́ли прямы́е/невью́щиеся во́лосы; **hold your back ~!** вы́прямите спи́ну!; **keep your knees ~!** не сгиба́йте коле́ни!; **I couldn't keep a ~ face** я не мог удержа́ться от улы́бки. **2.** (*level*) ро́вный; **are the pictures ~?** карти́ны вися́т ро́вно?; (*symmetrical*) симметри́чный; (*neat, in order*) в поря́дке; **he never puts his room ~** он никогда́ не убира́ет свою́ ко́мнату; **put one's hat ~** попр|авля́ть, -а́вить шля́пу; **is my tie ~?** как мой га́лстук — не коси́т?; **put the record ~** (*fig.*) внести́ (*pf.*) попра́вку/уточне́ние; **let's get this ~** дава́йте внесём определённость по э́тому вопро́су. **3.** (*direct, honest*) прямо́й, че́стный; **he is as ~ as a die** он абсолю́тно/безукори́зненно че́стен; **~ dealings** че́стность, прямота́; **~ fight** че́стный бой; борьба́ ме́жду двумя́ кандида́тами *и т.п.*; **~ tip** ве́рный сове́т. **4.** (*orthodox*): **~ play** (*theatr.*) (чи́стая) дра́ма; (*heterosexual*) гетеросексуа́льный; не гомосексуа́льный. **5.** (*undiluted*) неразба́вленный; (*unbroken; in a row*): **ten ~ wins** де́сять вы́игрышей подря́д; **~ flush** (*cards*) «королёвский цвет», флеш-роя́ль (*m.*).

adv. **1.** пря́мо; **the smoke goes ~ upwards** дым поднима́ется пря́мо вверх; **he can't walk ~** он не мо́жет идти́ по прямо́й; **sit (up) ~!** сиди́(те); **keep ~ on!** иди́те пря́мо/напрями́к!; (*directly*): **I am going ~ to Paris** я е́ду пря́мо в Пари́ж; **I will come ~ to the point** я приступлю́ пря́мо к де́лу; **I gave it him ~ from the shoulder** я ему́ так и отруби́л; я ему́ сказа́л напрями́к; **I told him ~ (out)** я сказа́л ему́ пря́мо. **2.** (*in the right direction or manner*): **he can't shoot ~** он не уме́ет (ме́тко) стреля́ть; **he promised to go ~ in future** он обеща́л впредь вести́ себя́ че́стно; **he can't see ~** (*coll.*) у него́ в глаза́х двои́тся; **can't you see ~?** вы что, осле́пли?; **I can't think ~** я не могу́ сосредото́читься. **3.**: **~ away, off** сра́зу, то́тчас, неме́дленно; **she went ~ off to her lawyer** она́ то́тчас (*or* тут же) пошла́ к (своему́) адвока́ту.

cpds. **~away** *adj.* (*US*) (*direct*) прямо́й, просто́й; (*immediate*) неме́дленный; **~-cut** *adj.* (*of tobacco*) продо́льно наре́занный; **~forward** *adj.* (*frank*) открове́нный, прямо́й; (*honest*) че́стный; (*uncomplicated*) просто́й, несло́жный; **~forwardness** *n.* открове́нность, прямота́; че́стность; простота́, несло́жность.

straighten ['streɪt(ə)n] *v.t.* **1.** выпрямля́ть, вы́прямить; **he ~ed his back** он вы́прямился; он распрями́л спи́ну. **2.** (*put in order*) попр|авля́ть, -а́вить; прив|оди́ть, -ести́ в поря́док; ула́|живать, -дить; **he ~ed out his affairs** он привёл свои́ дела́ в поря́док; **I will try to ~ things out** я постара́юсь всё ула́дить.

v.i. выпрямля́ться, вы́прямиться; распрям|ля́ться, -и́ться; (*become orderly*) испр|авля́ться, -а́виться; ула́|живаться, -диться.

strain [streɪn] *n.* **1.** (*tension*) натяже́ние; **the rope broke under the ~** верёвка не вы́держала натяже́ния и ло́пнула; (*wearing effect*): **she suffered the ~ of sleepless nights** она́ переутоми́лась из-за бессо́нных ноче́й; **the ~s of modern life** напряжённость/стресс совреме́нной жи́зни; **he is under ~** у него́ сли́шком больша́я нагру́зка; (*nervous fatigue*): **he is suffering from ~** у него́ не́рвное переутомле́ние; (*muscular ~*) растяже́ние (жил); (*effort, exertion*) напряже́ние; **it was a great ~ to climb the ladder** подъём по ле́стнице оказа́лся большо́й нагру́зкой; (*demand, load*): **his education is a ~ on my resources** его́ образова́ние си́льно ударя́ет по моему́ карма́ну (*or* сто́ит мне о́чень мно́го). **2.** (*of music*) напе́в, мело́дия; **we heard the ~s of a waltz** до нас доноси́лись зву́ки ва́льса. **3.** (*tone, style*) тон, стиль (*m.*); **he continued in the same ~** он продолжа́л в том же ду́хе/ро́де. **4.** (*breed, stock*) род, происхожде́ние; **he comes of a noble ~** он происхо́дит из зна́тного ро́да; он благоро́дного происхожде́ния; (*of animals, plants*) поро́да; **a hardy ~ of rose** выно́сливый сорт роз; (*biol.*) штамм. **5.** (*inherited feature*) насле́дственность; **there is a ~ of insanity in his family** в его́ роду́ име́ется насле́дственное психи́ческое заболева́ние; (*trace, tendency*) черта́, скло́нность, элеме́нт; **I detected a ~ of sentimentality in his writing** я обнару́жил (не́который) налёт сентимента́льности в его́ писа́ниях.

v.t. **1.** (*make taut*) натя́|гивать, -ну́ть. **2.** (*exert*) напр|яга́ть, -я́чь; **I ~ed my ears to catch his words** я напря́г слух, что́бы улови́ть его́ слова́; **we must ~ every nerve** нам сле́дует напря́чь все си́лы. **3.** (*over-exert*): **~ one's eyes** переутомля́ть (*impf.*) глаза́; по́ртить (*impf.*) зре́ние; **~ a tendon** растя́|гивать, -ну́ть сухожи́лие; **don't ~ yourself** смотри́те, не надорви́тесь. **4.** (*overtax, presume too much on*): **~ s.o.'s patience** испы́тывать (*impf.*) чьё-н. терпе́ние; **~ed relations** натя́нутые отноше́ния. **5.** (*force, pervert*) де́лать, с- натя́жку в+*p.*; **~ the meaning of a word** иска|жа́ть, -зи́ть смысл (како́го-н.) сло́ва; **~ed merriment** напускно́е весе́лье. **6.** (*clasp*): **she ~ed the child to her breast** она́ прижа́ла ребёнка к груди́. **7.** (*filter, also ~ off*) проце́|живать, -ди́ть; отце́|живать, -ди́ть.

v.i. **1.** (*exert o.s.*) напр|яга́ться, -я́чься; **the swimmer was ~ing to reach the shore** плове́ц напряга́л все си́лы, что́бы дости́чь бе́рега; **~ at a rope** тяну́ть (*impf.*) верёвку изо всех сил; **~ at the oars** нал|ега́ть, -е́чь на вёсла; **~ at the leash** (*of hound*) рва́ться (*impf.*) с поводка́; (*fig., of pers.*) рва́ться (*impf.*) в бой; **the masts were ~ing** ма́чты гну́лись; **plants ~ towards the light** расте́ния тя́нутся к све́ту. **2.**: **~ at a gnat** (*fig.*) крохобо́рствовать (*impf.*); переоце́нивать (*impf.*) ме́лочи.

strainer ['streɪnə(r)] *n.* си́то, си́течко, цеди́лка.

strait [streɪt] *n.* **1.** (*of water*) проли́в; **S~ of Dover/Gibraltar** Ду́врский/Гибралта́рский проли́в. **2.** (*liter.*, *difficult situation*; *need*) затрудни́тельное положе́ние; нужда́; **in great, dire ~s** в отча́янном положе́нии; в стеснённых обстоя́тельствах.

cpds. **~-jacket** *n.* смири́тельная руба́шка; **~-laced** *adj.* (*fig.*) пурита́нский.

straitened ['streɪtənd] *adj.*: **~ circumstances** стеснённые обстоя́тельства.

strand[1] [strænd] *n.* (*shore*) побере́жье, взмо́рье, пляж.

v.t. (*ship or pers.*) сажа́ть, посади́ть на мель; **I was ~ed in Paris** я очути́лся в Пари́же соверше́нно на мели́.

v.i. (*of ship*) сади́ться, сесть на мель.

strand[2] [strænd] *n.* (*fibre*, *thread*) прядь, стре́нга, нить; (*fig.*): **there are several ~s to the plot of this novel** в э́том рома́не не́сколько сюже́тных ли́ний.

strange [streɪndʒ] *adj.* **1.** (*unfamiliar*, *unknown*) незнако́мый, неизве́стный. **2.** (*of pers.*, *unused*) не знако́мый (с+*i.*); **he is still ~ to the work** он ещё не привы́к к э́той рабо́те (*or* не осво́ился с э́той рабо́той). **3.** (*foreign*, *alien*) чужо́й, чужезе́мный; **he loves to visit ~ lands** он лю́бит е́здить в чужи́е края́/стра́ны; **follow ~ gods** моли́ться (*impf.*) чужи́м бога́м. **4.** (*remarkable*, *unusual*) стра́нный, необыкнове́нный, необы́чный; **how ~ that you should ask that** как стра́нно, что вы (и́менно) об э́том спроси́ли!; **~ to say (*or* ~ly enough) he loves her** как (э́то) ни стра́нно, он лю́бит её; **he was ~ly silent about his family** непоня́тно почему́ он не хоте́л говори́ть о свое́й семье́; **she wears the ~est clothes** она́ чудно́ одева́ется; **~r things have happened** и не тако́е случа́лось; **I feel ~** (*dizzy*) мне не по себе́; меня́ мути́т.

strangeness ['streɪndʒnɪs] *n.* стра́нность, непривы́чность.

stranger ['streɪndʒə(r)] *n.* **1.** (*unknown pers.*) незнако́м|ец (*fem.* -ка); посторо́нний (челове́к); **he is shy with ~s** он стесня́ется посторо́нних; **you're quite a ~** вы совсе́м пропа́ли! **2.: a ~ to** (*unfamiliar with*) незнако́мый с+*i.*; чу́ждый +*d.*; **she is no ~ to poverty** она́ знако́ма с бе́дностью; бе́дность ей не в нови́нку; **I am a ~ to your way of thinking** мне чужд ваш о́браз мышле́ния. **3.** (*alien*, *foreigner*) чужестра́н|ец (*fem.* -ка); **I am a ~ here** я здесь чужо́й.

strangle ['stræŋg(ə)l] *v.t.* души́ть, за-; удави́ть (*pf.*); **this collar is strangling me** э́тот воротничо́к меня́ ду́шит; (*fig.*): **a ~d cry** сда́вленный крик; **death by strangling** смерть че́рез удуше́ние.

cpd. **~hold** *n.* (*lit.*, *fig.*) заси́лье; **have a ~hold on s.o.** держа́ть (*impf.*) кого́-н. мёртвой хва́ткой (*or* (*coll.*) за гло́тку).

strangler ['stræŋglə(r)] *n.* души́тель (*m.*).

strangulate ['stræŋgjʊ,leɪt] *v.t.* (*med.*): **~d hernia** ущемлённая гры́жа.

strangulation [,stræŋgjʊ'leɪʃ(ə)n] *n.* удуше́ние; (*med.*) зажима́ние, перехва́тывание, ущемле́ние.

strap [stræp] *n.* **1.** реме́нь (*m.*), ремешо́к; (*of dress*) брете́лька. **2.** (*thrashing*): **give s.o. the ~** поро́ть, вы- кого́-н. ремнём; **get the ~** получ|а́ть, -и́ть по́рку (ремнём).

v.t. **1.** (*secure with ~*) стя́|гивать, -ну́ть ремнём; **he was ~ped to a chair** он был привя́зан к сту́лу ремня́ми; (*bind wound etc.*): бинтова́ть, за-; на|кла́дывать, -ложи́ть ли́пкий пла́стырь на+*a.* **2.** (*beat with ~*) поро́ть, вы́- ремнём.

cpds. **~-hanger** *n.* стоя́щий пассажи́р; **~-work** *n.* переплета́ющийся орна́мент.

strapping ['stræpɪŋ] *adj.* ро́слый, си́льный, здоро́вый.

Strasb(o)urg ['stræzbɜːg] *n.* Страсбу́рг.

stratagem ['strætədʒəm] *n.* уло́вка; (вое́нная) хи́трость.

strategic [strə'tiːdʒɪk] *adj.* стратеги́ческий.

strategist ['strætɪdʒɪst] *n.* страте́г.

strategy ['strætɪdʒɪ] *n.* страте́гия; операти́вное иску́сство.

stratification [,strætɪfɪ'keɪʃ(ə)n] *n.* стратифика́ция, расслое́ние, напластова́ние, наслое́ние, залега́ние.

stratif|y ['strætɪ,faɪ] *v.t.* (*arrange in strata*) насл|а́ивать, -ои́ть; (*deposit in strata*) напласто́в|ывать, -а́ть; **~ied rock** слои́стый ка́мень.

strato-cumulus [,strætəʊ'kjuːmjʊləs] *n.* слои́сто-кучевы́е облака́.

adj. слои́сто-кучево́й.

stratosphere ['strætə,sfɪə(r)] *n.* стратосфе́ра.

stratospheric [,strætə'sferɪk] *adj.* стратосфе́рный.

strat|um ['strɑːtəm, 'streɪ-] *n.* **1.** (*geol.*) пласт, слой, напластова́ние, форма́ция. **2.: social ~a** слой о́бщества.

stratus ['streɪtəs, 'strɑː-] *n.* слои́стое о́блако.

straw [strɔː] *n.* **1.** (*collect.*) соло́ма; (*attr.*) соло́менный; **~ hat** соло́менная шля́п(к)а; **man of ~** (*fig.*) подставно́е/фикти́вное лицо́; (*man of no substance*) ненадёжный/несерьёзный челове́к. **2.** (*single ~*) соло́мин(к)а; **drink lemonade through a ~** пить (*impf.*) лимона́д че́рез соло́минку; **catch, clutch at a ~** (*fig.*) хвата́ться, схвати́ться за соло́минку; **not care a ~ (for)** наплева́ть (*pf.*) (на+*a.*); относи́ться (*impf.*) соверше́нно безразли́чно к+*d.*; **his promises are not worth a ~** его́ обеща́ниям грош цена́; **that was the last ~** э́то бы́ло после́дней ка́плей; **~ in the wind** (*fig.*) намёк; предупрежде́ние; при́знак; **~ vote** неофициа́льный опро́с.

cpds. **~-board** *n.* соло́менный карто́н; **~-coloured** *adj.* соло́менного цве́та.

strawberry ['strɔːbərɪ] *n.* (*pl.*, *collect.*) клубни́ка; (*wild*) земляни́ка; **a ~** я́года клубни́ки/земляни́ки; (*attr.*) клубни́чный, земляни́чный; **~ blonde** рыжева́тая блонди́нка; **~ ice** клубни́чное моро́женое.

cpd. **~-mark** *n.* роди́мое пятно́.

stray [streɪ] *adj.* **1.** (*wandering*, *lost*) заблуди́вшийся, бездо́мный; **~ sheep** отби́вшаяся от ста́да овца́; **~ dog** бродя́чая соба́ка; (*as n.*): **waifs and ~s** беспризо́рники (*m. pl.*). **2.** (*sporadic*): **~ instances** отде́льные слу́чаи; **a ~ bullet** шальна́я пу́ля.

v.i. **1.** (*wander*, *deviate*) заблуди́ться (*pf.*); сби́ться (*pf.*) с пути́; **the sheep ~ed on to the road** о́вцы забрели́ на доро́гу; **we must not ~ too far from the path** мы не должны́ отклоня́ться сли́шком далеко́ от тропи́нки; **she ~ed from the path of virtue** она́ сби́лась с пути́ и́стинного. **2.** (*roam*, *rove*) броди́ть (*impf.*); стра́нствовать (*impf.*). **3.** (*of thoughts*, *affections*) блужда́ть (*impf.*); **~ from the subject** отклон|я́ться, -и́ться от те́мы.

streak [striːk] *n.* **1.** поло́ска, прожи́лка, просло́йка; **~ of lightning** вспы́шка мо́лнии; **like a ~ of lightning** (*fig.*) с быстрото́й мо́лнии. **2.** (*fig.*, *trace*, *tendency*) черта́, накло́нность; **he has a cruel/yellow ~** в его́ хара́ктере есть жесто́кая/трусли́вая жи́лка; он скло́нен к жесто́кости/тру́сости.

v.t.: **~ed with red** с кра́сными поло́сками.

v.i. (*coll.*, *move rapidly*) мча́ться, про-; прон|оси́ться, -ести́сь.

streaker ['striːkə(r)] *n.* (*coll.*) «стри́кер», го́лый бегу́н.

streaky ['striːkɪ] *adj.* полоса́тый; с просло́йками.

stream [striːm] *n.* **1.** (*rivulet*, *brook*) руче́й, ре́чка, пото́к; (*branch of river*) рука́в. **2.** (*flow*) пото́к, тече́ние; **~ of blood/lava/water** пото́к кро́ви/ла́вы/воды́; **in a ~ (*or* ~s)** пото́ком, ручья́ми (*m. pl.*); (*fig.*) пото́к; **a ~ of people** людско́й пото́к; **~ of consciousness** пото́к созна́ния; **~ of abuse** пото́к руга́тельств (*nt. pl.*)/бра́ни. **3.** (*lit.*, *fig.*, *current*, *direction of flow*): **with the ~** по тече́нию; **against the ~** про́тив тече́ния. **4.** (*in school*): **he was put in the A ~** он попа́л в класс «А»; **remedial ~** пото́к/кла́ссы (*m. pl.*) для отстаю́щих.

v.t. **1.: his wounds ~ed blood** из его́ ран струи́лась кровь. **2.: the pupils were ~ed** ученико́в распредели́ли по кла́ссам (в зави́симости от спосо́бностей); **~ing** *n.* систе́ма пото́ков.

v.i. **1.** (*flow*) течь, струи́ться, ли́ться (*all impf.*); **blood was ~ing from his nose** из но́су у него́ текла́ кровь; **tears ~ed down her cheeks** слёзы струи́лись/лили́сь/текли́ у неё по щека́м; **light ~ed in at the window** свет струи́лся в окно́; **refugees were ~ing over the fields** бе́женцы несконча́емым пото́ком шли по поля́м; **he had a ~ing cold** у него́ был стра́шный на́сморк; **her eyes were ~ing** слёзы так и лили́сь у неё из глаз; **the windows were ~ing with rain** по стёклам струи́лся дождь. **2.: with**

hair ~ing in the wind с развева́ющимися на ветру́ (*or* по ве́тру) волоса́ми.

cpds. **~line** *n.* обтека́емая фо́рма; *v.t.* прид|ава́ть, -а́ть обтека́емую фо́рму +*d.*; (*fig.*) упро|ща́ть, -сти́ть; **~lined** *adj.* стро́йный, элега́нтный; упрощённый; **~lined car** автомаши́на/автомоби́ль (*m.*) обтека́емой фо́рмы.

streamer ['stri:mə(r)] *n.* вы́мпел; ле́нта.

streamlet ['stri:mlɪt] *n.* ручеёк, ре́чка.

street [stri:t] *n.* **1.** у́лица; **he lives in the next ~ (to us)** он живёт на сосе́дней (с на́ми) у́лице; **everyone had to be off the ~s by 10 p.m.** всем бы́ло приказа́но разойти́сь по дома́м к десяти́ ве́чера; **don't play in the ~** (*roadway*) не игра́й на мостово́й; **man in the ~** обыва́тель (*m.*); просто́й челове́к; **she went on the ~s** она́ пошла́ на пане́ль (*or* сде́лалась проститу́ткой); **they were turned out on to the ~** их вы́селили и́з дому (*or* вы́гнали на у́лицу); **this novel is not in the same ~ as his others** э́тот рома́н значи́тельно слабе́е остальны́х его́ произведе́ний; **he is ~s ahead of the other pupils** он на́ голову вы́ше свои́х соученико́в; **this is just up your ~** э́то как раз по ва́шей ча́сти. **2.** (*attr.*) у́личный; **~ arab** беспризо́рник; **~ cries** кри́ки (у́личных) разно́счиков; **~ door** пара́дное, пара́дная дверь; **at ~ level** на пе́рвом этаже́; **~ trader** у́личный разно́счик/лото́чник; **~ trading** у́личная торго́вля; **~ lighting** у́личное освеще́ние.

cpds. **~car** *n.* (*US*) трамва́й; **~-lamp** *n.* у́личный фона́рь; **~-singer** *n.* у́личный певе́ц; **~sweeper** *n.* дво́рник, подмета́льщик; (*machine*) маши́на для подмета́ния у́лиц; **~-walker** *n.* проститу́тка.

strength [streŋθ, streŋkθ] *n.* **1.** си́ла; **~ of mind/will** си́ла ду́ха/во́ли; **~ of purpose** реши́мость; **his ~ lies in lucid exposition** его́ си́ла —в я́сности изложе́ния (*might*): **the ~ of a fortress** мощь/непристу́пность кре́пости; (*of structure or solution*): **~ of a beam/wine/poison** кре́пость ба́лки/вина́/я́да; (*of a colour*) усто́йчивость; (*of material*) про́чность, сопротивле́ние; **I haven't the ~ to go on** я не в си́лах да́льше идти́; **it taxed his ~ severely** э́то вы́мотало все его́ си́лы; **recover, regain one's ~** восстан|а́вливать, -ови́ть си́лы; **acquire new ~, build up one's ~** наб|ира́ться, -ра́ться сил; **lose ~** теря́ть (*impf.*) си́лы; **argue from ~** спо́рить (*impf.*) с пози́ции си́лы; **he went from ~ to ~** он дви́гался вперёд гига́нтскими/семими́льными шага́ми. **2.** (*basis*): **on the ~ of** в си́лу +*g.*; на основа́нии +*g.*; **I resigned on the ~ of your promise** я ушёл в отста́вку, полага́ясь на ва́ше обеща́ние. **3.** (*numerical ~*) чи́сленность; **the enemy were in great ~** си́лы врага́ бы́ли велики́; **in full ~** в по́лном соста́ве; **up to ~** по́лностью укомплекто́ванный; **below ~** недоукомплекто́ванный; **bring up to ~** (до)укомплекто́вать (*pf.*); **on the ~** в шта́те; **be on the ~** чи́слиться (*impf.*) в соста́ве.

strengthen ['streŋθ(ə)n, -ŋkθ(ə)n] *v.t.* укреп|ля́ть, -и́ть; уси́ли|вать, -ть; упро́чи|вать, -ть; **~ a garrison** поп|олня́ть, -о́лнить соста́в гарнизо́на; **~ s.o.'s hand** укреп|ля́ть, -и́ть чью-н. пози́цию; поддержа́ть (*pf.*) кого́-н.; **~ a law** уси́ли|вать, -ть зако́н; **~ a solution** де́лать, с- раство́р бо́лее концентри́рованным; **his answer ~ed my conviction** его́ отве́т укрепи́л меня́ в моём убежде́нии.

v.i. укреп|ля́ться, -и́ться; уси́ли|ваться, -ться; упро́чи|ваться, -ться.

strenuous ['strenjʊəs] *adj.* (*of pers.*) энерги́чный, де́ятельный; (*of effort*) напряжённый, уси́ленный; (*of work*) тру́дный.

streptococcus [ˌstreptə'kɒkəs] *n.* стрептоко́кк.

stress [stres] *n.* **1.** (*tension*) напряже́ние; (*pressure*) давле́ние; нажи́м; **time of ~** тяжёлое вре́мя; **under the ~ of poverty** под гнётом нищеты́; **subject s.o. to ~** ока́з|ывать, -а́ть на кого́-н. давле́ние; (*psych.*) стресс; **a situation of ~** стре́ссовая ситуа́ция; **~ of weather** непого́да; **~ of war** тя́готы (*f. pl.*) войны́. **2.** (*emphasis*) ударе́ние; **lay ~ on** (*lit.*, *fig.*) де́лать, с- ударе́ние на+*p.*; (*fig.*) прид|ава́ть, -а́ть осо́бое значе́ние +*d.*; **the ~ is on the second syllable** ударе́ние па́дает на второ́й слог. **3.** (*mus.*) акце́нт. **4.** (*eng.*) напряже́ние; **breaking ~** преде́льное напряже́ние.

v.t. **1.** (*subject to ~*) подв|ерга́ть, -е́ргнуть напряже́нию. **2.** (*emphasize*) подчёрк|ивать, -ну́ть; де́лать, с- упо́р на+*a.* **3.** (*accentuate*) ста́вить, по- ударе́ние на+*a.*

stressful ['stresfʊl] *adj.* напряжённый; стре́ссовый.

stretch [stretʃ] *n.* **1.** (*extension*) вытя́гивание, растя́гивание; **the cat woke and gave a ~** ко́шка просну́лась и потяну́лась; **at full ~** (*fully extended*) преде́льно; (*lengthening*) удлине́ние; **at a ~** с натя́жкой; **by any ~ of the imagination** при са́мом ди́ком полёте фанта́зии; **~ of authority** превыше́ние вла́сти. **2.** (*elasticity*) растяжи́мость; **the rubber has no ~ in it** рези́на не тя́нется; **~ fabric** эласти́чная мате́рия; **~ socks** безразме́рные носки́. **3.** (*expanse*, *tract*) протяже́ние, простра́нство, уча́сток; **a fine ~ of country** великоле́пная приро́да; **a dusty ~ of road** пы́льный отре́зок/уча́сток доро́ги. **4.** (*of time*): **he works 8 hours at a ~** он рабо́тает во́семь часо́в подря́д. **5.** (*coll.*, *of imprisonment*): **he is doing a five-year ~** он отбыва́ет пятиле́тний срок (*заключения*).

v.t. **1.** (*lengthen*) вытя́гивать, вы́тянуть; (*broaden*) растя́|гивать, -ну́ть. **2.** (*pull to fullest extent*): **~ a rope between two posts** натя́|гивать, -ну́ть верёвку ме́жду двумя́ столба́ми; **a wire was ~ed across the road** попере́к доро́ги была́ натя́нута про́волока; **he wouldn't ~ out an arm to help me** (*fig.*) он не хоте́л протяну́ть мне ру́ку по́мощи; **~ o.s.** потя́|гиваться, -ну́ться; **~ one's legs** разм|ина́ть, -я́ть но́ги; **I found him ~ed (out) on the floor** я заста́л его́ распростёртым на полу́. **3.** (*strain*, *exert*): **~ a point** де́лать, с- (*or* допус|ка́ть, -ти́ть) натя́жку/усту́пку; **~ one's memory** напр|яга́ть, -я́чь па́мять; **~ the truth** преувели́чи|вать, -ть; (*coll.*) прив|ира́ть, -ра́ть.

v.i. **1.** (*be elastic*) растя́|гиваться, -ну́ться. **2.** (*extend*) прост|ира́ться, -ере́ться; раски́|дываться, -ну́ться; **the plain ~es for miles** равни́на простира́ется на мно́го миль; (*of time*) дли́ться, про-. **3.** (*reach*): **the rope will not ~ to the post** верёвку не дотяну́ть до столба́; **a rainbow ~ed across the sky** ра́дуга простёрлась по не́бу. **4.** (**~** *o.s.*) потя́|гиваться, -ну́ться.

stretcher ['stretʃə(r)] *n.* **1.** (*for carrying injured*) носи́л|ки (*pl.*, *g.* -ок); **~ case** лежа́чий/носи́лочный ра́неный. **2.** (*for shoes*) коло́дка. **3.** (*in boat*) упо́р для ног гребца́. **4.** (*of brick or stone*) ложо́к. **5.** (*for canvas*) подра́мник.

cpds. **~-bearer** *n.* санита́р-носи́льщик; **~-party** *n.* санита́рный отря́д.

strew [stru:] *v.t.* **1.** (*scatter*) разбр|а́сывать, -оса́ть; расст|ила́ть, -ла́ть; уст|ила́ть, -ла́ть. **2.** (*cover by scattering*) пос|ыпа́ть, -ы́пать; **~ a grave with flowers** ус|ыпа́ть, -ы́пать моги́лу цвета́ми.

striate(d) ['straɪt; 'straɪeɪtɪd] *adj.* полоса́тый, боро́здчатый.

stricken ['strɪkən] *adj.* **1.** (*lit.*, *fig.*) ра́неный; поражённый; **~ with fear** поражённый у́жасом; **~ with fever** сражённый лихора́дкой; **~ with paralysis** разби́тый параличо́м. **2.**: **~ in years** престаре́лый; в года́х; **3.** (*US*, *deleted*): **~ from the record** вы́черкнутый из протоко́ла.

strict [strɪkt] *adj.* **1.** (*precise*) стро́гий, то́чный; **the ~ truth** и́стинная пра́вда; **~ accuracy** абсолю́тная то́чность. **2.** (*stringent*): **in ~ confidence** в строжа́йшей та́йне. **3.** (*rigorous*, *stern*) стро́гий, взыска́тельный.

strictness ['strɪktnɪs] *n.* стро́гость, то́чность.

stricture ['strɪktʃə(r)] *n.* **1.** (*med.*) стрикту́ра, суже́ние сосу́дов. **2.** (*censure*) осужде́ние; **~s were passed on his conduct** ему́ бы́ло вы́несено порица́ние.

stride [straɪd] *n.* (*long pace*, *step*) (широ́кий) шаг; (*gait*) по́ступь; **he has an easy ~** у него́ лёгкая по́ступь; (*fig.*): **science has made great ~s** нау́ка сде́лала больши́е успе́хи; **he took the exam in his ~** он с лёгкостью одоле́л/сдал экза́мен; **he took the news in his ~** он споко́йно при́нял э́ту весть/но́вость; **get into one's ~** входи́ть, войти́ в колею́; бра́ться, взя́ться за де́ло.

v.i. шага́ть (*impf.*); **he strode across the ditch** он шагну́л че́рез (*or* перешагну́л) кана́ву.

stridency ['straɪd(ə)nsɪ] *n.* ре́зкость, пронзи́тельность.

strident ['straɪd(ə)nt] *adj.* ре́зкий, пронзи́тельный.

strife [straɪf] *n.* борьба́, вражда́, спор.

strike [straɪk] *n.* **1.** (*of workers*) забасто́вка, ста́чка; **general** ~ всео́бщая забасто́вка; **sympathetic** ~ забасто́вка солида́рности; ~ **committee** ста́чечный комите́т; ~ **pay** посо́бие басту́ющим; **be on** ~ бастова́ть (*impf.*); **go (***or* **come out) on** ~ забастова́ть (*pf.*); объяв|ля́ть, -и́ть забасто́вку. **2.** (*of gold, oil etc.*) нахо́дка/откры́тие месторожде́ния. **3.** (*attack; blow*) нападе́ние; уда́р; **our aircraft carried out a** ~ **on enemy shipping** на́ша авиа́ция соверши́ла налёт на неприя́тельские суда́. **4. he has two** ~**s against him** (*coll., fig.*) у него́ два ми́нуса.

v.t. **1.** (*hit*) уд|аря́ть, -а́рить (*чем по чему; что обо что; кого чем*); **he struck the table with his hand** он уда́рил/сту́кнул руко́й по́ столу; **he failed to** ~ **the ball** ему́ не удало́сь уда́рить по мячу́; **he struck his head on the table** он сту́кнулся/ уда́рился голово́й об стол; **a falling stone struck his head** па́дающий ка́мень уда́рил его́ по голове́; **the bullet struck the tree** пу́ля попа́ло в де́рево; **lightning struck the tree** мо́лния попа́ла/уда́рила в де́рево; **the ship struck a rock** кора́бль наскочи́л на скалу́; **she struck the knife out of his hand** она́ вы́била нож у него́ из руки́. **2.** (*deliver*): ~ **a blow** нан|оси́ть, -ести́ уда́р (*кому*); **who struck the first blow?** кто на́чал (дра́ку/ссо́ру)?; кто зачи́нщик?; ~ **a blow for freedom** выступа́ть/вы́ступить в защи́ту свобо́ды. **3.** (*plunge*): **she struck a knife into his back** она́ вонзи́ла ему́ нож в спи́ну; (*fig., instil*) всел|я́ть, -и́ть; **the lion's roar struck panic into them** льви́ный рёв вы́звал у них пани́ческий страх. **4.** (*fig., impress*) пора|жа́ть, -зи́ть; каза́ться, по- +*d.*; **he was struck by her beauty** он был поражён её красото́й; **how does the new play** ~ **you?** как вам показа́лась/нра́вится но́вая пьеса; **the idea** ~**s me as a good one** э́та мысль ка́жется мне хоро́шей; **an idea struck me** мне пришла́ в го́лову (*or* меня́ осени́ла) мысль; **the humour of the situation struck me** мне вдруг предста́вилась вся коми́чность ситуа́ции. **5.** (*fig., come upon, find, discover*) напада́ть, напа́сть на+*a.*; нат|ыка́ться, -кну́ться на+*a.*; на|ходи́ть, -йти́; откр|ыва́ть, -ы́ть; **we struck a good place for a holiday** мы откры́ли хоро́шее ме́сто для о́тдыха; **I struck a serious difficulty** я столкну́лся с серьёзным затрудне́нием; **they struck oil** они откры́ли нефтяно́е месторожде́ние; ~ **gold** на|ходи́ть, -йти́ зо́лото; ~ **it rich** (*coll.*) напа́сть (*pf.*) на жи́лу; **we shall soon** ~ **the main road** мы ско́ро вы́йдем/попадём на гла́вную доро́гу. **6.** (*produce by striking*): ~ **a light** высека́ть, вы́сечь ого́нь; зажига́ть, заже́чь спи́чку; ~ **sparks from a flint** высека́ть, вы́сечь и́скры из кремня́. **7.:** ~ **a match** чи́ркнуть (*pf.*) спи́чкой; ~ **a coin/medal** выбива́ть, вы́бить (*or* чека́нить, от-) моне́ту/меда́ль; ~ **a chord** (*lit.*) брать, взять акко́рд; (*fig.*): **his name** ~**s a chord** его́ и́мя мне что́-то говори́т/напомина́ет; ~ **a note** (*lit.*) уда́рить (*pf.*) по кла́више/струне́; (*fig.*) взять (*pf.*) тон; ~ **root** пус|ка́ть, -ти́ть ко́рни. **8.** (*of bell, clock etc.*) бить (*impf.*), отбива́ть (*impf.*); **this clock** ~**s the hours and quarters** э́ти часы́ отбива́ют часы́ и че́тверти; **it has just struck four** то́лько что про́било четы́ре; **the clock struck midnight** часы́ уда́рили по́лночь. **9.** (*arrive at*): ~ **a bargain** заключ|а́ть, -и́ть сде́лку; ~ **a balance** подв|оди́ть, -ести́ бала́нс/ито́ги; (*fig.*) на|ходи́ть, -йти́ компроми́сс; ~ **an average** выводи́ть, вы́вести сре́днее число́; ~ **a happy medium** найти́ (*pf.*) золоту́ю середи́ну. **10.** (*suddenly make*): ~ **s.o. blind** ослеп|ля́ть, -и́ть кого́-н; ~ **s.o. dumb** (*fig.*) ошара́шить (*pf.*) кого́-н.; **he was struck dumb** у него́ язы́к прили́п к го́ртани (*or* отня́лся); он онеме́л; ~ **me pink!** (*sl.*) мать родна́я; ~ **s.o. dead** порази́ть (*pf.*) кого́-н. на смерть. **11.** (*assume*): ~ **an attitude** вста|ва́ть, -ть в (*or* прин|има́ть, -я́ть) по́зу. **12.** (*lower, take down*): ~ **one's flag** спус|ка́ть, -ти́ть флаг; ~ **a sail** уб|ира́ть, -ра́ть па́рус; ~ **camp** сн|има́ться, -я́ться с ла́геря.

v.i. **1.** (*hit*) уд|аря́ть, -а́рить; **the disease struck without warning** боле́знь вспы́хнула неожи́данно; ~ **while the iron is hot** (*prov.*) куй желе́зо, пока́ горячо́; ~ (*aim a blow*) **at s.o.** зама́х|иваться, -ну́ться на кого́-н.; (*fig.*): ~ **at the root of the trouble** искорен|я́ть, -и́ть исто́чник зла; ~ **at the foundations of sth.** подрыв|а́ть, -орва́ть осно́вы чего́-н.; **the disease** ~**s at children** э́та боле́знь поража́ет дете́й. **2.:** ~ **against** (*collide with*) уд|аря́ться, -а́риться о+*a.* **3.** (*direct one's course; penetrate*): **we struck to the right** мы взя́ли напра́во; **the explorers struck inland** иссле́дователи напра́вились внутрь/вглубь страны́; **damp** ~**s through the walls** сы́рость проника́ет сквозь сте́ны́; **the insult struck home** оскорбле́ние заде́ло его́ за живо́е. **4.** (*take root*) прин|има́ться, -я́ться. **5.** (*of clock etc.*) бить, про-; **his hour has struck** (*fig.*) его́ час проби́л. **6.: the match won't** ~ спи́чка не зажига́ется. **7.** (*go on* ~) бастова́ть, за- (**for:** что́бы доби́ться +*g.*). **8.: struck on** (*coll.*) влюблённый в+*a.*

with advs.: ~ **back** *v.i.* (*retaliate*) нанести́ (*pf.*) отве́тный уда́р; ~ **down** *v.t.* (*fell*) сби|ва́ть, -ть с ног; сра|жа́ть, -зи́ть; (*of illness etc.*) сва́л|ивать, -и́ть; сра|жа́ть, -зи́ть; ~ **in** *v.i.* (*of disease*) прон|ика́ть, -и́кнуть внутрь; (*interrupt*) переб|ива́ть, -и́ть; ~ **off** *v.t.* отруб|а́ть, -и́ть; ~ **off s.o.'s head** обезгла́в|ливать, -ить кого́-н.; отруби́ть (*pf.*) кому́-н. го́лову; ~ **s.o. (***or* **s.o.'s name) off (list etc.)** вычёркивать, вы́черкнуть кого́-н. (*or* чьё-н. и́мя) (из спи́ска); (*print*): ~ **off 1,000 copies** отпеча́тать (*pf.*) ты́сячу экземпля́ров; ~ **out** *v.t.* (*delete*): ~ **out a word** вычёркивать, вы́черкнуть сло́во; (*originate*) изобре|та́ть, -сти́; *v.i.* (*aim blow*) нан|оси́ть, -ести́ уда́р; уд|аря́ть, -а́рить; (*of swimmer*): ~ **out for the shore** (бы́стро) плыть (*det.*) к бе́регу; (*fig.*): ~ **out on one's own** пойти́ (*pf.*) свои́м путём; ~ **through** *v.t.* (*cross out*) зачёркивать, зачеркну́ть; ~ **up** *v.t. & i.*: ~ **up a song** затя́|гивать, -ну́ть пе́сню; ~ **up an acquaintance** завя́з|ывать, -а́ть знако́мство; *v.i.* (*begin playing/singing*) заигра́ть, запе́ть (*both pf.*).

cpds. ~**-bound** *adj.* поражённый забасто́вкой; ~**-breaker** *n.* штрейкбре́хер; ~**-breaking** *n.* штрейкбре́херство.

striker ['straɪkə(r)] *n.* **1.** (*pers. on strike*) забасто́вщи|к (*fem.* -ца). **2.** (*in gun*) уда́рник; (*used with flint*) огни́во.

striking ['straɪkɪŋ] *adj.* **1.** (*forceful*) порази́тельный; ~ **resemblance** рази́тельное схо́дство; (*remarkable*) замеча́тельный; (*interesting*) интере́сный. **2.** (*of clock*) с бо́ем. **3.:** ~ **distance** досяга́емость, расстоя́ние возмо́жного уда́ра; ~ **force** (*mil.*) уда́рная гру́ппа; уда́рное соедине́ние.

Strine [straɪn] *n.* (*coll.*) австрали́йский язы́к.

string [strɪŋ] *n.* **1.** верёвка, бечёвка, шпага́т; **ball of** ~ клубо́к бечёвки/верёвки; ~ **bag** се́тка, (*coll.*) аво́ська; ~ **vest** се́тка; (*of apron, bonnet etc.*) завя́зка, тесёмка, шнуро́к; (*fig.*): **have s.o. on a** ~ держа́ть/вести́ (*impf.*) кого́-н. на поводу́; **pull the** ~**s** быть и́стинным заправи́лой (чего́); **pull** ~**s** наж|има́ть, -а́ть на все кно́пки; **with no** ~**s attached** (*fig.*) без каки́х бы то ни́ было усло́вий. **2.** (*of bow*) тетива́; **he has two** ~**s to his bow** (*fig.*) у него́ есть вы́бор ме́жду двумя́ сре́дствами; он де́ржит ко́е-что про запа́с. **3.** (*of mus. instrument, racket*) струна́; **the** ~**s** (*of orchestra*) стру́нные инструме́нты (*m. pl.*); ~ **of a violin** скрипи́чная струна́; ~ **band/quartet** стру́нный орке́стр/кварте́т; **harp on one** ~ (*fig.*) тяну́ть (*impf.*) одну́ и ту же пе́сню; (*fig.*): **second** ~ (*pers.*) втора́я скри́пка, дублёр; (*thg.*) запасно́е сре́дство, друга́я возмо́жность. **4.** (~*y substance, fibre e.g. in bean*) волокно́; ~ **bean** фасо́ль; (*in meat*) жи́ла. **5.** (*set of objects*): ~ **of beads** бу́с|ы (*pl., g.* —); ~ **of pearls** ни́тка же́мчуга; ~ **of onions/sausages** свя́зка лу́ка/соси́сок; ~ **of boats/houses/medals** ряд ло́док/домо́в/меда́лей; ~ **of cars/tourists** верени́ца автомоби́лей/тури́стов; ~ **of oaths** пото́к руга́тельств; ~ **of race-horses** скаковы́е ло́шади, принадлежа́щие одному́ владе́льцу.

v.t. **1.** (*furnish with* ~): ~ **a bow** натя́|гивать, -ну́ть тетиву́ на лук; ~ **a racket** натя́|гивать, -ну́ть стру́ны на раке́тку. **2.** (*thread on* ~) низа́ть (*or* нани́зывать), на-. **3.** (*remove* ~*y fibre from*): ~ **beans** чи́стить, по- стручки́ фасо́ли.

with advs.: ~ **along** *v.t.* (*coll., deceive*) води́ть (*impf.*) за́ нос; *v.i.*: ~ **along with s.o.** (*coll., accompany*) сопрово|жда́ть, -ди́ть кого́-н.; ~ **out** *v.t. & i.* (*extend*) растя́|гивать(ся), -ну́ть(ся); **the houses were strung out along the beach** дома́ тяну́лись вдоль побере́жья; ~ **together** *v.t.* низа́ть, на-; (*fig.*): **he is good at** ~**ing words**

together у него́ язы́к хорошо́ подве́шен; ~ **up** *v.t.* (*hang*): **the ham was strung up to the ceiling** о́корок был подве́шен под са́мый потоло́к; (*coll.*, *execute by hanging*) ве́шать, пове́сить; вздёрнуть (*pf.*) на ви́селицу; (*make tense*): **I am all strung up** я в большо́м напряже́нии; я взви́нчен.

stringed [strɪŋd] *adj.* стру́нный.

stringency ['strɪndʒ(ə)nsɪ] *n.* стро́гость; **credit** ~ стеснённый креди́т.

stringent ['strɪndʒ(ə)nt] *adj.* (*strict*, *precise*) стро́гий, то́чный.

stringer ['strɪŋə(r)] *n.* (*coll.*) внешта́тный корреспонде́нт.

stringy ['strɪŋɪ] *adj.* **1.** (*fibrous*): ~ **beans** волокни́стая фасо́ль; ~ **meat** жили́стое мя́со. **2.** (*of glue*) тягу́чий, вя́зкий.

strip[1] [strɪp] *n.* полоса́; (*of cloth*) поло́ска, ле́нта; ~ **of land** поло́ска земли́; **paper hung in ~s from the walls** обо́и полоса́ми свиса́ли со стен; **a ~ of wood** деревя́нная пла́нка/ре́йка; ~ **cartoon** расска́з в карти́нках; ~ **lighting** нео́новое освеще́ние; **tear s.o. off a** ~ (*coll.*) сн|има́ть, -ять стру́жку с кого́-н.

strip[2] [strɪp] *v.t.* (*tear off*) сдира́ть, содра́ть; **the bark was ~ped from the tree** (*or* **the tree was ~ped of its bark**) де́рево бы́ло обо́драно; с де́рева содра́ли кору́; **she ~ped the blankets off the bed** она́ стяну́ла/сняла́ одея́ла с крова́ти; **a tool for ~ping paint** инструме́нт для соска́бливания кра́ски; **he ~ped the thread of the screw** он сорва́л резьбу́ винта́. **2.** (*denude*) разд|ева́ть, -е́ть; **he was ~ped of his clothes** с него́ сорва́ли/сня́ли оде́жду; его́ разде́ли; **the room was ~ped bare** из ко́мнаты вы́несли всю ме́бель; **the birds ~ped the fruit bushes** пти́цы обклева́ли я́годы с кусто́в; **we had to ~ the walls** нам пришло́сь содра́ть обо́и/кра́ску со стен; ~ **(down) a machine/weapon** раз|бира́ть, -обра́ть (*or* демонти́ровать (*impf.*, *pf.*)) маши́ну/ору́жие; **the locusts ~ped the fields** саранча́ опустоши́ла поля́; (*fig.*, *deprive*) лиш|а́ть, -и́ть (*кого чего*); **he was ~ped of his rank** его́ лиши́ли зва́ния; **the authorities ~ped him of his property** вла́сти отобра́ли у него́ всё иму́щество.

v.i.: ~ **(naked),** ~ **off** разд|ева́ться, -е́ться (донага́).

with advs.: ~ **away,** ~ **off** *vv.t.* (*lit.*) *see v.t.* **1.**; (*fig.*, *remove*) от|бира́ть, -обра́ть; ~ **down** *v.t.* (*machine etc.*) раз|бира́ть, -обра́ть; демонти́ровать (*impf.*, *pf.*).

cpds. **~-club** *n.* клуб с пока́зом стрипти́за; **~-tease** *n.* стрипти́з; **~teaser** *n.* исполни́тель (*fem.* -ница) стрипти́за.

stripe [straɪp] *n.* **1.** полоса́, поло́ска. **2.** (*mil.*) наши́вка, шевро́н; **get a** ~ получ|а́ть, -и́ть очередно́е зва́ние; **lose a** ~ быть разжа́лованным. **3.** (*US*, *type*) тип, хара́ктер, род.

striped [straɪpt] *adj.* (*e.g. tiger*) полоса́тый; ~ **fabric** мате́рия в поло́ску, полоса́тая мате́рия; ~ **trousers** брю́ки в се́рую и чёрную поло́ску (к визи́тке).

stripling ['strɪplɪŋ] *n.* юне́ц.

stripper ['strɪpə(r)] *n.* (*solvent*) раство́р для удале́ния кра́ски; (*artiste*) исполни́тельница стрипти́за.

stripy ['straɪpɪ] *adj.* полоса́тый, в поло́ску.

strive [straɪv] *v.i.* **1.** стреми́ться (*impf.*) (**after, for:** к+*d.*); **they strove for victory** они́ стреми́лись к побе́де; **I strove to understand what he said** я стара́лся поня́ть, что он говори́т. **2.** (*fight*) боро́ться (*impf.*); **they strove with each other for mastery** они́ боро́лись друг с дру́гом за власть.

stroke[1] [strəʊk] *n.* **1.** уда́р; ~ **of lightning** уда́р мо́лнии; **six ~s of the cane** шесть уда́ров па́лкой; **at a** ~ (*fig.*) с одного́ маху́; одни́м уда́ром/ма́хом **2.** (*of clock*) уда́р, бой; **on the** ~ **of 9** ро́вно в де́вять. **3.** (*paralytic attack*) парали́ч; уда́р; **he had a** ~ его́ хвати́л уда́р; его́ разби́л парали́ч; **he died of a** ~ он у́мер от уда́ра. **4.** (*single movement of series*): ~ **of a piston** ход по́ршня; ~ **of an oar** взмах весла́, гребо́к; **row a slow** ~ ме́дленно грести́ (*impf.*); **put s.o. off his** ~ (*fig.*) сби|ва́ть, -ть кого́-н. с то́лку. **5.** (*in swimming*) стиль (*m.*); **what ~ does she use?** каки́м сти́лем она́ пла́вает? **6.** (*single action or instance*): **he has not done a** ~ **(of work)** он па́льцем о па́лец не уда́рил; ~ **of business** сде́лка; ~ **of genius** гениа́льный ход; гениа́льная мысль; ~ **of luck** (неожи́данная) уда́ча; везе́ние. **7.** (*with pen*, *pencil etc.*) штрих; **with, at a** ~ **of the pen** (*lit.*, *fig.*) одни́м ро́счерком пера́; **he dashed off the picture in a few ~s** он не́сколькими штриха́ми наброса́л карти́ну; (*with brush*) мазо́к; **thick/thin ~s** жи́рные/то́нкие мазки́; **put the finishing ~s to one's work** нанести́ (*pf.*) после́дние штрихи́; заверши́ть (*pf.*) свою́ рабо́ту. **8.** (*typ.*, *oblique* ~) дробь, коса́я черта́. **9.** (*oarsman*) загребно́й; **row** ~ (*also* ~ **a boat**) задава́ть (*impf.*) темп гребца́м.

stroke[2] [strəʊk] *n.*: **he gave her hand a** ~ он погла́дил её по руке́.

v.t. **1.** гла́дить (*or* поглаживать), по-; **she ~d the horse's head** она́ погла́дила ло́шадь по голове́. **2.** *see* **stroke**[1] **9.**

stroll [strəʊl] *n.* прогу́лка; **have, take, go for a** ~ идти́ (*det.*) на прогу́лку (*or* прогуля́ться).

v.i. гуля́ть (*impf.*); прогу́л|иваться, -я́ться; (*wander*) броди́ть (*impf.*); **~ing players** бродя́чие актёры, бродя́чая тру́ппа.

strong [strɒŋ] *adj.* **1.** (*powerful*, *forceful*) си́льный, кре́пкий; ~ **as a horse** си́льный как ло́шадь; ≃ здоро́в как бык; ~ **man** сила́ч; **a ~ly fortified city** хорошо́ укреплённый го́род; ~ **character** си́льная нату́ра; ~ **wind** си́льный/кре́пкий ве́тер; ~ **tide** си́льный прили́в; ~ **attraction** больша́я привлека́тельность (*or* притяга́тельная си́ла); ~ **measures** круты́е ме́ры; ~ **argument** ве́ский аргуме́нт; ~ **evidence** убеди́тельное доказа́тельство; ~ **protest** энерги́чный проте́ст; ~ **warning** серьёзное предупрежде́ние; ~ **suspicion** си́льное подозре́ние; **I am ~ly inclined to go** я о́чень/весьма́ скло́нен пойти́; ~ **words** си́льные выраже́ния; ~ **language** брань. **2.** (*stout*, *tough*; *durable*) кре́пкий; про́чный; ~ **cloth** кре́пкая мате́рия; ~ **walls** про́чные сте́ны; ~ **foundations** про́чные основа́ния. **3.** (*robust*, *healthy*) кре́пкий, здоро́вый; ~ **constitution** кре́пкое здоро́вье; **he is quite ~ again** он уже́ вполне́ окре́п; **he has never been very** ~ он никогда́ не отлича́лся кре́пким здоро́вьем; **she is feeling ~er** она́ чу́вствует себя́ лу́чше. **4.** (*firm*) твёрдый, кре́пкий; ~ **conviction** твёрдое убежде́ние; ~ **supporter** ре́вностный сторо́нник; ~ **faith** твёрдая ве́ра; **the market is** ~ ры́нок усто́йчив. **5.** (*of faculties*): ~ **mind** хоро́шая голова́; ~ **memory** о́страя па́мять; **he is ~ in Latin** он силён в латы́ни; **oratory is his ~ point** его́ си́ла в красноре́чии. **6.** (*of smell*, *taste etc.*): ~ **flavour** о́стрый/ре́зкий при́вкус; ~ **cheese** о́стрый сыр; ~ **onions** е́дкий лук; ~ **meat** (*fig.*) пи́ща для си́льных умо́в; **a** ~ (*unconventional*) **play** сме́лая пье́са; ~ **breath** дурно́й за́пах изо рта. **7.** (*concentrated*): ~ **drink** кре́пкий напи́ток; **a ~ cup of tea** ча́шка кре́пкого ча́я. **8.** (*sharply defined*) ре́зкий; ~ **light** ре́зкий свет; ~ **colour** я́ркий цвет; ~ **shadow** густа́я тень; ~ **accent** (*in speech*) си́льный акце́нт; ~ **likeness** большо́е схо́дство. **9.** (*well-supported*): ~ **candidate** кандида́т, облада́ющий больши́м ша́нсом на успе́х; ~ **favourite** би́тый фавори́т; **a** ~ (*well-chosen*) **team** си́льная/отбо́рная кома́нда. **10.** (*numerous*) чи́сленный; **a ~ contingent** многочи́сленный континге́нт; **a company 200** ~ ро́та чи́сленностью в 200 челове́к. **11.** (*cards*): **a ~ hand** беру́щая ка́рта; **my ~est suit** моя́ са́мая си́льная масть. **12.** (*gram.*): ~ **verb** си́льный глаго́л.

adv.: **going** ~ в прекра́сной фо́рме.

cpds. **~-arm** *adj.*: **~-arm tactics** та́ктика примене́ния си́лы; **~box** *n.* сейф; **~hold** *n.* кре́пость, цитаде́ль, тверды́ня, опло́т; **~-minded** *adj.* твёрдый, реши́тельный; **~-room** *n.* стальна́я ка́мера; **~-willed** *adj.* реши́тельный, волево́й.

strontium ['strɒntɪəm] *n.* стро́нций.

strop [strɒp] *n.* (*for razor etc.*) реме́нь (*m.*) для пра́вки бритв.

v.t. пра́вить (*impf.*) (*бритву*).

strophe ['strəʊfɪ] *n.* строфа́.

strophic ['strəʊfɪk, 'strɒ-] *adj.* строфи́ческий.

stroppy ['strɒpɪ] *adj.* (*coll.*) несгово́рчивый, сварли́вый, строптивый.

structural ['strʌktʃər(ə)l] *adj.*: ~ **geology/linguistics**

структу́рная геоло́гия/лингви́стика; ~ **defects** дефе́кты в констру́кции; ~ **engineer** инжене́р-строи́тель (*m.*); ~ **engineering** строи́тельная те́хника.

structuralism ['strʌktʃərə,lɪz(ə)m] *n.* структурали́зм.

structuralist ['strʌktʃərəlɪst] *n.* структурали́ст.

structure ['strʌktʃə(r)] *n.* **1.** (*abstr.*) структу́ра, стро́й, строе́ние, организа́ция; ~ **of a building** архитекто́ника зда́ния; ~ **of rocks, of a cell** структу́ра скал (*or* го́рных поро́д)/кле́тки; ~ **of a sentence** структу́ра предложе́ния; ~ **of a language** строй языка́. **2.** (*concr.*) строе́ние, сооруже́ние; **a top-heavy** ~ громо́здкое сооруже́ние; (*building*) зда́ние.

v.t. стро́ить, по-; организова́ть (*impf., pf.*).

struggle ['strʌg(ə)l] *n.* (*lit., fig.*) борьба́; ~ **for existence** борьба́ за существова́ние; (*tussle*) схва́тка, потасо́вка; **without a** ~ без бо́я/борьбы́/сопротивле́ния; (*attempt, effort*); **a violent** ~ **to escape** отча́янная попы́тка к бе́гству.

v.i. **1.** (*fight*) боро́ться (*impf.*); би́ться (*impf.*); **the rabbit** ~**d to escape from the snare** кро́лик би́лся в силка́х. **2.** (*fig., grapple*) би́ться (*impf.*) (*над чем*); **we** ~**d with this problem for a long time** мы до́лго би́лись над э́той пробле́мой. **3.** (*move convulsively*) би́ться (*impf.*); **the child** ~**d and kicked** ребёнок вырыва́лся и бил нога́ми; **he** ~**d for a while and then died** он сде́лал не́сколько су́дорожных движе́ний и у́мер. **4.** (*make strenuous efforts*) боро́ться (*impf.*); стара́ться (*impf.*) изо всех сил; **he** ~**d to make himself heard** он изо всех сил пыта́лся перекрича́ть други́х; **he** ~**d for breath** он хвата́л ртом во́здух; (*fig., move with difficulty*): **he** ~**d to his feet** он с трудо́м подня́лся на́ ноги; **a struggling artist** непри́знанный худо́жник.

strum [strʌm] *n.* бренча́ние, тре́ньканье.

v.t. & i. бренча́ть, тре́нькать (*both impf.*) (на+*p.*).

strumpet ['strʌmpɪt] *n.* (*arch.*) потаску́ха, шлю́ха.

strut[1] [strʌt] *n.* (*gait*) ва́жная похо́дка.

v.i. ходи́ть (*indet.*) с ва́жным/напы́щенным ви́дом.

strut[2] [strʌt] *n.* (*support*) стро́йка, подко́с, распо́рка.

strychnine ['strɪkni:n] *n.* стрихни́н; ~ **poisoning** отравле́ние стрихни́ном.

stub [stʌb] *n.* (*of tooth*) пенёк; (*of pencil*) огры́зок; (*of cigarette*) оку́рок; (*of dog's tail*) обру́бок; (*of cheque etc.*) корешо́к.

v.t. **1.** ~ **(up)** вырыва́ть, вы́рвать с ко́рнем; корчева́ть (*or* выкорчёвывать), вы-. **2.** ~ **(out) a cigarette** гаси́ть, по- папиро́су. **3.:** ~ **one's toe on sth.** спот|ыка́ться, -кну́ться о(бо) что-н.

stubble ['stʌb(ə)l] *n.* жнивьё, по́жня, стерня́; (*of beard*) щети́на.

stubbly ['stʌblɪ] *adj.*: ~ **field** пожни́вное по́ле; ~ **chin** щети́нистый подборо́док.

stubborn ['stʌbən] *adj.* (*obstinate*) упря́мый; (*tenacious*) упо́рный; (*unyielding, intractable*) неподатливый; **a** ~ **fight** упо́рный бой; ~ **soil** непода́тливая по́чва.

stubbornness ['stʌbənnɪs] *n.* упря́мство; упо́рство; непода́тливость.

stucco ['stʌkəʊ] *n.* штукату́рка; (*attr.*) лепно́й; ~ **moulding** лепно́е украше́ние, лепни́на.

v.t. штукату́рить, о-.

stuck-up ['stʌk'ʌp] *adj.* (*coll., haughty, conceited*) чванли́вый, зано́счивый.

stud[1] [stʌd] *n.* (*of horses*) ко́нный заво́д; коню́шня; племенна́я фе́рма.

cpds. ~**-book** *n.* племенна́я кни́га; ~**-farm** *n.* ко́нный заво́д; ~**-groom** *n.* (ста́рший) ко́нюх; ~**-horse** *n.* племенно́й жеребе́ц; ~**-mare** *n.* племенна́я кобы́ла.

stud[2] [stʌd] *n.* **1.** (*nail, boss etc.*) гвоздь (*m.*) с большо́й шля́пкой; кно́пка. **2.** (*collar-*~) за́понка.

v.t.: ~**ded boots** боти́нки на шипа́х; **a sky** ~**ded with stars** не́бо, усе́янное звёздами; **a dress** ~**ded with jewels** пла́тье, усы́панное драгоце́нными камня́ми.

student ['stju:d(ə)nt] *n.* студе́нт (*fem.* -ка); (*attr.*) студе́нческий; **medical** ~ студе́нт-ме́дик; (*fem.*) студе́нтка-меди́чка; (*pupil*) учени́к, уча́щийся; ~ **interpreter** перево́дчик-стажёр; ~ **of languages** изуча́ющий языки́; **engineering** ~ студе́нт-техно́лог; **law** ~ студе́нт (*fem.* -ка) юриди́ческого факульте́та.

studentship ['stju:dəntʃɪp] *n.* стипе́ндия.

studied ['stʌdɪd] *adj.* (*deliberate*): ~ **indifference** напускно́е/де́ланное равноду́шие/безразли́чие; ~ **insult** умы́шленное оскорбле́ние.

studio ['stju:dɪəʊ] *n.* **1.** (*of artist, photographer etc.*) мастерска́я, сту́дия, ателье́ (*indecl.*); ~ **couch** дива́н-крова́ть. **2.** (*broadcasting* ~) радиосту́дия. **3.** (*cin.*) съёмочный павильо́н; киносту́дия.

studious ['stju:dɪəs] *adj.* **1.** (*fond of study*) лю́бящий нау́ку. **2.** (*deliberate*) нарочи́тый; ~ **politeness** нарочи́тая/подчёркнутая ве́жливость; **he** ~**ly ignored me** он стара́тельно меня́ игнори́ровал. **3.** (*liter., anxious, zealous*) усе́рдный, стара́тельный; **he is** ~ **to forestall our wishes** он стара́ется предупреди́ть все на́ши жела́ния.

stud|y ['stʌdɪ] *n.* **1.** (*learning, investigation*) изуче́ние, учёба, нау́ка; ~**ies** заня́тия (*nt. pl.*); **department of Slavonic** ~**ies** отделе́ние/ка́федра слави́стики; **he gives all his time to** ~**y** он всё своё вре́мя отдаёт нау́ке/заня́тиям; **make a** ~**y of** (тща́тельно) изуч|а́ть, -и́ть; **my** ~**ies have convinced me** мои́ иссле́дования убеди́ли меня́. **2.** (*endeavour*): **her chief** ~**y is to please him** гла́вная её забо́та — угоди́ть ему́; **3.** (*sketch; mus.*) этю́д; **his face was a** ~**y** на его́ лицо́ сто́ило посмотре́ть. **4.** (*room*) кабине́т. **5.: in a brown** ~**y** в глубо́кой заду́мчивости; в глубо́ком разду́мье/размышле́нии.

v.t. **1.** (*learn, investigate*) изуч|а́ть, -и́ть; иссле́довать (*impf., pf.*); прораб|а́тывать, -о́тать; **occupied in** ~**ying local conditions** за́нятый изуче́нием ме́стных усло́вий; **Greek is not** ~**ied** не изуча́ют гре́ческий (язы́к) (*or* не занима́ются гре́ческим (языко́м)). **2.** (*scrutinize*) (внима́тельно) рассм|а́тривать, -отре́ть; **I** ~**ied his face** я испыту́юще посмотре́л на его́ лицо́. **3.** (*commit to memory*): ~**y a part** учи́ть (*impf.*) роль. **4.** (*pay regard to*) забо́титься, по- о+*p.*; **he** ~**ies his own interests** он счита́ется лишь с со́бственными интере́сами.

v.i. учи́ться (*impf.*); **he is** ~**ying for the Church** он гото́вится стать свяще́нником.

stuff [stʌf] *n.* **1.** (*material, substance*) материа́л, вещество́, вещь; **the** ~ **they make beer out of** (*coll.*) то, из чего́ приготовля́ют пи́во; **he is not the** ~ **heroes are made of** из таки́х геро́и не выхо́дят; **there's some good** ~ **in this book** в э́той кни́ге есть ко́е-что поле́зное/хоро́шее; **his poems are poor** ~ его́ стихи́ — дрянь; **green** ~ (*vegetables*) зе́лень, о́вощ|и (*pl., g.* -е́й). **2.** (*coll., things*) ве́щи (*f. pl.*); (*pej., rubbish*): **what shall I do with this** ~ **from the cupboard?** что мне де́лать с э́тим хла́мом из шка́фа?; **do you call this** ~ **beer?** (и) вы э́ту дрянь называ́ете пи́вом?; ~ **and nonsense!** чепуха́!; ерунда́! **3.** (*coll., business*): **do one's** ~ де́лать, с- своё де́ло; **know one's** ~ знать (*impf.*) своё де́ло; **that's the** ~ **(to give 'em)!** вот то, что на́до!; э́то-то и на́до!; **I don't want any rough** ~ пожа́луйста, без дра́ки.

v.t. **1.** (*pack, fill*) наб|ива́ть, -и́ть (*что чем*); **he** ~**ed the sacks with straw** он наби́л мешки́ соло́мой; **the box was** ~**ed with old clothes** сунду́к был наби́т ста́рым тряпьём; **the taxidermist** ~**s dead birds** таксидерми́ст набива́ет чу́чела птиц; **a** ~**ed eagle** чу́чело орла́; (*cul.*) фарширова́ть, за-; начин|я́ть, -и́ть; ~ **a duck with sage and onions** начин|я́ть, -и́ть у́тку шалфе́ем и лу́ком; **he** ~**ed his head with useless facts** он заби́л себе́ го́лову вся́кими нену́жными све́дениями; ~ **o.s.** (*overeat*) объ|еда́ться, -е́сться; об|жира́ться, -ожра́ться; ~**ed shirt** (*fig., coll.*) наду́тый индю́к; **get** ~**ed!** (*vulg.*) иди́ ты!; фиг тебе́!; **my nose is** ~**ed up** у меня́ нос зало́жен. **2.** (*cram, push*) запи́х|ивать, -а́ть/-ну́ть (*что во что*); **she** ~**ed her clothes into a case** она́ запихну́ла свою́ оде́жду в чемода́н; **he** ~**ed the note behind a cushion** он запихну́л/засу́нул запи́ску за поду́шку.

stuffiness ['stʌfɪnɪs] *n.* духота́, спёртость; (*of pers.*) чо́порность.

stuffing ['stʌfɪŋ] *n.* **1.** (*of cushion, doll etc.*) наби́вка; **knock the** ~ **out of s.o.** (*deflate*) сбить (*pf.*) с кого́-н. спесь;

(*enfeeble*) ослабить (*pf.*) кого-н.; (*thrash*) колотить, по-. **2.** (*cul.*) начинка, фарш.

stuffy ['stʌfɪ] *adj.* (*of room*) душный; (*of atmosphere*) душный, спёртый; (*of pers.*) чопорный.

stultif|y ['stʌltɪ,faɪ] *v.t.* (*render futile*): **our efforts were ~ied** наши усилия были сведены на нет.

stumbl|e ['stʌmb(ə)l] *n.* спотыкание; (*in speech*) запинка.

v.i. **1.** (*miss one's footing*) оступ|аться, -иться; спот|ыкаться, -кнуться; **he ~ed against, over a stone** он споткнулся о камень; **~ing gait** ковыляющая походка; **~ing-block** камень (*m.*) преткновения; **a ~ing-block to faith** помеха вере; **the ~ing-blocks of Russian grammar** трудности русской грамматики. **2.** (*speak haltingly*) зап|инаться, -нуться; спот|ыкаться, -кнуться; **he ~es over his words** он запинается/спотыкается на каждом слове; **he ~ed through his speech** он кое-как произнёс свою речь. **3.: ~e across, upon** (*find by chance*) нат|алкиваться, -олкнуться на+*a.*; нат|ыкаться, -кнуться на+*a.*; нап|адать, -асть на+*a.*

stumer ['stju:mə(r)] *n.* (*sl.*) фальшивый банкнот *и m.n.*

stump [stʌmp] *n.* **1.** (*of tree*) пень (*m.*), обрубок; **~ oratory** демагогия; (*of tooth*) пенёк; (*of limb*) культя; **stir one's ~s** (*coll.*) поторапливаться, пошевеливаться (*both impf.*); (*of cigar*) окурок; (*of pencil*) огрызок. **2.** (*used in drawing*) растушёвка. **3.** (*cricket*) столбик.

v.t. **1.** (*floor*) ставить, по- в тупик; озадачи|вать, -ть; **I was ~ed by the question** этот вопрос поставил меня впросак. **2.** (*drawing etc.*) тушевать, рас-. **3.** (*tour, making speeches*): **he ~ed the country** он совершил агитационную поездку (по стране); он объездил всю страну, выступая с речами.

v.i. (*walk clumsily*) топать (*impf.*), тяжело ступать (*impf.*); **he ~ed across the room** он протопал по комнате.

with adv.: **~ up** *v.t. & i.* (*coll.*) выкладывать, выложить (деньги); **I had to ~ up for the meal** мне пришлось заплатить за еду.

stumpy ['stʌmpɪ] *adj.* коренастый, приземистый.

stun [stʌn] *v.t.* **1.** (*knock unconscious*) оглуш|ать, -ить. **2.** (*amaze, astound*) пора|жать, -зить; ошелом|лять, -ить; **a ~ning dress** потрясающее/сногсшибательное платье (*coll.*).

stunt [stʌnt] *n.* трюк, номер; **~ man** (*cin.*) каскадёр; трюкач.

v.t.: **~ growth** задерж|ивать, -ать рост; **~ed trees** низкорослые деревья.

stupefaction [,stju:pɪ'fækʃ(ə)n] *n.* оглушение, ошеломление, оцепенение.

stupefy ['stju:pɪ,faɪ] *v.t.* оглуш|ать, -ить; (*amaze*) ошелом|лять, -ить.

stupendous [stju:'pendəs] *adj.* изумительный; (*in size*) огромный, колоссальный.

stupid ['stju:pɪd] *adj.* глупый, тупой; (*in state of stupor*) остолбенелый, оцепенелый; **~ with sleep** осоловелый; **~ person** глупый человек, дурак (*fem.* дура); глупец; тупица (*c.g.*).

stupidity [,stju:'pɪdɪtɪ] *n.* глупость, тупость.

stupor ['stju:pə(r)] *n.* остолбенение, оцепенение.

sturdiness ['stɜ:dɪnɪs] *n.* крепость, сила.

sturdy ['stɜ:dɪ] *adj.* крепкий, сильный; **a ~ youngster** крепкий парень, крепыш; **a ~ oak** могучий дуб.

sturgeon ['stɜ:dʒ(ə)n] *n.* осётр; (*as food*) осётр, осетрина.

stutter ['stʌtə(r)] *n.* заикание; **he has a terrible ~** он ужасно заикается.

v.t. произн|осить, -ести заикаясь.

v.i. заикаться (*impf.*).

stutterer ['stʌtərə(r)] *n.* заика (*c.g.*).

sty[1] [staɪ] *n.* (**pig ~**; *lit. fig.*) хлев, свинарник.

sty[2], **stye** [staɪ] *n.* (*on eye*) ячмень (*m.*).

Stygian ['stɪdʒɪən] *adj.* стигийский, адский, мрачный; **~ gloom** адский мрак.

style [staɪl] *n.* **1.** (*manner*) стиль (*m.*), манера; (*of writing*) стиль, слог; **written in a florid ~** написанный витиеватым слогом; **the ~ in which they live** их образ жизни; **the ~ of Rubens** манера Рубенса; **flattery is not his ~** лесть не в его духе/стиле; **in Southern ~** по-южному; **cramp s.o.'s ~** мешать (*impf.*) кому-н.; **in fine ~** с блеском; **~ sheet** издательская инструкция. **2.** (*elegance, taste, luxury*): **she has ~** у неё есть вкус; **in ~** с шиком; **live in ~** жить (*impf.*) широко (*or* на широкую ногу). **3.** (*fashion*) мода, фасон; **in the latest ~** по последней моде; **the latest ~s from Paris** последние парижские моды. **4.** (*sort, kind*) род, тип, сорт; **just the ~ of dinner I detest** как раз тот род банкета, какой я терпеть не могу; **what ~ of house do you require?** какого типа дом вы хотели бы приобрести? **5.** (*mode of address*) титул, титулование; **what is the proper ~ of a bishop?** как следует величать епископа? **6.** (*of dates*): **Old/New S~** старый/новый стиль; (*adv.*) по старому/новому стилю. **7.** (*engraving tool*) гравировальная игла.

v.t. **1.** (*designate*) наз|ывать, -вать; **self-~d** самозванный. **2.** (*design*): **she had her hair ~d** она сделала себе причёску.

stylish ['staɪlɪʃ] *adj.* (*fashionable*) модный; **a coat of ~ cut** пальто модного покроя; (*smart*) элегантный, стильный, изящный.

stylishness ['staɪlɪʃnɪs] *n.* элегантность, изящество.

stylist ['staɪlɪst] *n.* стилист; **hair ~** парикмахер-модельер.

stylistic [staɪ'lɪstɪk] *adj.* стилистический.

stylize ['staɪlaɪz] *v.t.* стилизовать (*impf., pf.*).

stylus ['staɪləs] *n.* **1.** (*engraving tool*) гравировальная игла; резец. **2.** (*for making or playing records*) (граммофонная) иголка.

stymie ['staɪmɪ] *v.t.* (*fig.*) мешать (*impf.*) +*d.*; препятствовать (*impf.*) +*d.*

styptic ['stɪptɪk] *adj.*: **~ pencil** кровоостанавливающий карандаш.

Styria ['stɪərɪə] *n.* Штирия.

Styx [stɪks] *n.* Стикс.

suasion ['sweɪʒ(ə)n] *n.* уговаривание; **moral ~** увещевание.

suave [swɑ:v] *adj.* гладкий, лощёный, обходительный; (*of wine etc.*) мягкий.

suavity ['swɑ:vɪtɪ] *n.* гладкость, обходительность.

sub [sʌb] *n.* (*coll.*) *abbr. of* **1. submarine** подлодка. **2. substitute** замена; врио (*m. indecl.*) (временно исполняющий обязанности). **3. subscription** подписка. **4. subaltern** младший офицер; *see also* **sub-edit, sub-editor**

subacid [sʌb'æsɪd] *adj.* слабокислотный.

subacute [,sʌbə'kju:t] *adj.* подострый.

subaltern ['sʌbəlt(ə)n] *n.* младший офицер.

adj. низший (*по чину и т.п.*).

subaqu|atic [,sʌbə'kwætɪk], **-eous** [sʌb'eɪkwɪəs] *adjs.* подводный.

subarctic [sʌb'ɑ:ktɪk] *adj.* субарктический.

subcategory ['sʌb,kætɪgərɪ] *n.* подсекция, подвид.

subcommittee ['sʌbkə,mɪtɪ] *n.* подкомиссия; подкомитет.

subconscious [sʌb'kɒnʃəs] *n.* (*the* ~) подсознательное.

adj. подсознательный.

subcontinent ['sʌb,kɒntɪnənt] *n.* субконтинент.

subcontract[1] [sʌb'kɒntrækt] *n.* субподряд, субдоговор.

subcontract[2] [,sʌbkən'trækt] *v.i.* заключ|ать, -ить субдоговор.

subcontractor [,sʌbkən'træktə(r)] *n.* субподрядчик, завод-смежник.

subcutaneous [,sʌbkju:'teɪnɪəs] *adj.* подкожный.

subdivide ['sʌbdɪ,vaɪd, -'vaɪd] *v.t. & i.* подраздел|ять(ся), -ить(ся).

subdivisible [,sʌbdɪ'vɪzɪb(ə)l] *adj.* поддающийся подразделению.

subdivision ['sʌbdɪ,vɪʒ(ə)n, -'vɪʒ(ə)n] *n.* подразделение.

subdominant [sʌb'dɒmɪnənt] *n.* субдоминанта.

subdue [səb'dju:] *v.t.* **1.** (*conquer, subjugate*) подав|лять, -ить; **~ one's enemies** покор|ять, -ить врагов; (*tame, discipline*): **~ one's passions** подав|лять, -ить (*or* укро|щать, -тить) страсти. **2.** (*reduce*) ум|еньшать, -еньшить; (*soften*) смягч|ать, -ить; **~d light** мягкий свет; (*weaken*) осл|аблять, -абить; (*sound etc.*) приглуш|ать, -ить; пон|ижать, -изить; **in ~d voices** приглушёнными голосами. **3.** (*restrain*): **with an air of ~d satisfaction** со сдержанным удовлетворением; **he seems ~d today** он сегодня что-то притих.

sub-edit [sʌb'edɪt] *v.t.* произ|водить, -ести (*or* делать, с-) техническое редактирование +*g.*; готовить (*impf.*) к набору.

sub-editor [sʌb'edɪtə(r)] *n.* помощник редактора; технический редактор (*abbr.* техред).

subfamily ['sʌb,fæmɪlɪ] *n.* подсемейство.

subfusc ['sʌbfʌsk] *adj.* тёмный.

subglacial [sʌb'gleɪʃ(ə)l, -sɪəl] *adj.* подледниковый.

subgroup ['sʌbgru:p] *n.* подгруппа.

subheading ['sʌbhedɪŋ] *n.* подзаголовок.

subhuman [sʌb'hju:mən] *n.* недочеловек.

adj. нечеловеческий; принадлежащей к низшей расе.

subjacent [sʌb'dʒeɪs(ə)nt] *adj.* нижележащий.

subject[1] ['sʌbdʒɪkt] *n.* **1.** (*pol.*) подданный. **2.** (*gram.*) подлежащий. **3.** (*phil.*) субъект. **4.** (*theme, matter*) тема, предмет; **the ~ of the book** тема книги; **he was made the ~ of an experiment** его сделали объектом опыта; из него сделали объект для опыта; **he talked on the ~ of bees** он говорил о пчёлах; **change the ~** перев|одить, -ести разговор на другую тему; **return to the ~** вернуться (*pf.*) к прерванному разговору; **a painter who treats biblical ~s** живописец/художник, пишущий (картины на) библейские сюжеты; **you are treating the ~ very lightly** вы недостаточно серьёзно относитесь к этому вопросу; **while we're on the ~** поскольку зашёл разговор об этом; раз уж мы заговорили об этом (*or* на эту тему). **5.** (*branch of study*) предмет, дисциплина; **~ library** отраслевая/специальная библиотека; **he passed in four ~s** он прошёл по четырём предметам. **6.** (*cause, occasion*) повод; **a ~ of rejoicing** повод для веселья (*or* к веселью). **7.** (*type of pers.*): **a hysterical ~** истерический субъект.

adj. **1.** (*subordinate*) подчинённый; зависимый; **~ to a foreign power** подвластный иностранному государству; находящийся под иностранным владычеством; **all citizens are ~ to the law** закон распространяется на всех граждан; **bodies are ~ to gravity** тела подчиняются закону тяготения. **2.** (*liable, prone, inclined*): **he is ~ to changes of mood** он подвержен (быстрым) сменам настроения; **are you ~ to colds?** вы подвержены простуде?; **trains are ~ to delay** возможны опоздания поездов. **3.**: **~ to** (*conditional upon*) подлежащий +*d.*; **the fare is ~ to alteration** стоимость проезда может быть изменена; **the treaty is ~ to ratification** договор подлежит ратификации; **the price is ~ to market fluctuations** цена зависит от колебаний рынка.

adv.: **~ to** при условии (*чего*); (однако) с учётом (*чего*); поскольку иное не содержится/предусматривается в+*p.*; **~ to the following provision** с соблюдением нижеследующего положения; **~ to your approval** если вы одобрите; **~ to your rights** поскольку это допускают ваши права; **~ to your views** если вы не возражаете; если это не противоречит вашему мнению.

cpds. **~-heading** *n.* рубрика, (под)заголовок; **~-matter** *n.* содержание, предмет (*чего*).

subject[2] [səb'dʒekt] *v.t.* **1.** (*make subordinate*) подчин|ять, -ить; **they were ~ed to the rule of one power** они были подчинены господству одной державы. **2.** (*expose, make liable*) подв|ергать, -ергнуть (*кого/что чему*); **the machine was ~ed to tests** машину подвергли испытаниям; **he was ~ed to insult** его подвергли оскорблению.

subjection [səb'dʒekʃ(ə)n] *n.* подчинение; **bring into ~** подчин|ять, -ить; покор|ять, -ить.

subjective [səb'dʒektɪv] *adj.* субъективный; (*gram.*): **~ case** именительный падеж.

subjectivism [səb'dʒektɪ,vɪz(ə)m] *n.* субъективизм.

subjectivist [səb'dʒektɪvɪst] *n.* субъективист.

subjectivity [,sʌbdʒek'tɪvɪtɪ] *n.* субъективность.

subjoin [sʌb'dʒɔɪn] *v.t.* присовокуп|лять, -ить; прил|агать, -ожить.

sub judice [sʌb 'dʒu:dɪsɪ, sʊb 'ju:dɪ,keɪ] *adj.* находящийся в производстве (*or* на рассмотрении (суда)).

subjugate ['sʌbdʒʊ,geɪt] *v.t.* (*enslave*) порабо|щать, -тить; (*subdue*) покор|ять, -ить; (*subject*) подчин|ять, -ить.

subjugation [,sʌbdʒʊ'geɪʃ(ə)n] *n.* порабощение; покорение; подчинение.

subjunctive [səb'dʒʌŋktɪv] *n.* **(~ mood)** сослагательное наклонение.

adj. сослагательный.

sublease ['sʌbli:s] *n.* субаренда, поднаём.

v.t. **1.** (*of lessor*; *also* **sublet**) перед|авать, -ать в субаренду. **2.** (*of lessee*) брать, взять в субаренду.

sublessee [,sʌble'si:] *n.* субарендатор, поднаниматель (*m.*).

sublessor [,sʌble'sɔ:(r)] *n.* отдающий в субаренду.

sublet ['sʌblet] = **sublease** *v.t.* **1.**

sublibrarian [,sʌblaɪ'breərɪən] *n.* помощни|к (*fem.* -ица) библиотекаря.

sublieutenant [,sʌblef'tenənt] *n.* младший лейтенант.

sublimate[1] ['sʌblɪmət] *n.* сублимат, возгон; **corrosive ~** сулема.

adj. сублимированный; возогнанный.

sublimate[2] ['sʌblɪ,meɪt] *v.t.* (*chem.*) сублимировать (*impf., pf.; also fig.*); воз|гонять, -огнать.

sublimation [,sʌblɪ'meɪʃ(ə)n] *n.* сублимация, возгонка.

sublime [sə'blaɪm] *n.* (*the ~*) великое, возвышенное; **it is only a step from the ~ to the ridiculous** от великого до смешного один шаг.

adj. (*majestic*) величественный; **the S~ Porte** (*hist.*) Блистательная/Высокая Порта; (*lofty*) возвышенный; **a ~ genius** величайший гений; **~ contempt** гордое презрение; **~ ignorance** великолепное неведение.

subliminal [səb'lɪmɪn(ə)l] *adj.* подсознательный; действующий на подсознание.

sublimity [səb'lɪmɪtɪ] *n.* возвышенность, величественность.

sublunary [sʌb'lu:nərɪ, -'lju:nərɪ] *adj.* (*earthly*) земной.

sub-machine gun [,sʌbmə'ʃi:n gʌn] *n.* пистолет-пулемёт; автомат.

sub-machine gunner [,sʌbmə'ʃi:n ,gʌnə(r)] *n.* автоматчик.

sub-man ['sʌbmæn] *n.* недочеловек.

submarine [,sʌbmə'ri:n, 'sʌb-] *n.* подводная лодка; **~ base** база для подводных лодок; **~ chaser** морской охотник.

adj. подводный.

submerge [səb'mɜ:dʒ] *v.t. & i.* погру|жать(ся), -зить(ся); затоп|лять(ся), -ить(ся).

submer|gence [səb'mɜ:dʒəns], **-sion** [səb'mɜ:ʃ(ə)n] *nn.* погружение в воду; затопление.

submission [səb'mɪʃ(ə)n] *n.* **1.** (*subjection*) подчинение; (*obedience*) повиновение; (*humility*) смирение; (*submissiveness*) покорность; (*capitulation*) капитуляция; **starve into ~** голодом довести (*pf.*) до капитуляции. **2.** (*presentation*) представление, предъявление; **~ of proof** представление доказательств.

submissive [səb'mɪsɪv] *adj.* покорный, смиренный, безропотный, послушный.

submit [səb'mɪt] *v.t.* **1.** (*yield*) подчин|ять, -ить; покор|ять, -ить; **~ o.s. to s.o.'s authority** покор|яться, -иться чьей-н. власти; отд|аваться, -аться на чью-н. власть. **2.** (*present, e.g. a dissertation*) предст|авлять, -авить. **3.** (*suggest, maintain*): **I ~ that your proposal is contrary to the statutes** я смею утверждать, что ваше предложение противоречит уставу.

v.i. подчин|яться, -иться; покор|яться, -иться; **I will not ~ to being insulted** я не позволю себя оскорблять.

subnormal [sʌb'nɔ:m(ə)l] *adj.* ниже нормального; **a ~ child** дефективный (*or* умственно отсталый) ребёнок.

sub-order ['sʌb,ɔ:də(r)] *n.* подотряд.

subordinate[1] [sə'bɔ:dɪnət] *n.* подчинённый.

adj. **1.** (*in rank or importance*) подчинённый; низший по чину; (*secondary*) второстепенный; **the regiment has three ~ battalions** в состав полка входят три подчинённых батальона; **he plays a ~ role** он играет второстепенную роль. **2.** (*gram.*) придаточный; **~ clause** придаточное предложение.

subordinat|e[2] [sə'bɔ:dɪ,neɪt] *v.t.* (*make subservient*) подчин|ять, -ить; (*place in less important position*) ставить, по- в подчинённое/зависимое положение; **~ing conjunction** подчинительный союз.

subordination [sə,bɔːdɪ'neɪʃ(ə)n] *n.* подчине́ние, подчинённость, субордина́ция.

suborn [sə'bɔːn] *v.t.* склон|я́ть, -и́ть к преступле́нию; (*bribe*) подкуп|а́ть, -и́ть.

sub-plot ['sʌbplɒt] *n.* побо́чная сюже́тная ли́ния.

subpoena [səb'piːnə, sə'piːnə] *n.* пове́стка в суд.

v.t. вызыва́ть, вы́звать в суд.

sub rosa [sʌb 'rəʊzə] *adj.* та́йный, секре́тный.

adv. та́йно, без огла́ски.

subscribe [səb'skraɪb] *v.t.* **1.** (*write below*) подпи́с|ывать, -а́ть; **he ~s himself 'yours truly'** он подпи́сывается «пре́данный Вам». **2.** (*contribute*) же́ртвовать, по-; **he ~s money to charities** он же́ртвует де́ньги на благотвори́тельные це́ли.

v.i. **1.** (*pay or take out subscription*): **~ to a journal** подпи́с|ываться, -а́ться на журна́л; **~ to a library** запи́с|ываться, -а́ться в пла́тную библиоте́ку; (*contribute*): **~ to a loan** подпи́с|ываться, -а́ться на заём. **2.** (*agree, assent*) присоедин|я́ться, -и́ться; **I cannot ~ to that view** я не могу́ согласи́ться с э́тим мне́нием.

subscriber [səb'skraɪbə(r)] *n.* (*of document*) подписа́вшийся; (*to publication etc.*) подпи́счик; (*contributor to fund*) же́ртвователь (*fem.* -ница); дона́тор; (*telephone ~*) абоне́нт; (*to library*) чита́тель (*fem.* -ница), абоне́нт пла́тной библиоте́ки.

subscription [səb'skrɪpʃ(ə)n] *n.* **1.** (*signature*) по́дпись. **2.** (*to library etc.*) абонеме́нт в+*a.*, абони́рование +*g.*; (*fee*) взнос, поже́ртвование; **~ to a society** чле́нский взнос в о́бщество; **~ to a newspaper** подпи́ска на газе́ту; **take out a ~** подпи́с|ываться, -а́ться (на+*a.*); **get up a ~** соб|ира́ть, -ра́ть де́ньги по подпи́ске; **the monument was erected by public ~** па́мятник был воздви́гнут на поже́ртвования гра́ждан; **~ form** подписно́й лист; **~ concert** конце́рт, сбор от кото́рого идёт в по́льзу кого́-н./чего́-н.

subsection ['sʌb,sekʃ(ə)n] *n.* подсе́кция.

subsequent ['sʌbsɪkwənt] *adj.* после́дующий, сле́дующий; **~ to his death** (име́ющий ме́сто) по́сле его́ сме́рти; **~ly** впосле́дствии; зате́м.

subserve [səb'sɜːv] *v.t.* соде́йствовать (*impf., pf.*) +*d.*

subservience [səb'sɜːvɪəns] *n.* соде́йствие; раболе́пие, послуша́ние.

subservient [səb'sɜːvɪənt] *adj.* **1.** (*serving as means*) соде́йствующий +*d.*; слу́жащий +*d.*; **his marriage was ~ to his ambition** брак был для него́ (лишь) сре́дством для достиже́ния свои́х це́лей. **2.** (*servile*) раболе́пный, послу́шный.

subside [səb'saɪd] *v.i.* **1.** (*of sediment*) ос|еда́ть, -е́сть; (*of liquid*) пон|ижа́ться, -и́зиться. **2.** (*of ground or building*) ос|еда́ть, -е́сть; **the ground ~d** земля́ осе́ла. **3.** (*of water*) па́дать, упа́сть; спа|да́ть, -сть; **the floods ~d** наводне́ние спа́ло; (*of blister*) оп|ада́ть, -а́сть. **4.** (*of fever*) па́дать, упа́сть; (*of wind, storm etc.*) ут|иха́ть, -и́хнуть; **the laughter ~d** смех ути́х; **the noise ~d** шум смолк; **passions ~d** стра́сти улегли́сь. **5.** (*of pers.*): **~ into an armchair** опус|ка́ться, -ти́ться в кре́сло; **he ran for 5 minutes, then ~d into a walk** он бежа́л пять мину́т, пото́м перешёл на шаг.

subsidence [səb'saɪd(ə)ns, 'sʌbsɪd(ə)ns] *n.* (*of ground*) оседа́ние, оса́дка.

subsidiary [səb'sɪdɪərɪ] *n.* (*comm.*) филиа́л.

adj. вспомога́тельный, подсо́бный; **~ company** подконтро́льная/ доче́рняя компа́ния.

subsidize ['sʌbsɪ,daɪz] *v.t.* субсиди́ровать (*impf., pf.*).

subsidy ['sʌbsɪdɪ] *n.* субси́дия, посо́бие, дота́ция.

subsist [səb'sɪst] *v.i.* (*exist*) существова́ть (*impf.*); (*survive*) жить, про-.

subsistence [səb'sɪst(ə)ns] *n.* (*existence*) существова́ние; бытие́; (*means of supporting life*) сре́дства (*nt. pl.*) к существова́нию; пропита́ние; **~ allowance, money** командиро́вочные (де́ньги); ава́нс; **~ farming** натура́льное хозя́йство; **~ wage** прожи́точный ми́нимум.

subsoil ['sʌbsɔɪl] *n.* подпо́чва.

subsonic [sʌb'sɒnɪk] *adj.* дозвуково́й.

subspecies ['sʌb,spiːʃiːz, -ʃɪz] *n.* подви́д, разнови́дность.

substance ['sʌbst(ə)ns] *n.* **1.** (*essence, reality*) субста́нция, мате́рия, реа́льность. **2.** (*essential elements*) суть, содержа́ние, су́щность, существо́; **he told me the ~ of his speech** он пересказа́л мне основно́е содержа́ние свое́й ре́чи; **in ~** по существу́. **3.** (*piece, type of matter*) вещество́. **4.** (*solidity*) пло́тность, содержа́ние; **the fabric lacks ~** э́тот материа́л недоста́точно пло́тный; **a piece of writing that lacks ~** сочине́ние, лишённое содержа́ния; **there is no ~ in the rumour** э́тот слух лишён како́го то ни́ было основа́ния. **5.** (*possessions*) состоя́ние; **waste one's ~** растра́|чивать, -тить своё состоя́ние; **a man of ~** состоя́тельный челове́к.

substandard [sʌb'stændəd] *adj.* нестанда́ртный, низкока́чественный; (*of language*) нелитерату́рный, просторе́чный.

substantial [səb'stænʃ(ə)l] *adj.* **1.** (*material*) веще́ственный, реа́льный; **a ~ being** реа́льное/живо́е существо́. **2.** (*solid, stout, sturdy*) кре́пкий; **a man of ~ build** челове́к кре́пкого телосложе́ния; **a ~ building** соли́дное зда́ние; **a ~ dinner** сы́тный обе́д. **3.** (*considerable*): **a ~ sum** поря́дочная/внуши́тельная су́мма; **a ~ contribution** большо́й/ва́жный вклад; **a ~ improvement** значи́тельное/заме́тное/суще́ственное улучше́ние. **4.** (*possessing resources*) состоя́тельный, зажи́точный. **5.** (*essential, overall*) по существу́/су́ти; **I am in ~ agreement** я согла́сен по существу́ (*or* в основно́м).

substantiate [səb'stænʃɪ,eɪt] *v.t.* обосно́в|ывать, -а́ть; дока́з|ывать, -а́ть.

substantiation [səb,stænʃɪ'eɪʃ(ə)n] *n.* обоснова́ние, доказа́тельство.

substantival [səb,stæn'taɪv(ə)l] *adj.* субстанти́вный.

substantive [səb'stæntɪv] *n.* и́мя существи́тельное.

adj. **1.** (*existing independently*) субстанти́вный, незави́симый, самостоя́тельный. **2.** (*pert. to subject matter*): **I have no ~ comments** у меня́ нет замеча́ний по существу́ (де́ла, вопро́са *и т.п.*); **~ provisions** резолюти́вная/операти́вная часть (*документа и т.п.*). **3.** (*mil.*): **~ rank** действи́тельное зва́ние.

substation ['sʌb,steɪʃ(ə)n] *n.* (*elec.*) подста́нция.

substitute ['sʌbstɪ,tjuːt] *n.* заме́на; (*pers.*) замести́тель (*m.*); (*thg.*) замени́тель (*m.*), суррога́т, эрза́ц; **butter ~** замени́тель/суррога́т ма́сла.

v.t. испо́льзовать (*impf., pf.*) (*что*) вме́сто (*чего*); **~ one word for another** замен|я́ть, -и́ть одно́ сло́во други́м; подст|авля́ть, -а́вить одно́ сло́во вме́сто друго́го; **a forgery was ~d for the original** оригина́л был подменён фальши́вкой/ко́пией; вме́сто оригина́ла подсу́нули фальши́вку/ко́пию.

v.i.: **~ for** заме|ща́ть, -сти́ть; подмен|я́ть, -и́ть (*кого*).

substitution [,sʌbstɪ'tjuːʃ(ə)n] *n.* заме́на, замеще́ние, подме́на; (*math.*) подстано́вка.

substratum ['sʌb,strɑːtəm, -,streɪtəm] *n.* основа́ние; ни́жний слой; (*geol.*) подпо́чва, субстра́т; (*phil.*) субстра́т.

substructure ['sʌb,strʌktʃə(r)] *n.* фунда́мент; ни́жнее строе́ние (доро́ги).

subsume [səb'sjuːm] *v.t.* включ|а́ть, -и́ть в каку́ю-н. катего́рию; отн|оси́ть, -ести́ к како́й-н. катего́рии, гру́ппе *и т.п.*

subtenancy [sʌb'tenənsɪ] *n.* субаре́нда, поднаём.

subtenant ['sʌb,tenənt] *n.* субарендáтор, поднанима́тель (*m.*).

subtend [səb'tend] *v.t.* (*an angle*) противолежа́ть (*impf.*) +*d.*; (*an arc*) стя́гивать (*impf.*) (*дугу*).

subterfuge ['sʌbtə,fjuːdʒ] *n.* уло́вка, хи́трость.

subterranean [,sʌbtə'reɪnɪən] *adj.* подзе́мный.

subtilize ['sʌtɪ,laɪz] *v.i.* (*reason subtly*) вдава́ться (*impf.*) в то́нкости; мудри́ть, на-; перемудри́ть (*pf.*).

subtitle ['sʌb,taɪt(ə)l] *n.* подзаголо́вок; (*cin.*) субти́тр.

subtle ['sʌt(ə)l] *adj.* **1.** (*fine, elusive*) то́нкий, неуловимый; (*refined*) уто́нчённый; **~ perfume** не́жный/то́нкий (*or* е́ле ощути́мый) за́пах/арома́т; **~ distinction** то́нкое разли́чие; **~ charm** неулови́мое обая́ние; **~ delight** изы́сканное удово́льствие; **~ power** таи́нственная си́ла. **2.** (*perceptive*) то́нкий; (*acute*) о́стрый; **~ remark** то́нкое замеча́ние; **~ mind** о́стрый ум; **~ observer**

проницательный челове́к; ~ **senses** обострённые чу́вства. **3.** (*ingenious*, *deft*): ~ **artist** то́нкий худо́жник; ~ **fingers** ло́вкие па́льцы; ~ **device** иску́сный трюк; ~ **argument** хитроу́мный до́вод. **4.** (*crafty*, *cunning*) иску́сный, хи́трый; ~ **enemy** кова́рный враг.

subtlety ['sʌtəltɪ] *n.* то́нкость; уто́нчённость; острота́; хи́трость; то́нкое разли́чие.

subtonic [sʌb'tɒnɪk] *n.* ни́жний вво́дный тон.

subtract [səb'trækt] *v.t.* вычита́ть, вы́честь.

subtraction [səb'trækʃ(ə)n] *n.* вычита́ние.

subtropical [sʌb'trɒpɪk(ə)l] *adj.* субтропи́ческий.

sub-unit ['sʌbju:nɪt] *n.* (*mil.*) подразделе́ние.

suburb ['sʌbɜ:b] *n.* при́город, предме́стье.

suburban [sə'bɜ:bən] *adj.* при́городный; (*fig.*) меща́нский, провинциа́льный.

suburbanite [sə'bɜ:bənaɪt] *n.* жи́тель (*fem.* -ница) при́города; за́городный жи́тель.

suburbia [sə'bɜ:bɪə] *n.* (*pej.*) ≃ меща́нство, провинциали́зм; ≃ обыва́тели (*m. pl.*).

subvention [səb'venʃ(ə)n] *n.* субси́дия, дота́ция.

subversion [səb'vɜ:ʃ(ə)n] *n.* подры́в; подрывна́я де́ятельность.

subversive [səb'vɜ:sɪv] *adj.* подрывно́й, разруши́тельный.

subvert [səb'vɜ:t] *v.t.* под|рыва́ть, -орва́ть; разр|уша́ть, -у́шить.

subway ['sʌbweɪ] *n.* (*passage under road*) подзе́мный перехо́д; (*US*, *railway*) подзе́мка, метро́ (*indecl.*).

subzero [sʌb'zɪərəʊ] *adj.*: ~ **temperatures** ми́нусовые температу́ры.

succeed [sək'si:d] *v.t.* **1.** (*follow*) сле́довать (*impf.*) за+*i.*; **night ~s day** ночь сменя́ет день. **2.** (*as heir*) насле́довать (*impf.*, *pf.*) +*d.*; **Mary was ~ed by Elizabeth I** по́сле Мари́и воцари́лась Елизаве́та I; (*as replacement*) смен|я́ть, -и́ть; **who ~ed him as President?** кто был сле́дующим президе́нтом?

v.i. **1.** (*follow*) после́довать (*pf.*) (за+*i.*); **~ing ages** после́дующие века́. **2.** (*as heir etc.*): **he ~ed to his father's estate** он унасле́довал (*or* получи́л в насле́дство) име́ние отца́; **he ~ed to the premiership** он за́нял пост премье́р-мини́стра. **3.** (*be*, *become successful*) преусп|ева́ть, -е́ть; доб|ива́ться, -и́ться успе́ха/своего́; **he is bound to ~ in life** он наверняка́ преуспе́ет в жи́зни (*or* сде́лает карье́ру); **he ~ed as a lawyer** он име́л успе́х в ка́честве адвока́та; **the attack ~ed beyond all expectation** ата́ка удала́сь сверх вся́ких ожида́ний; **he ~ed in tricking us all** ему́ удало́сь всех нас обману́ть.

success [sək'ses] *n.* успе́х, уда́ча; **his efforts were crowned with ~** его́ уси́лия увенча́лись успе́хом; **I tried to get in, but without ~** я пыта́лся войти́ (*or* туда́ попа́сть), но безуспе́шно; **I have had no ~ so far** пока́мест я не мог доби́ться успе́ха (*or* дости́гнуть це́ли); **nothing succeeds like ~** одна́ уда́ча влечёт за собо́й другу́ю; **he was not a ~ as a doctor** он был нева́жным врачо́м; он не по́льзовался успе́хом как врач; **my holidays were not a ~ this year** мои́ кани́кулы в э́том году́ бы́ли неуда́чными; **that book is among his ~es** э́та кни́га — одна́ из его́ уда́ч; **a series of military ~es** ряд вое́нных успе́хов; ~ **story** головокружи́тельная карье́ра.

successful [sək'sesfʊl] *adj.* успе́шный, уда́чный; **a ~ attempt** успе́шная попы́тка; **a ~ speech** уда́чная речь; **I tried to persuade him, but was not ~** я пыта́лся убеди́ть его́, но мне э́то не удало́сь; **a list of ~ candidates** спи́сок и́збранных/проше́дших кандида́тов; (*fortunate*) преуспева́ющий; уда́чливый; **he had the appearance of a ~ man** у него́ был вид преуспева́ющего челове́ка; **he was ~ in business** он был уда́члив в дела́х.

succession [sək'seʃ(ə)n] *n.* **1.** (*sequence*) последова́тельность; **in ~** подря́д; **they rode past in rapid ~** они промча́лись оди́н за други́м. **2.** (*series*) ряд, цепь; **a ~ of victories** цепь побе́д. **3.** (*succeeding to office etc.*) насле́дство, насле́ди, насле́дование; **the king's right of ~ was disputed** пра́во престолонасле́дия короля́ оспа́ривалось; **the ~ was broken** преє́мственность была́ нару́шена; **Apostolic ~** переда́ча апо́стольской благода́ти; **War of the Spanish S ~** война́ за Испа́нское насле́дство.

successive [sək'sesɪv] *adj.* после́довательный; сле́дующий оди́н за други́м; **on three ~ occasions** три ра́за подря́д.

successively [sək'sesɪvlɪ] *adj.* подря́д, после́довательно, поочерёдно.

successor [sək'sesə(r)] *n.* прее́мни|к (*fem.* -ца), насле́дни|к (*fem.* -ца); **he was the obvious ~ of, to his father** он я́вно заслу́живал стать прее́мником своего́ отца́; **the summer before last was hotter than its ~** позапро́шлое ле́то бы́ло жа́рче про́шлого.

succinct [sək'sɪŋkt] *adj.* (*concise*) сжа́тый; (*brief*) кра́ткий.

succinctness [sək'sɪŋktnɪs] *n.* сжа́тость, кра́ткость.

succour ['sʌkə(r)] (*liter.*) *n.* по́мощь.

v.t. при|ходи́ть, -йти́ на по́мощь +*d.*; выруча́ть, вы́ручить.

succulence ['sʌkjʊləns] *n.* со́чность.

succulent ['sʌkjʊlənt] *adj.* со́чный; (*bot.*) мяси́стый.

succumb [sə'kʌm] *v.i.* уступ|а́ть, -и́ть; подд|ава́ться, -а́ться; **they ~ed to the enemy's superior force** они́ уступи́ли превосходя́щей си́ле проти́вника; **she did not ~ to temptation** она́ не подда́лась искуше́нию; (*die*) сконча́ться (*pf.*); **he ~ed to his injuries** он сконча́лся от (полу́ченных) ран.

such [sʌtʃ] *pron.* **1.** (*that*) э́то; ~ **was not my intention** э́то не бы́ло мои́м наме́рением; ~ **being the case** в тако́м слу́чае; **he is a good scholar and is recognised as ~** он хоро́ший учёный и при́знан таковы́м. **2.**: **as ~** (*without qualification*) вообще́; как тако́вой. **3.** ~ (*people*) **as** те, кото́рые.

adj. **1.** (*of the kind mentioned*; *of this*, *that kind*) тако́й; **I know of no ~ place** я не слыха́л о тако́м ме́сте; **I have never seen ~ a sight** я никогда́ не ви́дел подо́бного зре́лища; **I said no ~ thing** я ничего́ подо́бного не говори́л; **some ~ thing** что́-то в э́том ро́де; **no ~ luck!** увы́!; е́сли бы!; **how could you do ~ a thing?** как вы могли́ так поступи́ть? **2.**: ~ **as** (*of a kind* …): ~ **grapes as you never saw** тако́й виногра́д, како́го вы в жи́зни не ви́дывали; **the difference was not ~ as to affect the result** ра́зница была́ не так велика́, что́бы повлия́ть на результа́т; **I am not ~ a fool as to believe him** я не тако́й дура́к, что́бы пове́рить ему́; (*like*): **people ~ as these** таки́е лю́ди; лю́ди, подо́бные э́тим; **a picture ~ as that is valuable** тако́го ро́да карти́ны це́нятся высоко́; **small objects ~ as diamonds** ме́лкие предме́ты, как наприме́р бриллиа́нты; **there is ~ a thing as politeness** существу́ет така́я вещь, как ве́жливость; **you can share my meal, ~ as it is** вы мо́жете раздели́ть со мно́ю мой у́жин, како́в он ни на есть. **3.** (*pred.*) тако́в; ~ **was the force of the gale** такова́ была́ си́ла урагана́; ~ **is life!** такова́ жизнь!

cpds. **~-and-~** *adj.* тако́й-то, (*pl.*) ко́е-каки́е; **~like** *pron.* & *adj.* подо́бный; **theatres, cinemas and ~like** теа́тры, кино́ и тому́ подо́бное.

suck [sʌk] *n.* соса́ние; **take a ~ at** пососа́ть (*pf.*); **the ~ of a whirlpool** заса́сывание водоворо́та; **give ~ to a child** корми́ть (*impf.*) ребёнка гру́дью.

v.t. **1.** соса́ть (*impf.*); **he was ~ing (at) an orange** он поса́сывал апельси́н; **he ~ed the orange dry** он вы́сосал весь сок из апельси́на; ~ **the breast** соса́ть (*impf.*) грудь; (~ *in*, *imbibe*) вс|а́сывать, -оса́ть; тяну́ть (*impf.*); **bees ~ nectar** пчёлы втя́гивают некта́р; **he was ~ing fruit juice through a straw** он тяну́л фрукто́вый сок че́рез соло́минку; (~ *out*) выса́сывать, вы́сосать; **he ~ed the blood from the poisoned wound** он вы́сосал кровь из отра́вленной ра́ны. **2.** (*squeeze or dissolve in mouth*) соса́ть (*impf.*); поса́сывать (*impf.*); **she was always ~ing lozenges** она́ ве́чно coса́ла леденцы́; **the baby likes to ~ its thumb** младе́нец лю́бит соса́ть па́лец.

v.i. соса́ть (*impf.*); ~ **at, on a pipe** поса́сывать/потя́гивать (*impf.*) тру́бку; **~ing-pig** моло́чный поросёнок; **~ing child** грудно́й ребёнок.

with advs.: ~ **in** *v.t.* вс|а́сывать, -оса́ть; (*engulf*) зас|а́сывать, -оса́ть; **he was ~ed in by the quicksand** его́ засоса́ла тряси́на; (*fig.*) впит|ывать, -а́ть (в себя́); ~ **out** *v.t.* выса́сывать, вы́сосать; ~ **up** *v.t.* выса́сывать, вы́сосать; (*absorb*) впи́тывать, -а́ть; *v.i.*: ~ **up to s.o.** (*coll.*) подли́з|ываться, -а́ться к кому́-н.

sucker ['sʌkə(r)] *n.* **1.** (*organ, device*) присóсок, присóска. **2.** (*bot.*) отрóсток, боковóй побéг. **3.** (*sl., gullible pers.*) простá|к (*fem.* -чка).

suckl|e ['sʌk(ə)l] *v.t.* вск|áрмливать, -ормúть; (*of pers.*) кормúть (*impf.*) грýдью; **the cow was ~ing the calf** телёнок сосáл мáтку.

suckling ['sʌklɪŋ] *n.* (*child*) груднóй ребёнок; сосунóк; (*animal*) сосýн, сосунóк; **~ pig** (*US*) молóчный поросёнок.

sucrose ['su:krəʊz, 'sju:-] *n.* сахарóза.

suction ['sʌkʃ(ə)n] *n.* сосáние, всáсывание, присáсывание; **~ pump** всáсывающий насóс.

Sudan [su:'dɑ:n, -'dæn] *n.* Судáн.

Sudanese [,su:də'ni:z] *n.* судáн|ец (*fem.* -ка).

adj. судáнский.

sudden ['sʌd(ə)n] *n.*: **(all) of a ~** внезáпно, вдруг.

adj. (*unexpected*) внезáпный, неожúданный; **he made a ~ movement** он сдéлал рéзкое движéние; **~ death** скоропостúжная смерть.

suddenly ['sʌd(ə)nlɪ] *adv.* внезáпно, вдруг.

suddenness ['sʌd(ə)nnɪs] *n.* внезáпность, неожúданность.

Sudetenland [su:'deɪt(ə)n,lænd] *n.* Судéтская óбласть.

sudorific [,sju:də'rɪfɪk] *n.* потогóнное срéдство.

adj. потогóнный.

suds [sʌdz] *n. pl.* мы́льная пéна.

sue [su:, sju:] *v.t.* возбу|ждáть, -дúть иск/дéло прóтив+*g.*; под|авáть, -áть в суд на+*a.*; (**for libel** за клеветý; **for damages** о возмещéнии убы́тков).

v.i. **1.** (*take legal action*) под|авáть, -áть в суд (на+*a.*). **2.** (*make entreaties*): **~ for peace** просúть (*impf.*) мúра; **~ for a woman's hand** доб|ивáться, -úться чьей-н. рукú.

suede [sweɪd] *n.* зáмша.

adj. зáмшевый.

suet ['su:ɪt, 'sju:ɪt] *n.* нутрянóе сáло; пóчечный жир.

Suez ['su:ɪz] *n.* Суэ́ц; **~ Canal** Суэ́цкий канáл.

suffer ['sʌfə(r)] *v.t.* **1.** (*experience*) испы́т|ывать, -áть; терпéть, по-; претерп|евáть, -éть; **she did not ~ much pain** онá недóлго мýчилась; **he ~ed many hardships** он перенёс/претерпéл мнóжество лишéний; **~ death** умерéть (*pf.*). **2.** (*permit*) позв|олять, -óлить; (*tolerate*) терпéть, по-/с-; сн|осúть, -ести́; **I will not ~ such conduct** я не потерплю́ такóго поведéния; **he does not ~ fools gladly** он не выносúт дуракóв; **~ the children to come to me** пустúте детéй приходúть ко мне.

v.i. страдáть (*impf.*) (от+*g.*); **he learnt to ~ without complaining** он научúлся безрóпотно переносúть страдáние; **he ~s from shyness** он (óчень) застéнчив; **he is ~ing from measles** он болéет кóрью; у негó корь; **he is ~ing from loss of appetite** он страдáет отсýтствием аппетúта; **he did not ~ much in the accident** он не óчень пострадáл во врéмя авáрии; **his reputation will ~ greatly** егó репутáция сúльно пострадáет; **he ~ed for his folly** он был накáзан за свою глýпость; **I ~ed for it** я за э́то поплатúлся.

sufferance ['sʌfərəns] *n.*: **on ~** из мúлости; с молчалúвого соглáсия.

sufferer ['sʌfrə(r)] *n.* страдéлец; **women are the greatest ~s** хýже всегó приходúться/достаётся жéнщинам; **be a ~ from ill-health** имéть (*impf.*) слáбое здорóвье; (*from accident*) пострадáвший, потерпéвший.

suffering ['sʌfrɪŋ] *n.* страдáние.

suffice [sə'faɪs] *v.t.* удовлетвор|я́ть, -úть; **one meal a day ~s her** ей достáточно есть одúн раз в день.

v.i. быть достáточным; хват|áть, -úть; **a brief statement will ~ for my purpose** мне потрéбуется лишь крáткое заявлéние; **that ~s to prove my case** э́то слýжит вполнé достáточным подтверждéнием моéй правоты́; **~ it to say that ...** достáточно сказáть, что…

sufficiency [sə'fɪʃənsɪ] *n.* достáточность, достáток; **we have a ~ of provisions** у нас достáточно провúзии.

sufficient [sə'fɪʃ(ə)nt] *n.*: **have you had ~ (to eat)?** вы сы́ты?

adj. достáточный, подходя́щий; **the sum is ~ for the journey** э́тих дéнег хвáтит на дорóгу; **lack ~ food** испы́тывать (*impf.*) недостáток в пúще; **he is ~ of an expert to realize ...** он достáточно осведомлён/свéдущ, чтóбы понять…; **~ unto the day is the evil thereof** довлéет днéви злóба егó.

suffix ['sʌfɪks] *n.* сýффикс.

v.t. приб|авля́ть, -áвить.

suffocat|e ['sʌfə,keɪt] *v.t.* душúть, за-; **I was ~ed by the close atmosphere** я задыхáлся в духотé; **he was ~ed by poisonous fumes** он задохнýлся/задóхся в ядовúтом ды́ме; **~ing heat** удýшливая жарá.

v.i. зад|ыхáться, -охнýться.

suffocation [,sʌfə'keɪʃ(ə)n] *n.* удушéние, удýшье.

suffragan ['sʌfrəgən] *n.* **(~ bishop)** викáрий; викáрный епúскоп.

suffrage ['sʌfrɪdʒ] *n.* (*vote*) гóлос; (*right to vote*) избирáтельное прáво; **female ~** избирáтельное прáво для жéнщин; **universal ~** всеóбщее избирáтельное прáво.

suffragette [,sʌfrə'dʒet] *n.* (*hist.*) суфражúстка.

suffuse [sə'fju:z] *v.t.* зал|ивáть, -úть; **a blush ~d her cheeks** её щёки залúл румя́нец.

suffusion [sə'fju:ʒ(ə)n] *n.* (*med.*) кровоподтёк, суффýзия.

Sufi ['su:fɪ] *n.* суфúст.

Sufism ['su:fɪz(ə)m] *n.* суфúзм.

sugar ['ʃʊgə(r)] *n.* сáхар; **granulated/caster ~** (сáхарный) песóк; **icing ~** сáхарная пýдра; **brown ~** корúчневый сáхар; неочúщенный сáхарный песóк; **beet ~** свекловúчный сáхар; **cane ~** тростникóвый сáхар; **lump ~** кусковóй сáхар, (сáхар-)рафинáд; (*in cubes*) пилёный сáхар.

v.t. **1.** (*lit., fig., sweeten*) подслá|щивать, -стúть. **2.** (*sprinkle with ~*) пос|ыпáть, -ы́пать сáхаром; посáхарить (*pf.*).

cpds. **~-basin, ~-bowl** *nn.* сáхарница; **~-beet** *n.* сáхарная свёкла; **~-candy** *n.* леденéц; **~-cane** *n.* сáхарный тростнúк; **~-coated** *adj.* обсáхаренный; **~-daddy** *n.* (*coll.*) покровúтель (*m.*); **~-loaf** *n.* сáхарная головá; **~-mill** *n.* сáхарный завóд; **~-plantation** *n.* сáхарная плантáция; **~-plum** *n.* крýглый леденéц; **~-refinery** *n.* рафинáдный завóд; **~-tongs** *n. pl.* щипц|ы́ (*pl., g.* -óв) для сáхара.

sugarless ['ʃʊgəlɪs] *adj.* без сáхара.

sugary ['ʃʊgərɪ] *adj.* **1.** сáхарный, сахарúстый; **go ~** (*of jam etc.*) засáхари|ваться, -ться. **2.** (*fig., of tone, smile etc.*) слáдкий, слащáвый.

suggest [sə'dʒest] *v.t.* **1.** (*propose*) пред|лагáть, -ожúть; совéтовать, по-; выдвигáть, вы́двинуть предложéние (*чтобы…*); **he ~ed (going for) a walk** он предложúл пойтú прогуля́ться; **he ~ed that I should follow him** он предложúл/ посовéтовал мне слéдовать за ним; **I ~ you try again** я совéтую вам попрóбовать ещё раз(óк); **all sorts of plans were ~ed** предлагáлись всевозмóжные плáны; (*with inanimate subject*): **what ~ed that idea to you?** что навелó вас на э́ту мысль?; **experience ~ed the right solution** óпыт подсказáл (*or* натолкнýл на) прáвильное решéние. **2.** (*evoke, call to mind*) вызывáть, вы́звать; **what does this shape ~?** что напоминáет э́та фóрма?; **does the name ~ nothing to you?** э́то úмя вам ничегó не говорúт? **3.** (*imply, indicate*) говорúть (*impf.*) о+*p.*; свидéтельствовать (*impf.*) о+*p.*; **his skill ~s long practice** егó мастерствó говорúт о длúтельной прáктике; **his tone ~ed impatience** в егó тóне чýвствовалось нетерпéние. **4.** (*instil an idea*) внуш|áть, -úть; **he had the power of ~ing to his audience that he was infallible** он умéл внушúть слýшателям мысль о егó непогрешúмости. **5.** (*advance as possible or likely*): **I ~ that the calculation is (or may be) wrong** по-мóему, здесь ошúбка в расчёте; **they ~ed improper motives on his part** онú вы́сказали подозрéние в чистотé егó мотúвов; **I ~ that you knew all the time** я утверждáю, что вы с сáмого начáла знáли об э́том; **do you ~ that I am lying?** вы хотúте сказáть, что я лгу?

suggestible [sə'dʒestɪb(ə)l] *adj.* (*of pers.*) внушáемый.

suggestion [sə'dʒestʃ(ə)n] *n.* **1.** (*proposal*) предложéние, совéт; **make a ~** внестú (*pf.*) предложéние; подáть (*pf.*) идéю/мысль; **I acted on his ~** я воспóльзовался егó совéтом/идéей. **2.** (*implication*) намёк, дóля; (*tinge*) оттéнок; **there was a ~ of regret in his voice** в егó гóлосе

звуча́ла но́тка сожале́ния; **a ~ of a foreign accent** чуть заме́тный иностра́нный акце́нт. **3.** (*hypnotic etc.*) внуше́ние.
suggestive [sə'dʒestɪv] *adj.* **1. ~ of** напомина́ющий. **2.** (*providing food for thought*) наводя́щий на размышле́ния. **3.** (*improper*) пика́нтный, непристо́йный, риско́ванный.
suicidal [ˌsu:ɪ'saɪd(ə)l, ˌsju:-] *adj.* **1.** (*pert. to suicide*) самоуби́йственный. **2.** (*leading to suicide*): **~ tendencies** скло́нность к самоуби́йству. **3.** (*of pers.*) скло́нный к самоуби́йству; суицида́льный. **4.** (*fig., fatal*) губи́тельный, ги́бельный; **~ policy** рокова́я/па́губная поли́тика.
suicide ['su:ɪˌsaɪd, 'sju:-] *n.* **1.** (*also fig.*) самоуби́йство; **commit ~** конча́ть, (по)ко́нчить с собо́й, ко́нчить, по-(жизнь) самоуби́йством. **2.** (*pers.*) самоуби́йца (*c.g.*); **~ pact** группово́е самоуби́йство по сго́вору; **~ pilot** (пило́т-)сме́ртник.
sui generis [ˌsju:aɪ 'dʒenərɪs, ˌsu:ɪ 'gen-] *adj.* своеобра́зный, уника́льный.
suit [su:t, sju:t] *n.* **1.** (*arch., petition*) проше́ние; **grant s.o.'s ~** исп|олня́ть, -о́лнить чью-н. про́сьбу; удовлетвор|я́ть, -и́ть чьё-н. проше́ние; (*for marriage*) сватовство́; **press one's ~** сва́таться (*impf.*) (*к кому*). **2.** (*leg.*) иск, де́ло; **civil/criminal ~** гражда́нский/уголо́вный иск; **bring (a) ~ against s.o.** предъяв|ля́ть, -и́ть иск кому́-н. **3.** (*of clothes*) костю́м; **two-piece ~** костю́м-дво́йка; (*woman's*) костю́м, ю́бка с жаке́том; **~ of armour** доспе́хи (*m. pl.*), ла́т|ы (*pl., g.* —). **4.** (*of cards*) масть; **follow ~** ходи́ть (*indet.*) в масть; (*fig.*) сле́довать (*impf.*) за+*i.*; сле́довать (*impf.*) чьему́-н. приме́ру; **politics are his strong ~** в поли́тике он соба́ку съел; **politeness is not his strong ~** он не отлича́ется любе́зностью/ве́жливостью.
v.t. **1.** (*accommodate, adapt*) приспос|а́бливать, -о́бить (*что к чему*); согласо́в|ывать, -а́ть (*что с чем*); **he ~s his speech to his audience** он приспоса́бливает свою́ речь к аудито́рии; **~ the action to the word** подкреп|ля́ть, -и́ть сло́во де́йствием; **he is not ~ed to be an engineer** он не годи́тся в инжене́ры; из него́ инжене́р(а) не вы́йдет; **they are ~ed to one another** они́ подхо́дят друг дру́гу. **2.** (*be satisfactory, convenient to*): **the plan ~s me** э́тот план меня́ устра́ивает; **will it ~ you to finish now?** удо́бно ли вам ко́нчить на э́том?; **he tries to ~ everybody** он стара́ется всем угоди́ть; **~ yourself!** как хоти́те!; де́лайте как зна́ете!; во́ля ва́ша! **3.** (*be good for, agree with*): **coffee does not ~ me** мне от ко́фе де́лается нехорошо́; ко́фе мне вре́ден; **the English climate does not ~ everyone** не всем подхо́дит англи́йский кли́мат. **4.** (*befit*) под|ходи́ть, -ойти́ +*d.*; **the role does not ~ him** э́та роль ему́ не подхо́дит; **buffoonery does not ~ an old man** шутовство́ не приста́ло старику́; **that hat ~s her** э́та шля́па ей идёт (*or* ей к лицу́).
v.i. под|ходи́ть, -ойти́; годи́ться (*impf.*).
cpd. **~case** *n.* (небольшо́й) чемода́н.
suitability [ˌsu:tə'bɪlɪtɪ, ˌsju:-] *n.* го́дность, приго́дность.
suitable ['su:təb(ə)l, 'sju:-] *adj.* подходя́щий, го́дный, соотве́тствующий, соотве́тственный; уда́чный; **he is ~ for the job** он подхо́дит для э́той до́лжности; **clothes ~ to the occasion** оде́жда, подходя́щая к (*or* соотве́тствующая/прили́чествующая) слу́чаю; **these clothes are hardly ~ for wet weather** э́та оде́жда едва́ ли годи́тся для дождли́вой пого́ды; **reading ~ to her age** чте́ние, соотве́тствующее её во́зрасту.
suitably ['su:təblɪ, 'sju:-] *adv.* соотве́тственно, пра́вильно; как сле́дует.
suite [swi:t] *n.* **1.** (*retinue*) сви́та. **2.** (*set*): **~ of furniture** гарниту́р ме́бели, ме́бельный гарниту́р; **bedroom ~** спа́льный гарниту́р; **~ of rooms** апарта́менты (*m. pl.*); (*in hotel*) (но́мер-)люкс. **3.** (*mus.*) сюи́та.
suitor ['su:tə(r), 'sju:-] *n.* (*wooer*) жени́х, покло́нник.
sulf- ['sʌlf] = **sulph-**
sulk [sʌlk] *n.* дурно́е настрое́ние; **a fit of the ~s** при́ступ дурно́го настрое́ния.
v.i. быть в дурно́м настрое́нии; **~ at s.o.** ду́ться (*impf.*) на кого́-н.
sulky[1] ['sʌlkɪ] *n.* одноме́стная коля́ска, двуко́лка.
sulky[2] ['sʌlkɪ] *adj.* наду́тый, оби́женный.
sullen ['sʌlən] *adj.* (*sulky*) наду́тый; (*morose*) угрю́мый; (*sombre*) мра́чный.
sullenness ['sʌlənnɪs] *n.* наду́тость; угрю́мость; мра́чность.
sully ['sʌlɪ] *v.t.* (*liter.*) пятна́ть, за-.
sulphate ['sʌlfeɪt] *n.* сульфа́т; **copper/iron/zinc ~** ме́дный/желе́зный/ци́нковый купоро́с.
sulphide ['sʌlfaɪd] *n.* сульфи́д; **copper ~** серни́стая медь.
sulphite ['sʌlfaɪt] *n.* сульфи́т; **copper ~** сернистоки́слая медь.
sulphonamide [sʌl'fɒnəˌmaɪd] *n.* сульфами́д.
sulphur ['sʌlfə(r)] (*US* **sulfur**) *n.* се́ра; **flowers of ~** се́рный цвет.
adj. (*colour*) зеленова́то-жёлтый.
sulphurate ['sʌlfjʊˌreɪt] *v.t.* (*impregnate*) пропи́т|ывать, -а́ть се́рой; (*fumigate*) оку́р|ивать, -и́ть се́рой.
sulphureous [sʌl'fjʊərɪəs] *adj.* се́рный; зеленова́то-жёлтый.
sulphuretted [ˌsʌlfjʊ'retɪd] *adj.* сульфи́рованный; **~ hydrogen** сероводоро́д.
sulphuric [sʌl'fjʊərɪk] *adj.* се́рный; **~ acid** се́рная кислота́.
sulphurous ['sʌlfərəs] *adj.* серни́стый.
sultan ['sʌlt(ə)n] *n.* султа́н.
sultana [sʌl'tɑ:nə] *n.* (*pers.*) султа́ница; (*fruit*) изю́минка, (*collect.*) кишми́ш.
sultanate ['sʌltəˌneɪt] *n.* (*state, institution*) султа́нство, султана́т.
sultriness ['sʌltrɪnɪs] *n.* духота́, зно́йность, зной.
sultry ['sʌltrɪ] *adj.* **1.** (*of atmosphere, weather*) зно́йный, ду́шный; **~ heat** зной. **2.** (*of temper or pers.*) зно́йный, стра́стный, ю́жный.
sum [sʌm] *n.* **1.** (*total*) ито́г; **~ total** о́бщая су́мма, о́бщий ито́г; **the ~ total of his demands was ...** в о́бщей сло́жности его́ тре́бования своди́лись к+*d.* **2.** (*amount*) су́мма; **his debts amounted to the ~ of £2,000** его́ долги́ достига́ли (су́ммы в) 2 000 фу́нтов; **he had a large ~ on him** у него́ с собо́й была́ больша́я су́мма де́нег. **3. ~** (*liter. substance, essence*) су́щность, суть; **in ~** (одни́м) сло́вом; **the ~ of all my wishes** ито́г/верши́на мои́х стремле́ний. **4.** (*problem*) (арифмети́ческая) зада́ча; **he gave me a ~ to do** он за́дал мне зада́чу; **he did the ~ in his head** он реши́л зада́чу в уме́; **he is good at ~s** он силён в арифме́тике.
v.t. (*usu.* **~ up**) **1.** (*reckon up*) подсчи́т|ывать, -а́ть; скла́дывать, сложи́ть. **2.** (*summarize*) сумми́ровать (*impf.*); подв|оди́ть, -ести́ ито́г +*g./d.*; резюми́ровать (*impf., pf.*); **the argument can be ~med up in one word** весь вопро́с сво́дится к одному́ сло́ву; (*form judgement of*): **he ~med up the situation at a glance** он оцени́л положе́ние с пе́рвого взгля́да; **she quickly ~med him up** она́ оцени́ла его́ сра́зу же по досто́инству.
v.i.: **~ up** сумми́ровать (*impf., pf.*); резюми́ровать (*impf., pf.*); **the judge's ~ming-up** заключи́тельная речь судьи́; **to ~ up, ...** сло́вом,...
sumac(h) ['su:mæk, 'ʃu:-, 'sju:-] *n.* сума́х.
Sumatra [sʊ'mɑ:trə] *n.* Сума́тра.
Sumatran [sʊ'mɑ:trən] *n.* жи́тель (*fem.* -ница) Сума́тры.
adj. суматри́йский.
summarily ['sʌmərɪlɪ] *adv.* бесцеремо́нно.
summarize ['sʌməˌraɪz] *v.t.* сумми́ровать (*impf., pf.*); резюми́ровать (*impf., pf.*); подв|оди́ть, -ести́ ито́г +*g./d.*
summary ['sʌmərɪ] *n.* резюме́ (*indecl.*), сво́дка.
adj. **1.** (*brief*) сумма́рный, кра́ткий; **~ account** сумма́рное изложе́ние, кра́ткий отчёт. **2.** (*rapid, sweeping*) бесцеремо́нный; **a ~ judgement** пове́рхностное сужде́ние; **~ methods** огу́льные ме́тоды. **3.** (*leg.*) ускоре́нный; **~ conviction** осужде́ние в поря́дке сумма́рного произво́дства; **~ jurisdiction** упрощённое/сумма́рное произво́дство.
summation [sə'meɪʃ(ə)n] *n.* (*addition*) подведе́ние ито́га; (*summing-up*) резюме́ (*indecl.*).
summer ['sʌmə(r)] *n.* **1.** ле́то; **in ~** ле́том; **a girl of some 20 ~s** (*liter.*) де́вушка лет двадцати́; **Indian (or St Martin's) ~** ба́бье ле́то. **2.** (*fig., prime*) расцве́т.
adj. ле́тний; **~ dress** ле́тнее пла́тье; **dressed in ~ clothes** оде́тый по-ле́тнему; **~ lightning** зарни́ца; **~**

school лéтний университéт; ~ **time** (*daylight saving*) лéтнее врéмя.

v.i. (*spend* ~) пров|одúть, -естú лéто.

cpds. ~**house** *n.* бесéдка; ~**time** *n.* лéтняя порá; ~**-weight** *adj.* лёгкий, лéтний.

summery ['sʌmərɪ] *adj.*: ~ **weather** лéтняя/тёплая погóда; ~ **clothes** лёгкая/лéтняя одéжда.

summit ['sʌmɪt] *n.* (*lit., fig.*) вершúна, верх; (*fig.*) зенúт, апогéй; **the ~ of his ambition** вершúна егó честолю́бия; ~ **(conference, talks)** совещáние на вы́сшем ýровне.

summon ['sʌmən] *v.t.* **1.** (*send for*) приз|ывáть, -вáть; (*also leg.*) вызывáть, вы́звать. **2.** (*order*) приз|ывать, -вáть; **she ~ed the children to dinner** онá позвалá детéй обéдать; **they ~ed the garrison to surrender** онú потрéбовали сдать крéпость/гóрод. **3.**: ~ **a meeting** соз|ывáть, -вáть собрáние; ~ **up one's energy/courage** соб|ирáться, -рáться с сúлами/дýхом.

summons ['sʌmənz] *n.* вы́зов; (*leg.*) судéбная повéстка, вы́зов в суд; **answer a ~** яв|ля́ться, -úться по повéстке; **serve a ~ on s.o.** вруч|áть, -úть комý-н. судéбную повéстку; (*mil.*): ~ **to surrender** ультимáтум о сдáче.

v.t. вызывáть, вы́звать в суд.

summum bonum [ˌsʊməm 'bɒnəm, 'bəʊ-] *n.* величáйшее благо.

sump [sʌmp] *n.* (*for waste liquid, sewage etc.*) выгребнáя я́ма; (*for engine oil*) маслосбóрник; поддóн кáртера; (*for sludge*) грязевúк.

sumptuary ['sʌmptjʊərɪ] *adj.*: ~ **law** закóн, огранúчивающий приобретéние предмéтов рóскоши.

sumptuous ['sʌmptjʊəs] *adj.* роскóшный, великолéпный.

sumptuousness ['sʌmptjʊəsnɪs] *n.* рóскошь, великолéпие.

sun [sʌn] *n.* сóлнце; (*astron.*) Сóлнце; **the ~ rises** сóлнце восхóдит/всхóдит; **the ~ sets** сóлнце захóдит/садúтся; **his ~ is set** егó звездá закатúлась; **before the ~ goes down** до захóда сóлнца; **the ~ is up** сóлнце встáло; **the ~ is out** (*shining*) сóлнце/сóлнышко свéтит; **when the ~ comes out** когдá вы́йдет сóлнце; **when the ~ goes in** когдá скрóется сóлнце; **against the ~** (*counter-clockwise*) прóтив часовóй стрéлки; **with the ~** (*clockwise*) по часовóй стрéлке; **rise with the ~** вст|авáть, -ать с сóлнцем (*or* чуть свет *or* ни свет ни заря́); **lie in the ~** лежáть (*impf.*) на сóлнце; **a place in the ~** (*fig.*) мéсто под сóлнцем; тёпленькое местéчко; **everything under the ~** всё на свéте; **have the ~ in one's eyes** (*at games*) игрáть (*impf.*) прóтив сóлнца/свéта; **the ~ is in my eyes** сóлнце бьёт мне в глазá; меня́ сóлнце слепúт; **this flower-bed catches the ~** на э́ту клýмбу пáдает сóлнце; **you have caught the ~** (*become sunburnt*) вы загорéли; **get a touch of the ~** (*sunstroke*) перегрéться (*pf.*) на сóлнце; получúть (*pf.*) сóлнечный удáр; **in the full blaze of the ~** на (сáмом) солнцепёке.

v.t.: ~ **o.s.** грéться (*impf.*) на сóлнце/сóлнышке.

cpds. ~**-baked** *adj.* вы́сушенный на сóлнце; ~**bathe** *v.i.* загорáть (*impf.*); принимáть (*impf.*) сóлнечные вáнны; приня́ть (*pf.*) сóлнечную вáнну; ~**bather** *n.* загорáющий; ~**beam** *n.* сóлнечный луч; ~**-blind** *n.* (*awning*) маркúза; жалюзú (*nt. indecl.*); (*roller-blind*) штóра; ~**-bonnet** *n.* панáм(к)а; ~**burn** *n.* (*tan*) загáр; (*inflammation*) сóлнечный ожóг; **he got a nasty ~burn** он стрáшно обгорéл; ~**burn lotion** крем для загáра; ~**burnt** *adj.* загорéлый; **get ~burnt** загорéть (*pf.*); **S~day** *see separate entry*; ~**-deck** *n.* вéрхняя пáлуба; ~**dial** *n.* сóлнечные часы́ (*m. pl.*); ~**down** *n.* захóд сóлнца; ~**downer** *n.* (*Austral., tramp*) бродя́га (*m.*); (*drink*) рю́мка, выпивáемая вéчером; ~**-drenched** *adj.* напоённый сóлнцем; ~**-dress** *n.* сарафáн; ~**-dried** *adj.* (*of fruit*) вы́сушенный на сóлнце, вя́леный; ~**flower** *n.* подсóлнух, подсóлнечник; ~**flower oil** подсóлнечное мáсло; ~**flower seed** подсóлнух, сéмечки (*nt. pl.*); ~**-glasses** *n. pl.* очкú от сóлнца; ~**-god** *n.* бог сóлнца; ~**-hat** *n.* шля́па от сóлнца, панáм(к)а; ~**-helmet** *n.* прóбковый шлем; ~**-lamp** *n.* квáрцевая лáмпа; ~**light** *n.* сóлнечный свет; ~**lit** *adj.* освещённый/зáлитый сóлнцем; ~**-lounge,** ~**-parlour** *nn.* соля́рий; застеклённая террáса; ~**-rays** *n. pl.* (*beams*) сóлнечные лучú (*m. pl.*); (*ultra-violet rays*) ультрафиолéтовые лучú; ~**rise** *n.* восхóд (сóлнца); **at ~rise** на зарé; ~**set** *n.* захóд сóлнца, закáт; **at ~set** на закáте; ~**shade** *n.* (*parasol*) (сóлнечный) зóнтик; (*awning*) навéс, маркúза, тент; ~**shine** *n.* сóлнечный свет; (*fig., cheer*) рáдость; **the ~shine went out of her life** счáстье ушлó из её жúзни; ~**shine roof** (*of car*) раздвижнáя кры́ша; ~**spot** *n.* пятнó на сóлнце; ~**stroke** *n.* сóлнечный удáр; ~**-suit** *n.* пля́жный костю́м; ~**-tan** *n.* загáр; ~**-tan lotion** крем для загáра; ~**-trap** *n.* соля́рий; ~**-up** *n.* (*US*) восхóд (сóлнца); ~**-worship** *n.* солнцепоклóнничество; культ сóлнца.

sundae ['sʌndeɪ, -dɪ] *n.* морóженое с фрýктами/орéхами (*и т.п.*).

Sunday ['sʌndeɪ, -dɪ] *n.* воскресéнье; **on ~s** по воскресéньям; **not in a month of ~s** ≃ пóсле дóждичка в четвéрг; когдá рак свúстнет; ~ **school** воскрéсная шкóла; **in one's ~ best** в выходнóм плáтье; в прáздничном наря́де.

sunder ['sʌndə(r)] *v.t.* (*liter.*) разлуч|áть, -úть; разъедин|я́ть, -úть.

sundries ['sʌndrɪz] *n.* рáзное.

sundry ['sʌndrɪ] *adj.* рáзный, различный; **all and ~** всё и вся; все без исключéния.

sunken ['sʌŋkən] *adj.* (*of eyes etc.*) впáлый, запáвший; (*submerged*) подвóдный, затóпленный.

sunless ['sʌnlɪs] *adj.* тёмный, мрáчный, без сóлнца.

sunny ['sʌnɪ] *adj.* сóлнечный; **a ~ room** сóлнечная кóмната; **look on the ~ side of things** вúдеть (*impf.*) свéтлую стóрону вещéй; **a ~ disposition** жизнерáдостный харáктер; **a ~ smile** сия́ющая улы́бка.

sup [sʌp] *n.*: **neither bite nor ~** (*arch.*) ни мáковой росúнки.

v.i. ýжинать, по-.

super ['su:pə(r), 'sju:-] (*coll.*) *n.* **1.** (*actor*) статúст (*fem.* -ка). **2.** = **superintendent**

adj. замечáтельный, превосхóдный; ~**!** здóрово!

superable ['su:pərəb(ə)l, 'sju:-] *adj.* преодолúмый.

superabundance [ˌsu:pərə'bʌnd(ə)ns, ˌsju:-] (чрезмéрное) изобúлие.

superabundant [ˌsu:pərə'bʌnd(ə)nt, ˌsju:-] *adj.* изобúльный; избы́точный.

superadd [ˌsu:pər'æd, ˌsju:-] *v.t.* доб|авля́ть, -áвить.

superannuate [ˌsu:pər'ænjʊˌeɪt, ˌsju:-] *v.t.* перев|одúть, -естú на пéнсию по стáрости; ~**d** (*of pers.*) вы́шедший на пéнсию; (*fig.*) престарéлый; (*of thg.*) устарéлый.

superannuation [ˌsu:pərˌænjʊ'eɪʃ(ə)n, ˌsju:-] *n.* перевóд на пéнсию по стáрости; (*payment*) пéнсия по стáрости.

superb [su:'pɜ:b, sju:-] *adj.* превосхóдный, великолéпный.

supercargo ['su:pəˌkɑ:gəʊ, 'sju:-] *n.* суперкáрго (*m. indecl.*).

supercharge ['su:pəˌtʃɑ:dʒ, 'sju:-] *v.t.* (*overload*) перегру|жáть, -зúть; ~**d engine** двúгатель (*m.*) с наддýвом.

supercharger ['su:pəˌtʃɑ:dʒə(r), 'sju:-] *n.* нагнетáтель (*m.*); компрéссор наддýва.

supercilious [ˌsu:pə'sɪlɪəs, ˌsju:-] *adj.* высокомéрный, надмéнный, презрúтельный.

superciliousness [ˌsu:pə'sɪlɪəsnɪs, ˌsju:-] *n.* высокомéрие, надмéнность, презрúтельность.

supercomputer [ˌsu:pəkəm'pju:tə(r)] *n.* сверхбольшáя ЭВМ, сýпер-ЭВМ, сýпер-компью́тер.

supercontinent ['su:pəˌkɒntɪnənt] *n.* протоконтинéнт.

supercooled ['su:pəˌku:ld, -'ku:ld, 'sju:-] *adj.* переохлаждённый.

superego [ˌsu:pər'i:gəʊ, -'egəʊ, ˌsju:-] *n.* сверх-я́ (*nt. indecl.*).

supererogation [ˌsu:pərˌerə'geɪʃ(ə)n, ˌsju:-] *n.*: **works of ~** сверхдóлжные дóбрые делá.

supererogatory [ˌsu:pərɪ'rɒgətərɪ, ˌsju:-] *adj.* излúшний; превышáющий трéбование дóлга.

superfatted [ˌsu:pə'fætɪd, ˌsju:-] *adj.* пережúренный.

superficial [ˌsu:pə'fɪʃ(ə)l, ˌsju:-] *adj.* (*lit., fig.*) повéрхностный.

superficiality [ˌsu:pəfɪʃɪ'ælɪtɪ, ˌsju:-] *n.* повéрхностность.

superfine ['su:pəˌfaɪn, 'sju:-] *adj.* (*highly refined*) тончáйший; (*of high quality*) (наи)вы́сшего кáчества.

superfluity [ˌsu:pə'flu:ɪtɪ, ˌsju:-] *n.* излúшек.

superfluous [su:'pɜ:flʊəs, sju:-] *adj.* излúшний.

superheat [ˌsu:pə'hi:t, ˌsju:-] *v.t.* перегр|евáть, -éть.

superheater [ˌsuːpəˈhiːtə(r), ˌsjuː-] *n.* пароперегрева́тель (*m.*).
superhet(erodyne) [ˌsuːpəˈhetərəʊˌdaɪn, ˌsjuː-] *n.* супергетероди́нный приёмник.
superhuman [ˌsuːpəˈhjuːmən, ˌsjuː-] *adj.* сверхчелове́ческий.
superimpose [ˌsuːpərɪmˈpəʊz, ˌsjuː-] *v.t.* на|кла́дывать, -ложи́ть (*что на что*).
superintend [ˌsuːpərɪnˈtend, ˌsjuː-] *v.t. & i.* заве́довать (*impf.*) (*чем*); управля́ть (*impf.*) (*кем/чем*); руководи́ть (*impf.*) (*чем/кем*); наблюда́ть (*impf.*) за (*кем/чем*); (*impf.*) надзира́ть за (*кем/чем*).
superintendence [ˌsuːpərɪnˈtend(ə)ns, ˌsjuː-] *n.* заве́дование (+*i.*); управле́ние (+*i.*); надзо́р (за+*i.*).
superintendent [ˌsuːpərɪnˈtend(ə)nt, ˌsjuː-] *n.* заве́дующий, управля́ющий, нача́льник, руководи́тель (*m.*).
superior [suːˈpɪərɪə(r), sjuː-, sʊ-] *n.* **1.** (*pers. of higher rank*) ста́рший, нача́льник; **he looks up to his ~s** он почита́ет ста́рших по положе́нию; (*better*): **he is his brother's ~ in every way** он во всём превосхо́дит своего́ бра́та. **2.** (*relig.*) настоя́тель (*fem.* -ница); **father ~** (оте́ц-)игу́мен; **mother ~** (мать-)игу́менья.
adj. **1.** (*of higher rank or status*) ста́рший, вы́сший; **~ officer** ста́рший офице́р; **~ court** вы́сшая (суде́бная) инста́нция. **2.** (*of better quality, better*) превосхо́дный, превосходя́щий; вы́сшего ка́чества; **~ skill** вы́сшее мастерство́; **he was ~ to me in wisdom** он был мудре́е меня́; он превосходи́л меня́ му́дростью; **this cloth is ~ to that** э́то сукно́ лу́чше того́ (*or* бо́лее высо́кого ка́чества, чем то); **a ~ (type of) man** отбо́рный челове́к. **3.** (*conscious of superiority, supercilious*): **a ~ smile** презри́тельная улы́бка; улы́бка превосхо́дства; **don't look so ~!** бро́сьте э́ту ва́шу высокоме́рную мане́ру! **4.** (*greater in number*) превосходя́щий. **5.: ~ to** (*rising above, not yielding to*) стоя́щий вы́ше+*g.*; **he proved ~ to temptation** он оказа́лся вы́ше собла́зна; **he rose ~ to his troubles** он смог подня́ться над свои́ми ли́чными тру́дностями. **6.** (*typ.*) надстро́чный. **7.: Lake S~** Ве́рхнее о́зеро.
superiority [suːˌpɪərɪˈɒrɪtɪ, sjuː-, sʊ-] *n.* (*of rank*) старшинство́; (*of quality or quantity*) превосхо́дство.
superlative [suːˈpɜːlətɪv, sjuː-] *n.* (*gram.*) превосхо́дная сте́пень; **talk in ~s** говори́ть (*impf.*) в преувели́ченных выраже́ниях.
adj. **1.** (*excellent*) велича́йший, высоча́йший; **~ beauty** необыкнове́нная красота́. **2.** (*gram.*) превосхо́дный.
superman [ˈsuːpəˌmæn, ˈsjuː-] *n.* сверхчелове́к, суперме́н.
supermarket [ˈsuːpəˌmɑːkɪt, ˈsjuː-] *n.* магази́н самообслу́живания, универса́м.
supernatural [ˌsuːpəˈnætʃər(ə)l, ˌsjuː-] *n.*: **a belief in the ~** ве́ра в сверхъестесте́ственное.
adj. сверхъесте́ственный.
supernormal [ˌsuːpəˈnɔːm(ə)l, ˌsjuː-] *adj.* превыша́ющий но́рму.
supernova [ˌsuːpəˈnəʊvə, ˌsjuː-] *n.* сверхно́вая (звезда́).
supernumerary [ˌsuːpəˈnjuːmərərɪ, ˌsjuː-] *n.* сверхшта́тный рабо́тник; (*actor*) стати́ст (*fem.* -ка).
adj. сверхшта́тный.
superphosphate [ˌsuːpəˈfɒsfeɪt, ˌsjuː-] *n.* суперфосфа́т.
superpower [ˈsuːpəˌpaʊə(r), ˈsjuː-] *n.* сверхдержа́ва.
supersaturate [ˌsuːpəˈsætʃəˌreɪt, ˌsjuː-, -tjʊˌreɪt] *v.t.* перес|ыща́ть, -ы́тить.
superscript [ˈsuːpəskrɪpt, ˈsjuː-] *adj.* (*math. etc.*) надстро́чный.
superscription [ˌsuːpəˈskrɪpʃ(ə)n, ˌsjuː-] *n.* (*inscription*) на́дпись.
supersede [ˌsuːpəˈsiːd, ˌsjuː-] *v.t.* (*replace*) смен|я́ть, -и́ть; замен|я́ть, -и́ть; (*remove from post etc.*) сме|ща́ть, -сти́ть.
supersensitive [ˌsuːpəˈsensɪtɪv] *adj.* сверхчувстви́тельный.
supersession [ˌsuːpəˈseʃ(ə)n, ˌsjuː-] *n.* заме́на, замеще́ние.
supersonic [ˌsuːpəˈsɒnɪk, ˌsjuː-] *adj.* сверхзвуково́й.
superstar [ˈsuːpəˌstɑː(r)] *n.* суперзвезда́.
superstate [ˈsuːpəsteɪt] *n.* сверхдержа́ва.
superstition [ˌsuːpəˈstɪʃ(ə)n, ˌsjuː-] *n.* суеве́рие, (религио́зный) предрассу́док.
superstitious [ˌsuːpəˈstɪʃəs, ˌsjuː-] *adj.* суеве́рный.
superstratum [ˈsuːpəˌstrɑːtəm, ˈsjuː-] *n.* вышележа́щий пласт/слой.
superstructure [ˈsuːpəˌstrʌktʃə(r), ˈsjuː-] *n.* надстро́йка.
supertanker [ˈsuːpəˌtæŋkə(r), ˈsjuː-] *n.* суперта́нкер.
supertax [ˈsuːpəˌtæks, ˈsjuː-] *n.* дополни́тельный подохо́дный нало́г.
supertonic [ˌsuːpəˈtɒnɪk, ˌsjuː-] *n.* ве́рхний вво́дный тон.
supervene [ˌsuːpəˈviːn, ˌsjuː-] *v.i.* наступ|а́ть, -и́ть.
supervise [ˈsuːpəˌvaɪz, ˈsjuː-] *v.t.* надзира́ть (*impf.*) за+*i.*; наблюда́ть (*impf.*) за+*i.*
supervision [ˌsuːpəˈvɪʒ(ə)n, ˌsjuː-] *n.* надсмо́тр/надзо́р (за+*i.*).
supervisor [ˈsuːpəˌvaɪzə(r), ˈsjuː-] *n.* надсмо́трщи|к (*fem.* -ца); надзира́тель (*fem.* -ница); (*acad.*) (нау́чный) руководи́тель (*fem.* -ница).
supervisory [ˈsuːpəˌvaɪzərɪ, ˈsjuː-] *adj.* контро́льный, надзира́ющий, наблюда́ющий; **~ council** контро́льный сове́т; **~ duties** обя́занности по надзо́ру.
supine [ˈsuːpaɪn, ˈsjuː-] *n.* (*gram.*) супи́н.
adj. (*face up*) лежа́щий на́взничь; (*fig.*) безде́ятельный, ине́ртный, вя́лый.
supper [ˈsʌpə(r)] *n.* у́жин; **have ~** у́жинать, по-; **the Last S~** Та́йная ве́черя.
supplant [səˈplɑːnt] *v.t.* (*replace*) вытесня́ть, вы́теснить; (*oust*) выжива́ть, вы́жить.
supple [ˈsʌp(ə)l] *adj.* (*flexible, pliant*) ги́бкий; **~ limbs** ги́бкие чле́ны; (*soft*) мя́гкий; **~ leather** мя́гкая ко́жа; (*amenable*) ги́бкий, пода́тливый.
supplement[1] [ˈsʌplɪmənt] *n.* **1.** (*addition*) добавле́ние, дополне́ние. **2.** (*of book etc.*) приложе́ние. **3.** (*geom.*) дополни́тельный у́гол.
supplement[2] [ˈsʌplɪmənt, ˌsʌplɪˈment] *v.t.* доп|олня́ть, -о́лнить; поп|олня́ть, -о́лнить.
supplementary [ˌsʌplɪˈmentərɪ] *adj.* дополни́тельный, доба́вочный.
suppleness [ˈsʌpəlnɪs] *n.* ги́бкость, мя́гкость.
suppliant [ˈsʌplɪənt] *n.* проси́тель (*fem.* -ница).
adj. проси́тельный, умоля́ющий.
supplicate [ˈsʌplɪˌkeɪt] *v.t.* моли́ть, умоля́ть (*impf.*).
v.i. моли́ть, умоля́ть (*both impf.*); **~ for mercy** моли́ть (*impf.*) о поща́де.
supplication [ˌsʌplɪˈkeɪʃ(ə)n] *n.* мольба́, про́сьба.
supplier [səˈplaɪə(r)] *n.* поставщи́|к (*fem.* -ца).
suppl|y [səˈplaɪ] *n.* **1.** (*providing*) снабже́ние (*чем*); пита́ние (*чем*); поста́вка, подво́д. **2.** (*thg. supplied, stock*) запа́с; **have you a good ~y of food?** у вас доста́точно продово́льствия/провиа́нта?; **water ~y** водоснабже́ние; **take, lay in a ~y of sth.** запас|а́ться, -ти́сь (*or* запр|авля́ться, -а́виться) чем-н.; **bread is in short ~y** хлеб в дефици́те; **a commodity in short ~y** дефици́тный това́р; (*pl., mil.*) (бое)припа́сы (*m. pl.*), боево́е пита́ние. **3.** (*econ.*): **~y and demand** спро́с и предложе́ние. **4. ~y teacher** вре́менный учи́тель; **teach on ~y** (вре́менно) замеща́ть (*impf.*) преподава́теля.
v.t. **1.** (*furnish, equip*) снаб|жа́ть, -ди́ть; снаря|жа́ть, -ди́ть; обеспе́чи|вать, -ть (*all кого/что чем*); пита́ть (*impf.*); **the farm ~ies us with potatoes** фе́рма обеспе́чивает/снабжа́ет нас карто́фелем; **~y a city with electricity** пита́ть (*impf.*) го́род электроэне́ргией; **the room was ~ied with bookshelves** ко́мната была́ обору́дована кни́жными по́лками; **keep s.o. ~ied** бесперебо́йно снабжа́ть (*impf.*) кого́-н.; **arteries ~y the heart with blood** арте́рии доставля́ют кро́вь к се́рдцу. **2.** (*give, yield*) да|ва́ть, -ть; дост|авля́ть, -а́вить (*что кому/чему*); пост|авля́ть, -а́вить; **cows ~y milk** коро́вы даю́т молоко́; **I wrote the music, he ~ied the words** я написа́л му́зыку, он сочини́л слова́ (к ней); **can you ~y a reason?** вы мо́жете привезти́ до́вод?; **catalogue ~ied on request** катало́г выдаётся по тре́бованию. **3.** (*meet need*): **~y a deficiency** возме|ща́ть, -сти́ть недоста́ток; **that will ~y everybody's needs** э́то удовлетворя́ет всех (*or* ну́жды всего́ о́бщества). **4.** (*fill*): **~y the gaps in s.o.'s knowledge** восп|олня́ть, -о́лнить пробе́лы в чьих-н. зна́ниях; **~y a vacancy** запо́лнить (*pf.*) вака́нсию.
support [səˈpɔːt] *n.* **1.** (*aid*) подде́ржка; **walk without ~** ходи́ть (*indet.*) без подде́ржки; **I hope for your ~** я наде́юсь/рассчи́тываю на ва́шу подде́ржку; **give, lend ~** ока́з|ывать, -а́ть подде́ржку/подкрепле́ние +*d.*;

подкреп|ля́ть, -и́ть; **in ~ of** в подде́ржку/подкрепле́ние +*g.*; **without visible means of ~** без определённых средств к существова́нию. **2.** (*lit., fig., prop*) опо́ра; **shelf ~** кронште́йн для по́лки; **the sole ~ of his family** еди́нственная опо́ра семьи́.

v.t. **1.** (*hold up, prop up*) подде́рж|ива́ть, -а́ть; подп|ира́ть, -ере́ть; **pillars ~ing the roof** коло́нны, подде́рживающие кры́шу; **he ~ed his chin on his hand** он подпира́л руко́й подборо́док; **~ o.s. with a stick** оп|ира́ться, -ере́ться на па́лку; (*fig., assist by deed or word*): **which party do you ~?** каку́ю па́ртию вы подде́рживаете?; **~ing actor** актёр вспомога́тельного соста́ва (*or* на вторы́х роля́х); **~ing film** кинофи́льм, демонстри́рующийся в дополне́ние к основно́му; (*sustain*): **air is necessary to ~ life** во́здух необходи́м для поддержа́ния жи́зни. **2.** (*provide subsistence for*) содержа́ть (*impf.*); **he cannot ~ a family** он не в состоя́нии содержа́ть семью́; **hospitals ~ed by voluntary contributions** больни́цы, содержа́щиеся на доброво́льные поже́ртвования. **3.** (*confirm*) подкреп|ля́ть, -и́ть; **his theory is not ~ed by the facts** его́ тео́рия не подкрепля́ется фа́ктами. **4.** (*endure*) выде́рживать, вы́держать; **I cannot ~ his insolence** я не выношу́ его́ высокоме́рия.

supporter [sə'pɔːtə(r)] *n.* (*of cause, motion etc.*) сторо́нни|к (*fem.* -ца), приве́рженец; (*of sports team*) боле́льщи|к (*fem.* -ца).

supportive [sə'pɔːtɪv] *adj.* подде́рживающий, лоя́льный.

suppose [sə'pəʊz] *v.t.* **1.** (*assume*) предпол|ага́ть, -ожи́ть; допус|ка́ть, -ти́ть; **let us ~ what you say is true** предполо́жим, что вы говори́те пра́вду; **supposing he came, what would you say?** е́сли бы он пришёл, что бы вы сказа́ли?; допу́стим/предполо́жим, что он придёт, что вы (тогда́)ска́жете?; **~ it rains?** а что е́сли пойдёт до́ждь?; **~ they find out?** а вдруг они узна́ют?; **always supposing he is alive** е́сли то́лько он жив; **everyone is ~d to know the rules** предполага́ется, что все знако́мы с пра́вилами. **2.** (*imagine, believe*): **I ~ him to be about sixty** я полага́ю, что ему́ лет шестьдеся́т; **I never ~d him to he a hero** я никогда́ не счита́л его́ геро́ем; **he is ~d to be rich** счита́ется/говоря́т, что он бога́т; **I ~ you like Moscow** вам, наве́рное, нра́вится Москва́; **I don't ~ he will mind that** не ду́маю, что он бу́дет про́тив э́того (*or* что ему́ э́то бу́дет неприя́тно); **what do you ~ he meant?** как по-ва́шему, что́ он име́л в виду́?; **I ~ so** наве́рное; должно́ быть; **'He's no fool.' — 'No, I ~ not'** «Он не дура́к» — «Да уж на́до полага́ть, что нет»; **it is not to be ~d that ...** не сле́дует ду́мать, бу́дто... **3.** (*expr. suggestion*): **~ we take a holiday?** дава́йте возьмём о́тпуск?; **~ you lend me a pound?** не дади́те ли вы мне фунт взаймы? **4.** (*presuppose*): **success ~s ability and training** успе́х невозмо́жен без спосо́бностей и соотве́тствующей подгото́вки. **5.** (*pass., be expected, required*): **this is ~d to help you sleep** э́то должно́ помо́чь вам засну́ть; **he is ~d to wash the dishes** ему́ поло́жено мыть посу́ду (*or* мытьё посу́ды); в его́ обя́занность вхо́дит мыть посу́ду; **he was ~d to lock the door** он должен был запере́ть дверь; **you are ~d to hold the cup like this** ча́шку сле́дует держа́ть (вот) так; **you are not ~d to talk in the library** в библиоте́ке не полага́ется разгова́ривать; **how was I ~d to know?** отку́да мне бы́ло знать? **6.** (*p.p., presumed*) предполага́емый, мни́мый.

supposition [ˌsʌpə'zɪʃ(ə)n] *n.* предположе́ние, гипо́теза, дога́дка.

supposititious [səˌpɒzɪ'tɪʃəs] *adj.* мни́мый, ло́жный, фальши́вый.

suppository [sə'pɒzɪtərɪ] *n.* суппозито́рий.

suppress [sə'pres] *v.t.* **1.** подав|ля́ть, -и́ть; сде́рж|ива́ть, -а́ть; **the rebellion was ~ed** восста́ние бы́ло пода́влено; **the heckler was ~ed** крикуна́ заста́вили замолча́ть (*or* утихоми́рили); **she could hardly ~ a smile** она́ с трудо́м подави́ла/сдержа́ла улы́бку; **~ing a yawn** подавля́я зево́ту; (*crush*) разда́в|ливать, -и́ть; **~ a heresy** громи́ть, раз- е́ресь. **2.** (*stop publication of*) запре|ща́ть, -ти́ть; **his article was ~ed** была́ запрещена́ публика́ция его́ статьи́; (*eliminate*): **~ a phrase** из|ыма́ть,-ъя́ть фра́зу. **3.** (*conceal*) скры|ва́ть, -ть; зам|а́лчивать, -олча́ть; ум|а́лчивать, -олча́ть о+*p.*; **they succeeded in ~ing the truth** им удало́сь скры́ть/замолча́ть пра́вду.

suppression [sə'preʃ(ə)n] *n.* (*restraining*) подавле́ние, сде́рживание; (*quelling*) подавле́ние; (*crushing*) разгро́м; (*banning*) запреще́ние; (*silencing*) зама́лчивание.

suppressio veri [səˌpresɪəʊ 'veəraɪ] *n.* сокры́тие и́стины.

suppressor [sə'presə(r)] *n.*: **noise ~** глуши́тель (*m.*).

suppurate ['sʌpjəˌreɪt] *v.i.* гнои́ться, за-/на-.

suppuration [ˌsʌpjə'reɪʃ(ə)n] *n.* нагное́ние.

supra- ['suːprə, 'sjuː-] *pref.* сверх(ъ)...

supranational [ˌsuːprə'næʃən(ə)l, ˌsjuː-] *adj.* наднациона́льный, надгосуда́рственный.

supremacist [suː'preməsɪst, sjuː-] *n.*: **white ~** сторо́нник госпо́дства бе́лых.

supremacy [suː'preməsɪ, sjuː-] *n.* верхове́нство, госпо́дство, превосхо́дство.

supreme [suː'priːm, sjuː-] *adj.* **1.** (*of authority*) верхо́вный; **S~ Soviet of the USSR** Верхо́вный Сове́т СССР; **~ power** верхо́вная власть; **he reigned ~** он вла́ствовал безразде́льно. **2.** (*utmost, greatest, highest*): **the ~ sacrifice** же́ртва со́бственной жи́знью; **~ goodness** высоча́йшая доброде́тель; **~ test of fidelity** вы́сшее испыта́ние ве́рности; **he was ~ly confident** он был в вы́сшей сте́пени (*or* чрезвыча́йно) (само)уве́рен; **~ly happy** на верху́ блаже́нства.

supremo [suː'priːməʊ, sjuː-] *n.* верхо́вный глава́; дикта́тор.

Supt. [ˌsuːpərɪn'tend(ə)nt, ˌsjuː-] *n.* (*abbr. of* **Superintendent**) коменда́нт, управля́ющий.

surcharge[1] ['sɜːtʃɑːdʒ] *n.* **1.** (*extra load*) доба́вочная нагру́зка; перегру́зка; (*of electricity*) перезаря́дка. **2.** (*extra fee*) допла́та, припла́та. **3.** (*penalty*) штраф, пе́ня. **4.** (*on postage-stamp*) надпеча́тка.

surcharge[2] ['sɜːtʃɑːdʒ, -'tʃɑːdʒ] *v.t.* **1.** (*overload*) перегру|жа́ть, -зи́ть. **2.** (*exact ~*[1] *from*) взыск|ивать, -а́ть с+*g.*; взима́ть (*impf.*) у+*g.* **3.** (*overstamp*) надпеча́т|ывать, -ать.

surcingle ['sɜːˌsɪŋg(ə)l] *n.* подпру́га.

surd [sɜːd] *n.* (*math.*) иррациона́льное число́; (*phon.*) глухо́й согла́сный.

sure [ʃʊə(r), ʃɔː(r)] *adj.* **1.** (*convinced, certain, confident*) уве́ренный, убеждённый; **a ~ hand** твёрдая рука́; **a ~ step** уве́ренный шаг; **feel ~ of sth.** чу́вствовать/испы́тывать (*impf.*) уве́ренность в чём-н.; **he is ~** (*confident*) **of success** он уве́рен в (своём) успе́хе; **if he comes he is ~ of a welcome** е́сли он придёт, он мо́жет не сомнева́ться в тёплом приёме; **you can be ~ of one thing ...** в одно́м мо́жно быть уве́ренным...; одно́ несомне́нно; **he is very ~ of himself** он о́чень самоуве́рен; **I'm ~ you are right** я уве́рен (*or* не сомнева́юсь), что вы пра́вы; **I'm not so ~ about that** я в э́том не уве́рен (*or* сомнева́юсь); **I'm not ~ whether I can come** я не зна́ю, смогу́ ли прийти́; **I'm not ~ whether to go or not** я не зна́ю, пойти́ и́ли нет; **I'm ~ I didn't mean to hurt you** пра́во, я не хоте́л вас оби́деть; **sorry, I'm ~** (*iron.*) ах, ах, прости́те!; **how can I be ~ he is honest?** отку́да я зна́ю, что он че́стен?; **don't be too ~** как бы вам не ошиби́ться!; **well, I'm ~!** (*expr. surprise*) вот те раз!; ну и ну! **2.** (*safe, reliable, trusty, unfailing*) ве́рный, надёжный; **a ~ shot** ме́ткий стрело́к; **a ~ way to break one's neck** ве́рный спо́соб слома́ть себе́ ше́ю; **he has ~ grounds for believing ...** у него́ все основа́ния ве́рить, что...; **there can be no ~ proof** абсолю́тных доказа́тельств не мо́жет быть. **3.** (*with inf, certain, to be relied on*): **he is ~ to come** он непреме́нно придёт; **be ~ to lock the door** не забу́дьте запере́ть дверь!; **be ~ and write to me** смотри́те напиши́те мне!; **it is ~ to be wet** наверняка́ бу́дет дождли́во; **you would be ~ to dislike him** вам бы он наверняка́ не понра́вился; **~ thing!** (*coll.*) коне́чно!; обяза́тельно!; ещё бы! **4.** (*undoubtedly true*) несомне́нный, уве́ренный; **one thing is ~** в одно́м мо́жно не сомнева́ться. **5.: for ~** несомне́нно, непреме́нно; то́чно, наверняка́; **to be ~** (*concessive*) коне́чно, разуме́ется, пра́вда; (*confirmatory*) в са́мом де́ле; **you have done well, to be ~** вы прекра́сно спра́вились, слов нет. **6.: make ~** (*convince, satisfy o.s.*) убе|жда́ться, -ди́ться; ув|еря́ться, -е́риться; удостов|еря́ться, -е́риться (*all* в чём); **you must make ~ of your facts** вы должны́ прове́рить все фа́кты; **I made ~ no-one was following me** я (сперва́) удостове́рился в том, что за мной никто́ не идёт; **I made ~** (*felt certain*) **that he would come** я был уве́рен, что он придёт. **7.: I made ~** (*ensured*) **that he would come** я позабо́тился о том, что́бы он (непреме́нно) пришёл; **we must make ~ of a house before winter** мы должны́ обеспе́чить себе́ жильё до наступле́ния зимы́.

adv.: **as ~ as fate** наверняка́, де́ло ве́рное (*coll.*) как пить дать; **~ enough** действи́тельно, коне́чно; **he will come ~ enough** он придёт, не беспоко́йтесь; **and ~ enough he fell down** и, коне́чно/разуме́ется, он упа́л; **it ~ was cold!** (*US*) до чего́ же бы́ло хо́лодно!

cpds. **~-fire** *adj.* безоши́бочный, ве́рный, надёжный; **~-footed** *adj.* стоя́щий твёрдо на нога́х; не спотыка́ющийся; с уве́ренной похо́дкой.

surely [ˈʃʊəlɪ] *adv.* **1.** (*securely*) надёжно; **slowly but ~** ме́дленно, но ве́рно. **2.** (*without doubt*) несомне́нно, ве́рно, наверняка́. **3.** (*expr. strong hope or belief*): **it ~ cannot have been he** не мо́жет быть, что́бы э́то был он; **this must ~ be his last appearance** уж э́то должно́ быть наверняка́ после́днее его́ выступле́ние; **~ I have met you before** я уве́рен, что (где́-то) ви́дел вас пре́жде; **~ you don't mean to say that ...** не хоти́те же вы сказа́ть, что...; **~ you saw him?** неуже́ли вы его́ не ви́дели; **~ you weren't offended?** неуже́ли вы не оби́делись?; **you ~ don't want to disappoint him** ведь вы не захоти́те его́ разочарова́ть(, не пра́вда ли)?; **~ the drought can't last much longer** не мо́жет быть, что́бы за́суха затяну́лась надо́лго. **4.** (*as answer, certainly*) коне́чно, непреме́нно.

surety [ˈʃʊərɪtɪ, ˈʃʊətɪ] *n.* **1.** (*liter., certainty*): **of a ~** наве́рное, несомне́нно. **2.** (*pledge*) зало́г. **3.** (*pers.*) поручи́тель (*fem.* -ница); **stand ~ for s.o.** руча́ться, поручи́ться за кого́-н.; брать, взять кого́-н. на пору́ки.

surf [sɜːf] *n.* прибо́й, буруны́ (*m. pl.*).

v.i. занима́ться (*impf.*) сёрфингом.

cpds. **~-board** *n.* доска́ для сёрфинга; **~-boat** *n.* прибо́йная шлю́пка; **~-riding** *n.* сёрфинг.

surface [ˈsɜːfɪs] *n.* **1.** пове́рхность; (*exterior*) вне́шность; **the earth's ~** пове́рхность земли́; **beneath the ~** (*lit.*) под пове́рхности; (*fig.*) за вне́шностью; **come to the ~** (*lit.*) всплы|ва́ть, -ть (на пове́рхность); (*fig.*) обнару́жи|ваться, -ться; **his politeness is only on the ~** его́ любе́зность чи́сто вне́шняя. **2.** (*attr.*) пове́рхностный, вне́шний; **~ mail** обы́чная по́чта; **~ impressions** пове́рхностные/о́бщие впечатле́ния; **~ politeness** показна́я ве́жливость; **~ tension** пове́рхностное натяже́ние; **~ vessel** надво́дное су́дно.

v.t. **1.: ~ paper** обраб|а́тывать, -о́тать пове́рхность бума́ги; **~ wood** о(б)тёс|ывать, -а́ть де́рево; **~ a road** покр|ыва́ть, -ы́ть доро́гу асфа́льтом (*u m.n.*). **2.: ~ a submarine** подн|има́ть, -я́ть подво́дную ло́дку на пове́рхность.

v.i. (*of submarine, swimmer etc.*) вспл|ыва́ть, -ыть на пове́рхность.

cpd. **~-to-air** *adj.* зени́тный, ти́па «земля́-во́здух».

surfeit [ˈsɜːfɪt] *n.* (*excess of eating etc.*) изли́шество, избы́ток; (*repletion, satiety; also fig.*) насыще́ние, пресыще́ние.

v.t. (*overfeed*) перек|а́рмливать, -орми́ть; (*satiate*) прес|ыща́ть, -ы́тить.

surfer [ˈsɜːfə(r)] *n.* сёрфинги́ст.

surfing [ˈsɜːfɪŋ] *n.* сёрфинг.

surge [sɜːdʒ] *n.* (*of waves, water*) во́лны (*f. pl.*); вал; (*of crowd, emotion etc.*) волна́, прили́в; (*of elec. current*) и́мпульс.

v.i. **1.** (*of waves, water*) вздыма́ться (*impf.*); набе|га́ть, -жа́ть. **2.** (*of crowd*) волнова́ться (*impf.*); **the crowd ~d forward** толпа́ подала́сь вперёд. **3.** (*of emotions*) нахлы́нуть (*pf.*); **anger ~d within her** в душе́ у неё поднима́лся/закипа́л гнев.

surgeon [ˈsɜːdʒ(ə)n] *n.* хиру́рг; **dental ~** зубно́й врач; (хиру́рг-)стомато́лог; (*mil.*) вое́нный врач, офице́р медици́нской слу́жбы.

surgery [ˈsɜːdʒərɪ] *n.* **1.** (*treatment*) хирурги́я; **minor/major ~** ма́лая/больша́я хирурги́я; **plastic ~** пласти́ческая хирурги́я; **spare-part ~** трансплантацио́нная хирурги́я; (*operation*) опера́ция. **2.** (*office*) приёмная/кабине́т (врача́); амбулато́рия; **in ~ hours** в приёмные часы́; **the doctor holds a ~ every morning** врач принима́ет ка́ждое у́тро.

surgical [ˈsɜːdʒɪk(ə)l] *adj.* хирурги́ческий; **~ instruments** хирурги́ческие инструме́нты; **~ boot** ортопеди́ческий боти́нок; **~ spirit** медици́нский спирт.

surliness [ˈsɜːlɪnɪs] *n.* гру́бость, неприве́тливость.

surly [ˈsɜːlɪ] *adj.* неприве́тливый, хму́рый, угрю́мый.

surmise [səˈmaɪz] *n.* (*conjecture*) дога́дка; (*supposition*) предположе́ние.

v.t. предпол|ага́ть, -ожи́ть; (*suspect*) подозрева́ть, заподо́зрить.

v.i. дога́д|ываться, -а́ться.

surmount [səˈmaʊnt] *v.t.* **1.** (*overcome*) преодол|ева́ть, -е́ть. **2.: peaks ~ed with snow** го́рные верши́ны, уве́нчанные сне́гом; **a table ~ed by a clock** стол, на кото́ром стоя́т часы́.

surmountable [səˈmaʊntəb(ə)l] *adj.* преодоли́мый.

surname [ˈsɜːneɪm] *n.* фами́лия.

v.t. (*arch.*): **Charles, ~d the Great** Карл, про́званный Вели́ким.

surpass [səˈpɑːs] *v.t.* прев|осходи́ть, -зойти́; **he ~ed everyone in strength** он превосходи́л всех си́лой; **a woman of ~ing beauty** же́нщина непревзойдённой красоты́.

surplice [ˈsɜːplɪs] *n.* стиха́рь (*m.*).

surplus [ˈsɜːpləs] *n.* (*excess*) изли́шек; (*residue*) оста́ток; **in ~** в избы́тке.

adj. **1.** (*excess*) изли́шный, избы́точный; **~ energy** избы́точная эне́ргия; **~ food** изли́шки (*m. pl.*) продово́льствия; **~ to our requirements** бо́льше, чем (нам) тре́буется; **~ population** избы́точное населе́ние. **2.** (*remaining*) оста́точный; **~ value** приба́вочная сто́имость.

surprise [səˈpraɪz] *n.* **1.** (*wonder, astonishment*) удивле́ние; **show ~** выка́зывать, вы́казать удивле́ние; удив|ля́ться, -и́ться; **to my great ~** к моему́ велича́йшему удивле́нию; **he looked up in ~** он удивлённо вски́нул глаза́. **2.** (*unexpected events, news, gift etc.*) неожи́данность, сюрпри́з; **his arrival was a ~ to us all** его́ прие́зд был для нас всех неожи́данность; **I had the ~ of my life** я был соверше́нно поражён; **give s.o. a ~** устро́ить (*pf.*) кому́-н. сюрпри́з; **I have a ~ for you in my bag** у меня́ в су́мке для вас (есть) сюрпри́з. **3.** (*unexpected action*): **catch, take s.o. by ~** засти́чь (*pf.*) кого́-н. врасплох́; **the fort was taken by ~** кре́пость была́ взята́/захва́чена внеза́пным уда́ром. **4.** (*attr.*) неожи́данный, внеза́пный; **~ visit** неожи́данный визи́т; **~ attack** внеза́пная ата́ка; **~ factor** фа́ктор внеза́пности; **~ package, packet** сюрпри́з; **~ party** импровизи́рованная вечери́нка; неожи́данный прихо́д госте́й с со́бственным угоще́нием.

v.t. **1.** (*astonish*) удив|ля́ть, -и́ть; пора|жа́ть, -зи́ть; **I'm ~d at you!** вы меня́ удивля́ете!; я э́того от вас не ожида́л; **I was ~d to hear you had been ill** я с удивле́нием узна́л, что вы бы́ли больны́ (*or* боле́ли); **you'd be ~d how much it costs** вы не пове́рите, до чего́ э́то до́рого; **I'm ~d you didn't know that already** удивля́юсь, как вы э́того не зна́ли; **it's nothing to be ~d at** в э́том нет ничего́ удиви́тельного; **I shouldn't be ~d if ...** я (ниско́лько) не удивлю́сь, е́сли...; **it may ~ you to learn that ...** быть мо́жет, вам неизве́стно, что... **2.** (*by unexpected gift etc.*) сде́лать/устро́ить/приподнести́ (*pf.*) сюрпри́з +*d.* **3.** (*capture by ~*) захват|ыва́ть, -и́ть врасплох́; (*liter., take by ~*) заст|ига́ть, -и́чь (*or* заст|ава́ть, -а́ть) (врасплох́); **we ~d him in the act of stealing** мы его́ пойма́ли с поли́чным; **the storm ~d us when we were half-way home** бу́ря засти́гла нас на полпути́ домо́й. **4. he was ~d into an admission** он призна́лся от неожи́данности.

surprising [səˈpraɪzɪŋ] *adj.* удиви́тельный, порази́тельный; **that is hardly ~** в э́том ма́ло удиви́тельного; **~ though it**

may seem как ни удиви́тельно; **he eats ~ly little** он удиви́тельно/порази́тельно (*or* до смешно́го) ма́ло ест.

surrealism [səˈrɪəˌlɪz(ə)m] *n.* сюрреали́зм.

surrealist [səˈrɪəlɪst] *n.* сюрреали́ст.

adj. сюрреалисти́ческий.

surrender [səˈrendə(r)] *n.* (*handing over*) сда́ча; (*giving up*) отка́з (от+*g.*); усту́пка; **~ value** (*of policy*) су́мма, возвраща́емая лицу́, отказа́вшемуся от страхово́го по́лиса; (*capitulation*) капитуля́ция; **no ~!** не сдава́ться!; **unconditional ~** безоговоро́чная капитуля́ция.

v.t. **1.** (*yield*) сда|ва́ть, -ть; **the fort was ~ed to the enemy** кре́пость была́ сдана́ неприя́телю. **2.** (*give up*) отказ|ыва́ться, -а́ться от+*g.*; уступ|а́ть, -и́ть. **3. ~ o.s.: he ~ed himself to justice** он отда́лся в ру́ки правосу́дия; **she ~ed herself to despair** она предала́сь отча́янию.

v.i. сд|ава́ться, -а́ться; капитули́ровать (*impf.*, *pf.*).

surreptitious [ˌsʌrəpˈtɪʃəs] *adj.* та́йный; сде́ланный исподтишка́.

surrogate [ˈsʌrəgət] *n.* суррога́т.

surround [səˈraʊnd] *n.* бордю́р, окаймле́ние; (*of a carpet*) кро́мка ковра́.

v.t. окруж|а́ть, -и́ть; обступ|а́ть, -и́ть; **the ~ing countryside** окружа́ющая ме́стность; окре́стности (*f. pl.*); **the troops were ~ed** войска́ бы́ли окружены́.

surroundings [səˈraʊndɪŋz] *n.* (*material environment*) ме́стность, окре́стности (*f. pl.*); обстано́вка; (*intellectual environment*) среда́, окруже́ние.

surtax [ˈsɜːtæks] *n.* доба́вочный подохо́дный нало́г.

surveillance [sɜːˈveɪləns] *n.* надзо́р; **under ~** под надзо́ром (поли́ции); под (полице́йским) надзо́ром.

survey[1] [ˈsɜːveɪ] *n.* **1.** (*general view*) обзо́р, обозре́ние, осмо́тр; (*inspection, investigation*) иссле́дование, обсле́дование, опро́с; **we are carrying out a ~ on the dangers of smoking** мы прово́дим иссле́дование по вопро́су о вреде́ куре́ния. **2.** (*of land*) межева́ние, съёмка, проме́р; **they are making a ~ of our village** произво́дится (топографи́ческая/землеме́рная) съёмка на́шего села́. **3.** (*plan, map*) план, ка́рта; *see also* **ordnance**

survey[2] [səˈveɪ] *v.t.* **1.** (*view*) обозр|ева́ть, -е́ть. **2.** (*review, consider*) иссле́довать (*impf.*); обсле́довать (*impf.*, *pf.*); рассм|а́тривать, -отре́ть. **3.** (*inspect*) осм|а́тривать, -отре́ть. **4.** (*land etc.*) межева́ть (*impf.*); ме́рить, с-; произв|оди́ть, -ести́ съёмку +*g.*; **the house was ~ed and valued** бы́ли произведены́ осмо́тр и оце́нка до́ма.

surveying [sɜːˈveɪɪŋ] *n.* (топографи́ческая) съёмка; съёмка; **photographic ~** фотосъёмка; **~ instruments** геодези́ческие прибо́ры.

surveyor [səˈveɪə(r)] *n.* **1.** (*official inspector*) инспе́ктор, контролёр; **~ of weights and measures** контролёр мер и весо́в. **2.** (*of land etc.*) землеме́р, топо́граф, геодези́ст; **~'s chain** ме́рная цепь.

survival [səˈvaɪv(ə)l] *n.* **1.** (*living on*) выжива́ние; **~ after death** посме́ртная/потусторо́нняя жизнь; **~ of the fittest** выжива́ние наибо́лее приспосо́бленных; есте́ственный отбо́р; **their ~ depended on us** их жизнь зависе́ла от нас; **~ kit** авари́йный компле́кт (средств жизнеобеспе́чения); **~ rate** выжива́емость. **2.** (*relic*) пережи́ток; **a ~ of, from the Middle Ages** пережи́ток средневеко́вья.

survive [səˈvaɪv] *v.t.* **1.** (*outlive*) переж|ива́ть, -и́ть; **he will ~ us all** он нас всех переживёт; **this knife has ~ its usefulness** э́тот нож пришёл в него́дность. **2.** (*come alive through*): **~ an illness** перен|оси́ть, -ести́ боле́знь; **they ~d the shipwreck** они́ оста́лись в живы́х по́сле кораблекруше́ния; (*joc.*): **I see you ~d the exam** а, так вы жи́вы и невреди́мы по́сле экза́мена!

v.i. (*continue to live*) выжива́ть, вы́жить; **not one of the family has ~d** из всей семьи́ никого́ не оста́лось (в живы́х); (*be preserved*): сохрани́ться, уцеле́ть (*both pf.*); **the custom still ~s** э́тот обы́чай ещё сохрани́лся.

survivor [səˈvaɪvə(r)] *n.* уцеле́вший; **the ~s of the earthquake** уцеле́вшие от землетрясе́ния; **he was the sole ~** он оди́н оста́лся в живы́х.

susceptibilit|y [səˌseptɪˈbɪlɪtɪ] *n.* **1.** (*to disease etc.*) восприи́мчивость (к боле́зни *и т. п.*). **2.** (*pl.*, *feelings*) чувстви́тельность; **he tried not to wound any ~ies** он стара́лся никого́ не задева́ть/ра́нить.

susceptible [səˈseptɪb(ə)l] *adj.* **1.** (*impressionable*) впечатли́тельный, восприи́мчивый; **a ~ bachelor** влю́бчивый холостя́к; (*sensitive*) чувстви́тельный. **2.: ~ to** восприи́мчивый к+*d.*; па́дкий на+*a.*; **he is ~ to colds** он подве́ржен просту́де; **he is ~ to flattery** он па́док на лесть. **3.: ~ of** поддаю́щийся +*d.*; **the facts are not ~ of proof** фа́кты не поддаю́тся доказа́тельству.

suspect[1] [ˈsʌspekt] *n.* подозрева́емый.

adj. подозри́тельный; не внуша́ющий дове́рия.

suspect[2] [səˈspekt] *v.t.* **1.** подозрева́ть, заподо́зрить; (*apprehend*) предчу́вствовать (*impf.*); предпол|ага́ть, -ожи́ть; **they ~ed a plot** они́ подозрева́ли/заподо́зрили за́говор; **I went in, ~ing nothing** я вошёл, ничего́ не подозрева́я (*or* ни о чём не дога́дываясь); **I ~ it will rain before long** я подозрева́ю, что ско́ро пойдёт дождь; **you, I ~, don't care** вам, я полага́ю/подозрева́ю, всё равно́; **I ~ed him to be lying** я подозрева́л, что он лжёт; я заподо́зрил его́ во лжи; **a ~ed criminal** подозрева́емый; **a ~ed connection between them** подозрева́емая/предполага́емая связь ме́жду ни́ми. **2.** (*disbelieve, doubt*) сомнева́ться, усомни́ться +*p.*; **I ~ed (the truth of) his story** я сомнева́лся в и́стинности его́ расска́за.

suspend [səˈspend] *v.t.* **1.** (*hang up*) подве́|шивать, -сить; **the cage was ~ed from the ceiling** кле́тка была́ подве́шена к потолку́ (*or* свиса́ла с потолка́); **the balloon was ~ed in mid-air** возду́шный шар пови́с в во́здухе; **particles of dust ~ed in the air** части́цы пы́ли, взве́шенные в во́здухе; **salt ~ed in water** соль, взве́шенная в воде́. **2.** (*postpone, delay, stop for a time*) вре́менно прекра|ща́ть, -ти́ть; приостан|а́вливать, -ови́ть; **~ a meeting** прер|ыва́ть, -ва́ть собра́ние; **~ judgement** от|кла́дывать, -ложи́ть вынесе́ние суде́бного реше́ния; (*fig.*) возде́рж|иваться, -а́ться от сужде́ния; **~ payment** приостан|а́вливать, -ови́ть платежи́; **~ hostilities** приостанови́ть (*pf.*) вое́нные де́йствия; **state of ~ed animation** состоя́ние бесчу́вствия; **~ed sentence** усло́вный пригово́р. **3.** (*debar temporarily from office etc.*) вре́менно отстран|я́ть, -и́ть; вре́менно исключ|а́ть, -и́ть; **the player was ~ed for three months** игрока́ отстрани́ли на три ме́сяца.

suspender [səˈspendə(r)] *n.* **1.** (*for hose*) подвя́зка. **2.** (*US, pl., braces*) подтя́жки (*pl.*, *g.* -ек); по́мочи (*pl.*, *g.* -е́й).

cpd. **~-belt** *n.* (же́нский) по́яс с подвя́зками.

suspense [səˈspens] *n.* **1.** напряже́ние, напряжённость; **keep s.o. in ~** держа́ть (*impf.*) кого́-н. в неизве́стности; **I can't stand the ~** я не в состоя́нии вы́нести напряже́ние/неизве́стность/неопределённость. **2.** (*leg.*) приостановле́ние. **3.** (*comm.*): **~ account** счёт переходя́щих сумм.

suspenseful [səˈspensfʊl] *adj.* трево́жный; (*film etc.*) захва́тывающий, завлека́тельный.

suspension [səˈspenʃ(ə)n] *n.* **1.** (*hanging*) подве́шивание; **~ bridge** подвесно́й/вися́чий мост. **2.** (*of vehicle etc.*) подве́с. **3.** (*mus.*) задержа́ние. **4.** (*chem.*) взве́шенное вещество́, суспе́нзия, взвесь. **5.** (*stoppage*) приостановле́ние; **~ of nuclear tests** вре́менное прекраще́ние испыта́ний я́дерного ору́жия. **6.** (*debarring from office etc.*) отстране́ние; **their goalkeeper faces ~** их вратарю́ грози́т (вре́менное) исключе́ние из кома́нды.

suspensive [səˈspensɪv] *adj.*: **~ veto** вре́менный запре́т, вре́менное ве́то.

suspensory [səˈspensərɪ] *adj.* (*med.*) подве́шивающий.

suspicion [səˈspɪʃ(ə)n] *n.* **1.** подозре́ние; **I had no ~ he was there** я не подозрева́л, что он там; **I have grave ~s of his honesty** у меня́ си́льные подозре́ния относи́тельно его́ че́стности; **he was looked upon with ~** к нему́ относи́лись подозри́тельно (*or* с подозре́нием); **arouse ~** возбу|жда́ть, -ди́ть подозре́ния; **his behaviour awakened my ~s** его́ поведе́ние вы́звало у меня́ (*or* пробуди́ло мои́) подозре́ния; **above ~** вы́ше/вне подозре́ний; **under ~** под подозре́нием; **on ~ of murder** по подозре́нию в уби́йстве; **lull s.o.'s ~s** усып|ля́ть, -и́ть чьи-н. подозре́ния. **2.** (*trace, nuance*) при́вкус, отте́нок; **a ~ of**

garlic зáпах/прíвкус чеснокá; **a ~ of irony** тень ирóнии; **a ~ of arrogance in his tone** нóтки (*f. pl.*) высокомéрия в егó тóне.

suspicious [sə'spɪʃəs] *adj.* **1.** (*mistrustful*) подозрíтельный, недовéрчивый (к+*d.*); **his silence made me ~** егó молчáние застáвило меня насторожиться; **I became ~** я заподóзрил нелáдное. **2.** (*arousing suspicion*) подозрíтельный.

sustain [sə'steɪn] *v.t.* **1.** (*lit., fig.: support*) поддéрж|ивать, -áть; **an arch ~ed by pillars** áрка, поддéрживаемая колóннами; **his diet was barely sufficient to ~ life** пищи едвá хватáло, чтóбы емý не умерéть с гóлоду; **hope alone ~ed him** он жил однóй надéждой. **2.** (*bear, endure*): **the bridge will not ~ heavy loads** мост не выдéрживает больших нагрýзок; **they ~ed the attack** онí вы́держали атáку; онí вы́стояли. **3.** (*undergo, suffer*) потерпéть (*pf.*); понестí (*pf.*); **the enemy ~ed heavy losses** протíвник понёс тяжёлые потéри; **~ an injury** перенестí (*pf.*) трáвму; получíть (*pf.*) увéчье. **4.** (*keep going, maintain*): **~ a role** выдéрживать, вы́держать роль; **~ one's efforts** не ослаблять (*impf.*) усилий; **a ~ed effort** длíтельное/непреры́вное усíлие; **~ed defence** долговрéменная оборóна; **tension was ~ed to the end** напряжéние не ослабевáло до концá; **~ a note** (*mus.*) держáть (*impf.*) нóту. **5.** (*uphold*) подтвер|ждáть, -дíть; **~ an objection** прин|имáть, -я́ть возражéние.

sustenance ['sʌstɪnəns] *n.* (*nourishment*) питáние, пища; (*support*) поддéржка.

susurration [ˌsju:sə'reɪʃ(ə)n, ˌsu:-] *n.* (*liter., rustling*) шóрох, шéлест.

sutler ['sʌtlə(r)] *n.* (*hist.*) маркитáнт (*fem.* -ка).

suture ['su:tʃə(r)] *n.* **1.** (*anat.*) шов. **2.** (*surg., stitching*) наложéние шва; (*thread*) нить (для сшивáния рáны); материáл для шва.

v.t. на|клáдывать, -ложíть шов на+*a.*; заш|ивáть, -íть (*рану*).

suzerain ['su:zərən] *n.* сюзерéн.

suzerainty ['su:zərəntɪ] *n.* сюзеренитéт.

s.v. (*abbr. of* ***sub voce***) под слóвом.

svelte [svelt] *adj.* стрóйный, гíбкий.

swab [swɒb] *n.* **1.** (*mop etc.*) швáбра. **2.** (*surg.*) тампóн. **3.** (*med., specimen*) мазóк.

v.t. мыть, вы- швáброй; подт|ирáть, -ерéть; дрáить, вы́-.

swaddl|e ['swɒd(ə)l] *v.t.* пеленáть, с-; сви|вáть, -ть; **~ing-clothes** пелёнки (*f. pl.*), свивáльник.

swag [swæg] *n.* (*festoon*) гирля́нда (*из цветов, плодов и m.n.*); (*sl., booty*) награбленная добы́ча; (*Austral., bundle*) пожíтк|и (*pl., g.* -ов), поклáжа.

swagger ['swægə(r)] *n.* (*gait*) вáжная похóдка; **walk with a ~** расхáживать (*impf.*) с вáжным вíдом; (*of manner*) самодовóльная/самоувéренная манéра держáться.

adj. (*coll.*) шикáрный, щегольскóй.

v.i. **1.** (*of walk*) расхáживать (*impf.*) с вáжным вíдом. **2.** (*of manner*) вáжничать (*impf.*). **3.** (*boast*) хвáстать(ся) (*impf.*).

cpds. **~-cane, ~-stick** *nn.* стек, офицéрская трóсточка.

Swahili [swə'hi:lɪ, swɑ:'hi:lɪ] *n.* (*people, language*) суахíли (*m. indecl.*).

swain [sweɪn] *n.* (*arch. or joc.*) **1.** (*shepherd*) пастушóк. **2.** (*lover*) ухажёр, обожáтель (*m.*), воздыхáтель (*m.*). **3.** (*rustic*) деревéнский пáрень.

swallow[1] ['swɒləʊ] *n.* (*bird*) лáсточка; **one ~ does not make a summer** однá лáсточка (ещё) не дéлает весны́.

cpds. **~-dive** (*US* **swan-dive**) *n.* прыжóк в вóду лáсточкой; **~-tail** *n.* (*butterfly*) бáбочка-пáрусник; **~-tailed** *adj.* с раздвоённым хвостóм; **~-tailed coat** фрак, визíтка.

swallow[2] ['swɒləʊ] *n.* (*act of ~ing*) глотáние, заглáтывание; (*amount ~ed, gulp*) глотóк; **at one ~** одним глоткóм; зáлпом.

v.t. **1.** проглáтывать, -отíть; загл|áтывать, -отáть; **he ~ed the vodka at one go** он вы́пил вóдку зáлпом; **~ the bait** (*fig.*) попáсться (*pf.*) на ýдочку; **~ sth. the wrong way** подавíться (*pf.*), поперхнýться (*pf.*); **I made him ~ his words** я застáвил егó взять свои словá назáд; **he had to ~ his pride** емý пришлóсь проглотíть своё самолю́бие; **he ~s every insult** он проглáтывает все оскорблéния; **she will ~ the most outrageous tales** онá готóва повéрить сáмым фантастíческим рóссказням. **2.** (*usu.* **~ up:** *engulf, absorb*) погло|щáть, -тíть; **the expenses ~ed up the earnings** расхóды поглотíли весь зáработок; **she wished the earth would ~ her up** онá былá готóва провалíться сквозь зéмлю; **death is ~ed up in victory** поглощенá смерть побéдою.

v.i. глотáть (*impf.*); **he ~ed** он сглотнýл.

swamp [swɒmp] *n.* болóто, топь.

v.t. **1.** (*fill, cover with water*) затоп|ля́ть, -íть; зал|ивáть, -íть; **a wave ~ed the boat** волнá затопíла/залилá лóдку. **2.** (*fig., overwhelm, inundate*) наводн|я́ть, -íть; зас|ыпáть, -ы́пать; **we were ~ed with applications** мы бы́ли завáлены заявлéниями/прóсьбами.

swampy ['swɒmpɪ] *adj.* болóтистый, тóпкий.

swan [swɒn] *n.* лéбедь (*m.*); (*coll., leisurely trip*) прогýлка.

v.i. шатáться (*impf.*) (*coll.*).

cpds. **~-dive** *n.* (*US*) = **swallow-dive; ~-maiden** *n.* царéвна-лéбедь; **~sdown** *n.* лебя́жий пух; **~-song** *n.* лебедíная песнь.

swank [swæŋk] (*coll.*) *n.* выставлéние напокáз, показýха; **do sth. for ~** дéлать,с- что-н. напокáз.

v.i.: **~ about sth.** выставля́ть (*impf.*) что-н. напокáз; хвáстать (*impf.*) чем-н.

swannery ['swɒnərɪ] *n.* садóк для лебедéй.

swap, swop [swɒp] (*coll.*) *n.* обмéн; **do a ~** совершíть (*pf.*) обмéн.

v.t. меня́ть, с-; махнýться (*pf.*) +*i.*; **will you ~ places with me?** вы соглáсны со мной поменя́ться местáми?; давáйте поменя́емся местáми!; **let's ~ watches** махнёмся часáми?; **they were ~ping jokes** онí обмéнивались анекдóтами; **~ horses in mid-stream** (*fig.*) меня́ть (*impf.*) курс на полпутí.

sward [swɔ:d] *n.* (*liter.*) газóн, дёрн.

swarm[1] [swɔ:m] *n.*: **~ of ants/bees** муравьи́ный/пчели́ный рой; **~ of locusts** стáя саранчí; **~ of tourists** толпá турíстов; **~ of children** стáйка детéй.

v.i. **1.** (*of bees, ants etc.*) роíться (*impf.*). **2.** (*of people*): **children came ~ing round him** дéти столпíлись вокрýг негó; **a crowd of people ~ed into the square** огрóмная толпá хлы́нула на плóщадь. **3.** (*teem*) кишéть (*impf.*) +*i.*; **the town is ~ing with tourists** гóрод кишíт турíстами.

swarm[2] [swɔ:m] *v.t. & i.* карáбкаться, вс-; **the sailors ~ed (up) the ropes** матрóсы вскарáбкались по вáнтам.

swarthy ['swɔ:ðɪ] *adj.* смýглый.

swash [swɒʃ] *v.i.* (*of water*) плескáться (*impf.*).

swashbuckler ['swɒʃˌbʌklə(r)] *n.* сорвиголовá (*m.*).

swashbuckling ['swɒʃˌbʌklɪŋ] *adj.* лихóй, задиристый.

swastika ['swɒstɪkə] *n.* свáстика.

swat [swɒt] *v.t.* бить (*impf.*); прихлóп|ывать, -нуть.

swatch [swɒtʃ] *n.* образéц, обрáзчик; образцы́ (*m. pl.*).

swath(e) [sweɪð] *n.* прокóс; полосá скóшенной травы́.

swathe [sweɪð] *v.t.* бинтовáть, за-; закýт|ывать, -ать.

swatter ['swɒtə(r)] *n.* хлопýшка (для мух), мухобóйка.

sway [sweɪ] *n.* **1.** (*~ing motion*) качáние, колебáние. **2.** (*influence*) влия́ние; (*authority*) авторитéт; (*rule*) власть; **have, hold ~ over s.o.** держáть (*impf.*) когó-н. в подчинéнии; **bring s.o. under one's ~** подчинíть (*pf.*) когó-н. себé.

v.t. **1.** (*rock*) качáть (*impf.*); колебáть, по-; **~ the balance in s.o.'s favour** поколебáть/склонíть (*pf.*) весы́ в чью-н. пóльзу. **2.** (*influence, move*) влия́ть, по-; колебáть, по-; **passions which ~ the minds of men** стрáсти, ведýщие на поводý человéческий рáзум; **he cannot be ~ed by such arguments** егó нельзя́ поколебáть такíми дóводами; **his speech ~ed votes** егó речь повлия́ла на исхóд голосовáния. **3.** (*rule*): **~ the realm** прáвить (*impf.*) цáрством; цáрствовать (*impf.*).

v.i. качáться (*impf.*); колебáться, по-.

Swaziland ['swɑ:zɪˌlænd] *n.* Свазилéнд.

swear [sweə(r)] *v.t. & i.* **1.** (*pronounce, promise solemnly*) кля́сться (*impf.*); божíться (*impf.*); **he swore allegiance to the king** он покля́лся в вéрности королю́; **they swore**

eternal friendship они́ покляли́сь в ве́чной дру́жбе; ~ **an oath** прин|оси́ть, -ести́ (*or* да|ва́ть, -ть) кля́тву; ~ **an accusation against s.o.** обвин|я́ть, -и́ть кого́-н. под прися́гой; **I ~ to God (that) ...** кляну́сь (Го́сподом) Бо́гом, что...; **I ~ by all that's sacred** кляну́сь всем святы́м; **he will ~ that black is white** он гото́в божи́ться, что чёрное — бе́лое. **2.** (*bind by an oath*) прив|оди́ть, -ести́ к прися́ге; **the jury was sworn in** прися́жных привели́ к прися́ге; **he was sworn to secrecy** с него́ взя́ли кля́тву о неразглаше́нии та́йны; его́ заста́вили покля́сться, что он бу́дет храни́ть та́йну; **sworn enemies** закля́тые враги́.

v.i. **1.** (*take an oath*) кля́сться, по-; (*fig.*): **he ~s by aspirin** он мо́лится на аспири́н; ~ **off** (*abjure*): **he swore off smoking** он дал заро́к не кури́ть; **he swore to having seen the crime** он заяви́л под прися́гой, что был свиде́телем преступле́ния; **we may have met before, but I can't ~ to it** мы, ка́жется знако́мы, впро́чем, поручи́ться не могу́. **2.** (*use bad language, curse*) брани́ться (*impf.*); чертых|а́ться, -ну́ться; скверносло́вить (*impf.*); **~ing** брань, ру́гань; ~ **like a trooper** руга́ться (*impf.*) как изво́зчик; **it's enough to make one ~** э́то чёрт зна́ет что тако́е; э́то хоть кого́ из терпе́ния вы́ведет; **he swore at me for making him late** он руга́л меня́ на все ко́рки за то, что я заста́вил его́ опозда́ть.

cpd. **~-word** *n.* руга́тельство, нецензу́рное сло́во.

sweat [swet] *n.* **1.** пот, испа́рина; **by the ~ of one's brow** в по́те лица́ своего́; **his brows were running, dripping with ~** у него́ со лба пот ли́лся ручьём; **his shirt was dripping with ~** вся его́ руба́шка была́ по́тная, хоть выжима́й. **2.** (*state or process of ~ing*) поте́ние, пот; **a good ~ will cure a cold** е́сли хороше́нько пропоте́ть, просту́да пройдёт; **he was in a ~** (*lit., fig.*) он был (весь) в поту́; **a cold ~** холо́дный пот. **3.** (*coll., drudgery*): **it is a ~ compiling a dictionary** составля́ть слова́рь, нелёгкая рабо́та; что́бы соста́вить слова́рь, прихо́дится попоте́ть. **4.** (*moisture, condensation*) запотева́ние. **5. old ~** (*veteran*) тёртый кола́ч (*coll.*).

v.t. **1.** (*exude*) поте́ть (*impf.*) +*i.*; **he was trying to ~ out a cold** он стара́лся (как сле́дует) пропоте́ть, что́бы изба́виться от просту́ды; ~ **blood** (*fig.*) рабо́тать (*impf.*) до крова́вого по́та. **2.** (*force hard work from*): **he ~s his workers** он выжима́ет пот из свои́х рабо́чих; **~ed labour** потого́нный труд; ~ **a horse** заг|оня́ть, -на́ть ло́шадь.

v.i. (*lit., fig.*) поте́ть, вс-; **~ing-room** пари́льня, парна́я; **he was ~ing with fear** он был в холо́дном поту́ от стра́ха.

cpds. **~-band** *n.* вну́тренняя ле́нта шля́пы; (*sportsman's*) потничо́к; **~-gland** *n.* потова́я железа́; **~-shirt** *n.* бума́жный (спорти́вный) сви́тер, футбо́лка; **~-shop** *n.* предприя́тие, на кото́ром существу́ет потого́нная систе́ма; **~suit** *n.* трениро́вочный костю́м.

sweater ['swetə(r)] *n.* сви́тер.

sweaty ['swetı] *adj.*: ~ **hands** по́тные ру́ки; ~ **clothes** пропи́танная по́том (*or* по́тная/пропете́вшая) оде́жда; ~ **odour** за́пах по́та.

Swede [swi:d] *n.* (*pers.*) швед (*fem.* -ка); (*s~*: *vegetable*) брю́ква.

Sweden ['swi:dən] *n.* Шве́ция.

Swedish ['swi:dıʃ] *n.* (*language*) шве́дский язы́к.

adj. шве́дский; ~ **drill** шве́дская гимна́стика.

sweep [swi:p] *n.* **1.** (*with broom etc.*): **give a room a good ~** хороше́нько подмести́ (*pf.*) ко́мнату; (*fig.*): **make a clean ~** забра́ть/вы́мести (*pf.*) всё под метёлку; **they made a clean ~ of the table** они́ съе́ли всё подчисту́ю; **the thieves made a clean ~** во́ры обчи́стили кварти́ру. **2.** (*steady movement*) ше́ствие, движе́ние; (*~ing movement*) взмах, разма́х; **the onward ~ of civilization** поступа́тельное ше́ствие цивилиза́ции; ~ **of a scythe/sword** взмах серпа́/меча́; ~ **of the arm** взмах руки́; **with one ~** одни́м ма́хом. **3.** (*range, reach*) разма́х, широта́, диапазо́н. **4.** (*long flowing curve*) изги́б; ~ **of a river** изги́б/излу́чина реки́; **the driver made a wide ~ on a bend** води́тель пла́вно разверну́лся на поворо́те (*or* сде́лал широ́кий разворо́т). **5. (chimney-~)** трубочи́ст.

v.t. **1.** (*rush over*): **the waves swept the shore** во́лны набега́ли на бе́рег; **the storm swept the countryside** бу́ря пронесла́сь над всей окру́гой; **the new fashion ~ing the country** но́вая мо́да, охвати́вшая страну́. **2.** (*carry forcefully*): **a wave swept him overboard** его́ смы́ло волно́й (за́ борт); **he swept her off her feet** (*lit.*) он подхвати́л её на ру́ки; (*fig.*) он вскружи́л ей го́лову. **3.** (*touch, brush*): **he swept his hand across the table** он провёл руко́й по́ столу; ~ **the keys (of a piano)** пробежа́ть (*pf.*) по кла́вишам руко́й. **4.** (*pass searchingly over*): **he swept the horizon with a telescope** он обша́рил горизо́нт подзо́рной трубо́й; **his eyes swept the faces of his audience** он оки́нул взгля́дом ли́ца слу́шателей; **the search vessels swept the sea** разве́дывательные корабли́ борозди́ли мо́ре. **5.** (*clean*) подме|та́ть, -сти́; чи́стить, вы́-; ~ **a chimney** проч|ища́ть, -и́стить трубу́; ~ **the board** (*fig., win all stakes*) забра́ть (*pf.*) все ста́вки. **6.** (*brush*): **he swept the litter into a corner** он замёл му́сор в у́гол; **her dress swept the ground** её пла́тье волочи́лось по земле́; (*fig.*): ~ **sth. under the carpet** заме|та́ть, -сти́ что-н. под ковёр; **he swept all before him** он преодоле́л все препя́тствия.

v.i. **1.** (*rush, dash*) прон|оси́ться, -ести́сь; **a plague swept over the land** чума́ пронесла́сь/промча́лась по стране́; **rain swept across the country** дождь прошёл по всей стране́; **fear swept over him** страх охвати́л/обуя́л его́. **2.** (*walk majestically*): **she swept into the room** она́ вели́чественно вошла́ в ко́мнату. **3.** (*curve*) из|гиба́ться, -огну́ться; **the coastline ~s to the right** берегова́я ли́ния изгиба́ется впра́во. **4.** (*clean, brush*) мести́ (*impf.*); подме|та́ть, -сти́; **a new broom ~s clean** (*fig.*) но́вая метла́ чи́сто метёт.

with advs.: ~ **along** *v.t.* нести́ (*det.*); увл|ека́ть, -е́чь; **the boat was swept along by the current** ло́дку несло́/уноси́ло тече́нием; **a good speaker ~s his audience along** хоро́ший ора́тор увлека́ет за собо́й аудито́рию; *v.i.* проше́ствовать (*impf.*); ~ **aside** *v.t.*: **he swept the curtain aside** он ре́зко отодви́нул занаве́ску; **she swept him aside** она́ отстрани́ла его́; **he swept aside my protestations** он не стал слу́шать мои́ возраже́ния; ~ **away** *v.t.* сме|та́ть, -сти́; **they were ~ing the snow away** они́ сгреба́ли снег; **the storm swept everything away** бу́ря всё смела́; **the bridge was swept away by the rains** мост смы́ло дождя́ми; (*fig., abolish*) поко́нчить (*pf.*) с+*i.*; уничт|ожа́ть, -о́жить; отмен|я́ть, -и́ть; **they swept away the old laws** они́ вы́бросили ста́рые зако́ны на сва́лку; ~ **down** *v.t.*: **the river ~s the logs down to the mill** река́ несёт брёвна к ме́льнице; *v.i.*: **the enemy swept down on us** враг обру́шился на нас; **the hills ~ down to the sea** холмы́ сбега́ют к мо́рю; ~ **in** *v.i.*: **the wind ~s in at the door** ве́тер врыва́ется в дверь; ~ **off** *v.t.* срыва́ть, сорва́ть; **the roof was swept off in the gale** кры́шу сорва́ло урага́ном; ~ **out** *v.t.*: **the maid was ~ing out the cupboards** служа́нка вымета́ла шкафы́; *v.i.*: **she swept out (of the room etc.)** она́ вели́чественно удали́лась; ~ **up** *v.t.*: **I have to ~ up the kitchen** я до́лжен подмести́ ку́хню; **be sure and ~ up all the dirt** смотри́те вы́метите весь му́сор как сле́дует; **she ~s her hair up into a bun** она́ забира́ет во́лосы вверх в у́зел; *v.i.*: **I had to ~ up after them** мне пришло́сь по́сле них убира́ть; **the car swept up to the house** маши́на подрули́ла к до́му; **the road ~s up to the church** доро́га поднима́ется к це́ркви.

cpds. **~-back** *n.* (*aeron.*) пряма́я стрелови́дность (кры́льев); **~-net** *n.* не́вод; **~stake** *n.* ≃ лотере́я, тотализа́тор.

sweeper ['swi:pə(r)] *n.* (*pers.*) подмета́льщик, мете́льщик; (*device*) подмета́льная маши́на.

sweeping ['swi:pıŋ] *adj.* **1.** (*of motion etc.*): **a ~ bow** широ́кий покло́н; ~ **gesture** разма́шистый жест; ~ **lines** стреми́тельные ли́нии. **2.** (*comprehensive*) всеобъе́млющий, всесторо́нний; (*thoroughgoing*) реши́тельный, исче́рпывающий; ~ **changes** радика́льные измене́ния; (*wholesale*) безусло́вный, огу́льный; **a ~ statement** огу́льное утвержде́ние; **he is too ~ in his condemnation** он изли́шне категори́чен в своём осужде́нии.

sweepings ['swi:pıŋz] *n.* му́сор, сор; ~ **of the gutter** (*fig.*)

отре́бье, сор, подо́нки (*m. pl.*).

sweet [swi:t] *n.* **1.** (*~meat*) конфе́та, (*pl.*) сла́сти (*f. pl.*). **2.** (*dish*) сла́дкое, тре́тье. **3.** (*pl., delight*): **the ~s of office** пре́лести (*f. pl.*) слу́жбы. **4.** (*beloved*): **my ~** (мой) ми́лый, (моя́) ми́лая.

adj. **1.** (*to taste*) сла́дкий; **I am not fond of ~ foods** я не люблю́ сла́достей; **I like my tea very ~** я пью о́чень сла́дкий чай; **my brother has a ~ tooth** мой брат сластёна; **this wine is too ~ for my taste** э́то вино́ сли́шком сла́дкое на мой вкус; э́то сли́шком сла́дкое вино́ для меня́; **make ~** сласти́ть, по-; **~ corn** кукуру́за; **~ potato** бата́т; **~** (*fresh, pure*) **water** све́жая/пре́сная вода́. **2.** (*fragrant*) сла́дкий, души́стый; **how ~ the roses smell!** каки́е души́стые ро́зы!; как сла́дко па́хнут ро́зы!; **~ peas** души́стый горо́шек. **3.** (*melodious*): **~ voice** прия́тный/мелоди́чный го́лос; **~ singer** сладкогла́сный пев́ец; **~ melody** сла́дкая/преле́стная мело́дия. **4.** (*agreeable*): **~ words** ла́сковые слова́; **~ nothings** не́жности (*f. pl.*); **~ sleep** сла́дкий сон; **praise was ~ to him** он упива́лся похвало́й; **a ~ face** ми́лое лицо́; **a ~** (*gentle*) **temper** мя́гкий нрав/хара́ктер; **a ~ woman** ми́лая/преле́стная же́нщина; (*coll., charming, nice*) ми́лый; **a ~ frock** ми́ленькое пла́тьице; **a ~ little dog** симпати́чная соба́чка; **they were perfectly ~ to us** они́ бы́ли чрезвыча́йно ми́лы с на́ми; **keep s.o. ~** (*coll.*) подма́з|ываться, -аться к кому́-н. **5.: he is ~ on her** (*sl.*) он в неё влюблён; **at one's own ~ will** когда́/как взду́мается; **go one's own ~ way** де́лать (*impf.*) что тебе́ уго́дно.

cpds. **~-and-sour** *adj.* ки́сло-сла́дкий; **~bread** *n.* «сла́дкое мя́со»; **~heart** *n.* возлю́бленн|ый (*fem.* -ая); дружо́к; (*as address*) ду́шенька; **they were childhood ~hearts** они́ в де́тстве (*or* с де́тства) бы́ли влюблены́ друг в дру́га; **~meat** *n.* = **~** *n.* **1.**; **~-scented** *adj.* благоуха́нный; **~-shop** *n.* конди́терская; **~-talk** (*US coll.*) *n.* лесть, ума́сливание; *v.t.* загова́ривать (*impf.*) кому́-н. зу́бы; **~-tempered** *adj.* с мя́гким хара́ктером, мя́гкого нра́ва; **~-william** *n.* туре́цкая гвозди́ка.

sweeten ['swi:t(ə)n] *v.t.* **1.** подсла́|щивать (*or* подслаща́ть), -сти́ть. **2.** (*fig.*): **~ s.o.'s temper** смягч|а́ть, -и́ть чей-н. гнев; **flowers ~ the air** цветы́ освежа́ют во́здух; **her laughter ~ed his life** её смех скра́шивал ему́ жизнь; **he ~ed the caretaker with a bribe** он задо́брил смотри́теля взя́ткой.

sweetener ['swi:tənə(r)] *n.* (*sugar substitute*) замени́тель (*m.*) са́хара; (*bribe*) взя́тка, «благода́рность».

sweetening ['swi:tənɪŋ] *n.* подсла́щивание; то, что придаёт сла́дость.

sweetness ['swi:tnɪs] *n.* сла́дость; све́жость; прия́тность.

swell [swel] *n.* **1.** (*of sea*) зыбь. **2.** (*mus.*) крещéндо (*indecl.*). **3.** (*coll., dandy*) франт, щёголь (*m.*); (*coll., bigwig*) ши́шка; ва́жная персо́на.

adj. (*first-rate*) шика́рный, миро́вой (*coll.*).

v.t. **1.** (*increase size or volume of*) разд|ува́ть, -у́ть; **the wind ~ed the sails** ве́тер наду́л паруса́; **rivers swollen by melting snow** ре́ки, взду́вшиеся от та́лого сне́га; **my finger is swollen** у меня́ па́лец опу́х/распу́х; **the book was ~ed by appendices** кни́га разбу́хла от приложе́ний. **2.** (*increase number of*) увели́чи|вать, -ть; **the population was ~ed by refugees** населе́ние увели́чилось благодаря́ бе́женцам. **3.** (*make arrogant*): **he was swollen with pride** он весь наду́лся/разду́лся от го́рдости; **~ed/swollen head** (*fig., coll.*) самомне́ние.

v.i. **1.** (*expand, dilate: also* **~ up**) над|ува́ться, -у́ться; разд|ува́ться, -у́ться; (*of part of body*) оп|уха́ть, -у́хнуть; расп|уха́ть, -у́хнуть. **2.** (*increase in size or volume*) выраста́ть, вы́расти; разбуха́ть, -у́хнуть; взд|ува́ться, -у́ться; **the crowd ~ed to over six thousand** толпа́ увели́чилась до шести́ с ли́шним ты́сяч (челове́к); **the novel ~ed to enormous size** рома́н разбу́х до огро́много разме́ра; **the rivers have ~ed since the thaw** ре́ки взду́лись по́сле о́ттепели. **3.** (*of pers., with pride etc.*) над|ува́ться, -у́ться; **~ with indignation** чуть не ло́пнуть (*pf.*) от негодова́ния; **hatred ~ed up in him** в нём клокота́ла не́нависть; **my heart ~ed with pride** се́рдце моё испо́лнилось/напо́лнилось го́рдостью. **4.** (*of sound*) нараста́ть (*impf.*); **the murmur ~ed into a roar** ро́пот перерос в рёв.

swelling ['swelɪŋ] *n.* (*on body*) о́пухоль, опуха́ние; (*on other object*) вы́пуклость.

swelter ['sweltə(r)] *v.i.* (*of pers.*) изнемога́ть (*impf.*) от жары́/зноя́/духоты́; **~ing** (*of atmosphere etc.*) нестерпи́мо жа́ркий.

swerve [swɜ:v] *n.* отклоне́ние, поворо́т.

v.i. (кру́то) пов|ора́чиваться, -ерну́ться; свёртывать, -ну́ть; отклон|я́ться, -и́ться; **the car ~d to avoid an accident** маши́на кру́то сверну́ла, что́бы избежа́ть ава́рии.

swift [swɪft] *n.* (*bird*) стриж.

adj. (*rapid*) бы́стрый; **a ~ movement** бы́строе движе́ние; **~ flight** стреми́тельный полёт; **~ of foot** быстроно́гий; (*prompt*) ско́рый; **a ~ reply** ско́рый отве́т; **~ to anger** вспы́льчивый.

cpd. **~-acting** *adj.* быстроде́йствующий.

swiftness ['swɪftnɪs] *n.* быстрота́, ско́рость, стреми́тельность.

swig [swɪg] (*coll.*) *n.* глото́к; **have, take a ~ of sth** сде́лать (*pf.*) глото́к чего́-н.; глотну́ть (*pf.*) чего́-н.; хлебну́ть (*pf.*) чего́-н.

v.t. хлеба́ть (*impf.*).

swill [swɪl] *n.* (*lit., fig.*) по́йло; (*pig-food*) помо́|и (*pl., g.* -ев).

v.t. **1.** (*wash, rinse*) мыть, вы́-; полоска́ть, вы́-; спол|а́скивать, -осну́ть. **2.** (*drink heavily*) лака́ть, хлеба́ть, хлеста́ть (*all impf., coll.*).

swim [swɪm] *n.* **1. have, go for a ~** купа́ться, ис-. **2.** (*main current of affairs*): **be in the ~** быть в ку́рсе дел; сле́довать (*impf.*) мо́де.

v.t. **1.** (*cross by ~ming*) перепл|ыва́ть, -ы́ть. **2.** (*cover by ~ming*): **~ a mile** пропл|ыва́ть, -ы́ть ми́лю. **3.** (*cause to ~*): **~ a horse across a river** пус|ка́ть, -ти́ть (*or* перепр|авля́ть, -а́вить) ло́шадь вплавь че́рез ре́ку.

v.i. **1.** пла́вать (*indet.*), плыть (*det.*), по-; **he can ~ on his back** он уме́ет пла́вать на спине́; **he ~s like a fish** он пла́вает как ры́ба; **she swam for the shore** она́ поплыла́ к бе́регу; **he had to ~ for his life** ему́ пришло́сь плыть изо всех сил; **~ with the tide** (*lit., fig.*) плыть (*det.*) по тече́нию; **~ against the tide** плыть (*det.*) про́тив тече́ния. **2.** (*of things: float*) пла́вать (*indet.*); **vegetables ~ming in butter** о́вощи пла́вающие в ма́сле. **3.** (*fig., reel, swirl*): **the noise made my head ~** от шу́ма у меня́ закружи́лась голова́; **everything was ~ming before my eyes** всё поплы́ло у меня́ пе́ред глаза́ми. **4.: her eyes swam with tears** её глаза́ бы́ли полны́ слёз.

swimmer ['swɪmə(r)] *n.* плов|е́ц (*fem.* -чи́ха); **a good, strong/poor ~** си́льный/сла́бый плове́ц.

swimming ['swɪmɪŋ] *n.* пла́вание; **he took ~ lessons** он брал уро́ки пла́вания; **~ contest, match** состяза́ние в пла́вании.

cpds. **~-bath, ~-pool** *nn.* (пла́вательный) бассе́йн; **~-costume** *n.* купа́льный костю́м, купа́льник; **~-trunks** *n. pl.* купа́льные трус|ы́ (*pl., g.* -о́в), пла́в|ки (*pl., g.* -ок).

swimmingly ['swɪmɪŋlɪ] *adj.*: **everything went ~** всё шло как по ма́слу (*or* гла́дко *or* без поме́х); **get on ~ with s.o.** найти́ (*pf.*) о́бщий язы́к (*or* сойти́сь (*pf.*)) с кем-н.

swindle ['swɪnd(ə)l] *n.* жу́льничество, моше́нничество, надува́тельство.

v.t. обма́н|ывать, -у́ть; **she ~d him out of the inheritance** она́ обма́нным путём (*or* обма́ном) получи́ла его́ насле́дство; **you've been ~d** вас наду́ли; **~ money out of s.o.** выма́нивать, вы́манить у кого́-н. де́ньги.

v.i. жу́льничать (*impf.*); моше́нничать (*impf.*).

swindler ['swɪndlə(r)] *n.* жу́лик, моше́нник.

swine [swaɪn] *n.* (*lit., fig.*) свинья́; **herd of ~** ста́до свине́й.

cpds. **~-breeding** *n.* свинові́дство; **~-fever** *n.* чума́ свине́й; **~herd** *n.* свинопа́с.

swing [swɪŋ] *n.* **1.** (*movement*) кача́ние, колеба́ние; **~ of the pendulum** кача́ние/разма́х ма́ятника; (*in boxing*) свинг, боково́й уда́р с разма́хом; **he took a ~ at the ball** он уда́рил по мячу́ с разма́ху; **in full ~** (*fig.*) в (по́лном) разга́ре. **2.** (*shift*): **the polls showed a ~ to the left** вы́боры показа́ли ре́зкий поворо́т/крен вле́во. **3.** (*of gait or* *rhythm*) ритм; **he walks with a ~** у него́ энерги́чная похо́дка; **his verse goes with a ~** его́ стиха́м сво́йствен мо́щный ритм; **the party went with a ~** вечери́нка вы́шла на сла́ву; **I couldn't get into the ~ of things** я ника́к не мог включи́ться в де́ло (*or* войти́ в курс де́ла). **4.** (*mus.*) суи́нг. **5.** (*seat slung on rope*) каче́л|и (*pl.*, *g.* -ей); **he gave the boy a (go on the) ~** он раскача́л ма́льчика на каче́лях.

v.t. **1.** (*apply circular motion to*): **~ a cane** пома́хивать (*impf.*) тро́сточкой; **~ one's arms** разма́хивать (*impf.*) рука́ми; **~ one's hips** пока́чивать (*impf.*) бёдрами; (*brandish*): **he swung the sword above his head** он взмахну́л шпа́гой над голово́й; **there's not enough room to ~ a cat** (*coll.*) здесь поверну́ться не́где; здесь я́блоку не́где упа́сть. **2.** (*dangle, suspend*): **~ a bag from one's arm** нести́ (*pf.*) су́мку на руке́; **~ the lead** (*sl.*) симули́ровать (*impf.*); приду́риваться (*impf.*). **3.** (*cause to turn, pivot*) пов|ора́чивать, -ерну́ть; разв|ора́чивать, -ерну́ть; **the tide swung the boat round** прили́в поверну́л ло́дку круго́м. **4.** (*sling, hoist*) вски́|дывать, -нуть; **he swung her on to his shoulders** он броско́м посади́л её себе́ на пле́чи; **he swung himself into the saddle** он вскочи́л в седло́; **they swung the cargo ashore** они́ перебро́сили груз на бе́рег. **5.** (*give rhythmic motion to*) кача́ть (*impf.*); колеба́ть (*impf.*). **6.** (*influence*): **his speech swung the jury in her favour** его́ речь склони́ла симпа́тии прися́жных на её сто́рону.

v.i. **1.** (*sway, oscillate*) кача́ться, колеба́ться, пока́чиваться, колыха́ться (*all impf.*); (*dangle*) висе́ть, свиса́ть, болта́ться (*all impf.*); **let one's legs ~** болта́ть (*impf.*) нога́ми; **he could ~ from a branch with one hand** он мог раска́чиваться на ве́тке одно́й руко́й; **the meat swung from a hook** мя́со висе́ло на крюке́; **a lamp swung from the ceiling** с потолка́ све́шивалась ла́мпа; **the children were ~ing in the park** де́ти кача́лись на каче́лях в па́рке. **2.** (*turn, pivot*) пов|ора́чиваться, -ерну́ться; враща́ться (*impf.*); **the door swung open in the wind** дверь распахну́лась от ве́тра; **the window swung to** окно́ захло́пнулось; **the ship is ~ing round** кора́бль повора́чивает; **he swung round on his heel** он (ре́зко) поверну́лся на каблука́х. **3.** (*move rhythmically*): **the band swung down the street** орке́стр (про)ше́ствовал по у́лице; **a ~ing stride** ме́рный шаг; **the monkeys swung from bough to bough** обезья́ны раска́чивались на ветвя́х; **~ing** (*lively, zestful*) жизнера́достный. **4.** (*sl., hang*): **he will ~ for this murder** его́ вздёрнут (*or* ждёт пе́тля) за э́то уби́йство.

cpds. **~-boat** *n.* ло́дка-каче́л|и (*pl.*, *g.* -ей); **~-bridge** *n.* разводно́й мост; **~-doors** *n. pl.* свобо́дно распа́хивающаяся (двустворча́тая) дверь; **~-wing** *adj.*: **~-wing aircraft** самолёт, име́ющий крыло́ с изменя́емой геоме́трией.

swingeing [ˈswɪndʒɪŋ] *adj.* (*coll.*): **a ~ blow** ошеломля́ющий уда́р; **a ~ majority** подавля́ющее большинство́; **a ~ lie** вопию́щая/на́глая ложь; **a ~ fine** грома́дный/здорове́нный штраф.

swinish [ˈswaɪnɪʃ] *adj.* сви́нский, ско́тский.

swipe [swaɪp] (*coll.*) *n.*: **take a ~ at s.o.** замахну́ться (*pf.*) на кого́-н.; **he took a ~ at the ball** он с си́лой/разма́ху уда́рил по мячу́.

v.t. (*hit*) с си́лой уд|аря́ть, -а́рить по+*d.*; (*steal*) сти́брить (*pf.*); стяну́ть (*pf.*) (*coll.*).

swirl [swɜːl] *n.* (*of water*) водоворо́т; (*of snow*) вихрь (*m.*); **~ of dust** столб пы́ли.

v.i. (*of water*) крути́ться (*impf.*) в водоворо́те; (*of snow*) ви́хриться (*impf.*); (*of leaves etc.*) кружи́ться, за-; (*of dust*) подн|има́ться, -я́ться столбо́м; (*fig.*): **my head is ~ing** у меня́ голова́ идёт кру́гом.

swish [swɪʃ] *n.* (*of water*) всплеск; (*of whip*) свист; (*of scythe etc.*) свист; взмах со сви́стом; (*of dress etc.*) шурша́ние, ше́лест.

adj. (*coll.*) шика́рный.

v.t. (*flick*) взма́х|ивать, -ну́ть +*i.*; **the cow ~ed her tail** коро́ва маха́ла/пома́хивала/взмахну́ла хвосто́м.

v.i. (*of fabric*) шурша́ть (*impf.*); шелесте́ть (*impf.*); (*of cane etc.*) расс|ека́ть, -е́чь во́здух (со сви́стом); (*of whip*) сви́стнуть (*pf.*); просвисте́ть (*pf.*); (*of scythe*) свисте́ть (*impf.*); **the wheels ~ed through the mud** колёса прошуме́ли по гря́зи.

Swiss [swɪs] *n.* швейца́р|ец (*fem.* -ка); **the ~** (*pl.*) швейца́рцы (*m. pl.*); **a German/French/Italian ~** герма́но-/фра́нко-/ита́ло-швейца́рец.

adj. швейца́рский; **~ German** (*ling.*) швейца́рский диале́кт неме́цкого языка́; **~ roll** руле́т с варе́ньем.

switch [swɪtʃ] *n.* **1.** (*twig, rod*) прут; (*riding-~*) хлыст. **2.** (*false hair*) накла́дка, фальши́вая коса́. **3.** (*rail.*) стре́лка. **4.** (*elec.*) выключа́тель (*m.*), переключа́тель (*m.*); (*knife-switch*) руби́льник. **5.** (*change of position, role, tactics etc.*) поворо́т, переме́на.

v.t. **1.** (*transfer*) перев|оди́ть, -ести́; переключ|а́ть, -и́ть. **2.** (*lash*): **the horse ~ed its tail** ло́шадь пома́хивала хвосто́м; **he ~ed the horse** он хлестну́л ло́шадь.

v.i.: **he ~ed from one extreme to the other** он перешёл/бро́сился из одно́й кра́йности в другу́ю.

with advs.: **~ off** *v.t.* выключа́ть, вы́ключить; **~ off a lamp** гаси́ть, по- ла́мпу; *v.i.* (*coll., withdraw one's attention*) отключи́ться (*pf.*); вы́ключиться (*pf.*); **~ on** *v.t.* включ|а́ть, -и́ть; (*light*) заж|ига́ть, -е́чь; **~ over** *v.t. & i.* переключ|а́ть(ся), -и́ть(ся); пере|ходи́ть, -йти́.

cpds. **~back** *n.* (*in amusement park*) америка́нские го́ры (*f. pl.*); **a ~back road** доро́га с круты́ми подъёмами и спу́сками; **~blade** *n.* пружи́нный нож, автомати́чески открыва́ющийся нож; **~board** *n.* коммута́тор; распредели́тельный/коммутацио́нный щит; щит управле́ния; **~board operator** телефони́ст (*fem.* -ка); **~man** *n.* стре́лочник; **~-plug** *n.* ште́псель (*m.*).

Switzerland [ˈswɪtsər,lænd] *n.* Швейца́рия.

swivel [ˈswɪv(ə)l] *n.* вертлю́г, шарни́рное соедине́ние; (*attr.*) враща́ющийся, поворо́тный; шарни́рный, вертлю́жный.

v.t. & i. пов|ора́чивать(ся), -ерну́ть(ся) (на шарни́рах).

cpds. **~-chair** *n.* поворо́тное/враща́ющееся сиде́нье; **~-eyed** *adj.* (*coll.*) косо́й, косогла́зый; **~-gun** *n.* ору́дие с поворо́тным устро́йством.

swiz(zle) [ˈswɪz(ə)l] *n.* (*coll.*) (*fraud*) моше́нничество; (*disappointment*) большо́е разочарова́ние.

swollen-headed [ˈswəʊlən] *adj.* чванли́вый, напы́щенный.

swoon [swuːn] *n.* о́бморок; **fall into a ~** упа́сть (*pf.*) в о́бморок.

v.i. па́дать, упа́сть в о́бморок.

swoop [swuːp] *n.* **1.** (*of bird etc.*) паде́ние вниз. **2.** (*sudden attack*) налёт; **at one fell ~** еди́ным уда́ром/ма́хом.

v.i. (*aeron.*) пики́ровать, с-; **the eagle ~ed (down) on its prey** орёл ри́нулся на свою́ же́ртву; **the enemy ~ed on the town** неприя́тель соверши́л внеза́пный налёт на го́род.

swop [swɒp] = **swap**

sword [sɔːd] *n.* шпа́га; (*liter., or fig.*) меч; **cavalry ~** са́бля, ша́шка; **~ of Damocles** Дамо́клов меч; **draw one's ~** обнажи́ть (*pf.*) меч; **sheathe, put up one's ~** вложи́ть (*pf.*) меч в но́жны; **cross ~s with s.o.** (*lit., fig.*) скрести́ть (*pf.*) шпа́ги с кем-н.; **put to the ~** пред|ава́ть, -а́ть мечу́; **at the ~'s point** (*fig.*) си́лой ору́жия; путём наси́лия; **beat ~s into ploughshares** перекова́ть (*pf.*) мечи́ на ора́ла.

cpds. **~-arm** *n.* пра́вая рука́; **~-bayonet** *n.* клинко́вый штык, штык-теса́к; **~-bearer** *n.* мечено́сец; **~-belt** *n.* портупе́я; **~-cut** *n.* ре́заная ра́на; (*scar*) рубе́ц; **~-dance** *n.* та́нец с са́блями; **~fish** *n.* меч-ры́ба; **~-guard** *n.* ча́шка шпа́ги; **~-hilt** *n.* эфе́с; **~-knot** *n.* темля́к; **~-play** *n.* фехтова́ние; (*fig., repartee*) пикиро́вка; **~sman** *n.* фехтова́льщик; **~smanship** *n.* иску́сство фехтова́ния; **~-stick** *n.* трость с вкладно́й шпа́гой; **~-swallower** *n.* шпагоглота́тель (*m.*).

swot [swɒt] *n.* (*pers.*) зубри́л(к)а (*c.g.*); (*study*) зубрёжка.

v.t.: **~ up a subject** зубри́ть, под-/вы́- предме́т.

v.i. зубри́ть (*impf.*).

sybarite [ˈsɪbə,raɪt] *n.* сибари́т (*fem.* -ка).

sybaritic [,sɪbəˈrɪtɪk] *adj.* сибари́тский.

sycamore [ˈsɪkə,mɔː(r)] *n.* сикамо́р анти́чный; (*maple*) я́вор; (*US, plane-tree*) плата́н, чина́р.

sycophancy [ˈsɪkə,fænsɪ] *n.* подхали́мство, лесть.

sycophant [ˈsɪkə,fænt] *n.* подхали́м, льстец.

sycophantic [,sɪkəˈfæntɪk] *adj.* подхали́мский, льсти́вый.

Sydney ['sɪdnɪ] *n.* Сидне́й.
syllabary ['sɪləbərɪ] *n.* слогова́я а́збука.
syllabic [sɪ'læbɪk] *adj.* силлаби́ческий, слогово́й.
syllabi(fi)cation [ˌsɪlæbɪ'keɪʃ(ə)n] *n.* разделе́ние на сло́ги.
syllab|ify [sɪ'læbɪˌfaɪ], **-ize** ['sɪləˌbaɪz] *v.t.* раздел|я́ть, -и́ть на сло́ги; произн|оси́ть, -ести́ по слога́м.
syllable ['sɪləb(ə)l] *n.* слог; **in words of one ~** (*fig.*) досту́пным языко́м; (*bluntly*) без обиняко́в; **he never uttered a ~** он не произнёс ни зву́ка.
syllabus ['sɪləbəs] *n.* (*programme*) програ́мма; уче́бный план; (*conspectus*) план, конспе́кт; (*time-table*) расписа́ние.
syllogism ['sɪləˌdʒɪz(ə)m] *n.* силлоги́зм.
syllogistic [ˌsɪlə'dʒɪstɪk] *adj.* силлогисти́ческий.
sylph [sɪlf] *n.* сильф (*fem.* -и́да).
cpd. **~-like** *adj.* грацио́зный.
sylvan ['sɪlv(ə)n] = **silvan**
sylviculture ['sɪlvɪˌkʌltʃə(r)] = **silviculture**
symbiosis [ˌsɪmbaɪ'əʊsɪs, ˌsɪmbɪ-] *n.* симбио́з.
symbiotic [ˌsɪmbaɪ'ɒtɪk, ˌsɪmbɪ-] *adj.* симбиоти́ческий.
symbol ['sɪmb(ə)l] *n.* си́мвол; (*emblem*) эмбле́ма; (*sign, e.g. math.*) знак.
symbolic(al) [sɪm'bɒlɪk(ə)l] *adj.* символи́ческий, символи́чный.
symbolism ['sɪmbəˌlɪz(ə)m] *n.* символи́зм.
symbolist ['sɪmbəlɪst] *n.* символи́ст (*fem.* -ка).
adj. символи́стский.
symbolization [ˌsɪmbəlaɪ'zeɪʃ(ə)n] *n.* символиза́ция.
symbolize ['sɪmbəˌlaɪz] *v.t.* символизи́ровать (*impf., pf.*).
symmetric(al) [ˌsɪ'metrɪk(ə)l] *adj.* симметри́чный, симметри́ческий.
symmetry ['sɪmɪtrɪ] *n.* симметри́я, симметри́чность.
sympathetic [ˌsɪmpə'θetɪk] *adj.* **1.** (*compassionate*) сочу́вственный; **a ~ look** сочу́вственный взгляд; **lend a ~ ear to** сочу́вственно выслу́шивать, вы́слушать; **~ words** по́лные сочу́вствия слова́. **2.** (*favourable, supportive*): **I am ~ towards his ideas** его́ иде́и мне близки́; **~ strike** забасто́вка солида́рности. **3.** (*physiol. etc.*): **~ nerve** симпати́ческий нерв; **~ ink** симпати́ческие черни́ла.
sympathize ['sɪmpəˌθaɪz] *v.i.* сочу́вствовать (*impf.*) (+*d.*); симпатизи́ровать (*impf.*); **he ~d with me in my grief** он сочу́вствовал моему́ го́рю; **I ~ with your viewpoint** мне поня́тна ва́ша пози́ция.
sympathizer ['sɪmpəˌθaɪzə(r)] *n.* сочу́вствующий, сторо́нник; (*comforter*) утеши́тель (*fem.* -ница).
sympathy ['sɪmpəθɪ] *n.* **1.** (*compassion, commiseration, fellow-feeling*) сочу́вствие, сострада́ние; (*agreement*) согла́сие; **feel ~ for s.o.** испы́тывать (*impf.*) сочу́вствие к кому́-н.; **evoke (*or* stir up) ~ for s.o.** вызыва́ть, вы́звать сочу́вствие к кому́-н.; **he had small ~ with idleness** он не одобря́л безде́лья; **we are in ~ with your ideas** мы сочу́вствуем ва́шим иде́ям; **the power workers came out in ~** рабо́тники электроста́нции забастова́ли в знак солида́рности; **my sympathies are with the miners** все мои́ симпа́тии на стороне́ шахтёров; **they were out of ~ with each other** они́ друг дру́га не понима́ли; **perfect ~ exists between them** ме́жду ни́ми цари́т по́лное согла́сие.
symphonic [sɪm'fɒnɪk] *adj.* симфони́ческий.
symphonist ['sɪmfənɪst] *n.* а́втор/сочини́тель (*m.*) симфони́ческой му́зыки.
symphony ['sɪmfənɪ] *n.* симфо́ния; **~ orchestra/concert** симфони́ческий орке́стр/конце́рт.
symposium [sɪm'pəʊzɪəm] *n.* (*discussion*) симпо́зиум; (*collection of essays etc.*) сбо́рник стате́й (и т.п.); **S~** (*work by Plato*) Пир.
symptom ['sɪmptəm] *n.* симпто́м; (*sign*) при́знак; **develop ~s** прояв|ля́ть, -и́ть симпто́мы; **he showed ~s of fear** он вы́казал при́знаки стра́ха.
symptomatic [ˌsɪmptə'mætɪk] *adj.* симптомати́чный, симптомати́ческий; **fever is ~ of many diseases** лихора́дка явля́ется симпто́мом мно́гих боле́зней.
synaesthesia [ˌsɪni:s'θi:zɪə] *n.* синестезия.
synagogue ['sɪnəˌgɒg] *n.* синаго́га.
sync(h) [sɪŋk] *n.* (*coll.*): **out of ~** несинхро́нный.
synchromesh ['sɪŋkrəʊˌmeʃ] *n.* синхрониза́тор; (*attr.*) синхронизи́рующий.
synchronism ['sɪŋkrəˌnɪz(ə)m] *n.* (*cin., TV*) синхрони́зм.
synchronization [ˌsɪŋkrənaɪ'zeɪʃ(ə)n] *n.* синхрониза́ция.
synchronize ['sɪŋkrəˌnaɪz] *v.t.* синхронизи́ровать (*impf., pf.*); **~d swimming** худо́жественное пла́вание.
v.i. (*of events*) совпада́ть (*impf.*) во вре́мени; (*of clocks*) пока́зывать (*impf.*) одина́ковое вре́мя.
synchronous ['sɪŋkrənəs] *adj.* синхро́нный; **~ satellite** геостациона́рный спу́тник.
synchrotron ['sɪŋkrəˌtrɒn] *n.* синхротро́н.
syncopate ['sɪŋkəˌpeɪt] *v.t.* (*gram., mus.*) синкопи́ровать (*impf., pf.*).
syncopation [ˌsɪŋkə'peɪʃ(ə)n] *n.* синко́па.
syncope ['sɪŋkəpɪ] *n.* (*gram.*) синко́па; (*med.*) о́бморок.
syncretism ['sɪŋkrəˌtɪz(ə)m] *n.* синкрети́зм.
syndic ['sɪndɪk] *n.* си́ндик.
syndicalism ['sɪndɪkəˌlɪz(ə)m] *n.* синдикали́зм.
syndicalist ['sɪndɪkəlɪst] *n.* синдикали́ст (*fem.* -ка).
syndicate[1] ['sɪndɪkət] *n.* синдика́т.
syndicate[2] ['sɪndɪˌkeɪt] *v.t.* синдици́ровать (*impf., pf.*).
syndrome ['sɪndrəʊm] *n.* синдро́м.
synecdoche [sɪ'nekdəkɪ] *n.* сине́кдоха.
synod ['sɪnəd] *n.* сино́д.
synod|al ['sɪnəd(ə)l], **-ic** [sɪ'nɒdɪk], **-ical** [sɪ'nɒdɪk(ə)l] *adjs.* синода́льный.
synonym ['sɪnənɪm] *n.* сино́ним.
synonymity [ˌsɪnə'nɪmɪtɪ] *n.* синоними́чность.
synonymous [sɪ'nɒnɪməs] *adj.* синоними́чный; синоними́ческий; (*fig.*) равнозна́чный (+*d.*).
synopsis [sɪ'nɒpsɪs] *n.* сино́псис; **~ of a thesis** (*acad.*) авторефера́т диссерта́ции.
synoptic [sɪ'nɒptɪk] *adj.* синопти́ческий.
synovitis [ˌsaɪnəʊ'vaɪtɪs, sɪn-] *n.* воспале́ние синовиа́льной оболо́чки.
syntactic(al) [sɪn'tæktɪkəl] *adj.* синтакси́ческий.
syntax ['sɪntæks] *n.* си́нтаксис.
synthesis ['sɪnθɪsɪs] *n.* си́нтез.
synthe|sist ['sɪnθɪsɪst], **-tist** ['sɪnθɪtɪst] *n.* синте́тик.
synthe|size ['sɪnθɪˌsaɪz], **-tize** ['sɪnθɪˌtaɪz] *v.t.* синтези́ровать (*impf., pf.*).
synthesizer ['sɪnθɪˌsaɪzə(r)] *n.* синтеза́тор.
synthetic(al) [sɪn'θetɪk(əl)] *adj.* (*chem., ling.*) синтети́ческий; (*artificial*) иску́сственный.
synthet|ist ['sɪnθɪtɪst], **-ize** ['sɪnθɪˌtaɪz] = **synthes|ist, -ize**
syphilis ['sɪfɪlɪs] *n.* си́филис.
syphilitic [ˌsɪfɪ'lɪtɪk] *adj.* сифилити́ческий.
syphon ['saɪf(ə)n] = **siphon**
Syracuse ['saɪrəˌkju:z] *n.* (*hist.*) Сираку́з|ы (*pl., g.* —).
Syria ['sɪrɪə] *n.* Си́рия.
Syriac ['sɪrɪˌæk] *n.* древнесири́йский язы́к.
adj. древнесири́йский.
Syrian ['sɪrɪən] *n.* сири́|ец (*fem.* -йка).
adj. сири́йский.
syringa [sɪ'rɪŋgə] *n.* сире́нь обыкнове́нная; жасми́н садо́вый.
syringe [sɪ'rɪndʒ, 'sɪr-] *n.* шприц, спринцо́вка; **hypodermic ~** шприц для подко́жных впры́скиваний.
v.t. (*ears etc.*) спринцева́ть (*impf.*); впры́с|кивать, -нуть; (*plants etc.*) опры́ск|ивать, -ать.
syrinx ['sɪrɪŋks] *n.* фле́йта Па́на.
syrup ['sɪrəp] *n.* сиро́п; (*treacle*) па́тока; **golden ~** све́тлая па́тока.
syrupy ['sɪrəpɪ] *adj.* (*fig.*) слаща́вый.
system ['sɪstəm] *n.* **1.** (*complex*) систе́ма; **solar ~** со́лнечная систе́ма; **digestive ~** пищевари́тельная систе́ма; **~ analysis** систе́мный ана́лиз. **2.** (*network*) сеть; **railway ~** железнодоро́жная сеть. **3.** (*body as a whole*) органи́зм; **the poison passed into his ~** яд прони́к в его́ органи́зм; **get sth. out of one's ~** (*fig.*) оч|ища́ться, -и́ститься от чего́-н. **4.** (*method*) систе́ма; **what ~ do you use?** како́й систе́мы вы приде́рживаетесь?; **~ of government** систе́ма правле́ния, госуда́рственный строй. **5.** (*methodical behaviour*) системати́чность.
systematic [ˌsɪstə'mætɪk] *adj.* системати́ческий, системати́чный.
systematization [ˌsɪstəmətaɪ'zeɪʃ(ə)n] *n.* систематиза́ция.

systematize ['sɪstəmə,taɪz] *v.t.* систематизи́ровать (*impf., pf.*)

systemic [sɪ'stemɪk] *adj.* системати́ческий, сомати́ческий; ~ **poison** общеядови́тое отравля́ющее вещество́.

systole ['sɪstəlɪ] *n.* си́стола, сокраще́ние се́рдца.

syzygy ['sɪzɪdʒɪ] *n.* (*astron.*) сизи́гия.

T

T [ti:] *n.*: **this suits me to a** ~ э́то меня́ вполне́ устра́ивает.

cpds. **~-junction** *n.* Т-обра́зный перекрёсток; **~-shaped** *adj.* Т-обра́зный; **~-shirt** *n.* ма́йка(-полурука́вка); футбо́лка (с коро́ткими рукава́ми); **~-square** *n.* рейсши́на.

TA (*abbr. of* ***Territorial Army***) территориа́льная а́рмия.

ta [tɑ:] *nt.* (*coll.*) спаси́бо.

tab [tæb] *n.* **1.** (*label on garment etc.*) наши́вка; (*for hanging clothes*) ве́шалка; пе́телька; (*insignia on collar*) петли́ца. **2.** (*coll., check*): **the police are keeping ~s on him** поли́ция присма́тривает за ним (*or* де́ржит его́ на заме́тке).

tabard ['tæbəd] *n.* костю́м геро́льда.

tabby ['tæbɪ] *n.* (*also* ~ **cat**) (се́рая) полоса́тая ко́шка.

tabernacle ['tæbə,næk(ə)l] *n.* **1.** (*bibl.*) ски́ния; киво́т; **Feast of T~s** (*Jewish*) пра́здник ку́щей. **2.** (*place of worship*) моле́льня.

table ['teɪb(ə)l] *n.* **1.** стол; **at** ~ за столо́м; **he has good ~ manners** он уме́ет держа́ться за столо́м; **he can drink me under the** ~ он меня́ перепьёт; **he laid his cards on the** ~ (*fig.*) он откры́л свои́ ка́рты; **he turned the ~s on his adversary** он поби́л проти́вника его́ же ору́жием; **T~ Bay** бу́хта Столо́вая; **a ~ for three** (*at restaurant*) сто́лик на трёх челове́к; (*fig., company at* ~) стол, компа́ния; **he keeps the ~ amused** он развлека́ет госте́й за столо́м; (*fig., food*) стол, ку́хня; **he keeps a good** ~ он хлебосо́льный хозя́ин. **2.** (*tablet*) плита́; **the ~s of the law** (*bibl.*) скрижа́ли (*f. pl.*) зако́на. **3.** (*arrangement of data*) табли́ца; ~ **of contents** оглавле́ние, содержа́ние; **he knows his twelve times** ~ он уме́ет умножа́ть на двена́дцать.

v.t.: ~ (*propose*) **an amendment** вн|оси́ть, -ести́ попра́вку.

cpds. **~cloth** *n.* ска́терть; **~-knife** *n.* столо́вый нож; **~-lamp** *n.* насто́льная ла́мпа; **~land** *n.* плато́ (*indecl.*), плоского́рье; **~-linen** *n.* столо́вое бельё; **~-mat** *n.* подста́вка (*под блюдо и т.п.*); **~-napkin** *n.* салфе́тка; **~spoon** *n.* столо́вая ло́жка; **~-talk** *n.* засто́льный разгово́р; **~-tennis** *n.* насто́льный те́ннис, пинг-по́нг; **~-turning** *n.* (*spiritualism*) столоверче́ние; **~ware** *n.* столо́вая посу́да; **~-water** *n.* минера́льная вода́; **~-wine** *n.* столо́вое вино́.

tableau ['tæbləʊ] *n.* жива́я карти́на, живопи́сная сце́на.

table d'hôte [,tɑ:b(ə)l 'dəʊt] *n.* табльдо́т; ~ **dinner** у́жин табльдо́т.

tablet ['tæblɪt] *n.* **1.** (*block for writing on*) (вощёная) доще́чка. **2.** (*inscribed plate or stone*) мемориа́льная доска́. **3.** (*of chocolate*) пли́тка; (*of soap*) кусо́к. **4.** (*pill*) табле́тка.

tabloid ['tæblɔɪd] *n.* малоформа́тная газе́та; (*pej.*) бульва́рная газе́та.

tab|oo, -u [tə'bu:] *n.* (*lit., fig.*) табу́ (*nt. indecl.*); (*prohibition*) запре́т.

adj.: **the subject is** ~ э́то запрещённая те́ма.

v.t. запре|ща́ть, -ти́ть.

tabor ['teɪbə(r)] *n.* ма́ленький бараба́н.

tabouret ['tæbərɪt] *n.* (*seat*) табуре́т, скаме́ечка; (*embroidery-frame*) пя́льц|ы (*pl., g.* -ев).

tabu [tə'bu:] = **taboo**

tabular ['tæbjʊlə(r)] *adj.* в ви́де табли́ц; табли́чный.

tabulate ['tæbjʊ,leɪt] *v.t.* табули́ровать (*impf.*); сост|авля́ть, -а́вить табли́цу из+*g.*

tabulation [,tæbjʊ'leɪʃ(ə)n] *n.* табули́рование; составле́ние табли́ц.

tabulator ['tæbjʊ,leɪtə(r)] *n.* (*machine*) табуля́тор.

tachometer [tə'kɒmɪtə(r)] *n.* taхо́метр.

tacit ['tæsɪt] *adj.* подразумева́емый; **a ~ spectator** молчали́вый зри́тель; ~ **agreement** молчали́вое согла́сие.

taciturn ['tæsɪ,tɜ:n] *adj.* неразгово́рчивый.

taciturnity [,tæsɪ'tɜ:nɪtɪ] *n.* неразгово́рчивость.

Tacitus ['tæsɪtəs] *n.* Та́цит.

tack [tæk] *n.* **1.** (*small nail*) гво́здик; **let's get down to brass ~s** (*fig.*) дава́йте разберёмся, что к чему́. **2.** (*long, loose stitch*) намётка. **3.** (*direction of vessel*) галс; **on the starboard** ~ пра́вым га́лсом; (*fig.*) курс, ли́ния; **he is on the wrong** ~ он на неве́рном пути́. **4. hard** ~ морско́й суха́рь.

v.t. **1.** (*fasten*) прикреп|ля́ть, -и́ть гво́здиками; приб|ива́ть, -и́ть. **2.** (*stitch*) сши|ва́ть, -ть; **she ~ed the dress together** она́ смета́ла пла́тье на живу́ю ни́тку. **3.** ~ **on** (*fig., add*) доб|авля́ть, -а́вить.

v.i. пов|ора́чивать, -ерну́ть на друго́й галс; **the ship ~ed before the wind** кора́бль сде́лал поворо́т оверշта́г.

tackle ['tæk(ə)l] *n.* **1.** (*rope-and-pulley mechanism*) полиспа́ст; сло́жный блок. **2.** (*equipment*) принадле́жности (*f. pl.*), обору́дивание; **fishing** ~ рыболо́вные сна́сти (*f. pl.*); **the workman arrived with all his** ~ рабо́чий прихвати́л с собо́й весь инструме́нт. **3.** (*football*) блокиро́вка.

v.t. (*grapple with*) бра́ться, взя́ться за+*a.*; **I don't know how to ~ this problem** я не зна́ю, как взя́ться за реше́ние э́той пробле́мы; **I went and ~d him on the subject** я пошёл к нему́ и возбуди́л э́тот вопро́с; (*football*) блоки́ровать.

cpd. **~-block** *n.* полиспа́ст, таль.

tackling ['tæklɪŋ] *n.* (*gear*) обору́дование, снаряже́ние.

tacky ['tækɪ] *adj.* (*sticky*) ли́пкий, кле́йкий.

tact [tækt] *n.* такт, такти́чность.

tactful ['tæktfʊl] *adj.* такти́чный.

tactfulness ['tæktfʊlnɪs] *n.* такти́чность.

tactic ['tæktɪk] = **tactic(s)**

tactical ['tæktɪk(ə)l] *adj.* такти́ческий.

tactician [tæk'tɪʃ(ə)n] *n.* та́ктик.

tactic(s) ['tæktɪks] *n.* та́ктика.

tactile ['tæktaɪl] *adj.* осяза́тельный, такти́льный.

tactless ['tæktlɪs] *adj.* беста́ктный.

tactlessness ['tæktlɪsnɪs] *n.* беста́ктность.

tadpole ['tædpəʊl] *n.* голова́стик.

Tadzhikistan [,tædʒɪkɪ'stɑ:n] *n.* Таджикиста́н.

taffeta ['tæfɪtə] *n.* тафта́; (*attr.*) тафтяно́й.

taffrail ['tæfreɪl] *n.* гакабо́рт.

tag [tæg] *n.* **1.** (*metal tip to shoe-lace*) металли́ческий наконе́чник. **2.** (*loop of boot etc.*) пе́тля; ушко́. **3.** (*label*) ярлы́к; **price** ~ ярлы́к с обозна́ченной цено́й, це́нник; (*fig.*) цена́. **4.** (*loose or ragged end*): **at the ~ end of the procession** в хвосте́ проце́ссии. **5.** (*stock phrase*) изби́тая фра́за/ цита́та. **6.** (*child's game*) (игра́ в) са́л|ки (*pl. g.* -ок).

v.t. **1.** (*fasten ~ to*) наве́|шивать, -сить ярлы́к на+*a.* **2.** (*attach*) соедин|я́ть, -и́ть.

v.i. (*follow*): **the children ~ged along behind** де́ти тащи́лись сза́ди; **he ~ged on to the group** он примкну́л к гру́ппе.

Tagus ['teɪgəs] *n.* Та́хо (*indecl.*), Те́жу (*indecl.*) (*both f.*).

Tahiti [tə'hi:tɪ] *n.* Таи́ти (*m. indecl.*).

Tahitian [tə'hi:ʃ(ə)n] *n.* таитя́н|ин (*fem.* -ка).

adj. таитя́нский.

taiga ['taɪgə] *n.* тайга́.

tail [teɪl] *n.* **1.** (*of animal*) хвост; (*dim.*) хво́стик; **the dog wagged its** ~ соба́ка виля́ла хвосто́м; **with his ~ between his legs** поджа́в хвост; (*fig.*) с ви́дом поби́той соба́ки; **with his ~ in the air** (*fig.*) окрылённый; **they turned** ~

and ran они́ поверну́ли и бро́сились наутёк. **2.** (*fig.*): **the ~ of a kite** хвост возду́шного зме́я; **at the ~ end** в са́мом конце́; **he saw the rabbit out of the ~ of his eye** он уви́дел кро́лика кра́ешком/уголко́м глаза́; **I can't make head or ~ of it** я ника́к тут не разберу́сь. **3.** (*of a coin*) ре́шка. **4.**: **~s** (*coat*) фрак.

v.t. **1.** (*follow closely*) висе́ть (*impf.*) на хвосте́ у+*g.* **2.** (*remove ~ of*): **she ~ed the gooseberries** она́ отре́зала хво́стики у крыжо́вника; **the sheep had been ~ed** о́вцам отре́зали хво́стики.

v.i. **1.** (*follow*) тащи́ться (*impf.*) за+*i.*; плести́сь (*impf.*) за+*i.*; **he ~ed after her** он ходи́л за ней по пята́м. **2.** (*dwindle*) уб|ыва́ть, -ы́ть; **the attendance figures ~ed off** посеща́емость упа́ла; **his voice ~ed away into silence** его́ го́лос (постепе́нно) зати́х; **the work ~ed off** рабо́та постепе́нно пошла́ на нет.

cpds. **~board** *n.* откидна́я доска́; откидно́й борт; **~-coat** *n.* фрак; **~-end** *n.* коне́ц, хвост; заключи́тельная часть; **~-fin** *n.* хвостово́й плавни́к; **~-gate** *n.* за́дняя две́рца, пика́п; **~-lamp, ~-light** *nn.* за́дний фона́рь; стоп-сигна́л; **~piece** *n.* (*at end of chapter*) винье́тка; (*conclusion*) концо́вка; **~plane** *n.* (*aeron.*) хвостово́й стабилиза́тор; **~-spin** *n.* (*aeron.*) норма́льный што́пор; (*fig.*) па́ника; **~-wheel** *n.* (*aeron.*) хвостово́е колесо́.

tailor ['teɪlə(r)] *n.* портно́й.

v.t.: **a well-~ed coat** хорошо́ сши́тое пальто́; (*fig.*) приспос|а́бливать, -о́бить; **his speech was ~ed to the situation** его́ речь была́ соста́влена с учётом ситуа́ции.

v.i. портня́жничать (*impf.*).

cpd. **~-made** *adj.* сде́ланный по зака́зу.

taint [teɪnt] *n.* пятно́, изъя́н, червото́чина; (*trace*) налёт, при́месь; (*infection*) зара́за.

v.t. по́ртить, ис-; **~ed meat** несве́жее мя́со; **~ed money** нечи́стые де́ньги; **~ed reputation** подмо́ченная репута́ция.

Taipei ['taɪ'peɪ] *n.* Тайбе́й.

Taiwan ['taɪ'wɑːn] *n.* Тайва́нь (*m.*).

take [teɪk] *n.* **1.** (*amount caught*) уло́в. **2.** (*money taken, e.g. at box office*) сбор, вы́ручка. **3.** (*cin.*) монта́жный кадр; (*repetition*) дубль (*m.*).

v.t. **1.** (*pick up, lay hold of, grasp*) брать, взять; **he took his pen and began to write** он взял ру́чку и на́чал писа́ть; **~ my arm!** возьми́те меня́ по́д руку!; **he took her in his arms** он её обня́л; **he took her by the hand** он взял её за́ руку; **he took me by the throat** он взял/схвати́л меня́ за го́рло; (*remove*): **the doctor took him off penicillin** врач снял его́ с пеницилли́на; **she took a coin out of her purse** она́ вы́нула моне́ту из кошелька́; **~ your hands out of your pockets!** вы́ньте ру́ки из карма́нов!; **~ 5 from 10** отними́те 5 от 10; **it took the courage out of him** э́то лиши́ло его́ му́жества; **the last mile took it out of me** на после́дней ми́ле я вы́дохся. **2.** (*catch*) лови́ть, пойма́ть; **the hare was ~n in a trap** за́яц попа́л в капка́н; (*shoot*): **they took a score of pheasants** они́ настреля́ли деся́тка два фаза́нов; (*come upon*): **I was ~n by surprise** я был засти́гнут врасплох. **3.** (*capture*): **the city was ~n by storm** го́род взя́ли шту́рмом; **they took several prisoners** они́ взя́ли не́сколько пле́нных; **he was ~n captive** он попа́л в плен; **I ~ your queen** (*chess*) я беру́ ва́шу короле́ву; (*assume*) прин|има́ть, -я́ть на себя́; **you must ~ the initiative** вы должны́ взять на себя́ инициати́ву; **he took the lead** (*in an enterprise*) он взял на себя́ руково́дство; **the Italians took the lead** (*racing*) италья́нцы вы́рвались вперёд; **he took it upon himself to refuse** он взял на себя́ сме́лость отказа́ть; **he took control** он взял управле́ние в свои́ ру́ки; (*win, gain*) выи́грывать, вы́играть; **we took 9 tricks** (*cards*) мы взя́ли 9 взя́ток; **she took first prize** она́ получи́ла пе́рвый приз; (*captivate*) нра́виться, по- +*d.*; **that ~s my fancy** мне э́то нра́вится/улыба́ется; **I was ~n by the house** дом меня́ очарова́л. **4.** (*acquire; obtain possession of*): **he decided to ~ a wife** он реши́л жени́ться; **he took a partner** он взял компаньо́на; (*for money*): **I have ~n a flat in town** я снял кварти́ру в го́роде; **these seats are ~n** э́ти места́ за́няты; (*in payment*): **they took £50 in one evening** они́ вы́ручили 50 фу́нтов за оди́н ве́чер; (*by enquiry or examination*): определ|я́ть, -и́ть; **the tailor took his measurements** портно́й снял с него́ ме́рку; **the doctor took my temperature** до́ктор изме́рил мне температу́ру; **the police took his name and address** поли́ция записа́ла его́ фами́лию и а́дрес; (*unlawfully or without consent*): **the thieves took all her jewellery** во́ры забра́ли все её драгоце́нности; **they were caught taking apples** их пойма́ли, когда́ они́ ворова́ли я́блоки. **5.** (*avail o.s. of*) воспо́льзоваться (*pf.*) +*i.*; **please ~ a seat** пожа́луйста, сади́тесь; **I'm taking a day's leave** я беру́ выходно́й день; **I ~ leave to differ** я позво́лю себе́ не согласи́ться; **~ your time!** спеши́ть не́куда; не торопи́тесь!; (*board, travel by*): **let's ~ a taxi** дава́йте возьмём такси́; **he took a bus to the station** он пое́хал авто́бусом до ста́нции. **6.** (*occupy*) зан|има́ть, -я́ть; **will you ~ the chair?** (*at meeting*) вы не хоти́те быть председа́телем?; **I am taking his place** я его́ замеща́ю; **that ~s first place** э́то (должно́ быть) на пе́рвом ме́сте. **7.** (*adopt, choose*): **I don't wish to ~ sides** я не жела́ю станови́ться ни на чью сто́рону; **I don't ~ the same view** у меня́ друга́я то́чка зре́ния; **~ me, for instance!** возьми́те меня́, наприме́р! **8.** (*accept*) прин|има́ть, -я́ть; **will you ~ a cheque?** я могу́ расплати́ться че́ком?; **will you ~ £50 for it?** вы отдади́те э́то за 50 фу́нтов?; **he never ~s bets** он никогда́ не идёт на пари́; **~ my advice!** послу́шайте меня́!; **he will ~ orders from no-one** ему́ никто́ не ука́з; **I ~ responsibility** я беру́ на себя́ отве́тственность; **he took his defeat well** он сто́йко перенёс пораже́ние; **he took the blame for everything** он взял на себя́ вину́ за всё; **you must ~ us as you find us** принима́йте нас таки́ми, каки́е мы есть; ≃ чем бога́ты, тем и ра́ды; **he ~s everything for granted** он воспринима́ет всё как само́ собо́й разуме́ющееся; **can't you ~ a joke?** что вы, шу́ток не понима́ете?; **I'll ~ no nonsense from you** я не потерплю́ от вас никаки́х глу́постей; **he would not ~ no for an answer** он не при́нял отка́за; он не сдава́лся; **I wouldn't ~ it as a gift** мне э́того и да́ром не на́до; **~ it from me!** (*believe me!*) пове́рьте мне!; я́ вам говорю́; **~ it easy!** не волну́йтесь!; не стара́йтесь!; потихо́ньку!; осторо́жно!; **they took a beating** (*coll.*) они́ получи́ли взбу́чку; (*bear*) выде́рживать, вы́держать; **he took his punishment like a man** он перенёс наказа́ние, как подоба́ет мужчи́не; **'Britain can ~ it!'** «Брита́ния с э́тим спра́вится!»; **I won't ~ this lying down** я не сда́мся без бо́я; (*respond to*): **she took three curtain calls** она́ три ра́за выходи́ла на аплодисме́нты; (*receive*) брать (*impf.*); **she ~s lessons in Spanish** она́ берёт уро́ки испа́нского языка́; **we ~ the Times** мы выпи́сываем «Таймс»; **she ~s paying guests** она́ де́ржит постоя́льцев; **I took him into my confidence** я ему́ дове́рился; **I shall have to ~ you in hand** мне придётся прибра́ть вас к рука́м; (*derive*): **the street ~s its name from a general** у́лица на́звана по и́мени одного́ генера́ла; (*qualify for*): **he took his degree** он получи́л дипло́м/сте́пень; (*submit to*): **when do you ~ your exams?** когда́ вы сдаёте экза́мены?; **you are taking a risk** вы риску́ете; **you must ~ your chance** вам на́до рискну́ть. **9.** (*use regularly; esp. food or drink*) прин|има́ть, -я́ть; **he has begun to ~ drugs** он на́чал принима́ть нарко́тики; **do you ~ sugar in your tea?** вы пьёте чай с са́харом?; (*of size in clothes*): **I ~ tens in shoes** у меня́ деся́тый разме́р боти́нок. **10.** (*apprehend*) пон|има́ть, -я́ть; **do you ~ my meaning?** вы понима́ете, что я хочу́ сказа́ть?; **what do you ~ that to mean?** как вы э́то понима́ете?; (*assume*) счита́ть (*impf.*); **I ~ him to be an honest man** я счита́ю его́ че́стным челове́ком; (*accept*): **I took him for a man of his word** он мне показа́лся челове́ком сло́ва; **what do you ~ me for?** за кого́ вы меня́ принима́ете?; (*mistake*): **I took her for her mother** я при́нял её за её мать. **11.** (*conceive, evince*) проявл|я́ть, -и́ть; **he has ~n a dislike to me** он меня́ невзлюби́л; **I began to ~ an interest** я на́чал проявля́ть интере́с. **12.** (*exert, exercise*): **~ care!** бу́дьте осторо́жны!; **he took no notice** он не обрати́л никако́го внима́ния. **13.** (*of single finite actions: give, have, make*): **~ a look at this!** взгляни́те-ка на э́то!; **I took a deep breath** я сде́лал глубо́кий вдох; **he took a shot at me** он вы́стрелил в меня́; **he took a bite out of the apple** он откусил яблоко; (*of longer, but finite, activity*: *have*): **I took a bath** я принял ванну; **let us ~ a walk!** давайте прогуляемся!; **he believes in taking exercise** он верит в пользу физических упражнений; (*partake of, consume*) есть, по-; **will you ~ tea with us?** вы выпьете с нами чаю?; **he took some refreshment** он немного подкрепился. **14.** (*make or obtain from original source*): **may we ~ notes?** можно нам делать заметки?; **I took an impression of the key** я сделал оттиск ключа; **may I ~ your photograph?** позвольте мне вас сфотографировать?; **~ a letter!** (*from dictation*) я вам продиктую письмо. **15.** (*convey*) отн|осить, -ести; брать (*impf.*); перед|авать, -ать; **he took the letter to the post** он отнёс письмо на почту; **~ my luggage upstairs please** отнесите мой багаж наверх, пожалуйста; **the train will ~ you there in an hour** поезд довезёт вас туда за час; **I'm taking the dog for a walk** я пойду выведу собаку; **he was ~n to hospital** его доставили в больницу; **she ~s the children to school** она отводит/отвозит детей в школу; **where will this road ~ us?** куда нас выведет эта дорога?; **he is taking the class through Hamlet** он сейчас проходит с учениками «Гамлета»; (*travel with*): **I shall ~ my warmest clothes** я возьму самые тёплые вещи. **16.** (*conduct, carry out*) вести (*det.*); **the class was ~n by the headmaster** директор вёл урок в этом классе; **the curate took the service** викарий отслужил молебен. **17.** (*contract, fall victim to*) подхват|ывать, -ить; **she ~s cold easily** она подвержена простуде. **18.** (*need, require*): **the job will ~ a long time** работа займёт много времени; **how long does it ~ to get there?** сколько (времени) туда добираться?; **it took us 3 hours to get there** мы добрались туда за три часа; **that ~s courage** это требует мужества; **it ~s some doing** это совсем не просто; **it took ten men to build the wall** потребовалось десять человек, чтобы построить эту стену; **he's got what it ~s** (*coll.*) у него есть для этого все задатки; (*gram., govern*) управлять (*impf.*) +*i.*; **this verb ~s the dative** этот глагол требует дательного падежа.

v.i. **1.** (~ *effect*; *succeed*): **the vaccination has not ~n** вакцина не привилась; **his new novel didn't ~** его новый роман не произвёл впечатления. **2.** (*photograph*): **he doesn't ~ well** он не фотогеничен. **3.** (*become*): **he took sick** он заболел/занемог. **4. ~ after** (*resemble*): **he ~s after his father** он похож на отца. **5. ~ from** (*detract from, decrease*): ум|еньшать, -еньшить; **this does not ~ from his credit** это не умаляет его заслуг. **6. ~ to** (*resort to*) приб|егать, -егнуть к+*d.*; **she took to her bed** она слегла; **the crew took to the boats** команда пересела в лодки; **he took to drink** он запил; **he has ~n to getting up early** он стал рано вставать; **he took to interrupting their work** он повадился отвлекать их от работы; (*feel (well-)disposed towards*) **~ to s.o.** почувствовать (*pf.*) к кому-н.; **I took to him from the start** он мне сразу понравился; **she does not ~ kindly to change** она плохо переносит перемену обстановки.

with advs.: **~ along** *v.t.* брать (*impf.*); прив|одить, -ести; (*by vehicle*) прив|озить, -езти; **I took my wife along to the meeting** я привёл жену на собрание; **~ apart** *v.t.* (*dismantle*) раз|бирать, -обрать; **~ aside** *v.t.* отв|одить, -ести в сторону; **~ away** *v.t.* (*remove*) уб|ирать, -рать; заб|ирать, -рать; **the police took his gun away** полиция отобрала у него пистолет; **he was ~n away to prison** его отвели в тюрьму; (*subtract*) вычитать, вычесть; отн|имать, -ять; (*~ home*): **hot meals to ~ away** горячая еда на вынос; **~ back** *v.t.* (*return*) возвра|щать, -тить; **I took the book back to the library** я вернул книгу в библиотеку; (*retrieve*) брать, взять обратно; **may I ~ back my pen** можно мне взять свою ручку назад?; (*retract*): **I ~ back everything I said** я беру назад всё, что сказал; **~ down** *v.t.* (*remove*) сн|имать, -ять; **she took down the curtains** она сняла занавески; (*lengthen*): **she took her dress down an inch** она отпустила платье на дюйм; (*dismantle*) сн|осить, -ести; **the shed was ~n down** сарай снесли; (*drop*) сн|имать, -ять; **~ down your trousers!** снимите брюки!; (*write down*) запис|ывать, -ать; **they took down my name and address** они записали мою фамилию и адрес; **she took down the speech in shorthand** она застенографировала речь; (*reduce in importance*): **that will ~ him down a peg** это его малость осадит; **~ in** *v.t.* (*lit.*) вн|осить, -ести; (*give shelter to*): **they took him in when he was starving** они приютили его, когда он голодал; (*let accommodation to*): **she ~s in lodgers** она берёт постояльцев/квартирантов; (*receive to work on at home*): **she ~s in washing** она берёт на дом стирку; (*make smaller*): **she took in her dress** она ушила платье; (*furl*) уб|ирать, -рать (*паруса*); (*include, encompass*) включ|ать, -ить; **this map ~s in the whole of London** это карта всего Лондона; **shall we ~ in a show this evening?** не пойти ли нам в театр сегодня вечером?; **this plan ~s in every contingency** этот план учитывает все возможности; (*comprehend, assimilate*) усв|аивать, -оить; **I could not ~ in all the details** я не мог удержать все подробности; (*deceive*) обман|ывать, -уть; **I was completely ~n in** меня здорово провели; **~ off** *v.t.* (*remove*) сн|имать, -ять; **he took off his hat** он снял шляпу; **shall I ~ off my clothes?** мне нужно раздеться?; **I took myself off to the races** я отправился на скачки; (*from menu*): **the steak has been ~n off** бифштекс вычеркнули из меню; (*deduct from price*): **I will ~ 10% off for cash** если вы платите наличными, я скину/сброшу 10%; (*lead away*) ув|одить, -ести; **he was ~n away screaming** когда его забирали, он кричал; **she was ~n off to hospital** её увезли в больницу; (*coll., impersonate, mimic*) имитировать (*impf.*); **he is good at taking off the Prime Minister** он хорошо копирует премьер-министра; *v.i.* (*become airborne*) взлет|ать, -еть; **the plane took off an hour late** самолёт взлетел с опозданием на час; **~ on** *v.t.* (*hire*) брать, взять; нан|имать, -ять; **more workers were ~n on** наняли/взяли новых рабочих; (*undertake*) брать, взять на себя; **he took on too much** он взял на себя слишком много; (*assume, acquire*) приобре|тать, -сти; **the word took on a new meaning** слово обрело новое значение; (*compete against*): **will you ~ me on at chess?** вы сыграете со мной в шахматы?; *v.i.* (*become agitated*) волноваться, раз-; **don't ~ on so!** (*coll.*) да не волнуйтесь вы так!; (*become popular*) прив|иваться, -иться; **the fashion is taking on** мода прививается; **~ out** *v.t.* (*extract*) вынимать, вынуть; **he took out his wallet** он вынул бумажник; **he had all his teeth ~n out** ему удалили все зубы; (*borrow from library*) брать, взять (в библиотеке); (*cause to go out for recreation etc.*) выводить, вывести; **she took the baby out for a walk** она пошла с ребёнком погулять; **he took his secretary out to dinner** он повёл свою секретаршу в ресторан; (*remove*) выводить, вывести; **how can I ~ out these stains?** чем можно вывести эти пятна?; (*coll., destroy*) уничт|ожать, -ожить; (*put into effect by writing*): **I must ~ out a new subscription** я должен возобновить подписку; **~ out a policy** брать, взять страховой полис; **~ out British nationality** получ|ать, -ить британское гражданство; (*obtain recompense for*): **I can't pay you, but you may ~ it out in vouchers** я не могу вам заплатить, но могу дать вам чеки; (*vent one's feelings*): **he took it out on his wife** он сорвал всё на своей жене; (*at cards*): **he took me out of that suit** он меня выбил из этой масти; **~ over** *v.t.* (*row across*): **the boatman took us over to the island** лодочник перевёз нас на остров; *v.t. & i.* (*assume control (of)*) прин|имать, -ять руководство (+*i.*); *v.i.* (*replace s.o.*): **let me ~ over!** я вас сменю!; **~ up** *v.t.* (*lift; lay hold of*) подн|имать, -ять; **he took up his bag and left** он взял свой чемодан и ушёл; **the rebels took up arms** повстанцы взялись за оружие; (*accept*) прин|имать, -ять; **will he ~ up the challenge?** он примет вызов?; (*carry upstairs*): **will you ~ up my bags, please?** пожалуйста, отнесите наверх мой вещи; (*remove from floor*): **the carpet has been ~n up** ковёр сняли/свернули; (*unearth*) выкапывать, выкопать; **the bulbs were ~n up after flowering** луковицы выкопали после того, как цветы отцвели; (*allow to enter vehicle*) подбирать, подобрать; **the bus stopped to ~ up passengers** автобус остановился, чтобы взять пассажи́ров; (*shorten*): **she had to ~ up her dress** ей пришло́сь укороти́ть пла́тье; **wind in the rope and ~ up the slack!** смота́йте верёвку и натяни́те её!; (*absorb*): **blotting-paper ~s up ink** промока́тельная бума́га впи́тывает черни́ла; (*occupy*): **this table ~s up too much room** э́тот стол занима́ет сли́шком мно́го ме́ста; **sport ~s up all my spare time** я спо́рту отдаю́ всё своё свобо́дное вре́мя; **I'm very ~n up at the moment** я сейча́с о́чень за́нят; **he is very ~n up with his new lady-friend** он сейча́с поглощён свое́й но́вой знако́мой; (*promote*): **his cause was ~n up by his MP** депута́т поддержа́л его́ де́ло; (*pursue*): **I shall ~ the matter up with the Minister** я обращу́сь с э́тим де́лом к мини́стру; (*accept challenge or offer*): **I'll ~ you up on that!** я ловлю́ вас на сло́ве; (*resume*): **he took up the subject where he left off** он продо́лжил разгово́р с того́ ме́ста, на кото́ром он останови́лся; (*interest o.s. in*) взя́ться (*impf.*) за+*a.*; **she has ~n up knitting** она́ заняла́сь вяза́нием; *v.i.* (*consort*): **he has ~n up with some dubious acquaintances** у него завели́сь подозри́тельные знако́мые.

cpds. **~-away** *adj.*: **a ~-away meal** еда́ на вы́нос; **~-home** *adj.*: **~-home pay** чи́стый за́работок; **~-off** *n.* (*impersonation*) подража́ние, паро́дия; (*of aircraft*; *also fig.*) взлёт; **~-over** *n.* (*comm.*) «поглоще́ние» (*како́й-н. компа́нии друго́й компа́нией*).

taker ['teɪkə(r)] *n.* беру́щий; **there were no ~s** никто́ не при́нял пари́; жела́ющих не́ было.

taking ['teɪkɪŋ] *n.* взя́тие; овладе́ние; **the money was there for the ~** де́ньги текли́ пря́мо в ру́ки; (*pl.*, *money taken*): **the ~s were lower than expected** сбор оказа́лся ме́ньше, чем рассчи́тывали.

adj. привлека́тельный; покоря́ющий; **she has ~ ways** она́ обая́тельна.

talc(um) ['tælkəm] *n.* слюда́; (**~ powder**) тальк.

tale [teɪl] *n.* **1.** (*story*) расска́з, по́весть; **fairy ~** ска́зка; **old wives' ~s** «ба́бушкины ска́зки»; **let me tell my own ~** дава́йте я сам расскажу́; **it tells its own ~** (*speaks for itself*) э́то говори́т сам за себя́. **2.** (*malicious or idle report*) спле́тни (*f. pl.*); вы́думки (*f. pl.*); **there is a ~ going about, that ...** погова́ривают, что…; **you've been telling ~s about me** вы на меня́ нагова́риваете; **tell ~s out of school** (*fig.*) я́бедничать (*impf.*).

cpds. **~-bearer, ~-teller** *nn.* я́беда (*c.g.*), я́бедни|к (*fem.* -ца); **~-bearing** *n.* спле́тничание.

talent ['tælənt] *n.* **1.** (*aptitude*, *ability*) тала́нт, дар; **a man of great ~s** исключи́тельно тала́нтливый челове́к; **he has a ~ for upsetting others** у него́ про́сто дар обижа́ть люде́й; (*persons of ability*) тала́нтливые лю́ди; **local ~** ме́стные тала́нты; **~ scout** открыва́тель (*m.*) тала́нтов. **2.** (*hist.*: *measure*, *sum*) тала́нт.

talented ['tæləntɪd] *adj.* тала́нтливый.

talisman ['tælɪzmən] *n.* талисма́н.

talk [tɔːk] *n.* **1.** (*speech*, *conversation*) разгово́р, бесе́да; **we had a long ~** мы до́лго бесе́довали/разгова́ривали; **I'd better have a ~ with him** мне бы на́до с ни́м поговори́ть; **he is all ~** он то́лько ме́лет языко́м; **~ programme, show** переда́ча в фо́рме бесе́ды; **small ~** све́тская болтовня́; **his actions caused much ~** его́ де́йствия вы́звали мно́го разгово́ров/то́лков; **they became the ~ of the town** они́ сде́лались при́тчей во язы́цех. **2.** (*address*, *lecture*) ле́кция; докла́д; **give a ~** прочита́ть (*pf.*) ле́кцию.

v.t. **1.** (*express*) говори́ть (*impf.*); **you are ~ing nonsense** вы говори́те чепуху́; **~ sense!** говори́те де́ло! **2.** (*discuss*) обсу|жда́ть, -ди́ть; разгова́ривать (*impf.*) о+*p.*; **they were ~ing politics** они́ говори́ли о поли́тике. **3.**: **~ French** говори́ть (*impf.*) по-францу́зски. **4.** (*bring or make by ~ing*): **he ~ed himself hoarse** он договори́лся до хрипоты́; **he can ~ the hind leg off a donkey** он мо́жет заговори́ть до́ смерти; **he ~ed me into it** он уговори́л меня́ сде́лать э́то; **he ~ed himself into the job** он заговори́л им зу́бы, и получи́л ме́сто; **I tried to ~ her out of it** я пыта́лся отговори́ть её от э́того; **I ~ed him round to my view** я склони́л его́ на свою́ сто́рону.

v.i. говори́ть (*impf.*); **baby is just learning to ~** ребёнок ещё то́лько у́чится говори́ть; **a ~ing parrot** говоря́щий попуга́й; **we got ~ing** мы разговори́лись; **we ~ed back and forth for hours** мы обсужда́ли э́то часа́ми; **~ about hard luck!** ну и не везёт же нам!; **he ~s about going abroad** он говори́т, что собира́ется за грани́цу; **you will get yourself ~ed about** о вас пойду́т то́лки; **people are beginning to ~** уже́ пошли́ разгово́ры/то́лки; **he ~ed at me for an hour** он це́лый час мне выгова́ривал; **~ into a microphone** говори́ть пе́ред микрофо́ном; **they were ~ing nineteen to the dozen** они́ без у́молку треща́ли; **~ing of students, how's your brother?** кста́ти о студе́нтах — как пожива́ет ваш брат?; **~ of the devil!** лёгок на поми́не!; **we ~ed round and round the subject** мы э́то подро́бно обсуди́ли; **~ing-point** до́вод, резо́н; **he is ~ing through his hat** он говори́т ерунду́; **I shall have to ~ to** (*reprimand*) **that boy** мне придётся отчита́ть э́того мальчи́шку; **he is always ~ing big** (*boasting/exaggerating*) он ве́чно хва́лится/преувели́чивает; **now you're ~ing!** (*coll.*) вот тепе́рь вы говори́те де́ло!; **he refused to ~** (*coll.*, *give information*) он не хоте́л ничего́ расска́зывать.

with advs.: **~ away** *v.t.*: **we ~ed the hours away** мы проговори́ли не́сколько часо́в; **I tried to ~ away his doubts** я пыта́лся рассе́ять его́ сомне́ния; *v.i.*: **while we were ~ing away, the bus left** пока́ мы болта́ли, авто́бус уе́хал; **~ back** *v.i.* огрыза́ться, дерзи́ть, возража́ть (*all impf.*); **I gave him no chance to ~ back** я не дал ему́ возмо́жности возрази́ть; **~ down** *v.t.* (*outshout*) перекри́|кивать, -ча́ть; (*aeron.*): **the pilot was ~ed down** пило́та напра́вили на переса́дку по ра́дио; *v.i.*: **children dislike being ~ed down to** де́ти не лю́бят, когда́ к ним подла́живаются; **~ out** *v.t.*: **the Opposition ~ed out the bill** оппози́ция затяну́ла пре́ния, так что не оста́лось вре́мени на голосова́ние по законопрое́кту; **~ over** *v.t.* (*discuss*) обсу|жда́ть, -ди́ть; (*persuade*) убе|жда́ть, -ди́ть.

talkative ['tɔːkətɪv] *adj.* разгово́рчивый, болтли́вый.

talker ['tɔːkə(r)] *n.* разгово́рчивый челове́к, болту́н; **he is a good ~** он хорошо́ говори́т; **he is a great ~** он лю́бит поговори́ть.

talkie ['tɔːkɪ] *n.* (*coll.*) звуково́й фильм.

talking ['tɔːkɪŋ] *adj.* говоря́щий; (*film*) звуково́й.

talking-to ['tɔːkɪŋ] *n.* вы́говор.

tall [tɔːl] *adj.* **1.** высо́кий, высо́кого ро́ста; **how ~ are you?** како́го вы ро́ста?; **six feet ~** ро́стом в шесть фу́тов. **2.** (*coll.*, *extravagant*, *unreasonable*) преувели́ченный, приукра́шенный; **a ~ story** небыли́ца, вы́думка; **that's a ~ order** э́то тру́дная зада́ча.

cpd. **~boy** *n.* высо́кий комо́д.

Tallin(n) ['tælɪn] *n.* Та́ллин; (*attr.*) та́ллинский.

tallness ['tɔːlnɪs] *n.* (высо́кий) рост, стан.

tallow ['tæləʊ] *n.* жир; са́ло.

tally ['tælɪ] *n.* **1.** (*notched stick*) па́лочка с надре́зами, обознача́ющими су́мму до́лга. **2.** (*account*, *score*) счёт; (*total*) ито́г.

v.i. соотве́тствовать (*impf.*); **their versions do not ~** их ве́рсии не совпада́ют.

cpd. **~-clerk** *n.* учётчик.

tally-ho [ˌtælɪ'həʊ] *int.* ату́!

Talmud ['tælmʊd, -məd] *n.* Талму́д.

Talmudic [ˌtæl'mʊdɪk] *adj.* талмуди́ческий.

talon ['tælən] *n.* ко́готь (*m.*).

tamarisk ['tæmərɪsk] *n.* тамари́ск.

tambour ['tæmbʊə(r)] *n.* (*embroidery frame*) кру́глые пя́льц|ы (*pl.*, *g.* -ев).

tambourine [ˌtæmbə'riːn] *n.* тамбури́н.

tame [teɪm] *adj.* (*not wild*; *domesticated*) ручно́й, дома́шний, приручённый; (*submissive*, *spiritless*) послу́шный, ручно́й; (*dull*, *boring*) пре́сный, ску́чный.

v.t. приру|ча́ть, -чи́ть; (*of savage animals*) укро|ща́ть, -ти́ть; **the settlers ~d the forest land** поселе́нцы осво́или леси́стую ме́стность; **his ardour was soon ~d** его́ пыл вско́ре остуди́ли.

tameable ['teɪməb(ə)l] *adj.* укроти́мый.

tamer ['teɪmə(r)] *n.* укроти́тель (*m.*).

Tamil ['tæmɪl] *n.* (*pers.*) тами́л (*fem.* -ка); (*language*) тами́льский язы́к.

adj. тами́льский.

tam o' shanter [ˌtæməˈʃæntə(r)], (*coll.*) **tammy** [ˈtæmɪ] *nn.* шотла́ндский бере́т.

tamp [tæmp] *v.t.* наб|ива́ть, -и́ть; за|кла́дывать, -ложи́ть; (*ram down*) трамбова́ть, у-.

tamper [ˈtæmpə(r)] *v.i.*: ~ **with** (*meddle in*) вме́ш|иваться, -а́ться в+*a.*; сова́ться (*impf.*) в+*a.*; **someone has been ~ing with the lock** кто-то ковыря́лся в замке́; **he ~ed with the document** он подде́лал докуме́нт; **the witness has been ~ed with** свиде́теля обрабо́тали.

tampon [ˈtæmpɒn] *n.* тампо́н.

tan [tæn] *n.* **1.** (*bark*) дуби́льное корьё. **2.** (*colour*) цвет бро́нзы; (*tint of skin*) зага́р; **he went to Spain to get a ~** он пое́хал загора́ть в Испа́нию.

v.t. **1.** (*convert to leather*) дуби́ть (*impf.*); **I'll ~ your hide** (*fig.*) я тебе́ зада́м. **2.** (*make brown*): **a ~ned face** загоре́лое лицо́.

v.i.: **she ~s easily** она́ бы́стро загора́ет.

tandem [ˈtændəm] *n.* **1.** (~ **carriage**) упря́жка цу́гом; (~ *bicycle*) па́рный велосипе́д. **2.**: **in ~** гусько́м, цу́гом.

tang [tæŋ] *n.* (*sharp taste or smell*) о́стрый/те́рпкий при́вкус/за́пах; **the ~ of sea air** за́пах мо́ря.

tangent [ˈtændʒ(ə)nt] *n.* (*geom.*) каса́тельная; (*fig.*): **he went off at a ~** он отклони́лся от те́мы; (*trig.*) та́нгенс.

tangential [tænˈdʒenʃ(ə)l] *adj.* тангенциа́льный; (*fig.*) отклоня́ющийся от те́мы.

tangerine [ˈtændʒəˌriːn] *n.* мандари́н.

tangible [ˈtændʒɪb(ə)l] *adj.* осяза́емый; (*fig.*) осяза́емый, ощути́мый; ~ **advantages** ощути́мые преиму́щества; ~ **assets** осяза́емые/реа́льные сре́дства.

Tangier [tænˈdʒɪə(r)] *n.* Танже́р.

tangle [ˈtæŋg(ə)l] *n.* сплете́ние; (*fig.*) пу́таница, неразбери́ха; **his affairs were in a ~** он запу́тался в свои́х дела́х.

v.t. спу́т|ывать, -ать; **the wool had got ~d up** ни́тки спу́тались; (*fig.*) усложн|я́ть, -и́ть; запу́т|ывать, -ать.

v.i. (*coll.*) свя́з|ываться, -а́ться; **you had better not ~ with him** вы с ним лу́чше не свя́зывайтесь.

tango [ˈtæŋgəʊ] *n.* та́нго (*indecl.*).

v.i. танцева́ть, с- та́нго.

tangy [ˈtæŋɪ] *adj.* о́стрый, те́рпкий.

tank [tæŋk] *n.* **1.** (*container*) бак, цисте́рна; **petrol ~** бензоба́к; **water ~** бак для воды́. **2.** (*armoured vehicle*) танк; **the T~ Corps** бронета́нковые войска́; ~ **trap** противота́нковая лову́шка; ~ **warfare** та́нковые сраже́ния; **he is in the T~s** он танки́ст.

v.i.: ~ **up** (*with petrol*) запр|авля́ться, -а́виться; **he is ~ed up** он подзаложи́л (*coll.*).

tankage [ˈtæŋkɪdʒ] *n.* (*capacity*) ёмкость ба́ка/цисте́рны; (*storage in tanks*) хране́ние в ба́ках/цисте́рнах.

tankard [ˈtæŋkəd] *n.* высо́кая пивна́я кру́жка.

tanker [ˈtæŋkə(r)] *n.* (*vessel*) та́нкер; (*vehicle*) автоцисте́рна.

tanner [ˈtænə(r)] *n.* (*of skins*) коже́вник, дуби́льщик.

tannery [ˈtænərɪ] *n.* коже́венный заво́д.

tannic [ˈtænɪk] *adj.* дуби́льный.

tannin [ˈtænɪn] *n.* тани́н.

tansy [ˈtænzɪ] *n.* пи́жма.

tantalize [ˈtæntəˌlaɪz] *v.t.* дразни́ть (*impf.*); терза́ть (*impf.*).

tantamount [ˈtæntəˌmaʊnt] *adj.* равноси́льный.

tantrum [ˈtæntrəm] *n.* вспы́шка раздраже́ния; **he is in one of his ~s** у него́ очередно́й при́ступ раздраже́ния; **the child is in a ~** ребёнок капри́зничает; **he flew into** (*or* **threw**) **a ~** он разора́лся/разбушева́лся.

Tanzania [ˌtænzəˈniːə] *n.* Танза́ния.

Tanzanian [ˌtænzəˈniːən] *adj.* танзани́йский.

Taoism [ˈtaʊɪz(ə)m, ˈtɑːəʊ-] *n.* даоси́зм.

tap[1] [tæp] *n.* кран; **don't leave the ~s running** закро́йте кра́ны; **there is plenty of wine on ~** разливно́го вина́ полно́; **he always has a few jokes on ~** у него́ всегда́ шу́тка наготове́.

v.t. **1.** (*pierce to extract liquid*): **the cask was ~ped** бочо́нок откры́ли; **they ~ped the trees for resin** они́ подсочи́ли дере́вья, что́бы собра́ть смолу́; (*fig.*); **the line is being ~ped** разгово́р подслу́шивают. **2.** (*fig., use*) испо́льзовать (*impf.*).

cpds. **~-room** *n.* пивна́я; **~-root** *n.* гла́вный/стержнево́й ко́рень.

tap[2] [tæp] *n.* **1.** (*light blow*) лёгкий уда́р; стук; **there came a ~ at the window** разда́лся стук в окно́. **2.** (*pl., US, lights-out signal*) отбо́й.

v.t. легко́ уд|аря́ть, -а́рить; сту́к|ать, -нуть; **he ~ped me on the shoulder** он тро́нул меня́ за плечо́.

v.i. стуча́ться, по-; **he ~ped on the door** он постуча́лся в дверь; **the branches ~ped against the window** ве́тки посту́кивали о стекло́; **his toes were ~ping to the rhythm** он отбива́л ритм нога́ми.

with adv.: ~ **out** *v.t.*: **he ~ped out his pipe** он вы́бил тру́бку; **he ~ped out a message** он вы́стукал сообще́ние.

cpds. **~-dance, ~-dancing** *nn.* чечётка; **~-dancer** *n.* танцо́р, отбива́ющий чечётку.

tape [teɪp] *n.* (*strip of fabric etc.*) тесьма́, ле́нта; (*in race*) фи́нишная ле́нточка; **breast the ~** каса́ться ле́нточки; **adhesive ~** ли́пкая ле́нта; (*magnetic ~*) магнитофо́нная ле́нта; плёнка; ~ **deck** (магнитофо́нная) де́ка; ~ **library** магнитоте́ка; **put sth. on ~** запи́с|ывать, -а́ть что-н. на плёнку; **he was playing over his old ~s** он прои́грывал ста́рые за́писи/плёнки.

v.t. **1.** (*bind with ~*) свя́з|ывать, -а́ть тесьмо́й; **have you ~d up the parcel?** вы завяза́ли посы́лку? **2.** (*coll., sum up, master*) оце́н|ивать, -и́ть; **I've got him ~d** я зна́ю ему́ це́ну. **3.** (*record*) запи́с|ывать, -а́ть на плёнку.

cpds. **~-measure** *n.* руле́тка, сантиме́тр; **~-recorder** *n.* магнитофо́н; **~-recording** *n.* магнитофо́нная за́пись; **~-streamer** *n.* (*comput.*) стри́мер; **~worm** *n.* ле́нточный червь.

taper [ˈteɪpə(r)] *n.* то́нкая свеча́.

v.t. & i. (*narrow off*) сужа́ть(ся), су́зить(ся).

tapestry [ˈtæpɪstrɪ] *n.* гобеле́н.

tapioca [ˌtæpɪˈəʊkə] *n.* тапио́ка.

tapir [ˈteɪpə(r), -pɪə(r)] *n.* тапи́р.

tapster [ˈtæpstə(r)] *n.* ба́рмен, каба́тчик.

tar[1] [tɑː(r)] *n.* (*substance*) дёготь (*m.*).

v.t. ма́зать, на- дёгтем; смоли́ть, вы́-/о-; **a ~red road** гудрони́рованная доро́га; **they are ~red with the same brush** (*fig.*) они́ одного́ по́ля я́годы; они́ одни́м ми́ром ма́заны.

cpd. **~-brush** *n.*: **there is a touch of the ~-brush in that family** в их роду́ есть при́месь негритя́нской кро́ви.

tar[2] [tɑː(r)] *n.* (*coll., sailor*) матро́с, моря́к.

taradiddle [ˈtærəˌdɪd(ə)l] *n.* (*coll.*) ложь, (*pl.*) вра́ки (*pl.*, *g.* —).

tarantella [ˌtærənˈtelə] *n.* таранте́лла.

tarantula [təˈræntjʊlə] *n.* тара́нтул.

tarboosh [tɑːˈbuːʃ] *n.* фе́ска.

tardiness [ˈtɑːdɪnɪs] *n.* медли́тельность; опозда́ние.

tardy [ˈtɑːdɪ] *adj.* (*slow-moving*) медли́тельный; (*late in coming, belated*) запозда́вший, запозда́лый; (*reluctant*) неохо́тный.

tare[1] [teə(r)] *n.* (*bot.*) ви́ка; (*pl., weeds*) сорня́к|и́ (*pl., g.* -о́в); (*bibl.*) пле́вел|ы (*pl., g.* —).

tare[2] [teə(r)] *n.* (*allowance for weight*) та́ра.

target [ˈtɑːgɪt] *n.* (*for shooting etc.*) мише́нь, цель; **his shots were off the ~** он стреля́л ми́мо це́ли; **bombing ~** объе́кт бомбардиро́вки; ~ **practice** уче́бная стрельба́; (*fig.*) **he became a ~ for abuse** он стал мише́нью для оскорбле́ний; (*objective*) цель; **we hope to reach the ~ of £1,000** мы наде́емся собра́ть наме́ченную су́мму в 1000 фу́нтов.

tariff [ˈtærɪf] *n.* **1.** (*duty*) тари́ф; ~ **reform** протекциони́стская рефо́рма; ~ **wall** тари́фный барье́р. **2.** (*list of charges*) тари́ф; (*for goods*) прейскура́нт.

tarmac [ˈtɑːmæk] *n.* гудрони́рованное шоссе́; (*aeron.*) преданга́рная бетони́рованная площа́дка.

v.t. гудрони́ровать (*impf., pf.*).

tarn [tɑːn] *n.* го́рное о́зеро.

tarnish [ˈtɑːnɪʃ] *n.* ту́склость, ту́склая пове́рхность.

v.t.: **~ed by damp** потускне́вший от вла́ги; (*fig.*) пятна́ть, за-; **he has a ~ed reputation** он запятна́л свою́ репута́цию.

v.i. тускне́ть, по-; окисл|я́ться, -и́ться.

tarpaulin [tɑːˈpɔːlɪn] *n.* (*material*) брезе́нт; (*hat*) непромока́емая матро́сская ша́пка.

tarragon ['tærəgən] *n.* полы́нь, эстраго́н.

tarry[1] ['tɑːrɪ] *adj.* (*of or like tar*) смоли́стый.

tarry[2] ['tærɪ] *v.i.* (*liter.*) (*remain, stay*) ост|ава́ться, -а́ться; пребыва́ть (*impf.*); (*delay*) заде́рж|иваться, -а́ться; ме́длить; (*impf.*).

tart[1] [tɑːt] *n.* **1.** (*flat pie*) откры́тый пиро́г с фру́ктами. **2.** (*sl., prostitute*) у́личная де́вка, шлю́ха.

v.t.: **~ up** (*coll., embellish*) прикра́|шивать, -сить; **she was all ~ed up** она́ была́ вся разоде́та/расфуфы́рена.

tart[2] [tɑːt] *adj.* (*of taste*) ки́слый; (*fig.*) ко́лкий, ехи́дный.

tartan ['tɑːt(ə)n] *n.* **1.** (*fabric*) шотла́ндка; **~ silk** шотла́ндский набивно́й шёлк. **2.** (*design*) клетча́тый рису́нок.

tartar[1] ['tɑːtə(r)] *n.* **1.** (*incrustation from wine*) ви́нный ка́мень; **cream of ~** ки́слый ви́нный ка́мень. **2.** (*on teeth*) (зубно́й) ка́мень.

Tartar[2] ['tɑːtə(r)] *n.* **1.** (*also* **Tatar**) тата́р|ин (*fem.* -ка). **2.** (*fig., troublesome or intractable pers.*): **you young ~!** ах ты, несно́сный ребёнок!; **he caught a ~** он встре́тил проти́вника не по си́лам; ≃ нашла́ коса́ на ка́мень; **our boss is a ~** у нас нача́льник — су́щий зверь.

tartish ['tɑːtɪʃ] *adj.* (*coll.*) (*meretricious*) вызыва́ющий; (*gaudy*) я́ркий, крича́щий.

tartlet ['tɑːtlɪt] *n.* тартале́тка.

tartness ['tɑːtnɪs] *n.* кислота́; ки́слый вкус; (*fig.*) ко́лкость, ехи́дство.

Tashkent [tæʃ'kent] *n.* Ташке́нт.

task [tɑːsk] *n.* зада́ча, зада́ние; **he was set a difficult ~** пе́ред ним поста́вили тру́дную зада́чу; **housework is an irksome ~** рабо́та по до́му — де́ло ску́чное; **take s.o. to ~ for carelessness** проб|ира́ть, -ра́ть кого́-н. за хала́тность; **~ force** (*mil.*) операти́вная гру́ппа.

cpd. **~master** *n.*: **he is a hard ~master** он из тебя́ все со́ки выжима́ет.

Tasmania [tæz'meɪnɪə] *n.* Тасма́ния.

Tasmanian [tæz'meɪnɪən] *n.* тасма́н|ец (*fem.* -ка).

adj. тасма́нский **~ devil** (*zool.*) су́мчатый дья́вол.

TASS [tæs] *n.* (*abbr. of* ***Telegraph Agency of the Soviet Union***) ТАСС, (Телегра́фное аге́нтство Сове́тского Сою́за).

tassel ['tæs(ə)l] *n.* ки́сточка.

taste [teɪst] *n.* (*sense; flavour*) вкус; **the fruit was sweet to the ~** плод был сла́док на вкус; **I have lost my ~ for whisky** я потеря́л вкус к ви́ски; **this fish has a queer ~** у э́той ры́бы стра́нный вкус; **it leaves a bad ~ in the mouth** (*fig.*) э́то оставля́ет неприя́тный оса́док; (*act of tasting; small portion for tasting*): **have a ~ of this!** попро́буйте/отве́дайте э́того!; **I gave him a ~ of his own medicine** (*fig.*) я оплати́л ему́ тем же (*or* той же моне́той); (*fig., liking*): **Wagner is not to everybody's ~** Ва́гнер нра́вится далеко́ не всем; **there is no accounting for ~s** о вку́сах не спо́рят; **she has expensive ~s in clothes** она́ лю́бит носи́ть дороги́е ве́щи; **add salt and pepper to ~** (*in recipe*) доба́вьте со́ли и пе́рца по вку́су; (*fig., discernment, judgement*) понима́ние; **he is a man of ~** он челове́к со вку́сом; **bad ~** дурно́й вкус; **a piece of bad ~** безвку́сица.

v.t. **1.** (*perceive flavour of*) различ|а́ть, -и́ть; **can you ~ the garlic in this dish?** вы чу́вствуете чесно́к в э́том блю́де? **2.** (*professionally*) дегусти́ровать (*impf., pf.*). **3.** (*eat small amount of*) есть, по-; **~ this and say if you like it** попро́буйте и скажи́те, нра́вится вам или нет; **they had not ~d food for 3 days** у них 3 дня не́ было ничего́ во рту. **4.** (*experience*) вку|ша́ть, -си́ть; изве́д|ывать, -ать; **they have ~d freedom** они́ вкуси́ли свобо́ду.

v.i.: **the meat ~s horrible** у мя́са проти́вный вкус; **~ of** име́ть (*impf.*) при́вкус +*g.*; отдава́ть (*impf.*) +*i.*; **the wine ~s of the cork** вино́ отдаёт про́бкой; **what does it ~ like?** како́го оно́ на вкус?

cpd. **~-bud** *n.* вкусова́я лу́ковица.

tasteful ['teɪstfʊl] *adj.* изя́щный; со вку́сом.

tastefulness ['teɪstfʊlnɪs] *n.* изя́щество; то́нкий вкус.

tasteless ['teɪstlɪs] *adj.* (*insipid*) безвку́сный, пре́сный; (*showing want of taste*) безвку́сный; (*in bad taste*) беста́ктный; в дурно́м то́не.

tastelessness ['teɪstlɪsnɪs] *n.* (*lit.*) пре́сность; (*fig.*) безвку́сица, безвку́сие; беста́ктность, дурно́й тон.

taster ['teɪstə(r)] *n.* (*sampler of wines etc.*) дегуста́тор.

tasty ['teɪstɪ] *adj.* вку́сный, пря́ный.

ta-ta [tæ'tɑː] *int.* пока́! (*coll.*).

Tatar ['tɑːtə(r)] = **Tartar**[2]

tatterdemalion [ˌtætədɪ'meɪlɪən] *n.* оборва́нец.

tattered ['tætəd] *adj.* по́рванный, разо́рванный; в кло́чьях.

tatters ['tætəz] *n.* кло́чь|я (*pl., g.* -ев), лохмо́ть|я (*pl., g.* -ев); **his shirt was in ~** от его́ руба́хи оста́лись кло́чья; **they tore him to ~** (*fig.*) они́ разнесли́ его́ в пух и прах.

tatting ['tætɪŋ] *n.* плетёное кру́жево.

tattle ['tæt(ə)l] *n.* спле́тня, болтовня́.

v.i. болта́ть (*impf.*); спле́тничать, по-; суда́чить, по-.

tattler ['tætlə(r)] *n.* болту́н, спле́тник.

tattoo[1] [tæ'tuː, tæ-] *n.* (*on skin*) татуиро́вка.

v.t. татуи́ровать, вы́-.

tattoo[2] [tə'tuː, tæ-] *n.* **1.** (*mil. signal*) сигна́л пове́стки пе́ред отбо́ем; (*fig.*) стук; **the rain beat a ~ on the roof** дождь бараба́нил по кры́ше. **2.** (*entertainment*) показа́тельные выступле́ния военнослу́жащих.

tatty ['tætɪ] *adj.* (*coll.*) потрёпанный, обша́рпанный.

taunt [tɔːnt] *n.* насме́шка, издёвка.

v.t. дразни́ть (*impf.*); **he was ~ed with cowardice** над ним насмеха́лись, называ́я его́ тру́сом.

Taurus ['tɔːrəs] *n.* (*astron.*) Теле́ц.

taut [tɔːt] *adj.* туго́й, ту́го натя́нутый; **he pulled the rope ~** он ту́го натяну́л верёвку; (*fig., of nerves etc.*) напряжённый, натя́нутый.

tautness ['tɔːtnɪs] *n.* натя́нутость; напряжённость.

tautological [ˌtɔːtə'lɒdʒɪk(ə)l] *adj.* тавтологи́ческий.

tautology [tɔː'tɒlədʒɪ] *n.* тавтоло́гия.

tavern ['tæv(ə)n] *n.* таве́рна.

tawdriness ['tɔːdrɪnɪs] *n.* крикли́вость, безвку́сица.

tawdry ['tɔːdrɪ] *adj.* крича́щий, безвку́сный, лубо́чный.

tawny ['tɔːnɪ] *adj.* кори́чнево-жёлтый; загоре́лый, сму́глый.

tax [tæks] *n.* **1.** (*levy*) нало́г; **a ~ is levied on profits** при́быль облага́ется нало́гом; **income ~** подохо́дный нало́г; **purchase ~** нало́г на поку́пки; **after ~** за вы́четом нало́га. **2.** (*fig., strain, demand*) испыта́ние; нагру́зка, бре́мя; **it was a great ~ on her strength** э́то подрыва́ло её си́лы.

v.t. **1.** обл|ага́ть, -ожи́ть нало́гом; (*fig.*): **he ~es my patience** он испы́тывает моё терпе́ние; **it ~es my memory** э́то тре́бует от меня́ напряже́ния па́мяти. **2.** (*charge*) обвин|я́ть, -и́ть (*кого в чём*); **he ~ed me with neglecting my work** он попрекну́л меня́ хала́тным отноше́нием к рабо́те.

cpds. **~-collector** *n.* сбо́рщик нало́гов; **~-deductible** *adj.* необлага́емый нало́гом; **~-free** *adj.* освобождённый от упла́ты нало́гов; **~man** *n.* (*coll.*) нало́говый инспе́ктор; **~payer** *n.* налогоплате́льщик.

taxable ['tæksəb(ə)l] *adj.* подлежа́щий обложе́нию нало́гов.

taxation [tæk'seɪʃ(ə)n] *n.* налогообложе́ние.

taxi ['tæksɪ] *n.* такси́ (*nt. indecl.*).

v.i. **1.** (*ride by ~*) е́хать (*det.*) на такси́. **2.** (*of aircraft*) рули́ть (*impf.*).

cpds. **~cab** *n.* такси́ (*nt. indecl.*); **~-driver** *n.* шофёр такси́; **~-meter** *n.* таксо́метр; **~-rank** *n.* стоя́нка такси́.

taxidermist ['tæksɪˌdɜːmɪst] *n.* таксидерми́ст.

taxidermy ['tæksɪˌdɜːmɪ] *n.* таксиде́рмия.

taxonomist [tæk'sɒnəmɪst] *n.* бота́ник/зоо́лог-система́тик.

taxonomy [tæk'sɒnəmɪ] *n.* система́тика, таксоно́мия.

TB (*abbr. of* **tuberculosis**) туберкулёз.

Tbilisi [təbɪ'liːsɪ] *n.* Тбили́си (*m. indecl.*).

tea [tiː] *n.* (*plant, beverage*) чай; (*meal*) чай, по́лдник; **make (the) ~** зава́р|ивать, -и́ть чай; **have, take ~** пить, вы́-; **I have lemon with my ~** я пью чай с лимо́ном; **a strong cup of ~** ча́шка кре́пкого ча́ю; **high ~** ра́нний у́жин с ча́ем; **that's not my cup of ~** (*coll.*) э́то не по мне; э́то не в моём вку́се.

cpds. **~-bag** *n.* мешо́чек с зава́ркой ча́я; **~-break** *n.* переры́в на чай; **~-caddy** *n.* ча́йница; **~-cake** *n.* ≃ бу́лочка; **~-chest** *n.* я́щик для ча́я; **~cloth** *n.* (*for table*) ска́терть; (*for washing-up*) ча́йное полоте́нце; **~-cosy** *n.* чехо́льчик (на ча́йник); (*in form of doll*) ба́ба; **~cup** *n.* ча́йная ча́шка; **storm in a ~cup** бу́ря в стака́не воды́; **~-garden** *n.* ча́йная на откры́том во́здухе; **~-house** *n.* ча́йная, чайхана́; **~-leaf** *n.* ча́йный лист, чаи́нка; **she read the ~-leaves for her friends** ≃ она́ гада́ла друзья́м на кофе́йной гу́ще; **~-maker** *n.* (*machine*) электросамова́р; **~-party** *n.* зва́ный чай; **~pot** *n.* ча́йник (для зава́рки); **~-room** *n.* кафе́-конди́терская; **~-rose** *n.* ча́йная ро́за; **~-service, ~-set** *nn.* ча́йный серви́з; **~shop** *n.* кафе́ (*indecl.*); **~spoon** *n.* ча́йная ло́жечка; **~spoonful** *n.* одна́/це́лая ча́йная ло́жечка; **~-strainer** *n.* ча́йное си́точко; **~-table** *n.* ча́йный сто́лик; **~-things** *n. pl.* ча́йный серви́з (*m. pl.*); **~time** *n.* ра́нний ве́чер; **~-towel** *n.* ча́йное полоте́нце; **~-tray** *n.* ча́йный подно́с; **~-trolley, ~-wagon** *nn.* сто́лик на колёсиках; **~-urn** *n.* кипяти́льник, тита́н; самова́р.

teach [ti:tʃ] *v.t.* **1.** (*instruct*) учи́ть, на-; обуч|а́ть, -и́ть; **she taught me Russian** она́ учи́ла меня́ ру́сскому языку́; **I taught myself English** я самостоя́тельно вы́учился англи́йскому языку́. **2.** (*v.t. & i., give instruction*) (*school etc.*) учи́ть (*impf.*); (*university etc.*) преподава́ть (*impf.*); **he ~es science for a living** он зараба́тывает на жизнь преподава́нием то́чных нау́к; **do you want to ~?** (*become a ~er*) вы хоти́те стать учи́телем/преподава́телем?; **~ing staff** преподава́тельский соста́в. **3.** (*ellipt.*): **that will ~ you!** э́то вас нау́чит уму́-ра́зуму!; **I'll ~ you (a lesson)!** я вас проучу́! **4.** (*enjoin*) научи́ть (*pf.*); внуш|а́ть, -и́ть; **Christ taught men to love one another** Христо́с учи́л люде́й люби́ть друг дру́га.

cpd. **~-in** *n.* семина́р, уче́бный сбор.

teachable ['ti:tʃəb(ə)l] *adj.* (*pers.*) поня́тливый, приле́жный; (*skill*) благоприобре́тенный.

teacher ['ti:tʃə(r)] *n.* учи́тель (*fem.* -ница); педаго́г; **~ training college** педагоги́ческий институ́т; (*school*) **~s** учителя́; **~s** *of doctrine etc.* учи́тели.

teaching ['ti:tʃɪŋ] *n.* **1.** (*precept*) уче́ние, доктри́на. **2.** (*activity*) преподава́ние, обуче́ние; **~ aid** уче́бное посо́бие. **3.** (*profession*) преподава́ние; **she intends to take up ~** она́ собира́ется преподава́ть. **4.** (*science*) педаго́гика.

teak [ti:k] *n.* (*wood*) тик; (*tree*) тик, ти́ковое де́рево.

teal [ti:l] *n.* чиро́к.

team [ti:m] *n.* (*of horses etc.*) упря́жка; (*games*) кома́нда; (*representative ~*) сбо́рная; **home ~** кома́нда хозя́ев по́ля; **visiting ~** кома́нда госте́й; **a ~ event** кома́ндное соревнова́ние; (*of workers etc.*) брига́да; **~ of scientists** гру́ппа учёных; (*of researchers etc.*) коллекти́в.

v.t.: **they were ~ed together** их запрягли́ в одну́ упря́жку; их включи́ли в одну́ брига́ду.

v.i.: **we ~ed up with our neighbours** мы объедини́лись с сосе́дями.

cpds. **~-spirit** *n.* коллективи́зм; чу́вство ло́ктя; срабо́танность; **~-work** *n.* коллекти́вная рабо́та; сы́гранность.

teamster ['ti:mstə(r)] *n.* (*US, lorry-driver*) води́тель (*m.*) грузовика́.

tear[1] [tɪə(r)] *n.* (**~-drop**) слеза́; **~s ran down her cheeks** слёзы текли́ по её щека́м; **I found her in ~s** я заста́л её в слеза́х; **she wept bitter ~s** она́ пла́кала го́рькими слеза́ми; **burst into ~s** распла́каться (*pf.*); **the audience was moved to ~s** пу́блика была́ тро́нута до слёз; **I laughed till the ~s came** я смея́лся до слёз.

cpds. **~-duct** *n.* слёзный прото́к; **~-gas** *n.* слезоточи́вый газ; **~jerker** *n.* (*sl.*) слезли́вый фильм (*u m.n.*).

tear[2] [teə(r)] *n.* (*rent*) разры́в, проре́ха.

v.t. **1.** (*rip, rend*) разрыва́ть, -орва́ть; рвать; **I tore my shirt on a nail** я порва́л руба́шку о гвоздь; **she tore a hole in her dress** она́ порвала́ пла́тье; **he tore the paper in two** он разорва́л бума́гу попола́м; **he tore open the envelope** он разорва́л/вскрыл конве́рт; **the book is badly torn** кни́га си́льно растрёпана; **he tore his finger on a nail** он пора́нил па́лец о гвоздь; (*fig.*): **my argument was torn to shreds** мой аргуме́нт разби́ли в пух и прах; **a country torn by strife** страна́, раздира́емая враждо́й; **she was torn by emotions** её раздира́ли (разли́чные) чу́вства; **I was torn, not knowing which to prefer** я разрыва́лся, не зная, что предпоче́сть; **that's torn it!** (*sl.*) из-за э́того всё срыва́ется. **2.** (*snatch; remove by force*) от|рыва́ть, -орва́ть; срыва́ть, сорва́ть; **the wind ~s branches from the trees** ве́тер срыва́ет ве́тви с дере́вьев; **she tore the baby from his arms** она́ вы́рвала ребёнка у него́ из рук. **3.** (*pull violently*) вырыва́ть, вы́рвать; **it makes one ~ one's hair** (*fig.*) от э́того хо́чется рвать на себе́ во́лосы.

v.i. **1.** (*pull violently*): **he tore at the wrapping-paper** он бро́сился срыва́ть обёрточную бума́гу. **2.** (*become torn*) рва́ться (*impf.*); **this material ~s easily** э́тот материа́л легко́ рвётся. **3.** (*rush*) мча́ться, по-; нести́сь, по-; **why are you in such a ~ing hurry?** куда́ вы так спеши́те?

with advs.: **we simply tore along** ну и мча́лись же мы!; **I could not ~ myself away** я не мог оторва́ться; **he tore the book away from me** он вы́рвал/вы́хватил у меня́ кни́гу; **the notice had been torn down** объявле́ние сорва́ли; **the old buildings are to be torn down** ста́рые зда́ния бу́дут сноси́ть; **he tore me off a strip** он дал мне прикури́ть (*coll.*); **he tore off on his bicycle** он помча́лся прочь на велосипе́де; **several pages had been torn out** не́сколько страни́ц бы́ло вы́рвано; **the children came ~ing out of school** де́ти стремгла́в вы́бежали из шко́лы; **the plants have been torn up** расте́ния вы́рвали с ко́рнем; **the street had been torn up to lay a new cable** у́лицу раскопа́ли для того́, что́бы уложи́ть но́вый ка́бель; **the letter was torn up** письмо́ порва́ли.

cpd. **~away** *n.* (*sl.*) сорвиголова́ (*c.g.*); у́харь (*m.*).

tearful ['tɪəfʊl] *adj.* по́лный слёз; пла́чущий, запла́канный.

tease [ti:z] *n.* (*pers.*) зади́ра (*c.g.*), насме́шни|к (*fem.* -ца).

v.t. **1.** (*comb out, fluff up*) чеса́ть, вы́-; ворсова́ть, на-. **2.** (*make fun of, irritate*) дразни́ть (*impf.*); издева́ться (*impf.*) над+*i.* **3.** (*pester*) пристава́ть (*impf.*) к+*d.*; доводи́ть (*impf.*).

tea|sel, -zel, -zle ['ti:z(ə)l] *n.* ворся́нка.

teaser ['ti:zə(r)] *n.* (*pers.*) = **tease**; (*coll., puzzle, problem*) головоло́мка.

teat [ti:t] *n.* сосо́к.

teaz|el, -le ['ti:z(ə)l] = **teasel**

tec [tek] (*coll.*) = **detective**

tec(h) [tek] (*coll.*) = **technical college**

technical ['teknɪk(ə)l] *adj.* техни́ческий; **~ college** техни́ческий вуз, те́хникум; **~ term** специа́льный те́рмин; **he is ~ly guilty of assault** форма́льно он вино́вен в нападе́нии.

technicality [,teknɪ'kælɪtɪ] *n.* (*detail*) техни́ческая дета́ль, форма́льность; (*term*) специа́льный те́рмин.

technician [tek'nɪʃ(ə)n] *n.* те́хник.

technique [tek'ni:k] *n.* (*skill*) те́хника, уче́ние; (*method*) техни́ческий приём, мето́дика.

technocracy [tek'nɒkrəsɪ] *n.* технокра́тия.

technocrat ['teknə,kræt] *n.* технокра́т.

technological [,teknə'lɒdʒɪk(ə)l] *adj.* технологи́ческий, техни́ческий.

technologist [tek'nɒlədʒɪst] *n.* техно́лог.

technology [tek'nɒlədʒɪ] *n.* те́хника, техноло́гия.

tectonic [tek'tɒnɪk] *adj.* тектони́ческий; архитекту́рный.

tectonics [tek'tɒnɪks] *n.* текто́ника; архитекту́ра.

ted [ted] *v.t.* вороши́ть (*impf.*) (*сено*).

teddy-bear ['tedɪ] *n.* плю́шевый медвежо́нок/ми́шка.

teddy-boy ['tedɪ] *n.* стиля́га (*m.*).

tedious ['ti:dɪəs] *adj.* утоми́тельный, ску́чный, ну́дный.

tedi|ousness ['ti:dɪəsnɪs], **-um** ['ti:dɪəm] *nn.* утоми́тельность, ску́ка.

tee [ti:] *n.* (*peg*) ко́лышек.

v.t.: **~ a ball** класть (*pf.*) мяч для пе́рвого уда́ра (*гольф*).

v.i.: **~ off** де́лать, с- пе́рвый уда́р.

tee-hee [ti:'hi:] *int.* хи-хи́!

teem [ti:m] *v.i.* **1.** (*reproduce in great numbers*) оби́льно размножа́ться (*impf.*); **fish ~ in these lakes** э́ти озёра изоби́луют ры́бой. **2.** (*be full, swarm*) кише́ть (*impf.*); изоби́ловать (*impf.*); **the house is ~ing with ants** дом киши́т муравья́ми; **his head ~s with new ideas** он по́лон но́вых иде́й; **it was ~ing with rain** (*coll.*) лило́ как из ведра́.

teen [ti:n] *n.*: **he is in his ~s** ему́ ещё нет двадцати́ лет; он подро́сток.

cpds. **~-age** *adj.* ю́ношеский, несовершеннолетний; **~ager** *n.* ю́ноша (*m.*)/де́вушка до двадцати́ лет.

teeny(-weeny) ['ti:nɪ] *adj.* (*coll.*) малю́сенький.

teeter ['ti:tə(r)] *v.i.* кача́ться (*impf.*); (*fig.*) колеба́ться (*impf.*).

teeth|e [ti:ð] *v.i.*: **baby is ~ing** у ребёнка ре́жутся зу́бы; **~ing troubles** (*fig.*) «де́тские боле́зни» (*f. pl.*); **~ing ring** зубно́е кольцо́.

teetotal [ti:'təʊt(ə)l] *adj.* непью́щий.

teetotalism [ti:'təʊtə,lɪz(ə)m] *n.* воздержа́ние от спиртны́х напи́тков.

teetotaller [ti:'təʊtələ(r)] *n.* тре́звенник.

teetotum [ti:'təʊtəm] *n.* верту́шка; волчо́к.

Teh(e)ran [teə'rɑ:n, -'ræn] *n.* Тегера́н.

Tel Aviv ['tel ə'vi:v] *n.* Тель-Ави́в.

telecamera ['telɪ,kæmrə, -mərə] *n.* телека́мера.

telecast ['telɪ,kɑ:st] *n.* телевизио́нная переда́ча, телепереда́ча.

v.t. перед|ава́ть, -а́ть по телеви́дению.

telecommunication [,telɪkə,mju:nɪ'keɪʃ(ə)n] *n.*: **~ satellite** спу́тник свя́зи; **~s** да́льняя связь; телегра́ф и телефо́н.

telegenic [,telɪ'dʒenɪk] *adj.* телегени́чный.

telegram ['telɪ,græm] *n.* телегра́мма.

telegraph ['telɪ,grɑ:f, -,græf] *n.* телегра́ф.

v.t. & i. телеграфи́ровать (*impf., pf.*; *pf. also* про-).

cpds. **~-key** *n.* телегра́фный ключ; **~-pole** *n.* телегра́фный столб; **~-wire** *n.* телегра́фный про́вод.

telegraph|er ['telɪ,grɑ:fə(r), tɪ'legrəfə(r)], **-ist** [tɪ'legrəfɪst] *nn.* телеграфи́ст (*fem.* -ка).

telegraphese [,telɪgrə'fi:z] *n.* телегра́фный стиль.

telegraphic [,telɪ'græfɪk] *adj.* телегра́фный.

telegraphist [tɪ'legrəfɪst] = **telegrapher**

telegraphy [tɪ'legrəfɪ] *n.* телеграфи́я; **wireless ~** беспро́волочный телегра́ф, радиотелегра́ф.

telekinesis [,telɪkaɪ'ni:sɪs, -kɪ'ni:sɪs] *n.* телепорта́ция.

telemark ['telɪ,mɑ:k] *n.* поворо́т (на лы́жах) с вы́падом.

telemeter ['telɪ,mi:tə(r), tɪ'lemɪtə(r)] *n.* телеме́тр.

v.t. телеметри́ровать (*impf., pf.*).

telemetry [tɪ'lemətrɪ] *n.* телеметри́я.

teleological [,telɪə'lɒdʒɪk(ə)l, ,ti:-] *adj.* телеологи́ческий.

teleology [,telɪ'ɒlədʒɪ, ,ti:-] *n.* телеоло́гия.

telepathic [,telɪ'pæθɪk] *adj.* телепати́ческий.

telepathy [tɪ'lepəθɪ] *n.* телепа́тия.

telephone ['telɪ,fəʊn] *n.* телефо́н; **are you on the ~?** у вас есть телефо́н?; **he is (talking) on the ~** он разгова́ривает по телефо́ну; **someone wants you on the ~** вас про́сят к телефо́ну; **he picked up the ~** он по́днял тру́бку; **~ call** телефо́нный звоно́к; **~ exchange** телефо́нная ста́нция; **~ number** телефо́нный но́мер, (*coll.*) телефо́н; **~ operator** телефони́ст (*fem.* -ка); **~ set** телефо́нный аппара́т; **public ~** телефо́н-автома́т.

v.t. & i. звони́ть, по- (*кому*) по телефону; телефони́ровать (*impf., pf.*) (*что кому*) (*pf. also* про-).

telephonic [,telɪ'fɒnɪk] *adj.* телефо́нный.

telephonist [tɪ'lefənɪst] *n.* телефони́ст (*fem.* -ка).

telephony [tɪ'lefənɪ] *n.* телефони́я.

telephoto(graphic) [,telɪ,fəʊtə'græfɪk] *adj.* телефотографи́ческий.

teleprinter ['telɪ,prɪntə(r)] *n.* телета́йп.

teleprompter ['telɪ,prɒmptə(r)] *n.* текстова́я приста́вка к телека́мере, «телесуфлёр».

telerecord ['telɪrɪ,kɔ:d] *v.t.* запи́с|ывать, -а́ть на видеоплёнку.

telescope ['telɪ,skəʊp] *n.* телеско́п.

v.t. & i. (*fig.*): **two coaches were ~d** два ваго́на вреза́лись друг в дру́га; **two words ~d into one** два сло́ва, сли́тые в одно́.

telescopic [,telɪ'skɒpɪk] *adj.* **1.** (*of or constituting a telescope*) телескопи́ческий; **~ lens** телескопи́ческий объекти́в; **~ sight** телескопи́ческий прице́л. **2.** (*visible only by telescope*) ви́димый посре́дством телеско́па. **3.** (*consisting of retracting and extending sections*) складно́й, выдвижно́й; **~ aerial** выдвижна́я анте́нна.

telescreen ['telɪskri:n] *n.* экра́н телеви́зора.

telethon ['telə,θɒn] *n.* (благотвори́тельный) телемарафо́н.

teletype ['telɪ,taɪp] *n.* телета́йп.

v.t. перед|ава́ть, -а́ть по телета́йпу.

televiewer ['telɪ,vju:ə(r)] *n.* телезри́тель (*m.*) (*fem.* -ница).

televise ['telɪ,vaɪz] *v.t.* пока́з|ывать, -а́ть по телеви́дению.

television ['telɪ,vɪʒ(ə)n, -'vɪʒ(ə)n] *n.* (*system, process*) телеви́дение; **colour ~** цветно́е телеви́дение; **black-and-white ~** телеви́дение чёрно-бе́лого изображе́ния; **what's on ~?** что пока́зывается по телеви́дению?; (**~ receiver, set**) телеви́зор; **~ programme** телевизио́нная переда́ча, телепереда́ча, телепрогра́мма; **~ studio** телесту́дия; **closed-circuit ~** ка́бельное телеви́дение.

telex ['teleks] *n.* те́лекс.

tell [tel] *v.t.* **1.** (*relate; inform of; make known*) расска́з|ывать, -а́ть; сообщ|а́ть, -и́ть; ука́з|ывать, -а́ть; **~ me all about it!** расскажи́те мне всё как есть/бы́ло; **the tale lost nothing in the ~ing** исто́рия ничего́ не потеря́ла в переска́зе; **I'll ~ you a secret** я расскажу́ вам секре́т; **don't ~ me he's gone** да неуже́ли он ушёл!; **I can't ~ you how glad I am** не могу́ вы́разить вам, как я дово́лен; **(I'll) ~ you what, let's both go!** зна́ете что, дава́йте пойдём вме́сте!; **you're ~ing me!** (*coll.*) кому́ вы расска́зываете?; без вас зна́ю!; **can you ~ me the time?** вы не зна́ете, кото́рый час?; **can you ~ me of a good dentist?** мо́жете ли вы указа́ть/назва́ть мне хоро́шего зубно́го врача́? **2.** (*speak, say*) говори́ть, сказа́ть; **are you ~ing the truth?** вы говори́те пра́вду? **3.** (*decide, determine, know*) определ|я́ть, -и́ть; узн|ава́ть, -а́ть; **how do you ~ which button to press?** отку́да изве́стно, каку́ю кно́пку на́до нажима́ть?; **there's no ~ing what may happen** кто знает, что мо́жет произойти́; **can she ~ the time yet?** она́ уже́ уме́ет определя́ть вре́мя? (*or* узнава́ть по часа́м, кото́рый час?); **you never can ~** никогда́ не зна́ешь. **4.** (*distinguish*) отлич|а́ть, -и́ть; различ|а́ть, -и́ть; **I can't ~ them apart** я не могу́ их различи́ть; **I can't ~ one wine from another** я не разбира́юсь в ви́нах; **how do you ~ the difference?** как вы их отлича́ете/различа́ете? **5.** (*assure*) зав|еря́ть, -е́рить; **I can ~ you** пове́рьте мне; пря́мо ска́жем. **6.** (*count*): **the old woman was ~ing her beads** стару́ха перебира́ла чётки; **there were seven all told** в о́бщей сло́жности их бы́ло семь/се́меро. **7.** (*direct, instruct*) прика́з|ывать, -а́ть; объясн|я́ть, -и́ть; **he was told to wait outside** ему́ веле́ли подожда́ть за две́рью; **~ him not to wait** скажи́те ему́, что́бы он не ждал. **8.** (*predict*) предска́з|ывать, -а́ть; **I told you so!** я вам говори́л!; **can you ~ my fortune?** мо́жете мне погада́ть?

v.i. **1.** (*give information*) расска́з|ывать, -а́ть; **he told of his adventures** он рассказа́л о свои́х приключе́ниях; **I have never heard ~ of that** я никогда́ об э́том не слы́шал; **don't ~ on me!** (*coll.*) не выдава́й меня́!; **he promised not to ~** (*divulge secret*) он обеща́л молча́ть; **time will ~** вре́мя пока́жет. **2.** (*have an effect*) ска́з|ываться, -а́ться; **every blow ~s** ка́ждый уда́р ощути́м; не оди́н уда́р не прохо́дит бессле́дно.

with adv.: **~ off** (*detail*) назн|ача́ть, -а́чить; **he was told off for special duty** ему́ поручи́ли осо́бое зада́ние; (*sl., reprove*) отчи́т|ывать, -а́ть; **he got a good ~ing-off** его́ здо́рово отчита́ли.

cpd. **~-tale** *n.* сплётник, я́беда (*c.g.*); (*attr.*) преда́тельский, многоговоря́щий; **~-tale wrinkles** преда́тельские морщи́ны; (*tech.*) сигна́льный, контро́льный.

teller ['telə(r)] *n.* (*narrator*) расска́зчик; (*counter of votes*) счётчик голосо́в; (*cashier*) касси́р.

telling ['telɪŋ] *adj.* эффекти́вный, си́льный; **a ~ argument** ве́ский/убеди́тельный до́вод; **a ~ example** нагля́дный приме́р; **a ~ blow** ощути́мый уда́р.

tellurium [te'ljʊərɪəm] *n.* теллу́р.

telly ['telɪ] *n.* (*television set*) те́лик (*coll.*).

telpher ['telfə(r)] *n.* те́льфер; **~ train** по́езд подвесно́й доро́ги.

temerity [tɪ'merɪtɪ] *n.* сме́лость, безрассу́дство.

temp [temp] *n.* (*coll.*) рабо́тающ|ий (*fem.* -ая) вре́менно.

v.i. рабо́тать (*impf.*) вре́менно.

temper ['tempə(r)] *n.* **1.** (*composition of substance*) соста́в; (*hardness of metal*) зака́лка. **2.** (*disposition of mind*) нрав; настрое́ние; **he has a quick ~** он вспы́льчив(ый); **he lost his ~** он потеря́л самооблада́ние; он разозли́лся; он вы́шел из себя́; **this put him in a bad ~** э́то его́ рассерди́ло; **don't lose your ~!** держи́те себя́ в рука́х!; не серди́тесь!; **I had difficulty keeping my ~** я с трудо́м сде́рживался. **3.** (*irritation, anger*) вспы́льчивость; несде́ржанность; **he flew into a ~** он вспыли́л; **he left in a ~** он разозли́лся и ушёл; он ушёл в сердца́х.

v.t. **1.** (*metall.*) зака́л|ивать, -и́ть. **2.** (*mitigate*) умеря́ть (*impf.*); смягч|а́ть, -и́ть; **we must ~ justice with mercy** справедли́вость должна́ сочета́ться с милосе́рдием. **3.** (*mus.*) темпери́ровать (*impf., pf.*).

tempera ['tempərə] *n.* те́мпера.

temperament ['temprəmənt] *n.* темпера́мент, нрав; (*mus.*) темпера́ция.

temperamental [,temprə'ment(ə)l] *adj.* **1.** (*of temperament*) органи́ческий, (*innate*) приро́дный. **2.** (*subject to moods*) неуравнове́шенный; с но́ровом; (*of a machine*) капри́зный.

temperance ['tempərəns] *n.* **1.** (*moderation*) воздержа́ние, уме́ренность. **2.** (*abstinence from alcohol*) тре́звость; воздержа́ние от спиртны́х напи́тков; **~ society** о́бщество тре́звости.

temperate ['tempərət] *adj.* возде́ржанный, уме́ренный; **the ~ zone** уме́ренный по́яс.

temperature ['temprɪtʃə(r)] *n.* температу́ра; (*fever*) жар; **he has (*or* is running) a ~** у него́ температу́ра/жар; **let me take your ~** дава́йте я вам изме́рю температу́ру.

tempest ['tempɪst] *n.* (*lit., fig.*) бу́ря; **~ in a teapot** бу́ря в стака́не воды́.

tempestuous [tem'pestjʊəs] *adj.* бу́рный, бу́йный.

tempestuousness [tem'pestjʊəsnɪs] *n.* бу́рность, бу́йство.

template ['templɪt, -pleɪt] *n.* шабло́н.

temple[1] ['temp(ə)l] *n.* (*relig.*) храм, святи́лище.

temple[2] ['temp(ə)l] *n.* (*anat.*) висо́к.

tempo ['tempəʊ] *n.* (*lit., fig.*) темп, ритм.

temporal ['tempər(ə)l] *adj.* (*of time*) временно́й; (*of this life; secular*) мирско́й, све́тский; (*anat.*) висо́чный.

temporary ['tempərərɪ] *n.* **(~ employee)** вре́менный слу́жащий.

adj. вре́менный.

tempori|ze, -se ['tempə,raɪz] *v.i.* тяну́ть (*impf.*) вре́мя; ме́длить (*impf.*).

tempt [tempt] *v.t.* соблазн|я́ть, -и́ть; иску|ша́ть, -си́ть; **he was ~ed into bad ways** он сби́лся (*or* его́ сби́ли) с пути́ и́стинного; **I was ~ed to agree with him** я был скло́нен с ним согласи́ться.

temptation [temp'teɪʃ(ə)n] *n.* собла́зн, искуше́ние; **she yielded to ~** она́ подда́ла́сь собла́зну; **the sight of food was a strong ~** еда́ вы́глядела о́чень зама́нчиво; **don't put ~ in his way!** не искуша́йте его́!

tempter ['temptə(r)] *n.* искуси́тель (*m.*); соблазни́тель (*m.*); **the T~** сатана́ (*m.*); дья́вол-искуси́тель.

temptress ['temptrɪs] *n.* искуси́тельница, соблазни́тельница.

ten [ten] *n.* де́сять; (**~** *people*) де́сятеро, де́сять челове́к; **he eats enough for ~** он ест за десятеры́х; **~ each** по десяти́; **in ~s, ~ at a time** по десяти́, деся́тками; (*figure; thg. numbered 10; group of* ~) деся́тка; **~ of spades** деся́тка пик; **the ~s** (*column*) деся́тки (*m. pl.*); **~s of thousands** деся́тки (*m. pl.*) ты́сяч; (*with var. nn. expr. or understood: cf. examples under* **five**): (~ *penny piece*) десятипе́нсовая моне́та; **~ to one** (*almost certainly*) почти́ наверняка́; **~ to ~** (*o'clock*) без десяти́ де́сять; **the upper ~** верху́шка о́бщества.

adj. де́сять +*g. pl.*; **~ eggs** (*as purchase*) деся́ток яи́ц; **~ threes are thirty** де́сятью три — три́дцать.

cpds. **~-copeck** *adj.*: **~-copeck piece** гри́венник; **~fold** *adj.* десятикра́тный; **~pins** *n. pl.* ке́гл|и (*pl., g.* -ей); **~-tonner** *n.* (*vehicle*) десятито́нка; **~-week, ~-year** (*etc.*) *adjs.* десятинеде́льный, десятиле́тний (*и т.п.*).

tenable ['tenəb(ə)l] *adj.* **1.** (*defensible*) обороноспосо́бный; (*fig.*) здра́вый, прие́млемый; **a ~ argument** разу́мный до́вод. **2.** (*to be held*): **the office is ~ for three years** срок полномо́чий — три го́да.

tenacious [tɪ'neɪʃəs] *adj.* це́пкий, насто́йчивый; **a ~ memory** це́пкая па́мять; **the dog held on ~ly** соба́ка кре́пко вцепи́лась; **~ of his rights** цепля́ющийся за свои́ права́.

tenacity [tɪ'næsɪtɪ] *n.* це́пкость, насто́йчивость.

tenancy ['tenənsɪ] *n.* **1.** (*renting*) наём помеще́ния; (*period*) срок на́йма/аре́нды; **during his ~** в пери́од его́ прожива́ния. **2.** (*ownership*) владе́ние.

tenant ['tenənt] *n.* (*one renting from landlord*) жиле́ц, квартира́нт; аренда́тор; (*leg., owner of real property*) (земле)владе́лец.

tenantry ['tenəntrɪ] *n.* аренда́торы (*m. pl.*); нанима́тели (*m. pl.*).

tench [tentʃ] *n.* линь (*m.*).

tend[1] [tend] *v.t.* (*look after*) присм|а́тривать, -отре́ть за+*i.*; уха́живать (*impf.*) за+*i.*; **the shepherds ~ed their flocks** пастухи́ пасли́ свои́ стада́; **she ~ed her invalid mother** она́ уха́живала за больно́й ма́терью; **the machine needs constant ~ing** маши́на тре́бует постоя́нного ухо́да.

tend[2] [tend] *v.i.* (*be inclined*) склоня́ться (*impf.*) (*к чему*); **I am ~ing towards your view** я склоня́юсь к ва́шей то́чке зре́ния; **he ~s to get excited** он легко́ возбужда́ется.

tendency ['tendənsɪ] *n.* тенде́нция; **an upward ~ in the market** тенде́нция к повыше́нию на ры́нке; **he has a ~ to forget** он забы́вчив(ый).

tendentious [ten'denʃəs] *adj.* тенденцио́зный.

tendentiousness [ten'denʃəsnɪs] *n.* тенденцио́зность.

tender[1] ['tendə(r)] *n.* (*ship*) посы́льное су́дно; (*wagon*) те́ндер.

tender[2] ['tendə(r)] *n.* **1.** (*offer*) предложе́ние; **~s are invited for the contract** принима́ются зая́вки на подря́д. **2.** (*currency*): **legal ~** зако́нное платёжное сре́дство.

v.t. предл|ага́ть, -ожи́ть; **he ~ed his resignation** он по́дал заявле́ние об отста́вке.

v.i.: **he ~ed for the contract** он предложи́л себя́ в подря́дчики.

tender[3] ['tendə(r)] *adj.* **1.** (*sensitive*) не́жный; **of ~ years** ю́ный, в не́жном во́зрасте; **he has a ~ conscience** он челове́к со́вестливый; **my finger is still ~** мой па́лец всё ещё боли́т; **it is a ~ subject with him** для него́ э́то больно́й/делика́тный вопро́с. **2.** (*loving, solicitous*) не́жный, ла́сковый, лю́бящий. **3.** (*not tough*): **a ~ steak** мя́гкий бифште́кс.

cpds. **~foot** *n.* (*coll.*) новичо́к; **~-hearted** *adj.* мягкосерде́чный; **~loin** *n.* вы́резка.

tenderness ['tendənɪs] *n.* не́жность; (*of meat etc.*) мя́гкость.

tendon ['tend(ə)n] *n.* сухожи́лие.

tendril ['tendrɪl] *n.* у́сик.

tenement ['tenɪmənt] *n.* (*cheap apartment*) (неблаго-устро́енное) жили́ще; **~ house** многокварти́рный дом (бара́чного ти́па).

Tenerife [,tenə'ri:f] *n.* Тенери́фе (*m. indecl.*).

tenet ['tenɪt, 'ti:net] *n.* до́гмат, при́нцип, доктри́на.

tenner ['tenə(r)] *n.* (*coll.*) деся́тка.

tennis ['tenɪs] *n.* те́ннис; **~ elbow** «те́ннисный» ло́коть (*травма*).

cpds. **~-court** *n.* те́ннисный корт; **~-player** *n.* теннисист (*fem.* -ка); **~-racket** *n.* те́ннисная раке́тка; **~-shoes** *n. pl.* паруси́новые ту́фли (*f. pl.*).

tenon ['tenən] *n.* шип.

cpds. **~-joint** *n.* соедине́ние на вставны́х шпи́льках; **~-saw** *n.* шипоре́зная пила́.

tenor[1] ['tenə(r)] *n.* (*course, direction*) направле́ние, напра́вленность; **the ~ of his ways** укла́д (*or* заведённый поря́док) его́ жи́зни; (*of speech etc.*); (*purport*) смысл, содержа́ние.

tenor[2] ['tenə(r)] *n.* (*mus.*) те́нор; **he sings ~** он поёт те́нором; **the melody is in the ~** мело́дию ведёт те́нор; (*attr.*) теноро́вый; **~ part** па́ртия те́нора; **~ saxophone** саксофо́н-те́нор; **~ voice** те́нор.

tense[1] [tens] *n.* (*gram.*) вре́мя (*nt.*).

tense[2] [tens] *adj.* натя́нутый, напряжённый; **~ nerves** натя́нутые не́рвы; **a moment of ~ excitement** моме́нт не́рвного возбужде́ния.

v.t. натя́|гивать, -ну́ть; напр|яга́ть, -я́чь; **he ~d his muscles** он напря́г му́скулы; **I was all ~d up** я был в напряжённом состоянии.

v.i. напр|ягáться, -ячься.

tenseness ['tensnɪs] *n.* (*lit.*, *fig.*) натянутость, напряжённость.

tensile ['tensaɪl] *adj.* растяжи́мый; ~ **strength** преде́л про́чности при растяже́нии.

tension ['tenʃ(ə)n] *n.* **1.** (*stretching*; *being stretched*) напряже́ние, растяже́ние; (*stretched state*) напряжённое состоя́ние; (*mental strain*, *excitement*) натя́нутость, напряжённость, **racial** ~ напряжённые ра́совые отноше́ния. **2.** (*voltage*): **high/low** ~ высо́кое/ни́зкое напряже́ние.

tent [tent] *n.* пала́тка; шатёр.

cpd. ~**-peg** *n.* ко́лышек для пала́тки.

tentacle ['tentək(ə)l] *n.* щу́пальце.

tentative ['tentətɪv] *adj.* про́бный, эксперимента́льный; предвари́тельный; ~**ly** ориентиро́вочно.

tenterhooks ['tentə,hʊks] *n.*: **I was on** ~ я сиде́л как на иго́лках.

tenth [tenθ] *n.* **1.** (*date*) деся́тое число́; **on the** ~ **of May** деся́того ма́я. **2.** (*fraction*) деся́тая часть; **one** ~ одна́ деся́тая.

adj. деся́тый.

cpd. ~**-rate** *adj.* ни́зшего со́рта.

tenuity [tɪ'nju:ɪtɪ] *n.* то́нкость.

tenuous ['tenjʊəs] *adj.* то́нкий; ~ **atmosphere** разряжённая атмосфе́ра; (*fig.*): **a** ~ **excuse** неубеди́тельная отгово́рка; **a** ~ **argument** сла́бый/неубеди́тельный аргуме́нт.

tenure ['tenjə(r)] *n.* (*of office*) пребыва́ние в до́лжности; срок полномо́чий; (*of property*) усло́вия (*nt. pl.*)/срок владе́ния иму́ществом.

tepee ['ti:pi:] *n.* вигва́м.

tepid ['tepɪd] *adj.* теплова́тый; (*fig.*) прохла́дный, равноду́шный.

tepid|ity [tɪ'pɪdɪtɪ], **-ness** ['tepɪdnɪs] *nn.* теплова́тость; (*fig.*) равноду́шие.

tepidly ['tepɪdlɪ] *adv.* с прохла́дцем/прохла́дцей.

teratogenic [,terətə'dʒenɪk] *adj.* тератоге́нный.

tercenten|ary [,tɜ:sen'ti:nərɪ, -'tenərɪ, tɜ:'sentɪnərɪ], **-nial** [,tɜ:sen'tenɪəl] *nn.* трёхсотле́тие.

adj. трёхсотле́тний.

tergiversation [,tɜ:dʒɪvɜ:'seɪʃ(ə)n] *n.* (*evasion*, *contradiction*) увиливание; мета́ние (из стороны́ в сто́рону).

term [tɜ:m] *n.* **1.** (*fixed or limited period*) пери́од; ~ **of office** должностно́й срок, срок полномо́чия, манда́т (полномо́чия); **a long** ~ **of imprisonment** дли́тельный срок заключе́ния; (*in school*, *university etc.*) триме́стр, уче́бная че́тверть; (*in law courts*) се́ссия. **2.** (*math.*, *logic*) элеме́нт, член. **3.** (*expression*) те́рмин; (*gram.*) вока́була; ~ **of abuse** бра́нное выраже́ние; **contradiction in** ~**s** противоречи́вое утвержде́ние/поня́тие; **he spoke of you in flattering** ~**s** он говори́л о вас в ле́стных выраже́ниях; **in** ~**s of** с то́чки зре́ния +*g.*; в смы́сле +*g.*; что каса́ется +*g.*; **in metric** ~**s** в метри́ческом выраже́нии; **he thinks of everything in** ~**s of money** он всё перево́дит на де́ньги. **4.** (*pl.*, *conditions*) усло́вия (*nt. pl.*); **will you accept my** ~**s?** вы принима́ете мои́ усло́вия?; ~**s of surrender** усло́вия капитуля́ции; **they came to** ~**s** они́ пришли́ к соглаше́нию; ~**s of reference** круг полномо́чий; (*charges*) усло́вия опла́ты; **what are your** ~**s?** каковы́ ва́ши усло́вия? **5.** (*pl.*, *relations*) отноше́ния (*nt. pl.*); **I kept on good** ~**s with him** я подде́рживал с ним хоро́шие отноше́ния; **we are on the best of** ~**s** мы в прекра́сных отноше́ниях; **they are not on speaking** ~**s** они́ не разгова́ривают друг с дру́гом; **they met on equal** ~**s** они́ встре́тились на ра́вных.

v.t. наз|ыва́ть, -ва́ть.

termagant ['tɜ:məgənt] *n.* меге́ра, фу́рия.

terminable ['tɜ:mɪnəb(ə)l] *adj.* могу́щий быть прекращённым; с ограни́ченным сро́ком.

terminal ['tɜ:mɪn(ə)l] *n.* **1.** (*of transport*) коне́чный пункт; (*rail*) вокза́л; **air** ~ (*in city*) (городско́й) аэровокза́л. **2.** (*elec.*) кле́мма, зажи́м.

adj. **1.** (*coming to or forming the end point*) коне́чный; после́дний; ~ **illness** смерте́льная боле́знь; ~ **patient** неизлечи́мый больно́й. **2.** (*occurring each term*) триместро́вый, семестро́вый, четвертно́й.

terminate ['tɜ:mɪ,neɪt] *v.t.* заверш|а́ть, -и́ть; класть, положи́ть коне́ц +*d.*; **they** ~**d his contract** они́ растóргли с ним контра́кт.

v.i. зак|а́нчиваться, -о́нчиться; заверш|а́ться, -и́ться; **words which** ~ **in a vowel** слова́, ока́нчивающиеся на гла́сную.

termination [,tɜ:mɪ'neɪʃ(ə)n] *n.* заверше́ние; прекраще́ние; коне́ц; (*of a word*) оконча́ние; ~ **of pregnancy** прекраще́ние бере́менности; або́рт.

terminological [,tɜ:mɪnə'lɒdʒɪk(ə)l] *adj.* терминологи́ческий.

terminology [,tɜ:mɪ'nɒlədʒɪ] *n.* терминоло́гия, номенклату́ра.

terminus ['tɜ:mɪnəs] *n.* коне́чный пункт; (*rail*) вокза́л.

termite ['tɜ:maɪt] *n.* терми́т.

tern [tɜ:n] *n.* кра́чка.

terpsichorean [,tɜ:psɪkə'ri:ən] *adj.*: **the** ~ **art** иску́сство та́нца.

terra [,terə] *n.*: ~ ***firma*** ['fɜ:mə] су́ша; ~ ***incognita*** [ɪŋ'kɒgnɪtə, ,ɪnkɒg'ni:tə] (*fig.*) неизве́данная о́бласть зна́ний (*u m.n.*).

terrace ['terəs, -rɪs] *n.* (*raised area*) терра́са, усту́п; (*row of houses*) ряд домо́в, постро́енных вплотну́ю.

v.t. террасúровать (*impf.*, *pf.*).

terracotta [,terə'kɒtə] *n.* террако́та; (*attr.*) террако́товый.

terrain [te'reɪn, tə-] *n.* ме́стность, релье́ф, райо́н.

terrapin ['terəpɪn] *n.* водяна́я черепа́ха.

terrestrial [tə'restrɪəl, tɪ-] *adj.* (*of the earth*) земно́й; (*living on dry land*) сухопу́тный; живу́щий на/в земле́.

terrible ['terɪb(ə)l] *adj.* (*inspiring fear*) стра́шный; **Ivan the T**~ Ива́н Гро́зный; (*coll.*, *very unpleasant or bad*) ужа́сный, жу́ткий, стра́шный; **I had a** ~ **time with him** я с ним хлебну́л го́ря.

terribly ['terɪblɪ] *adv.* (*coll.*, *extremely*) ужа́сно, стра́шно.

terrier ['terɪə(r)] *n.* терье́р; **bull** ~ бультерье́р; **fox** ~ фокстерье́р.

terrific [tə'rɪfɪk] *adj.* (*terrifying*) ужаса́ющий; (*coll.*, *huge*) колосса́льный; (*coll.*, *marvellous*) потряса́ющий.

terrify ['terɪ,faɪ] *v.t.* ужас|а́ть, -ну́ть; всел|я́ть, -и́ть страх/у́жас в+*a.*

terrine [tə'ri:n] *n.* паште́т, продава́емый в гли́няной посу́де.

territorial [,terɪ'tɔ:rɪəl] *n.* военнослу́жащий территориа́льной а́рмии.

adj. территориа́льный.

territory ['terɪtərɪ, -trɪ] *n.* террито́рия, райо́н; (*fig.*) о́бласть, сфе́ра.

terror ['terə(r)] *n.* (*fear*) у́жас, страх; **he went in** ~ **of his life** он жил под стра́хом сме́рти; **the thought struck** ~ **into me** э́та мысль привела́ меня́ в у́жас; (*pol.*, *hist.*) терро́р; (*coll.*, *pers.*) «гроза́», дья́вол, зара́за; (*child*) чертёнок.

cpds. ~**-stricken**, ~**-struck** *adjs.* объя́тый стра́хом/у́жасом.

terrorism ['terə,rɪz(ə)m] *n.* терро́р; террори́зм.

terrorist ['terərɪst] *n.* террори́ст (*fem.* -ка); (*attr.*) террористи́ческий.

terrorization [,terəraɪ'zeɪʃ(ə)n] *n.* терроризи́рование.

terrorize ['terə,raɪz] *v.t.* терроризи́ровать (*impf.*, *pf.*).

terse [tɜ:s] *adj.* кра́ткий, сжа́тый.

terseness ['tɜ:snɪs] *n.* кра́ткость, сжа́тость.

tertian ['tɜ:ʃ(ə)n] *n.* (~ **fever**) трёхдне́вная лихора́дка.

adj. трёхдне́вный; обостря́ющийся на тре́тий день.

tertiary ['tɜ:ʃərɪ] *n.* (*of monastic order*) принадлежа́щий к тре́тьему о́рдену мона́шеского бра́тства.

adj. (*geol. etc.*) трети́чный.

Terylene ['terɪ,li:n] *n.* (*propr.*) терилéн.

terza rima [,teətsə 'ri:mə] *n.* терци́на.

tessellated ['tesə,leɪtɪd] *adj.* моза́ичный; кле́тчатый.

tessera ['tesərə] *n.* (*in mosaic*) тессе́ра, моза́ика, ку́бик.

test [test] *n.* испыта́ние, про́ба, контро́ль (*m.*); ~ **case** показа́тельный слу́чай; **endurance** ~ испыта́ние выно́сливости; **his promises were put to the** ~ его́ обеща́ния подве́рглись прове́рке в де́ле; **these methods have stood the** ~ **of time** э́ти ме́тоды вы́держали прове́рку вре́менем; (*examination*) экза́мен; контро́льная рабо́та; (*oral*) опро́с; **he took a** ~ **in English** он сдава́л экза́мен/испыта́ние по англи́йскому языку́; (*chem.*) ана́лиз; о́пыт; иссле́дование; **(nuclear)** ~ **ban** запреще́ние испыта́ний я́дерного ору́жия; **a ~ for sugar** ана́лиз на содержа́ние са́хара; **blood ~** ана́лиз кро́ви; (*cricket*) = **~-match**

v.t. **1.** (*make trial of*) подв|ерга́ть, -е́ргнуть испыта́нию; пров|еря́ть, -е́рить; **his patience was severely ~ed** его́ терпе́ние подве́рглось суро́вому испыта́нию. **2.** (*subject to ~s*) пров|еря́ть, -е́рить; (*tech.*) опро́бовать (*pf.*); **the pupils were ~ed in arithmetic** ученика́м да́ли контро́льную рабо́ту по арифме́тике; **his job is to ~ (out) new designs** он ведёт испыта́ния но́вых констру́кций.

cpds. **~-bench** *n.* испыта́тельный стенд; **~-match** *n.* междунаро́дный кри́кетный матч; **~-pilot** *n.* лётчик-испыта́тель (*m.*); **~-tube** *n.* проби́рка; **~-tube baby** ребёнок «из проби́рки» (*зачатый вне материнского чрева*).

testament [ˈtestəmənt] *n.* (*will*) завеща́ние; (*bibl.*) заве́т; **the Old T~** Ве́тхий заве́т; **New T~** (*attr.*) новозаве́тный.

testamentary [ˌtestəˈmentərɪ] *adj.* завеща́тельный.

testator [teˈsteɪtə(r)] *n.* завеща́тель (*m.*).

testatrix [teˈsteɪtrɪks] *n.* завеща́тельница.

tester [ˈtestə(r)] *n.* (*pers.*) испыта́тель (*m.*); лабора́нт; (*device*) испыта́тельный прибо́р.

testicle [ˈtestɪk(ə)l] *n.* яи́чко.

testify [ˈtestɪˌfaɪ] *v.t. & i.* **1.** (*affirm*) свиде́тельствовать (*impf.*); да|ва́ть, -ть показа́ния; **will you ~ to my innocence?** вы подтверди́те мою́ невино́вность? **2.: ~ to** (*be evidence of*) свиде́тельствовать (*impf.*) о+*p.*

testimonial [ˌtestɪˈməʊnɪəl] *n.* (*certificate of conduct etc.*) рекоменда́ция, характери́стика; (*gift*) награ́да.

testimony [ˈtestɪmənɪ] *n.* показа́ния (*nt. pl.*); (*sign*) при́знак, свиде́тельство.

testiness [ˈtestɪnɪs] *n.* вспы́льчивость, раздражи́тельность.

testis [ˈtestɪs] = **testicle**

testy [ˈtestɪ] *adj.* вспы́льчивый, раздражи́тельный.

tetanus [ˈtetənəs] *n.* столбня́к, те́танус.

tetchiness [ˈtetʃɪnɪs] *n.* раздражи́тельность, оби́дчивость.

tetchy [ˈtetʃɪ] *adj.* раздражи́тельный, оби́дчивый.

tête-à-tête [ˌteɪtɑːˈteɪt] *n.* тет-а-те́т.

adv. тет-а-те́т; с глазу на глаз; вдвоём.

tether [ˈteðə(r)] *n.* при́вязь, пу́т|ы (*pl., g.* —); (*fig.*) грани́ца, преде́л; **he was at the end of his ~** он дошёл до ру́чки.

v.t. привя́з|ывать, -а́ть.

tetrahedron [ˌtetrəˈhiːdrən, -ˈhedrən] *n.* четырёхгра́нник, тетра́эдр.

tetrameter [tɪˈtræmɪtə(r)] *n.* тетра́метр.

Teuton [ˈtjuːt(ə)n] *n.* тевто́н, герма́нец.

Teutonic [tjuːˈtɒnɪk] *adj.* тевто́нский, герма́нский.

text [tekst] *n.* (*original words*) текст; (*quoted passage*) отры́вок; (*subject, theme*) те́ма.

cpd. **~-book** *n.* уче́бник, руково́дство; (*fig.*): **a ~-book example** хрестомати́йный приме́р.

textile [ˈtekstaɪl] *n.* ткань; (*pl.*) тексти́ль (*m.*).

adj. пряди́льный, тексти́льный; **~ workers** тексти́льщики.

textual [ˈtekstjʊəl] *adj.* текстово́й; **~ criticism** текстоло́гия.

textural [ˈtekstʃərəl] *adj.* структу́рный.

texture [ˈtekstʃə(r)] *n.* (*of fabric*) строе́ние (тка́ни), тексту́ра; (*fig., structure, arrangement*) склад, строе́ние; **the ~ of the skin** тип/ка́чество ко́жи; **the ~ of his writing** факту́ра его́ произведе́ний.

Thai [taɪ] *n.* таила́нд|ец (*fem.* -ка).

adj. та́йский.

cpd. **~land** *n.* Таила́нд

thalidomide [θəˈlɪdəˌmaɪd] *n.* (*pharm.*) талидоми́д; **~ babies** же́ртвы (*f. pl.*) талидоми́да.

Thames [temz] *n.* Те́мза; **he won't set the ~ on fire** он по́роха не вы́думает; он звёзд с не́ба не хвата́ет.

than [ðən, ðæn] *conj.* чем; **he is taller ~ I** он вы́ше меня́; **can't you walk faster ~ that?** вы не мо́жете идти́ быстре́е?; **it is later ~ you think** по́зже, чем вы ду́маете; **I would do anything rather ~ have him return** я гото́в на всё — лишь бы он не возвраща́лся; **the visitor was no other ~ his father** посети́телем был не кто ино́й, как его́ оте́ц; **I want nothing better ~ to relax** мне ничего́ так не хо́чется, как отдохну́ть.

thank [θæŋk] *v.t.* благодари́ть, от-; **~ you** спаси́бо; благодарю́ вас; **how can I ~ you?** как вы́разить вам свою́ благода́рность?; **I will ~ you to mind your own business** я проси́л бы вас не вме́шиваться не в своё де́ло; **he has only himself to ~** он сам во всём винова́т; **~ God you are safe** сла́ва Бо́гу, вы в безопа́сности.

cpds. **~-offering** *n.* благода́рственная же́ртва; **~-you** *n.*: **he left without as much as a ~-you** он ушёл, да́же не сказа́в спаси́бо; *adj.*: **~-you letter** благода́рственное письмо́.

thankful [ˈθæŋkfʊl] *adj.* благода́рный.

thankfulness [ˈθæŋkfʊlnɪs] *n.* благода́рность.

thankless [ˈθæŋklɪs] *adj.* (*ungrateful; unrewarding*) неблагода́рный.

thanks [θæŋks] *n. pl.* благода́рность; **let us give ~ to God** возблагодари́м Бо́га; **~ for everything** спаси́бо за всё; **many ~** большо́е спаси́бо!; **~ to** благодаря́+*d.*; **we won, no ~ to you** мы вы́играли, но отню́дь не благодаря́ вам; **you will get no ~ for it** вам никто́ за э́то спаси́бо не ска́жет; **vote of ~** вынесе́ние коллекти́вной благода́рности; **letter of ~** благода́рственное письмо́.

cpd. **~giving** *n.* (*expression of gratitude*) благодаре́ние; (*service*) благода́рственный моле́бен; **T~giving Day** день благодаре́ния.

that [ðæt] *pron.* **1.** (*demonstrative*) э́то; **~'s him!** вот (э́то) он!; **those are the boys I saw** э́то те ма́льчики, кото́рых я ви́дел; **those were the days!** вот э́то бы́ли времена́!; **what is ~?** что э́то тако́е?; **who is ~** кто э́то?; (*on the telephone*) кто говори́т?; **what's ~ for?** э́то к чему́ (*or* заче́м)?; **~'s a nice hat!** кака́я краси́вая шля́пка!; **look at ~!** вы то́лько посмотри́те!; **just think of ~!** вы то́лько поду́майте!; **~'s it!** (*sc. the point*) вот и́менно!; (*sc. right*) пра́вильно!; так!; **~'s just it, I can't swim** в то́м-то и де́ло, что я не уме́ю пла́вать; **it's not ~** не в э́том де́ло; **~ is how the war began** вот как начала́сь война́; **~'s right!** пра́вильно!; ве́рно!; (*iron.*) э́то уж то́чно!; **~'s all** вот и всё!; **what happened after ~?** что произошло́ пото́м?; **he's like ~, never satisfied** тако́й уж он челове́к — всегда́ недово́лен; **don't be like ~!** (*coll.*) ну, переста́ньте!; **how's ~ for a score?** ничего́ счёт, а?; **~'s ~, then: now we can go** ну, всё, тепе́рь мы мо́жем идти́; **... and ~'s ~!** ...и ла́дно!; **I'm going, and ~'s ~** я ухожу́, вот и всё; **with ~ he ended his speech** на э́том он ко́нчил свою́ речь; **~ is (to say)** то́ есть; **we talked of this and ~** мы говори́ли о том, о сём; **for all ~, he's a good husband** и при всём при э́том он хоро́ший муж; **the climate is like ~ of France** кли́мат тако́й же, как во Фра́нции; **'Did you beat him?' — 'T~ I did!'** «Вы у него́ вы́играли?» — «Ещё как!»; (*pl., as antecedent*): **there are those who say ...** есть таки́е, что говоря́т...; ко́е-кто говори́т; **at ~** (*moreover*) к тому́ же; вдоба́вок; **he's only a journalist, and a poor one at ~** он всего́ лишь журнали́ст, и при э́том нева́жный; (*either*): **he's not so tall at ~** он не тако́й уж высо́кий. **2.** (*rel.*) кото́рый; **the book ~ I am talking about** кни́га, о кото́рой я говорю́; **he was the best man ~ I ever knew** он был са́мым лу́чшим челове́ком, како́го я знал; **the year ~ my father died** год, в кото́ром сконча́лся мой оте́ц.

adj. э́тот, тот; **I'll take ~ one** я возьму́ вот э́тот; **from ~ day forward** начиная́/впредь с того́ дня; **at ~ time** в то вре́мя; **~ son of yours!** ох, уж э́тот ваш сын!

adv.: **~ much I know** э́то-то я зна́ю; э́то всё, что я зна́ю; **I can't walk ~ far** я не могу́ сто́лько ходи́ть; **I was ~ angry!** (*vulg.*) я так рассерди́лся; **it is not all ~ cold** не так уж хо́лодно.

conj. что; (*expr. wish*) что́бы; **would ~ it were not so!** каби́ э́то бы́ло не так!; (*expr. purpose*) (для того́) что́бы; (*var.*): **what have I done ~ you should scold me** что я сде́лал тако́го, что вы меня́ руга́ете?; **it's just ~ I have no time** де́ло в том, что у меня́ про́сто нет вре́мени; **it's not ~ I don't like him** не то, что́бы он мне не нра́вился; **now ~** раз уж; **now ~ I have more time** поско́льку у меня́ сейча́с бо́льше вре́мени; **it was there ~ I first saw her** там я и уви́дел её впервы́е; **he differs in ~ he likes reading** он отлича́ется тем, что он лю́бит чита́ть.

thatch [θætʃ] *n.* солóма, тростни́к; (*coll., hair*) копнá волóс.
v.t. крыть, по- солóмой; **a ~ed roof** солóменная/тростникóвая кры́ша.
thaw [θɔː] *n.* óттепель; **a ~ set in** начала́сь óттепель.
v.t. топи́ть, рас-.
v.i. тáять, рас-/от-; (*fig.*) смягч|áться, -и́ться; добрéть, по-.
the [ðɪ, ðə, ðiː] *def. art., usu. untranslated*; (*if more emphatic*) э́тот, тот (сáмый); **~ cheek of it!** какóе нахáльство!; **~ one with ~ blue handle** тот, что с голубóй ру́чкой; **something of ~ sort** чтó-то в э́том рóде; **he is ~ man for ~ job** он сáмый подходя́щий человéк для э́той рабóты; **I returned with ~ feeling that I had had a bad dream** я вернýлся с таки́м чу́вством, как бýдто я ви́дел плохóй сон; **not *the* Mr Smith?** неужéли тот сáмый ми́стер Смит?; **Turkey is *the* place this year** в э́том годý сáмое мóдное мéсто — Тýрция.
adv.: **~ more ~ better** чем бóльше, тем лýчше; **he was none ~ worse (for it)** он (при э́том) нискóлько не пострадáл; **that makes it all ~ worse** от э́того тóлько хýже; **so much ~ worse for him** тем хýже для негó.
theatre [ˈθɪətə(r)] *n.* **1.** (*playhouse*) теáтр; **~ ticket** билéт в теáтр. **2.** (*dramatic literature*) драматурги́я; теáтр; (*drama*) театрáльное искýсство; **the ~ of the absurd** теáтр абсýрда; **~ group** драмкружóк; **his novel would not make good ~** егó ромáн трýдно постáвить на сцéне. **3.** (*hall for lectures etc.*) зал; **operating ~** операциóнная; **~ sister** операциóнная сестрá. **4.** (*scene of operation*) пóле дéйствий; **~ of war** теáтр воéнных дéйствий.
cpds. **~-goer** *n.* театрáл; **~-going** *n.* посещéние теáтров; **~-land** *n.* райóн теáтров.
theatrical [θɪˈætrɪk(ə)l] *adj.* (*of the theatre*) театрáльный; (*showy, affected*) театрáльный, показнóй; (*of pers.*) манéрный.
theatricals [θɪˈætrɪk(ə)ls] *n.* спектáкль (*m.*); постанóвка; **amateur ~** люби́тельский спектáкль; театрáльная самодéятельность.
Theban [ˈθiːbən] *adj.* фиви́йский.
Thebes [θiːbz] *n.* Фи́в|ы (*pl., g.* —).
theft [θeft] *n.* крáжа.
their [ðeə(r)] *adj.* их; (*referring to gram. subject*) свой; **they lost ~ rights** они́ лиши́лись свои́х прав; **they want a house of ~ own** они́ хотя́т имéть сóбственный дом; **they broke ~ legs** они́ сломáли себé нóги; **nobody in ~ senses** никтó в здрáвом умé.
theirs [ðeəz] *pron.* их, свой (*cf.* **their**); **the money was ~ by right** дéньги принадлежáли им по прáву; **it is a habit of ~** у них такáя привы́чка; **he added his protest to ~** он присоедини́лся к их протéсту.
theism [ˈθiːɪz(ə)m] *n.* теи́зм.
theist [ˈθiːɪst] *n.* теи́ст.
theistic [θiːˈɪstɪk] *adj.* теисти́ческий.
thematic [θɪˈmætɪk] *adj.* темати́ческий.
theme [θiːm] *n.* (*subject: also mus.*) тéма; **~ park** темати́ческий парк; **~ song, tune** лейтмоти́в.
themselves [ðəmˈselvz] *pron.* **1.** (*refl.*) себя́, себé; -ся, -сь; **they have only ~ to blame** они́ сáми виновáты; **they live by ~** они́ живýт одни́; **they did it by ~** (*unaided*) они́ сдéлали э́то сáми/самостоя́тельно. **2.** (*emph.*): **they did the work ~** они́ сáми сдéлали э́ту рабóту.
then [ðen] *n.*: **before ~** до э́того/тогó врéмени; **by ~** к э́тому/томý врéмени; **since ~** с тех пор; **till ~** до тех пор.
adj. тогдáшний; **the ~ king** тогдáшний корóль.
adv. **1.** (*at that time*) тогдá; **~ and there** тут же, срáзу же; **now and ~** врéмя от врéмени; инóй раз. **2.** (*next; after that*) дáльше, дáлее. **3.** (*furthermore*) крóме тогó; опя́ть-таки. **4.** (*in that case*) тогдá; **~ what *do* you want?** чегó же вы в такóм слýчае хоти́те?; **till tomorrow, ~!** ну, тогдá до зáвтра!; (*introducing apodosis*) то. **5.** (*in resumption*) знáчит; и так. **6.** (*emph.*) итáк; **now ~, let's see what you've brought** ну что ж, давáйте посмóтрим, что вы принесли́; **now ~!** (*warning*) ну-нý!; **well ~, we can go tomorrow** знáчит (*or* стáло быть), мы мóжем пойти́ зáвтра.

thence [ðens] *adv.* (*from that place*) оттýда; (*from that source, for that reason*) отсю́да, из э́того.
cpds. **~forth, ~forward** *advs.* с тех пор.
theocracy [θɪˈɒkrəsɪ] *n.* теокрáтия.
theocratic [θɪəˈkrætɪk] *adj.* теократи́ческий.
theodolite [θɪˈɒdəˌlaɪt] *n.* теодоли́т.
theologian [θɪəˈləʊdʒɪən, -dʒ(ə)n] *n.* богослóв.
theological [θɪəˈlɒdʒɪk(ə)l] *adj.* богослóвский, теологи́ческий.
theology [θɪˈɒlədʒɪ] *n.* богослóвие, теолóгия.
theorem [ˈθɪərəm] *n.* теорéма.
theoretical [θɪəˈretɪk(ə)l] *adj.* теорети́ческий.
theor|etician [ˌθɪərɪˈtɪʃ(ə)n], **-ist** [ˈθɪərɪst] *nn.* теорéтик.
theorize [ˈθɪəraɪz] *v.i.* теоретизи́ровать (*impf.*).
theory [ˈθɪərɪ] *n.* теóрия; **in ~** в теóрии; теорети́чески.
theosophical [θɪəˈsɒfɪk(ə)l] *adj.* теосóфский.
theosophist [θɪˈɒsəfɪst] *n.* теосóф (*fem.* -ка).
theosophy [θɪˈɒsəfɪ] *n.* теосóфия.
therapeutic(al) [ˌθerəˈpjuːtɪk(əl)] *adj.* терапевти́ческий.
therapeutics [ˌθerəˈpjuːtɪks] *n.* терапéвтика.
therapist [ˈθerəpɪst] *n.* терапéвт.
therapy [ˈθerəpɪ] *n.* терапи́я; **occupational ~** трудотерапи́я; **shock ~** шокотерапи́я.
there [ðeə(r)] *adv.* **1.** (*in or at that place*) там; вон; вон тáм; **that man ~ is my uncle** тот человéк — мой дя́дя; **hey, you ~!** эй, ты!; **he's not all ~** у негó не все дóма (*coll.*). **2.** (*to that place*) тудá; **when shall we get ~?** когдá мы тудá доберёмся?; **we went ~ and back in a day** мы съéздили/сходи́ли тудá и обрáтно за оди́н день; **put it ~!** (*shaking hands*) дай пять! (*coll.*). **3.** (*of destination in general*): **the train gets you ~ quicker** на пóезде быстрée. **4.** (*at that point or stage*) тут, здесь; **~ he stopped reading** на э́том мéсте он перестáл читáть; **~ the matter ended** на э́том дéло и кóнчилось; **I wrote to him ~ and then** я тут же написáл емý. **5.** (*in that respect*) здесь; в э́том отношéнии; **~ I agree with you** здесь я с вáми соглáсен; **you're wrong ~** тут вы непрáвы. **6.** (*demonstr.*): **~ goes the bell!** а вот и звонóк!; **~ you go again!** опя́ть вы своё!; **I don't like it, but ~ it is** не нрáвится мне э́то, да ничегó не подéлаешь; **~ you are, take it!** вот вам, держи́те!; **~ you are; I told you so!** ну, вот! а я вам что говори́л?; **oh, ~ you are; I was looking for you** ах, вы тут! а я вас искáл; **don't tell anyone, ~'s a good chap!** не расскáзывайте никомý об э́том, лáдно?; **~'s gratitude for you!** вот вам людскáя благодáрность! **7.** (*in existence*): **the church isn't ~ any more** э́той цéркви бóльше нет. **8.** (*with v. to be, expr. presence, availability etc.*): **~'s a fly in my soup** у меня́ в сýпе мýха; **is ~ a doctor here?** тут есть врач?; **~'s no time to lose** нельзя́ не теря́ть ни минýты; **~'s no holding him** ýдержу на негó нет; **I don't want ~ to be any misunderstanding** я не хочý никаки́х недоразумéний; **~ seems to have been a mistake** тут, кáжется, произошлá оши́бка; **~ was plenty to eat** еды́ бы́ло полнó; **what is ~ to say?** что тут мóжно сказáть?
int.: **~! what did I tell you?** ну вот! что я вам говори́л?; **~, ~!** (*comforting child etc.*) ну! ну!
thereabouts [ˈðeərəˌbaʊts, -ˈbaʊts] *adv.* (*nearby*) поблизости; (*approximately*) óколо э́того; приблизи́тельно; **£5 or ~** 5 фýнтов и́ли óколо э́того.
thereafter [ðeərˈɑːftə(r)] *adv.* пóсле тогó; впредь.
thereby [ðeəˈbaɪ, ˈðeə-] *adv.* э́тим; таки́м óбразом.
therefore [ˈðeəfɔː(r)] *adv.* поэ́тому, слéдовательно.
therefrom [ðeəˈfrɒm] *adv.* от э́того/них; оттогó.
therein [ðeərˈɪn] *adv.* там; в э́том/том/них.
thereof [ðeərˈɒv] *adv.* (из) э́того; (из) тогó; (*of them*) их, из них.
thereon [ðeərˈɒn] *adv.* на э́том/том/них.
thereto [ðeəˈtuː] *adv.* к э́тому/томý/ним.
thereunder [ðeərˈʌndə(r)] *adv.* ни́же; под э́тим/тем/ни́ми.
thereupon [ˌðeərəˈpɒn] *adv.* срáзу же; тут; вслéдствие тогó.
therewith [ðeəˈwɪð] *adv.* с э́тим/тем/ни́ми.
therm [θɜːm] *n.* терм.
thermal [ˈθɜːm(ə)l] *n.* (*aeron.*) восходя́щий потóк тёплого вóздуха.
adj.: **~ capacity** теплоёмкость; **~ reactor** реáктор на тепловы́х нейтрóнах; **~ springs** горя́чие истóчники.

thermodynamics [ˌθɜːməʊdaɪˈnæmɪks] *n.* термодина́мика.
thermometer [θəˈmɒmɪtə(r)] *n.* термо́метр.
thermonuclear [ˌθɜːməʊˈnjuːklɪə(r)] *adj.* термоя́дерный; **~ device** термоя́дерное устро́йство.
thermoplastic [ˌθɜːməʊˈplæstɪk] *n.* термопла́ст.
adj. термопласти́ческий.
Thermopylae [θəˈmɒpəˌliː] *n.* Фермопи́л|ы (*pl.*, *g.* —).
thermos [ˈθɜːməs] *n.* **(~ flask)** те́рмос.
thermostat [ˈθɜːməˌstæt] *n.* термоста́т, терморегуля́тор.
thermostatic [ˌθɜːməˈstætɪk] *adj.* термостати́ческий.
thesaurus [θɪˈsɔːrəs] *n.* теза́урус; слова́рь, соста́вленный из смысловы́х гнёзд.
thesis [ˈθiːsɪs] *n.* (*dissertation*) диссерта́ция; (*contention*) те́зис.
Thespian [ˈθespɪən] *n.* (*joc.*) актёр, актри́са.
they [ðeɪ] *pron.* они́; **~ who ...** те, кото́рые/кто…; **both of them** они́ о́ба.
thick [θɪk] *n.*: **in the ~ of the fighting** в са́мом пе́кле боя́; **he stood by me through ~ and thin** он стоя́л за меня́ гру́дью.
adj. **1.** (*of solid substance*) то́лстый; (*of liquid*) густо́й; **a ~ overcoat** тяжёлое пальто́; **a ~ coat of paint** то́лстый слой кра́ски; **the dust lay an inch ~** пыль лежа́ла толщино́й в дюйм; **the room was ~ with dust** ко́мната была́ полна́ пы́ли; **~ soup** густо́й суп. **2.** (*close together*, *dense*) густо́й; (*of population*) пло́тный; **~ hair** густы́е во́лосы; **a ~ forest** густо́й/ча́стый лес; **the fog is getting ~** тума́н густе́ет; **the air was ~ with smoke** стоя́л густо́й дым. **3.** (*coll.*, *stupid*) тупо́й. **4.** (*coll.*, *intimate*) **they are as ~ as thieves** они́ снюха́лись. **5.** (*dull*, *indistinct*): **I woke with a ~ head** я просну́лся с тяжёлой голово́й; **he spoke with a ~ voice** он говори́л хри́плым го́лосом; у него́ язы́к заплета́лся; (*pronounced*, *extreme*): **he has a ~ accent** у него́ си́льный акце́нт. **6.: that's a bit ~!** (*coll.*, *of impertinence etc.*) ну, э́то уже́ чересчу́р/сли́шком!
adv. гу́сто, ча́сто; **the blows came ~ and fast** уда́ры сы́пались оди́н за други́м; **he laid it on ~** (*coll.*, *of flattery*) он переборщи́л; он хвати́л че́рез край.
cpds. **~head** *n.* тупи́ца (*c.g.*); **~-headed** *adj.* тупоголо́вый; **~set** *adj.* (*stocky*) корена́стый, кря́жистый; (*closely planted*) гу́сто заса́женный; **~-skinned** *adj.* (*lit.*, *fig.*) толстоко́жий.
thicken [ˈθɪkən] *v.t.* утол|ща́ть, -сти́ть; де́лать, с- бо́лее густы́м.
v.i. утол|ща́ться, -сти́ться; усложн|я́ться, -и́ться; уплотн|я́ться, -и́ться.
thicket [ˈθɪkɪt] *n.* ча́ща; за́росл|и (*pl.*, *g.* -ей).
thickness [ˈθɪknɪs] *n.* толщина́, густота́; (*layer*) слой.
thief [θiːf] *n.* вор; **stop ~!** держи́ во́ра!; **set a ~ to catch a ~** вор во́ра скоре́е пойма́ет; **honour among thieves** воровска́я честь.
thiev|e [θiːv] *v.i.* красть, у-; ворова́ть, у-/с-; **a ~ing fellow** ворова́тый тип.
thievery [ˈθiːvərɪ] *n.* кра́жа, воровство́.
thievish [ˈθiːvɪʃ] *adj.* ворова́тый; нечи́стый на́ руку.
thievishness [ˈθiːvɪʃnɪs] *n.* ворова́тость.
thigh [θaɪ] *n.* бедро́.
cpd. **~-bone** *n.* бе́дренная кость.
thimble [ˈθɪmb(ə)l] *n.* напёрсток.
thimbleful [ˈθɪmb(ə)lˌfʊl] *n.* (*fig.*) глото́чек.
thin [θɪn] *adj.* **1.** (*of measurement between surfaces*) то́нкий; **his coat had worn ~ at the elbows** его́ пальто́ протёрлось на локтя́х. **2.** (*not dense*) ре́дкий; жи́дкий; **your hair is getting ~ on top** у вас во́лосы реде́ют на маку́шке; **he vanished into ~ air** его́ как ве́тром сду́ло; **our troops are ~ on the ground** нам не хвата́ет войск; **a ~ audience** немногочи́сленная аудито́рия. **3.** (*not fat*) то́нкий, худо́й; **~ in the face** с худы́м лицо́м; **she has become ~** она́ похуде́ла; **as ~ as a lath** худо́й как ще́пка. **4.** (*of liquids*) жи́дкий; разба́вленный. **5.** (*flimsy*, *inadequate*) сла́бый; ша́ткий; **the play has a ~ plot** в пье́се почти́ нет фа́булы; **a ~ excuse** неубеди́тельная отгово́рка. **6.** (*coll.*, *uncomfortable*): **I had a ~ time** я скве́рно провёл вре́мя.
adv. то́нко; **don't cut the bread so ~!** не на́до ре́зать хлеб так то́нко!
v.t. де́лать, с- то́нким; разб|авля́ть, -а́вить; **she ~ned the gravy** она́ разба́вила подли́вку; **these plants should be ~ned (out)** э́ти расте́ния ну́жно прореди́ть.
v.i. станови́ться (*impf.*) жи́дким; сокра|ща́ться, -ти́ться; **when the fog ~s** когда́ тума́н рассе́ется; **the crowd ~ned out** толпа́ поре́дела; **his hair is ~ning** у него́ реде́ют во́лосы.
cpd. **~-skinned** *adj.* (*lit.*) тонкоко́жий; (*fig.*) уязви́мый; оби́дчивый.
thine [ðaɪn] *pron.* & *adj.* (*arch.*) твой.
thing [θɪŋ] *n.* **1.** (*object*) вещь, предме́т; **what is that black ~?** что э́то за чёрная шту́ка?; **you must be seeing ~s!** (*coll.*) вам что́-то мере́щится!; **there's no such ~ as ghosts** привиде́ний не существу́ет; при́зраков не быва́ет. **2.** (*pl.*, *belongings*) иму́щество; ве́щи (*f. pl.*); **pack up your ~s!** упаку́йте/собери́те свои́ ве́щи! **3.** (*pl.*, *clothes*) оде́жда, ве́щи; **take your ~s off!** (*sc. outer clothing*) раздева́йтесь! **4.** (*pl.*, *food*) еда́; **I don't care for sweet ~s** я не люблю́ сла́дкого. **5.** (*pl.*, *equipment*) принадле́жности (*f. pl.*); **she got out the tea ~s** она́ вы́ставила ча́йный серви́з. **6.** (*matter*, *affair*) де́ло; вещь; **~s of importance** ва́жные дела́; **~s of the mind** духо́вные це́нности (*f. pl.*); **~s Japanese** всё япо́нское; **for one ~, he's too old** нача́ть с того́, что он сли́шком стар; **you had better leave ~s as they are** лу́чше оста́вить всё как есть; **how are ~s?** как дела́?; **it will only make ~s worse** э́то то́лько уху́дшит ситуа́цию; **other ~s being equal** при про́чих ра́вных усло́виях; **all ~s considered** принима́я во внима́ние всё; **as ~s go** при ны́нешним положе́нии дел; **above all ~s** пре́жде/превы́ше всего́; **among other ~s** среди́ про́чего; **taking one ~ with another** взве́сив всё; **she was told to take ~s easy** ей веле́ли не перенапряга́ться/перетружда́ться; **let's talk ~s over** дава́йте э́то обсу́дим; **it was just one of those ~s** (*coll.*) ничего́ нельзя́ бы́ло поде́лать; **it comes to the same ~** э́то сво́дится к тому́ же са́мому; **well, of all ~s!** поду́мать то́лько! **7.** (*act*) де́йствие; посту́пок; **it's the worst ~ you could have done** э́то са́мое плохо́е, что вы могли́ сде́лать; **that was a silly ~ to do** э́то был глу́пый посту́пок; **I have some ~s to do** у меня́ есть ко́е-каки́е дела́. **8.** (*course of action*): **the only ~ now is to take a cab** еди́нственное, что мо́жно сейча́с сде́лать, э́то взять такси́; **the best ~ for you would be to marry** лу́чше всего́ вам бы бы́ло жени́ться. **9.** (*event*) собы́тие; **what a terrible ~ to happen!** како́е ужа́сное несча́стье!; **and a good ~ too!** так ему́/ей/им и на́до!; вот и прекра́сно!; **first ~** пе́рвым де́лом; в пе́рвую о́чередь; **last ~** в после́днюю о́чередь, напосле́док; **last ~ at night** на́ ночь; пе́ред сном; **it was a close, near ~** всё чуть не сорвало́сь. **10.** (*word*, *remark*): **what a ~ to say!** как мо́жно сказа́ть тако́е!; **he said nice ~s about you** он о́чень хорошо́ о вас отозва́лся. **11.** (*fact*): **I could tell you a ~ or two** я мог бы вам рассказа́ть ко́е-что. **12.** (*issue*): **the ~ is, can you afford it?** хва́тит ли у вас на э́то де́нег? — вот в чём де́ло. **13.** (*coll.*, *obsession*) навя́зчивая иде́я; (*aversion*): **she has a ~ about cats** она́ не выно́сит ко́шек. **14.** (*literary*, *musical work etc.*) произведе́ние; **it's a little ~ I wrote myself** э́ту вещи́цу я написа́л сам. **15.** **(a ~:** *something*; *with neg.*: *nothing*): **it's a ~ I have never done before** я э́того никогда́ ра́ньше не де́лал; **I don't know a ~ (*or* the first ~) about physics** я по фи́зике ни в зуб ного́й (*coll.*); **I can't see a ~** я ничего́ не ви́жу. **16.** (*creature*) существо́; **all living ~s** все живы́е существа́. **17.** (*emotively*, *of persons or animals*) созда́ние, тварь; **don't be such a mean ~** не бу́дьте тако́й ска́редой!; **poor ~** бедня́га, бедня́жка; (*both c.g.*); **she's a sweet little ~** она́ така́я мила́шка; **there's a wasp; kill the horrid ~!** смотри́, оса́! убе́й э́ту га́дость!; **old ~** (*sl.*, *old chap*) стари́к, старина́ (*m.*). **18.: the ~** (*var. idioms*): **it's the done ~** так при́нято; **it's not the ~ (to do)** так не поступа́ют; **it's the very ~ for my wife** мое́й жене́ э́то в са́мый раз; **just the ~!** то, что на́до!; **it's not quite the ~** э́то не совсе́м то; **I don't feel quite the ~ today** мне сего́дня ка́к-то не по себе́; **he did the right ~ by us** он с на́ми хорошо́ обошёлся; **he always says the right ~** он всегда́ зна́ет, что сказа́ть; **books and ~s** кни́ги и тому́ подо́бное (*or* и так да́лее).

thing|amy ['θɪŋəmɪ], **-umabob** ['θɪŋəmə,bɒb], **-umajig** ['θɪŋəmə,dʒɪg], **-ummy** ['θɪŋəmɪ] *nn.* (*coll.*) штукóвина; (*of people*) как (бишь) егó/её?

think [θɪŋk] *n.*: **I must have a ~** мне нáдо подýмать; **he's got another ~ coming** емý придётся ещё раз подýмать.

v.t. & i. (*opine*) дýмать, по-; полагáть (*impf.*); считáть (*impf.*); **I ~** (я) дýмаю; кáжется; по-мóему; мне дýмается; **I don't ~ so** не дýмаю; **what do you ~?** как вы дýмаете?; **yes, I ~ so** да, пожáлуй; **I ~ I'll go** я, пожáлуй, пойдý; **how could you ~ that?** как вам э́то моглó прийти́ на ум?; **where do you ~ he can be?** как вы дýмаете, кудá он мог девáться?; **when do you ~ you'll be back?** когдá вы дýмаете вернýться?; **I don't know what to ~** я не знáю, что и подýмать; **I ~ I'm going to sneeze** я, кáжется, сейчáс чихнý; **you're a great help, I don't ~!** ну и помóщничек же вы!; (*judge*): **it suits me, don't you ~?** вы не нахóдите, что э́то мне идёт?; **do you ~ she's pretty?** вы считáете её хорóшенькой?; **do what you ~ fit** поступáйте так, как вы считáете нýжным; **I thought it better to stay** я реши́л, что лýчше остáться; (*reflect*) дýмать, по-; мы́слить (*impf.*); **~ for o.s.** дýмать самостоя́тельно; **you will ~ yourself silly** у вас ум за рáзум зайдёт; **to ~ that he's only 12!** подýмать тóлько, емý всегó 12 лет!; **when I ~ what I've missed!** как подýмаю, что я упусти́л!; **it makes you ~, doesn't it?** э́то заставля́ет задýматься, не так ли?; **don't you ever ~?** вы что, совсéм перестáли дýмать?; **~ well!** подýмайте хорошéнько!; **let me ~, what was his name?** дáйте вспóмнить, как же егó зовýт?; **just ~!** вы тóлько подýмайте!; **I can't ~ straight today** у меня́ сегóдня головá не рабóтает; **I should ~ twice before agreeing** нáдо бы хорошéнько/двáжды подýмать, прéжде чем согласи́ться; (*expect*) дýмать (*impf.*); предполагáть (*impf.*); **I thought as much** так я и дýмал; (*imagine*): **I can't ~ how he does it** я не могý себé представить, как он э́то дéлает; **what do you ~? I've won a prize!** вы мóжете себé представить, я вы́играл приз!; **who would have thought it?** кто б мог подýмать?; **I would never have thought it of him** я бы никогдá в жи́зни егó в э́том не заподóзрил!; (*with inf.*): **if he ~s to deceive us** (*arch.*) éсли он собирáется нас обхитри́ть; **I never thought to ask** мне не пришлó в гóлову спроси́ть; (*with preps.* **about, of**): **I have other things to ~ about** у меня́ мнóго други́х забóт; **it has given me something to ~ about** э́то мне дáло пи́щу для размышлéний; **if I catch him, I'll give him something to ~ about** éсли я егó поймáю, емý достáнется от меня́; **have you thought about going to the police?** вы не дýмали пойти́ в поли́цию?; **what do you ~ about having a meal?** как насчёт тогó, чтóбы перекуси́ть?; **it doesn't bear ~ing about** стрáшно подýмать об э́том; **I was just ~ing of going to bed** я как раз собирáлся идти́ спать; **~ of a number!** задýмайте/загадáйте числó!; **I couldn't ~ of his name** я не мог вспóмнить, как егó зовýт; **I couldn't ~ of letting you pay** я бы не мог допусти́ть, чтóбы вы заплати́ли; **I would never have thought of doing that** я никогдá бы не догадáлся сдéлать такóе; **can you ~ of a good place to eat?** вы знáете, где мóжно хорошó поéсть?; **I thought of an excuse** я придýмал предлóг; **who first thought of the idea?** комý пéрвому э́та идéя пришлá на ум?; **what can he be ~ing of?** с чегó э́то он вдруг?; что э́то емý взбрелó в гóлову?; **it's not much when you ~ of it** э́то немнóго, éсли вдýматься; **I can't ~ of anything to say** я не знáю, что сказáть; **what do you ~ of the plan?** что вы дýмаете (*or* какóго вы мнéния) об э́том плáне?; **his employers ~ well of him** он на хорóшем счетý у свои́х работодáтелей; **he is well thought of in the City** егó уважáют в Си́ти; **I don't ~ much of him as a teacher** я невысокó ценю́ егó как преподовáтеля; **I was going to sell my house, but I thought better of it** я собирáлся продавáть свой дом, а потóм раздýмал; **~ nothing of it!** (*in reply to thanks*) не стóит!; **he ~s nothing of a 20-mile walk** емý прогýлка в 20 миль нипочём; **while I ~ of it** кстáти; мéжду прóчим.

with advs.: **he tried to ~ the pain away** он пытáлся о чём-нибýдь дýмать, чтóбы заглуши́ть боль; **the matter needs ~ing out** э́то дéло нáдо обмозговáть; **his arguments are well thought out** егó аргумéнты хорошó продýманы; **~ it over!** обдýмайте э́то!; **he never ~s his ideas through** он никогдá не додýмывает свои́ идéи до концá; **~ up** (*devise*) придýм|ывать, -ать; (*invent*) выдýмывать, вы́думать.

cpds. **~-piece** *n.* (*coll.*) обзóрная статья́; **~-tank** *n.* (*coll.*) «мозговóй центр».

thinkable ['θɪŋkəb(ə)l] *adj.* мы́слимый; возмóжный; **such an idea is barely ~** э́то почти́ немы́слимо.

thinker ['θɪŋkə(r)] *n.* мысли́тель (*m.*); **he is a quick ~** он бы́стро соображáет.

thinking ['θɪŋkɪŋ] *n.* **1.** (*cogitation*) размышлéние; дýмы (*f. pl.*); **we have some hard ~ to do** нам нáдо как слéдует поразмы́слить. **2.** (*opinion*) мнéние; **to my way of ~** на мой взгляд; **I brought him round to my way of ~** я склони́л егó к моéй тóчке зрéния.

adj. дýмающий; **the ~ public** дýмающие/мы́слящие лю́ди.

cpd. **~-cap** *n.*: **I must put my ~-cap on** (*coll.*) мне придётся пораски́нуть мозгáми.

thinness ['θɪnnɪs] *n.* тóнкость.

third [θɜːd] *n.* **1.** (*date*) трéтье числó; **my birthday is on the ~** мой день рождéния трéтьего. **2.** (*fraction*) треть; **two ~s** две трéти. **3.** (*mus.*) тéрция.

adj. трéтий; **~ degree** (*coll.*) допрóс «с пристрáстием»; **~ party, person** (*leg. etc.*) трéтья сторонá; **~ person** (*gram.*) трéтье лицó; **the T~ World** трéтий мир.

adv.: **he travelled ~** (*sc.* **~-class**) он путешéствовал трéтьим клáссом.

cpds. **~-class** *adj.* (*rail etc.*) третьеклáссный; (**~-rate**) третьесóртный; **~-degree** *adj.*: **~-degree burns** ожóги трéтьей стéпени; **~-party** *adj.*: **~-party insurance** страхóвка, возмещáющая убы́тки трéтьих лиц; **~-rate** *adj.* третьесóртный.

thirdly ['θɜːdlɪ] *adv.* в-трéтьих.

thirst [θɜːst] *n.* (*lit., fig.*) жáжда; **they died of ~** они́ ýмерли от жáжды; **~ for knowledge** жáжда знáний.

v.i. (*fig.*) жáждать (*impf.*) (*чего*); **he ~ed for revenge** он жáждал мéсти.

thirsty ['θɜːstɪ] *adj.* испы́тывающий жáжду; **I am, feel ~** мне хóчется (*or* я хочý) пить; **digging is ~ work** когдá рóешь зéмлю, хóчется пить; (*fig., of soil*) иссóхший.

thirteen [θɜː'tiːn, 'θɜː-] *n.* тринáдцать.

adj. тринáдцать +*g. pl.*

thirteenth [θɜː'tiːnθ, 'θɜːtɪnθ] *n.* (*date*) тринáдцатое числó; (*fraction*) однá тринáдцатая.

adj. тринáдцатый.

thirtieth ['θɜːtɪɪθ] *n.* (*date*) тридцáтое числó; (*fraction*) однá тридцáтая.

adj. тридцáтый.

thirt|y ['θɜːtɪ] *n.* три́дцать; **it happened in the ~ies** э́то случи́лось в тридцáтых годáх; **he is in his ~ies** емý за три́дцать.

adj. три́дцать +*g. pl.*

this [ðɪs] *pron.* э́то; (*liter.*) послéднее; **~ is what I think** вот что я дýмаю; **are these your shoes?** э́то вáши тýфли?; **we talked of ~ and that** мы говори́ли о том, о всём; **he should have been here before ~** емý бы порá ужé быть здесь; **do it like ~** сдéлайте э́то так (*or* слéдующим óбразом); **it was like ~** вот как э́то бы́ло; **~ is it** (*coll., the difficulty etc.*) вот и́менно!; в тóм-то и дéло!

adj. э́тот; дáнный; **~ book here** вот э́та кни́га; **~ country of ours** э́та нáша странá; **~ very day** сегóдня же; **~ day week** рóвно чéрез недéлю; в э́тот же день на бýдущей недéле; **~ time last week** в э́то же врéмя на прóшлой недéле; **come here ~ minute!** иди́ сюдá сию́ же минýту!; **these days** (*nowadays*) в настоя́щее врéмя, ны́нче; **he has been ill these three weeks** он был бóлен послéдние три недéли; **~ one or that** тот и́ли другóй; **he turned to ~ doctor and that** он обращáлся к рáзным врачáм (*or* то к одномý, то к другóму врачý).

adv.: **about ~ high** примéрно такóй высоты́; такóго примéрно рóста; **can you give me ~ much?** вы мóжете дать мне стóлько?; **I know ~ much** мне извéстно однó.

thistle ['θɪs(ə)l] *n.* чертополо́х.
cpd. **~down** *n.* пушо́к, пух.
thither ['ðɪðə(r)] *adv.* туда́.
tho' [ðəʊ] = **though**
thole(-pin) [θəʊl] *n.* уклю́чина, ко́лышек.
Thomas [ˌtɒməs] *n.*: **doubting ~** Фома́ неве́рный.
Thomism ['təʊmɪz(ə)m] *n.* уче́ние Фомы́ Акви́нского.
thong [θɒŋ] *n.* реме́нь (*m.*).
thorax ['θɔːræks] *n.* грудна́я кле́тка, то́ракс.
thorn [θɔːn] *n.* **1.** колю́чка, шип; **he is a ~ in my flesh** он сиди́т у меня́ в печёнках. **2.** (*prickly plant*) колю́чее расте́ние.
thorny ['θɔːnɪ] *adj.* колю́чий; (*fig.*): **a ~ path** терни́стый путь; **a ~ problem** о́страя пробле́ма.
thorough ['θʌrə] *adj.* (*comprehensive*) подро́бный, обстоя́тельный; (*conscientious*) добросо́вестный, аккура́тный; **a ~ worker** добросо́вестный рабо́тник; **he made a ~ job of it** он тща́тельно вы́полнил свою́ рабо́ту; (*fundamental*) основа́тельный; **you need a ~ change** вам ну́жно по́лностью смени́ть обстано́вку; (*out-and-out*): **he is a ~ scoundrel** он стопроце́нтный/зако́нченный негодя́й.
cpds. **~bred** *n.* чистопоро́дное живо́тное; *adj.* чистокро́вный, чистопоро́дный, поро́дистый; **~fare** *n.* тра́нспо́ртная магистра́ль; **'No T~fare'** «прохо́да/прое́зда нет»; **~going** *adj.* доскона́льный, тща́тельный, после́довательный.
thoroughly ['θʌrəlɪ] *adv.* вполне́, соверше́нно, по́лностью, вконе́ц.
thou [ðaʊ] *pron.* ты; **they say '~' to each other** они́ друг с дру́гом на «ты».
though [ðəʊ] *adv. & conj.* хотя́, хоть; несмотря́ на то, что…; **~ annoyed, I consented** хотя́ э́то меня́ раздража́ло, я вы́разил согла́сие; **~ not a music-lover, I …** хотя́ я и не большо́й люби́тель му́зыки, я…; **~ severe, he is just** он строг, но справедли́в; **even ~ it's late** пусть уже́ по́здно, но…; **a flaw, even ~ small** изъя́н, пусть и ма́лый; **strange ~ it may seem** как э́то ни стра́нно; **what ~ he be poor?** что из того́, что он бе́ден?; **he said he would come; he didn't, ~** он сказа́л, что придёт; одна́ко же, не пришёл; **as ~** как бу́дто бы; сло́вно; **it looks as ~ he will lose** похо́же на то, что он проигра́ет; **it's not as ~ you had no money** ведь де́ньги-то у вас есть.
thought [θɔːt] *n.* **1.** (*way, instance or body of thinking*) мысль, ду́ма; **modern scientific ~** совреме́нная нау́чная мысль. **2.** (*reflection*) мышле́ние, разду́мье, размышле́ние; **he spends hours in ~** он прово́дит це́лые часы́ в разду́мье; **deep, lost in ~** погружённый в мы́сли; **quick as ~** вмиг; **he acted without a moment's ~** он де́йствовал, не заду́мываясь; **I gave serious ~ to the matter** я мно́го ду́мал об э́том; **don't give it a ~!** вы́киньте э́то из головы́!; **on second ~s** поду́мав, поразмы́слив; по зре́лом размышле́нии; **second ~s are best** ≃ семь раз отме́рь — оди́н отре́жь; **collect one's ~s** соб|ира́ться, -ра́ться с мы́слями. **3.** (*consideration*): **take ~ for** забо́титься (*impf.*) о+*p.* **4.** (*idea, opinion*) мысль, иде́я, соображе́ние; **the ~ struck me** мне пришло́ в го́лову; **let me have your ~s on the subject** вы́скажите мне ва́ши соображе́ния на э́ту те́му; **he keeps his ~s to himself** он де́ржит свои́ мы́сли при себе́; **a penny for your ~s!** о чём заду́мались?; **you are much in my ~s** я мно́го о вас ду́маю; **his one ~ was to escape** он ду́мал то́лько о том, как бы убежа́ть. **5.** (*intention*): **she gave up all ~ of marrying** она́ отказа́лась от вся́кой мы́сли о заму́жестве; **I had some ~ of resigning** я поду́мывал об отста́вке; **I had no ~ of offending him** я и не ду́мал его́ обижа́ть. **6.**: **a ~** (*liter., a little*) чу́точку.
cpds. **~-read** *v.i.* чита́ть (*impf.*) чужи́е мы́сли; **~-reader** *n.* челове́к, чита́ющий чужи́е мы́сли; **~-reading** *n.* чте́ние чужи́х мы́слей; **~-transference** *n.* переда́ча мы́сли (на расстоя́нии), телепа́тия.
thoughtful ['θɔːtfʊl] *adj.* **1.** (*meditative*) заду́мчивый. **2.** (*well-considered, profound*): **a ~ essay** вду́мчивое/содержа́тельное эссе́. **3.** (*considerate*) внима́тельный, чу́ткий, предупреди́тельный.
thoughtfulness ['θɔːtfʊlnɪs] *n.* заду́мчивость; проду́манность; внима́тельность, чу́ткость, предупреди́тельность.
thoughtless ['θɔːtlɪs] *adj.* (*careless*) безду́мный, неосмотри́тельный; (*inconsiderate*) невнима́тельный, нечу́ткий.
thoughtlessness ['θɔːtlɪsnɪs] *n.* безду́мность, неосмотри́тельность; невнима́тельность, нечу́ткость.
thousand ['θaʊz(ə)nd] *n. & adj.* ты́сяча; **a ~ people** ты́сяча люде́й; **with £1,000** с ты́сячью фу́нтами; **a ~-to-one chance** оди́н шанс из ты́сячи; **he is a man in a ~** таки́е как он встреча́ются оди́н на ты́сячу; **I have a ~ and one things to do** у меня́ ты́сяча дел; **a ~ thanks!** огро́мнейшее спаси́бо!
cpd. **~fold** *adj.* тысячекра́тный; *adv.* в ты́сячу раз бо́льше.
thousandth ['θaʊzəndθ] *n.* ты́сячная часть.
adj. ты́сячный.
Thrace [θreɪs] *n.* Фра́кия.
Thracian ['θreɪʃɪən] *n.* фраки́ец.
adj. фраки́йский.
thraldom ['θrɔːldəm] *n.* (*liter.*) ра́бство.
thrall [θrɔːl] *n.* (*liter.*): **he was in ~ to his passions** он был рабо́м свои́х страсте́й.
thrash [θræʃ] *v.t.* **1.** (*beat*) поро́ть, вы́-; хлеста́ть, от-; **I'll ~ the life out of you!** я из тебя́ дух вы́шибу!; (*fig., defeat*) побе|жда́ть, -ди́ть; разн|оси́ть, -ести́; **he got a ~ing in the final round** ему́ си́льно доста́лось в фина́льном ра́унде. **2.** (*also* **thresh:** *make turbulent by beating*) колоти́ть (*impf.*); ударя́ть (*impf.*); **the whale ~ed the water with its tail** кит бил хвосто́м по воде́. **3.** = **thresh 1.**
v.i. (*also* **thresh**) мета́ться (*impf.*); **the swimmer ~ed about in the water** пловéц колоти́л рука́ми и нога́ми по воде́; **he ~ed about in bed** он мета́лся в посте́ли.
with adv.: **~ out** *v.t.* (*fig.*) обстоя́тельно обсу|жда́ть, -ди́ть; **let us ~ out this problem** разберём э́тот вопро́с по ко́сточкам; **they ~ed out a solution** они́ вы́работали реше́ние.
thrasher ['θræʃə(r)] = **thresher**
thread [θred] *n.* **1.** (*spun fibre; length of this*) ни́тка; **a reel of ~** кату́шка ни́ток; **his life hung by a ~** его́ жизнь висе́ла на воло́ске; (*fig.*) связь; нить; **a ~ of light** у́зкая поло́ска све́та; **there's not a ~ of evidence** нет ни мале́йшего доказа́тельства; **he lost the ~ of his argument** он потеря́л нить рассужде́ния; **he took up the ~ of his story** он продо́лжил свой расска́з; **it was hard for them to pick up the ~s after such a long separation** тру́дно бы́ло им притере́ться по́сле до́лгой разлу́ки. **2.** (*of a screw etc.*) резьба́.
v.t. прод|ева́ть, -е́ть ни́тку в+*a.*; нани́з|ывать, -а́ть; **can you ~ this needle?** вы мо́жете проде́ть ни́тку в э́ту иглу́?; **she was ~ing beads** она́ нани́зывала бу́сы.
cpd. **~bare** *adj.* потёртый, изно́шенный, потрёпанный.
threat [θret] *n.* угро́за; **there was a ~ of rain** собира́лся дождь.
threaten ['θret(ə)n] *v.t. & i.* угрожа́ть (*impf.*) +*d.*; грози́ть, по- +*d.*; грози́ться (*impf.*); **he ~ed me with a stick** он погрози́л мне па́лкой; **I was ~ed with expulsion** мне грози́ли исключе́нием; **I was ~ed with bankruptcy** мне грози́ло/угрожа́ло банкро́тство; **they ~ed revenge** они угрожа́ли мще́нием; **the clouds ~ed rain** ту́чи/облака́ предвеща́ли дождь; **he ~ed to leave** он угрожа́л тем, что уйдёт; он грози́лся уйти́; **war ~ed** нави́сла угро́за войны́; **rain was ~ing** надвига́лся дождь.
three [θriː] *n.* (число́/но́мер) три; (~ *people*) тро́е; **~ of us went** нас тро́е пошло́; мы пошли́ втроём; нас пошло́ три челове́ка; **~ each** по́ три; **~ at a time, in ~s** по́ три/тро́е; тро́йками; (*figure, thg. numbered 3; group of ~*) тро́йка; **the Big T~** «Больша́я тро́йка»; (*cut, divide*) **in ~** на́трое; **fold in ~** сложи́ть (*pf.*) втрое; (*with n. expr. or understood; cf. also examples under* **two**): **~ times ~** (*cheer*) девятикра́тное ура́.
adj. три +*g. sg.*; (*for people and pluralia tantum, also*) тро́е +*g. pl.* (*cf. examples under* **two**); **he and ~ others** он с тремя́ други́ми; **~ fours are twelve** три́жды (*or* три на) четы́ре — двена́дцать; **~ times as good** втрое лу́чше; ~

times as much втрóе бóльше; втройнé; ~ **quarters** три чéтверти; (*adv.*) нá три чéтверти.

cpds. **~-cornered** *adj.* треугóльный; **a ~-cornered fight** трёхсторóнняя борьбá; **~-D** (*coll.*) *n.* (*cin.*) стереокинó (*indecl.*); *adj.* трёхмéрный; **a ~-D film** стереоскопи́ческий фильм; **~-day** *adj.* трёхднéвный; **~-decker** *n.* (*ship*) трёхпáлубное сýдно; **~-dimensional** *adj.* (*lit.*) трёхмéрный; в трёх измерéниях; (*fig., of characters in a book etc.*) вы́пуклый; (*stereoscopic*) стереоскопи́ческий; **~-field** *adj.*: **~-field system** трёхпóлье; **~-figure** *adj.* трёхзначный; **~fold** *adj.* тройнóй; троекрáтный; *adv.* втройнé, втрóе, троекрáтно; **~-handed** *adj.* (*of card game*) с учáстием трёх игрокóв; **~-hour** *adj.* трёхчасовóй; **~-hundredth** *adj.* трёхсóтый; **~-lane** *adj.* трёхколéйный; **~-legged** *adj.* (*of table etc.*) на трёх нóжках; **~-legged race** бег пáрами; **~-piece** *adj.*: **~-piece suit** (костю́м-)трóйка; **~-piece suite** дивáн с двумя́ крéслами; **~-ply** *adj.* (*of timber, wool etc.*) трёхслóйный; **~-point** *adj.* трёхтóчечный; **~-point landing** (*aeron.*) посáдка на три тóчки; **~-point turn** разворóт с применéнием зáднего хóда; **~-quarter** *adj.* трёхчетвертнóй; **~-quarter portrait** портрéт в три чéтверти; **~score** *adj.*: **~score and ten** сéмьдесят (лет); **~-seater** *adj.* трёхмéстный; **~some** *n.* (*persons*) трóе, трóйка; (*game*) игрá втроём; **~-speed** *adj.*: **~-speed gear** трёхскоростнáя передáча; **~-storey** *adj.* трёхэтáжный; **~-ton** *adj.*: **~-ton lorry** (*also* **~-tonner** *n.*) трёхтóнка; **~-wheel(ed)** *adj.* трёхколёсный; **~-year** *adj.* трёхгоди́чный, трёхлéтний; **~-year-old** *adj.* трёхгодовáлый, трёхлéтний.

threnody [ˈθrenədɪ] *n.* надгрóбная песнь.

thresh [θreʃ] *v.t.* **1.** (*also* **thrash:** *beat grain from*) молоти́ть (*impf.*). **2.** = **thrash** *v.t.* **2.**

v.i. = **thrash** *v.i.*

thresher [ˈθreʃə(r)], **thrasher** [ˈθræʃə(r)] *nn.* (*worker*) молоти́льщик; (*machine*) молоти́лка.

threshing [ˈθreʃɪŋ], **thrashing** [ˈθræʃɪŋ] *nn.* молотьбá.

cpds. **~-floor** *n.* ток, гумнó; **~-machine** *n.* молоти́лка.

threshold [ˈθreʃəʊld, -həʊld] *n.* (*lit.*) порóг; (*fig.*) порóг, предвéрие; **on the ~** на порóге, в предвéрии.

thrice [θraɪs] *adv.* (*liter.*) (*three times*) три́жды, троекрáтно; (*fig., highly*) в вы́сшей стéпени.

thrift [θrɪft] *n.* **1.** (*frugality*) бережли́вость, экономность. **2.** (*bot.*) армéрия.

thriftless [ˈθrɪftlɪs] *adj.* расточи́тельный, неэконóмный.

thriftlessness [ˈθrɪftlɪsnɪs] *n.* расточи́тельность.

thrifty [ˈθrɪftɪ] *adj.* бережли́вый, экономный.

thrill [θrɪl] *n.* (*physical sensation*) дрожь, трéпет; (*excitement*) востóрг, восхищéние; **it gave me a ~** э́то привелó меня́ в востóрг/восхищéние.

v.t. восхи|щáть, -ти́ть; **she was ~ed to death** онá былá в ди́ком востóрге; **a ~ing finish** захвáтывающий конéц.

v.i.: **we ~ed at the good news** мы обрáдовались хорóшим вестя́м; **she ~ed with delight/horror** онá затрепетáла от рáдости/ýжаса; **fear ~ed through his veins** егó тряслó от стрáха.

thriller [ˈθrɪlə(r)] *n.* (*coll., play or story*) приключéнческий/детекти́вный ромáн/фильм.

thrive [θraɪv] *v.i.* (*prosper*) процветáть (*impf.*); преуспевáть (*impf.*); (*grow vigorously*) разраст|áться, -и́сь.

throat [θrəʊt] *n.* гóрло; (*gullet*) гортáнь, глóтка; **he took me by the ~** он схвати́л меня́ за глóтку; **he tried to cut his ~** он пытáлся перерéзать себé гóрло; **you are cutting your own ~** (*fig.*) вы рýбите сук, на котóром сиди́те; **I have a sore ~** у меня́ боли́т гóрло; **he cleared his ~** он откáшлялся; **he tries to force his ideas down one's ~** он пытáется навязáть свои́ идéи; **don't jump down my ~!** не затыкáйте мне рот!; **the words stuck in my ~** словá застря́ли у меня́ в гóрле; **a lump came into my ~** комóк подступи́л у меня́ к гóрлу.

throaty [ˈθrəʊtɪ] *adj.* (*guttural*) гортáнный, хри́плый.

throb [θrɒb] *n.* биéние, пульсáция; (*fig.*) волнéние, трéпет.

v.i. (*beat*) стучáть (*impf.*); си́льно би́ться (*impf.*); (*fig., quiver*) трепетáть, пульси́ровать, волновáться (*all impf.*); **his heart ~bed** сéрдце егó (учащённо) би́лось; **his head ~bed** у негó гудéла головá.

throe [θrəʊ] *n.* сýдорога, спазм; **~s of childbirth** родовы́е мýки (*f. pl.*); **I was in the ~s of packing** я лихорáдочно упакóвывал вéщи.

thrombosis [θrɒmˈbəʊsɪs] *n.* тромбóз.

throne [θrəʊn] *n.* (*lit., fig.*) трон, престóл; **he came to the ~** он вступи́л на престóл; **he lost his ~** егó свéргли с престóла.

throng [θrɒŋ] *n.* толпá; толчея́.

v.i. толпи́ться (*impf.*).

throttle [ˈθrɒt(ə)l] *n.* дрóссель (*m.*); **at full ~** на пóлном газý; **he opened the ~** он прибáвил газ; он газанýл.

v.t. **1.** (*strangle*) души́ть, за-/у-. **2.** (*control with ~*) дроссели́ровать (*impf.*); **he ~d the engine back, down** он сбáвил газ; он сни́зил оборóты мотóра.

through [θruː] *adj.* **1.** прямóй; сквознóй; **~ traffic** сквознóе движéние; **no ~ road** (*as notice*) нет проéзда; **a ~ train** прямóй пóезд. **2.** (*var. pred. uses*): **his trousers were ~** (*threadbare*) **at the knee** егó брю́ки протёрлись на колéнях; **you must wait till I'm ~** (*finished*) **with the paper** вам придётся подождáть, покá я кóнчу читáть газéту; **she told him she was ~ with him** онá емý сказáла, что мéжду ни́ми всё кóнчено; **you're ~** (*connected*), **caller!** говори́те, абонéнт!

adv. (*from beginning to end; completely*) до концá; **I was there all ~** я был там до концá; **have you read it ~?** вы всё прочитáли?; **he is a Briton ~ and ~** он бритáнец до мóзга костéй; **you will get wet ~** вы промóкнете наскво́зь; **the whole night ~** всю ночь напролёт; (*all the way*) пря́мо; до мéста; **the train goes ~ to Paris** пóезд идёт пря́мо до Пари́жа.

prep. **1.** (*across; from end to end or side to side of*) чéрез+*a.*; (*esp. suggesting difficulty*) сквозь+*a.*; **he came ~ the door** он прошёл чéрез дверь; **visible ~ smoke** ви́димый сквозь дым; (*into, in at*) в+*a.*; **he looked ~ the telescope** он посмотрéл в телескóп; **look ~ the window!** посмотри́те в óкно!; **the stone went ~ the window** кáмень влетéл в окнó; **I could see him ~ the fog** я мог разглядéть егó в тумáне; **I don't like driving ~ fog** я не люблю́ éздить, когдá тумáн; **the thought went ~ my mind** у меня́ промелькнýла мысль; **the stone flew ~ the air** кáмень летéл по вóздуху; (*via*): **we travelled ~ Germany** мы éхали чéрез Гермáнию. **2.** (*from beginning to end of*): **he won't live ~ the night** он не доживёт до утрá. **3.** (*during*) в течéние +*g.*; **the dog doesn't bark ~ the day** днём собáка не лáет. **4.** (*US, up to and including*): **from Monday ~ Saturday** с понедéльника по суббóту (включи́тельно). **5.** (*over the area of*): **the news spread ~ the town** весть распространи́лась по гóроду. **6.** (*through the medium of*): **the order was passed ~ him** прикáз был пéредан чéрез негó; **I heard of you ~ your sister** я слы́шал о вас от вáшей сестры́; **~ the newspaper** чéрез газéту. **7.** (*from, because of*) из-за+*g.*; по+*d.*; **~ laziness** из-за лéни; **~ stupidity** по глýпости; **~ no fault of mine** не по моéй винé; **it was ~ you that I caught cold** из-зá вас я простуди́лась; **he succeeded ~ his own efforts** он добился своегó свои́ми си́лами; (*of desirable result*) благодаря́+*d.*

cpds. **~put** *n.* пропускнáя спосóбность; **~-way** *n.* (*US*) автострáда.

throughout [θruːˈaʊt] *adv.* (*in every part*) вездé; повсю́ду; (*in all respects*) во всех отношéниях; во всём.

prep. (*from end to end of*) чéрез+*a.*; **~ the country** по всей странé; (*for the duration of*): **it rained ~ the night** всю ночь шёл дождь.

throw [θrəʊ] *n.* **1.** (*act of ~ing*) бросáние, метáние; **~ of dice** бросáние костéй; (*distance ~n*) бросóк; **a stone's ~ from here** (*fig.*) отсю́да рукóй подáть. **2.** (*in wrestling*) бросóк; (*from horse*) падéние с лóшади.

v.t. **1.** бр|осáть, -óсить; кидáть, ки́нуть; швыр|я́ть, -нýть; **~ sth. 100 yards** брóсить что-н. нá сто я́рдов; **~ me my towel!** брóсьте/ки́ньте мне полотéнце!; **he threw the ball into the air** он подбрóсил мяч в вóздух; **don't ~ stones at the dog** не кидáйтесь камня́ми в собáку; **his horse threw him** лóшадь сбрóсила егó; **he was thrown to the ground by the explosion** егó брóсило на зéмлю от взры́ва; **the**

trees ~ shadows деревья отбрасывают тень; **he threw me an angry look** он бросил на меня сердитый взгляд; **he threw her a kiss** он послал ей воздушный поцелуй; **~ing a cloak over his shoulders ...** накинув плащ на плечи,...; **the news threw them into a panic** сообщение подвергло их в панику; **he was ~n (up)on his own resources** ему пришлось рассчитывать только на себя; **he was ~n off balance** (*lit.*) он потерял равновесие; (*fig.*) он пришёл в замешательство; **the news threw me** (*coll.*) известие меня потрясло; **this ~s light on the problem** это проливает свет на проблему; **he threw himself at me** он бросился на меня; **she threw herself at him** (*fig.*) она вешалась к нему на шею; **he threw himself into the job** он с головой ушёл в работу; **he threw his arms round her** он её обнял; **he threw himself on their mercy** он сдался им на милость. **2.** (*dice*) выбрасывать, выбросить. **3.** (*shed*): **the snake ~s its skin** змея меняет кожу (*or* линяет). **4.** (*shape, e.g. pots on wheel*) обраб|атывать, -отать (на гончарном круге). **5.** ~ (*reverse*) **a switch** повернуть (*pf.*) выключатель обратно. **6.** (*coll., have*) устр|аивать, -оить; **let's ~ a party** давайте устроим вечеринку; **he would ~ a fit if he knew** если бы он знал, он бы закатил истерику.

with advs.: ~ **about** *v.t.* (*scatter*) разбр|асывать, -осить; **don't ~ litter about** не сорите; не разбрасывайте мусор; (*lavish*): **he ~s his money about** он бросается деньгами; (*obtrude*): **he likes to ~ his weight about** он любит задаваться; ~ **across** *v.t.*: **he threw the rope across to me** он перебросил мне верёвку; ~ **away** *v.t.* (*discard*) выбрасывать, выбросить; **I have ~n the letter away** я выбросил письмо; (*forgo*) упус|кать, -тить; **don't ~ away this chance** не упустите эту возможность (*or* этот шанс); ~ **back** *v.t.* отбр|асывать, -осить назад; **he was ~n back by the explosion** его отбросило взрывом; **he threw his shoulders back** он распрямил плечи; **he was ~n back on his own resources** ему пришлось (снова) полагаться на собственные средства; ~ **down** *v.t.* бр|осать, -осить на землю; **he threw himself down** он бросился на землю; (*fig.*): **the enemy threw down their arms** враг сложил оружие; **the workmen threw down their tools** рабочие забастовали; ~ **in** *v.t.* вбр|асывать, -осить; (*fig.*) (*include*) доб|авлять, -авить; **I'll ~ in the cushions for a pound** за фунт я дам в придачу подушки; (*contribute*): **may I ~ in a suggestion?** можно мне внести предложение?; ~ **in one's lot with** соедин|ять, -ить свою судьбу с+*i.*; ~ **in one's hand** (*surrender*) сд|аваться, -аться; (*abandon contest*) выходить, выйти из игры; ~ **off** *v.t.*: **they threw off the yoke of slavery** они сбросили с себя ярмо рабства; **he threw off his clothes** он сбросил с себя одежду; **he threw off his pursuers** он избавился от своих преследователей; **I can't ~ this cold off** я никак не могу избавиться от этого насморка; **he could ~ off a poem in half an hour** он мог набросать стихотворение за полчаса; ~ **on** *v.t.*: **he threw on a coat** он набросил/накинул пальто (на плечи); ~ **open** *v.t.*: **the gardens were ~n open to the public** сады были открыты для публики; **he threw open the door** он распахнул дверь; ~ **out** *v.t.* выбросать; выбросить; (*proffer*) предл|агать, -ожить; **I threw out a remark** я отпустил замечание; **he threw out a challenge** он бросил вызов; (*put out*): **they threw out a feeler** они пустили пробный шар; **the tree threw out new leaves** дерево дало новые листья; (*build on*) пристр|аивать, -оить; **the college has ~n out a new wing** к колледжу пристроен новый флигель; (*reject*) отклон|ять, -ить; **the bill was ~n out** (*parl.*) законопроект отклонили; (*expel*) исключ|ать, -ить; выбрасывать, выбросить; **the club threw him out** его исключили из клуба; (*upset*) сб|ивать, -ить; путать (*impf.*); **you will ~ me out in my calculations** вы собьёте меня со счёта; ~ **over** *v.t.* (*lit.*) бр|осать, -осить; ~ **my jacket over!** бросьте мне пиджак!; (*abandon*) пок|идать, -инуть; ост|авлять, -авить; (*reject*) отказ|ываться, -аться от+*g.*; **she threw him over after a week** через неделю она его бросила; ~ **together** *v.t.* (*compile*) компилировать, с-; **a book hastily ~n together** наспех составленная книга; (*bring into contact*) соб|ирать, -рать вместе; **they were ~n together a lot** им много случалось сталкиваться; ~ **up** *v.t.* (*lit.*) подбр|асывать, -осить; вски|дывать, -нуть; **he threw the ball up** он подбросил мяч; (*raise*): **she threw up the window** она распахнула окно; **he threw up his hands in horror** он вскинул руки от ужаса; (*give up*): **he intends to ~ up his job** он собирается бросить работу; *v.i.* (*vomit*): **he threw up** его вырвало; **I felt like ~ing up** меня тошнило.

cpds. **~away** *adj.* выбрасываемый по использовании; **a ~away line** как бы невзначай оброненные слова; **~back** *n.* проявление атавизма; возврат к предкам.

thrower ['θrəʊə(r)] *n.* метатель (*m.*).

thrum [θrʌm] *v.i.* бренчать (*impf.*); **he ~med on the table** он барабанил пальцами по столу.

thrush[1] [θrʌʃ] *n.* (*bird*) дрозд.

thrush[2] [θrʌʃ] *n.* (*disease*) молочница; автозный стоматит.

thrust [θrʌst] *n.* толчок; (*mil.*) наступление, удар; (*in fencing*) укол; (*fig.*): **the cut and ~ of debate** пикировка в споре.

v.t. толк|ать, -нуть; **he ~ a note into my hand** он сунул мне в руку записку; **he ~ his hands into his pockets** он засунул руки в карманы; **he ~ his hand out** он выбросил руку вперёд; **he ~ his sword home** он вонзил меч по самую рукоятку; **they ~ their way through the crowd** они пробились сквозь толпу; (*fig., impose*) навяз|ывать, -ать.

v.i. толкаться (*impf.*); пробиваться (*impf.*); **he ~ past us** он растолкал нас и прошёл.

thruster ['θrʌstə(r)] *n.* напористый/пробивной человек.

Thucydides [θu:'sɪdɪ,di:z] *n.* Фукидид.

thud [θʌd] *n.* глухой звук; стук.

v.i. уд|аряться, -ариться со стуком.

thug [θʌg] *n.* бандит, головорез, хулиган.

thuggery ['θʌgərɪ] *n.* бандитизм, хулиганство.

thumb [θʌm] *n.* большой палец (руки); **~s up!** ладно!; хорош!; идёт!; добро!; **he was given the ~s up sign to begin** ему дали сигнал к началу; **he works by rule of ~** он работает кустарным способом (*or* на глазок); **he is completely under her ~** он у неё полностью под каблуком; **I'm all (fingers and) ~s** у меня руки как крюки.

v.t. **1.** (*turn over with ~*) перелист|ывать, -ать; **he ~ed over, through the pages** он перелистал страницы; **a well-~ed volume** замусоленный/захватанный том. **2.:** ~ **a lift** (*coll.*) «голосовать» (*impf.*); **he ~ed a lift in a lorry** он приехал на попутном грузовике. **3.:** ~ **one's nose at** показать (*pf.*) нос +*d.*

cpds. **~-index** *n.* буквенный указатель (*на переднем обрезе словаря и т.п.*); **~-mark** *n.* = **~-print**; **~nail** *n.* ноготь (*m.*) большого пальца; **~nail sketch** набросок; краткое описание; **~-print** *n.* отпечаток большого пальца; **~screw** *n.* тиск|и (*pl., g.* -ов) для больших пальцев (*орудие пыток*); **~-stall** *n.* напёрсток, напальчник; **~-tack** *n.* (*US*) кнопка.

thump [θʌmp] *n.* (*blow*) тяжёлый удар; (*noise*) глухой стук/шум.

v.t. бить (*impf.*); колотить (*impf.*); **he ~ed me on the back** он сильно ударил меня по спине; **she ~ed the cushion** она взбила подушку; **he was ~ing the (piano) keys** он колотил/барабанил по клавишам; **he can ~ out a tune** он может пробарабанить мотив.

v.i. биться (*impf.*); колотиться (*impf.*); **someone ~ed on the door** кто-то колотил в дверь; **my heart began to ~** у меня заколотилось сердце.

thumping ['θʌmpɪŋ] *adj.* & *adv.* (*coll.*) громадный, ужасающий; **a ~ lie** наглая ложь.

thunder ['θʌndə(r)] *n.* гром; **a peal, crash of ~** удар грома; **there is ~ in the air** в воздухе пахнет грозой; (*fig.*) грохот, гром; **the ~ of the waves** шум волн; **a ~ of applause** гром аплодисментов.

v.t. греметь, про-; **'Get out!' he ~ed** «убирайтесь отсюда!», прогремел он.

v.i. (*lit.*) греметь, громыхать, грохотать (*all impf.*); **it is ~ing** гром гремит; **it has been ~ing all day** весь день гремела гроза; (*fig.*): **he ~ed at the door** он колотил в дверь; **the train ~ed past** поезд с грохотом пронёсся мимо; **he ~ed against the Pope** он произносил громовые ре́чи про́тив па́пы ри́мского.

cpds. **~bolt** *n.* уда́р мо́лнии, гром; **~clap** *n.* уда́р гро́ма; **~cloud** *n.* грозова́я ту́ча; **~storm** *n.* гроза́; **~struck** *adj.* (*fig.*) как гро́мом поражённый; ошеломлённый.

thundering [ˈθʌndərɪŋ] *adj. & adv.* грома́дный; **a ~ nuisance** ужа́сная неприя́тность; **a ~ great fish** огро́мная ры́ба.

thunderous [ˈθʌndərəs] *adj.* (*loud*) громово́й; **~ applause** бу́рные аплодисме́нты.

thundery [ˈθʌndərɪ] *adj.*: **it is ~ weather** пого́да (пред)грозова́я.

thurible [ˈθjʊərɪb(ə)l] *n.* кади́ло.

Thursday [ˈθɜːzdeɪ, -dɪ] *n.* четве́рг; **Maundy T~** Страстно́й/Вели́кий Четве́рг.

thus [ðʌs] *adv.* (*in this way*) таки́м о́бразом; (*accordingly*) сле́довательно, таки́м о́бразом; (*to this extent*) насто́лько; **~ far and no farther** до сих пор и ни ша́гу да́льше.

thwack [θwæk] *n.* си́льный уда́р.

v.t. колошма́тить, от-; поро́ть, вы́-.

thwart[1] [θwɔːt] *n.* (*bench*) ба́нка, скамья́ (*гребцов в лодке*).

thwart[2] [θwɔːt] *v.t.* меша́ть, по- *+d.*; **~ s.o.'s plans** расстр|а́ивать, -о́ить чьи-н. пла́ны.

thy [ðaɪ] *adj.* (*arch.*) твой; **~self** себя́; **thou ~self** ты сам.

thyme [taɪm] *n.* тимья́н.

thyroid [ˈθaɪrɔɪd] *n.* (**~ gland**) щитови́дная железа́.

adj. щитови́дный.

tiara [tɪˈɑːrə] *n.* тиа́ра, диаде́ма.

Tiber [ˈtaɪbə(r)] *n.* Тибр.

Tibet [tɪˈbet] *n.* Тибе́т.

Tibetan [tɪˈbet(ə)n] *n.* тибе́т|ец (*fem.* -ка.).

adj. тибе́тский.

tibia [ˈtɪbɪə] *n.* большеберцо́вая кость.

tic [tɪk] *n.* тик.

tick[1] [tɪk] *n.* **1.** (*of clock etc.*) ти́канье; **~, tock** тик-та́к. **2.** (*coll., moment*) секу́нда; мину́та, миг; **just a ~!** одну́ секу́нду/мину́ту! **3.** (*checking mark*) га́лочка, пти́чка.

v.t. отм|еча́ть, -е́тить га́лочкой.

v.i. ти́кать (*impf.*); **what makes him ~?** (*coll.*) что им дви́жет?

with advs.: **the meter was ~ing away** счётчик продолжа́л рабо́тать; **she ~ed off the items as I read them out** я перечисля́л предме́ты, а она́ отмеча́ла га́лочками; **he got ~ed off** (*coll., reprimanded*) ему́ да́ли нагоня́й; **I left the engine ~ing over** я оста́вил мото́р на холосто́м ходу́.

tick[2] [tɪk] *n.* (*parasite*) клещ; (*insignificant pers.*) вошь; ме́лкая со́шка.

tick[3] [tɪk] *n.* (*coll., credit*) креди́т; **I got some groceries on ~** я купи́л ко́е-каки́е проду́кты в креди́т.

ticker [ˈtɪkə(r)] *n.* (*coll.*) (*US, teleprinter*) ти́ккер, телегра́фный аппара́т; (*watch*) час|ы́ (*pl., g.* -о́в); (*heart*) се́рдце.

cpd. **~-tape** *n.* серпанти́н из ти́ккерной ле́нты.

ticket [ˈtɪkɪt] *n.* (*for travel, seating etc.*) биле́т; **a return ~ to London** обра́тный биле́т до Ло́ндона; (*tag*) ярлы́к; **price ~** этике́тка с ценой; це́нник; (*US, list of election candidates*) спи́сок кандида́тов на вы́борах; (*printed notice of offence*) пове́стка в суд за наруше́ние; **he got a ~ for speeding** он получи́л штраф за превыше́ние ско́рости; (*var. uses*): **~ of leave** досро́чное освобожде́ние заключённого; **work one's ~** (*get discharge from services*) демобилизова́ться (*impf., pf.*); (*pay for passage by working on ship*) отраб|а́тывать, -о́тать свой прое́зд на корабле́; **that's the ~!** (*coll.*) вот э́то то, что на́до!

v.t. снаб|жа́ть, -ди́ть ярлыко́м/этике́ткой.

cpds. **~-collector** *n.* контролёр; **~-machine** *n.* биле́тный автома́т; **~-office** *n.* биле́тная ка́сса; **~-punch** *n.* компо́стер.

ticking [ˈtɪkɪŋ] *n.* (*fabric*) тик.

tickle [ˈtɪk(ə)l] *n.* щекота́ние; **she gave the baby a ~** она́ пощекота́ла ребёнка; **he felt a ~ in his throat** у него́ запершило в го́рле.

v.t. щекота́ть, по-; **~ trout** лови́ть, пойма́ть форе́ль рука́ми; (*fig., amuse*) смеши́ть, рас-; забавля́ть, позаба́вить; **it ~d my fancy** э́то дразни́ло моё воображе́ние; **I was ~d to death** (*or* **~d pink**) (*coll.*) я чуть не ло́пнул со́ смеху.

v.i. чеса́ться (*impf.*); **this blanket ~s** э́то одея́ло шерсти́т; **my nose ~s** у меня́ щеко́чет в носу́.

ticklish [ˈtɪklɪʃ] *adj.* (*sensitive to tickling*) боя́щийся щеко́тки; (*requiring careful handling*) делика́тный, щекотли́вый.

tidal [ˈtaɪd(ə)l] *adj.* свя́занный с прили́вом и отли́вом; **~ river** прили́во-отли́вная река́; **~ wave** прили́вная волна́; (*fig.*) волна́ увлече́ния; взрыв о́бщего чу́вства.

tidbit [ˈtɪdbɪt] = **titbit**

tiddler [ˈtɪdlə(r)] *n.* (*small fish*) ко́люшка.

tiddl(e)y [ˈtɪdlɪ] *adj.* (*tipsy*) «под мухо́й» (*sl.*); (*small, trifling*) ма́ленький, малю́сенький.

tiddl(e)y-winks [ˈtɪdlɪwɪŋks] *n.* игра́ в бло́шки.

tide [taɪd] *n.* морско́й прили́в (и отли́в); **high ~** по́лная вода́; вы́сшая то́чка прили́ва; **low ~** ма́лая вода́; ни́зшая то́чка прили́ва; **neap ~** квадрату́рный прили́в; **spring ~** сизиги́йный прили́в; **the ~ is coming in** начался́ прили́в; **the ~ has gone out** (*or* **is out**) сейча́с отли́в; (*fig.*) волна́, тече́ние; **the rising ~ of excitement** уси́ливающееся возбужде́ние; **it was the turn of the ~** э́то бы́ло переломным пу́нктом.

v.t.: **this will ~ me over till next month** благодаря́ э́тому я перебью́сь до сле́дующего ме́сяца.

cpds. **~-mark** *n.* отме́тка у́ровня по́лной воды́; **~way** *n.* ру́сло прили́ва.

tidiness [ˈtaɪdɪnɪs] *n.* аккура́тность, опря́тность.

tidings [ˈtaɪdɪŋz] *n.* (*liter. and joc.*) ве́сти (*f. pl.*), но́вости (*f. pl.*); **have you heard the glad ~?** вы слы́шали ра́достную весть?

tidy [ˈtaɪdɪ] *adj.* (*neat, orderly*) аккура́тный, опря́тный; (*of room etc.*) аккура́тно при́бранный; (*considerable*) поря́дочный, значи́тельный; **a ~ sum** прили́чная/кру́гленькая су́мма.

v.t. (*also* **~ up**) прив|оди́ть, -ести́ в поря́док; приб|ира́ть, -ра́ть.

v.i.: **~ up** нав|оди́ть, -ести́ поря́док; приб|ира́ться, -ра́ться.

tie [taɪ] *n.* **1.** (**neck ~**) га́лстук. **2.** (*part that fastens or connects*) скре́па; шнур; ле́нта. **3.** (*fig., bond*) у́з|ы (*pl., g.* —); **~s of friendship** у́зы дру́жбы; **family ~s** семе́йные у́зы. **4.** (*fig., restriction*) обу́за; тягота́; **don't you find your children a ~?** де́ти вас не (сли́шком) свя́зывают? **4.** (*mus.*) ли́га. **5.** (*equal score*) ра́вное число́ очко́в; **the match ended in a ~** матч зако́нчился вничью́; **in the event of a ~** при ра́вных результа́тах у проти́вников.

v.t. **1.** (*fasten*) свя́з|ывать, -а́ть; привя́з|ывать, -а́ть; **he was ~d to the mast** его́ привяза́ли к ма́чте; (*fig.*): **he is ~d to her apron-strings** он де́ржится за её ю́бку; **my hands are ~d** у меня́ свя́заны ру́ки; **~d house** дом, закреплённый за рабо́тником на срок его́ рабо́ты; (*public house*) бар, отпуска́ющий пи́во то́лько определённого заво́да. **2.** (*arrange in bow or knot*) перевя́з|ывать, -а́ть; завя́з|ывать, -а́ть; шнурова́ть, за-; **he learnt to ~ his shoe-laces** он научи́лся шнурова́ть боти́нки; **can you ~ a knot in this string?** вы мо́жете завяза́ть у́зел на э́той верёвке?

v.i. **1.** (*fasten*) завя́з|ываться, -а́ться; **does this sash ~ at the front?** э́тот по́яс завя́зывается спе́реди? **2.** (*make equal score*) равня́ть, с- счёт; игра́ть, сыгра́ть в ничью́; **we ~d with them for first place** мы подели́ли с ни́ми пе́рвое ме́сто; **the runners ~d** сопе́рники пришли́ к фи́нишу одновре́ме́нно.

with advs.: **~ back** *v.t.* подвя́з|ывать, -а́ть; **I ~d back the roses** я подвяза́л ро́зы; **she wore her hair ~d back** она́ зачёсывала во́лосы наза́д; **~ down** *v.t.* (*lit.*) привя́з|ывать, -а́ть; (*fig., restrict*) свя́з|ывать, -а́ть; **I don't want to ~ myself down to a date** я не хочу́ быть свя́занным определённой да́той; **~ in** *v.i.* соотве́тствовать (*impf.*); согласо́в|ываться, -а́ться; **this ~s in with what I was saying** э́то согласу́ется с тем, что я говори́л; **~ on** *v.t.* привя́з|ывать, -а́ть; **~ up** *v.t.* (*lit.*) привя́з|ывать, -а́ть; свя́з|ывать, -а́ть; **the dog was ~d up** соба́ка была́ на при́вязи; **can you ~ up this parcel?** вы мо́жете перевяза́ть э́ту посы́лку?; **your shoe needs tying up** вам на́до затяну́ть шнуро́к на боти́нке; (*fig.*): **his firm is ~d up with the Ministry** его́ фи́рма свя́зана с министе́рством; **I'm rather ~d up this week** я дово́льно си́льно за́нят на э́той неде́ле; **his capital is ~d up** его́ капита́л заморо́жен.

cpds. **~-breaker** *n.* реша́ющая игра́; **~-on** *adj.*: **~-on label** привязно́й ярлы́к; **~pin** *n.* була́вка для га́лстука; **~-up** *n.* (*link*) связь; (*merger*) слия́ние.

tier [tɪə(r)] *n.* ряд; я́рус; **a wedding-cake with three ~s** трёхсло́йный сва́дебный торт.

Tierra del Fuego [tɪ'erə del 'fweɪɡəʊ] *n.* О́гненная Земля́.

tiff [tɪf] *n.* размо́лвка.

tiger ['taɪɡə(r)] *n.* тигр; (*fig.*): **he is a ~ for work** он рабо́тает как одержи́мый.

cpds. **~-cat** *n.* су́мчатая куни́ца; **~-cub** *n.* тигрёнок; **~-moth** *n.* ба́бочка-медве́дица.

tigerish ['taɪɡərɪʃ] *adj.* свире́пый, кровожа́дный.

tight [taɪt] *adj.* **1.** (*closely fixed or fitting*) те́сный; облега́ющий; **the dress was a ~ fit** пла́тье бы́ло те́сно; **it was a ~ squeeze getting into the car** мы е́ле уме́сти́лись в маши́не; **this knot is very ~** э́тот у́зел о́чень туго́й; **the cork is very ~** про́бка пло́тно при́гнано; **my shoes are too ~** мои́ ту́фли жмут. **2.** (*packed as full as possible*) наби́тый. **3.** (*taut*) стро́гий; **keep a ~ rein on your spending** вы должны́ стро́го следи́ть за те́м, что́бы не тра́тить ли́шнего. **4.** (*under pressure*; *difficult*) тру́дный; тяжёлый; **in a ~ corner** в тру́дном положе́нии; **I have a ~ schedule** у меня́ жёсткое расписа́ние. **5.** (*miserly*) прижи́мистый, скупо́й; **he is very ~ with his money** он о́чень скуп. **6.** (*in short supply*) тру́дно добыва́емый; **money is ~** с деньга́ми ту́го/тугова́то. **7.** (*evenly contested*): **a ~ race** состяза́ние ра́вных. **8.** (*coll.*, *drunk*) навеселе́; **he went out and got ~** он пошёл и напи́лся.

adv. кре́пко; пло́тно; **hold ~!** держи́тесь кре́пко!; **shut your eyes ~!** кре́пко зажму́рьте глаза́!; **the door was ~ shut** дверь была́ пло́тно закры́та; **I sat ~ and waited** я стоя́л на своём и выжида́л.

cpds. **~-fisted** *adj.* скупо́й, прижи́мистый; **~(ly)-fitting** *adj.* пло́тно облега́ющий; **~-lipped** *adj.* (*lit.*) с поджа́тыми губа́ми; (*fig.*, *secretive*) скры́тный; **~rope** *n.* натя́нутый кана́т; **he is walking a ~rope** (*fig.*) он хо́дит по острию́ ножа́; **~rope-walker** *n.* канатохо́дец; **~wad** *n.* скупе́ц.

tighten ['taɪt(ə)n] *v.t.* (*also* **~ up**) сжима́ть (*impf.*); закрепля́ть (*impf.*); **the screws need ~ing (up)** на́до затяну́ть болты́; **we must ~ our belts** (*fig.*) мы должны́ поту́же затяну́ть пояса́; нам придётся пойти́ на лише́ния; **the rules were ~ed** пра́вила ста́ли стро́же.

tightness ['taɪtnɪs] *n.* напряжённость; стеснённость.

tights [taɪts] *n.* колго́т|ки (*pl.*, *g.* -ок), трико́ (*indecl.*).

tigress ['taɪɡrɪs] *n.* тигри́ца.

Tigris ['taɪɡrɪs] *n.* Тигр.

tike [taɪk] = **tyke**

tilde ['tɪldə] *n.* ти́льда.

tile [taɪl] *n.* (*for roof*) черепи́ца; **he was (out) on the ~s last night** (*sl.*) он вчера́ кути́л; (*decorative*, *for wall etc.*) ка́фель (*m.*), пли́тка, изразе́ц.

v.t. крыть, по- черепи́цей/ка́фелем.

till[1] [tɪl] *n.* ка́сса.

till[2] [tɪl] *v.t.*: **~ the ground** обраба́тывать (*impf.*) зе́млю.

till[3] [tɪl] (*see also* **until**) *prep.* до+*g.*; **~ then** до того́ вре́мени; **he will not come ~ after dinner** он придёт то́лько по́сле у́жина; **I never saw him ~ now** я его́ впервы́е ви́жу.

conj. пока́… (не); до тех пор, пока́; **~ we meet again!** до сле́дующей встре́чи!; **let's wait ~ the rain stops** дава́йте переждём дождь; **don't go ~ I come back** не уходи́те, пока́ я не верну́сь (*or*, *coll.*, пока́ я верну́сь); **it was not ~ he spoke that I saw him** то́лько когда́ он заговори́л, я уви́дел его́; **not ~ Tuesday** не ра́ньше вто́рника.

tillage ['tɪlɪdʒ] *n.* (*ploughing*) обрабо́тка по́чвы; (*ploughed land*) па́шня.

tiller[1] ['tɪlə(r)] *n.* (*for steering*) ру́мпель (*m.*); рукоя́тка.

tiller[2] ['tɪlə(r)] n. (*of the soil*) земледе́лец.

tilt [tɪlt] *n.* **1.** (*sloping position*) накло́н, склон; **the table is on the ~** стол стои́т кри́во. **2.** (*attack*): **he came at me full ~** он я́ростно набро́сился на меня́.

v.t. наклон|я́ть, -и́ть; **he ~ed the chair back** он наклони́л стул наза́д; **he ~ed his cap backwards** он заломи́л ша́пку (на заты́лок).

v.i. **1.** (*slope*) наклон|я́ться, -и́ться; **the table was ~ing dangerously** стол опа́сно накрени́лся. **2.:** **~ at** (*attack*) боро́ться/сража́ться (*both impf.*) с+*i.*; **his book ~ed at present-day manners** в свое́й кни́ге он напада́л на совреме́нные нра́вы; **he is ~ing at windmills** он вою́ет с ветряны́ми ме́льницами.

cpd. **~yard** *n.* аре́на для турни́ров, риста́лище.

tilth [tɪlθ] *n.* (*tillage*) обрабо́тка по́чвы, па́хота; (*depth of soil*) вспа́ханный слой земли́.

timber ['tɪmbə(r)] *n.* (*substance*) лесоматериа́л, древеси́на; (*trees grown for felling*) строево́й лес; (*beam of roof*, *ship etc.*) бревно́.

cpd. **~-yard** *n.* дровяно́й склад.

timbre ['tæmbə(r), 'tæbrə] *n.* тембр.

timbrel ['tɪmbr(ə)l] *n.* тамбури́н.

time [taɪm] *n.* **1.** вре́мя (*nt.*); **we are working against ~** мы стара́емся ко́нчить рабо́ту в срок, хотя́ вре́мени в обре́з; **for all ~** навсегда́; **from the beginning of ~** испоко́н веко́в; с сотворе́ния ми́ра; **in (the) course of ~, with ~** с тече́нием вре́мени; **to the end of ~** ве́чно; **(Old) Father T~** де́душка-вре́мя; **~ flies** вре́мя бежи́т; **~ hangs heavy on my hands** вре́мя тя́нется ме́дленно; **kill ~** уб|ива́ть, -и́ть вре́мя; **~ has passed him by** жизнь прошла́ ми́мо его́; **~ is running out** срок истека́ет; **~ is on our side** вре́мя рабо́тает на нас; **~ will tell** вре́мя пока́жет; **it has stood the test of ~** э́то вы́держало испыта́ние вре́менем; **~ waits for no man** вре́мя не ждёт. **2.** (*system of measurement*): **Greenwich Mean T~** гринви́чское сре́днее вре́мя; **local ~** ме́стное вре́мя. **3.** (*duration*, *period*, *opportunity*): **after a ~** че́рез не́которое вре́мя; **all the ~** всегда́, постоя́нно; **you had all the ~ in the world to do it** у вас была́ у́йма вре́мени э́то сде́лать; **he has done ~** (*coll.*, *been in prison*) он своё отсиде́л; **he stayed for a ~** он про́был не́которое вре́мя; **I have been here for some ~** я здесь уже́ дово́льно до́лго; **he tried to gain ~** он пыта́лся вы́играть вре́мя; **given ~, he will succeed** дай срок, и он добьётся успе́ха; **all in good ~** всему́ своё вре́мя; **in good ~** заблаговре́менно; **I could do it in half the ~** я бы мог э́то сде́лать вдво́е быстре́е; **half the ~ he was asleep** он спал почти́ всё вре́мя; **I have no ~ for him** (*fig.*) мне с ним не́чего де́лать; **that is all I have ~ for** у меня́ нет ни на что бо́льше вре́мени; **I have no ~ to lose** мне нельзя́ теря́ть ни мину́ты; **I shall get used to it in ~** со вре́менем я к э́тому привы́кну; **in no ~ (at all)** момента́льно; **I could do it in no ~** я бы мог э́то сде́лать в два счёта; **do it in your own ~** сде́лайте э́то в нерабо́чее вре́мя; **I haven't seen him for a long ~** я его́ давно́ не ви́дел; **long ~ no see!** (*coll.*) ско́лько лет, ско́лько зим!; **he is a long ~ coming** что-то его́ до́лго нет; **a long ~ ago** давно́; **you must make ~ to do the job** вам придётся найти́ вре́мя, что́бы сде́лать э́ту рабо́ту; **make up for lost ~** нав|ёрстывать, -ерста́ть упу́щенное/потеря́нное вре́мя; **he lost no ~ in reading the book** он то́тчас же при́нялся чита́ть э́ту кни́гу; **pass the ~** пров|оди́ть, -ести́ вре́мя; **play for ~** оття́|гивать, -ну́ть вре́мя; **I am pressed for ~** у меня́ ма́ло вре́мени; меня́ поджима́ют сро́ки; **for some ~ now** с не́которого вре́мени; **it will he some ~ before he is well** он ещё не так ско́ро попра́вится; **we shall need some ~ to pack** нам потре́буется не́которое вре́мя на сбо́ры; **in one's spare ~** на досу́ге; **take your ~!** не торопи́тесь!; **it will take ~** э́то займёт вре́мя; **he asked for ~ off** он отпроси́лся с рабо́ты; **I want some ~ to myself** мне хо́чется побы́ть одному́; **your ~ is up** ва́ше вре́мя истекло́; **what a waste of ~!** кака́я пуста́я тра́та вре́мени!; **~ and motion study** хронометра́ж движе́ний рабо́чего. **4.** (*life-span*) пери́од жи́зни; век; **it will last my ~ (out)** э́того на мой век хва́тит; **if I had my ~ over again** е́сли бы мо́жно бы́ло нача́ть жизнь сно́ва. **5.** (*measuring progress or speed*): **this watch keeps good ~** э́ти часы́ хорошо́ иду́т; **what was his ~ for the race?** за ско́лько он прошёл/пробежа́л диста́нцию?; **he finished in record ~** он поби́л реко́рд. **6.** (*experience*): **he gave us a bad ~** он доста́вил нам неприя́тность; **they gave us a good ~** они́ нас хорошо́ при́няли; **have a good ~!** повесели́тесь как сле́дует!; **we had the ~ of our lives** мы отли́чно провели́ вре́мя; мы отли́чно повесели́лись; **I had a trying ~** я пережи́л тру́дный пери́од; **what sort of (a) ~ did you have?** вы хорошо́ провели́ вре́мя? **7.** (*~ of day or night*) час; **what's the ~?** кото́рый час?; **what ~ do you make it?** ско́лько на ва́ших (часа́х)?; **the ~ is 8 o'clock** сейча́с 8 часо́в; **can he tell the ~ yet?** он уже́ понима́ет вре́мя по часа́м?; **we passed the ~ of day** (*greeted each other*) мы поздоро́вались; **at that ~** (*hour*) в э́тот час; **at what ~?** в кото́ром часу́?; **what are you doing here at this ~ of night?** что вы тут де́лаете в тако́е вре́мя но́чи?; **what ~ do you go to bed?** в кото́ром часу́ вы ложи́тесь спать? **8.** (*moment*): **I was away at the ~** меня́ тогда́ (*or* в то вре́мя) не́ было; **at the right ~** в ну́жный/подходя́щий моме́нт; **at that ~** в то вре́мя; **at the same ~** (*simultaneously*) в то же (са́мое) вре́мя; (*notwithstanding*) тем не ме́нее; вме́сте с тем; **at ~s** иногда́, времена́ми; **at all ~s** всегда́; во всех слу́чаях; **at different ~s** в ра́зное вре́мя; **at no ~** никогда́; **at other ~s** в други́х слу́чаях; **you've finished, and not before ~!** вы наконе́ц-то ко́нчили!; **before ~** заблаговре́менно, преждевре́менно; **behind ~** с опозда́нием; **by the ~ I got back he had gone** (к тому́ вре́мени,) когда́ я верну́лся, его́ уже́ не́ было; **the ~ was ripe for change** наступи́ло вре́мя для переме́н; **shall we fix a ~?** дава́йте назна́чим вре́мя!; **from ~ to ~** иногда́, вре́мя от вре́мени; **it's ~ for bed** пора́ спать; **it's ~ I went** мне пора́ идти́; **T~, gentlemen, please!** ≃ закрыва́ем!; **~'s up** вре́мя истекло́; пора́ конча́ть; **there's a ~ for everything** всему́ своё вре́мя; **will he arrive in ~ for dinner?** он поспе́ет к у́жину?; **he got there in the nick of ~** он подоспе́л туда́ в са́мую после́днюю мину́ту; **there's no ~ like the present** ≃ лови́ моме́нт; по́льзуйся слу́чаем; **she is near her ~** (*to give birth*) ей ско́ро рожа́ть; она́ на сно́сях; **the train was on ~** по́езд пришёл во́время; **are the trains running to ~?** поезда́ хо́дят (то́чно) по расписа́нию? **9.** (*instance, occasion*) раз; **~ and (~) again; ~ after ~** сно́ва и сно́ва; ты́сячу раз; раз за ра́зом; **I've told you ~ and again** ско́лько раз я вам говори́л!; кото́рый раз я вам говорю́!; **~s without number** несчётное число́ раз; **several ~s over** мно́го раз; ты́сячу раз; **nine ~s out of ten** в девяти́ слу́чаях из десяти́; **six ~s running (*or* in a row)** шесть раз подря́д; **the ~ before** в про́шлый раз; **at one ~ or another** неоднокра́тно; **another ~** когда́-то; когда́-нибу́дь; в друго́й раз; **one at a ~!** по одному́; не все сра́зу!; **every ~ I go out it rains** ка́ждый раз, когда́ я выхожу́, идёт дождь; **give me Italian music every ~** италья́нскую му́зыку я предпочту́ любо́й друго́й; **the first ~ I saw him** когда́ я уви́дел его́ впервы́е (*or* в пе́рвый раз); **it's the first ~ we've met** э́то на́ша пе́рвая встре́ча; **it's the last ~ I'll lend him money** я никогда́ бо́льше не дам ему́ де́нег взаймы́; **for the last ~, will you shut up?** я тебе́ в после́дний раз говорю́ — заткни́сь!/замолчи́!; **many a ~, many ~s** мно́го раз, ча́сто, часте́нько; **next ~** в сле́дующий раз; **there may not be a next ~** второ́го слу́чая мо́жет не предста́виться; **a second oath, this ~ to Tsar Nicholas** втора́я прися́га, тепе́рь уже́ царю́ Никола́ю; **I'll let you off this ~** на сей раз я вас проща́ю. **10.** (*in multiplication*): **6 ~s 2 is 12** 6 (умно́жить) на 2 — 12; ше́стью два — двена́дцать; **ten ~s as easy** в де́сять раз ле́гче. **11.** (*period, age*) времена́ (*nt. pl.*), эпо́ха; **in the ~ of Queen Elizabeth** в эпо́ху короле́вы Елизаве́ты, в Елизаветинские времена́; **in olden ~s** в ста́рые времена́; в ста́рое вре́мя; в дре́вности; во вре́мя о́но; **at one ~** одно́ вре́мя, когда́-то, не́когда; **as a thinker he was ahead of his ~** как мысли́тель он опереди́л свою́ эпо́ху; **he was born before his ~** он роди́лся сли́шком ра́но; **that was before my ~** э́то бы́ло до меня́; **at my ~ of life** в моём во́зрасте. **12.** (*circumstances*): **we have seen good and bad ~s** мы пережи́ли и хоро́шее и плохо́е; **~s are not what they were** не те времена́ пошли́, что ра́ньше; **she is behind the ~s** она́ отста́ла от жи́зни; **he is irritating at the best of ~s** он раздража́ет да́же в лу́чшие мину́ты. **13.** (*mus.*) такт, ритм; **in quick ~** в бы́стром те́мпе; **in double-quick ~** (*fig.*) в два счёта; **you are not keeping ~** вы сбива́етесь с ри́тма; **they clapped in ~ with the music** они́ хло́пали в такт му́зыке; **beat ~** (*as conductor*) дирижи́ровать (*impf.*); (*with foot etc.*) отбива́ть (*impf.*) такт (*ногой и т.п.*); **common ~** четырёхча́стный та́ктовый разме́р; **in waltz ~** в те́мпе ва́льса; **mark ~** (*lit.*) марширова́ть (*impf.*) на ме́сте; (*fig.*) топта́ться (*impf.*) на ме́сте; **the job is marking ~** рабо́та застря́ла.

v.t. **1.** (*do at a chosen ~*) выбира́ть, вы́брать вре́мя +*g.*; рассчи́т|ывать, -а́ть вре́мя +*g.*; **you must ~ your blows carefully** вы должны́ осторо́жно выбира́ть моме́нт для нанесе́ния уда́ра; **his remarks were ill ~d** его́ замеча́ния бы́ли некста́ти. **2.** (*measure ~ of or for*) зас|ека́ть, -е́чь вре́мя +*g.*; отм|еча́ть, -е́тить по часа́м; хронометри́ровать (*impf., pf.*); **they ~d him over the mile** они́ засекли́ вре́мя, за кото́рое он пробежа́л одну́ ми́лю. **3.** (*schedule*): **the train was ~d to leave at 6** по́езд до́лжен был отойти́ в 6 часо́в.

cpds. **~-bomb** *n.* бо́мба заме́дленного де́йствия; **~-card, ~-sheet** *nn.* хронока́рта; **~-expired** *adj.* вы́служивший срок; **~-exposure** *n.* вы́держка; **~-fuse** *n.* дистанцио́нный взрыва́тель; **~-honoured** *adj.* освящённый века́ми; **~-keeper** *n.* (*pers.*) та́бельщик, хронометри́ст; **he is a good ~-keeper** (*at work*) он то́чно прихо́дит на рабо́ту; **this watch is a good ~-keeper** э́ти часы́ хорошо́ иду́т; **~-lag** *n.* запа́здывание; **~-limit** *n.* преде́льный срок; **~piece** *n.* час|ы́ (*pl., g.* -о́в), хроно́метр; **~-saving** *n.* эконо́мия вре́мени; *adj.* эконо́мящий вре́мя; **~-server** *n.* приспособле́нец, временщи́к; **~-serving** *n.* приспособле́нчество; *adj.* приспоса́бливающийся; **~-sheet** *n.* = **~-card; ~-signal** *n.* сигна́л вре́мени; **~-study** *n.* хронометра́ж; **~-switch** *n.* переключа́тель (*m.*) вре́мени; **~-table** *n.* расписа́ние; гра́фик; **~-wasting** *adj.* напра́сный, ли́шний; **~-work** *n.* почасова́я рабо́та; **~-worn** *adj.* обветша́лый.

timeless ['taɪmlɪs] *adj.* (*eternal*) ве́чный, непреходя́щий; (*unmarked by time*) неподвла́стный вре́мени, неустарева́ющий.

timeliness ['taɪmlɪnɪs] *n.* своевре́менность.

timely ['taɪmlɪ] *adj.* своевре́менный.

timer ['taɪmə(r)] *n.* (*pers.*) хронометражи́ст; (*device*) отме́тчик вре́мени, та́ймер.

timid ['tɪmɪd] *adj.* ро́бкий, пугли́вый; (*shy*) засте́нчивый.

timid|ity [ˌtɪ'mɪdɪtɪ], **-ness** ['tɪmɪdnɪs] *nn.* ро́бость, пугли́вость; засте́нчивость.

timing ['taɪmɪŋ] *n.* вы́бор (наибо́лее подходя́щего/удо́бного) вре́мени; распределе́ние вре́мени; плани́рование; темп; хронометра́ж.

timorous ['tɪmərəs] *adj.* боязли́вый, пугли́вый.

timorousness ['tɪmərəsnɪs] *n.* боязли́вость, пугли́вость.

timpani, tympani ['tɪmpənɪ] *n.* лита́вры (*f. pl.*)

timpanist, tympanist ['tɪmpənɪst] *n.* литаври́ст.

tin [tɪn] *n.* **1.** (*metal*) о́лово; (*attr.*) оловя́нный; **~ can** консе́рвная ба́нка; **~ hat** (*coll.*) стально́й шлем; **little ~ god** (*coll.*) «гли́няный и́дол»; ду́тая величина́. **2.** (*container, can*) жестя́нка, консе́рвная ба́нка; **~ of beans** ба́нка фасо́ли; **they eat out of ~s** они́ живу́т на консе́рвах. **3.** (*sl., money*) «ба́шл|и» (*pl., g.* -ей).

v.t. **1.** (*coat with ~*) покр|ыва́ть, -ы́ть о́ловом. **2.** (*pack in ~s*) консерви́ровать (*impf.*); **~ned goods** консерви́рованные проду́кты; консе́рв|ы (*pl., g.* -ов); **~ned fish** ры́бные консе́рвы.

cpds. **~foil** *n.* оловя́нная фо́льга; **~-opener** *n.* консе́рвный нож; **~-plate** *n.* бе́лая жесть; **~pot** *adj.* (*coll.*) дешёвый; никуды́шный; **a ~pot dictator** ме́лкий дикта́тор; **~smith** *n.* луди́льщик; жестя́нщик; **~-tack** *n.* лужёный гво́здик.

tincture ['tɪŋktjə(r), -tʃə(r)] *n.* раство́р; тинкту́ра; (*fig., slight flavour*) при́вкус, налёт.

tinder ['tɪndə(r)] *n.* трут.

cpd. **~-box** *n.* тру́тница.

tine [taɪn] *n.* (*of fork*) зубе́ц; (*of antler*) о́стрый отро́сток.

ting [tɪŋ] *n.* звон; дзи́ньканье.
v.i. звене́ть (*impf.*); дзи́нькать (*impf.*).

tinge [tɪndʒ] *n.* лёгкая окра́ска, отте́нок; (*fig.*) при́месь, налёт, отте́нок.
v.t. слегка́ окра́|шивать, -сить; (*fig.*): **her voice was ~d with regret** в её го́лосе звуча́ло лёгкое сожале́ние.

tingl|e ['tɪŋg(ə)l], **-ing** ['tɪŋglɪŋ] *nn.* пощи́пывание; тре́пет.
v.i.: **the slap made his hand ~e** его́ рука́ зуде́ла от уда́ра; **they were ~ing with excitement** они́ дрожа́ли от возбужде́ния.

tinker ['tɪŋkə(r)] *n.* ме́дник; луди́льщик; **I don't give a ~'s curse** мне наплева́ть; а мне до ла́мпочки (*coll.*).
v.i. (*meddle etc.*) вози́ться (*impf.*) (*с чем*); ковыря́ться (*impf.*) (*в чём*).

tinkle ['tɪŋk(ə)l] *n.* (*sound*) звон; звя́канье; (*coll.*, *telephone call*) телефо́нный звоно́к; **give me a ~ some time** звя́кните мне ка́к-нибу́дь.
v.t.: **he ~d the bell** он зазвони́л в колоко́льчик.
v.i.: **the bell ~d** колоко́льчик зазвене́л.

tinnitus [tɪ'naɪtəs] *n.* шум в уша́х.

tinny ['tɪnɪ] *adj.* (*of sound*) металли́ческий, жестяно́й; (*of taste*) металли́ческий.

tinsel ['tɪns(ə)l] *n.* блёст|ки (*pl.*, *g.* -ок); мишура́ (*also fig.*).
adj. (*fig.*) мишу́рный.

tint [tɪnt] *n.* отте́нок; тон; **autumn ~s** осе́нние кра́ски (*f. pl.*)/цвета́/тона́.
v.t.: **~ed glasses** тёмные очки́; **she ~s her hair** она́ подкра́шивает во́лосы.

tintinnabulation [,tɪntɪ,næbjʊ'leɪʃ(ə)n] *n.* звон колоколо́в.

tiny ['taɪnɪ] *adj.* кро́шечный.

tip[1] [tɪp] *n.* (*pointed end*) ко́нчик; верху́шка; **~ of the iceberg** (*lit.*, *fig.*) верху́шка а́йсберга; **use only the ~ of the brush** каса́йтесь одни́м ко́нчиком ки́сти; **the ~s of my fingers are freezing** у меня́ мёрзнут ко́нчики па́льцев; **I had his name on the ~ of my tongue** его́ и́мя верте́лось у меня́ на языке́.
v.t.: **arrows ~ped with bronze** стре́лы, уснащённые ме́дными наконе́чниками; **~ped cigarettes** папиро́сы с фи́льтром.
cpds. **~toe** *n.*: **on ~toe(s)** на цы́почках; (*fig.*): **on ~toe with excitement** вне себя́ от волне́ния; *v.i.* ходи́ть (*indet.*) на цы́почках; **she ~toed out of the room** она́ вы́шла из ко́мнаты на цы́почках; **~-top** *adj.* первокла́ссный; **in ~-top condition** в прекра́сном/превосхо́дном состоя́нии.

tip[2] [tɪp] *n.* (*dumping-ground*) сва́лка.
v.t. **1.** (*strike lightly*) зад|ева́ть, -е́ть; **he ~ped the ball** он сре́зал мяч; **a ~-and-run raid** внеза́пный/молниено́сный налёт; **he ~ped his hat to me** он приве́тствовал меня́, поднеся́ ру́ку к шля́пе. **2.** (*tilt*) наклон|я́ть, -и́ть; **he ~s the scale at 12 stone** он ве́сит (*or* тя́нет на) 168 фу́нтов; **this will ~ the scale** (*fig.*) **in their favour** э́то склони́т ча́шу весо́в в их по́льзу; **a ~ping lorry** самосва́л. **3.** (*overturn*, *empty*) выва́ливать, вы́валить; опорожн|я́ть, -и́ть; **~ the rubbish into the bin!** вы́валите му́сор в я́щик!
with advs.: **~ out** *v.t.* выва́ливать, вы́валить; **the car overturned and the occupants were ~ped out** маши́на переверну́лась и пассажи́ры вы́валились; **~ over** *v.t. & i.* опроки́|дывать(ся), -нуть(ся); **he ~ped the cup over** он опроки́нул ча́шку; **the boat ~ped over** ло́дка переверну́лась; **~ up** *v.t. & i.* наклон|я́ть(ся), -и́ть(ся); **he ~ped his plate up** он наклони́л таре́лку.
cpds. **~-cart** *n.* опроки́дывающаяся теле́жка; **~-up** *adj.*: **a ~-up seat** откидно́е сиде́ние.

tip[3] [tɪp] *n.* **1.** (*piece of advice*, *recommendation*) сове́т, намёк; **shall I give you a ~?** хоти́те сове́т?; **take my ~ and stay at home!** послу́шайте меня́ и сиди́те до́ма! **2.** (*gratuity*) чаев|ы́е (*pl.*, *g.* -ы́х); **I gave the porter a ~** я дал носи́льщику на чай.
v.t. **1.** (*coll.*, *give*): **~ me the wink when you're ready** да́йте мне знак, когда́ вы бу́дете гото́вы. **2.** (*mention as likely winner*): **he always ~ped the winner** он всегда́ уга́дывал победи́теля; **the horse was ~ped to win** большинство́ ста́вило на э́ту ло́шадь. **3.** (*remunerate*) да|ва́ть, -ть на чай +*d.*; **the driver expects to be ~ped** шофёр рассчи́тывает на чаевы́е; **'no ~ping allowed'** «чаевы́е запрещены́».
with adv.: **~ off** (*coll.*) предупре|жда́ть, -ди́ть.
cpd. **~-off** *n.*: **the police had a ~-off** поли́ции настуча́ли (*coll.*).

tipper[1] ['tɪpə(r)] *n.* (*vehicle*) самосва́л.

tipper[2] ['tɪpə(r)] *n.*: **he is a generous ~** он ще́дро раздаёт чаевы́е.

tippet ['tɪpɪt] *n.* (*woman's*) мехова́я пелери́на/наки́дка; (*official's*) паланти́н.

tipple ['tɪp(ə)l] *n.* питьё, напи́ток.
v.i. выпива́ть (*impf.*).

tippler ['tɪplə(r)] *n.* пьянчу́жка (*c.g.*).

tipsiness ['tɪpsɪnɪs] *n.* лёгкое опьяне́ние.

tipster ['tɪpstə(r)] *n.* (*at races*) «жучо́к»; (*informer*) осведоми́тель (*m.*).

tipsy ['tɪpsɪ] *adj.* подвы́пивший, навеселе́, под хмелько́м.

tirade [taɪ'reɪd, tɪ-] *n.* тира́да.

tire[1] ['taɪə(r)] (*US*) = **tyre**

tire[2] ['taɪə(r)] *v.t.* утом|ля́ть, -и́ть; надо|еда́ть, -е́сть +*d.*; **the walk ~d me** я уста́л от прогу́лки; **I'm ~d out** я совсе́м вы́мотан; **you will soon get ~d of him** он вам ско́ро надое́ст; **I had a tiring day** у меня́ был тру́дный день; **I am ~d of being idle** мне прие́лась пра́здность.
v.i. утом|ля́ться, -и́ться; уст|ава́ть, -а́ть; **she ~s easily** она́ бы́стро устаёт; **I shall never ~ of that music** э́та му́зыка мне никогда́ не надое́ст.

tiredness ['taɪədnɪs] *n.* уста́лость.

tireless ['taɪəlɪs] *adj.* неутоми́мый.

tiresome ['taɪəsəm] *adj.* надое́дливый, ну́дный.

tiro, tyro ['taɪə,rəʊ] *n.* новичо́к.

Tirol ['tɪrəl] = **Tyrol**

tissue ['tɪʃuː, 'tɪsjuː] *n.* **1.** (*text.*, *biol.*) ткань; **~ paper** то́нкая обёрточная бума́га; папиро́сная бума́га; **face ~** бума́жная салфе́тка; **toilet ~** туале́тная бума́га. **2.** (*fig.*) паути́на; сеть; **a ~ of lies** паути́на лжи.

tit[1] [tɪt] *n.* (*bird*) сини́ца.

tit[2] [tɪt] *n.* (*nipple*, *breast*) си́ська, ти́тька (*sl.*).

tit[3] [tɪt] *n.*: **~ for tat** «зуб за́ зуб».

Titan ['taɪt(ə)n] *n.* (*myth.*) Тита́н; (*fig.*) тита́н.

titanic [taɪ'tænɪk, tɪ-] *adj.* (*fig.*) титани́ческий, колосса́льный.

titanium [taɪ'teɪnɪəm, tɪ-] *n.* тита́н.

titbit ['tɪtbɪt] (*US* **tidbit**) *n.* ла́комый кусо́чек; (*fig.*): **a ~ of news** пика́нтная но́вость.

titch [tɪtʃ] *n.* коротышка, недоро́сток.

titchy ['tɪtʃɪ] *adj.* низкоро́слый.

tithe [taɪð] *n.* (*tax*) десяти́на; (*tenth part*) деся́тая часть.

titillate ['tɪtɪ,leɪt] *v.t.* щекота́ть (*impf.*); прия́тно возбу|жда́ть, -ди́ть.

titillation [,tɪtɪ'leɪʃ(ə)n] *n.* прия́тное возбужде́ние.

titivate, tittivate ['tɪtɪ,veɪt] *v.i.* прихора́шиваться (*impf.*); наря|жа́ться, -ди́ться.

title ['taɪt(ə)l] *n.* **1.** (*name of book etc.*) загла́вие; назва́ние. **2.** (*indicator of rank*, *occupation*, *status etc.*) зва́ние, ти́тул; **courtesy ~** почётный ти́тул; **they fought for the ~ of champion** они́ боро́лись за зва́ние чемпио́на. **3.** (*legal right or claim*) пра́во; **what is his ~ to the property?** на како́м основа́нии он претенду́ет на э́ту со́бственность?
cpds. **~-deed** *n.* докуме́нт, подтвержда́ющий пра́во со́бственности; **~-holder** *n.* чемпио́н; **~-page** *n.* ти́тульный лист; **~-role** *n.* загла́вная роль.

titled ['taɪt(ə)ld] *adj.* титуло́ванный.

titmouse ['tɪtmaʊs] *n.* сини́ца.

titter ['tɪtə(r)] *n.* хихи́канье.
v.i. хихи́кать (*impf.*).

tittivate ['tɪtɪ,veɪt] = **titivate**

tittle ['tɪt(ə)l] *n.*: **not one jot or ~** ни ка́пельки.
cpd. **~-tattle** *n.* спле́тн|и (*pl.*, *g.* -ен); *v.i.* спле́тничать (*impf.*).

tittup ['tɪtəp] *v.i.* (*prance*) подпры́гивать (*impf.*).

titular ['tɪtjʊlə(r)] *adj.* **1.** (*pert. to title*): **~ possessions** владе́ния, полага́ющиеся по ти́тулу; **a ~ bishop** епи́скоп ликвиди́рованной епа́рхии. **2.** (*in name only*) номина́льный.

tiz(zy) ['tɪzɪ] *n.* ажиота́ж (*coll.*); **she got into a ~** она́ распсихова́лась (*coll.*).

TNT (*abbr. of* **trinitrotoluene**) ТНТ, (тринитротолуóл).

to [tə, *before a vowel* tʊ, *emph.* tu:] *adv.* **1.** (*into closed position*): **draw the curtains ~!** задёрните занавéски! **2.:** **~ and fro** тудá и сюдá; взад и вперёд.

prep. **1.** (*expr. ind. obj., recipient*): *usu. expr. by d. case*; **a letter ~ my wife** письмó моéй женé; **let that be a lesson ~ you** пусть э́то бýдет для вас урóком; **it was a surprise ~ him** для негó э́то бы́ло неожи́данностью; **~ me that is absurd** по-мóему э́то нелéпо; **I'm not Vanya ~ you** какóй я вам Вáня?; **what's that ~ him?** а емý какóе дéло до э́того?; **a monument ~ Pushkin** пáмятник Пýшкину; (*expr. support*): **a toast ~ the workers** тост за рабóтников; **here's ~ our victory** за нáшу побéду. **2.** (*expr. destination*) a) (*with place-names, countries, areas, buildings, institutions, places of study or entertainment*) в+*a.*; **~ Moscow** в Москвý; **~ Russia** в Росси́ю; **~ the Crimea** в Крым; **~ the theatre** в теáтр; **~ school** в шкóлу; **he was elected ~ the council** егó вы́брали в совéт; (*expr. direction*): **the road ~ Berlin** дорóга на Берли́н; b) (*with islands, peninsulas, mountain areas of Russia, planets, points of the compass, left and right, places considered as activity or function, places of employment*) на+*a.*; **~ Ceylon** на Цейлóн; **~ the Caucasus** на Кавкáз; **back ~ earth** обрáтно на зéмлю; **turn ~ the right!** поверни́те напрáво!; **~ a concert** на концéрт; **~ war** на войнý; **~ the factory** на фáбрику; к фáбрике; **~ the station** на стáнцию; к стáнции; **he was appointed ~ a new post** егó назнáчили на нóвое мéсто; **he set the lines ~ music** он положи́л э́ти стихи́ на мýзыку; c) (*with persons, types of shop, objects approached but not entered*) к+*d.*; **he went ~ his parents'** он отпрáвился к свои́м роди́телям; **they came ~ the shore** они́ подошли́ к бéрегу; **pull the chair up ~ the table!** пододви́ньте стул к столý! **3.** (*expr. limit or extent of movement*: *up to*, *as far as*, *until*) до+*g.*; на+*a.*; по+*a.*; **is it far ~ town?** до гóрода далекó?; **we stayed ~ the end** мы прóбыли до концá; **he was in the water (up) ~ his waist** он стоя́л по пóяс в воде́; **you will get soaked ~ the skin** вы промóкните до костéй/ни́тки; **~ the bottom** на сáмое дно; **correct ~ 3 places of decimals** с тóчностью до ты́сячной; **he did it ~ perfection** он вы́полнил э́то превосхóдно; **they stood by him ~ a man** егó поддержáли все до одногó человéка; **from 10 ~ 4** с десяти́ до четырёх; **from morning ~ night** с утрá дó ночи; **from one end ~ the other** с одногó концá до другóго; **ten (minutes) ~ six** без десяти́ (минýт) шесть. **4.** (*expr. end state*): **torn ~ shreds** разóрванный в клóчья (*or* на куски́); **from bad ~ worse** всё хýже и хýже. **5.** (*expr. response*) на+*a.*; к+*d.*; **an answer ~ my letter** отвéт на моё письмó; **what do you say ~ that?** что вы на э́то скáжете?; **deaf ~ entreaty** глухóй к мольбáм. **6.** (*expr. result or reaction*) к+*d.*; **~ my surprise** к моемý удивлéнию; **~ everyone's disappointment** ко всеóбщему разочаровáнию; **~ that end** с э́той цéлью; для э́того; **it is ~ your advantage** э́то в вáших интерéсах; **~ no avail** напрáсно. **7.** (*expr. appurtenance, attachment, suitability*) к+*d.*; от+*g.*; в+*a.*; **the preface ~ the book** предисловие к кни́ге; **the key ~ the door** ключ от двéри; **the key ~ his heart** ключ к егó сéрдцу; **there's nothing ~ it** (*coll., it presents no problem*) ничегó трýдного; э́то пáра пустякóв. **8.** (*expr. reference or relationship*): **he is good ~ his employees** он хорошó отнóсится к свои́м сотрýдникам; **soft ~ the touch** мя́гкий на óщупь; **attention ~ detail** внимáние к подрóбностям; **ready ~ hand** (находя́щийся) под рукóй; **a benefactor ~ the nation** благодéтель нарóда; **a traitor ~ the cause** измéнник дéлу; **secretary ~ the director** секретáрь дирéктора; **close ~** бли́зкий к+*d.* **9.** (*expr. comparison*) по сравнéнию с+*i.*; **the expense is nothing ~ what it might have been** расхóд ничтóжен по сравнéнию с тем, каки́м он мог бы быть. **10.** (*expr. ratio or proportion*): **as 3 is ~ 4** как три отнóсится к четырём; **ten ~ one he won't succeed** дéсять прóтив одногó, что э́то емý не удáстся; **this car does 30 (miles) ~ the gallon** э́та маши́на дéлает 30 миль на галлóн; **there are 9 francs ~ the pound** оди́н фунт рáвен девяти́ фрáнкам. **11.** (*expr. score*) на+*a.*; **we won by six goals ~ four** мы вы́играли со счётом 6–4. **12.** (*expr. accompaniment*): **I fell asleep ~ the sound of lively conversation** я заснýл под оживлённый разговóр; **he tapped his foot ~ the music** слýшая мýзыку, он отбивáл такт ногóй. **13.** (*expr. position*): **~ my right** спрáва от меня́; **~ the south of London** к ю́гу от Лóндона; **~ the left of centre** (*in politics*) слéва от цéнтра.

particle with v. forming inf. **1.** (*as subj. or obj. of v.*): **~ err is human** человéку свóйственно ошибáться; **he learnt ~ swim** он научи́лся плáвать. **2.** (*as extension of adj.*): **easy ~ read** удобочитáемый; **too hot ~ touch** такóй горя́чий, что не дотрóнуться. **3.** (*expr. purpose*) (с тем *or* для тогó), чтóбы…; (*with inf. only*): **I came ~ help** я пришёл помóчь (*or* на пóмощь); **I have come ~ talk to you** я пришёл поговори́ть с вáми; (*expr. result, sequel*): **I arrived only ~ find him gone** когдá я приéхал, оказáлось, что егó ужé нет; **he disappeared, never ~ return** он исчéз, и никогдá ужé не возвращáлся. **4.** (*as substitute for rel. clause*): **he was first ~ arrive and last ~ leave** он при́был пéрвым и уéхал послéдним; **the captain was the next man ~ die** слéдующим ýмер капитáн. **5.** (*as substitute for complete inf.*): **I was going ~ write but I forgot ~** я собирáлся написáть, но забы́л.

toad [təʊd] *n.* жáба.

cpds. **~-in-the-hole** *n.* соси́ска, запечённая в тéсте; **~stool** *n.* погáнка.

toady ['təʊdɪ] *n.* лизоблю́д, подхали́м.

v.i. подли́зываться (*impf.*) (*к кому*); выслýживаться (*impf.*) (*перед кем*).

toast[1] [təʊst] *n.* гренóк, поджáренный хлеб; **as warm as ~** теплёхонький; **I had him on ~** (*coll.*) он был у меня́ на крючкé.

v.t. поджáри|вать, -ть; **~ed cheese** гренóк с сы́ром; **~ing fork** дли́нная ви́лка; **he ~ed his toes by the fire** он грел нóги уками́на.

cpd. **~-rack** *n.* подстáвка для гренкóв.

toast[2] [təʊst] *n.* (*drinking of health*) тост, здрáвица; **propose a ~ to** произнести́/провозгласи́ть/предложи́ть (*pf.*) тост/здрáвицу за+*a.*; **drink a ~ to sth.** вы́пить (*pf.*) за что-н.; **she was the ~ of the town** онá былá всеóбщей люби́мицей.

v.t. пить, вы́- за (*чьё-н.*) здорóвье.

cpd. **~-master** *n.* слугá, провозглашáющий тóсты.

toaster ['təʊstə(r)] *n.* (*machine*) тóстер.

tobacco [tə'bækəʊ] *n.* табáк.

cpd. **~-pouch** *n.* кисéт.

tobacconist [tə'bækənɪst] *n.* торгóвец табáчными издéлиями.

toboggan [tə'bɒgən] *n.* тобóгган; сáн|и (*pl.*, *g.* -éй).

v.i. катáться (*impf.*) на саня́х.

cpd. **~-slide** *n.* горá для катáния на тобóггане.

toccata [tə'kɑ:tə] *n.* токкáта.

tocsin ['tɒksɪn] *n.* набáт.

today [tə'deɪ] *n.* & *adv.* сегóдняшний день; сегóдня; **what's ~?** какóй день сегóдня?; **~'s newspaper** сегóдняшняя газéта; **from ~ on** с сегóдняшнего дня; (*fig., the present time*) настоя́щее врéмя, совремéнность; **young people of ~** совремéнная/ны́нешняя молодёжь.

toddle ['tɒd(ə)l] *v.i.* ковыля́ть (*impf.*); (*coll., walk*) прогýл|иваться, -я́ться; **I'll just ~ down to the shop** я тóлько сбéгаю в магази́н; я пройдýсь до магази́на.

toddler ['tɒdlə(r)] *n.* ребёнок, начинáющий ходи́ть.

toddy ['tɒdɪ] *n.* тóдди (*nt. indecl.*), пунш; **(palm ~)** арáк.

to-do [tə'du:] *n.* шум; суетá; **what's all the ~?** из-за чегó весь э́тот шум?; **he made a great ~ about answering the invitation** он устрóил цéлое дéло из своегó отвéта на приглашéние.

toe [təʊ] *n.* **1.** (*of foot*) пáлец (ноги́); **big ~** большóй пáлец (ноги́); **little ~** мизи́нец (ноги́); **tread on s.o.'s ~s** (*fig., offend*) наступи́ть (*pf.*) на люби́мую мозóль (*кому*); **on one's ~s** (*fig.*) начекý. **2.** (*of shoe or sock*) носóк.

v.t.: **the runners ~d the starting-line** учáстники забéга встáли на старт; **~ the line** (*fig., conform*) ходи́ть (*indet.*) по стрýнке.

cpds. **~-cap** *n.* носóк; **~-hold** *n.* опóра; тóчка опóры; **~-in** *n.* (*of vehicle*) сходи́мость перéдних колёс; **~-nail**

n. но́готь (*m.*) на па́льце ноги́.
toff [tɒf] *n.* (*sl.*) ба́рин, джентльме́н.
toff|ee, -y ['tɒfɪ] *n.* то́ффи (*nt. indecl.*); ири́с(ка); тяну́чка; **a** ~ ири́ска; **he can't shoot for** ~ (*coll.*) он никуды́шний стрело́к.
tofu ['təʊfu:] *n.* со́евый творо́г.
tog [tɒg] (*coll.*) *n.* (*pl. only*) оде́жда.
v.t. with advs. над|ева́ть, -е́ть; **we got him** ~**ged out for school** мы снаряди́ли его́ в шко́лу; **he** ~**ged himself up in a dinner-jacket** он вы́рядился в смо́кинг.
toga ['təʊgə] *n.* то́га.
together [tə'geðə(r)] *adv.* **1.** (*in company*) вме́сте, сообща́; **they get on well** ~ они́ ла́дят друг с дру́гом; **they were living** ~ (*as man and wife*) они́ жи́ли друг с дру́гом; ~ **with** (*in addition to*) вме́сте с+*i.* **2.** (*simultaneously*) одновре́ме́нно. **3.** (*in succession*) подря́д, непреры́вно; **he was away for weeks** ~ он был в разъе́здах неде́лями. **4.:** *for other phrasal vv. see relevant entries.*
togetherness [tə'geðənɪs] *n.* бли́зость; това́рищество.
toggle ['tɒg(ə)l] *n.* (*e.g. on a coat*) деревя́нная застёжка.
toil [tɔɪl] *n.* (тяжёлый) труд.
v.i. **1.** (*work hard or long*) труди́ться (*impf.*); **she was** ~**ing at the stove** она́ усе́рдно хлопота́ла у плиты́. **2.** (*move with difficulty*) тащи́ться (*impf.*); **they** ~**ed up the hill** они втащи́лись на холм.
toiler ['tɔɪlə(r)] *n.* тру́жени|к (*fem.* -ца).
toilet ['tɔɪlɪt] *n.* **1.** (*process of dressing, arranging hair etc.*) туале́т; ~ **articles** туале́тные принадле́жности; ~ **soap** туале́тное мы́ло. **2.** (*lavatory*) туале́т, убо́рная.
cpds. ~**-paper** *n.* туале́тная бума́га; ~**-powder** *n.* тальк; ~**-roll** *n.* руло́н туале́тной бума́ги.
toiletries ['tɔɪlɪtrɪz] *n. pl.* туале́тные принадле́жности.
toilette [twɑ:'let] *n.* туале́т.
toils [tɔɪlz] *n. pl.* сеть; **he was caught in the** ~ **of the law** он запу́тался в сетя́х зако́на.
toilsome ['tɔɪlsəm] *adj.* тру́дный, утоми́тельный.
Tokay [tə'keɪ] *n.* тока́йское (вино́).
token ['təʊkən] *n.* **1.** (*sign, evidence, guarantee*) знак, си́мвол; **in** ~ **of my friendship** в знак мое́й дру́жбы; **by the same** ~ к тому́ же; по той же причи́не. **2.** (*keepsake, memento*) сувени́р, па́мятный пода́рок. **3.** (*substitute for coin*) жето́н. **4.** (*attr.*) символи́ческий; ~ **money** де́нежные зна́ки; символи́ческие де́ньги; **they put up a** ~ **resistance** они́ оказа́ли лишь ви́димость сопротивле́ния.
Tokyo ['təʊkjəʊ, -kɪˌəʊ] *n.* То́кио (*m. indecl.*); (*attr.*) токи́йский.
tolerable ['tɒlərəb(ə)l] *adj.* (*endurable*) терпи́мый, выноси́мый; (*fairly good*) терпи́мый, сно́сный.
tolerance ['tɒlərəns] *n.* (*forbearance*) терпи́мость; (*resistance to adverse conditions, drugs etc.*) выно́сливость; (*tech., permissible variation*) до́пуск; допусти́мое отклоне́ние.
tolerant ['tɒlərənt] *adj.* терпи́мый; **he is not very** ~ **of criticism** он не о́чень лю́бит кри́тику.
tolerate ['tɒləˌreɪt] *v.t.* (*endure*) терпе́ть (*impf.*); (*permit*) допус|ка́ть, -ти́ть; (*sustain without harm*) перен|оси́ть, -ести́.
toleration [ˌtɒlə'reɪʃ(ə)n] *n.* терпи́мость.
toll[1] [təʊl] *n.* (*tax*) по́шлина, сбор; ~ **call** междугоро́дный разгово́р; (*fig.*) дань; **age is taking its** ~ во́зраст начина́ет ска́зываться; года́ беру́т своё; **the** ~ **of the road** (*accident rate*) чи́сленность жертв доро́жных происше́ствий.
cpds. ~**-bar,** ~**-gate** *nn.* заста́ва; ~**-bridge** *n.* мост, где взима́ется сбор; ~**-house** *n.* пост у заста́вы, где взима́ется сбор.
toll[2] [təʊl] *n.* (*of bell*) колоко́льный звон; бла́говест.
v.t. & i. звони́ть (*impf.*) в ко́локо́л; **the bell** ~**ed the hours** ко́локол отбива́л часы́; **they** ~**ed the bells** они́ звони́ли в колокола́.
Tom [tɒm] *n.* **1.: any** ~**, Dick or Harry** ка́ждый; пе́рвый встре́чный; **peeping** ~ согляда́тай. **2.** (**t**~: *male cat*) кот.
cpds. **t**~**boy** *n.* девчо́нка-сорване́ц; **t**~**cat** *n.* кот; **t**~**fool** *n.* дура́к, шут; *v.i.* дура́читься (*impf.*); **t**~**foolery** *n.* дура́чество, шутовство́; **t**~**tit** *n.* сини́ца.
tomahawk ['tɒməˌhɔ:k] *n.* томага́вк.
v.t. уд|аря́ть, -а́рить (*or* уб|ива́ть, -и́ть) томага́вком.
tomato [tə'mɑ:təʊ] *n.* помидо́р; ~ **purée** тома́т; ~ **sauce/juice** тома́тный со́ус/сок.
tomb [tu:m] *n.* моги́ла; (*monument*) мавзоле́й; **the** ~ (*fig., death*) смерть; (~**stone**) надгро́бный па́мятник; надгро́бная плита́.
tombola [tɒm'bəʊlə] *n.* лотере́я.
tome [təʊm] *n.* том.
tommy ['tɒmɪ] *n.* **1.** (**T**~: *private soldier*) (англи́йский) рядово́й. **2.** (*provisions, esp. in lieu of wages*) проду́кты (*m. pl.*), выдава́емые рабо́чим вме́сто зарпла́ты.
cpds. ~**-gun** *n.* автома́т, пистоле́т-пулемёт; ~**-rot** *n.* (*coll.*): **talk** ~**-rot** поро́ть (*impf.*) дичь.
tomorrow [tə'mɒrəʊ] *n. & adv.* за́втрашний день; за́втра; ~ **morning** за́втра у́тром; **the day after** ~ послеза́втра; **until** ~ до за́втра; ~**'s weather** за́втрашняя пого́да; ~ **week** че́рез 8 дней; (*fig., future*) бу́дущее.
tomtom ['tɒmtɒm] *n.* тамта́м.
ton [tʌn] *n.* **1.** то́нна; (*fig.*): **he has** ~**s of money** у него́ ку́ча де́нег; **he came down on me like a** ~ **of bricks** он так на меня́ и обру́шился. **2.** (*sl., 100 mph*): **he did a** ~ **on the motorway** он е́хал по автостра́де со ско́ростью 100 миль в час.
tonal ['təʊn(ə)l] *adj.* (*mus.; of colours*) тона́льный.
tonality [tə'nælɪtɪ] *n.* тона́льность.
tone [təʊn] *n.* **1.** (*quality of sound*) тон; (*mus. interval*) звук, тон; (*intonation*) го́лос, тон; *pl.* -ы *in these senses.* **2.** (*character*) хара́ктер, стиль (*m.*); **the debate took on a serious** ~ диску́ссия приобрела́ серьёзный хара́ктер. **3.** (*distinction*) тон; **his presence lent** ~ **to the occasion** его́ прису́тствие прида́ло осо́бый вес собы́тию. **4.** (*shade of colour*) отте́нок, тон (*pl.* -а́). **5.** (*med.*) то́нус.
v.i. гармони́ровать (*impf.*).
with advs.: ~ **down** *v.t.* смягч|а́ть, -и́ть; осл|абля́ть, -а́бить; ~ **in** *v.i.* гармони́ровать (*impf.*); ~ **up** *v.t.* укреп|ля́ть, -и́ть; тонизи́ровать (*impf.*); **these exercises will** ~ **up your muscles** ва́ши мы́шцы окре́пнут от э́тих упражне́ний.
cpds. ~**-arm** *n.* звукосвнима́тель (*m.*); ~**-deaf** *adj.* лишённый музыка́льного слу́ха; ~**-poem** *n.* симфони́ческая поэ́ма.
toneless ['təʊnlɪs] *adj.* моното́нный, невырази́тельный.
toner ['təʊnə(r)] *n.* (*xerographic*) кра́сящий порошо́к.
tongs [tɒŋz] *n.* щипц|ы́ (*pl., g.* -о́в).
tongue [tʌŋ] *n.* **1.** (*lit., and as food*) язы́к; **put, stick one's** ~ **out** высо́вывать, вы́сунуть (*or* пока́з|ывать, -а́ть) язы́к; (*dim., e.g. baby's*) язычо́к. **2.** (*fig., article so shaped*) язычо́к; ~**s of flame** язычки́ пла́мени; **the** ~ **of a shoe** язычо́к боти́нка; ~ **of land** коса́. **3.** (*fig., faculty or manner of speech*) язы́к, речь; **she has a sharp** ~ у неё о́стрый язы́к; **he spoke with his** ~ **in his cheek** он говори́л со скры́той иро́нией; **have you lost your** ~**?** вы что, язы́к проглоти́ли?; **keep a civil** ~ **in your head!** не груби́те!; **hold your** ~**!** молчи́те!; **the hounds gave** ~ го́нчие по́дали го́лос. **4.** (*language*) язы́к; **mother** ~ родно́й язы́к; **gift of** ~**s** спосо́бность к языка́м.
cpds. ~**-lashing** *n.* разно́с; ~**-tied** *adj.* косноязы́чный; лиши́вшийся да́ра ре́чи; **he was** ~**-tied** он как язы́к проглоти́л; ~**-twister** *n.* скорогово́рка.
tonic ['tɒnɪk] *n.* **1.** (*medicine*) тонизи́рующее сре́дство; (*fig.*) подде́ржка, утеше́ние; **the news was a** ~ **to us all** но́вость нас всех подбодри́ла. **2.** (~ **water**): напи́ток «то́ник». **3.** (*mus.*) то́ника.
adj.: **the** ~ **quality of sea air** тонизи́рующее сво́йство морско́го во́здуха; ~ **accent** ударе́ние; ~ **solfa** сольфе́джио (*indecl.*).
tonight [tə'naɪt] *n.* сего́дняшний ве́чер.
adj. сего́дня ве́чером.
tonnage ['tʌnɪdʒ] *n.* (*internal capacity*) тонна́ж; (*cargo-carrying capacity*) грузоподъёмность в то́ннах; (*total freightage*) суда́ (*pl.*), тонна́ж судо́в; (*duty; charge per ton*) тонна́жный сбор.
tonne [tʌn] *n.* метри́ческая то́нна.
tonsil ['tɒns(ə)l, -sɪl] *n.* минда́лина, миндалеви́дная железа́; **has he had his** ~**s out?** ему́ вы́резали/удали́ли гла́нды?
tonsillectomy [ˌtɒnsɪ'lektəmɪ] *n.* тонзиллэктоми́я, удале́ние минда́лин.
tonsillitis [ˌtɒnsɪ'laɪtɪs] *n.* воспале́ние минда́лин, тонзилли́т.

tonsorial [tɒn'sɔ:rɪəl] *adj.* парикма́херский.

tonsure ['tɒnsjə(r), 'tɒnʃə(r)] *n.* тонзу́ра.
v.t. выбрива́ть, вы́брить тонзу́ру +*d*.

too [tu:] *adv.* **1.** (*also*) та́кже, то́же. **2.** (*moreover*) к тому́ же; бо́лее того́; **there was a frost last night, and in May ~!** вчера́ но́чью уда́рил моро́з, и э́то в ма́е!; **and him a married man, ~!** а ещё жена́тый! **3.** (*US coll., indeed*) действи́тельно; **'You haven't washed!' — 'I have ~!'** «Ты не вы́мылся!» — «Нет, вы́мылся!». **4.** (*excessively*) сли́шком; **it's ~ cold for swimming** сли́шком хо́лодно, что́бы купа́ться; **the weather's ~ fine to last** пого́да сли́шком хороша́, что́бы удержа́ться; **am I ~ late for dinner?** я не опозда́л к у́жину?; **I've had ~ much to eat** я объе́лся; **all ~ soon** сли́шком ско́ро; **that is ~ much!** э́то уж сли́шком/чересчу́р!; **he had one (drink) ~ many** он вы́пил ли́шнего; **you will do that once ~ often** когда́-нибудь вы нарвётесь. **5.** (*very*) о́чень; кра́йне; **you are ~ kind** вы о́чень до́бры; **I'm not ~ sure** я бы не поручи́лся; **~ bad!** (о́чень) жаль!

tool [tu:l] *n.* **1.** (*implement*) инструме́нт, ору́дие; (*pl., collect.*) инструме́нт; **~s of one's trade** (*fig.*) ору́дия труда́; **sarcasm is a two-edged ~** сарка́зм — обоюдоо́строе ору́жие; **a bad workman blames his ~s** у плохо́го ма́стера всегда́ инструме́нт винова́т; **(machine-~)** стано́к; (*cutting part of lathe etc.*) резе́ц. **2.** (*fig., means, aid*) ору́дие. **3.** (*fig., pers. used by another*) ору́дие; марионе́тка; **he was a mere ~ in their hands** он был лишь ору́дием в их рука́х.
v.t. **1.** (*ornament*) вытисня́ть, вы́тиснить узо́р на+*p.*; де́лать, с- тисне́ние на+*p.*; **the book was finely ~ed** переплёт кни́ги был укра́шен изя́щным тисне́нием. **2.** (*equip with machinery*) обору́довать (*impf., pf.*) инструме́нтом; **the factory was ~ed up for new production** фа́брику оснасти́ли/обору́довали для вы́пуска но́вой проду́кции.
cpds. **~-bag** *n.* су́мка для инструме́нтов; **~-box, ~-chest** *nn.* я́щик для инструме́нтов; **~-shed** *n.* сара́й для инструме́нтов.

tooling ['tu:lɪŋ] *n.* (*on book-cover*) ручно́е тисне́ние.

toot [tu:t] *n.* гудо́к; свисто́к; сигна́л.
v.t.: **he ~ed the horn** он погуде́л; он дал сигна́л.
v.i. гуде́ть (*impf.*); свист|е́ть, -нуть; дать, из- гудо́к.

tooth [tu:θ] *n.* **1.** зуб; (*dim., e.g. baby's*) зу́бик, зубо́к; **false teeth** иску́сственные зу́бы; **she has a sweet ~** она́ сластёна/сладкое́жка; **he has all his (own) teeth** у него́ все зу́бы свои́; **I have a ~ loose** у меня́ шата́ется зуб; **he went to have a ~ out** он пошёл удали́ть зуб; **my ~ aches** у меня́ боли́т зуб; **have you cleaned your teeth?** ты чи́стил зу́бы?; **the baby is cutting its first ~** у младе́нца проре́зывается пе́рвый зуб; **the dog got its teeth into his leg** соба́ка вцепи́лась зуба́ми ему́ в но́гу. **2.** (*fig.*): **armed to the teeth** вооружённый до зубо́в; **fed up to the (back) teeth** сыт по го́рло; **he cast her family in her teeth** он попрека́л её семьёй; **in the teeth of heavy opposition** несмотря́ на серьёзное сопротивле́ние; **he sailed into the teeth of the gale** он поплы́л пря́мо про́тив си́льного ве́тра; **I can't wait to get my teeth into the job** не те́рпится скоре́е приня́ться за рабо́ту; **he got away by the skin of his teeth** он чу́дом уцеле́л; ему́ е́ле удало́сь убежа́ть/отде́латься; **they were fighting ~ and nail** они́ дра́лись не на жи́знь, а на смерть; **he's a bit long in the ~** он уже́ не пе́рвой мо́лодости; **this will put teeth into the law** э́то прида́ст зако́ну настоя́щую си́лу; **it sets my teeth on edge** (*lit.*) от э́того у меня́ сво́дит рот; э́то оставля́ет оско́мину во рту; (*fig.*) от э́того меня́ передёргивает; **it was not long before he showed his teeth** он вско́ре показа́л ко́гти. **3.** (*of a saw, gear, comb etc.*) зуб, зубе́ц.
cpds. **~ache** *n.* зубна́я боль; **he had a bad ~ache** у него́ о́чень боле́ли зу́бы; **~-brush** *n.* зубна́я щётка; **~-comb** *n.*: **I've been through this book with a fine ~-comb** я проштуди́ровал э́ту кни́гу о́чень основа́тельно; **~paste** *n.* зубна́я па́ста; **~pick** *n.* зубочи́стка.

toothsome ['tu:θsəm] *adj.* вку́сный, ла́комый.

toothy ['tu:θɪ] *adj.* зуба́стый.

top[1] [tɒp] *n.* **1.** (*summit; highest or upper part*) верх (*pl.* -и́); верху́шка, верши́на; маку́шка; **at the ~ of the hill** на верши́не холма́; **the ~s of the trees** верху́шки дере́вьев; **they climbed to the very ~** они́ взобра́лись на са́мый верх; **the soldiers went over the ~** солда́ты пошли́ в ата́ку из транше́й; **at the ~ of the page** в нача́ле страни́цы; **his name was (at the) ~ of the list** его́ и́мя бы́ло пе́рвым в спи́ске; **he has reached the ~ of the tree, ladder** (*fig.*) он дости́г вы́сших степене́й; **she cleaned the house from ~ to bottom** она́ убрала́ дом све́рху до́низу; **~ of the milk** сли́в|ки (*pl., g.* -ок); (*of the head*) маку́шка; **he has no hair on (the) ~ (of his head)** у него́ (на маку́шке) плешь; **he blew his ~** (*sl.*) он вы́шел из себя́; он распсихова́лся; **from ~ to toe** с ног до головы́; с головы́ до пят. **2.** (*fig., highest rank, foremost place*) вы́сший ранг; пе́рвое ме́сто; **he came ~ of the form** он стал пе́рвым в кла́ссе; **they put him at the ~ of the table** его́ посади́ли во главе́ стола́; **he reached the ~ of his profession** он за́нял ве́дущее положе́ние в свое́й о́бласти. **3.** (*fig., utmost degree, height*) верх; **the ~ of my ambition** преде́л мои́х мечта́ний; **at the ~ of his voice** во весь го́лос; **to the ~ of one's bent** ско́лько душе́ уго́дно; **he was at the ~ of his form** (*of athlete etc.*) он был в прекра́сной фо́рме; **(the) ~s** (*coll., the very best*) верх соверше́нства. **4.** (*upper surface*) пове́рхность; верх; **wood floats to the ~** де́рево всплыва́ет наве́рх; **on ~** (*lit.*) наверху́; **he put the book on ~** он положи́л кни́гу наве́рх/све́рху; (*fig.*): **I feel on ~ of the world** я чу́вствую себя́ на седьмо́м не́бе; **I'm getting on ~ of my work** я начина́ю справля́ться с рабо́той; **in every argument he comes out on ~** во всех спо́рах он оде́рживает верх; **on ~ of everything I caught a cold** вдоба́вок ко всему́ я ещё простуди́лся. **5.** (*lid, cover*) верх; кры́шка; (*hood of car*) кры́ша; **I can't get the ~ off this jar** я не могу́ снять кры́шку с э́той ба́нки; **I've lost the ~ to my pen** я потеря́л колпачо́к от ру́чки; **a bus with an open ~** авто́бус с откры́тым ве́рхом. **6.** (*upper leaves of plant*) ботва́; **turnip ~s** ботва́ ре́пы. **7. (~ gear)** вы́сшая/пряма́я переда́ча; **the car won't take this hill in ~** маши́на не возьмёт э́тот подъём на прямо́й переда́че. **8.: the big ~** (*circus tent*) шапито́ (*indecl.*). **9.** (*attr.; see also cpds.*): **~ copy** пе́рвый экземпля́р; **~ dog** (*coll.*) гла́вный; **~ drawer** ве́рхний я́щик; (*fig.*): **his family comes out of the ~ drawer** его́ семья́ принадлежи́т к вы́сшему кла́ссу; **~ hat** цили́ндр; **~ note** верх (*pl.* -и́/-а́); **~ people** верхи́ (*m. pl.*); **~ secret** *adj.* «соверше́нно секре́тный»; **~ sergeant** (*US*) старшина́ ро́ты; **at ~ speed** во всю мочь; **~ table** стол почётных госте́й.
v.t. **1.** (*serve as ~ to*): **a church ~ped by a steeple** це́рковь, уве́нчанная шпи́лем. **2.** (*remove ~ of*) ср|еза́ть, -е́зать верху́шку +*g.*; **~ and tail gooseberries** чи́стить, по- крыжо́вник. **3.** (*reach ~ of*) дост|ига́ть, -и́гнуть верши́ны +*g.* **4.** (*be higher than; exceed*) прев|ыша́ть, -ы́сить; **the mountains ~ 5,000 ft.** го́ры вы́ше пяти́ ты́сяч фу́тов; **he ~ped 60 mph** он де́лал бо́льше шести́десяти миль в час; (*fig., surpass*): **it ~ped all my expectations** э́то превзошло́ все мои́ ожида́ния.
with advs.: **~ out** *v.i.* пра́здновать, от- оконча́ние строи́тельства зда́ния; **~ up** *v.t.* дол|ива́ть, -и́ть; нап|олня́ть, -о́лнить; **may I ~ up your glass (or ~ you up)?** позво́льте доли́ть?; мо́жно я вам долью́?; *v.i.* запр|авля́ться, -а́виться; **he stopped to ~ up and drove on** он останови́лся запра́виться, и пое́хал да́льше.
cpds. **~-boot** *n.* сапо́г; **~-coat** *n.* (*garment*) пальто́ (*indecl.*); (*of paint*) ве́рхний слой; **~-dressing** *n.* подко́рмка; **~-flight** *adj.* первокла́ссный, наилу́чший; **~-gallant** *n.* брам-сте́ньга; **~-heavy** *adj.* неусто́йчивый; переве́шивающий в ве́рхней ча́сти; **~-hole** *adj.* (*coll.*) превосхо́дный, первокла́ссный; **~-knot** *n.* чуб; пучо́к воло́с/пе́рьев; **~mast** *n.* сте́ньга; **~-notch** *adj.* превосхо́дный, первокла́ссный; **~-ranking** *adj.* вы́сшего ра́нга; высокопоста́вленный; **~-sail** *n.* то́псель (*m.*); **~side** *n.* (*of beef*) говя́жья груди́нка; **~soil** *n.* па́хотный слой.

top[2] [tɒp] *n.* (*toy*) волчо́к; **my head was spinning like a ~** у меня́ голова́ шла кру́гом; **I slept like a ~** я спал как уби́тый.

topaz ['təʊpæz] *n.* топа́з; (*attr.*) топа́зовый.

top|ee, -i ['təʊpɪ] *n.* тропи́ческий шлем.
toper ['təʊpə(r)] *n.* пья́ница (*c.g.*).
topi ['təʊpɪ] = **topee**
topiary ['təʊpɪərɪ] *adj.*: **the ~ art** фигу́рная стри́жка кусто́в.
topic ['tɒpɪk] *n.* те́ма; предме́т обсужде́ния.
topical ['tɒpɪk(ə)l] *adj.* актуа́льный; злободне́вный.
topless ['tɒplɪs] *adj.* **1.** (*of unlimited height*) о́чень высо́кий. **2.** (*of dress*) без ли́фа, обнажа́ющий грудь; (*of pers.*) с обнажённой гру́дью.
topmost ['tɒpməʊst] *adj.* са́мый ве́рхний/ва́жный.
topographic(al) [ˌtɒpə'græfɪk(ə)l] *adj.* топографи́ческий.
topography [tə'pɒgrəfɪ] *n.* топогра́фия.
topology [tə'pɒlədʒɪ] *n.* тополо́гия.
topper ['tɒpə(r)] *n.* (*coll.*, *hat*) цили́ндр.
topping ['tɒpɪŋ] *adj.* (*coll.*) превосхо́дный, замеча́тельный.
topple ['tɒp(ə)l] *v.t.* вали́ть, с-; **the dictator was ~d (from power)** дикта́тора сбро́сили.
v.i. опроки́|дываться, -нуться; вали́ться, с-.
topsy-turvy [ˌtɒpsɪ'tɜːvɪ] *adj.* перевёрнутый верх дном.
adv. вверх дном; ши́ворот-навы́ворот.
toque [təʊk] *n.* (*woman's hat*) ток.
tor [tɔː(r)] *n.* холм.
Torah ['tɔːrə] *n.* то́ра.
torch [tɔːtʃ] *n.* фа́кел; (*fig.*) све́точ; зна́мя; **the ~ of learning was handed on** фа́кел зна́ний передава́лся из поколе́ния в поколе́ние; **she carried a ~ for him** она́ по нему́ со́хла (*coll.*); **(electric ~)** электри́ческий фона́рь; (*welding ~*) сва́рочная горе́лка.
cpds. **~-bearer** *n.* фа́кельщик; (*fig.*) просвети́тель (*m.*); **~light** *n.* свет фа́кела/фонаря́; **~-singer** *n.* исполни́тельница «жесто́ких рома́нсов».
toreador ['tɒrɪəˌdɔː(r)] *n.* тореадо́р.
torment[1] ['tɔːment] *n.* муче́ние; **a soul in ~** душа́, раздира́емая му́ками; **he suffered the ~s of the damned** он испы́тывал а́дские му́ки.
torment[2] [tɔː'ment] *v.t.* му́чить (*impf.*); причиня́ть (*impf.*) страда́ния +*d.*; **the child was ~ing the cat** ребёнок му́чил ко́шку; **he was ~ed with jealousy** он терза́лся ре́вностью.
tormentor [tɔː'mentə(r)] *n.* мучи́тель (*fem.* -ница).
tornado [tɔː'neɪdəʊ] *n.* торна́до (*indecl.*); (*fig.*) взрыв; вихрь (*m.*); **a ~ of applause** бу́ря аплодисме́нтов.
torpedo [tɔː'piːdəʊ] *n.* торпе́да.
v.t. (*lit.*) торпеди́ровать (*impf.*); (*fig.*) под|рыва́ть, -орва́ть; срыва́ть, сорва́ть.
cpds. **~-boat** *n.* торпе́дный ка́тер; **~-net** *n.* противоми́нная сеть; **~-tube** *n.* труба́ торпе́дного аппара́та.
torpid ['tɔːpɪd] *adj.* вя́лый, апати́чный; (*in hibernation*) находя́щийся в состоя́нии спя́чки.
torp|idity [tɔː'pɪdɪtɪ], **-or** ['tɔːpə(r)] *nn.* вя́лость, апа́тия.
torque [tɔːk] *n.* (*circlet*) металли́ческий брасле́т; (*mech.*) враща́ющий моме́нт.
torrent ['tɒrənt] *n.* (*lit.*, *fig.*) пото́к; **the rain fell in ~s** шёл проливно́й дождь; дождь лил как из ведра́; **he was met by a ~ of abuse** его́ встре́тил пото́к оскорбле́ний.
torrential [tə'renʃ(ə)l] *adj.* стреми́тельно теку́щий; проливно́й; **~ rain** проливно́й дождь.
torrid ['tɒrɪd] *adj.* жа́ркий, зно́йный; **~ zone** тропи́ческий по́яс.
torsion ['tɔːʃ(ə)n] *n.* (*process*) скру́чивание; (*state*) скру́ченность.
torso ['tɔːsəʊ] *n.* ту́ловище, торс.
tort [tɔːt] *n.* гражда́нско-правово́й дели́кт.
tortoise ['tɔːtəs] *n.* черепа́ха; (*attr.*) черепа́ший.
cpd. **~shell** *n.* (*as material*) черепа́ха; *adj.* черепа́ховый.
tortuous ['tɔːtjʊəs] *adj.* изви́листый; (*fig.*) укло́нчивый, нейскренний.
tortu|ousness ['tɔːtjʊəsnɪs], **-osity** [ˌtɔːtjʊ'ɒsɪtɪ] *nn.* изви́листость; (*fig.*) укло́нчивость, нейскренность.
torture ['tɔːtʃə(r)] *n.* (*physical*) пы́тка; **he was put to the ~** его́ подве́ргли пы́ткам; (*mental*) му́ки (*f. pl.*).
v.t. пыта́ть (*impf.*); му́чить (*impf.*); **she was ~d with anxiety** её му́чила трево́га; **a ~d expression** выраже́ние му́ки; (*fig.*, *distort*) иска|жа́ть, -зи́ть; **the meaning of the words was ~d** смысл слов изврати́ли/искази́ли.
torturer ['tɔːtʃərə(r)] *n.* мучи́тель (*m.*); пала́ч.
Tory ['tɔːrɪ] *n.* (*coll.*) то́ри (*m. indecl.*), консерва́тор; **the ~ party** консервати́вная па́ртия; **~ leaders** ли́деры то́ри.
tosh [tɒʃ] *n.* (*coll.*) вздор, чепуха́.
toss [tɒs] *n.* (*throw*) бросо́к; (*jerk*) толчо́к; **with a ~ of her head, she ...** тряхну́в голово́й (*or* вски́нув го́лову), она́...; **he took a nasty ~** он упа́л с ло́шади и си́льно ушибся.
v.t. **1.** (*throw*) бр|оса́ть, -о́сить; кида́ть, ки́нуть; **he was ~ed by a bull** бык по́днял его́ на рога́; **the horse ~ed its rider** ло́шадь сбро́сила седока́; **he ~ed a coin to the beggar** он бро́сил ни́щему моне́ту; **they ~ed a coin to decide** они́ подки́нули моне́ту, что́бы реши́ть исхо́д де́ла; **he ~ed a remark into the debate** в хо́де диску́ссии он бро́сил замеча́ние. **2.** (*rock*, *agitate*) швыр|я́ть, -ну́ть; **the ship was ~ed by the waves** во́лны подки́дывали су́дно вверх и вниз.
v.i. мета́ться (*impf.*); **the child ~ed in its sleep** ребёнок мета́лся во сне; **a ship was ~ing on the waves** кора́бль кача́лся на волна́х; **~ing branches** колы́шущиеся ве́тки.
with advs.: **~ about** *v.i.* мета́ться (*impf.*); **~ aside, ~ away** *vv.t.* отбр|а́сывать, -о́сить; **~ off** *v.t.* выпива́ть, вы́пить за́лпом; де́лать, с- на́спех; **he ~ed off a glass of vodka** он пропусти́л сто́пку во́дки; **he can ~ off an article in five minutes** он спосо́бен наброса́ть статью́ за пять мину́т; **~ up** *v.t.* подбр|а́сывать, -о́сить; *v.i.*: **shall we ~ up to see who goes?** дава́йте бро́сим жре́бий, кому́ идти́.
cpd. **~-up** *n.* нея́сный исхо́д; де́ло слу́чая.
tot[1] [tɒt] *n.* (*child*) малы́ш; (*of liquor*) глото́к.
tot[2] [tɒt] *v.t. with adv.* **up** сост|авля́ть, -а́вить (*сумму*); **he ~ted up the figures** он подвёл ито́г.
v.i.: **his expenses ~ted up to £5** его́ расхо́ды соста́вили 5 фу́нтов.
total ['təʊt(ə)l] *n.* су́мма, ито́г; **the grand ~ came to £200** о́бщая су́мма соста́вила £200.
adj. це́лый, о́бщий, по́лный; **~ eclipse** по́лное затме́ние; **~ failure** по́лный прова́л; **the ~ figure** о́бщая ци́фра; **he remained in ~ ignorance** он остава́лся в по́лном неве́дении; **~ war** тота́льная война́.
v.t. & i. (*reckon*, *also* **~ up**) подсчи́т|ывать, -а́ть; подв|оди́ть, -ести́ ито́г; **he ~led (up) the bills** он подсчита́л счета́; **the visitors ~led several hundred** число́ посети́телей дости́гло не́скольких со́тен.
totalitarian [təʊˌtælɪ'teərɪən] *adj.* тоталита́рный.
totalitarianism [təʊˌtælɪ'teərɪənɪz(ə)m] *n.* тоталитари́зм.
totality [təʊ'tælɪtɪ] *n.* вся су́мма, всё коли́чество; всео́бщность, тота́льность; (*astron.*) вре́мя по́лного затме́ния.
totalizator ['təʊtəlaɪˌzeɪtə(r)] *n.* тотализа́тор.
totally ['təʊtəlɪ] *adv.* соверше́нно, абсолю́тно, по́лностью.
tote[1] [təʊt] (*coll.*) = **totalizator**
tote[2] [təʊt] *v.t.* (*US coll.*) носи́ть, нести́ (*груз, оружие и т.п.*).
totem ['təʊtəm] *n.* тоте́м.
cpd. **~-pole** *n.* тоте́мный столб.
totter ['tɒtə(r)] *v.i.* (*walk unsteadily*) ковыля́ть (*impf.*); (*fig.*) шата́ться, пошатну́ться; (*be about to fall*) разруша́ться (*impf.*); разва́ливаться (*impf.*).
tottery ['tɒtərɪ] *adj.* неусто́йчивый; на гра́ни паде́ния.
toucan ['tuːkən] *n.* тука́н.
touch [tʌtʃ] *n.* **1.** (*contact*; *light pressure of hand etc.*) прикоснове́ние; **I felt a ~ on my shoulder** я почу́вствовал лёгкое прикоснове́ние к своему́ плечу́; **the instrument responded to the slightest ~** инструме́нт реаги́ровал на мале́йшее прикоснове́ние. **2.** (*sense*) осяза́ние; **the blind man recognized me by ~** слепо́й узна́л меня́ на о́щупь; **soft to the ~** мя́гкий на о́щупь. **3.** (*light stroke of pen or brush*) штрих; **he was putting the finishing ~es to the picture** он наноси́л после́дние мазки́ (на карти́ну). **4.** (*tinge*, *trace*) чу́точка, отте́нок, налёт; **a ~ of frost in the air** лёгкий моро́зец; **I caught a ~ of the sun** я получи́л лёгкий со́лнечный уда́р; **I had a ~ of rheumatism** у меня́ был небольшо́й при́ступ ревмати́зма; **this soup needs a ~ of salt** в су́пе чу́точку не хвата́ет со́ли; **there was a ~ of irony in his voice** в его́ го́лосе чу́вствовалось лёгкая иро́ния. **5.** (*artist's or performer's style*) худо́жественная мане́ра; стиль (*m.*); **he has a light ~ on the piano** у него́

лёгкое туше́ (на фортепья́но); (*fig.*): **he brought a personal ~ to all he did** на всём, что он де́лал, лежа́л отпеча́ток его́ ли́чности; **you must have lost your ~** вы я́вно утра́тили (бы́лую) хва́тку. **6.** (*communication*) обще́ние; **we must keep in ~** мы должны́ подде́рживать конта́кт друг с дру́гом; **we have been out of ~ for so long** мы так до́лго не обща́лись; **how can I get in ~ with you?** как мо́жно с ва́ми связа́ться?; **he put me in ~ with the situation** он ознако́мил меня́ с положе́нием веще́й; **we lost ~ with him** мы потеря́ли с ним конта́кт/связь. **7.** (*football*) пло́щадь, лежа́щая за боковы́ми ли́ниями по́ля; **the ball was in ~** мяч находи́лся в преде́лах боково́й ли́нии по́ля. **8.** (*child's game*) са́лки (*f. pl.*). **9.** (*sl.*, *potential source of money*): **he is a soft (*or* an easy) ~** у него́ легко́ вы́удить де́ньги.

v.t. **1.** (*contact physically*) тро́|гать, -нуть; прик|аса́ться, -осну́ться к+*d.*; **he ~ed her (on the) arm** он косну́лся её руки́; **don't ~ the paint** не дотра́гивайтесь до кра́ски; **the cars just ~ed each other** маши́ны едва́ косну́лись друг дру́га; **he ~ed his cap** он поднёс ру́ку к фура́жке; **it was ~ and go** исхо́д был неизве́стен до са́мого конца́; **~ wood!** тьфу-тьфу́, не сгла́зить! **2.** (*actuate*): **I ~ed the bell** я нажа́л звоно́к; (*fig.*): **he ~ed a tender chord in her** он косну́лся чувстви́тельной стру́нки в её се́рдце. **3.** (*reach*) дост|ига́ть, -и́гнуть +*g.*; **can you ~ the top of the door?** вы мо́жете дотяну́ться до ве́рха две́ри?; **the thermometer ~ed ninety** термо́метр подня́лся до девяно́ста гра́дусов; **I can just ~ bottom** я е́ле достаю до дна; **his fortunes ~ed bottom** он дошёл до дна. **4.** (*approach in excellence*; *compare with*) равня́ться (*impf.*) с+*i.*; идти́ (*det.*) в сравне́ние с+*i.*; **no-one can ~ him for eloquence** никто́ не мо́жет сравни́ться с ним в красноре́чии. **5.** (*affect*) тро́гать (*impf.*); волнова́ть, вз-; **it ~ed me to the heart (*or* ~ed my heart)** я был глубоко́ тро́нут; **his remarks ~ed me on the raw** его́ замеча́ния заде́ли меня́ за живо́е; **I find her innocence ~ing** меня́ тро́гает её наи́вность; **we were very ~ed by his speech** его́ речь о́чень взволнова́ла нас. **6.** (*taste*) притр|а́гиваться, -о́нуться; **I haven't ~ed food for two days** я не прикаса́лся к еде́ це́лых два дня; **I never ~ a drop** (*of alcohol*) я совсе́м не пью; я не пью ни ка́пли. **7.** (*injure slightly*) нан|оси́ть, -ести́ уще́рб +*d.*; **the flowers were ~ed by the frost** цветы́ бы́ли тро́нуты моро́зом; (*fig.*): **he must be a little ~ed** (*slightly mad*) он, должно́ быть, немно́го поме́шан/тро́нут. **8.** (*deal with*; *cope with*) спр|авля́ться, -а́виться с+*i.*; **nothing will ~ these stains** э́ти пя́тна ниче́м не вы́ведешь; **I couldn't ~ the maths paper** я ника́к не мог взя́ться (*or* приня́ться) за контро́льную по матема́тике. **9.** (*concern*) име́ть отноше́ние к+*d.*; каса́ться (*impf.*) +*g.*; **it ~es us all** э́то каса́ется нас всех; **I heard some news ~ing your son** (*liter.*) я слы́шал ко́е-что́, каса́ющееся ва́шего сы́на. **10.** (*have to do with*) зан|има́ться, -я́ться +*i.*; **I refuse to ~ your schemes** я не хочу́ име́ть ничего́ о́бщего с ва́шими пла́нами. **11.** (*treat lightly*; *also v.i. with prep.* **on**) затр|а́гивать, -о́нуть; **he ~ed (on) the subject of race** он косну́лся ра́сового вопро́са. **12.** (*prevail on for loan*): **can I ~ you for a fiver?** могу́ я стрельну́ть (*coll.*) у вас пятёрку?

v.i. **1.** (*make contact*) соприк|аса́ться, -осну́ться; **our hands ~ed** на́ши ру́ки встре́тились; **their lips ~d** их гу́бы слили́сь в поцелу́е; **if the wires ~ there will be an explosion** е́сли провода́ соприкосну́тся, бу́дет взрыв. **2.** (*of a vessel*: *call*, *put in*) за|ходи́ть, -йти́; **we ~ed at Gibraltar** на́ше су́дно зашло́ в Гибралта́р. **3. ~ on:** *see v.t.* **11.**

with advs.: **~ in** *v.t.*: **the features were ~ed in by another hand** лицо́ бы́ло дописа́но други́м худо́жником; **~ off** *v.t.* (*sketch*) набр|оса́ть, -о́сить; (*cause*) вызыва́ть, вы́звать; **~ up** *v.t.* испр|авля́ть, -а́вить; зак|а́нчивать, -о́нчить; **I'll just ~ it up** я чуть ко́е-где подпра́влю; **the photographs had been ~ed up** фотогра́фии бы́ли отретуши́рованы.

cpds. **~-and-go** *adj.* с непредсказу́емым исхо́дом; **~-down** *n.* (*football*) гол; (*aeron.*) поса́дка; **~line** *n.* бокова́я ли́ния по́ля; **~stone** *n.* (*fig.*) крите́рий; про́бный ка́мень; осело́к; **~-typist** *n.* машини́стка, рабо́тающая по слепо́му ме́тоду; **~wood** *n.* трут.

touchable ['tʌtʃəb(ə)l] *adj.* осяза́тельный, осяза́емый.

touché [tu:'ʃeɪ] *int.* туше́!

touched [tʌtʃd] *adj.* (*emotionally*) растро́ганный; (*coll.*, *mentally*) слегка́ поме́шанный, «тро́нутый».

touchiness ['tʌtʃɪnɪs] *n.* оби́дчивость.

touching ['tʌtʃɪŋ] *adj.* тро́гательный.

prep. относи́тельно+*g.*

touchy ['tʌtʃɪ] *adj.* оби́дчивый.

tough [tʌf] *n.* хулига́н, блатно́й.

adj. **1.** (*resistant to cutting or chewing*) жёсткий; упру́гий; **this steak is as ~ as leather** э́тот бифште́кс жёсткий как подо́шва. **2.** (*strong*, *sturdy*, *hardy*) кре́пкий; пло́тный; про́чный; выно́сливый; **you need a ~ pair of shoes** вам нужна́ кре́пкая о́бувь. **3.** (*difficult*) тру́дный; упря́мый; **I am finding it a ~ job** э́та рабо́та ока́зывается не из лёгких; **he is a ~ nut, customer** (*coll.*) он кре́пкий оре́шек. **4.** (*coll.*, *severe*, *uncompromising*) круто́й; жёсткий; упря́мый; несгово́рчивый; **you must take a ~ line with the children** с э́тими детьми́ ну́жно быть постро́же; **don't try and get ~ with me!** си́лой вы от меня́ ничего́ не добьётесь! **5.** (*coll.*, *painful*): **it was ~ on him when his father died** смерть отца́ была́ тя́жким уда́ром для него́; **~ luck!** вот незада́ча!; не везёт! **6.** (*ruffianly*) хулига́нский.

toughen ['tʌfən] *v.t.* & *i.* де́лать(ся), с- жёстким; **a ~ing-up course** курс трениро́вок с больши́ми нагру́зками.

toughness ['tʌfnɪs] *n.* (*of food etc.*) жёсткость; (*strength*; *hardiness*) про́чность; выно́сливость; (*uncompromising nature*) несгово́рчивость; упря́мство.

toupee ['tu:peɪ] *n.* небольшо́й пари́к, накла́дка.

tour [tʊə(r)] *n.* **1.** (*extended visit*) путеше́ствие, пое́здка; экску́рсия; **we are going on a ~ of Europe** мы собира́емся путеше́ствовать по Евро́пе; **the duty officer made a ~ of the building** дежу́рный осмотре́л всё зда́ние; **grand ~** (*hist.*) пое́здка по Евро́пе для заверше́ния образова́ния. **2.** (*theatr.*) турне́ (*indecl.*); гастро́ли (*f. pl.*); **the company was on ~** тру́ппа гастроли́ровала (*or* находи́лась на гастро́лях). **3.** (*period of duty*) срок слу́жбы; **have you done an overseas ~?** вы служи́ли за грани́цей?

v.t. & *i.* соверш|а́ть, -и́ть экску́рсию (по+*d.*); **we have been ~ing Scotland** мы объе́здили Шотла́ндию.

tour de force [ˌtʊə də 'fɔ:s] *n.* проявле́ние си́лы; ло́вкая шту́ка; **a ~ of memory** проявле́ние феномена́льной па́мяти.

tourism ['tʊərɪz(ə)m] *n.* тури́зм.

tourist ['tʊərɪst] *n.* тури́ст; **~ agency** туристи́ческое аге́нтство, бюро́ (*indecl.*) путеше́ствий; **~ class** второ́й класс; **the ~ industry** индустри́я тури́зма.

tourn|ament ['tʊənəmənt], **-ey** ['tʊənɪ] *nn.* турни́р; спорти́вное соревнова́ние.

tourniquet ['tʊənɪˌkeɪ] *n.* турнике́т.

tousle ['taʊz(ə)l] *v.t.* прив|оди́ть, -ести́ в беспоря́док; еро́шить, -взъ-.

tout [taʊt] *n.* зазыва́ла (*m.*); **ticket ~** «жучо́к».

v.i. навя́з|ывать, -а́ть това́р; зазыва́ть (*impf.*) покупа́телей.

tout court [tu: 'kʊə(r)] *adv.* про́сто, по́просту.

tow[1] [təʊ] *n.*: **can I give you a ~?** взять вас на букси́р?; **he had his family in ~** он привёл с собо́й всю семью́.

v.t. букси́ровать (*impf.*); **the ship was ~ed into harbour** кора́бль вошёл в га́вань на букси́ре; **they ~ed the car away** маши́ну отбукси́ровали.

cpds. **~(ing-)path** *n.* бечевни́к; **~-rope** *n.* бечева́; букси́рный трос/кана́т.

tow[2] [təʊ] *n.* (*material*) па́кля.

toward(s) [tə'wɔ:dz, twɔ:dz, tɔ:dz] *prep.* **1.** (*in the direction of*) к+*d.*; на+*a.*; по направле́нию к+*d.*; **he stood with his back ~ me** он стоя́л ко мне спино́й; **a move ~ peace** шаг на пути́ к ми́ру; **efforts ~ reconciliation** уси́лия, напра́вленные к примире́нию. **2.** (*in relation to*) по отноше́нию к+*d.*; относи́тельно+*g.*; **what is his attitude ~ education?** как он отно́сится к пробле́ме образова́ния?; **they seemed friendly ~ us** каза́лось, что они́ к нам дру́жески располо́жены; **responsibility ~ his family** отве́тственность пе́ред семьёй. **3.** (*for the purpose of*) для+*g*; **they were saving ~ buying a house** они́ копи́ли де́ньги на поку́пку до́ма; **I gave him something ~ the price** я ему́ дал часть де́нег на э́ту поку́пку. **4.** (*near*) к+*d*.; о́коло+*g*; **~ evening** к ве́черу, под ве́чер, пе́ред ве́чером; **I'm getting ~ the end of my supply** мои́ запа́сы подхо́дят к концу́.

towel ['taʊəl] *n.* полоте́нце; **throw in the ~** (*lit.*) вы́бросить (*pf.*) на ринг полоте́нце; (*fig.*) призна́ть (*pf.*) себя́ побеждённым.

v.t. вытира́ть, вы́тереть полоте́нцем; **give yourself a good ~ling!** вы́тритесь хороше́нько!

cpds. **~-horse, ~-rail** *nn.* ве́шалка для полоте́нец.

towelling ['taʊəlɪŋ] *n.* (*material*) махро́вая ткань.

tower ['taʊə(r)] *n.* ба́шня; (*fig.*): **a ~ of strength** опло́т; надёжная опо́ра.

v.i. вы́ситься, возвыша́ться (*both impf.*); **the building ~ed above us** зда́ние уходи́ло высо́ко́ в не́бо; (*fig.*): **he ~s above his fellows** он намно́го (*or* на це́лую го́лову) превосхо́дит свои́х колле́г; **a ~ing rage** си́льная/неи́стовая я́рость.

cpd. **~-block** *n.* многоэта́жный/высо́тный дом.

town [taʊn] *n.* **1.** го́род; **he is out of ~** он уе́хал за́ город; **are you going down ~?** (*US, to the business quarter*) вы собира́етесь в центр/го́род?; **let's go out on the ~!** дава́йте как сле́дует погуля́ем!; **go to ~** (*coll.*) разверну́ться (*pf.*) вовсю́; **man about ~** све́тский челове́к. **2.** (*attr.*) городско́й; **~ clerk** секрета́рь городско́й корпора́ции; **~ council** мэ́рия; **~ crier** глаша́тай; **~ hall** мэ́рия; ра́туша; **~ house** особня́к; **~ planning** планиро́вка городо́в; градострои́тельство.

cpds. **~scape** *n.* урбанисти́ческий ландша́фт; вид го́рода; **~sfolk, ~speople** *nn. pl.* горожа́не (*m. pl.*); **~sman** *n.* горожа́нин; **my fellow-~sman** ≃ мой земля́к; **fellow-~smen!** сограждане!

townee [taʊ'ni:] *n.* ≃ обыва́тель (*m.*), мещани́н.

township ['taʊnʃɪp] *n.* **1.** (*small town*) посёлок, городо́к. **2.** (*US*) райо́н.

tox(a)emia [tɒk'si:mɪə] *n.* зараже́ние кро́ви.

toxic ['tɒksɪk] *adj.* ядови́тый, токси́ческий.

toxicologist [,tɒksɪ'kɒlədʒɪst] *n.* токсико́лог.

toxicology [,tɒksɪ'kɒlədʒɪ] *n.* токсиколо́гия.

toxin ['tɒksɪn] *n.* токси́н; яд.

toy [tɔɪ] *n.* игру́шка; **~ boy** молодо́й любо́вник; **~ dog** игру́шечная соба́чка; (*lap-dog*) боло́нка; **~ soldier** оловя́нный солда́тик.

v.i.: **he ~ed with his pencil** он верте́л в рука́х каранда́ш; **I have been ~ing with the idea** я забавля́лся э́той иде́ей; **he ~ed with her affections** он игра́л её чу́вствами.

cpd. **~shop** *n.* игру́шечный магази́н.

trace[1] [treɪs] *n.* **1.** (*track*) след; отпеча́ток. **2.** (*vestige; sign of previous existence*) след; **he went away leaving no ~** он исче́з, не оста́вив и следа́; **the police could find no ~ of him** поли́ции не удало́сь напа́сть на его́ след; **I have lost all ~ of my family** я растеря́л всех родны́х; **the ship disappeared without ~** кора́бль пропа́л/исче́з бессле́дно; **there are ~s of French influence** чу́вствуется не́которое францу́зское влия́ние. **3.** (*small quantity*) ма́лое коли́чество; следы́ (*в анализе*); **~ elements** микроэлеме́нты.

v.t. **1.** (*delineate*) набр|а́сывать, -оса́ть; черти́ть, на-; **he ~d (out) his route on the map** он начерти́л маршру́т на ка́рте; (*with transparent paper or carbon*) копи́ровать, с-; **tracing paper** воско́вка; (*write laboriously*): **I helped him to ~ (out) the letters** я помо́г ему́ вы́писать/вы́вести бу́квы. **2.** (*follow the tracks of*) высле́живать, вы́следить; **the thief was ~d to London** следы́ во́ра вели́ в Ло́ндон; **he ~s his descent from Charlemagne** он ведёт свой род от Ка́рла Вели́кого; **the rumour was ~d to its source** исто́чник слу́хов был устано́влен. **3.** (*discover by search; discern*) устан|а́вливать, -ови́ть; просле́|живать, -ди́ть; **I cannot ~ your letter** я не могу́ разыска́ть ва́ше письмо́; **they ~d the site of the city walls** они́ установи́ли местоположе́ние ста́рой городско́й стены́.

trace[2] [treɪs] *n.* (*of harness*) постро́мка; **kick over the ~s** (*fig.*) вы́йти (*pf.*) из повинове́ния; взбунтова́ться (*pf.*); пусти́ться (*impf.*) во все тя́жкие.

traceable ['treɪsəb(ə)l] *adj.* просле́живаемый.

tracer ['treɪsə(r)] *n.* **(~ bullet)** трасси́рующая пу́ля; **(~ element)** ме́ченый а́том.

tracery ['treɪsərɪ] *n.* узо́р(ы), рису́нок.

trachea [trə'ki:ə, 'treɪkɪə] *n.* трахе́я.

tracheotomy [,trækɪ'ɒtəmɪ] *n.* трахеотоми́я.

trachoma [trə'kəʊmə] *n.* трахо́ма.

track [træk] *n.* **1.** (*mark of passage*) след; **the fox left ~s in the snow** лиси́ца оста́вила след на снегу́; **we followed in his ~s** мы шли по его́ следа́м; **the ~ of a vessel** след су́дна; **the police were on his ~** поли́ция напа́ла на его́ след; **we lost ~ of him** мы потеря́ли его́ след; (*fig.*): **I think I'm on the ~ of something big** я, ка́жется, на пути́ к большо́му откры́тию; **he covered his ~s successfully** он успе́шно замёл следы́; **he fell dead in his ~s** он так и у́мер на бегу́; **make ~s** улизну́ть (*pf., coll.*). **2.** (*path*) путь (*m.*), доро́жка; **the beaten ~** проторённая доро́жка; **off the beaten ~** вдали́ от прое́зжей доро́ги; **he is on the wrong ~** он на ло́жном пути́. **3.** (*for racing etc.*) (бегова́я) доро́жка; **cinder ~** га́ревая доро́жка; **hard ~** жёсткая доро́жка; **~ events** соревнова́ния по лёгкой атле́тике. **4.** (*rail*) колея́, полотно́; **single ~** одноколе́йный путь. **5.** (*of tank etc.*) гу́сеница; **~ed vehicle** гу́сеничный тра́нспорт. **6.** (*distance between vehicle's wheels*) ширина́ коле́й.

v.t. следи́ть за+*i*.; высле́живать, вы́следить; **the animal was ~ed to its den** зве́ря вы́следили до са́мой берло́ги; **the aircraft was ~ed by radar** путь самолёта проследи́ли с по́мощью рада́ра; **~ing station** ста́нция слеже́ния.

v.i. (*of camera*) панорами́ровать (*impf.*); **~ing shot** (*cin.*) пано́ра́мный кадр.

with adv.: **~ down** *v.t.*: **have you ~ed down the cause of the disease?** вы докопа́лись до причи́ны боле́зни?

cpds. **~-racing** *n.* го́нки по тре́ку; **~-shoes** *n. pl.* кроссо́вки (*f. pl.*); **~-suit** *n.* трениро́вочный костю́м.

tracker ['trækə(r)] *n.* (*hunter*) охо́тник; **~ dog** соба́ка-ище́йка.

tract[1] [trækt] *n.* (*region*) уча́сток, райо́н; **a desolate ~** забро́шенный райо́н; (*anat.*) тракт; **respiratory ~** дыха́тельные пути́ (*m. pl.*).

tract[2] [trækt] *n.* (*pamphlet*) памфле́т.

tractability [,træktə'bɪlɪtɪ] *n.* послуша́ние, сгово́рчивость.

tractable ['træktəb(ə)l] *adj.* послу́шный, сгово́рчивый.

traction ['trækʃ(ə)n] *n.* тя́га; **~ engine** тя́говый дви́гатель (*m.*); тяга́ч.

tractor ['træktə(r)] *n.* тра́ктор.

cpds. **~-driven** *adj.* на тра́кторной тя́ге; **~-driver** *n.* тракторист (*fem.* -ка).

trade [treɪd] *n.* **1.** (*business, occupation*) род заня́тий; ремесло́; профе́ссия; **the building ~** строи́тельная промы́шленность; **he is a builder by ~** он по профе́ссии строи́тель; **jack of all ~s** ма́стер на все ру́ки; **he is up to every trick of the ~** (*fig.*) он зна́ет все ходы́ и вы́ходы. **2.** (*commerce; exchange of goods*) торго́вля; **foreign ~** вне́шняя торго́вля; **winter is good for ~** зима́ — хоро́шее вре́мя для торго́вли; **~ is bad** торго́вля идёт пло́хо; **he is in ~** он торго́вец; он рабо́тает по торго́вой ча́сти; **he is doing a roaring ~** его́ торго́вля идёт о́чень успе́шно; **~ discount** ски́дка ро́зничным торго́вцам; **~ figures** да́нные о торго́вле; **~ gap** дефици́т торго́вого бала́нса; **~ secret** профессиона́льный секре́т; **~ price** опто́вая цена́; **~ show** (*of film*) закры́тый просмо́тр (для покупа́телей фи́льма); **~ wind** пасса́т.

v.t. (*exchange*) меня́ть (*impf.*); обме́н|ивать, -я́ть; **they ~d furs for food** они́ меня́ли шку́ры на проду́кты.

v.i. **1.** торгова́ть (*impf.*); **he ~s in sables** он торгу́ет соболя́ми; **trading estate** промы́шленная зо́на. **2.: ~ on** (*take advantage of*) испо́льзовать (*impf., pf.*) в свои́х интере́сах; извлека́ть (*impf.*) вы́году из+*g*.; **he ~s on my generosity** он злоупотребля́ет мое́й ще́дростью; **he ~s on his reputation** он спекули́рует на свое́й сла́ве/репута́ции.

with adv.: **~ in** *v.t.*: **I ~d in my old car for a new one** я сдал ста́рую маши́ну в счёт поку́пки но́вой.

cpds. **~-mark** *n.* (*lit.*) фабри́чная ма́рка; (*fig.*) отличи́тельный знак; отличи́тельная осо́бенность; **~-name** *n.* назва́ние фи́рмы; торго́вое/фи́рменное назва́ние това́ра; **~sman** *n.* торго́вец; ла́вочник; **~smen's entrance** чёрный ход; **~speople** *n. pl.* ла́вочники (*m. pl.*); торго́вое сосло́вие; **~(s) union** *n.* тред-юнио́н; профсою́з; **T~s Union Congress** (*Br.*) Конгре́сс тред-юнио́нов; **~-unionism** *n.* тред-юниони́зм; **~-unionist** *n.* тред-юниони́ст (*fem.* -ка); член профсою́за.

trader ['treɪdə(r)] *n.* (*merchant*) торго́вец, купе́ц; (*vessel*) торго́вое су́дно.

tradition [trə'dɪʃ(ə)n] *n.* тради́ция.

traditional [trə'dɪʃən(ə)l] *adj.* традицио́нный, общепри́нятый.

traditionalism [trə'dɪʃənə,lɪz(ə)m] *n.* приве́рженность тради́циям.

traditionalist [trə'dɪʃənəlɪst] *n.* приве́рженец тради́ции.

traduce [trə'dju:s] *v.t.* (*liter.*) клевета́ть (*impf.*) на+*a.*; черни́ть, о-; оклевета́ть (*pf.*).

traffic ['træfɪk] *n.* **1.** (*movement of vehicles etc.*) движе́ние, тра́нспорт; **heavy ~** большо́е/интенси́вное движе́ние; **~ circle** (*US*) кольцева́я тра́нспортная развя́зка; **~ cop** (*US coll.*) регулиро́вщик; госуда́рственный автомоби́льный инспе́ктор, «гаи́шник»; **~ indicator** указа́тель (*m.*) поворо́та; **~ lights** светофо́р; **~ warden** ≃ инспе́ктор доро́жного движе́ния. **2.** (*trade*) торго́вля; **the drug ~** торго́вля нарко́тиками.

v.i. торгова́ть (*чем*).

trafficator ['træfɪ,keɪtə(r)] *n.* указа́тель (*m.*) поворо́та.

trafficker ['træfɪkə(r)] *n.* (*pej.*) торга́ш; деле́ц.

tragedian [trə'dʒi:dɪən] *n.* (*actor*) тра́гик; (*author*) а́втор траге́дий.

tragedienne [trə,dʒi:dɪ'en] *n.* траги́ческая актри́са.

tragedy ['trædʒɪdɪ] *n.* (*lit. fig.*) траге́дия; **~ actor** тра́гик; **he appears in ~** он игра́ет в траге́диях.

tragic ['trædʒɪk] *adj.* траги́ческий.

tragicomedy [,trædʒɪ'kɒmɪdɪ] *n.* трагикоме́дия.

tragicomic [,trædʒɪ'kɒmɪk] *adj.* трагикоми́ческий.

trail [treɪl] *n.* **1.** след; **the storm left a ~ of destruction** бу́ря оста́вила после себя́ (следы́) разруше́ния; **a ~ of smoke** о́блако ды́ма; **the police were on his ~** поли́ция напа́ла на его́ след. **2.** (*mil.*): **at the ~** с ору́жием напереве́с.

v.t. **1.** (*draw or drag behind*) тащи́ть (*impf.*); волочи́ть (*impf.*); **she ~ed her skirt in the mud** её ю́бка волочи́лась по гря́зи; **the rowers ~ed their oars** гребцы́ держа́ли вёсла по бо́рту; **he was ~ing his coat** (*fig.*) он лез в дра́ку. **2.** (*pursue*) идти́ (*det.*) по сле́ду +*g.*; **they ~ed the beast to its lair** они́ проследи́ли зве́ря до берло́ги. **3.** (*mil.*): **~ arms** на́ руку!

v.i. **1.** (*be drawn or dragged*) тащи́ться (*impf.*); волочи́ться (*impf.*); **the rope ~ed on the ground** верёвка волочи́лась по земле́; **smoke ~ed from the chimney** дым тяну́лся из трубы́. **2.** (*straggle, follow wearily*) плести́сь (*impf.*); идти́ (*det.*) сза́ди; **they ~ed along behind him** они́ плели́сь за ним; **her voice ~ed away** её го́лос постепе́нно затиха́л. **3.** (*grow or hang loosely*) све́шиваться (*impf.*); стели́ться (*impf.*); **the roses ~ed over the wall** ро́зы обвива́ли сте́ну; **her hair ~ed down over her shoulders** во́лосы па́дали ей на пле́чи.

trailer ['treɪlə(r)] *n.* **1.** (*vehicle*) прице́п. **2.** (*cin.*) вы́держки (*f. pl.*) из реклами́руемого фи́льма; рекла́мный ро́лик. **3.** (*plant*) вью́щееся расте́ние.

train [treɪn] *n.* **1.** (*rail*) по́езд; **I came by ~** я прие́хал по́ездом; **hurry if you want to catch your ~** на́до поторопи́ться, е́сли вы хоти́те поспе́ть на по́езд; **the ~ is already in** по́езд уже́ при́был. **2.** (*line of moving vehicles, animals etc.*) проце́ссия; карава́н; (*mil.*) обо́з. **3.** (*retinue*) сви́та. **4.** (*fig.*) ряд, цепь; **~ of events** цепь/верени́ца/ряд собы́тий; **the war brought famine in its ~** война́ принесла́ с собо́й го́лод; **I don't follow your ~ of thought** мне тру́дно улови́ть ход ва́ших мы́слей. **5.** (*of dress etc.*) шлейф.

v.t. **1.** (*give instruction to*) обуч|а́ть, -и́ть; приуч|а́ть, -и́ть; **he was ~ed (up) for the ministry** его́ гото́вили в свяще́нники; **a ~ed nurse** медици́нская сестра́; **I have ~ed my dog to do tricks** я обучи́л соба́ку трю́кам; **he ~s horses** он дрессиру́ет лошаде́й. **2.** (*cause to grow*): **peaches can be ~ed up a wall** пе́рсиковые дере́вья мо́жно заста́вить ви́ться по стене́. **3.** (*direct*) нав|оди́ть, -ести́; наце́ли|вать, -ть; **they ~ed their guns on the ship** они́ навели́ ору́дия на кора́бль.

v.i. **1.** (*undertake preparation*) гото́виться (*impf.*); тренирова́ться (*impf.*); **she is ~ing to be a teacher** она́ гото́вится стать учи́тельницей; **the crew ~ed on beef-steaks** во вре́мя трениро́вки кома́нда пита́лась бифште́ксами. **2.** (*coll., travel by ~*) е́здить (*det.*), е́хать, по- (*indet.*) (*or* путеше́ствовать (*impf.*)) по́ездом (*or* на по́езде).

cpds. **~-bearer** *n.* паж; **~-driver** *n.* машини́ст; **~-ferry** *n.* железнодоро́жный паро́м; **~man** *n.* (*US*) проводни́к; **~-ride** *n.* пое́здка по́ездом; **~-set** *n.* игру́шечная моде́ль желе́зной доро́ги; **~-sick** *adj.* страда́ющий тошното́й в по́езде; **he was ~-sick** в по́езде его́ укача́ло.

trainee [treɪ'ni:] *n.* стажёр (*fem.* -ка); учени́|к (*fem.* -ца).

trainer ['treɪnə(r)] *n.* **1.** тре́нер; (*of horses etc.*) дрессиро́вщи|к (*fem.* -ца). **2.** (*sports shoe*) кроссо́вка, адида́ска.

training ['treɪnɪŋ] *n.* **1.** (*study, instruction*) подгото́вка, обуче́ние. **2.** (*physical preparation*) трениро́вка; **he went into ~** он на́чал тренирова́ться; **he is out of ~** он не в фо́рме. **3.** (*of animals*) дрессиро́вка.

cpds. **~-college** *n.* педагоги́ческий институ́т; **~-ship** *n.* уче́бное су́дно; **~-shoes** *n. pl.* (спорти́вные) та́почки (*f. pl.*).

traipse [treɪps] *v.i.* (*coll.*) таска́ться (*impf.*).

trait [treɪ, treɪt] *n.* осо́бенность, сво́йство; черта́.

traitor ['treɪtə(r)] *n.* преда́тель (*m.*), изме́нник; **he turned ~** он стал преда́телем.

traitorous ['treɪtərəs] *adj.* преда́тельский, изме́ннический, вероло́мный.

traitress ['treɪtrɪs] *n.* преда́тельница, изме́нница.

trajectory [trə'dʒektərɪ, 'trædʒɪk-] *n.* траекто́рия.

tram [træm] *n.* (*public vehicle*) трамва́й; (*mine-car*) рудни́чная ваго́нетка.

cpds. **~car** *n.* трамва́йный ваго́н; **~-lines** *n. pl.* трамва́йные ре́льсы (*m. pl.*).

trammel ['træm(ə)l] *n.* (*fig. usu. pl.*) пу́т|ы (*pl. g.* —).

v.t. меша́ть, по-; служи́ть, по- поме́хой.

tramp [træmp] *n.* (*sound of steps*) то́пот; (*long walk*) дли́тельный похо́д; (*vagrant*) бродя́га; (*steamer*) трамп; (*US coll., prostitute*) шлю́ха.

v.t.: **he ~ed the streets looking for work** он исходи́л весь го́род в по́исках рабо́ты; **we ~ed the hills together** мы с ним мно́го ходи́ли по гора́м.

v.i. **1.** (*walk heavily*) то́пать (*impf.*); **I heard him ~ing about** я слы́шал, как он тяжело́ ступа́л; **the soldiers ~ed down the road** солда́ты гро́мко прото́пали по у́лице. **2.** (*walk a long distance*) шага́ть, про-. **3.** (*be a vagrant*) бродя́жничать (*impf.*).

trample ['træmp(ə)l] *v.t.* топта́ть (*or* растáптывать), рас-; **the children ~d down the flowers** де́ти вы́топтали цветы́; **I was almost ~d underfoot** меня́ чуть не растопта́ли.

v.i. тяжело́ ступа́ть (*impf.*); (*fig.*): **~ on** поп|ира́ть, -ра́ть; **he ~d on everyone's feelings** он не счита́лся ни с чьи́ми чу́вствами.

trampoline ['træmpə,li:n] *n.* трампли́н, бату́т.

trampolining ['træmpə,li:nɪŋ] *n.* бату́тный спорт.

trampolinist ['træmpə,li:nɪst] *n.* батути́ст (*fem.*, -ка).

trance [trɑ:ns] *n.* транс.

tranquil ['træŋkwɪl] *adj.* споко́йный, ми́рный.

tranquillity [træŋ'kwɪlɪtɪ] *n.* споко́йствие.

tranquillize ['træŋkwɪ,laɪz] *v.t.* успок|а́ивать, -о́ить.

tranquillizer ['træŋkwɪ,laɪzə(r)] *n.* успока́ивающее сре́дство, транквилиза́тор.

transact [træn'zækt, trɑ:n-, -'sækt] *v.t.* вести́ (*det.*) (*дела*); заключ|а́ть, -и́ть (*сделку*).

transaction [træn'zækʃ(ə)n, trɑ:n-, -'sækʃ(ə)n] *n.* **1.**: **~ of business** веде́ние дел. **2.** (*deal*) сде́лка. **3.** (*pl., proceedings*) труды́ (*m. pl.*); протоко́лы (*m. pl.*); (*in title of journal*) ве́домости (*f. pl.*).

transatlantic [,trænzət'læntɪk, ,trɑ:n-, -sət'læntɪk] *adj.* трансатланти́ческий; (*American*) америка́нский.

Transcaucasia [,trænskɔ:'keɪzjə] *n.* Закавка́зье.

Transcaucasian [ˌtrænskɔːˈkeɪzjən] *adj.* закавка́зский.
transceiver [trænˈsiːvə(r), trɑːn-] *n.* приёмо-переда́тчик.
transcend [trænˈsend, trɑːn-] *v.t.* прев|ыша́ть, -ы́сить; выходи́ть, вы́йти за преде́лы +*g*.
transcendence [trænˈsend(ə)ns, trɑːn-] *n.* превыше́ние; (*excellence*) превосхо́дство.
transcendent [trænˈsend(ə)nt, trɑːn-] *adj.* **1.** (*surpassing*) превосхо́дный, выдаю́щийся. **2.** (*phil.*) трансценде́нтный.
transcendental [ˌtrænsenˈdent(ə)l, ˌtrɑːn-] *adj.* (*phil.*) трансцендента́льный; (*abstract*, *vague*) нея́сный, тума́нный; сверхабстра́ктный.
transcontinental [trænzˌkɒntɪˈnent(ə)l, trɑːnz-, træns-, trɑːns-] *adj.* межконтинента́льный, трансконтинента́льный.
transcribe [trænˈskraɪb, trɑːn-] *v.t.* перепи́с|ывать, -а́ть; транскриби́ровать (*impf.*, *pf.*).
transcript [ˈtrænskrɪpt, ˈtrɑːn-] *n.* ко́пия; расшифро́вка.
transcription [ˌtrænˈskrɪpʃ(ə)n, ˈtrɑːn-] *n.* перепи́сывание; ко́пия, транскри́пция; **the ~ of notes** расшифро́вка за́писи; **phonetic ~** фонети́ческая транскри́пция.
transept [ˈtrænsept, ˈtrɑːn-] *n.* трансе́пт.
transfer[1] [ˈtrænsfɜː(r), ˈtrɑːns-] *n.* **1.** (*conveyance*; *move*) переда́ча; перенесе́ние, перено́с; перево́д; **~ of property** переда́ча иму́щества; **the ~ of a football player** перево́д игрока́ в другу́ю футбо́льную кома́нду. **2.** (*drawing etc.*) переводна́я карти́нка. **3.** (*US*, **~** *ticket*) переса́дочный биле́т.
transfer[2] [trænsˈfɜː(r), trɑːns-] *v.t.* **1.** (*move*) перен|оси́ть, -ести́. **2.** (*hand over*) перед|ава́ть, -а́ть. **3.** (*convey from one surface to another*) перев|оди́ть, -ести́; перен|оси́ть, -ести́ (*рисунок*).
v.i. (*move*) перев|оди́ться, -ести́сь; пере|ходи́ть, -йти́; (*change from one vehicle to another*) перес|а́живаться, -е́сть.
transferable [trænsˈfɜːrəb(ə)l, trɑːns-, ˈtr-] *adj.* допуска́ющий заме́ну; переводи́мый.
transference [ˈtrænsfərəns, ˈtrɑː-] *n.* **1.** перенесе́ние; перево́д; **thought ~** переда́ча мы́сли на расстоя́нии. **2.** (*psych.*) замеще́ние.
transfiguration [trænsˌfɪgjʊˈreɪʃ(ə)n, trɑː-] *n.* видоизмене́ние; (*relig.*) **the T~** Преображе́ние.
transfigure [trænsˈfɪgə(r), trɑː-] *v.t.* видоизмен|я́ть, -и́ть; (*with joy etc.*) преобра|жа́ть, -зи́ть.
transfix [trænsˈfɪks, trɑː-] *v.t.* **1.** (*impale*) пронз|а́ть, -и́ть; прок|а́лывать, -оло́ть. **2.** (*fig.*, *root to the spot*) прико́в|ывать, -а́ть к ме́сту; **he was ~ed with horror** он оцепене́л от у́жаса; он не мог сдви́нуться с ме́ста от у́жаса.
transform [trænsˈfɔːm, trɑː-] *v.t.* (*change*) измен|я́ть, -и́ть; преобразо́в|ывать, -а́ть; (*make unrecognizable*) меня́ть, измени́ть до неузнава́емости.
transformation [ˌtrænsfəˈmeɪʃ(ə)n, ˌtrɑː-] *n.* превраще́ние, переворо́т; метаморфо́за, трансформа́ция.
transformer [trænsˈfɔːmə(r), trɑː-, -zˈfɔːmə(r)] *n.* (*elec.*) трансформа́тор.
transfuse [trænsˈfjuːz, trɑː-] *v.t.* перел|ива́ть, -и́ть; де́лать, с- перелива́ние кро́ви.
transfusion [trænsˈfjuːʒ(ə)n, trɑː-] *n.* перелива́ние (кро́ви).
transgress [trænzˈgres, trɑː-, -sˈgres] *v.t.* & *i.* (*infringe*) пере|ходи́ть, -йти́ грани́цы +*g.*; нар|уша́ть, -у́шить (*закон и т.п.*); (*sin*) греши́ть, со-.
transgression [trænzˈgreʃ(ə)n, trɑː-] *n.* (*infringement*) просту́пок; наруше́ние; (*sin*) грех.
transgressor [trænzˈgresə(r), trɑː-, -sˈgresə(r)] *n.* правонаруши́тель (*fem.* -ница), гре́шни|к (*fem.* -ца).
tranship [trænˈʃɪp, trɑː-, trænz-] (*also* **transship**) *v.t.* (*goods*) перегру|жа́ть, -зи́ть с одного́ су́дна на друго́е; (*persons*) перес|а́живать, -ди́ть с одного́ су́дна на друго́е.
transhipment [trænˈʃɪpmənt, trɑː-] (*also* **transshipment**) *n.* (*of goods*) перегру́зка; (*of persons*) переса́дка.
transhumance [trænsˈhjuːməns, trɑː-] *n.* сезо́нный перего́н скота́ на но́вые па́стбища.
transience [ˈtrænziəns, ˈtrɑː-, -sɪəns] *n.* быстроте́чность; мимолётность.
transient [ˈtrænziənt, ˈtrɑː-, -sɪənt] *n.* (*US*, *temporary lodger*) вре́менный жиле́ц.
adj. (*impermanent*) вре́менный; (*brief*, *momentary*) мимолётный, преходя́щий.
transistor [trænˈzɪstə(r), trɑː-, -ˈsɪstə(r)] *n.* (*electronic component*) кристаллотрио́д; **(~ radio)** транзи́сторный радио-приёмник, транзи́стор.
transit [ˈtrænzɪt, ˈtrɑː-, -sɪt] *n.* **1.** (*conveyance*, *passage*) транзи́т, перево́зка; **the ~ of goods** перево́зка това́ров/ гру́зов; **lost in ~** потёрянный при перево́зке; **~ camp** транзи́тный ла́герь. **2.** (*astron.*) прохожде́ние (че́рез меридиа́н). **3.** (*US*, *public transport*) городско́й тра́нспорт. **4.: in ~** транзи́том.
transition [trænˈzɪʃ(ə)n, trɑː-, -ˈsɪʃ(ə)n] *n.* **1.** (*change*) перехо́д; (*period of change*) перехо́дный пери́од. **2.** (*mus.*) модуля́ция.
transitional [trænˈzɪʃənəl, trɑː-, -ˈsɪʃənəl] *adj.* перехо́дный; промежу́точный.
transitive [ˈtrænsɪtɪv, ˈtrɑː-, -zɪtɪv] *adj.* перехо́дный
transitory [ˈtrænsɪtərɪ, ˈtrɑː-, -zɪtərɪ] *adj.* преходя́щий, мимолётный.
translatable [trænˈsleɪtəb(ə)l, trɑː-, -ˈzleɪtəb(ə)l] *adj.* переводи́мый.
translate [trænˈsleɪt, trɑː-, -ˈzleɪt] *v.t.* & *i.* **1.** (*express in another language*) перев|оди́ть, -ести́; **he ~s from Russian into English** он перево́дит с ру́сского на англи́йский; **have his works been ~d?** его́ произведе́ния переводи́лись?; **these poems do not ~ well** э́ти стихотворе́ния не поддаю́тся перево́ду. **2.** (*convert*): **promises must be ~d into action** обеща́ния ну́жно претворя́ть в жизнь. **3.** (*interpret*) толкова́ть, ис-; объясн|я́ть, -и́ть; интерпрети́ровать (*impf.*, *pf.*). **4.** (*eccles.*, *transfer*) перев|оди́ть, -ести́; **the bishop was ~d** епи́скопа перевели́ в другу́ю епа́рхию.
translation [trænsˈleɪʃ(ə)n, trɑː-, -zˈleɪʃ(ə)n] *n.* перево́д; **machine/simultaneous ~** маши́нный/синхро́нный перево́д; **a novel in ~** перево́дный рома́н; (*interpretation*) объясне́ние; толкова́ние; (*removal*) перемеще́ние.
translator [trænsˈleɪtə(r), trɑː-, -zˈleɪtə(r)] *n.* перево́дчи|к (*fem.* -ца).
transliterate [trænzˈlɪtəˌreɪt, trɑː-, -sˈlɪtəˌreɪt] *v.t.* транслитери́ровать (*impf.*, *pf.*).
transliteration [trænzˌlɪtəˈreɪʃ(ə)n, trɑː-, -sˌlɪtəˈreɪʃ(ə)n] *n.* транслитера́ция.
translucenc|e [trænzˈluːs(ə)ns, trɑː-, -ˈljuːs(ə)ns, -sˈl-], **-y** [trænzˈluːs(ə)nsɪ, trɑː-, -ˈljuːs(ə)nsɪ, -sˈl-] *nn.* просве́чиваемость, полупрозра́чность.
translucent [trænzˈluːs(ə)nt, trɑː-, -ˈljuːs(ə)nt, -sˈl-] *adj.* просве́чивающий(ся), полупрозра́чный.
transmigration [ˌtrænzmaɪˈgreɪʃ(ə)n, ˌtrɑː-, -smaɪˈgreɪʃ(ə)n] *n.* переселе́ние.
transmissible [trænzˈmɪsəb(ə)l, trɑː-, -sˈmɪsəb(ə)l] *adj.* передаю́щийся; **a ~ disease** зара́зная боле́знь.
transmission [trænzˈmɪʃ(ə)n, trɑː-, -sˈmɪʃ(ə)n] *n.* переда́ча, трансми́ссия; **there are news ~s every hour** но́вости передаю́тся ка́ждый час; **the ~ of racial characteristics** переда́ча ра́совых осо́бенностей; **~ of parcels** пересы́лка паке́тов.
transmit [trænzˈmɪt, trɑː-, -sˈmɪt] *v.t.* & *i.* сообщ|а́ть, -и́ть; перед|ава́ть, -а́ть; **she ~ted her musical gift to her son** сын унасле́довал её музыка́льный дар; **the plague was ~ted by rats** чуму́ разнесли́ кры́сы; **iron ~s heat** желе́зо прово́дит тепло́; **wires ~ electric current** электри́ческий ток идёт по провода́м; **the fire was ~ting no heat** ого́нь не грел; **my set will receive but not ~** моё ра́дио мо́жет вести́ приём, а не переда́чу.
transmitter [trænsˈmɪtə(r), trɑː-, -zˈmɪtə(r)] *n.* переда́тчик; передаю́щая радиоста́нция; **portable ~** ра́ция; **~ aerial** передаю́щая анте́нна; **metals are good ~s of heat** мета́лл — хоро́ший проводни́к тепла́.
transmogrification [trænzˌmɒgrɪfɪˈkeɪʃ(ə)n, trɑː-, -sˌmɒgrɪfɪˈkeɪʃ(ə)n] *n.* (*joc.*) превраще́ние.
transmogrify [trænzˈmɒgrɪˌfaɪ, trɑː-, -sˈmɒgrɪˌfaɪ] *v.t.* (*joc.*) превра|ща́ть, -ти́ть.
transmutation [trænzˌmjuːˈteɪʃ(ə)n, trɑː-, -sˌmjuːˈteɪʃ(ə)n] *n.* превраще́ние, преобразова́ние.
transmute [trænzˈmjuːt, trɑː-, -sˈmjuːt] *v.t.* превра|ща́ть, -ти́ть;

преобразо́в|ывать, -а́ть.

transnational [trænz'næʃən(ə)l, trɑː-, -s'næʃən(ə)l] *adj.* транснациона́льный, межнациона́льный; многосторо́нний; многонациона́льный.

transoceanic [trænz,əʊʃɪ'ænɪk, trɑː-, -s,əʊʃɪ'ænɪk] *adj.* заокеа́нский; ~ **countries** замо́рские/заокеа́нские стра́ны; ~ **flight** межконтинента́льный полёт.

transom ['trænsəm] *n.* фраму́га; ~ **window** откидно́е окно́; фраму́га.

transparence [træns'pærəns, trɑː-, -'peərəns] *n.* прозра́чность.

transparency [træns'pærənsɪ, trɑː-, -'peərənsɪ] *n.* **1.** = **transparence. 2.** (*picture*) транспара́нт.

transparent [træns'pærənt, trɑː-, -'peərənt] *adj.* прозра́чный; (*fig.*) я́вный, очеви́дный; **a ~ lie** я́вная ложь; **his motives are ~** его́ побужде́ния очеви́дны.

transpierce [træns'pɪəs, trɑː-] *v.t.* пронз|а́ть, -и́ть насквозь.

transpiration [,trænspɪ'reɪʃ(ə)n, trɑː-] *n.* испа́рина.

transpire [træn'spaɪə(r), trɑː-] *v.i.* (*exude moisture*) испар|я́ться, -и́ться; (*come to be known*) обнару́жи|ваться, -ться; (*coll., happen*) случ|а́ться, -и́ться.

transplant[1] ['trænsplɑːnt, 'trɑː-] *n.* **1.** расса́да; (*sapling*) са́женец; **these cabbages are ~s** э́ту капу́сту пересади́ли. **2.: heart ~** переса́дка се́рдца.

transplant[2] [træns'plɑːnt, trɑː-] *v.t. & i.* переса́|живать, -ди́ть; **the lettuces need ~ing** сала́т необходи́мо пересади́ть; **this species does not ~ easily** э́тот вид пло́хо перено́сит переса́дку; (*fig.*) пересел|я́ть, -и́ть; **they were ~ed into modern flats** их пересели́ли в совреме́нные кварти́ры; **the doctors ~ed skin from his back** врачи́ сде́лали ему́ переса́дку ко́жи со спины́.

transplantation [træns,plɑː'nteɪʃ(ə)n, trɑː-] *n.* переса́дка, транспланта́ция; (*fig.*) переселе́ние.

transport[1] ['trænspɔːt, 'trɑː-] *n.* **1.** (*conveyance*) перево́зка, тра́нспорт. **2.** (*means of conveyance*) тра́нспорт; ~ **café** доро́жное кафе́; **public ~** городско́й/obще́ственный тра́нспорт; **have you got ~?** вы на колёсах? **3.** (*ship*) тра́нспортное су́дно; (*aircraft*) тра́нспортный самолёт; **troop ~** войсково́й тра́нспорт. **4.** (*emotion*) поры́в (чувств); **in ~s of delight** вне себя́ от ра́дости.

transport[2] [træns'pɔːt, trɑː-] *v.t.* **1.** (*convey*) перев|ози́ть, -езти́; транспорти́ровать (*impf., pf.*). **2.** (*send to penal colony*) отпр|авля́ть, -а́вить на ка́торгу. **3.** (*of emotion*): **~ed with delight** вне себя́ от ра́дости.

transportable [træns'pɔːtəb(ə)l, trɑː-] *adj.* перевози́мый, передвижно́й; (*of a sick pers.*) транспорта́бельный.

transportation [,trænspɔː'teɪʃ(ə)n, ,trɑː-] *n.* (*of goods etc.*) перево́зка, транспорти́рование; (*of a convict*) ссы́лка, транспорта́ция.

transporter [træns'pɔːtə(r), trɑː-] *n.* транспортиро́вщик; транспортёр; ~ **bridge** навесно́й мост.

transpose [træns'pəʊz, trɑː-, -z'pəʊz] *v.t.* перест|авля́ть, -а́вить; меня́ть, по- места́ми; (*mus.*) транспони́ровать (*impf., pf.*).

transposition [,trænspə'zɪʃ(ə)n, ,trɑː-, -zpə'zɪʃ(ə)n] *n.* перестано́вка; перегруппиро́вка; (*mus.*) транспози́ция.

transsexual [trænz'seksjʊəl] *n.* транссексуали́ст.

adj. транссексуа́льный.

transship [træn'ʃɪp, trɑː-, trænz-], **-ment** [træn'ʃɪpmənt, trɑː-, trænz-] = **tranship, -ment**

Trans-Siberian [trænz,saɪ'bɪərɪən] *adj.*: ~ **Railway** транссиби́рская желе́зная доро́га.

transubstantiation [,trænsəb,stænʃɪ'eɪʃ(ə)n, ,trɑː-] *n.* пресуществле́ние.

Transvaal [trænz'vɑːl, trɑː-] *n.* Трансваа́ль (*m.*).

transverse ['trænzvɜːs, 'trɑː-, -'vɜːs, -ns-] *adj.* попере́чный; косо́й.

transvestism [trænz'vestɪz(ə)m, trɑː-, -s'vestɪz(ə)m] *n.* трансвести́зм.

transvestite [trænz'vestaɪt, trɑː-, -s'vestaɪt] *n.* трансвести́т.

Transylvania [,trænsɪl'veɪnɪə] *n.* Трансильва́ния.

Transylvanian [,trænsɪl'veɪnɪən] *adj.* трансильва́нский.

trap [træp] *n.* **1.** (*for animals etc.*) капка́н, западня́; **I shall set a ~ for the mice** я поста́влю мышело́вку; (*fig.*) лову́шка; **he fell into the ~** он попа́л в лову́шку; **set a ~ for s.o.** устро́ить (*pf.*) лову́шку кому́-н.; расста́вить (*pf.*) се́ти кому́-н. **2.** (*light vehicle*) рессо́рная двуко́лка. **3.** (*mouth*) гло́тка, пасть (*sl.*); **shut your ~!** заткни́сь!; закро́й гло́тку!; **keep your ~ shut!** молчи́ в тря́почку! (*sl.*).

v.t. лови́ть, пойма́ть в лову́шку/капка́н; (*fig., catch*): **his fingers were ~ped in the door** он защеми́л па́льцы две́рью; **there is some air ~ped in the pipes** в труба́х образова́лись возду́шные про́бки; **he felt ~ped** он почу́вствовал, что зажа́т в у́гол.

cpd. **~-door** *n.* люк.

trapeze [trə'piːz] *n.* трапе́ция; ~ **artist** акроба́т.

trapezium [trə'piːzɪəm] *n.* трапе́ция.

trapezoid ['træpɪ,zɔɪd] *n.* трапецо́ид.

trapper ['træpə(r)] *n.* тра́ппер; охо́тник, ста́вящий капка́ны.

trappings ['træpɪŋz] *n.* (*harness*) сбру́я; (*fig.*): **the ~ of office** вне́шние атрибу́ты (*m. pl.*) вла́сти.

Trappist ['træpɪst] *n.* член о́рдена трапи́стов.

traps [træps] *n.* (*coll., belongings*) пожи́тк|и (*pl., g.* -ов).

trash [træʃ] *n.* **1.** (*rubbishy material, writing etc.*) халту́ра, чти́во, макулату́ра. **2.** (*US, refuse*) му́сор, отхо́ды (*m. pl.*), отбро́сы (*m. pl.*). **3.: white ~** (*US coll.*) «бе́лая шваль».

cpds. **~-can** *n.* (*US*) му́сорное ведро́; му́сорный бак.

trashy ['træʃɪ] *adj.* низкопро́бный; дрянно́й.

trauma ['trɔːmə, 'traʊ-] *n.* тра́вма.

traumatic [trɔː'mætɪk, traʊ-] *adj.* травмати́ческий.

travail ['træveɪl] *n.* му́ки (*f. pl.*); **a woman in ~** же́нщина в ро́дах.

travel ['træv(ə)l] *n.* **1.** (*journeying*) путеше́ствие, пое́здка; **~ broadens the mind** путеше́ствие расширя́ет кругозо́р; **~ agent** заве́дующий бюро́ путеше́ствий (*or* туристи́ческим аге́нтством); **~ bureau** бюро́ путеше́ствий, туристи́ческое аге́нтство; **~ literature** (*accounts of journeys*) описа́ние путеше́ствий; (*holiday brochures*) туристи́ческие проспе́кты; **~ nerves** чемода́нное настрое́ние; беспоко́йство/волне́ние пе́ред доро́гой; **he suffers from ~ sickness** он пло́хо перено́сит путеше́ствие/доро́гу. **2.** (*movement of a part or mechanism*) ход.

v.t. путеше́ствовать (*impf.*) по+*d.*; е́здить (*indet.*) по+*d.*; **I have ~led the whole of England** я изъе́здил всю А́нглию; **he ~led a thousand miles to see her** он пое́хал за ты́сячу миль, что́бы её повида́ть.

v.i. путеше́ствовать (*impf.*); е́здить, съ-; **he has been ~ling since yesterday** он со вчера́шнего дня в пути́; (*as a salesman*) е́здить (*impf.*) в ка́честве коммивояжёра; (*move*) дви́гаться (*impf.*); перемеща́ться (*impf.*); **bad news ~s fast** плохи́е ве́сти бы́стро дохо́дят; **light ~s faster than sound** ско́рость све́та превыша́ет ско́рость зву́ка; **his eye ~led over the scene** он обвёл глаза́ми всю сце́ну; **we were really ~ling** (*coll., going fast*) мы мча́лись на всех пара́х.

cpds. **~-stained** *adj.* в доро́жной пыли́; **~-worn** *adj.* измо́танный пое́здками.

travel(l)ator ['trævə,leɪt(ə)r] *n.* дви́жущийся тротуа́р.

travelled ['træv(ə)ld] *adj.* мно́го путеше́ствовавший, быва́лый.

traveller ['trævələ(r)] *n.* **1.** путеше́ственник; **~'s cheque** тури́стский чек, аккредити́в; **~'s joy** ломоно́с; **~'s tales** (*fig.*) охо́тничьи расска́зы. **2.** (*commercial ~*) коммивояжёр.

travelling ['trævəlɪŋ] *n.* путеше́ствие.

adj. путеше́ствующий; ~ **crane** передвижно́й кран; ~ **library** передвижна́я библиоте́ка; ~ **salesman** коммивояжёр.

cpds. **~-bag** *n.* чемода́нчик, ручно́й бага́ж; **~-clock** *n.* доро́жные час|ы́ (*pl., g.* -о́в).

travelogue ['trævə,lɒg] *n.* ле́кция/фильм о путеше́ствиях; путево́й о́черк.

traverse ['trævəs, trə'vɜːs] *n.* (*in mountaineering*) попере́чина, тра́верс; (*naut.*) зигзагообра́зный курс; манёвр «зигза́г».

v.t. **1.** перес|ека́ть, -е́чь; **the railway ~s miles of desert** желе́зная доро́га пересека́ет обши́рную пусты́ню; **the**

searchlight ~d the sky прожéктор обшáривал нéбо. **2.** (*leg., deny; thwart*) отрицáть (*impf.*); перéчить (*impf.*) +*d.*

travesty ['trævɪstɪ] *n.* шарж, парóдия, травестú (*nt. indecl.*); **~ of justice** парóдия на справедлúвость.

v.t. пародúровать (*impf.*).

trawl [trɔ:l] *n.* (**~-net**) трал; дóнный нéвод.

v.t. & *i.* трáлить (*impf.*); ловúть (*impf.*) рыбу трáловыми сетями; **the fishermen ~ed their nets** рыбакú тащúли сéти по дну; **they ~ed for herring** онú отлáвливали сельдь (трáлом).

trawler ['trɔ:lə(r)] *n.* (*vessel*) трáулер.

tray [treɪ] *n.* (*for tea etc.*) поднóс; (*for correspondence*) корзúнка; (*in trunk*) лотóк.

trayful ['treɪfʊl] *n.* цéлый поднóс; **a ~ of glasses** поднóс со стакáнами.

treacherous ['tretʃərəs] *adj.* (*lit., fig.*) предáтельский, измéннический; веролóмный, ковáрный; (*undependable*) ненадёжный; **~ weather** ковáрная погóда; **the roads are ~** дорóги опáсны; **my memory is ~** на моЮ пáмять надéжда плохáя; пáмять мне изменяéт.

treacher|ousness ['tretʃərəsnɪs], **-y** ['tretʃərɪ] *nn.* предáтельство, измéна, веролóмство.

treacle ['tri:k(ə)l] *n.* пáтока.

treacly ['tri:klɪ] *adj.* лúпкий, вязкий; (*fig.*) прúторный, елéйный; **~ sentiment** слащáвость.

tread [tred] *n.* **1.** (*step*) пóступь; шагú (*m. pl.*). **2.** (*manner or sound of walking*) похóдка. **3.** (*of tyre*) протéктор.

v.t. **1.** (*walk on*) ступáть (*impf.*) по+*d.*; шагáть (*impf.*) по+*d.*; **a well-trodden path** (*lit.*) протóптанная тропúнка; (*fig.*) проторённая дорóжка; **his ambition was to ~ the boards** (*be an actor*) он мечтáл о теáтре. **2.** (*dance*): **~ a measure** (*arch.*) исп|олнять, -óлнить тáнец. **3.** (*trample on*) топтáть, по-; давúть, раз-; **the peasants were ~ing the grapes** крестьяне давúли виногрáд; (*fig.*): **the slaves were trodden under foot** рабы бы́ли совершéнно бесправны.

v.i.: **~ on that spider!** растопчúте/раздавúте э́того паукá!; **don't ~ on the grass** по травé не ходúть; (*fig.*): **he trod in his father's footsteps** он шёл по стопáм отцá; **he ~s on everybody's toes** он вéчно наступáет лЮдям на любúмую мозóль; **I won the race, but he trod hard on my heels** я пришёл пéрвым, но он бежáл за мной по пятáм; **I was ~ing on air** я ног под собóй не чýял от счáстья; **we must ~ lightly in this matter** в э́той ситуáции мы должны́ дéйствовать осторóжно.

with advs.: **he trod down the earth** он утрамбовáл зéмлю; **keep off the carpet, or you will ~ the mud in** не ходúте по коврý, а то он совсéм запáчкается; **they trod out the fire** онú затоптáли огóнь.

cpd. **~mill** *n.* (*lit.*) топчáк; (*fig.*) однообрáзная рабóта.

treadle ['tred(ə)l] *n.* педáль; ножнóй привóд.

treason ['tri:z(ə)n] *n.* (госудáрственная) измéна.

treasonable ['tri:zənəb(ə)l] *adj.* измéннический.

treasure ['treʒə(r)] *n.* (*precious object or pers.*) сокрóвище; (**~ trove**) клад; **art ~s** сокрóвища искýсства; **our maid is a ~** нáша прислýга — сýщее сокрóвище; нáшей прислýге цены́ нет.

v.t. (*store up, esp. in memory*) хранúть, со-; **~d memories** дорогúе воспоминáния; **I ~ his words** я свято хранЮ в пáмяти егó словá; (*value highly*) высокó ценúть (*impf.*).

cpd. **~-house** *n.* сокрóвищница; (*fig.*): **a ~-house of knowledge** сокрóвищница знáний.

treasurer ['treʒərə(r)] *n.* казначéй.

treasury ['treʒərɪ] *n.* (*lit., fig.*) сокрóвищница; (*public revenue department*) казнá; **~ bill** краткосрóчный казначéйский вéксель; **~ note** казначéйский билéт.

treat [tri:t] *n.* **1.** (*pleasure*) большóе (*or* ни с чем не сравнúмое) удовóльствие; **it's a ~ to listen to him** слýшать егó — однó удовóльствие; **school ~** пикнúк, экскýрсия. **2.** (*defrayal of entertainment*): **he stood ~ for them all** он всех угощáл; **it's my ~!** я угощáю!

v.t. **1.** (*behave towards*) обращáться (*impf.*) с+*i.*; **he ~s me like a child** он обращáется со мной, как с ребёнком; **the prisoners were well ~ed** с заключёнными обращáлись коррéктно; **how is the world ~ing you?** как жизнь?; как вы поживáете?; как вам живётся? **2.** (*deem, regard*) рассмáтривать (*impf.*); отн|осúться, -естúсь к+*d.*; **he ~ed it as a joke** он отнёсся к э́тому, как к шýтке; **we will ~ the application as valid** мы бýдем считáть э́то заявлéние дéйствительным. **3.** (*deal with; discuss*) трактовáть (*impf.*); рассмáтривать (*impf.*); **he ~ed the subject in detail** он подрóбно осветúл тéму. **4.** (*give medical care to*) лечúть (*impf.*); **how would you ~ a sprained ankle?** как вы лéчите растяжéние голеностóпного сухожúлия?; **he was ~ed for burns** егó лечúли от ожóгов. **5.** (*apply chemical process to*) обрабáт|ывать, -óтать; **the wood was ~ed with creosote** древесúну обработáли креозóтом. **6.** (*make a free partaker*) уго|щáть, -стúть; **he ~ed me to a drink** он поднёс мне рЮмку; **I shall ~ myself to a holiday** я устрóю себé канúкулы/óтпуск.

v.i. **1.** (*give an account*): **this book ~s of many subjects** в э́той кнúге говорúтся о мнóгих вещáх. **2.** (*negotiate*) вестú (*det.*) переговóры; **we ~ed with them on equal terms** мы велú с нúми переговóры на рáвных начáлах.

treatise ['tri:tɪs, -ɪz] *n.* трактáт; наýчный труд.

treatment ['tri:tmənt] *n.* **1.** (*handling*) обращéние; трактóвка; **his ~ of colour is masterly** он мастерскú владéет цвéтом; **the subject received only superficial ~** э́той тéмы коснýлись лишь повéрхностно. **2.** (*chem. etc.*) обрабóтка; **heat ~** термúческая обрабóтка. **3.** (*med.*) лечéние, процедýра; **she is still under ~** онá всё ещё лéчится.

treaty ['tri:tɪ] *n.* договóр.

treble ['treb(ə)l] *n.* (*voice*) дúскант; (*attr.*) дискантóвый; **~ clef** скрипúчный ключ.

adj. тройнóй; **~ knock** троекрáтный стук; **he earns ~ my money** он зарабáтывает втрóе бóльше меня.

v.t. & *i.* утр|áивать(ся), -óит(ся).

trecento [treɪ'tʃentəʊ] *n.* тречéнто (*indecl.*).

tree [tri:] *n.* дéрево; **family ~** родослóвное дéрево; родослóвная; **he is at the top of the ~** (*fig.*) он занимáет (сáмое) высóкое положéние; **he found himself up a (gum-)~** (*coll., in a fix*) он попáл в переплёт; егó припёрли к стéнке.

cpds. **~-fern** *n.* древовúдный пáпоротник; **~-surgery** *n.* обрéзка дерéвьев на омоложéние; **~-top** *n.* верхýшка дéрева.

treeless ['tri:lɪs] *adj.* лишённый дерéвьев.

trefoil ['trefɔɪl, 'tri:-] *n.* (*plant*) клéвер; (*decoration*) трилúстник.

trek [trek] *n.* (*migration*) переселéние; (*arduous journey*) похóд; перехóд.

v.i. пересел|яться, -úться.

trellis ['trelɪs] *n.* шпалéра, трельяж.

cpd. **~-work** *n.* решётка.

trembl|e ['tremb(ə)l] *n.* дрожь; **she was all of a ~e** (*coll.*) онá дрожáла как осúновый лист.

v.i. дрожáть (*impf.*); трястúсь (*impf.*); **he was ~ing with excitement** он дрожáл от волнéния; (*fig.*): **she ~ed for his safety** онá дрожáла за негó; **I ~e to think what may happen** меня бросáет в дрожь при мы́сли, что мóжет случúться; **in fear and ~ing** в стрáхе и трéпете.

tremendous [trɪ'mendəs] *adj.* громáдный; стрáшный; (*coll., very great; splendid*) огрóмный, потрясáющий; **this is a ~ help** э́то огрóмная пóмощь.

tremolo ['tremələʊ] *n.* трéмоло (*indecl.*).

tremor ['tremə(r)] *n.* (*trembling*) сотрясéние, содрогáние, дрожь; **there was a ~ in his voice** егó гóлос дрожáл; **earth ~** подзéмный толчóк.

tremulous ['tremjʊləs] *adj.* **1.** (*trembling*) дрожáщий; **in a ~ voice** с дрóжью в гóлосе. **2.** (*timid*) боязлúвый, трепéщущий.

trench [trentʃ] *n.* ров, канáва; (*mil.*) окóп, траншéя; **~ coat** шинéль; **~ fever** сыпнóй тиф; **~ foot** траншéйная стопá; **~ mortar** миномёт; **~ warfare** окóпная войнá.

v.t. (*make ~es in*) перек|áпывать, -опáть.

trenchant ['trentʃ(ə)nt] *adj.* óстрый, кóлкий, рéзкий.

trencher ['trentʃə(r)] *n.* (*arch.*) деревянное блЮдо.

cpd. **~man** *n.*: **a good ~man** хорóший едóк.

trend [trend] *n.* направле́ние, тенде́нция; **set a ~** вв|оди́ть, -ести́ но́вый стиль.

v.i. име́ть (*impf.*) тенде́нцию (*к чему*); склоня́ться (*impf.*) (*в каком-н. направлении*).

cpd. **~-setter** *n.* законода́тель (*fem.* -ница) мод/сти́ля.

trendy ['trendɪ] *adj.* (*coll.*) мо́дный, «всегда́ на у́ровне».

trepan [trɪ'pæn] *v.t.* (*surg.*) трепани́ровать (*impf.*, *pf.*).

trepidation [ˌtrepɪ'deɪʃ(ə)n] *n.* трево́га, тре́пет, дрожь; **in ~** трепеща́.

trespass ['trespəs] *n.* **1.** (*leg.*, *offence*) правонаруше́ние; (*intrusion on property*) наруше́ние владе́ния; вторже́ние в чужи́е владе́ния. **2.** (*relig.*) прегреше́ние; **forgive us our ~es** оста́ви нам до́лги на́ши.

v.i. **1.** (*intrude*) вт|орга́ться, -о́ргнуться в чужи́е владе́ния; **no ~ing** вход воспрещён; (*fig.*): **I have no wish to ~ on your hospitality** я не хочу́ злоупотребля́ть ва́шим гостеприи́мством. **2.** (*relig.*) греши́ть, со-; **those that ~ against us** те, кто про́тив нас согреша́ют; должники́ на́ши.

trespasser ['trespəsə(r)] *n.* правонаруши́тель (*fem.* -ница); лицо́, вторга́ющееся в чужи́е владе́ния; **~s will be prosecuted** наруши́тели бу́дут пресле́доваться.

tress [tres] *n.* ло́кон; коса́.

trestle ['tres(ə)l] *n.* ко́з|лы (*pl.*, *g.* -ел).

cpds. **~-bridge** *n.* мост на деревя́нных опо́рах; **~-table** *n.* стол на ко́злах.

trews [tru:z] *n.* ≃ клéтчатые штан|ы́ (*pl.*, *g.* -о́в).

tri- [traɪ] *comb. form* трёх..., тре...

triad ['traɪæd] *n.* (*group of three*) тро́ица, тро́йка; (*math.*) триа́да; (*mus.*) трезву́чие.

trial ['traɪəl] *n.* **1.** (*testing*, *test*) испыта́ние, про́ба; **it was a ~ of strength between them** э́то была́ про́ба их сил; **I discovered the truth by ~ and error** я откры́л пра́вду эмпири́ческим путём; **why not give him a ~?** почему́ бы не взять его́ на испыта́тельный срок?; **he took the car on a week's ~** он взял автомаши́ну на неде́льное испыта́ние; **the ship passed its ~s** кора́бль прошёл испыта́ния. **2.** (*attr.*) про́бный; **~ balloon** про́бный шар; **~ match** отбо́рочный матч; **~ order** (*of goods*) зака́з на про́бную па́ртию; **~ run** испыта́тельный пробе́г; **~ voyage** про́бный рейс. **3.** (*judicial examination*) суде́бное разбира́тельство; суде́бный проце́сс; **he went on ~ for murder** его́ суди́ли за уби́йство; **bring to (*or* put on) ~** привл|ека́ть, -е́чь к суду́; **he was given a fair ~** его́ суди́ли в соотве́тствии с зако́ном; **he stands his ~ next month** суд над ним состои́тся в сле́дующем ме́сяце; **the case came up for ~** наступи́л день суда́. **4.** (*annoyance*, *ordeal*) пережива́ние, испыта́ние; **he is a sore ~ to me** он — мой крест; **old age has its ~s** ста́рость не ра́дость.

triangle ['traɪˌæŋg(ə)l] *n.* (*geom.*, *mus.*, *fig.*) треуго́льник; **the eternal ~** изве́чный/любо́вный треуго́льник.

triangular [traɪ'æŋgjʊlə(r)] *adj.* треуго́льный; **a ~ argument** спор ме́жду тремя́ ли́цами.

triangulation [traɪˌæŋgjʊ'leɪʃ(ə)n] *n.* триангуля́ция; **~ point** топографи́ческая вы́шка.

Triassic [traɪ'æsɪk] *adj.* триа́совый.

tribadism ['trɪbədˌɪz(ə)m] *n.* лесби́йская любо́вь.

tribal ['traɪb(ə)l] *adj.* племенно́й.

tribalism ['traɪbəˌlɪz(ə)m] *n.* племенно́й строй.

tribe [traɪb] *n.* **1.** (*racial group*) пле́мя (*nt.*), род, коле́но; **the twelve ~s of Israel** двена́дцать коле́н изра́илевых. **2.** (*pej.*, *group*, *body*) ша́тия, компа́ния, братва́.

cpd. **~sman** *n.* член пле́мени.

tribulation [ˌtrɪbjʊ'leɪʃ(ə)n] *n.* страда́ние, го́ре, беда́.

tribunal [traɪ'bju:n(ə)l, trɪ-] *n.* трибуна́л, суд.

tribune ['trɪbju:n] *n.* (*pers.*) трибу́н; (*platform*) трибу́на, эстра́да.

tributary ['trɪbjʊtərɪ] *n.* (*state/pers.*) госуда́рство/лицо́, платя́щее дань; (*stream*) прито́к.

adj. платя́щий дань; явля́ющийся прито́ком.

tribute ['trɪbju:t] *n.* (*payment*) дань; (*token of respect etc.*) дань; до́лжное; **he paid ~ to his wife's help** он вы́разил благода́рность свое́й жене́ за по́мощь; **floral ~s** цвето́чные подноше́ния.

trice [traɪs] *n.* (*liter.*): **in a ~** вмиг, ми́гом.

trick [trɪk] *n.* **1.** (*dodge*, *device*) шту́ка, приём, хи́трости (*f. pl.*); **he knows all the ~s of the trade** он зна́ет все ходы́ и вы́ходы; **he tried every ~ in the book** он примени́л все изве́стные приёмы; **I know a ~ worth two of that** я зна́ю шту́ку похитре́е. **2.** (*deception*, *mischievous act*) шу́тка; обма́н, трюк; **he is always playing ~s on me** он всегда́ надо мной подшу́чивает; **he is up to his old ~s again** он сно́ва принялся́ за свои́ проде́лки; **a ~ of the light** опти́ческий обма́н; **a dirty ~** по́длость; **play a dirty ~ on s.o.** подложи́ть (*pf.*) кому́-н. свинью́; **he is good at card ~s** он ло́вко де́лает ка́рточные фо́кусы. **3.** (*feat*) шту́ка; **their dog can do a lot of ~s** их соба́ка зна́ет мно́го кома́нд; **you can't teach him any new ~s** его́ невозмо́жно научи́ть ничему́ но́вому; **that will do the ~** э́то срабо́тает наверняка́; **there's no ~ to it** э́то немудрено́ (*coll.*); не шту́ка; **~ cyclist** (*lit.*) цирково́й велосипеди́ст; (*joc.*, *psychiatrist*) психиа́тр. **4.** (*knack*) хва́тка; **there's a ~ to operating this machine** что́бы обраща́ться с э́той маши́ной, нужна́ осо́бая сноро́вка. **5.** (*mannerism*) привы́чка, мане́ра; **he has a ~ of repeating himself** у него́ осо́бая мане́ра повторя́ться. **6.** (*at cards*) взя́тка; **we won by the odd ~** мы вы́играли, благодаря́ реша́ющей взя́тке; **he never misses a ~** (*fig.*) он никогда́ не упу́стит слу́чая; он всегда́ на чеку́.

v.t. **1.** (*cheat*, *beguile*) обма́н|ывать, -у́ть; над|ува́ть, -у́ть; **they ~ed him out of a fortune** они́ вы́манили у него́ ма́ссу де́нег; **she was ~ed into marriage** её обма́нным путём втяну́ли в заму́жество. **2. ~ out, up** (*adorn*) укр|аша́ть, -а́сить; наря|жа́ть, -ди́ть; **~ed out in all her finery** разоде́тая в пух и прах.

trickery ['trɪkərɪ] *n.* обма́н, надува́тельство.

trickle ['trɪk(ə)l] *n.* стру́йка.

v.t. ка́пать (*impf.*).

v.i. сочи́ться (*impf.*); ка́пать (*impf.*); (*fig.*): **the news ~d out** но́вости просочи́лись; **the crowd began to ~ away** толпа́ начала́ постепе́нно расходи́ться.

trickster ['trɪkstə(r)] *n.* обма́нщик, ловка́ч.

tricksy ['trɪksɪ] *adj.* шаловли́вый, игри́вый.

tricky ['trɪkɪ] *adj.* (*crafty*, *deceitful*) хи́трый; (*awkward*) сло́жный, мудрёный, замысловатый.

tricolour ['trɪkələ(r), 'traɪˌkʌlə(r)] *n.* (*flag*) трёхцве́тный флаг; (*French*) францу́зский флаг.

tricot ['trɪkəʊ, 'tri:-] *n.* трико́ (*indecl.*).

tricycle ['traɪsɪk(ə)l] *n.* трёхколёсный велосипе́д.

trident ['traɪd(ə)nt] *n.* трезу́бец.

tried ['traɪd] *adj.* (*tested*) испы́танный, прове́ренный; надёжный, ве́рный.

triennial [traɪ'enɪəl] *adj.* продолжа́ющийся три го́да; повторя́ющийся че́рез ка́ждые три го́да.

trier ['traɪə(r)] *n.* (*persevering pers.*) стара́тельный челове́к.

trifle ['traɪf(ə)l] *n.* **1.** (*thg. of small value or importance*) пустя́к, ме́лочь; **she gets upset over ~s** она́ огорча́ется по пустяка́м; (*small sum*) небольша́я су́мма; **I paid the merest ~ for this book** я заплати́л су́щий пустя́к за э́ту кни́гу. **2. a ~** (*as adv.*) немно́го; са́мую ма́лость; **I was just a ~ angry** я чу́точку рассерди́лся. **3.** (*sweet dish*) бискви́т со сби́тыми сли́вками.

v.i. относи́ться (*impf.*) несерьёзно к+*d.*; **he ~d with her affections** он игра́л её чу́вствами; **he ~d with his food** он лени́во ковыря́лся в таре́лке; **he is not a man to be ~d with** с ним шу́тки пло́хи.

with adv.: **he ~d away his money** он по́пусту растра́тил де́ньги.

trifler ['traɪflə(r)] *n.* ветрого́н, пусто́й ма́лый.

trifling ['traɪflɪŋ] *adj.* пустяко́вый; незначи́тельный.

triforium [traɪ'fɔ:rɪəm] *n.* трифо́рий.

trigger ['trɪgə(r)] *n.* спусково́й крючо́к; **he was quick on the ~** (*fig.*) у него́ бы́ли молниено́сные реа́кции.

v.t. (*usu.* **~ off**) вызыва́ть, вы́звать; да|ва́ть, -ть нача́ло +*d.*; **his action ~ed off a chain of events** его́ посту́пок повлёк за собо́й цепь собы́тий.

cpds. **~-finger** *n.* указа́тельный па́лец (пра́вой руки́); **~-happy** *adj.* (*coll.*) стреля́ющий без разбо́ра.

trigonometrical [ˌtrɪgənə'metrɪk(ə)l] *adj.* тригонометри́ческий.

trigonometry [ˌtrɪgə'nɒmɪtrɪ] *n.* тригономе́трия.

trilateral [traɪ'lætər(ə)l] *adj.* трёхсторо́нний.

trilby ['trɪlbɪ] *n.* мя́гкая фе́тровая шля́па.

trill [trɪl] *n.* (*of bird, voice or instrument*) трель; (*of letter r*) вибри́рующее/раска́тистое «р».

v.t.: **the Italians ~ their 'r's** италья́нцы произно́сят «р» с вибра́цией.

v.i.: **the birds were ~ing** пти́цы залива́лись тре́лью.

trillion ['trɪljən] *n.* (10^{18}) квинтильо́н; (*US*, 10^{12}) триллио́н.

trilogy ['trɪlədʒɪ] *n.* трило́гия.

trim [trɪm] *n.* **1.** (*order, fitness*) поря́док; состоя́ние гото́вности; **the champion was in fighting ~** чемпио́н был в превосхо́дной фо́рме; **everything was in good ~** всё бы́ло/находи́лось в образцо́вом поря́дке; **we must get into ~ before the race** нам ну́жно прийти́ в фо́рму пе́ред соревнова́нием. **2.** (*light cut*) подре́зка, стри́жка; **your hair needs a ~** вам ну́жно подровня́ть во́лосы; **I must give the lawn a ~** на́до подстри́чь траву́.

adj. аккура́тный, опря́тный; **she has a ~ figure** у неё стро́йная фигу́рка; **he keeps his garden ~** он соде́ржит сад в образцо́вом поря́дке.

v.t. **1.** (*cut back to desired shape or size*) подр|еза́ть, -е́зать; подр|а́внивать, -овня́ть; **he was ~ming the hedge** он подра́внивал и́згородь; **the lamp needs ~ming** ну́жно подре́зать фити́ль; **he ~s his beard every day** он подра́внивает бо́роду ка́ждый день. **2.** (*decorate*) отде́л|ывать, -ать; отор|а́чивать, -очи́ть; **a hat ~med with fur** ша́пка, отде́ланная/оторо́ченная ме́хом. **3.** (*adjust balance or setting of*) уравнове́шивать (*impf.*); разме|ща́ть, -сти́ть балла́ст +*g.*; **they ~med the sails** они́ поста́вили паруса́ по ве́тру; **he ~med his sails to the wind** (*fig.*) он держа́л нос по ве́тру; он знал, отку́да ве́тер ду́ет.

with advs.: **~ away, ~ off** *vv.t.* подстр|ига́ть, -и́чь; подре́з|ывать (*or* подреза́ть), -ать.

trimaran ['traɪmə,ræn] *n.* тримара́н.

trimmer ['trɪmə(r)] *n.* (*time-server*) приспособле́нец; (*tech.*) обрезно́й стано́к.

trimming ['trɪmɪŋ] *n.* (*on dress etc.*) отде́лка; (*coll., accessory*) гарни́р, припра́ва; **roast duck and all the ~s** жа́реная у́тка с гарни́ром.

Trinitarian [,trɪnɪ'teərɪən] *n.* триипоста́сник.

trinitrotoluene [traɪ,naɪtrə'tɒljʊ,i:n] = **TNT**

trinity ['trɪnɪtɪ] *n.* тро́ица; **T~ Sunday** Тро́ицын день.

trinket ['trɪŋkɪt] *n.* безделу́шка; брело́к.

trio ['tri:əʊ] *n.* (*group of three*) тро́йка; (*mus.*) три́о (*indecl.*).

trip [trɪp] *n.* **1.** (*excursion*) пое́здка, путеше́ствие, прогу́лка; **he has gone on a ~ to Paris** он пое́хал (ненадо́лго) в Пари́ж; **the round ~ costs £10** пое́здка в о́ба конца́ сто́ит 10 фу́нтов; (*coll., psychedelic experience*) наркоти́ческое состоя́ние; кейф. **2.** (*stumble*) спотыка́ние.

v.t. **1.** (*cause to stumble; also* **~ up**) ста́вить, по- подно́жку +*d.*; (*fig.*) запу́т|ывать, -ать; **counsel tried to ~ the witness up** адвока́т пыта́лся сбить свиде́теля. **2.** (*release from catch*) расцепля́ть (*impf.*); выключа́ть (*impf*).

v.i. **1.** (*run or dance lightly*) пританцо́вывать (*impf.*) вприпля́ску; **she came ~ping down the stairs** она́ легко́ сбежа́ла вниз по ле́стнице. **2.** (*stumble; also* **~ up**) спот|ыка́ться, -кну́ться; **he ~ped over the rug** он споткну́лся о ковёр; (*fig., commit error*) ошиб|а́ться, -и́ться; **I ~ped up badly in my estimate** я здо́рово оши́бся в свои́х расчётах.

cpds. **~-hammer** *n.* па́дающий мо́лот; **~-wire** *n.* ми́нная про́волока; «спотыка́ч».

tripartite [traɪ'pɑ:taɪt] *adj.* трёхсторо́нний.

tripe [traɪp] *n.* (*offal*) требуха́; (*coll., rubbish*) чепуха́, вздор.

triple ['trɪp(ə)l] *adj.* тройно́й, утро́енный; **T~ Alliance** Тро́йственный сою́з; **~ time** (*mus.*) трёхдо́льный разме́р.

v.t. & i. утр|а́ивать(ся), -о́ить(ся).

triplet ['trɪplɪt] *n.* **1.** (*set of three*) тро́йка. **2.** (*one of three children born together*) тройня́шка; **~s** (*children*) тро́йня (*sg.*). **3.** (*mus.*) трио́ль.

triplex ['trɪpleks] *adj.*: **~ glass** три́плекс, безоско́лочное стекло́.

triplicate ['trɪplɪkət] *n.*: **in ~** в трёх экземпля́рах.

adj. тройно́й.

tripod ['traɪpɒd] *n.* трено́га, трено́жник.

tripos ['traɪpɒs] *n.* экза́мен для получе́ния дипло́ма бакала́вра (*в Кэмбридже*).

tripper ['trɪpə(r)] *n.* экскурса́нт (*fem.* -ка).

triptych ['trɪptɪk] *n.* три́птих.

trireme ['traɪri:m] *n.* трире́ма.

trisect [traɪ'sekt] *v.t.* дели́ть, раз- на три ра́вные ча́сти.

trisyllabic [,traɪsɪ'læbɪk, trɪ-] *adj.* трёхсло́жный.

trisyllable [traɪ'sɪləb(ə)l, trɪ-] *n.* трёхсло́жное сло́во.

trite [traɪt] *adj.* бана́льный, изби́тый.

triteness ['traɪtnɪs] *n.* бана́льность.

triumph ['traɪəmf, -ʌmf] *n.* торжество́; **they came home in ~** они́ верну́лись с побе́дой; (*hist.*) триу́мф.

v.i. **1.** (*be victorious*) побе|жда́ть, -ди́ть; **justice will ~ in the end** в конце́ концо́в справедли́вость восторжеству́ет; **he ~ed over adversity** он одоле́л невзго́ды. **2.** (*exult*) ликова́ть (*impf.*); торжествова́ть (*impf.*); **he ~ed in his enemy's defeat** он ликова́л/торжествова́л по слу́чаю пораже́ния врага́.

triumphal [traɪ'ʌmf(ə)l] *adj.* триумфа́льный.

triumphant [traɪ'ʌmf(ə)nt] *adj.* (*victorious*) победоно́сный; (*exultant*) торжеству́ющий, лику́ющий.

triumvir ['traɪəmvɪə(r), -'ʌmvə(r)] *n.* триумви́р.

triumvirate [traɪ'ʌmvɪrət] *n.* триумвира́т.

triune ['traɪju:n] *adj.* триеди́ный.

trivet ['trɪvɪt] *n.* (*tripod*) подста́вка; (*bracket*) тага́н; **as right as a ~** в по́лном поря́дке.

trivia ['trɪvɪə] *n.* ме́лочи (*f. pl.*).

trivial ['trɪvɪəl] *adj.* (*trifling*) ме́лкий; незначи́тельный; (*commonplace, everyday*) обы́денный; **the ~ round** повседне́вные дела́; (*shallow, artificial*) тривиа́льный, пове́рхностный.

triviality [,trɪvɪ'ælɪtɪ] *n.* незначи́тельность, тривиа́льность.

trivialize ['trɪvɪə,laɪz] *v.t.* оп|ошля́ть, -о́шлить.

trochaic [trə'keɪɪk] *adj.* трохеи́ческий.

trochee ['trəʊki:, -kɪ] *n.* хоре́й, трохе́й.

troglodyte ['trɒglə,daɪt] *n.* троглоди́т.

troglodytic [,trɒglə'dɪtɪk] *adj.* троглоди́тский.

troika ['trɔɪkə] *n.* тро́йка.

Trojan ['trəʊdʒ(ə)n] *n.* троя́н|ец (*fem.* -ка); (*fig.*): **he worked like a ~** он до́блестно труди́лся; он рабо́тал как вол.

adj. троя́нский; **~ horse** (*fig.*) троя́нский конь; **~ War** Троя́нская война́.

troll[1] [trəʊl] *n.* (*myth.*) тролль (*m.*).

troll[2] [trəʊl] *n.* (*fishing reel*) блесна́.

v.t. & i. лови́ть (*impf.*) (ры́бу) на блесну́.

troll[3] [trəʊl] *v.t. & i.* (*sing*) распева́ть (*impf.*); напева́ть (*impf.*).

trolley ['trɒlɪ] *n.* (*handcart*) теле́жка; (*table on wheels*) сто́лик на колёсиках; (*rail-car*) дрези́на; (*US, street-car*) трамва́й; **off one's ~** (*coll.*) с приве́том.

cpds. **~-bus** *n.* тролле́йбус; **~-car** *n.* (*US*) трамва́й.

trollop ['trɒləp] *n.* (*slattern*) растрёпа, неря́ха; (*prostitute*) проститу́тка, шлю́ха.

trombone [trɒm'bəʊn] *n.* тромбо́н.

trombonist [trɒm'bəʊnɪst] *n.* тромбони́ст.

troop [tru:p] *n.* **1.** (*assembled group of persons*) отря́д; (*of animals*) ста́до. **2.** (*mil. unit*) батаре́я; ро́та; **~ of horse** кавалери́йский отря́д. **3.** (*pl., soldiers*) войск|а́ (*pl., g.* —); **that's the stuff to give the ~s** (*joc.*) э́то как раз то, что на́до.

v.t.: **~ing the colour** церемо́ния вы́носа зна́мени.

v.i. дви́|гаться, -нуться толпо́й; **the children ~ed out of school** де́ти стро́ем вы́шли из шко́лы; **the deputation ~ed into the office** депута́ция цепо́чкой вошла́ в кабине́т.

cpds. **~-carrier** *n.* (*mil.*) транспортёр для перево́зки ли́чного соста́ва; (*aeron.*) тра́нспортно-деса́нтный самолёт; **~ship** *n.* тра́нспорт для перево́зки войск.

trooper ['tru:pə(r)] *n.* **1.** (*soldier*) кавалери́ст; танки́ст; **he swore like a ~** он руга́лся как изво́зчик. **2.** (*US, policeman*) полице́йский.

trope [trəʊp] *n.* троп.

trophy ['trəʊfɪ] *n.* трофе́й; (*prize, also*) приз.

tropic ['trɒpɪk] *n.* тро́пик; **T~ of Cancer** тро́пик Ра́ка; **T~ of Capricorn** тро́пик Козеро́га; **in the ~s** в тро́пиках.

tropical ['trɒpɪk(ə)l] *adj.* тропи́ческий; (*fig.*) горя́чий; стра́стный; бу́йный.

troposphere ['trɒpəˌsfɪə(r), 'trəʊ-] *n.* тропосфе́ра.

trot [trɒt] *n.* **1.** (*gait, pace*) рысь; **at a gentle ~** лёгкой ры́сью; (*fig.*) **he keeps me on the ~** (*constantly busy*) он всё вре́мя гоня́ет меня́; **I have been on the ~ all day** (*moving about*) я был на нога́х це́лый день; (*afflicted with diarrhoea*) я це́лый день «бе́гал». **2.** (*run or ride at this pace*) прогу́лка, пробе́жка; **she took her horse for a ~** она́ взяла́ ло́шадь на вы́ездку; **he does a ten-minute ~ every morning** ка́ждое у́тро он де́лает десятимину́тную пробе́жку.
v.t. **1.** (*exercise*) выгу́ливать (*impf.*); прогу́ливать (*impf.*); **he ~ted his horse in the park** он прогу́ливал ло́шадь в па́рке; **he ~ted me off my feet** он загоня́л меня́ до́ сме́рти.
v.i. (*of a horse*) идти́ (*det.*) ры́сью; (*of pers.*) семени́ть (*impf.*); **he ~ted after his wife** он семени́л за жено́й.
with advs. **~ along, ~ off** *vv.i.* (*coll.*) отпр|авля́ться, -а́виться; **I must be ~ting off home** мне пора́ (отправля́ться) домо́й; **~ out** *v.t.* (*coll.*) демонстри́ровать (*impf.*); **he ~ted out all his photographs** он продемонстри́ровал все свои́ фотогра́фии; **he ~ted out the usual excuses** он, как всегда́, вы́ставил ма́ссу отгово́рок.

troth [trəʊθ] *n.* ве́рность, (че́стное) сло́во.

Trotskyism ['trɒtskɪˌɪz(ə)m] *n.* троцки́зм.

Trotsky|ist ['trɒtskɪɪst], **-ite** ['trɒtskɪaɪt] *nn.* троцки́ст (*fem.* -ка).

trotter ['trɒtə(r)] *n.* (*horse*) рыси́стая ло́шадь; (*animal's foot*) но́жка; **pig's ~s** свины́е но́жки.

troubadour ['tru:bəˌdɔ:(r)] *n.* трубаду́р.

trouble ['trʌb(ə)l] *n.* **1.** (*grief, anxiety*) волне́ние, трево́га; беспоко́йство; **her heart was full of ~** се́рдце её бы́ло не на ме́сте; (*misfortune, affliction*) го́ре, беда́; **his ~s are over** тепе́рь все его́ несча́стья позади́; **I have ~s of my own!** мне бы ва́ши забо́ты!; **there is ~ brewing** ждать беды́; быть беде́. **2.** (*difficulty, difficulties*) хлоп|о́ты (*pl.*, *g.* -о́т); затрудне́ние; **family ~s** семе́йные неприя́тности/тру́дности (*both fem.*) /хло́поты; **money ~s** де́нежные затрудне́ния; **I am having ~ with the car** у меня́ непола́дки (*f. pl.*) с маши́ной; **don't make ~ for me** не создава́йте мне ли́шних тру́дностей; **what's the ~?** в чём де́ло?; **the ~ is (that) ...** беда́ в том, что...; **that's the ~** вот в чём беда́; в то́м-то и беда́; **without any ~** легко́; **the ~ with him is that ...** его́ беда́/недоста́ток в том, что... **3.** (*predicament*): **he's always getting into ~** он ве́чно попада́ет в исто́рии; **he is in ~ with the police** у него́ неприя́тности с поли́цией; **his brother got him into ~** брат навлёк неприя́тности на его́ го́лову; **he found himself in ~** он влип (*coll.*); **I got him out of ~** я вы́зволил его́ из беды́; **ask for ~** лезть (*det.*) на рожо́н; **that's asking for ~** э́так то́лько нарвёшься на неприя́тности; **he got her into ~** (*pregnant*) он сде́лал ей ребёнка. **4.** (*inconvenience*): **I don't want to put you to any ~** я не хочу́ вас затрудня́ть; **it will be no ~ at all** э́то меня́ нисколько не затрудни́т; **he saved me the ~** он изба́вил меня́ от э́той необходи́мости. **5.** (*disorder, mess*) неуря́дица. **6.** (*pains, care, effort*) забо́та, труд, хлоп|о́ты (*pl.*, *g.* -о́т); **she took a lot of ~ over the cake** она́ приложи́ла мно́го стара́ния для приготовле́ния пирога́; **he didn't even take the ~ to write** он да́же не потруди́лся написа́ть; **thank you for all your ~** спаси́бо за все ва́ши хло́поты; **it is not worth the ~** не сто́ит хлопо́т. **7.** (*disease, ailment*) неду́г, боле́знь; **he has heart ~** у него́ больно́е се́рдце; **mental ~** психи́ческое расстро́йство. **8.** (*unrest, civil commotion*) волне́ния (*nt. pl.*); беспоря́дки (*m. pl.*); **labour ~s** волне́ния среди́ рабо́чих; **~ spot** горя́чая то́чка.
v.t. **1.** (*agitate, disturb, worry*) трево́жить (*impf.*); волнова́ть (*impf.*); **he was ~d about money** он волнова́лся из-за́ де́нег; **don't let it ~ you** не принима́йте э́то бли́зко к се́рдцу; **a ~d countenance** обеспоко́енный вид; **~d times** сму́тные времена́; **he is fishing in ~d waters** (*fig.*) он ло́вит ры́бку в му́тной воде́. **2.** (*afflict*) беспоко́ить (*impf.*); му́чить (*impf.*); **he is ~d with a cough** его́ му́чит ка́шель; **my back ~s me** у меня́ боли́т спина́. **3.** (*put to inconvenience*) затрудн|я́ть, -и́ть; **may I ~ you for a match?** мо́жно попроси́ть у вас спи́чку?; **don't ~ yourself** не беспоко́йтесь; **sorry to ~ you!** прости́те за беспоко́йство!; **I'll ~ you to mind your own business** я бы попроси́л вас не лезть в чужи́е дела́.
v.i. труди́ться (*impf.*); беспоко́иться (*impf.*); **don't ~ about that** не беспоко́йтесь об э́том; **don't ~ to come and meet me** не сто́ит меня́ встреча́ть; **why should I ~ to explain?** с како́й ста́ти я до́лжен входи́ть в объясне́ния?
cpds. **~-free** *adj.* (*carefree*) беззабо́тный; (*reliable*) надёжный; безотка́зный; **~-maker** *n.* склю́чни|к (*fem.* -ца); (*instigator of ~*) смутья́н (*fem.* -ка); **~-shooter** *n.* авари́йный монтёр; (*fig.*) уполномо́ченный по ула́живанию конфли́ктов.

troublesome ['trʌb(ə)lsəm] *adj.* тру́дный; хло́потный; **a ~ child** тру́дный ребёнок; **a ~ cough** мучи́тельный ка́шель.

troublous ['trʌbləs] *adj.* (*liter.*) сму́тный, трево́жный.

trough [trɒf] *n.* **1.** (*for animals*) коры́то, корму́шка; (*for dough*) квашня́; (*for water*) жёлоб, лото́к. **2.** (*meteor.*) фронт ни́зкого давле́ния. **3.** (*between waves*) подо́шва волны́.

trounce [traʊns] *v.t.* (*thrash*) поро́ть, вы́-; сечь, вы́-; (*defeat*) разб|ива́ть, -и́ть.

troupe [tru:p] *n.* тру́ппа.

trouper ['tru:pə(r)] *n.* член тру́ппы; актёр, актри́са.

trousered ['traʊzəd] *adj.* в брю́ках.

trouser|s ['traʊzəz] *n.* штан|ы́ (*pl.*, *g.* -о́в), брю́ки (*pl.*, *g.* —); **a pair of ~s** па́ра брюк; **he has gone into long ~s** он уже́ на́чал носи́ть дли́нные брю́ки; **his wife wears the ~s** (*fig.*) его́ жена́ заправля́ет всем (*or* верхово́дит) в до́ме.
cpds. **~-button** *n.* брю́чная пу́говица; **~-leg** *n.* штани́на; **~-suit** *n.* брю́чный костю́м.

trousseau ['tru:səʊ] *n.* прида́ное.

trout [traʊt] *n.* (*fish*) форе́ль; (*sl., old woman*) стару́шка.

trouvaille ['tru:vaɪl] *n.* (счастли́вая/уда́чная) нахо́дка.

trowel ['traʊəl] *n.* (*for bricklaying etc.*) мастеро́к; **he laid it on with a ~** (*fig., of flattery*) он гру́бо льстил; (*for gardening*) (садо́вый) садо́к, лопа́тка.

truancy ['tru:ənsɪ] *n.* прогу́л.

truant ['tru:ənt] *n.* прогу́льщик; **did you ever play ~?** вы когда́-нибудь прогу́ливали уро́ки?
adj. (*fig.*) пра́здный, лени́вый.

truce [tru:s] *n.* переми́рие; (*respite*) переды́шка; (*fig., liter.*): **a ~ to jesting!** дово́льно шу́ток!

truck[1] [trʌk] *n.* (*railway wagon*) откры́тая това́рная платфо́рма; (*lorry*) грузови́к; (*barrow*) теле́жка.

truck[2] [trʌk] *n.* **1.** (*barter*) ме́на; товарообме́н; **I'll have no ~ with him** (*fig.*) я не жела́ю име́ть с ним никаки́х дел. **2.** (*US, market garden produce*) о́вощ|и (*pl.*, *g.* -е́й).

truckle ['trʌk(ə)l] *v.i.*: **~ to s.o.** раболе́пствовать (*impf.*) пе́ред кем-н.

truckle-bed ['trʌk(ə)l] *n.* ни́зкая крова́ть на колёсиках.

truculence ['trʌkjʊləns] *n.* агресси́вность, драчли́вость.

truculent ['trʌkjʊlənt] *adj.* агресси́вный, драчли́вый.

trudge [trʌdʒ] *n.* дли́нный/тру́дный путь.
v.i. тащи́ться (*impf.*).

true [tru:] *n.* (*alignment, adjustment*): **the wheel is out of ~** колесо́ пло́хо устано́влено.
adj. **1.** (*in accordance with fact*) ве́рный, правди́вый; **a ~ story** правди́вый расска́з; **is it ~ that he is married?** э́то пра́вда, что он жена́т?; **all my dreams came ~** все мои́ мечты́ сбы́лись/осуществи́лись; **it is only too ~** увы́, э́то чисте́йшая пра́вда; (*concessive*): **~, it will cost more** разуме́ется, э́то бу́дет сто́ить бо́льше. **2.** (*in accordance with reason, principle, standard; genuine*) правди́вый; настоя́щий; по́длинный, и́стинный; **it is not a ~ comparison** э́то ло́жное сравне́ние; **the ~ price is much higher** действи́тельная/настоя́щая цена́ намно́го вы́ше; **he is a ~ Briton** он настоя́щий брита́нец; **the ~ heir** зако́нный насле́дник. **3.** (*conforming accurately*) пра́вильный; **~ to life** реалисти́ческий; **~ to type** типи́чный, характе́рный. **4.** (*loyal, faithful; dependable*) пре́данный, ве́рный; надёжный; **he was always a ~ friend to me** он был мне всегда́ пре́данным дру́гом; **he remained**

~ to his word он сдержа́л сло́во; **a ~ sign of rain** ве́рный при́знак дождя́. **5.** (*mus., in tune*) ве́рный (*тон и т.п.*). **6.** (*accurately adjusted or positioned*) то́чно при́гнанный/устано́вленный.

adv. пра́вильно, ве́рно; **his story rings ~** его́ расска́з звучи́т убеди́тельно; **he aimed ~** он то́чно прице́лился.

cpds. **~-blue** *adj.* че́стный; сто́йкий; (*pol.*) консервати́вный; **~-born** *adj.* прирождённый, настоя́щий; **~-bred** *adj.* чистокро́вный; **~-hearted** *adj.* и́скренний; **~-love** *n.* (*sweetheart*) возлю́бленн|ый, -ая.

truffle ['trʌf(ə)l] *n.* трю́фель (*m.*).

trug [trʌg] *n.* садо́вая корзи́нка.

truism ['tru:ɪz(ə)m] *n.* трюи́зм.

truly ['tru:lɪ] *adv.* **1.** (*accurately; truthfully*) и́скренне; правди́во. **2.** (*loyally*) ве́рно. **3.** (*sincerely*) и́скренне; **yours ~** (*at end of letter*) пре́данный Вам; (*coll., myself*) ваш поко́рный слуга́; **I am ~ grateful** я и́скренне благода́рен. **4.** (*genuinely*) и́скренне; действи́тельно; **a ~ memorable occasion** пои́стине незабыва́емое собы́тие.

trump[1] [trʌmp] *n.* **1.** (**~ card**) ко́зырь (*m.*), козырна́я ка́рта; **we cut for ~s** мы сня́ли коло́ду, что́бы определи́ть козы́рную масть; **hearts are ~s** че́рви — ко́зыри; (*fig.*): **he played his ~ card** он вы́ложил свой ко́зырь; **the weather turned up ~s** нам (неожи́данно) повезло́ с пого́дой. **2.** (*coll., excellent fellow*) сла́вный па́рень.

v.t. бить, по- ко́зырем.

with adv.: **~ up** *v.t.* фабрикова́ть, с-.

trump[2] [trʌmp] *n.* (*trumpet sound*) труба́; **the Last T~** арха́нгельская труба́; тру́бный глас.

trumpery ['trʌmpərɪ] *n.* мишура́.

adj. мишу́рный.

trumpet ['trʌmpɪt] *n.* **1.** (*instrument*) труба́; **blow one's own ~** (*fig.*) хвали́ться (*impf.*). **2.** (*object so shaped*) тру́бка; **ear-~** слухова́я тру́бка; (*of flower*) тру́бчатый ве́нчик.

v.t. & i. **1.** (*proclaim*) труби́ть, про-; **his praises were ~ed abroad** повсю́ду труби́ли о нём хвалу́. **2.** (*of an elephant*) реве́ть, про-.

cpd. **~-call** *n.* (*lit.*) звук трубы́; (*fig.*) призы́вный звук (трубы́).

trumpeter ['trʌmpɪtə(r)] *n.* труба́ч.

truncate [trʌŋ'keɪt, 'trʌŋ-] *v.t.* ус|ека́ть, -е́чь; сокра|ща́ть, -ти́ть; **a ~d cone** усечённый ко́нус; **his speech was ~d** его́ ре́чь уре́зали.

truncheon ['trʌntʃ(ə)n] *n.* полице́йская дуби́нка.

trundle ['trʌnd(ə)l] *v.t. & i.* кати́ть(ся) (*impf.*).

trunk [trʌŋk] *n.* **1.** (*of tree*) ствол. **2.** (*of body*) ту́ловище. **3.** (*box*) сунду́к. **4.** (*of elephant*) хо́бот. **5.** (*pl., garment*) трус|ы́ (*pl., g.* -о́в); пла́в|ки (*pl., g.* -ок). **6.** (*US, boot of car*) бага́жник.

cpds. **~-call** *n.* вы́зов по междугоро́дному телефо́ну; **~-line** *n.* (*rail.*) магистра́ль; (*teleph.*) междугоро́дная связь; **~-road** *n.* магистра́льная доро́га.

truss [trʌs] *n.* **1.** (*structural support*) стропи́льная фе́рма. **2.** (*surgical support*) грыжево́й банда́ж. **3.** (*of hay*) пук, свя́зка.

v.t. **1.** (*support*) укреп|ля́ть, -и́ть; свя́з|ывать, -а́ть. **2.** (*tie up; also* **~ up**) свя́з|ывать, -а́ть; скру́|чивать, -ти́ть; **she ~ed the chicken** она́ связа́ла кры́лышки и но́жки цыплёнка пе́ред гото́вкой.

trust [trʌst] *n.* **1.** (*firm belief; confidence*) дове́рие; ве́ра; **put your ~ in God** положи́тесь на во́лю бо́жью; **I place perfect ~ in him** я доверя́ю ему́ по́лностью; **he takes everything on ~** он всё принима́ет на ве́ру. **2.** (*credit*) креди́т; **goods supplied on ~** това́ры, предоста́вленные в креди́т. **3.** (*pers. or object confided in*) наде́жда; **he is our sole ~** он на́ша еди́нственная наде́жда. **4.** (*responsibility*) отве́тственность; **a position of ~** отве́тственный пост; **he proved unworthy of his ~** он не оправда́л дове́рия. **5.** (*leg.*) довери́тельная со́бственность; **property held in ~** иму́щество, управля́емое по дове́ренности. **6.** (*association of companies*) трест; **~ territory** (*UN*) подопе́чная террито́рия.

v.t. **1.** (*have confidence in, rely on*) дов|еря́ть, -е́рить *+d.*; **he is not to be ~ed** ему́ нельзя́ доверя́ть; **I wouldn't ~ him with my money** я бы ему́ свои́х де́нег не дове́рил; **I can't ~ myself not to laugh** не зна́ю, смогу́ ли я удержа́ться от сме́ха; **he can be ~ed to do a good job** мо́жно быть уве́ренным, что он хорошо́ спра́вится с рабо́той; **~ him to make a mistake!** он, как всегда́, оши́бся!; **I can't ~ him out of my sight** его́ нельзя́ выпуска́ть из по́ля зре́ния. **2.** (*entrust*) вв|еря́ть, -е́рить. **3.** (*allow credit to*) да|ва́ть, -ть креди́т *+d.* **4.** (*earnestly hope*) наде́яться (*impf.*); полага́ть (*impf.*); **I ~ I see you well** я наде́юсь, вы в до́бром здра́вии.

v.i. **1.** (*have faith, confidence*) дов|еря́ться, -е́риться; **she ~ed in God** она́ отдала́сь на во́лю бо́жью. **2.** (*commit o.s. with confidence*) дов|еря́ться, -е́риться; наде́яться (*impf.*); **he ~ed to luck** он (по)наде́ялся на сча́стье; **it is unwise to ~ to memory** на па́мять полага́ться опа́сно.

trustee [trʌs'ti:] *n.* довери́тельный со́бственник; опеку́н.

trusteeship [trʌs'ti:ʃɪp] *n.* до́лжность опекуна́; опе́ка, попечи́тельство; **T~ Council** (*UN*) Сове́т по Опе́ке.

trustful ['trʌstfʊl] *adj.* дове́рчивый.

trustfulness ['trʌstθfʊlnɪs] *n.* дове́рчивость.

trusting ['trʌstɪŋ] *adj.* дове́рчивый; наи́вный.

trustworthiness ['trʌst,wɜ:ðɪnɪs] *n.* надёжность; достове́рность.

trustworthy ['trʌst,wɜ:ðɪ] *adj.* надёжный, достове́рный.

trusty ['trʌstɪ] *n.* (*privileged convict*) приду́рок (*coll.*).

adj. ве́рный, надёжный.

truth [tru:θ] *n.* пра́вда; (*verity, true saying*) и́стина; **the ~ is; to tell the ~** по пра́вде сказа́ть; **there's not a word of ~ in it** в э́том нет ни сло́ва пра́вды; **the whole ~ and nothing but the ~** вся пра́вда и ничего́ кро́ме пра́вды; **in ~** в са́мом де́ле; **a lover of ~** приве́рженец пра́вды; правдолю́бец; **~ to nature** реали́зм; то́чность воспроизведе́ния.

truthful ['tru:θfʊl] *adj.* (*of pers.*) правди́вый; (*of statement etc., also*) ве́рный, то́чный.

truthfulness ['tru:θfʊlnɪs] *n.* правди́вость; ве́рность, то́чность.

try [traɪ] *n.* **1.** (*attempt*) попы́тка; **he made several tries, but failed** он сде́лал не́сколько попы́ток, но все неуда́чно; **he had a good ~** он стара́лся, как мог. **2.** (*test*) испыта́ние; про́ба; **why not give it a ~?** а почему́ бы не попро́бовать? **3.** (*Rugby football*) прохо́д с мячо́м.

v.t. **1.** (*attempt*) пыта́ться, по-; стара́ться, по-; **he tried his best** он стара́лся изо всех сил; **he tried hard** он о́чень стара́лся. **2.** (*sample*) про́бовать, по-; (*taste*) отве́д|ывать, -ать; (*experiment with, assay*) **have you tried aspirin?** вы аспири́н про́бовали?; **~ how far you can jump** посмотри́те, как далеко́ вы мо́жете пры́гнуть. **3.** (*leg.*): **he was tried for murder** его́ суди́ли за уби́йство; **the judge tried the case** судья́ вёл проце́сс; **the case will be tried tomorrow** суд начина́ется за́втра. **4.** (*subject to strain*) утом|ля́ть, -и́ть; раздража́ть (*impf.*); му́чить (*impf.*); **he tries my patience** он испы́тывает моё терпе́ние; **fine print is ~ing to the eyes** ме́лкий шрифт утоми́телен для глаз; **a ~ing situation** тру́дное положе́ние; **a ~ing child** тру́дный ребёнок. **5.** (*test*) испы́т|ывать, -а́ть; пров|еря́ть, -е́рить; подв|ерга́ть, -е́ргнуть испыта́нию; про́бовать, по-; **I shall ~ my luck again** я ещё раз попыта́ю сча́стья; **he tried his hand at several occupations** он перепро́бовал не́сколько заня́тий; **a tried remedy** испы́танное сре́дство.

v.i.: **~ harder next time!** в сле́дующий раз приложи́те бо́льше уси́лий!; **I tried for a prize** я добива́лся при́за; я претендова́л на приз.

with advs.: **~ on** *v.t.* прим|еря́ть, -е́рить; **she tried on several dresses** она́ приме́рила не́сколько пла́тьев; (*fig.*) **it's no use ~ing it on with me** со мной э́тот но́мер не пройдёт (*coll.*); **~ out** *v.t.* испы́т|ывать, -а́ть; опро́бовать (*pf.*); **he tried out the idea on his friends** он подели́лся свои́м за́мыслом с друзья́ми, что́бы узна́ть их реа́кцию.

cpds. **~-on** *n.* приме́рка; (*coll.*) попы́тка обману́ть; **~-out** *n.* прове́рка, про́ба; **~-sail** *n.* три́сель (*m.*); **~-square** *n.* уго́льник.

tryst [trɪst] *n.* назна́ченная встре́ча, свида́ние.

tsar, tzar [zɑ:(r)] *n.* царь (*m.*).

tsardom [zɑ:dəm] *n.* (*territory*) ца́рство; (*régime*) цари́зм.

tsarina, tzarina [zɑ:'ri:nə] *n.* цари́ца.

tsarism ['zɑ:rɪz(ə)m] *n.* цари́зм.

tsarist ['zɑːrɪst] *adj.* ца́рский.

tsetse(-fly) ['tsetsɪ, 'tetsɪ] *n.* му́ха цеце́ (*indecl.*).

tub [tʌb] *n.* **1.** лоха́нь, уша́т. **2.** (*bath*) ва́нна; **he took a cold ~ before breakfast** он при́нял холо́дную ва́нну пе́ред за́втраком. **3.** (*coll., old boat*) ста́рая кало́ша, ста́рое коры́то.

v.i. мы́ться/купа́ться (*impf.*) в ва́нне.

cpd. **~-thumper** *n.* говору́н, вити́я (*m.*).

tuba ['tjuːbə] *n.* ту́ба.

tubby ['tʌbɪ] *adj.* (*of pers.*) коротконо́гий и то́лстый.

tube [tjuːb] *n.* **1.** (*of metal, glass etc.*) труба́, тру́бка; **(test-~)** проби́рка. **2.** (*of paint, toothpaste etc.*) тю́бик. **3.** (*inner ~ of tyre*) ка́мера (ши́ны). **4.** (*organ of body*) бронх; **bronchial ~s** ме́лкие бро́нхи. **5.** (*underground railway*) метро́ (*indecl.*); **we met on the ~** мы встре́тились в метро́; **travel by ~** е́хать (*det.*) на метро́.

cpd. **~-station** *n.* ста́нция метро́.

tuber ['tjuːbə(r)] *n.* (*bot.*) клу́бень (*m.*).

tubercle ['tjuːbək(ə)l] *n.* ме́лкий клу́бень; тубе́ркул.

tubercular [tjʊ'bɜːkjʊlə(r)] *adj.* туберкулёзный.

tuberculosis [tjʊˌbɜːkjʊ'ləʊsɪs] *n.* туберкулёз.

tuberose ['tjuːbəˌrəʊs] *n.* тубеpо́за.

tubular ['tjuːbjʊlə(r)] *adj.* тру́бчатый.

TUC (*abbr. of* ***Trades Union Congress***) Всебрита́нский конгре́сс тредюнио́нов.

tuck[1] [tʌk] *n.* (*fold in garment*) скла́дка, сбо́рка; **she put ~s in the sleeves** она́ сде́лала на рукава́х сбо́рки.

v.t. (*stow*) пря́тать, с-; под|бира́ть, -обра́ть (под себя́); **he ~ed his legs under the table** он спря́тал но́ги под стол; **the bird ~ed its head under its wing** пти́ца спря́тала го́лову под крыло́.

with advs.: **~ away** *v.t.* запря́т|ывать, -ать; **~ in** *v.t.* запр|авля́ть, -а́вить; **~ your shirt in** запра́вьте руба́шку; **~ up** *v.t.* под|гиба́ть, -огну́ть; под|вёртывать, -верну́ть; **he ~ed up his shirt sleeves** он засучи́л рукава́; **she ~ed up her skirt** она́ подобрала́ ю́бку; **they ~ed the children up (in bed)** дете́й уложи́ли в крова́ть (и подоткну́ли одея́ло).

tuck[2] [tʌk] *n.* (*coll., eatables*) сла́сти (*f. pl.*).

v.i.: **they ~ed into their supper** они́ уплета́ли у́жин за о́бе щеки́; **~ in!** нава́ливайтесь!

cpds. **~-box** *n.* коро́бка для сла́достей; **~-in** *n.* закусо́н (*sl.*); **~-shop** *n.* конди́терская.

tucker ['tʌkə(r)] *n.*: **he was wearing his best bib and ~** (*joc.*) он был оде́т в выходно́й костю́м.

Tudor ['tjuːdə(r)] *n.* представи́тель (*fem.* -ница) дина́стии Тюдо́ров.

adj. эпо́хи Тюдо́ров; (*archit.*) позднеготи́ческий.

Tuesday ['tjuːzdeɪ, -dɪ] *n.* вто́рник.

tufa ['tjuːfə] *n.* известко́вый туф.

tuffet ['tʌfɪt] *n.* бугоро́к.

tuft [tʌft] *n.* (*of grass, hair etc.*) пучо́к; (*beard*) боро́дка кли́нышком.

tufted ['tʌftɪd] *adj.*: (*of bird*) с хохолко́м; **a ~ mattress** стёганый матра́ц.

tug [tʌg] *n.* **1.** (*pull*) рыво́к, дёрганье; **he gave a ~ at the rope** он дёрнул за верёвку. **2.** (*boat*) букси́р.

v.t. тащи́ть (*impf.*); тяну́ть (*impf.*); **the dogs ~ged a sledge** соба́ки тяну́ли/тащи́ли са́ни.

v.i. дёргать; **he ~ged at my sleeve** он дёрнул меня́ за рука́в.

cpd. **~-of-war** *n.* перетя́гивание на кана́те; (*fig.*) тя́жба; ожесточённое соревнова́ние.

tuition [tjuː'ɪʃ(ə)n] *n.* обуче́ние.

tulip ['tjuːlɪp] *n.* тюльпа́н.

tulle [tjuːl] *n.* тюль (*m.*).

tum [tʌm] = **tummy**

tumble ['tʌmb(ə)l] *n.* **1.** (*fall*) паде́ние; **take a ~** упа́сть (*pf.*). **2.** (*acrobatic feat*) кувырка́нье; акробати́ческий прыжо́к. **3.** (*confusion*): **things were all in a ~** всё бы́ло в по́лном беспоря́дке.

v.t. **1.** (*cause to fall; fling*) бр|оса́ть, -о́сить; опроки́|дывать, -нуть; **we were all ~d out of the bus** нас вы́бросило из авто́буса; **he ~d the clothes into a cupboard** он су́нул оде́жду в шкаф. **2.** (*disorder, rumple*) прив|оди́ть, -ести́ в беспоря́док; **her hair was ~d by the wind** ве́тер растрепа́л ей во́лосы.

v.i. **1.** (*fall*) свали́ться (*pf.*); скати́ться (*pf.*); **the child ~d downstairs** ребёнок скати́лся с ле́стницы; **he ~d into bed** он бро́сился в крова́ть. **2.** (*roll*) валя́ться; ката́ться; мета́ться (*all impf.*); **the sick man ~d in his sleep** больно́й мета́лся во сне; **~ in the hay** (*fig.*) балова́ться, шали́ть (*both impf.*). **3.** (*fig.*): **when the order was given the men ~d to it** (*coll.*) прика́з был о́тдан и солда́ты его́ неме́дленно вы́полнили; **I ~d to his meaning** до меня́ дошло́, что он име́л в виду́.

with advs.: **the puppies ~d about on the floor** щеня́та кувырка́лись на полу́; **the cart ~d along** теле́га подпры́гивала на ходу́; **the house seemed about to ~ down** дом, каза́лось, вот-во́т разва́лится; **he often ~s over** он ча́сто спотыка́ется.

cpds. **~down** *adj.* развали́вшийся; полуразру́шенный; **~-weed** *n.* перекати́-по́ле.

tumbler ['tʌmblə(r)] *n.* **1.** (*drinking-vessel*) стака́н. **2.** (*mechanism*) реверси́вный механи́зм; **~ switch** выключа́тель с перекидно́й голо́вкой. **3.** (*acrobat*) акроба́т. **4.** (*pigeon*) ту́рман.

tumbr|el ['tʌmbr(ə)l], **-il** ['tʌmbrɪl] *n.* (самосва́льная) теле́жка.

tumescence [tjʊ'mes(ə)ns] *n.* опуха́ние, распуха́ние.

tumescent [tjʊ'mes(ə)nt] *adj.* опуха́ющий, распуха́ющий.

tumid ['tjuːmɪd] *adj.* распу́хший; (*fig.*) напы́щенный.

tumidity [ˌtjuː'mɪdɪtɪ] *n.* распуха́ние; (*fig.*) напы́щенность.

tummy ['tʌmɪ] *n.* (*coll.*) живо́т; (*dim., e.g. baby's*) живо́тик.

cpds. **~-ache** *n.* боль в живо́те; **~-button** *n.* пупо́к.

tumour ['tjuːmə(r)] *n.* о́пухоль.

tump ['tʌmp] *n.* холм, бугоро́к.

tumult ['tjuːmʌlt] *n.* шум; сумато́ха; (*fig.*) си́льное волне́ние; смяте́ние чувств; **when the ~ within him subsided** по́сле того́, как он успоко́ился.

tumultuous [tjʊ'mʌltjʊəs] *adj.* шу́мный, беспоко́йный; **he received a ~ welcome** ему́ устро́или бу́рную встре́чу.

tumulus ['tjuːmjʊləs] *n.* моги́льный холм/курга́н.

tun [tʌn] *n.* больша́я бо́чка.

tuna ['tjuːnə] *n.* (голубо́й) туне́ц.

tundra ['tʌndrə] *n.* ту́ндра.

tune [tjuːn] *n.* **1.** (*melody*) мело́дия; моти́в; **the ~ goes like this** моти́в тако́й; (*fig.*) тон; **he will soon change his ~** он ско́ро запоёт ина́че; **I paid up, to the ~ of £30** я заплати́л це́лых 30 фу́нтов. **2.** (*correct pitch; consonance*) строй; настро́енность; **you are not singing in ~** вы фальши́вите; **the piano is out of ~** фортепья́но расстро́ено; (*fig.*) согла́сие; гармо́ния; **he felt in ~ with his surroundings** он ощуща́л гармо́нию с окружа́ющим ми́ром.

v.t. **1.** (*bring to right pitch*) настр|а́ивать, -о́ить; **the instrument needs tuning** инструме́нт нужда́ется в настро́йке; **tuning-fork** камерто́н. **2.** (*adjust running of*) настр|а́ивать, -о́ить; регули́ровать (*impf.*); **the engine has been ~d** мото́р/дви́гатель был отрегули́рован.

with advs.: **~ in** *v.t. & i.* настр|а́ивать(ся), -о́ить(ся); **the radio is not ~d in properly** приёмник пло́хо настро́ен; **he ~d in to the BBC** он настро́ил свой приёмник на Би-Би-Си́; **~ out** *v.t.*: **~ out interference** устран|я́ть, -и́ть поме́хи; **~ up** настр|а́ивать(ся), -о́ить(ся); **he ~d up his guitar** он настро́ил гита́ру; **the orchestra was tuning up** оркестра́нты настра́ивали инструме́нты.

tuneful ['tjuːnfʊl] *adj.* музыка́льный, мелоди́чный.

tunefulness ['tjuːnfʊlnɪs] *n.* музыка́льность, мелоди́чность.

tuneless ['tjuːnlɪs] *adj.* немузыка́льный, немелоди́чный.

tunelessness ['tjuːnlɪsnɪs] *n.* немузыка́льность, немелоди́чность.

tuner ['tjuːnə(r)] *n.* (*of pianos etc.*) настро́йщик; (*radio component*) механи́зм настро́йки.

tung-oil [tʌŋ] *n.* ту́нговое ма́сло.

tungsten ['tʌŋst(ə)n] *n.* вольфра́м; (*attr.*) вольфра́мовый.

tunic ['tjuːnɪk] *n.* (*ancient garment*) туни́ка; (*woman's blouse*) блу́зка, со́бранная в та́лии; (*part of uniform*) ки́тель (*m.*).

tuning ['tjuːnɪŋ] *n.* настро́йка, регулиро́вка.

Tunis [tjuː'nɪs] *n.* Туни́с.

Tunisia [tjuː'nɪzɪə] *n.* Туни́с.

Tunisian [tju:ˈnɪzɪən] *n.* туни́с|ец (*fem.* -ка).
adj. туни́сский.

tunnel [ˈtʌn(ə)l] *n.* тонне́ль (*m.*), тунне́ль (*m.*).
v.t.: **they ~led their way out (of prison)** они́ сде́лали подко́п и бежа́ли.
v.i. про|кла́дывать, -ложи́ть тонне́ль; **they had to ~ through solid rock** им пришло́сь вести́ прохо́дку тонне́ля в твёрдой поро́де.

tunny(-fish) [ˈtʌnɪ] *n.* туне́ц.

tup [tʌp] *n.* (*ram*) бара́н.

tuppence [ˈtʌpəns] *n.* (*coll.*) два пе́нса; **I don't care ~** мне наплева́ть (*coll.*).

tuppenny [ˈtʌpənɪ] *adj.* (*coll.*) двухпе́нсовый; **I don't give a ~ damn** мне наплева́ть (*coll.*).
cpd. **~-ha'penny** *adj.* (*fig.*) грошо́вый, ничто́жный.

tu quoque [tu: ˈkwɒkweɪ, -kwi:] *n.* ре́плика ти́па «сам тако́й-то»; «посмотри́ на себя́».

turban [ˈtɜ:bən] *n.* (*male headgear*) тюрба́н, чалма́; (*woman's hat*) тюрба́н.

turbid [ˈtɜ:bɪd] *adj.* му́тный; (*fig.*) тума́нный; нея́сный.

turbid|ity [ˌtɜ:ˈbɪdɪtɪ], **-ness** [ˈtɜ:bɪdnɪs] *nn.* му́тность; (*fig.*) тума́нность; нея́сность.

turbine [ˈtɜ:baɪn] *n.* турби́на.

turbo-jet [ˈtɜ:bəʊˌdʒet] *n.* турбореакти́вный самолёт.

turbo-prop [ˈtɜ:bəʊˌprɒp] *n.* турбовинтово́й самолёт.

turbot [ˈtɜ:bət] *n.* белоко́рый па́лтус.

turbo-train [ˈtɜ:bəʊˌtreɪn] *n.* (скоростно́й) турбопо́езд.

turbulence [ˈtɜ:bjʊləns] *n.* бу́рность; (*aeron.*) турбуле́нтность, (*coll.*) болта́нка; (*fig.*) беспоко́йство.

turbulent [ˈtɜ:bjʊlənt] *adj.* бу́рный; (*fig.*) беспоко́йный, неукроти́мый.

turd [tɜ:d] *n.* (*vulg.*) **1.** (*lump of excrement*) кака́шка. **2.** (*objectionable pers.*) подо́нок.

tureen [tjʊəˈri:n, tə-] *n.* су́пница; су́пник.

turf [tɜ:f] *n.* **1.** (*grassy topsoil*) дёрн, дерни́на; (*peat*) торф; **a cottage thatched with turves** до́мик под земляно́й кры́шей. **2.** (*racing*): **a devotee of the ~** завсегда́тай бего́в; **~ accountant** букме́кер.
v.t. **1.** (*cover with ~; also ~ over*) покр|ыва́ть, -ы́ть дёрном. **2. ~ out** (*coll., eject*) выбра́сывать, вы́бросить; вышвы́ривать, вы́швырнуть.

turgid [ˈtɜ:dʒɪd] *adj.* (*fig.*) напы́щенный.

turgidity [tɜ:ˈdʒɪdɪtɪ] *n.* (*fig.*) напы́щенность.

Turk [tɜ:k] *n.* (*native of Turkey*) ту́р|ок (*fem.* -ча́нка); (*coll., rascal*) негодни́к; **you young T~!** а́х ты, озорни́к!

Turkey [ˈtɜ:kɪ] *n.* **1.** (*country*) Ту́рция. **2.** (**t~:** *bird*) инд|ю́к (*fem.* -е́йка); (*as food*) индю́шка; **cold t~** (*US sl., plain speaking*) разгово́р без обиняко́в.
cpds. **t~-cock** *n.* индю́к; **t~-hen** *n.* инде́йка; **t~-poult** *n.* индюшо́нок.

Turkic [ˈtɜ:kɪk] *adj.* тю́ркский.

Turkish [ˈtɜ:kɪʃ] *n.* туре́цкий язы́к.
adj. туре́цкий; **~ bath** туре́цкие ба́ни (*f. pl.*); **~ delight**раха́т-луку́м; **~ towel** мохна́тое/махро́вое полоте́нце.

Turkmen [ˈtɜ:kmən] *n.* (*pers.*) туркме́н (*fem.* -ка); (*language*) туркме́нский язы́к.
adj. туркме́нский.

Turkmenistan [tɜ:kmenɪˈstɑ:n] *n.* Туркмениста́н.

turmeric [ˈtɜ:mərɪk] *n.* курку́ма.

turmoil [ˈtɜ:mɔɪl] *n.* беспоря́док; смяте́ние.

turn [tɜ:n] *n.* **1.** (*rotation*) поворо́т, оборо́т; **a ~ of the handle** поворо́т ру́чки; **with a ~ of the wrist** поворо́том ки́сти/руки́; **the meat was done to a ~** мя́со бы́ло поджа́рено как раз в ме́ру; **it was one further ~ of the screw** (*fig.*) э́то бы́ло но́вым зави́нчиванием га́ек. **2.** (*change of direction*) измене́ние направле́ния; поворо́т; **a ~ in the road** поворо́т доро́ги; **I took a right ~** я поверну́л напра́во; **he made an about ~ in policy** он сде́лал поворо́т на 180° в поли́тике; **at every ~** (*fig.*) на ка́ждом шагу́; **at the ~ of the century** в нача́ле ве́ка; на рубеже́ двух столе́тий. **3.** (*change in condition*) переме́на; поворо́т; **his luck is on the ~** он вступа́ет в полосу́ везе́ния; **the ~ of the tide** (*lit.*) сме́на прили́во-отливно́го тече́ния; (*fig.*) измене́ние форту́ны; **the milk is on the ~** молоко́ скиса́ет; **his condition took a ~ for the worse** его́ состоя́ние уху́дшилось. **4.** (*opportunity of doing sth. in proper order*) о́чередь; **it's your ~ next** вы сле́дующий; **my ~ will come** придёт и мой черёд; бу́дет и на мое́й у́лице пра́здник; **I missed my ~** я пропусти́л свою́ о́чередь; **they worked ~ and ~ about** они́ рабо́тали по о́череди; **she went hot and cold by ~s** её броса́ло то в жар, то в хо́лод; **they all spoke in ~ (*or* took ~s to speak)** они́ выступа́ли/говори́ли по о́череди; **don't talk out of ~** (*fig., presumptuously*) не вступа́йте в разгово́р, пока́ вас не про́сят. **5.** (*service*) услу́га; **he did me a good ~** он оказа́л мне до́брую услу́гу; **one good ~ deserves another** долг платежо́м кра́сен. **6.** (*tendency, capability*): **he has a practical ~ of mind** он челове́к практи́ческого скла́да; **the car has a fine ~ of speed** маши́на даёт хоро́шую ско́рость; **a witty ~ of phrase** остроу́мный оборо́т. **7.** (*purpose*): **this will serve my ~** э́то мне вполне́ подойдёт. **8.** (*short spell*): **shall I take a ~ at the wheel?** дава́йте я вас сменю́ за рулём?; **I'm going to take a ~ in the garden** пойду́ прогуля́юсь по са́ду. **9.** (*short stage performance*) вы́ход; но́мер (програ́ммы); **the comedian did his ~** ко́мик испо́лнил свой но́мер; **star ~** гвоздь (*m.*) програ́ммы. **10.** (*coll., nervous shock*) потрясе́ние; припа́док; **you gave me quite a ~** вы меня́ поря́дком испуга́ли; **she had one of her ~s** с ней случи́лся припа́док.
v.t. **1.** (*cause to move round*) пов|ора́чивать, -ерну́ть; **he ~ed the key (in the lock)** он поверну́л ключ; **he ~ed the wheel sharply** он ре́зко поверну́л руль; **he ~ed his head** он поверну́л го́лову; он оберну́лся; **he ~ed his back on me** он поверну́лся ко мне спино́й; он отверну́лся от меня́; **she ~ed the pages** она́ перелиста́ла страни́цы; **he ~ed the scale at 12 stone** он ве́сил 168 фу́нтов; **this battle ~ed the scale** э́та би́тва реши́ла исхо́д де́ла. **2.** (*direct*) напр|авля́ть, -а́вить; **they ~ed the hose on to the flames** шланг напра́вили на пла́мя; **he ~ed the dogs on to the intruders** он натрави́л соба́к на незва́ных посети́телей; **he ~ed the full force of his sarcasm on me** весь его́ сарка́зм был напра́влен про́тив меня́; **I ~ed my mind to other things** я сосредото́чился на друго́м; **he can ~ his hand to anything** он всё уме́ет; он ма́стер на все ру́ки; **he ~ed a blind eye** он закры́л глаза́ (на+*a.*); **he ~ed a deaf ear to my request** он игнори́ровал мою́ про́сьбу; (*adapt*): **he ~ed his skill to good use, account** он уме́ло испо́льзовал своё мастерство́; (*incline*): **the accident ~ed me against driving** катастро́фа отби́ла у меня́ охо́ту води́ть маши́ну. **3.** (*pass round or beyond*): **slow down as you ~ the corner** при поворо́те за́ угол сба́вьте ско́рость; **they ~ed the enemy's flank** они́ обошли́ проти́вника с фла́нга; **it has ~ed two o'clock** уже́ два часа́; **he has ~ed fifty** ему́ испо́лнилось 50 лет. **4.** (*transform*) превра|ща́ть, -ти́ть; **he ~ed the water into wine** он обрати́л во́ду в вино́; **his joy was ~ed to sorrow** его́ ра́дость оберну́лась печа́лью; **he ~ed himself into an expert** он сде́лался специали́стом; **thunder ~s the milk** молоко́ в грозу́ скиса́ет; **grief ~ed his brain** он помеша́лся от го́ря; **it's enough to ~ one's stomach** от э́того мо́жет затошни́ть; **success ~ed his head** успе́х вскружи́л ему́ го́лову; (*translate*) перев|оди́ть, -ести́; **he ~ed Homer into English verse** он перевёл Гоме́ра на англи́йский стиха́ми. **5.** (*cause to become*): **the shock ~ed his hair white** он поседе́л от потрясе́ния; **shall we ~ the dogs loose?** спу́стим соба́к с це́пи? **6.** (*reverse*) перев|ора́чивать, -ерну́ть; меня́ть (*impf.*) на противополо́жное; **she ~ed her dress** она́ перелицева́ла пла́тье; **he ~ed his coat** (*fig., changed sides*) он перешёл в ла́герь врага́/проти́вника; **the picture was ~ed upside down** карти́ну переверну́ли вверх нога́ми; **the room was ~ed upside down** (*ransacked*) в ко́мнате всё переверну́ли вверх дном; **I ~ed the tables on him** (*fig.*) я отплати́л ему́ то́й же моне́той; **he did not ~ a hair** он и гла́зом не моргну́л. **7.** (*send forcibly*) прог|оня́ть, -на́ть; **he was ~ed out of the house** его́ вы́гнали из дому; **they will ~ you off the grass** они́ сго́нят вас с газо́на; **the boat was ~ed adrift** ло́дку пусти́ли по во́ле волн (*or* по тече́нию); **he never ~s a beggar from his door** он никогда́ не прого́нит ни́щего со двора́; (*deflect*) отвра|ща́ть, -ти́ть; **he will not be ~ed from his**

purpose его́ не собьёшь с и́збранного ку́рса; **his armour ~ed the bullet** его́ броня́ отрази́ла пу́лю. **8.** (*shape*): **the bowl was ~ed on the lathe** ку́бок/ча́шу обточи́ли на тока́рном станке́; (*fig.*): **he can ~ a witty phrase** он ма́стер на остроу́мные выраже́ния; **a well ~ed ankle** точёная но́жка. **9.** (*execute by ~ing*): **the children were ~ing somersaults** ребяти́шки кувырка́лись (*or* ходи́ли колесо́м); **the wheel has ~ed full circle** колесо́ сде́лало по́лный оборо́т; (*fig.*) положе́ние кардина́льно измени́лось.

v.i. **1.** (*move round*) пов|ора́чиваться, -ерну́ться; враща́ться (*impf.*); **the earth ~s on its axis** земля́ враща́ется вокру́г свое́й о́си; **the key won't ~** ключ не повора́чивается; **he ~ed as he spoke** заговори́в, он поверну́лся; **he ~ed on his heel** он кру́то поверну́лся; **~ing to me, he said ...** поверну́вшись ко мне, он сказа́л...; (*fig.*): **this will make him ~ in his grave** он от э́того в гробу́ перевернётся; (*depend*) зави́сеть (*impf.*); **everything ~s on his answer** всё зави́сит от его́ отве́та; (*revolve*): **the discussion ~ed upon the meaning of democracy** спор враща́лся вокру́г по́длинного значе́ния демокра́тии. **2.** (*change direction*) направля́ться (*impf.*); **we ~ (to the) left here** тут мы повора́чиваем нале́во; **right ~!** напра́во!; **we ~ed off the main road down a lane** мы сверну́ли с гла́вной доро́ги на тропи́нку; (*fig.*) обра|ща́ться, -ти́ться; **she hardly knew which way to ~** она́ не зна́ла, что ей де́лать; **who can I ~ to?** к кому́ я могу́ обрати́ться?; **I ~ to more serious topics** я перейду́ к бо́лее серьёзным вопро́сам; **the people ~ed against their rulers** наро́д восста́л про́тив прави́телей; **I've ~ed against meat** мне опроти́вело мя́со; **he ~ed on his attackers** он бро́сился на свои́х оби́дчиков; **he ~ed on me with reproaches** он засы́пал меня́ упрёками. **3.** (*change*) превра|ща́ться, -ти́ться; **the tadpoles ~ed into frogs** голова́стики преврати́лись в лягу́шек; **he ~ed into a miser** он стал скря́гой; **his pleasure ~ed to disgust** чу́вство удово́льствия перешло́ у него́ в отвраще́ние; (*change colour*): **the leaves have ~ed** ли́стья пожелте́ли. **4.** (*become*) ста|нови́ться, -ть; де́латься, с-; **she ~ed pale** она́ побледне́ла; **he ~ed traitor** он стал преда́телем; **it has ~ed warm** потепле́ло; (*become sour*): **the milk has ~ed** молоко́ прокисло/сверну́лось. **5.** (*on lathe etc.*): **this wood ~s easily** э́то де́рево легко́ обта́чивается. *See also* **turning**

with advs.: **~ about** *v.t.* (*reverse*) пов|ора́чивать, -ерну́ть; *v.i.* (*change to opposite direction*) поверну́ться (*pf.*) на 180°; **about ~!** круго́м!; **~ aside** *v.t. & i.* отклон|я́ть(ся), -и́ть(ся); **~ away** *v.t.* (*avert*): **he ~ed his head away** он поверну́л го́лову в сто́рону; (*deflect*): **a soft answer ~eth away wrath** кро́ткий отве́т га́сит гнев; (*refuse admittance to*) прог|оня́ть, -на́ть; не пус|ка́ть, -ти́ть; **hundreds were ~ed away from the stadium** со́тни не смогли́ попа́сть на стадио́н; *v.i.*: **she ~ed away in disgust** она́ с отвраще́нием отверну́лась; **~ back** *v.t.* (*repel*) от|сыла́ть, -осла́ть наза́д; **we were ~ed back at the frontier** нас верну́ли с грани́цы; (*fold back*) отв|ора́чивать, -ерну́ть; от|гиба́ть, -огну́ть; **his cuffs were ~ed back** его́ манже́ты бы́ли завёрнуты; (*return to former position*): **he ~ed back the pages** он стал листа́ть кни́гу в обра́тном поря́дке; **he ~ed the clock back** (*lit.*) он перевёл часы́ наза́д; **we cannot ~ the clock back** (*fig.*) мы не мо́жем поверну́ть вре́мя вспять; *v.i.* пов|ора́чивать, -ерну́ть наза́д; пойти́ (*pf.*) обра́тно; **~ down** *v.t.* (*fold down*): **his collar was ~ed down** у него́ воротни́к был отвёрнут; (*reduce by ~ing*) уб|авля́ть, -а́вить; **~ down the gas!** уба́вьте газ!; прикрути́те газ!; **~ the volume down!** (*TV etc.*) уба́вьте звук!; (*reject*) отка́з|ываться, -а́ться от+*g.*; **I was ~ed down for the job** мне отказа́ли в рабо́те; **my offer was ~ed down** моё предложе́ние бы́ло отве́ргнуто; **~ in** *v.t.*: **he ~ed in his toes** он ста́вил но́ги носка́ми внутрь; (*surrender*; *hand over*) сда|ва́ть, -ть; **they had to ~ in their arms** им пришло́сь сдать ору́жие; **he ~ed himself in to the police** он сда́лся поли́ции; **~ it in!** (*sl.*, *stop it!*) да брось!; *v.i.* (*incline inwards*) св|ёртываться, -ерну́ться внутрь; (*go to bed*) отпра́виться (*pf.*) на бокову́ю (*coll.*); **~ inside out** *v.t. & i.* вывора́чивать(ся), вы́вернуть(ся) наизна́нку; **~ off** *v.t.* (*e.g. light*, *engine*) выключа́ть, вы́ключить; гаси́ть, по-; **~ off the light!** погаси́те/вы́ключите свет!; (*tap*) закр|ыва́ть, -ы́ть; **the water was ~ed off at the main** во́ду отключи́ли; *v.i.* (*make a diversion*) св|ора́чивать, -ерну́ть; **we ~ed off to call at a farm** мы сверну́ли, что́бы зае́хать на фе́рму; **~ on** *v.t.* (*e.g. light*, *engine*, *radio*) включ|а́ть, -и́ть; (*tap*) откр|ыва́ть, -ы́ть; (*fig.*): **she ~ed on all her charm** она́ пусти́ла в ход всё своё обая́ние; **this music ~s me on** (*coll.*) э́то му́зыка меня́ возбужда́ет; **~ out** *v.t.* (*expel*) прог|оня́ть, -на́ть; исключ|а́ть, -и́ть; **the tenants were ~ed out on to the street** жильцо́в вы́гнали на у́лицу; (*switch off*) гаси́ть, по-; **the lights were ~ed out** свет был поту́шен; (*produce*) выпуска́ть, вы́пустить; произв|оди́ть, -ести́; **the factory ~s out 500 cars a day** фа́брика выпуска́ет 500 маши́н в день; **the school ~s out some first-rate scholars** шко́ла выпуска́ет первокла́ссных учёных; (*fig.*) укра|ша́ть, -си́ть; **he is always well ~ed out** он всегда́ хорошо́ оде́т; (*empty*) вывора́чивать, вы́вернуть; **he ~ed out his pockets** он вы́вернул карма́ны; (*tidy*) уб|ира́ть, ра́ть; **the room gets ~ed out once a month** ко́мнату убира́ют раз в ме́сяц; (*assemble for duty*) вызыва́ть, вы́звать; **the guard was ~ed out for inspection** охра́ну/карау́л вы́вели для прове́рки; *v.i.* (*prove*) ока́з|ываться, -а́ться; **let us see how things ~ out** посмо́трим, как пойду́т дела́; **as it ~ed out I was not required** как оказа́лось, я не пона́добился; **he ~ed out to be a liar** он оказа́лся лжецо́м; **it ~ed out that he was right** получи́лось, что он был прав; (*become*): **such children often ~ out criminals** из таки́х дете́й ча́сто выхо́дят престу́пники; **after a wet morning, it ~ed out a fine day** по́сле дождли́вого у́тра день вы́дался хоро́шим; (*assemble*) соб|ира́ться, -ра́ться; **the whole village ~ed out to welcome him** вся дере́вня вы́сыпала его́ приве́тствовать; (*go out of doors*): **I had to ~ out in the cold** мне пришло́сь вы́йти на хо́лод; **~ over** *v.t.* (*overturn*) перев|ора́чивать, -ерну́ть; опроки́|дывать, -нуть; (*reverse position of*): **I ~ed over the page** я переверну́л страни́цу; **the soil should be ~ed over** зе́млю на́до перекопа́ть; (*revolve*) запус|ка́ть, -ти́ть; **he ~ed over the engine by hand** он завёл мото́р вручну́ю; **I must ~ it over in my mind** я до́лжен э́то обду́мать; (*transfer*; *hand over*) перед|ава́ть, -а́ть; **he ~ed over the business to his partner** он пе́редал де́ло своему́ партнёру; **he was ~ed over to the authorities** его́ пе́редали властя́м; *v.i.* (*overturn*) перев|ора́чиваться, -ерну́ться; **the boat ~ed over and sank** ло́дка переверну́лась и зато́ну́ла; (*change position*) воро́чаться (*impf.*); переверну́ться (*pf.*); **he ~ed over (in bed)** он переверну́лся на друго́й бок; (*revolve*): **is the engine ~ing over?** дви́гатель повора́чивается; **~ round** *v.t.* (*change or reverse position of*) перев|ора́чивать, -ерну́ть; **~ your chair round this way** поверни́те стул в э́ту сто́рону; **he ~ed his car round** он разверну́л маши́ну; *v.i.* (*change position*): **he ~ed round to look** он оберну́лся, что́бы посмотре́ть; **his policy has ~ed completely round** он по́лностью измени́л свою́ поли́тику; (*revolve*) враща́ться (*impf.*); **the weather-vane ~s round in the wind** флю́гер враща́ется/ве́ртится на ветру́; **~ to** *v.i.* (*join in*, *help*) бра́ться/взя́ться за де́ло; **everyone ~ed to** все взя́ли́сь за рабо́ту; **~ up** *v.t.* (*increase flow of*) приб|авля́ть, -а́вить; усили|вать, -ть; **~ up the gas!** приба́вьте га́зу!; (*disinter*) выка́пывать, вы́копать; отк|а́пывать, -опа́ть; **the workmen ~ed up some bones** рабо́чие вы́копали не́сколько косте́й; (*put in higher position*) подн|има́ть, -я́ть вверх; **he ~ed his collar up** он по́днял воротни́к; **don't ~ your nose up at the offer** не вороти́те нос от тако́го предложе́ния; (*coll.*, *cause to vomit*): **the smell is enough to ~ you up** от одного́ за́паха мо́жет стошни́ть; *v.i.* (*arrive*) появ|ля́ться, -и́ться; **look who's ~ed up!** смотри́те, кто пришёл!; кого́ мы ви́дим!; (*be found*; *occur*) ока́з|ываться, -а́ться; подв|ёртываться, -ерну́ться; **don't look for your pen now; it may ~ up later** бро́сьте иска́ть ру́чку — сама́ найдётся; (*happen*; *become available*) подверну́ться (*pf.*); **he is waiting for a suitable job to ~ up** он ждёт, пока́ ему́ подвернётся подходя́щая рабо́та; **~ upside down** *v.t. & i.* перев|ора́чивать(ся),

-ерну́ть(ся) вверх дном; (*fig.*); **she ~ed the room upside down to find her ring** она́ переры́ла всю ко́мнату в по́исках кольца́.

cpds. **~coat** *n.* ренега́т; преда́тель (*fem.* -ница); **~-down** *adj.* отложно́й; **~key** *n.* тюре́мщик, надзира́тель (*m.*); **~out** *n.* (*assembly*) собра́ние, сбор; **there was a very good ~out** собра́ло́сь о́чень мно́го наро́ду; (*cleaning, tidying*) чи́стка, убо́рка; **his bedroom needs a good ~out** его́ спа́льню ну́жно хороше́нько убра́ть; его́ спа́льня нужда́ется в генера́льной убо́рке; (*equipage*) вы́езд; **~over** *n.* (*in business*) оборо́т (капита́ла); (*rate of renewal*) теку́честь; (*pie*) пиро́г с начи́нкой; **~pike** *n.* доро́жная заста́ва; (*road*) шоссе́ (*indecl.*); **~-round** *n.* (*of ship etc.*) оборо́т; (*reversal of policy, opinion etc.*) поворо́т на 180°; **~stile** *n.* турнике́т; **~table** *n.* (*rail.*) поворо́тный круг; (*of record player*) верту́шка; **~-up** *n.* (*of trouser*) манже́та, отворо́т; (*coll., surprise*) неожи́данность.

turner ['tɜːnə(r)] *n.* то́карь (*m.*).

turnery ['tɜːnərɪ] *n.* (*craft*) тока́рное ремесло́; (*products*) тока́рные изде́лия.

turning ['tɜːnɪŋ] *n.* (*bend; junction*) поворо́т; перекрёсток; **the first ~ on the right** пе́рвый поворо́т напра́во.

cpd. **~-point** *n.* (*lit.*) поворо́тный пункт; (*fig.*) кри́зис, перело́м; эта́пное собы́тие; **it was a ~-point in his career** э́то был реша́ющий моме́нт в его́ карье́ре.

turnip ['tɜːnɪp] *n.* ре́па, турне́пс; **~-tops** (*pl.*) ботва́ молодо́й ре́пы.

turpentine ['tɜːpən,taɪn] *n.* терпенти́н, скипида́р.

turpitude ['tɜːpɪ,tjuːd] *n.* поро́чность, ни́зость.

turps [tɜːps] (*coll.*) = **turpentine**

turquoise ['tɜːkwɔɪz, -kwɑːz] *n.* бирюза́; (*colour*) бирюзо́вый цвет.

turret ['tʌrɪt] *n.* (*tower*) ба́шенка; (*of tank etc.*) брониро́ванная/оруди́йная ба́шня; **~-lathe** револьве́рный стано́к.

turtle ['tɜːt(ə)l] *n.* **1.** черепа́ха. **2.: turn ~** перев|ора́чиваться, -ерну́ться вверх дном.

cpd. **~-neck** *adj.*: **~-neck sweater** (сви́тер-)водола́зка; битло́вка.

turtle-dove ['tɜt(ə)l,dʌv] *n.* ди́кий го́лубь.

tush [tʌʃ] *int.* фу!; тьфу!

tusk [tʌsk] *n.* клык, би́вень (*m.*).

tussle ['tʌs(ə)l] *n.* борьба́, дра́ка.

v.i. боро́ться (*impf.*); дра́ться (*impf.*); **they ~d together** они́ схвати́лись друг с дру́гом; (*fig.*) би́ться (*impf.*); **I ~d with the problem all night** я би́лся над э́той зада́чей всю ночь.

tussock ['tʌsək] *n.* ко́чка.

tussore ['tʌsɔː(r), 'tʌsə(r)] *n.* туссо́р.

tut [tʌt] (*also* **~-tut**) *v.i.* цо́кать (*impf.*) языко́м (, выража́я неодобре́ние).

int. а́х ты!; ай-я́й-я́й!

tutelage ['tjuːtɪlɪdʒ] *n.* попечи́тельство; опе́ка.

tutelary ['tjuːtɪlərɪ] *adj.* опеку́нский, опека́ющий.

tutor ['tjuːtə(r)] *n.* (*private teacher*) репети́тор; (*university teacher*) преподава́тель (*fem.* -ница); (*manual*) учёбник; **piano-~** учи́тель (*fem.* -ница) му́зыки.

v.t. & i. (*instruct*) дава́ть (*impf.*) ча́стные уро́ки +*d.*; обуч|а́ть, -и́ть (*кого чему*).

tutorial [tjuː'tɔːrɪəl] *n.* ≃ семина́р, консульта́ция.

adj. наста́внический; опеку́нский.

tutti ['tʊtɪ] *n.* (*mus.*) ту́тти (*nt. indecl.*).

tutti-frutti [,tuːtɪ'fruːtɪ] *n.* моро́женое с фру́ктами.

tutu ['tuːtuː] *n.* па́чка.

tu-whit tu-whoo [tʊ,wɪt tʊ'wuː] *n.* крик совы́.

tuxedo [tʌk'siːdəʊ] *n.* (*US*) смо́кинг.

TV (*abbr. of* **television**) ТВ, (телеви́дение); (*set*) телеви́зор, (*coll.*) те́лик; **~ addict** телема́н; **closed-circuit ~** за́мкнутое телеви́дение.

twaddle ['twɒd(ə)l] *n.* чепуха́; болтовня́.

twain [tweɪn] *n.* (*arch.*) два, дво́е; **in ~** попола́м, на́ двое.

twang [twæŋ] *n.* (*sound of plucked string*) звук натя́нутой струны́; (*nasal tone of voice*) гнуса́вый го́лос.

v.t.: **he ~ed the guitar** он тре́нькал на гита́ре; **the bow ~ed** тетива́ зазвене́ла.

twat [twɒt] *n.* пизда́ (*vulg.*).

tweak [twiːk] *n.* щипо́к.

v.t. ущипну́ть (*pf.*).

twee [twiː] *adj.* при́торный.

tweed [twiːd] *n.* (*material*) твид; **a ~ jacket** пиджа́к из тви́да; тви́довый пиджа́к; (*pl.*) оде́жда из тви́да; тви́довый костю́м.

tweet [twiːt] *n.* ще́бет, чири́канье.

v.i. щебета́ть (*impf.*); чири́кать (*impf.*).

tweezer ['twiːzə(r)] *n.* (*usu. pl.*) пинце́т; щи́пчик|и (*pl., g.* -ов).

twelfth [twelfθ] *n.* (*date*) двена́дцатое число́; (*fraction*) одна́ двена́дцатая.

adj. двена́дцатый; **T~ Night** кану́н Креще́ния; (*play title*) «Двена́дцатая ночь».

twelve [twelv] *n.* двена́дцать; **chapter ~** двена́дцатая глава́.

adj. двена́дцать +*g. pl.*; **12 times 12** двена́дцатью (*or* двена́дцать на) двена́дцать; **~ times as long** в двена́дцать раз длинне́е; (*with nn. expr. or understood*): **~ (o'clock)** (*midday*) по́лдень (*m.*); (*midnight*) по́лночь; **quarter to ~** без че́тверти двена́дцать; **quarter/half past ~** че́тверть/полови́на пе́рвого; **a boy of ~** двенадцатиле́тний ма́льчик; **the T~ (Apostles)** двена́дцать апо́столов.

cpd. **~month** *n.* год.

twentieth ['twentɪɪθ] *n.* (*date*) двадца́тое число́; (*fraction*) одна́ двадца́тая.

adj. двадца́тый.

twent|y ['twentɪ] *n.* два́дцать; **at (the age of) ~y** в два́дцать лет; в двадцатиле́тнем во́зрасте; **the ~ies** (*decade*) двадца́тые го́ды; **she is still in her ~ies** ей ещё нет тридцати́.

adj. два́дцать +*g. pl.*

cpd. **~-copeck** *adj.*: **a ~-copeck piece** двугри́венник.

twerp, twirp [twɜːp] *n.* (*coll.*) ничто́жество.

twice [twaɪs] *adv.* два́жды; вдво́е; два ра́за; **~ two is four** два́жды два — четы́ре; **he is ~ my age** он вдво́е ста́рше меня́; **~ as much** в два ра́за (*or* вдво́е) бо́льше; **that made him think ~** э́то заста́вило его́ заду́маться; **I would have thought ~ before buying that** я бы ещё поду́мал, сто́ит ли э́то покупа́ть; **he is ~ the man his brother is** его́ брат ему́ в подмётки не годи́тся.

cpd. **~-told** *adj.*: **a ~-told tale** ста́рая исто́рия.

twiddl|e ['twɪd(ə)l] *v.t.* верте́ть (*impf.*); крути́ть (*impf.*); **he sat there ~ing his thumbs** он бил баклу́ши; он безде́льничал; **he was ~ing with his watchchain** он теребі́л цепо́чку от часо́в.

twig[1] [twɪg] *n.* (*bot.*) ве́тка; прут.

twig[2] [twɪg] *v.t. & i.* (*coll.*) смек|а́ть, -ну́ть.

twilight ['twaɪlaɪt] *n.* су́мер|ки (*pl., g.* -ек); полумра́к; (*fig., decline*) упа́док; **T~ of the Gods** Зака́т/Ги́бель бого́в.

twill [twɪl] *n.* твил, са́ржа.

v.t.: **~ed cloth** кручёная ткань.

twin [twɪn] *n.* близне́ц, двойня́шка; (*pl.*) близнецы́, дво́йня (*f. sg.*); **I have a ~ sister** у меня́ сестра́ — мы с ней близнецы́; **she gave birth to ~s** она́ родила́ дво́йню; у неё роди́лись близнецы́; **identical ~s** однояйцевые/иденти́чные близнецы́; (*one of a pair*): **have you seen the ~ to this glove?** вы не ви́дели втору́ю перча́тку от э́той па́ры (*or* па́ру к э́той перча́тке)?

adj. похо́жий; одина́ковый; **they are ~ brothers** они́ (бра́тья)-близнецы́; **~ beds** две односпа́льные крова́ти; **~ propellers** двойно́й пропе́ллер.

v.t. (*fig.*) соедин|я́ть, -и́ть; **Cheltenham is ~ned with Sochi** Че́лтнем и Со́чи — города́-побрати́мы.

cpd. **~-set** *n.* шерстяно́й гарниту́р, «дво́йка» (*тонкий свитер и кофта*).

twine [twaɪn] *n.* бечёвка, шнуро́к.

v.t. & i. ви́ть(ся) (*impf.*); обв|ива́ть(ся), -и́ть(ся); **she ~d her arms round his neck** она́ обвила́ его́ ше́ю рука́ми; **the ivy ~d round the tree** плющ ви́лся вокру́г де́рева.

twinge [twɪndʒ] *n.* при́ступ о́строй бо́ли; (*fig.*) му́ка; **a ~ of conscience** угрызе́ние со́вести.

twinkl|e ['twɪŋk(ə)l] *n.* мерца́ние; огонёк; **there was a ~e in his eye** в его́ глаза́х вспы́хнул озорно́й огонёк.

v.i. мерца́ть (*impf.*); сверка́ть (*impf.*); **the lights of the town ~ed** мерца́ли огни́ го́рода; **his eyes ~ed with**

amusement его́ глаза́ ве́село блесте́ли; **in the ~ing of an eye** в мгнове́ние о́ка.

twirl [twɜːl] *n.* враще́ние; (*with pen etc.*) завиту́шка.

v.t. верте́ть (*impf.*); крути́ть (*impf.*); **he ~ed his walking-stick** он верте́л тро́стью/па́лкой; **he ~ed his moustache** он крути́л ус.

twirp [twɜːp] = **twerp**

twist [twɪst] *n.* **1.** (*jerk; sharp turning motion*) круче́ние; рыво́к; **he gave the handle a ~** он поверну́л ру́чку; **I gave my leg a ~** я вы́вихнул но́гу. **2.** (*sharp change of direction*) изги́б, поворо́т; **the lane was all ~s and turns** тропи́нка была́ о́чень изви́листой; **a ~ in the plot** круто́й поворо́т сюже́та. **3.** (*sth. ~ed or spiral in shape*) пе́тля; у́зел; **the rope was full of ~s** верёвка была́ вся в узла́х; **a ~ of paper** скру́ченный бума́жный кулёк; **a ~ of tobacco** пли́тка табака́; **a ~ of thread** скру́тка ните́й. **4.** (*peculiar tendency*) отклоне́ние, извраще́ние; **he had a criminal ~** в нём бы́ло что́-то поро́чное. **5.** (*dance*) твист.

v.t. **1.** (*screw round*) крути́ть (*or* скру́чивать), с-; **he tried to ~ my arm** (*lit.*) он пыта́лся вы́вернуть мне ру́ку; (*fig., coerce me*) он пыта́лся на меня́ дави́ть; **I ~ed my ankle** я подверну́л (себе́) но́гу. **2.** (*contort*) искрив|ля́ть, -и́ть; **his face was ~ed with hatred** его́ лицо́ бы́ло искаженó не́навистью; **a ~ed smile** крива́я улы́бка; (*fig.*) иска|жа́ть, -зи́ть; **don't try to ~ my meaning** не искажа́йте мои́ слова́. **3.** (*wind, twine*) обв|ива́ть, -и́ть; обм|а́тывать, -ота́ть; **they ~ed the flowers into a garland** они́ сплета́ли цветы́ в гирля́нду; **she ~ed her hair round her finger** она́ накру́чивала во́лосы на па́лец; **he can ~ you round his little finger** он мо́жет из вас верёвки вить. **4.** (*give curving motion to*) скру́|чивать, -ти́ть; закру́|чивать, -ти́ть; **he can ~ the ball well** он уме́ет хорошо́ подре́зать мяч. **5.** (*coll., cheat*) обма́н|ывать, -у́ть; **are you trying to ~ me?** вы пыта́етесь меня́ наду́ть?

v.i. **1.** (*wriggle*) ко́рчиться (*impf.*); извива́ться (*impf.*); **he ~ed about, trying to get away** он извива́лся, стара́ясь вы́рваться. **2.** (*twine; grow spirally*) обв|ива́ться, -и́ться; **the tendrils ~ed round their support** у́сики расте́ния вили́сь вокру́г жёрдочки. **3.** (*dance*) танцева́ть (*impf.*) твист.

with advs.: **~ off** *v.t.* откру́|чивать, -ти́ть; отви́н|чивать, -ти́ть; **he ~ed off the top of the bottle** он отвинти́л кры́шечку от буты́лки; **~ up** *v.t.* запу́т|ывать, -ать; **the string was all ~ed up** верёвка была́ вся в узла́х; (*fig.*) перепу́т|ывать, -ать; иска|жа́ть, -зи́ть; **he got the story all ~ed up** он перепу́тал всю исто́рию.

twister ['twɪstə(r)] *n.* (*dishonest pers.*) обма́нщик, моше́нник; (*problem; conundrum*) зада́ча; головоло́мка.

twisty ['twɪstɪ] *adj.* изви́листый; (*fig., devious*) нече́стный, укло́нчивый.

twit[1] [twɪt] *n.* ничто́жество, пусто́е ме́сто (*coll.*).

twit[2] [twɪt] *v.t.* поддр|а́знивать, -азни́ть.

twitch [twɪtʃ] *n.* (*jerk*) дёрганье; (*spasm*) су́дорога; подёргивание.

v.t. **1.** (*jerk*) дёргать (*impf.*); выдёргивать (*impf.*); **he ~ed the paper from my hand** он вы́рвал бума́гу у меня́ из рук. **2.** (*move spasmodically*) подёргивать (*impf.*) +*i.*; **the dog ~ed its ears** соба́ка повела́ уша́ми.

v.i. дёргаться (*impf.*); **my nose is ~ing** у меня́ дёргается нос.

twitter ['twɪtə(r)] *n.* **1.** (*chirping*) ще́бет, щебета́ние. **2.** (*rapid chatter*) ще́бет, болтовня́. **3. she was all of a ~** (*coll.*) она́ вся трепета́ла.

v.i. (*chirp*) щебета́ть (*impf.*); чири́кать (*impf.*); (*talk rapidly*) щебета́ть (*impf.*); болта́ть (*impf.*).

two [tuː] *n.* **1.** (число́/но́мер) два; (*~ people*) дво́е; **we ~** мы о́ба; **the ~** э́ти два/дво́е; о́ба +*g. sg.*; **there were ~ of us** нас бы́ло дво́е (*or* два челове́ка); **(the) ~ of us went** мы пошли́ вдвоём; нас пошло́ дво́е (*or* два челове́ка); **~ each, in ~s, ~ at a time, ~ by ~** по́ два/дво́е; **in ~s and threes** небольши́ми гру́ппами; (*cut, divide*) **in ~** на́ двое/попола́м; **fold in ~** сложи́ть (*pf.*) вдво́е; **the plate broke in ~** таре́лка разби́лась попола́м; (*figure, thg. numbered 2*) дво́йка; **~ and ~ are four** два плюс/и два — четы́ре; (*with var. nn. expr. or understood*): **chapter ~** втора́я глава́; **volume ~** том второ́й; **page ~** страни́ца два; **room ~** ко́мната но́мер два; второ́й но́мер; **size ~** второ́й разме́р/но́мер; **he lives at No. ~** он живёт в до́ме но́мер 2; **a No. ~ (bus)** дво́йка, второ́й но́мер; **~ of spades** дво́йка пик; **at ~ (o'clock)** в два (часа́); **~ p.m.** два часа́ дня; **an hour or ~** ча́с(ик)-друго́й; **in an hour or ~** че́рез час-друго́й; **a month or ~** ме́сяц-друго́й; (*of age*): **he is ~** ему́ два го́да; **at ~** в два го́да, в двухле́тнем во́зрасте; **a boy of ~** двухле́тний ма́льчик; (*idioms*): **~'s company, three's none** тре́тий — ли́шний; **~ can play at that game** ≃ я могу́ отплати́ть той же моне́той; посмо́трим ещё, чья возьмёт; **I put ~ and ~ together** я сообрази́л, что к чему́; я смекну́л в чём де́ло; **in ~ ~s** в два счёта; **that makes ~ of us** вот и я то́же; **degrees are ~ a penny** дипло́мами хоть пруд пруди́.

adj. два +*g. sg.*; (*for people and* pluralia tantum, *also*) дво́е +*g. pl.*; **~ students** два студе́нта, дво́е студе́нтов; **~ patients** дво́е больны́х; **~ children** дво́е дете́й; два ребёнка; **~ watches** дво́е часо́в; **~ whole glasses** це́лых два стака́на; **the ~ carriages** о́ба ваго́на; **he and ~ others** он с двумя́ други́ми; **~ fives are ten** два́жды пять — де́сять; **~ coffees** (*as order*) два ра́за ко́фе.

cpds. **~-day** *adj.* двухдне́вный; **~-digit** *adj.* двузна́чный; **~-dimensional** *adj.* двухме́рный, двупла́нный; **~-edged** *adj.* (*lit., fig.*) обоюдоо́стрый; **~-faced** *adj.* (*fig.*) двули́чный; **~fold** *adj.* двойно́й; *adv.* вдво́е; **~-handed** *adj.* двуру́чный; **~-hour** *adj.* двухчасово́й; **~-lane** *adj.* двухколе́йный; **~-legged** *adj.* двуно́гий; **~pence** *n.* два пе́нса; двухпе́нсовая моне́та; *see also* **tuppence; ~penny** *adj.* двухпе́нсовый; **~penny piece** двухпе́нсовая моне́та; **~penny-halfpenny** *adj.* (*coll., rubbishy*) грошо́вый; *see also* **tuppenny; ~-piece** *n.* (*suit*) (костю́м)-дво́йка; **~-ply** *adj.* двойно́й, двухсло́йный; **~-seater** *n.* двухме́стный автомоби́ль/самолёт; **~-sided** *adj.* двусторо́нний; **~-speed** *adj.* двухскоростно́й; **~-step** *n.* тусте́п; **~-storey(ed)** *adj.* двухэта́жный; **~-stroke** *adj.* двухта́ктный; **~-time** *v.t.* (*US sl.*) обма́н|ывать, -у́ть; изменя́ть (*impf.*) (жене́/му́жу); **~-timer** *n.* (*US sl.*) двуру́шник; **~-way** *adj.* (*e.g. traffic*) двусторо́нний; **~-way radio** приёмо-передаю́щая радиоста́нция; **~-year** *adj.* двухгоди́чный, двухле́тний; **~-year-old** *adj.* двухгодова́лый, двухле́тний.

tycoon [taɪ'kuːn] *n.* (*business magnate*) магна́т; кру́пный заправи́ла; тайку́н.

tyke, tike [taɪk] *n.* (*cur*) дворня́жка; (*low fellow*) хам; грубия́н.

tympan|i ['tɪmpənɪ], **-ist** ['tɪmpənɪst] = **timpan|i, -ist**

tympanum ['tɪmpənəm] *n.* (*eardrum*) бараба́нная перепо́нка; (*middle ear*) сре́днее у́хо.

type [taɪp] *n.* **1.** (*example*) тип; типи́чный образе́ц. **2.** (*class*) род, класс; **he is running true to ~** он типи́чный представи́тель своего́ кла́сса (*и т.п.*). **3.** (*letters for printing*) шрифт; **standing ~** набо́р; **in large/heavy ~** кру́пным/жи́рным шри́фтом.

v.t. **1.** (*classify*) классифици́ровать (*impf., pf.*); определ|я́ть, -и́ть. **2.** (*write with ~writer*) печа́тать, от- (*or* писа́ть, на-) (на маши́нке); **a ~d letter** письмо́, напеча́танное на маши́нке.

v.i. печа́тать (*impf.*) (на маши́нке); **typing** (*as n.*) маши́нопись; перепи́ска на маши́нке; **typing error** опеча́тка; **typing pool** машинопи́сное бюро́; **typing school** шко́ла маши́нописи.

cpds. **~cast** *adj.*: **he is ~cast as the butler** он всегда́ игра́ет роль дворе́цкого; **~-face** *n.* шрифт; **~script** *n.* машинопи́сный текст; маши́нопись; ру́копись (на маши́нке); **~setter** *n.* (*person*) набо́рщик; (*machine*) фотонабо́рная маши́на; **~setting** *n.* типогра́фский набо́р; **~write** *v.t.* печа́тать, на- на маши́нке; **a ~written letter** письмо́, напеча́танное на маши́нке; **~writer** *n.* (пи́шущая) маши́нка.

typhoid ['taɪfɔɪd] *n.* (*also* **~ fever**) брюшно́й тиф.

adj. тифо́зный.

typhoon [taɪ'fuːn] *n.* тайфу́н.

typhus ['taɪfəs] *n.* сыпно́й тиф.

typical ['tɪpɪk(ə)l] *adj.* типи́чный; **that is ~ of him** э́то для него́ типи́чно.

typify ['tɪpɪ,faɪ] *v.t.* быть типи́чным представи́телем *+g.*; олицетвор|я́ть, -и́ть.

typist ['taɪpɪst] *n.* (*fem.*) машини́стка; **he is a ~** он печа́тает на маши́нке; он зараба́тывает маши́нописью.

typographer [taɪ'pɒgrəfə(r)] *n.* печа́тник.

typographic(al) [,taɪpə'græfɪk(ə)l] *adj.* типогра́фский.

typography [taɪ'pɒgrəfɪ] *n.* книгопеча́тание; (*printed type*) шрифт.

typological [,taɪpə'lɒdʒɪk(ə)l] *adj.* типологи́ческий.

typology [taɪ'pɒlədʒɪ] *n.* типоло́гия.

tyrannical [tɪ'rænɪk(ə)l] *adj.* тирани́ческий, деспоти́чный.

tyrannicide [tɪ'rænɪ,saɪd] *n.* тираноуби́йство.

tyrannize ['tɪrə,naɪz] *v.t. & i.* тира́нствовать (*impf.*); тира́нить (*impf.*); **he ~s (over) his family** он тира́нит свою́ семью́.

tyrannous ['tɪrənəs] *adj.* тирани́ческий, деспоти́чный.

tyranny ['tɪrənɪ] *n.* (*despotic power*) тирани́я, деспоти́зм; (*tyrannical behaviour*) тира́нство; жесто́кость.

tyrant ['taɪərənt] *n.* тира́н, де́спот.

tyre ['taɪə(r)] (*US* **tire**) *n.* ши́на; **I have a flat ~** у меня́ спусти́лась ши́на.
cpd. **~-lever** *n.* монтиро́вочная лопа́тка.

tyro ['taɪə,rəʊ] = **tiro**

Tyrol, Tirol ['tɪrəl] *n.* Тиро́ль (*m.*).

Tyrol|ean [,tɪrə'li:ən], **-ese** [,tɪrə'li:z] *n.* тиро́л|ец (*fem.* -ька).
adj. тиро́льский.

tzar [zɑ:(r)] *etc.* = **tsar** *etc.*

tzigane [tsɪ'gɑ:n] *n.* цыга́н (*fem.* -ка).

U

U [u:] *cpds.* **~-boat** *n.* неме́цкая подво́дная ло́дка; **~-turn** *n.* разворо́т; (*fig.*) ре́зкое измене́ние поли́тики; поворо́т на 180°.

UAE (*abbr. of* ***United Arab Emirates***) ОАЭ, (Объединённые ара́бские эмира́ты).

ubiquitous [ju:'bɪkwɪtəs] *adj.* вездесу́щий.

ubiquity [ju:'bɪkwɪtɪ] *n.* вездесу́щность.

UDA (*abbr. of* ***Ulster Defence Association***) Ассоциа́ция защи́ты О́льстера.

udder ['ʌdə(r)] *n.* вы́мя (*nt.*).

UDI (*abbr. of* ***Unilateral Declaration of Independence***) Односторо́ннее провозглаше́ние незави́симости.

UDR (*abbr. of* ***Ulster Defence Regiment***) Полк защи́ты О́льстера.

UFO (*abbr. of* ***unidentified flying object***) НЛО, (неопо́знанный лета́ющий объе́кт).

ufologist [ju:'fɒlədʒɪst] *n.* нло́лог, уфи́ст.

Uganda [ju:'gændə] *n.* Уга́нда.

Ugandan [ju:'gændən] *n.* уга́нд|ец (*fem.* -ка).
adj. уга́ндский.

ugh [əx, ʌg, ʌx] *int.* брр!; ах!; тьфу!

ugliness ['ʌglɪnɪs] *n.* уро́дство; некраси́вая вне́шность; безобра́зность; (*fig.*) гну́сность.

ugly ['ʌglɪ] *adj.* **1.** (*unsightly*) некраси́вый, уро́дливый, безобра́зный; **~ duckling** га́дкий утёнок. **2.** (*unpleasant*) проти́вный, скве́рный; **an ~ wound** скве́рная ра́на. **3.** (*threatening*) опа́сный; **an ~ customer** гну́сный/опа́сный тип/субъе́кт; **an ~ rumour** неприя́тный слух; **an ~ sky** гро́зное не́бо; **he was in an ~ mood** он был в гро́зном настрое́нии.

uhlan ['u:lɑ:n, 'ju:lən] *n.* ула́н.

UK (*abbr. of* ***United Kingdom***) Соединённое Короле́вство (Великобрита́нии и Се́верной Ирла́ндии).
adj. (велико)брита́нский.

ukase [ju:'keɪz] *n.* ука́з.

Ukraine [ju:'kreɪn] *n.* Украи́на; **in (the) ~** на Украи́не.

Ukrainian [ju:'kreɪnɪən] *n.* (*pers.*) украи́н|ец (*fem.* -ка); (*language*) украи́нский язы́к.
adj. украи́нский.

ukulele [ju:kə'leɪlɪ] *n.* гава́йская гита́ра.

Ulan Bator [u'lɑ:n 'bɑ:tɔ:(r)] *n.* Ула́н-Ба́тор.

ulcer ['ʌlsə(r)] *n.* я́зва (желу́дка); (*fig.*) я́зва.

ulcerate ['ʌlsə,reɪt] *v.t.*: **~d feelings** уязвлённые чу́вства.

ulceration [,ʌlsə'reɪʃ(ə)n] *n.* изъязвле́ние.

ulcerous ['ʌlsərəs] *adj.* я́звенный.

ullage ['ʌlɪdʒ] *n.* (*space in cask*) незапо́лненный объём бо́чки; (*dregs*) оса́док.

ulna ['ʌlnə] *n.* локтева́я кость.

ulnar ['ʌlnə(r)] *adj.* локтево́й.

Ulster ['ʌlstə(r)] *n.* **1.** (*province*) О́льстер. **2.** (**u~**: *coat*) о́льстер, дли́нное свобо́дное пальто́ (*indecl.*).
cpds. **~man, woman** *nn.* жи́тель(ница) (*or* уроже́н|ец, *fem.* -ка) О́льстера.

ult. ['ʌltɪ,məʊ] = **ultimo**

ulterior [ʌl'tɪərɪə(r)] *adj.* скры́тый, невы́раженный; **~ motive** скры́тый моти́в; за́дняя мысль.

ultimate ['ʌltɪmət] *adj.* после́дний, оконча́тельный; **~ end, purpose** коне́чная цель.

ultimatum [,ʌltɪ'meɪtəm] *n.* ультима́тум.

ult(imo) ['ʌltɪ,məʊ] *n.* про́шлого ме́сяца.

ultra[1] ['ʌltrə] *n.* (*extremist*) челове́к кра́йних взгля́дов; ультра́ (*m. indecl.*).

ultra-[2] ['ʌltrə] *comb. form* ультра..., сверх(ъ)...

ultramarine [,ʌltrəmə'ri:n] *n.* (*pigment*) ультрамари́н.
adj. ультрамари́новый.

ultramontane [,ʌltrə'mɒnteɪn] *n.* (*relig.*) сторо́нник абсолю́тной вла́сти ри́мского па́пы.

ultrasonic [,ʌltrə'sɒnɪk] *n.* сверхзвуково́й, ультразвуково́й.

ultra-violet [,ʌltrə'vaɪələt] *adj.* ультрафиоле́товый; **~ rays** ультрафиоле́товые лучи́.

ultra vires [,ʌltrə 'vaɪə,ri:z, ,ʊltrɑ: 'vi:reɪz] *adj. & adv.* вне компете́нции, за преде́лами полномо́чий (*кого*).

ululate ['ju:lʊ,leɪt] *v.i.* выть (*impf.*); завыва́ть (*impf.*).

ululation [,ju:lʊ'leɪʃ(ə)n] *n.* вой, завыва́ние.

Ulysses ['ju:lɪ,si:z, ju:'lɪsi:z] *n.* Ули́сс, Одиссе́й.

umbelliferous [,ʌmbə'lɪfərəs] *adj.* зо́нтичный.

umber ['ʌmbə(r)] *n.* у́мбра.
adj. тёмно-кори́чневый.

umbilical [ʌm'bɪlɪk(ə)l, ,ʌmbɪ'laɪk(ə)l] *adj.* пупо́чный; **~ cord** пупови́на.

umbrage ['ʌmbrɪdʒ] *n.* оби́да; **take ~ (at)** об|ижа́ться, -и́деться (на+*a.*).

umbrella [ʌm'brelə] *n.* **1.** зо́нтик, зонт. **2.** (*fig., protection*) (авиацио́нное) прикры́тие; **an ~ of fighter aircraft** прикры́тие истреби́телями; **nuclear ~** я́дерный зо́нтик. **3.** (*fig., general heading*) ру́брика; **~ organisation** головна́я/возглавля́ющая организа́ция.
cpd. **~-stand** *n.* подста́вка для зонто́в.

umlaut ['ʊmlaʊt] *n.* умля́ут.

umpire ['ʌmpaɪə(r)] *n.* (*arbitrator*) посре́дник; трете́йский судья́; (*in games*) судья́ (*m.*); рефери́ (*m. indecl.*).
v.t. & i.: **he ~d (in) both matches** он суди́л о́ба ма́тча.

umpteen [ʌmp'ti:n] *adj.* (*coll.*) бесчи́сленное коли́чество *+g.*

umpteenth [ʌmp'ti:nθ] *adj.* (*coll.*) э́нный; **I have told you for the ~ time** ско́лько раз я тебе́ говори́л!

UN (*abbr. of* ***United Nations (Organization)***): **the ~** ООН (*f. indecl.*), (Организа́ция Объединённых На́ций).
adj. (*coll.*) оо́новский.

un- [ʌn] *neg. pref.*: *oft. expr. by pref.* не... (*e.g.* **unable**) *or* без..., бес... (*e.g.* **unashamed**).

unabashed [,ʌnə'bæʃt] *adj.* без смуще́ния; не растеря́вшийся.

unabated [,ʌnə'beɪtɪd] *adj.* неосла́бленный.

unabbreviated [,ʌnə'bri:vɪ,eɪtɪd] *adj.* несокращённый, по́лный.

unable [ʌn'eɪb(ə)l] *adj.* неспосо́бный; **he is ~ to swim** он не уме́ет пла́вать; **I am ~ to say** я не могу́ сказа́ть; **I shall be ~ to come** я не смогу́ прийти́.

unabridged [,ʌnə'brɪdʒd] *adj.* несокращённый, по́лный.

unaccented [ˌʌnæk'sentɪd] *adj.* безуда́рный, неуда́рный.
unacceptable [ˌʌnək'septəb(ə)l] *adj.* неприе́млемый.
unaccompanied [ˌʌnə'kʌmpənɪd] *adj.* не сопровожда́емый; **she came** ~ она́ пришла́ одна́ (*or* без сопровожде́ния); (*mus.*) без аккомпанеме́нта.
unaccomplished [ˌʌnə'kʌmplɪʃt, -'kɒmplɪʃt] *adj.* **1.** (*not fulfilled*) незавершённый, незако́нченный; **his mission was** ~ он не заверши́л свое́й ми́ссии. **2.** (*mediocre, unskilful*) посре́дственный, неиску́сный.
unaccountable [ˌʌnə'kaʊntəb(ə)l] *adj.* (*inexplicable*) необъясни́мый, непоня́тный, непостижи́мый; (*irrational*) безотчётный; (*not obliged to render an account of o.s.*) безотчётный.
unaccounted-for [ˌʌnə'kaʊntɪd fɔ:] *adj.* (*unexplained*) нея́сный, необъяснённый, непоня́тный; (*not included in account*) не ука́занный в отчёте.
unaccustomed [ˌʌnə'kʌstəmd] *adj.* **1.** (*unused*) непривы́кший; ~ **as I am to public speaking** хотя́ я и не привы́к выступа́ть. **2.** (*unusual*) необы́чный; **he spoke with** ~ **warmth** он говори́л с несво́йственной ему́ горя́чностью.
unachievable [ˌʌnə'tʃi:vəb(ə)l] *adj.* недосяга́емый, недостижи́мый, невыполни́мый.
unachieved [ˌʌnə'tʃi:vd] *adj.* недости́гнутый, незавершённый.
unacknowledged [ˌʌnək'nɒlɪdʒd] *adj.* **1.** (*unrecognized*) непри́знанный; **his work went** ~ никто́ не отме́тил его́ рабо́ты. **2.** (*without reply*) оста́вшийся без отве́та; **my letter was** ~ я не получи́л подтвержде́ния о получе́нии письма́.
unacquainted [ˌʌnə'kweɪntɪd] *adj.* незнако́мый; **I am** ~ **with the quality of his work** я не могу́ суди́ть о ка́честве его́ рабо́ты.
unactable [ˌʌn'æktəb(ə)l] *adj.* (*of a play*) несцени́чный.
unadaptable [ˌʌnə'dæptəb(ə)l] *adj.* (*of pers.*) неги́бкий, не приспосо́бленный к чему́-н.
unadorned [ˌʌnə'dɔ:nd] *adj.* неприкра́шенный, неукра́шенный.
unadulterated [ˌʌnə'dʌltəˌreɪtɪd] *adj.* настоя́щий, неподде́льный; ~ (*undiluted*) **milk** неразба́вленное молоко́; ~ **nonsense** чисте́йший вздор; **the** ~ **truth** чи́стая пра́вда.
unadventurous [ˌʌnəd'ventʃərəs] *adj.* непредприи́мчивый, несме́лый; (*uneventful*) без приключе́ний, споко́йный.
unaffected [ˌʌnə'fektɪd] *adj.* **1.** (*without affectation*) непринуждённый, есте́ственный, непритво́рный, лишённый аффекта́ции; **she has an** ~ **manner** она́ де́ржится про́сто/есте́ственно/непринуждённо. **2.** (*not harmed or influenced*): **the cargo was** ~ **by damp** груз не пострада́л от сы́рости; **our plans were** ~ **by the weather** пого́да не измени́ла на́ших пла́нов; **he was** ~ **by my entreaties** он остава́лся безуча́стным к мои́м мольба́м.
unafraid [ˌʌnə'freɪd] *adj.* незапу́ганный.
unaided [ʌn'eɪdɪd] *adj.* без посторо́нней по́мощи; **my** ~ **efforts** мои́ одино́кие уси́лия.
unaligned [ˌʌnə'laɪnd] *adj.*: **the** ~ **countries** неприсоедини́вшиеся стра́ны.
unalleviated [ˌʌnə'li:vɪˌeɪtɪd] *adj.* несмягчённый, необлегчённый; ~ **gloom** непрогля́дный мрак.
unalloyed [ˌʌnə'lɔɪd, ʌn'æl-] *adj.* нелеги́рованный; (*fig.*): ~ **pleasure** ниче́м не омрачённая ра́дость.
unalterable [ʌn'ɔ:ltərəb(ə)l, ʌn'ɒl-] *adj.* неизме́нный, непрело́жный.
unambiguous [ˌʌnæm'bɪgjʊəs] *adj.* недвусмы́сленный, я́сный, чёткий, то́чно вы́раженный.
unambitious [ˌʌnæm'bɪʃəs] *adj.* непритяза́тельный, скро́мный.
un-American [ˌʌnə'merɪkən] *adj.* чу́ждый америка́нским обы́чаям и поня́тиям; антиамерика́нский.
unamiable [ʌn'eɪmɪəb(ə)l] *adj.* неприве́тливый.
unanimity [ju:nə'nɪmɪtɪ] *n.* единоду́шие.
unanimous [ju:'nænɪməs] *adj.* единоду́шный, единогла́сный; **they were** ~ **in condemning him** они́ единоду́шно его́ порица́ли; **the resolution was passed** ~**ly** резолю́ция была́ принята́ единогла́сно.
unannounced [ˌʌnə'naʊnst] *adj.* необъя́вленный; без докла́да.
unanswerable [ʌn'ɑ:nsərəb(ə)l] *adj.*: **an** ~ **argument** неопровержи́мый до́вод; **an** ~ **question** вопро́с, на кото́рый невозмо́жно отве́тить.
unanswered [ʌn'ɑ:nsəd] *adj.* неотве́ченный, оста́вшийся без отве́та; (*unrequited*) без взаи́мности.
unanticipated [ˌʌnæn'tɪsɪˌpeɪtɪd] *adj.* (*unexpected*) непредви́денный, неожи́данный.
unapparent [ˌʌnə'pærənt] *adj.* нея́вный, скры́тый.
unappealing [ˌʌnə'pi:lɪŋ] *adj.* неприя́тный, непривлека́тельный.
unappeasable [ˌʌnə'pi:zəb(ə)l] *adj.* непримири́мый.
unappetizing [ʌn'æpɪˌtaɪzɪŋ] *adj.* неаппети́тный.
unappreciated [ˌʌnə'pri:ʃɪˌeɪtɪd] *adj.* непри́знанный, недооценённый.
unappreciative [ˌʌnə'pri:ʃətɪv] *adj.* неблагода́рный.
unapprehensive [ʌnˌæprɪ'hensɪv] *adj.* (*without fear*) бесстра́шный.
unapproachable [ˌʌnə'prəʊtʃəb(ə)l] *adj.* (*also of pers.*) недосту́пный.
unarmed [ʌn'ɑ:md] *adj.* невооружённый, безору́жный; ~ **combat** самозащи́та без ору́жия; (*abbr.* са́мбо (*indecl.*)).
unartistic [ˌʌnɑ:'tɪstɪk] *adj.* нехудо́жественный; (*insensitive to art*) лишённый худо́жественного вку́са; не име́ющий скло́нности к иску́сству.
unashamed [ˌʌnə'ʃeɪmd] *adj.* бессты́дный; без со́вести/стесне́ния.
unasked [ʌn'ɑ:skt] *adj.* непро́шенный; **she did it** ~ она́ сде́лала э́то по свое́й инициати́ве; (*uninvited*) незва́ный; без приглаше́ния.
unassailable [ˌʌnə'seɪləb(ə)l] *adj.*: **an** ~ **fortress** непристу́пная кре́пость; **an** ~ **argument** неопровержи́мый до́вод.
unassisted [ˌʌnə'sɪstɪd] *adj.* без (посторо́нней) по́мощи.
unassuming [ˌʌnə'sju:mɪŋ] *adj.* непритяза́тельный, скро́мный.
unattached [ˌʌnə'tætʃt] *adj.* не привя́занный/прикреплённый (*к чему*); **she is** ~ она́ одино́ка.
unattainable [ˌʌnə'teɪnəb(ə)l] *adj.* недосяга́емый.
unattended [ˌʌnə'tendɪd] *adj.* **1.** (*without escort*) без слуг/сви́ты; (*unaccompanied*) несопровожда́емый. **2.** (*without care*) оста́вленный без надзо́ра/присмо́тра; **the children were left** ~ дете́й оста́вили одни́х (без надзо́ра); **his business was** ~ его́ де́лом никто́ не занима́лся; **the shop is** ~ в магази́не нет продавца́.
unattractive [ˌʌnə'træktɪv] *adj.* непривлека́тельный, малопривлека́тельный, несимпати́чный; **the idea is most** ~ **to me** мне э́та иде́я совсе́м не нра́вится.
unauthenticated [ˌʌnɔ:'θentɪˌkeɪtɪd] *adj.* неудостове́ренный.
unauthorized [ʌn'ɔ:θəˌraɪzd] *adj.* неразрешённый; (*pers.*) посторо́нний; ~ **absence** самово́льная отлу́чка.
unavailable [ˌʌnə'veɪləb(ə)l] *adj.* не име́ющийся в нали́чии; **he was** ~ он был недосяга́ем/за́нят.
unavailing [ˌʌnə'veɪlɪŋ] *adj.* бесполе́зный, напра́сный, тще́тный.
unavoidabl|e [ˌʌnə'vɔɪdəb(ə)l] *adj.* (*sure to happen*) неизбе́жный, немину́емый; **I was** ~**y detained** я не мог освободи́ться (ра́ньше).
unawakened [ˌʌnə'weɪkənd] *adj.* неразбу́женный, непробуждённый.
unaware [ˌʌnə'weə(r)] *adj.* незна́ющий, неподозрева́ющий; **he was** ~ **of my presence** он не подозрева́л о моём прису́тствии; **I was** ~ **that he was married** я не знал, что он жена́т.
unawares [ˌʌnə'weəz] *adv.* неча́янно; врасплох́; **she dropped her purse** ~ она́ неча́янно урони́ла кошелёк; **I was taken** ~ **by his question** его́ вопро́с засти́г меня́ врасплох́.
unbacked [ʌn'bækt] *adj.* (*without support*): **an** ~ **assertion** голосло́вное утвержде́ние; **an** ~ **cheque** необеспе́ченный чек.
unbalanced [ʌn'bælənsd] *adj.* неравноме́рный, односторо́нний; (*mentally*) неуравнове́шенный, неусто́йчивый.
unbar [ʌn'bɑ:(r)] *v.t.*: ~ **a door** отодв|ига́ть, -и́нуть засо́в на две́ри; (*fig.*) откр|ыва́ть, -ы́ть.
unbearable [ʌn'beərəb(ə)l] *adj.* невыноси́мый.
unbeaten [ʌn'bi:t(ə)n] *adj.* неби́тый; (*unsurpassed*) непревзойдённый.
unbecoming [ˌʌnbɪ'kʌmɪŋ] *adj.* (*inappropriate*) неподходя́щий; (*indecorous*) неподоба́ющий (+*d.*), неприли́чный (для+*g.*); неприли́чествующий (*кому*); **conduct** ~ **an officer** поведе́ние, недосто́йное офице́ра (*or* неподоба́ющее офице́ру).

unbefitting [ˌʌnbɪˈfɪtɪŋ] *adj.* неподоба́ющий, неподходя́щий (для+*g.*).

unbeknown [ˌʌnbɪˈnəʊn] (*coll.* **unbeknownst**) *adv.*: **he did it ~ to me** он сде́лал э́то без моего́ ве́дома.

unbelief [ˌʌnbɪˈliːf] *n.* (*scepticism*) скептици́зм; (*lack of faith*) неве́рие.

unbelievable [ˌʌnbɪˈliːvəb(ə)l] *adj.* (*coll., amazing*) невероя́тный, неимове́рный.

unbeliever [ˌʌnbɪˈliːvə(r)] *n.* (*sceptic*) ске́птик; (*relig.*) неве́рующий.

unbelieving [ˌʌnbɪˈliːvɪŋ] *adj.* (*incredulous*) скепти́ческий; (*lacking faith*) неве́рующий.

unbend [ʌnˈbend] *v.t.* выпрямля́ть, вы́прямить; раз|гиба́ть, -огну́ть.

v.i. (*fig., relax*) смягч|а́ться, -и́ться; рассл|абля́ться, -а́биться; отбро́сить (*pf.*) чо́порность.

unbending [ʌnˈbendɪŋ] *adj.* (*fig.*) непреклóнный, суро́вый, неги́бкий.

unbiassed [ʌnˈbaɪəst] *adj.* непредвзя́тый; непредубеждённый; беспристра́стный.

unbidden [ʌnˈbɪd(ə)n] *adj.* непро́шенный; (*as adv., voluntarily*) доброво́льно; по свое́й во́ле.

unbind [ʌnˈbaɪnd] *v.t.* развя́з|ывать, -а́ть; (*hair*) распус|ка́ть, -ти́ть; (*wound*) разбинто́в|ывать, -а́ть.

unblemished [ʌnˈblemɪʃt] *adj.* чи́стый; (*fig.*) незапя́тнанный; безупре́чный; непоро́чный.

unblock [ʌnˈblɒk] *v.t.* **1.: the plumber ~ed the drain** водопрово́дчик прочи́стил водосто́к. **2.** (*of funds etc.*) разблоки́ровать (*pf.*).

unblushing [ʌnˈblʌʃɪŋ] *adj.* беззасте́нчивый, бессты́дный.

unbolt [ʌnˈbəʊlt] *v.t.* отп|ира́ть, -ере́ть.

unborn [ʌnˈbɔːn] *adj.*: **her ~ child** её ещё не рождённое (*or* её бу́дущее) дитя́; **generations yet ~** бу́дущие поколе́ния.

unbosom [ʌnˈbʊz(ə)m] *v.t.*: **~ o.s. to s.o.** откр|ыва́ть, -ы́ть (*or* изл|ива́ть, -и́ть) (свою́) ду́шу кому́-н.

unbound [ʌnˈbaʊnd] *adj.* (*of book*) непереплетённый.

unbounded [ʌnˈbaʊndɪd] *adj.* неограни́ченный, безграни́чный, безме́рный.

unbowed [ʌnˈbaʊd] *adj.* несо́гнутый; непокорённый; **his head was ~** (*fig.*) он не покори́лся; он не склони́л головы́.

unbridled [ʌnˈbraɪdəld] *adj.* (*fig.*) необу́зданный, разну́зданный.

unbroken [ʌnˈbrəʊkən] *adj.* неразби́тый, несло́мленный; **only one plate was ~** то́лько одна́ таре́лка уцеле́ла; **his spirit remained ~** дух его́ не́ был сло́млен; **an ~ record** непревзойдённый/непоби́тый реко́рд; **an ~ horse** необъе́зженный конь; **~ sleep** непреры́вный сон; **in ~ succession** в непреры́вной после́довательности.

unbrotherly [ʌnˈbrʌðəlɪ] *adj.* небра́тский.

unbuckle [ʌnˈbʌk(ə)l] *v.t.* расстёг|ивать, -ну́ть; (*sword*) отстёг|ивать, -ну́ть.

unburden [ʌnˈbɜːd(ə)n] *v.t.*: **he ~ed his soul to me** он изли́л мне ду́шу.

unbusinesslike [ʌnˈbɪznɪsˌlaɪk] *adj.* неделово́й, непракти́чный; не по-делово́му.

unbutton [ʌnˈbʌt(ə)n] *v.t.* расстёг|ивать, -ну́ть.

v.i. (*fig., relax*) отта́|ивать, -ять; держа́ть (*impf.*) себя́ свобо́дно/непринуждённо.

uncage [ʌnˈkeɪdʒ] *v.t.* выпуска́ть, вы́пустить из клётки.

uncalled-for [ʌnˈkɔːldfɔː(r)] *adj.* (*unasked-for*) непро́шенный; (*inappropriate*) неуме́стный; (*excessive*) изли́шний; (*undeserved*) незаслу́женный.

uncanny [ʌnˈkænɪ] *adj.* сверхъесте́ственный, жу́ткий; стра́нный, необъясни́мый; **an ~ phenomenon** стра́нное/таи́нственное явле́ние.

uncared-for [ʌnˈkeədfɔː(r)] *adj.* забро́шенный, запу́щенный.

uncarpeted [ʌnˈkɑːpɪtɪd] *adj.* без ковра́, непокры́тый ковро́м.

unceasing [ʌnˈsiːsɪŋ] *adj.* беспреры́вный, непреры́вный, беспреста́нный.

uncensored [ʌnˈsensəd] *adj.* не проше́дший цензу́ру; (*exempt from censorship*) неподцензу́рный.

unceremonious [ˌʌnserɪˈməʊnɪəs] *adj.* (*abrupt, discourteous*) бесцеремо́нный.

uncertain [ʌnˈsɜːt(ə)n] *adj.* **1.** (*hesitant, in doubt*) неуве́ренный, нереши́тельный; **he was ~ what to do/think** он не знал, что де́лать/ду́мать; **I am ~ what he wants** я не могу́ поня́ть, чего́ он хо́чет; **I am still ~** я всё ещё сомнева́юсь/коле́блюсь. **2.** (*not clear*) нея́сный, неопределённый; **in no ~ terms** без обиняко́в, весьма́ недвусмы́сленно; **a lady of ~ age** да́ма неопределённого во́зраста. **3.** (*changeable, unreliable*): **the weather is ~** пого́да изме́нчива; **he has an ~ temper** у него́ капри́зный нрав/хара́ктер; **~ friends** ненадёжные друзья́; **his grammar is ~** он нетвёрд в грамма́тике; **my position is ~** (*shaky*) у меня́ ша́ткое положе́ние.

uncertaint|y [ʌnˈsɜːtəntɪ] *n.* **1.** (*hesitation*) неуве́ренность, нереши́тельность; **be in a state of ~y** сомнева́ться (*impf.*); колеба́ться (*impf.*). **2.** (*lack of clarity*) нея́сность, неизве́стность, неопределённость. **3.** (*unreliable or unpredictable nature*) изме́нчивость; **the ~ies of life** превра́тности (*f. pl.*) судьбы́; **the future is full of ~y** бу́дущее полно́ неопределённости.

unchain [ʌnˈtʃeɪn] *v.t.* спус|ка́ть, -ти́ть с це́пи; сн|има́ть, -ять око́вы с+*g.*; **~ the door** сн|има́ть, -ять цепо́чку с две́ри.

unchallengeable [ʌnˈtʃælɪndʒəb(ə)l] *adj.* неоспори́мый, неопровержи́мый.

unchallenged [ʌnˈtʃælɪndʒd] *adj.* все́ми при́знанный; **I let his remark go ~** я не стал оспа́ривать его́ замеча́ние.

unchangeable [ʌnˈtʃeɪndʒəb(ə)l] *adj.* неизменя́емый, неизме́нный.

unchanged [ʌnˈtʃeɪndʒd] *adj.* неизмени́вшийся; **the patient's condition is ~** состоя́ние больно́го без переме́н/измене́ний.

uncharitable [ʌnˈtʃærɪtəb(ə)l] *adj.* зло́бный; чрезме́рно стро́гий, приди́рчивый.

uncharted [ʌnˈtʃɑːtɪd] *adj.* не отме́ченный на ка́рте; неиссле́дованный; неизве́данный.

unchaste [ʌnˈtʃeɪst] *adj.* нецелому́дренный.

unchastity [ʌnˈtʃæstɪtɪ] *n.* нецелому́дренность, нецелому́дрие; непристо́йность.

unchecked [ʌnˈtʃekt] *adj.*: **~ accounts** непрове́ренные счета́; **an ~ advance** (*mil.*) беспрепя́тственное продвиже́ние.

unchivalrous [ʌnˈʃɪvəlrəs] *adj.* неры́царский, неблагоро́дный.

unchristian [ʌnˈkrɪstjən] *adj.* нехристиа́нский, неподоба́ющий христиани́ну; (*coll., outrageous*): **I had to get up at an ~ hour** мне пришло́сь встать безбо́жно ра́но.

uncircumcised [ʌnˈsɜːkəmˌsaɪzd] *adj.* необре́занный.

uncivil [ʌnˈsɪvɪl] *adj.* неве́жливый, гру́бый.

uncivilized [ʌnˈsɪvɪˌlaɪzd] *adj.* нецивилизо́ванный, некульту́рный; **~ races** ди́кие племена́; **~ behaviour** некульту́рное поведе́ние.

unclad [ʌnˈklæd] *adj.* неоде́тый, го́лый.

unclaimed [ʌnˈkleɪmd] *adj.* невостре́бованный.

unclasp [ʌnˈklɑːsp] *v.t.* (*loosen clasp of*) расстёг|ивать, -ну́ть; (*release grip on*) разж|има́ть, -а́ть; **he ~ed his hands** он разжа́л ру́ки.

unclassifiable [ʌnˈklæsɪˌfaɪəb(ə)l] *adj.* не поддаю́щийся классифика́ции.

unclassified [ʌnˈklæsɪˌfaɪd] *adj.* неклассифици́рованный; (*without security grading*) несекре́тный.

uncle [ˈʌŋk(ə)l] *n.* дя́дя (*m.*); **at my ~'s** (*sl., in pawn*) в закла́де.

unclean [ʌnˈkliːn] *adj.* (*impure*) нечи́стый; пога́ный.

uncleanness [ʌnˈkliːnnɪs] *n.* нечистота́.

uncloak [ʌnˈkləʊk] *v.t.* (*fig.*) разоблач|а́ть, -и́ть.

unclothed [ʌnˈkləʊðd] *adj.* разде́тый, неоде́тый.

unclouded [ʌnˈklaʊdɪd] *adj.* (*lit., fig.*) безо́блачный; **an ~ brow** неомрачённое чело́.

uncoil [ʌnˈkɔɪl] *v.t.* & *i.* разм|а́тывать(ся), -ота́ть(ся).

uncoloured [ʌnˈkʌləd] *adj.* бесцве́тный, неокра́шенный; **his views are ~ by prejudice** он челове́к непредвзя́тый/беспристра́стный; **an ~ description** просто́е/неприукра́шенное описа́ние.

uncome-at-able [ˌʌnkʌmˈætəb(ə)l] *adj.* (*coll.*) неулови́мый, недостижи́мый.

uncomfortable [ʌn'kʌmftəb(ə)l] *adj.* (*lit., fig.*) неудóбный; нелóвкий.

uncommitted [ˌʌnkə'mɪtɪd] *adj.* нейтрáльный; не связáвший себя́; (*pol., unaligned*) неприсоедини́вшийся.

uncommon [ʌn'kɒmən] *adj.* рéдкий; необы́чный, незауря́дный; **he showed ~ generosity** он прояви́л необыкновéнную щéдрость; **that is ~ly good of you** вы чрезвычáйно дóбры/любéзны.

uncommunicative [ˌʌnkə'mju:nɪkətɪv] *adj.* неразговóрчивый, сдéржанный, скры́тный.

uncompanionable [ˌʌnkəm'pænjənəb(ə)l] *adj.* необщи́тельный.

uncomplaining [ˌʌnkəm'pleɪnɪŋ] *adj.* безрóпотный, терпели́вый.

uncomplimentary [ˌʌnkɒmplɪ'mentərɪ] *adj.* нелéстный.

uncompromising [ʌn'kɒmprəˌmaɪzɪŋ] *adj.* бескомпроми́ссный, неусту́пчивый, твёрдый.

unconcealed [ˌʌnkən'si:ld] *adj.* нескры́тый, нескрывáемый, я́вный.

unconcern [ˌʌnkən'sɜ:n] *n.* беззабóтность, беспéчность; безразли́чие, равноду́шие.

unconcerned [ˌʌnkən'sɜ:nd] *adj.* (*carefree*) беззабóтный, беспéчный; (*indifferent*) безразли́чный, равноду́шный; **~ with politics** не интересу́ющийся поли́тикой; **his manner was ~** он держáлся безучáстно.

unconditional [ˌʌnkən'dɪʃən(ə)l] *adj.* безуслóвный, безоговóрочный; **~ surrender** безоговóрочная капитуля́ция.

unconditioned [ˌʌnkən'dɪʃ(ə)nd] *adj.* необуслóвленный, безуслóвный; **~ reflex** безуслóвный рефлéкс.

unconfined [ˌʌnkən'faɪnd] *adj.* неограни́ченный; (*fig.*) свобóдный, нестеснённый.

unconfirmed [ˌʌnkən'fɜ:md] *adj.* неподтверждённый.

uncongenial [ˌʌnkən'dʒi:nɪəl] *adj.* неприя́тный; неблагоприя́тный; чу́ждый/чужóй (по ду́ху).

unconnected [ˌʌnkə'nektɪd] *adj.* не свя́занный; **the wires were ~** проводá нé были соединены́; **a series of ~ statements** ряд не свя́занных друг с дру́гом заявлéний.

unconquerable [ʌn'kɒŋkərəb(ə)l] *adj.* непобеди́мый, непокори́мый.

unconquered [ʌn'kɒŋkəd] *adj.* непобеждённый, непокорённый.

unconscionable [ʌn'kɒnʃənəb(ə)l] *adj.*: **an ~ liar** отъя́вленный/невозмóжный лгун; **he was away an ~ time** он пропадáл безбóжно дóлго.

unconscious [ʌn'kɒnʃəs] *n.*: **the ~** (*psych.*) подсознáние.
adj. **1.** (*senseless*) потеря́вший сознáние; в (глубóком) óбмороке; **he was knocked ~** он потеря́л сознáние от удáра. **2.** (*unaware*) не сознаю́щий; **he was ~ of having done wrong** он не сознавáл, что поступи́л плóхо; **he seemed ~ of my presence** казáлось, что он не замечáл моегó прису́тствия. **3.** (*unintentional*) невóльный; **he spoke with ~ irony** он говори́л с бессознáтельной ирóнией.

unconsciousness [ʌn'kɒnʃəsnɪs] *n.* (*physical*) бессознáтельное состоя́ние; (*unawareness*) отсу́тствие (о)сознáния.

unconsidered [ˌʌnkən'sɪdəd] *adj.* необду́манный, непроду́манный; **an ~ remark** необду́манное/случáйное замечáние.

unconstitutional [ˌʌnkɒnstɪ'tju:ʃən(ə)l] *adj.* противорéчащий конститу́ции.

unconstrained [ˌʌnkən'streɪnd] *adj.* невы́нужденный; непринуждённый.

unconsumed [ˌʌnkən'sju:md] *adj.* (*of supplies, food etc.*) неизрасхóдованный; (*by fire etc.*) неуничтóженный.

uncontaminated [ˌʌnkən'tæmɪˌneɪtɪd] *adj.* незаражённый, незагрязнённый.

uncontemplated [ˌʌn'kɒntəmˌpleɪtɪd] *adj.* непредви́денный.

uncontrollable [ˌʌnkən'trəʊləb(ə)l] *adj.*: **an ~ temper** неукроти́мый нрав; **an ~ child** неуправля́емый ребёнок; **an ~ influx of refugees** неконтроли́руемый/бесконтрóльный прили́в бéженцев.

uncontrolled [ˌʌnkən'trəʊld] *adj.* неконтроли́руемый, бесконтрóльный, неуправля́емый.

unconventional [ˌʌnkən'venʃən(ə)l] *adj.* нешаблóнный, нетрадициóнный, эксцентри́чный.

unconverted [ˌʌnkən'vɜ:tɪd] *adj.* **1.** (*econ.*) неконверти́рованный. **2.** (*relig.*) необращённый; **after hearing his arguments I was still ~** вы́слушав егó дóводы, я не измени́л свои́х воззрéний.

unconvince [ˌʌnkən'vɪns] *v.t.* разубе|ждáть, -ди́ть; разув|еря́ть, -éрить.

unconvinced [ˌʌnkən'vɪnsd] *adj.* неубеждённый.

unconvincing [ˌʌnkən'vɪnsɪŋ] *adj.* неубеди́тельный.

uncooked [ʌn'kʊkt] *adj.* сырóй; неприготóвленный; несвари́вшийся.

uncooperative [ˌʌnkəʊ'ɒpərətɪv] *adj.* не проявля́ющий готóвность помóчь; не желáющий учáствовать в совмéстных дéйствиях.

uncork [ʌn'kɔ:k] *v.t.* раску́пори|вать, -ть; отку́пори|вать, -ть.

uncorrected [ˌʌnkə'rektɪd] *adj.* неисправленный; **an ~ MS** невы́правленная ру́копись.

uncorroborated [ˌʌnkə'rɒbəˌreɪtɪd] *adj.* неподтверждённый.

uncorrupted [ˌʌnkə'rʌptɪd] *adj.* неиспóрченный; (*unbribed*) неподку́пный.

uncountable [ʌn'kaʊntəb(ə)l] *adj.* (*innumerable*) бесчи́сленный, неисчисли́мый; (*gram.*) неисчисля́емый.

uncounted [ʌn'kaʊntɪd] *adj.* (*innumerable*) несчётный, бессчётный, бесчи́сленный.

uncouple [ʌn'kʌp(ə)l] *v.t.* (*rail carriages*) расцеп|ля́ть, -и́ть; (*dogs*) спус|кáть, -ти́ть со свóры.

uncouth [ʌn'ku:θ] *adj.* гру́бый, неотёсанный.

uncouthness [ʌn'ku:θnɪs] *n.* гру́бость, неотёсанность.

uncover [ʌn'kʌvə(r)] *v.t.* сн|имáть, -ять; **he ~ed his head** он обнажи́л гóлову; (*fig.*) раскр|ывáть, -ы́ть; обнару́жи|вать, -ть; **the conspiracy was ~ed** зáговор раскры́ли; **their flank was ~ed** их фланг нé был защищён (*or* был обнажён *or* был остáвлен без прикры́тия).

uncritical [ʌn'krɪtɪk(ə)l] *adj.* некрити́чный, некрити́ческий.

uncrossed [ʌn'krɒsd] *adj.*: **an ~ cheque** некросси́рованный чек.

uncrowned [ʌn'kraʊnd] *adj.*: **~ king** (*lit., fig.*) некоронóванный корóль.

uncrushable [ʌn'krʌʃəb(ə)l] *adj.* (*of material*) немну́щийся; (*irrepressible*) неугомóнный.

UNCTAD ['ʌŋktæd] *n.* (*abbr. of* ***United Nations Conference on Trade and Development***) ЮНКТАД, (Конферéнция ООН по торгóвле и разви́тию).

unction ['ʌŋkʃ(ə)n] *n.* **1.** (*anointing*) помáзание; **extreme ~** собóрование. **2.** (*gusto*) вкус, смак. **3.** (*fig., oiliness*) елéйность.

unctuous ['ʌŋktjʊəs] *adj.* (*fig., oily*) елéйный.

uncultivated [ʌn'kʌltɪˌveɪtɪd] *adj.* (*of land*) необрабóтанный, невоздéланный; (*of pers.*) неразвитóй, некульту́рный.

uncultured [ʌn'kʌltʃəd] *adj.* некульту́рный.

uncurtained [ʌn'kɜ:t(ə)nd] *adj.* незанавéшенный, без занавéсок.

uncut [ʌn'kʌt] *adj.* неразрéзанный; неподстри́женный; **~ pages** неразрéзанные листы́/страни́цы; **his hair was ~** вóлосы у негó бы́ли неподстри́жены; **the film was shown ~** фильм показáли целикóм (*or* без сокращéний/купю́р).

undamaged [ʌn'dæmɪdʒd] *adj.* неповреждённый.

undated [ʌn'deɪtɪd] *adj.* недати́рованный.

undaunted [ʌn'dɔ:ntɪd] *adj.* неустраши́мый.

undeceive [ˌʌndɪ'si:v] *v.t.* выводи́ть, вы́вести из заблуждéния.

undecided [ˌʌndɪ'saɪdɪd] *adj.* нерешённый; нереши́тельный; **the battle was ~** исхóд би́твы был нея́сен; **I am ~ whether to go or stay** я не знáю, идти́ мне и́ли нет.

undecipherable [ˌʌndɪ'saɪfərəb(ə)l] *adj.* (*of code*) не поддаю́щийся расшифрóвке; (*of handwriting etc.*) неразбóрчивый.

undeclared [ˌʌndɪ'kleəd] *adj.* необъя́вленный, непровозглашённый; **a state of ~ war** состоя́ние войны́ без объявлéния (*or* необъя́вленной войны́).

undefended [ˌʌndɪ'fendɪd] *adj.* незащищённый; **they left the city ~** они́ остáвили гóрод без прикры́тия; **an ~ suit** (*leg.*) иск, не оспáриваемый отвéтчиком.

undefiled [ˌʌndɪ'faɪld] *adj.* чи́стый, незапáчканный, неосквернённый, незагрязнённый.

undefined [ˌʌndɪˈfaɪnd] *adj.* неопределённый.
undelivered [ˌʌndɪˈlɪvəd] *adj.*: **an ~ letter** недоста́вленное письмо́; **an ~ speech** непроизнесённая речь.
undemonstrative [ˌʌndɪˈmɒnstrətɪv] *adj.* сде́ржанный.
undeniable [ˌʌndɪˈnaɪəb(ə)l] *adj.* неоспори́мый, я́вный.
undenominational [ˌʌndɪˌnɒmɪˈneɪʃ(ə)nəl] *adj.* неконфессиона́льный; не относя́щийся к како́му-нибудь вероисповеда́нию.
undependable [ˌʌndɪˈpendəb(ə)l] *adj.* ненадёжный.
under [ˈʌndə(r)] *adv.* вниз; **the ship went ~** кора́бль затону́л; **he dived and stayed ~ for a minute** он нырну́л и продержа́лся под водо́й (одну́) мину́ту; **the people were kept ~** наро́д держа́ли под гнётом.
prep. **1.** под+*i.*; (*of motion*) под+*a.*; **(out) from ~** из-под+*g.* **2.** (*less than*) ме́ньше+*g.*; ни́же+*g.*; **he earns ~ £40 a week** он зараба́тывает ме́ньше сорока́ фу́нтов в неде́лю; **he was ~ age** он не дости́г совершеннолетия; **children ~ 14** де́ти моло́же (*or* в во́зрасте до) четы́рнадцати лет; **I can get there in ~ an hour** я могу́ добра́ться туда́ ме́ньше, чем за час; **no-one ~ the rank of major** никто́ в чи́не ни́же майо́ра. **3.** (*var. uses*): **~ arms** под ружём; **you are ~ arrest** вы аресто́ваны; **~ the circumstances** при сложи́вшихся обстоя́тельствах; **~ cultivation** обраба́тываемый; **~ a delusion** в заблужде́нии; **~ discussion** обсужда́емый; **~ oath** под прися́гой; **~ pain of death** под стра́хом сме́рти; **~ pressure** под давле́нием; **~ repair** в ремо́нте; **~ sail** под паруса́ми; **~ suspicion** под подозре́нием; **~ torture** под пы́тками; **~ way** на ходу́; **land ~ wheat** земля́ под пшени́цей; (**~** *authority of*): **he served ~ me** он служи́л под мои́м руково́дством; **he studied ~ a professor** он учи́лся/занима́лся у профе́ссора; **~ the tsars** при царя́х; **England ~ the Stuarts** А́нглия в ца́рствование Стю́артов; (*according to*): **~ the terms of the agreement** по усло́виям соглаше́ния; **~ orders** по прика́зу; **~ the rules** согла́сно уста́ву; (*classified with*): **they come ~ the same heading** они́ отно́сятся к той же ру́брике; **see ~ 'General Remarks'** смотри́ в пара́графе (*or* под ру́брикой) «О́бщие замеча́ния».
underact [ˌʌndərˈækt] *v.t.* & *i.* недоигр|ывать, -а́ть.
underarm [ˈʌndərˌɑːm] *adj.* & *adv.*: **an ~ shot** уда́р предпле́чьем.
under-belly [ˈʌndəˌbelɪ] *n.* низ живота́.
underbid [ˈʌndəˌbɪd; *v.* ʌndəˈbɪd] *n.* предложе́ние по бо́лее ни́зкой цене́.
v.i. сби|ва́ть, -ть це́ну.
underbred [ˌʌndəˈbred] *adj.* (*pers.*) невоспи́танный; (*animal*) нечистокро́вный, непоро́дистый.
underbrush [ˈʌndəˌbrʌʃ] *n.* подле́сок.
undercarriage [ˈʌndəˌkærɪdʒ] *n.* (*of aircraft*) шасси́ (*nt. indecl.*).
undercharge [ˌʌndəˈtʃɑːdʒ] *v.i.* брать, взять (*or* назн|ача́ть, -а́чить) сли́шком ни́зкую це́ну.
undercloth|es [ˈʌndəˌkləʊðz, -ˌkləʊz], **-ing** [ˈʌndəˌkləʊðɪŋ] *nn.* ни́жнее бельё.
undercoat [ˈʌndəˌkəʊt] *n.* (*of paint*) грунто́вка.
under-cover [ˌʌndəˈkʌvə(r), ˈʌn-] *adj.* та́йный.
undercurrent [ˈʌndəˌkʌrənt] *n.* подво́дное тече́ние; (*fig.*) скры́тая тенде́нция; **an ~ of melancholy** затаённая грусть.
undercut[1] [ˈʌndəˌkʌt] *n.* (*of meat*) вы́резка.
undercut[2] [ˌʌndəˈkʌt] *v.t.*: **'How much are you charging for the work? I don't want to ~ you'** «Ско́лько вы запра́шиваете за э́ту рабо́ту? Я не хочу́ сбива́ть це́ну.»
under-developed [ˌʌndədɪˈveləpt] *adj.* недора́звитый; **~ countries** слабора́звитые стра́ны; **~ muscles** слабора́звитые му́скулы; недора́звитая мускулату́ра; **~ photographs** недопроя́вленные сни́мки.
underdog [ˈʌndəˌdɒg] *n.* (*fig.*) побеждённая сторона́; обездо́ленный челове́к; неуда́чник.
underdone [ˌʌndəˈdʌn, ˈʌn-] *adj.* (*of food*) недожа́ренный, недова́ренный.
underemployment [ˌʌndərɪmˈplɔɪmənt] *n.* непо́лная за́нятость.
underestimate[1] [ˌʌndərˈestɪmət] *n.* недооце́нка.
underestimate[2] [ˌʌndərˈestɪˌmeɪt] *v.t.* недооце́н|ивать, -и́ть.
underestimation [ˌʌndərestɪˈmeɪʃ(ə)n] *n.* недооце́нка.
underexpose [ˌʌndərɪkˈspəʊz] *v.t.* (*phot.*) недодерж|ивать, -а́ть.
underexposure [ˌʌndərɪkˈspəʊʒə(r)] (*phot.*) недоста́точная вы́держка.
underfed [ˌʌndəˈfed] *adj.* недоко́рмленный.
underfelt [ˈʌndəˌfelt] *n.* грунт ковра́.
underfoot [ˌʌndəˈfʊt] *adv.* под нога́ми.
undergarments [ˈʌndəˌgɑːmənts] *n. pl.* ни́жнее бельё.
undergo [ˌʌndəˈgəʊ] *v.t.* испы́т|ывать, -а́ть; перен|оси́ть, -ести́; подв|ерга́ться, -е́ргнуться +*d.*; **the word has ~ne many changes** э́то сло́во претерпе́ло мно́го измене́ний; **he has to ~ an operation** ему́ предстои́т опера́ция.
undergraduate [ˌʌndəˈgrædjʊət] *n.* студе́нт (*fem.* -ка); (*attr.*) студе́нческий.
underground [ˈʌndəˌgraʊnd] *n.* **1.** (**~** *railway*) метро́ (*indecl.*); **on the U~** в метро́. **2.** (**~** *movement*) подпо́лье.
adj. подзе́мный; (*fig.*, *secret*, *subversive*) подпо́льный; **an ~ newspaper** подпо́льная газе́та.
adv. под землёй/зе́млю; (*fig.*) подпо́льно; **the former leader went ~** бы́вший ли́дер ушёл в подпо́лье.
undergrowth [ˈʌndəˌgrəʊθ] *n.* подле́сок.
underhand [ˈʌndəˌhænd] *adj.* (*secret*, *deceitful*) закули́сный, та́йный; **~ methods** закули́сные махина́ции; та́йные про́иски.
adv. тайко́м.
underhung [ˈʌndəˌhʌŋ, -ˈhʌŋ] *adj.*: **an ~ jaw** выступа́ющая вперёд че́люсть.
underlay [ˈʌndəˌlaɪ] *n.* (*fabric*) подкла́дка, подсти́лка.
underl|ie [ˌʌndəˈlaɪ] *v.t.* **1.** (*lit.*) лежа́ть (*impf.*) под+*i.*; **~ying stratum** ни́жний слой. **2.** (*fig.*) лежа́ть в осно́ве +*g.*; **~ying causes** причи́ны, лежа́щие в осно́ве (*чего*).
underline [ˌʌndəˈlaɪn] *v.t.* (*lit.*, *fig.*) подч|ёркивать, -еркну́ть.
underling [ˈʌndəlɪŋ] *n.* ме́лкий чино́вник; (*coll.*) ме́лкая со́шка.
underlining [ˌʌndəˈlaɪnɪŋ] *n.* (*e.g. of text*) подчёркивание.
underlip [ˈʌndəlɪp] *n.* ни́жняя губа́.
undermanned [ˌʌndəˈmænd] *adj.* испы́тывающий недоста́ток в рабо́чей си́ле; неукомплекто́ванный.
undermentioned [ˌʌndəˈmenʃ(ə)nd, ˈʌn-] *adj.* нижеупомя́нутый.
undermine [ˌʌndəˈmaɪn] *v.t.* подк|а́пывать, -опа́ть; (*by water*) подм|ыва́ть, -ы́ть; (*fig.*) разр|уша́ть, -у́шить; подт|а́чивать, -очи́ть; **his health was ~d by drink** алкого́ль подорва́л его́ здоро́вье; **his authority is ~d** его́ авторите́т вся́чески подрыва́ют.
undermost [ˈʌndəˌməʊst] *adj.* ни́зший.
underneath [ˌʌndəˈniːθ] *adv.* внизу́, ни́же.
prep. под+*i.*; (*of motion*) под+*a.*
undernourished [ˌʌndəˈnʌrɪʃt] *adj.* недоко́рмленный, недоеда́ющий.
undernourishment [ˌʌndəˈnʌrɪʃmənt] *n.* недоеда́ние.
underpants [ˈʌndəˌpænts] *n. pl.* (*long*) кальсо́н|ы (*pl.*, *g.* —); (*short*) (мужски́е) трус|ы́ (*pl.*, *g.* -о́в).
underpass [ˈʌndəˌpɑːs] *n.* прое́зд под полотно́м желе́зной доро́ги; (у́личный) тонне́ль (*m.*).
underpa|y [ˌʌndəˈpeɪ] *v.t.* сли́шком ни́зко опла́|чивать, -ти́ть; недопла́|чивать, -ти́ть; **the workers are ~id** рабо́чим ма́ло пла́тят.
underpayment [ˌʌndəˈpeɪmənt] *n.* сли́шком ни́зкая опла́та; недопла́та.
underpin [ˌʌndəˈpɪn] *v.t.* подв|оди́ть, -ести́ фунда́мент под+*a.*; (*fig.*) подде́рж|ивать, -а́ть.
underplot [ˈʌndəˌplɒt] *n.* побо́чная интри́га.
under-populated [ˌʌndəˈpɒpjʊˈleɪtɪd] *adj.* малонаселённый.
under-privileged [ˌʌndəˈprɪvɪlɪdʒd] *adj.* неиму́щий; по́льзующийся ме́ньшими права́ми.
under-production [ˌʌndəprəˈdʌkʃ(ə)n] *n.* недопроизво́дство.
underquote [ˌʌndəˈkwəʊt] *v.t.* (*goods*) назн|ача́ть, -а́чить бо́лее ни́зкую це́ну на+*a.*
underrate [ˌʌndəˈreɪt] *v.t.* недооце́н|ивать, -и́ть.
underripe [ˌʌndəˈraɪp] *adj.* недозре́лый, неспе́лый.
underscore [ˌʌndəˈskɔː(r)] *v.t.* подч|ёркивать, -еркну́ть.
under-secretary [ˌʌndəˈsekrətərɪ] *n.* замести́тель (*m.*)/помо́щник мини́стра; (*at UN*) замести́тель Генера́льного Секретаря́; **permanent ~** несменя́емый помо́щник мини́стра.

undersell [ˌʌndəˈsel] *v.t.* (*goods*) прод|авать, -ать по пониженной цене (*or* ниже стоимости).

undersexed [ˌʌndəˈsekst] *adj.* сексуально холодный.

under-sheriff [ˈʌndəˌʃerɪf] *n.* заместитель (*m.*) шерифа.

under|shirt [ˈʌndəˌʃɜːt], **-vest** [ˈʌndəˌvest] *nn.* майка; (*with sleeves*) нижняя рубашка/сорочка.

undersh|oot [ˌʌndəˈʃuːt] *v.t.* & *i.* стрелять (*impf.*) с недолётами; **the aircraft ~ot the runway** самолёт недотянул при посадке.

under-side [ˈʌndəˌsaɪd] *n.* низ; нижняя сторона/поверхность.

undersign [ˈʌndəˌsaɪn, -ˌʌndəˈsaɪn] *v.t.*: **we, the ~ed** мы, нижеподписавшиеся.

undersized [ˈʌndəˌsaɪzd, -ˈsaɪzd] *adj.* (*of pers.*) низкорослый.

underskirt [ˈʌndəˌskɜːt] *n.* нижняя юбка.

underslung [ˈʌndəˌslʌŋ] *adj.* подвесной; подвешенный ниже оси.

understaffed [ˌʌndəˈstɑːft] *adj.* испытывающий недостаток рабочей силы; неукомплектованный.

understand [ˌʌndəˈstænd] *v.t.* **1.** (*comprehend*) пон|имать, -ять; пост|игать, -игнуть; (*coll.*) смыслить (*impf.*); **he ~s French** он понимает по-французски; **he ~s finance** он разбирается в финансовых вопросах; **now I ~!** теперь всё понятно; **he can make himself understood in English** он может объясняться по-английски; **I hope I make myself understood** надеюсь, вы меня поняли; **let us ~ each other** поймём же друг друга; **he ~s children** он умеет обращаться с детьми; **I can ~ his wanting to leave** я понимаю его желание уйти; **I understood him to say he would come** насколько я понял, он обещал прийти; **am I to ~ you refuse?** иначе говоря (*or* надо понимать), вы отказываетесь?; **he gave me to ~ he was single** он дал мне понять, что он холост; **what are we to ~ from such an act?** как мы должны понять/истолковать такой поступок? **2.** (*gather, be informed*): **I ~ you are leaving** я слышал, что вы уезжаете; **you were, I ~, alone** вы были, насколько я понял, одни; **I ~ he is the best doctor in town** говорят/кажется, он лучший врач в городе. **3.** (*agree, accept*): **it is (an) understood (thing)** само собой разумеется; установлено; понятно без слов; (*custom*) так заведено; **it was understood that we should meet at 10** было установлено/договорено, что мы встретимся в 10 часов; **it is understood, then, that we meet tomorrow** итак, решено: мы встречаемся завтра. **4.** (*gram.*): **the verb is understood** глагол подразумевается.

understandable [ˌʌndəˈstændəb(ə)l] *adj.* (*comprehensible*) понятный; (*reasonable, justifiable*) понятный, оправданный.

understanding [ˌʌndəˈstændɪŋ] *n.* **1.** (*intellect*) ум; **it passes my ~** это выше моего понимания. **2.** (*comprehension*): **he has a clear ~ of the problem** он прекрасно понимает проблему; **he has a good ~ of economics** он хорошо разбирается в экономике; **it was my ~ that we were to meet here** насколько я понял, мы должны были встретиться здесь. **3.** (*sympathy*) понимание, отзывчивость, чуткость; **he showed ~ for my position** он вошёл в моё положение. **4.** (*agreement*) соглашение, договорённость; **on the clear ~ that ...** только при (*or* на том) условии, что...; **they came to an ~** они пришли к соглашению.

adj. отзывчивый, чуткий, тонкий; **~ parents** разумные родители.

understate [ˌʌndəˈsteɪt] *v.t.* преум|еньшать, -еньшить; недосказ|ывать, -ать.

understatement [ˌʌndəˈsteɪtmənt, ˈʌndə-] *n.* преуменьшение, недосказ.

understocked [ˌʌndəˈstɒkt] *adj.* плохо снабжённый (*чем*).

understudy [ˈʌndəˌstʌdɪ] *n.* дублёр (*fem.* -ша).

v.t. дублировать (*impf.*).

undertak|e [ˌʌndəˈteɪk] *v.t.* **1.** (*take on*) предприн|имать, -ять; брать, взять на себя; **you are ~ing a heavy responsibility** вы берёте на себя большую ответственность; **he has ~en the job of secretary** он принял на себя должность секретаря. **2.** (*pledge o.s., promise*) обяз|ываться, -аться. **3.** (*guarantee*) ручаться (*impf.*); гарантировать (*impf.*).

undertaker [ˈʌndəˌteɪkə(r)] *n.* гробовщик; заведующий/владелец похоронного бюро.

undertaking [ˌʌndəˈteɪkɪŋ] *n.* (*enterprise*) предприятие; (*pledge, guarantee*) обязательство, гарантия.

under-the-table [ˈʌndə(r)] *adj.* (*coll.*) тайный, незаконный.

undertone [ˈʌndəˌtəʊn] *n.* полутон; **in an ~** вполголоса; (*fig.*) подтекст.

undertow [ˈʌndəˌtəʊ] *n.* откат.

undervaluation [ˌʌndəvæljuːˈeɪʃ(ə)n] *n.* недооценка.

undervalue [ˌʌndəˈvæljuː] *v.t.* недооцен|ивать, -ить.

undervest [ˈʌndəˌvest] = **undershirt**

underwater [ˌʌndəˈwɔːtə(r)] *adj.* подводный.

underwear [ˈʌndəˌweə(r)] *n.* бельё.

underworld [ˈʌndəˌwɜːld] *n.* (*myth.*) преисподняя; (*criminal society*) подонк|и (*pl., g.* -ов)/дно общества; преступный мир.

underwrite [ˌʌndəˈraɪt, ˈʌn-] *v.t.* **1.: ~ a marine insurance policy** подпис|ывать, -ать полис морского страхования; прин|имать, -ять судно/груз на страх. **2.: ~ a loan** гарантировать (*impf., pf.*) размещение займа. **3.** (*support*) (финансово) поддерж|ивать, -ать.

underwriter [ˈʌndəˌraɪtə(r)] *n.* (морской) страховщик.

undeserved [ˌʌndɪˈzɜːvd] *adj.* незаслуженный.

undeserving [ˌʌndɪˈzɜːvɪŋ] *adj.* не заслуживающий (*чего*), недостойный.

undesigned [ˌʌndɪˈzaɪnd] *adj.* непреднамеренный, неумышленный.

undesirability [ˌʌndɪzaɪərəˈbɪlɪtɪ] *n.* нежелательность, нецелесообразность.

undesirable [ˌʌndɪˈzaɪərəb(ə)l] *n.* (*pers.*) нежелательный элемент.

adj. нежелательный, нецелесообразный.

undesirous [ˌʌndɪˈzaɪərəs] *adj.* нежелающий; **~ of fame** не жаждущий славы.

undetected [ˌʌndɪˈtektɪd] *adj.* необнаруженный.

undetermined [ˌʌndɪˈtɜːmɪnd] *adj.* неопределённый, нерешённый.

undeterred [ˌʌndɪˈtɜːd] *adj.* не поколебленный/отпугнутый/остановленный (*чем*).

undeveloped [ˌʌndɪˈveləpt] *adj.* неразвитой; **an ~ idea** неразработанная идея; **an ~ country** слаборазвитая страна; **~ land** необработанная земля; **the photographs were ~** фотографии не были проявлены.

undeviating [ʌnˈdiːvɪˌeɪtɪŋ] *adj.* неуклонный; постоянный.

undies [ˈʌndɪz] *n. pl.* (*coll.*) (женское) нижнее бельё.

undifferentiated [ˌʌndɪfəˈrenʃɪˌeɪtɪd] *adj.* недифференцированный.

undigested [ˌʌndɪˈdʒestɪd, ˌʌndaɪ-] *adj.* (*lit., fig.*) неусвоенный; **~ food** непереваренная пища; **~ facts** факты, не приведённые в систему.

undignified [ʌnˈdɪgnɪˌfaɪd] *adj.* недостойный, лишённый благородства; унизительный.

undiluted [ˌʌndaɪˈljuːtɪd] *adj.* неразбавленный; (*fig.*): **~ nonsense** чепуха в чистом виде; совершеннейший вздор.

undiminished [ˌʌndɪˈmɪnɪʃt] *adj.* неуменьшенный; **with ~ ardour** с неослабевающим рвением; **stocks are ~** запасы не сократились.

undiplomatic [ˌʌndɪpləˈmætɪk] *adj.* недипломатичный.

undiscerning [ˌʌndɪˈsɜːnɪŋ] *adj.* непроницательный, непрозорливый.

undischarged [ˌʌndɪsˈtʃɑːdʒd] *adj.* (*not executed*) невыполненный; (*not unloaded*) не выгруженный; **an ~ debt** неуплаченный долг; **an ~ bankrupt** не восстановленный в правах банкрот.

undisciplined [ʌnˈdɪsɪplɪnd] *adj.* необученный; недисциплинированный; **an ~ style** хаотичный стиль.

undisclosed [ˌʌndɪsˈkləʊzd] *adj.* неразоблачённый, нераскрытый.

undiscovered [ˌʌndɪˈskʌvəd] *adj.* неоткрытый, неисследованный.

undiscriminating [ˌʌndɪˈskrɪmɪˌneɪtɪŋ] *adj.* недискриминирующий; не разбирающийся, неразборчивый.

undisguised [ˌʌndɪsˈgaɪzd] *adj.* незамаскированный; явный; **with ~ relief** с явным/нескрываемым облегчением.

undismayed [ˌʌndɪsˈmeɪd] *adj.* неустрашённый.

undisputed [ˌʌndɪˈspjuːtɪd] *adj.* неоспа́риваемый; неоспори́мый, бесспо́рный.
undistinguished [ˌʌndɪˈstɪŋgwɪʃt] *adj.* (*of pers.*) посре́дственный, невзра́чный, (*coll.*) се́рый.
undistracted [ˌʌndɪˈstræktɪd] *adj.* нерассе́янный, сосредото́ченный.
undisturbed [ˌʌndɪˈstɜːbd] *adj.* невстрево́женный, споко́йный; **he was ~ by the news** но́вость его́ не взволнова́ла.
undivided [ˌʌndɪˈvaɪdɪd] *adj.* неразде́льный; **~ attention** неразде́льное внима́ние.
undivulged [ˌʌndaɪˈvʌldʒd, ˌʌndɪ-] *adj.* неразглашённый, та́йный.
undo [ʌnˈduː] *v.t.* **1.** (*unfasten*) развя́з|ывать, -а́ть; **my bootlace came ~ne** у меня́ развяза́лся шнуро́к на боти́нке. **2.** (*annul*) уничт|ожа́ть, -о́жить; аннули́ровать (*impf., pf.*); **he tried to ~ the work of his predecessor** он пыта́лся перечеркну́ть рабо́ту своего́ предше́ственника. **3.** (*ruin*) губи́ть, по-; **I am ~ne** я пропа́л/поги́б; **drink was his ~ing** пья́нство его́ погуби́ло; **we left much ~ne** у нас оста́лось мно́го недоде́ланного.
undomesticated [ˌʌndəˈmestɪˌkeɪtɪd] *adj.* неприру́ченный.
undoubted [ʌnˈdaʊtɪd] *adj.* несомне́нный; **an ~ success** несомне́нный/бесспо́рный успе́х; **you are ~ly right** вы несомне́нно/безусло́вно пра́вы.
undoubting [ʌnˈdaʊtɪŋ] *adj.* несомнева́ющийся.
undramatic [ʌndrəˈmætɪk] *adj.* недramати́ческий, несцени́чный; (*unexciting*) лишённый драмати́зма.
undraped [ʌnˈdreɪpt] *adj.* незадрапиро́ванный; (*nude*) обнажённый.
undreamed-of [ʌnˈdriːmd, ʌnˈdremt], **undreamt-of** [ʌnˈdremt] *adj.* не сни́вшийся; невообрази́мый; **such a thing was ~ when I was young** когда́ я был мо́лод, об э́том никто́ и ду́мать не мог; **~ riches** немы́слимое бога́тство.
undress [ʌnˈdres] *n.*: **in a state of ~** полуоде́тый; (*naked*) в го́лом ви́де; **~ uniform** повседне́вная фо́рма.
v.t. & i. разд|ева́ть(ся), -е́ть(ся).
undressed [ʌnˈdrest] *adj.* (*without clothes*) разде́тый; (*untreated*) необрабо́танный; **~ leather** невы́деланная ко́жа; **an ~ wound** неперевя́занная/необрабо́танная ра́на.
undrinkable [ʌnˈdrɪŋkəb(ə)l] *adj.* неприго́дный для питья́.
undue [ʌnˈdjuː] *adj.* (*excessive*) чрезме́рный, изли́шний; (*improper*) неподоба́ющий; **~ influence** неправоме́рное влия́ние.
undulat|e [ˈʌndjʊˌleɪt] *v.i.* волнова́ться (*impf.*); колыха́ться (*impf.*); **an ~ing landscape** холми́стый пейза́ж.
undulation [ˌʌndjʊˈleɪʃ(ə)n] *n.* волни́стость; волнообра́зное движе́ние; холми́стость.
unduly [ʌnˈdjuːlɪ] *adv.* чрезме́рно; непра́вильно.
undutiful [ʌnˈdjuːtɪˌfʊl] *adj.* непоко́рный; **an ~ daughter** непослу́шная/плоха́я дочь.
undying [ʌnˈdaɪɪŋ] *adj.* бесме́ртный; **he won ~ glory** он завоева́л себе́ ве́чную сла́ву; **you have earned my ~ gratitude** я вам обя́зан до гробово́й доски́.
unearned [ʌnˈɜːnd] *adj.* незарабо́танный; **~ income** нетрудовы́е дохо́ды (*m. pl.*); непроизво́дственный/ре́нтный дохо́д; (*undeserved*) незаслу́женный.
unearth [ʌnˈɜːθ] *v.t.* выка́пывать, вы́копать; **the body was ~ed** те́ло вы́копали; (*fig., discover*) раск|а́пывать, -опа́ть.
unearthly [ʌnˈɜːθlɪ] *adj.* **1.** (*supernatural*) неземно́й; сверхъесте́ственный. **2.** (*ghostly*) при́зрачный; **~ pallor** смерте́льная бле́дность. **3.** (*coll., unreasonable*) абсу́рдный; **why do you wake me at this ~ hour?** заче́м вы меня́ бу́дите в таку́ю рань (*or* ни свет, ни заря́)?
unease [ʌnˈiːz] *n.* нело́вкость; стеснённость.
uneasiness [ʌnˈiːzɪnɪs] *n.* нело́вкость; стеснённость; беспоко́йство, трево́га.
uneasy [ʌnˈiːzɪ] *adj.* **1.** (*physically uncomfortable*): **she spent an ~ night** она́ провела́ беспоко́йную/трево́жную ночь. **2.** (*anxious*) беспоко́йный, трево́жный; **she was ~ about her daughter** она́ беспоко́илась за дочь. **3.** (*ill at ease*) стеснённый, нело́вкий, не по себе́.
uneatable [ʌnˈiːtəb(ə)l] *adj.* несъедо́бный.
uneaten [ʌnˈiːt(ə)n] *adj.* несъе́денный.
uneconomic [ˌʌniːkəˈnɒmɪk, ˌʌnek-] *adj.* неэконо́мный; нерента́бельный; **an ~ rent** невы́годная ре́нта.
uneconomical [ˌʌniːkəˈnɒmɪk(ə)l, ˌʌnek-] *adj.* (*wasteful*) неэконо́мный; бесхозя́йственный.
unedifying [ʌnˈedɪˌfaɪɪŋ] *adj.* непристо́йный, малопривлека́тельный; не досто́йный подража́ния.
unedited [ʌnˈedɪtɪd] *adj.* неотредакти́рованный.
uneducated [ʌnˈedjʊˌkeɪtɪd] *adj.* необразо́ванный.
unemotional [ˌʌnɪˈməʊʃən(ə)l] *adj.* неэмоциона́льный; бесстра́стный.
unemployable [ˌʌnɪmˈplɔɪəb(ə)l] *adj.* нетрудоспосо́бный.
unemployed [ˌʌnɪmˈplɔɪd] *adj.* **1.** (*out of work*) безрабо́тный; (*as n.*: **the ~**) безрабо́тные (*pl.*). **2.** (*unused, e.g. resources*) неиспо́льзованный.
unemployment [ˌʌnɪmˈplɔɪmənt] *n.* безрабо́тица; **~ benefit** посо́бие по безрабо́тице; **~ has risen/fallen** число́ безрабо́тных возросло́/сни́зилось.
unenclosed [ˌʌnɪnˈkləʊzd] *adj.* (*of land*) неогоро́женный.
unencumbered [ˌʌnɪnˈkʌmbəd] *adj.* свобо́дный; (*with debt*) не обременённый долга́ми; **an ~ estate** незало́женное иму́щество/име́ние/поме́стье.
unending [ʌnˈendɪŋ] *adj.* несконча́емый, бесконе́чный.
unendowed [ˌʌnɪnˈdaʊd] *adj.* (*fig.*): **~ with intelligence** не наделённый ра́зумом.
unendurable [ˌʌnɪnˈdjʊərəb(ə)l] *adj.* невыноси́мый, нестерпи́мый.
un-English [ʌnˈɪŋglɪʃ] *adj.* не типи́чный для англича́нина; недосто́йный англича́нина.
unenlightened [ˌʌnɪnˈlaɪt(ə)nd] *adj.* непросвещённый, неосведомлённый.
unenterprising [ʌnˈentəˌpraɪzɪŋ] *adj.* непредприи́мчивый.
unenthusiastic [ˌʌnɪnˌθjuːzɪˈæstɪk, ˌʌnɪnˌθuː-] *adj.* невосто́рженный; **he was ~ about the idea** он не́ был в восто́рге от э́той иде́и.
unenviable [ʌnˈenvɪəb(ə)l] *adj.* неза́видный.
unequal [ʌnˈiːkw(ə)l] *adj.* нера́вный; **~ in length, of ~ length** разли́чной/неодина́ковой длины́; **he was ~ to the task** зада́ча была́ ему́ не по плечу́; **his style is ~** у него́ неро́вный стиль; **~ treaty** неравнопра́вный/несправедли́вый догово́р.
unequalled [ʌnˈiːkw(ə)ld] *adj.* несравне́нный, непревзойдённый.
unequipped [ˌʌnɪˈkwɪpt] *adj.* неподгото́вленный, неприспосо́бленный; **they were ~ to deal with such a large crowd** они́ не́ были (доста́точно) подгото́влены для того́, что́бы спра́виться с таки́м наплы́вом люде́й.
unequivocal [ˌʌnɪˈkwɪvək(ə)l] *adj.* недвусмы́сленный, несомне́нный.
unerring [ʌnˈɜːrɪŋ] *adj.* безоши́бочный; **~ aim** то́чный прице́л.
unescapable [ˌʌnɪˈskeɪpəb(ə)l] *adj.* неизбе́жный.
UNESCO [juːˈneskəʊ] *n.* (*abbr. of* **United Nations Educational, Scientific and Cultural Organization**) ЮНЕСКО, (Организа́ция Объединённых На́ций по вопро́сам образова́ния, нау́ки и культу́ры).
unethical [ʌnˈeθɪk(ə)l] *adj.* неэти́чный.
uneven [ʌnˈiːv(ə)n] *adj.* неро́вный; неравноме́рный; **an ~ surface** неро́вная пове́рхность; **an ~ temper** неро́вный/неуравнове́шенный хара́ктер; **~ progress** неравноме́рный прогре́сс.
uneventful [ˌʌnɪˈventfʊl] *adj.* ти́хий; без (осо́бых) приключе́ний/собы́тий.
unexampled [ˌʌnɪgˈzɑːmp(ə)ld] *adj.* бесприме́рный.
unexcelled [ˌʌnɪkˈseld] *adj.* непревзойдённый.
unexceptionable [ˌʌnɪkˈsepʃənəb(ə)l] *adj.* безупре́чный, безукори́зненный.
unexceptional [ˌʌnɪkˈsepʃən(ə)l] *adj.* неисключи́тельный, зауря́дный.
unexpected [ˌʌnɪkˈspektɪd] *adj.* неожи́данный, нежда́нный, непредви́денный, внеза́пный.
unexpired [ˌʌnɪkˈspaɪəd] *adj.* неисте́кший.
unexplored [ˌʌnɪkˈsplɔːd] *adj.* неизве́данный; неиссле́дованный.
unexposed [ˌʌnɪkˈspəʊzd] *adj.* укры́тый, укро́мный, защищённый; (*film*) неэкспони́рованный.

unexpressed [ˌʌnɪk'sprest] *adj.* невы́раженный, невы́сказанный.
unexpurgated [ʌn'ekspəˌgeɪtɪd] *adj.* без купю́р/про́пусков.
unfading [ʌn'feɪdɪŋ] *adj.* **1.:** ~ **dyes** нелиня́ющие кра́ски. **2.** (*fig.*) неувяда́емый, неувяда́ющий.
unfailing [ʌn'feɪlɪŋ] *adj.* ве́рный, надёжный, неизме́нный; **an ~ source** неиссяка́емый исто́чник; **his ~ support** его́ неизме́нная подде́ржка.
unfair [ʌn'feə(r)] *adj.* непоря́дочный, несправедли́вый, недобросо́вестный; **~ advantage** незако́нное преиму́щество; **an ~ opponent** нече́стный проти́вник.
unfairness [ʌn'feənɪs] *n.* несправедли́вость.
unfaithful [ʌn'feɪθfʊl] *adj.* неве́рный, вероло́мный, преда́тельский; **an ~ friend** вероло́мный друг; **his wife was ~ to him** жена́ ему́ измени́ла; **an ~ rendering** нето́чное воспроизведе́ние.
unfaithfulness [ʌn'feɪθfʊlnɪs] *n.* неве́рность, вероло́мство, преда́тельство.
unfaltering [ʌn'fɔːltərɪŋ, ʌn'fɒl-] *adj.* твёрдый, реши́тельный; непоколеби́мый; **an ~ voice** недро́гнувший го́лос.
unfamiliar [ˌʌnfə'mɪljə(r)] *adj.* незнако́мый; **his face is ~ to me** его́ лицо́ мне незнако́мо; **I am ~ with the district** я не зна́ю э́того райо́на.
unfamiliarity [ˌʌnfəmɪlɪ'ærɪtɪ] *n.* незна́ние; незнако́мство (*с чем*).
unfashionabl|e [ʌn'fæʃənəb(ə)l] *adj.* немо́дный; старомо́дный; **~y** не по мо́де.
unfashioned [ʌn'fæʃ(ə)nd] *adj.* (*unwrought, e.g. a jewel*) необрабо́танный.
unfasten [ʌn'fɑːs(ə)n] *v.t.* открепл|я́ть, -и́ть; (*untie*) отвя́з|ывать, -а́ть; развя́з|ывать, -а́ть; расшнуро́в|ывать, -а́ть; (*unbutton, unclasp*) отстёг|ивать, -ну́ть; расстёг|ивать, -ну́ть; (*open*) откр|ыва́ть, -ы́ть; **I found the door ~ed** я нашёл дверь отперто́й (*or* незаперто́й).
unfathom|able [ʌn'fæðəməb(ə)l], **-ed** [ʌn'fæðəmd] *adjs.* неизмери́мый, бездо́нный; безме́рный; (*incomprehensible*) непостижи́мый.
unfavourable [ʌn'feɪvərəb(ə)l] *adj.* неблагоприя́тный, неблагоскло́нный.
unfeeling [ʌn'fiːlɪŋ] *adj.* бесчу́вственный; жесто́кий.
unfeigned [ʌn'feɪnd] *adj.* неподде́льный, непритво́рный.
unfeminine [ʌn'femɪnɪn] *adj.* неже́нский, неже́нственный.
unfetter [ʌn'fetə(r)] *v.t.* (*lit., fig.*) сн|има́ть, -ять око́вы *c+g.*; освобо|жда́ть, -ди́ть; **~ed** свобо́дный.
unfilial [ʌn'fɪlɪəl] *adj.* неподоба́ющий сы́ну/до́чери.
unfinished [ʌn'fɪnɪʃt] *adj.* незако́нченный, незавершённый; **U~ Symphony** Неоко́нченная симфо́ния; **~ letter** недопи́санное письмо́; **~ goods** полуфабрика́ты.
unfit [ʌn'fɪt] *adj.* неподходя́щий, него́дный; **food ~ for (human) consumption** него́дная к потребле́нию пи́ща; **~ to rule** неспосо́бный пра́вить; **the doctor pronounced him ~** врач призна́л его́ больны́м (*for mil. service*: него́дным).
v.t. де́лать, с- него́дным.
unfix [ʌn'fɪks] *v.t.*: **~ bayonets** (*mil.*) от|мыка́ть, -омкну́ть штыки́.
unfixed [ʌn'fɪkst] *adj.* (*not certain*) неустано́вленный.
unflagging [ʌn'flægɪŋ] *adj.* неослабева́ющий, неосла́бный.
unflappable [ʌn'flæpəb(ə)l] *adj.* (*coll.*) невозмути́мый.
unflattering [ʌn'flætərɪŋ] *adj.* неле́стный.
unfledged [ʌn'fledʒd] *adj.* (*lit., fig.*) неопери́вшийся; (*fig.*) нео́пытный, незре́лый.
unfold [ʌn'fəʊld] *v.t.* развёр|тывать, -ну́ть; (*fig.*) раскр|ыва́ть, -ы́ть.
v.i. развёр|тываться, -ну́ться; расстила́ться (*impf.*); **the landscape ~ed before us** пе́ред на́ми расстила́лся пейза́ж; **as the story ~s** с дальне́йшим разви́тием повествова́ния.
unforced [ʌn'fɔːst] *adj.* (*voluntary*) доброво́льный, невы́нужденный; (*spontaneous*) непринуждённый.
unforeseen [ˌʌnfɔː'siːn] *adj.* непредви́денный.
unforgettable [ˌʌnfə'getəb(ə)l] *adj.* незабыва́емый, незабве́нный.
unforgivable [ˌʌnfə'gɪvəb(ə)l] *adj.* непрости́тельный.
unforgiven [ˌʌnfə'gɪv(ə)n] *adj.* непрощённый.
unforgiving [ˌʌnfə'gɪvɪŋ] *adj.* непроща́ющий; неумоли́мый.
unforgotten [ˌʌnfə'gɒt(ə)n] *adj.* незабы́тый.
unfortunate [ʌn'fɔːtjʊnət, -tʃənət] *n.* неуда́чни|к (*fem.* -ца); несчастли́в|ец (*fem.* -ица).
adj. несча́стный, неуда́чный; **an ~ coincidence** доса́дное совпаде́ние; **an ~ remark** неуда́чное замеча́ние; **it was ~ that I came in just then** как неуда́чно, что я вошёл и́менно тогда́!
unfortunately [ʌn'fɔːtjʊnətlɪ, -tʃənətlɪ] *adv.* к сожале́нию, к несча́стью.
unfounded [ʌn'faʊndɪd] *adj.* необосно́ванный.
unfreeze [ʌn'friːz] *v.t.* (*also fig., of assets*) размор|а́живать, -о́зить.
v.i. (*get warm*) размор|а́живаться, -о́зиться; (*fig., lose reserve of manner*) оття́ять (*pf.*).
unfrequented [ˌʌnfrɪ'kwentɪd] *adj.* малопосеща́емый.
unfriendliness [ʌn'frendlɪnɪs] *adj.* недружелю́бие, неприя́знь.
unfriendly [ʌn'frendlɪ] *adj.* недружелю́бный, неприя́зненный; **an ~ act** недру́жественный посту́пок; вражде́бный акт.
unfrock [ʌn'frɒk] *v.t.* лиш|а́ть, -и́ть духо́вного са́на.
unfruitful [ʌn'fruːtfʊl] *adj.* неплодоно́сный, неплодоро́дный; (*fig.*) беспло́дный; (*vain*) напра́сный, тще́тный; (*useless*) бесполе́зный.
unfruitfulness [ʌn'fruːtfʊlnɪs] *n.* беспло́дие; (*fig.*) тще́тность.
unfulfilled [ˌʌnfʊl'fɪld] *adj.* (*of task, aim etc.*) невы́полненный, неосуществлённый; (*of pers.*) неудовлетворённый.
unfurl [ʌn'fɜːl] *v.t.* развёр|тывать, -ну́ть; распус|ка́ть, -ти́ть.
unfurnished [ʌn'fɜːnɪʃt] *adj.* немеблиро́ванный; **an ~ letting** сда́ча жилья́ без ме́бели.
ungainliness [ʌn'geɪnlɪnɪs] *n.* нело́вкость, неуклю́жесть.
ungainly [ʌn'geɪnlɪ] *adj.* нело́вкий, неуклю́жий.
ungallant [ʌn'gælənt] *adj.* негала́нтный, нелюбе́зный.
ungarnished [ʌn'gɑːnɪʃd] *adj.* без украше́ний; без гарни́ра; (*fig.*) без прикра́с.
ungenerous [ʌn'dʒenərəs] *adj.* (*petty*) неблагоро́дный, ме́лочный; (*stingy*) нще́дрый, скупо́й.
ungentle [ʌn'dʒent(ə)l] *adj.* неделика́тный, гру́бый.
ungentlemanly [ʌn'dʒentəlmənlɪ] *adj.* неджентльме́нский, не досто́йный джентльме́на; неблагоро́дный.
unget-at-able [ˌʌnget'ætəb(ə)l] *adj.* (*coll.*) недосту́пный.
ungifted [ʌn'gɪftɪd] *adj.* неодарённый, незала́нтливый.
unglazed [ʌn'gleɪzd] *adj.* неглазуро́ванный, незастеклённый; **an ~ window** незастеклённое окно́, окно́ без стёкол.
ungloved [ʌn'glʌvd] *adj.* без перча́ток.
ungodliness [ʌn'gɒdlɪnɪs] *n.* непра́ведность, нече́стие, нечести́вость.
ungodly [ʌn'gɒdlɪ] *adj.* непра́ведный, нечести́вый; (*coll., frightful*): **an ~ noise** ужа́сный шум.
ungovernable [ʌn'gʌvənəb(ə)l] *adj.* непослу́шный, неуправля́емый; **an ~ temper** неукроти́мый нрав.
ungraceful [ʌn'greɪsfʊl] *adj.* неграцио́зный, нескла́дный, неуклю́жий.
ungracious [ʌn'greɪʃəs] *adj.* неве́жливый, нелюбе́зный.
ungraciousness [ʌn'greɪʃəsnɪs] *n.* неве́жливость, нелюбе́зность.
ungrammatical [ˌʌngrə'mætɪk(ə)l] *adj.* негра́мотный; (*of languages, also*) безгра́мотный.
ungrateful [ʌn'greɪtfʊl] *adj.* (*unthankful, unrewarding*) неблагода́рный; **an ~ task** неблагода́рный труд; неприя́тная рабо́та.
ungratefulness [ʌn'greɪtfʊlnɪs] *n.* неблагода́рность.
ungrudging [ʌn'grʌdʒɪŋ] *adj.* ще́дрый; до́брый; широ́кий; **he gave ~ly of his time** он ще́дро (*or* не скупя́сь) дари́л своё вре́мя.
unguarded [ʌn'gɑːdɪd] *adj.* (*e.g. town*) незащищённый; (*e.g. prisoner*) неохраня́емый; (*careless*) неосторо́жный, неосмотри́тельный.
unguent ['ʌŋgwənt] *n.* мазь.
ungulate ['ʌŋgjʊlət, -ˌleɪt] *adj.* копы́тный.
unhackneyed [ʌn'hæknɪd] *adj.* неизби́тый, небана́льный; све́жий, оригина́льный.
unhallowed [ʌn'hæləʊd] *adj.* (*unconsecrated*) неосвящённый;

(*impious*) гре́шный, безнра́вственный.
unhampered [ʌn'hæmpəd] *adj.* беспрепя́тственный; свобо́дный (от+*g.*).
unhandy [ʌn'hændɪ] *adj.* (*clumsy*) нело́вкий, неуклю́жий.
unhappily [ʌn'hæpɪlɪ] *adv.* **1.** (*without happiness*) несча́стливо; **they were ~ married** их брак был несчастли́вый. **2.** (*unfortunately*) к несча́стью.
unhappiness [ʌn'hæpɪnɪs] *n.* несча́стье, го́ре, грусть.
unhappy [ʌn'hæpɪ] *adj.* (*sorrowful*) несчастли́вый, несча́стный, гру́стный; (*unfortunate*) неуда́чный, незада́чливый.
unharmed [ʌn'hɑːmd] *adj.* неповреждённый; (*pred.*) цел и невреди́м.
unharness [ʌn'hɑːnɪs] *v.t.* распр|яга́ть, -я́чь.
unhatched [ʌn'hætʃt] *adj.* (*of chickens etc.*) невы́сиженный.
unhealthy [ʌn'helθɪ] *adj.* **1.** (*in or indicating ill-health*) нездоро́вый, боле́зненный; **an ~ pallor** нездоро́вая бле́дность. **2.** (*coll., dangerous*) вре́дный.
unheard [ʌn'hɜːd] *adj.* неуслы́шанный, неслы́шный, невы́слушанный; **his pleas went ~** его́ мольбы́ оста́лись без отве́та.
unheard-of [ʌn'hɜːdɒv] *adj.* (*unknown*) неслы́ханный; (*unexampled, also*) беспрецеде́нтный.
unheeded [ʌn'hiːdɪd] *adj.* незаме́ченный; **his advice went ~** к его́ сове́там не прислу́шались.
unheed|ful [ʌn'hiːdfʊl], **-ing** [ʌn'hiːdɪŋ] *adjs.* невнима́тельный.
unhelpful [ʌn'helpfʊl] *adj.* бесполе́зный; (*pers.*) неотзы́вчивый.
unhelpfulness [ʌn'helpfʊlnɪs] *n.* бесполе́зность; неотзы́вчивость.
unheralded [ʌn'herəldɪd] *adj.* невозвещённый; неожи́данный.
unheroic [ˌʌnhɪ'rəʊɪk] *adj.* негерои́ческий, негеро́йский; (*of pers.*) трусли́вый, малоду́шный.
unhesitating [ʌn'hezɪˌteɪtɪŋ] *adj.* неколе́блющийся, реши́тельный.
unhinge [ʌn'hɪndʒ] *v.t.* (*lit.*) сн|има́ть, -ять с пе́тель; (*fig.*) расстр|а́ивать, -о́ить; **the tragedy ~d his mind** от пе́режи́той траге́дии он помеша́лся (*coll.*) тро́нулся (в уме́).
unhistorical [ˌʌnhɪ'stɒrɪk(ə)l] *adj.* неистори́ческий.
unhitch [ʌn'hɪtʃ] *v.t.* отвя́з|ывать, -а́ть; распр|яга́ть, -я́чь.
unholy [ʌn'həʊlɪ] *adj.* нечести́вый; поро́чный; (*coll., frightful*) ужа́сный, жу́ткий; **an ~ row** ужа́сный/жу́ткий сканда́л.
unhook [ʌn'hʊk] *v.t.* **1.** (*unfasten hooks of*) расстёг|ивать, -ну́ть; **she ~ed her dress** она́ расстегну́ла крючки́ у пла́тья. **2.** (*release from hook etc.*) отцеп|ля́ть, -и́ть.
unhoped-for [ʌn'həʊptfɔː(r)] *adj.* неожи́данный, нежда́нный.
unhorse [ʌn'hɔːs] *v.t.* сбр|а́сывать, -о́сить с ло́шади.
unhurried [ʌn'hʌrɪd] *adj.* нетороплúвый, неспе́шный.
unhurt [ʌn'hɜːt] *adj.* невреди́мый.
unhygienic [ˌʌnhaɪ'dʒiːnɪk] *adj.* нездоро́вый, негигиени́чный.
uni- ['juːnɪ] *comb. form* одно́..., едино...
Uniat ['juːnɪˌæt, -ɪət] *n.* униа́т (*fem.* -ка).
UNICEF ['juːnɪˌsef] *n.* (*abbr. of* **United Nations Children's Fund**) ЮНИСЕФ, (Де́тский фонд ООН).
unicorn ['juːnɪˌkɔːn] *n.* единоро́г.
unidentifiable [ˌʌnaɪ'dentɪˌfaɪəb(ə)l] *adj.* не поддаю́щийся опозна́нию.
unidentified [ˌʌnaɪ'dentɪˌfaɪd] *adj.* неопо́знанный; **~ flying object (UFO)** неопо́знанный лета́ющий объе́кт (НЛО).
unification [juːnɪfɪ'keɪʃ(ə)n] *n.* объедине́ние; унифика́ция.
uniform ['juːnɪˌfɔːm] *n.* фо́рма, фо́рменная оде́жда; (*esp. mil.*) мунди́р.
adj. однообра́зный, одноро́дный; одина́ковый, еди́ный; станда́ртный; **at a ~ temperature** при постоя́нной температу́ре; **a ~ blue-grey colour** ро́вный се́ро-голубо́й цвет; **his books are ~ly interesting** его́ кни́ги всегда́ интере́сны.
uniformed ['juːnɪˌfɔːmd] *adj.* оде́тый в фо́рму; в мунди́ре.
uniformity [juːnɪ'fɔːmɪtɪ] *n.* единообра́зие, одноро́дность.
unify ['juːnɪˌfaɪ] *v.t.* (*unite*) объедин|я́ть, -и́ть; (*make uniform*) унифици́ровать (*impf.*).
unilateral [juːnɪ'lætər(ə)l] *adj.* односторо́нний.
unimaginable [ˌʌnɪ'mædʒɪnəb(ə)l] *adj.* невообрази́мый.
unimaginative [ˌʌnɪ'mædʒɪnətɪv] *adj.* лишённый воображе́ния; прозаи́чный.
unimpaired [ˌʌnɪm'peəd] *adj.* неосла́бленный; незатро́нутый; непострада́вший.
unimpassioned [ˌʌnɪm'pæʃ(ə)nd] *adj.* бесстра́стный, споко́йный.
unimpeachable [ˌʌnɪm'piːtʃəb(ə)l] *adj.* безупре́чный, безукори́зненный.
unimpeded [ˌʌnɪm'piːdɪd] *adj.* беспрепя́тственный; не остано́вленный (*чем*).
unimportance [ˌʌnɪm'pɔːt(ə)ns] *n.* нева́жность, незначи́тельность.
unimportant [ˌʌnɪm'pɔːt(ə)nt] *adj.* нева́жный, незначи́тельный.
unimposing [ˌʌnɪm'pəʊzɪŋ] *adj.* неимпоза́нтный, невнуши́тельный, скро́мный.
unimpressed [ˌʌnɪm'prest] *adj.*: **I was ~ by his threats** его́ угро́зы не произвели́ на меня́ никако́го впечатле́ния.
unimpressive [ˌʌnɪm'presɪv] *adj.* невпечатля́ющий.
uninfluenced [ʌn'ɪnflʊənst] *adj.* не находя́щийся под влия́нием (*кого/чего*); непредупреждённый.
uninformed [ˌʌnɪn'fɔːmd] *adj.* неосведомлённый, неинформи́рованный, несве́дущий.
uninhabitable [ˌʌnɪn'hæbɪtəb(ə)l] *adj.* неприго́дный для жилья́.
uninhabited [ˌʌnɪn'hæbɪtɪd] *adj.* необита́емый.
uninhibited [ˌʌnɪn'hɪbɪtɪd] *adj.* откры́тый, нестесни́тельный, свобо́дный.
uninitiated [ˌʌnɪ'nɪʃɪˌeɪtɪd] *adj.* непосвящённый.
uninjured [ʌn'ɪndʒəd] *adj.* непострада́вший; **he was ~ by his fall** при паде́нии он не получи́л поврежде́ний
uninspired [ˌʌnɪn'spaɪəd] *adj.* невдохновлённый; без подъёма.
uninspiring [ˌʌnɪn'spaɪərɪŋ] *adj.* не вдохновля́ющий.
uninsured [ˌʌnɪn'ʃʊəd] *adj.* незастрахо́ванный.
unintelligent [ˌʌnɪn'telɪdʒ(ə)nt] *adj.* неу́мный.
unintelligibility [ˌʌnɪnˌtelɪdʒɪ'bɪlɪtɪ] *n.* неразбо́рчивость, невня́тность.
unintelligible [ˌʌnɪn'telɪdʒɪb(ə)l] *adj.* неразбо́рчивый, невня́тный.
unintended [ˌʌnɪn'tendɪd] *adj.* ненаме́ренный, нево́льный; (*unforeseen*) непредусмо́тренный.
unintentional [ˌʌnɪn'tenʃən(ə)l] *adj.* ненаме́ренный, нево́льный.
uninterested [ʌn'ɪntrəstɪd, -trɪstɪd] *adj.* безразли́чный (к+*d.*); не заинтересо́ванный (*чем*); **he is ~ in history** он не интересу́ется исто́рией.
uninteresting [ʌn'ɪntrəstɪŋ, -trɪstɪŋ] *adj.* неинтере́сный.
uninterrupted [ˌʌnɪntə'rʌptɪd] *adj.* непрерыва́емый, непреры́вный.
uninventive [ˌʌnɪn'ventɪv] *adj.* неизобрета́тельный.
uninvited [ˌʌnɪn'vaɪtɪd] *adj.* неприглашённый, незва́ный.
uninviting [ˌʌnɪn'vaɪtɪŋ] *adj.* непривлека́тельный, неаппети́тный; **an ~ prospect** неприя́тная перспекти́ва.
union ['juːnjən, -nɪən] *n.* **1.** (*joining, uniting*) объедине́ние, сою́з; **the ~ of England and Scotland** у́ния А́нглии с Шотла́ндией. **2.** (*association*) сою́з; **U~ of Soviet Socialist Republics** Сою́з Сове́тских Социалисти́ческих Респу́блик; **U~ Republic** (*of former USSR*) Сою́зная респу́блика; **the U~** (*United States*) Соединённые Шта́ты (Аме́рики); **U~ Jack** госуда́рственный флаг Великобрита́нии; **students' ~** студе́нческий сою́з; (*building*) студе́нческий клуб. **3.** **(trade ~)** профессиона́льный сою́з, профсою́з; **~ card** профсою́зный биле́т. **4.** (*state of harmony*) гармо́ния; согла́сие; **they live in perfect ~** они́ живу́т в по́лном согла́сии; **the ~ of two hearts** сою́з лю́бящих серде́ц. **5.: ~ suit** (*US*) мужско́й нате́льный комбинезо́н.
unionist ['juːnjənɪst, 'juːnɪən-] *n.* **1.** (*member of trade union*) член профсою́за. **2.** (**U~:** *Br. pol.*) унионист.
unique [jʊ'niːk, juː'niːk] *adj.* уника́льный, еди́нственный (в своём ро́де); замеча́тельный, исключи́тельный; **~ object** у́никум.
unisex ['juːnɪˌseks] *adj.*: **~ clothes** одина́ковая оде́жда для

обо́их поло́в.
unisexual [ju:nɪ'seksʊəl] *adj.* (*bot.*) однопо́лый.
unison ['ju:nɪs(ə)n] *n.* (*mus.*) унисо́н; (*fig.*) гармо́ния; **they acted in perfect ~** они́ де́йствовали в по́лном согла́сии.
unit ['ju:nɪt] *n.* **1.** (*single entity*) едини́ца; це́лое; **the family is the ~ of society** семья́ — яче́йка о́бщества. **2.** (*math., and of measurement*) едини́ца; **~ of length** едини́ца длины́; **~ of currency, monetary ~** де́нежная едини́ца; **~ trust** довери́тельный паево́й фонд. **3.** (*mil.*) часть; (*large ~, formation*) соедине́ние; (*small ~, sub-~*) подразделе́ние; (*detachment*) отря́д. **4.** (*of furniture etc.*) се́кция; **kitchen ~s** се́кции для ку́хонного комба́йна. **5.** (*tech.*) агрега́т.
Unitarian [ju:nɪ'teərɪən] *n.* унита́рий.
adj. унита́рный.
unite [jʊ'naɪt, ju:-] *v.t.* соедин|я́ть, -и́ть; объедин|я́ть, -и́ть; **the country is ~d behind the President** вся страна́ сплоти́лась вокру́г президе́нта; **they were ~d in marriage** они́ сочета́лись у́зами бра́ка; **a ~d family** дру́жная семья́; **they made a ~d effort** они́ объедини́лись для совме́стных уси́лий; **the U~d Nations** (*organization*) Организа́ция Объединённых На́ций; **the U~d Kingdom** Соединённое Короле́вство; **the U~d States** Соединённые Шта́ты.
v.i. соедин|я́ться, -и́ться; объедин|я́ться, -и́ться; спл|а́чиваться, -оти́ться; **they ~d in condemning him** они́ единоду́шно его́ осуди́ли; **workers of the world, ~!** пролета́рии всех стран, соединя́йтесь!; **~d front** еди́ный фронт.
unit|y ['ju:nɪtɪ] *n.* **1.** (*oneness; coherence*) еди́нство; сплочённость; **~y of purpose** еди́нство це́ли; **national ~y** национа́льное еди́нство; **the (dramatic) ~ies** еди́нство вре́мени, ме́ста и де́йствия. **2.** (*concord*) согла́сие; **dwell in ~y** жить (*impf.*) в согла́сии. **3.** (*math.*) едини́ца.
universal [ju:nɪ'vɜ:s(ə)l] *n.* (*phil.*) универса́лия.
adj. всео́бщий, универса́льный; **his proposal met with ~ approval** его́ предложе́ние встре́тило всео́бщее одобре́ние; **~ joint** (*tech.*) универса́льный шарни́р; **a ~ remedy** универса́льное сре́дство; **~ suffrage** всео́бщее избира́тельное пра́во; **U~ Postal Union** Всеми́рный почто́вый сою́з.
universality [ju:nɪvɜ:'sælɪtɪ] *n.* универса́льность.
universe ['ju:nɪ,vɜ:s] *n.* вселе́нная, мир.
university [ju:nɪ'vɜ:sɪtɪ] *n.* университе́т; **~ sport** студе́нческий спорт; **~ town** университе́тский го́род/городо́к.
unjust [ʌn'dʒʌst] *adj.* несправедли́вый.
unjustifiable [ʌn'dʒʌstɪ,faɪəb(ə)l] *adj.* непрости́тельный.
unjustified [ʌn'dʒʌstɪ,faɪd] *adj.* неопра́вданный.
unkempt [ʌn'kempt] *adj.* нечёсаный, взлохма́ченный, растрёпанный.
unkind [ʌn'kaɪnd] *adj.* недо́брый, злой, нелюбе́зный; **be ~ to s.o.** пло́хо обраща́ться (*impf.*) с кем-н. (*or* относи́ться (*impf.*) к кому́-н.); **don't take it ~ly** не обижа́йтесь.
unkindness [ʌn'kaɪndnɪs] *n.* жесто́кость, злость, нелюбе́зность.
unknowable [ʌn'nəʊəb(ə)l] *adj.* непознава́емый.
unknowing [ʌn'nəʊɪŋ] *adj.* незна́ющий, несве́дущий, неосведомлённый.
unknown [ʌn'nəʊn] *n.* неизве́стное; **fear of the ~** страх пе́ред неизве́стностью; (*math.*) неизве́стная величина́.
adj. неизве́стный; **an ~ quantity** неизве́стная величина́; **the U~ Soldier** Неизве́стный солда́т.
adv.: **he did it ~ to me** он сде́лал э́то без моего́ ве́дома.
unlace [ʌn'leɪs] *v.t.* расшнуро́в|ывать, -а́ть.
unladen [ʌn'leɪd(ə)n] *adj.* (*without load or cargo*) поро́жний, без гру́за.
unladylike [ʌn'leɪdɪ,laɪk] *adj.* неподоба́ющий воспи́танной же́нщине; вульга́рный.
unlamented [,ʌnlə'mentɪd] *adj.* неопла́киваемый, неопла́канный.
unlatch [ʌn'lætʃ] *v.t.* сн|има́ть, -ять запо́р с+*g.*; отп|ира́ть, -ере́ть.
unlawful [ʌn'lɔ:fʊl] *adj.* незако́нный.
unleaded [ʌn'ledɪd] *adj.*: **~ petrol** нэтили́рованный бензи́н.
unlearn [ʌn'lɜ:n] *v.t.* разучи́ться (*pf.*) (+*inf.*); отучи́ться (*pf.*) от+*g.*; отв|ыка́ть, -ы́кнуть от+*g.*
unlearned [ʌn'lɜ:nɪd] *adj.* нео́бученный, неучёный.
unleash [ʌn'li:ʃ] *v.t.* спус|ка́ть, -ти́ть со сво́ры (*or* с це́пи); (*fig.*) да|ва́ть, -ть во́лю +*d.*; **~ a war** развяза́ть (*pf.*) войну́; **his fury was ~ed** он был в бе́шенстве.
unleavened [ʌn'lev(ə)nd] *adj.* незаква́шенный, пре́сный.
unless [ʌn'les, ən'les] *conj.* е́сли (то́лько) не; пока́ не; ра́зве (то́лько); **I shall go ~ it rains** я пойду́, е́сли не бу́дет дождя́; **I don't know why he is late, ~ he has lost his way** не зна́ю, почему́ он опа́здывает — ра́зве что заблуди́лся; **~ and until** то́лько когда́/е́сли.
unlettered [ʌn'letəd] *adj.* негра́мотный, необразо́ванный.
unlike [ʌn'laɪk] *adj. & adv.* непохо́жий, ра́зный; **~ poles** (*elec.*) разноимённые по́люсы; **~ signs** (*math.*) ра́зные зна́ки; **they are utterly ~** они́ соверше́нно ра́зные лю́ди (*or* не похо́жи друг на дру́га); **he is ~ his sister** он не похо́ж на свою́ сестру́; **that** (*conduct etc.*) **is ~ him** э́то на него́ не похо́же; **he talks ~ anyone I have ever heard** я никогда́ не слы́шал, что́бы так говори́ли (, как он); **~ the others, he works hard** не в приме́р други́м (*or* в отли́чие от остальны́х), он усе́рдно рабо́тает.
unlikeable [ʌn'laɪkəb(ə)l] *adj.* непривлека́тельный, несимпати́чный.
unlikelihood [ʌn'laɪklɪhʊd] *n.* неправдоподо́бие.
unlikely [ʌn'laɪklɪ] *adj.* неправдоподо́бный; **it is ~ he will recover** маловероя́тно, что он попра́вится; вряд ли он попра́вится.
unlimited [ʌn'lɪmɪtɪd] *adj.* неограни́ченный.
unlined [ʌn'laɪnd] *adj.* **1.: ~ paper** нелино́ванная бума́га; **an ~ face** лицо́ без морщи́н. **2.: an ~ coat** пальто́ без подкла́дки.
unlit [ʌn'lɪt] *adj.* неосвещённый, незажжённый; **~ streets** неосвещённые у́лицы; **the lamp was ~** ла́мпу не зажгли́; ла́мпа стоя́ла незажжённая.
unload [ʌn'ləʊd] *v.t.* выгружа́ть, вы́грузить; разгру|жа́ть, -зи́ть; **she ~ed her worries on to him** она́ излила́ пе́ред ним ду́шу; она́ переложи́ла свои́ забо́ты на него́; **he ~ed his shares** он сбыл (*coll.*) свои́ а́кции.
v.i. разгру|жа́ться, -зи́ться.
unloaded [ʌn'ləʊdɪd] *adj.* незаря́женный, пусто́й; **his gun was ~** его́ ружьё не́ было заря́жено.
unlock [ʌn'lɒk] *v.t.* отп|ира́ть, -ере́ть (ключо́м); откр|ыва́ть, -ы́ть.
unlocked [ʌn'lɒkt] *adj.* откры́тый, о́тпертый, неза́пертый.
unlooked-for [ʌn'lʊktfɔ:(r)] *adj.* неожи́данный, непредви́денный.
unloose [ʌn'lu:s] *v.t.* (*slacken; untie*) осл|абля́ть, -а́бить; отвя́з|ывать, -а́ть; (*release*) освобо|жда́ть, -ди́ть.
unlovable [ʌn'lʌvəb(ə)l] *adj.* неприя́тный, непривлека́тельный, несимпати́чный.
unloved [ʌn'lʌvd] *adj.* нелюби́мый.
unlovely [ʌn'lʌvlɪ] *adj.* неприя́тный, проти́вный, некраси́вый.
unloving [ʌn'lʌvɪŋ] *adj.* нелю́бящий.
unluckily [ʌn'lʌkɪlɪ] *adv.* к несча́стью.
unluck|y [ʌn'lʌkɪ] *adj.* неуда́чный, невезу́чий, незада́чливый; **he is ~y at cards** ему́ не везёт в ка́ртах; **it is ~y to spill salt** просы́пать соль — не к добру́ (*or* плоха́я приме́та); **~y number** несчастли́вое число́; **~ily for him** к несча́стью для него́.
unmade [ʌn'meɪd] *adj.*: **an ~ bed** незасте́ленная посте́ль.
unmaidenly [ʌn'meɪdənlɪ] *adj.* недеви́ческий; не подоба́ющий де́вушке; нескро́мный.
unman [ʌn'mæn] *v.t.* лиш|а́ть, -и́ть му́жества.
unmanageable [ʌn'mænɪdʒəb(ə)l] *adj.* неуправля́емый; непоко́рный; не поддаю́щийся контро́лю; (*of child*) тру́дный, непоко́рный.
unmanly [ʌn'mænlɪ] *adj.* нему́жественный, недосто́йный мужчи́ны; трусли́вый.
unmanned [ʌn'mænd] *adj.* не укомплекто́ванный людьми́; **an ~ satellite** спу́тник, управля́емый автомати́чески.
unmannerly [ʌn'mænəlɪ] *adj.* невоспи́танный.
unmarked [ʌn'mɑ:kt] *adj.* (*without markings*) неотме́ченный, неме́ченный; (*unobserved*) незаме́ченный.

unmarketable [ʌn'mɑ:kɪtəb(ə)l] *adj.* не подходя́щий для ры́нка.

unmarred [ʌn'mɑ:d] *adj.* незапя́тнанный; неиспо́рченный.

unmarried [ʌn'mærɪd] *adj.* нежена́тый, холосто́й; незаму́жняя; **he is** ~ он не жена́т; он холосто́й/нежена́тый; **she is** ~ она́ не за́мужем; ~ **mother** мать-одино́чка.

unmask [ʌn'mɑ:sk] *v.t.* (*fig.*) разоблач|а́ть, -и́ть; срыва́ть, сорва́ть ма́ску с+*g.*; (*mil.*) демаски́ровать (*impf.*, *pf.*).
v.i. (*lit.*) сн|има́ть, -ять ма́ску.

unmatched [ʌn'mætʃt] *adj.* (*without an equal*) непревзойдённый; бесподо́бный; (*glove etc.*) непа́рный, разро́зненный.

unmeaning [ʌn'mi:nɪŋ] *adj.* бессмы́сленный; незначи́тельный.

unmeant [ʌn'ment] *adj.* неумы́шленный, нево́льный.

unmeasured [ʌn'meʒəd] *adj.* (*fig.*, *boundless*, *immoderate*) безграни́чный, чрезме́рный.

unmentionable [ʌn'menʃənəb(ə)l] *adj.* неприли́чный, запре́тный.

unmerciful [ʌn'mɜ:sɪˌfʊl] *adj.* немилосе́рдный, безжа́лостный.

unmerited [ʌn'merɪtɪd] *adj.* незаслу́женный.

unmindful [ʌn'maɪndfʊl] *adj.* невнима́тельный, забы́вчивый; ~ **of his duty** забы́в о до́лге.

unmistakabl|e [ˌʌnmɪ'steɪkəb(ə)l] *adj.* ве́рный, я́сный, очеви́дный, несомне́нный; типи́чный, характе́рный; ~**y** несомне́нно, безусло́вно; **he is** ~**y a sailor** сра́зу ви́дно, что он моря́к.

unmitigated [ʌn'mɪtɪˌgeɪtɪd] *adj.* (*not softened*) несмягчённый, неосла́бленный; (*arrant*) зако́нченный, отъя́вленный, я́вный.

unmixed [ʌn'mɪkst] *adj.* несме́шанный; чи́стый.

unmolested [ˌʌnmə'lestɪd] *adj.* невреди́мый; оста́вленный в поко́е.

unmoor [ʌn'mʊə(r), ʌn'mɔ:(r)] *v.t.* & *i.* сн|има́ть(ся), -ять(ся) с я́коря.

unmounted [ʌn'maʊntɪd] *adj.* **1.** (*on foot*) пе́ший. **2.** (*of precious stone*) неопра́вленный. **3.** (*of photograph etc.*) неоканто́ванный.

unmourned [ʌn'mɔ:nd] *adj.* неопла́канный.

unmoved [ʌn'mu:vd] *adj.* (*unaffected by emotion*) бесчу́вственный; оста́вшийся равноду́шным; (*unbending*) непреклóнный.

unmusical [ʌn'mju:zɪk(ə)l] *adj.*: **an** ~ **noise** неприя́тный шум; **he is** ~ он не музыка́лен.

unmuzzle [ʌn'mʌz(ə)l] *v.t.* сн|има́ть, -ять намо́рдник с+*g.*; (*fig.*): **he** ~**d the press** он отмени́л цензу́ру в печа́ти.

unnameable [ʌn'neɪməb(ə)l] *adj.* гну́сный, ужа́сный, отврати́тельный.

unnamed [ʌn'neɪmd] *adj.* нена́званный, неупомя́нутый; (*unidentified*) неизве́стный.

unnatural [ʌn'nætʃər(ə)l] *adj.* неесте́ственный, противоесте́ственный; **an** ~ **father** бессерде́чный оте́ц; ~ **vice** извраще́ние; **he displayed** ~ **energy** он прояви́л неимове́рную/чудо́вищную эне́ргию; **not** ~**ly** есте́ственно.

unnavigable [ʌn'nævɪgəb(ə)l] *adj.* несудохо́дный; (*aeron.*) нелётный; (*of a balloon*) неуправля́емый.

unnecessary [ʌn'nesəsərɪ] *adj.* нену́жный, ли́шний; (*excessive*) изли́шний.

unneighbourly [ʌn'neɪbəlɪ] *adj.* недобрососе́дский.

unnerv|e [ʌn'nɜ:v] *v.t.* обесси́ли|вать, -ть; лиш|а́ть, -и́ть (*кого*) му́жества; **an** ~**ing experience** си́льное/неприя́тное/жу́ткое пережива́ние.

unnoted [ʌn'nəʊtɪd] *adj.* неотме́ченный, незаме́ченный.

unnoticeable [ʌn'nəʊtɪsəb(ə)l] *adj.* незаме́тный.

unnoticed [ʌn'nəʊtɪst] *adj.* незаме́ченный; **his appearance went** ~ его́ появле́ние прошло́ незаме́ченным; **I let his remarks pass** ~ я оста́вил его́ замеча́ния без внима́ния.

unnumbered [ʌn'nʌmbəd] *adj.* **1.** (*countless*) бесчётный, несме́тный; **on** ~ **occasions** мно́жество раз. **2.** (*without numbering*) ненумеро́ванный, без но́мера; ~ **pages** непронумеро́ванные страни́цы.

UNO ['ju:nəʊ] = **UN**

unobjectionable [ˌʌnəb'dʒekʃənəb(ə)l] *adj.* прие́млемый.

unobliging [ʌnə'blaɪdʒɪŋ] *adj.* нелюбе́зный, неуслу́жливый.

unobservant [ˌʌnəb'zɜ:v(ə)nt] *adj.* ненаблюда́тельный.

unobserved [ˌʌnəb'zɜ:vd] *adj.* незаме́ченный.

unobstructed [ˌʌnəb'strʌktɪd] *adj.* (*of road*) незагоро́женный, непреграждённый; (*of view*) незагоро́женный, ниче́м не заслонённый; ~ **progress** беспрепя́тственное (про)движе́ние.

unobtainable [ˌʌnəb'teɪnəb(ə)l] *adj.* недосту́пный, недостижи́мый.

unobtrusive [ˌʌnəb'tru:sɪv] *adj.* скро́мный, ненавя́зчивый.

unobtrusiveness [ˌʌnəb'tru:sɪvnɪs] *adj.* скро́мность, ненавя́зчивость.

unoccupied [ʌn'ɒkjʊˌpaɪd] *adj.* неза́нятый, свобо́дный; **an** ~ **house** пусто́й дом; ~ **seats** неза́нятые/свобо́дные места́.

unoffending [ˌʌnə'fendɪŋ] *adj.* (*harmless*) безвре́дный, безоби́дный; (*innocent*) неви́нный.

unofficial [ˌʌnə'fɪʃ(ə)l] *adj.* неофициа́льный.

unopposed [ˌʌnə'pəʊzd] *adj.* не встреча́ющий/встре́тивший сопротивле́ния; **the landing was** ~ вы́садившийся деса́нт не встре́тил сопротивле́ния; **his candidature was** ~ он был еди́нственным кандида́том.

unorganized [ʌn'ɔ:gəˌnaɪzd] *adj.* неорганизо́ванный; (*coll.*): **we are leaving tonight and I am still quite** ~ мы сего́дня ве́чером уезжа́ем, а я совсе́м ещё не гото́в/собра́лся.

unoriginal [ˌʌnə'rɪdʒɪn(ə)l] *adj.* неоригина́льный; заи́мствованный.

unorthodox [ʌn'ɔ:θəˌdɒks] *adj.* неортодокса́льный, неправове́рный; (*unconventional*) необщепри́нятый.

unorthodoxy [ʌn'ɔ:θəˌdɒksɪ] *n.* неортодокса́льность.

unostentatious [ˌʌnɒsten'teɪʃəs] *adj.* непоказно́й, не броса́ющийся в глаза́; скро́мный, ненавя́зчивый.

unpacified [ʌn'pæsɪfaɪd] *adj.* неумиротворённый; неусмирённый.

unpack [ʌn'pæk] *v.t.* & *i.* распако́в|ывать(ся), -а́ть(ся).

unpaid [ʌn'peɪd] *adj.* **1.** неопла́ченный; (*of debt*, *bill etc.*) неупла́ченный; ~ **work** беспла́тная рабо́та; **the men were** ~ рабо́чим не заплати́ли. **2.** (*of pers.*, *unsalaried*) не получа́ющий пла́ту/жа́лованье.

unpalatable [ʌn'pælətəb(ə)l] *adj.* невку́сный; (*fig.*) неприя́тный; **an** ~ **truth** го́рькая и́стина.

unparalleled [ʌn'pærəˌleld] *adj.* несравни́мый, несравне́нный; бесподо́бный; **the war was** ~ **in history** э́та война́ была́ беспримéрной в исто́рии.

unpardonable [ʌn'pɑ:dənəb(ə)l] *adj.* непрости́тельный.

unparliamentary [ˌʌnpɑ:lə'mentərɪ] *adj.*: ~ **language** «непарла́ментские»/ре́зкие выраже́ния.

unpatriotic [ˌʌnpætrɪ'ɒtɪk, ˌʌnpeɪt-] *adj.* непатриоти́ческий.

unpatronized [ʌ'pætrəˌnaɪzd] *adj.* непопуля́рный; малопосеща́емый.

unpaved [ʌn'peɪvd] *adj.* немощёный.

unpeg [ʌn'peg] *v.t.* **1.** откреп|ля́ть, -и́ть; **she** ~**ged the clothes** она́ сняла́ оде́жду с ве́шалки/крючка́. **2.:** ~ **prices** прекра|ща́ть, -ти́ть иску́сственную стабилиза́цию цен.

unpeopled [ʌn'pi:pəld] *adj.* ненаселённый, безлю́дный.

unperceived [ʌnpə'si:vd] *adj.* невоспри́нятый, неосо́знанный; незаме́ченный.

unperformed [ˌʌnpə'fɔ:md] *adj.* невы́полненный, неосуществлённый; **an** ~ **duty** невы́полненный долг; **the symphony remained** ~ симфо́ния (так и) не исполня́лась.

unperson ['ʌnˌpɜ:s(ə)n] *n.* ≃ бы́вшая персо́на.

unpersuaded [ˌʌnpə'sweɪdɪd] *adj.* неубеждённый.

unpersuasive [ˌʌnpə'sweɪsɪv] *adj.* неубеди́тельный.

unperturbed [ˌʌnpə'tɜ:bd] *adj.* невозмути́мый.

unpick [ʌn'pɪk] *v.t.* расп|а́рывать, -оро́ть.

unpin [ʌn'pɪn] *v.t.* отк|а́лывать, -оло́ть; вынима́ть, вы́нуть була́вки/шпи́льки из+*g.*

unpitying [ʌn'pɪtɪɪŋ] *adj.* безжа́лостный.

unplaced [ʌn'pleɪst] *adj.* (*of horse*) не заня́вший ни одного из пе́рвых трёх мест.

unplait [ʌn'plæt] *v.t.* расплe|та́ть, -сти́.

unplanned [ʌn'plænd] *adj.* незаплани́рованный; неожи́данный; **an** ~ **departure** неожи́данный отъе́зд; **an** ~ **economy** внепла́новая/непла́новая эконо́мика.

unplayable [ʌn'pleɪəb(ə)l] *adj.* (*of sports ground*) неподходя́щий для игры́; (*of music*) него́дный для исполне́ния.

unpleasant [ʌn'plez(ə)nt] *adj.* неприя́тный, отта́лкивающий, нелюбе́зный.
unpleasantness [ʌn'plezəntnɪs] *n.* непривлека́тельность, неприя́тность, нелюбе́зность; (*dispute*) ссо́ра, неприя́тность.
unpleasing [ʌn'pli:zɪŋ] *adj.* неприя́тный.
unplug [ʌn'plʌg] *v.t.* (*remove obstruction from*) отку́пори|вать, -ть; разблоки́ровать (*pf.*); (*disconnect*) отключ|а́ть, -и́ть; разъедин|я́ть, -и́ть.
unplumbed [ʌn'plʌmd] *adj.*: ~ **depths of depravity** неизмери́мая глубина́ паде́ния.
unpolluted [ˌʌnpə'lu:tɪd] *adj.* незагрязнённый; (*fig.*) неосквернённый.
unpopular [ʌn'pɒpjʊlə(r)] *adj.* непопуля́рный.
unpopularity [ˌʌnpɒpjʊ'lærɪtɪ] *n.* непопуля́рность.
unpractical [ʌn'præktɪk(ə)l] *adj.* (*solution etc.*) нецелесообра́зный; (*pers.*) непракти́чный.
unpractised [ʌn'præktɪst] *adj.* (*inexperienced, unskilled*) нео́пытный.
unprecedented [ʌn'presɪˌdentɪd] *adj.* беспрецеде́нтный.
unprejudiced [ʌn'predʒʊdɪst] *adj.* непредвзя́тый, непредубеждённый.
unpremeditated [ˌʌnprɪ'medɪˌteɪtɪd] *adj.* непреднаме́ренный; непредумы́шленный.
unprepared [ˌʌnprɪ'peəd] *adj.* неподгото́вленный; **his speech was** ~ он произнёс свою речь экспро́мтом; **I was** ~ **for his reply** его́ отве́т был для меня́ неожи́данностью.
unpreparedness [ˌʌnprɪ'peədnɪs] *n.* неподгото́вленность.
unprepossessing [ˌʌnpri:pə'zesɪŋ] *adj.* нерасполага́ющий.
unpresentable [ˌʌnprɪ'zentəb(ə)l] *adj.* непрезента́бельный, невзра́чный.
unpretentious [ˌʌnprɪ'tenʃəs] *adj.* непретенцио́зный, скро́мный, просто́й.
unpretentiousness [ˌʌnprɪ'tenʃəsnɪs] *n.* скро́мность, простота́.
unpreventable [ˌʌnprɪ'ventəb(ə)l] *adj.* неизбе́жный, неотврати́мый.
unpriced [ʌn'praɪst] *adj.* без определённой цены́; без указа́ния цены́.
unprincipled [ʌn'prɪnsɪp(ə)ld] *adj.* беспринци́пный.
unprintable [ʌn'prɪntəb(ə)l] *adj.* нецензу́рный, непеча́тный.
unprivileged [ʌn'prɪvɪlɪdʒd] *adj.* непривилеги́рованный.
unprocurable [ˌʌnprə'kjʊərəb(ə)l] *adj.* недосту́пный.
unproductive [ˌʌnprə'dʌktɪv] *adj.* непродукти́вный, непроизводи́тельный; ~ **capital** мёртвый капита́л; ~ **labour** непроизводи́тельный труд; **an** ~**argument** бесполе́зный спор.
unprofessional [ˌʌnprə'feʃən(ə)l] *adj.* непрофессиона́льный; ~ **conduct** наруше́ние профессиона́льной э́тики; (*amateur*): ~ **work** люби́тельская рабо́та.
unprofitable [ʌn'prɒfɪtəb(ə)l] *adj.* нерента́бельный, невы́годный, неприбы́льный; (*useless*) бессмы́сленный, бесполе́зный.
unpromising [ʌn'prɒmɪsɪŋ] *adj.* малообеща́ющий.
unprompted [ʌn'prɒmptɪd] *adj.* неподска́занный.
unpronounceable [ˌʌnprə'naʊnsəb(ə)l] *adj.* непроизноси́мый.
unpropitious [ˌʌnprə'pɪʃəs] *adj.* неблагоприя́тный.
unprotected [ˌʌnprə'tektɪd] *adj.* незащищённый, беззащи́тный.
unprovable [ʌn'pru:vəb(ə)l] *adj.* недоказу́емый.
unprove|d [ʌn'pru:vd], **-n** [ʌn'pru:v(ə)n] *adjs.* недока́занный.
unprovided [ˌʌnprə'vaɪdɪd] *adj.* неснабже́нный; не обеспе́ченный материа́льно; **a house** ~ **with bathrooms** дом без ва́нных (ко́мнат); **she was left** ~ **for** она́ оста́лась без средств к существова́нию.
unprovoked [ˌʌnprə'vəʊkt] *adj.* неспровоци́рованный; ниче́м не вы́званный; **she was** ~ **by his taunts** она́ не подда́лась его́ провока́циям; ему́ не удало́сь подде́ть её свои́ми насме́шками.
unpublished [ʌn'pʌblɪʃt] *adj.* неопублико́ванный, неизда́нный.
unpunished [ʌn'pʌnɪʃt] *adj.* безнака́занный, ненака́занный.
unputdownable [ˌʌnpʊt'daʊnəb(ə)l] *adj.* (*coll.*) захва́тывающий, «не оторвёшься».
unqualified [ʌn'kwɒlɪˌfaɪd] *adj.* **1.** (*without reservations*) безоговоро́чный; ~ **praise** безграни́чная хвала́; **an** ~ **refusal** реши́тельный отка́з. **2.** (*not competent*) некомпете́нтный, неквалифици́рованный; **I am** ~ **to judge** я недоста́точно компете́нтен, что́бы суди́ть; ~ **in medicine** не име́ющий медици́нской подгото́вки.
unquenchable [ʌn'kwentʃəb(ə)l] *adj.* (*of thirst*) неутоли́мый; (*of fire*) неугаси́мый; (*fig.*) неиссяка́емый, неистощи́мый.
unquestionabl|e [ʌn'kwestʃənəb(ə)l] *adj.* (*undoubted*) несомне́нный; (*indisputable*) неоспори́мый, беспо́рный; ~**e evidence** неоспори́мое доказа́тельство; **you are** ~**y right** вы безусло́вно пра́вы.
unquestioned [ʌn'kwestʃ(ə)nd] *adj.* беспо́рный, при́знанный; **I could not let his statement go** ~ я не мог пропусти́ть его́ выска́зывание без возраже́ний.
unquestioning [ʌn'kwestʃənɪŋ] *adj.*: ~ **obedience** безоговоро́чное/по́лное/слепо́е повинове́ние.
unquiet [ʌn'kwaɪət] *adj.* (*restless*) беспоко́йный; (*disturbed*) взволно́ванный, трево́жный.
unquotable [ʌn'kwəʊtəb(ə)l] *adj.* (*not fit for repetition*) нецензу́рный.
unquote [ʌn'kwəʊt] *v.t.* (*imper. only*): **'quote ...** ~**'** «откры́ть кавы́чки... закры́ть кавы́чки».
unravel [ʌn'ræv(ə)l] *v.t.* распу́т|ывать, -ать; **the wool was** ~**led** шерсть распу́тали; (*fig.*) разга́д|ывать, -а́ть.
unreachable [ʌn'ri:tʃəb(ə)l] *adj.*: **he was** ~ **at his office** его́ нельзя́ бы́ло заста́ть в конто́ре.
unread [ʌn'red] *adj.* (*of book etc.*) непрочи́танный; (*of writer*) кото́рого никто́ не чита́ет.
unreadable [ʌn'ri:dəb(ə)l] *adj.* (*illegible*) неразбо́рчивый; (*tedious*) нечита́бельный.
unreadiness [ʌn'redɪnɪs] *n.* негото́вность, отсу́тствие гото́вности.
unready [ʌn'redɪ] *adj.* негото́вый; (*hist., as title*) Ме́шкотный; **he has an** ~ **tongue** у него́ язы́к пло́хо подве́шен/приве́шен.
unreal [ʌn'rɪəl] *adj.* нереа́льный; иску́сственный; фантасти́ческий; ото́рванный от действи́тельности; ~ **condition** (*gram.*) нереа́льное усло́вие.
unrealistic [ˌʌnrɪə'lɪstɪk] *adj.* **1.** (*unpractical, unreasonable*) нереа́льный. **2.** (*of art*) нереалисти́чный, нереалисти́ческий.
unreality [ˌʌnrɪ'ælɪtɪ] *n.* нереа́льность; ото́рванность от действи́тельности/жи́зни.
unrealizable [ʌn'rɪəlaɪzəb(ə)l] *adj.* неосуществи́мый; (*comm.*) не могу́щий быть реализо́ванным.
unrealized [ʌn'rɪəlaɪzd] *adj.* неосуществлённый; неосо́знанный; (*comm.*) нереализо́ванный.
unreason [ʌn'ri:z(ə)n] *n.* неразу́мность, безрассу́дство.
unreasonable [ʌn'ri:zənəb(ə)l] *adj.* безрассу́дный; не(благо)разу́мный; **don't be** ~**!** бу́дьте благоразу́мны!; не упря́мьтесь!; (*excessive*) чрезме́рный; ~ **demands** необосно́ванные тре́бования; ~ **prices** завы́шенные це́ны.
unreasoning [ʌn'ri:zənɪŋ] *adj.* неразу́мный, нерассужда́ющий, безрассу́дный.
unreciprocated [ˌʌnrɪ'sɪprəˌkeɪtɪd] *adj.* без (*or* не встреча́ющий) взаи́мности.
unreclaimed [ˌʌnrɪ'kleɪmd] *adj.*: ~ **land** неосво́енная земля́; ~ **property** незатре́бованное иму́щество.
unrecognizable [ʌn'rekəgˌnaɪzəb(ə)l] *adj.* неузнава́емый.
unrecognized [ʌn'rekəgˌnaɪzd] *adj.* неу́знанный; непри́знанный; **he moved in the crowd** ~ **by anyone** он дви́гался в толпе́, нике́м не у́знанный; **his genius was** ~ его́ ге́ний не получи́л призна́ния; **the possibilities were** ~ **at the time** в своё вре́мя э́тих возмо́жностей не распозна́ли.
unreconciled [ʌn'rekənˌsaɪld] *adj.* непримири́вшийся.
unrecorded [ˌʌnrɪ'kɔ:dɪd] *adj.* незапи́санный, незафикси́рованный; **what became of him is** ~ что с ним случи́лось поздне́е — неизве́стно.
unredeemed [ˌʌnrɪ'di:md] *adj.* (*of pawned object*) невы́купленный; (*unpaid*) неопла́ченный, непога́шенный; **an** ~ **bill** неопла́ченная тра́та; **an** ~ **promise** невы́полненное обеща́ние; **his crime was** ~ **by any generous motive** за его́ преступле́нием не стоя́ло како́го-либо благоро́дного моти́ва.

unrefined [ˌʌnrɪˈfaɪnd] *adj.* неочи́щенный, нерафини́рованный; **~ gold** неочи́щенное зо́лото; **~ language** гру́бые выраже́ния.

unreflecting [ˌʌnrɪˈflektɪŋ] *adj.* (*of surface etc.*) неотража́ющий; (*unthinking*) незаду́мывающийся, неразмышля́ющий; безду́мный.

unregarded [ˌʌnrɪˈgɑːdɪd] *adj.* игнори́руемый; оста́вленный без внима́ния.

unregenerate [ˌʌnrɪˈdʒenərət] *adj.* не обновлённый духо́вно; нераска́явшийся.

unrehearsed [ˌʌnrɪˈhɜːst] *adj.* неподгото́вленный; неотрепети́рованный.

adv. экспро́мптом; без подгото́вки.

unrelated [ˌʌnrɪˈleɪtɪd] *adj.* **1.** (*not connected*) несвя́занный (с+*i.*); не име́ющий отноше́ния (к+*d.*); **an ~ participle** обосо́бленный прича́стный оборо́т. **2.** (*not kin*): **he is ~ to me** он мне не ро́дственник.

unrelenting [ˌʌnrɪˈlentɪŋ] *adj.* (*inexorable*) неумоли́мый; (*assiduous*) неосла́бный.

unreliability [ˌʌnrɪˌlaɪəˈbɪlɪtɪ] *n.* ненадёжность, недостове́рность; безотве́тственность.

unreliable [ˌʌnrɪˈlaɪəb(ə)l] *adj.* ненадёжный, недостове́рный; (*of pers.*) безотве́тственный; **he is ~** на него́ нельзя́ положи́ться.

unrelieved [ˌʌnrɪˈliːvd] *adj.* **1.** не освобождённый (*от чего*); не получи́вший по́мощи. **2.** однообра́зный; **the landscape was ~ by trees** ни еди́ное де́рево не оживля́ло пейза́ж; **~ gloom** беспросве́тный мрак.

unremarkable [ˌʌnrɪˈmɑːkəb(ə)l] *adj.* невыдаю́щийся; ниче́м не примеча́тельный.

unremarked [ˌʌnrɪˈmɑːkt] *adj.* незаме́ченный.

unremitting [ˌʌnrɪˈmɪtɪŋ] *adj.* неосла́бный; (*incessant*) беспреста́нный.

unrepeatable [ˌʌnrɪˈpiːtəb(ə)l] *adj.* неповтори́мый; (*improper*) нецензу́рный.

unrepentant [ˌʌnrɪˈpent(ə)nt] *adj.* нераска́явшийся; нека́ющийся, нераска́янный; упо́рствующий (в заблужде́ниях *и т.п.*).

unrepresentative [ˌʌnreprɪˈzentətɪv] *adj.* непоказа́тельный, нетипи́чный.

unrequited [ˌʌnrɪˈkwaɪtɪd] *adj.* не по́льзующийся взаи́мностью; **~ love** любо́вь без взаи́мности; неразделённая/безотве́тная любо́вь; **an ~ service** односторо́нняя услу́га.

unreserved [ˌʌnrɪˈzɜːvd] *adj.* (*not set aside*) незаброни́рованый; (*open, frank*) открове́нный, откры́тый; (*whole-hearted*) по́лный; **I agree with you ~ly** я по́лностью с ва́ми согла́сен.

unresisting [ˌʌnrɪˈzɪstɪŋ] *adj.* несопротивля́ющийся; усту́пчивый.

unresolved [ˌʌnrɪˈzɒlvd] *adj.* нереши́тельный; **he was ~ how to act** он не мог реши́ть, как поступи́ть; **an ~ problem** нерешённая пробле́ма; **my doubts were ~** мои́ сомне́ния не рассе́ялись.

unresponsive [ˌʌnrɪˈspɒnsɪv] *adj.* неотзы́вчивый; невосприи́мчивый; **he was ~ to my suggestion** он не реаги́ровал на моё предложе́ние; **the illness was ~ to treatment** боле́знь не поддава́лась лече́нию.

unrest [ʌnˈrest] *n.* (*disquiet*) беспоко́йство; (*social, political*) волне́ния (*nt. pl.*); беспоря́дки (*m. pl.*).

unrestful [ʌnˈrestfʊl] *adj.* беспоко́йный.

unresting [ʌnˈrestɪŋ] *adj.* неутоми́мый.

unrestrained [ˌʌnrɪˈstreɪnd] *adj.* несде́ржанный; необу́зданный; непринуждённый.

unrestricted [ˌʌnrɪˈstrɪktɪd] *adj.* неограни́ченный.

unrewarded [ˌʌnrɪˈwɔːdɪd] *adj.* невознаграждённый; **his efforts were ~ by success** его́ уси́лия не увенча́лись успе́хом.

unrewarding [ˌʌnrɪˈwɔːdɪŋ] *adj.* неблагода́рный.

unriddle [ʌnˈrɪd(ə)l] *v.t.* разга́д|ывать, -а́ть; объясн|я́ть, -и́ть.

unrighteous [ʌnˈraɪtʃəs] *adj.* несправедли́вый, непра́ведный; (*bibl.*) нечести́вый.

unrighteousness [ʌnˈraɪtʃəsnɪs] *n.* несправедли́вость, непра́ведность; нечести́вость.

unripe [ʌnˈraɪp] *adj.* неспе́лый, незре́лый (*also fig.*).

unrisen [ʌnˈrɪz(ə)n] *adj.*: **~ bread** не подня́вшийся хлеб.

unrivalled [ʌnˈraɪv(ə)ld] *adj.* непревзойдённый; вне конкуре́нции; **an ~ opportunity** уника́льная возмо́жность.

unroll [ʌnˈrəʊl] *v.t.* & *i.* развёр|тывать(ся), -ну́ть(ся).

unromantic [ˌʌnrəˈmæntɪk] *adj.* нероманти́ческий, нероманти́чный.

unruffled [ʌnˈrʌf(ə)ld] *adj.* гла́дкий, споко́йный; (*fig.*) невозмути́мый.

unruliness [ʌnˈruːlɪnɪs] *n.* непоко́рность, непослуша́ние.

unruly [ʌnˈruːlɪ] *adj.* непоко́рный, непослу́шный; бу́йный, бу́рный.

unsaddle [ʌnˈsæd(ə)l] *v.t.* рассёдл|ывать, -а́ть.

unsafe [ʌnˈseɪf] *adj.* риско́ванный, ненадёжный, опа́сный.

unsaid [ʌnˈsed] *adj.*: **some things are better left ~** есть ве́щи, о кото́рых лу́чше умолча́ть (*or* не говори́ть).

unsalaried [ʌnˈsælərɪd] *adj.* не получа́ющий (*or* без) жа́лованья/зарпла́ты.

unsaleable [ʌnˈseɪləb(ə)l] *adj.* нехо́дкий, не коти́рующийся.

unsatisfactory [ˌʌnsætɪsˈfæktərɪ] *adj.* неудовлетвори́тельный, неудовлетворя́ющий.

unsatisfied [ʌnˈsætɪsˌfaɪd] *adj.* неудовлетворённый; **I am ~with the results** я не удовлетворён результа́тами.

unsaturated [ʌnˈsætʃəˌreɪtɪd, -tjʊˌreɪtɪd] *adj.* ненасы́щенный.

unsavoury [ʌnˈseɪvərɪ] *adj.* (*lit.*) невку́сный; (*fig.*) неприя́тный, неприглядный; **an ~ reputation** дурна́я сла́ва; сомни́тельная репута́ция.

unsay [ʌnˈseɪ] *v.t.* брать, взять (*свои слова*) наза́д.

unscalable [ʌnˈskeɪləb(ə)l] *adj.* непристу́пный.

unscathed [ʌnˈskeɪðd] *adj.* невреди́мый; (*pred.*) цел и невреди́м.

unscheduled [ʌnˈʃedjuːld] *adj.* незаплани́рованный; **an ~ flight** полёт вне расписа́ния.

unscholarly [ʌnˈskɒləlɪ] *adj.* неэруди́рованный; не сво́йственный учёному, недосто́йный учёного.

unscientific [ˌʌnsaɪənˈtɪfɪk] *adj.* ненау́чный.

unscramble [ʌnˈskræmb(ə)l] *v.t.* **1.** (*teleph. conversation*) раскоди́ровать (*impf., pf.*). **2.** (*coll., analyse, sort out*) расшифро́в|ывать, -а́ть; разъясн|я́ть, -и́ть; раз|бира́ть, -обра́ть.

unscrew [ʌnˈskruː] *v.t.* & *i.* отви́н|чивать(ся), -ти́ть(ся); разви́н|чивать(ся), -ти́ть(ся).

unscripted [ʌnˈskrɪptɪd] *adj.*: **an ~ talk** импровизи́рованное выступле́ние.

unscrupulous [ʌnˈskruːpjʊləs] *adj.* беспринци́пный, недобросо́вестный.

unscrupulousness [ʌnˈskruːpjʊləsnɪs] *n.* беспринци́пность, недобросо́вестность.

unseal [ʌnˈsiːl] *v.t.* распеча́т|ывать, -ать; вскры|ва́ть, -ть.

unsealed [ʌnˈsiːld] *adj.*: **an ~ envelope** незапеча́танный конве́рт.

unseasonable [ʌnˈsiːzənəb(ə)l] *adj.* не по сезо́ну; **~ weather** пого́да не по сезо́ну; (*fig., untimely*) несвоевре́менный, неуме́стный, неуро́чный.

unseasoned [ʌnˈsiːz(ə)nd] *adj.*: **~ food** неприпра́вленная еда́; **~ timber** невы́держанная древеси́на; (*fig., inexperienced*) неприу́ченный, необстре́лянный.

unseat [ʌnˈsiːt] *v.t.* сса́|живать, -ди́ть; ст|а́лкивать, -олкну́ть; **the horse ~ed its rider** ло́шадь сбро́сила седока́; (*fig.*): **he was ~ed at the last election** его́ лиши́ли парла́ментского манда́та на после́дних вы́борах.

unseated [ʌnˈsiːtɪd] *adj.* (*standing*) стоя́щий, сто́я; без ме́ста; **he remained ~** он остава́лся на нога́х.

unseaworthiness [ʌnˈsiːˌwɜːðɪnɪs] *n.* неприго́дность к пла́ванию, неморехо́дность.

unseaworthy [ʌnˈsiːˌwɜːðɪ] *adj.* неприго́дный к пла́ванию.

unsecured [ˌʌnsɪˈkjʊəd] *adj.* (*of a box, parcel etc.*) незакреплённый, neза́пертый; (*of loan etc.*) необеспе́ченный, негаранти́рованный.

unseeing [ʌnˈsiːɪŋ] *adj.* незря́чий, неви́дящий.

unseemliness [ʌnˈsiːmlɪnɪs] *n.* непристо́йность, неприли́чие.

unseemly [ʌnˈsiːmlɪ] *adj.* неподоба́ющий, непристо́йный, неприли́чный.

unseen [ʌnˈsiːn] *n.* **1.: the ~** (*spiritual world*) духо́вный мир. **2.** (*translation*) перево́д с листа́.

adj. неви́димый, неви́данный; ~ **dangers** скры́тые опа́сности; **he remained** ~ он остава́лся незаме́ченным.
unselective [ˌʌnsɪˈlektɪv] *adj.* неразбо́рчивый.
unselfish [ʌnˈselfɪʃ] *adj.* бескоры́стный, самоотве́рженный.
unselfishness [ʌnˈselfɪʃnɪs] *n.* бескоры́стие; самоотве́рженность.
unserviceable [ʌnˈsɜːvɪsəb(ə)l] *adj.* него́дный, неиспра́вный.
unsettle [ʌnˈset(ə)l] *v.t.* (*fig.*) выбива́ть, вы́бить из коле́й; расстр|а́ивать, -о́ить.
unsettled [ʌnˈset(ə)ld] *adj.* неусто́йчивый; беспоко́йный; ~ **weather** неусто́йчивая пого́да; **an** ~ **account** незапла́ченный счёт; **the argument was** ~ спор не́ был решён; ~ **territory** незаселённая террито́рия.
unshackle [ʌnˈʃæk(ə)l] *v.t.* сн|има́ть, -ять кандалы́ c+*g.*; освобо|жда́ть, -ди́ть.
unshaded [ʌnˈʃeɪdɪd] *adj.* без те́ни; незаслонённый; (*without curtains or blinds*) незаве́шенный; без што́р; (*of a lamp*) без абажу́ра; (*without hatching*) незаштрихо́ванный.
unshadowed [ʌnˈʃædəʊd] *adj.* (*fig.*): ~ **prosperity** безо́блачное благополу́чие.
unshakeable [ʌnˈʃeɪkəb(ə)l] *adj.* непоколеби́мый.
unshaken [ʌnˈʃeɪkən] *adj.* (*resolute*) непоколе́бленный.
unshaven [ʌnˈʃeɪv(ə)n] *adj.* небри́тый.
unsheathe [ʌnˈʃiːð] *v.t.* вынима́ть, вы́нуть из но́жен; **he** ~**d his sword** он обнажи́л меч.
unsheltered [ʌnˈʃeltəd] *adj.* неприкры́тый, незащищённый.
unship [ʌnˈʃɪp] *v.t.* **1.** (*unload*) выгружа́ть, вы́грузить. **2.**: **they** ~**ped the mast** они́ убра́ли ма́чту.
unshod [ʌnˈʃɒd] *adj.* босо́й, необу́тый; (*of horse*) неподко́ванный.
unshrinkable [ʌnˈʃrɪŋkəb(ə)l] *adj.* безуса́дочный.
unshrinking [ʌnˈʃrɪŋkɪŋ] *adj.* (*intrepid*) непоколеби́мый, неустраши́мый.
unsifted [ʌnˈsɪftɪd] *adj.* (*lit.*) непросе́янный; (*fig.*, *of evidence etc.*) непросмо́тренный, нерассмо́тренный, непроанализи́рованный.
unsighted [ʌnˈsaɪtɪd] *adj.* (*of gun*) не име́ющий (*or* без) прице́ла; (*of shot*) неприце́льный.
unsightliness [ʌnˈsaɪtlɪnɪs] *n.* уро́дливость, непригля́дность.
unsightly [ʌnˈsaɪtlɪ] *adj.* некраси́вый, уро́дливый, непригля́дный.
unsigned [ʌnˈsaɪnd] *adj.* неподпи́санный.
unsisterly [ʌnˈsɪstəlɪ] *adj.* неподоба́ющий сестре́.
unskilful [ʌnˈskɪlfʊl] *adj.* неуме́лый, неиску́сный, неуклю́жий.
unskilfulness [ʌnˈskɪlfʊlnɪs] *n.* неуме́лость, неиску́сность, неуклю́жесть.
unskilled [ʌnˈskɪld] *adj.* неквалифици́рованный.
unsleeping [ʌnˈsliːpɪŋ] *adj.* неусы́пный, недре́млющий.
unsociability [ʌnˌsəʊʃəˈbɪlɪtɪ] *n.* необщи́тельность, нелюди́мость.
unsociable [ʌnˈsəʊʃəb(ə)l] *adj.* необщи́тельный, нелюди́мый.
unsocial [ʌnˈsəʊʃ(ə)l] *adj.* (*not given to association*) необщи́тельный; (*anti-social*) антиобще́ственный; ~ **hours (of work)** не общепри́нятые часы́ рабо́ты.
unsold [ʌnˈsəʊld] *adj.* непро́данный; залежа́вшийся.
unsoldierly [ʌnˈsəʊldʒəlɪ] *adj.* недосто́йный солда́та.
unsolicited [ˌʌnsəˈlɪsɪtɪd] *adj.* предоста́вленный/да́нный доброво́льно; непро́шенный.
unsolved [ʌnˈsɒlvd] *adj.* нерешённый, неразга́данный.
unsophisticated [ˌʌnsəˈfɪstɪˌkeɪtɪd] *adj.* просто́й, простоду́шный; безыску́сный; наи́вный, бесхи́тростный.
unsought [ʌnˈsɔːt] *adj.* непро́шенный.
unsound [ʌnˈsaʊnd] *adj.* (*bad, rotten*) испо́рченный, гнило́й; (*unwholesome*) нездоро́вый; (*unstable*) ша́ткий, непро́чный, нетвёрдый; ~ **views** неве́рные/необосно́ванные взгля́ды; **of** ~ **mind** душевнобольно́й; **a man of** ~ **judgement** челове́к, лишённый здра́вого смы́сла.
unsown [ʌnˈsəʊn] *adj.* незасе́янный.
unsparing [ʌnˈspeərɪŋ] *adj.* ще́дрый; усе́рдный; ~ **in his efforts** не щадя́щий сил; ~ **of praise** ще́дрый на похвалу́.
unspeakable [ʌnˈspiːkəb(ə)l] *adj.* невырази́мый; отврати́тельный; ~ **joy** невырази́мая ра́дость; **he is an** ~ **bore** он ужа́сный зану́да.
unspecialized [ʌnˈspeʃəˌlaɪzd] *adj.* неспециализи́рованный.
unspecified [ʌnˈspesɪˌfaɪd] *adj.* то́чно не определённый/ука́занный/устано́вленный.
unspent [ʌnˈspent] *adj.* (*of money*) неистра́ченный.
unspoil|ed [ʌnˈspɔɪld], **-t** [ʌnˈspɔɪlt] *adj.* неиспо́рченный; (*of pers.*) неизбало́ванный.
unspoken [ʌnˈspəʊkən] *adj.* невы́сказанный.
unsport|ing [ʌnˈspɔːtɪŋ], **-smanlike** [ʌnˈspɔːtsmənˌlaɪk] *adjs.* нече́стный; недосто́йный спортсме́на; **he behaved unsportingly** он вёл себя́ неспорти́вно.
unspotted [ʌnˈspɒtɪd] *adj.* (*fig.*): ~ **reputation** незапя́тнанная репута́ция.
unsprung [ʌnˈsprʌŋ] *adj.* безрессо́рный, без рессо́р.
unstable [ʌnˈsteɪb(ə)l] *adj.* нетвёрдый, неусто́йчивый; (*fig.*) изме́нчивый; **an** ~ **personality** неуравнове́шенная ли́чность.
unstained [ʌnˈsteɪnd] *adj.* (*fig.*) незапя́тнанный.
unstamped [ʌnˈstæmpt] *adj.*: **an** ~ **letter** письмо́ без ма́рки.
unstatesmanlike [ʌnˈsteɪtsmənˌlaɪk] *adj.* неподоба́ющий госуда́рственному де́ятелю.
unsteadiness [ʌnˈstedɪnɪs] *n.* неусто́йчивость, ша́ткость; непостоя́нство, изме́нчивость.
unsteady [ʌnˈstedɪ] *adj.* нетвёрдый; неусто́йчивый, ша́ткий; **the table was** ~ стол шата́лся; **he was** ~ **on his legs** он нетвёрдо стоя́л/держа́лся на нога́х; он шёл, шата́ясь; (*of character*) непостоя́нный, изме́нчивый.
unstick [ʌnˈstɪk] *v.t.* откле́и|вать, -ть.
unstinted [ʌnˈstɪntɪd] *adj.* (*limitless*) ще́дрый; безграни́чный, безме́рный.
unstinting [ʌnˈstɪntɪŋ] *adj.* (*generous*) ще́дрый.
unstop [ʌnˈstɒp] *v.t.*: **the plumber** ~**ped the pipe** водопрово́дчик прочи́стил трубу́.
unstrained [ʌnˈstreɪnd] *adj.* (*of liquids*) непроце́женный; (*effortless, spontaneous*) непринуждённый.
unstrap [ʌnˈstræp] *v.t.* отстёг|ивать, -ну́ть; расстёг|ивать, -ну́ть.
unstressed [ʌnˈstrest] *adj.* (*without emphasis*) неподчёркнутый; (*phon.*) безуда́рный.
unstrung [ʌnˈstrʌŋ] *adj.*: **an** ~ **violin** скри́пка с ненатя́нутыми стру́нами; (*fig.*): **he was** ~ он си́льно расстро́ился.
unstuck [ʌnˈstʌk] *adj.* откле́енный, ото́дранный; **the stamp came** ~ ма́рка откле́илась; (*fig.*, *coll.*): **my schemes came** ~ мои́ пла́ны провали́лись.
unstudied [ʌnˈstʌdɪd] *adj.* (*not learnt*) невы́ученный; (*unaffected*) непринуждённый.
unsubstantial [ˌʌnsəbˈstænʃ(ə)l] *adj.* несуще́ственный, нереа́льный; **an** ~ **dinner** несы́тный обе́д.
unsubstantiated [ˌʌnsəbˈstænʃɪˌeɪtɪd] *adj.* недока́занный, неподтверждённый, необосно́ванный.
unsuccessful [ˌʌnsəkˈsesfʊl] *adj.* безуспе́шный, неуда́чный; **he was** ~ **in the exam** он не вы́держал экза́мена.
unsuitability [ʌnˌsuːtəˈbɪlɪtɪ, ʌnˈsjuː-] *n.* неприго́дность.
unsuitable [ʌnˈsuːtəb(ə)l, ʌnˈsjuː-] *adj.* неподходя́щий, неприго́дный.
unsuited [ʌnˈsuːtɪd, ʌnˈsjuː-] *adj.* неподходя́щий; **he is** ~ **to the post** он не подхо́дит/годи́тся для э́той до́лжности.
unsullied [ʌnˈsʌlɪd] *adj.* (*fig.*) незапя́тнанный.
unsung [ʌnˈsʌŋ] *adj.*: **an** ~ **hero** геро́й, невоспе́тый поэ́том.
unsure [ʌnˈʃʊə(r), ʌnˈʃɔː(r)] *adj.* ненадёжный; неуве́ренный; **he is** ~ **on his feet** он нетвёрдо стои́т/де́ржится на нога́х; **he was** ~ **of his ground** он не чу́вствовал твёрдой по́чвы под нога́ми; он не чу́вствовал себя́ компете́нтным; **I am** ~ **if he will come** я не уве́рен, что он придёт; ~ **of o.s.** неуве́ренный в себе́.
unsurpass|able [ˌʌnsəˈpɑːsəb(ə)l], **-ed** [ˌʌnsəˈpɑːst] *adjs.* непревзойдённый.
unsuspected [ˌʌnsəˈspektɪd] *adj.* неподозрева́емый, незаподо́зренный.
unsusp|ecting [ˌʌnsəˈspektɪŋ], **-icious** [ˌʌnsəˈspɪʃəs] *adjs.* неподозрева́ющий, дове́рчивый.
unswayed [ʌnˈsweɪd] *adj.*: ~ **by public opinion** не подда́вшийся влия́нию обще́ственного мне́ния.
unswerving [ʌnˈswɜːvɪŋ] *adj.* (*fig.*) непоколеби́мый.

unsympathetic [ˌʌnsɪmpəˈθetɪk] *adj.* чёрствый, несочу́вствующий.
unsystematic [ˌʌnsɪstəˈmætɪk] *adj.* несистемати́ческий, несистемати́чный.
untameable [ʌnˈteɪməb(ə)l] *adj.* неукроти́мый; необу́зданный; (*of animal*) не поддаю́щийся прируче́нию.
untamed [ʌnˈteɪmd] *adj.* (*of animal*) неприру́ченный; (*of passion*) необу́зданный; (*of territory*) ди́кий.
untangle [ʌnˈtæŋg(ə)l] *v.t.* распу́т|ывать, -ать; **she ~d the wool** она́ распу́тала клубо́к ше́рсти; (*fig.*): **the confusion was finally ~d** в конце концо́в удало́сь разобра́ться в э́той пу́танице.
untanned [ʌnˈtænd] *adj.* (*of leather*) недублёный; (*by the sun*) незагоре́вший, незагоре́лый.
untarnished [ʌnˈtɑːnɪʃt] *adj.* непотускне́вший; (*fig.*) незапя́тнанный; **his honour was ~** его́ честь оста́лась незапя́тнанной/безупре́чной.
untasted [ʌnˈteɪstɪd] *adj.*: **he left the food ~** он не притро́нулся к еде́.
untaught [ʌnˈtɔːt] *adj.* (*uneducated*) неве́жественный, необразо́ванный; (*spontaneous*) врождённый, инстинкти́вный, есте́ственный.
untaxed [ʌnˈtækst] *adj.* свобо́дный от нало́гов; не обло́женный нало́гом.
unteachable [ʌnˈtiːtʃəb(ə)l] *adj.* (*of pers.*) не поддаю́щийся обуче́нию.
untempered [ʌnˈtempəd] *adj.* **1.: ~ steel** незакалённая сталь. **2.** (*fig.*) неуме́ренный, несмягчённый.
untenable [ʌnˈtenəb(ə)l] *adj.* несостоя́тельный, неприе́млемый; **~ arguments** неубеди́тельные до́воды; **an ~ position** (*mil.*) незащити́мая/невы́годная пози́ция.
untenanted [ʌnˈtenəntɪd] *adj.* пусто́й, нежило́й, незаселённый.
untended [ʌnˈtendɪd] *adj.* забро́шенный, неухо́женный.
untether [ʌnˈteðə(r)] *v.t.* отвя́з|ывать, -а́ть.
unthinkable [ʌnˈθɪŋkəb(ə)l] *adj.* (*unimaginable*) невообрази́мый, немы́слимый; (*inadmissible*) недопусти́мый; (*incredible*) невероя́тный.
unthinking [ʌnˈθɪŋkɪŋ] *adj.* (*thoughtless*) безду́мный; (*inadvertent*) неча́янный; машина́льный.
unthought-of [ʌnˈθɔːtɒv] *adj.* непредви́денный, неожи́данный.
unthread [ʌnˈθred] *v.t.*: **~ a needle** вынима́ть, вы́нуть ни́тку из иго́лки.
unthrifty [ʌnˈθrɪftɪ] *adj.* расточи́тельный, небере́жливый.
untidiness [ʌnˈtaɪdɪnɪs] *n.* неопря́тность, неаккура́тность.
untidy [ʌnˈtaɪdɪ] *adj.* неопря́тный, неаккура́тный; **an ~ person** неря́ха (*c.g.*); **his room was ~** его́ ко́мната была́ неу́брана; в его́ ко́мнате цари́л беспоря́док.
untie [ʌnˈtaɪ] *v.t.* развя́з|ывать, -а́ть; отвя́з|ывать, -а́ть; расшнуро́в|ывать, -а́ть.
until [ənˈtɪl, ʌn-] = **till; unless and ~** то́лько когда́/е́сли.
untimeliness [ʌnˈtaɪmlɪnɪs] *n.* преждевре́менность, несвоевре́менность; неуме́стность.
untimely [ʌnˈtaɪmlɪ] *adj.* (*premature*) преждевре́менный; (*unseasonable*) несвоевре́менный; (*ill-timed, inappropriate*) неуме́стный.
untinged [ʌnˈtɪndʒd] *adj.*: **~ by remorse** без следа́ раская́ния.
untiring [ʌnˈtaɪərɪŋ] *adj.* неутоми́мый, неосла́бный, неуста́нный.
unto [ˈʌntʊ, ˈʌntə] (*arch.*) = **to**
untold [ʌnˈtəʊld] *adj.* **1.** (*not told*) нерасска́занный; **he left his secret ~** он у́мер, так и не откры́в свою та́йну. **2.** (*inestimable*) бессчётный; **~ wealth** несме́тные бога́тства.
untouchable [ʌnˈtʌtʃəb(ə)l] *n.* неприкаса́емый, хариджа́н.
adj. (*unattainable*) недосяга́емый, недосту́пный; (*impossible to compete with*) недосяга́емый.
untouched [ʌnˈtʌtʃt] *adj.* нетро́нутый; **fruit ~ by hand** фру́кты, к кото́рым не прикаса́лись рука́ми; **his reserves were ~** он не прикосну́лся к свои́м запа́сам.
untoward [ˌʌntəˈwɔːd, ʌnˈtəʊəd] *adj.* (*inconvenient; adverse*) неблагоприя́тный; неуда́чный; **nothing ~ happened** ничего́ плохо́го не случи́лось; никаки́х неприя́тностей не́ было.
untraceable [ʌnˈtreɪsəb(ə)l] *adj.* непросле́живаемый; **his relatives were ~** не удало́сь напа́сть на след его́ ро́дственников.
untrained [ʌnˈtreɪnd] *adj.* необу́ченный, неквалифици́рованный, неподгото́вленный, нетрениро́ванный.
untrammelled [ʌnˈtræm(ə)ld] *adj.* несвя́занный, нско́ванный, свобо́дный.
untransferable [ˌʌntrænsˈfɜːrəb(ə)l, ˌʌntrɑːns-, ʌnˈt-] *adj.* без пра́ва переда́чи.
untranslatable [ˌʌntrænsˈleɪtəb(ə)l, ˌʌntrɑːn-, -zˈleɪtəb(ə)l] *adj.* непереводи́мый.
untravelled [ʌnˈtræv(ə)ld] *adj.* не/ма́ло е́здивший по све́ту; **~ wastes** неизве́данные пусты́ни.
untried [ʌnˈtraɪd] *adj.* (*inexperienced*) нео́пытный; (*untested*) неиспы́танный, непрове́ренный.
untrodden [ʌnˈtrɒd(ə)n] *adj.* неисхо́женный, нетро́нутый.
untroubled [ʌnˈtrʌb(ə)ld] *adj.* необеспоко́йный, невозмути́мый, споко́йный.
untrue [ʌnˈtruː] *adj.* (*inaccurate*) неве́рный, ло́жный, непра́вильный; (*unfaithful*) неве́рный.
untrustworthiness [ʌnˈtrʌstˌwɜːðɪnɪs] *n.* ненадёжность.
untrustworthy [ʌnˈtrʌstˌwɜːðɪ] *adj.* (*unreliable*) ненадёжный; (*undeserving of confidence*) не заслу́живающий дове́рия.
untruth [ʌnˈtruːθ] *n.* непра́вда, ложь; **he told an ~** он солга́л; он сказа́л непра́вду.
untruthful [ʌnˈtruːθfʊl] *adj.* (*of thg.*) неве́рный, ло́жный; (*of pers. or thg.*) лжи́вый.
untruthfulness [ʌnˈtruːθfʊlnɪs] *n.* неве́рность, ло́жность, лжи́вость.
untutored [ʌnˈtjuːtəd] *adj.* необу́ченный; инстинкти́вный.
untwine [ʌnˈtwaɪn] *v.t.* распу́т|ывать, -ать; расплe|та́ть, -сти́.
untwist [ʌnˈtwɪst] *v.t.* раскру́|чивать, -ти́ть.
unusable [ʌnˈjuːzəb(ə)l] *adj.* неприго́дный, неподходя́щий.
unused[1] [ʌnˈjuːzd] *adj.* (*not put to use*) неиспо́льзованный; **my ticket was ~** я не испо́льзовал свой биле́т.
unused[2] [ʌnˈjuːst] *adj.* (*unaccustomed*) непривы́кший (к+*d.*); **I am ~ to this** я к э́тому не привы́к.
unusual [ʌnˈjuːʒʊəl] *adj.* необыкнове́нный, необы́чный; **~ly** осо́бенно, исключи́тельно.
unutterable [ʌnˈʌtərəb(ə)l] *adj.* невырази́мый, несказа́нный, неопису́емый.
unvalued [ʌnˈvæljuːd] *adj.* (*not subjected to valuation*) неоценённый; (*unesteemed*) недооценённый.
unvaried [ʌnˈveərɪd] *adj.* неизме́нный, постоя́нный, однообра́зный.
unvarnished [ʌnˈvɑːnɪʃt] *adj.* (*fig.*): **the ~ truth** неприкра́шенная/го́лая пра́вда.
unvarying [ʌnˈveərɪɪŋ] *adj.* неизменя́ющийся, неизме́нный.
unveil [ʌnˈveɪl] *v.t.*: **the statue was ~ed on Sunday** торже́ственное откры́тие па́мятника состоя́лось в воскресе́нье; **he ~ed his designs** он раскры́л свои́ пла́ны.
unverifiable [ʌnˈverɪˌfaɪəb(ə)l] *adj.* не поддаю́щийся прове́рке.
unverified [ʌnˈverɪˌfaɪd] *adj.* непрове́ренный.
unversed [ʌnˈvɜːst] *adj.* несве́дующий (*в чём*), неискушённый (*в чём*); **he is ~ in mathematics** он профа́н в матема́тике.
unvoiced [ʌnˈvɔɪst] *adj.* невы́сказанный; (*phon.*) глухо́й.
unwanted [ʌnˈwɒntɪd] *adj.* нежела́нный, непро́шенный; **an ~ child** нежела́нный ребёнок; **they made me feel ~** они́ да́ли мне почу́вствовать, что я ли́шний среди́ них.
unwariness [ʌnˈweərɪnɪs] *n.* неосмотри́тельность, неосторо́жность.
unwarlike [ʌnˈwɔːlaɪk] *adj.* невои́нственный, миролюби́вый.
unwarrantable [ʌnˈwɒrəntəb(ə)l] *adj.* неопра́вданный, недопусти́мый.
unwarranted [ʌnˈwɒrəntɪd] *adj.* недозво́ленный; неразрешённый; необосно́ванный.
unwary [ʌnˈweərɪ] *adj.* неосмотри́тельный, неосторо́жный.
unwashed [ʌnˈwɒʃt] *adj.* немы́тый; нести́ранный.
unwatered [ʌnˈwɔːtəd] *adj.* **1.** (*e.g. desert*) неороша́емый. **2.: ~ plants** неполи́тые цветы́. **3.** (*undiluted*) неразба́вленный.
unwavering [ʌnˈweɪvərɪŋ] *adj.* непоколеби́мый; неизме́нный; твёрдый.
unweaned [ʌnˈwiːnd] *adj.* не о́тнятый от гру́ди.
unwearable [ʌnˈweərəb(ə)l] *adj.* него́дный для но́ски.

unwear|ied [ʌn'wɪərɪd], **-ying** [ʌn'wɪərɪɪŋ] *adjs.* неутоми́мый; насто́йчивый, неуста́нный.
unwedded [ʌn'wedɪd] *adj.* незаму́жняя; ~ **wife** неве́нчанная жена́.
unwelcome [ʌn'welkəm] *adj.* неприя́тный; нежела́тельный; **he is ~ here** он здесь ли́шний; его́ прису́тствие здесь нежела́тельно.
unwell [ʌn'wel] *adj.* нездоро́вый; **I felt ~** мне нездоро́вилось; **I have been ~** я был нездоро́в.
unwept [ʌn'wept] *adj.* неопла́канный; невы́плаканный.
unwholesome [ʌn'həʊlsəm] *adj.* нездоро́вый, вре́дный.
unwieldiness [ʌn'wiːldɪnɪs] *n.* громо́здкость, тяжелове́сность.
unwieldy [ʌn'wiːldɪ] *adj.* громо́здкий, тяжелове́сный.
unwifely [ʌn'waɪflɪ] *adj.* не подоба́ющий супру́ге.
unwilling [ʌn'wɪlɪŋ] *adj.* нежела́ющий; нескло́нный; нерасполо́женный; **he was ~ to agree** он не пожела́л согласи́ться; ~**ly** неохо́тно.
unwind [ʌn'waɪnd] *v.t.* & *i.* разм|а́тывать(ся), -ота́ть(ся); раскру́|чивать(ся), -ти́ть(ся); (*fig.*): **as the plot ~s** по ме́ре разви́тия сюже́та; **the drink helped him to ~** вино́ помогло́ ему́ рассла́биться.
unwinking [ʌn'wɪŋkɪŋ] *adj.* (*fig.*) бди́тельный.
unwisdom [ʌn'wɪzdəm] *n.* неблагоразу́мие.
unwise [ʌn'waɪz] *adj.* не(благо)разу́мный.
unwished-for [ʌn'wɪʃt] *adj.* нежела́нный.
unwitting [ʌn'wɪtɪŋ] *adj.* неча́янный.
unwomanly [ʌn'wʊmənlɪ] *adj.* неже́нский, неже́нственный.
unwonted [ʌn'wəʊntɪd] *adj.* (*liter.*) неприв́ычный, необы́чный.
unworkable [ʌn'wɜːkəb(ə)l] *adj.* нереа́льный, неосуществи́мый, неисполни́мый.
unworldly [ʌn'wɜːldlɪ] *adj.* неземно́й, не от ми́ра сего́; (*disinterested*) бескоры́стный; (*unsophisticated*) наи́вный, безыску́сственный.
unworn [ʌn'wɔːn] *adj.* (*never worn*) нено́шенный; (*not showing wear*) неизно́шенный.
unworthy [ʌn'wɜːðɪ] *adj.* (*undeserving*) недосто́йный (*кого/чего*); (*base*) по́длый, ни́зкий; **an ~ suspicion** гну́сное подозре́ние.
unwound [ʌn'waʊnd] *adj.* незаведённый; размо́танный.
unwrap [ʌn'ræp] *v.t.* разв|ора́чивать, (*or* разв|ёртывать), -ерну́ть.
unwritten [ʌn'rɪt(ə)n] *adj.*: **an ~ law** непи́саный зако́н.
unwrought [ʌn'rɔːt] *adj.* необрабо́танный.
unyielding [ʌn'jiːldɪŋ] *adj.* непреклóнный, упо́рный.
unyoke [ʌn'jəʊk] *v.t.* выпряга́ть, вы́прячь из ярма́.
unzip [ʌn'zɪp] *v.t.* расстёг|ивать, -ну́ть; раскр|ыва́ть, -ы́ть.
up [ʌp] *n.*: **~s and downs** (*of fortune*) взлёты (*m. pl.*) и паде́ния (*nt. pl.*); превра́тности (*f. pl.*) судьбы́; **his career has had its ~s and downs** в его́ карье́ре бы́ли взлёты (*m. pl.*) и паде́ния; **business is on the ~ and ~** дела́ пошли́ в го́ру.
adj.: **on the ~ stroke** (*of piston*) при хо́де (по́ршня) вверх; **~ train** по́езд, иду́щий в Ло́ндон.
adv. **1.** (*in a high or higher position*) вверх, наве́рх; **high ~ in the sky** высоко́ в не́бе; **'this side ~'** «верх!»; **they live 3 floors ~ from us** они́ живу́т тремя́ этажа́ми вы́ше нас; **she had her umbrella ~** зо́нтик у неё был раскры́т; **the window was ~** окно́ бы́ло откры́то; **the blinds were ~** што́ры бы́ли по́дняты; **the notice was ~ on the board** на доске́ висе́ло объявле́ние; **they played 101 ~** они́ игра́ли до ста одного́ очка́; **his spirits were ~ one minute, down the next** у него́ беспреста́нно меня́лось настрое́ние; **prices are ~ and will stay ~** це́ны подняли́сь и уже́ бо́льше не упаду́т; (*advanced*): **he was ~ in the lead** он был среди́ пе́рвых; **he is 20 points ~ on his opponent** он впереди́ проти́вника на два́дцать очко́в; **he is well ~ in his subject** он прекра́сно зна́ет свой предме́т; (*with greater intensity*): **sing ~! speak ~!** гро́мче!; (*at univ.*): **he is ~ at Oxford** он у́чится в О́ксфорде. **2.** (*into a higher position*) вверх; **hands ~!** ру́ки вверх!; (*~wards*) вы́ше, бо́льше; **children from the age of 12 ~** де́ти двена́дцати лет и ста́рше; (*expr. support*): **~ (with) the workers!** да здра́вствуют рабо́чие! **3.** (*out of bed; standing; active*): **he was ~ on his feet at once** он момента́льно вскочи́л на́ ноги; **I must be ~ and doing** мне пора́ приня́ться за рабо́ту; **he was already ~ when I called** когда́ я пришёл, он уже́ встал; **she was soon ~ and about again** она́ вско́ре опра́вилась; **I was ~ all night with the baby** я всю ночь провози́лся с ребёнком; **I was ~ late last night** я вчера́ о́чень по́здно лёг; я вчера́ до́лго не ложи́лся; **the house is not ~ (*built*) yet** дом ещё не постро́ен. **4.** (*roused*): **his blood was ~** он был взбешён; **they were ~ in arms against the new proposal** они́ встре́тили но́вое предложе́ние в штыки́. **5.** (*of agenda*): **the house is ~ for sale** дом продаётся; **he was ~ for trial** он находи́лся под судо́м; **the case was ~ before the court** де́ло рассма́тривалось в суде́. **6.** (*expr. completion or expiry*): **time's ~** вре́мя истекло́; **when is your leave ~?** когда́ конча́ется ваш о́тпуск?; **it's all ~ with them** с ни́ми всё ко́нчено; **the game is ~!** ка́рта би́та! **7.** (*coll., happening; amiss*): **what's ~?** в чём де́ло?; что тут происхо́дит?; **there's something ~ with the radio** (радио)приёмник барахли́т (*or* не в поря́дке). **8. ~ against** (*in contact with*): **the table was (right) ~ against the wall** стол стоя́л у стены́ (*or* вплотну́ю к стене́); (*confronted by*): **you are ~ against stiff opposition** вы име́ете де́ло с упо́рным сопротивле́нием; **he was ~ against it** он был в тру́дном положе́нии. **9. ~ to** (*equal to*): **I don't feel ~ to it** я не чу́вствую себя́ в си́лах; **he is not ~ to his work** он не справля́ется с рабо́той; (*on a par with*): **the book is ~ to expectations** кни́га оправда́ет ожида́ния; (*as far as*) до+*g.*; **~ to, ~ till now** до сих пор; **the book was brought ~ to date** в кни́гу включи́ли все после́дние да́нные; **I am ~ to chapter 3** я дочита́л до тре́тьей главы́; **he was in the affair ~ to his neck** он в э́том де́ле увя́з по са́мые у́шки; **his work is not ~ to scratch** его́ рабо́та оставля́ет жела́ть лу́чшего; (*incumbent upon*): **it is ~ to us to help** э́то мы должны́ помо́чь; **it's ~ to you now** тепе́рь реша́ть вам; тепе́рь э́то от вас зави́сит; (*occupied with*): **what is he ~ to?** чем он занима́ется?; что там у него́ происхо́дит?; **what are the children ~ to?** что там де́ти зате́яли?; **he is ~ to no good** он замы́слил что́-то недо́брое; он него́дник.
prep.: **they live ~ the hill** они́ живу́т на горе́/холме́; **he ran ~ the hill** он взбежа́л на́ гору, на хо́лм; **the cat was ~ a tree** кот взобра́лся на де́рево; **he went ~ the stairs** он подня́лся по ле́стнице; **they live ~ (*further along*) the street** они́ живу́т по/на э́той у́лице; **he is known ~ and down the land** его́ зна́ют по всей стране́.
v.i. (*coll.*): **she ~(ped) and said ...** она́ взяла́ и сказа́ла...
up-and-coming [ˌʌpən'kʌmɪŋ] *adj.* подаю́щий наде́жды; перспекти́вный, многообеща́ющий.
upas ['juːpəs] *n.* анча́р.
upbeat ['ʌpbiːt] *n.* сла́бая до́ля та́кта.
upbraid [ʌp'breɪd] *v.t.* укор|я́ть, -и́ть; порица́ть (*impf.*); брани́ть, вы-.
upbringing ['ʌpˌbrɪŋɪŋ] *n.* воспита́ние.
up-country [ʌp'kʌntrɪ, 'ʌp-] *adj.* вну́тренний.
adv. внутри́ страны́; во вну́тренних райо́нах страны́; (*expr. direction*) вглубь страны́.
update [ʌp'deɪt] *v.t.* модернизи́ровать (*impf., pf.*); пересмотре́ть и допо́лнить (*both pf.*) (*книгу*); ревизова́ть (*impf., pf.*).
up-end [ʌp'end] *v.t.* поста́вить (*pf.*) перпендикуля́рно (*or coll.* «на попа́»).
upgrade ['ʌpgreɪd] *n.* подъём; **on the ~** на подъёме.
v.t. пов|ыша́ть, -ы́сить в до́лжности; придава́ть (*impf.*) бо́льшее значе́ние +*d.*
upheaval [ʌp'hiːv(ə)l] *n.* (*earthquake etc.*) сдвиг, смеще́ние пласто́в; (*fig.*) переворо́т.
uphill ['ʌphɪl] *adj.* иду́щий в го́ру; **an ~ road** крута́я доро́га; **an ~ task** тяжёлая зада́ча.
adv. в го́ру.
uphold [ʌp'həʊld] *v.t.* (*support, lit., fig.*) подде́рж|ивать, -а́ть; отст|а́ивать, -оя́ть; (*confirm*) подтвер|жда́ть, -ди́ть; утвер|жда́ть, -ди́ть; **~ a protest** прин|има́ть, -я́ть проте́ст.
upholster [ʌp'həʊlstə(r)] *v.t.* об|ива́ть, и́ть; подб|ива́ть, и́ть; **an ~ed chair** кре́сло с мя́гкой оби́вкой; **well-~ed** (*coll., plump*) то́лстый.

upholsterer [ʌp'həʊlstərə(r)] *n.* обо́йщик, драпиро́вщик.
upholstery [ʌp'həʊlstərɪ] *n.* оби́вка.
upkeep ['ʌpki:p] *n.* содержа́ние, ремо́нт, ухо́д (за+*i.*); (*of pers.*) содержа́ние.
upland ['ʌplənd] *n.* нагорье; гори́стая часть страны́.
adj. наго́рный.
uplift[1] ['ʌplɪft] *n.* (*moral elevation*) духо́вный подъём.
uplift[2] [ʌp'lɪft] *v.t.* подн|има́ть, -я́ть; возв|ыша́ть, -ы́сить.
up-market [ʌp'mɑ:kɪt] *adj.* элита́рный, для шика́рной пу́блики.
upmost ['ʌpməʊst] = **uppermost**
upon [ə'pɒn] *prep.* **1.** *see* **on. 2.: once ~ a time** одна́жды; **once ~ a time there lived ...** жи́л(и)-бы́л(и)...; **~ my word, soul!** (*expr. surprise etc.*) Го́споди!; **~ my honour!** че́стное сло́во!; **the holidays are ~ us** приближа́ются кани́кулы; **the enemy is ~ us** враг уже́ бли́зок; **letter ~ letter** письмо́ за письмо́м.
upper ['ʌpə(r)] *n.* передо́к боти́нка; **he was on his ~s** (*coll.*) он оста́лся без гроша́.
adj. ве́рхний; вы́сший; **~ arm** плечо́; **~ classes** вы́сшие кла́ссы; **he got the ~ hand** он одержа́л верх; **U~ House** (*in UK*) пала́та ло́рдов; (*in USA*) сена́т; **~ lip** ве́рхняя губа́.
cpds. **~-case** *adj.* прописно́й; **~-class, -crust** *adjs.* относя́щийся к вы́сшему о́бществу; **~cut** *n.* апперко́т; **~most** (*also* **upmost**) *adj.* са́мый ве́рхний, вы́сший; **it was ~most in my mind** э́то бо́льше всего́ занима́ло мои́ мы́сли; **he said the first thing that came ~most** он сказа́л пе́рвое, что ему́ пришло́ в го́лову; *adv.*: **blade ~most** остриём вверх.
uppi|sh ['ʌpɪʃ], **-ty** ['ʌpɪtɪ] *adjs.* (*coll.*) на́глый, де́рзкий.
uppishness ['ʌpɪʃnɪs] *n.* (*coll.*) на́глость, де́рзкость.
uppity ['ʌpɪtɪ] = **uppish**
upright ['ʌpraɪt] *n.* (*beam, pillar etc.*) столб; **(~ piano)** пиани́но (*indecl.*).
adj. (*erect*) вертика́льный, прямо́й; (*honourable*) че́стный, прямо́й.
adv.: **stand ~** стоя́ть (*impf.*) пря́мо.
uprightness ['ʌpraɪtnɪs] *n.* че́стность, прямота́.
uprising ['ʌpˌraɪzɪŋ] *n.* восста́ние.
up-river ['ʌprɪvə(r)] = **upstream**
uproar ['ʌprɔ:(r)] *n.* (*noise*) шум, (*coll.*) гам; (*tumult, confusion*) возмуще́ние, волне́ние.
uproarious [ʌp'rɔ:rɪəs] *adj.* (*noisy*) шу́мный, бу́рный, бу́йный; (*funny*) ужа́сно/невозмо́жно смешно́й.
uproot [ʌp'ru:t] *v.t.* корчева́ть, вы́-; вырыва́ть, вы́рвать с ко́рнем; (*fig., displace*) выселя́ть, вы́селить; пересел|я́ть, -и́ть; (*fig., eradicate, e.g. customs*) искорен|я́ть, -и́ть.
uprush ['ʌprʌʃ] *n.* стреми́тельное движе́ние вверх; **~ of feelings** наплы́в чувств.
upset[1] ['ʌpset] *n.* **1.** (*physical*) недомога́ние; **stomach ~** расстро́йство желу́дка. **2.** (*emotional shock, confusion*) огорче́ние; (*pl.*) неприя́тности (*f. pl.*). **3.** (*unexpected result in sport*) неожи́данный результа́т.
upset[2] [ʌp'set] *v.t.* опроки́|дывать, -нуть; **he ~ the milk** он опроки́нул молоко́; **the news ~ her** но́вость её расстро́ила; **rich food ~s my stomach** от жи́рной пи́щи у меня́ расстра́ивается желу́док.
upshot ['ʌpʃɒt] *n.* развя́зка; заключе́ние; результа́т; **in the ~** в конце́ концо́в.
upside down [ˌʌpsaɪd 'daʊn] *adv.* вверх дном/(*coll.*) тарма́шками.
upstage [ʌp'steɪdʒ] *adv.* в глубине́ сце́ны.
v.t. (*coll.*) затм|ева́ть, -и́ть.
upstairs [ʌp'steəz] *adv.* наверху́, вве́рх; **he ran ~** он вбежа́л наве́рх; (*attr.*): **the ~ rooms** ве́рхние ко́мнаты.
upstanding [ʌp'stændɪŋ] *adj.* **1.** (*sturdy*) кре́пкий. **2.** прямо́й; **be ~!** вста́ньте!
upstart ['ʌpstɑ:t] *n.* вы́скочка (*c.g.*).
upstream ['ʌpstri:m], **up-river** ['ʌp'rɪvə(r)] *advs.* (*of place*) вверх по тече́нию; (*of motion*) про́тив тече́ния; **~ of** вы́ше+*g.*
upsurge ['ʌpsɜ:dʒ] *n.* подъём; наплы́в.
upswing ['ʌpswɪŋ] *n.* (*fig.*) подъём.
uptake ['ʌpteɪk] *n.*: **quick in the ~** (*coll.*) сметли́вый, сообрази́тельный.
uptight [ʌp'taɪt, 'ʌptaɪt] *adj.* (*coll., tense, angry*) напряжённый, нерво́зный.
up-to-date [ʌptə'deɪt] *adj.* совреме́нный, тепе́решний; нове́йший, (са́мый) после́дний.
up-to-the-minute [ˌʌptəðə'mɪnɪt] *adj.* сиюмину́тный; са́мый после́дний.
up-town ['ʌptaʊn] *adj.* & *adv.* (*US*) (располо́женный) в жилы́х кварта́лах го́рода.
upturn ['ʌptɜ:n] *n.* (*fig.*) сдвиг (к лу́чшему); улучше́ние.
upward ['ʌpwəd] *adj.* напра́вленный верх; **an ~ trend in prices** тенде́нция к повыше́нию цен.
adv. (*also* **~s**) вверх; **~s of** (*over*) **£100** свы́ше ста фу́нтов.
up-wind ['ʌpwɪnd] *adv.* про́тив ве́тра.
ur(a)emia [jʊ'ri:mɪə] *n.* уреми́я.
Urals ['jʊər(ə)lz] *n.* Ура́льские го́ры (*f. pl.*), Ура́л.
uranium [jʊ'reɪnɪəm] *n.* ура́н; (*attr.*) ура́новый.
Uranus ['jʊərənəs, jʊ'reɪnəs] *n.* Ура́н.
urban ['ɜ:bən] *adj.* городско́й.
urbane [ɜ:'beɪn] *adj.* све́тский, учти́вый.
urbanism ['ɜ:bəˌnɪz(ə)m] *n.* урбани́зм.
urbanist ['ɜ:bənɪst] *n.* градострои́тель (*m.*).
urbanity [ɜ:'bænɪtɪ] *n.* све́тскость, учти́вость.
urbanization [ˌɜ:bənaɪ'zeɪʃ(ə)n] *n.* урбаниза́ция; рост городо́в.
urbanize ['ɜ:bəˌnaɪz] *v.t.* урбанизи́ровать (*impf., pf.*).
urchin ['ɜ:tʃɪn] *n.* **1.** мальчи́шка (*m.*), (*coll.*) постре́л. **2.** (*zool.*) морско́й ёж.
Urdu ['ʊədu:, 'ɜ:-] *n.* язы́к урду́.
adj.: **~ script** шрифт (языка́) урду́.
urea ['jʊərɪə, -'ri:ə] *n.* мочеви́на.
uremia [jʊ'ri:mɪə] (*US*) = **ur(a)emia**
ureter [jʊə'ri:tə(r)] *n.* мочето́чник.
urethra [jʊə'ri:θrə] *n.* уре́тра.
urge [ɜ:dʒ] *n.* побужде́ние, стремле́ние; **I felt an ~ to go back** меня́ потяну́ло верну́ться/наза́д.
v.t. **1.** (*impel*; *also* **~ on, ~ forward**) гнать (*impf.*); под|гоня́ть, -огна́ть; **he ~d his horse up the hill** он гнал коня́ в го́ру. **2.** (*exhort*) взыва́ть, возва́ть (*кого к чему*); приз|ыва́ть, -ва́ть (*кого к чему*); угова́ривать (*impf.*); **he needed no urging** он не заста́вил себя́ угова́ривать. **3.** (*impress*): **he ~d on me the need to save money** он настоя́тельно убежда́л меня́ в необходи́мости де́лать сбереже́ния (*or* откла́дывать де́ньги).
urgency ['ɜ:dʒ(ə)nsɪ] *n.* **1.** (*need for prompt action*) сро́чность, безотлага́тельность, неотло́жность; **as a matter of ~** в сро́чном поря́дке. **2.** (*importunity*) насто́йчивость.
urgent ['ɜ:dʒ(ə)nt] *adj.* **1.** (*brooking no delay*) сро́чный, безотлага́тельный, неотло́жный; **he is in ~ need of money** он кра́йне нужда́ется в деньга́х. **2.** (*pressing, importunate*) настоя́тельный, насто́йчивый.
uric ['jʊərɪk] *adj.*: **~ acid** мочева́я кислота́.
urinal [jʊə'raɪn(ə)l, 'jʊərɪn(ə)l] *n.* (*for public use*) писсуа́р; (*vessel*) мочеприёмник, «у́тка».
urinary ['jʊərɪnərɪ] *adj.* мочево́й.
urinate ['jʊərɪˌneɪt] *v.i.* мочи́ться (*impf.*).
urination [jʊərɪ'neɪʃ(ə)n] *n.* мочеиспуска́ние.
urine ['jʊərɪn] *n.* моча́.
urn [ɜ:n] *n.* **1.** (*vase for ashes etc.*) у́рна, ва́за; **Grecian ~** гре́ческая ва́за. **2.** (*for tea, coffee etc.*) куб.
Ursa [ˌɜ:sə] *n.* (*astron.*): **~ Major/Minor** Больша́я/Ма́лая Медве́дица.
urticaria [ˌɜ:tɪ'keərɪə] *n.* крапи́вница, крапи́вная лихора́дка.
Uruguay ['jʊərəˌgwaɪ] *n.* Уругва́й.
Uruguayan [jʊərə'gwaɪən] *n.* уругва́|ец (*fem.* -йка).
adj. уругва́йский.
US(A) (*abbr. of* **United States of America**) США (*pl., indecl.*), (Соединённые Шта́ты Аме́рики).
adj. америка́нский; **US Army** а́рмия США.
usable ['ju:zəb(ə)l] *adj.* примени́мый, удо́бный, (при)го́дный.
usage ['ju:sɪdʒ] *n.* **1.** (*manner of treatment*) обраще́ние;

rough ~ гру́бое обраще́ние. **2.** (*habitual process*) обыкнове́ние; **a guide to English** ~ уче́бник англи́йского словоупотребле́ния; **sanctified by** ~ освящённый обы́чаем.

use[1] [ju:s] *n.* **1.** (*utilization*) употребле́ние, по́льзование +*i.*; **the telephone is in** ~ телефо́н за́нят; **this book is in constant** ~ э́та кни́га нахо́дится в постоя́нном по́льзовании; **make good** ~ **of your time!** хороше́нько испо́льзуйте ва́ше вре́мя!; **he is making** ~ **of you** он вас испо́льзует (в свои́х це́лях); **he put his talents to good** ~ он пра́вильно испо́льзовал свои́ спосо́бности; **a room for the** ~ **of the public** ко́мната о́бщего по́льзования; **these coins came into** ~ **last year** э́ти моне́ты вошли́ в обраще́ние в про́шлом году́. **2.** (*purpose*; *profitable application*) назначе́ние; примене́ние; **this tool has many** ~**s** э́тот инструме́нт применя́ется для разли́чных це́лей; **I shall find a** ~ **for it** я найду́ э́тому примене́ние; **I have no further** ~ **for it** мне э́то бо́льше не пона́добится; **I have no** ~ **for him** (*coll.*) мне с ним не́чего де́лать. **3.** (*value, advantage*) по́льза, толк; **this machine is no longer (of) any** ~ э́та маши́на бо́льше не годи́тся; **will this be of** ~ **to you?** вам э́то пригоди́тся?; **it's no** ~ **grumbling** что то́лку ворча́ть?; ворча́нием/жа́лобами де́лу не помо́жешь. **4.** (*power of using*): спосо́бность по́льзования (*чем*); **he lost the** ~ **of his legs** он утра́тил спосо́бность ходи́ть. **5.** (*right to use*): **I gave him the** ~ **of my car** я разреши́л ему́ по́льзоваться мое́й маши́ной; **'with** ~ **of kitchen'** с пра́вом по́льзования ку́хней. **6.** (*consumption*) потребле́ние, расхо́дование. **7.** (*arch., custom*) привы́чка, обыкнове́ние.

use[2] [ju:z] *v.t.* **1.** (*make use of, employ*) употреб|ля́ть, -и́ть; по́льзоваться, вос- +*i.*; (*apply*) примен|я́ть, -и́ть; **are you using this knife?** вам сейча́с ну́жен э́тот нож?; **oil is** ~**d for frying potatoes** карто́фель жа́рят на расти́тельном ма́сле; ~ **your head!** пораски́нь мозга́ми!; ~ **your eyes!** смотри́те как сле́дует!; ~ **force** приб|ега́ть, -е́гнуть к наси́лию; ~ **your own discretion!** де́йствуйте по со́бственному разуме́нию; **may I** ~ **your name?** могу́ я на вас сосла́ться?; **a** ~**d car** поде́ржанная маши́на; ~**d towels** испо́льзованные/гря́зные полоте́нца. **2.** (~ **up,** *consume*): испо́льзовать (*impf., pf.*); расхо́довать, из-; тра́тить, по-; изв|оди́ть, -ести́; **how much flour do you** ~ **per week?** ско́лько у вас идёт муки́ в неде́лю?; **the car** ~**s a lot of petrol** э́та маши́на берёт/расхо́дует мно́го бензи́на. **3.** (*treat*) обраща́ться (*impf.*), обходи́ться (*impf.*) с+*i.* **4.** (*exploit*): **I feel as if I have been** ~**d** я чу́вствую, что меня́ испо́льзовали в чьи́х-то це́лях.

use[3] [ju:z] *v.t. & i.* **1.** (*accustom*): **get** ~**d to** прив|ыка́ть, -ы́кнуть к+*d.*; **he is** ~**d to it** он к э́тому привы́к; **he is** ~**d to dining late** он (обы́чно) обе́дает (*or* привы́к обе́дать) по́здно. **2.** (*be accustomed*): **he** ~**d to be a teacher** он ра́ньше был учи́телем; **I** ~**d not to like him** пре́жде он мне не нра́вился; **he** ~**d to say** он говар́ивал; **I** ~**ed to go** я пре́жде/быва́ло ходи́л.

useful ['ju:sfʊl] *adj.* поле́зный; **he gave me a** ~ **tip** он дал мне поле́зный сове́т; **make yourself** ~! займи́тесь че́м-нибудь поле́зным!; **he is very** ~ **about the house** он о́чень мно́го помога́ет по до́му; **he is a** ~ **footballer** он спосо́бный футболи́ст.

usefulness ['ju:sfʊlnɪs] *n.* по́льза; **this book has outlived its** ~ э́та кни́га устаре́ла.

useless ['ju:slɪs] *adj.* (*worthless*) непригодный; (*futile*) бесполе́зный; (*vain*) тще́тный; (*coll., incompetent*): **he is** ~ **at tennis** он никуды́шный теннис́ист.

uselessness ['ju:slɪsnɪs] *n.* непригодность; бесполе́зность; тще́тность.

user ['ju:zə(r)] *n.* (*one who uses*) употребля́ющий; потреби́тель (*m.*); (*leg., use*) пра́во по́льзования; по́льзование (*чем*).

cpd. ~**-friendly** *adj.* удо́бный в употребле́нии; (*comput.*) дру́жественный.

usher ['ʌʃə(r)] *n.* (*court etc.*) швейца́р; (*pers. showing people to seats*) билетёр.

v.t. (*also* ~ **in**) вв|оди́ть, -ести́; **I was** ~**ed into his presence** меня́ ввели́ к нему́; (*fig.*) возве|ща́ть, -сти́ть; **the new year** ~**ed in many changes** но́вый год принёс с собо́й мно́жество переме́н.

usherette [,ʌʃə'ret] *n.* билетёрша.

USSR (*abbr. of* ***Union of Soviet Socialist Republics***) СССР, (Сою́з Сове́тских Социалисти́ческих Респу́блик).

usual ['ju:ʒʊəl] *adj.* обыкнове́нный, обы́чный; **the** ~ **crowd gathered** как обы́чно, собрала́сь толпа́; **with his** ~ **alacrity** со сво́йственной ему́ жи́востью; **it is** ~ **to remove one's hat** при́нято снима́ть шля́пу; **he is late as** ~ он, по обыкнове́нию (*or* как всегда́), опа́здывает; **the bus was fuller than** ~ авто́бус был перепо́лен бо́льше обы́чного.

usufruct ['ju:zju:,frʌkt] *n.* узуфру́кт.

usurer ['ju:ʒərə(r)] *n.* ростовщи́|к (*fem.*-ца).

usurious [jʊ'ʒʊərɪəs] *adj.* ростовщи́ческий.

usurp [jʊ'zɜ:p] *v.t.* узурпи́ровать (*impf., pf.*).

usurpation [,ju:zə'peɪʃ(ə)n] *n.* узурпа́ция.

usurper [jʊ'zɜ:pə(r)] *n.* узурпа́тор.

usury ['ju:ʒərɪ] *n.* ростовщи́чество.

utensil [ju:'tens(ə)l] *n.* инструме́нт; (*pl., collect.*) посу́да, у́тварь.

uterine ['ju:tə,raɪn, -rɪn] *adj.* ма́точный; ~ **brother** единоутро́бный брат.

uterus ['ju:tərəs] *n.* ма́тка.

utilitarian [jʊtɪlɪ'teərɪən] *n.* утилитари́ст (*fem.* -ка), сторо́нни|к (*fem.* -ца) утилитари́зма.

adj. утилита́рный.

utilitarianism [jʊtɪlɪ'teərɪə,nɪz(ə)m] *n.* утилитари́зм.

utilit|y [ju:'tɪlɪtɪ] *n.* **1.** (*usefulness*) поле́зность, практи́чность, вы́годность, вы́года, по́льза. **2.:** **public** ~**ies** коммуна́льные услу́ги (*f. pl.*)/предприя́тия (*nt. pl.*)/сооруже́ния (*nt. pl.*).

utilizable ['ju:tɪ,laɪzəb(ə)l] *adj.* приго́дный к употребле́нию.

utilization [ju:tɪlaɪ'zeɪʃ(ə)n] *n.* испо́льзование, утилиза́ция.

utilize ['ju:tɪ,laɪz] *v.t.* испо́льзовать (*impf., pf.*); утилизи́ровать (*impf., pf.*).

utmost ['ʌtməʊst], **uttermost** ['ʌtə,məʊst] *nn.* преде́л возмо́жного; **he did his** ~ **to avoid defeat** орн сде́лал всё возмо́жное, что́бы избежа́ть пораже́ния; **he exerts himself to the** ~ он стара́ется изо всех сил.

adjs. кра́йний; преде́льный.

Utopia [ju:'təʊpɪə] *n.* уто́пия.

Utopian [ju:'təʊpɪən] *adj.* утопи́ческий.

utter[1] ['ʌtə(r)] *adj.* по́лный, абсолю́тный, соверше́нный; ~ **darkness** абсолю́тная темнота́; **an** ~ **scoundrel** отъя́вленный негодя́й.

utter[2] ['ʌtə(r)] *v.t.* **1.** (*pronounce, emit*) изд|ава́ть, -а́ть; произн|оси́ть, -ести́; **she** ~**ed a moan** она́ издала́ стон; **he could not** ~ **a word** он не мог вы́говорить ни сло́ва. **2.** (*put into circulation*) пус|ка́ть, -ти́ть в обраще́ние.

utterance ['ʌtərəns] *n.* **1.** (*diction, speech*) произноше́ние, ди́кция; **defective** ~ дефе́кт ре́чи. **2.** (*expression*) выраже́ние; **he gave** ~ **to his anger** он вы́разил свой гнев. **3.** (*pronouncement*) выска́зывание.

uttermost ['ʌtə,məʊst] = **utmost**

uvula ['ju:vjʊlə] *n.* язычо́к.

uvular ['ju:vjʊlə(r)] *adj.* (*anat.*) язычко́вый; (*phon.*): ~ **'r'** увуля́рное «р».

uxorious [ʌk'sɔ:rɪəs] *adj.* чрезме́рно привя́занный к жене́.

uxoriousness [ʌk'sɔ:rɪəsnɪs] *n.* чрезме́рная привя́занность к жене́.

Uzbek ['ʌzbek, 'ʊz-] *n.* (*pers.*) узбе́|к (*fem.* -чка); (*language*) узбе́кский язы́к.

Uzbekistan [,ʌzbekɪ'stɑ:n, ,ʊz-] *n.* Узбекиста́н.

V

V [vi:] *n.*: **~-1/2** ракéта ФАУ-1/2.

cpd. **~-neck** *n. & adj.* вы́рез мы́сиком; **~-neck sweater** сви́тер с вы́резом в ви́де бу́квы «V».

v. *abbr. of* **1. volt(s)** [vɒlt(z), vəʊlt(z)] В, (вольт). **2. versus** ['vɜ:səs] про́тив; **England ~ France** А́нглия про́тив Фра́нции.

vac [væk] = **vacation** *n.* **2.**

vacanc|y ['veɪkənsɪ] *n.* **1.** (*emptiness*) пустота́, незапо́лненность. **2.** (*of mind*) ту́пость. **3.** (*job*) вака́нсия; (*place on course etc.*) ме́сто; (*room*): **no ~ies** (свобо́дных) ко́мнат нет.

vacant ['veɪkənt] *adj.* **1.** (*empty*) пусто́й. **2.** (*unoccupied*) неза́нятый, свобо́дный; **a ~ chair** свобо́дный стул; **a ~ post** неза́нятая/вака́нтная до́лжность, вака́нсия. **3.** (*of mind, expression etc.*) безду́мный, отсу́тствующий; бессмы́сленный.

vacate [və'keɪt, veɪ-] *v.t.* освобо|жда́ть, -ди́ть; **he ~d his chair** он встал со сту́ла; **the flat had been ~d** жильцы́ съе́хали с кварти́ры (*or* освободи́ли кварти́ру); **he will ~ the post in May** он освободи́т ме́сто (*or* уйдёт с до́лжности) в ма́е.

vacation [və'keɪʃ(ə)n] *n.* **1.** (*leaving empty*) освобожде́ние. **2.** (*at university, courts etc.*) кани́кул|ы (*pl., g.* —); **long ~** ле́тние кани́кулы. **3.** (*US, holiday*) о́тпуск, о́тдых; **when will you take your ~?** когда́ вы идёте в о́тпуск?; **on ~** в о́тпуске, (*coll.*) в отпуску́.

vaccinate ['væksɪ,neɪt] *v.t.* де́лать, с- приви́вку +*d.*; прив|ива́ть, -и́ть о́спу +*d.*; **have you been ~d?** вам сде́лали приви́вку?

vaccination [,væksɪ'neɪʃ(ə)n] *n.* приви́вка, оспопривива́ние; **~ mark** о́спа, о́спина.

vaccine ['væksi:n] *n.* вакци́на.

vacillate ['væsɪ,leɪt] *v.i.* колеба́ться (*impf.*), проявля́ть (*impf.*) нереши́тельность.

vacillation [,væsɪ'leɪʃ(ə)n] *n.* колеба́ние, нереши́тельность.

vacuity [və'kju:ɪtɪ] *n.* пустота́, пра́здность; бессодержа́тельность, бессмы́сленность.

vacuous ['vækjʊəs] *adj.* пусто́й, пра́здный; бессодержа́тельный, бессмы́сленный.

vacuum ['vækjʊəm] *n.* **1.** (*empty or airless place*) ва́куум; безвозду́шное простра́нство; (*fig.*) пустота́; **his death left a ~** его́ смерть была́ неисполни́мой утра́той (*or* оста́вила невосполни́мую пустоту́); **~ flask** те́рмос. **2.** (*coll.*, **~-cleaner**) пылесо́с.

v.t. & i. (*coll., clean with* **~** (**2.**)) пылесо́сить (*impf., pf.*).

vade-mecum [,vɑ:dɪ'meɪkəm, ,veɪdɪ'mi:kəm] *n.* (карма́нный) спра́вочник.

vagabond ['vægə,bɒnd] *n.* (*vagrant*) бродя́га (*c.g.*), скита́лец.

adj. бродя́чий, скита́льческий.

vagary ['veɪgərɪ] *n.* причу́да, капри́з.

vagina [və'dʒaɪnə] *n.* влага́лище.

vaginal [və'dʒaɪnəl] *adj.* влага́лищный.

vagrancy ['veɪgrənsɪ] *n.* бродя́жничество.

vagrant ['veɪgrənt] *n.* бродя́га (*c.g.*).

adj. бродя́чий; **~ thoughts** рассе́янные/пра́здные мы́сли.

vague [veɪg] *adj.* неопределённый, сму́тный, нея́сный; **a ~ resemblance** неулови́мое/отдалённое схо́дство; **~ rumours** неопределённые/сму́тные слу́хи; **he was rather ~ about his plans** он выска́зывался о свои́х пла́нах дово́льно уклóнчиво; **I haven't the ~st idea** не име́ю ни мале́йшего поня́тия/представле́ния.

vagueness ['veɪgnɪs] *n.* неопределённость, сму́тность, нея́сность.

vain [veɪn] *adj.* **1.** (*unavailing; fruitless*) тще́тный, напра́сный; **a ~ attempt** тще́тная попы́тка; **~ hopes** напра́сные наде́жды; **they tried in ~ to get a seat** они́ безуспе́шно пыта́лись найти́ ме́сто. **2.** (*empty*) пусто́й; **~ boasts** пуста́я похвальба́; **he took God's name in ~** он всу́е употребля́л и́мя госпо́дне. **3.** (*conceited*) тщесла́вный.

cpds. **~glorious** *adj.* тщесла́вный; **~glory** *n.* тщесла́вие.

val|ance ['væləns], **-ence** ['veɪləns] *n.* (*curtain, frill*) подзо́р, обо́рка, сбо́рка.

vale [veɪl] *n.* доли́на, дол; **~ of tears** юдо́ль слёз.

valediction [,vælɪ'dɪkʃ(ə)n] *n.* проща́ние.

valedictory [,vælɪ'dɪktərɪ] *adj.* проща́льный; (*US, as n.*) речь на вы́пуске (*учащихся*).

valence[1] ['veɪləns] = **valance**

valenc|e[2] ['veɪləns], **-y** ['veɪlənsɪ] *nn.* (*chem.*) вале́нтность.

valentine ['vælən,taɪn] *n.* (*missive*) ≃ любо́вное посла́ние.

valerian [və'lɪərɪən] *n.* (*bot.*) валериа́на; **~ drops** валериа́новые ка́пли, валерья́нка.

valet ['vælɪt, -leɪ] *n.* камерди́нер, слуга́ (*m.*).

v.t. служи́ть (*impf.*) камерди́нером +*d.*; **~ s.o.** следи́ть (*impf.*) за чьей-н. оде́ждой.

valetudinarian [,vælɪ,tju:dɪ'neərɪən] *n.* ипохо́ндрик; мни́тельный челове́к.

Valhalla [væl'hælə] *n.* Ва́льха́лла, Ва́льга́лла, Ва́лга́лла; (*fig.*) пантео́н.

valiant ['væljənt] *adj.* до́блестный, хра́брый; (*of effort*) герои́ческий.

valid ['vælɪd] *adj.* **1.** (*sound*) ве́ский, обосно́ванный; **~ objections** убеди́тельные возраже́ния; **~ reasons** ве́ские до́воды. **2.** (*leg.*) действи́тельный; **a ~ claim** зако́нная прете́нзия; **a ticket ~ for 3 months** биле́т, действи́тельный на три ме́сяца.

validate ['vælɪ,deɪt] *v.t.* утвер|жда́ть, -ди́ть; подтвер|жда́ть, -ди́ть.

validation [,vælɪ'deɪʃ(ə)n] *n.* утвержде́ние, подтвержде́ние.

validity [və'lɪdɪtɪ] *n.* зако́нность, ве́скость; **the ~ of his argument** ве́скость его́ до́вода; **the ~ of their marriage** зако́нность их бра́ка.

valise [və'li:z] *n.* (*US*) саквоя́ж, чемода́н.

Valkyrie [væl'kɪərɪ, 'vælkɪrɪ] *n.* валькирия.

valley ['vælɪ] *n.* доли́на.

valorous ['vælərəs] *adj.* до́блестный.

valour ['vælə(r)] *n.* до́блесть.

valuable ['væljʊəb(ə)l] *n.* (*usu. pl.*) це́нности (*f. pl.*); драгоце́нности (*f. pl.*).

adj. це́нный, поле́зный, ва́жный.

valuation [,væljʊ'eɪʃ(ə)n] *n.* оце́нка; определе́ние сто́имости; **people take you at your own ~** ≃ всё зави́сит от того, как себя пода́ть.

value ['vælju:] *n.* **1.** (*worth; advantageousness*) це́нность, ва́жность; **the ~ of exercise** по́льза моцио́на; **his advice was of great ~** его́ сове́т о́чень пригоди́лся (*or* оказа́лся о́чень поле́зным); **he sets a high ~ on his time** он о́чень дорожи́т свои́м вре́менем; он до́рого це́нит своё вре́мя. **2.** (*in money etc.*) це́нность, сто́имость; **the ~ of the pound** покупа́тельная си́ла фу́нта; **property is rising in ~** недви́жимое иму́щество поднима́ется в цене́; **the book is good ~ for money** э́та кни́га — вы́годная поку́пка; **~ added tax** нало́г на доба́вленную/прираще́нную сто́имость. **3.** (*mus.*) дли́тельность но́ты; **give each note its full ~** да|ва́ть, -ть ка́ждой но́те прозвуча́ть по́лностью. **4.** (*painting*) вале́р. **5.** (*denomination of coin, card etc.*) досто́инство. **6.** (*math.*) величина́. **7.** (*pl., standards*) (*духовные и т.п.*) це́нности (*f. pl.*).

v.t. **1.** (*estimate ~ of*) оце́н|ивать, -и́ть; **the house was ~d at £20,000** дом оцени́ли в 20 000 фу́нтов. **2.** (*regard highly*) дорожи́ть (*impf.*); цени́ть (*impf.*); **I ~ my leisure time** я ценю́ свой досу́г; **his ~d advice** его́ це́нное мне́ние; **a ~d friend of mine** друг, кото́рый мне о́чень до́рог.

valueless ['væljʊlɪs] *adj.* ничего́ не сто́ящий;

недействи́тельный, бесполе́зный; **a ~ promise** пусто́е обеща́ние.
valuer ['væljʊə(r)] *n.* оце́нщик.
valve [vælv] *n.* (*tech.*) кла́пан, ве́нтиль (*m.*); (*anat., mus.*) кла́пан; (*radio*) электро́нная ла́мпа.
valvular ['vælvjʊlə(r)] *adj.* кла́пановый; **~ defect** поро́к кла́панов (се́рдца).
vamoose [və'mu:s] *v.i.* см|ыва́ться, -ы́ться (*US sl.*).
vamp[1] [væmp] *n.* (*part of shoe*) передо́к/голо́вка/сою́зка боти́нка.
v.t.: **~ up** (*fig., renovate; improvise*) мастери́ть, с- на ско́рую ру́ку.
v.i. (*mus.*) импровизи́ровать (*impf., pf.*); бренча́ть, про-.
vamp[2] [væmp] *n.* (*adventuress*) (же́нщина-)вамп; сире́на; обольсти́тельница.
v.t. соблазн|я́ть, -и́ть.
vampire ['væmpaɪə(r)] *n.* **1.** (**~ bat**) вампи́р, упы́рь (*m.*). **2.** (*human creature*) вампи́р, кровопи́йца (*c.g.*).
van[1] [væn] *n.* **1.** (*motor vehicle*) (авто)фурго́н; **furniture ~** ме́бельный фурго́н. **2.** (*railway truck*) бага́жный ваго́н.
cpds. **~man, ~-driver** *nn.* води́тель (*m.*) фурго́на.
van[2] [væn] *n.* (*of army etc.*) головно́й отря́д; (*fig.*) аванга́рд; **in the ~ of civilization** в аванга́рде цивилиза́ции.
cpd. **~guard** *n.* аванга́рд; передово́й отря́д; (*fig.*) веду́щее звено́; аванга́рд.
vanadium [və'neɪdɪəm] *n.* вана́дий.
Vandal ['vænd(ə)l] *n.* (*hist.*) ванда́л; (**v~**, *fig.*) ванда́л, хулига́н.
vandalism ['vændə,lɪz(ə)m] *n.* вандали́зм.
vandalize ['vændə,laɪz] *v.t.* изуро́довать (*pf.*); разр|уша́ть, -у́шить.
Van Dyck [væn 'daɪk] *n.* Ван-Дейк.
Vandyke [væn'daɪk] *n.* (**~ beard**) боро́дка кли́нышком.
vane [veɪn] *n.* (*weathercock*) флю́гер; (*of windmill*) крыло́; (*of propeller, turbine*) ло́пасть.
Van Eyck [væn 'aɪk] *n.* Ван-Эйк.
Van Gogh [væn 'gɒf] *n.* Ван-Гог.
vanilla [və'nɪlə] *n.* вани́ль.
vanish ['vænɪʃ] *v.i.* исч|еза́ть, -е́знуть; проп|ада́ть, -а́сть; **~ing cream** крем под пу́дру; дневно́й крем; **~ing-point** то́чка схожде́ния паралле́льных (*в перспективе*); **his courage was reduced to ~ing-point** му́жество на́чисто поки́нуло его́; **his hopes of success ~ed** его́ наде́жды на успе́х улетучи́лись; он потеря́л вся́кую наде́жду на успе́х.
vanity ['vænɪtɪ] *n.* **1.** (*conceit*) тщесла́вие; **~ bag** да́мская су́мочка; космети́чка. **2.** (*futility; worthlessness*) суета́, тщета́; **~ of vanities** суета́ сує́т; **V~ Fair** я́рмарка тщесла́вия.
vanquish ['væŋkwɪʃ] *v.t.* побе|жда́ть, -ди́ть; покор|я́ть, -и́ть; (*fig.*) преодол|ева́ть, -е́ть; подав|ля́ть, -и́ть.
vantage ['vɑ:ntɪdʒ] *n.* преиму́щество.
cpds. **~-ground, ~-point** *nn.* вы́годная пози́ция.
vapid ['væpɪd] *adj.* (*fig.*) пло́ский, пре́сный; **~ conversation** пусто́й/бессодержа́тельный разгово́р.
vaporization [,veɪpəraɪ'zeɪʃ(ə)n] *n.* испаре́ние, парообразова́ние.
vaporize ['veɪpə,raɪz] *v.t. & i.* испар|я́ть, -и́ть; выпа́ривать, вы́парить; превра|ща́ть, -ти́ть в пар.
vaporous ['veɪpərəs] *adj.* (*lit., fig.*) тума́нный; (*filmy*) прозра́чный.
vapour ['veɪpə(r)] *n.* **1.** (*steam*) пар; **~ bath** парова́я ба́ня/ва́нна. **2.** (*mist*) тума́н. **3.** (*gaseous manifestation*) испаре́ние; **~ trail** инверсио́нный след.
v.i. (*talk pompously*) разглаго́льствовать (*impf.*).
Varangian [və'rændʒɪən] *n.* варя́г.
adj. варя́жкий.
variability [,veərɪə'bɪlɪtɪ] *n.* изме́нчивость, непостоя́нство.
variable ['veərɪəb(ə)l] *n.* (*math.*) переме́нная величина́.
adj. изме́нчивый, непостоя́нный; **~ winds** ве́тры переме́нных направле́ний; **~ moods** переме́нчивые настрое́ния; **~ standards** меня́ющиеся крите́рии.
variance ['veərɪəns] *n.* измене́ние; расхожде́ние; **this is at ~ with what we heard** э́то противоре́чит тому́, что мы слы́шали; **they were at ~** они́ спо́рили; ме́жду ни́ми был разла́д.
variant ['veərɪənt] *n.* вариа́нт.
adj. **1.** (*different; alternative*) разли́чный, ино́й; **~ reading** разночте́ние. **2.** (*changing*) переме́нчивый.
variation [,veərɪ'eɪʃ(ə)n] *n.* **1.** (*fluctuation*) измене́ние; **~s of temperature** колеба́ния (*nt. pl.*) температу́ры. **2.** (*divergence*) отклоне́ние; **~ from the norm** отклоне́ние от но́рмы; **magnetic ~** измене́ние магни́тного склоне́ния. **3.** (*biol. etc.: variant form*) аберра́ция, мута́ция. **4.** (*variant; also mus.*) вариа́ция; **~s on a theme** вариа́ции на те́му.
varicoloured ['veərɪ,kʌləd] *adj.* многоцве́тный, разноцве́тный.
varicose ['værɪ,kəʊs] *adj.* варико́зный; **~ veins** расшире́ние вен.
varied ['veərɪd] *adj.* (*diverse*) ра́зный, разнообра́зный, разли́чный.
variegated ['veərɪ,geɪtɪd, -rɪə,geɪtɪd] *adj.* разноцве́тный, пёстрый.
variety [və'raɪətɪ] *n.* **1.** (*diversity; many-sidedness*) разнообра́зие; **~ is the spice of life** пре́лесть жи́зни в (её) разнообра́зии; **the ~ of his achievements** его́ многочи́сленные достиже́ния. **2.** (*number of different things*) ряд; мно́жество; **for a ~ of reasons** по це́лому ря́ду соображе́ний. **3.** (**~ entertainment**) варьете́ (*indecl.*); **~ artist** эстра́дный арти́ст (*fem.* -ка); **~ show** эстра́дное представле́ние. **4.** (*biol.*) разнови́дность, вид, сорт.
variorum [,veərɪ'ɔ:rəm] *n.*: **~ edition** изда́ние с коммента́риями и вариа́нтами.
various ['veərɪəs] *adj.* **1.** (*diverse*) разли́чный, ра́зный, разнообра́зный. **2.** (*with pl., several*) мно́гие (*pl.*); ра́зные (*pl.*); **at ~ times** в ра́зное вре́мя.
varlet ['vɑ:lɪt] *n.* (*arch.*) негодя́й, плут.
varmint ['vɑ:mɪnt] *n.* (*US*) (*pers.*) шалопа́й, него́дник (*coll.*).
varnish ['vɑ:nɪʃ] *n.* лак; (*fig.*) лоск.
v.t. лакирова́ть, от-.
varsity ['vɑ:sɪtɪ] (*coll.*) = **university**
var|y ['veərɪ] *v.t.* меня́ть (*impf.*); измен|я́ть, -и́ть; разнообра́зить (*impf.*).
v.i. **1.** (*change*) меня́ться (*impf.*); **the menu never ~ies** меню́ никогда́ не меня́ется. **2.** (*differ*) ра|сходи́ться, -зойти́сь; отлич|а́ться, -и́ться; ра́зниться (*impf.*); **opinions ~y** мне́ния расхо́дятся; **with ~ying success** с переме́нным успе́хом.
vascular ['væskjʊlə(r)] *adj.* сосу́дистый.
vase [vɑ:z] *n.* ва́за.
vasectomy [və'sektəmɪ] *n.* вазэктоми́я.
Vaseline ['væsɪ,li:n] *n.* (*propr.*) вазели́н.
vassal ['væs(ə)l] *n.* васса́л; (*attr.*) васса́льный.
vassalage ['væsəlɪdʒ] *n.* вассалите́т; васса́льная зави́симость.
vast [vɑ:st] *adj.* обши́рный, просто́рный, грома́дный; огро́мный; (*grandiose*) грандио́зный; **~ plains** необозри́мые равни́ны.
vastly ['vɑ:stlɪ] *adv.* о́чень, кра́йне.
vastness ['vɑ:stnɪs] *n.* ширь, просто́р; огро́мность; грандио́зность.
VAT [,vi:eɪ'ti:, væt] *n.* (*Br., abbr. of* **value added tax**) нало́г на доба́вленную/приращённую сто́имость.
vat [væt] *n.* бо́чка, чан.
Vatican ['vætɪkən] *n.* Ватика́н; **~ City** (госуда́рство-го́род) Ватика́н.
adj. ватика́нский.
vaticination [væ,tɪsɪ'neɪʃ(ə)n] *n.* проро́чество.
vaudeville ['vɔ:dəvɪl, 'vəʊ-] *n.* водеви́ль (*m.*).
vault[1] [vɔ:lt, vɒlt] *n.* **1.** (*arched roof*) свод; (*fig.*): **the ~ of heaven** небосво́д. **2.** (*underground room or chamber*) подва́л, по́греб; (*of a bank*) храни́лище; (*of art gallery*) запа́сник; **wine ~** ви́нный по́греб; **family ~** (*tomb*) фами́льный склеп.
vault[2] [vɔ:lt, vɒlt] *n.* (*leap*) прыжо́к, скачо́к.
v.t. & i. перепры́г|ивать, -нуть; **he ~ed (over) the fence** он перепры́гнул че́рез забо́р; **~ing-horse** гимнасти́ческий конь.
vaulted ['vɔ:ltɪd, 'vɒltɪd] *adj.* сво́дчатый.

vaulting ['vɔ:ltɪŋ, 'vɒltɪŋ] *n.* (*archit.*) возведéние свóда; свод; своды (*m. pl.*).

vaunt [vɔ:nt] *n.* хвастовствó, похвальбá.

v.t. & i. хвáстать(ся), по-; похвал|я́ться, -и́ться (+*i.*).

VC = **Victoria Cross**

VCR (*abbr. of* ***video cassette recorder***) видеомагнитофóн.

VD (*abbr. of* ***venereal disease***) венери́ческая болéзнь.

VDU (*abbr. of* ***visual display unit***) дисплéй.

VE (*abbr. of* ***Victory in Europe***): ~ **Day** день побéды в Еврóпе.

veal [vi:l] *n.* теля́тина.

vector ['vektə(r)] *n.* (*math.*) вéктор; (*of disease*) перенóсчик/носи́тель (*m.*) инфéкции; (*aeron.*) курс, направлéние.

v.t. напр|авля́ть, -áвить; нав|оди́ть, -ести́.

vectorial [,vek'tɔ:rɪəl] *adj.* вéкторный.

Veda ['veɪdə, 'vi:-] *n.*: **the** ~**s** Вéд|ы (*pl.*, *g.* —).

vedette [vɪ'det] *n.* (*mounted sentry*) кóнный часовóй; (*patrol boat*) торпéдный кáтер.

Vedic ['veɪdɪk, 'vi:-] *adj.* (*ling.*) веди́йский; (*relig.*) веди́ческий.

veer [vɪə(r)] *v.i.* измен|я́ть, -и́ть направлéние; пов|орáчивать(ся), -ерну́ть(ся); **the wind is** ~**ing (round)** вéтер меня́ется; (*fig.*) измен|я́ть, -и́ть курс; измен|я́ться, -и́ться; **public opinion is** ~**ing in his favour** óбщественное мнéние меня́ется в егó пóльзу; ~ **to the left** (*pol.*) полевéть (*pf.*); ~ **to the right** поправéть (*pf.*).

vegan ['vi:gən] *n.* стрóгий вегетариáнец; (*attr.*) стрóго вегетариáнский.

veganism ['vi:gənɪz(ə)m] *n.* стрóгое вегетариáнство.

vegetable ['vedʒɪtəb(ə)l, 'vedʒtəb(ə)l] *n.* óвощ; **green** ~**s** зéлень, óвощи; **I don't want to become a** ~ я не хочу́ вести́ расти́тельное существовáние.

adj. овощнóй; ~ **diet** овощнáя диéта; **the** ~ **kingdom** расти́тельное цáрство; ~ **oils** расти́тельные маслá; ~ **marrow** кабачóк.

vegetarian [,vedʒɪ'teərɪən] *n.* вегетариáн|ец (*fem.* -ка); (*attr.*) вегетариáнский.

vegetarianism [,vedʒɪ'teərɪə,nɪz(ə)m] *n.* вегетариáнство.

vegetate ['vedʒɪ,teɪt] *v.i.* (*lit.*, *fig.*) прозябáть (*impf.*); (*fig.*) вести́ (*impf.*) расти́тельный óбраз жи́зни.

vegetation [,vedʒɪ'teɪʃ(ə)n] *n.* (*plant life*) расти́тельность.

vegetative ['vedʒɪtətɪv] *adj.* расти́тельный; (*bot.*) вегетациóнный.

vehemence ['vi:əməns] *n.* си́ла, стрáстность, я́рость.

vehement ['vi:əmənt] *adj.* си́льный, стрáстный, я́ростный.

vehicle ['vi:ɪk(ə)l, 'vɪək(ə)l] *n.* **1.** (*conveyance*) трáнспортное срéдство; **space** ~ косми́ческий корáбль. **2.** (*fig.*) проводни́к; срéдство распространéния/передáчи; **propaganda** ~ ору́дие пропагáнды.

vehicular [vɪ'hɪkjʊlə(r)] *adj.* перевóзочный; ~ **traffic** движéние автотрáнспорта; ~ **transport** автогужевóй трáнспорт.

veil [veɪl] *n.* вуáль; **she took the** ~ (*fig.*) онá постри́глась в монáхини; **let us draw a** ~ **over the consequences** обойдём молчáнием послéдствия; **under a** ~ **of secrecy** под покрóвом тáйны.

v.t. (*lit.*, *fig.*) вуали́ровать, за-; ~**ed threat** скры́тая угрóза.

vein [veɪn] *n.* **1.** (*anat.*) вéна. **2.** (*of leaf*) жи́лка. **3.** (*of rock*) жи́ла; **a** ~ **of gold** прожи́лка зóлота; золотáя жи́ла. **4.** (*mood*) настроéние, расположéние; **he was in humorous** ~ он был в игри́вом настроéнии; **in the same** ~ в тóм же ду́хе/тóне/сти́ле.

veined [veɪnd] *adj.*: **her hands were** ~ у неё выступáли вéны/жи́лы на рукáх; ~ **marble** мрáмор в прожи́лках.

velar ['vi:lə(r)] *adj.* задненёбный, велáрный.

Velcro ['velkrəʊ] *n.* (*propr.*): ~ **fastener** застёжка «вéлкро», липу́чка, замóк-отры́вок.

veld(t) [velt] *n.* вельд.

velleity [ve'li:ɪtɪ] *n.* пасси́вное желáние.

vellum ['veləm] *n.* тóнкий пергáмент; ~ **paper** велéновая бумáга.

velocity [vɪ'lɒsɪtɪ] *n.* скóрость, быстротá.

velodrome ['velə,drəʊm] *n.* велодрóм.

velour(s) [və'lʊə(r)] *n.* велю́р.

velum ['vi:ləm] *n.* пáрус, парусови́дная перепóнка.

velvet ['velvɪt] *n.* бáрхат; **a** ~ **dress** бáрхатное плáтье; **on** ~ (*fig.*) как у Христá за пáзухой; **the iron hand in the** ~ **glove** (*fig.*) мя́гкая, но реши́тельная поли́тика.

velveteen [,velvɪ'ti:n] *n.* вельвéт.

velvety ['velvɪtɪ] *adj.* бáрхатный, бархати́стый.

venal ['vi:n(ə)l] *adj.* продáжный, подку́пный.

venality [,vi:'nælɪtɪ] *n.* продáжность, подку́пность.

vendetta [ven'detə] *n.* вендéтта.

vending-machine ['vendɪŋ] *n.* автомáт.

vendor ['vendə(r), -dɔ:(r)] *n.* продав|éц (*fem.* -щи́ца).

veneer [vɪ'nɪə(r)] *n.* шпон, фанéра; (*fig.*) вне́шний лоск; **a** ~ **of politeness** показнáя вéжливость.

v.t. обш|ивáть, -и́ть фанéрой; ~**ed with walnut** отдéланный под орéх; фанерóванный орéхом.

venerable ['venərəb(ə)l] *adj.* **1.** (*revered*) почтéнный; ~ **ruins** дрéвние/свящéнные развáлины. **2.:** **V**~ (*as title*) преподóбный; **the V**~ **Bede** Бéда достопочтéнный.

venerate ['venə,reɪt] *v.t.* чтить (*impf.*); почитáть (*impf.*); благовéть (*impf.*) пéред+*i.*

veneration [,venə'reɪʃ(ə)n] *n.* почтéние, благоговéние.

venereal [vɪ'nɪərɪəl] *adj.* венери́ческий; ~ **disease** венери́ческая болéзнь.

venery ['venərɪ] *n.* (*arch.*) **1.** (*hunting*) псóвая охóта. **2.** (*sexual*) распу́тство.

Venetian [vɪ'ni:ʃ(ə)n] *n.* венециáн|ец (*fem.* -ка).

adj. венециáнский; ~ **blinds** жалюзи́ (*nt. pl.*, *indecl.*).

Venezuela [,venɪ'zweɪlə] *n.* Венесуэ́ла.

Venezuelan [,venɪ'zweɪlən] *n.* венесуэ́л|ец (*fem.* -ка).

adj. венесуэ́льский.

vengeance ['vendʒ(ə)ns] *n.* месть; (*bibl.*) отмщéние; **he sought** ~ **for the wrong done him** он хотéл отомсти́ть за причинённую емý оби́ду/несправедли́вость; **he swore to take** ~ **on me** он покля́лся отомсти́ть мне. **2.:** **with a** ~ (*coll.*, *in a high degree*) вовсю́, с лихвóй; **the rain came down with a** ~ дождь поли́л как из ведрá; **this is punctuality with a** ~**!** вот э́то пунктуáльность!; э́то пря́мо-таки сверхпунктуáльность!

vengeful ['vendʒfʊl] *adj.* мсти́тельный.

venial ['vi:nɪəl] *adj.* прости́тельный.

Venice ['venɪs] *n.* Венéция.

venison ['venɪs(ə)n, -z(ə)n] *n.* олéнина.

venom ['venəm] *n.* яд; (*fig.*) яд, злóба.

venomous ['venəməs] *adj.* ядови́тый; (*fig.*) ядови́тый, злóбный.

vent [vent] *n.* **1.** (*opening*) выходнóе отвéрстие; (*of wind instrument*) боковóе отвéрстие; (*flue*) дымохóд; (*in jacket*) разрéз. **2.** (*of animal*) зáдний прохóд. **3.** (*fig.*, *outlet*) вы́ход; выражéние; отду́шина; **he gave** ~ **to his feelings** он дал вóлю свои́м чу́вствам.

v.t. (*fig.*) изл|ивáть, -и́ть; да|вáть, -ть вы́ход +*d.*; **he** ~**ed his ill-temper on his secretary** он сорвáл своё дурнóе настроéние на секретáрше.

ventilate ['ventɪ,leɪt] *v.t.* провéтри|вать, -ть; вентили́ровать, про-; (*fig.*) обсу|ждáть, -ди́ть; **the question has been thoroughly** ~**d** э́тот вопрóс тщáтельно обсуждáлся.

ventilation [,ventɪ'leɪʃ(ə)n] *n.* **1.** вентиля́ция; ~ **shaft** вентиляциóнная шáхта. **2.** (*fig.*) (публи́чное) обсуждéние.

ventilator ['ventɪ,leɪtə(r)] *n.* вентиля́тор (*also med.*).

ventricle ['ventrɪk(ə)l] *n.* желу́дочек (сéрдца/мóзга).

ventriloquism [ven'trɪlə,kwɪz(ə)m] *n.* чревовещáние.

ventriloquist [ven'trɪlə,kwɪst] *n.* чревовещáтель (*m.*).

venture ['ventʃə(r)] *n.* **1.** (*risky undertaking*) рискóванное предприя́тие. **2.** (*commercial speculation*) спекуля́ция. **3.:** **at a** ~ наудáчу; наугáд.

v.t. (*risk*, *bet*) риск|овáть, -ну́ть +*i.*; стáвить, по- на кáрту; **I will** ~ **£5** я постáвлю 5 фу́нтов.

v.i. (*dare*) осмéли|ваться, -ться; отвáжиться (*pf.*); **I did not** ~ **to stop him** я не осмéлился егó останови́ть; **I** ~ **to suggest** я бы посовéтовал/рекомендовáл; **don't** ~ **too near the edge** не подходи́те сли́шком бли́зко к краю́; **nothing** ~**, nothing win** волкóв боя́ться — в лес не ходи́ть; попы́тка не пы́тка.

venturesome ['ventʃəsəm] *adj.* (*daring*) предприи́мчивый;

(*risky*) рискóванный.
venue ['venju:] *n.* мéсто сбóра/встрéчи/соревновáний.
Venus ['vi:nəs] *n.* (*myth.*, *astron.*) Венéра.
veracious [və'reɪʃəs] *adj.* правдúвый, достовéрный.
veracity [və'ræsɪtɪ] *n.* правдúвость; достовéрность (информáции).
veranda(h) [və'rændə] *n.* верáнда.
verb [vɜ:b] *n.* глагóл.
verbal ['vɜ:b(ə)l] *adj.* **1.** (*of or in words*) словéсный; ~ **subtleties** тóнкости языкá/словоупотреблéния. **2.** (*oral*) ýстный; **~ly** (тóлько) на словáх. **3.** (*literal*) буквáльный, дослóвный. **4.** (*gram.*): ~ **noun** отглагóльное существúтельное.
verbalize ['vɜ:bə,laɪz] *v.t.* (*put into words*) выражáть, вы́разить словáми.
verbatim [vɜ:'beɪtɪm] *adv.* дослóвно; слóво в слóво.
verbena [vɜ:'bi:nə] *n.* вербéна.
verbiage ['vɜ:bɪɪdʒ] *n.* многослóвие; пустослóвие.
verbose [vɜ:'bəʊs] *adj.* многослóвный.
verbos|eness [vɜ:'bəʊsnɪs], **-ity** [vɜ:'bɒsɪtɪ] *nn.* многослóвие.
verdant ['vɜ:d(ə)nt] *adj.* (*liter.*) зелёный, зеленéющий.
verdict ['vɜ:dɪkt] *n.* (*leg.*) вердúкт; **the jury brought in a ~ of guilty** суд присяжных признáл подсудúмого винóвным; (*fig.*, *decision*, *judgement*) заключéние, решéние, приговóр; **what's the ~?** какóв приговóр?; что вы скáжете?; **the popular ~** общéственное мнéние.
verdigris ['vɜ:dɪgrɪs, -,gri:s] *n.* ярь-медянка.
verdure ['vɜ:djə(r)] *n.* зéлень.
verge [vɜ:dʒ] *n.* край; (*of road*) обóчина; (*of forest*) опýшка; **the ~ of the cliff** край скалы́; обры́в; **a grass ~** бордю́р из дёрна; (*fig.*): **on the ~ of destruction** на краю́ гúбели; **on the ~ of tears** на грáни слёз; **she is on the ~ of 40** ей без мáлого сóрок; **he was on the ~ of betraying his secret** он чуть не вы́дал свою́ тáйну.
v.i.: **it ~s on madness** э́то гранúчит с безýмием.
verger ['vɜ:dʒə(r)] *n.* (*church official*) ≃ дьячóк.
Vergil ['vɜ:dʒɪl] = **Virgil**
veridical [vɪ'rɪdɪk(ə)l] *adj.* правдúвый, достовéрный.
veriest ['verɪɪst] *adj.* (*liter.*) сáмый, настоя́щий, сýщий, крáйный; **the ~ fool knows that** сáмый послéдний дурáк э́то знáет.
verifiable ['verɪ,faɪəb(ə)l] *adj.* поддаю́щийся провéрке.
verification [,verɪfɪ'keɪʃ(ə)n] *n.* провéрка, подтверждéние.
verify ['verɪ,faɪ] *v.t.* (*check accuracy of*) пров|еря́ть, -éрить; выверя́ть, вы́верить; св|еря́ть, -éрить; (*bear out*, *confirm*) подтвер|ждáть, -дúть.
verily ['verɪlɪ] *adv.* (*arch.*) úстинно, поúстине.
verisimilitude [,verɪsɪ'mɪlɪ,tju:d] *n.* правдоподóбие, вероя́тность.
veritable ['verɪtəb(ə)l] *adj.* настоя́щий, подлúнный, сýщий.
verit|y ['verɪtɪ] *n.* úстина; **eternal ~ies** вéчные úстины.
Vermeer [veə'mɪə] *n.*: **~ van Delft** Вермéр дéлфтский.
vermeil ['vɜ:meɪl, -mɪl] *n.* (*silver-gilt*) позолóченное серебрó; позолóченная брóнза.
vermicelli [,vɜ:mɪ'selɪ, -'tʃelɪ] *n.* вермишéль.
vermiform ['vɜ:mɪ,fɔ:m] *adj.*: ~ **appendix** (*anat.*) червеобрáзный отрóсток, аппéндикс.
vermilion [və'mɪljən] *n.* (*pigment*; *colour*) вермильóн, кúноварь.
adj. я́рко-крáсный; áлый.
vermin ['vɜ:mɪn] *n.* **1.** (*animal pests*) вредúтели (*m. pl.*); мéлкие хúщники (*m. pl.*). **2.** (*parasitic insects*) паразúты (*m. pl.*). **3.** (*fig.*, *obnoxious persons*) подóнки (*m. pl.*); сброд.
verminous [vɜ:'mɪvərəs] *adj.* (*infested with vermin*) кишáщий паразúтами, вшúвый.
vermouth ['vɜ:məθ, və'mu:θ] *n.* вéрмут.
vernacular [və'nækjʊlə(r)] *n.* **1.** (*local language*): **Latin gave place to the ~** латы́нь уступúла мéсто национáльным языкáм. **2.** (*dialect*) диалéкт; нарéчие. **3.** (*slang*) жаргóн, аргó (*indecl.*). **4.** (*homely speech*) просторéчие.
adj. национáльный, мéстный, просторéчный.
vernal ['vɜ:n(ə)l] *adj.* весéнний; (*poet.*) вéшний.
vernier ['vɜ:nɪə(r)] *n.* верньéр.
veronal ['verən(ə)l] *n.* веронáл.
veronica [və'rɒnɪkə] *n.* (*bot.*) верóника.
Versailles [veə'saɪ] *n.* Версáль (*m.*); **Treaty of ~** Версáльский (мúрный) договóр.
versatile ['vɜ:sə,taɪl] *adj.* разносторóнний, многосторóнний, универсáльный.
versatility [,vɜ:sə'tɪlɪtɪ] *n.* разносторóнность, многосторóнность, универсáльность.
verse [vɜ:s] *n.* **1.** (*line of ~*) строкá. **2.** (*stanza*) строфá. **3.** (*of Bible*) стих. **4.** (*sg. or pl.*, *poems*) стихú (*m. pl.*); стихотворéния (*nt. pl.*); **free ~** вóльные стихú; **light ~** куплéты (*m. pl.*); **blank ~** бéлые стихú; **prose and ~** прóза и поэ́зия; **he wrote in ~** он писáл в стихáх (*or* стихáми).
versed [vɜ:st] *adj.* (*well-informed*) свéдующий (в+*p.*); (*skilful*) óпытный, искушённый.
versification [,vɜ:sɪfɪ'keɪʃ(ə)n] *n.* версификáция, стихосложéние.
versifier ['vɜ:sɪ,faɪə(r)] *n.* рифмоплёт.
versify ['vɜ:sɪ,faɪ] *v.t.* перел|агáть. -ожúть в стихú.
version ['vɜ:ʃ(ə)n] *n.* **1.** (*individual account*) вéрсия, расскáз; **according to his ~** по егó словáм; **an idealized ~ of s.o.'s life** идеализúрованная биогрáфия когó-н. **2.** (*translation*) перевóд; **an English ~ of the Bible** бúблия на англúйском языкé; **a French ~ of Shakespeare** Шекспúр в францýзском перевóде. **3.** (*form or variant of text etc.*) вариáнт, текст; **original ~** пóдлинник, первоначáльный текст; **the Russian ~ is authentic** рýсский текст аутентúчен; (*adaptation*) переложéние, передéлка; **silent ~** (*cin.*) немóй вариáнт; **screen ~** экранизáция; **stage ~** инсценирóвка.
vers libre [veə 'li:brə] *n.* верлúбр.
verso ['vɜ:səʊ] *n.* оборóтная сторонá; оборóт; чётная/лéвая странúца.
verst [vɜ:st] *n.* верстá.
versus ['vɜ:səs] *prep.* **1.** (*leg.*) ·прóтив+*g.* **2.** (*sport*): **Manchester ~ Chelsea** матч Мáнчестер — Чéлси. **3.** (*compared or contrasted with*) в сравнéнии с+*i.*; **the question of free trade ~ protection** вопрóс о преимýществе свобóдной торгóвли пéред протекционúзмом.
vertebra ['vɜ:tɪbrə] *n.* позвонóк.
vertebrate ['vɜ:tɪbrət, -,breɪt] *n.* позвонóчное (живóтное).
adj. позвонóчный.
vertex ['vɜ:teks] *n.* (*top*, *apex*) вершúна; (*of the head*) тéмя (*nt.*), макýшка.
vertical ['vɜ:tɪk(ə)l] *n.* (*line*) вертикáль; вертикáльная лúния; перпендикуля́р.
adj. вертикáльный, отвéсный, перпендикуля́рный; **a ~ cliff** отвéсный утёс.
vertiginous [və'tɪdʒɪnəs] *adj.* головокружúтельный.
vertigo ['vɜ:tɪ,gəʊ] *n.* головокружéние.
verve [vɜ:v] *n.* жúвость, энéргия, сúла; огóнь (*m.*), огонёк.
very ['verɪ] *adj.* **1.** (*real*; *absolute*) настоя́щий, абсолю́тный. **2.** (*exact*; *identical*) тот сáмый; **this ~ day** сегóдня же; **at that ~ moment** в тот же момéнт; **this is the ~ thing for me** э́то как раз то, что мне нýжно; **those were his ~ words** э́то егó словá в тóчности; он так и сказáл. **3.** (*extreme*) сáмый; **at the ~ end** в сáмом концé. **4.** (*in emphasis*): **the ~ idea of it** однá мысль об э́том; **the ~ idea!** подýмать тóлько!; **his ~ words betray him** егó сóбственные словá выдаю́т егó с головóй; **the ~ fact of his being there is suspicious** (ужé) одúн факт егó присýтствия подозрúтелен.
adv. **1.** (*exceedingly*) óчень; **I don't feel ~ well** я чýвствую себя́ невáжно; **I can't sing ~ well** я довóльно плóхо пою́; **~ well, you can go** ну, хорошó, мóжете идтú; **~ good, sir** слýшаюсь; есть! **2.** (*emph.*, *with superl. etc.*) сáмый; **the ~ best** сáмый лýчший; наилýчший; **the ~ next day** на слéдующий же день; **you may keep it for your ~ own** мóжете э́то взять себé насовсéм.
Very ['verɪ, 'vɪərɪ] (*also* **Verey**) **light** *n.* сигнáльная ракéта Верú.
vesicular [vɪ'sɪkjʊlə(r)] *adj.*: **~ fever** пузырчáтка.
vesper|s ['vespə(r)s] *n.* вечéрня; вечéрняя молúтва; **~(-bell)** вечéрний звон.
vessel ['ves(ə)l] *n.* **1.** (*receptacle*) сосýд. **2.** (*ship*) сýдно,

корáбль (*m.*). **3.** (*anat.*) сосýд; **blood ~** кровенóсный сосýд. **4.** (*bibl.*): **the weaker ~** сосýд скудéльный; **a chosen ~** и́збранный сосýд.

vest[1] [vest] *n.* (*undergarment*) мáйка; (*US, waistcoat*) жилéт.

v.i. (*put on robes*) облач|áться, -и́ться.

cpd. **~-pocket** *n.* жилéтный кармáн.

vest[2] [vest] *v.t.* **1.** (*endow, furnish*) надел|я́ть, -и́ть; обл|екáть, -éчь; **be ~ed with a right** имéть (*impf.*) прáво; пóльзоваться (*impf.*) прáвом; **~ with power to act** упономóчи|вать, -ть; **~ s.o. with a function** возл|агáть, -ожи́ть на когó-н. обя́занность. **2.** (*place, establish*): **this right is ~ed in the Crown** э́то прáво принадлежи́т корóне; **authority ~ed in him** власть, котóрой он облечён; **~ed interest** имýщественное прáво, закреплённое закóном; крóвная заинтересóванность.

v.i.: **the estate ~s in him** имýщество перехóдит к немý.

vestal ['vest(ə)l] *n.* (**~ virgin**) вестáлка.

vestibule ['vestɪˌbju:l] *n.* (*lobby; porch*) вестибю́ль (*m.*); (*US, of corridor train*) тáмбур.

vestige ['vestɪdʒ] *n.* **1.** (*trace*) след; малéйший при́знак; **not a ~ of evidence** ни малéйшего доказáтельства. **2.** (*biol.*) остáток.

vestigial [ve'stɪdʒɪəl, -dʒ(ə)l] *adj.* остáточный, рудиментáрный.

vestment ['vestmənt] *n.* облачéние, ри́за.

vestry ['vestrɪ] *n.* (*room*) ри́зница.

Vesuvius [vɪ'su:vɪəs] *n.* Везýвий.

vet [vet] *n.* (*coll., veterinary surgeon*) ветврáч, ветеринáр.

v.t. (*check health of*) подв|ергáть, -éргнуть ветеринáрному осмóтру; (*coll., investigate*) пров|еря́ть, -éрить.

vetch [vetʃ] *n.* ви́ка.

veteran ['vetərən] *n.* (*lit., fig.*) ветерáн.

adj. многоóпытный, старéйший; **a ~ car** автомоби́ль-ветерáн.

veterinarian [ˌvetərɪ'neərɪən] *n.* ветеринáр.

veterinary ['vetəˌrɪnərɪ] *adj.* ветеринáрный; **~ surgeon** ветеринáрный врач.

veto ['vi:təʊ] *n.* вéто (*indecl.*); **he put a ~ on the suggestion** он наложи́л вéто на то предложéние; **the President exercised his ~** президéнт воспóльзовался свои́м прáвом вéто.

v.t. нал|агáть, -ожи́ть вéто на+*a.*; **my proposal was ~ed** моё предложéние бы́ло отвéргнуто.

vex [veks] *v.t.* доса|ждáть, -ди́ть; раздраж|áть, -и́ть; **how ~ing!** такáя/э́кая досáда!; **he seemed ~ed** он казáлся серди́тым; **a ~ed question** больнóй вопрóс.

vexation [vek'seɪʃ(ə)n] *n.* досáда; огорчéние.

vexatious [vek'seɪʃ(ə)s] *adj.* досáдный, огорчи́тельный.

via ['vaɪə] *prep.* чéрез+*a.*

viability [ˌvaɪə'bɪlɪtɪ] *n.* жизнеспосóбность, осуществи́мость.

viable ['vaɪəb(ə)l] *adj.* (*able to survive or exist*) жизнеспосóбный; (*coll., feasible*) осуществи́мый.

viaduct ['vaɪəˌdʌkt] *n.* виадýк, путепровóд.

vial ['vaɪəl] *n.* (*arch.*) пузырёк, флакóн; **pour out the ~s of one's wrath** (*liter.*) изли́ть (*pf.*) свой гнев.

viands ['vaɪəndz] *n.* (*arch.*) провиáнт.

viaticum [vaɪ'ætɪkəm] *n.* (*last rites*) послéднее причáстие.

vibes [vaɪbz] *n.* (*coll.*) (*vibraphone*) вибрафóн; (*vibrations*) вибрáции (*f. pl.*).

vibrant ['vaɪbrənt] *adj.* (*vibrating*) вибри́рующий; (*thrilling*) трепéщущий, дрожáщий; (*resonant*) резони́рующий.

vibraphone ['vaɪbrəˌfəʊn] *n.* вибрафóн.

vibrat|e [vaɪ'breɪt] *v.t.* заст|авля́ть, -áвить вибри́ровать (*impf.*).

v.i. вибри́ровать, дрожáть, колебáться (*all impf.*); **the whole house ~es** весь дом сотрясáется; **a voice ~ing with passion** гóлос, дрожáщий от стрáсти.

vibration [vaɪ'breɪʃ(ə)n] *n.* вибрáция, дрожь, колебáние.

vibrato [vɪ'brɑ:təʊ] *n. & adv.* вибрáто (*indecl.*).

vibrator [vaɪ'breɪtə(r)] *n.* (*for massage*) вибрáтор.

vibratory ['vaɪbrətərɪ, -'breɪtərɪ] *adj.* вибри́рующий.

viburnum [vaɪ'bɜ:nəm, vɪ-] *n.* кали́на.

vicar ['vɪkə(r)] *n.* (*clergyman*) прихóдский свящéнник; (*eccl., representative*) замести́тель (*m.*); викáрий; **V~ of Christ** намéстник Христá.

vicarage ['vɪkərɪdʒ] *n.* дом свящéнника.

vicarious [vɪ'keərɪəs] *adj.* кóсвенный; **~ punishment** наказáние за чужýю винý (*or* чужи́е грехи́); **feel ~ pleasure** пережи́вáть (*impf.*) чужýю рáдость.

vice[1] [vaɪs] *n.* **1.** (*evil doing*) порóк; **sunk in ~** погря́зший в порóке; **haunt of ~** злáчное мéсто; **~ squad** отря́д поли́ции нрáвов. **2.** (*particular fault*) порóк, слáбость, недостáток; **smoking is not among my ~s** курéние не вхóдит в числó мои́х порóков; (*of a horse*) нóров; (*of style etc.*) дефéкт, изъя́н, порóк.

vice[2] [vaɪs] (*US* **vise**) *n.* (*tool*) тиск|и́ (*pl., g.* -ов); клéщ|и (*pl., g.* -éй); **he had a grip like a ~** у негó былá желéзная хвáтка.

vice[3] [vaɪs] *n.* (*coll., deputy*) замести́тель (*m.*).

cpds. **~-admiral** *n.* ви́це-адмирáл; **~-chairman** *n.* замести́тель (*m.*) председáтеля; **~-chancellor** *n.* рéктор; ви́це-кáнцлер; **~-consul** *n.* ви́це-кóнсул; **~-president** *n.* ви́це-президéнт.

vice[4] [vaɪs] *prep.* вмéсто+*g.*; взамéн+*g.*

vicegerent [vaɪs'dʒerənt] *n.* намéстник.

vicennial [vaɪ'senɪəl] *adj.* двадцатилéтний; происходя́щий кáждые двáдцать лет.

viceregal [vaɪs'ri:g(ə)l] *adj.* вице-королéвский.

vicereine ['vaɪsreɪn] *n.* супрýга королéвского намéстника; (*hist.*) супрýга генерáл-губернáтора И́ндии.

viceroy ['vaɪsrɔɪ] *n.* королéвский намéстник; ви́це-корóль (*m.*); (*hist.*) генерáл-губернáтор И́ндии.

vice versa [ˌvaɪsɪ 'vɜ:sə] *adv.* наоборóт; **the cat stole the dog's dinner and ~** кóшка стащи́ла у собáки едý, а собáка — у кóшки.

vicinity [vɪ'sɪnɪtɪ] *n.* (*nearness*) бли́зость, сосéдство; (*neighbourhood*) окрýга, окрéстность.

vicious ['vɪʃəs] *adj.* **1.** (*marked by vice*) порóчный. **2.** (*spiteful*) злой, злóбный. **3.** (*of an animal*) злой, опáсный, норови́стый. **4.** (*faulty*) дефéктный, оши́бочный; **a ~ argument** неосновáтельный дóвод; **a ~ circle** порóчный круг. **5.**: **a ~ headache** жесточáйшая головнáя боль.

viciousness ['vɪʃəsnɪs] *n.* (*evil*) порóчность; (*spite*) злóбность; (*of an animal*) нóров, злóбность.

vicissitude [vɪ'sɪsɪˌtju:d, vaɪ-] *n.* преврáтность.

victim ['vɪktɪm] *n.* жéртва; (*of accident*) пострадáвший; **fall ~ to** дéлаться, с- (*or* пá|дать, -сть) жéртвой +*g.*

victimization [ˌvɪktɪmaɪ'zeɪʃ(ə)n] *n.* преслéдование; обмáн.

victimize ['vɪktɪˌmaɪz] *v.t.* подв|ергáть, -éргнуть преслéдованию; (*deceive*) обмáн|ывать, -ýть.

victor ['vɪktə(r)] *n.* победи́тель (*m.*).

Victoria Cross [vɪk'tɔ:rɪə] (*Br., mil.*) *n.* крест Виктóрии.

Victorian [vɪk'tɔ:rɪən] *n.* викториáн|ец (*fem.* -ка).

adj. викториáнский; (*fig.*) старомóдный.

victorious [vɪk'tɔ:rɪəs] *adj.* победонóсный, побéдный, торжествýющий.

victory ['vɪktərɪ] *n.* побéда.

victual ['vɪt(ə)l] *n.* (*pl. only*) пи́ща; съестны́е припáс|ы (*pl., g.* -ов).

v.t. снаб|жáть, -ди́ть продовóльствием.

victualler ['vɪtlə(r)] *n.* снабжéнец; постaвщи́к продовóльствия; **licensed ~** тракти́рщик.

vide ['vɪdeɪ, 'vi:-, 'vaɪdɪ] *v.tr. imper.* смотри́, (*abbr.* см.).

video ['vɪdɪəʊ] *n.*: **~ cassette** видеокассéта; **~ cassette recorder** видеомагнитофóн; **~ games machine** телеавтомáт; **~ recording** видеозáпись; **~ rental club** видеотéка; **~ tape** видеолéнта; **~ telephone** видеотелефóн.

v.t. запи́с|ывать, -áть на ви́део.

vie [vaɪ] *v.i.* состязáться (*impf.*); сопéрничать (*impf.*); **they ~d with each other for first place** они́ борóлись друг с дрýгом за пéрвое мéсто.

Vienna [vɪ'enə] *n.* Вéна.

Viennese [vɪə'ni:z] *n.* вéн|ец (*fem.* -ка).

adj. вéнский.

Vietnam [ˌvjet'næm] *n.* Вьетнáм.

Vietnamese [ˌvɪetnə'mi:z] *n.* (*pers.*) вьетнáм|ец (*fem.* -ка); (*language*) вьетнáмский язы́к.

adj. вьетнáмский.

view [vju:] *n.* **1.** (*sight; field of vision*) вид; пóле зрéния; **the mountains came into ~** показáлись гóры; **a ~ of the sea**

вид на мо́ре; **we came within ~ of the sea** (нам) откры́лось мо́ре; **he was lost to ~** он исче́з из по́ля зре́ния; **the procession passed from ~** проце́ссия скры́лось и́з виду/глаз; **in full ~ of the audience** на виду́ у пу́блики; **~ halloo!** ату́! **2.** (*fig.*): **I want to get a clear ~ of the situation** я хочу́ соста́вить себе́ я́сное представле́ние о ситуа́ции; **look at it from my point of ~** посмотри́те на э́то с моей то́чки зре́ния. **3.** (*inspection*) смотр, просмо́тр; **on a closer ~** при ближа́йшем рассмотре́нии; **the pictures are on ~ all week** вы́ставка карти́н бу́дет откры́та всю неде́лю; **private ~** закры́тый просмо́тр; (*of exhibition*) верниса́ж; **~ day** (*preparatory to auction sale*) де́нь (*m.*) предвари́тельного осмо́тра. **4.** (*scene, prospect*) вид; пейза́ж; **you get a good ~ from here** отсю́да хоро́ший вид. **5.** (*depicted scene*) вид, изображе́ние; **~s on sale at the door** откры́тки с ви́дами продаю́тся у вхо́да. **6.** (*mental attitude or opinion*) взгляд, мне́ние; **she has strong ~s on the subject** у неё на э́тот счёт твёрдые убежде́ния; **he holds extreme ~s** он челове́к кра́йних убежде́ний/взгля́дов; **in my ~** по-мо́ему; по моему́ мне́нию; **I take a different ~** у меня́ друга́я то́чка зре́ния; **he took a poor ~ of it** (*coll.*) ему́ э́то о́чень не понра́вилось; **I am ready to fall in with your ~s** я гото́в с ва́ми согласи́ться. **7.** (*intention*) наме́рение; **I am saving with a ~ to buying a house** я коплю́ де́ньги, что́бы купи́ть дом; **what have you in ~?** что вы име́ете в виду́? **8.** (*consideration*): **in ~ of** ввиду́+*g.*; **he was excused in ~ of his youth** его́ прости́ли по мо́лодости (*or*, учи́тывая его́ ю́ный во́зраст); **in ~ of recent developments** в све́те после́дних происше́ствий.

v.t. **1.** (*survey; gaze on*) смотре́ть (*impf.*); рассм|а́тривать, -отре́ть; **he ~ed the landscape through binoculars** он обозрева́л ме́стность в бино́кль. **2.** (*inspect*) осм|а́тривать, -отре́ть; **order to ~** смотрово́й о́рдер. **3.** (*fig., consider*) рассм|а́тривать, -отре́ть; оце́н|ивать, -и́ть; **he ~ed it in a different light** он ина́че смотре́л на э́то; **the request was ~ed unfavourably** к про́сьбе отнесли́сь отрица́тельно.

cpds. **~-finder** *n.* видоиска́тель (*m.*); **~point** *n.* то́чка зре́ния.

viewer ['vju:ə(r)] *n.* **1.** (*onlooker*) зри́тель (*fem.* -ница). **2.** (*of TV*) телезри́тель (*fem.* -ница). **3.** (*instrument*) прибо́р для просмо́тра диапозити́вов.

vigil ['vɪdʒɪl] *n.* **1.** (*staying awake*) бде́ние; **she kept ~ over the invalid** она́ не отходи́ла от посте́ли больно́го. **2.** (*eve of festival*) кану́н.

vigilance ['vɪdʒɪləns] *n.* бди́тельность; **~ committee** (*US*) ≃ дружи́на.

vigilant ['vɪdʒɪlənt] *adj.* бди́тельный.

vigilante [,vɪdʒɪ'læntɪ] *n.* ≃ дружи́нник.

vignette [vi:'njet] *n.* (*ornamental design*) винье́тка; (*character sketch*) набро́сок.

vigorous ['vɪgərəs] *adj.* си́льный, бо́дрый; **a ~ speech** энерги́чная речь.

vigour ['vɪgə(r)] *n.* си́ла, бо́дрость; (*of language, style etc.*) жи́вость, энерги́чность, эне́ргия.

Viking ['vaɪkɪŋ] *n.* ви́кинг.

vile [vaɪl] *adj.* гну́сный, ни́зкий, ме́рзкий.

vilification [,vɪlɪfɪ'keɪʃ(ə)n] *n.* поноше́ние, очерне́ние.

vilify ['vɪlɪ,faɪ] *v.t.* понос́ить (*impf.*); черни́ть, о-.

villa ['vɪlə] *n.* (*country residence*) ви́лла, да́ча; (*suburban house*) ви́лла, до́м(ик).

village ['vɪlɪdʒ] *n.* дере́вня, село́; (*attr.*) дереве́нский; **~ hall** се́льский клуб.

villager ['vɪlɪdʒə(r)] *n.* жи́тель (*fem.* -ница) дере́вни; крестья́н|ин (*fem.* -ка).

villain ['vɪlən] *n.* **1.** (*man of base character*) злоде́й, негодя́й; (*theatr.*) отрица́тельный геро́й; **he played the ~** он игра́л роль злоде́я; **he was the ~ of the piece** (*fig.*) он был гла́вным вино́вником. **2.** (*coll., criminal*) престу́пник.

villainess ['vɪlənɪs] *n.* злоде́йка, престу́пница.

villainous ['vɪlənəs] *adj.* (*scoundrelly*) по́длый, ни́зкий, гну́сный; (*coll., wretched*) отврати́тельный, ме́рзкий.

villainy ['vɪlənɪ] *n.* злоде́йство, по́длость.

villein ['vɪlɪn] *n.* (*hist.*) вилла́н.

Vilnius ['vɪlnɪəs] *n.* Ви́льнюс; (*attr.*) ви́льнюсский.

vim [vɪm] *n.* эне́ргия, си́ла, напо́р.

vinaigrette [,vɪnɪ'gret] *n.* подли́вка из у́ксуса и прова́нского ма́сла.

vindicate ['vɪndɪ,keɪt] *v.t.* (*defend successfully*) отст|а́ивать, -оя́ть; защи|ща́ть, -ти́ть; дока́з|ывать, -а́ть; (*justify*) опра́вд|ывать, -а́ть.

vindication [,vɪndɪ'keɪʃ(ə)n] *n.* защи́та; доказа́тельство; оправда́ние.

vindictive [vɪn'dɪktɪv] *adj.* мсти́тельный; **~ damages** штраф за убы́тки.

vindictiveness [vɪn'dɪktɪvnɪs] *n.* мсти́тельность.

vine [vaɪn] *n.* (*grape-~*) виногра́дная лоза́; (*any climbing or trailing plant*) вью́щееся/ползу́чее расте́ние.

cpds. **~-dresser, ~-grower** *nn.* виногра́дарь (*m.*), виноде́л; **~-growing** *adj.* виноде́льческий; **~yard** *n.* виногра́дник.

vinegar ['vɪnɪgə(r)] *n.* у́ксус.

vinegar|ish ['vɪnɪgərɪʃ], **-y** ['vɪnɪgərɪ] *adjs.* у́ксусный; ки́слый (*also fig.*).

vinery ['vaɪnərɪ] *n.* виногра́дная тепли́ца.

viniculture ['vɪnɪ,kʌltʃə(r)] *n.* виногра́дарство.

vinous ['vaɪnəs] *adj.* (*of wine*) ви́нный; **~ eloquence** пьяное/хмельно́е красноре́чие.

vintage ['vɪntɪdʒ] *n.* **1.** (*grape harvest*) сбор виногра́да; **the 1950 ~** (*sc. wine*) вино́ урожа́я (*or* из сбо́ра) ты́сяча девятьсо́т пятидеся́того го́да; **a rare ~** ре́дкое вино́; **this is a good ~** э́то хоро́ший год; **~ wine** ма́рочное вино́; **~ port** ста́рый/вы́держанный портве́йн. **2.** (*fig.*): **a ~ car** автомоби́ль (*m.*) ста́рой ма́рки; **of the same ~** (*sc. age*) того́ же вы́пуска; **a ~ Agatha Christie** рома́н са́мого плодотво́рного пери́ода тво́рчества Ага́ты Кри́сти.

vintner ['vɪntnə(r)] *n.* виноторго́вец.

vinyl ['vaɪnɪl] *n.* вини́л.

adj. вини́ловый.

viol ['vaɪəl] *n.* вио́ла; **~ da gamba** вио́ла да га́мба.

viola[1] [vɪ'əʊlə] *n.* (*mus.*) альт.

viola[2] ['vaɪələ] *n.* (*bot.*) вио́ла.

violate ['vaɪə,leɪt] *v.t.* **1.** (*infringe, transgress*) нар|уша́ть, -у́шить; поп|ира́ть, -ра́ть; преступ|а́ть, -и́ть; **this ~s the spirit of the agreement** э́то противоре́чит ду́ху соглаше́ния; **~ one's conscience** де́йствовать (*impf.*) вопреки́ свое́й со́вести. **2.** (*profane*) оскверн|я́ть, -и́ть. **3.** (*injure*) оскорб|ля́ть, -и́ть. **4.** (*break, e.g. silence*) нар|уша́ть, -у́шить. **5.** (*rape*) наси́ловать, из-.

violation [,vaɪə'leɪʃ(ə)n] *n.* наруше́ние, оскверне́ние, оскорбле́ние; **~ of territory** вторже́ние на чужу́ю террито́рию; (*rape*) изнаси́лование.

violator ['vaɪə,leɪtə(r)] *n.* наруши́тель (*fem.* -ница).

violence ['vaɪələns] *n.* си́ла, наси́лие, неи́стовство, я́рость, ожесточённость; **he resorted to ~** он примени́л си́лу; он прибе́гнул к наси́лию; **robbery with ~** грабёж с наси́лием; **it would do ~ to his principles** э́то противоре́чило бы его́ при́нципам; **do ~ to a text** иска|жа́ть, -зи́ть смысл те́кста; **a ~ to language** наси́лие над языко́м.

violent ['vaɪələnt] *adj.* **1.** (*strong, forceful*) си́льный, неи́стовый, я́ростный; ожесточённый; **a ~ storm** жесто́кий/си́льный што́рм; **~ pain** о́страя боль; **a ~ cough** сильне́йший ка́шель; **a ~ contrast** вопию́щее/ре́зкое противоре́чие; **~ colours** ре́зкие/крича́щие цвета́; **~ passions** неи́стовые стра́сти; **a ~ scene** бу́рная сце́на; **I took a ~ dislike to him** он вы́звал во мне ре́зкое отвраще́ние; **he was in a ~ temper** он был вне себя́ от бе́шенства; **he made a ~ speech** он произнёс горя́чую/гне́вную речь. **2.** (*using or involving force*): **~ blows** си́льные уда́ры; **he became ~** он на́чал бу́йствовать; **he laid ~ hands on her** он изби́л её; **he died a ~ death** он у́мер наси́льственной сме́ртью.

violet ['vaɪələt] *n.* (*bot.*) фиа́лка; (*colour*) фиоле́товый/ лило́вый цвет.

adj. (*of colour*) фиоле́товый, лило́вый.

violin [,vaɪə'lɪn] *n.* скри́пка; (*player*) скрипа́ч; **first ~** пе́рвая скри́пка.

violinist [vaɪə'lɪnɪst] *n.* скрипа́ч (*fem.* -ка).

violoncellist [,vaɪələn'tʃelɪst, ,vi:ə-] *n.* виолончели́ст (*fem.* -ка).

violoncello [ˌvaɪələnˈtʃeləʊ, ˌviːə-] *n.* виолонче́ль.
VIP (*abbr. of* ***very important person***) высокопоста́вленное лицо́, высо́кий гость.
viper [ˈvaɪpə(r)] *n.* гадю́ка; випе́ра; (*fig.*) змея́, гад, гадю́ка, га́дина.
virago [vɪˈrɑːgəʊ, -ˈreɪgəʊ] *n.* меге́ра.
Virgil [ˈvɜːdʒɪl] *n.* Верги́лий.
Virgilian [vɜːˈdʒɪlɪən] *adj.* верги́лиев, сво́йственный Верги́лию.
virgin [ˈvɜːdʒɪn] *n.* де́ва, де́вственница; (*male*) де́вственник; **the (Blessed) V~** де́ва Мари́я; **the wise and foolish ~s** му́дрые и неразу́мные де́вы; **the V~ Queen** короле́ва-де́вственница; **she is still a ~** она́ ещё де́вушка/деви́ца; **~ birth** рожде́ние от де́вы; (*of insects etc.*) партеногене́з; **~ modesty** де́вичий стыд; (*pure*; *undefiled*) чи́стый, нетро́нутый; **~ soil** целина́; **~ forest** де́вственный/первобы́тный лес.
virginal[1]**(s)** [ˈvɜːdʒɪn(ə)l] *n.* (*mus.*) клавеси́н.
virginal[2] [ˈvɜːdʒɪn(ə)l] *adj.* де́вственный, де́вичий; непоро́чный, неви́нный.
Virginia [vəˈdʒɪnɪə] *n.*: **~ tobacco** вирги́нский таба́к; **~ creeper** ди́кий виногра́д.
virginity [vəˈdʒɪnɪtɪ] *n.* де́вственность, непоро́чность; **lose one's ~** теря́ть, по- неви́нность; **take s.o.'s ~** лиш|а́ть, -и́ть кого́-н. неви́нности.
Virgo [ˈvɜːgəʊ] *n.* Де́ва.
viridian [vɪˈrɪdɪən] *n.* (*pigment*) виридиа́н; о́кись хро́ма.
virile [ˈvɪraɪl] *adj.* **1.** (*sexually potent*) вири́льный; облада́ющий мужско́й си́лой/поте́нцией. **2.** (*manly, robust*) му́жественный, энерги́чный; **a ~ handshake** мужско́е рукопожа́тие.
virility [vɪˈrɪlɪtɪ] *n.* му́жество; полова́я поте́нция; му́жественность, эне́ргия.
virology [vaɪˈrɒlədʒɪ] *n.* вирусоло́гия.
virtu [vɜːˈtuː] *n.*: **objects of ~** худо́жественные ре́дкости (*f. pl.*); рарите́ты (*m. pl.*).
virtual [ˈvɜːtjʊəl] *adj.* факти́ческий; **the dress was ~ly new** э́то бы́ло практи́чески но́вое пла́тье; **he is a ~ stranger to me** я его́, в су́щности, не зна́ю.
virtue [ˈvɜːtjuː, -tʃuː] *n.* **1.** (*moral excellence*) доброде́тель; **~ is its own reward** доброде́тель не нужда́ется в награ́де; (*specific*): **make a ~ of necessity** из нужды́ сде́лать (*pf.*) доброде́тель; **his great ~ is patience** его́ гла́вная доброде́тель —терпе́ние. **2.** (*chastity*) целому́дрие; **a woman of easy ~** досту́пная же́нщина. **3.** (*good quality*; *advantage*) досто́инство, преиму́щество; **his scheme had the ~ of being practicable** преиму́щество его́ пла́на состоя́ло в том, что он был выполни́м. **4.** (*consideration*) основа́ние; **by ~ of his long service** на основа́нии (*or* ввиду́) его́ долголе́тней слу́жбы.
virtuosity [ˌvɜːtjuːˈɒsɪtɪ, -tʃuːˈɒsɪtɪ] *n.* виртуо́зность.
virtuoso [ˌvɜːtjʊˈəʊsəʊ, -zəʊ] *n.* виртуо́з; **a ~ performance** виртуо́зное исполне́ние.
virtuous [ˈvɜːtjʊəs, -tʃʊəs] *adj.* доброде́тельный; (*chaste*) целому́дренный; **~ indignation** благоро́дное негодова́ние.
virulence [ˈvɪrʊləns, ˈvɪrjʊ-] *n.* (*of poison*) си́ла, смерте́льность; (*of disease*) вируле́нтность, свире́пость; (*of temper, speech etc.*) зло́ба, зло́бность, я́рость.
virulent [ˈvɪrʊlənt, ˈvɪrjʊ-] *adj.* (*of poison*) сильноде́йствующий; смерте́льный; (*of disease*) вируле́нтный, свире́пый; (*of temper, words etc.*) зло́бный, я́ростный; **~ pen** отра́вленное перо́.
virus [ˈvaɪərəs] *n.* ви́рус; **a ~ disease** ви́русное заболева́ние; (*fig.*) отра́ва, зара́за, ви́рус.
visa [ˈviːzə] *n.* ви́за.
v.t. визи́ровать (*impf., pf.*); **I have to get my passport ~ed** мне ну́жно поста́вит ви́зу в па́спорте.
visage [ˈvɪzɪdʒ] *n.* (*liter.*) лицо́; выраже́ние лица́; вид.
vis-à-vis [ˌviːzɑːˈviː] *adv.* визави́.
prep. (*in relation to*) по отноше́нию к+*d.*; в отноше́нии+*g.*; пе́ред+*i.*
viscera [ˈvɪsərə] *n.* вну́тренности (*f. pl.*); потроха́ (*m. pl.*); кишки́ (*f. pl.*).
visceral [ˈvɪsər(ə)l] *adj.* вну́тренний; **~ cavity** по́лость те́ла; **~ hatred** глубо́кая/органи́ческая не́нависть.
viscose [ˈvɪskəʊz, -kəʊs] *n.* виско́за.
viscosity [vɪˈskɒsɪtɪ] *n.* ли́пкость, кле́йкость, вя́зкость.
viscount [ˈvaɪkaʊnt] *n.* вико́нт.
viscountess [ˈvaɪkaʊntɪs] *n.* виконте́сса.
viscous [ˈvɪskəs] *adj.* ли́пкий, кле́йкий, вя́зкий.
vise [vaɪs] = **vice**[2]
visibility [ˌvɪzɪˈbɪlɪtɪ] *n.* ви́димость.
visibl|e [ˈvɪzɪb(ə)l] *adj.* **1.** (*perceptible by eye*) ви́димый. **2.** (*apparent*; *obvious*) я́вный, очеви́дный; **he has no ~e means of support** у него́ нет определённых средств к существова́нию; **she was ~y annoyed** она́ была́ заме́тно раздражена́.
Visigoth [ˈvɪzɪˌgɒθ] *n.* вестго́т.
Visigothic [ˌvɪzɪˈgɒθɪk] *adj.* вестго́тский.
vision [ˈvɪʒ(ə)n] *n.* **1.** (*faculty of sight*) зре́ние; **field of ~** по́ле зре́ния. **2.** (*imaginative insight*) проница́тельность; **a man of ~** прови́дец; дальнови́дный челове́к; челове́к с широ́ким кругозо́ром. **3.** (*apparition*) при́зрак; привиде́ние. **4.** (*sth. imagined or dreamed of*) мечта́; о́браз; **I had ~s of something better than this** я представля́л себе́ не́что друго́е — лу́чшее.
visionary [ˈvɪʒənərɪ] *n.* мечта́тель (*fem.* -ница); прови́д|ец (*fem.* -ица).
adj. (*unreal*) вообража́емый, при́зрачный; (*unpractical*) неосуществи́мый, нереа́льный.
visit [ˈvɪzɪt] *n.* (*call*) визи́т, посеще́ние; (*US, talk*) бесе́да; (*trip, stay*) пое́здка, пребыва́ние; побы́вка; (*of ship*) осмо́тр, о́быск; **make, pay a ~ to s.o.** посе|ща́ть, -ти́ть (*or* наве|ща́ть, -сти́ть) кого́-н.; **we had a ~ from our neighbours** нас посети́ли (*or* у нас бы́ли в гостя́х) на́ши сосе́ди; **we had a ~ from a policeman** к нам приходи́л полице́йский; **~ to a museum** посеще́ние музе́я; **~ to the scene of the crime** вы́езд на ме́сто преступле́ния; **pay us a ~** прове́дайте нас; **he is here on a ~** он гости́т здесь; он прие́зжий; **during my ~ to the States** во вре́мя моего́ пребыва́ния в Шта́тах; **we rarely have ~s from friends** к нам ре́дко наве́дываются друзья́.
v.t. **1.** посе|ща́ть, -ти́ть; наве|ща́ть, -сти́ть; наве́д|ываться, -аться к+*d.*; **he ~ed Europe** он побыва́л в Евро́пе; он съе́здил в Евро́пу; **I have never ~ed New York** я никогда́ не быва́л в Нью-Йо́рке. **2.** (*for inspection*) осм|а́тривать, -отре́ть; **the club was ~ed by the police** в клуб наве́далась поли́ция. **3.** (*of disease etc.*) пост|ига́ть, -и́чь; пора|жа́ть, -зи́ть. **4.** (*bibl., avenge*): **the sins of the fathers shall be ~ed on the children** де́ти бу́дут нака́заны за грехи́ отцо́в; грехи́ отцо́в паду́т на го́ловы дете́й; **~ing card** визи́тная ка́рточка; **~ing hours** приёмные часы́; часы́ посеще́ния.
v.i. (*US*): **~ with** пообща́ться (*pf.*) (*or* вида́ться, по-, *or* бесе́довать (*impf.*)) с+*i.*
visitant [ˈvɪzɪt(ə)nt] *n.* (*visitor*) гость (*m.*), прише́лец (из друго́го ми́ра); (*bird*) перелётная пти́ца.
visitation [ˌvɪzɪˈteɪʃ(ə)n] *n.* (*official visit*) обхо́д; (*coll., protracted visit*) затяну́вшийся визи́т; (*affliction*) ка́ра, наказа́ние (бо́жье).
visitor [ˈvɪzɪtə(r)] *n.* гость (*m.*), посети́тель (*m.*); **the town is full of ~s** го́род по́лон прие́зжих; **~s' book** кни́га посети́телей.
vi|sor, -zor [ˈvaɪzə(r)] *n.* (*hist.*) забра́ло; (*of cap*) козырёк; (*of windscreen*) солнцезащи́тный щито́к.
vista [ˈvɪstə] *n.* перспекти́ва, вид; (*fig.*) перспекти́вы (*f. pl.*); **this opened up new ~s** э́то откры́ло но́вые перспекти́вы.
Vistula [ˈvɪstjʊlə] *n.* Ви́сла.
visual [ˈvɪzjʊəl, ˈvɪʒj-] *adj.* (*concerned with seeing*) зри́тельный, визуа́льный; **~ nerve** зри́тельный нерв; **~ image** зри́тельный о́браз; **~ memory** зри́тельная/визуа́льная па́мять; **~ aids** нагля́дные посо́бия.
visualize [ˈvɪzjʊəˌlaɪz, ˈvɪʒj-] *v.t.* (*make visible*) де́лать, с- ви́димым; (*imagine*) предст|авля́ть, -а́вить себе́.
vital [ˈvaɪt(ə)l] *adj* **1.** (*concerned with life*) жи́зненный; **~ force** жи́зненная си́ла; **~ principle** жи́зненное нача́ло; **~ spark** и́скра бо́жья; **wounded in a ~ part** получи́вший смерте́льное ране́ние; **~ statistics** демографи́ческая стати́стика; (*joc., woman's measurements*) объём груди́,

та́лии и бёдер. **2.** (*essential*; *indispensable*) насу́щный; (кра́йне) необходи́мый; жи́зненно ва́жный; **a ~ question** суще́ственный/животрепе́щущий вопро́с; **it is of ~ importance** э́то вопро́с/де́ло первостепе́нной ва́жности; **speed was ~ to success** ско́рость была́ гла́вным зало́гом успе́ха. **3.** (*lively*; *having vitality*) энерги́чный, живо́й.

vitality [vaɪˈtælɪtɪ] *n.* (*vital power*) жи́зненная си́ла; (*viability*) жизнеспосо́бность; (*energy*; *liveliness*) эне́ргия, жи́вость.

vitalize [ˈvaɪtəˌlaɪz] *v.t.* ожив|ля́ть, -и́ть.

vitals [ˈvaɪt(ə)lz] *n.* жи́зненно ва́жные о́рганы (*m. pl.*); (*of ship*) подво́дная часть.

vitamin [ˈvɪtəmɪn, ˈvaɪt-] *n.* витами́н; (*attr.*) витами́нный; **V~ C** витами́н С (*pr.* це).

vitiate [ˈvɪʃɪˌeɪt] *v.t.* по́ртить, ис-; (*fig.*, *invalidate*) де́лать, с- недействи́тельным; под|рыва́ть, -орва́ть.

viticulture [ˈvɪtɪˌkʌltʃə(r)] *n.* виногра́дарство.

vitreous [ˈvɪtrɪəs] *adj.* стекля́нный.

vitrify [ˈvɪtrɪˌfaɪ] *v.t. & i.* превра|ща́ть(ся), -ти́ть(ся) в стекло́.

vitriol [ˈvɪtrɪəl] *n.* **1.** купоро́с; **blue ~** ме́дный купоро́с. **2.** (*fig.*) яд.

vitriolic [ˌvɪtrɪˈɒlɪk] *adj.* купоро́сный; (*fig.*) е́дкий, ядови́тый.

vituperate [vɪˈtjuːpəˌreɪt, vaɪ-] *v.t.* поноси́ть, брани́ть, хули́ть (*all impf.*).

vituperation [vɪˌtjuːpəˈreɪʃ(ə)n, vaɪ-] *n.* пороше́ние, брань, хула́.

vituperative [vɪˈtjuːpərətɪv, vaɪ-] *adj.* бра́нный, зло́бный.

viva [ˈvaɪvə] = **viva voce**

vivace [vɪˈvɑːtʃɪ] *adv.* вива́че; оживлённо.

vivacious [vɪˈveɪʃəs] *adj.* живо́й, оживлённый.

vivacity [vɪˈvæsɪtɪ] *n.* жи́вость, оживле́ние.

vivarium [vaɪˈveərɪəm, vɪ-] *n.* вива́рий.

viva voce [ˌvaɪvə ˈvəʊtʃɪ, ˈvəʊsɪ] *n.* (*also coll.* **viva**) у́стный экза́мен.

adj. у́стный.

adv. вслух.

vivid [ˈvɪvɪd] *adj.* **1.** (*bright*) я́ркий. **2.** (*lively*) живо́й; пы́лкий; **a ~ imagination** пы́лкое воображе́ние. **3.** (*clear and distinct*) чёткий, я́сный.

vividness [ˈvɪvɪdnɪs] *n.* я́ркость, жи́вость, чёткость.

viviparous [vɪˈvɪpərəs, vaɪ-] *adj.* живородя́щий.

vivisect [ˈvɪvɪˌsekt] *v.t.* подв|ерга́ть, -е́ргнуть вивисе́кции.

vivisection [ˌvɪvɪˈsekʃ(ə)n] *n.* вивисе́кция.

vivisectionist [ˌvɪvɪˈsekʃ(ə)nɪst] *n.* вивисе́ктор.

vixen [ˈvɪks(ə)n] *n.* лиси́ца(-са́мка); (*fig.*) ве́дьма, меге́ра.

viz. [vɪz] *adv.* а и́менно.

vizier [vɪˈzɪə(r), ˈvɪzɪə(r)] *n.* визи́рь (*m.*).

vizor [ˈvaɪzə(r)] = **visor**

vocabulary [vəˈkæbjʊlərɪ] *n.* (*range of words*) слова́рь (*m.*), запа́с слов, лексико́н; (*of a language*) слова́рный соста́в; (*of a subject*) номенклату́ра; (*list of words*) слова́рь (*m.*), сло́вник, спи́сок слов.

vocal [ˈvəʊk(ə)l] *adj.* **1.** (*of or using the voice*) голосово́й, речево́й; **~ cords** голосовы́е свя́зки; **~ music** вока́льная му́зыка. **2.** (*eloquent*) красноречи́вый.

vocalic [vəˈkælɪk] *adj.*: **~ harmony** гармо́ния гла́сных, сингармони́зм.

vocalist [ˈvəʊkəlɪst] *n.* вокали́ст; пев|е́ц (*fem.* -и́ца).

vocalize [ˈvəʊkəˌlaɪz] *v.i.* (*mus.*) исп|олня́ть, -о́лнить вокали́зы.

vocation [vəˈkeɪʃ(ə)n] *n.* (*calling*, *aptitude*) призва́ние; (*trade*, *profession*) профе́ссия.

vocational [vəˈkeɪʃən(ə)l] *adj.* профессиона́льный.

vocative [ˈvɒkətɪv] *n. & adj.* зва́тельный (паде́ж).

vociferate [vəˈsɪfəˌreɪt] *v.t. & i.* крича́ть (*impf.*); горла́нить (*impf.*).

vociferous [vəˈsɪfərəs] *adj.* гро́мкий, горла́стый, шу́мный.

vodka [ˈvɒdkə] *n.* во́дка.

vogue [vəʊg] *n.* мо́да; **in ~** в мо́де.

voice [vɔɪs] *n.* **1.** го́лос; звук; **I did not recognise his ~** я не узна́л его́ го́лос; **he is in good ~** он в го́лосе; **he shouted at the top of his ~** он крича́л во всё го́рло; **keep your ~ down!** не разгова́ривайте (*or* не говори́те) так гро́мко!; **I lost my ~** я потеря́л го́лос; **he raised his ~** он повы́сил го́лос. **2.** (*expression of opinion*) мне́ние; го́лос; **we must speak with one ~** мы должны́ говори́ть одно́ и то же; **not a ~ was raised against him** не оди́н челове́к не по́днял го́лос про́тив него́; **I have no ~ in the matter** моё мне́ние ничего́ не зна́чит в э́том де́ле. **3.** (*gram.*) зало́г.

v.t. **1.** (*utter*) выража́ть, вы́разить. **2.** (*phon.*) произн|оси́ть, -ести́ зво́нко; **a ~ed consonant** зво́нкий согла́сный.

cpds. **~-over** *n.* (*TV etc.*) го́лос за ка́дром, зака́дровый го́лос; **~-print** *n.* спектрогра́мма го́лоса/ре́чи, «отпеча́ток го́лоса».

voiceless [ˈvɔɪslɪs] *adj.* (*mute*) безгла́сный, безмо́лвный; (*phon.*) глухо́й.

void [vɔɪd] *n.* пустота́; пробе́л; пусто́е простра́нство; **his death left an aching ~ in my heart** с его́ сме́ртью я понёс невосполни́мую утра́ту.

adj. **1.** (*empty*; *bereft*) пусто́й; лишённый (*чего*); **the subject was ~ of interest** те́ма не представля́ла никако́го интере́са. **2.** (*invalid*) недействи́тельный; **the contract is null and ~** контра́кт не име́ет си́лы.

v.t. (*make invalid*) аннули́ровать (*impf.*, *pf.*); (*emit from body*) выделя́ть, вы́делить; изв|ерга́ть, -е́ргнуть.

voile [vɔɪl, vwɑːl] *n.* вуа́ль.

volatile [ˈvɒləˌtaɪl] *adj.* (*of liquid*) лету́чий; (*fig.*, *of pers.*) непостоя́нный, изме́нчивый, капри́зный.

volatility [ˌvɒləˈtɪlɪtɪ] *n.* лету́честь; (*fig.*) непостоя́нство, изме́нчивость, капри́зность.

vol-au-vent [ˈvɒləʊˌvɑ̃] *n.* волова́н (*слоеный пирожок*).

volcanic [vɒlˈkænɪk] *adj.* вулкани́ческий; (*fig.*) вулкани́ческий, бу́рный.

volcano [vɒlˈkeɪnəʊ] *n.* вулка́н.

vole [vəʊl] *n.* полёвка.

Volga [ˈvɒlgə] *n.* Во́лга; **~ boatmen** во́лжские бурлаки́.

volition [vəˈlɪʃ(ə)n] *n.* во́ля; **I went of my own ~** я пошёл по свое́й во́ле.

volley [ˈvɒlɪ] *n.* **1.** (*simultaneous discharge*) залп; (*fig.*): **a ~ of oaths** пото́к бра́ни. **2.** (*tennis etc.*) уда́р с лёта; **half ~** уда́р с отско́ка.

v.t. уда́рить (*pf.*) с лёта.

cpd. **~-ball** *n.* волейбо́л.

volt [vəʊlt] *n.* вольт.

voltage [ˈvəʊltɪdʒ] *n.* вольта́ж; **what is the ~ here?** како́е здесь напряже́ние?

voltaic [vɒlˈteɪɪk] *adj.* гальвани́ческий.

volte-face [vɒltˈfɑːs] *n.* (*about-turn*) поворо́т круго́м; (*fig.*, *complete reversal*) круто́й поворо́т; поворо́т на 180° гра́дусов.

voltmeter [ˈvəʊltˌmiːtə(r)] *n.* вольтме́тр.

volubility [ˌvɒljʊˈbɪlɪtɪ] *n.* говорли́вость, разгово́рчивость.

voluble [ˈvɒljʊb(ə)l] *adj.* говорли́вый, разгово́рчивый.

volume [ˈvɒljuːm] *n.* **1.** (*tome*) том; **it speaks ~s for his honesty** э́то лу́чшее доказа́тельство его́ че́стности. **2.** (*size*) объём. **3.** (*of sound*) си́ла; **~ control** регуля́тор гро́мкости; **turn the ~ down!** сде́лайте звук поти́ше!

volumetric [ˌvɒljʊˈmetrɪk] *adj.* объёмный.

voluminous [vəˈljuːmɪnəs, vəˈluː-] *adj.* огро́мный; **~ folds** пы́шные скла́дки; **a ~ work** объёмистое произведе́ние; **a ~ writer** плодови́тый писа́тель.

voluntary [ˈvɒləntərɪ] *n.* (*organ solo*) со́ло (*indecl.*) на орга́не.

adj. **1.** (*acting or done without compulsion*) доброво́льный, доброво́льческий; **~ worker** обще́ственный рабо́тник. **2.** (*maintained by ~ effort*) содержа́щийся на доброво́льные взно́сы. **3.** (*controlled by will*) созна́тельный, умы́шленный; **~ muscle** произво́льная мы́шца.

volunteer [ˌvɒlənˈtɪə(r)] *n.* доброво́лец, охо́тник; (*attr.*) доброво́льческий.

v.t. предл|ага́ть, -ожи́ть; де́лать, с- доброво́льно; **he ~ed his services** он предложи́л свои́ услу́ги.

v.i. вызыва́ться, вы́зваться сде́лать что-н.; **no-one ~ed** охо́тника не нашло́сь; **were you conscripted or did you ~?** вас призва́ли на вое́нную слу́жбу и́ли вы пошли́ доброво́льцем/са́ми?

voluptuary [vəˈlʌptjʊərɪ] *n.* сладостра́стник, гедони́ст.

voluptuous [vəˈlʌptjʊəs] *adj.* сладостра́стный; (*sensual*) чу́вственный; (*luxurious*) пы́шный, роско́шный.

voluptuousness [və'lʌptjʊəsnɪs] *n.* сладостра́стие; чу́вственность; пы́шность.

volute [və'lju:t] *n.* волю́та.

vomit ['vɒmɪt] *n.* рво́та, блево́тина.

v.t.: **he ~ed blood** его́ вы́рвало/рва́ло кро́вью; **the chimney ~ed smoke** труба́ изверга́ла дым.

v.i.: **he ~ed** его́ вы́рвало; **an attack of ~ing** при́ступ рво́ты.

voodoo ['vu:du:], **-ism** ['vu:du:ɪz(ə)m] *nn.* колдовство́, шама́нство.

voracious [və'reɪʃəs] *adj.* прожо́рливый, жа́дный; (*fig.*): **a ~ reader** ненасы́тный чита́тель.

vorac|iousness [və'reɪʃəsnɪs], **-ity** [və'ræsɪtɪ] *nn.* прожо́рливость, жа́дность, ненасы́тность.

vortex ['vɔ:teks] *n.* (*lit.*, *fig.*) вихрь (*m.*), водоворо́т.

votar|y ['vəʊtərɪ] (*fem.* **-ess**) ['vəʊtərɪs] *nn.* побо́рни|к (*fem.* -ца), приве́ржен|ец (*fem.* -ка).

vote [vəʊt] *n.* **1.** (*act of voting*) голосова́ние; **shall we put it to the ~?** поста́вим э́то на голосова́ние?; **proxy ~** голосова́ние по дове́ренности. **2.** (*~ cast*) го́лос; **I shall give my ~ to Labour** я отда́м свой го́лос лейбори́стам; **the chairman has the casting ~** у председа́теля реша́ющий го́лос; **affirmative ~** го́лос за; **negative ~** го́лос про́тив. **3.** (*affirmation*) во́тум; **the Prime Minister received a ~ of confidence** премье́р-мини́стр получи́л во́тум дове́рия; **I beg to move a ~ of thanks** предлага́ю вы́разить благода́рность; **pass a ~** прин|има́ть, -я́ть резолю́цию. **4.** (*right to ~*) пра́во го́лоса; избира́тельное пра́во; **when did women get the ~?** когда́ же́нщины получи́ли пра́во го́лоса?; **delegate without a ~** делега́т с совеща́тельным го́лосом. **5.** (*number of ~s cast*) коли́чество голосова́вшихся; **the Tories increased their ~** консерва́торы завоева́ли бо́льше голосо́в, чем на предыду́щих вы́борах. **6.** (*money granted by ~*): **the Army ~** ассигнова́ния (*nt. pl.*) на а́рмию.

v.t.: **they were ~d back into power** их сно́ва избра́ли в прави́тельство; (*allocate by ~*) ассигнова́ть (*impf.*, *pf.*); **a large sum was ~d for defence** больша́я су́мма была́ вы́делена на оборо́ну; (*declare*): **he was ~d a fine fellow** его́ объяви́ли сла́вным ма́лым; (*coll.*, *propose*): **I ~ we go home** я предлага́ю (*or* я за то, что́бы) пойти́ домо́й.

v.i. голосова́ть, про-; **they are voting on the resolution** они́ голосу́ют резолю́цию.

with advs.: **the measure was ~d down, out** предложе́ние отклони́ли/провали́ли; **they were ~d in by a large majority** их избра́ли реша́ющим большинство́м голосо́в; **the bill was ~d through** зако́н прошёл (*or* был при́нят).

voteless ['vəʊtlɪs] *adj.* лишённый избира́тельных прав; без го́лоса.

voter ['vəʊtə(r)] *n.* избира́тель (*m.*).

voting ['vəʊtɪŋ] *n.* голосова́ние, баллотиро́вка; (*attr.*): **~ qualification** избира́тельный ценз; **~ paper** избира́тельный бюллете́нь.

votive ['vəʊtɪv] *adj.* испо́лненный по обе́ту; **a ~ offering** жертвоприноше́ние (по обе́ту); благода́рная же́ртва.

vouch [vaʊtʃ] *v.i.* руча́ться, поручи́ться; **I can ~ for his honesty** я гото́в поручи́ться за его́ че́стность; **I will ~ for the truth of his story** я могу́ подтверди́ть, что он говори́т пра́вду.

voucher ['vaʊtʃə(r)] *n.* (*receipt*) распи́ска; (*token*) (льго́тный) тало́н; биле́т, бо́на; **luncheon ~** тало́н на обе́д.

vouchsafe [vaʊtʃ'seɪf] *v.t.* (*accord*) удост|а́ивать, -о́ить (*кого чем*); (*condescend*) соизво́лить (*pf.*); сни|сходи́ть, -зойти́.

vow [vaʊ] *n.* обе́т, кля́тва; **the monks were under a ~ of silence** мона́хи бы́ли свя́заны обе́том молча́ния; **he broke his marriage ~s** он нару́шил бра́чный обе́т.

v.t. кля́сться, по-; **they ~ed obedience** они́ да́ли обе́т послуша́ния; **he ~ed** (*resolved*) **never to return** он покля́лся не возвраща́ться; **he ~ed not to smoke** он дал заро́к не кури́ть; (*coll.*) он заре́кся кури́ть.

vowel ['vaʊəl] *n.* гла́сный.

voyage ['vɔɪɪdʒ] *n.* путеше́ствие (водо́й); рейс; (*by sea*) пла́вание; (*by air*) полёт; **on the ~ home** на обра́тном пути́.

v.i. путеше́ствовать (*impf.*).

voyager ['vɔɪɪdʒə(r)] *n.* путеше́ственник; морепла́ватель (*m.*); (*in space*) воздухопла́ватель (*fem.* -ница).

voyeur [vwɑ:'jɜ:(r)] *n.* челове́к, получа́ющий полово́е удовлетворе́ние от созерца́ния эроти́ческих сцен.

V-sign ['vi:saɪn] *n.* **1.** (*gesture of contempt*) ≃ ку́киш. **2.** (*for victory*) знак побе́ды.

vulcanite ['vʌlkə,naɪt] *n.* вулканизи́рованная рези́на; эбони́т.

vulcanize ['vʌlkə,naɪz] *v.t.* вулканизи́ровать (*impf.*).

vulgar ['vʌlgə(r)] *n.*: **the ~** простонаро́дье.

adj. **1.** (*plebeian*) простонаро́дный; плебе́йский; **the ~ herd** чернь; **the ~ tongue** наро́дный/родно́й язы́к. **2.** (*low*, *coarse*, *in bad taste*) вульга́рный, по́шлый, гру́бый; **~ language** гру́бый/у́личный язы́к. **3.** (*ordinary*, *widespread*) распространённый; **~ superstitions** распространённые предрассу́дки; **~ fraction** проста́я дробь.

vulgarian [vʌl'geərɪən] *n.* пошля́|к (*fem.* -чка).

vulgarism ['vʌlgə,rɪz(ə)m] *n.* вульгари́зм.

vulgarity [vʌl'gærɪtɪ] *n.* вульга́рность, по́шлость, гру́бость.

vulgarization [,vʌlgəraɪ'zeɪʃ(ə)n] *n.* вульгариза́ция.

vulgarize ['vʌlgə,raɪz] *v.t.* вульгаризи́ровать (*impf.*, *pf.*).

Vulgate ['vʌlgeɪt, -gət] *n.* (би́блия-)вульга́та.

vulnerability [,vʌlnərə'bɪlɪtɪ] *n.* уязви́мость, рани́мость; беззащи́тность.

vulnerable ['vʌlnərəb(ə)l] *adj.* **1.** уязви́мый, рани́мый; (*defenceless*) беззащи́тный; **~ to air attack** не защищённый от нападе́ния с во́здуха; **he is ~ to criticism** он представля́ет собо́й удо́бную мише́нь для крити́ческих замеча́ний. **2.** (*at bridge*) в зо́не.

vulpine ['vʌlpaɪn] *adj.* ли́сий, хи́трый.

vulture ['vʌltʃə(r)] *n.* гриф; (*fig.*) стервя́тник.

vulva ['vʌlvə] *n.* ву́льва.

W

wacky ['wækɪ] *adj.* (*sl.*) сумасше́дший, чо́кнутый.

wad [wɒd] *n.* **1.** (*pad*, *plug etc.*) комо́к; пыж. **2.** (*of papers*, *esp. banknotes*) па́чка.

v.t. (*line with wadding etc.*) подб|ива́ть, -и́ть ва́той; **~ded jacket** стёганый жаке́т; ва́тник; жаке́т на вати́не.

wadding ['wɒdɪŋ] *n.* ва́та; (*sheet ~*) вати́н.

waddle ['wɒd(ə)l] *n.* похо́дка вразва́лку; **she walks with a ~** она́ хо́дит перева́ливаясь.

v.i. ходи́ть (*indet.*) вразва́лку; перева́ливаться (*impf.*) (с бо́ку на́ бок).

wade [weɪd] *v.t.* пере|ходи́ть, -йти́ вброд; **we shall have to ~ the stream** нам придётся перейти́ ре́ку вброд.

v.i. проб|ира́ться, -ра́ться; **wading bird** боло́тная пти́ца; **we ~d through the mud** мы шли, увяза́я в грязи́; (*fig.*): **he ~d through blood to the throne** его́ путь к тро́ну был усе́ян тру́пами; он шёл к тро́ну по коле́но в крови́; **I have ~d through all his novels** я (с трудо́м) одоле́л все его́ рома́ны; **I ~d into the argument** я ри́нулся в спор.

with advs.: **~ in** *v.i.* (*lit.*) входи́ть, войти́ в во́ду; (*coll.*) набр|а́сываться, -о́ситься (*на кого/что*); (*fig.*): **he found them fighting and ~d in** он уви́дел деру́щихся и ри́нулся в схва́тку; **~ out** *v.i.*: **we had to ~ out to the boat** к ло́дке пришло́сь добира́ться по воде́.

wader ['weɪdə(r)] *n.* (*bird*) боло́тная пти́ца; (*pl.*, *waterproof boots*) боло́тные сапоги́ (*m. pl.*).

wafer ['weɪfə(r)] *n.* **1.** (*thin biscuit*) ва́фля. **2.** (*Communion *bread*) облáтка. **3.** (*representing seal*) сургýчная печáть.

waffle[1] ['wɒf(ə)l] *n.* (*cul.*) вáфля.

cpd. **~-iron** *n.* вáфельница.

waffle[2] ['wɒf(ə)l] *n.* (*coll., verbiage*) водá.

v.i. (*also* **~ on**) вóду лить (*impf.*).

waffler ['wɒflə(r)] *n.* (*coll.*) водолéй.

waffly ['wɒflɪ] *adj.* (*coll.*) водяни́стый.

waft [wɒft, wɑːft] *n.* (*whiff; breath*) дуновéние.

v.t. дон|оси́ть, -ести́; **the leaves were ~ed by the breeze** ветерóк гнáл ли́стья; **their voices were ~ed over to us** их голосá доноси́лись до нас.

wag[1] [wæg] *n.* (*shake*): **with a ~ of his tail** вильнýв хвостóм.

v.t. мах|áть, -нýть +*i.*; качáть, по- +*i.*; **the dog ~ged its tail** собáка вильнýла хвостóм; **he ~ged his finger at me** он погрози́л мне пáльцем; **he ~ged his head** он (тóлько) мотнýл головóй.

v.i.: **this will set tongues ~ging** э́то даст пóвод к сплéтням; э́то вы́зовет тóлки.

cpd. **~tail** *n.* трясогýзка.

wag[2] [wæg] *n.* (*jocular pers.*) остря́к, шутни́к.

wage[1] [weɪdʒ] *n.* **1.** зáработная плáта; (*coll.*) зарплáта; **he gets good ~s** он хорошó зарабáтывает; **his ~s are £40 a week** он зарабáтывает 40 фýнтов в недéлю; **a living ~** прожи́точный ми́нимум; **a fair day's ~** прили́чная зарплáта; **~ increase** повышéние зáработной плáты. **2.** (*pl., fig.*) возмéздие, плáта, расплáта; **~s of sin** плáта за грехи́.

cpds. **~-earner** *n.* наёмный рабóчий; (*breadwinner*) корми́л|ец (*fem.* -ица); **~-freeze** *n.* заморáживание зáработной плáты; **~-packet** *n.* (*fig.*) зарплáта, получка; **~-slave** *n.* (*fig.*) подёнщи|к (*fem.* -ца).

wage[2] [weɪdʒ] *v.t.* вести́, проводи́ть (*both impf.*).

wager ['weɪdʒə(r)] *n.* пари́ (*nt. indecl.*); **lay a ~** би́ться (*impf.*) об заклáд; держáть (*impf.*) пари́; **you will lose your ~** вы проигрáете пари́.

v.t.: **he ~ed £10 on a horse** он постáвил 10 фýнтов на лóшадь; **I ~ you 5 to 1 you can't do it** стáвлю пять прóтив одногó, что э́то вам не удáстся.

waggery ['wægərɪ] *n.* рóзыгрыш, подшýчивание.

waggish ['wægɪʃ] *adj.* шутли́вый, шýточный, игри́вый.

waggle ['wæg(ə)l] *v.t.* & *i.* помáх|ивать, -áть +*i.*; покáч|ивать, -áть +*i.*; **he ~d his head** он качáл ((*coll.*) мотáл) головóй.

wag(g)on ['wægən] *n.* **1.** (*horse-drawn*) повóзка, телéга; фургóн; **he hitched his ~ to a star** он был вдохновлён высóкой цéлью. **2.** (*on railway*) вагóн-платфóрма. **3.**: **he is on the ~** (*fig., not drinking alcohol*) он брóсил пить; он бóльше не пьёт.

wag(g)oner ['wægənə(r)] *n.* вóзчик.

wagon-lit [ˌvægɔ̃'liː] *n.* спáльный вагóн.

waif [weɪf] *n.* бездóмный; бродя́га (*c.g.*); **~s and strays** (*children*) беспризóрники (*m. pl.*); беспризóрные (*pl.*).

wail [weɪl] *n.* (*cry, howl*) вопль (*m.*); вой; (*of pain*) крик; (*lament*) причитáние; (*fig., of the wind*) завывáние, вой; (*of sirens, saxophones etc.*) вой.

v.i. (*cry, howl*) вопи́ть (*impf.*); выть (*impf.*); **the W~ing Wall** Стенá плáча.

wain [weɪn] *n.* (*arch.*) телéга.

wainscot ['weɪnskət], **-ing** ['weɪnskətɪŋ] *nn.* стеннáя панéль; обши́вка.

v.t. обш|ивáть, -и́ть (*стены*) панéлью.

waist [weɪst] *n.* (*of body or dress*) тáлия; **he stripped to the ~** он раздéлся до пóяса; **he put his arm round her ~** он óбнял её за тáлию; **she has no ~** у неё нет тáлии; (*fig.*) сужéние, перехвáт; **~ of a violin** перехвáт скри́пки; **~ of a ship** срéдняя часть сýдна, шкафýт.

cpds. **~-band** *n.* пóяс ю́бки/брю́к; корсáж; **~coat** *n.* жилéт; **~-deep, ~-high** *adjs.* по пóяс; **~line** *n.*: **I must watch my ~line** мне прихóдится следи́ть за своéй фигýрой.

wait [weɪt] *n.* **1.** (*act or time of ~ing*) ожидáние; **we had a long ~ for the bus** мы дóлго ждáли автóбуса. **2.** (*ambush*) засáда; **the robbers lay in ~ for their victim** разбóйники/граби́тели подстерегáли свою́ жéртву. **3.** (*pl., carol singers*) рождéственский хор.

v.t. **1.** (**~** *for; await*) ждать (*impf.*); выжидáть (*impf.*); **you must ~ your turn** вáша óчередь ещё не наступи́ла. **2.** (*defer*): **don't ~ dinner for me** не ждите меня́ с обéдом.

v.i. **1.** (*refrain from movement or action*) ждать, подо-; **we must ~ and see what happens** подождём — уви́дим, что бýдет дáльше; **he adopted a ~ and see policy** он зáнял выжидáтельную пози́цию; **it can/must ~ till tomorrow** э́то обождёт (*or* э́то придётся отложи́ть) до зáвтра; **I could hardly ~ to ...** я сгорáл от нетерпéния +*inf.*; **I ~ed for the rain to stop** я ждал, когдá окóнчится дождь; **everything comes to him who ~s** кто ждёт, тот дождётся; **I don't like to be kept ~ing** не люблю́, когдá меня́ заставля́ют ждать; **'No W~ing'** (*notice*) «стоя́нка запрещенá»; **~ing-list** спи́сок (*кандидатов, очередников и т.п.*); óчередь; **I'll put you on the ~ing-list** я вас занесý в óчередь; **~ing-room** (*doctor's etc.*) приёмная; (*on station*) зал ожидáния; **repairs while you ~** ремóнт в присýтствии закáзчика. **2.** (*act as servant*): **she ~s on him hand and foot** онá при нём как прислýга; **he ~ed at table** он рабóтал официáнтом; он прислýживал за столóм; **who is ~ing at this table?** кто подаёт за э́тим столóм?; кто обслýживает э́тот стол? **3.**: **~ up: she ~ed up for him** онá не ложи́лась (спать) до егó прихóда.

waiter ['weɪtə(r)] *n.* официáнт.

waitress ['weɪtrɪs] *n.* официáнтка; подавáльщица.

waive [weɪv] *v.t.* (*forgo*) откáз|ываться, -áться от+*g.*; **he ~d his privileges** он отказáлся от свои́х привилéгий; (*not insist on*) воздéрж|иваться, -áться от+*g.*; не соблю|дáть, -сти́ +*g.*; **on this occasion we will ~ the regulations** на сей раз мы пренебрежём прáвилами.

waiver ['weɪvə(r)] *n.* откáз (от+*g.*).

wake[1] [weɪk] *n.* (*funeral observance*) бдéние у грóба; поми́н|ки (*pl., g.* -ок).

wake[2] [weɪk] *n.* (*track of vessel*) попýтная струя́; кильвáтер; (*fig.*): **he drove away with the police in his ~** он умчáлся, преслéдуемый поли́цией; **there was havoc in the ~ of the storm** послéдствия штóрма бы́ли разруши́тельны; **his action brought trouble in its ~** егó поведéние повлеклó за собóй неприя́тности.

wake[3] [weɪk] *v.t.* буди́ть, раз-; **they made enough noise to ~ the dead** от их шýма и мёртвый проснýлся бы; **their shouts woke echoes in the valley** их кри́ки разбуди́ли э́хо в доли́не; **the letter woke memories of the past** письмó пробуди́ло/вы́звало воспоминáния о прóшлом.

v.i. (*also* **~ up**) прос|ыпáться, -нýться; **she woke with a start** онá внезáпно проснýлась; **she woke from a long sleep** онá проснýлась пóсле дóлгого сна; **~ up!** (*lit., fig.*) просни́тесь!

wakeful ['weɪkfʊl] *adj.*: **I was ~ last night** у меня́ былá бессóнница прóшлой нóчью; **the child was ~** ребёнок то и дéло просыпáлся; **we had a ~ night** мы провели́ бессóнную ночь.

wakefulness ['weɪkfʊlnɪs] *n.* бессóнница.

waken ['weɪkən] *v.t.* (*lit., fig.*) буди́ть, раз-; пробу|ждáть, -ди́ть.

waking ['weɪkɪŋ] *adj.* бессóнный; бóдрствующий; **in his ~ hours** когдá он не спал; в часы́ бóдрствования; **a ~ dream** сон наявý; мечтá; **~ and sleeping** во сне и наявý.

Wales [weɪlz] *n.* Уэ́льс.

walk [wɔːk] *n.* **1.** (*action of ~ing*) ходьбá; **a short ~ away** в нéскольких шагáх отсю́да/оттýда. **2.** (*excursion*) (пéшая) прогýлка; **shall we take a ~?** пойдёмте гуля́ть!; хоти́те погуля́ть?; **I'm going for a ~** я пойдý прогуля́юсь; **will you take the children for a ~?** вы погуля́ете с детьми́?; вы поведёте детéй на прогýлку?; **I went on a ten-mile ~** я прошёл дéсять миль пешкóм. **3.** (*~ing pace*) шаг; **the horse slowed to a ~** лóшадь перешлá на шаг. **4.** (*gait*) похóдка, пóступь. **5.** (*route for ~ing*): **there are some pleasant ~s round here** здесь есть прия́тные местá для прогýлок. **6.** (*path*) тропá, дорóжка; **garden ~s** садóвые дорóжки. **7.** (*contest*): **long-distance ~** (спорти́вная) ходьбá на дли́нную дистáнцию. **8.** (*~ of life, profession*) заня́тие, профéссия; **people from all ~s of life** представи́тели всех слоёв óбщества.

v.t. **1.** (*traverse*): **I ~ed these lanes in my youth** я исходи́л э́ти дорóги в мóлодости. **2.** (*cause to ~*): **he ~ed his**

horse up the hill он пусти́л ло́шадь ша́гом в го́ру; он повёл ло́шадь в го́ру под уздцы́; **he ~ed me off my feet** он меня́ си́льно утоми́л прогу́лкой; (*accompany*) сопрово|жда́ть, -ди́ть; прово|жа́ть, -ди́ть; **he offered to ~ her home** он вы́звался проводи́ть её домо́й; **he ~ed the boy up to the headmaster's study** он повёл ма́льчика к кабине́ту дире́ктора; (*take for a ~*) выводи́ть, вы́вести на прогу́лку; прогу́л|ивать, -я́ть.

v.i. **1.** (*go, come, move about, on foot*) ходи́ть (*indet.*), идти́ (*det.*); проха́живаться (*impf.*); прогу́ливаться (*impf.*); **I was ~ing along the road** я шёл по доро́ге; **I ~ed ten miles** я прошёл/проде́лал де́сять миль; **I ~ed here in an hour** я дошёл сюда́ за час; **he ~s with a stick** он хо́дит с па́лкой; **the baby is learning to ~** ребёнок у́чится ходи́ть; **I ~ed into a shop** я вошёл в магази́н; **he ~ed into a puddle** он ступи́л в лу́жу; **guess who I ~ed into** (*met accidentally*) **today** отгада́йте, на кого́ я сего́дня наткну́лся; **they ~ed into** (*entered unwarily*) **an ambush** они́ попа́ли в заса́ду; **I feel as if I was ~ing on air** я не чу́ю ног под собо́й; **he ~ed over the estate** он обошёл/исходи́л всё име́ние; **they ~ed all over us** (*coll., defeated us heavily*) они́ разби́ли нас на́голову; **he ~ed into a trap** он попа́лся в лову́шку. **2.** (*opp. ride*): **on fine days I ~ to the office** в хоро́шую пого́ду я хожу́ на рабо́ту пешко́м. **3.** (*opp. run*): **he ~ed the last 100 metres** после́дние сто ме́тров он прошёл ша́гом; **at a ~ing pace** ша́гом; со ско́ростью пешехо́да. **4.** (*take exercise, holiday etc. on foot*) ходи́ть (*indet.*) пешко́м; гуля́ть (*impf.*), прогу́ливаться (*impf.*); **I spent 2 weeks ~ing in Scotland** я броди́л две неде́ли по Шотла́ндии; **a ~ing tour** туристи́ческий похо́д; **a ~ing race** соревнова́ние по спорти́вной ходьбе́; **~ing shoes** обувь для ходьбы́; **~ing-stick** трость, па́лка; *see also* **walking. 5.** (*take part in procession*) ше́ствовать (*impf.*).

with advs.: **~ about** *v.i.* прогу́ливаться; проха́живаться; расха́живать (*all impf.*); **~ away** *v.i.* уходи́ть, уйти́; **he ~ed away from** (*outdistanced*) **all his competitors** он оста́вил далеко́ позади́ всех свои́х сопе́рников; **he ~ed away with several prizes** он без труда́ завоева́л не́сколько призо́в; **~ back** *v.i.* возвраща́ться, верну́ться пешко́м; **~ down** *v.i.* спус|ка́ться, -ти́ться; **~ in** *v.i.* входи́ть, войти́; **~ off** *v.t.* (*annul by ~ing*): **I must ~ off my fat** я до́лжен согна́ть ходьбо́й жир; **he was ~ing off a heavy lunch** он прогу́ливался по́сле сы́тного обе́да; *v.i.* уходи́ть, уйти́; **someone ~ed off with my hat** кто́-то стащи́л мою́ шля́пу; **he always ~s off with first prize** он всегда́ берёт пе́рвый приз; **~ on** *v.i.* (*continue ~ing*) продолжа́ть (*impf.*) идти́; идти́ (*det.*) да́льше; (*~ ahead*) идти́ (*det.*) вперёд; (*theatr.*) выходи́ть, вы́йти на сце́ну; **~ out** *v.i.* выходи́ть, вы́йти; **the delegates ~ed out in protest** делега́ты поки́нули зал (*or* вы́шли из за́ла) в знак проте́ста; **the men are threatening to ~ out** (*strike*) рабо́чие грозя́т забасто́вкой; **she is ~ing out with a policeman** она́ гуля́ет с полице́йским; **~ing-out dress** (*mil.*) выходна́я фо́рма оде́жды; **~ out on s.o.** (*coll.*) бр|оса́ть, -о́сить кого́-н.; **~ up** *v.i.* (*approach*): **~ up! ~ up!** сюда́! сюда́!; **I ~ed up to him** я подошёл к нему́; (*climb*): **'Did you use the lift?' — 'No, I ~ed up'** «Вы прие́хали на ли́фте?» — «Нет, я подня́лся по ле́стнице».

cpds. **~about** *n.* (*fig., coll.*) обще́ние знамени́тости с наро́дом; **~-on** *n.*: **a ~-on part** нема́я роль; **~-out** *n.* (*as protest*) демонстрати́вный ухо́д; (*strike*) забасто́вка; **~over** *n.* лёгкая побе́да; **~-up** *n.* (*US*) дом без ли́фта; **~way** *n.* широ́кая пешехо́дная доро́жка, алле́я.

walker ['wɔ:kə(r)] *n.* **1.** (*one who walks*) ходо́к; (*athlete*) скорохо́д; **I'm not a very good ~** я нева́жный ходо́к; **a hostel for ~s** общежи́тие для пе́ших тури́стов. **2.** (*device for handicapped pers.*) ходунки́ (*m. pl.*).

walkie-talkie [,wɔ:kı'tɔ:kı] *n.* ра́ция.

walking ['wɔ:kıŋ] *n.* ходьба́; *see also* **walk** *v.i.* **4.**

adj. ходя́чий, шага́ющий; **a ~ encyclopaedia** ходя́чая энциклопе́дия; **~ wounded** ходя́чие ра́неные.

Walkman ['wɔ:kmən] *n.* (*propr.*) во́кмен, плеер.

wall [wɔ:l] *n.* (*lit., fig.*) стена́, сте́нка; **town ~s** городски́е сте́ны; **Hadrian's ~** вал Адриа́на; **there were pictures on the ~** на стене́ висе́ли карти́ны; **within these four ~s** (*fig.*) (стро́го) ме́жду на́ми; **~s have ears** у стен есть у́ши; **he stood with his back to the ~** (*lit.*) он стоя́л у стены́; **they had their backs to the ~** (*fig.*) их прижа́ли/припёрли к сте́нке; **go up the ~** (*coll.*) лезть, по- на сте́н(к)у; **it's enough to send, drive you up the ~** (*coll.*) э́то хоть кого́ заста́вит на сте́нку лезть; **a blank ~** (*lit., fig.*) глуха́я стена́; **it's like banging, running one's head against a brick ~** всё равно́, что прошиба́ть сте́ну лбом; **he can see through a brick ~** он на три арши́на под землёй ви́дит; **the weakest goes to the ~** ≃ го́ре побеждённым; **a mountain ~** отве́сная скала́; **cylinder ~** сте́нка цили́ндра дви́гателя; **~ of the womb** сте́нка ма́тки; **~ clock** насте́нные час|ы́ (*pl., g.* -о́в); **~ map** насте́нная ка́рта; **~ painting** стенна́я ро́спись; фре́ска.

v.t. обн|оси́ть, -ести́ стено́й; огор|а́живать, -оди́ть; **~ed garden** обнесённый стено́й сад.

with advs.: **~ in** *v.t.* обн|оси́ть, -ести́ стено́й; (*immure*) замуро́в|ывать, -а́ть; **~ off** *v.t.* отгор|а́живать, -оди́ть (стено́й); **~ up** *v.t.* заде́л|ывать, -ать (*дверь, окно*); замуро́в|ывать, -а́ть.

cpds. **~-board** *n.* (насте́нная) облицо́вочная пане́ль; **~flower** *n.* желтофио́ль; (*at dance*) да́ма, оста́вшаяся без партнёра; **~paper** *n.* обо́|и (*pl., g.* -ев); *v.t.* обкле́и|вать, -ть обо́ями; **~-to-~** *adj.*: **~-to-~ carpeting** ковёр, покрыва́ющий весь пол.

wallaby ['wɒləbı] *n.* кенгуру́-валлаби (*m. indecl.*).

wallet ['wɒlıt] *n.* (*pocket-book*) бума́жник.

wall-eye ['wɔ:laı] *n.* глаз с бельмо́м.

wall-eyed ['wɔ:laıd] *adj.* с бельмо́м на глазу́; криво́й.

Walloon [wɒ'lu:n] *n.* валло́н (*fem.* -ка).

adj. валло́нский.

wallop ['wɒləp] (*coll.*) *n.* (*blow*) уда́р; (*crash*) шум, гро́хот; (*sl., beer*) пи́во.

v.t. (*thrash*) дуба́сить, от- (*coll.*); (*defeat*) разгроми́ть (*pf.*); **we got a ~ing in our last game** нам здо́рово доста́лось в после́дней игре́.

wallow ['wɒləʊ] *v.i.* валя́ться (*impf.*); ката́ться (*impf.*); (*fig.*) купа́ться (*impf.*) (*в чём*); **~ in luxury** купа́ться (*impf.*) в ро́скоши; **~ in grief** упива́ться (*impf.*) свои́м го́рем.

wally ['wɒlı] *n.* (*coll.*) дурале́й, неумёха.

walnut ['wɔ:lnʌt] *n.* гре́цкий оре́х; (*tree*) оре́ховое де́рево; (*wood*) оре́х.

adj. оре́ховый.

walrus ['wɔ:lrəs, 'wɒl-] *n.* морж; **~ moustache** дли́нные свиса́ющие усы́ (*m. pl.*).

waltz [wɔ:ls, wɔ:lts, wɒ-] *n.* вальс; **in ~ time** в ри́тме ва́льса; **a ~ tune** мело́дия ва́льса.

v.t. (*coll.*): **he ~ed her round the room** он закружи́лся с ней по ко́мнате.

v.i. танцева́ть (*impf.*) вальс; (*fig.*) пританцо́вывать (*impf.*); **she ~ed into the room** она́ впорхну́ла в ко́мнату.

wampum ['wɒmpəm] *n.* ва́мпум; ожере́лье из раку́шек.

wan [wɒn] *adj.* бле́дный, изнурённый; **a ~ light** сла́бый/ту́склый свет; **a ~ smile** сла́бая улы́бка; **his face looked ~** он осу́нулся.

wand [wɒnd] *n.* (волше́бная) па́лочка; **with a wave of his ~** по мановéнию (волше́бной) па́лочки; (*staff of authority*) жезл.

wander ['wɒndə(r)] *n.*: **I had a ~ round the shops** я прошёлся по магази́нам.

v.t. броди́ть; стра́нствовать; скита́ться (*all impf.*) по+*d.*; **condemned to ~ the earth** обречённый скита́ться по све́ту.

v.i. **1.** (*roam; go aimlessly or unhurriedly*) броди́ть (*impf.*); идти́ (*det.*) нетороплúво; **the W~ing Jew** Ве́чный жид; **a ~ing minstrel** бродя́чий пе́вец; **the car was ~ing all over the road** маши́на виля́ла из стороны́ в сто́рону; **I ~ed into the nearest pub** я забрёл в ближа́йший бар; **her ~ing gaze** её блужда́ющий взгляд; **his mind was ~ing** (*absent-mindedly*) его́ мы́сли пу́тались/блужда́ли; (*in delirium*) он бре́дил. **2.** (*stray*) заблу|жда́ться, -ди́ться; (*lit., fig.*) отклон|я́ться, -и́ться; **we ~ed from the track** мы сби́лись с тропы́; **don't let your attention ~** не отвлека́йтесь; **he ~ed from the**

point он отклони́лся от те́мы.

with advs.: ~ **about** *v.i.* слоня́ться (*impf.*); шля́ться (*impf.*); ~ **along** *v.i.* проха́живаться (*impf.*); забре|да́ть, -сти́ куда́-н.; ~ **away** *v.i.*: **she tried to stop the children ~ing away** она́ пыта́лась не дать де́тям разбрести́сь; ~ **in** *v.i.* забре|да́ть, -сти́; случа́йно за|ходи́ть, -йти́; ~ **off** *v.i.* побрести́ (*pf.*) куда́-н.; поплести́сь (*pf.*); ~ **on** *v.i.* прод|олжа́ть, -о́лжить; **he ~ed on** (*speaking*) он продолжа́л бубни́ть; ~ **over** *v.i.*: **he ~ed over to hear the news** он приплёлся узна́ть но́вости; ~ **up** *v.i.*: **he ~ed up to us** он подошёл к нам вя́лой похо́дкой.

wanderer ['wɒndərə(r)] *n.* стра́нник, скита́лец.

wandering ['wɒndərɪŋ] *n.* стра́нствие; (*pl., of speech*) бессвя́зная речь.

wanderlust ['wɒndə,lʌst, 'vændə,lʊst] *n.* страсть к путеше́ствиям; охо́та к переме́не мест.

wane [weɪn] *n.*: **be on the ~** (*lit., fig.*) убыва́ть (*impf.*); быть на исхо́де.

v.i. (*of the moon*) убыва́ть (*impf.*); быть на ущёрбе; (*fig., decline*) ослабева́ть (*impf.*); угаса́ть (*impf.*); идти́ (*det.*) на убы́ль; па́дать (*impf.*).

wangle ['wæŋg(ə)l] *v.t.* (*obtain by scheming*) заполучи́ть (*pf.*) хи́тростью; **he ~d £5 out of me** он вы́клянчил (*coll.*) у меня́ 5 фу́нтов; (*falsify in one's favour*): **he ~d the results** он подтасова́л результа́ты.

wank [wæŋk] *n.* (*vulg.*): **have a ~** подрочи́ть.

v.i. дрочи́ть (*impf.*).

wanker ['wæŋkə(r)] *n.* (*vulg.*) дрочи́ла (*c.g.*); (*fig.*) муда́к, долбоёб.

wanness ['wɒnnɪs] *n.* бле́дность, изнурённость.

want [wɒnt] *n.* **1.** (*lack*) недоста́ток, отсу́тствие; **for ~ of** за недоста́тком/неиме́нием *+g.*; **I took this for ~ of anything better** я взял э́то за неиме́нием лу́чшего. **2.** (*need*) нужда́; необходи́мость; **he was always in ~ of money** он всегда́ нужда́лся в деньга́х; **the house is in ~ of repair** дом нужда́ется в ремо́нте. **3.** (*penury*) бе́дность, нужда́. **4.** (*desire; requirement*) потре́бность, запро́сы (*m. pl.*), жела́ние; **it meets a long-felt ~** э́то восполня́ет давно́ ощути́мый пробе́л; **they can supply all your ~s** они́ мо́гут удовлетвори́ть все ва́ши запро́сы.

v.t. **1.** (*need; require*) нужда́ться (*impf.*) в+*p.*; **we badly ~ rain** нам о́чень ну́жен дождь; **what do you ~?** что вы хоти́те?; что вам на́до?; **the floor ~s polishing** пол на́до натере́ть; **your hair ~s cutting** вам пора́ постри́чься; **he ~s a good hiding** ему́ сле́дует хороше́нько всыпа́ть (*coll.*); его́ ма́ло би́ли; **I shan't ~ you today** вы мне сего́дня не пона́добитесь; **he is ~ed by the police** его́ разы́скивает поли́ция; **W~ed: a housekeeper** Тре́буется эконо́мка; **you're ~ed on the telephone** вас (про́сят) к телефо́ну; **you are ~ed at the office** вас вызыва́ют на рабо́ту; **what do you ~ with him?** что вам от него́ ну́жно?; **it only ~s someone to volunteer, and everyone would follow** заяви́сь оди́н доброво́лец, и все пойду́т за ним вслед. **2.** (*desire; wish for*) хоте́ть (*impf.*) *+g. or inf.*; жела́ть (*impf.*) *+g. or inf.*; **she ~s to go away** она́ хо́чет уе́хать/уйти́; **she ~s me to go away** она́ хо́чет, что́бы я уе́хал/ушёл; **I don't ~ him meddling in my affairs** я не хочу́, что́бы он вме́шивался в мои́ дела́; **I don't ~ any bread today** сего́дня мне хлеб не ну́жен; **I ~ it done immediately** я тре́бую, что́бы э́то бы́ло сде́лано неме́дленно; **you don't ~ to** (*ought not to*) **overdo it** вам не сле́дует переутомля́ться; **what do I ~ with all these books?** заче́м (*or* для чего́) мне все э́ти кни́ги?

v.i. (*liter., be in need*): **they ~ for nothing** они́ ни в чём не нужда́ются.

wanting ['wɒntɪŋ] *adj.* (*missing*) отсу́тствующий; недостаю́щий; (*lacking*): **he is ~ in courtesy** он неучти́в; (*inadequate*) недоста́точный; неполноце́нный; **he was tried and found ~** он не вы́держал испыта́ния.

wanton ['wɒnt(ə)n] *n.* распу́тница.

adj. **1.** (*playful*) ре́звый, игри́вый, шаловли́вый. **2.** (*wild; luxuriant*) бу́рный, бу́йный. **3.** (*wilful; ruthless*) своенра́вный, своево́льный; **~ cruelty** бессмы́сленная жесто́кость. **4.** (*licentious; immoral*) распу́тный.

v.i. (*trifle, play*) резви́ться (*impf.*); **the wind ~ed with her hair** ве́тер игра́л её волоса́ми.

wantonness ['wɒntənnɪs] *n.* ре́звость, игри́вость, шаловли́вость; (*wilfulness*) своенра́вие; (*unchastity*) распу́тство.

wapiti ['wɒpɪtɪ] *n.* кана́дский оле́нь, вапи́ти (*m. indecl.*).

war [wɔː(r)] *n.* **1.** война́; **the art of ~** вое́нное иску́сство; **~ of aggression** агресси́вная война́; **~ of attrition** война́ на истоще́ние; **~ of nerves** война́ не́рвов; психологи́ческая война́; **~ to the knife** война́ на истребле́ние; борьба́ не на жизнь, а на смерть; **civil ~** гражда́нская война́; **cold ~** холо́дная война́; **the Great W~** Пе́рвая мирова́я война́; **the W~s of the Roses** во́йны А́лой и Бе́лой ро́зы; **~ of independence** война́ за незави́симость; **the ~ between man and nature** борьба́ челове́ка с приро́дой; **price ~** «война́ цен», ценова́я конкуре́нция; **shooting ~** настоя́щая/«горя́чая» война́; **a country at ~** вою́ющая война́; страна́ в состоя́нии войны́; **their countries were at ~** их стра́ны воева́ли друг с дру́гом; **what did you do in the ~?** что вы де́лали во вре́мя войны́? (*or* в войну́); **you've been in the ~s!** (*fig.*) ну и доста́лось же вам!; **England went to ~ with Germany** А́нглия вступи́ла в войну́ с Герма́нией; **declare ~ on** объяв|ля́ть, -и́ть войну́ *+d.*; **make, wage ~ on** вести́ (*det.*) войну́ (*or* воева́ть (*impf.*)) с+*i.*; **they carried the ~ into the enemy's camp** (*fig.*) они́ перешли́ в наступле́ние. **2.** (*attr.*) вое́нный (*see also cpds.*); **~ baby** дитя́ войны́; **~ bonds** облига́ции вое́нных за́ймов; **~ cabinet** вое́нный кабине́т; **~ correspondent** вое́нный корреспонде́нт; **~ criminal** вое́нный престу́пник; **~ damage** разруше́ния (*nt. pl.*) (*or* поте́ри (*f. pl.*)), нанесённые войно́й; **~ debt** вое́нный долг; **~ decoration** боева́я награ́да; **W~ Department** вое́нное министе́рство; **help the ~ effort** рабо́тать (*impf.*) для нужд фро́нта; **on a ~ footing** на вое́нном положе́нии; **~ graves** солда́тские моги́лы; **~ guilt** вина́ за развя́зывание войны́; **~ loan** вое́нный заём; **~ memorial** па́мятник геро́ям войны́; **W~ Office** вое́нное министе́рство; **~ risk** (*insurance*) страхова́ние от поте́рь, причинённых войно́й; **~ service** слу́жба в де́йствующей а́рмии; **~ widow** вдова́ поги́бшего на войне́; **~ work** рабо́та для нужд фро́нта.

v.i. боро́ться (*impf.*); сража́ться (*impf.*); **~ring ideologies** бо́рющиеся идеоло́гии.

cpds. **~-cloud** *n.*: **~-clouds are gathering** сгуща́ются ту́чи войны́; **~-cry** *n.* боево́й клич; **~-dance** *n.* вои́нственный та́нец; **~-game** *n.* вое́нная игра́; **~-god** *n.* бог войны́; **~head** *n.* боева́я часть, боеголо́вка; **~-horse** *n.* (*lit.*) боево́й конь; (*fig.*) быва́лый солда́т, ветера́н; **~like** *adj.* (*martial*) вои́нственный; (*military*) вое́нный; **~-lord** *n.* полково́дец; **~monger** *n.* поджига́тель (*m.*) войны́; **~mongering** *n.* разжига́ние войны́; **~-paint** *n.* (*of savage*) раскра́ска; (*coll., ceremonial costume*) пара́дная фо́рма; **~-path** *n.* (*lit.*) тропа́ войны́; **on the ~-path** (*fig.*) в вои́нственном настрое́нии; **~-plane** *n.* вое́нный самолёт; **~ship** *n.* вое́нный кора́бль; **~time** *n.* вое́нное вре́мя; **~-torn** *adj.* раздира́емый/опустошённый войно́й; **~-weary** *adj.* изнурённый/изму́ченный войно́й; **~-whoop** *n.* боево́й клич; **~-worn** *adj.* изму́ченный/изнурённый войно́й.

warble ['wɔːb(ə)l] *n.* (*song*) трель; пе́ние птиц.

v.i. (*of birds*) издава́ть (*impf.*) тре́ли; залива́ться (*impf.*); (*of pers.*) залива́ться (*impf.*) пе́сней; распева́ть (*impf.*).

warbler ['wɔːblə(r)] *n.* (*bird*) пе́вчая пти́ца.

ward [wɔːd] *n.* **1.** (*arch., guard*): **keep watch and ~ over** бди́тельно охраня́ть (*impf.*). **2.** (*leg., custody*): **a child in ~** ребёнок, находя́щийся под опе́кой. **3.** (*pers. under guardianship*) подопе́чный; **~ of court** несовершенноле́тний/душевнобольно́й под опе́кой суда́. **4.** (*urban division*) о́круг. **5.** (*in hospital etc.*) пала́та; **isolation ~** изоля́тор; **casual ~** ночле́жка; **walk the ~s** об|ходи́ть, -йти́ больны́х/пала́ты; (*fig.*) про|ходи́ть, -йти́ пра́ктику в больни́це. **6.** (*in prison*) ка́мера. **7.** (*pl., of a key or lock*) вы́ступы (*m. pl.*) и вы́емки (*f. pl.*).

v.t.: **~ off** (*a blow*) отра|жа́ть, -зи́ть; пари́ровать (*impf., pf.*); **~ off danger** отвра|ща́ть, -ти́ть опа́сность.

cpds. **~room** *n.* офице́рская каю́т-компа́ния; **~-sister** *n.* пала́тная сестра́.

warden ['wɔ:d(ə)n] *n.* **1.** (*of college*) ре́ктор; (*of hostel*) коменда́нт; (*of prison*) нача́льник тюрьмы́. **2.: air-raid ~** уполномо́ченный гражда́нской оборо́ны; **game ~** инспе́ктор по охра́не ди́чи; **traffic ~** контролёр счётчиков на автомоби́льных стоя́нках.

warder ['wɔ:də(r)] *n.* (*in prison*) надзира́тель (*m.*), тюре́мщик.

wardress ['wɔ:drɪs] *n.* надзира́тельница, тюре́мница.

wardrobe ['wɔ:drəʊb] *n.* **1.** платяно́й шкаф, гардеро́б; (*stock of clothes*) гардеро́б, запа́с оде́жды; **~ dealer** торго́вец поно́шенным пла́тьем. **2.** (*theatr.*) костюме́рная; **~ mistress** одева́льщица.

wardship ['wɔ:dʃɪp] *n.* опе́ка, попечи́тельство.

ware[1] [weə(r)] *n.* **1.** (*collect., usu. comb. form, manufactured articles*) това́р; изде́лия (*nt. pl.*); (*pottery*): **Delft~** фая́нс. **2.** (*pl., articles offered for sale*) това́ры (*m. pl.*); изде́лия (*nt. pl.*); **peddle one's ~s** (*lit.*) предлага́ть (*impf.*) това́ры на прода́жу; (*fig.*) занима́ться (*impf.*) само净рекла́мой.

cpds. **~house** *n.* (това́рный) склад; *v.t.* храни́ть (*impf.*) на скла́де; **~houseman** *n.* кладовщи́к.

ware[2] [weə(r)] *v.t.* (*imper.*) береги́сь +*g.*; **~ wire!** осторо́жно, про́волока!

warfare ['wɔ:feə(r)] *n.* война́; боевы́е де́йствия; **germ ~** бактериологи́ческая война́; **guerrilla ~** партиза́нская война́; **they were in a state of constant ~** (*fig.*) они́ постоя́нно враждова́ли.

wariness ['weərɪnɪs] *n.* осторо́жность, осмотри́тельность, насторо́жённость.

warlock ['wɔ:lɒk] *n.* колду́н, маг.

warm [wɔ:m] *n.* **1.** (*act of ~ing*): **come and have a ~ by the fire** иди́те погре́йтесь у ками́на. **2.: British ~** (*greatcoat*) коро́ткая зи́мняя шине́ль.

adj. тёплый; **a ~ day** тёплый день; **a ~ fire** жа́ркий ого́нь; **~ countries** жа́ркие/тёплые стра́ны/края́; **I can't keep ~ in this weather** в э́ту пого́ду я ника́к не могу́ согре́ться; **I got very ~ playing tennis** от игры́ в те́ннис я си́льно разгорячи́лся; (*fig.*) тёплый, серде́чный; **they got a ~** (*iron.*) **welcome** им устро́или тёпленькую встре́чу; **they made things ~ for him** (*coll.*) они́ со́здали для него́ невыноси́мую обстано́вку; **accept my ~est thanks** прими́те мою́ горя́чую благода́рность; **his plan was ~ly approved** его́ план горячо́ поддержа́ли; **a ~ friendship developed** ме́жду ни́ми возни́кла горя́чая дру́жба; **he has a ~ heart** он отзы́вчивый челове́к; **~ with wine** разгорячённый вино́м; **the argument grew ~** спор разгоре́лся не на шу́тку; **the scent was still ~** след ещё не осты́л; **am I getting ~?** (*fig.*) я бли́зок к пра́вде?

v.t. греть, со-; подогр|ева́ть, -е́ть; нагр|ева́ть, -е́ть; отогр|ева́ть, -е́ть; разогр|ева́ть, -е́ть; согр|ева́ть, -е́ть; **~ o.s. at the fire** гре́ться (*impf.*) у ками́на/огня́; **that fire will not ~ the room** э́тот ками́н не обогре́ет ко́мнату; **will you have your milk ~ed?** вам подогре́ть молоко́?; **~ing-pan** гре́лка.

v.i. нагр|ева́ться, -е́ться; отогр|ева́ться, -е́ться; разогр|ева́ться, -е́ться; согр|ева́ться, -е́ться; (*fig.*): **he ~ed to the subject as he went on** по ме́ре расска́за он всё бо́льше воодушевля́лся; **I ~ed to(wards) him as I got to know him** чем бли́же я его́ узнава́л, тем бо́льше он мне нра́вился.

with advs.: **~ over** *v.t.* разогр|ева́ть, -е́ть; **~ up** *v.t.* отогр|ева́ть, -е́ть; разогр|ева́ть, -е́ть; согр|ева́ть, -е́ть; **a fire will ~ up the room** ками́н нагре́ет ко́мнату; **his dinner had been ~ed up** ему́ разогре́ли у́жин; **a drink will ~ you up** вино́ вас согре́ет; **this engine needs a lot of ~ing up** э́тот мото́р прихо́дится до́лго прогрева́ть; **he told a few jokes to ~ up the audience** что́бы расшевели́ть пу́блику, он рассказа́л два-три анекдо́та; *v.i.* согр|ева́ться, -е́ться; отогр|ева́ться, -е́ться; **the house takes a long time to ~ up** э́тот дом тру́дно прогре́ть; **the TV is ~ing up** телеви́зор нагрева́ется; **the conversation ~ed up** разгово́р оживи́лся; **he ~ed up before the race** он сде́лал разми́нку пе́ред нача́лом соревнова́ния.

cpds. **~-air** *adj.*: **~-air heating system** возду́шное центра́льное отопле́ние; **~-blooded** *adj.* теплокро́вный; **~-hearted** *adj.* серде́чный, уча́стливый; **~-up** *n.* разми́нка.

warmish ['wɔ:mɪʃ] *adj.* теплова́тый.

warmth [wɔ:mθ] *n.* теплота́, тепло́; (*fig.*) серде́чность; (*temper*) горя́чность.

warn [wɔ:n] *v.t.* **1.** (*caution*) предупре|жда́ть, -ди́ть; предостер|ега́ть, -е́чь; **I ~ed her not to go out alone** я говори́л ей, что́бы она́ одна́ не выходи́ла; **you have been ~ed!** ≃ име́ющий у́ши да слы́шит; **we were ~ed against pickpockets** нас предостерегли́ от карма́нных воро́в; **he was ~ed off drink** ему́ запрети́ли пить. **2.** (*admonish*): **I shan't ~ you again** э́то моё после́днее предупрежде́ние. **3.** (*give notice*) изве|ща́ть, -сти́ть; опове|ща́ть, -сти́ть.

with adv.: **~ off** *v.t.*: **he was ~ed off** (*sc. the racecourse*) ему́ запрети́ли явля́ться на ипподро́м.

warning ['wɔ:nɪŋ] *n.* предупрежде́ние, предостереже́ние; **gale ~** штормово́е предупрежде́ние; **early ~** (*system*) (*mil.*) ра́ннее предупрежде́ние; да́льнее обнару́жение; **give ~ of** предупре|жда́ть, -ди́ть о+*p.*; **take ~ from sth.** уч|и́тывать, -е́сть неблагоприя́тные после́дствия чего́-н.; **let this be a ~ to you** пусть э́то послу́жит вам предостереже́нием; **he was let off with a ~** он отде́лался (одни́м лишь) предупрежде́нием; **without ~** без предупрежде́ния; вдруг; соверше́нно неожи́данно.

adj. предупрежда́ющий; предостерега́ющий; **he gave a ~ look** он бро́сил предостерега́ющий взгляд; **he fired a ~ shot** он дал предупреди́тельный вы́стрел.

warp [wɔ:p] *n.* (*weaving*) осно́ва; (*distortion*) искривле́ние; деформа́ция.

v.t. **1.** (*distort*) коро́бить, по-; искрив|ля́ть, -и́ть; **damp ~s the binding** переплёт коро́бит от сы́рости. **2.** (*fig.*) по́ртить, ис-; **a ~ed sense of humour** извращённое чу́вство ю́мора.

v.i. (*become distorted*) коро́биться, по-; деформи́роваться (*impf., pf.*).

warrant ['wɒrənt] *n.* **1.** (*justification; authority*) оправда́ние, основа́ние, руча́тельство; **I will be your ~** я бу́ду ва́шим поручи́телем. **2.** (*written authorization*) о́рдер; суде́бное распоряже́ние; **search ~** о́рдер на о́быск; **travel ~** ли́тер (на прое́зд); **~ officer** старшина́ (*m.*); **a ~ is out for his arrest** вы́писан о́рдер на его́ аре́ст; **death ~** (*fig.*) сме́ртный пригово́р.

v.t. **1.** (*justify*) опра́вд|ывать, -а́ть; обосно́в|ывать, -а́ть. **2.** (*guarantee*) гаранти́ровать (*impf., pf.*); руча́ться, поручи́ться за+*a.*; **I can ~ him to be reliable** я руча́юсь за его́ надёжность; **he will be back I('ll) ~ you** он вернётся, уверя́ю вас (*or* вот увиди́те).

warrantor ['wɒrəntə(r)] *n.* поручи́тель (*m.*); гара́нт.

warranty ['wɒrəntɪ] *n.* **1.** (*authority*) оправда́ние, основа́ние, руча́тельство. **2.** (*guarantee*) гара́нтия; **this watch is under ~** э́ти часы́ с гара́нтией.

warren ['wɒrən] *n.* кро́личья нора́; (*man-made*) садо́к для кро́ликов; (*fig.*) мураве́йник, лабири́нт.

warrior ['wɒrɪə(r)] *n.* во́ин; **the Unknown W~** Неизве́стный солда́т; **a ~ race** вои́нственный наро́д.

Warsaw ['wɔ:sɔ:] *n.* Варша́ва; **~ Pact** Варша́вский догово́р.

wart [wɔ:t] *n.* борода́вка; **~s and all** (*fig.*) без прикра́с.

cpd. **~-hog** *n.* африка́нский каба́н; борода́вочник.

wary ['weərɪ] *adj.* осторо́жный, осмотри́тельный, насторо́жённый; **be ~ of** остерега́ться (*impf.*) +*g.*; относи́ться (*impf.*) насторо́жённо к+*d.*

wash [wɒʃ] *n.* **1.** (*act of ~ing*) мытьё; **I must have, get a ~** мне на́до помы́ться/умы́ться; **she gave the floor a good ~** она́ хороше́нько вы́мыла пол. **2.** (*laundering; laundry*) сти́рка; **send to the ~** отд|ава́ть, -а́ть в сти́рку; **my shirts are all at the ~** все мои́ руба́шки в сти́рке; **she does a big ~ on Mondays** по понеде́льникам у неё больша́я сти́рка; **this tablecloth needs a ~** э́ту ска́терть не меша́ло бы постира́ть; **it will all come out in the ~** (*fig.*) всё ула́дится/образу́ется/утрясётся. **3.** (*motion of water etc.*) прибо́й; волна́; **the vessel made a big ~** от корабля́ пошла́ си́льная волна́; **the ~ of waves on the shore** плеск волн, разбива́ющихся о бе́рег. **4.** (*alluvium*) аллю́вий. **5.** (*garbage for pigs*) по́йло для свине́й. **6.** (*solution of paint*) то́нкий слой акваре́ли; **a ~ drawing** рису́нок ту́шью размы́вкой. **7.** (*lotion*; *liquid toilet preparation*) примо́чка; туале́тная вода́; лосьо́н.

v.t. **1.** (*cleanse with water etc.*) мыть, по-/об-/вы́; стира́ть, вы́-; ~ **one's hands and face** вы́мыть (*pf.*) ру́ки и лицо́; ~ **one's eyes** промы́ть (*pf.*) глаза́; ~ **dishes** мыть, вы́- посу́ду; **he ~ed himself in the stream** он помы́лся/обмы́лся в ручье́; ~ **one's mouth** полоска́ть, про- рот; **this fabric must be ~ed in cold water** э́ту ткань сле́дует стира́ть в холо́дной воде́; (*fig.*): ~ **one's hands of sth.** умы́ть (*pf.*) ру́ки; ~ **one's dirty linen in public** выноси́ть (*impf.*) сор из избы́. **2.** (*of water*; *flow past*) омыва́ть (*impf.*); (*sweep away*) сн|оси́ть, -ести́; **he was ~ed overboard by a wave** его́ смы́ло волно́й за́ борт; (*scoop out*; *erode*) разм|ыва́ть, -ы́ть; **the stream ~ed a channel in the sand** пото́к промы́л кана́ву в песке́. **3.** (*coat with thin paint*) покр|ыва́ть, -ы́ть то́нким сло́ем кра́ски.

v.i. **1.** (~ *o.s.*) мы́ться, вы́-; ум|ыва́ться, -ы́ться. **2.** (~ *clothes*) стира́ть, вы́-. **3.** (*of fabric*: *stand up to ~ing*) стира́ться (*impf.*); (*fig.*): **that excuse won't** ~ э́та отгово́рка не пройдёт. **4.** (*of water*) плеска́ться (*impf.*); **waves ~ed over the deck** во́лны перека́тывались по па́лубе.

with advs.: ~ **away** *v.t.* (*remove*: *stains etc.*) смы|ва́ть, -ть (*or* отм|ыва́ть, -ы́ть) (*пятна*); (*erode*: *cliffs etc.*) разм|ыва́ть, -ы́ть (*or* подм|ыва́ть, -ы́ть) (*утёсы*); ~ **down** *v.t.* мыть, вы́-; сн|оси́ть, -ести́; зап|ива́ть, -и́ть (*что чем*); **I had a sandwich, ~ed down with beer** я съел бутербро́д и запи́л его́ пи́вом; ~ **off** *v.t.* & *i.* смы|ва́ть(ся), -ы́ть(ся); отмы|ва́ть(ся), -ы́ть(ся); отсти́р|ывать(ся), -а́ть(ся); ~ **out** *v.t.* (*e.g. stains*) смы|ва́ть, -ть; отм|ыва́ть, -ы́ть; (*a garment*) стира́ть, вы́-; (*a stain*) отсти́р|ывать, -а́ть; (*of colour*) линя́ть, по-/вы́-; **you look ~ed out** у вас утомлённый вид; **the game was ~ed out (by rain)** пришло́сь прекрати́ть игру́ из-за дождя́; ~ **up** *v.t.* (*dishes*) мыть, вы́- (*посуду*); (*on to shore*) выбра́сывать, вы́бросить на бе́рег; **a chest ~ed up by the tide** сунду́к, вы́брошенный мо́рем/прили́вом; **~ed up** (*exhausted*) уста́лый, разби́тый; (*ruined*) ко́нченый; (*coll.*) пропа́щий.

cpds. **~-basin, ~-bowl** *nn.* ра́ковина; **~board** *n.* стира́льная доска́; **~-boiler** *n.* бак для кипяче́ния белья́; **~-bowl** *n.* = **~-basin**; **~-day** *n.* день (*m.*) сти́рки; **~-down** *n.* мытьё, мо́йка; **~-hand stand** *n.* умыва́льник; **~-house** *n.* пра́чечная; **~leather** *n.* мо́ющаяся за́мша; **~-out** *n.* (*result of flood or rain*) размы́в; (*coll., fiasco*) прова́л; (*coll., failure*) неуда́ча; **~-room** *n.* убо́рная; **~-stand** *n.* умыва́льник; **~-tub** *n.* лоха́нь; коры́то.

washable ['wɒʃəb(ə)l] *adj.* мо́ющийся.

washer ['wɒʃə(r)] *n.* (*washing-machine*) стира́льная маши́на; (*machine component*) прокла́дка.

cpd. **~woman** *n.* пра́чка.

washing ['wɒʃɪŋ] *n.* **1.** (*action*) мытьё, умыва́ние, сти́рка. **2.** (*clothes*) бельё; **hang out the** ~ ве́шать, пове́сить (*or* разве́|шивать, -сить) бельё; **take in** ~ брать (*impf.*) бельё в сти́рку; рабо́тать (*impf.*) пра́чкой.

cpds. **~-day** *n.* день (*m.*) сти́рки; **~-machine** *n.* стира́льная маши́на; **~-powder** *n.* стира́льный порошо́к; **~-soda** *n.* стира́льная со́да; **~-up** *n.*: **do the ~-up** мыть, вы́- посу́ду.

Washington ['wɒʃɪŋt(ə)n] *n.* Вашингто́н; (*attr.*) вашингто́нский.

washy ['wɒʃɪ] *adj.* (*of liquid*) водяни́стый, жи́дкий; (*of colour or complexion*) бле́дный, блёклый, линя́лый; (*of character etc.*) сла́бый, вя́лый.

wasp [wɒsp] *n.* оса́.

cpds. **~-sting** *n.* уку́с осы́; **~-waisted** *adj.* с оси́ной та́лией.

waspish ['wɒspɪʃ] *adj.* язви́тельный, ко́лкий.

waspishness ['wɒspɪʃnɪs] *n.* язви́тельность, ко́лкость.

wassail ['wɒseɪl, 'wɒs(ə)l] *n.* (*arch., festivity*) пир; пи́ршество.

v.t. пирова́ть (*impf.*); бра́жничать (*impf.*).

wastage ['weɪstɪdʒ] *n.* убы́ток, уте́чка.

waste [weɪst] *n.* **1.** (*purposeless or extravagant use*; *failure to use*) (рас)тра́та, расточи́тельство, растра́чивание; ~ **of money** пуста́я тра́та де́нег; вы́брошенные де́ньги; **it would be a ~ of time** э́то бы́ло бы напра́сной тра́той вре́мени; ~ **of fuel** перерасхо́д то́плива; **there was an enormous ~ of young lives in the war** война́ поглоти́ла огро́мное коли́чество молоды́х жи́зней; **go, run to** ~ тра́титься (*impf.*) по́пусту; (*coll.*) идти́ (*det.*) псу под хвост. **2.** (*refuse*) отхо́ды (*m. pl.*), отбро́сы (*m. pl.*), му́сор; ~ **collection** вы́воз му́сора. **3.** (*superfluous material*) отхо́ды (*m. pl.*), отбро́сы (*m. pl.*), обре́зки (*m. pl.*); **atomic** ~ отхо́ды а́томной промы́шленности; **cotton** ~ уга́р, очёски (*m. pl.*); **metallic** ~ металли́ческий лом. **4.** (*desert area*) пусты́ня; ~ **of waters** морско́й просто́р.

adj. **1.** (*superfluous, unwanted*) ли́шний, нену́жный; (*left over after manufacture*) отрабо́танный; (*rejected*; *thrown away*) брако́ванный; ~ **products** отхо́ды (*m. pl.*); ~ **paper** макулату́ра; нену́жная бума́га. **2.** (*of land*: *desolate, desert*) пусты́нный; (*uninhabited*) незаселённый, опустошённый; (*uncultivated*) невозде́ланный; ~ **ground** неплодоро́дная/невозде́ланная земля́; ~ **land** пусты́рь (*m.*), пу́стошь; (*unproductive*) непроизводи́тельный; **lay** ~ опустош|а́ть, -и́ть; разор|я́ть, -и́ть; **lie** ~ быть невозде́ланной (*о земле*); (*fig., featureless*) невырази́тельный, безцве́тный.

v.t. **1.** (*make no use of, use to no purpose, squander*) тра́тить, ис-/по- да́ром/зря/по́пусту; растра́|чивать, -тить; мота́ть, про-; **be ~d** проп|ада́ть, -а́сть (да́ром); ~ **one's life** бесполе́зно прожи́ть (*pf.*) жизнь; ~ **one's chance** упусти́ть (*pf.*) слу́чай; **a ~d talent** растра́ченный по́пусту тала́нт; **my joke was ~d on him** он не оцени́л моеи́ шу́тки; моя́ шу́тка до него́ не дошла́; ~ **one's breath, words** говори́ть (*impf.*) на ве́тер; ~ **not, want not** ≃ мотовство́ до нужды́ доведёт. **2.** (*lay* ~; *ravage*) опустош|а́ть, -и́ть; разор|я́ть, -и́ть. **3.** (*wear away*) изнур|я́ть, -и́ть; истощ|а́ть, -и́ть; **his body was ~d by sickness** его́ те́ло бы́ло истощено́/изнурено́ боле́знью; **a wasting disease** изнури́тельная боле́знь.

v.i. (*usu.* ~ **away**: *become weak*; *wither*) исс|яка́ть, -я́кнуть; истощ|а́ться, -и́ться; ча́хнуть, за-; **wasting assets** истощи́мые акти́вы; изна́шиваемое иму́щество.

cpds. **~-basket** *n.* му́сорная корзи́на; **~-bin** *n.* му́сорное ведро́; му́сорный я́щик; **~-disposal** *n.*: **~-disposal unit** мусородроби́лка; **~-paper-basket** *n.* корзи́н(к)а для (нену́жной) бума́ги; **~-pipe** *n.* сливна́я/водоотво́дная труба́.

wasteful ['weɪstfʊl] *adj.* расточи́тельный; неэконо́мный.

wastefulness ['weɪstfʊlnɪs] *n.* расточи́тельность, неэконо́мность.

waster ['weɪstə(r)] *n.* (*coll.*) никуды́шный/никчёмный челове́к; безде́льник.

wastrel ['weɪstr(ə)l] *n.* (*arch., good-for-nothing*) безде́льник; расточи́тель (*m.*).

watch[1] [wɒtʃ] *n.* **1.** (*alert state*) надзо́р, присмо́тр, наблюде́ние; **keep** ~ стоя́ть (*impf.*) на ва́хте; **the dog keeps ~ on, over the house** соба́ка карау́лит/сторожи́т дом; **on the** ~ начеку́; **she is on the ~ for a bargain** она́ подстерега́ет слу́чай купи́ть по дешёвке. **2.** (*liter.*): **in the ~es of the night** в бессо́нные (ночны́е) часы́. **3.** (*hist., night guardian or patrol* (*collect.*)) стра́жа; (ночно́й) дозо́р; карау́л; патру́ль (*m.*). **4.** (*duty period at sea*) ва́хта; **be on** ~ нести́ (*det.*) ва́хту; стоя́ть (*impf.*) на ва́хте; **first/middle** ~ пе́рвая/ночна́я ва́хта; **dog** ~ полува́хта; (*in general, e.g. for signal operators*) дежу́рство; **I was on ~ from 6 to 12** я дежу́рил с шести́ до двена́дцати; **who's doing the evening ~?** кто на ночно́м дежу́рстве?

v.t. **1.** (*look at*; *keep eyes on*) смотре́ть (*impf.*); **he was ~ing TV** он смотре́л телеви́зор; **I ~ed him draw** я смотре́л, как он рису́ет. **2.** (*keep under observation*) следи́ть (*impf.*) за+*i.*; смотре́ть (*impf.*) за+*i.*; **he is being ~ed by the police** поли́ция следи́т/наблюда́ет за ним; (*be careful of*) следи́ть (*impf.*) за+*i.*; **I have to ~ my weight** мне ну́жно следи́ть за ве́сом/фигу́рой; ~ **your step!** (*lit.*) не оступи́тесь!; (*fig.*; *also, coll.*, ~ **it!**) бу́дьте осторо́жны!; осторо́жно!; береги́тесь!; **I shall have to ~ myself** мне придётся впредь быть осмотри́тельнее. **3.** (*guard*) сторожи́ть; карау́лить; стере́чь (*all impf.*); **he was set to ~ sheep** его́ поста́вили пасти́ ове́ц.

v.i. **1.** смотре́ть, наблюда́ть, следи́ть (*all impf.*); **he was**

content to ~ он дово́льствовался ро́лью просто́го наблюда́теля; **she ~ed by his bedside** она́ дежу́рила у его́ посте́ли; **he ~ed for his opportunity** он (напряжённо) ждал/поджида́л удо́бную возмо́жность; **he ~ ed for the postman** он сторожи́л почтальо́на; **will you ~ over my things?** вы не присмо́трите за мои́ми веща́ми?; **he ~ ed over her interests** он стоя́л на стра́же её интере́сов. **2.** (*be careful*): ~ **how you cross the street** бу́дьте осторо́жны (*or* смотри́те) при перехо́де у́лицы.

with adv.: ~ **out** *v.i.* (*beware*) остерега́ться (+*g.*); берéчься (+*g.*); опаса́ться (+*g.*) (*all impf.*); **you'll fall if you don't ~ out** вы упадёте, е́сли не бу́дете осторо́жны; ~ **out for the signal!** жди́те сигна́ла!

cpds. **~-dog** *n.* (*lit.*) сторожева́я соба́ка; (*fig.*) наблюда́тель (*m.*); **~-fire** *n.* сигна́льный/бива́чный костёр; **~man** *n.* сто́рож, вахтёр; **~-night** *n.* (*service*) новогóдняя всéнощная; **~tower** *n.* сторожева́я ба́шня; **~word** *n.* (*slogan*) призы́в, ло́зунг, деви́з; (*password*) паро́ль (*m.*).

watch[2] [wɒtʃ] *n.* (*timepiece*) час|ы́ (*pl.*, *g.*, -о́в); **two ~es** дво́е часо́в; **set one's** ~ ста́вить, по- часы́; **what time is it by your ~?** ско́лько на ва́ших часа́х?

cpds. **~-case** *n.* ко́рпус часо́в; **~-chain, ~-guard** *nn.* цепо́чка для часо́в; **~-glass** (*US* **~-crystal**) *n.* часово́е стекло́; **~-maker** *n.* часовщи́к; **~-spring** *n.* часова́я пружи́на; **~-strap** *n.* ремешо́к для часо́в; (*metal*) брасле́т.

watcher [wɒtʃə(r)] *n.* наблюда́тель (*m.*).

watchful ['wɒtʃfʊl] *adj.* внима́тельный; бди́тельный; насторо́женный.

watchfulness ['wɒtʃfʊlnɪs] *n.* внима́тельность; бди́тельность; насторо́женность.

water ['wɔːtə(r)] *n.* **1.** вода́; **we went there by** ~ мы пое́хали туда́ по воде́ (*or* во́дным путём); **we are going on the ~ today** сего́дня мы пойдём ката́ться на ло́дке; **our friends from across, over the** ~ на́ши замо́рские/заокеа́нские друзья́; **at the ~'s edge** у са́мой воды́; **the ~ has been cut off** во́ду отключи́ли; **she turned on the** ~ она́ пусти́ла во́ду (*or* откры́ла кран); **a house with ~ laid on** дом с водопрово́дом; **the road is under** ~ доро́га зато́плена; **he spends money like** ~ он сори́т деньга́ми. **2.** (*attr.*) (*see also cpds.*): ~ **bus** речно́й трамва́й; ~ **power** гидроэне́ргия; ~ **sports** во́дный спорт; ~ **supply** водоснабже́ние. **3.** (*fig. phrr.*): **in deep** ~ в беде́/го́ре; в опа́сном положе́нии; **in low** ~ на мели́ (*coll.*); **get into hot** ~ вл|ипа́ть, -и́пнуть; **still ~s run deep** в ти́хом о́муте че́рти во́дятся; **keep one's head above** ~ св|оди́ть, -ести́ концы́ с конца́ми; **pour, throw cold ~ on** раскритикова́ть (*pf.*); ~ **under the bridge** невозвра́тное про́шлое; **the argument won't hold** ~ э́тот до́вод ниче́м не обосно́ван (*or* ни на чём не осно́ван). **4.** (*pl.*, *areas of sea*; *reaches of river*) во́ды (*f. pl.*); **in Icelandic ~s** в исла́ндских во́дах; **in home ~s** в свои́х во́дах; **the head ~s of the Nile** исто́ки (*m. pl.*) Ни́ла; **the upper ~s of the Thames** ве́рхнее тече́ние Те́мзы; (*pl.*, *mineral ~s*) минера́льные во́ды; **they went to the spa to take the ~s** они́ пое́хали (лечи́ться) на во́ды. **5.** (*urine*) моча́; **make, pass** ~ мочи́ться, по-; (*fluid*): ~ **on the brain** водя́нка мо́зга; гидросефали́я; ~ **on the knee** жи́дкость в коле́нной ча́шечке. **6.** (*state of tide*): у́ровень (*m.*) воды́; **high/low** ~ прили́в/отли́в. **7.** (*quality of diamond*) вода́; **of the first** ~ (*lit.*) чи́стой воды́; (*fig.*) чисте́йшей воды́.

v.t. **1.** (*sprinkle ~ on*) пол|ива́ть, -и́ть водо́й; сбры́з|гивать, -нуть. **2.** (*dilute*) разб|авля́ть, -а́вить; **the milk has been ~ed** молоко́ разба́влено. **3.** (*provide with ~*) пои́ть, на-; **he stopped to ~ his horse** он останови́лся напои́ть ло́шадь. **4.**: **~ed silk** муари́рованный шёлк; муа́р.

v.i. (*exude ~*) выделя́ть, вы́делить во́ду; слези́ться (*impf.*); **his eyes were ~ing with the wind** от ве́тра у него́ слези́лись глаза́; **the sight of food made my mouth** ~ при ви́де еды́ у меня́ потекли́ слю́нки; **the wound is still ~ing** ра́на всё ещё не подсо́хла.

with adv.: ~ **down** *v.t.* (*lit.*) разб|авля́ть, -а́вить; (*fig.*) смягч|а́ть, -и́ть; осл|абля́ть, -а́бить.

cpds. **~-biscuit** *n.* пече́нье на воде́; **~-blister** *n.* пузы́рь (*m.*), волды́рь (*m.*); **~-borne** *adj.* (*of freight*) доставля́емый водо́й; перевози́мый по воде́; **~-bottle** *n.* (*soldier's*) фля́жка; (*carafe*) графи́н; (*for heating bed*) гре́лка; **~-buffalo** *n.* буйво́л; **~-butt** *n.* ка́дка; **~-cannon** *n.* брандспо́йт, гидропу́льт; **~-cart** *n.* бо́чка водово́за; **~-chute** *n.* водяны́е го́ры (*f. pl.*); **~-closet** *n.* ватерклозе́т; **~-colour** *n.* (*paint*) акваре́ль; акваре́льные кра́ски (*f. pl.*); (*painting*) акваре́ль; **~-cooled** *adj.* с водяны́м охлажде́нием; **~course** *n.* пото́к; ру́сло; **~cress** *n.* кресс водяно́й; **~-diviner** *n.* иска́тель (*m.*) воды́; **~-divining** *n.* по́иски (*m. pl.*) воды́; **~ed-down** *adj.* (*fig.*) осла́бленный; **~fall** *n.* водопа́д; **~fowl** *n.* водопла́вающая пти́ца; **~front** *n.* часть го́рода, примыка́ющая к бе́регу; **~-gauge** *n.* водоме́р; **~-glass** *n.* (*utensil*) стака́н; **~-heater** *n.* кипяти́льник; **~-hen** *n.* ку́рочка водяна́я; **~-hole** *n.* пруд, ключ, исто́чник; **~-ice** *n.* шербе́т; **~-jacket** *n.* водяна́я руба́шка; **~-jump** *n.* во́дный рубе́ж на ска́чках; ров с водо́й; **~-level** *n.* у́ровень (*m.*) воды́; (*instrument*) ватерпа́с; **~-lily** *n.* водяна́я ли́лия, кувши́нка; **~-line** *n.* (*naut.*) ватерли́ния; **~logged** *adj.* (*of wood*) мо́крый; (*of ship*) (полу)зато́пленный; (*of ground*) заболо́ченный; **~-main** *n.* водопрово́дная магистра́ль; **~man** *n.* (*boatman*) ло́дочник; **~mark** *n.* водяно́й знак; **~meadow** *n.* заливно́й луг; **~-melon** *n.* арбу́з; **~-meter** *n.* водоме́р; **~-mill** *n.* водяна́я ме́льница; **~-nymph** *n.* речна́я ни́мфа, руса́лка; **~-pipe** *n.* водопрово́дная труба́; **~-pistol** *n.* игру́шечный водяно́й пистоле́т; **~-polo** *n.* во́дное по́ло (*indecl.*); **~proof** *n.* & *adj.* непромока́емый (плащ); *v.t.* обраб|а́тывать, -о́тать водонепроница́емым соста́вом; **~-rat** *n.* водяна́я кры́са; **~-rate** *n.* нало́г на во́ду; пла́та за во́ду; **~-repellent** *adj.* водооттáлкивающий; **~side** *n.* бе́рег; **~-skiing** *n.* воднолы́жный спо́рт; **~-skis** *n. pl.* во́дные лы́жи (*f. pl.*); **~-softener** *n.* водоумягчи́тель (*m.*); **~spout** *n.* (*phenomenon*) водяно́й смерч; (*conduit*) водосто́чная труба́; **~-tank** *n.* резервуа́р; бак для воды́; **~-tap** *n.* водопрово́дный кран; **~tight** *adj.* (*lit.*) водонепроница́емый; (*fig.*, *of argument etc.*) неопровержи́мый, убеди́тельный; **~-tower** *n.* водонапо́рная ба́шня; **~-trough** *n.* пои́лка для скота́; **~-wag(g)on** *n.* пово́зка водово́за; **go on the ~-wag(g)on** (*fig.*) дать (*pf.*) заро́к не пить; **~way** *n.* во́дный путь; **~-weed** *n.* во́доросль; **~-wheel** *n.* водяно́е колесо́; **~-wings** *n. pl.* пла́вательные пузыри́ (*m. pl.*); **~works** *n. pl.* (*lit.*) систе́ма водоснабже́ния; (*fig.*, *coll.*: *urinary system*) по́чки (*f. pl.*); (*fig.*, *tears*): **she turned on the ~works** она́ разреве́лась; она распусти́ла ню́ни (*coll.*).

watering ['wɔːtərɪŋ] *n.* поли́вка; **the roses need** ~ ну́жно поли́ть ро́зы.

cpds. **~-can** *n.* ле́йка; **~-cart** *n.* поли́вочная маши́на; **~-place** *n.* (*for animals*) водопо́й; (*resort*) (во́дный) куро́рт; во́ды (*f. pl.*); **~-pot** *n.* ле́йка.

Waterloo [ˌwɔːtə'luː] *n.* Ватерло́о (*indecl.*); **the Battle of** ~ сраже́ние у Ватерло́о; **meet one's** ~ потерпе́ть (*pf.*) оконча́тельное пораже́ние.

watershed ['wɔːtəˌʃed] *n.* (*lit.*, *fig.*) водоразде́л.

watery ['wɔːtərɪ] *adj.* водяни́стый, жи́дкий; ~ **vegetables** разва́ренные о́вощи; ~ **eyes** слезя́щиеся глаза́; **a ~ sky** не́бо, суля́щее дождь; ~ **colour** бле́дный/размы́тый/водяни́стый цвет; ~ **garments** промо́кшая оде́жда; **a ~ grave** водяна́я моги́ла.

watt [wɒt] *n.* ватт.

wattage ['wɒtɪdʒ] *n.* мо́щность в ва́ттах.

wattle[1] ['wɒt(ə)l] *n.* **1.** (*interlaced sticks*) пру́тья (*m. pl.*), пле́тень (*m.*); ~ **and daub hut** ма́занка. **2.** (*plant*) ака́ция.

wattle[2] ['wɒt(ə)l] *n.* (*of bird*) боро́дка.

wave [weɪv] *n.* **1.** (*ridge of water*) волна́; вал; **life on the ocean** ~ морска́я жизнь. **2.** (*fig.*, *of persons advancing*) волна́; **the infantry attacked in ~s** пехо́та наступа́ла эшело́нами. **3.** (*fig.*, *temporary increase or spread*) подъём, волна́; ~ **of enthusiasm** волна́/взрыв энтузиа́зма; **crime** ~ ре́зкий рост престу́пности; **heat** ~ жара́; полоса́/пери́од си́льной жары́. **4.** (*phys.*) волна́; **short/medium/long ~s** коро́ткие/сре́дние/дли́нные во́лны; ~ **theory**

волнова́я тео́рия. **5.** (*undulation*): **her hair has a natural ~** у неё (от приро́ды) вью́щиеся во́лосы; **the rain took the ~ out of her hair** от дождя́ у неё распрями́лись во́лосы; **permanent ~** шестиме́сячная зави́вка; перманéнт. **6.** (*gesture*) взмах, жест (руки́); **she gave a ~ of her hand** она́ помаха́ла/взмахну́ла руко́й; **at the ~ of a wand** по мановéнию па́лочки.

v.t. **1.** (*move to and fro or up and down*) разма́хивать (*impf.*) +*i.*; маха́ть, по- +*i.*; **the children were waving flags** де́ти разма́хивали флажка́ми; **she ~d her handkerchief at me** она́ помаха́ла мне платко́м; **he ~d his hand** (*as a signal*) он по́дал знак (*or* махну́л) руко́й; **he ~d his sword** он взмахну́л мечо́м/са́блей. **2.** (*express by hand-waving*): **~ a greeting** помаха́ть (*pf.*) руко́й в знак приве́тствия; **~ goodbye** помаха́ть (*pf.*) руко́й на проща́ние; прости́ться (*pf.*) взма́хом руки́. **3.** (*set in ~s*) зав|ива́ть, -и́ть; **she had her hair ~d** она́ зави́ла во́лосы.

v.i. **1.** (*move to and fro or up and down*) развева́ться (*impf.*); кача́ться (*impf.*); **waving branches** кача́ющиеся ве́тви; **waving corn** волну́ющаяся под ве́тром пшени́ца; **the flags were waving in the breeze** фла́ги развева́лись на ветру́. **2.** (*~ one's hand*) маха́ть, по-; **~ at s.o.** маха́ть, по- кому́-н. **3.** (*undulate*; *be wavy*) ви́ться (*impf.*); волнова́ться (*impf.*).

with advs.: **~ aside** *v.t.* отстран|я́ть, -и́ть жéстом; **he ~d my objections aside** он отмахну́лся от мои́х возраже́ний; **~ away** *v.t.* отстран|я́ть, -и́ть же́стом; **~ down** *v.t.* остан|а́вливать, -ови́ть; **the policeman ~d us down** полице́йский сде́лал знак руко́й, что́бы мы останови́лись; **~ on** *v.t.*: **the officer ~d his men on** офице́р взма́хом руки́ дал солда́там сигна́л к наступле́нию; **when our passports had been checked we were ~d on** прове́рив на́ши паспорта́, нам махну́ли: «Проезжа́йте!».

cpds. **~band** *n.* диапазо́н волн; **~length** *n.* длина́ волны́; **he and I are on the same ~length** (*fig.*) мы с ним настро́ены на одну́ волну́; мы одина́ково смо́трим на ве́щи; **~-meter** *n.* волноме́р.

waver [ˈweɪvə(r)] *v.i.* **1.** (*flicker*) колыха́ться (*impf.*). **2.** (*falter*; *become unsteady*) дрожа́ть, за-; дро́гнуть (*pf.*); **the front line ~ed** пере́дний край дро́гнул; **his voice ~ed** его́ го́лос задрожа́л. **3.** (*hesitate*; *be irresolute*) колеба́ться (*impf.*).

waverer [ˈweɪvərə(r)] *n.* коле́блющийся.

wavy [ˈweɪvɪ] *adj.* волнообра́зный, волни́стый, извива́ющийся; **a ~ line** волни́стая ли́ния/черта́; **~ hair** вью́щиеся во́лосы.

wax[1] [wæks] *n.* **1.** воск; (*in the ears*) ушна́я се́ра; **paraffin ~** твёрдый парафи́н; **he is like ~ in her hands** она́ из него́ верёвки вьёт. **2.** (*attr.*) восково́й (*see also cpds.*).

v.t. вощи́ть, на-; нат|ира́ть, -ере́ть (во́ском); **~ one's moustaches** фа́брить, на- усы́; **~ed thread** вощёная ни́тка.

cpds. **~-chandler** *n.* свечно́й фабрика́нт; торго́вец свеча́ми; **~-paper** *n.* воща́нка, воско́вка; **~work** *n.* (*model*) восковая фигу́ра; восково́й муля́ж; **~works** *n.* (*exhibition*) галере́я восковы́х фигу́р.

wax[2] [wæks] *v.i.* **1.** (*of moon*) прибыва́ть (*impf.*). **2.** (*liter.*, *grow*) де́латься (*impf.*); станови́ться (*impf.*); **~ fat** жире́ть, раз-; **~ merry** развесели́ться (*pf.*); **~ eloquent** де́латься, с- красноречи́вым; **~ angry** разгнева́ться; разозли́ться; рассерди́ться (*all pf.*).

waxen [ˈwæks(ə)n] *adj.* восково́й; **~ complexion** восковая бле́дность лица́.

waxy [ˈwæksɪ] *adj.* восково́й; **~ potatoes** водяни́стая карто́шка.

way [weɪ] *n.* **1.** (*road, path*) доро́га, путь (*m.*); (*track*) тропа́; (*specific*): **Appian W~** А́ппиева доро́га; **Milky W~** Мле́чный путь; **W~ of the Cross** кре́стный путь; **over the ~** напро́тив. **2.** (*route, journey*): **which is the best ~ to London?** как лу́чше пройти́/прое́хать в Ло́ндон?; **he lost his ~** он заблуди́лся; он сби́лся с пути́; **he went (on) his ~** он пошёл да́льше; он удали́лся; **he went the ~ of all flesh** он испыта́л уде́л всего́ земно́го; **they went their own ~s** ка́ждый пошёл свои́м путём; **go down the wrong ~** (*of food etc.*) попа́сть (*pf.*) не в то го́рло; **lead the ~** (*lit.*) идти́ (*det.*) вперёд; пока́з|ывать, -а́ть доро́гу; (*fig.*) под|ава́ть, -а́ть приме́р; **feel one's ~** дви́гаться (*impf.*) осмотри́тельно (*or* на о́щупь); **the longest ~ round is the shortest ~ home** ≃ ти́ше е́дешь, да́льше бу́дешь; **we made our ~ to the dining-room** мы прошли́ в столо́вую; **you must make your own ~ to the station** вам придётся добира́ться до ста́нции самому́; **they made their ~ across mountains** они́ проби́лись че́рез го́ры; **he made his ~ in the world** он проби́л себе́ доро́гу в жи́зни; он преуспе́л в жи́зни; **pay one's ~** (*lit.*) (*of pers.*) опла́|чивать, -ти́ть свою́ доро́гу; е́хать (*det.*) на свои́ де́ньги; жить (*impf.*) на со́бственные сре́дства (*or* по сре́дствам); (*of thg.*) окуп|а́ться, -и́ться; опра́вдывать (*impf.*) себя́; **he worked his ~ through college** он учи́лся в колле́дже и одновреме́нно рабо́тал; (*with preps.*): **by ~ of London** че́рез Ло́ндон; **by the ~** по доро́ге; в пути́; попу́тно; (*incidentally*) кста́ти; ме́жду про́чим; **by ~ of** *see also* **11.**; **(for) once in a ~** и́зредка; хотя́ бы одна́жды; **in the ~** *see* **9.**; **on the ~** по доро́ге; на/по пути́; **he was on his ~ to the bank** он шёл в банк; **a letter is on its ~** письмо́ (нахо́дится) в пути́; **I must be on my ~** мне пора́; **on your ~!** (*sl.*) проходи́!; **I sent him on his ~** я его́ отпра́вил; **they have another child on the ~** они́ ожида́ют ещё одного́ ребёнка; **be on the ~ in/out** (*of fashion*) входи́ть (*impf.*) в мо́ду, вы́ходить (*impf.*) из мо́ды; **the hall is well on the ~ to completion** строи́тельство за́ла бли́зится к концу́; **he is well on the ~ to being a professor** у него́ все ша́нсы стать профе́ссором; **he went out of his ~ to help me** он прояви́л нема́лое усе́рдие, что́бы мне помо́чь; **out of the ~** (*remote*) в стороне́; далеко́; **the price is nothing out of the ~** цена́ не осо́бенно высо́кая; (*inappropriate*) неуме́стно, беста́ктно, изли́шне; *see also* **9.**; (*with adv. indicating direction*): **~ across** перехо́д; **~ in** вход; **~ out** (*lit.*, *fig.*) вы́ход; **can you find the ~ back?** вы не заблу́дитесь на обра́тном пути́?; вы найдёте доро́гу наза́д?; **the ~ ahead will be difficult** нам предстои́т тру́дная доро́га; **~ through** прохо́д; **~ round** око́льный путь; (*fig.*, *loophole*) лазе́йка; **he knows his ~ around** он зна́ет, что к чему́. **3.** (*door*): **he came in by the front ~ and went out by the back** он вошёл с пара́дного хо́да, а вы́шел с чёрного. **4.** (*direction*) сторона́, направле́ние; **which ~ did they go?** в каку́ю сто́рону они́ пошли́?; **this ~** сюда́; **are you going my ~?** вам со мной по пути́?; вы в мою́ сто́рону?; **come s.o.'s ~** дост|ава́ться, -а́ться кому́-н.; дов|оди́ться, -ести́сь кому́-н.; **look the other ~** (*fig.*) смотре́ть (*impf.*) сквозь па́льцы; **I travelled by bus both ~s** я е́хал авто́бусом туда́ и обра́тно (*or* в о́ба конца́); **you can't have it both ~s** ли́бо одно́, ли́бо друго́е; что́-нибудь одно́; **it cuts both ~s** э́то па́лка о двух конца́х; **no two ~s about it** э́то несомне́нно; об э́том не мо́жет быть двух мне́ний; **I put him in the ~ of a job** я помо́г ему́ устро́иться на рабо́ту; **I don't know which ~ to turn** я не зна́ю, что де́лать (*or* как быть). **5.** (*of reversible thgs.*): **his hat is on the wrong ~ round** он наде́л шля́пу за́дом наперёд; **the picture is the wrong ~ up** карти́на пове́шена вверх нога́ми; **is the flag the right ~ up?** пра́вильно ли пове́шен флаг?; **the other ~ round** наоборо́т, напро́тив. **6.** (*neighbourhood, area*): **down your ~** в ва́ших края́х; **he lives somewhere Plymouth ~** он живёт где-то в райо́не Пли́мута. **7.** (*distance*) расстоя́ние; **a long ~ off** (*away*) далеко́; **a little, short ~** недалеко́; **quite a ~** дово́льно далеко́; **a long ~ from one's country** вдали́ от ро́дины; **it is only a little ~ to the shops** до магази́нов совсе́м недалеко́ (*or* два шага́); **we walked all the ~ here** всю доро́гу сюда́ мы прошли́ пешко́м; **all the ~ to the Pacific** до са́мого Ти́хого океа́на; **I went part of the ~ to meet him** (*lit.*) я вы́шел ему́ навстре́чу; (*fig.*) я пошёл ему́ навстре́чу; **better by a long ~** куда́/гора́здо/намно́го лу́чше; **it will go some ~ to restore confidence** э́то в како́й-то ме́ре помо́жет восстанови́ть дове́рие; **all the ~** всю доро́гу; (*fig.*) по́лностью. **8.** (*US coll.*) (*a long ~*) далеко́; **~ back** (*long ago*) давны́м-давно́; **~ ahead of the others** намно́го впереди́ остальны́х; **~ out** (*coll*, *exceptional*) замеча́тельный, потряса́ющий. **9.** (*clear passage*; *space or freedom to proceed*) прое́зд, прохо́д;

right of ~ право проезда; **clear the ~** расч|ищать, -истить путь; **fight one's ~ through the crowd** прод|ираться, -раться сквозь толпу; **get in the ~** мешать, по- (*кому*); путаться (*impf.*) (*у кого*) под ногами; **this chair is always getting in the ~** этот стул вечно торчит на дороге; **get out of the ~!** (прочь) с дороги!; дайте пройти!; **get sth. out of the ~** (*lit.*) уб|ирать, -рать что-н. с дороги; (*fig., dispose of*) свал|ивать, -ить что-н.; кончить, по- с чем-н.; изб|авляться, -авиться от чего-н.; раздел|ываться, -аться с чем-н.; **make ~ for the President!** дорогу президенту!; **he made ~ for his successor** он уступил место своему преемнику; **I put the vase out of harm's ~** я убрал вазу от греха подальше; **put out of the ~** устран|ять, -ить; **you are standing in the ~** вы загораживаете дорогу; **I shan't stand in your ~** я не буду стоять на вашем пути (*or* вам мешать/препятствовать); **I can't see my ~ to doing that** боюсь, что не смогу это сделать; **give ~** (*fail to resist*) подд|аваться, -аться; (*collapse*) провал|иваться, -иться; раз|рываться, -орваться; ломаться, с-; рухнуть (*pf.*); **his legs gave ~** у него подкосились ноги; (*retreat*) отступ|ать, -ить; (*make concessions*) уступ|ать, -ить; (*allow precedence*) уступ|ать, -ить дорогу; (*surrender, abandon o.s.*) сд|аваться, -аться; пред|аваться, -аться; **give ~ to tears** дать (*pf.*) волю слезам. **10.** (*means, method*) средство, метод, приём; **he found a ~ to keep food warm** он нашёл способ/средство сохранять пищу горячей; **there is no ~ to** нет никакой возможностей; **W~s and Means Committee** бюджетная комиссия; **there are ~s and means** есть всякие пути и возможности; **you will soon get into the ~ of it** вы вскоре научитесь. **11.** (*manner, fashion*) средство, способ, образ, метод, приём, подход; **in this ~** таким образом; **is this the ~ to do it?** так это делается?; **do it your own ~!** делайте по-своему!; **in a polite ~** вежливо; **I'll miss her in a ~** мне, пожалуй, будет её недоставать; **one ~ or another** так или иначе; тем или иным способом; **the right ~** так; правильно; надлежащим образом; **the wrong ~** не так, неправильно; **in the same ~** (точно) так же; таким же образом; **I love the ~ he smiles** мне очень нравится его улыбка; **it's disgraceful the ~ he drinks** безобразие, что он так пьёт; **I don't like the ~ you said that** мне не нравится, как вы это сказали; **~ of thinking** взгляды (*m. pl.*); образ мыслей; **to my ~ of thinking** как мне кажется; на мой взгляд; по-моему; **try to see it my ~** попытайтесь встать на мою точку зрения; **let's put it this ~** скажем так; **that's all right in its ~** по-своему (*or* в своём роде) это неплохо; **either ~** (*in either fashion*) любым из двух способов; (*in either case or event*) в обоих случаях; **whichever ~ you look at it** куда ни кинь; **by ~ of** (*in order to*) с тем, чтобы; дабы; с целью; **by ~ of a change** для разнообразия; **by ~ of a joke** шутки ради; (*in the guise of*) в виде/порядке/качестве; вместо; взамен (*all +g.*); **he is by ~ of being an authority** он считается авторитетом; **he is by ~ of being a musician** у него музыкальные склонности; (*manner of behaving*): **she has a winning ~** у неё обаятельная манера; **he has a ~ with him** у него к каждому есть подход; **it's only his ~** у него просто такая манера; есть всего лишь его манера; **he has a ~ with the ladies** он умеет нравится дамам; (*preference*): **have it your own ~!** будь по-вашему!; **have, get one's own ~** доб|иваться, -иться своего; **things went my ~** дела сложились в мою пользу (*or* так, как я хотел). **12.** (*habit, custom*) обычай, привычка, повадка; **~ of life** образ жизни; **it is not my ~ to deceive** не в моём обычае/характере обманывать; **he has a ~ of not paying his bills** у него привычка не платить по счетам; **that's always the ~ with him** он всегда так; **that's the ~ of the world** так уж заведено/водится на свете; **mend one's ~s** испр|авляться, -авиться; **fall into bad ~s** пойти (*pf.*) по плохой/дурной дорожке; **these ideas have a ~ of turning out badly** эти идеи обычно выходят боком. **13.** (*state, condition*) положение, состояние; **things are in a bad ~** плохо дело; дела из рук вон плохи; **she was in a terrible ~** (*ill*) она была очень больна; (*angry*) она была ужасно сердита; **in the family ~** в (интересном) положении. **14.** (*scale, degree*): **in a small ~** скромно; **in a big ~** в широком/большом масштабе; кардинально; **he is a printer in a small ~** у него небольшая типография; **he went in for photography in a big ~** он стал заниматься фотографией всерьёз (*or* с энтузиазмом). **15.** (*sense, respect*) смысл, отношение; **in a ~** в некотором отношении; в известном смысле; **in some ~s** в некоторых отношениях; **in one ~** в одном смысле; **in no ~** ничуть; никоим образом; **were you involved in any ~?** были ли вы сколько-нибудь в этом замешаны?; **one ~ and another** во всех отношениях; по разным причинам. **16.** (*line, course*): **what have we in the ~ of food?** что у нас есть по части еды?; **he called there in the ~ of business** он зашёл туда по делу. **17.** (*of ship etc.*): **under ~** (*also* **weigh**) на ходу, в пути; **have ~ on** продвигаться (*impf.*); **gather ~** наб|ирать, -рать ход; **lose ~** уб|авлять, -авить ход; **preparations are under ~** (сейчас) идут приготовления. **18. (slip~)** стапель (*m.*). **19.: permanent ~** полотно; верхнее строение пути. **20.** (*US*): **~ station** промежуточная станция, полустанок; **~ train** поезд, идущий со всеми остановками.

cpds. **~bill** *n.* (*list of goods*) транспортная накладная; **~farer** *n.* путник, странник; **~lay** *v.t.* подстер|егать, -ечь; устр|аивать, -оить засаду *+d.*; **~-leave** *n.* право прокладывать кабель (*m.*)/трубы *и т.п.*; **~mark** *n.* веха; **~-out** *adj.* (*coll.*) замечательный, не от мира сего; **~side** *n.* обочина (дороги); (*attr.*) придорожный; **fall by the ~side** (*fig.*) выбывать, выбыть из строя.

wayward ['weɪwəd] *adj.* своенравный, своевольный, непокорный.

waywardness ['weɪwədnɪs] *n.* своенравие, своеволие, непокорность.

WC (*abbr. of* **water-closet**) уборная.

we [wi:, wɪ] *pron.* мы (*also royal, editorial*); **~ lawyers** мы, адвокаты; **give us a rest!** дайте человеку отдохнуть!; **how are ~ feeling today?** как мы сегодня себя чувствуем?; **~ don't inform on people** у нас не принято доносить.

weak [wi:k] *adj.* **1.** (*infirm; feeble*) слабый; **a ~ constitution** хрупкое сложение; **he has a ~ heart** у него слабое сердце; **a ~ imagination** бедное воображение; **I feel ~ in the legs** у меня ноги подкашиваются от слабости; **a ~ old man** дряхлый старик; **he's a bit ~ in the head** он придурковат; **their cries grew ~er** их крики слабели/ослабевали; **a ~ hand** (*at cards*) плохие карты; **his ~ point is spelling** он слаб в орфографии; орфография — его слабое место; **the ~est go to the wall** слабых бьют; **the ~er sex** слабый пол. **2.** (*unconvincing*) неубедительный, неосновательный; **the argument is too ~ to stand up** этот довод совершенно неубедителен; **they put up a ~ case** они привели слабые доводы. **3.** (*of morals or will*) безвольный, слабовольный, неустойчивый; **a ~ man/character** слабый/нерешительный человек/характер; **the ~er brethren** немощные братья; **in a ~ moment** в минуту слабости. **4.** (*diluted; thin*) жидкий, слабый; **do you like your tea ~?** вы любите некрепкий/слабый чай? **5.** (*gram.*) слабый. **6.** (*of style*) вялый; **a ~ ending to a story** вялый конец рассказа.

cpds. **~-headed** *adj.* слабоумный; **~-kneed** *adj.* (*fig.*) малодушный, нерешительный; **~-minded** *adj.* слабоумный; **~-sighted** *adj.* со слабым зрением; **~-spirited** *adj.* малодушный; **~-willed** *adj.* слабовольный.

weaken ['wi:kən] *v.t.* осл|аблять, -абить; **his resolve was ~ed** его решимость была поколеблена; **~ one's grip** ослабить (*pf.*) хватку.

v.i. слабеть, ослабнуть; **the frost showed no signs of ~ing** мороз упорствовал.

weakling ['wi:klɪŋ] *n.* слабый человек; хилый/слабенький ребёнок *и т.п.*

weakly ['wi:klɪ] *adj.* хилый, болезненный.

weakness ['wi:knɪs] *n.* слабость, хилость; **the tests revealed ~es in the structure** испытания выявили структурные дефекты; **there is a ~ in his logic** в его логике есть изъян; **she has a ~ for him** она питает к нему слабость.

weal[1] [wi:l] *n.* (*liter.*) бла́го, благосостоя́ние; **the common, public** ~ бла́го о́бщества; о́бщее бла́го; **in** ~ **and woe** в сча́стье и в го́ре/беде́.

weal[2] [wi:l] *n.* (*mark on skin*) рубе́ц.

wealth [welθ] *n.* бога́тство; **a man of** ~ бога́ч; состоя́тельный челове́к; **he possesses great** ~ он о́чень бога́тый челове́к; **the** ~ **of the Indies** бога́тства И́ндии; ~ **tax** нало́г на иму́щество; (*fig., profusion*) оби́лие, изоби́лие; **a** ~ **of illustrations** оби́лие иллюстра́ций; **a** ~ **of detail** мно́жество подро́бностей/дета́лей; **a** ~ **of experience** богате́йший о́пыт; **a** ~ **of material** огро́мный материа́л; **a** ~ **of imagery** огро́мное бога́тство о́бразов.

wealthy ['welθɪ] *adj.* бога́тый, состоя́тельный; **the** ~ богачи́ (*m. pl.*); бога́тые, иму́щие; **she has a** ~ **appearance** у неё вид бога́той же́нщины; су́дя по ви́ду, она́ бога́та.

wean [wi:n] *v.t.* отн|има́ть, -я́ть (*or* отлуч|а́ть, -и́ть) от груди́; отлуч|а́ть, -и́ть от ма́тери; (*fig.*) отуч|а́ть, -и́ть (*от чего*).

weanling ['wi:nlɪŋ] *n.* ребёнок (*и т.п.*), (неда́вно) о́тнятый от груди́.

weapon ['wepən] *n.* ору́жие; **guided** ~**s** управля́емые снаря́ды (*m. pl.*)/раке́ты (*f. pl.*); ~ **of war** боево́е сре́дство; (*fig.*) ору́дие, сре́дство; **the strike was their last** ~ **of defence** забасто́вка была́ их после́дним сре́дством защи́ты.

weaponry ['wepənrɪ] *n.* ору́жие, вооруже́ние.

wear [weə(r)] *n.* **1.** (*articles or type of clothing*) оде́жда, пла́тье; **beach** ~ оде́жда для пля́жа; купа́льные костю́мы (*m. pl.*); **children's** ~ де́тская оде́жда, де́тское пла́тье; (~*ing of clothes*) но́ска, ноше́ние; **in general** ~ в ходу́; **a suit for everyday** ~ бу́дничный/повседне́вный костю́м. **2.** (*continued use as causing damage or loss of quality*) изно́с, снос; **this material stands up to hard** ~ э́тот материа́л прекра́сно но́сится; **show signs of** ~ име́ть (*impf.*) поно́шенный/потёртый/потрёпанный вид; **fair** ~ **and tear** (*leg.*) норма́льная у́быль и норма́льный изно́с; **the** ~ **and tear of life** жи́зненные передря́ги (*f. pl.*). **3.** (*resistance to* ~) но́скость; **these shoes have a lot of** ~ **left in them** э́ти боти́нки мо́жно ещё до́лго носи́ть (*or* ещё до́лго бу́дут носи́ться).

v.t. **1.** (*of garments or accessories*) носи́ть (*indet.*); над|ева́ть, -е́ть; **what shall I** ~**?** что мне наде́ть?; **she was** ~**ing light blue** она́ была́ в голубо́м (пла́тье); **he** ~**s galoshes** он но́сит гало́ши; **he always wore a hat** он всегда́ ходи́л в шля́пе; **she** ~**s scent** она́ ду́шится; **scarves are being worn this year** в э́том году́ но́сят (*or* мо́дно носи́ть) ша́рфы; **are you** ~**ing a watch?** у вас есть часы́?; вы при часа́х?; **worn** (*used*) **clothes** (из)но́шенная/ста́рая оде́жда; (*of hair*): ~ **one's hair long** носи́ть (*indet.*) дли́нные во́лосы; ~ **one's hair short** ко́ротко стри́чься (*impf.*); **he** ~**s his hair brushed back** он зачёсывает во́лосы наза́д; **they all wore beards** они́ все носи́ли бо́роды; у них у всех бы́ли бо́роды; ~ **mourning** ходи́ть (*indet.*) в тра́уре; (*fig.*): ~**ing a smile** с улы́бкой (на лице́); ~**ing a frown** насу́пившись; **his face** ~**s a worried look** у него́ озабо́ченный вид; **the house wore an air of neglect** дом вы́глядел запу́щенным/забро́шенным; **he** ~**s his years well** он вы́глядит моложа́во (*or* моло́же свои́х лет). **2.** (*coll., usu. with neg., tolerate*): **he won't** ~ **that excuse** така́я отгово́рка у него́ не пройдёт. **3.** (*injure surface of; abrade; damage by use*) ст|ира́ть, -ере́ть; прот|ира́ть, -ере́ть; **the steps are worn** ступе́ни стёрлись; **his cuffs are badly worn** его́ манже́ты обтрёпаны; **he** ~**s his socks into holes** он изна́шивает носки́ до дыр; **a well-worn suit** си́льно поно́шенный костю́м; **the waves have worn the stone** во́лны обточи́ли/отшлифова́ли ка́мень; (*fig.*): **she was worn to a shadow with worry** от постоя́нной забо́ты она́ преврати́лась в тень; **I had a** ~**ing day** у меня́ был тяжёлый день; **a well-worn theme** изби́тая те́ма. **4.** (*produce by friction*): **the stream wore a channel in the sand** пото́к проры́л кана́ву в песке́; **you've worn a hole in your trousers** вы протёрли брю́ки (до дыр); **a well-worn track** проторённая доро́жка; **they wore a path across the field** они́ протопта́ли/протори́ли тропи́нку че́рез по́ле.

v.i. **1.** (*stand up to* ~) (хорошо́) носи́ться (*indet.*); быть про́чным; **the play** ~**s well after 50 years** э́та пье́са и 50 лет спустя́ отли́чно смо́трится. **2.** (*show effects of* ~): ~ **thin, threadbare** изн|а́шиваться, -оси́ться; истрёп|ываться, -а́ться; (*fig.*): **his patience wore thin** его́ терпе́ние бы́ло на исхо́де; **that excuse has worn thin** э́то оправда́ние звучи́т неубеди́тельно. **3.** (*progress*) подвига́ться (*impf.*); **his life wore towards its close** его́ жизнь бли́зилась к концу́.

with advs.: ~ **away** *v.t. & i.* ст|ира́ть(ся), -ере́ть(ся); **weather had worn away the inscription** ве́тры и дожди́ стёрли на́дпись; **the cliffs were worn away in places** ска́лы места́ми вы́ветрились; ~ **down** *v.t. & i.* изн|а́шивать(ся), -оси́ть(ся); **the teeth were worn down to stumps** от зубо́в оста́лись одни́ ко́рни; **the heels have worn down very quickly** каблуки́ сноси́лись о́чень бы́стро; (*fig.*): **he wore down her opposition** он преодоле́л её сопротивле́ние; **they wore down the enemy's resistance** они́ сломи́ли сопротивле́ние проти́вника; ~ **in** *v.t.* (*shoes*) разн|а́шивать, -оси́ть (*боти́нки*); ~ **off** *v.t. & i.* ст|ира́ть(ся), -ере́ть(ся); **the pattern wore off** узо́р стёрся; (*fig.*) (постепе́нно) проходи́ть (*impf.*); **the novelty soon wore off** вско́ре новизна́ вы́ветрилась; ~ **on** *v.i.*: **as the evening wore on** к концу́ ве́чера; ~ **out** *v.t. & i.* изн|а́шивать(ся), -оси́ть(ся); истрёп|ывать(ся), -а́ть(ся); **the machine wore out** маши́на срабо́талась; (*fig.*) изнур|я́ть(ся), -и́ть(ся); **the children wore me out** де́ти меня́ заму́чили/изму́чили; **you look worn out** у вас изму́ченный вид; **worn-out** (*of clothes etc.*) изно́шенный, сноси́вшийся, истёртый, потёртый.

wearable ['weərəb(ə)l] *adj.* приго́дный для но́ски.

wearer ['weərə(r)] *n.* владе́лец, носи́тель (*fem.* -ница).

weariness ['wɪərɪnɪs] *n.* утомле́ние; ску́ка.

wearing ['weərɪŋ] *adj.* утоми́тельный, надое́дливый.

wearisome ['wɪərɪsəm] *adj.* надое́дливый, ску́чный, ну́дный.

weary ['wɪərɪ] *adj.* **1.** (*tired*) уста́лый, утомлённый; ~ **in body and mind** уста́вший душо́й и те́лом (*or* физи́чески и духо́вно); ~ **of walking** уста́вший от ходьбы́; **the journey made him** ~ путеше́ствие его́ утоми́ло. **2.** (*tiring*) утоми́тельный; **a** ~ **wait** томи́тельное ожида́ние; **ten** ~ **miles** де́сять до́лгих миль. **3.** (*showing tiredness*) уста́вший; **he gave a** ~ **sigh** он уста́ло вздохну́л. **4.**: ~ **of** (*fed up with*) уста́вший от (*чего*); **I was** ~ **of his complaints** мне надое́ли/наску́чили его́ жа́лобы.

v.t. & i. утом|ля́ть(ся), -и́ть(ся); **I shall never** ~ **of hearing that tale** мне никогда́ не надое́ст/наску́чит э́та исто́рия.

weasel ['wi:z(ə)l] *n.* ла́ска; ~ **words** (*fig.*) обма́нчивые слова́.

v.i.: ~ **out of sth.** (*fig., coll.*) увильну́ть/уклони́ться/устрани́ться (*pf.*) от чего́-н.

weather ['weðə(r)] *n.* пого́да; **bad** ~ плоха́я пого́да, нена́стье; **rough** ~ непого́да; **wet** ~ дождли́вая пого́да; **in all** ~**s** в любу́ю (*or* во вся́кую) пого́ду; **what's the** ~ **like?** кака́я сего́дня пого́да?; **the** ~ **was bad** пого́ды не́ было; ~ **permitting** при благоприя́тной пого́де; **make heavy** ~ **of sth.** (*fig.*) осложн|я́ть, -и́ть де́ло; разд|ува́ть, -у́ть (*coll.*) (*or* преувели́чи|вать, -ть) тру́дности; **under stress of** ~ вследствие неблагоприя́тной пого́ды; **protection against the** ~ защи́та от непого́ды; **fly above the** ~ лете́ть (*det.*) над облака́ми; **be, feel under the** ~ (*fig.*) нева́жно себя́ чу́вствовать (*impf.*); **on the** ~ **side, beam, bow, quarter** (*naut.*) с наве́тренной стороны́; **keep a** ~ **eye open** смотре́ть (*impf.*) в о́ба; держа́ть (*impf.*) у́хо востро́; ~ **bureau** бюро́ (*indecl.*) пого́ды; ~ **chart/map** синопти́ческая/метеорологи́ческая ка́рта; ~ **forecast** прогно́з пого́ды.

v.t. **1.** (*survive; circumvent*) выде́рживать, вы́держать; переж|ива́ть, -и́ть; перен|оси́ть, -ести́; выноси́ть, вы́нести; ~ **a storm** вы́держать (*pf.*) шторм; ~ **a crisis** перенести́/вы́держать (*pf.*) кри́зис. **2.** (*expose to atmosphere*) подв|ерга́ть, -е́ргнуть атмосфе́рным влия́ниям; (*discolour or wear away by exposure*) изн|а́шивать, -оси́ть.

cpds. ~**-beaten** *adj.* обве́тренный; потрёпанный ве́трами; ~**-board** *n.* обши́вочная доска́; ~**-bound** *adj.* заде́ржанный непого́дой; ~**cock** *n.* флю́гер; ~**-glass** *n.*

баро́метр; **~man** *n.* метеоро́лог; **~-proof** *adj.* погодоусто́йчивый; защища́ющий от непого́ды; *v.t.* защи|ща́ть, -ти́ть от непого́ды; **~ prophet** *n.* предсказа́тель (*m.*) пого́ды; **~-service** *n.* метеорологи́ческая слу́жба; **~-ship** *n.* метеорологи́ческое су́дно; **~-station** *n.* метеорологи́ческая ста́нция; **~-strip** *n.* во́йлочная прокла́дка; **~-vane** *n.* флю́гер; **~-wise** *adj.* уме́ющий предсказывать пого́ду; **~-worn** *adj.* пострада́вший от непого́ды.

weav|e [wi:v] *n.* тка́цкое переплете́ние; вы́работка тка́ни.

v.t. **1.** (*thread, flowers etc.*) плести́, с-; спле|та́ть, -сти́; впле|та́ть, -сти́; (*fig.*): **he wove these incidents into his novel** он вплёл э́ти эпизо́ды в ткань своего́ рома́на. **2.** (*cloth, basket etc.*) плести́, с-; ткать, со-; (*fig.*): **~e a web of intrigue** плести́, с- сеть интри́г; **the story was woven around one girl's life** расска́з был постро́ен на материа́ле биогра́фии одно́й де́вушки.

v.i. **1.** (*work at loom*) ткать (*impf.*); **engaged in ~ing** занима́ющийся тка́чеством. **2.** (*twist and turn*) снова́ть (*impf.*), идти́ (*det.*) непрямы́м путём. **3. get ~ing!** (*coll., get busy*) за рабо́ту!

weaver ['wi:və(r)] *n.* (*pers.*) ткач (*fem.* -и́ха); (*bird*) тка́чик.

web [web] *n.* **1.** (*woven fabric*) ткань. **2. (spider's ~)** паути́на; (*fig.*) сеть, паути́на, сплете́ние. **3.** (*membrane*) перепо́нка.

cpd. **~-footed** *adj.* перепо́нчатый, водопла́вающий, ла́пчатый.

webbing ['webɪŋ] *n.* тка́нный реме́нь; тка́ная ле́нта.

wed [wed] *v.t. & i.* (*liter.*) **1.** (*of man*) жени́ться (*impf., pf.*) на+*p.*; **his ~ded wife** его́ зако́нная супру́га. **2.** (*of woman*) выходи́ть, вы́йти (за́муж) за+*a.* **3.** (*of couple*) пожени́ться (*pf.*); венча́ться, об-/по-; вступ|а́ть, -и́ть в брак; сочета́ться (*impf., pf.*) бра́ком. **4.** (*of parent*) выдава́ть, вы́дать (за́муж). **5.** (*of celebrant*) венча́ть, об-/по-; сочета́ть (*impf., pf.*) бра́ком; **the newly ~ded pair** новобра́чные (*pl.*), молодожёны (*m. pl.*). **6.** (*fig.*): **he is ~ded to his job** он (всеце́ло) пре́дан свое́й рабо́те; **he is ~ded to his opinion** он упо́рно де́ржится своего́ взгля́да.

wedding ['wedɪŋ] *n.* сва́дьба, бракосочета́ние; (*in church*) венча́ние; **where shall we have the ~?** где мы отпра́зднуем сва́дьбу?; **silver/golden ~** серебряная/золота́я сва́дьба; **~ anniversary** годовщи́на сва́дьбы; **~ breakfast** приём по́сле бракосочета́ния; сва́дебный за́втрак; **~ march** сва́дебный марш.

cpds. **~-cake** *n.* сва́дебный торт; **~-day** *n.* день (*m.*) сва́дьбы; **~-dress** *n.* подвене́чный/венча́льный/сва́дебный наря́д; **~-night** *n.* пе́рвая бра́чная ночь; **~-ring** *n.* обруча́льное кольцо́.

wedge [wedʒ] *n.* клин; **drive (in) a ~** (*lit., fig.*) вби|ва́ть, -ть клин (ме́жду+*i.*); **it's the thin end of the ~** ≃ э́то цвето́чки, а я́годки (бу́дут) впереди́; **a ~ of cake** кусо́к то́рта; **the seats were arranged in ~s** кре́сла бы́ли располо́жены кли́ньями; **~ formation** (*mil.*) боево́й «клин».

v.t. закреп|ля́ть, -и́ть кли́ном; закли́н|ивать, -и́ть; **~ in** вкли́н|ивать, -и́ть; **I ~d in some packing to stop the draught** я наби́л в щель па́клю от сквозняка́; **we were ~d in** нас сти́снули со всех сторо́н.

cpds. **~-heeled** *adj.*: **~-heeled shoe** танке́тка; **~-shaped** *adj.* клинови́дный, клинообра́зный.

wedlock ['wedlɒk] *n.* брак, супру́жество; **born in ~** законорождённый; **holy ~** свяще́нные у́з|ы (*pl., g.* —) бра́ка.

Wednesday ['wenzdeɪ, -dɪ] *n.* среда́; **Ash ~** пе́пельная среда́ (*первый день великого поста*).

wee [wi:] *adj.* (*Sc. & coll.*) кро́шечный, ма́хонький, малю́сенький; **a ~ drop of brandy** глото́чек/ка́пелька коньяку́; **she's a ~ bit jealous** она́ чу́точку ревну́ет.

weed [wi:d] *n.* (*in garden or field*) сорня́к; **the garden ran to ~s** сад заро́с сорняка́ми; (*in water*) во́доросль; **the ~** (*tobacco*) таба́к; (*marijuana*) марихуа́на, «тра́вка»; (*fig., lanky or weak looking pers.*) то́щий/долговя́зый челове́к.

v.t. (*clear of ~s*) поло́ть, вы́-; проп|а́лывать, -оло́ть; **the garden needs ~ing** сад необходи́мо прополо́ть (*or* очи́стить от сорняко́в).

with adv.: **~ out** *v.t.* (*eradicate, remove*) удал|я́ть, -и́ть; устран|я́ть, -и́ть; искорен|я́ть, -и́ть; **he ~ed out unwanted books from the library** он освободи́л библиоте́ку от нену́жных книг.

cpds. **~-grown, ~-infested** *adjs.* заро́сший сорняка́ми; **~-killer** *n.* гербици́д.

weeds [wi:dʒ] *n.*: **widow's ~** вдо́вий трау́р/наря́д.

weedy ['wi:dɪ] *adj.* (*overgrown with weeds*) заро́сший сорняка́ми; (*lanky, weakly*) худосо́чный, сла́бый, то́щий, долговя́зый.

week [wi:k] *n.* неде́ля; **what day of the ~ is it?** како́й сего́дня день (неде́ли)?; **the ~ before last** позапро́шлая неде́ля; **the ~ after next** че́рез две неде́ли; **in the last ~ of August** в после́дних чи́слах а́вгуста; **Easter W~** пасха́льная неде́ля; **Low W~** Фомина́ неде́ля; **a ~ (from) today** (*or* **today ~**, *or* **this day ~**) ро́вно че́рез неде́лю; **two ~s (from) tomorrow** че́рез две неде́ли, счита́я с за́втрашнего дня; **(on) Monday ~** че́рез понеде́льник; **last Monday ~** в позапро́шлый понеде́льник; **in a ~** че́рез неде́лю; в неде́льный срок; **I haven't seen him in, for ~s** я его́ давно́ не ви́дел; **he stays away for ~s** он неде́лями отсу́тствует; **six ~s** шесть неде́ль, полтора́ ме́сяца; **from one ~ to the next** из неде́ли в неде́лю; **~ in, ~ out** (це́лыми) неде́лями; по неде́лям; **three times a ~** три ра́за в неде́лю; **the news is a ~ old** э́та но́вость неде́льной да́вности; **you're a ~ late with the rent** вы задержа́ли квартпла́ту на неде́лю; **at the end of the ~** в конце́ неде́ли; **I'm not at home during the ~** в рабо́чие дни меня́ не быва́ет до́ма; **I'll come some time during the ~** я ка́к-нибудь загляну́ на неде́ле; **~'s wages** неде́льное жа́лованье; **work a 40-hour ~** рабо́тать (*impf.*) со́рок часо́в в неде́лю; быть на сорокачасово́й неде́ле; **working ~** рабо́чая неде́ля; **I'm off on a ~'s holiday** я уезжа́ю на неде́лю в о́тпуск.

cpds. **~day** *n.* бу́дний/рабо́чий день; **~day closing is on Wednesday(s)** выходно́й день — среда́; **my ~day clothes** моя́ бу́дничная оде́жда; **~end** *n.* коне́ц неде́ли, уике́нд; **we get up late at the ~end** по суббо́там и воскресе́ньям мы встаём по́здно; **~-long** *adj.* продолжа́ющийся неде́лю; неде́льный; **~-night** *n.* бу́дний ве́чер; **~-old** *adj.* неде́льной да́вности.

weekly ['wi:klɪ] *n.* еженеде́льник.

adj. (*once a week*) еженеде́льный.

adv. еженеде́льно; ка́ждую неде́лю.

weeny ['wi:nɪ] *adj.* (*coll.*) кро́хотный, малю́сенький.

weep [wi:p] *n.* плач, рыда́ние; **she had a good ~** она́ как сле́дует (*or* хороше́нько) вы́плакалась; **she had a quiet ~ to herself** она́ ти́хонько всплакну́ла.

v.t. пла́кать, за-; **she wept bitter tears** она́ го́рько пла́кала; она́ пролила́ го́рькие слёзы; **he wept himself to sleep** он пла́кал, пока́ не усну́л; он засну́л в слеза́х.

v.i. **1.** (*shed tears*) пла́кать, за-; **I wept to see him go** мне бы́ло жа́лко до слёз, что он ушёл/уе́хал; **she wept over her misfortune** она́ опла́кивала своё несча́стье; **he was ~ing** (*mourning*) **for his mother** он горева́л по свое́й ма́тери; **the child was ~ing for its mother** ребёнок пла́кал и призыва́л свою́ мать. **2.**: **~ing willow** плаку́чая и́ва. **3.** (*exude moisture*) выделя́ть, вы́делить вла́гу.

with adv.: **~ out** *v.t.*: **~ one's eyes, heart out** го́рько рыда́ть (*impf.*); вы́плакать (*pf.*) (все) глаза́.

weeper ['wi:pə(r)] *n.* (*hired mourner*) пла́кальщи|к (*fem.* -ца).

weepie ['wi:pɪ] *n.* (*coll.*) душещипа́тельный фильм, расска́з *и т.п.*

weepy ['wi:pɪ] *adj.* (*coll.*): **I feel ~** у меня́ в глаза́х защипа́ло.

weevil ['wi:vɪl] *n.* долгоно́сик.

wee-wee ['wi:wi:] *n.* пи-пи́ (*nt. indecl.*) (*coll.*).

v.i. де́лать, с- пи-пи́; ходи́ть, с- по-ма́ленькому; пи́сать, на-/по-.

w.e.f. (*abbr. of* **with effect from**) вступа́ющий в си́лу с+*g.*

weft [weft] *n.* уто́к.

weigh [weɪ] *n.*: **under ~** (*naut.*) *see* **way** *n.* **17.**

v.t. **1.** (*find or test weight of*) взве́|шивать, -сить; **~ sth. in one's hand** взве́шивать (*impf.*) что-н. в руке́; **~ o.s.** взве́|шиваться, -ситься; (*fig., consider; assess; compare*) взве́|шивать, -сить; обду́м|ывать, -ать; оце́н|ивать, -и́ть; **~ the consequences** взве́сить (*pf.*) после́дствия; **~ one's**

words взвéшивать (*impf.*) (свой) словá. **2.** (*of* ~*ed object*: *amount to*) вéсить (*impf.*); **my luggage** ~**s 20 kilos** мой багáж вéсит 20 килó; **what do you** ~**?** скóлько вы вéсите?; какóй у вас вес?; **I** ~ **too much** я вéшу слúшком мнóго; у меня́ слúшком большóй вес. **3.**: ~ **anchor** подн|имáть, -я́ть я́корь; сн|имáться, -я́ться с я́коря.

v.i. **1.** (*indicate weight*) покáз|ывать, -áть вес; **these scales** ~ **accurately** э́ти весы́ тóчные; ~**ing machine** весы́(-автомáт). **2.** (*fig.*, *be a burden*) давúть (*impf.*); **there is something** ~**ing on his mind** он чем-то подáвлен; **the crime** ~**ed heavy on his conscience** преступлéние лежáло тя́жким брéменем/кáмнем на егó сóвести. **3.** (*fig.*, *have influence or importance*) имéть (*impf.*) вес/значéние/влия́ние; **this is the consideration which** ~**s with me** (úменно) э́то соображéние для меня́ чрезвычáйно вáжно; **her evidence will** ~ **against him** её показáния бýдут не в егó пóльзу.

with advs.: ~**(t) down** *v.t.* (*burden*) отяго|щáть, -тúть; **the branches were** ~**ed down with, by fruit** вéтви гнýлись под тя́жестью плодóв; (*fig.*) угнетáть (*impf.*); тяготúть (*impf.*); **he was** ~**ed down with care** он был угнетён/подáвлен забóтой (*or* обременён забóтами); ~ **in** *v.i.* (*be* ~*ed before contest*) взвé|шиваться, -ситься пéред соревновáнием; (*coll.*, *intervene forcefully*): **they** ~**ed in with a powerful argument** онú вы́двинули сúльный аргумéнт/дóвод; ~ **out** *v.t.* отвé|шивать, -сить; **he** ~**ed out half a pound of cheese** он отвéсил полуфýнта сы́ра; *v.i.* (*of jockey*) взвé|шиваться, -ситься пóсле состязáния; ~ **up** *v.t.* (*lit.*, *fig.*) взвé|шивать, -сить; (*fig.*) оцéн|ивать, -úть.

cpds. ~**bridge** *n.* весы́-платфóрма; мостовы́е весы́; ~**-house** *n.* весовáя; ~**-in** *n.* (*sport*) взвéшивание боксёра/жокéя пéред состязáнием.

weight [weɪt] *n.* **1.** (*phys.*, *gravitational force*; *relative mass*; *this expressed on a scale*) вес; **3lbs in** ~ вéсом в три фýнта; **goods sold by** ~ товáр, продаю́щийся на вес (*or*, *coll.*, вразвеснýю); **he gave me short** ~ он меня́ обвéсил; **what is your** ~**?** скóлько вы вéсите?; какóй у вас вес?; **we are the same** ~ у нас одинáковый вес; **I have to watch my** ~ мне прихóдится следúть за фигýрой/вéсом; **gain, put on** ~ приб|авля́ть, -áвить в вéсе; толстéть, по-; попр|авля́ться, -áвиться; **lose** ~ теря́ть, по- в вéсе; худéть, по-; **he is under/over** ~ он вéсит слúшком мáло/мнóго; он недовéшивает/перевéшивает; **he is worth his** ~ **in gold** такúе как он — на вес зóлота; э́то зóлото, а не человéк; **pull one's** ~ (*fig.*) выполня́ть, вы́полнить свою́ дóлю рабóты; **throw one's** ~ **about** (*fig.*) распоряжáться (*impf.*); комáндовать (*impf.*). **2.** (*load*) тя́жесть, груз; (*fig.*) брéмя (*nt.*); **the pillars take all the** ~ колóнны несýт всю нагрýзку; **that chair won't take, stand your** ~ э́тот стул не вы́держит вáшего вéса; **don't put too much** ~ **on that shelf** не перегружáйте э́ту пóлку; **take the** ~ **off your feet** (*coll.*, *sit down*) прися́дьте; **it was a great** ~ **off my mind** у меня́ кáмень с душú свалúлся; ~ **of responsibility** брéмя ответственности; **dead** ~ мёртвый груз; (*pressure*) нажúм; **you put too much** ~ **on the pen** вы слúшком (сúльно) нажимáете на перó; (*impact*) сúла удáра; **they bore the main** ~ **of the attack** онú прúняли (на себя́) глáвный удáр. **3.** (*object for weighing or* ~*ing*) гúря; **a 2lb** ~ двухфунтóвая гúря. **4.** (*importance*; *influence*) вес; влия́ние; авторитéт; **the** ~ **of evidence is against him** все свидéтельства, в основнóм, прóтив негó; **his arguments are without** ~ егó дóводы неосновáтельны; **his opinion carries great** ~ с егó мнéнием óчень считáются; он пóльзуется большúм влия́нием/авторитéтом; **this adds** ~ **to his words** э́то придаёт вес егó словáм.

v.t. **1.** (*attach a* ~ *to*; *make heavier*) утяжел|я́ть, -úть; **a stick** ~**ed with lead** пáлка, утяжелённая свинцóм; (*reinforce*, *of fabric*) утяжел|я́ть, -úть. **2.** (*add compensatory factor to*): **salary** ~**ed by allowances** зарплáта, допóлненная финáнсовыми льгóтами; **London** ~**ing** тарúфная надбáвка для рабóтающих в Лóндоне; **the system was** ~**ed in their favour** систéма предоставля́ла им привилéгии.

with adv.: ~ **down** *v.t.* = **weigh down**

cpds. ~**-lifter** *n.* штангúст (*fem.* -ка); ~**-lifting** *n.* поднятие тя́жестей; ~**-watcher** *n.* человéк, стремя́щийся сбрóсить лúшний вес; человéк, следя́щий за своéй фигýрой; ~**-watching** *n.* контрóль (*m.*) за своúм вéсом.

weightless [ˈweɪtlɪs] *adj.* невесóмый.

weightlessness [ˈweɪtlɪsnɪs] *n.* невесóмость.

weighty [ˈweɪtɪ] *adj.* (*heavy*) тяжёлый, грýзный; (*important*) вáжный, вéский, весóмый; (*influential*) влия́тельный, авторитéтный.

weir [wɪə(r)] *n.* плотúна, водослúв.

weird [wɪəd] *n.* (*Sc.*): **dree one's** ~ смир|я́ться, -úться с судьбóй.

adj. **1.** (*unearthly*, *uncanny*) таúнственный, сверхъестéственный; **the** ~ **sisters** (*witches*) вéдьмы (*f. pl.*). **2.** (*strange*, *frightening*) стрáнный, жýткий.

weirdness [ˈwɪədnɪs] *n.* таúнственность, стрáнность; жýткость.

weirdo [ˈwɪədəʊ] *n.* псих (*coll.*).

Welch [weltʃ] = **Welsh**

welcome [ˈwelkəm] *n.* приём, привéтствие; **bid s.o.** ~ привéтствовать (*impf.*) когó-н.; **he got a great** ~ **from the audience** пýблика оказáла емý горя́чий приём; **they gave us a warm** ~ онú нас радýшно прúняли; **he outstayed his** ~ он пересидéл; он злоупотребúл гостеприúмством (своúх) хозя́ев; он надоéл (своúм) хозя́евам.

adj. **1.** (*gladly received*) желáнный; **a** ~ **guest** желáнный/дорогóй гость; **this is** ~ **news** э́то рáдостное/прия́тное извéстие; **make s.o. (feel)** ~ окáз|ывать, -áть комý-н. радýшный приём; **a** ~ **gift** подáрок, пришéдшийся кстáти (*or* комý-н. по вкýсу). **2.** (*pred.*, *ungrudgingly permitted*): **you are** ~ **to take it** пожáлуйста, берúте!; **anyone is** ~ **to my share** я с удовóльствием уступлю́ свою́ дóлю комý угóдно; **you may have it and** ~ берúте себé на здорóвье; **if you think you can do better you're** ~ **to try** éсли дýмаете, что у вас вы́йдет лýчше — пожáлуйста, (по)прóбуйте; **you're** ~**!** (*esp. US*: *no thanks are required*) пожáлуйста!; нé за что!; на здорóвье!

v.t. привéтствовать (*impf.*); охóтно прин|имáть, -я́ть; встр|ечáть, -éтить теплó/радýшно; **she** ~**d her guests at the door** онá привéтствовала гостéй в двеpя́х; **a welcoming smile** привéтливая улы́бка; **I** ~ **the suggestion** я привéтствую э́то предложéние; **I would** ~ **the opportunity** я был бы рад (такóму) слýчаю; **I** ~**d his action** я был довóлен егó постýпком; **his arrival was** ~**d by all** все рáдовались егó приéзду/появлéнию; **they were** ~**d by gunfire** их встрéтили артиллерúйским огнём.

int. добрó пожáловать!; мúлости прóсим!

weld [weld] *n.* сварнóе соединéние; сварнóй шов.

v.t. & i. свáр|ивать(ся), -úть(ся); пая́ть (*impf.*); (*fig.*) спл|áчивать, -отúть; объедин|я́ть, -úть.

with advs.: ~ **on** *v.t.* привáр|ивать, -úть; припá|ивать, -я́ть; ~ **together** *v.t.* (*lit.*, *fig.*) свáр|ивать, -úть; спá|ивать, -я́ть; (*fig.*) спл|áчивать, -отúть; объедин|я́ть, -úть.

welder [ˈweldə(r)] *n.* свáрщик.

welding [ˈweldɪŋ] *n.* свáрка; **arc** ~ дуговáя свáрка; ~ **torch** свáрочная горéлка.

welfare [ˈwelfeə(r)] *n.* (*well-being*) благосостоя́ние; (*organized provision for social needs*) социáльное обеспéчение; **the W**~ **State** государство всеóбщего благосостоя́ния/благодéнствия; ~ **work** рабóта по улучшéнию бытовы́х услóвий; благотворúтельность.

welkin [ˈwelkɪn] *n.* (*arch.*): **their cries made the** ~ **ring** их крúки сотрясáли небесá/вóздух.

well[1] [wel] *n.* (*for water*) колóдец; (*for oil*) нефтянáя сквáжина; (*mineral spring*) истóчник; (*fig.*, *source*) роднúк; **(stair-**~**)** пролёт лéстницы; лéстничная клéтка.

v.i. (*spring up*; *gush*) бить (*impf.*) ключóм; хлы́нуть (*pf.*); **blood** ~**ed out of the wound** кровь хлы́нула из рáны; **tears** ~**ed up in her eyes** её глазá напóлнились слезáми.

cpds. ~**-deck** *n.* колóдезная пáлуба; ~**-head**, ~**spring** *nn.* (*source*) истóчник, роднúк, ключ; ~**-water** *n.* роднúкóвая/колóдезная водá.

well[2] [wel] *adj.* (*usu. pred.*) **1.** (*in good health*) здорóвый; **I haven't been** ~ мне нездорóвилось; **I am quite** ~ **again** я совсе́м вы́здоровел/попра́вился; **he is not a ~ man** он челове́к боле́зненный; **you don't look ~** вы пло́хо вы́глядите. **2.** (*right, satisfactory*): **all's ~** всё хорошо́/прекра́сно; всё в поря́дке; **all is not ~ in that family** в э́той семье́ не всё благополу́чно; **~ and good** (ну и) прекра́сно; тем лу́чше; ла́дно; хорошо́; пусть так. **3.** (*well off, fortunate*): **you are ~ out of his company** ва́ше сча́стье, что вы (бо́льше) с ним не обща́етесь/во́дитесь. **4.** (*as n.*): **leave ~ alone** от добра́ добра́ не и́щут; лу́чшее — враг хоро́шего. **5.: (just) (as) ~** (*advisable*): **it would be (as) ~ to ask** не меша́ло бы (*or* сто́ило бы) спроси́ть; **it may be as ~ to explain** пожа́луй, сто́ит объясни́ть; (*fortunate*): **'I'll pay' — 'That's just as ~, because I have no money'** «Я заплачу́» — «Отли́чно — тем бо́лее, что я без де́нег»; *see also adv.*, **10.**. **6.: ~ enough; all very ~** (*tolerable*) вполне́ го́дный; сно́сный; неплохо́й; по-сво́ему хоро́ший; **margarine is ~ enough in its way, but I prefer butter** маргари́н — вещь неплоха́я, но я предпочита́ю ма́сло; **smoking is all very ~ in moderation** уме́ренное куре́ние — вещь сно́сная; **that's all very ~, but ...** всё так (*or* э́то прекра́сно), но... **7.: all very ~** (*easy, convenient*): **it's all very ~ for you, you're not a woman** ва́м-то что — вы не же́нщина!; **it's all very ~ to say that afterwards** легко́ говори́ть за́дним число́м.

adv. **1.** (*satisfactorily*) хорошо́; **I did not sleep ~** я пло́хо спал; **~ done!** здо́рово!; молоде́ц!; **~ begun is half done** лиха́ беда́ нача́ло; **extremely ~** отли́чно; **perfectly ~** прекра́сно; **pretty ~** вполне́ хорошо́; сно́сно; (*nearly*) почти́; (*considerably*) значи́тельно. **2.** (*very, thoroughly; properly*) о́чень, весьма́, хороше́нько; как сле́дует; **I was ~ pleased** я был о́чень дово́лен; **~ done** (*of food*) (хорошо́) прожа́ренный; **I am ~ aware of it** я э́то прекра́сно зна́ю; **~ and truly** оконча́тельно, реши́тельно; **they were ~ and truly beaten** они́ бы́ли разби́ты на́голову (*or* в пух и прах); **you are ~ able to do this yourself** вы прекра́сно мо́жете с э́тим спра́виться са́ми; **the picture was ~ worth £2000** э́та карти́на вполне́ сто́ила двух ты́сяч фу́нтов; **he can't leave ~ alone** он ве́чно перестара́ется/перемудри́т. **3.** (*considerably: esp. with advs. & preps.*) гора́здо, далеко́; **~ on in life** в года́х; немолодо́й, пожило́й; **~ up in the list** в са́мом нача́ле спи́ска; **~ over retiring age** мно́го ста́рше пенсио́нного во́зраста; **~ past 40** далеко́ за со́рок; **~ in the lead** мно́го впереди́; **~ into the night** далеко́ за́ полночь. **4.** (*favourably*): **~ off** бога́тый; состоя́тельный; зажи́точный; **~ off for** обеспе́ченный *+i.*; **he doesn't know when he's ~ off** он не зна́ет своего́ сча́стья; **I wish him ~** я ему́ жела́ю благополу́чия; **his teacher thinks ~ of him** учи́тель о нём хоро́шего мне́ния; **his manners speak ~ for his upbringing** по его́ мане́рам ви́дно, что он получи́л хоро́шее воспита́ние; **it speaks ~ for his courage** э́то свиде́тельствует о его́ хра́брости. **5.** (*fortunately, successfully*) уда́чно, благополу́чно; **all went ~** всё прошло́/сошло́ благополу́чно; **he did very ~ for himself** он прекра́сно устро́ил свои́ дела́; **some firms did ~ out of the war** не́которые фи́рмы нажи́ли́сь на войне́; **~ met!** уда́чная встре́ча! **6.** (*comfortably, affluently*): **live ~** жить (*impf.*) в доста́тке; **do o.s. ~** ни в чём себе́ не отка́зывать (*impf.*). **7.** (*wisely*) разу́мно, пра́вильно; **he did ~ to ask for his money back** он пра́вильно сде́лал, что попроси́л де́ньги наза́д; **you would do ~ to insure your luggage** вам бы сле́довало застрахова́ть свой бага́ж; **you would be ~ advised to stay** бы́ло бы благоразу́мно с ва́шей стороны́ оста́ться (*or* не уезжа́ть/уходи́ть). **8.** (*probably, indeed, reasonably*): **it may ~ be true** э́то вполне́ возмо́жно; не исключено́, что э́то так; **you may ~ ask** вопро́с нели́шний; **one cannot ~ refuse** неудо́бно отказа́ть; как здесь отка́жешь?; **you may ~ be surprised** вы име́ете все основа́ния удивля́ться; **we might ~ try** о́чень сто́ит попыта́ться/попро́бовать. **9.: as ~** (*in addition*) вдоба́вок; сверх того́; то́же; та́кже; заодно́; **there was meat as ~ as fish** там была́ не то́лько ры́ба, но и мя́со; там бы́ли и ры́ба и мя́со. **10.: as ~** (*with equal reason or profit*) с таки́м же основа́нием/успе́хом; **(you, he** *etc.*) **may, might as ~** (*expr. recommendation*) не меша́ло бы; пожа́луй; почему́ бы не; **you may as ~ take an umbrella** на вся́кий слу́чай прихвати́те (*or* сто́ит захвати́ть) зо́нтик с собо́й; **as you've bought the book, you may as ~ use it** поско́льку вы купи́ли кни́гу, почему́ бы вам е́ю не по́льзоваться?; *cf. adj.*, **5.**

int. ну; ну а; (*expr. surprise*) ну!; вот те ра́з!; **~, I never!** вот те на́!; поду́мать то́лько!; вот каки́е дела́!; **~, ~!** ну и ну!; **~, of all the cheek!** ну и наха́льство же!; (*expr. expectation*): **~ then?** ну как?; ну так что же?; (*impatient or emphatic interrogation*): **~, what do you want?** ну, так чего́ вы хоти́те?; **~, what's it about?** да в чём де́ло?; (*agreement*): **very ~, I'll do it** хорошо́, я э́то сде́лаю; (*qualified acceptance*): **~, but what about my wife?** ну, а как насчёт жены́?; (*concession*): **~, you can come if you like** что ж(е), е́сли хоти́те, приходи́те; **~, you may be right** что ж(е), мо́жет вы и пра́вы; **ah, ~, in that case** ах, ну, в тако́м слу́чае (*or* раз так); (*resignation*): **oh ~, it can't be helped** (ну) что ж, ничего́ не поде́лаешь; (*summing up*) ну (вот); **~ then** (ну) так вот; (*resumption*): **~, as I was saying** ита́к, как я говори́л; (*indecision, explanation*) да...; **~, I'm not sure** ви́дите ли, я не уве́рен; **~, I only arrived today** ви́дите ли, я то́лько сего́дня прие́хал; **~, he says he must see you** да вот, он говори́т, что ему́ необходи́мо с ва́ми повида́ться.

cpds. **~-advised** *adj.* благоразу́мный, му́дрый; **~-aimed** *adj.* ме́ткий; **~-appointed** *adj.* хорошо́ обору́дованный/снаряжённый; **~-balanced** *adj.* уравнове́шенный, разу́мный; сбаланси́рованный; **a ~-balanced diet** рациона́льная дие́та; **~-behaved** *adj.* (благо)воспи́танный; хоро́шего поведе́ния; **~-being** *n.* благополу́чие, благосостоя́ние; **~-beloved** *adj.* люби́мый, возлю́бленный; **~-born** *adj.* хоро́шего/благоро́дного/аристократи́ческого происхожде́ния; родови́тый; **~-bred** *adj.* (благо)воспи́танный; (*horse*) поро́дистый; чистокро́вный; хоро́ших крове́й; **~-built** *adj.* (*pers.*) хорошо́ сложённый; **~-chosen** *adj.* уда́чно подо́бранный; **~-conducted** *adj.* хорошо́ поста́вленный/организо́ванный; **~-connected** *adj.* име́ющий (ро́дственные) свя́зи (в вы́сшем све́те); **~-defined** *adj.* отчётливый, определённый; стро́го очерченный; **~-deserved** *adj.* заслу́женный; **~-directed** *adj.* ме́ткий; то́чный; то́чно напра́вленный; **~-disposed** *adj.* благожела́тельный; благоскло́нный; **~-earned** *adj.* заслу́женный; **~-educated** *adj.* образо́ванный; **~-favoured** *adj.* краси́вый, привлека́тельный; **~-fed** *adj.* отко́рмленный, сы́тый, то́лстый; **~-found** *adj.* хорошо́ обору́дованный/снаряжённый; **~-founded, ~-grounded** *adjs.* обосно́ванный, аргументи́рованный; **~-groomed** *adj.* ухо́женный, хо́леный; **~-grounded** *adj.* = **~-founded; ~-grown** *adj.* ро́слый; развито́й; **~-heeled** *adj.* (*coll.*) состоя́тельный; **~-informed** *adj.* зна́ющий; све́дущий; хорошо́ осведомлённый; **~-intentioned** *adj.* де́йствующий/сде́ланный из лу́чших побужде́ний; **~judged** *adj.* проду́манный, разу́мный; **~-kept, ~-run** *adjs.* содержа́щийся в поря́дке; **the date was a ~-kept secret** да́та держа́лась (до сих пор) в глубо́кой та́йне; **~-knit** *adj.* (*fig.*) сплочённый, кре́пкий; **~-known** *adj.* (*of pers.*) изве́стный; знамени́тый; (*of facts*) (обще-)изве́стный; **~-looking** *adj.* здоро́вый на вид; **~-made** *adj.* хорошо́/иску́сно/мастерски́ сде́ланный; **a ~-made suit** хорошо́ скро́енный костю́м; **~-mannered** *adj.* воспи́танный; с хоро́шими мане́рами; **~-marked** *adj.* отчётливый, заме́тный; **~-matched** *adj.* подходя́щий; **a ~-matched couple** подходя́чая па́ра; **~-meaning** *adj.* (*of pers.*) де́йствующий из лу́чших побужде́ний; **~-meant** *adj.* сде́ланный/ска́занный из лу́чших побужде́ний; **~-nigh** *adv.* (*liter.*) почти́; **~-off** *adj.* состоя́тельный; зажи́точный; обеспе́ченный; **~-oiled** *adj.* (*drunk*) косо́й (*coll.*); подвы́пивший; **~-ordered, ~-regulated, ~-run** *adjs.* хорошо́ организо́ванный/поста́вленный; **~-paid** *adj.* хорошо́ опла́чиваемый; высокоопла́чиваемый; **~-preserved** *adj.* (*of pers.*) хорошо́ сохрани́вшийся; **~-proportioned** *adj.* пропорциона́льный; с хоро́шими пропо́рциями; **~-read** *adj.* начи́танный; эруди́рованный; **~-regulated** *adj.* = **~-ordered; ~-remembered** *adj.*

памя́тный; незабве́нный; **~-rounded** *adj.* окру́глый; (*fig.*) закруглённый; **~-run** *adj.* = **~-ordered, ~-kept; ~-set-up** *adj.* скла́дный; **~-situated** *adj.* хорошо́/удо́бно располо́женный; **~-spent** *adj.* потра́ченный не зря (*or* с то́лком); **~-spoken** *adj.* учти́вый; **~-taken** *adj.* ме́ткий; **~-thought-of** *adj.* уважа́емый, почита́емый, по́льзующийся хоро́шей репута́цией; **~-thought-out** *adj.* проду́манный; **~-thumbed** *adj.* захва́танный, (*coll.*) замусо́ленный; **~-timed** *adj.* то́чно/хорошо́ рассчи́танный; своевре́менный; ска́занный/сде́ланный кста́ти; **~-to-do** *adj.* состоя́тельный; зажи́точный; обеспе́ченный; **~-trained** *adj.* вы́ученный, вы́школенный, обу́ченный; **~-tried** *adj.* испы́танный, прове́ренный; **~-trodden** *adj.* проторённый, исхо́женный; **~-turned** *adj.* (*of speech etc.*) отто́ченный, уда́чно вы́раженный; **~-wisher** *n.* доброжела́тель (*fem.* -ница); **~-worn** *adj.* (*lit.*) поно́шенный; (*fig.*, *trite*) изби́тый, иста́сканный.

wellington [ˈwelɪŋt(ə)n] *n.* **1.** (*hist.*) высо́кий сапо́г. **2.** (*pl.*) рези́новые сапоги́ (*m. pl.*).

Welsh[1] [welʃ] *n.* **1.: the ~** (*pl.*, *people*) валли́йцы (*m. pl.*), уэ́льсцы (*m. pl.*). **2.** (*language*) валли́йский язы́к.

adj. валли́йский, уэ́льский; **~ rabbit, rarebit** грено́к с сы́ром.

cpds. **~man** *n.* валли́ец, уэ́льсец; **~woman** *n.* валли́йка, уроже́нка Уэ́льса.

welsh[2] [welʃ] *v.i.* (*coll.*) скр|ыва́ться, -ы́ться не уплати́в (*долга, проигрыша*); **~ on s.o.** обст|авля́ть, -а́вить кого́-н.

welsher [ˈwelʃə(r)] *n.* жу́лик.

welt [welt] *n.* (*of shoe*) рант; (*weal*) рубе́ц (*от удара плетью и т.п.*); (*heavy blow*) си́льный уда́р; (*border of garment*) обши́вка, оторо́чка.

v.t. (*shoe*) шить, с- на ранту́.

Weltanschauung [ˌveltɑːnˈʃaʊʊŋ] *n.* мировоззре́ние.

welter [ˈweltə(r)] *n.* (*confusion*) сумбу́р, пу́таница; (*disorderly mixture*) мешани́на; хао́с; **a ~ of new ideas** це́лый водоворо́т но́вых иде́й.

v.i. (*roll*; *wallow*) валя́ться (*impf.*); бара́хтаться (*impf.*); **~ in one's blood** лежа́ть (*impf.*) в лу́же кро́ви.

cpd. **~-weight** *n.* боксёр/боре́ц второ́го полусре́днего ве́са.

Weltschmerz [ˈveltʃmeəts] *n.* мирова́я скорбь.

wen [wen] *n.* жирови́к, жирова́я ши́шка.

Wenceslas [ˈwensɪsləs] *n.* (*Czech hist.*) Ва́цлав.

wench [wentʃ] *n.* де́вка.

wend [wend] *v.t.*: **~ one's way** держа́ть (*impf.*) путь.

werewolf [ˈwɪəwʊlf, ˈweə-] *n.* челове́к-волк; о́боротень (*m.*).

west [west] *n.* за́пад; **in the ~** на за́паде; **to the ~ of** к за́паду от+*g.*; за́паднее +*g.*; **the W~** (*pol.*) За́пад; (*western USA*) за́падные шта́ты (*m. pl.*); **the Wild W~** ди́кий за́пад; **W~ country** за́падная часть А́нглии; **W~ End** Уэст-Э́нд; **W~ Side** Уэст-Са́йд; **~ wind** за́падный ве́тер.

adv. к за́паду; на за́пад; **due ~ of** пря́мо на за́пад от+*g.*; **go ~** (*fig.*) (*coll.*, *fig.*) умере́ть, исче́знуть, пропа́сть (*all pf.*).

cpds. **~bound** *adj.* дви́жущийся на за́пад; **~-by-north** *adv.* вест-тень-но́рд; **~-by-south** *adv.* вест-тень-зю́йд; **~-north-~** *adv.* вест-норд-ве́ст; **~-south-~** *adv.* вест-зюйд-ве́ст.

westering [ˈwestərɪŋ] *adj.* (*of sun*) зака́тывающийся.

westerly [ˈwestəlɪ] *n.* (*wind*) за́падный ве́тер.

adj. за́падный; (*of wind*) с за́пада.

adv. (*westwards*) к за́паду, на за́пад.

western [ˈwest(ə)n] *n.* ве́стерн, ковбо́йский рома́н/фильм.

adj. за́падный.

cpd. **~most** *adj.* са́мый за́падный.

westerner [ˈwestənə(r)] *n.* жи́тель (*m.*) за́пада.

westernization [ˌwestənaɪˈzeɪʃ(ə)n] *n.* внедре́ние за́падного о́браза жи́зни.

westernize [ˈwestəˌnaɪz] *v.t.* внедр|я́ть, -и́ть за́падный о́браз жи́зни в+*a.*

westward [ˈwestwəd] *n.*: **to (the) ~** к за́паду, на за́пад.

adj. за́падный.

westwards [ˈwestwədz] *adv.* к за́паду; на за́пад.

wet [wet] *n.* **1.** (*liquid*; *moisture*): **there is some ~ on the floor** на полу́ кака́я-то вода́. **2.** (*rain*): **come in out of the ~** входи́те, не сто́йте под дождём!

adj. **1.** (*covered, soaked or splashed with water etc.*) мо́крый, сыро́й, вла́жный; **~ through (or to the skin)** промо́кший до ни́тки; **grass ~ with dew** роси́стая трава́; трава́, покры́тая росо́й; **her cheeks were ~ with tears** её лицо́ бы́ло мокры́м от слёз; **my feet are ~** у меня́ промо́кли но́ги; **get ~** промо́кнуть (*pf.*); **I got my suit ~** мой костю́м промо́к; **the baby is ~** ребёнок мо́крый; **~ dock** мо́крый док; приливно́й бассе́йн; **~ dream** (*coll.*) эроти́ческий сон, вызыва́ющий поллю́цию; **~ fish** све́жая (некопчёная) ры́ба; **~ mud** жи́дкая грязь; **~ pack** вла́жное обёртывание; **~ suit** гидрокостю́м; **wringing ~** мо́крый, хоть выжима́й; **he's still ~ behind the ears** (*coll.*) у него́ молоко́ ещё на губа́х не обсо́хло. **2.** (*rainy*) дождли́вый; **it looks like being ~ today** похо́же, что день бу́дет дождли́вым; **we are in for a ~ spell** начина́ется/наступа́ет пери́од дожде́й. **3.** (*in liquid state*) сыро́й, жи́дкий; **~ paint** све́жая кра́ска; **'W~ Paint'** «осторо́жно, окра́шено!»; **the ink was still ~** черни́ла ещё не просо́хли. **4.** (*allowing sale of liquor*) не приня́вший сухо́го зако́на; **a ~ state** «мо́крый» штат (*где разрешается продажа алкогольных напитков*). **5.** (*coll.*, *inept*; *spineless*) вя́лый, малоду́шный, мягкоте́лый.

v.t. (*make ~*) мочи́ть, на-; см|а́чивать, -очи́ть; увлажн|я́ть, -и́ть; **~ting agent** увлажни́тель (*m.*); **the child ~ itself** ребёнок обмочи́лся/опи́сался; **the child ~ its bed** ребёнок опи́сал/напи́сал в посте́ль; **the child ~s its bed** ребёнок мо́чится в посте́ли; (*fig.*): **~ one's whistle** (*coll.*) промочи́ть (*pf.*) го́рло; **~ a bargain** вспры́ск|ивать, -нуть сде́лку.

cpd. **~-nurse** *n.* корми́лица; *v.t.* корми́ть (*impf.*) гру́дью; (*fig.*) ня́ньчиться (*impf.*) с+*i.*

wether [ˈweðə(r)] *n.* валу́х; кастри́рованный бара́н.

wetness [ˈwetnɪs] *n.* вла́жность, сы́рость.

WEU (*abbr. of* **Western European Union**) ЗЕС, (Западноевропе́йский сою́з).

whack [wæk] *n.* (*blow*; *sound of blow*) уда́р; звук уда́ра; (*coll.*, *share*) зако́нная/причита́ющая до́ля; (*coll.*, *attempt*): **have a ~** пыта́ться, по-.

v.t. **1.** (*coll.*, *beat*) бить, по-; колоти́ть, от-; **I feel ~ed** (*exhausted*) я чу́вствую себя́ вконе́ц разби́тым. **2. ~ up** (*coll.*, *produce by energetic action*) произв|оди́ть, -ести́; **I'll just ~ up a meal** я на́скоро что́-нибудь состря́паю.

whacking [ˈwækɪŋ] *n.* по́рка.

adj. & adv. (*sl.*) здоро́вый, здорове́нный; **a ~ (great) lie** чудо́вищная ложь.

whacko [ˈwækəʊ] *int.* здо́рово!; блеск! (*coll.*).

whale [weɪl] *n.* **1.** кит. **2.: a ~ of a ...** (*coll.*) огро́мный; замеча́тельный; **we had a ~ of a time** мы потряса́юще/здо́рово провели́ вре́мя.

cpds. **~-boat** *n.* китобо́йное су́дно; **~bone** *n.* кито́вый ус; **~-oil** *n.* кито́вый жир; во́рвань.

whaler [ˈweɪlə(r)] *n.* (*man*) китоло́в, китобо́й; (*ship*) китобо́йное су́дно.

whaling [ˈweɪlɪŋ] *n.* охо́та на кито́в; китобо́йный про́мысел.

cpd. **~-gun** *n.* гарпу́нная пу́шка.

wham [wæm] (*also* **whang**) *n. & int.* уда́р; бум!; хлоп!

v.t. уд|аря́ть, -а́рить в+*a.*

wharf [wɔːf] *n.* при́стань, на́бережная.

v.t. (*moor at ~*) швартова́ть, при- у при́стани.

wharfage [ˈwɔːfɪdʒ] *n.* (*accommodation*) при́станское устро́йство; (*charge*) при́станские сбо́ры (*m. pl.*).

wharfinger [ˈwɔːfɪndʒə(r)] *n.* владе́лец при́стани.

what [wɒt] *pron.* **1.** (*interrog.*) что?; что же?; **~'s that?** что э́то (тако́е)?; **~ (did you say)?** как (вы сказа́ли)?; что?; **~, me?** как, я?; кто, я?; **~, you here again!** как, вы опя́ть здесь?; **~'s that to you?** а вам како́е (*or* что за) де́ло (до э́того)?; а ва́м-то что?; **~ is that in Russian?** как э́то по-ру́сски?; **~ is it?; ~'s the matter?** в чём де́ло?; **~ stung me?** кто меня́ укуси́л?; **~ is he?** (*by occupation*) чем он занима́ется?; кто он?; кем он рабо́тает?; **~ is she like?** (*in appearance*) кака́я она́ из себя́? (*or* вне́шне); как она́ вы́глядит?; (*in character*) кака́я она́?; что она́ собо́й представля́ет?; **~ do you want to be?** (*to a child*) кем ты хо́чешь стать?; **~ (sex) is their new baby?** кто у них роди́лся?; **~'s the weather like?** кака́я пого́да?; **~ does it look like?** как э́то вы́глядит?; **~ does it taste like?** каково́ э́то на вкус?; **~ was the film like?** ну, как фильм?; **~ is the price?; ~ does it cost?** ско́лько э́то сто́ит?; **~ are potatoes today?** почём сего́дня карто́шка?; **~'s the date?** како́е/кото́рое сего́дня число́?; **~ is his name?** как его́ зову́т?; как его́ фами́лия?; **~ are their names?** назови́те их фами́лии; **~'s the news?** каки́е но́вости?; что слы́шно но́вого?; **~ do you think?** как вы ду́маете?; каково́ ва́ше мне́ние?; **~ do you think about this?** что вы ду́маете об э́том?; **~ the devil!** како́го чёрта!; **~ about money?** а де́ньги?; как насчёт де́нег?; **~ about the cat?** ну, а как ко́шка?; как быть с ко́шкой?; **~ about it?** (*what relevance has it?*) ну и что из э́того?; (*shall we?*) ну так как?; **~ about a walk?** не пройти́сь ли нам?; **~ of it?** ну и (да́льше) что?; ну, и так что ж?; **~ does it matter?** како́е э́то име́ет значе́ние?; не всё ли равно́?; **~ more can I say?** что я могу́ ещё сказа́ть?; **~ are you looking at?** на что вы смо́трите?; **~ for?** заче́м?; к чему́?; **~ do you take me for?** за кого́ вы меня́ принима́ете?; **~ is this box for?** для чего́ э́та коро́бка?; **~ (ever) did you come for?** заче́м (то́лько) вы пришли́?; **~ do I want this money for?** на что мне э́ти де́ньги?; **I'll give you ~ for!** я вам покажу́/дам!; **~ are you talking about?** о чём вы говори́те?; **~ has it to do with me?** при чём тут я?; **~ do I care?** како́е мне де́ло?; **~'s up?** (*coll.*) в чём де́ло?; что случи́лось?; **~'s the use of trying?** како́й смысл (*or* к чему́) стара́ться?; **~ exactly?** что и́менно?; **~ next!** ещё чего́!; до чего́ дошли́!; **~ then?** (*in that case*); (*coll.*) **so ~?** ну и что?; (**~** *do we do then?*) что тогда́ (де́лать)?; (**~** *happened then?*) а да́льше что?; **~ though we are poor?** что из того́, что мы бе́дны?; **~ if ...?** а что, как..?; **~ if he refuses (after all)?** а вдруг он отка́жется?; **are you trying to be funny or ~?** вы что, шу́тите?; **~ ho!** (*greeting*) приве́т!; (*toast*) ва́ше здоро́вье!; **... and ~ not, and ~ have you** (*coll.*) и так да́лее; и тому́ подо́бнее; и всё тако́е про́чее. **2.** (*rel.: that which; the things which*) (то), что; **~ is so annoying is ...** что осо́бенно доса́дно, э́то...; **and, ~ is more ...** к тому́ же...; бо́льше/ма́ло того́,...; **~ I like is music** что я люблю́, так э́то му́зыку; **~ is missing is a guarantee** чего́ нет (*or* не хвата́ет) — э́то гара́нтии; **~ followed is unknown** дальне́йшее неизве́стно; **he is sorry for ~ happened** он жале́ет о случи́вшемся; **this is ~ I mean** вот что я име́ю в виду́; **~ is called a truce** так называ́емое переми́рие; **tell me ~ you remember** расскажи́те мне всё, что по́мните; **give me ~ you can** да́йте мне́ ско́лько мо́жете; **she knows ~'s ~** она́ зна́ет, что к чему́; **I'll see ~ I can do** я постара́юсь сде́лать, что могу́; **(do) you know ~?; I'll tell you ~!** зна́ете что?; что я вам скажу́!; у меня́ иде́я!; **not but ~ he sympathized** не то́, что́бы он не сочу́вствовал; **I don't know but ~ I shall go** как знать, мо́жет я и пойду́; я не уве́рен, что не пойду́; **~ with one thing and another** из-за одного́, то из-за друго́го; **~ with all these interruptions, we never got finished** со всеми э́тими поме́хами мы ника́к не могли́ ко́нчить. **3.** (*whatever*): **I will do ~ I can** я сде́лаю (всё), что могу́; **say ~ you like, I think it's unfair** что бы вы ни говори́ли, по-мо́ему э́то несправедли́во; **come ~ may** что бы ни произошло́; будь что бу́дет. **4.** (*exclamatory*): **~ it is to have a good wife!** что зна́чит име́ть хоро́шую жену́!; **~ I wouldn't give for a cup of tea!** я бы всё отда́л за ча́шку ча́я; **~ she must have suffered!** что она́ должна́ была́ пережи́ть!; **~ didn't we do!** чего́ мы то́лько не де́лали!; **~ a lot of ...** ско́лько +*g*.!

adj. **1.** (*interrog.*) како́й; како́в?; **~ colour are his eyes?** како́го цве́та у него́ глаза́?; **~ chance is there of success?** каковы́ ша́нсы на успе́х?; **~ kind of (a)** како́й; **~ kind of a man are you?** что вы за челове́к?; **~ news is there?** что но́вого?; каки́е но́вости?; **~ time is it?** кото́рый час?; **~'s the use?** что то́лку?; како́й смысл?; **find out ~ trains there are** узна́ть (*pf.*), каки́е есть поезда́. **2.** (*rel.*): **~ friends I make is no concern of yours** не ва́ше де́ло, с кем я дружу́; **I have brought ~ food I need for the journey** я взял с собо́й сто́лько еды́, ско́лько мне пона́добится на вре́мя пое́здки; **~ little he published** то немно́гое, что он напеча́тал; **I gave him ~ money I had** я о́тдал ему́ все де́ньги, каки́е у меня́ бы́ли. **3.** (*exclamatory*): **~ a fool he is!** ну и дура́к же он!; **~ an idea!** что за иде́я!; **~ impudence!** кака́я/какова́ на́глость!; **~ a pity/shame!** кака́я жа́лость/доса́да; **~ weather!** кака́я (*or* что за *or* ну и) пого́да!; пого́да кака́я!; **~ partial judges we are!** до чего́ мы пристра́стны!; **~ was his surprise when ...** каково́ бы́ло его́ удивле́ние, когда́...; **~ lovely soup!** како́й прекра́сный суп; **useful, ~!** (*coll.*) поле́зно, а?

cpds. **~-d'ye-call-him, ~'s-his-name, ~-you-may-call-him** *nn.* как его́ там?; как бишь его́?; **~-d'ye-call-it, ~'s it, ~-you-may-call-it** *nn.* как его́; э́то са́мое...; **~not** *n.* (*trivial thg.*) безделу́шка, шту́чка, штуко́вина; (*article of furniture*) этаже́рка.

whatever [wɒt'evə(r)] *pron.* **1.** (*anything that*): **do ~ you like** де́лайте, что хоти́те; де́лайте всё, что вам уго́дно; **~ I have is yours** всё моё — ва́ше. **2.** (*no matter what*): **~ happens** что бы ни случи́лось; **or ~** (*coll.*) и́ли что там (ещё). **3.** (*what ever*): **~ are you doing?** чем вы там за́няты?; **~ did you do that for?** ну, заче́м вы э́то сде́лали?; **~ is wrong?** в чём (же) де́ло?; **~ next?** ещё чего́ захоте́ли/вы́думали!

adj. **1.** (*any*): **he took ~ food he could find** он забра́л всю пи́щу, каку́ю то́лько мог найти́. **2.** (*no matter what*) како́й/каково́й бы ни; **~ friends we may offend** пусть ины́е друзья́ и обижа́ются. **3.** (*emphasising neg. or interrog.*): **there is no doubt ~ of his guilt** в его́ вино́вности нет ни мале́йшего сомне́ния; **is there any chance ~ that he may recover?** есть ли хоть како́й-нибу́дь шанс, что он попра́вится?; **no one ~** ни одна́ душа́; **he will see no one ~** он абсолю́тно никого́ не принима́ет.

whatsoever [ˌwɒtsəʊ'evə(r)] *pron.* = **whatever** *pron.* **1., 2.**

adj. = **whatever** *adj.*

wheat [wi:t] *n.* пшени́ца; **summer/winter ~** яровая́/ози́мая пшени́ца.

Wheatstone bridge ['wi:tstəʊn] *n.* (*electr.*) мо́ст(ик) сопротивле́ния.

wheedle ['wi:d(ə)l] *v.t.* подоль|ща́ться, -сти́ться к+*d.*; **~ sth. out of s.o.** выпра́шивать, вы́просить что-н. у кого́-н.; выма́нивать, вы́манить что-н. у кого́-н. ле́стью.

wheel [wi:l] *n.* **1.** колесо́; **spare ~** запасно́е колесо́; **change a ~** (*on car*) меня́ть, по- (*or* смен|я́ть, -и́ть) колесо́; **take the ~** сади́ться, сесть за руль; **he was at the ~** (*driving*) **for 12 hours** он сиде́л за рулём 12 часо́в; **man at the ~** (*on ship*) штурва́льный; (*fig., in command*) ко́рмчий; **go on ~s** (*fig., proceed smoothly*) идти́ (*det.*) как по ма́слу; **~s down** (*of aircraft*) с вы́пущенным шасси́; **big ~** (*on fairground*) колесо́ обозре́ния; чёртово колесо́; (*sl., bigwig*) (больша́я) ши́шка; **fifth ~** (*fig.*) пя́тое колесо́ в теле́ге; **break on the ~** колесова́ть (*impf., pf.*); **break a butterfly on a ~** (*fig.*) стреля́ть (*impf.*) из пу́шек по воробья́м; **turn a pot on the ~** де́лать, с- горшо́к на гонча́рном кру́ге; **put one's shoulder to the ~** (*fig.*) взя́ться/приня́ться (*pf.*) энерги́чно за де́ло; **oil the ~s** (*fig., bribe*) подма́з|ывать, -ать кого́-н.; **put a spoke in s.o.'s ~** (*fig.*) вст|авля́ть, -а́вить кому́-н. па́лки в колёса; **~s within ~s** (*fig.*) сло́жные интри́ги (*f. pl.*); та́йные пружи́ны (*f. pl.*)/влия́ния. **2.** (*mil.*): **they carried out a right ~** они́ сде́лали поворо́т впра́во; **right ~!** ле́вое плечо́ вперёд — марш!

v.t. ката́ть, вози́ть (*both indet.*); кати́ть (*det.*); везти́ (*det.*); **she ~ed the baby/barrow/pram** она́ кати́ла/везла́ ребёнка/та́чку/коля́ску; **he ~ed his bicycle up the hill** он вкати́л велосипе́д на́ гору; **he was ~ed in in an invalid chair** его́ вкати́ли/ввезли́ на инвали́дной коля́ске.

v.i. верте́ться; враща́ться; кружи́ть(ся) (*all impf.*); **gulls were ~ing overhead** ча́йки кружи́ли(сь) над голово́й; **the troops ~ed about** войска́ измени́ли направле́ние движе́ния; **he ~ed round to face me** он кру́то поверну́лся ко мне (*or* в мою́ сто́рону).

cpds. **~barrow** *n.* та́чка; **~base** *n.* колёсная ба́за; **~-chair** *n.* ката́лка; инвали́дное кре́сло; **~-house** *n.* рулева́я ру́бка; **~-spin** *n.* пробуксо́вка колёс; **~wright** *n.* колёсник; колёсный ма́стер.

wheeled [wi:ld] *adj.* колёсный, на колёсах.

wheeler-dealer ['wi:lə(r)] *n.* (*coll.*) (кру́пный) деле́ц.

wheeze [wi:z] *n.* (*chesty breathing*) хрип; пыхте́ние; сопе́ние; (*sl., bright idea; scheme*) уда́чная мысль; ло́вкий трюк.

v.i. сопе́ть (*impf.*); хрипе́ть (*impf.*); дыша́ть (*impf.*) с при́свистом.

wheezy ['wi:zɪ] *adj.* хри́плый; пыхтя́щий; страда́ющий оды́шкой.

whelk [welk] *n.* (*mollusc*) брюхоно́гий моллю́ск.

whelp [welp] *n.* (*puppy, also fig.*) щено́к; (*young of other animal*) детёныш; (*fig., ill-bred youth*) щено́к.

v.i. щени́ться, о-.

when [wen] *adv.* **1.** (*interrog.*) когда́; **~ has he ever refused?** а когда́ он отка́зывал(ся)?; ра́зве он когда́-нибудь отка́зывал(ся)?; **say ~!** (*to s.o. pouring a drink*) скажи́те, когда́ дово́льно. **2.** (*rel.*): **there have been occasions ~** бы́ли слу́чаи, когда́...; **the day ~ I met you** день, когда́ (*or* кото́рый) я вас встре́тил.

with preps.: **~ do you have to be there by?** к како́му ча́су вам ну́жно там быть?; **~ must it be ready for?** когда́ э́то должно́ быть гото́во?; **~ does it date from?** к како́му вре́мени э́то отно́сится?; **since ~?** как давно́?; с каки́х (э́то) пор?; с како́го вре́мени?; **till, until ~?** до каки́х пор?; до како́го вре́мени?

conj. когда́; как (то́лько); по́сле, того́ как; тогда́, когда́; (*by the time that*) пока́; **~ she saw him, she ...** уви́дев его́, она́...; **~ he was grown up, he ...** бу́дучи взро́слым (*or* когда́ он вы́рос), он...; **~ passing** проходя́ ми́мо; **~ young** в мо́лодости; (*and then*) и тогда́; как (вдруг); да вдруг; (*although*) хотя́; (*whereas*) а; в то вре́мя как; **how can he buy it ~ he has no money?** как он мо́жет э́то купи́ть, е́сли у него́ нет де́нег?; **you shall have it ~ you ask politely** попроси́ ве́жливо, и тогда́ полу́чишь.

whence [wens] *adv.* & *conj.* (*liter.*) (*interrog.*) (*also* **from ~**) отку́да; **~ this confusion?** отчего́/почему́ тако́е смяте́ние; **~ comes it that ...** как э́то получа́ется, что...?; (*rel.*): **return it ~ it came** верни́те э́то по принадле́жности; **~ I conclude that ...** из чего́ я заключа́ю, что...

whencesoever [ˌwenssəʊ'evə(r)] *adv.* (*liter.*): **~ he comes** отку́да бы он ни пришёл.

whenever [wen'evə(r)] *adv.* & *conj.* **1.** (*at whatever time*) когда́; **come ~ you like** приходи́те, когда́ то́лько захоти́те; **~ he comes** когда́ бы он ни пришёл. **2.** (*on every occasion when*) ка́ждый/вся́кий раз, когда́; **~ he speaks he stammers** он всегда́ заика́ется, когда́ говори́т. **3. or ~** (*coll., at any time*) и́ли ещё когда́. **4.** (*when ever?*) когда́ же (наконе́ц); **~ did you find time?** как то́лько вы нашли́ вре́мя?

whensoever [ˌwensəʊ'evə(r)] *adv.* & *conj.* (*arch.*) = **whenever 1., 2.**

where [weə(r)] *adv.* **1.** (*direct or indirect question*) где; (*whither*) куда́; **~ should we be without you?** что бы мы без вас де́лали?; **~'s the sense in that?** како́й (же) в э́том смы́сл?; **~ can the harm be in our going there?** что плохо́го, е́сли мы туда́ пойдём?; **~ will you be if that happens?** что с ва́ми бу́дет, е́сли э́то случи́тся?; **~ did he hit you?** куда́ он вас уда́рил?; **~ are you wounded?** куда́ вы ра́нены?; где у вас ра́на? **2.** (*rel.*) где; **the hotel ~ we stopped** гости́ница, в кото́рой мы останови́лись; **we came home, ~ we had dinner** мы пришли́ домо́й, (где) и пообе́дали; (*without antecedent*) там, где; **that's not ~ I left my coat** я не здесь/там оста́вил пальто́; **that's ~ you're wrong** здесь-то вы и ошиба́етесь; **you can go ~ you please** мо́жете идти́, куда́ уго́дно; **making changes ~ necessary** де́лая исправле́ния там, где э́то необходи́мо; **~ he is weakest is in facts** его́ са́мое сла́бое ме́сто — э́то фа́кты; **send him ~ he will be well taken care of** отпра́вьте его́ туда́, где за ним бу́дет хоро́ший уход. **3.** (*US coll., that*): **I see in the paper ~** в газе́те говори́тся, что/бу́дто... **4.** (*whereas*) тогда́, как; ме́жду тем, как; в то вре́мя как; **(in cases ~)** в тех слу́чаях, когда́.

with preps.: **~ from?** отку́да; (*of origin*): **~ does he come from?** отку́да он (ро́дом)?; из каки́х он мест?; **that's not far from ~ I live** э́то недалеко́ от того́ ме́ста, где я живу́; **~ to?** куда́?; **~ have you got to in the story?** до како́го ме́ста вы дочита́ли/дошли́?; **I've no idea ~ he can have got to** поня́тия не име́ю, куда́ он мог де́ться; **carry on to ~ the road forks** вам на́до дое́хать до разви́лки.

whereabouts ['weərəˌbaʊts] *n.* местонахожде́ние, местопребыва́ние.

adv. где; **~ did you find it?** где вы э́то нашли́?; **can you tell me ~ to look?** вы мо́жете мне сказа́ть, где (приблизи́тельно) иска́ть?

whereas [weər'æz] *n.*: **~es** деклара́ти́вная часть (догово́ра *и т.п.*).

conj. **1.** (*while*) тогда́ как; в то вре́мя как; а; хотя́; ме́жду тем, как. **2.** (*leg., since*) в виду́ того́, что; поско́льку; принима́я во внима́ние, что; учи́тывая, что.

whereat [weər'æt] *adv.* (*liter.*) где; и тогда́; на э́то.

whereby [weə'baɪ] *adv.* (*liter.*) тем; чем; посре́дством кото́рого; **he lacked the means ~ to travel** у него́ не́ было средств для путеше́ствий; **he devised a plan ~ he might escape** он вы́работал план, с по́мощью кото́рого он собира́лся соверши́ть побе́г; **there is a rule ~ ...** существу́ет пра́вило, согла́сно кото́рому...

wherefore ['weəfɔ:(r), -'fɔ:(r)] *n.*: **he wanted to know the why(s) and ~(s)** он хоте́л знать, как и почему́.

adv. (*arch., why?*) почему́?

wherein [weər'ɪn] *adv.* (*interrog., rel.*) где; в кото́ром; в чём.

whereof [weər'ɒv] *rel. adv.* (*liter.*) из кото́рого; о ком; о чём; **the substance ~ it was made** вещество́, из кото́рого э́то сде́лано; **the person ~ I spoke** лицо́, о кото́ром я говори́л.

whereon [weər'ɒn] *rel. adv.* (*liter.*) на кото́ром.

wheresoever [ˌweəsəʊ'evə(r)] *adv.* & *conj.* (*arch.*) = **wherever**

whereto [weə'tu:] *rel. adv.* (*liter.*) к кото́рому.

whereupon [ˌweərə'pɒn, 'weər-] *adv.* (*and then*) по́сле чего́; всле́дствие чего́; тогда́; на э́то.

wherever [weər'evə(r)] *adj.* & *conj.* (*also* (*arch.*) **wheresoever**) где; куда́; **sit ~ you like** сади́тесь, куда́ уго́дно; **~ he goes he makes friends** где бы он ни оказа́лся, он приобрета́ет друзе́й; **or ~** (*coll.*) и́ли ещё где; и́ли где бы то ни́ было; (*where ever*): **~ are you going?** куда́ же вы идёте?

wherewith [weə'wɪð] *rel. adv.* (*liter.*) чем; с по́мощью кото́рого; **I have nothing ~ to pay them** у меня́ нет де́нег, что́бы с ним рассчита́ться; мне не́чем с ни́ми расплати́ться.

wherewithal ['weəwɪˌðɔ:l] *n.* (*coll.*) необходи́мые сре́дства; **I haven't the ~ to pay him** мне не́чем с ним расплати́ться.

wherry ['werɪ] *n.* ло́дка, я́лик; ба́ржа, ба́рка.

cpd. **~man** *n.* ло́дочник.

whet [wet] *v.t.* точи́ть, на-; (*fig.*) обостр|я́ть, -и́ть; возбу|жда́ть, -ди́ть.

cpd. **~stone** *n.* точи́льный ка́мень; (*lit., fig.*) осело́к.

whether ['weðə(r)] *conj.* **1.** (*introducing indirect question*) ли; **I asked ~ he was coming with us** я спроси́л, пойдёт ли он с на́ми; **I don't know ~ she will come (or not)** я не зна́ю, придёт ли она́ (*or* придёт она́ и́ли нет); **the question is ~ to go or stay** вопро́с в том — идти́ и́ли остава́ться; **I doubt ~ you understand** я не уве́рен, что вы понима́ете; я сомнева́юсь, что́бы вы понима́ли; **it depends on ~ I am free tonight** э́то зави́сит от того́, бу́ду ли я свобо́ден сего́дня ве́чером; **I am not interested in ~ you agree** меня́ не интересу́ет, согла́сны вы и́ли нет. **2.** (*introducing alternative hypotheses*): **~ you like it or not, I shall go** нра́вится вам э́то и́ли нет, а я пойду́; **he was ignored, ~ by accident or design** случа́йно ли, и́ли наме́ренно, но его́ забы́ли; **~ or no** всё равно́; во вся́ком (*or* в любо́м) слу́чае.

whew [hwju:] *int.* уф!

whey [weɪ] *n.* сы́воротка.

which [wɪtʃ] *pron.* **1.** (*interrog.*) како́й, кото́рый; (*of pers.*) кто; **~ is the right answer?** како́й отве́т пра́вильный?; **~ is the way to the museum?** как пройти́ в музе́й?; **~ of you?** кто/кото́рый из вас?; **~ of these bags is the heavier?** кото́рая из э́тих су́мок тяжеле́е?; **~ is the taller, John or Susan?** кто вы́ше — Джон и́ли Сюза́нна?; **I cannot tell**

~ is ~ (*of persons*) я ника́к не могу́ разобра́ться, кто из них кто; **~ do you want, milk or cream?** что вы предпочита́ете — молоко́ и́ли сли́вки? **2.** (*rel., in defining and non-defining senses*) кото́рый; **the book (~) I was reading has gone** кни́га, кото́рую я чита́л, пропа́ла; **Cappriccio, ~ was Strauss's last opera** «Капри́ччио», после́дняя о́пера Штра́уса; **he passed in Latin, ~ he had learnt inside a year** он сдал экза́мен по латы́ни, кото́рую он изучи́л за оди́н год; **the hotel at ~ we stayed** гости́ница, в кото́рой (*or* где) мы жи́ли/останови́лись; **the club of ~ I am a member** клуб, чле́ном кото́рого я явля́юсь; (*with adj. or descriptive n. as antecedent*): **he looked like a boxer, ~ indeed he was** он был похо́ж на боксёра, каковы́м он, со́бственно, и явля́лся; **he seemed overwrought, ~ in fact he was** он каза́лся кра́йне расстро́енным, да так оно́ на са́мом де́ле и бы́ло; (*with clause as antecedent*) что; **he refused, ~ I had expected** он отказа́л, чего́ я, со́бственно, и ожида́л.

adj. **1.** (*direct or indirect question*) кото́рый; **~ shoes are yours?** каки́е тут боти́нки/ту́фли ва́ши?; **~ film do you mean?** како́й фильм вы име́ете в виду́?; о како́м фи́льме вы говори́те?; **~ brother runs the business?** кото́рый из бра́тьев возглавля́ет де́ло?; **~ party does he belong to?** к како́й па́ртии он принадлежи́т?; **do you know ~ horse won?** вы (не) зна́ете, кака́я ло́шадь вы́играла? **2.** (*rel.*) како́й; кото́рый; каково́й; **come between 1 and 2, at ~ time I am always in** приходи́те ме́жду ча́сом и двумя́, в э́то вре́мя я всегда́ до́ма; **10 years, during ~ time he spoke to nobody** де́сять лет, в тече́ние кото́рых он ни с кем не говори́л.

which(so)ever [ˌwɪtʃsəʊ'evə(r)] *pron. & adj.* **1.** како́й бы ни; **take ~ book you like** бери́те любу́ю кни́гу, каку́ю хоти́те; **~ of you comes in first wins the prize** кто из вас придёт пе́рвым, полу́чит приз; **~ way you go, you'll have plenty of time** како́й бы доро́гой вы ни пошли́, вы вполне́ успе́ете; **~ way you look at it** куда́ ни кинь; **do it by ~ method seems easiest** де́лайте э́то тем спо́собом, како́й вам ка́жется наибо́лее просты́м. **2.** (*which ever*): **~ way did he go?** куда́ то́лько его́ занесло́?

whiff [wɪf] *n.* дунове́ние; (*pleasant smell*) лёгкий арома́т; (*unpleasant*) душо́к; (*of smoke etc.*) за́пах, дымо́к; **a ~ of chloroform** глото́к хлорофо́рма; **he took a ~** (*of cigarette etc.*) он сде́лал затя́жку; он затяну́лся; **there was a ~ of scandal about the business** де́ло попа́хивало/отдава́ло моше́нничеством; **I caught the ~ of a cigar** я почу́ял за́пах сига́ры; **he stepped out for a ~ of fresh air** он вы́шел подыша́ть (све́жим во́здухом).

Whig [wɪg] *n.* (*hist.*) виг.

while [waɪl] *n.* вре́мя; **where have you been all this ~?** где вы бы́ли всё э́то вре́мя?; **after a ~** вско́ре; че́рез не́которое вре́мя; **between ~s** в промежу́тках; ме́жду де́лом; **I am going away for a ~** я уезжа́ю ненадо́лго (*or* на коро́ткое/недо́лгое/не́которое вре́мя, *or* на коро́ткий срок); **I haven't seen you for a long ~** я вас давно́ не ви́дел; **a long, great, good ~ ago** давны́м-давно́; **a short ~ before** незадо́лго до (э́того); **a short ~ ago, back** неда́вно; **in a little, short ~** ско́ро, вско́ре; в ско́ром вре́мени; вско́рости; **it may take some (*or* quite a) ~** возмо́жно, что э́то бу́дет неско́ро; **once in a ~** и́зредка; вре́мя от вре́мени; от слу́чая к слу́чаю; **it was well worth ~** э́то сто́ило (затра́ченного вре́мени/труда́); **I will make it worth his ~** я постара́юсь, чтобы он не оста́лся в накла́де; **he went on reading the ~** (*liter.*) (всё э́то вре́мя) он продолжа́л чита́ть.

v.t.: ~ (*also* **wile**) **away:** пров|оди́ть, -ести́ (*or* корота́ть, с-, *or* уб|ива́ть, -и́ть) (*время*).

conj. (*also* **whilst**) **1.** (*during the time that*) пока́; в то вре́мя, как; во вре́мя того́, как; **be good ~ I'm away!** веди́ себя́ хорошо́, пока́ меня́ нет до́ма; **don't talk ~ you're eating** не разгова́ривай за столо́м; **~ reading he fell asleep** за чте́нием (*or* чита́я) он засну́л; **~ asleep** во сне; **write ~ I dictate** пиши́те, а я бу́ду диктова́ть; **~ in Paris I visited the Louvre** во вре́мя (моего́) пребыва́ния в Пари́же, я пошёл в Лувр. **2.** (*whereas*) а; тогда́ как; ме́жду тем, как; хотя́. **3.** (*although*) хотя́; **~ not wishing to be awkward, I must object** не жела́я создава́ть тру́дности, я всё же вы́нужден протестова́ть.

whilst [waɪlst] = **while** *conj.*

whim [wɪm] *n.* при́хоть, капри́з.

whimper ['wɪmpə(r)] *n.* хны́канье, поску́ливание.

v.t. & i. (*of pers.*) хны́кать, по-; (*of a dog*) скули́ть (*impf.*).

whimsey ['wɪmzɪ] = **whimsy**

whimsical ['wɪmzɪk(ə)l] *adj.* причу́дливый; капри́зный; эксцентри́чный; игри́вый.

whimsicality [ˌwɪmzɪ'kælɪtɪ] *n.* причу́дливость; капри́зность; игри́вость.

whims|y, -ey ['wɪmzɪ] *n.* при́хоть, причу́да, капри́з.

whin|e [waɪn] *n.* вой; хны́канье; нытьё; **he spoke in a ~e** он говори́л плакси́вым/но́ющим/хны́чущим го́лосом; **the ~e of a shell** вой снаря́да; **the ~e of machinery** гул маши́н.

v.i. скули́ть (*impf.*); хны́кать (*impf.*); **the dog was ~ing to come in** соба́ка скули́ла у две́ри, что́бы её впусти́ли; (*fig., complain*) хны́кать (*impf.*); ныть (*impf.*); **you're always ~ing about something!** всегда́-то вы но́ете!

whiner ['waɪnə(r)] *n.* ны́тик.

whinge [wɪndʒ] = **whine** *v.i.* (*complain*).

whinny ['wɪnɪ] *n.* ти́хое/ра́достное ржа́ние.

v.i. ти́хо/ра́достно ржа́ть, за-.

whip [wɪp] *n.* **1.** (*lash*) плеть, плётка, кнут, хлыст; **use the ~ on s.o.** поро́ть, вы́- кого́-н.; **have the ~ hand over s.o.** (*fig.*) име́ть (*impf.*) кого́-н. в по́лном подчине́нии. **2.** (*hunt official, also* **~per-in**) выжля́тник, доезжа́чий. **3.** (*party official*) организа́тор парла́ментской фра́кции; (*notice issued by him*) инстру́кция по пода́че голосо́в.

v.t. **1.** (*flog*) поро́ть, вы́-; хлеста́ть, от-; сечь, вы́-; **that boy deserves a good ~ping** э́того мальчи́шку сле́довало бы хороше́нько вы́пороть/отхлеста́ть; **~ a top** запус|ка́ть, -ти́ть волчо́к; **~ping-boy** (*fig., scapegoat*) «ма́льчик для битья́»; козёл отпуще́ния; **~ping-post** позо́рный столб; **~ping-top** юла́, волчо́к; (*fig.*): **the wind ~ped the waves into a fury** во́лны я́ростно вздыма́лись под ве́тром; (*fig., defeat*) разби́ть, поби́ть, победи́ть (*all pf.*). **2.** (*beat into froth*) взб|ива́ть, -и́ть; **~ped cream** взби́тые сли́вки. **3.** (*coll., move rapidly*): **as I entered he ~ped the papers into a drawer** когда́ я вошёл, он бы́стро су́нул бума́ги в я́щик; **she ~ped the cake out of the oven** она́ бы́стро вы́тащила торт из пе́чи/духо́вки.

v.i. (*coll., move rapidly*) рвану́ться, бро́ситься, ри́нуться (*all pf.*); **he ~ped into the shop** он влете́л в магази́н.

with advs.: **~ back** *v.t.*: **he ~ped back the dogs** он отогна́л соба́к плёткой; *v.i.*: **the branch ~ped back in my face** пле́тка разогну́лась и хлестну́ла меня́ по лицу́; **~ off** *v.t.* (*coll.*): **the wind ~ped off my hat** ве́тром сби́ло мою́ шля́пу; **~ on** *v.t.* (*urge on with ~*) под|гоня́ть, -огна́ть; подхлёст|ывать, -ну́ть; (*coll.*): **he ~ped on his overcoat** он бы́стро наки́нул пальто́; **~ out** *v.t.* (*coll.*): **~ping out a knife** выхва́тив нож; *v.i.* (*coll.*): **he ~ped out for a breath of air** он вы́скочил на мину́ту глотну́ть све́жего во́здуха; **~ round** *v.i.* (*coll.*): **he ~ped round to face me** он стреми́тельно/кру́то оберну́лся ко мне; **~ up** *v.t.* (*beat into froth*) взб|ива́ть, -и́ть; (*fig., stimulate*): **~ up enthusiasm** возбу|жда́ть, -ди́ть (*or* разж|ига́ть, -е́чь) энтузиа́зм; (*coll., improvise*) де́лать, с- на ско́рую ру́ку; **she ~ped up a nice supper** она́ бы́стро состря́пала вку́сный у́жин.

cpds. **~cord** *n.* (*cord*) бечёвка; (*fabric*) габарди́н; **~lash** *n.* реме́нь (*m.*) (кнута́), бечева́ (пле́ти); **~-round** *n.* (*coll., collection*) сбор де́нег (на благотвори́тельные це́ли).

whipper-snapper ['wɪpəˌsnæpə(r)] *n.* молокосо́с, щено́к.

whippet ['wɪpɪt] *n.* го́нчая (соба́ка).

whippoorwill ['wɪpʊəˌwɪl] *n.* козодо́й жа́лобный.

whir [wɜː(r)] = **whir(r)**

whirl [wɜːl] *n.* **1.** (*revolving or eddying movement*) круже́ние, оборо́т; (*fig.*) смяте́ние, неразбери́ха, вихрь (*m.*); **my brain is in a ~** у меня́ голова́ идёт круго́м. **2.** (*bustling activity*) водоворо́т, вихрь (*m.*); **a ~ of social engagements** водоворо́т, вихрь све́тской жи́зни.

v.t. & i. **1.** (*swing round and round*) верте́ть(ся) (*impf.*); кружи́ть(ся) (*impf.*); **she found herself ~ed round in his**

arms он закружи́л её в объя́тиях; **the leaves ~ed about in the wind** ли́стья кружи́лись на ветру́; **my head was ~ing** у меня́ кружи́лась голова́. **2.** (*hurry*; *dash*) нести́сь (*impf.*); **the trees and hedges ~ed past** дере́вья и кусты́ проноси́лись ми́мо; **they were ~ed away in his car** он умча́л их в свое́й маши́не.

cpds. **~pool** *n.* водоворо́т; **~wind** *n.* вихрь (*m.*), урага́н; **sow the wind and reap the ~wind** (*prov.*) посе́ешь ве́тер — пожнёшь бу́рю; (*fig.*, *attr.*) стра́стный, бу́рный; **a ~wind courtship** бу́рный рома́н.

whirligig ['wɜːlɪgɪg] *n.* **1.** (*top*) юла́, куба́рь (*m.*), волчо́к. **2.** (*roundabout*) карусе́ль. **3.** (*fig.*) водоворо́т, вихрь (*m.*), круговоро́т; **the ~ of time** превра́тности (*f. pl.*) судьбы́.

whirlybird ['wɜːlɪˌbɜːd] *n.* (*coll.*) вертолёт.

whir(r) [wɜː(r)] *n.* жужжа́ние, стрекота́ние; **the ~ of wings** шум кры́льев.

v.i. жужжа́ть; стрекота́ть; шуме́ть (*all impf.*).

whisk [wɪsk] *n.* **1.** (*small brush or similar device*) ве́ничек, метёлочка, ки́сточка. **2.** (*for beating eggs, cream etc.*) муто́вка. **3.** (*light brushing movement*) взмах; **with a ~ of its tail** взмахну́в хвосто́м.

v.t. **1.** (*flap*; *brush*) сма́х|ивать, -ну́ть; от|гоня́ть, -огна́ть; **she ~ed the dust under the carpet** она́ бы́стро замела́ пыль под ковёр. **2.** (*beat, e.g. eggs*) взб|ива́ть, -ить.

v.i. (*move briskly*) мча́ться, по-; **the mouse ~ed into its hole** мышь юркну́ла в нору́.

with advs.: **~ about** *v.t.* (*wave*; *brandish*) маха́ть (*impf.*); **the cow stood ~ing its tail about** коро́ва стоя́ла, пома́хивая хвосто́м; **~ away** *v.t.*: **he ~ed away the flies with his handkerchief** он отогна́л мух платко́м; **~ off** *v.t.* (*convey quickly*) бы́стро ун|оси́ть, -ести́ (*or* ув|оди́ть, -ести́); **he was ~ed off in an ambulance** его́ умча́ла каре́та ско́рой по́мощи.

whisker ['wɪskə(r)] *n.* (*pl.*, *facial hair*) ба́к|и (*pl.*, *g.* —); ба́ч|ки (*pl.*, *g.* -ек); бакенба́рды (*f. pl.*); (*of animal*) усы́ (*m. pl.*); **he came within a ~ of success** (*coll.*) он был на поро́ге успе́ха.

whiskered ['wɪskəd] *adj.* (*of pers.*) нося́щий ба́ки; с бакенба́рдами/ба́чками; (*of cat etc.*) уса́тый.

whisk(e)y ['wɪskɪ] *n.* ви́ски (*nt. indecl.*); **~ and soda** ви́ски с со́довой.

whisper ['wɪspə(r)] *n.* шёпот; **he spoke in a ~** он говори́л шёпотом; **stage ~** театра́льный шёпот; **not a ~ of this will escape my lips** я ни слове́чка об э́том не пророню́; (*rumour*) слух, молва́; **there are ~s of a coalition** хо́дят слу́хи о возмо́жности созда́ния) коали́ции; (*sibilant sound*) шо́рох, ше́лест.

v.t. & i. **1.** (*speak, say in ~s*) шепта́ть(ся) (*impf.*); говори́ть (*impf.*) шёпотом; **they were ~ing together** они́ шушу́кались ме́жду собо́й; **she ~ed her secret to me** она́ шепну́ла/прошепта́ла мне свою́ та́йну на́ ухо; **he ~ed (to) me to come outside** он шёпотом пригласи́л меня́ вы́йти; **~ing gallery** акусти́ческий свод; **it is ~ed that ...** хо́дит слух, что...; **~ing campaign** та́йная/клеветни́ческая кампа́ния; поли́тика инсинуа́ций. **2.** (*make ~ing noise*) шелесте́ть (*impf.*); шурша́ть (*impf.*); **the wind ~ed in the pines** ве́тер шелесте́л в со́снах.

whist [wɪst] *n.* (*card game*) вист.

whistl|e ['wɪs(ə)l] *n.* **1.** (*sound*) свист, свисто́к. **2.** (*instrument*) свисто́к; (*factory ~*) гудо́к; **he played a tune on his tin ~e** он сыгра́л мело́дию на свое́й свисту́льке; **blow the/a ~e** св|исте́ть, -и́стнуть; **the ~e's gone!** (*in football match*) свисто́к прозвуча́л! **3.** (*fig.*) **wet one's ~e** (*coll.*) промочи́ть (*pf.*) го́рло.

v.t. **1.** (*call by ~ing*) сви́стнуть (*pf.*); **he ~ed his dog back** он сви́стом подозва́л (к себе́) соба́ку. **2.** (*produce by ~ing*) св|исте́ть, -и́стнуть; **can you ~e the tune?** вы мо́жете насвисте́ть моти́в э́той пе́сни?

v.i. **1.** св|исте́ть, про-, сви́стнуть; да|ва́ть, -ть свисто́к; **he came along ~ing** он шёл посви́стывая; **he can ~e for his money** (*coll.*) не вида́ть ему́ свои́х де́нег (как свои́х уше́й); **the train ~ed as it entered the tunnel** при вхо́де в тунне́ль по́езд дал свисто́к (*or* просвисте́л); **the wind ~es in the chimney** ве́тер завыва́ет в трубе́; **when the kettle ~es** когда́ ча́йник засвисти́т; **a bullet ~ed past him** пу́ля просвисте́ла ми́мо него́. **2.: he had ~ed past before I could stop him** (*coll.*) он так бы́стро пронёсся ми́мо, что я не успе́л его́ останови́ть.

cpd. **~e-stop** *n.* полуста́нок; **a ~e-stop tour** разъездна́я агитацио́нная кампа́ния (кандида́та на вы́борах).

whit[1] [wɪt] *n.* (*arch.*) ка́пля, йо́та; **he was not a ~ (*or* no ~) disturbed** э́то его́ ничу́ть не смути́ло.

Whit[2] [wɪt] *adj.*: **~ Monday** Ду́хов день; **~ Sunday** = **Whitsun**; **~ week** неде́ля ме́жду воскресе́ньем Свято́го Ду́ха и Тро́ицыным днём.

white [waɪt] *n.* **1.** (*colour*) бе́лый цвет; белизна́; **pure ~** чи́стый бе́лый цвет; (*as adj.*) белосне́жный; **a dirty ~** гря́зно-бе́лый цвет; **off ~** (*adj.*) белова́тый; (*clothes*): **she was wearing ~** она́ была́ в бе́лом; **dressed in ~** оде́тый в бе́лое; (*paint*) бе́лая кра́ска; бели́л|а (*pl.*, *g.* —); **Chinese ~** кита́йские бели́ла. **2.** (*of the eyes*) бело́к. **3.** (*of an egg*) бело́к. **4.** (*racial type*) белоко́жий, бе́лый; **poor ~s** бе́лая беднота́. **5.** (*butterfly*) капу́стница. **6.** (*loaf*) бе́лый бато́н. **7.** (*chess*) бе́лые (*pl.*); **it was W~'s move** был ход бе́лых. **8.** (*billiard ball*) «свой» шар. **9.** (*pl.*, *sl.*, *leucorrhea*) бе́л|и (*pl.*, *g.* -ей).

adj. бе́лый; **grow ~** беле́ть, по-; **his face went as ~ as a sheet** он сде́лался бе́лым как полотно́; **his hair turned ~** он поседе́л; **he turned ~** он побледне́л; **his creditors bled him ~** кредито́ры обобра́ли его́ до ни́тки; **a ~ Christmas** Рождество́ со сне́гом; **~ coffee** ко́фе с молоко́м; **W~ Ensign** брита́нский вое́нно-морско́й флаг; **~ frost** и́ней; и́зморозь; **~ heat** бе́лое кале́ние; **~ horses** (*waves*) бара́шки (*m. pl.*); **the W~ House** Бе́лый дом; **~ lead** свинцо́вые бели́ла; **a ~ lie** ложь во спасе́ние; **~ metal** баббит; **W~ Paper** Бе́лая кни́га; **W~ Russia** Белору́ссия; **a W~ Russian** (*Byelorussian*) белору́с (*fem.* -ка); (*émigré*) бе́лый эмигра́нт (*fem.* бе́лая эмигра́нтка); **~ slave traffic** торго́вля живы́м това́ром; **~ spirit** уайт-спи́рит; **~ sugar** (са́хар-)рафина́д; рафини́рованный са́хар; **~ tie and tails** фрак.

v.t.: **a ~d sepulchre** (*fig.*) гроб пова́пленный; ханжа́ (*c.g.*), лицеме́р.

cpds. **~bait** *n.* малёк; **~-collar** *adj.*: **~-collar worker** *n.* слу́жащий; **~-haired, ~-headed** *adjs.* белоголо́вый; седо́й; **~-hot** *adj.* раскалённый добела́; **~-livered** *adj.* малоду́шный, трусли́вый; **~-out** *n.* бе́лая мгла; **~thorn** *n.* боя́рышник колю́чий; **~wash** *n.* побе́лка; (*fig.*) лакиро́вка; обеле́ние; зама́зывание (недоста́тков); *v.t.* бели́ть, по-; (*fig.*) обел|я́ть, -и́ть; зама́з|ывать, -ать; лакирова́ть (*impf.*).

whiten ['waɪt(ə)n] *v.t.* бели́ть, по-; (*fig.*, *whitewash*) обел|я́ть, -и́ть; опра́вд|ывать, -а́ть.

whitener ['waɪt(ə)nə(r)] *n.*: **coffee ~** осветли́тель (*m.*) ко́фе.

whiteness ['waɪtnɪs] *n.* белизна́; бе́лый цвет.

whitening ['waɪtnɪŋ] = **whiting 1.**

whither ['wɪðə(r)] *adv.* (*liter.*) куда́; **~ away?** куда́ де́ржите путь?; **~ Europe?** куда́ идёт Евро́па?

whithersoever [ˌwɪðəsəʊ'evə(r)] *adv.* (*liter.*) куда́ бы ни.

whiting ['waɪtɪŋ] *n.* **1.** (*also* **whitening**: *powdered chalk*) мел. **2.** (*fish*) хек; мерла́нг.

whitish ['waɪtɪʃ] *adj.* белёсый; блёдный; белова́тый.

cpd. **~-brown** *adj.* све́тло-кори́чневый.

whitlow ['wɪtləʊ] *n.* ногтоеда, панари́ций.

Whitsun ['wɪts(ə)n] *n.* (*Whit Sunday*) Тро́ицын день, Тро́ица; Пятидеся́тница; *see also* **Whit**[2]

whittle ['wɪt(ə)l] *v.t.* строга́ть, вы-; обстру́г|ивать, -а́ть; **~ a pencil** чини́ть, о- каранда́ш; **he ~d a twig into a whistle** он вы́строгал (себе́) свисто́к из ве́тки; **this pipe was ~d out of cherrywood** э́та тру́бка вы́резана из ви́шнёвого де́рева.

with advs.: **~ away** *v.t.* сostру́г|ивать, -а́ть; ст|а́чивать, -очи́ть; (*fig.*) ум|еньша́ть, -е́ньшить; сокра|ща́ть, -ти́ть; св|оди́ть, -ести́ на нет; **his savings were ~d away** его́ сбереже́ния постепе́нно исся́кли; **~ down** *v.t.* состру́г|ивать, -а́ть; (*fig.*) сн|ижа́ть, -и́зить; смягч|а́ть, -и́ть.

whity ['waɪtɪ] = **whitish**

whiz(z) [wɪz] *n.* свист.

v.i. прон|оси́ться, -ести́сь со сви́стом; мча́ться, про-; просвисте́ть (*pf.*).

cpds. **~-bang** *n.* снаря́д, грана́та; **~-kid** *n.* (*coll.*) ≃ восходя́щая звезда́.

WHO[1] (*abbr. of* **World Health Organization**) ВОЗ, (Всеми́рная организа́ция здравоохране́ния).

who[2] [hu:] *pron.* **1.** (*interrog.*) кто; **~ is he?** кто он (тако́й)?; э́то кто?; **~ (else) but Smith?** сам Смит (свое́й со́бственной персо́ной); **~ is he when he's at home?** (*coll.*) э́та что за пти́ца?; како́й он на са́мом де́ле?; **~ does he think he is?** что он о себе́ вообража́ет?; **~'s it** (*coll., what's his name*) как бишь его́?; **~ am I to object?** како́е я име́ю пра́во возража́ть?; **~ goes there?** (*mil.*) кто идёт?; **~(m)ever do you mean?** кого́ же вы име́ете в виду́?; **he knows ~'s ~** он зна́ет, кто есть кто (*or* что ка́ждый собо́й представля́ет); **W~'s W~** (*directory*) биографи́ческий спра́вочник; «Кто есть кто»; **W~ was W~** «Кто кем был». **2.** (*rel.*) кото́рый, како́й, кто; **those ~** те, кто/кото́рые; **anyone ~** вся́кий, кто; **the sort of people ~m we need** таки́е лю́ди, каки́е нам нужны́; **~m the gods love die young** те, кого́ возлю́бят бо́ги, умира́ют молоды́ми; **as ~ should say** как бы говоря́; **Mr. X, ~ is my uncle** г-н X, мой дя́дя; **it was given to my sister, ~ passed it on to me** э́то да́ли мое́й сестре́, а она́ передала́ мне.

whoa, wo [wəʊ] *int.* тпру!

whodunit [hu:'dʌnɪt] *n.* (*sl.*) детекти́вный рома́н/фильм.

whoever [hu:'evə(r)] *pron.* **1.** (*anyone who; no matter who; also arch.* **whosoever**) кто бы ни; **~ comes will be welcome** кто бы ни пришёл, бу́дет жела́нным го́стем; **~ else objects, I do not** пусть там други́е как хотя́т (*or* не зна́ю, как други́е), а я не возража́ю. **2.** (*who ever*) кто то́лько; **~ heard of such a thing?** слы́ханное ли де́ло?; **~ would have thought it?** кто бы мог поду́мать?

whole [həʊl] *n.* (*single entity*) це́лое; **nature is a ~** приро́да есть еди́ное це́лое; (*totality*) все, всё; **the ~ of the audience** вся аудито́рия; **you haven't heard the ~ of the story** э́то ещё не всё; **taken as a ~** в це́лом; **on the ~** в о́бщем (и це́лом); в основно́м.

adj. **1.** (*intact; unbroken; undamaged*) це́лый, невреди́мый; **after the raid there was not one building left ~** по́сле налёта не оста́лось ни одного́ це́лого зда́ния; **he escaped with a ~ skin** он вы́шел (из э́той исто́рии) цел и невреди́м. **2.** (*in one piece*) целико́м; **the ox was roasted ~** быка́ зажа́рили целико́м. **3.** (*full; complete; entire*) весь, це́лый, це́льный; **he ate a ~ chicken** он съел це́лого цыплёнка; **two ~ glasses** це́лых два стака́на; **I was there for a ~ hour** я был там целый час; **the ~ lot** всё; (*people*) все; **a ~ number** це́лое число́; **~ milk** це́льное молоко́; **the ~ world** весь мир; **his ~ life through** на протяже́нии всей его́ жи́зни.

cpds. **~-hearted** *adj.* беззаве́тный, пре́данный; **~-heartedly** *adv.* от всей души́; **~-length** *adj.*: **a ~-length portrait** портре́т во весь рост; **~meal** *adj.*: **a ~meal loaf** буха́нка хле́ба из непросе́янной муки́; **~sale** *n.* опто́вая торго́вля; **sell sth. by (*US* at) ~sale** прод|ава́ть, -а́ть о́птом; **a ~sale dealer** оптови́к; *adj.* опто́вый; (*fig.*) ма́ссовый; **our business is ~sale only** мы торгу́ем то́лько о́птом; **I can get it for you ~sale** я могу́ вам э́то доста́ть по опто́вой цене́; *adv.* о́птом; (*fig.*) в ма́ссовом масшта́бе; **~saler** *n.* оптови́к; **~-time** *adj.*: **a ~-time job** рабо́та на по́лную ста́вку; рабо́та, рассчи́танная на по́лный рабо́чий день; **a ~-time worker** челове́к, рабо́тающий на по́лную ста́вку (*or* рабо́тающий по́лную рабо́чую неде́лю); **~-tone** *adj.*: **~-tone scale** га́мма на це́лых но́тах.

wholefood ['həʊlfu:d] *n.* натура́льные проду́кты.

adj. натура́льный.

wholefooder ['həʊlfu:də(r)] *n.* натури́ст.

wholeness ['həʊlnɪs] *n.* (*integrality*) це́льность, це́лость.

wholesome ['həʊlsəm] *adj.* **1.** (*promoting health*) поле́зный, цели́тельный, здоро́вый, благотво́рный; **~ food** здоро́вая пи́ща. **2.** (*sound; prudent*) здра́вый, благотво́рный; **I gave him some ~ advice** я ему́ дал здра́вый/поле́зный сове́т; **he has a ~ respect for his teacher** он испо́лнен надлежа́щего почте́ния к (своему́) учи́телю.

wholesomeness ['həʊlsəmnɪs] (*of food*) поле́зность; (*fig.*) здра́вость.

wholly ['həʊllɪ] *adv.* по́лностью; всеце́ло; целико́м; сплошь; **I am ~ at a loss** я в по́лном/соверше́нном недоуме́нии; **it cannot be ~ bad** не мо́жет быть, что́бы э́то было сплошь пло́хо.

whoop [hu:p, wu:p] *n.* во́зглас; вопль (*m.*); **with a ~ of joy** с ра́достным кри́ком.

v.i. **1.** издава́ть (*impf.*) во́пли; зака́т|ываться, -и́ться ка́шлем; **~ing-cough** коклю́ш. **2.: ~ it up** (*sl.*) бу́рно весели́ться (*impf.*); кути́ть (*impf.*).

whoopee ['wʊpɪ] *n.*: **make ~** (*sl.*) кути́ть (*impf.*).

whoops [wʊps] *int.* (*coll.*) оп!

whop [wɒp] *v.t.* (*sl.*) (*thrash*) взду|ва́ть, -ть; колошма́тить, от-; (*defeat*) разб|ива́ть, -и́ть в пух и прах.

whopper ['wɒpə(r)] *n.* (*sl.*) **1.** (*anything very large*) грома́дина, махи́на; **a ~ of a fish** огро́мная ры́бина. **2.** (*outrageous lie*) чудо́вищная ложь.

whopping ['wɒpɪŋ] (*sl.*) *adj.* (*also* **~ great**) огро́мный, чудо́вищный, здорове́нный.

whore [hɔ:(r)] *n.* шлю́ха; **the W~ of Babylon** вавило́нская блудни́ца.

v.i. распу́тничать (*impf.*).

cpds. **~-house** *n.* барда́к, борде́ль (*m.*); **~monger** *n.* (*arch.*) блудни́к.

whorl [wɔ:l, wɜ:l] *n.* вито́к, завиту́шка, завито́к; (*bot.*) мутовка; (*of finger-prints*) пальцево́й узо́р.

whortleberry ['wɜ:t(ə)lˌberɪ] *n.* черни́ка (*collect.*); я́года че́рники.

whose [hu:z] *pron.* (*interrog.*) чей; **~ partner are you?** чей вы партнёр?; (*rel.*) чей, кото́рого; **for ~ sake** ра́ди кото́рого; **the people ~ house we bought** лю́ди, у кото́рых мы купи́ли дом.

whosoever [ˌhu:səʊ'evə(r)] *pron.* (*arch.*) = **whoever 1.**

why [waɪ] *n.* причи́на; **all the ~s and wherefores** все э́ти почему́ да отчего́.

adv. почему́, отчего́, заче́м; **'Are you married?' — 'No, ~?'** «вы жена́ты?» — «Нет, а что?»; **~ so?** что так?; почему́?; **~ not?** почему́?; почему́ бы нет?; **~ not let me help you?** дава́йте я вам помогу́; **the reasons ~ …** соображе́ния, по кото́рым…; **he shall pay me, or I'll know the reason ~** пусть он то́лько попро́бует мне не заплати́ть!

int. да; ведь; да ведь; **~, of course** да, коне́чно; **~, what's the harm in it?** а что в э́том плохо́го?; **~ yes, I suppose so** да наве́рное э́то так; **~, you must remember Mary!** ах, да неуже́ли вы не по́мните Мэ́ри!; **if the worst came to the worst, ~, we'd have to start again** на худо́й коне́ц — что ж, (*or* ну,) придётся нача́ть (всё) с нача́ла.

wick [wɪk] *n.* фити́ль (*m.*).

wicked ['wɪkɪd] *adj.* (*depraved*) гре́шный, бессо́вестный, поро́чный; **(there's) no peace for the ~!** (*humorous acceptance of trouble*) нет гре́шнику поко́я!; (*malicious*) злой, зло́бный; (*roguish*) лука́вый, плутовско́й; **she gave him a ~ glance** она́ лука́во взгляну́ла на него́; (*coll., disgraceful*) ужа́сный, безобра́зный; **a ~ shame** безобра́зие; **a ~ waste** чудо́вищное расточи́тельство.

wickedness ['wɪkɪdnɪs] *n.* (*depravity*) грех, бессо́вестность, поро́чность; (*malice*) зло́ба.

wicker ['wɪkə(r)] *n.* пру́тья (*m. pl.*) для плете́ния; **~ chair** плетёное кре́сло.

cpd. **~work** *n.* плете́ние; плетёные изде́лия.

wicket ['wɪkɪt] *n.* **1.** **(~-gate)** кали́тка. **2.** (*at cricket*) воро́тц|а (*pl., g.* -ев); (*fig.*): **he is on a sticky ~** он в невы́годном положе́нии.

cpd. **~-keeper** *n.* ловя́щий мяч за воро́тцами (*в крикете*).

widdershins ['wɪdəʃɪnz] = **withershins**

wide [waɪd] *n.*: **to the ~** (*coll.*): **broke to the ~** (абсолю́тно) без гроша́; разорён вконе́ц.

adj. **1.** широ́кий; (*in measuring*) ширино́й в+*a.*, **the table is 3 feet ~** стол ширино́й в 3 фу́та; стол име́ет 3 фу́та ширины́ (*or* в ширину́). **2.** (*fig., liberal*) широ́кий. **3.** (*extensive*) большо́й, широ́кий, обши́рный, просто́рный; **~ experience** большо́й/бога́тый о́пыт; **~ interests** широ́кий круг интере́сов; **a ~ choice** широ́кий вы́бор; **a ~ difference** огро́мная ра́зница; **his reading has been ~**

он начи́танный челове́к; **the ~ world over** во всём ми́ре; по всему́ (бе́лому) све́ту; **the world is ~** мир вели́к. **4.** (*off target*): **his answer was ~ of the mark** он попа́л па́льцем в не́бо. **5.** (*artful*): **~ boy** лихо́й па́рень; ло́вкий ма́лый; про́йда (*m.*), пройдо́ха (*m.*) (*coll.*).

adv. **1.** (*extensively*): **far and ~** повсю́ду; вдоль и поперёк. **2.** (*to full extent*): **open the door ~!** откро́йте дверь на́стежь!; **he is ~ awake** у него́ сна ни в одно́м глазу́; **his mouth was ~ open** рот его́ был широ́ко́ раскры́т. **3.** (*off target*) ми́мо це́ли; **shoot ~** стреля́ть (*impf.*) ми́мо це́ли; (*miss*) ма́зать, про-; **the bullet went ~** пу́ля пролете́ла ми́мо це́ли.

cpds. **~-angle** *adj.*: **~-angle lens** широкоуго́льная ли́нза; **~awake** *n.* (*hat*) широкопо́лая шля́па; **~-awake** *adj.* недре́млющий, бди́тельный, начеку́; **~-eyed** *adj.* (*surprised*) изумлённый; (*naive*) наи́вный; **~-ranging** *adj.* (*intellect etc.*) разносторо́нний; **~-screen** *adj.*: **~-screen film** широкоэкра́нный фильм; **~spread** *adj.* распространённый.

widely ['waɪdlɪ] *adv.* **1.** (*to a large extent*) широ́ко́; **~ differing opinions** ре́зко расходя́щиеся мне́ния; **he is ~ read** (*has read a lot*) он о́чень начи́тан; (*many people read him*) его́ кни́ги о́чень популя́рны. **2.** (*over a large area*) далеко́; **~ scattered** разбро́санный; **it is ~ known** широ́ко́ изве́стно; **it is ~ believed that ...** мно́гие счита́ют, что...

widen ['waɪd(ə)n] *v.t. & i.* расш|иря́ть(ся), -и́рить(ся); **they are ~ing the road** веду́тся рабо́ты по расшире́нию доро́ги; **the gap between them ~s daily** разры́в ме́жду ни́ми увели́чивается с ка́ждым днём.

widgeon ['wɪdʒ(ə)n] *n.* ди́кая у́тка.

widow ['wɪdəʊ] *n.* вдова́; **become a ~** стать (*pf.*) вдово́й; овдове́ть (*pf.*); **the ~'s mite** (*bibl.*) ле́пта вдови́цы; вдо́вья ле́пта; **~'s peak** во́лосы (*m. pl.*), расту́щие мы́сиком на лбу́; **~'s weeds** вдо́вий тра́ур; **grass ~** соло́менная вдова́; **war ~** же́нщина, потеря́вшая му́жа на войне́.

v.t. де́лать, с- вдово́й; **she was ~ed by the war** война́ отняла́ у неё му́жа.

widower ['wɪdəʊə(r)] *n.* вдове́ц.

widowhood ['wɪdəʊ,hʊd] *n.* вдовство́.

width [wɪtθ, wɪdθ] *n.* **1.** (*measurement*) ширина́; **the river is 2 miles in ~** ширина́ реки́ 2 ми́ли; река́ име́ет 2 ми́ли ширины́ (*or* в ширину́). **2.** (*piece of material*) поло́тнище. **3.** (*wide extent*) широта́.

cpds. **~ways, ~wise** *advs.* в ширину́.

wield [wi:ld] *v.t.* держа́ть (*impf.*) в рука́х; владе́ть (*impf.*) +*i.*; **~ an axe** рабо́тать (*impf.*) топоро́м; **~ a sword** владе́ть (*impf.*) шпа́гой; **~ authority** по́льзоваться (*impf.*) вла́стью.

Wiener schnitzel ['vi:nə ʃnɪts(ə)l] *n.* шни́цель (*m.*) по-ве́нски.

wife [waɪf] *n.* **1.** (*spouse*) жена́; **take to ~** (*arch.*) взять (*pf.*) в жёны; **he made her his ~** он на ней жени́лся; **the President's ~** супру́га президе́нта; **the ~** (*my ~*) моя́ жена́; (*coll.*) стару́ха; **all the world and his ~ were there** там был весь свет; **common-law ~** гражда́нская/неве́нчанная жена́; подру́га. **2.** (*arch., old woman*) стару́ха, ба́бка; **old wives' tales** ба́бьи ска́зки (*f. pl.*); ро́сскazн|и (*pl., g.* -ей).

wifely ['waɪflɪ] *adj.* подоба́ющий/сво́йственный жене́; **~ duties** же́нские обя́занности.

wig [wɪg] *n.* пари́к; **~s on the green** (*arch.*) о́бщая сва́лка; ку́ча мала́.

cpds. **~-block** *n.* парикма́херский болва́н; **~-maker** *n.* парикма́хер.

wigging ['wɪgɪŋ] *n.* (*coll.*) разно́с, нагоня́й, взбу́чка, нахлобу́чка; **give s.o. a ~** зад|ава́ть, -а́ть кому́-н. взбу́чку/нахлобу́чку; де́лать, с-кому́-н. разно́с.

wiggle ['wɪg(ə)l] *n.* пока́чивание, ёрзание; **walk with a ~** идти́ (*det.*) вихля́ющей похо́дкой; **get a ~ on** (*sl., hurry up*) потора́пливайтесь!; пошеве́ливаетесь!

v.t. пока́чивать (*impf.*); виля́ть (*impf.*); **she ~s her hips** она́ вихля́ет бёдрами; **the baby ~d its toes** ребёнок шевели́л па́льцами ног.

v.i. (*e.g. a loose tooth*) шата́ться (*impf.*), кача́ться (*impf.*).

wiggly ['wɪglɪ] *adj.*: **a ~ line** волни́стая ли́ния; **a ~ tooth** кача́ющийся/шата́ющийся зуб.

Wight [waɪt] *n.*: **the Isle of ~** о́стров (*abbr.* о́-в) Уа́йт.

wigwag ['wɪgwæg] *v.i.* (*signal*) сигнализи́ровать, профлажка́ми; семафо́рить (*impf.*).

wigwam ['wɪgwæm] *n.* вигва́м.

wild [waɪld] *n.* **1.** (*~ state*): **this animal is not found in the ~** э́то живо́тное не во́дится на во́ле. **2.** (*pl., desert or uncultivated tract*) де́бр|и (*pl., g.* -ей); пусты́ня; **the ~s of Africa** де́бри А́фрики; **(out) in the ~s** на отши́бе; вдали́ от цивилиза́ции.

adj. **1.** (*not domesticated; not cultivated*) ди́кий; **~ boar** каба́н; ди́кая свинья́; **~ flower** полево́й цвето́к; **~ goose chase** (*fig.*) бессмы́сленное предприя́тие; пого́ня за химе́рами; бессмы́сленная зате́я; **~ rose** ди́кая ро́за, шипо́вник; **in the ~ state** в ди́ком состоя́нии/ви́де, на во́ле. **2.** (*not civilized*) ди́кий; **~ man** (*savage*) дика́рь (*m.*); (*political extremist*) кра́йний, экстреми́ст. **3.** (*of scenery: desolate, uninhabited*) ди́кий, пусты́нный. **4.** (*of birds etc.: easily startled*) пугли́вый. **5.** (*unrestrained, wayward, disorderly*) необу́зданный, нei̮стовый, бу́рный, бу́йный; (*dissolute*) разгу́льный; **a ~ fellow** пове́са (*m.*); **your hair looks (rather) ~** у вас во́лосы растрепа́лись; **everything was in ~ confusion** (там) цари́л стра́шный беспоря́док; **she lets her children run ~** она́ распуска́ет свои́х дете́й доне́льзя; **he let the garden run ~** он запусти́л сад. **6.** (*tempestuous*) бу́рный, бу́йный; **it was a ~ sea** мо́ре бушева́ло (*or* бы́ло о́чень бу́рным). **7.** (*excited, passionate, frantic*) вне себя́; исступлённый; **~ with rage/delight** вне себя́ от я́рости/восто́рга; **he drives me ~** он меня́ из себя́ выво́дит; **it made her ~** э́то приводи́ло её в нei̮стовство; **he is ~ with impatience** он гори́т нетерпе́нием; **they were ~ about him** они́ бы́ли в (ди́ком) восто́рге от него́; **~ laughter** бе́шеный хо́хот. **8.** (*reckless; ill-aimed; ill-considered*) безу́мный; неле́пый; ди́кий; **a ~ scheme** сумасбро́дная/безу́мная зате́я; **a ~ shot** вы́стрел наута́д; шальна́я пу́ля.

adv. наобу́м; науга́д; **shoot ~** стреля́ть (*impf.*) наобу́м.

cpds. **~-cat** *adj.* риско́ванный; **~-cat strike** неофициа́льная забасто́вка; **~fire** *n.*: **the news/disease spread like ~fire** но́вость/боле́знь распространи́лась с молниено́сной быстрото́й; **~fowl** *n.* дичь.

wildebeest ['wɪldə,bi:st, 'vɪl-] *n.* гну (*m. indecl.*).

wilderness ['wɪldənɪs] *n.* ди́кая ме́стность; пусты́ня; **a voice crying in the ~** (*fig.*) глас вопию́щего в пусты́не; **in the ~** (*pol.*) не удел, в опа́ле; (*neglected garden*) запу́щенный/невозде́ланный сад; **a ~ of roofs** мо́ре крыш.

wildlife ['waɪldlaɪf] *n.* жива́я приро́да; **~ sanctuary** запове́дник; **~ photographer** фотоохо́тник; **~ photography** фотоохо́та.

wildness ['waɪldnɪs] *n.* (*of behaviour, character*) ди́кость, необу́зданность.

wile [waɪl] *n.* (*liter.*) хи́трость, уло́вка; (*pl.*) ухищре́ния (*nt. pl.*); **fall victim to s.o.'s ~s** пасть (*pf.*) же́ртвой чьих-н. ко́зней (*or* чьего́-н. обма́на/кова́рства).

v.t.: **she ~d him into consenting** она хи́тростью вы́нудила его́ согласи́ться.

with adv.: **~ away** *see* **while** *v.t.*

wilful ['wɪlfʊl] (*US* **willful**) *adj.* **1.** (*of pers., headstrong, refractory*) своенра́вный, упря́мый. **2.** (*intentional*) умы́шленный, преднаме́ренный, зло́стный; **~ disobedience** созна́тельное неповинове́ние; **~ murder** предумы́шленное уби́йство.

wilfulness ['wɪlfʊlnɪs] (*US* **willfulness**) *n.* своенра́вие, упря́мство; преднаме́ренность.

wiliness ['waɪlɪnɪs] *n.* хи́трость, кова́рство, лука́вство.

will[1] [wɪl] *n.* **1.** (*faculty; its exercise; determination, intent*) во́ля; **free ~** свобо́да во́ли; **he has a ~ of his own** он челове́к упря́мый/своево́льный; **he has no ~ of his own** он легко́ подчиня́ется чужи́м влия́ниям; **against my ~** вопреки́ моему́ влия́нию; во́лей-нево́лей; **lack of ~** безво́лие, отсу́тствие си́лы во́ли; **the ~ to live** во́ля к жи́зни; **where there's a ~ there's a way** где хоте́ние, там и уме́ние; **take the ~ for the deed** суди́ть (*impf.*) по наме́рениям; **of one's own free ~** доброво́льно, по со́бственной во́ле; **Thy ~ be done** да бу́дет во́ля Твоя́;

he had his ~ of her (*liter.*) он овладе́л е́ю. **2.** (*energy; enthusiasm*) эне́ргия; **go to work with a ~** рабо́тать (*impf.*) энерги́чно (*or* с душо́й). **3.** (*discretion, desire*) жела́ние, во́ля; **he came and went at ~** он приходи́л и уходи́л, когда́ хоте́л. **4.** (*disposition*) расположе́ние; **I feel no ill ~ towards him** я на него́ не в оби́де; я не пита́ю злых чувств к нему́; **men of good ~** лю́ди до́брой во́ли. **5.** (*disposition of property*) завеща́ние; **last ~ and testament** после́дняя во́ля; **make, draw up one's ~** сде́лать (*pf.*) завеща́ние; **he died without making a ~** он у́мер, не оста́вив завеща́ния.

v.t. **1.** (*compel*) заст|авля́ть, -а́вить; **he ~ed himself to stay (*or* into staying) awake** (уси́лием во́ли) он заста́вил себя́ бо́дрствовать; **you cannot ~ success** одни́м хоте́нием успе́ха не добьёшся. **2.: God ~ing** е́сли на то бу́дет во́ля бо́жья. **3.** (*bequeath*) завеща́ть (*impf., pf.*).

cpd. **~-power** *n.* си́ла во́ли.

will[2] [wɪl] *v.t. & i.* (*see also* **would**) **1.** (*expr. future*): **he ~ be president** он бу́дет президе́нтом; **in five minutes it ~ be midnight** че́рез пять мину́т насту́пит по́лночь; **tomorrow ~ be Tuesday** за́втра — вто́рник; **he said he would be back by 3** он сказа́л, что вернётся к трём; **I won't do it again** я бо́льше не бу́ду. **2.** (*expr. wish, insistence*): **let him do what he ~** пусть де́лает, что хо́чет; **come when you ~** приходи́те, когда́ уго́дно; **he ~ always have his own way** он всегда́ насто́ит на своём. **3.** (*expr. willingness*): **I ~ come with you** я пойду́ с ва́ми; **~ (*or* won't) you come in?** войди́те, пожа́луйста!; **pass the salt, ~ (*or* would) you?** бу́дьте любе́зны, переда́йте соль; **'Tell me your name!' — 'No, I won't'** «Скажи́те, как вас зову́т?» — «Не скажу́!»; **he won't help me** он не хо́чет мне помо́чь; **the dog wouldn't come when I called** соба́ка не шла, когда́ я её звал; **the window won't open** окно́ ника́к не открыва́ется. **4.** (*expr. inevitability*): **boys ~ be boys** ма́льчики есть ма́льчики; **accidents ~ happen** несча́стных слу́чаев не избежа́ть. **5.** (*expr. habit*): **he ~/would sit there for hours on end** он проси́живает/проси́живал там часа́ми; **he would often come to see me** он ча́сто заходи́л ко мне. **6.** (*expr. surmise, probability*): **this ~ be the book you're looking for** вот, ве́рно, кни́га, кото́рую вы и́щете; **she would have been about 60 when she died** ей бы́ло, должно́ быть, о́коло шести́десяти, когда́ она́ умерла́.

willful ['wɪlfʊl] = **wilful**

William ['wɪljəm] *n.* (*hist.*) Вильге́льм; **~ the Conqueror** Вильге́льм Завоева́тель; **~ of Orange** Вильге́льм Ора́нский.

willies ['wɪlɪz] *n.* (*sl.*): **it gives me the ~** меня́ от э́того броса́ет в дрожь; меня́ о́торопь берёт; у меня́ от э́того мура́шки по спине́ (бе́гают).

willing ['wɪlɪŋ] *adj.* **1.** (*readily disposed*) скло́нный, располо́женный; **~ workers** усе́рдные рабо́тники; **he is her ~ slave** он её послу́шный раб; **a ~ horse** (*fig.*) работя́га (*c.g.*), рабо́чая лоша́дка; **I am ~ to admit ...** я гото́в призна́ть...; **are you ~ that he should join us?** вы согла́сны, что́бы он к нам присоедини́лся?; **he was not ~ to accept responsibility** он не хоте́л брать на себя́ отве́тственность; **show ~** прояв|ля́ть, -и́ть гото́вность; **'Will you do me a favour?' — 'W~ly!'** «Вы мо́жете сде́лать мне одолже́ние?» — «Охо́тно!». **2.** (*readily given or shown*) доброво́льный; **~ obedience** доброво́льное повинове́ние; **he lent a ~ ear to their request** он благоскло́нно вы́слушал их про́сьбу/пожела́ние.

willingness ['wɪlɪŋnɪs] *n.* гото́вность, жела́ние.

will-o'-the-wisp [ˌwɪləðə'wɪsp] *n.* блужда́ющий огонёк; (*fig., elusive pers.*) неулови́мый челове́к; (*fig., delusive hope or plan*) несбы́точная наде́жда/мечта́; иллю́зия.

willow ['wɪləʊ] *n.* **1.** (*tree*) и́ва; **the ~ family** семе́йство и́вовых; **pussy ~** ве́рба; **weeping ~** плаку́чая и́ва; **thicket of ~** и́вовая за́росль, ивня́к. **2.** (*fig., cricket-bat*) бита́.

cpds. **~-herb** *n.* кипре́й, ива́н-ча́й; **~-pattern** (*china*) *n.* посу́да с си́ним трафаре́тным кита́йским рису́нком; **~-warbler** *n.* пе́ночка-весни́чка.

willowy ['wɪləʊɪ] *adj.* (*lithe*) то́нкий, ги́бкий, стро́йный.

willy ['wɪlɪ] *n.* (*coll.*) член, со́лоп.

willy-nilly [ˌwɪlɪ'nɪlɪ] *adv.* во́лей-нево́лей; хо́чешь не хо́чешь.

wilt [wɪlt] *v.i.* (*lit., fig.*) ни́кнуть, по-; пон|ика́ть, -и́кнуть; сн|ика́ть, -и́кнуть; **~ing enthusiasm** ослабева́ющий энтузиа́зм.

wily ['waɪlɪ] *adj.* хи́трый, кова́рный, лука́вый; **a ~ old bird** (*coll.*) стре́ляный воробе́й; **a ~ old fox** ста́рая лиса́.

wimp [wɪmp] *n.* слизня́к, сопля́к.

wimpish ['wɪmpɪʃ] *adj.* бесхара́ктерный.

wimple ['wɪmp(ə)l] *n.* (*nun's*) апо́стольник, плат.

win [wɪn] *n.* (*gain*) вы́игрыш; (*victory*) побе́да; **a ~ at cards** вы́игрыш в ка́ртах; картёжный вы́игрыш; **we had 5 home and 2 away ~s** мы одержа́ли 5 побе́д на своём по́ле и 2 на чужо́м; **it was an easy ~ for them** они́ с лёгкостью вы́играли.

v.t. **1.** (*be victorious in*) выи́грывать, вы́играть; **the Allies won the war** сою́зники вы́играли войну́; **~ a race** побе|жда́ть, -ди́ть в забе́ге; **he won every race** он победи́л во всех соревнова́ниях по бе́гу; **who won the election?** кто вы́играл на вы́борах?; **the game was won outright** игра́ сра́зу же око́нчилась побе́дой; **~ the day, field** одержа́ть (*pf.*) побе́ду. **2.** (*gain*) получ|а́ть, -и́ть; выи́грывать, вы́играть; **he won £5 from me** он вы́играл у меня́ 5 фу́нтов; **~ a medal/competition** завоёв|ывать, -а́ть меда́ль/пе́рвенство; **~ a prize** вы́играть/взять (*pf.*) приз; **~ one's spurs** (*lit.*) получи́ть (*pf.*) ры́царское зва́ние; (*fig.*) получи́ть (*pf.*) призна́ние; **~ s.o.'s affection** сни́ск|ивать, -а́ть чью-н. любо́вь; **~ s.o.'s heart** покор|я́ть, -и́ть чьё-н. се́рдце; **~ s.o.'s confidence** сни́ск|ивать, -а́ть (*or* войти́ (*pf.*) в) чьё-н. дове́рие; **he won my consent** он доби́лся моего́ согла́сия; **this work won her many friends** благодаря́ э́той рабо́те она́ приобрела́ мно́го друзе́й.

v.i.: **~ hands down** вы́играть (*pf.*) без труда́ (*or* с лёгкостью); **~ on points** вы́играть (*pf.*) по очка́м; **~ by 4 goals to 1** вы́играть (*pf.*) со счётом 4:1.

with advs.: **~ back** *v.t.* возвраща́ть, верну́ть себе́; оты́гр|ывать, -а́ть; отвоёв|ывать, -а́ть; **~ out** *v.i.* одержа́ть (*pf.*) побе́ду/верх; преодоле́ть (*pf.*) все тру́дности; **~ over, ~ round** *vv.t.* угов|а́ривать, -ори́ть; **we won him over to our side** мы уговори́ли его́ перейти́ на на́шу сто́рону; **he cannot be won round** его́ нельзя́/невозмо́жно уговори́ть; **~ through** *v.i.* проб|ива́ться, -и́ться.

wince [wɪns] *n.*: **with a ~** вздро́гнув.

v.i. содрог|а́ться, -ну́ться; мо́рщиться, по-.

winch [wɪntʃ] *n.* лебёдка, во́рот; **~ truck** автолебёдка.

v.t. (*usu. with advs.*) подн|има́ть, -я́ть с по́мощью лебёдки; **the glider was ~ed off the ground** планёр запусти́ли в во́здух с по́мощью лебёдки.

wind[1] [wɪnd] *n.* **1.** ве́тер; **high ~** си́льный ве́тер; **fair ~** попу́тный ве́тер; **strong ~** ре́зкий ве́тер; **there's not much ~ about** ве́тра почти́ нет; **the ~ is in the east** ве́тер ду́ет с восто́ка; **the ~ is rising** ве́тер уси́ливается/поднима́ется; **the ~ blew hard** дул кре́пкий ве́тер; **sail before the ~** плыть (*det.*) с попу́тным ве́тром; **you will have the ~ in your face** вам придётся идти́ про́тив ве́тра; **the ~ was behind us** ве́тер дул нам в спи́ну; **in the ~'s eye** (*naut.*) пря́мо про́тив ве́тра; **open to the four ~s** откры́тый всем ве́трам; **exposed to ~ and weather** откры́тый непого́дам; **he is sailing close to the ~** (*lit.*) он идёт кру́то к ве́тру; (*fig.*) он ведёт себя́ на гра́ни дозво́ленного; **the deer were down ~ of us** оле́ни находи́лись в подве́тренной стороне́ от нас; **get, catch ~ of** чу́ять, по-; (*fig.*) прове́д|ывать, -ать; пронюх|ивать, -ать. **2.** (*var. fig. uses*): **between ~ and water** не в бровь, а в глаз; по (са́мому) больно́му ме́сту; **raise the ~** (*coll.*) раздобы́ть (*pf.*) де́нег; **gone with the ~** безвозвра́тно уше́дший; **he ran like the ~** он мча́лся как ве́тер; **fling caution to the ~s** отбро́сить/забы́ть (*pf.*) вся́кую осторо́жность; **scattered to the four ~s** разбро́санный повсю́ду (*or* по всему́ све́ту); **I must see how the ~ blows** мне ну́жно поня́ть, куда́ ве́тер ду́ет; **it took the ~ out of his sails** (*fig.*) э́то вы́било по́чву у него́ из-под ног; э́то обескура́жило его́; **~ of change** (*fig.*) ве́тер переме́н; но́вое ве́яние; **he's all ~** (*empty* *talk*) он пустобрёх; **get the ~ up** (*sl.*) тру́сить, с-; **the noise put the ~ up me** (*sl.*) э́тот шум меня́ испуга́л/напуга́л; **there is something in the ~** что́-то назрева́ет/затева́ется; **it's an ill ~ that blows nobody good** нет ху́да без добра́. **3.** (*breath*) дыха́ние; **out of ~** запыха́вшись; **lose one's ~** запыха́ться (*pf.*); **get back** (*or* **recover) one's ~** отдыша́ться (*pf.*); **get one's second ~** обре|та́ть, -сти́ второ́е дыха́ние; **knock the ~ out of s.o.** (*fig.*) ошелом|ля́ть, -и́ть кого́-н.; **sound in ~ and limb** соверше́нно здоро́вый. **4.** (*in bowels etc.*) ве́тры (*m. pl.*); га́зы (*m. pl.*); **I've got ~** меня́ распира́ют га́зы; у меня́ живо́т пу́чит; **bring a baby's ~ up** масси́ровать (*impf.*) ребёнка, чтобы освободи́ть от га́зов; **break ~** по́ртить, ис- во́здух. **5.** (**~** *instruments*) духовы́е инструме́нты (*m. pl.*); **~ quintet** духово́й квинте́т.

v.t. **1.** (*detect by smell*) чу́ять, по-/у-. **2.** (*deprive of breath*): **the blow ~ed him** от уда́ра у него́ дух захвати́ло; **I was ~ed by the climb** от подъёма я запыха́лся; **he ~ed me** он уда́рил меня́ под вздох. **3.: ~ a horse** да|ва́ть, -ть ло́шади передохну́ть.

cpds. **~bag** *n.* (*coll.*) пустоме́ля (*c.g.*), краснобай́; **~-break** *n.* ветроло́м; ветрозащи́тные насажде́ния; **~-cheater** (*US* **-breaker)** *nn.* ветронепроница́емая ку́ртка; штормо́вка; **~-driven** *adj.*: **~-driven sand** песо́к, гони́мый ве́тром; **~-driven machinery** механи́зм, рабо́тающий от ве́тра; **~fall** *n.* (*of fruit*) па́данец; (*of good fortune*) непредви́денный дохо́д; неожи́данное везе́ние/сча́стье; **~-flower** *n.* анемо́н; **~-gauge** *n.* анемо́метр; **~hover** *n.* пустельга́; **~-jammer** *n.* (торго́вый) па́русник; **~mill** *n.* ветряна́я ме́льница; **tilt at ~mills** (*fig.*) сража́ться (*impf.*) с ветряны́ми ме́льницами; **~pipe** *n.* дыха́тельное го́рло; **~screen** (*US* **~shield)** *nn.* пере́днее/ветрово́е стекло́; **~screen wiper** стеклоочисти́тель (*m.*), «дво́рник»; **~-sleeve, ~-sock** *nn.* ветрово́й ко́нус; **~swept** *adj.* (*of terrain*) откры́тый ве́тру; (*of hair etc.*) растрёпанный; **~-tunnel** *n.* аэродинами́ческая труба́; **~-vane** *n.* флю́гер.

wind[2] [wɪnd] *v.t.* (*sound by blowing*): **~ a (blast on the) horn** затруби́ть (*pf.*) в рог.

wind[3] [waɪnd] *n.* **1.** (*single turn*) вито́к; **there were 25 ~s on the coil** на кату́шке бы́ло 25 витко́в. **2.** (*bend*) поворо́т, изги́б.

v.t. **1.** (*cause to encircle, curve or curl*): **she wound the wool into a ball** она́ смота́ла шерсть в клубо́к; **the thread was wound on to a reel** ни́тка была́ намо́тана на кату́шку; **a rope was wound round the pole** на шест была́ намо́тана верёвка; **the chain had wound itself round the wheel** цепь обвила́сь вокру́г колеса́; **the hedgehog ~s itself into a ball** ёжик свёртывается клубко́м (*or* в клубо́к); **she can ~ you round her little finger** (*fig.*) она́ из вас верёвки вьёт; она́ ве́ртит ва́ми, как хо́чет. **2.** (*fold, wrap*) уку́т|ывать, -ать; **she wound a shawl round the baby; she wound the baby in a shawl** она́ уку́тала/заверну́ла ребёнка в плато́к; **~ing-sheet** са́ван. **3.** (*rotate*) верте́ть (*impf.*); крути́ть (*impf.*). **4.: ~ a clock** зав|оди́ть, -ести́ часы́; **~ing-engine** подъёмная маши́на. **5.: the river ~s its way to the sea** река́, извива́ясь, течёт к мо́рю; **she wound her way into his affections** она́ постепе́нно овладе́ла его́ се́рдцем.

v.i. (*twist*) ви́ться (*impf.*); извива́ться (*impf.*); **the path ~s up the hill** доро́жка/тропи́нка зме́йкой поднима́ется в го́ру; **~ing staircase** винтова́я ле́стница; **a ~ing road** изви́листая доро́га.

with advs.: **~ about** *v.i.*: **the road ~s about** доро́га вьётся; **~ down** *v.t.* опус|ка́ть, -ти́ть; *v.i.*: **the clock spring ~s down in 7 days** у э́тих часо́в семидне́вный заво́д; **~ in** *v.t.*: **~ in a fishing line** см|а́тывать, -ота́ть у́дочку; **he wound in a large salmon** он вы́тянул кру́пного ло́сося; **~ up** *v.t.*: **~ up the bucket from the well** подн|има́ть, -я́ть ведро́ из коло́дца; **~ up a clock** зав|оди́ть, -ести́ часы́; (*fig., arouse*) взви́н|чивать, -ти́ть; **he gets very wound up at times** иногда́ он ужа́сно взви́нчивается; **he wound himself up to make a speech** он настро́ил себя́ на выступле́ние; (*fig., settle*) заверш|а́ть, -и́ть; **I am ~ing up my affairs** я свёртываю свои́ дела́; (*fig., terminate*) зак|а́нчивать, -о́нчить; **they wound up the meeting with a prayer** они́ зако́нчили собра́ние моли́твой; *v.i.* (*conclude*) заключ|а́ть, -и́ть; заверш|а́ть, -и́ть; **he wound up for the Opposition** он произнёс заключи́тельную речь от и́мени оппози́ции; **if you go on like that you will ~ up in prison** е́сли вы бу́дете продолжа́ть в том же ду́хе, вы ко́нчите тюрьмо́й; **he wound up by shooting himself** он ко́нчил тем, что застрели́лся.

windlass ['wɪndləs] *n.* лебёдка, во́рот.

windless ['wɪndlɪs] *adj.* безве́тренный.

window ['wɪndəʊ] *n.* **1.** окно́; (*dim., also cashier's etc.*) око́шко; **he looked through the ~** он смотре́л в окно́; он вы́глянул из окна́; **double ~s** двойны́е ра́мы (*f. pl.*); **French ~** балко́нная дверь; двуство́рчатое окно́; стекля́нные ство́рчатые две́ри (*f. pl.*); **(shop-~)** витри́на; **keep all one's goods in the ~** (*fig.*) выставля́ть, вы́ставить всё напока́з; пока́з|ывать, -а́ть това́р лицо́м; **a ~ on the world** окно́ в мир. **2.** (*attr.*) око́нный; **~ envelope** конве́рт с прозра́чным прямоуго́льником для а́дреса.

cpds. **~-blind** *n.* што́ра; жалюзи́ (*nt. indecl.*); **~-box** *n.* нару́жный я́щик для цвето́в; **~-catch** *n.* око́нный затво́р, шпингале́т; **~-cleaner** *n.* мо́йщик о́кон; **~-dressing** *n.* (*lit.*) оформле́ние витри́н; (*fig.*) очковтира́тельство; **~-ledge** *n.* (нару́жный) подоко́нник; **~-pane** *n.* око́нное стекло́; **~-seat** *n.* дива́н у окна́; **~-shopping** *n.* рассма́тривание витри́н; **~-sill** *n.* подоко́нник.

windsurfer ['wɪnd,sɜːfə(r)] *n.* виндсёрфинги́ст.

windsurfing ['wɪnd,sɜːfɪŋ] *n.* виндсёрфинг.

windward ['wɪndwəd] *n.* наве́тренная сторона́; **get to ~ of** (*fig.*) об|ходи́ть, -ойти́; обскака́ть (*pf.*).

adj. наве́тренный.

windy ['wɪndɪ] *adj.* **1.** (*characterized by wind*) ве́треный; **a ~ night** ве́треная ночь. **2.** (*exposed to wind*) обдува́емый ве́тром; откры́тый ве́трам. **3.** (*verbose*) многосло́вный, пусто́й; **a ~ speaker** велере́чивый ора́тор/докла́дчик; пустоме́ля (*c.g.*), краснобай́; **~ eloquence** пустосло́вие, краснобай́ство. **4.** (*flatulent*) вызыва́ющий пу́чение; **~ food** пи́ща, от кото́рой пу́чит (живо́т). **5.** (*coll., scared*): **are you getting ~?** вы тру́сите?

wine [waɪn] *n.* **1.** (виногра́дное) вино́; **dry, medium dry, sweet ~** сухо́е/полусухо́е/сла́дкое вино́; **sparkling ~** игри́стое вино́; **table ~** столо́вое вино́; **good ~ needs no bush** хоро́ший това́р сам себя́ хва́лит; **new ~ in old bottles** (*bibl.*) молодо́е вино́ в меха́х ве́тхих. **2.** (*from other fruit or plant*) нали́вка.

v.t.: **he was ~d and dined** его́ угости́ли на сла́ву; его́ корми́ли-пои́ли; его́ по́тчевали.

cpds. **~-bibber** *n.* пья́ница (*c.g.*); **~-bottle** *n.* ви́нная буты́лка; **~-cellar** *n.* ви́нный по́греб; **~-coloured** *adj.* тёмно-кра́сный; бордо́вый; вишнёвый; **~-cooler** *n.* ведёрко со льдом (для охлажде́ния вина́); **~-glass** *n.* бока́л, рю́мка; **~-grower** *n.* виноде́л; виногра́дарь (*m.*); **~-growing** *n.* виноде́лие; виногра́дарство; *adj.* виногра́дарский, виноде́льческий; **~-list** *n.* ка́рта вин; **~-press** *n.* дави́льный пресс; **~skin** *n.* мех для вина́; **~-taster** *n.* дегуста́тор вин; **~-tasting** *n.* дегуста́ция вин; **~-vault** *n.* ви́нный по́греб; **~-waiter** *n.* официа́нт, ве́дающий ви́нами.

winery ['waɪnərɪ] *n.* ви́нный заво́д, виноде́льня.

wing [wɪŋ] *n.* **1.** (*of bird, insect or aircraft*) крыло́; **on the ~** в полёте; **shoot a bird on the ~** подстрели́ть (*pf.*) пти́цу на лету́; **on the ~s of the wind** на кры́льях (*or* с быстрото́й) ве́тра; **clip s.o.'s ~s** (*fig.*) подр|еза́ть, -е́зать кому́-н. кры́лышки; **spread, stretch one's ~s** (*fig.*) распр|авля́ть, -а́вить кры́лья; **take ~** (*lit.*) улет|а́ть, -е́ть; лете́ть, по-; взлет|а́ть, -е́ть; (*fig.*) см|ыва́ться, -ы́ться; исч|еза́ть, -е́знуть; улету́чи|ваться, -ться; **take under one's ~** (*fig.*) брать, взять под своё кры́лышко. **2.** (*of building*) крыло́, фли́гель (*m.*). **3.** (*of vehicle*) крыло́. **4.** (*of diptych etc.*) ство́рка. **5.** (*of mil. formation*) фланг; крыло́; край. **6.** (*of political party*) крыло́; **the left/right ~** ле́вое/пра́вое крыло́. **7.** (*of football or hockey team*) фланг; край; (*player in this position*) кра́йний напада́ющий. **8.** (*air force formation*) (авиа-)крыло́. **9.** (*pl., of stage*) кули́сы (*f. pl.*); **wait in the ~s** (*lit.*) ждать (*impf.*) своего́ вы́хода на сце́ну; (*fig.*) ждать (*impf.*) своего́ ча́са; быть наготове. **10.** (*pl.,* *emblem on uniform*) «кры́лья».

v.t. **1.** (*equip with ~s*): **~ed words** крыла́тые слова́; **fear ~ed his steps** страх подгоня́л его́ (*or* прида́л ему́ кры́лья). **2.: ~ one's way** лете́ть (*impf.*). **3.** (*wound in ~*) ра́нить (*impf.*, *pf.*) в крыло́; подстре́л|ивать, -и́ть; (*wound in arm*) ра́нить (*impf.*, *pf.*) в ру́ку.

cpds. **~-beat** *n.* взмах кры́льев; **~-case** *n.* надкры́лье; **~-collar** *n.* стоя́чий воротни́к с отворо́тами; **~-commander** *n.* подполко́вник авиа́ции; **~-half** *n.* полузащи́тник; **~-mirror** *n.* боково́е зе́ркало; **~-sheath** *n.* = **-case; ~-span, ~-spread** *nn.* разма́х крыла́; **~-tip** *n.* коне́ц крыла́.

wingding ['wɪŋdɪŋ] *n.* (*US sl., party*) кутёж, попо́йка.

winger ['wɪŋə(r)] *n.* (*player*) кра́йний напада́ющий.

wingless ['wɪŋlɪs] *adj.* бескры́лый.

wink [wɪŋk] *n.* **1.: give s.o. a ~** подми́г|ивать, -ну́ть кому́-н.; **tip s.o. the ~** (*fig.*) намек|а́ть, -ну́ть кому́-н.; предупре|жда́ть, -ди́ть кого́-н.; **a nod is as good as a ~** доста́точно намёка; **I didn't sleep a ~** (*or* **didn't have a ~ of sleep**) я всю ночь не сомкну́л глаз; **have, take forty ~s** (*coll.*) вздремну́ть (*pf.*). **2.** (*coll., very short time*) миг; **in a ~** сию́ мину́ту; момента́льно; ми́гом.

v.t.: **~ one's eye** подми́г|ивать, -ну́ть; морг|а́ть, -ну́ть; **he ~ed away a tear** он сморгну́л слезу́.

v.i.: **~ at s.o.** подми́г|ивать, -ну́ть кому́-н.; **~ at sth.** (*connive at*) смотре́ть (*impf.*) сквозь па́льцы на что-н.; **it's as easy as ~ing** э́то раз плю́нуть; э́то ле́гче лёгкого; (*of star, light etc.*) мига́ть (*impf.*); мерца́ть (*impf.*); **~ing lights** (*on car*) мига́ющие огни́.

winker ['wɪŋkə(r)] *n.* (*indicator light*) мига́лка, индика́тор поворо́та.

winkle ['wɪŋk(ə)l] *n.* морска́я ули́тка.

v.t.: **~ out** (*fig.*) извл|ека́ть, -е́чь; выковы́ривать, вы́ковырять; выта́скивать, вы́тащить.

winner ['wɪnə(r)] *n.* победи́тель (*fem.* -ница), призёр (*fem., coll.* -ша), лауреа́т (*fem.* -ка); **who was the ~?** кто вы́играл/победи́л?; **he backed three ~s** он три ра́за ста́вил на пра́вильную ло́шадь; (*successful thg.*) верня́к (*coll.*); **her new book is a ~** её но́вая кни́га име́ет потряса́ющий успе́х; **he comes out with a ~ every time** вся́кий раз у него́ уда́ча.

winning ['wɪnɪŋ] *adj.* **1.** (*victorious*) вы́игравший, победи́вший; **the ~ team** кома́нда-победи́тельница. **2.** (*bringing about a win*) выи́грывающий, принося́щий вы́игрыш; **~ card** вы́игрышная ка́рта; **~ stroke** реша́ющий уда́р. **3.** (*persuasive, attractive*) привлека́тельный, обая́тельный; **~ ways** прия́тные мане́ры; **a ~ smile** обая́тельная/подкупа́ющая улы́бка.

cpd. **~-post** *n.* фи́нишный столб.

winnings ['wɪnɪŋz] *n. pl.* вы́игрыш.

winnow ['wɪnəʊ] *v.t.* ве́ять (*impf.*); отве́|ивать, -ять; (*fig.*) отсе́|ивать, -ять; просе́|ивать, -ять; пров|еря́ть, -е́рить; **~ truth from fiction** отдел|я́ть, -и́ть пра́вду от вы́мысла.

with advs.: **~ away, ~ out chaff from grain** отве́|ивать, -ять поло́ву/мяки́ну от зерна́.

winsome ['wɪnsəm] *adj.* привлека́тельный, обая́тельный; подкупа́ющий, располага́ющий.

winter ['wɪntə(r)] *n.* зима́; **in ~** зимо́й; (*attr.*) зи́мний; **~ crop** ози́мая культу́ра; **~ garden** зи́мний сад; **~ quarters** зи́мние кварти́ры; **~ sleep** зи́мняя спя́чка; **~ sports** зи́мные ви́ды спо́рта; **W~'s Tale** (*play title*) «Зи́мняя ска́зка».

v.i. зимова́ть, пере-.

cpds. **~-time** *n.* зима́; **~-weight** *adj.* зи́мний, тёплый.

wintry ['wɪntrɪ] *adj.* зи́мний, моро́зный; (*fig.*) холо́дный, ледяно́й, неприве́тливый.

wipe [waɪp] *n.*: **give this plate a ~!** вы́трите э́ту таре́лку!; **she gave the baby's face a ~** она́ вы́терла ребёнку лицо́.

v.t. **1.** (*rub clean or dry*) вытира́ть, вы́тереть; прот|ира́ть, -ере́ть; обт|ира́ть, -ере́ть; **~ s.o.'s nose** вы́тереть (*pf.*) кому́-н. нос; **~ one's eyes** утере́ть (*pf.*) слёзы; **she ~d the dishes** она́ вы́терла посу́ду; **he ~d the floor** он протёр пол; **~ the floor with s.o.** (*fig., coll.*) утере́ть (*pf.*) нос кому́-н.; **~ your shoes on the mat!** оботри́те но́ги/боти́нки о ко́врик!; **~ sth. dry** на́сухо вы́тереть (*pf.*) что-н. **2.** (*efface*) ст|ира́ть, -ере́ть; ликвиди́ровать (*impf.*, *pf.*); **~ a mark off the wall** стере́ть (*pf.*) пятно́ со стены́.

with advs.: **~ away** *v.t.* ст|ира́ть, -ере́ть; ут|ира́ть, -ере́ть; **she ~d away a tear** она́ смахну́ла слезу́; **~ down** *v.t.* прот|ира́ть, -ере́ть; **~ off** *v.t.* ст|ира́ть, -ере́ть; **this debt will take years to ~ off** что́бы погаси́ть э́тот долг, потре́буются го́ды; **the town was ~d off the map** го́род был стёрт с лица́ земли́; **~ out** *v.t.* (*clean*) вытира́ть, вы́тереть; прот|ира́ть, -ере́ть; (*expunge*): **~ out an insult** смыть (*pf.*) оскорбле́ние; **I can't ~ out the memory** я не могу́ отогна́ть воспомина́ние; (*destroy*) уничт|ожа́ть, -о́жить; **the disease ~d out the entire population** эпиде́мия по́лностью уничто́жила населе́ние; **~ over** *v.t.* (слегка́) прот|ира́ть, -ере́ть; пройти́сь (*pf.*) тря́пкой по+*d.*; **~ up** *v.t.* подт|ира́ть, -ере́ть.

wiper ['waɪpə(r)] (*coll.*) = **windscreen-wiper**

wire ['waɪə(r)] *n.* **1.** (*fine-drawn metal; a length of this*) про́волока; про́вод (*pl.* -а́); **barbed ~** колю́чая про́волока; **chicken ~** про́волочная се́тка; **pull ~s** (*fig., exert influence*) пуска́ть (*impf.*) в ход свя́зи; **~ mattress** пружи́нный матра́ц; **~ netting** про́волочная се́тка; **~ rope** трос; **~ wool** про́волочная моча́лка; ёж(ик). **2.** (*as mil. defence*) про́волочные загражде́ния; (*as barrier, fencing etc.*) про́волочная се́тка. **3.** (*elec.*) про́вод; **fuse ~** пла́вкий предохрани́тель; **telephone ~** телефо́нный ка́бель; **send a message by ~** сообщи́ть (*pf.*) что-н. телегра́ммой (*or* по телегра́фу); посла́ть (*pf.*) телегра́мму; телеграфи́ровать (*impf.*, *pf.*); **live ~** (*lit.*) про́вод под напряже́нием/то́ком; (*fig., of pers.*) (челове́к-)ого́нь, живчик; **get one's ~s crossed** (*fig.*) запу́таться (*pf.*); неве́рно поня́ть (*pf.*) что-н. **4.** (*coll., telegram*) телегра́мма.

v.t. **1.** (*provide, strengthen or fasten with ~*) свя́з|ывать, -а́ть (*or* скреп|ля́ть, -и́ть) про́волокой. **2.** (*snare with ~*) лови́ть (*impf.*) в про́волочные силки́. **3.** (*coll., send telegram to*) телеграфи́ровать (*impf.*, *pf.*) +*d.* **4.** (*elec.*): **they ~d the house** они́ сде́лали прово́дку в до́ме.

v.i. (*coll., telegraph*) телеграфи́ровать (*impf.*, *pf.*); **they ~d for him to come** они́ вы́звали его́ телегра́ммой.

with advs.: **~ together** *v.t.* скреп|ля́ть, -и́ть про́волокой; **~ up** *v.t.* (*connect*) подключ|а́ть, -и́ть.

cpds. **~-brush** *n.* про́волочная щётка; **~-cutters** *n. pl.* куса́ч|ки (*pl., g.* -ек); **~-gauge** *n.* (*instrument*) про́волочный кали́бр; **~-haired** *adj.* жесткошёрст(н)ый; **~-puller** *n.* (*coll.*) ма́стер закули́сных махина́ций; ловка́ч; **~-tapping** *n.* подслу́шивание телефо́нных разгово́ров; подслу́шка; **~worm** *n.* жук-щелку́н.

wireless ['waɪəlɪs] *n.* **1.** (**~** *telegraphy*) беспро́волочный телегра́ф; **~ officer** ради́ст. **2.** (*sound radio*) ра́дио (*indecl.*); **~ enthusiast** радиолюби́тель (*m.*); **I heard it on the ~** я э́то слы́шал по ра́дио. **3.** (*broadcast receiver: also* **~ set**) (радио)приёмник; ра́дио.

v.t. (*send by ~*) ради́ровать (*impf.*, *pf.*) (*что кому*); опове|ща́ть, -сти́ть (*кого*) по ра́дио.

wiring ['waɪərɪŋ] *n.* (*elec.*) электропрово́дка; **~ diagram** монта́жная схе́ма.

wiry ['waɪərɪ] *adj.* (*of pers.*) жи́листый, двужи́льный.

wisdom ['wɪzdəm] *n.* му́дрость; (*prudence*) благоразу́мие, разу́мность; **~ tooth** зуб му́дрости; **the W~ of Solomon** Кни́га прему́дрости Соломо́на; **worldly ~** жите́йская му́дрость.

wise[1] [waɪz] *n.* (*arch.*) о́браз, спо́соб; **in no ~** нико́им о́бразом; **in, on this ~** таки́м о́бразом/спо́собом.

wise[2] [waɪz] *adj.* **1.** (*sage*) му́дрый; **~ counsel** му́дрый сове́т; **the W~ Men** (*bibl.*) волхвы́ (*m. pl.*); **get, grow ~r** умне́ть, по-; **he nodded ~ly** он глубокомы́сленно кива́л голово́й. **2.** (*sensible, prudent*) у́мный, благоразу́мный; **~ after the event** за́дним умо́м кре́пок; **you were ~ not to attempt it** вы пра́вильно сде́лали, что не ста́ли пыта́ться; **it's not ~ to bathe on this coast** не рекоменду́ется/сто́ит купа́ться на э́том берегу́; **he ~ly refused** он име́л му́дрость отказа́ться. **3.** (*well-informed*) осведомлённый; **now that you've told me I am none the ~r** да́же по́сле ва́шего объясне́ния я ма́ло чего́ понима́ю; **you could**

sneak in without anyone's being the ~r вы мо́жете тихо́нько войти́, и никто́ не заме́тит; **~ guy** (*US sl.*) «у́мник»; всезна́йка (*c.g.*); **put s.o. ~ to sth.** (*coll.*) ввести́ (*pf.*) кого́-н. в курс де́ла; откры́ть (*pf.*) кому́-н. глаза́ на что-н.; **be ~ to sth.** (*coll.*) быть в ку́рсе дел; ви́деть (*impf.*) что-н. наскво́зь; **get ~ to** (*coll.*) подм|еча́ть, -е́тить; пон|има́ть, -я́ть; прове́дать (*pf.*). **4.** (*arch., having occult power*): **~ woman** зна́харка; гада́лка.

v.t.: **~ up** (*US sl.*) надоу́мить (*pf.*).

cpds. **~acre** *n.* у́мник, всезна́йка (*c.g.*); **~crack** (*coll.*) *n.* шу́тка, острота́; *v.i.* остри́ть (*impf.*).

wish [wɪʃ] *n.* **1.** (*desire*) жела́ние, во́ля; (*request*) про́сьба; **I have no ~ to interfere** я не собира́юсь вме́шиваться; **the ~ is often father to the thought** лю́ди охо́тно принима́ют жела́емое за действи́тельное; **if ~es were horses, beggars would ride** (*prov.*) е́сли бы да кабы́, во рту росли́ грибы́; **make a ~!** загада́йте жела́ние!; **he expressed the ~ that** он вы́разил жела́ние, что́бы; **you acted against my ~es** вы де́йствовали/поступи́ли про́тив мое́й во́ли. **2.** (*thg. ~ed for or requested*) предме́т жела́ний; мечта́; **he got his ~** его́ жела́ние сбыло́сь; его́ мечта́ сбыла́сь. **3.** (*hope on another's behalf*) пожела́ние; **best ~es!** всего́ наилу́чшего!; **with every good ~** с наилу́чшими пожела́ниями.

v.t. **1.** (*want, require*) жела́ть (*impf.*); хоте́ть (*impf.*) (*both +a. or g., inf. or* что́бы). **2.** (*expr. unfulfilled desire*): **I ~ I'd never been born** ах, заче́м то́лько меня́ мать родила́!; **I ~ I hadn't gone there** я жале́ю, что пошёл туда́; **I only ~ I knew** е́сли бы я то́лько знал; хотел бы я знать; **I ~ you'd be quiet** нельзя́ ли не шуме́ть?; не шуми́те, пожа́луйста!; **I ~ he was alive** кабы́ он был жив!; **he ~ed himself dead** он мечта́л о сме́рти; ему́ не хоте́лось жить; **I could have ~ed him further** (*coll.*) я бы охо́тно посла́л его́ пода́льше (*or* ко всем чертя́м); **she ~ed she had stayed at home** она пожале́ла, что не оста́лась до́ма; **I ~ he hadn't left so soon** как жаль, что он ушёл так ра́но. **3.** (*with double object*): **I ~ him well** я жела́ю ему́ добра́; **I ~ed him good morning** я пожела́л ему́ до́брого утра́; я поздоро́вался с ним; **I ~ you many happy returns** поздравля́ю вас с днём рожде́ния; **I ~ed him goodbye** я попроща́лся с ним. **4.** (*coll., inflict*) навя́з|ывать, -а́ть; **I had the job ~ed on me** мне навяза́ли э́ту рабо́ту; **I wouldn't ~ this headache on anyone** тако́й головно́й бо́ли и врагу́ своему́ не пожела́ю.

v.i: **she has everything a woman could ~ for** у неё есть всё, о чём то́лько же́нщина мо́жет мечта́ть; **~ing will get you nowhere** от хоте́ния то́лку ма́ло.

cpds. **~-bone** *n.* ду́жка; **~-fulfilment** *n.* исполне́ние (та́йных/подсозна́тельных) жела́ний.

wishful ['wɪʃfʊl] *adj.*: **he is ~ of ...** ему́ хо́чется *+inf.*; **~ thinking** самообольще́ние; приня́тие жела́емого за действи́тельное.

wishy-washy ['wɪʃɪ,wɒʃɪ] *adj.* (*of liquid*) жи́дкий, сла́бый; (*of pers.*) вя́лый; (*sentimental*) сентимента́льный; (*of style*) вя́лый, водяни́стый.

wisp [wɪsp] *n.* пучо́к, клок; **a ~ of hay** пучо́к се́на; **a ~ of hair** прядь воло́с; **a ~ of smoke** стру́йка ды́ма; **a ~ of a girl** то́ненькая де́вушка.

wispy ['wɪspɪ] *adj.* лёгкий, то́нкий; **~ hair** ре́дкие растрёпанные во́лосы.

wist|aria [wɪ'steərɪə], **-eria** [wɪ'stɪərɪə] *n.* глици́ния.

wistful ['wɪstfʊl] *adj.* тоску́ющий, тоскли́вый; **a ~ smile** мечта́тельная улы́бка; **the child looked ~ly at the cake** ребёнок мечта́тельно (*or* с тоско́й) смотре́л на пиро́жное.

wistfulness ['wɪstfʊlnɪs] *n.* тоска́, мечта́тельность.

wit[1] [wɪt] *n.* **1.** (*intelligence*) ум, ра́зум, соображе́ние; **he hadn't the ~(s) (*or* ~ enough) to realise what had happened** у него́ не доста́ло ума́ поня́ть, что случи́лось; **at one's ~'s end** в отча́янии; **I am at my ~'s end to know what to do** про́сто ума́ не приложу́, что де́лать; **you will drive me out of my ~s** вы меня́ сведёте с ума́; **he was out of his ~s with worry** он был сам не свой от трево́ги; **he has a ready ~** он за сло́вом в карма́н не поле́зет; **keep one's ~s about one** не растеря́ться (*pf.*); **he lives by his ~s** он авантюри́ст; **he was scared out of his ~s** он был до́ сме́рти напу́ган. **2.** (*verbal ingenuity*) остроу́мие. **3.** (*pers.*) остря́|к (*fem. coll.* -чка).

wit[2] [wɪt] *v.* (*arch.*): **to ~** то есть; а и́менно.

witch [wɪtʃ] *n.* **1.** (*sorceress*) ве́дьма; **~es' sabbath** ша́баш ведьм. **2.** (*charmer*) чаровни́ца. **3.** (*hag*) ве́дьма, ста́рая карга́.

v.t. (*arch.*): **the ~ing hour** глуха́я по́лночь.

cpds. **~craft** *n.* чёрная ма́гия, колдовство́; **~-doctor** *n.* зна́харь (*m.*); **~-elm, -hazel** *nn.* = **wych-elm, -hazel; ~-hunt** *n.* (*lit., fig.*) охо́та за ве́дьмами.

witchery ['wɪtʃərɪ] *n.* (*witchcraft*) колдовство́; (*fascination*) ча́р|ы (*pl., g.* —).

with [wɪð] *prep.* **1.** (*expr. accompaniment*) *usu.* c+*i.*; **come ~ me!** пойдёмте со мной!; **she has no-one to play ~** ей не́ с кем игра́ть; **he is ~ the manager** он у заве́дующего; **he is ~ Shell** он рабо́тает в компа́нии «Шелл»; **~ no hat on** без шля́пы; **~ his charm he will go far** с таки́м обая́нием он далеко́ пойдёт; **meat ~ tomato sauce** мя́со в тома́тном со́усе; **a film ~ Greta Garbo** фильм с уча́стием Гре́ты Га́рбо; **he came ~ the rest** он пришёл вме́сте с остальны́ми. **2.** (*expr. agreement or sympathy*): **he that is not ~ us is against us** кто не с на́ми, тот про́тив нас; **I'm ~ you** (*in understanding*) понима́ю; (*in opinion*) я с ва́ми согла́сен; (*in support*) я на ва́шей стороне́; **he is ~ it** (*sl.*) он в ку́рсе; он зна́ет, что к чему́; **get ~ it!** очни́сь! (*sl.*). **3.**: **I lost patience ~ him** я потеря́л с ним вся́кое терпе́ние; **don't be rough ~ the cat!** не обраща́йтесь так гру́бо с ко́шкой!; **are you pleased ~ the result?** вы дово́льны результа́том?; **what do you want ~ me?** что вы от меня́ хоти́те?; **what has it to do ~ him?** при чём тут он?; како́е э́то име́ет к нему́ отноше́ние?; **I have business ~ him** у меня́ есть де́ло к нему́; **influence ~ the President** влия́ние на президе́нта. **4.** (*expr. antagonism or separation*): **don't argue ~ me** не спо́рьте со мной; **at war ~** в состоя́нии войны́ c+*i.*; **a break ~ tradition** отхо́д от тради́ции. **5.** (*in the case of*) у+*g.*; c+*i.*; **it's a habit ~ me** у меня́ така́я привы́чка; **~ children it's different** с детьми́ совсе́м друго́е де́ло; **it's a holiday ~ us** у нас сейча́с пра́здник. **6.** (*denoting host or pers. in charge, possession etc.*): **we stayed ~ our friends** мы жи́ли у друзе́й; **the boy was left ~ his aunt** ма́льчика оста́вили у тётки (*or* с тёткой); **I have no money ~ me** у меня́ нет с собо́й (*or* при себе́) де́нег; **the next move is ~ you** сле́дующий ход за ва́ми. **7.** (*denoting instrument or means*): **I am writing ~ a pen** я пишу́ перо́м; **he walks ~ a stick** он хо́дит с па́лкой; (*by means of*) с по́мощью (*or* при по́мощи) +*g.*; посре́дством+*g.*; **the word begins/ends ~ an A** э́то сло́во начина́ется/конча́ется на «А»; **it is written ~ a hyphen** э́то пи́шется че́рез дефи́с; **I bought a suit ~ the £100** на э́ти сто фу́нтов я купи́л себе́ костю́м; **they fought ~ swords** они́ дра́лись на шпа́гах. **8.** (*denoting cause*) от+*g.*; **she was shaking ~ fright** она́ дрожа́ла от стра́ха; **he went down ~ flu** он заболе́л гри́ппом; **I am delighted ~ him** я в восто́рге от него́. **9.** (*denoting characteristic*): **a girl ~ blue eyes** голубогла́зая де́вушка; де́вушка с голубы́ми глаза́ми; **~ child** (*pregnant*) бере́менная; **a dressing-gown ~ a blue lining** хала́т на голубо́й подкла́дке; **a tie ~ blue spots** га́лстук в си́них кра́пинках; **a suit ~ grey stripes** костю́м в се́рую поло́ску. **10.** (*denoting manner etc.*): **~ pleasure** с удово́льствием; **~ care** осторо́жно; **he replied ~ a smile** он отве́тил с улы́бкой; **he bore it ~ courage** он перенёс э́то му́жественно. **11.** (*in the same direction or degree as; at the same time as*): **the rainfall varies ~ the season** коли́чество атмосфе́рных оса́дков меня́ется в зави́симости от вре́мени го́да; **~ the approach of spring** с наступле́нием весны́; **one must move ~ the times** на́до идти́ в но́гу с вре́менем; **I could barely keep up ~ him** я е́ле за ним поспева́л. **12.** (*denoting attendant circumstance*): **I sleep ~ the window open** я сплю с откры́тым окно́м; **he walked off ~ his hands in his pockets** он ушёл, засу́нув ру́ки в карма́ны; **a holiday ~ all expenses paid** по́лностью опла́ченный о́тпуск; **~ your permission** с ва́шего разреше́ния; **ten minutes went by ~ no sign of the leader** прошло́ де́сять мину́т, а руководи́тель всё не появля́лся; ~ **a good secretary this would never have happened** при хоро́шем секретаре́ э́того бы не случи́лось. **13.** (*despite*) несмотря́ на+*a.*; при+*p.*; ~ **all his faults he's a gentleman** несмотря́ на все его́ недоста́тки, он джентльме́н; ~ **the best will in the world** при всём жела́нии. **14.** (*in excl. or command*): **away ~ him!** гони́ его!; **down ~ the door!** взлома́йте дверь!; **down ~ tyranny!** доло́й произво́л!; **off ~ you!** убира́йтесь!; **off ~ your coat!** (доло́й) пальто́!; **out ~ it!** расска́зывайте!; не тайте(сь)!

withal [wɪ'ðɔːl] *adv.* (*arch.*) к тому́ же, вдоба́вок.

withdraw [wɪð'drɔː] *v.t.* отн|има́ть, -я́ть; сн|има́ть, -ять; уб|ира́ть, -ра́ть; ~ **one's hand** отдёр|гивать, -нуть (*or* отн|има́ть, -я́ть) ру́ку; ~ **one's eyes** отв|оди́ть, -ести́ взгляд/глаза́; ~ **a child from school** заб|ира́ть, -ра́ть ребёнка из шко́лы; ~ **a coin from circulation** из|ыма́ть, -ъя́ть моне́ту из обраще́ния; ~ **money from the bank** брать, взять де́ньги из ба́нка; ~ **a horse from a race** сн|има́ть, -я́ть ло́шадь с забе́га; ~ **an ambassador** от|зыва́ть, -озва́ть посла́; ~ **troops** от|води́ть, -вести́ войска́; ~ **an offer** брать, взять обра́тно/наза́д предложе́ние; ~ **a statement** отка́з|ываться, -а́ться от заявле́ния; **a ~n character** за́мкнутый/нелюди́мый челове́к.

v.i. удал|я́ться, -и́ться; ретирова́ться (*impf., pf.*); ~ **from a competition** выбыва́ть, вы́быть из соревнова́ния; ~ **from an enterprise** уходи́ть, уйти́ с предприя́тия; ~ **into o.s.** зам|ыка́ться, -кну́ться в себе́; (*mil.*) от|ходи́ть, -ойти́; **the army withdrew to prepared positions** войска́ отошли́ на зара́нее подгото́вленные пози́ции.

withdrawal [wɪð'drɔːəl] *n.* отня́тие, сня́тие; (*of coinage*) изъя́тие; (*of statement*) отка́з от свои́х слов; (*mil.*) отво́д; (*absenting o.s.*) вы́ход, ухо́д; (*of ambassador*) отозва́ние, отзы́в; (*of drugs*) прекраще́ние приёма нарко́тиков; ~ **symptoms** абстине́нтный синдро́м.

withe [wɪθ, wɪð, waɪð] = withy

wither ['wɪðə(r)] *v.t.* **1.** иссуш|а́ть, -и́ть; **blossom ~ed by frost** цветы́, загу́бленные моро́зом; **~ed leaves** увя́дшие ли́стья; **a ~ed arm** суха́я рука́. **2.** (*fig.*) губи́ть, по-; **she gave me a ~ing glance** она́ бро́сила на меня́ уничтожа́ющий взгляд; она́ меня́ испепели́ла взгля́дом; **~ing scorn** убийственное презре́ние/пренебреже́ние.

v.i. вя́нуть, за-; отс|ыха́ть, -о́хнуть; блёкнуть, по-; **the flowers ~ed in the sun** цветы́ завя́ли на со́лнце; **her beauty ~ed with age** с года́ми её красота́ увя́ла.

with advs.: ~ **away** *v.i.* отс|ыха́ть, -о́хнуть; ча́хнуть, за-; (*of the state*) отм|ира́ть, -ере́ть; ~ **up** *v.i.* отс|ыха́ть, -о́хнуть.

withers ['wɪðəz] *n.* хо́лка, загри́вок; **my ~ are unwrung** (*fig.*) э́то меня́ не тро́гает.

withershins ['wɪðəʃɪnz], **widdershins** ['wɪdəʃɪnz] *adv.* про́тив движе́ния со́лнца.

withhold [wɪð'həʊld] *v.t.* **1.** (*refuse to give*) отка́з|ывать, -а́ть в (*чём*); возде́рж|иваться, -а́ться от (*чего*); ~ **one's consent** не да|ва́ть, -ть согла́сия; ~ **support** не ока́з|ывать, -а́ть подде́ржки; ~ **payment** уде́рж|ивать, -а́ть (*or* заде́рж|ивать, -а́ть) опла́ту; ~ **a visa** не да|ва́ть, -ть ви́зы; ~ **information** ута́|ивать, -и́ть информа́цию. **2.** (*restrain*) уде́рж|ивать, -а́ть.

within [wɪ'ðɪn] *adv.* внутри́; **from ~** изнутри́; **he is outwardly calm but raging ~** вне́шне он споко́ен, но в душе́ его́ всё кипи́т.

prep. **1.** (*inside*) в+*p.*; внутри́+*g.*; **you can talk safely ~ these walls** в э́тих стена́х вы мо́жете говори́ть свобо́дно; ~ **doors** (*liter.*) до́ма, в помеще́нии; **a voice ~ him said 'no'** вну́тренний го́лос сказа́л ему́ «нет»; **my heart sank ~ me** у меня́ упа́ло се́рдце; **'he's lying,' I thought ~ myself** «он врёт», поду́мал я про себя́. **2.** (*nor farther than; accessible to*) в преде́лах +*g.*; **there are 3 stations ~ a (radius of a) mile** в ра́диусе одно́й ми́ли име́ются 3 ста́нции; **the library is ~ walking distance** до библиоте́ки мо́жно дойти́ пешко́м; ~ **earshot** в преде́лах слы́шимости; на расстоя́нии слы́шимости (го́лоса); **we are ~ sight of our goal** мы почти́ дости́гли це́ли; ~ **reach** в зо́не/преде́лах досяга́емости; ~ **sight** в преде́лах ви́димости; **we kept ~ sight of land** мы плы́ли, не теря́я из виду бе́рега; **he came ~ an ace of death** он был на волосо́к от сме́рти; он чуть не у́мер. **3.** (*of time*) в тече́ние +*g.*; на протяже́нии +*g.*; за+*a.*; ~ **(the next) three days** в тече́ние (ближа́йших) трёх дней; не по́зже, чем че́рез три дня; в трёхдне́вный срок; **I can finish the job ~ a week** я могу́ ко́нчить э́ту рабо́ту за неде́лю; **they died ~ a year of each other** они́ у́мерли оди́н за други́м в тече́ние го́да; ~ **a year of his death** (*sc. after*) ме́ньше чем че́рез год по́сле его́ сме́рти; не прошло́ и го́да с его́ сме́рти, как…; (*sc. before*) ме́ньше чем за́ год до его́ сме́рти; **the letters came ~ a few days of each other** пи́сьма пришли́ одно́ за други́м с промежу́тком в не́сколько дней. **4.** (~ *limits of*) в преде́лах/ра́мках +*g.*; **live ~ one's income** жить (*impf.*) по сре́дствам; ~ **one's rights** по пра́ву; **it is ~ his powers** э́то ему́ по си́лам; э́то вхо́дит в его́ компете́нцию; **it comes ~ their jurisdiction** э́то подпада́ет под их юрисди́кцию; **keep ~ the law** держа́ться (*impf.*) в ра́мках зако́на; **keep ~ the speed limit** не превыша́ть (*impf.*) устано́вленной ско́рости; **he will tell you your weight ~ a pound** он определи́т ваш вес с то́чностью до фу́нта; ~ **limits** до изве́стной сте́пени.

without [wɪ'ðaʊt] *adv.* (*arch., liter.*) снару́жи; за две́рью; на дворе́.

prep. **1.** (*arch., outside*) вне+*g.*; ~ **the city wall** за̀ городско́й стено́й. **2.** (*not having; lacking; free from*) без+*g.*; ~ **delay** сра́зу же; безотлага́тельно; то́тчас (же); ~ **doubt** без сомне́ния; ~ **fail** непреме́нно; ~ **success** безуспе́шно; **times ~ number** бессчётное число́ раз; ~ **regard to the consequences** несмотря́ на после́дствия; не заду́мываясь о после́дствиях; **it goes ~ saying** само́ собо́й разуме́ется; (*with n. understood*): **the gas was cut off and we were ~ for several hours** газ отключи́ли, и нам пришло́сь обходи́ться без него́ не́сколько часо́в; **even in hard times they have never gone ~** да́же в са́мые тяжёлые времена́ они́ не голода́ли; **if you can't afford cigarettes, then do ~** е́сли у вас нет де́нег на сигаре́ты, не кури́те; (*with gerund*): ~ **thinking** не ду́мая; не поду́мав; **he did it ~ being caught** ему удало́сь э́то сде́лать и не попа́сться; **he did it ~ anyone finding out** он э́то сде́лал так, что никто́ не узна́л; **he left ~ so much as saying goodbye** он ушёл, да́же не прости́вшись; **he left ~ my seeing him** он ушёл, а я так с ним и не повида́лся.

withstand [wɪð'stænd] *v.t.* устоя́ть (*pf.*) пе́ред+*i.*; выде́рживать, вы́держать; сопротивля́ться (*impf.*) +*d.*; ~ **a siege** вы́держать (*pf.*) оса́ду; ~ **temptation** устоя́ть (*pf.*) пе́ред собла́зном; не подда́ться (*pf.*) собла́зну.

v.i. выста́ивать, вы́стоять.

with|y ['wɪðɪ], **-e** [wɪθ, wɪð, waɪð] *n.* жгут; и́вовый прут.

witless ['wɪtlɪs] *adj.* (*of pers.*) безмо́зглый, глу́пый; (*of action*) бесмы́сленный.

witlessness ['wɪtlɪsnɪs] *n.* бессмы́сленность.

witness ['wɪtnɪs] *n.* **1.** (*eye-*) очеви́д|ец (*fem.* -ица); свиде́тель (*fem.* -ница); **as God is my ~** ви́дит Бог. **2.** (*in court of law*) свиде́тель (*fem.* -ница); (*present at search, inventory etc.*) понято́й. **3.** (*testimony*) свиде́тельство; **bear ~** свиде́тельствовать (*impf.*); дава́ть (*impf.*) показа́ния; (*speak in support of*) подтвержда́ть (*impf.*); руча́ться, поручи́ться за+*a.*; **bear false ~** лжесвиде́тельствовать (*impf.*); **call to ~** приз|ыва́ть, -ва́ть (*кого*) в свиде́тели; ссыла́ться, сосла́ться на+*a.*; **in ~ whereof** в подтвержде́ние/доказа́тельство чего́; (*fig.*): **his clothes are a ~ to his vanity** его́ мане́ра одева́ться свиде́тельствует/говори́т о его́ тщесла́вии; **(as) ~ my poverty** о чём свиде́тельствует моя́ нищета́.

v.t. **1.** (*be spectator of*) быть свиде́телем/очеви́дцем +*g.*; **the race was ~ed by a large crowd** на ска́чках прису́тствовало мно́жество наро́ду; **no-one ~ed the accident** никто́ не ви́дел, как произошла́ катастро́фа; **Europe ~ed many wars** Евро́па повида́ла нема́ло войн. **2.** (*be evidence of*) свиде́тельствовать (*impf.*) о+*p.* **3.:** ~ **s.o.'s signature** зав|еря́ть, -е́рить чью-н. по́дпись.

v.i.: **I can ~ to the truth of that** я могу́ засвиде́тельствовать, что э́то пра́вда; **he ~ed to having**

known the accused он показа́л, что был знако́м с обвиня́емым.

cpds. **~-box, ~-stand** *nn.* ме́сто для да́чи свиде́тельских показа́ний; **take the ~-stand** (*fig.*) выступа́ть, вы́ступить в ка́честве свиде́теля.

witticism [ˈwɪtɪˌsɪz(ə)m] *n.* острота́.

wittiness [ˈwɪtɪnɪs] *n.* остроу́мие.

wittingly [ˈwɪtɪŋlɪ] *adv.* заве́домо, созна́тельно, умы́шленно.

witty [ˈwɪtɪ] *adj.* остроу́мный.

wizard [ˈwɪzəd] *n.* (*magician*) колду́н, куде́сник; (*fig.*) волше́бник; **a financial ~** фина́нсовый ге́ний.

adj. (*sl.*) чуде́сный.

wizardry [ˈwɪzədrɪ] *n.* колдовство́; (*fig.*) ча́р|ы (*pl.*, *g.* —).

wizen(ed) [ˈwɪz(ə)nd] *adj.* вы́сохший, иссо́хший, морщи́нистый, смо́рщенный.

wo [wəʊ] = **whoa**

woad [wəʊd] *n.* (*plant*) ва́йда; (*dye*) сини́ль.

wobble [ˈwɒb(ə)l] *n.* кача́ние, поша́тывание; **front-wheel ~** вихля́ние пере́дних колёс.

v.t. (*also* **~ about**) шата́ть (*impf.*).

v.i. (*also* **~ about**) шата́ться; ковыля́ть; кача́ться; колыха́ться; вихля́ть (*all impf.*); (*fig.*, *vacillate*) колеба́ться (*impf.*); (*quaver*): **she ~s on the top notes** на высо́ких но́тах у неё дрожи́т го́лос.

wobbly [ˈwɒblɪ] *adj.* (*lit.*, *fig.*) ша́ткий, неусто́йчивый; **he is still ~ after his fall** он всё ещё нетвёрдо де́ржится на нога́х по́сле паде́ния.

wodge [wɒdʒ] *n.* (*coll.*) ком, кусо́к.

woe [wəʊ] *n.* **1.** (*grief*, *distress*) го́ре, скорбь; **tale of ~** го́рестная исто́рия; **~ is me!** (*liter. or joc.*) го́ре мне!; увы́ (мне)! **2.** (*pl.*, *troubles*) бе́ды (*f. pl.*), неприя́тности (*f. pl.*); **he had a cure for all the world's ~s** у него́ был гото́в реце́пт про́тив всех невзго́д ми́ра.

cpd. **~begone** *adj.* удручённый, го́рестный.

woeful [ˈwəʊfʊl] *adj.* ско́рбный, го́рестный, жа́лкий, уны́лый; **a ~ countenance** ско́рбное лицо́; **~ ignorance** вопию́щее неве́жество.

wog [wɒg] *n.* (*sl.*, *pej.*) черномазый.

wok [wɒk] *n.* котело́к (с вы́пуклым дни́щем).

wold [wəʊld] *n.* пусты́нное наго́рье.

wolf [wʊlf] *n.* (*animal*) волк; **(she-~)** волчи́ца; **cry ~** (*fig.*) подн|има́ть, -я́ть ло́жную трево́гу; **keep the ~ from the door** (*fig.*) зараба́тывать (*impf.*) на пропита́ние; перебива́ться (*impf.*); **lone ~** (*fig.*) единоли́чни|к (*fem.* -ца), индивидуали́ст (*fem.* -ка); **~ in sheep's clothing** (*fig.*) волк в ове́чьей шку́ре; **throw s.o. to the wolves** (*fig.*) бр|оса́ть, -о́сить кого́-н. на произво́л судьбы́; (*rapacious or greedy pers.*) волк, хи́щник; (*coll.*, *sexually aggressive male*) кобе́ль (*m.*), ба́бник.

v.t. (*coll.*, *also* **~ down**) прогл|а́тывать, -оти́ть с жа́дностью.

cpds. **~-cub** *n.* волчо́нок; **~-dog** *n.* волкода́в; **~hound** *n.* волкода́в; **~-pack** *n.* ста́я волко́в; во́лчья ста́я; **~-whistle** *n.* (*coll.*) свист при ви́де краси́вой де́вушки.

wolfish [ˈwʊlfɪʃ] *adj.* во́лчий, зве́рский.

wolfram [ˈwʊlfrəm] *n.* вольфра́м.

wolverine [ˈwʊlvəˌriːn] *n.* росома́ха.

woman [ˈwʊmən] *n.* **1.** же́нщина; **my good ~** ми́лая; **kept ~** содержа́нка; **the little ~** (*joc.*, *my wife*) жёнушка, хозя́йка; **old ~** (*lit.*) стару́ха; (*coll.*, *wife*) жена́, хозя́йка; **the 'other ~'** (*in sexual triangle*) любо́вница, разлу́чница; **single ~** незаму́жняя же́нщина; **~ of the town** у́личная же́нщина; **~ of the world** све́тская/быва́лая же́нщина; **play the ~** вести́ (*det.*) себя́ как ба́ба; **a ~'s place is in the home** ме́сто же́нщины — до́ма (*or* у очага́); **women's rights** же́нское равнопра́вие; **man born of ~** (*bibl.*) сме́ртный; рождённый же́нщиной. **2.** (*femininity*): **there is little of the ~ in her** в ней ма́ло же́нственности; **all the ~ in her rebelled** вся её же́нская суть восста́ла про́тив э́того. **3.** (*coll.*, *charwoman*): **daily ~** приходя́щая домрабо́тница. **4.** (*arch.*, *female attendant*) камери́стка, фре́йлина. **5.** (*illicit sexual partner*) любо́вница. **6.** (*man with feminine characteristics*) ба́ба; **he is an old ~** он настоя́щая ба́ба; **~ doctor** же́нщина-врач; **~ friend** подру́га, прия́тельница.

cpds. **womenfolk** *n. pl.* же́нщины (*f. pl.*); (*of household*) же́нская полови́на; **~-hater** *n.* женоненави́стник; **~kind** *n.* же́нщины (*f. pl.*); же́нская полови́на; **~-servant** *n.* служа́нка.

womanhood [ˈwʊmənˌhʊd] *n.* **1.** (*maturity*) же́нская зре́лость; **grow to (*or* reach) ~** созр|ева́ть, -е́ть. **2.** (*instinct*) же́нственность; же́нские ка́чества.

womanish [ˈwʊmənɪʃ] *adj.* женоподо́бный, же́нственный.

womanize [ˈwʊməˌnaɪz] *v.t.* (*make effeminate*) прид|ава́ть, -а́ть же́нские черты́ +*d*.

v.i. (*coll.*, *philander*) пу́таться (*impf.*) с ба́бами; волочи́ться/гоня́ться (*both impf.*) за ю́бками.

womanizer [ˈwʊməˌnaɪzə(r)] *n.* (*coll.*) женолю́б, ба́бник, волоки́та (*m.*).

womanliness [ˈwʊmənlɪnɪs] *n.* же́нственность.

womanly [ˈwʊmənlɪ] *adj.* же́нственный, же́нский; не́жный, мя́гкий.

womb [wuːm] *n.* **1.** ма́тка; (*fig.*) утро́ба; **fruit of the ~** (*liter.*) плод чре́ва; ребёнок. **2.** (*fig.*): **nations yet in the ~ of time** ещё не рождённые наро́ды.

wombat [ˈwɒmbæt] *n.* вомба́т.

Women's Libber [ˈwɪmɪnz ˈlɪbə(r)] *n.* эмансипи́рованная же́нщина, эмансипе́.

Women's Liberation [ˈwɪmɪnz lɪbəˈreɪʃ(ə)n] *n.* эмансипа́ция же́нщин; **~ movement** движе́ние за эмансипа́цию же́нщин.

wonder [ˈwʌndə(r)] *n.* **1.** (*miracle*, *marvel*) чу́до; **work ~s** твори́ть, со- чудеса́; **vitamin C does ~s** витами́н C — чудоде́йственное сре́дство; (*marvel*): **nine days ~** кратковре́менная сенса́ция; **~s will never cease** (*joc.*) чудеса́ в решете́; чудеса́, да и то́лько!; **that child is a little ~** э́тот ребёнок настоя́щий/су́щий вундерки́нд; (*surprising thg.*): **the ~ is that ...** удиви́тельно, что...; что удиви́тельно/стра́нно, э́то то, что...; **for a ~** как ни стра́нно; **small ~ that ...** неудиви́тельно, что...; **no ~ he was angry!** неудиви́тельно, что он рассерди́лся!; ещё бы ему́ не рассерди́ться! **2.** (*amazement*, *admiration*) изумле́ние, восхище́ние; **the sight filled him with ~** зре́лище его́ порази́ло/изуми́ло; **I looked at him in ~** я смотре́л на него́, рази́нув рот (*or* с удивле́нием); **they were struck with ~** они́ бы́ли потрясены́/поражены́.

v.t. **1.** (*be surprised*): **I ~ he wasn't killed** удиви́тельно, что он оста́лся в живы́х; **he will be out, I shouldn't ~** вполне́ возмо́жно, что его́ не ока́жется до́ма; **I shouldn't ~ if it rained** я не удивлю́сь, е́сли пойдёт дождь. **2.** (*deliberate*, *desire to know*): **I ~ who that was** интере́сно/любопы́тно (*or* хоте́лось бы знать), кто бы э́то мог быть; **he ~ed if she was coming** он гада́л, придёт она́ и́ли нет; **you will ~ why I said that** вы спро́сите, почему́ я э́то сказа́л; **I was ~ing whether to invite him** я не мог реши́ть, приглаша́ть его́ и́ли нет; **it makes you ~ where they find the money** не понима́ю (*or* удиви́тельно), отку́да то́лько у них де́ньги беру́тся; **I ~ if I might open the window** вы не возража́ете, е́сли я откро́ю окно́? *See also v.i.*

v.i. **1.** (*feel surprised*) удив|ля́ться, -и́ться (*чему*); пора|жа́ться, -зи́ться (*чему*); диви́ться (*impf*) (*чему*); **I ~ed at his foolishness** я был поражён его́ легкомы́слием; **this is not to be ~ed at** здесь не́чему удивля́ться; в э́том нет ничего́ удиви́тельного; **can you ~ that he got hurt?** неудиви́тельно, что он ушиб́ся. **2.** (*feel curiosity*) интересова́ться (*impf.*); **I was ~ing about that** я и сам разду́мывал об э́том; **'Why do you ask?' — 'I just ~ed'** «Почему́ вы спра́шиваете?» — «Про́сто так». **3.** (*expr. doubt*): **I ~** я не уве́рен; сомнева́юсь; **you tell me he's clever. I ~!** вы утвержда́ете, что он спосо́бный. Не зна́ю, не зна́ю — мо́жет быть.

cpds. **~land** *n.* страна́ чуде́с; **~-stricken, ~-struck** *adjs.* поражённый, изумлённый; **~-worker** *n.* чудотво́рец.

wonderful [ˈwʌndəˌfʊl] *adj.* изуми́тельный, удиви́тельный, порази́тельный; **what ~ weather!** кака́я чу́дная пого́да!; **you have a ~ memory** у вас замеча́тельная па́мять; **she is ~ with children** у неё замеча́тельный подхо́д к де́тям; она́ удиви́тельно (хорошо́) уме́ет обраща́ться с детьми́.

wonderment ['wʌndəmənt] *n.* удивле́ние, изумле́ние.
wondrous ['wʌndrəs] (*arch. or liter.*) *adj.* ди́вный.
adv. удиви́тельно, необыча́йно; на ре́дкость.
wonky ['wɒŋkɪ] *adj.* (*sl.*) (*unstable*) ша́ткий; (*of pers., groggy*) нетвёрдый на нога́х.
wont [wəʊnt] (*arch. or liter.*) *n.* обыкнове́ние, привы́чка; **as is his ~** по своему́ обыкнове́нию; **earlier than his ~** ра́ньше его́ обы́чного вре́мени.
adj. привы́чный, обы́чный; **as he was ~ to say** как он люби́л говори́ть (*or* говари́вал).
wonted ['wəʊntɪd] *adj.* обы́чный, привы́чный, обыкнове́нный.
woo [wu:] *v.t.* **1.** (*court*) уха́живать (*impf.*) за+*i.* **2.** (*fig., try to win*) добива́ться (*impf.*) +*g.*; завоёвывать (*impf.*); **he ~ed sleep in vain** он напра́сно стара́лся засну́ть. **3.** (*fig., coax*) обха́живать (*impf.*); **both candidates were ~ing the voters** о́ба кандида́та пыта́лись завоева́ть расположе́ние избира́телей.
wood [wʊd] *n.* **1.** (*forest*) лес; **the road went through the ~s** доро́га шла че́рез лес (*or* ле́сом); **~ed country** леси́стая ме́стность; **~ anemone** ве́треница лесна́я; (*fig.*): **he can't see the ~ for trees** он за дере́вьями ле́са не ви́дит; **we're not out of the ~ yet** ещё не все опа́сности/тру́дности преодолены́; ещё не всё позади́; **don't halloo till you are out of the ~** не скажи́ «гоп», пока́ не перепры́гнешь; **~ spirit** (*myth.*) ле́ший. **2.** (*substance*) де́рево; **work in ~** ре́зать (*impf.*) по де́реву; **touch** (*US* **knock on**) **~** тьфу, тьфу! (чтоб не сгла́зить!); **~ alcohol, ~ spirit** мети́ловый/дре́весный спирт; **~ block** (*for paving*) торе́ц; **~ carving** деревя́нная скульпту́ра/резьба́; **~ pavement** торцо́вая мостова́я; **~ pulp** древеси́на; **~ demon** (*Russ. myth.*) ле́ший. **3.** (*as fuel or kindling*) дров|а́ (*pl., g.* —); **I chopped some ~ for the fire** я наколо́л дров для ками́на; **~ smoke** дым от горя́щего де́рева. **4.: the ~** (*cask*) бочо́нок; **wine/beer drawn from the ~** разливно́е вино́/пи́во. **5.** (*in game of bowls*) шар. **6.** (*golf-club*) деревя́нная клю́шка.
cpds. **~bine** *n.* (ди́кая) жи́молость; **~-carver** *n.* ре́зчик по де́реву; **~cock** *n.* ва́льдшнеп; **~craft** *n.* (*knowledge of forest conditions*) зна́ние ле́са; (*~working*) ремесло́ деревообде́лочника; **~cut** *n.* гравю́ра на де́реве, ксилогра́фия; **~cutter** *n.* дровосе́к; **~-engraver** *n.* гравёр, ксило́граф; **~-engraving** *n.* (*process*) гравиро́вка на де́реве; ксилогра́фия; (*product*) гравю́ра на де́реве; ксилогра́фия; **~land** *n.* леси́стая ме́стность; (*attr.*) лесно́й; **~-louse** *n.* мокри́ца; **~man** *n.* лесни́к, лесору́б; **~-nymph** *n.* дриа́да; **~pecker** *n.* дя́тел; **~-pigeon** *n.* вя́хирь (*m.*), го́рлица; **~-pile** *n.* шта́бель (*m.*) дров; поле́нница; **~-shed** *n.* дровяно́й сара́й; **~sman** *n.* лесно́й жи́тель; **~-wind** *n.* (*collect.*) деревя́нные духовы́е инструме́нты (*m. pl.*); **~work** *n.* (*carpentry*) столя́рная рабо́та; (*articles*) деревя́нные изде́лия; **~worker** *n.* пло́тник, столя́р; **~working** *n.* обрабо́тка древеси́ны; **~working machine** деревообде́лочный стано́к; **the ~working industry** лесообраба́тывающая промы́шленность; **~worm** *n.* личи́нка древото́чца; **~-yard** *n.* дровяно́й склад.
woodchuck ['wʊdtʃʌk] *n.* суро́к лесно́й.
wooded ['wʊdɪd] *adj.* леси́стый.
wooden ['wʊd(ə)n] *adj.* деревя́нный; (*fig., awkward, stiff, clumsy*) деревя́нный, топо́рный.
cpd. **~-headed** *adj.* тупо́й, тупоу́мный.
woody ['wʊdɪ] *adj.* (*wooded*) леси́стый; (*of or like wood*) деревя́нный.
wooer ['wu:ə(r)] *n.* ухажёр, жени́х, покло́нник.
woof[1] [wu:f] *n.* (*weft*) уто́к.
woof[2] [wʊf] *n.* (*dog's bark*) га́вканье, лай.
v.t. га́вкать (*impf.*); ла́ять (*impf.*).
woofer ['wu:fə(r)] *n.* (*radio*) репроду́ктор ни́зкого то́на.
wool [wʊl] *n.* **1.** (*on sheep etc.*) шерсть, руно́; **pull the ~ over s.o.'s eyes** (*fig.*) вв|оди́ть, -ести́ кого́-н. в заблужде́ние; пус|ка́ть, -ти́ть пыль в глаза́ кому́-н.; **~ merchant** торго́вец ше́рстью; **the ~ trade** торго́вля ше́рстью; **knitting ~** шерсть для вяза́ния; **mending, darning ~** шерсть для што́пки; **I wear ~ next to my skin** я ношу́ шерстяно́е бельё. **2.** (*similar substance*): **cotton ~** ва́та; **steel ~** ёжик. **3.** (*joc., hair*): **lose one's ~** выходи́ть, вы́йти из себя́; (*coll.*) лезть, по-/за- в буты́лку.
cpds. **~-carding, ~-combing** *nn.* чеса́ние ше́рсти; **~-gathering** *n.* (*fig.*) рассе́янность, мечта́тельность; (*pres. part.*): **he is ~-gathering** он замечта́лся; **W~ sack** *n.* (*fig., Lord Chancellorship*) пост ло́рда-ка́нцлера.
woollen ['wʊlən] (*US* **woolen**) *n.* шерстяна́я ткань/пря́жа; (*pl.*) шерстяна́я оде́жда.
adj. шерстяно́й; **~ goods** суко́нный това́р; **~ cloth** сукно́.
cpd. **~-draper** *n.* суко́нщик.
woolliness ['wʊlɪnɪs] *n.* (*fig.*) расплы́вчатость, му́тность, нея́сность, нечёткость, тума́нность.
woolly ['wʊlɪ] *n.* сви́тер; (*pl., woollen underclothes*) шерстяно́е бельё.
adj. **1.** (*bearing or covered with wool*) покры́тый ше́рстью; шерсти́стый; (*furry*) мохна́тый; (*downy*) пуши́стый, шерсти́стый; **~ clouds** пуши́стые облака́; **~ hair** густы́е курча́вые во́лосы. **2.** (*of sound*) глухо́й; (*fig., lacking definition*) расплы́вчатый, му́тный; (*of mind, argument etc.*) нея́сный, нечёткий, му́тный, тума́нный.
woozy ['wu:zɪ] *adj.* (*coll., tipsy*) косо́й, окосе́вший; (*from blow etc.*) обалде́вший, в обалде́нии.
wop [wɒp] *n.* (*sl., pej.*) италья́шка (*m.*).
word [wɜ:d] *n.* **1.** сло́во; **I don't believe a ~ of it** по-мо́ему э́то чи́стый вы́мысел; ни за что не пове́рю; **he didn't say a ~ about it** он об э́том (да́же) не заикну́лся; **those are big ~s** э́то сли́шком гро́мкие слова́; **he doesn't know a ~ of English** он совсе́м не зна́ет англи́йского; **by ~ of mouth** у́стно, на слова́х; **eat one's ~s** взять (*pf.*) свои́ слова́ наза́д; призна́ться (*pf.*), что (был) непра́в; **~s fail me** не нахожу́ слов; **from the ~ go** с са́мого нача́ла; **I couldn't get a ~ in (edgeways)** мне не удало́сь вста́вить ни слове́чка; **a kind ~ and she was happy** одно́ ла́сковое слове́чко — и она́ была́ сча́стли́ва; **you can't get a ~ out of him** слове́чка от него́ не добъёшься; **he hasn't a good ~ to say for it** он не признаёт за э́тим никаки́х досто́инств; **he never has a good ~ for anyone** он ни о ком до́брого сло́ва не ска́жет; **those are hard ~s** (чересчу́р) си́льно ска́зано; **may I have a ~ with you?** мо́жно вас на полсло́ва?; **beyond ~s** неопису́емый, не поддаю́щийся описа́нию; **I have no ~s for (*or* to express) it** я не зна́ю, как э́то назва́ть; **high ~s** разгово́р в повы́шенном то́не; кру́пный разгово́р; **in a ~** (одни́м) сло́вом; коро́че говоря́; **in a few ~s** в не́скольких слова́х; вкра́тце; **in other ~s** и́наче говоря́, други́ми слова́ми; **in so many ~s** пря́мо, напрями́к; буква́льно, досло́вно; **he told me in so many ~s that I was a liar** он пря́мо так и сказа́л, что я лгу; **in ~s of one syllable** (*fig.*) са́мыми просты́ми слова́ми; **in Byron's ~s** как сказа́л Ба́йрон; слова́ми Ба́йрона; по выраже́нию Ба́йрона; **in ~ and deed** сло́вом и де́лом; **last ~s** после́дние/предсме́ртные слова́; **this book is the last ~ on the subject** э́та кни́га — лу́чшее, что напи́сано на э́ту те́му; **the last ~ in fashion** после́дний крик мо́ды; **our coaches are the last ~ in comfort** на́ши авто́бусы — са́мые комфорта́бельные в ми́ре; **he had the last ~** после́днее сло́во оста́лось за ним; **bold in ~s only** хра́брый то́лько на слова́х; **be at a loss for ~s** не находи́ть (*impf.*) слов; **a man of few ~s** немногосло́вный челове́к; **a man of many ~s** многосло́вный/велеречи́вый челове́к; **not a ~!** ни сло́ва!; **not a ~ of it is true** в э́том нет ни сло́ва пра́вды; **comfort's not the ~ for it!** комфо́рт — э́то не то сло́во; **play on ~s** игра́ слов, каламбу́р; **put into ~s** выража́ть, вы́разить слова́ми; **put in a good ~ for s.o.** замо́лвить (*pf.*) слове́чко за кого́-н.; **you are putting ~s into my mouth** вы припи́сываете мне слова́, каки́х я не говори́л; **say a few ~s** (*sc. a brief speech*) сказа́ть (*pf.*) не́сколько слов; **you took the ~s out of my mouth** э́то как раз то, что я хоте́л сказа́ть; **he is too greedy for ~s** он невероя́тно жа́ден; **~ for ~** сло́во в сло́во; **translate ~ for ~** перев|оди́ть, -ести́ досло́вно/буква́льно; **were those his very ~s?** он так и́менно и сказа́л?; **waste ~s** говори́ть (*impf.*) на ве́тер; тра́тить (*impf.*) по́пусту слова́; **a ~ in season** своевре́менный сове́т; во́время ска́занное сло́во; **a ~ in your ear** я хочу́ вам ко́е-что сказа́ть. **2.** (*pl., disputation,*

quarrel) ссо́ра; **they had ~s; ~s passed between them** они́ побрани́лись; у них был кру́пный разгово́р. **3.** (*pl., text set to music*) текст, слова́ (*nt. pl.*); **set, put ~s to music** положи́ть (*pf*) слова́ на му́зыку. **4.** (*pl., actors part*) роль, текст. **5.** (*bibl.*): **the W~** Сло́во; **God's W~** сло́во госпо́дне; свяще́нное писа́ние. **6.** (*news; information*) изве́стие, сообще́ние; **send ~ of sth.** изве|ща́ть, -сти́ть (*or* да|ва́ть, -ть знать) о чём-н.; **he sent, left ~ that he was not coming** он переда́л, что не смо́жет прийти́; **~ came that he had been killed** пришло́ сообще́ние (*or* дошло́ изве́стие), что он поги́б; **the ~ got round that ...** ста́ло изве́стно, что...; **what's the good ~?** (*joc.*) что слы́шно хоро́шенького? **7.** (*promise; assurance*) сло́во, обеща́ние; **give, pledge one's ~** да|ва́ть, -ть сло́во; обеща́ть (*impf., pf.*); **I give you my ~** даю́ вам сло́во; **keep one's ~** держа́ть, с- сло́во; **~ of honour!** че́стное сло́во!; **a man of his ~** челове́к сло́ва; **he was as good as his ~** он сдержа́л сло́во; **his ~ is as good as his bond** на его́ сло́во мо́жно положи́ться; его́ сло́во кре́пкое; **take s.o. at his ~** пойма́ть (*pf.*) кого́-н. на сло́ве; **you must take my ~ for it** вам придётся пове́рить мне на сло́во; **upon my ~** (*asseveration*) ей-Бо́гу!; ей-ей!; (*exclamation*) вот э́то да!; ну и ну! **8.** (*command*) сло́во, прика́з; **at the ~ of command** по кома́нде; **at the ~ 'go', start running!** по кома́нде «марш!», беги́те!; **give the ~** отда́ть (*pf.*) приказа́ние/распоряже́ние; **just say the ~!** то́лько прикажи́те!

v.t. формули́ровать, с-; выража́ть, вы́разить; сост|авля́ть, -а́вить; **that might have been differently ~ed** э́то мо́жно бы́ло сказа́ть/вы́разить ина́че.

cpds. **~-blind** *adj.* страда́ющий слове́сной слепото́й; **~-break, ~-division** *nn.* (*typ.*) перено́с; **~-game** *n.* слове́сная игра́ (*скрэбл и т.п.*); **~-perfect** *adj.* зна́ющий (*что*) на зубо́к; **~-picture** *n.* о́бразное описа́ние; **~-play** *n.* игра́ слов; каламбу́р; **~-processor** *n.* электро́нный печа́тающий автома́т.

wordiness ['wɜːdɪnɪs] *n.* многосло́вие, велере́чи́вость.

wording ['wɜːdɪŋ] *n.* реда́кция; фо́рмула, формулиро́вка.

wordless ['wɜːdlɪs] *adj.* безмо́лвный; **~ grief** безмо́лвное го́ре.

wordy ['wɜːdɪ] *adj.* многосло́вный, велере́чи́вый.

work [wɜːk] *n.* **1.** (*mental or physical labour, task*) рабо́та, труд; (*official, professional*) слу́жба; (*school etc.*) заня́тия (*nt. pl.*); (*activity*) де́ятельность; **job of ~** де́ло; **he's got some ~ on** он за́нят де́лом; **he is at ~** он сейча́с рабо́тает; **he is at (his place of) ~** он на рабо́те/слу́жбе; **he is at ~ on a dictionary** он рабо́тает над словарём; **all in the day's ~** в поря́дке веще́й, норма́льно; **the right to ~** пра́во на труд; **forces at ~** де́йствующие/дви́жущие си́лы; **~s of mercy** благотвори́тельность; **creative ~** тво́рческая де́ятельность; **good ~s** до́брые дела́; **public ~s** обще́ственные рабо́ты (*f. pl.*); **~ for peace** борьба́ за мир; **his life's ~** де́ло его́ жи́зни; **he does his ~ well** он хоро́ший рабо́тник; **we have done a good day's ~** мы сего́дня успе́шно порабо́тали; **he is doing some ~ on the house** он занима́ется ремо́нтом до́ма; **he is doing some ~ on the Stuarts** он рабо́тает над исто́рией дина́стии Стю́артов; **there is plenty of ~ to be done** здесь мно́го рабо́ты; здесь предстои́т больша́я рабо́та; **I have ~ to do** мне на́до рабо́тать; я за́нят; **you will have your ~ cut out** вы хлопо́т не оберётесь; **get to ~ on** нача́ть (*pf.*) рабо́ту над+*i.*; **get down to ~** приня́ться/взя́ться/засе́сть (*pf.*) за рабо́ту/де́ло; **it's hard ~ digging clay** копа́ть гли́ну — тя́жкий труд (*or* тяжело́ *or* нелёгкое де́ло); **you are making hard ~ of it** вы де́лаете из э́того це́лую исто́рию; вы преувели́чиваете тру́дности; **make short ~ of** бы́стро/жи́во распра́виться (*pf.*) с+*i.*; **many hands make light ~** когда́ рук мно́го, рабо́та спо́рится; **set s.o. to ~** засади́ть (*pf.*) кого́-н. за рабо́ту. **2.** (*activity, not necessarily productive*) де́йствие, посту́пок; **it was the ~ of a moment** э́то бы́ло де́лом одно́й мину́ты; **the ~ of a madman** де́ло рук сумаше́дшего; **dirty ~** (*difficult, unpleasant*) чёрная рабо́та; (*nefarious*) по́длость; **there's been some dirty ~ here** тут де́ло нечи́сто; **nice ~!** (*coll.*) отли́чно!; здо́рово; **the mice have been at ~** тут порабо́тали мы́ши. **3.** (*employment*) рабо́та, слу́жба; **it is hard to find ~** тру́дно найти́ рабо́ту; **in ~** рабо́тающий; **out of ~** без рабо́ты; **he was put out of ~** он лиши́лся рабо́ты; **~ force** рабо́чие (*m. pl.*), рабо́чая си́ла. **4.** (*materials etc.; handicraft*): **she took her ~ with her on holiday** она́ пое́хала в о́тпуск со свои́м рукоде́лием; **fancy ~** (*carving*) резьба́; (*embroidery*) худо́жественная вы́шивка; **embossed ~** чека́нка. **5.** (*workmanship*) мастерство́, отде́лка; **an excellent piece of ~** прекра́сная/отли́чная рабо́та. **6.** (*finished product*) произведе́ние, изде́лие; **sale of ~** прода́жа изде́лий. **7.** (*literary or artistic composition*) произведе́ние, сочине́ние; (*esp. academic*) труд; (*collect.*) тво́рчество; (*publication*) изда́ние; **the (complete) ~s of Shakespeare** (по́лное) собра́ние сочине́ний Шекспи́ра; **~s on art** кни́ги по иску́сству; **~ of reference** спра́вочник, спра́вочное изда́ние; **he knew all the ~s of Chopin** он знал все произведе́ния Шопе́на; **~ in progress** теку́щая рабо́та; **this cake is a ~ of art** э́тот пиро́г — настоя́щее произведе́ние иску́сства. **8.** (*pl., parts of machine*) механи́зм; **the ~s of a clock** часово́й механи́зм; **something is wrong with the ~s** механи́зм испо́ртился; (*fig.*): **gum up the ~s** засто́порить (*pf.*) рабо́ту (*coll.*); **I asked them a simple question and I got the whole ~s** (*coll.*) я зада́л им просто́й вопро́с, а они́ меня́ заму́чили подро́бностями; **give s.o. the ~s** (*sl.*) обраб|а́тывать, -о́тать кого́-н.; брать, взять кого́-н. в рабо́ту. **9.** (*pl., factory or similar installation*) заво́д, фа́брика, предприя́тие; **engineering ~s** машинострои́тельный заво́д; **steel ~s** сталелите́йный заво́д; **sewage ~s** канализацио́нная систе́ма; **~s committee, council** заводско́й/фабри́чный комите́т; сове́т предприя́тия; рабо́чий сове́т; **~s manager** дире́ктор заво́да/ фа́брики. **10.** (*pl., operations*): **public ~s** обще́ственные рабо́ты (*f. pl.*); **clerk of the ~s** производи́тель (*m.*) рабо́т; прора́б. **11.** (*pl., defensive structures; fortifications*) фортифика́ция (*f. pl.*), укрепле́ния (*nt. pl.*), сооруже́ния (*nt. pl.*); **defensive ~s** оборони́тельные сооруже́ния.

v.t. **1.** (*cause to ~, exact ~ from*): **he ~s his men hard** он заставля́ет люде́й рабо́тать, не поклада́я рук; **he ~ed himself to death** он извёл себя́ рабо́той; **he ~ed his wife to death** он совсе́м загоня́л жену́; **that idea has been ~ed to death** э́то изби́тая/зата́сканная иде́я; **~ one's fingers to the bone** труди́ться/рабо́тать (*impf.*) до седьмо́го по́та. **2.** (*set in motion, actuate*) прив|оди́ть, -ести́ в движе́ние/де́йствие; **~ a lever** наж|има́ть, -а́ть на рыча́г; управля́ть (*impf.*) рычаго́м; перевести́ (*pf.*) рыча́г; **how do you ~ this machine?** как рабо́тает э́то маши́на? **3.** (*effect*): **~ wonders** твори́ть, со- чудеса́; **he ~ed it so that he was off duty** (*coll.*) он так подстро́ил, что ему́ не приходи́лось дежу́рить. **4.** (*achieve by ~ing*): **~ one's passage** отраб|а́тывать, -о́тать свой прое́зд; **he ~ed his way through university** все го́ды студе́нчества он зараба́тывал себе́ на жизнь; **he ~ed his way up to the rank of manager** из просты́х рабо́чих он проби́лся в директора́; **~ one's way forward** пробира́ться/ пробива́ться (*impf.*) вперёд. **5.** (*operate, manage: a mine, land etc.*) разраба́тывать, обраба́тывать, эксплуати́ровать (*all impf.*); **the mine was ~ed by Italians** на ша́хте рабо́тали италья́нцы; **our salesman who ~s the north-west** наш коммивояжёр, обслу́живающий се́веро-за́падный райо́н. **6.** (*move, bring by degrees*): **~ sth. into place** вти́с|кивать, -нуть что-н. куда́-н.; **he ~ed the conversation round to his favourite subject** он постепе́нно подвёл разгово́р к свое́й излю́бленной те́ме; **he ~ed this theme into his story** он ввёл/ вплёл э́ту те́му в свой расска́з. **7.** (*shape, manipulate; see also* **wrought**) обраб|а́тывать, -о́тать; **~ butter** сби|ва́ть, -ть ма́сло; **~ clay/dough** меси́ть, за- гли́ну/те́сто. **8.** (*excite*) возбу|жда́ть, -ди́ть; **he ~ed the crowd into a frenzy** он довёл толпу́ до неи́стовства; **~ o.s. into a rage** дов|оди́ть, -ести́ себя́ до исступле́ния. **9.** (*make by stitching etc.*) вышива́ть, вы́шить; **a design of flowers was ~ed in silk on the tablecloth** ска́терть была́ вы́шита шёлковым цвето́чным узо́ром.

v.i. **1.** (*labour, be employed*) рабо́тать, труди́ться, служи́ть (*all impf.*); **~ like a horse** (*fig.*) рабо́тать как вол; рабо́тать, не разгиба́я спины́; **he ~ed for 6 hours** он прорабо́тал 6 часо́в; ~ **against time** стара́ться (*impf.*) ко́нчить к определённому сро́ку; ~ **at a problem** рабо́тать/би́ться (*impf.*) над зада́чей; ~ **at Latin** занима́ться (*impf.*) латы́нью; ~ **at a lathe** рабо́тать (*impf.*) на тока́рном станке́; ~ **for the government** рабо́тать (*impf.*) на госуда́рственной слу́жбе; ~ **for peace** боро́ться (*impf.*) за мир; ~ **for a living** зараба́тывать (*impf.*) себе́ на жизнь; **he ~s in leather** он рабо́тает по ко́же; **he ~s in oils** он пи́шет ма́слом; **he is ~ing on a novel** он рабо́тает над рома́ном; **he ~ed through the theorems of Euclid** он прошёл теоре́мы Евкли́да; ~ **to a budget** держа́ться (*impf.*) в преде́лах бюдже́та; укла́дываться (*impf.*) в бюдже́т; ~ **to rule** пров|оди́ть, -ести́ италья́нскую забасто́вку; ~ **with s.o.** сотру́дничать (*impf.*) с кем-н.; ~ **to a tight schedule** приде́рживаться (*impf.*) стро́гого расписа́ния. **2.** (*operate*, *function*) рабо́тать (*impf.*); де́йствовать (*impf.*); **the brake won't ~** то́рмоз отказа́л; **my watch stopped ~ing** мои́ часы́ переста́ли идти́; **the machine ~s by electricity** э́тот аппара́т рабо́тает на электри́честве; **everything was ~ing smoothly** всё шло как по ма́слу. **3.** (*produce desired effect*): **the plan ~ed** план уда́лся; **the medicine ~ed** лека́рство помогло́/поде́йствовало; **the method ~s well** э́тот ме́тод уда́чен/эффекти́вен; **her charm ~ed** обая́нием она́ доби́лась своего́. **4.** (*exert influence*) рабо́тать, де́йствовать (*both impf.*); ока́зывать (*impf.*) влия́ние; ~ **against** меша́ть (*impf.*) +*d.*; служи́ть (*impf.*) поме́хой +*d.*; ~ **(up)on s.o.** обраба́тывать (*impf.*) кого́-н.; порабо́тать (*pf.*) над кем-н.; ~ **towards** спосо́бствовать (*impf.*) +*d.*; стреми́ться (*impf.*) к+*d.* **5.** (*ferment*) броди́ть (*impf.*); **she left the yeast to ~** она́ поста́вила дро́жжи (, что́бы они́ подошли́). **6.** (*move gradually*): **a screw ~ed loose** винт осла́б; **his shirt ~ed out of his trousers** руба́шка вы́билась/вы́лезла у него́ из брюк; **the damp ~ed through the plaster** сы́рость прошла́/прони́кла че́рез штукату́рку; **he ~ed round to his subject by degrees** он испо́дволь подошёл к свое́й те́ме.

with advs.: ~ **around** *v.i.* = ~ **round;** ~ **away** *v.i.* труди́ться (*impf.*); (*coll.*) корпе́ть (*impf.*) (*над чем*); ~ **back** *v.i.*: **I ~ed back through last year's newspapers** я просмотре́л номера́ газе́т за про́шлый год (в обра́тном поря́дке); ~ **down** *v.i.*: **my socks ~ down as I walk** когда́ я хожу́, у меня́ соска́льзывают носки́; ~ **in** *v.t.*: **mix butter, sugar and eggs, then ~ in the dry ingredients** смеша́йте я́йца с ма́слом и са́харом, пото́м доба́вьте сухи́е ингредие́нты; **the audience were delighted when he ~ed in some local allusions** пу́блика была́ в восто́рге, когда́ он затро́нул в свое́й програ́мме ме́стные те́мы; *v.i.*: **the ink stain has ~ed in** черни́ла прошли́ насквозь; ~ **off** *v.t.*: **he ran round the house to ~ off some of his energy** он пробежа́лся вокру́г до́ма, что́бы дать вы́ход свое́й эне́ргии; **don't ~ off your irritation on me** не срыва́йте своё раздраже́ние на мне; **I shall never be able to ~ off this debt** я никогда́ не смогу́ погаси́ть э́тот долг; **I'm trying to ~ off my arrears of correspondence** я пыта́юсь разде́латься с накопи́вшейся корреспонде́нцией; ~ **out** *v.t.* (*devise*) разраб|а́тывать, -о́тать; (*calculate*) вычисля́ть, вы́числить; подсчи́т|ывать, -а́ть; **you must ~ out the answer yourself** вы должны́ са́ми найти́ отве́т; (*solve*) разреш|а́ть, -и́ть; ула́|живать, -дить; ~ **things out** раз|бира́ться, -обра́ться; **all this will ~ itself out** всё э́то ула́дится/образу́ется; **the mine is ~ed out** рудни́к истощи́лся; *v.i.* (*turn out*) ока́з|ываться, -а́ться; получ|а́ться, -и́ться; конча́ться, ко́нчиться; (*turn out satisfactorily*): **our marriage hasn't ~ed out** наш брак оказа́лся неуда́чным; (*be solved*) разреш|а́ться, -и́ться; **the sum won't ~ out** зада́ча не выхо́дит/получа́ется; (*of calculation*): **the expenses ~ out at £70** изде́ржки составля́ют £70; **his share ~s out at £5** его́ до́ля сво́дится к пяти́ фу́нтам; (*train, of an athlete*) тренирова́ться (*impf.*); ~ **over** *v.t.* перераб|а́тывать, -о́тать; (*beat up*): **the gang gave him a ~ing-over** (*coll.*) ша́йка его́ разби́ла до полусме́рти; ~ **round** *v.i.* пов|ора́чиваться, -ерну́ться; **his tie ~ed round till it was under his ear** его́ га́лстук сби́лся на́ сто́рону, и был где́-то уже́ у са́мого у́ха; **I was just ~ing round to that point** я как раз подходи́л к э́тому (вопро́су); ~ **up** *v.t.* (*transform by ~ing*): **he ~ed the clay up into its final shape** он прида́л гли́не оконча́тельную фо́рму; (*elaborate*) перераб|а́тывать, -о́тать; **these ideas are worth ~ing up into a book** над э́тими иде́ями сто́ит порабо́тать и вы́пустить их (отде́льной) кни́гой; (*raise, develop*): **he ~ed up a profitable business** он разверну́л при́быльное де́ло; **he ~ed up a market for his products** он завоева́л ры́нок для свои́х това́ров; **the agent ~ed up support for the candidate** избира́тельный аге́нт доби́лся подде́ржки своему́ кандида́ту; **I can't ~ up any interest in economics** я ника́к не могу́ пробуди́ть в себе́ интере́с к эконо́мике; **I went for a short walk to ~ up an appetite** я вы́шел немно́го пройти́сь, что́бы нагуля́ть себе́ аппети́т; (*arouse, excite*): **he ~ed himself up** он взвинти́л себя́; **he ~ed up his listeners to a pitch of fury** он довёл свои́х слу́шателей до неи́стовства; (*pred.*): **~ed up** (*excited*) взволно́ван, возбуждён; (*worried*) расстро́ен; **get o.s. ~ed up** расстр|а́иваться, -о́иться; *v.i.*: **he ~ed up to a climax** он подходи́л к кульмина́ции; он подводи́л слу́шателей к кульминацио́нному пу́нкту; **events were ~ing up to a climax** собы́тия нараста́ли; **she realised that he was ~ing up to a proposal** она́ поняла́, что он собира́ется ей сде́лать предложе́ние.

cpds. **~-bag, ~-basket** *nn.* су́мка/корзи́нка с рукоде́лием; **~-bench** *n.* верста́к; **~-book** *n.* журна́л учёта вы́полненной рабо́ты; тетра́дь для упражне́ний; **~-box** *n.* рабо́чий я́щик; **~day** *n.* (*unit of payment*) трудоде́нь (*m.*); **~-force** *n.* рабо́чие (*pl.*), рабо́тники (*m. pl.*); рабо́чая си́ла; **~-horse** *n.* (*lit.*) рабо́чая ло́шадь; (*fig.*) рабо́чая лоша́дка/ло́шадь; **~house** *n.* (*Br.*) рабо́тный дом; (*US*) исправи́тельная тюрьма́; **~-load** *n.* нагру́зка; **~man** *n.* рабо́тник; **~manlike** *adj.* иску́сный, де́льный; **~manship** *n.* иску́сство, мастерство́; **~mate** *n.* сотру́дни|к (*fem.* -ца), колле́га (*c.g.*); **~-out** *n.* трениро́вка, размі́нка; **~people** *n. pl.* рабо́чие (*pl.*), трудя́щиеся; **~-room** *n.* рабо́чая ко́мната/мастерска́я; **~-sheet** *n.* рабо́чий листо́к; рабо́чая ка́рта; **~shop** *n.* мастерска́я, цех; **~-shy** *adj.* (*coll.*) лени́вый; **~-table** *n.* рабо́чий стол; **~-top** *n.* (*surface for working*) рабо́чий стол; (*in kitchen*) ве́рхняя пане́ль; **~-to-rule** *n.* ≃ италья́нская забасто́вка; **~-woman** *n.* рабо́тница.

workable [ˈwɜːkəb(ə)l] *adj.* **1.** (*of mine etc.*) рента́бельный. **2.** (*feasible*) выполни́мый, реа́льный, осуществи́мый.

workaday [ˈwɜːkəˌdeɪ] *adj.* бу́дний, повседне́вный.

workaholic [ˌwɜːkəˈhɒlɪk] *n.* работома́н, трудого́лик.

worker [ˈwɜːkə(r)] *n.* рабо́тник, трудя́щийся; (*manual*) рабо́чий; **~s of the world, unite!** пролета́рии всех стран, соединя́йтесь!; **hard ~** тру́жени|к (*fem.* -ца), работя́га (*c.g.*); **office ~** слу́жащий; **party ~** парти́йный активи́ст (*fem.* -ка); **social ~** обще́ственный рабо́тник, обще́ственни|к (*fem.* -ца); **~ bee** рабо́чая пчела́.

working [ˈwɜːkɪŋ] *n.* **1.** (*mine, quarry etc.*) рудни́к, вы́работки (*f. pl.*). **2.** (*usu. pl.*; *operation*) рабо́та, де́йствие; **the ~s of the human mind** мысли́тельный проце́сс челове́ка. **3.** (*attr., pert. to work*) рабо́чий; **~ capital** оборо́тный капита́л; **~ clothes** рабо́чая оде́жда, спецо́вка; **~ conditions** усло́вия труда́; **~ day** (*part of day devoted to work*) рабо́чий день; (*opp. to rest day*) рабо́чий/бу́дний день; **~ drawing** рабо́чий чертёж; **~ hours** рабо́чее вре́мя/рабо́чие часы́; **~ knowledge** о́бщее знако́мство (с+*i.*); **all his ~ life** вся его́ трудова́я жизнь; **~ lunch** делово́й обе́д; **~ majority** доста́точное коли́чество голосо́в; **in ~ order** в испра́вности.

adj. рабо́чий; **~ man** рабо́тник, рабо́чий; **~ men's club** рабо́чий клуб; **~ class** рабо́чий класс; **~ model** де́йствующая моде́ль; **~ party** рабо́чая гру́ппа; **~ woman** рабо́тающая же́нщина; же́нщина, име́ющая специа́льность.

cpds. **~-class** *adj.* рабо́чий, характе́рный для представи́теля рабо́чего кла́сса; **~-class families** се́мьи рабо́чих; **~-out** *n.* (*elaboration*) дета́льная разрабо́тка.

world [wɜːld] *n.* **1.** (*universe, system*) мир, вселе́нная; **the**

ancient ~ анти́чный мир; **new** ~ но́вый мир; **come into the, this** ~ ро|жда́ться, -ди́ться (*or* появ|ля́ться, -и́ться) на свет; **bring into the** ~ (*give birth to*; *deliver*) произв|оди́ть, -ести́ на свет; ро|жа́ть, -ди́ть; **he is not long for this** ~ он не жиле́ц (на э́том све́те); **out of this** ~ (*coll.*, *stupendous*) потряса́ющий; **not of this** ~ не от ми́ра сего́; **in this** ~ на э́том све́те; **the other, next** ~; **the** ~ **to come** тот свет; мир ино́й; **in the next** ~; на том све́те; **the end of the** ~ (*i.e. of time*) коне́ц све́та, светопредставле́ние; ~ **without end** (*for ever*) на ве́ки ве́чные/веко́в; **get the best of both** ~**s** ≃ и де́ньги загрести́, и неви́нность соблюсти́; **a** ~ **of troubles** про́пасть хлопо́т. **2.** (*intensive and other fig. uses*): **how in the** ~ **did you know?** как вы то́лько умудри́лись (э́то) узна́ть?; **what in the** ~ **has happened?** да что же, наконе́ц, случи́лось?; **why in the** ~ **didn't you tell me?** ну почему́ же вы мне не сказа́ли?; **he is the** ~**'s worst tennis-player** тако́го скве́рного тенниси́ста во всём ми́ре (*or* днём с огнём) не сы́щешь; **for all the** ~ **as if ...** то́чно так (*or* точь-в-точь), как е́сли бы...; **not for the** ~ ни на что на све́те; (*coll.*) ни за каки́е коври́жки; **the** ~ **of dreams** ца́рство грёз; **the** ~**, the flesh and the devil** всевозмо́жные искуше́ния; **he renounced the** ~ он отрёкся от ми́ра; **I wouldn't hurt him for the** ~ я его́ ни за что (на све́те) не стал бы обижа́ть; **she's all the** ~ **to me** она для меня́ — всё; **the boss thinks the** ~ **of him** он у хозя́ина на о́чень высо́ком счету́; **I would give the** ~ **to know** я бы всё отда́л, то́лько бы узна́ть; **dead to the** ~ без созна́ния; в по́лном изнеможе́нии; **I felt on top of the** ~ я был на верши́не благополу́чия/сча́стья; я был в превосхо́дном настрое́нии. **3.** (*infinite amount or extent*) мно́го, у́йма; **there is a** ~ **of meaning in that phrase** э́та фра́за полна́ глубо́кого значе́ния; **a** ~ **of difference** огро́мная ра́зница; **there was a** ~ **of difference between them** они́ отлича́лись друг от дру́га как земля́ и не́бо; **it will do him a** ~ **of good** э́то ему́ о́чень да́же пойдёт на по́льзу; **I was** ~**s away** мои мы́сли вита́ли где́-то за три́девять земе́ль. **4.** (*geog.*; *the earth's countries and peoples*) мир, свет; **is there life on other** ~**s?** есть ли жизнь на други́х плане́тах?; **a journey round the** ~ путеше́ствие вокру́г све́та; кругосве́тное путеше́ствие; **go round the** ~ объе́хать (*pf.*) весь свет; **all the** ~**'s a stage** весь мир — теа́тр; **the** ~ **is wide** свет не кли́ном сошёлся; **the** ~**'s his oyster** весь мир у его́ ног; **his** ~ **is a very narrow one** его́ миро́к о́чень у́зок; у него́ о́чень у́зкий кругозо́р; **the whole** (*or* **all the**) ~ **knows** всем (*or* всему́ ми́ру) изве́стно; **(all) the** ~ **over** в це́лом ми́ре; по всему́ све́ту; (по)всю́ду; повсеме́стно; **to the** ~**'s end** на кра́й све́та; **the Old/New W**~ Ста́рый/Но́вый свет; **the Roman** ~ мир дре́вних ри́млян; **the English-speaking** ~ англоязы́чные стра́ны (*f. pl.*); **the Third W**~ тре́тий мир; **citizen of the** ~ космополи́т; граждани́н ми́ра; ~ **affairs** междунаро́дные дела́; **W**~ **Bank** Междунаро́дный Банк; ~ **champion** чемпио́н ми́ра; ~ **championship** чемпиона́т ми́ра; **W**~ **Cup** кубо́к ми́ра по футбо́лу; **W**~**'s Fair** всеми́рная вы́ставка; ~ **peace** мир во всём ми́ре; ~ **politics** мирова́я поли́тика; **a** ~ **power** вели́кая держа́ва; ~ **record** мирово́й реко́рд; ~ **service of the BBC** междунаро́дная слу́жба Би-Би-Си́; ~ **war** мирова́я война́; **W**~ **War I/II** пе́рвая/втора́я мирова́я война́. **5.** (*human affairs*; *active life*) жизнь; **how goes the** ~ **with you?** как жизнь/дела́/пожива́ете?; **he has seen something of the** ~ он име́ет не́которое представле́ние о жи́зни; **a man of the** ~ све́тский/быва́лый челове́к; **all's right with the** ~ в ми́ре всё прекра́сно; **get on in the** ~ вы́йти́ (*pf.*) в лю́ди; **come up in the** ~ сде́лать (*pf.*) карье́ру; **go down in the** ~ утра́тить (*pf.*) было́е положе́ние; **know the** ~ знать (*impf.*) жизнь. **6.** (*society*) о́бщество, свет; **the great** ~ вы́сший свет; **what will the** ~ **say?** что ска́жет свет?; что ска́жут лю́ди? **7.** (*sphere*; *domain*) мир; сфе́ра; **the** ~ **of nature** ца́рство приро́ды; **the scientific** ~ нау́чные круги́ (*m. pl.*); **the animal** ~ живо́тный мир; **the sporting** ~ мир спо́рта, спорти́вный мир; **the** ~ **of art** мир иску́сства.

cpds. ~**-beater** *n.* (*pers.*) ма́стер вы́сшего кла́сса; (*thg.*) что-н. первокла́ссное; ~**-famous** *adj.* всеми́рно изве́стный; ~**-shaking** *adj.* име́ющий мирово́е значе́ние; ~**-view** *n.* мировоззре́ние; ~**-weary** *adj.* разочаро́ванный; пресы́щенный жи́знью; ~**-wide** *adj.* всеми́рный, мирово́й; *adv.* по всему́ све́ту/ми́ру.

worldliness ['wɜ:ldlɪnɪs] *n.* посюсторо́нность, су́етность.

worldly ['wɜ:ldlɪ] *adj.* **1.** (*material*) земно́й, материа́льный; ~ **goods** иму́щество. **2.** (*of this world*; *secular*) земно́й, мирско́й; ~ **wisdom** жите́йская му́дрость. **3.: a** ~ **person** су́етный челове́к; челове́к, поглощённый земны́ми дела́ми/интере́сами.

cpds. ~**-minded** *adj.* посюсторо́нний, су́етный; ~**-wise** *adj.* о́пытный; облада́ющий жи́зненным о́пытом.

worm [wɜ:m] *n.* **1.** (*earth* ~) червь (*m.*), червя́к. **2.** (*maggot*; *grub*) гу́сеница, личи́нка. **3.** (*parasite*) глист; **have** ~**s** име́ть (*impf.*) глисты́; (*fig.*, *liter.*): **the** ~ **of remorse** угрызе́ния (*nt. pl.*) со́вести. **4.** (*abject pers.*) ничто́жный червь; раб; ничто́жество; **even a** ~ **will turn** раб, и тот взбунту́ется. **5.** (*of screw*) червя́к, шнек; червя́чный винт.

v.t. **1.** (*insinuate*): **he** ~**ed his way (or himself) through the bushes** он пропо́лз ме́жду куста́ми; **he** ~**ed himself into her confidence** он вкра́лся к ней в дове́рие. **2.** (*extract*) выпы́тывать, вы́пытать; **they** ~**ed the secret out of him** они́ вы́ведали его́ та́йну. **3.** (*rid of parasites*) гнать (*impf.*) глисты́ у+*g.*

cpds. ~**-cast** *n.* земля́, вы́брошенная земляны́м червём; ~**-eaten** *adj.* черви́вый, зачерви́вевший; (*fig.*) устаре́вший; ~**-hole** *n.* червото́чина; ~**-powder** *n.* глистого́нное сре́дство; ~**-wheel** *n.* червя́чное колесо́.

wormwood ['wɜ:mwʊd] *n.* полы́нь; (*fig.*) го́речь; **the thought was** ~ **to him** э́то мысль была́ для него́ ху́же го́рькой ре́дьки.

worn [wɔ:n] *see* **wear** *v.t. and* **wear out**

worrier ['wʌrɪə(r)] *n.* (*pers.*) беспоко́йный челове́к; **he's a** ~ он ве́чно беспоко́ится; он у нас паникёр.

worrisome ['wʌrɪsəm] *adj.* (*causing worry*) беспоко́йный, трево́жный; (*given to worrying*) беспоко́йный, мни́тельный.

worr|y ['wʌrɪ] *n.* **1.** (*anxiety*) неприя́тность, трево́га, забо́та. **2.** (*sth. causing anxiety*) неприя́тность, забо́та; **he is a** ~**y to me** я с ним му́чаюсь; **money** ~**ies** де́нежные забо́ты (*f. pl.*); ~ **beads** чёт|ки (*pl.*, *g.* -ок) для не́рвных.

v.t. **1.** (*cause anxiety or discomfort to*) беспоко́ить (*impf.*); волнова́ть (*impf.*); **what is** ~**ying you?** что вас беспоко́ит?; чем вы озабо́чены?; **I'm** ~**ied about my son** я беспоко́юсь за сы́на; меня́ беспоко́ит сын; **I am** ~**ied about his health** я озабо́чен состоя́нием его́ здоро́вья; **don't** ~**y yourself** не беспоко́йтесь; **she** ~**ies herself sick** она́ изво́дит себя́ трево́гой. **2.** (*trouble*; *bother*) надоеда́ть (*impf.*) +*d.*; пристава́ть (*impf.*) к+*d.*; **he keeps** ~**ying me to read him a story** он приста́ёт ко мне, что́бы я ему́ почита́л; **he** ~**ied me with questions** он одолева́л меня́ вопро́сами; **the noise doesn't** ~**y me** мне шум не меша́ет. **3.** (*of dog*) рвать (*impf.*) зуба́ми; трепа́ть (*impf.*); грызть (*impf.*); **your dog has been** ~**ying my sheep** ва́ша соба́ка броса́лась на мои́х ове́ц.

v.i. беспоко́иться, волнова́ться, расстра́иваться; му́читься; терза́ться (*all impf.*); **you are** ~**ying over nothing** вы напра́сно (*or* по пустяка́м) расстра́иваетесь/волну́етесь; **why** ~**?** (*let's be cheerful*) сто́ит ли (*or* к чему́) волнова́ться/трево́житься?; **I should** ~**!** (*coll.*) а мне како́е де́ло?; а мне-то что?; **not to** ~**!** (*coll.*) не волну́йтесь!; не беда́!; всё устро́ится.

worse [wɜ:s] *n.* ху́дшее; **there is** ~ **to come** э́то ещё не всё; э́то ещё цвето́чки (, а я́годки впереди́); **a change for the** ~ переме́на к ху́дшему; **things went from bad to** ~ положе́ние час о́т часу станови́лось ху́же.

adj. ху́дший; **we couldn't have picked a** ~ **day** тру́дно бы́ло бы вы́брать бо́лее неуда́чный день; **my trouble is** ~ **than yours** моя́ беда́ похуже ва́шей; **you will only make matters** ~ вы то́лько усугу́бите/уху́дшите положе́ние; **or** ~ и́ли ещё что-н. похуже; **I can't think of anything** ~ не могу́ себе́ предста́вить ничего́ ху́же; **he was none the** ~ **for his adventure** он вы́шел це́лым и невреди́м из э́того приключе́ния; **these cushions are the** ~ **for wear** э́ти поду́шки поистрепа́лись; **he looked the ~ for wear** у него́ был си́льно потрёпанный вид; **~ luck!** увы́!; к сожале́нию; к несча́стью; (*in health*) ху́же; **the patient is ~ today** больно́му сего́дня ху́же; **his condition is ~** его́ состоя́ние уху́дшилось.

adv. ху́же; **we played ~ than ever** так скве́рно мы никогда́ не игра́ли; **it is raining ~ than it was an hour ago** дождь идёт сильне́е, чем час наза́д; **you might do ~ than accept** мо́жет быть, и сто́ит приня́ть; **she hates me ~ than before** она́ ненави́дит меня́ пу́ще пре́жнего; **they are ~ off than we** они́ в ху́дшем положе́нии, чем мы; (*financially*) они́ ме́нее состоя́тельны, чем мы.

worsen ['wɜːs(ə)n] *v.t. & i.* ух|удша́ться, -у́дшиться.

worship ['wɜːʃɪp] *n.* **1.** (*relig.*) культ, поклоне́ние, почита́ние; **public ~, act of ~** богослуже́ние, церко́вная слу́жба; **forms of ~** религио́зные обря́ды; **freedom of ~** свобо́да со́вести/вероисповеда́ния; свобо́да отправле́ния религио́зных ку́льтов; **place of ~** це́рковь, храм. **2.** (*of pers. etc.*) поклоне́ние; **~ of success** преклоне́ние пе́ред успе́хом; **he gazed at her with ~ in his eyes** он смотре́л на неё с обожа́нием; **Your W~** Ва́ша ми́лость.

v.t. & i. поклоня́ться (*impf.*) +*d.*; преклоня́ться (*impf.*) (пе́ред+*i.*); почита́ть (*impf.*); **~ God** моли́ться (*impf.*) Бо́гу; **~ strange gods** поклоня́ться чужи́м бога́м; **the church where he ~ped** це́рковь, в кото́рую он ходи́л; **he ~s the ground she treads on** он боготвори́т её.

worshipful ['wɜːʃɪp,fʊl] *adj.* (*entitled to respect*) уважа́емый, почте́нный; (*reverential*) благогове́йный.

worshipper ['wɜːʃɪpə(r)] *n.* (*pers. attending service*) моля́щийся; (*fig.*) покло́нни|к (*fem.* -ца).

worst [wɜːst] *n.* наиху́дшее; са́мое плохо́е; **the ~ of the storm is over** шторм начина́ет утиха́ть; **the ~ of it is that ...** ху́же всего́ то, что...; **that's the ~ of being clever** в то́м-то и беда́/го́ре у́мников; **if the ~ should happen** е́сли произойдёт са́мое стра́шное; **if the ~ comes to the ~** в са́мом ху́дшем слу́чае; на худо́й коне́ц; е́сли де́ло бу́дет совсе́м пло́хо; **we must prepare for the ~** мы должны́ быть гото́вы ко всему́ (*or* к ху́дшему); **when things were at their ~** когда́ положе́ние каза́лось безнадёжным; **you saw him at his ~** вы ви́дели его́ в о́чень неудо́бный моме́нт; **at (the) ~ you may have to pay a fine** в кра́йнем слу́чае вам придётся уплати́ть штраф; **get, have the ~ of it** понести́ (*pf.*) пораже́ние; **let him do his ~** пусть себе́ де́лает, что хо́чет (никто́ его́ не бои́тся!).

adj. наиху́дший; са́мый плохо́й; **my ~ enemy** мой зле́йший/пе́рвый враг; **that was his ~ mistake** э́то была́ его́ са́мая серьёзная оши́бка; **he is a bore of the ~ kind** он зану́да, каки́х ма́ло; **it is the ~ winter in living memory** тако́й плохо́й зимы́ никто́ не упо́мнит; **you came at the ~ possible time** вы пришли́ в са́мое неподходя́щее вре́мя; **I had the ~ job of all — clearing up** мне доста́лось са́мая проти́вная рабо́та — убо́рка.

adv. ху́же всего́/всех; **he fared ~ of all** ему́ пришло́сь ху́же, чем всем остальны́м; **who did ~ in the exam?** кто ху́же всех сдал экза́мен?

v.t. (*liter.*) побе|жда́ть, -ди́ть; нан|оси́ть, -ести́ пораже́ние +*d.*

worsted ['wʊstɪd] *n.* (*yarn*) гребенна́я шерсть; (*cloth*) ткань из гребенно́й ше́рсти; шерстяна́я мате́рия.

worth [wɜːθ] *n.* (*value*) це́нность; (*merit*) досто́инство; **of great ~** значи́тельный; **of little ~** незначи́тельный; **a man of ~** досто́йный челове́к; челове́к, заслу́живающий уваже́ния; **his true ~ was appreciated by few** лишь немно́гие цени́ли его́ по досто́инству; (*quantity of specified value*): **give me a pound's ~ of sweets** да́йте мне конфе́т на (оди́н) фунт.

pred. adj. **1.** (*of value equal to*): **it's ~ about £1** э́то сто́ит о́коло одного́ фу́нта; **what is your house ~?** во ско́лько оце́нивается ваш дом?; **I paid £3000 for the car, but it's ~ more** я заплати́л 3000 фу́нтов за э́ту маши́ну, но по существу́ она́ сто́ит бо́льше; **what's it ~ to you if I tell you?** что вы дади́те за то, что́бы узна́ть?; **this isn't ~ much today** сейча́с за э́то мно́го не возьмёшь; **it's ~ a lot to me** для меня́ э́то о́чень це́нно/ва́жно (*or* мно́го зна́чит); **our money is ~ less every day** с ка́ждым днём на́ши де́ньги обесце́ниваются; **I tell you this for what it's ~** за что купи́л, за то и продаю́; **he is ~ his weight in gold** таки́е, как он, це́нятся на вес зо́лота. **2.** (*deserving of*) сто́ящий, заслу́живающий; **if a thing is ~ doing, it's ~ doing well** е́сли уж де́лать что-то, так де́лать как сле́дует; **I thought it was ~ a try** я счита́л, что име́ет смысл (*or* сто́ит) попро́бовать; **it's not ~ the trouble of asking** не сто́ит спра́шивать; **I'll make it ~ your while** я бу́ду вам благода́рен; вы в накла́де не оста́нетесь; **it is ~ while** не меша́ет; не ли́шнее; **it is well ~ while** о́чень да́же сто́ит; **it is ~ noticing** э́то заслу́живает внима́ния; **it's hardly ~ mentioning** об э́том вряд ли сто́ит упомина́ть; **it's well ~ the money** э́то вполне́ сто́ящая вещь; э́то вполне́ опра́вданная затра́та; **well ~ having** о́чень сто́ящий/поле́зный; **is life ~ living?** сто́ит ли жить? **3.** (*possessed of*): **he died ~ a million** он оста́вил миллио́н; **what is the old man ~?** ско́лько у старика́ за душо́й?; (*fig.*): **he ran for all he was ~** он мча́лся во весь дух (*or* изо всех сил).

cpd. **~while** *adj.* **a ~while person** досто́йный/сто́ящий челове́к; **a ~while undertaking** сто́ящее де́ло; **a ~while experiment** интере́сный о́пыт.

worthiness ['wɜːðɪnɪs] *n.* досто́инство.

worthless ['wɜːθlɪs] *adj.* ничего́ не сто́ящий; никуды́шный; ничто́жный, никчёмный.

worthlessness ['wɜːθlɪsnɪs] *n.* ничто́жность, никчёмность.

worthy ['wɜːðɪ] *n.* (*arch. or joc.*) почте́нный челове́к/муж; **local worthies** ме́стная знать.

adj. **1.** (*estimable; meritorious; deserving respect*) досто́йный, почте́нный; **a ~ man** досто́йный челове́к; **a ~ life** че́стно про́житая жизнь; **a ~ cause** пра́вое де́ло. **2.** (*deserving*): **~ of note** досто́йный внима́ния; **~ of (*or* to have) a place in the team** досто́йный быть чле́ном кома́нды; **~ of remembrance** досто́йный па́мяти; **a cause ~ of support** де́ло, заслу́живающее подде́ржки. **3.** (*matching up or appropriate*): **~ of the occasion** подоба́ющий слу́чаю; **he is not ~ of her** он её не сто́ит.

wot [wɒt] *int.* (*joc. form of* **what**) как?!; что?!

Wotan ['vəʊtɑːn, 'wəʊ-] *n.* Вота́н.

wotcher ['wɒtʃə(r)] *int.* (*sl.*) здоро́во!

would [wʊd, wəd] *v. aux.* (*see also* **will**) **1.** (*conditional*): **he ~ be angry if he knew** он бы рассерди́лся, е́сли бы узна́л; **I ~ like to know** я хоте́л бы знать; **I ~n't know** отку́да мне знать? **2.** (*expr. wish*): **I ~ rather** я бы предпочёл; **~ that it were otherwise!** ах, кабы́ э́то бы́ло не так!; **~ to God I had never seen him!** заче́м то́лько я с ним повстреча́лся!; **I ~ point out that ...** я бы хоте́л указа́ть на то, что... **3.** (*of typical action etc.*): **you ~ do that!** с тебя́ ста́нется!; **of course it ~ rain today** ну коне́чно же, и́менно сего́дня до́лжен был пойти́ дождь; **of course he ~ say that** ну коне́чно, он э́то ска́жет. **4.** (*of habitual action*): *see* **will**[2] **5.**

cpd. **~-be** *adj.* претенду́ющий (*на что*); **a ~-be writer** мечта́ющий стать писа́телем; претенду́ющий на зва́ние писа́теля; **a ~-be gentleman** стро́ящий из себя́ джентльме́на; **a ~-be smart saying** так называ́емая острота́.

wound [wuːnd] *n.* ра́на, ране́ние; **receive a ~** получи́ть (*pf.*) ране́ние; **he inflicted several knife ~s** он нанёс не́сколько ножевы́х уда́ров; **lick one's ~s** (*lit., fig.*) зали́з|ывать, -а́ть ра́ны; **knife ~** ножева́я ра́на; (*fig.*) душе́вная ра́на; оби́да; **the rebuff was a severe ~ to his vanity** ре́зкий отка́з бо́льно ра́нил его́ самолю́бие.

v.t. ра́нить (*impf., pf.*); **he was ~ed in the leg** его́ ра́нило в но́гу; **there were many ~ed** бы́ло мно́го ра́неных; (*fig.*) ра́нить (*impf., pf.*); зад|ева́ть, -е́ть; об|ижа́ть, -и́деть; **~ s.o.'s feelings** оскорб|ля́ть, -и́ть чьи-н. чу́вства; **~ed pride** уязвлённое самолю́бие.

wove [wəʊv] *adj.* (*of paper*) веле́невый.

wow [waʊ] *n.* (*sl.*): **the show was a ~** спекта́кль прошёл с огро́мным успе́хом.

v.t. (*sl.*) прив|оди́ть, -ести́ в восто́рг.

int. здо́рово!; вот э́то да!; ух!; блеск!

WPC (*abbr. of* ***woman police constable***) же́нщина-полице́йский.

wrack [ræk] *n.* **1.** (*seaweed*) во́доросл|и (*pl.*, *g.* -ей). **2.** = **rack**[3]. **3.** = **rack**[4]

wraith [reɪθ] *n.* при́зрак, привиде́ние, дух.

wrangle ['ræŋg(ə)l] *n.* пререка́ние, ссо́ра, спор.

v.i. пререка́ться; ссо́риться; спо́рить (*all impf.*).

wrangler ['ræŋglə(r)] *n.* спо́рщик, скло́чник; **senior** ~ отли́чник по матема́тике.

wrap [ræp] *n.* **1.** (*lit.*) (*shawl*) шаль, плато́к; (*cloak*) наки́дка, пелери́на; (*rug*) плед. **2.** (*fig.*, *covering*): **under ~s** (*fig.*) стро́го засекре́ченный; **take the ~s off** (*fig.*) рассекре́|чивать, -тить.

v.t. **1.** (*cover*; *enclose*) завёр|тывать, -ну́ть; обёр|тывать, -ну́ть; ~ **o.s. in a blanket** завёр|тываться, -ну́ться (*or* заку́т|ываться, -аться) в одея́ло; **she ~ped the baby in a shawl** она́ заверну́ла ребёнка в шаль; **the brooch was ~ped in cotton wool** бро́шка была́ обёрнута ва́той; **they were ~ping presents** они́ завёртывали пода́рки; (*fig.*) обвола́кивать (*impf.*); скры|ва́ть, -ть; **~ped in mystery** оку́танный та́йной; **the mountain was ~ped in mist** гора́ была́ оку́тана тума́ном. **2.** (*wind or fold as a covering*) свёр|тывать, -ну́ть; скла́дывать, сложи́ть; ~ **one's coat round one** заверну́ться/запахну́ться/закута́ться (*pf.*) в пальто́; **we ~ sacking round the pipes in winter** зимо́й мы об(в)ёртываем тру́бы мешкови́ной; **he ~ped his arms around her** он заключи́л её в объя́тия; он о́бнял её.

with advs.: ~ **over** *v.i.* (*of garment*) запа́хиваться (*impf.*); ~ **up** *v.t.* (*cover up*) об(в)ёр|тывать, -ну́ть; завёр|тывать, -ну́ть; запако́в|ывать, -а́ть; заку́т|ывать, -ать; **don't ~ up the boy in cotton-wool!** не ку́тайте ребёнка в ва́ту!; **he ~s up his meaning in high-flown language** он облека́ет свою́ мысль в пы́шные выраже́ния; (*conclude*) закругл|я́ть, -и́ть (*coll.*); (*dispose of*; *summarize*) кра́тко сумми́ровать (*impf.*); **he ~ped up the whole question in a few words** он изложи́л существо́ вопро́са в не́скольких слова́х; (*obscure*) скры|ва́ть, -ть; (*pass.*, *be engrossed*) уйти́/погрузи́ться (*pf.*) (*во что*); **he is ~ped up in his studies** он поглощён заня́тиями; **she is ~ped up in her children** она́ поглощена́ свои́ми детьми́; *v.i.* (*put on extra clothes*) заку́таться (*pf.*); ~ **up well when you go out!** оде́ньтесь потепле́е (*or* заку́тайтесь хороше́нько), когда́ бу́дете выходи́ть!

cpd. **~-up** *n.* (*coll.*, *summary*) сво́дка.

wrapper ['ræpə(r)] *n.* **1.** (*of foodstuff*, *sweet etc.*) обёртка; (*of book*) суперобло́жка; (*of newspaper sent by post*) бандеро́ль. **2.** (*house-coat*) хала́т, пеньюа́р.

wrapping ['ræpɪŋ] *n.* (*cover*) обёртка, упако́вка; (*packing material*) упако́вочный/обёрточный материа́л.

cpd. **~-paper** *n.* обёрточная бума́га.

wrath [rɒθ, rɔːθ] *n.* (*liter.*) гнев; **day of** ~ стра́шный суд, су́дный день; **slow to** ~ ме́дленный на гнев; **vent one's ~ on** обру́ши|вать, -ть гнев на+*a.*

wrathful ['rɒθfʊl] *adj.* гне́вный, я́ростный.

wreak [riːk] *v.t.* нан|оси́ть, -ести́; ~ **vengeance on** мсти́ть, ото- +*d.*

wreath [riːθ] *n.* вено́к, вене́ц, гирля́нда; ~ **of roses** вено́к из роз; **lay a ~ on s.o.'s grave** возложи́ть (*pf.*) вено́к на чью-н. моги́лу; (*fig.*): ~ **of smoke** кольцо́/завито́к ды́ма.

wreathe [riːð] *v.t.* **1.** (*encircle*) окруж|а́ть, -и́ть; обв|ива́ть, -и́ть; **the hills were ~d in mist** над гора́ми клуби́лся тума́н; **the porch was ~d with roses** крыльцо́ бы́ло уви́то ро́зами; **her face was ~d in smiles** её лицо́ сия́ло улы́бкой. **2.** (*twine*) спле|та́ть, -сти́; сви|ва́ть, -ть; **the snake ~d itself round his neck** змея́ обвила́сь вокру́г его́ ше́и.

v.i. (*of smoke*) клуби́ться (*impf.*).

wreck [rek] *n.* **1.** (*ruin*, *destruction*, *esp. of ship*) (корабле)круше́ние, ава́рия, катастро́фа; **the gales caused many ~s** от што́рмов мно́жество судо́в потерпе́ло круше́ние; (*fig.*) ги́бель, крах, разоре́ние. **2.** (*~ed ship*) затону́вший (*or* потерпе́вший круше́ние) кора́бль; **the shores were strewn with ~s** берега́ бы́ли усе́яны оста́тками кораблекруше́ний. **3.** (*damaged or disabled vehicle, building, pers. etc.*) разва́лина; **his car was a ~ after the collision** по́сле ава́рии его́ маши́на пришла́ в по́лную него́дность; **he is a physical and mental** ~ он соверше́нная разва́лина, как физи́чески, так и у́мственно; **she became a nervous** ~ у неё не́рвы совсе́м сда́ли; **I look a** ~ я вы́гляжу ужа́сно; **the house was a ~ after the party** по́сле вечери́нки в до́ме бы́ло всё вверх дном.

v.t. **1.** (*sink*) топи́ть, по-; **the ship was ~ed** су́дно потерпе́ло круше́ние. **2.**: ~ **a train** вызыва́ть, вы́звать круше́ние по́езда; ~ **a building** сн|оси́ть, -ести́ зда́ние. **3.** (*fig.*, *ruin*, *destroy*) разр|уша́ть, -у́шить; разор|я́ть, -и́ть; губи́ть, по-; по́ртить, ис-; срыва́ть, сорва́ть.

wreckage ['rekɪdʒ] *n.* (*wrecking*, *lit.*, *fig.*) круше́ние; (*remains*) обло́мки (*m. pl.*) (круше́ния *и m.n.*).

wrecker ['rekə(r)] *n.* **1.** (*hist.*) граби́тель (*m.*) разби́тых судо́в. **2.** (*salvager*) спаса́тель (*m.*). **3.** (*demolition worker*) рабо́чий по сно́су домо́в. **4.** (*US*, *repairer*) рабо́чий авари́йно-ремо́нтной брига́ды; (*vehicle*) маши́на техни́ческой по́мощи.

Wren[1] [ren] *n.* военнослу́жащая же́нской вспомога́тельной вое́нно-морско́й слу́жбы.

wren[2] [ren] *n.* вьюро́к, королёк; крапи́вник.

wrench [rentʃ] *n.* **1.** (*violent twist or pull*) дёрганье, рыво́к; **he gave my arm a** ~ он дёрнул меня́ за плечо́; **he gave his ankle a** ~ он вы́вихнул но́гу; **he got the lid off with a** ~ он ре́зко сорва́л кры́шку. **2.** (*fig.*) тоска́, боль, надры́в; **leaving our old home was a** ~ покида́я родно́й дом, мы испы́тывали о́струю боль. **3.** (*tool*) га́ечный ключ.

v.t. дёр|гать, -нуть; рвать, со-; **he ~ed the door open** он ре́зко рвану́л к себе́ дверь; **he ~ed the paper out of my hand** он вы́рвал/вы́дернул бума́гу из мои́х рук; (*fig.*, *distort*) иска|жа́ть, -зи́ть; извра|ща́ть, -ти́ть; **he ~ed at the door handle** он дёрнул (за) дверну́ю ру́чку.

with advs.: ~ **off**, ~ **out** *vv.t.* от|рыва́ть, -орва́ть; вырыва́ть, вы́рвать; выдёргивать, вы́дернуть.

wrest [rest] *v.t.* **1.** (*take away or extract by force*) вырыва́ть, вы́рвать (си́лой); **they ~ed a confession of guilt from him** они́ принуди́ли его́ призна́ться в свое́й вине́; **they ~ed a living from the land** они́ с трудо́м добива́ли себе́ пропита́ние на э́той ску́дной земле́. **2.** (*twist*; *pervert*) иска|жа́ть, -зи́ть; извра|ща́ть, -ти́ть.

wrestle ['res(ə)l] *n.* борьба́; (*bout*, *match*) схва́тка, встре́ча, соревнова́ние (по борьбе́).

v.i. боро́ться (*impf.*); (*fig.*): ~ **with a problem** би́ться (*impf.*) над зада́чей; **he ~d with his conscience** он боро́лся со свое́й со́вестью.

wrestler ['reslə(r)] *n.* бор|е́ц (*fem.* -чи́ха); **free-style** ~ боре́ц по во́льной борьбе́; **Greco-Roman** ~ боре́ц по класси́ческой борьбе́.

wrestling ['reslɪŋ] *n.* борьба́.

cpds. **~-bout**, **~-match** *nn.* встре́ча/схва́тка по борьбе́.

wretch [retʃ] *n.* (*sad or unfortunate pers.*) несча́стный; жа́лкий челове́к; (*contemptible pers.*) негодя́й; (*joc.*) него́дник; **little** ~ (*of a child*) чертёнок, бесёнок; **poor** ~ бедня́га (*c.g.*).

wretched ['retʃɪd] *adj.* (*miserable*, *unhappy*) несча́стный, жа́лкий; **a ~ hovel** жа́лкая лачу́га; (*inferior*) никуды́шный, скве́рный; **this coffee is ~ stuff** э́тот ко́фе пить невозмо́жно; ~ **food** отврати́тельная еда́; (*unpleasant*): **I've had a ~ day** у меня́ был ужа́сный день; ~ **weather** ме́рзкая/проти́вная пого́да; **a ~ toothache** отча́янная зубна́я боль; (*as expletive*): **owing to his ~ stupidity** благодаря́/из-за его́ дура́цкой ту́пости; **I can't find the ~ key** не зна́ю, куда́ запропасти́лся э́тот прокля́тый/несча́стный/проти́вный ключ.

wretchedness ['retʃɪdnɪs] *n.* (*misery*) страда́ние, го́ре, муче́ние, несча́стье; (*poor quality*) него́дность.

wrick [rɪk] = **rick**[2]

wriggle ['rɪg(ə)l] *n.* изги́б, изви́в.

v.t. (*also* ~ **about**): ~ **one's toes** шевели́ть (*impf.*) па́льцами ног; **he ~d (himself) free** он вы́вернулся/вы́скользнул; **he ~d his way out of the cave** он ползко́м, извива́ясь, вы́брался из пеще́ры.

v.i. (*also* ~ **about**) изгиба́ться (*impf.*); извива́ться (*impf.*); **a wriggling worm** извива́ющийся червь; **don't ~ in your seat** переста́нь ёрзать!; **the baby ~d out of my**

arms ребёнок вы́скользнул у меня́ из рук; ~ **out of a difficulty** вы́вернуться (*pf.*) из затрудни́тельного положе́ния; ~ **out of a responsibility** увильну́ть (*pf.*) от отве́тственности.

wring [rɪŋ] *n.*: **she gave the clothes another** ~ она́ ещё раз отжа́ла бельё.

v.t. **1.** (*squeeze*) пож|има́ть, -а́ть; сж|има́ть, -ать; **he wrung my hand** он кре́пко пожа́л мне ру́ку; **he wrung his hands in despair** он в отча́янии лома́л ру́ки; (*squeeze out by twisting*) выжима́ть, вы́жать; отж|има́ть, -а́ть; ~ **clothes dry** выжима́ть, вы́жать бельё до́суха; ~**ing wet** мо́крый, хоть вы́жми; (*twist round*) скру́|чивать, -ти́ть; ~ **a chicken's neck** сверну́ть (*pf.*) ку́рице го́лову; **I'll** ~ **your neck!** я тебе́ ше́ю сверну́! **2.** (*fig., extract by force*) ист|орга́ть, -о́ргнуть; **the story wrung tears from his eyes** расска́з заста́вил его́ прослези́ться; **I wrung a promise from him** я вы́рвал у него́ обеща́ние; **they tried to** ~ **a confession out of him** они́ пыта́лись вы́рвать у него́ призна́ние. **3.** (*fig., torture; distress*) терза́ть (*impf.*); **her tears wrung his heart** её слёзы терза́ли ему́ ду́шу.

with adv.: ~ **out** *v.t.*: (*clothes*) выжима́ть, вы́жать; (*water*) отж|има́ть, -а́ть; (*fig.*) ~ **out a confession** вырыва́ть, вы́рвать призна́ние.

wringer ['rɪŋə(r)] *n.* пресс для отжима́ния белья́.

wrinkle ['rɪŋk(ə)l] *n.* **1.** (*on skin*) морщи́на; (*on dress*) скла́дка; **the dress fits without a** ~ пла́тье (сиди́т) как влито́е. **2.** (*coll., useful hint*) сове́т, намёк.

v.t.: ~ **one's brow** мо́рщить, на- лоб; ~ **one's nose** мо́рщить, с- нос.

v.i. мя́ться (*impf.*); смина́ться (*impf.*); **this material** ~**s easily** э́тот материа́л о́чень мнётся/мну́щийся.

with adv.: ~ **up** *v.t.* мо́рщить, с-.

wrinkl|ed ['rɪŋk(ə)ld], **-y** ['rɪŋklɪ] *adjs.* морщи́нистый, смо́рщенный.

wrist [rɪst] *n.* запя́стье; (*of dress or glove*) манже́та, обшла́г, кра́га.

cpds. ~**-band** *n.* (*of watch*) брасле́т; ~**-watch** *n.* нару́чные час|ы́ (*pl., g.* -о́в).

wristlet ['rɪstlɪt] *n.* брасле́т; ремешо́к для нару́чных часо́в.

writ [rɪt] *n.* **1.** (*written injunction or summons*) пове́стка; исково́е заявле́ние; ~ **of execution** исполни́тельный лист; **serve a** ~ **on s.o.** вруч|а́ть, -и́ть кому́-н. пове́стку; **his** ~ **does not run here** (*fig.*) его́ власть не распространя́ется на э́ту о́бласть. **2.**: **Holy W**~ свяще́нное писа́ние.

write [raɪt] *v.t.* **1.** писа́ть, на-; **he** ~**s a good hand** у него́ хоро́ший по́черк; **she can** ~ **shorthand** она́ зна́ет стеногра́фию; она мо́жет стенографи́ровать; **the word is written with a hyphen, with a 'y'** э́то сло́во пи́шется че́рез дефи́с/«у»; **honesty is written all over his face** у него́ на лице́ напи́сано, что он че́стный челове́к; **writ large** (*liter.*) в увели́ченном ви́де. **2.**: ~ **a cheque** выпи́сывать, вы́писать чек. **3.** (*compose*) писа́ть, на-; сочин|я́ть, -и́ть; **he** ~**s plays** он пи́шет пье́сы; **Beethoven wrote nine symphonies** Бетхо́вен сочини́л де́вять симфо́ний. **4.** (*convey by letter*): **he wrote me all the news** он сообщи́л мне в письме́ все но́вости; он написа́л мне обо всех новостя́х. *See also* **written**

v.i. **1.** писа́ть (*impf.*); **please** ~ **larger/smaller** пиши́те, пожа́луйста, крупне́е/ме́льче. **2.** (*compose*) сочин|я́ть, -и́ть; писа́ть, на-; **he** ~**s for 'The Times'** он сотру́дничает в газе́те «Таймс»; **he** ~**s a bit** он попи́сывает; ~ **for a living** быть писа́телем(-профессиона́лом); зараба́тывать (*impf.*) перо́м; писа́ть (*impf.*) для за́работка; **she wants to** ~ она́ хо́чет стать писа́тельницей; ~ **for the screen/stage** писа́ть сцена́рии/пье́сы; **he** ~**s home every week** он пи́шет домо́й ка́ждую неде́лю; **don't forget to** ~! пиши́те!; **nothing to** ~ **home about** (*coll.*) ничего́ осо́бенного.

with advs.: ~ **away,** ~ **off** *vv.i.*: **he wrote away, off for a catalogue** он вы́писал себе́ катало́г; ~ **back** *v.i.* отв|еча́ть, -е́тить (письмо́м); ~ **down** *v.t.* (*make a note of*): ~ **the address down before you forget it** запиши́те а́дрес, а то забу́дете; (*designate*): **I would** ~ **him down as a fool** я бы сказа́л, что он дура́к; (*underplay*): **the incident was written down in the press** в пре́ссе э́тот инциде́нт был замя́т; (*reduce value*): **the old stock has been written down** залежа́вшийся това́р был уценён; *v.i.* (*condescend*): **he** ~**s down to his public** он подде́лывается под вку́сы пу́блики; ~ **in** *v.t.* впи́с|ывать, -а́ть; вст|авля́ть, -а́вить; **his name was written in afterwards** его́ и́мя вписа́ли поздне́е; *v.i.* обра|ща́ться, -ти́ться с пи́сьмами (*куда-н.*); ~ **in for a free sample!** закажи́те (по по́чте) беспла́тный образе́ц; ~ **off** *v.t.* (*compose quickly*) писа́ть (*impf.*) с лёгкостью; **he wrote off 3 articles in one evening** он наката́л (*coll.*) три статьи́ за оди́н ве́чер; (*cancel*): ~ **off a debt** спи́с|ывать, -а́ть долг; (*recognize annulment or loss of*): ~ **off £500 for depreciation** списа́ть (*pf.*) 500 фу́нтов на амортиза́цию; **the car had to be written off** маши́ну пришло́сь сакти́ровать; **you may as well** ~ **it off** пиши́ пропа́ло; **I wrote him off** я на нём поста́вил крест; *v.i.* = ~ **away;** ~ **out** *v.t.* выпи́сывать, вы́писать; ~ **out your homework again!** перепиши́ дома́шнее зада́ние!; ~ **out a cheque for £20** вы́писать (*pf.*) чек на 20 фу́нтов; **he has written himself out** он исписа́лся; **this character was written out after three episodes** а́втор се́рии вы́кинул э́тот персона́ж по́сле трёх эпизо́дов; ~ **up** *v.t.*: **I must** ~ **up my diary** мне ну́жно довести́ дневни́к до сего́дняшнего дня; **the journalist wrote up the incident** журнали́ст подро́бно описа́л инциде́нт; **the critics wrote him up as an actor of promise** кри́тики расхвали́ли его́ как актёра с больши́м бу́дущим.

cpds. ~**-in** *n.* (*US*) кандида́т, дополни́тельно внесённый в избира́тельный бюллете́нь; ~**-off** *n.*: **the car was a** ~**-off** маши́ну списа́ли на слом; ~**-up** *n.* отчёт в пре́ссе.

writer ['raɪtə(r)] *n.* **1.** (*pers. writing*) а́втор; **this (***or* **the present)** ~ нижеподписа́вшийся; пи́шущий э́ти стро́ки. **2.** (*author*) писа́тель (*fem.* -ница); ~**'s cramp** су́дорога от писа́ния.

writhe [raɪð] *v.i.* ко́рчиться (*impf.*); извива́ться (*impf.*); (*fig.*): ~ **with shame** ко́рчиться (*impf.*) от стыда́; ~ **under an insult** терза́ться (*impf.*) оби́дой.

writing ['raɪtɪŋ] *n.* **1.** (*act, process*) (на)писа́ние; **at this** ~ в то вре́мя, когда́ пи́шутся э́ти стро́ки. **2.** (*ability, art*) письмо́, гра́мота; **reading and** ~ чте́ние и письмо́; **the art of** ~ иску́сство сло́ва. **3.** (*written words*): **in** ~ пи́сьменно; в пи́сьменном ви́де; в пи́сьменной фо́рме; **commit to** ~ запи́с|ывать, -а́ть; изл|ага́ть, -ожи́ть на бума́ге. **4.** (*script, system of* ~) письмо́, пи́сьменность. **5.**: **sacred** ~**s** свяще́нные кни́ги (*f. pl.*); **the** ~ **on the wall** (*fig.*) злове́щее предзнаменова́ние. **6.** (*literary composition*) произведе́ние, сочине́ния (*nt. pl.*); **the** ~**s of Plato** произведе́ния Плато́на. **7.** (*profession*) писа́тельский труд; **take up** ~ зан|има́ться, -я́ться литерату́рой/сочини́тельством. **8.** (*style*) стиль (*m.*); язы́к; мане́ра (письма́); **fine** ~ (чересчу́р) краси́вый стиль; **a good piece of** ~ прекра́сная про́за.

cpds. ~**-block** *n.* блокно́т; ~**-case** *n.* несессе́р для пи́сьменных принадле́жностей; ~**-desk** *n.* пи́сьменный стол; ~**-pad** *n.* блокно́т; ~**-paper** *n.* почто́вая/пи́счая бума́га; ~**-table** *n.* пи́сьменный стол.

written ['rɪt(ə)n] *adj.* (*not oral, not typed*) пи́сьменный, пи́саный, рукопи́сный; **the** ~ **word** пи́сьменная речь; (*printed, typed*) печа́тное сло́во; *see also* **write**

wrong [rɒŋ] *n.* **1.** (*moral* ~) зло; **do** ~ греши́ть, со-; непра́вильно/нехорошо́/пло́хо поступа́ть (*impf.*); заблужда́ться (*impf.*); **know the difference between right and** ~ различа́ть (*impf.*) добро́ и зло; **two** ~**s don't make a right** злом зла не попра́вишь. **2.** (*unjust action or its result*) несправедли́вость, оби́да; **do** ~ **to** об|ижа́ть, -и́деть; быть несправедли́вым к+*d.*; **they did him a great** ~ они́ его́ кре́пко оби́дели; **the** ~**s of Ireland** несправедли́вости, причинённые Ирла́ндии; **right a** ~ испр|авля́ть, -а́вить зло/несправедли́вость; **you do** ~ **to accuse him** вы его́ напра́сно обвиня́ете. **3.** (*state of error*): **you are in the** ~ вы непра́вы/винова́ты; **put s.o. in the** ~ свали́ть (*pf.*) вину́ на кого́-н.; ста́вить, по- кого́-н. в положе́ние оби́дчика.

adj. **1.** (*contrary to morality*) гре́шный; (*reprehensible*) предосуди́тельный; **it is ~ to steal** ворова́ть нельзя́/грешно́/нехорошо́; **that was very ~ of you** э́то с ва́шей стороны́ бы́ло о́чень нехорошо́/ду́рно. **2.** (*mistaken*) непра́вый; **I was ~ to let him do it** я не до́лжен был (*or* мне не сле́довало) разреша́ть ему́ э́то; **you are ~** вы непра́вы/ошиба́етесь; **prove ~** опров|ерга́ть, -е́ргнуть (*кого/что*). **3.** (*incorrect, erroneous, unsuitable, improper*) непра́вильный, неве́рный, оши́бочный, неподходя́щий; не тот; **at the ~ time** в неподходя́щее вре́мя; **in/to the ~ place** не там/туда́; **get hold of the ~ end of the stick** непра́вильно поня́ть (*pf.*) (*or* превра́тно истолкова́ть (*pf.*)) что-н.; **take the ~ turning** (*lit.*) сверну́ть (*pf.*) не туда́; (*fig.*) сби́ться (*pf.*) с пути́; **you're going the ~ way** вы идёте непра́вильно (*or* не туда́); **my food went down the ~ way** еда́ попа́ло не в то го́рло; **that's the ~ way to go about it** э́то де́лается не так; **back the ~ horse** (*fig.*) поста́вить (*pf.*) не на ту ло́шадь; **this shirt is the ~ size/colour** э́та руба́шка не того́ разме́ра/цве́та; **~ side out** наизна́нку; **the ~ way round** наоборо́т; **the clock is ~** часы́ врут; **everything went ~** всё сложи́лось неуда́чно; **the ~ track** ло́жный/неве́рный след; **the letter went to the ~ address** письмо́ попа́ло не по а́дресу; **you have the ~ number** вы не туда́ попа́ли; **he began at the ~ end** он на́чал не с того́ конца́; **what's ~ with it?** (*what is the harm in it?*) что в э́том плохо́го? **4.** (*out of order; causing concern*) нела́дный; **is (there) anything ~?** что́(-нибудь) случи́лось?; **there's something ~ with my car** что́-то с мое́й маши́ной не в поря́дке; **what's ~ with Britain?** что произошло́ с А́нглией? **5.** (*of food*): **can you taste anything ~ with this fish?** вам не ка́жется, что у э́той ры́бы стра́нный вкус? **6.** (*of health*): **the doctor asked me what was ~** врач спроси́л, на что я жа́луюсь; **he found nothing ~ with me** он никаки́х боле́зней у меня́ не нашёл.

adv. (*incorrectly*) непра́вильно, не так; **don't get me ~** (*coll.*) пойми́те меня́ пра́вильно; не пойми́те меня́ превра́тно; **you've got it all ~** вы всё перепу́тали; **I got in ~ with him** (*coll.*) я навлёк на себя́ его́ недово́льство; **the clock went ~** часы́ испо́ртились; **our plans went ~** на́ши пла́ны спу́тались; **his daughter went ~** его́ дочь сби́лась с пути́; **we went ~ at the last crossroads** на после́днем перекрёстке мы не туда́ поверну́ли; **where did we go ~** (*make a mistake*)? в чём мы ошибли́сь?; **everything went ~ for us** нам во всём сопу́тствовала неуда́ча; **I guessed ~** я не угада́л; **he never puts a foot ~** он никогда́ не де́лает неве́рного ша́га.

v.t. (*treat unjustly*) быть несправедли́вым к+*d.*; об|ижа́ть, -и́деть; **you ~ me if you think that** е́сли вы так счита́ете, вы ко мне несправедли́вы.

cpds. **~doer** *n.* гре́шни|к (*fem.* -ца), нечести́в|ец (*fem.* -ица); престу́пни|к (*fem.* -ца), правонаруши́тель (*fem.* -ница); **~doing** *n.* грех, преступле́ние, правонаруше́ние; **~-headed** *adj.* упо́рствующий в своём заблужде́нии.

wrongful [ˈrɒŋfʊl] *adj.* (*unjust*) несправедли́вый; (*unlawful*) незако́нный, неправоме́рный; **~ dismissal** незако́нное увольне́ние.

wroth [rəʊθ, rɒθ] *pred. adj.* (*liter.*) разгне́ванный.

wrought [rɔːt] *adj.* (*cf.* **work** *v.t.* **7.**): **~ iron** сва́рочная/мя́гкая/ко́вкая сталь.

cpd. **~-up** *adj.* взви́нченный.

wry [raɪ] *adj.* криво́й, переко́шенный; **a ~ smile** крива́я улы́бка; **make a ~ face** сostро́ить (*pf.*) ки́слую физионо́мию; скриви́ться, смо́рщиться (*both pf.*).

cpd. **~neck** *n.* дубоно́с, вертише́йка.

wych-elm [ˈwɪtʃelm] *n.* ильм го́рный.

wych-hazel [ˈwɪtʃˌheɪz(ə)l] *n.* гамаме́лис, лещи́на вирги́нская.

wyvern [ˈwaɪv(ə)n] *n.* крыла́тый драко́н.

X

X [eks] *n.* (*unknown quantity or pers.*) X, икс; **let ~ be the number of hours worked** пусть X равня́ется числу́ рабо́чих часо́в; **the correspondent, Mr ~** корреспонде́нт, г-н N; **~ marks the spot where the body was found** кресто́м обозна́чено ме́сто, где был на́йден труп; **he signed with an ~** он поста́вил кре́стик вме́сто по́дписи; **an X film** фильм катего́рии X (*только для взрослых*).

cpd. **~-ray** *n.* (*pl.*) рентге́новы лучи́, икс-лучи́ (*m. pl.*); (*sg., picture*) рентгеногра́мма; рентге́новский сни́мок; **~-ray therapy** рентгенотерапи́я; *v.t.* просве́|чивать, -ти́ть рентге́новскими луча́ми; де́лать, с- рентге́н +*g.*

xanthic [ˈzænθɪk] *adj.*: **~ acid** ксантоге́новая кислота́.

xenogamy [zeˈnɒgəmɪ] *n.* ксеного́мия.

xenophobe [ˈzenəˌfəʊb] *n.* ксенофо́б.

xenophobia [ˌzenəˈfəʊbɪə] *n.* ксенофо́бия.

xenophobic [ˌzenəˈfəʊbɪk] *adj.* отлича́ющийся ксенофо́бией.

xerography [zɪəˈrɒgrəfɪ, ze-] *n.* ксерогра́фия.

Xerox [ˈzɪərɒks, ˈze-] *n.* ксе́рокс, фотоко́пия.

v.t. де́лать, с- ксе́рокс +*g.*; ксерографи́ровать (*impf., pf.*).

Xerxes [ˈzɜːksiːz] *n.* Ксеркс.

Xmas [ˈkrɪsməs, ˈeksməs] = **Christmas**

xylophone [ˈzaɪləˌfəʊn] *n.* ксилофо́н.

Y

Y [waɪ] *n.* (*math.*) и́грек.

cpd. **~-shaped** *adj.* вилкообра́зный, У-обра́зный.

yacht [jɒt] *n.* я́хта.

v.i. пла́вать/ходи́ть/ката́ться (*indet.*) на я́хте.

cpds. **~-club** *n.* яхт-клу́б; **~sman** *n.* яхтсме́н; **~swoman** *n.* яхтсме́нка.

yachting [ˈjɒtɪŋ] *n.* пла́вание/ката́ние на я́хтах; па́русный/я́хтенный спорт.

yack [jæk] *v.i.* (*coll.*) болта́ть (*impf.*).

yah [jɑː] *int.* ха!; э-э!

yahoo [jəˈhuː, jɑː-] *n.* **1.** (*in Swift's novel*) иеху (*m. indecl.*). **2.** хам.

Yahveh [ˈjɑːveɪ] *n.* Я́хве (*m. indecl.*).

yak [jæk] *n.* як; (*attr.*) я́чий.

Yakut [jæˈkuːt] *n.* (*pers.*) яку́т (*fem.* -ка); (*language*) яку́тский язы́к.

adj. яку́тский.

Yale lock [jeɪl] *n.* (*propr.*) цилиндри́ческий/автомати́ческий/америка́нский замо́к.

Yalta [ˈjæltə] *n.* Я́лта; (*attr.*) я́лтинский.

yam [jæm] *n.* ямс, диоскоре́я, бата́т.

Yangtze [ˈjæŋksɪ, ˈjæŋktsɪ] *n.* Янцзы́ (*f. indecl.*), Чанцзя́н.

Yank[1] [jæŋk], **yankee** [ˈjæŋkɪ] (*coll.*) *n.* я́нки (*m. indecl.*); северя́нин (*в США*).

adj. америка́нский; се́верный.

yank[2] [jæŋk] (*coll., pull*) *n.* рыво́к, дёрганье.
v.t. дёр|гать, -нуть.
with advs.: ~ **off** *v.t.* срыва́ть, сорва́ть; ~ **out** *v.t.* вырыва́ть, вы́рвать; выта́скивать, вы́тащить.
yap [jæp] *n.* тя́вканье; трёп, болтовня́.
v.i. (*of dogs*) тя́вк|ать, -нуть; (*chatter*) точи́ть (*impf.*) ля́сы (*impf.*); трепа́ться (*impf.*).
yard[1] [jɑːd] *n.* **1.** (*unit of measure*) ярд; **this material is sold by the** ~ э́то сукно́ продаётся на я́рды; **he writes poetry by the** ~ он пи́шет несме́тное/невоя́тное коли́чество стихо́в. **2.** (*naut.*) рей.
cpds. ~**-arm** *n.* нок ре́я; ~**stick** *n.* (*lit.*) измери́тельная лине́йка (длино́й в оди́н ярд); (*fig.*) мери́ло, ме́рка, крите́рий; **measure others by one's own** ~**stick** ме́рить (*impf.*) всех на свой арши́н.
yard[2] [jɑːd] *n.* **1.** (*of house*; **court**~) двор. **2.** (*for industrial purposes*): **timber** ~ лесно́й склад; **builder's** ~ строи́тельная площа́дка; **railway** ~ парк; **goods** ~ грузово́й парк. **3.** (*for cattle*) заго́н.
yarmulka [ˈjɑːməlkə] *n.* ермо́лка.
yarn [jɑːn] *n.* **1.** (*spun thread*) пря́жа; (*for knitting*) ни́тка. **2.** (*coll., story*) анекдо́т, расска́з, «ба́йка».
v.i. (*coll.*) болта́ть (*impf.*); трепа́ться (*impf.*).
yarovization [jærəvaɪˈzeɪʃ(ə)n] *n.* (*Russ. agric.*) яровиза́ция.
yarovize [ˈjærəˌvaɪz] *v.t.* (*Russ. agric.*) яровизи́ровать (*impf., pf.*).
yashmak [ˈjæʃmæk] *n.* чадра́, яшма́к.
yataghan [ˈjætəˌgæn] *n.* ятага́н.
yaw [jɔː] *v.i.* ры́скать (*impf.*), отклоня́ться (*impf.*) от ку́рса.
yawl [jɔːl] *n.* (*ship's boat*) ял.
yawn [jɔːn] *n.* зево́та, зево́к.
v.i. зев|а́ть, -ну́ть; **he was** ~**ing his head off** он отча́янно зева́л; (*fig, of chasm*) зия́ть (*impf.*); разв|ерза́ться, -е́рзнуться.
yaws [jɔːz] *n. pl.* фрамбе́зия.
ye [jiː] *pron.* (*arch.*) вы; ~ **Gods!** о бо́ги!
yea [jeɪ] *n.* (*affirmative vote*): **the** ~**s have it** большинство́ «за».
adv. (*yes*) да; (*indeed, moreover*) бо́льше/бо́лее того́.
yeah [jeə] *adv.* (*coll.*) да; ага́; **oh** ~**?** неуже́ли?; ну да?; ах так?
year [jɪə(r), jɜː(r)] *n.* **1.** год; **last** ~ в про́шлом году́; **he was only 40 years old** ему́ бы́ло всего́ со́рок лет; **in the** ~**s of my youth** в го́ды мое́й ю́ности; **I have known him for ten** ~**s** вот уже де́сять лет, как я его́ зна́ю; **twice a** ~ два ра́за (*or* два́жды) в год; **every** ~ **the exam gets harder** с ка́ждым го́дом экза́мен стано́вится трудне́е; ~ **in,** ~ **out** из го́да в год; ~ **after** ~ год за го́дом; ~ **by** ~ с ка́ждым го́дом; **all the** ~ **round** кру́глый год; **he is in his twentieth** ~ ему́ пошёл двадца́тый год; **Happy New Y**~**!** с Но́вым го́дом!; **New Y**~**'s Day** день Но́вого го́да; **New Y**~**'s Eve** нового́дняя ночь, кану́н Но́вого го́да; **he was chosen sportsman of the** ~ его́ провозгласи́ли лу́чшим спортсме́ном го́да; **in the** ~ **dot** (*coll.*) во вре́мя о́но; **in this** ~ **of grace** в на́ши дни, в наш век; **he is in his third** ~ (*as student*) он на тре́тьем ку́рсе; **he is in my** ~ мы с ним однoку́рсники. **2.** (*pl., a long time*): **it is** ~**s since I saw him** я его́ це́лую ве́чность не ви́дел. **3.** (*pl., age*): **he looks young for his** ~**s** он мо́лодо вы́глядит для свои́х лет; **he wears his** ~**s well** он хорошо́ сохрани́лся; **advanced in** ~**s** в года́х/лета́х; **he is getting on in** ~**s** он (уже́) в во́зрасте; **a man of his** ~**s** челове́к его́ во́зраста; ~**s of discretion** созна́тельный во́зраст.
cpds. ~**-book** *n.* ежего́дник; ~**-long** *adj.* годи́чный; для́щийся це́лый год; ~**-old** *adj.* годова́лый; ~**-round** *adj.* круглогодово́й, круглогоди́чный.
yearling [ˈjɪəlɪŋ, ˈjɜː-] *n.* годови́к, годовичо́к; (*horse*) годова́лая ло́шадь.
adj. годова́лый.
yearly [ˈjɪəlɪ, ˈjɜː-] *adj.* (*happening once a year*) ежего́дный, годи́чный; (*pert. to a year*) годово́й; ~ **income** годово́й дохо́д; ~ **report** годово́й отчёт.
adv. (*once a year*) раз в год; (*every year*) ка́ждый год.
yearn [jɜːn] *v.i.* **1.:** ~ **for** тоскова́ть (*impf.*) по+*d.*; изголода́ть (*impf.*) по+*d.*; жа́ждать (*impf.*) +*g.* **2.:** ~ **to, towards: he has long** ~**ed to see her** он уже́ давно́ мечта́ет уви́деться с ней.
yearning [ˈjɜːnɪŋ] *n.* тоска́ (*по чему*); жа́жда (+*g.*); си́льное жела́ние (+*g.*);
yeast [jiːst] *n.* дро́жж|и (*pl., g.* -е́й); заква́ска; (*attr.*) дрожжево́й.
yeasty [ˈjiːstɪ] *adj.* (*frothy*) пе́нистый.
yell [jel] *n.* (пронзи́тельный) крик; **give a** ~ вскри́к|ивать, -нуть; закрича́ть (*pf.*).
v.t. & i. вопи́ть, за-; кр|ича́ть, -и́кнуть; **he** ~**ed abuse at me** он обру́шил на меня́ пото́к бра́ни.
yellow [ˈjeləʊ] *n.* **1.** (*colour*) желтизна́; жёлтый цвет; **she was dressed in** ~ она́ была́ оде́та в жёлтое. **2.** (*of egg*) желто́к. **3.** (*pigment*) жёлтая кра́ска.
adj. **1.** жёлтый; **go, turn** ~ желте́ть, по-; ~ **fever** жёлтая лихора́дка; **the** ~ **press** жёлтая пре́сса. **2.** (*coll., cowardly*) трусли́вый; **there was a** ~ **streak in him** он был трусова́т. **3.** (*envious*) зави́стливый.
v.t. (*make or paint* ~) желти́ть, вы́-; ~**ed leaves** пожелте́лые ли́стья; **paper** ~**ed with age** бума́га, пожелте́вшая от вре́мени.
v.i. желте́ть, по-.
cpds. ~**back** *n.* бульва́рный рома́н; ~**-beaked** *adj.* с жёлтым клю́вом; ~**-bellied** *adj.* (*coll.*) трусли́вый; ~**-hammer** *n.* овся́нка; ~**-leaved** *adj.* с жёлтыми/пожелте́вшими ли́стьями.
yellowing [ˈjeləʊɪŋ] *n.* пожелте́ние.
yellowish [ˈjeləʊɪʃ] *adj.* желтова́тый.
yellowness [ˈjeləʊnɪs] *n.* желтизна́; (*cowardice*) тру́сость.
Yellow River [jeləʊ ˈrɪvə(r)] *n.* Хуанхэ́ (*f. indecl.*).
yelp [jelp] *n.* визг.
v.i. визжа́ть, взви́згнуть.
Yemen [ˈjemən] *n.* Йе́мен.
Yemeni [ˈjemənɪ] *n.* йе́мен|ец (*fem.* -ка).
adj. йе́менский.
yen[1] [jen] *n.* (*unit of currency*) ие́на.
yen[2] [jen] *n.* (*coll., yearning*) тоска́ (*по чему*).
v.i. тоскова́ть (*impf.*) (*по чему*).
yeoman [ˈjəʊmən] *n.* **1.** (*hist.*) йо́мен. **2.** (*small landowner*) ме́лкий землевладе́лец, фе́рмер. **3.** (*nav.*): ~ **of signals** старшина́(*m.*)-сигна́льщик. **4.: Y**~ **of the Guard** ≃ лейб-гварде́ец. **5.: do** ~ **service** ока́з|ывать, -а́ть по́длинную по́мощь.
yeomanry [ˈjəʊmənrɪ] *n.* (*hist.*) сосло́вие йо́менов; (*cavalry force*) территориа́льная ко́нница.
yes [jes] *n.* (*affirmation*) утвержде́ние; (*vote in favour*) го́лос «за».
adv. да; (*in reply to neg. statement or command*) нет; ~, **sir** слу́шаюсь!; (*mil.*) так то́чно!; есть!
cpd. ~**-man** *n.* подпева́ла (*m.*).
yesterday [ˈjestəˌdeɪ] *n.* вчера́шний день; ~**'s paper** вчера́шняя газе́та; ~ **was my birthday** вчера́ был мой день рожде́ния; **since** ~ со вчера́шнего дня; **the day before** ~ позавчера́, тре́тьего дня.
adv. вчера́; ~ **morning/evening** вчера́ у́тром/ве́чером; ~ **week** во́семь дней (тому́) наза́д; **I wasn't born** ~ я не ма́ленький; я не вчера́ роди́лся.
yester-year [ˈjestəjɪə(r)] *n.* (*liter.*) про́шлый год.
yet [jet] *adv.* **1.** (*so far, up to now, to date*) до сих пор; пока́; **the biggest shark** ~ **caught** са́мая кру́пная аку́ла, каку́ю когда́-либо (*or* до сих пор) удава́лось пойма́ть; **as** ~ пока́, поку́да; **as** ~ **nothing has been done** ничего́ пока́ не сде́лано; (*with neg.*) ещё; **he has not read the book** ~ он ещё не чита́л кни́ги; **I have never** ~ **seen him** я ещё ни ра́зу не ви́дел его́; **it's not time** ~ ещё ра́но; ещё не вре́мя; (*with interrog.*): **has the post arrived** ~**?** по́чта ещё не пришла́?; **can I come in** ~**?** мо́жно уже́ войти́? **2.** (*some day; before all is over*) ещё; **he will win** ~ он ещё победи́т; **I'll catch you** ~ вы у меня́ ещё попадётесь. **3.** (*still*): **he has** ~ **to learn of the disaster** он ещё не зна́ет о катастро́фе; **while there is** ~ **time** пока́ ещё есть вре́мя; пока́ ещё не по́здно; **I can see him** ~ (*fig.*) он таки́м у меня́ и оста́лся в па́мяти; **if I hadn't called you, you would have been asleep** ~ е́сли б я вас не разбуди́л, вы бы до сих пор (*or* и по сию́ по́ру *or* и сейча́с) (ещё) спа́ли. **4.** (*so early*) уже́; **need you go** ~**?**

вам ужé порá (идти́)?; **let's not give up ~!** ещё рáно отчáиваться!; **it won't happen just ~** э́то ещё не сейчáс случи́тся; **shall we go? Not just ~** пойдёмте? Чуть попóзже. **5.** (*with comp.*, *even*) дáже, ещё; **this book is ~ more interesting** э́та кни́га (дáже) ещё интерéснее; **he will not accept help, nor ~ advice** он не принимáет ни пóмощи, ни дáже совéта. **6.** (*again, in addition*) ещё; **there is ~ another reason** есть ещё и другáя причи́на; **~ once more** ещё (оди́н) раз; **he came back ~ again** он снóва/опя́ть (*or* ещё раз) вернýлся. **7.** (*nevertheless*) тем не мéнее; всё-таки; всё-же; **it is strange ~ true** э́то стрáнно, но тем не мéнее вéрно/так.

conj. однáко; **he is good to me, ~ I dislike him** он ко мне хорошó отнóсится, и, однáко, я егó не люблю́.

yeti [ˈjetɪ] *n.* снéжный человéк, йéти (*m. indecl.*).

yew [ju:] *n.* (*tree*) тис; (*wood*) древеси́на ти́сового дéрева.

adj. ти́совый.

Yid [jɪd] *n.* жид (*pej.*) (*fem.* -óвка).

Yiddish [ˈjɪdɪʃ] *n.* и́диш, еврéйский язы́к.

adj.: **a ~ newspaper** газéта на и́дише.

yield [ji:ld] *n.* **1.** (*crop*) урожáй; **a poor ~** скýдный урожáй. **2.** (*return*) дохóд, дохóдность; **~ of bonds** процéнты (*m. pl.*) по облигáциям. **3.** (*quantity produced*) вы́ход; (*of milk*) надóй; (*of mine*) добы́ча; (*of fish*) улóв. **4.** (*tech.*, *of metal*): **~ temperature** температýра текýчести; **~ point** предéл текýчести.

v.t. **1.** (*bring in*; *produce*) прин|оси́ть, -ести́; произв|оди́ть, -ести́; (с)да|вáть, -ть; **this land ~s a good harvest** э́та земля́ даёт хорóший урожáй; **research ~ed no result** исслéдование оказáлось безрезультати́вным (*or* ничегó нé дало). **2.** (*give up*) уступ|áть, -и́ть; **he was unwilling to ~ his rights** он не желáл поступи́ться свои́ми правáми; **~ o.s.** сда|вáться, -ться; **~ the floor** (*parl.*) уступ|áть, -и́ть трибýну; **~ ground** сда|вáть, -ть террито́рию; (*fig.*) сда|вáть, -ть (свои́) пози́ции; **he ~ed the point** в э́том пýнкте он согласи́лся.

v.i. уступ|áть, -и́ть; подд|авáться, -áться; под|авáться, -áться; **the door ~ed to a strong push** под си́льным напóром дверь подалáсь; **the ground ~ed under their feet** пóчва оседáла под их ногáми; **I ~ to none in my admiration for him** никтó не восхищáется им бóльше моегó; **he ~s to none in bravery** он никомý не уступáет в хрáбрости; **he would not ~ to persuasion** он не поддавáлся никаки́м уговóрам; **he ~ed to the temptation** он не смог устоя́ть пéред соблáзном; **we will never ~ to force** мы ни за что не подчини́мся наси́лию (*or* отстýпим пéред наси́лием); **the disease ~ed to treatment** болéзнь поддалáсь лечéнию; **the sea ~ed up its treasures** мóре óтдало свои́ сокрóвища.

yielding [ˈji:ldɪŋ] *adj.* (*of ground etc.*) подáтливый, мя́гкий; (*compliant*) поклáдистый, устýпчивый, подáтливый; **in a ~ moment** в минýту слáбости.

yippee [ˈjɪpi:, -ˈpi:] *int.* урá!

YMCA (*abbr. of* ***Young Men's Christian Association***) Христиáнский сою́з молоды́х людéй.

yob(bo) [ˈjɒbəʊ] *n.* (*sl.*) хулигáн, грубия́н.

yodel [ˈjəʊd(ə)l] *v.i.* петь, про- на тирóльский лад (*or* йóдлем).

yoga [ˈjəʊgə] *n.* йóга.

yog(h)urt [ˈjɒgət] *n.* йогýрт.

yogi [ˈjəʊgɪ] *n.* йог.

yo-heave-ho [ˈjəʊhi:vˌhəʊ] *int.* (раз, два,) взя́ли!; дрýжно!

yoicks [jɔɪks] *int.* улюлю́!

yoke [jəʊk] *n.* **1.** (*fitted to oxen etc.*) ярмó. **2.** (*fig.*) и́го, ярмó; **the Ta(r)tar ~** (*hist.*) татáрское и́го; **endure the ~** нести́ (*det.*) и́го; **come under the ~** подпáсть (*pf.*) под и́го; **shake off the ~** сбр|áсывать, -óсить и́го/ярмó; **~ of servitude** ýз|ы (*pl.*, *g.* —) рáбства. **3.**: **~** (*pair*) **of oxen** упря́жка волóв. **4.** (*for carrying pails etc.*) коромы́сло. **5.** (*of dress*) кокéтка.

v.t. (*lit.*) впря|гáть, -чь в ярмó; (*fig.*, *link*) соедин|я́ть, -и́ть; сочетáть (*impf.*, *pf.*).

cpd. **~-fellow** *n.* (*joc.*) супрýг, супрýга; напáрник, товáрищ по рабóте.

yokel [ˈjəʊk(ə)l] *n.* деревéнщина (*c.g.*).

yolk [jəʊk] *n.* желтóк; **~ sac** (*biol.*) желтóчный мешóк (зарóдыша).

yon(der) [ˈjɒndə(r)] *adj.* вон тот.

adv. вон там.

yore [jɔ:(r)] *n.* (*liter.*): **knights of ~** ры́цари стародáвнего врéмени; **in days of ~** давны́м-давнó; во врéмя óно.

you [ju:] *pron.* **1.** вы; (*familiar sg.*) ты; **~ and I** мы с тобóй/вáми; **~ and he** вы с ним; **this is for ~** э́то для вас, э́то вам; **~ silly fool!** (вот) дурáк!; **~ darling!** ми́лая моя́!; как ты мил(á)!; **~ lawyers** вы, юри́сты; ваш брат, юри́сты; **don't ~ go away** не взду́майте уйти́. **2.** (*one, anyone*): **~ never can tell** как знать?; **~ soon get used to it** к э́тому скóро привыкáешь; **there's a book for ~!** (*sc. a fine one*) вот э́то кни́га (, так кни́га)!; **what are ~ to do with a child like that?** что дéлать с таки́м ребёнком?

cpd. **~-know-who** *n.* (*coll.*) нéкто; э́тот сáмый.

young [jʌŋ] *n.*: **the ~** молодёжь; (**~** *animals*) детёныши (*m. pl.*); (*birds*) птенцы́, птéнчики (*m. pl.*); **with ~** (*of bitch etc.*) щённая; (*of cow*) стéльная; (*of mare*) жерёбая; (*of sow*) супорóс(н)ая.

adj. **1.** молодóй, ю́ный; **~ man** молодóй человéк, ю́ноша (*m.*); **her ~ man** (*sweetheart*) её возлю́бленный/ми́лый; **~** (*child*) **musicians** ю́ные музыкáнты; **~ children** мáленькие дéти; **~ people** молодёжь; **~ ones** (*children*) дéт|и (*pl.*, g. -éй); (*animals*) детёныши; **a ~ nation** нóвое (*or* недáвно образовáвшееся) госудáрство; молодáя странá; **he is ~ for his years** он ещё неóпытный; **in my ~ days** в дни моéй ю́ности; в мóлодости; когдá я был молоды́м/мóлод; **he is ~er than I** он молóже меня́; **~ Smith; the ~er Smith** Смит млáдший; **the night is ~** дéтское врéмя; **when the century was ~** в (сáмом) начáле вéка.

cpd. **~-looking** *adj.* моложáвый.

youngish [ˈjʌŋɪʃ] *adj.* довóльно молодóй.

youngster [ˈjʌŋstə(r)] *n.* (*child*) мáльчик, подрóсток; (*youth*) юнéц; (*pl.*, *collect.*) молодёжь.

your [jɔ:(r), jʊə(r)] *adj.* **1.** ваш; (*familiar sg.*) твой; (*referring to subj. of clause*) свой. **2.** (*pej.*): **that's ~ politician for you!** вот они́, (вáши) поли́тики!

yours [jɔ:z, jʊəz] *pron.* ваш; твой; свой; **my father and ~** мой отéц и ваш; **my teacher and ~** (*2 people*) нáши с вáми учителя́; (*1 pers.*) наш с вáми учи́тель; **he is no friend of ~** какóй он вам друг!; **a friend of ~** оди́н из вáших прия́телей; **here is my hat — have you found ~?** вот моя́ шля́па, (а) вы свою́ нашли́?

pred. adj. ваш; **~ of the 10th** Вáше письмó от 10-ого; **~ truly** прéданный Вам; (*joc.*) ваш покóрный слугá; **what's ~?** что вы бýдете пить?; **I'd like to read something of ~** я бы хотéл прочитáть чтó-нибудь из тогó, что вы написáли; **that cough of ~** э́тот ваш кáшель.

yourself [jɔ:ˈself, jʊə-] *pron.* **1.** (*refl.*) себя́; **don't deceive ~!** не обмáнывайте (самогó) себя́!; не обмáнывайтесь! **2.** (*emph.*) сам; **you wrote to him ~** вы сáми емý писáли. **3.** (*after preps.*): **you brought this trouble on ~** вы сáми на себя́ навлекли́ э́ту неприя́тность; **why are you sitting by ~?** почемý вы сиди́те в одинóчестве?; **did you do it all by ~?** вы э́то сдéлали сáми (*or* без посторóнней пóмощи)? **4.**: **you don't look ~ today** вы невáжно вы́глядите сегóдня.

youth [ju:θ] *n.* **1.** (*state or period*) мóлодость; (*liter.*) ю́ность; **in my ~** в (моéй) мóлодости; когдá я был молоды́м. **2.** (*young man*) ю́ноша (*m.*); **as a ~ he was studious** в мóлодости он был прилéжен (в заня́тиях). **3.** (*young people*) молодёжь; **the ~ of our country** молодёжь нáшей страны́; **~ club** молодёжный клуб; **~ hostel** молодёжная бáза/гости́ница.

youthful [ˈju:θfʊl] *adj.* ю́ный, ю́ношеский; **~ strength** ю́ношеская си́ла; **~ dreams** мечты́ мóлодости; (*of face, pers. etc.*) молодóй, ю́ный; **he had a ~ appearance** он вы́глядел мóлодо/моложáво; у негó моложáвый вид.

youthfulness [ˈju:θfʊlnɪs] *n.* мóлодость; (*of appearance*) моложáвость.

yowl [jaʊl] *n.* вой.

v.i. выть (*impf.*).

yo-yo [ˈjəʊjəʊ] *n.* йо-йó (*indecl.*); диáболо (*indecl.*).

ytterbium [ɪ'tɜ:bɪəm] *n.* иттéрбий.
yttrium ['ɪtrɪəm] *n.* и́ттрий.
yucca ['jʌkə] *n.* ю́кка.
yucky ['jʌkɪ] *adj.* (*sl.*) гря́зный, га́дкий.
Yugoslav ['ju:gəˌslɑ:v], **-ian** [ju:gə'slɑ:vɪən] *nn.* югосла́в (*fem.* -ка).
adj. югосла́вский.
Yugoslavia [ju:gə'slɑ:vɪə] *n.* Югосла́вия.
Yugoslavian [ju:gə'slɑ:vɪən] = **Yugoslav**
yule [ju:l] *n.* (*arch.*) Рождество́; свя́т|ки (*pl.*, *g.* -ок).
yummy ['jʌmɪ] *adj.* (*coll.*) вку́сный.
yum-yum [jʌm'jʌm] *int.* ням-ня́м!
yurt [jʊət] *n.* ю́рта.
YWCA (*abbr. of* ***Young Women's Christian Association***) Христиа́нский сою́з же́нской молодёжи.

Z

Z [zed] *n.* зет; **from A to ~** от а́льфы до оме́ги; от «а» до «я»; с са́мого нача́ла до са́мого конца́.
Zachariah [zækə'raɪə] *n.* (*bibl.*) Заха́рия (*m.*).
Zaire [zɑ:'ɪə(r)] *n.* Заи́р.
Zairean [zɑ:'ɪərɪən] *n.* заи́р|ец (*fem.* -ка).
adj. заи́рский.
Zambia ['zæmbɪə] *n.* За́мбия.
Zambian ['zæmbɪən] *n.* замби́|ец (*fem.* -йка).
adj. замби́йский.
zany ['zeɪnɪ] *n.* шут, кло́ун.
adj. смешно́й, фигля́рский.
Zanzibar ['zænzɪˌbɑ:(r)] *n.* Занзиба́р.
Zarathustra [zærə'θu:strə] = **Zoroaster**
zeal [zi:l] *n.* усе́рдие, рве́ние; энтузиа́зм, пыл.
Zealand ['zi:lænd] *n.* Зела́ндия.
zealot ['zelət] *n.* фан|а́тик (*fem.* -ати́чка); ревни́тель (*fem.* -ница); энтузиа́ст (*fem.* -ка).
zealous ['zeləs] *adj.* усе́рдный, рья́ный, ре́вностный; **a ~ supporter** горя́чий сторо́нник (*fem.* горя́чая сторо́нница).
zebra ['zebrə, 'zi:-] *n.* зе́бра; (*attr.*) зе́бровый; **~ crossing** перехо́д «зе́бра».
zebu ['zi:bu:] *n.* зе́бу (*m. indecl.*).
Zen [zen] *n.* дзэн.
zenith ['zenɪθ, 'zi:-] *n.* (*lit.*, *fig.*) зени́т; (*fig.*) вы́сшая то́чка; расцве́т.
zephyr ['zefə(r)] *n.* зефи́р.
Zeppelin ['zepəlɪn] *n.* цеппели́н.
zero ['zɪərəʊ] *n.* нуль (*m.*), ноль (*m.*); нулева́я то́чка; **absolute ~** абсолю́тный нуль; **ten degrees below ~** ми́нус де́сять гра́дусов; де́сять гра́дусов ни́же нуля́; **~ hour** час «Ч»; **~ altitude** нулева́я высота́; **~ option** (*pol.*) нулево́й вариа́нт.
v.t.: **~ an instrument** устан|а́вливать, -ови́ть прибо́р на нуль.
v.i.: **~ in on a target** пристре́л|иваться, -я́ться.
zest [zest] *n.* пыл; энтузиа́зм; **add ~ to** прид|ава́ть, -а́ть вкус/пика́нтность/интере́с/остроту́ *+d.*; **he entered into the project with ~** он с жа́ром/увлече́нием взя́лся за э́ту иде́ю; **~ for life** жизнера́достность, жизнелю́бие.
zeugma ['zju:gmə] *n.* зе́вгма.
Zeus [zju:s] *n.* Зевс.
ziggurat ['zɪgəˌræt] *n.* зиккура́т.
zigzag ['zɪgzæg] *n.* зигза́г.
adj. зигзагообра́зный.
v.i. идти́ (*det.*) зигза́гом; де́лать, с- зигза́ги.
Zimbabwe [zɪm'bɑ:bwɪ, -weɪ] *n.* Зимба́бве (*indecl.*).
Zimbabwean [zɪm'bɑ:bwɪən, -weɪən] *n.* зимбабви́|ец (*fem.* -йка).
adj. зимбабви́йский.
zinc [zɪŋk] *n.* цинк; **flowers of ~** ци́нковые бели́ла.
adj. ци́нковый.
v.t. цинкова́ть, о-.
zinnia ['zɪnɪə] *n.* ци́нния.
Zion ['zaɪən] *n.* Сио́н.
Zionism ['zaɪəˌnɪz(ə)m] *n.* сиони́зм.
Zionist ['zaɪənɪst] *n.* сиони́ст (*fem.* -ка).
zip [zɪp] *n.* **1.** (**~**-*fastener*, *also* **~per**) (застёжка-)мо́лния. **2.** (*sound of bullet*) свист (пу́ли); (*sound of tearing of cloth*) треск. **3.** (*coll.*, *energy*) пыл, эне́ргия. **4.: Z~ code** (*US*) (почто́вый) и́ндекс.
v.t. (*usu.* **~ up**) застёг|ивать, -ну́ть (на мо́лнию).
v.i. (*of bullet etc.*) свисте́ть, про-; прон|оси́ться, -ести́сь со сви́стом.
cpd. **~-fastener** *n.* (застёжка-)мо́лния.
zirconium [zə'kəʊnɪəm] *n.* цирко́ний.
zit [zɪt] *n.* (*coll.*) пры́щ, хоти́мчик.
zither ['zɪðə(r)] *n.* ци́тра.
zloty ['zlɒtɪ] *n.* зло́тый.
zodiac ['zəʊdɪˌæk] *n.* зодиа́к.
zodiacal [zə'daɪək(ə)l] *adj.* зодиака́льный.
zombie ['zɒmbɪ] *n.* (*fig.*, *coll.*) ску́чный/вя́лый челове́к; живо́й труп.
zonal ['zəʊnəl] *adj.* зона́льный.
zone [zəʊn] *n.* зо́на, по́яс, полоса́, райо́н; **danger ~** опа́сная зо́на; (*geog.*): **torrid ~** тропи́ческий по́яс; **frigid ~** аркти́ческий по́яс; **temperate ~s** уме́ренные пояса́; **free ~** во́льная га́вань; **~ time** поясно́е вре́мя.
v.t. (*divide into ~s*) райони́ровать (*impf.*, *pf.*); разб|ива́ть, -и́ть на зо́ны.
zoo [zu:] *n.* зооса́д, зоопа́рк.
zoological [ˌzəʊə'lɒdʒɪk(ə)l, *disp.* ˌzu:ə-] *adj.* зоологи́ческий; **~ gardens** зоологи́ческий сад.
zoologist [zəʊ'ɒlədʒɪst, *disp.* ˌzu:-] *n.* зоо́лог.
zoology [zəʊ'ɒlədʒɪ, *disp.* ˌzu:-] *n.* зооло́гия.
zoom [zu:m] *n.* **1.** (*aeron.*) свеча́, го́рка. **2.** (*sound*) жужжа́ние, гул. **3.** (*attr.*) **~ lens** объекти́в с переме́нным фо́кусным расстоя́нием.
v.i. **1.** (*aeron.*) де́лать, с- свечу́/го́рку; (*fig.*): **prices ~ed** це́ны ре́зко повы́сились. **2.** (*make buzzing noise*) жужжа́ть, про-.
zoophyte ['zəʊəˌfaɪt] *n.* зоофи́т.
Zoroaster [ˌzɒrəʊ'æstə(r)], **Zarathustra** [ˌzærə'θu:strə] *n.* Зороа́стр, Зарату́стра (*m.*).
Zoroastrian [ˌzɒrəʊ'æstrɪən] *n.* после́дователь (*fem.* -ница) Зороа́стра/Зарату́стры.
zouave [zu:'ɑ:v, zwɑ:v] *n.* зуа́в.
Zulu ['zu:lu:] *n.* зулу́с (*fem.* -ка).
adj. зулу́сский.
Zurich ['zjʊərɪk] *n.* Цю́рих.
zygoma [zaɪ'gəʊmə, zɪ-] *n.* скулова́я кость.
zygote ['zaɪgəʊt] *n.* зиго́та.
zymosis [zaɪ'məʊsɪs, zɪ-] *n.* (*fermentation*) броже́ние, фермента́ция; (*infection*) зара́за, инфе́кция.
zymotic [zaɪ'mɒtɪk, zɪ-] *adj.* (*fermented*) броди́льный; (*infectious*) инфекцио́нный, зара́зный.

The Oxford Russian Dictionary

Revised Edition

Russian–English

EDITED BY MARCUS WHEELER
AND BORIS UNBEGAUN

English–Russian

EDITED BY PAUL FALLA

REVISED AND UPDATED
BY COLIN HOWLETT

Oxford New York
OXFORD UNIVERSITY PRESS
1997

Oxford University Press, Great Clarendon Street, Oxford OX2 6DP
Oxford New York
Athens Auckland Bangkok Bogota Bombay
Buenos Aires Calcutta Cape Town Dar es Salaam
Delhi Florence Hong Kong Istanbul Karachi
Kuala Lumpur Madras Madrid Melbourne
Mexico City Nairobi Paris Singapore
Taipei Tokyo Toronto Warsaw
and associated companies in
Berlin Ibadan

First revised 1993
This further revised edition 1997

British Library Cataloguing in Publication Data
Data available

Library of Congress Cataloging in Publication Data
Data available
ISBN 0–19–860153–0

1 3 5 7 9 10 8 6 4 2

Printed in Spain by
Mateu Cromo Artes Graficas S.A.
Madrid